**Summer 2016** Volume 28, Number 2

P9-EEI-696

# State
## YELLOW BOOK

who's who in
the executive and
legislative branches
of the 50 state
governments

LEADERSHIP DIRECTORIES, INC.

www.leadershipdirectories.com
info@leadershipdirectories.com

New York Office
1407 Broadway, Suite 318
New York, NY 10018
(212) 627-4140
Fax (212) 645-0931

Washington, DC Office
1667 K Street, NW, Suite 801
Washington, DC 20006
(202) 347-7757
Fax (202) 628-3430

## Congressional
YELLOW BOOK
who's who in congress,
including committees and key staff

## Federal
YELLOW BOOK
who's who in federal departments and agencies

## State
YELLOW BOOK
who's who in the executive and legislative branches
of the 50 state governments

## Municipal
YELLOW BOOK
who's who in the leading city and county governments
and local authorities

## Federal Regional
YELLOW BOOK
who's who in the federal government's departments,
agencies, diplomatic missions, military installations
and service academies outside of Washington, DC

## Judicial
YELLOW BOOK
who's who in federal and state courts

## Corporate
YELLOW BOOK
who's who at the leading U.S. companies

## Financial
YELLOW BOOK
who's who at the leading U.S. financial institutions

## News Media
YELLOW BOOK
who's who among reporters, writers, editors
and producers in the leading national news media

## Associations
YELLOW BOOK
who's who at the leading U.S.
trade and professional associations

## Law Firms
YELLOW BOOK
who's who in the management
of the leading U.S. law firms

## Government Affairs
YELLOW BOOK
who's who in government affairs

## Foreign Representatives
YELLOW BOOK
who's who in the U.S. offices of foreign corporations,
foreign nations, the foreign press and
intergovernmental organizations

## Nonprofit Sector
YELLOW BOOK
who's who in the management of the leading
foundations, universities, museums,
and other nonprofit organizations

## The Leadership Library®
who's who in the leadership of the United States

## Leadership Directories, Inc.
STATE YELLOW BOOK

Summer 2016, Volume 28, Number 2

Drew Wheatley, *Team Leader and Content Manager*
Nzinga Kelliebrew, *Content Manager*
Elizabeth Tierney, *Content Manager*

William W. Cressey, *Chairman of the Board*
Gretchen Teichgraeber, *President and Chief Executive Officer*
James M. Petrie, *Secretary*

*Sales, Marketing, and Customer Service*
Sean Doyle, *Senior Vice President, Sales and Licensing*
William Schneider, *Vice President, Business Development*
Jacqueline Johnson, *Fulfillment Manager*
Stefan Andersen; Michele Anderson; Laurie Consoli;
Anne Marie Del Vecchio; Heather Donegal; Ed Faas;
Melissa Kaus; Nancy Scholem;
Wanda Speight-Bridgers; Nicole Tamang

*Products, Marketing, and Content*
Sue Healy, *Executive Vice President, Products and Marketing*
Tom Zurla, *Vice President, Content*
Carmela Makabali, *Senior Director, Content and Database Management*
Harris Beringer, *Manager, Product Marketing*
Michela Shoucair, *Marketing Manager*
Dave Marmon, *Senior Product Specialist*
Gareth Sparks, *Manager, Content Development and Quality*
Brendan Timmons, *Product Specialist*

*Information Technology*
Brian F. Hanley, *Chief Information Officer*
Jill McLoughlin, *Project Leader/DBA*
Cynthia Cordova, *Network Administrator*
Rabeya Khandaker, *Senior Software Engineer*

*Administration and Finance*
James Gee, *Vice President for Administration and Treasurer*
Shai Tzach, *Controller*
Alan Fan; Elvis A. Perez

ISBN: 978-0-87289-429-7

Printed in the United States of America.

The *State Yellow Book* (ISSN 0899-2207) is published
quarterly by Leadership Directories, Inc., 1407 Broadway,
Suite 318, New York, NY 10018. Annual subscription: $635.
Additional subscriptions delivered to the same individual and
address: $477. For air mail postage: Canada and Mexico add
$75 per subscription. Outside North America add $100 per
subscription. Periodicals postage paid at New York, NY and
additional mailing offices.

POSTMASTER: Send address changes to
*State Yellow Book*, Leadership Directories, Inc.,
1407 Broadway, Suite 318, New York, NY 10018.

For additional information, including details about
other Leadership Directories, Inc. publications, please
call (212) 627-4140.

# State

## YELLOW BOOK

Summer 2016

# Table of Contents

## Section I: Executive Branch

*(continued on next page)*

## Section II: Legislative Branch

# State Capitol
## SPOTLIGHT

By Drew Wheatley
Team Leader and Content Manager, *State Yellow Book*

May 23, 2016

This edition of the *State Yellow Book* contains senior personnel and organizational changes that have taken place in the fifty states – as well as in the governments of the District of Columbia, American Samoa, Guam, Puerto Rico and the Virgin Islands – between February 2016 and May 2016. Highlighted below are some items of interest.

### The Leadership® Content Commitment

Leadership Directories provides high quality, accurate and up to date information on the key leaders in government, business, legal, media and nonprofit organizations in the United States. Every item of information on more than 750,000 people and 150,000 organizations has been verified at the source.

### State Yellow Book Online

*Leadership® State-Muni Premium* is the online version of the *State Yellow Book*. It is available as an annual subscription and includes daily updates and additional content not available in the print directory, plus searching, list-building, and exporting capabilities. For more information, please contact us at (212) 627-4140.

### Legislative Vacancies

#### Michigan

There is one vacancy in the Michigan Senate. State Senator Virgil Smith Jr. (D-District 4) resigned from office. A general election to fill this legislative vacancy will be held on November 8, 2016.

There is one vacancy in the Michigan House of Representatives. State Representative Derek Miller (D-District 28) resigned from office to serve of Treasurer of Macomb County, Michigan. A general election to fill this legislative vacancy will be held on November 8, 2016.

#### Mississippi

There is one vacancy in the Mississippi House of Representatives. State Representative Linda Coleman (D-District 29) resigned from office to serve as a Judge of the Eleventh Judicial District of Mississippi. A general election to fill this legislative vacancy will be held on November 8, 2016.

#### Missouri

There are two vacancies in the Missouri State Senate. State Senator Paul LeVota (D-District 11) and State Senator Tom Dempsey (R-District 23) resigned from office. A general election to fill these legislative vacancies will be held on November 8, 2016.

There is one vacancy in the Missouri House of Representatives. State Representative Don Gosen (R-District 101) resigned from office. A general election to fill this legislative vacancy will be held on November 8, 2016.

*(continued on next page)*

## Legislative Vacancies—continued

### Nevada

There are two vacancies in the Nevada Senate. State Senator Debbie Smith (D-District 13) is deceased. State Senator Greg Brower (R-District 15) resigned from office. A general election to fill these legislative vacancies will be held on November 8, 2016.

There are three vacancies in the Nevada Assembly. State Assembly Member Marilyn Kirkpatrick (D-District 1) resigned from office to serve on the Clark County Board of Commissioners. State Assembly Member Erven Nelson (R-District 5) resigned from office. State Assembly Member Pat Hickey (R-District 25) resigned from office to serve on the State Board of Education. A general election to fill these legislative vacancies will be held on November 8, 2016.

### New Hampshire

There are three vacancies in the New Hampshire House of Representatives. State Representatives Robert Luther (R-Belknap-3) and Marcia Moody (D-Rockingham-17) are deceased. State Representative Kyle Tasker (R-Rockingham-2) resigned from office. A general election to fill these legislative vacancies will be held on November 8, 2016.

### New Jersey

There is one vacancy in the New Jersey General Assembly. State Assembly Member Patrick Diegnan (R-District 18) resigned from office to serve in the New Jersey State Senate. The Democratic Committee has not yet chosen a successor to fill this legislative vacancy.

### New York

There are two vacancies in the New York State Assembly. State Assembly Member Todd Kaminsky (D-District 20) resigned from office to serve in the New York State Senate. State Assembly Member Barbara Clark (D-District 33) is deceased. A general election to fill this legislative vacancies will be held on November 8, 2016.

### Pennsylvania

There is one vacancy in the Pennsylvania House of Representatives. State Representative Thomas Killion (R-District 168) resigned from office to serve in the Pennsylvania Senate. A special election to fill this legislative vacancy will be held on July 12, 2016.

### Rhode Island

There is one vacancy in the Rhode Island House of Representatives. State Representative Raymond Gallison (D-District 69) resigned from office. A general election to fill this legislative vacancy will be held on November 8, 2016.

### South Carolina

There are two vacancies in the South Carolina House of Representatives. State Representative Edward Southard (R-District 100) resigned from office. A special election to fill this legislative vacancy will be held on August 30, 2016. State Representative Michael Gambrell (R-District 7) resigned from office to serve in the South Carolina Senate. A special election date has not yet been determined to fill this legislative vacancy.

### Texas

There is one vacancy in the Texas House of Representatives. State Representative Ruth McClendon (D-District 120) resigned from office. A special runoff election to fill this legislative vacancy will be held on August 2, 2016.

## Legislative Vacancies—continued

### Virginia

There is one vacancy in the Virginia Senate. State Senator John C. Miller (D-District 1) is deceased. A special election to fill this legislative vacancy will be held on November 8, 2016.

### Washington

There is one vacancy in the Washington House of Representatives. State Representative Hans Dunshee (D-District 44) resigned from office to serve on the Snohomish County Council. The Democratic Party has not yet chosen a successor to fill this legislative vacancy.

## Party Affiliation Statistics (As of May 25, 2016)

| Governors | | Control of the Legislature | |
|---|---|---|---|
| Democrats | 18 | Democrats | 11 |
| Republicans | 31 | Republicans | 30 |
| Independents | 1 | Nonpartisan | 1 |
| | | Party Control Divided | 8 |

As always, the editors of the *State Yellow Book* extend our sincere thanks to the hundreds of contacts who help us maintain the high quality of the information in our products by consistently taking time out of their busy schedules to provide accurate and timely updates. We welcome your comments and invite you to call us at (212) 627-4140 or send an email to info@leadershipdirectories.com.

# Party Control of State Government — listed by branch

| State | Governor | Senate | House |
|---|---|---|---|
| Alabama | Republican | Republican | Republican |
| Alaska | Independent | Republican | Republican |
| American Samoa | Independent | Nonpartisan | Nonpartisan |
| Arizona | Republican | Republican | Republican |
| Arkansas | Republican | Republican | Republican |
| California | Democratic | Democratic | Democratic |
| Colorado | Democratic | Republican | Democratic |
| Connecticut | Democratic | Democratic | Democratic |
| Delaware | Democratic | Democratic | Democratic |
| Florida | Republican | Republican | Republican |
| Georgia | Republican | Republican | Republican |
| Guam | Republican | Democratic | N/A |
| Hawaii | Democratic | Democratic | Democratic |
| Idaho | Republican | Republican | Republican |
| Illinois | Republican | Democratic | Democratic |
| Indiana | Republican | Republican | Republican |
| Iowa | Republican | Democratic | Republican |
| Kansas | Republican | Republican | Republican |
| Kentucky | Republican | Republican | Democratic |
| Louisiana | Democratic | Republican | Republican |
| Maine | Republican | Republican | Democratic |
| Maryland | Republican | Democratic | Democratic |
| Massachusetts | Republican | Democratic | Democratic |
| Michigan | Republican | Republican | Republican |
| Minnesota | Democrat | Democratic | Republican |
| Mississippi | Republican | Republican | Republican |
| Missouri | Democratic | Republican | Republican |
| Montana | Democratic | Republican | Republican |
| Nebraska | Republican | Nonpartisan | N/A |
| Nevada | Republican | Republican | Republican |
| New Hampshire | Democratic | Republican | Republican |
| New Jersey | Republican | Democratic | Democratic |
| New Mexico | Republican | Democratic | Republican |
| New York | Democratic | Republican | Democratic |
| North Carolina | Republican | Republican | Republican |
| North Dakota | Republican | Republican | Republican |
| Ohio | Republican | Republican | Republican |
| Oklahoma | Republican | Republican | Republican |
| Oregon | Democratic | Democratic | Democratic |
| Pennsylvania | Democratic | Republican | Republican |
| Puerto Rico | Popular Democratic Party | Popular Democratic Party | Popular Democratic Party |
| Rhode Island | Democratic | Democratic | Democratic |
| South Carolina | Republican | Republican | Republican |
| South Dakota | Republican | Republican | Republican |
| Tennessee | Republican | Republican | Republican |
| Texas | Republican | Republican | Republican |
| Utah | Republican | Republican | Republican |
| Vermont | Democratic | Democratic | Democratic |
| Virgin Islands | Independent | Democratic | N/A |
| Virginia | Democratic | Republican | Republican |
| Washington | Democratic | Republican | Democratic |
| West Virginia | Democratic | Republican | Republican |
| Wisconsin | Republican | Republican | Republican |
| Wyoming | Republican | Republican | Republican |

# Governors and Their Reelection Years

| State | Governor | Election Year | State | Governor | Election Year |
|---|---|---|---|---|---|
| Alabama | Robert J. Bentley (R)* | 2018 | Nebraska | John Peter "Pete" (R) Ricketts | 2018 |
| Alaska | William M. "Bill" Walker (I) | 2018 | | | |
| American Samoa | Lolo Matasi Moliga (I) | 2016 | Nevada | Brian E. Sandoval (R)* | 2018 |
| Arizona | Douglas "Doug" Ducey (R) | 2018 | New Hampshire | Margaret W. "Maggie" Hassan (D)** | 2016 |
| Arkansas | W. Asa Hutchinson (R) | 2018 | | | |
| California | Jerry E. Brown (D)* | 2018 | New Jersey | Christopher J. "Chris" Christie (R)* | 2017 |
| Colorado | John W. Hickenlooper (D)* | 2018 | | | |
| Connecticut | Dannel P. "Dan" Malloy (D)* | 2018 | New Mexico | Susana Martinez (R)* | 2018 |
| Delaware | Jack A. Markell (D)* | 2016 | New York | Andrew M. Cuomo (D) | 2018 |
| Florida | Rick L. Scott (R)* | 2018 | North Carolina | Patrick L. "Pat" McCrory (R) | 2016 |
| Georgia | Nathan Deal (R)* | 2018 | North Dakota | John S. Dalrymple (R)** | 2016 |
| Guam | Edward "Eddie" Calvo (R)* | 2018 | Ohio | John R. Kasich (R)* | 2018 |
| Hawaii | David Y. Ige (D) | 2018 | Oklahoma | Mary Fallin (R)* | 2018 |
| Idaho | C.L. "Butch" Otter (R) | 2018 | Oregon | Kate Brown (D) | 2016 |
| Illinois | Bruce V. Rauner (R) | 2018 | Pennsylvania | Thomas W. "Tom" Wolf (D) | 2018 |
| Indiana | Mike Pence (R) | 2016 | Puerto Rico | Alejandro J. García Padilla** (PDP) | 2016 |
| Iowa | Terry E. Branstad (R) | 2018 | | | |
| Kansas | Samuel D. Brownback (R)* | 2018 | Rhode Island | Gina M. Raimondo (D) | 2018 |
| Kentucky | Matt Bevin (R)* | 2019 | South Carolina | Nikki R. Haley (R)* | 2018 |
| Louisiana | John Bel Edwards (D) | 2019 | South Dakota | Dennis M. Daugaard (R)* | 2018 |
| Maine | Paul R. LePage (R)* | 2018 | Tennessee | William E. "Bill" Haslam (R)* | 2018 |
| Maryland | Lawrence "Larry" Hogan (R) | 2018 | | | |
| | | | Texas | Greg Abbott (R) | 2018 |
| Massachusetts | Charles "Charlie" Baker (R) | 2018 | Utah | Gary R. Herbert (R) | 2016 |
| Michigan | Richard D. "Rick" Snyder (R)* | 2018 | Vermont | Peter Shumlin (D)** | 2016 |
| | | | Virgin Islands | Kenneth Mapp (I) | 2018 |
| Minnesota | Mark Dayton (D) | 2018 | Virginia | Terence "Terry" McAuliffe (D)* | 2017 |
| Mississippi | Phil Bryant (R)* | 2019 | | | |
| Missouri | Jeremiah W. "Jay" Nixon (D)* | 2016 | Washington | Jay Inslee (D) | 2016 |
| | | | West Virginia | Earl R. Tomblin (D)* | 2016 |
| Montana | Steve Bullock (D) | 2016 | Wisconsin | Scott Walker (R) | 2018 |
| | | | Wyoming | Matthew "Matt" Mead (R)* | 2018 |

*Governor will not be running for reelection due to state term limits
**Governor will not be seeking reelection

# 2016 Legislative Calendar

| State | Convenes | Adjourns | State | Convenes | Adjourns |
|---|---|---|---|---|---|
| Alabama | February 2 | May 18 | Montana | *** | *** |
| Alaska | January 19 | April 17 | Nebraska | January 6 | March 6 |
| American Samoa | January 11 | ** | Nevada | *** | *** |
| Arizona | January 11 | ** | New Hampshire | January 6 | July 1 |
| Arkansas | April 13 | May 12 | New Jersey | January 12 | * |
| California | January 4 | August 31 | New Mexico | January 19 | February 18 |
| Colorado | January 13 | May 11 | New York | January 6 | * |
| Connecticut | February 3 | May 4 | North Carolina | April 25 | ** |
| Delaware | January 12 | June 30 | North Dakota | *** | *** |
| Florida | January 12 | May 1 | Ohio | January 5 | * |
| Georgia | January 11 | ** | Oklahoma | February 1 | May 27 |
| Guam | January 11 | * | Oregon | February 1 | March 6 |
| Hawaii | January 20 | March 19 | Pennsylvania | January 5 | * |
| Idaho | January 11 | ** | Puerto Rico | January 11 | May 11 |
| Illinois | January 13 | * | Rhode Island | January 5 | ** |
| Indiana | January 12 | March 14 | South Carolina | January 12 | June 2 |
| Iowa | January 11 | April 19 | South Dakota | January 12 | March 29 |
| Kansas | January 11 | April 10 | Tennessee | January 12 | ** |
| Kentucky | January 5 | April 12 | Texas | *** | *** |
| Louisiana | March 14 | June 6 | Utah | January 25 | March 10 |
| Maine | January 6 | April 20 | Vermont | January 5 | *** |
| Maryland | January 13 | April 11 | Virgin Islands | January 11 | * |
| Massachusetts | January 6 | * | Virginia | January 13 | March 12 |
| Michigan | January 13 | * | Washington | January 11 | March 10 |
| Minnesota | March 8 | May 23 | West Virginia | January 12 | March 11 |
| Mississippi | January 5 | May 8 | Wisconsin | January 12 | * |
| Missouri | January 6 | May 30 | Wyoming | February 8 | ** |

*Legislature meets throughout the year
**Date Unknown
***No regular session in 2016

# States with Term Limits

| State | Enacted | Senate | House | Year of Impact |
|-------|---------|--------|-------|----------------|
| Arizona | 1992 | Four consecutive 2-year terms | Four consecutive 2-year terms | 2000 |
| Arkansas | 1992; modified in 2014 | 16-year cumulative total | 16-year cumulative total | 1998 |
| California | 1990; modified in 2012 | 12-year cumulative total | 12-year cumulative total | 1996 |
| Colorado | 1990 | Two 4-year terms | Four 2-year terms | Senate: 2000 House: 1998 |
| Florida | 1992 | Restricts members from serving more than 8 consecutive years. | Restricts members from serving more than 8 consecutive years. | Senate: 2002 House: 2000 |
| Louisiana | 1995 | Three consecutive 4-year terms | Three consecutive 4-year terms | 2007 |
| Maine | 1993 | Four consecutive 2-year terms | Four consecutive 2-year terms | 1996 |
| Michigan | 1992 | Two 4-year terms | Three 2-year terms | 1998 |
| Missouri | 1992 | Members can serve 8 years in one body; no more than 16 years of service. | Members can serve 8 years in one body; no more than 16 years of service. | 2000 |
| Montana | 1992 | Members are limited to 8 years of service in a 16-year period. | Members are limited to 8 years of service in a 16-year period. | 1998 |
| Nebraska | 2000 | Members will be limited to two consecutive four year terms. | | 2008 |
| Nevada | 1996 | Three 4-year terms | Six 2-year terms | 2010 |
| Ohio | 1992 | Two consecutive terms | Four consecutive terms | Senate: 2002 House: 2000 |
| Oklahoma | 1990 | Restricts members to no more than 12 years of service. | Restricts members to no more than 12 years of service. | 2004 |
| South Dakota | 1992 | Four consecutive 2-year terms | Four consecutive 2-year terms | 2002 |

# User's Guide

The *State Yellow Book* is designed to give you direct access to more than 43,000 leaders in the Executive and Legislative branches of government for the 50 states, the District of Columbia, American Samoa, Guam, Puerto Rico, and the Virgin Islands. The *State Yellow Book* is divided into the following sections:

## ▶Executive Section

Each state lists the Governor's Office and the Lieutenant Governor's Office, followed by departments, commissions, boards and other major agencies of the state government, in alphabetical order by office name. Each office is structured to show the hierarchy by office and job titles. Each state entry includes:

**1 Government Information**, including terms of Governor and Legislature, next election, electoral votes, and state seal.

**2 Office Name**, with mailing address, general information telephone number, fax number, TTY number (for the hearing impaired), and e-mail and Internet addresses, when available.

**3 Photographs** of each Governor with biographical information, including date of service, date of birth, home, education, profession, and religion.

**4** Names and job titles of **Personnel** listed hierarchically by job title, as well as direct-dial telephone and fax numbers, and e-mail address, when available. When an individual's address is different from the main bold heading, it is included directly under that person's name.

**5 Educational Background** stating school name, year graduated, and degree(s), when available.

**6 Special Coded Symbols** preceding an individual's title are used to identify elected officials, and department or agency heads appointed by either the Governor, Legislature, Board, Commission or State Supreme Court.

## ►Legislative Section

Each state lists the leadership of state legislatures, all members with committee assignments, and a complete listing of standing committees. Legislative sessions vary among states. We therefore list district, business and residential telephone numbers, as well as district addresses when available. Each state entry includes:

**1 Name of the Legislature**, with a general information telephone number, fax number, bill status number, and e-mail and Internet addresses, when available.

**2 A Mailing Address**, general information telephone number, fax number, and e-mail and Internet addresses for the Senate and House, if different from the one listed under the main heading.

**3 Photographs** of the President of the Senate and Speaker of the House, when available. Biographical information includes reelection year, date of service, birth date, home, educational background, profession, and religion.

**4 Leadership** of the Senate and House.

**5 Party Affiliation** statistics show the political division of each state Senate and House by party membership (Democrat; Republican; Independent; Vacancy).

**6 A complete list of all Senators** and **Representatives** in alphabetical order with committee assignments. Each member has a party affiliation, district number, and counties represented. Individual telephone numbers (capitol, district, and residential numbers), fax numbers, e-mail addresses, and district addresses have been included, when available.

**7 Standing Committees** for the Senate and House in alphabetical order, listing the chairperson, vice chairperson, members, and key staff. Each committee lists members in alphabetical order, with the majority in the left column, the minority in the right column.

## Indexes

▶**Subject Index**

Lists departments, agencies and offices alphabetically under a subject heading. Gives state abbreviations and the page number on which each entry is found.

▶**Name Index**

Alphabetical listing of every name found in the *State Yellow Book*.

# Executive Branch

# Alabama

Tel: (334) 242-7100 (State Information)  Internet: www.alabama.gov

**Number of U.S. Congressional Delegates:** 2 Senators; 7 Representatives  **Governor's Term:** 4 years
**Legislature Description:** 35 member Senate; 105 member House of Representatives; Term - Senate 4 years, House 4 years  **Next Election:** Governor November 2018; Legislature November 2018
**Number of Electoral Votes:** 9  **Official Name:** State of Alabama (name of Indian tribe)
**Nickname:** The Heart of Dixie  **Motto:** We Dare Defend Our Rights

**Population:** 4,858,979 (2015); Rank 24  **Fiscal Year:** 2014  **Budget:** $13,576,828,000

## Office of the Governor

State Capitol, 600 Dexter Avenue, Montgomery, AL 36130
Tel: (334) 242-7100  Fax: (334) 353-0004

**Employees:** 33  **Fiscal Year:** 2015  **Budget:** $1,890,000

**Robert Julian Bentley**
Governor

Began Service: January 17, 2011
Term Expires: January 2019
Date of Birth: February 3, 1943
Education: Alabama 1964 BS; Medical Col (AL) 1968 MD
Home: Tuscaloosa
Religion: Baptist
Career: State Representative (R-AL, District 63), Alabama House of Representatives (2002-2010); Founding Partner and President, Alabama Dermatology Associates, P.C.

★ Governor **Robert Julian Bentley** (R) . . . . . . . . . . . . . . . . (334) 242-7210
  E-mail: info@governor.alabama.gov
  Executive Assistant to the Governor **Rachel Gandy** . . . . . (334) 242-7100
  Aide-de-Camp **Jake Jacobs** . . . . . . . . . . . . . . . . . . . . . . . (334) 242-7100
Chief of Staff **(Vacant)** . . . . . . . . . . . . . . . . . . . . . . . . . . . (334) 242-7100
Deputy Chief of Staff, Administration **Blake Hardwich** . . . (334) 242-7151
  Executive Assistant to the Deputy Chief of Staff
    **Faye McCall** . . . . . . . . . . . . . . . . . . . . . . . . . . . . . . . . . (334) 242-7911
    E-mail: faye.mccall@governor.alabama.gov
Deputy Chief of Staff, Policy **Jon Barganier** . . . . . . . . . . . (334) 242-7911
Administration Director **Cheryl Lynn Fondon** . . . . . . . . . . (334) 353-7510
  E-mail: cheryl.fondon@governor.alabama.gov
  Education: Pensacola Christian 1989 BSEd
Appointments Director **Will Edwards** . . . . . . . . . . . . . . . . (334) 242-3300
  Assistant Appointments Director **Patrick Bond** . . . . . . . . (334) 242-3300
Communications Director **Jennifer Ardis** . . . . . . . . . . . . . (334) 242-7100
  Note: Until June 16, 2016.
  E-mail: jennifer.ardis@governor.alabama.gov
  Press Secretary and NGA Coordinator
    **Yasamie August** . . . . . . . . . . . . . . . . . . . . . . . . . . . . . . (334) 242-7150
    E-mail: yasamine.august@governor.alabama.gov
Constituent Services Director **Pam Bye** . . . . . . . . . . . . . . . (334) 242-7100
  E-mail: pam.bye@governor.alabama.gov
Education Policy Director **John Barganier** . . . . . . . . . . . . . (334) 242-7100
Legislative Affairs Director **Derek Trotter** . . . . . . . . . . . . . (334) 242-7100
Federal and Local Government Relations Director
  **Zach Lee** . . . . . . . . . . . . . . . . . . . . . . . . . . . . . . . . . . . . (334) 242-4738
Scheduling Director **Alexandra Rice** . . . . . . . . . . . . . . . . . (334) 242-7151
Chief Fiscal Officer **Becca Crawford** . . . . . . . . . . . . . . . . . (334) 353-7510
Chief Legal Advisor **David B. Byrne** . . . . . . . . . . . . . . . . . (334) 242-7100
Chief Political Advisor **(Vacant)** . . . . . . . . . . . . . . . . . . . . (334) 242-7100

## Governors Office of Minority Affairs [GOMA]

Director **Nichelle Nix** . . . . . . . . . . . . . . . . . . . . . . . . . . . . . (334) 242-7100

## Alabama Department of Archives and History [ADAH]

624 Washington Avenue, Montgomery, AL 36130-0100
P.O. Box 300100, Montgomery, AL 36130-0100
Tel: (334) 242-4435  Fax: (334) 240-3433
Internet: www.archives.alabama.gov

**Employees:** 46  **Fiscal Year:** 2015  **Budget:** $6,404,000
▲ Director **Steve Murray** . . . . . . . . . . . . . . . . . . . . . . . . . . (334) 242-4441
  E-mail: steve.murray@archives.alabama.gov
  Executive Secretary **Tunisia Thomas** . . . . . . . . . . . . . . . (334) 242-4441

## Banking Department

401 Adams Avenue, Suite 680, Montgomery, AL 36130
P.O. Box 4600, Montgomery, AL 36103-4600
Tel: (334) 242-3452  Tel: (866) 465-2279 (Toll Free)  Fax: (334) 242-3500
Internet: www.banking.alabama.gov

**Employees:** 102  **Fiscal Year:** 2015  **Budget:** $14,305,000
■ Superintendent **John D. Harrison** . . . . . . . . . . . . . . . . . . (334) 242-3452
  E-mail: john.harrison@banking.alabama.gov
  Education: Troy State 1967 BS
Deputy Superintendent **Hobart F. "Trabo" Reed, Jr.** . . . . . . (334) 242-3452
  E-mail: trabo.reed@banking.alabama.gov
  Education: Alabama 1979 BS

## Department of Early Childhood Education [ADECE]

135 South Union Street, Suite 215, Montgomery, AL 36130-2755
P.O. Box 302755, Montgomery, AL 36130-2735
Tel: (334) 353-2700  Internet: www.children.alabama.gov

**Employees:** 62  **Fiscal Year:** 2014  **Budget:** $39,956,000
■ Commissioner **Jeana Ross** . . . . . . . . . . . . . . . . . . . . . . . . (334) 353-2700
  E-mail: jeana.ross@dca.alabama.gov
  Education: Alabama Birmingham BS; Alabama MA

## Department of Commerce [ADO]

401 Adams Avenue, 6th Floor, Montgomery, AL 36104
Tel: (800) 248-0033  Tel: (334) 242-0400
Fax: (334) 242-5669  E-mail: adoinfo@commerce.alabama.gov
Internet: www.madeinalabama.com

■ Secretary of Commerce **Greg Canfield** . . . . . . . . . . . . . . . (334) 242-0421
  E-mail: greg.canfield@commerce.alabama.gov
  Education: Alabama 1983 BS
  Special Assistant to the Secretary **Stefania C. Yuhas** . . . . (334) 242-0421
Deputy Secretary of Commerce, Business Development
  Division **Angela Till** . . . . . . . . . . . . . . . . . . . . . . . . . . . (334) 353-0221
  Education: Auburn (Montgomery)
Deputy Secretary of Commerce, Workforce Development
  Division **Ed Castile** . . . . . . . . . . . . . . . . . . . . . . . . . . . . (334) 242-4158
                                      Fax: (334) 242-0299
Executive Secretary **Rosalyn Frank** . . . . . . . . . . . . . . . . . . (334) 242-0475
Administrative Assistant **Anne Williams** . . . . . . . . . . . . . . (334) 242-0400
Incentives Manager **Angela Smith** . . . . . . . . . . . . . . . . . . . (334) 353-8113

---

★ Elected Official     ■ Appointed by Governor     ● Appointed by Legislature     ▲ Appointed by Board or Commission     ◆ Appointed by State Supreme Court

EXECUTIVE BRANCH

# Alabama Department of Conservation and Natural Resources [ADCNR]

P.O. Box 301450, Montgomery, AL 36130-1450
Tel: (800) 262-3151  E-mail: dcnr.media@dcnr.alabama.gov
Internet: www.outdooralabama.com

**Employees:** 918  **Fiscal Year:** 2015  **Budget:** $235,696,000

■Commissioner **N. Gunter Guy, Jr.** . . . . . . . . . . . . . . . . . . (334) 242-3486
   E-mail: dcnr.commissioner@dcnr.alabama.gov
   Education: Auburn 1978 BS; Cumberland 1982 JD
■Deputy Commissioner **Curtis Jones** . . . . . . . . . . . . . . . . (334) 242-3486
   E-mail: curtis.jones@dcnr.alabama.gov
Legal Counsel **William A. Gunter** . . . . . . . . . . . . . . . . . . (334) 242-3165
   E-mail: william.gunter@dcnr.alabama.gov

# Department of Corrections [DOC]

P.O. Box 301501, Montgomery, AL 36130-1501
Tel: (334) 353-3883  Fax: (334) 353-3967

**Employees:** 6,377  **Fiscal Year:** 2015  **Budget:** $473,607,000

■Commissioner
   **Col Jefferson S. "Jeff" Dunn, USAF (Ret)** . . . . . . . . . . (334) 353-3883
   E-mail: jeff.dunn@governor.alabama.gov
Governmental Relations Deputy Commissioner
   **Jeffery Williams** . . . . . . . . . . . . . . . . . . . . . . . . . . (334) 353-4633
Women's Services Deputy Commissioner
   **Wendy Williams** . . . . . . . . . . . . . . . . . . . . . . . . . . (334) 353-3313
Industries Director **Dr. Andy Farquhar** . . . . . . . . . . . . . . (334) 261-3600
   1400 Lloyd Street, Montgomery, AL 36107
   Education: Auburn 1975 BS, 1978 MS; Iowa State 1985 PhD
Investigations and Intelligence Division Director
   **Arnaldo Mercado** . . . . . . . . . . . . . . . . . . . . . . . . . (334) 353-8912
   E-mail: arnaldo.mercado@doc.alabama.gov
Public Information Division Director
   **Robert "Bob" Horton** . . . . . . . . . . . . . . . . . . . . . . . (334) 353-4053
   E-mail: bob.horton@doc.alabama.gov
Victim's Services Division Director (Acting)
   **Janet LeJune** . . . . . . . . . . . . . . . . . . . . . . . . . . . . (334) 353-3871
General Counsel **Anne Adams Hill** . . . . . . . . . . . . . . . . . (334) 353-3885

# Alabama Department of Economic and Community Affairs [ADECA]

401 Adams Avenue, Montgomery, AL 36130
P.O. Box 5690, Montgomery, AL 36103-5690
Tel: (334) 242-5100  TTY: (334) 242-2408  Fax: (334) 242-5099

**Employees:** 225  **Fiscal Year:** 2015  **Budget:** $206,399,000

■Director **Jim Byard, Jr.** . . . . . . . . . . . . . . . . . . . . . . . (334) 242-5591
   Education: Troy State BA
   Executive Secretary **Pamela B. Gates** . . . . . . . . . . . . . (334) 242-8672
■Assistant Director **Gina Smith** . . . . . . . . . . . . . . . . . . . (334) 242-5591
General Counsel **Claudia K. Smith** . . . . . . . . . . . . . . . . . (334) 242-5256
   E-mail: claudia.smith@adeca.alabama.gov
Community and Economic Development Division
   Director **Beatrice M. Forniss** . . . . . . . . . . . . . . . . . . (334) 242-5370
                                              Fax: (334) 242-4203

# Department of Finance

State Capitol, 600 Dexter Avenue, Suite N105, Montgomery, AL 36130
Tel: (334) 242-7160  Fax: (334) 353-3300

**Employees:** 457  **Fiscal Year:** 2015  **Budget:** $127,407,000

■Director (Acting) **Bill Newton** . . . . . . . . . . . . . . . . . . . (334) 242-7160
   E-mail: bill.newton@budget.alabama.gov
   Education: Alabama MBA; Faulkner JD

# Alabama Department of Forensic Sciences [ADFS]

1051 Wire Road, Auburn, AL 36832
Tel: (334) 844-4648  Fax: (334) 887-7531

**Employees:** 189  **Fiscal Year:** 2015  **Budget:** $24,861,000

■Director **Michael F. Sparks** . . . . . . . . . . . . . . . . (334) 844-4648 ext. 235
   E-mail: michael.sparks@adfs.alabama.gov

Deputy Director **Roderick J. Kennette** . . . . . . . . . . (334) 844-4648 ext. 250
Administrative Services Officer **Sam Mitchell** . . . . (334) 844-4648 ext. 239
   E-mail: samuel.mitchell@adfs.alabama.gov
Data Processing Manager **James D. Foster** . . . . . . (334) 844-4648 ext. 232
   E-mail: james.foster@adfs.alabama.gov
Personnel Manager **Sandra Webster** . . . . . . . . . . (334) 844-4648 ext. 241

# Alabama Law Enforcement Agency [ALEA]

P.O. Box 304115, Montgomery, AL 36130-4115
Tel: (334) 517-2800  Fax: (334) 353-3071
E-mail: information@dhs.alabama.gov  Internet: www.alea.gov

**Employees:** 15  **Fiscal Year:** 2015  **Budget:** $121,614,000

■Secretary (Acting) **Stan Stabler** . . . . . . . . . . . . . . . . . (334) 517-2800
   E-mail: stan.stabler@le.alabama.gov
   Executive Assistant **Merritt Hays** . . . . . . . . . . . . . . . . (334) 517-2889
■Chief of Staff **Hal Taylor** . . . . . . . . . . . . . . . . . . . . . . (334) 517-2847
   E-mail: hal.taylor@dhs.alabama.gov
■Homeland Security Director **Shirrell Roberts** . . . . . . . . . . (334) 517-2812
   E-mail: shirrell.roberts@dhs.alabama.gov
Public Information Officer **Anna Morris** . . . . . . . . . . . . . (334) 517-2800
   E-mail: anna.morris@le.alabama.gov

# Department of Public Safety [DPS]

301 South Ripley Street, Montgomery, AL 36104
P.O. Box 1511, Montgomery, AL 36102
Tel: (334) 242-4371  Tel: (334) 242-4400 (Driver License Information)
Fax: (334) 353-8477

**Employees:** 1,178  **Fiscal Year:** 2015  **Budget:** $42,397,000

■Director **Col. John E. Richardson** . . . . . . . . . . . . . . . . . (334) 242-4394
   E-mail: john.richardson@dps.alabama.gov
■Assistant Director **Lt. Col. Jack Clark** . . . . . . . . . . . . . . (334) 242-4703
   E-mail: jack.clark@dps.alabama.gov

# Criminal Justice Information Commission

201 South Union Street, Suite 300, Montgomery, AL 36104
Tel: (334) 517-2400  Fax: (334) 517-2740

▲Director **Kevin Wright** . . . . . . . . . . . . . . . . . . . . . . . (334) 517-2800
   E-mail: kwright@alacop.gov

# Alabama Department of Insurance [ALDOI]

201 Monroe Street, Suite 502, Montgomery, AL 36130-3351
P.O. Box 303351, Montgomery, AL 36130-3351
Tel: (334) 269-3550  Fax: (334) 241-4192
E-mail: insdept@insurance.alabama.gov  Internet: www.aldoi.gov

**Employees:** 140  **Fiscal Year:** 2014  **Budget:** $14,839,000

■Insurance Commissioner **Jim L. Ridling** . . . . . . . . . . . . . (334) 269-3550
   E-mail: jim.ridling@insurance.alabama.gov
   Education: U Ozarks
   Executive Secretary **Angela Slade** . . . . . . . . . . . . . . . (334) 241-4101
Chief of Staff **Mark Fowler** . . . . . . . . . . . . . . . . . . . . . (334) 269-3550
                                              Fax: (334) 956-7931

# Department of Labor

649 Monroe Street, Montgomery, AL 36131
P.O. Box 303500, Montgomery, AL 36130
Fax: (334) 242-3960

**Employees:** 968  **Fiscal Year:** 2015  **Budget:** $80,796,000

■Commissioner **Fitzgerald Washington** . . . . . . . . . . . . . . (334) 242-8055
Chief Child Labor Inspector **Robin Wilburn** . . . . . . . . . . (205) 613-3611
   E-mail: robin.wilburn@labor.alabama.gov
Chief Elevator and Boiler Inspector (Acting)
   **Marvin Byrum** . . . . . . . . . . . . . . . . . . . . . . . . . . . (334) 242-3066
   E-mail: marvin.byrum@labor.alabama.gov
   Administrative Assistant **Michael Barnett** . . . . . . . . . . (334) 242-8990
Assistant Director **(Vacant)** . . . . . . . . . . . . . . . . . . . . . (334) 242-8475
Public Information Manager **Tara Hutchison** . . . . . . . . . . (334) 242-8616
   E-mail: tara.hutchison@labor.alabama.gov

---

★ Elected Official   ■ Appointed by Governor   ● Appointed by Legislature   ▲ Appointed by Board or Commission   ◆ Appointed by State Supreme Court

# Alabama Department of Mental Health [ADMH]

100 North Union Street, Suite 520, Montgomery, AL 36130
P.O. Box 301410, Montgomery, AL 36130-1410
Tel: (334) 242-3417 Tel: (800) 367-0955 (In State) Fax: (334) 242-0684
E-mail: dmhmr@mh.alabama.gov Internet: www.mh.alabama.gov

**Employees:** 2,576 **Fiscal Year:** 2015 **Budget:** $898,435,000

■Commissioner **James V. "Jim" Perdue** . . . . . . . . . . . . . . . (334) 242-3640
  Executive Assistant **Lynn Frost** . . . . . . . . . . . . . . . . . . . . (334) 242-3107

## Personnel Department

300 Folsom Administrative Building, 64 North Union Street,
Montgomery, AL 36130-4100
Tel: (334) 242-3389 Fax: (334) 242-1110

**Employees:** 83 **Fiscal Year:** 2015 **Budget:** $8,310,000

▲Director **Jackie B. Graham** . . . . . . . . . . . . . . . . . . . . . . . (334) 242-3709
  E-mail: jackie.graham@personnel.alabama.gov
Deputy Director **Alice Ann Byrne** . . . . . . . . . . . . . . . . . . . . (334) 242-3450
Chief Counsel **Alice Ann Byrne** . . . . . . . . . . . . . . . . . . . . . (334) 242-3450
  E-mail: aliceann.byrne@personnel.alabama.gov
Certification Manager **Thomas Patterson** . . . . . . . . . . . . . (334) 242-3389
Classification and Pay Manager **Darby Forrester** . . . . . . . (334) 353-4076
Examinations Manager **Christy Kelley** . . . . . . . . . . . . . . . (334) 242-3389
Information Systems Manager **Mike Bruner** . . . . . . . . . . . (334) 242-3671
  E-mail: mbruner@alabama.gov
Payroll Audit and Records Manager **Sherry Grable** . . . . . . (334) 242-3099
Hearing Officer **Randy C. Sallé** . . . . . . . . . . . . . . . . . . . . (334) 242-8353
Training Coordinator **(Vacant)** . . . . . . . . . . . . . . . . . . . . . (334) 242-3494

## Alabama Department of Public Health [ADPH]

RSA Tower, 201 Monroe Street, Montgomery, AL 36104
P.O. Box 303017, Montgomery, AL 36130-3017
Tel: (334) 206-5300 Tel: (800) 252-1818 (Toll Free) Fax: (334) 206-5534
Internet: www.adph.org

**Employees:** 2,932 **Fiscal Year:** 2015 **Budget:** $640,502,000

▲State Health Officer **(Vacant)** . . . . . . . . . . . . . . . . . . . . . (334) 206-5200
  Executive Assistant **Patricia Vinson** . . . . . . . . . . . . . . . . (334) 206-5200

## Alabama Department of Rehabilitation Services [ADRS]

602 S. Lawrence Street, Montgomery, AL 36104
Tel: (334) 293-7500 Tel: (800) 441-7607 (Toll Free) Fax: (334) 293-7383

**Employees:** 706 **Fiscal Year:** 2015 **Budget:** $151,790,000

▲Commissioner **Dr. Cary F. Boswell** . . . . . . . . . . . . . . . . . (334) 293-7200
  E-mail: cary.boswell@rehab.alabama.gov
Deputy Commissioner **(Vacant)** . . . . . . . . . . . . . . . . . . . . (334) 293-7035
  Executive Secretary **LeAnne Bull** . . . . . . . . . . . . . . . . . . (334) 293-7201
Chief Financial Officer **Suzette Taylor** . . . . . . . . . . . . . . . (334) 293-7150
Chief Legal Counsel **Steve Simpson** . . . . . . . . . . . . . . . . . (334) 293-7187
  Education: Auburn 1979 BS; Alabama 1982 JD
Computer Services Director **David Rainey** . . . . . . . . . . . . . (334) 293-7114
  E-mail: david.rainey@rehab.alabama.gov
Human Resources Director **Jane Elizabeth Burdeshaw** . . (334) 293-7032
Internal Auditor Manager **Frank Snyder** . . . . . . . . . . . . . . (334) 293-7246
Program Evaluation **Michael Quinn** . . . . . . . . . . . . . . . . . (334) 293-7127

## Vocational Rehabilitation Service

Assistant Commissioner **James Myrick** . . . . . . . . . . . . . . . (334) 293-7174
Client Assistance Program Director **Rachel Hughes** . . . . . . (334) 263-2749
Statewide Technology Access and Response (STAR)
  Director **Helen L. Baker** . . . . . . . . . . . . . . . . . . . . . . . . (334) 293-7012
  E-mail: helen.baker@rehab.alabama.gov
Consumer Relations Coordinator **Graham Sisson** . . . . . . . (334) 293-7189
  E-mail: graham.sisson@rehab.alabama.gov
Employers Services Coordinator **Peggy Anderson** . . . . . . . (205) 290-4457
  P.O. Box 19888, Birmingham, AL 35219-0888

Head Injury Services Coordinator **Maria Crowley** . . . . . . . (205) 290-4590
  P.O. Box 19888, Birmingham, AL 35219-0888
Independent Living State Coordinator **Lisa Alford** . . . . . . . (334) 293-7040
Supported Employment Coordinator **Tina Dortch** . . . . . . . (334) 293-7257
Learning Disabilities Specialist **Karen Jenkins** . . . . . . . . . (334) 293-7108
Psychological Specialist **(Vacant)** . . . . . . . . . . . . . . . . . . (334) 293-7500
Quality Assurance Specialist and Welfare to Work
  **(Vacant)** . . . . . . . . . . . . . . . . . . . . . . . . . . . . . . . . . . (334) 293-7500
Social Security Specialist **Donna Bowden** . . . . . . . . . . . . (334) 293-7026
Transition Services Specialist **Tina Dortch** . . . . . . . . . . . . (334) 293-7257

# Alabama Department of Revenue [ADOR]

Gordon Persons Office Building, 50 North Ripley Street,
Montgomery, AL 36132
Tel: (334) 242-1175 Fax: (334) 242-0550

**Employees:** 1,416 **Fiscal Year:** 2015 **Budget:** $135,764,000

■Commissioner **Julie P. Magee** . . . . . . . . . . . . . . . . . . . . . (334) 242-1175
  E-mail: julie.magee@revenue.alabama.gov
  Education: South Alabama 1991 BA
Public Information Manager **Frank Miles** . . . . . . . . . . . . . . (334) 242-1175
  E-mail: frank.miles@revenue.alabama.gov

## Office of the Deputy Commissioner

Deputy Commissioner **Brenda Coone** . . . . . . . . . . . . . . . . (334) 242-1175
Deputy Commissioner **Joe Garrett** . . . . . . . . . . . . . . . . . . (334) 242-1175
Deputy Commissioner **Curtis E. Stewart** . . . . . . . . . . . . . . (334) 242-1175

# Alabama Department of Senior Services [ADSS]

RSA Tower, 201 Monroe Street, Suite 350, Montgomery, AL 36130-3351
Tel: (334) 242-5743 Tel: (877) 425-2243 Fax: (334) 242-5594

**Employees:** 46 **Fiscal Year:** 2015 **Budget:** $126,181,000

■Commissioner **Neal Morrison** . . . . . . . . . . . . . . . . . . . . . (334) 242-4985
  E-mail: neal.morrison@adss.alabama.gov
  Education: Athens State BSBA; Birmingham JD
Nursing Home State Ombudsman **Virginia Bell** . . . . . . . . . (334) 242-5753
Emergency Management Coordinator **Russ Black** . . . . . . . (334) 353-8457
Medicaid Waiver Services Coordinator **Jean Stone** . . . . . . (334) 353-8288
Public Information Manager **(Vacant)** . . . . . . . . . . . . . . . . (334) 242-5743

# Alabama Department of Transportation [ALDOT]

1409 Coliseum Boulevard, Montgomery, AL 36110
P.O. Box 303050, Montgomery, AL 36130-3050
Tel: (334) 242-6358 Fax: (334) 353-2677
E-mail: aldotinfo@dot.state.al.us Internet: www.dot.state.al.us

**Fiscal Year:** 2015 **Budget:** $1,707,962,000

■Director **John R. Cooper** . . . . . . . . . . . . . . . . . . . . . . . . . (334) 242-6776
  E-mail: cooperjr@dot.state.al.us
  Education: Alabama

# Alabama Tourism Department [ATD]

401 Adams Avenue, Montgomery, AL 36130
P.O. Box 4927, Montgomery, AL 36103-4927
Tel: (334) 242-4169 Tel: (800) 252-2262 Fax: (334) 242-4554
E-mail: info@tourism.alabama.gov

■Director **Lee Sentell** . . . . . . . . . . . . . . . . . . . . . . . . . . . . (334) 242-4169
  E-mail: lee.sentell@tourism.alabama.gov
  Education: Auburn BA
  Executive Secretary **Cynthia Flowers** . . . . . . . . . . . . . . . (334) 242-4169

# Department of Youth Services [DYS]

P.O. Box 66, Mount Meigs, AL 36057-0001
Tel: (334) 215-3800 Fax: (334) 215-1453 E-mail: info@dys.alabama.gov
Internet: http://dys.alabama.gov

**Employees:** 313 **Fiscal Year:** 2015 **Budget:** $100,983,000

▲Executive Director **Steven P. Lafreniere** . . . . . . . . . . . . . (334) 215-3800
  E-mail: steven.lafreniere@dys.alabama.gov

*(continued on next page)*

---

★ Elected Official   ■ Appointed by Governor   ● Appointed by Legislature   ▲ Appointed by Board or Commission   ◆ Appointed by State Supreme Court

**Department of Youth Services** *continued*

Executive Assistant to the Director **Marcia Calendar** .... (334) 215-3802
Education Superintendent **Dr. Rafael Richardson** ........ (334) 215-3859
Administration Deputy Director **David Rogers** ...........(334) 215-3854
　E-mail: david.rodgers@dys.alabama.gov
Programs and Client Services Deputy Director
　**Tim Davis** ................................................(334) 215-3809
Institutional Services Administrator **James V. Kent** ...... (334) 215-3810
　E-mail: james.kent@dys.alabama.gov
Treatment Coordinator **Alesia Allen** ..................(334) 245-3836

## Alabama National Guard

1720 Congressman W.L. Dickinson Drive, Montgomery, AL 36109
P.O. Box 3711, Montgomery, AL 36109-0711
Tel: (334) 271-7400  Fax: (334) 213-7511

■Adjutant General **MG Perry G. Smith, ARNG** ..........(334) 271-7400
　E-mail: perry.g.smith@us.army.mil
　Education: Auburn 1973 BS; Troy State 1996 MSHRM
Information Management (DCSIM) Deputy Chief of Staff
　**COL Steven T. Grigsby, ARNG** ...................(334) 270-2947
　E-mail: steven.t.grigsby.mil@mail.mil
Logistics (DCSLOG) Deputy Chief of Staff
　**COL Allen Rigsby, ARNG** ...................... (334) 213-7730
Plans Operations and Training Chief
　**COL Jeffery Smithermen, ARNG** .................(334) 271-7234
Public Affairs Office Chief
　**LTC Shannon Hancock, ARNG** ..................(334) 271-7400
　E-mail: shannon.hancock@alabama.gov
Director of Staff **(Vacant)** ..........................(334) 271-7346
Army Personnel and Administration Division Chief
　**COL Christopher J. "Chris" Morgan, ARNG** ........ (334) 271-7314
　E-mail: cmorgan@alabama.gov
Budget and Fiscal Officer **(Vacant)** ..................(334) 271-7308
Human Resources Officer **COL Dennis Butters, ARNG** ... (334) 271-7216
State Property and Dispersing Chief
　**COL Mark Weeks, ARNG** .......................(334) 271-7275
　Education: Auburn BS

## Office of Prosecution Services

515 South Perry Street, Montgomery, AL 36104-4615
Tel: (334) 242-4191  Fax: (334) 240-3186

**Employees:** 7  **Fiscal Year:** 2015  **Budget:** $6,311,000

▲Executive Director **Randall I. "Randy" Hillman** ........(334) 242-4191
　E-mail: randy.hillman@alabamada.gov
Executive Assistant and Conference Coordinator
　**Debbie J. Wright** .............................(334) 242-4191
　E-mail: debbie.wright@alabamada.gov
Deputy Director and Chief Prosecutor **Barry Matson** ..... (334) 242-4191
Fiscal Officer **Melissa B. Gargus** ...................(334) 242-4191
General Counsel **Beau Brown** ......................(334) 242-4191
Grant Coordinator **Brooke Grigsby** ..................(334) 242-4191
Account Clerk **Debra Montesano** ....................(334) 242-4191
Administrative Assistant **Chris Sustarich** ..............(334) 242-4191
Traffic Safety Resource Prosecutor
　**William "Bill" Lindsey** ........................(334) 242-4191

## Emergency Management Agency [EMA]

5898 County Road 41, Clanton, AL 35046-2160
P.O. Drawer 2160, Clanton, AL 35046-2160
Tel: (205) 280-2200  TTY: (205) 280-0405  Fax: (205) 208-0495
E-mail: info@ema.alabama.gov  Internet: ema.alabama.gov

**Employees:** 84  **Fiscal Year:** 2015  **Budget:** $68,290,000

■Director **Art Faulkner** .............................(205) 280-2201
Assistant Director **Jimmy Plier** .....................(205) 280-2277
State Public Information Manager **Brian Corbett** ........(205) 280-2275
　E-mail: brian.corbett@doc.alabama.gov　　　Fax: (205) 280-2448
Executive Operations Officer **Jeff Byard** ..............(205) 280-2204
　　　　　　　　　　　　　　　　　　　　Fax: (205) 280-2493

## State Health Planning and Development Agency [SHPDA]

100 North Union Street, Suite 870, Montgomery, AL 36104
P.O. Box 303025, Montgomery, AL 36130-3025
Tel: (334) 242-4103  Fax: (334) 242-4113  Internet: www.shpda.state.al.us

**Employees:** 7  **Fiscal Year:** 2015  **Budget:** $853,000

■Executive Director **Alva M. Lambert** .................(334) 242-4103
　E-mail: alva.lambert@shpda.alabama.gov
　Education: Alabama BA; Jones Law JD; Auburn (Montgomery) MPS
　Executive Secretary **Nicole Horn** ...................(334) 242-4512

## Alabama Medicaid Agency

P.O. Box 5625, Montgomery, AL 36103-5625
Tel: (334) 242-5000  E-mail: almedicaid@medicaid.alabama.gov
Internet: www.medicaid.alabama.gov

**Employees:** 514  **Fiscal Year:** 2015  **Budget:** $6,073,280,000

■Commissioner (Acting) **Stephanie "McGee" Azar** .......(334) 242-5600
　Executive Assistant **Kathleen Hudson** ..............(334) 242-5600
Health Information Technology Coordinator
　**Paul Brannan** ................................(334) 242-5000

## Alabama Credit Union Administration [ACUA]

100 N. Union Street, Suite 650, Montgomery, AL 36104
Fax: (334) 353-5795  Internet: www.acua.alabama.gov

■Administrator **Sarah H. Moore** ......................(334) 353-5770
　E-mail: sarah.moore@acua.alabama.gov
　Education: Auburn 1987 BS
　Executive Secretary **Christy Ealum** .................(334) 353-5770
Assistant Administrator **Lloyd H. Moore** ..............(334) 353-5770
　E-mail: lloyd.moore@acua.alabama.gov

## Commission on Higher Education

100 North Union Street, Montgomery, AL 36130-2000
P.O. Box 302000, Montgomery, AL 36130-2000
Tel: (334) 242-1998  Fax: (334) 242-0268

**Employees:** 28  **Fiscal Year:** 2015  **Budget:** $20,793,000

■Chair **Larry J. Hughes** (District 3) ................. (334) 396-6930
　Term Expires: August 31, 2016　　　　　　Fax: (334) 396-6929
　Education: Auburn MPA
■Vice Chair **Charles E. Ball** (At-Large) ................ (205) 264-8401
　Term Expires: August 31, 2019
　Education: Auburn 1992 MCP; Birmingham-Southern 1983 BA
■Commissioner **Miranda Boudin Frost** (District 5) ........(256) 533-5789
　Term Expires: August 31, 2024
●Commissioner **Charles Buntin** (District 2) .............(334) 794-0328
　Term Expires: August 31, 2024
■Commissioner **Karen Calametti** (District 1) ...........(251) 639-1300
　Term Expires: August 31, 2020　　　　　　Fax: (251) 639-1380
■Commissioner **Darius Foster** (District 7) .............(205) 276-8044
　Term Expires: August 31, 2020　　　　　　Fax: (205) 933-5001
■Commissioner **Timothy Gyan** (District 6) .............(205) 264-7412
　Term Expires: August 31, 2024
■Commissioner **William Jones** (At-Large) ..............(334) 467-5353
　Term Expires: August 31, 2018　　　　　　Fax: (256) 533-2501
■Commissioner **Patricia McGriff** (District 4) ...........(256) 796-7022
　Term Expires: August 31, 2020
■Commissioner **Stan R. Plyant** (At-Large) .............(256) 533-1919
　Term Expires: August 31, 2023　　　　　　Fax: (256) 535-9300
■Commissioner **Sydney G. Raine** (At-Large) ......(251) 432-0909 ext. 148
　Term Expires: August 31, 2018　　　　　　Fax: (251) 432-1004
■Commissioner **Charles E. Sanders, Jr.** (At-Large) ....... (205) 322-0457
　Term Expires: August 31, 2021　　　　　　Fax: (205) 322-8481
　Education: Rhodes BA; Alabama JD

## Commission Staff

Executive Director **Gregory G. Fitch** .................(334) 242-2123
　Education: Emporia State MA; Nebraska PhD

---

★ Elected Official　■ Appointed by Governor　● Appointed by Legislature　▲ Appointed by Board or Commission　◆ Appointed by State Supreme Court

## Alabama Housing Finance Authority [AHFA]

7460 Halcyon Pointe Drive, Suite 200, Montgomery, AL 36117
P.O. Box 242928, Montgomery, AL 36124-2928
Tel: (334) 244-9200  Tel: (800) 325-2432 (Toll Free)  Fax: (334) 244-9214

Executive Director **Robert L. Strickland** . . . . . . . . . . . . . . (334) 244-9200

## Alabama Securities Commission [ASC]

401 Adams Avenue, Suite 280, Montgomery, AL 36104
P.O. Box 304700, Montgomery, AL 36130-4700
Tel: (334) 242-2984  Tel: (800) 222-1253  Fax: (334) 242-0240
E-mail: asc@asc.alabama.gov

**Employees:** 33  **Fiscal Year:** 2015  **Budget:** $5,982,000

▲Director **Joseph P. "Joe" Borg** . . . . . . . . . . . . . . . . . . . . (334) 242-2386
   E-mail: joseph.borg@asc.alabama.gov

## Alcoholic Beverage Control Board

2715 Gunter Park Drive West, Montgomery, AL 36109-1021
Tel: (334) 271-3840  Fax: (334) 277-2150  Internet: www.abc.alabama.gov

**Employees:** 888  **Fiscal Year:** 2015  **Budget:** $70,582,000

▲Administrator **Hannibal McNeil "Mac" Gipson, Jr.** . . . . . . (334) 271-3840
   E-mail: administrator@abc.alabama.gov
   Education: Troy U

## State Board of Education

Gordon Persons Building, 50 North Ripley Street, P.O. Box 302101,
Montgomery, AL 36130-2101
Tel: (334) 242-9700  Fax: (334) 242-9708

President **Robert Julian Bentley** . . . . . . . . . . . . . . . . . . . (334) 242-7100
   Affiliation: Governor, Office of the Governor, State    Fax: (334) 242-0937
   of Alabama
   State Capitol, 600 Dexter Avenue, Montgomery, AL 36130
★President Pro Tem
   **Yvette Richardson** (D-Fourth District) . . . . . . . . . . . . . (205) 923-7262
   Term Expires: 2019                                     Fax: (205) 923-7262
   7125 Westmoreland Drive, Fairfield, AL 35064
★Vice President **Jeffery Newman** (R-Seventh District) . . . . (334) 242-9700
   Term Expires: 2017
   Education: Auburn BSEd; Mississippi State MEd; West Alabama MEd
★Member **Ella B. Bell** (D-Fifth District) . . . . . . . . . . . . . . . (334) 834-2811
   Term Expires: 2017
   2634 Airwood Drive, Montgomery, AL 36108
   E-mail: stateboard5@hotmail.com
   Education: Tuskegee 1969 BS; Alabama State 1974 MEd
★Member **Stephanie W. Bell** (R-Third District) . . . . . . . . . (334) 272-2777
   Term Expires: 2017                                     Fax: (334) 260-0100
   3218 Lancaster Lane, Montgomery, AL 36106
   E-mail: stephaniewbell@gmail.com
   Education: Auburn BA
★Member **Matthew Brown** (First District) . . . . . . . . . . . . . (334) 610-1283
   Term Expires: 2017
   Education: Pensacola Christian 2007; Cumberland 2011 JD
★Member **Mary Scott Hunter** (R-Eighth District) . . . . . . . . (888) 531-1312
   Term Expires: 2019
   P.O. Box 18903, Huntsville, AL 35804
   E-mail: hunter@maryscotthunter.com
★Member **Cynthia McCarty** (R-Sixth District) . . . . . . . . . . . (256) 310-6048
   Term Expires: 2019
   E-mail: csmccarty60@gmail.com
★Member **Betty J. Peters** (R-Second District) . . . . . . . . . . . (334) 794-8024
   Term Expires: 2019
   526 Beatrice Road, Kinsey, AL 36303
   E-mail: bpetersfaulk@gmail.com
   Education: Troy State (Dothan) 1983 BS
▲Secretary and Executive Officer **Dr. Philip Cleveland** . . . . (334) 242-9700
   5114 Gordon Persons Building, Montgomery, AL 36130
   Affiliation: State Superintendent (Interim), Alabama State Department
   of Education, State Board of Education, State of Alabama
   50 North Ripley Street, Montgomery, AL 36132
   Education: Auburn; Nova Southeastern EdD
Executive Secretary **Ann Starks** . . . . . . . . . . . . . . . . . . . (334) 242-9700

## Alabama State Department of Education [ALSDE]

50 North Ripley Street, Montgomery, AL 36132
P.O. Box 302101, Montgomery, AL 36104

**Employees:** 882  **Fiscal Year:** 2015  **Budget:** $1,146,264,000

▲State Superintendent (Interim) **Dr. Philip Cleveland** . . . . . . (334) 242-9700
   E-mail: pcleveland@alsde.edu
Deputy Superintendent **Andy Craig** . . . . . . . . . . . . . . . . . . . (334) 242-9755
Career and Technical Education Deputy Superintendent
   **Dr. Philip Cleveland** . . . . . . . . . . . . . . . . . . . . . . . . . (334) 242-9960
Instructional Services Deputy Superintendent
   **Sherrill Parris** . . . . . . . . . . . . . . . . . . . . . . . . . . . . . . (334) 353-1389
External Affairs Assistant Superintendent **Jeff Langham** . . (334) 242-9960
Research, Information, and Data Services Deputy
   Superintendent **Dr. Melinda Maddox** . . . . . . . . . . . . . . (334) 242-9716
   E-mail: mmaddox@alsde.edu
Alabama Reading Initiative Coordinator **Judy S. Stone** . . . (334) 353-1389
Assessment and Accountability Coordinator
   **Rebecca Mims** . . . . . . . . . . . . . . . . . . . . . . . . . . . . . . (334) 242-8038
   E-mail: rmims@alsde.edu
General Counsel **Juliana Teixeira Dean** . . . . . . . . . . . . . . (334) 242-1899
   E-mail: jdean@alsde.edu
   Education: Alabama 2002 LLM
Child Nutrition Programs Director **June Barrett, SNS** . . . . (334) 242-1988
   E-mail: jbarrett@alsde.edu
Communication Director **Michael O. Sibley** . . . . . . . . . . . (334) 242-9950
Instructional Services Director **Robin Nelson** . . . . . . . . . . (334) 242-9743
Data and Development Director
   **Dominique "Dom" Martel** . . . . . . . . . . . . . . . . . . . . (334) 353-7018
   E-mail: dmartel@alsde.edu
Disability Determination Director **Jim Methvin** . . . . . . . . . (205) 989-2100
   P.O. Box 830300, Birmingham, AL 35283
Federal Programs Director **Edmond Moore** . . . . . . . . . . . . (334) 242-8215
   E-mail: emoore@alsde.edu
Human Resources Director **Belinda Cooley** . . . . . . . . . . . . (334) 242-9900
Networking and Operations Director **Scott Crews** . . . . . . . (334) 353-7018
   E-mail: screws@alsde.edu
Office of Student Learning Director
   **Dr. Shanthia Washington, EdD** . . . . . . . . . . . . . . . . . (334) 535-1608
Prevention and Support Services Director **Marilyn Lewis** . . (334) 242-0076
Pupil Transportation Director **Kevin Snowden** . . . . . . . . . (334) 242-9730
School Architect Director **Ethan Perry Taylor** . . . . . . . . . (334) 242-9731
Special Education Services Director **Crystal Richardson** . . (334) 242-8114
Teacher Education and Certification Director
   **Dr. Jayne A. Meyer** . . . . . . . . . . . . . . . . . . . . . . . . . . (334) 242-9560
Technology Initiative Director **Earlene Patton** . . . . . . . . . . (334) 242-9594
   E-mail: epatton@alsde.edu
Legislative Services Liaison **Tracey A. Meyer** . . . . . . . . . . (334) 353-1600
   E-mail: tmeyer@alsde.edu
Chief Fiscal Officer **Vera Guettler** . . . . . . . . . . . . . . . . . . (334) 242-9774

## Department of Postsecondary Education [DPE]

135 South Union Street, Montgomery, AL 36104
P.O. Box 302130, Montgomery, AL 36130-2130
Tel: (334) 293-4500  Fax: (334) 293-4526

**Employees:** 60  **Fiscal Year:** 2015  **Budget:** $47,403,000

▲Chancellor **Dr. Mark Heinrich** . . . . . . . . . . . . . . . . . . . . (334) 293-4524
   E-mail: mark.heinrich@dpe.edu
   Education: Tennessee Tech BS, MA; Alabama PhD
Legal and Human Resources Vice Chancellor (Acting)
   **Jeff Miller** . . . . . . . . . . . . . . . . . . . . . . . . . . . . . . . . . (334) 293-4603
Instructional and Student Services Deputy Chancellor
   **Susan Price** . . . . . . . . . . . . . . . . . . . . . . . . . . . . . . . . (334) 293-4551
   Education: Virginia 1988 JD
GED Administrator (Interim) **Mo Jones** . . . . . . . . . . . . . . (334) 293-4571
   E-mail: mo.jones@dpe.edu
Facilities Coordinator **Frank Barnes** . . . . . . . . . . . . . . . . (334) 293-4741
Internal Audit Director **Alvena Williams** . . . . . . . . . . . . . . (334) 293-4531
Workforce and Economic Development Senior Executive
   Director **Terry Waters** . . . . . . . . . . . . . . . . . . . . . . . . . (334) 293-4708

---

★ Elected Official    ■ Appointed by Governor    ● Appointed by Legislature    ▲ Appointed by Board or Commission    ◆ Appointed by State Supreme Court

**EXECUTIVE BRANCH**

## Board of Pardons and Paroles

301 South Ripley Street, Montgomery, AL 36130
Tel: (334) 335-2405  Fax: (334) 242-1809
Internet: www.paroles.state.al.us

**Employees:** 626  **Fiscal Year:** 2015  **Budget:** $40,561,000

■Chairman **Cliff Walker** ................................... (334) 242-8700
■Associate Board Member **Eddie Cook, Jr.** ............... (334) 242-8700
  E-mail: eddie.cook@alabpp.gov
  Education: Alabama State 1987 BS
■Associate Board Member **William W. "Bill" Wynne, Jr.** ... (334) 335-7771
  Education: Alabama 1975 BS, 1976 MS
Executive Director **Cynthia S. Dillard** ................. (334) 242-8713
  E-mail: cynthia.dillard@paroles.alabama.gov
  Education: Georgia 1975 BA

## State Employees' Insurance Board

201 South Union Street, Suite 200, Montgomery, AL 36104
P.O. Box 304900, Montgomery, AL 36130
Tel: (334) 263-8341  Tel: (866) 836-9737  Fax: (334) 263-8541
Internet: www.alseib.org

Chief Executive Officer **William Ashmore, CPA** ........ (334) 263-8404
  E-mail: washmore@alseib.org
  Education: Auburn 1983 BSBA

## Board of Veterans Affairs

Chairman **Robert Julian Bentley** .................... (334) 242-5077
Vice Chair **Dolores "Dee" Hardin** .................. (334) 242-5077
Deputy Vice Chair **Chad Richmond** ................. (334) 242-5077
Member **Robert Baker** .............................. (334) 242-5077
Member **Jeffrey Brown** ............................. (334) 242-5077
Member **Wayne Dial** ................................. (334) 242-5077
Member **Patrick Downing** ........................... (334) 242-5077
Member **Don Fisher** ................................ (334) 242-5077
Member **Willis Frazier** ............................ (334) 242-5077
Member **James Graves** .............................. (334) 242-5077
Member **John R. New** ............................... (334) 242-5077
Member **Ken Rollins** ............................... (334) 242-5077
Member **Charles Stephens** .......................... (334) 242-5077
Member **Sandra Thompson** ........................... (334) 242-5077
Member **Debra Walker** .............................. (334) 242-5077
Member **Cynthia Jean Watson** ....................... (334) 242-5077
Member **William Wyatt** ............................. (334) 242-5077

## Alabama Department of Veterans Affairs

RSA Plaza Building, 770 Washington Avenue, Suite 470,
Montgomery, AL 36104
Tel: (334) 242-5077  Fax: (334) 242-5102  Internet: www.va.state.al.us

**Employees:** 104

▲Commissioner **RADM W. Clyde Marsh, USN (Ret)** ...... (334) 242-5077
  E-mail: clyde.marsh@va.alabama.gov
  Education: Alabama A&M 1973 BA; Troy State 1988 MS
Assistant Commissioner, Personnel and Administration
  **Michael E. Northcutt** ............................ (334) 242-5077
  E-mail: mike.northcutt@va.alabama.gov
  Education: Troy State 2003 BS, 2005 MS
Assistant Commissioner, Education Services **(Vacant)** ..... (334) 242-5077
General Counsel **(Vacant)** .......................... (334) 242-5077
Public Information Officer **Jana Ingels** .............. (334) 242-5077
Administrative Assistant **Tomeca Jones** .............. (334) 242-5077
Executive Assistant **Wendi Findley** ................. (334) 242-5077
Personnel Assistant **Rhonda Armstrong** .............. (334) 242-5077
Senior Accountant **Dixie Black** ..................... (334) 242-5077
Staff Accountant **Mary Ann Green** ................... (334) 242-5077
Receptionist **Shayla Santiago** ...................... (334) 242-5077
Computer Operations IT Systems Technician
  **Brandon Baker** .................................. (334) 242-5077
  E-mail: brandon.baker@va.alabama.gov

## Alabama Public Library Service [APLS]

6030 Monticello Drive, Montgomery, AL 36130
Tel: (334) 213-3900  TTY: (334) 213-3905  Fax: (334) 213-3993
Internet: www.statelibrary.alabama.gov

**Employees:** 44  **Fiscal Year:** 2015  **Budget:** $9,214,000

▲Director (Interim) **Kelyn Ralya** ..................... (334) 213-3976
  E-mail: kralya@apls.state.al.us
Assistant Director **Kelyn Ralya** ..................... (334) 213-3976
  Confidential Assistant **Scott Burbank** ............. (334) 213-3929
  Executive Secretary **Vanessa Carr** ................ (334) 213-3902
Blind and Physically Handicapped Division Head
  **Ruth Evans** ..................................... (334) 213-3921
Chief Information Officer **Kevin Goff** ................ (334) 213-3922
  E-mail: kgoff@apls.state.al.us
Public Relations **Stephanie Taylor** .................. (334) 213-3943
  E-mail: staylor@apls.state.al.us

## Retirement Systems of Alabama [RSA]

201 South Union Street, Montgomery, AL 36104
P.O. Box 302150, Montgomery, AL 36130-2150
Tel: (334) 517-7000  Fax: (877) 517-0021
E-mail: communications@rsa-al.gov  Internet: www.rsa-al.gov

Chief Executive Officer **David G. Bronner** ........... (334) 517-7000
  Education: Alabama JD, PhD
Deputy Secretary and Treasurer **Donald Yancey** ....... (334) 517-7000
General Counsel **Leura Garrett Canary** .............. (334) 517-7000
  Education: Huntington Col BA; Alabama JD

## Office of the Secretary of Information Technology

100 North Union Street, Suite 980, Montgomery, AL 36134
Tel: (334) 242-7100  Fax: (334) 242-7331

■Secretary (Acting) **Dr. Joanne Hale** ................. (334) 242-7100
  E-mail: joanne.hale@alabama.gov
  Education: Missouri BSIE, MSc; Texas Tech PhD
Deputy Secretary **Cheri Martin** ..................... (334) 242-7100
  E-mail: cheri.martin@dhr.alabama.gov
IT Strategic Planning and Policy Director
  **Mason L. Tanaka** ................................ (334) 242-7100
  E-mail: mason.tanaka@governor.alabama.gov
Executive Assistant **Jane Claire Carter** ............. (334) 242-7100

## Office of Broadband Development

Tel: (334) 242-7100

Director **Kathy Johnson** ............................ (334) 242-7100

## Office of the Lieutenant Governor

Alabama State House, 11 South Union Street, Suite 725,
Montgomery, AL 36130-6050
Tel: (334) 242-7900  Fax: (334) 242-4661
E-mail: info@ltgov.alabama.gov

**Employees:** 13  **Fiscal Year:** 2015  **Budget:** $649,000

★Lieutenant Governor **Kay Ivey** (R) ................. (334) 242-7900
  Term Expires: January 2019
  E-mail: kay.ivey@ltgov.alabama.gov
  Education: Auburn 1967 BS
  Career: Assistant Director, Alabama Development Office, State of
  Alabama; Government Relations and Communications Director,
  Commission on Higher Education, State of Alabama; State Treasurer
  (R-AL), State of Alabama (2003-2011)
Chief of Staff **Steve Pelham** ........................ (334) 242-7900
Deputy Chief of Staff **Taylor Nichols** .............. (334) 242-7900
  E-mail: taylor.nichols@ltgov.alabama.gov
Executive Assistant **Barbara Kelley** ................. (334) 242-7900
Public and Constituent Affairs Director **Katy Solhuff** ..... (334) 242-7900
Senior Accountant **June Rogers** ..................... (334) 242-7900

---

★ Elected Official    ■ Appointed by Governor    ● Appointed by Legislature    ▲ Appointed by Board or Commission    ◆ Appointed by State Supreme Court

# Office of the Secretary of State

State Capitol, 600 Dexter Avenue, Montgomery, AL 36130
P.O. Box 5616, Montgomery, AL 36103-5616
Tel: (334) 242-7200 TTY: (334) 242-5748 Fax: (334) 242-4993

**Employees:** 47 **Fiscal Year:** 2015 **Budget:** $14,186,000

★Secretary of State **John H. Merrill** (R) .................. (334) 242-7200
  Term Expires: January 2019
  Education: Alabama 1990 BA
  Career: Director of Community Relations and Community Education,
  Tuscaloosa County Board of Education (1994-2010)
  Confidential Assistant **Barbie Sawyer** ................. (334) 242-7223
Chief of Staff **David Brewer** ......................... (334) 242-7207
  Assistant to the Chief of Staff **John C. Bennett** ........ (334) 242-4133
Office Manager **Stephanie Vaught** .................... (334) 353-2171
General Counsel **Joel Laird, Jr.** ...................... (334) 242-0447
Public Information Officer **Tamara Cofield** ............. (334) 242-7228
  E-mail: tamara.cofield@sos.alabama.gov
Elections Analyst **Brittany Hamilton** ................. (334) 242-7205
Mail/Warehouse Clerk **Bernard McCaster** ............. (334) 265-7150
  E-mail: bernard.mccaster@sos.alabama.gov
  Executive Assistant **Stacey K. Waller-Dakwa** ......... (334) 242-7223

# Office of the Attorney General

501 Washington Avenue, Montgomery, AL 36130
Tel: (334) 242-7300 Fax: (334) 242-7458

**Employees:** 175 **Fiscal Year:** 2015 **Budget:** $21,790,000

★Attorney General **Luther J. Strange** (R) .............. (334) 242-7300
  Term Expires: January 2019
  Education: Tulane 1975 BA, 1979 JD
  Career: Director, Federal Affairs, Sonat, Inc. (1985-1994); Partner and
  Chair, Government Affairs Practice Group, Bradley Arant Rose &
  White LLP
  Communications Director **Michael C. "Mike" Lewis** ..... (334) 353-2199
  E-mail: mikelewis@ago.state.al.us
  Education: Troy State 1986 BA
Press Secretary **Joy Patterson** ....................... (334) 242-7491
  E-mail: pressoffice@ago.state.al.us
Scheduler **Sandy McLure** ............................ (334) 242-7447
  E-mail: smclure@ago.state.al.us

# Office of the State Treasurer

600 Dexter Avenue, Room S-106, Montgomery, AL 36130
Tel: (334) 242-7500 Fax: (334) 242-7592
E-mail: alatreas@treasury.alabama.gov

**Fiscal Year:** 2015 **Budget:** $3,720,000

★State Treasurer **Young J. Boozer III** (R) ............. (334) 242-7500
  Term Expires: January 2019
  E-mail: young.boozer@treasury.alabama.gov
  Education: Stanford 1971 BA; Wharton 1973 MBA
  Career: Executive Vice President, Risk Management, and General
  Auditor, The Colonial BancGroup, Inc. (1985-2007); Assistant Finance
  Director, Office of the Assistant Finance Director for Information and
  Administrative Services, Department of Finance, State of Alabama
  (2009-2010)
Deputy Treasurer **Glenda Allred** ..................... (334) 242-7505
  Executive Assistant **Brittany Matthews** ............. (334) 242-7523
Assistant State Treasurer **Daria Story** ............... (334) 242-7506
                                                Fax: (334) 353-4080

# Office of the State Auditor

600 Dexter Avenue, Montgomery, AL 36130
Tel: (334) 242-7010 Fax: (334) 242-7650

**Employees:** 9 **Fiscal Year:** 2015 **Budget:** $930,000

★State Auditor **Jim Zeigler** (R) ...................... (334) 242-7010
  Term Expires: January 2019
  Education: Alabama 1972 BPA; Jones Law 1978 JD

# Department of Agriculture and Industries

1445 Federal Drive, Montgomery, AL 36107-1123
Tel: (334) 240-7100 Fax: (334) 240-7190 Internet: www.agi.alabama.gov

**Employees:** 362 **Fiscal Year:** 2015 **Budget:** $33,501,000

★Commissioner **John McMillan** (R) ................... (334) 240-7100
  Term Expires: January 2019
  E-mail: john.mcmillan@agi.alabama.gov
  Education: Baldwin County High (Bay Minette, Alabama);
  Rhodes 1963 BA
  Executive Assistant to the Commissioner **Cindy Wright** .. (334) 240-7105
Chief of Staff **Daniel J. Autrey** ..................... (334) 240-7285
Deputy Commissioner **Brett Hall** ..................... (334) 240-7101
  Education: Trinity U 1970 BA
Deputy Commissioner **Wayne Walker** ................. (334) 240-7109
Assistant Commissioner **Glen Zorn** ................... (334) 240-6594
Accounting Director **Gwen Barnett** .................. (334) 240-7112
                                                Fax: (334) 240-7166
Information Technology Section Director **Mark Green** .... (334) 240-7200
  E-mail: mark.green@agi.alabama.gov       Fax: (334) 240-7169
Legal Section Attorney **Patrick Moody** ............... (334) 240-3898
Petroleum Commodities Section Director **Karen Wurtz** .... (334) 240-7127
                                                Fax: (334) 240-7271
Procurement Director **Kathy Childree** ................ (334) 240-7152
                                                Fax: (334) 240-7193
Public Relations Director **Amy Belcher** .............. (334) 240-7126
  E-mail: amy.belcher@agi.alabama.gov
State Veterinarian **Dr. Tony Frazier** ................. (334) 240-7255
                                                Fax: (334) 223-7352
General Services Supervisor **Michael Frazier** .......... (334) 240-6587
  E-mail: michael.frazier@agi.alabama.gov  Fax: (334) 240-7174
Personnel Officer **Teresa Brunson** ................... (334) 240-7120
                                                Fax: (334) 240-3724

# Farmers Market Authority

Richard Beard Building, 1445 Federal Drive, Suite 003,
Montgomery, AL 36107-1123
Tel: (334) 240-7247 Fax: (334) 240-3723 E-mail: fma@agi.alabama.gov
Internet: www.buylocalalabama.gov

**Employees:** 4 **Fiscal Year:** 2015 **Budget:** $2,250,000

Director **Don Wambles** ............................. (334) 240-7249
Administrative Support Assistant III **Rebecca Brown** ..... (334) 240-7251
Administrative Support Assistant III **Belinda Mulder** .... (334) 240-7110
Agriculture Marketing Specialist **John Willoughby** ...... (334) 240-7248
Agriculture Marketing Specialist **(Vacant)** ............. (334) 353-7505

# Alabama Public Service Commission [APSC]

P.O. Box 304260, Montgomery, AL 36130
Tel: (334) 242-5218 Fax: (334) 242-0509 Internet: www.psc.state.al.us

**Employees:** 73

★President **Twinkle Andress Cavanaugh** (R) ........... (334) 242-5203
  Term Expires: November 2016
  E-mail: twinkle.cavanaugh@psc.alabama.gov
★Associate Commissioner **Chris "Chip" Beeker, Jr.** (R) .... (334) 242-5191
  Term Expires: November 2018
  Education: West Alabama
★Associate Commissioner **Jeremy H. Oden** (R) .......... (334) 242-5218
  Term Expires: November 2018
  Education: Asbury Col BA; Asbury Sem

---

★ Elected Official  ■ Appointed by Governor  ● Appointed by Legislature  ▲ Appointed by Board or Commission  ◆ Appointed by State Supreme Court

EXECUTIVE BRANCH

# Alaska

Tel: (907) 465-2111 (State Information)

**Number of U.S. Congressional Delegates:** 2 Senators; 1 Representative  **Governor's Term:** 4 years
**Legislature Description:** 20 member Senate; 40 member House of Representatives; Term - Senate 4 years, House 2 years  **Next Election:** Governor November 2018; Legislature November 2018
**Number of Electoral Votes:** 3  **Official Name:** State of Alaska (Aleut: Great Land)
**Nickname:** Land of the Midnight Sun  **Motto:** North to the Future

**Population:** 738,432 (2015); Rank 48  **Fiscal Year:** 2014  **Budget:** $7,967,836,000

## Office of the Governor

State Capitol, Third Floor, Juneau, AK 99801
Tel: (907) 465-3500  Fax: (907) 465-3532
**Fiscal Year:** 2015  **Budget:** $31,425,700

**William M. "Bill" Walker**
Governor

Term Expires: December 2018
Date of Birth: April 16, 1951
Education: Lewis & Clark 1973 BSBA;
U Puget Sound 1983 JD
Home: Anchorage
Career: Mayor (R-AK), City of Valdez, Alaska
(1979-1980); Attorney, Hughes, Thorsness, Gantz,
Powell & Brundin, LLC (1983-1995)

★Governor **William M. "Bill" Walker** (I) . . . . . . . . . . . . . . . (907) 465-3500
  E-mail: bill.walker@alaska.gov
Chief of Staff **Norris "Jim" Whitaker** . . . . . . . . . . . . . . (907) 465-3500
Administrative Services Director **Guy Bell** . . . . . . . . . . . . (907) 465-3876
  E-mail: guy.bell@alaska.gov
Legislative Director **Darwin Peterson** . . . . . . . . . . . . . . (907) 465-3500
  E-mail: darwin.peterson@alaska.gov
Governor's Scheduler **Janice Mason** . . . . . . . . . . . . . . . (907) 465-3500
  E-mail: janice.mason@alaska.gov

## Anchorage Office

550 West Seventh Avenue, Suite 1700, Anchorage, AK 99501
Tel: (907) 269-7450  Fax: (907) 269-7461
Deputy Chief of Staff **Marcia Davis** . . . . . . . . . . . . . . . (907) 269-7450
  E-mail: marcia.davis@alaska.gov
Spokesperson **Grace Jang** . . . . . . . . . . . . . . . . . . . . . (907) 269-7450
  E-mail: grace.jang@alaska.gov
Press Secretary **Katie Marquette** . . . . . . . . . . . . . . . . (907) 269-7450
  E-mail: katie.marquette@alaska.gov
Senior Advisor on Rural Business and Intergovernmental
  Affairs **Gerad Godfrey** . . . . . . . . . . . . . . . . . . . . . (907) 269-7450
  E-mail: gerad.godfrey@alaska.gov
Special Advisor for Arctic Policy **Craig Fleener** . . . . . . . . (907) 269-7450
  E-mail: craig.fleener@alaska.gov
Special Advisor for Crime Policy and Prevention
  **Amanda Price** . . . . . . . . . . . . . . . . . . . . . . . . . (907) 269-7450
  E-mail: amanda.price@alaska.gov

## Fairbanks Office

675 Seventh Avenue, Suite H5, Fairbanks, AK 99701
Tel: (907) 451-2920  Fax: (907) 451-2858
Director **Melissa Stepovich** . . . . . . . . . . . . . . . . . . . (907) 451-2920
  E-mail: melissa.stepovich@alaska.gov

## Matanuska Susitna Office [MATSU]

Palmer State Office Building, 515 East Dahlia Avenue, Suite 140,
Palmer, AK 99645
Tel: (907) 761-5690  Fax: (907) 761-5908
Director **Sarah Heath** . . . . . . . . . . . . . . . . . . . . . . . (907) 761-5690
  E-mail: sarah.heath@alaska.gov
  Education: Alaska; Texas Wesleyan U JD

## Washington Office

444 North Capitol Street, NW, Suite 336, Washington, DC 20001-1512
Tel: (202) 624-5858  Fax: (202) 624-5857
Associate Director **Nathan Butzlaff** . . . . . . . . . . . . . . . (202) 654-5858
  E-mail: nathan.butzlaff@alaska.gov
  Education: Georgetown BS
Research Analyst **Amy Dobson** . . . . . . . . . . . . . . . . . . (202) 624-5858
  E-mail: amy.dobson@alaska.gov

## Office of Management and Budget

P.O. Box 110020, Juneau, AK 99811-0020
Tel: (907) 465-4660  Fax: (907) 465-2090
Director **Pat Pitney** . . . . . . . . . . . . . . . . . . . . . . . (907) 465-4660
  E-mail: pat.pitney@alaska.gov
  Education: Alaska (Fairbanks) 1991 MBA
Chief Budget Analyst **Kelly O'Sullivan** . . . . . . . . . . . . . (907) 465-4681
Economist **(Vacant)** . . . . . . . . . . . . . . . . . . . . . . . (907) 465-4677

## Department of Administration

P.O. Box 110200, Juneau, AK 99811-0200
Tel: (907) 465-2200  Fax: (907) 465-2135
**Employees:** 1,128  **Fiscal Year:** 2015  **Budget:** $329,129,300
■Commissioner **Sheldon Allred Fisher, Sr.** . . . . . . . . . . . (907) 269-6293
  E-mail: sheldon.fisher@alaska.gov
  Education: BYU 1987 BA; Yale 1990 JD
  Executive Secretary **Chad Medel** . . . . . . . . . . . . . . . (907) 465-2200
  Special Assistant to the Commissioner **Megan Collie** . . . . (907) 269-6293
  Special Assistant to the Commissioner **(Vacant)** . . . . . . (907) 465-2200
Deputy Commissioner **John Boucher** . . . . . . . . . . . . . . . (907) 465-4677
  E-mail: john.boucher@alaska.gov
  Education: Notre Dame
Deputy Commissioner **Leslie Ridle** . . . . . . . . . . . . . . . (907) 465-2200
  E-mail: leslie.ridle@alaska.gov

## Division of Administrative Services

P.O. Box 110208, Juneau, AK 99811
Tel: (907) 465-2277  Fax: (907) 465-2194
Director **Cheryl Lowenstein** . . . . . . . . . . . . . . . . . . . (907) 465-2277
  E-mail: cheryl.lowenstein@alaska.gov

## Division of Enterprise Technology Services [ETS]

P.O. Box 110206, Juneau, AK 99811-0206
Tel: (907) 465-2220  Fax: (907) 465-3450
Director **Jim Steele** . . . . . . . . . . . . . . . . . . . . . . . (907) 465-2220
  E-mail: jim.steele@alaska.gov

---

★ Elected Official     ■ Appointed by Governor     ● Appointed by Legislature     ▲ Appointed by Board or Commission     ◆ Appointed by State Supreme Court

## Division of Finance

P.O. Box 110204, Juneau, AK 99811-0204
Tel: (907) 465-2240  Fax: (907) 465-2169

Director **Scot Arehart** . . . . . . . . . . . . . . . . . . . . . . . . . . . (907) 465-3435
Deputy Direct Reporting Program Manager (DRPM) and
  Technical Director **Lisa Pusich** . . . . . . . . . . . . . . . . . . (907) 465-2240
Administrative Officer **Nicole Wery-Tagaban** . . . . . . . . . . (907) 465-5615
  E-mail: nicole.wery-tagaban@alaska.gov
Accounting Services Supervisor **Tara Jeans** . . . . . . . . . . . . (907) 465-5608
State Payroll Manager **Kelly Baines** . . . . . . . . . . . . . . . . . (907) 465-5625
State Travel Manager **Danielle Meier** . . . . . . . . . . . . . . . (907) 465-6534

## Division of General Services

P.O. Box 110210, Juneau, AK 99811-0210
Tel: (907) 465-2250  Fax: (907) 465-2189  TTY: (907) 465-2205

Director and Chief Procurement Officer
  **Thomas "Tom" Mayer** . . . . . . . . . . . . . . . . . . . . . . . . (907) 465-5677
State Leasing and Facilities Manager **Tanci Mintz** . . . . . . . (907) 269-0300

## Division of Motor Vehicles

1300 West Benson Boulevard, Anchorage, AK 99503
Tel: (907) 269-5551

Director **Amy Erickson** . . . . . . . . . . . . . . . . . . . . . . . . . . . (907) 269-5559
  E-mail: amy.erickson@alaska.gov
  Education: Arizona State 1997 BA
Operations Manager **Amy Johnson** . . . . . . . . . . . . . . . . . (907) 269-5566
  E-mail: amy.johnson1@alaska.gov
Driver Licensing Manager **Nichole Tham** . . . . . . . . . . . . . (907) 269-3775
  E-mail: nichole.tham@alaska.gov

## Division of Personnel and Labor Relations

P.O. Box 110201, Juneau, AK 99811-0201
Tel: (907) 465-4430  TTY: (907) 465-3415

Director **Kate Sheehan** . . . . . . . . . . . . . . . . . . . . . . . . . . (907) 465-4403
Deputy Director of Labor Relations **Emily Wright** . . . . . . . (907) 465-4429
  E-mail: emily.wright@alaska.gov  Fax: (907) 465-3412
Deputy Director of Personnel **Nancy Sutch** . . . . . . . . . . . . (907) 465-3794

## Division of Retirement and Benefits

P.O. Box 110203, Juneau, AK 99811-0203
Tel: (907) 465-4460  TTY: (907) 465-2805  Fax: (907) 465-3086

Chief Pension Officer **Kathleen "Kathy" Lea** . . . . . . . . . . . (907) 465-3326
Chief Health Official **Michele Michaud** . . . . . . . . . . . . . . . (907) 465-3225
Chief Operating Officer **Jim Puckett** . . . . . . . . . . . . . . . . (907) 465-4471
Chief Financial Officer **Kevin Worley** . . . . . . . . . . . . . . . . (907) 465-5703

## Division of Risk Management

P.O. Box 110218, Juneau, AK 99811-0218
Tel: (907) 465-2180  Fax: (907) 465-3690

Director **Scott Jordan** . . . . . . . . . . . . . . . . . . . . . . . . . . . (907) 465-5723
Risk Manager **Leasa Davis** . . . . . . . . . . . . . . . . . . . . . . . . (907) 465-5724

## Office of Administrative Hearings

P.O. Box 110231, Juneau, AK 99811-0231
550 West Seventh Avenue, Suite 1940, Anchorage, AK 99501
Tel: (907) 269-8170

Chief Administrative Law Judge **Kathleen A. Frederick** . . . (907) 269-8170
  Education: Gettysburg BA; Villanova JD
Deputy Chief Administrative Law Judge
  **Christopher M. Kennedy** . . . . . . . . . . . . . . . . . . . . . . . (907) 269-8170

## Office of Public Advocacy

900 West Fifth Avenue, Suite 525, Anchorage, AK 99501-2090
Tel: (907) 269-3500  Fax: (907) 269-3535

Director **Richard "Rick" Allen** . . . . . . . . . . . . . . . . . . . . . (907) 269-3500
Deputy Director **Chad Holt** . . . . . . . . . . . . . . . . . . . . . . . (907) 269-3500

## Public Defender Agency

900 West Fifth Avenue, Suite 200, Anchorage, AK 99501-2090
Tel: (907) 334-4400  Fax: (907) 269-5746

■Director **Quinlan G. Steiner** . . . . . . . . . . . . . . . . . . . . . (907) 334-4400
  E-mail: quinlan.steiner@alaska.gov
  Education: Seattle BBA; Lewis & Clark JD

## Department of Commerce, Community and Economic Development

550 West Seventh Avenue, Suite 1535, Anchorage, AK 99501
State Office Building, 9th Floor, Juneau, AK 99811-0800
P.O. Box 110800, Juneau, AK 99811-0800
Tel: (907) 269-1800 (Anchorage Office)
Fax: (907) 269-8125 (Anchorage Office)
Tel: (907) 465-2500 (Juneau Office)
TTY: (907) 465-5437 (Juneau Office)
Fax: (907) 465-5442 (Juneau Office)  E-mail: questions@alaska.gov
Internet: www.commerce.state.ak.us

**Employees:** 539  **Fiscal Year:** 2015  **Budget:** $198,710,800

■Commissioner **Chris Hladick** . . . . . . . . . . . . . . . . . . . . . (907) 465-2500
  E-mail: chris.hladick@alaska.gov
Deputy Commissioner **Fred E. Parady** . . . . . . . . . . . . . . . (907) 269-1800
  Education: Idaho BS; Montana State MS
Executive Secretary **Linda Mattson** . . . . . . . . . . . . . . . . . (907) 465-2500
Special Assistant **Abigail Enghirst** . . . . . . . . . . . . . . . . . . (907) 269-8159
Legislative Liaison **Micaela Fowler** . . . . . . . . . . . . . . . . . (907) 465-2503
  E-mail: micaela.fowler@alaska.gov

## Regulatory Commission of Alaska [RCA]

701 West Eighth Avenue, Suite 300, Anchorage, AK 99501
Tel: (907) 276-6222  Fax: (907) 276-0160

■Chair **Robert M. "Bob" Pickett** . . . . . . . . . . . . . . . . . . . (907) 263-2102
  Term Expires: March 1, 2020
  E-mail: bob.pickett@alaska.gov
  Education: Idaho BA
■Commissioner **Stephen McAlpine** . . . . . . . . . . . . . . . . . (907) 263-2115
  Term Expires: March 1, 2021
  E-mail: stephen.mcalpine@alaska.gov
■Commissioner **Rebecca L. Pauli** . . . . . . . . . . . . . . . . . . (907) 276-6222
  Term Expires: March 1, 2022
  E-mail: rebecca.pauli@alaska.gov
■Commissioner **Norman Rokeberg** . . . . . . . . . . . . . . . . . (907) 263-2106
  Term Expires: March 1, 2019
  E-mail: norman.rokeberg@alaska.gov
  Education: Willamette 1971 BA
■Commissioner **Janis "Jan" Wilson** . . . . . . . . . . . . . . . . . (907) 263-2130
  Term Expires: March 1, 2018
  E-mail: janis.wilson@alaska.gov

## Alaska Energy Authority

813 West Northern Lights Boulevard, Anchorage, AK 99503
Tel: (907) 771-3000  Fax: (907) 771-3044
Internet: www.akenergyauthority.org

Executive Director **Sara Fisher-Goad** . . . . . . . . . . . . . . . . (907) 771-3000
  Executive Assistant **Teri Webster** . . . . . . . . . . . . . . . . . (907) 771-3074
Chief Financial Officer **Michael E. Lamb** . . . . . . . . . . . . . . (907) 771-3000
Chief Operating Officer and Project Implementation
  Director **Kirk Warren** . . . . . . . . . . . . . . . . . . . . . . . . . . (907) 771-3072
Chief Procurement Officer **Tom Erickson** . . . . . . . . . . . . . (907) 771-3000
Energy Policy and Outreach Director **(Vacant)** . . . . . . . . . (907) 771-3000
  Energy Policy and Outreach Manager **Emily Ford** . . . . . . (907) 771-3000
Human Resources Director **Jennifer Haldane** . . . . . . . . . . (907) 771-3000
Policy and Programs Director **Sean Skaling** . . . . . . . . . . . (907) 771-3000
  Education: Colby; Colorado

---

★ Elected Official   ■ Appointed by Governor   ● Appointed by Legislature   ▲ Appointed by Board or Commission   ◆ Appointed by State Supreme Court

## Alaska Industrial Development and Export Authority [AIDEA]

813 West Northern Lights Boulevard, Anchorage, AK 99503
Tel: (907) 771-3000   Fax: (907) 771-3044   Internet: www.aidea.org

Executive Director **John Springsteen** . . . . . . . . . . . . . . . . . (907) 771-3008
    Education: MIT 1991 BSCE; Kellogg MBA
Commercial Finance Director
    **Christine "Chris" Anderson** . . . . . . . . . . . . . . . . . (907) 771-3030
Chief Financial Officer **Michael E. Lamb** . . . . . . . . . . . . .(907) 771-3009
Chief Infrastructure Development Officer **Mark Davis** . . . . .(907) 771-3080
    Education: Stanford JD
Project Development and Asset Management Director
    **James Hemsath** . . . . . . . . . . . . . . . . . . . . . . . . . . (907) 771-3040
Business Development and Communications Officer
    **Michael "Mike" Catsi** . . . . . . . . . . . . . . . . . . . . . . (907) 771-3060
External Affairs Officer **Karsten Rodvik** . . . . . . . . . . . . . (907) 771-3024
Human Resources Director **Jennifer Haldane** . . . . . . . . . . (907) 771-3011

## Alaska Railroad Corporation

327 West Ship Creek Avenue, Anchorage, AK 99501
P.O. Box 107500, Anchorage, AK 99510-7500
Tel: (907) 265-2300   Fax: (907) 265-2312

■Chairman **Linda Leary** . . . . . . . . . . . . . . . . . . . . . . . . (907) 265-2403
    Education: Maine; Alaska
■Vice Chair **William J. "Bill" Sheffield** . . . . . . . . . . . . . .(907) 265-2403
■Member **John E. Binkley** . . . . . . . . . . . . . . . . . . . . . . (907) 265-2403
    Affiliation: President, Alaska Cruise Association
    360 K Street, Suite 300, Anchorage, AK 99501-2308
    Education: Alaska (Fairbanks) 2005 AS
■Member **Jack Burton** . . . . . . . . . . . . . . . . . . . . . . . . . (907) 265-2403
■Member **Jon Cook** . . . . . . . . . . . . . . . . . . . . . . . . . . . (907) 265-2403
■Member **Chris Hladick** . . . . . . . . . . . . . . . . . . . . . . . . (907) 465-2500
    Affiliation: Commissioner, Department of Commerce, Community and
    Economic Development, State of Alaska
    State Office Building, 9th Floor, Juneau, AK 99811-0800
■Member **Marc A. Luiken** . . . . . . . . . . . . . . . . . . . . . . . (907) 465-3900
    Affiliation: Commissioner, Department of Transportation and Public
    Facilities, State of Alaska
    3132 Channel Drive, Juneau, AK 99801-7898
    Education: Air Force Acad 1981 BS; Air Command Col 1996;
    Joint Forces Staff Col 1996; Troy State 1996 MS; Air War Col 2000,
    2004 MSS

### Executive Management Team

▲President and Chief Executive Officer
    **William G. "Bill" O'Leary, CPA** . . . . . . . . . . . . . . . . (907) 265-2403
    E-mail: olearyb@akrr.com
    Education: Alaska (Fairbanks) BAcc
Chief Financial Officer **Barbara Amy** . . . . . . . . . . . . . . .(907) 265-3924
    Education: Connecticut BBA; Chicago MBA
Chief Information Officer **James Ratchford** . . . . . . . . . . . (907) 265-2300
    Education: Maryland
Chief Operating Officer **Doug Engebretson** . . . . . . . . . . . (907) 265-2556
Vice President, Advanced Train Control Systems and
    Technology **Eileen Reilly** . . . . . . . . . . . . . . . . . . . . (907) 265-2655
    E-mail: reillye@akrr.com
    Education: Rutgers BS
Vice President, Business Management and Corporate
    Affairs **Wendy Lindskoog** . . . . . . . . . . . . . . . . . . . (907) 265-2498
    Education: Colorado BS
Vice President, Corporate Planning and Real Estate
    **James W. Kubitz** . . . . . . . . . . . . . . . . . . . . . . . . . (907) 265-2428
    Education: Willamette BA
Vice President, Engineering **Clark Hopp** . . . . . . . . . . . . . (907) 265-2342
Vice President and General Counsel **William Hupprich** . . . (907) 265-2455
Vice President, Marketing and Customer Services
    **Dale Wade** . . . . . . . . . . . . . . . . . . . . . . . . . . . . . (907) 265-2464

## Alaska Seafood Marketing Institute [ASMI]

311 North Franklin Street, Suite 200, Juneau, AK 99801-1147
Tel: (907) 465-5560   Fax: (907) 465-5572
E-mail: info@alaskaseafood.org   Internet: www.alaskaseafood.org

Executive Director **Alexa Tonkovich** . . . . . . . . . . . . . . . . (907) 465-5560

## Alcoholic Beverage Control Board

550 West Seventh Avenue, Suite 1600, Anchorage, AK 99501
Tel: (907) 269-0350   Fax: (907) 334-2285
Internet: www.commerce.alaska.gov/dnn/abc

■Director **Cynthia A. Franklin** . . . . . . . . . . . . . . . . . . . .(907) 269-0351
    E-mail: cynthia.franklin@alaska.gov

## Serve Alaska

550 West Seventh Avenue, Suite 1770, Anchorage, AK 99501
Tel: (907) 269-4637   Fax: (907) 269-5666
E-mail: serve.alaska@alaska.gov

Executive Director **Paula Pawlowski** . . . . . . . . . . . . . . . . (907) 269-4637

## Department of Corrections [DOC]

550 West Seventh Avenue, Suite 1800, Anchorage, AK 99501
P.O. Box 112000, Juneau, AK 99811-2000
802 Third Street, Douglas, AK 99824
Tel: (907) 465-4652   Tel: (907) 269-7397 (Anchorage)
Fax: (907) 465-3390   Fax: (907) 269-7390 (Anchorage Fax)
Internet: www.correct.state.ak.us

**Employees:** 1,879   **Fiscal Year:** 2015   **Budget:** $316,323,100

■Commissioner **Dean Williams** . . . . . . . . . . . . . . . . . . . .(907) 269-7397
    E-mail: dean.williams@alaska.gov
    Executive Secretary **Kay Hoover** . . . . . . . . . . . . . . (907) 269-7397
    Administrative Assistant **Anna Satre** . . . . . . . . . . . . (907) 465-4652
Deputy Commissioner of Institutions **Clare Sullivan** . . . . . (907) 465-4652

## Department of Environmental Conservation [DEC]

410 Willoughby Avenue, Suite 303, Juneau, AK 99801-1795
P.O. Box 111800, Juneau, AK 99811-1800
Tel: (907) 465-5065 (Juneau)   Fax: (907) 465-5070 (Juneau)
Tel: (907) 269-7500 (Anchorage)   Tel: (907) 451-2100 (Fairbanks)

**Employees:** 558   **Fiscal Year:** 2015   **Budget:** $76,776,000

■Commissioner **Lawrence L. "Larry" Hartig** . . . . . . . . . . . (907) 465-5065
    E-mail: dec.commissioner@alaska.gov
    Education: Utah BA; Lewis & Clark JD
Deputy Commissioner **Alice Edwards** . . . . . . . . . . . . . . . (907) 465-5066
    Executive Secretary **Claire Fishwick** . . . . . . . . . . . . (907) 465-5066
Legislative Liaison **Alida Bus** . . . . . . . . . . . . . . . . . . . . (907) 465-5871
    E-mail: alida.bus@alaska.gov
Media and Publications Officer **Candice Bressler** . . . . . . . (907) 465-5009
    E-mail: candice.bressler@alaska.gov

## Department of Fish and Game

1255 West 8th Street, Juneau, AK 99801
P.O. Box 115526, Juneau, AK 99811-5526
Tel: (907) 465-4100   TTY: (800) 478-3648   Fax: (907) 465-2332
E-mail: dfg.commissioner@alaska.gov

**Employees:** 1,711   **Fiscal Year:** 2015   **Budget:** $191,916,600

■Commissioner **Sam Cotten** . . . . . . . . . . . . . . . . . . . . . .(907) 465-4100
    E-mail: dfg.commissioner@alaska.gov
    Commissioner's Secretary **Abby Smith** . . . . . . . . . . . (907) 465-6141
Deputy Commissioner **Kevin A. Brooks** . . . . . . . . . . . . . . (907) 465-6138
    Education: Michigan 1983 BA; Alaska 1989 MBA
Deputy Commissioner **Charles O. Swanton** . . . . . . . . . . . (907) 465-4115
    Special Assistant **Jill Klein** . . . . . . . . . . . . . . . . . . (907) 267-2228
    Federal Fisheries Coordinator **(Vacant)** . . . . . . . . . . (907) 267-2111
Legislative Liaison **(Vacant)** . . . . . . . . . . . . . . . . . . . . (907) 267-2311
Librarian **Celia Rozen** . . . . . . . . . . . . . . . . . . . . . . . . (907) 267-2314
                       Fax: (907) 267-2464

---

# Alaska Department of Health and Social Services [DHSS]

3601 C Street, Suite 902, Anchorage, AK 99503
P.O. Box 240249, Anchorage, AK 99503
Tel: (907) 269-7800  Fax: (907) 269-0060

**Employees:** 3,650  **Fiscal Year:** 2015  **Budget:** $2,520,694,900

■Commissioner **Valerie Davidson**...................(907) 269-7800
 E-mail: val.davidson@alaska.gov
 Education: Alaska Southeast; New Mexico JD
 Special Assistant to the Commissioner **Tara Horton**.....(907) 269-8021
Rate Review Executive Director **Jared C. Kosin**........(907) 334-2447
 3601 C Street, Room 978,          Fax: (907) 563-7309
 Anchorage, AK 99524-0249
Communications Manager **Clay Butcher**..............(907) 269-7867
 E-mail: clay.butcher@alaska.gov
Legislative Liaison **(Vacant)**.........................(907) 465-1611
Executive Secretary III **(Vacant)**....................(907) 269-7801

## Office of the Deputy Commissioner for Family, Community and Integrated Services

Deputy Commissioner **Karen Forrest**.................(907) 465-1610

### Division of Juvenile Justice [DJJ]

240 Main Street, Suite 700, Juneau, AK 99801
P.O. Box 110635, Juneau, AK 99811-0635
Tel: (907) 465-2212  Fax: (907) 465-2333  E-mail: hss.djj@alaska.gov

Director **Leonard "Rob" Wood**.....................(907) 465-2112
Operations Deputy Director **Dennis Weston**...........(907) 261-4388
Statewide Programs and Administrative Deputy Director
 **Barbara Murray**.................................(907) 465-2116
 E-mail: barbara.murray@alaska.gov

### Office of Children's Services

P.O. Box 110630, Juneau, AK 99811-0630
751 Old Richardson Highway, Suite 300, Fairbanks, AK 99701-7802
Tel: (907) 465-3191  Tel: (907) 451-2650 (Fairbanks Office)
Fax: (907) 465-3397  Fax: (907) 451-2616 (Fairbanks Office)

Director **Christy Lawton**...........................(907) 465-3011
                                   Tel: (907) 451-2096
Deputy Director **Tracy Spartz-Campbell**..............(907) 465-2145
Children's Services Manager (Acting) **Sara Childress**....(907) 269-3903
 323 East Fourth Avenue, Anchorage, AK 99503    Fax: (907) 269-3901
Community Relations Manager **Scott Heaton**..........(907) 465-3191
                                   Fax: (907) 465-3548
Early Childhood Comprehensive Systems Manager
 **Tracy Spartz-Campbell**..........................(907) 465-3191
Early Intervention/Infant Learning Program Manager
 **Tracy Spartz-Campbell**..........................(907) 465-3191
 E-mail: tracy.spartz-campbell@alaska.gov
Child Welfare Administrator **Kim Guay**..............(907) 451-3478
 323 East Fourth Avenue, Anchorage, AK 99501    Fax: (907) 451-3901
 E-mail: kim.guay@alaska.gov
Division Operations Manager **Travis Erickson**..........(907) 269-3903
                                   Fax: (907) 269-3988
Social Services Program Officer **Barbara Cosolito**.......(907) 465-3209
 E-mail: barbara.cosolito@alaska.gov        Fax: (907) 465-2061
Social Services Program Officer **Yvonne Hill**..........(907) 465-3458
 E-mail: yvonne.hill@alaska.gov
Online Resources for Children of Alaska Project
 Manager **Ilya Stepanov**..........................(907) 465-3633
 E-mail: ilya.stepanov@alaska.gov

### Division of Behavioral Health

3601 C Street, Suite 934, Anchorage, AK 99503
P.O. Box 110620, Juneau, AK 99811-0620
Tel: (907) 269-3600 (Anchorage Office)
Tel: (907) 451-5045 (Fairbanks Office)
Tel: (907) 465-3370 (Juneau Office)  Fax: (907) 465-2668 (Juneau Office)

Director **Randall Burns**...........................(907) 269-5948
Division Operations Manager **Stacy Toner**.............(907) 465-3370

Administrative Operations Manager II **Linda Brazak**....(907) 465-8202
 E-mail: linda.brazak@alaska.gov
Alaska Psychiatric Institute Chief Executive Officer
 **Melissa Ring, PhD**..............................(907) 269-7101
 3700 Piper Street, Anchorage, AK 99508    Fax: (907) 269-7251
Risk and Research Management Chief **Shaun Wilhelm**...(907) 269-3408

## Office of the Deputy Commissioner for Medicaid and Health Care Policy

Deputy Commissioner **Jon Sherwood**................(907) 465-5830
Medicaid Expansion Project Director **(Vacant)**..........(907) 269-7800
Medicaid Program Integrity Manager **Douglas Jones**.....(907) 269-0361
 Building K, 4601 Business Park Boulevard,    Fax: (907) 269-3460
 Anchorage, AK 99503-7167

### Division of Health Care Services

Building L, 4501 Business Park Boulevard, Suite 24,
Anchorage, AK 99503-7167
P.O. Box 110660, Juneau, AK 99811-0660
Tel: (907) 334-2400  Fax: (907) 561-1684

Director **Margaret Brodie**..........................(907) 334-2520
Accounting and Recovery Manager **Punipuao Pedro**.....(907) 334-2452
Administrative Operations Manager **Bobby Miles**........(907) 334-2409
 E-mail: bobby.miles@alaska.gov
Division Operations Manager **Lori Campbell**...........(907) 334-2406
EPSDT Coordinator **Carrie Truett**...................(907) 269-4576
Pharmacy Program and Ancillary Services Manager
 **Erin Narus**....................................(907) 334-2425
Provider Services Manager **Cindy Christensen**..........(907) 334-2430
Quality Assurance Manager **(Vacant)**.................(907) 375-6468
Systems and Analysis Manager **Linda Walsh**...........(907) 334-2441
State Children's Health Insurance Program (SCHIP)
 Coordinator **Barbara Hale**.......................(907) 465-5833
 E-mail: barbara.hale@alaska.gov        Fax: (907) 465-2204
Tribal Health Program Manager **Renee Gayhart**........(907) 465-1619
 E-mail: renee.gayhart@alaska.gov
Legislative Liaison **Courtney King**...................(907) 334-8653
 E-mail: courtney.king@alaska.gov        Fax: (907) 561-1684

### Division of Public Assistance [DPA]

3601 C Street, Anchorage, AK 99503
350 Main Street, Juneau, AK 99801
P.O. Box 110640, Juneau, AK 99811-0640
Tel: (907) 465-3347  Fax: (907) 465-5154

Director **Sean O'Brien**............................(907) 465-5847
Field Services Chief (Acting) **Tammie Walker**...........(907) 269-7875
                                   Tel: (907) 465-4986
                                   (Juneau Office)
                                   Fax: (907) 269-3099
Public Assistant Program Office **Erin Walker-Tolles**......(907) 465-6161
Program Integrity and Analysis Chief **Elaine Rich**........(907) 465-4952
                                   Fax: (907) 465-5254
Program and Policy Development Chief **Monica Mitchell**.........(907) 465-5835
                                   Fax: (907) 465-5254
Central Regional Manager **Mark Armstrong**...........(907) 269-6547
 400 Gambell Street, Suite 304,          Fax: (907) 269-6532
 Anchorage, AK 99501
 E-mail: mark.armstrong@alaska.gov
Coastal Regional Manager **Marjorie Tiedje**............(907) 269-8974
                                   Fax: (907) 563-0767
Northern Regional Manager
 **Michael "Mike" Thibodeau**......................(907) 451-2801
 675 Seventh Avenue, Station D,          Fax: (907) 451-5177
 Fairbanks, AK 99701-4592
Southeast Regional Manager (Acting) **Victoria O'Brien**...(907) 228-7105
 2030 Sea Level Drive, Suite 301,         Fax: (907) 225-7381
 Ketchikan, AK 99901
Family Nutrition and Women, Infants and Children
 (WIC) Health Program Manager **Kathleen Wayne**......(907) 465-8636
 Goldstein Building, 130 Seward Street, 5th Floor,  Fax: (907) 465-3416
 Juneau, AK 99811
 E-mail: kathleen.wayne@alaska.gov

## Division of Senior and Disabilities Services

550 West Eight Street, Anchorage, AK 99501 (Anchorage Office)
751 Old Richardson Highway, Suite 100a, Fairbanks, AK 99701-7802
(Fairbanks Office)
Tel: (907) 269-3666 (Anchorage Office)
Fax: (907) 269-3688 (Anchorage Office)
Tel: (907) 451-5045 (Fairbanks Office)
Fax: (907) 451-5046 (Fairbanks Office)
Tel: (907) 465-3372 (Juneau Office)  Fax: (907) 465-1170 (Juneau Office)

Director **Duane Mayes** . . . . . . . . . . . . . . . . . . . . . . . . . . . . .(907) 269-2083
Fax: (907) 269-3690
Deputy Director **Deb Etheridge** . . . . . . . . . . . . . . . . . . . . .(907) 465-5481
Fax: (907) 465-1170
Grants Program Manager **Lisa Morley** . . . . . . . . . . . . . . . .(907) 465-4996
P.O. Box 110680, Juneau, AK 99811-0680      Fax: (907) 465-2677
E-mail: lisa.morley@alaska.gov
Operations and Training Unit Manager **Andy Sandusky** . . (907) 465-3448
Personal Care Assistance Unit Manager **Rodney George** . . (907) 269-3453
E-mail: rodney.george@alaska.gov      Fax: (907) 269-8164
Policy and Programs Development Unit Manager
  **Jetta Whittaker** . . . . . . . . . . . . . . . . . . . . . . . . . . . . . . . .(907) 465-1605
Fax: (907) 465-1170
Provider Certification and Compliance Unit Manager
  **Cheri Herman** . . . . . . . . . . . . . . . . . . . . . . . . . . . . . . . . . .(907) 269-4139
Fax: (907) 269-3690
Quality Assurance Unit Manager **Caroline Hogan** . . . . . . . .(907) 269-3666
Fax: (907) 269-3690
Research and Analysis Unit Manager
  **Anastasiya Podunovich** . . . . . . . . . . . . . . . . . . . . . . . . . .(907) 269-3477
Waiver and PCA Program Units Manager **Lisa McGuire** . . .(907) 269-3681
Fax: (907) 269-3639
Medicare Information Officer **Judith Bendersky, MPH** . . . (907) 269-3680
E-mail: judith.bendersky@alaska.gov      Tel: (800) 478-6065
Fax: (907) 269-2045

## Office of the Assistant Commissioner for Finance and Management Services

350 Main Street, Juneau, AK 99801
Alaska Office Building, P.O. Box 110650, Juneau, AK 99811-0650
Tel: (907) 465-3082  Fax: (907) 465-2499

Assistant Commissioner **Sana Efird** Room 129 . . . . . . . . . . (907) 465-1630
E-mail: sana.efird@alaska.gov
Deputy Director **Myra Pugh** . . . . . . . . . . . . . . . . . . . . . . . . (907) 465-3469
E-mail: myra.pugh@alaska.gov
Administrative Operations Manager **Debbie Vanslyke** . . . . (907) 465-4636
E-mail: debbie.vanslyke@alaska.gov
Audit Manager **Torrey Jacobson** Suite 509 . . . . . . . . . . . . (907) 465-3121
Fax: (907) 465-2499
Budget Manager **Melissa Ordner** . . . . . . . . . . . . . . . . . . . . (907) 465-1629
Fax: (907) 465-1850
Data Processing Manager **Timothy "Tim" Banaszak**
  Room 18 . . . . . . . . . . . . . . . . . . . . . . . . . . . . . . . . . . . . . . (907) 465-3610
E-mail: timothy.banaszak@alaska.gov      Fax: (907) 465-3034
Facilities Section Manager **Michael Frawley** . . . . . . . . . . . (907) 465-1870
Federal Allocations Manager **Linnea Osborne** . . . . . . . . . . (907) 465-6333
E-mail: linnea.osborne@alaska.gov
Grants and Procurement Manager **Darla Madden** . . . . . . . (907) 465-1624
333 Wiloughby Avenue, Room 760,      Fax: (907) 465-6421
Juneau, AK 99811-0650
Human Resources Manager **(Vacant)** . . . . . . . . . . . . . . . . . (907) 465-2308
240 Main Street, Suite 501, Juneau, AK 99801
Revenue Manager **Valeria Buschfort** Room 412 . . . . . . . . (907) 465-1216
Finance Officer **James Farley** Room 414 . . . . . . . . . . . . . . (907) 465-1690

## Division of Public Health

3601 C Street, Anchorage, AK 99503
350 Main Street, Room 508, Juneau, AK 99801
P.O. Box 110610, Juneau, AK 99811-0610
Tel: (907) 465-3090  Fax: (907) 465-4632

Chief Medical Officer and Director of Public Health
  **Dr. Jay C. Butler, MD** . . . . . . . . . . . . . . . . . . . . . . . . . . .(907) 269-8000
Education: North Carolina MD
Deputy Director **Jill Lewis** Suite 214 . . . . . . . . . . . . . . . . .(907) 465-8617

## Department of Labor and Workforce Development

1111 West Eighth Street, Juneau, AK 99801
P.O. Box 111149, Juneau, AK 99811-1149
Tel: (907) 465-2700  Fax: (907) 465-2784
E-mail: commissioner.labor@alaska.gov  Internet: www.labor.state.ak.us

**Employees: 992  Fiscal Year: 2015  Budget: $148,225,300**
■Commissioner **Heidi Drygas** . . . . . . . . . . . . . . . . . . . . . . . (907) 465-2700
E-mail: commissioner.labor@alaska.gov
Education: Alaska (Fairbanks); Willamette JD
Deputy Commissioner **Greg Cashen** . . . . . . . . . . . . . . . . . (907) 465-2700
E-mail: greg.cashen@alaska.gov
Education: Northern Arizona
Deputy Commissioner **Joe J. Thomas** . . . . . . . . . . . . . . . . (907) 465-2700
E-mail: joe.thomas@alaska.gov
Education: West Virginia BA
Special Assistant **Michelle Zenger** . . . . . . . . . . . . . . . . . . (907) 465-5673
E-mail: michelle.zenger@alaska.gov

## Alaska Labor Relations Agency

3301 Eagle Street, Suite 206, Anchorage, AK 99503
P.O. Box 107026, Anchorage, AK 99510-7026
Tel: (907) 269-4895  Fax: (907) 269-4898

Administrator/Hearing Examiner **Mark Torgerson** . . . . . . . (907) 269-4895
E-mail: mark.torgerson@alaska.gov

## Department of Law

Dimond Courthouse, 123 - 4th Street, 6th Floor, P.O. Box 110300,
Juneau, AK 99811-0300
Tel: (907) 465-2133  Fax: (907) 465-2075  Internet: www.law.alaska.gov

## Office of the Attorney General

P.O. Box 110300, Juneau, AK 99811-0300
Tel: (907) 269-5100  Fax: (907) 465-2075

**Employees: 574  Fiscal Year: 2015  Budget: $95,765,300**
■Attorney General **Craig W. Richards** . . . . . . . . . . . . . . . . . (907) 465-2133
E-mail: craig.richards@alaska.gov
Education: Washington and Lee JD; Duke MBA; Virginia

## Department of Military and Veterans Affairs

P.O. Box 5800, Joint Base Elmendorf-Richardson, AK 99505-5800
Tel: (907) 428-6003  Fax: (907) 428-6019

**Employees: 343  Fiscal Year: 2015  Budget: $54,045,200**
■Commissioner **BG Laurel Hummel, USA (Ret)** . . . . . . . . . (907) 428-6008
E-mail: laurie.hummel@alaska.gov
Education: West Point 1982
Deputy Commissioner **Col Robert Doehl, ANG** . . . . . . . . . (907) 428-6003
Special Assistant **Marty Meyer** . . . . . . . . . . . . . . . . . . . . . (907) 428-6003
Alaska Naval Militia Commander
  **CPT Roger A. Motzko, ARNG** . . . . . . . . . . . . . . . . . . . . (907) 428-6014
Alaska State Defense Force Commander
  **BG Roger E. Holl, ARNG** . . . . . . . . . . . . . . . . . . . . . . . . (907) 428-6850
Military Youth Academy Director **Bob Roses** . . . . . . . . . . (907) 384-6017
Fax: (907) 384-6007
Public Affairs Director **LtCol Candis Olmstead, ANG** . . . . (907) 249-1342
E-mail: candis.olmstead@akanch.ang.af.mil      Tel: (907) 428-7091
Veterans Affairs Office Director **Verdie Bowen** . . . . . . . . . (907) 428-6016
E-mail: verdie.bowen@alaska.gov

## Alaska National Guard

Building 5900, Camp Denali,
Joint Base Elmendorf-Richardson, AK 99505-5800
P.O. Box 5800, Joint Base Elmendorf-Richardson, AK 99505-5800
Tel: (907) 384-1110

■Adjutant General **BG Laurel Hummel, USA (Ret)** . . . . . . . (907) 428-6008
E-mail: laurie.hummel@alaska.gov
Staff Judge Advocate **(Vacant)** . . . . . . . . . . . . . . . . . . . . . (907) 428-6020
State Command Sergeant Major
  **CSM Pamela Harrington, ARNG** . . . . . . . . . . . . . . . . . . . (907) 428-6056

---

★ Elected Official      ■ Appointed by Governor      ● Appointed by Legislature      ▲ Appointed by Board or Commission      ◆ Appointed by State Supreme Court

Joint Staff Director **(Vacant)** . . . . . . . . . . . . . . . . . . . . . . (907) 428-6450
Information Technology Manager **Timothy R. Crawford** . . (907) 428-6204
  E-mail: timothy.r.crawford6.civ@mail.mil
Inspector General **Col David R. Wille, ANG** . . . . . . . . . . . (907) 428-6060
  E-mail: david.r.wille.mil@mail.mil
US Property and Fiscal Officer
  **COL Michael Williams, ARNG** . . . . . . . . . . . . . . . . . . . (907) 428-6850

## Alaska Air National Guard

5005 Raspberry Road, Anchorage, AK 99502
Tel: (907) 249-1176  Fax: (907) 249-1467  Internet: airguard.alaska.gov

Commander/Assistant Adjutant General
  **Col Karen E. Mansfield, ANG** . . . . . . . . . . . . . . . . . . . (907) 428-6072
168th Wing Commander **Col Mark A. Hedlund, ANG** . . . . (907) 428-6850
  Eielson AFB, AK 99702
176th Wing Commander
  **BrigGen Donald S. Wenke, ANG** . . . . . . . . . . . . . . . . (907) 249-1176
  Kulis Air National Guard Base, 5005 Raspberry Road,
  Anchorage, AK 99502-1998

## Alaska Army National Guard

Building 5900, Camp Denali,
Joint Base Elmendorf-Richardson, AK 99505-5800
P.O. Box 5800, Joint Base Elmendorf-Richardson, AK 99505-5800
Internet: armyguard.alaska.gov

Commander/Assistant Adjutant General
  **COL Joseph J. Streff, USA** . . . . . . . . . . . . . . . . . . . . . (907) 428-6075

## Alaska Department of Natural Resources

550 West 7th Avenue, Suite 1400, Anchorage, AK 99501
Tel: (907) 269-8431  Fax: (907) 269-8918  E-mail: dnr.pic@alaska.gov
Internet: dnr.alaska.gov

**Employees:** 1,099  **Fiscal Year:** 2015  **Budget:** $224,867,400

■Commissioner (Acting) **Marty K. Rutherford** . . . . . . . . . . (907) 269-8431
  E-mail: marty.rutherford@alaska.gov
  Executive Secretary **Mary Kay Ryckman** . . . . . . . . . . . . (907) 269-8426
Deputy Commissioner **Edmund J. "Ed" Fogels** . . . . . . . . (907) 269-8431
  E-mail: ed.fogels@alaska.gov
  Education: Virginia 1979 BS
Deputy Commissioner **(Vacant)** . . . . . . . . . . . . . . . . . . . . (907) 269-8431
Intergovernmental Coordinator **John Crowther** . . . . . . . . . (907) 269-8431
Mental Health Trust Land Office Executive Director
  **Marcie Menefee** . . . . . . . . . . . . . . . . . . . . . . . . . . . . (907) 269-8753
  2600 Cordova Street, Suite 100,      Fax: (907) 269-8905
  Anchorage, AK 99503
Special Projects Assistant **Jim Shine** . . . . . . . . . . . . . . . . (907) 269-8431
  Education: Western State Col BA; Denver JD
State Pipeline Coordinator **David de Gruyter** . . . . . . . . . . . (907) 269-6403
  3651 Penland Parkway, Anchorage, AK 99508      Fax: (907) 269-6880
  E-mail: david.degruyter@alaska.gov
Public Information Center Chief
  **Kathleen "Kathy" Johnson** . . . . . . . . . . . . . . . . . . . . (907) 269-8415
  550 West Seventh Avenue, Suite 1260, Anchorage, AK 99501
  E-mail: kathy.johnson@alaska.gov
Legislative Liaison **Courtney Sanborn** . . . . . . . . . . . . . . . (907) 269-8431
  E-mail: courtney.sanborn@alaska.gov
Communications Coordinator **Elizabeth Bluemink** . . . . . . . (907) 269-8434
  E-mail: elizabeth.bluemink@alaska.gov

## Division of Agriculture

1800 Glenn Highway, Suite 12, Palmer, AK 99645-6736
Tel: (907) 745-7200  Fax: (907) 745-7112

Director **Arthur Keyes** . . . . . . . . . . . . . . . . . . . . . . . . . . (907) 761-3867
Administrative Officer II **Curt Sandvik** . . . . . . . . . . . . . . . (907) 761-3866
  E-mail: curt.sandvik@alaska.gov
Administrative Officer I **Lora Haralson** . . . . . . . . . . . . . . . (907) 761-3851
Agricultural Revolving Loan Fund Manager/Loan Officer
  **Amanda Swanson** . . . . . . . . . . . . . . . . . . . . . . . . . . . (907) 761-3869
Inspection Manager/Development Specialist II
  **David Driscoll** . . . . . . . . . . . . . . . . . . . . . . . . . . . . . (907) 761-3861
  E-mail: david.driscoll@alaska.gov

Marketing Manager/Development Specialist II
  **David Driscoll** . . . . . . . . . . . . . . . . . . . . . . . . . . . . . (907) 761-3861
Mt. McKinley Meat and Sausage Plant Production
  Manager **Francis "Frank" Huffman** . . . . . . . . . . . . . . (907) 745-5232
  385 Inner Springer LP, Palmer, AK 99645      Fax: (907) 746-0575
Plant Materials Center Program Manager
  **Brianne Blackburn** . . . . . . . . . . . . . . . . . . . . . . . . . (907) 745-8785
  5310 South Bodenburg Spur, Palmer, AK 99645      Fax: (907) 746-1568
  E-mail: brianne.blackburn@alaska.gov

## Division of Forestry

550 West Seventh Avenue, Suite 1450, Anchorage, AK 99501
Tel: (907) 269-8463  Fax: (907) 269-8931

State Forester **John C. "Chris" Maisch** . . . . . . . . . . . . . . (907) 451-2660
Deputy State Forester **Dean Brown** . . . . . . . . . . . . . . . . . (907) 269-8476
Administrative Services Manager **Karlyn Herrera** . . . . . . . . (907) 269-8477
  E-mail: keri.hubbard@alaska.gov
Fire Program Manager **Tom Kurth** . . . . . . . . . . . . . . . . . . (907) 269-8463
  E-mail: tom.kurth@alaska.gov
Forest Resources Program Manager **Jim Eleazer** . . . . . . . . (907) 269-8473
  E-mail: jim.eleazer@alaska.gov
Operation Forester **Robert Schmoll** . . . . . . . . . . . . . . . . . (907) 356-5850
                                              Fax: (907) 356-5855
Safety Officer **Rocky Ansell** . . . . . . . . . . . . . . . . . . . . . . (907) 761-6247
Coastal Regional Forester **Michael "Mike" Curran** . . . . . . (907) 225-3070
  2417 Tongass Avenue, Suite 213,      Fax: (907) 247-3070
  Ketchikan, AK 99901
Northern Regional Forester **Tim Dabney** . . . . . . . . . . . . . (907) 451-2670
  3700 Airport Way, Fairbanks, AK 99709      Fax: (907) 451-2690

## Division of Geological and Geophysical Surveys

3354 College Road, Fairbanks, AK 99709
Tel: (907) 269-8400  Fax: (907) 451-5050  Internet: www.dggs.alaska.gov

Director and State Geologist **Steve Masterman** . . . . . . . . (907) 451-5007
Division Operations Manager **Kenneth R. Papp** . . . . . . . . (907) 754-3595
  Education: Cincinnati BS; Alaska (Fairbanks) MS
  Administrative Officer **Shelly L. Showalter** . . . . . . . . . (907) 451-5002
  E-mail: shelly.showalter@alaska.gov
Energy Resources Section Chief **David LePain** . . . . . . . . (907) 451-5085
  E-mail: david.lepain@alaska.gov
Engineering Geology Section Chief **Deanne Stevens** . . . . (907) 451-5014
  E-mail: deanne.stevens@alaska.gov
Geologic Communications Section Chief **Paula Davis** . . . . (907) 451-5053
  E-mail: paula.davis@alaska.gov
Mineral Resources Section Chief **Lawrence K. Freeman** . . (907) 451-5027
Geologic Materials Center Curator **(Vacant)** . . . . . . . . . . . (907) 754-3595

## Division of Mining, Land and Water

550 West Seventh Avenue, Suite 1070, Anchorage, AK 99501
Tel: (907) 269-8600  Fax: (907) 269-8904

Director **Brent Goodrum** . . . . . . . . . . . . . . . . . . . . . . . . (907) 269-8600
  E-mail: brent.goodrum@alaska.gov
Deputy Director **Martin "Marty" Parsons** . . . . . . . . . . . . (907) 269-8532
  E-mail: marty.parsons@alaska.gov
Operations Chief **Wyn Menefee** . . . . . . . . . . . . . . . . . . . (907) 269-8501
  E-mail: wyn.menefee@alaska.gov
Administrative Officer **Melissa Richie** . . . . . . . . . . . . . . . (907) 269-8627
  E-mail: melissa.richie@alaska.gov
Mining Section Manager **Scott Pexton** . . . . . . . . . . . . . . . (907) 269-8621
  E-mail: scott.pexton@alaska.gov      Fax: (907) 269-8949
Resource Assessment and Development Manager
  **(Vacant)** . . . . . . . . . . . . . . . . . . . . . . . . . . . . . . . . . (907) 269-8592
                                              Fax: (907) 269-8915
Realty Services Section Manager **Jerri Sansone** . . . . . . . . (907) 269-2552
Water Resources Section Manager **David W. Schade** . . . . . (907) 269-8645
  E-mail: david.w.schade@alaska.gov

## Division of Oil and Gas

550 West Seventh Avenue, Suite 1100, Anchorage, AK 99501
Tel: (907) 269-8800  Fax: (907) 269-8938  Internet: dog.dnr.alaska.gov

Director **Corri Feige** . . . . . . . . . . . . . . . . . . . . . . . . . . . (907) 269-7493
  E-mail: corri.feige@alaska.gov

*(continued on next page)*

★ Elected Official   ■ Appointed by Governor   ● Appointed by Legislature   ▲ Appointed by Board or Commission   ◆ Appointed by State Supreme Court

**Division of Oil and Gas** *continued*

Deputy Director **Jim Beckham** . . . . . . . . . . . . . . . . . . . . . . . (907) 269-8775
 E-mail: jim.beckham@alaska.gov
 Education: US Coast Guard Acad BS
Administrative Operations Manager I **Brenda Muller** . . . . . (907) 269-8820
 E-mail: brenda.muller@alaska.gov
Petroleum Land Manager **Saree Timmons** . . . . . . . . . . . . . .(907) 375-7751
 E-mail: saree.timmons@alaska.gov
Permitting Manager **Kim Kruse** . . . . . . . . . . . . . . . . . . . . . . (907) 375-7754
 E-mail: kim.kruse@alaska.gov
Pipeline Coordinator **Jason Walsh** . . . . . . . . . . . . . . . . . . . . (907) 269-6419
Resource Evaluation Manager **Paul Decker** . . . . . . . . . . . . . (907) 269-8791
 E-mail: paul.decker@alaska.gov
 Education: Fort Lewis BS; Wisconsin MS, PhD
Commercial Analyst **James "Jim" Stouffer** . . . . . . . . . . . . (907) 269-8796
 E-mail: jim.stouffer@alaska.gov
Commercial Manager **Alex Nouvakhov** . . . . . . . . . . . . . . . (907) 375-8233
Units Manager **Temple Davidson** . . . . . . . . . . . . . . . . . . . . (907) 269-8784

## Division of Parks and Outdoor Recreation

550 West Seventh Avenue, Suite 1380, Anchorage, AK 99501
Tel: (907) 269-8700 Fax: (907) 269-8917 Internet: dnr.alaska.gov/parks
Director **Ben Ellis** . . . . . . . . . . . . . . . . . . . . . . . . . . . . . . . . (907) 269-8700
 E-mail: ben.ellis@alaska.gov
Design and Construction Chief **Rys Miranda** . . . . . . . . . . . (907) 269-8736
 E-mail: rys.miranda@alaska.gov
Field Operations Chief **Claire LeClair** . . . . . . . . . . . . . . . . (907) 269-8702
Grants and Administration Services Chief **Jamie Walker** . . (907) 269-8703
 E-mail: jamie.walker@alaska.gov
History/Archaeology and Historical Commission Chief
 **Judy Bittner** . . . . . . . . . . . . . . . . . . . . . . . . . . . . . . . . (907) 269-8715
 Fax: (907) 269-8908

## Division of Support Services

Tel: (907) 465-2422 Fax: (907) 465-3886 Internet: dnr.alaska.gov/ssd
Director **Jeanmarie Davis** . . . . . . . . . . . . . . . . . . . . . . . . . (907) 465-2422
 Fax: (907) 465-2102
Operations Manager **Fabienne Peter-Contesse** . . . . . . . . . (907) 465-3379
Finance Officer **William "Bill" Andrews** . . . . . . . . . . . . . (907) 465-3503
Procurement Officer **Marlys Hagen** . . . . . . . . . . . . . . . . . . (907) 269-8666
 Fax: (907) 269-8909
Revenue Officer **Cristin Cowles-Brunton** . . . . . . . . . . . . . (907) 269-8677
 Fax: (907) 269-8911
State Recorder **Vicky Backus** . . . . . . . . . . . . . . . . . . . . . . . (907) 269-8882
 E-mail: vicky.backus@alaska.gov Fax: (907) 269-8912
Land Records Information Chief **Chris Hamilton** . . . . . . . . (907) 269-8836
 E-mail: christopher.hamilton@alaska.gov Fax: (907) 269-8920

## Alaska Department of Public Safety

5700 East Tudor Road, Anchorage, AK 99507-1221
Tel: (907) 269-5511 Fax: (907) 269-5033 Internet: www.dps.alaska.gov

**Employees:** 904 **Fiscal Year:** 2015 **Budget:** $193,091,600

■Commissioner **Col. Gary Folger** . . . . . . . . . . . . . . . . . . . . (907) 269-5086
 Note: Until May 31, 2016.
 E-mail: gary.folger@alaska.gov
■Commissioner **Walter Monegan III** . . . . . . . . . . . . . . . . . .(907) 269-5086
 Note: Effective June 1, 2016.
 Executive Secretary **Vickie Miller** . . . . . . . . . . . . . . . . .(907) 269-5086
 E-mail: vickie.miller@alaska.gov
Deputy Commissioner **William Comer** . . . . . . . . . . . . . . . (907) 465-4322
 Special Assistant **Allison Hanzawa** . . . . . . . . . . . . . . . . (907) 465-5505
 E-mail: allison.hanzawa@alaska.gov
 Legislative Liaison **Kelly Howell** . . . . . . . . . . . . . . . . . (907) 269-5591
 E-mail: kelly.howell@alaska.gov
 Education: Alaska 1992 BA
Administrative Assistant II **Tanya Silva** . . . . . . . . . . . . . . .(907) 465-4322

## Department of Revenue

State Office Building, 333 West Willoughby Avenue, 11th Floor,
Juneau, AK 99801
P.O. Box 110400, Juneau, AK 99811-0400
Tel: (907) 465-2300 TTY: (907) 465-3679 Fax: (907) 465-2389
Internet: www.dor.alaska.gov

**Employees:** 873 **Fiscal Year:** 2015 **Budget:** $321,866,200

■Commissioner **Randall Hoffbeck** . . . . . . . . . . . . . . . . . . . .(907) 465-2301
 E-mail: randall.hoffbeck@alaska.gov
 Special Assistant to the Commissioner
 **Stephanie Alexander** . . . . . . . . . . . . . . . . . . . . . . . . . (907) 465-6829
Deputy Commissioner **Jerry Burnett** . . . . . . . . . . . . . . . . . (907) 465-3669
 Education: Central Washington BS; Alaska MBA, MPA
Deputy Commissioner **Dona B. Keppers** . . . . . . . . . . . . . . (907) 269-1034
 550 West Seventh Avenue, Suite 670, Anchorage, AK 99501
Alaska Municipal Bond Bank Authority Executive
 Director **Deven Mitchell** . . . . . . . . . . . . . . . . . . . . . . . . (907) 465-3750
 Fax: (907) 465-2902

## Department of Transportation and Public Facilities

3132 Channel Drive, Juneau, AK 99801-7898
P.O. Box 112500, Juneau, AK 99811-2500
Tel: (907) 465-3900 Fax: (907) 586-8365
E-mail: dot.commissioner@alaska.gov Internet: www.dot.state.ak.us

**Employees:** 3,500 **Fiscal Year:** 2015 **Budget:** $625,371,100

■Commissioner **Marc A. Luiken** . . . . . . . . . . . . . . . . . . . . . (907) 465-3900
 E-mail: dot.commissioner@alaska.gov
 Executive Secretary **Caro Rosier-Polley** . . . . . . . . . . . . . (907) 465-3900
Deputy Commissioner **Steven D. Hatter** . . . . . . . . . . . . . . (907) 465-3900
Design and Engineering Services Chief Engineer
 **D. Lance Mearig** . . . . . . . . . . . . . . . . . . . . . . . . . . . . . (907) 465-6958
Administrative Services Director **Amanda Holland** . . . . . . .(907) 465-3911
 E-mail: amanda.holland@alaska.gov
 Finance Officer **June Gotschall** . . . . . . . . . . . . . . . . . . . (907) 465-8829
Program Development Director **Michael "Mike" Vigue** . . . (907) 465-6971
 E-mail: mike.vigue@alaska.gov
Internal Review Chief **Robert Janes** . . . . . . . . . . . . . . . . . .(907) 465-2080
Information Systems and Services Division Director
 **William Anker** . . . . . . . . . . . . . . . . . . . . . . . . . . . . . . . (907) 465-2956
 E-mail: william.anker@alaska.gov
Transportation Management and Security Chief **(Vacant)** . . (907) 465-1762
Public Information Officer **Jeremy Woodrow** . . . . . . . . . . (907) 465-8994
 E-mail: jeremy.woodrow@alaska.gov
Chief Contracts Officer **Charlie Deininger** . . . . . . . . . . . . . (907) 465-8946
 E-mail: charlie.deininger@alaska.gov
Legislative Liaison **Mike Lesmann** . . . . . . . . . . . . . . . . . . (907) 465-4772
 E-mail: mike.lesmann@alaska.gov

## Board of Education and Early Development

801 West Tenth Street, Suite 200, Juneau, AK 99801-0500
P.O. Box 110500, Juneau, AK 99811-0500
Tel: (907) 465-2802 Fax: (907) 465-4156

■Chair **James K. Fields** . . . . . . . . . . . . . . . . . . . . . . . . . . . (907) 822-5913
 Term Expires: March 1, 2018
 P.O. Box 397, Glennallen, AK 99588
 E-mail: james@avak.biz
■First Vice-Chair **Sue Hull** (Fourth Judicial District) . . . . . . (907) 378-7139
 Term Expires: February 18, 2018
 1630 Washington Drive, Fairbanks, AK 99709
 E-mail: hull@gci.net
■Second Vice-Chair **Barbara A. Thompson** (At-Large) . . . . (907) 465-2802
 Term Expires: February 28, 2019
 Education: San Diego State BA; Alaska Pacific MAT
■Member **Alec Burris** . . . . . . . . . . . . . . . . . . . . . . . . . . . . (907) 352-0400
 Term Expires: June 30, 2016
 2472 North Seward Meridian Parkway, Wasilla, AK 99654
■Member **Kenny Gallahorn** (Second Judicial District) . . . . . (907) 465-2802
 Term Expires: February 28, 2019
 P.O. Box 946, Kotzebue, AK 99752
 E-mail: kennygallahorn@gmail.com

---

★ Elected Official ■ Appointed by Governor ● Appointed by Legislature ▲ Appointed by Board or Commission ◆ Appointed by State Supreme Court

■Member **Dr. Keith Hamilton** (At-Large) . . . . . . . . (907) 260-7422 ext. 101
  Term Expires: March 1, 2020
  35109 Royal Place, Soldotna, AK 99669
  E-mail: khamilton@alaskacc.edu
■Member **John Harmon** (Third Judicial District) . . . . . . . . (907) 273-1503
  Term Expires: March 1, 2020
  P.O. Box 2926, Palmer, AK 99645
  E-mail: jharmon@lumenchristiak.com
  Education: Houghton BA; St Joseph's Col (ME) MSEd; Capital U JD
■Member **Rebecca Himschoot** (First Judicial District) . . . . . (907) 617-5481
  Term Expires: March 1, 2021
  E-mail: alaskaeducator@gmail.com
  Education: Western Washington BA

## Department of Education and Early Development

P.O. Box 110500, Juneau, AK 99811-0500
Tel: (907) 465-2800  Fax: (907) 465-4156  TTY: (907) 465-2815
Internet: www.education.alaska.gov

**Employees:** 367  **Fiscal Year:** 2015  **Budget:** $1,613,666,700

▲Commissioner (Interim) **Dr. Susan A. McCauley** . . . . . . . . (907) 465-8677
  E-mail: susan.mccauley@alaska.gov
Education Deputy Commissioner (Interim)
  **Betty Walters** . . . . . . . . . . . . . . . . . . . . . . . . . . (907) 465-2802
  Education: Marywood U
Legislative Liaison **Marcy Herman** . . . . . . . . . . . . . . . . . . (907) 465-2803
  E-mail: marcy.herman@alaska.gov
Executive Secretary **Shawn Sypeck** . . . . . . . . . . . . . . . (907) 465-2802
Rural Education Coordinator **Chris Simon** . . . . . . . . . . . . (907) 500-2189
Public Information Officer **Eric Fry** . . . . . . . . . . . . . . . . . (907) 465-2851
  E-mail: eric.fry@alaska.gov

## Libraries, Archives and Museums Division

P.O. Box 110571 M/S 0571, Juneau, AK 99811-0571
Tel: (907) 465-2910  Fax: (907) 465-2151  E-mail: asl@alaska.gov

Director/State Librarian **Linda Thibodeau** . . . . . . . . . . . . (907) 465-2911
  Note: Until June 30, 2016.
Director/State Librarian **Patience Frederiksen** . . . . . . . . . . (907) 269-6566
  Note: Effective July 1, 2016.
  Education: Carnegie Mellon; Syracuse MLS
Deputy Director **Bob Banghart** . . . . . . . . . . . . . . . . . . (907) 465-2912
Administrative Officer **Debbie McBride** . . . . . . . . . . . . . . (907) 465-2929
  E-mail: debbie.mcbride@alaska.gov
Alaska State Museum Chief Curator **Addison Field** . . . . . . (907) 465-4866
  P.O. Box 110525, Juneau, AK 99811       Fax: (907) 465-2976
  395 Whittier Street, Juneau, AK 99801
  E-mail: addison.field@alaska.gov
Museum Services Curator **Scott Carrlee** . . . . . . . . . . . . . . (907) 465-4806
Sheldon Jackson Museum Curator
  **Jacqueline Fernandez** . . . . . . . . . . . . . . . . . . (907) 747-8904
  104 College Dr., Sitka, AK 99835-7657       Fax: (907) 747-3004
  E-mail: jacqueline.fernandez@alaska.gov
State Archivist **Dean Dawson** . . . . . . . . . . . . . . . . . . . . . (907) 465-2275
  141 Willoughby Avenue, Juneau, AK 99801    Fax: (907) 465-2465
Exhibits Specialist **Aaron Elmore** . . . . . . . . . . . . . . . . . . (907) 465-4820
Government Publications Librarian **Maeghan Kearney** . . . . (907) 465-1300
Government Services Coordinator **Daniel Cornwall** . . . . . . (907) 465-6332
  E-mail: dan.cornwall@alaska.gov
Grants/State Data Coordinator **Patience Frederiksen** . . . . . (907) 269-6566
  Note: Until June 30, 2016.
  E-mail: patience.frederiksen@alaska.gov
Historical Collections **James "Jim" Simard** . . . . . . . . . . . (907) 465-2926
Information Services Head **Freya Anderson** . . . . . . . . . . . (907) 465-1315
Library Development **Patience Frederiksen** . . . . . . . . . . . (907) 269-6566
  Note: Until June 30, 2016.
Museum Registrar **Andrew Washburn** . . . . . . . . . . . . . . (907) 465-4829

## School Finance Division

Tel: (907) 465-2891  Fax: (907) 463-5279

Director **Elizabeth Nudelman** . . . . . . . . . . . . . . . . . . . . (907) 465-8679
Administrative Assistant **(Vacant)** . . . . . . . . . . . . . . . . . . (907) 465-2891

## Teaching and Learning Support Division

Tel: (907) 465-2830  Fax: (907) 465-3396
Director **Dr. Susan A. McCauley** . . . . . . . . . . . . . . . . . . (907) 465-2857
                                          Fax: (907) 465-6760
Deputy Director **Paul Prussing** . . . . . . . . . . . . . . . . . . . (907) 465-8721
Assessment, Accountability and Information Management
  Director **Margaret McKinen** . . . . . . . . . . . . . . . . . (907) 465-2970
Special Education Director **Donald "Don" Enoch** . . . . . . . (907) 465-2972
Teacher Education and Certification Administrator
  **Sondra Meredith** . . . . . . . . . . . . . . . . . . . . . . . . (907) 465-8663
  E-mail: sondra.meredith@alaska.gov       Fax: (907) 465-2441
Head Start Education Specialist **Melora Gaber** . . . . . . . . . (907) 465-8707
                                          TTY: (907) 465-2815
Head Start Education Specialist **Paul Sugar** . . . . . . . . . . . (907) 465-1862
                                          TTY: (907) 465-2815

## Office of the Lieutenant Governor

State Capitol Building, Third Floor, Juneau, AK 99801
Tel: (907) 465-3520  Fax: (907) 465-5400

★Lieutenant Governor **Byron I. Mallott** (D) . . . . . . . . . . . . (907) 465-3520
  Term Expires: December 2018
  E-mail: byron.mallott@alaska.gov
  Career: Chief Executive Officer, Sealaka Corporation (1982-1992);
  Executive Director, Alaska Permanent Fund Corporation (1995-1999)
Scheduler **Shari Paul** . . . . . . . . . . . . . . . . . . . . . . . . . . (907) 465-3520
  E-mail: shari.paul@state.co.us

## Division of Elections

240 Main Street, 4th Floor, Juneau, AK 99801
P.O. Box 110017, Juneau, AK 99811-0017
Tel: (907) 465-4611  TTY: (907) 465-3020  E-mail: elections@alaska.gov

Director **Josephine "Josie" Bahnke** . . . . . . . . . . . . . . . . (907) 465-4611
Election Program Manager **Brian Jackson** . . . . . . . . . . . . (907) 465-4611
Election Coordinator **Sharon Forrest** . . . . . . . . . . . . . . . (907) 465-4611
Administrative Officer **Kristi DiCostanzo** . . . . . . . . . . . . . (907) 465-4611
  E-mail: kristi.dicostanzo@alaska.gov
Language Assistance Compliance Manager
  **Indra Arriaga Delgado** . . . . . . . . . . . . . . . . . . . (907) 522-8683
  2525 Gambell Street, Suite 100, Anchorage, AK 99503-2838
Yup'ik Language Assistant Program Coordinator
  **John Toopetlook** . . . . . . . . . . . . . . . . . . . . . . . . (907) 374-3717

★ Elected Official    ■ Appointed by Governor    ● Appointed by Legislature    ▲ Appointed by Board or Commission    ◆ Appointed by State Supreme Court

*State Yellow Book*                    © Leadership Directories, Inc.                    Summer 2016

# American Samoa

Internet: www.americansamoa.gov

**Number of U.S. Congressional Delegates:** 1 Nonvoting Delegate  **Governor's Term:** 4 years
**Legislature Description:** 18 member Senate; 21 member House of Representatives; Term - Senate 4 years, House 2 years  **Next Election:** Governor November 2016; Legislature November 2016
**Official Name:** American Samoa  **Motto:** Samoa-Muamua le Atua (Samoa, God is first)

**Population:** 54,517 (2014)

## Office of the Governor

A.P. Lutali Executive Office Building, Pago Pago, AS 96799
Tel: (684) 633-4116  Fax: (684) 633-2269

**Lolo Matalasi Moliga**
Governor

Began Service: January 4, 2013
Term Expires: January 4, 2017
Education: Chadron State BEd;
San Diego State 2012 MPA
Career: State Representative (I-AS), American Samoa House of Representatives; Chief Procurement Officer, Procurement Office, American Samoa; President of the Senate, American Samoa Senate (2005-2009); State Senator (I-AS, District 2), American Samoa Senate (2005-2009); President, Development Bank of American Samoa, American Samoa (2009-2012)

★Governor **Lolo Matalasi Moliga** (I) . . . . . . . . . . . . . . . . . . (684) 633-4116
  E-mail: lolomoliga@gmail.com
Executive Assistant to the Governor
  **Iulogologo Joseph M. Pereira** . . . . . . . . . . . . . . . . . . (684) 633-4116
  E-mail: josephpereira48@hotmail.com
Chief of Staff **Fiu Johnny Saelua** . . . . . . . . . . . . . . (684) 633-4116
  Senior Administrative Assistant **Melesete G. Haleck** . . . . (684) 633-4116
  E-mail: melesete.haleck@go.as.gov
Deputy Chief of Staff **Taimalelagi P. "Minnie" Tuia** . . . . . . (684) 633-4116
  E-mail: minnie.tuia@go.as.gov
Chief Legal Counsel **Steven H. Watson** . . . . . . . . . . . . . . (684) 633-4116
  E-mail: stevew@blueskynet.as
Federal Programs Director **Jerome Ierome** . . . . . . . . . . . . . (684) 633-4116
  E-mail: jerome.ierome.asg.govoffice@gmail.com
Chief Protocol Officer **(Vacant)** . . . . . . . . . . . . . . . . . . . . . (684) 633-4116
Finance Officer **Don Fa'ai'usao** . . . . . . . . . . . . . . . . . . . . (684) 633-4116
  E-mail: don.faaiuaso@go.as.gov
Communications Director **(Vacant)** . . . . . . . . . . . . . . . . . . (684) 633-4116
Press Officer **(Vacant)** . . . . . . . . . . . . . . . . . . . . . . . . . . (684) 633-4116

## Hawaii Office

1427 Dillingham Boulevard, Suite 210, Honolulu, HI 96817
Tel: (808) 847-1998  Fax: (808) 845-3420  E-mail: ahawaiioff@aol.com

Director **Soloalii Falepo** . . . . . . . . . . . . . . . . . . . . . . . . . . (808) 847-1998
Deputy Director **Bonnelly Liu-Pauulu** . . . . . . . . . . . . . . . . (808) 847-1998
  E-mail: bliupauulu.asgoffice.hawaii@gmail.com

## Office of the Lieutenant Governor

A.P. Lutali Executive Office Building, Pago Pago, AS 96799
Tel: (684) 633-4116  Fax: (684) 633-2269

★Lieutenant Governor **Lemanu Peleti Mauga** (I) . . . . . . . . . (684) 633-4116
  Term Expires: January 4, 2017
  E-mail: lemanu.mauga@go.as.gov
  Education: Hawaii; San Diego State 2013 MPA

## Office of the Administrative Law Judge

Tel: (684) 633-7712  Fax: (684) 633-7725  E-mail: alj@as.gov
Law Judge **Toetagata Albert Mailo** . . . . . . . . . . . . . . . (684) 633-7712
Deputy Law Judge **Marie Alailima** . . . . . . . . . . . . . . . . . (684) 633-7712

## Office of the Territorial Auditor

Tel: (684) 633-5191  Fax: (684) 633-1039
Territorial Auditor (Acting) **Liua Fatuesi** . . . . . . . . . . . . . (684) 633-5191
Deputy Director **(Vacant)** . . . . . . . . . . . . . . . . . . . . . . . . (684) 633-5191

## Office of the Public Defender

P.O. Box 4030, Pago Pago, AS 96799
Tel: (684) 633-1286  Fax: (684) 633-4745
Public Defender **Marc Douglas Fiaui** . . . . . . . . . . . . . . . . (684) 633-1286

## Department of Administrative Services

Executive Office Building, Utulei, Pago Pago, AS 96799
Tel: (684) 633-4156  Fax: (684) 633-1841
Director **Malemo Tausaga** . . . . . . . . . . . . . . . . . . . . . . . .(684) 633-4158
  E-mail: malemo.tausaga@das.as.gov
Deputy Director **Eliki Afalava** . . . . . . . . . . . . . . . . . . . . . (684) 633-4158
  E-mail: elike.afalava@das.as.gov

## Department of Agriculture [DOA]

Tel: (684) 699-9272  Fax: (684) 699-4031
Director **Lealao Melila Purcell** . . . . . . . . . . . . . . . . . . . . . (684) 699-9272
Deputy Director **Peter Gurr** . . . . . . . . . . . . . . . . . . . . . . . (684) 699-9272

## Department of Commerce [DOC]

Tel: (684) 633-5155  Fax: (684) 633-4195
E-mail: doc@americansamoa.gov
Director **Keniseli Lafaele** . . . . . . . . . . . . . . . . . . . . . . . . . (684) 633-5155
Deputy Director **Uili Leauanae** . . . . . . . . . . . . . . . . . . . . (684) 633-5155

## Department of Education [DOE]

P.O. Box DOE, Pago Pago, AS 96799
Tel: (684) 633-5237  Fax: (684) 633-4240
Director **Dr. Vaitinasa Salu Hunkin-Finau** . . . . . . . . . . . . (684) 633-5237
  Education: BYU (HI) 1968 BA; BYU 1974 MAED; Hawaii 1986 EdD
Deputy Director **Philo Jennings** . . . . . . . . . . . . . . . . . . . . (684) 633-5237
Deputy Director **Faaui Vaitautolu** . . . . . . . . . . . . . . . . . . (684) 633-5237
Deputy Director of Finance **(Vacant)** . . . . . . . . . . . . . . . . (684) 633-5237
GED (General Education Development) Administrator
  **Samuel Uhrle** . . . . . . . . . . . . . . . . . . . . . . . . . . . . . . . (684) 633-5237

## American Samoa Department of Homeland Security [ASDHS]

Tel: (684) 699-0414  Fax: (684) 699-5329
Director **Utualii Iuniasolua Tului Savusa** . . . . . . . . . . . . . (684) 699-0414
  Education: Kemper Military 1989 AA
Deputy Director **Jacinta Brown** . . . . . . . . . . . . . . . . . . . . (684) 699-0414

---

★ Elected Official    ■ Appointed by Governor    ● Appointed by Legislature    ▲ Appointed by Board or Commission    ◆ Appointed by State Supreme Court

State Registrar **Taifita Solomona** . . . . . . . . . . . . . . . . . . . . (684) 633-1405
P.O. Box 6894, Pago Pago, AS 96799          Fax: (684) 633-7910

## Department of Human Resources
Tel: (684) 633-4485  Fax: (684) 633-1139
Director **Lei S. Thompson** . . . . . . . . . . . . . . . . . . . . . . (684) 633-4485
Education: Southern Illinois 1979 BSEd; Chapman 1986 MS
Deputy Director **Eseneiaso Liu** . . . . . . . . . . . . . . . . . . . . (684) 633-4485

## Department of Human and Social Services [DHSS]
Tel: (684) 633-7506  Tel: (684) 633-1405 (Vital Records)
Fax: (684) 633-5944
■Director **Dr. Taeaoafua Meki Solomona** . . . . . . . . . . . . (684) 633-7506
E-mail: mtsolomona@dhss.as
Deputy Director **Mauvaefa'atasi "John" Suisala** . . . . . . . (684) 633-7506

## Department of Legal Affairs
American Samoa Government, Pago Pago, AS 96799
P.O. Box 7, Pago Pago, AS 96799
Tel: (684) 633-4163  Fax: (684) 633-1838
Attorney General **Talauega Eleasalo Ale** . . . . . . . . . . . . . (684) 633-4163
E-mail: eleasalo.ale@la.as.gov
Assistant Attorney General **Mitzie Jessop-Folau** . . . . . . . . (684) 633-4163
Education: Utah 1992 BA; J Reuben Clark Law 1995 JD

## Department of Local Government
Tel: (684) 633-5201  Fax: (684) 633-5590
Secretary of Samoan Affairs **Mauga Tasi Asuega** . . . . . . . (684) 633-5201
Deputy Secretary **Tuiagamoa Tavai** . . . . . . . . . . . . . . . . (684) 633-5201

## Department of Marine and Wildlife Resources
Tel: (684) 633-4456  Fax: (684) 633-5944
Director **Ruth Tofiga-Matagi** . . . . . . . . . . . . . . . . . . . . (684) 633-4456
Deputy Director **Selaina V. Tuimavave** . . . . . . . . . . . . . (684) 633-4456

## Department of Parks and Recreation
Tel: (684) 699-9513  Fax: (684) 699-4427
Director **Tamaaiga P. Gaoteote** . . . . . . . . . . . . . . . . . . . (684) 699-9513
E-mail: piligaoteote@yahoo.com
Deputy Director **Ken Tupua** . . . . . . . . . . . . . . . . . . . . . . (684) 699-9513
E-mail: kennethtupua@gmail.com

## Department of Planning and Budget
Tel: (684) 633-4207  Fax: (684) 633-1148
■Director **Catherine D. Aigamaua-Saelua** . . . . . . . . . . . . (684) 633-4207
E-mail: catherine.saelua@obp.as.gov
■Deputy Director **Aokuso Satia** . . . . . . . . . . . . . . . . . . . (684) 633-4207
E-mail: aokuso.satia@obp.as.gov

## Department of Port Administration
Tel: (684) 633-4251  Fax: (684) 633-5281
Director **Dr. Taimalelagi "Claire" Tuia-Poumele** . . . . . . . (684) 633-4251
Deputy Director **Chris King** . . . . . . . . . . . . . . . . . . . . . . (684) 633-4251

## Department of Procurement
Tel: (684) 699-1170  Fax: (684) 699-2387
Chief Procurement Officer **Oreta Crichton** . . . . . . . . . . . . (684) 699-1170
Deputy Chief Procurement Officer **Sapi Ma'o-Ena** . . . . . . . (684) 699-1170

## Department of Public Health
American Samoa Government, Pago Pago, AS 96799
Tel: (684) 633-4606  Fax: (684) 633-5379
Director **Motusa Tuileama Nua** . . . . . . . . . . . . . . . . . . . (684) 633-4606
Deputy Director **Fara Utu** . . . . . . . . . . . . . . . . . . . . . . . (684) 633-4606

## Department of Public Information
Tel: (684) 633-4191  Fax: (684) 633-4369
Director **Fagafaga D. Langkilde** . . . . . . . . . . . . . . . . . . . (684) 633-4191
E-mail: fagafaga.langkilde@opi.as.gov
Deputy Director **Vincent Iuli** . . . . . . . . . . . . . . . . . . . . . (684) 633-4191
E-mail: vincent.iuli@opi.as.gov

## Department of Public Safety [DPS]
P.O. Box 1086, Pago Pago, AS 96799
Tel: (684) 633-1111  Fax: (684) 633-7296
■Commissioner **Save Liuato Tuitele** . . . . . . . . . . . . . . . . (684) 633-1111
E-mail: ziontuitele@yahoo.com
Deputy Commissioner **Vaimaga Maiava** . . . . . . . . . . . . . (684) 633-1111

## Department of Public Works
Tel: (684) 699-9921  Fax: (684) 699-9913
Director **Faleosina Voigt** . . . . . . . . . . . . . . . . . . . . . . . (684) 699-9921
Deputy Director **Laupule Tilei** . . . . . . . . . . . . . . . . . . . . (684) 699-9921

## Department of Treasury
Tel: (684) 633-4155  Fax: (684) 633-4100
Treasurer **Ueligitone Tonumaipe'a** . . . . . . . . . . . . . . . . . (684) 633-4155
Deputy Treasurer **Tina Vaa** . . . . . . . . . . . . . . . . . . . . . . (684) 633-4155

## Department of Youth and Women's Affairs
Tel: (684) 644-2836
Director **Jonathan Fanene** . . . . . . . . . . . . . . . . . . . . . . . (684) 644-2836
E-mail: jonathan.fanene@dywa.as.gov
Deputy Director **Pa'u Roy T. Ausage** . . . . . . . . . . . . . . . . (684) 644-2836
E-mail: roy.ausage@dywa.as.gov

## Election Office
Tel: (684) 699-3570  Fax: (684) 699-3574  E-mail: info@eo.as.gov
E-mail: asgelect@samoatelco.com
■Chief Election Officer **Dr. Uiagalelei L. Uiagalelei** . . . . . . (684) 699-3570
Deputy Director **Meleisea Vai Filiga** . . . . . . . . . . . . . . . . (684) 699-3570

## Insurance Office
Tel: (684) 633-4116  Fax: (684) 633-2269
■Insurance Commissioner **Tau Tanuvasa** . . . . . . . . . . . . . (684) 633-4116
E-mail: tanuvasa_t@yahoo.com
Assistant **Elizabeth Perri** . . . . . . . . . . . . . . . . . . . . . . . (684) 633-4116

## Office of Property Management
Tel: (684) 699-6505  Fax: (694) 699-6535
Chief of Property Management **Malo Niumata** . . . . . . . . . . (684) 699-6505
Assistant Chief **Poleen Asalele** . . . . . . . . . . . . . . . . . . . (684) 699-6505

## Office of Protection and Advocacy for the Disabled
P.O. Box 3937, Pago Pago, AS 96799
Tel: (684) 699-2441  Fax: (684) 699-7286
■Director **Dr. Matautu "Peter" Tinitali** . . . . . . . . . . . . . . (684) 699-2441
E-mail: uta.opad@americansamoa.gov
Deputy Director **Tapumanaia Galu Satele** . . . . . . . . . . . . (684) 699-2441

## Territorial Energy Office
Tel: (684) 699-1101  Fax: (684) 699-2835  Internet: www.asgteo.com
Director **Aliitama Sotoa** . . . . . . . . . . . . . . . . . . . . . . . . (684) 699-1101
Deputy Director **Taliga Vaiolo** . . . . . . . . . . . . . . . . . . . . (684) 699-1101

★ Elected Official      ■ Appointed by Governor      ● Appointed by Legislature      ▲ Appointed by Board or Commission      ◆ Appointed by State Supreme Court

EXECUTIVE BRANCH

## Office of Disaster Assistance and Petroleum Management [ODAPM]

Tel: (684) 699-1329  Tel: (684) 699-1330  Fax: (684) 699-5005
E-mail: tofr@as.gov
Director **Alfonso P. Galea'i** .......................... (684) 699-1329
Deputy Director **Salu Tuigamala** ..................... (684) 699-1329

## Veterans and Military Affairs Office

Tel: (684) 699-2910  Fax: (684) 633-2269
Director **Taua'a Sam Vaouli** ......................... (684) 633-2910

## American Samoa Environmental Protection Agency [ASEPA]

Tel: (684) 633-2304  Fax: (684) 633-5801  E-mail: info@epa.as.gov
Executive Director **Ameko Pato** ..................... (684) 633-2304
Deputy Director **Fa'amao Asalele, Jr.** ............... (684) 633-2304

## American Samoa Power Authority [ASPA]

Tel: (684) 699-5282  Fax: (684) 699-7067
Chief Executive Officer **Utu Abe Malae** .............. (684) 699-5282
Chief Operations Officer **Reno Vivao** ............... (684) 699-5282
Chief Financial Officer **Susana Faiivae** ............ (684) 699-5282

## American Samoa Telecommunications Authority [ASTCA]

Tel: (684) 633-1121  Fax: (684) 633-9032
Chief Executive Officer **Aleki Sene, Jr.** ............ (684) 633-1121

## Criminal Justice Planning Agency

Tel: (684) 633-5221  Fax: (684) 633-7552  E-mail: cjpa@as.gov
Director **Keith Gebauer** ............................ (684) 633-5221
    E-mail: keith.gebauer@cjpa.as.gov
Deputy Director **Leonard Seumanutafa** .............. (684) 633-5221

## Medical Services Authority

Tel: (684) 633-4818  Fax: (684) 633-5086
Chief Executive Officer **Taufete'e John Faumuina, Jr.** ... (684) 633-4818
    Education: Boston Col 1972 BA
Medical Services Chief **Dr. Iotamo Saleapaga** ......... (684) 633-4818

## Alcoholic Beverage Control Board

Tel: (684) 633-5155
Chairman **(Vacant)** ................................. (684) 633-5155

## American Samoa Community College [ASCC]

P.O. Box 2609, Pago Pago, AS 96799
Tel: (684) 699-9155  Fax: (684) 699-6259  E-mail: info@amsamoa.edu
President **Dr. Seth Galea'i** ........................ (684) 699-9155

## Board of Higher Education

Tel: (684) 699-9155  Fax: (684) 699-6259
Chairman **Rev. Sekuini Sevaaetasi** ................. (684) 699-9155

## Development Bank of American Samoa [DBAS]

Tel: (684) 633-4456  Fax: (684) 633-1163  E-mail: dbasinfo@dbas.org
President **Ruth Matagi-fa'atili** .................... (684) 633-4456
    E-mail: ruth@dbas.org

## Territorial Administration on Aging [TAOA]

Tel: (684) 633-1251  Fax: (684) 633-2533
Director **Ale Tifimalae Ale** ........................ (684) 633-1251
Deputy Director **Kuresa Paopao** .................... (684) 633-1251

---

★ Elected Official   ■ Appointed by Governor   ● Appointed by Legislature   ▲ Appointed by Board or Commission   ◆ Appointed by State Supreme Court

# Arizona

Tel: (602) 542-4331 (Governor)   Internet: www.az.gov

**Number of U.S. Congressional Delegates:** 2 Senators; 9 Representatives   **Governor's Term:** 4 years
**Legislature Description:** 30 member Senate; 60 member House of Representatives; Term - Senate 2
years, House 2 years   **Next Election:** Governor November 2018; Legislature November 2016
**Number of Electoral Votes:** 11   **Official Name:** State of Arizona (O'odham: Little Spring)
**Nickname:** The Grand Canyon State   **Motto:** Ditat Deus (God Enriches)

**Population:** 6,828,065 (2015); Rank 14   **Fiscal Year:** 2015   **Budget:** $9,083,913,500

## Office of the Governor

1700 West Washington Street, Phoenix, AZ 85007
Tel: (602) 542-4331   Fax: (602) 542-1381   Internet: www.azgovernor.gov

**Fiscal Year:** 2015   **Budget:** $4,954,800

**Douglas A. "Doug" Ducey**
Governor

Began Service: January 5, 2015
Term Expires: 2019
Date of Birth: April 9, 1964
Education: Arizona State 1982 BS
Religion: Roman Catholic
Career: Sales and Marketing Executive, The
Procter & Gamble Company (1986-1993);
Chief Executive Officer/Chairman, Cold Stone
Creamery (1995-2007); State Treasurer, Office of
the State Treasurer Doug Ducey, State of Arizona
(2011-2015)

★ Governor **Douglas A. "Doug" Ducey** (R) . . . . . . . . . . . . . (602) 542-4331
   E-mail: dducey@az.gov
   Senior Executive Assistant **Barb Conley** . . . . . . . . . . . . (602) 542-4331
   E-mail: bconley@az.gov
Chief of Staff **Kirk D. Adams** . . . . . . . . . . . . . . . . . . . . (602) 542-4331
   E-mail: kadams@az.gov
   Education: U Phoenix BS
Deputy Chief of Staff for Communications
   **Daniel Scarpinato** . . . . . . . . . . . . . . . . . . . . . . . . . . (602) 542-2661
   E-mail: dscarpinato@az.gov
   Education: Arizona 2004
Deputy Chief of Staff for External Affairs and Policy
   Development **Daniel "Danny" Seiden** . . . . . . . . . . . . . (602) 542-3439
   E-mail: dseiden@az.gov
   Education: Pepperdine 2003 BA; Arizona State 2008 JD
Deputy Chief of Staff for Policy and Budget
   **Victor Riches** . . . . . . . . . . . . . . . . . . . . . . . . . . . . . . (602) 542-3465
   E-mail: vriches@az.gov
Chief of Operations **Henry R. Darwin** . . . . . . . . . . . . . . (602) 542-1327
   E-mail: hdarwin@az.gov
   Senior Advisor to Chief of Operations **Sean Price** . . . . . . (602) 542-1308
   E-mail: sprice@az.gov
Senior Advisor **Sara Mueller** . . . . . . . . . . . . . . . . . . . . . (602) 542-4331
   E-mail: smueller@az.gov
Senior Advisor **J. P. Twist** . . . . . . . . . . . . . . . . . . . . . . (602) 542-1626
Director of Legislative Affairs **Gretchen Martinez** . . . . . . . (602) 542-4331
   E-mail: gmartinez@az.gov
   Education: Arizona BA
Director of Scheduling **Samantha Brooks** . . . . . . . . . . . . (602) 542-1315
   E-mail: sbrooks@az.gov
Senior Press Secretary **Annie Dockendorff** . . . . . . . . . . . (602) 542-7029
   E-mail: adockendorff@az.gov
Digital Press Secretary **Torunn Sinclair** . . . . . . . . . . . . . (602) 542-4331
   E-mail: tsinclair@az.gov
Press and Digital Coordinator **Blake Wilson** . . . . . . . . . . (602) 542-1272
   E-mail: bwilson@az.gov
   Education: Arizona State BA, BS
General Counsel **Mike Liburdi** . . . . . . . . . . . . . . . . . . . (602) 542-1371
   E-mail: mliburdi@az.gov

Deputy General Counsel **Kate King** . . . . . . . . . . . . . . . . . (602) 542-1455
   E-mail: kking@az.gov
Education Policy Advisor **Dawn Wallace** . . . . . . . . . . . . . (602) 542-1316
   E-mail: dwallace@az.gov
Government and Transportation Policy Advisor
   **Rene Guillen** . . . . . . . . . . . . . . . . . . . . . . . . . . . . . (602) 542-1256
   E-mail: rguillen@az.gov
Health and Human Services Policy Advisor
   **Christina Corieri** . . . . . . . . . . . . . . . . . . . . . . . . . . (602) 542-3394
   E-mail: ccorieri@az.gov
Native American Affairs Policy Advisor
   **Kristine Fire Thunder** . . . . . . . . . . . . . . . . . . . . . . . (602) 542-4421
   E-mail: kfirethunder@az.gov
Natural Resources Policy Advisor **Hunter Moore** . . . . . . . (602) 542-1782
   E-mail: hmoore@az.gov
Public Safety Policy Advisor **Joe Cuffari** . . . . . . . . . . . . . (602) 542-3391
   E-mail: jcuffari@az.gov

## Accounting Office

Tel: (602) 542-1339   Fax: (602) 542-1329

Comptroller **John McCleve** . . . . . . . . . . . . . . . . . . . . . . (602) 542-1339
   E-mail: jmccleve@az.gov

## Governor's Office of Children, Youth and Families [GOCYF]

Tel: (602) 542-4043   Fax: (602) 542-3423

Executive Director **Debbie Moak** . . . . . . . . . . . . . . . . . . (602) 542-4043
   E-mail: dmoak@az.gov

## Governor's Office of Equal Opportunity

Tel: (602) 542-3711   Fax: (602) 542-3712

**Employees:** 4   **Fiscal Year:** 2015   **Budget:** $188,300

Director **Barry Wong** . . . . . . . . . . . . . . . . . . . . . . . . . . (602) 542-3711
   E-mail: equalopportunity@az.gov
   Education: Arizona 1981 BS, 1984 JD

## Governor's Office of Highway Safety [GOHS]

3030 North Central Avenue, Suite 1550, Phoenix, AZ 85012
Tel: (602) 255-3216

Highway Safety Director **Alberto Gutier** . . . . . . . . . . . . . (602) 255-3216
   E-mail: directorsoffice@azgohs.gov
   Education: Christian Brothers (Cuba); Florida BS
Executive Assistant **Mari Hembeck** . . . . . . . . . . . . . . . . (602) 255-3216
   E-mail: marihembeck@azgohs.gov

## Governor's Southern Arizona Office

400 West Congress, Suite 504, Tucson, AZ 85701
Tel: (520) 628-6580   Fax: (520) 628-6512

■ Director **Juan Ciscomani** . . . . . . . . . . . . . . . . . . . . . . (520) 628-6580
   E-mail: jciscomani@az.gov
■ Deputy Director **Becky Barry** . . . . . . . . . . . . . . . . . . . (520) 628-6580

---

★ Elected Official   ■ Appointed by Governor   ● Appointed by Legislature   ▲ Appointed by Board or Commission   ◆ Appointed by State Supreme Court

**EXECUTIVE BRANCH**

# Office of Strategic Planning and Budgeting

Tel: (602) 542-5381  Fax: (602) 542-0868  E-mail: ospb@az.gov
Internet: www.ospb.state.az.us

**Employees:** 22  **Fiscal Year:** 2015  **Budget:** $1,994,000

Director **Lorenzo Romero** . . . . . . . . . . . . . . . . . . . . . (602) 542-5383
  E-mail: romero@az.gov
  Education: Arizona State
Office Manager **Pamela Ray** . . . . . . . . . . . . . . . . . . . (602) 542-5381
  E-mail: pray@az.gov
Assistant Director **Bret Cloninger** . . . . . . . . . . . . . . . . (602) 542-5823
  E-mail: bcloninger@az.gov
Assistant Director **Bill Greeney** . . . . . . . . . . . . . . . . . (602) 542-5822
  E-mail: bgreeney@az.gov
Budget and Project Manager **Scott Selin** . . . . . . . . . . . . (602) 542-5384
  E-mail: sselin@az.gov
Budget and Project Manager **Laura Johnson** . . . . . . . . . . (602) 542-0866
  E-mail: ljohnson@az.gov
Senior Analyst **(Vacant)** . . . . . . . . . . . . . . . . . . . . . (602) 542-0866
Senior Analyst **Charles Martin** . . . . . . . . . . . . . . . . . (602) 542-6192
  E-mail: cmartin@az.gov
Operations Analyst **Michael Williams** . . . . . . . . . . . . . (602) 542-3801
  E-mail: mwilliams@az.gov
Economist **Glenn Farley** . . . . . . . . . . . . . . . . . . . . . (602) 542-3476
  E-mail: gfarley@az.gov

# Arizona-Mexico Commission [AMC]

Tel: (602) 542-1370  Fax: (602) 542-1411  Internet: www.azmc.org

Executive Director **Marcos Garay** . . . . . . . . . . . . . . . . (602) 542-1370
  E-mail: mgaray@az.gov
  Education: Thunderbird Global MBA
Deputy Executive Director **(Vacant)** . . . . . . . . . . . . . . (602) 542-1370

# Boards and Commissions

Tel: (602) 542-2449  Fax: (602) 542-0758

Director **LCpl Ryan D. Peters, USMC (Ret)** . . . . . . . . . . (602) 542-1743
  Education: Arizona 2008

# Constituent Services

Tel: (602) 542-1318  Fax: (602) 542-1381

Director **LCpl Ryan D. Peters, USMC (Ret)** . . . . . . . . . . (602) 542-1318

# Office of the Auditor General

2910 North 44th Street, Suite 410, Phoenix, AZ 85018
Tel: (602) 553-0333  Fax: (602) 553-0051
E-mail: webmaster@azauditor.gov  Internet: www.azauditor.gov

**Employees:** 185  **Fiscal Year:** 2015  **Budget:** $18,246,000

● Auditor General
  **Debra K. "Debbie" Davenport, CPA, CGFM, CFE** . . . . . (602) 553-0333
  E-mail: ddavenport@azauditor.gov
  Education: Arizona State BSBA
Deputy Auditor General **Melanie M. Chesney** . . . . . . . . . (602) 553-0333
  Education: Wisconsin (Green Bay) BS; Arizona State MS
General Counsel **Jeffrey P. "Jeff" Larson** . . . . . . . . . . . (602) 553-0333
  Education: Arizona State BS, JD
Information Technology Director
  **Joseph D. "Joe" Moore** . . . . . . . . . . . . . . . . . . . (602) 553-0333
  E-mail: jmoore@azauditor.gov
  Education: Niagara 1982 BA; SUNY (Albany) 1985 MPA
Professional Practice Director **Donna Miller, CPA** . . . . . . . (602) 553-0333
  Education: Arizona BS

# Arizona Department of Administration [AZDOA]

100 North Fifteenth Avenue, Suite 401, Phoenix, AZ 85007
Tel: (602) 542-1500  Internet: www.azdoa.gov

**Employees:** 533  **Fiscal Year:** 2015  **Budget:** $180,298,000

■ Director **Craig C. Brown** . . . . . . . . . . . . . . . . . . . . (602) 542-1500
  Education: Utah State 1982 BA
  Executive Staff Assistant **Heather Ryan** . . . . . . . . . . (602) 542-1500

Deputy Director **Kevin Donnellan** . . . . . . . . . . . . . . . . (602) 542-0878
  E-mail: kevin.donnellan@azdoa.gov
Associate Director **Judy Wente** . . . . . . . . . . . . . . . . . (602) 542-0878
  E-mail: judy.wente@azdoa.gov
Budget and Resource Planning Assistant Director/
  State of Arizona Labor Market Information Director
  **Paul Shannon** . . . . . . . . . . . . . . . . . . . . . . . . (602) 542-0878
  E-mail: paul.shannon@azdoa.gov
Communications Director **Megan Rose** . . . . . . . . . . . . . (602) 542-0027
  E-mail: megan.rose@azdoa.gov
Assistant Legislative Liaison -Project Manager
  **Cherie Stone** . . . . . . . . . . . . . . . . . . . . . . . . . (602) 542-0167
  E-mail: cherie.stone@azdoa.gov
General Counsel **Nicole Ong** . . . . . . . . . . . . . . . . . . . (602) 542-2181
Security Administrator **(Vacant)** . . . . . . . . . . . . . . . . (602) 542-1605
Comptroller **Joe Whitmer** . . . . . . . . . . . . . . . . . . . . (602) 542-1924

# Arizona State Mine Inspector [ASMI]

Tel: (602) 542-5971

**Employees:** 15  **Fiscal Year:** 2016  **Budget:** $1,215,000

★ State Mine Inspector **Joe Hart** (R) . . . . . . . . . . . . . . . (602) 542-5971
  Term Expires: January 2019
Deputy Director **Laurie Swartzbaugh** . . . . . . . . . . . . . . (602) 542-5971
  E-mail: lswartzbaugh@asmi.az.gov
  Business Manager **Esther Olivas** . . . . . . . . . . . . . . (602) 542-5971
  E-mail: eolivas@asmi.az.gov

# Arizona Department of Agriculture [AZDA]

1688 West Adams, Phoenix, AZ 85007
Tel: (602) 542-4373  Internet: www.azda.gov

**Employees:** 200  **Fiscal Year:** 2015  **Budget:** $24,669,000

■ Director **Mark W. Killian** . . . . . . . . . . . . . . . . . . . . (602) 542-3575
  E-mail: mkillian@azda.gov
  Education: Arizona State 1981 BS
Deputy Director **Jeffrey D. Grant** . . . . . . . . . . . . . . . . (602) 542-0997
  Education: Arizona State 1982 BA
Executive Staff Assistant **Anita Landy** . . . . . . . . . . . . . (602) 542-0990
Agricultural Consultation and Training Assistant Director
  **Brett Cameron** . . . . . . . . . . . . . . . . . . . . . . . . (602) 542-0984
Citrus Fruit and Vegetable Standardization Assistant
  Director **Ed Foster** . . . . . . . . . . . . . . . . . . . . . . (602) 542-0947
State Agricultural Laboratory Assistant Director
  **Doug Marsh** . . . . . . . . . . . . . . . . . . . . . . . . . (602) 744-4924
  State Veterinarian **Susan Gale** . . . . . . . . . . . . . . . (602) 542-0960
Public Information Officer **Laura Oxley** . . . . . . . . . . . . . (602) 542-4313
Webmaster **David Hall** . . . . . . . . . . . . . . . . . . . . . . (602) 542-0938

# Arizona Department of Weights and Measures [ADWM]

1688 West Adams Street, Phoenix, AZ 85007
Tel: (602) 771-4920  Tel: (800) 277-6675 (In State)  Fax: (602) 939-8586
Internet: www.dwm.az.gov

**Employees:** 36  **Fiscal Year:** 2015  **Budget:** $1,362,000

**Note:** On June 1, 2016, The Department of Weights and Measures will become the Weights and Measures Division under the Arizona Department of Agriculture.

■ Director (Interim) **Mark W. Killian** . . . . . . . . . . . . . . . (602) 542-5729
  Assistant to the Director **Roger Fisk** . . . . . . . . . . . . (602) 771-4922
  E-mail: rfisk@azda.gov
Administrative Division Director **(Vacant)** . . . . . . . . . . . (602) 771-4927
Financial Services and Accounts Payable Director
  **(Vacant)** . . . . . . . . . . . . . . . . . . . . . . . . . . . (602) 771-4927
Fuel Inspection and Regulatory Programs Director
  **Damien DeSantiago** . . . . . . . . . . . . . . . . . . . . . (602) 771-4948
Environmental Programs Manager **Michelle Wilson** . . . . . . (602) 771-4933
  E-mail: mwilson@azda.gov
Systems Network Engineer **Mackenzie Smith** . . . . . . . . . (602) 771-4926
  E-mail: msmith@azda.gov
State Metrologist **Brian Sellers** . . . . . . . . . . . . . . . . . (602) 771-4938
  4425 West Olive Avenue, Suite 134, Glendale, AZ 85302

---

★ Elected Official  ■ Appointed by Governor  ● Appointed by Legislature  ▲ Appointed by Board or Commission  ◆ Appointed by State Supreme Court

Assistant State Metrologist **Eric Gaedert** . . . . . . . . . . . . . (602) 771-4928
    4425 West Olive Avenue, Glendale, AZ 85302
Administrative Assistant **Michele Mellott** . . . . . . . . . . . . . (602) 771-4934
Legislative Liaison and Public Information Officer
    **(Vacant)** . . . . . . . . . . . . . . . . . . . . . . . . . . . . . . . . . . (602) 771-4929

## Arizona Department of Child Safety [DCS]

P.O. Box 6030, Phoenix, AZ 85005-6030
Tel: (602) 255-2500

Director **Gregory A. McKay** . . . . . . . . . . . . . . . . . . . . . . (602) 542-3981
Deputy Director **Michael "Mike" Dellner** . . . . . . . . . . . . . (602) 542-3981

## Arizona Department of Corrections [ADC]

1601 West Jefferson, Phoenix, AZ 85007
Tel: (602) 542-5497  Fax: (602) 542-2859
E-mail: media@azcorrections.gov  Internet: www.azcorrections.gov

**Employees:** 9,180  **Fiscal Year:** 2016  **Budget:** $1,082,241,000

■Director **Charles L. Ryan** . . . . . . . . . . . . . . . . . . . . . . . . (602) 542-5225
    E-mail: cryan@azcorrections.gov
    Education: Arizona State BS; Western International MPA
    Executive Assistant **Amy Funari** . . . . . . . . . . . . . . . . . (602) 542-5225
Deputy Director **Jeffrey Hood** . . . . . . . . . . . . . . . . . . . . . (602) 542-5225
General Counsel **Brad Keogh** . . . . . . . . . . . . . . . . . . . . . (602) 542-1532
Legislative Liaison **Art Harding** . . . . . . . . . . . . . . . . . . . (602) 542-3568
    E-mail: aharding@azcorrections.gov
Emergency Preparedness Administrator **Robert Church** . . . (602) 364-0652

## Arizona Department of Economic Security [DES]

1789 West Jefferson, Petrified Forest National Park, AZ 85007
P.O. Box 6123, Phoenix, AZ 85005
Tel: (602) 542-4791  Fax: (602) 542-5339  E-mail: webmaster@azdes.gov
Internet: www.azdes.gov

**Employees:** 7,735  **Fiscal Year:** 2016  **Budget:** $2,463,640,000

■Director **Timothy "Tim" Jeffries** . . . . . . . . . . . . . . . . . . (602) 542-5757
    E-mail: director@azdes.gov
    Education: Santa Clara U BS; Duke MBA
Ombudsman **Lane Organ** . . . . . . . . . . . . . . . . . . . . . . . . (602) 364-2860
Communications Director **Tasya Peterson** . . . . . . . . . . . . (602) 542-4296
    E-mail: pio@azdes.gov
Legislative Services Director **Kathy Ber** . . . . . . . . . . . . . (602) 542-4669
    E-mail: kber@azdes.gov
Operations and Special Projects Deputy Director
    **Todd Bright** . . . . . . . . . . . . . . . . . . . . . . . . . . . . . . . (602) 542-3873
Programs Deputy Director **Clark Collier** . . . . . . . . . . . . . (602) 542-3937

## Department of Emergency and Military Affairs [DEMA]

5636 East McDowell Road, Phoenix, AZ 85008-3495
Tel: (602) 267-2700  Fax: (602) 267-2954  Internet: https://dema.az.gov/

**Employees:** 66  **Fiscal Year:** 2015  **Budget:** $5,378,000

■Director **MajGen Michael T. "Mick" McGuire, ANG** . . . . (602) 267-2710
    E-mail: michael.t.mcguire14.mil@mail.mil
Joint Staff Director
    **BrigGen Kerry L. Muehlenbeck, ANG** . . . . . . . . . . . . . (602) 267-2787
    E-mail: kerry.l.muehlenbeck.mil@mail.mil
Emergency Management Division Director
    **Wendy Smith-Reeve** . . . . . . . . . . . . . . . . . . . . . . . . . (602) 464-6203
Administrative Services Officer
    **COL Roland D. Aut, ARNG** . . . . . . . . . . . . . . . . . . . . (602) 267-2721
    E-mail: roland.d.aut.mil@mail.mil
Public Affairs Officer **Candace N. Park** . . . . . . . . . . . . . (602) 267-2619
    E-mail: candace.n.park.mil@mail.mil

## Arizona National Guard

5636 East McDowell Road, Phoenix, AZ 85008-3495
Tel: (602) 267-2759

■Adjutant General
    **MajGen Michael T. "Mick" McGuire, ANG** . . . . . . . . . (602) 267-2710

## Arizona Air National Guard

5636 East McDowell Road, Phoenix, AZ 85008-3495
Tel: (602) 267-2660

Commander **BrigGen Edward P. Maxwell, USAF** . . . . . . . (602) 267-2660
    Education: Air Force Acad 1984 BA

## Arizona Army National Guard

5636 East McDowell Road, Phoenix, AZ 85008-3495
Tel: (602) 267-2710

Land Component Commander **BG John Hoefert, ARNG** . . (602) 267-2717
Information Technology Director
    **COL Kenneth W. Stice, ARNG** . . . . . . . . . . . . . . . . . . (602) 267-2014
    E-mail: kenneth.w.stice2.mil@mail.mil

## Arizona Department of Environmental Quality [ADEQ]

1110 West Washington Street, Phoenix, AZ 85007
Tel: (602) 771-2300  TTY: (602) 771-4829  Fax: (602) 771-2218
Internet: www.azdeq.gov

**Employees:** 420  **Fiscal Year:** 2014  **Budget:** $7,000,000

■Director **Misael Cabrera, PE** . . . . . . . . . . . . . . . . . . . . . (602) 771-2203
    E-mail: cabrera.misael@azdeq.gov
Deputy Director **Bret H. Parke** . . . . . . . . . . . . . . . . . . . . (602) 771-2204
Chief Policy and Legislative Affairs Director
    **Amanda Stone** . . . . . . . . . . . . . . . . . . . . . . . . . . . . . (520) 628-6883
    E-mail: stone.amanda@azdeq.gov
Communication Director **Ian Bingham** . . . . . . . . . . . . . . . (602) 771-2300
    E-mail: ian.bingham@azdeq.gov
Public Information Office **Caroline Oppleman** . . . . . . . . . (602) 771-2215
    E-mail: oppleman.caroline@azdeq.gov    Fax: (602) 771-2270
Financial Services Director **(Vacant)** . . . . . . . . . . . . . . . . (602) 771-2356
Administrative Counsel **Sherri Zendri** . . . . . . . . . . . . . . . (602) 771-2242
General and Laboratory Services Section Manager
    **Dan Borns** . . . . . . . . . . . . . . . . . . . . . . . . . . . . . . . . (602) 771-4720
                                                              Fax: (602) 771-4719

## Department of Fire, Building and Life Safety

1110 West Washington, Suite 100, Phoenix, AZ 85007-2935
Tel: (602) 364-1003  Fax: (602) 364-1052

**Employees:** 27  **Fiscal Year:** 2015  **Budget:** $1,917,000

■Director (Interim) **Debra Blake** . . . . . . . . . . . . . . . . . . . (602) 364-1003
    E-mail: debra.blake@dfbls.az.gov
    Executive Assistant **Amy Michaels** . . . . . . . . . . . . . . . (602) 364-1003
Deputy Director for Administration **(Vacant)** . . . . . . . . . . (602) 364-1033

## Office of the State Fire Marshal

Tel: (602) 364-1003

State Fire Marshal **(Vacant)** . . . . . . . . . . . . . . . . . . . . . . (602) 364-1003
Assistant State Fire Marshal **Fred Durham** . . . . . . . . . . . (602) 364-1003
    E-mail: fred.durham@dfbls.az.gov

## Arizona Department of Gaming

1110 West Washington, 450, Phoenix, AZ 85007
Tel: (602) 771-4263  Fax: (602) 255-3883  Internet: gaming.az.gov

**Employees:** 115

■Director **Daniel Bergin** . . . . . . . . . . . . . . . . . . . . . . . . . (602) 771-4263
    E-mail: dbergin@azgaming.gov
    Education: Arizona State 1985 BS, 1988 JD
Self Exclusion Administrator **Dawn Revere** . . . . . . . . . . . (602) 771-4263

**EXECUTIVE BRANCH**

---

★ Elected Official    ■ Appointed by Governor    ● Appointed by Legislature    ▲ Appointed by Board or Commission    ◆ Appointed by State Supreme Court

## Arizona Division of Racing

1110 West Washington, Suite 260, Phoenix, AZ 85007
Tel: (602) 364-1700  Fax: (602) 364-1703  E-mail: ador@azracing.gov
Internet: www.racing.az.gov

**Employees:** 41  **Fiscal Year:** 2015  **Budget:** $2,014,000

■Director **Rudy Casillas** . . . . . . . . . . . . . . . . . . . . . . . . . . . (602) 364-1726
   E-mail: rcasillas@azracing.gov
Deputy Director **Rudy Casillas** . . . . . . . . . . . . . . . . . . . . (602) 364-1726
   E-mail: rcasillas@azracing.gov
Administrative Hearing and Services Coordinator
   **Sherrie Koss** . . . . . . . . . . . . . . . . . . . . . . . . . . . . . . . . . (602) 364-1730
   E-mail: skoss@azgaming.gov
Program Coordinator **Rudy Casillas** . . . . . . . . . . . . . . . . . (602) 364-1714

## Arizona Department of Health Services [ADHS]

150 North 18th Avenue, Phoenix, AZ 85007
1818 West Adams Street, Phoenix, AZ 85007 (Vital Records)
Tel: (602) 542-1025  Tel: (602) 364-1300 (Vital Records)
Fax: (602) 542-1062  Fax: (602) 249-3040 (Vital Records)
Internet: www.azhealth.gov

**Employees:** 1,177  **Fiscal Year:** 2014  **Budget:** $611,180,000

■Director **Cara Christ, MD** . . . . . . . . . . . . . . . . . . . . . . . . .(602) 542-1140
   E-mail: cara.christ@azdhs.gov
   Education: Arizona State 2000; Arizona 2005 MD
   Executive Staff Assistant **Wendy Synder** . . . . . . . . . . . . . (602) 542-1140
Deputy Director **(Vacant)** . . . . . . . . . . . . . . . . . . . . . . . . . . (602) 364-4566
   Executive Staff Assistant **Anne Rubio** . . . . . . . . . . . . . . . (602) 364-4566
Communications Director **Holly Ward** . . . . . . . . . . . . . . . .(602) 542-1094
   E-mail: holly.ward@azdhs.gov
Legislative Liaison **Colby Bower** . . . . . . . . . . . . . . . . . . . . (602) 542-1032
   E-mail: colby.bower@azdhs.gov
State Epidemiologist **Ken Komatsu** . . . . . . . . . . . . . . . . . .(602) 364-3587
Workforce Development Trainer **Libby Puccio** . . . . . . . . . . (602) 542-1101
   Education: Arizona State 2006 BA; U Phoenix 2009 MA

## Arizona Department of Homeland Security [AZDOHS]

1700 West Washington, Phoenix, AZ 85007
Tel: (602) 542-7013  Fax: (602) 542-1729  E-mail: HS@azdohs.gov

■Director **Gilbert M. Orrantia** . . . . . . . . . . . . . . . . . . . . . . .(602) 542-7013
   E-mail: gorrantia@azdohs.gov
   Education: Arizona State BA
Deputy Director **Tim Roemer** . . . . . . . . . . . . . . . . . . . . . . . (602) 542-7006
   Executive Assistant **Linda Singhurse** . . . . . . . . . . . . . . . (602) 542-7013
Preparedness Assistant Director **Cheryl Kennedy** . . . . . . . . (602) 542-7077

## Arizona Department of Housing

1110 West Washington, Suite 280, Phoenix, AZ 85007
Tel: (602) 771-1000  TTY: (602) 771-1001  Fax: (602) 771-1002
E-mail: info@azhousing.gov

**Employees:** 65  **Fiscal Year:** 2015-2016  **Budget:** $93,570,000

■Director **Michael Trailor** . . . . . . . . . . . . . . . . . . . . . . . . . .(602) 771-1007
   E-mail: michael.trailor@azhousing.gov
   Education: Arizona State

## Arizona Department of Insurance [ADOI]

2910 North 44th Street, Suite 210, Phoenix, AZ 85018-7269
Tel: (602) 364-3100  Fax: (602) 364-2400  E-mail: info@azinsurance.gov

**Employees:** 86  **Fiscal Year:** 2015  **Budget:** $5,883,000

■Director (Interim) **Leslie Hess** . . . . . . . . . . . . . . . . . . . . . (602) 364-3471
   Education: George Washington JD
Deputy Director **(Vacant)** . . . . . . . . . . . . . . . . . . . . . . . . . . (602) 364-3471
Chief Information Officer **Eugene P. Glover** . . . . . . . . . . . (602) 364-2983
   E-mail: eglover@azinsurance.gov
Chief Operating Officer **Scott B. Greenberg** . . . . . . . . . . . (602) 364-3471
   Education: Arizona State 1986 BS, 1988 MBA
Public Information Officer **(Vacant)** . . . . . . . . . . . . . . . . . . (602) 364-3761

---

Legislative Liaison **Steven Briggs** . . . . . . . . . . . . . . . . . . . (602) 364-3471
   E-mail: sbriggs@azinsurance.gov

## Arizona Department of Juvenile Corrections [ADJC]

1624 West Adams Street, Phoenix, AZ 85007
Tel: (602) 542-4302  Fax: (602) 542-5156  Internet: www.azdjc.gov

**Employees:** 739  **Fiscal Year:** 2015  **Budget:** $40,762,000

■Director **Dona Marie Markley** . . . . . . . . . . . . . . . . . . . . . .(602) 364-4051
   E-mail: dmmarkley@azdjc.gov
   Executive Assistant **Jackie Ruble** . . . . . . . . . . . . . . . . . (602) 364-4051
Assistant Director **(Vacant)** . . . . . . . . . . . . . . . . . . . . . . . . (602) 364-0622
Inspector General **Doug Sargent** . . . . . . . . . . . . . . . . . . . . (602) 542-5490
Medical Director **Dr. Robert D. Jones, MD** . . . . . . . . . . . . (602) 364-4051
Community Corrections Bureau Administrator
   **Sandra Acosta** . . . . . . . . . . . . . . . . . . . . . . . . . . . . . . . (602) 542-4685
Investigations Bureau Administrator **(Vacant)** . . . . . . . . . . .(602) 542-5490
Legal Services Bureau Administrator **James Mapp** . . . . . . . (602) 364-3508
   E-mail: jmapp@azdjc.gov                    Fax: (602) 364-3524
Government Affairs and Public Relations Administrator
   **Matthew Contorelli** . . . . . . . . . . . . . . . . . . . . . . . . . . . (602) 542-2564
Secure Care Operations Bureau Administrator **(Vacant)** . . . (623) 869-9050
Secure Care Programs Chief Administrator
   **Peter Luszczak** . . . . . . . . . . . . . . . . . . . . . . . . . . . . . . (602) 525-6544
   E-mail: pluszczak@azdjc.gov
   Education: Kingston Poly U (UK) BA; York (UK) MA
Education Superintendent **Adam Henning** . . . . . . (602) 582-1180 ext. 4102

## Arizona State Land Department

1616 West Adams Street, Room 305, Phoenix, AZ 85007
Tel: (602) 542-4631  Fax: (602) 542-2508  E-mail: inquiry@azland.gov

**Employees:** 129  **Fiscal Year:** 2016  **Budget:** $15,158,000

■Commissioner **Lisa A. Atkins** . . . . . . . . . . . . . . . . . . . . . . (602) 542-4621
   E-mail: latkins@azland.gov
   Education: Arizona
Deputy Land Commissioner **Wesley Mehl** . . . . . . . . . . . . . (602) 542-4621
   E-mail: wmehl@azland.gov
Administration Director **Jill Pernice** . . . . . . . . . . . . . . . . . .(602) 542-3179
   E-mail: jpernice@azland.gov
Information Technology Director **Evan Brom** . . . . . . . . . . . (602) 542-2605
   E-mail: ebrom@azland.gov
Natural Resources Director **Fred Breedlove** . . . . . . . . . . . . (602) 542-2693
   Natural Resources Assistant Director **(Vacant)** . . . . . . . . (602) 542-2657
Real Estate Director **Max Masel** . . . . . . . . . . . . . . . . . . . . .(602) 542-4017
Appraisal Manager **Mark Fast** . . . . . . . . . . . . . . . . . . . . . . (602) 364-2684
   E-mail: mfast@azland.gov
Minerals Section Manager **Joe Dixon** . . . . . . . . . . . . . . . . (602) 542-2685
   E-mail: jdixon@azland.gov
Planning and Engineering Section Manager
   **Mark Edelman** . . . . . . . . . . . . . . . . . . . . . . . . . . . . . . .(602) 542-6331
   E-mail: medelman@azland.gov
Range Section Manager **(Vacant)** . . . . . . . . . . . . . . . . . . . (602) 542-2696
Legislative Policy Administrator **Molly Bonsall** . . . . . . . . . (602) 542-2626
   E-mail: mbonsall@azland.gov

## Arizona Department of Liquor Licenses and Control

800 West Washington Street, 5th Floor, Phoenix, AZ 85007
Tel: (602) 542-5141  TTY: (602) 542-9024  Fax: (602) 542-5707
E-mail: answers@azliquor.gov  Internet: www.azliquor.gov

**Employees:** 45  **Fiscal Year:** 2015  **Budget:** $2,963,000

■Director **John Cocca** . . . . . . . . . . . . . . . . . . . . . . . . . . . . . (602) 542-9020
   E-mail: john.cocca@azliquor.gov
Deputy Director **Michael Rosenberger** . . . . . . . . . . . . . . . (602) 542-9076
Administration Assistant Director **Pearlette J. Ramos** . . . . (602) 542-9021
   E-mail: pearlette.ramos@azliquor.gov
Communications Director and Human Resources
   Manager **Lee A. Hill** . . . . . . . . . . . . . . . . . . . . . . . . . . (602) 542-1936
Licensing Assistant Director **Lee A. Hill** . . . . . . . . . . . . . . (602) 542-1936
Compliance Officer **Robert Dorn** . . . . . . . . . . . . . . . . . . . .(602) 542-9045

---

★ Elected Official   ■ Appointed by Governor   ● Appointed by Legislature   ▲ Appointed by Board or Commission   ◆ Appointed by State Supreme Court

## Arizona Department of Public Safety [AZDPS]

2102 West Encanto Boulevard, Phoenix, AZ 85005-6638
P.O. Box 6638, Phoenix, AZ 85005-6638
Tel: (602) 223-2000  Fax: (602) 223-2917  Internet: www.azdps.gov

**Employees:** 1,905  **Fiscal Year:** 2014  **Budget:** $50,802,100

■Director **Frank L. Milstead** . . . . . . . . . . . . . . . . . . . . . . . . . (602) 223-2359
  E-mail: fmilstead@azdps.gov
  Education: U Phoenix
Deputy Director **Heston Silbert** . . . . . . . . . . . . . . . . . . . . . (602) 223-2080
Chief Financial Officer **Phil Case** . . . . . . . . . . . . . . . . . . . . (602) 223-2463

## Arizona Department of Real Estate [ADRE]

2910 North 44th Street, Suite 100, Phoenix, AZ 85018
Tel: (602) 771-7799  Fax: (602) 468-0562  Internet: www.azre.gov

**Employees:** 32  **Fiscal Year:** 2015  **Budget:** $2,989,000

■Commissioner **Judy Lowe** . . . . . . . . . . . . . . . . . . . . . . . . . . (602) 771-7760
  E-mail: jlowe@azre.gov
Deputy Commissioner **Louis Dettorre** . . . . . . . . . . . . . . . . (602) 771-7769
Legislative Liaison **Louis Dettorre** . . . . . . . . . . . . . . . . . . (602) 771-7769
  E-mail: ldettorre@azre.gov
Enforcement and Compliance Manager **Daniel Y. Jones** . . . (602) 771-7760
Real Estate Auditing and Investigations Manager
  **Robin King** . . . . . . . . . . . . . . . . . . . . . . . . . . . . . . . . . . . (602) 771-7760

## Arizona Department of Revenue [AZDOR]

1600 West Monroe, Phoenix, AZ 85007
Tel: (602) 716-6090  Fax: (602) 542-4772  Internet: www.azdor.gov

**Employees:** 750  **Fiscal Year:** 2015  **Budget:** $73,653,000

■Director **David Briant** . . . . . . . . . . . . . . . . . . . . . . . . . . . . (602) 716-6090
  Executive Assistant **Loretta Bowdish** . . . . . . . . . . . . . . . (602) 716-6913
Deputy Director **Carlton Woodruff** . . . . . . . . . . . . . . . . . . (602) 716-6090
Administrative Services Assistant Director **Lisa Cross** . . . . (602) 716-6936
  E-mail: lcross@azdor.gov
Audit Division Assistant Director **Ronald T. Johnson** . . . . (602) 716-6552
Collections Division Assistant Director **Frank Bouche** . . . . (602) 716-6892
Information Technology Assistant Director/Chief
  Information Officer **(Vacant)** . . . . . . . . . . . . . . . . . . . . . . (602) 716-6119
Processing Administration Assistant Director
  **Lynette Nowlan** . . . . . . . . . . . . . . . . . . . . . . . . . . . . . . (602) 716-6281
  E-mail: lnowlan@azdor.gov
  Education: Arizona State BS
Property Tax Division Assistant Director **Frank Boucek** . . . (602) 716-6807
Taxpayer and External Services Director
  **Anthony Forschino** . . . . . . . . . . . . . . . . . . . . . . . . . . . . (602) 716-6921
  Education: Grand Canyon BS
Tax Policy and Research Assistant Director
  **Frank Boucek** . . . . . . . . . . . . . . . . . . . . . . . . . . . . . . . (602) 716-6807
Legislative Liaison **Sean Laux** . . . . . . . . . . . . . . . . . . . . . . (602) 716-6132
  E-mail: slaux@azdor.gov
Public Information Officer **Sean Laux** . . . . . . . . . . . . . . . . (602) 716-6882
  E-mail: slaux@azdor.gov

## Arizona Department of Transportation [ADOT]

206 South 17th Avenue, Phoenix, AZ 85007-3212
Tel: (602) 712-7011  Fax: (602) 712-6941  E-mail: info@azdot.gov
Internet: www.azdot.gov

**Employees:** 4,548  **Fiscal Year:** 2015  **Budget:** $360,618,000

■Director **John S. Halikowski** . . . . . . . . . . . . . . . . . . . . . . (602) 712-7227
  E-mail: director@azdot.gov
  Education: Arizona State BA
Chief Financial Officer **Kristine Ward** . . . . . . . . . . . . . . . . (602) 712-7011
  Education: Bowie State BSA; Arizona State MA
Executive Assistant **Lila Trimmer** . . . . . . . . . . . . . . . . . . . (602) 712-7227
  E-mail: ltrimmer@azdot.gov

ITG Programmer **Cyndi Striegler** . . . . . . . . . . . . . . . . . . . . (602) 712-7661
  E-mail: cstriegler@azdot.gov
Communications Director **Timothy Tait** . . . . . . . . . . . . . . . (602) 712-7070

## Arizona Department of Veterans' Services [AZDVS]

3839 North Third Street, Suite 209, Phoenix, AZ 85012-2069
Tel: (602) 255-3373  Fax: (602) 255-1038  Internet: www.dvs.az..gov

**Employees:** 366  **Fiscal Year:** 2015  **Budget:** $5,218,000

■Director **COL Wanda A. Wright, ARNG (Ret)** . . . . . . . . . (602) 255-3373
  E-mail: director@azdvs.gov
  Education: Arizona 1997 MPA; Arizona State 2013 MEd
  Executive Assistant to Director **Tera Scherer** . . . . . . . . . (602) 234-8415
Deputy Director **Robert M. Barnes** . . . . . . . . . . . . . . . . . . (602) 255-3373
Assistant Deputy Director **John F. Scott** . . . . . . . . . . . . . . (602) 255-3373
Operations Assistant Deputy Director **(Vacant)** . . . . . . . . (602) 255-3373
Arizona State Veteran Home Phoenix Administrator
  **Jim Dugger** . . . . . . . . . . . . . . . . . . . . . . . . . . . . . . . . . . (602) 248-1550
  4141 North Herrera Way, Phoenix, AZ 85012-1814
  E-mail: jdugger@azdvs.gov
Arizona State Veteran Home Tucson Administrator
  **James Ross** . . . . . . . . . . . . . . . . . . . . . . . . . . . . . . . . . . (520) 638-2155
  E-mail: jross@azdvs.gov
Veterans Education Office Administrator/State Approving
  Agent **Leanna DeKing** . . . . . . . . . . . . . . . . . . . . . . . . . . (602) 255-5395
  E-mail: ldeking@azdvs.gov
Information Technology Manager (Acting)
  **Lauren Quebbeman** . . . . . . . . . . . . . . . . . . . . . . . . . . . (602) 263-1829
  E-mail: lquebbeman@azdvs.gov
Chief Financial Officer **Luis A. Marquez, C.P.M.** . . . . . . . . (602) 234-8419
  Education: Puerto Rico BA
Public Information Officer **Dave Hampton** . . . . . . . . . . . . (602) 255-3373
  E-mail: dhampton@azdvs.gov
State Veterans Fiduciary **Lori Braddock** . . . . . . . . . . . . . . (602) 248-1554
Administrative Secretary **Judy Smith** . . . . . . . . . . . . . . . . (602) 234-8406

## Arizona Department of Water Resources [ADWR]

3550 North Central Avenue, Second Floor, Phoenix, AZ 85012
Tel: (602) 771-8500  Internet: www.azwater.gov

**Employees:** 90  **Fiscal Year:** 2015  **Budget:** $11,809,000

■Director **Thomas Buschatzke** . . . . . . . . . . . . . . . . . . . . . . (602) 771-8500
  E-mail: tbuschatzke@azwater.gov
  Education: SUNY (Cortland) 1977 BS
■Deputy Director **Lynne Smith** . . . . . . . . . . . . . . . . . . . . . . (602) 771-1301
  E-mail: ljsmith@azwater.gov
  Education: Occidental BA; Arizona MPA
Executive Assistant **Colleen K. Lane** . . . . . . . . . . . . . . . . . (602) 771-8426
  E-mail: cklane@azwater.gov
Chief Counsel **Kenneth C. Slowinski** . . . . . . . . . . . . . . . . (602) 771-8472
Legislative Liaison and Ombudsman **Doug Dunham** . . . . . (602) 364-2650
  E-mail: dwdunham@azwater.gov
Public Information Officer **Michelle Moreno** . . . . . . . . . . . (602) 771-8530
  E-mail: mamoreno@azwater.gov
Chief Financial Officer **(Vacant)** . . . . . . . . . . . . . . . . . . . . (602) 771-8508
Human Resources Administrator **Lupe Beimer** . . . . . . . . . (602) 771-8505

## Arizona Registrar of Contractors [AZROC]

Arizona State Capitol Executive Tower, 1700 West Washington Street,
Suite 105, Phoenix, AZ 85007
Tel: (602) 542-1525  Tel: (877) 692-9762 (In State)  Fax: (602) 542-1599
E-mail: webmaster@azroc.gov  Internet: www.azroc.gov

**Employees:** 104

■Director **Jeffrey Fleetham** . . . . . . . . . . . . . . . . . . . . . . . . . (602) 542-1525
  E-mail: jeffrey.fleetham@azroc.gov
  Executive Assistant to Director and Agency
  Administration Coordinator **Lisa Gray** . . . . . . . . . . . . . . (602) 542-1525
  E-mail: lisa.gray@azroc.gov

*(continued on next page)*

---

★ Elected Official    ■ Appointed by Governor    ● Appointed by Legislature    ▲ Appointed by Board or Commission    ◆ Appointed by State Supreme Court

**Arizona Registrar of Contractors** *continued*

Licensing and Finance Assistant Director
Wilma Dengavi . . . . . . . . . . . . . . . . . . . . . . . . . . . . (602) 542-1525
E-mail: wilma.dengavi@azroc.gov
Chief of Staff **(Vacant)** . . . . . . . . . . . . . . . . . . . . . . (602) 542-1525
Chief Information Officer **Sergio Gallegos** . . . . . . . . . (602) 542-1525
Chief of Investigations **(Vacant)** . . . . . . . . . . . . . . . (602) 542-1525
Assistant Director Legal and Recovery Fund
James Hanson . . . . . . . . . . . . . . . . . . . . . . . . . . . . . (602) 542-1525
Assistant Director of Compliance **Jeff Wills** . . . . . . . . . (602) 542-1525
Human Resources Manager **Laura Hamisch** . . . . . . . . . (602) 542-1525
Public Information Officer, Legislative Liaison and
Ombudsman **Jim Knupp** . . . . . . . . . . . . . . . . . . . . . (602) 542-1525

## Residential Utility Consumer Office [RUCO]

1110 West Washington Street, Suite 220, Phoenix, AZ 85007
Tel: (602) 364-4835  Fax: (602) 364-4846  Internet: www.azruco.gov

**Employees:** 8  **Fiscal Year:** 2016  **Budget:** $1,335,000

■Director **David Tenney** . . . . . . . . . . . . . . . . . . . . . . . (602) 364-4838
E-mail: dtenney@azruco.gov
Chief Counsel **Daniel Pozefsky** . . . . . . . . . . . . . . . . . (602) 364-4839
Education: SUNY (Buffalo) 1983 BS, 1987 JD
Attorney **(Vacant)** . . . . . . . . . . . . . . . . . . . . . . . . . . (602) 364-4841
Accounting and Rates Chief **Robert Mease** . . . . . . . . . . (602) 364-4842
E-mail: rmease@azruco.gov
Public Utilities Analyst **John Cassidy** . . . . . . . . . . . . . . (602) 364-4843
E-mail: jcassidy@azruco.gov
Public Utilities Analyst **Timothy Coley** . . . . . . . . . . . . (602) 364-4844
E-mail: tcoley@azruco.gov
Education: Troy State 1985 BS; West Georgia Col 1997 MPA
Public Utilities Analyst **Jeffrey Michlik** . . . . . . . . . . . . (602) 364-4837
E-mail: jmichlik@azruco.gov
Administrative Services Officer II **Cheryl Fraulob** . . . . . . . (602) 364-4845
E-mail: cfraulob@azruco.gov
Special Projects Advisor **Jordy Fuentes** . . . . . . . . . . . . (602) 364-4840

## State Boards Office

1400 West Washington Street, Suite 230, Phoenix, AZ 85007
Tel: (602) 542-3095  Fax: (602) 542-3093

**Employees:** 2

Administrator **Susan "Susie" Myers** . . . . . . . . . . . . . . (602) 542-5629
▲Acupuncture Board Executive Director
Pedro "Pete" Gonzalez . . . . . . . . . . . . . . . . . . . . . (602) 364-0145
E-mail: petegonzalez@azacupunctureboard.us
▲Dispensing Opticians Board Executive Director
Lori D. Scott . . . . . . . . . . . . . . . . . . . . . . . . . . . . (602) 542-8158
E-mail: director@asbdo.state.az.us
▲Funeral Directors & Embalmers Board Executive
Director **Rudolfo "Rudy" Thomas** . . . . . . . . . . . . . (602) 542-3095
E-mail: rudy.thomas@azfuneralboard.us
▲Homeopathic Physicians Examiners Board Executive
Director **Christine Springer** . . . . . . . . . . . . . . . . . (602) 542-8154
E-mail: chris.springer@azhomeopathbd.az.gov
Education: Northern Colorado 1975 BFA
▲Massage Therapy Board Executive Director
Kathleen Phillips . . . . . . . . . . . . . . . . . . . . . . . . . (602) 542-8604
E-mail: kathleen.phillips@massageboard.az.gov
▲Naturopathic Physicians Board Medical Examiners
Executive Director **Gail Anthony** . . . . . . . . . . . . . . (602) 542-8242
E-mail: gail.anthony@aznd.gov
▲Nursing Care Institution Administrators and Assisted
Living Facility Managers Board of Examiners
Executive Director **Allen Imig** . . . . . . . . . . . . . . . . (602) 364-8156
▲Optometry Board Executive Director **Margaret Whelan** . . . (602) 542-8155
E-mail: margaret.whelan@optometry.az.gov
▲Podiatry Examiners Board Executive Director
Ryan P. Edmonson . . . . . . . . . . . . . . . . . . . . . (602) 542-3095 ext. 7
E-mail: ryan.edmonson@podiatry.az.gov

## Arizona Office of Tourism [AOT]

1110 West Washington Street, Suite 155, Phoenix, AZ 85007-2957
Tel: (602) 364-3700  Fax: (602) 364-3701  Internet: www.azot.gov

**Employees:** 28  **Fiscal Year:** 2015  **Budget:** $9,104,000

■Director **Debbie Johnson** . . . . . . . . . . . . . . . . . . . . . (602) 364-3717
E-mail: djohnson@tourism.az.gov
Executive Assistant and Office Manager **Sandra Groh** . . . (602) 364-3717
Deputy Director **Stephanie Dowling** . . . . . . . . . . . . . . (602) 364-3704
Education: South Dakota 2006 BS

## Arizona Radiation Regulatory Agency [ARRA]

4814 South 40th Street, Phoenix, AZ 85040
Tel: (602) 255-4845  Fax: (602) 437-0705  E-mail: info@azrra.gov

**Employees:** 34  **Fiscal Year:** 2015  **Budget:** $1,467,000

■Director **Aubrey V. Godwin** . . . . . . . . . . . . . . . . . . . (602) 255-4822
E-mail: agodwin@azrra.gov
Education: Mississippi 1961 BA; Michigan 1966 MS
Business Manager **Kari Watkins** . . . . . . . . . . . . . . . . . (602) 255-4841
E-mail: kwatkins@azrra.gov

## Arizona Corporation Commission

1200 West Washington Street, Phoenix, AZ 85007
Tel: (602) 542-3026  Fax: (602) 542-4111  E-mail: mailmaster@azcc.gov

**Employees:** 264  **Fiscal Year:** 2016  **Budget:** $27,753,000

★Chairman **Doug Little** (R) . . . . . . . . . . . . . . . . . . . . . (602) 542-0745
Term Expires: January 2019
★Commissioner **Robert "Bob" Burns** (R) . . . . . . . . . . . . (602) 542-3682
Term Expires: January 2017
★Commissioner **Thomas "Tom" Forese** (R) . . . . . . . . . . . (602) 542-3933
Term Expires: January 2019
Education: BYU (Idaho) (Attended)
★Commissioner **Bob Stump** (R) . . . . . . . . . . . . . . . . . . (602) 542-3935
Term Expires: January 2017
Education: UC Berkeley 1993 AB; Harvard 1997 MTS
★Commissioner **Andrew M. "Andy" Tobin** (R) . . . . . . . . . (602) 542-3026

## Office of the Executive Director

Executive Director **Jodi Jerich** . . . . . . . . . . . . . . . . . . (602) 542-3931
E-mail: jjerich@azcc.gov
Education: Indiana BA, JD

## Game and Fish Commission

5000 West Carefree Highway, Phoenix, AZ 85086-5000
Tel: (602) 942-3000

■Chairman **Kurt R. Davis** . . . . . . . . . . . . . . . . . . . . . . (602) 942-3000
Education: Northern Arizona 1984 BS
■Member **James R. Ammons** . . . . . . . . . . . . . . . . . . . . (602) 942-3000
■Member **Edward "Pat" Madden** . . . . . . . . . . . . . . . . . (602) 942-3000
■Member **Eric S. Sparks** . . . . . . . . . . . . . . . . . . . . . . (602) 942-3000
■Member **James S. "Jim" Zieler** . . . . . . . . . . . . . . . . . (602) 942-3000

## Game and Fish Department

Tel: (602) 942-3000 (Information, Customer Service or Phone Directory)
Tel: (623) 236-7701 (Fishing Information)
Tel: (623) 236-7702 (Hunting Information)
Tel: (623) 236-7700 (Wildlife News)  TTY: (800) 367-8938
Fax: (623) 236-7924  Internet: www.azgfd.gov

**Employees:** 274

▲Director **Larry D. Voyles** . . . . . . . . . . . . . . . . . . . . . (623) 236-7278
E-mail: lvoyles@azgfd.gov
Deputy Director **Ty Gray** . . . . . . . . . . . . . . . . . . . . . . (623) 236-7100
Legislative Liaison **Jorge Canaca** . . . . . . . . . . . . . . . . (623) 236-7280
E-mail: jcanaca@azgfd.gov
Chief of Information **Bill Andres** . . . . . . . . . . . . . . . . . (623) 236-7223
E-mail: bandres@azgfd.gov                  Fax: (623) 236-7903
Government Affairs Legislative Specialist
David Fernandez . . . . . . . . . . . . . . . . . . . . . . . . . . (623) 236-7334
E-mail: dfernandez@azgfd.gov

---

★ Elected Official    ■ Appointed by Governor    ● Appointed by Legislature    ▲ Appointed by Board or Commission    ◆ Appointed by State Supreme Court

# Arizona Commission for Postsecondary Education [ACPE]

2020 North Central Avenue, Suite 650, Phoenix, AZ 85004-4590
Tel: (602) 258-2435  Fax: (602) 258-2483  Internet: www.highered.az.gov

**Employees:** 6  **Fiscal Year:** 2015  **Budget:** $1,396,800

Executive Director **Dr. April L. Osborn** . . . . . . . . (602) 258-2435 ext. 106
  Education: Ohio State 1974 BS; Northern Arizona 1978 MA;
  Arizona State 1988 EdD
State Student Financial Assistance Associate
  Director **Daniel Helm** . . . . . . . . . . . . . . . . . . (602) 258-2435 ext. 104

# Arizona Commerce Authority

1700 West Washington Street, Suite 600, Phoenix, AZ 85007
Tel: (602) 845-1200  TTY: (602) 280-1301  Fax: (602) 771-1200
E-mail: frontdesk@azcommerce.com  Internet: www.azcommerce.com

■President and Chief Executive Officer **Sandra Watson** . . . . (602) 771-1160
  E-mail: sandraw@azcommerce.com
■Chief Administrative Officer and General Counsel
  **Greg Linaman** . . . . . . . . . . . . . . . . . . . . . . . . . . (602) 845-1255
  E-mail: gregl@azcommerce.com
■Chief Financial Officer **Wayne Holder** . . . . . . . . . . . . . . (602) 845-1229
  E-mail: wayneh@azcommerce.com
Business Development Senior Vice President
  **Brian Sherman** . . . . . . . . . . . . . . . . . . . . . . . . . (602) 845-1218
General Business Attractions Senior Vice President
  **Kevin Sullivan** . . . . . . . . . . . . . . . . . . . . . . . . . (602) 845-1261
Rural Business Attraction Senior Vice President
  **Keith Watkins** . . . . . . . . . . . . . . . . . . . . . . . . . (602) 845-1278
Community and Marketing Affairs Director **Susan Marie** . . . . . . . . . (602) 845-1238

# Arizona State Lottery Commission

4740 East University Drive, Phoenix, AZ 85034
Tel: (480) 921-4400  TTY: (480) 894-5317  Fax: (480) 921-4512
E-mail: feedback@lottery.state.az.us  Internet: www.arizonalottery.com

**Employees:** 68

■Executive Director **Gregory Edgar** . . . . . . . . . . . . . . . . . (480) 921-4505
  E-mail: gedgar@azlottery.gov
  Education: Arizona State BA
Deputy Director **(Vacant)** . . . . . . . . . . . . . . . . . . . . . . . (480) 921-4437

# Arizona State Parks

23751 N. 23rd Avenue, Suite 190, Phoenix, AZ 85085
Tel: (602) 542-4174  TTY: (602) 542-4174  Fax: (602) 542-4188
Internet: www.azstateparks.com

▲Executive Director **Susan "Sue" Black** . . . . . . . . . . . . . . (602) 542-4174
  E-mail: sblack@azstateparks.gov
Executive Assistant **Shawn Schmidt** . . . . . . . . . . . . . . . . (602) 542-7107
  E-mail: sschmidt@azstateparks.gov
Administrative Services Deputy Director
  **James "Jim" Keegan** . . . . . . . . . . . . . . . . . . . . . (602) 542-6920
  E-mail: jkeegan@azstateparks.gov
Parks Deputy Director/Legislative Liaison **Kelly Moffitt** . . . (602) 542-7103
  E-mail: kmoffitt@azstateparks.gov
Development Chief **Russell Moore** . . . . . . . . . . . . . . . . . . (602) 542-6944
  E-mail: rmoore@azstateparks.gov
Park Operations Chief **Randy Furnish** . . . . . . . . . . . . . . (602) 542-7150
  E-mail: rfurnish@azstateparks.gov
Research and Marketing Chief **Glenn Schlottman** . . . . . . . (602) 542-7105
Resources and Public Programs Chief **Dawn Collins** . . . . . . (602) 542-2138
  E-mail: dcollins@azstateparks.gov
Public Information Officer/Marketing **Monica Enriquez** . . . (602) 542-1996
  E-mail: menriquez@azstateparks.gov
State Historic Preservation Officer **James Garrison** . . . . . . (602) 542-4009

# Office of the Secretary of State

1700 West Washington Street, Seventh Floor, Phoenix, AZ 85007
Tel: (602) 542-0681  Fax: (602) 542-1575  Internet: www.azsos.gov

**Fiscal Year:** 2015  **Budget:** $14,469,000

★Secretary of State **Michele Reagan** (R) . . . . . . . . . . . . . . (602) 542-0681
  Term Expires: January 2019
  Education: Illinois State 1991 BA
Deputy Secretary of State **Lee Miller** . . . . . . . . . . . . . . . . (602) 542-4919
Chief Financial Officer **Elizabeth "Liz" Atkinson** . . . . . . . (602) 542-6171
Chief Information Officer **Bill Maaske** . . . . . . . . . . . . . . . (602) 926-3603
Communications Director **Matthew Roberts** . . . . . . . . . . . (602) 542-2228

# Office of the State Treasurer

1700 West Washington Street, First Floor, Phoenix, AZ 85007
Tel: (602) 542-7888  Fax: (602) 542-7176  E-mail: info@aztreasury.gov

**Fiscal Year:** 2015  **Budget:** $778,000

★State Treasurer **Jeff DeWit** (R) . . . . . . . . . . . . . . . . . . . (602) 388-1333
  Term Expires: January 2019
  Education: USC
Deputy Treasurer of Administration **Sean Dollman** . . . . . . (602) 542-7880
  E-mail: seand@aztreasury.gov
Deputy Treasurer of Operations **Lorraine Jones** . . . . . . . . (602) 542-7818
Deputy Treasurer of Policy and Research
  **Mark Swenson** . . . . . . . . . . . . . . . . . . . . . . . . . (602) 542-7877
  E-mail: marks@aztreasury.gov
Chief Investment Officer **Patty Humbert** . . . . . . . . . . . . . (602) 542-7841
Human Resources Director **Ken Price** . . . . . . . . . . . . . . . (602) 542-7875

# Department of Financial Institutions [AZDFI]

2910 North 44th Street, Suite 310, Phoenix, AZ 85018
Tel: (602) 771-2800  Fax: (602) 381-1225  Internet: www.azdfi.gov

**Employees:** 58  **Fiscal Year:** 2015  **Budget:** $3,005,000

■Superintendent **(Vacant)** . . . . . . . . . . . . . . . . . . . (602) 771-2800 ext. 12770
Administrative Assistant Superintendent
  **Michael Fowler** . . . . . . . . . . . . . . . . . . . . (602) 771-2800 ext. 12781
  E-mail: mfowler@azdfi.gov
Financial Services Division Superintendent
  **Robert "Bob" Charlton** . . . . . . . . . . . . . . . (602) 771-2800 ext. 12777
  Education: Kansas BA

# Office of the Attorney General

1275 West Washington Street, Phoenix, AZ 85007
Tel: (602) 542-5025  Internet: www.azag.gov

**Fiscal Year:** 2015  **Budget:** $23,243,000

★Attorney General **Mark Brnovich** (R) . . . . . . . . . . . . . . (602) 542-5025
  Term Expires: January 2019
  Education: Arizona State BS; San Diego JD
  Career: Assistant U.S. Attorney, Criminal Division, Arizona District,
  United States Department of Justice (2007-2009); Director, Arizona
  Department of Gaming, State of Arizona (2009-2013)
Chief Deputy and Chief of Staff **Michael Bailey** . . . . . . . . (602) 542-5025
Director of Communications **Ryan Anderson** . . . . . . . . . . (602) 542-5025
  E-mail: ryan.anderson@azdoa.gov
Director of Community Outreach and Education
  **Amilyn Pierce** . . . . . . . . . . . . . . . . . . . . . . . . . (602) 542-5025
Director of Legislative Affairs **Courtney McKinstry** . . . . . . (602) 542-7922
Director of Operations **Leslie Welch** . . . . . . . . . . . . . . . (602) 542-8046
  E-mail: leslie.welch@azag.gov
Press Secretary **Mia Garcia** . . . . . . . . . . . . . . . . . . . . . (602) 542-8019
  E-mail: mia.garcia@azag.gov

★ Elected Official    ■Appointed by Governor    ●Appointed by Legislature    ▲Appointed by Board or Commission    ◆Appointed by State Supreme Court

*State Yellow Book*    © Leadership Directories, Inc.    Summer 2016

# Arizona Department of Education [ADE]

1535 West Jefferson, Bin 2, Phoenix, AZ 85007
Tel: (602) 542-4361  Tel: (602) 542-5393  Fax: (602) 542-5440
E-mail: adeinbox@azed.gov

**Employees:** 300  **Fiscal Year:** 2014  **Budget:** $3,779,600,000

★ Superintendent of Public Instruction **Diane Douglas** (R) . . (602) 542-5460
   E-mail: diane.douglas@azed.gov
   Education: Rutgers 1985 BS
Chief of Staff **Michael Bradley** . . . . . . . . . . . . . . . . . . . . . . . (602) 364-1952
Deputy Superintendent **Shari Zara** . . . . . . . . . . . . . . . . . . . . (602) 364-2347
Associate Superintendent **Cecilia Johnson** . . . . . . . . . . . . . (602) 364-1957
Associate Superintendent **Carol Lippert** . . . . . . . . . . . . . . . . (602) 364-1985
Associate Superintendent **Leila Williams** . . . . . . . . . . . . . . (602) 364-2811
Associate Superintendent **(Vacant)** . . . . . . . . . . . . . . . . . . . (602) 364-4288
Deputy Associate Superintendent of Exceptional Student
   Services **(Vacant)** . . . . . . . . . . . . . . . . . . . . . . . . . . . . . . . . (602) 542-4013
Chief Information Officer **Mark Masterson** . . . . . . . . . . . . . (602) 542-3541
   E-mail: mark.masterson@azed.gov
Public Information Officer **Sally Stewart** . . . . . . . . . . . . . . . (602) 542-5072
   E-mail: sally.stewart@azed.gov
Organization Development Director **Pat Childress** . . . . . . . . (602) 542-3069
Policy Development and Government Relations Director
   **Ashley Berg** . . . . . . . . . . . . . . . . . . . . . . . . . . . . . . . . . . . . . (602) 364-1967

# State Board of Education

1535 West Jefferson Street, Bin 11, Phoenix, AZ 85007
Tel: (602) 542-5057  Fax: (602) 542-3046

■ President **Gregory A. Miller** . . . . . . . . . . . . . . . . . . . . . . . . (602) 542-5057
   Term Expires: January 16, 2017
■ Vice President
   **Reginald M. "Reg" Ballantyne III, FACHE** . . . . . . . . . . (602) 542-5057
   Term Expires: January 16, 2017
   Education: Cornell 1967 MBA
■ Member **Tim Carter** . . . . . . . . . . . . . . . . . . . . . . . . . . . . . . . (602) 542-5057
   Term Expires: January 20, 2018
■ Member-Designate **Dr. Michael M. Crow** . . . . . . . . . . . . . . (602) 542-5057
   Term Expires: January 21, 2019
   Education: Iowa State 1977 BA; Syracuse 1985 PhD
■ Member **Christopher Clark "Chris" Deschene** . . . . . . . . . (602) 542-5057
   Term Expires: January 16, 2017
   Education: Naval Acad 1993 BS; Arizona State 2005 JD, 2005 MSME
   Member **Diane Douglas** . . . . . . . . . . . . . . . . . . . . . . . . . . . . (602) 542-3813
   Term Expires: (Concurrent with term of office)
■ Member **Amy Hamilton** . . . . . . . . . . . . . . . . . . . . . . . . . . . . (602) 542-5057
   Term Expires: January 18, 2016
■ Member **Roger Jacks** . . . . . . . . . . . . . . . . . . . . . . . . . . . . . . (602) 542-5057
   Term Expires: January 18, 2016
   Education: Northern Colorado BA; Pepperdine MA;
   Nova Southeastern MS
■ Member **James D. "J.D." Rottweiler** . . . . . . . . . . . . . . . . . (602) 542-5057
   Term Expires: January 16, 2017
■ Member **Chuck Schmidt** . . . . . . . . . . . . . . . . . . . . . . . . . . . (602) 542-5057
   Term Expires: January 21, 2019
■ Member **Jared Taylor** . . . . . . . . . . . . . . . . . . . . . . . . . . . . . . (602) 542-5057
   Term Expires: January 21, 2018
   Executive Director **Christine Thompson** . . . . . . . . . . . . . . (602) 542-5057

---

★ Elected Official　　■ Appointed by Governor　　● Appointed by Legislature　　▲ Appointed by Board or Commission　　◆ Appointed by State Supreme Court

# Arkansas

Tel: (501) 682-3000 (State Information)

**Number of U.S. Congressional Delegates:** 2 Senators; 4 Representatives **Governor's Term:** 4 years
**Legislature Description:** General Assembly - 35 member Senate; 100 member House of Representatives;
Term - Senate 4 years, House 2 years **Next Election:** Governor November 2018; Legislature November
2016 **Number of Electoral Votes:** 6 **Official Name:** State of Arkansas (Sioux: South-Wind People)
**Nickname:** The Natural State **Motto:** Regnat Populus (The People Rule)

**Population:** 2,978,204 (2015); Rank 33 **Fiscal Year:** 2014 **Budget:** $26,855,751,183

## Office of the Governor

State Capitol, 500 Woodlane Street, Suite 250, Little Rock, AR 72201
Tel: (501) 682-2345 TTY: (501) 682-7515 Fax: (501) 682-1382
E-mail: info@governor.arkansas.gov

**Employees:** 53 **Fiscal Year:** 2014 **Budget:**

### W. Asa Hutchinson
Governor

Began Service: January 13, 2015
Term Expires: January 2019
Date of Birth: December 3, 1950
Education: Bob Jones U 1972 BS;
Arkansas 1975 JD
Home: Little Rock
Religion: Baptist
Career: U.S. Attorney, Arkansas - Western
District, Executive Office for United States
Attorneys, United States Department of Justice
(1982-1985); U.S. Representative (R-AR, District
3), Office of Representative W. Asa Hutchinson,
United States House of Representatives
(1997-2001); Director, Drug Enforcement
Administration, United States Department of
Justice (2001-2003); Under Secretary, Border
and Transportation Security, United States
Department of Homeland Security, George W.
Bush Administration (2003-2005)

★ Governor **W. Asa Hutchinson** (R) . . . . . . . . . . . . . . . . . . . (501) 682-2345
Chief of Staff **Michael Lamoureux** . . . . . . . . . . . . . . . . . (501) 683-6408
  Note: Until the end of May 2016.
  E-mail: michael.lamoureux@governor.arkansas.gov
Chief of Staff **Alison Williams** . . . . . . . . . . . . . . . . . . . . . (501) 682-2345
  Note: Effective June 1, 2016.
  Education: Arkansas 1999 BA; Virginia MBA
Deputy Chief of Staff **Jon Gilmore** . . . . . . . . . . . . . . . . . (501) 683-6467
Senior Advisor **Marjorie L. Greenberg** . . . . . . . . . . . . . . . (501) 683-6414
  E-mail: majorie.greenberg@governor.arkansas.gov
  Education: Harvard 1992 AB; Michigan 1996 MBA
Senior Advisor **Betty Anderson Guhman** . . . . . . . . . . . . . (501) 683-6407
  E-mail: betty.guhman@governor.arkansas.gov
Chief Legal Counsel **Justin Tate** . . . . . . . . . . . . . . . . . . . (501) 682-8040
  E-mail: justin.tate@governor.arkansas.gov
Communications Director **J.R. Davis** . . . . . . . . . . . . . . . . (501) 683-6412
  E-mail: jr.davis@governor.arkansas.gov
  Education: Arkansas Tech 2008 AB
Budget Director **(Vacant)** . . . . . . . . . . . . . . . . . . . . . . . . . (501) 683-6442
Director of Constituent Services **Ateca Williams** . . . . . . . . (501) 683-6847
  E-mail: ateca.williams@governor.arkansas.gov
Director of Correspondence **Tory Freeman** . . . . . . . . . . . . (501) 683-6457
  E-mail: tory.freeman@governor.arkansas.gov
Director of Legislative Affairs **Rett Hatcher** . . . . . . . . . . . (501) 683-6428
  E-mail: rett.hatcher@governor.arkansas.gov
Director of Scheduling **Kyndall Rogers** . . . . . . . . . . . . . . (501) 683-6416
  E-mail: kyndall.rogers@governor.arkansas.gov
Policy Director **Kelly Eichler** . . . . . . . . . . . . . . . . . . . . . . (501) 683-6439
  E-mail: kelly.eichler@governor.arkansas.gov
  Education: Arkansas; Arkansas (Little Rock) JD

Policy Advisor **Christian Olson** . . . . . . . . . . . . . . . . . . . . (501) 683-6426
  E-mail: christian.olson@governor.arkansas.gov
Senior Health Policy Advisor **John Martin** . . . . . . . . . . . . (501) 682-2345
Energy Policy Advisor **Tori Gordon** . . . . . . . . . . . . . . . . . (501) 683-6432
  E-mail: tori.gordon@governor.arkansas.gov
Economic Liaison **Katie Beck** . . . . . . . . . . . . . . . . . . . . . (501) 683-6400
  E-mail: katie.beck@governor.arkansas.gov

## Washington Office

444 North Capitol Street, NW, Washington, DC 20001

Director of State-Federal Relations **Alison Williams** . . . . . . (501) 682-2345
  Note: Until May 31, 2016.

## Arkansas Department of Aeronautics

2315 Crisp Drive, Hangar 8, Little Rock, AR 72202
Tel: (501) 376-6781 Fax: (501) 378-0820

**Employees:** 4 **Fiscal Year:** 2016 **Budget:** $15,623,559

■ Director **Jerry Chism** . . . . . . . . . . . . . . . . . . . . . . . . . . (501) 376-6781
  E-mail: jerry.chism@arkansas.gov
  Executive Assistant to the Director **Kay Groce** . . . . . . . . (501) 376-6781
Assistant Director **Lily Roberts** . . . . . . . . . . . . . . . . . . . (501) 376-6781
State Airport Engineer **Richard Mills** . . . . . . . . . . . . . . . . (501) 376-6781
  E-mail: richard.mills@arkansas.gov
Grants Coordinator **McCall Harriman** . . . . . . . . . . . . . . . (501) 376-6781

## Arkansas Agriculture Department [AAD]

1 Natural Resources Drive, Little Rock, AR 72205
Tel: (501) 683-4851 Fax: (501) 683-4852

**Employees:** 568 **Fiscal Year:** 2014 **Budget:** $63,798,471

■ Secretary **Wes Ward** . . . . . . . . . . . . . . . . . . . . . . . . . . . (501) 683-4851
  E-mail: wes.ward@aad.ar.gov
  Education: Arkansas State BS; Arkansas JD, LLM
  Executive Assistant **Melissa Lambert** . . . . . . . . . . . . . . (501) 683-4851
Deputy Secretary **Cynthia Edwards** . . . . . . . . . . . . . . . . (501) 219-6362
Chief Financial Officer **DeeVee Pearson** . . . . . . . . . . . . . (501) 219-6361
Communications Director **Adriane Barnes** . . . . . . . . . . . . (501) 516-6255
  E-mail: adriane.barnes@arkansas.gov
Human Resources Administrator **Paula Jones** . . . . . . . . . . (501) 219-6370
Marketing Director **Christian Olsen** . . . . . . . . . . . . . . . . (501) 219-6324
  E-mail: christian.olson@aad.ar.gov

## Arkansas Assessment Coordination Department [ACD]

1614 West Third Street, Little Rock, AR 72201
Tel: (501) 324-9240 Fax: (501) 324-9242 Internet: www.arkansas.gov/acd

**Employees:** 34 **Fiscal Year:** 2014 **Budget:** $18,896,195

■ Director **Glenn Allen "Bear" Chaney** . . . . . . . . . . . . . . . (501) 324-9100
  E-mail: gchaney@arkansasonline.com
Deputy Director **Faye Tate** . . . . . . . . . . . . . . . . . . . . . . . (501) 324-9113
Staff Attorney **John Nichols** . . . . . . . . . . . . . . . . . . . . . . (501) 324-9109

---

★ Elected Official    ■ Appointed by Governor    ● Appointed by Legislature    ▲ Appointed by Board or Commission    ◆ Appointed by State Supreme Court

EXECUTIVE BRANCH

# Arkansas State Bank Department

400 Hardin Road, Suite 100, Little Rock, AR 72211
Fax: (501) 324-9028   E-mail: asbd@banking.state.ar.us

**Employees:** 72   **Fiscal Year:** 2015   **Budget:** $9,013,210

■Commissioner **Candace A. Franks** . . . . . . . . . . . . . . . . . . (501) 324-9019
  Term Expires: June 13, 2019
  E-mail: cfranks@banking.state.ar.us
  Education: Arkansas State BA, MA; Arkansas (Little Rock) JD
Deputy Commissioner **Luther Guinn** . . . . . . . . . . . . . . . . (501) 324-9019
  E-mail: lguinn@banking.state.ar.us
Deputy Commissioner **Susannah T. Marshall** . . . . . . . . . . (501) 324-9019
  E-mail: smarshall@banking.state.ar.us
Assistant Deputy Commissioner **Richard Buzbee** . . . . . . . (501) 324-9019
  E-mail: rbuzbee@banking.state.ar.us
Assistant Deputy Commissioner **Wilks Marshall** . . . . . . . . (501) 324-9019
  E-mail: wmarshall@banking.state.ar.us
Assistant Deputy Commissioner **Baker Moseley** . . . . . . . . (501) 324-9019
  E-mail: bmoseley@banking.state.ar.us
Assistant Deputy Commissioner **Michael G. Saunders** . . . (501) 324-9019
  E-mail: msaunders@banking.state.ar.us

# Arkansas Department of Career Education [ACE]

Luther Hardin Building, Three Capitol Mall, Little Rock, AR 72201-1083
Tel: (501) 682-1500   Fax: (501) 682-1509

**Employees:** 93   **Fiscal Year:** 2014   **Budget:** $165,495,616

▲Director **Dr. Charisse Childers** . . . . . . . . . . . . . . . . . . . (501) 682-1500
  E-mail: charisse.childers@arkansas.gov
  Education: Arkansas State 1988 BS; Arkansas PhD
Deputy Director for Career and Technical Education
  **Kathi Turner** . . . . . . . . . . . . . . . . . . . . . . . . . . . (501) 682-1040
  Education: Austin Peay State BS; Arkansas MS    Fax: (501) 682-1805
Associate Director for Career and Technical Education
  **Dr. Cheryl Wiedmaier** . . . . . . . . . . . . . . . . . . . . . (501) 683-4434
  Education: Northwest Missouri State BA; Missouri PhD
Associate Director for CTE-Special Projects
  **Sonja Wright-McMurray** . . . . . . . . . . . . . . . . . . . (501) 683-4432
Chief Financial Officer **Lorna Claudio** . . . . . . . . . . . . . . (501) 682-1848
Chief Information Officer **(Vacant)** . . . . . . . . . . . . . . . . (501) 682-1500
Communications Director **Kathy Edgerton** . . . . . . . . . . . (501) 682-1701
  E-mail: kathy.edgerton@arkansas.gov
Human Resources Manager **DeCarlia Smith** . . . . . . . . . . (501) 682-1500

# Arkansas Rehabilitation Services [ARS]

525 West Capitol Avenue, Little Rock, AR 72201
Tel: (501) 296-1600   Fax: (501) 296-1655

Commissioner **Alan McClain** . . . . . . . . . . . . . . . . . . . . . (501) 296-1616
  E-mail: alan.mcclain@arkansas.gov
  Education: Hendrix 1987 BA; Arkansas (Little Rock) 1993 MPA
Associate Commissioner of Access and Accommodations
  **Linda Morgan** . . . . . . . . . . . . . . . . . . . . . . . . . . (501) 296-1600
  Education: Arkansas BA; Central Arkansas MS
Chief of Field Services **Carl E. Daughtery** . . . . . . . . . . . (501) 296-1600
  E-mail: carl.daughtery@arkansas.gov
  Education: Philander Smith BA; Webster MPA
Chief of Financial Management **Joseph "Joe" Baxter** . . . . (501) 296-1600
  Education: Florida A&M BS
Director of Program Planning, Development and
  Evaluation **Robert P. Treviño** . . . . . . . . . . . . . . . . (501) 296-1600
  Education: LSU (Shreveport) BA; Arkansas (Little Rock) MPA
Director of Transition Services **Judy Smith** . . . . . . . . . . . (501) 296-1600

# Division of Adult Education

Tel: (501) 682-1970

Deputy Director **Dr. Trenia Miles** . . . . . . . . . . . . . . . . . . (501) 682-1970
GED (General Education Development) Administrator
  **Janice Hanlon** . . . . . . . . . . . . . . . . . . . . . . . . . . (501) 682-1980
  E-mail: janice.hanlon@arkansas.gov

# Arkansas Department of Emergency Management [ADEM]

Building 9501, Camp Joseph T. Robinson,
North Little Rock, AR 72199-9600
Tel: (501) 683-6700   Fax: (501) 683-7890
E-mail: adem@adem.arkansas.gov   Internet: www.adem.arkansas.gov

**Employees:** 104   **Fiscal Year:** 2014   **Budget:** $148,929,561

■Director and State Homeland Security Adviser
  **David Maxwell** . . . . . . . . . . . . . . . . . . . . . . . . . . (501) 683-6700
  E-mail: david.maxwell@adem.arkansas.gov
  Executive Assistant to the Director **Kerri Phillips** . . . . . . . (501) 683-6700
Deputy Director **Tina Owens** . . . . . . . . . . . . . . . . . . . . (501) 683-6700
Training and Branch Manager **Mark Hooker** . . . . . . . . . . . (501) 683-6700
Exercise Section Chief **Steve Moore** . . . . . . . . . . . . . . . (501) 683-6700
Administration Division Director **Bobbie Ann Merkel** . . . . (501) 683-6700
  E-mail: bobbieann.merkel@adem.arkansas.gov
Communications Division Director **(Vacant)** . . . . . . . . . . (501) 683-6700
Response and Recovery Division Director **Scott Bass** . . . . (501) 683-6700
Preparedness Division Director **Sheila Annable** . . . . . . . . (501) 683-6700
Law Enforcement Coordinator **David Bertelin** . . . . . . . . . (501) 683-6700
Public Education Coordinator **(Vacant)** . . . . . . . . . . . . . (501) 683-6700
Public Information Officer Chief **Whitney Green** . . . . . . . (501) 683-6700
  E-mail: whitney.green@adem.arkansas.gov

# Arkansas Department of Environmental Quality [ADEQ]

5301 North Shore Drive, North Little Rock, AR 72118
Tel: (501) 682-0744   Fax: (501) 682-0880   E-mail: adeq@state.ar.us
Internet: www.adeq.state.ar.us

**Employees:** 420   **Fiscal Year:** 2014   **Budget:** $102,927,734

■Director **Becky Keogh** . . . . . . . . . . . . . . . . . . . . . . . . (501) 682-0959
  E-mail: keogh@adeq.state.ar.us
  Executive Assistant to the Director **Beth Thompson** . . . . (501) 682-0959
General Counsel **Julie Chapman** . . . . . . . . . . . . . . . . . . (501) 682-6347
Public Information Officer **Katherine Benenati** . . . . . . . . . (501) 682-0821
  E-mail: benenati@adeq.state.ar.us
Executive Secretary **Patricia Lowry** . . . . . . . . . . . . . . . . (501) 682-0959

# Arkansas Department of Finance and Administration [DFA]

P.O. Box 3278, Little Rock, AR 72203-3278
DFA Building, 1509 West Seventh Street, Room 401,
Little Rock, AR 72201
Tel: (501) 682-2242   Fax: (501) 682-1029

**Fiscal Year:** 2014   **Budget:** $494,022,675

■Director **Larry W. Walther** . . . . . . . . . . . . . . . . . . . . . (501) 682-2242
  E-mail: larry.walther@dfa.arkansas.gov
  Education: Arkansas (Monticello) BS
  Executive Assistant **Jamie Levinsky** . . . . . . . . . . . . . (501) 682-2242
Deputy Director **Timothy J. Leathers** . . . . . . . . . . . . . . . (501) 682-2242
  E-mail: tim.leathers@dfa.arkansas.gov
  Executive Assistant **Rachel Jones** . . . . . . . . . . . . . . . (501) 682-2242
Economic Analysis and Tax Research Administrator
  **John Shelnutt** . . . . . . . . . . . . . . . . . . . . . . . . . . (501) 682-1688
  E-mail: john.shelnutt@dfa.arkansas.gov
Criminal Detention Facilities Review Committees
  Coordinator **J. Sterling Penix** . . . . . . . . . . . . . . . . (501) 324-9493
  1515 Building, 1515 West Seventh Street,    Fax: (501) 683-6919
  Suite 222, Little Rock, AR 72201

# Accounting Office

DFA Building, 1509 West Seventh Street, Room 403,
Little Rock, AR 72201
Fax: (501) 683-0823

Administrator **Paul Louthian** . . . . . . . . . . . . . . . . . . . . . (501) 682-1675
  E-mail: paul.louthian@dfa.arkansas.gov

---

★ Elected Official   ■ Appointed by Governor   ● Appointed by Legislature   ▲ Appointed by Board or Commission   ◆ Appointed by State Supreme Court

## Administrative Services Office

1515 Building, 1515 West Seventh Street, Room 700,
Little Rock, AR 72201
P.O. Box 2485, Little Rock, AR 72203
Fax: (501) 324-9070
Administrator **Carla Haugen** . . . . . . . . . . . . . . . . . . . . . . . (501) 324-9057
E-mail: carla.haugen@dfa.arkansas.gov

## Alcoholic Beverage Control - Administration Office

1515 Building, 1515 West Seventh Street, Room 503,
Little Rock, AR 72201
Fax: (501) 682-2221
Director **Gary "Bud" Roberts** . . . . . . . . . . . . . . . . . . . . . .(501) 682-1105

## Alcoholic Beverage Control - Enforcement Office

1515 Building, 1515 West Seventh Street, Room 204,
Little Rock, AR 72201
P.O. Box 2259, Little Rock, AR 72203
Fax: (501) 682-3874
Director **Boyce Hamlet** . . . . . . . . . . . . . . . . . . . . . . . . . . . . (501) 682-8174

## Budget Office

DFA Building, 1509 West Seventh Street, Room 402,
Little Rock, AR 72201
Fax: (501) 682-1086
Administrator **Duncan Baird** . . . . . . . . . . . . . . . . . . . . . . . . (501) 682-1941
E-mail: duncan.baird@dfa.arkansas.gov

## Division of Building Authority

501 Woodlane, Suite 101N, Little Rock, AR 72201
Tel: (501) 682-1833 TTY: (501) 682-1487 Fax: (501) 682-5589
E-mail: info@aba.arkansas.gov
■Director **Anne Laidlaw** . . . . . . . . . . . . . . . . . . . . . . . . . . . (501) 682-1833
E-mail: anne.laidlaw@dfa.arkansas.gov

## Intergovernmental Services Office

1515 Building, 1515 West Seventh Street, Suite 400,
Little Rock, AR 72201
Fax: (501) 683-2598
Office Administrator **Doris Smith** . . . . . . . . . . . . . . . . . . . . (501) 682-1074
E-mail: doris.smith@dfa.arkansas.gov

## Office of the Arkansas Lottery

P.O. Box 3238, Little Rock, AR 72203-3238
Tel: (501) 683-2000
Director **Bishop Woosley** . . . . . . . . . . . . . . . . . . . . . . . . . . (501) 683-2000
Chief Fiscal Officer **Jerry Fetzer** . . . . . . . . . . . . . . . . . . . . .(501) 683-2000

## Personnel Management Office

DFA Building, 1509 West Seventh Street, 2nd Floor,
Little Rock, AR 72201
Fax: (501) 682-5104
Administrator **Kay Barnhill** . . . . . . . . . . . . . . . . . . . . . . . . . (501) 682-8197
E-mail: kay.terry@dfa.arkansas.gov

## Procurement Office

DFA Building, 1509 West Seventh Street, 3rd Floor,
Little Rock, AR 72201
Fax: (501) 324-9311
Administrator **Camber Thompson** . . . . . . . . . . . . . . . . . . . .(501) 324-9316
E-mail: camber.thompson@dfa.arkansas.gov

## Revenue Division

P.O. Box 1272, Little Rock, AR 72203
Ragland Building, 1900 West 7th Street, Room 2047,
Little Rock, AR 72201
Tel: (501) 682-7025 Fax: (501) 682-1683
Operations and Administration Assistant Commissioner
**Walter Anger** . . . . . . . . . . . . . . . . . . . . . . . . . . . . . . . . . . (501) 682-7025
E-mail: walter.anger@dfa.arkansas.gov

Administrative Assistant **Cherry Williams** . . . . . . . . . . . . .(501) 682-8969
Policy & Legal Assistant Commissioner **John Theis** . . . . . .(501) 682-7000
Ledbetter Building, 1816 West 7th Street, Room 2440,
Little Rock, AR 72201
Administrative Assistant **Wendy Spadoni** . . . . . . . . . . . . .(501) 682-7000
Problem Resolution and Tax Information Officer
**Will Keadle** . . . . . . . . . . . . . . . . . . . . . . . . . . . . . . . . . . (501) 682-7751
Problem Resolution and Tax Information Officer
**David Rector** . . . . . . . . . . . . . . . . . . . . . . . . . . . . . . . . . . (501) 682-7751

## Department of Arkansas Heritage

1500 Tower Building, 323 Center Street, Little Rock, AR 72201
Tel: (501) 324-9150 TTY: (501) 324-9811 Fax: (501) 324-9154
E-mail: info@arkansasheritage.com Internet: www.arkansasheritage.com

**Employees:** 28 **Fiscal Year:** 2014 **Budget:** $22,129,875
■Director **Stacy Hurst** . . . . . . . . . . . . . . . . . . . . . . . . . . . . (501) 324-9155
E-mail: stacy.hurst@arkansasheritage.org
Education: Arkansas BA
Deputy Director/General Counsel **Rebecca Burkes** . . . . . . .(501) 324-9157
Communications Director **Melissa Whitfield** . . . . . . . . . . . .(501) 324-9611
E-mail: melissaw@arkansasheritage.org
Fiscal and Personnel Manager **Rick Pruitt** . . . . . . . . . . . . . .(501) 324-9586
Education Coordinator **Allison Reavis** . . . . . . . . . . . . . . . . (501) 324-9346

## Arkansas Department of Health [ADH]

4815 West Markham Street, Little Rock, AR 72205-3867
4815 West Markham Street, Slot 44, Little Rock, AR 72205 (Vital
Records)
Tel: (501) 661-2000 Tel: (501) 661-2336 (Vital Records)
Fax: (501) 661-2717 (Vital Records) Internet: www.healthy.arkansas.gov

**Employees:** 2,937 **Fiscal Year:** 2014 **Budget:** $370,000,000
■Director and State Health Officer
**Nathaniel "Nate" Smith, MD, MPH** . . . . . . . . . . . . . . .(501) 661-2400
E-mail: nathaniel.smith@arkansas.gov      Fax: (501) 671-1450
Education: Rice 1986 BA; Dallas Sem 1991 MA;
Baylor Col Medicine 1991 MD; Texas 1996 MPH
State Epidemiologist **Dr. Dirk Haselow, MD, PhD** . . . . . . . .(501) 661-2142

## Office of the Deputy State Health Officer and Chief Science Officer

Deputy State Health and Chief Science Officer
**Joseph H. "Joe" Bates, MD, MS** . . . . . . . . . . . . . . . . . .(501) 661-2412
Education: Hendrix 1964 BA
Deputy Chief Science Officer
**Namvar Zohoori, PhD, MPH** . . . . . . . . . . . . . . . . . . . . . .(501) 280-4346
Education: U West Indies (Jamaica) 1978 BSc, 1982 MD;
Johns Hopkins 1988 MPH; North Carolina 1993 PhD

## Office of the Deputy Director for Administration

Deputy Director for Administration **Ann Purvis, JD** . . . . . .(501) 280-4235
E-mail: ann.purvis@arkansas.gov
Human Resources and Professional Development Director
**Xavier Heard** . . . . . . . . . . . . . . . . . . . . . . . . . . . . . . . . . . (501) 683-5749
Building/Supply Manager **James Joiner, PE** . . . . . . . . . . . .(501) 661-2364
Internal Audit Manager **Bob Berry, CPA** . . . . . . . . . . . . . . .(501) 280-4477
Chief Information Officer **Michael Kincaid** . . . . . . . . . . . . . (501) 661-2180
E-mail: michael.kincaid@arkansas.gov

## Office of the Deputy Director for Public Health Programs

Tel: (501) 280-4663 Fax: (501) 671-1450
Deputy Director **Stephanie C. Williams, MPH** . . . . . . . . . .(501) 661-2919
Chief Medical Officer **Dr. J. Gary Wheeler, MD** . . . . . . . . .(501) 661-2797
Health Communications Director **Marisha DiCarlo** . . . . . . .(501) 661-2474
E-mail: marisha.dicarlo@arkansas.gov
Minority Health and Health Disparities Director
**Michelle Smith, PhD, MPH** . . . . . . . . . . . . . . . . . . . . . . .(501) 280-4192

---

★ Elected Official   ■ Appointed by Governor   ● Appointed by Legislature   ▲ Appointed by Board or Commission   ◆ Appointed by State Supreme Court

## Arkansas Department of Higher Education [ADHE]

423 Main Street, Suite 400, Little Rock, AR 72201
Tel: (501) 371-2000 Fax: (501) 371-2001 Internet: www.adhe.edu

**Employees:** 50 **Fiscal Year:** 2014 **Budget:** $77,168,609

▲ Director **Dr. Brett Powell** . . . . . . . . . . . . . . . . . . . . . . . . . . (501) 371-2031
  Note: Until July 31, 2016.
  E-mail: brett.powell@adhe.edu
  Education: Arkansas (Little Rock) 2009 EdD
Senior Associate Director of Academic Affairs
  **Ann V. Clemmer** . . . . . . . . . . . . . . . . . . . . . . . . . . . . . (501) 371-2216
Senior Associate Director of Administration and Finance
  **Harold Criswell** . . . . . . . . . . . . . . . . . . . . . . . . . . . . . (501) 371-2029
Senior Associate Director of Institutional Finance
  **Tara Smith** . . . . . . . . . . . . . . . . . . . . . . . . . . . . . . . . (501) 371-2026
Senior Associate Director of Research and Technology
  **Dr. Marla Strecker** . . . . . . . . . . . . . . . . . . . . . . . . . . (501) 682-1602
Federal Program Coordinator **Monieca West** . . . . . . . . . . . (501) 683-2079
Financial Aid Coordinator **Elyse Price** . . . . . . . . . . . . . . . (501) 371-2054
NCLB (No Child Left Behind) Coordinator
  **Suzanne Mitchell** . . . . . . . . . . . . . . . . . . . . . . . . . . . (501) 371-2062
  E-mail: suzanne.mitchell@adhe.edu
  Education: Arkansas State 1969 BS; Arkansas 1975 MEd;
  Missouri (Kansas City) 1991 EdS, 1998 PhD

## Arkansas State Highway Commission [AHTD]

P.O. Box 2261, Little Rock, AR 72203-2261
Tel: (501) 569-2000 Fax: (501) 569-2400

■ Chairman **Dick Trammel** . . . . . . . . . . . . . . . . . . . . . . . . (501) 569-2244
  Term Expires: January 14, 2019
  E-mail: dick.trammel@arkansashighways.com
  Affiliation: Executive Vice President, Arvest Bank Group, Inc.
  Education: Arkansas 1960 BS
■ Vice Chairman **Tom Schueck** . . . . . . . . . . . . . . . . . . . . (501) 569-2244
  Term Expires: January 14, 2021
■ Commissioner **Alec Farmer** . . . . . . . . . . . . . . . . . . . . . . (501) 569-2244
  Term Expires: January 14, 2025
■ Commissioner **Robert S. Moore, Jr.** . . . . . . . . . . . . . . . . (501) 569-2244
  Term Expires: January 14, 2023
  Education: Ouachita Baptist 1966 BA; Arkansas 1973 JD
■ Commissioner **Frank D. Scott** . . . . . . . . . . . . . . . . . . . . (501) 569-2244
  Term Expires: January 14, 2017
  Education: Arkansas (Little Rock) MBA

## Arkansas State Highway and Transportation Department [AHTD]

P.O. Box 2261, Little Rock, AR 72203-2261
Tel: (501) 569-2000 Fax: (501) 569-2400
E-mail: info@arkansashighways.com

**Employees:** 3,589 **Fiscal Year:** 2014 **Budget:** $2,236,940,408

▲ Director **Scott E. Bennett** . . . . . . . . . . . . . . . . . . . . . . . (501) 569-2211
  E-mail: scott.bennett@arkansashighways.com
  Education: Arkansas 1989 BSCE, 1994 MSCE
Internal Audit Chief Auditor **Judy Robertson** . . . . . . . . . . (501) 569-2237
Chief Legal Counsel **Rita Looney** . . . . . . . . . . . . . . . . . . (501) 569-2112

## Office of the Deputy Director and Chief Engineer

Tel: (501) 569-2214

Deputy Director and Chief Engineer **Emanuel Banks** . . . . . (501) 569-2214
  E-mail: emanuel.banks@ahtd.ar.gov
  Education: Arkansas 1987 MSCE

## Arkansas Department of Human Services [DHS]

P.O. Box 1437, Little Rock, AR 72203-1437
Tel: (501) 682-1001 TTY: (501) 682-1001 Fax: (501) 682-6836

**Employees:** 8,325 **Fiscal Year:** 2014 **Budget:** $7,430,624,664

■ Director **Cynthia D. "Cindy" Gillespie** . . . . . . . . . . . . . . (501) 682-8650
  Education: Trevecca Nazarene Col 1979 BA; Auburn 1983 MA
  Administrative Assistant **Pamela "Pam" Lambert** . . . . . . (501) 682-8650
Client Protection and Advocacy Director **Patricia Nation** . . (501) 682-8650
Emergency Services Director **Edwin Lyons** . . . . . . . . . . . (501) 683-1739
  Fax: (501) 682-1597
Policy and Planning Director **(Vacant)** . . . . . . . . . . . . . . . (501) 682-8650
Human Capital Manager **Geania Dickey** . . . . . . . . . . . . . . (501) 682-6366
Research Analysis Manager **Bob Darling** . . . . . . . . . . . . . (501) 682-7953
Senior Policy Analyst **Rachael Veregge** . . . . . . . . . . . . . . (501) 682-8650
Communications Director **Amy Webb** . . . . . . . . . . . . . . . . (501) 682-8650
  E-mail: amy.webb@dhs.arkansas.gov
Public Information Coordinator **Kimberly Rusley** . . . . . . . (501) 682-8650

## Department of Information Systems [DIS]

P.O. Box 3155, Little Rock, AR 72203-3155
Tel: (501) 682-9990 TTY: (501) 682-3001 Fax: (501) 682-4310
E-mail: dis@arkansas.gov Internet: www.dis.arkansas.gov

**Employees:** 251 **Fiscal Year:** 2014 **Budget:** $111,607,031

■ Director and Chief Technology Officer **Mark E. Myers** . . . . (501) 682-4976
  E-mail: mark.e.myers@arkansas.gov
  Education: Arkansas
Deputy Director **Yessica Jones** . . . . . . . . . . . . . . . . . . . . (501) 683-1620
  E-mail: yessica.jones@arkansas.gov
  Education: Harding BS, MBA
Chief Operating Officer **Jeff Dean** . . . . . . . . . . . . . . . . . . (501) 682-2810
  Executive Assistant **Leslie McCarty** . . . . . . . . . . . . . . . (501) 682-4976
AWIN (Arkansas Wireless Information Network) Director
  **Penny Rubow** . . . . . . . . . . . . . . . . . . . . . . . . . . . . . (501) 682-5358
  E-mail: penny.rubow@arkansas.gov
Chief Enterprise Architect **Scott Utley** . . . . . . . . . . . . . . (501) 682-4429
  E-mail: scott.utley@arkansas.gov
Chief Financial Officer **Jerry Pack** . . . . . . . . . . . . . . . . . (501) 682-4022
Customer Relationship Management **Nancy Jauernig** . . . . (501) 682-4030
Enterprise Systems Management **Ali Yavuzer** . . . . . . . . . . (501) 683-3150
  E-mail: ali.yavuzer@arkansas.gov
Enterprise Network Support **Don McDaniel** . . . . . . . . . . . (501) 682-5027
Enterprise Operations **Brian Fortson** . . . . . . . . . . . . . . . (501) 682-4034
  E-mail: brian.fortson@arkansas.gov
General Counsel **Anthony Black** . . . . . . . . . . . . . . . . . . . (501) 682-1011
State Chief Security Officer **Frank Andrews** . . . . . . . . . . . (501) 682-4550
  E-mail: frank.andrews@arkansas.gov

## Arkansas Insurance Department [AID]

1200 West Third Street, Little Rock, AR 72201-1904
Tel: (501) 371-2600 Tel: (800) 282-9134 Fax: (501) 371-2618
E-mail: insurance@arkansas.gov Internet: www.insurance.arkansas.gov

**Employees:** 200 **Fiscal Year:** 2014 **Budget:** $122,379,562

■ Commissioner **Allen Kerr** . . . . . . . . . . . . . . . . . . . . . . . (501) 371-2623
  E-mail: allen.kerr@arkansas.gov

## Arkansas Department of Labor

10421 West Markham, Little Rock, AR 72205
Tel: (501) 682-4534 TTY: (800) 285-1131 Fax: (501) 682-4535

**Employees:** 98 **Fiscal Year:** 2014 **Budget:** $7,283,419

■ Director **Leon Jones, Jr.** . . . . . . . . . . . . . . . . . . . . . . . . (501) 682-4541
  E-mail: leon.jones@arkansas.gov
  Executive Assistant **Rosalyn Miller** . . . . . . . . . . . . . . . (501) 682-4541

---

★ Elected Official ■ Appointed by Governor ● Appointed by Legislature ▲ Appointed by Board or Commission ◆ Appointed by State Supreme Court

# Arkansas Military Department

Camp Robinson, North Little Rock, AR 72199-9600
Tel: (501) 212-5001  Fax: (501) 212-5009  Internet: www.arguard.org

**Employees:** 539  **Fiscal Year:** 2014  **Budget:** $94,443,767

■Adjutant General **MajGen Mark H. Berry, ANG** . . . . . . . . . (501) 212-5001
  Education: Embry-Riddle 1983; Golden Gate 1984 MPA
  Executive Assistant
    **SSG Jennifer D. Champion, ARNG** . . . . . . . . . . . . . (501) 212-5001
Deputy Adjutant General
  **COL Gregrey C. Bacon, ARNG** . . . . . . . . . . . . . . . . . . (501) 212-5002
Chief of Staff **COL Christopher S. Stanger, ARNG** . . . . . . (501) 212-6061
Military Support Director **COL Damon N. Cluck, ARNG** . . (501) 212-5475
                                  Fax: (501) 212-5479
Education Officer **LTC Richard D. Garringer, ARNG** . . . . . (501) 212-4021
Information Management Officer
  **LTC James W. Mann, ARNG** . . . . . . . . . . . . . . . . . . . (501) 212-5902
  E-mail: james.w.mann5.mil@mail.mil    Fax: (501) 212-5909
Safety Officer **COL Phillip A. Hogue, ARNG** . . . . . . . . . . . (501) 212-5092
                                    Fax: (501) 212-5099

# Arkansas Department of Parks and Tourism

One Capitol Mall, Little Rock, AR 72201
Tel: (501) 682-7777  TTY: (501) 682-7777  TTY: (501) 682-1191 (Parks)
Fax: (501) 682-1364  E-mail: info@arkansas.com
Internet: www.arkansas.com

**Employees:** 702  **Fiscal Year:** 2014  **Budget:** $130,099,848

■Executive Director **Kane Webb** . . . . . . . . . . . . . . . . . . . . . (501) 682-2535
  E-mail: kane.webb@arkansas.gov
  Executive Secretary **Savannah Mitchell** . . . . . . . . . . . . . (501) 682-2535
    E-mail: savannah.mitchell@arkansas.gov
  Executive Assistant **Kris Richardson** . . . . . . . . . . . . . . (501) 682-7614
    E-mail: kris.richardson@arkansas.gov
Internal Auditor **Richard Scott** . . . . . . . . . . . . . . . . . . . . (501) 682-2160
  E-mail: richard.scott@arkansas.gov
Personnel Director **David Flake** . . . . . . . . . . . . . . . . . . . . (501) 682-6888
  E-mail: david.flake@arkansas.gov
  Assistant Personnel Director **Heather Reese** . . . . . . . . . . (501) 682-7742
    E-mail: heather.reese@arkansas.gov

# Arkansas Securities Department [ASD]

Heritage West Building, 201 East Markham, Room 300,
Little Rock, AR 72201
Tel: (501) 324-9260  Tel: (800) 981-4429 (Investor Protection Hotline)
Fax: (501) 324-9268  Internet: www.securities.arkansas.gov

**Employees:** 39  **Fiscal Year:** 2014  **Budget:** $3,511,785

■Commissioner **B. Edmond Waters** . . . . . . . . . . . . . . . . . (501) 324-9260
  E-mail: ewaters@securities.arkansas.gov
  Education: Arkansas (Little Rock)
Deputy Commissioner **Ann McDougal** . . . . . . . . . . . . . . . (501) 324-8685
Deputy Commissioner for Mortgage, Money Services and
  Perpetual Care Cemeteries **Karyn Tierney** . . . . . . . . . . . (501) 324-8671
  E-mail: ktierney@securities.arkansas.gov
  Education: Guilford Col 1999 BA; Arkansas (Little Rock) 2003 JD
Chief Counsel **David Smith** . . . . . . . . . . . . . . . . . . . . . . . (501) 324-8694
Broker Dealer Registration Supervisor **Bradd Worden** . . . . (501) 324-8690
Securities Registration/Exemption Supervisor
  **Felicia West** . . . . . . . . . . . . . . . . . . . . . . . . . . . . . . . . (501) 324-8697

# Arkansas Department of Veterans Affairs [ADVA]

501 Woodlane Street, Suite 230C, Little Rock, AR 72201
Tel: (501) 370-3820  TTY: (800) 285-1131  Fax: (501) 370-3829
Internet: www.veterans.arkansas.gov

**Employees:** 137  **Fiscal Year:** 2015  **Budget:** $17,770,208

■Director **LTC Matt Snead, ARNG** . . . . . . . . . . . . . . . . . (501) 683-1376
  E-mail: matt.snead@arkansas.gov
  Education: Henderson State

Deputy Director **Edward L. "Lane" Bailey** . . . . . . . . . . . . (501) 683-5371
  Education: Ouachita Baptist BA; Brown U MA;
  Arkansas (Little Rock) MPA
Finance Manager **Karen E. Watkins** . . . . . . . . . . . . . . . . . (501) 683-1643
                                    Fax: (501) 682-4833
Personnel Manager **Sara Terry** . . . . . . . . . . . . . . . . . . . . . (501) 683-1386

# Arkansas Department of Workforce Services [DWS]

#2 Capitol Mall, Little Rock, AR 72201
Tel: (501) 682-2121  Fax: (501) 682-8845
Internet: www.dws.arkansas.gov

**Employees:** 800  **Fiscal Year:** 2014  **Budget:** $727,263,869

■Director **Daryl E. Bassett** . . . . . . . . . . . . . . . . . . . . . . . . (501) 682-3394
  E-mail: daryl.bassett@arkansas.gov
  Education: Harding 1978 BA
Deputy Director **Ron Snead** . . . . . . . . . . . . . . . . . . . . . . . (501) 682-2033
  E-mail: ron.snead@arkansas.gov
Board of Review Chair **Sommer Faulkenberry** . . . . . . . . . (501) 682-1063
  E-mail: sommer.faulkenberry@arkansas.gov
General Counsel **Don Denton** . . . . . . . . . . . . . . . . . . . . . . (501) 682-3250
  E-mail: don.denton@arkansas.gov
Employment Assistance Assistant Director **Cindy Varner** . . (501) 371-1028
  E-mail: cindy.varner@arkansas.gov
Financial Management Assistant Director **Bryan Hicks** . . . . (501) 682-3108
  E-mail: bryan.hicks@arkansas.gov
Information Technology Assistant Director
  **Earnest L. Sweat III** . . . . . . . . . . . . . . . . . . . . . . . . . . (501) 682-5668
  E-mail: earnest.sweat@arkansas.gov
TANF (Temporary Assistance for Needy Families)
  Assistant Director **Phil Harris** . . . . . . . . . . . . . . . . . . . (501) 683-5370
  E-mail: phil.harris@arkansas.gov
Unemployment Insurance Assistant Director
  **Ronald "Ron" Calkins** . . . . . . . . . . . . . . . . . . . . . . . . (501) 682-3200
New Hire Registry Assistant Director **Steve Guntharp** . . . . (501) 682-3378
  Education: Arkansas 1997 BS

# Board of Corrections

P.O. Box 20550, White Hall, AR 71612
Tel: (870) 267-6754  Fax: (870) 267-6756

■Chair **Benny Magness** . . . . . . . . . . . . . . . . . . . . . . . . . . (870) 267-6754
  Term Expires: December 31, 2018
■Vice Chair **Dr. Mary Parker-Reed** . . . . . . . . . . . . . . . . . (870) 267-6754
  Term Expires: December 31, 2016
■Member **Tyrone Broomfield** . . . . . . . . . . . . . . . . . . . . . . (870) 267-6754
  Term Expires: September 31, 2017
■Member **Dr. William "Dubs" Byers** . . . . . . . . . . . . . . . . (870) 267-6754
  Term Expires: December 31, 2021
■Member **Earl "Buddy" Chadick** . . . . . . . . . . . . . . . . . . . (870) 267-6754
  Term Expires: December 31, 2019
■Member **John Felts** . . . . . . . . . . . . . . . . . . . . . . . . . . . . (870) 267-6754
  Term Expires: November 14, 2019
■Member **Bobby Glover** . . . . . . . . . . . . . . . . . . . . . . . . . . (870) 267-6754
  Term Expires: December 31, 2020

# Arkansas Department of Community Correction

105 West Capitol Avenue, Little Rock, AR 72201
Internet: www.dcc.arkansas.gov

■Director **Sheila Sharp** . . . . . . . . . . . . . . . . . . . . . . . . . . (501) 682-9566
  E-mail: sheila.sharp@arkansas.gov
  Education: Arkansas (Little Rock) 1991 MA
Chief Deputy Director **Kevin K. Murphy** . . . . . . . . . . . . . (501) 683-5793
  E-mail: kevin.murphy@arkansas.gov
Deputy Director for Administrative Services
  **Chad Brown** . . . . . . . . . . . . . . . . . . . . . . . . . . . . . . . . (501) 837-6930
  E-mail: chad.brown@arkansas.gov
Deputy Director of Communications and Public Affairs
  **Dina Tyler** . . . . . . . . . . . . . . . . . . . . . . . . . . . . . . . . . (501) 682-9510
Deputy Director for Parole/Probation Services
  **Dan Roberts** . . . . . . . . . . . . . . . . . . . . . . . . . . . . . . . . (501) 682-9588
Deputy Director for Residential Services **(Vacant)** . . . . . . . (501) 682-9577
Internal Affairs Administrator **Dicky Johnson** . . . . . . . . . . (501) 837-3060

*(continued on next page)*

---

★ Elected Official   ■ Appointed by Governor   ● Appointed by Legislature   ▲ Appointed by Board or Commission   ◆ Appointed by State Supreme Court

**Arkansas Department of Community Correction** *continued*

Internal Auditor **Anne Geddings** . . . . . . . . . . . . . . . . . . . (501) 682-9542
Public Relations Manager **Rhonda Sharp** . . . . . . . . . . . . .(501) 682-9593
  E-mail: rhonda.sharp@arkansas.gov
Legal Counsel **Wade Hodge** . . . . . . . . . . . . . . . . . . . . . . . (501) 747-3783

# Arkansas Department of Correction [ADC]

P.O. 8707, Pine Bluff, AR 71611
Tel: (870) 267-6999   Fax: (870) 267-6244
E-mail: adc.webmaster@arkansas.gov

**Employees:** 4,326  **Fiscal Year:** 2014  **Budget:** $391,855,499

▲ Director **Wendy L. Kelley** . . . . . . . . . . . . . . . . . . . . . . . . . (870) 267-6200
  E-mail: wendy.l.kelley@arkansas.gov
  Education: Arkansas 1984 BA; Arkansas (Little Rock) 1987 JD
  Executive Assistant **Jada Lawrence** . . . . . . . . . . . . . . . . .(870) 267-6209
Assistant Director **Jim DePriest** . . . . . . . . . . . . . . . . . . . . (870) 267-6999
Chief Deputy Director of Institutions **Dale Reed** . . . . . . . . (870) 267-6300
Deputy Director, Health and Correctional Programs
  **Rory Griffin** . . . . . . . . . . . . . . . . . . . . . . . . . . . . . . . . (870) 267-6361
Deputy Director, Operations **Dexter Payne** . . . . . . . . . . . . (870) 267-6302
Assistant Director, Administrative Services
  **Mike Carraway** . . . . . . . . . . . . . . . . . . . . . . . . . . . . . (870) 850-8719
  E-mail: mike.carraway@arkansas.gov
Assistant Director, Construction and Maintenance
  **Gail Mainard** . . . . . . . . . . . . . . . . . . . . . . . . . . . . . . . (870) 267-6625
Chaplaincy Services Administrator **Joshua Mayfield** . . . . . (870) 267-6236
  E-mail: joshua.mayfield@arkansas.gov
Classification Administrator **Shelli Hamilton** . . . . . . . . . . .(870) 267-6482
  E-mail: shelly.hamilton@ark.org
Warehouse Administrator **Kay Skillen** . . . . . . . . . . . . . . . . (870) 267-6600
  E-mail: kay.skillen@arkansas.gov
Farm Administrator **David Farabough** . . . . . . . . . . . . . . . (870) 850-8454
Human Resources Administrator
  **Stacia Wood-Lenderman** . . . . . . . . . . . . . . . . . . . . . .(870) 850-8524
  E-mail: stacia.wood-lenderman@arkansas.gov
Information Systems Administrator **Rhonda Patterson** . . . .(870) 850-8521
  E-mail: rhonda.westerman@arkansas.gov
Industry Administrator **Robert Carter** . . . . . . . . . . . . . . . .(870) 850-8430
  E-mail: robert.carter@arkansas.gov
Internal Affairs and Disciplinary Hearing Administrator
  **Raymond Naylor** . . . . . . . . . . . . . . . . . . . . . . . . . . . . (870) 267-6218
  E-mail: raymond.naylor@arkansas.gov
Medical Services Administrator **George Wilson** . . . . . . . . . (870) 267-6331
Mental Health Services Administrator **Bob Parker** . . . . . . .(870) 267-6325
Research and Planning Administrator **Tiffanye Compton** . . (870) 267-6310
Training Academy Administrator **Fred Campbell** . . . . . . . (501) 467-3507
  E-mail: fred.campbell@arkansas.gov
Assistant Chief Financial Officer **Keith Leathers** . . . . . . . .(870) 850-8498
Accounting Operations Manager **Rick Norton** . . . . . . . . . . (870) 850-8577
Budget Manager **Sonja Wallace** . . . . . . . . . . . . . . . . . . . . (870) 267-6287
Procurement Manager **Teresa Funderburg** . . . . . . . . . . . . (870) 850-8500
Chief Legal Counsel **Jim DePriest** . . . . . . . . . . . . . . . . . . (870) 267-6371
  E-mail: jim.depriest@arkansas.gov
Constituency Officer **(Vacant)** . . . . . . . . . . . . . . . . . . . . . . (870) 267-6999
Equal Employment Opportunity and Grievance Officer
  **Donna Stout** . . . . . . . . . . . . . . . . . . . . . . . . . . . . . . . (870) 267-6370
Communications Administrator **Cathy Frye** . . . . . . . . . . . . (870) 267-6205
  E-mail: cathy.frye@arkansas.gov
  Education: North Texas State 1993 ABJ

# State Board of Education

Arch Ford Education Building, Four Capitol Mall, Room 305A,
Little Rock, AR 72201-1071
Tel: (501) 683-0205   Fax: (501) 682-1079

■ Chair **Toyce Newton** . . . . . . . . . . . . . . . . . . . . . . . . . . . (501) 683-0205
  Term Expires: June 30, 2016
  P.O. Box 274, Crossett, AR 71635
  E-mail: tnewton@phoenixyouth.com
■ Vice-Chair **Mireya Reith** . . . . . . . . . . . . . . . . . . . . . . . . (501) 683-0205
  Term Expires: June 30, 2018
  1819 North Hunters Ridge, Fayetteville, AR 72701
  E-mail: mireya.reith@gmail.com

■ Member **Dr. Jay Barth** . . . . . . . . . . . . . . . . . . . . . . . . . . (501) 683-0205
  Term Expires: June 30, 2019
  E-mail: jay@jaybarth.org
■ Member **Joe Black** . . . . . . . . . . . . . . . . . . . . . . . . . . . . .(501) 683-0205
  Term Expires: June 30, 2018
  4141 Jackson 21, Newport, AR 72112
  E-mail: jblack07@earthlink.net
■ Member **M. Susan Chambers** . . . . . . . . . . . . . . . . . . . . .(501) 683-0205
  Term Expires: June 30, 2021
  E-mail: susan.chambers@walmart.com
  Education: William Jewell BS
■ Member **Charisse Dean** . . . . . . . . . . . . . . . . . . . . . . . . . (501) 683-0205
  Term Expires: June 30, 2022
  E-mail: charissedean18@gmail.com
■ Member **Vicki Saviers** . . . . . . . . . . . . . . . . . . . . . . . . . . (501) 683-0205
  Term Expires: June 30, 2016
  Eight Edgehill Road, Little Rock, AR 72207
  E-mail: vsaviers@gmail.com
■ Member **R. Brett Williamson** . . . . . . . . . . . . . . . . . . . . . (501) 683-0205
  Term Expires: June 30, 2022
  E-mail: brett.williamson@murphyoffices.com
  Education: Ouachita Baptist BABA
■ Member **Diane Zook** . . . . . . . . . . . . . . . . . . . . . . . . . . . (501) 683-0205
  Term Expires: June 30, 2020
  E-mail: ddzook@aol.com

# Arkansas Department of Education [ADE]

Arch Ford Education Building, Four Capitol Mall,
Little Rock, AR 72201-1071
Tel: (501) 682-4475

**Employees:** 360  **Fiscal Year:** 2016  **Budget:** $3,906,108,690

▲ Commissioner **Johnny Key** . . . . . . . . . . . . . . . . . . . . . . . (501) 682-4203
  E-mail: johnny.key@arkansas.gov
  Education: Arkansas 1991 BS
Deputy Commissioner **Dr. T. Mark Gotcher** . . . . . . . . . . . (501) 682-4205
Chief of Staff **Deborah Coffman** . . . . . . . . . . . . . . . . . . . (501) 683-0205
Academic Accountability Assistant Commissioner
  **Annette M. Barnes** . . . . . . . . . . . . . . . . . . . . . . . . . . .(501) 682-1298
Fiscal and Administrative Services Assistant
  Commissioner **Greg Rogers** . . . . . . . . . . . . . . . . . . . . . (501) 682-4476
  E-mail: greg.rogers@arkansas.gov
Educator Effectiveness and Licensure Assistant
  Commissioner **Ivy Pfeffer** . . . . . . . . . . . . . . . . . . . . . . (501) 682-4210
  Education: Arkansas State BS; Walden MS
Learning Services Assistant Commissioner **Stacy Smith** . . (501) 682-1991
  Education: Arkansas (Little Rock) BSElEd
Research and Technology Assistant Commissioner
  **Dr. Eric Saunders** . . . . . . . . . . . . . . . . . . . . . . . . . . . .(501) 371-5005
  E-mail: eric.saunders@arkansas.gov
  Education: Oklahoma State BS; Harding DEd
General Counsel **Kendra Clay** . . . . . . . . . . . . . . . . . . . . . (501) 682-4227
  E-mail: kendra.clay@arkansas.gov
Legislative Services Director **Michelle Griffin** . . . . . . . . . . . (501) 682-4251
  E-mail: michelle.griffin@arkansas.gov
  Education: Arkansas (Little Rock); Webster
Communications Director **Kimberly Friedman** . . . . . . . . . . (501) 683-4788
  E-mail: kimberly.friedman@arkansas.gov
Communications Manager **Gayle Morris** . . . . . . . . . . . . . .(501) 682-4217
  E-mail: gayle.morris@arkansas.gov
Special Education Director **Lisa Haley** . . . . . . . . . . . . . . . .(501) 682-4221

# Arkansas Economic Development Commission [AEDC]

900 West Capitol Avenue, Suite 400, Little Rock, AR 72201
Tel: (501) 682-1121   Fax: (501) 682-7499

**Employees:** 91  **Fiscal Year:** 2014  **Budget:** $322,191,139

■ Executive Director **Mike Preston** . . . . . . . . . . . . . . . . . . . (501) 682-7351
  E-mail: mpreston@arkansasedc.com
  Education: Florida 2005

---

★ Elected Official   ■ Appointed by Governor   ● Appointed by Legislature   ▲ Appointed by Board or Commission   ◆ Appointed by State Supreme Court

## Arkansas Game and Fish Commission [AGFC]

Two Natural Resources Drive, Little Rock, AR 72205
Tel: (501) 223-6300  Fax: (501) 223-6465  Internet: www.agfc.com

**Fiscal Year:** 2014  **Budget:** $88,123,246

▲Director **Mike Knoedl** ...........................(501) 223-6305
  Note: Mike Knoedl announced his retirement from the Arkansas Game
  and Fish Commission effective July 1, 2016.
  E-mail: mike.knoedl@agfc.ar.gov
▲Director **Jeff Crow** ...............................(501) 223-6300
  Note: Effective July 1, 2016.
  E-mail: jeffrey.crow@agfc.ar.gov

## Arkansas Workers' Compensation Commission [AWCC]

324 South Spring Street, Little Rock, AR 72203
P.O. Box 950, Little Rock, AR 72203-0950
Tel: (501) 682-3930  TTY: (800) 285-1131  Internet: www.awcc.state.ar.us

■Chairman **Scotty Dale Douthit** ......................(501) 683-3412
  Term Expires: December 5, 2020
  E-mail: ddouthit@awcc.state.ar.us
■Commissioner **Philip Alan Hood** .....................(501) 324-9560
  Term Expires: December 5, 2018
  E-mail: phood@awcc.state.ar.us
  Education: Grambling State BS
■Commissioner **Karen H. McKinney** ...................(501) 324-9560
  Term Expires: December 5, 2016
  E-mail: kmckinney@awcc.state.ar.us
  Education: Henderson State 1989; Arkansas 1992 JD
■Chief Executive Officer **Barbara Webb** ..............(501) 682-3930
  E-mail: bwebb@awcc.state.ar.us

## Arkansas State Police [ASP]

One State Police Plaza Drive, Little Rock, AR 72209
Tel: (501) 618-8000  Fax: (501) 618-8222  Internet: www.asp.arkansas.gov
E-mail: info@asp.arkansas.gov

**Fiscal Year:** 2014  **Budget:** $142,795,198

■Director **William "Bill" Bryant** ....................(501) 618-8299
  E-mail: bill.bryant@asp.arkansas.gov
  Executive Secretary **Donna Humphries** ..............(501) 618-8299
  Legal Counsel **Gregory C. Downs** ...................(501) 618-8350
  Education: Arkansas (Little Rock) 2005 JD

## Office of the Lieutenant Governor

State Capitol, 500 Woodlane Street, Suite 270, Little Rock, AR 72201
Tel: (501) 682-2144  Fax: (501) 682-2894  E-mail: lg.staff@arkansas.gov
Internet: www.ltgovernor.arkansas.gov

**Fiscal Year:** 2014  **Budget:** $398,405

★Lieutenant Governor
  **LTC J. Timothy "Tim" Griffin, USAR** (R) ...........(501) 682-2144
  Term Expires: January 2019
  E-mail: tim.griffin@ark.org
  Education: Hendrix 1990 BA; Tulane 1994 JD
  Career: Special Assistant to the President and Deputy Director, Office
  of Political Affairs, Executive Office of the President (2005); Acting
  U.S. Attorney, Arkansas - Eastern District, Executive Office for United
  States Attorneys, United States Department of Justice (2007); U.S.
  Representative (R-AR, District 2), Office of Representative Tim Griffin,
  United States House of Representatives (2011-2015)
Chief of Staff and Legal Counsel **Scott Burton** ..........(501) 682-2144
Deputy Legal Counsel and Communications Director
  **Katie Grygar** ....................................(501) 682-2144
  E-mail: katie.grygar@arkansas.gov
  Education: Northwestern; Washington U (MO) JD
Senior Advisor **Kelsi Daniell** ........................(501) 682-2144
  Education: Ouachita Baptist

## Office of the Secretary of State

State Capitol, Room 256, Little Rock, AR 72201
Tel: (501) 682-1010  TTY: (501) 682-3420  Fax: (501) 682-3510
E-mail: general_info@sos.arkansas.gov

**Fiscal Year:** 2014  **Budget:** $27,314,843

★Secretary of State **Mark Martin** (R) ................(501) 682-3013
  Term Expires: January 2019
  Education: Arkansas 1998 BSME
  Career: State Representative (R-AR, District 87), Arkansas House of
  Representatives (2005-2011)
  Executive Administrative Assistant **Lyndajo Jones** ......(501) 682-3013
Chief Deputy Secretary of State **Kelly Boyd** ............(501) 682-3013
Deputy Secretary of State **Joseph Wood** ...............(501) 682-3013
  E-mail: joseph.wood@sos.arkansas.gov
Legal Services Deputy Secretary of State **A. J. Kelly** ......(501) 682-6787
State Capitol Police Chief **Darrell Hedden** .............(501) 682-5173
Strategic Initiatives Director **(Vacant)** ...................(501) 682-1010

## Office of the Attorney General

323 Center Street, Suite 200, Little Rock, AR 72201
Tel: (501) 682-2007  Tel: (800) 448-3014 (Crime Victim's Hotline)
TTY: (501) 682-6073  Fax: (501) 682-8084  E-mail: oag@arkansasag.gov

**Employees:** 167  **Fiscal Year:** 2014  **Budget:** $22,191,419,000

★Attorney General **Leslie Rutledge** (R) ...............(501) 682-2007
  Term Expires: January 2019
  Education: Arkansas (Little Rock) 2001 JD
Chief of Staff **Carl Vogelpohl** .......................(501) 682-2007
  Education: Arkansas
Chief Deputy Attorney General **Julie Benafield** ........(501) 682-2007
  Education: Ouachita Baptist 1985 BA; Arkansas (Little Rock) 1989 JD
Deputy Attorney General for Civil Department
  **Ryan W. Owsley** ..................................(501) 682-1681
  Education: Ouachita Baptist; Arkansas (Little Rock) JD
Deputy Attorney General for Criminal Department
  **Darnisa Johnson** .................................(501) 682-8075
Deputy Attorney General for Medicaid Fraud
  **Lloyd Warford** ..................................(501) 682-1320
Deputy Attorney General for Public Protection
  **Sarah Page Tacker** ...............................(501) 682-1321
Deputy Attorney General for State Agencies
  **Meredith Blaise Rebsamen** ........................(501) 682-1316
  Education: Arkansas (Little Rock) JD
Legislative Director **Cory Cox** .......................(501) 682-2007
  E-mail: cory.cox@arkansasag.gov
Solicitor General **Lee Rudofsky** ......................(501) 682-2007
  Education: Cornell 2001 BS, 2002 MPA; Harvard 2005 JD
Communications Director **Judd Deere** .................(501) 317-9880
  E-mail: judd.deere@arkansasag.gov
  Education: Lyon 2010 BA
Network Administrator **Paul Goldner** .................(501) 682-6318
  E-mail: paul.goldner@arkansasag.gov

## Office of the State Treasurer

State Capitol Building, 500 Woodlane Street, Suite 220,
Little Rock, AR 72201
Tel: (501) 682-5888  Fax: (501) 682-3842

**Fiscal Year:** 2013-2014  **Budget:**

★State Treasurer **Dennis Milligan** (R) ..................(501) 682-5888
  Term Expires: January 2019
  Career: Chairman, Arkansas Republican Party (2007-2008)
  Executive Assistant to the Treasurer **Holly Beaver** ......(501) 682-5888
Chief of Staff **Jim Harris** ...........................(501) 682-5888
Deputy Chief of Staff **Jason Brady** ...................(501) 682-5888
  Education: Arkansas State 1994 BS

## Office of the Auditor of State

1401 West Capitol Avenue, Suite 325, Little Rock, AR 72201
Tel: (501) 682-6000  Fax: (501) 682-2521  E-mail: info@auditor.ar.gov

★Auditor of State **Andrea Lea** (R) .....................(501) 682-6030
  Term Expires: January 2019
  Education: Arkansas Tech

*(continued on next page)*

---

★ Elected Official  ■ Appointed by Governor  ● Appointed by Legislature  ▲ Appointed by Board or Commission  ◆ Appointed by State Supreme Court

**Office of the Auditor of State** *continued*

Chief Deputy Auditor **Wesley Smith** . . . . . . . . . . . . . . . .(501) 682-6029
Chief of Staff **(Vacant)** . . . . . . . . . . . . . . . . . . . . . . . . . .(501) 371-2103

# Office of the Commissioner of State Lands [COSL]

State Capitol Building, 500 Woodlane Street, Suite 109,
Little Rock, AR 72201
Tel: (501) 324-9422  Fax: (501) 682-1996  E-mail: land@cosl.org
Internet: www.cosl.org

★Commissioner of State Lands **John M. Thurston** (R) . . . . .(501) 324-9422
  Term Expires: January 2019
  Education: Henderson State (Attended)

# Health Services Permit Agency

5800 West 10th Street, Suite 805, Little Rock, AR 72204
Tel: (501) 661-2509  Fax: (501) 661-2399  Internet: www.arhspa.org

■Director **Tracy L. Steele** . . . . . . . . . . . . . . . . . . . . . . . . . .(501) 661-2509
  E-mail: tracy.steele@arkansas.gov
  Education: Rice BA
Planning Specialist **Roxann Walker** . . . . . . . . . . . . . . . . . .(501) 280-4918
  E-mail: roxann.walker@arkansas.gov
Management Project Analyst **Jennifer Cooper** . . . . . . . . . .(501) 661-2501
  E-mail: jennifer.cooper@arkansas.gov
Operations Manager **Latreasa F. Mullins** . . . . . . . . . . . . . .(501) 661-2197

# Arkansas Development Finance Authority [ADFA]

900 West Capitol Avenue, Suite 310, Little Rock, AR 72201
P.O. Box 8023, Little Rock, AR 72203-8023
Tel: (501) 682-5900  TTY: (501) 682-2877  Fax: (501) 682-5859

■President **Aaron Burkes** . . . . . . . . . . . . . . . . . . . . . . . . . .(501) 682-3339
  E-mail: aaron.burkes@adfa.arkansas.gov
Vice President and General Counsel **Layne Anderson** . . . .(501) 682-5464
Development Finance Vice President **Brad Henry** . . . . . . . .(501) 682-5905
Finance and Administration Vice President
  **Cheryl Schluterman** . . . . . . . . . . . . . . . . . . . . . . . . . . . .(501) 682-5995
  E-mail: cheryl.schluterman@adfa.arkansas.gov
Housing Vice President **Ben Van Kleef** . . . . . . . . . . . . . . . .(501) 682-5927
Internal Audit Vice President **Patrick Patton** . . . . . . . . . . . .(501) 682-5902
Public Finance Officer **Robert "Ro" Arrington** . . . . . . . . . .(501) 682-5910
Public Information Officer **Derrick Rose** . . . . . . . . . . . . . . .(501) 682-5904
  E-mail: derrick.rose@adfa.arkansas.gov

---

★ Elected Official   ■ Appointed by Governor   ● Appointed by Legislature   ▲ Appointed by Board or Commission   ◆ Appointed by State Supreme Court

# California

Tel: (800) 807-6755 (State Information)  Internet: www.ca.gov

**Number of U.S. Congressional Delegates:** 2 Senators; 53 Representatives  **Governor's Term:** 4 years
**Legislature Description:** 40 member Senate; 80 member Assembly; Term - Senate 4 years, Assembly 2 years  **Next Election:** Governor November 2018; Legislature November 2016  **Number of Electoral Votes:** 55  **Official Name:** State of California (name of island in Las Sergas de Esplanadian)
**Nickname:** The Golden State  **Motto:** Eureka (I have found it)

**Population:** 39,144,818 (2015); Rank 1  **Fiscal Year:** 2015-2016  **Budget:** $122,609,000,000

## Office of the Governor

State Capitol, Suite 1173, Sacramento, CA 95814
Tel: (916) 445-2841  Fax: (916) 558-3160

**Fiscal Year:** 2015-2016  **Budget:** $13,452,000

### Edmund Gerald "Jerry" Brown, Jr.
Governor

Began Service: January 3, 2011
Term Expires: January 2019
Date of Birth: April 7, 1938
Education: UC Berkeley 1961 BA; Yale 1964 LLB
Home: Oakland
Religion: Roman Catholic
Career: Secretary of State, State of California (1970-1974); Governor (D-CA), State of California (1974-1982); Counsel, Reavis and McGrath (1983-1989); Chairman, California Democratic Party (1989-1991); Radio Program Host (1994-1997); Mayor, Office of the Mayor, City of Oakland, California (1999-2007); Attorney General (D-CA), Office of Attorney General Jerry Brown, Justice Department, State of California (2007-2011)

★Governor **Edmund Gerald "Jerry" Brown, Jr.** (D) . . . . . . (916) 445-2841
Director **Ned Ruthrauff** . . . . . . . . . . . . . . . . . . . . . . . . . . (916) 445-2841
  E-mail: ned.ruthrauff@gov.ca.gov
  Executive Secretary **Nancy E. McFadden** . . . . . . . . . . . . (916) 445-2841
    E-mail: nancy.mcfadden@gov.ca.gov
    Education: San José State BA; Virginia JD
Special Counsel **Anne Gust Brown** . . . . . . . . . . . . . . . . . (916) 445-2841
  E-mail: anne.brown@gov.ca.gov
  Education: Stanford 1980 BA; Michigan 1983 JD
Immigrant Integration Director **Daniel Torres** . . . . . . . . . . (916) 445-2841
  Education: UC Davis JD
Constituent Affairs Director **Adrian Mata** . . . . . . . . . . . . (916) 445-2841
  E-mail: adrian.mata@gov.ca.gov
Operations Director **Julie Lee** . . . . . . . . . . . . . . . . . . . . (916) 445-1682
  E-mail: julie.lee@gov.ca.gov
Scheduling Director **Kathy Baldree** . . . . . . . . . . . . . . . . . (916) 324-7745
  E-mail: kathy.baldree@gov.ca.gov
Chief Fiscal Officer **Sandra Sharrer** . . . . . . . . . . . . . . . . (916) 322-0242
  E-mail: sandra.sharrer@gov.ca.gov
Chief Personnel Officer **Esther Jimenez** . . . . . . . . . . . . . (916) 445-1697
  E-mail: esther.jimenez@gov.ca.gov
Business Services Officer **(Vacant)** . . . . . . . . . . . . . . . . . (916) 445-0446
Appointments Secretary **Mona Pasquil** . . . . . . . . . . . . . . (916) 445-4541
  E-mail: mona.pasquil@gov.ca.gov
Chief Deputy Appointments Secretary **Bob Franzoia** . . . . . (916) 445-4541
  E-mail: bob.franzoia@gov.ca.gov
  Education: Cal State (Chico)
Deputy Appointments Secretary **Veronica Ortiz-Torres** . . . . (916) 445-4541
  E-mail: veronica.ortiz-torres@gov.ca.gov
Information Technology Unit Manager **Becky Curler** . . . . . . (916) 324-0404
  E-mail: becky.curler@gov.ca.gov
Cabinet Secretary **Keely Bosler** . . . . . . . . . . . . . . . . . . . (916) 324-2472
  E-mail: keely.bosler@gov.ca.gov
  Education: Cornell MS

Deputy Cabinet Secretary **Wade Crowfoot** . . . . . . . . . . . . (916) 445-6533
  E-mail: wade.crowfoot@gov.ca.gov
Energy and Environment Senior Advisor
  **Cliff Rechtschaffen, JD** . . . . . . . . . . . . . . . . . . . . . . . (916) 445-2841
    E-mail: cliff.rechtschaffen@gov.ca.gov
    Education: Princeton AB; Yale JD
Jobs and Business Senior Advisor **Michael E. Rossi** . . . . . . (916) 445-2841
Policy and Judicial Appointments Senior Advisor
  **Joshua Groban** . . . . . . . . . . . . . . . . . . . . . . . . . . . . . (916) 445-2841
    E-mail: joshua.groban@gov.ca.gov
Policy Senior Advisor **Lark Park** . . . . . . . . . . . . . . . . . . . (916) 445-2841
  E-mail: lark.park@gov.ca.gov
  Education: UC Berkeley BA
Special Advisor **Nettie Sabelhaus** . . . . . . . . . . . . . . . . . . (916) 445-2841
  E-mail: nettie.sabelhaus@gov.ca.gov
Tribal Negotiations Senior Advisor **Joginder Dhillon** . . . . . (916) 445-2841
  Education: Houston ML; Harvard JD
Tribal Advisor **Cynthia Gomez** . . . . . . . . . . . . . . . . . . . . (916) 653-4082
  E-mail: cynthia.gomez@gov.ca.gov
Education Policy Advisor **Karen Stapf Walters** . . . . . . . . . (916) 445-2841
  E-mail: kwalters@cde.ca.gov
External Affairs Director **Jamie Callahan** . . . . . . . . . . . . (916) 324-2472
  E-mail: jamie.callahan@gov.ca.gov
  Education: George Mason MPP
Press Secretary **Evan Westrup** . . . . . . . . . . . . . . . . . . . . (916) 445-4571
  E-mail: evan.westrup@gov.ca.gov
  Education: Edinburgh (Scotland) MA
  Deputy Press Secretary **Deborah Hoffman** . . . . . . . . . . . (916) 445-4571
    E-mail: deborah.hoffman@gov.ca.gov
  Deputy Press Secretary **Gareth Lacy** . . . . . . . . . . . . . . . (916) 445-4571
    E-mail: gareth.lacy@gov.ca.gov

## Washington Office

444 North Capitol Street, NW, Suite 134, Washington, DC 20014
Fax: (202) 624-5280

■Director **Katie Wheeler Mathews** . . . . . . . . . . . . . . . . . (202) 624-5270
  E-mail: katie.wheelermathews@wdc.ca.gov

## Legal Affairs Office

Tel: (916) 445-0873  Fax: (916) 558-3160

Chief Deputy Legal Affairs Secretary **Peter Southworth** . . (916) 445-0873
  Education: Columbia JD
Deputy Legal Affairs Secretary **Daniel J. Calabretta** . . . . . (916) 445-0873
  Education: Chicago JD
Deputy Legal Affairs Secretary **Gabriel Sanchez** . . . . . . . . (916) 445-0873

## Legislative Affairs Office

Tel: (916) 445-4341  Fax: (916) 558-3177

Legislative Affairs Secretary **Camille Wagner** . . . . . . . . . . (916) 445-4341
  E-mail: camille.wagner@gov.ca.gov
Chief Deputy Legislative Secretary **Tom Dyer** . . . . . . . . . . (916) 445-4341
  E-mail: tom.dyer@dof.ca.gov
Deputy Legislative Secretary **Donna Campbell** . . . . . . . . . (916) 445-4341
  E-mail: donna.campbell@gov.ca.gov
Deputy Legislative Secretary **Michael R. O. Martinez** . . . . (916) 445-4341
  E-mail: michael.martinez@gov.ca.gov
  Education: Stanford AB

---

★ Elected Official    ■ Appointed by Governor    ● Appointed by Legislature    ▲ Appointed by Board or Commission    ◆ Appointed by State Supreme Court

EXECUTIVE BRANCH

## Office of Business and Economic Development [GOBIZ]

1325 J Street, Suite 1800, Sacramento, CA 95822
Tel: (916) 322-0694

Director **Panorea Avdis** .............................. (916) 322-0694
Chief Deputy Director **Will Koch** ..................... (916) 322-0694
Business Investment Services Deputy Director
  **Leslie McBride** ................................. (916) 322-0694
California Competes Tax Credit Program Deputy Director
  **Kristen Kane** .................................. (916) 322-0694
  Education: San Diego JD
Communications Deputy Director **Brook Taylor** ......... (916) 322-0667
  E-mail: brook.taylor@gov.ca.gov
External Affairs Deputy Director **(Vacant)** ........... (916) 322-0694
Innovation and Entrepreneurship Deputy Director
  **Louis Stewart** ................................. (916) 322-0694
International Affairs and Business Development Deputy
  Director **Brian Peck** ........................... (916) 322-0694
  Education: San Diego JD
■Legal Affairs Deputy Director
  **Grace Arupo Rodriguez, JD** ..................... (916) 322-0694
  E-mail: grace.arupo-rodriguez@gov.ca.gov
  Education: UCLA BA; UC Davis JD
Legislative and Inter-Governmental Affairs Deputy
  Director **Andrew Sturmself** ..................... (916) 322-0694
Zero Emission Vehicle Infrastructure Deputy Director
  **Tyson Eckerle** ................................. (916) 322-0694
  Education: UC Santa Barbara 2009 MS
Small Business Deputy Director **Jesse Torres** ......... (916) 322-0694
Senior Permit Assistance Specialist **Frank Ramirez** ... (916) 322-0694
Senior Business Development Specialist
  **Gilbert Gonzales** .............................. (916) 322-0694

## Office of Planning and Research [OPR]

1400 10th Street, Suite 100, Sacramento, CA 95814
Tel: (916) 322-2318  Fax: (916) 324-9936  Internet: opr.ca.gov

Director **Ken Alex** .................................. (916) 322-2318
  E-mail: ken.alex@gov.ca.gov
Chief Deputy Director **Louise Bedsworth** ............. (916) 322-2318
State Clearinghouse Director **Scott Morgan** .......... (916) 445-0613
                                              Fax: (916) 323-3018

## Business, Consumer Services and Housing Agency

915 Capitol Mall, Suite 350-A, Sacramento, CA 95814
Tel: (916) 653-4090  E-mail: info@bcsh.ca.gov  Internet: www.bcsh.ca.gov

■Secretary (Acting) **Alexis Podesta** ................. (916) 653-4090
  E-mail: alexis.podesta@bcsh.ca.gov
  ■Assistant to the Secretary **Gladys Lopez** ........ (916) 653-4090
    E-mail: gladys.lopez@bcsh.ca.gov
■Undersecretary **(Vacant)** .......................... (916) 653-4090
  ■Assistant to the Undersecretary **Patricia "Patti" Ochoa** .. (916) 653-4090
    E-mail: patricia.ochoa@bcsh.ca.gov
■Deputy Secretary of Business and Consumer Relations
  **Sonya Logman** .................................. (916) 653-4090
  E-mail: sonya.logman@bcsh.ca.gov
■Deputy Secretary of Communications **(Vacant)** ....... (916) 653-4090
■Deputy Secretary of Fiscal Policy and Administration
  **Tina Daley** .................................... (916) 653-4090
  E-mail: tina.daley@bcsh.ca.gov
■Deputy Secretary and General Counsel
  **Peter M. Williams** ............................. (916) 653-4090
  E-mail: peter.williams@bcsh.ca.gov
■Deputy Secretary, Housing Policy **(Vacant)** ......... (916) 653-4090
■Deputy Secretary of Legislation **Reginald "Reggie" Fair** .. (916) 653-4090
  E-mail: reginald.fair@bcsh.ca.gov
  Education: UC Santa Barbara MA
Administrative Operations Manager **Anna Pozdyn** ....... (916) 653-4090
  E-mail: anna.pozdyn@bcsh.ca.gov
Chief Information Officer **Andrew Armani** ............. (916) 653-4090
  E-mail: andrew.armani@bcsh.ca.gov
  Education: Cal State (Chico) BS

Planning and Policy Special Assistant
  **Nkiruka Catherine Ohaegbu, MBA** ................ (916) 653-4090
  Education: Cal State (Sacramento) 2014 MBA

## Department of Alcoholic Beverage Control [ABC]

3927 Lennane Drive, Suite 100, Sacramento, CA 95834
Tel: (916) 419-2500  Fax: (916) 419-2599  Internet: www.abc.ca.gov

**Employees: 449  Fiscal Year: 2015-2016  Budget: $60,670,000**
■Director (Acting) **Mona Prieto** ..................... (916) 419-2510
  E-mail: mona.prieto@abc.ca.gov
  Administrative Assistant **Jennifer Smiley** ....... (916) 419-2510
■Chief Deputy Director **(Vacant)** .................... (916) 419-2510
Administration Division Chief **Randall Deems** ........ (916) 419-2510
General Counsel **Matthew Botting** .................... (916) 928-9806
  Education: Otago (NZ) 1990 BL
Legislative Officer **Adriana Ruelas** ................. (916) 928-6821
  E-mail: adriana.ruelas@abc.ca.gov
Media Contact **John Carr** ............................ (916) 419-2525
  Education: San Diego State 1979 BA

## Alcoholic Beverage Control Appeals Board

300 Capitol Mall, Suite 1245, Sacramento, CA 95814
Tel: (916) 445-4005  Fax: (916) 323-2760
E-mail: abcboard@abcappeals.ca.gov

■Chairman **Baxter Rice** .............................. (916) 445-4005
■Member **Fred Hiestand** .............................. (916) 445-4005
■Member **Peter Roddy** ................................ (916) 445-4005
Chief Counsel/Executive Officer **Esteban Almanza** ..... (916) 445-4005
Attorney I **Sarah M. Smith** .......................... (916) 445-4005
Attorney III **Linda A. Mathes** ....................... (916) 445-4005
Legal Secretary **Liliana Chavez** ..................... (916) 445-4005
Legal Secretary **Kristi Jones** ....................... (916) 445-4005

## Department of Business Oversight

1515 K Street, Suite 200, Sacramento, CA 95814
1810 13th Street, Sacramento, CA 95811
Tel: (916) 445-7205  Fax: (916) 445-2123  Internet: www.dbo.ca.gov

■Commissioner **Jan Lynn Owen** ........................ (916) 324-9011
  E-mail: janlynn.owen@dbo.ca.gov
  Education: Cal State (Fresno) 1987 BEc
  Policy and Planning Deputy Commissioner
    **Tom Dresslar** ................................ (916) 322-5967
■Chief Deputy Commissioner **(Vacant)** ................ (916) 322-5967
Administration Deputy Commissioner **Jennifer Chavez** ... (916) 322-5969
  E-mail: jennifer.chavez@dbo.ca.gov
Legislation Deputy Commissioner **Indira McDonald** ...... (916) 445-7205
  E-mail: indira.mcdonald@dbo.ca.gov
Los Angeles Region Deputy Commissioner **John Ross** .... (213) 897-8952
  300 South Spring Street, Suite 15513, Los Angeles, CA 90013
  E-mail: john.ross@dbo.ca.gov
Northern Area Region Deputy Commissioner **(Vacant)** .... (415) 263-8507
  45 Fremont Street, Suite 1100, San Francisco, CA 94105
General Counsel **Scott Wyckoff, JD** .................. (916) 327-0309
  E-mail: scott.wyckoff@dbo.ca.gov
Assistant General Counsel **Bret Ladine** .............. (916) 322-5858
  E-mail: bret.ladine@dbo.ca.gov
  Education: Yale 2003 BA
Assistant General Counsel **Stephen Lau** .............. (916) 322-7910
  E-mail: stephen.lau@dbo.ca.gov
  Education: UC Berkeley 1997 BA; UC Davis 2002 JD
Communications Director **Mark Leyes** ................. (916) 322-7180
  E-mail: mark.leyes@dbo.ca.gov
  Education: Cal State (Fullerton) BA, MA

## Department of Consumer Affairs [DCA]

1625 North Market Boulevard, Sacramento, CA 95834
Tel: (916) 574-8200  Tel: (800) 952-5210  TTY: (916) 322-1700
Fax: (916) 574-8613  E-mail: dca@dca.ca.gov  Internet: www.dca.ca.gov

■Director **Awet Kidane** .............................. (916) 574-8200
  E-mail: awet.kidane@dca.ca.gov

---

★ Elected Official   ■ Appointed by Governor   ● Appointed by Legislature   ▲ Appointed by Board or Commission   ◆ Appointed by State Supreme Court

■Chief Deputy Director **(Vacant)** . . . . . . . . . . . . . . . . . . . . . (916) 574-8200

■Board and Bureau Relations Deputy Director
  **Christine J. Lally** . . . . . . . . . . . . . . . . . . . . . . . . . . (916) 574-8200
  E-mail: christine.lally@dca.ca.gov
  Education: Cal State (Sacramento) BA
Communications Deputy Director **Veronica Harms** . . . . . . (916) 574-8171
Legal Affairs Deputy Director **Doreathea Johnson** . . . . . . (916) 574-8220
■Legislative and Policy Review Deputy Director
  **Tracy Montez** . . . . . . . . . . . . . . . . . . . . . . . . . . . . . . (916) 574-7800
  E-mail: tracy.montez@dca.ca.gov
■Legislative and Regulatory Review Deputy Director
  **(Vacant)** . . . . . . . . . . . . . . . . . . . . . . . . . . . . . . . . . . (916) 574-7800
■Legislative and Regulatory Review Assistant Deputy
  Director **Adam Quinonez** . . . . . . . . . . . . . . . . . . . . . (916) 574-7800
Chief Information Officer **Jason Piccione** . . . . . . . . . . . . (916) 574-8004
  E-mail: jason.piccione@dca.ca.gov
Assistant Chief Counsel **(Vacant)** . . . . . . . . . . . . . . . . . . (916) 574-8220

## Department of Fair Employment and Housing [DFEH]

2218 Kausen Drive, Suite 100, Elk Grove, CA 95758
Tel: (916) 478-7251  Fax: (888) 382-5293  Internet: www.dfeh.ca.gov

**Employees:** 190

■Director **Kevin Kish** . . . . . . . . . . . . . . . . . . . . . . . . . . . (916) 478-7251
  E-mail: kevin.kish@dfeh.ca.gov
Chief Deputy Director **Joan Keegan** . . . . . . . . . . . . . . . . (916) 478-7251
Administration Deputy Director **DeLesa Swanigan** . . . . . (916) 478-7251
  E-mail: delesa.swanigan@dfeh.ca.gov
Communications Deputy Director **Fahizah Alim** . . . . . . . . (916) 478-7251
  E-mail: fahizah.alim@dfeh.ca.gov
Chief Counsel **Jon Ichinaga** . . . . . . . . . . . . . . . . . . . . . (916) 478-7251
Chief of Dispute Resolution **Annmarie Billotti** . . . . . . . . (916) 478-7151
  E-mail: annmarie.billotti@dfeh.ca.gov
Chief of Enforcement **Mary Bonilla** . . . . . . . . . . . . . . . . (916) 478-7251
Chief of Public Policy and Education **Nelson Chan** . . . . . . (916) 478-7251
Chief Information Officer **PJ Bajwa** . . . . . . . . . . . . . . . . (916) 478-7251

## Department of Housing and Community Development

P.O. Box 952051, Sacramento, CA 94252-2051
2020 W. El Camino Avenue, Sacramento, CA 95833
Fax: (916) 263-7417  Internet: www.hcd.ca.gov

**Employees:** 570  **Fiscal Year:** 2015-2016  **Budget:** $355,370,000

■Director **Benjamin T. Metcalf** . . . . . . . . . . . . . . . . . . . (916) 263-7400
Chief Deputy Director **John Hiber** . . . . . . . . . . . . . . . . . (916) 263-7400
General Counsel/Deputy Director **Tad Egawa** . . . . . . . . . . (916) 263-2769
  E-mail: tad.egawa@hcd.ca.gov
Deputy General Counsel **Anthony Pane** . . . . . . . . . . . . . . (916) 653-4090
Legislation Director **Diane Richardson** . . . . . . . . . . . . . . (916) 263-3206
Audit and Evaluation Deputy Director **Marc A. Wilson** . . . (916) 263-3396
Codes and Standards Deputy Director **Richard Weinert** . . . (916) 445-9471
  E-mail: rweinert@hcd.ca.gov            Tel: (916) 323-9224
                                              (Mobilehome
                                           Registration and
                                            Titling Program)

Communications Office Deputy Director
  **Evan Gerberding** . . . . . . . . . . . . . . . . . . . . . . . . . . . (916) 263-7400
■Financial Assistance Division Deputy Director
  **Laura Whittall-Scherfee** . . . . . . . . . . . . . . . . . . . . . (916) 263-2771
  E-mail: lscherfee@hcd.ca.gov
External Affairs Assistant Director **Karen Naungayan** . . . . (916) 653-4090
Homeless and Housing Policy Assistant Director
  **Cindy Cavanaugh** . . . . . . . . . . . . . . . . . . . . . . . . . . (916) 263-7400
Housing Policy Development Deputy Director **Lisa Bates** . . (916) 263-2911
  E-mail: lbates@hcd.ca.gov
Tribal Liaison External Affairs Deputy Director
  **Evan Gerberding** . . . . . . . . . . . . . . . . . . . . . . . . . . . (916) 263-7400
Intergovernmental Affairs Assistant Director
  **Linda Wheaton** . . . . . . . . . . . . . . . . . . . . . . . . . . . . (916) 263-7400
Housing Standards Assistant Chief **Shawn Huff** . . . . . . . . (916) 445-9471
  E-mail: shuff@hcd.ca.gov
Information Technology Branch Chief **David Chase** . . . . . . (916) 263-6575
  E-mail: dchase@hcd.ca.gov

Webmaster **Richard Withers** . . . . . . . . . . . . . . . . . . . . . (916) 263-6237

## California Environmental Protection Agency [CalEPA]

Office of the Secretary, 1001 I Street, 25th Floor,
Sacramento, CA 95812-4015
Tel: (916) 323-2514  Fax: (916) 324-0908
E-mail: cepacomm@calepa.ca.gov  Internet: www.calepa.ca.gov

**Employees:** 5,008  **Fiscal Year:** 2015-2016  **Budget:** $4,285,033,000

■Secretary **Matthew "Matt" Rodriquez** . . . . . . . . . . . . . . (916) 324-9214
  E-mail: matthew.rodriquez@calepa.ca.gov
  Education: UC Berkeley BA; Hastings 1980 JD
■Administrative Assistant **Chona V. Sarte** . . . . . . . . . . . . (916) 324-9214
  E-mail: chona.sarte@calepa.ca.gov
■Undersecretary **Gordon Burns** . . . . . . . . . . . . . . . . . . . (916) 324-3708
  E-mail: gordon.burns@calepa.ca.gov
■Border and Intergovernmental Affairs Deputy Secretary
  **Aimee Barnes** . . . . . . . . . . . . . . . . . . . . . . . . . . . . . (916) 324-7316
  E-mail: aimee.barnes@calepa.ca.gov
  Education: Dartmouth 2004 BA; Columbia 2007 MPA
■Business Operations Chief **Eric Jarvis** . . . . . . . . . . . . . . (916) 341-2658
Climate Policy Change Deputy Secretary
  **Ashley Conrad-Saydah** . . . . . . . . . . . . . . . . . . . . . . . (916) 322-2628
  Education: Princeton 1999 BS; UC Santa Barbara MEn
■Communications and External Affairs Deputy Secretary
  **Alex Barnum** . . . . . . . . . . . . . . . . . . . . . . . . . . . . . . (916) 324-9670
  E-mail: alex.barnum@calepa.ca.gov
  Education: Columbia 1987 MSJ; Antioch U 1983 BA
■Environmental Policy Deputy Secretary **Grant Cope** . . . . (916) 324-3708
Legislative Affairs Deputy Secretary
  **Catalina Hayes-Bautista** . . . . . . . . . . . . . . . . . . . . . . (916) 323-2514
Science and Health Deputy Secretary **Gina Solomon** . . . . (916) 324-8735
Education and Quality Programs Assistant Secretary
  **(Vacant)** . . . . . . . . . . . . . . . . . . . . . . . . . . . . . . . . . . (916) 322-7179
Environmental Justice Assistant Secretary
  **Arsenio Mataka** . . . . . . . . . . . . . . . . . . . . . . . . . . . . (916) 323-2559
Fiscal and Administration Assistant Secretary **Eric Jarvis** . . (916) 323-2658
  E-mail: eric.jarvis@calepa.ca.gov
■Law Enforcement Deputy Secretary and Counsel
  **Alice Busching Reynolds** . . . . . . . . . . . . . . . . . . . . . (916) 322-2893
  E-mail: alice.reynolds@calepa.ca.gov
Local Program Coordination and Emergency Response
  Assistant Secretary **Jim Bohon** . . . . . . . . . . . . . . . . . (916) 322-8284
Agency Chief Information Officer **Sergio Gutierrez** . . . . . (916) 322-1620
  E-mail: sgutierrez@calepa.ca.gov
Assistant General Counsel for Enforcement
  **Christie Henke Vosburg** . . . . . . . . . . . . . . . . . . . . . . (916) 322-7310
  Education: UC Davis 2001 BA; Berkeley Law 2009 JD
Assistant General Counsel **Kristin Peer** . . . . . . . . . . . . . . (916) 322-7310

## Department of Pesticide Regulation [DPR]

1001 I Street, P.O. Box 4015, Sacramento, CA 95812-4015
Tel: (916) 445-4300  Fax: (916) 324-1491  Internet: www.cdpr.ca.gov

**Employees:** 390  **Fiscal Year:** 2015-2016  **Budget:** $90,911,000

■Director **Brian Leahy** . . . . . . . . . . . . . . . . . . . . . . . . . (916) 445-4000
  E-mail: brian.leahy@cdpr.ca.gov
■Chief Deputy Director **Christopher Reardon** . . . . . . . . . . (916) 445-4000
  E-mail: christopher.reardon@cdpr.ca.gov
■Deputy Director for Legislation and Policy
  **Jesse Cuevas** . . . . . . . . . . . . . . . . . . . . . . . . . . . . . . (916) 445-3976
  E-mail: jesse.cuevas@cdpr.ca.gov
Communications Assistant Director **Charlotte Fadipe** . . . . (916) 445-3974
  E-mail: charlotte.fadipe@cdpr.ca.gov
  Education: Oxford (UK) BSChem; UC Berkeley MJ
Outreach and Public Engagement Assistant Director
  **Paul Verke** . . . . . . . . . . . . . . . . . . . . . . . . . . . . . . . . (916) 445-3974
Legal Affairs Office Chief Counsel **Polly Frenkel** . . . . . . . (916) 324-2666
Regulations Coordinator **Linda Irokawa-Otani** . . . . . . . . (916) 445-3991
Equal Employment Opportunity Officer **Lisa Zwicky** . . . . (916) 322-1987

---

★ Elected Official   ■ Appointed by Governor   ● Appointed by Legislature   ▲ Appointed by Board or Commission   ◆ Appointed by State Supreme Court

## Administrative Services Division

Fax: (916) 445-4149

Assistant Director **Anise Severns** . . . . . . . . . . . . . . . . . . . (916) 650-6957
  E-mail: anise.severns@cdpr.ca.gov

Fiscal Services and Business Operations Branch Chief
  **Lu Saephanh** . . . . . . . . . . . . . . . . . . . . . . . . . . . . . . . (916) 324-1350

Personnel Services Branch Chief **Lisa Zwicky** . . . . . . . . . . (916) 322-4327
                                               Fax: (916) 445-6416

## Pesticide Programs Division

Assistant Director **George Farnsworth** . . . . . . . . . . . . . . . .(916) 445-3984
                                               Fax: (916) 324-1452

Assistant Director **Marylou Verder-Carlos** . . . . . . . . . . . . . (916) 445-3984
                                               Fax: (916) 324-1452

Enforcement Branch Chief **Donna Marciano** . . . . . . . . . . . . (916) 324-4100
                                               Fax: (916) 445-3907

Environmental Monitoring Branch Chief **David Duncan** . . (916) 324-4039
                                               Fax: (916) 324-4088

Medical Toxicology Branch Chief **Sheryl Beauvais** . . . . . . (916) 445-4233
                                               Fax: (916) 324-3506

Pest Management and Licensing Branch Chief
  **Joe Damiano** . . . . . . . . . . . . . . . . . . . . . . . . . . . . . . . (916) 445-3914
                                               Fax: (916) 324-4033

Pesticide Registration Branch Chief **Ann Prichard** . . . . . . . (916) 445-4400
                                               Fax: (916) 324-1719

Product Compliance Branch Chief **Susan McCarthy** . . . . . (916) 445-4159
                                               Fax: (916) 445-6100

Worker Health and Safety Branch Chief **Lisa Ross** . . . . . . . (916) 445-4222

County/State Liaison **Joe Marade** . . . . . . . . . . . . . . . . . . . (916) 445-3906

## Department of Resources, Recycling and Recovery [CalRecycle]

801 K Street, MS 19-01, Sacramento, CA 95814

Tel: (916) 341-6646

■Director **Scott Smithline** . . . . . . . . . . . . . . . . . . . . . . . .(916) 322-4032
  E-mail: scott.smithline@calrecycle.ca.gov      Fax: (916) 319-7227
  Education: Golden Gate 2000 JD

■Chief Deputy Director **Ken DaRosa** . . . . . . . . . . . . . . . . . (916) 341-6544
  E-mail: ken.darosa@calrecycle.ca.gov

■Chief Counsel **Elliott Block** . . . . . . . . . . . . . . . . . . . . . . . (916) 322-6080
  E-mail: elliot.block@calrecycle.ca.gov
  Education: UCLA BA; UC Davis JD

■Policy and Planning Assistant Director **(Vacant)** . . . . . . . . (916) 322-4032

■Legislative Affairs Deputy Director **Mindy McIntyre** . . . . . (916) 341-6583
  Education: UC Davis BS

Audits Office Manager **Josephine Urban** . . . . . . . . . . . (916) 341-6646
  Education: Cal State (Sacramento) BSAcc, MST

■Policy and Analysis Deputy Director **Christine Hironaka** . . (916) 341-6583
  E-mail: christine.hironaka@calrecycle.ca.gov
  Education: Stanford BA

■External Affairs Manager **(Vacant)** . . . . . . . . . . . . . . . . . (916) 341-6583

■Public Affairs Office Communications Director
  **Mark Oldfield** . . . . . . . . . . . . . . . . . . . . . . . . . . . . . . . (916) 341-9942
  E-mail: mark.oldfield@calrecycle.ca.gov

■Public Affairs Supervisor **Jeffrey Danzinger** . . . . . . . . . . . (916) 341-6298
  E-mail: jeffrey.danzinger@calrecycle.ca.gov
  Education: Texas A&M

## Department of Toxic Substances Control [DTSC]

1001 I Street, Sacramento, CA 95814

Tel: (916) 324-1826  Fax: (916) 324-3158  Internet: www.dtsc.ca.gov

**Employees:** 941  **Fiscal Year:** 2015-2016  **Budget:** $216,889,000

Director **Barbara Lee** . . . . . . . . . . . . . . . . . . . . . . . . . . . (916) 322-0504
  Administrative Assistant II **Kim Smith** . . . . . . . . . . . . . (916) 322-0504
  Executive Assistant **Erik Erreca** . . . . . . . . . . . . . . . . . .(916) 322-0504

Chief Deputy Director **Francesca Negri** . . . . . . . . . . . . . . . (916) 322-0504

■Administrative/Fiscal Deputy Director **Andrew Collada** . . . (916) 327-6097
  E-mail: acollada@dtsc.ca.gov                   Fax: (916) 445-9549

Brownfields and Environmental Restoration (Cleanups)
  Program Deputy Director **Zolaikha Taghvaei Bayar** . . . . (916) 255-3366
  Education: New Mexico MSCE                      Fax: (916) 327-0978

---

Cost and Recovery Deputy Director **Terri Hardy** . . . . . . . . . (916) 324-1826

■Enforcement Deputy Director **(Vacant)** . . . . . . . . . . . . . . . (916) 324-2997
                                               Fax: (916) 323-3391

Environmental Information Management Deputy Director
  **George Okamoto** . . . . . . . . . . . . . . . . . . . . . . . . . . . . . (916) 327-2508
  E-mail: george.okamoto@dtsc.ca.gov           Fax: (916) 322-0978

Environmental Justice Assistant Director
  **Ana Mascareñas** . . . . . . . . . . . . . . . . . . . . . . . . . . . . . (916) 324-1826
  Education: Brown U BA; Cal State (Los Angeles) MPH

■External Affairs Deputy Director **Jim Marxen** . . . . . . . . . . (916) 324-8295
  E-mail: jim.marxen@dtsc.ca.gov               Fax: (916) 327-0978

■Office of Policy Legislative Director **(Vacant)** . . . . . . . . . . (916) 327-1186
                                               Fax: (916) 324-1808

Chief Scientist **(Vacant)** . . . . . . . . . . . . . . . . . . . . . . . . . (916) 322-5244
                                               Fax: (510) 540-3937

Environmental Chemistry Lab (ECL) Chief
  **Bruce La Belle** . . . . . . . . . . . . . . . . . . . . . . . . . . . . . . . (510) 540-3112
                                               Fax: (510) 540-2305

Civil Rights Office Chief **(Vacant)** . . . . . . . . . . . . . . . . . . . (916) 324-6544

■Chief Counsel **Fran McChesney** . . . . . . . . . . . . . . . . . . . . (916) 323-3380
  E-mail: frances.mcchesney@dtsc.ca.gov

## Office of Environmental Health Hazard Assessment [OEHHA]

1001 I Street, Sacramento, CA 95814

Tel: (916) 324-7572  Tel: (916) 445-6900 (Proposition 65 Implementation)
Fax: (916) 327-1097  Internet: www.oehha.ca.gov

**Employees:** 125  **Fiscal Year:** 2015-2016  **Budget:** $21,882,000

■Director (Acting) **Lauren Zeise, PhD** . . . . . . . . . . . . . . . . . (916) 322-6325
  E-mail: lauren.zeise@oehha.ca.gov

Chief Deputy Director **Allan Hirsch** . . . . . . . . . . . . . . . . . . (916) 322-6325

Administration and Program Support Deputy Director
  **Susan Villa** . . . . . . . . . . . . . . . . . . . . . . . . . . . . . . . . . (916) 327-8044
  E-mail: susan.villa@oehha.ca.gov

External and Legislative Affairs Deputy Director
  **Sam Delson** . . . . . . . . . . . . . . . . . . . . . . . . . . . . . . . . . (916) 324-0955
  E-mail: sam.delson@oehha.ca.gov
  Education: Stanford 1999 MA; Harvard 2000 MPA

Scientific Affairs Deputy Director **Melanie Marty, PhD** . . . . (510) 622-3195
  1515 Clay Street, 16th Floor, Oakland, CA 94612

Air, Community, and Environmental Research Branch
  Chief **(Vacant)** . . . . . . . . . . . . . . . . . . . . . . . . . . . . . . . (916) 322-5624

Pesticide and Environmental Toxicology Branch Chief
  **David Ting** . . . . . . . . . . . . . . . . . . . . . . . . . . . . . . . . . . (510) 622-3226
  1515 Clay Street, 16th Floor, Oakland, CA 94612

Reproductive and Cancer Hazard Assessment Branch
  Chief **Martha S. Sandy** . . . . . . . . . . . . . . . . . . . . . . . . . (510) 622-3192
  1515 Clay St., 16th Floor, Oakland, CA 94612

Special Assistant **Julian Leichty** . . . . . . . . . . . . . . . . . . . . (916) 324-7572

Chief Counsel **Carol Monahan-Cummings, JD** . . . . . . . . . (916) 322-0493
  Education: Empire Col JD

## Emergency Services [Cal OES]

3650 Schriever Avenue, Mather, CA 95655

Tel: (916) 845-8510  Fax: (916) 845-8910

■Director **Mark S. Ghilarducci** . . . . . . . . . . . . . . . . . . . . . (916) 845-8506
  E-mail: mark.ghilarducci@caloes.ca.gov

■Chief Deputy Director **Nancy L. Ward** . . . . . . . . . . . . . . . (916) 845-8506
  E-mail: nancy.ward@caloes.ca.gov

Crisis Communications and Public Affairs Deputy
  Director **Kelly Huston** . . . . . . . . . . . . . . . . . . . . . . . . . .(916) 845-8506
  E-mail: kelly.huston@caloes.ca.gov

Finance and Administration Deputy Director
  **Lona "Grace" Koch** . . . . . . . . . . . . . . . . . . . . . . . . . . . (916) 845-8506
  E-mail: grace.koch@caloes.ca.gov

Logistic Management Deputy Director
  **Mitch Medigovich** . . . . . . . . . . . . . . . . . . . . . . . . . . . .(916) 845-8552

■Planning, Preparedness and Prevention Deputy Director
  **Christina "Tina" Curry** . . . . . . . . . . . . . . . . . . . . . . . . . (916) 845-8506
  E-mail: christina.curry@caloes.ca.gov

Recovery Assistant Director **Charles Rabamad** . . . . . . . . . . (916) 845-8201

■Response Assistant Director **Danjel "Dan" Bout** . . . . . . . . (916) 845-8506
  E-mail: dan.bout@caloes.ca.gov

---

★ Elected Official   ■ Appointed by Governor   ● Appointed by Legislature   ▲ Appointed by Board or Commission   ◆ Appointed by State Supreme Court

Chief Technology Officer **Carla Simmons** . . . . . . . . . . . . . (916) 845-8316
E-mail: carla.simmons@caloes.ca.gov
Fire and Rescue Branch Chief **Kim Zagaris** . . . . . . . . . . . (916) 845-8726
Law Enforcement Branch Chief **Mark N. Pazin** . . . . . . . . . (916) 845-8700
Preparedness Division Chief **Moustafa Abou-Taleb** . . . . . . (916) 845-8791
Chief of Legislative and External Affairs
**M. Reginald "Reggie" Salvador** . . . . . . . . . . . . . . . . (916) 845-8473
E-mail: reggie.salvador@caloes.ca.gov
Chief Legal Counsel **Jill Talley** . . . . . . . . . . . . . . . . . . (916) 845-8543
Education: Pepperdine JD
Special Advisor **(Vacant)** . . . . . . . . . . . . . . . . . . . . . . (916) 845-8506

# California Government Operations Agency [CalGovOps]

915 Capitol Mall, Suite 200, Sacramento, CA 95814
Tel: (916) 651-9011  Fax: (916) 651-9071

■ Secretary **Marybel Batjer** . . . . . . . . . . . . . . . . . . . . . (916) 651-9011
E-mail: marybel.batjer@govops.ca.gov
Education: Mills 1976 BA
■ Communications Deputy Secretary **Lynda Gledhill** . . . . . . (916) 651-9011
E-mail: lynda.gledhill@govops.ca.gov
Education: Missouri MAJ
Fiscal Policy and Administration Deputy Secretary
**Jennifer Osborn** . . . . . . . . . . . . . . . . . . . . . . . . . . (916) 651-9011
Government Innovation and Accountability Deputy
Secretary **Stuart Drown** . . . . . . . . . . . . . . . . . . . . . (916) 651-9011
Education: UC Berkeley 1982 BA, 1986 MPP
Legislation Deputy Secretary **Khaim Morton** . . . . . . . . . . (916) 651-9011
Sustainability Deputy Secretary **Matt Henigan** . . . . . . . . . (916) 651-9011
General Counsel **Holly Pearson** . . . . . . . . . . . . . . . . . . (916) 651-9011
Education: USC 1986 BA; McGeorge 1991 JD
Human Resources Deputy Secretary **David Rechs** . . . . . . . (916) 651-9011

# Department of General Services [DGS]

707 Third Street, 8th Floor, West Sacramento, CA 95605-2811
Tel: (916) 376-5000  Fax: (916) 376-5018  Internet: www.dgs.ca.gov

**Employees:** 3,562  **Fiscal Year:** 2015-2016  **Budget:** $1,065,428,000

■ Director **Daniel C. Kim** . . . . . . . . . . . . . . . . . . . . . . . (916) 376-5012
E-mail: daniel.kim@dgs.ca.gov
Administrative Assistant **Carmen Llamas** . . . . . . . . . . . . (916) 376-5012
■ Chief Deputy Director **Jeff McGuire** . . . . . . . . . . . . . . . (916) 376-5023
■ Chief Counsel, Office of Legal Services **(Vacant)** . . . . . . . (916) 376-5038
Administration Division Deputy Director **Miles Burnett** . . . (916) 376-5020
E-mail: miles.burnett@dgs.ca.gov
■ Interagency Support Division Deputy Director
**Brent Jamison, JD** . . . . . . . . . . . . . . . . . . . . . . . . (916) 376-5000
E-mail: brent.jamison@dgs.ca.gov
Education: Santa Clara U 1997 BS; McGeorge 2000 JD
Strategic Planning, Policy and Research Deputy Director
**Jason Kenney** . . . . . . . . . . . . . . . . . . . . . . . . . . . (916) 376-5004
■ Public Affairs Deputy Director **Brian Ferguson** . . . . . . . . (916) 376-5038
E-mail: brian.ferguson@dgs.ca.gov
Education: Syracuse MA
■ Business Development Program Manager **Tanya Little** . . . . (916) 324-8401
E-mail: tanya.little@dgs.ca.gov
Chief Information Officer **Rebecca Skarr** . . . . . . . . . . . . (916) 375-4695
E-mail: rebecca.skarr@dgs.ca.gov
Equal Employment Opportunity Officer
**Michelle Armitage** . . . . . . . . . . . . . . . . . . . . . . . . (916) 376-5122
Facility Management Deputy Director **Jemahl Åmen** . . . . . (916) 376-5000
■ Special Projects Deputy Director **Juan Vasquez** . . . . . . . . (916) 376-9812
E-mail: juan.vasquez@dgs.ca.gov

# Office of Administrative Hearings

2349 Gateway Oaks, Suite 200, Sacramento, CA 95833
Tel: (916) 263-0550  Fax: (916) 263-0554

Director and Chief Administrative Law Judge
**Zackery P. Morazzini** . . . . . . . . . . . . . . . . . . . . . . (916) 263-0653
Fax: (916) 263-0545
Assistant Director **Melissa Crowell** . . . . . . . . . . . . . . . . (916) 263-0550
Fax: (916) 263-0545

General Jurisdiction Division Presiding Administrative
Law Judge **Alan Alvord** . . . . . . . . . . . . . . . . . . . . . (619) 525-4475
1350 Front Street, Suite 6022,          Fax: (619) 525-4419
San Diego, CA 92191
General Jurisdiction Division Presiding Administrative
Law Judge **Dian M. Vorters** . . . . . . . . . . . . . . . . . . . (213) 576-7200
General Jurisdiction Division Presiding Administrative
Law Judge **Jonathan Lew** . . . . . . . . . . . . . . . . . . . . (916) 263-0550
2349 Gateway Oaks Drive, Suite 200, Sacramento, CA 95833
General Jurisdiction Division Presiding Administrative
Law Judge **Cheryl R. Tompkin** . . . . . . . . . . . . . . . . . (510) 622-2732
1515 Clay Street, Suite 206,           Fax: (510) 622-2743
Oakland, CA 94612-1413
Special Education Division Presiding Administrative Law
Judge **Richard T. Breen** . . . . . . . . . . . . . . . . . . . . . (949) 598-5850
23046 Avenida De La Carlota, Suite 750, Laguna Hills, CA 92653
Special Education Division Presiding Administrative Law
Judge **Peter Paul Castillo** . . . . . . . . . . . . . . . . . . . . (916) 263-0880
Fax: (916) 263-0890
Special Education Division Presiding Administrative Law
Judge **Bob Varma** . . . . . . . . . . . . . . . . . . . . . . . . . (818) 904-2383
15350 Sherman Way, Suite 300,         Fax: (818) 904-2360
Van Nuys, CA 91406

# Fiscal Services Office

707 Third Street, West Sacramento, CA 95605
Tel: (916) 376-5143  Internet: www.ofs.dgs.ca.gov

Chief **Rhonda Basarich** . . . . . . . . . . . . . . . . . . . . . . . (916) 376-5133

# Fleet Administration and Asset Management Office

1700 National Drive, Sacramento, CA 95834
Tel: (916) 928-2550  Fax: (916) 327-2076  Internet: www.dgs.ca.gov/ofa

Chief **Robert Stroud** . . . . . . . . . . . . . . . . . . . . . . . . . (916) 928-9863

# Office of Human Resources

707 Third Street, Suite 7-130, West Sacramento, CA 95605
Tel: (916) 376-5400  Fax: (916) 376-5390  Internet: www.dgs.ca.gov/ohr

Chief **Estela Gonzales** . . . . . . . . . . . . . . . . . . . . . . . . (916) 376-5413

# Legal Services Office

707 Third Street, Suite 7-330, West Sacramento, CA 95605
Tel: (916) 376-5080  Fax: (916) 376-5088  Internet: www.dgs.ca.gov/ols

■ Chief Counsel and Deputy Director **Leslie R. Lopez** . . . . . . (916) 376-5085
E-mail: leslie.lopez@dgs.ca.gov
Education: San José State BA; Santa Clara U JD

# Office of Public School Construction

707 Third Street, Suite 400, West Sacramento, CA 95691
Tel: (916) 445-3160  Fax: (916) 445-5526  Internet: www.opsc.dgs.ca.gov

Executive Officer **Lisa Silverman** . . . . . . . . . . . . . . . . . (916) 375-5959
Deputy Executive Officer **Barbara Kampmeinert** . . . . . . . (916) 375-4732

# State Allocation Board

707 Third Street, Suite 400, West Sacramento, CA 95691
Tel: (916) 375-4751

■ Chair **Michael Cohen** . . . . . . . . . . . . . . . . . . . . . . . . (916) 445-8582
Education: Stanford BA; Texas MPA
■ Vice Chair **Carol Liu** . . . . . . . . . . . . . . . . . . . . . . . . (916) 651-4025
Education: San José State Col 1963 BAE
■ Member **Susan Bonilla** . . . . . . . . . . . . . . . . . . . . . . . (916) 319-2014
Education: Azusa Pacific 1982 BA
■ Member **Rocky J. Chávez** . . . . . . . . . . . . . . . . . . . . . (916) 319-2076
Education: Cal State (Chico) 1973 BA; Marine Corps Command U;
Air War Col
■ Member **Cesar Diaz** . . . . . . . . . . . . . . . . . . . . . . . . . (916) 651-4027
■ Member **Loni Hancock** . . . . . . . . . . . . . . . . . . . . . . . (916) 651-4009
Education: Ithaca 1963 BA; Wright Inst 1977 MA
■ Member **Robert "Bob" Huff** . . . . . . . . . . . . . . . . . . . . (916) 651-4029
Education: Westmont BA
■ Member **Daniel C. Kim** . . . . . . . . . . . . . . . . . . . . . . . (916) 376-5023
■ Member **Adrin Nazarian** . . . . . . . . . . . . . . . . . . . . . . (916) 319-2046
Education: UCLA 1986 BA

*(continued on next page)*

---

★ Elected Official   ■ Appointed by Governor   ● Appointed by Legislature   ▲ Appointed by Board or Commission   ◆ Appointed by State Supreme Court

**Office of Public School Construction** *continued*

- Member **Thomas "Tom" Torlakson** .................... (916) 651-4027
  Education: UC Berkeley 1971 BA
- Member **(Vacant)** ........................................ (916) 376-5023
Executive Officer **Lisa Silverman** ...................... (916) 375-4751

## Risk and Insurance Management Office
707 Third Street, 1st Floor, West Sacramento, CA 95605
Tel: (916) 376-5300  Fax: (916) 376-5277  Internet: www.orim.dgs.ca.gov
Chief **Kim Hunt** ........................................... (916) 376-5271

## State Publishing Office
344 North Seventh Street, Sacramento, CA 95814-0212
Tel: (916) 322-1031  Fax: (916) 323-0308  Internet: www.dgs.ca.gov/osp
State Printer **David "Jerry" Hill** ...................... (916) 445-5378

## Division of the State Architect
1130 K Street, Suite 101, Sacramento, CA 95814
Tel: (916) 445-8100  Fax: (916) 445-3521  Internet: www.dsa.dgs.ca.gov
- State Architect **Chester A. "Chet" Widom, FAIA** ........ (916) 322-4866
  E-mail: chester.widom@dgs.ca.gov
  Education: USC 1962 BARCH
- Deputy State Architect **Robert Chase** ................. (916) 323-7344
  E-mail: bob.chase@dgs.ca.gov
  Education: Boston Arch

## Procurement Division
707 Third Street, 2nd Floor, West Sacramento, CA 95605
Tel: (800) 559-5529  Fax: (916) 375-4421
Fax: (916) 375-4444 (Customer Service and General Information)
Internet: www.dgs.ca.gov/pd
Deputy Director **James "Jim" Butler** ................. (916) 375-4445

## Real Estate Services Division
707 Third Street, West Sacramento, CA 95605
Fax: (916) 376-1895  Internet: www.dgs.ca.gov/resd
Deputy Director (Acting) **Jacque Roberts** ............. (916) 376-5000
Assistant Deputy Director **(Vacant)** ................. (916) 376-1695
Real Estate Services Assistant Deputy Director **(Vacant)** ... (916) 376-1695
Asset Management Branch Chief **Jim Martone** .......... (916) 376-1692
Building and Property Management Branch Chief
  (Acting) **Greg Simmons** ............................. (619) 688-0200
                                          Fax: (619) 688-0203
Construction Services Branch Chief (Acting)
  **Doug Brenning** ..................................... (916) 696-3007
Project Services and Project Management Branch Chief
  **Faizi Pourhosseini** ................................ (916) 375-4257

## California Department of Human Resources [CalHR]
North Building, 1515 S Street, Suite 500, Sacramento, CA 95811
Tel: (916) 324-0455  TTY: (800) 735-2929  Fax: (916) 322-8376
Internet: www.calhr.ca.gov
**Employees: 289  Fiscal Year: 2015-2016  Budget: $96,855,000**
- Director **Richard Gillihan** ......................... (916) 322-5193
  E-mail: richard_gillihan@calpers.ca.gov
  Assistant to the Director **Julie Taylor** ........... (916) 322-5193
- Deputy Director of Operations **Katie Hagen** ........ (916) 322-5193
  E-mail: katie_hagen@calpers.ca.gov
  Assistant to the Chief Deputy Director **Elaine Martin** ... (916) 322-5193
Communications Deputy Secretary **Lynda Gledhill** ...... (916) 651-9028
  E-mail: lynda.gledhill@govops.ca.gov
Labor Relations Deputy Director **Pam Manwiller** ....... (916) 324-0476
  Labor Relations Assistant Deputy Director **(Vacant)** ..... (916) 324-0476
- Legislative Director **Danny Brown** .................. (916) 323-8490
  E-mail: danny.brown@calhr.ca.gov
- Legislative Affairs Deputy Director **Jodi LeSubre** ..... (916) 323-8490
Chief Counsel (Acting) **Frolan R. Aguiling** .......... (916) 324-0512
  E-mail: frolan.aguiling@calhr.ca.gov
  Deputy Chief Counsel **Frolan R. Aguiling** .......... (916) 324-0512

Administration Division Chief **Mark Rodriguez** ........ (916) 322-6351
  E-mail: mark_rodriguez@calpers.ca.gov
Benefits Division Chief **Belinda Collins** ............. (916) 324-9366
  1800 - 15th St., Sacramento, CA 95814-7243   Fax: (916) 322-3769
Information Technology Chief **Chad Crowe** ............. (916) 324-0501
  E-mail: chad.crowe@calhr.ca.gov
Personnel Management Division Chief **Bryan Baldwin** .... (916) 323-8495
Selection Division Chief **Adria Jenkins-Jones** ........ (916) 322-6351
Statewide Workforce Development Programs and Special
  Projects Chief **Jeff Douglas** ...................... (916) 324-0455
Savings Plus Program Administrator
  **Michelle Berklacich** .............................. (916) 324-0536
  E-mail: michelle_berklacich@calpers.ca.gov
- Principal Labor Relations Officer **Candace Murch** ....... (916) 324-0455
  E-mail: candace_murch@calpers.ca.gov

## Department of Technology
1325 J Street, Suite 1600, Sacramento, CA 95822
Tel: (916) 319-9223  E-mail: askcio@cio.ca.gov  Internet: www.cio.ca.gov
- Director and State Chief Information Officer (Acting)
  **Amy Tong** .......................................... (916) 319-9223
  E-mail: amy.tong@state.ca.gov
- Chief Deputy Director of Operations **Chris Cruz** ......... (916) 319-9223
  E-mail: chris.cruz@state.ca.gov
- Chief Deputy Director of Policy
  **Andrea Wallin-Rohmann** ............................. (916) 319-9223
  E-mail: andrea.wallin-rohmann@state.ca.gov
- Deputy Director of Broadband and Digital Literacy
  **Adelina Zendejas** .................................. (916) 431-5354
  E-mail: adelina.zendejas@state.ca.gov
- Deputy Director of Enterprise Solutions **Scott Paterson** .. (916) 319-9223
  E-mail: scott.paterson@state.ca.gov
- Deputy Director of External Affairs and Communication
  **Teala Schaff** ...................................... (916) 319-9223
  E-mail: teala.schaff@state.ca.gov
Legislation Assistant Deputy Assistant Deputy
  **Shanda Chaudhry** ................................... (916) 319-9223
Deputy Director of the Information Technology Project
  Oversight Division **Rebecca Stilling** .............. (916) 319-9223
  E-mail: rebecca.stilling@state.ca.gov
  Education: Cal State (Fullerton) MA
- Legal Services Deputy Director/Chief Counsel
  **Anthony Lewis** ..................................... (916) 319-9223
  E-mail: anthony.lewis@state.ca.gov
- State Chief Information Security Office Director
  **(Vacant)** .......................................... (916) 319-9223

## Office of Technology Services
P.O. Box 1810, Rancho Cordova, CA 95741
Tel: (916) 464-7547  Fax: (916) 464-4025  Internet: www.dts.ca.gov
E-mail: info@dts.ca.gov
- Chief **Robert Schmidt** .............................. (916) 228-6512
  E-mail: robert.schmidt@state.ca.gov
  Education: Cal State (Chico) BS; Cal State (Sacramento) MBA
Assistant Chief **Ellen Ishimoto** ..................... (916) 228-6512
Customer Delivery Division Deputy Director
  **Rolundia Mitchell** ................................ (916) 454-7225
Financial Officer **Melissa Matsuura** ................. (916) 739-7760
Public Information Officer **Teala Schaff** ............ (916) 319-9223
Statewide Telecommunications and Network Division
  Director **Barbara Garrett** ......................... (916) 464-7547
  E-mail: barbara.garrett@state.ca.gov

## Office of Digital Innovation and Technology Engagement
Chief **Scott Gregory** ................................ (916) 431-5449
  E-mail: scott.gregory@state.ca.gov

---

# California Public Employees' Retirement System [CalPERS]

400 Q Street, Sacramento, CA 95811
Tel: (916) 795-3829  Fax: (916) 795-3410  Internet: www.calpers.ca.gov

▲Chief Executive Officer **Anne Stausboll** . . . . . . . . . . . . . (916) 795-3829
Note: Until June 30, 2016.
E-mail: anne_stausboll@calpers.ca.gov
Education: Oberlin BA; UC Davis 1984 JD

Chief Financial Officer Deputy Executive Officer
**Cheryl Eason** . . . . . . . . . . . . . . . . . . . . . . . . . . . . . . (916) 795-3829
Education: Royal Roads (Canada) MBA; Dalhousie AA

Benefits Programs Policy and Planning Deputy Executive
Director **Doug P. McKeever** . . . . . . . . . . . . . . . . . . . . (916) 795-3829

Customer Services and Support Deputy Executive Officer
**Donna Lum** . . . . . . . . . . . . . . . . . . . . . . . . . . . . . . . . (916) 795-3822

Operations and Technology Deputy Executive Officer
**W. Douglas Hoffner** . . . . . . . . . . . . . . . . . . . . . . . . (916) 795-1251
Education: Art Inst Southern Cal BA

Information Technology Services Branch Chief
Information Officer **Liana Bailey-Crimmins** . . . . . . . . . . (916) 765-3829
E-mail: liana_bailey-crimmins@calpers.ca.gov

Chief Actuary **Alan W. Milligan** . . . . . . . . . . . . . . . . (916) 795-4177
General Counsel **Matthew G. Jacobs, JD** . . . . . . . . . . . . (916) 795-3797
Education: UC Berkeley BS

Senior Portfolio Manager for Global Governance
**Anne Simpson** . . . . . . . . . . . . . . . . . . . . . . . . . . . . (916) 795-3829

Communications and Stakeholder Relations Deputy
Executive Officer **Brad W. Pacheco** . . . . . . . . . . . . . . (916) 795-3850

Chief Investment Officer
**Theodore H. "Ted" Eliopoulos** . . . . . . . . . . . . . . . . (916) 795-3829
Education: Dartmouth 1986 AB; Virginia 1989 JD

Public Information Officer **Joe DeAnda** . . . . . . . . . . . . . (916) 795-3829

## Board of Administration

■President **Rob Feckner** . . . . . . . . . . . . . . . . . . . . . . . (916) 795-3829
E-mail: Rob_Feckner@calpers.ca.gov

Vice President **Henry Jones** . . . . . . . . . . . . . . . . . . . . (916) 795-3829
Member **Michael Bilbrey** . . . . . . . . . . . . . . . . . . . . . (916) 795-3829
■Member **Dana Hollinger** . . . . . . . . . . . . . . . . . . . . . (916) 795-3829
Member **Joseph "J.J." Jelincic** . . . . . . . . . . . . . . . . (916) 795-3829
●Member **Ron Lind** . . . . . . . . . . . . . . . . . . . . . . . . . . (916) 795-3829
Member **Priya Sara Mathur** . . . . . . . . . . . . . . . . . . . (916) 795-3829
Education: Haas MBA

■Member **Bill Slaton** . . . . . . . . . . . . . . . . . . . . . . . . (916) 795-3829
Education: Texas BBA

Member **Theresa Taylor** . . . . . . . . . . . . . . . . . . . . . . (916) 795-3829
Member (Ex Officio) **John Chiang** . . . . . . . . . . . . . . . (916) 795-3829
Education: Central Florida BA; Georgetown 1987 JD

Member (Ex Officio) **Richard Costigan III** . . . . . . . . . . (916) 795-3829
Affiliation: Member, State Personnel Board, California Government
Operations Agency, State of California
801 Capitol Mall, Sacramento, CA 95814
Education: Georgia 1988 BA; Cumberland 1991 JD

Member (Ex Officio) **Richard Gillihan** . . . . . . . . . . . . . (916) 795-3829

## State Personnel Board

801 Capitol Mall, Sacramento, CA 95814
Tel: (916) 653-1028  Fax: (916) 653-8147  Internet: www.spb.ca.gov

**Employees:** 70

President **Kimiko Burton** . . . . . . . . . . . . . . . . . . . . . (916) 653-1028
Vice President **Lauri M. Shanahan** . . . . . . . . . . . . . . . (916) 653-1028
Education: UCLA JD

Member **Patricia T. "Pat" Clarey** . . . . . . . . . . . . . . . (916) 653-1028
Education: Union Col (NY) BS; Harvard 1983 MPA

Member **Richard Costigan III** . . . . . . . . . . . . . . . . . . (916) 653-1028
Member **Maeley L. Tom** . . . . . . . . . . . . . . . . . . . . . . (916) 653-1028
Education: San Francisco State U BA

▲Executive Officer **Suzanne Ambrose** . . . . . . . . . . . . . (916) 653-1028
E-mail: suzanne.ambrose@spb.ca.gov

Chief Counsel **Alvin Gittisriboongul** . . . . . . . . . . . . . (916) 653-1403
E-mail: alvin.gittisriboongul@spb.ca.gov

Chief Administrative Law Judge **Paul Ramsey** . . . . . . . . (916) 651-3899

Policy and Compliance Review Division Chief
**Lori Gillihan** . . . . . . . . . . . . . . . . . . . . . . . . . . . . . (916) 651-0924
E-mail: lori.gillihan@spb.ca.gov

Communications Deputy Secretary **Lynda Gledhill** . . . . . . (916) 651-9028
E-mail: lynda.gledhill@govops.ca.gov

# Franchise Tax Board

P.O. Box 1468, Sacramento, CA 95812-1468
Tel: (800) 852-5711
Tel: (800) 338-0505 (F.A.S.T. [Fast Answers about State Taxes])
Tel: (916) 845-6500 (F.A.S.T. From outside of the United States)
Tel: (800) 822-6268 (For Speaking Impaired)  TTY: (800) 822-6268
Fax: (916) 845-4505  Internet: www.ftb.ca.gov

**Employees:** 5,095.3  **Fiscal Year:** 2015-2016  **Budget:** $726,956,000

Chair **Betty T. Yee** . . . . . . . . . . . . . . . . . . . . . . . . . (916) 445-2636
Education: UC Berkeley BA; Golden Gate MPA

Member **Michael Cohen** . . . . . . . . . . . . . . . . . . . . . . (916) 445-3878
Member **Fiona Ma** . . . . . . . . . . . . . . . . . . . . . . . . . . (916) 644-4154
Executive Officer **Selvi Stanislaus** . . . . . . . . . . . . . . . (916) 845-4543

# Health and Human Services Agency [CHHS]

1600 Ninth Street, Room 460, Sacramento, CA 95814
Tel: (916) 654-3454  Fax: (916) 654-3343  Internet: www.chhs.ca.gov
Internet: www.dhs.ca.gov/chs (Vital Records)

**Employees:** 32,297  **Fiscal Year:** 2015-2016  **Budget:** $52,335,611,000

■Secretary **Diana S. Dooley** . . . . . . . . . . . . . . . . . . . . (916) 654-3454
E-mail: diana.dooley@chhs.ca.gov
Administrative Assistant **Maria Campos-Vergara** . . . . . . (916) 654-3454
Deputy Secretary for Health Information **(Vacant)** . . . . . . (916) 654-3454

■Undersecretary **Michael Wilkening** . . . . . . . . . . . . . . . (916) 654-3454
E-mail: michael.wilkening@chhs.ca.gov
Education: UC Davis BA, MA
Special Projects Deputy Secretary **Katie Heidorn** . . . . . . . (916) 654-3454
E-mail: katie.heidorn@chhs.ca.gov

Program and Fiscal Affairs Assistant Secretary
**Robert Ducay** . . . . . . . . . . . . . . . . . . . . . . . . . . . . (916) 654-3454

Program and Fiscal Affairs Assistant Secretary
**Sandra Gallardo** . . . . . . . . . . . . . . . . . . . . . . . . . . (916) 653-1975

■Program and Fiscal Affairs Assistant Secretary
**Kristopher Kent** . . . . . . . . . . . . . . . . . . . . . . . . . . (916) 654-3454
E-mail: kkent@chhs.ca.gov

■Program and Fiscal Affairs Assistant Secretary
**Marko Mijic** . . . . . . . . . . . . . . . . . . . . . . . . . . . . . (916) 654-3454
E-mail: marko.mijic@chhs.ca.gov

Program and Fiscal Affairs Assistant Secretary
**Janne Olson-Morgan** . . . . . . . . . . . . . . . . . . . . . . . (916) 654-3454
Education: Pomona 2002 BA; South Carolina 2011 MPP

Program and Fiscal Affairs Assistant Secretary
**John Wordlaw** . . . . . . . . . . . . . . . . . . . . . . . . . . . . (916) 654-3454

Communications Deputy Secretary **Karin Caves** . . . . . . . (916) 654-3454
E-mail: karin.caves@chhs.ca.gov

External Affairs Office Deputy Secretary **Scott Murray** . . . (916) 654-3454

■Legislative Affairs Deputy Secretary **Kiyomi Burchill** . . . . (916) 654-3454
E-mail: kburchil@chhs.ca.gov
Education: Stanford 2006; South Carolina 2011

Olmstead Activities Assistant Secretary **Kiyomi Burchill** . . . (916) 654-3454

■Administrative and Financial Services Chief
**Sonia Fernandez-Herrera** . . . . . . . . . . . . . . . . . . . . (916) 654-3459
E-mail: sherrera@chhs.ca.gov

■External Affairs Office Associate Secretary
**Jim Suennen** . . . . . . . . . . . . . . . . . . . . . . . . . . . . . (916) 654-3454
E-mail: jim.suennen@chhs.ca.gov

General Counsel **Douglas M. Press** . . . . . . . . . . . . . . . (916) 654-3454

# Department of Aging [CDA]

1300 National Drive, Suite 200, Sacramento, CA 95834
Tel: (916) 419-7500  Fax: (916) 928-2267  Internet: www.aging.ca.gov

**Employees:** 116  **Fiscal Year:** 2015-2016  **Budget:** $199,109,000

■Director **Lora Connolly** . . . . . . . . . . . . . . . . . . . . . . (916) 419-7500
E-mail: lora.connolly@aging.ca.gov
Education: USC MA

*(continued on next page)*

---

★ Elected Official   ■ Appointed by Governor   ● Appointed by Legislature   ▲ Appointed by Board or Commission   ◆ Appointed by State Supreme Court

**Department of Aging** *continued*

Chief Deputy Director (Acting) **Lora Connolly** . . . . . . . . . . (916) 419-7500
Legislation and Public Affairs Assistant Director
  **Christin Hemann** . . . . . . . . . . . . . . . . . . . . . . . . . . . . (916) 419-7500
Administration Division Deputy Director
  **Jeannine Fenton** . . . . . . . . . . . . . . . . . . . . . . . . . . . . . (916) 419-7500
Long Term Care & Aging Services Division Deputy
  Director **Edmond P. Long** . . . . . . . . . . . . . . . . . . . . . . (916) 419-7500
Chief Counsel **Chisorom Okwuosa** . . . . . . . . . . . . . . . . . (916) 419-7500
State Long-Term Care Ombudsman
  **Joseph "Joe" Rodrigues** . . . . . . . . . . . . . . . . . . . . . . (916) 419-7500
    Education: St Patrick's BA, MDiv

## Department of Child Support Services [DCSS]

P.O. Box 419064, Rancho Cordova, CA 95741-9064 (Mail Stop 100)
Fax: (916) 464-5211

**Employees:** 594 **Fiscal Year:** 2015-2016 **Budget:** $1,001,127,000

■Director **Alisha Griffin** . . . . . . . . . . . . . . . . . . . . . . . . . (916) 464-5300
  E-mail: alisha.griffin@dcss.ca.gov
  Education: Bridgeport 1976 MS
■Chief Deputy Director **Mark Beckley** . . . . . . . . . . . . . . . (916) 464-5300
  E-mail: mark.beckley@dcss.ca.gov
  Education: USC MPP
■Chief Counsel **Kathleen Hrepich** . . . . . . . . . . . . . . . . . . (916) 464-5300
  E-mail: kathleen.hrepich@dcss.ca.gov
  Education: Lincoln Law JD
Communications and Public Affairs Assistant Director
  **Dana Christine Simas** . . . . . . . . . . . . . . . . . . . . . . . . (916) 464-3220

## Department of Community Services and Development

2389 Gatway Oaks Drive, Sacramento, CA 95833
Tel: (916) 576-7109 Fax: (916) 263-1406 Internet: www.csd.ca.gov

**Employees:** 111 **Fiscal Year:** 2015-2016 **Budget:** $264,032,000

■Director **Linné K. Stout** . . . . . . . . . . . . . . . . . . . . . . . . . (916) 576-7110
  E-mail: lstout@csd.ca.gov
■Chief Deputy Director **Jason Wimbley** . . . . . . . . . . . . . . (916) 576-7219
  E-mail: jwimbley@csd.ca.gov
Community Services Block Grant Program Manager
  **Sylmia Britt** . . . . . . . . . . . . . . . . . . . . . . . . . . . . . . . . (916) 576-7188
Community Services Block Grant Central Region
  Program Manager **Sylmia Britt** . . . . . . . . . . . . . . . . . (916) 576-7188
Community Services Block Grant Northern Region
  Program Manager **Sylmia Britt** . . . . . . . . . . . . . . . . . (916) 576-7188
Lead Hazard Control Program Manager
  **Lorraine Yamada** . . . . . . . . . . . . . . . . . . . . . . . . . . . . (916) 576-7154
Energy, Weatherization Assistance Program Manager
  **Leslie Campanella** . . . . . . . . . . . . . . . . . . . . . . . . . . (916) 576-7131
Public Information Officer **Rob McAndrews** . . . . . . . . . . . (916) 576-7117
  E-mail: rob.mcandrews@csd.ca.gov

## California Department of Developmental Services [DDS]

P.O. Box 944202, Sacramento, CA 94244-2020
Tel: (916) 654-1690 Fax: (916) 654-2167 Internet: www.dds.ca.gov

**Employees:** 5,179 **Fiscal Year:** 2015-2016 **Budget:** $264,032,000

■Director **Nancy Bargmann** . . . . . . . . . . . . . . . . . . . . . . . (916) 654-1897
  E-mail: nancy.bargmann@dds.ca.gov
  Education: Pepperdine MBA; San Diego State MSSW
■Chief Deputy Director **John Doyle** . . . . . . . . . . . . . . . . . (916) 654-1897
  E-mail: john.doyle@dds.ca.gov
Chief Counsel **Hiren Patel** . . . . . . . . . . . . . . . . . . . . . . . (916) 654-3405
Administration Division Deputy Director **Jean Johnson** . . (916) 654-3432
  E-mail: jean.johnson@dds.ca.gov
■Community Services Division Deputy Director (Acting)
  **Brian Winfield** . . . . . . . . . . . . . . . . . . . . . . . . . . . . . . (916) 654-1958
  E-mail: brian.winfield@dds.ca.gov
Developmental Centers Division Deputy Director
  **Dwayne Lafon** . . . . . . . . . . . . . . . . . . . . . . . . . . . . . . (916) 654-1963

Information Technology Division Deputy Director
  **Beverly Humphrey** . . . . . . . . . . . . . . . . . . . . . . . . . . (916) 654-1826
■Communications Assistant Director **Nancy Lungren** . . . . . (916) 654-1884
  E-mail: nancy.lungren@dds.ca.gov
Legislation Office Assistant Director **Eric Gelber** . . . . . . . . (916) 654-1884
  E-mail: eric.gelber@dds.ca.gov

## Department of Health Care Services [DHCS]

1501 Capitol Avenue, Suite 6001, Sacramento, CA 95814
P.O. Box 997413, Sacramento, CA 95899-7413
Tel: (916) 440-7400 Fax: (916) 440-7404 Internet: www.dhcs.ca.gov

**Employees:** 3,502 **Fiscal Year:** 2015-2016 **Budget:** $93,658,398,000

■Director **Jennifer Kent** . . . . . . . . . . . . . . . . . . . . . . . . . (916) 440-7400
  E-mail: jennifer.kent@dhcs.ca.gov
Chief Deputy Director **Karen Johnson** . . . . . . . . . . . . . . . (916) 440-7400
  E-mail: karen.johnson@dhcs.ca.gov
  Education: Saint Louis U BAA
■Chief Deputy Director, Health Care Programs
  **Mari Cantwell** . . . . . . . . . . . . . . . . . . . . . . . . . . . . . . (916) 440-7400
  E-mail: marianne.cantwell@dhcs.ca.gov
  Education: Brown U 1998 BA; UCLA 2000 MPP
Deputy Director and Chief Counsel **Jared Goldman** . . . . . . (916) 440-7400
Policy Associate Director **Anastasia Dodson** . . . . . . . . . . (916) 440-7400
  Education: UC Berkeley MPP
Medical Director **Dr. Neal Kohatsu, MD** . . . . . . . . . . . . . (916) 440-7400
Administration Deputy Director **Adam Weintraub** . . . . . . . (916) 440-7400
  E-mail: adam.weintraub@dhcs.ca.gov
Audits and Investigations Deputy Director **Bruce Lim** . . . . . (916) 440-7550
  E-mail: bruce.lim@dhcs.ca.gov
Civil Rights Deputy Director **Johnathan Clarkson** . . . . . . . (916) 440-7370
Quality Care Director **Sarah Brooks** . . . . . . . . . . . . . . . . (916) 440-7400
  Education: UC Berkeley MSW
Health Care Financing Deputy Director **(Vacant)** . . . . . . . . (916) 440-7525
Health Information Technology Office Chief
  **Raul Ramirez** . . . . . . . . . . . . . . . . . . . . . . . . . . . . . . (916) 440-7340
  E-mail: raul.ramirez@dhcs.ca.gov
■Legal Services Deputy Director and Chief Counsel/ Chief
  Information Officer **Douglas M. Press** . . . . . . . . . . . . . (916) 440-7700
  E-mail: douglas.press@dhcs.ca.gov
■Office of Public Affairs Deputy Director
  **Norman Williams** . . . . . . . . . . . . . . . . . . . . . . . . . . . (916) 440-7660
  E-mail: Norman.Williams@dhcs.ca.gov
SUD Prevention, Treatment and Recovery Division Chief
  **Don Braeger** . . . . . . . . . . . . . . . . . . . . . . . . . . . . . . . (916) 322-7012
Grants Management Office Chief **Allen Scott** . . . . . . . . . . (916) 324-8903

## Department of Managed Health Care

980 Ninth Street, Suite 500, Sacramento, CA 95814-2725
Tel: (888) 466-2219 Fax: (916) 322-2579 E-mail: geninfo@dmhc.ca.gov

**Employees:** 374

■Director **Michelle "Shelley" Rouillard** . . . . . . . . . . . . . . (916) 322-2314
  E-mail: shelley.rouillard@dmhc.ca.gov
  Education: Rutgers BASW
  Assistant to the Director **Linda Stall** . . . . . . . . . . . . . . (916) 322-2314
■Chief Deputy Director **Marta Green** . . . . . . . . . . . . . . . . (916) 327-0098
  E-mail: mgreen@dmhc.ca.gov
Communications and Planning Deputy Director
  **Rachel Arrezola** . . . . . . . . . . . . . . . . . . . . . . . . . . . . (916) 445-7442
■Legislative Affairs Deputy Director **Jenny Mae Phillips** . . . (888) 466-2219
Stakeholder and Policy Relations Deputy Director
  **Mary Watanabe** . . . . . . . . . . . . . . . . . . . . . . . . . . . . (916) 322-1583

## California Department of Public Health [CDPH]

1615 Capitol Avenue, MS 0500, Sacramento, CA 95814
P.O. Box 997377, MS 0500, Sacramento, CA 95899-7377
Tel: (916) 558-1700 Internet: www.cdph.ca.gov

■Director/State Public Health Officer **Karen L. Smith** . . . . . (916) 558-1700
  E-mail: karen.smith@cdph.ca.gov
  Education: Stanford MD; Johns Hopkins MPH

---

★ Elected Official   ■ Appointed by Governor   ● Appointed by Legislature   ▲ Appointed by Board or Commission   ◆ Appointed by State Supreme Court

Assistant Director **Susan Fanelli** . . . . . . . . . . . . . . . . . . . . . .(916) 650-6710
Education: UC Davis MA
Administration Deputy Director **Alan Lum** . . . . . . . . . . . . . . (916) 558-1700
E-mail: alan.lum@cdph.ca.gov
Center for Health Statistics and Informatics Deputy
Director **James Greene** . . . . . . . . . . . . . . . . . . . . . . . . . . (916) 552-8092
Vital Statistics State Registrar **Tony Agurto** . . . . . . . . . . .(510) 620-3129
Deputy Director and Chief Counsel **Karin S. Schwartz** . . . (916) 558-1700
Education: Bryn Mawr 1986 AB; Stanford JD
■Office of Public Affairs Deputy Director **Ali Bay** . . . . . . . . .(916) 440-7259
E-mail: ali.bay@cdph.ca.gov
■Operations Chief Deputy Director **Brandon Nunes** . . . . . . .(916) 558-1700
E-mail: brandon.nunes@cdph.ca.gov
■Policy and Programs Chief Deputy Director
**Claudia Crist** . . . . . . . . . . . . . . . . . . . . . . . . . . . . . . . . (916) 558-1700
E-mail: claudia.crist@dhcs.ca.gov
Education: Bellevue U BS; USC 2006 MHA

## Center for Chronic Disease Prevention and Health Promotion
■Deputy Director **Mark Starr, DVM** . . . . . . . . . . . . . . . . . . . . (916) 445-0661
E-mail: mark.starr@cdph.ca.gov
Education: UC Davis MS, DVM
Chronic Disease and Injury Control Chief (Acting)
**Caroline Peck** . . . . . . . . . . . . . . . . . . . . . . . . . . . . . . . .(916) 449-5700
Environmental and Occupational Disease Control Chief
**Rick Kreutzer, MD** . . . . . . . . . . . . . . . . . . . . . . . . . . . . .(510) 620-3130
Education: Pennsylvania 1982 MD

## Center for Environmental Health
Deputy Director **Mark Starr, DVM** . . . . . . . . . . . . . . . . . . . . (916) 445-0275
Food, Drug and Radiation Safety Chief **Steve Woods** . . . . (916) 449-5624

## Center for Health Care Quality
■Deputy Director **Jean Iacino** . . . . . . . . . . . . . . . . . . . . . . . . . (916) 324-6630
E-mail: jean.iacino@cdph.ca.gov
Education: Duke MA

## Center for Infectious Diseases
1616 Capitol Avenue, Suite 74318, Sacramento, CA 95814
Deputy Director
**Dr. Gilberto F. "Gil" Chavez, MPH, MD** . . . . . . . . . . . . (916) 445-0062
Education: San Diego State MPH
Communicable Disease Control Chief
**Dr. James Watt, MD** . . . . . . . . . . . . . . . . . . . . . . . . . . . (916) 552-9700
E-mail: james.watt@cdph.ca.gov            Fax: (916) 552-8973
Office of AIDS Chief **Dr. Karen Mark, MD** . . . . . . . . . . . . (916) 449-5905

## Department of Rehabilitation [DOR]
721 Capitol Mall, Sacramento, CA 95814
Tel: (916) 354-1313  TTY: (916) 558-5807  Fax: (916) 558-5806
Internet: www.dor.ca.gov

**Employees:** 1,823  **Fiscal Year:** 2015-2016  **Budget:** $435,609,000
■Director **Joseph "Joe" Xavier** . . . . . . . . . . . . . . . . . . . . . . . (916) 558-5800
E-mail: joe.xavier@dor.ca.gov
■Chief Deputy Director **Juney Lee** . . . . . . . . . . . . . . . . . . . . (916) 558-5802
Note: Until June 1, 2016.
E-mail: juney.lee@dor.ca.gov
■Chief Deputy Director-Designate **Kelly Hargreaves** . . . . . . (916) 558-5802
Note: Effective June 1, 2016.
E-mail: khargrea@dor.ca.gov
Legal Affairs Chief Counsel **Kelly Hargreaves** . . . . . . . . . (916) 558-5828
Note: Until June 1, 2016.
Administrative Services Division Deputy Director
**Theresa Correale** . . . . . . . . . . . . . . . . . . . . . . . . . . . . . . (916) 558-5808
E-mail: theresa.correale@dor.ca.gov
■Independent Living and Community Access Division
Deputy Director **Irene Mary Walela** . . . . . . . . . . . . . . . . (916) 558-5817
Informational Technology Service Division Deputy
Director **Jon Kirkham** . . . . . . . . . . . . . . . . . . . . . . . . . . (916) 650-0485
E-mail: jon.kirkham@dor.ca.gov
Specialized Services Division Deputy Director
**Elena Gomez** . . . . . . . . . . . . . . . . . . . . . . . . . . . . . . . . . (916) 558-5820

Specialized Services Assistant Deputy Director
**Rosa Gomez** . . . . . . . . . . . . . . . . . . . . . . . . . . . . . . . . . (916) 558-5820
Vocational Rehabilitation Employment Division Deputy
Director **William "Bill" Moore** . . . . . . . . . . . . . . . . . . . . (916) 558-5442
■Legislation and External Affairs Assistant Director
**(Vacant)** . . . . . . . . . . . . . . . . . . . . . . . . . . . . . . . . . . . . (916) 558-5792
■Operations and Accountability Officer **Suzanne Chan** . . . . (916) 354-1393
E-mail: suzanne.chan@dor.ca.gov
Education: U San Francisco MPA
Public Information Officer **Michelle Basso Reynolds** . . . . .(916) 558-5870
E-mail: michelle.reynold@dor.ca.gov

## State Rehabilitation Council [SRC]
721 Capitol Mall, Sacramento, CA 95814
Tel: (916) 558-5868  TTY: (916) 558-5807  Fax: (916) 558-5879
Chair **David Deleonardis** . . . . . . . . . . . . . . . . . . . . . . . . . . (916) 558-5868
Vice Chair **Danielle Anderson** . . . . . . . . . . . . . . . . . . . . . . (916) 558-5868
Treasurer **Patricia Collins-Day** . . . . . . . . . . . . . . . . . . . . . .(916) 558-5868
Member **Victoria Benson** . . . . . . . . . . . . . . . . . . . . . . . . . .(916) 558-5868
Member **Patricia Collins-Day** . . . . . . . . . . . . . . . . . . . . . . (916) 558-5868
Member **Manuel Cons** . . . . . . . . . . . . . . . . . . . . . . . . . . . (916) 558-5868
Member **Inez de Ocio** . . . . . . . . . . . . . . . . . . . . . . . . . . . .(916) 558-5868
Education: Cal State (Fresno) MS
Member **Marc Espino** . . . . . . . . . . . . . . . . . . . . . . . . . . . . (916) 558-5868
Member **Lesley Ann Gibbons** . . . . . . . . . . . . . . . . . . . . . . .(916) 558-5868
Member **Abby Snay** . . . . . . . . . . . . . . . . . . . . . . . . . . . . . (916) 558-5868
Member **Deanna Strachan** . . . . . . . . . . . . . . . . . . . . . . . . (916) 558-5868
Member **Michael Torres** . . . . . . . . . . . . . . . . . . . . . . . . . . (916) 558-5868
Member **La Quita Wallace** . . . . . . . . . . . . . . . . . . . . . . . . (916) 558-5868
Member **(Vacant)** . . . . . . . . . . . . . . . . . . . . . . . . . . . . . . .(916) 558-5868
Member **(Vacant)** . . . . . . . . . . . . . . . . . . . . . . . . . . . . . . .(916) 558-5868
Ex-Officio Member **Joseph "Joe" Xavier** . . . . . . . . . . . . . .(916) 558-5868
Executive Officer **Stacy Cervenka** . . . . . . . . . . . . . . . . . . (916) 558-5595
E-mail: stacy.cervenka@dor.ca.gov

## Department of Social Services
744 P Street, Room MS 8-17-11, Sacramento, CA 95814
Tel: (916) 657-2598  Fax: (916) 654-6012

**Employees:** 4,093  **Fiscal Year:** 2015-2016  **Budget:** $22,410,901,000
■Director **William "Will" Lightbourne** . . . . . . . . . . . . . . . . (916) 657-2598
E-mail: will.lightbourne@dss.ca.gov
Chief Deputy Director **Pat Leary** . . . . . . . . . . . . . . . . . . . (916) 657-2598
Legislation Office Deputy Director **(Vacant)** . . . . . . . . . . . .(916) 657-2623
                                       Fax: (916) 653-1695
Public Affairs and Outreach Programs Deputy Director
**Michael Weston** . . . . . . . . . . . . . . . . . . . . . . . . . . . . . . (916) 657-2268
Adult Programs Division Deputy Director **Eileen Carroll** . . (916) 653-5403
                                       Fax: (916) 653-1693
Children and Family Services Division Deputy Director
**Greg Rose** . . . . . . . . . . . . . . . . . . . . . . . . . . . . . . . . . . (916) 657-2614
                                       Fax: (916) 657-2049
Community Care Licensing Division Deputy Director
**Pam Dickfoss** . . . . . . . . . . . . . . . . . . . . . . . . . . . . . . . .(916) 657-2346
                                       Fax: (916) 657-3783
Disability Determination Service Division Deputy
Director **Eva Lopez** . . . . . . . . . . . . . . . . . . . . . . . . . . . . (916) 657-2265
                                       Fax: (916) 653-8690
Information Systems Division Deputy Director
**Karen Cagle** . . . . . . . . . . . . . . . . . . . . . . . . . . . . . . . . .(916) 654-1039
E-mail: karen.cagle@dss.ca.gov          Fax: (916) 651-8280
State Hearings Division Deputy Director/Chief
Administrative Law Judge **Manuel A. Romero** . . . . . . . .(916) 657-3550
                                       Fax: (916) 651-6258
Welfare to Work Division Deputy Director
**Todd R. Bland** . . . . . . . . . . . . . . . . . . . . . . . . . . . . . . . (916) 657-3546
Education: Yale 1984 BA; Harvard 1989 MPP
Benefits and Services Program Chief Deputy Director
**Peter Cervinka** . . . . . . . . . . . . . . . . . . . . . . . . . . . . . . .(916) 657-2598
■Chief Counsel and Legal Division Deputy Director
**Torene L.M. Schwab** . . . . . . . . . . . . . . . . . . . . . . . . . . (916) 657-2353
E-mail: tory.schwab@dss.ca.gov
Senior Assistant Chief Counsel **(Vacant)** . . . . . . . . . . . . . (916) 651-6804

*(continued on next page)*

---

★ Elected Official   ■ Appointed by Governor   ● Appointed by Legislature     ▲ Appointed by Board or Commission   ◆ Appointed by State Supreme Court

EXECUTIVE BRANCH

**Department of Social Services** *continued*

Ombudsman for Foster Care **(Vacant)** ................. (916) 653-4296
Fax: (916) 651-6568

Immigration Branch Chief **(Vacant)** ................... (916) 657-3456

# California Department of State Hospitals

1600 Ninth Street, Sacramento, CA 95814-6404
Tel: (916) 654-2309  Fax: (916) 654-3198
E-mail: dsh.ombudsman@dsh.ca.gov  Internet: www.dsh.ca.gov

**Employees:** 10.823  **Fiscal Year:** 2015-2016  **Budget:** $1,795,329,000

■Director **Pamela A. Ahlin** .......................... (916) 654-2309
E-mail: pam.ahlin@dsh.ca.gov

■Chief Deputy Director **Stephanie Clendenin** ........... (916) 654-2309
E-mail: stephanie.clendenin@dsh.ca.gov

Medical Director **Katherine Warburton** ............... (916) 654-2309

Administrative Services Deputy Director
**Lupe Alonzo-Diaz** ................................ (916) 651-5329

Information Technology Deputy Director **Rogene Sears** ... (916) 651-3084
E-mail: rogene.sears@dsh.ca.gov

■Communications Chief **Ken August** .................. (916) 654-2309
E-mail: ken.august@dsh.ca.gov

■Legislation Assistant Director **Thomas Dey** ............. (916) 654-2309
E-mail: thomas.dey@dsh.ca.gov

Chief Counsel **Pamela Holmes** ...................... (916) 654-2309

# Labor and Workforce Development Agency [LWDA]

800 Capitol Mall, MIC-55, Sacramento, CA 95814
Tel: (916) 653-9900  Fax: (916) 327-9158  Internet: www.labor.ca.gov

**Employees:** 11,813  **Fiscal Year:** 2015-2016  **Budget:** $898,058,000

■Secretary **David Lanier** ............................. (916) 653-9900
E-mail: david.lanier@labor.ca.gov

■Undersecretary **Andre Schoorl** ...................... (916) 653-9900
E-mail: andre.schoorl@labor.ca.gov

Administrative Assistant **Wendy Bryant** .............. (916) 653-9900
E-mail: wendy.bryant@labor.ca.gov

■Communications Deputy Secretary **Garin Casaleggio** ..... (916) 653-9900
E-mail: garin.casaleggio@labor.ca.gov

General Counsel **Mark Woo-Sam** .................... (916) 653-9900

■Director of Legislation **Ralph Lightstone** ............. (916) 653-9900
E-mail: ralph.lightstone@labor.ca.gov

# Employment Development Department [EDD]

722 Capitol Mall, Room 5098, Sacramento, CA 95814
Tel: (916) 654-8210  Fax: (916) 657-5294  Internet: www.edd.ca.gov

**Employees:** 8,385  **Fiscal Year:** 2015-2016  **Budget:** $13,763,710,000

■Director **Patrick W. Henning, Jr.** .................... (916) 654-8212
E-mail: patrick.henning@edd.ca.gov

■Chief Deputy Director **Sharon Hilliard** ............... (916) 654-8210
E-mail: sharon.hilliard@edd.ca.gov

■Legal Office General Counsel **Sandra V. Clifton** ........ (916) 654-8410
E-mail: sandra.clifton@edd.ca.gov

Assistant Chief Legal Counsel **Barbara Kaufman** ........ (916) 654-8410
E-mail: barbara.kaufman@edd.ca.gov

■Information Officer II **Patti Roberts** ................. (916) 657-5125
E-mail: patti.roberts@edd.ca.gov

Administration Branch Deputy Director **Greg Williams** ... (916) 654-8187
E-mail: greg.williams@edd.ca.gov

Disability Insurance Branch Deputy Director **(Vacant)** .... (916) 654-8914

Information Technology Branch Deputy Director
**Gail Overhouse** ................................. (916) 653-8546
E-mail: gail.overhouse@edd.ca.gov

Policy Accountability and Compliance Branch Deputy
Director **Gregory Riggs** .......................... (916) 654-7014
E-mail: greg.riggs@edd.ca.gov

Public Affairs Branch Deputy Director **Loree Levy** ....... (916) 657-0694
E-mail: loree.levy@edd.ca.gov

Tax Branch Deputy Director **Lisa Wheeler** .............. (916) 653-1528
E-mail: lisa.wheeler@edd.ca.gov

Unemployment Insurance Branch Deputy Director
**Sabrina Reed** ................................... (916) 654-9140

# Department of Industrial Relations [DIR]

1515 Clay Street, 17th Floor, Oakland, CA 94612
Tel: (844) 286-7087  Fax: (510) 622-3265  E-mail: dirinfo@dir.ca.gov
Internet: www.dir.ca.gov

**Employees:** 2,790  **Fiscal Year:** 2015-2016  **Budget:** $619,691,000

■Director **Christine Baker** .......................... (510) 286-7087
E-mail: cbaker@dir.ca.gov

Communication Deputy Director **Erika Monterroza** ...... (510) 286-1161
E-mail: emonterroza@dir.ca.gov         Fax: (510) 286-1165

Special Counsel to the Director **John Cumming**
17th Floor ....................................... (510) 286-7087
E-mail: jcumming@dir.ca.gov

Administration Division Chief **Clifford Okamoto** ........ (510) 286-7087
E-mail: cokamoto@dir.ca.gov

Apprenticeship Standards Division Chief **Diane Ravnik** ... (415) 703-4920
E-mail: dravnik@dir.ca.gov

Labor Standards Enforcement Labor Commissioner
**Julie Su** ........................................ (415) 703-4810
E-mail: jsu@dir.ca.gov

■Special Counsel to the Labor Commissioner
**Christina Chung** ................................ (510) 622-3273
E-mail: cchung@dir.ca.gov

Chief Information Officer **Jim Culbeaux** ............... (510) 286-6801
E-mail: jculbeaux@dir.ca.gov

Office of Insurance Plans Chief **(Vacant)** .............. (916) 464-7000
11050 Olson Drive Suite, 230, Rancho Cordova, CA 95670

Chief Counsel **Christopher Jagard** .................... (510) 286-7087
E-mail: cjagard@dir.ca.gov

# Workers' Compensation Division [DWC]

Tel: (800) 736-7401

■Administrative Director **Destie Overpeck** .............. (510) 286-7100
E-mail: doverpeck@dir.ca.gov

Executive Medical Director **(Vacant)** .................. (800) 736-7401

# Natural Resources Agency

California Natural Resources Agency, 1725 23rd Street, Suite 1311,
Sacramento, CA 95816
Tel: (916) 653-5656  Fax: (916) 263-0648  Internet: www.resources.ca.gov

**Employees:** 19,214  **Fiscal Year:** 2015-2016  **Budget:** $4,882,750,000

■Secretary **John Laird** ............................... (916) 653-5656
E-mail: john.laird@resources.ca.gov

■Administrative Assistant **Kimberly Goncalves** ......... (916) 653-7310
E-mail: kimberly.goncalves@resources.ca.gov

■Undersecretary **Janelle Beland** ...................... (916) 653-5314
E-mail: janelle.beland@resources.ca.gov
Education: American River 1989

Deputy Secretary and General Counsel
**Thomas "Tom" Gibson** ........................... (916) 653-5481
E-mail: thomas.gibson@resources.ca.gov
Education: Lewis & Clark JD

■Assistant General Counsel **Heather Baugh** ............. (916) 653-8152
E-mail: heather.baugh@resources.ca.gov
Education: Arizona BA; U Pacific JD

■Communications Deputy Secretary **Nancy Vogel** ........ (916) 653-9402
E-mail: nancy.vogel@resources.ca.gov
Education: UC Berkeley BS

■Communications Associate Director **Samuel Chiu** ....... (916) 653-9402
E-mail: samuel.chiu@resources.ca.gov
Education: Stanford MPP

■Communications and Outreach Advisor **Erin Mellon** ...... (916) 653-5656

Climate Change and Energy Special Assistant
**J.R. Delarosa** ................................... (916) 651-7591
E-mail: jr.delarosa@resources.ca.gov

■Energy Deputy Secretary **Saúl Gómez** ................ (916) 653-5656

---

★ Elected Official   ■ Appointed by Governor   ● Appointed by Legislature     ▲ Appointed by Board or Commission     ◆ Appointed by State Supreme Court

■External Affairs Deputy Secretary **Todd Ferrara** . . . . . . . . . (916) 653-5792
  E-mail: todd.ferrara@resources.ca.gov
■Legislation Deputy Secretary **Kealii Bright** . . . . . . . . . . . . . (916) 654-2753
  E-mail: kealii.bright@resources.ca.gov
Ocean and Coastal Policy Deputy Secretary
  **Deborah Halberstadt** . . . . . . . . . . . . . . . . . . . . . . . . . . . (916) 653-5656
  E-mail: deborah.halberstadt@resources.ca.gov
■Ocean Protection Council Deputy Director **Amy Vierra** . . (916) 651-8738
  E-mail: amy.vierra@resources.ca.gov
Policy Implementation Deputy Secretary **(Vacant)** . . . . . . . . (916) 653-5656
Administration and Finance Assistant Secretary
  **Patrick Kemp** . . . . . . . . . . . . . . . . . . . . . . . . . . . . . . . . . (916) 653-5656
  E-mail: patrick.kemp@resources.ca.gov
Bonds and Grants Deputy Assistant Secretary
  **Bryan Cash** . . . . . . . . . . . . . . . . . . . . . . . . . . . . . . . . . . . (916) 653-6381
  E-mail: bryan.cash@resources.ca.gov
Bonds and Grants Deputy Assistant Secretary **Julie Alvis** . . (916) 653-9264
  E-mail: julie.alvis@resources.ca.gov
Federal Water Policy Assistant Secretary
  **Emanuel Joaquin Esquivel** . . . . . . . . . . . . . . . . . . . . . . (202) 624-5270
Chief Information Officer **Tim Garza** . . . . . . . . . . . . . . . . (916) 653-6931
  E-mail: tim.garza@resources.ca.gov

# Department of Conservation

801 K St., MS 24-01, Sacramento, CA 95814
TTY: (916) 324-2555  Fax: (916) 445-0732
Internet: www.conservation.ca.gov

**Employees:** 544  **Fiscal Year:** 2015-2016  **Budget:** $102,524,000

■Director **David A. Bunn** . . . . . . . . . . . . . . . . . . . . . . . . . . (916) 322-1080
  E-mail: dbunn@conservation.ca.gov
  Education: UC Davis MS, PhD
Chief Deputy Director **Jason Marshall** . . . . . . . . . . . . . . . (916) 322-1080
  E-mail: jason.marshall@conservation.ca.gov
Administration Division Deputy Director **Clayton Haas** . . . (916) 323-2950
  E-mail: clayton.haas@conservation.ca.gov
State Geologist **John G. Parrish** . . . . . . . . . . . . . . . . . . . . (916) 445-1923
State Mining and Geology Board Executive Officer
  **(Vacant)** . . . . . . . . . . . . . . . . . . . . . . . . . . . . . . . . . . . . . (916) 322-1082
                                                        Fax: (916) 445-0738
Communications Assistant Director **Teresa Schilling** . . . . . (916) 323-1886
  E-mail: teresa.schilling@conservation.ca.gov
Governmental and Environmental Relations Assistant
  Director **Benjamin Turner** . . . . . . . . . . . . . . . . . . . . . . . (916) 445-8733
  E-mail: benjamin.turner@conservation.ca.gov
  Education: UC Santa Barbara MA
Land Resource Protection Assistant Director
  **John Lowrie** . . . . . . . . . . . . . . . . . . . . . . . . . . . . . . . . . . (916) 324-0850
Mine Reclamation Assistant Director **Pat Perez** . . . . . . . . . (916) 323-9198
  E-mail: pat.perez@conservation.ca.gov
Chief Information Officer **Terese Matchim** . . . . . . . . . . . . (916) 324-2555
State Oil and Gas Supervisor **Ken Harris** . . . . . . . . . . . . . . (916) 445-9686
Special Assistant **Brady J. Van Engelen** . . . . . . . . . . . . . . (916) 323-0413
  E-mail: alan.vanengelen@conservation.ca.gov
Webmaster **Donald L. Drysdale** . . . . . . . . . . . . . . . . . . . . (916) 445-0633
  E-mail: donald.l.drysdale@conservation.ca.gov
Webmaster **Krista Watson** . . . . . . . . . . . . . . . . . . . . . . . . (916) 445-0608
  E-mail: krista.watson@conservation.ca.gov
Chief Counsel **Bruce Reeves** . . . . . . . . . . . . . . . . . . . . . . . (916) 323-6733

# Department of Fish and Wildlife [DFG]

Resources Building, 1416 Ninth Street, 12th Floor,
Sacramento, CA 95814
Tel: (916) 653-7667  Fax: (916) 653-7387

**Employees:** 2,541  **Fiscal Year:** 2015-2016  **Budget:** $486,470,000

■Director **Charlton H. "Chuck" Bonham** . . . . . . . . . . . . . (916) 653-7667
  E-mail: director@wildlife.ca.gov
  Administrative Assistant to the Director **Jan Ortiz** . . . . . . (916) 653-7667
  E-mail: jan.ortiz@wildlife.ca.gov
■Chief Deputy Director **Kevin Hunting** . . . . . . . . . . . . . . . (916) 653-7667
  E-mail: kevin.hunting@wildlife.ca.gov
  Administrative Assistant **Gem Laoyan** . . . . . . . . . . . . . . . (916) 653-7667
  ■Aquaculture Coordinator **Randolph Lovell** . . . . . . . . . . . (916) 445-2008
  E-mail: randy.lovell@wildlife.ca.gov

Wildlife Conservation Board Executive Director
  **John Donnelly** . . . . . . . . . . . . . . . . . . . . . . . . . . . . . . . . (916) 445-0137
  E-mail: john.donnelly@wildlife.ca.gov          Fax: (916) 323-0280
■General Counsel **Wendy Bogdan** . . . . . . . . . . . . . . . . . . . (916) 654-5295
  Administrative Deputy Director **Gabriel Tiffany** . . . . . . . . (916) 653-4425
  E-mail: gabe.tiffany@wildlife.ca.gov          Fax: (916) 651-8763
■Communications Deputy Director **Jordan Traverso** . . . . . . (916) 654-9937
  E-mail: jordan.traverso@wildlife.ca.gov
  Communications, Education and Outreach Assistant
  Director **Clark Blanchard** . . . . . . . . . . . . . . . . . . . . . . . (916) 657-4607
  E-mail: clark.blanchard@resources.ca.gov
Law Enforcement Division Deputy Director **David Bess** . . . (916) 657-4607
                                                        Fax: (916) 653-3772
■Legislation Deputy Director **Susan LaGrande** . . . . . . . . . . (916) 651-6719
  E-mail: susan.lagrande@wildlife.ca.gov
Ecosystem Conservation Division Deputy Director
  **Sandra Morey** . . . . . . . . . . . . . . . . . . . . . . . . . . . . . . . . (916) 653-4207
                                                        Fax: (916) 653-3673
Wildlife and Fisheries Division Deputy Director **(Vacant)** . . (916) 653-4207
                                                        Fax: (916) 653-9890
■Office of Oil Spill Prevention and Response
  Administrator **Thomas Cullen** . . . . . . . . . . . . . . . . . . . . (916) 445-9326
  E-mail: thomas.cullen@wildlife.ca.gov
  Education: US Coast Guard Acad 1983 BS; Purdue 1997 MS
■Office of Oil Spill Prevention and Response Assistant
  Administrator **(Vacant)** . . . . . . . . . . . . . . . . . . . . . . . . . (916) 445-9326

## Regional Offices

Region 1 Regional Manager **Neil Manji** . . . . . . . . . . . . . . . (530) 225-2360
  601 Locust Street, Redding, CA 96001        Fax: (530) 225-2381
Region 2 Sacramento Valley-Central Sierra Region
  Headquarters Regional Manager **Tina Bartlett** . . . . . . . . (916) 358-1075
  1701 Nimbus Rd., Ste. A,                    Fax: (916) 358-2912
  Rancho Cordova, CA 95670
Region 3 Bay Delta Regional Manager **Scott Wilson** . . . . . (707) 944-5518
  7329 Silverado Trail, Napa, CA 94558        Fax: (707) 944-5563
Region 4 Central Regional Manager **Julie Vance** . . (559) 243-4005 ext. 154
  1234 E. Shaw Avenue, Fresno, CA 93710       Fax: (559) 243-4022
Region 5 South Coast Region Headquarters Regional
  Manager **Edmond "Ed" Pert** . . . . . . . . . . . . . . . . . . . . . (858) 467-2702
  3883 Ruffin Road, San Diego, CA 92123       Fax: (858) 467-4299
Region 6 Inland Deserts Region Manager
  **Leslie MacNair** . . . . . . . . . . . . . . . . . . . . . . . . . . . . . . . (562) 799-3629
  3602 Inland Empire Boulevard, Suite C-220,  Fax: (909) 481-2945
  Ontario, CA 91764
Region 7 Marine Region Headquarters Regional Manager
  **Craig Shuman** . . . . . . . . . . . . . . . . . . . . . . . . . . . . . . . . (562) 342-7139
  20 Lower Ragsdale Drive, Suite 100,         Fax: (831) 649-2894
  Monterey, CA 93940

# California Department of Forestry and Fire Protection [CAL FIRE]

P.O. Box 944246, Sacramento, CA 94244-2460
1416 Ninth Street, Room 1505, Sacramento, CA 95814
Tel: (916) 653-5123  Fax: (916) 653-4171  Internet: www.fire.ca.gov

**Employees:** 7,451  **Fiscal Year:** 2015-2016  **Budget:** $1,773,154,000

■Director **Ken Pimlott** . . . . . . . . . . . . . . . . . . . . . . . . . . . (916) 653-7772
  E-mail: ken.pimlott@fire.ca.gov
■State Fire Marshal **Tonya L. Hoover** . . . . . . . . . . . . . . . . (916) 445-8200
  E-mail: tonya.hoover@fire.ca.gov
■Assistant State Fire Marshal **Michael "Mike" Richwine** . . .(916) 445-8200
■Chief Legal Counsel **Stephanie Shimazu** . . . . . . . . . . . . . (916) 653-4153
  E-mail: stephanie.shimazu@fire.ca.gov
  Education: UC Davis BA; San Francisco Law JD
Communications Director **Janet Upton** . . . . . . . . . . . . . . . (916) 653-7772
■Chief Deputy Director **Janet Barentson** . . . . . . . . . . . . . . (916) 653-7772
  E-mail: janet.barentson@fire.ca.gov
Fire Protection Deputy Director **Dave Teter, EMT-P** . . . . . .(916) 653-7772
■Legislation Deputy Director **Caroline Godkin** . . . . . . . . . . (916) 653-7772
  E-mail: caroline.godkin@fire.ca.gov
Management Services Deputy Director
  **Anthony P. "Tony" Favro** . . . . . . . . . . . . . . . . . . . . . . . (916) 653-7772
  E-mail: tony.favro@fire.ca.gov
  Education: Santa Clara U BA

*(continued on next page)*

---

★ Elected Official  ■ Appointed by Governor  ● Appointed by Legislature  ▲ Appointed by Board or Commission  ◆ Appointed by State Supreme Court

EXECUTIVE BRANCH

**California Department of Forestry and Fire Protection** *continued*

Resource Management Deputy Director **Helge Eng** . . . . . . . (916) 653-7772
  E-mail: helge.eng@fire.ca.gov
Equal Employment Opportunity Chief **Allison Lyman** . . . . (916) 653-5123

# Department of Parks and Recreation

1416 Ninth Street, Sacramento, CA 95814
Tel: (916) 653-6995  Fax: (916) 654-6374  E-mail: info@parks.ca.gov
Internet: www.parks.ca.gov

**Employees:** 3,878  **Fiscal Year:** 2015-2016  **Budget:** $630,935,000

■Director **Lisa Ann L. Mangat** . . . . . . . . . . . . . . . . . . . . . . . (916) 653-8380
  E-mail: lisa.mangat@parks.ca.gov
  Administrative Assistant **Lynn Black** . . . . . . . . . . . . . . . (916) 653-8380
Chief Deputy Director **Elizabeth McGuirk** . . . . . . . . . . . (916) 653-8380
  E-mail: liz.mcguirk@parks.ca.gov
■Chief Counsel **Tara Lynch** . . . . . . . . . . . . . . . . . . . . . . . . (916) 653-6884
  E-mail: tara.lynch@parks.ca.gov
  Education: McGeorge JD
Acquisitions and Development Deputy Director
  **Kathleen Amann** . . . . . . . . . . . . . . . . . . . . . . . . . . . . . .(916) 445-7961
  E-mail: kathleen.amann@parks.ca.gov
Administrative Services Division Deputy Director
  **Helen Carriker** . . . . . . . . . . . . . . . . . . . . . . . . . . . . . . .(916) 653-0528
  E-mail: helen.carriker@parks.ca.gov
External Affairs Deputy Director **Sedrick V. Mitchell** . . . . . (916) 653-8380
  Education: Cal State (Stanislaus) BA
■Public Affairs Deputy Director **Gloria Sandoval** . . . . . . . . (916) 653-8380
  E-mail: gloria.sandoval@parks.ca.gov
Legislation Deputy Director **Marivel Barajas** . . . . . . . . . . . (916) 653-8380
  E-mail: marivel.barajas@parks.ca.gov
■Off-Highway Motor Vehicle Recreation Deputy Director
  (Acting) **Maria Mowrey** . . . . . . . . . . . . . . . . . . . . . . . . (916) 324-5801
  E-mail: maria.mowrey@parks.ca.gov
Facilities Management Division Chief **Karl Knapp** . . . . . . . . (916) 324-0487
  E-mail: karl.knapp@parks.ca.gov
Natural Resources Division Chief **Jay Chamberlin** . . . . . . . (916) 653-9542
  E-mail: jay.chamberlin@parks.ca.gov
Marketing and Business Development (Acting)
  **Andy Vasquez** . . . . . . . . . . . . . . . . . . . . . . . . . . . . . . . (916) 653-7733
Northern Division Chief **Dana Jones** . . . . . . . . . . . . . . . . . (916) 657-4042
  E-mail: dana.jones@parks.ca.gov
Southern Division Chief **Brian Ketterer** . . . . . . . . . . . . . . (916) 657-4042
  E-mail: brian.ketterer@parks.ca.gov
Public Information Officer **Jeremiah Harvey** . . . . . . . . . (916) 653-7585

## Division of Boating and Waterways [DBW]

One Capitol Mall, Suite 500, Sacramento, CA 95814
Tel: (916) 327-1916  Tel: (888) 326-2822  Fax: (916) 327-1770
E-mail: pubinfo@parks.ca.gov  Internet: www.dbw.ca.gov

■Deputy Director **Lynn Sadler** . . . . . . . . . . . . . . . . . . . . . . .(916) 327-1776
  E-mail: lynn.sadler@parks.ca.gov
  Administrative Liaison **Jared Zucker** . . . . . . . . . . . . . . . . (916) 327-1777
  E-mail: jared.zucker@parks.ca.gov
Boating Operations Division Chief **Ramona Fernandez** . . . (916) 327-1823
Communications Information Officer **Dennis Weber** . . . . . .(916) 653-5115
  E-mail: dennis.waters@parks.ca.gov

## Department of Water Resources

1725 23rd Street, 11th Floor, Sacramento, CA 95816
P.O. Box 942836, Sacramento, CA 94236-0001
Tel: (916) 653-5791  Fax: (916) 653-5028

**Employees:** 3,496  **Fiscal Year:** 2015-2016  **Budget:** $3,826,022,000

■Director **Mark W. Cowin** . . . . . . . . . . . . . . . . . . . . . . . . . (916) 653-7007
  E-mail: mcowin@water.ca.gov
  Education: Stanford 1980 BSCE
  Administrative Assistant **Janiene Friend** . . . . . . . . . . . . (916) 653-7007
  Assistant Chief Deputy Director **Cindy Messer** . . . . . . . . (916) 653-5791
■State Water Project Chief Deputy Director
  **Carl Torgersen** . . . . . . . . . . . . . . . . . . . . . . . . . . . . . . . .(916) 653-6055
  E-mail: carlt@water.ca.gov
  Education: Cal State (Sacramento) BSME

Business Operations Deputy Director **Kathie Kishaba** . . . . (916) 654-9412
  E-mail: kkishaba@water.ca.gov
■Energy Resources Scheduling Division Deputy Director
  **John Pacheco** . . . . . . . . . . . . . . . . . . . . . . . . . . . . . . . . (916) 543-6812
  E-mail: jpacheco@water.ca.gov          Fax: (916) 574-2512
Integrated Water Management Deputy Director
  **Gary Bardini** . . . . . . . . . . . . . . . . . . . . . . . . . . . . . . . . (916) 653-8045
Special Initiatives Deputy Director **Taryn Ravazzini** . . . . . . (916) 653-5791
■State Water Project Deputy Director **(Vacant)** . . . . . . . . . (916) 653-8043
Statewide Emergency Preparedness and Security Deputy
  Director **Bill Croyle** . . . . . . . . . . . . . . . . . . . . . . . . . . . (916) 654-6135
  Education: Cal State (Sacramento) BS
■Legislative Affairs Assistant Director **Kasey Schimke** . . . . (916) 653-0488
  E-mail: kschimke@water.ca.gov
■Public Affairs Director **Ed Wilson** . . . . . . . . . . . . . . . . . .(916) 651-7512
                                          Fax: (916) 653-4684
■Public Affairs Deputy Assistant Director **(Vacant)** . . . . . . .(916) 651-7512
                                          Fax: (916) 653-4684
■Chief Counsel **Spencer Kenner** . . . . . . . . . . . . . . . . . . . . (916) 653-7084
  E-mail: skenner@water.ca.gov
Engineering Division Chief **Jeanne Kuttel** . . . . . . . . . . . . . (916) 653-3927
Environmental Services Division Chief **Dean Messer** . . . . . (916) 651-0168
Flood Management Division Chief **Keith Swanson** . . . . . . . (916) 574-0601
Management Services Division Chief **Kim Oliphint** . . . . . . (916) 653-4827
Operations and Maintenance Division Chief
  **David Starks** . . . . . . . . . . . . . . . . . . . . . . . . . . . . . . . . (530) 534-2370
Planning and Local Assistance Division Chief
  **Kamyar Guivetchi** . . . . . . . . . . . . . . . . . . . . . . . . . . . . (916) 653-3937
  901 P Street, Sacramento, CA 95814
Safety of Dams Division Chief **David Gutierrez** . . . . . . . . . (916) 227-4660
  2200 X Street, Sacramento, CA 95818
Technology Services Division Chief **Tim Garza** . . . . . . . . . (916) 653-8364
Bay-Delta Office Chief **Paul Marshall** . . . . . . . . . . . . . . . (916) 653-1099
  Education: Cal State (Sacramento) 1988 MSCE
Fiscal Services Office Chief **Perla Netto-Brown** . . . . . . . . (916) 653-9836
State Water Project Analysis Office Chief **(Vacant)** . . . . . . (916) 653-4313

# Energy Resources Conservation and Development Commission

1516 Ninth Street, MS-29, Sacramento, CA 95814-5512
Tel: (916) 654-4930  Fax: (916) 654-3478
E-mail: mediaoffice@energy.ca.gov  Internet: www.energy.ca.gov

**Employees:** 670  **Fiscal Year:** 2015-2016  **Budget:** $422,944,000

■Chairman **Robert B. Weisenmiller, PhD** . . . . . . . . . . . . . . (916) 654-5036
■Commissioner **Karen Douglas, JD** . . . . . . . . . . . . . . . . . .(916) 654-4930
  Education: Colorado 1998 MPP; Stanford 2001 JD
■Commissioner **David Hochschild** . . . . . . . . . . . . . . . . . . . (916) 654-3992
  Education: Swarthmore BA; JFK School Govt MPP
■Commissioner **Andrew McAllister** . . . . . . . . . . . . . . . . . . (916) 654-3787
  Education: UC Berkeley MS
■Commissioner **Janea Ashanti Scott** . . . . . . . . . . . . . . . . . .(916) 654-4930
  E-mail: janea.scott@energy.ca.gov
  Education: Stanford 1996 BA; Colorado 2000 JD

# California Conservation Corps

1719 24th Street, Sacramento, CA 95816
Tel: (916) 341-3100  Internet: www.ccc.ca.gov

**Employees:** 351  **Fiscal Year:** 2015-2016  **Budget:** $100,538,000

■Director **Bruce Saito** . . . . . . . . . . . . . . . . . . . . . . . . . . . .(916) 341-3207
  E-mail: bruce.saito@ccc.ca.gov
Chief Counsel **Jeffrey Schwarzschild** . . . . . . . . . . . . . . . . (916) 341-3133
External Affairs Director **Martha Diepenbrock** . . . . . . . . . .(916) 341-3105
Chief Deputy Director **Amy Cameron** . . . . . . . . . . . . . . . . (916) 321-3233
Energy Program Development Director
  **William McNamara** . . . . . . . . . . . . . . . . . . . . . . . . . . . (916) 341-3100
  Education: Northeastern 1973 (Attended)
Administrative Division Chief **Dawne Bortolazzo** . . . . . . . .(916) 341-3137
  E-mail: dawne.bortolazzo@ccc.ca.gov
Regional Deputy - Region 1 **Virginia Clark** . . . . . . . . . . . . (916) 341-3147
Regional Deputy - Region 2 **Larry Notheis** . . . . . . . . . . . . (916) 341-3141
Program Development Chief **Martha Diepenbrock** . . . . . . . (916) 341-3105

---

Information Systems Manager **Rita Gass** . . . . . . . . . . . . . (916) 341-3244
E-mail: rita.gass@ccc.ca.gov
Public Information Officer **Susanne Levitsky** . . . . . . . . . . (916) 341-3145

# Coastal Conservancy
1330 Broadway, 13th Floor, Oakland, CA 94612
Tel: (510) 286-1015  Fax: (510) 286-0470  Internet: www.scc.ca.gov

**Employees:** 65  **Fiscal Year:** 2015-2016  **Budget:** $75,226,000

Executive Officer **Samuel "Sam" Schuchat** . . . . . . . . . . .(510) 286-0523
E-mail: sam.schuchat@scc.ca.gov
Education: Williams 1983 BA; San Francisco State U 1989 MA
Chief Deputy Executive Officer **Mary Small** . . . . . . . . . . . (510) 286-4176
E-mail: mary.small@scc.ca.gov
Deputy Executive Officer **Amy Hutzel** . . . . . . . . . . . . . . . (510) 286-4181
E-mail: amy.hutzel@scc.ca.gov

# California State Transportation Agency
915 Capitol Mall, Suite 350-B, Sacramento, CA 95814
Tel: (916) 323-5400  Internet: www.calsta.ca.gov

■Secretary **Brian P. Kelly** . . . . . . . . . . . . . . . . . . . . . . . . . . (916) 323-5401
E-mail: brian.kelly@calsta.ca.gov
■Undersecretary **Brian C. Annis** . . . . . . . . . . . . . . . . . . . . . (916) 323-5485
E-mail: brian.annis@calsta.ca.gov
Education: U Washington MA
Assistant Secretary for Rail and Ports **Ben De Alba** . . . . . . (916) 324-7516
Deputy Secretary for Communications and Strategic
Planning **Melissa Figueroa** . . . . . . . . . . . . . . . . . . . . . .(916) 445-3545
E-mail: melissa.figueroa@calsta.ca.gov
Education: Cal Poly San Luis Obispo 2002 BS
Deputy Secretary and General Counsel **Alicia Fowler** . . . . . (916) 324-7501
Deputy Secretary for Environmental Policy and Housing
Coordination **Kate White** . . . . . . . . . . . . . . . . . . . . . . . . (916) 324-7505
Deputy Secretary for Legislation **Ronda Paschal** . . . . . . . . (916) 323-5416
E-mail: ronda.paschal@calsta.ca.gov
■Deputy Secretary of Policy Coordination
**Carol D. Farris** Suite 350 . . . . . . . . . . . . . . . . . . . . . . . .(916) 323-5401
E-mail: carol.farris@calsta.ca.gov
■Deputy Secretary for Budget and Finance **Russia Chavis** . . (916) 327-3370
E-mail: russia.chavis@calsta.ca.gov
Education: USC MPP

# Department of Motor Vehicles [DMV]
2415 First Avenue, Sacramento, CA 94232
P.O. Box 932382, Sacramento, CA 94232-3820
Fax: (916) 657-5716  Internet: www.dmv.ca.gov

**Employees:** 8,209  **Fiscal Year:** 2015-2016  **Budget:** $1,112,383,000

■Director **Jean M. Shiomoto** . . . . . . . . . . . . . . . . . . . . . . . . .(916) 657-6941
E-mail: jean.shiomoto@dmv.ca.gov
■Chief Deputy Director **Bill Davidson** . . . . . . . . . . . . . . . . . (916) 657-6940
E-mail: bill.davidson@dmv.ca.gov
Administrative Services Deputy Director **Pam Mizukami** . . (916) 657-6486
E-mail: pam.mizukami@dmv.ca.gov
Communications/Public Affairs Deputy Director
**Armando Botello** . . . . . . . . . . . . . . . . . . . . . . . . . . . . . . . (916) 657-6437
E-mail: armando.botello@dmv.ca.gov
Communication Programs Division Deputy Director
**Rico Rubiono** . . . . . . . . . . . . . . . . . . . . . . . . . . . . . . . . . .(916) 657-7722
Enterprise Risk Management Deputy Director
**Bernard C. Soriano** . . . . . . . . . . . . . . . . . . . . . . . . . . . . .(916) 657-7626
E-mail: bernard.soriano@dmv.ca.gov
Field Operations Deputy Director **Bill Davidson** . . . . . . . . (916) 657-7061
Legislative Deputy Director (Acting) **Patrick Barrett** . . . . . .(916) 657-6518
E-mail: patrick.barrettpatrick@dmv.ca.gov
Information Systems Division Deputy Director
**Stacy Cockrum** . . . . . . . . . . . . . . . . . . . . . . . . . . . . . . . . (916) 657-8762
E-mail: stacy.cockrum@dmv.ca.gov
Education: Cal State (Sacramento) 2000
Investigations Deputy Director **Frank Alvarez** . . . . . . . . . . (916) 657-8377
Deputy Director and Chief Counsel **Brian Soublet** . . . . . . .(916) 323-5400
Registration Operations Deputy Director **Kathleen Rose** . . (916) 657-8135
E-mail: kathleen.rose@dmv.ca.gov

■Special Projects Deputy Director **(Vacant)** . . . . . . . . . . . . . (916) 654-5266
■Strategic Planning and Policy Deputy Director
**Mike McGowan** . . . . . . . . . . . . . . . . . . . . . . . . . . . . . . . .(916) 654-5266
E-mail: mike.mcgowan@dmv.ca.gov
Audits Chief **David Saika** . . . . . . . . . . . . . . . . . . . . . . . . . (916) 657-6480
■Chief of Enterprise Planning and Performance
**Stephanie Dougherty** . . . . . . . . . . . . . . . . . . . . . . . . . . . (916) 657-8814
E-mail: stephanie.dougherty@dmv.ca.gov
Chief Privacy Officer **(Vacant)** . . . . . . . . . . . . . . . . . . . . . .(916) 657-6626

## Licensing Operations Division
Deputy Director **Wesley Goo** . . . . . . . . . . . . . . . . . . . . . . . (916) 657-6721
Driver Licensing Branch Chief **Coleen Solomon** . . . . . . . . (916) 657-8504
Driver Safety Branch Chief **Ila Parisek** . . . . . . . . . . . . . . . (916) 657-7023
Occupational Licensing Branch Chief **Timothy Corcoran** . . (916) 657-7464

# California Department of Transportation [CALTRANS]
1120 N Street, Sacramento, CA 95814
Tel: (916) 654-5266  Fax: (916) 653-5776  Internet: www.dot.ca.gov

**Employees:** 39,070  **Fiscal Year:** 2015-2016  **Budget:** $10,494,654,000

■Director **Malcolm Dougherty** . . . . . . . . . . . . . . . . . . . . . . .(916) 654-6130
E-mail: malcolm.dougherty@dot.ca.gov
Education: Rutgers 1991 BSCE
Administrative Assistant **Shari Mannering** . . . . . . . . . . . . (916) 654-5267
■Chief Deputy Director **Kome Ajise** . . . . . . . . . . . . . . . . . . .(916) 654-5791
E-mail: kome.ajise@dmv.ca.gov
Administrative Assistant **JoAnne Valdivia** . . . . . . . . . . . . (916) 654-4852
Chief Counsel **Jean Scherer** . . . . . . . . . . . . . . . . . . . . . . . (916) 654-2630
Chief of Staff **Dara Wheeler** . . . . . . . . . . . . . . . . . . . . . . . (916) 654-3660
Administration Deputy Director **Christina "Cris" Rojas** . . . (916) 654-3910
E-mail: cris.rojas@dot.ca.gov
Audits and Investigations Assistant Deputy Director
**William E. Lewis** . . . . . . . . . . . . . . . . . . . . . . . . . . . . . . .(916) 323-7112
E-mail: william.lewis@dot.ca.gov
■External Affairs Deputy Director **Will Shuck** . . . . . . . . . . . (916) 653-5451
E-mail: will.shuck@dot.ca.gov
Legislative Affairs Assistant Deputy Director
**Melanie Perron** . . . . . . . . . . . . . . . . . . . . . . . . . . . . . . . . (916) 654-2936
E-mail: melanie.perron@dot.ca.gov
■Public Affairs Assistant Deputy Director
**Tamie McGowen** . . . . . . . . . . . . . . . . . . . . . . . . . . . . . . . .(916) 654-8782
E-mail: tamie.mcgowen@dot.ca.gov
Chief Information Officer **George Akiyama** . . . . . . . . . . . . .(916) 654-6282
E-mail: george.akiyama@dot.ca.gov
Chief Engineer **Karla Sutliff** . . . . . . . . . . . . . . . . . . . . . . . (916) 654-4923

## Business and Economic Opportunity
Deputy Director (Acting) **Janice Salais** . . . . . . . . . . . . . . . (916) 324-0449

## Finance
Deputy Director/Chief Financial Officer **Norma Ortega** . . . (916) 654-5429
Accounting Services Division Chief **Clark Paulsen** . . . . . . . (916) 227-9000
P.O. Box 942874, Sacramento, CA 94274
Budgets Division Chief **Steven Keck** . . . . . . . . . . . . . . . . . (916) 654-4556
Transportation Programming Division Chief
**Bruce de Terra** . . . . . . . . . . . . . . . . . . . . . . . . . . . . . . . . (916) 654-4013

## Maintenance and Operations
Deputy Director **Steve Takigawa** . . . . . . . . . . . . . . . . . . . . (916) 654-6823
Maintenance Division Chief **Tony Tavares** . . . . . . . . . . . . . (916) 654-5849
E-mail: tony.tavares@dot.ca.gov
Equipment Services Division Chief **Larry Orcutt** . . . . . . . . (916) 227-9600
P.O. Box 160048, Sacramento, CA 95816
E-mail: larry.orcutt@dot.ca.gov
Research and Innovation Division Chief
**Dr. James R. "Jim" Appleton** . . . . . . . . . . . . . . . . . . . . . (916) 654-8877
E-mail: james.appleton@dot.ca.gov
Education: Wheaton (IL) 1958 BA; Michigan 1965 MA, 1965 PhD
Traffic Operations Division Chief **Tom Hallenbeck** . . . . . . . (916) 654-2352

★ Elected Official   ■ Appointed by Governor   ● Appointed by Legislature   ▲ Appointed by Board or Commission   ◆ Appointed by State Supreme Court

*State Yellow Book*           © Leadership Directories, Inc.           Summer 2016

## Planning and Modal Programs

1120 N Street, Sacramento, CA 95814
Tel: (916) 654-6592  Fax: (916) 654-6608

■Deputy Director **Coco Briseno** . . . . . . . . . . . . . . . . . . . . . . (916) 654-6592
   E-mail: coco.brisneo@dot.ca.gov
Aeronautics Division Chief **Gary Cathey** . . . . . . . . . . . . . . (916) 654-5470
Local Assistance Division Chief **Rihui Zhang** . . . . . . . . . . (916) 653-1776
   E-mail: rihui_zhang@dot.ca.gov
Rail and Mass Transportation Division Chief
   **Bruce Roberts** . . . . . . . . . . . . . . . . . . . . . . . . . . . . . . . . (916) 654-6542
Research, Innovation and System Information Division
   Chief **Dr. James R. "Jim" Appleton** . . . . . . . . . . . . . (916) 654-6228
   E-mail: james.appleton@dot.ca.gov
Transportation Planning Division Chief **Katie Benouar** . . . .(916) 653-1818
   E-mail: katie_benouar@dot.ca.gov

## Project Delivery

Fax: (916) 653-6456

Project Management Division Chief **James "Jim" Davis** . .(916) 654-2494
   E-mail: james_davis@dot.ca.gov
Construction Division Chief **Rachel Falsetti** . . . . . . . . . . . (916) 654-2157
   E-mail: rachel.falsetti@dot.ca.gov
Design Division Chief **Tim Craggs** . . . . . . . . . . . . . . . . . . . (916) 654-3858
Engineering Services Division Chief **Mike Keever** . . . . . . . (916) 227-8800
   P.O. Box 942874, Sacramento, CA 94274
   E-mail: mike.keever@dot.ca.gov
Environmental Analysis Division Chief **Katrina Pierce** . . . . (916) 653-7136
Right of Way Division Chief **Jennifer Lowden** . . . . . . . . . . (916) 654-5075

## California High Speed Rail Authority

770 L Street, Suite 800, Sacramento, CA 95814
Tel: (916) 324-1541  Fax: (916) 322-0827
Internet: www.cahighspeedrail.ca.gov

**Employees:** 151  **Fiscal Year:** 2015-2016  **Budget:** $3,088,986,000

●Chair **Dan Richard** . . . . . . . . . . . . . . . . . . . . . . . . . . . . . . . (916) 324-1541
■Vice Chair **Thomas Richards** . . . . . . . . . . . . . . . . . . . . . . . (916) 324-1541
●Member **Jose Luis "Lou" Correa, JD** . . . . . . . . . . . . . . . (916) 324-1541
   Education: Cal State (Fullerton) BEc; UCLA MBA, JD
●Member **Daniel Curtin** . . . . . . . . . . . . . . . . . . . . . . . . . . . . (916) 324-1541
●Member **Bonnie Lowenthal** . . . . . . . . . . . . . . . . . . . . . . . . (916) 324-1541
●Member **Lorraine Paskett** . . . . . . . . . . . . . . . . . . . . . . . . . (916) 324-1541
■Member **Michael E. Rossi** . . . . . . . . . . . . . . . . . . . . . . . . . (916) 324-1541
■Member **The Honorable Lynn Schenk** . . . . . . . . . . . . . . . (916) 324-1541
   E-mail: lynn.schenk@hsr.ca.gov
   Education: UCLA 1967 BA; San Diego 1970 JD
●Member **(Vacant)** . . . . . . . . . . . . . . . . . . . . . . . . . . . . . . . . . (916) 324-1541

## Executive Staff

▲Chief Executive Officer **Jeffrey "Jeff" Morales** . . . . . . . . . (916) 324-1541
   E-mail: jeff.morales@hsr.ca.gov
Chief Deputy Director **Dennis A. Trujillo** . . . . . . . . . . . . . . (916) 324-1541
Planning and Integration Director **Melissa DuMond** . . . . . .(916) 324-1541
   Education: North Carolina Wilmington
Chief Counsel **Thomas "Tom" Fellenz** . . . . . . . . . . . . . . . (916) 324-1541
Assistant Chief Counsel **James Andrew** . . . . . . . . . . . . . . (916) 324-1541
   E-mail: james.andrew@hsr.ca.gov
▲Chief Administrative Officer **Deborah Harper** . . . . . . . . . . (916) 324-1541
   E-mail: deborah.harper@hsr.ca.gov
Chief Engineer **Scott Jarvis** . . . . . . . . . . . . . . . . . . . . . . . . (916) 324-1541
Engineering Director **Kevin Thompson** . . . . . . . . . . . . . . . . (916) 324-1541
   Education: Arizona State 1983 BE
Operations and Maintenance Director **Bruce Armistead** . . .(916) 324-1541
Real Property Director **Alan Glen** . . . . . . . . . . . . . . . . . . . . (916) 324-1541
Multimedia Manager **Justin Chechourka** . . . . . . . . . . . . . . (916) 324-1541
Senior Legislative Analyst **William Robinson** . . . . . . . . . . . (916) 324-1541
   E-mail: william.robinson@hsr.ca.gov
Communications Chief **Lisa Marie Alley** . . . . . . . . . . . . . . (916) 324-1541
   E-mail: lisa.alley@hsr.ca.gov

## Office of Traffic Safety

2208 Kausen Drive, Suite 300, Elk Grove, CA 95758
Tel: (916) 509-3030  Fax: (916) 509-3055  E-mail: contactots@ots.ca.gov
Internet: www.ots.ca.gov

Director **Rhonda Craft** . . . . . . . . . . . . . . . . . . . . . . . . . . . . (916) 509-3066
   E-mail: rhonda.craft@ots.ca.gov
   Secretary to the Director **Lisa Baker** . . . . . . . . . . . . . . (916) 509-3038
   E-mail: lisa.baker@ots.ca.gov
Public Information Officer **Christopher Cochran** . . . . . . . . (916) 509-3063
   E-mail: chris.cochran@ots.ca.gov
Administration Assistant Director **Robert Nelson** . . . . . . . . (916) 509-3030
   E-mail: robert.nelson@ots.ca.gov

## California Highway Patrol [CHP]

601 North 7th Street, Sacramento, CA 95811
P.O. Box 942898, Sacramento, CA 94298-0001
Tel: (916) 843-3000  TTY: (800) 735-2929  Fax: (916) 843-3264
Internet: www.chp.ca.gov

**Employees:** 11,053  **Fiscal Year:** 2015-2016  **Budget:** $2,390,641,000

■Commissioner **Joseph A. Farrow** . . . . . . . . . . . . . . . . . . . (916) 843-3001
   E-mail: jfarrow@chp.ca.gov
   Education: Cal State (Sacramento) BA; San Diego State MA
Deputy Commissioner **Warren Stanley** . . . . . . . . . . . . . . . (916) 843-3001
   Administrative Assistant **James Mann** . . . . . . . . . . . . . (916) 843-3001
Assistant Commissioner **Scott Silbee** . . . . . . . . . . . . . . . . (916) 843-3002
   Executive Assistant **Jim Jacobs** . . . . . . . . . . . . . . . . . . (916) 843-3004
   Executive Assistant **Tom McCreary** . . . . . . . . . . . . . . . (818) 240-8200
Staff Assistant Commissioner **Capt. Avery A. Browne** . . . .(916) 843-3004
   Executive Assistant **Brent Newman** . . . . . . . . . . . . . . . (916) 843-3003
Employee Relations Office Commander **Ryan Okashima** . . (916) 843-3100
Media Relations Office Commander
   **Capt. Joshua Brooke Ehlers** . . . . . . . . . . . . . . . . . . . . (916) 843-3310
                                                   Fax: (916) 657-8639
Administrative Services Division Chief **Bob Jones** . . . . . . . (916) 843-3500
   E-mail: bjones@chp.ca.gov
Enforcement and Planning Division Chief
   **Robert Maynard** . . . . . . . . . . . . . . . . . . . . . . . . . . . . . . (916) 843-3330
   E-mail: rmaynard@chp.ca.gov
Information Management Division Chief
   **Scott R. Howland** . . . . . . . . . . . . . . . . . . . . . . . . . . . . . (916) 843-4000
   E-mail: showland@chp.ca.gov
Protective Services Division Deputy Chief
   **Assistant Chief Chris Main** . . . . . . . . . . . . . . . .(916) 323-1514 ext. 451
   Executive Assistant **Greg Klingenberg** . . . . . . . . . . . . . (916) 843-3005
Legislation Coordinator **Richard Desmond** . . . . . . . . . . . . (916) 843-3200
   E-mail: rdesmond@chp.ca.gov
Headquarters Librarian **Mary Guido** . . . . . . . . . . . . . . . . . (916) 843-3464
Special Counsel **Susan Mosier** . . . . . . . . . . . . . . . . . . . . . (916) 843-3050

## California Transportation Commission [CTC]

1120 N Street, MS-52, Sacramento, CA 95814
Tel: (916) 654-4245  Fax: (916) 653-2134  Internet: www.catc.ca.gov

**Employees:** 18  **Fiscal Year:** 2015-2016  **Budget:** $28,831,000

■Chair **Robert "Bob" Alvarado** . . . . . . . . . . . . . . . . . . . . . (916) 654-4245
   Term Expires: February 1, 2018
■Vice Chair **Frances Lee "Fran" Inman** . . . . . . . . . . . . . . (916) 654-4245
   Term Expires: February 1, 2018
■Commissioner **Yvonne Brathwaite Burke** . . . . . . . . . . . . (916) 654-4245
   Term Expires: February 1, 2017
   Education: UCLA 1953 BA; USC 1956 JD
■Commissioner **Lucetta A. "Lucy" Dunn** . . . . . . . . . . . . . (916) 654-4245
   Term Expires: February 1, 2020
   Education: Cal State (Fullerton) BA; Western State U San Diego JD
■Commissioner **James Earp** . . . . . . . . . . . . . . . . . . . . . . . (916) 654-4245
   Term Expires: February 1, 2019
■Commissioner **James C. Ghielmetti** . . . . . . . . . . . . . . . . (916) 654-4245
   Term Expires: January 1, 2016
   Education: Denver BS
■Commissioner **Carl Guardino** . . . . . . . . . . . . . . . . . . . . . (916) 654-4245
   Term Expires: February 1, 2019
   Education: San José State BA

---

★ Elected Official   ■ Appointed by Governor   ● Appointed by Legislature   ▲ Appointed by Board or Commission   ◆ Appointed by State Supreme Court

● Commissioner **Christine Kehoe** . . . . . . . . . . . . . . . . (916) 654-4245
   Term Expires: January 1, 2020
■ Commissioner **James Madaffer** . . . . . . . . . . . . . . . . (916) 654-4245
   Term Expires: February 1, 2019
■ Commissioner **Joseph Tavaglione** . . . . . . . . . . . . . . (916) 654-4245
   Term Expires: February 1, 2017
■ Commissioner **(Vacant)** . . . . . . . . . . . . . . . . . . . . . . (916) 654-4245
   Ex Officio **James T. "Jim" Beall, Jr.** . . . . . . . . . . . . (916) 654-4245
   Education: San José State BA
   Ex Officio **Jim Frazier** . . . . . . . . . . . . . . . . . . . . . . (916) 654-4245

## Executive Staff

▲ Executive Director **Susan Bransen** . . . . . . . . . . . . . (916) 654-4245
   E-mail: susan.bransen@dot.ca.gov
Chief Deputy Director **(Vacant)** . . . . . . . . . . . . . . . . (916) 654-4245
Deputy Director **Garth Hopkins** . . . . . . . . . . . . . . . . (916) 653-3148
Deputy Director **Laurel Janssen** . . . . . . . . . . . . . . . . (916) 651-6145
Deputy Director **Eric Thronson** . . . . . . . . . . . . . . . . (916) 654-7179
Deputy Director **Mitchell Weiss** . . . . . . . . . . . . . . . . (916) 653-2072
Deputy Director and Chief Engineer **Stephen Maller** . . . . . (916) 653-2070
   E-mail: stephen.maller@dot.ca.gov
Assistant Deputy Director **Dawn Cheser** . . . . . . . . . (916) 653-7665
Assistant Deputy Director **Teresa Favila** . . . . . . . . . (916) 653-2064
Assistant Deputy Director **Jose Oseguera** . . . . . . . . (916) 654-4245
Associate Deputy Director **Laura Pennebaker** . . . . . . . . (916) 653-7121
Associate Deputy Director **Laurie Waters** . . . . . . . . . (916) 651-6145
Administrative Officer **Rosemary Mejia** . . . . . . . . . . . (916) 653-2128
   E-mail: rosemary.mejia@dot.ca.gov
Associate Governmental Program Analyst
   **Anne Johnson** . . . . . . . . . . . . . . . . . . . . . . . . . . . (916) 653-2096
   E-mail: anne.johnson@dot.ca.gov
Associate Governmental Program Analyst
   **Douglas Remedios** . . . . . . . . . . . . . . . . . . . . . . . (916) 653-2066
   E-mail: douglas.remedios@dot.ca.gov
Associate Governmental Program Analyst
   **Deborah Trujillo-Mckee** . . . . . . . . . . . . . . . . . . . (916) 653-3159
   E-mail: deborah.mckee@dot.ca.gov
Administrative Assistant **Jennifer Velasco** . . . . . . . . . . (916) 653-2094
   E-mail: jennifer.velasco@dot.ca.gov

## Department of Corrections and Rehabilitation [CDCR]

1515 S Street, Sacramento, CA 95811-7243
P.O. Box 942883, Sacramento, CA 94283-0001
Tel: (916) 323-6001  Fax: (916) 442-2637  Internet: www.cdcr.ca.gov

**Employees:** 59,937  **Fiscal Year:** 2015-2016  **Budget:** $10,699,939,000

■ Secretary **Scott Kernan** . . . . . . . . . . . . . . . . . . . . . (916) 323-6001
   E-mail: scott.kernan@cdcr.ca.gov
   Administrative Assistant **Kathy Gaddi** . . . . . . . . . . . (916) 341-7010
   Special Assistant to the Secretary
   **Maricarmen Peoples** . . . . . . . . . . . . . . . . . . . . . (916) 323-6001
   Health Care Services Undersecretary **Diana Toche, DDS** . . (916) 323-6001
   E-mail: diana.toche@cdcr.ca.gov
   Education: Fresno Pacific BA; U Pacific DDS
   Operations Undersecretary **Ralph M. Diaz** . . . . . . . . . (916) 323-6001
   Office of Public and Employee Communications Assistant
   Secretary **Jeffrey Callison** . . . . . . . . . . . . . . . . . . . (916) 323-6001
   E-mail: jeffrey.callison@cdcr.ca.gov
■ External Communications Deputy Assistant Secretary
   (Acting) **Albert Rivas** . . . . . . . . . . . . . . . . . . . . . . (916) 445-4950
   Education: UC Davis 2003 BS
■ Administration and Offender Services Undersecretary
   **Kenneth Pogue** . . . . . . . . . . . . . . . . . . . . . . . . . . (916) 323-6001
   E-mail: kenneth.pogue@cdcr.ca.gov
■ Legislative Affairs Assistant Secretary
   **Kristoffer Applegate** . . . . . . . . . . . . . . . . . . . . . . (916) 445-4737
   Education: McGeorge JD
   Superintendent of Education, Juvenile Programs Division
   **Tami Mckee-Sani** . . . . . . . . . . . . . . . . . . . . . . . . (916) 324-5018
■ Correctional Safety Chief **Derrick Marion** . . . . . . . . . (916) 327-3268
   Rehabilitative Programs Division Director **Jay Virbel** . . . . . (916) 323-6001

Enterprise Information Services Director
   **Russell "Russ" Nichols** . . . . . . . . . . . . . . . . . . . . (916) 358-2318
   E-mail: russ.nichols@cdcr.ca.gov
   Education: Cal State (Sacramento) 1993 BS
Facilities, Construction, and Management Director
   **Deborah Hysen** . . . . . . . . . . . . . . . . . . . . . . . . . (916) 255-2601
Internal Oversight and Research Director **Bryan Beyer** . . . . (916) 324-5305
Juvenile Justice Director **Michael "Mike" Minor** . . . . . . (916) 322-5333
■ Statewide Dental Director **Morton Rosenberg** . . . . . . . . (916) 323-2848
   E-mail: morton.rosenberg@cdcr.ca.gov
■ Correctional Health Care Services Division Director
   **(Vacant)** . . . . . . . . . . . . . . . . . . . . . . . . . . . . . . (916) 445-1116
   Audits and Compliance Deputy Director **L. D. Zamora** . . . . (916) 358-2621
   E-mail: lori.zamora@cdcr.ca.gov
■ Internal Affairs Deputy Director **David Grant** . . . . . . . . (916) 255-0860
   E-mail: david.grant@cdcr.ca.gov
   Facility Planning, Construction, and Management Deputy
   Director **Dean Borg** . . . . . . . . . . . . . . . . . . . . . . . (916) 255-2601
■ Fiscal Services Deputy Director **Jason Lopez** . . . . . . . . . (916) 323-0218
   Juvenile Programs Division Deputy Director
   **Anthony Lucero** . . . . . . . . . . . . . . . . . . . . . . . . . (916) 324-4217
■ Rehabilitative Programs Deputy Director **Kevin Hoffman** . . (916) 323-2848
   E-mail: kevin.hoffman@cdcr.ca.gov
   Research Office Deputy Director **Wayne Babby** . . . . . . . . (916) 323-2919
   E-mail: wayne.babby@cdcr.ca.gov
■ Budget Management Associate Director **Jason Lopez** . . . . . (916) 323-2848
   E-mail: jason.lopez@cdcr.ca.gov
■ High Security Institutions Associate Director (Acting)
   **Sandra Alfaro** . . . . . . . . . . . . . . . . . . . . . . . . . . (916) 445-2165
■ Contract Beds Unit Chief **Joe Moss** . . . . . . . . . . . . . (916) 255-2601
   E-mail: joseph.moss@cdcr.ca.gov
■ Labor Relations Chief **(Vacant)** . . . . . . . . . . . . . . . . (916) 445-1008
■ Policy Standardization Chief **Natalie Fransham** . . . . . . . (916) 324-4214
   E-mail: natalie.fransham@cdcr.ca.gov
   Office of Victim Services Chief **Nolice Edwards** . . . . . . (916) 323-4185
   Ombudsman Office Chief **Sara Malone** . . . . . . . . . . . (916) 445-1748
■ Legal Affairs Assistant Secretary **Patrick McKinney II** . . . . (916) 323-6001
   Education: Hastings JD
   Chief Deputy General Counsel **Howard E. Moseley** . . . . . (916) 323-6001
   Chief Deputy General Counsel **Simone Renteria** . . . . . . . (916) 323-6001
   Education: Southwestern Law JD
■ Inspector General **Robert A. Barton** . . . . . . . . . . . . . (916) 323-2848
   E-mail: robert.barton@cdcr.ca.gov
   Education: UC Davis JD
   Information Security Officer **(Vacant)** . . . . . . . . . . . . (916) 358-1959
■ Press Secretary of Media Relations **Vicky Waters** . . . . . . (916) 445-4950
   E-mail: vicky.waters@cdcr.ca.gov

## Division of Administrative Services
Director **Alene Shimazu** . . . . . . . . . . . . . . . . . . . . . . (916) 323-6001
   E-mail: alene.shimazu@cdcr.ca.gov

## Division of Adult Institutions
■ Adult Institutions Division Director **Kathleen Allison** . . . . (916) 445-7688
   E-mail: kathleen.allison@cdcr.ca.gov
■ Facility Operations Deputy Director **Connie Gipson** . . . . . (916) 445-7688
   E-mail: connie.gipson@cdcr.ca.gov
■ Facility Support Deputy Director **Jeffrey Macomber** . . . . . (916) 327-9523
   E-mail: jeffrey.macomber@cdcr.ca.gov
■ Reception Center Institutions Associate Director
   **Amy Miller** . . . . . . . . . . . . . . . . . . . . . . . . . . . . (916) 323-4108
   E-mail: amy.miller@cdcr.ca.gov
■ Female Offender Programs Associate Director **(Vacant)** . . . (916) 322-8055

## Department of Finance
State Capitol, Room 1145, Sacramento, CA 95814
Tel: (916) 445-3878  TTY: (916) 324-6547  Internet: www.dof.ca.gov

■ Director **Michael Cohen** . . . . . . . . . . . . . . . . . . . . . (916) 445-4141
   E-mail: michael.cohen@dof.ca.gov
   Administrative Assistant **Chastity Benson** . . . . . . . . . . (916) 445-4924
■ Chief Deputy Director, Budget **Amy Costa** . . . . . . . . . . (916) 445-9862
■ Chief Deputy Director, Policy **Eraina Ortega** . . . . . . . . . (916) 445-8582
   E-mail: eraina.ortega@dof.ca.gov
   Education: UC Irvine BA; Harvard MPP

*(continued on next page)*

---

★ Elected Official     ■ Appointed by Governor     ● Appointed by Legislature     ▲ Appointed by Board or Commission     ◆ Appointed by State Supreme Court

**Department of Finance** continued

Chief Operating Officer **Todd Jerue** . . . . . . . . . . . . . . . . (916) 445-4923
External Affairs Deputy Director **H. D. Palmer** . . . . . . . . . (916) 323-0648
  Education: Maryland BA
■Legislative Director **Jacqueline Wong-Hernandez** . . . . . . (916) 445-8610
Chief Counsel **Kari Lynn Krogseng** . . . . . . . . . . . . . . . . . (916) 324-4856
  E-mail: kari.krogseng@dof.ca.gov
  Education: Berkeley Law JD

# Department of Food and Agriculture [CDFA]

1220 N Street, Suite 400, Sacramento, CA 95814
Tel: (916) 654-0433  Fax: (916) 653-4723
E-mail: officeofpublicaffairs@cdfa.ca.gov  Internet: www.cdfa.ca.gov

**Employees:** 1,982  **Fiscal Year:** 2015-2016  **Budget:** $414,430,000

■Secretary **Karen Ross** . . . . . . . . . . . . . . . . . . . . . . . . . . (916) 654-0433
  E-mail: secretary.ross@cdfa.ca.gov
  Education: Nebraska BA
■Undersecretary **Jim Houston** . . . . . . . . . . . . . . . . . . . . . (916) 654-0433
  E-mail: jim.houston@cdfa.ca.gov
■Deputy Secretary **Jennifer Lester Moffitt** . . . . . . . . . . . . (916) 654-0433
  E-mail: jenny.lestermoffitt@cdfa.ca.gov
Finance and Administration Deputy Secretary
  **Kevin Masuhara** . . . . . . . . . . . . . . . . . . . . . . . . . . . . (916) 654-0433
  E-mail: kevin.masuhara@cdfa.ca.gov
■Legislation and Public Engagement Deputy Secretary
  **(Vacant)** . . . . . . . . . . . . . . . . . . . . . . . . . . . . . . . . . . (916) 654-0433
Agency Information Officer **Mary Winkley** . . . . . . . . . . . . (916) 654-0442
  E-mail: mary.winkley@cdfa.ca.gov
Public Affairs Director **Steve Lyle** . . . . . . . . . . . . . . . . . . (916) 654-0462
State Veterinarian **Annette Jones** . . . . . . . . . . . . . . . . . . (916) 900-5000
  Education: UC Davis BS, DVM
EEO (Equal Employment Opportunity) Officer
  **Cathy D'Ambrosio** . . . . . . . . . . . . . . . . . . . . . . . . . . . (916) 654-1005
Statewide Coordinator **Robert L. Wynn, Jr.** . . . . . . . . . . . (916) 651-0253
Principal Assistant **Carol Tate** . . . . . . . . . . . . . . . . . . . . (916) 654-0433
■Chief Counsel **Michele Dias** . . . . . . . . . . . . . . . . . . . . . (916) 654-0433
  E-mail: michele.dias@cdfa.ca.gov
County Liaison **Gary Leslie** . . . . . . . . . . . . . . . . . . . . . . . (916) 653-6649

## Administrative Services Division

Director **Kari Morrow** . . . . . . . . . . . . . . . . . . . . . . . . . . . (916) 654-1020
  E-mail: kari.morrow@cdfa.ca.gov
Assistant Director **Jody Lusby** . . . . . . . . . . . . . . . . . . . . . (916) 654-1020
  E-mail: jody.lusby@cdfa.ca.gov
Audit Office Chief **Ron Shackelford** . . . . . . . . . . . . . . . . (916) 900-5026
Department Services Chief **Melissa Eidson** . . . . . . . . . . . (916) 651-8183
  E-mail: melissa.eidson@cdfa.ca.gov
Financial Services Chief **Debbie Ackerman** . . . . . . . . . . . (916) 403-6060
Human Resources Chief **Gay Faivre** . . . . . . . . . . . . . . . . (916) 403-6582
Budget Officer **Nathan Johnson** . . . . . . . . . . . . . . . . . . (916) 403-6505
Chief Financial Officer **Debbie Ackerman** . . . . . . . . . . . . (916) 654-0424
Labor Relations Human Resources Officer
  **Hank Jennings** . . . . . . . . . . . . . . . . . . . . . . . . . . . . . (916) 403-6578
Training Officer **Teresa Swafford** . . . . . . . . . . . . . . . . . . (916) 403-6615

## Animal Health and Food Safety Services Division

Director **Annette Jones** . . . . . . . . . . . . . . . . . . . . . . . . . (916) 900-5000
Assistant Director **David Preciado** . . . . . . . . . . . . . . . . . (916) 900-5034
Animal Health Chief **Kent Fowler** . . . . . . . . . . . . . . . . . (916) 900-5002
Livestock Identifications Chief **John Suther** . . . . . . . . . . (916) 900-5006
Meat and Poultry Chief **Douglas Hepper** . . . . . . . . . . . . (916) 900-5059
Milk and Dairy Food Safety Chief
  **Dr. Stephen Beam, PhD** . . . . . . . . . . . . . . . . . . . . . . (916) 900-5008

## Fairs and Expositions Division

1010 Hurley Way, Suite 200, Sacramento, CA 95825
Tel: (916) 999-3000  Fax: (916) 263-2969

Branch Chief **John Quiroz** . . . . . . . . . . . . . . . . . . . . . . . (916) 900-5025

# Inspection Services Division

1220 N Street, Sacramento, CA 95814
Tel: (916) 900-5020  Fax: (916) 900-5344
E-mail: inspection_services@cdfa.ca.gov  Internet: www.cdfa.ca.gov/is

Director **Rick Jensen** . . . . . . . . . . . . . . . . . . . . . . . . . . . (916) 900-5020
  2800 Gateway Oaks Drive, Suite 100, Sacramento, CA 95833
  E-mail: rick.jensen@cdfa.ca.gov
Special Assistant **Natalie Krout-Greenberg** . . . . . . . . . . . (916) 900-5020
Center for Analytical Chemistry Branch Chief
  **Nirmal Saini** . . . . . . . . . . . . . . . . . . . . . . . . . . . . . . . (916) 262-1434
  3292 Meadowview Rd., Sacramento, CA 95832    Fax: (916) 262-1572
Feed, Fertilizer, Livestock Drugs and Egg Regulatory
  Services Branch Chief **Amadou Ba** . . . . . . . . . . . . . . . (916) 900-5022
  E-mail: amadou.ba@cdfa.ca.gov    Fax: (916) 900-5349
Inspection and Compliance Branch Chief **Steve Patton** . . . (916) 944-5218
  2800 Gateway Oaks Drive, Suite 100,    Fax: (916) 900-5345
  Sacramento, CA 95833
  E-mail: steve.patton@cdfa.ca.gov

# Marketing Services Division

2800 Gateway Oaks Drive, Suite 150, Sacramento, CA 95833
Internet: www.cdfa.ca.gov/mkt

Director **Jeff Cesca** . . . . . . . . . . . . . . . . . . . . . . . . . . . . (916) 900-5011
Assistant Director **Kathy Diaz-Cretu** . . . . . . . . . . . . . . . . (916) 900-5093
Agriculture Statistics Chief
  **Christina S. "Chris" Messer** . . . . . . . . . . . . . . . . . . . (916) 498-5161
  E-mail: chris.messer@nass.usda.gov
Dairy Marketing Branch Chief **Don Shippelhoute** . . . . . . (916) 900-5014
Market Enforcement Branch Chief **Nancy Iljana** . . . . . . . . (916) 900-5016
Marketing Branch Chief **Robert Maxie** . . . . . . . . . . . . . . (916) 900-5179
Milk Pooling Branch Chief **John Lee** . . . . . . . . . . . . . . . . (916) 900-5012

# Measurement Standards Division

6790 Florin Perkins Road, Suite 100, Sacramento, CA 95828-0812
Internet: www.cdfa.ca.gov/dms

Director **Kristin Macey** . . . . . . . . . . . . . . . . . . . . . . . . . . (916) 229-3000
Assistant Director **(Vacant)** . . . . . . . . . . . . . . . . . . . . . . (916) 229-3000
Principal State Metrologist **Greg Boers** . . . . . . . . . . . . . (916) 229-3022
Enforcement Branch Chief **Kathy DeContreras** . . . . . . . . (916) 229-3047
  E-mail: katherine.decontreras@cdfa.ca.gov
Measurement Services Program Supervisor **Andrea Alley** . . (916) 229-3000
  E-mail: andrea.alley@cdfa.ca.gov
Petroleum Products/Weighmaster Enforcement Branch
  Chief **Allan Morrison** . . . . . . . . . . . . . . . . . . . . . . . . . (916) 229-3050

# Plant Health and Pest Prevention Services Division

Director **Nick Condos** . . . . . . . . . . . . . . . . . . . . . . . . . . (916) 654-0317
Assistant Director **Stephen Brown** . . . . . . . . . . . . . . . . . (916) 654-0317
Integrated Pest Control Branch Chief **Patrick Akers** . . . . . (916) 403-6655
Pest Detection/Emergency Projects Branch Chief
  **Debby Tanouye** . . . . . . . . . . . . . . . . . . . . . . . . . . . . (916) 654-1211
Pest Exclusion Branch Chief **Duane Schnabel** . . . . . . . . . (916) 654-0312
Plant Pest Diagnostics Branch Chief **Umesh Kodira** . . . . . (916) 262-1100

# Military Department

9800 Goethe Road, Sacramento, CA 95826
P.O. Box 269101, Sacramento, CA 95826-9101
Tel: (916) 854-3000  Fax: (916) 854-3671

**Employees:** 813  **Fiscal Year:** 2015-2016  **Budget:** $190,515,000

■Adjutant General **MG David Baldwin, ARNG** . . . . . . . . . (916) 854-3500
  E-mail: david.s.baldwin.mil@mail.mil
■Deputy Adjutant General **BG Matthew Beevers, ARNG** . . (916) 854-3500
  E-mail: matthew.beevers.mil@mail.mil
Joint Staff Director **COL Robert Spano, ARNG** . . . . . . . . (916) 854-3500
Personnel and Human Resources Director
  **COL Jon Lathrop, ARNG** . . . . . . . . . . . . . . . . . . . . . (916) 854-3500
Chief State Policy and Liaison
  **LTC Darrin Bender, ARNG** . . . . . . . . . . . . . . . . . . . . (916) 854-3705
Public Affairs Officer **Peter B. Cross** . . . . . . . . . . . . . . . . (916) 854-3304
Administrative Office Assistant **Carmen Sannebeck** . . . . . (916) 854-3500

---

★ Elected Official   ■ Appointed by Governor   ● Appointed by Legislature   ▲ Appointed by Board or Commission   ◆ Appointed by State Supreme Court

# California National Guard

9800 Goethe Road, Sacramento, CA 95826
Tel: (916) 854-3000
- Adjutant General **MG David Baldwin, ARNG** . . . . . . . . . . (916) 854-3500
  E-mail: david.s.baldwin.mil@mail.mil

# California Air National Guard

9800 Goethe Road, Sacramento, CA 95826
Tel: (916) 854-3000

Deputy Adjutant General
  **BrigGen Nathaniel Reddicks, ANG** . . . . . . . . . . . . . . . (916) 854-3573

# California Army National Guard

9800 Goethe Road, Sacramento, CA 95826
Tel: (916) 854-3000

Deputy Adjutant General
  **MG Lawrence Haskins, ARNG** . . . . . . . . . . . . . . . . . . (916) 854-3056
Information Management Director
  **LTC Peter Barajas, ARNG** . . . . . . . . . . . . . . . . . . . . . (916) 854-3498

# California Department of Veterans Affairs [CDVA]

P.O. Box 942895, Sacramento, CA 94295-0001
1227 O Street, Sacramento, CA 95814
Tel: (800) 221-8998  Tel: (800) 952-5626 (In State)  TTY: (916) 653-1966
Fax: (916) 653-2456  E-mail: webmaster@calvet.ca.gov

**Employees:** 3,035  **Fiscal Year:** 2015-2016  **Budget:** $433,147,000
- Secretary **Dr. Vito D. Imbasciani, MD** . . . . . . . . . . . . . . (916) 653-2158
  E-mail: vito.imbasciani@calvet.ca.gov
- Undersecretary **Russell Atterberry** . . . . . . . . . . . . . . . . . (916) 653-2158
  E-mail: russell.atterberry@calvet.ca.gov
  - Special Assistant to the Undersecretary
    **Thomas Jay Martin** . . . . . . . . . . . . . . . . . . . . . . . . (916) 653-1969
    E-mail: thomas.martin@calvet.ca.gov
- Administrative Services Deputy Secretary
  **Sherri Gastinell** . . . . . . . . . . . . . . . . . . . . . . . . . . . . . (916) 503-8060
  E-mail: sherri.gastinell@calvet.ca.gov
- Communications Deputy Secretary **Paul Sullivan** . . . . . . . . (916) 653-1969
  E-mail: paul.sullivan@calvet.ca.gov
- Legislation and Government Relations Deputy Secretary
  **John Peter "J.P." Tremblay** . . . . . . . . . . . . . . . . . . . . . (916) 653-2192
  E-mail: jp.tremblay@calvet.ca.gov
  Veterans Homes Assistant Deputy Secretary
    **Thomas Jay Martin** . . . . . . . . . . . . . . . . . . . . . . . . (916) 653-2293
- Veterans Services Deputy Secretary **Keith Boylan** . . . . . . . (800) 221-8998
  E-mail: keith.boylan@calvet.ca.gov
- Minority Veterans Affairs Deputy Secretary
  **Ricardo Reyes** . . . . . . . . . . . . . . . . . . . . . . . . . . . . . . (916) 651-5040
- Women Veterans Deputy Secretary **Lindsey Sin** . . . . . . . . (916) 653-2158
  E-mail: lindsey.sin@calvet.ca.gov
- Chief Counsel **Todd Irby** . . . . . . . . . . . . . . . . . . . . . . . . (916) 653-2539
  E-mail: todd.irby@calvet.ca.gov
  Education: Pepperdine JD
Bond Finance Division Chief **Eric Tiche** . . . . . . . . . . . . . . . (916) 653-2081
Farm and Home Purchases Division (Cal-vet) Chief and
  Deputy Secretary **Theresa Gunn** . . . . . . . . . . . . . . . . . (916) 503-8318
  E-mail: theresa.gunn@calvet.ca.gov
Financial Services Division Chief **(Vacant)** . . . . . . . . . . . . . (916) 653-2327
Information Services Division Chief **Lisa Senitte** . . . . . . . . (916) 653-1924
  E-mail: lisa.senitte@calvet.ca.gov
Personnel Management Division Chief **Karen Escobar** . . . . (916) 653-2194
Education Administrator **(Vacant)** . . . . . . . . . . . . . . . . . . (916) 503-8317
Equal Employment Opportunity Officer **Sue Rose** . . . . . . . (916) 653-2194

# Veterans Home of California - Barstow

100 East Veterans Parkway, Barstow, CA 92311
Tel: (760) 252-6200  Tel: (800) 746-0606
Tel: (760) 252-6281 (Admissions)  TTY: (760) 252-6243

Administrator **James Sullivan** . . . . . . . . . . . . . . . . . . . . . (760) 252-6250
Skilled Nursing Facility Administrator **Kevin McGuire** . . . . (760) 252-6200

# Veterans Home of California - Chula Vista [VHC-Chula Vista]

700 East Naples Court, Chula Vista, CA 91911
Tel: (619) 482-6010  Tel: (888) 857-2146
- Administrator **Lael Hepworth** . . . . . . . . . . . . . . . . . . . . (619) 482-6032
  E-mail: lael.hepworth@calvet.ca.gov
  Education: Boise State 2001 BBA; U Phoenix 2004 MBA
Assistant Administrator **Richard Thomas** . . . . . . . . . . . . . (619) 482-6032
  E-mail: richard.thomas@calvet.ca.gov

# Veterans Home of California - West Los Angeles

11500 Nimitz Avenue, Los Angeles, CA 90049-4704
Tel: (877) 605-1332  Tel: (424) 832-8200

Deputy Director **Chris Walter** . . . . . . . . . . . . . . . . . . . . . (877) 605-1332
Administrator **Julian Manalo** . . . . . . . . . . . . . . . . . . . . . (877) 605-1332
  E-mail: julian.manalo@calvet.ca.gov
Deputy Administrator **Peter Kim** . . . . . . . . . . . . . . . . . . . (877) 605-1332
  E-mail: peter.kim@calvet.ca.gov
  Education: Trident International MBA
Skilled Nursing Facility Administrator **Donna Santos** . . . . (877) 605-1332
  E-mail: donna.santos@calvet.ca.gov

# Veterans Home of California - Yountville

P.O. Box 1200, Yountville, CA 94599-1297
Tel: (707) 944-4600  Tel: (800) 404-8387 (Pre-Admissions)
Fax: (707) 944-5005
- Administrator **Donald Veverka** . . . . . . . . . . . . . . . . . . . . (707) 944-4500
  E-mail: donald.veverka@calvet.ca.gov
Deputy Administrator **Alan Jessen** . . . . . . . . . . . . . . . . . . (707) 944-4502
  E-mail: alan.jessen@calvet.ca.gov
Nursing Director **Monica Diaz** . . . . . . . . . . . . . . . . . . . . (707) 944-4508
Chief Medical Officer **Dr. Paul Chin** . . . . . . . . . . . . . . . . (707) 944-4506
Public Affairs Officer **Terri Mejorado** . . . . . . . . . . . . . . . (707) 933-4536
  E-mail: terri.mejorado@calvet.ca.gov

# Office of the Inspector General

10111 Old Placerville Road, Suite 110, Sacramento, CA 95827
Tel: (916) 255-1102  Internet: www.oig.ca.gov
- Inspector General **Robert A. Barton** . . . . . . . . . . . . . . . . (916) 255-1102
  Executive Assistant to the Inspector General
    **Rita Biddle** . . . . . . . . . . . . . . . . . . . . . . . . . . . . . . (916) 255-1102
Chief Deputy Inspector General **Roy W. Wesley** . . . . . . . . (916) 255-1102
Chief Counsel **James Spurling** . . . . . . . . . . . . . . . . . . . . (916) 255-1102
  Education: McGeorge JD
Public Information Officer **Shaun Spillane** . . . . . . . . . . . . (916) 255-1102
  E-mail: spillanes@oig.ca.gov
- Executive Director-C-ROB **Misty Polasik** . . . . . . . . . . . . . (916) 255-1102
  E-mail: misty.polasik@oig.ca.gov
Legal Analyst **Linda Whitney** . . . . . . . . . . . . . . . . . . . . . (916) 255-1102
  E-mail: whitneyl@oig.ca.gov

# Office of the State Public Defender

1111 Broadway, Suite 1000, Oakland, CA 94607
Tel: (510) 267-3300  Fax: (510) 452-8712  Internet: www.ospd.ca.gov
- State Public Defender **Mary Katherine McComb** . . . . . . . . (510) 267-3300
  E-mail: mccomb@ospd.ca.gov
  Education: Stanford JD

# California State Auditor

621 Capitol Mall, Suite 1200, Sacramento, CA 95814
Tel: (916) 445-0255  Tel: (800) 952-5665 (Whistleblower's Hotline)
TTY: (916) 445-0033  TTY: (866) 293-8729 (Whistleblower's Hotline)
Fax: (916) 323-0913  Fax: (916) 322-2603 (Investigations/Whistleblower)

**Employees:** 170  **Fiscal Year:** 2015-2016  **Budget:** $30,727,000
- State Auditor **Elaine M. Howle, CPA, CGFM** . . . . . . . . . . (916) 445-0255
  E-mail: elaineh@auditor.ca.gov
  Education: UMass (Amherst) BS; Cal State (Sacramento) MBA

*(continued on next page)*

---

★ Elected Official   ■ Appointed by Governor   ● Appointed by Legislature   ▲ Appointed by Board or Commission   ◆ Appointed by State Supreme Court

**California State Auditor** *continued*

Chief Deputy State Auditor **Doug Cordiner** . . . . . . . . . . . .(916) 445-0255
  Education: Cal State (Sacramento) BS
Deputy State Auditor/Administration **(Vacant)** . . .(916) 445-0255 ext. 123
Deputy State Auditor/Audits **Ben M. Belnap, CIA** . . . . . .(916) 445-0255
Deputy State Auditor/Audits
  **John Collins II, CPA**. . . . . . . . . . . . . . . . . . . . .(916) 445-0255 ext. 329
    Education: Thomas Aquinas Col BA
Deputy State Auditor/Audits **Karen McKenna, CPA** . . . . .(916) 445-0255
Chief Counsel **Donna L. Neville**. . . . . . . . . . . . . . . . . . .(916) 445-0255
Chief of Investigations **(Vacant)** . . . . . . . . . . . . . . . . . . .(916) 445-0255
Chief of Legislative and Governmental Affairs
  **Paul A. Navarro** . . . . . . . . . . . . . . . . . . . . . . . . . . . . .(916) 445-2841
  E-mail: pauln@auditor.ca.gov      Tel: (916) 445-0255
  Education: UC Berkeley BA;             ext. 292
  U Washington 1990 MPA
Chief of Public Affairs
  **Margarita Fernandez, CPA, CGFM** . . . . . . . . . .(916) 445-0255 ext. 343
    Education: Cal State (Sacramento) BS
Manager/Resource Coordinator **(Vacant)**. . . . . . . . . . . . . .(916) 445-0255
Information Privacy Officer
  **Stephanie Ramirez-Ridgeway** . . . . . . . . . . .(916) 445-0255 ext. 266
Information Security Officer **Jeremy Evans** . . . . . .(916) 445-0255 ext. 440

# California Gambling Control Commission

2399 Gateway Oaks Drive, Suite 220, Sacramento, CA 95833-4231
Tel: (916) 263-0700   Fax: (916) 263-0499
E-mail: commission@cgcc.ca.gov

**Employees:** 35   **Fiscal Year:** 2015-2016   **Budget:** $103,091,000

Chairman **Jim Evans** . . . . . . . . . . . . . . . . . . . . . . . . . . .(916) 263-0493
Commissioner **Tiffany E. Conklin** . . . . . . . . . . . . . . . . . .(916) 263-0493
Commissioner **Roger Dunstan** . . . . . . . . . . . . . . . . . . . .(916) 263-0493
Commissioner **Lauren Hammond** . . . . . . . . . . . . . . . . . .(916) 263-0493
Commissioner **Trang To** . . . . . . . . . . . . . . . . . . . . . . . . .(916) 263-0493
Executive Director **Stacey Luna Baxter** . . . . . . . . . . . . .(916) 263-0493
  E-mail: slunabaxter@cgcc.ca.gov

# California State Lands Commission

100 Howe Avenue, Suite 100 South, Sacramento, CA 95825-8202
Tel: (916) 574-1800   Fax: (916) 574-1810   TTY: (800) 735-2929

**Employees:** 229   **Fiscal Year:** 2015-2016   **Budget:** $34,127,000

Commissioner **Michael Cohen** . . . . . . . . . . . . . . . . . . . .(916) 574-1800
Commissioner **Gavin Christopher Newsom** . . . . . . . . . . .(916) 574-1800
  Education: Santa Clara U 1989 BA
Commissioner **Betty T. Yee** . . . . . . . . . . . . . . . . . . . . . .(916) 574-1800
Executive Officer **Jennifer Lucchesi** . . . . . . . . . . . . . . . .(916) 574-1800

# California State Lottery Commission

700 North 10th Street, Sacramento, CA 95814-0393
Tel: (916) 822-8131   TTY: (800) 345-4275   Fax: (916) 737-5985
Internet: www.calottery.com

■Chair **Nathaniel "Nate" Kirtman III** . . . . . . . . . . . . . . .(916) 822-8110
  Education: Pomona 1992
■Vice Chair **Gregory J. Ahern** . . . . . . . . . . . . . . . . . . . .(916) 822-8110
■Commissioner **Rowena T. Libang-Bobila**. . . . . . . . . . . . .(916) 822-8110
  Education: Hastings JD
■Commissioner **Connie M. Perez** . . . . . . . . . . . . . . . . . .(916) 822-8110
■Commissioner **John Smolin** . . . . . . . . . . . . . . . . . . . . .(916) 822-8110
■Director **Hugo López** . . . . . . . . . . . . . . . . . . . . . . . . . .(916) 822-8110
  Education: Cal State (Sacramento) 1976 BS

## Security and Law Enforcement Division

Internet: www.calottery.com/sled

Assistant Deputy Director **(Vacant)** . . . . . . . . . . . . . . . . .(916) 822-8131

Deputy Director **Stephen A. Tacchini** . . . . . . . . . . . . . . .(916) 822-8131
  Education: San Mateo 1975 AA; San Francisco State U 1996 BA

# California Public Utilities Commission [CPUC]

505 Van Ness Avenue, San Francisco, CA 94102-3298
Tel: (415) 703-2782   Tel: (800) 848-5580   TTY: (415) 703-2032
Fax: (415) 703-1758   Internet: www.cpuc.ca.gov

■President **Michael Picker** . . . . . . . . . . . . . . . . . . . . . . .(415) 703-3703
  E-mail: michael.picker@cpuc.ca.gov
  Education: Immaculate Heart BA; UC Davis MBA
  Chief of Staff **Nicolas L. Chaset** . . . . . . . . . . . . . . . . .(415) 703-1556
    E-mail: nlc@cpuc.ca.gov
■Commissioner **Mike Florio** . . . . . . . . . . . . . . . . . . . . . .(415) 703-2440
  E-mail: mike.florio@cpuc.ca.gov
■Commissioner **Catherine J. Kissee-Sandoval** . . . . . . . . . .(415) 703-2444
  E-mail: catherine.sandoval@cpuc.ca.gov
  Education: Yale 1984 BA; Oxford (UK) 1990 MLITT;
  Stanford 1990 JD
■Commissioner **Carla J. Peterman** . . . . . . . . . . . . . . . . .(415) 703-2444
  E-mail: carla.peterman@cpuc.ca.gov
■Commissioner **Liane M. Randolph** . . . . . . . . . . . . . . . . .(415) 703-2444
  E-mail: liane.randolph@cpuc.ca.gov
  Education: UCLA 1990 BA, 1993 JD
■Deputy Executive Director **Maryam Ebke** . . . . . . . . . . . .(415) 703-2782
  E-mail: maryam.ebke@cpuc.ca.gov

# California Student Aid Commission [CSAC]

P.O. Box 419026, Rancho Cordova, CA 95741-9026
Tel: (916) 464-8271   Tel: (888) 224-7268   Fax: (916) 464-8033
E-mail: studentsupport@csac.ca.gov   Internet: www.csac.ca.gov

**Employees:** 120   **Fiscal Year:** 2015-2016   **Budget:** $2,151,753,000

■Chair **Hal Geiogue** . . . . . . . . . . . . . . . . . . . . . . . . . . . .(916) 464-8271
  Note: General Public Representative
  E-mail: hal.geiogue@csac.ca.gov
■Vice Chair **Lande Ajose**. . . . . . . . . . . . . . . . . . . . . . . . .(916) 464-8271
  Note: General Public Representative
  E-mail: lande.ajose@csac.ca.gov
■Secretary **Dr. Wm. Gregory Sawyer** . . . . . . . . . . . . . . .(916) 464-8271
  Note: General Public Representative
  Education: Mount Union BA; Eastern New Mexico MA;
  North Texas PhD
■Member **Nancy Rose Anton** . . . . . . . . . . . . . . . . . . . . .(916) 464-8271
  Note: General Public Representative
  E-mail: nancy.anton@csac.ca.gov
■Member **Glen T. Becerra** . . . . . . . . . . . . . . . . . . . . . . .(916) 464-8271
  Note: Public, Proprietary, Non-Profit Representative
  Education: UC Berkeley 1993 BA
■Member **Harry Le Grande** . . . . . . . . . . . . . . . . . . . . . .(916) 464-8271
  Note: University California Representatives
  E-mail: harry.legrande@csac.ca.gov
  Education: UC Irvine BA; Oregon State MEd
■Member **Debra Maxie** . . . . . . . . . . . . . . . . . . . . . . . . . .(916) 464-8271
  Note: Public, Proprietary, Non-Profit Representative; Note: General
  Public Representative
■Member **Jamillah Moore** . . . . . . . . . . . . . . . . . . . . . . . .(916) 464-8271
  Note: California Community College Representative
●Member **Maria S. Salinas** . . . . . . . . . . . . . . . . . . . . . . .(916) 464-8271
  Note: General Public Representative
●Member **Jose Solorio** . . . . . . . . . . . . . . . . . . . . . . . . . .(916) 464-8271
  Note: General Public Representative
●Member **David Valladolid** . . . . . . . . . . . . . . . . . . . . . . .(916) 464-8271
  Note: General Public Representative
■Member **(Vacant)** . . . . . . . . . . . . . . . . . . . . . . . . . . . . . .(916) 464-8271
  Note: Independent California Colleges and Universities Representatives
■Member **(Vacant)** . . . . . . . . . . . . . . . . . . . . . . . . . . . . . .(916) 464-8271
  Note: California Secondary Schools Representative
■Student Representative **Jessica Foresti** . . . . . . . . . . . . . .(916) 464-8271
■Student Representative **Devon Graves** . . . . . . . . . . . . . .(916) 464-8271

---

# Emergency Medical Services Authority [EMSA]

10901 Gold Center Drive, Suite 400, Rancho Cordova, CA 95670
Tel: (916) 322-4336  Fax: (916) 322-8765  Internet: www.emsa.ca.gov

**Employees:** 80  **Fiscal Year:** 2015-2016  **Budget:** $32,192,000

Director **Dr. Howard Backer, MD, MPH, FACEP** . . (916) 322-4336 ext. 432
Chief Deputy Director **Daniel R. Smiley** . . . . . . . . . . . . . . (916) 431-3672
   Education: Cal State (Fresno) BS; U San Francisco MPA
Legislative and External Affairs Deputy Director
   **Jennifer Lim** . . . . . . . . . . . . . . . . . . . . . . . . . . . . . . (916) 431-3700
   E-mail: jennifer.lim@emsa.ca.gov
Legal Counsel **Steven McGee** . . . . . . . . . . . . . . . . . . . . . .(916) 431-3693
Administration Division Chief **Rick Trussell** . . . . . . . . . . . .(916) 431-3737
   E-mail: rick.trussell@emsa.ca.gov
Disaster Medical Services Division Chief **(Vacant)** . . . . . . . (916) 431-3676
Emergency Medical Services' Personnel Division
   Chief **Sean Trask** . . . . . . . . . . . . . . . . . . . . . . . . . (916) 431-3689 ext. 429
Emergency Medical Services' Systems Division Chief
   **Tom McGinnis** . . . . . . . . . . . . . . . . . . . . . . . . . . . . (916) 431-3695
   E-mail: tom.mcginnis@emsa.ca.gov
Chief Information Officer **(Vacant)** . . . . . . . . . . . . . . . . . . (916) 431-3739
Enforcement Manager **Michael Smith** . . . . . . . . . . . . . . . . (916) 431-3703

# California State Library

California State Library, 914 Capitol Mall, Sacramento, CA 95814
P.O. Box 942837, Sacramento, CA 94237-0001
Tel: (916) 323-9759  Fax: (916) 654-0064  Internet: www.library.ca.gov

**Employees:** 138  **Fiscal Year:** 2015-2016  **Budget:** $51,888,000

## Office of the State Librarian

■State Librarian **Greg Lucas** . . . . . . . . . . . . . . . . . . . . . . . (916) 323-9759
   E-mail: greg.lucas@library.ca.gov
   Education: USC MA
■Deputy State Librarian **Gerald "Gerry" Maginnity** . . . . . . (916) 323-9759
   E-mail: gerald.maginnity@library.ca.gov
   Special Assistant **Karina Robinson** . . . . . . . . . . . . . . . . (916) 653-0217

# Office of the Lieutenant Governor

State Capitol, Suite 1114, Sacramento, CA 95814
Tel: (916) 445-8994  Fax: (916) 323-4998

**Fiscal Year:** 2015-2016  **Budget:** $1,068,000

★Lieutenant Governor **Gavin Christopher Newsom** (D) . . . (916) 445-8994
   Term Expires: January 1, 2019
   E-mail: gavin.newsom@ltg.ca.gov
   Affiliation: Commissioner, California State Lands Commission, State of
   California
   100 Howe Avenue, Suite 100 South, Sacramento, CA 95825-8202;
   President of the Senate, California State Senate
   State Capitol, 1020 N Street, Sacramento, CA 95814-4900
Chief of Staff **Rhys Williams** . . . . . . . . . . . . . . . . . . . . . . (916) 445-8994

# Office of the Secretary of State

1500 11th Street, Sacramento, CA 95814
Tel: (916) 653-6814  Fax: (916) 653-4620
E-mail: constituent.affairs@sos.ca.gov  Internet: www.sos.ca.gov

**Employees:** 559  **Fiscal Year:** 2015-2016  **Budget:** $127,016,000

★Secretary of State **Alejandro "Alex" Padilla** (D) . . . . . . . . (916) 653-7244
   Term Expires: January 2019
   Education: MIT 1994 BS
   Career: Council Member, Office of the City Council, City of Los
   Angeles, California; Director, National League of Cities; State Senator
   (D-CA, District 20), California State Senate (2006-2014)
Chief Deputy Secretary of State **Bill Mabie** . . . . . . . . . . . . (916) 653-7244

# Office of the State Treasurer

915 Capitol Mall, Room 110, Sacramento, CA 95814
P.O. Box 942809, Sacramento, CA 94209
Tel: (916) 653-2995  Fax: (916) 653-3125  Internet: www.treasurer.ca.gov

**Employees:** 400  **Fiscal Year:** 2015-2016  **Budget:** $33,283,000

★State Treasurer **John Chiang** (D) . . . . . . . . . . . . . . . . . . . . (916) 653-2995
   Term Expires: January 2019
Chief of Staff **Collin Wong-Martinusen** . . . . . . . . . . . . . . (916) 653-2995
Retirement Security and Health Care Deputy Treasurer
   **Grant Boyken** . . . . . . . . . . . . . . . . . . . . . . . . . . . . . (916) 653-2995
Administration and Fiscal Policy Deputy Treasurer
   **Vince Brown** . . . . . . . . . . . . . . . . . . . . . . . . . . . . . . (916) 653-2995
   E-mail: vince.brown@treasurer.ca.gov
Legislation and Infrastructure Financing Deputy Treasurer
   **Alan Gordon** . . . . . . . . . . . . . . . . . . . . . . . . . . . . . . (916) 653-2995
   E-mail: alan.gordon@treasurer.ca.gov
Public Finance Deputy Treasurer **Tim Schaefer** . . . . . . . . . . (916) 653-2995
General Counsel **Mark Paxson** . . . . . . . . . . . . . . . . . . . . . (916) 653-2995
Communications Director **Marc Lifsher** . . . . . . . . . . . . . . . (916) 653-2995
   E-mail: mlifsher@treasurer.ca.gov

# Office of the State Controller

P.O. Box 942850, Sacramento, CA 94250-5872
Tel: (916) 445-2636  Fax: (916) 322-4404  Internet: www.sco.ca.gov

★State Controller **Betty T. Yee** (D) . . . . . . . . . . . . . . . . . . . .(916) 445-2636
   Term Expires: January 2019
   E-mail: byee@hsr.ca.gov
Chief of Staff **Karen Greene-Ross** . . . . . . . . . . . . . . . . . . . (916) 445-2636
Deputy State Controller for Communications
   **Nicole Winger** . . . . . . . . . . . . . . . . . . . . . . . . . . . . . (916) 445-2636
   E-mail: nicole.winger@sco.ca.gov
   Education: Whittier 1995 BA; Cal State (Sacramento) 1996
Deputy State Controller for Environmental Policy
   **Anne Baker** . . . . . . . . . . . . . . . . . . . . . . . . . . . . . . . (916) 445-2636
   E-mail: anne.baker@sco.ca.gov
   Education: JFK School Govt MPA
Deputy State Controller for Legislative Affairs
   **Evan L. Goldberg** . . . . . . . . . . . . . . . . . . . . . . . . . . . (916) 445-2636
   E-mail: evan.goldberg@sco.ca.gov
Deputy State Controller for Taxation **Yvette Stowers** . . . . .(916) 445-2636
   E-mail: yvette.stowers@sco.ca.gov
   Education: San José State BSAcc; Golden Gate MT
Assistant Deputy State Controller **Becca Doten** . . . . . . . . . (916) 445-2636
   E-mail: becca.doten@sco.ca.gov
   Education: USC BA
Senior Financial Advisor **Lynn E Paquin** . . . . . . . . . . . . . . (916) 445-2636
   Education: Boston U BSJ; Columbia MPPA
Deputy State Controller for Health Policy **Alan LoFaso** . . . (916) 445-2636
   E-mail: alan.lofaso@sco.ca.gov
   Education: McGeorge JD

## Accounting and Reporting Division

3301 C Street, Suite 700, Sacramento, CA 95816
Tel: (916) 327-4144  Fax: (916) 323-4807

Division Chief **Cassandra Moore-Hudnall** . . . . . . . . . . . . . (916) 445-5834
Assistant Chief Local Operations **Jill Kanemasu** . . . . . . . . .(916) 322-9891
Transition Bureau Chief **Jocelyn Boubique** . . . . . . . . . . . . (916) 322-7748
State Government Reporting Bureau Chief **Carlos Diaz** . . . .(916) 327-8830
Administrative Assistant **Reyna Santana** . . . . . . . . . . . . . . (916) 327-4144

## Administration and Disbursements Division

300 Capitol Mall, 15th Floor, Sacramento, CA 95814
Tel: (916) 323-8314  Fax: (916) 327-0597

Division Chief **Larry Norris** . . . . . . . . . . . . . . . . . . . . . . . (916) 323-8314
   E-mail: lnorris@sco.ca.gov
Disbursements Bureau Chief **Allan Watson** . . . . . . . . . . . . (916) 323-5166
Budgets and Contracts Bureau Chief **(Vacant)** . . . . . . . . . . (916) 323-8314
Administrative Assistant **Terra Evans** . . . . . . . . . . . . . . . . (916) 324-9742

---

★ Elected Official    ■ Appointed by Governor    ● Appointed by Legislature    ▲ Appointed by Board or Commission    ◆ Appointed by State Supreme Court

EXECUTIVE BRANCH

## Audits Division

3301 C Street, Suite 715, Sacramento, CA 95816
Tel: (916) 324-8907  Fax: (916) 327-0832

Division Chief **Jeffrey V. "Jeff" Brownfield** . . . . . . . . . . . . . (916) 324-8907
Community Related Audits Bureau Chief **Lisa Hughes** . . . . (916) 323-1770
Financial Audits Bureau Chief **Carolyn Baez** . . . . . . . . . . (916) 322-7656
Local Government Bureau Chief **Mike Spalj** . . . . . . . . . . . (916) 324-7226
Local Government Compliance Bureau Chief
  **Liz Gonzalez** . . . . . . . . . . . . . . . . . . . . . . . . . . . . . . . (916) 324-0622
Management Analysis and Technical Support Bureau
  Chief **Gilda Carpenter** . . . . . . . . . . . . . . . . . . . . . . . (916) 322-7518
Mandated Costs Bureau Chief **Jim Spano** . . . . . . . . . . . (916) 323-1828
Operations Bureau Chief **Miguel Gonzalez** . . . . . . . . . . . (916) 445-3060
State Agency Bureau Chief **Andrew Finlayson** . . . . . . . . . (916) 324-6310
Administrative Assistant **Catherine Graves** . . . . . . . . . . . (916) 324-2940

## Information Systems Division

300 Capitol Mall, 7th Floor, Sacramento, CA 95814
Tel: (916) 322-3030

Division Chief **Todd Boltjes** . . . . . . . . . . . . . . . . . . . . . . (916) 445-8245
Administrative Assistant **(Vacant)** . . . . . . . . . . . . . . . . . . (916) 322-3030

## Personnel/Payroll Services Division

300 Capitol Mall, 10th Floor, Sacramento, CA 95814
Tel: (916) 322-6367  Fax: (916) 322-6493

Division Chief **Debra Spellman** . . . . . . . . . . . . . . . . . . . . (916) 322-8104
Operations Bureau Chief **Debra Spellman** . . . . . . . . . . . . (916) 322-8104
Management Analysis Bureau Chief **Michelle Ezray** . . . . . . (916) 322-6367
  E-mail: mezray@sco.ca.gov

## Unclaimed Property Division

10600 White Rock Road, Suite 141, Rancho Cordova, CA 95670
Tel: (916) 464-0641  Fax: (916) 464-6222

Division Chief **Gary Qualset** . . . . . . . . . . . . . . . . . . . . . . (916) 464-6281
Assistant Chief **Cathleen Dinubilo** . . . . . . . . . . . . . . . . . (916) 464-6263
  Administrative Analyst **Celeste Amour** . . . . . . . . . . . . . (916) 464-6281

## Department of Insurance

300 Capitol Mall, 17th Floor, Sacramento, CA 95814
Tel: (916) 492-3500  TTY: (800) 482-4833  Fax: (916) 445-5280
Internet: www.insurance.ca.gov

**Employees:** 1,397  **Fiscal Year:** 2015-2016  **Budget:** $250,000,000

★ Insurance Commissioner **Dave Jones** (D) . . . . . . . . . . . . . (916) 492-3500
  Term Expires: January 2019             Fax: (916) 445-2043
  Education: Harvard JD
  Scheduling Director **Roberta Potter** . . . . . . . . . . . . . . . (916) 492-3609
Chief Deputy Commissioner **Nettie Hoge** . . . . . . . . . . . . . (415) 538-4010
  45 Fremont Street, 23rd Floor,          Fax: (415) 904-5889
  San Francisco, CA 94105
Health Policy and Reform Branch, Deputy Commissioner
  **Janice Rocco** . . . . . . . . . . . . . . . . . . . . . . . . . . . . . . . (916) 492-3576
                                          Fax: (916) 445-5280
Legislative Branch, Legislative Director and Deputy
  Commissioner **Robert Herrell** . . . . . . . . . . . . . . . . . . . (916) 492-3573
  E-mail: robert.herrell@insurance.ca.gov    Fax: (916) 322-7294
  Education: UC Irvine 1990 BA, 1991 MBA
Administration and Licensing Services Branch, Deputy
  Commissioner **Erika Sperbeck** . . . . . . . . . . . . . . . . . . . (916) 492-3618
  E-mail: erika.sperbeck@insurance.ca.gov    Fax: (916) 327-3482
Communications and Press Relations Branch, Deputy
  Commissioner **Byron Tucker** . . . . . . . . . . . . . . . . . . . . (213) 346-6363
  300 South Spring Street, 14th Floor,   Fax: (916) 897-9051
  Los Angeles, CA 90013
  E-mail: byron.tucker@insurance.ca.gov
Community Programs and Policy Initiatives Branch,
  Deputy Commissioner **Chris Shultz** . . . . . . . . . . . . . . . (916) 492-3589
                                          Fax: (916) 445-5280
Consumer Services and Market Conduct Branch, Deputy
  Commissioner **Anthony "Tony" Cignarale** . . . . . . . . . . (213) 346-6360
  300 South Spring Street, 14th Floor,   Fax: (213) 897-6041
  Los Angeles, CA 90013

Enforcement Branch, Deputy Commissioner
  **George Mueller** . . . . . . . . . . . . . . . . . . . . . . . . . . . . . (916) 854-5760
  Education: USC BPA, MPA               Fax: (916) 255-3202
Enforcement Branch-Fraud Division Chief
  **Martin Gonzalez** . . . . . . . . . . . . . . . . . . . . . . . . . . . . (916) 854-5760
                                          Fax: (916) 255-3202
Financial Surveillance Branch, Deputy Commissioner
  **Susan Bernard** . . . . . . . . . . . . . . . . . . . . . . . . . . . . . (415) 538-4073
  45 Fremont Street, 23rd Floor,          Fax: (415) 904-5889
  San Francisco, CA 94105
  E-mail: susan.bernard@insurance.ca.gov
Legal Branch, General Counsel and Deputy
  Commissioner **John F. Finston** . . . . . . . . . . . . . . . . . . (415) 904-4379
  45 Fremont Street, 23rd Floor,          Fax: (415) 904-5889
  San Francisco, CA 94105
  Education: Johns Hopkins 1977 BES; St John's U (NY) 1980 JD
Litigation, Deputy General Counsel **Michael J. Levy** . . . . . (916) 492-3572
Rate Regulation Branch, Deputy Commissioner
  **Joel Laucher** . . . . . . . . . . . . . . . . . . . . . . . . . . . . . . . (415) 538-4381
  45 Fremont Street, 23rd Floor,          Fax: (213) 897-6041
  San Francisco, CA 94105
Regulatory and Legal Services, Deputy General Counsel
  **Susan Stapp** . . . . . . . . . . . . . . . . . . . . . . . . . . . . . . . (415) 438-4403
                                          Fax: (415) 904-5889
Special Counsel and Deputy Commissioner
  **Geoff Margolis** . . . . . . . . . . . . . . . . . . . . . . . . . . . . . (916) 492-3574
Enforcement Branch-Investigations Division, Chief
  **Kim Johnson-Woods** . . . . . . . . . . . . . . . . . . . . . . . . . (916) 854-5777
  9342 Tech Center Drive, Suite 100,     Fax: (916) 255-3344
  Sacramento, CA 95826
Information Technology Division, Chief
  **David Noronha** 14th Floor . . . . . . . . . . . . . . . . . . . . . (916) 492-3294
  E-mail: david.noronha@insurance.ca.gov    Fax: (916) 327-3481
Conservation and Liquidation Office/ Chief Executive
  Officer **David E. Wilson** . . . . . . . . . . . . . . . . . . . . . . . (415) 676-5000
  425 Market Street, 23rd Floor,          Fax: (415) 676-5001
  San Francisco, CA 94105
Ethics and Operational Compliance Officer
  **George Mendoza** 13th Floor . . . . . . . . . . . . . . . . . . . . (916) 492-3510
California Organized Investment Network/Chair
  **Stacie Olivares-Castain** . . . . . . . . . . . . . . . . . . . . . . . (213) 346-6869
                                          Fax: (916) 323-1944
Press Secretary **Nancy Kincaid** . . . . . . . . . . . . . . . . . . . (916) 492-3542
  E-mail: nancy.kincaid@insurance.ca.gov    Fax: (916) 445-2043

## Department of Justice

P.O. Box 944255, Sacramento, CA 94244-2550
Tel: (916) 322-3360  Fax: (916) 323-5341

**Employees:** 4,716  **Fiscal Year:** 2015-2016  **Budget:** $794,134,000

## Office of the Attorney General

1300 I Street, Sacramento, CA 95814
Tel: (916) 445-9555  TTY: (916) 324-5564  TTY: (800) 952-5548
Fax: (916) 323-9569  E-mail: piu@doj.ca.gov

★ Attorney General **Kamala Devi Harris, JD** (D) . . . . . . . . . (916) 324-5437
  Term Expires: January 2019
  Education: Howard U 1986 BA; Hastings 1990 JD
Associate Attorney General **Venus Johnson** . . . . . . . . . . . (916) 324-5435
  E-mail: venus.johnson@doj.ca.gov
Chief Deputy Attorney General **Nathan R. Barankin** . . . . . (916) 324-5435
Chief of Policy **Daniel R. Suvor** . . . . . . . . . . . . . . . . . . . (213) 897-2737
  Education: USC 2004 BA; George Washington 2008 JD

## Administrative Services Division

Director **Tammy Lopes** . . . . . . . . . . . . . . . . . . . . . . . . . . (916) 324-4404
  E-mail: tammy.lopes@doj.ca.gov
Deputy Director **Dave Harper** . . . . . . . . . . . . . . . . . . . . . (916) 322-2332
  E-mail: dave.harper@doj.ca.gov
Law Practice Support Section Manager **Megan Sato** . . . . . (916) 445-1939
Legal Support Operations Manager **Laurie Denny** . . . . . . . (916) 327-7887
Accounting Office Officer **Sumi Thomison** . . . . . . . . . . . . (916) 324-5066
Budget Office Officer **Michael Fong** . . . . . . . . . . . . . . . . (916) 445-8215
Personnel Officer **Arwen Flint** . . . . . . . . . . . . . . . . . . . . (916) 324-3825
Law Librarian **Dragomir Cosanici** . . . . . . . . . . . . . . . . . (916) 445-9940

---

★ Elected Official    ■ Appointed by Governor    ● Appointed by Legislature    ▲ Appointed by Board or Commission    ◆ Appointed by State Supreme Court

## California Justice Information Services Division

4949 Broadway, Sacramento, CA 95820
P.O. Box 953417, Sacramento, CA 94203-4170
Tel: (916) 227-3882

Director **Joe Dominic** .............................. (916) 227-3043
  E-mail: joe.dominic@doj.ca.gov
Criminal Identification and Investigative Services Bureau
  Chief **Jenny Reich**.................................. (916) 227-5372
  E-mail: jenny.reich@doj.ca.gov
Criminal Justice IT Services Bureau Chief **(Vacant)** ...... (916) 227-1353
Criminal Information and Analysis Bureau Chief
  **Julie Basco** ..................................... (916) 227-3541
  E-mail: Julie.Basco@doj.ca.gov
Departmental Technology Services Bureau CIO and Chief
  **Adrian Farley** .................................. (916) 227-3122
  E-mail: adrian.farley@doj.ca.gov
  Education: Pitzer
Technology Support Bureau Chief **Nancy Johnson**....... (916) 227-5882
  E-mail: nancy.johnson@doj.ca.gov

## Civil Law Division

Chief Assistant Attorney General **Kathleen Kenealy**...... (916) 324-5431
Business and Tax Section Senior Assistant Attorney
  General **Diane Spencer Shaw** ..................... (213) 897-2468
  300 South Spring Street, Los Angeles, CA 90013-1230
Correctional Law Section Senior Assistant Attorney
  General **Jonathan Wolff**.......................... (415) 703-1113
  455 Golden Gate Avenue, Suite 11000, San Francisco, CA 94102-3664
Employment and Administrative Mandate Senior
  Assistant Attorney General **Chris Knudsen** ........... (916) 645-3060
  E-mail: chris.knudsen@doj.ca.gov
Government Law Section Senior Assistant Attorney
  General **Douglas Woods** .......................... (916) 324-4663
Health, Education and Welfare Section Senior Assistant
  Attorney General **Julie Weng-Gutierrez** .............. (916) 445-8223
  E-mail: julie.wenggutierrez@doj.ca.gov
Health Quality Enforcement Senior Assistant Attorney
  General **Gloria Castro** ............................ (213) 897-6804
  300 South Spring Street, Los Angeles, CA 90013-1230
  E-mail: gloria.castro@doj.ca.gov
Licensing Law Senior Assistant Attorney General
  **Linda K. Schneider** .............................. (619) 645-3037
  110 West A Street, San Diego, CA 92101
  E-mail: linda.schneider@doj.ca.gov
Tort and Condemnation Law Senior Assistant Attorney
  General **Kristin Hogue** ........................... (619) 645-2024

## Criminal Law Division

Chief Assistant Attorney General **Gerald Engler** ........ (916) 324-5261
Senior Assistant Attorney General **Michael Farrell** ....... (916) 324-5246
Senior Assistant Attorney General **Julie Garland** ........ (619) 645-2604
  110 West A Street, Suite 700, San Diego, CA 92101
Senior Assistant Attorney General **Jeff Laurence** ....... (415) 703-5897
Senior Assistant Attorney General **Lance Winters**........ (213) 897-2382
  300 S. Spring Street, Los Angeles, CA 90013
Senior Assistant Attorney General/Capital Case
  Coordinator **Ronald Matthias** ..................... (415) 703-5858
  445 Golden Gate Avenue, San Francisco, CA 94102
Correctional Writs and Appeals Senior Assistant Attorney
  General **Jennifer Neill**............................ (916) 324-1456
  Education: McGeorge JD
eCrime Unit Senior Assistant Attorney General
  **Robert M. Morgester** ............................ (916) 445-9330
  E-mail: robert.morgester@doj.ca.gov
Financial Fraud and Prosecution Unit Senior Assistant
  Attorney General **Jim Root**........................ (213) 897-2365
Native American Affairs Office Chief **Olin Jones** ........ (916) 322-2767
Medi-Cal Fraud and Elder Abuse Bureau Director/ Senior
  Assistant Attorney General **Saralyn Ang-Olson** ....... (916) 621-1821
Victim's Services Office Special Counsel **Deborah Bain** .. (916) 324-9945

## Law Enforcement Division

1300 I Street, Suite 1100, Sacramento, CA 95814
P.O. Box 903281, Sacramento, CA 94203-2810
Tel: (916) 319-8220

Director **Larry Wallace** ............................(916) 319-8200
Adjutant to the Director **Jeff Wall** ...................(916) 319-8223
Firearms Bureau Chief **Steve Lindley**................(916) 227-4001
Gambling Control Bureau Chief **Wayne Quint** ...... (916) 227-3021
Investigation Bureau Chief **John Marsh** ............... (916) 319-9570

### Forensic Services Bureau

Tel: (916) 322-6185

Bureau Chief **John Yoshida**.........................(916) 322-7122

### Toxicology

Supervisor **Dan Coleman**...........................(916) 227-3620
Supervisor **Nathan Sato** ...........................(916) 227-3620

## Public Rights Division

Chief Assistant Attorney General **Mark Breckler** ........ (916) 322-8150
  E-mail: mark.breckler@doj.ca.gov
Antitrust Law Section Senior Assistant Attorney General
  **Kathleen Foote** .................................(415) 703-5555
  455 Golden Gate Avenue, Suite 11000, San Francisco, CA 94102-7004
Charitable Trusts Section Senior Assistant Attorney
  General **Tania Ibanaez** .......................... (415) 703-1120
  455 Golden Gate Avenue, Suite 11000, San Francisco, CA 94102-7004
  E-mail: tania.ibanez@doj.ca.gov
Civil Rights Enforcement Section Senior Assistant
  Attorney General **Angela Sierra**...................(213) 620-6312
  300 S. Spring St., Los Angeles, CA 90013-1230
  E-mail: angela.sierra@doj.ca.gov
Consumer Law Section Senior Assistant Attorney
  General **Nicklas Akers** .......................... (415) 703-5505
  455 Golden Gate Avenue, San Francisco, CA 94102-7004
Corporate Fraud Section Senior Assistant Attorney
  General **Martin Goyette** .......................... (415) 703-5569
  445 Golden Gate Avenue, San Francisco, CA 94102
Environment Law Senior Assistant Attorney General
  **Sally Magnani**...................................(916) 322-1802
  1515 Clay Street, Oakland, CA 94612
Indian and Gaming Law Section Senior Assistant
  Attorney General **Sara Drake** ..................... (916) 324-5375
Land Law Senior Assistant Attorney General
  **John Saurenman** ................................ (213) 897-2702
  300 South Spring Street, Los Angeles, CA 90013-1230
Natural Resources Senior Assistant Attorney General
  **Robert Byrne** ...................................(415) 703-5860
  445 Golden Gate Avenue, San Francisco, CA 94102
Tobacco Litigation and Enforcement Senior Assistant
  Attorney General **Karen Leaf** ..................... (916) 323-3804
  E-mail: karen.leaf@doj.ca.gov
Registry of Charitable Trusts Registrar **David Eller** ....... (916) 324-5498

## State Board of Education [SBE]

1430 N Street, Room 5111, Sacramento, CA 95814
Tel: (916) 319-0827 Fax: (916) 319-0175 E-mail: sbe@cde.ca.gov
Internet: www.cde.ca.gov/be

■President **Dr. Michael W. Kirst** ...................... (916) 319-0827
■Vice President **Dr. Ilene Straus** .................... (916) 319-0827
■Member **Sue Burr** ................................ (916) 319-0827
■Member **Bruce L. Holaday** ....................... (916) 319-0827
  Education: Illinois; Indiana
■Member **Feliza Ortiz-Licon** ....................... (916) 319-0827
■Member **Patricia Ann Rucker** ..................... (916) 319-0827
■Member **Dr. Nicolasa Sandoval** ................... (916) 319-0827
■Member **Olivia Sison** ............................. (916) 319-0827
■Member **Ting Lan Sun** ............................(916) 319-0827
  Education: Stanford MA; UC Davis PhD
■Member **Trish Boyd Williams** ..................... (916) 319-0827
■Student Member **Michael McFarland** ................. (916) 319-0827

---

★ Elected Official   ■ Appointed by Governor   ● Appointed by Legislature   ▲ Appointed by Board or Commission   ◆ Appointed by State Supreme Court

## Staff

■Executive Director **Karen Stapf Walters** . . . . . . . . . . . . . . . (916) 319-0699
  E-mail: kwalters@cde.ca.gov
  Executive Assistant **(Vacant)** . . . . . . . . . . . . . . . . . . . . . . . . (916) 319-0705
■Deputy Executive Director **Patricia de Cos** . . . . . . . . . . . . . (916) 319-0702
  E-mail: pdecos@cde.ca.gov
■Chief Counsel **Judy M. Cias** . . . . . . . . . . . . . . . . . . . . . . . . . (916) 319-0696
  E-mail: jcias@cde.ca.gov

# Department of Education [CDE]

1430 N Street, Suite 5602, Sacramento, CA 95814-5901
Tel: (916) 319-0800  Internet: www.cde.ca.gov

**Employees: 2,557  Fiscal Year: 2015-2016  Budget: $794,134,000**

★State Superintendent of Public Instruction
  **Thomas "Tom" Torlakson** (D) . . . . . . . . . . . . . . . . . . . . . (916) 319-0800
  Term Expires: January 2019
  E-mail: superintendent@cde.ca.gov
  Scheduler **Cindy Quiralte** . . . . . . . . . . . . . . . . . . . . . . . . . . (916) 319-0583
  Principal Advisor **Jason Spencer** . . . . . . . . . . . . . . . . . . . . (916) 319-0521
  Chief Deputy Superintendent of Public Instruction
  **Glen Price** . . . . . . . . . . . . . . . . . . . . . . . . . . . . . . . . . . . . . (916) 319-0794
  Chief Deputy Superintendent of Public Instruction
  **Michelle Zumot** . . . . . . . . . . . . . . . . . . . . . . . . . . . . . . . . . (916) 319-0794
  Executive Assistant **Kathy Dobson** . . . . . . . . . . . . . . . . . . (916) 319-0793
  Communications Director **Bill Ainsworth** . . . . . . . . . . . . . . (916) 319-0691
  E-mail: bill.ainsworth@cde.ca.gov
  Government Affairs Director **Debra Brown** . . . . . . . . . . . . . (916) 319-0821
                                                        Fax: (916) 319-0156
  Federal Policy Liaison **John Hooper III** . . . . . . . . . . . . . . . (916) 319-0650
                                                        Fax: (916) 319-0111

# Board of Equalization

450 N Street, Sacramento, CA 94279-0073
Tel: (916) 445-6464  TTY: (916) 327-4975  Fax: (916) 324-2586
Internet: www.boe.ca.gov

★Chairman **Jerome E. Horton** (D-District 3) . . . . . . . . . . . . . (916) 445-4154
  Term Expires: January 6, 2019
  Education: Cal State (Dominguez) BS
★Vice Chair **George C. Runner** (R-District 1) . . . . . . . . . . . . (916) 445-2181
  Term Expires: January 6, 2019
  Education: U Redlands BS
★Member **Diane L. Harkey** (R-District 4) . . . . . . . . . . . . . . . (916) 323-9794
  Term Expires: January 6, 2019
  Education: UC Irvine BEc
★Member **Fiona Ma** (D-District 2) . . . . . . . . . . . . . . . . . . . . (916) 445-6464
  Term Expires: January 6, 2019
  Ex-Officio Member **Betty T. Yee** . . . . . . . . . . . . . . . . . . . . . (916) 445-2636
  Executive Director **David Gau** . . . . . . . . . . . . . . . . . . . . . . (916) 327-4975
  Chief Deputy Director **(Vacant)** . . . . . . . . . . . . . . . . . . . . . (916) 322-9070

★ Elected Official   ■Appointed by Governor   ●Appointed by Legislature   ▲Appointed by Board or Commission   ◆Appointed by State Supreme Court

Summer 2016                © Leadership Directories, Inc.                State Yellow Book

EXECUTIVE BRANCH

# Colorado

Tel: (303) 866-5000 (State Operator)  Internet: www.colorado.gov

**Number of U.S. Congressional Delegates:** 2 Senators; 7 Representatives  **Governor's Term:** 4 years
**Legislature Description:** General Assembly - 35 member Senate; 65 member House of Representatives;
Term - Senate 4 years, House 2 years  **Next Election:** Governor November 2018; Legislature
November 2016  **Number of Electoral Votes:** 9  **Official Name:** State of Colorado (Spanish: Red)
**Nickname:** Centennial State  **Motto:** Nil sine numine (Nothing without providence)

**Population:** 5,456,574 (2015); Rank 22  **Fiscal Year:** 2013-2014  **Budget:** $23,010,060,163

## Office of the Governor

136 State Capitol, Denver, CO 80203-1792
Tel: (303) 866-2471  Fax: (303) 866-2003

**Governor John Hickenlooper**
Governor

Began Service: January 11, 2011
Term Expires: January 2019
Date of Birth: February 7, 1952
Education: Wesleyan U 1974 BA, 1980 MA
Home: Denver
Religion: Quaker
Career: Geologist; Mayor, City and County of
Denver, Colorado (2003-2011)

★Governor **Governor John Hickenlooper** (D) . . . . . . . . . . . (303) 866-2471
Chief of Staff **Douglas J. "Doug" Friednash** . . . . . . . . . . (303) 866-2471
  Education: UC Santa Barbara 1984 BA; San Diego 1987 JD
Deputy Chief of Staff **David Padrino** . . . . . . . . . . . . . . . . (303) 866-2417
Deputy Chief of Staff and Chief Administrative Officer
  **(Vacant)** . . . . . . . . . . . . . . . . . . . . . . . . . . . . . . . . . (303) 866-2471
Chief Legal Counsel **Jacki Cooper Melmed** . . . . . . . . . . . (303) 866-3788
  E-mail: jackie.melmed@state.co.us
  Education: Michigan 1992 BA; Chicago 1997 MA; Colorado 2003 JD
Chief Recovery Officer **Molly Urbina** . . . . . . . . . . . . . . . (303) 866-4917
  E-mail: molly.urbina@state.co.us
Communications Director **Kathy Green** . . . . . . . . . . . . . . (303) 866-6324
  E-mail: kathy.green@state.co.us
Marijuana Coordination Director **Andrew S. Freedman** . . . (303) 866-4969
  E-mail: andrew.freedman@state.co.us
  Education: Harvard 2010 JD
Senior Advisor **Jamie Van Leeuwen** . . . . . . . . . . . . . . . . (303) 866-3906
  E-mail: jamie.vanleeuwen@state.co.us
  Education: Creighton 1996 BA; Tulane 1997 MPH;
  Colorado (Denver) 1999 MA, 2007 PhD

## Office of Economic Development and International Trade [OEDIT]

1625 Broadway, Suite 2700, Denver, CO 80202
Tel: (303) 892-3840  Fax: (303) 892-3848

■Executive Director **Fiona Arnold** . . . . . . . . . . . . . . . . . . . (303) 892-3840
  E-mail: fiona.arnold@state.co.us
  Education: U Tasmania (Australia); U Adelaide (Australia) BLL;
  Southern Methodist ML
Communications Director **Holly Shrewsbury** . . . . . . . . . . (303) 892-3840
  E-mail: holly.shrewsbury@state.co.us
Legislative Liaison **Eloise Hirsch** . . . . . . . . . . . . . . . . . . (303) 892-3840
  E-mail: eloise.hirsch@state.co.us
Senior Advisor **(Vacant)** . . . . . . . . . . . . . . . . . . . . . . . . . (303) 892-3840

## Colorado Creative Industries

1625 Broadway, Suite 2700, Denver, CO 80202
Tel: (303) 892-3802  Fax: (303) 892-3848

Director **Margaret Hunt** . . . . . . . . . . . . . . . . . . . . . . . . . (303) 892-3870
Deputy Director **Sheila Sears** . . . . . . . . . . . . . . . . . . . . . (303) 892-3852
Program Manager **Christy Costello** . . . . . . . . . . . . . . . . (303) 892-3724
  E-mail: christine.costello@state.co.us

Program Manager **Ruth Bruno** . . . . . . . . . . . . . . . . . . . . . (303) 892-3813
  E-mail: ruth.bruno@state.co.us
Program Administrator **Amanda Flores** . . . . . . . . . . . . . . (303) 892-3832
  E-mail: amanda.flores@state.co.us
Program Administrator **Benjamin Litwin** . . . . . . . . . . . . . (303) 892-3822
  E-mail: benjamin.litwin@state.co.us

## Colorado Tourism Office [CTO]

1625 Broadway, Suite 2700, Denver, CO 80202
Tel: (303) 892-3840  Fax: (303) 892-3848

Director **Cathy Ritter** . . . . . . . . . . . . . . . . . . . . . . . . . . . (303) 892-3856
Associate Director **(Vacant)** . . . . . . . . . . . . . . . . . . . . . . (303) 892-3840
Deputy Director of International Tourism
  **Janet Christopher** . . . . . . . . . . . . . . . . . . . . . . . . . . . (303) 892-3840
Director of Heritage and Agritourism Program
  **Laura Grey** . . . . . . . . . . . . . . . . . . . . . . . . . . . . . . . . (303) 892-3840
  E-mail: laura.grey@state.co.us
  Education: Denver 2008 BA
Director of U.S. Marketing **Amber Kollman** . . . . . . . . . . . (303) 892-3717
Director of Visitor Services **Kelly Barbello** . . . . . . . . . . . (303) 892-3840
Communications Manager **Kirstin P. Graber** . . . . . . . . . . (303) 892-3840
  E-mail: kirstin.graber@state.co.us
Operations Manager **(Vacant)** . . . . . . . . . . . . . . . . . . . . . (303) 892-3840

## Office of Information Technology

601 East 18th Avenue, Suite 250, Denver, CO 80203
Tel: (303) 764-7700  Fax: (303) 764-7725  E-mail: oit@state.co.us
Internet: www.colorado.gov/oit

**Fiscal Year:** 2013-2014  **Budget:** $57,947,616

■Secretary of Technology and Chief Information Officer
  **Sumana "Suma" Nallapati** . . . . . . . . . . . . . . . . . . . . . (303) 764-7700
  E-mail: sumana.nallapati@state.co.us
  Education: Andhra U (India)
Deputy Chief Information Officer and Chief Financial
  Officer **Brenda Berlin** . . . . . . . . . . . . . . . . . . . . . . . . (303) 764-7928
  E-mail: brenda.berlin@state.co.us
Chief Communications Officer and Public Information
  Officer **Tauna Lockhart** . . . . . . . . . . . . . . . . . . . . . . . (303) 764-7716
  E-mail: tauna.lockhart@state.co.us
  Education: Dartmouth BA
Chief Customer Officer **William M. Chumley** . . . . . . . . . . (303) 764-7896
  E-mail: william.chumley@state.co.us
Chief Data Officer **(Vacant)** . . . . . . . . . . . . . . . . . . . . . . (303) 764-7700
Chief Strategy Officer **Monica M. Coughlin** . . . . . . . . . . . (303) 764-7710
  E-mail: monica.coughlin@state.co.us
Chief Technology Officer **David McCurdy** . . . . . . . . . . . . (303) 764-7834
  E-mail: david.mccurdy@state.co.us
Human Resources Director **Karen Wilcox** . . . . . . . . . . . . (303) 764-7906

## Office of Policy, Research and Legislative Affairs

Tel: (303) 866-2471

Chief Strategy Officer and Director **Alan B. Salazar** . . . . . (303) 866-2471
  E-mail: alan.salazar@state.co.us
  Education: Colorado 1980 BA, 1984 JD
Deputy Director of Strategic Operations **Lisa Carpenter** . . . (303) 866-5800
  E-mail: lisa.carpenter@state.co.us

*(continued on next page)*

---

★ Elected Official  ■ Appointed by Governor  ● Appointed by Legislature  ▲ Appointed by Board or Commission  ◆ Appointed by State Supreme Court

**Office of Policy, Research and Legislative Affairs** *continued*

Legislative Director **Kurtis T. Morrison** . . . . . . . . . . . . . . . . (303) 866-2471
E-mail: kurtis.morrison@state.co.us
Education: Creighton 2002 BA
Deputy Legislative Director **(Vacant)** . . . . . . . . . . . . . . . . . . (303) 866-2471
Legislative Assistant **Adam Zarrin** . . . . . . . . . . . . . . . . . . . . (303) 866-6290
E-mail: adam.zarrin@state.co.us
Senior Policy Director **Simon N. Tafoya** . . . . . . . . . . . . . . (303) 866-2989
E-mail: simon.tafoya@state.co.us
Education: Colorado Col BA; Princeton 2007 MPAUP
Senior Policy Advisor **Adrienne Russman** . . . . . . . . . . . . . (303) 866-2471
Note: Criminal Justice, Public Safety, Military and Veteran Affairs, and
Transportation
E-mail: adrienne.russman@state.co.us
Policy Advisor **Kyle M. Brown** . . . . . . . . . . . . . . . . . . . . . . . (303) 866-2471
Note: Health and Human Services
E-mail: kyle.brown@state.co.us
Education: Georgetown 2004 BS; Harvard 2009 PhD
Policy Advisor **Matt Hastings** . . . . . . . . . . . . . . . . . . . . . . . . (303) 866-2471
Note: Agriculture, Local Affairs, and Personnel and Administration,
and Economic Development
E-mail: matt.hastings@state.co.us
Policy Advisor **Zachary M. Pierce** . . . . . . . . . . . . . . . . . . . . (303) 866-2471
Note: Natural Resources and Energy
E-mail: zachary.pierce@state.co.us
Policy Advisor **Evy Valencia** . . . . . . . . . . . . . . . . . . . . . . . . (303) 866-2471
Note: Education and Human Services
E-mail: evy.valencia@state.co.us

## Office of State Planning and Budgeting

200 East Colfax Avenue, Room 111, Denver, CO 80203
Tel: (303) 866-3317  Fax: (303) 866-3044

Director **Henry Sobanet** . . . . . . . . . . . . . . . . . . . . . . . . . . . . (303) 866-3317
E-mail: henry.sobanet@state.co.us
Deputy Director **Erick Scheminske** . . . . . . . . . . . . . . . . . . . (303) 866-3024
E-mail: erick.scheminske@state.co.us
Chief Economist **Jason Schrock** . . . . . . . . . . . . . . . . . . . . . . (303) 866-3174
Economist **Michael Yeadon** . . . . . . . . . . . . . . . . . . . . . . . . . (303) 866-2765
Economist **Greg Lestikow** . . . . . . . . . . . . . . . . . . . . . . . . . . (303) 866-2628
Office Manager **Cate Stanek** . . . . . . . . . . . . . . . . . . . . . . . . (303) 866-3317

## Department of Agriculture [CDA]

305 Interlocken Parkway, Broomfield, CO 80021
Tel: (303) 869-9000  E-mail: comments@state.co.us
Internet: www.colorado.gov/ag

**Employees: 274  Fiscal Year: 2013-2014  Budget: $42,670**

■Commissioner **Donald C. Brown** . . . . . . . . . . . . . . . . . . . . (303) 869-9007
E-mail: don.brown@state.co.us
Deputy Commissioner **Chris Wiseman** . . . . . . . . . . . . . . . . (303) 869-9007
Education: Colorado State Pueblo BS
Chief Administrative Officer **Jenifer Gurr** . . . . . . . . . . . . (303) 869-9002
E-mail: jenifer.gurr@state.co.us
Chief Financial Officer **Joy Huse** . . . . . . . . . . . . . . . . . . . . (303) 869-9020
Communications Director **Christi Lightcap** . . . . . . . . . . . . (303) 869-9005
E-mail: christi.lightcap@state.co.us
Contract Legislative Liaison **Danny TomLinson** . . . . . . . . (303) 660-6036
E-mail: dtomlinson@msn.com
Human Resources Manager **Jenifer Gurr** . . . . . . . . . . . . . (303) 869-9002
Controller **(Vacant)** . . . . . . . . . . . . . . . . . . . . . . . . . . . . . . . (303) 869-9023
Purchasing Agent **Rob Archer** . . . . . . . . . . . . . . . . . . . . . . . (303) 869-9027

## Department of Corrections [DOC]

1250 Academy Park Loop, Colorado Springs, CO 80910
Tel: (719) 579-9580  Fax: (719) 226-4755  TTY: (719) 579-9580

**Employees: 6,019**

■Executive Director **Rick Raemisch** . . . . . . . . . . . . . . . . . . (719) 226-4701
E-mail: rick.raemisch@state.co.us
Education: Wisconsin (Stevens Point) BS; Wisconsin 1988 JD
Deputy Executive Director **Kellie Wasko** . . . . . . . . . . . . . (719) 579-9580
Clinical and Correctional Services Director
**Renae E. Jordan** . . . . . . . . . . . . . . . . . . . . . . . . . . . . . . (719) 579-9580
Education: Southern Colorado BS; Bellevue U MS

Finance and Administration Director **Jennifer Bennett** . . . . (719) 226-4751
E-mail: jennifer.bennett@state.co.us
Information Technology Director **Rick Vyncke** . . . . . . . . . . (719) 226-4825
E-mail: rick.vyncke@state.co.us
Parole Director **Melissa Roberts** . . . . . . . . . . . . . . . . . . . . . (303) 763-2422
Parole Deputy Director **Alison Morgan** . . . . . . . . . . . . . . . (719) 226-4723
Prisons Director **Steve Hager** . . . . . . . . . . . . . . . . . . . . . . . (719) 226-4775
Prisons Deputy Director **John L. Davis** . . . . . . . . . . . . . . . (719) 226-4775
Prisons Deputy Director **Frances Falk** . . . . . . . . . . . . . . . . (719) 226-4736
Chief Human Resource Officer **Rick Thompkins** . . . . . . . . (719) 226-4401
Inspector General **Jay Kirby** . . . . . . . . . . . . . . . . . . . . . . . . (719) 226-4678
E-mail: jay.kirby@state.co.us
Private Prison Monitoring Assistant Director
**Paul Hollenbeck** . . . . . . . . . . . . . . . . . . . . . . . . . . . . . . . (719) 226-4903

## Colorado State Board of Parole

Building 54, 1600 West 24th Street, Pueblo, CO 81003
Tel: (719) 583-5800  Fax: (719) 583-5805
E-mail: pbchair@doc.state.co.us

■Chairperson **Joe Morales** . . . . . . . . . . . . . . . . . . . . . . . . . . (719) 583-5800
Term Expires: July 1, 2016
■Vice Chairperson **Rebecca L. Oakes** . . . . . . . . . . . . . . . . . (719) 583-5800
Term Expires: July 1, 2017
■Member **Denise K. Balazic** . . . . . . . . . . . . . . . . . . . . . . . . (719) 583-5800
Term Expires: July 1, 2017
Education: Southern Illinois BS
■Member **John O'Dell** . . . . . . . . . . . . . . . . . . . . . . . . . . . . . (719) 583-5800
Term Expires: July 1, 2015
■Member **Alfredo Enrique Pena** . . . . . . . . . . . . . . . . . . . . . (719) 583-5800
Term Expires: July 1, 2017
Education: Texas; Denver JD
■Member **Alexandra J. Walker** . . . . . . . . . . . . . . . . . . . . . . (719) 583-5800
Term Expires: July 1, 2016
■Member **(Vacant)** . . . . . . . . . . . . . . . . . . . . . . . . . . . . . . . . (719) 583-5800

## Department of Health Care Policy and Financing

1570 Grant Street, Denver, CO 80203-1818
Tel: (303) 866-2993  Tel: (800) 221-3943  TTY: (303) 866-3883
Fax: (303) 866-4411

**Employees: 358**

■Executive Director **Susan "Sue" Birch** . . . . . . . . . . . . . . . (303) 866-3871
E-mail: susan.birch@state.co.us          Fax: (303) 866-2828
Education: Colorado 1982 BSN, 1988 MBA

### Client and Clinical Care Office

Director/Chief Medical Officer **Judy T. Zerzan** . . . . . . . . . (303) 866-3410
Education: Willamette 1993 BA; Oregon Health 1998 MD;
North Carolina 1999 MPH
Chief Client Officer **Antoinette Taranto** . . . . . . . . . . . . . . (303) 866-5005
Education: Penn State BS
Data Analysis Section Manager **(Vacant)** . . . . . . . . . . . . . . (303) 866-2567
Quality and Health Improvement Unit Manager
**Camille Harding** . . . . . . . . . . . . . . . . . . . . . . . . . . . . . . . (303) 866-5879
Pharmacy Benefits Section Manager **Cathy Traugott** . . . . . (303) 866-6338
Grants Management **Leah Spielberg** . . . . . . . . . . . . . . . . . . (303) 866-5903

### Community Living Office

Fax: (303) 866-2786

Director **Jed Ziegenhagen** . . . . . . . . . . . . . . . . . . . . . . . . . . (303) 866-3200

### Finance Office

Fax: (303) 866-4411

Director/Deputy Executive Director **John Bartholomew** . . (303) 866-2854
Education: UC Santa Barbara          Fax: (216) 636-6958

### Health Information Office

Director **Chris W. Underwood** . . . . . . . . . . . . . . . . . . . . . . (303) 866-4766
Education: Colorado BEc, MEc
Provider Operations Director **(Vacant)** . . . . . . . . . . . . . . . . (303) 866-4766
Purchasing and Contracting Section Manager
**Cindy Ward** . . . . . . . . . . . . . . . . . . . . . . . . . . . . . . . . . . . (303) 866-3456

---

★ Elected Official   ■ Appointed by Governor   ● Appointed by Legislature   ▲ Appointed by Board or Commission   ◆ Appointed by State Supreme Court

EXECUTIVE BRANCH

## Health Programs Office

Medicaid Director and Health Programs Office Director
**Gretchen Hammer** . . . . . . . . . . . . . . . . . . . . . . . . . (303) 866-5929
Education: Colorado Col BA; U Washington MPH
Deputy Medicaid Director **Laurel Karabatsos** . . . . . . . . . . (303) 866-2445
Education: Colorado
Benefits Section Manager **Valeria Baker-Easley** . . . . . . . . (303) 866-3684
Primary Care Case Management Systems Section
Manager **Marceil Case** . . . . . . . . . . . . . . . . . . . . . . . (303) 866-3054
Provider Relations and Dental Program Division Director
**William "Bill" Heller** . . . . . . . . . . . . . . . . . . . . . . . (303) 866-3244

## Policy, Communications, and Administration Office

Fax: (303) 866-2828
Director **Tom Massey** . . . . . . . . . . . . . . . . . . . . . . . . . (303) 866-6657
E-mail: tom.massey@state.co.us
Deputy Director **Carrie Cortiglio** . . . . . . . . . . . . . . . . . . (303) 866-3972
E-mail: carrie.cortiglio@state.co.us
Operations Manager/Governor's Advocate
**Diane Rodriguez** . . . . . . . . . . . . . . . . . . . . . . . . . . (303) 866-2868
E-mail: diane.rodriguez@state.co.us
Facility Coordinator **Heather Allen** . . . . . . . . . . . . . . . . . (303) 866-6092
Legislative Liaison **Mary Kathryn Hurd** . . . . . . . . . . . . . . (303) 866-4324
E-mail: mk.hurd@state.co.us
Client Services Division Director **Christine Comer** . . . . . . (303) 866-5410
External Relations Division Director **Rachel Reiter** . . . . . . (303) 866-3140
E-mail: rachel.reiter@state.co.us
Human Resources Section Manager **Janice Smuda** . . . . . (303) 866-3143
Federal Policy and Rules Officer **Barbara Prehmus** . . . . . . (303) 866-2991

## Department of Higher Education

1560 Broadway, Suite 1600, Denver, CO 80202
Tel: (303) 862-3001 Fax: (303) 996-1329 Internet: highered.colorado.gov

**Employees:** 22,842 **Fiscal Year:** 2013-2014 **Budget:** $3,233,189,910

■Executive Director (Acting) **Jennifer Sobanet** . . . . . . . . . (303) 862-3001
Note: Until the end of May 2016.
E-mail: jennifer.sobanet@dhe.state.co.us
E-mail: executivedirector@dhe.state.co.us
Executive Assistant and Office Manager
**Suzanne Stark** . . . . . . . . . . . . . . . . . . . . . . . . . . . (303) 866-2723
GEAR UP Program Director **Dr. Timothy J. Flanagan** . . (303) 866-3001
Education: SUNY (Albany) PhD
Chief Operating Officer **Jennifer Sobanet** . . . . . . . . . . . . (303) 866-2723
Note: Until the end of May 2016.
E-mail: jennifer.sobanet@dhe.state.co.us
Chief Policy Officer **Kachina Weaver** . . . . . . . . . . . . . . . (303) 866-2723
E-mail: kachina.weaver@dhe.state.co.us
Human Resources Manager **Cynthia "Cindy" Langen** . . . . (720) 264-8575

## Colorado Commission on Higher Education [CCHE]

Tel: (303) 862-3001 Fax: (303) 996-1329

■Chair
**Dr. Monte Moses, PhD** (6th Congressional Dist. Rep.) . . (303) 862-3001
Term Expires: July 1, 2019
E-mail: monte.moses@yahoo.com
■Vice Chair **Luis A. Colón** (4th Congressional Dist. Rep.) . . (303) 862-3001
Term Expires: July 1, 2017
E-mail: lcolon@xcelenteglobal.com
Education: Michigan MBA
■Commissioner
**John L. Anderson** (3rd Congressional Dist. Rep.) . . . . . . (303) 862-3001
Term Expires: July 1, 2019
E-mail: anderson@frontier.net
■Commissioner
**Maia A. Babbs, CFA** (7th Congressional Dist. Rep.) . . . . (303) 862-3001
Term Expires: July 1, 2019
E-mail: maia@obermeyerwood.com
Affiliation: Research Analyst, Janus Capital Group Inc.
151 Detroit Street, Denver, CO 80206-4923
Education: Virginia BA; Fletcher Law & Diplomacy MA

■Commissioner
**Renny Fagan** (7th Congressional Dist. Rep.) . . . . . . . . . (303) 862-3001
Term Expires: July 1, 2019
E-mail: rfagan@coloradononprofits.org
Education: Chicago BA; Northwestern JD
■Commissioner **Jeanette Autobee Garcia**
(3rd Congressional Dist. Rep.) . . . . . . . . . . . . . . . . . . . (303) 862-3001
Term Expires: July 1, 2019
E-mail: autobeegarcia@gmail.com
■Commissioner
**Richard C. Kaufman** (6th Congressional Dist. Rep.) . . . . (303) 862-3001
Term Expires: July 12, 2016
E-mail: rkaufman@rcalaw.com
Education: Indiana State 1972 BS; Emory 1976 JD
■Commissioner
**Vanecia B. Kerr** (6th Congressional Dist. Rep.) . . . . . . . (303) 862-3001
Term Expires: July 1, 2018
E-mail: vkerr@cityyear.org
Education: Hampton BA; Baruch Col MPA
■Commissioner
**Tom McGimpsey** (2nd Congressional Dist. Rep.) . . . . . . (303) 862-3001
Term Expires: July 1, 2019
E-mail: tom.mcgimpsey@aei.com
■Commissioner
**Paula E. Sandoval** (1st Congressional Dist. Rep.) . . . . . . (303) 862-3001
Term Expires: July 1, 2018
Education: Colorado BA; Colorado (Denver) MPA
■Commissioner
**Barbara J. "BJ" Scott** (5th Congressional Dist. Rep.) . . (719) 630-6474
Term Expires: June 30, 2016
E-mail: bjscott@peakvista.org
Affiliation: Executive Director, Peak Vista Community Health Centers
Foundation, Peak Vista Community Health Centers
722 South Wahsatch Avenue, Colorado Springs, CO 80903
Education: Luther Col BA

## Colorado Department of Human Services [CDHS]

1575 Sherman Street, 8th Floor, Denver, CO 80203-1714
Tel: (303) 866-5700 Fax: (303) 866-4047

**Employees:** 4,875

■Executive Director **Reginald "Reggie" Bicha** . . . . . . . . . . (303) 866-3475
E-mail: reginald.bicha@state.co.us
Education: Wisconsin (Eau Claire) 1992 BSW; Minnesota MSW
Deputy Executive Director for Community Partnerships
**Julie Krow** . . . . . . . . . . . . . . . . . . . . . . . . . . . . . . (303) 866-5414
Deputy Executive Director of Operations **Nikki Hatch** . . . . (303) 866-3988
Deputy Executive Director of Strategic Communications
and Legislative Affairs **Dee Martinez** . . . . . . . . . . . . . (303) 866-5700
Communications Director **Alicia Caldwell** . . . . . . . . . . . . (303) 866-3411
Education: Northwestern
Legislative Liaison **Jen Politi-Corrigan** . . . . . . . . . . . . . . (303) 866-4479
E-mail: jennifer.corrigan@state.co.us

## Department of Labor and Employment [CDLE]

633 17th Street, Suite 1200, Denver, CO 80202
Tel: (888) 390-7936 Fax: (303) 318-8000

**Employees:** 1,013

■Executive Director **Ellen Golombek** . . . . . . . . . . . . . . . . (303) 318-8020
E-mail: ellen.golombek@state.co.us
Deputy Executive Director **Kristin Corash** . . . . . . . . . . . . (303) 318-8035
Human Resources Director **Glenda C. Barry** . . . . . . . . . . (303) 318-8202
Webmaster **Amanda Neal** . . . . . . . . . . . . . . . . . . . . . . (303) 318-8238

---

★ Elected Official    ■ Appointed by Governor    ● Appointed by Legislature    ▲ Appointed by Board or Commission    ◆ Appointed by State Supreme Court

## Department of Local Affairs [DOLA]

1313 Sherman Street, Room 521, Denver, CO 80203
Tel: (303) 864-7720  TTY: (303) 866-5300  Fax: (303) 866-7879
E-mail: dola.helpdesk@state.co.us  Internet: www.dola.state.co.us

**Employees:** 164

- Executive Director
  **MajGen Irving L. "Irv" Halter, Jr., USAF (Ret)** . . . . . . . (303) 864-7720
    E-mail: irv.halter@state.co.us
    Education: Air Force Acad 1977 BS; Troy State 1990 MS;
    Air Command Col 1990
  Executive Assistant **Melissa Nord** . . . . . . . . . . . . . . . . . . (303) 864-7720
  Deputy Executive Director **Patrick Coyle** . . . . . . . . . . . . (303) 866-2239
  Budget Director **James McCoy** . . . . . . . . . . . . . . . . . . . . . (303) 866-4099
  Controller **Janet Miks** . . . . . . . . . . . . . . . . . . . . . . . . . . . (303) 866-2252
    Fax: (303) 866-4202
  Legislative Liaison **Bruce A. Eisenhauer** . . . . . . . . . . . . . . (303) 864-7720
    E-mail: bruce.eisenhauer@state.co.us
  Communications Director **Denise Stepto** . . . . . . . . . . . . . . (303) 864-7707
    E-mail: denise.stepto@state.co.us
  Human Resources Director **Jennifer L. Clayman** . . . . . . . . (303) 864-7865
    Fax: (303) 866-2251
  Public Information Officer **Patrick Collins** . . . . . . . . . . . . (303) 866-7864
    Education: Colorado 2008 BA

## Department of Military and Veterans Affairs [DMVA]

6848 South Revere Parkway, Centennial, CO 80112-6709
Tel: (720) 250-1500  Fax: (720) 250-1519

**Employees:** 1,390  **Fiscal Year:** 2013-2014  **Budget:** $223,858,252

- Executive Director
  **MajGen H. Michael "Mike" Edwards, ANG** . . . . . . . . . (720) 250-1500
    E-mail: tag.assistant@dmva.state.co.us
    Education: Air Force Acad 1973 BS; Air War Col 1977
  Executive Assistant **Jean Schjodt** . . . . . . . . . . . . . . . . . . (720) 250-1500
  Deputy Executive Director **Michael T. "Mickey" Hunt** . . . . (720) 250-1510
  Legislative Liaison **Greg Dorman** . . . . . . . . . . . . . . . . . . (720) 250-1511
    E-mail: greg.dorman@dmva.state.co.us
  Controller **Will Thomson** . . . . . . . . . . . . . . . . . . . . . . . . (720) 250-1530
  Human Resources Director **Tamy Calahan** . . . . . . . . . . . . (720) 250-1520
  Information Technology Director **Steve Holland** . . . . . . . . (720) 250-1513
  Purchasing and Contracts Director **Janet Jones** . . . . . . . . (720) 250-1541
    Purchasing Agent **Allison Gard** . . . . . . . . . . . . . . . . . . (720) 250-1540
  Facilities Maintenance Supervisor **Larry Brown** . . . . . . . . (720) 250-1373

## Colorado National Guard

6848 South Revere Parkway, Centennial, CO 80112-6709
Tel: (720) 250-1500

- Adjutant General
  **MajGen H. Michael "Mike" Edwards, ANG** . . . . . . . . . (720) 250-1500
    E-mail: tag.assistant@dmva.state.co.us
  Senior Enlisted Leader **CSM William D. Woods, ARNG** . . (720) 250-1500

## Colorado Air National Guard

84 North Aspen Street, Centennial, CO 80011
Tel: (720) 847-9955

Assistant Adjutant General **Jerome P. Limoge, Jr.** . . . . . . . . (720) 847-9955
  Education: South Carolina 1988 MD
Command Chief Master Sergeant
  **CMSgt James B. Whitlow, ANG** . . . . . . . . . . . . . . . . . . (720) 847-9955
Wing Commander **Col Floyd W. Dunstan, ANG** . . . . . . . (720) 847-9955
Vice Commander **Col Timothy Conklin, ANG** . . . . . . . . . (720) 847-9955
  Education: Air Force Acad 1988 BS

## Colorado Army National Guard

6848 South Revere Parkway, Centennial, CO 80112-6709
Tel: (720) 250-1020

Assistant Adjutant General and Commander
  **BG Donald Laucirica, ARNG** . . . . . . . . . . . . . . . . . . . . (720) 250-1020
    Education: Utah 1985 BS; Webster 2007 MS
Command Chief Warrant Officer
  **CW5 Sefer S. Imeraj, ARNG** . . . . . . . . . . . . . . . . . . . . (720) 250-1020

## Department of Natural Resources

1313 Sherman Street, Room 718, Denver, CO 80203
Tel: (303) 866-3311  Fax: (303) 866-2115  Internet: www.dnr.state.co.us

**Fiscal Year:** 2013-2014  **Budget:** $277,509,241

- Executive Director (Interim)
  **Robert "Bob" Randall** . . . . . . . . . . . . . . . . . . . . (303) 866-3311 ext. 8668
    E-mail: robert.randall@state.co.us
    Education: Missouri; Lewis & Clark JD
  Deputy Director **Robert "Bob" Randall** . . . . . . . . (303) 866-3311 ext. 8668
    E-mail: robert.randall@state.co.us
  Assistant Director for Energy and Minerals
    **Kathleen Staks** . . . . . . . . . . . . . . . . . . . . . . . . (303) 866-3311 ext. 8658
    Education: Denver JD
  Assistant Director for Parks, Wildlife and Lands
    **Madeleine West** . . . . . . . . . . . . . . . . . . . . . . . (303) 866-3311 ext. 8666
    Education: Bates BS; Colorado (Denver) MPA
  Assistant Director for Water **Lauren Ris** . . . . . . . . (303) 866-3311 ext. 8663
    Education: Willamette; Michigan MEP
  Policy Adviser **(Vacant)** . . . . . . . . . . . . . . . . . . . . . . . . (303) 866-3311
  Controller **Susan Borup** . . . . . . . . . . . . . . . . . . (303) 866-3292 ext. 8634
  Budget Director **William H. "Bill" Levine** . . . . . . (303) 866-3311 ext. 8667
    E-mail: bill.levine@state.co.us
    Education: Michigan 1995 MPP
  Communications Director **Todd Hartman** . . . . . . . (303) 866-3311 ext. 8665
    E-mail: todd.hartman@state.co.us
  Human Resources Director **Tina Miller** . . . . . . . . (303) 866-2667 ext. 8648
  Legislative Liaison **Gaspar Perricone** . . . . . . . . . (303) 866-3311 ext. 8664
    E-mail: gaspar.perricone@state.co.us
    Education: Utah 2007

## State Board of Land Commissioners

1127 Sherman Street, Denver, CO 80203
Tel: (303) 866-3454  Fax: (303) 866-3152

- President **Gary Butterworth** . . . . . . . . . . . . . . . . . . . . . . (303) 866-3454
    Term Expires: March 30, 2017
    E-mail: gary.butterworth@state.co.us
    Education: Yale 1994 BA
- Vice Chair **Buck Blessing** . . . . . . . . . . . . . . . . . . . . . . . (303) 866-3454
    Term Expires: June 30, 2017
    E-mail: buck.blessing@state.co.us
- Commissioner **Robert Bledsoe** . . . . . . . . . . . . . . . . . . . . (303) 866-3454
    Term Expires: March 30, 2017
    E-mail: bob.bledsoe@state.co.us
- Commissioner **Barbara King Bynum** . . . . . . . . . . . . . . . . (303) 866-3454
    Term Expires: June 30, 2019
    E-mail: barbara.bynum@state.co.us
- Commissioner **Greg Moffet** . . . . . . . . . . . . . . . . . . . . . . (303) 866-3454
    Term Expires: June 30, 2019
    E-mail: greg.moffet@state.co.us

## Department of Personnel and Administration [DPA]

1525 Sherman Street, Denver, CO 80203
Tel: (303) 866-3000  Fax: (303) 866-2102
Internet: www.colorado.gov/dpa

**Employees:** 393

- Executive Director **P. June Taylor** . . . . . . . . . . . . . . . . . . (303) 866-4434
    Education: New Mexico BA; Denver 1998 JD
    Executive Assistant **(Vacant)** . . . . . . . . . . . . . . . . . . . . (303) 866-6559
  Deputy Executive Director **Kara Veitch** . . . . . . . . . . . . . . (303) 866-4434
    Education: Colorado BA, 2000 JD
  State Archives Director **George F. Orlowski** . . . . . . . . . . . (303) 866-2329
    Education: Illinois State 1983 (Attended);
    Wilbur Wright 1985 (Attended); Columbia Col Chicago 1987 BA
  Chief Operations Officer **Kristin F. Rozansky** . . . . . . . . . . (303) 866-5044
    Education: Colorado State; Colorado JD
  Budget Policy and Analysis Director **Adrian Leiter** . . . . . . (303) 866-4022
  Human Resources Director **Susan A. Rafferty** . . . . . . . . . . (303) 866-2284
  Communications Director **Adrian Schulte** . . . . . . . . . . . . . (303) 866-6555
    E-mail: adrian.schulte@state.co.us
  Legislative Liaison **Jack Wylie** . . . . . . . . . . . . . . . . . . . . (303) 866-3539
    E-mail: jack.wylie@state.co.us

---

★ Elected Official  ■ Appointed by Governor  ● Appointed by Legislature  ▲ Appointed by Board or Commission  ◆ Appointed by State Supreme Court

# Colorado Department of Public Health and Environment [CDPHE]

4300 Cherry Creek Drive, South, Denver, CO 80246-1530
Tel: (303) 692-2000  Tel: (303) 692-2200 (Vital Records)
TTY: (303) 691-7700  Fax: (303) 691-7702
Fax: (800) 423-1108 (Vital Records)
E-mail: cdphe.information@state.co.us
E-mail: vital.records@state.co.us (Vital Records)

**Employees:** 1,241  **Fiscal Year:** 2014-2015  **Budget:** $525,821,265

■Executive Director and Chief Medical Officer
  **Larry Wolk, MD, MSPH** . . . . . . . . . . . . . . . . . . . . . . . . . . . (303) 692-2012
    Education: Pennsylvania 1984 BA; Vermont 1988 MD;
    Colorado Health MPH
  Executive Assistant **Patricia Marnette** . . . . . . . . . . . . . . . (303) 692-2011
Legislative Liaison **Eliza Schultz** . . . . . . . . . . . . . . . . . . . . (303) 692-3471
    E-mail: eliza.schultz@state.co.us
Deputy Director **Karin Lisa McGowan** . . . . . . . . . . . . . . . . (303) 692-3473
Deputy Chief Medical Officer **Tista Ghosh, MD, MPH** . . . (303) 692-2657
    Education: Yale MPH
  Program Assistant **Julie Perez** . . . . . . . . . . . . . . . . . . . . . (303) 692-2614
Human Resources and Support Services Director
  **Mona F. Heustis** . . . . . . . . . . . . . . . . . . . . . . . . . . . . . . . (303) 692-2063

# Colorado Department of Public Safety [CDPS]

700 Kipling Street, Suite 1000, Denver, CO 80215-5865
Tel: (303) 239-4400  TTY: (303) 239-4505  Fax: (303) 239-4670

**Employees:** 1,616

■Executive Director **Stan Hilkey** . . . . . . . . . . . . . . . . . . . . . (303) 239-4398
    E-mail: stan.hilkey@state.co.us
Deputy Executive Director **Rebecca Spiess** . . . . . . . . . . . . (303) 239-4398
    E-mail: rebecca.spiess@state.co.us
    Education: Penn State; Colorado
Public Information Officer **(Vacant)** . . . . . . . . . . . . . . . . . . (303) 239-4415

## Division of Criminal Justice

Tel: (303) 239-4442  Fax: (303) 239-4491  Internet: www.dcj.state.co.us

Director **Jeanne M. Smith** . . . . . . . . . . . . . . . . . . . . . . . . . (303) 239-4451
    E-mail: jeanne.smith@state.co.us

## Division of Fire Prevention and Control

690 Kipling Street, Suite 2000, Lakewood, CO 80215
Tel: (303) 239-4600  Fax: (303) 239-5887  Internet: www.dfs.state.co.us

Director **Paul L. Cooke** . . . . . . . . . . . . . . . . . . . . . . . . . . . . (303) 239-5865
Deputy Director **Theresa Staples** . . . . . . . . . . . . . . . . . . . . (303) 239-4600

## Division of Homeland Security and Emergency Management

9195 East Mineral Avenue, Suite 200, Centennial, CO 80112
Tel: (720) 852-6600  Fax: (720) 852-6750

Director **Kevin Klein** . . . . . . . . . . . . . . . . . . . . . . . . . . . . . . (303) 239-4655
Grant Program Manager **Ezzie Michaels** . . . . . . . . . . . . . . (720) 852-6607
State Community Preparedness Program Manager
  **Cathy Prudhomme** . . . . . . . . . . . . . . . . . . . . . . . . . . . . . . (720) 852-6650
Financial Officer **Bill Archambault** . . . . . . . . . . . . . . . . . . . (720) 852-6601

## Colorado Bureau of Investigation

690 Kipling Street, Denver, CO 80215
Fax: (303) 239-4201

Director **Michael S. Rankin** . . . . . . . . . . . . . . . . . . . . . . . . (303) 239-4300
Deputy Director of Criminal Justice Information Systems
  **Chris Andrist** . . . . . . . . . . . . . . . . . . . . . . . . . . . . . . . . . . (303) 239-4308
    Education: Kansas
Deputy Director of Investigations **Ted Mink** . . . . . . . . . . . (303) 239-4221
    Education: Northern Colorado 1972 BA
Deputy Director of Forensic Services **Janet M. Girten** . . . . (303) 239-4210
Public Information Officer **Susan Medina** . . . . . . . . . . . . . (303) 239-4423
    E-mail: susan.medina@state.co.us

# Colorado State Patrol

Tel: (303) 239-4500  TTY: (303) 239-4505  Fax: (303) 239-4485
Internet: www.csp.state.co.us

■Chief **Col. Scott G. Hernandez** . . . . . . . . . . . . . . . . . . . . . (303) 239-4406
    E-mail: scott.hernandez@state.co.us

# Department of Regulatory Agencies [DORA]

1560 Broadway, Suite 1550, Denver, CO 80202
Tel: (303) 894-7855  Fax: (303) 894-7885  E-mail: dora_edo@state.co.us
Internet: www.colorado.gov/dora

**Employees:** 548

■Executive Director **Joseph D. "Joe" Neguse** . . . . . . . . . . (303) 894-7866
    E-mail: dora_edo@state.co.us
    Education: Colorado 2005 BA, 2009 JD
Deputy Director **Michelle Pedersen** . . . . . . . . . . . . . . . . . . (303) 894-2116
Communications Director/Public Information Officer
  **Rebecca Laurie** . . . . . . . . . . . . . . . . . . . . . . . . . . . . . . . . (303) 894-2338
    E-mail: rebecca.laurie@state.co.us
Operations Manager **Megan Ripko** . . . . . . . . . . . . . . . . . . . (303) 894-7866

## Office of Consumer Counsel

1560 Broadway Street, Suite 200, Denver, CO 80202
E-mail: OCC@dora.state.co.us  Internet: www.dora.state.co.us/occ

Director **Cindy Schonhaut** . . . . . . . . . . . . . . . . . . . . . . . . . (303) 894-2224
    Education: Syracuse; Miami JD

## Office of Policy, Research and Regulatory Reform

1560 Broadway, Suite 1550, Denver, CO 80202
Fax: (303) 894-7885  E-mail: opr@dora.state.co.us
Internet: www.dora.state.co.us/opr

Director **Bruce Harrelson** . . . . . . . . . . . . . . . . . . . . . . . . . . (303) 894-2992
    Education: U Phoenix 1987 BA

## Division of Banking

1560 Broadway, Suite 975, Denver, CO 80202
Tel: (303) 894-7575  Fax: (303) 894-7570
E-mail: dora_bankingwebsite@state.co.us

Commissioner **Chris Myklebust** . . . . . . . . . . . . . . . . . . . . . (303) 894-7575
    E-mail: chris.myklebust@state.co.us
    Education: Regis U
Deputy Commissioner **Ken Boldt** . . . . . . . . . . . . . . . . . . . . (303) 894-3011
    E-mail: kenneth.boldt@state.co.us
Examinations Director **Mary Stanfield** . . . . . . . . . . . . . . . . (303) 894-7578
    E-mail: mary.stanfield@state.co.us
    Education: Colorado 1983 BS, 1987 MBA
Operations Manager **Kara Hunter** . . . . . . . . . . . . . . . . . . . . (303) 894-7586
    Education: Augustana (SD) 1989 BA

## Colorado Civil Rights Division

1560 Broadway, Suite 1050, Denver, CO 80202
Tel: (303) 894-2997  Fax: (303) 894-7830  E-mail: dora_ccrd@state.co.us
Internet: www.dora.state.co.us/civil-rights

■Director (Interim) **Jennifer McPherson** . . . . . . . . . . . . . . . (303) 894-7816

## Division of Financial Services

1560 Broadway, Suite 950, Denver, CO 80202
Tel: (303) 894-2336  Fax: (303) 894-7886
E-mail: dora_financialservices_website@state.co.us
Internet: www.dora.state.co.us/financial-services

Commissioner **Patricia Salazar** . . . . . . . . . . . . . . . . . . . . . (303) 894-7741
    E-mail: patty.salazar@state.co.us
    Education: USC 2007 MPA
Deputy Commissioner **Mark Valente** . . . . . . . . . . . . . . . . . (303) 894-7742

---

★ Elected Official   ■ Appointed by Governor   ● Appointed by Legislature   ▲ Appointed by Board or Commission   ◆ Appointed by State Supreme Court

EXECUTIVE BRANCH

## Division of Insurance
1560 Broadway, Suite 850, Denver, CO 80202
Tel: (303) 894-7499  Fax: (303) 894-7455
E-mail: dora_ins_website@state.co.us
Internet: www.dora.state.co.us/insurance
■Insurance Commissioner **Marguerite Salazar** . . . . . . . . . . (303) 894-7480
  E-mail: marguerite.salazar@state.co.us
  Education: Adams State 1975 BA, 1976 MA
Deputy Commissioner - Consumer Affairs **Peg Brown** . . . . (303) 894-7501
Deputy Commissioner - Finance and Administration
  **John J. Postolowski**. . . . . . . . . . . . . . . . . . . . . . . .(303) 894-7532
  E-mail: john.postolowski@state.co.us
Financial Affairs Chief **Scott Lloyd** . . . . . . . . . . . . . . . . . (303) 894-7537
Financial Examination Chief Examiner **Henry Freaney** . . . .(303) 894-7488
  E-mail: henry.freaney@state.co.us
Investigations Supervisor **Steven Giampaolo** . . . . . . . . . . (303) 894-2241

## Division of Real Estate
1560 Broadway Street, Suite 925, Denver, CO 80202
Tel: (303) 894-2166  Fax: (303) 894-2683
E-mail: dora_realestate_website@state.co.us
Internet: www.dora.state.co.us/real-estate
Director **Marcia Waters**. . . . . . . . . . . . . . . . . . . . . . . . . .(303) 894-2422
Deputy Director **(Vacant)**. . . . . . . . . . . . . . . . . . . . . . . . .(303) 894-2545

## Division of Professions and Occupations
1560 Broadway, Suite 1350, Denver, CO 80202
Tel: (303) 894-7855  Fax: (303) 894-7693
E-mail: dora_opr_website@state.co.us
Director **Lauren Larson** . . . . . . . . . . . . . . . . . . . . . . . . . (303) 894-7711
  E-mail: lauren.larson@state.co.us
  Education: Syracuse BA; Michigan MPP
Deputy Director for Business and Inspection **(Vacant)**. . . . .(303) 894-2465
                              Fax: (303) 894-2310
Deputy Director for Health Care **Ronne M. Hines** . . . . . . . (303) 894-7770
                              Fax: (303) 894-7764
Deputy Director for Management **Michael W. Skorupka** . . (303) 894-2372
                              Fax: (303) 894-7693
Accountancy Program Director **Ofelia Duran** . . . . . . . . . . . (303) 894-7794
                              Fax: (303) 894-2310
Acupuncturists Registration Program Director
  **Leanne Duffy**. . . . . . . . . . . . . . . . . . . . . . . . . . . . . .(303) 894-7796
  E-mail: dora_acupunctureboard@state.co.us
Audiologist and Hearing Aid Providers Registration
  Program Director **Maulid Miskell** . . . . . . . . . . . . . . .(303) 894-7761
                              Fax: (303) 894-7764
Barber and Cosmetologist Licensing Board Program
  Director **Ofelia Duran** . . . . . . . . . . . . . . . . . . . . . . . .(303) 894-7794
                              Fax: (303) 894-7764
Chiropractic Examiners Board Program Director
  **Tony Munoz**. . . . . . . . . . . . . . . . . . . . . . . . . . . . . . . .(303) 894-7898
                              Fax: (303) 894-7764
Dental Examiners Board Program Director
  **Maulid Miskell** . . . . . . . . . . . . . . . . . . . . . . . . . . . .(303) 894-7761
                              Fax: (303) 894-7764
Electrical Board Program Director **Mark Browne** . . . . . . . (303) 894-2309
                              Fax: (303) 894-2310
Examiners of Architects Board Program Director
  **Joyce J. Young** . . . . . . . . . . . . . . . . . . . . . . . . . . . . .(303) 894-7781
                              Fax: (303) 894-2310
Medical Examiners Board Program Director
  **Karen McGovern**. . . . . . . . . . . . . . . . . . . . . . . . . . . .(303) 894-7704
                              Fax: (303) 894-7692
Mental Health Occupations Registration Program Director
  **Catherine Rodriguez** . . . . . . . . . . . . . . . . . . . . . . . . .(303) 894-2987
                              Fax: (303) 894-7764
Midwives Registration Program Director **Andrea Faley** . . . .(303) 894-7754
                              Fax: (303) 894-7764
Nursing Board Program Director **Georgia Roberts, Esq.** . . (303) 894-2819
  E-mail: dora_nursingboard@state.co.us      Fax: (303) 894-2821
Nursing Home Administrators Board Program Director
  **Leanne Duffy**. . . . . . . . . . . . . . . . . . . . . . . . . . . . . .(303) 894-7796
                              Fax: (303) 894-7764

Optometric Examiners Board Program Director
  **Leanne Duffy** . . . . . . . . . . . . . . . . . . . . . . . . . . . . . .(303) 894-7796
                              Fax: (303) 894-7692
Outfitters Registration Program Director **Ofelia Duran** . . . .(303) 894-7794
                              Fax: (303) 894-7764
Physical Therapy Licensure Program Director (Interim)
  **Maulid Miskell** . . . . . . . . . . . . . . . . . . . . . . . . . . . . .(303) 894-7761
                              Fax: (303) 894-7764
Plumbers Examining Board Program Director
  **Mark Browne**. . . . . . . . . . . . . . . . . . . . . . . . . . . . . . .(303) 894-2309
                              Fax: (303) 894-2310
Podiatry Board Program Director **Leanne Duffy** . . . . . . . . (303) 894-7796
                              Fax: (303) 894-7692
Professional Engineers and Professional Land Surveyors
  Program Director **Joyce J. Young** . . . . . . . . . . . . . . . .(303) 894-7781
                              Fax: (303) 894-2310
Respiratory Therapist Licensure Program Director
  **Leanne Duffy** . . . . . . . . . . . . . . . . . . . . . . . . . . . . . .(303) 894-7796
                              Fax: (303) 894-7764
Veterinary Medicine Board Program Director
  **Tony Munoz**. . . . . . . . . . . . . . . . . . . . . . . . . . . . . . . .(303) 894-7898
                              Fax: (303) 894-7764

## Division of Securities
1560 Broadway, Suite 900, Denver, CO 80202
Tel: (303) 894-2320  Fax: (303) 861-2126
E-mail: dora_securitieswebsite@state.co.us
Internet: www.dora.state.co.us/securities
Commissioner **Gerald Rome** . . . . . . . . . . . . . . . . . . . . . . .(303) 894-2320
  Education: Colorado BA; Denver JD

## Colorado Public Utilities Commission [PUC]
1560 Broadway, Suite 250, Denver, CO 80202
Tel: (303) 894-2000  Fax: (303) 894-2065
E-mail: dora_puc_website@state.co.us
■Chairman **Joshua B. Epel** . . . . . . . . . . . . . . . . . . . . . . . .(303) 894-2007
  Term Expires: January 7, 2019
  E-mail: joshua.epel@state.co.us
  Education: Michigan (Attended); McGill (Canada) (Attended);
  Grand Valley State; New Hampshire 1980 JD
■Commissioner **Frances Ann Koncilja** . . . . . . . . . . . . . . . .(303) 894-2007
  Education: Southern Colorado BA; Colorado JD
■Commissioner **Glenn Vaad** . . . . . . . . . . . . . . . . . . . . . . . (303) 894-2914
  Term Expires: January 2017
  E-mail: glenn.vaad@state.co.us

## Department of Revenue
1375 Sherman Street, Denver, CO 80261
Tel: (303) 866-3091  Fax: (303) 866-2400

**Employees:** 1,242  **Fiscal Year:** 2013-2014  **Budget:** $302,095,503

■Executive Director **Barbara J. Brohl**. . . . . . . . . . . . . . . . .(303) 866-5610
  E-mail: dor.edo@state.co.us
  Education: Regis U; Denver 1995 JD
  Executive Assistant **Christine Lovato** . . . . . . . . . . . . . . (303) 866-5610
Deputy Director **Heidi Humphreys**. . . . . . . . . . . . . . . . . . (303) 866-5610
Internal Auditor **Robert R. Gates** . . . . . . . . . . . . . . . . . . .(303) 866-5596
Accounting and Financial Services Director
  **Trinka Mullin** . . . . . . . . . . . . . . . . . . . . . . . . . . . . . .(303) 866-3726
Taxation Unit Senior Director **John Vecchiarelli** . . . . . . . (303) 866-3714
Legislative Liaison **(Vacant)** . . . . . . . . . . . . . . . . . . . . . . (303) 866-2819
Tax Audit and Compliance Division Director
  **Chris Muntean** . . . . . . . . . . . . . . . . . . . . . . . . . . . . . (303) 866-5586
Chief Hearing Officer **Mike Williams** . . . . . . . . . . . . . . . . (303) 205-5705
                              Fax: (303) 205-5700
Information Technology Chief Information Officer
  **Dannette Matthis** . . . . . . . . . . . . . . . . . . . . . . . . . . . .(303) 866-2215
  E-mail: dannette.mathis@state.co.us
Citizens Advocate **Melissa Martinez** . . . . . . . . . . . . . . . . .(303) 866-4622
Media Relations Director **Daria Serna** . . . . . . . . . . . . . . . .(303) 866-5303

★ Elected Official    ■ Appointed by Governor    ● Appointed by Legislature    ▲ Appointed by Board or Commission    ◆ Appointed by State Supreme Court

Summer 2016                © Leadership Directories, Inc.                *State Yellow Book*

# Colorado Lottery

212 West 3rd Street, Suite 210, Pueblo, CO 81003
Fax: (303) 759-6847  Internet: www.coloradolottery.com

■Chair **Charles Dennis Maes** . . . . . . . . . . . . . . . . . . . . . . . (303) 759-6816
  Term Expires: July 1, 2017
■Vice-Chair **Michael D. Weatherwax, CPA** . . . . . . . . . . . . . (303) 759-6816
  Term Expires: July 1, 2018
■Commissioner **The Honorable Jim "Jimmy" Bensberg** . . (303) 759-6816
  Term Expires: July 1, 2018
  Education: Colorado State 1984 JBA
■Commissioner **James Howard Davis** . . . . . . . . . . . . . . . . (303) 759-6816
  Term Expires: July 1, 2019
■Commissioner **Stella Peterson** . . . . . . . . . . . . . . . . . . . . . (303) 759-6816
  Term Expires: July 1, 2016

# State Board of Education

201 East Colfax Avenue, Denver, CO 80203
Tel: (303) 866-6817  Fax: (303) 830-0793
E-mail: state.board@cde.state.co.us

★Chairman **Steve Durham** (R-Fifth Congressional) . . . . . . . (303) 866-6817
  Term Expires: January 2017
★Vice Chairman
  **Angelika Schroeder** (D-Second Congressional) . . . . . . . . (303) 866-6817
  Term Expires: January 2019
  Education: Colorado BAM, MBA, PhD
★Member **Dr. Val Flores** (D-First Congressional) . . . . . . . . . (303) 866-6817
  Term Expires: January 2021
★Member **Jane Goff** (D-Seventh Congressional) . . . . . . . . . (303) 866-6817
  Term Expires: January 2021
★Member
  **Pamela "Pam" Mazanec** (R-Fourth Congressional) . . . . (303) 866-6817
  Term Expires: January 2019
★Member **Joyce Rankin** (R-Third Congressional) . . . . . . . . . (303) 866-6817
  Term Expires: January 2017
★Member **Debora Scheffel** (R-Sixth Congressional) . . . . . . . (303) 866-6817
  Term Expires: January 2017

# Colorado Department of Education [CDE]

201 East Colfax Avenue, Denver, CO 80203
Tel: (303) 866-6600
Tel: (303) 866-6628 (Educator Licensing and Certification Information)
Internet: www.cde.state.co.us

▲Commissioner (Interim) **Katy Anthes** . . . . . . . . . . . . . . . . . (303) 866-6600
  E-mail: commissioner@cde.state.co.us
  E-mail: anthes_k@cde.state.co.us
  Education: Colorado (Denver) PhD
  Special Assistant to the Commissioner **(Vacant)** . . . . . . . (303) 866-6901
  Executive Assistant to the Commissioner
  **Jessica Fuller** . . . . . . . . . . . . . . . . . . . . . . . . . . . . . . . (303) 866-6646
Chief of Staff **(Vacant)** . . . . . . . . . . . . . . . . . . . . . . . . . . . . (303) 866-6857
Associate Commissioner of Accountability, Performance
  and Support (Interim) **Alyssa Pearson** . . . . . . . . . . . . . (303) 866-6099
Associate Commissioner of Innovation **(Vacant)** . . . . . . . . (303) 866-6938
Associate Commissioner of Quality Instruction and
  Leadership **Barbara Hickman** . . . . . . . . . . . . . . . . . . . . . (303) 866-6600
  Education: Minnesota BA; St Mary's Col (CA) MA
Associate Commissioner of School Finance and
  Operations **Leanne Emm** . . . . . . . . . . . . . . . . . . . . . . . . (303) 866-6202
Associate Commissioner of Strategic Partnerships
  **Roseyn Hood** . . . . . . . . . . . . . . . . . . . . . . . . . . . . . . . . . (303) 866-6600
  Education: Duke BA
Legislative Liaison **Jennifer Mello** . . . . . . . . . . . . . . . . . . . (303) 866-4247
  E-mail: jennifer.mello@state.co.us
Chief Communications Officer **(Vacant)** . . . . . . . . . . . . . . . (303) 866-6822

# Transportation Commission

4201 East Arkansas Avenue, Room 270, Denver, CO 80222-3406
Tel: (303) 757-9025  Fax: (303) 757-9717

■Chair **Kathy I. Connell** (District 6) . . . . . . . . . . . . . . . . . . (303) 757-9025
  Term Expires: July 1, 2019
  E-mail: commissioner.connell@state.co.us

■Vice Chair **Gary M. Reiff** (District 3) . . . . . . . . . . . . . . . . . (303) 757-9025
  Term Expires: July 1, 2017
  E-mail: commissioner.reiff@state.co.us
  Education: Stanford 1981 BA, 1981 MA; Harvard 1984 JD
■Commissioner **Heather M. Barry** (District 4) . . . . . . . . . . . (303) 757-9025
  Term Expires: July 1, 2017
  E-mail: commissioner.barry@state.co.us
■Commissioner **Shannon Gifford** (District 1) . . . . . . . . . . . (303) 757-9025
  Term Expires: July 1, 2017
  E-mail: commissioner.gifford@state.co.us
■Commissioner **Kathleen R. Gilliland** (District 5) . . . . . . . . (303) 757-9025
  Term Expires: July 1, 2019
  E-mail: commissioner.gilliland@state.co.us
■Commissioner **Kathy Hall** (District 7) . . . . . . . . . . . . . . . . (303) 757-9025
  Term Expires: July 1, 2019
  E-mail: commissioner.hall@state.co.us
■Commissioner **Steven Hofmeister** (District 11) . . . . . . . . . (303) 757-9025
  Term Expires: July 1, 2019
  E-mail: commissioner.hofmeister@state.co.us
■Commissioner **Edward James Peterson** (District 2) . . . . . (303) 757-9025
  Term Expires: July 1, 2019
  E-mail: commissioner.peterson@state.co.us
■Commissioner **Nolan Schriner** (District 9) . . . . . . . . . . . . . (303) 757-9025
  Term Expires: July 1, 2019
  E-mail: commissioner.schriner@state.co.us
■Commissioner **William "Bill" Thiebaut** (District 10) . . . . . (303) 757-9025
  Term Expires: July 1, 2017
  E-mail: commissioner.thiebaut@state.co.us
■Commissioner **Sidny Zink, CPA** (District 8) . . . . . . . . . . . . (303) 757-9025
  Term Expires: July 1, 2017
  E-mail: commissioner.zink@state.co.us

# Department of Transportation [CDOT]

4201 East Arkansas Avenue, Denver, CO 80222-3406
Tel: (303) 757-9011  TTY: (303) 757-9087  Fax: (303) 757-9656

**Employees:** 3,318  **Fiscal Year:** 2013-2014  **Budget:** $1,267,747,364

■Executive Director **Shailen P. Bhatt** . . . . . . . . . . . . . . . . . . (303) 757-9201
  E-mail: shailen.bhatt@state.co.us
  Education: Western Kentucky BA
Deputy Executive Director **Michael Peter "Mike" Lewis** . . (303) 512-5204
  Education: Vermont BS
Chief Transportation Counsel **Kathy Young** . . . . . . . . . . . . (720) 508-6628
  E-mail: kathy.young@state.co.us
Office of Emergency Management Director **Chad Ray** . . . . (303) 512-4034

# Office of the Lieutenant Governor

130 State Capitol, Denver, CO 80203
Tel: (303) 866-2087  Fax: (303) 866-5469

★Lieutenant Governor **Donna Lynne, DrPH** (D) . . . . . . . . . . (303) 866-2087
  Term Expires: January 2019
  Education: New Hampshire BA; George Washington MPA;
  Columbia DrPH
  Career: Executive Vice President and Chief Operating Officer, Group
  Health Incorporated (1998-2005); President, Kaiser Foundation Health
  Plan of Colorado, Inc., Kaiser Permanente
Chief of Staff **Scott J. Wasserman** . . . . . . . . . . . . . . . . . . . (303) 866-2526
Deputy Chief of Staff **Antonio Mendez** . . . . . . . . . . . . . . . (303) 866-6325

# Office of the Attorney General

1300 Broadway, 10th Floor, Denver, CO 80203
Tel: (720) 508-6000  Fax: (720) 508-6030
E-mail: attorney.general@state.co.us

**Employees:** 447

★Attorney General **Cynthia H. Coffman** (R) . . . . . . . . . . . . . (720) 508-6000
  Term Expires: January 2019
  Education: Missouri 1983 BA; Georgia State 1991 JD
  Career: Chief Deputy Attorney General, Office of Attorney General
  John Suthers, State of Colorado (2005-2015)
Chief of Staff **Melanie J. Snyder** . . . . . . . . . . . . . . . . . . . . . (720) 508-6000
  Education: Arizona BA; San Diego JD
Chief Deputy **David C. Blake** . . . . . . . . . . . . . . . . . . . . . . . (720) 508-6000
  Education: Virginia Tech 1996 BA; George Mason 2007 JD
Chief Investigator **Larry Adkisson** . . . . . . . . . . . . . . . . . . . (720) 508-6000

*(continued on next page)*

---

★ Elected Official   ■ Appointed by Governor   ● Appointed by Legislature   ▲ Appointed by Board or Commission   ◆ Appointed by State Supreme Court

**Office of the Attorney General** *continued*

Deputy Attorney General for Business and Licensing
**Russell B. Klein** . . . . . . . . . . . . . . . . . . . . . . . . . . . . (720) 508-6421
Education: SUNY (Buffalo) 1999 JD
Deputy Attorney General for Civil Litigation and
Employment **Vincent E. Morscher** . . . . . . . . . . . . . . . . (720) 508-6594
Deputy Attorney General of Consumer Protection
**Alissa Gardenswartz** . . . . . . . . . . . . . . . . . . . . . . . . (720) 508-6000
Education: UCLA 1992; Chicago 1996 JD
Deputy Attorney General for Criminal Justice
**Scott Turner** . . . . . . . . . . . . . . . . . . . . . . . . . . . . . . (720) 508-6722
Education: Missouri (Kansas City) 1989 JD
Medicaid Fraud Control Unit Director (Interim)
**Cynthia J. Kowert** . . . . . . . . . . . . . . . . . . . . . . . . . (720) 508-6687
Deputy Attorney General for Natural Resources and
Environment **Casey A. Shpall** . . . . . . . . . . . . . . . . . . (720) 508-6290
E-mail: casey.shpall@coag.gov
Deputy Attorney General for Revenue and Utilities
**Eric T. Meyer** . . . . . . . . . . . . . . . . . . . . . . . . . . . . . (720) 508-6000
Deputy Attorney General for State Services
**Melody Mirbaba** . . . . . . . . . . . . . . . . . . . . . . . . . . . (720) 508-6163
Education: Southern Methodist 1996 BA; Denver 1999 JD
Director of Legislative Affairs **Jennifer M. Anderson** . . . . (720) 508-6000
E-mail: jennifer.anderson@coag.gov
Education: Denver; New Mexico JD
Solicitor General **Frederick R. Yarger** . . . . . . . . . . . . . . (720) 508-6000
Education: Dartmouth BA; Chicago JD
Deputy Solicitor General **Glenn E. Roper** . . . . . . . . . . . (720) 508-6000
Education: BYU 2002 BA; J Reuben Clark Law 2005 JD
Office of Community Engagement Director
**José A. Esquibel** . . . . . . . . . . . . . . . . . . . . . . . . . . . (720) 508-6565
Education: New Mexico BA
Senior Counsel of Consumer Resources **Jan Zavislan** . . . . (720) 508-6000
Education: Northern Colorado BA; Denver JD
Public Information Officer/Communications Director
**Roger Hudson** . . . . . . . . . . . . . . . . . . . . . . . . . . . . (720) 508-6553
E-mail: roger.hudson@coag.gov

# Office of the Secretary of State

1700 Broadway, Second Floor, Denver, CO 80290
Tel: (303) 894-2200  TTY: (303) 894-4860  Fax: (303) 869-4871
E-mail: secretary@sos.state.co.us

**Employees: 120**

★ Secretary of State **Wayne W. Williams** (R) . . . . . . . . . . . (303) 894-2200
Term Expires: January 2019
Deputy Secretary of State **Suzanne Staiert** . . . . . . . . . . . (303) 894-2200
Legislative Liaison **Tim Griesmer** . . . . . . . . . . . . . . . . . (303) 860-6903
E-mail: tim.griesmer@sos.state.co.us
Communications Director **Lynn Bartels** . . . . . . . . . . . . . (303) 894-2200
Education: Cottey 1977 AA; Northern Arizona 1980 BSJ

# Business and Licensing Division

Fax: (303) 869-4864  E-mail: sos.business@sos.state.co.us

Director **Mike Hardin** . . . . . . . . . . . . . . . . . . . . . . . . (303) 894-2200
E-mail: mike.hardin@sos.state.co.us
Deputy Director **D. J. Davis** . . . . . . . . . . . . . . . . . . . . (303) 894-2200
Manager **Alberta Bennett** . . . . . . . . . . . . . (303) 894-2200 ext. 6202
Administrative Rules Program Manager
**Deanna Maiolo** . . . . . . . . . . . . . . . . . . . . (303) 894-2200 ext. 6404
Charities Program Manager **Chris Cash** . . . . . . . . . . . . . (303) 894-2200
Lobbyist Registration Program Manager
**Angela Lawson** . . . . . . . . . . . . . . . . . . . . (303) 894-2200 ext. 6304
Education: UC Berkeley BA; Colorado (Denver) MPA, MS;
Georgetown MPP
Notary Public Program Manager
**Deanna Maiolo** . . . . . . . . . . . . . . . . . . . . (303) 894-2200 ext. 6404

# Elections Division

Fax: (303) 869-4861  E-mail: sos.elections@sos.state.co.us

Elections Director **Judd Choate** . . . . . . . . . . . . . (303) 894-2200 ext. 6307
Education: Fort Hays State 1992 AB; Purdue 1994 AM, 1997 DPhil;
Colorado 2006 Dr Jur
Deputy Director **Hilary Rudy** . . . . . . . . . . . . . . (303) 894-2200 ext. 6302

Campaign Finance Manager
**Stephen M. "Steve" Bouey** . . . . . . . . . . . . . (303) 894-2200 ext. 6383
County Regulation and Support Manager
**Dwight Shellman** . . . . . . . . . . . . . . . . . . . (303) 894-2200 ext. 6313
Legal, Policy, and Rulemaking Manager
**Ben Schler** . . . . . . . . . . . . . . . . . . . . . . . (303) 894-2200 ext. 6342
Voter Registration Manager **Minerva Padron** . . . . (303) 894-2200 ext. 6332

# Information Systems Division

Fax: (303) 869-4866

Chief Information Officer **Trevor Timmons** . . . . . (303) 894-2200 ext. 6602
E-mail: trevor.timmons@sos.state.co.us
Deputy Director **Jeff Oliver** . . . . . . . . . . . . . . . . . . . . (303) 894-2200
E-mail: jeff.oliver@sos.state.co.us

# Office of the Treasurer

200 East Colfax Avenue, Room 140, Denver, CO 80203
Tel: (303) 866-2441  Fax: (303) 866-2123

**Employees: 32**

★ State Treasurer **Walker R. Stapleton** (R) . . . . . . . . . . . . (303) 866-2441
Term Expires: January 2019
E-mail: walker.stapleton@state.co.us
Education: Williams 1996; London School Econ (UK) MBS;
Harvard 2003 MBA
Administrative Assistant **Erin Gallegos** . . . . . . . . . . . . (303) 866-2441
Deputy Treasurer **Jonathan J. Forbes** . . . . . . . . . . . . . . (303) 866-4951

## Accounting Division
Chief Financial Officer **Charles Scheibe** . . . . . . . . . . . . . (303) 866-5826

## Cash Management Division
Cash Manager **Sandy Tan** . . . . . . . . . . . . . . . . . . . . . . (303) 866-3253

## Investment Division
Chief Investment Officer **Helen DiBartolomeo** . . . . . . . . . (303) 866-5651
E-mail: helen.dibartolomeo@state.co.us
Education: SUNY (Potsdam) 1973 BA
Investment Officer **Edward H. "Ted" Frost** . . . . . . . . . . . (303) 866-2758
Investment Officer **Jamila Loftis** . . . . . . . . . . . . . . . . . . (303) 866-2440

# Colorado Housing and Finance Authority [CHFA]

1981 Blake Street, Denver, CO 80202-1272
Tel: (303) 297-2432  Fax: (303) 297-2615  Internet: www.chfainfo.com

Executive Director and Chief Executive Officer
**Cris A. White** . . . . . . . . . . . . . . . . . . . . . . . . . . . . . . (303) 297-7400
Education: Regis U BS
Executive Administrative Coordinator **Alison Medina** . . . (303) 297-7302
E-mail: amedina@chfainfo.com
Chief Financial Officer **Patricia Hippe** . . . . . . . . . . . . . . (303) 297-7399
Education: Minnesota BBA; U St Thomas (MN) MBA
Chief Operating Officer **Jaime Gomez** . . . . . . . . . . . . . . (303) 297-7440
Education: Colorado BS
Community Development Director **Steve Johnson** . . . . . . . (303) 297-7363
General Counsel **Charles K. Knight** . . . . . . . . . . . . . . . . (303) 297-7314
E-mail: cknight@chfainfo.com
Home Finance Director **Dan McMahon** . . . . . . . . . . . . . (303) 297-7405
Marketing and Community Relations Director
**Jerilynn Martinez** . . . . . . . . . . . . . . . . . . . . . . . . . . (303) 297-7427
E-mail: jmartinez@chfainfo.com

---

★ Elected Official   ■ Appointed by Governor   ● Appointed by Legislature   ▲ Appointed by Board or Commission   ◆ Appointed by State Supreme Court

# Connecticut

Tel: (800) 406-1527 (State Information)

**Number of U.S. Congressional Delegates:** 2 Senators; 5 Representatives  **Governor's Term:** 4 years
**Legislature Description:** General Assembly - 36 member Senate; 151 member House of Representatives;
Term - Senate 2 years, House 2 years  **Next Election:** Governor November 2018; Legislature November
2016  **Number of Electoral Votes:** 7  **Official Name:** State of Connecticut (Mohican: Long River Place)
**Nickname:** The Constitution State  **Motto:** Qui transtulit sustinet (He who transplanted still sustains)

**Population:** 3,590,886 (2015); Rank 29  **Fiscal Year:** 2014-2015  **Budget:** $34,840,100,000

## Office of the Governor

State Capitol, 210 Capitol Avenue, Hartford, CT 06106
Tel: (860) 566-4840  Tel: (800) 406-1527 (Toll-Free)
TTY: (860) 524-7397  Fax: (860) 524-7395

**Dannel P. "Dan" Malloy**
Governor

Began Service: January 5, 2011
Term Expires: 2019
Date of Birth: July 21, 1955
Education: Boston Col 1977 BA, 1980 JD
Home: Stamford
Religion: Roman Catholic
Career: Assistant District Attorney, Office of the
District Attorney, County of Kings, New York
(1980-1984); Partner, Abate & Fox (1984-1995);
Mayor, Mayor, City of Stamford, Connecticut
(1995-2009)

★ Governor **Dannel P. "Dan" Malloy** (D) . . . . . . . . . . . . . . (860) 566-4840
  E-mail: governor.malloy@po.state.ct.us
Chief of Staff **Brian Durand** . . . . . . . . . . . . . . . . . . . . . . . (860) 566-4840
Communications Director **Mark Bergman** . . . . . . . . . . . . . (860) 566-4840
Executive Office Administrator **Kathryn Damato** . . . . . . . . (860) 566-4840
  E-mail: kathryn.damato@ct.gov
Director of Policy **Elizabeth "Liz" Donohue** . . . . . . . . . . . (860) 566-4840
  E-mail: liz.donohue@ct.gov
Government Affairs Director **Paul H. Mounds, Jr.** . . . . . . . (860) 566-4840
  E-mail: paul.mounds@cga.ct.gov
  Education: Trinity Col (CT) 2007 BA
Legislative Liaison **Paul H. Mounds, Jr.** . . . . . . . . . . . . . . (860) 566-4840
General Counsel **Karen K. Buffkin** . . . . . . . . . . . . . . . . . . (860) 566-4840
Legal Counsel **(Vacant)** . . . . . . . . . . . . . . . . . . . . . . . . . . (860) 566-4840
Deputy Legal Counsel **Eleanor Michael** . . . . . . . . . . . . . . (860) 566-4840
  E-mail: eleanor.michael@cga.ct.gov
Communications Director **Devon Puglia** . . . . . . . . . . . . . . (860) 524-7314
  E-mail: devon.puglia@ct.gov
Deputy Press Secretary **David Bednarz** . . . . . . . . . . . . . . (860) 566-4840
  E-mail: david.bednarz@ct.gov
Community Non-Profit Human Services Cabinet
  **Terry Edelstein** . . . . . . . . . . . . . . . . . . . . . . . . . . . . . . (860) 566-4840
Governor's Liaison to the Disability Community
  **Jonathan Slifka** . . . . . . . . . . . . . . . . . . . . . . . . . . . . . . (860) 566-4840

## Washington Office

444 North Capitol Street, NW, Suite 317, Washington, DC 20001
Fax: (202) 347-7151

■ Director **Dan DeSimone** . . . . . . . . . . . . . . . . . . . . . . . . . (202) 347-4535
  E-mail: dan.desimone@ct.gov

## Office of the Chief Medical Examiner [OCME]

11 Shuttle Road, Farmington, CT 06032
Tel: (860) 679-3980  Fax: (860) 679-1257
Tel: (800) 842-8820 (Connecticut Only)  Internet: http://www.ct.gov/ocme

**Employees:** 53  **Fiscal Year:** 2015-2016  **Budget:** $6,072,000

▲ Chief Medical Examiner **Dr. James R. Gill** . . . . . . . . . . . . (860) 679-3980
  E-mail: jgill@ocme.org
  Education: MIT BS; Connecticut 1992 MD
▲ Deputy Chief Medical Examiner **Dr. Maura DeJoseph** . . . (860) 679-3980
  E-mail: mdejoseph@ocme.org
Associate Medical Examiner **Frank Evangelista, MD** . . . . . (860) 679-3980
Associate Medical Examiner **Angela McGuire** . . . . . . . . . . (860) 679-3980
Associate Medical Examiner **Christina Stanley** . . . . . . . . . (860) 679-3980
Associate Medical Examiner **Gregory Vincent, MD** . . . . . . (860) 679-3980
Associate Medical Examiner **Susan S. Williams, MD** . . . . (860) 679-3980
Administrator **Lincoln Dwayne Gordon** . . . . . . . . . . . . . . (860) 679-3980
  E-mail: ligordon@ocme.org
  Executive Secretary **Linda Sylvia** . . . . . . . . . . . . . . . . . (860) 679-3980
Lead Investigator **Holly Ohlko** . . . . . . . . . . . . . . . . . . . . . (860) 679-3980
Human Resources Specialist **Nicole Norman** . . . . . . . . . . (860) 679-3980
Data Processing Technical Analyst **Gerry Levesque** . . . . . (860) 679-3980
  E-mail: glevesque@ocme.org
Forensic Technician Supervisor **Angel Negron** . . . . . . . . . (860) 679-3980
Forensic Photographer **Mary Catherine Sonntag** . . . . . . . (860) 679-3980
Anthropologist **Kristen Harnett-McCann** . . . . . . . . . . . . . (860) 679-3980

## Office of Consumer Counsel [OCC]

Ten Franklin Square, New Britain, CT 06051-2605
Tel: (860) 827-2900  Fax: (860) 827-2929  E-mail: occ.info@ct.gov

**Employees:** 14  **Fiscal Year:** 2016  **Budget:** $3,431,000

■ Consumer Counsel **Elin Swanson Katz** . . . . . . . . . . . . . . (860) 827-2900
  E-mail: elin.katz@ct.gov
  Education: Cornell BS; Boston U 1990 JD

## Office of Policy and Management [OPM]

280 Trumbull Street, Hartford, CT 06103
Tel: (860) 418-6200  Tel: (800) 286-2214 (In State)  TTY: (860) 418-6456
Fax: (860) 418-6487

**Employees:** 114  **Fiscal Year:** 2015  **Budget:** $351,457,000

■ Secretary **Benjamin Barnes** . . . . . . . . . . . . . . . . . . . . . . (860) 418-6500
  E-mail: ben.barnes@ct.gov
  Executive Secretary **Laura Mirante** . . . . . . . . . . . . . . . . (860) 418-6379
Deputy Secretary **Susan Weisselberg** . . . . . . . . . . . . . . . (860) 418-6501

## Department of Administrative Services [DAS]

165 Capitol Avenue, Hartford, CT 06106
Tel: (860) 713-5100  Fax: (860) 713-7481  TTY: (860) 713-7463

**Employees:** 649  **Fiscal Year:** 2014-2015  **Budget:** $146,547,000

■ Commissioner **Melody A. Currey** . . . . . . . . . . . . . . . . . . (860) 713-5100
  E-mail: melody.currey@po.state.ct.us

*(continued on next page)*

---

★ Elected Official    ■ Appointed by Governor    ● Appointed by Legislature    ▲ Appointed by Board or Commission    ◆ Appointed by State Supreme Court

EXECUTIVE BRANCH

**Department of Administrative Services** *continued*

■Deputy Commissioner **Toni Fatone** . . . . . . . . . . . . . . . . . . . (860) 713-5100
  E-mail: toni.fatone@ct.gov
Staff Counsel and Director of Communications
  **Jeffrey R. Beckham** . . . . . . . . . . . . . . . . . . . . . . . . . . . . . (860) 713-5195
  E-mail: jeffrey.beckham@ct.gov
Fleet Operations Director **Frank Sanzo** . . . . . . . . . . . . . . . (860) 713-5155
  E-mail: frank.sanzo@ct.gov
Management Information Solutions Director **(Vacant)** . . . . . (860) 713-5013
Procurement Services Manager **Carol Wilson** . . . . . . . . . . . (860) 713-5093
  E-mail: carol.wilson@ct.gov
State and Federal Property Distribution Center Manager
  **Juan Carlos "Carlos" Velez** . . . . . . . . . . . . . . . . . . . . . . (860) 713-5092
  E-mail: carlos.velez@ct.gov
Legal Counsel and Legislative Liaison **Erin Choquette** . . . . (860) 713-5276
  E-mail: erin.choquette@ct.gov
Affirmative Action Officer **Alicia Nunez** . . . . . . . . . . . . . . . (860) 713-5308
Bureau of Properties and Facilities Management Director
  **Douglas Moore** . . . . . . . . . . . . . . . . . . . . . . . . . . . . . . . (860) 713-5800
State Marshal Commission Manager **Douglas Rinaldi** . . . . . (860) 716-5372
  Fax: (860) 713-5377
Claims Commissioner **Christy Scott** . . . . . . . . . . . . . . . . . . (860) 713-5501
  Education: Smith BA; Connecticut JD
State Properties Review Board Director **Brian Dillon** . . . . . (860) 713-6400
State Insurance Risk and Management Board Director
  **Daria Cirish** . . . . . . . . . . . . . . . . . . . . . . . . . . . . . . . . . . (860) 713-5223
  Fax: (860) 713-7444

## Business Office

Tel: (860) 713-5024  Fax: (860) 713-7494
Director **Jean Michael** . . . . . . . . . . . . . . . . . . . . . . . . . . . . (860) 713-5115
  E-mail: jean.michael@ct.gov
Collection Services Manager **JoAnn Figueiredo** . . . . . . . . . (860) 713-5400
  E-mail: joann.figueiredo@ct.gov          Fax: (860) 713-5124

## Division of Construction Services

165 Capitol Avenue, Hartford, CT 06106
Tel: (860) 713-5100  Fax: (860) 713-7255
Deputy Commissioner **Pasquale J. Salemi** . . . . . . . . . . . . . (860) 713-5850
Chief Architect **David Barkin** . . . . . . . . . . . . . . . . . . . . . . . (860) 713-5631
Chief Engineer **Allen Herring** . . . . . . . . . . . . . . . . . . . . . . . (860) 713-5691
Design and Construction Office Director
  **Joseph Cassidy** . . . . . . . . . . . . . . . . . . . . . . . . . . . . . . . (860) 713-5705
Managing Attorney **Kevin Kopetz** . . . . . . . . . . . . . . . . . . . (860) 713-5886

## Division of Statewide Human Resources Management

Tel: (860) 713-5205  Fax: (860) 713-7471
Director (Interim) **Shari Grzyb** . . . . . . . . . . . . . . . . . . . . . . (860) 713-5204
Workers' Compensation and Master Insurance Program
  Administrator **Douglas Rinaldi** . . . . . . . . . . . . . . . . . . . (860) 713-5002

## Department of Agriculture

165 Capitol Avenue, Hartford, CT 06106
Tel: (860) 713-2500  Tel: (800) 861-9939 (Toll Free)  Fax: (860) 713-2514
E-mail: ctdeptag@ct.gov

**Employees:** 53  **Fiscal Year:** 2015  **Budget:** $6,224,000

■Commissioner **Steven K. Reviczky** . . . . . . . . . . . . . . . . . . (860) 713-2501
  E-mail: steven.reviczky@ct.gov
  Executive Assistant **Jason Bowsza** . . . . . . . . . . . . . . . . . (860) 713-2501
Legislative Program Manager and Chief of Staff
  **George E. Krivda, Jr.** . . . . . . . . . . . . . . . . . . . . . . . . . . . (860) 713-2573
  E-mail: george.krivda@ct.gov

## Agricultural Development and Resource Preservation Bureau

Tel: (860) 713-2530  Fax: (860) 713-2516
Director **Linda Piotrowicz** . . . . . . . . . . . . . . . . . . . . . . . . . (860) 713-2558
Farmland Preservation Director **Cameron Weimar** . . . . . . . (860) 713-2530

## Aquaculture and Laboratory Services Bureau

190 Rogers Avenue, Milford, CT 06460
P.O. Box 97, Milford, CT 06460
Tel: (203) 874-0696  Fax: (203) 783-9976  E-mail: dept.agric@snet.net
Director **David H. Carey** . . . . . . . . . . . . . . . . . . . . . . (203) 874-0696 ext. 103

## Regulation and Inspection Bureau

Fax: (860) 713-2515  E-mail: regandinsp.ctdeptag@ct.gov
Director **Dr. Bruce A. Sherman** . . . . . . . . . . . . . . . . . . . . . (860) 713-2504
Assistant Director **Wayne Kasacek** . . . . . . . . . . . . . . . . . . . (860) 713-2508
State Veterinarian **Mary Jane Lis** . . . . . . . . . . . . . . . . . . . . (860) 713-2505
  E-mail: mary.lis@ct.gov

## Department of Banking

260 Constitution Plaza, Hartford, CT 06103-1800
Tel: (860) 240-8299  Tel: (800) 831-7225 (Toll Free)
Tel: (877) 472-8313 (Foreclosure Assistance Hotline)
Fax: (860) 240-8178  Internet: www.ct.gov/dob

**Employees:** 109  **Fiscal Year:** 2014-2015  **Budget:** $20,727,000

■Commissioner **Jorge L. Perez** . . . . . . . . . . . . . . . . . . . . . . (860) 240-8100
  Secretary **Jeanne M. Charbonneau** . . . . . . . . . . . . . . . . (860) 240-8103

## Department of Children and Families [DCF]

505 Hudson Street, Hartford, CT 06106-7107
Tel: (860) 550-6305  Tel: (800) 842-6348 (Adoption Information)
Tel: (860) 550-6578 (Adoption Information [in State])
Tel: (860) 842-2288 (Child Abuse & Neglect Hotline)
Tel: (888) 543-4376 (Foster Care Recruitment)
Tel: (888) 285-2210 (Mentor Program)  TTY: (800) 982-6373
Fax: (860) 566-7947  Internet: www.state.ct.us/dcf

**Employees:** 2,585  **Fiscal Year:** 2015  **Budget:** $793,045,000

■Commissioner **Joette Katz** . . . . . . . . . . . . . . . . . . . . . . . . (860) 550-6300
  E-mail: commissioner.dcf@ct.gov
  Education: Brandeis 1974 BA; Connecticut 1977 JD
  Executive Secretary **Cindy Conklin** . . . . . . . . . . . . . . . . (860) 550-6354
Chief of Staff **Elizabeth Duryea** . . . . . . . . . . . . . . . . . . . . . (860) 550-6314
■Operations Deputy Commissioner **Michael Williams** . . . . . (860) 550-6657
  E-mail: michael.williams@ct.gov
■Administration Deputy Commissioner **Fernando Muniz** . . . (860) 550-6657
  E-mail: fernando.muniz@ct.gov

## Department of Consumer Protection

165 Capitol Avenue, Hartford, CT 06106
Tel: (860) 713-6100 (Consumer Information / Complaints)
TTY: (860) 713-7240  Fax: (860) 706-1203  Internet: www.ct.gov/dcp

**Employees:** 220  **Fiscal Year:** 2014-2015  **Budget:** $23,109,000

■Commissioner **Jonathan A. Harris** . . . . . . . . . . . . . . . . . . (860) 713-6053
  E-mail: jonathan.harris@ct.gov          Fax: (860) 706-1239
  Education: Brandeis 1986 BA; NYU 1990 JD
Deputy Commissioner **Michelle H. Seagull** . . . . . . . . . . . . (860) 713-6057
  Fax: (860) 706-1276
Legislative Program Manager **Gary W. Berner** . . . . . . . . . . (860) 713-6208
  Fax: (860) 706-1215

## Department of Correction

24 Wolcott Hill Road, Wethersfield, CT 06109
Tel: (860) 692-7480  E-mail: doc.pio@ct.gov

**Employees:** 6,625  **Fiscal Year:** 2014-2015  **Budget:** $711,467,000

■Commissioner **Scott Semple** . . . . . . . . . . . . . . . . . . . . . . . (860) 692-7482
  E-mail: scott.semple@ct.gov
Affirmative Action Division Director **Holly Darin** . . . . . . . . (860) 692-7633
  Fax: (860) 692-7639
External Affairs Division Director (Acting)
  **Karen Martucci** . . . . . . . . . . . . . . . . . . . . . . . . . . . . . . . (860) 692-7780
  Fax: (860) 692-7783
Public Information Officer **Andrius Banevicius** . . . . . . . . . . (860) 692-7780
  E-mail: doc.pio@ct.gov

---

★ Elected Official   ■ Appointed by Governor   ● Appointed by Legislature   ▲ Appointed by Board or Commission   ◆ Appointed by State Supreme Court

Parole and Community Services Director
**Joseph Haggan** . . . . . . . . . . . . . . . . . . . . . . . . (860) 297-4400
300 Sheldon Street, Hartford, CT 06106    Fax: (860) 297-6599

## Administration Division

Deputy Commissioner **Cheryl Cepelak, IPMA-CS** . . . . . . . (860) 692-7871
E-mail: cheryl.cepelak@ct.gov    Fax: (860) 692-7876

Best Practices Unit Director **Patrick Hynes** . . . . . . . . . . . (860) 692-7817

Engineering and Facilities Management Services Director
**Stephen Link** . . . . . . . . . . . . . . . . . . . . . . . . . (860) 692-7554
E-mail: stephen.link@ct.gov    Fax: (860) 692-7556

Fiscal Services Chief **Michelle Schott** . . . . . . . . . . . . . (860) 692-7700
Tel: (860) 692-7702

Human Resources Director **Suzanne Smedes** . . . . . . . . . . (860) 692-6804
Fax: (860) 692-6894

Management Information Systems Director
**Robert Cosgrove** . . . . . . . . . . . . . . . . . . . . . . (860) 692-7688
E-mail: bob.cosgrove@ct.gov    Fax: (860) 692-7669

Nutrition and Food Services Director **Michael Bibens** . . . . (860) 691-6989
Fax: (860) 691-6874

Training and Staff Development Director **Lauren Powers** . . (203) 271-5100
275 Jarvis Street, Cheshire, CT 06410    Fax: (203) 271-5179

## Internal Security Division

Director **Christine Whidden** . . . . . . . . . . . . . . . . . . . (860) 692-7507
Fax: (860) 692-7499

## Operations Division

Deputy Commissioner **(Vacant)** . . . . . . . . . . . . . . . . . (860) 692-7487
Fax: (860) 692-7488

District One Administrator **Angel Quiros** . . . . . . . . . . . . (860) 763-8017
3 Walker Drive, Enfield, CT 06082

District Two Administrator **Michael P. Lajoie** . . . . . . . . . . (203) 250-3161
944 Highland Avenue, Cheshire, CT 06410

Bridgeport Correctional Center Warden **Allison Black** . . . . . (203) 579-6131
1106 North Avenue, Bridgeport, CT 06604    Fax: (203) 579-6693

Brooklyn Correctional Institution Warden **Jonathan Hall** . . (860) 779-4500
59 Hartford Road, Brooklyn, CT 06234    Fax: (860) 779-4557

Cheshire Correctional Institution Warden
**Jon Brighthaupt** . . . . . . . . . . . . . . . . . . . . . . (203) 651-6100
900 Highland Ave., Cheshire, CT 06410    Fax: (203) 651-6069

Corrigan-Radgowski Correctional Center Warden
**Scott Erfe** . . . . . . . . . . . . . . . . . . . . . . . . . . (860) 848-5700
986 Norwich-New London Turnpike,    Fax: (860) 848-5821
Uncasville, CT 06382

Enfield Correctional Institution Warden **Peter Murphy** . . . . (860) 763-7300
289 Shaker Rd., Enfield, CT 06082    Fax: (860) 763-7350

Garner Correctional Institution Warden **Henry Falcone** . . . (203) 270-2800
50 Nunnawauk Road, Newtown, CT 06470    Fax: (203) 270-1826

Hartford Correctional Center Warden **Walter Ford** . . . . . . (860) 240-1800
177 Weston Street, Hartford, CT 06120    Fax: (860) 566-2725

MacDougall-Walker Correctional Institution Warden
**Carol Chapdelaine** . . . . . . . . . . . . . . . . . . . . (860) 627-2100
1153 East St. South, Suffield, CT 06078    Fax: (860) 627-2144

Manson Youth Institution Warden **John Alves** . . . . . . . . . (203) 806-2500
42 Jarvis Street, Cheshire, CT 06410    Fax: (203) 699-1845

New Haven Correctional Center Warden **Jose Feliciano** . . . (203) 974-4111
245 Whalley Ave., New Haven, CT 06530    Fax: (203) 974-4167

Northern Correctional Institution Warden
**Anne Cournoyer** . . . . . . . . . . . . . . . . . . . . . . (860) 763-8600
287 Bilton Rd., Somers, CT 06071    Fax: (860) 763-8651

Osborn Correctional Institution Warden
**Edward Maldonado** . . . . . . . . . . . . . . . . . . . . (860) 814-4600
335 Bilton Rd., Somers, CT 06071    Fax: (860) 814-4826

Robinson Correctional Institution Warden **Kimberly Weir** . . (860) 253-8000
285 Shaker Road, Enfield, CT 06082    Fax: (860) 253-8317

Willard-Cybulksi Correctional Institution Warden
**John Tarascio** . . . . . . . . . . . . . . . . . . . . . . . . (860) 763-6100
391 Shaker Rd., Enfield, CT 06082    Fax: (860) 763-6111

York Correctional Institution Warden **Stephen Faucher** . . . (860) 691-6700
201 West Main Street, Niantic, CT 06357    Fax: (860) 691-6800

Tactical Operation Director **William Colon** . . . . . . . . . . . (860) 692-7503
Fax: (860) 692-7513

## Programs and Treatment Division

District 3 Administrator **Monica Rinaldi** . . . . . . . . . . . . . (860) 692-7494
Fax: (860) 692-7495

Offender Program and Addiction Services Director
**Linda Kendrick** . . . . . . . . . . . . . . . . . . . . . . . (860) 692-7651

Correctional Education Superintendent (Acting)
**Kim Holley** . . . . . . . . . . . . . . . . . . . . . . . . . . (860) 692-7536
Fax: (860) 692-7538

Correctional Enterprises of Connecticut Director
**David A. Brown** . . . . . . . . . . . . . . . . . . . . . . . (860) 692-6839
Fax: (860) 263-6838

Offender Classification and Population Management
Director **Karl G. Lewis** . . . . . . . . . . . . . . . . . . . (860) 292-3412
Fax: (860) 292-3422

Victim Services Director **David Snyder** . . . . . . . . . . . . . (860) 692-7642
Tel: (860) 692-7586

Religious Services Director **Anthony Bruno** . . . . . . . . . . (860) 692-7577
Fax: (860) 692-6263

Volunteer Services Director **Douglas Kulmacz** . . . . . . . . . (860) 692-7580
Fax: (860) 692-6263

## Department of Developmental Services [DDS]

460 Capitol Avenue, Hartford, CT 06106
Tel: (860) 418-6000   TTY: (860) 418-6079   Fax: (860) 418-6001
E-mail: ddsct.co@ct.gov   Internet: www.ct.gov/dds

**Employees: 3,805   Fiscal Year: 2014-2015   Budget: $1,112,607,000**

■Commissioner **Morna A. Murray** . . . . . . . . . . . . . . . . (860) 418-6011
E-mail: morna.murray@ct.gov    Fax: (860) 418-6009
Education: George Washington 1982 AB, 1986 JD

Executive Secretary **Margaret Castonguay** . . . . . . . . . . (860) 418-6010

Chief of Staff **Kathryn Rock-Burns** . . . . . . . . . . . . . . . (860) 418-8762

Communications and Strategy Director
**Nicole M. Cadovius** . . . . . . . . . . . . . . . . . . . . (860) 418-6044
E-mail: nicole.cadovius@ct.gov

Equal Employment Opportunity Assurance Director
**Carl Jordan** . . . . . . . . . . . . . . . . . . . . . . . . . . (860) 418-6144
Fax: (860) 418-6004

Fiscal Administrator (Acting) **Cres Secchiaroli** . . . . . . . . . (860) 418-8712

Human Resources Administrator **Thomas Donlon** . . . . . . . (860) 418-6124
E-mail: thomas.donlon@ct.gov

Investigations Director **Kendres Lally** 2nd Floor . . . . . . . . (860) 418-8725
E-mail: kendres.lally@ct.gov    Fax: (860) 920-3182

Legislative and Executive Affairs Director
**Christine Pollio** . . . . . . . . . . . . . . . . . . . . . . . (860) 418-6066
E-mail: christine.pollio@ct.gov

Quality Management Services Director **Dan Micari** . . . . . . (860) 418-6081
Fax: (860) 418-6002

Ombudsman **Edward R. Mambruno** . . . . . . . . . . . . . . . (860) 418-6047
Education: Connecticut BS, MPA

Southbury Training School Director **Eugene Harvey** . . . . . . (203) 586-2602
Fax: (203) 586-2720

## Family and Community Services

Deputy Commissioner **Jordan A. Scheff** . . . . . . . . . . . . . (860) 418-6015
Executive Secretary **(Vacant)** . . . . . . . . . . . . . . . . (860) 418-6014

Birth to Three Program Director (Acting)
**Lynn Skene Johnson** . . . . . . . . . . . . . . . . . . . . (860) 418-6141

Operations Center Director **Peter Mason** . . . . . . . . . . . . (860) 418-6077

Waiver, Policy and Enrollment Director
**Siobhan C. Morgan** . . . . . . . . . . . . . . . . . . . . . (860) 418-8723

Aging Services Coordinator **Robert C. Smith** . . . . . . . . . . (860) 418-6041
Fax: (860) 418-6004

Health Services Director **(Vacant)** . . . . . . . . . . . . . . . . (860) 418-6083

## Finance and Information Technology Services

Chief Financial Officer **Mary Fuller** . . . . . . . . . . . . . . . (860) 418-6163

Audit, Billing and Rate Setting **Shawn Boisclair** . . . . . . . . (860) 418-6109

Budget Director **Kevin Lawton** . . . . . . . . . . . . . . . . . . (860) 418-6023

Engineering and Facilities Management Director
**Warren Schilling** . . . . . . . . . . . . . . . . . . . . . . . (860) 418-6031

*(continued on next page)*

---

★ Elected Official    ■ Appointed by Governor    ● Appointed by Legislature    ▲ Appointed by Board or Commission    ◆ Appointed by State Supreme Court

**Finance and Information Technology Services** *continued*

Information Technology Director **Tina Good** . . . . . . . . . . . (860) 418-6071
 E-mail: tina.good@ct.gov

## Legal and Government Affairs

Director **M. J. McCarthy, Esq.** . . . . . . . . . . . . . . . . . . . . (860) 418-6170
 Education: Yale 1979 PA          Fax: (860) 418-6112
Assistant Director **Marjorie Wakeman** . . . . . . . . . . . . . . (860) 418-6059
Eligibility Services Director **Kathleen Murphy** . . . . . . . (860) 418-6000
Litigation Management Coordinator **(Vacant)** . . . . . . . . . (860) 418-6095
          Fax: (860) 418-6009
Abuse/Neglect Registry **(Vacant)** . . . . . . . . . . . . . . . . . (860) 418-6048
Paralegal Specialist **Donna Patrick** . . . . . . . . . . . . . . . . (860) 418-6085

## Department of Economic and Community Development [DECD]

505 Hudson Street, Hartford, CT 06106-7106
Tel: (860) 270-8000  Fax: (860) 270-8188  E-mail: decd@ct.gov
Internet: www.decd.org

**Employees:** 118  **Fiscal Year:** 2016  **Budget:** $39,711,000

■Commissioner **Catherine H. Smith** . . . . . . . . . . . . . . . . (860) 270-8010
 E-mail: catherine.smith@ct.gov
 Education: Hampshire 1976 BA; Yale 1983 MPPM
Deputy Commissioner **Bart Kollen** . . . . . . . . . . . . . . . . . (860) 270-8020
Deputy Commissioner **Tim Sullivan** . . . . . . . . . . . . . . . . (860) 270-8040
Business and Industry Development Executive Director
 **Beatriz Gutierrez** . . . . . . . . . . . . . . . . . . . . . . . . . . . (860) 270-8013
Communications Director **James Watson** . . . . . . . . . . . . (860) 270-8182
 E-mail: jim.watson@ct.gov
Legislative Affairs Director **Rob Michalik** . . . . . . . . . . . (860) 270-8186
 E-mail: rob.michalik@ct.gov

## Offices of Culture and Tourism

One Constitution Plaza, 2nd Floor, Hartford, CT 06103
Tel: (860) 256-2800  Fax: (860) 256-2811

**Employees:** 48

■Deputy Commissioner **Christopher "Kip" Bergstrom** . . . . (860) 256-2727
 E-mail: kip.bergstrom@ct.gov
 Assistant to Deputy Commissioner **Leigh Johnson** . . . . . (860) 256-2727
Receptionist and Clerk **German Rivera** . . . . . . . . . . . . . . (860) 256-2800
Director of Culture **Kristina Newman-Scott** . . . . . . . . . . (860) 256-2753

## Department of Emergency Services and Public Protection [DPS]

1111 Country Club Road, Middletown, CT 06457-2389
Tel: (860) 685-8000  TTY: (860) 524-5781  Fax: (860) 685-8354

**Employees:** 1,654  **Fiscal Year:** 2014-2015  **Budget:** $175,476,000

■Commissioner **Dora B. Schrio** . . . . . . . . . . . . . . . . . . . . (860) 685-8000
 Education: Northeastern 1974 BA; UMass (Boston) 1976 MS;
 Columbia 1983 EdD; Saint Louis U 2002 JD
■Deputy Commissioner **Col. Brian Meraviglia** . . . . . . . . . (860) 685-8000
 E-mail: brian.meraviglia@ct.gov

## Department of Energy and Environmental Protection [DEEP]

79 Elm Street, Hartford, CT 06106
Tel: (860) 424-3000

■Commissioner **Robert Klee** . . . . . . . . . . . . . . . . . . . . . . (860) 424-3001
 Executive Secretary **Carmen I. Colón** . . . . . . . . . . . . . (860) 424-3571
Deputy Commissioner for Energy
 **Katherine M. "Katie" Scharf Dykes** . . . . . . . . . . . . . (860) 827-2807
 Education: Yale 2000 BA, 2006 MA, 2006 JD
Deputy Commissioner for Environmental Conservation
 **Susan Whalen** . . . . . . . . . . . . . . . . . . . . . . . . . . . . . . (860) 424-3005
 Education: Colby 1979 BA
 Natural Resources Bureau Chief **William A. Hyatt** . . . . . (860) 424-3487
          Fax: (860) 424-4070
 Outdoor Recreation Bureau Chief **(Vacant)** . . . . . . . . . (860) 424-3030
Deputy Commissioner for Environmental Quality
 **(Vacant)** . . . . . . . . . . . . . . . . . . . . . . . . . . . . . . . . . . (860) 424-3009

Air Management Bureau Chief **Anne R. Gobin** . . . . . . . . (860) 424-3026
Materials Management and Compliance Assurance
 Bureau Chief **Yvonne P. Bolton** . . . . . . . . . . . . . . . . . (860) 424-3021
Water Protection and Land Reuse Bureau Chief
 **Betsey C. Wingfield** . . . . . . . . . . . . . . . . . . . . . . . . . (860) 424-3704
Chief of Staff **(Vacant)** . . . . . . . . . . . . . . . . . . . . . . . . . (860) 424-3203
Financial and Support Services Bureau Chief **(Vacant)** . . . . (860) 424-3100
Communications Director **Dennis S. Schain** . . . . . . . . . . (860) 424-3110
 E-mail: dennis.schain@ct.gov
Affirmative Action Office Director **(Vacant)** . . . . . . . . . . (860) 424-3051
Planning and Program Development Office Director
 **Robert E. Kaliszewski** . . . . . . . . . . . . . . . . . . . . . . . (860) 424-3003
Information Management Office Director **(Vacant)** . . . . . . (860) 424-3642
Adjudications Office Director **Janice B. Deshais** . . . . . . . (860) 424-3037
Legal Counsel Office Director **Melinda M. Decker** . . . . . . (860) 424-3859

## Insurance Department

P.O. Box 816, Hartford, CT 06142-0816
Tel: (860) 297-3800  Fax: (860) 566-7410  Internet: www.ct.gov/cid

**Employees:** 148  **Fiscal Year:** 2014-2015  **Budget:** $28,791,000

■Insurance Commissioner **Katharine L. "Katie" Wade** . . . . (860) 297-3801
 E-mail: katharine.wade@ct.gov
 Executive Secretary **Patricia Butler** . . . . . . . . . . . . . . (860) 297-3801
Deputy Commissioner **John C. Thomson** . . . . . . . . . . . . (860) 297-3995
 E-mail: john.thomson@ct.gov
Communications Director **Donna Tommelleo** . . . . . . . . . . (860) 297-3958
 E-mail: donna.tommelleo@ct.gov     Fax: (860) 297-3491
Financial Regulation Division Director **Kathryn Belfi** . . . . (860) 297-3814
          Fax: (860) 297-3978
 Actuary **(Vacant)** . . . . . . . . . . . . . . . . . . . . . . . . . . . . (860) 297-3814
          Fax: (860) 297-3978
Life and Health Division Director **Danny Albert** . . . . . . . (860) 297-3863
          Fax: (860) 297-3941
Property and Casualty Division Director
 **George Bradner** . . . . . . . . . . . . . . . . . . . . . . . . . . . . (860) 297-3841
          Fax: (860) 297-3941
Business Office Manager **(Vacant)** . . . . . . . . . . . . . . . . . (860) 297-3995
          Fax: (860) 297-3941
Captive Insurance Unit Manager **Janet Grace** . . . . . . . . . (860) 297-3800
Consumer Affairs Program Manager **Gerard O'Sullivan** . . . (860) 297-3900
          Fax: (860) 297-3972
Market Conduct/Fraud Investigation and Licensing
 Division Director **Kurt Swan** . . . . . . . . . . . . . . . . . . . (860) 297-3898
          Fax: (860) 267-3872

## Department of Labor [DOL]

200 Folly Brook Boulevard, Wethersfield, CT 06109-1114
Tel: (860) 263-6000  Internet: www.ct.gov/dol

**Employees:** 710  **Fiscal Year:** 2014-2015  **Budget:** $195,174,000

■Commissioner **Scott Jackson** . . . . . . . . . . . . . . . . . . . . . (860) 263-6511
 E-mail: scott.jackson@ct.gov
 Education: Cornell
■Deputy Commissioner **Kurt Westby** . . . . . . . . . . . . . . . . (860) 263-6511
Appeals Chairperson **Lynne Knox** . . . . . . . . . . . . . . . . . (860) 566-3045
 E-mail: lynne.knox@ct.gov
Communications Director **Nancy Steffens** . . . . . . . . . . . . (860) 263-6535
 E-mail: nancy.steffens@ct.gov
Human Resources Director **(Vacant)** . . . . . . . . . . . . . . . . (860) 263-6685
Project Management and Technology Support Director
 **John Matteis** . . . . . . . . . . . . . . . . . . . . . . . . . . . . . . . (860) 263-6046
 E-mail: john.matteis@ct.gov
Information Technologies Director **Tracey Jackson** . . . . . . (860) 263-6145
 E-mail: tracey.jackson@ct.gov
Labor Relations Director **Katherine Foley** . . . . . . . . . . . . (860) 566-7535
 38 Wolcott Hill Road, Wethersfield, CT 06109
 E-mail: katherine.foley@ct.gov
OSHA (Occupational Safety and Health Administration)
 Director **Ken Tucker** . . . . . . . . . . . . . . . . . . . . . . . . . (860) 263-6900
 38 Wolcott Hill Road, Wethersfield, CT 06109
Program Policy Director **(Vacant)** . . . . . . . . . . . . . . . . . . (860) 263-6762
Labor Operations Director **Ram Aberasturia** . . . . . . . . . . (860) 263-6502
Research and Information Director **Andrew Condon** . . . . . (860) 263-6261
 E-mail: andrew.condon@ct.gov

---

★ Elected Official     ■ Appointed by Governor     ● Appointed by Legislature     ▲ Appointed by Board or Commission     ◆ Appointed by State Supreme Court

Tax Director **Carl Guzzardi** .................... (860) 263-6452
Unemployment Compensation Director **(Vacant)** ......... (860) 263-6784
Wage and Workplace Standards Director **Gary Pechie** ..... (860) 263-6376
E-mail: gary.pechie@ct.gov
Education: Marietta 1974 BA
Chief Fiscal Officer **Robert J. Merola** ............... (860) 263-6048
Education: Connecticut 1975 BS
Affirmative Action Administrator **Marla Shiller** ......... (860) 263-6520
Office of Workforce Competitiveness Director
**Kathleen Marioni** ................................ (860) 263-6526

## Department of Mental Health and Addiction Services [DMHAS]
410 Capitol Avenue, Fourth Floor, Hartford, CT 06134
P.O. Box 341431, Hartford, CT 06134
Tel: (860) 418-7000  Fax: (860) 418-6691  TTY: (860) 418-6999
Internet: www.ct.gov/dmhas

**Employees:** 3,446  **Fiscal Year:** 2014-2015  **Budget:** $680,729,000

■Commissioner **Miriam E. Delphin-Rittmon** ............ (860) 418-6959
E-mail: miriam.delphin-rittmon@ct.gov
Education: Hofstra 1989 BA; Purdue 1992 MS, 2001 PhD
Chief of Staff **Michael Michaud** ..................... (860) 418-6900

## Military Department
William A. O'Neill Armory, 360 Broad Street, Hartford, CT 06105-3706
Tel: (860) 524-4953  Fax: (860) 524-4898  Internet: www.mil.state.ct.us

**Employees:** 70  **Fiscal Year:** 2015  **Budget:** $6,153,000

■Adjutant General **MajGen Thaddeus J. Martin, ANG** .... (860) 524-4953
E-mail: thaddeus.j.martin.mil@mail.mil
Assistant Adjutant General **Mark Russo** ............... (860) 524-4957
Information Technologies Director
**COL John Whitford, ARNG** ...................... (860) 524-4916

## Connecticut Air National Guard
360 Broad Street, Hartford, CT 06105-3706
Tel: (860) 524-4953

■Adjutant General **BrigGen Jon Mott, ANG** ........... (860) 524-4953

## Department of Motor Vehicles [DMV]
60 State Street, Wethersfield, CT 06161
Tel: (860) 263-5700  Tel: (800) 842-8222 (In State)
E-mail: dmv.phonecenter@ct.gov

**Employees:** 747  **Fiscal Year:** 2014-2015  **Budget:** $68,838,000

■Commissioner **Michael Bzdyra** ..................... (860) 263-5015
Deputy Commissioner **Victor M. Diaz** ............... (860) 263-5015
Center for Teen Safe Driving Director
**William K. Seymour** ............................ (860) 263-5024
E-mail: william.seymour@ct.gov
Corporate and Public Relations Director **Ernie Bertothy** ... (860) 263-5034
E-mail: ernie.bertothy@ct.gov                    Fax: (203) 263-5553

## Department of Public Health [DPH]
410 Capitol Avenue, Hartford, CT 06106
P.O. Box 340308, Hartford, CT 06134-0308
Tel: (860) 509-8000  Tel: (860) 509-7700 (Vital Records)
Fax: (860) 509-7286  Fax: (860) 509-7964 (Vital Records)

**Employees:** 710  **Fiscal Year:** 2014-2015  **Budget:** $278,993,000

■Commissioner **Raul Pino, MD, MPH** ................ (860) 509-7101
E-mail: dph.commissioner@ct.gov
Executive Secretary **D. Jensen** ..................... (860) 509-7101
Executive Assistant **D. Ward** ...................... (860) 509-7101
Deputy Commissioner **Janet M. Brancifort, MPH** ....... (860) 509-7101
Deputy Commissioner **(Vacant)** ..................... (860) 509-7101
Executive Secretary **Rebecca Foreman** ............... (860) 509-7101

## Department of Rehabilitation Services [DRS]
25 Sigourney Street, Hartford, CT 06106
Tel: (860) 424-4844  Tel: (800) 537-2549  E-mail: brs.dss@ct.gov

**Employees:** 356  **Fiscal Year:** 2014-2015  **Budget:** $81,496,000

Commissioner **Amy Porter** .......................... (860) 424-4864
Fax: (860) 424-4850

## Bureau of Education and Services for the Blind [BESB]
184 Windsor Avenue, Windsor, CT 06095
Tel: (860) 602-4000  TTY: (860) 602-4221  Fax: (860) 602-4020
E-mail: besb@ct.gov

**Employees:** 120

■Director **Brian S. Sigman** .......................... (860) 602-4008
E-mail: brian.sigman@ct.gov
Volunteer Program Coordinator **Lori St. Amand** ........ (860) 602-4129
Tel: (800) 842-4510
ext. 4129

## Bureau of Rehabilitation Services
25 Sigourney Street, 11th Floor, Hartford, CT 06106
Tel: (860) 424-4844  Tel: (800) 537-2549
Tel: (860) 920-7163 (Video Phone)  Fax: (860) 424-4850
E-mail: brs.dss@ct.gov
Bureau Chief **Dave Doukas** ......................... (860) 424-4862

## Deaf and Hard of Hearing Services
67 Prospect Avenue, 3rd Floor, West Hartford, CT 06133
P.O. Box 330730, West Hartford, CT 06133-0730
Tel: (800) 537-2549  TTY: (860) 231-8169
Tel: (860) 231-8756 ext. 4 (Counceling Services)
Tel: (860) 231-1690 ext. 5 (Interpreting Unit)  Fax: (860) 231-8746
E-mail: cdhi@ct.gov  Internet: www.ct.gov/cdhi

**Employees:** 48

Interpreter Coordinator **Patricia Clark** ........... (860) 231-1690 ext. 309
Interpreter Coordinator **Sara Gerhold** ...... (860) 899-1647 (Video Phone)
Office Assistant **Jacqueline Medina** ........... (860) 231-1690 ext. 307
Financial Administrative Assistant
**Phuong Nguyen** .......................... (860) 231-1690 ext. 320
Clerk Typist **Judith Dandrow** ..................... (860) 231-8169
Clerk Typist **Tina Tyson** ................... (860) 231-1690 ext. 306
Counselor for the Deaf and
Hard of Hearing **Mary Ann
Dayton-Fitzgerald, LPC** ......... (860) 231-8756 ext. 318 (Video Phone)
Tel: (860) 899-1648
(Video Phone)

Counselor for the Deaf
and Hard of Hearing
**Melissa Dennis, LPC** ........... (860) 231-8756 ext. 313 (Video Phone)
Tel: (860) 899-1818
(Video Phone)

## Department of Revenue Services [DRS]
25 Sigourney Street, Hartford, CT 06106
Tel: (860) 297-5962  Fax: (860) 297-5714  TTY: (860) 297-5742
E-mail: drs@po.state.ct.us  Internet: www.ct.gov/drs

**Employees:** 635  **Fiscal Year:** 2014-2015  **Budget:** $68,691,000

■Commissioner **Kevin B. Sullivan** .................... (860) 297-4900
E-mail: kevin.b.sullivan@po.state.ct.us
Education: Trinity Col (CT) 1971 BA; Connecticut 1982 JD
Executive Secretary **Patricia Hicks** ................. (860) 297-5601
Deputy Commissioner **Joseph Mooney** ............... (860) 297-5801
First Assistant Commissioner and General Counsel
**Louis Bucari** ................................. (860) 297-5798
Chief of Staff **(Vacant)** ........................... (860) 297-5620
Revenue Services Bureau Chief, Administration
**Gary Dowling** ................................ (860) 297-4732
E-mail: gary.dowling@po.state.ct.us

*(continued on next page)*

EXECUTIVE BRANCH

**Department of Revenue Services** *continued*

Revenue Services Bureau Chief, Operations
**Pamela Doolan** . . . . . . . . . . . . . . . . . . . . . . . . . . (860) 541-3226
Communications Director **Sarah Kaufman** . . . . . . . . . . . . . (860) 297-5610
Taxpayer Services Director **Peter Santagata** . . . . . . . . . . . (860) 297-4924
Appellate Division Director **Scot Anderson** . . . . . . . . . . . (860) 297-4773
Audit and Compliance Director **John Kutsukos** . . . . . . . (860) 541-4561
Information Services Division Director **Real Lavigne** . . . . . (860) 297-5820
   E-mail: real.lavigne@po.state.ct.us
Legal Division Director **Marilee Clark** . . . . . . . . . . . . . . . (860) 297-5634

## Department of Social Services [DSS]

55 Farmington Avenue, Hartford, CT 06105-3730
Tel: (800) 842-1508 (In State)  Fax: (860) 424-5192
TTY: (800) 842-4524  E-mail: pgr.dss@ct.gov  Internet: www.ct.gov/dss

**Employees:** 1,212  **Fiscal Year:** 2015  **Budget:** $3,065,738,000

■Commissioner **Roderick L. Bremby** . . . . . . . . . . . . . (860) 424-5054
   E-mail: roderick.bremby@ct.gov       Fax: (860) 424-5057
   Education: Kansas 1982 BA, 1984 MPA
  Administration Deputy Commissioner
   **Kathleen Brennan** . . . . . . . . . . . . . . . . . . . . . . (860) 424-5693
   E-mail: kathleen.brennan@ct.gov     Fax: (860) 424-5900
  Programs Deputy Commissioner **(Vacant)** . . . . . . . . . . . . . (860) 424-5105
                         Fax: (860) 424-4899
  Chief of Staff **Astread Ferron-Poole** . . . . . . . . . . . . . . (860) 424-5501
                         Fax: (860) 566-2022
  Medicaid Director **Kate McEvoy** . . . . . . . . . . . . . . . . (860) 424-5067
   E-mail: kate.mcevoy@ct.gov
  SNAP Director **Ronald Roberts** . . . . . . . . . . . . . . . . (860) 424-5135

## Workers' Compensation Commission

21 Oak Street, 4th Floor, Hartford, CT 06106
Tel: (860) 493-1500  Fax: (860) 247-1361

**Employees:** 97  **Fiscal Year:** 2014-2015  **Budget:** $22,715,000

■Chairman **John A. Mastropietro** . . . . . . . . . . . . . . . . (860) 493-1500
   E-mail: john.mastropietro@ct.gov
   Education: Connecticut 1975 BA; Western New England 1978 JD
   Executive Secretary **Tara Remillard** . . . . . . . . . . . . . . (860) 493-1579
■Member **Scott A. Barton** . . . . . . . . . . . . . . . . . . . . (860) 493-1500
   Term Expires: November 30, 2015
■Member **Randy L. Cohen** . . . . . . . . . . . . . . . . . . . . (860) 493-1500
   Term Expires: February 20, 2018
■Member **Stephen B. Delaney** . . . . . . . . . . . . . . . . . . (860) 493-1500
   Term Expires: March 12, 2017
■Member **Daniel E. Dilzer** . . . . . . . . . . . . . . . . . . . . (860) 493-1500
   Term Expires: May 6, 2018
■Member **Christine L. Engel** . . . . . . . . . . . . . . . . . . . (860) 493-1500
   Term Expires: March 5, 2018
■Member **Jack R. Goldberg** . . . . . . . . . . . . . . . . . . . (860) 493-1500
   Term Expires: April 25, 2017
   Education: Northeastern 1975 BA; Connecticut 1992 JD
■Member **Jodi Murray Gregg** . . . . . . . . . . . . . . . . . . (860) 493-1500
   Term Expires: February 20, 2018
■Member **Peter C. Mlynarczyk** . . . . . . . . . . . . . . . . . (860) 493-1500
   Term Expires: March 7, 2017
■Member **Stephen Morelli** . . . . . . . . . . . . . . . . . . . . (860) 493-1500
   Term Expires: 2018
   Education: Connecticut 1983 BA, 1986 JD
■Member **Nancy E. Salerno** . . . . . . . . . . . . . . . . . . . (860) 493-1500
   Term Expires: March 2, 2019
■Member **David W. Schoolcraft** . . . . . . . . . . . . . . . . . (860) 493-1500
   Term Expires: May 7, 2018
■Member **Charles F. Senich** . . . . . . . . . . . . . . . . . . . (860) 493-1500
   Term Expires: March 7, 2017
■Member **Michelle D. Truglia** . . . . . . . . . . . . . . . . . . (860) 493-1500
   Term Expires: March 17, 2018
■Member **Ernie R. Walker** . . . . . . . . . . . . . . . . . . . . (860) 493-1500
   Term Expires: March 11, 2019

## Connecticut Department of Transportation [ConnDOT]

2800 Berlin Turnpike, Newington, CT 06131
P.O. Box 317546, Newington, CT 06131-7546
Tel: (860) 594-3000  Fax: (860) 594-3008

**Employees:** 3,556  **Fiscal Year:** 2014-2015  **Budget:** $603,762,000

■Commissioner **James P. "Jim" Redeker** . . . . . . . . . . . (860) 594-3001
   E-mail: james.redeker@ct.gov
   Executive Secretary **Angela Brault** . . . . . . . . . . . . . . (860) 594-3002
■Deputy Commissioner **Anna Barry** . . . . . . . . . . . . . . (860) 594-3000
   E-mail: anna.barry@ct.gov
   Executive Secretary **Sandra Guerra** . . . . . . . . . . . . . (860) 594-3011

## Department of Veterans' Affairs [DVA]

287 West Street, Rocky Hill, CT 06067
Tel: (860) 616-3600  Fax: (860) 616-3604  Internet: www.ct.gov/ctva

**Employees:** 289  **Fiscal Year:** 2015  **Budget:** $28,246,000

■Commissioner **LTC Sean M. Connolly, USAR** . . . . . . . . . (860) 616-3601
   E-mail: sean.connolly@ct.gov
   Education: Bryant U 1996 BA; Columbus Law 1999 JD
   Executive Assistant **Fausto Parra** . . . . . . . . . . . . . . . (860) 616-3607
■Deputy Commissioner **(Vacant)** . . . . . . . . . . . . . . . . (860) 616-3603
Chief of Staff and General Counsel **Thomas J. Saadi** . . . . (860) 616-3604
Healthcare Administrator **Suzanne Krassler** . . . . . . . . . . (860) 616-3701
   E-mail: suzanne.krassler@ct.gov     Fax: (860) 616-3703
Communications Director **Emily Hein** . . . . . . . . . . . . . (860) 616-3605
   E-mail: emily.hein@ct.gov
Food Services Director **Paul LaPierre** . . . . . . . . . . . . . (860) 616-3860
Planning Director **Babatunde Green** . . . . . . . . . . . . . . (860) 721-3606
                         Fax: (860) 721-5984
Residential and Rehab Services Director **Maria Cheney** . . . (860) 616-3801
                         Fax: (860) 616-3803
Safety and Security Director **Hugo C. Adams** . . . . . . . . . (860) 616-3611

## Criminal Justice Commission

300 Corporate Place, Rocky Hill, CT 06067
Tel: (860) 258-5800  Fax: (860) 258-5858  E-mail: conndcj@ct.gov
Internet: www.ct.gov/cjc

■Chairman **Richard N. Palmer** . . . . . . . . . . . . . . . . . (860) 258-5800
   Affiliation: Associate Justice, Chambers of Associate Justice Richard N.
   Palmer, Connecticut Supreme Court
   Supreme Court Building, 231 Capitol Avenue, Hartford, CT 06106
   Education: Trinity Col (CT) 1972 BA; Connecticut 1977 JD
■Member **Juliett L. Crawford** . . . . . . . . . . . . . . . . . . (860) 258-5800
■Member **Mary M. Galvin** . . . . . . . . . . . . . . . . . . . . (860) 258-5800
■Member **Maura Hughes Horan** . . . . . . . . . . . . . . . . (860) 258-5800
   Education: UC San Diego 1984 BA; Connecticut 1988 JD
■Member **Moy Ogilvie** . . . . . . . . . . . . . . . . . . . . . . (860) 258-5800
   Education: Bowdoin 1990 BA; Boston U 1995 JD
■Member **Ann G. Taylor** . . . . . . . . . . . . . . . . . . . . . (860) 258-5800
   Affiliation: General Counsel, Connecticut Children's Medical Center
   282 Washington Street, Hartford, CT 06106
   Education: Catholic U BA; Western New England JD
Ex-Officio Member **Kevin T. Kane** . . . . . . . . . . . . . . . (860) 258-5800
   Affiliation: Chief State's Attorney, Criminal Justice Division, Criminal
   Justice Commission, State of Connecticut
   300 Corporate Place, Rocky Hill, CT 06067
   Education: Marquette 1965 BA; Connecticut 1968 JD

## Criminal Justice Division

Tel: (860) 258-5800  Fax: (860) 258-5858  E-mail: conndcj@ct.gov
Internet: www.ct.gov/csao

**Employees:** 480  **Fiscal Year:** 2015  **Budget:** $53,195,581,000

▲Chief State's Attorney **Kevin T. Kane** . . . . . . . . . . . . . (860) 258-5800
   E-mail: conndcj@ct.gov
▲Deputy Chief State's Attorney (Administration)
   **John J. Russotto** . . . . . . . . . . . . . . . . . . . . . . (860) 258-5800
   E-mail: john.russotto@ct.gov
   Education: Fairfield 1987 BA; Boston U 1990 JD

---

★ Elected Official    ■ Appointed by Governor    ● Appointed by Legislature    ▲ Appointed by Board or Commission    ◆ Appointed by State Supreme Court

▲Deputy Chief State's Attorney (Operations)
**Leonard C. Boyle** . . . . . . . . . . . . . . . . . . . . . . . . . . (860) 258-5800
E-mail: leonard.boyle@ct.gov
Education: Hartford 1980; Connecticut 1983 JD
Executive Assistant State's Attorney **Brian Austin, Jr.** . . . . (860) 258-5800
Executive Assistant State's Attorney **Michael A. Gailor** . . . (860) 258-5800
Education: Cornell 1984 BA; Connecticut Col 1987 JD

## Medicaid Fraud Control Unit
300 Corporate Place, Rocky Hill, CT 06067
Tel: (860) 258-5986  Fax: (860) 258-5838

Director **Christopher Godialis** . . . . . . . . . . . . . . . . . . . . (860) 258-5986

## State Board of Education
165 Capitol Avenue, Room 301, Hartford, CT 06106
Tel: (860) 713-6510  Fax: (860) 713-7002  Internet: www.sde.ct.gov

■Chairperson **Allan B. Taylor** . . . . . . . . . . . . . . . . . . . . . (860) 713-6510
Term Expires: February 28, 2017
Education: Harvard, MPP, JD
■Vice Chair **Theresa Hopkins-Staten** . . . . . . . . . . . . . . . (860) 713-6510
Term Expires: February 28, 2017
Education: Connecticut 1984
■Member **Erin Benham** . . . . . . . . . . . . . . . . . . . . . . . . . (860) 713-6510
Term Expires: February 28, 2019
Education: Southern Connecticut State U MS
■Member **Erik Clemons** . . . . . . . . . . . . . . . . . . . . . . . . . (860) 713-6510
■Member **William P. Davenport** . . . . . . . . . . . . . . . . . . . (860) 713-6510
■Member **Terry H. Jones** . . . . . . . . . . . . . . . . . . . . . . . . (860) 713-6510
Term Expires: February 28, 2019
■Member **Dr. Estela R. López** . . . . . . . . . . . . . . . . . . . . (860) 713-6510
Term Expires: February 28, 2019
Affiliation: Senior Associate, Excelencia in Education
1752 N Street, NW, Sixth Floor, Washington, DC 20036
Education: Columbia MA, PhD
■Member **Maria I. Mojica** . . . . . . . . . . . . . . . . . . . . . . . (860) 713-6510
Education: Yale 1978 BA, 1983 MPH
■Member **Malia Sieve** . . . . . . . . . . . . . . . . . . . . . . . . . . (860) 713-6510
■Member **Joseph Vrabely** . . . . . . . . . . . . . . . . . . . . . . . (860) 713-6510
Term Expires: February 28, 2019
■Member **Stephen P. Wright** . . . . . . . . . . . . . . . . . . . . . (860) 713-6510
Term Expires: February 28, 2019
Student Member **Susannah M. Beyl** . . . . . . . . . . . . . . . . (860) 713-6510
Term Expires: June 2016
Student Member **Timothy J. "TJ" Noel-Sullivan** . . . . . . . (860) 713-6510
Term Expires: June 2016
Ex Officio Member **Mark E. Ojakian** . . . . . . . . . . . . . . . (860) 947-1801
Education: St Anselm 1975 BA; American U 1977 MA
Ex Officio Member **Dianna Roberge-Wentzell** . . . . . . . . . (860) 947-1801
Education: Mount Holyoke; UMass (Amherst); Hartford PhD
Ex Officio Member **Robert J. "Bob" Trefry** . . . . . . . . . . . (860) 947-1801
Education: George Washington 1974 MA

## State Department of Education
165 Capitol Avenue, Hartford, CT 06106
P. O. Box 2219, Hartford, CT 06145
Tel: (860) 713-6543  Fax: (860) 713-7005  Internet: www.sde.ct.gov

**Employees:** 1,691  **Fiscal Year:** 2015  **Budget:** $3,014,582,000

▲Commissioner **Dianna Roberge-Wentzell** . . . . . . . . . . . . (860) 713-6500
E-mail: dianna.roberge-wentzell@ct.gov
Chief Academic Officer **(Vacant)** . . . . . . . . . . . . . . . . . . (860) 713-6775
Chief Operating Officer **Charlene M. Russell-Tucker** . . . . . (860) 716-6550
Chief Talent Officer **Sarah Barzee** . . . . . . . . . . . . . . . . . (860) 713-6848
Chief Turnaround Officer **Desi Nesmith** . . . . . . . . . . . . . (860) 713-6848

## State Library
231 Capitol Avenue, Hartford, CT 06106
Tel: (860) 757-6500  Fax: (860) 757-6503  E-mail: isref@cslib.org
Internet: www.cslib.org  Internet: www.iconn.org (Digital Library)

**Employees:** 97  **Fiscal Year:** 2015  **Budget:** $12,205,000

▲State Librarian **Kendall F. Wiggin** . . . . . . . . . . . . . . . . (860) 757-6510
E-mail: kendall.wiggin@ct.gov
Executive Secretary **Jane A. Beaudoin** . . . . . . . . . . . . . . (860) 757-6510

Library for the Blind and Physically Handicapped
Director **Gordon Reddick** . . . . . . . . . . . . . . . . . . . . . . . (860) 721-2021
Fax: (860) 721-2056
Fiscal Services **Mark Smith** . . . . . . . . . . . . . . . . . . . . . . (860) 424-3311
Fax: (860) 424-3920
Library Development Division Director **Dawn LaValle** . . . . (860) 757-6665
Museum of Connecticut History Administrator
**Dean Nelson** . . . . . . . . . . . . . . . . . . . . . . . . . . . . . . (860) 757-6532
Fax: (860) 757-6533
Public Records **LeAnn Power** . . . . . . . . . . . . . . . . . . . . . (860) 757-6540
State Archivist **Lizette Pelletier** . . . . . . . . . . . . . . . . . . . (860) 757-6511
State Data Coordinator **Thomas "Tom" Newman** . . . . . . . (860) 757-6573
E-mail: tom.newman@ct.gov
Web Resources Librarian **(Vacant)** . . . . . . . . . . . . . . . . . (860) 757-6584

## Connecticut Lottery Corporation
777 Brook Street, Rocky Hill, CT 06067
Tel: (860) 713-2700  Fax: (860) 713-2805  E-mail: ctlottery@ctlottery.org
Internet: www.ctlottery.org

▲President and Chief Executive Officer **Anne M. Noble** . . . . (860) 713-2815
E-mail: anne.noble@ctlottery.org
Executive Secretary **(Vacant)** . . . . . . . . . . . . . . . . . . . . . (860) 713-2816
▲Marketing and Sales Vice President **Diane Patterson** . . . . . (860) 713-2819
E-mail: diane.patterson@ctlottery.org

## Office of the Lieutenant Governor
State Capitol, 210 Capitol Avenue, Room 304, Hartford, CT 06106
Tel: (860) 524-7384  Fax: (860) 524-7304

★Lieutenant Governor **Nancy Wyman** (D) . . . . . . . . . . . . . (860) 524-7384
Term Expires: January 2019
E-mail: ltgovernor.wyman@ct.gov
Career: Chair, Education, Standing Joint Committees, Connecticut
General Assembly; State Representative (D-CT, District 53),
Connecticut House of Representatives (1987-1995); Comptroller
(D-CT), Office of State Comptroller Nancy Wyman, State of
Connecticut (1995-2011)
Chief of Staff **Bettye Jo Pakulis** . . . . . . . . . . . . . . . . . . . (860) 524-7341
Senior Advisor **Martin L. Heft** . . . . . . . . . . . . . . . . . . . . (860) 524-7317
Communications Director **Juliet S. Manalan** . . . . . . . . . . . (860) 524-7377
Special Assistant **Jennifer Putetti** . . . . . . . . . . . . . . . . . . (860) 524-7371

## Office of the Secretary of State
State Capitol, 210 Capitol Avenue, Room 104, Hartford, CT 06106
Tel: (860) 509-6200  Fax: (860) 509-6209

★Secretary of State **Denise W. Merrill** (D) . . . . . . . . . . . . . (860) 509-6200
Term Expires: 2019
E-mail: denise.merrill@ct.gov
Education: Connecticut
Career: Deputy Majority Leader, Connecticut House of Representatives;
Member-at-Large, Executive Committee, National Conference of State
Legislatures (2006-2009); State Representative (D-CT, District 54),
Connecticut House of Representatives (1992-2011)
Chief of Staff **Shannon Wegele** . . . . . . . . . . . . . . . . . . . (860) 509-6228
Administrative Assistant **Ilona Havrilla** . . . . . . . . . . . . . . (860) 509-6212

## Administrative Offices
30 Trinity Street, Hartford, CT 06115
P.O. Box 150470, Hartford, CT 06115-0470
Fax: (860) 509-6131

■Deputy Secretary of State **James Field Spallone** . . . . . . . . (860) 509-6200
E-mail: james.spallone@ct.gov
Education: Williams 1987 BA; Connecticut 1992 JD
Commercial Recording Division Director **Seth Klaskin** . . . (860) 509-6059
Legislative and Election Administrative Division Director
**Margaret "Peggy" Reeves** . . . . . . . . . . . . . . . . . . . . . (860) 509-6123
E-mail: peggy.reeves@ct.gov            Fax: (860) 509-6127
Education: Connecticut Col BA; Pace JD
Communications Director **(Vacant)** . . . . . . . . . . . . . . . . . (860) 509-6255
Fiscal Administrative Manager
**Blanche H. Reeves-Tucker** . . . . . . . . . . . . . . . . . . . . (860) 509-6166
Fax: (860) 509-6175
Human Resource Associate **Gloria Sparveri** . . . . . . . . . . . (860) 509-6171
Fax: (860) 509-6236

*(continued on next page)*

★ Elected Official   ■ Appointed by Governor   ● Appointed by Legislature   ▲ Appointed by Board or Commission   ◆ Appointed by State Supreme Court

**Administrative Offices** *continued*

Legislative Liaison **Lewis Button III** . . . . . . . . . . . . . . . (860) 509-6110
  E-mail: lewis.button@ct.gov
Revenue Accountant **David Pritchard** . . . . . . . . . . . . . . (860) 509-6154
                                                    Fax: (860) 509-6175

# Office of the Attorney General

55 Elm Street, Hartford, CT 06106
Tel: (860) 808-5318  Fax: (860) 808-5387
E-mail: attorney.general@ct.gov

**Employees:** 315

★Attorney General **George C. Jepsen** (D) . . . . . . . . . . . . . . (860) 808-5318
  Term Expires: 2019
  Education: Dartmouth 1976 BA; Harvard 1982 MPP, 1982 JD
  Career: State Senator (D-CT, District 27), Connecticut State Senate
  (1991-2003); Chairman, Connecticut Democrats, Democratic National
  Committee (2003-2005); Of Counsel, Cowdery, Ecker & Murphy,
  L.L.C. (2003-2011)
Deputy Attorney General **Perry Zinn-Rowthorn** . . . . . . . . (860) 808-5320
Information Technology Manager **Scott Eliasson** . . . . . . . . (860) 808-5318
  E-mail: scott.eliasson@ct.gov

## Antitrust and Government Program Fund

Fax: (860) 808-5033
Assistant Attorney General **Michael E. Cole** . . . . . . . . . . . (860) 808-5040

## Child Protection

110 Sherman Street, Hartford, CT 06105
Fax: (860) 808-5590
Assistant Attorney General **Benjamin Zivyon** . . . . . . . . . . (860) 808-5480
  E-mail: benjamin.zivyon@ct.gov

## Civil Rights/Torts

Fax: (860) 808-5384
Assistant Attorney General **(Vacant)** . . . . . . . . . . . . . . . . (860) 808-5160

## Collections and Child Support

Fax: (860) 808-5389
Assistant Attorney General **Sean O. Kehoe** . . . . . . . . . . . (860) 808-5150
  E-mail: sean.kehoe@ct.gov

## Consumer Protection

110 Sherman Street, Hartford, CT 06105
Fax: (860) 808-5593
Assistant Attorney General **(Vacant)** . . . . . . . . . . . . . . . . (860) 808-5400

## Employment Rights

Fax: (860) 808-5383
Assistant Attorney General **Ann Lynch** . . . . . . . . . . . . . . (860) 808-5340
  E-mail: ann.lynch@ct.gov

## Energy

Fax: (860) 827-2893
Assistant Attorney General **Clare Kindall** . . . . . . . . . . . . . (860) 827-2620

## Environment

Fax: (860) 808-5386
Assistant Attorney General **Kimberly Massicotte** . . . . . . . . (860) 808-5250

## Finance and Public Utilities

Fax: (860) 808-5385
Assistant Attorney General **Matthew Budzik** . . . . . . . . . . . (860) 827-5270

## Health and Education

Fax: (860) 808-5385
Assistant Attorney General **Henry A. Salton** . . . . . . . . . . . (860) 808-5210
  E-mail: henry.salton@ct.gov

# Public Safety and Special Revenue

110 Sherman Street, Hartford, CT 06105
Fax: (860) 808-5591
Assistant Attorney General **Terrence M. O'Neill** . . . . . . . . (860) 808-5450
  E-mail: terrence.oneill@ct.gov

## Special Litigation

Fax: (860) 808-5347
Assistant Attorney General **Mark F. Kohler** . . . . . . . . . . . (860) 808-5020

## Transportation

Fax: (860) 808-5384
Assistant Attorney General **(Vacant)** . . . . . . . . . . . . . . . . (860) 808-5090

## Workers' Compensation and Labor Relations

Fax: (860) 808-5388
Assistant Attorney General **Philip M. Schulz** . . . . . . . . . . (860) 808-5050

# Office of the State Comptroller

55 Elm Street, Hartford, CT 06106
Tel: (860) 702-3300  Fax: (860) 702-3319

★Comptroller **Kevin P. Lembo** (D) . . . . . . . . . . . . . . . . . . (860) 702-3301
  Term Expires: 2019
  E-mail: comptroller.lembo@ct.gov
  Career: Assistant Comptroller, Office of the State Comptroller, State of
  Connecticut; Healthcare Advocate, Office of the Healthcare Advocate,
  State of Connecticut (2005-2011)
Deputy Comptroller **Martha Carlson** . . . . . . . . . . . . . . . . (860) 702-3302

# Office of the State Treasurer

55 Elm Street, Hartford, CT 06106
Tel: (860) 618-3404

**Employees:** 131  **Fiscal Year:** 2015  **Budget:** $3,393,000

★State Treasurer **Denise L. Nappier** (D) . . . . . . . . . . . . . . (860) 702-3010
  Term Expires: 2019
  E-mail: state.treasurer@ct.gov
  Education: Virginia State BA; Cincinnati MCP
  Career: City Treasurer, Office of the City Treasurer, Town and City of
  Hartford, Connecticut
  Executive Secretary **Marianne Dziedzic** . . . . . . . . . . . . . (860) 702-3106
  External Relations Senior Executive Assistant
    **Gail M. Crockett** . . . . . . . . . . . . . . . . . . . . . . . . . . . (860) 702-3282
Deputy State Treasurer **Richard D. Gray** . . . . . . . . . . . . . (860) 702-3292
  Education: Connecticut 1972; New Haven MBA
Chief of Staff **(Vacant)** . . . . . . . . . . . . . . . . . . . . . . . . . (860) 702-3211
Chief Compliance Officer **Christine Shaw** . . . . . . . . . . . . (860) 618-3404
  Education: Connecticut BEc, MBA, JD
General Counsel **Catherine LaMarr** . . . . . . . . . . . . . . . . . (860) 702-3018
Communications Director **David S. Barrett** . . . . . . . . . . . (860) 702-3164
  E-mail: david.s.barrett@ct.gov
Financial Reporting and Controls Manager
  **Robert C. "Bob" Morgan** . . . . . . . . . . . . . . . . . . . . . . (860) 702-3290
Webmaster **Leon Rippel** . . . . . . . . . . . . . . . . . . . . . . . . (860) 702-3148

★ Elected Official   ■ Appointed by Governor   ● Appointed by Legislature   ▲ Appointed by Board or Commission   ◆ Appointed by State Supreme Court

Summer 2016               © Leadership Directories, Inc.               *State Yellow Book*

# Delaware

Tel: (800) 464-4357 (Delaware Help Line)  Internet: www.delaware.gov

**Number of U.S. Congressional Delegates:** 2 Senators; 1 Representatives  **Governor's Term:** 4 years
**Legislature Description:** General Assembly - 21 member Senate; 41 member House of Representatives;
Term - Senate 4 years, House 2 years  **Next Election:** Governor November 2016; Legislature November
2016  **Number of Electoral Votes:** 3  **Official Name:** State of Delaware (after Lord De La Warr)
**Nickname:** The First State  **Motto:** Liberty and Independence

**Population:** 945,934 (2015); Rank 45  **Employees:** 25,877  **Fiscal Year:** 2015  **Budget:** $1,372,536,000

## Office of the Governor

150 Martin Luther King Jr. Blvd. South, 2nd Floor, Dover, DE 19901
Tel: (302) 744-4101  Fax: (302) 739-2775

**Employees:** 25  **Fiscal Year:** 2015  **Budget:** $2,807,000

**Jack A. Markell**
Governor

Began Service: 2009
Term Expires: January 2017
Date of Birth: November 26, 1960
Education: Brown U 1982 BA;
Chicago 1985 MBA
Religion: Jewish
Career: Banker, First Chicago Corporation;
Consultant, McKinsey and Company, Inc.;
Senior Management, Comcast Corporation;
Senior Vice President, Corporate Development,
Nextel Communications, Inc.; Founder, Delaware
Money School; State Treasurer (D-DE), State of
Delaware (1998-2009)

★ Governor **Jack A. Markell** (D) . . . . . . . . . . . . . . . . . . . . (302) 744-4101
    E-mail: jack.markell@state.de.us
Chief of Staff **Michael "Mike" Barlow** . . . . . . . . . . . . . (302) 744-4101
Deputy Chief of Staff **Drewry "Drew" Fennell, Esq.** . . . . . (302) 744-4101
    E-mail: drew.fennell@state.de.us
Executive Assistant to the Governor
    **Victoria "Dee" Jones** . . . . . . . . . . . . . . . . . . . . . . . (302) 744-4102
    E-mail: victoria.jones@state.de.us
Chief Legal Counsel **Meredith Stewart Tweedie** . . . . . . . (302) 744-4223
Deputy Legal Counsel **Scott Perkins** . . . . . . . . . . . . . . . (302) 577-8640
    E-mail: scott.perkins@state.de.us
Boards and Commissions Director **Lydia Prigg** . . . . . . . . (302) 744-4235
    E-mail: lydia.prigg@state.de.us
Constituent Relations Director **Jennifer Hill** . . . . . . . . . (302) 577-3210
Communications Director **Jonathon Dworkin** . . . . . . . . . (302) 577-3210
    E-mail: jonathon.dworkin@state.de.us
    Education: Syracuse 2007 BS
Economic Development Policy Advisor
    **Damian DeStefano** . . . . . . . . . . . . . . . . . . . . . . . . . (302) 744-4101
    E-mail: damian.destefano@state.de.us
Education Policy Advisor **Meghan Wallace** . . . . . . . . . . . (302) 577-3210
    E-mail: meghan.wallace@state.de.us
Health Care Policy Advisor **(Vacant)** . . . . . . . . . . . . . . . (302) 577-3210
Scheduling Secretary **Amanda Galinskie** . . . . . . . . . . . . (302) 577-3210
    E-mail: amanda.tenshaw@state.de.us
Press Secretary **Courtney McGregor** . . . . . . . . . . . . . . . (302) 577-8229

## Washington Office

444 North Capitol Street, NW, Suite 230, Washington, DC 20001
Fax: (202) 624-5495

Director **Garth A. Spencer, Jr.** . . . . . . . . . . . . . . . . . . . (202) 624-7724
    E-mail: garth.spencer@state.de.us

## Delaware Economic Development Office [DEDO]

99 Kings Highway, Dover, DE 19901
Tel: (302) 739-4271  Fax: (302) 739-5749  Internet: www.state.de.us/dedo

**Employees:** 42  **Fiscal Year:** 2015  **Budget:** $24,242,000

Director **Bernice Whaley** . . . . . . . . . . . . . . . . . . . . . . . (302) 672-6808
    E-mail: bernice.whaley@state.de.us
    Executive Secretary **(Vacant)** . . . . . . . . . . . . . . . . . . (302) 672-6808
Deputy Director **(Vacant)** . . . . . . . . . . . . . . . . . . . . . . (302) 672-3811

## Technology and Information Department [DTI]

William Penn Building, 801 Silver Lake Boulevard, Dover, DE 19904
Tel: (302) 739-9600  Fax: (302) 739-6251

**Employees:** 232

Secretary and Chief Information Officer
    **James L. Collins** . . . . . . . . . . . . . . . . . . . . . . . . . . . (302) 739-9629
    E-mail: james.collins@state.de.us
    Education: Wesley Col (DE) 1997 BA
    Executive Assistant **Ronda Ramsburg** . . . . . . . . . . . . . (302) 739-9629
Chief Operations Officer **William "Bill" Hickox** . . . . . . (302) 739-9693
    E-mail: william.hickox@state.de.us
    Education: SUNY (Cortland) 1991 BA; Wilmington U 2000 MBA
Chief Security Officer **Elayne Starkey** . . . . . . . . . . . . . . (302) 739-9640
    E-mail: elayne.starkey@state.de.us
Chief Technology Officer **Matthew Payne** . . . . . . . . . . . (302) 739-9600
    E-mail: matthew.payne@state.de.us

## Pension Office

McArdel Building, 860 Silver Lake Boulevard, Suite 1, Dover, DE 19904
Tel: (302) 739-4208

Administrator **David C. Craik** . . . . . . . . . . . . . . . . . . . (302) 739-4208
    E-mail: david.craik@state.de.us

## Office of Management and Budget

Haslet Building, 122 Martin Luther King Jr. Boulevard S.,
Dover, DE 19901
Tel: (302) 739-4206  Fax: (302) 739-5661
Internet: www.state.de.us/budget

**Employees:** 413  **Fiscal Year:** 2015  **Budget:** $1,228,773,000

Director **Brian Maxwell** . . . . . . . . . . . . . . . . . . . . . . . (302) 739-4204
    E-mail: brian.maxwell@state.de.us
    Executive Assistant to the Director **Debra R. Gerardi** . . . (302) 739-4204
Deputy Director **(Vacant)** . . . . . . . . . . . . . . . . . . . . . . (302) 739-4206
Insurance Coverage Administrator **Debra Lawhead** . . . . . . (302) 739-4206
    E-mail: debra.lawhead@state.de.us
Policy and External Affairs Director
    **Robert L. Scoglietti** . . . . . . . . . . . . . . . . . . . . . . . . (302) 739-4206
Media Relations Manager **(Vacant)** . . . . . . . . . . . . . . . . (302) 739-4204
Payroll Human Resource State Technology Manager
    **Ruby Katcher** . . . . . . . . . . . . . . . . . . . . . . . . . . . . (302) 739-2260
    E-mail: ruby.katcher@state.de.us
Administration and Human Resources Director
    **Sally Wojcieszyn** . . . . . . . . . . . . . . . . . . . . . . . . . . (302) 672-6828
Human Resources and Finance Manager **Glynis Moore** . . . (302) 672-6829

---

★ Elected Official    ■ Appointed by Governor    ● Appointed by Legislature    ▲ Appointed by Board or Commission    ◆ Appointed by State Supreme Court

EXECUTIVE BRANCH

## Budget Development, Planning and Administration Division
Director **Meaghan Brennan** . . . . . . . . . . . . . . . . . . . . . . . . . (302) 739-4206
Deputy Director **Nicholas Johnson** . . . . . . . . . . . . . . . . . (302) 739-4206
Deputy Director **Benjamin Boettcher** . . . . . . . . . . . . . . . (302) 739-4206

## Facilities Management Division
540 South Dupont Highway, Suite 1, Dover, DE 19901
Tel: (302) 739-3613
Director **Dennis Groom** . . . . . . . . . . . . . . . . . . . . . . . . . . . . (302) 739-5644
Deputy Director **Chris Prosser** . . . . . . . . . . . . . . . . . . . . . (302) 739-5644
Engineering and Operations Chief **Mark DeVore, PE** . . . . . (302) 739-5644
   Education: US Coast Guard Acad 1985 BSCE; Illinois 1991 MSCE
Architectural Accessibility Board Administrator
   **Dan Muterspaw** . . . . . . . . . . . . . . . . . . . . . . . . . . . . . . (302) 739-5644
   E-mail: dan.muterspaw@state.de.us
Facilities Program Supervisor **Alisha McCullough** . . . . . . . (302) 739-5644
   E-mail: alisha.mccullough@state.de.us
Real Property Administrator **Donna Diaz** . . . . . . . . . . . . . (302) 739-5644
   E-mail: donna.diaz@state.de.us

## Government Support Services Division
100 Enterprise Drive, Suite Four, Dover, DE 19904
Tel: (302) 857-4500  Fax: (302) 739-2564
Internet: http://gss.omb.delaware.gov
Director **Dean W. Stotler** . . . . . . . . . . . . . . . . . . . . . . . . . . (302) 857-4501
   E-mail: dean.stotler@state.de.us
Deputy Director **Peter Korolyk** . . . . . . . . . . . . . . . . . . . . . (302) 857-4503
   E-mail: peter.korolyk@state.de.us
                                       Fax: (302) 739-2564
Fleet Administrator **Richard Cordrey** . . . . . . . . . . . . . . . . (302) 857-4531
   E-mail: richard.cordrey@state.de.us
Food Distribution and Surplus Property Administrator
   **Teresa Youngcourt** . . . . . . . . . . . . . . . . . . . . . . . . . . . . (302) 838-8060
   E-mail: teresa.youngcourt@state.de.us
                                       Fax: (302) 836-7642
Helpline Manager **David Weiss** . . . . . . . . . . . . . . . . . . . . . (302) 255-1811
Messenger Services Supervisor **Sherry Szcuka** . . . . . . . . . (302) 857-4570
   E-mail: sherry.szcuka@state.de.us
State Contract Procurement Administrator **(Vacant)** . . . . . . (302) 857-4559

## Human Resource Management and Statewide Benefits Division
Director **Brenda Lakeman** . . . . . . . . . . . . . . . . . . . . . . . . . (302) 739-4195
Deputy Director **Amy Bonner** . . . . . . . . . . . . . . . . . . . . . . (302) 739-4206
Statewide Benefits Deputy Director **Faith Rentz** . . . . . . . . (302) 739-8331

## Department of Agriculture [DDA]
2320 South DuPont Highway, Dover, DE 19901-5515
Tel: (302) 698-4500  Fax: (302) 697-6287
Internet: http://dda.delaware.gov
**Employees:** 143  **Fiscal Year:** 2015  **Budget:** $66,409,000
■Secretary **Edwin "Ed" Kee** . . . . . . . . . . . . . . . . . . . . . . . . (302) 698-4502
   E-mail: edwin.kee@state.de.us
   Education: Delaware MS
   Administrative Specialist III **Lisa Wildermuth** . . . . . . . . (302) 698-4501
Deputy Secretary **E. Austin Short III** . . . . . . . . . . . . . . . . (302) 698-4505
   Executive Assistant **Holly Porter** . . . . . . . . . . . . . . . . . (302) 698-4503
Controller **Brennon Fountain** . . . . . . . . . . . . . . . . . . . . . . (302) 698-4515
Food Products Inspection Administrator **Andrea Jackson** . .(302) 698-4545
   E-mail: andrea.jackson@state.de.us
Forestry Administrator **Michael Valenti** . . . . . . . . . . . . . . (302) 698-4550
   E-mail: michael.valenti@state.de.us
Nutrient Management Administrator **Chris Brosch** . . . . . . .(302) 698-4555
   E-mail: chris.brosch@state.de.us
Pesticides Compliance Administrator **Chris Wade** . . . . . . . (302) 698-4570
   E-mail: chris.wade@state.de.us
Plant Industries Administrator **Faith B. Kuehn, PhD** . . . . . (302) 698-4587
   E-mail: faith.kuehn@state.de.us
Poultry and Animal Health Administrator **Heather Hirst** . . (302) 698-4560
   E-mail: heather.hirst@state.de.us
Weights and Measures Administrator **Steve Connors** . . . . . (302) 698-4601
   E-mail: steve.connors@state.de.us

Agriculture Compliance Officer **Daniel Woodall** . . . . . . . . . (302) 698-4526
   E-mail: daniel.woodall@state.de.us
Community Relations Officer/Market & Product
   Development Administrator **Daniel "Dan" Shortridge** . . (302) 698-4520
   E-mail: daniel.shortridge@state.de.us
Educational Resource Specialist **(Vacant)** . . . . . . . . . . . . . (302) 698-4518

## Department of Correction [DOC]
Central Administration Building, 245 McKee Road, Dover, DE 19904
Tel: (302) 739-5601  Fax: (302) 739-8221

**Employees:** 2,562  **Fiscal Year:** 2015  **Budget:** $291,395,000
■Commissioner **Col. Robert M. Coupe** . . . . . . . . . . . . . . . (302) 739-5601
   E-mail: ropert.cape@state.de.us
Employee Development Center Director
   **Ronald "Ron" Sauls** . . . . . . . . . . . . . . . . . . . . . . . . . . (302) 857-5290
                                       Fax: (302) 739-5751
Human Resources Director **Jennifer Biddle** . . . . . . . . . . . .(302) 739-5298
Internal Affairs Director **Ron Drake** . . . . . . . . . . . . . . . . . (302) 659-6060
                                       Fax: (302) 653-2899
Community Relations Chief **(Vacant)** . . . . . . . . . . . . . . . . . (302) 857-5246
Media Relations Chief **(Vacant)** . . . . . . . . . . . . . . . . . . . . (302) 857-5232
Institutional Inspector **Joe Dudlek** . . . . . . . . . . . . . . . . . . (302) 857-5247

## Community Corrections Bureau
Tel: (302) 857-5250

**Employees:** 607  **Fiscal Year:** 2015  **Budget:** $50,401,000
Community Corrections Chief **Alan Grinstead** . . . . . . . . . (302) 857-5242
   Deputy Bureau Chief **Curt Shockley** . . . . . . . . . . . . . . (302) 857-5250
Home Confinement Director **Ken Brandon** . . . . . . . . . . . .(302) 674-7200
Probation and Parole Director **Jill Rush** . . . . . . . . . . . . . . (302) 857-5310
Morris Community Corrections Center Warden
   **Jim Hutchins** . . . . . . . . . . . . . . . . . . . . . . . . . . . . . . . (302) 739-4758
   300 Water St., Dover, DE 19904
Plummer Community Corrections Center Warden
   **Carole Evans** . . . . . . . . . . . . . . . . . . . . . . . . . . . . . . . (302) 577-3039
   38 Todds Lane, Wilmington, DE 19802   Tel: (302) 761-2800
Probation Center Central Violation Warden
   **Jim Hutchins** . . . . . . . . . . . . . . . . . . . . . . . . . . . . . . . (302) 659-6100
   875 Smyrna Landing Rd., Smyrna, DE 19977
Probation Center Sussex Violation Warden
   **William Oettel** . . . . . . . . . . . . . . . . . . . . . . . . . . . . . . (302) 856-5790
   Route 113, Georgetown, DE 19947

## Administrative Offices
Chief **Janet Durkee** . . . . . . . . . . . . . . . . . . . . . . . . . . . . . . (302) 857-5204
   E-mail: janet.durkee@state.de.us
Deputy Chief **Jodie Wedel** . . . . . . . . . . . . . . . . . . . . . . . . (302) 857-5347
   E-mail: jodie.wedel@state.de.us
Controller **Kim Girantino** . . . . . . . . . . . . . . . . . . . . . . . . . (302) 857-5263
Food Services Director **Wendall Lundy** . . . . . . . . . . . . . . (302) 857-5313
Facilities Maintenance/Capital Program Administrator
   **Eric Smeltzer** . . . . . . . . . . . . . . . . . . . . . . . . . . . . . . . (302) 857-5261
   E-mail: eric.smeltzer@state.de.us
Purchasing Administrator **(Vacant)** . . . . . . . . . . . . . . . . . . (302) 857-5262
Chief Information Officer **Phillip Winder** . . . . . . . . . . . . . (302) 857-5282
   E-mail: phillip.winder@state.de.us

## Prisons Bureau
**Employees:** 1,625  **Fiscal Year:** 2015  **Budget:** $159,883,000
Chief **Chris Klein** . . . . . . . . . . . . . . . . . . . . . . . . . . . . . . . . (302) 857-5221
   Deputy Chief **Robert May** . . . . . . . . . . . . . . . . . . . . . . (302) 857-5365
Adult Education Director **Thomas Keeton** . . . . . . . . . . . . . (302) 857-5276
Correctional Industries Director **Carl Barker** . . . . . . . . . . . (302) 857-5411
Arts Program Administrator **Carmita Kelley** . . . . . . . . . . . (302) 857-5277
   E-mail: carmita.kelley@state.de.us
Inmate Classification Administrator **Bill Evans** . . . . . . . . . (302) 857-5218
   E-mail: bill.evans@state.de.us
Concrete Design Systems Manager **Jack Evans** . . . . . . . . . (302) 653-4913
Special Operation Warden **David Hall** . . . . . . . . . . . . . . . . (302) 857-5258
James T Vaughn Correctional Center Warden
   **Dave Pierce** . . . . . . . . . . . . . . . . . . . . . . . . . . . . . . . . (302) 653-9261
   1181 Paddock Rd., Smyrna, DE 19977

---

★ Elected Official   ■ Appointed by Governor   ● Appointed by Legislature   ▲ Appointed by Board or Commission   ◆ Appointed by State Supreme Court

Delores J. Baylor Correctional Institution Warden
  **Wendi Caple** . . . . . . . . . . . . . . . . . . . . . . . . . . . . . . . (302) 577-3004
  660 Baylor Boulevard, New Castle, DE 19720
Howard R. Young Correctional Institution Warden
  **Steven Wesley** . . . . . . . . . . . . . . . . . . . . . . . . . . . . . . (302) 429-7747
  1301 E. 12th St., Wilmington, DE 19801
Sussex Correctional Institution Warden **G.R. Johnson** . . . . (302) 856-5280
  RD 1, Box 500, Georgetown, DE 19947

# Department of Education [DDOE]

401 Federal Street, Suite 2, Dover, DE 19901
Tel: (302) 735-4000  Tel: (877) 838-3787  Fax: (302) 739-4654
Internet: www.doe.k12.de.us

**Employees:** 13,874  **Fiscal Year:** 2015  **Budget:** $2,332,382,000

■Secretary **Steven H. Godowsky** . . . . . . . . . . . . . . . . . . . . . (302) 735-4000
  E-mail: steven.godowsky@doe.k12.de.us
Deputy Secretary **David Blowman** . . . . . . . . . . . . . . . . . . . (302) 735-4000
Policy and External Affairs Associate Secretary
  **Susan Keene Haberstroh** . . . . . . . . . . . . . . . . . . . (302) 857-3300
  Education: Delaware 2002 MPA
Adult Education and School Supports Associate
  Secretary **Karen Field Rogers** . . . . . . . . . . . . . . . . (302) 735-4040
Teaching and Learning Associate Secretary
  **Michael Watson** . . . . . . . . . . . . . . . . . . . . . . . . . . (302) 735-4180
Adult Education and Prison Education Resources
  Director **Maureen Whelan** . . . . . . . . . . . . . . . . . . . . (302) 857-3340
  E-mail: mwhelan@doe.k12.de.us
Early Development and Learning Resources Director
  **Susan Perry-Manning** . . . . . . . . . . . . . . . . . . . . . . (302) 735-4295
Education Associate, Private Business, Trade
  Schools and Veterans Affairs Programs
  Director **Patricia Keeton** . . . . . . . . . . . . . . . . . . (302) 857-3340 ext. 3313
Exceptional Children Resources Director
  **Mary Ann Mieczkowski** . . . . . . . . . . . . . . . . . . . . . . (302) 735-4210
Finance Office Director **Kimberly Wheatley** . . . . . . . . . . . (302) 735-4040
School Support Director **Linda Wolfe** . . . . . . . . . . . . . . . (302) 735-4060
  E-mail: lwolfe@doe.k12.de.us
Technology Resources and Data Development Director
  **Patrick Bush** . . . . . . . . . . . . . . . . . . . . . . . . . . . . (302) 735-4140
  E-mail: patrick.bush@doe.k12.de.us
Webmaster **Robert "Bob" Leuze** . . . . . . . . . . . . . . (302) 735-4140 ext. 4153
  E-mail: bob.leuze@doe.k12.de.us

# Delaware Higher Education Office [DHEO]

401 Federal Street, Suite 2, Dover, DE 19901
Tel: (302) 735-4120  Fax: (302) 739-5894

Director **Shana Payne** . . . . . . . . . . . . . . . . . . . . . . . . . . . (302) 735-4120

# Department of Finance [DOF]

Carvel State Office Building, 820 North French Street, 8th Floor,
Wilmington, DE 19801
Tel: (302) 577-8979  Fax: (302) 577-8982

**Employees:** 302  **Fiscal Year:** 2015  **Budget:** $126,802,000

■Secretary **Thomas J. Cook** . . . . . . . . . . . . . . . . . . . . . . . (302) 577-8984
  E-mail: tom.cook@state.de.us
Deputy Secretary **David M. Gregor** . . . . . . . . . . . . . . . . . (302) 577-8684
  Education: SUNY (Fredonia) 1985 BA; Syracuse 1987 MPA
Bond Finance Director **Stephanie Scola** . . . . . . . . . . . . . (302) 577-8988
Information Systems Director **James Courtney** . . (302) 323-5300 ext. 3002
  E-mail: james.courtney@state.de.us
Personnel Administrator **Mary Jane Donnelly** . . . . . . . . . . (302) 577-8955
  E-mail: maryjane.donnelly@state.de.us

# Accounting Division

820 Silver Lake Blvd., Suite 200, Dover, DE 19901
Fax: (302) 739-1200

**Employees:** 57  **Fiscal Year:** 2015  **Budget:** $3,321,000

Director **Kristopher Knight** . . . . . . . . . . . . . . . . . . . . . . . (302) 672-5500

# Revenue Division

Tel: (302) 577-8200  Fax: (302) 577-8656

**Employees:** 131  **Fiscal Year:** 2014  **Budget:** $16,689,000

Director **Patrick T. Carter** . . . . . . . . . . . . . . . . . . . . . . . . (302) 577-8686
  Education: Delaware 1981 BS; Indiana 1983 MBA
Business Tax Assistant Director **Michael Smith** . . . . . . . . (302) 577-8445
Personal Taxes Assistant Director **James Stewart** . . . . . . . (302) 577-8170

# State Lottery

McKee Business Park, 1575 McKee Road, Suite 102, Dover, DE 19904
Fax: (302) 739-6706  Internet: www.delottery.com

Director **Vernon Kirk** . . . . . . . . . . . . . . . . . . . . . . . . . . . (302) 739-5291

# Department of Health and Social Services [DHSS]

1901 North DuPont Highway, New Castle, DE 19720
Jesse S. Cooper Building, 417 Federal Street, Dover, DE 19901 (Vital
Records)
P.O. Box 637, Dover, DE 19903 (Vital Records)
Tel: (302) 255-9040  Tel: (302) 739-4721 (Vital Records)
Fax: (302) 255-4429

**Employees:** 4,251  **Fiscal Year:** 2015  **Budget:** $1,169,642,000

# Office of the Secretary

Tel: (302) 255-9040  Fax: (302) 255-4429

■Secretary **Rita M. Landgraf** . . . . . . . . . . . . . . . . . . . . . . (302) 255-9040
  E-mail: rita.landgraf@state.de.us
  Executive Secretary **Pamela Grimes** . . . . . . . . . . . . . . . (302) 255-9045
Deputy Secretary **Henry R. Smith III** . . . . . . . . . . . . . . . . (302) 255-9040
  Deputy Principal Assistant **Jay W. Lynch** . . . . . . . . . . (302) 255-9037
Chief Policy Advisor **Deborah I. Gottschalk, Esq.** . . . . . . (302) 255-9038
Communications Director **Jill Fredel** . . . . . . . . . . . . . . . . (302) 255-9047
  E-mail: jill.fredel@state.de.us
Constituent Relations Director **Kathleen Weiss** . . . . . . . . (302) 255-9048
  Education: North Carolina State 1976 BA
Office Manager **Allyson McGonigle** . . . . . . . . . . . . . . . . . (302) 255-9043
Administrative Specialist I **Tomeka Jones** . . . . . . . . . . . . (302) 255-9046
Administrative Specialist II **Sharon Ainsworth** . . . . . . . . . (302) 255-9044

# Delaware Health Care Commission [DHCC]

Margaret O'Neill Building, 410 Federal Street, Suite 7, Dover, DE 19901
Tel: (302) 739-2730  Fax: (302) 739-6927

**Employees:** 6

■Chairman **Dr. Nancy H. Fan, MD** . . . . . . . . . . . . . . . . . . (302) 739-2730
Member **Theodore W. Becker, Jr.** . . . . . . . . . . . . . . . . . . (302) 739-2730
Member **Thomas J. Cook** . . . . . . . . . . . . . . . . . . . . . . . . (302) 739-2730
Member **Susan Cycyk, MEd** . . . . . . . . . . . . . . . . . . . . . . (302) 739-2730
Member **A. Richard Heffron** . . . . . . . . . . . . . . . . . . . . . . (302) 739-2730
Member **Rita M. Landgraf** . . . . . . . . . . . . . . . . . . . . . . . . (302) 739-2730
  Affiliation: Secretary, Office of the Secretary, Department of Health and
  Social Services, State of Delaware
  1901 North DuPont Highway, New Castle, DE 19720
Member **Dr. Janice Lee, MD** . . . . . . . . . . . . . . . . . . . . . . (302) 739-2730
Member **Dr. Kathleen Sharon Matt, PhD** . . . . . . . . . . . . . (302) 739-2730
Member **Dr. Edmondo J. Robinson, MD, MBA** . . . . . . . . . (302) 739-2730
Member **Dennis Rochford** . . . . . . . . . . . . . . . . . . . . . . . . (302) 739-2730
Member **Karen Weldin Stewart** . . . . . . . . . . . . . . . . . . . . (302) 739-2730
  Affiliation: Insurance Commissioner, Department of Insurance, State of
  Delaware
  841 Silver Lake Boulevard, Dover, DE 19904
▲Executive Director **Laura Howard** . . . . . . . . . . . . . . . . . (302) 739-2730
  E-mail: laura.howard@state.de.us

EXECUTIVE BRANCH

# Department of Labor [DOL]

4425 North Market Street, Wilmington, DE 19802
Tel: (302) 761-8000  Fax: (302) 761-6621
Internet: www.delawareworks.com

**Employees:** 479  **Fiscal Year:** 2015  **Budget:** $77,699,000

■Secretary **Patrice Gilliam-Johnson, PhD** . . . . . . . . . . . . . .(302) 761-8001
   Education: Morgan State BA; Maryland MA, 1984 PhD
Deputy Principal Assistant **Leon Tucker** . . . . . . . . . . . . . . .(302) 761-8001
   E-mail: leon.tucker@state.de.us
   Administrative Assistant **Patricia Bistany** . . . . . . . . . . . .(302) 761-8001
     E-mail: patricia.bistany@state.de.us
Controller **Kris Brooks** . . . . . . . . . . . . . . . . . . . . . . . . . . . .(302) 761-8003

## Administration Support

Fax: (302) 761-6619

**Employees:** 43  **Fiscal Year:** 2015  **Budget:** $3,985,000

Director **Vanessa Phillips** . . . . . . . . . . . . . . . . . . . . . . . . .(302) 761-8013
   E-mail: vanessa.phillips@state.de.us

## Employment and Training Division

Tel: (302) 761-8085  Fax: (302) 761-6634  Internet: www.vcnet.net

**Employees:** 95  **Fiscal Year:** 2015  **Budget:** $21,679,000

■Director **Stacey Ling** . . . . . . . . . . . . . . . . . . . . . . . . . . . .(302) 761-8129
   E-mail: stacey.ling@state.de.us
Deputy Director **(Vacant)** . . . . . . . . . . . . . . . . . . . . . . . . . .(302) 761-8111

## Industrial Affairs Division

Fax: (302) 761-6601

**Employees:** 72  **Fiscal Year:** 2015  **Budget:** $11,467,000

■Director **(Vacant)** . . . . . . . . . . . . . . . . . . . . . . . . . . . . . . .(302) 761-8200
Apprenticeship and Training Manager **Kevin Calio** . . . . . . .(302) 451-3419
   E-mail: kevin.calio@state.de.us
Labor Law Enforcement Administrator
   **Anthony "Tony" Deluca** . . . . . . . . . . . . . . . . . . . . . . .(302) 761-8200
   E-mail: anthony.deluca@state.de.us
Occupational Safety and Health Consultation Manager
   **Traci Fraley** . . . . . . . . . . . . . . . . . . . . . . . . . . . . . . . .(302) 761-8219
   E-mail: traci.fraley@state.de.us
Workers' Compensation Manager **Stephanie Parker** . . . . . .(302) 761-8200

## Unemployment Insurance Division

Fax: (302) 761-6637

**Employees:** 132  **Fiscal Year:** 2015  **Budget:** $15,764,000

■Director **Thomas Ellis** . . . . . . . . . . . . . . . . . . . . . . . . . . .(302) 761-8350
   E-mail: thomas.ellis@state.de.us
Unemployment Insurance Administrator
   **Heather Comstock** . . . . . . . . . . . . . . . . . . . . . . . . . . .(302) 761-8360
   E-mail: heather.comstock@state.de.us
Unemployment Insurance Administrator **Carolyn Nasser** . .(302) 761-8357
   E-mail: carolyn.nasser@state.de.us
Unemployment Insurance Administrator **(Vacant)** . . . . . . . .(302) 761-8353
Deputy Principal Assistant **Bobbi DiVirgilio** . . . . . . . . . . . .(302) 761-8351

## Vocational Rehabilitation Division

Fax: (302) 761-6611

**Employees:** 137  **Fiscal Year:** 2015  **Budget:** $24,800,000

■Director **Andrea Guest** . . . . . . . . . . . . . . . . . . . . . . . . . . .(302) 761-8275
   E-mail: andrea.guest@state.de.us
Deputy Director and Client Services
   **Jocelyn C. Langrehr** . . . . . . . . . . . . . . . . . . . . . . . . . .(302) 761-8275
   E-mail: jocelyn.langrehr@state.de.us
Disability Determination Service Deputy Director
   **(Vacant)** . . . . . . . . . . . . . . . . . . . . . . . . . . . . . . . . . . .(302) 324-7600

# Department of Natural Resources and Environmental Control [DNREC]

89 Kings Highway, Dover, DE 19901
Tel: (302) 739-9000  Fax: (302) 739-6242
Internet: www.dnrec.delaware.gov

**Employees:** 789

## Office of the Secretary

Tel: (302) 739-9000

■Secretary **David S. Small** . . . . . . . . . . . . . . . . . . . . . . . . .(302) 739-9000
   E-mail: david.small@state.de.us
   Education: Randolph-Macon 1980 BA
Deputy Secretary **Kara S. Coats** . . . . . . . . . . . . . . . . . . . .(302) 739-9000
   E-mail: kara.coats@state.de.us
Executive Secretary **Casie Anthony** . . . . . . . . . . . . . . . . . .(302) 739-9000
Chief Operating Officer **Robert Zimmerman** . . . . . . . . . . .(302) 739-9000
Human Resources Manager **(Vacant)** . . . . . . . . . . . . . . . . .(302) 739-9901
Financial Assistance Branch Administrator **Terry Deputy** . .(302) 739-9941
Public Affairs Chief **Carol A. Riggs** . . . . . . . . . . . . . . . . . .(302) 739-9902

## Delaware National Guard

250 Airport Road, New Castle, DE 19720
Tel: (302) 326-7024  Fax: (302) 326-7029
Internet: delawarenationalguard.com

**Employees:** 109  **Fiscal Year:** 2015  **Budget:** $22,061,000

■Adjutant General
   **MG Francis D. "Frank" Vavala, ARNG** . . . . . . . . . . . . .(302) 326-7001
   E-mail: francis.d.vavala.mil@mail.mil
   Education: Wilmington Col (DE) 1984 BS
Chief of Staff **COL Albert Citro, ARNG** . . . . . . . . . . . . . .(302) 326-7005
State Command Sergeant Major
   **CSM Robert K. Miller, ARNG** . . . . . . . . . . . . . . . . . . .(302) 326-7004
Command Chief Master Sergeant **Patricia Ottinger** . . . . . . .(302) 326-7114
   2600 Spruance Drive, New Castle, DE 19720-1615
Command Chief Warrant Officer
   **CW5 David Dale, ARNG** . . . . . . . . . . . . . . . . . . . . . . .(302) 326-7050

## Delaware Air National Guard

2600 Spruance Drive, New Castle, DE 19720
Tel: (302) 323-3555

Assistant Adjutant General
   **BrigGen Carol Timmons, ANG** . . . . . . . . . . . . . . . . . .(302) 326-3362
                            Fax: (302) 323-3365

## Delaware Army National Guard

250 Airport Road, New Castle, DE 19720
Tel: (302) 326-7000

Assistant Adjutant General **BG James P. Begley, ARNG** . .(302) 326-7003
Information Technology Director
   **Vincent Michael Orlando** . . . . . . . . . . . . . . . . . . . . . . .(302) 326-7023
   E-mail: vincent.m.orlando.mil@mail.mil

# Department of Safety and Homeland Security [DSHS]

Public Safety Building, 303 Transportation Circle, Suite 220,
Dover, DE 19901
P.O. Box 818, Dover, DE 19903-0818 (Mailing)
Tel: (302) 744-2680  Internet: http://dshs.delaware.gov

**Employees:** 1,155  **Fiscal Year:** 2015  **Budget:** $181,725,000

■Secretary **James N. "Jim" Mosley** . . . . . . . . . . . . . . . . . .(302) 744-2680
   E-mail: de_homelandsecurity@state.de.us
Executive Secretary **Dee L. Rivard** . . . . . . . . . . . . . . . . . .(302) 744-2677
Administration Chief/Human Resource Manager
   **Joseph "Joe" Swiski** . . . . . . . . . . . . . . . . . . . . . . . . . .(302) 744-2670
   E-mail: joseph.swiski@state.de.us
Administrative Specialist III **Carol Lee** . . . . . . . . . . . . . . . .(302) 744-2693
Homeland Security Advisor **Raymond Holcomb** . . . . . . . .(302) 744-2678

---

★ Elected Official   ■ Appointed by Governor   ● Appointed by Legislature   ▲ Appointed by Board or Commission   ◆ Appointed by State Supreme Court

EXECUTIVE BRANCH

E-911 Administrator **Eric Wagner** . . . . . . . . . . . . . . . . . . . (302) 744-2682
E-mail: eric.wagner@state.de.us
Deputy Principal Assistant and Relief From Disabilities
Coordinator **Terry Pepper** . . . . . . . . . . . . . . . . . . . . . . (302) 744-2690
E-mail: terry.pepper@state.de.us
Deputy Principle Assistant **Kimberly Holland Chandler** . . (302) 744-2675
E-mail: randall.l.hughes@state.de.us
Community Relations Chief (Acting)
**Kimberly Holland Chandler** . . . . . . . . . . . . . . . . . . . (302) 744-2667
Administrative Specialist I **Sandy O'Brien** . . . . . . . . . . . . (302) 744-2680
Human Resources Specialist III - Payroll and Benefits
**Tonya M. Brady** . . . . . . . . . . . . . . . . . . . . . . . . . . . . (302) 744-2686
Human Resources Specialist II - Applicant Services
**Robin Harding** . . . . . . . . . . . . . . . . . . . . . . . . . . . . . (302) 744-2688

## Office of Highway Safety

Public Safety Building, 303 Transportation Circle, Suite 201,
Dover, DE 19901
P.O. Box 1321, Dover, DE 19903
Tel: (302) 744-2740  Fax: (302) 739-5995

■Director **Jana R. Simpler** . . . . . . . . . . . . . . . . . . . . . . . (302) 744-2740
E-mail: jana.simpler@state.de.us

## Alcohol and Tobacco Enforcement Division

Kent Aeropark, 34 Starlifter Avenue, Dover, DE 19901
Tel: (302) 741-2717  Fax: (302) 739-4770

**Employees:** 19  **Fiscal Year:** 2015  **Budget:** $1,993,000

Director **John Yeomans** . . . . . . . . . . . . . . . . . . . . . . . . . (302) 741-2719

## Capitol Police Division

150 East Water Street, Dover, DE 19901
Fax: (302) 739-2869

**Employees:** 75  **Fiscal Year:** 2015  **Budget:** $7,333,000

Chief **John Horsman** . . . . . . . . . . . . . . . . . . . . . . . . . . . (302) 739-4390

## Communications Division

3050 Upper King Road, Dover, DE 19904-6410
Fax: (302) 697-0355

Director **Mark A. Grubb** . . . . . . . . . . . . . . . . . . . . . . . . (302) 739-4207
E-mail: mark.grubb@state.de.us

## Forensic Sciences Division

200 S. Adams Street, Wilmington, DE 19801
Tel: (302) 577-3416

Director **Michael J. Wolf** . . . . . . . . . . . . . . . . . . . . . . . . (302) 744-2680
Education: Villanova BS; George Washington 1976 MS
Chief Medical Examiner **Gary L. Collins** . . . . . . . . . . . . . (302) 577-3420

## State Police Division

P.O. Box 430, Dover, DE 19903
Fax: (302) 739-5966

**Employees:** 954  **Fiscal Year:** 2015  **Budget:** $132,602,000

■Superintendent
**Col Nathaniel McQueen, Jr., USMC (Ret)** . . . . . . . . . . (302) 739-5911
E-mail: nathaniel.mcqueen@state.de.us
Education: Wilmington U BSBehavSci; Delaware State MSSW
Special Operations Officer **Lt. Col. Monroe Hudson** . . . . . (302) 739-5911
Communications Section Chief **Joseph Mulford** . . . . . . . . (302) 659-2340
E-mail: joseph.mulford@state.de.us
Information Technology and Communications Director
**Michael McDonald** . . . . . . . . . . . . . . . . . . . . . . . . . (302) 672-5444
E-mail: michael.mcdonald@state.de.us

## State Police Crime Lab

Director **Julie Willey** . . . . . . . . . . . . . . . . . . . . . . . . . . (302) 744-2680

## Delaware Emergency Management Agency

165 Brick Store Landing Road, Smyrna, DE 19977
Tel: (302) 659-3362  Fax: (302) 659-6855

■Director **James E. Turner III** . . . . . . . . . . . . . . . . . . . . (302) 659-3362
E-mail: jamie.turner@state.de.us
Deputy Director **Glenn Gillespie** . . . . . . . . . . . . . . . . . . (302) 659-2234
Administrative Specialist III **Faye L. Myers** . . . . . . . . . . . (302) 659-2242
E-mail: faye.myers@state.de.us

## Delaware Division of Gaming Enforcement [DGE]

Blue Hen Corporate Center, 655 S. Bay Road, Suite 1A,
Dover, DE 19901
Tel: (302) 526-5850

Director **Daniel J. Kelly** . . . . . . . . . . . . . . . . . . . . . . . . . (302) 526-5851

## Department of Services for Children, Youth and Their Families [DSCYF]

1825 Faulkland Road, Wilmington, DE 19805
Tel: (302) 633-2500  Fax: (302) 995-8290  E-mail: info.dscyf@state.de.us

**Employees:** 1,204  **Fiscal Year:** 2015  **Budget:** $193,553,000

■Secretary **Carla Benson-Green** . . . . . . . . . . . . . . . . . . . (302) 633-2500
E-mail: carla.benson-green@state.de.us
Education: Morgan State BS
Chief Policy Advisor **Steve Yeatman** . . . . . . . . . . . . . . . (302) 633-2505
Deputy Principal Assistant **Cara Sawyer** . . . . . . . . . . . . . (302) 633-2505
Executive Assistant **Eileen Welsh** . . . . . . . . . . . . . . . . . . (302) 633-2502
E-mail: eileen.welsh@state.de.us
Community Relations Coordinator **Dawn Thompson** . . . . . (302) 633-2501
E-mail: dawn.thompson@state.de.us

## Department of State

401 Federal Street, Suite 3, Dover, DE 19901
Tel: (302) 739-4111  Fax: (302) 739-3811

**Employees:** 609  **Fiscal Year:** 2015  **Budget:** $1,372,536,000

■Secretary of State **Jeffrey W. "Jeff" Bullock** . . . . . . . . . . (302) 739-4111
Education: Delaware
Chief Deputy Secretary of State
**Richard J. "Rick" Geisenberger** . . . . . . . . . . . . . . . . . (302) 739-4111
Community Relations Chief **Charles R. "C.R." McLeod** . . . (302) 744-5038
Administration Chief **Courtney Stewart** . . . . . . . . . . . . . (302) 739-4111
E-mail: courtney.stewart@state.de.us
Human Resources Manager **Deloris Hayes-Arrington** . . . . . (302) 739-4111
Board of Pardons Assistant **Judy A. Smith** . . . . . . . . . . . (302) 857-3658
Administrative Specialist II **Diane Crockett** . . . . . . . . . . . (302) 739-4111
Administrative Assistant **(Vacant)** . . . . . . . . . . . . . . . . . (302) 857-3651

## Wilmington Office

Carvel State Office Building, 820 North French Street, 4th Floor,
Wilmington, DE 19801
Fax: (302) 577-2694

Executive Secretary **Kathy Bradford** . . . . . . . . . . . . . . . . (302) 577-8767

## Division of the Arts

Carvel State Office Building, 820 North French Street, 4th Floor,
Wilmington, DE 19801
Tel: (302) 577-8278  Fax: (302) 577-6561  E-mail: delarts@state.de.us

**Employees:** 8  **Fiscal Year:** 2015  **Budget:** $4,091,000

Director **Paul Weagraff** . . . . . . . . . . . . . . . . . . . . . . . . . (302) 577-8278
Deputy Director **Kristin Pleasanton** . . . . . . . . . . . . . . . . (302) 577-8284
Administrative Specialist **Gwen Henderson** . . . . . . . . . . . (302) 577-8282
E-mail: gwen.henderson@state.de.us
Administrative Specialist **Dana Wise** . . . . . . . . . . . . . . . . (302) 577-8278
E-mail: dana.wise@state.de.us

*(continued on next page)*

---

★ Elected Official   ■ Appointed by Governor   ● Appointed by Legislature   ▲ Appointed by Board or Commission   ◆ Appointed by State Supreme Court

**Division of the Arts** *continued*

Communications Coordinator **Katie West** . . . . . . . . . . . . . . . (302) 577-8283
  E-mail: katie.west@state.de.us

## Division of Corporations

Tel: (302) 739-3073  Fax: (302) 739-3815

Corporations Section Administrator **April Wright** . . . . . . . . (302) 739-3073
Franchise Tax Section Administrator **June Bilbrough** . . . . . (302) 739-3073
Technical Support Section Administrator **Shawn Moore** . . (302) 857-3472
Marketing Director **Cynthia Kane** . . . . . . . . . . . . . . . . . . . . (302) 739-3073
Applications Development Manager **Dameon Deputy** . . . . (302) 739-3073
  E-mail: dameon.deputy@state.de.us

## Division of Historical and Cultural Affairs

21 The Green, Dover, DE 19901
Tel: (302) 736-7400  Fax: (302) 739-5660

**Employees:** 48  **Fiscal Year:** 2015  **Budget:** $4,771,000

Director/State Historic Officer **Timothy A. Slavin** . . . . . . . . (302) 736-7400

## Office of Human Relations

Carvel State Office Building, 820 North French Street, 4th Floor,
Wilmington, DE 19801
Fax: (302) 577-5050

Director **Romona S. Fullman** . . . . . . . . . . . . . . . . . . . . . . . (302) 577-5050

## Division of Libraries

121 Martin Luther King Jr. Boulevard North, Dover, DE 19901
Tel: (302) 739-4748  Fax: (302) 739-6787
E-mail: annie.norman@state.de.us

**Employees:** 15  **Fiscal Year:** 2015  **Budget:** $10,273,000

State Librarian and Director **Dr. Anne E.C. Norman** . . . . . . (302) 257-3001

## Professional Regulation Division

Cannon Building, 861 Silver Lake Boulevard, Suite 203, Dover, DE 19904
Tel: (302) 744-4500  Fax: (302) 739-2711
E-mail: customerservice.dpr@state.de.us

Director **David Mangler** . . . . . . . . . . . . . . . . . . . . . . . . . . . (302) 744-4500
  Education: Iowa BSN; Illinois (Chicago) ScM
Deputy Director **Shauna Slaughter** . . . . . . . . . . . . . . . . . . (302) 744-4500
Medical Executive Director **Devashree Brittingham** . . . . . (302) 744-4500
Nursing Executive Director **Peggy Mack** . . . . . . . . . . . . . . (302) 744-4500
  E-mail: peggy.mack@state.de.us
Pharmacy Executive Director **David Dryden** . . . . . . . . . . . (302) 744-4500

## Public Service Commission

Cannon Building, 861 Silver Lake Boulevard, Suite 100, Dover, DE 19904
Tel: (302) 736-7500  Fax: (302) 739-4849
Internet: www.depsc.delaware.gov

■Chair **Dallas Winslow** . . . . . . . . . . . . . . . . . . . . . . . . . . . (302) 736-7500
  Education: Dickinson Col 1966 BA; Duquesne 1972 JD
■Commissioner **Joann Conaway** . . . . . . . . . . . . . . . . . . . (302) 736-7500
■Commissioner **Kim Drexler** . . . . . . . . . . . . . . . . . . . . . . . (302) 736-7500
■Commissioner **Harold Gray** . . . . . . . . . . . . . . . . . . . . . . . (302) 736-7500
■Commissioner **Manubhai C. "Mike" Karia** . . . . . . . . . . . . (302) 736-7500
Executive Director **Robert Howatt** . . . . . . . . . . . . . . . . . . . (302) 736-7500

## Delaware Public Archives

P.O. Box 1401, Dover, DE 19903
121 Martin Luther King Jr. Boulevard North, Dover, DE 19901
Tel: (302) 744-5000  Fax: (302) 739-2578  E-mail: aarchives@state.de.us

**Employees:** 30  **Fiscal Year:** 2015  **Budget:** $2,245,000

Director and State Archivist **Stephen Marz** . . . . . . . . . . . . (302) 744-5000

## Office of the State Bank Commissioner

555 East Loockerman Street, Suite 210, Dover, DE 19901
Fax: (302) 739-3609

State Bank Commissioner **Robert A. Glen** . . . . . . . . . . . . . (302) 739-4235
  E-mail: robert.glen@state.de.us
  Education: Williams BA; NYU MS; Pennsylvania JD
Deputy Bank Commissioner **Kevin J. Urso** . . . . . . . . . . . . . (302) 739-4235

## Veterans Affairs Commission

Robbins Building, 802 Silver Lake Plaza, Suite 100, Dover, DE 19904
Tel: (302) 739-2792  Fax: (302) 739-2794

Executive Director
  **CMSgt Lawrence W. "Larry" Kirby, USAF (Ret)** . . . . . (302) 739-2792
  Education: Wilmington U BA; Bowie State MA

## Division of the Public Advocate [DPA]

Carvel State Office Building, 820 North French Street, 4th Floor,
Wilmington, DE 19801
29 South State Street, Dover, DE 19901
Tel: (302) 241-2555  Fax: (302) 577-3297
Internet: publicadvocate.delaware.gov

Public Advocate **David L. Bonar** . . . . . . . . . . . . . . . . . . . . (302) 577-5077
  Education: UC Berkeley 1967

## Department of Transportation [DelDOT]

800 Bay Road, Dover, DE 19901
P.O. Box 778, Dover, DE 19903
Tel: (302) 760-2000  Fax: (302) 739-4329  Internet: www.deldot.gov

**Employees:** 77  **Fiscal Year:** 2015  **Budget:** $8,440,000

■Secretary **Jennifer L. Cohan** . . . . . . . . . . . . . . . . . . . . . . (302) 760-2303
  E-mail: jennifer.cohan@state.de.us
  Administrative Assistant **Lesley Devine** . . . . . . . . . . . . . (302) 760-2197
Deputy Secretary **Nicole Majeski** . . . . . . . . . . . . . . . . . . . (302) 760-2715
  Administrative Assistant **Darlene Cox** . . . . . . . . . . . . . . (302) 760-2202
Deputy Attorney General **Annie C. Cordo** . . . . . . . . . . . . . (302) 760-2020
  E-mail: annie.cordo@state.de.us
  Education: Michigan State 2002 BA; Penn State Law 2005 JD
Financial Director **Hugh E. Curran** . . . . . . . . . . . . . . . . . . . (302) 760-2700
  Education: Delaware BS, MBA
Human Resources Director **Vanessa Phillips** . . . . . . . . . . . (302) 760-4831
Public Relations Director **Geoff Sundstrom** . . . . . . . . . . . (302) 760-2080
  E-mail: geoff.sundstrom@state.de.us
Legislative Liaison **Evan Park** . . . . . . . . . . . . . . . . . . . . . . (302) 760-2076
Chief Engineer **Robert McCleary** . . . . . . . . . . . . . . . . . . . (302) 760-2305
  E-mail: robert.mccleary@state.de.us
Special Assistant for Legislation, Budget and Policy
  **(Vacant)** . . . . . . . . . . . . . . . . . . . . . . . . . . . . . . . . . . . . (302) 760-2492
Transportation Solutions Deputy Director
  **Shante Hastings** . . . . . . . . . . . . . . . . . . . . . . . . . . . . . (302) 760-2835
Civil Rights Administrator **Kathrina Stroud** . . . . . . . . . . . . (302) 760-2555
  E-mail: kathrina.stroud@state.de.us
Audit Manager **Phillip Henry** . . . . . . . . . . . . . . . . . . . . . . . (302) 760-2059
Fiscal Officer **Jennifer Stubbs** . . . . . . . . . . . . . . . . . . . . . . (302) 760-2608

## Division of Motor Vehicles

P.O. Box 698, Dover, DE 19903-0698
Fax: (302) 739-2042  Internet: www.dmv.de.gov

**Employees:** 430  **Fiscal Year:** 2016  **Budget:** $39,868,000

Director **Scott Vien** . . . . . . . . . . . . . . . . . . . . . . . . . . . . . . (302) 744-2541
Customer Relations Chief **Mike Williams** . . . . . . . . . . . . . . (302) 744-2565
Driver Services Chief **Kami Beers** . . . . . . . . . . . . . . . . . . . (302) 744-2561
Toll Operations Chief **Victor Buono** . . . . . . . . . . . . . . . . . . (302) 366-7203
Vehicle Services Chief **Scott Clapper** . . . . . . . . . . . . . . . . (302) 744-2533

---

★ Elected Official  ■ Appointed by Governor  ● Appointed by Legislature  ▲ Appointed by Board or Commission  ◆ Appointed by State Supreme Court

## Maintenance and Operations

800 Bay Road, Dover, DE 19901
Tel: (302) 760-2201

**Employees: 710  Fiscal Year: 2016  Budget: $65,864,000**

Director **Mark Alexander**...............................(302) 760-2201
  E-mail: mark.alexander@state.de.us
Canal District Engineer **Kevin Canning** ..............(302) 326-4461
Central District Engineer **Thomas Greve**..............(302) 760-2429
  930 Public Safety Boulevard, Dover, DE 19901
  E-mail: thomas.greve@state.de.us
North District Engineer **Don Weber** ..................(302) 894-6300
  39 East Regal Boulevard, Newark, DE 19713
  E-mail: don.weber@state.de.us
South District Engineer **Jeff Reed** ..................(302) 853-1300
  23697 Dupont Boulevard, Georgetown, DE 19947
  E-mail: jeff.reed@state.de.us
Chief of Administration **Anne Brown**.................(302) 760-2092
  E-mail: anne.brown@state.de.us
Statewide Support Services Assistant Director
  **Brian Urbanek**......................................(302) 760-2536

## Planning

**Employees: 57  Fiscal Year: 2016  Budget: $5,650,000**

Director **Drew Boyce**..............................(302) 760-2111
Decision and Data Support Assistant Director **(Vacant)**....(302) 760-2121
Development Coordination Assistant Director **Marc Cote** ..(302) 760-2122
Local Systems Improvement Assistant Director
  **Jeff Niezgoda**......................................(302) 760-2121
Statewide and Regional Planning Assistant Director
  **Roberta Geier** .....................................(302) 760-2155

## Technology and Innovation

**Employees: 65  Fiscal Year: 2015  Budget: $22,230,000**

Director **LiWen Lin**................................(302) 760-2099
  Education: Delaware 1990 BA; Wilmington Col (DE) 2001 MPA
Office of Information Technology Manager **Barry Cowin** ..(302) 760-2600
  E-mail: barry.cowin@state.de.us
Contract Services Administrator **Jim Hoagland**.........(302) 760-2031
  E-mail: jim.hoagland@state.de.us
Facilities Manager **Karen Potter** .....................(302) 760-2300
  E-mail: karen.potter@state.de.us

## Transportation Solutions

**Employees: 454  Fiscal Year: 2015  Budget: $20,503,000**

Director **Robert McCleary**..........................(302) 760-2305
Bridge Assistant Director **Barry Benton** ..............(302) 760-2311
Construction Assistant Director **Javier Torrijos** ..........(302) 760-2420
Group II Construction Engineer **Jonathan Ledger** .......(302) 894-6340
  2233A N. duPont Hwy., Dover, DE 19901
  E-mail: jonathan.ledger@state.de.us
Performance Management Assistant Director
  **James Pappas**.......................................(302) 760-2379
Engineering Support Assistant Director **David Nicol** ......(302) 760-2264
Project Development Assistant Director (North Region)
  **Mark Tudor** ........................................(302) 760-2371
Project Development Assistant Director (South Region)
  **Mike Simmons**......................................(302) 760-2370
Traffic Assistant Director **Mark Luszcz** ...............(302) 659-4060
Transportation Solutions, Right of Way Assistant Director
  **Robert M. "Rob" Cunningham** ....................(302) 760-2228
  E-mail: robert.cunningham3@state.de.us

## Delaware Transit Corporation

900 Public Safety Boulevard, Dover, DE 19901
Internet: www.dartfirststate.com

Chief Executive Officer **John T. Sisson** ..............(302) 760-2833
Chief Human Resources Officer **Mary Beth Palermo** .....(302) 576-6020
Chief Financial Officer **Edward Taylor** ...............(302) 576-6110
Chief Operations Officer **Richard Paprcka** ............(302) 576-6050
Marketing and Public Affairs Chief **Julie Theyerl** ........(302) 760-2000

## Office of the Commissioner of Elections

905 South Governor's Avenue, Suite 170, Dover, DE 19904
Tel: (302) 739-4277  Tel: (800) 464-4357 (State Help Line [Delaware])
Tel: (800) 273-9500 (State Help Line [Outside of DE])
Fax: (302) 739-6794  E-mail: coe_vote@state.de.us
Internet: http://elections.delaware.gov

**Employees: 12  Fiscal Year: 2015  Budget: $2,311,000**

■Commissioner **Elaine Manlove**......................(302) 739-4277
  E-mail: elaine.manlove@state.de.us

## Office of Defense Services

Tel: (302) 577-5200  Fax: (302) 577-3995
■Public Defender **Brendan J. O'Neill**..................(302) 577-5200
  E-mail: brendan.oneill@state.de.us
Chief of Legal Services **Lisa Minutola** ...............(302) 577-5118

## Office of the Public Defender

Carvel State Office Building, 820 North French Street, 3rd Floor,
Wilmington, DE 19801
Tel: (302) 577-5200  Fax: (302) 577-3995

**Employees: 143  Fiscal Year: 2014  Budget: $21,277,500**

Chief Deputy Public Defender **Todd Conner** ...........(302) 577-5123

## Office of Conflicts Counsel

Chief Conflicts Counsel **Stephanie Volturo** ...........(302) 468-5075

## Delaware Solid Waste Authority [DSWA]

1128 South Bradford Street, Dover, DE 19904
P.O. Box 455, Dover, DE 19903-0455
Tel: (302) 739-5361  Tel: (800) 404-7080 (Citizens' Response Line)
Fax: (302) 739-4287  E-mail: wlp@dswa.com  Internet: www.dswa.com

▲Chief Executive Officer **Richard P. Watson, PE, BCEE**....(302) 739-5361
  Education: Clarkson U BCE; Delaware 1992 MCE
Chief Operating Officer **Robin M. Roddy, BCEE, PE** .....(302) 739-5361

## Delaware State Housing Authority [DSHA]

18 The Green, Dover, DE 19901
Tel: (888) 363-8808  TTY: (302) 739-7428
Tel: (888) 363-8808 (Toll Free)  Fax: (302) 739-6122
Internet: www.destatehousing.com

**Employees: 138  Fiscal Year: 2015  Budget: $17,937,000**

■Director **Anas Ben Addi** ...........................(888) 363-8808
  E-mail: anas@destatehousing.com
Executive Secretary **Shannon Keenan** .........(888) 363-8808 ext. 223
Policy and Planning Director **Marlena Gibson** ....(888) 363-8808 ext. 297
  E-mail: marlena@destatehousing.com
Chief Operating Officer **Cynthia A. Karnai** ......(888) 363-8808 ext. 235
Housing Development Director **R. Susan Eliason** ........(888) 363-8808
  E-mail: susane@destatehousing.com
Housing Asset Manager **Cynthia L. Deakyne** ....(888) 363-8808 ext. 291
  E-mail: cindy@destatehousing.com
Housing Finance Director **Matthew J. Heckles**..........(888) 363-8808
  E-mail: matthew@destatehousing.com        Fax: (302) 577-5021
Assistant Housing Finance Administrator **Patricia Conley** .........(888) 363-8808
  E-mail: tricia@destatehousing.com        Fax: (302) 577-5021
Housing Management Director **Chris A. Whaley**.........(888) 363-8808
  E-mail: chrisw@destatehousing.com
Public Relations Chief **Jonathan Starkey** .............(888) 363-8808

---

★ Elected Official    ■ Appointed by Governor    ● Appointed by Legislature    ▲ Appointed by Board or Commission    ◆ Appointed by State Supreme Court

**EXECUTIVE BRANCH**

# Delaware River and Bay Authority [DRBA]

P.O. Box 71, New Castle, DE 19720
Tel: (302) 571-6303  Fax: (302) 571-6367  Internet: www.drba.net

- Executive Director **Scott A. Green, Esq.** . . . . . . . . . . . . . (302) 571-6301
  E-mail: scott.green@drba.net
  Education: Washington College of Law 1980 JD
Deputy Executive Director **Frank W. Minor** . . . . . . . . . . . . (302) 571-6445
  Education: Syracuse BA
Chief Financial Officer **Victor A. Ferzetti** . . . . . . . . . . . . . (302) 571-6382
  Education: Geneva BS
Chief Human Resource Officer **Charlotte L. Crowell** . . . . . (302) 571-6397
  Education: Goldey-Beacom BS
Chief Information Officer
  **Geraldine Dinicola "Gerry" Owens** . . . . . . . . . . . . . . . (302) 571-6333
  E-mail: geraldine.owens@drba.net
  Education: Rowan BA
Chief Operations Officer **Vincent P. Meconi** . . . . . . . . . . . (302) 571-6394
  Education: Notre Dame BA; Delaware MPA
Police Administrator **Col. Richard H. Arroyo** . . . . . . . . . . (302) 571-6303
Deputy Police Administrator **Lt. Col. David E. Winch** . . . . (302) 571-6303
  Education: Wilmington Col (DE) 2000

# State Board of Education

Townsend Building, 401 Federal Street, Suite 2, Dover, DE 19901
Tel: (302) 735-4010  Fax: (302) 739-7768
Internet: www.destateboarded.k12.de.us

- President **Dr. Teri Quinn Gray** . . . . . . . . . . . . . . . . . . . (302) 735-4010
  Education: Jackson State U BS; Maryland PhD
- Vice President **Jorge L. Melendez** . . . . . . . . . . . . . . . . . (302) 735-4010
- Member **Nina Lou Bunting** . . . . . . . . . . . . . . . . . . . . . (302) 735-4010
- Member **Gregory B. "Greg" Coverdale, Jr.** . . . . . . . . . . (302) 735-4010
  Education: Delaware State 1999 BSBA
- Member **G. Patrick Heffernan** . . . . . . . . . . . . . . . . . . . (302) 735-4010
- Member **Barbara B. Rutt** . . . . . . . . . . . . . . . . . . . . . . . (302) 735-4010
- Member **Dr. Terry M. Whittaker** . . . . . . . . . . . . . . . . . . (302) 735-4010
  Education: Wisconsin BA; Minnesota MA; Delaware EdD
Executive Director **Donna R. Johnson** . . . . . . . . . . . . . . . (302) 735-4010
  E-mail: donna.johnson@state.de.us

# State Law Library

540 South Dupont Highway, Suite 3, Dover, DE 19901
Librarian **Patricia Burris** . . . . . . . . . . . . . . . . . . . . . . . (302) 739-5467
Librarian **Leah S. Chandler** . . . . . . . . . . . . . . . . . . . . . (302) 856-5483
Librarian **Alda Monsen** . . . . . . . . . . . . . . . . . . . . . . . . (302) 255-0847

# Office of the Lieutenant Governor

Tatnall Building, 150 William Penn Street, 3rd Floor, Dover, DE 19901
Tel: (302) 744-4333  Fax: (302) 739-6965

**Employees:** 6  **Fiscal Year:** 2015  **Budget:** $351,000

**Note:** Lieutenant Governor Matthew Denn resigned on January 6, 2015 to serve as Attorney General. The position will remain vacant for the remainder of the term, which expires in January 2017.

- ★ Lieutenant Governor **(Vacant)** . . . . . . . . . . . . . . . . . (302) 744-4333
  Term Expires: 2017

# Office of the Attorney General

Carvel State Office Building, 820 North French Street,
Wilmington, DE 19801
Tel: (302) 577-8400 (Civil Division)
Tel: (302) 577-8500 (Criminal Division)  TTY: (302) 577-5783
Fax: (302) 577-6630  Internet: attorneygeneral.delaware.gov
E-mail: attorney.general@state.de.us

**Employees:** 409  **Fiscal Year:** 2015  **Budget:** $68,080,000

- ★ Attorney General **Matthew P. "Matt" Denn** (D) . . . . . . . . (302) 577-8400
  Term Expires: January 2019
  Education: UC Berkeley; Yale 1991 JD
  Career: Insurance Commissioner (D-DE), Insurance Department, State of Delaware (2005-2009); Lieutenant Governor (D-DE), Office of the Lieutenant Governor, State of Delaware (2009-2015)
Information Technology Director **Jeff Reed** . . . . . . . . . . . (302) 577-8400

# Office of the State Treasurer

820 Silver Lake Boulevard, Suite 100, Dover, DE 19904
Tel: (302) 672-6700  Fax: (302) 739-5635
E-mail: statetreasurer@state.de.us  Internet: treasurer.delaware.gov

**Fiscal Year:** 2015  **Budget:** $617,700,000

- ★ State Treasurer **Ken Simpler** (R) . . . . . . . . . . . . . . . . . (302) 672-6700
  Term Expires: January 2019
  Education: Chicago JD, MBA

# Office of Auditor of Accounts

401 Federal Street, Suite 1, Dover, DE 19901
Tel: (302) 739-4241  Internet: auditor.delaware.gov

**Employees:** 27  **Fiscal Year:** 2015  **Budget:** $3,020,000

- ★ State Auditor **R. Thomas "Tom" Wagner, Jr., CFE, CGFM, CICA** (R) . . . . . . . . . . . . . . . . . . . . . . . . . (302) 739-5055
  Term Expires: January 2019
  E-mail: r.thomas.wagner@state.de.us
  Education: Richmond BS; Wilmington Col (DE) MBA
Chief Administrative Auditor
  **Kathleen Davies, CPA, CISA, CGFM, CGAP** . . . . . . . . (302) 857-3919

# Department of Insurance

841 Silver Lake Boulevard, Dover, DE 19904
Tel: (302) 674-7300  Fax: (302) 739-5280
E-mail: consumer@deins.state.de.us  Internet: www.delawareinsurance.gov

- ★ Insurance Commissioner **Karen Weldin Stewart** (D) . . . . . (302) 674-7300
  Term Expires: 2017
  Executive Assistant **Lorilee Harrison** . . . . . . . . . . . . . . (302) 674-7300
Deputy Commissioner **Hardy Drane** . . . . . . . . . . . . . . . . (302) 674-7300
Chief of Staff **Paul Reynolds** . . . . . . . . . . . . . . . . . . . . (302) 674-7300
Controller **Jenifer Vaughn** . . . . . . . . . . . . . . . . . . . . . . (302) 674-7300
Company Regulation Director **Dave Lonchar** . . . . . . . . . . (302) 674-7330
Fraud Prevention Bureau Director **Gerald Pepper** . . . . . . . (302) 674-7300
Information Technology Services Director (Acting)
  **Tim Li** . . . . . . . . . . . . . . . . . . . . . . . . . . . . . . . . . (302) 674-7300
  E-mail: tim.li@state.de.us
Investigations Office Director **Michael Gould** . . . . . . . . . . (302) 674-7300
Licensing Office Director **Fleur McKendell** . . . . . . . . . . . (302) 674-7300
Communications Director **Jerry Grant** . . . . . . . . . . . . . . . (302) 674-7300
  Education: Widener 1999 JD
Insurance Consumer Protection Enforcement Manager
  **Frank Pyle** . . . . . . . . . . . . . . . . . . . . . . . . . . . . . . (302) 674-7300

---

★ Elected Official   ■ Appointed by Governor   ● Appointed by Legislature   ▲ Appointed by Board or Commission   ◆ Appointed by State Supreme Court

# District of Columbia

Tel: (202) 737-4404 (State Information or call 311)  Internet: www.dc.gov

**Number of U.S. Congressional Delegates:** 1 Nonvoting Delegate  **Legislature Description:** Council of the District of Columbia (Unicameral) - 13 members; Term - 4 years  **Number of Electoral Votes:** 3
**Official Name:** District of Columbia  **Motto:** Justitia omnibus (Justice for all)

**Population:** 672,228 (2015); Rank 49

## Office of the Mayor

1350 Pennsylvania Avenue, NW, Washington, DC 20004
Tel: (202) 727-6300  Fax: (202) 727-0505  E-mail: eom@dc.gov
Internet: www.mayor.dc.gov

**Muriel Bowser**
Mayor

Began Service: January 2, 2015
Term Expires: January 2, 2019
Date of Birth: April 2, 1972
Education: Chatham BA; American U MPP
Career: Advisory Neighborhood Commissioner, District of Columbia (2004-2007); Council Member (D-DC, Ward 4), Council of the District of Columbia, District of Columbia (2007-2015)

★ Mayor **Muriel Bowser** (D) . . . . . . . . . . . . . . . . . . . . . . . . . . (202) 727-6300
Chief of Staff **John Falcicchio** . . . . . . . . . . . . . . . . . . (202) 727-6300
Deputy Chief of Staff **Lindsey Parker** . . . . . . . . . . . . . . . (202) 727-6300
  Education: Yale
Senior Advisor **Beverly L. Perry** . . . . . . . . . . . . . . . . . . . (202) 727-6300
  Education: George Washington; Georgetown 1981 JD
General Counsel **Elizabeth "Betsy" Cavendish** . . . . . . . . . (202) 727-6300
  Education: Yale 1982, 1988
Deputy General Counsel **Rob Hawkins** . . . . . . . . . . . . . (202) 727-6300
  Education: Virginia Tech 2002 BA; Pittsburgh 2007 JD
Director of Scheduling **Jason Fink** . . . . . . . . . . . . . . . . . . (202) 727-6300

## Office of the Attorney General

441 Fourth Streeet NW, Washington, DC 20001
Tel: (202) 727-3400  Fax: (202) 347-8922  E-mail: dc.oag@dc.gov
Internet: www.oag.dc.gov

**Employees:** 785  **Fiscal Year:** 2015  **Budget:** $85,738,000

★ Attorney General **Karl A. Racine** (D) . . . . . . . . . . . . . . . . (202) 727-3400
  Term Expires: January 2, 2019
  Education: Pennsylvania 1985 BA; Virginia 1989 JD
Chief of Staff **Kim M. Whatley** . . . . . . . . . . . . . . . . . . . (202) 727-3400
Chief Information Officer (Acting) **Kim M. Whatley** . . . . . (202) 727-3400
  E-mail: kim.whatley@dc.gov
Communications Director **Robert Marus** . . . . . . . . . . . . . . (202) 724-5646
  E-mail: robert.marus@dc.gov
Public Affairs Specialist **Andrew Phifer** . . . . . . . . . . . . . (202) 741-7652
Community Outreach Director **James "Tony" Towns** . . . . (202) 727-3400
  Education: Morehouse Col; Georgetown JD; Temple LLM
Legislative Affairs Director **James A. Pittman**
  Suite 1100S . . . . . . . . . . . . . . . . . . . . . . . . . . . . . . . (202) 727-3400
  Education: Alabama A&M BA; Howard U JD    Fax: (202) 730-1439
Senior Counsel **Stephanie Litos** . . . . . . . . . . . . . . . . . . (202) 727-3400
Senior Counsel **Elizabeth W. Wilkins** . . . . . . . . . . . . . . . (202) 727-3400
  Education: Yale BA, 2013 JD
Special Counsel on Juvenile Justice Reform
  **Seema Gajwani** . . . . . . . . . . . . . . . . . . . . . . . . . . . (202) 727-3400
  Education: Northwestern 1998; NYU 2001 JD

## Office of the Chief Deputy Attorney General

Chief Deputy Attorney General **Natalie O. Ludaway** . . . . . (202) 727-3400
  Education: Hunter BA, MA; George Washington 1986 JD

## Office of Cable Television, Film, Music and Entertainment

200 I Street SE, Washington, DC 20003
Tel: (202) 727-6608  Fax: (202) 727-3246  E-mail: film@dc.gov

Director **Angie M. Gates** . . . . . . . . . . . . . . . . . . . . . . . . (202) 727-6608
  E-mail: angie.gates@dc.gov
  Education: New Orleans MA
Deputy Director **Herbert Niles** . . . . . . . . . . . . . . . . . . . (202) 727-6608
  Education: Stanford 1987 BS
Chief of Staff **Derek Younger** . . . . . . . . . . . . . . . . . . . . (202) 671-0066
Director of Operations **Steven Johnson** . . . . . . . . . . . . . (202) 671-0066
Director of Programming **Karen Tolson** . . . . . . . . . . . . . (202) 671-0066
  Education: Howard Col BA
Communications Manager **Pharoh Martin** . . . . . . . . . . . . (202) 727-6608
  E-mail: pharoh.martin@dc.gov

## Office of the Inspector General

717 14th Street NW, 5th Floor, Washington, DC 20005
Tel: (202) 727-2540  Fax: (202) 727-9903  Internet: www.oig.dc.gov

**Employees:** 112

Inspector General **Daniel W. Lucas** . . . . . . . . . . . . . . . . . (202) 727-2540
  Education: Col Charleston 1994 BSBA; Oklahoma 2004
Principal Deputy Inspector General **Marie Hart** . . . . . . . . . (202) 727-2540
Deputy Inspector General for Business Management
  **Jaime Yarussi** . . . . . . . . . . . . . . . . . . . . . . . . . . . (202) 727-2540
Deputy Inspector General for Operations
  **Matt Wilcoxson** . . . . . . . . . . . . . . . . . . . . . . . . . . (202) 727-2540
Deputy Inspector General for Quality Management
  **Slemo Warigon** . . . . . . . . . . . . . . . . . . . . . . . . . . (202) 727-2540
Deputy Inspector General for Risk Assessment and
  Future Planning **James Duginske** . . . . . . . . . . . . . . . (202) 727-2540
General Counsel **Karen E. Branson** . . . . . . . . . . . . . . . . (202) 727-2540
Assistant Inspector General for Audits **Toayoa Aldridge** . . . (202) 727-7721
Assistant Inspector General for Inspections and
  Evaluations **Edward Farley** . . . . . . . . . . . . . . . . . . . (202) 727-2540
Assistant Inspector General for Investigations
  **Martin Kenney** . . . . . . . . . . . . . . . . . . . . . . . . . . . (202) 727-1083
Assistant Inspector General for Medicaid Fraud
  **Brentton Wolfingbarger** . . . . . . . . . . . . . . . . . . . . . (202) 727-2245
                                          Fax: (202) 727-5937

## Office of the Secretary of the District of Columbia

1350 Pennsylvania Avenue, NW, Room 419, Washington, DC 20004
Tel: (202) 727-6306  Fax: (202) 727-3582  E-mail: secretary@dc.gov

Secretary **Lauren C. Vaughan** . . . . . . . . . . . . . . . . . . . . (202) 727-6306
  E-mail: lauren.vaughan@dc.gov
  Education: Hampton; George Washington
Deputy Secretary **Joy Holland** . . . . . . . . . . . . . . . . . . . (202) 727-6306
  Executive Assistant **Arlethia Denise Thompson** . . . . . . . (202) 727-6306
    E-mail: arlethia.thompson@dc.gov

*(continued on next page)*

---

★ Elected Official   ■ Appointed by Governor   ● Appointed by Legislature   ▲ Appointed by Board or Commission   ◆ Appointed by State Supreme Court

**Office of the Secretary of the District of Columbia** *continued*

Special Assistant **(Vacant)** .......................... (202) 727-6306
Communications Director **(Vacant)** ................... (202) 727-6306
Ceremonial Services Office Director **Betty Akers** ........ (202) 727-5082
Administrator, Office of Documents **Victor Reid** ......... (202) 727-5090
  E-mail: victor.reid@dc.gov
Administrator, Office of Public Records **Rebecca Katz** .... (202) 671-1105
  E-mail: rebecca.katz@dc.gov
Notary and Authentication Unit Chief **Judi Gold** ......... (202) 727-3117
Protocol and International Affairs Officer
  **Patricia Elwood** .................................. (202) 727-6306

## Office on Asian and Pacific Islander Affairs [OAPIA]

441 4th Street NW, 805 South, Washington, DC 20001
Tel: (202) 727-3120  Fax: (202) 727-9655  E-mail: oapia@dc.gov
Internet: www.apia.dc.gov

Director **David Do** .................................. (202) 727-7984
  E-mail: david.do@dc.gov

## Executive Office of Communications

1350 Pennsylvania Avenue, NW, Washington, DC 20004
Tel: (202) 727-5011  Fax: (202) 727-9561

Communications Director **Michael Czin** ................ (202) 727-5011
  Note: Until the end of May 2016.
  E-mail: michael.czin@dc.gov
Senior Communications Officer **LaToya Foster** .......... (202) 727-9691
  E-mail: latoya.foster@dc.gov

## Mayor's Office of Community Affairs [MOCA]

1350 Pennsylvania Avenue NW, Suite 332, Washington, DC 20004
Tel: (202) 442-8150

Director **Charon P.W. Hines** ......................... (202) 442-8150
  Education: Mary Baldwin

## DC Youth Advisory Council [DCYAC]

Tel: (202) 727-7966  E-mail: dcyac@dc.gov

Executive Director **Dionne Burkett-Lewis** ............. (202) 727-7966
  E-mail: dionne.burkett@dc.gov

## Mayors Office on Volunteerism [Serve DC]

Frank D. Reeves Municipal Center, 2000 14th Street NW, Suite 101,
Washington, DC 20009
Tel: (202) 727-7925  TTY: (202) 727-8421

Chief Service Officer/Executive Director **Delano Hunter** .. (202) 727-7925
  Education: Delaware State BS
Deputy Director of Grants and Finance **Sareeta Spriggs** .. (202) 727-7925
  Education: Norfolk State BS; Strayer U MBA
Director of Communications and Special Initiatives
  **Janis D. Hazel** ................................. (202) 727-7972
  E-mail: janis.hazel@dc.gov
Communications and Outreach Specialist
  **Isha Foster-Lee** ............................... (202) 727-7925
Executive Assistant **Khadija Ismail** ................... (202) 727-7925

## Office on African Affairs [OAA]

Franklin D. Reeves Center of Municipal Affairs, 2000 14th Street, NW,
Suite 400, Washington, DC 20009
Tel: (202) 727-5634  Fax: (202) 727-2357

Director **Mamadou Samba** ............................ (202) 727-5634
  E-mail: mamadou.samba@dc.gov
  Education: South Carolina; Kennesaw State U MPA
Deputy Director **Heran Sereke-Brhan** ................. (202) 727-5634
  E-mail: heran.sereke-brhan@dc.gov
  Education: Michigan State PhD

## Office of Lesbian, Gay, Bisexual, Transgender and Questioning Affairs [LGBTQ]

John A. Wilson Building, 1350 Pennsylvania Avenue, NW, Suite 211,
Washington, DC 20001
Tel: (202) 727-9493  TTY: (202) 727-9493  Fax: (202) 727-5931
E-mail: lgbtq@dc.gov

Director **Sheila Alexander-Reid** ...................... (202) 442-5143
  E-mail: sheila.alexander-reid@dc.gov
Deputy Director **Terrance Laney** ..................... (202) 442-8150

## Office of Religious Affairs

1350 Pennsylvania Avenue, NW, Suite 332, Washington, DC 20004
Tel: (202) 698-4722  E-mail: onecongregationonefamily@dc.gov

Director **Donald L. Isaac, Sr.** ....................... (202) 442-8150
  Education: UDC BS; Southeastern U MPA

## Office on Returning Citizen Affairs [ORCA]

2100 Martin Luther King Jr. Avenue SE, Suite 100,
Washington, DC 20020
Tel: (202) 715-7670  Fax: (202) 715-7672  E-mail: orca@dc.gov

Director **Charles Thornton** .......................... (202) 715-7670
  E-mail: charles.thornton@dc.gov

## Office on Women's Policy and Initiatives

1350 Pennsylvania Avenue, NW, Suite 327, Washington, DC 20004
Tel: (202) 724-7690  Fax: (202) 727-2357  E-mail: women@dc.gov

Director **Kimberly A. Bassett** ........................ (202) 724-7690
  Education: North Carolina Central BA; North Carolina A&T MA

## Mayor's Office of Community Relations and Services [MOCRS]

1350 Pennsylvania Avenue, NW, Suite 332, Washington, DC 20004
Tel: (202) 442-8150  Fax: (202) 727-5931  E-mail: mocrs@dc.gov

Director **Gregory Jackson, Jr.** ....................... (202) 442-8150
  Education: Virginia BA
Executive Assistant **Jeanne Loeher** .................. (202) 727-3000
Mayor's Correspondence Unit Director **Jim Slattery** ..... (202) 545-3119
  E-mail: jim.slattery@dc.gov

## Mayor's Office of Federal and Regional Affairs

1350 Pennsylvania Avenue, NW, Washington, DC 20004

Director **Eugene Kinlow** ............................. (202) 724-5333
  Education: UDC
Senior Associate Director **Arlen E. Herrell** ............ (202) 727-6300

## Mayor's Office on Latino Affairs [OLA]

Reeves Center, 2000 - 14th Street, NW, 2nd Floor,
Washington, DC 20009
Tel: (202) 671-2825  Fax: (202) 673-4557  Internet: http://ola.dc.gov

Executive Director **Jackie Reyes** ..................... (202) 671-1896
  E-mail: jackie.reyes@dc.gov
Deputy Director **Julio Güity-Guevara** ................. (202) 478-1396
Community Outreach Specialist **Ingrid Gutierrez** ........ (202) 671-2823
Community Outreach Specialist **Olimpia Lopez** ......... (202) 673-4557
Advocacy and Language Access Coordinator
  **Cecilia Castillo** ............................... (202) 671-2824
Language Access Monitor **Henry Jimenez** ............. (202) 671-3005
Grants Management Specialist **Eduardo Perdomo** ....... (202) 340-7761
Grants Monitor **Carlene Forbes** ...................... (202) 478-1418
  E-mail: carlene.forbes@dc.gov
Grants Program Manager **(Vacant)** .................... (202) 671-2827
Administrative Officer **Melinda Salinas** ............... (202) 671-1724
  E-mail: melinda.salinas@dc.gov
Public Information Specialist **Susana Castillo** .......... (202) 478-1396
  E-mail: susana.castillo@dc.gov

---

★ Elected Official    ■ Appointed by Governor    ● Appointed by Legislature    ▲ Appointed by Board or Commission    ◆ Appointed by State Supreme Court

# Mayor's Office of Legal Counsel [MOLC]

Director **Mark H. Tuohey III** . . . . . . . . . . . . . . . . . . . . . (202) 727-6300
E-mail: mark.tuohey@dc.gov
Education: St Bonaventure 1968 BA; Fordham 1973 JD

# Mayor's Office of Talent and Appointments [MOTA]

1350 Pennsylvania Avenue NW, Suite 211, Washington, DC 20004
Tel: (202) 727-1372  Fax: (202) 727-2359  E-mail: mota@dc.gov
Internet: mota.dc.gov

Director **Steve Walker** . . . . . . . . . . . . . . . . . . . . . . . . . (202) 727-1372
E-mail: steve.walker@dc.gov
Education: Prairie View A&M

# Mayor's Office of Veterans Affairs [OVA]

441 Fourth Street, NW, Suite 870 North, Washington, DC 20001
Tel: (202) 724-5454  Fax: (202) 724-7117  E-mail: ova@dc.gov
Internet: www.ova.dc.gov

Director **Tammi Lambert** . . . . . . . . . . . . . . . . . . . . . . . . (202) 724-5454
E-mail: tammi.lambert@dc.gov
Deputy Director **Wanda Smith Battle** . . . . . . . . . . . . . . . (202) 724-5454

# Office of Policy and Legislative Affairs

1350 Pennsylvania Avenue, NW, Room 511, Washington, DC 20001
Tel: (202) 727-6979  Fax: (202) 727-3765

Director **Maia Hunt Estes** . . . . . . . . . . . . . . . . . . . . . . . (202) 727-6979
E-mail: maia.hunt.estes@dc.gov
Education: Spelman BA; Georgetown JD
Deputy Director **(Vacant)** . . . . . . . . . . . . . . . . . . . . . . . (202) 727-6979
Associate Director **John Coombs** . . . . . . . . . . . . . . . . . . (202) 727-6979
Legislative Services Director **Lolita Alston** . . . . . . . . . . . . (202) 727-6979
E-mail: lolita.alston@dc.gov
Policy Analyst **Hassan Christian** . . . . . . . . . . . . . . . . . . (202) 724-7680
Education: Morehouse Col 2001 BA
Policy Analyst **Chan Tei Durant** . . . . . . . . . . . . . . . . . . (202) 727-7938
Policy Analyst **Deborah George Johnson** . . . . . . . . . . . . (202) 727-6979

# Office of the City Administrator [OCA]

John A. Wilson Building, 1350 Pennsylvania Avenue, NW, Suite 513,
Washington, DC 20004
Tel: (202) 478-9200  Fax: (202) 535-1224

**Employees: 41  Fiscal Year: 2015  Budget: $5,027,000**

City Administrator **Rashad M. Young** . . . . . . . . . . . . . . . (202) 478-9200
E-mail: oca.eom@dc.gov
Education: Dayton 1998 BS, 2002 MBA
Special Assistant to the City Administrator
**Sean M. Garrick** . . . . . . . . . . . . . . . . . . . . . . . . . . . (202) 478-9200
Deputy City Administrator **Kevin Donahue** . . . . . . . . . . . (202) 478-9200
Education: Georgetown 1994 BA; Harvard 1999 MPP
Director of Agency Operations **(Vacant)** . . . . . . . . . . . . . (202) 478-9200
Chief Performance Officer and CapStat Director
**Jennifer Reed** . . . . . . . . . . . . . . . . . . . . . . . . . . . . . (202) 478-9200
Communications Director **Olivia Dedner** . . . . . . . . . . . . . (202) 478-9200
E-mail: olivia.dedner@dc.gov
General Counsel and Senior Policy Advisor
**Barry Kreiswirth** . . . . . . . . . . . . . . . . . . . . . . . . . . . (202) 478-9200

# Metropolitan Police Department [MPDC]

300 Indiana Avenue, NW, Washington, DC 20001
Tel: (202) 727-8599  Fax: (202) 727-9524  TTY: (202) 671-2864
E-mail: mail.chief-of-police@dc.gov

**Employees: 4,581  Fiscal Year: 2015  Budget: $525,631,000**

Chief of Police **Cathy L. Lanier** . . . . . . . . . . . . . . . . . . . (202) 727-4218
E-mail: cathy.lanier@dc.gov
Education: Johns Hopkins BA, MA; Naval Postgrad MA
Assistant Chief **(Vacant)** . . . . . . . . . . . . . . . . . . . . . . . (202) 727-4218

Homeland Security Bureau Assistant Chief
**Lamar Greene** . . . . . . . . . . . . . . . . . . . . . . . . . . . . . . (202) 727-4218
Internal Affairs Bureau Assistant Chief
**Kimberly Chisley-Missouri** . . . . . . . . . . . . . . . . . . . . . (202) 576-6600
801 Shepherd Street, NW, Washington, DC 20011-5822
Investigative Services Bureau Assistant Chief
**Peter Newsham** . . . . . . . . . . . . . . . . . . . . . . . . . . . . (202) 727-4295
Patrol Services and School Security Bureau Assistant
Chief **Diane Groomes** . . . . . . . . . . . . . . . . . . . . . . . . . (202) 727-4218
Training Division Commander **Daniel P. Hickson** . . . . . . . (202) 645-0073
Chief Operation Officer **Leeann Turner** . . . . . . . . . . . . . . (202) 727-4389
E-mail: leeann.turner@dc.gov
General Counsel **Terry Ryan** . . . . . . . . . . . . . . . . . . . . . (202) 727-4129
Public Information Director **(Vacant)** . . . . . . . . . . . . . . . (202) 727-9346

# Department of Motor Vehicles [DMV]

95 M Street, SW, Suite 300, Washington, DC 20024
Tel: (202) 737-4404  Fax: (202) 727-1010  E-mail: dmv@dc.gov

**Employees: 263  Fiscal Year: 2015  Budget: $38,215,000**

Director **Lucinda M. Babers** . . . . . . . . . . . . . . . . . . . . . (202) 727-2200
E-mail: lucinda.babers@dc.gov
Education: Georgia Tech BIE; Johns Hopkins MS

# Office of the Chief Medical Examiner [OCME]

401 E Street SW, 6th Floor, Washington, DC 20024
Tel: (202) 698-9000  Fax: (202) 698-9101  E-mail: ocme@dc.gov

Chief Medical Examiner **Dr. Roger A. Mitchell, Jr.** . . . . . . (202) 698-9001
Education: Howard U 1996 BS; U Medicine/Dentistry NJ 2003 MD
Executive Assistant to the Chief Medical Examiner
**Viola Hiers** . . . . . . . . . . . . . . . . . . . . . . . . . . . . . . . (202) 698-9000
Deputy Chief **Dr. Jan M. Gorniak, DO** . . . . . . . . . . . . . . (202) 698-9000
Chief of Staff **Beverly Fields** . . . . . . . . . . . . . . . . . . . . (202) 698-9006
Education: Howard U 1989
Medical Examiner **Constance D'Angelo** . . . . . . . . . . . . . (202) 698-9000
Medical Examiner **Mehdi Koolaee** . . . . . . . . . . . . . . . . . (202) 698-9000
Medical Examiner **Sasha Osbourne** . . . . . . . . . . . . . . . . (202) 698-9000
Medical Examiner **Terrell Tops** . . . . . . . . . . . . . . . . . . . (202) 698-9000
Freedom of Information Act (FOIA) Officer and General
Counsel **Mikelle L. Devillier** . . . . . . . . . . . . . . . . . . . . (202) 698-9005
Education: Loyola U (New Orleans) 2004 JD

# Office of Administrative Hearings [OAH]

441 Fourth Street, NW, Suite 450N, Washington, DC 20001-2714
Tel: (202) 442-9094  E-mail: oah@dc.gov  Internet: www.oah.dc.gov

**Employees: 77  Fiscal Year: 2015  Budget: $9,561,000**

Chief Administrative Law Judge **Eugene A. Adams** . . . . . . (202) 442-9099
Education: Wesleyan U; Connecticut JD
Principal Administrative Law Judge **John P. Dean** . . . . . . . (202) 727-8284
Principal Administrative Law Judge **Paul B. Handy** . . . . . . (202) 727-8282
Principal Administrative Law Judge **Samuel McClendon** . . (202) 727-3821
E-mail: samuel.mcclendon@dc.gov
Principal Administrative Law Judge **Erika L. Pierson** . . . . . (202) 478-1465
E-mail: erika.pierson@dc.gov
Education: Grinnell; Northern Illinois JD
Principal Administrative Law Judge **Robert Sharkey** . . . . . (202) 442-9092
E-mail: robert.sharkey@dc.gov
Principal Administrative Law Judge
**Arabella Wattles Teal** . . . . . . . . . . . . . . . . . . . . . . . . (202) 478-1414
E-mail: arabella.teal@dc.gov
Education: Harvard BA; Georgetown JD
Principal Administrative Law Judge **Wanda R. Tucker** . . . (202) 478-1413
E-mail: wanda.tucker@dc.gov
Principal Administrative Law Judge **Ann C. Yahner** . . . . . (202) 442-8168
Education: Wellesley; Harvard JD
Administrative Law Judge **Claudia Barber** . . . . . . . . . . . . (202) 724-5475
E-mail: claudia.barber@dc.gov
Administrative Law Judge **Sherri Beatty-Arthur** . . . . . . . . (202) 442-7290
E-mail: sherri.beatty-arthur@dc.gov
Administrative Law Judge **Eli Bruch** . . . . . . . . . . . . . . . . (202) 478-1413
E-mail: eli.bruch2@dc.gov

*(continued on next page)*

---

★ Elected Official   ■ Appointed by Governor   ● Appointed by Legislature   ▲ Appointed by Board or Commission   ◆ Appointed by State Supreme Court

**Office of Administrative Hearings** *continued*

Administrative Law Judge **Nicholas Cobbs** . . . . . . . . . . . . (202) 671-0135
  Education: Amherst; Pennsylvania JD
Administrative Law Judge **Claudia Crichlow** . . . . . . . . . . . (202) 741-5211
Administrative Law Judge **Joan Davenport** . . . . . . . . . . . . (202) 727-8280
  E-mail: joan.davenport@dc.gov
Administrative Law Judge **William L. England, Jr.** . . . . . . . (202) 442-9536
Administrative Law Judge **Elizabeth Figueroa** . . . . . . . . . (202) 724-5476
  E-mail: elizabeth.figueroa@dc.gov
Administrative Law Judge **Jesse Goode** . . . . . . . . . . . . . . (202) 442-5946
  E-mail: jesse.goode@dc.gov
Administrative Law Judge **Sharon Goodie** . . . . . . . . . . . . (202) 442-9101
  E-mail: sharon.goodie@dc.gov
Administrative Law Judge **James C. Harmon, Jr.** . . . . . . . (202) 442-8053
Administrative Law Judge **Scott Harvey** . . . . . . . . . . . . . (202) 442-9095
  E-mail: scott.harvey@dc.gov
Administrative Law Judge **Caryn Hines** . . . . . . . . . . . . . . (202) 671-0134
  E-mail: caryn.hines@dc.gov
Administrative Law Judge **Audrey Jenkins** . . . . . . . . . . . . (202) 724-9733
  E-mail: audrey.jenkins@dc.gov
Administrative Law Judge **E. Savannah Little** . . . . . . . . . . (202) 727-3356
Administrative Law Judge **Margaret Mangan** . . . . . . . . . . (202) 442-9102
  E-mail: margaret.mangan@dc.gov
Administrative Law Judge **Mary Masulla** . . . . . . . . . . . . . (202) 478-1464
  E-mail: mary.masulla@dc.gov
Administrative Law Judge **Calonette McDonald** . . . . . . . . (202) 727-3821
  E-mail: calonette.mcdonald@dc.gov
Administrative Law Judge **Beverly Sherman Nash** . . . . . . (202) 442-8165
  E-mail: beverly.nash@dc.gov
Administrative Law Judge **John Thomas Rooney** . . . . . . . (202) 724-7482
  E-mail: john.rooney2@dc.gov
Administrative Law Judge **Vytas V. Vergeer** . . . . . . . . . . . (202) 442-9099
  E-mail: vytas.vergeer@dc.gov
Administrative Law Judge **Bernard Weberman** . . . . . . . . . (202) 478-9169
  E-mail: bernard.weberman@dc.gov
Administrative Law Judge **N. Denise Wilson-Taylor** . . . . . (202) 671-0172
  E-mail: denise.wilson-taylor@dc.gov

## Office of Budget and Finance

Director **Matthew Brown** . . . . . . . . . . . . . . . . . . . . . . . (202) 478-9200
  E-mail: matthew.brown3@dc.gov
  Education: Texas Wesleyan U BA; George Washington MPA
Deputy Director for Capital Improvements Program
  **John McGaw** . . . . . . . . . . . . . . . . . . . . . . . . . . . . . (202) 727-1429

## Office of Human Rights [OHR]

One Judiciary Square, 441 Fourth Street, NW, Suite 570N,
Washington, DC 20001
Tel: (202) 727-4559  TTY: (202) 724-2050  Fax: (202) 727-9589

Director **Mónica Palacio, JD** . . . . . . . . . . . . . . . . . . . . . (202) 727-4559
  Education: Fordham 1990 BA; Georgetown 1993 JD

## Human Rights Commission

One Judiciary Square, 441 4th Street NW, Suite 290N,
Washington, DC 20001
Tel: (202) 727-0656  Fax: (202) 727-3781

Chair **Earl D. Fowlkes, Jr.** . . . . . . . . . . . . . . . . . . . . . . . (202) 727-0656
  Term Expires: December 31, 2017
Chief Administrative Law Judge **David Simmons** . . . . . . . (202) 727-0656
  E-mail: david.simmons@dc.gov
Administrative Law Judge **Dianne S. Harris** . . . . . . . . . . . (202) 727-2350
  E-mail: diannes.harris@dc.gov
Administrative Law Judge **J.P. Howard** . . . . . . . . . . . . . . (202) 741-7622
  E-mail: jp.howard@dc.gov

## Office of Labor Relations and Collective Bargaining [OLRCB]

441 4th Street NW, Suite 820N, Washington, DC 20001
Tel: (202) 724-4953  Fax: (202) 727-6887  E-mail: olrcb.eom@dc.gov

Director **Lionel Sims** . . . . . . . . . . . . . . . . . . . . . . . . . . (202) 724-4953
  E-mail: lionel.sims@dc.gov
  Education: Wayne State U BS; Detroit Mercy JD

## Office of Planning [OP]

1100 4th Street SW, Suite E650, Washington, DC 20024
Tel: (202) 442-7600  Fax: (202) 442-7638  E-mail: op@dc.gov

Director **Eric D. Shaw** . . . . . . . . . . . . . . . . . . . . . . . . . (202) 442-7600
  E-mail: eric.shaw@dc.gov
Deputy Director for Development Review and Historic
  Preservation **Jennifer Steingasser, AICP** . . . . . . . . . . . (202) 442-8808
  Education: Texas BS; Virginia MS
Deputy Director for Planning, Engagement and Design
  **Tanya Stern** . . . . . . . . . . . . . . . . . . . . . . . . . . . . . (202) 442-7635

## Office of Public-Private Partnerships [OP3]

Tel: (202) 478-9200

Director **Seth Miller Gabriel** . . . . . . . . . . . . . . . . . . . . (202) 478-9200
  Education: Washington Col; George Washington
Deputy Director **Judah Gluckman** . . . . . . . . . . . . . . . . . (202) 478-9200
  Education: Chicago; Washington College of Law JD

# Council of the District of Columbia

John A. Wilson Building, 1350 Pennsylvania Avenue, NW,
Washington, DC 20004
Tel: (202) 724-8000  TTY: (202) 347-5181  Fax: (202) 347-3070
Internet: www.dccouncil.us

★Chairman of the Council **Phil Mendelson** (D-At-Large) . . . (202) 724-8032
  Term Expires: January 2, 2019        Fax: (202) 724-8099
  Education: American U 1981 BA
★Council Member **Yvette M. Alexander** (D-Ward 7) . . . . . . (202) 724-8068
  Term Expires: January 2, 2017        Fax: (202) 741-0911
★Council Member **Charles Allen** (D-Ward 6) . . . . . . . . . . . (202) 724-8072
  Term Expires: January 2, 2019
★Council Member **Anita Bonds** (D-At-Large) . . . . . . . . . . . (202) 724-8064
  Term Expires: January 2, 2019        Fax: (202) 724-8086
★Council Member **Mary M. Cheh** (D-Ward 3) . . . . . . . . . . . (202) 724-8062
  Term Expires: January 2, 2019        Fax: (202) 724-8118
  Education: Douglass BA; Rutgers JD; Harvard 1977 LLM
★Council Member **Jack Evans** (D-Ward 2) . . . . . . . . . . . . . (202) 724-8058
  Term Expires: January 2, 2017        Fax: (202) 724-8023
  Education: Wharton 1975 BA; Pittsburgh 1978 JD
★Council Member **David Grosso** (I-At-Large) . . . . . . . . . . . (202) 724-8105
  Term Expires: January 2, 2017        Fax: (202) 724-8071
  Education: Earlham 1997 BP
★Council Member **LaRuby May** (D-Ward 8) . . . . . . . . . . . . (202) 724-8045
  Term Expires: January 2, 2017        Fax: (202) 724-8055
  Education: Eckerd BA; George Washington MA
★Council Member **Kenyan McDuffie** (D-Ward 5) . . . . . . . . . (202) 724-8028
  Term Expires: January 2, 2019        Fax: (202) 724-8076
  Education: Howard U BS; Maryland JD
★Council Member **Brianne Nadeau** (D-Ward 1) . . . . . . . . . (202) 724-8181
  Term Expires: January 2, 2019        Fax: (202) 724-8109
★Council Member **Vincent B. Orange, Sr.** (D-At-Large) . . . (202) 724-8174
  Term Expires: January 2, 2017        Fax: (202) 727-8210
  Education: U Pacific 1979 BS, 1980 BA; Howard U 1983 JD;
  Georgetown 1988 MLT
★Council Member **Elissa Silverman** (I-At-Large) . . . . . . . . (202) 724-7772
  Term Expires: January 2, 2019        Fax: (202) 724-8087
★Council Member **Brandon T. Todd** (D-Ward 4) . . . . . . . . . (202) 724-8052
  Term Expires: January 2, 2017        Fax: (202) 741-0908
  Education: Bowie State BS
Secretary to the Council **Nyasha Smith** . . . . . . . . . . . . . . (202) 724-8080
Assistant Secretary **Jamaine Taylor** . . . . . . . . . . . . . . . . (202) 724-8080
General Counsel **Ellen Efros** . . . . . . . . . . . . . . . . . . . . . (202) 724-8026
                               Fax: (202) 724-8129
Budget Director **Jennifer Budoff** . . . . . . . . . . . . . . . . . . (202) 724-5689
                               Fax: (202) 724-7819
Chief Information Officer **Chris Warren** . . . . . . . . . . . . . . (202) 724-8018
  E-mail: cwarren@dccouncil.us

---

# Office of the Chief Financial Officer [OCFO]

John A. Wilson Building, 1350 Pennsylvania Avenue, NW, Suite 203, Washington, DC 20004
Tel: (202) 727-2476  Fax: (202) 727-1643  E-mail: ocfo@dc.gov
Internet: cfo.dc.gov

**Employees:** 957  **Fiscal Year:** 2015  **Budget:** $136,336,000

Chief Financial Officer **Jeffrey S. DeWitt** . . . . . . . . . . . . . (202) 727-2476
  Term Expires: June 2017
  Education: Eastern Illinois BS; Southern Illinois MS
Deputy Chief Financial Officer and Chief of Staff
  **Angell Jacobs** . . . . . . . . . . . . . . . . . . . . . . . . . . . . (202) 727-2476
Continuous Improvement Officer **Baraka Ondiek** . . . . . . . (202) 727-2476
Chief Information Officer (Interim) **Richard Weil** . . . . . . . (202) 727-8775
Chief Risk Officer **Marshelle Richardson** . . . . . . . . . . . . (202) 727-2476
Public Affairs Officer **David Umansky** . . . . . . . . . . . . . . (202) 727-6391
  E-mail: david.umansky@dc.gov
General Counsel **David Tseng** . . . . . . . . . . . . . . . . . . . (202) 727-9528
  E-mail: david.tseng@dc.gov
Freedom of Information Act (FOIA) Officer
  **LaVerne Lee** . . . . . . . . . . . . . . . . . . . . . . . . . . . . . (202) 727-9528
  John A. Wilson Building, 441 Fourth Streeet NW,    Fax: (202) 724-4217
  Suite 200, Washington, DC 20001
Senior Advisor for Economic Development Finance
  **John Ross** . . . . . . . . . . . . . . . . . . . . . . . . . . . . . . . (202) 727-2421
  E-mail: john.ross@dc.gov
Senior Financial Policy Advisor **Darryl Street** . . . . . . . . . . (202) 727-2476
  E-mail: darryl.street@dc.gov

## Economic Development and Regulation Cluster

1100 4th Street SW, Suite E450, Washington, DC 20024
Fax: (202) 478-9261

Associate Chief Financial Officer **Cyril Byron, Jr.** . . . . . . . . (202) 442-8684
Controller **Dennis Ramprashad** . . . . . . . . . . . . . . . . . . (202) 478-9261
Chief, Management Operations **Joscaira Akhran** . . . . . . . . (202) 442-8923

## Government Operations Cluster

441 Fourth Streeet NW, Suite 890N, Washington, DC 20001
Tel: (202) 727-0333  Fax: (202) 727-2202

Associate Chief Financial Officer
  **Mohamed A. Mohamed** . . . . . . . . . . . . . . . . . . . . . . (202) 727-0333
Chief, Management Operations **Rhonda Cheatham** . . . . . . (202) 727-0333

## Government Services Cluster

2000 14th Street NW, Sixth Floor, Washington, DC 20009
Tel: (202) 671-2300

Associate Chief Financial Officer **George B. Dines, Jr.** . . . (202) 727-2476
  Education: Maryland 1981 BA; Washington U (MO) 1982 MA;
  Southeastern U 2007 MBA
Chief, Management Operations **Hillary Ferguson** . . . . . . . . (202) 671-2366

## Human Support Services Cluster

64 New York Avenue, NE, 6th Floor, Washington, DC 20002
Tel: (202) 671-4210  Fax: (202) 671-4203

Associate Chief Financial Officer **Delicia Moore** . . . . . . . . (202) 671-4220

## Primary and Secondary Education Cluster

1200 First Street, NE, 11th Floor, Washington, DC 20002
Tel: (202) 442-6078  Fax: (202) 442-5807

Associate Chief Financial Officer **Deloras A. Shepherd** . . . (202) 442-6078
  E-mail: deloras.shepherd@dc.gov

## Public Safety and Justice Cluster

Tel: (202) 673-3338

Associate Chief Financial Officer **Angelique R. Hayes** . . . . (202) 673-3347
  E-mail: angelique.hayes@dc.gov

# Office of Budget and Planning [OBP]

1350 Pennsylvania Avenue, NW, Suite 229, Washington, DC 20004
Tel: (202) 727-1239  Fax: (202) 724-5222

Deputy Chief Financial Officer **Gordon McDonald** . . . . . . . (202) 727-6343
  Education: Howard U BABA, MBA
Associate Deputy Chief Financial Officer **Jim Spaulding** . . (202) 727-1782
Director for Budget Administration **Eric M. Cannady** . . . . . (202) 727-1072
Director for Capital Improvements Program **David Clark** . . (202) 727-2055
Director for Financial Planning, Analysis, and
  Management Services **Leticia Stephenson** . . . . . . . . . . . (202) 727-1036

# Office of Finance and Treasury [OFT]

1101 Fourth Street SW, Eigth Floor, Washington, DC 20005
Fax: (202) 727-6049

Treasurer **Jeffrey Barnette** . . . . . . . . . . . . . . . . . . . . . . (202) 727-6055
Associate Treasurer for Asset Management **John Henry** . . . (202) 727-6288
  Education: Virginia State BA; Howard U MBA
Associate Treasurer for Banking and Operations
  **Clarice Wood** . . . . . . . . . . . . . . . . . . . . . . . . . . . . (202) 727-0760
  E-mail: clarice.wood@dc.gov
Associate Treasurer for Debt and Grants Management
  **Carmen Pigler** . . . . . . . . . . . . . . . . . . . . . . . . . . . . (202) 727-6055
  Education: Columbia MBA
Chief of Management Operations **Jeanne Marie Hoover** . . (202) 727-0911
  E-mail: jeanne.hoover@dc.gov
Director of Unclaimed Property **Gracie Musher** . . . . . . . . (202) 442-8195
Administrative Manager **Mallie C. Douglas** . . . . . . . . . . . (202) 727-6055
  E-mail: mallie.douglas@dc.gov

# Office of Financial Operations and Systems [OFOS]

1100 4th Street SW, Suite E800, Washington, DC 20024
Fax: (202) 442-8201

Deputy Chief Financial Officer **Bill Slack** . . . . . . . . . . . . . (202) 442-8200
Deputy Comptroller **Diji Omisore** . . . . . . . . . . . . . . . . . (202) 727-2476
  Education: Towson U

# Office of Integrity and Oversight

1100 4th Street SW, Suite 750E, Washington, DC 20024
Tel: (202) 442-6433

Executive Director **Timothy M. Barry** . . . . . . . . . . . . . . . (202) 442-6433
  E-mail: timothy.barry@dc.gov
  Education: Westfield State U; Scranton
Director of Audit Division **Mohamad K. Yusuff, CPA** . . . . (202) 442-8240
  Education: Howard U 1975; George Washington 1977 MBA
Director of Internal Security **James E. Glymph** . . . . . . . . . (202) 442-8280

# Office of Management and Administration

1101 Fourth Street SW, Suite 220W, Washington, DC 20005

Executive Director **Paul Lundquist** . . . . . . . . . . . . . . . . . (202) 442-6523
  E-mail: paul.lundquist@dc.gov
  Education: Yale 1985 MPPM

# Office of Revenue Analysis

1101 Fourth Street SW, Suite 770W, Washington, DC 20005
Tel: (202) 727-7775  E-mail: ora@dc.gov

Deputy Chief Financial Officer and Chief Economist
  **Fitzroy Lee** . . . . . . . . . . . . . . . . . . . . . . . . . . . . . . . (202) 727-7775
  Education: U West Indies (Jamaica) BS; Georgia State PhD
Economic Affairs Director **Farhad Niami** . . . . . . . . . . . . . (202) 727-7775
  Education: Oregon State PhD
Fiscal and Legislative Analysis Director **Yesim Yilmaz** . . . . (202) 727-7775
  Education: Bogaziçi U (Turkey) BA; George Mason PhD
Revenue Estimation Director **Steven Giachetti** . . . . . . . . . (202) 727-7775

---

★ Elected Official    ■ Appointed by Governor    ● Appointed by Legislature    ▲ Appointed by Board or Commission    ◆ Appointed by State Supreme Court

## Office of Tax and Revenue

West Building, 1101 4th Street SW, Washington, DC 20024
Tel: (202) 442-6200  Internet: www.otr.cfo.dc.gov

Deputy Chief Financial Officer **Stephen M. Cordi** . . . . . . . (202) 442-6383
  Education: Haverford 1965 BA; Georgetown 1968 JD;
  Johns Hopkins 1970 MLA
Chief Tax Appraiser **Stephen Cappello** . . . . . . . . . . . . . . . (202) 442-6760
Deputy Chief Tax Appraiser **Olufemi Omotoso** . . . . . . . . (202) 442-6731
Management Analyst **Andrea Holley** . . . . . . . . . . . . . . . . . (202) 442-6372

## Lottery and Charitable Games Control Board

2101 M. L. King, Jr. Avenue, SE, Washington, DC 20020
Tel: (202) 645-8000  Fax: (202) 645-3683  Internet: www.dclottery.com

Executive Director (Interim) **Tracey Cohen** . . . . . . . . . . . . (202) 645-8010
  E-mail: tracey.cohen@dc.gov
  Education: Pittsburgh BA, MPIA

## Office of the Deputy Mayor for Education [DME]

1350 Pennsylvania Avenue, NW, Suite 307, Washington, DC 20004
Tel: (202) 727-3636  Fax: (202) 727-8198  E-mail: dme@dc.gov

Deputy Mayor **Jennifer C. Niles** . . . . . . . . . . . . . . . . . . . . . (202) 727-0953
  E-mail: jennifer.niles@dc.gov
Chief of Staff **Margie Yeager** . . . . . . . . . . . . . . . . . . . . . . . (202) 727-0953
Executive Assistant **Tara Lynch** . . . . . . . . . . . . . . . . . . . . . . (202) 727-3636
Data Analyst **Cecilia Kaltz** . . . . . . . . . . . . . . . . . . . . . . . . . . (202) 727-3636

## Office of the State Superintendent of Education [OSSE]

810 First Street, NE, 9th Floor, Washington, DC 20002
Tel: (202) 727-6436  Fax: (202) 727-2019  Internet: http://osse.dc.gov

**Employees:** 360  **Fiscal Year:** 2015  **Budget:** $406,901,000

State Superintendent **Hanseul Kang** . . . . . . . . . . . . . . . . . (202) 727-6436
  E-mail: hanseul.kang@dc.gov
  Education: Georgetown; Harvard JD
Executive Assistant **Maisha Hayes** . . . . . . . . . . . . . . . . . . . (202) 727-3471
Chief of Staff **Shana Young** . . . . . . . . . . . . . . . . . . . . . . . . . (202) 727-6436
  Deputy Chief of Staff **Jessie Harteis** . . . . . . . . . . . . . . . (202) 344-9805
    E-mail: jessie.harteis@dc.gov
  Special Assistant for Policy **Bridget Kelly** . . . . . . . . . . . (202) 322-1727
    E-mail: bridget.kelly@dc.gov
Chief Operating Officer (Acting) **Gregory Ellis** . . . . . . . . . (202) 727-6436
Assistant Superintendent of Assessment, Data and
  Research **(Vacant)** . . . . . . . . . . . . . . . . . . . . . . . . . . . . . . (202) 727-6436
Assistant Superintendent of Early Learning
  **Elizabeth Groginsky** . . . . . . . . . . . . . . . . . . . . . . . . . . . . (202) 727-6436
  Education: Maryland; Colorado
Assistant Superintendent of Elementary, Secondary, and
  Specialized Education **Dr. Amy Maisterra** . . . . . . . . . . . (202) 727-6436
  Education: Smith MSW; Pennsylvania DEd
Assistant Superintendent of Health and Wellness
  **Donna Anthony** . . . . . . . . . . . . . . . . . . . . . . . . . . . . . . . . (202) 727-6436
Assistant Superintendent of Postsecondary and Career
  Education **Antoinette S. Mitchell** . . . . . . . . . . . . . . . . . (202) 727-6436
Chief Information Officer **Tom Fontenot** . . . . . . . . . . . . . . (202) 727-6436
  E-mail: thomas.fontenot@dc.gov
State GED (General Education Development)
  Administrator and Chief Examiner **Philip PremDas** . . . . . (202) 274-7173
    E-mail: philip.premdas@dc.gov
Agency Fiscal Officer **Paris Saunders** . . . . . . . . . . . . . . . . (202) 727-6436
Athletics Director **Clark E. Ray** . . . . . . . . . . . . . . . . . . . . . (202) 727-6436
  Education: Arkansas BS; Temple MEd
Director of Communications **Patience Peabody** . . . . . . . . (202) 654-6120
  E-mail: patience.peabody@dc.gov
Director of Operations **Gregory Ellis** . . . . . . . . . . . . . . . . . (202) 727-6436
  E-mail: gregory.ellis@dc.gov
Director of Student Transportation **Gretchen Brumley** . . . . (202) 724-5675
Director of Talent and Human Resources **Pete Siu** . . . . . . . (202) 727-6436
Director of Transportation **(Vacant)** . . . . . . . . . . . . . . . . . . (202) 727-6436

General Counsel (Interim) **Sarah Jane Forman** . . . . . . . . . (202) 727-6436
Community Outreach Specialist **Victoria L. Holmes** . . . . . . (202) 372-5415
  E-mail: victoria.holmes@dc.gov

## State Board of Education

441 Fourth Street, NW, Suite 723 North, Washington, DC 20001
Tel: (202) 741-0888  Fax: (202) 741-0879  Internet: http://sboe.dc.gov

★President **Jack N. Jacobson** (D-Ward 2) . . . . . . . . . . . . . . (202) 741-0888
  Term Expires: January 2, 2017
  E-mail: jack.jacobson@dc.gov
  Education: Augustana (IL) 2000 BA
★Vice President **Karen Williams** (D-Ward 7) . . . . . . . . . . . (202) 741-0888
  Term Expires: January 2, 2017
  E-mail: karen.williams5@dc.gov
  Education: George Washington BE
★Board Member **D. Kamili Anderson** (D-Ward 4) . . . . . . . (202) 257-3380
  Term Expires: January 2, 2017
  E-mail: kamili.anderson@dc.gov
★Board Member **Tierra Jolly** (Ward 8) . . . . . . . . . . . . . . . . (202) 812-1464
  Term Expires: January 2, 2017
  E-mail: tierra.jolly@dc.gov
★Board Member **Mark Jones** (Ward 5) . . . . . . . . . . . . . . . . (202) 302-7294
  Term Expires: January 2, 2019
  E-mail: mark.jones@dc.gov
★Board Member **Mary Lord** (D-At-Large) . . . . . . . . . . . . . . (202) 257-3226
  Term Expires: January 2, 2017
  E-mail: mary.lord@dc.gov
  Education: Harvard
★Board Member **Laura Wilson Phelan** (Ward 1) . . . . . . . . . (202) 276-5859
  Term Expires: January 2, 2019
  E-mail: laura.wilson.phelan@dc.gov
★Board Member **Ruth Wattenberg** (Ward 3) . . . . . . . . . . . . (202) 431-5379
  Term Expires: January 2, 2019
  E-mail: ruth.wattenberg@dc.gov
★Board Member **Joe Weedon** (Ward 6) . . . . . . . . . . . . . . . . (202) 431-5369
  Term Expires: January 2, 2019
  E-mail: joe.weedon@dc.gov
Executive Director **John-Paul C. Hayworth** . . . . . . . . . . . . (202) 741-0888
  E-mail: john-paul.hayworth@dc.gov
  Education: Baylor 2001 AB; Connecticut 2003 AM

## Department of Parks and Recreation [DPR]

1250 U Street NW, 2nd Floor, Washington, DC 20010
1480 Girard Street, NW, 4th Floor, Washington, DC 20009
Tel: (202) 673-7647  Fax: (202) 673-2087  Internet: www.dpr.dc.gov

**Employees:** 570  **Fiscal Year:** 2015  **Budget:** $42,223,000

Director **Keith A. Anderson** . . . . . . . . . . . . . . . . . . . . . . . . (202) 671-2321
  E-mail: keith.anderson@dc.gov
  Education: Hampton
Chief Operations Officer **(Vacant)** . . . . . . . . . . . . . . . . . . . (202) 316-4236
Chief of Staff **Jason Yuckenberg** . . . . . . . . . . . . . . . . . . . . (202) 273-2195
  E-mail: jason.yuckenberg@dc.gov
Recreational Services Deputy Director **Tony Thompson** . . . (202) 673-2143
  E-mail: tony.thompson@dc.gov
General Counsel **Amy Caspari** . . . . . . . . . . . . . . . . . . . . . . . (202) 671-2088
Communications and Community Affairs
  **Gwendolyn Crump** . . . . . . . . . . . . . . . . . . . . . . . . . . . . . (202) 288-6027
  E-mail: gwendolyn.crump@dc.gov
Financial Officer **Marjorie Edmonds** . . . . . . . . . . . . . . . . . (202) 673-2032
  E-mail: marjorie.edmonds@dc.gov

## DC Public School System [DCPS]

1200 First Street, NE, Washington, DC 20002
Tel: (202) 442-5885  Fax: (202) 442-5026

Chancellor **Kaya K. Henderson** . . . . . . . . . . . . . . . . . . . . . (202) 535-1581
  E-mail: kaya.henderson@dc.gov
  Education: Georgetown 1992
Senior Adviser **Kenneth S. Slaughter** . . . . . . . . . . . . . . . . (202) 442-5885
  Education: Georgetown 1976 JD
Chief Operating Officer **Nathaniel Savio Beers, MD** . . . . . (202) 442-5885
  Education: Rochester; George Washington MD; JFK School Govt MPA

---

★ Elected Official   ■ Appointed by Governor   ● Appointed by Legislature   ▲ Appointed by Board or Commission   ◆ Appointed by State Supreme Court

EXECUTIVE BRANCH

Chief of Staff **Peter Weber** . . . . . . . . . . . . . . . . . . . . . . (202) 442-5885
  E-mail: peter.weber@dc.gov
General Counsel **D. Scott Barash** . . . . . . . . . . . . . . . . . . (202) 442-5000
  E-mail: scott.barash@dc.gov
  Education: Yale 1985 BA; Chicago 1988 JD
Chief Financial Officer **Deloras A. Shepherd** . . . . . . . . . . (202) 442-5300
Chief of College and Career **Emily Durso** . . . . . . . . . . . . . (202) 442-5885
  Education: Georgetown; Catholic U
Chief of Innovation and Research
  **Dr. Robert W. Simmons III** . . . . . . . . . . . . . . . . . . . . . (202) 442-5885
  E-mail: robert.simmons@dc.gov
  Education: Western Michigan; Lawrence Tech MS
Chief of Instructional Practice **Jason Kamras** . . . . . . . . . . (202) 321-1248
  E-mail: jason.kamras@dc.gov
Chief of Schools **John Davis** . . . . . . . . . . . . . . . . . . . . . . (202) 442-5618
Chief of Talent and Culture **Crystal Jefferson** . . . . . . . . . . (202) 442-5417
Chief of Teaching and Learning **Brian Pick** . . . . . . . . . . . . (202) 442-5611
  Education: Princeton           Fax: (202) 442-5081
  Deputy Chief of Educational Technology and Library
  Programs **David Rose** . . . . . . . . . . . . . . . . . . . . . . . . . (202) 442-5885
  E-mail: david.rose@dc.gov
Family and Public Engagement Chief
  **Josephine Bias Robinson** . . . . . . . . . . . . . . . . . . . . . (202) 719-6613
  E-mail: josephine.robinson@dc.gov    Fax: (202) 442-5418
  Education: Georgetown 1991 BSFS
  Family and Public Engagement Deputy Chief
  **Sarah Parker** . . . . . . . . . . . . . . . . . . . . . . . . . . . . . . (202) 442-5308
Facilities and Technology Initiatives Deputy Chief
  **Bridget Stesney** . . . . . . . . . . . . . . . . . . . . . . . . . . . . (202) 576-8725
  E-mail: bridget.stesney@dc.gov
  Education: Central Michigan 1999 BS; Virginia Tech 2007 MURP
Food and Nutrition Services Director **Robert Jaber** . . . . . . (202) 442-5112
  Executive Assistant **Ursula Ferguson** . . . . . . . . . . . . . . (202) 535-1581
Athletic Director **Stephanie Evans** . . . . . . . . . . . . . . . . . (202) 442-5635
Budget Director **Donald Sink** . . . . . . . . . . . . . . . . . . . . . (202) 442-5300
Chief of Communications **Ernestine Walls Benedict** . . . . . (202) 442-8854
  E-mail: ernestine.benedict@dc.gov
  Education: Temple
  Press Secretary **Michelle Lerner** . . . . . . . . . . . . . . . . . . (202) 480-0860
  E-mail: michelle.lerner@dc.gov

## Office of Federal Grants and Programs
Director **Jocelyn Basley** . . . . . . . . . . . . . . . . . . . . . . . . . (202) 442-5149
  E-mail: jocelyn.basley@dc.gov       Fax: (202) 442-5529

## Language Acquisition Division
1200 S Street NW, Washington, DC 20009
Tel: (202) 671-0750
Executive Director **Elba Garcia** . . . . . . . . . . . . . . . . . . . . (202) 671-0750
Receptionist **Asuncion Alvarado** . . . . . . . . . . . . . . . . . . . (202) 671-0750

## Office of the Regional Superintendents
Cluster I **Harry Hughes** . . . . . . . . . . . . . . . . . . . . . . . . . (202) 939-4540
Cluster II **Angela Chapman** . . . . . . . . . . . . . . . . . . . . . . . (202) 939-4540
Cluster III **LaKimbre Brown** . . . . . . . . . . . . . . . . . . . . . . (202) 939-4540
Cluster IV (Interim) **Aileen Murphy** . . . . . . . . . . . . . . . . . (202) 729-3290
Cluster V **Janice Harris** . . . . . . . . . . . . . . . . . . . . . . . . . (202) 729-3290
Cluster VI **Shawn Stover** . . . . . . . . . . . . . . . . . . . . . . . . (202) 729-3290
Cluster VII **Eugene Pinkard** . . . . . . . . . . . . . . . . . . . . . . (202) 939-5290
Cluster VIII (Interim) **Dan Shea** . . . . . . . . . . . . . . . . . . . . (202) 939-5290
Cluster IX **David Pender** . . . . . . . . . . . . . . . . . . . . . . . . . (202) 939-5290

## Office of the Deputy Mayor for Greater Economic Opportunity
Deputy Mayor **Courtney Snowden** . . . . . . . . . . . . . . . . . . (202) 737-4404
  Education: Beloit 2000 BA

## Office on African American Affairs
Director **Rahman Branch** . . . . . . . . . . . . . . . . . . . . . . . . . (202) 442-8150

## Department of Employment Services [DOES]
4058 Minnesota Avenue NE, Suite 5000, Washington, DC 20019
Tel: (202) 671-1900  TTY: (202) 673-6994  Fax: (202) 673-6976
Internet: www.does.dc.gov

**Employees: 580  Fiscal Year: 2015  Budget: $113,796,000**

Director **Deborah A. Carroll** . . . . . . . . . . . . . . . . . . . . . . (202) 671-1900
  E-mail: does@dc.gov
  Education: Temple BS, JD
Chief of Staff **Rámon Pérez-Goizueta** . . . . . . . . . . . . . . . (202) 671-1673
  E-mail: ramon.perez-goizueta@dc.gov
Operations Deputy Director **Jerome Johnson** . . . . . . . . . . (202) 671-1900
General Counsel **Tonya Saap** . . . . . . . . . . . . . . . . . . . . . . (202) 671-1500
  E-mail: tonya.saap@dc.gov
Chief Financial Officer **Natalie Myers** . . . . . . . . . . . . . . . . (202) 671-1546
Strategic Communication Officer **(Vacant)** . . . . . . . . . . . . . (202) 671-2100
Apprenticeship Information and Training Director
  **Drew Hubbard** . . . . . . . . . . . . . . . . . . . . . . . . . . . . . (202) 698-5099
  E-mail: drew.hubbard@dc.gov
Employer Services Director **Sheree Finley** . . . . . . . . . . . . . (202) 698-3495
Ex-Offenders/Project Empowerment Associate Director
  **Charles Jones** . . . . . . . . . . . . . . . . . . . . . . . . . . . . . . (202) 698-6688
  E-mail: charles.jones@dc.gov

### A. Phillip Randolph One-Stop Career Center
6210 North Capitol Street, NW, Washington, DC 20011
Program Manager **Deborah Nelson** . . . . . . . . . . . . . . . . . . (202) 724-7000
  E-mail: deborah.nelson@dc.gov

### DC Workers Career Center
3720 Martin Luther King Avenue, SE, Washington, DC 20032
Program Manager **Dario Stewart** . . . . . . . . . . . . . . . . . . . . (202) 741-7747

### South Capitol CVS Pharmacy One-Stop Career Center
4049 South Capitol Street, SW, Washington, DC 20032
Program Manager **Deborah Nelson** . . . . . . . . . . . . . . . . . . (202) 645-4000
  E-mail: deborah.nelson@dc.gov

### Veteran's Affair Satellite One-Stop Career Center
609 H Street, NE, Washington, DC 20006
Program Manager **Christopher Rawlins** . . . . . . . . . . . . . . . (202) 530-9379
  E-mail: christopher.rawlins@dc.gov

### Labor Standards Bureau
64 New York Avenue, NE, Room 3123, Washington, DC 20002
Tel: (202) 671-1880
Associate Director **Mohammed R. Sheik** . . . . . . . . . . . . . . (202) 671-1532
  E-mail: mohammed.sheik@dc.gov
Wage-Hour Office Deputy Associate Director
  **Michael Watts** . . . . . . . . . . . . . . . . . . . . . . . . . . . . . (202) 671-1880
  E-mail: michael.watts@dc.gov
  Education: UDC 1994 BA
Workers' Compensation Office Associate Director
  **Lisa Baxter** . . . . . . . . . . . . . . . . . . . . . . . . . . . . . . . (202) 671-1555
  E-mail: lisa.baxter@dc.gov
Hearings and Adjudication Chief Administrative Law
  Judge **Henry McCoy** . . . . . . . . . . . . . . . . . . . . . . . . . (202) 671-2233
  609 H Street, NE, Washington, DC 20002
  E-mail: henry.mccoy@dc.gov
Occupational Safety and Health Office Supervisory
  Safety Specialist **John Cates** . . . . . . . . . . . . . . . . . . . . (202) 671-1800

---

★ Elected Official   ■ Appointed by Governor   ● Appointed by Legislature   ▲ Appointed by Board or Commission   ◆ Appointed by State Supreme Court

## Department of Small and Local Business Development [DSLBD]

One Judiciary Square, 441 Fourth Street, NW, Suite 850N, Washington, DC 20001
Tel: (202) 727-3900  Fax: (202) 724-3786  E-mail: dslbd@dc.gov

**Employees:** 37  **Fiscal Year:** 2015  **Budget:** $9,501,000

Director **Ana Recio Harvey** . . . . . . . . . . . . . . . . . . . . . . . . (202) 727-3900
  Education: Houston
Administrative Officer to the Director
  **Gabrielle Richards** . . . . . . . . . . . . . . . . . . . . . . . . . . . (202) 727-3900
  E-mail: gabrielle.richards@dc.gov
Deputy Director of Compliance Division
  **Ronnie Edwards** . . . . . . . . . . . . . . . . . . . . . . . . . . . . . (202) 727-3900
Policy and Planning Director **(Vacant)** . . . . . . . . . . . . . . . (202) 727-3900

## Office of the Deputy Mayor for Health and Human Services

1350 Pennsylvania Avenue, NW, Suite 223, Washington, DC 20004
Tel: (202) 727-7973  Fax: (202) 442-5066

Deputy Mayor **Brenda Donald** . . . . . . . . . . . . . . . . . . . . (202) 727-6300
  E-mail: brenda.donald@dc.gov
  Education: George Washington BA; Arkansas (Little Rock) MPA
Chief of Staff **Rachel Joseph** . . . . . . . . . . . . . . . . . . . . . (202) 727-7973
  E-mail: rachel.joseph@dc.gov
Senior Policy Advisor **Jenna Cevasco** . . . . . . . . . . . . . . . (202) 727-7973
  E-mail: jenna.cevasco@dc.gov

## Child and Family Services Agency [CFSA]

400 Sixth Street, SW, 5th Floor, Washington, DC 20024
Tel: (202) 442-6100  Fax: (202) 727-7700  Fax: (202) 727-6505
E-mail: cfsa@dc.gov

**Employees:** 793  **Fiscal Year:** 2015  **Budget:** $230,672,000

Director **Raymond C. Davidson** . . . . . . . . . . . . . . . . . . . (202) 442-6175
  E-mail: raymond.davidson@dc.gov
  Education: George Washington MBA
Executive Assistant **Verrita Kelly** . . . . . . . . . . . . . . . . . (202) 442-6175
  E-mail: verrita.kelly@dc.gov
Staff Assistant **Amber Tate** . . . . . . . . . . . . . . . . . . . . . . (202) 442-6175
  E-mail: amber.tate@dc.gov

### Program Operations

Clinical and Health Services Administration Deputy
  Director **Cheryl Durden** . . . . . . . . . . . . . . . . . . . . . . . . (202) 727-7049
  E-mail: cheryl.durden@dc.gov
Principal Deputy Director **Heather Stowe** . . . . . . . . . . . . (202) 442-6000
Planning Policy and Program Support Deputy Director
  **(Vacant)** . . . . . . . . . . . . . . . . . . . . . . . . . . . . . . . . . . . . (202) 442-6000
Well Being Deputy Director **Marie Morilus-Black** . . . . . . . (202) 442-6000
Program Specialist **Melissa Eversley** . . . . . . . . . . . . . . . (202) 715-7799
  E-mail: melissa.eversley@dc.gov

### Administration

Deputy Director **(Vacant)** . . . . . . . . . . . . . . . . . . . . . . . . (202) 442-6000
Chief Contracting Officer **Tara Sigamoni** . . . . . . . . . . . . (202) 442-6000
Chief of Staff **Michele Rosenberg** . . . . . . . . . . . . . . . . . (202) 442-6000
Communication Director **Mindy Good** . . . . . . . . . . . . . . . (202) 442-6000
  E-mail: mindy.good@dc.gov
Fiscal Officer **Justin Kopca** . . . . . . . . . . . . . . . . . . . . . . (202) 442-6000
  Education: Wisconsin MPP
General Counsel **(Vacant)** . . . . . . . . . . . . . . . . . . . . . . . . (202) 442-6000
Agency Performance Director **Mary Williams** . . . . . . . . . . (202) 727-7197
Information Systems Director **Brady Birdsong, CPM** . . . . . (202) 442-6000
  E-mail: brady.birdsong@dc.gov
  Education: Oklahoma MS

## Department of Behavioral Health

64 New York Avenue, NE, Third Floor, Washington, DC 20002
Tel: (202) 673-7440  Fax: (202) 673-3433  E-mail: dbh@dc.gov

Director **Dr. Tanya Royster** . . . . . . . . . . . . . . . . . . . . . . (202) 673-9219
  E-mail: tanya.royster@dc.gov
  Education: Case Western
Senior Deputy Director **Barbara J. Bazron, PhD** . . . . . . . . (202) 727-8946
Deputy Director **(Vacant)** . . . . . . . . . . . . . . . . . . . . . . . . (202) 727-8941
Prevention Services Program Manager **Judith Donovan** . . . (202) 727-7598
  E-mail: judith.donovan@dc.gov
Children and Youth Services Director **Denise Dunbar** . . . . (202) 671-2900
Consumer and Family Affairs Director
  **Raphaella Richardson** . . . . . . . . . . . . . . . . . . . . . . . . (202) 673-4377
Emergency Services Director **(Vacant)** . . . . . . . . . . . . . . . (202) 673-2200
Operations Deputy Director **Mark Lassiter** . . . . . . . . . . . (202) 727-9568
  1300 First Street N.E., Room 360, Washington, DC 20002
Provider Relations Director **Venida Hamilton** . . . . . . . . . . (202) 671-3155
Treatment Services Director **Javon Oliver** . . . . . . . . . . . . (202) 727-8473
  1300 First Street N.E., Room 303, Washington, DC 20002
Chief of Office of Certification **Gwendolyn Wills** . . . . . . . (202) 535-1054
  1300 First Street N.E., Room 200, Washington, DC 20002
  E-mail: gwendolyn.wills@dc.gov
Performance Manager **Alina McClerklin** . . . . . . . . . . . . . (202) 727-8464
  1300 First Street N.E., Room 305, Washington, DC 20002
Chief Clinical Officer **Marc E. Dalton** . . . . . . . . . . . . . . . (202) 673-2200
Quality Assurance Chief **Todd Menhinick** . . . . . . . . . . . . (202) 727-9478
  1300 First Street N.E., Room 303, Washington, DC 20002
Policy and Planning Chief **(Vacant)** . . . . . . . . . . . . . . . . . (202) 727-8857
Recovery Services Chief **Valerie Robinson** . . . . . . . . . . . . (202) 727-9032
General Counsel **Matthew W. Caspari** . . . . . . . . . . . . . . . (202) 673-7505
Public Information Officer **Phyllis Jones** . . . . . . . . . . . . . (202) 673-1937
  E-mail: phyllis.jones@dc.gov

## Department on Disability Services [DDS]

1125 - 15 Street, NW, Washington, DC 20005
Tel: (202) 730-1700  Fax: (202) 730-1843

**Employees:** 430  **Fiscal Year:** 2015  **Budget:** $156,255,000

Director (Interim) **Andrew Reese** . . . . . . . . . . . . . . . . . . (202) 730-1700
  E-mail: andrew.reese@dc.gov
Deputy Director of Administration **Deborah Bonsack** . . . . (202) 730-1715
  E-mail: deborah.bonsack@dc.gov

### Office of Consumer Affairs

Program Manager **(Vacant)** . . . . . . . . . . . . . . . . . . . . . . . (202) 730-1700

### Office of the General Counsel

General Counsel (Acting) **Mark Back** . . . . . . . . . . . . . . . . (202) 730-1592

### Office of the Agency Chief Financial Officer

Agency Chief Financial Officer **(Vacant)** . . . . . . . . . . . . . (202) 730-1700

## Department of Human Services [DHS]

64 New York Avenue, NE, 6th Floor, Washington, DC 20002
P.O. Box 54047, Washington, DC 20032
Tel: (202) 671-4200  TTY: (202) 671-4495  Fax: (202) 671-4326

**Employees:** 1,215  **Fiscal Year:** 2015  **Budget:** $397,845,000

Director **Laura Green Zeilinger** . . . . . . . . . . . . . . . . . . . (202) 671-4200
  E-mail: laura.zeilinger@dc.gov
  Education: Sarah Lawrence 1995 BA;
  Washington College of Law 2005 JD
Chief Operating Officer **Sharon Kershbaum** . . . . . . . . . . . (202) 671-4200
  Education: Pennsylvania 1992 BA; Wharton 1998 MBA
Senior Advisor for Policy and Program Support
  **Sakina Thompson** . . . . . . . . . . . . . . . . . . . . . . . . . . . (202) 671-4451
  E-mail: sakina.thompson@dc.gov
Family Services Administrator (Acting) **Kristi Greenwalt** . . (202) 698-4171
  E-mail: kristi.greenwalt@dc.gov
General Counsel **Monica J. Brown** . . . . . . . . . . . . . . . . . . (202) 671-4346
Administrative Support Office Chief **Brenda C. Perkins** . . . (202) 671-4385

---

★ Elected Official   ■ Appointed by Governor   ● Appointed by Legislature   ▲ Appointed by Board or Commission   ◆ Appointed by State Supreme Court

Information Systems Office Chief **Boyle Stuckey** . . . . . . . . (202) 442-3223

Program Review, Accountability Office Chief
**Christa Phillips** . . . . . . . . . . . . . . . . . . . . . . . . . . . . (202) 671-4493

Economic Security Administrator **Anthea Seymour** . . . . . . (202) 698-3900
  E-mail: anthea.seymour@dc.gov

Capital Projects Operations Manager **Lisa Franklin Kelly** . . (202) 671-4200

## Refugee Resettlement Office

2146 - 24th Place, NE, Washington, DC 20018
Fax: (202) 529-4365

State Coordinator **Debra Crawford** . . . . . . . . . . . . . . . . . . (202) 299-2153

## Department of Health [DOH]

899 North Capitol Street, NE, Washington, DC 20002
Tel: (202) 442-5955  Tel: (202) 442-9303 (Vital Records)
Fax: (202) 442-4795

**Employees:** 599  **Fiscal Year:** 2015  **Budget:** $266,124,000

Director **Dr. LaQuandra S. Nesbitt** . . . . . . . . . . . . . . . . . . (202) 442-5955
  E-mail: laquandra.nesbitt@dc.gov
  Education: Michigan BS; Wayne State U MD; Harvard MPH
Executive Assistant **Monique Johnson** . . . . . . . . . . . . . (202) 442-5955
General Counsel **Phillip Husband** . . . . . . . . . . . . . . . . . (202) 442-5970
  E-mail: phillip.husband@dc.gov          Fax: (202) 442-4797
Deputy General Counsel **(Vacant)** . . . . . . . . . . . . . . . . . (202) 442-5977
Director of Communications **Marcus Anthony Williams** . . (202) 724-7481
  E-mail: marcus.williams@dc.gov
  Education: Penn State 2007 BA; Georgetown 2010 MPS
Labor Management Liaison **Earl Murphy** . . . . . . . . . . . . . (202) 442-9189

## Center for Policy, Planning and Evaluation

825 North Capitol Street, NE, 2nd Floor, Washington, DC 20002
Tel: (202) 442-5865  Fax: (202) 442-4833

Senior Deputy Director **Fern Johnson-Clarke, PhD** . . . . . . (202) 442-9032
  E-mail: fern.johnson-clarke@dc.gov
  Education: Howard U PhD
Chief of Staff **Terrence Williams** . . . . . . . . . . . . . . . . . (202) 727-7790
State Planning Director **Amha Selassie** . . . . . . . . . . . . . . (202) 442-9355
  E-mail: amha.selassie@dc.gov
State Epidemiologist **Dr. John Davies Coles** . . . . . . . . . . (202) 442-9134
Vital Records Registrar **Terra Abrams** . . . . . . . . . . . . . . (202) 442-9029
                                                        Fax: (202) 442-4848
Vital Records System Coordinator **Sylvia Luna-Lopez** . . . . (202) 442-9298
                                                        Fax: (202) 442-4848
Administrative Officer **Jill Woods** . . . . . . . . . . . . . . . . . (202) 442-9026
  E-mail: jill.woods@dc.gov

## Community Health Administration

899 North Capitol Street NE, Suite 3000, Washington, DC 20002
Tel: (202) 442-5925  Fax: (202) 535-1710

Senior Deputy Director **Ryan Springer** . . . . . . . . . . . . . . (202) 727-8941
                                                        Fax: (202) 535-2397
Deputy Director for Operations **Sajeed Popat** . . . . . . . . . (202) 442-9340
                                                        Fax: (202) 442-4814
Grants Monitor Team Leader **Bryan Cheseman** . . . . . . . . (202) 442-9414
  E-mail: bryan.cheseman@dc.gov          Fax: (202) 442-4796
  Education: Howard U 1987

## Cancer and Chronic Disease Prevention Bureau Chief

899 North Capitol Street, NE, Washington, DC 20002
Tel: (202) 442-9170

Bureau Chief **Jason R. Brown** . . . . . . . . . . . . . . . . . . . . (202) 442-5895

## Child, Adolescent and School Health Bureau

Fax: (202) 442-4947
Bureau Chief **Sarah Lee** . . . . . . . . . . . . . . . . . . . . . . . . (202) 442-9338

## Nutrition and Physical Fitness Bureau

899 North Capitol Street NE, Suite 3000, Washington, DC 20002
Tel: (800) 345-1942 (Women, Infants and Children Hotline)
Fax: (202) 645-0497

Bureau Chief **Amelia Peterson-Kosecki** . . . . . . . . . . . . . (202) 442-9397
                                                        Fax: (202) 645-0516

Women, Infants and Children Special Supplemental
  Nutrition Program Director **Christi Dorsey** . . . . . . . . . . (202) 442-9397
                                                        Fax: (202) 535-1710

## Perinatal and Infant Health Bureau

Fax: (202) 698-7028
Bureau Chief **Karen P. Watts** . . . . . . . . . . . . . . . . . . . . . (202) 442-9405
                                                        Fax: (202) 671-0854

## Health Emergency Preparedness and Response Administration [EHMSA]

55 M Street SE, Washington, DC 20003
Fax: (202) 671-0707

Senior Deputy Director **Dr. Brian Amy, MD** . . . . . . . . . . . (202) 671-4222
ALS (Advanced Life Support) Coordinator
  **Sabrina Turner** . . . . . . . . . . . . . . . . . . . . . . . . . . . . (202) 671-4222

## Health Regulation and Licensing Administration [HRLA]

899 North Capitol Street NE, Washington, DC 20002
Tel: (202) 724-4900  Fax: (202) 724-5145  E-mail: hrla@dc.gov

Senior Deputy Director
  **Rikin S. Mehta, JD, PharmD, LLM** . . . . . . . . . . . . . . . (202) 724-8800

## Animal Disease Prevention Division

899 North Capitol Street, NE, Washington, DC 20002 (Administrative Office)
1350 Pennsylvania Avenue NW, Washington, DC 20004

Program Manager **Dr. Vito Del Vento** . . . . . . . . . . . . . . . (202) 535-2323
  E-mail: vito.delvento@dc.gov
Program Specialist **Joy McFarland-Mills** . . . . . . . . . . . . . (202) 442-4932
  E-mail: joy.mcfarland-mills@dc.gov
Investigator **Shakira Richardson** . . . . . . . . . . . . . . . . . . (202) 535-2321
Staff Assistant and Licensing Specialist
  **Lakisha Thompson** . . . . . . . . . . . . . . . . . . . . . . . . . . (202) 535-2323

## Food Safety and Hygiene Inspection Services Division [FSHISD]

899 North Capitol Street, NE, Washington, DC 20002
Tel: (202) 535-2180

Program Manager **Arian Gibson** . . . . . . . . . . . . . . . . . . . (202) 727-9856
Supervisory Sanitarian **Jacqueline Coleman** . . . . . . . . . . (202) 535-2186
Supervisory Sanitarian **Ronnie Taylor** . . . . . . . . . . . . . . (202) 535-2339
Staff Assistant **Lisa Davis** . . . . . . . . . . . . . . . . . . . . . . . (202) 535-2042

## Health Care Facilities Division

899 North Capitol Street NE, Washington, DC 20002
Tel: (202) 724-8800  Fax: (202) 442-9431

Program Manager **Dr. Sharon Lewis** . . . . . . . . . . . . . . . . (202) 442-4737
Supervisory Nurse Consultant **Cassandra Kingsberry** . . . . (202) 727-7487
Supervisory Nurse Consultant **Veronica Longstreth** . . . . . (202) 727-9861
Nurse Consultant **Olubukunola Alao** . . . . . . . . . . . . . . . (202) 724-7799
Nurse Consultant **Vanessa Edwards** . . . . . . . . . . . . . . . (202) 727-3627
Nurse Consultant **Tamara Freeman** . . . . . . . . . . . . . . . . (202) 727-7487
Nurse Consultant **Margaret Lewis** . . . . . . . . . . . . . . . . . (202) 727-5268
Nurse Consultant **Constance Mckoy** . . . . . . . . . . . . . . . (202) 442-9416
Nurse Consultant **Marcia Sampong** . . . . . . . . . . . . . . . . (202) 442-9016
Nurse Consultant **Tracy Spann-Downing** . . . . . . . . . . . . (202) 727-6409
Nurse Consultant **(Vacant)** . . . . . . . . . . . . . . . . . . . . . . (202) 727-6409
Nurse Consultant **(Vacant)** . . . . . . . . . . . . . . . . . . . . . . (202) 727-9859
Inspection and Compliance Specialist **Semret Tesfaye** . . . (202) 727-1740
Health Services Program Specialist **Charlotte Payne** . . . . . (202) 727-7487
Administrative Support Assistant **Carolyn Hammiel** . . . . . . (202) 727-9865

---

## Intermediate Care Facilities Division [ICFD]

899 North Capitol Street, NE, Washington, DC 20002
Tel: (202) 442-4751

Program Manager **Sharon H. Mebane** . . . . . . . . . . . . . . . .(202) 442-4751
  E-mail: sharon.mebane@dc.gov
Supervisory Health Services Program Specialist
  **Laura Hunte** . . . . . . . . . . . . . . . . . . . . . . . . . . . . . .(202) 442-4736
  E-mail: laura.hunte@dc.gov
Health Service Program Coordinator
  **Cynthia "Cindy" McGee** . . . . . . . . . . . . . . . . . . . .(202) 442-4749

## Pharmaceutical Control Division

899 North Capitol Street NE, 6th Floor, Washington, DC 20002
Tel: (202) 724-4900

Executive Director **Patricia D'Antonio** . . . . . . . . . . . . . . . .(202) 727-9856
Pharmacist Inspector **Jawara Kasimu-Graham** . . . . . . . . .(202) 442-5927
Attorney Advisor **Carla Williams** . . . . . . . . . . . . . . . . . .(202) 724-8687
Investigator **Debbie Moss** . . . . . . . . . . . . . . . . . . . . . . . .(202) 724-8809
Licensing Specialist **Karin Barron** . . . . . . . . . . . . . . . . . .(202) 724-8938

## Rodent and Vector Control Division

Program Manager **Gerard Brown** . . . . . . . . . . . . . . . . . . .(202) 535-2636
  E-mail: gerard.brown1@dc.gov

## HIV/AIDS, Hepatitis, STD, and TB Administration [HAHSTA]

899 North Capitol Street NE, Suite 4000, Washington, DC 20002
Fax: (202) 671-4860

Senior Deputy Director **Michael Kharfen** . . . . . . . . . . . . . .(202) 671-4900
  E-mail: michael.kharfen@dc.gov

## Department of Health Care Finance [DHCF]

441 Fourth Street, NW, Suite 900S, Washington, DC 20001
Tel: (202) 442-5988  Fax: (202) 442-4790

**Employees:** 217  **Fiscal Year:** 2015  **Budget:** $2,764,826,000

Director **Wayne M. Turnage, MPA** . . . . . . . . . . . . . . . . . .(202) 442-5988
  E-mail: wayne.turnage@dc.gov
  Education: North Carolina A&T 1980 BS; Ohio State 1982 MPA
Chief of Staff **Melisa Byrd** . . . . . . . . . . . . . . . . . . . . . . . .(202) 478-5809
Chief Operating Officer **Kenneth Evans** . . . . . . . . . . . . . .(202) 442-8436
Deputy Director of Finance **Sumita Chaudhuri, CPA** . . . . .(202) 478-5925
Medical Director **Dr. Lisa Fitzpatrick, MD** . . . . . . . . . . . .(202) 442-9077
Senior Deputy Director/Medicaid Director
  **Claudia Schlosberg** . . . . . . . . . . . . . . . . . . . . . . . . .(202) 442-9075
  Education: Union Col (NY) 1976 BA; Antioch Law 1981 JD
Agency Fiscal Officer **Darrin Shaffer** . . . . . . . . . . . . . . . .(202) 442-9079
Children Health Services Director **Colleen Sonosky** . . . . . .(202) 442-5913
Health Care Delivery Management Administration
  Director **Lisa Truitt** . . . . . . . . . . . . . . . . . . . . . . . . . .(202) 442-9109
  E-mail: lisa.triutt@dc.gov
Health Care Operations Administration Director
  **Donald Shearer** . . . . . . . . . . . . . . . . . . . . . . . . . . . .(202) 698-2007
                              Fax: (202) 610-3209
Long Term Care Administration Director **Ieisha Gray** . . . . .(202) 442-5818
  E-mail: ieisha.gray@dc.gov
Clinician, Pharmacy and Acute Provider Service Program
  Manager **Cavella Bishop** . . . . . . . . . . . . . . . . . . . . . .(202) 724-8936
  E-mail: cavella.bishop@dc.gov
Healthcare Operations Administration Program Manager
  **Laurie Rowe** . . . . . . . . . . . . . . . . . . . . . . . . . . . . . . .(202) 698-2044
State Children's Health Insurance Program (SCHIP)
  Coordinator **Colleen Sonosky** . . . . . . . . . . . . . . . . . .(202) 442-5913
Health Care Policy and Research Administration Director
  **Alice M. Weiss** . . . . . . . . . . . . . . . . . . . . . . . . . . . . .(202) 442-9107
  Education: Haverford 1991 AB; Northeastern 1997 JD
Chief Information Officer **David Sidransky** . . . . . . . . . . . .(202) 478-1375
General Counsel **Sheryl Johnson** . . . . . . . . . . . . . . . . . . .(202) 442-5976
Health Care Ombudsman **Maude Holt** . . . . . . . . . . . . . . .(202) 299-2114
  E-mail: maude.holt@dc.gov

## Department of Youth Rehabilitation Services [DYRS]

450 H Street NW, Washington, DC 20001
Tel: (202) 299-5362  Fax: (202) 299-5608  E-mail: dyrs@dc.gov

**Employees:** 558  **Fiscal Year:** 2015  **Budget:** $96,002,000

Director **Clinton Lacey** . . . . . . . . . . . . . . . . . . . . . . . . . . .(202) 299-5362
  E-mail: clinton.lacey@dc.gov
  Education: CCNY BA
Senior Deputy Director **Linda Harllee Harper** . . . . . . . . . .(202) 299-5362
Deputy Director for Secure Programs **Willie Fullilove** . . . . .(202) 299-5362
Deputy Director for Youth and Family Services
  **Garine Dalce** . . . . . . . . . . . . . . . . . . . . . . . . . . . . . .(202) 299-5362
Chief of Staff **(Vacant)** . . . . . . . . . . . . . . . . . . . . . . . . . .(202) 299-5362
Chief Administrative Officer **Hugo Tovar** . . . . . . . . . . . . .(202) 299-5362
  E-mail: hugo.tovar@dc.gov
Freedom of Information Act (FOIA) Officer **(Vacant)** . . . . .(202) 299-5362
  1000 Mount Olivet Road, NE, Washington, DC 20002
General Counsel (Acting) **Lindsey Appiah** . . . . . . . . . . . . .(202) 299-5362
Human Resources Director **Timothy Howell** . . . . . . . . . . .(202) 299-5362

## Office on Aging [DCOA]

500 K Street NE, Washington, DC 20002
Tel: (202) 727-6603  Fax: (202) 724-4979  E-mail: dcoa@dc.gov
Internet: www.dcoa.dc.gov

Executive Director (Acting) **Laura Newland** . . . . . . . . . . . .(202) 724-4382
  E-mail: laura.newland@dc.gov
  Education: Kalamazoo BA; Georgetown JD
Chief of Staff **Garret King** . . . . . . . . . . . . . . . . . . . . . . . . .(202) 727-8365
  Resource Allocation Officer **Eden Teklebrhane** . . . . . . .(202) 727-8372
Aging and Disability Division Manager and Executive
  Team Lead **Sara Tribe** . . . . . . . . . . . . . . . . . . . . . . . .(202) 535-1444
  Education: Colgate Darden 2001; Boston U 2007
Budget Analyst **Berthell Epes** . . . . . . . . . . . . . . . . . . . . . .(202) 724-5622
Budget Analyst **Nkwenti Sanga** . . . . . . . . . . . . . . . . . . . .(202) 727-6602
Communications Director **Darrell Jackson, Jr.** . . . . . . . . . .(202) 727-5622
  E-mail: darrell.jacksonjr@dc.gov
Community Relations Officer
  **Krystal Branton, MEd, MSW** . . . . . . . . . . . . . . . . . .(202) 727-8370
Customer and Information Services Specialist
  **Darlene Nowlin** . . . . . . . . . . . . . . . . . . . . . . . . . . . . .(202) 727-8364
Employment Specialist **Maria Anderson** . . . . . . . . . . . . . .(202) 727-0374
  E-mail: maria.anderson@dc.gov

## Office of Disability Rights

441 4th Street NW, Suite 729 North, Washington, DC 20001
Tel: (202) 724-5055

Director **Alexis P. Taylor** . . . . . . . . . . . . . . . . . . . . . . . . . .(202) 727-8005
  E-mail: alexis.taylor@dc.gov
  Education: Georgetown BSNE, JD; DePaul LLM
Attorney Advisor **Jessica Hunt** . . . . . . . . . . . . . . . . . . . . .(202) 727-0287

## Office of the Deputy Mayor for Planning and Economic Development [DMPED]

John A. Wilson Building, 1350 Pennsylvania Avenue, NW, Suite 317,
Washington, DC 20004
Tel: (202) 727-6365  Fax: (202) 727-6703  E-mail: dmped.eom@dc.gov

**Employees:** 80  **Fiscal Year:** 2015  **Budget:** $34,469,000

Deputy Mayor **Brian T. Kenner** . . . . . . . . . . . . . . . . . . . . .(202) 727-6365
  E-mail: brian.kenner@dc.gov
  Education: Iowa; Harvard MPP
Chief of Staff **Andrew Trueblood** . . . . . . . . . . . . . . . . . . .(202) 727-6365
Senior Advisor for Housing **(Vacant)** . . . . . . . . . . . . . . . . .(202) 727-6365
Director of Business Development and Strategy
  **Karima Woods** . . . . . . . . . . . . . . . . . . . . . . . . . . . . .(202) 727-6365
Director of Communications **Joaquin McPeek** . . . . . . . . . .(202) 727-6365
  E-mail: joaquin.mcpeek@dc.gov
  Education: Cal State (Sacramento)
Director of Contracts, Procurement, and Grant
  **Jacque McDonald** . . . . . . . . . . . . . . . . . . . . . . . . . . .(202) 727-6365

---

★ Elected Official  ■ Appointed by Governor  ● Appointed by Legislature  ▲ Appointed by Board or Commission  ◆ Appointed by State Supreme Court

Summer 2016         © Leadership Directories, Inc.         *State Yellow Book*

Deputy Chief of Staff and Director of Interagency Affairs
**Timothy White** . . . . . . . . . . . . . . . . . . . . . . . . . (202) 727-6365
Director of Operations **Sheila Cuthrell** . . . . . . . . . . . . . (202) 727-6365
Director of Real Estate **Sarosh Olpadwala** . . . . . . . . . . . (202) 727-6365
Executive Director of the Workforce Investment Council
**Odie Donald II** . . . . . . . . . . . . . . . . . . . . . . . . . (202) 727-6365
  Education: Georgia State BA, MBA
General Counsel **Susan Longstreet** . . . . . . . . . . . . . (202) 741-5085
  E-mail: susan.longstreet@dc.gov
Office Manager **David Howard** . . . . . . . . . . . . . . . . . (202) 727-6365
  Education: Florida 1977 BA

## Department of Consumer and Regulatory Affairs [DCRA]

1100 4th Street SW, Washington, DC 20024
Tel: (202) 442-4000  Fax: (202) 442-9445  Internet: http://dcra.dc.gov

**Employees:** 268

Director **Melinda M. Bolling** . . . . . . . . . . . . . . . . . . (202) 442-4000
  Education: Georgia Tech; Columbus Law JD
Chief Building Official **Jatinder Singh Khokhar** . . . . . . . (202) 442-8937
  Education: Punjab U (India) BSEE
  Staff Assistant **Kandice Taylor** . . . . . . . . . . . . . . (202) 442-8947
Support Service Deputy Director **Gilbert Davidson** . . . . . . (202) 442-8943
Integrity Officer **Tanya Williams** . . . . . . . . . . . . . . . (202) 442-8930
Chief of Staff **Lori Parris** . . . . . . . . . . . . . . . . . . . (202) 442-8947
  Education: Suffolk JD

## Office of the General Counsel

941 North Capitol Street, NE, Washington, DC 20002
Fax: (202) 442-9447

General Counsel **Charles Thomas** . . . . . . . . . . . . . . . (202) 442-8460
Deputy General Counsel **(Vacant)** . . . . . . . . . . . . . . (202) 442-8460

## Controller's Office

Fax: (202) 442-9444

Agency Fiscal Officer **Rebecca Berry** . . . . . . . . . . . . . (202) 442-8682

## Information Systems Office

Fax: (202) 442-8367

Director **Kevin Edwards** . . . . . . . . . . . . . . . . . . . . (202) 442-8340
  E-mail: kevin.edwards@dc.gov
  Education: Virginia BS; Georgia Tech MS

## Permit Operations Division

Fax: (202) 442-4863

Division Chief **Gary Englebert** . . . . . . . . . . . . . . . . . (202) 442-4533
Zoning Division Administrator **Matthew LeGrant** . . . . . . . (202) 442-4674
  E-mail: matthew.legrant@dc.gov

## Business and Professional Licensing Administration

Fax: (202) 442-4258

Administrator **Harriett Broadie** . . . . . . . . . . . . . . . . (202) 442-4311
Special Events & Vending Program Manager
**Vincent Parker II** . . . . . . . . . . . . . . . . . . . . . . (202) 535-2973
  E-mail: vincent.parker@dc.gov

## Department of Energy and the Environment [DOEE]

1200 First Street, NE, 5th Floor, Washington, DC 20002
Tel: (202) 535-2600  Fax: (202) 535-2881  E-mail: doee@dc.gov

**Employees:** 249

Director **Tommy Wells** . . . . . . . . . . . . . . . . . . . . . (202) 478-1417
  E-mail: tommy.wells@dc.gov
  Education: Alabama 1979 BA; Minnesota 1983 MA;
  Columbus Law 1991 JD
Chief of Staff **Adrianna Hochberg** . . . . . . . . . . . . . . (202) 478-1417
Administrative Services Deputy Director **Michelle Dee** . . . . (202) 481-3839
Energy Administration Deputy Director
**Teresa Lawrence** . . . . . . . . . . . . . . . . . . . . . . (202) 299-3339

Environmental Services Deputy Director
**Richard Jackson** . . . . . . . . . . . . . . . . . . . . . . (202) 673-6710
Energy Affordability Program Chief **Teresa Lawrence** . . . . (202) 442-4177
Natural Resources Deputy Director **Hamid Karimi** . . . . . . (202) 535-2600
Youth Conservation Program Coordinator
**Johnnie Philson** . . . . . . . . . . . . . . . . . . . . . . (202) 673-6700
Enforcement and Environmental Justice Chief
**Steve Kelton** . . . . . . . . . . . . . . . . . . . . . . . . (202) 673-6736
  E-mail: steve.kelton@dc.gov
Policy and Sustainable Solutions Chief (Interim)
**William Updike** . . . . . . . . . . . . . . . . . . . . . . . (202) 671-3307
Associate Director and Supervisory Environmental
  Protection Specialist **(Vacant)** . . . . . . . . . . . . . (202) 654-6017
Chief and Supervisory Environmental Protection
  Specialist **Mary Begin** . . . . . . . . . . . . . . . . . . (202) 535-2289
Supervisory Biologist and Supervisory Environmental
  Specialist **Bryan King** . . . . . . . . . . . . . . . . . . (202) 535-2260
Supervisory Public Affairs Specialist (Acting)
**Robin Graham** . . . . . . . . . . . . . . . . . . . . . . . (202) 535-2511
  E-mail: robin.graham@dc.gov
Chief Information Officer **Brian Robinson** . . . . . . . . . . (202) 535-1993
  E-mail: brian.robinson@dc.gov
Public Information Officer **Julia Christian** . . . . . . . . . . (202) 741-0842

## Department of Housing and Community Development [DHCD]

Anacostia Gateway Government Center,
1800 Martin Luther King Jr. Avenue, SE, Washington, DC 20020
Tel: (202) 442-7200  Fax: (202) 442-7078  Internet: www.dhcd.dc.gov

**Employees:** 152  **Fiscal Year:** 2015  **Budget:** $128,707,000

Director **Polly Donaldson** . . . . . . . . . . . . . . . . . . . (202) 442-7200
  E-mail: polly.donaldson@dc.gov
Chief of Staff **Allison Ladd** . . . . . . . . . . . . . . . . . . (202) 442-7230
Chief Administrative Officer **(Vacant)** . . . . . . . . . . . . (202) 442-7200
Chief Program Officer **Vonda J. Orders** . . . . . . . . . . . (202) 442-7200
  Education: Maryland 1996 BA, 2002 JD
Administrative Services Support Manager
**Laverne E. Law** . . . . . . . . . . . . . . . . . . . . . . . (202) 442-7170
  E-mail: laverne.law@dc.gov
Agency Fiscal Officer **Douglas A. Kemp** . . . . . . . . . . . (202) 442-7200
  Education: Adrian BA
Director of Communications and Community Outreach
**(Vacant)** . . . . . . . . . . . . . . . . . . . . . . . . . . . (202) 442-7253
General Counsel **(Vacant)** . . . . . . . . . . . . . . . . . . (202) 442-7220

## Development Finance Division

Fax: (202) 442-7079

Deputy Director **Oke Anyaegbunam** . . . . . . . . . . . . . (202) 442-7280

## Housing Regulation Administration

Fax: (202) 727-8852

Administrator (Interim) **Keith A. Anderson** . . . . . . . . . . (202) 442-7200
  E-mail: keith.anderson@dc.gov

## Rental Housing Commission

441 4th Street NW, Suite 1140B North, Washington, DC 20001
Fax: (202) 442-9446

Chair **Peter Szagedy-Maszak** . . . . . . . . . . . . . . . . . (202) 442-8949
Commissioner **Claudia McKoin** . . . . . . . . . . . . . . . . (202) 442-8949
Commissioner **(Vacant)** . . . . . . . . . . . . . . . . . . . . (202) 442-8949

## Residential and Community Services

Fax: (202) 442-7090

Residential and Community Services Deputy Director
**(Vacant)** . . . . . . . . . . . . . . . . . . . . . . . . . . . (202) 442-7290
Home Purchase Assistant Program Chief
**Janice Blassingame** . . . . . . . . . . . . . . . . . . . . (202) 442-7290
  E-mail: janice.blassingame@dc.gov
Information Technology Officer **Rene Snowden** . . . . . . . (202) 442-7290
  E-mail: rene.snowden@dc.gov

★ Elected Official    ■ Appointed by Governor    ● Appointed by Legislature    ▲ Appointed by Board or Commission    ◆ Appointed by State Supreme Court

*State Yellow Book*    © Leadership Directories, Inc.    Summer 2016

## Department of Insurance, Securities and Banking [DISB]

810 First Street, NE, Suite 701, Washington, DC 20002
Tel: (202) 727-8000  Fax: (202) 535-1207  E-mail: disb@dc.gov

**Employees:** 138  **Fiscal Year:** 2015  **Budget:** $18,531,000

Commissioner **Stephen C. Taylor** . . . . . . . . . . . . . . . . . . . . . (202) 442-7760
  Education: Fordham 1989 BS; Georgetown 1992 JD, 1996 LLM
Deputy Commissioner (Acting) **Dana Sheppard** . . . . . . . . (202) 442-7820
  E-mail: dana.sheppard@dc.gov
  Education: Texas 1991 JD; Georgetown 2004 LLM
Banking Associate Commissioner **Christopher Weaver** . . . (202) 442-7774
  E-mail: christopher.weaver@dc.gov
Chief of Administration and Policy **Katrice Purdie** . . . . . . . (202) 442-7773
  E-mail: katrice.purdie@dc.gov
Enforcement and Consumer Protection Division Associate
  Commissioner (Acting) **Greg Marsillo** . . . . . . . . . . . . . . . (202) 442-7109
Insurance Bureau Associate Commissioner
  **Philip Barlow, FSA, MAAA** . . . . . . . . . . . . . . . . . . . . . . (202) 442-7823
  E-mail: philip.barlow@dc.gov
  Education: Georgia State 1993 BBA
Risk Finance Bureau Associate Commissioner
  **Dana Sheppard** . . . . . . . . . . . . . . . . . . . . . . . . . . . . . . . (202) 442-7820
  E-mail: dana.sheppard@dc.gov
Securities Bureau Associate Commissioner
  **Theodore A. Miles** . . . . . . . . . . . . . . . . . . . . . . . . . . . . (202) 442-7800
  Education: Harvard 1959 BA; Howard U 1963 LLB
Agency Fiscal Officer **Bright A. Ahaiwe, CPA** . . . . . . . . . (202) 442-7822
  Education: Tennessee 1979 BS; Howard U 1982 MBA
Communications Director **Kathryn "Kate" Hartig** . . . . . . . (202) 442-7753
  E-mail: kathryn.hartig@dc.gov
General Counsel (Acting) **J. Carl Wilson** . . . . . . . . . . . . . . (202) 442-7758
  E-mail: carl.wilson@dc.gov

## District Department of Transportation [DDOT]

55 M Street SE, Suite 400, Washington, DC 20003
Tel: (202) 673-6813  TTY: (202) 673-6813  Fax: (202) 671-0127
Internet: www.ddot.dc.gov

**Employees:** 544  **Fiscal Year:** 2015  **Budget:** $91,506,000

Director **Leif A. Dormsjo** . . . . . . . . . . . . . . . . . . . . . . . . . . (202) 671-4097
  E-mail: leif.dormsjo@dc.gov
Deputy Director **Greer Johnson Gillis, PE** . . . . . . . . . . . . . (202) 671-4691
  Education: Georgia Tech BSCE, MSCE
Chief of Staff **Adrea Turner** . . . . . . . . . . . . . . . . . . . . . . . . (202) 673-6813
  E-mail: adrea.turner@dc.gov
  Education: Col Charleston BS, MPA
  Deputy Chief of Staff **(Vacant)** . . . . . . . . . . . . . . . . . . . . (202) 673-6813
General Counsel **Frank Seales, Jr.** . . . . . . . . . . . . . . . . . . . (202) 673-6813
  Education: Tennessee State BS; Indiana JD
Associate Director of Administrative Services **(Vacant)** . . . . (202) 673-6813
Associate Director of Policy, Planning and Sustainability
  Administration **Sam D. Zimbabwe** . . . . . . . . . . . . . . . . . (202) 673-6813
Associate Director of Public Space Regulation
  Administration **Matthew Marcou** . . . . . . . . . . . . . . . . . (202) 359-6497
  2217 14th Street, NW, Washington, DC 20009
Associate Director of Transportation Operations
  Administration **Suzette Robinson** . . . . . . . . . . . . . . . . . (202) 671-1366
Associate Director of Urban Forestry **(Vacant)** . . . . . . . . . . (202) 671-1490
  2217 14th Street, NW, Washington, DC 20009
Chief Administrative Officer **Dorinda R. Floyd** . . . . . . . . . . (202) 673-6813
Chief Engineer **(Vacant)** . . . . . . . . . . . . . . . . . . . . . . . . . . . (202) 673-6813
Chief Information Officer **José Colón** . . . . . . . . . . . . . . . . . (202) 741-8913
Chief Operations Officer **(Vacant)** . . . . . . . . . . . . . . . . . . . (202) 673-6813
Chief Performance Officer **John P. Thomas** . . . . . . . . . . . . (202) 673-6813
Public Information Officer **Terry Owens** . . . . . . . . . . . . . . . (202) 671-5124
  E-mail: terry.owens@dc.gov
  Education: Michigan State

## Taxicab Commission [DCTC]

2235 Shannon Place SE, Suite 3001, Washington, DC 20020
Tel: (202) 645-6018 (Driver Service)
Tel: (202) 645-6012 (Office of Taxicabs)  Fax: (202) 645-3555
Fax: (202) 889-3604  E-mail: dctc@dc.gov

Chairperson **Ernest Chrappah** . . . . . . . . . . . . . . . . . . . . . . (202) 645-6005
  E-mail: ernest.chrappah@dc.gov
  Education: Maryland MBA
Commissioner **Elliott Ferguson** . . . . . . . . . . . . . . . . . . . . . (202) 645-6018
Commissioner **Linwood Jolly** . . . . . . . . . . . . . . . . . . . . . . . (202) 645-6018
  E-mail: dctc.com6@dc.gov
Commissioner **Anthony Muhammed** . . . . . . . . . . . . . . . . . (202) 645-6018
Commissioner **Betty Smalls** . . . . . . . . . . . . . . . . . . . . . . . . (202) 645-6018
Commissioner **Stanley Tapscott** . . . . . . . . . . . . . . . . . . . . (202) 645-6018
Commissioner **Dotti L. Wade** . . . . . . . . . . . . . . . . . . . . . . . (202) 645-6018
Commissioner **Jon M. Zeitler** . . . . . . . . . . . . . . . . . . . . . . . (202) 645-6018
  Term Expires: May 4, 2019

### Administration
Chief Administrative Officer **(Vacant)** . . . . . . . . . . . . . . . . . (202) 645-6003
Mediation Officer **David Person** . . . . . . . . . . . . . . . . . . . . . (202) 542-6008

### Enforcement Division
Licensing and Enforcement Official **Dennis J. Starks** . . . . . (202) 645-0111
Assistant Supervisory Vehicle Enforcement Inspector
  **Mia Bowden** . . . . . . . . . . . . . . . . . . . . . . . . . . . . . . . . . (202) 645-6018
Assistant Supervisory Vehicle Enforcement Inspector
  **Carl Martin** . . . . . . . . . . . . . . . . . . . . . . . . . . . . . . . . . (202) 645-6018
Lead Public Vehicle Enforcement Inspector
  **Timothy Evans** . . . . . . . . . . . . . . . . . . . . . . . . . . . . . . (202) 645-6018
Public Vehicle Enforcement Inspector **Kalvin Bears** . . . . . . (202) 645-6018
Public Vehicle Enforcement Inspector **Adrea Benson** . . . . . (202) 645-6018
Public Vehicle Enforcement Inspector **Michael Conrad** . . . . (202) 645-6018
Public Vehicle Enforcement Inspector **Jonice Earle** . . . . . . (202) 645-6018
Public Vehicle Enforcement Inspector **Marques Hugins** . . . (202) 645-6018
Public Vehicle Enforcement Inspector **James Lane** . . . . . . . (202) 645-6018
Public Vehicle Enforcement Inspector **Thomas Lea** . . . . . . . (202) 645-6018
Public Vehicle Enforcement Inspector **Eilma McKennon** . . . (202) 645-6018
Public Vehicle Enforcement Specialist **Clarissa Edwards** . . (202) 645-6018

### Licensing Division
Senior Hearing Examiner **Roxanne D. Neloms** . . . . . . . . . . (202) 645-6013
  Education: Texas Southern 2001 JD
Manager Client Services **Linda A. Roberts** . . . . . . . . . . . . . (202) 645-6008
Procurement Analyst **Renee Hevor** . . . . . . . . . . . . . . . . . . (202) 645-6008
Program Support Specialist **Tiara Baber** . . . . . . . . . . . . . . . (202) 645-4092
Program Analyst **Sherry Tillman** . . . . . . . . . . . . . . . . . . . . (202) 645-6009
Staff Assistant **Wanda T. Goodwin** . . . . . . . . . . . . . . . . . . (202) 645-6012

## Office of the Deputy Mayor for Public Safety and Justice

Tel: (202) 724-7173

**Employees:** 21  **Fiscal Year:** 2015  **Budget:** $26,302,000

Deputy Mayor **Kevin Donahue** . . . . . . . . . . . . . . . . . . . . . . (202) 724-7173

## Fire and Emergency Medical Services Department [FEMS]

1923 Vermont Avenue, NW, Suite 201 South, Washington, DC 20001
Tel: (202) 673-3320  Fax: (202) 462-0807

**Employees:** 2,028

Chief **Gregory M. Dean** . . . . . . . . . . . . . . . . . . . . . . . . . . . (202) 673-3320
  E-mail: gregory.dean@dc.gov
  Education: U Phoenix BA
Assistant Chief of Emergency Medical Services
  **Edward R. Mills III** . . . . . . . . . . . . . . . . . . . . . . . . . . . . (202) 673-3320
Assistant Fire Chief of Services **David Foust** . . . . . . . . . . . (202) 673-3320
Chief Communications Officer **Doug Buchanan** . . . . . . . . . (202) 673-3320
  Education: Temple BAJ
Public Information Officer **Tim Wilson** . . . . . . . . . . . . . . . . (202) 673-3331
  E-mail: tim.wilson@dc.gov

---

★ Elected Official    ■ Appointed by Governor    ● Appointed by Legislature    ▲ Appointed by Board or Commission    ◆ Appointed by State Supreme Court

EXECUTIVE BRANCH

## Office of the Medical Director

Fax: (202) 462-0807

Medical Director **(Vacant)** .......................... (202) 673-3320

## Fire Prevention Division

1100 Fourth Street, SW, E-700, Washington, DC 20024
Tel: (202) 727-1614  Fax: (202) 727-3238

Fire Marshal **Mark Wynn** .......................... (202) 727-1600

## Homeland Security and Emergency Management Agency [HSEMA]

2720 Martin Luther King Jr. Avenue, SE, Washington, DC 20032
Tel: (202) 727-6161  TTY: (202) 730-0488  Fax: (202) 715-7288
E-mail: ema@dc.gov

**Employees:** 87  **Fiscal Year:** 2015  **Budget:** $74,994,000

Director **Christopher T. Geldart** ..................... (202) 727-6161
  E-mail: christopher.geldart@dc.gov
  Education: Maryland BA
Chief of Staff **Brian Baker** ......................... (202) 727-6161
Public Information Officer **Nicole Chapple** ........... (202) 727-6161
  E-mail: nicole.chapple@dc.gov
Emergency Operations Division Chief **Timothy Spriggs** .. (202) 727-6161
Emergency Operations Deputy Chief **Fred Goldsmith** .... (202) 727-6161
Exercise and Training Division Chief **Patrice White** ..... (202) 727-6161
Finance Division Chief **Johnny Greene** ............... (202) 727-6161
Telecommunications and COMSEC Chief
  **William "Bill" Curry** ............................ (202) 727-6161

## Office of the Chief Technology Officer [OCTO]

200 I Street SE, 5th Floor, Washington, DC 20003
Tel: (202) 727-2277  TTY: (202) 727-8673  Fax: (202) 727-6857
E-mail: octo@dc.gov

**Employees:** 283  **Fiscal Year:** 2015  **Budget:** $101,770,000

Chief Technology Officer **Archana Vemulapalli** ........ (202) 727-2277
  Education: Madras (India); Pennsylvania; Georgetown
Chief Data Officer **Dervel Reed** ..................... (202) 727-2277
  E-mail: dervel.reed@dc.gov
Chief of Staff (Interim) **Carol Washington** ........... (202) 727-2277
Geographic Information Systems Director (Acting)
  **Julie Kanzler** ................................... (202) 727-9307
  E-mail: julie.kanzler@dc.gov
Technology Innovation Director **(Vacant)** ............. (202) 727-2277
General Counsel **Christina Fleps** .................... (202) 727-0619
Infrastructure Services Deputy Chief Technology Officer
  **Lance Schine** ................................... (202) 727-2277
  E-mail: lance.schine@dc.gov
PMO Deputy Chief Technology Officer **David Bishop** .... (202) 727-2277
  E-mail: david.bishop@dc.gov
Communications Director **Michael Rupert** ............. (202) 724-5178
  E-mail: michael.rupert@dc.gov

## Office of Contracting and Procurement [OCP]

One Judiciary Square, 441 Fourth Street, NW, Suite 700 South,
Washington, DC 20001
Tel: (202) 727-0252  Fax: (202) 727-3229  E-mail: ocp@dc.gov
Internet: www.ocp.dc.gov

Chief Procurement Officer **George A. Schutter** ........ (202) 724-4242
  E-mail: george.schutter@dc.gov
  Education: Illinois Tech BSAcc; Naval Postgrad MS
Executive Assistant **Kimberly Diggs** ................. (202) 724-5262
Chief of Staff **Gina Toppin** ........................ (202) 724-4089
Assistant Director for Procurement **Sheila Mobley** ...... (202) 724-4388
Compliance and Integrity Officer **(Vacant)** ............ (202) 727-2095
General Counsel **Nancy K. Hapeman** ................. (202) 724-4391
Public Information Officer **Lauren Stephens** ........... (202) 724-4982
  E-mail: lauren.stephens@dc.gov
Chief Information Officer **(Vacant)** .................. (202) 724-4250

Chief Learning Officer **Michael "Mike" Wooten** ........ (202) 727-5557
Human Resources Officer **(Vacant)** .................. (202) 724-4365
Strategic Development and Analysis Officer **(Vacant)** ..... (202) 299-3951
Business Operations Manager **(Vacant)** ............... (202) 724-8759

## Office of Unified Communications [OUC]

2720 Martin Luther King Jr. Avenue, SE, Washington, DC 20032
Tel: (202) 730-0524  Fax: (202) 730-0504  E-mail: director.ouc@dc.gov
Internet: www.ouc.dc.gov

Director **Karima Holmes** .......................... (202) 730-0503
  E-mail: karima.holmes@dc.gov
  Education: Augusta State BA

## Department of Corrections [DOC]

Reese Building, 20009 14th Street NW, 7th Floor, Washington, DC 20001
Tel: (202) 673-7316  Fax: (202) 332-1470  Internet: http://doc.dc.gov

**Employees:** 863

Director **Thomas N. Faust** ......................... (202) 673-7316
  E-mail: thomas.faust@dc.gov
  Education: Virginia Tech 1976 BS; George Mason 1989 MPA
Executive Assistant **Sallie Thomas** .................. (202) 671-2314
Management Support Deputy Director **Quincy Booth** ..... (202) 671-2053
  E-mail: quincy.booth@dc.gov
Operations Deputy Director **Toni Perry** ............... (202) 671-2044
  Warden **William J. Smith** ......................... (202) 673-7316
General Counsel **Maria Amato** ...................... (202) 671-2042
  E-mail: maria.amato@dc.gov
Government and Public Affairs Coordinator **Sylvia Lane** .. (202) 671-2137
  E-mail: sylvia.lane@dc.gov
Case Management Services Administrator
  **Teresa Washington** .............................. (202) 698-4924
  E-mail: teresa.washington@dc.gov
Community Corrections Administrator
  **James F. Murphy, Sr.** ............................ (202) 671-2099
  E-mail: james.murphy2@dc.gov
Health Services Administrator
  **Beth Jordan Mynett, MD** ......................... (202) 698-6955
  E-mail: beth.mynett@dc.gov
  Education: Arizona MD
Management Information and Technology Administrator
  **Baron Hsu** ..................................... (202) 698-4899
Training Administrator **Ricardo Gradillas** ............. (202) 671-2565
  E-mail: ricardo.gradillas@dc.gov
Facilities Management Manager **(Vacant)** .............. (202) 673-8114
Internal Affairs Supervisor **Wanda Patten** ............. (202) 727-2700
Agency Chief Contracting Officer **Benjamin Collins** ...... (202) 727-2700
  E-mail: ben.collins@dc.gov
Chief Financial Officer **Antoinnette Hudson-Beckham** ... (202) 671-3030
Human Resource Management Chief **Desiree Townes** .... (202) 671-2131

## Department of General Services [DGS]

2000 14th Street, NW, 8th Floor, Washington, DC 20009
Tel: (202) 727-2800  Fax: (202) 727-9877

**Employees:** 651  **Fiscal Year:** 2015  **Budget:** $423,275,000

Director **RADM Christopher E. Weaver, USN (Ret)** ..... (202) 727-2800
  Education: Naval Acad 1971 BS; George Washington 1993 MPA
Chief of Staff **Latrina Owens** ...................... (202) 727-4400
  E-mail: latrina.owens@dc.gov
Chief Financial Officer **Massimo Marchiori** ........... (202) 727-2800
General Counsel **Camille Sabbakhan** ................. (202) 724-4170
  Education: Virginia BS; Richmond JD; VCU MURP

## Office of the Chief Operating Officer

Chief Operating Officer **Jonathan M. Kayne** ........... (202) 724-4400
  Education: Hartford BS; Johns Hopkins MS

## Capital Division

Deputy Director **Jeffrey Bonvechio** .................. (202) 724-4400

## Contracting and Procurement Division

Associate Director **Yinka Alao** ...................... (202) 724-4400

---

★ Elected Official  ■ Appointed by Governor  ● Appointed by Legislature  ▲ Appointed by Board or Commission  ◆ Appointed by State Supreme Court

### Facilities Division
Deputy Director **Spencer Davis** ........................ (202) 671-0588

### Portfolio Management Division
Associate Director **J. Forest Hayes** .................... (202) 724-4400

### Protective Services Division
Associate Director **Anthony W. Fortune** ............... (202) 698-8101

### Sustainability and Energy Division
Associate Director **Mark Chambers** ................... (202) 727-2800

## Department of Human Resources [DCHR]
One Judiciary Square, 441 Fourth Street, NW, Suite 330S,
Washington, DC 20001
Tel: (202) 442-9700  Fax: (202) 727-6827  Internet: www.dchr.dc.gov

**Employees:** 133  **Fiscal Year:** 2015  **Budget:** $15,973,000

Director **Ventris Cassandra Gibson** ................... (202) 442-9700
  Education: Maryland University Col
Deputy Director **(Vacant)** ............................ (202) 442-9700
Associate Director for Policy and Compliance
  **Justin Zimmerman** ................................. (202) 442-9700
Administrative Officer **Laverne Harvey** ............... (202) 442-9641
  E-mail: laverne.harvey-johnson@dc.gov
Benefits and Retirement Group Associate Director
  **Candice Ahwah-Gonzalez** .......................... (202) 442-9611
Learning and Development Associate Director (Interim)
  **Nicole Cook** ...................................... (202) 442-9654

## Department of Public Works [DPW]
2000 14th Street, NW, 6th Floor, Washington, DC 20009
Tel: (202) 673-6833  TTY: (202) 673-6833  Fax: (202) 671-0642
E-mail: dpw@dc.gov

**Employees:** 1,417  **Fiscal Year:** 2015  **Budget:** $155,141,000

Director (Interim) **Christopher Shorter** .............. (202) 673-6812
  Special Assistant **Viola McIver** ................... (202) 673-6812
Deputy Director **Karla Kirby** ........................ (202) 673-6833
Chief Financial Officer **Perry Fitzpatrick** ........... (202) 671-2300
                                            Fax: (202) 671-0626
Chief Information Officer **(Vacant)** ................. (202) 671-0096
                                            Fax: (202) 671-0637
Fleet Management Administrator **Edward Hamilton** ..... (202) 576-6799
  E-mail: edward.hamilton@dc.gov       Fax: (202) 576-7715
Parking Enforcement Management Administrator
  **Teri Adams** ...................................... (202) 541-6083
  E-mail: teri.doke@dc.gov             Fax: (202) 541-6113
  Education: Hampton; Howard U JD
Solid Waste Management Administrator
  **Jeffrey H. Powell** ................................ (202) 645-7044
  E-mail: jeffrey.powell@dc.gov        Fax: (202) 645-6040
  Education: Virginia State; Howard U MBA
Freedom of Information Act (FOIA) Officer
  **Christine Davis** .................................. (202) 673-2030
                                            Fax: (202) 673-4555
Public Information Officer **Linda Grant** ............. (202) 671-2375
  E-mail: linda.grant@dc.gov

## Office of the District of Columbia Auditor [ODCA]
717 14th Street NW, Washington, DC 20005
Tel: (202) 727-3600  TTY: (202) 855-1000  Fax: (202) 724-8814
E-mail: odca@dc.gov  Internet: www.dcauditor.org

Auditor **Kathleen "Kathy" Patterson** ............... (202) 727-3600
  Education: Northwestern 1970 BS; Georgetown 1990 MA
Deputy Auditor **Lawrence Perry** ..................... (202) 727-3600
Chief of Staff **Stacie Pittell** ..................... (202) 727-3600
General Counsel **Amy Bellanca** ...................... (202) 727-3600

## Office of Zoning [DCOZ]
441 4th Street NW, Suite 200 South, Washington, DC 20001
Tel: (202) 727-6311  Fax: (202) 727-6072  E-mail: dcoz@dc.gov

Director **Sara Bardin** .............................. (202) 727-5372
  Education: Dayton BFA

## Zoning Commission [ZC]
441 Fourth Street, NW, Romm 220 South, Washington, DC 20001
Internet: http://www.dcoz.dc.gov/zc/zc.shtm

Chairman **Anthony J. Hood** .......................... (202) 727-6311
  E-mail: anthony.hood@dc.gov
Vice Chairman **Marcie Cohen** ........................ (202) 727-6311
  E-mail: marcie.cohen@dc.gov
Commissioner **Peter G. May** ......................... (202) 727-6311
  Education: Georgetown BA; Maryland MAR
Commissioner **Robert Miller** ........................ (202) 727-6311
Commissioner **Michael G. Turnbull, FAIA** ............ (202) 727-6311
  Education: Illinois (Chicago) 1973 BArch

## Board of Zoning Adjustment
441 Fourth Street, NW, 220 South, Washington, DC 20001

Chairperson **Marnique Heath** ........................ (202) 727-6311
  Term Expires: September 30, 2016
Vice Chairperson **Anita Butani D'Souza** ............. (202) 727-6311
  Education: Wharton MBA
Member **Frederick L. Hill** .......................... (202) 727-6311
Member **Jeffrey L. Hinkle** .......................... (202) 727-6311

## DC Housing Finance Agency [DCHFA]
815 Florida Avenue, NW, Washington, DC 20001
Tel: (202) 777-1600  Fax: (202) 986-6736  Internet: www.dchfa.org

### Board of Directors
Chair **Buwa Binitie** ................................ (202) 777-1600
  Term Expires: 2017
  Education: NYU BS; Johns Hopkins MS
Vice Chair **Stephen M. Green** ....................... (202) 777-1600
  Term Expires: 2016
Member **Bryan "Scottie" Irving** .................... (202) 777-1600
  Term Expires: 2017
  Education: Central State BS
Member **Stanley Jackson** ............................ (202) 777-1600
  Term Expires: 2016
  Education: Fayetteville State BS; Howard U MBA

### Office of the Executive Director
Executive Director and CEO (Interim) **Todd A. Lee** ... (202) 777-1601
Deputy Executive Director **Fran D. Makle** ........... (202) 777-1636
Associate Executive Director **W. David Watts** ....... (202) 777-1600
Government Affairs Director **Nkosi C. Bradley** ...... (202) 777-1600
Public Relations Manager **Yolanda McCutchen** ........ (202) 777-1600
  E-mail: yolanda.mccutchen@dc.gov
Executive Assistant **Karen Harris** .................. (202) 777-1600

### Office of Administration
Human Resources Officer **Heather A. Hart** ........... (202) 777-1657
Procurement Officer **Jacqueline Reid** ............... (202) 777-1600
Facilities Manager **Marcus Thompson** ................ (202) 777-1600
Receptionist **Connell Young** ........................ (202) 777-1600
  E-mail: cyoung@dchfa.org

### Office of the General Counsel
General Counsel **Maria K. Day-Marshall** ............. (202) 777-1600
Deputy General Counsel **Michael Winter** ............. (202) 777-1600
Records Administrator **Lillian Johnson** ............. (202) 777-1600
  E-mail: ljohnson@dchfa.org
Associate General Counsel **Tracy Parker** ............ (202) 777-1600
Associate General Counsel **Daniel Nunez** ............ (202) 777-1600

---

★ Elected Official   ■ Appointed by Governor   ● Appointed by Legislature   ▲ Appointed by Board or Commission   ◆ Appointed by State Supreme Court

## Office of Public Finance

Director **Anthony L. Waddell** . . . . . . . . . . . . . . . . . . . . . . . (202) 777-1613
  Education: Johns Hopkins MS
Senior Development Officer **(Vacant)** . . . . . . . . . . . . . . . . (202) 777-1600
  Development Officer **Carolyn Fischer** . . . . . . . . . . . . . . . (202) 777-1600
  Development Officer **Martin Lucero** . . . . . . . . . . . . . . . . (202) 777-1600
  Development Analyst **Bobvala Tengen** . . . . . . . . . . . . . (202) 777-1600
Construction Engineer/Monitor **Sue Ghazi** . . . . . . . . . . . (202) 777-1600
Construction Engineer/Monitor **Birol Yilmaz** . . . . . . . . . . (202) 777-1600
Administrative Assistant (Acting) **Pat Thomas** . . . . . . . . (202) 777-1600

## Office of the Chief Financial Officer

Chief Financial Officer **(Vacant)** . . . . . . . . . . . . . . . . . . . . (202) 777-1620
Controller **Tatsiana Kurlovich** . . . . . . . . . . . . . . . . . . . . . . (202) 777-1600
Accounting Clerk **Valencia Anderson** . . . . . . . . . . . . . . . (202) 777-1600
Account Manager **Yong-ki Kim** . . . . . . . . . . . . . . . . . . . . . (202) 777-1600
General Ledger Accountant **Abiy Tamrat** . . . . . . . . . . . . . (202) 777-1600
Payroll Accountant **Gloria San-Gil** . . . . . . . . . . . . . . . . . . (202) 777-1600
Project Budget Analyst **Seyoum Gizaw** . . . . . . . . . . . . . . (202) 777-1600
Project Ledger Accountant **Brooks Harrison** . . . . . . . . . . (202) 777-1600
Financial Analyst Manager **(Vacant)** . . . . . . . . . . . . . . . . (202) 777-1600

## Single Family Programs

Director **Lisa G. Hensley** . . . . . . . . . . . . . . . . . . . . . . . . . . (202) 777-1600
Deputy Director **Bill Milko** . . . . . . . . . . . . . . . . . . . . . . . . . (202) 777-1600
Loan Processor **Chanita Haughton** . . . . . . . . . . . . . . . . . (202) 777-1600
Single Family Program Manager **Deborah Jones** . . . . . . . (202) 777-1600
Administrative Assistant **Sherray Gibson** . . . . . . . . . . . . . (202) 777-1600

## Office of Compliance and Asset Management

Director **Risha Williams** . . . . . . . . . . . . . . . . . . . . . . . . . . (202) 777-1600
Asset Manager **Jeree Turlington** . . . . . . . . . . . . . . . . . . . (202) 777-1600
Asset Manager **Jelani Whitt** . . . . . . . . . . . . . . . . . . . . . . . (202) 777-1600
Loan Servicer **Jackie Langeluttig** . . . . . . . . . . . . . . . . . . . (202) 777-1600
Compliance Coordinator **Fredericka Earle** . . . . . . . . . . . . (202) 777-1600

# Housing Authority [DCHA]

1133 North Capitol Street, NE, Suite 150, Washington, DC 20002-7599
Tel: (202) 535-1015  TTY: (202) 535-1691  Fax: (202) 535-1740
E-mail: dchousing@dchousingauth.org

Executive Director **Adrianne Todman** . . . . . . . . . . . . . . . (202) 535-1513
  E-mail: adrianne.todman@dc.gov
Senior Executive Assistant **Shenetta Haberman-Jones** . . . (202) 216-4466
Information Technology Division Director
  **Richard Congo** . . . . . . . . . . . . . . . . . . . . . . . . . . . . . . . (202) 535-1015
  E-mail: richard.congo@dc.gov
General Counsel **Kenneth S. Slaughter** . . . . . . . . . . . . . . (202) 535-2835
  E-mail: kenneth.slaughter@dc.gov

# District of Columbia Water and Sewer Authority [DC Water]

5000 Overlook Ave., SW, Washington, DC 20032
Tel: (202) 787-2000  Fax: (202) 787-2333  E-mail: info@dcwater.com

Chairman **Matthew Brown** . . . . . . . . . . . . . . . . . . . . . . . . . (202) 787-2330
  Affiliation: Director, Office of Budget and Finance, Office of the City
  Administrator, District of Columbia
  John A. Wilson Building, 1350 Pennsylvania Avenue, NW, Suite 513,
  Washington, DC 20004
Principal Member **Ellen O. Boardman** . . . . . . . . . . . . . . . (202) 787-2330
Principal Member **Rachna Butani** . . . . . . . . . . . . . . . . . . . (202) 787-2330
Principal Member **Elisabeth "Lisa" Feldt** . . . . . . . . . . . . . (202) 787-2330
  Affiliation: Director, Department of Environmental Protection, County
  of Montgomery, Maryland
  255 Rockville Pike, Suite 120, Rockville, MD 20850
  Education: Union Col (NY) 1980 BSCE;
  George Washington 1984 BSCE
Principal Member **Timothy L. Firestine** . . . . . . . . . . . . . . (202) 787-2330
Principal Member **Bradley W. Frome** . . . . . . . . . . . . . . . . (202) 787-2330
  Affiliation: Assistant Deputy Chief Administrative Officer for Economic
  Development and Public Infrastructure, Office of the County Executive,
  County of Prince George's, Maryland
  County Administration Building, 14741 Governor Oden Bowie Drive,
  5th Floor, Upper Marlboro, MD 20772

Principal Member **Nicholas A. Majett** . . . . . . . . . . . . . . . . (202) 787-2330
  Education: Howard U BS, 1985 JD
Principal Member **Obiora Menkiti** . . . . . . . . . . . . . . . . . . (202) 787-2330
Principal Member **James Patteson** . . . . . . . . . . . . . . . . . . (202) 787-2330
  Affiliation: Director, Public Works and Environmental Services
  Department, County of Fairfax, Virginia
  12055 Government Center Parkway, Suite 659, Fairfax, VA 22035-5502
Principal Member **(Vacant)** . . . . . . . . . . . . . . . . . . . . . . . . (202) 787-2330
Principal Member **(Vacant)** . . . . . . . . . . . . . . . . . . . . . . . . (202) 787-2330
Secretary to the Board **Linda R. Manley** . . . . . . . . . . . . . (202) 787-2330

## Management

Chief Executive Officer and General Manager
  **George S. Hawkins, Esq.** . . . . . . . . . . . . . . . . . . . . . . . (202) 787-2609
  E-mail: george.hawkins@dcwater.com
  Education: Princeton 1983 AB; Harvard 1987 JD
Chief of Staff **Mustaafa Dozier** . . . . . . . . . . . . . . . . . . . . (202) 787-2025
Chief Engineer **Leonard R. Benson** . . . . . . . . . . . . . . . . . (202) 787-2609
  E-mail: leonard.benson@dcwater.com
Chief Operating Officer **Biju George, PE** . . . . . . . . . . . . . (202) 787-2000
Engineering and Technical Services Director
  **Liliana Maldonado** . . . . . . . . . . . . . . . . . . . . . . . . . . . . (202) 787-2358
Risk Manager **Tanya L. DeLeon** . . . . . . . . . . . . . . . . . . . . (202) 787-2051
External Affairs Chief **John Lisle** . . . . . . . . . . . . . . . . . . . (202) 787-2616
  E-mail: john.lisle@dcwater.com
Human Capital Management Director
  **Arthur R. "Rick" Green** . . . . . . . . . . . . . . . . . . . . . . . . (202) 787-2213
Customer Service Director **Lauren A. Preston** . . . . . . . . . (202) 354-3700
Consumer Services Assistant General Manager
  **Charles W. Kiely** . . . . . . . . . . . . . . . . . . . . . . . . . . . . . (202) 787-2000
  E-mail: charles.kiely@dcwater.com
Chief Marketing Officer **Alan R. Heymann** . . . . . . . . . . . . (202) 787-2000
Chief Procurement Officer **John Bosley** . . . . . . . . . . . . . . (202) 787-2000
  Education: Maryland; Vermont Law JD
Procurement Director **Dan Bae** . . . . . . . . . . . . . . . . . . . . (202) 787-2025
Chief Financial Officer **Mark T. Kim, JD, PhD** . . . . . . . . . (202) 787-2000
  E-mail: mark.kim@dcwater.com
  Education: Northwestern BA; Cornell JD; Harvard PhD
Controller **John M. Madrid, CPA, MBA** . . . . . . . . . . . . . . . (202) 787-2159
Finance and Budget Director **Gail Alexander-Reeves** . . . . (202) 787-2158
Chief Information Officer **Thomas Kuczynski** . . . . . . . . . . (202) 787-2629
  E-mail: thomas.kuczynski@dcwater.com
  Education: LaSalle Col (Canada) 1983;
  Maryland University Col 2003 MBA
Distribution and Conveyance Systems Director
  **Charles R. "Chuck" Sweeney** . . . . . . . . . . . . . . . . . . . . (202) 354-3700
Facilities Director **Johnnie Walker** . . . . . . . . . . . . . . . . . . (202) 787-2565
Fleet Management Director **Timothy Fitzgerald** . . . . . . . . (202) 264-3803
Infrastructure and Operations Director
  **Joseph M. Edwards** . . . . . . . . . . . . . . . . . . . . . . . . . . . (202) 787-2000
Maintenance Services Director **Anthony Mack** . . . . . . . . . (202) 787-4045
Security Director **Steven P. "Steve" Caldwell** . . . . . . . . . (202) 787-2565
Security Manager **James C. Holloway** . . . . . . . . . . . . . . . (202) 787-7631
Sewer Services Director **Cuthbert A. Braveboy** . . . . . . . . (202) 264-3828
Assistant General Manager, Blue Plains
  **Aklile Tesfaye, PE** . . . . . . . . . . . . . . . . . . . . . . . . . . . . (202) 787-4172
  Education: Maryland MS
Assistant General Manager, Support Services
  **Rosalind R. Inge** . . . . . . . . . . . . . . . . . . . . . . . . . . . . . (202) 787-2609
  E-mail: rosalind.inge@dcwater.com
General Counsel **Henderson J. Brown** . . . . . . . . . . . . . . . (202) 787-2240
  Education: Amherst; Georgetown JD

# Public Service Commission of the District of Columbia [PSC]

1333 H Street, NW, Second Floor West Tower, Washington, DC 20005
Tel: (202) 626-5100  Fax: (202) 626-9174  TTY: (202) 628-2428
Internet: www.dcpsc.org

Chairperson **Betty Ann Kane** . . . . . . . . . . . . . . . . . . . . . . . (202) 626-5125
  Education: Middlebury BA; Yale 1964 MA
  Executive Assistant **Wendy Newkirk** . . . . . . . . . . . . . . . (202) 626-5119
Commissioner **Joanne Doddy Fort** . . . . . . . . . . . . . . . . . . (202) 626-5115
  Education: Bryn Mawr BA

*(continued on next page)*

---

★ Elected Official     ■ Appointed by Governor     ● Appointed by Legislature          ▲ Appointed by Board or Commission     ◆ Appointed by State Supreme Court

# 98
EXECUTIVE BRANCH

**Public Service Commission of the District of Columbia** *continued*

Executive Assistant **Mable Spears** . . . . . . . . . . . . . . . . . . (202) 626-5118
Commissioner **Willie L. Phillips** . . . . . . . . . . . . . . . . . . . . . (202) 626-9207
  Education: Montevallo 2000 BS; Howard U 2005 JD
Executive Assistant **LaWanda Hale** . . . . . . . . . . . . . . . . (202) 626-9207

## Alcoholic Beverage Regulation Administration Board [ABRA]

2000 14th Street NW, 4th Floor, Suite 400S, Washington, DC 20002
Tel: (202) 442-4423  Fax: (202) 442-9563  Internet: www.abra.dc.gov

Chairperson **Donovan Anderson** . . . . . . . . . . . . . . . . . . . (202) 442-4423
Member **Nick Alberti** . . . . . . . . . . . . . . . . . . . . . . . . . . . . . (202) 442-4423
Member **Ruthanne Miller** . . . . . . . . . . . . . . . . . . . . . . . . . (202) 442-4423
Member **James Short** . . . . . . . . . . . . . . . . . . . . . . . . . . . . (202) 442-4423
Member **Michael Silverstein** . . . . . . . . . . . . . . . . . . . . . . (202) 442-4423
Member **(Vacant)** . . . . . . . . . . . . . . . . . . . . . . . . . . . . . . . (202) 442-4423
Member **(Vacant)** . . . . . . . . . . . . . . . . . . . . . . . . . . . . . . . (202) 442-4423

## Alcoholic Beverage Regulation Administration

Director **Fred Moosally** . . . . . . . . . . . . . . . . . . . . . . . . . . (202) 442-4355

## Board of Elections [BOEE]

One Judiciary Square, 441 Fourth Street, NW, Suite 250 North,
Washington, DC 20001-2745
Tel: (202) 727-2525  TTY: (202) 639-8916  Fax: (202) 347-2648
Internet: www.dcboee.org

Chairman **David Michael Bennett** . . . . . . . . . . . . . . . . . (202) 727-2525
  Education: Duke 1977 BA; George Washington JD
Member **Michael "Mike" Gill** . . . . . . . . . . . . . . . . . . . . . (202) 727-2525
  Affiliation: Counsel, Government Affairs Group, Crowell & Moring
  LLP
  1001 Pennsylvania Avenue, N.W., 10th Floor (North Side),
  Washington, DC 20004-2595
  Education: Dayton BA; Johns Hopkins MA; Columbus Law JD
Member **Dionna Maria Lewis** . . . . . . . . . . . . . . . . . . . . . (202) 727-2525
Member-Designate **Andrew T. "Chip" Richardson** . . . . . . (202) 727-2525
  Note: Andrew Richardson's nomination must be confirmed by the City
  Council.
  Education: Purdue BA; William & Mary 1995 JD
Executive Director (Acting) **Terri Stroud** . . . . . . . . . . . . . (202) 727-2525
  Education: North Carolina; Georgetown JD

## Campaign Finance Office [OCF]

Reeves Municipal Building, 2000 - 14th Street, NW, Suite 420,
Washington, DC 20009
Fax: (202) 671-0658  Internet: www.ocf.dc.gov

Director **Cecily E. Collier-Montgomery** . . . . . . . . . . . . . (202) 671-0550
  E-mail: cecily.collier-montgomery@dc.gov
  Education: Howard U 1972 BA
Administrative Officer **Nadine Journiette** . . . . . . . . . . . . (202) 671-0547
  E-mail: nadine.journiette@dc.gov
Chief Technology Officer **(Vacant)** . . . . . . . . . . . . . . . . . (202) 671-0547

## Public Information and Records Management Division

Public Affairs Manager **S. Wesley Williams** . . . . . . . . . . . (202) 671-0551

## Reports and Analysis Division

Audit Manager **Renee Coleman** . . . . . . . . . . . . . . . . . . . (202) 671-0547

## Office of the General Counsel

General Counsel **William O. Sanford** . . . . . . . . . . . . . . . (202) 671-0658

## Public Employee Relations Board [PERB]

1100 4th Street SW, Suite 630, Washington, DC 20024
Tel: (202) 727-1822  Fax: (202) 727-9116  E-mail: perb@dc.gov

Chairperson **Charles J. Murphy** . . . . . . . . . . . . . . . . . . . (202) 727-1822
  Education: Morgan State BS; Wisconsin MBA
Board Member **Yvonne T. Dixon** . . . . . . . . . . . . . . . . . . (202) 727-1822
  Education: Earlham 1971 BA; NYU 1974 JD
Board Member **Ann F. Hoffman** . . . . . . . . . . . . . . . . . . . (202) 727-1822
Board Member **Barbara Somson** . . . . . . . . . . . . . . . . . . (202) 727-1822
Board Member **Douglas A. Warshof** . . . . . . . . . . . . . . . (202) 727-1822
Executive Director **Clarene Martin** . . . . . . . . . . . . . . . . . (202) 727-1822
Supervisory Attorney Advisor **E. Lindsey Maxwell** . . . . . . (202) 727-1822
  Attorney Advisor **Erica Balkum** . . . . . . . . . . . . . . . . . (202) 727-1822
  Attorney Advisor **Colby Harmon** . . . . . . . . . . . . . . . . (202) 727-1822
    Education: Utah 2003 BA, 2005 MPA; Suffolk 2008 JD
  Attorney Advisor **David McFadden** . . . . . . . . . . . . . . (202) 727-1822
Office Administrator **Patricia Waller** . . . . . . . . . . . . . . . (202) 727-1822

## District of Columbia National Guard

2001 East Capitol Street, SE, Washington, DC 20003

Commanding General **MG Errol R. Schwartz, ARNG** . . . . (202) 685-9798
  Education: UDC 1980 BS; Central Michigan 1984 MS;
  National Defense U 2000 MS
Army Land Component Commander **BG William Walker** . . (202) 685-9879
Adjutant General **BG Renwick L. Payne, ARNG** . . . . . . . . (202) 685-9802
  Education: Governors State BA

★ Elected Official  ■ Appointed by Governor  ● Appointed by Legislature  ▲ Appointed by Board or Commission  ◆ Appointed by State Supreme Court

22

# Florida

Tel: (850) 488-1234 (The Capitol)  Tel: (866) 693-6748 (State Information/ State Operator)
Internet: www.myflorida.com

**Number of U.S. Congressional Delegates:** 2 Senators; 27 Representatives  **Governor's Term:** 4 years
**Legislature Description:** 40 member Senate; 120 member House of Representatives; Term - Senate 4 years,
House 2 years  **Next Election:** Governor November 2018; Legislature November 2016  **Number of
Electoral Votes:** 29  **Official Name:** State of Florida (Spanish: flowery)  **Nickname:** The Sunshine State
**Motto:** In God We Trust

**Population:** 20,271,272 (2015); Rank 3  **Fiscal Year:** 2015-2016  **Budget:** $78,397,224,000

## Office of the Governor

The Capitol, Tallahassee, FL 32399-0001
Tel: (850) 488-7146  TTY: (850) 888-7146  Fax: (850) 487-0801

**Fiscal Year:** 2015-2016  **Budget:** $369,645,000

**Richard Lynn "Rick" Scott**
Governor

Began Service: January 4, 2011
Term Expires: January 6, 2019
Date of Birth: December 2, 1952
Education: Missouri (Kansas City) BS;
Southern Methodist 1978 JD
Home: Naples
Religion: Methodist
Career: Partner, Johnson & Swanson; Chief
Executive, Columbia Hospital Corporation
(1987-1997)

★Governor **Richard Lynn "Rick" Scott** (R) . . . . . . . . . . . . (850) 488-7146
  E-mail: rick.scott@eog.myflorida.com
Chief of Staff **Dr. Kim McDougal** . . . . . . . . . . . . . . . . (850) 488-5000
  Education: Tulane 1984 BE; Florida State 1985 MSE, 1991 PhD
Deputy Chief of Staff **Frank Collins III** . . . . . . . . . . . . . . (850) 488-7146
  E-mail: frank.collins@eog.myflorida.com
  Education: LSU BA
Deputy Chief of Staff **Karl N. Rasmussen** . . . . . . . . . . . . (850) 488-7146
  E-mail: karl.rasmussen@eog.myflorida.com
Deputy Chief of Staff and External Affairs Director
  **Bradley O. Piepenbrink** . . . . . . . . . . . . . . . . . . . . (850) 717-9207
  E-mail: brad.piepenbrink@eog.myflorida.com
  Education: Florida Gulf Coast 2008
Chief Inspector General **Melinda M. Miguel** . . . . . . . . . . (850) 717-9264
  E-mail: melinda.miguel@eog.myflorida.com
Cabinet Affairs Director **Kristin Olson** . . . . . . . . . . . . . (850) 488-7146
  E-mail: kristin.olson@eog.myflorida.com
Communications Director **Jackie Schutz** . . . . . . . . . . . . (850) 717-9282
  E-mail: media@eog.myflorida.com
Deputy Communications Director **McKinley Lewis** . . . . . (850) 717-9282
Executive Placement Director **(Vacant)** . . . . . . . . . . . . . (850) 717-9234
Information Technology Director **Allen Cash** . . . . . . . . . . (850) 717-9225
  E-mail: allen.cash@eog.myflorida.com
Legislative Affairs Director **Kevin Reilly** . . . . . . . . . . . . (850) 488-5000
  E-mail: kevin.reilly@eog.myflorida.com
  Education: Florida 2008 BA, 2009 MM
Policy Director **Jeffrey S. Woodburn** . . . . . . . . . . . . . . (850) 717-9510
  E-mail: jeff.woodburn@laspbs.state.fl.us
External Affairs Deputy Director **Leda D. Williams** . . . . . (850) 717-9207
  E-mail: leda.williams@eog.myflorida.com
Press Secretary **Jereima "Jeri" Bustamante** . . . . . . . . . (850) 488-7146
  E-mail: jeri.bustamante@eog.myflorida.com
  Education: Florida International
General Counsel **William Spicola** . . . . . . . . . . . . . . . . (850) 488-7146
Education Policy Advisor **Ashley Spicola** . . . . . . . . . . . (850) 488-7146
  E-mail: ashley.spicola@myflorida.com
Appointments Analyst **Megan M. Bailey** . . . . . . . . . . . (850) 717-9243
  E-mail: megan.bailey@eog.myflorida.com
  Education: Florida State 2009 BS

## Adoption and Child Protection Office

Tel: (850) 717-9261  Fax: (850) 921-0173
Director **Zackary Gibson** . . . . . . . . . . . . . . . . . . . . . . (850) 717-9261
  E-mail: zackary.gibson@eog.myflorida.com
Chief Child Advocate **Zackary Gibson** . . . . . . . . . . . . . (850) 717-9261

## Office of Policy and Budget

Director **Cynthia Kelly** . . . . . . . . . . . . . . . . . . . . . . . (850) 833-7587
  E-mail: cynthia.kelly@myflorida.com
Budget Management Policy Coordinator
  **Sharon Renee Tondee** . . . . . . . . . . . . . . . . . . . . . (850) 487-1880
Education Policy Coordinator **Ashley Spicola** . . . . . . . . . (850) 487-1880
  E-mail: ashley.spicola@myflorida.com
Environmental Policy Unit Coordinator **Julia Spespy** . . . . (850) 488-5551
Finance and Economic Analysis Policy Coordinator
  **Christian Weiss** . . . . . . . . . . . . . . . . . . . . . . . . . (850) 487-2814
General Government Coordinator **Laurie Grasel** . . . . . . . (850) 488-5184
Health and Human Services Policy Coordinator
  **Mary Beth Vickers** . . . . . . . . . . . . . . . . . . . . . . . (850) 488-7734
  E-mail: mary.vickers@floridahealth.gov
Public Safety Policy Unit Coordinator
  **Sara Katie Cunningham** . . . . . . . . . . . . . . . . . . . . (850) 922-4020
Systems Design and Development Policy Coordinator
  **Michael Jones** . . . . . . . . . . . . . . . . . . . . . . . . . . (850) 488-6955
  E-mail: michael.jones@laspbs.state.fl.us
Transportation and Economic Development Coordinator
  **Mark Kruse** . . . . . . . . . . . . . . . . . . . . . . . . . . . . (850) 717-9513
  E-mail: mark.kruse@laspbs.state.fl.us
Special Investigator for Finance and Tax **Patricia Nelson** . . (850) 488-7146

## Washington Office

444 North Capitol Street, NW, Suite 349, Washington, DC 20001
Tel: (202) 624-5885  Fax: (202) 624-5886
Office Liaison **Christine Diaz** . . . . . . . . . . . . . . . . . . . (202) 624-5885

## Department of Business and Professional Regulation [DBPR]

Northwood Ctr., 1940 N. Monroe St., Tallahassee, FL 32399-0750
Tel: (850) 487-1395  TTY: (800) 955-8771  Fax: (850) 488-1830
E-mail: communications@dbpr.state.fl.us

**Employees:** 1,612
■Secretary **Ken Lawson** . . . . . . . . . . . . . . . . . . . . . . (850) 413-0755
  E-mail: ken.lawson@myfloridalicense.com
  Education: Florida State, JD

## Florida Department of Children and Families [DCF]

1317 Winewood Boulevard, Tallahassee, FL 32399-0700
Tel: (850) 487-1111  Fax: (850) 922-2993
Internet: www.myflfamilies.com

**Employees:** 11,809  **Fiscal Year:** 2015-2016  **Budget:** $3,009,338,000
■Secretary **Mike Carroll** . . . . . . . . . . . . . . . . . . . . . . (850) 487-1111
  E-mail: mike.carroll@myflfamilies.com
  Inspector General **Keith Parks** . . . . . . . . . . . . . . . . (850) 488-1225
  E-mail: keith.parks@myflfamilies.com

*(continued on next page)*

★ Elected Official  ■ Appointed by Governor  ● Appointed by Legislature  ▲ Appointed by Board or Commission  ◆ Appointed by State Supreme Court

**EXECUTIVE BRANCH**

EXECUTIVE BRANCH

**Florida Department of Children and Families** *continued*

General Counsel **Rebecca Kapusta** . . . . . . . . . . . . . . . . . (850) 488-2381
E-mail: rebecca.kapusta@myflfamilies.com
Deputy Secretary **David Fairbanks** . . . . . . . . . . . . . . . . . (850) 487-1111
Southern Regional Managing Director
**Bronwyn Stanford** . . . . . . . . . . . . . . . . . . . . . . . . (850) 487-1111
Chief of Staff **Jane E. Johnson** . . . . . . . . . . . . . . . . . . . . (850) 487-1111
Education: Georgetown
Communications Director **Jessica Sims** . . . . . . . . . . . (850) 413-0771
E-mail: jessica.sims@myflfamilies.com
Legislative Affairs Director **Michael Wickersheim** . . . . . (850) 488-9410
E-mail: michael.wickersheim@myflfamilies.com
Press Secretary **Michelle Glady** . . . . . . . . . . . . . . . . . . . (850) 717-4611
E-mail: michelle.glady@myflfamilies.com

## Administration
Fax: (850) 922-4996
Assistant Secretary **Scott Stewart** . . . . . . . . . . . . . . . . . (850) 488-6062
E-mail: scott.stewart@myflfamilies.com
Chief Financial Officer **Kimberly McMurray, CPA** . . . . . . . (850) 717-4761
E-mail: kimberly.mcmurray@myflfamilies.com
General Services Director **Matthew "Matt" Howard** . . . . .(850) 717-4030
E-mail: matthew.howard@myflfamilies.com
Human Resources Director (Interim) **Shelby Jefferson** . . . (850) 921-8487

## Mental Health
Substance Abuse and Mental Health Assistant Secretary
**John Bryant** . . . . . . . . . . . . . . . . . . . . . . . . . . . . . . .(850) 487-1111

## Operations
Operations Assistant Secretary **Vicki Abrams** . . . . . . . . . . (850) 487-1111
Florida Abuse Hotline Director **Patricia Badland** . . . . . . . . (850) 487-6100
E-mail: patricia.badland@myflfamilies.com

## Programs
Adult Protective Services Director **Robert Anderson** . . . . . (850) 488-8922
E-mail: robert.anderson@myflfamilies.com
Child Care Services Director
**Samantha Wass de Czege** . . . . . . . . . . . . . . . . . . (850) 488-4900
E-mail: samantha.wassoleczege@myflfamilies.com
Child Welfare Assistant Secretary **JoShonda Guerrier** . . . . (850) 488-8762
Domestic Violence Director **(Vacant)** . . . . . . . . . . . . . . . . (850) 921-2168
Economic Self-Sufficiency Assistant Secretary
**Jerilyn D. "Jeri" Flora** . . . . . . . . . . . . . . . . . . . . . . (850) 717-4125
Family Safety Director **Elisa Cramer** . . . . . . . . . . . . . . . . (850) 488-8762
E-mail: elisa.cramer@myflfamilies.com

# Florida Department of Citrus [FDOC]
P.O. Box 9010, Bartow, FL 33831-9010
Tel: (863) 537-3999  Fax: (877) 352-2487

**Employees:** 57  **Fiscal Year:** 2015-2016  **Budget:** $41,832,000

▲Executive Director **Shannon Shepp** . . . . . . . . . . . . . . . . (863) 537-3950
E-mail: sshepp@citrus.myflorida.com
Executive Secretary **Heather Facey** . . . . . . . . . . . . . . . (863) 537-3950
Deputy Executive Director **(Vacant)** . . . . . . . . . . . . . . . (863) 537-3957
Brand and Public Relations Director **Samantha Land** . . . . (863) 537-3968
E-mail: david.steele@myflorida.com
Economic and Market Research Director
**Dr. Marisa Zansler** . . . . . . . . . . . . . . . . . . . . . . . . (863) 537-3999
International Marketing Director **Michael Schadler** . . . . . . (863) 537-3999
E-mail: mschadler@citrus.state.fl.us
Scientific Research Director **Rosa Walsh** . . . . . . . . . . . . (863) 956-2023
E-mail: rosa.walsh@myflorida.com
Administration and Finance Deputy Executive Director
**Christine Marion** . . . . . . . . . . . . . . . . . . . . . . . . . .(863) 537-3999
E-mail: cmarion@citrus.state.fl.us
Inspector General **Kevin Ray Eaton** . . . . . . . . . . . . . . . . (863) 537-3999

# Florida Department of Corrections
501 South Calhoun Street, Tallahassee, FL 32399
Tel: (850) 717-3030  Fax: (850) 922-2848  Internet: www.dc.state.fl.us

**Employees:** 23,729  **Fiscal Year:** 2015-2016  **Budget:** $2,363,223,000

■Secretary **Julie L. Jones** . . . . . . . . . . . . . . . . . . . . . . . (850) 717-3030
E-mail: jones.julie@mail.dc.state.fl.us
Education: Florida Atlantic BS, MS
Institutions Deputy Secretary
**Timothy H. "Tim" Cannon** . . . . . . . . . . . . . . . . . . . (850) 717-3018
Legal Counsel **Jennifer Parker** . . . . . . . . . . . . . . . . . . . (850) 717-3605
E-mail: parker.jennifer@mail.dc.state.fl.us
Legislative Affairs Director **Jared Torres** . . . . . . . . . . . . . (850) 717-3045
E-mail: torres.jared@mail.dc.state.fl.us
Public Affairs Director **(Vacant)** . . . . . . . . . . . . . . . . . . . (850) 487-7996

# Department of Economic Opportunity
Caldwell Building, 107 East Madison Street, Tallahassee, FL 32399-4120
Tel: (850) 245-7105  Fax: (850) 921-3223

■Executive Director **Cissy Proctor** . . . . . . . . . . . . . . . . . . (850) 245-7105
E-mail: cissy.proctor@deo.myflorida.com
Chief of Staff **Dean Izzo** . . . . . . . . . . . . . . . . . . . . . . . . (850) 717-7122
E-mail: dean.izzo@deo.myflorida.com
Education: Georgia State 1995 BBA
Chief Communications Officer **Erin Gillespie** . . . . . . . . . . (850) 245-7145
E-mail: erin.gillespie@deo.myflorida.com
Chief Financial Officer (Interim) **Damon Steffens** . . . . . . (850) 245-7119
Chief Information Officer **David Gilmore** . . . . . . . . . . . . . (850) 245-7305
E-mail: david.gilmore@deo.myflorida.com
General Counsel **James "Jim" Poppell** . . . . . . . . . . . . . . (850) 245-7160
E-mail: james.poppell@deo.myflorida.com
Legislative and Cabinet Affairs Director **Bill Wilson** . . . . . (850) 245-7370
E-mail: bill.wilson@deo.myflorida.com
Education: Florida International 2004 BBA
Inspector General **James E. "Jim" Landsberg** . . . . . . . . . (850) 245-7141
E-mail: james.landsberg@deo.myflorida.com
Press Secretary **Morgan L. McCord** . . . . . . . . . . . . . . . . (850) 245-7105
Education: Florida State

# Department of Elder Affairs [DOEA]
4040 Esplanade Way, Tallahassee, FL 32399-7000
TTY: (850) 414-2000  Fax: (850) 414-2004
E-mail: information@elderaffairs.org  Internet: elderaffairs.org

**Employees:** 451  **Fiscal Year:** 2015-2016  **Budget:** $295,807,000

■Secretary **Samuel P. Verghese** . . . . . . . . . . . . . . . . . . . (850) 414-2000
E-mail: vergheses@elderaffairs.org
Deputy Secretary and Chief of Staff **Richard Prudom** . . . (850) 414-2393
E-mail: prudomrm@elderaffairs.org
Education: Kent (UK)
Inspector General **Taroub King** . . . . . . . . . . . . . . . . . . . (850) 414-2013
General Counsel **(Vacant)** . . . . . . . . . . . . . . . . . . . . . . . (850) 414-2074
Communications Director **Ashley Chambers** . . . . . . . . . . (850) 414-2142
E-mail: marshalla@elderaffairs.org
Internal and External Affairs Director **Carol Carr** . . . . . . . (850) 414-2011
Legislative Affairs Director **Jo Morris** . . . . . . . . . . . . . . . (850) 414-2155
E-mail: morrisj@elderaffairs.org
Education: Florida State BA, MA
Statewide Community-Based Services Division Director
**Madeleine Nobles** . . . . . . . . . . . . . . . . . . . . . . . . (850) 414-2135
Chief Financial Officer **Jon Manalo** . . . . . . . . . . . . . . . . (850) 414-2077
Long Term Care Ombudsman **Leigh Davis** . . . . . . . . . . . (850) 414-2331
Office of Strategic Initiatives Manager **Mindy Sollisch** . . . (850) 414-2181

---

★ Elected Official   ■ Appointed by Governor   ● Appointed by Legislature   ▲ Appointed by Board or Commission   ◆ Appointed by State Supreme Court

EXECUTIVE BRANCH

# Department of Environmental Protection [DEP]

Marjory Stoneman Douglas Building, 3900 Commonwealth Boulevard, Tallahassee, FL 32399-3000
Tel: (850) 245-2118 (Citizen Services)  Fax: (850) 245-2128
Internet: www.floridadep.org

**Employees:** 3,231  **Fiscal Year:** 2015-2016  **Budget:** $1,441,985,000

■Secretary **Jonathan P. Steverson** .................. (850) 245-2011
   E-mail: jon.steverson@dep.state.fl.us          Fax: (850) 245-2021
   Executive Assistant **Belva Schmalfuss** ............... (850) 245-2035
                                                 Fax: (850) 245-2021
Inspector General **Candie Fuller** ..................... (850) 245-3151
Chief of Staff **Leonard C. "Lennie" Zeiler, Jr.** ......... (850) 245-2012
                                                 Fax: (850) 245-2021
General Counsel **Frederick Aschauer, Jr.** ............. (850) 245-2242
Environmental Education and Sustainable Initiatives
   Director **(Vacant)** ............................ (850) 245-2132
External Affairs Coordinator **Russell Budell** ........... (850) 245-2113
   E-mail: russell.budell@dep.state.fl.us
Ombudsman and Public Services Director **John Calhoun** .. (850) 245-2118
Press Secretary **Lori Elliott** ...................... (850) 778-7294
   E-mail: lori.elliott@dep.state.fl.us
Communications Coordinator **Lauren E. Engel** ......... (850) 245-2111
Webmaster **Leah Donaldson** ..................... (850) 245-2125
   E-mail: leah.donaldson@dep.state.fl.us

## Land and Recreational Services

Tel: (850) 245-2528  Fax: (850) 245-2048

Deputy Secretary **Gary F. Clark** ..................... (850) 245-2043
Planning Manager **Sophia Arteaga** .................. (850) 245-2043
   E-mail: sophia.arteaga@dep.state.fl.us

## Recreation and Parks Division

Fax: (850) 245-3041

Director **Donald Forgione** ........................ (850) 245-3029
   E-mail: donald.forgione@dep.state.fl.us
Operations Director **(Vacant)** ..................... (850) 245-2062
Assistant Director **Charles W. "Chuck" Hatcher** ....... (850) 245-3015
Assistant Director **Matthew M. "Matt" Mitchell** ....... (850) 245-3053
Design and Construction Services Chief
   **Michael W. Foster, Jr.** ...................... (850) 245-2694
   E-mail: michael.foster@dep.state.fl.us     Fax: (850) 921-6627
Natural and Cultural Resources Chief **Parks Small** ....... (850) 245-3104
   E-mail: parks.small@dep.state.fl.us         Fax: (850) 245-3114
Operational Services Chief **Jim Brooks** ............... (850) 245-3076
                                                 Fax: (850) 245-3091
Park Planning Chief **Sine Murray** ................... (850) 245-3058

## State Lands Division

Director **David A. Clark** .......................... (850) 245-2555
                                                 Fax: (850) 245-2572
Assistant Director **(Vacant)** ................. (850) 245-2025 ext. 4025
                                                 Fax: (850) 245-2572
Appraisal Chief **Douglas J. Dane** ........... (850) 245-2665 ext. 4663
                                                 Fax: (850) 245-2668
Florida Geological Survey Director
   **Nicholas "Nick" Campanile** ................. (850) 245-2642
                                                 Fax: (850) 412-0494
Land Acquisition Chief **Lynda Godfrey** ............... (850) 245-2680
                                                 Fax: (850) 245-2719
Public Land Administration Chief **Cheryl McCall** ........ (850) 245-2806
                                                 Fax: (850) 245-2761
Survey and Mapping Chief **Rod Maddox** .............. (850) 245-2642
                                                 Fax: (850) 245-2645
Environmental Services Office Bureau **(Vacant)** ......... (850) 245-2773
                                                 Fax: (850) 245-2786

## Water Policy and Ecosystem Restoration

Tel: (850) 245-3166  Fax: (850) 245-3145

Director **Tom Beck** ............................. (850) 245-3166

Deputy Secretary **Drew Bartlett** .................. (850) 245-3166
   Education: Georgia Tech BIE; Georgia State MBA
Ecosystems Director **Edward C. Smith** .............. (850) 245-3169

## Coastal and Aquatic Managed Areas Office

Fax: (850) 245-2110

Director **Kevin Claridge** .......................... (850) 245-2094
Budget Manager **(Vacant)** ........................ (850) 245-2097
Aquatic Preserve and Marine Program Planning Manager
   **Penny Isom** ............................... (850) 245-2109

## Administrative Services Division

Marjorie and Archie Carr Building, 3800 Commonwealth Boulevard, M.S.60, Tallahassee, FL 32399-3000
Tel: (850) 245-2307  Fax: (850) 245-2338

Director **Robert B. "Bob" Wilson** ................... (850) 245-2307
   E-mail: bob.wilson@dep.state.fl.us
Budget & Planning Chief **Sue Oshesky** .............. (850) 245-2340
                                                 Fax: (850) 245-2349
Finance & Accounting Chief **Darinda McLaughlin** ....... (850) 245-2420
                                                 Fax: (850) 245-2462
General Services Chief **Gwenn Godfrey** .............. (850) 245-2350
   E-mail: gwenn.godfrey@dep.state.fl.us       Fax: (850) 412-0765
Personnel Services Chief **(Vacant)** ................. (850) 245-2532
                                                 Fax: (850) 245-2545
Chief Information Officer **Warren Sponholtz** .......... (850) 245-7565
   E-mail: warren.sponholtz@dep.state.fl.us

## Environmental Assessment and Restoration Division

Fax: (850) 245-7524

Director **Tom Frick** ............................. (850) 245-7518
Laboratories Chief **William Coppenger** .............. (850) 245-8057
                                                 Fax: (850) 412-0441
Mercury Program Administrator **(Vacant)** ............. (850) 245-8072
Watershed Restoration Bureau Chief **(Vacant)** .......... (850) 245-7518

## Regulatory Programs

Fax: (850) 245-2048

Deputy Secretary **Paula L. Cobb** ................... (850) 245-2037
   Education: South Carolina 2007 JD; Vermont Law JD
Assistant Deputy Secretary **Mike P. Halpin** ........... (850) 245-2033
Executive Staff Director **Mary Alice McElheney** ........ (850) 245-2038
   E-mail: maryalice.mcelheney@dep.state.fl.us
   Personal Secretary **(Vacant)** .................. (850) 245-2016

## Air Resources Management Division

Fax: (850) 717-9001

Director **Justin B. Green** ......................... (850) 717-9000
Deputy Director **Jeff Koerner** ..................... (850) 717-9000
   Human Resources **Mary Fillingim** .............. (850) 717-9000
Budget, Training and Business Coordinator
   **John Hughes** .............................. (850) 717-9009
   E-mail: John.Hughes@dep.state.fl.us

## Waste Management Division

Bob Martinez Center, 2600 Blair Stone Road, MS#4500, Tallahassee, FL 32399-2400
Tel: (850) 245-8705  Fax: (850) 245-8703

Director **Joe Ullo** ............................. (850) 245-8705
   Administrative Assistant **Judith A. Pennington** ........ (850) 245-8705
Assistant Director **John Coates** .................... (850) 245-8705
Petroleum Storage Systems Chief **Diane Pickett** ........ (850) 245-8804
                                                 Fax: (850) 245-8831
Solid and Hazardous Waste Chief **Cory D. Dilmore** ...... (850) 245-8735
                                                 Fax: (850) 245-8803
Waste Cleanup Chief **Peter Cornais** ................ (850) 245-8930
                                                 Fax: (850) 245-8976

---

★ Elected Official   ■ Appointed by Governor   ● Appointed by Legislature   ▲ Appointed by Board or Commission   ◆ Appointed by State Supreme Court

## Water Resource Management Division

Fax: (850) 245-8336

Director **Frederick Aschauer, Jr.**.....................(850) 245-8336
  Administrative Assistant **Mayra Folsom** .............(850) 245-8676
Deputy Director **Jane Herndon**........................(850) 245-8337
Mining and Minerals Regulation Program
  Administrator **Orlando E. Rivera** ............ (850) 245-8336 ext. 5266
    E-mail: orlando.rivera@dep.state.fl.us        Fax: (850) 488-1254
State Revolving Fund Program Administrator
  **Tom Shiftlett** .......................................(850) 245-8394
                                                    Fax: (850) 245-8411

## Department of Health

4052 Bald Cypress Way, Bin #A00, Tallahassee, FL 32399-1701
P.O. Box 210, Jacksonville, FL 32231 (Vital Records)
Tel: (850) 245-4444  Tel: (904) 359-6900 (Vital Records)
Fax: (850) 487-3729  Fax: (904) 359-6993 (Vital Records)
E-mail: health@doh.state.fl.us
E-mail: vitalstats@flhealth.gov (Vital Statistics)
Internet: www.doh.state.fl.us

**Employees:** 16,549  **Fiscal Year:** 2015-2016  **Budget:** $2,821,749,000

■Surgeon General and Secretary **Dr. Celeste Philip, MD** ... (850) 245-4321
    E-mail: celeste_philip@doh.state.fl.us
  Assistant **Margaret Medina** .........................(850) 245-4210
    E-mail: margaret_medina@doh.state.fl.us
  Chief of Staff **Jennifer A. Tschetter** ................(850) 245-4479
  General Counsel **(Vacant)** ...........................(850) 245-4005
  Inspector General **James D. Boyd, CPA, MBA** .........(850) 245-4140
    Education: Florida State 1976 BS
  Equal Opportunity Director **Dee Dee McGee** ...........(850) 245-4002
  Minority Health Director **Michael Mason** .............(850) 245-4841
Administration Deputy Secretary
  **J. Martin "Marty" Stubblefield** ....................(850) 245-4343
    E-mail: marty_stubblefield@doh.state.fl.us
    Education: Southern Mississippi 1987
County Health Systems Deputy Secretary
  **Kim E. Barnhill** ...................................(850) 245-4243
    Note: On extended administrative leave
County Health Systems Deputy Secretary (Interim)
  **Paul D. Myers** .....................................(850) 245-4444
  Performance and Quality Improvement Director
    **Paul Coley** ......................................(850) 245-4007
  Health Deputy Secretary **Dr. Celeste Philip, MD** .......(850) 245-4259
    E-mail: celeste_philip@doh.state.fl.us
  Communications Director
    **Mara K. Gambineri** ................... (850) 245-4111 ext. 4112
      E-mail: mara.burger@flhealth.gov        Fax: (850) 245-4459
  Legislative Planning Director **Marco Paredes** .........(850) 245-4006
    E-mail: marco_paredes@doh.state.fl.us
  State Registrar **Kenneth T. "Ken" Jones** ..... (904) 359-6900 ext. 1001
                                                    Fax: (904) 359-6931
  Public Health Laboratory Bureau Chief
    **Susanne Crowe** ...................................(904) 791-1500
  State Epidemiologist **Dr. Anna Likos, MD** .............(850) 245-4356
  State Toxicologist **Dr. Kendra F. Goff** ...............(850) 488-6811
  Chief Deputy Registrar **(Vacant)** ............ (904) 359-6900 ext. 9000
                                                    Fax: (904) 359-6931
    Deputy Registrar **(Vacant)**........................(904) 359-6900
                                                    Fax: (904) 359-6931

### Administrative Division

Fax: (850) 487-4574

Director **Ed McEachron** ...............................(850) 245-4147
  E-mail: ed_mceachron@doh.state.fl.us
Budget Management Director **Michele Tallent** ..........(850) 245-4454
Finance & Accounting Chief **Joanne Lane** .............(850) 245-4494
General Services Chief **Roger Twitchell** ..............(850) 245-4003
  E-mail: roger_twitchell@doh.state.fl.us
Personnel and Human Resources Management Chief
  **Susan Veal** ........................................(850) 245-4188

## Community Health Promotion Division

Tel: (850) 245-4100  Fax: (850) 414-6091

Director (Acting) **Shannon Hughes** ...................(850) 245-4100
Child Nutrition Program Chief **Maria Williamson** ........(850) 245-4323
  E-mail: maria_williamson@doh.state.fl.us
Chronic Diseases Chief **(Vacant)** ............. (850) 245-4330 ext. 2800
Family and Health Services Chief
  **Kris-tena Albers** ............... (850) 245-4100 ext. 4467
WIC (Women, Infants and Children) and Nutrition
  Services Chief **(Vacant)** ...........................(850) 245-4202

## Disability Determination Division

Fax: (850) 922-8667

Director **Rhonda Wilson** ..............................(850) 488-3347

## Disease Control and Health Promotion Division

Tel: (850) 245-4300  Fax: (850) 922-9299

Director **Dr. Anna Likos, MD** .........................(850) 245-4300
Communicable Disease Chief
  **Robert "Sterling" Whisenhunt** ....................(850) 245-4303
Epidemiology Chief **(Vacant)** .........................(850) 245-4401

## Emergency Preparedness and Community Support Division

Tel: (850) 245-4440  Fax: (850) 921-8162

Director **Cynthia E. "Cindy" Dick** ...................(850) 245-4444
Trauma Office Director **(Vacant)** ............. (850) 245-4440 ext. 2760
Emergency Medical Program Manager **(Vacant)**.........(850) 245-4440
Radiation Control Chief **Cynthia Becker** .............(850) 245-4266

## Information Technology Division

Tel: (850) 245-4233  Fax: (850) 921-5149

Chief Information Officer **Tony K. Powell** .............(850) 245-4256
Deputy Chief Information Officer **Joseph Wright** ........(850) 245-4233
  E-mail: joe.wright@flhealth.gov
Deputy Director **(Vacant)** ............................(850) 617-5876

## Medical Quality Assurance Division

Tel: (850) 245-4224

Director **Lucy Gee** ...................................(850) 245-4224
Enforcement Bureau Chief **Mark Whitten** ..............(850) 245-4478
Health Care Practitioner Regulations Chief
  **Adrienne Rodgers** .................................(850) 245-4095
Operations Chief **Lola T. Pouncey** ...................(850) 245-4063

## Florida Department of Highway Safety and Motor Vehicles [DHSMV]

Neil Kirkman Building, 2900 Apalachee Parkway,
Tallahassee, FL 32399-0500
Tel: (850) 617-2000  E-mail: hsmv-info@flhsmv.gov

**Employees:** 4,414  **Fiscal Year:** 2015-2016  **Budget:** $453,933,000

■Executive Director **Terry Rhodes**.....................(850) 617-3100
  E-mail: terryrhodes@flhsmv.gov
Deputy Executive Director **Diana Vaughn** .............(850) 617-3197
Chief of Staff **(Vacant)** .............................(850) 617-3100
Inspector General **Julie Leftheris** ...................(850) 617-3129
Administrative Services Division Director
  **Steven Fielder** ...................................(850) 617-3406
  E-mail: stevenfielder@flhsmv.gov
Communications Director **Beth W. Frady** ..............(850) 617-3100
  E-mail: bethfrady@flhsmv.gov
Cyber Security Director
  **Mike Russo, CFE, CISSP, PMP, CGEIT, CISA** .........(850) 617-0157
    Education: Northeastern BS
Highway Patrol Division Director **Col. Gene Spaulding** .. (850) 617-2300
Information Systems Director
  **Clayton "Boyd" Dickerson-Walden** .................(850) 617-2012

---

★ Elected Official   ■ Appointed by Governor   ● Appointed by Legislature   ▲ Appointed by Board or Commission   ◆ Appointed by State Supreme Court

Summer 2016                    © Leadership Directories, Inc.                    *State Yellow Book*

Legislative Affairs Administrator **Jennifer Langston** . . . . . (850) 617-3195
E-mail: jenniferlangston@flhsmv.gov
Motorist Services Division Director **Robert Kynoch** . . . . . . (850) 617-2819
E-mail: robertkynoch@flhsmv.gov
Office of Workforce Services Director
**Teresa W. "Terry" Stepp** . . . . . . . . . . . . . . . . . . . . (850) 617-3259
Chief Financial Officer **Susan Carey** . . . . . . . . . . . . . . . (850) 617-3404
Chief Performance Officer **Larry J. Gowen** . . . . . . . . . . . (850) 617-2117
E-mail: larrygowen@flhsmv.gov
General Counsel **Steve Hurm** . . . . . . . . . . . . . . . . . . . . . (850) 617-3138

## Florida Department of Juvenile Justice [FDJJ]

2737 Centerview Drive, Tallahassee, FL 32399-3100
Tel: (850) 488-1850  Fax: (850) 922-2992  Internet: www.djj.state.fl.us

**Employees:** 3,501 **Fiscal Year:** 2015-2016 **Budget:** $540,307,000

■Secretary **Christina K. "Christy" Daly** . . . . . . . . . . . . (850) 413-7313
E-mail: christy.daly@djj.state.fl.us
Deputy Secretary **Tim Niermann** . . . . . . . . . . . . . . . . . . (850) 717-2702
General Counsel **Brian Berkowitz** . . . . . . . . . . . . . . . . . (850) 921-4129
E-mail: brian.berkowitz@djj.state.fl.us       Fax: (850) 921-4159
Inspector General **Robert A. Munson** . . . . . . . . . . . . . . (850) 921-6344
E-mail: robert.munson@djj.state.fl.us       Fax: (850) 414-7182
Chief of Staff **Fred W. Schuknecht** . . . . . . . . . . . . . . . . (850) 488-1850
Administrative Director **Vickie Harris** . . . . . . . . . . . . . . (850) 717-2303
Communications Director **Heather DiGiacomo** . . . . . . . (850) 921-5900
E-mail: heather.digiacomo@djj.state.fl.us       Fax: (850) 921-5907
Health Services Administrator
**Charles T. "Chuck" Corley** . . . . . . . . . . . . . . . . . . (850) 921-2630
Fax: (850) 922-0151
Detention Assistant Secretary **Dixie Fosler** . . . . . . . . . . . (850) 921-6292
Prevention and Victim Services Assistant Secretary
**Alice B. Sims** . . . . . . . . . . . . . . . . . . . . . . . . . . . . (850) 717-2433
Fax: (850) 922-6189
Probation and Community Intervention Assistant
Secretary **Paul Hatcher** . . . . . . . . . . . . . . . . . . . . . (850) 717-2571
Fax: (850) 413-0293
Residential Services Assistant Secretary
**Laura Moneyham** . . . . . . . . . . . . . . . . . . . . . . . . . (850) 921-4188
Fax: (850) 414-2264
Legislative Affairs Director **Meredith Stanfield** . . . . . . . . (850) 717-2716
E-mail: meredith.stanfield@djj.state.fl.us       Fax: (850) 921-5907
Education: Georgia 2006 BA

## Florida Department of Law Enforcement [FDLE]

2331 Phillips Road, Tallahassee, FL 32304
P.O. Box 1489, Tallahassee, FL 32302-1489
Tel: (850) 410-7000  Tel: (850) 488-0797 (Job Line)
TTY: (850) 488-6085  Fax: (850) 410-7022  Internet: www.fdle.state.fl.us

**Employees:** 1,814 **Fiscal Year:** 2015-2016 **Budget:** $270,024,000

■Commissioner **Richard L. "Rick" Swearingen** . . . . . . . . . (850) 410-7001
E-mail: rickswearingen@fdle.state.fl.us
Education: Auburn
Assistant Commissioner **Robert "Don" Ladner** . . . . . . . . . (850) 488-7001
E-mail: donladner@fdle.state.fl.us
■Assistant Commissioner **Jennifer Pritt** . . . . . . . . . . . . (850) 410-7001
E-mail: jenniferpritt@fdle.state.fl.us
General Counsel **Jason Jones** . . . . . . . . . . . . . . . . . . . . (850) 410-7676
Inspector General **Lourdes O. Howell-Thomas** . . . . . . . . (850) 410-7225
Business Support Program Director **Michelle Pyle** . . . . . . . (850) 410-7260
Criminal Justice Information Program Director
**Charles Schaeffer** . . . . . . . . . . . . . . . . . . . . . . . . (850) 410-7100
E-mail: charlesschaeffer@fdle.state.fl.us
Criminal Justice Professionalism Program Director
**Dean Register** . . . . . . . . . . . . . . . . . . . . . . . . . . . (850) 410-8600
Executive Investigations Director **Scott McInerney** . . . . . . (850) 410-8240
External Affairs Director **Ronald "Ron" Draa** . . . . . . . . . (850) 410-7001
E-mail: ronalddraa@fdle.state.fl.us
Information Resource Management Director
**Joey Hornsby** . . . . . . . . . . . . . . . . . . . . . . . . . . . (850) 410-8410
E-mail: joeyhornsby@fdle.state.fl.us

Investigations and Forensic Services Director
**Donna Uzzell** . . . . . . . . . . . . . . . . . . . . . . . . . . . . (850) 410-8390
Finance and Accounting Chief **Charlotte Fraser** . . . . . . . . (850) 410-7234
E-mail: charlottefraser@fdle.state.fl.us
General Services Chief **Sonya Avant** . . . . . . . . . . . . . . . (850) 410-7311
E-mail: sonyaavant@fdle.state.fl.us
Grants Program Chief **Petrina Herring** . . . . . . . . . . . . . (850) 410-8701
E-mail: petrinaherring@fdle.state.fl.us
Human Resources Chief **Joy Brady** . . . . . . . . . . . . . . . . (850) 410-7264
E-mail: joybrady@fdle.state.fl.us
Communications Director **Gretl Plessinger** . . . . . . . . . . . (850) 410-7000

## Department of the Lottery

250 Marriott Drive, Tallahassee, FL 32301
Tel: (850) 487-7777  TTY: (850) 487-7784  Fax: (850) 487-7709
E-mail: asklott@flalottery.com  Internet: www.flalottery.com

**Employees:** 423 **Fiscal Year:** 2015-2016 **Budget:** $169,616,000

■Secretary **Tom Delacensarie** . . . . . . . . . . . . . . (850) 487-7738 ext. 2773
E-mail: delacenseriet@flalottery.com
Deputy Secretary **(Vacant)** . . . . . . . . . . . . . . . . . . . . (850) 487-7738
Executive Assistant **Mimi Schmitzer** . . . . . . . . . . . . . . (850) 487-7728
Brand Management Chief **Shan Daniels** . . . . . . . . . . . . . (850) 487-7727
E-mail: danielss@flalottery.com
Chief of Staff **Daniel M. "Dan" Olson** . . . . . . . . (850) 487-7711 ext. 2207
General Counsel **Josie Tamayo** . . . . . . . . . . . . . . . . . . (850) 487-7724
Inspector General **Andy Mompeller** . . . . . . . . . . . . . . . (850) 487-7726
Human Resources Director **Nyla Davis** . . . . . . . . . . . . . (850) 487-7721
Legislative Affairs Director **Michael Manley** . . . . . . . . . . (850) 487-7729
E-mail: manleym@flalottery.com
Security Director **Ron Cave** . . . . . . . . . . . . . . . . . . . . (850) 487-7730

## Department of Management Services [DMS]

4050 Esplanade Way, Suite 280, Tallahassee, FL 32399-0950
Tel: (850) 488-2786  Fax: (850) 922-6149
E-mail: executive_office@dms.state.fl.us
Internet: www.dms.myflorida.com

**Employees:** 1,308 **Fiscal Year:** 2015-2016 **Budget:** $702,898,000

■Secretary **Chad Poppell** . . . . . . . . . . . . . . . . . . . . . (850) 414-1159
E-mail: chad.poppell@myflorida.com
Education: Valdosta State U
Chief of Staff **Ben Wolf** . . . . . . . . . . . . . . . . . . . . . . (850) 488-0018
Workforce Operations Deputy Secretary **Darren Brooks** . . . (850) 921-3788
E-mail: darren.brooks@dms.myflorida.com
Business Operations Deputy Secretary
**Erin Geraghty Rock** . . . . . . . . . . . . . . . . . . . . . . (850) 410-2954
E-mail: erin.rock@dms.myflorida.com
General Counsel **Drew Atkinson** . . . . . . . . . . . . . . . . . (850) 488-0229
E-mail: drew.atkinson@dms.myflorida.com
Inspector General (Interim) **Yolanda V. Lockett** . . . . . . . . (850) 488-5285
Communications Director **Maggie Mickler** . . . . . . . . . . . (850) 921-5266
Legislative Affairs Director **Taylor Hatch** . . . . . . . . . . . . (850) 488-6285
E-mail: taylor.hatch@dms.myflorida.com
Chief Information Officer **Robert "Bob" Ward** . . . . . . . . . (850) 488-2786

### Administration Division

Director **Debra Forbess** . . . . . . . . . . . . . . . . . . . . . . (850) 487-9911
E-mail: debra.forbess@dms.myflorida.com
Human Resources Director **Heather N. Tyndall-Best** . . . . . (850) 488-2410
Finance and Accountability Bureau Chief
**Kelly McMullen** . . . . . . . . . . . . . . . . . . . . . . . . . (850) 487-0950

### Administrative Hearings Division

1230 Apalachee Parkway, Tallahassee, FL 32399-3060
Tel: (850) 488-9675

Director/Chief Judge **Robert S. Cohen** . . . . . . . . . . . . . (850) 488-9675
Deputy Chief Judge **(Vacant)** . . . . . . . . . . . . . . . . . . . (850) 488-9675

---

★ Elected Official   ■ Appointed by Governor   ● Appointed by Legislature   ▲ Appointed by Board or Commission   ◆ Appointed by State Supreme Court

**EXECUTIVE BRANCH**

## Real Estate Development and Management Division

4050 Esplande Way, Suite 315, Tallahassee, FL 32399
Tel: (850) 488-2074

Director **Tom Berger** .................................... (850) 488-2074
Operations and Maintenance Bureau Chief **Michael Jara** . . (850) 488-0211

## Retirement Division

1317 Winewood Boulevard, Tallahassee, FL 32399-0700
P.O. Box 9000, Tallahassee, FL 32315-9000
Tel: (850) 488-0294  Fax: (850) 488-5290

Director **Dan Drake** ................................... (850) 488-5540
Fax: (850) 921-4528
Assistant Director **Elizabeth Stevens** .................. (850) 921-2131
Benefit Payments Bureau Chief **Shirley Beauford** ........ (850) 488-4742
Enrollment & Contributions Bureau Chief
  **Joyce Morgan** ...................................... (850) 488-8837
Local Retirement System Bureau Chief **Keith Brinkman** . . (850) 488-2784
Retirement Calculations Bureau Chief **(Vacant)** .......... (850) 488-6491

## State Group Insurance Division

4050 Esplanade Way, Suite 215, Tallahassee, FL 32399-0950
Tel: (850) 921-4600  Fax: (850) 488-0252  Fax: (850) 921-4528

Director **Tami Fillyaw** ................................. (850) 921-4600
Policy and Development Bureau Chief **Suzetta Furlong** . . . (850) 921-4600
  Education: Union U 1988 BA; Sarasota 2001 MAED

## Agency for State Technology

Tel: (850) 412-6050  Internet: http://www.ast.myflorida.com/

Chief Information Officer/Executive Director
  **Jason M. Allison** ...................................(850) 412-6050
  E-mail: jason.allison@ast.myflorida.com
  Education: Florida State 1998 BA
Deputy Executive Director **Curtis R. Unruh** ............. (850) 717-9506
  E-mail: curtis.unruh@ast.myflorida.com
Chief of Staff **Kristina L. Wiggins** .................... (850) 717-9506
  E-mail: kristina.wiggins@ast.myflorida.com
Chief Financial Officer **(Vacant)** ...................... (850) 412-6046
Chief Information Security Officer **Danielle M. Alvarez** . . . (850) 412-6049
Chief Operations Officer **Kevin Patten** ................. (850) 488-4989
Chief Planning Officer **Tara S. Kyvik** .................. (850) 412-6054
  E-mail: tara.kyvik@ast.myflorida.com
  Education: Florida State BS, MPA, MIS
Chief Technology Officer **Eric Larson** .................. (850) 412-6045
Procurement **Mark L. Hernandez** ....................... (850) 412-6023
  E-mail: mark.hernandez@ast.myflorida.com
Accounting **Ronda D. Pearson** ......................... (850) 412-6026
  E-mail: ronda.pearson@ast.myflorida.com
General Counsel **Anthony "Tony" Garcia, JD** .......... (850) 412-6066
Inspector General **Tabitha A. McNulty, CISA** .......... (850) 412-6022
  Education: Florida State BSAcc
Human Resource Officer **Pat Chandler** ................. (850) 412-6071
Fax: (850) 487-1183
External Affairs Manager **Erin Choy** ................... (850) 412-6041

## Department of Military Affairs

P.O. Box 1008 (St. Francis Barracks), St. Augustine, FL 32085-1008
Tel: (904) 823-0231  Fax: (904) 823-0152  Internet: www.dma.state.fl.us

**Employees:** 397  **Fiscal Year:** 2015-2016  **Budget:** $96,345,000
■Adjutant General
  **BG Michael A. Calhoun, ARNG** .......... (904) 823-0100 ext. 0100
  E-mail: michael.calhoun@us.army.mil
  Executive Assistant
    **COL Edmund W "Ned" Woolfolk, Jr., USA (Ret)** . . . (904) 823-0150
Assistant Adjutant General (Air)
  **BrigGen James O. "Jim" Eifert, ANG** .............. (904) 823-0110
  Education: Air Force Acad 1982 BS
Assistant Adjutant General(Army)
  **COL Perry L. Hagaman, ARNG** .................... (904) 823-0110

Chief of Staff and Legislative Affairs Director
  **Glenn W. Sutphin, Jr.** ........................... (850) 414-9049
  400 S. Monroe St., Tallahassee, FL 32399
  E-mail: glenn.sutphin@myflorida.com
Chief of Staff (National Guard) **Mike Canzoneri** ........ (904) 823-0120
Judge Advocate General
  **COL Elizabeth Masters, ARNG** ................... (904) 823-0131
53rd Infantry Brigade Commander
  **COL John Haas, ARNG** ........................... (904) 823-0400
Personnel Deputy Chief of Staff **Vaughn Brown** ........ (904) 823-0300
Executive Services Director
  **SGM Robert Hosford, ARNG** ..................... (904) 823-0154
State Quartermaster **Sondra Vaughn** .................. (904) 823-0200
Public Affairs Director **Maj M. Caitlin Brown, ANG** ..... (904) 823-0168

## Florida Department of Revenue

5050 West Tennessee Street, Tallahassee, FL 32399-0100
Tel: (850) 617-8600  TTY: (800) 955-8771 (Florida Relay Service)
Fax: (850) 488-0024

**Employees:** 5,155  **Fiscal Year:** 2015-2016  **Budget:** $574,219,000
■Executive Director **Leon M. Biegalski** ................. (850) 617-8600
  E-mail: leon.biegalski@myflorida.com
Deputy Executive Director **Andrea Moreland** ........... (850) 617-8600
  Education: Florida 1992 JD
Chief of Staff **(Vacant)** ............................... (850) 617-8600
Child Support Program Director: **Ann Coffin** ........... (800) 622-5437
  E-mail: ann.coffin@myflorida.com
  Child Support Program Deputy Director **Thomas Mato** ........ (850)
  717-7000
    E-mail: matot@dor.state.fl.us
GTA (General Tax Administration) Program Director
  **Maria Johnson** .................................. (800) 352-3671
Information Services Program Director
  **Damodaran "Damu" Kuttikrishnan** ................ (850) 617-8700
Legislative and Cabinet Services Director
  **Debra J. "Debbie" Longman** ..................... (850) 617-8600
Property Tax Oversight Program Director
  **Maurice Gogarty, PhD** ........................... (850) 717-6570
Property Tax Oversight Deputy Program Director
  **(Vacant)** ......................................... (850) 617-8850
Tax Research Director **Bob McKee** ..................... (850) 617-8322
Chief of Public Information **Renee Watters** ............. (850) 617-8600
  E-mail: wattersr@dor.state.fl.us
General Counsel **Tony Hamm** .......................... (850) 617-8347
Inspector General **Sharon Doredant** ................... (850) 617-8152
  Education: Florida State BA
Taxpayer Rights Advocate **Patrick Loebig** ............. (850) 617-8168
  Education: Iowa State 1983 BS; Nova 1986 JD

## Florida Department of State

500 South Bronough Street, Tallahassee, FL 32399-0250
Tel: (850) 245-6500  Fax: (850) 245-6125
Internet: www.dos.myflorida.com

**Employees:** 407  **Fiscal Year:** 2015-2016  **Budget:** $132,059,000
■Secretary of State **Kenneth W. "Ken" Detzner** ......... (850) 245-6524
  E-mail: secretaryofstate@dos.myflorida.com
  Education: Florida State
  Executive Assistant **Shelby Bishop** ................. (850) 245-6524
Deputy Secretary of State for Administrative Services,
  Corporations and Elections **John Boynton** ........... (850) 245-4605
Deputy Secretary of State for Cultural, Historical and
  Information Programs **Kerri Post** ................... (850) 245-6514
Assistant Secretary of State/Chief of Staff
  **Jennifer Kennedy** ................................ (850) 245-6524
Communications Director **Meredith Beatrice** ........... (850) 245-6522
  E-mail: meredith.beatrice@dos.myflorida.com
Legislative Affairs Director **Christie Fitz-Patrick** ........ (850) 245-6512
  E-mail: christie.burrus@myflorida.com
Inspector General **John Greene** ....................... (850) 245-6195

---

★ Elected Official  ■ Appointed by Governor  ● Appointed by Legislature  ▲ Appointed by Board or Commission  ◆ Appointed by State Supreme Court

## Administrative Services Division

Tel: (850) 245-6550   Fax: (850) 245-6597

Director **Wes Underwood** . . . . . . . . . . . . . . . . . . . . . . . . . . . . . (850) 245-6550
Budget and Financial Management Director **(Vacant)** . . . . . (850) 245-6550
Human Resources Director **Dave Tepper** . . . . . . . . . . . . . . . (850) 245-6550
Chief Information Officer **George Brown** . . . . . . . . . . . . . (850) 245-6106
   E-mail: george.brown@dos.myflorida.com

## Corporations Division

2661 Executive Center Circle, Tallahassee, FL 32301
Tel: (800) 755-5111   Fax: (850) 245-6014

Director **Brenda L. Vorsiek** . . . . . . . . . . . . . . . . . (850) 245-6001 ext. 4004
Commercial Information Services Chief **Lyn Shoffstall** . . . (850) 245-6862

## Cultural Affairs Division

500 South Bronough Street, Tallahassee, FL 32399
Tel: (850) 845-6470   Fax: (850) 245-6497   E-mail: info@florida-arts.org
Internet: www.florida-arts.org

Division Director **Sandy Shaughnessy** . . . . . . . . . . . . . . . (850) 245-6480
   Education: NYU BA
Associate Director of Arts Resources and Services
   **Gaylen Phillips** . . . . . . . . . . . . . . . . . . . . . . . . . . . . . . . . (850) 245-6482
Associate Director of Government and Finance
   **Patricia A. Warren** . . . . . . . . . . . . . . . . . . . . . . . . . . . . . (850) 245-6467
Museum of Florida History Director **Jeana Brunson** . . . . . (850) 245-6386

## Elections Division

Tel: (850) 245-6200   Fax: (850) 245-6217   E-mail: doe@dos.state.fl.us
Internet: election.dos.state.fl.us

Director **Maria I. Matthews** . . . . . . . . . . . . . . . . . . . . . . . (850) 245-6200
Administrative Code and Register Program Administrator
   **Ernest L. Reddick** . . . . . . . . . . . . . . . . . . . . . . . . . . . . . . (850) 245-6270

## Historical Resources Division

500 South Bronough Street, Tallahassee, FL 32399-0250
Tel: (850) 245-6300   Fax: (850) 245-6435   Internet: www.flheritage.com

Director **Timothy A. Parsons, PhD** . . . . . . . . . . . . . . . . . . (850) 245-6300
Historic Preservationist **Carl Shiver** . . . . . . . . . . . . . . . . . . (850) 245-6300
Historic Preservationist **(Vacant)** . . . . . . . . . . . . . . . . . . . . (850) 245-6300
Government Operations Specialist **Robert Taylor** . . . . . . . . (850) 245-6472

## Library and Information Services Division

R. A. Gray Building, Tallahassee, FL 32399-0250
Tel: (850) 488-2812   Fax: (850) 245-6735
E-mail: info@dos.myflorida.com

Director/State Librarian **Amy L. Johnson** . . . . . . . . . . . . . (850) 245-6600
Archives & Records Management Bureau Chief
   **Gerard Clark** . . . . . . . . . . . . . . . . . . . . . . . . . . . . . . . . . (850) 245-6639
State and Federal Grants Program Administrator
   **Marian Deeney** . . . . . . . . . . . . . . . . . . . . . . . . . . . . . . . (850) 245-6622
   E-mail: mdeeney@dos.state.fl.us
State Library Technical Services **Connie Garrett** . . . . . . . . (850) 245-6655
   E-mail: connie.garrett@dos.myflorida.com

# Florida Department of Transportation [FDOT]

605 Suwannee Street, Tallahassee, FL 32399-0450
Tel: (850) 414-5200   Fax: (850) 414-5201   E-mail: fdot.pio@dot.state.fl.us
Internet: www.dot.state.fl.us

**Employees:** 6,939   **Fiscal Year:** 2015-2016   **Budget:** $10,034,186,000

■Secretary **James "Jim" Boxold** . . . . . . . . . . . . . . . . . . . . (850) 414-5205
   E-mail: jim.boxold@dot.state.fl.us
Chief of Staff and Legislative Programs Director
   **Mike Dew** . . . . . . . . . . . . . . . . . . . . . . . . . . . . . . . . . . . (850) 414-5205
   Education: Ohio State
General Counsel **Tom Thomas** . . . . . . . . . . . . . . . . . . . . . (850) 414-5265
Inspector General **Bob Clift** . . . . . . . . . . . . . . . . . . . . . . . (850) 410-5800
Legislative Affairs Director **Tom DiGiacomo** . . . . . . . . . . . (850) 414-5231
   E-mail: tom.digiacomo@dot.state.fl.us

Turnpike Enterprise Director **Diane Gutierrez-Scaccetti** . . (407) 264-3100
                                              Fax: (407) 822-6679
Public Information Officer **Dick Kane** . . . . . . . . . . . . . . . . . (850) 414-4540
   E-mail: fdot.pio@dot.state.fl.us
Federal Programs Coordinator **Douglas D. Callaway** . . . . . (202) 624-5885
   444 N. Capitol Street, NW, Suite 349,      Fax: (202) 624-5886
   Washington, DC 20001

## District Operations

District Secretary **Tommy Barfield** (District 3) . . . . . . . . . (850) 330-1425
   P.O. Box 607, Chipley, FL 32428-0607
District Secretary **Noranne Downs** (District 5) . . . . . . . . . (386) 943-5475
   719 South Woodland Boulevard, DeLand, FL 32720
District Secretary **Greg Evans** (District 2) . . . . . . . . . . . . . (386) 961-7800
   1109 South Marion Avenue, Lake City, FL 32025-5874
District Secretary **Billy Hattaway** (District 1) . . . . . . . . . . . (863) 519-2201
   P.O. Box 1249, Bartow, FL 33831-1249
District Secretary **Gerard V. O'Reilly** (District 4) . . . . . . . . (954) 777-4110
   3400 W. Commercial Boulevard, Fort Lauderdale, FL 33309-3421
District Secretary **Gus Pego** (District 6) . . . . . . . . . . . . . . (305) 470-5197
   1000 NW 111th Avenue, Miami, FL 33172
District Secretary **Paul Steinman** (District 7) . . . . . . . . . . (813) 975-6000
   11201 N. Malcolm McKinley Drive, Tampa, FL 33612-6403
   Education: Michigan State 1989 BSCE

## Engineering and Operations

Fax: (850) 414-5201

Assistant Secretary **Brian Blanchard** . . . . . . . . . . . . . . . . . (850) 414-5220
   E-mail: brian.blanchard@dot.state.fl.us
Chief Engineer **Tom Byron** . . . . . . . . . . . . . . . . . . . . . . . . (850) 414-5240
   E-mail: tom.byron@dot.state.fl.us
Construction Director **David Sadler** . . . . . . . . . . . . . . . . . . (850) 414-4150
Design Director **Tim Lattner** . . . . . . . . . . . . . . . . . . . . . . . (850) 414-4175
Maintenance Director **Rudy Powell** . . . . . . . . . . . . . . . . . . (850) 410-5757
   E-mail: rudy.powell@dot.state.fl.us
Materials Director **Tim Ruelke** . . . . . . . . . . . . . . . . . . . . . (352) 955-6620
   E-mail: timothy.ruelke@dot.myflorida.com
Right of Way Director **Jim Spalla** . . . . . . . . . . . . . . . . . . . . (850) 414-4545
   State Traffic Operations Engineer **Mark Wilson** . . . . . . . . (850) 410-5413
     E-mail: mark.wilson@dot.state.fl.us
Chief Safety Officer **Lora B. Hollingsworth** . . . . . . . . . . . (850) 245-1504
   E-mail: lora.hollingsworth@dot.state.fl.us

## Finance and Administration

Fax: (850) 414-5201

Assistant Secretary **Rachel Davis Cone** . . . . . . . . . . . . . . . (850) 414-5215
   E-mail: rachel.cone@dot.state.fl.us

## Intermodal Systems Development [ISD]

Assistant Secretary **Richard Biter** . . . . . . . . . . . . . . . . . . . (850) 414-5235
   Education: Tri-State 1973 BA

## Transportation Commission

605 Suwannee Street, MS 9, Tallahassee, FL 32399-0450
Tel: (850) 414-4105   Fax: (850) 414-4234

■Chairman **Jay Trumbull, Sr.** . . . . . . . . . . . . . . . . . . . . . . . (850) 414-4105
■Vice Chairman **Kenneth W. Wright** . . . . . . . . . . . . . . . . . (850) 414-4105
   E-mail: kwright@shutts.com
   Education: South Florida 1970 BA; Cumberland 1974 JD
■Secretary **Beth R. Kigel** . . . . . . . . . . . . . . . . . . . . . . . . . . (850) 414-4105
■Member **John Browning** . . . . . . . . . . . . . . . . . . . . . . . . . . (850) 414-4105
   Education: Florida State BA
■Member **Donnie Ellington** . . . . . . . . . . . . . . . . . . . . . . . . (850) 415-4105
■Member **Maurice Ferre** . . . . . . . . . . . . . . . . . . . . . . . . . . (850) 414-4105
   Education: Lawrenceville (Lawrenceville, NJ) 1953;
   Miami 1957 BSAE, 1958 MBA
■Member **Ronald "Ron" Howse** . . . . . . . . . . . . . . . . . . . . . (850) 414-4105
■Member **Teresa Sarnoff** . . . . . . . . . . . . . . . . . . . . . . . . . . (850) 414-4105
■Member **Jim Sebesta** . . . . . . . . . . . . . . . . . . . . . . . . . . . . (850) 414-4105
   Education: Loyola U (Chicago) BS; DePaul MBA

---

★ Elected Official    ■ Appointed by Governor    ● Appointed by Legislature    ▲ Appointed by Board or Commission    ◆ Appointed by State Supreme Court

EXECUTIVE BRANCH

# Florida Department of Veterans Affairs

11351 Ulmerton Road, Suite 311-K, Largo, FL 33778-1630
Tel: (727) 518-3202  Fax: (727) 518-3407  Internet: www.floridavets.org

**Employees:** 1,089  **Fiscal Year:** 2015-2016  **Budget:** $108,470,000

■Executive Director (Interim) **Glenn W. Sutphin, Jr.** . . . . . . (850) 487-1533
  E-mail: exdir@fdva.state.fl.us
  Executive Assistant **John Rudy** . . . . . . . . . . . . . (727) 518-3202 ext. 5594
Executive Deputy Director **Al Carter** . . . . . . . . . . . . . . . . . (727) 518-3202
  E-mail: cartera@fdva.state.fl.us
General Counsel **Chuck Faircloth** . . . . . . . . . . . . (850) 487-1533 ext. 7705
Communications Director **Steve Murray** . . . . . . . . . . . . . . (850) 487-1533
  400 S. Monroe St., Suite 2105, Tallahassee, FL 32399
  E-mail: murrayr@fdva.state.fl.us
Legislative Affairs and Cabinet Affairs Director
  (Acting) **Jessica Kraynak** . . . . . . . . . . . . . . . . . (850) 487-1533 ext. 7712
  E-mail: kraynakj2@fdva.state.fl.us

## Administration and Public Information Division

Mary Grizzle Building, 11351 Ulmerton Road, Room 311-K,
Largo, FL 33778-1630
Tel: (727) 518-3202

Director **Leticia Nazario-Braddock** . . . . . . . . . . . (727) 518-3202 ext. 5538
  E-mail: nazario-braddock1@fdva.state.fl.us
Purchasing Director **Scott Gerke** . . . . . . . . . . . . . (727) 518-3202 ext. 5557
Account Services Administrator
  **Johanna Baynard** . . . . . . . . . . . . . . . . . . . . . (727) 518-3203 ext. 5571
Staff Development Administrator **Liliane Bitar** . . . (727) 518-3202 ext. 5547
  E-mail: bitarl@fdva.state.fl.us
Chief Information Officer **Christine Loso** . . . . . . . (727) 518-3202 ext. 5507
  E-mail: christine.loso@myflorida.com
  Education: Colorado Christian 2002 BS
Fiscal Officer **Linda Rizzo** . . . . . . . . . . . . . . . . . . (727) 518-3202 ext. 5515
Personnel Officer **James Uliasz** . . . . . . . . . . . . . . (727) 518-3202 ext. 5608
Inspector General **David Marzullo** . . . . . . . . . . . . (727) 518-3202 ext. 5570
  Management Analyst **Ronald Burke** . . . . . . . . . . . . . . . . . (727) 518-3202
  Management Analyst **John Rudy** . . . . . . . . . . . . . (727) 518-3202 ext. 5594

## Veterans' Benefits and Assistance Division

9500 Bay Pines Boulevard, Room 214, St. Petersburg, FL 33744
Tel: (727) 319-7400

Director **Ethel "Alene" Tarter** . . . . . . . . . . . . . . . . . . . . . (727) 319-7421
  Executive Assistant **Doug Walton** . . . . . . . . . . . . . . . . . . (727) 319-7427
State Approving Veterans' Training Bureau Chief
  **Betsy Wickham** . . . . . . . . . . . . . . . . . . . . . . . . . . . . . . . . (727) 319-7401
Veterans' Claims Services Bureau Chief **Jim Ansboury** . . . (727) 319-7403
Veterans' Field Services Bureau Chief
  **Andy McCormick** . . . . . . . . . . . . . . . . . . . . . . (321) 397-6584 ext. 4905

# Agency for Health Care Administration [AHCA]

2727 Mahan Drive, Tallahassee, FL 32308-7703
Tel: (850) 412-3600  Tel: (888) 419-3456 (Agency Call Center)
Fax: (850) 922-2897  Internet: ahca.myflorida.com

**Employees:** 1,544  **Fiscal Year:** 2015-2016  **Budget:** $25,512,030,000

■Secretary **Elizabeth "Liz" Dudek** . . . . . . . . . . . . . . . . . . (850) 412-3603
  E-mail: ahcasecretary@ahca.myflorida.com
  Education: Elmhurst 1973 BA
Health Quality Assurance Deputy Secretary
  **Molly Mckinstry** . . . . . . . . . . . . . . . . . . . . . . . . . . . . . . . (850) 412-4334
Health Quality Assurance Assistant Deputy Secretary
  **Polly Weaver** . . . . . . . . . . . . . . . . . . . . . . . . . . . . . . . . . (850) 412-4491
Operations Deputy Secretary **Tonya Kidd** . . . . . . . . . . . . . (850) 412-3811
  Education: Florida State 1989 BS
Chief of Staff **Timothy "Toby" Philpot, Jr., JD** . . . . . . . . (850) 412-3606
  Education: Florida; Florida Coastal JD
General Counsel **Stuart F. Williams** . . . . . . . . . . . . . . . . . (850) 412-3630
  E-mail: stuart.williams@ahca.myflorida.com

Inspector General **Eric W. Miller** . . . . . . . . . . . . . . . . . . . (850) 412-3990
Chief Financial Officer **Anita Hicks** . . . . . . . . . . . . . . . . . (850) 412-3815
Human Resources Chief **Cindy Mazzara** . . . . . . . . . . . . . (850) 412-3900
Florida Center for Health Information and Policy,
  Analysis Bureau Chief **Heidi Fox** . . . . . . . . . . . . . . . . . . (850) 412-3749
Support Services Chief **Jennifer Barrett** . . . . . . . . . . . . . . (850) 412-3887
  E-mail: jennifer.barrett@ahca.myflorida.com
Communications Director **Mallory Deason McManus** . . . . (850) 412-3620
  E-mail: mallory.mcmanus@ahca.myflorida.com
Deputy Chief of Staff **Joshua Spagnola** . . . . . . . . . . . . . . (850) 412-3612
  E-mail: joshua.spagnola@ahca.myflorida.com
Chief Information Officer **Scott Ward** . . . . . . . . . . . . . . . . (850) 412-4848
  E-mail: scott.ward@ahca.myflorida.com
Health Insurance Portability and Accountability Act
  Privacy Security Officer **Kathy Pilkenton** . . . . . . . . . . . (850) 412-3966

# Agency for Persons with Disabilities [APD]

4030 Esplanade Way, Suite 380, Tallahassee, FL 32399-0950
Tel: (850) 488-4257  Fax: (850) 922-6456
E-mail: apd_director@apd.state.fl.us  Internet: apdcares.org

■Executive Director **Barbara J. Palmer** . . . . . . . . . . . . . . . (850) 488-4879
  E-mail: barbara.palmer@apdcares.org
  Education: Florida State 1970 BS, 1974 MS
Deputy Director of Operations **Tom Rankin** . . . . . . . . . . . (850) 488-4257
  E-mail: tom.rankin@apdcares.org
Deputy Director for Programs **Denise Arnold** . . . . . . . . . . (850) 488-4257
  E-mail: denise.arnold@apdcares.org
Chief of Staff **Karen Hagan** . . . . . . . . . . . . . . . . . . . . . . . (850) 488-4879

# Office of the Auditor General

Claude Pepper Building, 111 West Madison Street, Room G-74,
Tallahassee, FL 32399-1450
Tel: (850) 412-2722  Fax: (850) 488-6975
E-mail: flaudgen@aud.state.fl.us

●Auditor General **Sherrill F. Norman** . . . . . . . . . . . . . . . . . (850) 412-2722
  E-mail: sherrillnorman@aud.state.fl.us
Deputy Auditor General **Gregory L. Centers** . . . . . . . . . . (850) 412-2889
Deputy Auditor General **Marilyn Rosetti** . . . . . . . . . . . . . (850) 412-2921
Deputy Auditor General **Matthew J. Tracy** . . . . . . . . . . . . (850) 412-2749
General Counsel **John H. Tenewitz** . . . . . . . . . . . . . . . . . (850) 412-2724
  Education: Florida State 1980 JD

# Office of the Public Counsel [OPC]

Claude Pepper Building, 111 West Madison Street, Suite 812,
Tallahassee, FL 32399-1400
Tel: (850) 488-9330  Fax: (850) 487-6419

▲Public Counsel **James R. "J.R." Kelly** . . . . . . . . . . . . . . . (850) 488-9330
  E-mail: james.kelly@myflorida.com
  Education: Florida State 1981 BSAcc, 1988 JD
Deputy Public Counsel **Charles Rehwinkel** . . . . . . . . . . . . (850) 488-9330
Office Manager/Legislative Analyst **Mike Jenkins** . . . . . . . (850) 488-9330
Executive Assistant **Monica Woods** . . . . . . . . . . . . . . . . . (850) 488-9330
  E-mail: monica.woods@myflorida.com

# Financial Services Commission

200 East Gaines Street, Tallahassee, FL 32399-0300
Tel: (800) 342-2762 (Consumer Hotline)

Commissioner **Jeffrey H. "Jeff" Atwater** . . . . . . . . . . . . . (850) 413-2850
  Education: Florida 1981 BA
Commissioner **Pamela J. "Pam" Bondi** . . . . . . . . . . . . . . (850) 245-0140
  Education: Florida 1987 BA; Stetson 1990 JD
Commissioner **Adam H. Putnam** . . . . . . . . . . . . . . . . . . . (850) 488-3022
  Education: Florida 1995 BS
Commissioner **Richard Lynn "Rick" Scott** . . . . . . . . . . . . (850) 488-4441

---

★ Elected Official  ■ Appointed by Governor  ● Appointed by Legislature  ▲ Appointed by Board or Commission  ◆ Appointed by State Supreme Court

## Office of Financial Regulation

200 East Gaines Street, Tallahassee, FL 32399
Internet: www.flofr.com

Commissioner **Drew J. Breakspear** . . . . . . . . . . . . . . . . (850) 410-9601
  E-mail: drew.breakspear@flofr.com
  Education: U Witwatersrand BCommerce; Harvard 1969 MBA
Deputy Commissioner **Pamela P. Epting** . . . . . . . . . . . . . (850) 410-9601
  E-mail: pam.epting@flofr.com
Inspector General **Karen Fisher** . . . . . . . . . . . . . . . . . . . (850) 410-9601
  E-mail: karen.fisher@flofr.com
Legislative and Cabinet Deputy Director
  **Meredith Hinshelwood** . . . . . . . . . . . . . . . . . . . . . . . (850) 410-9544
General Counsel **Colin Roopnarine** . . . . . . . . . . . . . . . . (850) 410-9655
  E-mail: general.counsel@flofr.com

## Office of Insurance Regulation

200 East Gaines Street, Tallahassee, FL 32399
Tel: (850) 413-3140  Fax: (850) 488-3334

▲Commissioner **Kevin M. McCarty** . . . . . . . . . . . . . . . . (850) 413-5914
  Note: Until late June 2016.
  E-mail: kevin.mccarty@floir.com
  Education: Florida BA, JD
▲Commissioner **David Altmaier** . . . . . . . . . . . . . . (850) 413-3101 ext. 5914
  E-mail: david.altmaier@floir.com
  Education: Western Kentucky 2004 BA
Chief of Staff **Belinda Miller** . . . . . . . . . . . . . . . . . . . . . (850) 413-5000
Deputy Chief of Staff **Caitlin Murray** . . . . . . . . . . . . . . (850) 413-5005
General Counsel **Anoush Brangaccio** . . . . . . . . . . . . . . . (850) 413-4116
Life and Health Deputy Commissioner **Rich Robleto** . . . . . (850) 413-5104
  Education: Temple BA; Delaware MBA
  Life and Health Financial Oversight Director
  **Carolyn Morgan** . . . . . . . . . . . . . . . . . . . . . . . . . . . (850) 413-5233
  Life and Health Product Review Director **Eric Johnson** . . (850) 413-5059
Property and Casualty Deputy Commissioner **(Vacant)** . . . . (850) 413-3849
  Property and Casualty Financial Oversight Director
  **Robert Ridenour** . . . . . . . . . . . . . . . . . . . . . . . . . . . (850) 413-3849
  Property and Casualty Product Review Director
  **Sandra Starnes** . . . . . . . . . . . . . . . . . . . . . . . . . . . . (850) 413-5344
Market Investigations Director **Susanne Murphy** . . . . . . . . (850) 413-4115

## Florida Fish and Wildlife Conservation Commission

620 South Meridian Street, Tallahassee, FL 32399-1600
Tel: (850) 488-4676  TTY: (850) 488-9542  Fax: (850) 921-5786
E-mail: fwc@myfwc.com  Internet: www.myfwc.com

**Employees:** 2,096  **Fiscal Year:** 2015-2016  **Budget:** $358,985,000

■Chairman **Brian Yablonski** . . . . . . . . . . . . . . . . . . . . . (305) 444-4648
  Term Expires: January 5, 2019
  Education: Wake Forest BA; Miami JD
■Vice Chairman **Aliese P. "Liesa" Priddy** . . . . . . . . . . . . . (850) 487-3796
  Term Expires: January 6, 2017
■Commissioner **Ronald M. Bergeron** . . . . . . . . . . . . . . . (850) 487-3796
  Term Expires: August 1, 2017
■Commissioner **Richard Hanas** . . . . . . . . . . . . . . . . . . . (850) 487-3796
  Term Expires: August 1, 2017
■Commissioner **Adrien "Bo" Rivard III** . . . . . . . . . . . . . . (850) 487-3796
  Term Expires: August 1, 2017
  Education: Florida; Samford JD
■Commissioner **Charles Roberts III** . . . . . . . . . . . . . . . . . (850) 487-3796
  Term Expires: August 1, 2016
■Commissioner **Robert A. Spottswood** . . . . . . . . . . . . . . . (850) 488-4676
  Term Expires: January 6, 2018
  Education: Florida 1979; Miami 1982 JD
■Commissioner **(Vacant)** . . . . . . . . . . . . . . . . . . . . . . . . (850) 487-3796
  Term Expires: August 1, 2017

## Florida Public Service Commission

2540 Shumard Oak Boulevard, Tallahassee, FL 32399-0850
Tel: (850) 413-6100  E-mail: contact@psc.state.fl.us
Internet: www.floridapsc.com

**Employees:** 286  **Fiscal Year:** 2015-2016  **Budget:** $25,137,000

■Chairman **Julie Imanuel Brown** . . . . . . . . . . . . . . . . . . . (850) 413-6042
  Term Expires: January 1, 2019
  E-mail: commissioner.brown@psc.state.fl.us
  Education: Florida JD
■Commissioner **Ronald A. "Ron" Brisé** . . . . . . . . . . . . . . (850) 413-6046
  Term Expires: January 1, 2018
  E-mail: commissioner.brise@psc.state.fl.us
  Education: Oakwood BS; American InterContinental 2005 MBA
■Commissioner **Arthur L. "Art" Graham** . . . . . . . . . . . . . (850) 413-6040
  Term Expires: January 1, 2018
■Commissioner **Lisa Polak Edgar** . . . . . . . . . . . . . . . . . . (850) 413-6044
  Term Expires: January 1, 2017
  E-mail: commissioner.edgar@psc.state.fl.us
  Education: Florida State 1985 BA, 1988 JD
■Commissioner **Jimmy T. Patronis** . . . . . . . . . . . . . . . . . (850) 413-6038
  Term Expires: January 1, 2019
  E-mail: jpatroni@psc.state.fl.us
  Education: Florida State 1996 BS

## State Board of Education

Turlington Building, 325 West Gaines Street, Suite 1514,
Tallahassee, FL 32399-0400
Tel: (850) 245-0505  Fax: (850) 245-9667  Internet: http://fldoe.org

■Chair **Marva Johnson** . . . . . . . . . . . . . . . . . . . . . . . . . (850) 245-9661
  Term Expires: December 31, 2017
  E-mail: marva.johnson@fldoe.org
■Vice Chair **John R. Padget** . . . . . . . . . . . . . . . . . . . . . . (850) 245-9661
  Term Expires: December 31, 2016
  E-mail: john.padget@fldoe.org
■Member **Gary R. Chartrand** . . . . . . . . . . . . . . . . . . . . . (850) 245-9661
  Term Expires: December 31, 2018
  E-mail: gary.chartrand@fldoe.org
■Member **Thomas "Tom" Grady** . . . . . . . . . . . . . . . . . . . (850) 245-9661
  Term Expires: December 31, 2018
  E-mail: tom.grady@fldoe.org
  Education: Florida State 1979 BS; Duke 1982 JD
■Member **Rebecca Fishman Lipsey** . . . . . . . . . . . . . . . . . (850) 245-9661
  Term Expires: December 31, 2017
  E-mail: rebecca.lipsey@fldoe.org
  Education: Pennsylvania 2003 BA; Bank Street MEd
■Member **Michael Olenick** . . . . . . . . . . . . . . . . . . . . . . . (850) 245-9661
  Term Expires: December 31, 2016
  E-mail: michael.olenick@fldoe.org
  Education: Lafayette; Nova Southeastern JD
■Member **Andy Tuck** . . . . . . . . . . . . . . . . . . . . . . . . . . . (850) 245-9661
  Term Expires: December 31, 2017
  E-mail: andy.tuck@fldoe.org

## Florida Department of Education [FLDOE]

Turlington Building, 325 West Gaines Street, Tallahassee, FL 32399-0400
Tel: (850) 245-0505  Fax: (850) 245-9667  Internet: www.fldoe.org

▲Commissioner **Pamela "Pam" Stewart** . . . . . . . . . . . . . . (850) 245-0505
  E-mail: commissioner@fldoe.org
  Education: South Florida BA, MEd
  Executive Assistant to the Commissioner **Aubrey Post** . . . (850) 245-7830
Chief of Staff **Kathy Hebda** . . . . . . . . . . . . . . . . . . . . . . (850) 245-9663
General Counsel **Matthew Mears** . . . . . . . . . . . . . . . . . . (850) 245-0442
Inspector General **Mike Blackburn** . . . . . . . . . . . . . . . . . (850) 245-9418
  E-mail: mike.blackburn@fldoe.org
Governmental Relations Director **Tanya Cooper** . . . . . . . . . (850) 245-9663
Independent Education and Parental Choice Executive
  Director **Adam Miller** . . . . . . . . . . . . . . . . . . . . . . . . (850) 245-0502
Communications Director **Meghan Speakes Collins** . . . . . . (850) 245-0413
  E-mail: meghan.collins@fldoe.org                Fax: (850) 245-9650
Chief Technology and Information Officer **(Vacant)** . . . . . . (850) 245-0510

---

★ Elected Official   ■ Appointed by Governor   ● Appointed by Legislature   ▲ Appointed by Board or Commission   ◆ Appointed by State Supreme Court

## Division of Blind Services

325 West Gaines Street, Room 1114, Tallahassee, FL 32399-0400
Tel: (850) 245-0300  Tel: (850) 245-0363

Director **Robert Doyle III** . . . . . . . . . . . . . . . . . . . . . . . . . . . (850) 245-0300

## Division of Career and Adult Education

325 West Gaines Street, Suite 744, Tallahassee, FL 32399-0400
Tel: (850) 245-0446  Fax: (850) 245-9052
E-mail: careerandadulted@fldoe.org

Chancellor **Roderic Duckworth** . . . . . . . . . . . . . . . . . . (850) 245-9463
  E-mail: rod.duckworth@fldoe.org
  Education: Southern Arkansas U 1987 BS
GED (General Education Development) Administrator
  **Tara Goodman** . . . . . . . . . . . . . . . . . . . . . . . . . . . . . (850) 245-9002
  E-mail: tara.goodman@fldoe.org

## Division of Florida Colleges

325 West Gaines Street, Room 1554, Tallahassee, FL 32399-0400
Tel: (850) 245-0407  Fax: (850) 245-9454

Chancellor **Madeline Pumareiga** . . . . . . . . . . . . . . . . . (850) 245-9449
Executive Vice Chancellor **Dr. Christopher M. Mullin** . . . . (850) 245-0458
  Education: Florida; Teachers Col Columbia U; Florida PhD
Financial Policy Associate Vice Chancellor **Scott Kittel** . . . (850) 245-9467
Research and Analytics Associate Vice Chancellor
  **Eric Godin** . . . . . . . . . . . . . . . . . . . . . . . . . . . . . . . (850) 245-9482
Student and Academic Affairs Associate Vice Chancellor
  **Karinda Barrett** . . . . . . . . . . . . . . . . . . . . . . . . . . . (850) 245-9492
Communications Coordinator **Cora Merritt** . . . . . . . . . . . (850) 245-0448
  E-mail: cora.merritt@fldoe.org
External Affairs Director **(Vacant)** . . . . . . . . . . . . . . . . (850) 245-9788
Governmental Affairs and Equity Director
  **Alexander Anderson** . . . . . . . . . . . . . . . . . . . . . . . . (850) 245-9455

## Division of Finance and Operations

Deputy Commissioner **Linda Champion** . . . . . . . . . . . . . (850) 245-0406

## Division of Public Schools

Turlington Building, 325 West Gaines Street, Room 1502,
Tallahassee, FL 32399-0400
Tel: (850) 245-0509  Fax: (850) 245-5036

Chancellor **Hershel Lyons** . . . . . . . . . . . . . . . . . . . . . . (850) 245-0509
Executive Vice Chancellor **Mary Jane Tappen** . . . . . . . . . (850) 245-0509
Educator Quality Deputy Chancellor **Brian Dassler** . . . . . . (850) 245-0509
Safe Schools Office Director **Brooks Rumenik** . . . . . . . . . (850) 245-0416
  E-mail: brooks.rumenik@fldoe.org
Race To The Top Projects Manager **Holly Edenfield** . . . . . (850) 245-0509

## Division of Vocational Rehabilitation

Building A, 2002 Old Saint Augustine Road, Tallahassee, FL 32301-4862
Tel: (850) 245-3399

Director **Aleisa McKinlay** . . . . . . . . . . . . . . . . . . . . . . . (850) 245-3400

## Office of the Lieutenant Governor

The Capitol, Suite: PL-05, Tallahassee, FL 32399-0001
Tel: (850) 717-9331  Fax: (850) 921-6114  E-mail: fl_ltgov@eog.state.fl.us

★Lieutenant Governor **Carlos C. Lopez-Cantera** (R) . . . . . . (850) 717-9331
  Term Expires: 2019
  E-mail: carlos.lopez-cantera@myflorida.com
  E-mail: clc@eog.myflorida.com
  Education: Miami 1996 BA

## Legal Affairs Department

The Capitol, Plaza Level One, Tallahassee, FL 32399-1050
Tel: (850) 414-3990  Tel: (866) 966-7226 (Fraud Hotline)
Fax: (850) 487-2564  Fax: (850) 410-1630 (Citizen Services)
Internet: http://myfloridalegal.com

**Employees:** 1,293  **Fiscal Year:** 2015-2016  **Budget:** $204,343,000

## Office of the Attorney General

The Capitol, Plaza Level One, Tallahassee, FL 32399-1050
Tel: (850) 414-3990  Fax: (850) 487-2564

**Employees:** 1,215

★Attorney General **Pamela J. "Pam" Bondi** (R) . . . . . . . . (850) 245-0140
  Term Expires: January 2019
Chief Deputy Attorney General **Tyler Cathey** . . . . . . . . . (850) 245-0140
  Education: Muhlenberg; Florida JD
Associate Deputy Attorney General **Trish Conners** . . . . . . (850) 245-0140
Associate Deputy Attorney General/General Counsel
  **Kent Perez** . . . . . . . . . . . . . . . . . . . . . . . . . . . . . . (850) 245-0140
Inspector General **Steve Rumph** . . . . . . . . . . . . . . . . . (850) 414-3300
Solicitor General **(Vacant)** . . . . . . . . . . . . . . . . . . . . . (850) 414-3300
Media Director **Whitney Ray** . . . . . . . . . . . . . . . . . . . . (850) 245-0150
  Education: Arkansas BA
Public Relations Director **Trey Stapleton** . . . . . . . . . . . . (850) 245-0150
  E-mail: trey.stapleton@myfloridalegal.com
  Education: North Texas

## Department of Financial Services

200 East Gaines Street, Tallahassee, FL 32399
Tel: (850) 413-2850  TTY: (850) 413-3262  Fax: (850) 413-2950
Internet: www.myfloridacfo.com

**Employees:** 2,603

★Chief Financial Officer **Jeffrey H. "Jeff" Atwater** (R) . . . . (863) 413-2806
  Term Expires: January 2019
  E-mail: jeff.atwater@myfloridacfo.com
Chief of Staff **Robert C. Kneip** . . . . . . . . . . . . . . . . . . (850) 413-4900
  Deputy Chief Financial Officer, Communications
  **Michelle M. D. Winokur** . . . . . . . . . . . . . . . . . . . . (850) 413-2851
  Deputy Chief Financial Officer, Fraud **Jay Etheridge** . . . (850) 413-2851
  Deputy Chief Financial Officer, Operations
  **Paul Whitfield** . . . . . . . . . . . . . . . . . . . . . . . . . . . (850) 413-2909
General Counsel **Drew Parker** . . . . . . . . . . . . . . . . . . . (850) 413-2840
Inspector General **Teresa Michael** . . . . . . . . . . . . . . . . (850) 413-4960
Cabinet Affairs Director **Robert Tornillo** . . . . . . . . . . . . (850) 413-2825
  Education: Florida State 1984 BS
Communications Director **Ashley Carr** . . . . . . . . . . . . . . (850) 413-2842
  E-mail: ashley.carr@myfloridacfo.com
Internal Operations and Appointments Director
  **Susan Miller** . . . . . . . . . . . . . . . . . . . . . . . . . . . . (850) 413-2806
  E-mail: susan.miller@myfloridacfo.com
Legislative Affairs Director **Elizabeth Boyd** . . . . . . . . . . (850) 413-2890
  E-mail: elizabeth.boyd@myfloridacfo.com
  Education: Florida State 2005 BS
Policy, Research and Legislative Affairs Director
  **Katie Hayden** . . . . . . . . . . . . . . . . . . . . . . . . . . . . (850) 413-2809
  E-mail: katie.hayden@myfloridacfo.com
Program Management Director **(Vacant)** . . . . . . . . . . . . . (850) 413-2907
Insurance Consumer Advocate **Sha'Ron James** . . . . . . . . (850) 413-5923
  Education: Florida A&M BEc; Syracuse MPA

## Division of Accounting and Auditing

200 East Gaines Street, Tallahassee, FL 32399-0318
Fax: (850) 413-5553  Internet: www.myfloridacfo.com

Director **Christina Smith** . . . . . . . . . . . . . . . . . . . . . . . (850) 413-5510
Assistant Director **Rachael Lieblick** . . . . . . . . . . . . . . . (850) 413-5510
Assistant Director **Rick Sweet** . . . . . . . . . . . . . . . . . . . (850) 413-5510

## Division of Administration

200 East Gaines Street, Tallahassee, FL 32399-0313
Tel: (850) 413-3100  Fax: (850) 922-2322

Director **Stephanie Iliff** . . . . . . . . . . . . . . . . . . . . . . . . (850) 413-2172
  E-mail: stephanie.iliff@myfloridacfo.com

---

★ Elected Official   ■ Appointed by Governor   ● Appointed by Legislature   ▲ Appointed by Board or Commission   ◆ Appointed by State Supreme Court

Summer 2016                    © Leadership Directories, Inc.                    *State Yellow Book*

## Division of Agents and Agency Services

200 East Gaines Street, Tallahassee, FL 32399-0318
Tel: (850) 413-3137  Tel: (850) 413-3136  Fax: (850) 922-3905

Director **Greg Thomas** . . . . . . . . . . . . . . . . . . . . . . . . . . . . . . (850) 413-5400
   E-mail: greg.thomas@myfloridacfo.com
Assistant Director **(Vacant)** . . . . . . . . . . . . . . . . . . . . . . . . . (850) 413-5416

## Division of Consumer Services

200 East Gaines Street, Tallahassee, FL 32399-0322
Tel: (850) 413-3089  Fax: (850) 922-5372

Director **Tasha Carter** . . . . . . . . . . . . . . . . . . . . . . . . . . . . . (850) 413-5800
Assistant Director **(Vacant)** . . . . . . . . . . . . . . . . . . . . . . . . . (850) 413-5800

## Division of Funeral, Cemetery and Consumer Services

200 East Gaines Street, Tallahassee, FL 32399-0361
Tel: (850) 413-3039

Director **Doug Shropshire** . . . . . . . . . . . . . . . . . . . . . . . . . . (850) 413-3039
Assistant Director **Ellen Simon** . . . . . . . . . . . . . . . . . . . . . . (850) 413-3039

## Division of Information Systems [DIS]

200 East Gaines Street, Tallahassee, FL 32399
Tel: (850) 413-3184  Fax: (850) 922-2035

Director **Charles Ghini** . . . . . . . . . . . . . . . . . . . . . . . . . . . . . (850) 413-3184
   E-mail: charles.ghini@myfloridacfo.com
   Education: Florida State 1995 BS
Assistant Director **Roosevelt Sawyer, Jr.** . . . . . . . . . . . . . (850) 413-3184
Accounting Systems Design Chief **Jennifer Grant** . . . . . . . (850) 413-3184
Customer Support Services Bureau Chief **Jon Yeaton** . . . . (850) 413-3184
   E-mail: jon.yeaton@myfloridacfo.com
Distributed Infrastructure Bureau Chief **Nicholas Platt** . . . . (850) 413-3184
Enterprise Applications Bureau Chief **Tabitha Hunter** . . . . (850) 413-3184
Payroll Design and Development Bureau Chief
   **Ron Ricks** . . . . . . . . . . . . . . . . . . . . . . . . . . . . . . . . . . . . . (850) 413-3184
   E-mail: ron.ricks@myfloridacfo.com
Administrative Services Manager **Sherry Faircloth** . . . . . . . (850) 413-3184
   E-mail: sherry.faircloth@myfloridacfo.com
Assistant Data Center Director **Clyde Gaskins** . . . . . . . . . . (850) 413-3184
   E-mail: clyde.gaskins@myfloridacfo.com
Enterprise Financial Support Services Deputy Director
   **Robin Kinsey** . . . . . . . . . . . . . . . . . . . . . . . . . . . . . . . . . . (850) 413-3184

## Division of Unclaimed Property

Director **Walter Graham** . . . . . . . . . . . . . . . . . . . . . . . . . . . (850) 413-5515

## Insurance Fraud Division

200 East Gaines Street, Tallahassee, FL 32399
Tel: (850) 413-3115  Fax: (850) 413-3996

Director **Simon Blank** . . . . . . . . . . . . . . . . . . (850) 413-4001 ext. 4001
   Education: U Duisburg-Essen MEc
Assistant Director **Major Timothy J. Cannon** . . . . . . . . . . (850) 413-4047

## General Fraud Bureau

Bureau Chief **Buddy Hand** . . . . . . . . . . . . . . . . . . . . . . . . (850) 413-4020
   E-mail: buddy.hand@myfloridacfo.com

## Workers' Compensation Fraud Bureau

Bureau Chief **John Dygon** . . . . . . . . . . . . . . . . . . . . . . . . . (954) 958-5412
   E-mail: john.dygon@myfloridacfo.com

## Operational Support Services Bureau

Law Enforcement Major **Ernie Stoll** . . . . . . . . . . . . . . . . . . (850) 413-4053
   E-mail: ernie.stoll@myfloridacfo.com

## Legal Services Division

200 East Gaines Street, Tallahassee, FL 32399
Fax: (850) 413-3029

Director **Linda K. Reel** . . . . . . . . . . . . . . . . . . . . . . . . . . . . (850) 413-4250

## Rehabilitation and Liquidation Division

2020 Capital Circle, South East, Tallahassee, FL 32301-0110
Tel: (850) 413-3179  Fax: (850) 413-3992

Director **Toma L. Wilkerson** . . . . . . . . . . . . . . . (850) 413-4477 ext. 3983
Administrative Assistant **Dana Green** . . . . . . . . . (850) 413-3111 ext. 5922

## Risk Management Division

200 East Gaines Street, Tallahassee, FL 32399
Tel: (850) 413-3120  Fax: (850) 413-2732

Director **Molly Merry, CPA** . . . . . . . . . . . . . . . . . . . . . . . . (850) 413-4700

## State Fire Marshal Division [SFM]

200 East Gaines Street, Tallahassee, FL 32399
Fax: (850) 413-3170

Director **Julius Halas** . . . . . . . . . . . . . . . . . . . . . . . . . . . . . (850) 413-3601
Assistant Director **Mark Sauls** . . . . . . . . . . . . . . . . . . . . . . (850) 413-3170

## Treasury Division

200 East Gaines Street, Tallahassee, FL 32399-0340
Tel: (850) 413-3301  Fax: (850) 488-4715

Director **Bert Wilkerson** . . . . . . . . . . . . . . . . . . . . . . . . . . . (850) 413-3301

## Workers' Compensation

200 East Gaines Street, Tallahassee, FL 32399-4220
Tel: (850) 413-1600  Fax: (850) 413-1973

Director **Tanner Holloman** . . . . . . . . . . . . . . . . . . . . . . . . . (850) 413-1600
   E-mail: tanner.holloman@myfloridacfo.com
Assistant Director **Andrew Sabolic** . . . . . . . . . . . . . . . . . . (850) 413-1600

# Department of Agriculture and Consumer Services

The Capitol, Room PL - 10, Tallahassee, FL 32399-0810
Tel: (850) 410-3800  Fax: (850) 617-7744

**Employees:** 3,577  **Fiscal Year:** 2015-2016  **Budget:** $1,529,394,000

★Commissioner **Adam H. Putnam (R)** . . . . . . . . . . . . . . . . . (850) 617-7700
   Term Expires: January 2019
   E-mail: adam.putnam@freshfromflorida.com
Assistant Commissioner and Chief of Staff **Mike Joyner** . . (850) 617-7700
Deputy Chief of Staff **Amanda Bevis** . . . . . . . . . . . . . . . . . (850) 617-7700
   E-mail: amanda.bevis@freshfromflorida.com
Deputy Commissioner **Lisa Conti** . . . . . . . . . . . . . . . . . . . . (850) 617-7700
   Education: Miami 1984 BA; Florida 1988 DVM;
   South Florida 1993 MPH
Deputy Commissioner **Jay S. Levenstein** . . . . . . . . . . . . . . (850) 617-7700
   Education: Florida BS; Miami JD
General Counsel **Lorena Holley** . . . . . . . . . . . . . . . . . . . . . (850) 245-1000
   407 S. Calhoun St., Room 520, Tallahassee, FL 32399-0800
Inspector General **Ron Russo** . . . . . . . . . . . . . . . . . . . . . . . (850) 245-1360
   2005 Apalachee Parkway, Tallahassee, FL 32399-6500
   E-mail: ron.russo@freshfromflorida.com
Agricultural Law Enforcement Director **Jerry Bryan** . . . . . . (850) 245-1300
   2005 Apalachee Parkway, Tallahassee, FL 32399-6500
Agricultural Water Policy Director
   **Steven E. "Steve" Dwinell** . . . . . . . . . . . . . . . . . . . . . . . (850) 617-1704
   1203 Governors Square Boulevard, Tallahassee, FL 32301
   E-mail: steven.dwinell@freshfromflorida.com
Cabinet Affairs Director **Brooke McKnight** . . . . . . . . . . . . . (850) 617-7700
   Education: South Florida 2004 BA; George Washington MA
Communications Director **Jennifer "Jenn" Meale** . . . . . . . (850) 617-7700
   E-mail: jennifer.meale@freshfromflorida.com
External Affairs Director **Cheryl Flood** . . . . . . . . . . . . . . . . (850) 617-7700
   Education: Florida 1999
Federal/State Relations Director **Matt Joyner** . . . . . . . . . . (850) 617-7700
   E-mail: matt.joyner@freshfromflorida.com
Legislative Affairs Director **Grace Lovett** . . . . . . . . . . . . . . (850) 617-7700
   E-mail: grace.lovett@freshfromflorida.com
Policy and Budgeting Director **Derek W. Buchanan** . . . . . . (850) 410-2293
                                                Fax: (850) 410-2275

Legal Section Librarian/Office Manager
   **Barbara Colston** . . . . . . . . . . . . . . . . . . . . . . . . . . . . . . . (850) 245-1000
                                                Fax: (850) 245-1001

---

★ Elected Official   ■ Appointed by Governor   ● Appointed by Legislature   ▲ Appointed by Board or Commission   ◆ Appointed by State Supreme Court

## Administration Division

407 South Calhoun Street, Room 509, Tallahassee, FL 32399-0800
Tel: (850) 617-7000  Fax: (850) 922-6967

Director **Alan Edwards** . . . . . . . . . . . . . . . . . . . . . . . . . . . . . (850) 617-7000
  E-mail: alan.edwards@freshfromflorida.com
Assistant Director **Joey Hicks** . . . . . . . . . . . . . . . . . . . . . . . (850) 617-7000
  E-mail: joey.hicks@freshfromflorida.com
Chief Information Officer **Michael Johnston** . . . . . . . . . . . (850) 245-1015
  E-mail: michael.johnston@freshfromflorida.com
Agriculture Programs Coordinator **Kristopher Browning** . . (850) 617-7014
  E-mail: kristopher.browning@freshfromflorida.com

## Agricultural Environmental Services Division

3125 Conner Boulevard, Room F-130, Tallahassee, FL 32399-1650
Tel: (850) 617-7900  Fax: (850) 617-7939  Internet: www.flaes.org

Director **Anderson H. "Andy" Rackley** . . . . . . . . . . . . . . . (850) 617-7900
Assistant Director **Kelly Friend** . . . . . . . . . . . . . . . . . . . . . (850) 617-7900
Program Planning Coordinator **Weldon Collier** . . . . . . . . . (850) 617-7900

## Animal Industry Division

407 South Calhoun Street, Room 335, Tallahassee, FL 32399-0800
Tel: (850) 410-0900  Fax: (850) 410-0946

Director **Dr. Michael A. "Mike" Short** . . . . . . . . . . . . . . . .(850) 410-0900
                                                        Fax: (850) 410-0915
Assistant Director **(Vacant)** . . . . . . . . . . . . . . . . . . . . . . . . (850) 410-0900

## Aquaculture Division

1203 Governors Square Boulevard, 5th Floor, Tallahassee, FL 32301
Tel: (850) 617-7600  Fax: (850) 617-7601
Internet: www.floridaaquaculture.com

Director **Kal Knickerbocker** . . . . . . . . . . . . . . . . . . . . . . . .(850) 617-7600
Aquaculture Development Assistant Director
  **Portia Sapp** . . . . . . . . . . . . . . . . . . . . . . . . . . . . . . . . . . . (850) 617-7600

## Consumer Service Division

2005 Apalachee Parkway, Tallahassee, FL 32399-6500
Tel: (850) 410-3800  Fax: (850) 410-3839  Internet: www.800helpfla.com

Chief **(Vacant)** . . . . . . . . . . . . . . . . . . . . . . . . . . . . . . . . . .(850) 410-3675
Director **Tom Steckler** . . . . . . . . . . . . . . . . . . . . . . . . . . . . (850) 410-3663
Assistant Director **Amy Topol** . . . . . . . . . . . . . . . . . . . . . . . (850) 410-3692
Compliance Chief **Liz E. Compton** . . . . . . . . . . . . . . . . . . . (850) 410-6735
Consumer Assistance Chief **(Vacant)** . . . . . . . . . . . . . . . . .(850) 410-3768
Fair Rides Inspection Bureau Chief **Allan Harrison** . . . . . . (850) 921-1537
Mediation and Enforcement Bureau Chief
  **Alan A Parkinson** . . . . . . . . . . . . . . . . . . . . . . . . . . . . . . (850) 410-3697
Standards Bureau Chief **Matthew D. Curran** . . . . . . . . . . . (850) 921-1560
Communications Service Program Manager
  **Gwendolyn Worlds** . . . . . . . . . . . . . . . . . . . . . . . . . . . . (850) 410-3702
  E-mail: gwendolyn.worlds@freshfromflorida.com

## Food, Nutrition and Wellness Division

Tel: (850) 617-7400  Fax: (850) 617-7402

Director **(Vacant)** . . . . . . . . . . . . . . . . . . . . . . . . . . . . . . . . (850) 617-7400
Assistant Director **Lakeisha Hood** . . . . . . . . . . . . . . . . . . . .(850) 617-7400
Food Distribution Bureau Chief
  **Christine "Christie" Meresse** . . . . . . . . . . . . . . . . . . . . . (850) 617-7427
Implementation and Accountability Bureau Chief
  **Erica Field** . . . . . . . . . . . . . . . . . . . . . . . . . . . . . . . . . . . (850) 617-7441

## Food Safety Division

3125 Conner Boulevard, Suite 181, Tallahassee, FL 32399-1650
Tel: (850) 245-5595  Fax: (850) 488-7946
E-mail: foodinsp@freshfromflorida.com

Director **Dr. Tiffiani Onifade** . . . . . . . . . . . . . . . . . . . . . . . (850) 245-5547
Assistant Director **Lee Cornman** . . . . . . . . . . . . . . . . . . . . . (850) 245-5595
Chemical Residue Bureau Chief **Jo Marie Cook** . . . . . . . . . (850) 617-7505
Dairy Bureau Chief **Zachary Conlin** . . . . . . . . . . . . . . . . . . (850) 245-5415
Food Laboratories Bureau Chief **Patty Lewandowski** . . . . .(850) 617-7555
                                                        Fax: (850) 487-6573
Food and Meat Inspection Bureau Chief **Brenda Morris** . . . (850) 245-5545

## Florida Forest Service

3125 Conner Boulevard, Room 228, Tallahassee, FL 32399-1650
Tel: (850) 410-5800  Fax: (850) 922-6855
E-mail: ffssupport@freshfromflorida.com

Director **James R. "Jim" Karels** . . . . . . . . . . . . . . . . . . . . (850) 681-5800
Assistant Director **(Vacant)** . . . . . . . . . . . . . . . . . . . . . . . . (850) 681-5800
Field Operations Bureau Chief **Jeff Vowell** . . . . . . . . . . . . (850) 681-5800
Forest Management Bureau Chief **Brad Ellis** . . . . . . . . . . . (850) 681-5800
Forest Protection Bureau Chief **John Fish** . . . . . . . . . . . . . (850) 681-5800
Forest Logistic and Support Chief **John Stys** . . . . . . . . . . .(850) 681-5800

## Fruit and Vegetables Division

P.O. Box 1072, Winter Haven, FL 33882-1072
Tel: (863) 297-3900  Fax: (863) 297-3969

Director **Carrie Porterfield** . . . . . . . . . . . . . . . . . (863) 578-1900 ext. 1931
Assistant Division Director **(Vacant)** . . . . . . . . . . (863) 578-1900 ext. 1931
Technical Control Bureau Information Officer **(Vacant)** . . . .(863) 297-3910
Inspection Bureau Chief **Marlon Clements** . . . . . . . . . . . . . (863) 291-5820

## Licensing and Enforcement Division

2520 North Monroe Street, Tallahassee, FL 32303
Tel: (850) 245-5500  Fax: (850) 245-5505

Director **Grea Bevis** . . . . . . . . . . . . . . . . . . . . . . . . . . . . . . (850) 245-5500
Assistant Director **Paul Pagano** . . . . . . . . . . . . . . . . . . . . . .(850) 245-5500
License Issuance Bureau Chief **Laura Galleger** . . . . . . . . . . (850) 245-5634
Regulation and Enforcement Bureau Chief **Ed Warren** . . . . (850) 245-5500
Support Services Bureau Chief **Mikah Ford** . . . . . . . . . . . . (850) 245-5500

## Marketing and Development Division

407 South Calhoun Street, Room 435, Tallahassee, FL 32399-0800
Tel: (850) 617-7300  Fax: (850) 922-2861
Internet: www.florida-agriculture.com

Director **Darica Smith** . . . . . . . . . . . . . . . . . . . . . . . . . . . . (850) 617-7300
Assistant Director **Christopher "Chris" Green** . . . . . . . . . . (850) 617-7300
                                                        Fax: (850) 617-7301
Development and Information Bureau Chief **(Vacant)** . . . . . (850) 617-7330
Education and Communications Bureau Chief
  **Walter "Walt" Land** . . . . . . . . . . . . . . . . . . . . . . . . . . . . (850) 617-7050
  E-mail: walter.land@freshfromflorida.com
Seafood and Aquaculture Bureau Chief **Martin May** . . . . . .(850) 617-7280
  2051 E. Dirac Drive, Tallahassee, FL 32310-3760
State Farmers' Markets Bureau Chief
  **Daniel "Danny" Raulerson, CPA** . . . . . . . . . . . . . . . . . . (850) 617-7380
  Education: Florida State 1979 BSAcc
Agricultural Statistics Service State Statistician
  **Candice Erick** . . . . . . . . . . . . . . . . . . . . . . . . . . . . . . . . .(407) 648-6013
  P.O. Box 530105, Orlando, FL 32853
  E-mail: candice.erick@freshfromflorida.com

## Plant Industry Division

P.O. Box 147100, Gainesville, FL 32614-7100
Tel: (352) 372-3505  Fax: (352) 334-0967

Director **Dr. Trevor R. Smith** . . . . . . . . . . . . . . . . . . . . . . .(352) 395-4628
  Education: Florida PhD
Assistant Director **Greg S. Hodges** . . . . . . . . . . . . . . . . . . .(352) 395-4627
Citrus Budwood Registration Bureau Chief
  **Michael Kesinger** . . . . . . . . . . . . . . . . . . . . . . . . . . . . . (863) 298-7712
  3027 Lake Alfred Road, Winter Haven, FL 33881-1438
  E-mail: michael.kesinger@freshfromflorida.com
Entomology, Nematology and Plant Pathology Bureau
  Chief **Leroy Whilby** . . . . . . . . . . . . . . . . . . . . . . . . . . . .(352) 395-4661
Methods Development and Biological Control
  Bureau Chief **Eric Rohrig** . . . . . . . . . . . . . . . . . (352) 395-4746 ext. 445
  E-mail: eric.rohrig@freshfromflorida.com
Pest Eradication and Control Bureau Chief
  **Caroline "Callie" Walker** . . . . . . . . . . . . . . . . . . . . . . . . (863) 298-7718
  3027 Lake Alfred Road, Winter Haven, FL 33881-1438
Plant and Apiary Inspection Bureau Chief **Tyson Emery** . . (352) 395-4709
DPI (Division of Plant Industry) Librarian **Beverly Pope** . . (352) 395-4721
                                                        Fax: (352) 955-2301

---

# Georgia

Tel: (404) 656-2000 (State Operator)

**Number of U.S. Congressional Delegates:** 2 Senators; 14 Representatives  **Governor's Term:** 4 years
**Legislature Description:** General Assembly - 56 member Senate; 180 member House of Representatives;
Term - Senate 2 years, House 2 years  **Next Election:** Governor November 2018; Legislature November
2016  **Number of Electoral Votes:** 16  **Official Name:** State of Georgia (after George II of England)
**Nickname:** Empire State of the South  **Motto:** Wisdom, Justice, and Moderation

**Population:** 10,214,860 (2015); Rank 8  **Fiscal Year:** 2015  **Budget:** $44,130,341,000

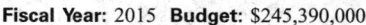

## Office of the Governor

203 State Capitol, Atlanta, GA 30334
Tel: (404) 656-1776  Fax: (404) 657-7332

**Fiscal Year:** 2015  **Budget:** $245,390,000

**Nathan Deal**
Governor

Began Service: January 10, 2011
Term Expires: January 2019
Date of Birth: August 25, 1942
Education: Mercer 1964 BA, 1966 JD
Home: Gainesville
Religion: Baptist
Career: Ranking Member, Subcommittee on
Health, Committee on Energy and Commerce,
United States House of Representatives
(2007-2010); Member, Subcommittee on
Communications, Technology and the Internet,
Committee on Energy and Commerce,
United States House of Representatives
(2007-2010); Member, Subcommittee on
Oversight and Investigations, Committee
on Energy and Commerce, United States
House of Representatives (2009-2010); U.S.
Representative (R-GA, District 9), Office of
Representative Nathan Deal, United States House
of Representatives (1993-2010)

★Governor **Nathan Deal** (R) . . . . . . . . . . . . . . . . . . . . . . . (404) 656-1776
Chief of Staff **Chris Riley** . . . . . . . . . . . . . . . . . . . . . . . . (404) 656-1776
Deputy Chief of Staff for Communications
  **Jen Talaber Ryan** . . . . . . . . . . . . . . . . . . . . . . . . . . . (404) 656-1776
  Education: Florida
Deputy Chief of Staff for Executive Office Operations
  **Carrie Ashbee** . . . . . . . . . . . . . . . . . . . . . . . . . . . . . (404) 656-1784
  E-mail: cashbee@georgia.gov
Deputy Chief of Staff for Legislative and External Affairs
  **Julia Ayers** . . . . . . . . . . . . . . . . . . . . . . . . . . . . . . . (404) 656-1784
  Education: Mississippi
Deputy Chief of Staff for Policy **Katie Childers** . . . . . . . . . (404) 656-1784
  Education: Georgia; Georgia Southern
Chief Operating Officer **David Werner** . . . . . . . . . . . . . . . (404) 656-1776
  E-mail: dwerner@georgia.gov
  Education: Georgia; Emory JD
State Accounting Officer **Alan Skelton, CPA** . . . . . . . . . . . (404) 656-1776
  Education: Florida State BA
Executive Counsel **W. Ryan Teague** . . . . . . . . . . . . . . . . (404) 656-1776
  Education: Clemson; Georgia 2003 JD
Constituent Services Director **Ben Smith** . . . . . . . . . . . . . (404) 656-1776
  E-mail: bsmith@georgia.gov
Deputy Communications Director **Merry Hunter Hipp** . . . . (404) 516-5376
Education Outreach Coordinator **Pam Williams** . . . . . . . . . (404) 656-1776
Policy Director **(Vacant)** . . . . . . . . . . . . . . . . . . . . . . . . . (404) 656-1784
Policy Advisor **Kristin Bernhard** . . . . . . . . . . . . . . . . . . . (404) 656-1784
  E-mail: kbernhard@georgia.gov

## Georgia Emergency Management Agency [GEMA]

935 East Confederate Avenue, SE, Atlanta, GA 30316
P.O. Box 18055, Atlanta, GA 30316-0055
Tel: (404) 635-7000  Tel: (800) 874-4362  Fax: (404) 635-7005

Director **MG James B. "Jim" Butterworth, ARNG** . . . . . (404) 635-7001
  E-mail: james.butterworth@ga.gov
  Education: Georgia BS
Deputy Director of Programs and Finance
  **Charley English** . . . . . . . . . . . . . . . . . . . . . . . . . . . . (404) 635-7000
  E-mail: charley.english@ga.gov
  Education: Georgia State BSCrimJ; Naval Postgrad
Deputy Director of Emergency Management **Gary Kelley** . . (404) 635-7000
  Operations Division Director **Charles Dawson** . . . . . . . . (404) 635-7000
  Hazard Mitigation Division Director **Terry Lunn** . . . . . . . (404) 635-7000
Deputy Director of Programs, Preparedness and Recovery
  **(Vacant)** . . . . . . . . . . . . . . . . . . . . . . . . . . . . . . . . . (404) 635-7000
Chief of Staff **Lauren Curry** . . . . . . . . . . . . . . . . . . . . . . (404) 635-7000
  Note: Until June 15, 2016.

### Homeland Security Division

Tel: (404) 635-7014

Director **Micah Hamrick** . . . . . . . . . . . . . . . . . . . . . . . . (404) 635-7014
  Education: Tennessee Temple (Attended)

## Office of the State Inspector General

Two Martin Luther King, Jr. Drive SW, 1102 West Tower,
Atlanta, GA 30334
Tel: (866) 435-7644  Fax: (404) 657-9716  Internet: www.oig.georgia.gov

Inspector General
  **Lt Cdr Deborah Wallace, CFE, USN (Ret)** . . . . . . . . . . (404) 656-7924
  E-mail: inspector.general@oig.ga.gov
  Education: Chaminade BS; Troy State MS
Deputy Inspector General **William Donaldson** . . . . . . . . . (866) 435-7644
Investigator **Austin Mayberry** . . . . . . . . . . . . . . . . . . . . (866) 435-7644
Investigator **Liana Rummel** . . . . . . . . . . . . . . . . . . . . . . (866) 435-7644
Investigator **Misti Williams** . . . . . . . . . . . . . . . . . . . . . . (866) 435-7644

## Office of the State Treasurer

West Tower, 200 Piedmont Avenue, Suite 1204, Atlanta, GA 30334
Tel: (404) 656-2168  Fax: (404) 656-9048  E-mail: otfs.web@otfs.ga.gov

■State Treasurer **Steve McCoy** . . . . . . . . . . . . . . . . . . . . (404) 656-2168
  Education: Georgia BBA; Georgia State MBA
  Career: Deputy State Treasurer and Chief Investment Officer, Office of
  the State Treasurer, State of Georgia (2011)
■Deputy State Treasurer **(Vacant)** . . . . . . . . . . . . . . . . . (404) 656-2168

## Washington Office

Hall of States, 1455 Pennsylvania Avenue, NW, Suite 400,
Washington, DC 20004
Tel: (202) 624-3680

Federal Affairs Director **Todd W. Smith** . . . . . . . . . . . . . (202) 652-2299
  E-mail: ts@rubicondc.com

---

★ Elected Official    ■ Appointed by Governor    ● Appointed by Legislature    ▲ Appointed by Board or Commission    ◆ Appointed by State Supreme Court

## Office of Planning and Budget [OPB]

270 Washington Street, SW, Suite 8066, Atlanta, GA 30334-8500
Tel: (404) 656-3820  Fax: (404) 656-7198

■ Director and Chief Financial Officer **Teresa MacCartney** . . (404) 656-3820
  E-mail: teresa.maccartney@opb.georgia.gov
  Education: Georgia Southern BS, MPA
  Executive Assistant **Tawana Guthrie** . . . . . . . . . . . . . . . (404) 656-3820
Deputy Director **Richard "Rick" Dunn** . . . . . . . . . . . . . . . (404) 656-3820
  Note: Until June 15, 2016.
Administration Director **Yvonne Turner** . . . . . . . . . . . . . (404) 656-3820
  E-mail: yvonne.turner@opb.state.ga.us
Budget Services Division Director **Stephanie Beck** . . . . . . (404) 656-3820
Capital Budgeting Director **Ron Nawrocki** . . . . . . . . . . . . (404) 656-6364
  Education: Rutgers 1975 BSCE; Georgia Tech 1976 MScE
Database and Technical Support Unit Director
  **Bruce Zents** . . . . . . . . . . . . . . . . . . . . . . . . . . . . . . . . (404) 656-3820
  E-mail: bruce.zents@opb.state.ga.us
Educational Development Director **Mike Kooi** . . . . . . . . . . (404) 463-3820
Human Development Director **(Vacant)** . . . . . . . . . . . . . . (404) 656-3820
Human Resource Director **Felicia Lowe** . . . . . . . . . . . . . (404) 657-7317
Physical and Economic Development Director **(Vacant)** . . . (404) 656-3820
Performance Management Director **Alice Zimmerman** . . . . (404) 657-7316
Public Safety Director **Joe Hood** . . . . . . . . . . . . . . . . . . . (404) 656-3820
Webmaster **Bruce Zents** . . . . . . . . . . . . . . . . . . . . . . . . . (404) 656-3820

## Department of Administrative Services [DOAS]

200 Piedmont Avenue, Suite 1804 West Tower, Atlanta, GA 30334
Tel: (404) 656-5514  Fax: (770) 657-4726

**Fiscal Year:** 2015  **Budget:** $200,623,000

■ Commissioner **Sid Johnson** . . . . . . . . . . . . . . . . . . . . . (404) 657-9441
  E-mail: sid.johnson@ga.gov
  Education: Tennessee BABA; Pennsylvania MA
  Executive Assistant **Gwen Middleton** . . . . . . . . . . . . . . (404) 657-9441
Operations Deputy Commissioner **Gina Tiedemann** . . . . . . (404) 463-5558
  E-mail: gina.tiedemann@doas.ga.gov
  Education: Georgia BBA
State Purchasing Deputy Commissioner **Lisa Eason** . . . . . . (404) 656-0934
  E-mail: lisa.eason@doas.ga.gov
State Human Resources Administration Deputy
  Commissioner **Candy Sarvis** . . . . . . . . . . . . . . . . . . . (404) 657-0591
  E-mail: candy.sarvis@doas.ga.gov
  Education: Texas (Arlington) BSE; Texas JD
  Compensation and Benefits Administration Director
    **Nicole Long** . . . . . . . . . . . . . . . . . . . . . . . . . . . . . (404) 651-5049
  Enterprise Services Director **Jacqui Lindsay** . . . . . . . . . . (404) 463-1284
    Education: Penn State BS
  Policy and Compliance Director **Katy Townsend** . . . . . . . (404) 657-2186
Assistant Commissioner and General Counsel
  **Rebecca Sullivan** . . . . . . . . . . . . . . . . . . . . . . . . . . . (404) 651-5935
  E-mail: rebecca.sullivan@doas.ga.gov
Fleet Management Director **Ed Finnegan** . . . . . . . . . . . . . (404) 651-7263
Human Resources Director **Robert Bender** . . . . . . . . . . . (404) 656-5418
  E-mail: robert.bender@doas.ga.gov
Risk Management Services Division Director
  **Wade Damron** . . . . . . . . . . . . . . . . . . . . . . . . . . . . . (404) 463-5458
  E-mail: wade.damron@doas.ga.gov
Surplus Property Division Director **Steve Ekin** . . . . . . . . . (404) 656-6871
  E-mail: steven.ekin@doas.ga.gov
State Cards Program Manager **John Thomason** . . . . . . . . (404) 656-5344
  Education: Auburn BS
Chief Financial Officer **Paulette Petty** . . . . . . . . . . . . . . . (404) 657-9410
  Education: DeVry U BS; Keller Grad School MBA
Chief Information Officer **John Barmann** . . . . . . . . . . . . . (404) 656-9480
  E-mail: john.barmann@doas.ga.gov
  Education: Cleveland State
Strategic Sourcing Director **Darryl Mitchell** . . . . . . . . . . . (404) 656-5342
  Education: Tuskegee BS; Georgia Col MBA

## Department of Banking and Finance [DBF]

2990 Brandywine Road, Suite 200, Atlanta, GA 30341-5565
Tel: (770) 986-1633  Fax: (770) 986-1654

**Fiscal Year:** 2015  **Budget:** $11,639,000

■ Commissioner **Kevin B. Hagler, CEM** . . . . . . . . . . . . . . . (770) 986-1628
  E-mail: khagler@dbf.state.ga.us
  Education: Auburn BS
Senior Deputy Commissioner **Steve Pleger, CEM** . . . . . . . (770) 986-1629
  E-mail: spleger@dbf.state.ga.us
Administration Deputy Commissioner
  **Renee Martin, CPA** . . . . . . . . . . . . . . . . . . . . . . . . . . (770) 986-1640
  E-mail: rmartin@dbf.state.ga.us         Fax: (770) 986-1274

## Department of Behavioral Health and Developmental Disabilities [DBHDD]

Two Peachtree Street, NW, Atlanta, GA 30303-3142
Tel: (404) 657-2252  Tel: (800) 715-4225 (Georgia Crisis & Access Line)
TTY: (800) 255-0056

Commissioner **Frank Berry** . . . . . . . . . . . . . . . . . . . . . . . (404) 657-2252
  E-mail: frank.berry@ga.gov
Deputy Commissioner and Chief Operations Officer
  **Jeff Minor** . . . . . . . . . . . . . . . . . . . . . . . . . . . . . . . . (404) 657-2252
  Education: Georgia Southern 1980 BS
Chief of Staff **Judy Fitzgerald** . . . . . . . . . . . . . . . . . . . . (404) 657-2252
Assistant Commissioner and Chief Medical Officer
  **Dr. Emile Risby, MD** . . . . . . . . . . . . . . . . . . . . . . . . . (404) 657-2254
Assistant Commissioner for Public Affairs
  **Lavin Gartland** . . . . . . . . . . . . . . . . . . . . . . . . . . . . . (404) 657-5964
Developmental Disabilities Division Director
  **Dan Howell** . . . . . . . . . . . . . . . . . . . . . . . . . . . . . . . (404) 657-2680
                                          Fax: (404) 342-7274
Mental Health Disabilities Division Director **Chris Gault** . . (404) 657-2273
Addictive Diseases Division Director **Cassandra Price** . . . . (404) 657-2331
                                          Fax: (404) 657-5812
Communications Director **Chris Bailey** . . . . . . . . . . . . . . . (404) 657-2252
                                          Fax: (770) 408-5467
Human Resources Director **Mark Green** . . . . . . . . . . . . . . (404) 657-2252
                                          Fax: (770) 359-5624
Multiple Offender Program Director **Scott Dunbar** . . . . . . . (404) 463-4274

## Department of Community Affairs [DCA]

60 Executive Park South, NE, Atlanta, GA 30329-2231
Tel: (404) 679-4940  Fax: (404) 679-0589

**Fiscal Year:** 2015  **Budget:** $327,760,000

▲ Commissioner **Camila Knowles** . . . . . . . . . . . . . . . . . . (404) 679-0585
  E-mail: camila.knowles@dca.ga.gov
  Education: Harvard 2001 AB; Georgetown 2007 JD
  Executive Assistant **Alyssa Nordin Justice** . . . . . . . . . . (404) 679-0585
Chief Operating Officer **Brian Dill** . . . . . . . . . . . . . . . . . . (404) 982-3579
Community Development and Finance Deputy
  Commissioner **Christopher Nunn** . . . . . . . . . . . . . . . . (404) 679-4940
Finance and Administration Deputy Commissioner
  **John Ellis** . . . . . . . . . . . . . . . . . . . . . . . . . . . . . . . . (404) 679-4833
  E-mail: john.ellis@dca.ga.gov         Fax: (404) 327-6869
Housing Deputy Commissioner **Carmen Chubb** . . . . . . . . . (404) 679-0607
  Education: Georgia 1988 BA         Fax: (404) 679-4837
Rental Assistance Division Assistant Director
  **Shawn Williams** . . . . . . . . . . . . . . . . . . . . . . . . . . . . (404) 679-0621
Intergovernmental Affairs Director **Seth Coker** . . . . . . . . . (706) 679-4912

## Department of Community Health [DCH]

Two Peachtree Street, NW, 40th Floor, Atlanta, GA 30303
Tel: (404) 656-4507  Fax: (404) 651-6880  Internet: www.dch.georgia.gov

**Fiscal Year:** 2015  **Budget:** $13,450,967,000

■ Commissioner **Clyde L. Reese III** . . . . . . . . . . . . . . . . . (404) 656-4507
  E-mail: clyde.reese@ga.gov
Chief of Staff **Sharon L. King** . . . . . . . . . . . . . . . . . . . . . (404) 656-4507

---

★ Elected Official   ■ Appointed by Governor   ● Appointed by Legislature   ▲ Appointed by Board or Commission   ◆ Appointed by State Supreme Court

Executive Assistant and Board Coordinator
**Danisha Williams** . . . . . . . . . . . . . . . . . . . . . . . (404) 656-7993
General Counsel **Marial Ellis** . . . . . . . . . . . . . . . . . . . (404) 657-7993
 E-mail: mellis@dch.ga.gov
Chief Financial Officer **Elizabeth Brady** . . . . . . . . (404) 657-4859
Chief Information Officer **Matthew Jarrard** . . . . . . . . . (404) 656-2343
 E-mail: vharris@dch.ga.gov
Chief Operating Officer **Marsha Hopkins** . . . . . . . . . . (404) 463-3050
Health Information Technology Director **Laura Ellis** . . . . . (404) 654-5700
 E-mail: lellis2@dch.ga.gov
Communications and Legislative Affairs Director
**Lisa Marie Shekell** . . . . . . . . . . . . . . . . . . . . . . . . (404) 657-9118
 E-mail: lshekell@dch.ga.gov        Fax: (404) 656-4164
 Education: St John Fisher BA
Rural Health Services Office Director **Patricia Whaley** . . . . (229) 401-3090

## Office of Health Planning

Two Peachtree Street, NW, 5th Floor, Atlanta, GA 30303
Tel: (404) 656-0409  Fax: (404) 656-0442

Executive Director **Rachel L. King** . . . . . . . . . . . . . . . . . (404) 656-0409
 E-mail: rking@dch.ga.gov

## Healthcare Facility Regulation Division

Tel: (404) 657-5700

Executive Director **Melanie Simon** . . . . . . . . . . . . . . . . . (404) 657-5700
Administrative Specialist **Yvonne Freeman** . . . . . . . . . . . (404) 656-7592

## Medical Assistance Plans Division

Tel: (404) 651-8681  Fax: (404) 677-3845  Internet: www.dch.georgia.gov

Division Chief **Dr. Linda Wiant** . . . . . . . . . . . . . . . . . . . (404) 651-8681
 Education: Mercer 1993 PharmD
 Confidential Administrator **Jacqueline Foster** . . . . . . . . (404) 651-8681
  E-mail: jfoster@dch.ga.gov
 Planning and Implementation Administrator
 **Kevin Tolmich** . . . . . . . . . . . . . . . . . . . . . . . . . . . (404) 651-8681
Executive Business Analyst **Mary Kathryn Scruggs** . . . . . . (404) 651-8681
 Education: Georgia State BA; Georgia JD
Associate Chief of Operations **Lynnette Rhodes** . . . . . . . . (404) 651-8681
 Managed Care and Contracts Assistant Chief
 **Woody Dahmer** . . . . . . . . . . . . . . . . . . . . . . . . . . (404) 651-8681
 Policy and Provider Services Assistant Chief
 **Marcey Alter** . . . . . . . . . . . . . . . . . . . . . . . . . . . (404) 651-8681
Member Services and Policy Assistant Chief
 **Jonathan Duttweiler** . . . . . . . . . . . . . . . . . . . . . . . (404) 651-8681
Performance, Quality, and Outcomes Assistant Chief
 **Dr. Janice Carson** . . . . . . . . . . . . . . . . . . . . . . . . (404) 651-8681
Regulatory Services and Compliance Assistant Chief
 **Heather Bond** . . . . . . . . . . . . . . . . . . . . . . . . . . . (404) 657-1502
State Children's Health Insurance Program (SCHIP)
 Director **Sheila Alexander** . . . . . . . . . . . . . . . . . . . . (404) 657-9506
  E-mail: salexander@dch.ga.gov.        Fax: (404) 656-8366
  Education: Emory 1988 BA; State U West Georgia 2004 MPA

## State Health Benefits Plan Division

State Health Benefit Plan Chief **Jeffrey T. Rickman** . . . . . . (404) 463-0826

## Department of Community Supervision

Two Martin Luther King, Jr. Drive SE, Suite 458,
Atlanta, GA 30334-4909
Tel: (404) 656-4661

■Commissioner **Michael W. Nail** . . . . . . . . . . . . . . . . . . (404) 656-4661
Assistant Commissioner **Scott Maurer** . . . . . . . . . . . . . . (404) 656-4661
Executive Operations Director **Sandra Thomas** . . . . . . . . (404) 656-4661
Public Affairs Director **Bert Flewellen** . . . . . . . . . . . . . (404) 309-7257

## Georgia Department of Corrections [GDC]

300 Patrol Road, Forsyth, GA 31029
Tel: (478) 992-5253  TTY: (478) 992-5259  E-mail: info@dcor.state.ga.us
Internet: www.dcor.state.ga.us

**Fiscal Year:** 2015  **Budget:** $1,200,533,000

■Commissioner **Col. Homer Bryson** . . . . . . . . . . . . . . . (478) 992-5253
 E-mail: homer.bryson@ga.gov
 Confidential Secretary **Peggy Chapman** . . . . . . . . . . . (478) 992-5253
Assistant Commissioner, Chief of Staff
 **Gregory C. Dozier** . . . . . . . . . . . . . . . . . . . . . . . . (478) 992-5261
Assistant Commissioner, Chief of Operations
 **Timothy C. Ward** . . . . . . . . . . . . . . . . . . . . . . . . (478) 992-5258
Assistant Commissioner, Education
 **Dr. L. C. "Buster" Evans** . . . . . . . . . . . . . . . . . . . . (478) 992-5253
  Education: Valdosta State Col BS, MS; Georgia 1991 EdD
General Counsel **Jennifer Ammons** . . . . . . . . . . . . . . . . (478) 992-5240
Correctional Industries Director **Norman Wilson** . . . . . . . (404) 244-5107
 2984 Clifton Springs Rd., Decatur, GA 30344
Business Operations Division Assistant Commissioner
 **Scott Poitevint** . . . . . . . . . . . . . . . . . . . . . . . . . . (478) 992-6323
Facilities Operations Deputy **Jack Koon** . . . . . . . . . . . . (478) 992-5101
Information Technology Director **Tom McMurry** . . . . . . . . (478) 992-5820
 E-mail: tom.mcmurry@ga.gov
Investigations and Compliance Office Director
 **Ricky Myrick** . . . . . . . . . . . . . . . . . . . . . . . . . . . (478) 992-5341
  E-mail: ricky.myrick@ga.gov
Board Liaison **Simone Juhmi** . . . . . . . . . . . . . . . . . . . (478) 992-5258
Webmaster **Elise Jones** . . . . . . . . . . . . . . . . . . . . . . . (478) 992-6002
 E-mail: elise.jones@ga.gov

## Defense Department

Building Two, 1000 Halsey Avenue, Marietta, GA 30061
P.O. Box 1970, Marietta, GA 30061-4277
Tel: (678) 569-6001  Fax: (678) 569-6005

**Fiscal Year:** 2015  **Budget:** $66,724,000

■Adjutant General **BrigGen Joe Jarrard, AUS (Ret)** . . . . . . (678) 569-6001
 E-mail: joe.jarrard@ga.gov
 Executive Officer **LTC Jason Baker, ARNG** . . . . . . . . . . (678) 569-6017
 Executive Assistant **Maria Dickerson** . . . . . . . . . . . . . . (678) 569-6001
Deputy Adjutant General **Joe Ferrero** . . . . . . . . . . . . . (678) 569-6102
Assistant to Deputy Adjutant General **Lainie Adams** . . . . . (678) 569-3932
State Defense Force Commander
 **BG Thomas Danielson, ARNG** . . . . . . . . . . . . . . . . . (678) 569-3932
Public Affairs Officer **LTC Tom Laslesnieski, ARNG** . . . . . (678) 569-3855

## Georgia National Guard

Tel: (678) 569-6001

■Adjutant General **BrigGen Joe Jarrard, AUS (Ret)** . . . . . . (678) 569-6001
 E-mail: joe.jarrard@ga.gov
Information Assurance Manager
 **CW3 Samuel Blaney, ARNG** . . . . . . . . . . . . . . . . . . . (678) 569-6001

## Georgia Air National Guard

Building 840, 1388 First Street, Dobbins AFB, GA 30069-5007

■Commander **BrigGen Jesse Simmons, ANG** . . . . . . . . . . (678) 569-5205
 E-mail: jesse.simmons@ang.af.mil
 Administrative Assistant **Sgt Nicholas Coney, ANG** . . . . . (678) 569-4040

## Georgia Army National Guard

Building Two, 1000 Halsey Avenue, Marietta, GA 30061
Tel: (678) 569-6001

■Commander **COL Thomas Carden, ARNG** . . . . . . . . . . . (678) 569-5003
 E-mail: thomas.carden@ga.gov

★ Elected Official  ■ Appointed by Governor  ● Appointed by Legislature  ▲ Appointed by Board or Commission  ◆ Appointed by State Supreme Court

*State Yellow Book*        © Leadership Directories, Inc.        Summer 2016

# Department of Driver Services [DDS]

2206 East View Parkway, Conyers, GA 30013
P.O. Box 80447, Conyers, GA 30013
Tel: (678) 413-8650  Internet: www.dds.ga.gov

**Fiscal Year:** 2015  **Budget:** $67,687,000

■Chairman **David W. Connell** . . . . . . . . . . . . . . . . . . . . . . (678) 413-8650
  Education: Auburn BS; Southern Mississippi MBA
Vice Chairman **Lynda Coker** . . . . . . . . . . . . . . . . . . . . . . (678) 413-8650
Secretary **Jeffrey G. Wigington** . . . . . . . . . . . . . . . . . . . (678) 413-8650
  Education: Wake Forest 1992 JD
Member **Dawn Cartee** . . . . . . . . . . . . . . . . . . . . . . . . . . (678) 413-8650
Member **Todd Cowan** . . . . . . . . . . . . . . . . . . . . . . . . . . (678) 413-8650
Member **Anthony Heath** . . . . . . . . . . . . . . . . . . . . . . . . (678) 413-8650
Member **Rachel Little** . . . . . . . . . . . . . . . . . . . . . . . . . . (678) 413-8650
Member **Jeff Markey** . . . . . . . . . . . . . . . . . . . . . . . . . . (678) 413-8650
Member **Hubert Parker** . . . . . . . . . . . . . . . . . . . . . . . . (678) 413-8650
■Commissioner **Bert Brantley** . . . . . . . . . . . . . . . . . . . . (678) 413-8660
  E-mail: bert.brantley@ga.gov
  Education: Georgia BA, MPA
Deputy Commissioner **Spencer R. Moore** . . . . . . . . . . . . (678) 413-8660
  E-mail: spencer.moore@ga.gov
  Education: Morehouse Col BA
General Counsel **Cassandra Williams** . . . . . . . . . . . . . . . (678) 413-8650

# Georgia Department of Early Care and Learning [DECAL]

745 East Tower, 2 Martin Luther King, Jr. Drive, SE, Atlanta, GA 30334
Tel: (404) 656-5957  Tel: (888) 442-7735  Fax: (404) 651-7184

Commissioner **Amy Jacobs** . . . . . . . . . . . . . . . . . . . . . . (404) 651-7432
  E-mail: amy.jacobs@decal.ga.gov

## Administrative Services

Tel: (404) 656-5957

Chief Communications Officer **Reg Griffin** . . . . . . . . . . . . (404) 656-5957
  E-mail: reg.griffin@decal.ga.gov
Chief Information Officer **Craig Detweiler** . . . . . . . . . . . . (404) 656-5957
  E-mail: craig.detweiler@decal.ga.gov
Deputy Commissioner for Finance and Administration
  **H. Ray Higgins** . . . . . . . . . . . . . . . . . . . . . . . . . . . . . (404) 656-5957
  E-mail: ray.higgins@decal.ga.gov
Finance Director **Sharon McPherson** . . . . . . . . . . . . . . . (404) 651-7198
Human Resources Director **Robin C. Stevens** . . . . . . . . . . (404) 651-7412

## Child Care Services

Tel: (404) 651-5562

Assistant Commissioner **Kristie Lewis** . . . . . . . . . . . . . . . (404) 651-5562
Child Care Services Division Director **Elisabetta Kasfir** . . . (404) 651-5562
Child Care Services Division Director **Rhonda Parker** . . . . (404) 651-5562

## Nutrition

Nutrition Services Director **Falita Flowers** . . . . . . . . . . . . (404) 656-5957

# Georgia Department of Economic Development [GDEcD]

75 Fifth Street, NW, Suite 1200, Atlanta, GA 30308
Tel: (404) 962-4000  Internet: www.georgia.org

**Fiscal Year:** 2015  **Budget:** $197,000,000

■Commissioner **Chris Carr** . . . . . . . . . . . . . . . . . . . . . . . (404) 962-4000
  E-mail: chris.carr@ga.gov
  Education: Georgia 1995 BBA, 1999 JD
  Executive Assistant to the Commissioner
  **Gina McKinney** . . . . . . . . . . . . . . . . . . . . . . . . . . . . . (404) 962-4003
Global Commerce Deputy Commissioner **Tom Croteau** . . . (404) 962-4013
                                          Fax: (404) 962-4021
International Relations Deputy Commissioner
  **Ember Bishop** . . . . . . . . . . . . . . . . . . . . . . . . . . . . . . (404) 962-4183
Marketing and Communications Deputy Commissioner
  **Greg Torre** . . . . . . . . . . . . . . . . . . . . . . . . . . . . . . . . (404) 962-4173

Film, Music and Digital Entertainment Division Deputy
  Commissioner **Lee Thomas** . . . . . . . . . . . . . . . . . . . . (404) 962-4048
  E-mail: lthomas@georgia.org              Fax: (404) 962-4053
Tourism Division Deputy Commissioner **Kevin Langston** . . . . . . . . . (404) 962-4082
  Education: Kansas State BArch; Georgia State MBA    Fax: (404) 962-4093
Chief Financial Officer **John Moffatt** . . . . . . . . . . . . . . . (404) 962-4007
Chief Operating Officer **Pat Wilson** . . . . . . . . . . . . . . . . (404) 962-4070

# Center of Innovation for Logistics [GCOI]

190 Technology Circle, Suite 173, Savannah, GA 31407
Tel: (912) 966-7867  Fax: (912) 963-2549
E-mail: logistics@georgiainnovation.org

Executive Director **Jannine Miller** . . . . . . . . . . . . . . . . . (912) 966-7867
  Education: Georgia State BA, MA

# Department of Human Services [DHS]

Two Peachtree Street, NW, Suite 29-250, Atlanta, GA 30303-3142
Tel: (404) 656-5680  Fax: (404) 651-8669

**Fiscal Year:** 2015  **Budget:** $1,722,718,000

■Commissioner **Robyn A. Crittenden** . . . . . . . . . . . . . . . (404) 656-5680
  Education: Yale 1986 BA; Michigan JD
  Executive Assistant **Stefanie Reese** . . . . . . . . . . . . . . . (404) 651-6314
Deputy Commissioner **Renorta Heard** . . . . . . . . . . . . . . (404) 656-2624
Deputy Commissioner **Lynn H. Vellinga** . . . . . . . . . . . . . (404) 656-2624
Assistant Commissioner **(Vacant)** . . . . . . . . . . . . . . . . . (404) 463-0097
Chief Financial Officer (Acting) **Demetrius Taylor** . . . . . . (404) 656-5680
Chief Information Officer **Venkat Krishnan** . . . . . . . . . . . (404) 657-3759
  E-mail: venkat.krishnan@ga.gov
General Counsel **Rachel King** . . . . . . . . . . . . . . . . . . . . (404) 656-4421
Human Resource Management Office Director
  **Rosemary Calhoun** . . . . . . . . . . . . . . . . . . . . . . . . . . (404) 656-6750
Legislative Affairs and Communications Director
  **Ashley Fielding** . . . . . . . . . . . . . . . . . . . . . . . . . . . . (404) 657-5102
  E-mail: ashely.fielding@dhs.ga.gov

## Office of Financial Services

Two Peachtree Street, NW, Suite 30-240, Atlanta, GA 30303-3142
Tel: (404) 656-2072

Assistant Chief Financial Officer **(Vacant)** . . . . . . . . . . . (404) 656-4472
Facilities & Support Services Director **Jim Bricker** . . . . . . (404) 656-4305
Financial Services Office Director **Bill Zisek** . . . . . . . . . . (404) 656-7999

## Division of Aging Services

Two Peachtree Street, NW, Suite 9-270, Atlanta, GA 30303-3142
Tel: (404) 657-5258

Director **Dr. James Bulot** . . . . . . . . . . . . . . . . . . . . . . . (404) 657-5258
Deputy Director **Jean O'Callaghan** . . . . . . . . . . . . . . . . (404) 657-5256
Policy and Planning Development Specialist
  **Allan Goldman** . . . . . . . . . . . . . . . . . . . . . . . . . . . . . (404) 657-5680

## Division of Child Support Services [DCSS]

Tel: (877) 423-4746

Director **Tanguler Gray-Johnson** . . . . . . . . . . . . . . . . . . (404) 657-0634
  E-mail: tsgray@dhr.state.ga.us

## Division of Family and Children Services [DFCS]

Two Peachtree Street, NW, Suite 29-250, Atlanta, GA 30303-3142
Tel: (404) 895-9724  Fax: (404) 657-5105

Director **Bobby Cagle** . . . . . . . . . . . . . . . . . . . . . . . . . (404) 651-8409
Deputy Director **Carol Christopher** . . . . . . . . . . . . . . . . (404) 657-5256
Deputy Director of Finance and Administration
  **Clifford "Cliff" O'Connor** . . . . . . . . . . . . . . . . . . . . . . (404) 657-7662
  E-mail: coconnor@dhr.state.ga.us

## Vocational Rehabilitation Agency

Tel: (404) 232-1978

Executive Director **Gregory A. Schmieg** . . . . . . . . . . . . . (404) 232-1998

---

★ Elected Official    ■ Appointed by Governor    ● Appointed by Legislature    ▲ Appointed by Board or Commission    ◆ Appointed by State Supreme Court

Field Services Director **Ed James** . . . . . . . . . . . . . . . . . . . (404) 232-1810
  E-mail: ed.james@gvra.ga.gov

# Department of Juvenile Justice [DJJ]

3408 Covington Highway, Decatur, GA 30032

Tel: (404) 508-6500  Fax: (404) 508-7289  Internet: www.djj.state.ga.us

**Fiscal Year:** 2015  **Budget:** $311,199,000

■Commissioner **Avery D. Niles** . . . . . . . . . . . . . . . . . . . . . . (404) 508-7200
  E-mail: averyniles@djj.state.ga.us

Assistant Commissioner and Chief of Staff **Mark Sexton** . . (404) 508-7200
  E-mail: marksexton@djj.state.ga.us

Assistant Commissioner **Keith Horton** . . . . . . . . . . . . . . (404) 508-7200

Administrative Services Deputy Commissioner
  **Shawanda Reynolds-Cobb** . . . . . . . . . . . . . . . . . . . . . (404) 508-6524
  E-mail: shawandareynolds-cobb@djj.state.ga.us
  Education: Georgia State 1994 BS; Central Michigan 1999 MPA

Community Services Deputy Commissioner **Joe Vignati** . . (404) 508-6554
  E-mail: joe.vignati@djj.state.ga.us
  Education: Augusta 1987 BA; Georgia State 1992 MPPA

Security Deputy Commissioner **Dewayne Orrick** . . . . . . . . (404) 508-7200
  E-mail: dewayne.orrick@djj.state.ga.us

Support Services Deputy Commissioner
  **Miguel Fernandez** . . . . . . . . . . . . . . . . . . . . . . . . . . . (404) 508-7280
  E-mail: miguelfernandez@djj.state.ga.us  Fax: (404) 508-7332

Communications Office Director **Jim Shuler** . . . . . . . . . . . (404) 508-7147

Continuous Improvement Office Director **Chris Saxton** . . . (404) 508-6566

Legal Services Director **Cindy Wang** . . . . . . . . . . . . . . . (404) 508-7239
  E-mail: cindywang@djj.state.ga.us

Operation and Compliance Deputy Commissioner
  **Sarah Draper** . . . . . . . . . . . . . . . . . . . . . . . . . . . . . (404) 253-7410
  E-mail: sarah.draper@ga.gov  Fax: (404) 508-7332

Training and Personnel Services Deputy Commissioner
  **Chris Thomas** . . . . . . . . . . . . . . . . . . . . . . . . . . . . . (404) 508-7281
  E-mail: chris.thomas@ga.gov  Fax: (404) 508-7332

# Department of Natural Resources [DNR]

Two Martin Luther King, Jr. Drive, Suite 1252 East,
Atlanta, GA 30334-9000

Tel: (404) 656-3500  Fax: (404) 656-0770  Internet: www.gadnr.org

**Fiscal Year:** 2015  **Budget:** $281,475,000

▲Commissioner **Mark Williams** . . . . . . . . . . . . . . . . . . . . (404) 656-3500
  Education: Georgia Col BS
  Executive Assistant **Cathy Barnette** . . . . . . . . . . . . . . . (404) 656-3500
Deputy Commissioner **Walter Rabon** . . . . . . . . . . . . . . . (404) 232-1377

## Coastal Resources Division

One Conservation Way, Brunswick, GA 31523-8600

Tel: (912) 264-7218  Internet: www.gadnr.org

Director **Spud Woodward** . . . . . . . . . . . . . . . . . . . . . . . (912) 264-7218
Ecological Services Chief **Brad Gane** . . . . . . . . . . . . . . . (912) 262-3130
Marine Fisheries Chief **Pat Geer** . . . . . . . . . . . . . . . . . . (912) 263-3121

## Environmental Protection Division

Two M. L. King, Jr. Drive SE, Suite 1456, Atlanta, GA 30334

Tel: (404) 656-4713  Internet: www.gadnr.org

▲Director **Judson H. "Jud" Turner** . . . . . . . . . . . . . . . . . (404) 656-4713
  Note: Until May 31, 2016.

▲Director (Interim) **Walter Rabon** . . . . . . . . . . . . . . . . . . (404) 656-4713
  Note: Effective June 1, 2016.

▲Director-Designate **Richard "Rick" Dunn** . . . . . . . . . . . (404) 656-4713
  Note: On May 23, 2016, Governor Nathan Deal nominated Richard
  Dunn to be Director of the Environmental Protection Division. Mr.
  Dunn's nomination must be confirmed by the Department of Natural
  Resources Board. He will begin acting in this position effective June
  15, 2016.

▲Deputy Director-Designate **Lauren Curry** . . . . . . . . . . . . . (404) 656-4713
  Note: On May 23, 2016, Governor Nathan Deal nominated Lauren
  Curry to be Deputy Director of the Environmental Protection Division.
  Ms. Curry's nomination must be confirmed by the Department of
  Natural Resources Board. She will begin acting in this position
  effective June 15, 2016.

Assistant Director for Operations **Mary Walker** . . . . . . . . . (404) 656-4713
  Note: Until June 15, 2016.
State Geologist **Jim Kennedy** . . . . . . . . . . . . . . . . . . . . . (404) 463-0679
Air Protection Branch Chief **Karen Hayes** . . . . . . . . . . . . (404) 363-7000
Land Protection Branch Chief **Jeff Cown** . . . . . . . . . . . . . (404) 656-7802
Watershed Protection Management Branch Chief
  **James Capp** . . . . . . . . . . . . . . . . . . . . . . . . . . . . . . . (404) 656-6232

## Historic Preservation Division

254 Washington Street, Ground Level, Atlanta, GA 30334

Tel: (770) 389-7844  Internet: www.gafhpo.org

Director **David Crass** . . . . . . . . . . . . . . . . . . . . . . . . . . (770) 389-7844

## Law Enforcement Division

Tel: (770) 918-6408

Division Director **Col. Eddie Henderson** . . . . . . . . . . . . : . (770) 918-6408
                                               Fax: (770) 918-6410
Assistant Division Director **Lt. Col. Jeff Weaver** . . . . . . . . (770) 918-6408

## Parks, Recreation and Historic Sites Division

2600 Highway 155 Southwest, Suite C, Stockbridge, GA 30281

Tel: (770) 389-7277  Internet: www.gastatepark.org

Director **Becky Kelley** . . . . . . . . . . . . . . . . . . . . . . . . . . (770) 389-7277
Assistant Director **Wally Woods** . . . . . . . . . . . . . . . . . . . (770) 389-7277
Engineering and Construction Chief **David Clark** . . . . . . . . (770) 389-7277
Park Operations Chief **(Vacant)** . . . . . . . . . . . . . . . . . . . (770) 389-7277

## Wildlife Resources Division

2070 US Highway 278, SE, Social Circle, GA 30025-4711

Tel: (770) 918-6400  Internet: www.gadnr.org

Director **Daniel "Dan" Forster** . . . . . . . . . . . . . . . . . . . . (770) 918-6400
Assistant Director **Mark Whitney** . . . . . . . . . . . . . . . . . . (770) 918-6401
Fisheries Management Branch Chief **John Biagi** . . . . . . . . (770) 918-6406
  E-mail: john.biagi@dnr.state.ga.us
Game Management Branch Chief **John Bowers** . . . . . . . . (770) 918-6404
  E-mail: john.bowers@dnr.state.ga.us
Non-Game/Heritage Branch Chief **Mike Harris** . . . . . . . . . (770) 761-3035

# Department of Public Health [DPH]

Two Peachtree Street, NW, Floor 15, Atlanta, GA 30303-3142

Tel: (404) 657-2700  Tel: (404) 679-4702 (Vital Records)
Fax: (404) 657-2715  Fax: (404) 679-4730 (Vital Records)

Commissioner and State Health Officer
  **Dr. Brenda Fitzgerald, MD** . . . . . . . . . . . . . . . . . . . . (404) 657-2700
  Education: Georgia State BS; Emory MD
Chief of Staff **James C. Howgate II** . . . . . . . . . . . . . . . . . (404) 657-2700
  Education: George Mason 1991 BS; George Washington 2000 MPH
Deputy Chief of Staff **Christine Greene** . . . . . . . . . . . . . . (404) 657-2700

# Department of Public Safety [DPS]

959 East Confederate Avenue, SE, Atlanta, GA 30316

P.O. Box 1456, Atlanta, GA 30371-1456

Tel: (404) 624-7597  Fax: (404) 624-7498  E-mail: publicinfo@gsp.net

Internet: dps.georgia.gov

**Fiscal Year:** 2015  **Budget:** $191,978,000

■Commissioner **Col. Mark W. McDonough** . . . . . . . . . . . . (404) 624-7477
  E-mail: mark.mcdonough@ga.gov
Deputy Commissioner **Lt. Col. Russell Powell** . . . . . . . . . (404) 624-7344
Commanding Officer **Major Tommy Waldrop** . . . . . . . . . . (404) 624-7451
Headquarters Adjutant **Major Hank Fielding** . . . . . . . . . . (404) 624-7016
Motor Carrier Compliance Division Chief
  **Major Johnnie Jones** . . . . . . . . . . . . . . . . . . . . . . . . (404) 624-7212
  E-mail: johnnie.jones@ga.gov
Administrative Services Division Director
  **Lt. Kevin Rexroat** . . . . . . . . . . . . . . . . . . . . . . . . . . . (404) 624-7582
  E-mail: kevin.rexroat@ga.gov
Investigative Services Division Director **Angie Holt** . . . . . . (404) 624-7523
  E-mail: angie.holt@ga.gov
Training Division Director **Capt. Scott Woodell** . . . . . . . . (478) 993-4531
  E-mail: scott.woodell@ga.gov

*(continued on next page)*

EXECUTIVE BRANCH

---

★ Elected Official  ■ Appointed by Governor  ● Appointed by Legislature  ▲ Appointed by Board or Commission  ◆ Appointed by State Supreme Court

**EXECUTIVE BRANCH**

**Department of Public Safety** *continued*

Public Information Director **Capt. Mark Perry** . . . . . . . . . . .(404) 624-7597
  E-mail: mark.perry@ga.gov
Capitol Police Services Unit **Capt. Lewis Young** . . . . . . . . (404) 656-4830

# Georgia Bureau of Investigation

3121 Panthersville Road, Decatur, GA 30034
Tel: (404) 244-2600

Director **Vernon M. Keenan** . . . . . . . . . . . . . . . . . . . . (404) 244-2501
  Confidential Secretary **Machelle Jones** . . . . . . . . . . . . . (404) 270-8299
Assistant Director **Dan Kirk** . . . . . . . . . . . . . . . . . . . . . (404) 270-8346
Executive Secretary **Natalie Ammons** . . . . . . . . . . . . . . . (404) 270-8346

# Department of Revenue [DOR]

1800 Century Boulevard, Atlanta, GA 30345-3205
Tel: (404) 417-4477
Tel: (877) 423-6711 (General Information and Taxpayer Assistance)
TTY: (404) 417-2160  Fax: (404) 417-2101  Internet: etax.dor.ga.gov

**Fiscal Year:** 2015  **Budget:** $206,333,000

■Commissioner **Lynne Riley** . . . . . . . . . . . . . . . . . . . . . . (404) 417-2100
  E-mail: lynne.riley@ga.gov
  Education: Northeastern; Bentley Col
Deputy Commissioner **Scott Graham** . . . . . . . . . . . . . . . . .(404) 417-2100
Office of Special Investigations Director **Staci Guest** . . . . . (404) 417-2180
                                                      Fax: (404) 417-2181
Legal Affairs and Tax Policy Office Director
  **Frank O'Connell** . . . . . . . . . . . . . . . . . . . . . . . . . . . (404) 417-2213
                                                      Fax: (404) 417-2293
Alcohol and Tobacco Tax Division Director
  **Howard Tyler** . . . . . . . . . . . . . . . . . . . . . . . . . . . . .(404) 417-4900
Compliance Division Director **Pete Donnelly** . . . . . . . . . . . (404) 417-6400
Local Government Services Division Director **Ellen Mills** . .(404) 724-7015
  4125 Welcome All Road, Atlanta, GA 30349
Processing Center Division Director **(Vacant)** . . . . . . . . . . .(404) 724-7510
Taxpayer Services Division Director
  **Ronald Johnson, Jr.** . . . . . . . . . . . . . . . . . . . . . . . . .(404) 417-2400
Motor Vehicle Division Director **Georgia Steele** . . . . . . . . .(855) 406-5222
  4125 Welcome All Road, Atlanta, GA 30349
Information Technology Division Director **Michael Long** . . (404) 724-6004
  E-mail: michael.long@dor.ga.gov

# Department of Veterans Service [GDVS]

Floyd Veterans Memorial Building, Suite E-970, Atlanta, GA 30334-4800
Tel: (404) 656-2300  Fax: (404) 656-7006
E-mail: gavetsvc@vs.state.ga.us  Internet: veterans.georgia.gov

**Fiscal Year:** 2015  **Budget:** $40,951,000

Commissioner **Mike Roby** . . . . . . . . . . . . . . . . . . . . . . . (404) 656-2300
                                                      Fax: (404) 656-9738
Administrative Services Assistant Commissioner
  **Dan Holtz** . . . . . . . . . . . . . . . . . . . . . . . . . . . . . . . .(404) 656-2307
  E-mail: dholtz@vs.state.ga.us
Field Operations and Appeals Assistant Commissioner
  **George Canavaggio** . . . . . . . . . . . . . . . . . . . . . . . . . .(404) 656-2305
Accounting and Financial Division Director
  **Chris Hambright** . . . . . . . . . . . . . . . . . . . . . . . . . . . (404) 656-5896
                                                      Fax: (404) 463-8620
Claims Division Director **Henry Torres** . . . . . . . . . . . . . . .(404) 929-5345
Operations Director **Richard A. "Rick" Graham** . . . . . . . .(404) 656-2307
Personnel and Human Resources Director **Wonda Jones** . . (404) 463-3076
Public Information Division Director **Jon Suggs** . . . . . . . . .(404) 656-5933
  E-mail: jsuggs@vs.state.ga.us
State Approving Agency, Education and Training
  Division Director **Larry Edwards** . . . . . . . . . . . . . . . . . (404) 656-2306
Budget Specialist **April Dodgen** . . . . . . . . . . . . . . . . . . (404) 463-0324
                                                      Fax: (404) 929-5347

# Technical College System of Georgia

1800 Century Place, NE, Suite 400, Atlanta, GA 30345-4304
Tel: (404) 679-1600  Fax: (404) 327-6932

**Fiscal Year:** 2015  **Budget:** $697,939,000

Commissioner **Gretchen Corbin** . . . . . . . . . . . . . . . . . . . (404) 679-1600
  E-mail: gretchen.corbin@ga.gov
  Education: Clemson; Oklahoma
  Executive Assistant **Darlene Smith** . . . . . . . . . . . . . . . . (404) 679-1602
Deputy Commissioner **Matt Arthur** . . . . . . . . . . . . . . . . . .(404) 679-1696
External Affairs Assistant Commissioner **(Vacant)** . . . . . . . .(404) 679-2924
Facilities Management Director **Sara Honeywill** . . . . . . . . . (404) 679-2925
General Counsel **Linda Osborne-Smith** . . . . . . . . . . . . . . . (404) 679-1607
State Board Operations Director **JoAnn Brown** . . . . . . . . . . (404) 679-1612
GED Administrator **Latanya Overby** . . . . . . . . . . . . . . . . . (404) 679-4959
  E-mail: loverby@tcsg.edu

## Administrative Services Office

Tel: (404) 679-1787  Fax: (404) 327-6928

Assistant Commissioner **Penni Haberly** . . . . . . . . . . . . . . . (404) 679-1752
  E-mail: phaberly@tcsg.edu

## Adult Education Office

Tel: (404) 679-1600  Fax: (404) 679-1630

Assistant Commissioner **Beverly Smith** . . . . . . . . . . . . . . . (404) 679-1647

## Data, Planning and Research Services

Tel: (404) 679-1600  Fax: (404) 327-6932

Assistant Commissioner **Andy Parsons** . . . . . . . . . . . . . . . (404) 982-3435

## Economic Development Office

Fax: (404) 253-2798

Assistant Commissioner **Jackie Rohosky** . . . . . . . . . . . . . . (404) 253-2801

## Technical Education Office

Tel: (404) 679-1660  Fax: (404) 982-3485

Assistant Commissioner **Dr. Kathryn Hornsby** . . . . . . . . . . .(404) 679-5281

# Georgia Drugs and Narcotics Agency [GDNA]

254 Washington Street, Suite G2000, Atlanta, GA 30334
Tel: (404) 656-5100  Tel: (800) 656-6568 (Toll Free)  Fax: (404) 651-8210

▲Director **C. Richard Allen** . . . . . . . . . . . . . . . . . . . . . .(404) 656-5100
  E-mail: allenr@gdna.ga.gov
Deputy Director **Dennis Troughton** . . . . . . . . . . . . . . . . . (404) 656-5100
Business Operation Specialist **Carla Leary** . . . . . . . . . . . . (404) 656-5100

# Georgia Commission on Equal Opportunity

7 Martin Luther King, Jr. Drive, SE, 3rd Floor, Suite 351,
Atlanta, GA 30334-9004
Tel: (404) 656-1736  Fax: (404) 656-4399  E-mail: gceo@state.ga.us
Internet: www.gceo.state.ga.us

■Executive Director and Administrator **Melvin Everson** . . . . (404) 232-1776
  E-mail: meverson@gceo.state.ga.us
  Education: Albany State U BSCor

# Georgia Government Transparency and Campaign Finance Commission [CFC]

200 Piedmont Avenue Southeast, Suite 1402 - West Tower,
Atlanta, GA 30334
Tel: (404) 463-1980  Fax: (404) 463-1988  E-mail: gaethics@ethics.ga.gov
Internet: www.ethics.ga.gov

▲Executive Director **Stefan Ritter** . . . . . . . . . . . . . . . . . . (404) 463-1980

---

★ Elected Official   ■ Appointed by Governor   ● Appointed by Legislature   ▲ Appointed by Board or Commission   ◆ Appointed by State Supreme Court

# Georgia State Financing and Investment Commission [GSFIC]

270 Washington Street, SW, Suite 2140, Atlanta, GA 30334-8500
Tel: (404) 463-5700  Fax: (404) 463-5720

Chief Executive Officer and Chairman **Nathan Deal** . . . . . . (404) 463-5700
Vice Chairman **Casey Cagle** . . . . . . . . . . . . . . . . . . . . . . (404) 463-5700
  Education: Georgia Southern (Attended)
Secretary and Treasurer **Greg Griffin** . . . . . . . . . . . . . . . . (404) 463-5700
Member **Gary W. Black** . . . . . . . . . . . . . . . . . . . . . . . . . (404) 463-5700
  Education: Georgia 1980
Member **Steve McCoy** . . . . . . . . . . . . . . . . . . . . . . . . . . (404) 463-5700
Member **Samuel S. "Sam" Olens** . . . . . . . . . . . . . . . . . . (404) 463-5700
  Education: American U 1978 BA, 1980 MA; Emory 1983 JD
Member **David Ralston** . . . . . . . . . . . . . . . . . . . . . . . . . . (404) 463-5700

## Construction Division

270 Washington Street, SW, 2nd Floor, Atlanta, GA 30334
Tel: (404) 463-5600  Fax: (404) 463-5611

▲ State Property Officer and Division Director
  **Steven L. "Steve" Stancil** . . . . . . . . . . . . . . . . . . . (404) 463-5600
Deputy Director **Marvin M. Woodward** . . . . . . . . . . . . . . (404) 463-5608
Communications Director **Paul L. Melvin** . . . . . . . . . . . . . (404) 463-1863
                                                    Fax: (404) 657-0337
Construction Services Director **Carmen Cureton** . . . . . . . . (404) 463-5757
Human Resources Director **Lisa Sharpton** . . . . . . . . . . . . (404) 463-5664
Information Technology Director
  **Andrew "Andy" Triemer** . . . . . . . . . . . . . . . . . . . . (404) 463-5798
  E-mail: andrew.triemer@gsfic.ga.gov
Legal Services Director **Cindy Presto** . . . . . . . . . . . . . . . . (404) 463-5640
                                                    Fax: (404) 463-5981
Procurement Director **Jeff Lacks** . . . . . . . . . . . . . . . . . . . (404) 463-5600
Chief Financial Officer **Alex Volodarski** . . . . . . . . . . . . . . (404) 463-5630
State ADA (American Disabilities Act) Coordinator
  **Manuel "Mike" Galifianakis III** . . . . . . . . . . . . . . . (404) 463-5645

## Finance and Investment Division

■ Director **Diana Pope, CPA** . . . . . . . . . . . . . . . . . . . . . . (404) 463-5701
  E-mail: diana.pope@gsfic.ga.gov
  Education: Hawaii BA
Accounting Director **Kim Site** . . . . . . . . . . . . . . . . . . . . . (404) 463-5708
Bond Finance Director **Lee McElhannon** . . . . . . . . . . . . . (404) 463-5711
  Education: Georgia State 1983 MBA

# Georgia Forestry Commission [GFC]

P.O. Box 819, Macon, GA 31202-0819
Tel: (478) 751-3500  Fax: (478) 751-3465  Internet: www.gatrees.org

**Fiscal Year:** 2015  **Budget:** $50,429,000

■ Director **Robert Farris** . . . . . . . . . . . . . . . . . . . . . . . . . (478) 751-3480
  E-mail: bfarris@gfc.state.ga.us
  Education: Georgia 1984 BS

# Georgia Professional Standards Commission [GAPSC]

Two Peachtree Street, Suite 6000, Atlanta, GA 30303
Tel: (404) 232-2500  Fax: (404) 232-2560  Internet: www.gapsc.com

Executive Secretary **Kelly Henson** . . . . . . . . . . . . . . . . . . (404) 232-2594

# Georgia Public Broadcasting [GPB]

Georgia Public Broadcasting, 260 -14th Street, NW,
Atlanta, GA 30318-5360
Tel: (404) 685-2400  Fax: (404) 685-2617  Tel: (800) 222-6006
Internet: www.gpb.org

■ President and Executive Director **Teya Ryan** . . . . . . . . . . (404) 685-2400
  E-mail: tryan@gpb.org
  Executive Assistant **Gwendolyn Clayton** . . . . . . . . . . (404) 685-2389
Deputy Director and Chief Financial Officer
  **Elizabeth LaPrade** . . . . . . . . . . . . . . . . . . . . . . . . (404) 685-2652
  E-mail: elaprade@gpb.org
Chief Operating Officer **(Vacant)** . . . . . . . . . . . . . . . . . . . (404) 685-2624

Information Technology Manager **Vicki Hamilton** . . . . . . . . (404) 362-4998
  E-mail: vicki.hamilton@ga.gov
Engineering Services Director **Robert "Bob" Butler** . . . . . (404) 685-2527
Human Resources Director **Veronica Daniels** . . . . . . . . . . (404) 685-2637
Marketing and Communications Vice President
  **Mandy Wilson** . . . . . . . . . . . . . . . . . . . . . . . . . . . (404) 685-2427
  E-mail: mandy.wilson@ga.gov

# Georgia Building Authority [GBA]

One Martin Luther King Jr. Drive, SW, Atlanta, GA 30334
Tel: (404) 656-3253  Fax: (404) 657-0337  Internet: www.gba.ga.gov

■ State Property Officer and Executive Director
  **Steven L. "Steve" Stancil** . . . . . . . . . . . . . . . . . . . (404) 656-3253
  E-mail: steve.stancil@spo.ga.gov
Deputy Executive Director **Steve Fanczi** . . . . . . . . . . . . . (404) 656-3253
  Education: Presbyterian Col 1984 BS; Georgia State 1986 MPA
Executive Assistant **(Vacant)** . . . . . . . . . . . . . . . . . . . . . (404) 656-3253
Deputy State Property Officer **Marvin M. Woodward** . . . . (404) 463-5608

## Facilities Management

Director **Debra Myers** . . . . . . . . . . . . . . . . . . . . . . . . . . (404) 463-7705
                                                    Fax: (404) 657-0337

## Shared Services

Chief Financial Officer **April King, CPA** . . . . . . . . . . . . . . (404) 463-1470
  Education: Georgia Tech 1989 BS

## Support Services

Assistant Executive Director **Charles Petty** . . . . . . . . . . . (404) 463-4685
Food Service Director **Charles Petty** . . . . . . . . . . . . . . . . (404) 463-4685

# Georgia Regional Transportation Authority [GRTA]

245 Peachtree Center Avenue, NE, Suite 800, Atlanta, GA 30303-1223
Tel: (404) 463-3000  Fax: (404) 463-3060  E-mail: comments@grta.org
Internet: www.grta.org

▲ Executive Director **Christopher "Chris" Tomlinson** . . . . . (404) 463-3070
  Education: Morehouse Col; Georgia State JD
Chief External Affairs Officer **Matt Markham** . . . . . . . . . . (404) 463-2118
  E-mail: mmarkham@grta.org
Information Technology Director **Charles Fleming** . . . . . . . (404) 463-3098
  E-mail: cfleming@grta.org
Chief Human Resources and Administrative Officer
  **Mitzi Williams** . . . . . . . . . . . . . . . . . . . . . . . . . . . (404) 463-3097
Chief Financial Officer **Mark Peoples** . . . . . . . . . . . . . . . (404) 463-3050
Chief Regional Transit Operations Director
  **Dionne Pittman** . . . . . . . . . . . . . . . . . . . . . . . . . . (404) 463-2035
Strategic Transportation Performance Deputy Chief
  **Rob Goodwin** . . . . . . . . . . . . . . . . . . . . . . . . . . . . (404) 463-2432
Transit Division Director **(Vacant)** . . . . . . . . . . . . . . . . . . (404) 463-3090
Planning and Policy Manager **Angela Sneed** . . . . . . . . . . (404) 463-2381
  E-mail: asneed@grta.org
Accounting Manager **Mark Peoples** . . . . . . . . . . . . . . . . . (404) 463-3050
Contracts and Procurement Manager **Angela Sneed** . . . . . (404) 463-2381
  E-mail: asneed@grta.org
Customer Relations Manager **(Vacant)** . . . . . . . . . . . . . . . (404) 463-3000
Principal Planner **Brian Borden** . . . . . . . . . . . . . . . . . . . . (404) 463-2429
  E-mail: bborden@grta.org
Program Manager **Dave Cassell** . . . . . . . . . . . . . . . . . . . (404) 463-3009

# State Road and Tollway Authority [SRTA]

47 Trinity Avenue, 4th Floor, Atlanta, GA 30334
Tel: (404) 893-6100  Fax: (404) 893-6144  E-mail: gsrta@georgiatolls.com
Internet: www.georgiatolls.com

Chairman **Nathan Deal** . . . . . . . . . . . . . . . . . . . . . . . . . . (404) 893-6100
Member **Mitchell Land** . . . . . . . . . . . . . . . . . . . . . . . . . . (404) 893-6100
Member **Teresa MacCartney** . . . . . . . . . . . . . . . . . . . . . (404) 893-6100
Member **Russell McMurry, PE** . . . . . . . . . . . . . . . . . . . . (404) 893-6100
Member **Joe T. Wood, Jr.** . . . . . . . . . . . . . . . . . . . . . . . . (404) 893-6100

---

★ Elected Official   ■ Appointed by Governor   ● Appointed by Legislature   ▲ Appointed by Board or Commission   ◆ Appointed by State Supreme Court

## Executive Staff

■Executive Director and Board Secretary
**Christopher "Chris" Tomlinson** . . . . . . . . . . . . . . . . . . (404) 893-6100
E-mail: ctomlinson@georgiatolls.com
Deputy Executive Director **Elmer Stancil** . . . . . . . . . . . (404) 893-6126
Chief External Affairs Officer **Matt Markham** . . . . . . . . . (404) 893-6103
E-mail: mmarkham@grta.org
Chief Financial Officer and Treasurer **Mark Peoples** . . . . . . (404) 893-3007

## Pardons and Paroles Board

East Tower, 2 Martin Luther King, Jr. Drive, SE, Suite 458,
Atlanta, GA 30334
Tel: (404) 656-5651  Fax: (404) 651-8502
E-mail: webmaster@pap.state.ga.us  Internet: www.pap.state.ga.us

**Fiscal Year:** 2015  **Budget:** $56,179,000

■Chairman **Terry E. Barnard** . . . . . . . . . . . . . . . . . . . . . . (404) 651-6667
Term Expires: December 31, 2017
■Vice Chairman **James W. Mills** . . . . . . . . . . . . . . . . . . . (404) 651-6695
Term Expires: December 31, 2018
Education: Mercer; New Orleans Baptist MDiv
■Member **Braxton Cotton** . . . . . . . . . . . . . . . . . . . . . . . . (404) 651-6695
Term Expires: December 31, 2019
Education: Georgia Military AA; St Leo U BSCrimJ
■Member **James E. Donald** . . . . . . . . . . . . . . . . . . . . . . . (404) 651-6597
Term Expires: December 31, 2015
Education: Mississippi 1970 BA; Missouri 1983 MPA
■Member **Albert Murray** . . . . . . . . . . . . . . . . . . . . . . . . . (404) 651-6599
Term Expires: December 31, 2016
Education: Tennessee State 1969 BS, 1973 MEd

## Board Staff

Executive Director **Christopher L. Barnett** . . . . . . . . . . . . (404) 651-6638
Education: Georgia Southern BA, MPA
Public Affairs Director **Steve Hayes** . . . . . . . . . . . . . . . . (404) 657-9450
Education: Murray State U 1984 BS

## State Board of Education

205 Jesse Hill Jr. Drive, Atlanta, GA 30334
Tel: (404) 657-7410  Fax: (404) 657-6978
E-mail: state.board@doe.k12.ga.us

■Chair **Mike Royal** (Seventh Congressional) . . . . . . . . . . . . . (404) 657-7410
Term Expires: 2018
E-mail: mroyal@doe.k12.ga.us
■Vice Chair **Lisa Kinnemore** (Fourth Congressional) . . . . . . (404) 657-7410
Term Expires: 2020
E-mail: lkinnemore@doe.k12.ga.us
■Member **James E. "Trey" Allen** (Twelfth Congressional) . . (404) 657-7410
■Member **Kevin Boyd** (Ninth Congressional) . . . . . . . . . . . . (404) 657-7410
Term Expires: 2014                              Fax: (404) 657-4978
E-mail: kevin.boyd@doe.k12.ga.us
■Member **Brian K. Burdette** (Tenth Congressional) . . . . . . . (404) 657-7410
Term Expires: 2014
E-mail: bburdette@doe.k12.ga.us
Education: Penn State BA
■Member **Barbara Hampton** (Sixth Congressional) . . . . . . . (404) 657-7410
Term Expires: 2018
E-mail: bahampton@doe.k12.ga.us
■Member **Scott Johnson** (Eleventh Congressional) . . . . . . . (404) 657-7410
Term Expires: 2020
E-mail: scjohnson@doe.k12.ga.us
■Member **Michael Long** (First Congressional) . . . . . . . . . . (404) 657-7410
Term Expires: 2020
E-mail: mlong@doe.k12.ga.us
■Member **Kenneth Mason** (Fifth Congressional) . . . . . . . . . (404) 657-7410
Term Expires: 2018
E-mail: kmason@doe.k12.ga.us
Education: Hendrix BS
■Member **Sandra Reed** (Eighth Congressional) . . . . . . . . . . (404) 657-7410
Term Expires: 2020
E-mail: sreed@doe.k12.ga.us
■Member **Helen Odom Rice** (Third Congressional) . . . . . . . (404) 657-7410
Term Expires: 2018
E-mail: hrice@doe.k12.ga.us
Education: Valdosta State U BA, MEd

■Member **Larry Winter** (Fourteenth Congressional) . . . . . . . . (706) 278-2834
Term Expires: 2020
E-mail: lwinter@doe.k12.ga.us
■Member **(Vacant)** (Second Congressional) . . . . . . . . . . . . . (404) 657-7410
■Member **(Vacant)** (Thirteenth Congressional) . . . . . . . . . . . (404) 657-7410
Chief Executive Officer **Richard Lee Woods** . . . . . . . . . . . (404) 656-2800
Fax: (404) 651-8737

## Department of Education [DOE]

2066 Twin Towers East, 205 Jesse Hill Drive, SW,
Atlanta, GA 30334-5001
Tel: (404) 656-2800  Fax: (404) 651-8737  TTY: (800) 255-0056
E-mail: webmaster@gadoe.org  Internet: www.doe.k12.ga.us

★State Superintendent **Richard Lee Woods** (D) . . . . . . . . . . (706) 656-2598
Term Expires: January 2019
E-mail: state.superintendent@doe.k12.ga.us
Chief of Staff (Acting) **Mike Buck** . . . . . . . . . . . . . . . . . . (404) 463-1158
Administrative Assistant **Stephen Castellow** . . . . . . . . . (404) 657-6165

## Office of Curriculum, Instruction and Assessment

1766 Twin Towers East, Atlanta, GA 30334-5030
Tel: (404) 656-2804  Fax: (404) 651-8507

Deputy State Superintendent **Caitlin McMunn Dooley** . . . . (404) 656-2804
Administrative Assistant **Laura Peace** . . . . . . . . . . . . . . (404) 656-2804
Education: Georgia State PhD
Chief Academic Officer **Mike Buck** . . . . . . . . . . . . . . . . . (404) 463-1158
Administrative Secretary **Lynn Dessauer** . . . . . . . . . . . . (404) 656-1158
Assessment and Accountability Associate Superintendent
**Melissa Fincher** . . . . . . . . . . . . . . . . . . . . . . . . . . . . . (404) 656-2688
1554 Twin Towers East, Atlanta, GA 30334-5040      Fax: (404) 656-5976
Career, Technical, and Agricultural Education Director
**David Turner** . . . . . . . . . . . . . . . . . . . . . . . . . . . . . . . (404) 657-8304
Curriculum and Instruction Director **Pamela H. Smith** . . . . (404) 657-4141
Twin Towers East, 1752, Atlanta, GA 30334-5040       Fax: (404) 656-5744
Special Education Services and Supports Director
**Debbie Gay** . . . . . . . . . . . . . . . . . . . . . . . . . . . . . . . . (404) 657-3963
E-mail: dgay@doe.k12.ga.us

## Office of External Affairs and Policy

2062 Twin Towers East, Atlanta, GA 30334-5001
Tel: (404) 651-7562  Fax: (404) 651-8737

Policy and Charter Schools Associate Superintendent
**Garry McGiboney** . . . . . . . . . . . . . . . . . . . . . . . . . . . . (404) 656-2965
1870 Twin Towers East, Atlanta, GA 30334-5040      Fax: (404) 463-0441
Administrative Assistant **Marie Jacob** . . . . . . . . . . . . . . (404) 651-7562
Fax: (678) 717-6536
Charter Schools Director **Louis Erste** . . . . . . . . . . . . . . . (404) 657-0515
Communications Director **Matt Cardoza** . . . . . . . . . . . . . (404) 651-7358
Excellence Recognition Program Coordinator
**Keisha Ford-Jenrette** . . . . . . . . . . . . . . . . . . . . . . . . . (404) 657-2949
E-mail: kford@doe.k12.ga.us
Governmental Affairs Director **Cal Newton** . . . . . . . . . . . (404) 859-5497
Georgia Foundation of Public Education Executive
Director **William Bradley "Brad" Bryant** . . . . . . . . . . . (404) 656-4689
2053 Twin Towers East, Atlanta, GA 30334
Education: Presbyterian Col BA; Georgia MBA; Mercer JD
Policy Director **Howard Hendley, EdD** . . . . . . . . . . . . . . (404) 657-2956

## Office of Finance and Business Operations

1666 Twin Towers East, Atlanta, GA 30334
Tel: (404) 656-2492  Fax: (404) 656-0816

Chief Financial Officer **Scott Austensen** . . . . . . . . . . . . . (404) 656-2492
Administrative Assistant **Linda Myers** . . . . . . . . . . . . . . (404) 656-2492
Facilities Superintendent **Mike Rowland** . . . . . . . . . . . . . (404) 656-4556
1670 Twin Towers East, Atlanta, GA 30334       Fax: (404) 651-7688
Human Resources Associate Superintendent **Erin Elmore** . . (404) 656-2510
2052 Twin Towers East, Atlanta, GA 30334-5010
Accounting Services Division Director **Randy Trowell** . . . . (404) 656-2497
1654 Twin Towers East, Atlanta, GA 30334-5050      Fax: (404) 657-5512
Financial Review Director **Louis Byars** . . . . . . . . . . . . . . (404) 656-2447

---

★ Elected Official    ■ Appointed by Governor    ● Appointed by Legislature    ▲ Appointed by Board or Commission    ◆ Appointed by State Supreme Court

Internal Support Services Director **David Childers**
  1662 Twin Towers East . . . . . . . . . . . . . . . . . . . . . . . . . . . (404) 656-8345
  E-mail: dchilders@doe.k12.ga.us
Pupil Transportation Services Director
  **Carlton "Turner" Allen** . . . . . . . . . . . . . . . . . . . . . . . . . . (404) 656-2467
                                                    Fax: (404) 657-1330
Assistant Budget Director **Denise Peterson** . . . . . . . . . . . . (404) 656-2492
School Nutrition Director **Nancy Rice, RD, LD, SNS** . . . . . (404) 651-9443
  1662 Twin Towers East, Atlanta, GA 30334      Fax: (404) 657-9188
  Education: Georgia BS, MEd

## Office of School Improvement

1854 Twin Towers East, Atlanta, GA 30334-5040
Tel: (404) 651-7277  Fax: (404) 657-0546

Deputy State Superintendent **Avis King** . . . . . . . . . . . . . . . (404) 651-7277
  Administrative Assistant **Debbie Moss** . . . . . . . . . . . . . (404) 651-7277
Federal Programs Associate Superintendent
  **Barbara Lunsford** . . . . . . . . . . . . . . . . . . . . . . . . . . . . . (404) 657-4209
  E-mail: blunsford@doe.k12.ga.us
Teacher and Leader Effectiveness Assistant
  Superintendent **Cindy Saxon** . . . . . . . . . . . . . . . . . . . . . (404) 463-5845
Schools Improvement Division Director **Cayanna Good** . . . (404) 463-3456
Governor's Honors Program Director **Dale Lyles** . . . . . . . . (404) 657-0183
  1866 Twin Towers East, Atlanta, GA 30334
  E-mail: dlyles@doe.k12.ga.us

## Office of School Turnaround

1566 Twin Towers East, 205 Jesse Hill Jr. Drive, SE, Atlanta, GA 30334
Tel: (404) 651-0810

Deputy Superintendent **Sylvia Hooker** . . . . . . . . . . . . . . . (404) 232-1431
Administrative Assistant **Tina Wolfe** . . . . . . . . . . . . . . . . (404) 232-1434

## Office of Technology Services

1966 Twin Towers East, Atlanta, GA 30334
Tel: (404) 463-0503  Fax: (404) 656-0978

Chief Information Officer and Deputy Superintendent
  **Robert "Bob" Swiggum** . . . . . . . . . . . . . . . . . . . . . . . . (404) 651-0810
  E-mail: rswiggum@doe.k12.ga.us
Chief Privacy Officer **Levette Williams** . . . . . . . . . . . . . . . (404) 463-0503
Administrative Assistant **Yolanda Yancy-Holmes** . . . . . . . (404) 651-0810
Internal Technology Director **Christina Clayton** . . . . . . . . (404) 463-0503
  E-mail: cclayton@doe.k12.ga.us

## State Board of Workers' Compensation [SBWC]

270 Peachtree Street, NW, Atlanta, GA 30303-1299
Tel: (404) 656-3818  Tel: (800) 533-0682  Internet: www.sbwc.georgia.gov

**Fiscal Year:** 2015  **Budget:** $18,085,000

■Chairman **Judge Frank R. McKay** . . . . . . . . . . . . . . . . . . (404) 656-2034
  Education: Clemson BA; Mercer JD
■Director **Judge Harrill L. Dawkins** . . . . . . . . . . . . . . . . . (404) 656-2038
  E-mail: harrill.dawkins@ga.gov
■Director **Judge Elizabeth D. Gobeil** . . . . . . . . . . . . . . . . (404) 656-2036
  E-mail: gobeile@sbwc.ga.gov

## Board Staff

▲Executive Director/Chief Operating Officer
  **Delece A. Brooks** . . . . . . . . . . . . . . . . . . . . . . . . . . . . . (404) 656-2048
  E-mail: brooksd@sbwc.ga.gov

## Georgia Lottery Corporation

250 Williams Street, Suite 3000, Atlanta, GA 30303
Tel: (404) 215-5000  Fax: (404) 215-8871  E-mail: glottery@galottery.org
Internet: www.galottery.com

▲President and Chief Executive Officer **Debbie D. Alford** . . . (404) 215-5000
  E-mail: debbie.alford@ga.gov
Corporate Affairs Vice President **J. B. Landroche** . . . . . . . . (404) 215-5014
  E-mail: jlandroche@galottery.org
Government Relations Vice President **Brad Bohannon** . . . . (404) 215-5168

## Office of the Lieutenant Governor

240 State Capitol, Atlanta, GA 30334
Tel: (404) 656-5030  Fax: (404) 656-6739  Internet: www.ltgov.ga.gov

**Fiscal Year:** 2015  **Budget:** $971,000

★Lieutenant Governor **Casey Cagle** (R) . . . . . . . . . . . . . . . (404) 656-5030
  Term Expires: January 2019
  E-mail: casey.cagle@ltgov.ga.gov
Chief of Staff **George W. "Bo" Butler** . . . . . . . . . . . . . . . (404) 656-5030
  Education: Mississippi 2009 BS
External Affairs Officer **Roy Neill** . . . . . . . . . . . . . . . . . . . (404) 656-5030
Communications Officer **Adam Ross** . . . . . . . . . . . . . . . . . (404) 656-5030
General Counsel/Policy Director **Irene Munn** . . . . . . . . . . (404) 656-5030
Constituent Services Coordinator **Kim Crowell** . . . . . . . . . (404) 656-5030
  E-mail: kim.crowell@ltgov.ga.gov
Field Representative **George Lee** . . . . . . . . . . . . . . . . . . . . (404) 656-5030
Field Representative **(Vacant)** . . . . . . . . . . . . . . . . . . . . . . (404) 656-5030
Legislative Liaison **Taylor Schindler** . . . . . . . . . . . . . . . . (404) 656-5030
  Education: Georgia
Office Manager **Cheryl Germany** . . . . . . . . . . . . . . . . . . . (404) 651-5259
Personal Assistant/Scheduler **Evelyn Thomas** . . . . . . . . . . (404) 656-5030
  E-mail: evelyn.thomas@ltgov.ga.gov
Policy Analyst **(Vacant)** . . . . . . . . . . . . . . . . . . . . . . . . . . (404) 656-5030

## Office of the Secretary of State

214 State Capitol, Atlanta, GA 30334
Tel: (844) 753-7825  TTY: (888) 265-1115  Fax: (404) 656-0513
E-mail: sosweb@sos.state.ga.us

**Fiscal Year:** 2015  **Budget:** $30,621,000

★Secretary of State **Brian P. Kemp** (R) . . . . . . . . . . . . . . . (844) 753-7825
  Term Expires: January 2019
  Education: Georgia
  Career: State Senator (R-GA, District 46), Georgia Senate (2002-2006);
  Director, Board of Directors, St. Mary's Health Care System Inc.
Deputy Secretary of State **Tim Fleming** . . . . . . . . . . . . . . . (844) 753-7825
  E-mail: tfleming@sos.state.ga.us
Administration Director **Lorri Smith** . . . . . . . . . . . . . . . . . (404) 467-5812
  Two Martin Luther King, Jr. Drive, SE, Suite 820,    Fax: (404) 657-7675
  Atlanta, GA 30334
  E-mail: lsmith@sos.state.ga.us
Corporations Division Director **Shawnzia Thomas** . . . . . . . (404) 656-2817
  West Tower, Two Martin Luther King, Jr. Drive, SE,    Fax: (404) 657-2248
  Suite 315, Atlanta, GA 30334
Elections Division Director **Chris Harvey** . . . . . . . . . . . . . . (844) 753-7825

## Archives and History Division

5800 Jonesboro Road, Morrow, GA 30260
Tel: (678) 364-3710  Fax: (678) 364-3856
E-mail: reference@sos.state.ga.us

Director **Christopher M. Davidson** . . . . . . . . . . . . . . . . . (678) 364-3710

## Professional Licensing Board

237 Coliseum Drive, Macon, GA 31217-3858
Tel: (478) 207-2440  Fax: (478) 207-1363  Internet: www.sos.state.ga.us

Director **Lisa Durden** . . . . . . . . . . . . . . . . . . . . . . . . . . . . (478) 207-2440

## Office of the Attorney General

40 Capitol Square, SW, Atlanta, GA 30334
Tel: (404) 656-3300  Fax: (404) 657-8733

**Employees:** 240

★Attorney General **Samuel S. "Sam" Olens** (R) . . . . . . . . . (404) 483-2477
  Term Expires: January 2019
  Counsel to the Attorney General **Daryl Robinson** . . . . . . (404) 656-3300
  Executive Assistant **Devaan Bernard** . . . . . . . . . . . . . . . (404) 656-3306
Chief Deputy Attorney General
  **Jeffrey L. "Jeff" Milsteen** . . . . . . . . . . . . . . . . . . . . . . (404) 656-3347
  Education: Johns Hopkins 1981 BA; Emory 1984 JD
Solicitor General **Britt C. Grant** . . . . . . . . . . . . . . . . . . . . (404) 656-3300
  Education: Stanford 2007 JD

*(continued on next page)*

---

★ Elected Official   ■ Appointed by Governor   ● Appointed by Legislature   ▲ Appointed by Board or Commission   ◆ Appointed by State Supreme Court

EXECUTIVE BRANCH

**Office of the Attorney General** *continued*

Commercial Transactions and Litigation Deputy Attorney
General **W. Wright Banks, Jr.** . . . . . . . . . . . . . . . . . . . . (404) 651-6107
Education: Georgia 1990 AB; Mercer 1993 JD
Criminal Justice Deputy Attorney General **Beth Burton** . . . (404) 656-3349
General Litigation Deputy Attorney General
**Kathleen Pacious** . . . . . . . . . . . . . . . . . . . . . . . . . . . . . (404) 656-9622
Education: Boston Col 1982 BA; Emory 1985 JD
Government Services and Employment Deputy Attorney
General **Dennis Dunn** . . . . . . . . . . . . . . . . . . . . . . . . . . (404) 656-5614
E-mail: ddunn@law.ga.gov
Education: Stetson 1980 BA; Emory 1983 JD
Regulated Industries and Professions Deputy Attorney
General **Isaac Byrd** . . . . . . . . . . . . . . . . . . . . . . . . . . . . (404) 656-3383
Education: Duke 1971 BS; Harvard 1974 JD
Special Prosecutions Senior Assistant Attorney General
**David McLaughlin** . . . . . . . . . . . . . . . . . . . . . . . . . . . . (404) 656-2218
Communications Director **Nicolas Genesi** . . . . . . . . . . . . (404) 656-3300
E-mail: ngenesi@law.ga.gov
Information Technology Director **Aracelis Caraballo** . . . . (404) 657-3244
E-mail: acaraballo@law.ga.gov
Medicaid Fraud Control Unit Director
**Irvan Alan "Van" Pearlberg** . . . . . . . . . . . . . . . . . . . . (404) 656-5400
Education: Long Island 1973; John Marshall 1976 JD
Legal Policy Counsel/Deputy Solicitor General
**Timothy A. Butler** . . . . . . . . . . . . . . . . . . . . . . . . . . . . (404) 656-3300
Operations Director **Ann Bentley** . . . . . . . . . . . . . . . . . (404) 651-9452

# Office of the Insurance and Safety Fire Commissioner

West Tower, Two M. L. King, Jr. Drive SE, 7th Floor, Atlanta, GA 30334
Tel: (404) 656-2070 Fax: (404) 657-8542 Internet: www.gainsurance.org

★Insurance Commissioner **Ralph T. Hudgens** (R) . . . . . . . . (404) 656-4700
Term Expires: January 2019      Fax: (404) 463-2279
E-mail: rhudgens@oci.ga.gov
Education: Georgia Military; Florida BS
Career: State Representative (R-GA, District 24), Georgia House of
Representatives (1996-2002); State Senator (R-GA, District 47),
Georgia Senate
Chief Deputy Insurance Commissioner
**Justin K. Durrance** . . . . . . . . . . . . . . . . . . . . . . . . . . . (404) 656-9140
Deputy Commissioner **(Vacant)** . . . . . . . . . . . . . . . . . . . (404) 656-2056
Assistant Deputy Commissioner **(Vacant)** . . . . . . . . . . . . (404) 656-2056
Chief Enforcement Attorney **Margaret Witten** . . . . . . . . . (404) 656-2060
Fax: (404) 657-9831
Chief Information Officer **Brett Brammer** . . . . . . . . . . . . (404) 656-5875
E-mail: bbrammer@oci.ga.gov      Fax: (404) 657-6399
Personnel Director **Loranda Allen** . . . . . . . . . . . . . . . . . (404) 656-2082
Fax: (404) 657-7493
Public Education Director **(Vacant)** . . . . . . . . . . . . . . . . (404) 657-2044
Communication Director **Glenn Allen** . . . . . . . . . . . . . . (404) 656-2092
E-mail: gallen@oci.ga.gov
Agents Licensing Division Director **Tammy Holmes** . . . . . (404) 656-2101
Fax: (404) 656-0874
Consumer Services Division Director **Greg Hawkins** . . . . . (404) 656-2070
Fiscal Division Director **Christopher Walker** . . . . . . . . . . (404) 656-2131
Fax: (404) 657-7493
Industrial Loan Division Director **Christopher Stephens** . (404) 656-2080
Fax: (404) 657-6931
Insurance Financial Oversight Director **Trey Sivley** . . . . . (404) 656-2074
Fax: (404) 657-7743
Premium Tax Division Director **M. Linda Brooks** . . . . . . . (404) 656-7553
Fax: (404) 657-2369
Examinations Chief Examiner **Mark Ossi** . . . . . . . . . . . . . (404) 656-0718
Fax: (404) 657-8291
Insurance Product Review **Steve Manders** . . . . . . . . . . . . (404) 656-2085
Fax: (404) 657-7679
Special Fraud Investigations **Sherry Mowell** . . . . . . . . . . (404) 656-2060
Fax: (404) 657-9831
State Fire Marshal **M. Dwayne Garriss** . . . . . . . . . . . . . . (404) 656-2064
Fax: (404) 657-6971
Deputy State Fire Marshal **Chris Stephens** . . . . . . . . . . . (404) 656-2064
Fax: (404) 657-6971

# Georgia Department of Agriculture

Agriculture Building, 19 MLK Jr. Drive, SW, Atlanta, GA 30334
Tel: (404) 656-3600 TTY: (404) 657-8387 Fax: (404) 651-7957
E-mail: info@agr.state.ga.us

**Fiscal Year:** 2015 **Budget:** $59,568,000

★Commissioner **Gary W. Black** (R) . . . . . . . . . . . . . . . . . (404) 656-3602
Term Expires: January 2019
E-mail: gary.black@agr.georgia.gov
Chief Information Officer **Dan Brown** . . . . . . . . . . . . . . (404) 656-3720
E-mail: dan.brown@agr.state.ga.us
Director of Operations **Dr. James D. Sutton** . . . . . . . . . . (404) 656-1264

## Administration Division

Director **Dan Brown** . . . . . . . . . . . . . . . . . . . . . . . . . . . (404) 656-3720
E-mail: dan.brown@agr.georgia.gov    Fax: (404) 463-0545
Personnel Director **Cora Potter** . . . . . . . . . . . . . . . . . . . (404) 656-3615
Press and Consumer Services Director
**Julie McPeake** . . . . . . . . . . . . . . . . . . . . . (855) 327-6829 ext. 6922
Chief Financial Officer **Kelly Dudley** . . . . . . . . . . . . . . . (404) 656-5645
Fiscal Director **Terressa Loggins** . . . . . . . . . . . . . . . . . (404) 656-3611
Procurement Officer **(Vacant)** . . . . . . . . . . . . . . . . . . . . (404) 656-5645
Farmers and Consumers Market Bulletin Editor
**Amy Carter** . . . . . . . . . . . . . . . . . . . . . . . . . . . . . . . . (404) 656-3682
E-mail: amy.carter@agr.georgia.gov

## Animal Industry Division

Director/State Veterinarian **Dr. Robert Cobb** . . . . . . . . . . (404) 656-3671
Assistant State Veterinarian **Wendy Cuevas-Espelid** . . . . . (404) 656-3667
Meat Inspection Director **Adam Buuck** . . . . . . . . . . . . . . (404) 656-3673
Equine Health Manager **Mark "Mat" Thompson** . . . . . . . (404) 656-3713
Livestock and Poultry Manager **Daniel Duncan** . . . . . . . . (404) 656-3665
Poultry Market News Editor **Arty Schronce** . . . . . . . . . . . (404) 656-3656

## Food Safety Division

Director **Natalie Adan** . . . . . . . . . . . . . . . . . . . . . . . . . . (404) 656-3625
Dairy Program Director (North) **Lane Skates** . . . . . . . . . . (404) 656-3625
Dairy Program Director (South) **Ronnie Lott** . . . . . . . . . . (404) 656-3628
Retail Food Program Manager **Bruce Varnadoe** . . . . . . . . (404) 656-3621

## Fuels and Measures Division

Director **Richard Lewis** . . . . . . . . . . . . . . . . . . . . . . . . . (404) 656-3605

## Marketing Division

Director **Jack Spruill** . . . . . . . . . . . . . . . . . . . . . . . . . . (404) 656-3368
Farmers' Markets Administrative Director
**Paul Thompson** . . . . . . . . . . . . . . . . . . . . . . . . . . . . . (404) 656-3680
Bonding Agricultural Manager **Johnny Hurst** . . . . . . . . . (404) 656-3725
Commodities Promotions Director **Andy Harrison** . . . . . . (404) 656-3678
Warehouse Agriculture Manager **Johnny Hurst** . . . . . . . . (404) 656-3725

## Plant Industry Division

Director **Tommy Gray** . . . . . . . . . . . . . . . . . . . . . . . . . . (404) 463-8617
Pesticides Regulatory Program Manager **Jennifer Wren** . . . (404) 656-4958
Plant Protection and Apiary Director **Mike Evans** . . . . . . . (404) 651-9486
Seed, Fertilizer and Feed Director **Alan Lowman** . . . . . . . (404) 656-3637
Structural Pests Control Director **Derrick Lastinger** . . . . . (404) 656-3641

---

★ Elected Official    ■ Appointed by Governor    ● Appointed by Legislature    ▲ Appointed by Board or Commission    ◆ Appointed by State Supreme Court

# Georgia Department of Labor [GDOL]

148 Andrew Young International Boulevard NE, Atlanta, GA 30303-1751
Tel: (404) 232-7300  Fax: (404) 657-9996
E-mail: commissioner@gdol.ga.gov  Internet: www.dol.state.ga.us

**Fiscal Year:** 2015  **Budget:** $127,062,000

★Commissioner **John Mark Butler** (R) . . . . . . . . . . . . . . . . . (404) 232-7300
  Term Expires: January 2019
  124 Briarwood Drive, Carrollton, GA 30117
  E-mail: commissioner@gdol.ga.gov
  Education: Auburn
  Career: Member, Economic Development and Tourism, House
  Standing Committees, Georgia House of Representatives; Vice Chair,
  Appropriations, House Standing Committees, Georgia House of
  Representatives (2007-2010)
Chief of Staff **Brooke Lucas** . . . . . . . . . . . . . . . . . . . . . . (404) 232-7323
Deputy Commissioner **Tim Evans** . . . . . . . . . . . . . . . . . . . (404) 232-7425
  E-mail: tim.evans@gdol.ga.gov
  Education: Georgia 1991 BBA
Communications Director **Sam Hall** . . . . . . . . . . . . . . . . . (404) 232-7440
  E-mail: sam.hall@gdol.ga.gov
  Education: Troy State 1972 BS, 1979 BS
Program Development Director **(Vacant)** . . . . . . . . . . . . . . (404) 232-7360
Marketing and Community Relations Director
  **Amanda Trice** . . . . . . . . . . . . . . . . . . . . . . . . . . . . . . (404) 232-7360
Legislative Liaison **(Vacant)** . . . . . . . . . . . . . . . . . . . . . . (404) 232-3789

## Administrative Services

Internet: www.vocrehabga.org

Director **Russell Gable** . . . . . . . . . . . . . . . . . . . . . . . . . . . (404) 232-3420
  E-mail: russell.gable@gdol.ga.gov
Facilities Management Director **Russell Gable** . . . . . . . . (404) 232-3420
Human Resources Director **Bo McDaniel** . . . . . . . . . . . . . (404) 232-3620
  Facilities Operations Manager **Donna Williams** . . . . . . . (404) 232-3400
    E-mail: donna.williams@gdol.ga.gov

## Employment Services

Director **Linda Manus** . . . . . . . . . . . . . . . . . . . . . . . . . . . . (404) 232-3505
  E-mail: linda.manus@ga.gov
Workforce Systems Manager **Alan Carson** . . . . . . . . . . . . (404) 232-3535
  E-mail: alan.carson@gdol.ga.gov
Jobs for Georgia Graduates Program Director
  **Nedra Wakefield** . . . . . . . . . . . . . . . . . . . . . . . . . . . . (404) 656-5567
  151 Ellis St., NE, Ste. 100, Atlanta, GA 30303-1751
  E-mail: nedra.wakefield@gdol.ga.gov
  Education: Bennett 1984 BA; South Carolina State 1985 MA

## Field Services

Director **Wayne Mack** . . . . . . . . . . . . . . . . . . . . . . . . . . . . (404) 232-3504
  E-mail: wayne.mack@gdol.ga.gov

## Financial Services

Director **Lisa Earls** . . . . . . . . . . . . . . . . . . . . . . . . . . . . . . (404) 232-3000
  Education: Savannah State 1983 BBA, 1987 MBA
Information Technology Chief Information Officer
  **Jeff May** . . . . . . . . . . . . . . . . . . . . . . . . . . . . . . . . . . . (404) 232-7563
  E-mail: jeff.may@gdol.ga.gov

## Policy and External Affairs

Chief **Denise Beckwith** . . . . . . . . . . . . . . . . . . . . . . . . . . . (404) 232-3180
  148 Andrew Young International Boulevard, Atlanta, GA 30303
  E-mail: denise.beckwith@gdol.ga.gov

## Unemployment Insurance

Director **Brenda Brown** . . . . . . . . . . . . . . . . . . . . . . . . . . . (404) 232-3990
Policy and Procedures Chief **Denise Beckwith** . . . . . . . . (404) 232-3196
Child Labor Manager **Genia Burnsed** . . . . . . . . . . . . . . . . (404) 232-3260
  E-mail: genia.burnsed@ga.gov
Claims Administration Chief **Alexi Henry** . . . . . . . . . . . . (404) 232-3559
  E-mail: alexi.henry@gdol.ga.gov
Quality Assurance Manager **Howard Smith** . . . . . . . . . . . (404) 232-3080

Review Board Chief **Nancy Fickling** . . . . . . . . . . . . . . . . . (404) 232-7480
  E-mail: nancy.fickling@gdol.ga.gov
  Appeals Chief **Alice Mitchell** . . . . . . . . . . . . . . . . . . . . (770) 909-7470
    E-mail: alice.mitchell@gdol.ga.gov
    Education: Alabama 1971 BS, 1974 JD; Central Oklahoma 1999 MS
Unemployment Insurance Legal Section Chief
  **Brock Timmons** . . . . . . . . . . . . . . . . . . . . . . . . . . . . . (404) 232-3310
  Education: Vanderbilt 1966 BA; Georgia 1969 JD
Unemployment Insurance Tax Administration Chief
  **Denise Samuel** . . . . . . . . . . . . . . . . . . . . . . . . . . . . . . (404) 232-3320
  Adjudication Manager **Leonard Lockett** . . . . . . . . . . . . (404) 232-3301
    E-mail: leonard.lockett@gdol.ga.gov
  Employer Accounts Manager **Tameka Goggins** . . . . . . . (404) 232-3346
    E-mail: tameka.goggins@gdol.ga.gov
USDOL (US Department of Labor) Veterans Employment
  and Training Services State Director **(Vacant)** . . . . . . . . . (404) 656-3127

# Georgia Public Service Commission [PSC]

244 Washington Street, SW, Suite 127, Atlanta, GA 30334-5701
Tel: (404) 656-4501  Fax: (404) 656-2341  TTY: (800) 255-0056
E-mail: gapsc@psc.state.ga.us  Internet: www.psc.state.ga.us

**Fiscal Year:** 2015  **Budget:** $9,553,000

★Chairman **Chuck Eaton** (R-District 3) . . . . . . . . . . . . . . . (404) 657-2020
  Term Expires: 2018
★Vice Chair **H. Doug Everett** (R-District 1) . . . . . . . . . . . . (404) 463-6745
  Term Expires: 2018
★Commissioner **Tim Echols** (R-District 2) . . . . . . . . . . . . . (404) 657-4574
  Term Expires: 2016
  Education: Georgia 1982 BA, 2009 MA
★Commissioner
  **Lauren "Bubba" McDonald, Jr.** (R-District 4) . . . . . . . . (404) 463-4261
  Term Expires: 2016
★Commissioner **Stan Wise** (R-District 5) . . . . . . . . . . . . . . (404) 463-0214
  Term Expires: 2018
  Education: Charleston Southern 1974 BS

## Commission Staff

▲Executive Director **Deborah K. Flannagan** . . . . . . . . . . . (404) 656-2141

## State Transportation Board

●Chairman **Emily Dunn** . . . . . . . . . . . . . . . . . . . . . . . . . . . (404) 631-1990
●Vice Chairman **Robert L. Brown, Jr.** . . . . . . . . . . . . . . . . (404) 631-1990
●Secretary **Jamie Boswell** . . . . . . . . . . . . . . . . . . . . . . . . . (404) 631-1990
●Member **Rudy Bowen** . . . . . . . . . . . . . . . . . . . . . . . . . . . (404) 631-1990
●Member **Mark Burkhalter** . . . . . . . . . . . . . . . . . . . . . . . . (404) 631-1990
  Education: Georgia BA, BA
●Member **Johnny Wilson Floyd** . . . . . . . . . . . . . . . . . . . . (404) 631-1990
●Member **Tim Golden** . . . . . . . . . . . . . . . . . . . . . . . . . . . . (404) 631-1990
  Education: Valdosta State U 1977 BA
●Member **Don A. Grantham** . . . . . . . . . . . . . . . . . . . . . . . (404) 631-1990
●Member **Stacey Key** . . . . . . . . . . . . . . . . . . . . . . . . . . . . (404) 631-1990
●Member **Dana Lemon** . . . . . . . . . . . . . . . . . . . . . . . . . . . (404) 631-1990
●Member **Jeffrey "Jeff" Lewis** . . . . . . . . . . . . . . . . . . . . . (404) 631-1990
●Member **Ann R. Purcell** . . . . . . . . . . . . . . . . . . . . . . . . . (404) 631-1990
  Education: Georgia Southern BS
●Member **Sam M. Wellborn** . . . . . . . . . . . . . . . . . . . . . . . (404) 631-1990
●Member **Roger Williams** . . . . . . . . . . . . . . . . . . . . . . . . . (404) 631-1990
  Education: North Georgia 1995 BS
Executive Secretary **Elizabeth Osmon** . . . . . . . . . . . . . . . (404) 656-2000

# Georgia Department of Transportation [GDOT]

One Georgia Center, 600 West Peachtree Street, NW, Atlanta, GA 30308
Tel: (404) 631-1990  Fax: (404) 631-1844

**Fiscal Year:** 2015  **Budget:** $2,467,798,000

▲Commissioner **Russell McMurry, PE** . . . . . . . . . . . . . . . . (404) 631-1005
  E-mail: russell.mcmurry@ga.gov
  Senior Executive Assistant to the Commissioner
  **Charis R. Madaris** . . . . . . . . . . . . . . . . . . . . . . . . . . . . (404) 631-1005

*(continued on next page)*

---

★ Elected Official    ■ Appointed by Governor    ● Appointed by Legislature    ▲ Appointed by Board or Commission    ◆ Appointed by State Supreme Court

**Georgia Department of Transportation** *continued*

Senior Policy Advisor **Joshua Waller** . . . . . . . . . . . . . . . . . . (404) 631-1927
  E-mail: joshua.waller@dot.ga.gov

★ Elected Official   ■ Appointed by Governor   ● Appointed by Legislature   ▲ Appointed by Board or Commission   ◆ Appointed by State Supreme Court

Summer 2016                    © Leadership Directories, Inc.                    *State Yellow Book*

# Guam

Internet: www.guam.gov

**Number of U.S. Congressional Delegates:** 1 Nonvoting Delegate **Governor's Term:** 4 years **Legislature Description:** Unicameral- 15 member Senate; Term - 2 years **Next Election:** Governor November 2018; Legislature November 2016 **Official Name:** Guam **Nickname:** Where America's Day Begins

**Population:** 161,000 (2014) **Fiscal Year:** 2014 **Budget:** $874,227,313

**EXECUTIVE BRANCH**

## Office of the Governor

P.O. Box 2950, Hagatna, GU 96932
Tel: (671) 472-8931 Fax: (671) 477-4826

**Edward Baza "Eddie" Calvo**
Governor

Began Service: January 2011
Term Expires: January 2019
Date of Birth: August 29, 1961
Education: Notre Dame 1983 BBA
Religion: Catholic
Career: General Manager, Pacific Construction Company; General Manager and Vice President, Pepsi Cola Bottling Company of Guam; Senator, Guam Legislature (1999-2011)

★ Governor **Edward Baza "Eddie" Calvo** (R) . . . . . . . . . . . . (671) 472-8931
    E-mail: governor@guam.gov
Chief of Staff **Mark Calvo** . . . . . . . . . . . . . . . . . . . . . . . . . (671) 472-8931
Chief Education Advisor **Vincent Leon Guerrero** . . . . . . . . (671) 472-8931
    E-mail: vincent.leonguerrero@guam.gov
Chief Fiscal Advisor **Bernadette "Bernie" Artero** . . . . . . . (671) 472-8931
    E-mail: bernadette.artero@guam.gov
    E-mail: cfa@guam.gov
Chief Policy Advisor **Arthur Clark, Esq.** . . . . . . . . . . . . . . (671) 472-8931
    E-mail: arthur.clark@guam.gov
Legal Counsel **Sandra Miller** . . . . . . . . . . . . . . . . . . . . . . . (671) 472-8931
    E-mail: sandra.miller@guam.gov
Communications Director **Oyaol Ngirairikl** . . . . . . . . . . . . (671) 472-8931
    E-mail: oya@guam.gov
Protocol Officer **Julie Dela Rosa** . . . . . . . . . . . . . . . . . . . (671) 472-8931
    E-mail: julie.delarosa@guam.gov
Staff Assistant for Constituent Services/Medical Referral
  **Evelyn Claros** . . . . . . . . . . . . . . . . . . . . . . . . . . . . . . (671) 472-8931
    E-mail: evelyn.claros@guam.gov
Special Assistant for Climate Change **Tricee Limtiaco** . . . . (671) 472-8931
    E-mail: tricee.limtiaco@guam.gov
Special Assistant for External Affairs
  **Christopher M. "Chris" Duenas** . . . . . . . . . . . . . . . . . . (671) 472-8931
    E-mail: chris.duenas@guam.gov
Special Assistant for Healthcare **Brian San Nicolas** . . . . . . (671) 472-8931
    E-mail: brian.sannicolas@guam.gov
Special Assistant for Military Buildup and Infrastructure
  **(Vacant)** . . . . . . . . . . . . . . . . . . . . . . . . . . . . . . . . . . (671) 472-8931

## Bureau of Budget and Management Research

P.O. Box 2950, Hagatna, GU 96932
Tel: (671) 475-9412 Fax: (671) 472-2825
Director **Jose "Joey" Calvo** . . . . . . . . . . . . . . . . . . . . . . . (671) 475-9412

## Bureau of Statistics and Plans

Ricardo J. Bordallo Governor's Complex, 513 West Marine Corps Drive, Hagatna, GU 96910
P.O. Box 2950, Hagatna, GU 96910
Tel: (671) 472-4201 Fax: (671) 477-1812 Internet: www.bsp.guam.gov
■ Director (Acting) **William Castro** . . . . . . . . . . . . . . . . . . (671) 475-9661
    E-mail: william.castro@guam.gov
Chief Economist **Albert M. Perez** . . . . . . . . . . . . . . . . . . . (671) 472-4201
Guam Coastal Management Program Administrator
  **Edwin J.C. Reyes** . . . . . . . . . . . . . . . . . . . . . . . . . . . . (671) 472-4201

## Department of Military Affairs

Building 300, 430 Army Drive, Barrigada, GU 96913-4421
Tel: (671) 735-0406 Fax: (671) 734-4081 Internet: http://dma.guam.gov
Adjutant General
  **BG Roderick R. Leon Guerrero, ARNG** . . . . . . . . . . . . . (671) 735-0403
Veterans Affairs Administrator **Martin Manglona** . . . . . . . (671) 475-8391
  P.O. Box 5178, Hagatna, GU 96932     Fax: (671) 475-8396

## Civil Service Commission

Phase II Complex, 777 Route 4, Suite 107, Sinajana, GU 96910
Tel: (671) 647-1855 Tel: (671) 647-1857 Fax: (671) 647-1867
Executive Director **Alberto A. "Tony" Lamorena V** . . . . . . (671) 647-1855
  Note: Until June 17, 2016.

## Guam Behavioral Health and Wellness Center [GBHWC]

790 Gov. Carlos G. Camacho Road, Tamuning, GU 96913
Tel: (671) 647-1901 Fax: (671) 647-6948
■ Director **Rey Vega** . . . . . . . . . . . . . . . . . . . . . . . . . . . . . (671) 647-1901
    E-mail: rey.vega@mail.dmhsa.guam.gov
■ Deputy Director **Benny Pinaula** . . . . . . . . . . . . . . . . . . . (671) 647-1901
    E-mail: benny.pinaula@gbhwc.guam.gov

## Guam Election Commission [GEC]

414 West Soledad Avenue, GCIC Building, Suite 200, Hagatna, GU 96910
Tel: (671) 477-9791 Fax: (671) 477-1895
▲ Executive Director **Maria T. Pangelinan** . . . . . . . . . . . . . (671) 477-9791
    E-mail: director@gec.guam.gov

## Guam Public Utilities Commission

414 West Soledad Avenue, GCIC Building, Suite 207, Hagatna, GU 96910
Tel: (671) 472-1907 Fax: (671) 472-1917 E-mail: info@guampuc.com
Chairman **Jeffrey C. Johnson** . . . . . . . . . . . . . . . . . . . . . . (671) 472-1907
Commissioner **Filomena Cantoria** . . . . . . . . . . . . . . . . . . (671) 472-1907
Commissioner **Joseph McDonald** . . . . . . . . . . . . . . . . . . . (671) 472-1907
Commissioner **Peter Montinola** . . . . . . . . . . . . . . . . . . . . (671) 472-1907
Commissioner **Andrew Niven** . . . . . . . . . . . . . . . . . . . . . . (671) 472-1907
Commissioner **Michael A. Pangelinan** . . . . . . . . . . . . . . . (671) 472-1907
  Term Expires: September 30, 2017
  E-mail: mpangelinan@calvofisher.com
  Education: UC Berkeley 1992 BA; Loyola Law 1995 JD
Commissioner **Rowena Perez** . . . . . . . . . . . . . . . . . . . . . . . (671) 472-1907
Administrator **Lourdes R. "Lou" Palomo** . . . . . . . . . . . . . (671) 472-1907

---

★ Elected Official   ■ Appointed by Governor   ● Appointed by Legislature   ▲ Appointed by Board or Commission   ◆ Appointed by State Supreme Court

## Government of Guam Retirement Fund

424 Rt. 8, Maite, GU 96910
Tel: (671) 475-8900  Fax: (671) 475-8922  Internet: www.ggrf.com
▲Director **Paula M. Blas**...........................(671) 475-8948
   E-mail: pmblas@ite.net

## Office of Technology

P.O. Box 2950, Hagatna, GU 96932
Tel: (671) 475-1229  Fax: (671) 472-9508
■Chief Technology Officer **Frank Lujan, Jr.**.............(671) 475-1229
   E-mail: frank.lujan@doa.guam.gov

## Office of the Lieutenant Governor

P.O. Box 2950, Hagatna, GU 96932
Tel: (671) 475-9380  Fax: (671) 477-2007
★Lieutenant Governor **Raymond S. "Ray" Tenorio** (R) ....(671) 475-9380
   Term Expires: 2019
   Education: U Guam 2000 BS
   Career: President, Denanche Security Agency (1995-2002); President,
   Trace Investigations Incorporated (1997-2002); Secretary of the
   Legislature, Guam Legislature (2007-2008)
Chief of Staff **Joseph W. Duenas** ...................(671) 475-9380
Deputy Chief of Staff **Jadeen Tuncap** ................(671) 475-9380
   E-mail: jadeen.tuncap@guam.gov
Office and Program Manager **Leila Uong**..............(671) 475-9380

## Office of the Attorney General

590 South Marine Corps Drive, Suite 706, Tamuning, GU 96913
Tel: (671) 475-3324  Tel: (671) 472-2493
★Attorney General **Elizabeth Barrett-Anderson** (I) .......(671) 475-3324
   Term Expires: 2019

## Department of Administration [DOA]

P.O. Box 884, Hagatna, GU 96932
590 South Marine Corps Drive, Tamuning, GU 96913
Tel: (671) 475-1250  Fax: (671) 472-4217  Internet: www.doa.guam.gov
Director (Acting) **Anthony "Tony" Blaz** ..............(671) 475-1101
   E-mail: anthony.blaz@doa.guam.gov
Deputy Director **Abigail Reyes**......................(671) 475-1101
   E-mail: abigail.reyes@guam.gov

## General Services Agency

148 Route 1 Marine Corps Drive, Piti, GU 96915
P.O. Box 884, Hagatna, GU 96932
Tel: (671) 475-1712  Fax: (671) 472-4217
Chief Procurement Officer **Claudia S. Acfalle** ..........(671) 475-1712

## Department of Agriculture

163 Dairy Road, Mangilao, GU 96913
Tel: (671) 734-3942  Fax: (671) 734-6569  Internet: www.doag.guam.gov
■Director **Matthew Sablan**.........................(671) 734-3943
   E-mail: matt.sablan12@yahoo.com
■Deputy Director **Jessie B. Palican** ...................(671) 734-3942
   E-mail: jessie.palican@gmail.com

## Department of Chamorro Affairs

194 Hernan Cortez Avenue, Terlaje Professional Building,
Hagatna, GU 96910
P.O. Box 2950, Hagatna, GU 96910
Tel: (671) 475-4278  Fax: (671) 475-4227  Internet: www.dca.guam.gov
President **Joseph Artero-Cameron**...................(671) 475-4279

## Guam Museum

194 Hernan Cortez Avenue, Terlaje Professional Building,
Hagatna, GU 96910
P.O. Box 518, Hagatna, GU 96932
Tel: (671) 475-4230  Fax: (671) 475-4227
Administrator **Leona M. Young**.....................(671) 475-4648

## Guam Council on the Arts and Humanities Agency

P.O. Box 2950, Hagatna, GU 96932
Tel: (671) 300-1204  Fax: (671) 300-1209  E-mail: info@caha.guam.gov
Director **Joseph Artero-Cameron** ...................(671) 475-2781

## Guam Public Library System [GPLS]

254 Martyr Street, Hagatna, GU 96910-5141
Tel: (671) 475-4754  Fax: (671) 477-9777  E-mail: gpls@gpls.guam.gov
President **Joseph Artero-Cameron**...................(671) 475-4278

## Department of Corrections [DOC]

P.O. Box 3236, Hagatna, GU 96932
Tel: (671) 735-5170  Fax: (671) 734-4490  Internet: www.doc.guam.gov
Director **MGySgt Jose A. San Agustin, USMC (Ret)** ...(671) 735-5176
   Note: Until June 10, 2016.
Director **Alberto A. "Tony" Lamorena V** .............(671) 735-5170
   Note: Effective June 20, 2016.
Deputy Director **Carleen Borja** ......................(671) 735-5173

## Department of Education

P.O. Box DE, Hagatna, GU 96932
Tel: (671) 300-1547  Fax: (671) 472-5001  Internet: www.gdoe.net
Superintendent **Jon J.P. Fernandez**..................(671) 300-1547
   Education: Arkansas; Georgetown JD; Harvard

## Guam Fire Department

P.O. Box 2950, Hagatna, GU 96910
DNA Building, 238 AFC Flores Street, Suite 1001, Hagatna, GU 96910
Tel: (671) 642-3311  Fax: (671) 642-2012  Internet: www.gfd.guam.gov
■Fire Chief **Lt. Joey Cruz San Nicolas** ................(671) 642-3321
   E-mail: joey.sannicolas@gfd.guam.gov
   Education: U Guam BBA

## Department of Integrated Services for Individuals with Disabilities [DISID]

238 AFC Flores Street, DNA Building, Suite 702, Hagatna, GU 96910
Tel: (671) 475-4646  Fax: (671) 477-2892  Internet: www.disid.guam.gov
Director **Benito Servino** ...........................(671) 475-4646

## Department of Labor/Agency for Human Resources Development [DOL/AHRD]

414 West Soledad Avenue, GCIC Building, Suite 400, Hagatna, GU 96910
Tel: (671) 300-4582  Fax: (671) 475-6811  Internet: www.dol.guam.gov
■Director **Maria S. Connelley**......................(671) 475-7083
   E-mail: maria.connelley@dol.guam.gov
■Deputy Director **Dr. Shirley A. "Sam" Mabini, PhD** .....(671) 475-7044
   E-mail: sam.mabini@dol.guam.gov

## Department of Land Management

P.O. Box 2950, Hagatna, GU 96932
590 South Marine Corps Drive, ITC Building, Suite 733,
Tamuning, GU 96913
Tel: (671) 649-5263  Fax: (671) 649-5383  Internet: www.dlm.guam.gov
Director **Michael J.B Borja** ...................(671) 649-5263 ext. 600
Deputy Director **David Camacho** ....................(671) 649-5263

## Department of Parks and Recreation

490 Chalan Palasyo, Agana, GU 96910
Tel: (671) 475-6296  Fax: (671) 477-0997
Director (Acting) **Robert Sanchez "Bob" Lizama** .......(671) 475-6296
   E-mail: robert.lizama@dpr.guam.gov
Deputy Director **William Reyes**.....................(671) 475-6296

---

★ Elected Official   ■ Appointed by Governor   ● Appointed by Legislature   ▲ Appointed by Board or Commission   ◆ Appointed by State Supreme Court

# Guam Police Department

233 Central Avenue, Tiyan, GU 96912
Building 13-16A, Mariner Avenue, Tiyan, GU 96913
Tel: (671) 475-8518  Fax: (671) 475-8460  Internet: http://gpd.guam.gov

■Chief of Police **Joseph I. Cruz** . . . . . . . . . . . . . . . . . . . . . . (671) 475-8508
  E-mail: chief@gpd.guam.gov
  E-mail: joseph.i.cruz@gpa.guam.gov

# Department of Public Health and Social Services

123 Chalan Kareta, Route 10, Mangilao, GU 96923
P.O. Box 2816, Hagatna, GU 96932 (Vital Records)
Tel: (671) 735-7101  Tel: (671) 735-7185 (Vital Records)
Fax: (671) 734-5910  Fax: (671) 734-5910 (Vital Records)
Internet: www.dphss.guam.gov

■Director **James W. Gillan, MS** . . . . . . . . . . . . . . . . . . . . (671) 735-7102
  E-mail: james.gillan@dphss.guam.gov
Deputy Director **Leo Casil** . . . . . . . . . . . . . . . . . . . . . . . . . (671) 735-7102
Medical Director **Dr. Anna Mathew, MD, FACP** . . . . . . . . (671) 735-7352
Human Services Program Administrator
  **Theresa L. Arcangel** . . . . . . . . . . . . . . . . . . . . . . . . . . (671) 735-7282
Nutrition Health Services Administrator
  **Charles H. Morris** . . . . . . . . . . . . . . . . . . . . . . . . . . . . (671) 475-0287
  E-mail: charles.morris@dphss.guam.gov
Vital Statistics Director **Carolyn Garrido** . . . (671) 735-7263 (Vital Records)

# Department of Public Works

542 North Marine Drive, Tamuning, GU 96913
Tel: (671) 646-3131  Fax: (671) 649-6178  Internet: www.dpw.guam.gov

Director **Glenn Leon Guerrero** . . . . . . . . . . . . . . . . . . . . . (671) 646-3131
Deputy Director **Felix Benavente** . . . . . . . . . . . . . . . . . . . (671) 646-3131

# Department of Revenue and Taxation

1240 Army Drive, Barrigada, GU 96913
P.O. Box 23607, GMF, GU 96921
Tel: (671) 635-1815  Fax: (671) 633-2643  Internet: www.guamtax.com

■Director **John Camacho** . . . . . . . . . . . . . . . . . . . . . . . . . (671) 475-1817
  E-mail: john.camacho@revtax.guam.gov
Deputy Director **Marie Benito** . . . . . . . . . . . . . . . . . . . . . . (671) 475-1817

# Guam Passport Office

1240 Army Drive, Barrigada, GU 96913
Tel: (671) 635-7699  Fax: (671) 635-7577

Chief Passport Officer **Maryann Palomo** . . . . . . . . . . . . . (671) 635-7699

# Department of Youth Affairs

P.O. Box 23672, GMF, GU 96921
Tel: (671) 735-5010  Fax: (671) 734-7536  Internet: www.dya.guam.gov

Director **Adonis J. Mendiola** . . . . . . . . . . . . . . . . . . . . . . . (671) 735-5010
Deputy Director **Peter Alexcis Ada** . . . . . . . . . . . . . . . . . (671) 735-5010

# Federal Programs Office

P.O. Box 2950, Hagatna, GU 96932
Fax: (671) 300-7575

■Federal Grants Administrator **Raymond F.Y. Blas, Sr.** . . . . . . (671) 475-9162
  E-mail: gcofpo@guam.gov

# Office of the Chief Medical Examiner [OCME]

325 Duenas Drive, Tamuning, GU 96913
Tel: (671) 646-9363  Fax: (671) 646-8860  E-mail: cme.guam@gmail.com

▲Chief Medical Examiner **Dr. Aurelio A. Espinola** . . . . . . . . (671) 646-9363
  E-mail: cme.guam@gmail.com

# Office of Public Accountability [OPA]

238 AFC Flores Street, Suite 401, Hagatna, GU 96910
Tel: (671) 475-0390  Fax: (671) 472-7951  Internet: www.guamopa.org

★Public Auditor **Doris Flores Brooks, CPA, CGFM** (R) . . . . (671) 475-0390

# Customs and Quarantine Agency

770 East Sunset Boulevard, Tiyan, GU 96913
P.O. Box 21828 GMF, Barrigada, GU 96921
Tel: (671) 475-6202  Fax: (671) 649-1755  Internet: www.cqa.guam.gov

Director **Pedro A. Leon Guerrero** . . . . . . . . . . . . . . . . . . (671) 475-6202
Chief of Customs **Raffaele M.J. Sgambelluri** . . . . . . . . . . (671) 475-6202

# Guam Environmental Protection Agency

Building 17-3304, Mariner Avenue, Barrigada, GU 96913
P.O. Box 22439, Barrigada, GU 96921
Tel: (671) 475-1658  Fax: (671) 475-8007

■Administrator **Eric Palacios** . . . . . . . . . . . . . . . . . . . . . . (671) 300-4759
  E-mail: gepa.administrator@epa.guam.gov
Deputy Administrator **Yvette Cruz** . . . . . . . . . . . . . . . . . . (671) 475-1658
Air and Land Division Administrator **Conchita Taitano** . . . (671) 300-4760
  Education: U San Francisco BS, MSEM
Environmental Monitoring and Surveillance Division
  Administrator **Jesse Cruz** . . . . . . . . . . . . . . . . . . . . . . . (671) 300-4795

# Guam Visitors Bureau

401 Pale San Vitores Road, Tamuning, GU 96913
Tel: (671) 646-5278  Fax: (671) 646-8861

▲General Manager **Jon Nathan Pangilinan Denight** . . . . . . (671) 646-5278
  E-mail: ndenight@visitguam.org
  Education: Santa Clara U 1999 BS
Deputy General Manager **Telo Taitague** . . . . . . . . . . . . . . (671) 646-5279

# Guam Economic Development Authority [GEDA]

GITC Building, 590 South Marine Corps Drive, Suite 511,
Tamuning, GU 96913
Tel: (671) 647-4332  Fax: (671) 649-4146

▲Administrator **John "Jay" Rojas** . . . . . . . . . . . . . (671) 647-4332 ext. 120
  E-mail: jay.rojas@guam.gov
Deputy Administrator **Mana Silva Taijeron** . . . . . . (671) 647-4332 ext. 121

# Guam International Airport Authority

P.O. Box 8770, Tamuning, GU 96931
Tel: (671) 646-0300  Fax: (671) 646-8823
Internet: www.guamairport.com

Executive Manager **Charles H. "Chuck" Ada II** . . . . . . . . . (671) 646-0300
Deputy Executive Manager **Pedro Roy Martinez** . . . . . . . . (671) 646-0300

# Port Authority of Guam

1026 Cabras Highway, Suite 201, Piti, GU 96915
Tel: (671) 477-5931  Fax: (671) 472-2689

▲General Manager **Joanne M. Salas Brown** . . . . . . . . . . . (671) 477-5931
  E-mail: jbrown@portguam.com
  Education: U Guam 1987 BS; Hawaii 1988 MA
Deputy General Manager **Felix Pangelinan** . . . . . . . . . . . (671) 472-7678
Deputy General Manager, Administration and Finance
  **(Vacant)** . . . . . . . . . . . . . . . . . . . . . . . . . . . . . . . . . . . (671) 472-7678

# Hawaii

Tel: (808) 586-2211 (State Operator)  Internet: www.hawaii.gov

**Number of U.S. Congressional Delegates:** 2 Senators; 2 Representatives  **Governor's Term:** 4 years
**Legislature Description:** 25 member Senate; 51 member House of Representatives; Term - Senate 4 years, House 2 years  **Next Election:** Governor November 2018; Legislature November 2016
**Number of Electoral Votes:** 4  **Official Name:** State of Hawaii (homeland)  **Nickname:** Aloha State
**Motto:** Ua mau ke ea o ka aina i ka pono (The life of the land is perpetuated in righteousness)

**Population:** 1,431,603 (2015); Rank 40  **Fiscal Year:** 2014  **Budget:** $11,819,318,188

## Office of the Governor

State Capitol, Honolulu, HI 96813
Tel: (808) 586-0034  Fax: (808) 586-0006
Internet: www.governor.hawaii.gov

**David Y. Ige**
Governor

Began Service: December 1, 2014
Term Expires: 2018
Date of Birth: January 15, 1957
Education: Hawaii 1979 BSEE, 1985 MBA
Home: Aiea
Career: State Representative (D-HI), Hawaii House of Representatives (1986-1993); State Senator (D-HI, District 16), Hawaii Senate (1994-2014)

★ Governor **David Y. Ige** (D) . . . . . . . . . . . . . . . . . . . (808) 586-0034
Chief of Staff **Michael "Mike" McCartney** . . . . . . . . . . . . (808) 586-0034
  E-mail: mike.mccartney@hawaii.gov
  Education: Pacific U 1982 BS
Deputy Chief of Staff **Laurel A. Johnston** . . . . . . . . . . . . (808) 586-0034
  E-mail: laurel.a.johnston@hawaii.gov
Communications Director **Cindy McMillan** . . . . . . . . . . . . (808) 586-0034
  E-mail: cindy.mcmillan@hawaii.gov
Communications Deputy Director and Press Secretary
  **Joanne C. "Jodi" Leong** . . . . . . . . . . . . . . . . . . . . (808) 586-0034
  Education: Hawaii BA
Digital Media Specialist **Yasmin Dar** . . . . . . . . . . . . . . . (808) 586-0034
Education Policy Analyst **(Vacant)** . . . . . . . . . . . . . . . . . (808) 586-0034
Protocol Officer and Deputy Military Affairs Liaison
  **CMSgt Rob Lee, ANG** . . . . . . . . . . . . . . . . . . . . . . (808) 586-0034
  Education: Wayland Baptist BS, MS
Deputy Military Affairs Liaison
  **Thomas Kahalu Lee, Jr.** . . . . . . . . . . . . . . . . . . . . . (808) 586-0034
Special Advisor **Elizabeth O. "Betsy" Kim** . . . . . . . . . . . (808) 586-0034
  Education: UCLA 2005 BA

## Executive Office of Early Learning

State Capitol, 415 South Beretania Street, Room 417, Honolulu, HI 96813
Tel: (808) 586-3811  E-mail: gov.earlylearning@hawaii.gov
Internet: www.earlylearning.hawaii.gov

Early Learning Director **Lauren Moriguchi** . . . . . . . . . . . (808) 305-9806
  E-mail: lauren_moriguchi@hawaiidoe.org
  Education: Idaho

## Office of Collective Bargaining [OCB]

235 South Beretania Street, Room 1201, Honolulu, HI 96813
Tel: (808) 587-6893  Fax: (808) 587-6894

■ Chief Negotiator **James K. Nishimoto** . . . . . . . . . . . . . . (808) 587-6893
  E-mail: james.nishimoto@hawaii.gov

## East Hawaii - Hilo Office

75 Aupuni Street, Suite 103A, Hilo, HI 96720
Tel: (808) 974-6262  Fax: (808) 974-6263  E-mail: hilogov@hawaii.gov
Governor's Liaison **Wil Okabe** . . . . . . . . . . . . . . . . . . . . (808) 974-6262
  E-mail: wil.m.okabe@hawaii.gov

## Kauai Office

3060 Eiwa Street, #106, Lihue, HI 96766
Tel: (808) 274-3102  Fax: (808) 274-3103  E-mail: kauaigov@hawaii.gov
Governor's Representative **Carrice Gardner** . . . . . . . . . . . (808) 274-3100
  E-mail: carrice.gardner@hawaii.gov

## Lanai Office

P.O. Box 630806, Lanai City, HI 96763
Tel: (808) 565-6380
Volunteer Governor's Representative **Jarrod Barfield** . . . . . (808) 565-6380

## Maui Office

2264 Aupuni Street, Suite 1, Wailuku, HI 96793
Tel: (808) 243-5795  Fax: (808) 243-5049  E-mail: mauigov@hawaii.gov
Governor's Liaison **Leah Belmonte** . . . . . . . . . . . . . . . . . (808) 243-5795

## Molokai Office

P.O. Box 88, Kaunakakai, HI 96748
Tel: (808) 553-9000
Volunteer Governor's Representative
  **Beverly Pauole-Moore** . . . . . . . . . . . . . . . . . . . . . . (808) 553-9000

## West Hawaii - Kona Office

Kuakini Towers, 75-5722 Kuakini Highway, Suite 215,
Kailua Kona, HI 96740
Tel: (808) 327-4953  Fax: (808) 327-4952  E-mail: konagov@hawaii.gov
Governor's Representative **Susan M. Kim** . . . . . . . . . . . . (808) 327-4593
  E-mail: susan.m.kim@hawaii.gov

## Office of the Lieutenant Governor

State Capitol, Honolulu, HI 96813
Tel: (808) 586-0255  Fax: (808) 586-0231

★ Lieutenant Governor **Shan S. Tsutsui** (D) . . . . . . . . . . . (808) 586-0255
  Term Expires: December 3, 2018
  E-mail: shan.tsutsui@hawaii.gov
  Education: Hawaii 1994 BA
  Career: State Senator (D-HI, District 5), Hawaii Senate (2003-2012)
Chief of Staff **Keira Kamiya** . . . . . . . . . . . . . . . . . . . . (808) 586-0255
Deputy Chief of Staff **Ross Tsukenjo** . . . . . . . . . . . . . . . (808) 586-0255
Senior Advisor to the Lieutenant Governor
  **Jayson M. Watts** . . . . . . . . . . . . . . . . . . . . . . . . . . (808) 586-0255

---

★ Elected Official  ■ Appointed by Governor  ● Appointed by Legislature  ▲ Appointed by Board or Commission  ◆ Appointed by State Supreme Court

# Department of the Attorney General

425 Queen Street, Honolulu, HI 96813
Tel: (808) 586-1500  TTY: (808) 586-1298  Fax: (808) 586-1239
E-mail: hawaiiag@hawaii.gov

**Employees:** 739  **Fiscal Year:** 2015  **Budget:** $78,356,000

■ Attorney General **Douglas S. Chin** . . . . . . . . . . . . . . . . . . . (808) 586-1282
  E-mail: douglas.s.chin@hawaii.gov
  Education: Stanford BA; Hawaii JD
First Deputy Attorney General **Russell A. Suzuki** . . . . . . . (808) 586-1292
  Education: Hawaii; Ohio State JD
  Special Assistant **Joshua A. Wisch, JD** . . . . . . . . . . . . (808) 586-1284
    Education: Carnegie Mellon; Georgetown 2002 JD
Solicitor General **Girard D. Lau, Esq.** . . . . . . . . . . . . . . . . (808) 586-1360
Administration Division Supervising Deputy Attorney
  General **Patricia T. Ohara** . . . . . . . . . . . . . . . . . . . . (808) 586-0618
  E-mail: patricia.t.ohara@hawaii.gov  Fax: (808) 586-1372
Appellate Division Supervising Deputy Attorney General
  **Girard D. Lau, Esq.** . . . . . . . . . . . . . . . . . . . . . . . . . (808) 586-1360
                        Fax: (808) 586-1237
Civil Recoveries Division Supervising Deputy Attorney
  General **Michael Vincent** . . . . . . . . . . . . . . . . . . . . . (808) 586-1100
                        Fax: (808) 586-8116
Civil Rights Litigation Division Supervising Deputy
  Attorney General **Caron M. Inagaki** . . . . . . . . . . . . . (808) 586-1494
                        Fax: (808) 586-1369
Commerce and Economic Development Division
  Supervising Deputy Attorney General **Bryan Yee** . . . . . . (808) 586-1180
                        Fax: (808) 586-1205
Criminal Justice Division Supervising Deputy Attorney
  General **Kevin K. Takata** . . . . . . . . . . . . . . . . . . . . . (808) 586-1160
  Melim Building, 333 Queen Street, Second Floor,  Fax: (808) 586-1375
  Honolulu, HI 96813
  Medicaid Fraud Control Unit Director
    **Christopher D. Young** . . . . . . . . . . . . . . . . . . . . . (808) 586-1169
Education Division Supervising Deputy Attorney General
  **Holly T. Shikada** . . . . . . . . . . . . . . . . . . . . . . . . . . (808) 586-1255
  235 South Beretania Street, Suite 304,  Fax: (808) 586-1488
  Honolulu, HI 96813
  E-mail: holly.t.shikada@hawaii.gov
Employment Law Division Supervising Deputy Attorney
  General **James Halvorson** . . . . . . . . . . . . . . . . . . . . (808) 587-2900
  Leiopapa A. Kamehameha Building,  Fax: (808) 587-2965
  235 South Beretania Street, Room 1501, Honolulu, HI 96813
  E-mail: james.e.halvorson@hawaii.gov
Family Law Division Supervising Deputy Attorney
  General **Mary Anne Magnier** . . . . . . . . . . . . . . . . . . (808) 693-7081
  1001 Kamokila Street, Suite 211,  Fax: (808) 693-7079
  Kapolei, HI 96707
  E-mail: maryanne.magnier@hawaii.gov
  Education: Hawaii 1983 JD
Health and Human Services Division Supervising Deputy
  Attorney General **Heidi M. Rian** . . . . . . . . . . . . . . . . (808) 587-3050
  Kekuanao'a Building, 465 South King Street,  Fax: (808) 587-3077
  2nd Floor, Honolulu, HI 96813
  E-mail: heidi.m.rian@hawaii.gov
Labor Division Supervising Deputy Attorney General
  **Frances E. H. Lum** . . . . . . . . . . . . . . . . . . . . . . . . . (808) 586-1450
  E-mail: frances.e.lum@hawaii.gov  Fax: (808) 586-1376
Land/Transportation Division Supervising Deputy
  Attorney General **William J. Wynhoff** . . . . . . . . . . . . (808) 587-2992
  Kekuanao'a Building, 465 South King Street,  Fax: (808) 587-2999
  3rd Floor, Honolulu, HI 96813
  E-mail: bill.j.wynhoff@hawaii.gov
Major Litigation Division Supervising Deputy Attorney
  General **Harvey E. Henderson, Jr.** . . . . . . . . . . . . . . (808) 586-1219
  Education: UC Berkeley; Hastings 1968 JD
Public Safety, Hawaiian Homelands and Housing
  Division Supervising Deputy Attorney General
  **Diane K. Taira** . . . . . . . . . . . . . . . . . . . . . . . . . . . . (808) 587-2978
  E-mail: diane.k.taira@hawaii.gov  Fax: (808) 586-1372
Tax and Charities Division Supervising Deputy Attorney
  General **Hugh R. Jones** . . . . . . . . . . . . . . . . . . . . . . (808) 586-1470
                        Fax: (808) 586-8116
Tort Litigation Division Supervising Deputy Attorney
  General **Caron M. Inagaki** . . . . . . . . . . . . . . . . . . . . (808) 586-1300
                        Fax: (808) 586-1369

Investigations Division Chief Investigator
  **Dan Hanagami** . . . . . . . . . . . . . . . . . . . . . . . . . . . (808) 586-1240
                        Fax: (808) 586-1371
Crime Prevention and Justice Assistance Division
  Administrator **Julie Y. Ebato** . . . . . . . . . . . . . . . . . . (808) 586-1150
  235 South Beretania Street, Suite 401,  Fax: (808) 586-1097
  Honolulu, HI 96813
Administrative Services Manager **David T. Moore** . . . . . . . (808) 586-1287
  E-mail: david.t.moore@hawaii.gov
Information Technology Manager **Victor Mau** . . . . . . . . . . (808) 586-1208
Librarian **William Stempel** . . . . . . . . . . . . . . . . . . . . . (808) 586-1220

## Office of Child Support Hearings

Kakuhihewa Building, 601 Kamokila Boulevard, Room 436,
Kapolei, HI 96707
Fax: (808) 692-7114
Supervisor **Erin N. Sugita** . . . . . . . . . . . . . . . . . . . . . . (808) 692-7110
  E-mail: erin.n.sugita@hawaii.gov

## Child Support Enforcement Agency [CSEA]

Kakuhihewa Building, 601 Kamokila Boulevard, Room 207,
Kapolei, HI 96707
Tel: (808) 692-8265  Fax: (808) 692-7134
Administrator **Lynette Lau** . . . . . . . . . . . . . . . . . . . . . . (808) 692-7000
  E-mail: csea.administration@hawaii.gov

## Hawaii Criminal Justice Data Center

Kekuanao'a Building, 465 South King Street, Room 101,
Honolulu, HI 96813
Tel: (808) 587-3110  Fax: (808) 587-3109
Administrator **Liane M. Moriyama** . . . . . . . . . . . . . . . . . (808) 587-3110

# Department of Accounting and General Services [DAGS]

Kalanimoku Building, 1151 Punchbowl Street, Honolulu, HI 96813
P.O. Box 119, Honolulu, HI 96810-0119
Tel: (808) 586-0400  Fax: (808) 586-0775  E-mail: dags@hawaii.gov
Internet: ags.hawaii.gov

**Employees:** 707  **Fiscal Year:** 2015  **Budget:** $215,795,000

■ Comptroller **Doug G. Murdock** . . . . . . . . . . . . . . . . . . (808) 586-0400
  E-mail: doug@gohta.net
■ Deputy Comptroller **Audrey Hidano** . . . . . . . . . . . . . . . (808) 586-0402
  E-mail: audrey.hidano@hawaii.gov  Fax: (808) 586-0707
  Education: Heald Col (Honolulu) AS
Data Processing Systems Manager **Glenn Y. Segawa** . . . . . (808) 586-0580
  E-mail: glenn.y.segawa@hawaii.gov  Fax: (808) 586-0707
  Education: Hawaii 1972 BA; Roosevelt 1984 BGS
Business Management Officer **Kerry K. Yoneshige** . . . . . . (808) 586-0696
  Education: Hawaii 1976 BBA  Fax: (808) 586-0707
Personnel Officer **Dianne F. Matsuura** . . . . . . . . . . . . . . (808) 586-0369
  Education: USC BS, MPA  Fax: (808) 586-0349
Risk Management Officer **Tracy S. Kitaoka** . . . . . . . . . . . (808) 586-0547
                        Fax: (808) 586-0553

## Office of Elections

802 Lehua Avenue, Pearl City, HI 96782
Tel: (808) 453-8683  Fax: (808) 453-6006  E-mail: elections@hawaii.gov
Internet: www.hawaii.gov/elections
Chief Election Officer **Scott T. Nago** . . . . . . . . . . . . . . . (808) 453-8683

## Office of Enterprise Technology Services [OIMT]

1177 Alakea Street, Room 305, Honolulu, HI 96813
Tel: (808) 586-1930  E-mail: oimt@hawaii.gov

■ Chief Information Officer **Todd Nacapuy** . . . . . . . . . . . . (808) 586-1930
Information Technology Development Officer
  **Michael Otsuji** . . . . . . . . . . . . . . . . . . . . . . . . . . . (808) 586-1930
Information Technology Operations Officer and Chief
  Technology Officer **Jim Miwa** . . . . . . . . . . . . . . . . . (808) 586-1930
Business Architect **Mark Choi** . . . . . . . . . . . . . . . . . . . (808) 586-1930

---

★ Elected Official  ■ Appointed by Governor  ● Appointed by Legislature  ▲ Appointed by Board or Commission  ◆ Appointed by State Supreme Court

## State Procurement Office

Kalanimoku Building, 1151 Punchbowl Street, Honolulu, HI 96813
P.O. Box 119, Honolulu, HI 96810-0119
Tel: (808) 587-4700  Fax: (808) 587-4703

■Administrator **Sarah Allen** . . . . . . . . . . . . . . . . . . . . . . . . (808) 587-4700
  E-mail: sarah.allen@hawaii.gov
  Education: U South Africa
Assistant Administrator **Paula A. Youngling** . . . . . . . . . . . (808) 586-0554
                                                          Fax: (808) 586-0570
Inventory Management Specialist **Michael Ong** . . . . . . . . . (808) 586-0562
Surplus Property Manager **Craig I. Kuraoka** . . . . . . . . . . . (808) 831-6757
                                                          Fax: (808) 831-6786
Health and Human Services Program Manager
  **Corinne Y. Higa** . . . . . . . . . . . . . . . . . . . . . . . . . . . . . (808) 587-4706
Hawaii Electronic Procurement System Program Manager
  **Mara Smith** . . . . . . . . . . . . . . . . . . . . . . . . . . . . . . . . (808) 587-4704
  Education: NYU BA
Purchasing Specialist **Lori Cervantes** . . . . . . . . . . . . . . . (808) 586-0563
Purchasing Specialist **Owen Kano** . . . . . . . . . . . . . . . . . . (808) 586-0766
Purchasing Specialist **Stacey L. Kauleinamoku** . . . . . . . . (808) 586-0571
Purchasing Specialist **Stanton D. Mato** . . . . . . . . . . . . . . (808) 586-0566
Purchasing Specialist **Shawn Richey** . . . . . . . . . . . . . . . . (808) 586-0577
Purchasing Specialist **Carey Ann R. Sasaki** . . . . . . . . . . . (808) 586-0575
Purchasing Specialist **Kevin S. Takaesu** . . . . . . . . . . . . . (808) 586-0568
Purchasing Specialist **Donna Tsuruda-Kashiwabara** . . . . . (808) 586-0565
Travel Services and pCard Manager **Bonnie A. Kahakui** . . (808) 587-4702

## Accounting Division

Tel: (808) 586-0600  Fax: (808) 586-0739

Division Head **Wayne M. Horie** . . . . . . . . . . . . . . . . . . . . (808) 586-0600
  Education: Hawaii BBA
Pre-Audit Branch Chief **Sheila K. Walters** . . . . . . . . . . . . . (808) 586-0650
  Education: Hawaii BBA
Systems Accounting Branch Chief **Kurt I. Muraoka** . . . . . . (808) 586-0610
  Education: Hawaii BBA
Uniform Accounting and Reporting Branch Chief
  **(Vacant)** . . . . . . . . . . . . . . . . . . . . . . . . . . . . . . . . . . (808) 586-0599

## Archives Division

Kekauluohi Building, Iolani Palace Grounds, 364 South King Street,
Honolulu, HI 96813
Tel: (808) 586-0329  Fax: (808) 586-0330  E-mail: archives@hawaii.gov

State Archivist (Acting) **Luella H. Kurkjian** . . . . . . . . . . . . (808) 586-0310
  Education: Syracuse 1967 BS; Hawaii 1990 MLIS, 1999 MPA
Historical Records Branch Chief **Luella H. Kurkjian** . . . . . . (808) 586-0320
Records Center Branch Chief (Acting)
  **Gina S. Vegara-Bautista** . . . . . . . . . . . . . . . . . . . . . . (808) 831-6780
  729B Kakoi Street, Honolulu, HI 96819            Fax: (808) 831-6777

## Audit Division

1151 Punchbowl Street, Room 230, Honolulu, HI 96813
Tel: (808) 586-0360  Fax: (808) 586-0738
E-mail: dagsaudit@exec.state.hi.us

Administrator (Acting) **Steven J. Lee** . . . . . . . . . . . . . . . . . (808) 586-0360
Supervising Auditor **(Vacant)** . . . . . . . . . . . . . . . . . . . . . . (808) 586-0364

## Automotive Management Division

869-A Punchbowl Street, Honolulu, HI 96813
P.O. Box 119, Honolulu, HI 96810-0119
Tel: (808) 586-0343  Fax: (808) 586-0354

Division Head **Brian Y. Saito** . . . . . . . . . . . . . . . . . . . . . . (808) 586-0343
  E-mail: brian.saito@hawaii.gov
Automotive Services Operations Supervisor
  **Richard F. Hung** . . . . . . . . . . . . . . . . . . . . . . . . . . . . . (808) 586-0351
Motor Pool Supervisor **Arthur Oshita** . . . . . . . . . . . . . . . (808) 586-0353
Parking Control Branch Supervisor **Keala C Irvine** . . . . . . (808) 586-0352
  E-mail: keala.c.irvine@hawaii.gov
Staff Services Supervisor **Hugh P. Sonoda** . . . . . . . . . . . . (808) 586-0350

## Central Services Division

729B Kakoi Street, Honolulu, HI 96819
Tel: (808) 831-6730  Fax: (808) 831-6750

Administrator **Dean H. Shimomura** . . . . . . . . . . . . . . . . . . (808) 831-6730
  E-mail: dean.h.shimomura@hawaii.gov
Procurement and Inventory Branch Chief
  **Glenn K. Nishimoto** . . . . . . . . . . . . . . . . . . . . . . . . . . (808) 831-6741
Public Building Management Services Branch Chief
  **James Hisano** . . . . . . . . . . . . . . . . . . . . . . . . . . . . . . (808) 831-6734
Public Buildings Repair and Alterations Chief
  **Dean H. Shimomura** . . . . . . . . . . . . . . . . . . . . . . . . . . (808) 831-6736

## Information and Communication Services Division

Kalanimoku Building, 1151 Punchbowl Street, Room B-10,
Honolulu, HI 96813
Tel: (808) 586-1920  Fax: (808) 586-1922

Administrator **(Vacant)** . . . . . . . . . . . . . . . . . . . . . . . . . . (808) 586-1910
Assistant Administrator **(Vacant)** . . . . . . . . . . . . . (808) 586-1920 ext. 308
Client Services Branch I Chief **(Vacant)** . . . . . . . . (808) 586-1850 ext. 752
                                                          Fax: (808) 586-1864
Client Services Branch II Chief
  **Dennis S. Uyesugi** . . . . . . . . . . . . . . . . . . . . . (808) 586-1855 ext. 702
  E-mail: dennis.s.uyesugi@hawaii.gov          Fax: (808) 586-2109
Planning and Project Management Office Chief
  **Sharon N. Wong** . . . . . . . . . . . . . . . . . . . . . . . (808) 586-1930 ext. 615
Production Services Branch Chief **Gerald I. Ouchi** . . . . . . . (808) 586-4747
  E-mail: gerald.i.ouchi@hawaii.gov              Fax: (808) 586-1882
Systems Services Branch Chief **(Vacant)** . . . . . . . . (808) 586-1940 ext. 343
Technology Support Services Branch Chief
  **(Vacant)** . . . . . . . . . . . . . . . . . . . . . . . . . . . (808) 586-1940 ext. 508
Telecommunications Services Branch Chief
  (Acting) **Sharon N. Wong** . . . . . . . . . . . . . . . . . (808) 586-1930 ext. 615
                                                          Fax: (808) 586-1962

## Land Survey Division

Kalanimoku Building, 1151 Punchbowl Street, Room 210,
Honolulu, HI 96813
Tel: (808) 586-0380  Fax: (808) 586-0383  E-mail: landsurvey@hawaii.gov

State Land Surveyor **Reid Siarot** . . . . . . . . . . . . . . . . . . . . (808) 586-0390
Assistant State Land Surveyor **Gerald Yonashiro** . . . . . . . . (808) 586-0380

## Public Works Division

Kalanimoku Building, 1151 Punchbowl Street, Room 426,
Honolulu, HI 96813
Tel: (808) 586-0526  Fax: (808) 586-0521  Internet: www.hawaii.gov/pwd

State Public Works Administrator **James K. Kurata** . . . . . . (808) 586-0526
Construction Management Branch Chief
  **Clyde K. Kumabe** Room 423 . . . . . . . . . . . . . . . . . . . . (808) 586-0414
Planning Branch Chief **(Vacant)** . . . . . . . . . . . . . . . . . . . . (808) 586-0500
                                                          Fax: (808) 586-0482
Project Management Branch Chief **Eric K. Nishimoto**
  Room 427 . . . . . . . . . . . . . . . . . . . . . . . . . . . . . . . . . . (808) 586-0460
  Education: Hawaii 1984 BS                       Fax: (808) 586-0530
Staff Services Office Chief **Lloyd T. Ogata** Room 422 . . . . (808) 586-0520
Technical Services Office Chief **Scott M. Ojiri**
  Room 428 . . . . . . . . . . . . . . . . . . . . . . . . . . . . . . . . . . (808) 586-0450
  E-mail: scott.m.ojiri@hawaii.gov               Fax: (808) 586-0745
Leasing Specialist **Ivan S. Nishiki** Room 429 . . . . . . . . . . (808) 586-0508
  Education: Hawaii 1974 BBA                      Fax: (808) 586-0779

## Department of Budget and Finance

P.O. Box 150, Honolulu, HI 96810-0150
Tel: (808) 586-1518  Fax: (808) 586-1976
E-mail: hi.budgetandfinance@hawaii.gov

**Employees: 361  Fiscal Year: 2015  Budget: $2,354,475,000**

■Director **Wesley K. Machida** . . . . . . . . . . . . . . . . . . . . . . (808) 586-1518
  E-mail: wesley.k.machida@hawaii.gov
■Deputy Director **Roderick K. Becker** . . . . . . . . . . . . . . . . (808) 586-1516
  Education: Hawaii BA

---

★ Elected Official    ■ Appointed by Governor    ● Appointed by Legislature    ▲ Appointed by Board or Commission    ◆ Appointed by State Supreme Court

## Office of the Public Defender

1130 North Nimitz Highway, Suite A-254, Honolulu, HI 96817
Fax: (808) 586-2222  Internet: www.publicdefender.hawaii.gov

State Public Defender **John M. Tonaki** ................(808) 586-2200
Chief Deputy **Timothy E. Ho** ......................(808) 586-2200

## Employees' Retirement System of the State of Hawaii [ERS]

201 Merchant Street, Suite 1400, Honolulu, HI 96813-2980
Tel: (808) 586-1735  Fax: (808) 586-5766

Executive Director **Thomas Williams** ..............(808) 586-1700
Assistant Administrator **Kanoe Margol** ............(808) 586-1636
Accounting Manager **Larry Wolfe** ..................(808) 586-1728
Benefits Manager **Karl Kaneshiro** .................(808) 586-1649
Staff Support Services Supervisor **(Vacant)** ......(808) 586-1682
Chief Investment Officer **Vijoy P. Chattergy** .......(808) 586-1727
Information Technology Manager **Keith Miyamoto** .......(808) 586-1713
  E-mail: miyamotok@hiers.org

## Hawaii Employer-Union Health Benefits Trust Fund [EUTF]

201 Merchant Street, Suite 1520, Honolulu, HI 96813
Tel: (808) 586-7390  Fax: (808) 586-2161  E-mail: eutf@hawaii.gov

Administrator **Derek Mizuno** ......................(808) 586-7390
Assistant Administrator **Donna Tonaki** ...........(808) 586-7390

## Department of Business, Economic Development and Tourism

One Capitol District Building, 250 South Hotel Street,
Diamond Head Wing, 5th Floor, Honolulu, HI 96813
P.O. Box 2359, Honolulu, HI 96804
Tel: (808) 586-2355  Fax: (808) 586-2377  Internet: dbedt.hawaii.gov

**Employees:** 298  **Fiscal Year:** 2013-2014  **Budget:** $301,943,904

■Director **Luis P. Salaveria** .......................(808) 586-2355
  Education: Hawaii 1993 BA
■Deputy Director **Mary Alice Evans** ................(808) 586-2355

## Department of Commerce and Consumer Affairs [DCCA]

P.O. Box 541, Honolulu, HI 96809
Tel: (808) 586-2850  Fax: (808) 586-2856  E-mail: dcca@dcca.hawaii.gov

**Employees:** 409  **Fiscal Year:** 2014-2015  **Budget:** $54,870,000

■Director **Catherine P. Awakuni Colón** .............(808) 586-2850
  E-mail: cawakuni@dcca.hawaii.gov
■Deputy Director **Jo Ann Uchida Takeuchi** ..........(808) 586-2855
  E-mail: juchida@dcca.hawaii.gov
  Education: Hawaii BA, 1981 JD

### Administrative Hearings Office

335 Merchant Street, Room 100, Honolulu, HI 96813
Tel: (808) 586-2828  E-mail: oah@dcca.hawaii.gov

Senior Hearings Officer **David H. Karlen** ...........(808) 586-2828
  Education: Chicago 1968 BA; Boalt Hall 1973 JD

### Administrative Services Office

Tel: (808) 586-2830  Fax: (808) 586-2877

Business Management Officer (Acting) **Kay M. Okimoto** ..(808) 586-2844
  E-mail: kay.m.okimoto@dcca.hawaii.gov

### Consumer Protection Office

235 South Beretania Street, Room 801, Honolulu, HI 96813
Tel: (808) 586-2630  Fax: (808) 586-2640

Executive Director **Stephen H. "Steve" Levins** .........(808) 586-2636
  Education: Rhode Island BA; Temple JD

### Regulated Industries Complaints Office

235 South Beretania Street, 9th Floor, Honolulu, HI 96813
Tel: (808) 587-4272 (Consumer Complaints)
Tel: (808) 587-4272 (Prior Complaints)  Fax: (808) 586-2670
E-mail: rico@dcca.hawaii.gov

Complaints and Enforcement Officer **Daria Loy-Goto** .....(808) 586-2666

### Business Registration Division

335 Merchant Street, Room 201, Honolulu, HI 96813
P.O. Box 40, Honolulu, HI 96810
Tel: (808) 586-2727  Fax: (808) 586-2733  E-mail: breg@dcca.hawaii.gov

Securities Commissioner **Ty Nohara** ..................(808) 586-2744

### Cable Television Division

335 Merchant Street, Room 101, Honolulu, HI 96813
Tel: (808) 586-2620  Fax: (808) 586-2625
E-mail: cabletv@dcca.hawaii.gov

Administrator **Ji Sook "Lisa" Kim** ..................(808) 586-2620

### Consumer Advocacy Division

Tel: (808) 586-2800  Fax: (808) 586-2780
E-mail: consumeradvocate@dcca.hawaii.gov

■Executive Director **Jeffrey T. Ono** ...................(808) 586-2770
  E-mail: dca@dcca.hawaii.gov
Utilities Administrator **Dean Nishina** ...............(808) 586-2800
  E-mail: dca@dcca.hawaii.gov

### Financial Institutions Division

335 Merchant Street, Room 221, Honolulu, HI 96813
P.O. Box 2054, Honolulu, HI 96805
Tel: (808) 586-2820  Fax: (808) 586-2818  E-mail: dfi@dcca.hawaii.gov

Commissioner **Iris K. Ikeda** .........................(808) 586-2820
  E-mail: iris.k.ikeda@dcca.hawaii.gov
Deputy Commissioner **Tara L. Murphy** ................(808) 586-2820
  E-mail: tara.l.murphy@dcca.hawaii.gov

### Insurance Division

335 Merchant Street, Room 213, Honolulu, HI 96813
P.O. Box 3614, Honolulu, HI 96811
Fax: (808) 586-2806  E-mail: insurance@dcca.hawaii.gov

Insurance Commissioner **Gordon I. Ito** ...............(808) 586-2799
  Education: Hawaii BA, JD
Deputy Commissioner **Kathleen H. Nakasone** ..........(808) 586-3040

### Professional and Vocational Licensing Division

335 Merchant Street, Room 301, Honolulu, HI 96813
P.O. Box 3469, Honolulu, HI 96801
Tel: (808) 586-3000  E-mail: pvl@dcca.hawaii.gov

Administrator **Celia Suzuki** ........................(808) 586-2690

## Hawaii Public Utilities Commission

465 South King Street, Suite 103, Honolulu, HI 96813
Tel: (808) 586-2020  Fax: (808) 586-2066  E-mail: hawaii.puc@hawaii.gov
Internet: www.puc.hawaii.gov

Chairman **Randall Y. "Randy" Iwase** ................(808) 586-2020
  E-mail: randy.y.iwase@hawaii.gov
  Education: Florida 1971 BA; San Francisco Law JD
Commissioner **Lorraine H. Akiba** ...................(808) 586-2020
  Term Expires: June 30, 2018
  E-mail: lorraine.h.akiba@hawaii.gov
  Education: UC Berkeley 1977 BA; Hastings 1981 JD
Commissioner **Michael E. Champley** ................(808) 586-2020
  Term Expires: June 30, 2016
  E-mail: michael.e.champley@hawaii.gov
  Education: Dayton BS; Indiana MBA
Administrative Director **Delmond J. Won** ............(808) 586-2020
  E-mail: delmond.j.won@hawaii.gov

★ Elected Official   ■ Appointed by Governor   ● Appointed by Legislature   ▲ Appointed by Board or Commission   ◆ Appointed by State Supreme Court

*State Yellow Book*          © Leadership Directories, Inc.          Summer 2016

# Department of Defense
3949 Diamond Head Road, Honolulu, HI 96816-4495
Tel: (808) 733-4258  Fax: (808) 733-4236
E-mail: webmaster@dod.state.hi.us

**Employees:** 243  **Fiscal Year:** 2015  **Budget:** $123,117,000

■Adjutant General
  **MG Arthur Joseph "Joe" Logan, ARNG** . . . . . . . . . . . . (808) 672-1202
    E-mail: arthur.j.logan.mil@mail.mil
Deputy Adjutant General **BG Kenneth Hara, ARNG** . . . . . .(808) 733-4244
  Plans and Operations Branch Chief **Victor Gustafson** . . . (808) 733-4300
Public Affairs Officer **LtCol Charles J. Anthony, ANG** . . . (808) 733-4258
    E-mail: charles.anthony@hickam.af.mil

## Hawaii National Guard
3949 Diamond Head Road, Honolulu, HI 96816-4495
Tel: (808) 672-1202

■Adjutant General
  **MG Arthur Joseph "Joe" Logan, ARNG** . . . . . . . . . . . (808) 672-1202
    E-mail: arthur.j.logan.mil@mail.mil

## Hawaii Air National Guard
3949 Diamond Head Road, Honolulu, HI 96816-4495
Tel: (808) 733-4232  Fax: (808) 733-7227

Chief of Staff and Commander
  **BrigGen Ryan T. Okahara, ANG** . . . . . . . . . . . . . . . . . .(808) 733-4232
    Education: Hawaii BS; Webster MA
Senior Enlisted Leader **(Vacant)** . . . . . . . . . . . . . . . . . . . . (808) 733-4232

## Hawaii Army National Guard
3949 Diamond Head Road, Honolulu, HI 96816-4495
Tel: (808) 672-1012  Fax: (808) 672-1252

Commander **BG Keith Y. Tamashiro, ARNG** . . . . . . . . . . . (808) 672-1014
Chief Information Officer **Col Reynold T. Hioki, ANG** . . . . (808) 672-1012

## Hawaii Emergency Management Agency
Administrator **MajGen Vern T. Miyagi, ANG** . . . . . . . . . . (808) 733-4300
Executive Officer **Toby L. Clairmont, RN, CEM** . . . . . . . . (808) 733-4300

# Department of Education
Queen Liliuokalani Building, 1390 Miller Street, Honolulu, HI 96813
P.O. Box 2360, Honolulu, HI 96804
Tel: (808) 586-3230  TTY: (808) 586-3232  Fax: (808) 586-3234
Internet: www.hawaiipublicschools.org

**Employees:** 19,975  **Fiscal Year:** 2015  **Budget:** $2,096,799,000

▲Superintendent **Kathryn S. Matayoshi** . . . . . . . . . . . . . .(808) 586-3313
    E-mail: kathryn_matayoshi@notes.k12.hi.us
    Education: Carleton; Hastings JD
Deputy Superintendent **Stephen Schatz** . . . . . . . . . . . . . .(808) 586-3313
    Education: UC Santa Cruz; Cal State (Dominguez)
Budget Director **Brian Hallett** . . . . . . . . . . . . . . . . . . . . (808) 586-3355
                                                    Fax: (808) 586-3360
Communications Director **Donalyn Dela Cruz** . . . . . . . . . .(808) 586-2332
    Education: Hawaii BA
Senior Assistant Superintendent **Amy Kunz** . . . . . . . . . . . . (808) 586-3230
    E-mail: amy_kunz@notes.k12.hi.us

## Office of Curriculum, Instruction and Student Support
Tel: (808) 586-3446  Fax: (808) 586-3429

Assistant Superintendent **Suzanne Mulcahy** . . . . . . . . . . . (808) 586-3446
Director **Sandra Goya** . . . . . . . . . . . . . . . . . (808) 203-5505 ext. 1303
State GED (General Education Development)
    Administrator **Annette Young-Ogata** . . . . . . . . . . . . . . (808) 203-5511
    E-mail: annette.young-ogata@hawaiidoe.org

## Office of Fiscal Services
Tel: (808) 586-3444  Fax: (808) 586-3445

Assistant Superintendent and Chief Financial Officer
  **Amy Kunz** . . . . . . . . . . . . . . . . . . . . . . . . . . . . . . . . (808) 586-3737
Accounting Director **Tom Ishimaru** . . . . . . . . . . . . . . . . .(808) 586-3450
                                                    Fax: (808) 586-3374

# Office of Human Resources
Fax: (808) 586-3419

Assistant Superintendent **Barbara A. Krieg** . . . . . . . . . . . .(808) 586-3400
    Education: Notre Dame BA; UCLA 1995 JD
Personnel Management Director **Kerry Tom** . . . . . . . . . . . (808) 586-3473

## Office of Information Technology Services
Fax: (808) 586-3645

Assistant Superintendent and Chief Information Officer
  **Clyde S. Sonobe** . . . . . . . . . . . . . . . . . . . . . . . . . . . .(808) 586-3307
    Education: USC BS
Enterprise Architecture Branch Director **(Vacant)** . . . . . . . .(808) 586-3212
Information Technology Project Management Branch
  Director **(Vacant)** . . . . . . . . . . . . . . . . . . . . . . . . . . . (808) 564-6037

## Office of School Facilities and Support Services
Tel: (808) 586-3444  Fax: (808) 586-3445

Assistant Superintendent
  **Col Dann S. Carlson, USAF (Ret)** . . . . . . . . . . . . . . . . (808) 586-3444

## Office of Strategy, Innovation and Performance
Tel: (808) 586-3800

Assistant Superintendent **Tammi Oyadomori-Chun, EdD** . .(808) 586-3800

# Department of Health
1250 Punchbowl Street, Honolulu, HI 96813
P.O. Box 3378, Honolulu, HI 96801
Tel: (808) 586-4400  Tel: (808) 586-4542 (Vital Records)
Fax: (808) 586-4368  Internet: www.health.hawaii.gov

**Employees:** 2,631  **Fiscal Year:** 2014-2015  **Budget:** $1,649,320,000

■Director **Dr. Virginia "Ginny" Pressler, MD** . . . . . . . . . . (808) 586-4410
    E-mail: virginia.pressler@hawaii.gov
Communications Director **Janice Okubo** . . . . . . . . . . . . . (808) 586-4442
    E-mail: janice.okubo@doh.hawaii.gov

## Executive Office on Aging
Number 1 Capitol District, 250 South Hotel Street, Suite 406,
Honolulu, HI 96813-2831
Tel: (808) 586-0100  Fax: (808) 586-0185

■Executive Director **Terri Byers** . . . . . . . . . . . . . . . . . . . .(808) 586-0100
    E-mail: terri.byers@doh.hawaii.gov

## District Health Offices
Hawaii District Health Officer **Aaron Ueno** . . . . . . . . . . . .(808) 974-6006
  75 Aupuni Street, Hilo, HI 96720          Fax: (808) 974-6000
Kauai District Health Officer **Dileep G. Bal, MD** . . . . . . . .(808) 241-3614
  3040 Umi Street, Lihue, HI 96766          Fax: (808) 241-3480
Maui District Health Officer **Lorrin Pang, MD** . . . . . . . . . .(808) 984-8200
  State Office Building, 54 High Street,      Fax: (808) 984-8222
  Wailuku, HI 96793

## Office of Environmental Quality Control
State Office Tower, 235 South Beretania Street, Suite 702,
Honolulu, HI 96813
Tel: (808) 586-4185  Fax: (808) 586-4186
E-mail: oeqchawaii@doh.hawaii.gov

■Director (Interim) **Scott Glenn** . . . . . . . . . . . . . . . . . . . .(808) 586-4185
    E-mail: scott.glenn@doh.hawaii.gov
    Education: Evansville 2000 BA; Hawaii 2009 MA

## State Health Planning and Development Agency
1177 Alakea Street, Suite 402, Honolulu, HI 96813
Tel: (808) 587-0788  Fax: (808) 587-0783
E-mail: doh.shpda@doh.hawaii.gov

Administrator **Romala S. Radcliffe** . . . . . . . . . . . . . . . . . .(808) 587-0788

---

★ Elected Official    ■ Appointed by Governor    ● Appointed by Legislature    ▲ Appointed by Board or Commission    ◆ Appointed by State Supreme Court

## Office of the Deputy Director of Health
Tel: (808) 586-4412  Fax: (808) 586-4368

■First Deputy Director **Keith Yamamoto** . . . . . . . . . . . . . . . (808) 586-4412
E-mail: keith.yamamoto@doh.hawaii.gov
Education: Hawaii MPA

## Behavioral Health Administration
Tel: (808) 586-4416  Fax: (808) 586-4368

Deputy Director **Lynn N. Fallin** . . . . . . . . . . . . . . . . . . . . . . (808) 586-4416

## Environmental Health Administration
Tel: (808) 586-4424  Fax: (808) 586-4368

Deputy Director **Keith E. Kawaoka** . . . . . . . . . . . . . . . . . (808) 586-4424
Environmental Resources Office Manager **Nancy Bartter** . . (808) 586-7567

## Health Resources Administration
Tel: (808) 586-4433  Fax: (808) 586-4444

Deputy Director **Danette Wong Tomiyasu** . . . . . . . . . . . . (808) 586-4433
Education: U Phoenix MSW

## Department of Human Resources Development
235 South Beretania Street, Honolulu, HI 96813
Tel: (808) 587-1100  Fax: (808) 587-1106  TTY: (808) 587-1148
E-mail: dhrd@hawaii.gov  Internet: dhrd.hawaii.gov

**Employees:** 91  **Fiscal Year:** 2015  **Budget:** $21,635,000

■Director **James K. Nishimoto** . . . . . . . . . . . . . . . . . . . . . . . . (808) 587-1100
E-mail: james.k.nishimoto@hawaii.gov
■Deputy Director **Cindy S. Inouye** . . . . . . . . . . . . . . . . . . . . (808) 587-1110
E-mail: cindy.s.inouye@hawaii.gov
Education: Hawaii BA, MA, JD

## Department of Human Services
1390 Miller Street, Room 209, Honolulu, HI 96813
P.O. Box 339, Honolulu, HI 96809-0339
Tel: (808) 586-4997  Fax: (808) 586-4890
Internet: humanservices.hawaii.gov

**Employees:** 2,215  **Fiscal Year:** 2015  **Budget:** $3,027,800,000

■Director **Rachael S. Wong, DrPH, MPH** . . . . . . . . . . . . . . (808) 586-4999
E-mail: dhs@dhs.hawaii.gov
Education: Princeton AB; Hawaii MPH
Administrative Assistant **Lisa Nakao** . . . . . . . . . . . . . . . (808) 586-4888
■Deputy Director **Pankaj Bhanot** . . . . . . . . . . . . . . . . . . . . . (808) 586-4999
E-mail: pbhanot@dhs.hawaii.gov
Education: U Delhi (India) BA, JD; Cornell ML;
Nottingham (UK) (Attended)
●Youth Services Executive Director (Acting)
**Merton Chinen** . . . . . . . . . . . . . . . . . . . . . . . . . . . . . . (808) 587-5700
E-mail: mchinen@dhs.hawaii.gov
Benefit, Employment and Support Services Division
Administrator (Acting) **Scott Nakasone** . . . . . . . . . . . . (808) 586-5230
E-mail: snakasone2@dhs.hawaii.gov
Supplemental Nutrition Assistance Program
Administrator **Pamela Higa** . . . . . . . . . . . . . . . . . . . . (808) 586-5722
Med-Quest Division Administrator **Judy Mohr Peterson** . . (808) 692-8050
Social Services Division Administrator **Mona Maehara** . . . (808) 586-5701
Vocational Rehabilitation and Services for the Blind
Division Administrator **Albert Perez** . . . . . . . . . . . . . . . (808) 586-9741
E-mail: aperez@dhs.hawaii.gov
Business Management Officer **Ken N. Kitamura**
Room 206 . . . . . . . . . . . . . . . . . . . . . . . . . . . . . . . . . . (808) 586-4856
E-mail: kkitamura@dhs.hawaii.gov
Business Management Officer **Paul Sasaki** . . . . . . . . . . . . (808) 586-4868
E-mail: psasaki@dhs.hawaii.gov
Personnel Officer **Brenna Hashimoto** . . . . . . . . . . . . . . . . (808) 586-4951
Homelessness Coordinator **Scott Morishige** . . . . . . . . . . . (808) 586-0974
E-mail: scott.s.morishige@hawaii.gov
Assistant Homelessness Coordinator **Brian Matson** . . . . . . (808) 586-7066
E-mail: brian.w.matson@hawaii.gov

## Department of Labor and Industrial Relations
830 Punchbowl Street, Honolulu, HI 96813
Tel: (808) 586-8842  Fax: (808) 586-9099  TTY: (808) 586-8847
E-mail: dlir.director@hawaii.gov  Internet: labor.hawaii.gov

**Employees:** 664  **Fiscal Year:** 2015  **Budget:** $464,868,000

■Director **Linda Chu-Takayama** . . . . . . . . . . . . . . . . . . . . . . (808) 586-8844
E-mail: linda.c.takayama@hawaii.gov
■Deputy Director **Leonard Hoshijo** . . . . . . . . . . . . . . . . . . . . (808) 586-8852
E-mail: leonard.hoshijo@hawaii.gov
Public Information Officer **William G. Kunstman** . . . . . . (808) 586-8845
E-mail: william.g.kunstman@hawaii.gov
Research and Statistics Office Chief **Phyllis Dayao** . . . . . . (808) 586-8996
Disability Compensation Division Administrator **(Vacant)** . . (808) 586-9151
Hawaii Occupational Safety and Health Administrator
**(Vacant)** . . . . . . . . . . . . . . . . . . . . . . . . . . . . . . . . . . . . (808) 586-9116
Unemployment Insurance Division Administrator
**Linda Y. Uesato** . . . . . . . . . . . . . . . . . . . . . . . . . . . . . . (808) 586-9069
Workforce Development Division Administrator
**Elaine N. Young** . . . . . . . . . . . . . . . . . . . . . . . . . . . . . (808) 586-8812
E-mail: elaine.n.young@hawaii.gov
Labor Law Enforcement Administrator
**Pamela B. Martin** . . . . . . . . . . . . . . . . . . . . . . . . . . . . (808) 586-8771
Business Management Officer **Norman Ahu** . . . . . . . . . . . (808) 586-8888
E-mail: norman.ahu@hawaii.gov
Employment Security Appeals Chief Referee
**Pamela A. Toguchi** . . . . . . . . . . . . . . . . . . . . . . . . . . . (808) 586-8935
E-mail: pamela.a.toguchi@hawaii.gov

## Department of Land and Natural Resources [DLNR]
Kalanimoku Building, 1151 Punchbowl Street, Honolulu, HI 96813
Tel: (808) 587-0400  Fax: (808) 587-0390  E-mail: dlnr@hawaii.gov

**Employees:** 760  **Fiscal Year:** 2015  **Budget:** $154,665,000

■Director **Suzanne Case** . . . . . . . . . . . . . . . . . . . . . . . . . . . . . (808) 587-0401
E-mail: suzanne.case@hawaii.gov
■First Deputy **Kekoa Kaluhiwa** . . . . . . . . . . . . . . . . . . . . . . . (808) 587-0402
E-mail: kekoa.kaluhiwa@hawaii.gov
Aquatic Resources Division Head
**Dr. Bruce Anderson, PhD** . . . . . . . . . . . . . . . . . . . . . . . (808) 587-0100
Education: Punahou (Honolulu, HI); Colorado Col 1974 BA;
Yale 1979 MPH; Hawaii 1981 PhD
Conservation and Resources Enforcement Division Chief
**Thomas "Tommy" Friel** . . . . . . . . . . . . . . . . . . . . . . . . (808) 587-0066
Education: Hawaii 1984 BS
Engineering Division Chief Engineer **Carty Chang** . . . . . . (808) 587-0230
Forestry and Wildlife Division Administrator
**David "Dave" Smith** . . . . . . . . . . . . . . . . . . . . . . . . . . (808) 587-0166
Land Division Administrator **Russell Y. Tsuji** . . . . . . . . . . (808) 587-0419
Conservation and Coastal Lands Office Administrator
**Samuel J. Lemmo** . . . . . . . . . . . . . . . . . . . . . . . . . . . . (808) 587-0378
Conveyances Bureau Registrar **Nicki Ann Thompson** . . . . (808) 587-0147
E-mail: nicki.thompson@hawaii.gov
Fiscal Management Officer **Cynthia Gomez** . . . . . . . . . . . (808) 587-0344
Information Technology Manager **Lila Loos** . . . . . . . . . . . (808) 587-0337
E-mail: lila.loos@hawaii.gov

## Department of Public Safety [PSD]
919 Ala Moana Boulevard, 4th Floor, Honolulu, HI 96814
Tel: (808) 587-1288  Fax: (808) 587-1282  Internet: dps.hawaii.gov

**Employees:** 2,663  **Fiscal Year:** 2015  **Budget:** $267,668,000

■Director **Nolan Espinda** . . . . . . . . . . . . . . . . . . . . . . . . . . . . (808) 587-1288
E-mail: nolan.espinda@doh.hawaii.gov          Fax: (808) 587-1421
Administrative Assistant **Joan Yanagihara** . . . . . . . . . . . (808) 587-1285
Chief Investigator (Acting) **Patrick K. Nakashima** . . . . . . (808) 587-1130
Civil Rights Compliance Officer **Oscar Hernandez** . . . . . . (808) 587-1228
E-mail: oscar.a.hernandez@hawaii.gov
Inspection and Investigation Officer **Alan M. Asato** . . . . . (808) 587-1335
E-mail: alan.m.asato@hawaii.gov
Litigation Coordination Officer **Shelley D. Nobriga** . . . . . (808) 587-1367
E-mail: shelley.d.nobriga@hawaii.gov
Education: Hawaii 1988 BSW, 2000 JD

★ Elected Official    ■ Appointed by Governor    ● Appointed by Legislature    ▲ Appointed by Board or Commission    ◆ Appointed by State Supreme Court

## Administration Division

■Deputy Director **Cathy Y. Ross** . . . . . . . . . . . . . . . . . . . . . (808) 587-1251
  E-mail: cathy.y.ross@hawaii.gov
  Education: Hawaii BA, MPH
Business Management Officer **Teresita V. Fernandez** . . . . (808) 587-1236
Fiscal Officer **Clifford N. Asato** . . . . . . . . . . . . . . . . . . . (808) 587-1186
Personnel Management Officer **Colleen O. Miyasato** . . . . . (808) 587-1221
Information Technology Administrator (Acting)
  **Judy Q. Yamada** . . . . . . . . . . . . . . . . . . . . . . . . . . . (808) 587-1181
  E-mail: judy.q.yamada@hawaii.gov
Training and Staff Development Administrator
  **Isaac U. Sagario** . . . . . . . . . . . . . . . . . . . . . . . . . . (808) 453-6080
  E-mail: isaac.u.sagario@hawaii.gov

## Corrections Division

■Deputy Director **Jodie Maesaka-Hirata** . . . . . . . . . . . . . . . (808) 587-1340
  E-mail: jodie.f.maesaka-hirata@hawaii.gov
  Education: Hawaii BS; Chaminade MS
Health Care Administrator **Wesley K. Mun** . . . . . . . . . . . (808) 587-1250
Classification Officer **Monica M. Lortz** . . . . . . . . . . . . . . (808) 587-2567

## Law Enforcement Division

Pier 20, Honolulu, HI 96817

■Deputy Director **Shawn H. Tsuha** . . . . . . . . . . . . . . . . . . (808) 587-2562
  E-mail: shawn.h.tsuha@hawaii.gov
  Education: U Phoenix; Hawaii AS
Narcotics Enforcement Division Administrator (Acting)
  **Derek J. Nakamura** . . . . . . . . . . . . . . . . . . . . . . . . (808) 837-8470
  3375 Koapaka Street, D100, Honolulu, HI 96819
  E-mail: derek.j.nakamura@hawaii.gov
Sheriff **Renee Sonobe Hong** . . . . . . . . . . . . . . . . . . . . . (808) 587-2648
  First Deputy **Lt. Albert X. Cummings** . . . . . . . . . . . . . . (808) 587-3628

## Department of Taxation

P.O. Box 259, Honolulu, HI 96809
Tel: (808) 587-4242  Fax: (808) 587-1506  Internet: tax.hawaii.gov

**Employees: 382  Fiscal Year: 2015  Budget: $24,550,217**

■Director **Maria E. Zielinski, CPA** . . . . . . . . . . . . . . . . . . (808) 587-1513
  E-mail: maria.e.zielinski@hawaii.gov
  Education: CUNY BS
  Private Secretary **Dana Remigio** . . . . . . . . . . . . . . . (808) 587-1540
Deputy Director **BrigGen Joseph K. "Joe" Kim, ANG** . . . (808) 587-1523
  Education: Air Force Acad 1982 BS;
  Bellevue Col (Washington) 1990 MBA
  Private Secretary **Sonny Kekipi** . . . . . . . . . . . . . . . (808) 587-1527
Compliance Division Chief **Kevin Wakayama** . . . . . . . . . . (808) 587-1460
Tax Services and Processing Division Chief (Acting)
  **Janyne Kaai** . . . . . . . . . . . . . . . . . . . . . . . . . . . . (808) 543-6811
Information Technology Manager **Robert Su** . . . . . . . . . . . (808) 587-1778
  E-mail: robert.l.su@hawaii.gov
Administrative Services Officer **Dexter Suzuki** . . . . . . . . . (808) 587-1500
  E-mail: dexter.t.suziki@hawaii.gov
Personnel Officer (Acting) **Gene Dumaran** . . . . . . . . . . . (808) 587-1503
Rules Officer **Ted S. Shiraishi** . . . . . . . . . . . . . . . . . . . (808) 587-1569
Tax Research and Planning Officer (Acting)
  **Yvonne Chow** . . . . . . . . . . . . . . . . . . . . . . . . . . . (808) 587-1447

## Department of Transportation [DOT]

869 Punchbowl Street, Honolulu, HI 96813
Tel: (808) 587-2150  Fax: (808) 587-2367  E-mail: dotpao@hawaii.gov
Internet: hidot.hawaii.gov

**Employees: 2,210  Fiscal Year: 2015  Budget: $1,656,366,000**

■Director **Ford Fuchigami** . . . . . . . . . . . . . . . . . . . . . . . (808) 587-2150
  E-mail: ford.fuchigami@hawaii.gov
■Administration Deputy Director **Jade Butay** . . . . . . . . . . . (808) 587-2154
  E-mail: jade.butay@hawaii.gov
  Education: Hawaii BA; Babson MA
■Highway Improvements Deputy Director
  **Edwin H. Sniffen** . . . . . . . . . . . . . . . . . . . . . . . . . (808) 587-2156
Business Management Officer **Lisa H. Dau** . . . . . . . . . . . . (808) 587-2133
Contracts Officer **Tammy L. Lee** . . . . . . . . . . . . . . . . . . (808) 587-2130
  E-mail: tammy.l.lee@hawaii.gov

Environmental Health Specialist **Chris Takeno** . . . . . . . . . . (808) 831-7997
Departmental Personnel Officer **Rey Domingo** . . . . . . . . . (808) 587-2145
Program Evaluation Manager **Clarita Barretto Hironaka** . . (808) 587-2211
Public Information Officer **Timothy Sakahara** . . . . . . . . . . (808) 587-2160
Information Technology Manager **Arthur Minagawa** . . . . . (808) 587-2369
  E-mail: arthur.minagawa@hawaii.gov
State Planner **Dean Nakagawa** . . . . . . . . . . . . . . . . . . . (808) 831-7973
  E-mail: dean.nakagawa@hawaii.gov
Civil Rights Manager **Cliffon N. Harty** . . . . . . . . . . . . . . (808) 587-2020
                                                    Fax: (808) 587-2025

## Airports Division

Honolulu International Airport, 400 Rodgers Boulevard, Suite 700,
Honolulu, HI 96819-1880
Tel: (808) 836-6411  Fax: (808) 838-8750

Administrator **Ross Higashi** . . . . . . . . . . . . . . . . . . . . . (808) 838-8704
Engineering Program Manager **Jeff Chang** . . . . . . . . . . . . (808) 838-8835
  E-mail: jeff.chang@hawaii.gov
Administrative Services Officer **Sidney A. Hayakawa** . . . . (808) 838-8706
  E-mail: sidney.a.hayakawa@hawaii.gov
Certification, Security and Safety Officer **Mary Kitsu** . . . . (808) 838-8703
General Aviation Officer **Henry P. Bruckner** . . . . . . . . . . (808) 838-8706
Operations Officer **Alex Tamorio** . . . . . . . . . . . . . . . . . (808) 838-8607

## Harbors Division

79 South Nimitz Highway, Honolulu, HI 96813-4898
Fax: (808) 587-1984

■Deputy Director **Darrell T. Young** . . . . . . . . . . . . . . . . . (808) 587-3651
  E-mail: darrell.t.young@hawaii.gov
  Education: Col Notre Dame (CA) BBA
Administrator **Davis K. Yogi** . . . . . . . . . . . . . . . . . . . . . (808) 587-1928
Secretary **Dreana Lee K. "Dre" Kalili** . . . . . . . . . . . . . . (808) 587-3651
Administrative Services Officer **Kendrick Yh Au** . . . . . . . . (808) 587-1933
  E-mail: kendrick.yh.au@hawaii.gov
Fiscal Officer **Kendrick Yh Au** . . . . . . . . . . . . . . . . . . . (808) 587-1893
                                                    Fax: (808) 587-3658
Budget Analyst **(Vacant)** . . . . . . . . . . . . . . . . . . . . . . . (808) 587-1922
Management Information Systems Manager
  **Lena L. Wang** . . . . . . . . . . . . . . . . . . . . . . . . . . . (808) 587-3653
  E-mail: lena.l.wang@hawaii.gov
Property Manager **Calvert Chun** . . . . . . . . . . . . . . . . . . (808) 587-1944
                                                    Fax: (808) 587-2504
Personnel Management Specialist **Beulah Olanolan** . . . . . (808) 587-1925
                                                    Fax: (808) 587-1936

## Highways Division

869 Punchbowl Street, Honolulu, HI 96813
Fax: (808) 587-2340

Administrator **Raymond J. "Ray" McCormick** . . . . . . . . . (808) 587-2221
Engineering Program Manager **Ferdinand Cajigal** . . . . . . . (808) 873-3538
  650 Palapala Drive, Kahului, HI 96732          Fax: (808) 873-3544
  E-mail: ferdinand.cajigal@hawaii.gov
Engineering Program Manager **Lawrence Dill** . . . . . . . . . . (808) 241-3000
                                                    Fax: (808) 241-3011
Engineering Program Manager **Pratt M. Kinimaka** . . . . . . . (808) 831-6703
  727 Kakoi Street, Honolulu, HI 96819           Fax: (808) 831-6725
  E-mail: pratt.kinimaka@hawaii.gov
Engineering Program Manager **Salvador Panem** . . . . . . . . (808) 933-8866
  50 Makaala Street, Hilo, HI 96720              Fax: (808) 933-8869
  E-mail: sal.panem@hawaii.gov

## State Board of Agriculture

1428 South King Street, Honolulu, HI 96814
Tel: (808) 973-9560  Fax: (808) 973-9613  E-mail: hdoa.info@hawaii.gov

■Chairperson **Scott Edward Enright** . . . . . . . . . . . . . . . . (808) 973-9560
  Affiliation: Director, Department of Agriculture, State Board of
  Agriculture, State of Hawaii
  1428 South King Street, Honolulu, HI 96814-2512
  Education: Hawaii (Hilo) BA; George Mason MS
■Member **Michelle Galimba** (At-Large) . . . . . . . . . . . . . . (808) 973-9560
■Member **Richard Ha** (Hawaii County) . . . . . . . . . . . . . . . (808) 973-9560
■Member **Clark Hashimoto** (At-Large) . . . . . . . . . . . . . . . (808) 973-9560
■Member **Glenn Hong** (At-Large) . . . . . . . . . . . . . . . . . . (808) 973-9560
■Member **Jerry Ornellas** (Kauai County) . . . . . . . . . . . . . (808) 973-9560

---

★ Elected Official    ■ Appointed by Governor    ● Appointed by Legislature    ▲ Appointed by Board or Commission    ◆ Appointed by State Supreme Court

■ Member **Simon Russell** (Maui County) . . . . . . . . . . . . . . (808) 973-9560
Member - Ex Officio (Voting) **Suzanne Case** . . . . . . . . . . . (808) 973-9560
Member - Ex Officio (Voting) **Dr. Maria Gallo** . . . . . . . . . (808) 973-9560
   Affiliation: Dean, College of Tropical Agriculture and Human
   Resources, University of Hawaii Manoa (Note: Until June 30, 2016.)
   2500 Campus Road, Honolulu, HI 96822
   Education: Cornell BS; North Carolina State MS, PhD
Member - Ex Officio (Voting) **Luis P. Salaveria** . . . . . . . . .(808) 973-9560

## Department of Agriculture

1428 South King Street, Honolulu, HI 96814-2512
Tel: (808) 973-9600  TTY: (808) 973-9479  Fax: (808) 973-9613
E-mail: hdoa.info@hawaii.gov

**Employees: 323  Fiscal Year: 2015  Budget: $50,918,000**

■ Director **Scott Edward Enright** . . . . . . . . . . . . . . . . . . . . . (808) 973-9550
Deputy Director **Phyllis Shimabukuro-Geiser** . . . . . . . . . (808) 973-9600
Public Information Officer **Janelle K. Saneishi** . . . . . . . . . (808) 973-9560
   E-mail: hdoa.info@hawaii.gov
Planner **Earl J. Yamamoto** . . . . . . . . . . . . . . . . . . . . . . . . (808) 973-9466

## Hawaiian Homes Commission

91-5420 Kapolei Parkway, Kapolei, HI 96707
Tel: (808) 620-9500

■ Chair **Jobie Masagatani** . . . . . . . . . . . . . . . . . . . . . . . . . (808) 620-9501
   Term Expires: December 31, 2014
   E-mail: dhhl.director@hawaii.gov
   Education: Kamehameha (Honolulu, Hawaii); Northwestern BS;
   Princeton MPAff
■ Member **Doreen Napua Canto** . . . . . . . . . . . . . . . . . . . . (808) 620-9500
   Term Expires: June 30, 2015
■ Member **Kathleen Puamae'ole Chin** . . . . . . . . . . . . . . . . (808) 620-9500
   Term Expires: June 30, 2017
■ Member **Gene Ross Davis** . . . . . . . . . . . . . . . . . . . . . . . . (808) 620-9500
   Term Expires: June 30, 2016
■ Member **Wallace A. Ishibashi, Jr.** . . . . . . . . . . . . . . . . . . (808) 620-9500
   Term Expires: June 30, 2017
■ Member **David Ka'apu** . . . . . . . . . . . . . . . . . . . . . . . . . . (808) 620-9500
   Term Expires: June 30, 2017
■ Member **Michael Puamamo Kahikina** . . . . . . . . . . . . . . . (808) 620-9500
   Term Expires: June 30, 2015
   Education: Hawaii 1990 BA
■ Member **Bill Richardson** . . . . . . . . . . . . . . . . . . . . . . . . . (808) 620-9500
   Term Expires: June 30, 2017
■ Member **Renwick Tassill** . . . . . . . . . . . . . . . . . . . . . . . . (808) 620-9500
   Term Expires: June 30, 2015

## Department of Hawaiian Home Lands [DHHL]

91-5420 Kapolei Parkway, Kapolei, HI 96707
P.O. Box 1879, Honolulu, HI 96805
Tel: (808) 620-9500  Fax: (808) 620-9529

**Employees: 170  Fiscal Year: 2015  Budget: $82,504,000**

■ Director **Jobie Masagatani** . . . . . . . . . . . . . . . . . . . . . . . (808) 620-9502
   E-mail: dhhl.director@hawaii.gov
■ Deputy Director **William J. Aila, Jr.** . . . . . . . . . . . . . . . . (808) 620-9502
   E-mail: william.j.ailajr@hawaii.gov
   Education: Hawaii 1980 BS
Legal Counsel **Craig Y. Iha** . . . . . . . . . . . . . . . . . . . . . . . (808) 620-9500

## Hawaii State Ethics Commission

1001 Biishop Street, Suite 970, Honolulu, HI 96813
Tel: (808) 587-0460  Fax: (808) 587-0470
E-mail: ethics@hawaiiethics.org

Chair **Susan N. DeGuzman** . . . . . . . . . . . . . . . . . . . . . . . (808) 587-0460
Vice Chair **David O'Neal** . . . . . . . . . . . . . . . . . . . . . . . . . (808) 587-0460
Commissioner **Reynaldo D. Graulty** . . . . . . . . . . . . . . . . (808) 587-0460
Commissioner **Ruth D. Tschumy** . . . . . . . . . . . . . . . . . . . (808) 587-0460
Commissioner **Melinda Wood** . . . . . . . . . . . . . . . . . . . . . (808) 587-0460
Executive Director and General Counsel **(Vacant)** . . . . . . . (808) 587-0460

# Office of Hawaiian Affairs [OHA]

711 Kapi'olani Boulevard, Suite 500, Honolulu, HI 96813
Tel: (808) 594-1835  Fax: (808) 594-1865  E-mail: kwo@oha.org
Internet: www.oha.org

★ Chairperson **Robert K. Lindsey, Jr.** (Hawai'i Island) . . . . . .(808) 594-1855
   Note: On medical leave.
   E-mail: robertl@oha.org
   Education: Hawaii 1970 BA
★ Trustee **Leina'ala Ahu Isa** (At-Large) . . . . . . . . . . . . . . . .(808) 594-1857
   E-mail: leia@oha.org
★ Trustee **Dan Ahuna** (Kaua'i and Ni'ihau) . . . . . . . . . . . . . .(808) 594-1751
   E-mail: dana@oha.org
   Education: Hawaii 1991 BS
★ Trustee **Rowena Noelani Akana** (At-Large) . . . . . . . . . . . .(808) 594-1860
   E-mail: rowenaa@oha.org
★ Trustee **Peter Apo** (O'ahu) . . . . . . . . . . . . . . . . . . . . . . . .(808) 594-1854
   E-mail: petera@oha.org
   Education: Georgetown 1955 JD
★ Trustee **S. Haunani Apoliona** (At-Large) . . . . . . . . . . . . . .(808) 594-1886
   E-mail: haunania@oha.org
   Education: Hawaii BA, MSW
★ Trustee **Carmen "Hulu" Lindsey** (Maui) . . . . . . . . . . . . . .(808) 594-1858
   E-mail: hulul@oha.org
★ Trustee **Colette Y. Machado** (D-Moloka'i and Lana'i) . . . .(808) 594-1837
   E-mail: colettem@oha.org
   Education: Hawaii
★ Trustee **John D. Waihe'e IV** (At-Large) . . . . . . . . . . . . . . .(808) 594-1876
   E-mail: johnw@oha.org
   Education: Loma Linda

## Administration

Tel: (808) 594-1835  E-mail: info@oha.org

Chief Executive Officer **Dr. Kamana'opono M. Crabbe** . . .(808) 594-1892
   E-mail: kamanaoc@oha.org
   Education: Hawaii, 2002 PhD
Chief Financial Officer **Hawley Iona** . . . . . . . . . . . . . . . . .(808) 594-1999
Chief Operating Officer **Lisa Victor** . . . . . . . . . . . . . . . . . (808) 594-1973
Chief Advocate **Kawika Riley** . . . . . . . . . . . . . . . . . . . . . . (808) 594-1970
   Education: Northern Colorado 2005 BA; George Washington 2007 MA
Community Engagement Director
   **Kehaunani Abad, PhD** . . . . . . . . . . . . . . . . . . . . . . . (808) 594-0262
Land and Property Director **Miles Nishijima** . . . . . . . . . . .(808) 594-1835
Research Director **Lisa Watkins-Victorino** . . . . . . . . . . . . .(808) 594-1769

# Idaho

Tel: (208) 334-2100 (State Information)

**Number of U.S. Congressional Delegates:** 2 Senators; 2 Representatives  **Governor's Term:** 4 years
**Legislature Description:** 35 member Senate; 70 member House of Representatives; Term - Senate 2
years, House 2 years  **Next Election:** Governor November 2018; Legislature November 2016
**Number of Electoral Votes:** 4  **Official Name:** State of Idaho (Shoshone: Sun coming down mountain)
**Nickname:** The Gem State  **Motto:** Esto perpetua (Let it be perpetual)

**Population:** 1,654,930 (2015); Rank 39  **Fiscal Year:** 2015  **Budget:** $7,432,000,000

## Office of the Governor

700 West Jefferson Street, 2nd Floor, West Wing, Boise, ID 83720-0080
P. O. Box 83720, Boise, ID 83720
Tel: (208) 334-2100  Fax: (208) 334-3454

**Employees:** 18  **Fiscal Year:** 2015  **Budget:** $1,910,000

### C. L. "Butch" Otter
Governor

Began Service: January 1, 2007
Term Expires: January 2019
Date of Birth: May 3, 1942
Education: Idaho 1967 BA
Religion: Catholic
Career: State Representative (R-ID), Idaho House
of Representatives (1972-1976); President,
Simplot Livestock, J.R. Simplot Company;
Lieutenant Governor (R-ID), State of Idaho
(1987-2000); U.S. Representative (R-ID, District
1), Office of Representative C. L. Otter, United
States House of Representatives (2001-2007)

★ Governor **C. L. "Butch" Otter** (R) . . . . . . . . . . . . . . . . . . (208) 334-2100
   E-mail: governor@gov.idaho.gov
   Special Assistant to the Governor
   **Claudia Simplot-Nally** . . . . . . . . . . . . . . . . . . . . (208) 334-2100
   E-mail: claudia.nally@gov.idaho.gov
   Scheduler and Assistant to the Governor
   **Bobbi-Jo Meuleman** . . . . . . . . . . . . . . . . . . . . . . (208) 334-2100
   E-mail: bobbi-jo.meuleman@gov.idaho.gov
Chief of Staff **David Hensley** . . . . . . . . . . . . . . . . . . . . (208) 334-2100
   E-mail: david.hensley@gov.idaho.gov
Legal Counsel **Tom Perry** . . . . . . . . . . . . . . . . . . . . . . . (208) 334-2100
   E-mail: tom.perry@gov.idaho.gov
Associate Counsel to the Governor and Public Records
   Ombudsman **Cally Younger** . . . . . . . . . . . . . . . . . . (208) 334-2100
   E-mail: cally.younger@gov.idaho.gov
Eastern Idaho Field Representative
   **Mike Webster** . . . . . . . . . . . . . . (208) 557-2500 ext. 3760
   E-mail: mike.webster@gov.idaho.gov
Northern Idaho Field Representative **Katie Brodie** . . . . . . . (208) 334-2100
   E-mail: katie.brodie@gov.idaho.gov
Director of Communications and Senior Special Assistant
   for Economic Development and Energy **Mark Warbis** . . . (208) 334-2100
   E-mail: mark.warbis@gov.idaho.gov
Senior Special Assistant for Education and Government
   Services **Marilyn Whitney** . . . . . . . . . . . . . . . . . . (208) 334-2100
Senior Special Assistant for Health and Social Services
   **Tammy Perkins** . . . . . . . . . . . . . . . . . . . . . . . . . (208) 334-2100
   E-mail: tammy.perkins@gov.idaho.gov
Special Assistant for Boards and Commissions
   **Ann Beebe** . . . . . . . . . . . . . . . . . . . . . . . . . . . . (208) 334-2100
   E-mail: ann.beebe@gov.idaho.gov
Special Assistant for Communications **Nicholas Stout** . . . . (208) 334-2100
   E-mail: nicholas.stout@gov.idaho.gov
Special Assistant for Health and Social Services
   **Kendra Knighten** . . . . . . . . . . . . . . . . . . . . . . . . (208) 334-2100
   E-mail: kendra.knighten@gov.idaho.gov

Special Assistant for Natural Resources
   **Stephen Goodson** . . . . . . . . . . . . . . . . . . . . . . . . (208) 334-2100
   E-mail: stephen.goodson@gov.idaho.gov
Staff Assistant **Katrine Franks** . . . . . . . . . . . . . . . . . . (208) 334-2100
   E-mail: katrine.franks@gov.idaho.gov
Spokesman/Press Secretary **Jon Hanian** . . . . . . . . . . . . (208) 334-2100
   E-mail: jon.hanian@gov.idaho.gov

## Endowment Fund/Investment Board

816 West Bannock Street, Suite 301, Boise, ID 83702
Tel: (208) 334-3311
Investment Manager **Larry Johnson** . . . . . . . . . . . . . . . (208) 334-3312

## Department of Administration

650 West State Street, Suite 100, Boise, ID 83702
P.O. Box 83720, Boise, ID 83720
Tel: (208) 332-1824  Fax: (208) 334-2307  Internet: www.adm.idaho.gov

**Employees:** 145  **Fiscal Year:** 2015  **Budget:** $46,428,000

■ Director **Robert L. "Bob" Geddes** . . . . . . . . . . . . . . . . (208) 332-1824
   Education: Utah State BS
   Human Resources Manager **Rebecca L. Fry** . . . . . . . . . . (208) 332-1831

## Office of the Chief Information Officer

P.O. Box 83720, Boise, ID 83702-0003
Internet: http://cio.idaho.gov

Chief Technology Officer **Greg Zickau** . . . . . . . . . . . . . (208) 332-1875
   E-mail: greg.zickau@cio.idaho.gov
Chief Information Security Officer **(Vacant)** . . . . . . . . . . . (208) 332-1851
Enterprise IT Infrastructure Manager **Jon Pope** . . . . . . . . (208) 332-1877
   E-mail: jon.pope@cio.idaho.gov
Geospatial Information Officer **Bill Farnsworth** . . . . . . . . (208) 332-1878
   E-mail: bill.farnsworth@cio.idaho.gov

## Insurance and Internal Support Division

P.O. Box 83720, Boise, ID 83702-0003
Tel: (208) 332-1860 (Group Insurance)
Tel: (208) 332-1869 (Risk Management)

Chief Financial Officer **D. Keith Reynolds** . . . . . . . . . . . (208) 332-1812
Administrative Rules Coordinator **Dennis Stevenson** . . . . . (208) 332-1822
   E-mail: dennis.stevenson@adm.idaho.gov
Group Insurance Administration **Jennifer Pike** . . . . . . . . . (208) 332-1865
   E-mail: jennifer.pike@adm.idaho.gov

## Public Works Division

502 North Fourth Street, Boise, ID 83702
P.O. Box 83720, Boise, ID 83702-0072

Administrator **Jan Frew** . . . . . . . . . . . . . . . . . . . . . . (208) 332-1911
Facilities Services Manager **Ric Johnston** . . . . . . . . . . . . (208) 332-1937
Project Management Manager **Barry Miller** . . . . . . . . . . . (208) 332-1916

## Purchasing Division

650 West State Street, Room B-15, Boise, ID 83702
P.O. Box 83720, Boise, ID 83720-0075
Tel: (208) 327-7465  Fax: (208) 327-7320

Administrator **Bill Burns** . . . . . . . . . . . . . . . . . . . . . . (208) 327-7465
State Purchasing Manager **Sarah Hilderbrand** . . . . . . . . . (208) 327-1611
Federal Surplus Property Manager **James Hollis** . . . . . . . . (208) 334-1627

---

★ Elected Official    ■ Appointed by Governor    ● Appointed by Legislature    ▲ Appointed by Board or Commission    ◆ Appointed by State Supreme Court

EXECUTIVE BRANCH

Postal Services Manager **Lewis Carroll**................(208) 332-1951

# Department of Commerce
700 West State Street, Boise, ID 83702-0093
P.O. Box 83720, Boise, ID 83720-0093
Tel: (208) 334-2470  Fax: (208) 334-2631
E-mail: info@commerce.idaho.gov

■Director **Megan Ronk**.....................(208) 781-5152
  E-mail: megan.ronk@commerce.idaho.gov
  Education: Albertson BA
Chief Business Development and Marketing Officer
  **Matt Borud**.......................(208) 287-0772
Chief Industry and Community Services Officer
  **Chrissy Bowers**..................(208) 780-5139
Chief Operations Officer **(Vacant)**.............(208) 334-2470
Business Attraction Manager **Susie Davidson**.........(208) 287-0783
Community Development Manager **Dennis Porter**......(208) 287-0782
International Trade Manager **Jennifer Verdon**..........(208) 287-3165
Tourism Manager **Diane Norton**...............(208) 287-0785
Idaho Global Entrepreneurial Mission Program Manager
  **Carmen Achabal**..................(208) 780-5146
Public Information Specialist **Megan Hill**.........(208) 287-0784
  E-mail: megan.hill@commerce.idaho.gov

## Idaho Rural Partnership [IRP]
1090 East Watertower Street, Suite 100, Meridian, ID 83642
Tel: (208) 332-1730

Executive Director (Acting) **Jon Barrett**...........(208) 332-1730
Administrative Assistant **Vickie Winkel**..........(208) 332-1730

# Department of Environmental Quality [DEQ]
1410 North Hilton, Boise, ID 83706-1255
Tel: (208) 373-0502  Fax: (208) 373-0417  Internet: www.deq.idaho.gov

**Employees:** 371  **Fiscal Year:** 2015  **Budget:** $54,856,000

■Director **John H. Tippets**................(208) 373-0240
  Education: BYU; Utah State MHR
Deputy Director **Jess Byrne**...............(208) 373-0114
Management Assistant **Rosie Alonzo**..........(208) 373-0240
Grants and Contracts Officer **Dave Sande**...........(208) 373-0410
Grants and Contracts Officer **(Vacant)**...........(208) 373-0286
Human Resources Manager **Sharon Haylatt**.........(208) 373-0242

## Air Quality Division
Administrator **Tiffany Floyd**................(208) 373-0552
Mobile and Area Source Manager **Robert Wilkosz**.......(208) 373-0302
Monitoring, Modeling and Emission Inventory Manager
  **Bruce Louks**....................(208) 373-0294
Stationary Source Manager **Mike Simon**.............(208) 373-0212

## Environmental Management and Information Division
Administrator **Mark Clough**................(208) 373-0158
  E-mail: mark.clough@deq.idaho.gov

## Technical Services Division
Administrator **Mark Dietrich**...............(208) 373-0204

## Waste Division
Administrator **Orville Green**................(208) 373-0148
Hazardous Waste Program Manager **Brian Monson**......(208) 373-0490
Mine Waste Program Manager **Rob Hanson**...........(208) 373-0290
Remediation Program Manager **Michael McCurdy**.......(208) 373-0188

## Water Quality Division
Administrator **Barry Burnell**................(208) 373-0194
Drinking Water Program Manager **Jerri Henry**..........(208) 373-0471
Ground Water Integrated Watershed Management
  Program Manager **Ed Hagan**.............(208) 373-0356
Loan Program Manager **Tim Wendland**............(208) 373-0439
  E-mail: tim.wendland@deq.idaho.gov

Surface Water Program Manager **Don Essig**............(208) 373-0119
Wastewater/Ground Water Program Manager **(Vacant)**.....(208) 373-0502

## Regional Offices
Boise Regional Office Administrator **Aaron Scheff**.......(208) 373-0550
Coeur d'Alene Regional Office Administrator
  **Dan Redline**....................(208) 666-4621
  2110 Ironwood Parkway, Suite 100, Coeur d'Alene, ID 83814
Idaho Falls Regional Office Administrator **Erick Neher**....(208) 528-2650
  900 North Skyline Drive, Suite B, Idaho Falls, ID 83402
Lewiston Regional Office Administrator **John Cardwell**...(208) 799-4370
  1118 F St., Lewiston, ID 83501
Pocatello Regional Office Administrator **Bruce Olenick**...(208) 236-6160
  444 Hospital Way, #300, Pocatello, ID 83201
Twin Falls Regional Office Administrator
  **Dave Anderson**...................(208) 736-2190
  1363 Fillmore Street, Suite 2, Twin Falls, ID 83301

# Department of Finance
800 Park Boulevard, Suite 200, Boise, ID 83712-7742
P.O. Box 83720, Boise, ID 83720-0031
Tel: (208) 332-8000  Fax: (208) 332-8098
E-mail: finance@finance.idaho.gov  Internet: http://finance.idaho.gov

**Employees:** 62  **Fiscal Year:** 2015  **Budget:** $6,728,000

■Director **Gavin M. Gee**..................(208) 332-8010
  E-mail: ggee@finance.idaho.gov
  Education: BYU 1974 BA; Idaho 1977 JD
  Administrative Assistant II **Lisa Baker**.............(208) 332-8011
Lead Deputy Attorney General **Joseph B. "Joe" Jones**..(208) 332-8016
  E-mail: joe.jones@finance.idaho.gov
  Education: Cal State (Long Beach) 1978 BS; Gonzaga 1981 JD
Deputy Attorney General **Alan Conilogue**...........(208) 332-8093
Deputy Attorney General **Brian Nicholas**..............(208) 332-8092
Consumer Finance Bureau Chief **Michael Larsen**.......(208) 332-8060
  Education: BYU 1981 BA; Idaho 1985 JD
Financial Institutions Bureau Chief **Mary E. Hughes**.....(208) 332-8030
  E-mail: mhughes@finance.idaho.gov
  Education: Western Illinois 1975 BA; Idaho 1979 JD
Securities Bureau Chief **Jim Burns**................(208) 332-8080
Supporting Services Bureau Chief **David Jensen**.........(208) 332-8020
  Education: Northwest Nazarene Col 1985 BBA
IT Manager **Blake Wickman**...............(208) 332-8026
  E-mail: bwickman@finance.idaho.gov

# Department of Health and Welfare [IDHW]
450 West State Street, Boise, ID 83702
P.O. Box 83720, Boise, ID 83720-0036
Tel: (208) 334-5500  Tel: (208) 334-5988 (Vital Records)
TTY: (208) 334-4921  Fax: (208) 332-7260
E-mail: questions@dhw.idaho.gov
Internet: www.healthandwelfare.idaho.gov

**Employees:** 2,860  **Fiscal Year:** 2015  **Budget:** $2,550,284,000

■Director **Richard M. "Dick" Armstrong**..............(208) 334-5500
  E-mail: armstrongr@dhw.idaho.gov
  Executive Assistant to the Director **Elsie Boyd**.........(208) 334-5502
Welfare and Family Services Deputy Director
  **Russ Barron**....................(208) 334-5500
Medicaid and Behavioral Health Deputy Director
  **Denise Chuckovich**.................(208) 334-5500
  E-mail: chuckovd@dhw.idaho.gov
Support Services Deputy Director **David N. Taylor**.......(208) 334-5500
Public Information Manager **Tom Shanahan**............(208) 334-0668
  E-mail: shanahat@dhw.idaho.gov
Domestic Violence Council Executive Director
  **Loann Dettman**...................(208) 332-1542

## Behavioral Health Division
Administrator **Ross B. Edmunds**.................(208) 334-5726
  E-mail: edmundsr@dhw.idaho.gov
  Management Assistant **Lynn Richter**.................(208) 334-6997
  E-mail: richterl@dhw.idaho.gov

*(continued on next page)*

**Behavioral Health Division** *continued*

Children's Mental Health Program Manager
**Casey Moyer** ............................ (208) 334-4916
E-mail: moyerc@dhw.idaho.gov
Substance Use Disorders Program Manager
**Rosie Andueza** .......................... (208) 334-5553
E-mail: anduezar@dhw.idaho.gov

## Family and Community Services Division
Tel: (208) 334-5700 Fax: (208) 332-7330

Administrator **Gary Moore** ................... (208) 334-0641
E-mail: mooreg@dhw.idaho.gov
Management Assistant **Aimee Prokupek** ........ (208) 334-0641
E-mail: prokupeka@dhw.idaho.gov
Bureau Chief **Cameron Gilliland** ............. (208) 334-5702
E-mail: gillilac@dhw.idaho.gov
Deaf and Hard of Hearing Council Executive Director
**Steve Snow** .............................. (208) 334-0803
Developmental Disabilities State Council Executive
Director **Christine Pisani** ................. (208) 334-2178
TTY: (208) 334-2179
Fax: (208) 334-3417
Adult and Children Developmental Disabilities Program
Manager **Chad Cardwell** ..................... (208) 334-5536
E-mail: cardwelc@dhw.idaho.gov
Fax: (208) 332-7331
Child Protection Program Manager **Miren Unsworth** ..... (208) 334-6618
E-mail: unswortm@dhw.idaho.gov
Fax: (208) 332-7331
Tribal Relations Program Specialist **Tanya McElfresh** ..... (208) 334-4941
Southwest Idaho Treatment Center (Acting)
**Dayna Wilhite-Grow** ....................... (208) 442-2812
Fax: (208) 467-0965
Early Childhood Information Clearinghouse and 211
Idaho CareLine Program Supervisor **Gretchan Heller** ... (208) 334-6955
Fax: (208) 334-5531

## Financial Services Division
Tel: (208) 334-5578 Fax: (208) 334-5694

Financial Executive Officer **Jodi Osborn** ............. (208) 334-6679
E-mail: osbornj@dhw.idaho.gov
Management Assistant **Sue Hill** .................... (208) 334-5578
Audits and Investigations Bureau Chief **Steve Bellomy** ... (208) 334-0609
E-mail: bellomys@dhw.idaho.gov
EPT (Electronic Payment System) Supervisor
**Alyce Porter** ............................. (208) 334-5820
E-mail: portera@dhw.idaho.gov

## Information and Technology Services Division
Tel: (208) 334-6598 Fax: (208) 334-0645

Administrator **Michael Farley** ................... (208) 334-6598
E-mail: farleym@dhw.idaho.gov
Management Assistant **Kimberlee Hall** ............. (208) 334-6598
E-mail: hallk@dhw.idaho.gov
Information Technology Applications Bureau Chief
**Brad Alvaro** .............................. (208) 334-4996
E-mail: alvarob@dhw.idaho.gov
Information Technology Infrastructure Programs Bureau
Chief **Alvino Artalejo** ...................... (208) 334-0640
E-mail: artaleja@dhw.idaho.gov
Information Technology Operations Support Programs
Bureau Chief **Mary Ostwinkle** ................ (208) 334-5602
E-mail: ostwinkm@dhw.idaho.gov

## Medicaid Division
Tel: (208) 334-5747 Fax: (208) 364-1811

Administrator **Lisa Hettinger** .................. (208) 334-5747
E-mail: hettingerl@dhw.idaho.gov
Management Assistant **Teresa Martin** ............. (208) 364-1804
Deputy Administrator **Dave Simnitt** ............. (208) 364-1939
E-mail: simnittd@dhw.idaho.gov
Policy Deputy Administrator **Matt Wimmer** ........... (208) 334-5747
E-mail: wimmerm@dhw.idaho.gov

Operations Deputy Administrator **Cathy Libby** .......... (208) 334-5747
E-mail: libbyc@dhw.idaho.gov
Medical Director **Dr. Mark Turner** ............... (208) 332-7952
Developmental Disability Services Bureau Chief
**Arthur Evans** ............................. (208) 364-1896
E-mail: evansa@dhw.idaho.gov
Financial Operations Bureau Chief **Sheila Pugatch** ....... (208) 287-1141
Long Term Care Bureau Chief **Elizabeth Kriete** ........ (208) 287-1179
E-mail: krietee@dhw.idaho.gov
Medical Care Bureau Chief **Tiffany Kinzler** .......... (208) 334-5747
E-mail: kinzlert@dhw.idaho.gov
Systems and Project Management Bureau Chief
**Rene Hughes** .............................. (208) 334-5747
E-mail: rene.hughes@doh.wa.gov
CHIP and EPSDT Coordinator **Cindy Brock** ........ (208) 364-1983

## Operational Services Division
Operational Services Division Administrator
**Paul Spannknebel** ......................... (208) 334-5912
E-mail: spannknp@dhw.idaho.gov
Management Assistant **Mary Barnett** ............. (208) 334-5912
Facilities Management and Field Services Bureau Chief
**George Taylor** ............................ (208) 334-5615

## Public Health Division
Tel: (208) 334-5945 Fax: (208) 334-6581

Administrator and State Health Official
**Elke Shaw-Tulloch** ........................ (208) 334-5932
E-mail: shawe@dhw.idaho.gov
Management Assistant **Nancy Panganiban** .......... (208) 334-6996
E-mail: panganiN@dhw.idaho.gov
Clinical and Preventive Services Bureau Chief
**Dieuwke Dizney-Spencer** ................... (208) 334-0670
Community and Environmental Health Bureau Chief
**Elke Shaw-Tulloch** ........................ (208) 334-5950
Emergency Medical Services Bureau Chief **(Vacant)** ...... (208) 334-4000
509 West Washington, Boise, ID 83702
Health Policy and Vital Statistics Bureau Chief
**James Aydelotte** .......................... (208) 334-4969
450 West State Street, Boise, ID 83720-0036        Fax: (866) 559-9629
E-mail: aydelotj@dhw.idaho.gov
Health Policy and Resource Development Bureau Chief
**Angela Wickham** .......................... (208) 334-6553
Fax: (208) 332-7262
Laboratories Bureau Chief **Dr. Christopher Ball** .. (208) 334-2235 ext. 268
2220 Old Penitentiary Road, Boise, ID 83712

## Welfare and Self Reliance Services Division
Tel: (208) 334-5815 Fax: (208) 334-5817

Administrator **Lori Wolff** ...................... (208) 334-5696
E-mail: wolffl@dhw.idaho.gov
Management Assistant **Rebecca Smith-Pitman** ........ (208) 334-5696
Deputy Administrator **Greg Kunz** ............... (208) 334-5714
E-mail: kunzg@dhw.idaho.gov
Deputy Administrator **(Vacant)** ................. (208) 334-5815
Child Support Bureau Chief **Kandee Yearsley** .......... (208) 334-0620
E-mail: yearslek@dhw.idaho.gov
Compliance and Support Bureau Chief **(Vacant)** ........ (208) 332-7396

## Department of Insurance [DOI]
700 West State Street, 3rd Floor, Boise, ID 83720
P.O. Box 83720, Boise, ID 83720-0043
Tel: (208) 334-4250 Fax: (208) 334-4398 Internet: www.doi.idaho.gov

**Employees:** 69 **Fiscal Year:** 2015 **Budget:** $6,891,000

■Director **Dean L. Cameron** .................... (208) 334-4250
Education: Ricks 1984 AA
Deputy Director **Thomas A. "Tom" Donovan** ........ (208) 334-4250
Deputy Attorney General **Richard Burleigh** ........... (208) 334-4250
State Fire Marshal **Knute Sandahl** .............. (208) 334-4377
Program Information Coordinator **Teresa Jones** ......... (208) 334-4373

---

★ Elected Official     ■ Appointed by Governor     ● Appointed by Legislature     ▲ Appointed by Board or Commission     ◆ Appointed by State Supreme Court

## Department of Labor

317 West Main Street, Boise, ID 83735-0001
Tel: (208) 332-3570  Fax: (208) 334-6430  E-mail: www@labor.idaho.gov
Internet: http://labor.idaho.gov

**Employees:** 674  **Fiscal Year:** 2015  **Budget:** $412,428,000

■ Director **Kenneth Edmunds** .............................. (208) 334-3110
  E-mail: kenneth.edmunds@labor.idaho.gov
  Education: BYU
  Administrative Assistant to the Director
    **Cheryl Ausman** .............................(208) 332-3570 ext. 3229
Chief Deputy Director **Jay Engstrom** ..........(208) 332-2121 ext. 3101
  E-mail: jay.engstrom@labor.idaho.gov
Communications and Research Deputy Director
  **Georgia Smith** ...............................(208) 332-3570 ext. 2102
  E-mail: georgia.smith@labor.idaho.gov
Workforce and Field Services Deputy Director
  **Rogelio "Roy" Valdez** ....................(208) 332-3570 ext. 3163
  E-mail: rogelio.valdez@labor.idaho.gov
  Education: Texas Pan American 1991 BA
Unemployment Insurance Administrator
  **Jay Engstrom** ................................(208) 332-3570 ext. 2121
  E-mail: jay.engstrom@labor.idaho.gov
Deputy Attorney General **Craig Bledsoe** ........(208) 332-3570 ext. 3232
  E-mail: craig.bledsoe@labor.idaho.gov

## Department of Lands [IDL]

300 North 6th Street, Suite 103, Boise, ID 83702
P.O. Box 83720, Boise, ID 83720-0050
Tel: (208) 334-0200  Tel: (208) 769-1525 (Coeur d'Alene)
Fax: (208) 334-3698  Internet: www.idl.idaho.gov

**Employees:** 482  **Fiscal Year:** 2015  **Budget:** $65,970,000

▲ Director **Thomas "Tom" Schultz** ..................(208) 334-0200
  Education: Virginia BA; Wyoming MS; Montana MF
State Forester and Forestry and Fire Division
  Administrator **David Groeschl** ....................(208) 769-1525
  3284 West Industrial Loop, Coeur d'Alene, ID 83815
  E-mail: dgroeschl@idl.idaho.gov
Public Information Officer **Sharla Arledge** ..........(208) 334-0286
  Fire Management Bureau Chief **Ken Ockfen** ..........(208) 769-1525
    3284 West Industrial Loop, Coeur d'Alene, ID 83815
  Forest Management Bureau Chief **Bob Helmer** .........(208) 769-1525
    3284 West Industrial Loop, Coeur d'Alene, ID 83815
  Forestry Assistance Bureau Chief **Craig Foss** ..........(208) 769-1525
    3284 West Industrial Loop, Coeur d'Alene, ID 83815
Lands and Waterways Division Director **Diane French** ....(208) 332-8819
  Endowment and Leasing Bureau Chief
    **Michael J. Murphy** ............................(208) 334-0200
Support Services Division Administrator
  **Donna Caldwell** .................................(208) 334-0200
Chief Operations Officer **Robert "Bob" Brammer** .......(208) 334-0200
  North Operations Chief **Eric Besaw** .................(208) 769-1525
    3284 West Industrial Loop, Coeur d'Alene, ID 83815
  South Operations Chief **(Vacant)** ..................(208) 334-0200
Fiscal Officer **Debbie Buck** ........................(208) 334-0225
Human Resources Officer **Andrea Ryan** ................(208) 769-1525

## Idaho Department of Parks and Recreation [IDPR]

5657 Warm Springs Avenue, Boise, ID 83716
P.O. Box 83720, Boise, ID 83720-0065
Tel: (208) 334-4199  TTY: (800) 377-3529  Fax: (208) 334-3741
Internet: www.parksandrecreation.idaho.gov

**Employees:** 397  **Fiscal Year:** 2015  **Budget:** $32,350,000

■ Director **David R. Langhorst** .........................(208) 514-2251
  E-mail: david.langhorst@idpr.idaho.gov
  Education: Auburn 1984 BA
Management Assistant **Betty Mills** ...................(208) 514-2251
  E-mail: betty.mills@idpr.idaho.gov
                                        Fax: (208) 334-5232
Communications Manager **Jennifer Okerlund** ...........(208) 514-2254
  E-mail: jennifer.okerlund@idpr.idaho.gov
Fiscal Officer **Steve Martin** ........................(208) 514-2460

## Idaho Department of Water Resources [IDWR]

322 East Front Street, 6th Floor, Boise, ID 83702
P.O. Box 83720, Boise, ID 83720-0098
Tel: (208) 287-4800  Fax: (208) 287-6700
E-mail: idwrinfo@idwr.idaho.gov

**Employees:** 148  **Fiscal Year:** 2015  **Budget:** $15,605,000

■ Director **Gary Spackman** ...........................(208) 287-4800
  E-mail: gary.spackman@idwr.idaho.gov
Deputy Director **Mathew "Mat" Weaver** ..............(208) 287-4914
Deputy Attorney General **Garrick Baxter** .............(208) 287-4800
Planning and Technical Services Division Administrator
  **Brian Patton** ..................................(208) 287-4841
Water Compliance Bureau Chief **Timothy "Tim" Luke** ...(208) 287-4959

## Idaho State Department of Agriculture [ISDA]

P.O. Box 790, Boise, ID 83701
Tel: (208) 332-8500  Fax: (208) 334-2170  Internet: www.agri.idaho.gov

**Employees:** 411  **Fiscal Year:** 2015  **Budget:** $32,851,000

■ Director **Celia R. Gould** ...........................(208) 332-8503
  E-mail: celia.gould@agri.idaho.gov
  Education: Boise State BA
■ Deputy Director **Brian Oakey** ......................(208) 332-8552
  E-mail: brian.oakey@agri.idaho.gov
Chief of Staff/Communications Director
  **Pamela "Pamm" Juker** ...........................(208) 332-8671
  E-mail: pamela.juker@agri.idaho.gov
  Education: Boise State MPPA
  Special Assistant **Chanel Tewalt** ..................(208) 332-8503
Legal Deputy Attorney General **Angela Kaufmann** ......(208) 332-8509
Finance Officer **Kelly Nielsen** ......................(208) 332-8514
Human Resource Senior Specialist **Hanna Hall** .........(208) 332-8522
Office Specialist **Sharon Henning** ...................(208) 332-8501

### Agricultural Inspections Division

Tel: (208) 332-8670  Fax: (208) 332-8670

Administrator **Cindy Stark** .........................(208) 332-8670

### Agricultural Resources Division

2270 Old Penitentiary Road, Boise, ID 83712

Administrator **George Robinson** .....................(208) 332-8531
Bureau Chief **Ben Miller** ...........................(208) 332-8593
Bureau Chief **Bob Spencer** ..........................(208) 332-8613

### Animal Industries Division

2270 Old Penitentiary Road, Boise, ID 83712

Administrator/State Veterinarian **Dr. Bill Barton** .....(208) 332-8540
Dairy/Concentrated Animal Feeding Operation (CAFO)
  Bureau Chief **Marv Patten** ........................(208) 332-8551
Office Support Supervisor **Denise Walters** .............(208) 332-8540

### Market Development Division

2270 Old Penitentiary Road, Boise, ID 83712

Administrator **Laura Johnson** ........................(208) 332-8530
Trade Specialist **Eric Boyington** ....................(208) 332-8537
Trade Specialist **Leah Clark** .......................(208) 332-8684
Trade Specialist **Skylar Jett** ......................(208) 332-8542
Trade Specialist **Emily Klodowski** ..................(208) 332-8532

### Plant Industries Division

2270 Old Penitentiary Road, Boise, ID 83712

Administrator **Lloyd Knight** ........................(208) 332-8620
Administrative Assistant **Gail Jorgensen** .............(208) 332-8626
Feeds and Plant Services Bureau Chief **Jared Stuart** .....(208) 332-8620

★ Elected Official   ■ Appointed by Governor   ● Appointed by Legislature   ▲ Appointed by Board or Commission   ◆ Appointed by State Supreme Court

*State Yellow Book*     © Leadership Directories, Inc.     Summer 2016

## Idaho Bureau of Occupational Licenses [IBOL]

JR Williams Building, 700 West State Street, Boise, ID 83702
P.O. 83720, Boise, ID 83720-0063
Tel: (208) 334-3233  Fax: (208) 334-3945  E-mail: ibol@ibol.idaho.gov
Internet: www.ibol.idaho.gov

■Chief **Tana Cory** . . . . . . . . . . . . . . . . . . . . . . . . . . . . . . . . . . . . . . . (208) 334-3233
   E-mail: tana.cory@ibol.idaho.gov
  Deputy Chief **Dawn Hall** . . . . . . . . . . . . . . . . . (208) 334-3233 ext. 2582
  Investigative Unit Manager **Lori Peel** . . . . . . . . . . (208) 334-3233 ext. 2597

## Division of Veterans Services

351 Collins Road, Boise, ID 83702
Tel: (208) 780-1300  Fax: (208) 577-2311
Internet: www.veterans.idaho.gov

**Employees:** 356  **Fiscal Year:** 2014  **Budget:** $27,796,000

■Administrator **David E. Brasuell** . . . . . . . . . . . . . . . . . . . . . . . (208) 780-1300
   E-mail: david.brasuell@veterans.idaho.gov
  Deputy Administrator **Tracy Schaner** . . . . . . . . . . . . . . . . (208) 780-1300
   E-mail: tracy.schaner@veterans.idaho.gov
  Idaho State Veterans (Boise) Cemetery Director
   **James Earp** . . . . . . . . . . . . . . . . . . . . . . . . . . . . . . . . . (208) 780-1340
                                Fax: (208) 577-2331
  Idaho State Veterans Home (Boise) Administrator
   **Randal Barns** . . . . . . . . . . . . . . . . . . . . . . . . . . . . . . . . (208) 780-1600
  Idaho State Veterans Home (Lewiston) Administrator
   **Kenneth Shull** . . . . . . . . . . . . . . . . . . . . . . . . . . . . . . . (208) 750-3600
   821 - 21st Avenue, Lewiston, ID 83501-6392
  Idaho State Veterans Home (Pocatello) Administrator
   **Josiah Dahlstrom** . . . . . . . . . . . . . . . . . . . . . . . . . . . . (208) 235-7800
   1957 Alvin Ricken Drive, Pocatello, ID 83201-2727
  Veterans Advocacy Office Program Supervisor
   **Bill Heyob** . . . . . . . . . . . . . . . . . . . . . . . . . . . . . . . . (208) 780-1380
   444 Fort Street, Boise, ID 83702        Fax: (208) 577-2333

## Fish and Game Commission

600 South Walnut, Boise, ID 83712
P.O. Box 25, Boise, ID 83707
Tel: (208) 334-3700  Fax: (208) 334-2148
E-mail: idfginfo@idfg.idaho.gov

■Chairman **Mark Doerr** . . . . . . . . . . . . . . . . . . . . . . . . . . . . . (208) 308-1852
  Term Expires: June 30, 2016
  E-mail: mark.doerr@idfg.idaho.gov
■Commissioner **Derick Attebury** . . . . . . . . . . . . . . . . . . . . . . (208) 521-4500
  Term Expires: June 30, 2019
  6890 Big Bend Drive, Idaho Falls, ID 83406
  E-mail: derick.attebury@gmail.com
■Commissioner **Daniel A. Blanco** . . . . . . . . . . . . . . . . . . . . . (208) 816-0746
  Term Expires: June 30, 2019
  P.O. Box 8805, Moscow, ID 83843
  E-mail: daniel.blanco@idfg.idaho.gov
■Commissioner **Lane Clezie** . . . . . . . . . . . . . . . . . . . . . . . . . (208) 317-4868
  Term Expires: June 30, 2018
  13542 West Trail Creek Road, Pocatello, ID 83204
  E-mail: lane.clezie@idfg.idaho.gov
■Commissioner **Brad Corkill** . . . . . . . . . . . . . . . . . . . . . . . . . (208) 682-3253
  Term Expires: June 30, 2017       Tel: (208) 682-4602
  2885 West Kathleen Avenue, Coeur d'Alene, ID 83815
  E-mail: bradcorkill@whitemanlumber.com
■Commissioner **Blake Fischer** . . . . . . . . . . . . . . . . . . . . . . . . (208) 867-2703
  Term Expires: June 30, 2018
  2863 South Teddy Avenue, Meridian, ID 83642
  E-mail: blake.fischer@idfg.idaho.gov
■Commissioner **Will Naillon**
  Term Expires: June 30, 2016
  987 Foothills Road, Challis, ID 83226
  E-mail: willnaillon@gmail.com

## Department of Fish and Game [IDFG]

600 South Walnut, Boise, ID 83712
P.O. Box 25, Boise, ID 83707
Tel: (208) 334-3771  Fax: (208) 334-2114
E-mail: idfginfo@idfg.idaho.gov

**Employees:** 945  **Fiscal Year:** 2015  **Budget:** $88,180,000

▲Director **Virgil Moore** . . . . . . . . . . . . . . . . . . . . . . . . . . . . (208) 334-5159
   E-mail: vmoore@idfg.idaho.gov     Fax: (208) 334-4885
  Programs and Policy Deputy Director **Sharon Kiefer** . . . (208) 334-3772
   Education: Austin State BS;       Fax: (208) 334-4885
   Texas State (San Marcos) MS
  Operations Deputy Director **Ed Schriever** . . . . . . . . . . . . . (208) 334-3772
                                Fax: (208) 334-4885
  Legal Deputy Attorney General **Dallas Burkhalter** . . . . . . . (208) 334-3771
                                Fax: (208) 334-2148
  Legal Deputy Attorney General **Kathleen Trever** . . . . . . . . (208) 334-3715
                                Fax: (208) 334-2148
  Administration Bureau Chief **Michael Pearson** . . . . . . . . . . (208) 334-3781
   E-mail: michael.pearson@idfg.idaho.gov   Fax: (208) 334-2148
  Communications Bureau Chief **Michael Keckler** . . . . . . . . . (208) 334-3746
   E-mail: mkeckler@idfg.idaho.gov
  Enforcement Bureau Chief **Greg Wooten** . . . . . . . . . . . . . (208) 334-3736
  Engineering Bureau Chief **Michael "Mike" Maffey** . . . . . . (208) 334-3730
                                Fax: (208) 334-2148
  Fisheries Bureau Chief **Jim Fredericks** . . . . . . . . . . . . . . . (208) 334-3791
  Information Systems Bureau Chief **Bob Ross** . . . . . . . . . . (208) 287-2851
   E-mail: bob.ross@idfg.idaho.gov     Fax: (208) 334-2148
  Wildlife Bureau Chief **Jeff Gould** . . . . . . . . . . . . . . . . . . . (208) 334-2920

## Idaho Public Utilities Commission [IPUC]

P.O. Box 83720, Boise, ID 83720-0074
Tel: (208) 334-0300  Fax: (208) 334-3762  Internet: www.puc.idaho.gov

**Employees:** 47  **Fiscal Year:** 2015  **Budget:** $5,159,000

■Commissioner **Eric R. Anderson** . . . . . . . . . . . . . . . . . . . . . (208) 334-3427
  Term Expires: January 2019
  Education: Eastern Washington 1979 BA
■Commissioner **Paul Kjellander** . . . . . . . . . . . . . . . . . . . . . . (208) 334-2898
  Term Expires: April 2016
  E-mail: paul.kjellander@puc.idaho.gov
  Education: Muskingum Col 1982 BA; Ohio MA
■Commissioner **Kristine Raper** . . . . . . . . . . . . . . . . . . . . . . . (208) 334-3912
  Term Expires: January 2021
  E-mail: kristine.sasser@puc.idaho.gov

### Commission Staff

Executive Administrator **Joe Leckie** . . . . . . . . . . . . . . . . . . . (208) 334-0330

## Idaho State Tax Commission

800 Park Boulevard, Boise, ID 83712-7742
P.O. Box 36, Boise, ID 83722-0410
Tel: (208) 334-7660  Fax: (208) 334-7664  TTY: (800) 377-3529
E-mail: taxrep@tax.idaho.gov  Internet: http://tax.idaho.gov

■Chairman **Ken A. Roberts** . . . . . . . . . . . . . . . . . . . . . . . . . . (208) 334-7500
  Term Expires: April 1, 2019
  E-mail: ken.roberts@tax.idaho.gov
■Commissioner **Richard "Rich" Jackson** . . . . . . . . . . . . . . . (208) 334-7500
  Term Expires: April 1, 2017
  E-mail: rich.jackson@tax.idaho.gov
■Commissioner **Tom Katsilometes** . . . . . . . . . . . . . . . . . . . . (208) 334-7500
  Term Expires: March 8, 2017
  E-mail: tom.katsilometes@tax.idaho.gov
■Commissioner **Elliot Werk** . . . . . . . . . . . . . . . . . . . . . . . . . (208) 334-7500
  Term Expires: March 8, 2021
  Education: Sonoma State BS

## Idaho State Board of Accountancy [ISBA]

3101 West Main Street, Suite 210, Boise, ID 83702-2099
P.O. Box 83720, Boise, ID 83720-0002
Tel: (208) 334-2490  Fax: (208) 334-2615

▲Executive Director **Kent Absec** . . . . . . . . . . . . . . . . . . . . . . (208) 334-2490
   E-mail: kent.absec@isba.idaho.gov

---

★ Elected Official   ■ Appointed by Governor   ● Appointed by Legislature   ▲ Appointed by Board or Commission   ◆ Appointed by State Supreme Court

## Board of Correction

1299 North Orchard, Suite 110, Boise, ID 83706
Tel: (208) 658-2000 Fax: (208) 327-7404 E-mail: board@idoc.idaho.gov
Internet: www.idoc.idaho.gov

■Chairman **Debbie S. Field** ............................ (208) 658-2000
  Term Expires: January 1, 2019
■Vice Chairman **Dr. David McClusky** ................. (208) 658-2000
  Term Expires: January 1, 2019
■Secretary **Cindy Wilson** ............................ (208) 658-2000
  Term Expires: January 1, 2017

## Department of Correction [IDOC]

1299 North Orchard, Suite 110, Boise, ID 83706
Tel: (208) 658-2000 E-mail: inquire@idoc.idaho.gov

**Employees:** 1,691

▲Director **Kevin Kempf** ............................ (208) 658-2000
  E-mail: kkempf@idoc.idaho.gov
Public Information Officer **Jeff Ray** .................. (208) 658-2141
  E-mail: jeray@idoc.idaho.gov
Lead Deputy Attorney General **Mark Kubinski** .......... (208) 658-2000
  E-mail: mkubinsk@idoc.idaho.gov
Deputy Attorney General **Emily MacMaster** ........... (208) 658-2097
  E-mail: emacmaster@idoc.idaho.gov
Deputy Attorney General **(Vacant)** ................. (208) 658-2098
Human Resources Director **Sharla Means** ............. (208) 658-2000
Administrative Assistant **Andrea Blades** ............. (208) 658-2048

## Division of Management Services

Division Chief **Pat Donaldson** ...................... (208) 658-2000
Correctional Industries General Manager **Marty Thomas** .. (208) 577-5551
Deputy Chief - Evaluation and Compliance **(Vacant)** ...... (208) 658-2108

## Information Technology Office

Senior Information Services Manager/Chief Information
  Officer **Randy Turner** .......................... (208) 658-2087
  E-mail: randy.turner@idoc.idaho.gov
Application and Database Information Technology
  Manager **Michele Tomlinson** .................... (208) 658-2076
  E-mail: jotomlin@idoc.idaho.gov
Information Technology Project Manager **(Vacant)** ....... (208) 658-2177
Operations Information Technology Manager
  **Jerry Hinshaw** ............................... (208) 658-2082
Quality Assurance Information Technology Manager
  **Michele Tomlinson** ........................... (208) 658-2076
  E-mail: jotomlin@idoc.idaho.gov

## Division of Prisons

Division Chief **Jeff Zmuda** ........................ (208) 658-2000
Idaho Correctional Institution - Orofino Warden
  **Terema Carlin** ............................... (208) 476-3655
  Hospital Drive North #23, Orofino, ID 83544
  E-mail: tcarlin@idoc.idaho.gov
Idaho State Correctional Institution Warden
  **Randy Blades** ....................... (208) 336-0740 ext. 4701
  13400 Pleasant Valley Road, Boise, ID 83707
  P.O. Box 14, Boise, ID 83707
North Idaho Correctional Institution Warden
  **Lynn Guyer** ....................... (208) 962-3276 ext. 102
  Star Route #3, Box 147, Cottonwood, ID 83522
Pocatello Women's Correctional Center Warden
  **Nancy Efpefeth** .............................. (208) 236-6360
  P.O. Box 6049, Pocatello, ID 83205-6049
  E-mail: nancy.efpefeth@idoc.idaho.gov
St. Anthony Work Camp Warden **Jim Woolf** ..... (208) 624-3775 ext. 204
  P.O. Box 246, St. Anthony, ID 83445
South Boise Women's Correctional Center Warden
  **Noel Barlow-Hust** ............................ (208) 334-2731
  13200 South Pleasant Valley Road, Kuna, ID 83634
South Idaho Correctional Institution Warden **Steve Little** .. (208) 336-1260
  13400 Pleasant Valley Road, Boise, ID 83707
  E-mail: slittle@idoc.idaho.gov
Idaho Maximum Security Institution Warden **Al Ramirez** .. (208) 338-1635

## Division of Probation and Parole

Operations Division Chief **Henry Atencio** ............. (208) 658-2000
Probation and Parole Deputy Division Chief
  **Terry Kirkham** ............................... (208) 658-2118
East Boise Women's Community Work Center Manager
  **Sue Wessels** ................................ (208) 334-3448
  2366 Old Penitentiary Road, Boise, ID 83720
Idaho Falls Community Work Center Manager
  **Mike Richman** ....................... (208) 525-7143 ext. 23
  3955 Bombardier Avenue, Idaho Falls, ID 83402
Nampa Community Work Center Manager **Monica Ford** .. (208) 465-8413
  2908 11th Avenue, North Extension, Nampa, ID 83651
South Idaho Correctional Institution Community
  Work Center Manager **Kapri Zmuda** ......... (208) 334-2241 ext. 6105
  2366 Old Penitentiary Road, Boise, ID 83720

## State Board of Education

P.O. Box 83720, Boise, ID 83720-0037
Tel: (208) 334-2270 TTY: (208) 334-2270 Fax: (208) 334-2632
E-mail: board@osbe.idaho.gov Internet: www.boardofed.idaho.gov

**Employees:** 36 **Fiscal Year:** 2015 **Budget:** $4,610,000

■President **Don Soltman** ........................... (208) 334-2270
  Term Expires: June 30, 2019
  Education: Air Force Acad BS; Baylor MHCA
■Vice President **Emma Atchley** ..................... (208) 334-2270
  Term Expires: June 30, 2020
  Education: Idaho; Claremont Grad
■Secretary **Dr. William H. "Bill" Goesling** ............. (208) 334-2270
  Term Expires: March 1, 2016
  Education: Montana BSChem; Naval Postgrad MASc; Idaho PhD
■Member **Dr. Linda Clark** .......................... (208) 334-2270
  Term Expires: June 30, 2020
  Education: Boise State BA; Idaho MEd; U San Francisco EdD
■Member **Debbie Critchfield** ....................... (208) 334-2270
  Term Expires: June 30, 2018
■Member **David Hill** .............................. (208) 334-2270
  Term Expires: June 30, 2017
■Member **Richard Westerberg** ...................... (208) 334-2270
  Term Expires: March 1, 2019
Ex-Officio Member **Sherri Ybarra** ................... (208) 332-6800
▲Executive Director **Matt Freeman** .................. (208) 332-1571
  E-mail: matt.freeman@osbe.idaho.gov

## Department of Education [SDE]

650 West State Street, Boise, ID 83720
P.O. Box 83720, Boise, ID 83720-0027
Tel: (208) 332-6800 Tel: (800) 432-4601 Fax: (208) 334-2228
E-mail: webmaster@sde.idaho.gov Internet: www.sde.idaho.gov

★State Superintendent **Sherri Ybarra** (R) ............... (208) 332-6800
  Term Expires: January 2019
  E-mail: sybarra@sde.idaho.gov

## Division of Educational Programs

Chief Deputy Superintendent **(Vacant)** ............... (208) 332-6815
Statewide System of Support Director **Greg Alexander** ... (208) 332-6869
Elementary and Secondary Education Act Programs
  Director **Marcia Beckman** ...................... (208) 332-6953
Special Education Director **Richard A. Henderson** ...... (208) 332-6806
Child Nutrition Director **Colleen Fillmore** ............. (208) 332-6823
  E-mail: crfillmore@sde.idaho.gov
Certification and Professional Standards Director
  **Lisa Colón** ................................. (208) 332-6886
Assessment Director **(Vacant)** ..................... (208) 332-6842
Content Director **Scott Cook** ....................... (208) 332-6927
Student Engagement and Postsecondary Readiness
  Director **Matt McCarter** ....................... (208) 332-6961

## Division of Public School Finance

Deputy Superintendent **Timothy Hill** ................. (208) 332-6843
  E-mail: tdhill@sde.idaho.gov

## Division of Transparent Accountability

Chief of Staff **(Vacant)** ........................... (208) 332-6814

*(continued on next page)*

---

★ Elected Official   ■ Appointed by Governor   ● Appointed by Legislature   ▲ Appointed by Board or Commission   ◆ Appointed by State Supreme Court

## EXECUTIVE BRANCH

**Division of Transparent Accountability** *continued*

Chief Communications Officer **Jeff Church** . . . . . . . . . . . . . (208) 332-6934
  E-mail: jchurch@sde.idaho.gov
Chief Information Officer **(Vacant)** . . . . . . . . . . . . . . . . . . (208) 332-6970
Chief Financial Officer **Louie Konkol** . . . . . . . . . . . . . . . . (208) 332-6874
Transportation Director **Doug Scott** . . . . . . . . . . . . . . . . (208) 332-6856

# Idaho Department of Juvenile Corrections [DJC]

954 West Jefferson Street, Boise, ID 83720
P.O. Box 83720, Boise, ID 83720-0285
Tel: (208) 334-5100 Fax: (208) 334-5120 Internet: www.idjc.idaho.gov

■Executive Director **Sharon Harrigfeld** . . . . . . (208) 334-5100 ext. 404
  E-mail: sgrigg@idahocities.org
  Education: Boise State; Col Idaho

## Board of Juvenile Corrections

954 West Jefferson Street, Boise, ID 83720
Tel: (208) 334-5100 Fax: (208) 334-5120 Internet: www.idjc.idaho.gov

■Chair **Denton C. Darrington** . . . . . . . . . . . . . . . . (208) 334-5100
  Education: Utah State 1963 BS
■Member **Barry Black** . . . . . . . . . . . . . . . . . . . . . . (208) 334-5100
■Member **Shawn Hill** . . . . . . . . . . . . . . . . . . . . . . . (208) 334-5100
■Member **Patti Anne Lodge** . . . . . . . . . . . . . . . . . . (208) 334-5100
  Education: Marylhurst 1964 BA
■Member **Richard Wills** . . . . . . . . . . . . . . . . . . . . . (208) 334-5100

## Idaho Board of Medicine

P.O. Box 83720, Boise, ID 83720-0058
Westgate Office Plaza, 1755 Westgate Drive, Suite 140, Boise, ID 83704
Tel: (208) 327-7000 Fax: (208) 327-7005 E-mail: info@bom.idaho.gov
Internet: bom.idaho.gov

▲Executive Director **Anne Lawler** . . . . . . . . . . . . . . . . . (208) 327-7000

## Idaho State Board of Tax Appeals

3380 Americana Terrace, Suite 110, Boise, ID 83706
P.O. Box 83720, Boise, ID 83720-0088
Tel: (208) 334-3354 Fax: (208) 334-4060 Internet: www.bta.idaho.gov

■Chairman **David Kinghorn** . . . . . . . . . . . . . . . . . . . . (208) 334-3354
■Member **Leland G. "Lee" Heinrich** . . . . . . . . . . . . . . (208) 334-3354
■Member **Linda Pike** . . . . . . . . . . . . . . . . . . . . . . . . (208) 334-3354
▲Director **Steven Wallace** . . . . . . . . . . . . . . . . . . . . (208) 334-3354
  E-mail: steve.wallace@bta.idaho.gov

## Idaho Transportation Board

3311 West State Street, Boise, ID 83703
P.O. Box 7129, Boise, ID 83707
Tel: (208) 334-8000 Fax: (208) 334-3858

■Chairman **Jerry Whitehead** . . . . . . . . . . . . . . . . . . . (208) 334-8808
■Vice Chairman **R. James "Jim" Coleman** (District 1) . . . . (208) 762-4704
  Term Expires: January 31, 2019
■Member **Julie DeLorenzo** (District 3) . . . . . . . . . . . . . (208) 703-4348
  Term Expires: January 31, 2015
■Member **Lee Gagner** (District 6) . . . . . . . . . . . . . . . . (208) 529-0700
  Term Expires: January 31, 2020
  Education: Minot State BS
■Member **Dwight Horsch** (District 5) . . . . . . . . . . . . . . (208) 221-4765
  Term Expires: January 31, 2017
  Education: Idaho; Kansas State 1968
■Member **Jim D. Kempton** (District 4) . . . . . . . . . . . . . (208) 673-6261
  Term Expires: January 31, 2018
  Education: Idaho BS, MS
■Member **Janice "Jan" Vassar** (District 2) . . . . . . . . . . . (208) 743-5093
  Term Expires: January 31, 2016

# Transportation Department [ITD]

3311 West State Street, Boise, ID 83703
P.O. Box 7129, Boise, ID 83707
Tel: (208) 334-8000 TTY: (208) 334-4458 Fax: (208) 334-3858

**Employees:** 1,688 **Fiscal Year:** 2015 **Budget:** $531,715,000

▲Director **Brian W. Ness** . . . . . . . . . . . . . . . . . . . . . (208) 334-8807
  E-mail: brian.ness@itd.idaho.gov
Chief Deputy **Scott Stokes** . . . . . . . . . . . . . . . . . . . . (208) 334-8027
  Management Assistant **Carla Anderson** . . . . . . . . . . . . (208) 334-8820
Lead Deputy Attorney General **Larry Allen** . . . . . . . . . . . (208) 334-8815
  E-mail: larry.allen@itd.idaho.gov
Chief Administrative Officer **Charlene McArthur** . . . . . . . (208) 334-8876
  E-mail: charlene.mcarthur@itd.idaho.gov
Chief Engineer and Engineering Plans and Products
  Administrator **Kimbol Allen** . . . . . . . . . . . . . . . . . . (208) 334-8802
Chief Human Resources Officer **Brenda Williams** . . . . . . . (208) 334-8010
  Human Resources Development Manager
    **Tony Loomer** . . . . . . . . . . . . . . . . . . . . . . . . . (208) 334-8496
Chief Operations Officer **Jim Carpenter** . . . . . . . . . . . . (208) 334-8839
Information Technology Administrator **(Vacant)** . . . . . . . . (208) 334-8771
Aeronautics Division Administrator **Mike Pape, CAM** . . . . (208) 334-8788
  E-mail: mike.pape@itd.idaho.gov
  Education: Embry-Riddle 1985 BSAv
Motor Vehicles Division Administrator **Alan Frew** . . . . . . (208) 334-4443
  E-mail: alan.frew@itd.idaho.gov
Communications Officer Manager **Vincent Trimboli** . . . . . (208) 334-8005
  E-mail: vincent.trimboli@itd.idaho.gov
Controller **Dave Tolman** . . . . . . . . . . . . . . . . . . . . . (208) 334-8525
Government Affairs Program Manager **Mollie McCarty** . . . (208) 334-8804
  E-mail: mollie.mccarty@itd.idaho.gov
Business and Support Manager **Michelle Doane** . . . . . . . (208) 334-8752
Internal Review Manager **(Vacant)** . . . . . . . . . . . . . . . (208) 334-8834
Executive Assistant to the Board **Sue S. Higgins** . . . . . . . (208) 334-8808

# State Police [ISP]

700 South Stratford Drive, Meridian, ID 83642
Tel: (208) 884-7000 Fax: (208) 884-7290

**Employees:** 535 **Fiscal Year:** 2015 **Budget:** $65,007,000

■Director **Col. Ralph Powell** . . . . . . . . . . . . . . . . . . . (208) 884-7003
  E-mail: ralph.powell@isp.idaho.gov
  Education: BYU (Idaho) AA; BYU BA; Boise State MPA
■Deputy Director **Lt. Col. Kedrick Wills** . . . . . . . . . . . . (208) 884-7003
  E-mail: kedrick.willis@isp.idaho.gov
Deputy Attorney General **Stephanie Altig** . . . . . . . . . . . (208) 884-7050
                                                         Fax: (208) 884-7228
Alcohol Beverage Control Bureau Chief
  **Lt. Russ Wheatly** . . . . . . . . . . . . . . . . . . . . . . . (208) 884-7062
                                                         Fax: (208) 884-7096
Financial Executive Officer
  **Elizabeth M. "Marsi" Woody, CGFM** . . . . . . . . . . . . (208) 884-7210
Financial Manager **Elizabeth J. Yturralde** . . . . . . . . . . . (208) 884-7025
Criminal Identification Bureau Manager **Dawn A. Peck** . . . (208) 884-7136
                                                         Fax: (208) 884-7193
Commercial Vehicle Safety Manager **Capt. Bill Reese** . . . . (208) 884-7222
                                                         Fax: (208) 884-7192
Human Resources Officer **Becky Harris** . . . . . . . . . . . . (208) 884-7016
                                                         Fax: (208) 884-7087
Laboratory Systems Director **Matthew Gamette** . . . . . . . (208) 884-7000
Police Services Manager **Major Kevin Hudgens** . . . . . . . . (208) 884-7205
Enforcement Operations Major **Steve Richardson** . . . . . . (208) 884-7207

# Peace Officer Standards and Training Academy [POST]

Fax: (208) 884-7295

Division Administrator **Victor McCraw** . . . . . . . . . . . . . (208) 884-7251

# Office of Drug Policy [ODP]

304 North 8th Street, Floor 4, Boise, ID 83720
Tel: (208) 854-3040

Administrator **Elisha Figueroa** . . . . . . . . . . . . . . . . . . (208) 854-3040
  E-mail: elisha.figueroa@odp.idaho.gov
  Education: Arizona State BA; Northwest Nazarene U MA

---

★ Elected Official   ■ Appointed by Governor   ● Appointed by Legislature   ▲ Appointed by Board or Commission   ◆ Appointed by State Supreme Court

Administrative Services Manager **Gayle Hines**..........(208) 854-3040
  E-mail: gayle.hines@odp.idaho.gov
Program and Communications Specialist **Bryan Norton** ...(208) 854-3040
  E-mail: bryan.norton@odp.idaho.gov

# Office of Energy Resources [OER]

304 North 8th Street, Boise, ID 83720
P.O. Box 83720, Boise, ID 83720-0036
Tel: (208) 332-1660 Fax: (208) 332-1661

Administrator **John Chatburn**........................(208) 332-1671
  E-mail: john.chatburn@oer.idaho.gov

# Fiscal Office

304 North 8th Street, Suite 250, Boise, ID 83720
P.O. Box 83720, Boise, ID 83720-0036
Tel: (208) 332-1660 Fax: (208) 332-1661

Financial Technician **Tammy Japhet**.................(208) 332-1663

# Division of Financial Management [DFM]

P.O. Box 83720, Boise, ID 83720-0032
304 North 8th Street, 3rd Floor, Boise, ID 83720
Tel: (208) 334-3900 Fax: (208) 334-2438 E-mail: info@dfm.idaho.gov
Internet: http://dfm.idaho.gov

**Employees:** 16 **Fiscal Year:** 2014 **Budget:** $1,521,000

Administrator **Jani Revier**..........................(208) 854-3053
  E-mail: jani.revier@dfm.idaho.gov

# Division of Human Resources

304 North 8th Street, Boise, ID 83720
P.O. Box 83720, Boise, ID 83720-0066
Tel: (208) 334-2263 Tel: (800) 554-5627 (Toll Free) Fax: (208) 854-3088
Internet: www.dhr.idaho.gov E-mail: idhr@dhr.idaho.gov

**Employees:** 12 **Fiscal Year:** 2015 **Budget:** $1,724,000

■Administrator **Susan Buxton**........................(208) 854-3076
  Education: Whitman; Idaho
Deputy Administrator **Kim Wherry Toryanski** ......(208) 854-3077
Human Resource Consultant **Michelle Peugh** .........(208) 854-3073
Human Resource Consultant **Shelli Rael**..............(208) 854-3083
Human Resource Consultant **Joe Webber** .............(208) 854-3056
Projects Manager **Sharon Duncan** ...................(208) 854-3087
  Compensation Specialist **Cari Markham** ...........(208) 854-3079
  Human Resources Associate **Chris Eismann** .........(208) 854-3065
Training Manager **Mark Fisher** ......................(208) 854-3081
  E-mail: mark.fisher@dhr.idaho.gov
  Training Specialist **Ashleigh Jensen** ...............(208) 854-3057

# Idaho State Liquor Division [ISLD]

1349 East Beechcraft Court, Boise, ID 83716
Tel: (208) 947-9400 Fax: (208) 947-9401 Internet: www.liquor.idaho.gov

**Employees:** 333 **Fiscal Year:** 2014 **Budget:** $16,576,000

Director **Jeffrey R. "Jeff" Anderson** ................(208) 947-9402
  Education: Cal State (Chico) BSBA
Chief Financial Officer **Tony Faraca** .................(208) 947-9414
Information Technology and Security Deputy Director
  **Jon Spence**.......................................(208) 947-9434
  E-mail: jon.spence@liquor.idaho.gov
Procurement, Distribution, and Retail Operations Deputy
  Director **Howard Wasserstein** ....................(208) 947-9456

# Military Division

Gowen Field, 4040 West Guard Street, Boise, ID 83705
Tel: (208) 422-5242

**Employees:** 319 **Fiscal Year:** 2014 **Budget:** $63,032,000

Adjutant General **MajGen Gary Sayler, ANG** ..........(208) 422-5242
  Education: North Dakota State 1971
  Executive Administrative Assistant **Gayla Crall** .......(208) 422-5242
Director of Staff **Col James Heuring, ANG** ...........(208) 422-5241

Public Affairs Officer **Maj Christopher Borders, ANG** ...(208) 422-5268
  E-mail: timothy.marsano@us.army.mil
State Accounting Officer **Mark Agenbroad** .............(208) 422-6001
Base Civil Engineer **LTC Sarin Schwartz, ARNG**.......(208) 422-5500
  E-mail: sschwartz@imd.idaho.gov
Base Installation Command **MajGen Gary Sayler, ANG** ..(208) 422-4268
Training Site Commander **LTC Charles Moore, ARNG**....(208) 272-4268

# Bureau of Homeland Security

Building 600, 4040 West Guard Street, Boise, ID 83705-5004
Tel: (208) 422-3040 Fax: (208) 422-3044

Chief **BrigGen William B. "Brad" Richy, ANG** .........(208) 422-3001
  Education: McKendree 1983 BBA
Grant Management Branch Chief **Karen Wallen** .........(208) 258-6518
Response and Recovery Branch Chief **Fred Abt**..........(208) 334-3012
Idaho E911 Program Coordinator **Craig Logan** ..........(208) 422-5234
Senior Training Specialist **Natalie Lahti**................(208) 334-3460
Training and Exercise Section Chief **Coleen Rice** .......(208) 422-3035

# Idaho National Guard

Building 440, 3882 West Ellsworth Street, Boise, ID 83705
Tel: (208) 272-5755 Fax: (208) 272-3560

Adjutant General **MajGen Gary Sayler, ANG** ...........(208) 422-5242

# Idaho Air National Guard

4474 South DeHaviland Street, Boise, ID 83705-8103
Tel: (208) 422-5398 Internet: www.idaho.ang.af.mil

Assistant Adjutant General
  **BrigGen Michael Nolan, ANG** ....................(208) 422-5241
  Education: Florida 1984 BS; National War Col 2009
Wing Command Chief Master Sergeant
  **CMSgt Tammy S. Ladley, ANG** ...................(208) 422-5398

# Idaho Army National Guard

Building 600, 4040 West Guard Street, Boise, ID 83705
Tel: (208) 272-5232

Assistant Adjutant General **BG John Goodale, ARNG**....(208) 422-5241
116th Calvary Brigade Commander
  **COL Don Blunk, ARNG** ..........................(208) 422-5242

# Office of the Lieutenant Governor [LGO]

State Capitol Building, 700 West Jefferson Street, Boise, ID 83720-0080
Tel: (208) 334-2200 Fax: (208) 334-3259

★Lieutenant Governor **Brad J. Little** (R) ................(208) 334-2200
  Term Expires: January 2019
  E-mail: brad.little@lgo.idaho.gov
  Education: Idaho 1977 BS
Chief of Staff **Greg Wilson** ..........................(208) 334-2200
Communications and Staff Assistant **Ann DeAngeli** ......(208) 334-2200
  E-mail: ann.deangeli@lgo.idaho.gov
Scheduling and Staff Assistant **Jennifer O'Kief** .........(208) 334-2200
  E-mail: jennifer.okief@lgo.idaho.gov

# Office of the Secretary of State

Idaho State Capitol Building, 700 West Jefferson Street, 2nd Floor,
Room E205, Boise, ID 83720-0080
P.O. Box 83720, Boise, ID 83720-0032
Tel: (208) 334-2300 TTY: (208) 334-2366 Fax: (208) 334-2282
E-mail: sosinfo@sos.idaho.gov Internet: www.sos.idaho.gov

**Employees:** 24 **Fiscal Year:** 2015 **Budget:** $2,081,000

★Secretary of State **Lawerence E. Denney** (R) ..........(208) 334-2300
  Term Expires: January 2019
  Education: Idaho 1970 BS

# Commercial Affairs

450 North Fourth Street, Boise, ID 83702

Commercial Affairs **Kim Hunter** ......................(208) 332-2819
Notary Public/Trademark Division Clerk
  **Debbie R. Farnsworth** ...........................(208) 332-2810

---

★ Elected Official    ■ Appointed by Governor    ● Appointed by Legislature    ▲ Appointed by Board or Commission    ◆ Appointed by State Supreme Court

## Code Commission

P.O. Box 83720, Boise, ID 83701-0080

■ Member **Daniel Bowen** . . . . . . . . . . . . . . . . . . . . . . . . . . . (208) 332-2814
■ Member **Andrew Doman** . . . . . . . . . . . . . . . . . . . . . . . . . . (208) 332-2814
■ Member **Jeremy Pisca** . . . . . . . . . . . . . . . . . . . . . . . . . . . . (208) 332-2814
Ex-Officio Secretary **Lawerence E. Denney** . . . . . . . . . . . (208) 332-2814

## Office of the Attorney General

P.O. Box 83720, Boise, ID 83720-0010

Tel: (208) 334-2400  Fax: (208) 854-8071  Internet: www.state.id.us/ag

**Employees:** 188  **Fiscal Year:** 2015  **Budget:** $20,386,000

★ Attorney General **Lawrence G. Wasden** (R) . . . . . . . . . . . (208) 334-2400
  Term Expires: January 2019
  E-mail: lawrence.wasden@ag.idaho.gov
  Education: BYU 1982 BA; Idaho 1985 JD
  Executive Assistant **Janet Carter** . . . . . . . . . . . . . . . . . . (208) 334-2400
Chief Deputy **Sherm Furey** . . . . . . . . . . . . . . . . . . . . . . . . (208) 334-2400
Assistant Chief Deputy **Brian Kane** . . . . . . . . . . . . . . . . . . (208) 334-2400
Administration & Budget Division Chief **Tara Orr** . . . . . . . (208) 334-2400
  E-mail: tara.orr@ag.idaho.gov
  Business Manager **Trudy Jackson** . . . . . . . . . . . . . . . . . (208) 334-2400
  Information Technology Manager **Dustin Russell** . . . . . . (208) 334-4133
    E-mail: dustin.russell@ag.idaho.gov

### Civil Litigation Division

Deputy Attorney General/Division Chief **Steven Olsen** . . . (208) 334-2400
Tax Commission Deputy Attorney General
  **William "Bill" von Tagen** . . . . . . . . . . . . . . . . . . . . . . . (208) 334-7530

### Consumer Protection Division

Fax: (208) 334-4151

Division Chief **Brett DeLange** . . . . . . . . . . . . . . . . . . . . . . (208) 334-2424
Finance Department Deputy Attorney General
  **Joseph B. "Joe" Jones** . . . . . . . . . . . . . . . . . . . . . . . . . (208) 332-8000
    E-mail: joseph.jones@finance.idaho.gov
Insurance Department Deputy Attorney General
  **Richard Burleigh** . . . . . . . . . . . . . . . . . . . . . . . . . . . . . (208) 334-4210

### Contracts and Administrative Law Division

Division Chief **S. Kay Christensen** . . . . . . . . . . . . . . . . . . (208) 334-2400
Industrial Commission Deputy Attorney General
  **Blair Jaynes** . . . . . . . . . . . . . . . . . . . . . . . . . . . . . . . . . (208) 334-6000
Labor Department Lead Deputy Attorney General
  **Craig Bledsoe** . . . . . . . . . . . . . . . . . . . . . . . . . . . . . . . (208) 332-3570
PERSI (Public Employees Retirement System of Idaho)
  Lead Deputy Attorney General **Joanna Guilfoy** . . . . . . . (208) 334-3365
Public Utilities Commission Deputy Attorney General
  **Donald Howell** . . . . . . . . . . . . . . . . . . . . . . . . . . . . . . . (208) 334-0312
State Board of Education Deputy Attorney General
  **Jenifer Marcus** . . . . . . . . . . . . . . . . . . . . . . . . . . . . . . . (208) 334-2270
Health and Welfare Deputy Attorney General
  **Nicole McKay** . . . . . . . . . . . . . . . . . . . . . . . . . . . . . . . (208) 334-5541
    E-mail: nmckay@agri.idaho.gov

### Criminal Law Division

Fax: (208) 854-8074

Deputy Attorney General/Division Chief **Paul Panther** . . . (208) 334-4545
Correction Department Deputy Attorney General
  **Mark Kubinski** . . . . . . . . . . . . . . . . . . . . . . . . . . . . . . . (208) 658-2097
  1299 North Orchard, Suite 110, Boise, ID 83706
Idaho State Police Deputy Attorney General
  **Stephanie Altig** . . . . . . . . . . . . . . . . . . . . . . . . . . . . . . (208) 884-7050
  P.O. Box 700, Meridian, ID 83680-0700
Juvenile Corrections Department Deputy Attorney
  General **(Vacant)** . . . . . . . . . . . . . . . . . . . . . . . . . . . . . (208) 334-5100
Medicaid Fraud Control Unit Deputy Attorney General
  **Rondee Blessing** . . . . . . . . . . . . . . . . . . . . . . . . . . . . . (208) 334-4100

### Natural Resources Division

Fax: (208) 854-8071

Deputy Attorney General/Division Chief **Clive Strong** . . . . (208) 334-2400
  E-mail: clive.strong@ag.idaho.gov
Agriculture Department Deputy Attorney General
  **Sean Costello** . . . . . . . . . . . . . . . . . . . . . . . . . . . . . . . (208) 332-8509
Environmental Quality Department Deputy Attorney
  General **Doug Conde** . . . . . . . . . . . . . . . . . . . . . . . . . . (208) 373-0494
Fish and Game Department Deputy Attorney General
  **Kathleen Trever** . . . . . . . . . . . . . . . . . . . . . . . . . . . . . (208) 287-2710
Lands Department Deputy Attorney General
  **Steve Schuster** . . . . . . . . . . . . . . . . . . . . . . . . . . . . . (208) 334-0243
    E-mail: steve.schuster@ag.idaho.gov
Water Resources Department Deputy Attorney General
  **Garrick Baxter** . . . . . . . . . . . . . . . . . . . . . . . . . . . . . . (208) 327-7920

## Office of the State Treasurer [STO]

700 West Jefferson Street, Suite 126, Boise, ID 83720-0080
P.O. Box 83720, Boise, ID 83720-0091
Tel: (208) 334-3200  Fax: (208) 332-2959
E-mail: idahotreasurer@sto.idaho.gov  Internet: sto.idaho.gov

**Employees:** 29  **Fiscal Year:** 2015  **Budget:** $4,605,000

★ State Treasurer **Ron G. Crane** (R) . . . . . . . . . . . . . . . . . . (208) 334-3200
  Term Expires: January 2019
  E-mail: ron.crane@sto.idaho.gov
  Career: State Representative (ID), Idaho House of Representatives
  (1982-1998)
Deputy Treasurer **Laura Steffler** . . . . . . . . . . . . . . . . . . . . (208) 332-2999
College Savings Plan Administrator **Christine Stoll** . . . . . . (208) 332-2935
Investment Pool Administrator **Chris Priest** . . . . . . . . . . . (208) 332-2955

## Office of the State Controller

700 West State Street, Boise, ID 83720
Tel: (208) 334-3100  Fax: (208) 334-2671  E-mail: scoinfo@sco.idaho.gov
Internet: www.sco.idaho.gov

**Employees:** 91  **Fiscal Year:** 2015  **Budget:** $14,094,000

★ State Controller **Brandon Woolf** (R) . . . . . . . . . . . . . . . . . (208) 334-3100
  Term Expires: January 2019
  Education: Utah State BA; Boise State MBA
  Career: Statewide Payroll Division Deputy Controller, Office of the
  State Controller, State of Idaho (2011); Administration Division Chief
  Deputy Controller, Office of the State Controller, State of Idaho
  (2011-2012)
Administration Division Chief Deputy Controller
  **Dan Goicoechea** . . . . . . . . . . . . . . . . . . . . . . . . . . . . . (208) 334-3100
    E-mail: dgoicoechea@sco.idaho.gov
Administration Division Assistant Chief Deputy/General
  Counsel **Brian Benjamin** . . . . . . . . . . . . . . . . . . . . . . . (208) 334-3100
    Education: Idaho 1993 BSB, 1996 JD
Boards and Commissions Deputy Controller
  **Scott Phillips** . . . . . . . . . . . . . . . . . . . . . . . . . . . . . . . (208) 334-3100
Computer Services Division Deputy Controller
  **Tammy Shipman** . . . . . . . . . . . . . . . . . . . . . . . . . . . . . (208) 334-2342
    E-mail: tshipman@sco.idaho.gov
Statewide Payroll Division Deputy Controller
  **Audrey Musgrave** . . . . . . . . . . . . . . . . . . . . . . . . . . . . (208) 334-2394
Statewide Accounting Division Administrator
  **Patrick Hodges** . . . . . . . . . . . . . . . . . . . . . . . . . . . . . . (208) 334-3150
    E-mail: phodges@sco.idaho.gov

---

★ Elected Official    ■ Appointed by Governor    ● Appointed by Legislature    ▲ Appointed by Board or Commission    ◆ Appointed by State Supreme Court

# Illinois

Tel: (217) 782-2000 (State Information Office)  Internet: www.illinois.gov

**Number of U.S. Congressional Delegates:** 2 Senators; 18 Representatives  **Governor's Term:** 4 years
**Legislature Description:** General Assembly - 59 member Senate; 118 member House of Representatives;
Term - Senate 4 years and 2 years, House 2 years  **Next Election:** Governor November 2018; Legislature
November 2016  **Number of Electoral Votes:** 20  **Official Name:** State of Illinois (Algonquian: man)
**Nickname:** The Prairie State  **Motto:** State Sovereignty-National Union

**Population:** 12,859,995 (2015); Rank 5  **Fiscal Year:** 2015  **Budget:** $58,602,226,000

## Office of the Governor

207 State Capitol Building, Springfield, IL 62706
Tel: (217) 782-6830  TTY: (217) 782-0244

**Employees:** 99  **Fiscal Year:** 2015  **Budget:** $5,094,000

**Bruce V. Rauner**
Governor

Began Service: January 12, 2015
Term Expires: 2019
Date of Birth: February 18, 1957
Education: Dartmouth 1978 BA;
Harvard 1981 MBA
Home: Winnetka
Career: Senior Principal, GTCR Golder Rauner,
LLC (1998-2012)

★Governor **Bruce V. Rauner** (R) . . . . . . . . . . . . . . . . . . . . (217) 782-6830
Deputy Governor **Trey Childress** . . . . . . . . . . . . . . . . . . . (217) 558-0883
  E-mail: trey.childress@illinois.gov
  Executive Assistant to the Governor **Holly Griff** . . . . . . . . (217) 782-6830
    E-mail: holly.griff@illinois.gov
  Special Assistant to the Governor
    **Jared Melamed Dubnow** . . . . . . . . . . . . . . . . . . . . (217) 558-3417
    E-mail: jared.dubnow@illinois.gov
    Education: Emory
Chief of Staff **Michael "Mike" Zolnierowicz** . . . . . . . . . . (217) 558-0881
  E-mail: michael.zolnierowicz@illinois.gov
  Education: Hope
Deputy Chief of Staff for Legislative Affairs
  **Richard "Rich" Goldberg** . . . . . . . . . . . . . . . . . . . . (217) 558-1030
    E-mail: richard.goldberg@illinois.gov
    Education: Northwestern 2004 BSJ
Deputy Chief of Staff for Outreach **Kelley Folino** . . . . . . . . (312) 814-1048
  E-mail: kelley.folino@illinois.gov
Deputy Chief of Staff for Policy **Aaron Winters** . . . . . . . . (217) 558-1026
  E-mail: aaron.winters@illinois.gov
Chief Financial Officer **(Vacant)** . . . . . . . . . . . . . . . . . . . . (217) 782-6830
Chief Information Officer **Hardik Bhatt** . . . . . . . . . . . . . . . (217) 524-7083
  E-mail: hardik.bhatt@illinois.gov
  Education: Maharaja Sayajirao U (India) BS; Kellogg 2005 MBA
Chief Operating Officer **Linda Lingle** . . . . . . . . . . . . . . . . (217) 782-6830
  E-mail: linda.lingle@illinois.gov
  Education: Cal State (Northridge) 1975 BA
Education Secretary **Elizabeth Delaney "Beth" Purvis** . . . (312) 814-2121
  E-mail: beth.purvis@illinois.gov
Government Transformation Director **David Wu** . . . . . . . . (312) 814-5674
  E-mail: david.wu@illinois.gov
  Education: Wesleyan U BA; Harvard MA; Wisconsin MA
General Counsel **Jason Barclay** . . . . . . . . . . . . . . . . . . . . (217) 558-1022
  E-mail: jason.barclay@illinois.gov
  Education: Duke BA; Virginia JD
Advance Director **Jared Melamed Dubnow** . . . . . . . . . . . (217) 524-0057
  E-mail: jared.dubnow@illinois.gov
Communications Director **Lance Trover** . . . . . . . . . . . . . . (217) 558-1015
  E-mail: lance.trover@illinois.gov
  Education: Southern Illinois 2006 JD
Constituent Affairs Director **Molly Kamykowski** . . . . . . . (217) 782-1101

Downstate Director **Randy D. Pollard** . . . . . . . . . . . . . . . . (217) 558-1018
  E-mail: randy.pollard@illinois.gov
Legislative Director **Jim Kaitschuk** . . . . . . . . . . . . . . . . . . (217) 782-8665
  E-mail: jim.kaitschuk@illinois.gov
Operations Director **Jared Melamed Dubnow** . . . . . . . . . . (217) 524-0057
  E-mail: jared.dubnow@illinois.gov
Research Director **Edward "Ed" Murphy** . . . . . . . . . . . . . (217) 557-4185
Scheduling Director **Morgan Kreitner** . . . . . . . . . . . . . . . (217) 782-6830
  E-mail: morgan.kreitner@illinois.gov
Special Projects Director **(Vacant)** . . . . . . . . . . . . . . . . . . (217) 782-6830
Press Secretary **Andrew Flach** . . . . . . . . . . . . . . . . . . . . (217) 782-6830
  E-mail: andrew.flach@illinois.gov
Press Secretary **Catherine "Cate" Kelly** . . . . . . . . . . . . . . (217) 782-6830
  E-mail: catherine.kelly@illinois.gov
Deputy Press Secretary **Alexandra "Allie" Bovis** . . . . . . . (217) 782-6830
Deputy Press Secretary **Lyndsey Walters** . . . . . . . . . . . . . (217) 782-6830
  Education: Drexel
Press Assistant **Jacquelyn Reineke** . . . . . . . . . . . . . . . . . (217) 782-6830
  E-mail: jacquelyn.reineke@illinois.gov
Economic Development Policy Adviser **(Vacant)** . . . . . . . . (217) 558-1029
Education Policy Adviser
  **Elizabeth Delaney "Beth" Purvis** . . . . . . . . . . . . . . . . (312) 814-2121
    E-mail: beth.purvis@illinois.gov
Efficiency and Metrics Policy Adviser **Joe Beyer** . . . . . . . . (217) 782-6830
  Education: Harvard JD, MBA
Environment and Energy Policy Adviser **Alec Messina** . . . . (217) 782-6830
  E-mail: alec.messina@illinois.gov
  Education: Southern Illinois JD
Infrastructure Policy Adviser **Brian Henry Oszakiewski** . . (217) 782-6830
  E-mail: brian.oszakiewski@illinois.gov
  Education: Creighton 2006 BA; Johns Hopkins MA
Public Safety Policy Adviser **Samantha Gaddy** . . . . . . . . . (217) 782-1219
  E-mail: samantha.gaddy@illinois.gov
Revenue and Pensions Policy Adviser **Michael Mahoney** . . (217) 782-1149
  E-mail: michael.mahoney@illinois.gov
Special Counsel to the Governor and Healthcare
  and Human Services Policy Adviser
  **Jennifer Walsh "Jen" Hammer** . . . . . . . . . . . . . . . . . . (217) 558-1025
    E-mail: jennifer.hammer@illinois.gov
    Education: Arizona State 2004 BS; Southern Illinois 2008 JD
Diversity and Recruitment Director **Janice Collier** . . . . . . (217) 782-6830
Latino Affairs Director **Marcos Peterson** . . . . . . . . . . . . . (312) 814-3967
  E-mail: marcos.peterson@illinois.gov
Coalitions Coordinator **Ashley Kalus** . . . . . . . . . . . . . . . . (312) 814-0021
  E-mail: ashley.kalus@illinois.gov
Outreach Coordinator **Dennis Jung** . . . . . . . . . . . . . . . . . (312) 814-8266
  E-mail: dennis.jung@illinois.gov
Special Counsel **Joseph H. "Joe" Hartzler** . . . . . . . . . . . (217) 558-3472
  E-mail: joseph.hartzler@illinois.gov
Deputy Counsel **Mitch Holzrichter** . . . . . . . . . . . . . . . . . (312) 814-6700
  E-mail: mitch.holzrichter@illinois.gov
Deputy Counsel **Dennis Murashko** . . . . . . . . . . . . . . . . . (312) 814-4185
  E-mail: dennis.murashko@illinois.gov
Associate Counsel **Emily Bastedo** . . . . . . . . . . . . . . . . . . (312) 814-5298
  E-mail: emily.bastedo@illinois.gov
Associate Counsel **Chasity Boyce** . . . . . . . . . . . . . . . . . . (312) 814-6778
  E-mail: chasity.boyce@illinois.gov
Associate Counsel **Emily Gibellina** . . . . . . . . . . . . . . . . . (312) 814-3758
  E-mail: emily.gibellina@illinois.gov

*(continued on next page)*

---

★ Elected Official  ■ Appointed by Governor  ● Appointed by Legislature  ▲ Appointed by Board or Commission  ◆ Appointed by State Supreme Court

**EXECUTIVE BRANCH**

**Office of the Governor** *continued*

Associate Counsel **Georgia Man** . . . . . . . . . . . . . . . . . . . . . . (312) 814-1181
  E-mail: georgia.man@illinois.gov
Associate Counsel **Christina McClernon** . . . . . . . . . . . . . . . (312) 814-5154
  E-mail: christina.mcclernon@illinois.gov

# Chicago Office

100 West Randolph Street, Suite 16-100, Chicago, IL 60601
Tel: (312) 814-2121  Fax: (312) 814-5512

■ Chief of Staff **Michael "Mike" Zolnierowicz** . . . . . . . . . . (312) 814-2411
  E-mail: michael.zolnierowicz@illinois.gov

# Washington Office

444 North Capitol Street, NW, Suite 400, Washington, DC 20001
Fax: (202) 724-0689

Director **Kathleen "Kathy" Lydon** . . . . . . . . . . . . . . . . . . . (202) 624-7760
  E-mail: kathy.lydon@illinois.gov
  Education: Georgetown 1977 BSFS; Chicago 1979 MBA

# Citizens' Action Office

222 South College, Springfield, IL 62704
Fax: (217) 524-4049

Co-Director **Lynda Delaforgue** . . . . . . . . . . . . . . . . . . . . . . . (217) 782-0244
Co-Director **William McNary** . . . . . . . . . . . . . . . . . . . . . . . . (217) 782-0244

# Homeland Security Office

2200 South Dirksen Parkway, Springfield, IL 62703
Internet: www.illinoishomelandsecurity.net

Public Safety Director **Rodger A. Heaton** . . . . . . . . . . . . . . (217) 782-2700
  E-mail: rodger.heaton@illinois.gov
  Education: Illinois 1981 BS; Indiana 1985 JD

# Office of Management and Budget

108 State House, Springfield, IL 62706
Tel: (217) 782-4520  Fax: (217) 524-1514

Director **Tim Nuding** . . . . . . . . . . . . . . . . . . . . . . . . . . . . . . (217) 782-5886
  E-mail: tim.nuding@illinois.gov

# Office of the Auditor General

Iles Park Plaza, 740 East Ash Street, Springfield, IL 62703-3154
Tel: (217) 782-6046  TTY: (888) 261-2887  Fax: (217) 785-8222
E-mail: oag.auditor@illinois.gov  Internet: www.auditor.illinois.gov

**Employees:** 104  **Fiscal Year:** 2015  **Budget:** $29,574,000

● Auditor General **Frank J. Mautino, Jr.** . . . . . . . . . . . . . . . (217) 782-3536
  E-mail: fmautino@auditor.illinois.gov
  Education: Illinois State 1984 BS
Chief of Staff **Dean Devert** . . . . . . . . . . . . . . . . . . . . . . . . . (217) 782-6046
Legal Counsel **Rebecca Patton** . . . . . . . . . . . . . . . . . . . . . . (217) 782-6698
Compliance Audit Director **Bruce Bullard** . . . . . . . . . . . . . (217) 782-0811
Information Systems Audit Director
  **William J. "Bill" Sampias** . . . . . . . . . . . . . . . . . . . . . (217) 785-5563
  E-mail: bsampias@auditor.illinois.gov
Performance Audit Director **Ameen Dada** . . . . . . . . . . . . . (217) 782-0812
Fiscal Officer **Terri Davis** . . . . . . . . . . . . . . . . . . . . . . . . . . (217) 782-9305

# Office of Executive Inspector General [OEIG]

69 W. Washington Street, Suite 3400, Chicago, IL 60602
Illinois Building, 607 East Adams Street, 14th Floor,
Springfield, IL 62701
Tel: (312) 814-5600  Tel: (217) 558-5600  Fax: (312) 814-5479
Fax: (217) 782-1605

**Employees:** 69  **Fiscal Year:** 2015  **Budget:** $7,538,100

■ Executive Inspector General **Maggie Hickey** . . . . . . . . . . (312) 814-5600
  E-mail: maggie.hickey@illinois.gov
  Education: Loyola U (Chicago) 1986 BA; DePaul 1991 JD
■ First Assistant Inspector General **Susan M. Haling** . . . . . . (312) 814-5600

Deputy Inspector General and Chief of Chicago Division
  **Fallon Opperman** . . . . . . . . . . . . . . . . . . . . . . . . . . . . (217) 558-5600
  Education: North Central Col BA; DePaul JD
Deputy Inspector General and Chief of Springfield
  Division **Thomas H. Klein** . . . . . . . . . . . . . . . . . . . . . . (217) 558-5600
  Education: Michigan 1999 JD
Deputy Inspector General and Chief of Regional Transit
  Board Division **Brandon Myers** . . . . . . . . . . . . . . . . . . (312) 814-5600
General Counsel **Daniel Hurtado** . . . . . . . . . . . . . . . . . . . . (312) 814-5600
  Education: Northwestern JD
Chief Administration Officer **Claudia Ortega** . . . . . . . . . . . (312) 814-5600
  E-mail: claudia.p.ortega@illinois.gov
  Education: DePaul BA
Human Resources Supervisor **Denise Zych Vieaux** . . . . . . . (312) 814-5600

# Department on Aging

One Natural Resources Way, Suite 100, Springfield, IL 62702-1271
Tel: (217) 785-2870  Tel: (800) 252-8966 (In State)  TTY: (888) 206-1327
Fax: (217) 785-4477  E-mail: ilsenior@aging.state.il.us
Internet: www.illinois.gov/aging

**Employees:** 160  **Fiscal Year:** 2015  **Budget:** $1,138,627,000

■ Director **Jean Bohnhoff** . . . . . . . . . . . . . . . . . . . . . . . . . . (217) 785-2870
Deputy Director **Jennifer Reif** . . . . . . . . . . . . . . (312) 814-4179 (Chicago)
  E-mail: jennifer.reif@illinois.gov        Tel: (217) 785-2870
                                              (Springfield)
Operations Chief of Staff **Matthew J. Ryan** . . . . . . . . . . . (312) 814-8449
Finance and Administration Division Chief Fiscal Officer
  **Jodi Becker** . . . . . . . . . . . . . . . . . . . . . . . . . . . . . . . . (217) 785-3381
Home and Community Services Director **Jose Jimenez** . . . (217) 785-3353
Community Relations and Outreach Division Manager
  **Elizabeth Delheimer** . . . . . . . . . . . . . . . . . . . . . . . . . (217) 785-3371
  E-mail: elizabeth.delheimer@illinois.gov
BEAM Division Manager **(Vacant)** . . . . . . . . . . . . . . . . . . . (217) 524-4009
Information Technology Division Manager
  **David Weibring** . . . . . . . . . . . . . . . . . . . . . . . . . . . . . (217) 558-3915
Planning, Research and Development
  Manager **Lora McCurdy** . . . . . . . . . . . . . (217) 558-3925 (Springfield)
                                                      Tel: (312) 814-1106
                                                          (Chicago)
Legislative Liaison **Alexander Burke** . . . . . . . . . . . . . . . . . (217) 785-8671
  E-mail: alexander.burke@illinois.gov
Webmaster **Dave Haley** . . . . . . . . . . . . . . . . . . . . . . . . . . . (217) 785-9258

# Department of Agriculture

P.O. Box 19281, Springfield, IL 62794-9281
Tel: (217) 782-2172  TTY: (217) 524-6858  Fax: (217) 785-4505
Internet: www.agr.state.il.us

**Employees:** 331  **Fiscal Year:** 2015  **Budget:** $82,218,000

■ Director **Raymond Poe** . . . . . . . . . . . . . . . . . . . . . . . . . . (217) 785-4789
  E-mail: raymond.poe@illinois.gov
  Education: DeVry Inst 1963 BA
Deputy Director **Warren Goetsch** . . . . . . . . . . . . . . . . . . . . (217) 785-4789
Chief of Staff **Grant Hammer** . . . . . . . . . . . . . . . . . . . . . . (217) 782-5051
  Education: Southern Illinois
Legal Counsel **Craig Sondgeroth** . . . . . . . . . . . . . . . . . . . (217) 558-0014
Legislative Liaison **Laura Sinclair** . . . . . . . . . . . . . . . . . . . (217) 782-9023
  E-mail: laura.sinclair@illinois.gov
Budget and Fiscal Services Bureau Chief
  **Richard Campbell** . . . . . . . . . . . . . . . . . . . . . . . . . . . (217) 785-4550
County Fairs and Horse Racing Bureau Chief **Kelly Beck** . . (217) 785-0106
DuQuoin State Fair Bureau Chief **(Vacant)** . . . . . . . . . . . . (618) 542-1515
                                                      Fax: (618) 542-1541
Human Resources Bureau Chief **Cheryl Bluhm** . . . . . . . . . (217) 524-5125
Illinois State Fair Bureau Chief **(Vacant)** . . . . . . . . . . . . . . (217) 785-4885
                                                      Fax: (217) 782-9115
Marketing, Promotion and Grants Bureau Chief
  **Karen Fraase** . . . . . . . . . . . . . . . . . . . . . . . . . . . . . . . (217) 524-3297
                                                      Fax: (217) 524-5960

# Administrative Services Division

Manager **Rebecca Clark Pitcher** . . . . . . . . . . . . . . . . . . . . (217) 785-5485
  E-mail: rebecca.clark@illinois.gov        Fax: (217) 557-5729

---

★ Elected Official    ■ Appointed by Governor    ● Appointed by Legislature    ▲ Appointed by Board or Commission    ◆ Appointed by State Supreme Court

Buildings and Grounds Bureau Chief **Vince Veseling** . . . . . (217) 782-0789
     Fax: (217) 524-1018
Computer Services Bureau Chief **Mark D. Kinkade** . . . . . . .(217) 558-3977
     E-mail: mark.kinkade@illinois.gov      Fax: (217) 558-4062

## Agricultural Industry Regulation Division
Tel: (217) 558-7041   Fax: (217) 524-7801

Manager **Chuck Cawley** . . . . . . . . . . . . . . . . . . . . . . . . . .(217) 558-7041
     E-mail: chuck.cawley@illinois.gov
Agricultural Products Inspection Bureau Chief
     **Gerald Kirbach** . . . . . . . . . . . . . . . . . . . . . . . . . . . . (217) 782-3817
     E-mail: gerald.kirbach@illinois.gov
Medicinal Plants Bureau Chief **Jack Campbell** . . . . . . . . . (217) 524-4190
Warehouses Bureau Chief **Stuart Selinger** . . . . . . . . . . . . .(217) 785-8308
Weights and Measures Bureau Chief **Doug Rathbun** . . . . . (217) 785-8301

## Food Safety and Animal Protection Division
Manager **Dr. Ray Hankes** . . . . . . . . . . . . . . . . . . . . . . . . . .(217) 785-5680
     Fax: (217) 524-7801
Animal Disease Laboratory Bureau Chief **Dale Webb** . . . . .(309) 344-2451
     2100 South Lake Storey Road, Galesburg, IL 61402    Fax: (309) 344-7358
Animal Health and Welfare Bureau Chief **Dr. Mark Ernst** . .(217) 782-4944
     Fax: (217) 524-7702
Meat and Poultry Inspection Bureau Chief
     **Kris Mazurczak** . . . . . . . . . . . . . . . . . . . . . . . . . . . . .(217) 782-6684
     Fax: (217) 524-7801

## Natural Resource Division
Manager **(Vacant)** . . . . . . . . . . . . . . . . . . . . . . . . . . . . . . .(217) 299-5204
Environmental Programs Bureau Chief **John Teefey** . . . . . .(217) 785-4754
Land and Water Resources Bureau Chief **Steve Chard** . . . .(217) 782-2661
     E-mail: steve.chard@illinois.gov

## Department of Central Management Services [CMS]
715 William G. Stratton Bldg., Springfield, IL 62706
JRTC 100 West Randolph, Suite 4-500, Chicago, IL 60601-3219
Tel: (217) 782-2141   TTY: (217) 785-3979   Fax: (217) 524-1880
E-mail: cmsinfo@pop.state.il.us   Internet: www.cms.illinois.gov

**Employees:** 1,370   **Fiscal Year:** 2015   **Budget:** $4,234,373,000

■Director (Acting) **Michael "Mike" Hoffman** . . . . . . . . . . . (312) 814-2648
Deputy Director, Business Enterprise Program
     **Paul H. Cerpa** . . . . . . . . . . . . . . . . . . . . . . . . . . . . . . (312) 814-4190
     100 West Randolph Street, 4th Floor, Chicago, IL 60601
Office Manager **Donna Lopez** . . . . . . . . . . . . . . . . . . . . . .(312) 814-2143
     E-mail: donna.lopez@illinois.gov
General Counsel **Michael Basil** . . . . . . . . . . . . . . . . . . . . . (312) 814-2322
Chief Administrative Officer **(Vacant)** . . . . . . . . . . . . . . . .(312) 814-0952
Budget Director **Karen Pape** . . . . . . . . . . . . . . . . . . . . . . . (217) 524-5323
Chief Internal Auditor (Illinois Office of Internal Audit)
     **Debbie Abbott** . . . . . . . . . . . . . . . . . . . . . . . . . . . . . . (217) 782-2645
Chief Operating Officer **(Vacant)** . . . . . . . . . . . . . . . . . . . .(312) 814-1900
Equal Opportunity Officer **Fred Stewart** . . . . . . . . . . . . . . (217) 558-6713

## Department of Children and Family Services [DCFS]
406 East Monroe Street, Springfield, IL 62701-1498
Tel: (217) 785-2509   Fax: (217) 524-0014

**Employees:** 2,600   **Fiscal Year:** 2015   **Budget:** $1,117,865,000

■Director **George H. Sheldon** . . . . . . . . . . . . . . . . . . . . . .(312) 814-6800
     E-mail: george.sheldon@illinois.gov
     Education: Florida State 1969 BA, 1978 JD
Chief of Staff **(Vacant)** . . . . . . . . . . . . . . . . . . . . . . . . . . . .(312) 814-6800
Child Protection Deputy Director **Chris Boyster** . . . . . . . . (312) 793-4676
Legislative Affairs Deputy Director **(Vacant)** . . . . . . . . . . . (217) 785-2504
Technology and Planning Division Director
     **Keith Schoonover** . . . . . . . . . . . . . . . . . . . . . . . . . . . .(217) 524-1510
     E-mail: keith.schoonover@illinois.gov

## Chicago Headquarters
100 West Randolph Street, 6th Floor, Chicago, IL 60601
TTY: (312) 814-6834   Fax: (312) 814-5986

Clinical Practice and Development Deputy Director
     **Larry Small** . . . . . . . . . . . . . . . . . . . . . . . . . . . . . . . . . (312) 814-4115
Communications Deputy Director **(Vacant)** . . . . . . . . . . . .(312) 814-6847
Bureau of Operations Deputy Director **Michael Ruppe** . . . . (312) 794-3500
Guardian and Advocacy/Guardianship Deputy Director
     **Debra Dyer-Webster** . . . . . . . . . . . . . . . . . . . . . . . . . .(312) 814-8600
     E-mail: debra.dyer-webster@illinois.gov
Human Resources Deputy Director **Tammy Grant** . . . . . . . (312) 814-1222
     E-mail: tammy.grant@illinois.gov
Quality Assurance and Research Deputy Director
     **Cynthia Richter-Jackson** . . . . . . . . . . . . . . . . . . . . . . (312) 814-5546
Legal Services Chief Counsel **Michelle D. Jackson** . . . . . . (312) 814-2367

## Illinois Department of Commerce and Economic Opportunity [DCEO]
500 East Monroe Street, Springfield, IL 62701-1643
100 West Randolph Street, Suite 3-400, Chicago, IL 60601
Tel: (217) 782-7500 (Springfield)   Tel: (312) 814-7179 (Chicago)
TTY: (800) 785-6055   Fax: (217) 524-0864 (Springfield)
Fax: (312) 814-4428 (Chicago)

**Employees:** 366   **Fiscal Year:** 2015   **Budget:** $748,799,000

■Director (Acting) **Sean McCarthy** . . . . . . . . . . . . (312) 814-2334 (Chicago)
     E-mail: sean.mccarthy@illinois.gov      Tel: (217) 785-6280
     Education: Stonehill BA; Dominican U (IL) MBA         (Springfield)
■Assistant Director **Andria Winters** . . . . . . . . . . . . . . . . . (312) 814-2811
     E-mail: andria.winters@illinois.gov
     Education: Michigan 2005 BA
Chief Accountability Officer (Acting) **Emily Monk** . . . . . . .(217) 524-4847
Chief Financial Officer **Travis March** . . . . . . . . . . . . . . . . (217) 524-4438
Chief Information Officer **Lisa Logan** . . . . . . . . . . . . . . . . .(217) 558-0424
     E-mail: lisa.logan@illinois.gov
Chief Internal Auditor **Natalie Covello** . . . . . . . . . . . . . . . (312) 814-8764
Chief Operating Officer **Brittany Ladd** . . . . . . . . . . . . . . . .(217) 782-7500
General Counsel **Justin Heather** . . . . . . . . . . . . . . . . . . . .(312) 814-6015
     E-mail: justin.heather@illinois.gov
Deputy General Counsel **Garrett Carter** . . . . . . . . . . . . . . (312) 814-6015
Chief of Staff **Anthony Esposito** . . . . . . . . . . . . . . . . . . . . (217) 782-7500
Deputy Chief of Staff **Kaitlyn Ezeocha** . . . . . . . . . . . . . . . (312) 814-6195
Human Resources Deputy Director **Teresa Smith** . . . . . . . (312) 814-5279
Office of Film Deputy Director **Christine T. Dudley** . . . . . .(312) 814-3600
Office of Film Assistant Deputy Director
     **Raul R. Esparza III** . . . . . . . . . . . . . . . . . . . . . . . . . . .(312) 814-7161
Legislative Affairs Deputy Director **Andrew Perkins** . . . . . (217) 785-6315
     E-mail: andrew.perkins@illinois.gov
Management Operations Deputy Director
     **Bonnie Van Tholen** . . . . . . . . . . . . . . . . . . . . . . . . . . (312) 814-6019
Policy Development, Planning and Research Office
     Deputy Director **(Vacant)** . . . . . . . . . . . . . . . . . . . . . . (312) 814-9407
Procurement Officer **Rick Rogers** . . . . . . . . . . . . . . . . . . .(217) 524-8148
Public Information Officer **Kyle Ann Sebastian** . . . . . . . . . (217) 782-7500

## Office of Business Development
100 W. Randolph Street, Suite 3, Chicago, IL 60601
Tel: (800) 252-2923 (First Stop Business Information Center)
Tel: (312) 814-1346

Deputy Director **Victor "Vic" Narusis** . . . . . . . . . . . . . . . .(312) 814-9592
Assistant Deputy Director **Antonio Baxton** . . . . . . . . . . . . (312) 814-3548
Business Finance Division Manager **Mark Gauss** . . . . . . . . (217) 785-6169

## Office of Community Development
Tel: (217) 785-6174

Deputy Director **David Wortman** . . . . . . . . . .(217) 558-4200 (Springfield)
     Tel: (312) 814-5701
        (Chicago)
Assistant Deputy Director **Wendy Bell** . . . . . . . . . . . . . . . .(217) 558-2838

## Energy Assistance Office
Deputy Director **Gail Hedges** . . . . . . . . . . . . . . . . . . . . . . (217) 784-1709

---

★ Elected Official    ■ Appointed by Governor    ● Appointed by Legislature    ▲ Appointed by Board or Commission    ◆ Appointed by State Supreme Court

*State Yellow Book*        © Leadership Directories, Inc.        Summer 2016

## Office of Employment and Training

Deputy Director **Julio Rodriguez** . . . . . . . . . . . . . . . . . . . . . . (312) 814-8421
E-mail: julio.rodriguez@illinois.gov

## Office of Energy and Recycling

Deputy Director **Marion "Molly" Lunn** . . . . . . . . . . . . . . (312) 814-2354

## Office of Entrepreneurship, Innovation and Technology

Deputy Director **Randy Kowalski** . . . . . . . . . . . . . . . . . (312) 814-8345
Assistant Deputy Director **Jennifer O'Rourke** . . . . . . . . . . (312) 814-8345

## Office of Grants Management

Deputy Director (Acting) **Mary Feagans** . . . . . . . . . . . . . (217) 785-2708

## Office of Marketing and Communications

Deputy Director **Tonya Lamia** . . . . . . . . . . . . . . . . . . . (312) 814-1182

## Office of Tourism

Fax: (312) 814-6175
■Deputy Director **Cory Jobe** . . . . . . . . . . . . . . . . . . . . . . (312) 814-4735
E-mail: cory.jobe@illinois.gov
Deputy Director **Jan Kemmerling** . . . . . . . . . . . . . . . . . . (217) 785-6351
620 East Adams Street, Springfield, IL 62701
Assistant Deputy Director **Eric Wagner** . . . . . . . . . . . . . . (312) 793-2369

## Department of Corrections [IDOC]

1301 Concordia Court, Springfield, IL 62794
P.O. Box 19277, Springfield, IL 62794-9277
Tel: (217) 558-2200  TTY: (800) 526-0844
Internet: www.illinois.gov/idoc

**Employees:** 10,800  **Fiscal Year:** 2015  **Budget:** $1,386,357,000

■Director (Acting) **John R. Baldwin** . . . . . . . . . . . . . . . . (217) 558-2200
Education: Iowa BBA; Iowa State MA
Secretary to the Director **(Vacant)** . . . . . . . . . . . . . . . . . (217) 558-2200
Assistant Director (Acting) **Gladyse Taylor** . . . . . (217) 557-6010 ext. 4002
Chief of Staff **Bryan Gleckler** . . . . . . . . . . . . . . . . . . . . (217) 558-2200
Chief Fiscal Officer **Jared Brunk** . . . . . . . . . . . . . . . . . . (217) 558-2200
Chief Information Officer **Steven A. Matthews** . . . . . . . . (217) 558-2200
E-mail: steven.matthews@doc.illinois.gov
Chief Legal Counsel **LaShonda A. Hunt** . . . . . . . . . . . . . (217) 558-2200
Education: Michigan 1995 JD
Chief Public Safety Officer **(Vacant)** . . . . . . . . . . . . . . . (217) 558-2200
Chief of Operations **Mike Warden Atchison** . . . . . . . . . . (217) 558-2200
Community Outreach Administrator **Marcus King** . . . . . . . (217) 558-2200
Intergovernmental Relations Chief **Michael R. Lane** . . . . . . (217) 558-2200
E-mail: michael.r.lane@doc.illinois.gov
Investigations and Intelligence Chief **Darryl L. Johnson** . . . (217) 558-2200
E-mail: darryl.johnson@illinois.gov
Parole Chief (Acting) **Tim Christianson** . . . . . . . . . . . . . (217) 558-2200
Programs and Support Services Chief **(Vacant)** . . . . . . . . . (217) 558-2200
Communications Director **Nicole Wilson** . . . . . . . . . . . . . (217) 558-2200

## Department of Employment Security [IDES]

33 South State Street, 9th Floor, Chicago, IL 60603
Tel: (800) 244-5631  TTY: (866) 322-8357  Fax: (312) 793-9834

**Employees:** 1,318  **Fiscal Year:** 2015  **Budget:** $228,494,000

■Director **Andrew Lockhart** . . . . . . . . . . . . . . . . . . . . . (312) 793-5022
Administration Deputy Director **Barbara Piwowarski** . . . . . (312) 793-9104
E-mail: barbara.piwowarski2@illinois.gov
Business Services Deputy Director **(Vacant)** . . . . . . . . . . . (312) 793-9842
Service Delivery Deputy Director **(Vacant)** . . . . . . . . . . . . (312) 793-1365
Chief Financial Officer **Linda DeMore** . . . . . . . . . . . . . . (312) 793-6255
Chief Information Officer **Monica Carranza** . . . . . . . . . . . (312) 793-2504
E-mail: monica.carranza@illinois.gov
Chief Legal Counsel **Joseph Mueller** . . . . . . . . . . . . . . . (312) 793-5704
850 East Madison, Springfield, IL 62702
E-mail: joseph.mueller@illinois.gov

## Department of Financial and Professional Regulation [IDFPR]

100 West Randolph Street, Suite 9-100, Chicago, IL 60601
Tel: (312) 814-4500  TTY: (217) 524-6735  Fax: (312) 814-2238
Internet: www.idfpr.com

**Employees:** 437  **Fiscal Year:** 2015  **Budget:** $79,540,000

■Secretary **Bryan A. Schneider** . . . . . . . . . . . . . . . . . . (312) 814-2837
E-mail: bryan.schneider@illinois.gov
General Counsel **Jessica Baer** . . . . . . . . . . . . . . . . . . . (312) 814-3230
Public Information Officer **Terry Horstman** . . . . . . . . . . . (217) 558-2953
E-mail: terry.horstman@illinois.gov

### Banking Division

Division Director **(Vacant)** . . . . . . . . . . . . . . . . . . . . . . (312) 793-1418
Banks and Thrift Assistant Director **Scott D. Clarke** . . . . . . (217) 785-1260
E-mail: scott.clarke@illinois.gov
Education: Western Illinois 1981 BA
Deputy General Counsel **Michael Diaz** . . . . . . . . . . . . . . (217) 524-4454

### Financial Institutions Division

Tel: (312) 814-2000  TTY: (312) 814-7138  Fax: (312) 814-5168
Internet: www.idfpr.com

Director **Francisco Menchaca** . . . . . . . . . . . . . . . . . . . (312) 814-5340
E-mail: francisco.menchaca@illinois.gov  Tel: (312) 814-2002

### Professional Regulation Division

Director **Jay Stewart** . . . . . . . . . . . . . . . . . . . . . . . . . (217) 782-9405
100 West Randolph, Room 9-100, Chicago, IL 60601
Assistant Director **Jeff Read** . . . . . . . . . . . . . . . . . . . . (217) 782-9405
General Counsel **Mark Thompson** . . . . . . . . . . . . . . . . . (312) 814-3079

## Illinois Department of Insurance [IDOI]

100 West Randolph Street, Suite 9-301, Chicago, IL 60601
Tel: (312) 814-2420  TTY: (312) 814-2603  Fax: (312) 814-5416
E-mail: director@ins.state.il.us

**Employees:** 260  **Fiscal Year:** 2015  **Budget:** $38,776,000

Director (Acting) **Anne Melissa Dowling** . . . . . . . . . . . . . (312) 814-5559
Education: Miss Porter's (Farmington, CT) 1976
Press Officer **Alissandra Calderon** . . . . . . . . . . . . . . . . (312) 814-5452

## Department of Healthcare and Family Services [HFS]

201 South Grand Avenue East, 3rd Floor, Springfield, IL 62763
Tel: (217) 782-1200  TTY: (800) 526-5812  Fax: (217) 524-7979
E-mail: hfs.webmaster@illinois.gov  Internet: www.hfs.illinois.gov

**Employees:** 2,103  **Fiscal Year:** 2015  **Budget:** $17,388,161,000

■Director **Felicia Norwood** . . . . . . . . . . . . . . . . . . . . . (217) 782-7755
E-mail: felicia.norwood@illinois.gov
E-mail: hfs.director@illinois.gov
Deputy Director **Michael D. Taylor** . . . . . . . . . . . . . . . . (217) 782-7755
Chief of Staff **Raymond "Ray" Marchiori** . . . . . . . . . . . . (217) 782-1200
Communications Director **John K. Hoffman** . . . . . . . . . . . (312) 793-6130
E-mail: john.k.hoffman@illinois.gov
Administrative Operations Deputy Director
**Richard Foxman** . . . . . . . . . . . . . . . . . . . . . . . . . . . (312) 793-4792
E-mail: richard.foxman@illinois.gov
Enterprise Architect **Edward "Ed" Carter** . . . . . . . . . . . . (217) 524-8350
E-mail: ed.carter@illinois.gov
Human Resources Deputy Director **(Vacant)** . . . . . . . . . . (217) 782-3323
New Initiatives and Quality Management Deputy Director
**Catina Latham** . . . . . . . . . . . . . . . . . . . . . . . . . . . (217) 782-1200
General Counsel **Mollie Zito** . . . . . . . . . . . . . . . . . . . . (312) 793-4792
Inspector General **Bradley Hart** . . . . . . . . . . . . . . . . . . (217) 785-7030
Tel: (312) 793-4053
All Kids Bureau Chief **Lynne Thomas** . . . . . . . . . . . . . . (217) 524-7156
Fax: (217) 557-4274
Legislative Affairs Chief **Shawn McGady** . . . . . . . . . . . . (217) 782-1212
E-mail: shawn.mcgady@illinois.gov

---

★ Elected Official   ■ Appointed by Governor   ● Appointed by Legislature   ▲ Appointed by Board or Commission   ◆ Appointed by State Supreme Court

Chief Information Officer **Julie Hagele** . . . . . . . . . . . . . . . (217) 557-9766
E-mail: julie.hagele@illinois.gov
Personnel Services Division Administrator **Terri Shawgo** . . (217) 558-4527
State Purchasing Officer **Lynette Schafer** . . . . . . . . . . . . . . (217) 558-3059
E-mail: lynette.schafer@illinois.gov
Child Support Services Division Administrator
**Pamela "Pam" Lowry** . . . . . . . . . . . . . . . . . . . . . . . . . . . (217) 782-1820
E-mail: pamela.lowry@illinois.gov
Finance Division Administrator **Mike Casey** . . . . . . . . . . . (217) 524-7480
E-mail: michael.p.casey@illinois.gov
Medical Programs Administrator **Teresa Hursey** . . . . . . . . (217) 782-2570
E-mail: teresa.hursey@illinois.gov                  Fax: (217) 782-5672
Managed Care Quality Manager **Ellen Amerson** . . . . . . . . (217) 558-1297
Webmaster **(Vacant)** . . . . . . . . . . . . . . . . . . . . . . . . . . . . . . (217) 785-9834

## Department of Human Rights [IDHR]

100 West Randolph Street, Suite 10-100, Chicago, IL 60601
Tel: (312) 814-6200  TTY: (312) 263-1579  Fax: (312) 814-1436
Internet: www2.illinois.gov/dhr

**Employees:** 32  **Fiscal Year:** 2015  **Budget:** $12,947,000

■Director **Rocco J. Claps** . . . . . . . . . . . . . . . . . . . . . . . . . . .(312) 814-6245
E-mail: rocco.claps@illinois.gov
Education: Illinois State 1983
Deputy Director **Bobbie Wanzo** . . . . . . . . . . . . . . . . . . . . (312) 814-6245
E-mail: bobbie.wanzo@illinois.gov
Chief Legal Counsel **Ngozi Okorafor** . . . . . . . . . . . . . . . . (312) 814-6262
E-mail: ngozi.okorafor@illinois.gov
Legislative Affairs **Hector Villagrana** . . . . . . . . . . . . . . . . (217) 785-5111
E-mail: hector.villagrana@illinois.gov
Charge Processing Division Manager **Brent Harzman** . . . . .(312) 814-6283
E-mail: brent.harzman@illinois.gov
Management Operations Manager **Burley Howard** . . . . . . .(312) 814-6259
E-mail: burley.howard@illinois.gov
Fiscal Officer **Marla Butler** . . . . . . . . . . . . . . . . . . . . . . . . (312) 814-6208

## Department of Human Services [DHS]

100 South Grand Avenue, East, Springfield, IL 62762
Tel: (800) 843-6154  TTY: (800) 447-6404  Fax: (217) 557-1647
Internet: www.dhs.state.il.us

**Employees:** 11,129  **Fiscal Year:** 2015  **Budget:** $6,419,211,000

■Secretary **James Dimas** . . . . . . . . . . . . . . . . . . . . . . . . . . .(312) 814-1547
Chief of Staff **Gregory M. "Greg" Bassi** . . . . . . . . . . . . . .(217) 557-1619
Communications Director **Marianne Manko** . . . . . . . . . . . (217) 558-1538
General Counsel **Fred Flather** . . . . . . . . . . . . . . . . . . . . . . (312) 814-2747
Grants Administration Director **Mary Jennings** . . . . . . . . .(800) 843-6154
Hispanic/Latino Affairs Director **(Vacant)** . . . . . . . . . . . . .(312) 793-4306
Human Resources Director **Scott Viniard** . . . . . . . . . . . . .(312) 793-2352
Innovation, Strategy and Performance Office Director
**Bruce Bendix** . . . . . . . . . . . . . . . . . . . . . . . . . . . . . . . . . (312) 793-3970
Legislative Affairs Director **Jennifer Aring** . . . . . . . . . . . . (217) 557-1551
E-mail: jennifer.aring@illinois.gov
Strategic Planning and Performance Director **(Vacant)** . . . . (217) 557-9363
Security and Emergency Preparedness Director (Acting)
**Kenneth "Ken" McCaffrey** . . . . . . . . . . . . . . . . . . . . . . . (217) 557-9363
Fax: (217) 557-9388
Senior Deputy General Counsel **Daniel Dyslin** . . . . . . . . . .(312) 814-6104
Division of Family and Community Services Associate
Director **Alan Summers** . . . . . . . . . . . . . . . . . . . . . . . . . (618) 993-7480

## Program Divisions

Assistant Secretary of Programs **(Vacant)** . . . . . . . . . . . . . (217) 524-0395
Alcoholism and Substance Abuse Division Director
**(Acting) Maria C. Bruni, PhD** . . . . . . . . . . . . . . . . . . . . (312) 814-2300
Education: Chicago 1997 PhD                  Tel: (217) 524-4138
Developmental Disabilities Division Director
**Gregory Fenton** . . . . . . . . . . . . . . . . . . . . . . . . . . . . . . . .(217) 524-7065
Family and Community Services Director
**Diane Grigsby Jackson** . . . . . . . . . . . . . . . . . . . . . . . . . . (312) 793-4627
Family and Community Services Assistant Director
**(Vacant)** . . . . . . . . . . . . . . . . . . . . . . . . . . . . . . . . . . . . . . (312) 793-4627
Rehabilitation Services Division Director **Kris Smith** . . . . . (217) 557-0401

### Mental Health Division

Mental Health Division Director **Diana Knaebe** . . . . . . . . . (312) 814-2300

## Operations

Operations Assistant Secretary **(Vacant)** . . . . . . . . . . . . . . (312) 793-1547
Chief Financial Officer **Robert Brock** . . . . . . . . . . . . . . . . .(217) 557-1543
Chief Operating Officer **Khari Hunt** . . . . . . . . . . . . . . . . . (312) 793-9954
Budget Director **Robert Brock** . . . . . . . . . . . . . . . . . . . . . .(217) 782-7522
Contract Administration Director **Brian Bertrand** . . . . . . . (800) 843-6154
Fiscal Services Division Director **(Vacant)** . . . . . . . . . . . . . (312) 793-9954
Chief Information Officer **Brad Long** . . . . . . . . . . . . . . . . . (217) 557-3166
E-mail: brad.long@illinois.gov
Customer Support Bureau Chief **(Vacant)** . . . . . . . . . . . . . (312) 793-1573
Business Services Director **Paul Hartman, Jr.** . . . . . . . . . . (217) 786-2168
E-mail: phartman@treasurer.il.gov
Clinical, Administrative and Program Support Office
Manager **(Vacant)** . . . . . . . . . . . . . . . . . . . . . . . . . . . . . (217) 557-9275
Procurement Officer **William Strahle** . . . . . . . . . . . . . . . . (217) 557-9298

## Department of Juvenile Justice [IDJJ]

707 North 15th Street, Springfield, IL 62702
Tel: (217) 557-1030  Internet: www.illinois.gov/idjj/

**Employees:** 962  **Fiscal Year:** 2015  **Budget:** $120,797,000

■Director **Candice Jones** . . . . . . . . . . . . . . . . . . . . . . . . . . .(312) 814-0085
E-mail: candice.jones@doc.illinois.gov
Education: Washington U (MO) BA; NYU JD
Deputy Director of Aftercare **Eva Moore** . . . . . . . . . . . . . .(312) 633-5219
Deputy Director of Operations **Jesse Montgomery** . . . . . . (630) 584-0506
Deputy Director of Programs **Heidi Mueller** . . . . . . . . . . . .(312) 814-3057
Chief Legal Counsel **Beth Compton** . . . . . . . . . . . . . . . . . (312) 814-5749
Chief of Staff **Jessica McMiller Baptiste** . . . . . . . . . . . . . . (312) 814-3308
Education: St Thomas U 2008
Chief of Mental Health Services **Dr. Jennifer Jaworski** . . . (630) 584-0506
Chief of Professional Development and Training
**Marna Goodman** . . . . . . . . . . . . . . . . . . . . . . . . . . . . . . (312) 814-6186
Chief of Intergovernmental Relations
**Sarah Myerscough-Mueller** . . . . . . . . . . . . . . . . . . . . . . (312) 814-1308
Labor Relations Administrator **Todd Creviston** . . . . . . . . . (630) 584-0506

## Department of Labor [IDOL]

160 North LaSalle Street, Suite C-1300, Chicago, IL 60601
Tel: (312) 793-2800  Fax: (312) 793-5257  E-mail: idol@illinois.gov
Internet: http://labor.illinois.gov/

**Employees:** 100  **Fiscal Year:** 2016  **Budget:** $35,521,000

■Director **Hugo Chaviano** . . . . . . . . . . . . . . . . . . . . . . . . . .(312) 793-2800
E-mail: hugo.chaviano@illinois.gov
Education: Rutgers 1975 BA; Northwestern 1978 JD
Assistant Director **Anna Hui** . . . . . . . . . . . . . . . . . . . . . . . (312) 793-1584
General Counsel **Helen J. Kim** . . . . . . . . . . . . . . . . . . . . . . (312) 793-1966
E-mail: helen.j.kim@illinois.gov
Carnival and Amusement Rides Division Manager
**Bill Szerletich** . . . . . . . . . . . . . . . . . . . . . . . . . . . . . . . . . (217) 782-9347
E-mail: bill.szerletich@illinois.gov
Fair Labor Standards Division Manager
**Beatriz Martorello** . . . . . . . . . . . . . . . . . . . . . . . . . . . . . (312) 793-1802
E-mail: beatriz.martorello@illinois.gov
Human Resources Director/Personnel Manager
**Ann Pufundt** . . . . . . . . . . . . . . . . . . . . . . . . . . . . . . . . . . (217) 557-0819
Safety Inspection and Education Division Manager
**Benjamin Noven** . . . . . . . . . . . . . . . . . . . . . . . . . . . . . . . (312) 793-0846
Legislative Liaison **Chris Wieneke** . . . . . . . . . . . . . . . . . . (217) 558-1270
E-mail: chris.wieneke@illinois.gov
Chief Financial Officer **Todd Miller** . . . . . . . . . . . . . . . . . . (217) 782-1709
Chief Information Officer **Krishna Brahmamdam** . . . . . . . (217) 792-3049
E-mail: krishna.brahmamdam@illinois.gov
Public Information Officer **Ben Noble** . . . . . . . . . . . . . . . . (312) 793-1626
E-mail: ben.noble@illinois.gov

★ Elected Official  ■ Appointed by Governor  ● Appointed by Legislature  ▲ Appointed by Board or Commission  ◆ Appointed by State Supreme Court

*State Yellow Book*                  © Leadership Directories, Inc.                  Summer 2016

# Illinois Lottery

122 S. Michigan Avenue, 19th Floor, Chicago, IL 60603
Tel: (217) 524-5240  Tel: (312) 793-3030  Fax: (312) 793-5514
Fax: (217) 785-3990  Internet: www.illinoislottery.com

■Director (Acting) **B.R. Lane** ........................... (312) 793-1681
  E-mail: b.r.lane@illinois.gov
Chief of Staff **Jayme Odom** ....................... (312) 793-1682
  E-mail: jayme.odom@illinois.gov
General Counsel **Nellie Ridsdale** 19th Floor ....... (312) 814-3512
Chief Financial Officer (Acting) **Brett A. Finley** ..... (217) 558-4817
Chief Operations and Technology Officer **Harold Mays** .. (312) 793-3048
  E-mail: harold.mays@illinois.gov
Communications Director **Stephen Rossi** ............. (312) 793-3034
  E-mail: stephen.rossi@illinois.gov

# Department of Military Affairs

1301 North MacArthur Boulevard, Springfield, IL 62702-2399
Tel: (217) 761-3500  TTY: (217) 761-3791  Fax: (217) 761-3736
E-mail: paoil@il.ngb.army.mil  Internet: www.il.ngb.army.mil

**Employees: 217  Fiscal Year: 2015  Budget: $37,021,000**

■Adjutant General **BG Richard J. Hayes, Jr., ARNG** ...... (217) 761-3500
Chief of Staff **COL Eric Little, ARNG** ................ (217) 761-3506
Joint Chief of Staff **COL Joseph Schweickert, ARNG** .... (217) 761-3506
Information Management Director
  **LTC Marc Sullivan, ARNG** ....................... (217) 761-1701
Staff Director (Air) **(Vacant)** ...................... (217) 761-3580
United States Property and Fiscal Officer
  **Melissa Beauman** ............................... (217) 761-3544
Joint Staff Director **BG Michael J. Glisson, ARNG** ...... (217) 761-3027
Webmaster **(Vacant)** ............................... (217) 761-1718

# Department of Natural Resources [IDNR]

One Natural Resources Way, Springfield, IL 62702-1271
Tel: (217) 782-6302  TTY: (217) 782-9175  Fax: (217) 785-9236
Internet: http://dnr.state.il.us

**Employees: 1,122  Fiscal Year: 2015  Budget: $191,298,000**

■Director **Wayne Arthur Rosenthal** ................(217) 785-0075
  E-mail: wayne.a.rosenthal@illinois.gov
  Education: Sangamon State 1974 BA
  Deputy Director **(Vacant)** ....................... (847) 608-3100
Chief of Staff **Jason Heffley** ...................... (217) 785-0075
Legal Services Office Director **Brett Krebbs** ........ (217) 782-1809
Legislation Office Director **(Vacant)** ............... (217) 785-0075
Human Resources Manager **Michele Cusumano** ........(217) 782-1274
Agency Procurement Officer **Karen Rueter** ........... (217) 782-0356
Chief Fiscal Officer **Doug Florence** ................. (217) 524-8538
Equal Employment Opportunity Officer **Jay Johnson** ..... (217) 782-2662

# Architecture, Engineering and Grants Office

Tel: (217) 782-2605

Division Manager **Bob Appleman** ................... (217) 782-3050

# Land Management Office

Director **Ronald "Rin" House** ..................... (217) 524-1265

# Law Enforcement Office

Director **Rafael Gutierrez** ........................ (217) 785-8403
  Education: Illinois BS

# Mines and Minerals Office

Tel: (217) 782-6791  TTY: (217) 524-4626  Fax: (217) 524-4819

Director **Jim Hafliger** ............................ (217) 782-6791
  E-mail: jim.hafliger@illinois.gov
Abandoned Mines Division Supervisor (Interim)
  **Greg Pinto** .................................... (217) 785-0398
Blasting and Explosives Division Operations Supervisor
  **Michael "Mike" Falter** ......................... (217) 785-9019
Land Reclamation Division Supervisor **Scott Fowler** ..... (217) 782-4970

Mine Safety and Training Division Manager **(Vacant)** .... (217) 558-1223
Oil and Gas Division Supervisor **Doug Shutt** ......... (217) 782-7756

# Realty and Environmental Planning Office

Director **Connie Waggoner** ........................(217) 524-5464
Eco Systems and Environment Manager (Acting)
  **Keith Shank** ...................................(217) 785-5500
Concession and Lease Management Division Manager
  **Bill Taft** ..................................... (217) 782-9633
Realty and Planning Division Manager (Acting)
  **Pat Brannan** ................................... (217) 782-7940

# Resource Conservation Office

Director **James "Jim" Herkert** .....................(217) 785-8272
Fisheries Division Chief **Dan Stephenson** ...........(217) 524-4111
  E-mail: dan.stephenson@illinois.gov
Natural Heritage Chief **Ann Holtrop** ................ (217) 785-4325
Wildlife Division Program Manager **John Buhnerkempe** ..(217) 782-6384

# Scientific Research and Analysis Office

Director **(Vacant)** ............................... (217) 524-9506
Illinois State Museum Director **Bonnie W. Styles** ........(217) 782-7475
  502 South Spring Street, Springfield, IL 62706    Fax: (217) 782-1254
  E-mail: bstyles@museum.state.il.us

# Strategic Services Offices

Tel: (217) 782-0179

Director **(Vacant)** ............................... (217) 524-4395
Agency Communications Coordinator
  **Shaun Stoutamyer** ..............................(217) 782-6232
  E-mail: shaun.stoutamyer@illinois.gov
Agency Vehicle Coordinator **Tom Dyson** ............. (217) 782-1533
  E-mail: tom.dyson@illinois.gov
Education Division Manager **Valerie Keener** .......... (217) 785-0973
Marketing Services Manager **Michelle Silver** ..........(217) 785-8610
Photographic Services Manager **Adele Hodde** .......... (217) 785-0064
  E-mail: adele.hodde@illinois.gov
Publication Services Manager **(Vacant)** ............. (217) 785-4193
Systems and Licensing Division Manager **(Vacant)** ...... (217) 782-6232

# Water Resources Office

Director **(Vacant)** ............................... (217) 785-3334
Administrative Assistant **Nicole Bergee** ............. (217) 782-1808
  E-mail: nicole.bergee@illinois.gov

# Illinois Department of Public Health [IDPH]

535 West Jefferson Street, Springfield, IL 62702
Tel: (217) 557-2556  Tel: (217) 557-3497 (Vital Records)
TTY: (800) 547-0466  Internet: www.idph.state.il.us

**Employees: 1,150  Fiscal Year: 2015  Budget: $405,115,000**

# Office of the Director

■Director **Dr. Nirav Dinesh Shah, MD** ................(217) 557-2556
  E-mail: nirav.shah@illinois.gov
  Senior Medical Advisor to the Director (Acting)
    **Arthur F. Kohrman** ...........................(312) 814-4846
                                          Fax: (312) 814-4845
  Assistant Director **Michelle Gentry-Wiseman** ........ (217) 557-2556
  Chief of Staff **Erik Rayman** ..................... (217) 557-2556
  Chief Legal Counsel **Kyle Stone** ................. (217) 782-2043
    E-mail: kyle.stone@illinois.gov
  Governmental Affairs Division Chief **Bryan Clow** ........ (217) 782-6187
    E-mail: bryan.clow@illinois.gov
  Minority Health Services Chief (Acting)
    **Veronica Halloway** ............................ (217) 785-4311
  State Medical Cannabis Statewide Program Coordinator
    **Joseph Wright** ................................ (312) 814-3803
    Education: Chicago-Kent JD

---

★ Elected Official   ■ Appointed by Governor   ● Appointed by Legislature   ▲ Appointed by Board or Commission   ◆ Appointed by State Supreme Court

EXECUTIVE BRANCH

## Finance and Administration Office

Tel: (217) 785-2033

Deputy Director **Vicki Wilson** ........................(217) 785-2033
E-mail: vicki.wilson@illinois.gov
Budget Manager **Ted Hasara** .......................(217) 785-2033
Physical Services Division Chief (Acting) **Vicki Wilson** . . . (217) 785-2033
E-mail: vicki.wilson@illinois.gov

## Health Care Regulation Office

Tel: (217) 782-5180  Fax: (217) 524-6292

Deputy Director (Acting) **Debra Bryars** ...............(217) 782-5180
Administrative Rules and Procedures Division Chief
(Acting) **Sean Dailey**............................(217) 785-5566
E-mail: sean.dailey@illinois.gov          Fax: (217) 524-0137
Assisted Living Division Chief **Lynda Kovarik**..........(217) 782-2448
E-mail: lynda.kovarik@illinois.gov          Fax: (217) 557-2432
Health Care Facilities and Programs Division Chief
(Acting) **Debra Bryars**..........................(217) 782-7412
E-mail: debra.bryars@illinois.gov
Life Safety and Construction Division Chief
**Henry Kowalenko**................................(217) 785-4264
Fax: (217) 782-0382
Long-Term Care Field Operations Division Chief
**Connie Jensen** ................................(217) 785-2692
E-mail: connie.jensen@illinois.gov          Fax: (217) 782-0382
Long-Term Care Quality Assurance Division Chief
**Darlene Harney**................................(217) 782-5180
E-mail: darlene.harney@illinois.gov          Fax: (217) 785-4200

## Health Promotion Office

Deputy Director (Acting) **Conny Moody** ...............(217) 782-3300
Division of Health Assessment and Screening Chief
(Acting) **Conny Moody**............................(217) 782-3300
Assistant Deputy Director **Joe Mitchell** ...............(217) 782-3300
Medical Cannabis Division Chief (Acting)
**Conny Moody**....................................(855) 636-3688

## Health Protection Office

Tel: (217) 782-3984  Fax: (217) 524-0802

Deputy Director **David W. Culp, PhD** .................(217) 782-3984
Medical Director (Acting) **Arthur F. Kohrman**..........(312) 814-4846
Fax: (312) 814-4844
Assistant Medical Director **(Vacant)** ..................(312) 814-4846
Fax: (312) 814-4844
State Epidemiologist **Dr. Connie Austin** ...............(312) 814-4846
Environmental Health Division Chief **Ken McCann**.......(217) 782-5830
Fax: (217) 785-0253
Food, Drugs and Dairies Division Chief **Molly Lamb** .....(217) 785-2439
Fax: (217) 782-0943
Infectious Diseases Division Chief
**Tal Holmes, PhD, MPH** ..........................(217) 782-3984
Fax: (217) 557-4049
Laboratories Division Chief (Acting) **Matt Charles** .......(217) 782-6562
Fax: (217) 524-7924
HIV/AIDS Section Chief (Acting)
**Tal Holmes, PhD, MPH** ..........................(217) 782-1207
State Public Health Veterinarian **Dr. Connie Austin**......(217) 785-7165

## Human Resources Office

Deputy Director **Siobhan Johnson** ..................(217) 785-2031

## Office of Policy, Planning and Statistics

Deputy Director **Bill Dart** ...........................(217) 785-2040
Epidemiological Studies Division Chief **Tiefu Shen** ......(217) 785-1873
Health Policy Division Chief **(Vacant)** .................(217) 782-6235
Health Statistics Center Chief **Bill Dart** ...............(217) 785-2040
Health Systems Development Division Chief and
Assistant Deputy Director (Acting) **Bill Dart** ..........(217) 785-2040
Rural Health Center Chief (Acting) **Bill Dart** ...........(217) 785-2040
Patient Safety and Quality Division Chief **(Vacant)** .......(312) 814-1097
Vital Records Division Chief **Joseph "Joe" Aiello**.......(217) 782-6554
925 East Ridgely Avenue,          Fax: (217) 785-3209
Springfield, IL 62702-2737

## Women's Health Office

Deputy Director and Title V Director
**Shannon R. Lightner-Gometz** ..........(217) 785-1050 (Springfield)
Tel: (312) 814-1884
(Chicago)
Maternal Child and Family Services Division Chief
**Andrea Palmer** .................................(312) 814-1884
Women's Health Services Division Chief **Joyce E. Hall** . . . (312) 793-1171
Population Health Management Division Chief (Acting)
**Sarah O'Connor-Bennett** .........................(217) 524-9297
E-mail: sarah.oconnor@illinois.gov

## State Board of Health

▲ Chairman **Babette Seligmann Sanders, PT** ...........(217) 782-6187

## Preparedness and Response Office

Deputy Director **Gina Swehla** .......................(217) 558-0560
Disaster Planning and Readiness Division Chief
(Acting) **Winfred C. Rawls** .......................(217) 558-0560
Emergency Medical Services and Highway Safety
Division Chief **Jack Fleeharty**....................(217) 557-3911

## Department of Revenue

101 West Jefferson Street, Springfield, IL 62702
Tel: (217) 782-3336  Fax: (217) 782-4217

**Employees:** 1,691  **Fiscal Year:** 2015  **Budget:** $674,703,000

■ Director **Constance "Connie" Beard**..................(217) 785-7570
E-mail: connie.beard@illinois.gov          Fax: (217) 782-6337
Education: Eastern Illinois 1976 BA; Illinois 1979 JD
Assistant to the Director **Paula Bell** ..................(217) 785-7570
Assistant Director **Ed Buckles** ......................(217) 785-2607
Chief of Staff **Kevin Conner** .......................(217) 785-2607
Legislative Office Manager **Jane McEnaney** ...........(217) 785-5918
E-mail: jane.mcenaney@illinois.gov
Chief Budget Officer **Cory Staley** ....................(217) 782-7288
Chief Information Officer **Tom Pantier** ................(217) 782-3804
General Counsel **Mark Dyckman** ....................(312) 814-3190
100 West Randolph Street, Chicago, IL 60601

## Department of Transportation [IDOT]

2300 South Dirksen Parkway, Springfield, IL 62764
Tel: (217) 782-7820  TTY: (217) 524-4875  Internet: www.dot.il.gov

**Employees:** 5,214  **Fiscal Year:** 2015  **Budget:** $2,320,729,000

■ Secretary **Randall S. Blankenhorn** ...................(217) 782-5597
E-mail: randy.blankenhorn@illinois.gov
■ Deputy Secretary **(Vacant)** .........................(217) 782-7820
■ Assistant Secretary **Rich Brauer** .....................(312) 793-2250
100 West Randolph Street, Chicago, IL 60601
E-mail: rich.brauer@illinois.gov
Chief of Staff **Matthew A. MaGalis**...................(217) 782-0692
Chief Communications Officer **(Vacant)** ...............(217) 782-7820
Chief Operating Officer **(Vacant)**.....................(217) 782-7820
Librarian **Karen Perrin** .............................(217) 782-6680

## Office of Business and Workforce Diversity

Director **Pamela Simon** ............................(217) 785-5395
Deputy Director (Acting) **Bruce A. Harmening** .........(312) 793-2966
Small Business Enterprises Bureau Chief **(Vacant)** .......(217) 785-5947

## Office of Chief Counsel

Chief Counsel **William "Bill" Barnes, Jr., JD** ..........(312) 793-2255
Education: Northwestern 1992 BA, 1999 JD
Deputy Chief Counsel **Richard Kabaker** ..............(312) 793-4838
Deputy Chief Counsel **Phillip Kaufmann** ..............(312) 793-2255
Claims Bureau Chief **James Sterr** ...................(217) 782-6263
Civil Rights Bureau Chief (Acting) **Karen Ward** ........(217) 785-2762
Fax: (217) 524-4063

## Office of Communications

Director **(Vacant)** .................................(217) 558-0665

*(continued on next page)*

---

★ Elected Official      ■ Appointed by Governor      ● Appointed by Legislature      ▲ Appointed by Board or Commission      ◆ Appointed by State Supreme Court

**Office of Communications** continued

Deputy Director **Guy Tridgell**..........................(312) 793-4199
  E-mail: guy.tridgell@illinois.gov
  Education: Drake 1994
Communications Services Bureau Chief **(Vacant)** ........(217) 782-5025

## Office of Finance and Administration
Director **Jeff Heck**.....................................(217) 524-4686
  E-mail: jeff.heck@illinois.gov
Deputy Director **(Vacant)**...............................(217) 782-4665
Deputy Director **(Vacant)**...............................(217) 557-0118
Budget and Fiscal Management Bureau Chief
  **Joanne Woodworth**...................................(217) 782-5434
Business Services Bureau Chief **Lori Campbell**.........(217) 524-8151
  E-mail: lori.campbell@illinois.gov
Information Processing Bureau Chief **Dan Wilcox**.......(217) 785-2400
  E-mail: dan.wilcox@illinois.gov
Personnel Management Bureau Chief **Dianna Taylor**......(217) 782-4665

## Office of Planning and Programming
Director (Interim) **Jeffrey "Jeff" South**...............(217) 782-6289
  E-mail: jeffrey.south@illinois.gov
Deputy Director **(Vacant)**...............................(312) 793-0493
Deputy Director **(Vacant)**...............................(217) 782-6332
Statewide Program Planning Bureau Chief
  **Jeffrey "Jeff" South**................................(217) 782-2755
  E-mail: jeffrey.south@illinois.gov
Urban Program Planning Bureau Chief **Karen Shoup**.....(217) 782-7868
  E-mail: karen.shoup@illinois.gov
Policy and Federal Affairs Bureau Chief **Jeff Bell**.......(217) 785-4050

## Office of Quality Compliance and Review
201 West Center Court, 1st Floor, Schaumburg, IL 61096
Director **Jeff Heck**.....................................(847) 221-3000
  E-mail: jeff.heck@illinois.gov

## Aeronautics Division
Capital Airport, Number One Langhorn Bond Drive, Springfield, IL 62707
Director **Steven Young**.................................(217) 785-8515
Deputy Director **(Vacant)**...............................(217) 782-7820
Administrative Services Bureau Chief **(Vacant)**..........(217) 785-8512
Air Operations Bureau Chief **Steven Young**.............(217) 785-8544
Airport Engineering Bureau Chief (Acting)
  **Steven J. Long**.....................................(217) 785-8514
Aviation Safety Bureau Chief **Linda Schumm**...........(217) 785-8516
  E-mail: linda.schumm@illinois.gov

## Highways Division
Director/Chief Engineer **Omer Osman**..................(217) 785-0888
  E-mail: omer.osman@illinois.gov
Deputy Director/Assistant Chief Engineer
  **Aaron Weatherholt**..................................(217) 782-2101
  E-mail: aaron.weatherholt@illinois.gov
Deputy Director (Acting) **Justan Mann**................(217) 782-2101
  E-mail: justan.mann@illinois.gov
Deputy Director/Region 1 Engineer **John Fortmann**.....(847) 705-4000
  E-mail: john.fortmann@illinois.gov
Deputy Director/Region 2 Engineer **Paul Loete**.........(815) 284-2271
  E-mail: paul.loete@illinois.gov
Deputy Director/Region 3 Engineer **Kensil E. Garnett**....(309) 671-3333
  E-mail: kensil.garnett@illinois.gov
Deputy Director/Region 4 Engineer **Roger L. Driskell**....(217) 342-3951
  E-mail: roger.driskell@illinois.gov
Deputy Director/Region 5 Engineer **Jeffrey Keirn**.......(618) 346-3110
Bridges and Structures Bureau Chief (Acting)
  **Carl Puzey**.........................................(217) 782-2124
  E-mail: carl.puzey@illinois.gov
Construction Bureau Chief (Acting) **Timothy Kell**......(217) 782-6667
  E-mail: tim.kell@illinois.gov
Design and Environmental Bureau Chief **Maureen Addis**..(217) 782-7526
Land Acquisition Bureau Chief (Acting)
  **Salmon O. Danmole**.................................(217) 782-6243
Local Roads and Streets Bureau Chief (Acting)
  **James "Jim" Klein**.................................(217) 782-3805

Materials and Physical Research Bureau Chief (Acting)
  **Laura Mlacnik**......................................(217) 782-7200
  E-mail: laura.mlacnik@illinois.gov
Operations Bureau Chief (Acting) **Amy Eller**...........(217) 782-7231
Safety Engineering Bureau Chief **Priscilla Tobias**.......(217) 782-3568
  E-mail: priscilla.tobias@illinois.gov

## Public and Intermodal Transportation Division
300 West Adams, Chicago, IL 60606
Fax: (312) 793-1251
Director **Beth McCluskey**..............................(312) 793-2111
Deputy Director **John E. Oimoen**......................(312) 793-4222
Deputy Director **David T. Spacek**......................(312) 793-2154
Create and Freight Rail Bureau Chief **Samuel Tuck**......(312) 793-3940
High Speed and Passenger Rail Bureau Chief **(Vacant)**....(217) 782-4133
Transit Capital Bureau Chief **Carlos Campos**...........(312) 793-2328
Transit Operations Bureau Chief **John Marrella**.........(312) 793-3616

## Traffic Safety Division
1340 North 9th Street, Springfield, IL 62702
P.O. Box 9484, Springfield, IL 62794
Fax: (217) 782-9159
Director **Jared Thornley**..............................(217) 558-5095
Administrative Services and Safety Programs Bureau
  Chief (Interim) **Ken Martin**.........................(217) 558-2499
Safety Data and Data Services Bureau Chief
  **Jessica Keldermans**.................................(217) 782-6518
  E-mail: jessica.keldermans@illinois.gov

## Department of Veterans Affairs [DVA]
833 South Spring Street, Springfield, IL 62794-9432
P.O. Box 19432, Springfield, IL 62794
Tel: (217) 782-6641
Tel: (217) 782-3564 (POW/MIA Veterans Scholarship Info)
Tel: (800) 437-9824 (Veterans Information)  Fax: (217) 524-0344

**Employees:** 1,208  **Fiscal Year:** 2015  **Budget:** $120,896,000

■Director **Erica Jeffries**...............................(217) 785-4114
  Education: West Point 1998 BS; Georgetown 2008 MA;
  Virginia Tech 2014 MBA
  Assistant to the Director **Edie Long**.................(217) 785-4114
■Assistant Director **Harry F. Sawyer**..................(815) 730-4327
  E-mail: harry.sawyer@illinois.gov
Human Resources Manager **Miguel Calderon**..........(217) 782-5765
Chief of Staff **Renysha Brown**........(217) 785-2775 (Springfield)
Chief Legal Counsel **Matthew Roberts**........(312) 814-5391 (Chicago)
State Approving Agency Administrator
  **Dan Wellman**.......................(217) 782-7838 (Springfield)
  E-mail: dan.wellman@illinois.gov         Tel: (312) 814-1121
                                                    (Chicago)
Legislative Liaison **Jaimee Ray**.......................(217) 524-7278
Veterans Education Specialist **Melissa Cushman**........(217) 785-4578

## Illinois Emergency Management Agency [IEMA]
2200 South Dirksen Parkway, Springfield, IL 62703
Tel: (217) 782-2700  Fax: (217) 524-7967
E-mail: iema_webmaster@state.il.us  Internet: www.state.il.us/iema

**Fiscal Year:** 2015  **Budget:** $155,882,000

■Director **James Joseph**...............................(217) 782-2700
  E-mail: james.joseph@illinois.gov
  Assistant to the Director **Sarah Plinski**.............(217) 558-4110
Assistant Director **Joseph G. Klinger**.................(217) 785-2700
  Education: Texas BS; Southwest Texas State MS
  Executive Secretary **Lori Beagles**...................(217) 785-9868
Operations Chief **(Vacant)**............................(217) 557-4794
Chief Legal Counsel **(Vacant)**.........................(217) 524-0770
Labor Relations Administrator **Kevin Moore**...........(217) 782-3184
  E-mail: kevin.moore@illinois.gov

★ Elected Official  ■ Appointed by Governor  ● Appointed by Legislature  ▲ Appointed by Board or Commission  ◆ Appointed by State Supreme Court

Summer 2016          © Leadership Directories, Inc.          State Yellow Book

Legislative Liaison **Eric Murphy** . . . . . . . . . . . . . . . . . . . . . . (217) 557-4828
  E-mail: eric.murphy@illinois.gov
  Education: Western Illinois 2008 BA
Public Information Officer **Patti Thompson** . . . . . . . . . . . .(217) 557-4756
  E-mail: patti.thompson@illinois.gov
Radiation Safety Bureau Chief **Adnan Khayyat** . . . . . . . . .(217) 782-1329

## Illinois Environmental Protection Agency [IEPA]

P.O. Box 19276, Springfield, IL 62794-9276
Tel: (217) 782-3397  TTY: (217) 782-9143  Fax: (217) 782-9039
Internet: www.epa.illinois.gov

**Employees:** 829  **Fiscal Year:** 2015  **Budget:** $211,002,000

■Director **Lisa Bonnett** . . . . . . . . . . . . . . . . . . . . . . . . . . . . . (217) 782-0547
  E-mail: lisa.bonnett@illinois.gov
Chief of Staff **Sherrie Elzinga** . . . . . . . . . . . . . . . . . . . . . . . (217) 782-3397
Chief Financial Officer **Carol Radwine** . . . . . . . . . . . . . . . (217) 524-4337
Public Information Officer (Acting)
  **Kimberly "Kim" Biggs** . . . . . . . . . . . . . . . . . . . . . . . . . . (217) 558-1536
  E-mail: kim.biggs@illinois.gov
Legislative Affairs Chief **Donovan Griffith** . . . . . . . . . . . (217) 782-0547
  E-mail: donovan.griffith@illinois.gov
Librarian **Tracy Pierceall** . . . . . . . . . . . . . . . . . . . . . . . . . . (217) 782-9691
Webmaster **Wally Hartshorn** . . . . . . . . . . . . . . . . . . . . . . . (217) 785-6882
  E-mail: wally.hartshorn@illinois.gov

## Environmental Operations and Administration

Deputy Director **Ryan McCreery** . . . . . . . . . . . . . . . . . . . . .(217) 782-0547
Laboratories Division Manager **Thomas Weiss** . . . . . . . . . .(217) 782-9780

## Legal Affairs, Community Relations and Pollution Prevention

Associate Director **(Vacant)** . . . . . . . . . . . . . . . . . . . . . . . . .(217) 557-7826
Legal Counsel Division General Counsel and Ethics
  Officer **John J. Kim** . . . . . . . . . . . . . . . . . . . . . . . . . . . . . (217) 782-5544
Community Relations Manager **Brad Frost** . . . . . . . . . . . . .(217) 782-5562

## Illinois Historic Preservation Agency [IHPA]

Old State Capitol, Springfield, IL 62701
Tel: (217) 782-4836  TTY: (217) 524-7128  Fax: (217) 785-7937
E-mail: hpa.info@illinois.gov

▲Director **Heidi Brown-McCreery** . . . . . . . . . . . . . . . . . . . .(217) 785-7930
  E-mail: heidi.brown-mccreery@illinois.gov
Deputy Director **(Vacant)** . . . . . . . . . . . . . . . . . . . . . . . . . . (217) 785-9045
Executive Office Manager **Cheryl Dawson** . . . . . . . . . . . . .(217) 785-1511
Legislative Director **Peggy Snyder** . . . . . . . . . . . . . . . . . . . (217) 785-9045
  E-mail: peggy.snyder@illinois.gov
Administrative Services Division Director
  **Michael Norris** . . . . . . . . . . . . . . . . . . . . . . . . . . . . . . . .(217) 785-9383
  E-mail: michael.norris@illinois.gov
Historic Sites Division Director **Ryan Prehn** . . . . . . . . . . .(217) 785-1584
Preservation Services Division Director
  **Rachel Leibowitz** . . . . . . . . . . . . . . . . . . . . . . . . . . . . . . (217) 785-5031
Administrative Assistant **Thomas Carlisle** . . . . . . . . . . . . . (217) 785-7929
Chief Legal Counsel **Garth Madison** . . . . . . . . . . . . . . . . . (217) 785-1511

## Office of the State Appellate Defender [OSAD]

400 West Monroe, Springfield, IL 62704
P.O. Box 5240, Springfield, IL 62705
TTY: (217) 782-5384  Fax: (217) 782-5385

**Employees:** 220  **Fiscal Year:** 2015  **Budget:** $19,908,000

◆State Appellate Defender **Michael J. Pelletier** . . . . . . . . . .(217) 782-7203
  E-mail: michael.pelletier@illinois.gov
  Education: Northern Illinois 1972 BA; John Marshall 1976 JD
Deputy State Appellate Defender **David Bergschneider** . . . (217) 782-7203
Deputy State Appellate Defender **James Chadd** . . . . . . . . . (312) 814-5472

Chief Fiscal Officer **Tonya L. Janecek** . . . . . . . . . . . . . . . . (217) 782-7203

## Illinois State's Attorneys Appellate Prosecutor [ILSAAP]

725 South Second Street, Springfield, IL 62704
Tel: (217) 782-1628  TTY: (217) 557-2618  Fax: (217) 782-6305

**Employees:** 81  **Fiscal Year:** 2015  **Budget:** $19,828,000

▲Director **Patrick J. Delfino** . . . . . . . . . . . . . . . . . . . . . . . . .(217) 782-1628
  E-mail: pdelfino@ilsaap.org
  Education: Notre Dame
Associate Director for Administration
  **Matthew "Matt" Jones** . . . . . . . . . . . . . . . . . . . . . . . . . .(217) 782-1628
  E-mail: mjones@ilsaap.org
  Education: Illinois 1988 BA, 1991 JD

## Office of the State Fire Marshal

1035 Stevenson Drive, Springfield, IL 62703-4259
Tel: (217) 785-0969  Fax: (217) 782-1062

**Employees:** 130  **Fiscal Year:** 2015  **Budget:** $27,624,000

■State Fire Marshal **Matthew Perez** . . . . . . . . . . . . . . . . . . .(312) 814-8959
  Education: Southern IL Edwardsville 2010 BS
  Executive Assistant **Katherine Nunes** . . . . . . . . . . . . . . .(312) 814-8959
Deputy Director **Les Albert** . . . . . . . . . . . . . . . . . . . . . . . . .(217) 558-1751
Chief of Operations **Kevin Schott** . . . . . . . . . . . . . . . . . . . .(217) 785-1030
Chief Counsel **Matt Taksin** . . . . . . . . . . . . . . . . . . . . . . . . . (217) 785-1519
Media Coordinator **Jacquelyn Reineke** . . . . . . . . . . . . . . . (312) 485-8227
  E-mail: jacquelyn.reineke@illinois.gov

## Illinois Criminal Justice Information Authority [ICJIA]

300 West Adams Street, Suite 700, Chicago, IL 60606
Tel: (312) 793-8550  TTY: (312) 793-4170  Fax: (312) 793-8422
E-mail: cja.info@illinois.gov  E-mail: cja.irc@illinois.gov
Internet: www.icjia.state.il.us

**Employees:** 75  **Fiscal Year:** 2015  **Budget:** $51,051,000

■Executive Director **John Maki** . . . . . . . . . . . . . . . . . . . . . . .(312) 793-8550
  E-mail: john.maki@illinois.gov
Deputy Director **Randy Kurtz** . . . . . . . . . . . . . . . . . . . . . . . (312) 793-8550
General Counsel **Lisa Stephens** . . . . . . . . . . . . . . . . . . . . . .(312) 793-8550
  E-mail: lisa.stephens@illinois.gov
Federal and State Grants Unit Associate Director
  **Kevin N. Givens** . . . . . . . . . . . . . . . . . . . . . . . . . . . . . . .(312) 793-1300
  Education: Southern U A&M BME; Xavier (LA) BS;
  Keller Grad School MBA
Human Resources Associate Director **Luz Agosto** . . . . . . . .(312) 793-8550
Information Systems Unit Associate Director
  **Tony Jenkins** . . . . . . . . . . . . . . . . . . . . . . . . . . . . . . . . . .(312) 793-8550
  E-mail: anthony.jenkins@illinois.gov
Research and Analysis Unit Associate Director
  **Megan Alderden** . . . . . . . . . . . . . . . . . . . . . . . . . . . . . . .(312) 793-8550
  E-mail: megan.alderden@illinois.gov

## Illinois Finance Authority [IFA]

160 North LaSalle Street, Suite C-1000, Chicago, IL 60601
P.O. Box 641249, Chicago, IL 60664
Tel: (312) 651-1300  Fax: (312) 651-1350  Internet: www.il-fa.com

■Executive Director **Christopher B. Meister** . . . . . . . . . . . . (312) 651-1310
  E-mail: cmeister@il-fa.com
Executive Assistant **Mari Money** . . . . . . . . . . . . . . . . . . . . .(312) 651-1300
  E-mail: mmoney@il-fa.com
General Counsel and FOIA Officer **Elizabeth Weber** . . . . .(312) 651-1340
Human Resources Officer **Ximena Granda** . . . . . . . . . . . . (312) 651-1300
  Education: Northeastern Illinois 2004 BAcc

---

★ Elected Official    ■ Appointed by Governor    ● Appointed by Legislature    ▲ Appointed by Board or Commission    ◆ Appointed by State Supreme Court

EXECUTIVE BRANCH

# Illinois Housing Development Authority [IHDA]

401 North Michigan Avenue, Suite 700, Chicago, IL 60611
Tel: (312) 836-5200  TTY: (312) 836-5222  Fax: (312) 832-2170
Internet: www.ihda.org

▲Executive Director **Audra Hamernik** . . . . . . . . . . . . . . . . . . (312) 836-5314
  E-mail: ahamernik@ihda.org
Chief of Staff **Debbie Olson** . . . . . . . . . . . . . . . . . . . . . . . . (312) 836-5344
General Counsel **Maureen G. Ohle** . . . . . . . . . . . . . . . . . . . (312) 836-5339
  E-mail: maohle@ihda.org
  Education: Illinois (Springfield) BA; Columbus Law JD
Chief Financial Officer/Assistant Treasurer
  **Nandini Natarajan** . . . . . . . . . . . . . . . . . . . . . . . . . . . . (312) 836-7345
  Education: UMass (Amherst) MS
Controller (Acting) **Ronald Gajos** . . . . . . . . . . . . . . . . . . . . (312) 836-5285

# State Toll Highway Authority

2700 Ogden Avenue, Downers Grove, IL 60515
Tel: (630) 241-6800  TTY: (630) 241-6898  Fax: (630) 241-6102
Internet: www.illinoistollway.com

■Chairperson **Robert Schillerstron** . . . . . . . . . . . (630) 241-6800 ext. 1100
Executive Director **Greg Bedalov** . . . . . . . . . . . . (630) 241-6800 ext. 1000
Chief of Administration **Deborah Allen** . . . . . . . . . . . . . . (630) 241-6800
Chief of Business Systems **Shana Whitehead** . . . . . . . . . (630) 241-6800
Chief of Communications **Cindy Klima** . . . . . . . . . . . . . (630) 241-6800
Chief of Diversity and Strategic Development
  **Gustavo Giraldo** . . . . . . . . . . . . . . . . . . . . . . . . . . . . . (630) 241-6800
Chief of Engineering **Paul D. Kovacs, PE** . . . . . . . . . . . . . (630) 241-6800
Chief of Finance **Michael Colsch** . . . . . . . . . . . . . . . . . . . (630) 241-6800
Chief of Information Technology **Joseph M. Kambich** . . . . (630) 241-6800
  E-mail: jkambich@getipass.com
Chief of Operations **David Wilson** . . . . . . . . . . . . . . . . . . (630) 241-6800
Chief Internal Auditor **Cassaundra Rouse** . . . . . . . . . . . . (630) 241-6800
General Counsel **David Goldberg** . . . . . . . . . . . . . . . . . . . (630) 241-6800

# Capital Development Board [CDB]

William G. Stratton Building, 401 South Spring Street,
Springfield, IL 62706
Tel: (217) 782-2864  TTY: (217) 524-4449  Fax: (217) 782-8625
E-mail: cdb.northreceptionist@illinois.gov

**Employees: 131  Fiscal Year: 2014-2015  Budget: $25,155,000**
Chairman **James R. Reilly** . . . . . . . . . . . . . . . . . . . . . . . . . (312) 787-9400
▲Executive Director **Jodi Golden** . . . . . . . . . . . . . . . . . . . (217) 782-8725
  E-mail: jodi.golden@illinois.gov

# State Board of Education

100 North First Street, Springfield, IL 62777-0001
Tel: (217) 782-4321  Tel: (866) 262-6663  Tel: (866) 326-0087 (TDD)
Fax: (217) 524-4928  Internet: www.isbe.net

■Board Chairman **James T. Meeks** . . . . . . . . . . . . . . . . . . (217) 557-6626
■Board Vice Chairman **Steven R. Gilford** . . . . . . . . . . . . . (217) 557-6626
  Education: Dartmouth 1974 AB; Duke 1978 MA, 1978 JD
■Board Member **Curt Bradshaw** . . . . . . . . . . . . . . . . . . . . (217) 557-6626
■Board Member **Lula Mae Ford** . . . . . . . . . . . . . . . . . . . . (217) 557-6626
■Board Member **Melinda A. LaBarre** . . . . . . . . . . . . . . . . (217) 557-6626
  Education: Southern Illinois 1963 BS; Illinois (Springfield) 1988 MA
■Board Member **Craig Lindvahl** . . . . . . . . . . . . . . . . . . . . (217) 557-6626
■Board Member **Eligio Cerda Pimentel** . . . . . . . . . . . . . . (217) 557-6626
■Board Member **John W. Sanders** . . . . . . . . . . . . . . . . . . (217) 557-6626
■Board Member **(Vacant)** . . . . . . . . . . . . . . . . . . . . . . . . . (217) 557-6626
▲State Superintendent of Education **Tony Smith, PhD** . . . . . (217) 782-2223
  E-mail: statesup@isbe.net
  Education: UC Berkeley 1992 BA, 1993 MA, 2002 PhD

# Fiscal Support Services

Chief Financial Officer **Robert Wolfe** . . . . . . . . . . . . . . . (217) 782-0249
  Budget and Financial Management Division
  Administrator **Marc Gibbs** . . . . . . . . . . . . . . . . . . . . . (217) 782-0249
  Fiscal and Procurement Services Division Administrator
  **Myong-Ae Kim** . . . . . . . . . . . . . . . . . . . . . . . . . . . . . (217) 785-8777

Funding and Disbursements Division Administrator
  **Tim Imler** . . . . . . . . . . . . . . . . . . . . . . . . . . . . . . . . . (217) 782-5256
  E-mail: timler@isbe.net

# Human Resources

Tel: (217) 782-6434  Fax: (217) 524-0396
Director **Anwar Johnson** . . . . . . . . . . . . . . . . . . . . . . . . . (217) 782-6434

# Public Information

Fax: (217) 782-3097
Communications Director **Laine Evans** . . . . . . . . . . . . . . . (217) 782-4648
  Education: Wofford 2008 BA; Georgetown

# School Support Services for All Schools

Assistant Superintendent **(Vacant)** . . . . . . . . . . . . . . . . . (217) 557-6763

# Special Education and Support Services

Fax: (217) 782-9224
Director **David Andel** . . . . . . . . . . . . . . . . . . . . . . . . . . . (217) 782-5589
Special Education Services (Chicago) Division
  Administrator **David Andel** . . . . . . . . . . . . . . . . . . . . . (217) 782-5589
  E-mail: dandel@isbe.net
Special Education Services (Springfield) Division
  Administrator **David Andel** . . . . . . . . . . . . . . . . . . . . . (217) 782-5589
  E-mail: dandel@isbe.net

# Teachers' Retirement System

2815 West Washington, Springfield, IL 62794-9253
P.O. Box 19253, Springfield, IL 62794
Tel: (800) 877-7896  TTY: (217) 753-0329  Fax: (217) 753-0967
E-mail: administration@trs.illinois.gov  Internet: http://trs.illinois.gov

Executive Director **Richard W. "Dick" Ingram** . . . . . . . . . (217) 753-0315
General Counsel **Marcy Dutton** . . . . . . . . . . . . . (217) 753-0375 ext. 2991
Deputy Executive Director **Sally Soderberg** . . . . . . . . . . . (800) 877-7896
  E-mail: deputy_executive_director@trs.illinois.gov
Chief Financial Officer **Jana Bergschneider** . . . . . . . . . . . (800) 877-7896
Chief Investment Officer **Stan Rupnik** . . . . . . . . . . . . . . . (217) 753-0370
Chief Technology Officer **Tom Smith** . . . . . . . . . . . . . . . . (800) 877-7896
Communications Director **Dave Urbanek** . . . . . . . . . . . . . (800) 877-7896
Chief Human Resources Officer **Gina Larkin** . . . . . . . . . . (800) 877-7896

# Teaching and Learning Services For All Children

Fax: (217) 782-5333
Assessments and Accountability Director
  **Angela Chamness** . . . . . . . . . . . . . . . . . . . . . . . . . . . (217) 782-0354
Career and Technical Education Administrator
  **Dora Welker** . . . . . . . . . . . . . . . . . . . . . . . . . . . . . . . (217) 782-4620

# State Board of Elections

2329 South MacArthur Boulevard, Springfield, IL 62704
Tel: (217) 782-4141  Fax: (217) 782-5959  Internet: www.elections.il.gov

**Employees: 76  Fiscal Year: 2015  Budget: $19,726,000**
Chairman **Charles W. Scholz** . . . . . . . . . . . . . . . . . . . . . . (217) 782-4141
  Education: Georgetown 1975 BA; Mercer 1978 JD
Vice Chair **Ernest L. Gowen** . . . . . . . . . . . . . . . . . . . . . . (217) 782-4141
Member **William J. "Bill" Cadigan** . . . . . . . . . . . . . . . . . (217) 782-4141
Member **Andrew Carruthers** . . . . . . . . . . . . . . . . . . . . . . (217) 782-4141
Member **Betty Coffrin** . . . . . . . . . . . . . . . . . . . . . . . . . . (217) 782-4141
Member **John R. Keith** . . . . . . . . . . . . . . . . . . . . . . . . . . (217) 782-4141
Member **William M. McGuffage** . . . . . . . . . . . . . . . . . . . (217) 782-4141
Member **Casandra B. Watson** . . . . . . . . . . . . . . . . . . . . . (217) 782-4141
▲Executive Director **Steven S. Sandvoss** . . . . . . . . . . . . . (217) 782-4141
  E-mail: ssandvoss@elections.il.gov

---

★ Elected Official   ■ Appointed by Governor   ● Appointed by Legislature   ▲ Appointed by Board or Commission   ◆ Appointed by State Supreme Court

## State Employees' Retirement System [SRS]

2101 South Veterans Parkway, Springfield, IL 62794-9255
P.O. Box 19255, Springfield, IL 62794
Tel: (217) 785-7444  TTY: (217) 785-7218  Fax: (217) 557-3943
E-mail: ser@mail.state.il.us  Internet: www.state.il.us/srs

**Fiscal Year:** 2015  **Budget:** $1,148,681,000

▲Executive Secretary **Timothy B. "Tim" Blair**............(217) 785-7016
  E-mail: tim.blair@srs.illinois.gov

## Illinois State Police [ISP]

801 South 7th Street, Suite 1100 S, Springfield, IL 62794-9461
P.O. Box 19461, Springfield, IL 62794
Tel: (217) 782-7263  TTY: (800) 255-3323  Internet: www.isp.state.il.us

**Employees:** 2,711  **Fiscal Year:** 2015  **Budget:** $428,177,000

■Director **Leo P. Schmitz**........................(217) 782-7263
  E-mail: leo_schmitz@isp.state.il.us
First Deputy Director **Chad Peterson**..................(217) 782-7263
Administration Division Deputy Director **Kelly Walter**....(217) 557-2040
Forensic Services Division Deputy Director **Jill Rizzs**.....(217) 785-7542
Internal Investigation Division Deputy Director
  **Deborah Simental**...............................(217) 782-5423
Operations Division Deputy Director **Tad Williams**......(217) 782-1320
Public Information Officer
  **M-Sgt. Matthew Boerwinkle**....................(217) 782-6637
  E-mail: matthew.boerwinkle@isp.state.il.us
911 Administrator **Cindy Barbera-Brelle**..............(217) 524-1762
911 Manager **Marci Elliott**........................(217) 524-1762

## Office of the Lieutenant Governor

214 State Capitol Building, Springfield, IL 62706
Tel: (312) 814-5240  Fax: (312) 814-5240

★Lieutenant Governor **Evelyn Sanguinetti** (R)..........(217) 558-3085
  Term Expires: January 2019
  Education: Florida International BA; John Marshall 1998 JD
Chief of Staff **Brian Colgan**........................(312) 814-5240
  Education: Illinois 2003

## Office of the Secretary of State

213 State Capitol Building, Springfield, IL 62756
Tel: (217) 782-2201  TTY: (800) 261-5280  Fax: (217) 785-0358
Internet: www.cyberdriveillinois.com

**Employees:** 3,702  **Fiscal Year:** 2015  **Budget:** $400,580,000

★Secretary of State **Jesse White** (D)..................(217) 782-2201
  Term Expires: January 2019
  Education: Alabama State 1957 BS
Chief of Staff **Thomas Benigno**.....................(217) 782-2201
Deputy Chief of Staff **Terri L. Coombes**...............(217) 782-0115
  E-mail: tcoombes@ilsos.net
General Counsel **Irene Lyons**.......................(217) 785-3094
Press Secretary **Dave Druker**.......................(217) 782-5984
  E-mail: ddruker@ilsos.net
Accounting Revenue Director **(Vacant)**................(217) 782-6823
Administrative Hearings Director **Thomas Rubbone**.....(217) 782-3296
  E-mail: trubbone@ilsos.net
Archives and Records Director **Dave Joens**............(217) 782-3492
Budget Director **Jacqueline Price**....................(217) 782-8892
Business Services Director **Ray Cachares**.............(217) 524-1159
  E-mail: rcachares@ilsos.net
Communications Director **Bob Yadgir**................(217) 782-5984
  E-mail: byadgir@ilsos.net
Court of Claims Director **(Vacant)**...................(217) 782-7102
Driver Services Director (Chicago Metro) **Rick Kurnick**...(312) 814-2975
  E-mail: slacey@treasurer.il.gov
Driver Services Director (Downstate) **Mike Mayer**.......(217) 785-0963
  E-mail: mmayer@ilsos.net
Index Director **David Weisbaum**.....................(217) 782-7107
Information Systems Services Director **Jeffrey L. Carter**..(217) 782-7236
  E-mail: jcarter@ilsos.net
Intergovernmental Affairs Director **Jill Zwick**...........(217) 557-5581

Legislative Affairs Director **H. W. Devlin**.............(217) 782-6640
  E-mail: hdevlin@ilsos.net
Personnel Director **Stephan Roth**...................(217) 782-1750
Physical Services Director **Daryl Vermillion**...........(217) 782-3896
Police Director **Sydney R. Roberts**..................(217) 782-7150
Programs and Policies Director **Terri L. Coombes**......(217) 782-0115
Securities Director **Tanya Solov**....................(217) 782-2256
Vehicles Director **Ernie Dannenberger**...............(217) 524-0416
  E-mail: edannenberger@ilsos.net

## State Library

300 South Second Street, Springfield, IL 62701-1796
Fax: (217) 785-5600
Director **Anne Craig**.............................(217) 782-2994

## Office of the Attorney General

500 South Second Street, Springfield, IL 62706
Tel: (217) 782-1090  TTY: (217) 785-2771  Fax: (217) 785-2551
E-mail: attorney_general@state.il.us

**Employees:** 742  **Fiscal Year:** 2015  **Budget:** $75,204,000

★Attorney General **Lisa Madigan** (D)..................(217) 782-9000
  Term Expires: January 2019
  E-mail: lmadigan@atg.state.il.us
  Education: Georgetown 1988 BA; Loyola U (Chicago) 1994 JD
  Counsel to the Attorney General **Michael J. Luke**......(217) 782-1974
  E-mail: mluke@atg.state.il.us
Chief Deputy Attorney General **Brent Stratton**.........(312) 814-2560
Chief of Staff **Ann Spillane**.......................(312) 814-5328
  Deputy Chief of Staff, Administration
  **Melissa Mahoney**...........................(312) 814-3489
  E-mail: mmahoney@atg.state.il.us
Attorney General's Senior Executive Assistant
  **Eva Stachon**...............................(312) 814-5328
Investigations Division Chief **Cameron Eugenis**.........(312) 814-2584
Child Support Enforcement Bureau Chief **Scott Black**....(217) 785-5793
Consumer Fraud Bureau Chief **Elizabeth Blackston**......(217) 782-1090
Environmental Law Bureau Chief **Andrew Armstrong**....(217) 782-7968
General Law Bureau Chief **Karen McNaught**...........(217) 782-1841
Revenue Litigation Bureau Chief **Rosalie Lowery**.......(217) 782-9022
Tobacco Enforcement Bureau Chief **Marilyn Kueper**.....(217) 785-8541
Workers' Compensation Bureau Chief **Gregory Riddle**...(217) 782-9062
  E-mail: griddle@atg.state.il.us
Public Access and Opinions Division Chief **Lynn Patton**..(217) 782-9070
Fiscal Affairs Deputy Director **Josiah Small**...........(217) 785-8127
Human Resources Director **Laura Mehan**.............(217) 524-9075
Library Services Director **(Vacant)**..................(217) 782-9044
Equal Employment Opportunity Officer **Laura Mehan**....(312) 814-5846

## Attorney General's Chicago Office

100 West Randolph Street, Suite 12, Chicago, IL 60601
Fax: (312) 814-2549

Child Support Enforcement Deputy Attorney General
  **(Vacant)**..................................(312) 814-5568
Civil Litigation Deputy Attorney General
  **Roger Flahaven**...........................(312) 814-1030
Criminal Justice Deputy Attorney General **(Vacant)**.......(312) 814-5376
Welfare Litigation Assistant Attorney General
  **Karen Konieczny**...........................(312) 793-2380
  Government and Community Relations Co-Director
  **Eileen Baumstark**..........................(312) 814-4215
  Government and Community Relations Co-Director
  **Lisa Thompson-Bennett**.....................(312) 814-1176
Chief Internal Auditor **J. Harold Wagner**.............(217) 524-4094
Inspector General **Diane Saltoun**...................(312) 814-2963
Solicitor General **Carolyn Shapiro**..................(312) 814-5584
Press Secretary **Maura Possley**.....................(312) 814-4632
  E-mail: mpossley@atg.state.il.us
Chief Fiscal Officer **David Boots**....................(217) 782-9058
Attorney Recruitment and Professional Development
  Director **Ruta Stropus**........................(312) 814-3695
Legislative Affairs Director **Caitlin Groh**.............(312) 814-8839
  E-mail: cgroh@atg.state.il.us

*(continued on next page)*

★ Elected Official  ■ Appointed by Governor  ● Appointed by Legislature  ▲ Appointed by Board or Commission  ◆ Appointed by State Supreme Court

*State Yellow Book*  © Leadership Directories, Inc.  Summer 2016

EXECUTIVE BRANCH

**Attorney General's Chicago Office** *continued*

Scheduling Director **Courtney Levy** . . . . . . . . . . . . . . . . . (312) 814-3000
Strategic Communications Director **(Vacant)** . . . . . . . . . . . (312) 814-4544
Budget and Fiscal Bureau Director **(Vacant)** . . . . . . . . . . . .(312) 793-3895
Office Services Bureau Senior Director **Rocco LaSalvia** . . .(312) 814-3667
Office Services Bureau Director **Rocco LaSalvia** . . . . . . . . (217) 782-9017
Policy Director **(Vacant)** . . . . . . . . . . . . . . . . . . . . . . . . .(312) 814-3873
Policy Deputy Chief of Staff **Mary Morrissey-Kochanny** . .(312) 814-8553
Civil Appeals Division Chief **Jan Hughes** . . . . . . . . . . . . .(312) 814-2129
Consumer Protection Division Chief
  **Deborah "Debbie" Hagan** . . . . . . . . . . . . . . . . . . . . . .(217) 814-2129
Crime Victims Services Division Chief **Cindy Hora** . . . . . .(312) 814-3749
Criminal Appeals Division Chief **Michael Glick** . . . . . . . . .(312) 814-2232
Criminal Enforcement Division Chief **Stephen Plazibat** . . .(312) 814-5023
Environmental Enforcement Division Chief
  **Matthew Dunn** . . . . . . . . . . . . . . . . . . . . . . . . . . . . . .(217) 524-1503
Government Representation Division Chief
  **Kathleen Flahaven** . . . . . . . . . . . . . . . . . . . . . . . . . . .(312) 814-2822
Public Interest Division Chief **Cara Hendrickson** . . . . . . . .(312) 814-1134
  E-mail: chendrickson@atg.state.il.us
Antitrust Bureau Chief **Robert W. Pratt** . . . . . . . . . . . . . .(312) 814-5610
  Education: Yale 1975 JD
Charitable Trusts Bureau Chief **Therese Harris** . . . . . . . . .(312) 814-3966
Child Welfare Litigation Bureau Chief
  **Barbara Greenspan** . . . . . . . . . . . . . . . . . . . . . . . . . .(312) 814-7087
  E-mail: barbara.greenspan@illinois.gov
Civil Rights Bureau Chief **Karyn Bass Ehler** . . . . . . . . . . .(312) 814-5968
  E-mail: kehler@atg.state.il.us
Consumer Fraud Bureau Chief **Susan Ellis** . . . . . . . . . . . .(312) 814-5018
Criminal Prosecution/Trial Assistance Bureau Chief
  **Bill Elward** . . . . . . . . . . . . . . . . . . . . . . . . . . . . . . . .(312) 814-3754
Disability Rights Bureau Chief **Laura Paul** . . . . . . . . . . . .(312) 814-8109
Environmental Crimes Bureau Chief **Collette Kennedy** . . .(312) 814-5282
Environmental Enforcement Bureau Chief
  **Elizabeth Wallace** . . . . . . . . . . . . . . . . . . . . . . . . . . .(312) 814-5396
Franchise Bureau Chief **Cassandra Halm** . . . . . . . . . . . . .(217) 782-2398
General Law Bureau Chief **David W. Van De Burgt** . . . . . .(312) 814-3650
Health Care Bureau Chief **Ray Threlkeld** . . . . . . . . . . . . .(312) 814-3789
High Tech Crimes Bureau Chief **David Haslett** . . . . . . . . .(312) 814-3505
Medicaid Fraud Bureau Chief **Frederick Crystal** . . . . . . . .(312) 814-1624
Military and Veterans Rights Bureau Chief (North)
  **Grant Swinger** . . . . . . . . . . . . . . . . . . . . . . . . . . . . . .(312) 814-3892
Military and Veterans Rights Bureau Chief (South)
  **Thomas Banning** . . . . . . . . . . . . . . . . . . . . . . . . . . . .(217) 732-4436
Public Utilities Bureau Chief **Janice Dale** . . . . . . . . . . . . .(312) 814-3736
  E-mail: jdale@atg.state.il.us
Revenue Litigation Bureau Chief **John Flores** . . . . . . . . . .(312) 814-6153
Sexually Violent Persons Bureau Chief **Joelle Marasco** . . .(312) 814-3530
Special Litigation Bureau Chief **Jeanne Witherspoon** . . . .(312) 814-4186
Special Prosecutions Bureau Chief **Edward Carter** . . . . . . .(312) 814-3738
Statewide Grand Jury Bureau Chief **John Kezdy** . . . . . . . .(312) 814-3037
Toll Highway Bureau Chief **Elizabeth Looby** . . . . . . . . . . .(630) 241-6800
  E-mail: elooby@atg.state.il.us
Unemployment Insurance Bureau Chief
  **Andrew Dryjanski** . . . . . . . . . . . . . . . . . . . . . . . . . . .(312) 793-6943
Workers' Compensation Bureau Chief **Jill Otte** . . . . . . . . .(312) 814-3675
  E-mail: jotte@atg.state.il.us
Women's Issues Senior Policy Advisor **Wendy H. Cohen** . .(312) 814-2699
  Education: Syracuse 1970
Regional Counsel **Regina Haasis** . . . . . . . . . . . . . . . . . . .(217) 278-3366
Information Technology Bureau Chief Technology Officer
  **Lora McDonald** . . . . . . . . . . . . . . . . . . . . . . . . . . . . .(217) 785-5020
  E-mail: lmcdonald@atg.state.il.us

## Office of the State Treasurer

219 State House, Springfield, IL 62706
Tel: (217) 782-2211  Fax: (217) 785-2777  Internet: www.treasurer.il.gov

**Fiscal Year:** 2015  **Budget:** $3,591,178,000

★State Treasurer **Michael W. "Mike" Frerichs** (D) . . . . . . . .(217) 782-2211
  Term Expires: January 2019
  Education: Yale 1995 BA

Deputy Treasurer **Jay Rowell** . . . . . . . . . . . . . . . . . . . . . . (217) 782-2211
  Education: Loyola U (Chicago) JD
Chief of Staff **Justin Cajindos** . . . . . . . . . . . . . . . . . . . . . (217) 782-2211
  Education: Illinois 2007 BA
Executive Director of Finance **(Vacant)** . . . . . . . . . . . . . . .(217) 782-2211
Director of Communication **Paris Ervin** . . . . . . . . . . . . . . .(217) 782-2211
  E-mail: ervin@treasurer.il.gov
Director of College Savings **Fernando Diaz** . . . . . . . . . . . .(217) 782-2211
Director of Human Resources **Aimee Pine** . . . . . . . . . . . .(217) 782-2211
Inspector General **David Wells** . . . . . . . . . . . . . . . . . . . . .(217) 782-2211
  Education: Elmhurst 1994 BS; Lewis U 1996 MS
General Information **Pat Dawson** . . . . . . . . . . . . . . . . . . . .(217) 782-2211
  E-mail: dawson@treasurer.il.gov
General Counsel **Keith Horton** . . . . . . . . . . . . . . . . . . . . .(217) 782-2211
Press Secretary **Greg Rivera** . . . . . . . . . . . . . . . . . . . . . . .(217) 782-2211
  E-mail: rivera@treasurer.il.gov
Chief Internal Auditor **Leighann Manning** . . . . . . . . . . . . .(217) 558-0010
Chief Procurement Officer **James "Jim" Underwood** . . . .(217) 782-2211
  Education: Antioch U BA

## Office of the Comptroller

201 State House, Springfield, IL 62706
Tel: (217) 782-6000  TTY: (217) 782-1308  Fax: (217) 782-7561
E-mail: webmaster@mail.ioc.state.il.us  Internet: www.ioc.state.il.us/

**Employees:** 257  **Fiscal Year:** 2015  **Budget:** $116,436,000

★Comptroller **Leslie Geissler Munger** (R) . . . . . . . . . . . . . .(312) 814-5913
  Education: Illinois BS; Kellogg MBA
  Executive Assistant (Chicago) **Lisa Post** . . . . . . . . . . . .(312) 814-5913
  100 West Randolph Street, Suite 15-500, Chicago, IL 60601-3252
Chief of Staff **Bradley C. Hahn** . . . . . . . . . . . . . . . . . . . .(312) 814-7055
Communications Director **Rich Carter** . . . . . . . . . . . . . . . .(312) 814-5707
Human Resources Director **Ryan Amerson** . . . . . . . . . . . .(217) 782-6084
Internal Audit Director **Tracy Allen** . . . . . . . . . . . . . . . . . .(217) 782-1003
Legislative Affairs Director **(Vacant)** . . . . . . . . . . . . . . . . .(312) 814-4981
Scheduler **Lisa Post** . . . . . . . . . . . . . . . . . . . . . . . . . . . . .(217) 782-6000
  E-mail: postlr@mail.ioc.state.il.us
Inspector General **Michael J. "Mike" Drake** . . . . . . . . . . .(217) 782-2103
Chief Legal Counsel **Alissa Camp** . . . . . . . . . . . . . . . . . . .(217) 782-0905

## Cemetery Care and Burial Trust

Director **Percy Lucina** . . . . . . . . . . . . . . . . . . . . . . . . . . . .(312) 814-0009
  Education: Iowa 1993 (Attended)
  Local Government Director **Lauren Shiliga** . . . . . . . . . . .(312) 814-5921

## Policy and Programs Division

Assistant Comptroller of Fiscal Policy and Information
  Technology **(Vacant)** . . . . . . . . . . . . . . . . . . . . . . . . . .(217) 782-6000
Funds Management Director **Kevin Fitzpatrick** . . . . . . . . . .(217) 785-4829
Public Accountability Project Director **(Vacant)** . . . . . . . . .(217) 524-5774

## Springfield Operations

Assistant Comptroller **Marvin Becker** . . . . . . . . . . . . . . . .(217) 558-3359
Administrative Services Director **Steve W. Klokkenga** . . . .(217) 558-2996
Budget and Procurement Director **Patty Allen** . . . . . . . . . .(312) 814-5709
  Education: Marian Col (WI) 1983 BBA
Financial Reporting Director **Kathleen Madonia** . . . . . . . .(217) 782-2052
Information Technology Director **John Haycraft** . . . . . . . . .(217) 782-5681
  E-mail: john.haycraft@mail.ioc.state.il.us
State Accounting Director **(Vacant)** . . . . . . . . . . . . . . . . . .(217) 782-7078
  Consumer Affairs Director **(Vacant)** . . . . . . . . . . . . . . . .(217) 782-2673

★ Elected Official   ■ Appointed by Governor   ● Appointed by Legislature   ▲ Appointed by Board or Commission   ◆ Appointed by State Supreme Court

Summer 2016                    © Leadership Directories, Inc.                    *State Yellow Book*

# Indiana

Tel: (317) 232-1000 (State Information)  Internet: www.in.gov

**Number of U.S. Congressional Delegates:** 2 Senators; 9 Representatives  **Governor's Term:** 4 years
**Legislature Description:** General Assembly - 50 member Senate; 100 member House of Representatives;
Term - Senate 4 years, House 2 years  **Next Election:** Governor November 2016; Legislature
November 2016  **Number of Electoral Votes:** 11  **Official Name:** State of Indiana (land of Indians)
**Nickname:** The Hoosier State  **Motto:** Crossroads of America

**Population:** 6,619,680 (2015); Rank 16  **Fiscal Year:** 2013-2014  **Budget:** $29,270,687,674

## Office of the Governor

State House, 200 West Washington Street, Room 206,
Indianapolis, IN 46204
Tel: (317) 232-4567  TTY: (317) 233-5614  Fax: (317) 232-3443

**Mike Pence**
Governor

Began Service: January 14, 2013
Term Expires: January 2017
Date of Birth: June 7, 1959
Education: Hanover 1981 BA; Indiana 1986 JD
Home: Columbus
Religion: Christian
Career: Attorney, Stark Doniger Mernitz and
Smith (1986-1991); President, Indiana Policy
Review Foundation (1991-1993); Talk Show Host,
"The Mike Pence Show" (1992-1999); U.S.
Representative (R-IN, District 6), Office of
Representative Mike Pence, United States House
of Representatives (2001-2013)

★ Governor **Mike Pence** (R) . . . . . . . . . . . . . . . . . . . . . . . (317) 232-4567
Chief of Staff **James "Jim" Atterholt** . . . . . . . . . . . . . . . .(317) 232-1800
  Education: Wisconsin 1986 BA
Deputy Chief of Staff **Danielle McGrath** . . . . . . . . . . . . . . (317) 234-5339
  E-mail: dmcgrath@gov.in.gov
  Education: DePauw; Indiana
Deputy Chief of Staff for Communications and Strategy
  **Matthew H. "Matt" Lloyd** . . . . . . . . . . . . . . . . . . . . . . (317) 232-4567
  E-mail: mlloyd@gov.in.gov
  Education: Illinois 1996 BA
Deputy Chief of Staff of Public Safety **John H. Hill** . . . . . . (317) 232-3986
  E-mail: jhill@gov.in.gov
  Education: Taylor 1973 BA
Deputy Chief of Staff of Policy and Strategy
  **Ryan T. Streeter** . . . . . . . . . . . . . . . . . . . . . . . . . . . . . (317) 232-4567
  E-mail: rstreeter@gov.in.gov
  Education: Moody Bible BA; Northern Illinois MA; Emory 1997 PhD
Education and Workforce Policy Director **(Vacant)** . . . . . . (317) 232-4567
Energy and Environment Policy Director **Dan Schmidt** . . (317) 232-4567
  E-mail: dschmidt@gov.in.gov
  Education: Colorado; Indiana JD
Health Care Policy Director **Brian S. Neale** . . . . . . . . . . (317) 232-4567
  E-mail: bneale@gov.in.gov
  Education: Indiana 2007 JD
Regulatory Policy Director **Adam H. Berry** . . . . . . . . . . . (317) 232-4567
  E-mail: aberry@gov.in.gov
  Education: Wabash Col 2004 BA; Indiana 2008 JD
Communications Director **Shelley Triol** . . . . . . . . . . . . . . .(317) 234-8835
  E-mail: striol@idoa.in.gov
Press Secretary **Kara Brooks** . . . . . . . . . . . . . . . . . . . . . .(317) 232-1622
  E-mail: kbrooks@gov.in.gov
Deputy Press Secretary **Stephanie Hodgin** . . . . . . . . . . . (317) 233-4721
  E-mail: shodgin@gov.in.gov
Community Relations Director **Zachary Christian Bauer** . . (317) 232-4567
  E-mail: zbauer@gov.in.gov
  Education: James Madison 2009 AB

Legislative Director **Brady Brookes** . . . . . . . . . . . . . . . . . . (317) 233-9690
  E-mail: bbrookes@gov.in.gov
  Education: Miami U (OH)
  Senior Advisor for Legislative Affairs
  **Jeffrey K. "Jeff" Espich** . . . . . . . . . . . . . . . . . . . . . . . . (317) 232-4567
  E-mail: jespich@gov.in.gov
  Education: Indiana 1966 BS
Operations Director **Jennifer L. Pavlik** . . . . . . . . . . . . . . . (317) 232-4567
  E-mail: jpavlik@gov.in.gov
  Education: Kansas 1999 BA
General Counsel **Mark G. Ahearn** . . . . . . . . . . . . . . . . . . .(317) 232-4567
  E-mail: mahearn@gov.in.gov
  Education: Indiana; Indiana (Indianapolis) 1982 JD
Special Assistant **Jackie Cissell** . . . . . . . . . . . . . . . . . . . . (317) 232-4567
  E-mail: jjoynerburroughs@gov.in.gov
Scheduler **Erin Norton** . . . . . . . . . . . . . . . . . . . . . . . . . . . (317) 232-0668
  E-mail: enorton@gov.in.gov
  Education: Anderson U 2013

## Washington Office

1455 Pennsylvania Avenue, NW, Suite 1140, Washington, DC 20004
Tel: (202) 624-1474  Fax: (202) 624-1475
Director **Josh Pitcock** . . . . . . . . . . . . . . . . . . . . . . . . . . . (202) 624-1474
  E-mail: josh.pitcock@in.gov
  Education: DePauw 1998 BA; Wake Forest 2001 JD
Deputy Federal Representative **Jordan Wicker** . . . . . . . . . .(202) 624-1474
  E-mail: jwicker@idem.in.gov

## Indiana Office of Inspector General

315 West Ohio Street, Room 104, Indianapolis, IN 46202
Tel: (317) 232-3850  Fax: (317) 232-0707  E-mail: info@ig.in.gov
Inspector General **Cynthia Carrasco** . . . . . . . . . . . . . . . . . (317) 232-3850
  E-mail: ccarrasco@ig.in.gov
  Education: Texas (El Paso); Indiana JD
Ethics Director **Jennifer Cooper** . . . . . . . . . . . . . . . . . . . . (317) 234-4108
Investigations Director **Darrell Boehmer** . . . . . . . . . . . . . . (317) 232-3850

## Office of the Adjutant General

Joint Forces Headquarters, 2002 South Holt Road,
Indianapolis, IN 46241-4839
Tel: (317) 247-3559  Fax: (317) 247-3146

**Fiscal Year:** 2013-2014  **Budget:** $92,076,779

■ Adjutant General **MG Courtney P. Carr, ARNG** . . . . . . . . . (317) 247-3559
  Education: West Point 1983 BS; Chicago 1994 MBA;
  Army War Col 2003 MS
Chief of Joint Staff **BG Ronald A. Westfall, ARNG** . . . . . . (317) 247-3276
Emergency Preparedness Director
  **LTC Dan Gilbert, ARNG** . . . . . . . . . . . . . . . . . . . . . . . (317) 247-3204
Public Affairs Officer **LTC Cathy A. Van Bree, ARNG** . . . . (317) 247-3105

## Indiana National Guard

Tel: (317) 247-3300

■ Adjutant General **MG Courtney P. Carr, ARNG** . . . . . . . . . (317) 247-3559
Command Chief Warrant Officer
  **CW5 Elizabeth A. Keene, ARNG** . . . . . . . . . . . . . . . . . (317) 247-3112
  Note: Until September 30, 2016.

*(continued on next page)*

---

★ Elected Official    ■ Appointed by Governor    ● Appointed by Legislature    ▲ Appointed by Board or Commission    ◆ Appointed by State Supreme Court

EXECUTIVE BRANCH

**Indiana National Guard** *continued*

Command Chief Warrant Officer
  **CW4 Christopher R. Jennings, ARNG** . . . . . . . . . . . . . (317) 247-3300
    Note: Effective September 30, 2016.
Command Sergeant Major
  **CSM James R. Gordon, ARNG** . . . . . . . . . . . . . . . . . . (317) 247-3280
Vice Chief of Staff **COL Timothy Thombleson, ARNG** . . (317) 247-3441
Information Management (J6) Director **Pete Nelson** . . . . . . (317) 247-3167
    E-mail: pete.nelson@us.army.mil

## Indiana Air National Guard

Tel: (317) 247-3272

Assistant Adjutant General
  **BrigGen Jeffrey W. Hauser, ANG** . . . . . . . . . . . . . . . . . .(812) 240-2072
    Education: Indiana State 1982 BS; Indiana Wesleyan 1988 MSBA;
    Air Command Col 1998; Air War Col 2001
Chief of Staff **Col Christopher H. Colbert, ANG** . . . . . . . (317) 496-2756
    Education: Indiana State 1983 BSSecEd; Air Command Col 1998;
    Air War Col 2004

## Indiana Army National Guard

Assistant Adjutant General and Senior Mission
  Commander **(Vacant)** . . . . . . . . . . . . . . . . . . . . . . . . . . . . .(812) 526-1500

# Indiana Department of Administration [IDOA]

Indiana Government Ctr. South, 402 West Washington Street,
Room W479, Indianapolis, IN 46204
Tel: (317) 232-3150   Fax: (317) 233-3153   Internet: www.in.gov/idoa

**Fiscal Year:** 2013-2014   **Budget:** $26,551,809

■Commissioner **Jessica Robertson** . . . . . . . . . . . . . . . . . . . (317) 233-1494
    E-mail: jrobertson@idoa.in.gov
    Education: Indiana State 2005 BS
    Executive Assistant **Marita Steltenpohl** . . . . . . . . . . . . . (317) 233-1494
      E-mail: masteltenpohl@idoa.in.gov
Facilities Deputy Commissioner **Brian Renner** . . . . . . . . . .(317) 232-6795
                                 Fax: (317) 233-3956
Minority and Women's Business Enterprise Deputy
  Commissioner **Terrie Daniel** . . . . . . . . . . . . . . . . . . . . (317) 234-2718
Procurement Deputy Commissioner **Debra Walker** . . . . . . . (317) 234-5584
                                 Fax: (317) 232-7312
General Counsel **Tim A. Grogg** . . . . . . . . . . . . . . . . . . . .(317) 234-1596
State Engineer **Martin Hurford** . . . . . . . . . . . . . . . . . . . . (317) 232-3004
                                 Fax: (317) 233-4613
Administrative Services Director **Todd Carr** . . . . . . . . . . . (317) 233-0394
    E-mail: tcarr@idoa.in.gov
Management Information Systems Director **Joe Starry** . . . . (317) 233-9864
    E-mail: jstarry@idoa.in.gov
State and Federal Surplus Property Director
  **Ramona Beaman** . . . . . . . . . . . . . . . . . . . . . . . . . . . . . . (317) 234-3690
    E-mail: rbeaman@idoa.in.gov
Vendor Management and Supplier Performance Director
  **Leila Sublett** . . . . . . . . . . . . . . . . . . . . . . . . . . . . . . . (317) 232-3279
                                 Fax: (317) 233-8252
Public Works Director **Martin Hurford** . . . . . . . . . . . . . . (317) 232-3004
                                 Fax: (317) 233-4613
  State Architect **(Vacant)** . . . . . . . . . . . . . . . . . . . . . . . . (317) 232-3018
                                 Fax: (317) 233-4613
Child Services Ombudsman **Alfreda Singleton-Smith** . . . . (317) 234-7295
Corrections Ombudsman **Charlene Burkett** . . . . . . . . . . . . (317) 234-3982

# Indiana Department of Child Services [DCS]

Indiana Government Center South, 302 West Washington Street,
Room E-306, Indianapolis, IN 46204
Tel: (317) 234-5437   Fax: (317) 234-4490   Internet: www.in.gov/dcs

■Director **Mary Beth Bonaventura** . . . . . . . . . . . . . . . . . (317) 234-1391
    E-mail: mary.bonaventura@dcs.in.gov
    Education: Marian U; Northern Illinois 1981 JD
    Executive Assistant **Briana Miles** . . . . . . . . . . . . . . . . (317) 234-1391
General Counsel **Wade Hornbacher** . . . . . . . . . . . . . . . . . (317) 234-3871
    E-mail: wade.hornbacher@dcs.in.gov

Chief of Staff **Doris Tolliver** . . . . . . . . . . . . . . . . . . . . . .(317) 232-4439
  Deputy Chief of Staff **Luke Bosso** . . . . . . . . . . . . . . . . (317) 234-6245
    E-mail: luke.bosso@dcs.in.gov
Chief Financial Officer **Rick Peterson** . . . . . . . . . . . . . . . (317) 234-6910
Chief Information Officer of Technology **Tony Bender** . . . . (317) 234-6457
    E-mail: tony.bender@dcs.in.gov
Child Support Deputy Director **Cynthia Longest** . . . . . . . . (317) 234-4482
    E-mail: cynthia.longest@dcs.in.gov
Communications Deputy Director **James Wide** . . . . . . . . . . (317) 234-3924
    E-mail: james.wide@dcs.in.gov
Field Operations Deputy Director **Jane Bisbee** . . . . . . . . . (317) 234-3999
    E-mail: jane.bisbee@dcs.in.gov
Human Resources Deputy Director **Aiesha Peterson** . . . . . (317) 234-1388
Legislative Director **Parvonay Stover** . . . . . . . . . . . . . . . .(317) 234-8031
    E-mail: parvonay.stover@dcs.in.gov
Permanency and Practice Support Deputy Director
  **Reba James** . . . . . . . . . . . . . . . . . . . . . . . . . . . . . . . . (317) 234-4631
    E-mail: reba.james@dcs.in.gov
Placement Support and Compliance Deputy Director
  **Corinne Gilchrist** . . . . . . . . . . . . . . . . . . . . . . . . . . . . .(317) 234-4443
    E-mail: corinne.gilchrist@dcs.in.gov
Programs and Services Deputy Director **Lisa Rich** . . . . . . . (317) 232-4497
    E-mail: lisa.rich@dcs.in.gov
Staff Development Deputy Director **LaTrece Thompson** . . (317) 234-4211

# Indiana Department of Correction [IDOC]

Indiana Government Ctr. South, 302 West Washington Street, Room E334,
Indianapolis, IN 46204
Tel: (317) 232-5711   Fax: (317) 232-6798

**Fiscal Year:** 2013-2014   **Budget:** $720,434,220

■Commissioner **Bruce Lemmon** . . . . . . . . . . . . . . . . . . . . (317) 232-5711
    E-mail: blemmon@idoc.in.gov
    Education: Indiana State
    Executive Assistant **Stephanie Lightfoot** . . . . . . . . . . . . (317) 232-5711
State Prison Superintendent **Ron Neal** . . . . . . . . . . . . . . . .(219) 874-7256
                                 Fax: (219) 874-0339
Chief Counsel **Robert Bugher** . . . . . . . . . . . . . . . . . . . . . .(317) 232-5718
    E-mail: rbugher@idoc.in.gov
Chief Communications Officer **Douglas Garrison** . . . . . . . .(317) 232-5780
    E-mail: dsgarrison@idoc.in.gov
Ombudsman **Charlene Burkett** . . . . . . . . . . . . . . . . . . . . . (317) 234-3982

## Administration

Chief of Staff **Randy Koester** . . . . . . . . . . . . . . . . . . . . . . (317) 233-5541
    E-mail: rkoester@idoc.in.gov
  Administrative Assistant to the Chief of Staff
    **Amanda Royston** . . . . . . . . . . . . . . . . . . . . . . . . . . . (317) 233-5541
Chief Financial Officer **Grant Knies** . . . . . . . . . . . . . . . . . (317) 232-5805
    Education: Indiana BSBA
Research and Technology Executive Director
  **Aaron Garner** . . . . . . . . . . . . . . . . . . . . . . . . . . . . . . . (317) 232-1757
                                 Fax: (317) 233-1474
Contract Compliance Director **John Schilling** . . . . . . . . . . (317) 233-6499
    E-mail: jschilling@idoc.in.gov
Construction Services Director **Kevin Orme** . . . . . . . . . . . .(317) 232-1195
Legislative Services Director **Jon Ferguson** . . . . . . . . . . . . .(317) 233-8861
    E-mail: jferguson1@idoc.in.gov
Medical Services Director **Dr. Michael Mitcheff** . . . . . . . . (317) 233-8593
Mental Health and Special Populations Executive
  Director **Mark Levenhagen** . . . . . . . . . . . . . . . . . . . . (317) 234-1926
Chief Investigator **Todd Tappy** . . . . . . . . . . . . . . . . . . . . .(317) 232-0270
Human Resources Executive Director **Jess Gibson** . . . . . . .(317) 233-5232
                                 Fax: (317) 233-0391
PREA Executive Director **Bryan Pearson** . . . . . . . . . . . . . (317) 232-5288
Policy Manager **Andy Dunigan** . . . . . . . . . . . . . . . . . . . . (317) 233-5236
    E-mail: adunigan@idoc.in.gov

## Operations

Deputy Commissioner **James Basinger** . . . . . . . . . . . . . . . (317) 232-5723
  Assistant to the Deputy Commissioner **Dana Wilson** . . . . (317) 232-5723
Adult Operations Executive Director **William Wilson** . . . . .(317) 234-0323

---

Classification Executive Director **Jack Hendrix** . . . . . . . . . (317) 232-2247
Fax: (317) 232-2255
Emergency Services Executive Director **Richard Curry** . . . . (317) 234-3906
Fax: (317) 234-1953
Staff Development and Training Executive Director
**Nancy Riley** . . . . . . . . . . . . . . . . . . . . . . . . . . . . . . . . . . (765) 521-0230
2050 North Country Road, New Castle, IN 47362
E-mail: nriley@idoc.in.gov
Inspector General **Michael Osburn** . . . . . . . . . . . . . . . . . . . (317) 232-5766
E-mail: mosburn@idoc.in.gov

## Re-Entry
Deputy Commissioner **Julie Lanham** . . . . . . . . . . . . . . . . (317) 233-6984
E-mail: jlanham@idoc.in.gov
Education: Indiana
Assistant to the Deputy Commissioner **Dana Wilson** . . . . (317) 233-5723
Education Director **John Nally** . . . . . . . . . . . . . . . . . . . . . (317) 234-1500
Health Care Services Director **Monica Gipson** . . . . . . . . . . (317) 233-8593
Parole and Release Services Director **Doug Huyvaert** . . . . . (317) 232-5757
Secretary to the Director **Denise Allen** . . . . . . . . . . . . . . (317) 232-5757
PEN (Prison Enterprises Network) Products Director
**Mike Herron** . . . . . . . . . . . . . . . . . . . . . . . . . . . . . . . . (317) 955-6800
2010 East New York Street, Indianapolis, IN 46201
E-mail: mherron@idoc.in.gov
Re-Entry and Medicaid Executive Director **Alexis Dean** . . . (317) 233-2286
Religious and Volunteer Services Director **David Liebel** . . . (317) 232-1545
E-mail: dliebel@idoc.in.gov
Fax: (317) 234-1953
Registration and Victim Services Director **Brent Myers** . . . (317) 233-8648
E-mail: bmyers@idoc.in.gov
Fax: (317) 233-4948
Transition Facilities and Community-Based Programs
Director **Michael "Mike" Lloyd** . . . . . . . . . . . . . . . . . . . (317) 233-3417
E-mail: mclloyd@idoc.in.gov
Fax: (317) 838-7548

## Youth Services
Executive Director **Christine Blessinger** . . . . . . . . . . . . . . (317) 234-2969
E-mail: cblessinger@idoc.in.gov
Administrative Assistant **(Vacant)** . . . . . . . . . . . . . . . . . . . (317) 232-5706
Juvenile Education Director **Susan Lockwood** . . . . . . . . . . (317) 234-1926
E-mail: slockwood@idoc.in.gov
Juvenile Reintegration Director **Stacy Doane-Selmier** . . . . (317) 234-3906
E-mail: sdoane-selmier@idoc.in.gov
Re-Entry and External Relations Director
**Kellie Whitcomb** . . . . . . . . . . . . . . . . . . . . . . . . . . . . . (317) 408-1482
E-mail: kwhitcomb@idoc.in.gov

## Indiana Department of Education [DOE]
228 State House, Indianapolis, IN 46204
Tel: (317) 232-6610  TTY: (317) 232-0570  Fax: (317) 232-8004

★ Indiana Superintendent of Public Instruction
**Glenda Ritz** (D) . . . . . . . . . . . . . . . . . . . . . . . . . . . . . . . (317) 232-6665
Term Expires: 2017
Education: Ball State BEd, MEd; IU-Purdue U Indianapolis
Executive Assistant **Megan Eckstein** . . . . . . . . . . . . . . . . (317) 232-6612
Special Assistant to the Superintendent **Joel Smith** . . . . . (317) 234-0959
Chief of Staff **Craig Hartzer** . . . . . . . . . . . . . . . . . . . . . . (317) 234-6790
Education: Indiana 1972 BA; Miami U (OH) 1978 PhD
Deputy Superintendent of Public Instruction
**Danielle Shockey** . . . . . . . . . . . . . . . . . . . . . . . . . . . . (317) 232-9010
Education: Ball State 1996 BS; IU-Purdue U (Ft Wayne) 2000 MS
Assistant Superintendent for School Support Services
**Risa Ann Regnier** . . . . . . . . . . . . . . . . . . . . . . . . . . . . (317) 232-0501
E-mail: rregnier@doe.in.gov
Education: Oberlin 1977 BA; Indiana (Indianapolis) 1988 JD
Chief Financial Officer **Beverly Flanagan** . . . . . . . . . . . . . (317) 232-0514
General Counsel **Bernice Corley** . . . . . . . . . . . . . . . . . . . . (317) 232-9153
E-mail: bcorley@doe.in.gov
Education: Drake 2000 JD
Executive Director of Communications **Daniel Altman** . . . . (317) 232-0550
E-mail: daltman@doe.in.gov
Executive Director of Finance and Business Operations
**Lisa L. Acobert** . . . . . . . . . . . . . . . . . . . . . . . . . . . . . . (317) 234-0205
E-mail: lacobert@doe.in.gov

Executive Director of Government and Public Affairs
**Scott E. Reske** . . . . . . . . . . . . . . . . . . . . . . . . . . . . . . . (317) 234-6014
E-mail: sreske@doe.in.gov
Education: Purdue 1983 BS; Seattle 1990 MPA;
Marine Corps Command U 2001
Director of Federal Relations **Jeffrey Coyne** . . . . . . . . . . . (317) 232-0551
Director of Legislative Affairs **John F. Barnes** . . . . . . . . . (317) 232-0576
E-mail: jbarnes@doe.in.gov
Education: Butler 1979 BA
Assistant Director of Government Affairs
**Cory Cochran** . . . . . . . . . . . . . . . . . . . . . . . . . . . . . . . (317) 232-6617
E-mail: ccochran@doe.in.gov
Human Resources Director **Kimberly A. "Kim" Allman** . . . (317) 232-9096
Director of Accountability **Maggie Paino** . . . . . . . . . . . . . . (317) 232-9185
Director of Accounting **Tracy Brown** . . . . . . . . . . . . . . . . (317) 232-6974
Director of External Affairs **Joshua E. Gillespie** . . . . . . . . (317) 232-9080
E-mail: jgillespie1@sboe.in.gov
Education: Purdue 2000 BA
Director of Information Technology **Joshua Towns** . . . . . . (317) 232-6845
E-mail: jtowns@doe.in.gov
Director of Policy and Research **Pete Weldy** . . . . . . . . . . . (317) 234-4703
E-mail: pweldy@doe.in.gov
Director of School Finance **Melissa K. Ambre** . . . . . . . . . . (317) 232-0841
Education: Indiana BS; Butler MBA

## Indiana Department of Environmental Management [IDEM]
Indiana Government Center North, 100 North Senate Avenue,
Indianapolis, IN 46204
Tel: (317) 232-8603  Tel: (800) 451-6027  TTY: (800) 743-3333
Fax: (317) 233-6647

■ Commissioner **Carol Comer** . . . . . . . . . . . . . . . . . . . . . . (317) 232-8611
E-mail: ccomer@idem.in.gov
Administrative Assistant **Mary Fields** . . . . . . . . . . . . . . . . (317) 232-8611
Chief of Staff **Bruno L. Pigott** . . . . . . . . . . . . . . . . . . . . . (317) 232-2550
Education: Michigan State; IU-Purdue U Indianapolis
Deputy Chief of Staff **Donald M. Snemis** . . . . . . . . . . . . . (317) 234-9581
Education: Ball State 1985 BS; Notre Dame 1988 JD
Government and Community Affairs Director
**Steve Howell** . . . . . . . . . . . . . . . . . . . . . . . . . . . . . . . . (317) 232-8587
E-mail: snhowell@idem.in.gov
Business and Legislative Liaison **Brian Rockensuess** . . . . . (317) 233-3386
E-mail: brockens@idem.in.gov

## Indiana Department of Financial Institutions [DFI]
30 South Meridian Street, Suite 300, Indianapolis, IN 46204
Tel: (317) 232-3955  Fax: (317) 232-7655

■ Director **Thomas C. Fite, CEM** . . . . . . . . . . . . . . . . . . . (317) 233-9460
E-mail: tfite@dfi.in.gov

## Administrative Division
Deputy Director **Gina Williams** . . . . . . . . . . . . . . . . . . . . (317) 232-5841
E-mail: gwilliams@dfi.in.gov
Education: Indiana State 1985 BS
Administration Supervisor **Troy D. Pogue** . . . . . . . . . . . . . (317) 233-6342
E-mail: tpogue@dfi.in.gov
Education: Ball State 1992 BS

## Depository Institutions Division
Deputy Director **(Vacant)** . . . . . . . . . . . . . . . . . . . . . . . . . (317) 453-2177
Bank Supervisor **(Vacant)** . . . . . . . . . . . . . . . . . . . . . . . . . (317) 232-5852
Credit Unions Division Supervisor **Mark Powell** . . . . . . . . (317) 232-5851
E-mail: mpowell@dfi.in.gov
Education: Ball State 1972 BS

## Non-Depository Institutions Division
Deputy Director **Mark B. Tarpey** . . . . . . . . . . . . . . . . . . . (317) 232-3961
E-mail: mtarpey@dfi.in.gov
Education: Marian Col (IN) 1970 BA
Assistant to the Deputy Director **Ryan E. Black** . . . . . . . . (317) 232-3955

---

★ Elected Official ■ Appointed by Governor ● Appointed by Legislature ▲ Appointed by Board or Commission ◆ Appointed by State Supreme Court

EXECUTIVE BRANCH

# Indiana State Department of Health [ISDH]

Two North Meridian Street, Indianapolis, IN 46204
P.O. Box 7125, Indianapolis, IN 46206 (Vital Records)
Tel: (317) 233-1325  Tel: (317) 233-2700 (Vital Records)
TTY: (317) 233-7859  Fax: (317) 233-7387  Internet: www.in.gov/isdh

**Fiscal Year:** 2013-2014  **Budget:** $305,943,226

■ State Health Commissioner **Dr. Jerome Adams** . . . . . . . . (317) 233-7400
  E-mail: jeadams@isdh.in.gov
  Education: Maryland Baltimore County; UC Berkeley MPH;
  Indiana MD
  Administrative Assistant **Tami Barrett** . . . . . . . . . . . . . . (317) 233-7400
Chief of Staff **Eric Miller** . . . . . . . . . . . . . . . . . . . . . . . . (317) 233-7200
  E-mail: erimiller@isdh.in.gov
Chief Medical Officer and State Liaison Officer
  **Dr. Joan Duwve, MD** . . . . . . . . . . . . . . . . . . . . . . . . . (317) 233-7164
Facilities Management Director (Interim) **Pamela Cowan** . .(317) 233-7852
                                                  Fax: (317) 233-7637
Grants Director **Rebecca Chauhan** . . . . . . . . . . . . . . . . . . (317) 233-7558
  E-mail: rchauhan1@isdh.in.gov
HIPAA (Health Insurance Portability and Accountability
  Act) Compliance Director **Christopher Rogers** . . . . . . . (317) 233-7655
  E-mail: chrogers@isdh.in.gov
Legal Affairs Director **Preston Black** . . . . . . . . . . . . . . . . (317) 233-7409
Legislative Affairs Director **(Vacant)** . . . . . . . . . . . . . . . . (317) 234-3808
Public Affairs Director **Jennifer O'Malley** . . . . . . . . . . . . (317) 233-7315

## Health and Human Services

Assistant Commissioner **Arthur L. Logsdon** . . . . . . . . . . . (317) 233-7679
Chronic Disease Prevention and Control Director
  **Ann Alley** . . . . . . . . . . . . . . . . . . . . . . . . . . . . . . . . . (317) 233-7451
Medical Director **Dr. T.S. Danielson** . . . . . . . . . . . . . . . . (317) 233-7428
Nutrition and Physical Activity Director **Eden Bezy** . . . . . (317) 233-7726
Human Immunodeficiency Virus & Sexually Transmitted
  Disease Director **(Vacant)** . . . . . . . . . . . . . . . . . . . . . . (317) 233-7476
Immunization Director **David E. "Dave" McCormick** . . . . (317) 233-7010
Local Health Department Outreach Director
  **David Hopper** . . . . . . . . . . . . . . . . . . . . . . . . . . . . . . (317) 234-6623
  E-mail: dahopper@isdh.in.gov
Newborn Screening Director **(Vacant)** . . . . . . . . . . . . . . . (317) 233-1231
Oral Health Services Director **James Miller, DDS** . . . . . . .(317) 233-7417
Primary Care Office Director **Ann Alley** . . . . . . . . . . . . . . (317) 233-8651
Women, Infants and Children (WIC) Director
  **Eldon Whetstone** . . . . . . . . . . . . . . . . . . . . . . . . . . . . (317) 233-7596
Trauma Registry and Injury Prevention Division Director
  **Katie Hokanson** . . . . . . . . . . . . . . . . . . . . . . . . . . . . (317) 234-2865
Women's Health Office Director **Laura Chavez** . . . . . . . . . (317) 233-7493

## Health Care Quality and Regulatory Services Commission

Tel: (317) 233-7621  Fax: (317) 233-7154

Assistant Commissioner **Terry L. Whitson** . . . . . . . . . . . . (317) 233-7022
  Education: Indiana JD
  Administrative Assistant **Teresa Watson** . . . . . . . . . . . . (317) 233-7621
Acute Care Director **Randall D. Snyder** . . . . . . . . . . . . . . (317) 233-1286
  CLIA (Clinical Laboratory Improvement Act)/Blood
  Center Director **Lorraine Switzer** . . . . . . . . . . . . . . . (317) 233-7502
  Weights & Measures Manager **Michael Miller** . . . . . . . . . (317) 356-7078
  2525 North Shadeland Avenue, Suite D-3,      TTY: (317) 356-7139
  Indianapolis, IN 46219-1791            Fax: (317) 351-2877
Hospitals, Ambulatory Surgery Centers Director
  **John Lee** . . . . . . . . . . . . . . . . . . . . . . . . . . . . . . . . . (317) 233-7487
Prison Health Director **Joyce Elder** . . . . . . . . . . . . . . . . . (317) 233-7485
Healthcare Quality and Training Director **Janelyn Kulik** . . .(317) 233-7480
Home Health, Hospice, Rural Health Centers & End
  Stage Renal Disease Director **Kelly Hemmelgarn, RN** . . .(317) 233-7742
Long Term Care Director **Kimberley K. Rhoades** . . . . . . . (317) 233-7442
  Long Term Care Deputy Director **Brenda Buroker, RN** . . (317) 234-7340
  Administrative Processing Director **Darlene Jones** . . . . . . (317) 233-7351
    E-mail: dkjones@isdh.in.gov
    Education: Ball State 1995 BSW

Complaints Director **Karen Smith** . . . . . . . . . . . . . . . . . . (317) 233-7709
  Education: Purdue 1982 BSN
Enforcement Director **Miriam L. Buffington** . . . . . . . . . . (317) 233-7613
Information Technology Director **Matt Doades** . . . . . . . . (317) 233-7364
  E-mail: mdoades@isdh.in.gov
Training Director **Gina Berkshire** . . . . . . . . . . . . . . . . . . (317) 233-4719
State Registrar **Brian Carnes** . . . . . . . . . . . . . . . . . . . . . . (317) 233-7523
                                             Tel: (317) 233-2700
                                             (Vital Records
                                          Customer Service)
                                          Fax: (317) 233-7210

## Operational Services Commission

Two North Meridian Street, Indianapolis, IN 46204

Deputy Chief of Staff and Chief Financial Officer
  **Joseph "Joe" Fistrovich** . . . . . . . . . . . . . . . . . . . . . . . (317) 233-7102
Administrative Services Director **Pamela Cowan** . . . . . . . . (317) 233-7852
  E-mail: pcowan@isdh.in.gov
Records Management Director **(Vacant)** . . . . . . . . . . . . . . (317) 233-7267

## Public Health Protection and Laboratory Services

550 West 16th Street, Indianapolis, IN 46206
Tel: (317) 921-5808

Assistant Commissioner **Judith C. Lovchik** . . . . . . . . . . . (317) 921-5808
Deputy Laboratory Director (Interim) **Mark Glazier** . . . . . (317) 921-5842
Epidemiology Resource Center Director **Pam Pontones** . . .(317) 233-7861
Public Health Preparedness and Emergency Response
  Director **Lee Christenson** . . . . . . . . . . . . . . . . . . . . . . (317) 233-5576

## Office of Technology and Compliance

Chief Technology and Compliance Officer
  **Christine Mickens** . . . . . . . . . . . . . . . . . . . . . . . . . . (317) 233-7673
  E-mail: cmickens@isdh.in.gov
State Health Data Center Director **Christine Mickens** . . . . (317) 233-7673
  E-mail: cmickens@isdh.in.gov

# Indiana Department of Homeland Security [IDHS]

302 West Washington Street, Room E208, Indianapolis, IN 46204
Tel: (317) 232-3980  Fax: (317) 232-3895  E-mail: pio@dhs.in.gov

■ Executive Director **David W. Kane** . . . . . . . . . . . . . . . . (317) 232-3986
  E-mail: dkane@dhs.in.gov
  Executive Administrative Assistant **(Vacant)** . . . . . . . . . (317) 232-6139
Administrative Law Judge **Justin Forkner** . . . . . . . . . . . . (317) 234-8917
  Education: Indiana (Indianapolis) 2010 JD
General Counsel **Jonathan Whitham** . . . . . . . . . . . . . . . .(317) 234-7752
Legal and Code Services Director and Chief Counsel
  **Mara J. Snyder** . . . . . . . . . . . . . . . . . . . . . . . . . . . . (317) 233-5341
Legal Counsel **Bradley "Brad" Gavin** . . . . . . . . . . . . . . . (317) 233-4928
                                              Fax: (317) 232-0146
Human Resources Director **Maria Limon** . . . . . . . . . . . . . (317) 233-4679
Senior Public Information Officer **John Erickson** . . . . . . . (317) 234-4214
  E-mail: jerickson@dhs.in.gov

## Emergency Response and Recovery Division

Director **Arvin Copeland** . . . . . . . . . . . . . . . . . . . . . . . . (317) 232-3834
  Education: Indiana Wesleyan BSBA
Assistant Director **Phil Brown** . . . . . . . . . . . . . . . . . . . . .(317) 232-3832
District Programs Section Chief **Kathy Dayhoff-Dwyer** . . . (317) 409-5759
Hazard Mitigation Director **Manuela Johnson** . . . . . . . . . (317) 233-4282
Individual Assistance Program Director **Briana Husband** . . (317) 232-3841
Mitigation Program Director **Mary Moran** . . . . . . . . . . . . (317) 232-3831
Public Assistance Program Director **Carmen Goodman** . . . (317) 234-8675
Recovery Program Director **Rosemary Petersen** . . . . . . . .(317) 233-6507

## Fire and Building Safety Division

Tel: (317) 232-2222

■ State Fire Marshal and Director **James L. Greeson** . . . . . (317) 232-2226
  E-mail: jgreeson@dhs.in.gov
Assistant Fire Marshal **Robert Johnson** . . . . . . . . . . . . . . (317) 233-0195

---

★ Elected Official    ■ Appointed by Governor    ● Appointed by Legislature    ▲ Appointed by Board or Commission    ◆ Appointed by State Supreme Court

Boiler and Pressure Vessel Director **Dean Illingworth** .... (317) 232-1927
  E-mail: dillingworth@dhs.in.gov
Code Enforcement Director **David "Dave" Smith** ........ (317) 232-7648
  E-mail: dsmith@dhs.in.gov
Elevator Safety Director **Tom Hendricks** .............. (317) 232-2054
  E-mail: thendricks@dhs.in.gov
Emergency Medical Services Branch Director
  **Michael S. "Mike" Garvey** .................. (317) 232-3983
Plan Review Branch Director **Bonnie Robinson** ........ (317) 232-1421
CBRNE Programs Section Chief **Catherine Dutton** ...... (317) 234-6510
Fire Investigations Chief **Bob Dean** .................. (317) 232-6434
  E-mail: bdean@dhs.in.gov

## Planning and Assessment Division
Director **(Vacant)** .................................. (317) 234-3969
Chief Financial Officer **Leann Walton** ................ (317) 234-7008
Information Technology and Data Management Director
  **Chuck Emsweller** .............................. (317) 232-6236
  E-mail: cemsweller@dhs.in.gov

## Training and Preparedness Division
Director **(Vacant)** .................................. (317) 234-3969
Certification Director **Michael S. "Mike" Garvey** ....... (317) 232-3983
Fire and Emergency Management Services Director
  **John Buckman** ................................ (317) 233-0498
Search and Rescue Training Manager **Lillian Hardy** ...... (800) 200-7424
State Exercise Officer **(Vacant)** .................... (317) 234-4787

# Indiana Department of Insurance [IDOI]
311 West Washington Street, Suite 103, Indianapolis, IN 46204-2787
Tel: (317) 232-2385  Tel: (800) 622-4461 (Interstate Hotline)
Fax: (317) 232-5251  E-mail: doi@in.gov  Internet: www.in.gov/idoi
■Commissioner **Stephen W. "Steve" Robertson** ........ (317) 232-3520
  E-mail: srobertson@idoi.in.gov
  Education: Nebraska BS, JD
  Executive Assistant **Dawn Bopp** .................... (317) 232-3520
Chief of Staff **Doug Webber** ...................... (317) 234-7734
Chief Financial Examiner **Cynthia D. "Cindy" Donovan** .. (317) 232-2408
Chief Financial Officer **Barb Lohman** ................ (317) 232-2405
Chief General Counsel **Tina Korty** .................. (317) 232-2417
Accident and Health Deputy Commissioner **(Vacant)** ..... (317) 234-7732
Consumer Services Chief Deputy Commissioner
  **Bettye Foy** .................................. (317) 232-1990
Enforcement Division Deputy General Counsel
  **Debra McNeil** ................................ (317) 232-2404
Producer and Agency Licensing Division Deputy
  Commissioner **Chet Pietras** .................... (317) 234-1138
Property and Casualty Product Lines Deputy
  Commissioner **Kate Kixmiller** .................. (317) 232-3495
State Health Insurance Assistant Program (SHIP)
  Director **Cheryl St. Clair** ...................... (317) 232-3640
Title Division Director **Randall Evans** .............. (317) 234-5881
Medical Malpractice Manager **Nancy Wilkins** .......... (317) 232-2401
Communication and Outreach Director **Jenifer Groth** ..... (317) 234-8582
  E-mail: jgroth@idoi.in.gov

# Indiana Department of Labor [DOL]
Indiana Government Center South, 402 West Washington Street,
Room W195, Indianapolis, IN 46204
Tel: (317) 232-2655  Fax: (317) 233-3790  Internet: www.in.gov/labor
■Commissioner **Rick J. Ruble** ...................... (317) 232-2655
  E-mail: rruble@dol.in.gov
  Education: Indiana, JD
Human Resource Director **Kimberly A. "Kim" Allman** ... (317) 232-2655
  E-mail: kallman@spd.in.gov
Controller and Chief Financial Officer **Ambat Babu** ...... (317) 232-2655
  E-mail: ababu@dol.in.gov
Quality, Metrics and Statistics Executive Director
  **Kenneth "K.R." Boucher** ...................... (317) 232-2655
  Education: Indiana BA
Public Information Officer **Amanda Stanley** ............ (317) 232-2379
  E-mail: astanley4@dor.in.gov

## Child Labor Bureau
Bureau Director **Michael Myers** .................... (317) 232-2655
  E-mail: childlabor@dol.in.gov
  E-mail: mmyers@dol.in.gov

# Indiana Occupational Safety and Health Administration [IOSHA]
Deputy Commissioner **Tim E. Maley** .................. (317) 232-2655
Mines Bureau Assistant Commissioner
  **Donald "Blink" McCorkle** .................... (812) 888-4514
  VU Technology Center, 1002 N. First Street, Vincennes, IN 47591
Construction Safety Director **Jerry Lander** ............ (317) 232-2655
Industrial Compliance, Discrimination and VPP Director
  **Julie Alexander** .............................. (317) 232-2655

# INSafe - Onsite OSHA Consultation
INSafe and QM&S Assistant Commissioner and
  Marketing Manager **Michelle Ellison** ............ (317) 233-2655
  Education: Indiana BSB

# Indiana Department of Natural Resources [DNR]
Indiana Government Center W256, 402 West Washington Street,
Indianapolis, IN 46204
Tel: (317) 232-4021  Fax: (317) 233-6811  E-mail: dnrweb@dnr.in.gov
Internet: www.in.gov/dnr
**Fiscal Year:** 2013-2014  **Budget:** $145,179,510
■Director **Cameron R. "Cam" Clark** .................. (317) 232-4021
  E-mail: cclark1@dnr.in.gov
  Education: Vanderbilt 1985 BA; Indiana 1990 JD
Communications Division Director **Phil Bloom** .......... (317) 233-3046
  E-mail: pbloom@dnr.in.gov
Law Enforcement Division Director **Lt. Col. Danny East** .. (317) 232-3846
Legislative Director **Samuel Hyer** .................. (317) 233-6904
  E-mail: shyer@dnr.in.gov
Executive Assistant/Constituent Services Assistant
  **Shelley Reeves** .............................. (317) 234-1072

## Administrative Management Team
Deputy Director **Mike Smith** ...................... (317) 234-7792
  E-mail: msmith@dnr.in.gov
Budget, Performance Management, Grants and Payroll
  Director **Jeffrey Saucerman** .................... (317) 234-1618
Fleet Facilities, Asset Management and Safety and ADA
  Compliance Director **Greg Sorrels** .............. (317) 232-4134
                                              Fax: (317) 233-0436
Human Resources Director **Amanda Foor** .............. (317) 232-4032
Internal Audit, Purchasing, Accounting and Customer
  Service Director **Chari Burke** .................. (317) 234-5227
  Education: Purdue 1997 BS
Management Information Systems Division Director
  **Timothy Ping** ................................ (317) 234-4796
  E-mail: tping@dnr.in.gov

## Land Management Team
Deputy Director **John M. Davis** .................... (317) 232-4025
  E-mail: jdavis@dnr.in.gov
Engineering Division Director **Dale Gick** ............ (317) 232-4148
  E-mail: dgick@dnr.in.gov
Fish and Wildlife Division Director **Mark Reiter** ........ (317) 232-8129
  E-mail: mreiter@dnr.in.gov          Fax: (317) 232-8150
Forestry Division Director **John Seifert** .............. (317) 232-4116
Land Acquisition Division Director **(Vacant)** .......... (317) 233-0441
Nature Preserves Division Director **John Bacone** ........ (317) 232-4054
  E-mail: jbacone@dnr.in.gov
  Education: Eastern Illinois 1971 BS; Illinois 1973 MS
Outdoor Recreation Division Director **Steve Morris** ...... (317) 232-4751
  E-mail: smorris@dnr.in.gov
State Parks and Reservoirs Division Director
  **Dan Bortner** ................................ (317) 232-4136
  E-mail: dbortner@dnr.in.gov

---

★ Elected Official   ■ Appointed by Governor   ● Appointed by Legislature   ▲ Appointed by Board or Commission   ◆ Appointed by State Supreme Court

EXECUTIVE BRANCH

## Regulatory Management Team

Fax: (317) 232-6811

Deputy Director **Chris Smith** . . . . . . . . . . . . . . . . . . . . . . . (317) 232-1557
E-mail: csmith@dnr.in.gov

Entomology and Plant Pathology Director
**Phil T. Marshall** . . . . . . . . . . . . . . . . . . . . . . . . . . . . . . (317) 232-4189
E-mail: pmarshall@dnr.in.gov

Historic Preservation and Archaeology Director
**Mitchell Zoll** . . . . . . . . . . . . . . . . . . . . . . . . . . . . . . . . (317) 232-3492
Education: Ball State MA

Oil and Gas Division Director **Herschel McDivitt** . . . . . . . (317) 232-4058
E-mail: hmcdivitt@dnr.in.gov

Reclamation Division Director **Steve Weinzapfel** . . . . . . . . (812) 665-2207
201 West Main Street, Jasonville, IN 47438-1408
P.O. Box 147, Jasonville, IN 47438-0147
E-mail: sweinzapfel@dnr.in.gov

Water Division Director **Mike Neyer** . . . . . . . . . . . . . . . . . (317) 232-4158
E-mail: mneyer@dnr.in.gov
Education: Rose-Hulman 1974 BSCE

## Chief Legal Counsel's Office

Chief Legal Counsel **Joseph "Joe" Hoage** . . . . . . . . . . . . . (317) 234-3869
E-mail: jhoage@dnr.in.gov
Education: Franklin Col (IN); Valparaiso 2006 JD

## Indiana State Personnel Department [SPD]

Indiana Government Center South, 402 West Washington Street,
Room W161, Indianapolis, IN 46204
Tel: (317) 232-3080  TTY: (317) 232-4555  Fax: (317) 232-3089
Fax: (317) 233-1979

**Fiscal Year:** 2013-2014  **Budget:** $3,072,000

■Director **Denny Darrow** . . . . . . . . . . . . . . . . . . . . . . . . (317) 232-4581
E-mail: jdarrow@spd.in.gov
Education: Purdue 1992

Deputy Director **John Bayse** . . . . . . . . . . . . . . . . . . . . . . (317) 232-3080

Deputy Director and Chief of Staff **Stefanie Krevda** . . . . . . (317) 232-4581
Education: Purdue 2009 BA

Communications Director **Ashley Hungate** . . . . . . . . . . . . (317) 234-4530
E-mail: ahungate@spd.in.gov

Compensation Director **Kristi L. Hall** . . . . . . . . . . . . . . . . (317) 234-2956

Disability/Benefits Director **Christy Tittle** . . . . . . . . . . . . (317) 232-3241

Employee Relations Director **Bruce Baxter** . . . . . . . . . . . . (317) 233-8796

Employee Engagement Director **(Vacant)** . . . . . . . . . . . . . (317) 234-3111

Recruitment Director **Nicole Russell** . . . . . . . . . . . . . . . . (317) 234-4148

Finance Division Director **Thomas "Tom" Michalak** . . . . . (317) 232-3058

HRMS/MIS Division Director **Melton Thomas** . . . . . . . . . (317) 234-7871
E-mail: melthomas@spd.in.gov

Legal Advisor **Keith Beesley** . . . . . . . . . . . . . . . . . . . . . . (317) 232-3062
E-mail: kbeesley@spd.in.gov

## Indiana Department of Transportation [INDOT]

Indiana Government Ctr. North, 100 North Senate Avenue, Room N758,
Indianapolis, IN 46204-2249
Tel: (317) 232-5525  Fax: (317) 234-8365

**Fiscal Year:** 2013-2014  **Budget:** $1,416,641,245

■Commissioner **Brandye L. Hendrickson** . . . . . . . . . . . . . (317) 232-5525
E-mail: bhendrickson@indot.in.gov

Executive Advisor to the Commissioner and
Construction Director **Robert F. "Bob" Tally, Jr.** . . . . . . (317) 234-8384
E-mail: rtally@indot.in.gov
Education: Louisville BS, ME

Executive Assistant to the Commissioner
**Jenny Ziemer** . . . . . . . . . . . . . . . . . . . . . . . . . . . . . . . (317) 232-3166

Chief of Staff **Chris Kiefer** . . . . . . . . . . . . . . . . . . . . . . . (317) 233-3601
Education: Indiana 2000 BA

Deputy Chief of Staff **Robert K. Alderman** . . . . . . . . . . . (317) 234-5136
E-mail: ralderman@indot.in.gov         Fax: (317) 232-5118

Chief Financial Officer **Daniel Brassard** . . . . . . . . . . . . . (317) 232-1472
Education: Evansville BS, MBA

Deputy Commissioner of Capital Program Management
**Samuel "Sam" Sarvis** . . . . . . . . . . . . . . . . . . . . . . . . . (317) 234-7173
E-mail: ssarvis@indot.in.gov
Education: Oakland U BS

Deputy Commissioner and Chief Legal Counsel
**Lori A. Torres** . . . . . . . . . . . . . . . . . . . . . . . . . . . . . . . (317) 232-5012
Education: Indiana 1982 BA, 1986 JD

Deputy Commissioner of Engineering and Asset
Management **James "Jim" Poturalski** . . . . . . . . . . . . . . (317) 234-0410

Deputy Commissioner of Innovative Project Delivery
**Jim Stark** . . . . . . . . . . . . . . . . . . . . . . . . . . . . . . . . . . (317) 232-0694
Education: Purdue BA

Deputy Commissioner of Operations **Ryan Gallagher** . . . (317) 234-8355
Education: Penn State BS

Accounting Director **Aaron Hood** . . . . . . . . . . . . . . . . . . (317) 232-0619

Chief Engineer and Construction Management Director
**Mark Miller** . . . . . . . . . . . . . . . . . . . . . . . . . . . . . . . . (317) 232-5456
E-mail: mrmiller@indot.in.gov

Emergency Planning and Response Director
**Tom Vanderpool** . . . . . . . . . . . . . . . . . . . . . . . . . . . . . (317) 234-3981

Environmental Services Director **Laura Hilden** . . . . . . . . . (317) 232-5018
E-mail: lhilden@indot.in.gov

Executive Communication Director
**Linda McGrannahan-Roberson** . . . . . . . . . . . . . . . . . . (317) 234-7175

Highway Design and Technical Services Director
**John Wright** . . . . . . . . . . . . . . . . . . . . . . . . . . . . . . . . (317) 232-5147

Internal Affairs Director **Ed King** . . . . . . . . . . . . . . . . . . (317) 232-5793
E-mail: eking@indot.in.gov

Management Information System Director **Joel Bump** . . . . (317) 234-3106
E-mail: jbump@indot.in.gov

Multimodal Director **Katie England** . . . . . . . . . . . . . . . . . (317) 234-7911

Procurement, Project Accounting and Budget Director
**Karen Hicks** . . . . . . . . . . . . . . . . . . . . . . . . . . . . . . . . (317) 232-5641

Statewide Technical Service Director **Louis Feagans** . . . . . (317) 232-5332
E-mail: lfeagans@indot.in.gov

Public Information Director **Will Wingfield** . . . . . . . . . . . . (317) 233-4675
E-mail: wwingfield@indot.in.gov

Real Estate Director **Michael Jett** . . . . . . . . . . . . . . . . . . (317) 232-5081

Research and Development Director
**Barry K. Partridge** . . . . . . . . . . . . . . . . . . . . . (765) 463-1521 ext. 251
E-mail: bpartridge@indot.in.gov

Traffic Support Director **Mike Bowman** . . . . . . . . . . . . . . (317) 899-8625

Contract Manager **Jeff Clanton** . . . . . . . . . . . . . . . . . . . . (317) 232-4198
E-mail: jclanton@indot.in.gov

## District Offices

Crawfordsville District Deputy Commissioner
**Alan Plunkett** . . . . . . . . . . . . . . . . . . . . . . . . . . . . . . . (765) 361-5201
41 West 300 North, Crawfordsville, IN 47933
Box 667, Crawfordsville, IN 47933

Fort Wayne District Deputy Commissioner
**Todd Johnson** . . . . . . . . . . . . . . . . . . . . . . . . . . . . . . . (260) 969-8206
5333 Hatfield Road, Fort Wayne, IN 46808

Greenfield District Deputy Commissioner
**Michael Smith** . . . . . . . . . . . . . . . . . . . . . . . . . . . . . . . (317) 467-3434
32 South Broadway Street, Greenfield, IN 46140-2247
P.O. Box 667, Greenfield, IN 46140

LaPorte District Deputy Commissioner **Rick Powers** . . . . . (219) 325-7472
315 East Boyd Boulevard, LaPorte, IN 46352      Fax: (219) 325-7434

Seymour District Deputy Commissioner
**Anthony McClellan** . . . . . . . . . . . . . . . . . . . . . . . . . . . (812) 524-3702
185 Agrico Lane, Seymour, IN 47274

Vincennes District Deputy Commissioner
**Russell "Rusty" Fowler** . . . . . . . . . . . . . . . . . . . . . . . . (812) 895-7301
3650 South U.S. 41, Vincennes, IN 47591

## Indiana Department of Veterans Affairs [DVA]

Indiana Government Ctr. South, 302 West Washington Street, Room E120,
Indianapolis, IN 46204-2738
Tel: (317) 232-3910  Fax: (317) 232-7721  E-mail: idva@dva.in.gov

**Fiscal Year:** 2013-2014  **Budget:** $1,830,077

■Director **CSM James M. Brown, ARNG** . . . . . . . . . . . . . (317) 232-3923
E-mail: jambrown@dva.in.gov

---

★ Elected Official   ■ Appointed by Governor   ● Appointed by Legislature      ▲ Appointed by Board or Commission      ◆ Appointed by State Supreme Court

Deputy Director **Chris Crabtree** . . . . . . . . . . . . . . . . . . (317) 232-3910
  Education: Indiana Wesleyan BS; Indiana JD
State Service Officer **Michael Hamm** . . . . . . . . . . . . . . . (317) 232-3921
State Approving Agency Director **Raymond Baker** . . . . . . . (317) 234-6061
State Approving Agency Deputy Director **(Vacant)** . . . . . . . (317) 234-6061
State Approving Agency Central Program Director
  **(Vacant)** . . . . . . . . . . . . . . . . . . . . . . . . . . . . . . . . . . (317) 232-3914
State Approving Agency Northeast Program Director
  **Fred Major** . . . . . . . . . . . . . . . . . . . . . . . . . . . . . . . . (317) 234-5865
State Approving Agency Northwest Program Coordinator
  **Summer G. Tacy** . . . . . . . . . . . . . . . . . . . . . . . . . . . . (317) 234-5658
State Approving Agency Southeast Program Director
  **Amber Mertens** . . . . . . . . . . . . . . . . . . . . . . . . . . . . . (317) 232-3917
State Approving Agency Southwest Program Director
  **(Vacant)** . . . . . . . . . . . . . . . . . . . . . . . . . . . . . . . . . . (317) 232-3916
State Approving Agency Program Coordinator
  **Tara Eggen** . . . . . . . . . . . . . . . . . . . . . . . . . . . . . . . . (317) 234-6062
Veterans Employment and Education Director
  **Deanna Pugh** . . . . . . . . . . . . . . . . . . . . . . . . . . . . . . . (317) 232-3910
Women's Veteran Coordinator
  **SMSgt Laura J. McKee, USAFR** . . . . . . . . . . . . . . . . . (317) 232-3910
  Education: Indiana

# Indiana Department of Workforce Development [DWD]

10 North Senate Avenue, Indianapolis, IN 46204
Tel: (888) 967-5663  Fax: (317) 233-1670

■Commissioner **Steven Braun** . . . . . . . . . . . . . . . . . . . . . (317) 232-7676
  E-mail: sbraun@dwd.in.gov
  Education: Harvard BS
  Executive Assistant **Cindy George** . . . . . . . . . . . . . . . . (317) 232-7676
General Counsel **Jeff Gill** . . . . . . . . . . . . . . . . . . . . . . . . (317) 233-5044
Chief of Staff and Chief Financial Officer
  **William "Bill" Nonte** . . . . . . . . . . . . . . . . . . . . . . . . . (317) 232-7675
Chief Operating Officer **Josh Richardson** . . . . . . . . . . . . (317) 232-2000
Chief Strategy Officer **Regina Ashley** . . . . . . . . . . . . . . . (317) 232-0204
Deputy Commissioner of Information **Steve Elliott** . . . . . . (317) 234-8371
  E-mail: selliott1@dwd.in.gov
Deputy Commissioner of Unemployment Insurance
  Operations **(Vacant)** . . . . . . . . . . . . . . . . . . . . . . . . . . (317) 232-7472
Marketing and Communications Director **Joseph Franks** . . (317) 234-7671
GED (General Education Development) Administrator
  **Terri Banks** . . . . . . . . . . . . . . . . . . . . . . . . . . . . . . . (317) 234-8339
  E-mail: tbanks@dwd.in.gov

# Office of Environmental Adjudication [OEA]

Indiana Government Ctr, North, 100 North Senate Avenue, N501,
Indianapolis, IN 46204
Tel: (317) 232-8591  Fax: (317) 233-9372

■Director and Chief Environmental Law Judge
  **Mary L. Davidsen** . . . . . . . . . . . . . . . . . . . . . . . . . . . (317) 232-8530
  E-mail: mdavidsen@oea.in.gov
Environmental Law Judge **Catherine Gibbs** . . . . . . . . . . . (317) 232-8591
Administrative Assistant **India Davidson** . . . . . . . . . . . . . (317) 232-8591

# Office of Management and Budget [OMB]

212 State House, 200 West Washington Street, Indianapolis, IN 46204
Tel: (317) 232-5610  Fax: (317) 233-3323  Internet: www.in.gov/omb

■Director **Micah Vincent** . . . . . . . . . . . . . . . . . . . . . . . . (317) 233-9204
  E-mail: mvincent@dlgf.in.gov
  Education: Purdue 2005 BS; Indiana (Indianapolis) 2008 JD
Operations Manager and Executive Assistant
  **Aaron Bennett** . . . . . . . . . . . . . . . . . . . . . . . . . . . . . . (317) 234-4411
Business Intelligence and Analytics Director **(Vacant)** . . . . (317) 234-4090
■General Counsel and Policy Director **Justin McAdam** . . . (317) 234-2285
  E-mail: jmcadam@gov.in.gov
Management Information Services Director **(Vacant)** . . . . . . (317) 232-3470
General Government Assistant Director **(Vacant)** . . . . . . . . (317) 232-5623

Health and Human Services Assistant Director
  **Joe Habig** . . . . . . . . . . . . . . . . . . . . . . . . . . . . . . . . . (317) 232-5611
  E-mail: johabig@sba.in.gov
Higher Education Assistant Director **Chad Timmerman** . . . (317) 232-5657
Public Safety, Conservation and Transportation Assistant
  Director **Ron Sobecki** . . . . . . . . . . . . . . . . . . . . . . . . . (317) 232-7221
Tax and Revenue Assistant Director **John Weinmann** . . . . (317) 232-3471

# Department of Government Efficiency and Financial Planning [GEFP]

One North Capitol Street, Suite 900, Indianapolis, IN 46204
Tel: (317) 233-4332  Fax: (317) 232-8872

■Executive Director **David Matusoff** . . . . . . . . . . . . . . . . (317) 234-8292
  E-mail: dmatusoff@gov.in.gov
Deputy Director **Joshua Martin** . . . . . . . . . . . . . . . . . . . (317) 234-8292

# Department of Local Government Finance [DLGF]

Indiana Government Center North, 100 North Senate Avenue,
Room N1058, Indianapolis, IN 46204
Tel: (317) 232-3777  Fax: (317) 974-1629  E-mail: gateway@dlgf.in.gov
Internet: www.in.gov/dlgf

■Commissioner **Courtney L. Schaafsma** . . . . . . . . . . . . . (317) 234-5720
  E-mail: cshaafsma@dlgf.in.gov
Operations and Finance Deputy Commissioner
  **Matt Parkinson** . . . . . . . . . . . . . . . . . . . . . . . . . . . . . (317) 232-3759
  Administrative Assistant **Linda Ebert** . . . . . . . . . . . . . . (317) 232-3775
General Counsel **Michael Duffy** . . . . . . . . . . . . . . . . . . . (317) 233-9219
  E-mail: mduffy@dlgf.in.gov
  Deputy General Counsel **David Marusarz** . . . . . . . . . . . (317) 233-6770
Communications Director **Jenny Banks** . . . . . . . . . . . . . . (317) 234-4376
  E-mail: jbanks@dlgf.in.gov

## Assessment Division

Director **J. Barry Wood** . . . . . . . . . . . . . . . . . . . . . . . . . (317) 232-3762
  E-mail: bwood@dlgf.in.gov
  Administrative Assistant **Donna Bratcher** . . . . . . . . . . . (317) 233-0166
Assessor/Auditor **Derek Grimes** . . . . . . . . . . . . . . . . . . . (317) 234-8889
Assessor/Auditor **Chirjeev Oberoi** . . . . . . . . . . . . . . . . . (317) 234-8888
Assessor/Auditor **Julie Waddell** . . . . . . . . . . . . . . . . . . . (317) 232-3765
Assessor/Auditor **Chris Wilkening** . . . . . . . . . . . . . . . . . (317) 234-8720
Senior Statistician and Application System Analyst
  **Deliverance Bougie** . . . . . . . . . . . . . . . . . . . . . . . . . . (317) 234-5861
Utility Specialist **Marlo Hayden** . . . . . . . . . . . . . . . . . . . (317) 232-3756
  E-mail: mhayden@dlgf.in.gov

## Budget Division

Director **(Vacant)** . . . . . . . . . . . . . . . . . . . . . . . . . . . . . (317) 234-3937
Assistant Director **Dan Jones** . . . . . . . . . . . . . . . . . . . . . (317) 232-0651

## Data Analysis Division

Director **Geoff Kuester** . . . . . . . . . . . . . . . . . . . . . . . . . (317) 232-3759
Assistant Director **James Johnson** . . . . . . . . . . . . . . . . . . (317) 233-8347

# Indiana Department of Revenue [DOR]

Indiana Government Ctr. North, 100 North Senate Avenue, Room N248,
Indianapolis, IN 46204
Tel: (317) 233-3242  TTY: (317) 233-5977  Fax: (317) 232-2103

**Fiscal Year:** 2013-2014  **Budget:** $74,222,485

■Commissioner **Andrew J. Kossack** . . . . . . . . . . . . . . . . . (317) 232-2109
  E-mail: akossack@dor.in.gov
  Education: Butler; Indiana 2007 JD
  Assistant to the Commissioner **Jane Graham** . . . . . . . . . (317) 232-8039
Chief Financial Officer **Valerie Hunt** . . . . . . . . . . . . . . . . (317) 232-2177
  Education: Indiana BS, MBA
Chief Information Officer **Kevin Gulley** . . . . . . . . . . . . . . (317) 233-1453
  E-mail: kgulley@dor.in.gov
  Education: Indiana BBA; Butler MBA
Collections Deputy Commissioner **Milton Cuevas** . . . . . . . (317) 232-5013
Enforcement Deputy Commissioner **Ron Broughton** . . . . . (317) 232-0564
Special Tax and Support Administration Deputy
  Commissioner **Jim Poe** . . . . . . . . . . . . . . . . . . . . . . . . (317) 232-8039

*(continued on next page)*

---

★ Elected Official    ■ Appointed by Governor    ● Appointed by Legislature    ▲ Appointed by Board or Commission    ◆ Appointed by State Supreme Court

**EXECUTIVE BRANCH**

**Indiana Department of Revenue** *continued*

Tax Administration Deputy Commissioner
**Robert "Bob" Dittmer** .............................(317) 234-3793
General Counsel **Asheesh Agarwal** ..................(317) 232-0610
  Education: Northwestern 1994 BA; Chicago 1997 JD
Inheritance Tax Administrator **Donald Hopper** ..........(317) 233-3293
                               Fax: (317) 233-6489
Protest Review Manager **Patrick Gallagher** .............(317) 233-3228
                               Fax: (317) 233-6489
Legal Division Administrative Law Judge **Bruce Kolb** .....(317) 232-2566
                               Fax: (317) 233-6489
Human Resources Director **Beverly "Bev" Bridget** .......(317) 232-2149
                               Fax: (317) 232-1061
Public Relations Director **Amanda Stanley** .............(317) 232-2379
  E-mail: astanley4@dor.in.gov
Tax Policy Director **Collin Davis** .....................(317) 615-7318
Field Audit Deputy Director **Mandi Shawarira** ..........(317) 233-5163
                               Fax: (317) 233-5167
Taxpayer Advocate and Ethics Officer
**Tammy Jones** .........................(317) 232-2345 ext. 11675
                               Fax: (317) 232-5425

## Indiana Board of Tax Review [IBTR]

100 North Senate Avenue, Room N1026, Indianapolis, IN 46204
Tel: (317) 232-3786  Fax: (317) 234-5589  Internet: www.in.gov/ibtr

■Chairman **Ted J. Holaday** .........................(317) 233-6767
  Term Expires: January 1, 2016
  E-mail: tholaday@ibtr.in.gov
  Education: DePauw; Indiana (Indianapolis) JD
■Commissioner **Betsy J. Brand** ......................(317) 232-3784
  Term Expires: January 1, 2015
  E-mail: bbrand@ibtr.in.gov
■Commissioner **Jonathan R. "Jon" Elrod** ..............(317) 232-3753
  Term Expires: January 1, 2015
  Education: Xavier (OH) 1999 BA; Indiana 2002 JD
Senior Administrative Law Judge
  **Thomas "Tom" Martindale** ....................(317) 234-8320
Senior Administrative Law Judge **David Pardo** ..........(317) 234-3733
Senior Administrative Law Judge **John J. Thompson** ....(317) 232-3783

## Indiana Finance Authority [IFA]

One North Capitol Avenue, Suite 900, Indianapolis, IN 46204-2226
Tel: (317) 233-4332  Fax: (317) 232-6786  Internet: www.in.gov/ifa

■Public Finance Director **Daniel Huge** .................(317) 233-2916
  E-mail: dhuge@ifa.in.gov
  Education: Purdue
  Executive Assistant to the Public Finance Director
  **(Vacant)** .......................................(317) 234-3507
Chief Operating Officer and Environmental Programs
  Director **Jim McGoff** .............................(317) 232-2972
Controller **Connie McAfee** ...........................(317) 234-4265
General Counsel **Andrew P. Seiwert** ..................(317) 234-4780
Debt Management Director **Mark Pascarella** ...........(317) 234-2228
Program/Office Manager **Cindy Herron** ...............(317) 233-4335
  E-mail: cherron@ifa.in.gov
Financial Resources Coordinator **Sara Westrick-Corbin** ...(317) 234-1688
Media Relations Coordinator **(Vacant)** ................(317) 234-3507

## Indiana Office of Technology [IOT]

100 North Senate Avenue, Room N551, Indianapolis, IN 46204
Tel: (317) 234-4357

Chief Information Officer **Dewand Neely** ..............(317) 234-0835
  E-mail: dneely@iot.in.gov
  Education: Purdue; Indiana Wesleyan MBA

## State Board of Accounts [SBOA]

Indiana Government Center South, 302 West Washington Street,
Room E418, Indianapolis, IN 46204
Tel: (317) 232-2513  Fax: (317) 232-4711

**Fiscal Year:** 2013-2014  **Budget:** $19,487,346

■State Examiner **Paul D. Joyce, CPA** ..................(317) 232-2524
  E-mail: pjoyce@sboa.in.gov
  Education: Indiana State 1991

■Deputy State Examiner **Michael H. Bozymski, CPA** ......(317) 232-2507
  E-mail: mbozymski@sboa.in.gov
  Education: Ball State 1985
■Deputy State Examiner **Tammy White** ................(317) 232-2513
  E-mail: twhite@sboa.in.gov
  Education: Indiana (Indianapolis)

## Indiana Public Retirement System [INPRS]

One North Capitol Street, Suite 001, Indianapolis, IN 46204
Tel: (888) 286-3544  Fax: (317) 232-3882  E-mail: inprs@inprs.in.gov

■Executive Director **Steven "Steve" Russo** .............(317) 232-3864
  E-mail: sterusso@inprs.in.gov
  Education: Purdue
Chief Operating Officer and Deputy Director
  **Steven Barley** ..................................(317) 233-4184
Chief Communication Officer **Jeffrey D. "Jeff" Hutson** ...(317) 234-3401
  E-mail: jhutson@inprs.in.gov
Chief Financial Officer **Donna Brown** .................(317) 234-2383
Chief Investment Officer (Interim) **Scott Davis** ..........(317) 234-6210
Chief Legal and Compliance Officer
  **Anthony "Tony" Green** .........................(317) 234-7319
Chief Technology Officer **Michael "Mike" Hineline** ......(317) 234-7889
  E-mail: mhineline@inprs.in.gov
Human Resources Director **Donna Grotz** ..............(317) 234-1130
Internal Audit Director **Teresa A. Snedigar, CIA** .........(317) 234-5681

## Office of State Based Initiatives

Executive Director **Luke Kenworthy** ..................(317) 234-2079

## Office of Utility Consumer Counselor [OUCC]

115 West Washington Street, 1500-South, Indianapolis, IN 46204
Tel: (317) 232-2494  Tel: (888) 441-2494  Fax: (317) 232-5923
E-mail: uccinfo@oucc.state.in.us  Internet: www.in.gov/oucc

Utility Consumer Counselor **David Stippler** .............(317) 232-2494
Federal Affairs Deputy Consumer Counselor
  **Robert Gordon Mork** ...........................(317) 232-2494
  Education: Yale 1988 BA; Indiana 1992 JD
State Affairs Deputy Consumer Counselor
  **Randall C. Helmen** .............................(317) 232-2494
Paralegal **Cheryl A. Williams** ........................(317) 232-2494

## Family and Social Services Administration [FSSA]

Indiana Government Center South, 402 West Washington Street,
Room W-461, Indianapolis, IN 46204-7083
Tel: (317) 233-4454  TTY: (317) 232-6478  Fax: (317) 233-4693
Internet: www.in.gov/fssa

■Secretary **John J. Wernert III, MD** ...................(317) 233-4690
  E-mail: john.wernert@fssa.in.gov
  Education: Louisville 1985 MD; Bellarmine U; Louisville
  Executive Assistant to the Secretary **Lisa Graham** ......(317) 233-4690
Chief of Staff **Chris Johnson** ........................(317) 234-8901
Deputy Secretary **(Vacant)** ..........................(317) 233-4690
General Counsel **Allison Taylor** ......................(317) 234-3884
                               Fax: (317) 232-1133
Chief Audit Executive **Roger Booth** ...................(317) 232-6859
                               Fax: (317) 233-9235
Communications and Media Director
  **James "Jim" Gavin** .............................(317) 234-0197
  E-mail: jim.gavin@fssa.in.gov
Contract Management Director **Greg McAloon** ..........(317) 234-6814
  E-mail: greg.mcaloon@fssa.in.gov
Human Resources Director **Marci Iaria** ................(317) 234-2873
                               Fax: (317) 232-1530
Senior Policy and Legislative Director
  **William "Gus" Habig** ...........................(317) 232-1164
  E-mail: william.habig@fssa.in.gov
Medicaid Director **Joseph W. Moser** ..................(317) 234-2407
  Education: Marian Col (IN) 2000 BS; Miami U (OH) 2001 MA
Aging Division Director **Yonda Snyder** ................(317) 232-1731

---

★ Elected Official    ■ Appointed by Governor    ● Appointed by Legislature    ▲ Appointed by Board or Commission    ◆ Appointed by State Supreme Court

Disability and Rehabilitative Services Division Director
**Kylee Hope** . . . . . . . . . . . . . . . . . . . . . . . . . . . . . . . . (317) 232-1147
Early Childhood and Out-of-School Learning Director
**Nicole Norvell** . . . . . . . . . . . . . . . . . . . . . . . . . . . . . (317) 234-3313
Family Resources Division Director **Adrienne Shields** . . . . (317) 234-2373
Mental Health and Addiction Division Director
**Kevin Moore** . . . . . . . . . . . . . . . . . . . . . . . . . . . . . . . (317) 232-7860
  Fax: (317) 233-3472
Rehabilitation Services Bureau Director
**Theresa Koleszar** . . . . . . . . . . . . . . . . . . . . . . . . . . . (317) 234-4475
Chief Compliance Officer **(Vacant)** . . . . . . . . . . . . . . . . . (317) 234-8826
Chief Financial Officer **Paul Bowling** . . . . . . . . . . . . . . . (317) 233-4451
Chief Information Officer and Technology Services
  Division Director **Jared Linder** . . . . . . . . . . . . . . . . . (317) 234-6998
    E-mail: jared.linder@fssa.in.gov
Chief Medical Officer **Dr. Ann Zerr** . . . . . . . . . . . . . . . . . (317) 234-7268
Chief Privacy and Security Officer **H. Cliff McCullough** . . . (317) 232-4732
    E-mail: h.cliff.mccullough@fssa.in.gov
Chief Quality Officer **Andrew VanZee** . . . . . . . . . . . . . . . (317) 232-1165
    Education: Knox (IL) BS; South Carolina MHCA
Special Counsel for Program Integrity **(Vacant)** . . . . . . . . (317) 233-1764
Strategic Initiatives Director **(Vacant)** . . . . . . . . . . . . . . (317) 233-5711

## Indiana Professional Licensing Agency [IPLA]

Indiana Government Ctr. South, 402 West Washington Street,
Room W072, Indianapolis, IN 46204
Tel: (317) 232-2960  Fax: (317) 233-4236

■Executive Director **Deborah Frye** . . . . . . . . . . . . . . . . . (317) 234-1981
    E-mail: defrye@pla.in.gov
  Administrative Assistant to the Executive Director
    **Katie Byers** . . . . . . . . . . . . . . . . . . . . . . . . . . . . . (317) 234-1981
Chief Legal Counsel **Michael Minglin** . . . . . . . . . . . . . . (317) 232-2912
Compliance and Investigations Director
  **Zaneta Nunnally** . . . . . . . . . . . . . . . . . . . . . . . . . . (317) 232-1120
    E-mail: znunnally@pla.in.gov
Comptroller and Operations Manager **Maureen Bennett** . . (317) 234-1983
Information Technology Director **Herb Price** . . . . . . . . . . (317) 234-1984
    E-mail: hprice@pla.in.gov
    Education: Ball State 1970 BS
Accountancy Board Director **Rae Harman** . . . . . . . . . . . . (317) 234-8800
Architects and Landscape Architects Board Director
  **Amy Hall** . . . . . . . . . . . . . . . . . . . . . . . . . . . . . . . . (317) 234-3022
Athletic Trainers Board Director **Amy Hall** . . . . . . . . . . . (317) 234-3048
Behavioral Health and Human Services Licensing Board
  Director **Cindy Vaught** . . . . . . . . . . . . . . . . . . . . . . . (317) 234-2054
Chiropractic Examiners Board Director **Cindy Vaught** . . . (317) 234-2054
    E-mail: pla8@pla.in.gov
    E-mail: cvaught@pla.in.gov
Cosmetology and Barber Examiners Board Director
  **Tracy Hicks** . . . . . . . . . . . . . . . . . . . . . . . . . . . . . . (317) 234-3031
Dentistry Board Director **Cindy Vaught** . . . . . . . . . . . . . (317) 234-2054
Dietitians Certification Board Director
  **Darren Covington** . . . . . . . . . . . . . . . . . . . . . . . . . . (317) 234-2060
    E-mail: dcovington@pla.in.gov
Engineering Board Director **Amy Hall** . . . . . . . . . . . . . . . (317) 234-3022
Funeral and Cemetery Service Board Director
  **Tracy Hicks** . . . . . . . . . . . . . . . . . . . . . . . . . . . . . . (317) 234-3031
Health Facility Administrators Board Director **Amy Hall** . . (317) 234-3022
    E-mail: pla10@pla.in.gov
Massage Therapy Board Director **Rae Harman** . . . . . . . . (317) 234-8800
Medical Licensing Board Director **Darren Covington** . . . . (317) 234-2060
    E-mail: pla3@pla.in.gov
    E-mail: dcovington@pla.in.gov
Nursing Board Director **Exton R. Cordingley** . . . . . . . . . (317) 234-1990
Occupational Therapy Committee Board Director
  **Rae Harman** . . . . . . . . . . . . . . . . . . . . . . . . . . . . . . (317) 234-8800
Optometry Board Director **Rae Harman** . . . . . . . . . . . . . (317) 234-8800
Physician Assistant Committee Board Director
  **Darren Covington** . . . . . . . . . . . . . . . . . . . . . . . . . . (317) 234-2060
Podiatric Medicine Board Director **Darren Covington** . . . (317) 234-2060
    E-mail: dcovington@pla.in.gov
Psychology Board Director **Exton R. Cordingley** . . . . . . . (317) 234-1990

Respiratory Care Committee Board Director
  **Cindy Vaught** . . . . . . . . . . . . . . . . . . . . . . . . . . . . . (317) 234-2054
    E-mail: cvaught@pla.in.gov
Speech Language Pathology Audiology Board Director
  **(Vacant)** . . . . . . . . . . . . . . . . . . . . . . . . . . . . . . . . . (317) 234-2067
Veterinary Medical Examiners Board Director
  **Cindy Vaught** . . . . . . . . . . . . . . . . . . . . . . . . . . . . . (317) 234-2054

## Indiana Bureau of Motor Vehicles [BMV]

Indiana Government Center North, 100 North Senate Avenue,
Room N440, Indianapolis, IN 46204
Tel: (888) 692-6841  Fax: (317) 234-3336

■Commissioner **Kent Abernathy** . . . . . . . . . . . . . . . . . . . (317) 232-5914
    E-mail: kabernathy@bmv.in.gov
    Education: West Point BS; Oakland City Col MS; Army War Col MS
  Assistant to the Commissioner **Laurel Pritt** . . . . . . . . . (317) 232-5914
Chief of Staff **Peter L. Lacy** . . . . . . . . . . . . . . . . . . . . . (317) 232-5914
    Education: Citadel; Xavier (OH) MBA
Chief Financial Officer **Jeff Moon** . . . . . . . . . . . . . . . . . (317) 233-1530
  Fax: (317) 233-4234
Chief Operating Officer **Kevin Garvey** . . . . . . . . . . . . . . (317) 232-4688
    E-mail: kgarvey@bmv.in.gov  Fax: (317) 233-3138
Branch Operations Deputy Commissioner **Noah Shelton** . . (317) 234-8075
  Fax: (317) 233-0189
Communications Deputy Commissioner **(Vacant)** . . . . . . . (317) 233-5323
  Fax: (317) 232-8762
Human Resources Executive Director **Teresa Steppe** . . . . (317) 232-1044
  Fax: (317) 233-2839
General Counsel **Adam Krupp** . . . . . . . . . . . . . . . . . . . . (317) 234-5217
  Fax: (317) 233-3135

## Indiana Economic Development Corporation [IEDC]

One North Capitol Avenue, Suite 700, Indianapolis, IN 46204
Tel: (317) 232-8800  TTY: (317) 233-5977  Fax: (317) 233-5123

■Secretary of Commerce **Victor P. Smith** . . . . . . . . . . . . . (317) 234-1359
    E-mail: vsmith@iedc.in.gov
    Education: Colgate 1990 BS; Columbus Law 1996 JD
■President **James A. "Jim" Schellinger** . . . . . . . . . . . . . (317) 234-3565
    E-mail: jschellinger@iedc.in.gov
    Education: Notre Dame BArch; Harvard (Attended)
Chief of Staff **Steve Akard** . . . . . . . . . . . . . . . . . . . . . . (317) 234-2083
Business Development Vice President **Kent Anderson** . . . . (317) 234-8002
  Fax: (317) 233-4146
General Counsel **Chris Cotterill** . . . . . . . . . . . . . . . . . . . (317) 233-4459
    Education: Wabash Col 1999 BA; Indiana 2002 JD  Fax: (317) 233-4146
Marketing Vice President **Kelly Nicholl** . . . . . . . . . . . . . (317) 232-4950
  Fax: (317) 233-9851
Chief Financial Officer **Mark Pishon** . . . . . . . . . . . . . . . (317) 232-8780
Motor Sports Director **Rollie Helmling** . . . . . . . . . . . . . . (317) 232-8894
  Fax: (317) 232-4146
Operations and Business Systems Director
  **Garth Brazelton** . . . . . . . . . . . . . . . . . . . . . . . . . . . (317) 234-4038
  Fax: (317) 234-1735
Policy Director **Eric Shields** . . . . . . . . . . . . . . . . . . . . . (317) 643-1965
  Fax: (317) 234-1735
Regulatory Affairs Director **(Vacant)** . . . . . . . . . . . . . . . (317) 232-8893
  Fax: (317) 232-4146

## Commission for Higher Education [CHE]

101 West Ohio Street, Suite 300, Indianapolis, IN 46204-1971
Tel: (317) 464-4400

▲Commissioner **Teresa S. Lubbers** . . . . . . . . . . . . . . . . . (317) 464-4400
    E-mail: tlubbers@che.in.gov
    Education: Indiana 1973 BA; JFK School Govt 1981 MPA
Chief Operating Officer and Chief Financial
  Officer **Matt Hawkins** . . . . . . . . . . . . . . . . . . . . (317) 464-4400 ext. 115
  Chief Information Officer **Michael Hawryluk** . . . . . . . . . (317) 232-2797
  Information Systems Manager **Basu Maharjan** . . . . . . . . (317) 233-4855
    E-mail: bmaharjan@che.in.gov

*(continued on next page)*

---

★ Elected Official   ■ Appointed by Governor   ● Appointed by Legislature   ▲ Appointed by Board or Commission   ◆ Appointed by State Supreme Court

**Commission for Higher Education** *continued*

Student Support Services Director **Colby Shank** . . . . . . . . (317) 232-1023
Senior Associate Commissioner and Chief Academic
  Officer **Dr. Kenneth Sauer** . . . . . . . . . . . . . . . . . . . . . . . (317) 232-1090
Associate Commissioner for Finance and Human
  Resources **Dominick Chase** . . . . . . . . . . . . . . . . . . . . . . (317) 232-1025
Associate Commissioner for Policy and Legislation
  **Sarah Ancel** . . . . . . . . . . . . . . . . . . . . . . . . . . . . . . . . . (317) 232-1070
  E-mail: sancel@che.in.gov
Associate Commissioner for Research and Analysis
  **Stacy Townsley** . . . . . . . . . . . . . . . . . . . . . . . . . . . . . . . (317) 232-1029
Associate Commissioner for Strategic Communications
  and Student Success Initiatives **Jason Bearce** . . . . . . . (317) 232-1060
  E-mail: jasonb@che.in.gov
  Communications Director **Stephanie Wilson** . . . . . . . . . (317) 232-1016
    E-mail: swilson@che.in.gov

## Indiana Archives and Records Administration [IARA]

402 West Washington Street, Room W472, Indianapolis, IN 46204
Tel: (317) 232-3380  Fax: (317) 233-1713

**Fiscal Year:** 2013-2014  **Budget:** $2,075,693

■Director and State Archivist **Jim Corridan** . . . . . . . . . . . . (317) 232-3380
  E-mail: jcorridan@icpr.in.gov
 Deputy Director **Patrick "Pat" Cochran** . . . . . . . . . . . . . (317) 232-3663
 Micrographics and Imaging Services Program Director
  **Brian Taylor** . . . . . . . . . . . . . . . . . . . . . . . . . . . . . . . . . (317) 233-3746
  100 North Senate Avenue, Room NO55,      Fax: (317) 233-0908
  Indianapolis, IN 46204
 State Archives Program Director **Alan F. January** . . . . . . . (317) 591-5222
  6440 East 30th Street, Indianapolis, IN 46219    Fax: (317) 591-5234
  Education: Wisconsin 1965 BA; Iowa 1976 PhD

## Indiana Utility Regulatory Commission [IURC]

National City Center, 101 West Washington Street, Suite 1500 E,
Indianapolis, IN 46204
Tel: (317) 232-2701  Tel: (800) 851-4268 (Utility Consumer Affairs)
TTY: (317) 232-8556  Fax: (317) 232-6758  Internet: www.in.gov/iurc

■Chairman **Carol A. Stephan** . . . . . . . . . . . . . . . . . . . . . . . (317) 234-4715
  Term Expires: February 2020
  E-mail: cstephan@urc.in.gov
  Education: Indiana; Indiana (Indianapolis) JD
■Commissioner **James F. "Jim" Huston** . . . . . . . . . . . . . . . (317) 232-2701
  Term Expires: March 31, 2017
  Education: Ball State
■Commissioner **Angela Weber** . . . . . . . . . . . . . . . . . . . . . . (317) 232-2706
  Term Expires: March 2018
  Education: Indiana, JD
■Commissioner **David E. Ziegner** . . . . . . . . . . . . . . . . . . . . (317) 232-4199
  Term Expires: April 2015
  E-mail: dziegner@urc.in.gov
  Education: Indiana 1976 BA, 1979 JD
■Commissioner **(Vacant)** . . . . . . . . . . . . . . . . . . . . . . . . . . (317) 232-2701

## Worker's Compensation Board of Indiana [WCB]

Indiana Government Center South, 402 West Washington Street,
Room W196, Indianapolis, IN 46204
Tel: (317) 233-3009  Fax: (317) 233-5493

■Chairman **Linda Hamilton** . . . . . . . . . . . . . . . . . . . . . . . . (317) 232-3811
  E-mail: lhamilton@wcb.in.gov
 Executive Administrator **Mary Taivalkoski** . . . . . . . . . . . . (317) 232-3811
 Second Injury Fund Administrator **Curtis Vickers** . . . . . . . (317) 232-3810
 Compliance Director **Alan Buckley** . . . . . . . . . . . . . . . . . . (317) 232-5922
 Information Technology Manager **Rob Howell** . . . . . . . . . . (317) 233-0396
  E-mail: rhowell@wcb.in.gov

## Indiana Criminal Justice Institute [ICJI]

101 West Washington Street, 1170-East, Indianapolis, IN 46204
Tel: (317) 232-1233  Tel: (800) 353-1484 (Victim Help Line)
Fax: (317) 232-4979  Internet: www.in.gov/cji

■Executive Director **David Reid Murtaugh** . . . . . . . . . . . . . (317) 232-1233
  E-mail: dmurtaugh@cji.in.gov
  Education: Vincennes AS; Indiana Northwest BGS
  Executive Assistant **Yvonne Stoner** . . . . . . . . . . . . . . . . . (317) 232-7608
 Deputy Director of Operations/General Counsel
  **Devon McDonald** . . . . . . . . . . . . . . . . . . . . . . . . . . . . . (317) 232-7611
 Deputy Director of Policy & Planning **Christina Trexler** . . . (317) 234-8891
 Legal Counsel **Gabrielle Owens** . . . . . . . . . . . . . . . . . . . . (317) 232-1292
 Drug and Crime Control Division Director
  **Andrew Rodeghero** . . . . . . . . . . . . . . . . . . . . . . . . . . . (317) 234-3324
 Research and Planning Division Director **Joshua Ross** . . . . (317) 234-2922
  E-mail: joross@cji.in.gov
  Education: Indiana 2000 BS, 2005 MA
 Substance Abuse Services Division Director
  **Sonya Carrico** . . . . . . . . . . . . . . . . . . . . . . . . . . . . . . . (317) 232-1289
  E-mail: scarrico@cji.in.gov
  Education: Taylor BS
 Traffic Safety Division Director **Steven Hillman** . . . . . . . . (317) 232-1296
 Victim Services Division Director **Jade Palin** . . . . . . . . . . (317) 232-2927
 Youth Division Director **Hannah Cowles** . . . . . . . . . . . . . (317) 233-3340
  E-mail: hcowles@cji.in.gov
 Communications Director **Adam J. Baker** . . . . . . . . . . . . . (317) 232-7609
  E-mail: adbaker@cji.in.gov
 Victim Compensation Supervisor **Nolan Jenkins** . . . . . . . . (317) 234-3523
  E-mail: njenkins@cji.in.gov

## Indiana Law Enforcement Academy

P.O. Box 313 - Law Enforcement Training Board,
Plainfield, IN 46168-0313
Tel: (317) 839-5191  Fax: (317) 839-9741  Internet: www.in.gov/ilea

▲Executive Director **Rusty K. Goodpaster** . . . . . . . . . . . . . (317) 839-5191
  E-mail: rgoodpaster@ilea.in.gov
  Education: Indianapolis BS
 Deputy Director **Michael J. Lindsay** . . . . . . . . . . . . . . . . . (317) 839-5191
  Education: Indiana BS
 Administrative Assistant **Janice Hardwick** . . . . . . . . . . . . (317) 839-5191

## Indiana State Library

140 North Senate Avenue, Indianapolis, IN 46204
Tel: (317) 232-3675  TTY: (317) 232-7763  Fax: (317) 232-3728

■State Librarian **Jacob Speer** . . . . . . . . . . . . . . . . . . . . . . . (317) 232-3693
  E-mail: jspeer@library.in.gov
 Statewide Library Services and Outreach Associate
  Director **Wendy Knapp** . . . . . . . . . . . . . . . . . . . . . . . . (317) 232-3718
 Director of Operations **Scott Lambert** . . . . . . . . . . . . . . . (317) 232-3701
 Communications Director **Ryan Brown** . . . . . . . . . . . . . . . (317) 753-9766
  E-mail: rybrown@library.in.gov
  Education: Ball State BA
 Law Library Consultant and General Counsel
  **Sylvia Watson** . . . . . . . . . . . . . . . . . . . . . . . . . . . . . . . (317) 232-3735
  E-mail: sywatson@library.in.gov
 Library Development Office Supervisor **Steven Schmidt** . . (317) 232-3675
 Management Information Systems Director **Jason Boyer** . . (317) 234-2128
  E-mail: jboyer@library.in.gov
 Professional Development Office Supervisor
  **Suzanne Walker** . . . . . . . . . . . . . . . . . . . . . . . . . . . . . (317) 234-5649

## Public and Support Services

Associate Director, Public Services **Connie Bruder** . . . . . . . (317) 232-3734
Indiana Collections Supervisor **Monique Howell** . . . . . . . . (317) 234-7270
Cataloguing Supervisor **Jocelyn Lewis** . . . . . . . . . . . . . . . (317) 232-3687
Genealogy Collections Supervisor **Stephanie Ashbury** . . . (317) 232-3724
Manuscripts and Rare Books Collection Supervisor
  **Bethany Fiechter** . . . . . . . . . . . . . . . . . . . . . . . . . . . . . (317) 232-3671
Reference and Government Services Supervisor **(Vacant)** . . (317) 232-3727
Talking Book and Braille Library Supervisor
  **Margaret "Maggie" Ansty** . . . . . . . . . . . . . . . . . . . . . . (317) 232-3738

State Data Center Coordinator
  **Katherine "Katie" Springer** . . . . . . . . . . . . . . . . . . . . . . . (317) 232-3678

# Indiana State Police [ISP]
Indiana Government Ctr. North, 100 North Senate Avenue, 3rd Floor,
Indianapolis, IN 46204
Tel: (317) 232-8248  Fax: (317) 232-0652

■Superintendent **Doug Carter** . . . . . . . . . . . . . . . . . . . . . . . . (317) 232-8241
  E-mail: dcarter@isp.in.gov
  Executive Assistant **Anna Clevenger** . . . . . . . . . . . . . . . . (317) 232-8242
Assistant Superintendent **Col. Mark A. French** . . . . . . . . . . (317) 232-8242

# Ports of Indiana Commission
150 West Market Street, Suite 100, Indianapolis, IN 46204
Tel: (317) 232-9200  Fax: (317) 232-0137
E-mail: info@portsofindiana.com  Internet: www.portsofindiana.com

■Chairman **Ken Kaczmarek, CPA** . . . . . . . . . . . . . . . . . . . . . (317) 232-9200
  Term Expires: June 1, 2015
  Education: Indiana 1968 BS, 1971 MBA
■Vice Chairman **Greg L. Gibson** . . . . . . . . . . . . . . . . . . . . . . . (317) 232-9200
  Education: Rose-Hulman BS
■Secretary/Treasurer **Jay K. Potesta** . . . . . . . . . . . . . . . . . . (317) 232-9200
  Education: VanderCook Music BA
■Commissioner **Ramon Arredondo** . . . . . . . . . . . . . . . . . . . . (317) 232-9200
  Education: Central Florida BA, MPP
■Commissioner **Marvin Ferguson** . . . . . . . . . . . . . . . . . . . . . (317) 232-9200
■Commissioner **Christine H. Keck** . . . . . . . . . . . . . . . . . . . . . (317) 232-9200
  Education: Indiana
■Commissioner **Philip W. McCauley II, CPA** . . . . . . . . . . . . (317) 232-9200
  Education: St Joseph Col 1965 BAcc
■Commissioner **Miriam E. Robeson** . . . . . . . . . . . . . . . . . . . . (317) 232-9200
  Term Expires: October 31, 2019

# Office of the Lieutenant Governor
200 West Washington Street, Suite 333, Indianapolis, IN 46204
Tel: (317) 232-4545  Fax: (317) 232-4788

★Lieutenant Governor **Eric Holcomb** (R) . . . . . . . . . . . . . . . (317) 232-4545
  Term Expires: 2017
  E-mail: eholcomb@lg.in.gov
Chief of Staff **Danny Lopez** . . . . . . . . . . . . . . . . . . . . . . . . . . (317) 232-4545
Deputy Chief of Staff and General Counsel
  **Mark Wuellner** . . . . . . . . . . . . . . . . . . . . . . . . . . . . . . . . . (317) 232-8831
Communications Director **Dennis Rosebrough** . . . . . . . . . (317) 234-3258
  E-mail: derosebrough@lg.in.gov
  Education: Valparaiso
Intergovernment Relations Director **Greg Wilson** . . . . . . . . (317) 232-4789
Public Relations Director **Emily Duncan** . . . . . . . . . . . . . . (317) 471-9048
  E-mail: eduncan@lg.in.gov
  Education: DePauw BA
Policy Director **Ryan Heater** . . . . . . . . . . . . . . . . . . . . . . . . . (317) 232-8915
Office of Small Business and Entrepreneurship Director
  **Jacob Schpok** . . . . . . . . . . . . . . . . . . . . . . . . . . . . . . . . . . (317) 232-8805
  Education: Ball State 2005 BS          Fax: (317) 232-8872

# Indiana Housing and Community Development Authority [IHCDA]
30 South Meridian Street, Suite 1000, Indianapolis, IN 46204
Tel: (317) 232-7777  Fax: (317) 232-7778

**Fiscal Year:** 2013-2014  **Budget:** $2,700,000

▲Executive Director **Jacob Sipe** . . . . . . . . . . . . . . . . . . . . . . (317) 233-1811
  E-mail: jsipe@ihcda.in.gov
Deputy Executive Director and Chief Real Estate
  Development Officer **Matt Rayburn** . . . . . . . . . . . . . . . . . (317) 233-9564
General Counsel **David Stewart** . . . . . . . . . . . . . . . . . . . . . . (317) 232-7777
  E-mail: dstewart2@ihcda.in.gov
Chief Community Programs Officer
  **Donna Billiard-Wright** . . . . . . . . . . . . . . . . . . . . . . . . . . (317) 233-5371
Chief Financial Officer and Finance Director
  **Blake Blanch** . . . . . . . . . . . . . . . . . . . . . . . . . . . . . . . . . . (317) 234-2114
Chief Operating Officer and Chief of Staff
  **Kyleen Welling** . . . . . . . . . . . . . . . . . . . . . . . . . . . . . . . . (317) 234-0934
Asset Preservation Director **Mark Neyland** . . . . . . . . . . . . (317) 234-6976

Community Programs Director **Lauren Perry** . . . . . . . . . . . (317) 234-6977
Community Services Deputy Director **Lori Dimick** . . . . . . . (317) 232-7117
Housing Choice Opportunities Deputy Director
  **Tamela Royston** . . . . . . . . . . . . . . . . . . . . . . . . . . . . . . . (317) 232-7777
Homeownership Director **Kim Harris** . . . . . . . . . . . . . . . . . (317) 233-5367
Human Resources Director **Amber Hughes** . . . . . . . . . . . . (317) 460-3847
Information Technology Manager **Jayson Conley** . . . . . . . (317) 232-5647
  E-mail: jconley@ihcda.in.gov
Legislative Affairs and Policy Director **Zachary Rice** . . . . . (317) 232-0624
  E-mail: zrice@ihcda.in.gov
Marketing and Communications Director
  **Bradley Meadows** . . . . . . . . . . . . . . . . . . . . . . . . . . . . . . (317) 234-1745
  E-mail: brmeadows@ihcda.in.gov
Placemaking Manager **Carmen Lethig** . . . . . . . . . . . . . . . (317) 234-6290
Research and Innovation Director **Joe Palus** . . . . . . . . . . . (317) 233-1813
  E-mail: jpalus@ihcda.in.gov
Controller **Ike Levy** . . . . . . . . . . . . . . . . . . . . . . . . . . . . . . . . (317) 232-3562

# Indiana State Department of Agriculture [ISDA]
One North Capitol Street, Suite 600, Indianapolis, IN 46204
Tel: (317) 232-8770  Fax: (317) 232-1362  Internet: www.in.gov/isda

■Director **Ted A. McKinney** . . . . . . . . . . . . . . . . . . . . . . . . . . (317) 233-1902
  E-mail: tmckinney@isda.in.gov
  Education: Purdue
  Executive Assistant **Hannah Ferguson** . . . . . . . . . . . . . . (317) 232-7707
Deputy Director **Melissa Rekeweg** . . . . . . . . . . . . . . . . . . . (317) 650-9877
  Education: Purdue
Communications Director **Ben Gavelek** . . . . . . . . . . . . . . . (317) 690-3303
  E-mail: bgavelek@isda.in.gov
  Press Secretary **DyNishia Miller** . . . . . . . . . . . . . . . . . . . (317) 605-6960
Policy and Regulatory Affairs Director **David Bausman** . . . (317) 232-8695
  E-mail: dbausman@isda.in.gov
Economic Development Division Director
  **Connie Neininger** . . . . . . . . . . . . . . . . . . . . . . . . . . . . . . (317) 517-7529
Soil Conservation Division Director **Jordan Seger** . . . . . . . (317) 695-4933
Future Farmers of America (FFA) and Indiana Young
  Farmers Director **Tamara Neighbors** . . . . . . . . . . . . . . . (317) 407-7926

# Office of the Attorney General
302 West Washington Street, 5th Floor, Indianapolis, IN 46204
Tel: (317) 232-6201  TTY: (800) 743-3333  Fax: (317) 232-7979
E-mail: constituent@atg.in.gov  Internet: www.in.gov/attorneygeneral

**Employees:** 403  **Fiscal Year:** 2013-2014  **Budget:** $43,763,382

★Attorney General **Gregory F. "Greg" Zoeller** (R) . . . . . . . (317) 232-6201
  Term Expires: 2017
  Education: Indiana 1982 JD
  Career: Chief Deputy Attorney General, Office of the Attorney General,
  State of Indiana (2005-2009)
Assistant Attorney General **Matthew J. "Matt" Light** . . . . (317) 232-6333
  Education: Indiana BA
Chief of Staff **Staci Schneider** . . . . . . . . . . . . . . . . . . . . . . . (317) 232-6351
Chief Deputy Attorney General **Gary Secrest** . . . . . . . . . . (317) 232-4866
  Education: Butler; Indiana (Indianapolis) JD
Deputy Attorney General **Richard Bramer** . . . . . . . . . . . . (317) 232-6201
  Education: Wabash Col 1988 BA; Indiana 1991 JD
Solicitor General **Thomas M. "Tom" Fisher** . . . . . . . . . . . (317) 232-6255
Victim Services Division Chief Counsel and Assistant
  Attorney General **Abigail Kuzma** . . . . . . . . . . . . . . . . . . (317) 232-6201
  E-mail: abigail.kuzma@atg.in.gov
Chief Counsel and Consumer Protection Director
  **Richard Bramer** . . . . . . . . . . . . . . . . . . . . . . . . . . . . . . . (317) 232-1008
Chief Counsel and Medicaid Fraud Director
  **Matthew Whitmire** . . . . . . . . . . . . . . . . . . . . . . . . . . . . . (317) 915-5303
Education and Training Director **Natalie Robinson** . . . . . . (317) 233-6143
Information Technology Director **Joey Hedrick** . . . . . . . . . (317) 234-7111
  E-mail: joey.hedrick@atg.in.gov
Chief Financial Officer **William Fulton** . . . . . . . . . . . . . . . (317) 883-4521
Victim Advocacy Programs Director **Jennifer Thuma** . . . . (317) 234-2339
Marketing Director **Jaime Barb** . . . . . . . . . . . . . . . . . . . . . (317) 234-8105
  E-mail: jaime.barb@atg.in.gov          Fax: (317) 233-2162

★ Elected Official   ■ Appointed by Governor   ● Appointed by Legislature   ▲ Appointed by Board or Commission   ◆ Appointed by State Supreme Court

# Office of the Secretary of State

201 Statehouse, 200 West Washington Street, Indianapolis, IN 46204-2790
Tel: (317) 232-6531  Fax: (317) 233-3283  E-mail: constituent@sos.in.gov

**Fiscal Year:** 2013-2014  **Budget:** $6,336,270

★Secretary of State **Connie Lawson** (R) . . . . . . . . . . . . . . . . . (317) 232-6532
　Term Expires: 2019
　Career: State Senator (R-IN, District 24), Indiana Senate (1996-2012)
　Executive Assistant **(Vacant)** . . . . . . . . . . . . . . . . . . . . . (317) 232-6536
Deputy Secretary of State and Chief of Staff
　**Brandon Clifton** . . . . . . . . . . . . . . . . . . . . . . . . . . . . (317) 234-7152
Deputy Chief of Staff and Communications Director
　**Valerie Warycha** . . . . . . . . . . . . . . . . . . . . . . . . . . . . (317) 233-8655
　E-mail: vwarycha@sos.in.gov
Chief Legal Counsel **Jerry Bonnet** . . . . . . . . . . . . . . . . . . (317) 232-6532
　Education: Indiana 1980 BA; Tennessee JD; New Orleans MBA;
　Texas MIB
Auto Dealer Services Director **Melissa Reynolds** . . . . . . . . (317) 232-6687
　E-mail: mereynolds@sos.in.gov
Business and Information Services Director
　**Rebecca Longfellow** . . . . . . . . . . . . . . . . . . . . . . . . . (317) 232-6691
　302 West Washington Street, Room E018, Indianapolis, IN 46204
　E-mail: rlongfellow@sos.in.gov
　Deputy Business Services Director **Beth Swindle** . . . . . . (317) 234-1553
　　302 West Washington Street, Room E018, Indianapolis, IN 46204
Operations Director **Marisa Smith** . . . . . . . . . . . . . . . . . . (317) 232-6590
Chief Information Officer **Tom Vessely** . . . . . . . . . . . . . . (317) 232-6695
　E-mail: tvessely@sos.in.gov
Office and Operation Specialist **Elizabeth Bryant** . . . . . . . (317) 234-8009

# Office of the State Auditor

240 State House, 200 West Washington Street,
Indianapolis, IN 46204-2793
Tel: (317) 232-3300  TTY: (317) 233-6220  Fax: (317) 234-1916
E-mail: comments@audlan.state.in.us  Internet: www.in.gov/auditor

**Fiscal Year:** 2013-2014  **Budget:** $5,234,737

■State Auditor **Suzanne Crouch** . . . . . . . . . . . . . . . . . . . (317) 232-3300
　Term Expires: 2019
　E-mail: scrouch@auditor.in.gov
　Education: Purdue BS
　Career: State Representative (R-IN, District 78), Indiana House of
　Representatives (2005-2014)
Deputy Auditor of Administration **Erin Sheridan** . . . . . . . . (317) 233-6010
　E-mail: esheridan@auditor.in.gov
Deputy Auditor of Operations **Courtney Everett** . . . . . . . . . (317) 233-9817
Director of Accounts Payable **Mary Reilly** . . . . . . . . . . . . . (317) 233-5763
Director of Human Resources **Colleen Tye** . . . . . . . . . . . . . (317) 232-3327
Director of Information Systems **Tracy Byrnes** . . . . . . . . . . (317) 234-1626
　200 West Washington Street, Room 240, Indianapolis, IN 46204-2790
　E-mail: tbarnes@auditor.in.gov
Director of Payroll **Brent Plunkett** . . . . . . . . . . . . . . . . . . (317) 232-3299
　Assistant Director of Payroll **Paula Hart** . . . . . . . . . . . . . (317) 232-4277
Director of Purchasing and Contracts **Beth Memmer** . . . . . (317) 232-3307
Director of Settlements **Fred Van Dorp** . . . . . . . . . . . . . . . (317) 234-1667
Communications Director **(Vacant)** . . . . . . . . . . . . . . . . . . (317) 233-3277
Finance Manager **Clay Jackson** . . . . . . . . . . . . . . . . . . . . (317) 232-3328

# Office of the Treasurer

200 West Washington Street, Room 242, Indianapolis, IN 46204
Tel: (317) 232-6386  Fax: (317) 233-1780

★State Treasurer **Kelly Mitchell** (R) . . . . . . . . . . . . . . . . . . (317) 232-8509
　Term Expires: December 31, 2018
　Education: Valparaiso BA; IU-Purdue U Indianapolis MA
Chief of Staff and General Counsel **Jillean Battle** . . . . . . . (317) 232-6388
Deputy Treasurer for Fiscal Operations **Kim Logan** . . . . . . (317) 233-0921
Deputy Treasurer and Investment Manager
　**Michael D. Frick** . . . . . . . . . . . . . . . . . . . . . . . . . . . (317) 232-0140
Chief Accountant **Vicki L. Pool** . . . . . . . . . . . . . . . . . . . . (317) 232-6260
　Education: Wisconsin 1982 BBA; Florida International 1990 MS
Communications Director **Caitlin Larson** . . . . . . . . . . . . . . (317) 232-6387
　E-mail: clarson1@tos.in.gov
　Assistant Communications Director and Scheduler
　**(Vacant)** . . . . . . . . . . . . . . . . . . . . . . . . . . . . . . . . (317) 232-6386

Local Government Investment Pool (TrustINdiana)
　Director **Cindy Barger** . . . . . . . . . . . . . . . . . . . . . . . . . (317) 232-0139

---

★ Elected Official　　■ Appointed by Governor　　● Appointed by Legislature　　▲ Appointed by Board or Commission　　◆ Appointed by State Supreme Court

# Iowa

Tel: (515) 281-5011 (State Operator)  Internet: www.iowa.gov

**Number of U.S. Congressional Delegates:** 2 Senators; 4 Representatives  **Governor's Term:** 4 years
**Legislature Description:** General Assembly - 50 member Senate; 100 member House of Representatives;
Term - Senate 4 years, House 2 years  **Next Election:** Governor November 2018; Legislature November
2016  **Number of Electoral Votes:** 6  **Official Name:** State of Iowa (Sioux: beautiful land)
**Nickname:** The Hawkeye State  **Motto:** Our liberties we prize and our rights we will maintain

**Population:** 3,123,899 (2015); Rank 30  **Fiscal Year:** 2015  **Budget:** $7,063,385,000

## Office of the Governor

State Capitol Building, Des Moines, IA 50319
1007 East Grand Avenue, Des Moines, IA 50319
Tel: (515) 281-5211  Fax: (515) 281-6611

**Employees:** 24  **Fiscal Year:** 2015  **Budget:** $2,289,566

**Terry E. Branstad**
Governor

Began Service: January 14, 2011
Term Expires: January 2019
Date of Birth: November 17, 1946
Education: Iowa 1969 BA; Drake 1974 JD
Religion: Roman Catholic
Career: Governor (R-IA), State of Iowa
(1983-1999); Founder, Branstad and Associates,
L.C.; Partner, Kaufman, Patee, Branstad & Miller;
President, Des Moines University (2003-2009)

★Governor **Terry E. Branstad** (R) . . . . . . . . . . . . . . . . . . . . (515) 281-5211
Chief of Staff **Michael Bousselot** . . . . . . . . . . . . . . . . . . . .(515) 281-5211
  Education: Northern Iowa 2006 BAcc; Drake 2009 JD
Communications Director **Ben Hammes** . . . . . . . . . . . . . . (515) 725-3516
  E-mail: ben.hammes@iowa.gov
  Education: Northern Iowa 2008 BA
Legal Counsel **Larry Johnson, Jr.** . . . . . . . . . . . . . . . . . . . .(515) 725-3505
  Education: Purdue BS; Creighton
Legislative Liaison **Ted Stopulos** . . . . . . . . . . . . . . . . . . (515) 725-3508
  Education: Iowa 2007; Drake 2010
Executive Scheduler **Alicia Freed** . . . . . . . . . . . . . . . . . . (515) 725-3510
  E-mail: alicia.freed@iowa.gov
Special Assistant for Education **Linda Lantor Fandel** . . . . .(515) 725-3522
  E-mail: linda.fandel@iowa.gov
Boards and Commissions Appointments Director
  **Tracie Gibler** . . . . . . . . . . . . . . . . . . . . . . . . . . . . . . . . (515) 725-3516
  Education: Northwestern; Drake JD

## Office of State-Federal Relations

400 North Capitol Street, NW, Suite 359, Washington, DC 20001
Fax: (202) 624-8189

Director **Doug Hoelscher** . . . . . . . . . . . . . . . . . . . . . . . (202) 624-5479
  E-mail: doug.hoelscher@iowa.gov
  Education: Iowa 1999 BA

## Office of Drug Control Policy

Ola Babcock Building, 112 East Grand Avenue, 2nd Floor,
Des Moines, IA 50319
Internet: www.iowa.gov/odcp

**Employees:** 4  **Fiscal Year:** 2015  **Budget:** $241,134

Director **Steven F. Lukan** . . . . . . . . . . . . . . . . . . . . . . . .(515) 725-0305
  E-mail: steve.lukan@iowa.gov
  Education: Loras 2003 BA

## Iowa Department of Administrative Services [DAS]

Hoover Building, 1305 East Walnut Street, Des Moines, IA 50319
Tel: (515) 242-5120  Fax: (515) 281-6140  Internet: www.das.iowa.gov

**Employees:** 345  **Fiscal Year:** 2014  **Budget:** $1,664,936,000

■Director **Janet E. Phipps** . . . . . . . . . . . . . . . . . . . . . . . . . (515) 281-5360
  E-mail: janet.phipps@iowa.gov
General Services Enterprise **Charlee Cross** . . . . . . . . . . . . (515) 725-2281
  E-mail: charlee.cross@iowa.gov
State Accounting Enterprise **Calvin McKelvogue** . . . . . . . . (515) 281-4877
Chief Financial Officer **Dave Heuton** . . . . . . . . . . . . . . . . (515) 725-0114
  Education: Iowa State 1985 BS
Legal Counsel/Human Resources Manager **Karin Gregor** . . (515) 281-5064
Marketing and Communications Legislative Liaison
  **Tami Wiencek** . . . . . . . . . . . . . . . . . . . . . . . . . . . . . . . (515) 725-2017

## Iowa Department on Aging [IDA]

510 East 12th Street, Suite 2, Des Moines, IA 50319
Tel: (515) 725-3333  TTY: (800) 735-2942

**Employees:** 33  **Fiscal Year:** 2014  **Budget:** $28,517,000

■Director **Donna Harvey** . . . . . . . . . . . . . . . . . . . . . . . . . (515) 725-3301
  E-mail: donna.harvey@iowa.gov
Assistant Director **Joel Wulf** . . . . . . . . . . . . . . . . . . . . . . (515) 725-3326
  E-mail: joel.wulf@iowa.gov
Executive Secretary **Danika Welsch** . . . . . . . . . . . . . . . . (515) 725-3302
State Long-Term Care Ombudsman
  **Deanna Clingan-Fischer** . . . . . . . . . . . . . . . . . . . . . . . (515) 725-3327
Policy and Planning Director **(Vacant)** . . . . . . . . . . . . . . . (515) 725-3025

## Iowa Department of Agriculture and Land Stewardship

Wallace Building, Des Moines, IA 50319
Tel: (515) 281-5321  Fax: (515) 281-6236
E-mail: agri@iowaagriculture.gov  Internet: www.iowaagriculture.gov

**Employees:** 328  **Fiscal Year:** 2015  **Budget:** $36,355,000

★Secretary **Bill Northey** (R) . . . . . . . . . . . . . . . . . . . . . . .(515) 281-5321
  Term Expires: January 2019
  Education: Iowa State 1981 BS; Southwest Minnesota State 2004 MBA
Deputy Secretary **Michael Naig** . . . . . . . . . . . . . . . . . . . . (515) 281-5681

### Administration Division

Director **Margaret Thomson** . . . . . . . . . . . . . . . . . . . . . . .(515) 725-1036
  E-mail: margaret.thomsen@iowaagriculture.gov
Accounting Bureau Chief **(Vacant)** . . . . . . . . . . . . . . . . . . (515) 281-8611
State Climatologist **Harry Hillaker** . . . . . . . . . . . . . . . . . .(515) 281-8981
  Education: Texas BA; Colorado MA
State Statistician **Greg Thessen** . . . . . . . . . . . . . . . . . . . (515) 284-4340
  Federal Building, 210 Walnut Street, Room 833, Des Moines, IA 50309

### Consumer Protection and Industry Services Division

Director **Stephen Moline** . . . . . . . . . . . . . . . . . . . . . . . . (515) 281-8610
Agricultural Division and Market Development Bureau
  Chief **Maury Wills** . . . . . . . . . . . . . . . . . . . . . . . . . . . . (515) 281-5783
  Education: Iowa State BA; Drake MS

*(continued on next page)*

---

★ Elected Official  ■ Appointed by Governor  ● Appointed by Legislature  ▲ Appointed by Board or Commission  ◆ Appointed by State Supreme Court

**EXECUTIVE BRANCH**

**Consumer Protection and Industry Services Division** *continued*

State Veterinarian **David Schmitt** . . . . . . . . . . . . . . . . . . . . (515) 281-5305
Education: Iowa State DVM

Animal Welfare Assistant State Veterinarian
**Jeff Kaisand** . . . . . . . . . . . . . . . . . . . . . . . . . . . . . . . . . (515) 281-6358

Horticulture and Farmers Market State Horticulturist
**(Vacant)** . . . . . . . . . . . . . . . . . . . . . . . . . . . . . . . . . . . . (515) 242-5043

Commercial Feed and Fertilizer Bureau Chief
**Randy Watts** . . . . . . . . . . . . . . . . . . . . . . . . . . . . . . . . (515) 281-8136

Dairy Products Control Bureau Chief
**David "Dave" Brown** . . . . . . . . . . . . . . . . . . . . . . . . . (515) 281-3545

Entomology and Plant Science Bureau Chief
**Robin Pruisner** . . . . . . . . . . . . . . . . . . . . . . . . . . . . . . (515) 725-1465

Grain Warehouse Bureau Chief **Richard Wahl** . . . . . . . . . . (515) 242-6338

Meat and Poultry Inspection Bureau Chief
**Dr. Randall Larsen** . . . . . . . . . . . . . . . . . . . . . . . . . . (515) 281-3338

Pesticide Bureau Chief **Gretchen Paluch** . . . . . . . . . . . . . (515) 281-8591

Weights and Measures Bureau Chief (Acting)
**Randy Watts** . . . . . . . . . . . . . . . . . . . . . . . . . . . . . . . . (515) 725-1493

Renewable Fuels and Co-Products Program Director
**Harold Hommes** . . . . . . . . . . . . . . . . . . . . . . . . . . . . . (515) 725-2258
Education: Iowa State BS

## Soil Conservation Division

Director **James Gillespie** . . . . . . . . . . . . . . . . . . . . . . . . . (515) 281-7043
Field Services Representative **Vince Sitzman** . . . . . . . . . . (515) 281-7818
Financial Incentives Bureau Chief **Matt McDonald** . . . . . . (515) 281-6153
Mines and Minerals Bureau Chief **Susan Kozak** . . . . . . . . (515) 281-6147
Water Resource Bureau Chief **Jacob Hansen** . . . . . . . . . . (515) 725-2962

## Iowa Department for the Blind

524 Fourth Street, Des Moines, IA 50309-2306
Tel: (515) 281-1333 TTY: (515) 281-1355 Fax: (515) 281-1263

▲Director **Richard Sorey** . . . . . . . . . . . . . . . . . . . . . . . . . (515) 281-1293
E-mail: ricahrd.sorey@blind.state.ia.us
Education: James Madison 1984 BS; Old Dominion 1995 MSEd

Deputy Director **Bruce K. Snethen** . . . . . . . . . . . . . . . . . . (515) 281-1293

## Iowa Department of Commerce

200 East Grand Avenue, Suite 370, Des Moines, IA 50309-1827
Tel: (515) 725-0505 Fax: (515) 725-0519

**Employees:** 329 **Fiscal Year:** 2014 **Budget:** $388,445,000

■Director **JoAnn M. Johnson** . . . . . . . . . . . . . . . . . . . . . . (515) 725-0505
E-mail: joann.johnson@iowa.gov
Education: Northern Iowa BA

## Alcoholic Beverages Division

1918 SE Hulsizer Road, Ankeny, IA 50021
Fax: (515) 281-7385 Internet: www.IowaABD.com

Administrator **Stephen Larson** . . . . . . . . . . . . . . . . . . . . . (515) 281-7402
E-mail: larson@iowaabd.com

Deputy Administrator **Timothy "Tim" Iversen** . . . . . . . . . (515) 281-7444
Deputy Director of Administration **Tyler Ackerson** . . . . . . (515) 281-7443
Information Technology **Bobby Bailey** . . . . . . . . . . . . . . . (515) 725-2260
E-mail: bailey@Iowaabd.com

Regulatory Affairs Deputy Administrator **Karen Freund** . . . (515) 281-7414
Compliance Officer **Heather Schaffer** . . . . . . . . . . . . . . . . (515) 281-7461

## Banking Division

200 East Grand Avenue, Suite 300, Des Moines, IA 50309
Fax: (515) 281-4862 Internet: www.idob.state.ia.us

Superintendent **Ron L. Hansen** . . . . . . . . . . . . . . . . . . . . . (515) 281-4014
Education: Arizona State BS

Bank Bureau Chief **Shauna Shields** . . . . . . . . . . . . . . . . . (515) 281-4014
Finance Bureau Chief **Rodney E. "Rod" Reed** . . . . . . . . . (515) 281-4014
Education: Iowa State 1982 BS

Chief Operating Officer **David Huang** . . . . . . . . . . . . . . . (515) 242-0273
Regional Manager **Tracy L. Bergmann, CEM** . . . . . . . . . . (515) 281-4862

## Credit Union Division

200 East Grand Avenue, Suite 370, Des Moines, IA 50309
Fax: (515) 725-0519

Superintendent **JoAnn M. Johnson** . . . . . . . . . . . . . . . . . (515) 725-0505
E-mail: joann.johnson@iowa.gov

Executive Officer **Jan Johnson** . . . . . . . . . . . . . . . . . . . . . (515) 725-0506
E-mail: jan.johnson@iowa.gov

## Insurance Division

330 Maple Street, Des Moines, IA 50319-0065
Fax: (515) 281-3059 Internet: www.iid.state.ia.us

■Insurance Commissioner **Nick Gerhart** . . . . . . . . . . . . . . (515) 281-5907
E-mail: nick.gerhart@iid.iowa.gov
Education: Northern Iowa 1998 BA; Saint Louis U 2001 JD,
2002 MHA

Assistant Commissioner **(Vacant)** . . . . . . . . . . . . . . . . . . (515) 281-4119
First Deputy Commissioner **(Vacant)** . . . . . . . . . . . . . . . . (515) 242-6836
Deputy Commissioner/Chief Financial Examiner
**Jim "Jim" Armstrong** . . . . . . . . . . . . . . . . . . . . . . . . . (515) 281-4412
E-mail: jim.armstrong@iid.iowa.gov
Education: Iowa Wesleyan 1984 BA

Consumer & Legal Affairs Assistant Commissioner
**Doug Ommen** . . . . . . . . . . . . . . . . . . . . . . . . . . . . . . . (515) 725-1220

Securities Counselor **Craig A. Goettsch** . . . . . . . . . . . . . (515) 281-8813
Education: Iowa 1972 BA, 1975 JD

Securities Superintendent **(Vacant)** . . . . . . . . . . . . . . . . . (515) 281-6836
Personnel Officer **Kimberly "Kim" Sacker** . . . . . . . . . . . (515) 281-4033
E-mail: kim.sacker@iid.iowa.gov

## Professional Licensing Bureau

1920 Southeast Hulsizer Road, Ankeny, IA 50021-3941
Tel: (515) 725-9022 Fax: (515) 281-7411

Bureau Chief **Rodney E. "Rod" Reed** . . . . . . . . . . . . . . . (515) 281-4014
Engineering and Land Surveying Examining Board
Executive Officer **Robert Lampe** . . . . . . . . . . . . . . . . . (515) 725-9024
E-mail: robert.lampe@iowa.gov

Interior Design Board Administrator (Interim) **Jeff Evans** . . (515) 725-9024
Landscape Architectural Examining Board Executive
Officer **Jill Simbro** . . . . . . . . . . . . . . . . . . . . . . . . . . . (515) 281-4014

Accounting Board Executive Officer **Robert Lampe** . . . . . . (515) 725-9024
E-mail: robert.lampe@iowa.gov

## Iowa Utilities Board [IUB]

1375 East Court Avenue, Room 69, Des Moines, IA 50319-0069
Tel: (515) 725-7300 Fax: (515) 725-7399 E-mail: iub@max.state.ia.us
Internet: www.state.ia.us/iub

■Chairperson **Geri D. Huser** . . . . . . . . . . . . . . . . . . . . . . . (515) 725-7888
Term Expires: April 30, 2021

■Board Member **Elizabeth S. "Libby" Jacobs** . . . . . . . . . . (515) 725-7313
Term Expires: April 30, 2017
Education: Nebraska BA; Drake MPA

■Board Member **Nick Wagner** . . . . . . . . . . . . . . . . . . . . . . (515) 725-7313
Term Expires: April 30, 2019

General Counsel **David Lynch** . . . . . . . . . . . . . . . . . . . . . (515) 725-7331
E-mail: david.lynch@iub.iowa.gov
Education: Yale 1980 BA; Iowa 1983 JD

Executive Secretary **Joan Conrad** . . . . . . . . . . . . . . . . . . . (515) 725-7334

## Iowa Department of Corrections [IDOC]

510 East 12th Street, Des Moines, IA 50319
Tel: (515) 725-5701 Fax: (515) 725-5799 Internet: www.doc.state.ia.us

**Employees:** 3,839 **Fiscal Year:** 2015 **Budget:** $404,519,000

■Director **Jerry Bartruff** . . . . . . . . . . . . . . . . . . . . . . . . . . (515) 725-5710
E-mail: jerry.bartruff@iowa.gov

Secretary **Diana Billhorn** . . . . . . . . . . . . . . . . . . . . . . . . . (515) 725-5708
Community-Based Corrections Deputy Director
**Sally Kreamer** . . . . . . . . . . . . . . . . . . . . . . . . . . . . . . . (515) 725-5701

Operations Deputy Director **Dan Craig** . . . . . . . . . . . . . . . (515) 725-5701
Inspector General **Diann Wilder-Tomlinson** . . . . . . . . . . . (515) 725-5726

---

★ Elected Official   ■ Appointed by Governor   ● Appointed by Legislature   ▲ Appointed by Board or Commission   ◆ Appointed by State Supreme Court

Media and Public Relations Assistant Director
**Fred Scaletta** . . . . . . . . . . . . . . . . . . . . . . . . . . . . (515) 725-5707
E-mail: fred.scaletta@iowa.gov
Offender Services Deputy Director
**Dorothy "Dot" Faust** . . . . . . . . . . . . . . . . . . . . . (515) 725-5713
Prison Industries Deputy Director **Daniel Clark** . . . . . . . . . (515) 725-5705
General Counsel **Michael Savala** . . . . . . . . . . . . . . . . . . . (515) 725-5715
E-mail: michael.savala@iowa.gov
Education: Augustana (IL) 1991 BA; Iowa 1994 JD
Information Technology Specialist **Kevin Vandewall** . . . . . . (515) 725-5720
E-mail: kevin.vandewall@iowa.gov

## Iowa Department of Cultural Affairs
New Historical Building, 600 East Locust, Des Moines, IA 50319
Tel: (515) 281-5111  Fax: (515) 242-6498
Internet: www.culturalaffairs.org

**Employees:** 57  **Fiscal Year:** 2014  **Budget:** $17,337,000
■Director **Mary Cownie** . . . . . . . . . . . . . . . . . . . . . . . . (515) 281-8741
E-mail: mary.cownie@iowa.gov
Executive Assistant **Chris Kramer** . . . . . . . . . . . . . . . . (515) 281-3223
Administrative Assistant **(Vacant)** . . . . . . . . . . . . . . . . . (515) 281-8741

## State Historical Society of Iowa
Tel: (515) 281-6412  Tel: (319) 335-3916 (Iowa City Historical Library)
Administrator **Susan Kloewer** . . . . . . . . . . . . . . . . . . . (515) 281-8749
E-mail: susan.kloewer@iowa.gov

## Iowa Department of Education
Grimes State Office Building, 400 East 14th Street,
Des Moines, IA 50319-0146
Tel: (515) 281-5294  Fax: (515) 242-5988

**Employees:** 732  **Fiscal Year:** 2014  **Budget:** $3,718,260,000
■Director **Ryan Wise** . . . . . . . . . . . . . . . . . . . . . . . . . . . (515) 281-3436
E-mail: ryan.wise@iowa.gov
Attorney **Nicole Proesch** . . . . . . . . . . . . . . . . . . . . . . . . (515) 281-8661

### Community Colleges Division
Tel: (515) 281-8260
Administrator **Jeremy Varner** . . . . . . . . . . . . . . . . . . . (515) 281-8260
E-mail: jeremy.varner@iowa.gov
State Director for Adult Education **Alex Harris** . . . . . . . . (515) 281-3640
E-mail: alex.harris@iowa.gov             Fax: (515) 242-5988
State Staff Development Consultant **(Vacant)** . . . . . . . . . (515) 281-4723
Federal Data Consultant **Lisa Gard** . . . . . . . . . . . . . . . . (515) 281-3125
E-mail: lisa.gard@iowa.gov

### Learning and Results Division
Deputy Director **David Tilly** . . . . . . . . . . . . . . . . . . . . . (515) 281-3333
E-mail: david.tilly@iowa.gov
Educator Quality Services Bureau Chief **Linda Carroll** . . . . (515) 725-2873
Information and Analysis Bureau Chief
**James "Jay" Pennington** . . . . . . . . . . . . . . . . . . . . (515) 281-4837
E-mail: jay.pennington@iowa.gov
Learning Strategies and Support Services Bureau Chief
**Sarah Brown** . . . . . . . . . . . . . . . . . . . . . . . . . . . . (515) 281-5735
School and Improvement Services Bureau Chief
**Amy Williamson** . . . . . . . . . . . . . . . . . . . . . . . . . (515) 725-2888
Standards and Curriculum Services Bureau Chief
**Erika Cook** . . . . . . . . . . . . . . . . . . . . . . . . . . . . . . (515) 281-4158

### Policy and Communication Division
Deputy Director **(Vacant)** . . . . . . . . . . . . . . . . . . . . . . . (515) 281-5296
Media and Communications Services Bureau Chief
**Staci Hupp** . . . . . . . . . . . . . . . . . . . . . . . . . . . . . . (515) 281-5651
E-mail: staci.hupp@iowa.gov

### School Finance and Support Services Division
Deputy Director **Jeff Berger** . . . . . . . . . . . . . . . . . . . . (515) 281-3968
E-mail: jeff.berger@iowa.gov
Education: Iowa 1983 SB; Wayne State Col 1987 MSE; Drake 1996;
Iowa State 2007 DEduc

Nutrition and Health Services Bureau Chief
**Ann Feilmann** . . . . . . . . . . . . . . . . . . . . . . . . . . . . (515) 281-4757
E-mail: ann.feilmann@iowa.gov
Office of Administrative Services Chief Financial Officer
**Jeff Berger** . . . . . . . . . . . . . . . . . . . . . . . . . . . . . . (515) 281-3968
E-mail: jeff.berger@iowa.gov

## Vocational Rehabilitation Services Division
Fax: (515) 281-4703
Administrator **David Mitchell** . . . . . . . . . . . . . . . . . . . (515) 281-4140
E-mail: david.mitchell@iowa.gov
Chief Financial Officer and Administrative Services
Bureau Chief **Matthew "Matt" Coulter** . . . . . . . . . . . (515) 281-4093
E-mail: matthew.coulter@iowa.gov    Fax: (515) 281-4149
Disability Determination Services Bureau Chief
**Elizabeth McLaren** . . . . . . . . . . . . . . . . . . . . . . . (515) 725-0702
E-mail: liz.mclaren@ssa.gov
Rehabilitation Services Bureau Chief **Kenda Jochimsen** . . . (515) 281-4154

## State Library of Iowa
1112 East Grand Avenue, Des Moines, IA 50319
Tel: (515) 281-4105  Fax: (515) 281-6191
State Librarian **Michael Scott** . . . . . . . . . . . . . . . . . . . (515) 281-4105
Information Specialist **Emily Bainter** . . . . . . . . . . . . . . (515) 281-7574
Specialized Library Services Program Director
**Barbara "Barb" Corson** . . . . . . . . . . . . . . . . . . . . (515) 281-4352
E-mail: barb.corson@lib.state.ia.us    Fax: (515) 252-6543
State Documents Librarian **Thomas "Tom" Keyser** . . . . (515) 242-6542
Fax: (515) 281-4118
State Data Center Coordinator **Gary Krob** . . . . . . . . . . . (515) 281-6618
E-mail: gary.krob@lib.state.ia.us    Fax: (515) 242-6543
State Law Library Librarian **Mandy Easter** . . . . . . . . . . (515) 281-4434

## Iowa Public Television
P.O. Box 6450, Johnston, IA 50131-6450
Tel: (515) 242-3100
Executive Director and General Manager
**Molly M. Phillips** . . . . . . . . . . . . . . . . . . . . . . . . . (515) 242-3120
Administrative Assistant **Karen Schaeffer** . . . . . . . . . . (515) 242-3117
Educational Services Division Director **Terry Rinehart** . . . . (515) 242-4180
Engineering and Technology Division Director
**William Hayes** . . . . . . . . . . . . . . . . . . . . . . . . . . . (515) 242-3116
Programming and Production Division Director
**Justin Beaupre** . . . . . . . . . . . . . . . . . . . . . . . . . . (515) 242-3205

## Iowa Department of Homeland Security and Emergency Management
7900 Hickman Road, Suite 500, Windsor Heights, IA 50324
Tel: (515) 725-3231  Fax: (515) 725-3260  E-mail: webmaster@iowa.gov
Internet: http://homelandsecurity.iowa.gov/

**Fiscal Year:** 2014  **Budget:** $350,808,000
■Director and Iowa Homeland Security Advisor
**Mark Schouten** . . . . . . . . . . . . . . . . . . . . . . . . . . . (515) 725-3231
E-mail: mark.schouten@iowa.gov
Education: Iowa State BA; Iowa JD
Executive Assistant **Michelle Matthes** . . . . . . . . . . . . . (515) 725-3230
E-mail: michelle.matthes@iowa.gov
Legislative Liaison **John Benson** . . . . . . . . . . . . . . . . . (515) 725-3208
E-mail: john.benson@iowa.gov
Public Information Officer **Stefanie Bond** . . . . . . . . . . . (515) 725-3207
E-mail: stefanie.bond@iowa.gov
Public Information Officer **Lucinda Parker** . . . . . . . . . . (515) 725-3239
E-mail: lucinda.parker@iowa.gov

### Operations Division
Administrator **Joyce Flinn** . . . . . . . . . . . . . . . . . . . . . . (515) 323-4313
Response Bureau Chief **Frank Klier** . . . . . . . . . . . . . . . (515) 323-4236
Communications and Infrastructure Bureau Chief
**Randy Goddard** . . . . . . . . . . . . . . . . . . . . . . . . . . . (515) 323-4238

## Planning and Finance Division

Administrator **Angela Chen** . . . . . . . . . . . . . . . . . . . . . . . . . . (515) 725-3231
Human Resources Officer **Amy Meston** . . . . . . . . . . . . . . . (515) 725-3236
Grants and Financials Bureau Chief **Mark Schouten** . . . . . (515) 725-3231
Planning and Training Bureau Chief **Susan Dixon** . . . . . . . (515) 725-3257

## Recovery Division

Administrator **Patrick Hall** . . . . . . . . . . . . . . . . . . . . . . . . . . . (515) 725-9325
Disaster Operations Bureau Chief **Aimee Bartlett** . . . . . . . . (515) 725-9364
Hazard Mitigation Bureau Chief **Dennis Harper** . . . . . . . . . (515) 725-9348
Public Assistance Bureau Chief **Katie Waters** . . . . . . . . . . . (515) 725-9314

## Iowa Department of Human Rights

Lucas State Office Building, 321 East 12th Street, Des Moines, IA 50319
Tel: (515) 242-5655  Fax: (515) 242-6119  E-mail: humanrights@iowa.gov

**Employees:** 45  **Fiscal Year:** 2014  **Budget:** $90,136,000

■Director **San Wong** . . . . . . . . . . . . . . . . . . . . . . . . . . . . . . . . (515) 242-5640
   E-mail: san.wong@iowa.gov
■Community Action Agency Division Administrator
   **William J. Brand** . . . . . . . . . . . . . . . . . . . . . . . . . . . . . . . . . . (515) 281-3268
   E-mail: bill.brand@iowa.gov
■Community Advocacy and Services Division
   Administrator **(Vacant)** . . . . . . . . . . . . . . . . . . . . . . . . . . . . . . (515) 281-7121
■Criminal and Juvenile Justice Planning Division
   Administrator **Steve Michael** . . . . . . . . . . . . . . . . . . . . . . . . . (515) 242-6122
   E-mail: steve.michael@iowa.gov

## Office of Persons with Disabilities

Tel: (888) 219-0471  Fax: (515) 242-6119
E-mail: dhr.disabilities@iowa.gov

Director **San Wong** . . . . . . . . . . . . . . . . . . . . . . . . . . . . . . . . . (515) 242-5640

## Office on the Status of Women

Tel: (515) 281-4461  Fax: (515) 242-6119  E-mail: women@iowa.gov
Internet: www.women.iowa.gov

■Division Administrator **Kristen Corey** . . . . . . . . . . . . . . . . . (515) 281-4470
   E-mail: kristen.corey@iowa.gov
Publications and Special Projects Coordinator **(Vacant)** . . . . (515) 281-4470
Program Planner **Kristen Corey** . . . . . . . . . . . . . . . . . . . . . . (515) 281-4470
   E-mail: kristen.corey@iowa.gov

## Iowa Department of Human Services

Hoover Building, 1305 East Walnut, Des Moines, IA 50319-0114
Tel: (515) 281-3147  Fax: (515) 281-4597  E-mail: tcrawfo@dhs.state.ia.us
Internet: www.dhs.state.ia.us

**Employees:** 4,800  **Fiscal Year:** 2014  **Budget:** $7,090,306,000

■Director **Charles M. Palmer** . . . . . . . . . . . . . . . . . . . . . . . . . (515) 281-5452
   E-mail: cpalmer1@dhs.state.ia.us
   Education: Grinnell 1961
Deputy Director **Sally Titus** . . . . . . . . . . . . . . . . . . . . . . . . . . (515) 281-5758
   Secretary **Trudy Crawford** . . . . . . . . . . . . . . . . . . . . . . . . . . (515) 281-5452

## Communications Office

Public Information Officer **Amy L. McCoy** . . . . . . . . . . . . . . (515) 281-4848
   E-mail: amccoy@dhs.state.ia.us

## Adult, Child and Family Services Division

Tel: (515) 281-8746

Administrator **Wendy Rickman** . . . . . . . . . . . . . . . . . . . . . . . (515) 281-5521
   E-mail: wrickma@dhs.state.ia.us
Child Care Bureau Chief **Chad Dahm** . . . . . . . . . . . . . . . . . (515) 281-6177
Child Welfare and Community Services Bureau Chief
   **Janee Harvey** . . . . . . . . . . . . . . . . . . . . . . . . . . . . . . . . . . . . (515) 281-6802
Financial and Work Supports Bureau Chief **Ann Wiebers** . . . . . . . . (515)
281-6080
   E-mail: awieber@dhs.state.ia.us

## Data Management Division

Tel: (515) 281-3409

Chief Information Officer **Lorrie Tritch** . . . . . . . . . . . . . . . . (515) 281-3409
   E-mail: ltritch@dhs.state.ia.us
Iowa Collection Reporting Systems for Child Support
   Bureau Chief **(Vacant)** . . . . . . . . . . . . . . . . . . . . . . . . . . . . . . (515) 281-7059
Income Maintenance Systems Bureau Chief **(Vacant)** . . . . . (515) 281-8328
Medical Systems and Data Warehousing Bureau Chief
   **Randall "Randy" Clemenson** . . . . . . . . . . . . . . . . . . . . . . . (515) 256-4690
   E-mail: rclemen@dhs.state.ia.us
Network Support Bureau Chief **Cathy McLuen** . . . . . . . . . (515) 281-5775
   E-mail: cmcluen@dhs.state.ia.us
Technology Support Bureau Chief **(Vacant)** . . . . . . . . . . . . . (515) 281-7059

## Field Operations

Tel: (515) 281-5758

Field Operations Division Administrator
   **Vern Armstrong** . . . . . . . . . . . . . . . . . . . . . . . . . . . . . . . . . (515) 281-6899
   E-mail: larmstr@dhs.state.ia.us
Child Support Recovery Bureau Chief **Carol Eaton** . . . . . . . (515) 281-5767
   E-mail: ceaton@dhs.state.ia.us

## Fiscal Management Division

Tel: (515) 281-6085

Chief Finance Officer **Jean Slaybaugh** . . . . . . . . . . . . . . . . . (515) 281-4987
Budget and Accounting Bureau Chief **Joe Havig** . . . . . . . . . (515) 281-6022
Child Support Payments Bureau Chief **Angela Lathrop** . . . (515) 281-7684
Purchase of Service Bureau Chief **Jon Wetlaufer** . . . . . . . . (515) 281-5970
Purchasing, Payment and Receipts Bureau Chief **(Vacant)** . . . . . . . . (515)
281-5482

## Mental Health and Disability Services Division

Administrator **Richard Shults** . . . . . . . . . . . . . . . . . . . . . . . . (515) 281-8580
   E-mail: rshults@dhs.state.ia.us
Targeted Case Management Chief **Diane Diamond** . . . . . . . (515) 281-7156
Community Services and Planning Bureau Chief
   **Theresa Armstrong** . . . . . . . . . . . . . . . . . . . . . . . . . . . . . . . (515) 281-0377
Refugee Programs Bureau Chief **(Vacant)** . . . . . . . . . . . . . . (515) 283-7904

## Iowa Department of Inspections and Appeals

321 East 12th Street, Des Moines, IA 50319-0083
Tel: (515) 281-7102  TTY: (515) 242-6515  Fax: (515) 242-6863
E-mail: webmaster@dia.iowa.gov  Internet: http://dia.iowa.gov

**Employees:** 532  **Fiscal Year:** 2014  **Budget:** $114,590,000

■Director **Rodney A. "Rod" Roberts** . . . . . . . . . . . . . . . . . . (515) 281-5457
   E-mail: rod.roberts@dia.iowa.gov
Deputy Director **Aaron D. Baack** . . . . . . . . . . . . . . . . . . . . . (515) 281-6442
   Executive Officer **Sara Throener** . . . . . . . . . . . . . . . . . . . . (515) 281-5457
■Public Defender **Adam Gregg** . . . . . . . . . . . . . . . . . . . . . . . (515) 242-6158
   E-mail: adam.gregg@ia.us
   Education: Central Col (IA) 2006 BA; Drake 2009 JD
Racing and Gaming Administrator **Brian Ohorilko** . . . . . . . (515) 281-7358
   E-mail: brian.ohorilko@iowa.gov
Child Advocacy Board Administrator **Jim Hennessey** . . . . (515) 242-6392
   E-mail: jim.hennessey@dia.iowa.gov
Employment Appeal Board Chair **Kim D. Schmett** . . . . . . . (515) 281-8115
   E-mail: kim.schmett@dia.iowa.gov
Food and Consumer Safety Bureau Chief
   **Steven Mandernach** . . . . . . . . . . . . . . . . . . . . . . . . . . . . . . . (515) 281-8587

## Racing and Gaming Commission

1300 Des Moines Street, Suite 100, Des Moines, IA 50309-5508
Tel: (515) 281-7352  Fax: (515) 242-6560  E-mail: irgc@iowa.gov
Internet: www.irgc.iowa.gov

■Commissioner **Richard D. Arnold** . . . . . . . . . . . . . . . . . . . . (641) 203-0298
   Term Expires: April 30, 2016
   26875 407th Street, Russell, IA 50238-7537
   E-mail: rcarnold@sirisonline.com

★ Elected Official    ■ Appointed by Governor    ● Appointed by Legislature    ▲ Appointed by Board or Commission    ◆ Appointed by State Supreme Court

Summer 2016                     © Leadership Directories, Inc.                     *State Yellow Book*

■Commissioner **Carl Heinrich** . . . . . . . . . . . . . . . . . . . . . . (712) 323-7253
   Term Expires: April 30, 2017
   816 Birchwood Circle, Council Bluffs, IA 51503-6700
■Commissioner **Kristine Kramer** . . . . . . . . . . . . . . . . . . . . (641) 394-3086
   Term Expires: April 30, 2018
   P.O. Box 263, New Hampton, IA 50659-0263
   E-mail: kandwmotors@iowatelecom.net
■Commissioner **Jeffrey M. "Jeff" Lamberti** . . . . . . . . . . . . (515) 964-8777
   Term Expires: April 30, 2017
   210 Northeast Delaware Avenue, Suite 200, Ankeny, IA 50021
   E-mail: jeff.lamberti@ankenylaw.com
   Affiliation: President and Managing Shareholder, Lamberti, Gocke &
   Luetje, P.C.
   210 NE Delaware Avenue, Suite 200, Ankeny, IA 50021
   Education: Drake 1985 BA, 1989 MBA, 1989 JD
■Commissioner **Delores Mertz** . . . . . . . . . . . . . . . . . . . . . . (515) 395-2952
   Term Expires: April 30, 2018
   1803 East Mound Street, Apt 8, Algona, IA 50511

## Iowa Department of Justice

1305 East Walnut Street, Des Moines, IA 50319
Tel: (515) 281-5164  Fax: (515) 281-4209

### Office of the Attorney General

Hoover Building, 2nd Floor, Des Moines, IA 50319
Tel: (515) 281-5164  Fax: (515) 281-4209
E-mail: webteam@ag.state.ia.us  Internet: www.iowaattorneygeneral.gov

**Employees:** 239  **Fiscal Year:** 2014  **Budget:** $130,199,000

★Attorney General **Thomas John "Tom" Miller** (D) . . . . . . (515) 281-8373
   Term Expires: January 2019
   E-mail: agtommiller@ag.state.ia.us
   Education: Loras 1966 BA; Harvard 1969 JD
   Executive Secretary **Jane Ambrozic** . . . . . . . . . . . . . . . (515) 281-8373
Deputy Attorney General **Tam Ormiston** . . . . . . . . . . . . . . (515) 281-5166
Chief Deputy Attorney General **Eric Tabor** . . . . . . . . . . . . . (515) 281-5166
First Assistant Attorney General **Kevin M. McCarthy** . . . . . (515) 281-5164
Solicitor General **Jeffrey S. Thompson** . . . . . . . . . . . . . . . (515) 281-5166
Area Prosecutions Division Director **Scott Brown** . . . . . . . (515) 281-3648
Consumer Protection Division Director **Jessica Whitney** . . (515) 281-5926
Criminal Appeals Division Director **Kevin Cmelik** . . . . . . . (515) 281-5976
Environmental Law Division Director **(Vacant)** . . . . . . . . . . (515) 281-5351
Licensing and Administrative Law Division Director
   **(Vacant)** . . . . . . . . . . . . . . . . . . . . . . . . . . . . . . . . . . (515) 281-6858
Regents and Human Services Division Director
   **Diane Stahle** . . . . . . . . . . . . . . . . . . . . . . . . . . . . . . . (515) 281-8330
Revenue Division Director **Donald Stanley** . . . . . . . . . . . . (515) 281-5846
Special Litigation Division Director **(Vacant)** . . . . . . . . . . . (515) 281-5881
Transportation Division Director **David Gorham** . . . . . . . . (515) 239-1509
   800 Lincoln Way, Ames, IA 50010
   E-mail: david.gorham@iowa.gov
Crime Victim Assistance Program Director
   **Janelle Melohn** . . . . . . . . . . . . . . . . . . . . . . . . . . . . . (515) 281-5044
   321 E. 12th St., Rm. 018, Des Moines, IA 50319
Prosecuting Attorneys' Training Council Director
   **Tom Ferguson** . . . . . . . . . . . . . . . . . . . . . . . . . . . . . (515) 281-5428
Consumer Advocate **Mark Schuling, CPA** . . . . . . . . . . . . . (515) 725-7200
   Education: Drake JD
Communications Director **Geoff Greenwood** . . . . . . . . . . (515) 281-6699
Information Technology Specialist **John Boccella** . . . . . . . (515) 281-4534
   E-mail: john.boccella@iowa.gov

## Iowa Department of Management [DOM]

State Capitol Building, Room 13, Des Moines, IA 50319
Tel: (515) 281-3322  Fax: (515) 242-5897

**Employees:** 22  **Fiscal Year:** 2016  **Budget:** $2,961,000

■Director **David Roederer** . . . . . . . . . . . . . . . . . . . . . . . . . (515) 281-3322
   E-mail: david.roederer@iowa.gov
   Education: Northern Iowa 1973 BA
   Secretary to the Director **Tammy Winters** . . . . . . . . . . . (515) 281-3322
■Chief Information Officer **Robert "Bob" von Wolffradt** . . (515) 745-4873
   E-mail: robert.vonwolffradt@iowa.gov

■State Budget Director **David Roederer** . . . . . . . . . . . . . . . (515) 281-3322
   E-mail: david.roederer@iowa.gov

## Iowa Department of Natural Resources [DNR]

Wallace Building, 502 East 9th Street, Des Moines, IA 50319-0034
Tel: (515) 725-8200  Fax: (515) 725-8201
E-mail: webmaster@dnr.state.ia.us  Internet: www.iowadnr.gov

**Employees:** 1,002  **Fiscal Year:** 2014  **Budget:** $393,075,000

■Director **Charles R. "Chuck" Gipp** . . . . . . . . . . . . . . . . . (515) 725-8282
   E-mail: chuck.gipp@dnr.iowa.gov
   Education: Luther Col 1970 BA
Deputy Director **Bruce Trautman** . . . . . . . . . . . . . . . . . . . (515) 725-8383
   E-mail: bruce.trautman@dnr.iowa.gov
Executive Secretary **Karen Fynaardt** . . . . . . . . . . . . . . . . (515) 725-8283
Legislative Liaison **Sharon Tahtinen** . . . . . . . . . . . . . . . . (515) 725-8299
   E-mail: sharon.tahtinen@dnr.iowa.gov
Communications Bureau Chief **(Vacant)** . . . . . . . . . . . . . . (515) 725-8288
Public Affairs Coordinator **Kevin Baskins** . . . . . . . . . . . . (515) 725-8388
Legal Services Bureau Chief **Ed Tormey** . . . . . . . . . . . . . (515) 725-8373
   E-mail: ed.tormey@dnr.iowa.gov
Budget and Finance Bureau Chief **Jennifer Nelson** . . . . . (515) 725-8220
Customer Services Bureau Chief **Dave Cretors** . . . . . . . . (515) 725-8283
Engineering Services Bureau Chief **Travis Baker** . . . . . . . (515) 725-8457
Realty Services Bureau Chief **Travis Baker** . . . . . . . . . . . (515) 725-8457

### Conservation and Recreation Division

Administrator **Kelley Myers** . . . . . . . . . . . . . . . . . . . . . . . (515) 725-8484
   E-mail: kelley.myers@dnr.iowa.gov
Fisheries Bureau Chief **Joe Larscheid** . . . . . . . . . . . . . . . (515) 725-8445
   E-mail: joe.larscheid@iowa.gov
Forestry Bureau Chief **Paul Tauke** . . . . . . . . . . . . . . . . . . (515) 725-8450
Law Enforcement Bureau Chief **Mark Sedlmayr** . . . . . . . . (515) 725-8479
   E-mail: mark.sedlmayr@dnr.iowa.gov
Parks Bureau Chief **Todd Coffelt** . . . . . . . . . . . . . . . . . . . (515) 725-8494
   E-mail: todd.coffelt@dnr.iowa.gov
   Education: Simpson (IA) BA; Iowa State MS
Wildlife Bureau Chief **Dale Garner** . . . . . . . . . . . . . . . . . . (515) 281-7127
   E-mail: dale.garner@dnr.iowa.gov

### Environmental Services Division

Administrator **William "Bill" Ehm** . . . . . . . . . . . . . . . . . . (515) 725-8300
   E-mail: william.ehm@dnr.iowa.gov

## Iowa Department of Public Defense

7105 NW 70th Avenue, Johnston, IA 50131-1824
Tel: (515) 252-4000  Fax: (515) 252-4787

**Employees:** 278  **Fiscal Year:** 2014  **Budget:** $48,346,000

■Adjutant General **MG Timothy E. Orr, ARNG** . . . . . . . . . . (515) 252-4211
   E-mail: timothy.e.orr4.mil@mail.mil
Command Sergeant Major
   **SgtMaj Rachel L. Fails, USMC** . . . . . . . . . . . . . . . . . (515) 252-4410
Chief of Staff **COL Michael Amundson, ARNG** . . . . . . . . (515) 252-4305
Public Affairs Officer **COL Greg Hapgood, ARNG** . . . . . . (515) 252-4582
   Education: Iowa 1988 BA; Creighton 2000 JD   Fax: (515) 252-4656

## Iowa National Guard

6100 Northwest 78th Avenue, Johnston, IA 50131
Tel: (515) 252-4582  E-mail: paoia@ng.army.mil
Internet: www.iowanationalguard.com

■Adjutant General **MG Timothy E. Orr, ARNG** . . . . . . . . . . (515) 252-4211
   E-mail: timothy.e.orr4.mil@mail.mil

## Iowa Air National Guard

6100 Northwest 78th Avenue, Johnston, IA 50131
Tel: (515) 252-4464

■Deputy Adjutant General
   **BrigGen William D. Dehaes, ANG** . . . . . . . . . . . . . . . (515) 252-4017
   E-mail: william.dehaes@iowa.gov
Senior Military Attorney
   **Col Michael Kuehn, USAF (Ret)** . . . . . . . . . . . . . . . . (515) 252-4296

---

★ Elected Official   ■ Appointed by Governor   ● Appointed by Legislature   ▲ Appointed by Board or Commission   ◆ Appointed by State Supreme Court

EXECUTIVE BRANCH

## Iowa Army National Guard

6100 Northwest 78th Avenue, Johnston, IA 50131
Tel: (515) 252-4242

■ Deputy Commanding General (Movement)
   **BG Steve Altman, ARNG** . . . . . . . . . . . . . . . . . . . . . . (515) 252-4020
   E-mail: steve.altman@lmco.com
■ Deputy Commanding General (Sustainment)
   **BG Randy Warm, ARNG** . . . . . . . . . . . . . . . . . . . . . . (515) 252-4786
   E-mail: randy.warm.mil@mail.mil
   Information Management Director
   **LTC James W. "Jim" White, ARNG** . . . . . . . . . . (515) 252-4242
   E-mail: james.w.white.mil@mail.mil

## Iowa Department of Public Health [IDPH]

Lucas State Office Building, 321 East 12th Street,
Des Moines, IA 50319-0075
Tel: (515) 281-7689  Tel: (800) 735-2942 (Deaf Relay)
Tel: (515) 281-4944 (Vital Records)  Fax: (515) 281-4958
TTY: (800) 735-2942  E-mail: webmaster@idph.state.ia.us
Internet: www.idph.state.ia.us

**Employees:** 427

■ Director **Gerd W. Clabaugh, MPA** . . . . . . . . . . . . . . . (515) 281-8474
   E-mail: gerd.clabaugh@idph.iowa.gov
   Education: Drake BA
   Deputy Director **(Vacant)** . . . . . . . . . . . . . . . . . . . . . . . (515) 281-4355
   Communications Director **Polly Carver-Kimm** . . . . . . . . . . (515) 281-6693
   E-mail: polly.carver-kimm@idph.iowa.gov
   State Epidemiologist
   **Patricia "Patty" Quinlisk, MPH, MD** . . . . . . . . . . . . . . (515) 281-4941

## Division of Acute Disease Prevention, Emergency Response, and Environmental Health

Director **Kenneth "Ken" Sharp** . . . . . . . . . . . . . . . . . . . (515) 281-5099
State Toxicologist **Stuart Schmitz** . . . . . . . . . . . . . . . . . (515) 281-8707
Technical Assistance Chief **Dale Anthony** . . . . . . . . . . . . (515) 281-6601

## Division of Administration and Professional Licensure

Tel: (515) 281-4955

Division Director **Marcia Spangler** . . . . . . . . . . . . . . . . . (515) 281-4955
   E-mail: marcia.spangler@idph.iowa.gov

## Division of Behavioral Health

Director **Kathy Stone** . . . . . . . . . . . . . . . . . . . . . . . . . . . (515) 281-4417

## Division of Health Promotion and Chronic Disease Prevention

Director (Interim) **Brenda Dobson** . . . . . . . . . . . . . . . . (515) 281-4355
                                                   Fax: (515) 242-6384

## Division of Tobacco Use Prevention and Control

Director **Jerilyn Oshel** . . . . . . . . . . . . . . . . . . . . . . . . . . (515) 281-8857

## Iowa Department of Public Safety [DPS]

Public Safety Building, 215 East 7th Street, Des Moines, IA 50319-0040
Tel: (515) 725-6001  Fax: (515) 725-6195

**Employees:** 880  **Fiscal Year:** 2014  **Budget:** $472,471,000

■ Commissioner **Roxann Ryan** . . . . . . . . . . . . . . . . . . . . . (515) 725-6182
   E-mail: rryan@dps.state.ia.us
   Education: Iowa PhD
   Executive Officer SAC **Capt. Jeff Ritzman** . . . . . . . . . . . (515) 725-6181
   Assistant Attorney General **John Lunquist** . . . . . . . . . . . (515) 281-3658
   Fire Marshal **Jeff Quigle** . . . . . . . . . . . . . . . . . . . . . . . . (515) 725-6145
   E-mail: jeffrey.quigle@iowa.gov

Administrative Services Division Director
   **Charis Paulson** . . . . . . . . . . . . . . . . . . . . . . . . . . . . . . (515) 725-6017
   E-mail: charis.paulson@iowa.gov
   Education: Buena Vista U 1990 BA; Drake 1992 MBA
Fusion Center and Intelligence Division Assistant
   Director **James Saunders** . . . . . . . . . . . . . . . . . . . . . . (515) 725-6330
Narcotics Enforcement Division Director
   **James Saunders** . . . . . . . . . . . . . . . . . . . . . . . . . . . . (515) 725-6305
   E-mail: saunders@dps.state.ia.us
Professional Development and Information Bureau Chief
   **Lt. Neil Wellner** . . . . . . . . . . . . . . . . . . . . . . . . . . . . . (515) 725-6276
   E-mail: neil.wellner@iowa.gov
Professional Standards Bureau Chief **Bret Braafhart** . . . . . . (515) 725-7265
State Patrol Division Chief **Michael Van Berkum** . . . . . . . . (515) 725-6090
Traffic Safety Bureau Administrator **Patrick Hoye** . . . . . . . . (515) 725-6120
   E-mail: patrick.hoye@iowa.gov

## Criminal Investigation Division

Criminal Investigation Division Director
   **James Saunders** . . . . . . . . . . . . . . . . . . . . . . . . . . . . (515) 725-6305

## Criminalistics Laboratory

Tel: (515) 725-1500  Fax: (515) 725-1518

Administrator **Bruce B. Reeve** . . . . . . . . . . . . . . . . . . . . (515) 559-7065
   E-mail: reeve@dps.state.ia.us
Toxicology Criminalist Supervisor **Jess Dunn** . . . . . . . . . . (515) 559-7052

## Iowa Department of Revenue

Hoover State Office Building, Des Moines, IA 50319
Tel: (515) 281-3114  TTY: (515) 242-5942  Fax: (515) 242-6040

**Employees:** 277  **Fiscal Year:** 2014  **Budget:** $3,130,343,000

■ Director **Courtney M. Kay-Decker** . . . . . . . . . . . . . . . . (515) 281-3204
   E-mail: courtney.decker@iowa.gov
   Education: Northwestern 1994 BA; Iowa 1997 JD
Internal Services Division Administrator
   **Jessica Holmes** . . . . . . . . . . . . . . . . . . . . . . . . . . . . . (515) 281-4908
   E-mail: jessica.holmes@iowa.gov
Property Tax Administrator **Julie Roisen** . . . . . . . . . . . . . . (515) 281-4040
   E-mail: julie.roisen@iowa.gov
Policy and Communications Division Administrator
   **Victoria Daniels** . . . . . . . . . . . . . . . . . . . . . . . . . . . . . (515) 281-8450
Research and Analyst Division Administrator
   **Amy Harris** . . . . . . . . . . . . . . . . . . . . . . . . . . . . . . . . . (515) 281-0196
Tax Management Division Administrator and Deputy
   Director **Adam Humes** . . . . . . . . . . . . . . . . . . . . . . . . (515) 281-5079
   E-mail: adam.humes@iowa.gov

## Iowa Department of Transportation

800 Lincoln Way, Ames, IA 50010
Tel: (515) 239-1101  TTY: (515) 239-1514  Fax: (515) 817-6508

■ Director **Paul Trombino III, PE** . . . . . . . . . . . . . . . . . . . (515) 239-1111
   E-mail: paul.trombino@dot.iowa.gov       Fax: (515) 239-1120
   Education: Wisconsin (Milwaukee) BS; Wisconsin BS
General Counsel/Special Assistant Attorney General
   **David Gorham** . . . . . . . . . . . . . . . . . . . . . . . . . . . . . . (515) 239-1509
   E-mail: david.gorham@dot.iowa.gov       Fax: (515) 239-1609

## Transportation Commission

Tel: (515) 239-1242  Fax: (515) 239-1120

■ Chair **Leonard L. Boswell** . . . . . . . . . . . . . . . . . . . . . . (515) 239-1242
   E-mail: boswell.leonard@gmail.com
   Education: Graceland Col 1969 BA
■ Vice Chair **Daniel Huber** . . . . . . . . . . . . . . . . . . . . . . . (515) 239-1242
   E-mail: dhuber@frontierhg.com
■ Commissioner **Kathleen Fehrman** . . . . . . . . . . . . . . . . (308) 530-5331
   E-mail: kathy.jo.fehrman@gmail.com
■ Commissioner **Loree R. Miles** . . . . . . . . . . . . . . . . . . . (515) 239-1242
   E-mail: loree@thewhitehousefarm.com
■ Commissioner **John Putney** . . . . . . . . . . . . . . . . . . . . . (515) 239-1242
   E-mail: jlputney@windstream.net
■ Commissioner **Amy L. Reasner** . . . . . . . . . . . . . . . . . . . (515) 239-1242
   E-mail: areasner@lynchdallas.com
■ Commissioner **David A. Rose** . . . . . . . . . . . . . . . . . . . . (515) 239-1242
   E-mail: rosesclinton@gmail.com

---

★ Elected Official   ■ Appointed by Governor   ● Appointed by Legislature   ▲ Appointed by Board or Commission   ◆ Appointed by State Supreme Court

■Commissioner **Charese E. Yanney** . . . . . . . . . . . . . . . . . . . . (515) 239-1242
   E-mail: ceydog@aol.com

## Highway Division
Director **Mitchell J. "Mitch" Dillavou** . . . . . . . . . . . . . . . (515) 239-1124
District 1 (Ames) Engineer **Scott Dockstader** . . . . . . . . . . (515) 239-1635
   1020 S. 4th St., Ames, IA 50010
   E-mail: scott.dockstader@dot.iowa.gov
District 2 (Mason City) Engineer **E. Jon Ranney** . . . . . . . . (641) 422-9465
   428 43rd Street NW, Mason City, IA 50401
   E-mail: ejon.ranney@dot.iowa.gov
District 3 (Sioux City) Engineer **Tony Lazarowicz** . . . . . . . (712) 276-1451
   2800 Gordon Drive, Sioux City, IA 51102-0987
   PO Box 987, Sioux City, IA 51102-0987
   E-mail: tony.lazarowicz@dot.iowa.gov
District 4 (Atlantic) Engineer **Troy Jerman, PE** . . . . . . . . . (712) 243-3355
   2210 East Seventh Street, Atlantic, IA 50022
   E-mail: troy.jerman@dot.iowa.gov
District 5 (Fairfield) Engineer **James "Jim" Armstrong** . . (641) 469-4005
   307 West Briggs, Fairfield, IA 52556
District 6 (Cedar Rapids) Engineer
   **Jim Schnoebelen, PE** . . . . . . . . . . . . . . . . . . . . . . . . . (319) 364-0235
   5455 Kirkwood Boulevard SW, Cedar Rapids, IA 52404
   E-mail: jim.schnoebelen@dot.iowa.gov

## Information Technology Division
Director **Annette Dunn** . . . . . . . . . . . . . . . . . . . . . . . . . . . (515) 239-1284
   E-mail: annette.dunn@dot.iowa.gov

## Motor Vehicle Division
6310 SE Convenience Blvd., Ankeny, IA 50021
Tel: (800) 532-1121  Internet: www.dot.state.ia.us/mvd/

Director **Mark D. Lowe** . . . . . . . . . . . . . . . . . . . . . . . . . . . (515) 237-3121
   E-mail: mark.lowe@dot.iowa.gov

## Operations and Finance Division
Tel: (515) 239-1340
Director **Lee Wilkinson** . . . . . . . . . . . . . . . . . . . . . . . . . . (515) 239-1340

## Planning, Programming and Modal Division
Tel: (515) 239-1661
Director **Stuart Anderson, PE** . . . . . . . . . . . . . . . . . . . . . (515) 239-1661
   Education: Iowa State 1991 BSCE

## Iowa Department of Veterans Affairs
Camp Dodge, Building 3465, 7105 NW 70th Avenue,
Johnston, IA 50131-1824
Tel: (515) 252-4698  Tel: (800) 838-4692  Fax: (515) 727-3713
E-mail: info@idva.state.ia.us

■Executive Director **Col Robert King, ANG (Ret)** . . . . . . . . (515) 727-3444
   E-mail: robert.king@iowa.gov
   Education: Upper Iowa BSBA
Outreach Coordinator **(Vacant)** . . . . . . . . . . . . . . . . . . . . (515) 727-3442
Secretary **Mari Mielke** . . . . . . . . . . . . . . . . . . . . . . . . . . . (515) 252-4698
Veterans Benefits Specialist **John Halstead** . . . . . . . . . . . (515) 727-3439
Veterans Benefits Specialist **David Heim** . . . . . . . . . . . . . (515) 362-7350
Executive Officer and Veterans Benefits Specialist
   **Robert "Bob" Steben** . . . . . . . . . . . . . . . . . . . . . . . . . (515) 727-3438
Trustfund Administrator **Missy Miller** . . . . . . . . . . . . . . . . (515) 727-3443

## Iowa Workforce Development
1000 East Grand Avenue, Des Moines, IA 50319
Tel: (515) 281-5387  Tel: (800) 562-4692 (Job Iowa)  Fax: (515) 281-4698
Internet: www.iowaworkforce.org  Internet: www.iowaworks.org
Internet: www.iowajobs.org

**Employees:** 674  **Fiscal Year:** 2014  **Budget:** $1,237,965,000

■Director **Beth Townsend** . . . . . . . . . . . . . . . . . . . . . . . . . (515) 281-5364
   E-mail: beth.townsend@iowa.gov
   Education: Nebraska (Kearney) JD
Executive Assistant **Diana Sisler** . . . . . . . . . . . . . . . . . . . (515) 281-5365

■Deputy Director **Edward "Ed" Wallace** . . . . . . . . . . . . . . (515) 281-5082
   E-mail: edward.wallace@iwd.iowa.gov
Communications Director **Courtney Greene** . . . . . . . . . . . (515) 281-9646
   E-mail: courtney.greene@iwd.iowa.gov
Webmaster **(Vacant)** . . . . . . . . . . . . . . . . . . . . . . . . . . . . . (515) 242-0057

## Iowa College Student Aid Commission
430 East Grand Ave, 3rd Floor, Des Moines, IA 50309-1920
Tel: (515) 725-3400  Fax: (515) 725-3401
E-mail: info@iowacollegeaid.gov  Internet: www.iowacollegeaid.gov

**Employees:** 35  **Fiscal Year:** 2014  **Budget:** $112,704,000

▲Executive Director **Karen Misjak** . . . . . . . . . . . . . . . . . . . (515) 725-3410
   E-mail: karen.misjak@iowa.gov
   Education: Missouri 1983 BS

## Iowa Telecommunications and Technology Commission [ITTC]
Grimes Building, 400 East 14th Street, Des Moines, IA 50319-1004
Tel: (515) 725-4692  Fax: (515) 725-4727  E-mail: icn.info@iowa.gov
Internet: www.icn.state.ia.us

■Chairperson **Richard "Dick" Bruner** . . . . . . . . . . . . . . . . (515) 725-1102
■Member **Kathleen Kohorst** . . . . . . . . . . . . . . . . . . . . . . . (515) 725-1102
■Member **Kelly Ann Lange** . . . . . . . . . . . . . . . . . . . . . . . . (515) 327-1306
   Education: Iowa 2003
■Member **Timothy L. Lapointe** . . . . . . . . . . . . . . . . . . . . . (515) 725-1102
■Member **Mary B. Sellers** . . . . . . . . . . . . . . . . . . . . . . . . . (515) 725-1102
   Education: Florida 1989 BS; Iowa 2007 MBA
Member - Ex Officio **Mary Mosiman, CPA** . . . . . . . . . . . . (515) 281-5835
   Education: Iowa State 1992 BAcc
Member - Ex Officio **Robert "Bob" von Wolffradt** . . . . . . (515) 281-3462
▲Executive Director **Ric Lumbard** . . . . . . . . . . . . . . . . . . . (515) 725-1102
   E-mail: ric.lumbard@icn.state.ia.us

## Iowa Economic Development Authority
200 East Grand Avenue, Des Moines, IA 50309
Tel: (515) 725-3000  Fax: (515) 725-3010

**Employees:** 112  **Fiscal Year:** 2014  **Budget:** $410,177,000

■Director **Deborah V. "Debi" Durham** . . . . . . . . . . . . . . . (515) 725-3022
   E-mail: debi.durham@iowa.gov
   Education: Missouri Southern State U BSBA
General Counsel/Chief Operations Officer
   **Rita C. Grimm** . . . . . . . . . . . . . . . . . . . . . . . . . . . . . . . (515) 725-3018

## Division of Business Development
Tel: (515) 725-3133  E-mail: business@iowa.gov

Division Administrator **Rita C. Grimm** . . . . . . . . . . . . . . . (515) 725-3018
Business Finance Administrator **Terry Roberson** . . . . . . . . (515) 725-3044

## Division of Community Development
Tel: (515) 725-3002  E-mail: community@iowa.gov

Division Administrator **Tim Waddell** . . . . . . . . . . . . . . . . . (515) 725-3002

## Iowa Agricultural Development Division [IADD]
2015 Grand Avenue, Des Moines, IA 50312
Tel: (515) 725-4919  Tel: (515) 725-4900  Fax: (515) 725-4901
E-mail: iada@iowa.gov  Internet: www.iada.state.ia.us

IA AG Program Specialist **Steven K. Ferguson** . . . . . . . . . (515) 725-4928
IA AG Program Specialist **Tammy Nebola** . . . . . . . . . . . . (515) 725-4919
   E-mail: tammy.nebola@iowa.gov

## Iowa Finance Authority [IFA]
2015 Grand Avenue, Des Moines, IA 50312
Tel: (515) 725-4900  Tel: (800) 432-7230  Fax: (515) 725-4901
Internet: www.iowafinanceauthority.gov

■Executive Director **David D. "Dave" Jamison** . . . . . . . . . . (515) 725-4977
   E-mail: dave.jamison@iowa.gov

*(continued on next page)*

---

★ Elected Official   ■ Appointed by Governor   ● Appointed by Legislature   ▲ Appointed by Board or Commission   ◆ Appointed by State Supreme Court

**Iowa Finance Authority** *continued*

Deputy Director **Cynthia "Cindy" Harris**............(515) 725-4976
Deputy Director **Carolann Jensen**...................(515) 725-4955
Title Guaranty Division Director **Tara Lawrence**........(515) 725-4904
Marketing and Communications Director **Ashley Jared**...(515) 725-4934

## Iowa State Board of Education

Grimes State Office Building, Des Moines, IA 50319-0146
Tel: (515) 281-5296  TTY: (800) 532-1486  Fax: (515) 281-4122

■President **Charles C. "Charlie" Edwards, Jr.**...........(515) 988-7206
  E-mail: charlescedwardsjr@gmail.com
  Education: Colorado BA
■Vice President **Michael Knedler**.....................(712) 323-9363
  E-mail: mlknedler@cox.net
■Member **Brooke Axiotis**............................(515) 664-6898
  E-mail: brooke.axiotis@gmail.com
  Education: Drake JD
■Member **Michael Bearden**...........................(641) 473-2902
  E-mail: mbearden@cgaconsultants.com
■Member **Bettie Bolar**..............................(515) 281-5296
  E-mail: bettie.bolar@gmail.com
■Member **Diane Crookham-Johnson**.....................(515) 281-5294
  E-mail: diane.crookham-johnson@musco.com
■Member **Angela English**............................(563) 875-7294
  E-mail: english@iowatelecom.net
■Member **William "Mike" May**........................(641) 753-5294
  E-mail: mmmay@mediacombb.net
■Member **Mary Ellen Miller**.........................(515) 281-5296
  E-mail: maryellen.miller@iowa.gov
  Education: Buena Vista U BBA
Student Member **Robert Nishimwe**....................(515) 281-5296
  E-mail: robertnishimwe@yahoo.com
Executive Director **Ryan Wise**......................(515) 281-3436

## Iowa Ethics and Campaign Disclosure Board

510 East 12th, Suite 1A, Des Moines, IA 50319
Tel: (515) 281-4028  Fax: (515) 281-4073  Internet: www.iowa.gov/ethics

▲Executive Director and Legal Counsel **Megan Tooker**.....(515) 281-3489
  E-mail: megan.tooker@iowa.gov

## Iowa Board of Parole [IBP]

Jessie M. Parker Building, 510 East 12th Street, Suite # 3,
Des Moines, IA 50319
Tel: (515) 725-5757  Fax: (515) 725-5762  Internet: www.bop.state.ia.us

**Employees:** 9  **Fiscal Year:** 2014  **Budget:** $1,232,000

■Chair **John Hodges**................................(515) 725-5757
  E-mail: john.hodges@iowa.gov
■Vice Chair **Norman L. "Norm" Granger**..............(515) 725-5750
  Term Expires: June 30, 2018
  E-mail: norm.granger@iowa.gov
■Member **Charles W. Larson, Sr.**....................(515) 725-5757
  E-mail: charles.larson@iowa.gov
  Education: Kansas State BA; Iowa JD
■Member **Susan Lerdal**..............................(515) 725-5757
■Member **Sheila Wilson**.............................(515) 725-5757
  E-mail: sheila.wilson@iowa.gov
Secretary **Angalea "Lea" Scaletta**..................(515) 725-5757
  E-mail: lea.scaletta@ibop.state.ia.us          Fax: (515) 725-5762

## Iowa Public Employees Retirement System [IPERS]

7401 Register Drive, Des Moines, IA 50321
P.O. Box 9117, Des Moines, IA 50306-9117
Tel: (515) 281-0020  TTY: (800) 735-2942  Fax: (515) 281-0053
E-mail: info@ipers.org  Internet: www.ipers.org

Chief Executive Officer **Donna Mueller**..............(515) 281-0070
  E-mail: ceo@ipers.org
  Education: Minnesota BA; Washington and Lee JD
General Counsel **Gregg Schochenmaier**...............(515) 281-0054
  E-mail: gregg.schochenmaier@ipers.org

Chief Benefits Officer **David Martin**...............(515) 281-0065
Chief Investment Officer **Karl C. Koch**.............(515) 281-0030
  E-mail: investments@ipers.org
Information Officer **Rick Hindman**..................(515) 281-0060
  E-mail: rick.hindman@ipers.org
Communications Director **Judith "Judy" Akre**.........(515) 281-0043

## Office of the Lieutenant Governor

State Capitol Building, Des Moines, IA 50319-0146
Tel: (515) 281-5211  Fax: (515) 725-3528

★Lieutenant Governor **Kimberly "Kim" Reynolds** (R).....(515) 281-5211
  Term Expires: January 2019
  Education: Northwest Missouri State
  Career: Treasurer, Office of the County Treasurer, County of Clarke,
  Iowa (1998-2006); State Senator (R-IA, District 48), Iowa Senate
  (2009-2010)

## Office of the Secretary of State

321 East 12th Street, First Floor, Des Moines, IA 50319
Tel: (515) 281-5204  Fax: (515) 242-5952  E-mail: sos@sos.iowa.gov
Internet: sos.iowa.gov

**Employees:** 26  **Fiscal Year:** 2014  **Budget:** $5,216,000

★Secretary of State **Paul D. Pate** (R)...................(515) 281-5204
  Term Expires: January 2019
Elections Director **Dawn Williams**..................(515) 281-5204
  E-mail: dawn.williams@sos.iowa.gov
Elections Deputy Secretary **Carol Olson**............(515) 281-5204
  E-mail: carol.olson@sos.iowa.gov
Election Administrator **Eric Gookin**................(515) 281-7550
  E-mail: eric.gookin@sos.iowa.gov
  Education: Drake 2012 JD
Executive Assistant **Deb Safford**...................(515) 281-6230
  E-mail: deb.safford@sos.iowa.gov

## Office of the State Treasurer

State Capitol Building, Des Moines, IA 50319-0005
Tel: (515) 281-5368  Fax: (515) 281-7562  E-mail: treasurer@iowa.gov

**Employees:** 27  **Fiscal Year:** 2014  **Budget:** $39,000,000

★State Treasurer **Michael L. Fitzgerald** (D)..............(515) 281-5368
  Term Expires: January 2019
  E-mail: treasurer@iowa.gov
  Education: Iowa 1974 BS
  Career: Marketing Analyst, Massey Ferguson Company (1974-1982)
  Executive Secretary to the Treasurer
    **GeorgAnna Madsen**...............................(515) 281-5368
    E-mail: georganna.madsen@iowa.gov
Deputy Treasurer **Karen Austin**.....................(515) 281-7677
  Education: Simpson (IA) 1991 BA
Deputy Treasurer **Stefanie Devin**...................(515) 281-5957
  Education: Iowa State 1983 BBA

## Office of the State Auditor

State Capitol Building, Room 111, Des Moines, IA 50319-0001
Tel: (515) 281-5834  Fax: (515) 242-6134  E-mail: info@auditor.state.ia.us
Internet: auditor.iowa.gov

**Employees:** 100  **Fiscal Year:** 2014  **Budget:** $9,600,000

★State Auditor **Mary Mosiman, CPA** (R)...............(515) 281-5835
  Term Expires: January 1, 2019
  E-mail: mary.mosiman@auditor.state.ia.us
Executive Assistant **Anna Hartzog**..................(515) 281-5835
Chief Deputy Auditor **Warren Jenkins, CPA**..........(515) 281-5835
  Education: Iowa State 1972 BS
Financial Audit Deputy **Andrew Nielsen, CPA**.........(515) 281-5834
  Education: Northern Iowa 1975 BA
Performance Investigation Deputy **Tami Kusian, CPA**.....(515) 281-5834
  Education: Northern Iowa 1981 BA
Chief of Staff and Legal Counsel
  **Bernardo Granwehr, JD**...........................(515) 281-5835

---

★ Elected Official   ■ Appointed by Governor   ● Appointed by Legislature   ▲ Appointed by Board or Commission   ◆ Appointed by State Supreme Court

# Kansas

Tel: (785) 296-5059 (State Information)  Internet: www.kansas.gov

**Number of U.S. Congressional Delegates:** 2 Senators; 4 Representatives  **Governor's Term:** 4 years
**Legislature Description:** 40 member Senate; 125 member House of Representatives; Term - Senate 4
years, House 2 years  **Next Election:** Governor November 2018; Legislature November 2016
**Number of Electoral Votes:** 6  **Official Name:** State of Kansas (Sioux: South-wind people)
**Nickname:** The Sunflower State  **Motto:** Ad astra per aspera (To the stars through difficulties)

**Population:** 2,911,641 (2015); Rank 34  **Employees:** 39,880  **Fiscal Year:** 2015  **Budget:** $15,089,052,377

## Office of the Governor

State Capitol, 2nd Floor, Topeka, KS 66612-1590
Tel: (785) 296-3232  Tel: (877) 579-6757  TTY: (800) 766-3777
Fax: (785) 296-7973

**Employees:** 33  **Fiscal Year:** 2015  **Budget:** $14,587,255

**Samuel Dale "Sam" Brownback**
Governor

Began Service: January 10, 2011
Term Expires: January 2019
Date of Birth: September 12, 1956
Education: Kansas State 1978 BS;
Kansas 1982 JD
Home: Topeka
Religion: Catholic
Career: Secretary, Department of Agriculture,
State of Kansas (1986-1993); White House
Fellow, Office of the United States Trade
Representative, Executive Office of the President,
George H.W. Bush Administration (1990-1991);
U.S. Representative (R-KS, District 2), Office
of Representative Sam Brownback, United
States House of Representatives (1994-1996);
U.S. Senator (R-KS), Office of Senator Sam
Brownback, United States Senate (1996-2011)

★Governor **Samuel Dale "Sam" Brownback** (R) . . . . . . . . (785) 296-3232
Chief of Staff **Jon Hummell** . . . . . . . . . . . . . . . . . . . . . . . . (785) 296-3232
Appointments Director **Kim Borchers** . . . . . . . . . . . . . . . . (785) 296-3232
  E-mail: gov.appointments@ks.gov
Communications Director and Press Secretary
  **Eileen Hawley** . . . . . . . . . . . . . . . . . . . . . . . . . . . . . . . (785) 296-3232
  E-mail: media@ks.gov
  Education: Houston 1994 BA; Seton Hall 2008 MA
Deputy Communications Director **Melika Willoughby** . . . (785) 296-3232
Constituent Services Director **Niomi Burget** . . . . . . . . . . . (785) 296-3232
  E-mail: niomi.burget@ks.gov
Operations Director **(Vacant)** . . . . . . . . . . . . . . . . . . . . . . (785) 296-3232
Policy Director **Brandon J. Smith** . . . . . . . . . . . . . . . . . . . (785) 296-3232
  Education: George Washington LLM
Scheduling Director **Denise Coatney** . . . . . . . . . . . . . . . . . (785) 296-3232
  E-mail: denise.coatney@ks.gov
Grants Office Administrator **Shawn Cowing** . . . . . . . . . . . (785) 296-3232
  E-mail: shawn.cowing@ks.gov
  Education: Kansas 1994 BA
Chief Counsel **Brant M. Laue** . . . . . . . . . . . . . . . . . . . . . . . (785) 296-3232
  Education: Oral Roberts 1983 BA; Cornell 1986 JD
Legislative Liaison **Timothy M. Shallenburger** . . . . . . . . . (785) 296-4839
  E-mail: tim.shallenburger@ks.gov
  Education: Pittsburg State (Attended)

## Washington Office

500 New Jersey Avenue Northwest, Suite 400, Washington, DC 20001
Tel: (202) 715-2923  Fax: (202) 638-1045

Director **Adam Nordstrom** . . . . . . . . . . . . . . . . . . . . . . . . . (202) 715-2923
  Education: George Washington BBA; George Mason JD

## Division of the Budget

900 Southwest Jackson Street, Room 504, Topeka, KS 66612-1225
Tel: (785) 296-2436  Fax: (785) 296-0231
E-mail: budget.info@budget.ks.gov  Internet: www.budget.ks.gov

Director **Shawn Sullivan** . . . . . . . . . . . . . . . . . . . . . . . . . . (785) 296-2436
  Topeka, KS 66612
  Education: Kansas State 1988 BS; North Texas 2000 MS
Deputy Director **Julie Thomas** . . . . . . . . . . . . . . . . . . . . . . (785) 296-2436

## Office of the Lieutenant Governor

State Capitol, 300 Southwest 10th Avenue, 2nd Floor, Topeka, KS 66612
Tel: (785) 296-2214  Fax: (785) 296-5669  E-mail: lt.governor@ks.gov

★Lieutenant Governor **Jeffrey W. "Jeff" Colyer, MD** (R) . . . (785) 296-2213
  Term Expires: January 2019
  E-mail: lt.governor@ks.gov
  Education: Georgetown 1981 BA; Cambridge 1982 MSt;
  Kansas 1986 MD
  Career: State Representative (R-KS, District 48), Kansas House of
  Representatives (2007-2009)
Chief of Staff **Chuck Knapp** . . . . . . . . . . . . . . . . . . . . . . . (785) 296-2213
  Education: Kansas 1988 BA

## Office of the Securities Commissioner

109 Southwest Ninth Street, Suite 600, Topeka, KS 66612-1215
Tel: (785) 296-3307  Fax: (785) 296-6872  E-mail: ksc@ksc.ks.gov

**Employees:** 30  **Fiscal Year:** 2015  **Budget:** $3,005,160

■Securities Commissioner **Joshua Ney** . . . . . . . . . . . . . . . . (785) 296-3307
  E-mail: josh.ney@ksc.ks.gov
  Education: Northwestern Col (MN) BA; Washburn 2009 JD
Chief Regulatory Officer **Steven C. Wassom, CPA** . . . . . . (785) 296-3309
  E-mail: steven.wassom@ksc.ks.gov
  Education: Kansas State, MBA

## Office of the State Bank Commissioner

700 SW Jackson Street, Suite 300, Topeka, KS 66603
Tel: (785) 296-2266  Fax: (785) 296-6037
E-mail: banking@osbckansas.org  Internet: www.osbckansas.org

**Employees:** 106  **Fiscal Year:** 2016  **Budget:** $10,774,285

■Bank Commissioner **Deryl Schuster** . . . . . . . . . . . . . . . . . (785) 296-1520
  E-mail: deryl.schuster@osbckansas.org
  Education: Southwestern Col (KS)

## Banking and Trust Division

Fax: (785) 296-6037

Deputy Bank Commissioner **Judi M. Stork** . . . . . . . . . . . . (785) 296-1515
  E-mail: judi.stork@osbckansas.org
  Education: Kansas State 1979 BS

## Consumer and Mortgage Lending Division

Fax: (785) 296-6037

Deputy Commissioner **Jennifer R. Cook** . . . . . . . . . . . . . . (785) 296-1532
  E-mail: jennifer.cook@osbckansas.org

---

★ Elected Official   ■ Appointed by Governor   ● Appointed by Legislature   ▲ Appointed by Board or Commission   ◆ Appointed by State Supreme Court

EXECUTIVE BRANCH

## Office of the State Fire Marshal [KSFM]

800 Southwest Jackson Street, Suite 104, Topeka, KS 66612-1216
Tel: (785) 296-3401  Fax: (785) 296-0151

**Employees:** 60.5

■State Fire Marshal **Douglass "Doug" Jorgensen** . . . . . . . (785) 296-3401
  E-mail: doug.jorgensen@ks.gov
Chief Deputy State Fire Marshal **(Vacant)** . . . . . . . . . . . . . (785) 296-3401
Legal Counsel and Assistant Attorney General **(Vacant)** . . . (785) 296-3401
Emergency Response Division Chief
  **Henry "Hank" DuPont, Jr.** . . . . . . . . . . . . . . . . . (785) 296-3401
Fire Investigation Division Chief **Wally Roberts** . . . . . . . . (785) 296-3401
Fire Prevention Division Chief **Brenda McNorton** . . . . . . . (785) 296-3401

## Adjutant General's Department

2800 Southwest Topeka Boulevard, Topeka, KS 66611
Tel: (785) 274-1000  Fax: (785) 274-1682
E-mail: ngksstaffpao@ng.army.mil

**Employees:** 449  **Fiscal Year:** 2015  **Budget:** $49,434,236

■Adjutant General **MG Lee E. Tafanelli, ARNG** . . . . . . . . . . (785) 274-1001
  E-mail: lee.e.tafanelli.mil@mail.mil
  Education: Pittsburg State 1982 BS; Army War Col MA;
  Kansas State 1999 MA
Chief of Staff **BG Scott A. Dold, ANG** . . . . . . . . . . . . . . . (785) 274-1007
Deputy Chief of Staff **COL Barry K. Taylor, ARNG** . . . . . . (785) 274-1011
Agency Comptroller **Cheri R. Froetschner** . . . . . . . . . . . . (785) 274-1451
National Guard and Reserve Benefits Adviser
  **Howard L. Steanson** . . . . . . . . . . . . . . . . . . . . . . . (785) 274-1188
  E-mail: howard.l.steanson.ctr@mail.mil
Director of Staff - Air **Lt. Col. Shelly Bausch** . . . . . . . . . . (785) 274-1472
Chief Information Officer and Director, J6
  **COL Chris A. Stratmann, ARNG** . . . . . . . . . . . . . . . . (785) 274-1031
  E-mail: christopher.a.stratmann.mil@mail.mil
Plans, Operations and Military Support Officer
  **LTC Paul W. Schneider, ARNG** . . . . . . . . . . . . . . . . . (785) 274-1193
Procurement Officer **Nancy K. Bisel-Hur** . . . . . . . . . . . . (785) 274-1457
Procurement Officer **(Vacant)** . . . . . . . . . . . . . . . . . . . . (785) 274-1454
Public Affairs Director **Ben Bauman** . . . . . . . . . . . . . . . (785) 646-1192
  Education: Washburn 1985 BA                    Fax: (785) 274-1622

### Division of Emergency Management [KDEM]

2800 Southwest Topeka Boulevard, Topeka, KS 66611

Director **MG Lee E. Tafanelli, ARNG** . . . . . . . . . . . . . . . (785) 274-1001
Deputy Director **Angelynn T. "Angee" Morgan** . . . . . . . . (785) 274-1403

### Division of Homeland Security

2800 Southwest Topeka Boulevard, Topeka, KS 66611

Director **MG Lee E. Tafanelli, ARNG** . . . . . . . . . . . . . . . (785) 274-1001
Deputy Director **(Vacant)** . . . . . . . . . . . . . . . . . . . . . . . (785) 274-1506

## Department of Administration

1000 Southwest Jackson, Suite 500, Topeka, KS 66612
Tel: (785) 296-3011  Fax: (785) 296-2702  Internet: www.admin.ks.gov

**Employees:** 575  **Fiscal Year:** 2015  **Budget:** $87,701,397

■Secretary **Sarah L. Shipman** . . . . . . . . . . . . . . . . . . . . (785) 296-3011
  E-mail: sarah.shipman@da.ks.gov
  Education: Southwestern Col (KS); Washburn JD
Assistant to the Secretary **Marcia Shuart** . . . . . . . . . . . . (785) 296-3011

### Office of Chief Counsel

Tel: (785) 296-6003

Chief Counsel **John Yeary** . . . . . . . . . . . . . . . . . . . . . . . (785) 296-6003
  SCOB, Suite 500, Topeka, KS 66612

### Office of Facilities and Property Management

Director **Mark McGivern** . . . . . . . . . . . . . . . . . . . . . . . . (785) 296-8070

## Kansas Department for Aging and Disability Services [KDADS]

503 South Kansas Avenue, Topeka, KS 66603-3404
Tel: (785) 296-4986  TTY: (785) 291-3167  Fax: (785) 296-0256
E-mail: wwwmail@kdads.ks.gov

**Employees:** 275  **Fiscal Year:** 2015  **Budget:** $1,515,112,630

■Secretary (Interim) **Tim Keck** . . . . . . . . . . . . . . . . . . . . (785) 296-4986
  Special Assistant to the Secretary **Megan Thompson** . . (785) 296-6681
Administrative Services Commissioner **Brad Ridley** . . . . . . (785) 296-6464
  E-mail: brad.ridley@kdads.ks.gov
Community Programs Commissioner **Brandt Haehn** . . . . . . (785) 296-3773
  Education: Fort Hays State; Wichita State MPA
Licensing, Certification and Evaluation Commissioner
  **Codi Thurness** . . . . . . . . . . . . . . . . . . . . . . . . . . . (785) 296-8366
  Education: Kansas State
Chief Counsel **Susan Andrews** . . . . . . . . . . . . . . . . . . . . (785) 206-0237
Communications Director **Angela de Rocha** . . . . . . . . . . . (785) 296-6154
Legislative and Policy Director **Kelli Ludlum** . . . . . . . . . . . (785) 296-4986
  E-mail: kelli.ludlum@kdads.ks.gov
Managed Care Director **James Bart** . . . . . . . . . . . . . . . . (785) 296-6270
  Education: Iowa; Creighton JD
Mental Health Commissioner **William "Bill" Rein** . . . . . . . (785) 296-4079
  Operations Director **Nikki Gilliland** . . . . . . . . . . . . . . (785) 368-6245
Procurement and Facilities Manager **Amanda Clayton** . . . . (785) 296-6450
KanCare Ombudsman **Kerrie Bacon**
  New England Building . . . . . . . . . . . . . . . . . . . . . . . (785) 296-4986
  Education: Baker U BS

## Kansas Department of Agriculture [KDA]

1320 Research Park Drive, Manhattan, KS 66502
Tel: (785) 564-6700  Fax: (785) 564-6777  E-mail: ksag@kda.ks.gov
Internet: www.agriculture.ks.gov

**Employees:** 320  **Fiscal Year:** 2015  **Budget:** $42,664,762

■Secretary **Jackie McClaskey** . . . . . . . . . . . . . . . . . . . . (785) 564-6700
  E-mail: jackie.mcclaskey@kda.ks.gov
Deputy Secretary **Chad Bontrager** . . . . . . . . . . . . . . . . . (785) 564-6700
Assistant Secretary **Susan Metzger** . . . . . . . . . . . . . . . . (785) 564-6700
  E-mail: susan.metzger@kda.ks.gov
  Education: U Mary Washington BS; Old Dominion MS
Assistant Secretary **Josh Roe** . . . . . . . . . . . . . . . . . . . . (785) 564-6700
  Education: Kansas State BS; Iowa State MS
Communications Director **Heather Lansdowne** . . . . . . . . . (785) 564-6706
  E-mail: heather.lansdowne@kda.ks.gov
Public Relations Director **Jason Walker** . . . . . . . . . . . . . . (785) 564-6700
  E-mail: jason.walker@kda.ks.gov
Kansas Agricultural Statistics Director **(Vacant)** . . . . . . . . (785) 233-2230
  632 SW Van Buren St., Rm. 200,          Fax: (785) 233-2518
  Topeka, KS 66601-3534
  P.O. Box 3534, Topeka, KS 66601-3534
  E-mail: nass-ks@nass.usda.gov
Marketing Director **Kerry Wefald** . . . . . . . . . . . . . . . . . . (785) 564-6700
Economist **Kellen Liebsch** . . . . . . . . . . . . . . . . . . . . . . (785) 564-6726
Agriculture Commodities Assurance Program Manager
  **(Vacant)** . . . . . . . . . . . . . . . . . . . . . . . . . . . . . . . (785) 564-6700
  Forbes Field Bldg. 282, P.O. Box 19282, Topeka, KS 66619-0282
Agriculture Laboratory Manager **Audra Gile** . . . . . . . . . . . (785) 862-0108
  P.O. Box 19323, Topeka, KS 66619-0323    Fax: (785) 862-0727
Food Safety Inspection Program Manager **Steve Moris** . . . (785) 564-6700
  E-mail: steve.moris@kda.ks.gov
Grain Warehouse Program Manager **Paul Heady** . . . . . . . . (785) 564-6686
Meat and Poultry Inspection Program Manager
  **Tony George** . . . . . . . . . . . . . . . . . . . . . . . . . . . . (785) 296-3511
  E-mail: tony.george@kda.ks.gov        Fax: (785) 296-0673
Pesticide and Fertilizer Use Program Manager
  **Gary Meyer** . . . . . . . . . . . . . . . . . . . . . . . . . . . . . (785) 564-6688
  E-mail: gary.meyer@kda.ks.gov         Fax: (785) 564-6779
Plant Protection and Weed Control Program Manager
  **Jeff Vogel** . . . . . . . . . . . . . . . . . . . . . . . . . . . . . . (785) 564-6699
  E-mail: jeff.vogel@kda.ks.gov
Weights and Measures Program Manager **Doug Musick** . . . (785) 564-6700
  E-mail: doug.musick@kda.ks.gov

---

★ Elected Official   ■ Appointed by Governor   ● Appointed by Legislature   ▲ Appointed by Board or Commission   ◆ Appointed by State Supreme Court

Chief Fiscal Officer **Justin Law** . . . . . . . . . . . . . . . . . . . . . (785) 564-6700
Fax: (785) 564-6779
Chief Legal Counsel **Robert Large** . . . . . . . . . . . . . . . . . . (785) 564-6715
Agribusiness Development Director **Lynne Hinrichsen** . . . . (785) 564-6700
Building Manager **Jennifer Brunkow** . . . . . . . . . . . . . . . . . (785) 564-6700
Executive Secretary **Kayla Stansbury** . . . . . . . . . . . . . . . . (785) 564-6797

# Department for Children and Families [DCF]

555 South Kansas Avenue, Topeka, KS 66603
Tel: (785) 296-3271  Fax: (785) 296-4685  TTY: (785) 296-3471

**Employees:** 2,530  **Fiscal Year:** 2015  **Budget:** $567,989,205

■Secretary **Phyllis Gilmore, LMSW** . . . . . . . . . . . . . . . . . (785) 296-3274
E-mail: phyllis.gilmore@dcf.ks.gov
Education: Vanderbilt 1967 BS; Washington U (MO) 1971 MSW
Deputy Secretary and Chief of Staff **Jeff Kahrs** . . . . . . . . . (785) 296-3271
Education: Wichita State BA; Washburn 1993 JD

# Kansas Department of Commerce

1000 Southwest Jackson Street, Suite 100, Topeka, KS 66612-1354
Tel: (785) 296-3481  Fax: (785) 296-5055  TTY: (785) 296-3487
Internet: www.kansascommerce.com

**Employees:** 269  **Fiscal Year:** 2015  **Budget:** $99,235,525

■Secretary **Antonio J. Soave** . . . . . . . . . . . . . . . . . . . . . . (785) 296-3481
Education: American U; Detroit Law JD; San Diego ML
Business and Community Development Deputy Secretary
**Steve Kelly** . . . . . . . . . . . . . . . . . . . . . . . . . . . . . . . . . . (785) 296-5298
Workforce Services Deputy Secretary **(Vacant)** . . . . . . . . . (785) 296-7834
Chief Financial Officer **Richard Martinez** . . . . . . . . . . . . . (785) 296-3736
Human Resources Director **Sandra "Sandy" Brown** . . . . . (785) 296-6742
Minority and Women-Owned Business Director
**Rhonda Harris** . . . . . . . . . . . . . . . . . . . . . . . . . . . . . . . (785) 296-3425
Communications Director **Nicole Randall** . . . . . . . . . . . . . (785) 296-3351
E-mail: nrandall@kansascommerce.com
Research Director **Matt Keith** . . . . . . . . . . . . . . . . . . . . . (785) 296-4931
Rural Opportunity Zones Manager **Darla Price** . . . . . . . . . (785) 296-5298

# Kansas Department of Corrections [KDOC]

714 Southwest Jackson Street, Suite 300, Topeka, KS 66603-3714
Tel: (785) 296-3317  Fax: (785) 296-0014  E-mail: kdocpub@doc.ks.gov

**Employees:** 480  **Fiscal Year:** 2015  **Budget:** $191,235,473

■Secretary **(Interim) Johnnie Goddard** . . . . . . . . . . . . . . . (785) 296-3317
E-mail: johng@doc.ks.gov
■Secretary **Joseph L. "Joe" Norwood** . . . . . . . . . . . . . . . (785) 296-3317
Note: On April 4, 2016, Governor Sam Brownback appointed Joseph
Norwood to serve as Secretary of the Department of Corrections,
effective May 30, 2016.
Education: Kansas BS
Legal Counsel **Linden Appel** . . . . . . . . . . . . . . . . . . . . . . (785) 296-7721
E-mail: lindena@doc.ks.gov
Education: Washburn JD
Community and Field Services Deputy Secretary
**(Interim) Teresa "Terri" Williams** . . . . . . . . . . . . . . . . . (785) 296-4520
Education: Washburn; Kansas MPA
Facility Management Division Deputy Secretary
**Johnnie Goddard** . . . . . . . . . . . . . . . . . . . . . . . . . . . . . (785) 296-0449
Juvenile Services Deputy Secretary
**Teresa "Terri" Williams** . . . . . . . . . . . . . . . . . . . . . . . . (785) 296-0042
Enforcement, Apprehensions and Investigations Director
**(Interim) Marcelle Cappel-Chmidling** . . . . . . . . . . . . . . . (785) 296-0200
E-mail: marcelle.chmidling@doc.ks.gov
Human Resources Director **Jan Clausing** . . . . . . . . . . . . . (785) 296-3101
Education: Wichita State MS
Information Technology Director **Harold Sass** . . . . . . . . . . (785) 231-1250
E-mail: harolds@doc.ks.gov
Programs, Contracts and Fiscal Services Director
**Keith Bradshaw** . . . . . . . . . . . . . . . . . . . . . . . . . . . . . . (785) 296-4522
Special Assistant and Communications Director
**Adam Pfannenstiel** . . . . . . . . . . . . . . . . . . . . . . . . . . . . (785) 215-2857
E-mail: adam.pfannenstiel@doc.ks.gov
Education: Fort Hays State 2007

Victim Services Director **Audrey Cress** . . . . . . . . . . . . . . . (785) 224-8773

# Kansas Department of Credit Unions [KDCU]

700 Southwest Jackson Street, Suite 803, Topeka, KS 66603
Tel: (785) 296-3021  Fax: (785) 296-6830
E-mail: kdcuoffice@kdcu.ks.gov  Internet: www.kdcu.ks.gov

**Employees:** 12  **Fiscal Year:** 2015  **Budget:** $1,059,615

■Administrator **Jerel Wright** . . . . . . . . . . . . . . . . . . . . . . . (785) 296-3021
E-mail: jerel.wright@ks.gov
Education: Washburn 1979 BBA, 1983 JD

# Kansas Department of Health and Environment [KDHE]

Curtis Office Building, 1000 Southwest Jackson, Topeka, KS 66612
Tel: (785) 296-1500  Tel: (785) 296-1400 (Vital Records)
Fax: (785) 296-8075 (Vital Records)  E-mail: info@kdhe.state.ks.us
E-mail: vital.records@kdheks.gov (Vital Records)

**Employees:** 671  **Fiscal Year:** 2015  **Budget:** $2,299,097,918

■Secretary **Dr. Susan Mosier, MD, MBA, FACS** . . . . . . . . . (785) 296-0461
E-mail: smosier@kdheks.gov              Fax: (785) 368-6368
Education: Kansas State 1980 BA; Texas MBA; Kansas MD
Deputy Secretary **Aaron Dunkel** . . . . . . . . . . . . . . . . . . . . (785) 296-0461
Deputy Secretary for Environment **Gary Mason** . . . . . . . . . (785) 296-0461
Policy Analyst and Legislative Liaison **John Monroe** . . . . . (785) 296-4577
E-mail: jpmonroe@kdheks.gov
Communications Director **Tanya Roman** . . . . . . . . . . . . . . (785) 296-5795
E-mail: troman@kdheks.gov
Deputy Chief Counsel **(Vacant)** . . . . . . . . . . . . . . . . . . . . (785) 296-1500
Human Resources Director **Karen Vandy** . . . . . . . . . . . . . (785) 291-3064
Information Technology Director **Glen Yancey** . . . . . . . . . . (785) 296-5643
E-mail: gyancey@kdheks.gov
Public Information Officer **Ashton Rucker** . . . . . . . . . . . . . (785) 291-3684
E-mail: arucker@kdheks.gov
Public Information Officer **Cassie Sparks** . . . . . . . . . . . . . (785) 368-8053
E-mail: csparks@kdheks.gov

## Division of Environment

Fax: (785) 296-8464
Director **John W. Mitchell** . . . . . . . . . . . . . . . . . . . . . . . . (785) 296-1534
Education: Kansas BS, MEH
Deputy Director **Leo Henning** . . . . . . . . . . . . . . . . . . . . . (785) 296-1660
Air Bureau Director **Rick Brunetti** . . . . . . . . . . . . . . . . . . (785) 296-1551
E-mail: rburnetti@kdheks.gov
Environmental Field Services Bureau Director
**April Dixon** . . . . . . . . . . . . . . . . . . . . . . . . . . . . . . . . . . (785) 296-0380
Environmental Remediation Bureau Director
**Leo Henning** . . . . . . . . . . . . . . . . . . . . . . . . . . . . . . . . . (785) 296-1660
Waste Management Bureau Director
**William "Bill" Bider** . . . . . . . . . . . . . . . . . . . . . . . . . . . (785) 296-1600
Education: Bethany (KS) 1976 BS; Kansas 1977 MS
Water Bureau Director **(Vacant)** . . . . . . . . . . . . . . . . . . . . (785) 296-5504

## Division of Health Care Finance

Tel: (785) 296-3512  Fax: (785) 296-4813
Director **Michael Randol** . . . . . . . . . . . . . . . . . . . . . . . . . (785) 269-3512
Data Policy and Evaluation Director **(Vacant)** . . . . . . . . . . (785) 368-3981
Medicaid Director **Dr. Susan Mosier, MD, MBA, FACS** . . . (785) 296-0461
Medicaid Director of Eligibility **(Vacant)** . . . . . . . . . . . . . (785) 296-8355
Projections, Financing and Estimation Director **(Vacant)** . . . (785) 296-3416
State Employee Health Benefits Plan Director
**Mike Michael** . . . . . . . . . . . . . . . . . . . . . . . . . . . . . . . . (785) 296-3981
Operations Director and Medicaid Deputy Director
**Christiane Swartz** . . . . . . . . . . . . . . . . . . . . . . . . . . . . . (785) 296-6280
General Counsel **Brian Vazquez** . . . . . . . . . . . . . . . . . . . . (785) 296-0696
Senior Administrative Specialist **Talysha Hickerson** . . . . . . (785) 296-3512

## Division of Public Health

Fax: (785) 296-1562
Director **Dr. Susan Mosier, MD, MBA, FACS** . . . . . . . . . . (785) 296-0461

*(continued on next page)*

*(continued on next page)*

★ Elected Official    ■ Appointed by Governor    ● Appointed by Legislature    ▲ Appointed by Board or Commission    ◆ Appointed by State Supreme Court

**Division of Public Health** *continued*

Community Health System Bureau Director
**Ashley Goss** . . . . . . . . . . . . . . . . . . . . . . . . . . (785) 296-7100
Family Health Bureau Director **Rachel Sisson** . . . . . . . . . . (785) 291-3368
Health Promotion Bureau Director **Brandon Skidmore** . . . (785) 296-8916
Nutrition and Women, Infants and Children (WIC)
Services Director **Dave Thomason** . . . . . . . . . . . . . . . . . (785) 296-1324
E-mail: dthomason@kdheks.gov

## Department of Labor [DOL]

401 SW Topeka Boulevard, Topeka, KS 66603-3182
Tel: (785) 296-5000  Fax: (785) 368-6294

**Employees:** 507  **Fiscal Year:** 2015  **Budget:** $340,654,100

■Secretary **Lana Gordon** . . . . . . . . . . . . . . . . . . . . . (785) 296-5000 ext. 2705
E-mail: lana.gordon@dol.ks.gov
Education: Kansas 1971 BS
Deputy Secretary and Chief Counsel
**Bradley Burke** . . . . . . . . . . . . . . . . . . . . . . . . (785) 296-5000 ext. 2569
Chief Financial Officer **Dawn Palmberg** . . . . . . . . (785) 296-5000 ext. 2551
Chief Information Officer **John Cahill** . . . . . . . . . (785) 296-5000 ext. 7580
E-mail: john.cahill@dol.ks.gov
Employment Standards Director **Tim Triggs** . . . . . (785) 296-5000 ext. 2547
Human Resources Director **Lacie Worcester** . . . . (785) 296-5000 ext. 2565
Industrial Safety and Health Director
**Terri Sanchez** . . . . . . . . . . . . . . . . . . . . . . . . (785) 296-5000 ext. 2310
Labor Market Information Services Director
**Justin McFarland** . . . . . . . . . . . . . . . . . . . . (785) 296-5000 ext. 2714
E-mail: justin.mcfarland@dol.ks.gov
Communications Director **Barbara Hersh** . . . . . . . (785) 296-5000 ext. 2542
Unemployment Insurance Director
**Brett Flachsbarth** . . . . . . . . . . . . . . . . . . . . (785) 296-5000 ext. 2507
Workers Compensation Director **Larry Karns** . . . . (785) 296-4000 ext. 2156
Kansas Unemployment Insurance Contact
Center Manager **Cheryl Jones** . . . . . . . . . . . . (785) 296-5000 ext. 2511
Legislative Liaison **Joyce Bishop** . . . . . . . . . . . . (785) 296-5000 ext. 2705
E-mail: joyce.bishop@dol.ks.gov
Procurement Officer **Gregory Layne** . . . . . . . . . . (785) 296-5000 ext. 2553

## Department of Revenue

Docking State Office Building, 915 Southwest Harrison,
Topeka, KS 66612-1588
Tel: (785) 368-8222  Fax: (785) 368-3892  Internet: www.ksrevenue.org

**Employees:** 1,072  **Fiscal Year:** 2015  **Budget:** $119,223,988

■Secretary **Nicholas M. "Nick" Jordan** . . . . . . . . . . . . . (785) 296-3041
E-mail: nick.jordan@ks.gov
Alcoholic Beverage Control Division Director
**LaVern Fields** . . . . . . . . . . . . . . . . . . . . . . . . . . . . (785) 296-7015
Property Valuation Division Director **David Harper** . . . . . . (785) 296-4218
Vehicle Division Director **Lisa Kaspar** . . . . . . . . . . . . . (785) 296-3601
E-mail: lisa.kaspar@kdor.ks.gov
Chief Information Officer **Kevin Chronister** . . . . . . . . . . . (785) 291-7087
E-mail: kevin.chronister@kdor.ks.gov
Legal Services Bureau General Counsel **David Clauser** . . . (785) 296-8679
Human Resources Director **(Vacant)** . . . . . . . . . . . . . . . (785) 296-3077
Policy and Research Director **Richard Cram** . . . . . . . . . . . (785) 296-3081
Resource Management Director **James "Jim" Conant** . . . . (785) 296-4007
Taxation Director **Steve Stotts** . . . . . . . . . . . . . . . . . . . (785) 296-6431
Tax Specialist **Mark Ciardullo** . . . . . . . . . . . . . . . . . . . (785) 296-5330
Legislative Liaison **Richard Carlson** . . . . . . . . . . . . . . . (785) 368-8222
E-mail: richard.carlson@kdor.ks.gov
Education: Kansas State 1968 BS
Audit Services **Mike Boekhaus** . . . . . . . . . . . . . . . . . . . (785) 291-3431
Collections **Jeffery Scott** . . . . . . . . . . . . . . . . . . . . . . . (785) 296-3321
Customer Relations **(Vacant)** . . . . . . . . . . . . . . . . . . . . (785) 296-2445

## Kansas Department of Transportation [KSDOT]

Eisenhower State Office Building, 700 Southwest Harrison,
Topeka, KS 66603
Tel: (785) 296-3566  Fax: (785) 368-7415  TTY: (785) 296-3585
E-mail: publicinfo@ksdot.org  Internet: www.ksdot.org

**Employees:** 2,738  **Fiscal Year:** 2015  **Budget:** $1,155,650,548

■Secretary **Mike King** . . . . . . . . . . . . . . . . . . . . . . . . . (785) 296-3461
E-mail: mking@ksdot.org
Education: John Brown 1981 BS
Deputy Secretary and State Transportation Engineer
**Jerry Younger** . . . . . . . . . . . . . . . . . . . . . . . . . . . (785) 296-3285
Chief Counsel **Barbara "Barb" Rankin** . . . . . . . . . . . . . . (785) 296-3831
E-mail: rankin@ksdot.org
Librarian **Marie Manthe** . . . . . . . . . . . . . . . . . . . . . . . (785) 291-3854
Fax: (785) 296-2526

### Division of Aviation

Fax: (785) 296-3833  E-mail: kdotaviation@ksdot.org
Director **Merrill Eisenhower Atwater** . . . . . . . . . . . . . . . (785) 296-2553
Education: Missouri Western State U

### Division of Engineering and Design

Tel: (785) 296-2270  Fax: (785) 291-3986
Director **Jim Kowach** . . . . . . . . . . . . . . . . . . . . . . . . . (785) 296-2270
E-mail: kowach@ksdot.org
Local Projects Bureau Chief **Ron Seitz** . . . . . . . . . . . . . . (785) 296-3861
E-mail: seitz@ksdot.org
Right-of-Way Bureau Chief **Rob Stork** . . . . . . . . . . . . . . (785) 296-3501
E-mail: rstork@ksdot.org
Road Design Bureau Chief **Scott King** . . . . . . . . . . . . . . (785) 296-3525
Structures/Geotechnical Services Bureau Chief
**Mark Hoppe** . . . . . . . . . . . . . . . . . . . . . . . . . . . . (785) 296-3525

### Division of Fiscal and Asset Management

Director **Chris Herrick** . . . . . . . . . . . . . . . . . . . . . . . . (785) 296-3640
Finance and Budget Office Chief **Ben Cleeves** . . . . . . . . . (785) 296-6044
Fiscal Services Bureau Chief **Rhonda Seitz** . . . . . . . . . . . (785) 296-3640

### Division of Operations

Tel: (785) 296-2235  Fax: (785) 296-2799
Director **Catherine Patrick** . . . . . . . . . . . . . . . . . . . . . (785) 296-2235
Construction and Materials Bureau Chief **Greg Schieber** . . (785) 296-3576
Maintenance Bureau Chief **Clay Adams** . . . . . . . . . . . . . (785) 296-3233
Research Bureau Chief **Rick Kreider** . . . . . . . . . . . . . . . (785) 296-3711
E-mail: rickk@ksdot.org

### Division of Partner Relations

Tel: (785) 296-3585  Fax: (785) 296-0287
Director **Wade Wiebe** . . . . . . . . . . . . . . . . . . . . . . . . . (785) 296-3585
E-mail: wwiebe@ksdot.org
Chief Information Officer **Jeff Neal** . . . . . . . . . . . . . . . . (785) 296-0310
E-mail: jfneal@ksdot.org
Personnel Services Bureau Chief **Denise Schwab** . . . . . . . (785) 296-0433
Support Services Bureau Chief **Robert "Bob" Stacks** . . . . (785) 368-7025
E-mail: bstacks@ksdot.org

### Division of Planning and Development

Tel: (785) 296-2252  Fax: (785) 296-7173
Director **Chris Herrick** . . . . . . . . . . . . . . . . . . . . . . . . (785) 296-2252
E-mail: chrish@ksdot.org
Assistant to the Director **(Vacant)** . . . . . . . . . . . . . . . . (785) 296-7451
Program and Project Management Bureau Chief
**Mark Taylor** . . . . . . . . . . . . . . . . . . . . . . . . . . . . (785) 296-3526
E-mail: markt@ksdot.org
Traffic Safety and Technology Bureau Chief
**Mike Floberg** . . . . . . . . . . . . . . . . . . . . . . . . . . . . (785) 296-3756
Transportation Planning Bureau Chief **Mike Moriarty** . . . . (785) 296-3841

---

★ Elected Official   ■ Appointed by Governor   ● Appointed by Legislature   ▲ Appointed by Board or Commission   ◆ Appointed by State Supreme Court

## Division of Policy

Tel: (785) 296-3585  Fax: (785) 296-0287

Director **Joel Skelley** . . . . . . . . . . . . . . . . . . . . . . . . . . . . . . . (785) 296-3585
  E-mail: joelsk@ksdot.org
Policy and Legislative Affairs Office Chief
  **Halee Lindstrom** . . . . . . . . . . . . . . . . . . . . . . . . . . . . . . (785) 296-3585
  E-mail: halee@ksdot.org
Public Affairs Bureau Chief **Steve Swartz** . . . . . . . . . . . . . (785) 296-3585
  Education: Kansas 1974 BA
Public Information Officer **Ann Williamson** . . . . . . . . . . . (785) 296-2669
  E-mail: annw@ksdot.org

## Kansas Department of Wildlife, Parks and Tourism

1020 South Kansas Avenue, Suite 200, Topeka, KS 66612
Tel: (785) 296-2281  E-mail: kdwpinfo@ksoutdoors.com

**Employees:** 341  **Fiscal Year:** 2015  **Budget:** $65,747,925

■Secretary **Robin Jennison** . . . . . . . . . . . . . . . . . . . . . . . . . (785) 296-2281
  E-mail: robin.jennison@ksoutdoors.com
Assistant Secretary for Administration **Todd Workman** . . . (785) 296-2281
  E-mail: todd.workman@ksoutdoors.com
Assistant Secretary for Parks and Tourism
  **Linda Craghead** . . . . . . . . . . . . . . . . . . . . . . . . . . . . . . . (785) 296-3870
  E-mail: linda.craghead@ksoutdoors.com
Tourism Division Director **(Vacant)** . . . . . . . . . . . . . . . . . . (785) 296-2281
Chief Legal Counsel **Christopher Tymeson** . . . . . . . . . . . (785) 296-2281
  Legal Counsel **Amy Thornton** . . . . . . . . . . . . . . . . . . . . (785) 296-2281
Chief Engineer **Chad Grisier** . . . . . . . . . . . . . . . . . . . . . . . (785) 296-2281
Natural Resources Coordinator **Steven Adams** . . . . . . . . . (785) 296-3048
  E-mail: steven.adams@ksoutdoors.com
Wildtrust Coordinator and Accountant **Donald Dilling** . . . . (620) 672-0755
  512 SE 25th Avenue, Pratt, KS 67124

## Operations Office

512 SE 25th Avenue, Pratt, KS 67124-8174
Fax: (316) 672-6020

Wildlife, Fisheries and Boating Assistant Secretary
  **Keith Sexson, Jr.** . . . . . . . . . . . . . . . . . . . . . . . . . . . . . (620) 672-5911
Administrative Services Division Director **Frank Jarmer** . . (620) 672-0754
  E-mail: frank.jarmer@ksoutdoors.com
Fish and Wildlife Division Director **(Vacant)** . . . . . (620) 672-5911 ext. 190
Information Services Division Director **Ron Kaufman** . . . . (785) 296-2281
  E-mail: ron.kaufman@ksoutdoors.com
Law Enforcement Division Director **Kevin Jones** . . . . . . . . (620) 672-0705
Parks Division Director **Linda Lanterman** . . . . . . . . . . . . . (620) 672-5911
  E-mail: linda.lanterman@ksoutdoors.com

## Kansas Corporation Commission [KCC]

1500 Southwest Arrowhead Road, Topeka, KS 66604
Tel: (785) 271-3100  Fax: (785) 271-3354
E-mail: public.affairs@kcc.ks.gov

**Employees:** 195  **Fiscal Year:** 2015  **Budget:** $18,918,988

■Chair **Jay Scott Emler** . . . . . . . . . . . . . . . . . . . . . . . . . . . (785) 271-3350
  Term Expires: March 15, 2019
  Education: Bethany (KS) 1971 BEd; Denver 1976 JD;
  Naval Postgrad 2008 MA
■Commissioner **Shari Fiest Albrecht** . . . . . . . . . . . . . . . . . (785) 271-3350
  Term Expires: March 15, 2016
  E-mail: s.feist.albrecht@kcc.ks.gov
  Education: Kansas 1981 BA; Washburn 1984 JD
■Commissioner **Pat Apple** . . . . . . . . . . . . . . . . . . . . . . . . . (785) 271-3166
  Term Expires: March 15, 2018

## Kansas Human Rights Commission [KHRC]

Landon State Office Building, 900 SW Jackson Street, Room 568 South,
Topeka, KS 66612-1252
Tel: (785) 296-3206  Tel: (888) 793-6874  TTY: (785) 296-0245
Fax: (785) 296-0589  E-mail: khrc@ink.org  Internet: www.khrc.net

**Employees:** 16  **Fiscal Year:** 2015  **Budget:** $1,437,714

■Chair **Melvin J. Neufeld** . . . . . . . . . . . . . . . . . . . . . . . . . (785) 296-3206
■Vice Chair **Terry Crowder** . . . . . . . . . . . . . . . . . . . . . . . . (785) 296-3206
■Commissioner **David Bryant** . . . . . . . . . . . . . . . . . . . . . . . (785) 296-3206
■Commissioner **Michael Kane** . . . . . . . . . . . . . . . . . . . . . . . (785) 296-3206
■Commissioner **Eric Laverentz** . . . . . . . . . . . . . . . . . . . . . . (785) 296-3206
■Commissioner **Harold F. Schorn II** . . . . . . . . . . . . . . . . . . (785) 296-3206
■Commissioner **(Vacant)** . . . . . . . . . . . . . . . . . . . . . . . . . . (785) 296-3206
▲Executive Director **Ruth Glover** . . . . . . . . . . . . . . . . . . . . (785) 296-3206
  E-mail: ruth.glover@khrc.state.ks.us

## Kansas Lottery Commission

128 North Kansas Avenue, Topeka, KS 66603
Tel: (785) 296-5700  Fax: (785) 296-5712  Internet: www.kslottery.com

**Employees:** 101  **Fiscal Year:** 2015  **Budget:** $335,251,277

■Chair **Catherine Moyer** . . . . . . . . . . . . . . . . . . . . . . . . . . (785) 296-5700
  Term Expires: March 15, 2019
  Affiliation: General Manager, Pioneer Communications
  120 West Kansas Avenue, Ulysses, KS 67880
  Education: Middlebury BA; Washburn JD
■Commissioner **Tom Roberts** . . . . . . . . . . . . . . . . . . . . . . . (785) 296-5700
  Term Expires: March 15, 2017
■Commissioner **Alana Roethle** . . . . . . . . . . . . . . . . . . . . . . (785) 296-5700
  Term Expires: March 15, 2019
  Education: Florida State; Minnesota MBA
■Commissioner **Jeffry A. Scharping** . . . . . . . . . . . . . . . . . . (785) 296-5700
  Term Expires: March 15, 2018
  Education: Kansas State; Wichita State
■Commissioner **James Washington** . . . . . . . . . . . . . . . . . . . (785) 296-5700
  Term Expires: January 15, 2017

### Commission Staff

■Executive Director **Terry Presta** . . . . . . . . . . . . . . . . . . . . (785) 296-5729
  E-mail: terry.presta@kslottery.net

## Commission on Veterans' Affairs

700 Southwest Jackson Street, Suite 1004, Topeka, KS 66603
Tel: (785) 296-3976  Fax: (785) 296-1462  Internet: www.kcva.ks.gov

▲Executive Director **Col Gregg Burden, USAF (Ret)** . . . . . . (785) 296-3976
  E-mail: gburden@kcva.ks.gov
  Education: Kansas State

## Kansas Highway Patrol

122 SW 7th Street, Topeka, KS 66603-3847
Tel: (785) 296-6800  Fax: (785) 296-5956  E-mail: info@khp.ks.gov
Internet: www.kansashighwaypatrol.org

**Employees:** 885  **Fiscal Year:** 2015  **Budget:** $81,645,664

■Superintendent **Col. Mark Bruce** . . . . . . . . . . . . . . . . . . . (785) 296-6800
  E-mail: mbruce@khp.ks.gov
Assistant Superintendent **Lt. Col. Randy Moon** . . . . . . . . . (785) 296-6800
Human Resources Director **Jesse Maddox** . . . . . . . . . . . . . (785) 296-6800
East Region Commander **Major Mark Goodloe** . . . . . . . . . (785) 296-6800
West Region Commander **Major Jason DeVore** . . . . . . . . . (785) 827-3065
Professional Standards Unit **Capt. Eric Pippin** . . . . . . . . . . (785) 296-6800
Legal Counsel **Tammie Lord** . . . . . . . . . . . . . . . . . . . . . . . (785) 296-6800
Legal Counsel **Sarah E. Washburn** . . . . . . . . . . . . . . . . . . (785) 296-6800
  Education: Washburn 2010 JD
Chief Fiscal Officer **Kim Torrey** . . . . . . . . . . . . . . . . . . . . (785) 296-6800
Emergency Management **Capt. Eric Sauer** . . . . . . . . . . . . . (785) 296-6800
Homeland Security Operations **Capt. Eric Sauer** . . . . . . . . (785) 296-6800
Public and Governmental Affairs
  **Capt. Joshua Kellerman** . . . . . . . . . . . . . . . . . . . . . . . . (785) 296-6800
Special Operations **Major John Eichkorn** . . . . . . . . . . . . . (785) 296-6800

*(continued on next page)*

---

★ Elected Official    ■ Appointed by Governor    ● Appointed by Legislature    ▲ Appointed by Board or Commission    ◆ Appointed by State Supreme Court

EXECUTIVE BRANCH

**Kansas Highway Patrol** *continued*

Support Services **Major Scott Harrington** . . . . . . . . . . . . . (785) 296-6800
E-mail: sharring@khp.ks.gov

## Kansas State Library

300 SW 10th Avenue, Room 312N, Topeka, KS 66612-1593
Tel: (785) 296-3296  TTY: (785) 296-2149  Fax: (785) 296-6650
E-mail: infodesk@library.ks.gov

**Employees:** 31  **Fiscal Year:** 2015  **Budget:** $6,677,117,000

■State Librarian **Joanne M. "Jo" Budler** . . . . . . . . . . . . . . (785) 296-3296
E-mail: jo.budler@library.ks.gov
Education: Iowa MLS, MFA
Director of Reference Services **Cindy Roupe** . . . . . . . . . . . (785) 296-5437
Director of Statewide Resource Sharing **Jeff Hixon** . . . . . . . (785) 296-3154
Talking Books Director **Hillary McHenry** . . . . . . . . . . . . . (620) 341-6287
ESU Memorial Union, 1200 Commercial Street, Emporia, KS 66801
Interlibrary Loan Librarian **Tom Roth** . . . . . . . . . . . . . . . (785) 296-4326

## Office of the Attorney General

120 Southwest 10th Avenue, 2nd Floor, Topeka, KS 66612-1597
Tel: (785) 296-2215  Fax: (785) 296-6296

**Employees:** 135  **Fiscal Year:** 2015  **Budget:** $20,335,339

★Attorney General **Derek Schmidt** (R) . . . . . . . . . . . . . . . (785) 296-2215
Term Expires: January 14, 2019
Education: Kansas 1990 BA; Georgetown 1996 JD
Career: Majority Leader, Kansas Senate (2005-2011); State Senator
(R-KS, District 15), Kansas Senate (2001-2011)
Chief of Staff **Eric Montgomery** . . . . . . . . . . . . . . . . . . . (785) 296-2215
Chief Deputy Attorney General **Jeff Chanay** . . . . . . . . . . . (785) 368-8435
Deputy Attorney General for Civil Litigation
**Dennis D. Depew** . . . . . . . . . . . . . . . . . . . . . . . . . . . (785) 296-2215
Deputy Attorney General for Criminal Litigation
**Vic Braden** . . . . . . . . . . . . . . . . . . . . . . . . . . . . . . . (785) 296-2215
Deputy Attorney General for Consumer Protection
**Jim Welch** . . . . . . . . . . . . . . . . . . . . . . . . . . . . . . . (785) 296-3751
Education: Washburn 1974 BA, 1977 JD    Fax: (785) 291-3699
Deputy Attorney General for Legal Opinions and
Government Counsel **Athena E. Andaya** . . . . . . . . . . . . . (785) 368-8401
Deputy Attorney General for Medicaid Fraud (Interim)
**Jackie Neil Williams** . . . . . . . . . . . . . . . . . . . . . . . . . (785) 368-8413
Education: Wichita State 1967 BBA; Washburn 1970 JD
Solicitor General **Stephen McAllister** . . . . . . . . . . . . . . . (785) 296-2215
Education: Kansas 1985 BA, 1988 JD
Division of Crime Victims Compensation Director
**Jeff Wagaman** . . . . . . . . . . . . . . . . . . . . . . . . . . . . . (785) 296-2359
Victim Services Director **Dorthy Stucky Halley** . . . . . . . . . (785) 291-3950

## Office of the Secretary of State

Memorial Hall, 120 S.W. 10th Avenue, Topeka, KS 66612-1594
Tel: (785) 296-4564  TTY: (800) 262-8683  Fax: (785) 296-4570
E-mail: kssos@sos.ks.gov

**Employees:** 40  **Fiscal Year:** 2015  **Budget:** $4,908,858

★Secretary of State **Kris W. Kobach, JD** (R) . . . . . . . . . . . (785) 296-4575
Term Expires: January 2019
Education: Harvard 1988 BA; Oxford (UK) 1990 MPhil, 1992 PhD;
Yale 1995 JD
Career: Counsel, Office of the Attorney General, United States
Department of Justice (2001-2003); Policy Advisor, Romney for
President, Inc. (2007-2008); State Chairman, Kansas Republican Party,
Republican National Committee (2007-2009)
Executive Assistant **(Vacant)** . . . . . . . . . . . . . . . . . . . . (785) 296-4575
Assistant to the Secretary of State **(Vacant)** . . . . . . . . . . . (785) 296-8542
Assistant Secretary of State **Eric Rucker** . . . . . . . . . . . . . (785) 296-2034
Administration Deputy Assistant Secretary of State and
Chief of Staff **Nancy Bryant** . . . . . . . . . . . . . . . . . . . . (785) 296-3033
E-mail: 622@sos.ks.gov
Education: Fort Hays State 1976 BS, 1986 MS
Business Services Deputy Assistant Secretary of State
**Kathy Sachs** . . . . . . . . . . . . . . . . . . . . . . . . . . . . . . (785) 296-3828
Education: Baker U 1995 BBA

Elections and Legislative Matters Deputy Assistant
Secretary of State **Bryan A. Caskey** . . . . . . . . . . . . . . . (785) 296-4561
E-mail: election@sos.ks.gov
Legal Counsel and Policy Deputy Assistant Secretary of
State **(Vacant)** . . . . . . . . . . . . . . . . . . . . . . . . . . . . (785) 296-4801
Public Affairs Director **Craig McCullah** . . . . . . . . . . . . . . (785) 296-4580
Human Resources Director **Craig McCullah** . . . . . . . . . . . (785) 296-4580
Fax: (785) 296-4570
Chief Information Officer **(Vacant)** . . . . . . . . . . . . . . . . . (785) 368-8025
E-mail: techsup@sos.ks.gov
Kansas Register **Lara Murphy** . . . . . . . . . . . . . . . . . . . . (785) 296-0082

## Office of the State Treasurer

Landon State Office Building, 900 Southwest Jackson Street, Suite 201,
Topeka, KS 66612-1235
Tel: (785) 296-3171  Tel: (785) 296-4165 (Unclaimed Property)
Fax: (785) 296-7950  E-mail: public@treasurer.state.ks.us

**Employees:** 46  **Fiscal Year:** 2015  **Budget:** $25,301,658

★State Treasurer **Ron Estes** (R) . . . . . . . . . . . . . . . . . . . (785) 296-3171
Term Expires: January 2019
E-mail: ron@treasurer.ks.gov
Education: Tennessee Tech BCE, MBA
Career: Treasurer, Office of the Treasurer, County of Sedgwick, Kansas
(2005-2011)
Special Assistant to the Treasurer
**Thomas "Tom" Treacy** . . . . . . . . . . . . . . . . . . . . . . (785) 296-4163
Assistant State Treasurer **Jennifer Hermann** . . . . . . . . . . . (785) 296-3171
Education: Friends
Communications and Financial Literacy Director
**Ashley Murdie** . . . . . . . . . . . . . . . . . . . . . . . . . . . . (785) 296-3538
E-mail: ashley@treasurer.ks.gov
Education: Kansas State BA
Cash Management Director **Lucinda Anstaett** . . . . . . . . . . (785) 296-3171
Information Technology Director **Cindy Hooper-Bears** . . . . (785) 296-3171
E-mail: cindy@treasurer.ks.gov
Learning Quest Savings Program Director **Scott Gates** . . . (785) 296-3171
Municipal Bond Services Director **Stan Jones** . . . . . . . . . (785) 296-3171
Unclaimed Property Director **Kathy Priest** . . . . . . . . . . . . (785) 296-3171
Executive Assistant **Mindy Forrer** . . . . . . . . . . . . . . . . . (785) 296-2565

## Kansas Insurance Department

420 Southwest Ninth Street, Topeka, KS 66612-1678
Tel: (785) 296-3071  Fax: (785) 296-7805  TTY: (877) 235-3151
Internet: www.ksinsurance.org

**Employees:** 110  **Fiscal Year:** 2015  **Budget:** $30,062,048

★Insurance Commissioner **Ken Selzer, CPA** (R) . . . . . . . . . (785) 296-3071
Term Expires: January 2019
Education: Kansas State BSAcc; USC MBA
Assistant and Scheduler **Lacey Kennett** . . . . . . . . . . . . . (785) 291-3299
E-mail: lkennett@ksinsurance.org
Assistant Commissioner **John Wine** . . . . . . . . . . . . . . . . (785) 296-7806
Comptroller **Charlotte Humburg** . . . . . . . . . . . . . . . . . . (785) 296-1840
Communications Director **Bob Hanson** . . . . . . . . . . . . . . (785) 296-7807
E-mail: bhanson@ksinsurance.org
Consumer Assistance Director **LeAnn Crow** . . . . . . . . . . (785) 296-7827
Information Technology Director **Linda Scott** . . . . . . . . . . (785) 368-6527
E-mail: lscott@ksinsurance.org
Public Outreach Director **Cindy Hermes** . . . . . . . . . . . . . (785) 296-7803
Human Resource and Building Services Director (Acting)
**John Wine** . . . . . . . . . . . . . . . . . . . . . . . . . . . . . . . (785) 296-7806
Anti-Fraud Division Director **Randy Adair** . . . . . . . . . . . . (785) 296-7802
Financial Surveillance Division Director **Ken Abitz, CIA** . . . (785) 296-7821
Education: Kansas State 1974 BS
Health and Life Division Director **Julie Holmes** . . . . . . . . . (785) 296-6410
Property and Casualty Division Director **Heather Droge** . . . (785) 296-7839
General Counsel **Diane Minear** . . . . . . . . . . . . . . . . . . . (785) 296-7847
Education: Kansas BGS, 2001 JD
Consulting Actuary **Mark Birdsall** . . . . . . . . . . . . . . . . . (785) 296-1056
Director of Government Affairs **Clark Shultz** . . . . . . . . . . . (785) 296-2752
E-mail: cshultz@ksinsurance.org
Education: Wichita State 1994 BGS

---

★ Elected Official    ■ Appointed by Governor    ● Appointed by Legislature    ▲ Appointed by Board or Commission    ◆ Appointed by State Supreme Court

## State Board of Education

120 Southeast 10th Avenue, Topeka, KS 66612
Tel: (785) 296-3201  Fax: (785) 291-3791  E-mail: pplamann@ksde.org
Internet: www.ksde.org

★Chair **Jim McNiece** (R-District 10) . . . . . . . . . . . . . . . . . . (316) 729-9742
  Term Expires: 2017
  1214 Manchester Court, Wichita, KS 67212
  E-mail: nemprin@yahoo.com
  Education: St Mary Plains 1971 BA; Fort Hays State 1977 MS

★Vice Chair **Carolyn L. Wims-Campbell** (D-District 4) . . . . (785) 266-3798
  Term Expires: 2017                         Fax: (785) 291-3791
  3824 Southeast Illinois Avenue, Topeka, KS 66609
  E-mail: campbell4ksboe@gmail.com

★Member **John Bacon** (R-District 3) . . . . . . . . . . . . . . . . . . (913) 660-0392
  Term Expires: 2019                         Fax: (913) 829-4213
  14183 West 157th Street, Olathe, KS 66062
  E-mail: jwmsbacon@aol.com

★Member **Kathy Busch** (R-District 8) . . . . . . . . . . . . . . . . . (316) 682-5718
  Term Expires: 2017
  238 North Ridgewood, Wichita, KS 67208
  E-mail: kathy.busch@ymail.com
  Education: Kansas State; Wichita State MS

★Member **Sally Cauble** (R-District 5) . . . . . . . . . . . . . . . . . (620) 629-5423
  Term Expires: 2019
  1104 Summerlon Ridge, Dodge City, KS 67801
  E-mail: scauble@swko.net

★Member **Deena L. Horst** (R-District 6) . . . . . . . . . . . . . . . (785) 827-8540
  Term Expires: 2017
  920 South 9th, Salina, KS 67401
  E-mail: deena@worldlinc.net

★Member **Jim Porter** (R-District 9) . . . . . . . . . . . . . . . . . . . (316) 617-6779
  Term Expires: 2019
  501 South 7th, Fredonia, KS 66736
  E-mail: jimporterksbe@gmail.com

★Member **Steve Roberts** (R-District 2) . . . . . . . . . . . . . . . . (913) 302-8185
  Term Expires: 2017
  6017 West 124th Terrace, Overland Park, KS 66209
  E-mail: mrxmath@gmail.com

★Member **Janet Waugh** (D-District 1) . . . . . . . . . . . . . . . . . (913) 287-5165
  Term Expires: 2019
  715 North 74th Street, Kansas City, KS 66112
  E-mail: jwaugh1052@aol.com

★Member **Kenneth R. Willard** (R-District 7) . . . . . . . . . . . (620) 669-0498
  Term Expires: 2019
  24 Dakota Drive, Hutchinson, KS 67502
  E-mail: kwillard48@gmail.com

## Kansas State Department of Education [KSDE]

900 Southwest Jackson Street, Topeka, KS 66612-1235
Tel: (785) 296-3201  Fax: (785) 296-7933  Internet: www.ksde.org

**Employees:** 255  **Fiscal Year:** 2015  **Budget:** $4,533,991,535

▲Commissioner **Dr. Randy Watson** . . . . . . . . . . . . . . . . . . (785) 296-3202
  E-mail: rwatson@ksde.org
  Executive Secretary **Penny Rice** . . . . . . . . . . . . . . . . . . (785) 296-3202
                                            Fax: (785) 291-3791
  General Counsel **Scott Gordon** . . . . . . . . . . . . . . . . . . . (785) 296-3204
  E-mail: sgordon@ksde.org              Fax: (785) 291-3791
  Human Resources Director **Wendy Fritz** . . . . . . . . . . . . . (785) 296-5363

### Fiscal and Administrative Services Division

Tel: (785) 296-3871
Deputy Commissioner **Dale M. Dennis** . . . . . . . . . . . . . . . (785) 296-3871
  E-mail: ddennis@ksde.org
  Executive Secretary **Tamara Milligan** . . . . . . . . . . . . . . . (785) 296-3871
Child Nutrition and Wellness Director **Cheryl Johnson** . . . (785) 296-2276
  E-mail: csjohnson@ksde.org
Communications and Recognition Programs Director
  **Denise Kahler** . . . . . . . . . . . . . . . . . . . . . . . . . . . . . . . (785) 296-4876
  E-mail: dkahler@ksde.org
Fiscal Auditing Director **Stephanie Smith** . . . . . . . . . . . . (785) 296-4976
Fiscal Services and Operations Director (**Vacant**) . . . . . . . . (785) 296-4962

Information Technology Services Director **Lane Wiley** . . . . (785) 296-7931
  E-mail: lwiley@ksde.org
School Finance Director **Craig Neuenswander** . . . . . . . . . (785) 296-3872
                                            Fax: (785) 296-0459

### Learning Services Division

Deputy Commissioner **Brad Neuenswander** . . . . . . . . . . . (785) 296-2303
  Education: Baker U 1987 BA; Kansas State 1994 MEd
Early Childhood, Special Education and Title Programs
  Director **Colleen Riley** . . . . . . . . . . . . . . . . . . . . . . . . . . (785) 291-3097
Research and Evaluation Director **Scott E. Smith** . . . . . . . (785) 296-3142
  E-mail: sesmith@ksde.org
Teacher Education and Licensure Director **Scott Myers** . . . (785) 296-3069

## Kansas Children's Cabinet and Trust Fund

Landon State Office Building, 900 SW Jackson, Room 152,
Topeka, KS 66612-1221
Tel: (785) 368-7044  Tel: (877) 204-5171  Fax: (785) 296-8694
Internet: www.kschildrenscabinet.org

▲Executive Director **Janice Suzanne Smith** . . . . . . . . . . . (785) 368-7044
  E-mail: janice.smith@dcf.ks.gov
  Education: Park BA; Wichita State MA
Program Consultant **Dyogga S.L. Adegbore, PHR** . . . . . . (785) 368-7044
  E-mail: dyogga.adegbore@dcf.ks.gov
  Education: Washburn BGS
Early Childhood Director **Amy Blosser** . . . . . . . . . . . . . . (785) 368-7044
  E-mail: amy.blosser@dcf.ks.gov
  Education: Kansas BA

## Kansas Development Finance Authority [KDFA]

555 South Kansas Avenue, Suite 202, Topeka, KS 66603
Tel: (785) 357-4445  Fax: (785) 357-4478  E-mail: kdfa@kdfa.org
Internet: www.kdfa.org

■President **Timothy M. Shallenburger** . . . . . . . . . . (785) 357-4445 ext. 302
  E-mail: tshallenburger@kdfa.org

---

★ Elected Official   ■ Appointed by Governor   ● Appointed by Legislature   ▲ Appointed by Board or Commission   ◆ Appointed by State Supreme Court

# Kentucky

Tel: (502) 564-2500 (State Operator)  Internet: www.kentucky.gov

**Number of U.S. Congressional Delegates:** 2 Senators; 6 Representatives  **Governor's Term:** 4 years
**Legislature Description:** General Assembly - 38 member Senate; 100 member House of Representatives;
Term - Senate 4 years, House 2 years  **Next Election:** Governor November 2019; Legislature November
2016  **Number of Electoral Votes:** 8  **Official Name:** Commonwealth of Kentucky (Wyandotte:
Meadowland)  **Nickname:** The Bluegrass State  **Motto:** United we stand, divided we fall

**Population:** 4,425,092 (2015); Rank 26  **Fiscal Year:** 2014-2016  **Budget:** $20,300,000,000

## Office of the Governor

700 Capital Avenue, Suite 102, Frankfort, KY 40601
Tel: (502) 564-2611  TTY: (502) 564-9551  Fax: (502) 564-2517
Internet: governor.ky.gov

**Fiscal Year:** 2015  **Budget:** $12,039,000

**Matt Bevin**
Governor

Began Service: December 8, 2015
Term Expires: December 2019
Date of Birth: January 9, 1967
Education: Washington and Lee 1989 BA;
Central Michigan (Attended)
Home: Louisville
Religion: Southern Baptist
Career: Republican Candidate for U.S. Senate,
Matt Bevin For Senate, Kentucky – U.S. Senate
Campaigns (2013-2014)

★Governor **Matt Bevin** (R) . . . . . . . . . . . . . . . . . . . . . . . . . . . . (502) 564-2611
  E-mail: governor@ky.gov
Chief of Staff **James Blake Brickman** . . . . . . . . . . . . . . . (502) 564-2611
  Education: Vanderbilt 2000 BA; Kentucky 2009 JD
  Deputy Chief of Staff for External Affairs
    **Catherine Gatewood Easley** . . . . . . . . . . . . . . . . . . . . . (502) 564-2611
    Education: Wake Forest 2006 BA
  Deputy Chief of Staff for Policy **Adam M. Meier** . . . . . . (502) 564-2611
    E-mail: adam.meier@ky.gov
General Counsel **M. Stephen Pitt** . . . . . . . . . . . . . . . . . . . . (502) 564-2611
  E-mail: steve.pitt@ky.gov
  Education: Western Kentucky 1968 BS; Kentucky 1971 JD
  Deputy General Counsel **S. Chad Meredith** . . . . . . . . . . (502) 564-2611
    E-mail: chad.meredith@ky.gov
    Education: Kentucky 2007 JD
Secretary of the Executive Cabinet **Scott W. Brinkman** . . . (502) 564-2611
  E-mail: scott.brinkman@ky.gov
  Education: Notre Dame BA; Cincinnati JD
Deputy Secretary of the Executive Cabinet
  **Nathan Haney** . . . . . . . . . . . . . . . . . . . . . . . . . . . . . . . . . . (502) 564-2611
  Education: Louisville 2006 BS, 2009 JD; Bellarmine U 2010 MBA
Senior Advisor **Andrew V. McNeill** . . . . . . . . . . . . . . . . . (502) 564-2611
Boards and Commissions Executive Director
  **Brett Gaspard** . . . . . . . . . . . . . . . . . . . . . . . . . . . . . . . . . . (502) 564-2611
Communications Director **Jessica Ditto** . . . . . . . . . . . . . . . (502) 564-2611
  E-mail: jessica.ditto@ky.gov
Legislative Director **Bryan Sunderland** . . . . . . . . . . . . . . . (502) 564-2611
Scheduling Director **Stephanie Nelson** . . . . . . . . . . . . . . . (502) 564-2611

## Washington Office

444 North Capitol Street, NW, Suite 532, Washington, DC 20001
Director **Leeann Veatch** . . . . . . . . . . . . . . . . . . . . . . . . . . . . . (202) 220-1350
  E-mail: leeann.veatch@ky.gov

## Cabinet for Economic Development

300 West Broadway, Frankfort, KY 40601
Tel: (502) 564-7140  Fax: (502) 564-3256  E-mail: econdev@ky.gov
Internet: www.thinkkentucky.com

**Employees:** 71  **Fiscal Year:** 2015  **Budget:** $26,657,000

■Secretary (Acting) **Erik Dunnigan** . . . . . . . . . . . . . . . . . . . (502) 564-7670
  E-mail: erik.dunnigan@ky.gov
  Chief of Staff **(Vacant)** . . . . . . . . . . . . . . . . . . . . . . . . . . . (502) 564-7670
  Staff Assistant **Tammy Hensley** . . . . . . . . . . . . . . . . . . . (502) 564-7670
Deputy Secretary **Erik Dunnigan** . . . . . . . . . . . . . . . . . . . . (502) 564-7670
  E-mail: erik.dunnigan@ky.gov
Executive Director **Caroline Boeh Baesler** . . . . . . . . . . . (502) 564-7670
  Education: Centre 1987 BS; Kentucky 1994 JD

## Office of Financial Services

Executive Director **Katie Smith** . . . . . . . . . . . . . . . . . . . . . . (502) 564-4554
  E-mail: katie.smith@ky.gov
Compliance Division Assistant Director **Bobby Aldridge** . . (502) 564-4554
Finance and Personnel Division Director **Lauren Moore** . . . (502) 564-4300
  Finance and Personnel Assistant Director **Jon Wertzler** . . (502) 564-4300
Incentive Assistance Division Director **Don Goodin** . . . . . . (502) 564-4554
Network Administration and Support Division
  Director **Ben "Bennie" Hall** . . . . . . . . . . . . . . . (502) 564-4300 ext. 4284
  E-mail: ben.hall@ky.gov
Bluegrass State Skills Corporation Executive Director
  **Joshua Benton** . . . . . . . . . . . . . . . . . . . . . . . . . . . . . . . . . (502) 564-2021

## Department for Business Development

Commissioner **Mandy Lambert** . . . . . . . . . . . . . . . . . . . . . (502) 564-7140
Deputy Commissioner **John Bevington** . . . . . . . . . . . . . . . (502) 564-7140

## Office of Research and Public Affairs

Tel: (502) 564-4886

Executive Director **Joe Lilly** . . . . . . . . . . . . . . . . . . . . . . . . (502) 564-4886
Deputy Executive Director **Karen Lefler** . . . . . . . . . . . . . . (502) 564-4886
Executive Assistant **Donna Jones** . . . . . . . . . . . . . . . . . . . (502) 564-4886
Database and Systems Development Division
  Director **Steven P. Vest** . . . . . . . . . . . . . . . . . (502) 564-4300 ext. 21996
  E-mail: steven.vest@ky.gov
  Education: Kentucky 1988 BS, 1999 MBA

## Education and Workforce Development Cabinet

Capital Plaza Tower, 500 Mero Street, 3rd Floor, Frankfort, KY 40601
Tel: (502) 564-0372  Fax: (502) 564-0651  Internet: ewdc.ky.gov

**Employees:** 2,549  **Fiscal Year:** 2015  **Budget:** $641,035,000

■Secretary **Hal Heiner** . . . . . . . . . . . . . . . . . . . . . . . . . . . . . (502) 564-0372
  E-mail: hal.heiner@ky.gov
  Education: Louisville, ME
Deputy Secretary **Beth A. Brinly** . . . . . . . . . . . . . . . . . . . . (502) 564-0372
  Education: Louisville 1986 BS; Penn State 2004 MA
Chief of Staff **James Andrew "Andy" Hightower** . . . . . . (502) 564-0372
  Education: Georgetown BA
General Counsel **Randy K. Justice** . . . . . . . . . . . . . . . . . . . (502) 564-6606

★ Elected Official    ■ Appointed by Governor    ● Appointed by Legislature    ▲ Appointed by Board or Commission    ◆ Appointed by State Supreme Court

Summer 2016                                   © Leadership Directories, Inc.                                   *State Yellow Book*

Communications Director **Woody Maglinger** . . . . . . . . . . . (502) 564-9908
  E-mail: woody.maglinger@ky.gov
Executive Assistant **Elizabeth Hack** . . . . . . . . . . . . . . . . . (502) 564-0651

## Council on Postsecondary Education [CPE]

1024 Capital Center Drive, Suite 320, Frankfort, KY 40601
Fax: (502) 573-1535  Internet: www.cpe.state.ky.us

Council Chair **Glenn Denton** . . . . . . . . . . . . . . . . . . . . . (502) 753-1555
  Education: Centre 1992; Salmon P Chase 1995 JD
■President **Robert L. "Bob" King** . . . . . . . . . . . . . . (502) 573-1555 ext. 239
  E-mail: robert.king@ky.gov
  Education: Trinity Col (CT) 1968 BA; Vanderbilt 1971 JD
  Executive Secretary **Mary B. Allison** . . . . . . . . . . (502) 573-1555 ext. 239
Executive Vice President **Aaron Thompson** . . . . . . (502) 573-1555 ext. 259
  E-mail: aaron.thompson@ky.gov
Academic Affairs Vice President and Chief
  Academic Officer **Jay Morgan** . . . . . . . . . . . . . . (502) 573-1555 ext. 313
  E-mail: jay.morgan@ky.gov
Budget and Finance Vice President **Bill Payne** . . . . (502) 573-1555 ext. 226
Innovation and E-Learning Vice President
  **Allen Lind** . . . . . . . . . . . . . . . . . . . . . . . . . . . (502) 573-1555 ext. 305
  E-mail: allen.lind@ky.gov
Kentucky Adult Education Vice President
  **Reecie D. Stagnolia** . . . . . . . . . . . . . . . . . . . . . (502) 573-5114 ext. 124
  Education: Kentucky 1982 BBA
Policy, Planning, and Operations Vice President
  **Lee Nimocks** . . . . . . . . . . . . . . . . . . . . . . . . . (502) 573-1555 ext. 244
  Executive Relations Associate
    **Heather Bingham** . . . . . . . . . . . . . . . . . . . . (502) 573-1555 ext. 256
    E-mail: heather.bingham@ky.gov
  Legislative Liaison Senior Fellow **Ron Carson** . . (502) 573-1555 ext. 269
    E-mail: ron.carson@ky.gov
General Counsel **Travis Powell** . . . . . . . . . . . . . . . (502) 573-1555 ext. 142

## Office of Educational Programs

Director **(Vacant)** . . . . . . . . . . . . . . . . . . . . . . . . . . . . . . (502) 564-0372

## Education Department

Fiscal Year: 2015  Budget: $4,852,359,000

▲Commissioner **Stephen Lynn Pruitt** . . . . . . . . . . . . . . . . . . (502) 564-0372
  Education: North Georgia; State U West Georgia 1996 MEd;
  Auburn PhD
  Secretary/Scheduler **Jody Smith** . . . . . . . . . . . . (502) 564-3141 ext. 4806
  Policy Coordinator **Mary Ann Miller** . . . . . . . . . . (502) 564-3141 ext. 4803
    E-mail: maryann.miller@education.ky.gov

## Office of Administration and Support

Associate Commissioner **Hiren Desai** . . . . . . . . . (502) 564-1976 ext. 4302
  E-mail: hiren.desai@education.ky.gov
Budget and Financial Management Division
  Director **Charlie Harman** . . . . . . . . . . . . . . . . . (502) 564-2351 ext. 4328
District Support Director **Kay Kennedy** . . . . . . . . (502) 564-3930 ext. 4433
Nutrition and Health Services Division Director
  **Deanna Tackett** . . . . . . . . . . . . . . . . . . . . . . . . (502) 564-5625 ext. 4929
Resource Management Division Director
  **Lynn McGowan-McNear** . . . . . . . . . . . . . . . . . (502) 564-3716 ext. 4311

## Office of Assessment and Accountability

Associate Commissioner **Ken Draut** . . . . . . . . . . . (502) 564-2256 ext. 4728
  E-mail: Ken.Draut@education.ky.gov
Assessment Design and Implementation
  Division Director **Kevin Hill** . . . . . . . . . . . . . . . (502) 564-9853 ext. 4712
Support and Research Division Director
  **Rhonda Sims** . . . . . . . . . . . . . . . . . . . . . . . . . . (502) 564-4394 ext. 4751
  E-mail: rhonda.sims@education.ky.gov

## Office of Guiding Support Services/General Counsel

Associate Commissioner and General Counsel
  **Kevin C. Brown** . . . . . . . . . . . . . . . . . . . . . . . . (502) 564-4474 ext. 4814
  E-mail: kevin.brown@education.ky.gov
Communications Division Director **Rebecca Blessing** . . . . (502) 564-2000
  E-mail: rebecca.blessing@education.ky.gov

Innovation and Partner Engagement Division Director
  **David Cook** . . . . . . . . . . . . . . . . . . . . . . . . . . . . . . . . . (502) 564-4832

## Office of Knowledge, Information, and Data Services

Associate Commissioner **David Couch** . . . . . . . . . (502) 564-2020 ext. 229
  E-mail: david.couch@education.ky.gov
Engineering and Managing Services Division
  Director **Mike Leadingham** . . . . . . . . . . . . . . . . (502) 564-2020 ext. 202
  E-mail: mike.leadingham@education.ky.gov
Enterprise Data Division Director **Dede Conner** . . . . . . . (502) 564-0372
  E-mail: dede.conner@education.ky.gov
Operations Services Division Director
  **Phil Coleman** . . . . . . . . . . . . . . . . . . . . . . . . . . (502) 564-2020 ext. 204

## Office of Next Generation Learners

Associate Commissioner **(Vacant)** . . . . . . . . . . . . . (502) 564-9850 ext. 4151
Program Standards Division Director **Karen Kidwell** . . . . . (502) 564-2106
Next Generation Professionals Division Director
  **Gregory Ross** . . . . . . . . . . . . . . . . . . . . . . . . . . . . . . . (502) 564-1479
Learning Services Division Director **Johnny Collett** . . . . . (502) 564-4970

## Office of Next Generation Schools and Districts

Associate Commissioner **Kelly Foster** . . . . . . . . . . (502) 564-5130 ext. 4001
  E-mail: kelly.foster@education.ky.gov
Student Success Division Director **Toya Robey** . . (502) 564-1479 ext. 4525
Consolidated Plans and Audits Division Director
  **Donna Tackett** . . . . . . . . . . . . . . . . . . . . . . . . . . . . . . (502) 564-3791
  E-mail: donna.tackett@education.ky.gov
Kentucky School for the Blind Principal **John Roberts** . . . (502) 897-1583
  1867 Frankfort Avenue, Louisville, KY 40206
Kentucky School for the Deaf Principal **Rodney Buis** . . . . . (859) 239-7017
  303 South Second Street, Danville, KY 40423-0027    Fax: (859) 239-7006
  P.O. Box 27, Danville, KY 40423-0027

## Kentucky Board of Education

Capital Plaza Tower, 500 Mero Street, Frankfort, KY 40601
Tel: (502) 564-3141  Fax: (502) 564-5680

■Chair **Roger L. Marcum** (Supreme Court District 1) . . . . . . (502) 564-3141
  Term Expires: April 14, 2018
  E-mail: rlmarcum22@gmail.com
  Education: Berea 1974 BA; Eastern Kentucky 1988 MA
■Vice Chair
  **William L. Twyman** (Supreme Court District 2) . . . . . . . (502) 564-3141
  Term Expires: April 14, 2018
  E-mail: wtwyman@scrtc.com
■Member **Grayson Boyd** (Supreme Court District 7) . . . . . . (502) 564-3141
  Term Expires: April 14, 2018
  E-mail: grboyd@bigsandybb.com
■Member **Ben Cundiff** (Supreme Court District 1) . . . . . . . (502) 564-3141
  Term Expires: April 14, 2018
■Member **Richard F. Gimmel** (At-Large) . . . . . . . . . . . . . (502) 564-3141
  Term Expires: April 14, 2020
■Member
  **Samuel D. Hinkle IV** (Supreme Court District 6) . . . . . (502) 564-3141
  Term Expires: April 14, 2018
  Education: Washington and Lee 1969 BA; Yale 1972 JD
■Member **Gary W. Houchens** (At-Large) . . . . . . . . . . . . . (502) 564-3141
  Term Expires: April 14, 2020
■Member **Alesa G. Johnson** (At-Large) . . . . . . . . . . . . . . (502) 564-3141
  Term Expires: April 14, 2020
■Member **Nawanna B. Privett** (Supreme Court District 5) . . (859) 227-7541
  Term Expires: April 14, 2018                          Res: (859) 224-3232
  E-mail: nawannap@aol.com                          Fax: (859) 276-1540
■Member **Milton C. Seymore** (At-Large) . . . . . . . . . . . . . (502) 564-3141
  Term Expires: April 14, 2020
■Member
  **Mary Gwen Wheeler** (Supreme Court District 4) . . . . . . (502) 564-3141
  Term Expires: April 14, 2018
  E-mail: marygwenw@cflouisville.org
Member - Ex Officio **Robert L. "Bob" King** . . . . . . . . . . . (502) 573-1555
  1024 Capital Center, Suite 320,                    Fax: (502) 573-1537
  Frankfort, KY 40601
  E-mail: robert.king@ky.gov

*(continued on next page)*

---

★ Elected Official    ■ Appointed by Governor    ● Appointed by Legislature        ▲ Appointed by Board or Commission    ◆ Appointed by State Supreme Court

**Kentucky Board of Education** *continued*

Member - Ex Officio **Stephen Lynn Pruitt** . . . . . . . . . . . . (502) 564-3141
  E-mail: stephen.pruitt@education.ky.gov
  Affiliation: Commissioner, Education Department, Education and
  Workforce Development Cabinet, Commonwealth of Kentucky
  Capital Plaza Tower, 500 Mero Street, 3rd Floor, Frankfort, KY 40601

## Department for Libraries and Archives [KDLA]

300 Coffee Tree Road, Frankfort, KY 40601
P.O. Box 537, Frankfort, KY 40602-0537
Fax: (502) 564-5773   Internet: www.kdla.ky.gov

**Fiscal Year:** 2015   **Budget:** $19,964,000

■State Librarian/Commissioner **Wayne Onkst** . . . . . . . . . . . . (502) 564-8300
  E-mail: wayne.onkst@ky.gov
  Education: Kentucky 1978 BA, 1979 MA
  Executive Staff Advisor **Paige Sexton** . . . . . . . . (502) 564-8300 ext. 315
    E-mail: paige.sexton@ky.gov
  Financial Services Branch Manager
    **Barbara Campbell** . . . . . . . . . . . . . . . . . . . . . (502) 564-8300 ext. 302
  Internal Policy Analyst/LSTA (Library
    Services and Technology Act) Coordinator
    **Nicole Bryan** . . . . . . . . . . . . . . . . . . . . . . . . . (502) 564-8300 ext. 304
    E-mail: nicole.bryan@ky.gov
  Field Services Division Director **Terry Manwel** . . . (502) 564-8300 ext. 230
    Data Analyst **Jay Bank** . . . . . . . . . . . . . . . . . . (502) 564-8300 ext. 263
    E-mail: jay.bank@ky.gov
  Public Records Division Director/Records
    Administrator/State Archivist **(Vacant)** . . . . . . . . (502) 564-8300 ext. 249
    State Publications Coordinator **(Vacant)** . . . . . . . (502) 564-8300 ext. 330
  State Library Services Division Director
    **Julie Scalos** . . . . . . . . . . . . . . . . . . . . . . . . . . (502) 564-8300 ext. 230
    Technical Services Branch Manager
    **William Shrout** . . . . . . . . . . . . . . . . . . . . . . . (502) 564-8300 ext. 229
    E-mail: william.shrout@ky.gov

## Department of Workforce Investment

Commissioner **Beth Kuhn** . . . . . . . . . . . . . . . . . . . . . . . . . (502) 564-0372
  E-mail: beth.kuhn@ky.gov

## Office for the Blind

275 East Main Street, Mail Stop 2-EJ, Frankfort, KY 40621
Fax: (502) 564-2951   TTY: (800) 321-6668

Executive Director **Allison Flanagan** . . . . . . . . . . . . . . . . . (502) 564-4754
  E-mail: allison.flanagan@ky.gov
Business Enterprise Division Assistant Director
  **Scott Fricano** . . . . . . . . . . . . . . . . . . . . . . . . . . . . . . . (502) 564-4754
Consumer Services Division Director **Becky Cabe** . . . . . . . (502) 564-4754
Charles W. McDowell Rehabilitation Center Manager
  **Stephen Deeley** . . . . . . . . . . . . . . . . . . . . . . . . . . . . . . (502) 429-4460
  8412 Westport Road, Louisville, KY 40242
  E-mail: stephen.deeley@ky.gov

## Career and Technical Education Office

Capital Plaza Tower, 500 Mero Street, 20th Floor, Frankfort, KY 40601
Tel: (502) 564-4286   Fax: (502) 564-4800   Internet: www.kytech.ky.gov
E-mail: wfddte.webmaster@mail.state.ky.us

Associate Commissioner (Interim) **Laura Arnold** . . . . . . . . (502) 564-4286
Division Director **Laura Arnold** . . . . . . . . . . . . . . . . . . . . (502) 564-4286
Division Director (Interim) **Matt Chaliff** . . . . . . . . . . . . . . (502) 564-4286

## Employment and Training Office

CHR Building, 2WB, 275 East Main Street, Frankfort, KY 40601
Tel: (502) 564-5331   Fax: (502) 564-7456
Internet: www.kentuckycareercenter.com

Executive Director **Jason Dunn** . . . . . . . . . . . . . . . . . . . . . (502) 564-5331
Unemployment Insurance Division Director (Acting)
  **Melissa A. Beasley** . . . . . . . . . . . . . . . . . . . . . . . . . . . (502) 564-2900
Workforce Services Division Director **Lori Collins** . . . . . . . (502) 564-5331
Communications Director **Holly Neal** . . . . . . . . . . . . . . . . (502) 564-5331
  E-mail: holly.neal@ky.gov

## Vocational Rehabilitation Office

275 East Main Street, Mail Stop 2-EK, Frankfort, KY 40621
Tel: (502) 564-4440   Tel: (800) 372-7172 (Toll Free)   Fax: (502) 564-6745

Executive Director **Buddy Hoskinson** . . . . . . . . . . . . . . . . (502) 564-4440
Community Relations Director **Jason Jones** . . . . . . . . . . . . (502) 564-4440
Carl D. Perkins Vocational Training Center Director
  **Barbara Burchett Pugh** . . . . . . . . . . . . . . . . . . . . . . . (606) 788-7080
  5659 Main Street, Thelma, KY 41260-8609    Tel: (800) 443-2187
                                              (Toll Free)
Program Services Director **(Vacant)** . . . . . . . . . . . . . . . . . (502) 564-4440
Program Services Assistant Director **Holly Hendricks** . . . . . (800) 372-7172
Administrative Services Branch Manager **(Vacant)** . . . . . . . (502) 564-4440
Rehabilitation Program Administrator **Susie Edwards** . . . . (502) 564-4440
  E-mail: susiem.edwards@ky.gov

## Kentucky Workforce Investment Board [KWIB]

275 East Main Street, 2WC, Frankfort, KY 40601
Fax: (502) 564-7452

Chairman **Edward J. "Ed" Holmes** . . . . . . . . . . . . . . . . . . (502) 564-0372
Executive Director **Thomas M. "Tom" West** . . . . . . . . . . . (502) 564-0372
Administrative Coordinator **Stephen Rosenberg** . . . . . . . . (502) 564-2919
  E-mail: steve.rosenberg@ag.ky.gov

## Kentucky Commission on the Deaf and Hard of Hearing [KCDHH]

632 Versailles Road, Frankfort, KY 40601
Tel: (502) 573-2604   Fax: (502) 573-3594   E-mail: kcdhh@kcdhh.ky.gov
Internet: www.kcdhh.ky.gov

**Fiscal Year:** 2015   **Budget:** $2,266,000

Executive Director **Virginia Moore** . . . . . . . . . . . . . . . . . . (502) 573-2604
Administrative Assistant **Blake Noland** . . . . . . . . . . . . . . . (502) 573-2604
Executive Secretary **Tashina Crowe** . . . . . . . . . . . . . . . . . (502) 573-2604
Executive Staff Advisor **Anita Dowd** . . . . . . . . . . . . . . . . . (502) 573-2604
Executive Staff Interpreter **Rachel Morgan** . . . . . . . . . . . . (502) 573-2604
Interpreter Referral Specialist **Rachel Rodgers** . . . . . . . . . (502) 573-2604
Information Program Coordinator **Emily Kimbell** . . . . . . . . (502) 573-2604
  Education: Gallaudet BA
Information Program Coordinator **(Vacant)** . . . . . . . . . . . . (502) 573-2604
TAP Coordinator **Cole Zulauf** . . . . . . . . . . . . . . . . . . . . . (502) 573-2604
Information Office Supervisor **(Vacant)** . . . . . . . . . . . . . . . (502) 573-2604
Network Analyst **Jim Rivard** . . . . . . . . . . . . . . . . . . . . . . (502) 573-2604
  E-mail: jim.rivard@ky.gov

## Education Professional Standards Board

100 Airport Road, 3rd Floor, Frankfort, KY 40601
Tel: (502) 564-4606   Tel: (888) 598-7667   Fax: (502) 564-7080

▲Executive Director (Acting) **Jimmy Adams** . . . . . . . . . . . . (502) 564-4606
  E-mail: jimmy.adams@ky.gov
Deputy Executive Director **(Vacant)** . . . . . . . . . . . . . . . . . (502) 564-4606
Executive Assistant **Ashley Abshire** . . . . . . . . . . . . . . . . . (502) 564-4606
Certification Director **John Fields** . . . . . . . . . . . . . . . . . . . (502) 564-4606
Educator Preparation Director **Ben Boggs** . . . . . . . . . . . . . (502) 564-5789
Professional Learning and Assessment Director
  **Donna Brockman** . . . . . . . . . . . . . . . . . . . . . . . . . . . . (502) 564-4606
General Counsel **Lisa Lang** . . . . . . . . . . . . . . . . . . . . . . . . (502) 564-4606

## Governor's Scholars Program

1024 Capital Center Drive, Suite 210, Frankfort, KY 40601
Fax: (502) 573-1641

Executive Director **Aristofanes "Arise" Cedeno** . . . . . . . . . (502) 573-1618
  E-mail: aristofanes.cedeno@ag.ky.gov
  Assistant to the Director **Danielle Moore** . . . . . . . . . . . . (502) 573-1618
Associate Director **Sarah Metzmeier** . . . . . . . . . . . . . . . . . (502) 564-0372
Fiscal Officer **Bonnie Mullin** . . . . . . . . . . . . . . . . . . . . . . . (502) 564-0372

## Kentucky Educational Television

600 Cooper Drive, Lexington, KY 40502
Tel: (859) 258-7000   Fax: (859) 258-7399   Internet: www.ket.org

**Fiscal Year:** 2015   **Budget:** $14,302,000

Executive Director **Shae Hopkins** . . . . . . . . . . . . . . . . . . . (859) 258-7100

---

★ Elected Official     ■ Appointed by Governor     ● Appointed by Legislature     ▲ Appointed by Board or Commission     ◆ Appointed by State Supreme Court

Summer 2016                         © Leadership Directories, Inc.                         *State Yellow Book*

Education Senior Director **Nancy Carpenter** . . . . . . . . . . . (859) 258-7260
Programming Senior Director **Craig Cornwell** . . . . . . . . . . (859) 258-7275
Business Director **Linda Hume** . . . . . . . . . . . . . . . . . . . . . . (859) 258-7107
Communications Director **(Vacant)** . . . . . . . . . . . . . . . . . . . (859) 258-7251
Personnel Director **(Vacant)** . . . . . . . . . . . . . . . . . . . . . . . . (859) 258-7030
Production Director **Mike Brower** . . . . . . . . . . . . . . . . . . . . (859) 258-7275
Technical Planning Director **(Vacant)** . . . . . . . . . . . . . . . . (859) 258-7254
Transmission Systems Director **Fred Engel** . . . . . . . . . . . . . (859) 258-7172

# Energy and Environment Cabinet [EEC]

Capital Plaza Tower, 500 Mero Street, 12th Floor, Frankfort, KY 40601
Tel: (502) 564-3350  Fax: (502) 564-7484
E-mail: cynthia.schafer@ky.gov

**Employees:** 1,669  **Fiscal Year:** 2015  **Budget:** $262,150,000

■Secretary **Charles G. Snavely** . . . . . . . . . . . . . . . . . . . . . (502) 564-3350
  E-mail: charles.snavely@ky.gov
  Executive Assistant **(Vacant)** . . . . . . . . . . . . . . . . . . . . . (502) 564-3350
Executive Advisor **(Vacant)** . . . . . . . . . . . . . . . . . . . . . . . (502) 564-3350
Communications and Public Outreach Executive Director
  **John Mura** . . . . . . . . . . . . . . . . . . . . . . . . . . . . . . . . . . (502) 564-5525
  E-mail: john.mura@ky.gov
Budget Officer **Melissa Highfield Smith** . . . . . . . . . . . . . (502) 564-2282
Legislative and Intergovernmental Affairs Executive
  Director **(Vacant)** . . . . . . . . . . . . . . . . . . . . . . . . . . . . (502) 564-3350
Environmental Scientific Consultant **Karen Wilson** . . . . . . (502) 564-3350
Administrative Specialist III **Christy Morris** . . . . . . . . . . . (502) 564-3350

## Office of Administrative Hearings

35-36 Fountain Place, Frankfort, KY 40601
Tel: (502) 564-7312  Internet: http://www.oah.ky.gov
Director and Chief Hearing Officer **Robert Layton** . . . . . . (502) 564-7312
Executive Secretary **Lisa Booth** . . . . . . . . . . . . . . . . . . . . . (502) 564-7312

## Office of the General Counsel

500 Mero Street, 12th Floor, Frankfort, KY 40601
Tel: (502) 564-3350  Fax: (502) 564-7484
General Counsel **John Horne** . . . . . . . . . . . . . . . . . . . . . . (502) 564-3350
  E-mail: john.horne@ky.gov
  Executive Secretary **Kari Sutherland** . . . . . . . . . . . . . . (502) 564-2356

## Office of the Inspector General

61 Wilkinson Boulevard, Frankfort, KY 40601
Tel: (502) 564-1985  Fax: (502) 564-0873  E-mail: eppc.oig@ky.gov
Inspector General **(Vacant)** . . . . . . . . . . . . . . . . . . . . . . . . (502) 564-1985

## Environmental Quality Commission

Capitol Plaza Tower, 500 Mero Street, 12th Floor, Frankfort, KY 40601
Tel: (502) 564-2674  Fax: (502) 564-2676  E-mail: eqc@ky.gov

**Fiscal Year:** 2015  **Budget:** $197,000

Executive Director **Arnita Gadson** . . . . . . . . . . . . . . . . . . (502) 564-2674
  Education: Webster 1996 MSHRMD

## Kentucky Public Service Commission

211 Sower Boulevard, Frankfort, KY 40602
P.O. Box 615, Frankfort, KY 40602
Tel: (502) 564-3940  Fax: (502) 564-3460  TTY: (800) 648-6057
Internet: http://psc.ky.gov

■Chairman **(Vacant)** . . . . . . . . . . . . . . . . . . . . . . . . . . . . . (502) 782-2554
■Vice Chairman **Daniel E. "Dan" Logsdon, Jr.** . . . . . . . . . . (502) 782-2553
  Term Expires: July 1, 2017
  E-mail: dan.logsdon@ky.gov
  Education: Murray State U BA
■Commissioner **Robert "Bob" Cicero** . . . . . . . . . . . . . . . . (502) 564-3940
  Term Expires: July 1, 2016
  E-mail: robert.cicero@ky.gov
  Education: Pittsburgh MBA

### Commission Staff
Executive Director **(Vacant)** . . . . . . . . . . . . . . . . . . . . . . . (502) 782-2560

## Worker's Compensation Board

2780 Research Park Drive, Lexington, KY 40511
Fax: (859) 246-2779
Chairman **Michael Alvey** . . . . . . . . . . . . . . . . . . . . . . . . . . (859) 246-2773
  Term Expires: January 4, 2018
Member **Rebekkah Rechter** . . . . . . . . . . . . . . . . . . . . . . . (859) 246-2773
  Education: Georgetown 2002 JD
Member **Franklin Stivers** . . . . . . . . . . . . . . . . . . . . . . . . . (859) 246-2773
  E-mail: franklin.stivers@ky.gov

## Department for Energy Development and Independence [DEDI]

Capital Plaza Tower, 500 Mero Street, 12th Floor, Frankfort, KY 40601
Tel: (502) 564-7192  Fax: (502) 564-7484  Fax: (502) 564-7406
Internet: www.energy.ky.gov
Commissioner (Acting) **Dr. Leonard K. "Len" Peters** . . . . (502) 564-3350
Deputy Commissioner **(Vacant)** . . . . . . . . . . . . . . . . . . . . (502) 564-7192
Budget and Personnel Officer **Amanda Cook** . . . . . (502) 564-7192 ext. 225
Grants and Contracts Manager **(Vacant)** . . . . . . . . (502) 564-7192 ext. 230
  Grants and Contracts Executive Advisor **Paul Brooks** . . . (502) 564-7192

## Department for Environmental Protection [DEP]

300 Fair Oaks, Frankfort, KY 40601
Tel: (502) 564-2150  Fax: (502) 564-4245  E-mail: envhelp@ky.gov

**Fiscal Year:** 2015  **Budget:** $117,564,000

■Commissioner **Bruce Scott** . . . . . . . . . . . . . . . . . . . . . . . (502) 564-2150
  E-mail: bruce.scott@ky.gov
  Executive Secretary **Denise Profitt** . . . . . . . . . . . . . . . . (502) 564-2150
Deputy Commissioner **Aaron Keatley** . . . . . . . . . . . . . . . . (502) 564-2150
  Executive Secretary **(Vacant)** . . . . . . . . . . . . . . . . . . . . (502) 564-2150
Administrative Support Branch Manager
  **Nina Hockensmith** . . . . . . . . . . . . . . . . . . . . . . . . . . . (502) 564-2150

### Division for Air Quality
200 Fair Oaks Lane, Frankfort, KY 40601
Tel: (502) 564-3999  Fax: (502) 573-3787  Internet: www.air.ky.gov
Director **Sean Alteri** . . . . . . . . . . . . . . . . . . . . . . . . . . . . . (502) 564-3999
Assistant Director **Andrea Smith** . . . . . . . . . . . . . . . . . . . (502) 564-3999

### Division of Waste Management
Tel: (502) 564-6716  Fax: (502) 564-4049  E-mail: waste@ky.gov
Internet: www.waste.ky.gov
Director (Acting) **Tony Hatton** . . . . . . . . . . . . . . . . . . . . . (502) 564-6716
Hazardous Waste Branch Manager **April Webb, PE** . . . . . . (502) 564-6716
  Education: Kentucky 1997 BS

### Division of Water
200 Fair Oaks Lane, Fourth Floor, Frankfort, KY 40601
Tel: (502) 564-3410  Fax: (502) 564-0111  E-mail: water@ky.gov
Internet: www.water.ky.gov
Director **Peter Goodmann** . . . . . . . . . . . . . . . . . . . . . . . . (502) 564-3410
Assistant Director **(Vacant)** . . . . . . . . . . . . . . . . . . . . . . . (502) 564-3410

## Department for Natural Resources [DNR]

Two Hudson Hollow, Frankfort, KY 40601
Tel: (502) 564-6940  Fax: (502) 564-6764
E-mail: naturalresources@ky.gov  Internet: www.dnr.ky.gov

**Fiscal Year:** 2015  **Budget:** $110,190,000

Commissioner **Steve Hohmann** . . . . . . . . . . . . . . . . . . . . (502) 564-6940
                                                    Fax: (502) 564-5698
Executive Secretary **Deneen Shannon** . . . . . . . . . . . . . . . (502) 564-6940
Executive Staff Advisor **(Vacant)** . . . . . . . . . . . . . . . . . . . (502) 564-6940

### Division of Abandoned Mine Lands
2521 Lawrenceburg Road, Frankfort, KY 40601
Tel: (502) 564-2141  Fax: (502) 564-6544
Director **Bob Scott** . . . . . . . . . . . . . . . . . . . . . . . . . . . . . (502) 564-2141

★ Elected Official   ■ Appointed by Governor   ● Appointed by Legislature   ▲ Appointed by Board or Commission   ◆ Appointed by State Supreme Court

*State Yellow Book*            © Leadership Directories, Inc.            Summer 2016

## Division of Conservation

2 Hudson Hollow, Frankfort, KY 40601
Tel: (502) 564-2320  Fax: (502) 564-6079  E-mail: conservation@ky.gov
Internet: www.conservation.ky.gov

Director **Kimberly "Kim" Richardson** . . . . . . . . . . . . . . . (502) 573-3080

## Division of Forestry

627 Comanche Trail, Frankfort, KY 40601
Tel: (502) 564-4496  Fax: (502) 564-6553  Internet: www.forestry.ky.gov

Director **Leah MacSwords** . . . . . . . . . . . . . . . . . . . . . . . (502) 564-4496

## Division of Mine Permits

Two Hudson Hollow, Frankfort, KY 40601
Tel: (502) 564-2320  Fax: (502) 564-6764

Director **Allen Luttrell** . . . . . . . . . . . . . . . . . . . . . . . . . . (502) 564-2320

## Division of Mine Reclamation and Enforcement

Fax: (502) 564-5848

Director **Billy Ratliff** . . . . . . . . . . . . . . . . . . . . . . . . . . . . (502) 564-2340
    E-mail: billy.ratliff@ky.gov

## Division of Mine Safety

1025 Capital Center Drive, Suite 201, Frankfort, KY 40602-2244
P.O. Box 2244, Frankfort, KY 40602
Tel: (502) 573-0142  Fax: (502) 573-0152

Director **John D. Small** . . . . . . . . . . . . . . . . . . (502) 573-0140 ext. 247
    E-mail: john.small@ky.gov
Executive Secretary **(Vacant)** . . . . . . . . . . . . . . . . . . . (502) 573-0140
General Counsel **C. Michael "Mike" Haines** . . . . . . . . . . . (502) 564-2356
    E-mail: mike.haines@ky.gov
    Education: Transylvania 1979 BA; Kentucky 1983 JD
Chief Mine Inspector (Electrical) **Danny Hurt** . . . . . . . . . (606) 285-3227
    P.O. Box 907, Martin, KY 41649
    E-mail: danny.hurt@ky.gov

## Division of Oil and Gas Conservation

1025 Capital Center Drive, Frankfort, KY 40601
Tel: (502) 573-0147  Fax: (502) 573-1099

Director **Kim Collings** . . . . . . . . . . . . . . . . . . . . . . . . . . (502) 573-0147
Assistant Director **Marvin Combs** . . . . . . . . . . . . . . . . . . (502) 573-0147

## Division of Technical and Administrative Support [DTAS]

Two Hudson Hollow, Frankfort, KY 40601
Tel: (502) 564-6940  Fax: (502) 564-5698

Assistant Director **Linda Potter** . . . . . . . . . . . . . . . . . . . (502) 564-6940
    E-mail: linda.potter@ky.gov

## Office of the Deputy Commissioner

Deputy Commissioner **Sandy Gruzesky** . . . . . . . . . . . . . (502) 564-6940
    E-mail: sandy.gruzesky@ky.gov

# Finance and Administration Cabinet [FAC]

Capitol Annex, 702 Capital Avenue, Room 383, Frankfort, KY 40601
Tel: (502) 564-4240  Fax: (502) 564-6785  Internet: www.finance.ky.gov

**Employees:** 2,587  **Fiscal Year:** 2015  **Budget:** $896,179,000

■Secretary **Col William M. Landrum III** . . . . . . . . . . . . . . . (502) 564-4240
    E-mail: william.landrum@ky.gov
    Education: VMI 1975 BA; Kentucky 1988 MBA; Army War Col 1996
Deputy Secretary **Robin Kinney** . . . . . . . . . . . . . . . . . . . (502) 564-4240
Deputy Secretary **Steve Rucker** . . . . . . . . . . . . . . . . . . . (502) 564-4240
Communications Director **Pamela Trautner** . . . . . . . . . . . (502) 564-4240
Inspector General **Kenneth F. Bohac** . . . . . . . . . . . . . . . (502) 564-4240
    Education: Western Illinois 1977 BA; Lewis U 1988 MBA

# Department for Facilities and Support Services

Bush Building, 403 Wapping Street, Room 340, Frankfort, KY 40601
Tel: (502) 564-3590  Fax: (502) 564-0569

**Fiscal Year:** 2015  **Budget:** $60,523,000

■Commissioner (Acting) **Charles Bush** . . . . . . . . . . . . . . . (502) 564-0402
    E-mail: charles.bush@ky.gov
Deputy Commissioner **(Vacant)** . . . . . . . . . . . . . . . . . . . (502) 564-2312
Building and Mechanical Services Office Executive
    Director **Paul McPherson** . . . . . . . . . . . . . . . . . . . . . (502) 782-0421
    701 Holmes Street, Frankfort, KY 40601
    Building Services Division Director **Butch Jacobs** . . . . . . (502) 782-0417
    Mechanical Services Division Director **(Vacant)** . . . . . . . (502) 782-0442
Facility Development and Efficiency Office Executive
    Director **Jennifer Linton** . . . . . . . . . . . . . . . . . . . . . . (502) 564-5697
Historic Properties Division Director and State Curator
    **David Buchta** . . . . . . . . . . . . . . . . . . . . . . . . . . . . . (502) 564-0900
    401 Wapping Street, Frankfort, KY 40601      Fax: (502) 564-7869
    Education: Kentucky 2005 MArch
Real Properties Division Director **Scott Aubrey** . . . . . . . . . (502) 564-2600
                                                   Fax: (502) 564-8108
Surplus Property Division Director **Dewey Blevins** . . . . . . . (502) 782-0442
                                                   Fax: (502) 573-2215

# Department of Revenue [DOR]

501 High Street, Frankfort, KY 40620
Tel: (502) 564-4581  Fax: (502) 564-3685  TTY: (502) 564-3058
Tel: (502) 564-1600 (Automated Refund Tax Information System)
Internet: http://revenue.ky.gov

**Fiscal Year:** 2015  **Budget:** $108,627,000

Commissioner **Daniel P. Bork** . . . . . . . . . . . . . . . . . . . . (502) 564-3226
    Education: Winona State; Minnesota      Fax: (502) 564-3875
Deputy Commissioner **Elyse Weigel** . . . . . . . . . . . . . . . . (502) 564-3226
                                                   Fax: (502) 564-3875
Staff Assistant **Stacy Ball** . . . . . . . . . . . . . . . . . . . . . . . (502) 564-3226

## Office of Income Taxation

Tel: (502) 564-5495

Executive Director **Bob Brooks** . . . . . . . . . . . . . . . . . . . (502) 564-5495

## Office of Processing and Enforcement

Executive Director **Mack Gillim** . . . . . . . . . . . . . (502) 564-3227 ext. 43228
                                               Fax: (502) 564-9565

Taxpayer Registration Branch Manager
    **Celeste Popplewell** . . . . . . . . . . . . . . . . . . . . . . . . (502) 564-3306
                                               Fax: (502) 227-0772
Collections Division Director **Tammy Watts** . . . . (502) 564-4921 ext. 4435
                                               Fax: (502) 564-7348
Data Integrity Division Director **Kathy Moreland** . . . . . . . . (502) 564-4581
    E-mail: kathy.moreland@ky.gov
Revenue Operations Division Director
    **Jerry McCarty** . . . . . . . . . . . . . . . . . . . . . (502) 564-9329 ext. 47868
                                               Fax: (502) 564-9897

## Office of Property Valuation

Fax: (502) 564-8368

Executive Director **David Gordon** . . . . . . . . . . . (502) 564-8338 ext. 47177
Mineral Resources Valuation Branch Manager
    **Carla Briscoe** . . . . . . . . . . . . . . . . . . . . . . . . . . . (502) 564-6993
State Valuation Branch Manager **Kellie Lang** . . . . . . . . . (502) 564-8180
                                               Fax: (502) 564-8192

## Office of Sales and Excise Taxes

Executive Director **Richard Dobson** . . . . . . . . . . (502) 564-5523 ext. 45523
                                               Fax: (502) 564-2906

Miscellaneous Taxes Division Director
    **Jim Oliver** . . . . . . . . . . . . . . . . . . . . . . . . . (502) 564-2935 ext. 42935
                                               Fax: (502) 564-2906
Sales and Use Tax Division Director
    **Ricky Haven** . . . . . . . . . . . . . . . . . . . . . . . . (502) 564-5170 ext. 46828
                                               Fax: (502) 564-2041

---

★ Elected Official     ■ Appointed by Governor     ● Appointed by Legislature     ▲ Appointed by Board or Commission     ◆ Appointed by State Supreme Court

## Office of the Taxpayer Ombudsman
Director **Cathy Freeman** .............................. (502) 564-7822
Fax: (502) 564-3875

## Office of Administrative Services
Capitol Annex Building, 702 Capitol Avenue, Room 183,
Frankfort, KY 40601
Tel: (502) 564-0410   Fax: (502) 564-4279

■Executive Director **Troy Robinson** .................... (502) 564-0410
E-mail: troy.robinson@ky.gov
Human Resources Division Director **Honor Barker** ....... (502) 782-1596
Capitol Annex, 700 Capitol Avenue, Suite 188,     Fax: (502) 564-2613
Frankfort, KY 40601
E-mail: honor.barker@ky.gov
Postal Services Division Director **Mark Simpson** ........ (502) 564-3769
1230 Wilkinson Boulevard, Frankfort, KY 40601
E-mail: markt.simpson@ky.gov

## Office of the Controller
Tel: (502) 564-2998

Executive Director **Edgar C. Ross** ..................... (502) 564-4240
Education: Kentucky 1957 BS
Assistant State Controller **Kim Moore** ................. (502) 564-7750
484 Capitol Annex, 702 Capital Avenue, Frankfort, KY 40601
Customer Resource Center Division Director
**Barbara Aldridge-Montfort** ........................ (502) 564-9641
Capitol Annex, 702 Capital Ave., 460, Frankfort, KY 40601
Statewide Accounting Services Office Executive
Director **Donald Sweasy** .......................... (502) 564-4240
Financial Management Office Executive Director
**Ryan Barrow** Room 76 ............................ (502) 564-2924
Policy and Audit Office Executive Director
**Gerald W. Hoppmann** ............................ (502) 564-7236
Education: Wyoming 1988 BS, 1989 MPA
Procurement Services Office Executive Director
**Don Speer** ............................ (502) 564-4510 ext. 232

## Turnpike Authority of Kentucky
702 Capitol Avenue, Suite 78, Frankfort, KY 40601
Fax: (502) 564-2653

▲Executive Director **Edgar C. Ross** .................... (502) 564-2998
E-mail: ed.ross@ky.gov
▲Secretary **Ryan Barrow** ............................. (502) 564-2924
E-mail: ryan.barrow@ky.gov
Administrative Assistant **Marcia Hutcherson** ........... (502) 564-2856
E-mail: marcia.hutcherson@ky.gov

## Office of Equal Employment Opportunity and Contract Compliance
Fax: (502) 564-1055

Executive Director **Yvette M. Smith** .................. (502) 564-2874
Capitol Annex, 702 Capital Ave., Frankfort, KY 40601
E-mail: yvette.smith@ky.gov
Education: Midway 2000 BA

## Office of the General Counsel
General Counsel **Geri Grigsby** ........................ (502) 564-6660
Legal Services for Finance and Technology Office
Executive Director **Stewart Douglas Hendrix** ......... (502) 564-6660
Legal Services for Revenue Office Executive Director
**Geri Grigsby** .................................... (502) 564-6660
Fax: (502) 564-4044
Protest Resolution Division Director **Brad Nilsson** ...... (502) 564-6660
Legal Services for Revenue Manager **Doug Dowell** ..... (502) 564-3112
Fax: (502) 564-4044

## Commonwealth Office of Technology [COT]
101 Cold Harbor Drive, Frankfort, KY 40601
Tel: (502) 564-1201

**Fiscal Year:** 2015  **Budget:** $132,547,000

Chief Information Officer **(Vacant)** ................... (502) 564-1201
Executive Secretary **Kim Meyer** ..................... (502) 564-1201
Deputy Commissioner **Jim Barnhart** ................. (502) 564-7777
E-mail: jim.barnhart@ky.gov
Commonwealth Office of Broadband Outreach and
Development **Brian E. Kiser** ...................... (502) 564-1635
E-mail: brian.kiser@ky.gov
Office of Enterprise Technology Executive Director
**Roy Terry** ...................................... (502) 564-1209
E-mail: roy.terry@ky.gov

## School Facility Construction Commission
Fax: (502) 564-3412

Executive Director **Kristi Culpepper** ................. (502) 564-5582

## Kentucky Higher Education Assistance Authority [KHEAA]
P.O. Box 798, Frankfort, KY 40602-0798
Tel: (502) 696-7200  Fax: (502) 696-7293  Internet: www.kheaa.com

Executive Director/Chief Executive Officer
**Carl P. Rollins II** ................................. (502) 696-7497
E-mail: crollins@kheaa.com
Education: Morehead State BBA; Kentucky MBA, PhD
General Counsel **Diana Barber** ...................... (502) 696-7298
E-mail: dbarber@kheaa.com
Asset Management Vice President **Chris Thacker** ....... (502) 329-7152
Customer Relations Senior Vice President **Ted Franzeim** .. (502) 696-7284
E-mail: tfranzeim@kheaa.com
Government Relations Vice President **Erin Klarer** ........ (502) 696-7442
Guarantor Operations Vice President **David Bailey** ....... (502) 696-7447
Chief Financial Officer **David Carlsen** ................ (502) 329-7149
Chief Information Officer **Mary Lou Skelton** .......... (502) 696-7335
E-mail: mskelton@kheaa.com

## Kentucky River Authority [KRA]
627 Wilkinson Boulevard, Frankfort, KY 40601
Fax: (502) 564-2681

■Executive Director **Jerry Graves** .................... (502) 564-2866
E-mail: jerry.graves@ky.gov

## Housing Corporation
1231 Louisville Road, Frankfort, KY 40601
Tel: (502) 564-7630

Chief Executive Officer **J. Kathryn Peters** ....... (502) 564-7630 ext. 299
Deputy Executive Director for Business Services
**Amy Smith** ................................ (502) 564-7630 ext. 369
E-mail: asmith@kyhousing.org
Deputy Executive Director for Finance and
Investments **James F. Statler** ............... (502) 564-7630 ext. 286
Deputy Executive Director for Housing
Production and Programs **Rob Ellis** ........... (502) 564-7630 ext. 257
Deputy Executive Director for Internal Audits
**Kevin Field** ............................... (502) 564-7630 ext. 237
Deputy Executive Director for Legal Services
and Compliance **Lisa Beran** ................. (502) 564-7630 ext. 722
E-mail: lberan@kyhousing.org
Executive Assistant **Karla Hale** ................. (502) 564-7630 ext. 341
Corporate Secretary **Lisa Beran** ................ (502) 564-7630 ext. 722

## Commonwealth Credit Union
417 High Street, Frankfort, KY 40601
P.O. Box 978, Frankfort, KY 40602-0978
Fax: (502) 564-8146  Tel: (800) 228-6420  Internet: www.ccuky.org

President **Karen Harbin** ............................. (502) 564-4775
Executive Vice President **David Young** ............... (502) 564-4775

*(continued on next page)*

---

**Commonwealth Credit Union** *continued*

Branch Manager **Kim Durrum** . . . . . . . . . . . . . . . . . . . . . . . (502) 564-4775
  108 Lawson Drive, Georgetown, KY 40324
  E-mail: kdurrum@cwcu.org

Branch Manager **Kim Jennings** . . . . . . . . . . . . . . . . . . . . . (502) 564-4775
  1015 Crossroads Drive, Lawrenceburg, KY 40342
  E-mail: kjennings@cwcu.org

Branch Manager **Danielle Luigart** . . . . . . . . . . . . . . . . . . . (502) 564-4775
  280 Meijer Way Branch, Lexington, KY 40503
  E-mail: dluigart@cwcu.org

Branch Manager **Bethany Patton** . . . . . . . . . . . . . . . . . . . (502) 564-4775
  1425 Louisville Rd., Louisville, KY 40602
  E-mail: bpatton@cwcu.org

Branch Manager **Missy Raizor** . . . . . . . . . . . . . . . . . . . . . (502) 564-4775
  E-mail: mraizor@cwcu.org

Branch Manager **Cindy Searcy** . . . . . . . . . . . . . . . . . . . . . (502) 564-4775
  101 Sower Blvd., Frankfort, KY 40601
  E-mail: cindy.searcy@ag.ky.gov

Branch Manager **Lynette Wooldridge** . . . . . . . . . . . . . . . (502) 564-4775
  2540 Sir Barton Way, Lexington, KY 40509
  E-mail: lwooldri@cwcu.org

# Kentucky Retirement Systems [KRS]

Perimeter Park West, 1260 Louisville Road, Frankfort, KY 40601-6124
Tel: (502) 696-8800  Tel: (800) 928-4646 (Toll Free)  Fax: (502) 696-8822
E-mail: krs.mail@kyret.ky.gov

**Fiscal Year:** 2015  **Budget:** $31,074,000

■ Chairman **Thomas K. Elliott** . . . . . . . . . . . . . . . . . . . . . . . (502) 696-8800
  Term Expires: March 31, 2019
  Education: Kentucky BA

▲ Executive Director **William A. Thielen** . . . . . . . . . . . . . . (502) 696-8888
  Note: Until September 1, 2016.
  E-mail: williama.thielen@ag.ky.gov

Chief Benefits Officer **Charlene Haydon** . . . . . . . . . . . . . (502) 696-8888

Chief Investments Officer (Interim) **David Peden, CFA** . . . . (502) 696-8888
  Education: Western Kentucky BA; Louisville MBA

Chief Operations Officer **Karen Roggenkamp** . . . . . . . . . . (502) 696-8888

Chief Security Officer **Mark McChesney** . . . . . . . . . . . . . . (502) 696-8800

Director of Accounting **Todd E. Coleman** . . . . . . . . . . . . . (502) 696-8800

Director of Fixed Income **David Peden, CFA** . . . . . . . . . . . (502) 696-8888

Information Technology Director
  **Jeff Luckett, CISA, CIA** . . . . . . . . . . . . . . . . . . . . . . . . . . (502) 696-8800
  E-mail: jeff.luckett@kyret.ky.gov
  Education: Louisville BS

General Counsel **Brian C. Thomas** . . . . . . . . . . . . . . . . . . (502) 696-8800
  Education: Georgetown Col BA; Kentucky JD

# Cabinet for Health and Family Services [CHFS]

275 East Main Street, 5W-A, Frankfort, KY 40621
Tel: (502) 564-7042  Internet: www.chfs.ky.gov

**Employees:** 7,450  **Fiscal Year:** 2015  **Budget:** $11,987,765,000

■ Secretary **Vickie Yates Brown Glisson** . . . . . . . . . . . . . . (502) 564-7042
  Education: Georgetown 1976 BA; Kentucky 1979 JD

Deputy Secretary **Tim E. Feeley** . . . . . . . . . . . . . . . . . . . . (502) 564-7042

Executive Advisor **Eric Clark** . . . . . . . . . . . . . . . . . . . . . . . (502) 564-7042

Policy Advisor **Dana C. Nickles** . . . . . . . . . . . . . . . . . . . . . (502) 564-7042

## Office of Administrative and Technology Services

275 East Main Street, 4E-C, Frankfort, KY 40621
Tel: (502) 564-0105  Fax: (502) 564-0302

Executive Director **Chris Clark** . . . . . . . . . . . . . . . . . . . . . . (502) 564-6478
  E-mail: christopher.clark@ky.gov

Executive Advisor **Stephen Smith** . . . . . . . . . . . . . . . . . . . (502) 564-0105

Accounting and Procurement Services Division Director
  **Lee Ann Brewer** . . . . . . . . . . . . . . . . . . . . . . . . . . . . . . . . (502) 564-0105

Facilities Management Division Director **Scott Baker** . . . . . (502) 564-0105

Medicaid Systems Division Director **Jennifer Harp** . . . . . . (502) 564-6479
  E-mail: jennifer.harp@ky.gov

Strategic Services Division Director **(Vacant)** . . . . . . . . . . . (502) 564-0105

Systems Management Division Director **(Vacant)** . . . . . . . . (502) 564-0105

## Office of Communications and Administrative Review

Executive Director (Interim) **Doug Hogan** . . . . . . (502) 564-6786 ext. 3465
  E-mail: doug.hogan@ky.gov
  Education: Western Kentucky BA

Administrative Hearings Division Director (Acting)
  **Dana C. Nickles** . . . . . . . . . . . . . . . . . . . . . . . . . . . . . . . (502) 564-6621
  E-mail: dana.nickles@ky.gov

## Office of Health Policy

275 East Main Street, 3W-E, Frankfort, KY 40621
Tel: (502) 564-9592  Fax: (502) 564-0302  Internet: http://chfs.ky.gov/ohp

Executive Director **(Vacant)** . . . . . . . . . . . . . . . . . . . . . . . . (502) 564-9592
                                                                        Fax: (502) 564-0302

Policy Advisor **Diona Mullins** . . . . . . . . . . . . . . . . . . . . . . (502) 564-9592

## Office of Human Resource Management

275 East Main Street, 5C-D, Frankfort, KY 40621
Tel: (502) 564-7770  Fax: (502) 564-0200

Executive Director **Alan Sisk** . . . . . . . . . . . . . . . . . . . . . . . (502) 564-7770

Deputy Executive Director **Tresa Straw** . . . . . . . . . . . . . . . (502) 564-7770

Personnel Administration Assistant Director **Kelly Black** . . . (502) 564-7770

Employee Management Division Staff Assistant
  **Jay Klein** . . . . . . . . . . . . . . . . . . . . . . . . . . . . . . . . . . . . . (502) 564-7770

## Office of the Inspector General

275 East Main Street, 5E-A, Frankfort, KY 40621
Fax: (502) 564-6546  Internet: chfs.ky.gov/oig

■ Inspector General **(Vacant)** . . . . . . . . . . . . . . . . . . . . . . . (502) 564-2888
  E-mail: maryellen.mynear@ky.gov

Deputy Inspector General **Connie Payne** . . . . . . . . . . . . . . (502) 564-2888
  E-mail: connie.payne@ky.gov

Audits and Investigations Division Director
  **Stephanie Hold** . . . . . . . . . . . . . . . . . . . . . . . . . . . . . . . . (502) 564-2815
  E-mail: stephanie.hold@ky.gov

  Audits and Investigations Assistant Division Director
    **Susan Selby** . . . . . . . . . . . . . . . . . . . . . . . . . . . . . . . . . (502) 564-2815

Health Care Division Director (Acting) **Connie Payne** . . . . (502) 564-7968

Regulated Childcare Division Director **Ideisha Bellamy** . . . (502) 564-7962
  E-mail: idesha.bellamy@ag.ky.gov

## Office of Legal Services

Tel: (502) 564-7905  Fax: (502) 564-7573

General Counsel **Christina Heavrin** . . . . . . . . . . . . . . . . . . (502) 564-7042

Deputy General Counsel **D. Brent Irvin** . . . . . . . . . . . . . . . (502) 564-7905

Deputy General Counsel **Mona S. Womack** . . . . . . . . . . . . (502) 564-7905

## Office of the Ombudsman

Tel: (800) 372-2973  TTY: (800) 627-4702  Fax: (502) 564-5080

Ombudsman Executive Director **Chip Ward** . . . . . . . . . . . . (502) 564-5497

Complaint Review Branch **Andrea T. Day** . . . . . . . . . . . . . (502) 564-5497

Performance Enhancement Branch **LaToya Payne** . . . . . . . (502) 564-5497
  E-mail: latoya.payne@ky.gov

## Office of Policy and Budget

275 East Main Street, 4E-A, Frankfort, KY 40621

Executive Director **Beth Jurek** . . . . . . . . . . . . . . . . . . . . . . (502) 564-7042

# Department for Aging and Independent Living [DAIL]

275 East Main Street, 3E-E, Frankfort, KY 40621
Tel: (502) 564-6930  Fax: (502) 564-4595

Commissioner **Deborah Anderson** . . . . . . . . . . . . . . . . . . (502) 564-6930
  E-mail: deborah.anderson2@ky.gov

Deputy Commissioner **Victoria Eldridge** . . . . . . . . . . . . . . (502) 564-6930

Long-Term Care Ombudsman **Sherry Culp** . . . . . . . . . . . . (859) 277-9215

---

★ Elected Official   ■ Appointed by Governor   ● Appointed by Legislature   ▲ Appointed by Board or Commission   ◆ Appointed by State Supreme Court

# Department for Behavioral Health, Developmental and Intellectual Disabilities [DBHDID]

275 East Main Street, Suite 4E-B, Frankfort, KY 40621
Tel: (502) 564-4527  Fax: (502) 564-5478

Commissioner (Acting) **Wendy Morris** . . . . . . . . . . . . . . . . (502) 564-4527
Deputy Commissioner **Kim Roush** . . . . . . . . . . . . . . . . . (502) 564-4527
Developmental Disabilities Council Executive Director
**Marylee Underwood** . . . . . . . . . . . . . . . . . . . . . . . . (502) 564-7841
Administration and Financial Management Division
Director **Stephanie Craycraft** . . . . . . . . . . . . . . . . . . (502) 564-4527
E-mail: stephanie.craycraft@ky.gov
Behavioral Health Division Director **Natalie Kelly** . . . . (502) 564-4527
Developmental and Intellectual Disabilities Division
Director **Tabitha Burkhart-Wilson** . . . . . . . . . . . . . . (502) 564-4527
Program Integrity Division Director **Sarah McCount** . . . . . (502) 564-4527

# Department for Community Based Services [DCBS]

275 East Main Street, 3W-A, Frankfort, KY 40621
Fax: (502) 564-6907

Commissioner **Adria Johnson** . . . . . . . . . . . . . . . . . . . (502) 564-3703
Deputy Commissioner **Kelly Staples** . . . . . . . . . . . . . . . (502) 564-3703
Deputy Commissioner **(Vacant)** . . . . . . . . . . . . . . . . . . (502) 564-3703
Administration and Financial Management Division
Director **(Vacant)** . . . . . . . . . . . . . . . . . . . . . . . . . (502) 564-7463
Administration and Financial Management Division
Deputy Director **Ariane Shouse** . . . . . . . . . . . . . . . (502) 564-7463
E-mail: ariane.shouse@ky.gov
Child Care Division Director **Marybeth Jackson** . . . . . . . (502) 564-2524
Family Support Division Director **(Vacant)** . . . . . . . . . . . (502) 564-3440
Permanency and Protection Division Director
**Pam Cotton** . . . . . . . . . . . . . . . . . . . . . . . . . . . . (502) 564-6852
Permanency and Protection Division Assistant Director
**Tina Webb** . . . . . . . . . . . . . . . . . . . . . . . . . . . . (502) 564-6852
Program Performance Division Director **(Vacant)** . . . . . . . (502) 564-3703
Service Regions Division Director **Lesa Dennis** . . . . . . . . (502) 564-3703

# Department for Income Support [DIS]

730 Schenkel Lane, Frankfort, KY 40602

Commissioner **Steven Veno** . . . . . . . . . . . . . . . . (502) 564-7941 ext. 4819
E-mail: stevenp.veno@ky.gov
Deputy Commissioner **Stephen Brooks** . . . . . . . . (502) 564-2285 ext. 4823
E-mail: steve.brooks@ky.gov
Child Support Enforcement Director
**Steven Veno** . . . . . . . . . . . . . . . . . . . . . . (502) 564-2285 ext. 4819
E-mail: stevenp.veno@ky.gov
Disability Determination Services **Staci Cain** . . . . . . . . . . . (502) 782-1504
E-mail: staci.cain@ky.gov

# Department for Medicaid Services [DMS]

275 East Main Street, 6W-A, Frankfort, KY 40621
Tel: (502) 564-8196  Fax: (502) 564-0509  Internet: www.chfs.ky.gov/dms

Commissioner **Stephen P. Miller, CPA** . . . . . . . . . . . . . . (502) 564-4321
Deputy Commissioner **Neville Wise** . . . . . . . . . . . . . . . . (502) 564-4321
E-mail: neville.wise@ky.gov
Fiscal Management Division Director **Tammy Branhan** . . . (502) 564-8196
E-mail: tammy.branham@ky.gov
Community Alternatives Division Director
**Leslie H. Hoffman** . . . . . . . . . . . . . . . . . . . . . . . . (502) 564-7540
Community Alternatives Division Assistant Director
**Earl Gresham** . . . . . . . . . . . . . . . . . . . . . . . . . . (502) 564-7540
E-mail: earl.gresham@ag.ky.gov
Member Services Division Director **Jill Hunter** . . . . . . . . (502) 564-8196
Policy and Operations Division Director **Lee Guice** . . . . . . (502) 564-6890
Fax: (502) 564-0509

# Department for Public Health [DOH]

275 East Main Street, HS1 W-A, Frankfort, KY 40621
275 East Main Street, 1E-A, Frankfort, KY 40621 (Vital Records)
Tel: (502) 564-3970  Tel: (502) 564-4212 (Vital Records)
Fax: (502) 564-9377  Fax: (866) 283-7477 (Vital Records)
Internet: chfs.ky.gov/dph

Commissioner
**Dr. Stephanie Mayfield Gibson, MD, FCAP** . . . . . . . . . (502) 564-3970

## Administration and Financial Management Division

Director and Policy Advisor (Acting)
**Ron Horseman** . . . . . . . . . . . . . . . . . . . . (502) 564-3970 ext. 4109

## Epidemiology and Health Planning Division

Tel: (502) 564-3418  Fax: (502) 564-0542

Director **Dr. Kraig Eckman Humbaugh** . . . . . . . . . . . . . . (502) 564-7243
Note: Until May 31, 2016.
Education: Yale 1989 MD

## Laboratory Services Division

Director **Dr. Paul Bachner** . . . . . . . . . . . . . . . . . . . . . . (502) 564-4446

## Maternal and Child Health Division

Director **Ruth Ann Shepherd** . . . . . . . . . . . . . . . . . . . . (502) 564-4830
E-mail: ruth.shepherd@ky.gov

## Public Health Protection and Safety Division

Director (Acting) **Kathy Fowler, RS** . . . . . . . . . . . . . . . . (502) 564-7398

# Commission for Children with Special Health Care Needs

310 Whittington Parkway, Suite 200, Louisville, KY 40222
Fax: (502) 429-4489

Executive Director **Jackie Richardson** . . . . . . . . . . . . . . . (502) 429-4430

# Justice and Public Safety Cabinet [JPSC]

125 Holmes Street, Frankfort, KY 40601-2638
Tel: (502) 564-7554  Fax: (502) 564-4840  Internet: www.justice.ky.gov

**Employees:** 7,660  **Fiscal Year:** 2015  **Budget:** $959,573,000

■Secretary **John C. Tilley** . . . . . . . . . . . . . . . . . . . . . . . (502) 564-7554
Education: Kentucky 1991 BA; Salmon P Chase 1996 JD
■Deputy Secretary **(Vacant)** . . . . . . . . . . . . . . . . . . . . . (502) 564-3279
Chief of Staff **Yvonne Board** . . . . . . . . . . . . . . . . . . . (502) 564-7554
General Counsel **(Vacant)** . . . . . . . . . . . . . . . . . . . . . . (502) 564-3279
Office of Legislative and Intergovernmental Services
Executive Director **Jennifer Feldman Brislin** . . . . . . . . (502) 564-7554
Office of Investigations Executive Director
**Barney Kinman** . . . . . . . . . . . . . . . . . . . . . . . . . . (502) 564-6688
E-mail: barney.kinman@ky.gov
Chief Medical Examiner **Tracey Corey** . . . . . . . . . . . . . (502) 852-5587
Parole Board Chairperson **Shannon Jones** . . . . . . . . . . . (502) 564-3620
Education: Eastern Kentucky BS
Director of Communications **(Vacant)** . . . . . . . . . . . . . . (502) 564-7554

# Office of Drug Control Policy

125 Holmes Street, 1st Floor, Frankfort, KY 40602
Tel: (502) 564-9564  Fax: (502) 564-6104

Executive Director **Van Ingram** . . . . . . . . . . . . . . . . . . . (502) 564-9564
Branch Manager **Heather Wainscott** . . . . . . . . . . . . . . . (502) 564-8240
Education: Kentucky BA

---

★ Elected Official    ■ Appointed by Governor    ● Appointed by Legislature    ▲ Appointed by Board or Commission    ◆ Appointed by State Supreme Court

## Department of Corrections [DOC]

Health Services Building, 275 East Main Street, Ground Floor,
Frankfort, KY 40602-2400
P.O. Box 2400, Frankfort, KY 40602
Tel: (502) 564-4726   Fax: (502) 564-5037

■Commissioner **Rodney Ballard** ...................... (502) 564-4726
  Education: Northern Kentucky BS
  Executive Secretary **MaryAnn Sullivan** .............. (502) 564-4726
General Counsel **Brenn Combs** ..................... (502) 564-4726
  Legal Secretary **Loreen Grant** ................... (502) 564-7554
Ombudsman **John Dunn** ........................... (502) 564-4726
Public Information Office Chief **Lisa Lamb** ......... (502) 564-4726
  E-mail: lisa.lamb@ky.gov
Special Investigations **Mark Wasson** ................ (502) 564-4726
                                 Fax: (502) 564-3520
Victim Services Program Administrator
  **Tammy Lou Wright** ........................... (502) 564-5061

### Adult Institutions

275 East Main Street, Frankfort, KY 40621
P.O. Box 2400, Frankfort, KY 40601
Fax: (502) 564-3520

Deputy Commissioner **James L. "Jim" Erwin** .......... (502) 564-2220
  275 East Main Street, Frankfort, KY 40601
  Education: Centre 1984 BA; Louisville 1987 MA
  Administrative Specialist **Valerie Moore** ........... (502) 564-2220
Program Administrator **Mary Godfrey** ............... (502) 564-7554
  Education: Louisville BA
  Administrative Specialist **Meredith Sanford** ........ (502) 564-2220
Clinical Director **Dr. Doug Crall** ................... (502) 564-2220
Correctional Industries Division Director **Tom Cannady** ... (502) 573-1040
  1041 Leestown Rd., Frankfort, KY 40601   Fax: (502) 573-1045
Operations and Programs Director **(Vacant)** ......... (502) 564-7554
Contract Management Branch Manager **Eric Buckley** ..... (502) 564-7023
Food Services Branch Manager **Susan Williams** ........ (502) 564-6490
  2439 Lawrenceburg Road, Frankfort, KY 40601
Education Program Services Administrator
  **Martha Slemp** ...................... (502) 564-4795 ext. 229
  2439 Lawrenceburg Road, Frankfort, KY 40601
  E-mail: martha.slemp@ky.gov
Law Enforcement Liaison Program Coordinator
  **Jeff Hulker** ................................ (502) 564-2220

### Community Services and Facilities

Fax: (502) 564-0401

Deputy Commissioner **Paula Holden** ................. (502) 564-7290
  275 East Main Street, Frankfort, KY 40601
Local Facilities Division Director **Jeff Burton** .......... (502) 564-7290
  2439 Lawrenceburg Road, Frankfort, KY 40601   Fax: (502) 564-9836
Fiscal Manager **(Vacant)** .......................... (502) 564-4726

### Personnel Services

125 Holmes Street, Frankfort, KY 40602
Tel: (502) 564-4636   Fax: (502) 564-2571

Personnel Director (Acting) **Bobbie Underwood** ........ (502) 564-4636
Personnel Branch Manager **Diana Eads** .............. (502) 564-4636
Recruitment Branch Manager **Teresa Harris** ........... (502) 564-4636
Payroll Manager **Rodney Moore** .................... (502) 564-4636

### Probation and Parole

Director **Roberto "Bob" Rodriguez** .................. (502) 564-7554
  Education: Hofstra BA
  Assistant Director **Cortney Shewmaker** ............. (502) 564-4221
Corrections Program Administrator
  **Leigh "Ambie" Ingram** ....................... (502) 564-7554
  Education: Western Kentucky BFA

### Support Services

275 East Main Street, Frankfort, KY 40621
Fax: (502) 564-5037

Deputy Commissioner **Kimberly Potter-Blair** ........... (502) 564-4726
  275 East Main Street, Frankfort, KY 40601

---

Administrative Services Director **Hilarye Dailey** ........ (502) 564-4726
  E-mail: hilarye.dailey@ag.ky.gov
  Administrative Services Assistant Director **(Vacant)** ..... (502) 564-4726
Mental Health Division Director **Kevin Pangburn** ....... (502) 564-6490
                                  Fax: (502) 564-0572
Population Management Director **Paula Holden** ......... (502) 564-2220
Capital Construction Branch Manager **Gunvant Shah** ..... (502) 564-2094
  2439 Lawrenceburg Road, Frankfort, KY 40601   Fax: (502) 564-1297
Offender Records Branch Manager **Johnathan Hall** ...... (502) 564-2433
                                  Fax: (502) 564-1471

### Information and Technology Branch

Tel: (502) 564-4360   Fax: (502) 564-5642

Information Technology Branch Manager **Terry Terrell** .... (502) 564-4360
  E-mail: terry.terrell@ky.gov
Information Technology Systems Consultant **Beth Moore** .. (502) 564-4360
  E-mail: beth.moore@ky.gov
Information Technology Systems Engineer **Scott Bailey** ... (502) 564-4360
  E-mail: scott.bailey@ky.gov
Information Systems Supervisor, Applications
  **Del Combs** .................................. (502) 564-4360
  E-mail: del.combs@ky.gov
  Analyst/Programmer III **Cedric Coleman** ........... (502) 564-4360
    E-mail: cedric.coleman@ky.gov
  Systems Analyst II **Nathan Brown** ................ (502) 564-4360
  Systems Analyst II **Zach Schadler** ............... (502) 564-4360
  Systems Analyst III **Amanda Sayle** ............... (502) 564-2433
    E-mail: amanda.sayle@ky.gov
Information Systems Supervisor, Network
  **Jeremy Shuck** ............................... (502) 564-4360
  E-mail: jeremy.shuck@ag.ky.gov
  Network Analyst I **Jesse Gritton** ................. (502) 564-4360
    E-mail: jesse.gritton@ky.gov
  Network Analyst I **Ryan Walters** ................. (502) 564-4360
    E-mail: ryan.walters@ky.gov
  Network Analyst II **Charles Columbia** ............. (502) 564-4360
    E-mail: charles.columbia@ky.gov
  Network Analyst II **Michael Meehan** .............. (502) 564-4360
    E-mail: michael.meehan@ky.gov
  Network Analyst II **Jeff Smith** ................... (502) 564-4360
    E-mail: jeff.smith@ky.gov
  Network Analyst III **Danny Milburn** .............. (502) 564-4360
    E-mail: danny.milburn@ky.gov

## Department of Criminal Justice Training [DOCJT]

Funderburk Building, 521 Lancaster Avenue, Richmond, KY 40475-3102
Tel: (859) 622-1328   Fax: (859) 622-2740

**Fiscal Year:** 2015   **Budget:** $57,132,000

Commissioner (Acting) **Jonathan Grate** ............... (859) 622-8081
  E-mail: jonathan.grate@ky.gov
Deputy Commissioner **Leslie Gannon** ................ (859) 622-6165
General Counsel **Gerald Ross** ...................... (859) 622-2214
Administrative Division Director **(Vacant)** ............ (859) 622-5002
Training Operation Division Director **James R. Brown** ... (859) 622-2221
Staff Advisor **Pam Smallwood** ..................... (859) 622-8560
Special Assistant **Kelly Foreman** ................... (859) 622-8552
Staff Assistant **Edliniae Sweat** .................... (859) 622-2912

## Department of Juvenile Justice [DJJ]

1025 Capital Center Drive, Third Floor, Frankfort, KY 40601
Tel: (502) 573-2738   Fax: (502) 573-4308   Internet: djj.ky.gov

**Fiscal Year:** 2015   **Budget:** $109,912,000

■Commissioner (Acting) **LaDonna Koebel** ............ (502) 573-2738
■Community and Mental Health Deputy Commissioner
  **Miranda Denney** ............................ (502) 429-7225
  E-mail: miranda.denney@ky.gov
■Operations Deputy Commissioner **Mark Cook** .......... (502) 573-2726
  E-mail: mark.cook@ky.gov
  Classification Branch Division Director
  **Monica Edmonds** ........................... (502) 573-2738
  Classification Branch Manager **Veronica Koontz** ...... (502) 573-2738

---

★ Elected Official    ■ Appointed by Governor    ● Appointed by Legislature    ▲ Appointed by Board or Commission    ◆ Appointed by State Supreme Court

Transportation Branch Manager **Lynn Lockridge** . . . . . . . (502) 429-3356
Administration Services Director **Cynthia Ann Watson** . . . (502) 573-2738
  E-mail: cynthia.watson@ky.gov          Fax: (502) 573-0307
Fiscal Branch Manager **Scott Whitaker** . . . . . . . . . . . . . (502) 573-3747
                                               Fax: (502) 573-0307
Information Systems Branch Manager **Bill May** . . . . . . . . (502) 573-2738
  E-mail: bill.may@ky.gov
Human Resources Manager **Kim Whitley** . . . . . . . . . . . . (502) 573-3747
                                               Fax: (502) 573-2031
Community Service Division Director
  **Samantha Woods** . . . . . . . . . . . . . . . . . . . . . . . . . . . . (606) 528-4050
                                               Fax: (606) 528-0404
Central Region Division Director **(Vacant)** . . . . . . . . . . . . (270) 526-3826
                                               Fax: (270) 526-2116
Eastern Region Division Director **Chris Mann** . . . . . . . . . . (606) 784-6421
                                               Fax: (606) 784-9983
Southeastern Region Division Director **(Vacant)** . . . . . . . . (859) 239-7064
                                               Fax: (859) 239-7066
Western Region Division Director **John Weyers III** . . . . . . . (270) 575-7095
Program Services Division Director **Stacy Floden** . . . . . . . (502) 573-2738
Ombudsman **Walter Wright** . . . . . . . . . . . . . . . . . . . . . . (502) 573-2738

## Department of Public Advocacy [DPA]

5 Mill Creek Park, Frankfort, KY 40601
Tel: (502) 564-8006   Fax: (502) 695-6767   Internet: dpa.ky.gov

**Fiscal Year:** 2015   **Budget:** $51,248,000

■Public Advocate **Col Edward C. Monahan, USAF** . . . . . . . (502) 564-8006
  E-mail: ed.monahan@ky.gov
  Education: Thomas More Col 1973; Columbus Law 1976 JD
  Administrative Specialist **Jessie Luscher** . . . . . . . . . . . . (502) 564-8006
Deputy Public Advocate **Damon L. Preston** . . . . . . . . . . . (502) 564-8006
Law Operations Division Director **Brad Holjater** . . . . . . . . (502) 564-8006
Post-Trial Division Director **Timothy G. Arnold** . . . . . . . . (502) 564-8006
Protection & Advocacy Division Director **Jeff Edwards** . . . (502) 564-8006
Trial Division Director **Glenda Edwards** . . . . . . . . . . . . . (502) 564-8006
Systems Administrator **Scott Richard** . . . . . . . . . . . . . . . (502) 564-8006
  E-mail: scott.richard@ky.gov
General Counsel **Scott West** . . . . . . . . . . . . . . . . . . . . . . (502) 564-8006

## State Police Department [KSP]

919 Versailles Road, Frankfort, KY 40601
Tel: (502) 782-1800   Fax: (502) 573-1479
Internet: www.kentuckystatepolice.org

**Fiscal Year:** 2015   **Budget:** $208,580,000

Commissioner **Richard W. "Rick" Sanders** . . . . . . . . . . . (502) 782-1793
  E-mail: richard.sanders@ky.gov       Fax: (502) 695-6341
  Education: Louisville BA, 1991 MJA
Deputy Commissioner **Major William Alexander Payne** . . (502) 782-1800
                                               Fax: (502) 695-6341
Administrative Division Director **Col. Scott Miller** . . . . . . . (502) 695-6323
  E-mail: scott.miller@ky.gov         Fax: (502) 782-1788
Operations Division Director **Lt. Col. Jack Miniard** . . . . . . (502) 782-1802
                                               Fax: (502) 695-6341
Technical Services Division Director
  **Lt. Col. John M. Bradley** . . . . . . . . . . . . . . . . . . . . . . (502) 695-6300
  E-mail: john.bradley@ky.gov
Chief Information Officer **Major Barry Shane Bates** . . . . . (502) 782-1804
  E-mail: barry.bates@ky.gov         Fax: (502) 695-6341
Strategic Planning Branch **Angela Parker** . . . . . . . . . . . . (502) 782-1848
                                               Fax: (502) 695-6377
Commercial Vehicle Enforcement
  **Lt. Col. Curtis O'Bannon** . . . . . . . . . . . . . . . . . . . . . . (502) 782-1806

## Kentucky Parole Board

Chair **Lelia "Lee" VanHoose** . . . . . . . . . . . . . . . . . . . . . (502) 564-7554
Member **Michael A. Bolcas** . . . . . . . . . . . . . . . . . . . . . . (502) 564-7554
  Education: Eastern Kentucky
Member **Larry R. Brock** . . . . . . . . . . . . . . . . . . . . . . . . . (502) 564-7554
Member **George Carson** . . . . . . . . . . . . . . . . . . . . . . . . . (502) 564-7554
Member **Sharon L. Hardesty** . . . . . . . . . . . . . . . . . . . . . (502) 564-7554
Member **Walter F. Maguire** . . . . . . . . . . . . . . . . . . . . . . . (502) 564-7554
Member **Caroline W. Mudd** . . . . . . . . . . . . . . . . . . . . . . . (502) 564-7554
  Education: Campbellsville Col BS

Member **Neeka Parks** . . . . . . . . . . . . . . . . . . . . . . . . . . . (502) 564-7554
Member **Amanda Spears** . . . . . . . . . . . . . . . . . . . . . . . . (502) 564-7554

## Labor Cabinet

1047 US Highway, 127 South, Suite 4, Frankfort, KY 40601
Tel: (502) 564-3070   Fax: (502) 564-5387   Internet: www.labor.ky.gov

**Employees:** 503   **Fiscal Year:** 2015   **Budget:** $216,900,000

■Secretary **Derrick Ramsey** . . . . . . . . . . . . . . . . . . . . . . (502) 564-3070
■Deputy Secretary **Mike Nemes** . . . . . . . . . . . . . . . . . . . (502) 564-4318
  E-mail: mike.nemes@ky.gov
General Counsel **Early "Chip" Smith** . . . . . . . . . . . . . . . (502) 564-3213
                                               Fax: (502) 564-5484

## Department of Workers' Claims [DWC]

657 Chamberlin Avenue, Frankfort, KY 40601
Tel: (502) 782-4578   Fax: (502) 564-5934

■Commissioner **Dwight T. Lovan** . . . . . . . . . . . . . . . . . . . (502) 564-4439
  E-mail: dwight.lovan@ky.gov
  Education: Kentucky JD

## Department of Workplace Standards

Fax: (502) 696-2248
Commissioner **Anthony Russell** . . . . . . . . . . . . . . . . . . . (502) 564-0977
Deputy Commissioner **Michael "Mike" Donta** . . . . . . . . . (502) 564-0977
Workers Compensation Fund Director
  **Robert L. "Bob" Whittaker** . . . . . . . . . . . . . . . . . . . . (502) 564-3083
Mediation Standards, Apprenticeship and Training
  Division Director **(Vacant)** . . . . . . . . . . . . . . . . . . . . . (502) 564-3534
Labor-Management Relations and Mediation Program
  Coordinator **Jodie M. Craig** . . . . . . . . . . . . . . . . . . . . (502) 564-3203
                                               Fax: (502) 696-1897

## Personnel Cabinet

Fax: (502) 564-7603   Internet: http://personnel.ky.gov

**Employees:** 220   **Fiscal Year:** 2015   **Budget:** $78,072,000

■Secretary **Thomas B. "Tom" Stephens** . . . . . . . . . . . . . (502) 564-7430
  Executive Assistant III **Joyce Wilcher** . . . . . . . . . . . . . . (502) 564-7430
Office of Diversity and Equality Executive Director
  **Christopher L. "Chris" Johnson** . . . . . . . . . . . . . . . . . (502) 564-8000

## Employee Insurance Department

501 High Street, Frankfort, KY 40601
Fax: (502) 564-5278
Commissioner **(Vacant)** . . . . . . . . . . . . . . . . . . . . . . . . . (502) 564-0358
Deputy Commissioner **Jenny Goins** . . . . . . . . . . . . . . . . (502) 564-0358
  Executive Secretary **Lubona "Lulu" Cisse** . . . . . . . . . . . (502) 564-0358
  Staff Assistant **Donna Cordier** . . . . . . . . . . . . . . . . . . . (502) 564-0358
Insurance Administration Division Director **Jeffreyn Barr** . . (502) 564-0358

## Department of Human Resources Administration

501 High Street, Frankfort, KY 40601
Fax: (502) 564-9249
Commissioner **Mary Elizabeth Harrod** . . . . . . . . . . . . . . (502) 564-7571
  Executive Secretary **Tammy R. McNew** . . . . . . . . . . . . . (502) 564-4610
Employee Management Division Assistant Director
  **Larry B. Gillis, IPMA-CP** . . . . . . . . . . . . . . . . . . . . . . (502) 564-6464
  Classification and Compensation Branch Personnel
    Program Manager **Dawn Moreland** . . . . . . . . . . . . . . (502) 564-5300
    E-mail: dawn.moreland@ky.gov      Fax: (502) 573-0324
  Payroll Branch Personnel Program Manager
    **Yvonne M. Richmond** . . . . . . . . . . . . . . . . . . . . . . . . (502) 564-6883
    E-mail: yvonnem.richmond@ky.gov
  Personnel Administration Branch Manager
    **Amanda Coulter** . . . . . . . . . . . . . . . . . . . . . . . . . . . . (502) 564-6873
    E-mail: amanda.coulter@ky.gov
Career Opportunities Division Director **Karen Mixson** . . . (502) 564-8030
Human Resource Certification Branch Manager
  **Scotty Barker** . . . . . . . . . . . . . . . . . . . . . . . . . . . . . . (502) 564-8030
  E-mail: scotty.barker@ky.gov

*(continued on next page)*

---

★ Elected Official    ■ Appointed by Governor    ● Appointed by Legislature    ▲ Appointed by Board or Commission    ◆ Appointed by State Supreme Court

EXECUTIVE BRANCH

**Department of Human Resources Administration** *continued*

Register Branch Personnel Program Manager
**Rick C. Davis** ................................. (502) 564-8030
E-mail: rickc.davis@ky.gov

## Administrative Services Office

Executive Director **(Vacant)** ........................ (502) 564-7430
Fiscal Manager **Sherry Kefauver** .....................(502) 564-7430
Human Resources Administrator **Tanya Lawrence** ........(502) 564-7430

## Employee Relations Office

Executive Director **Mary Hook** ...................... (502) 564-7911
Deputy Executive Director **(Vacant)** ................. (502) 564-7911
Program Manager **Nila Meeks** ....................... (502) 564-7430
Employees Recognition Branch Manager
**Linda C. Brown** ................................ (502) 564-5954
Life Insurance Branch **Joe M. Hughes** .............. (502) 564-4774
Workers Compensation Branch
**Matthew "Matt" Hutcherson** .................... (502) 564-6847
Workplace Relations Branch Manager
**Linda House Patrick** ........................... (502) 564-3433
Kentucky Safety Program **Dana Harvey** .............(502) 564-7911
Return to Work Program **Donna Shelton** ............ (502) 564-0348
E-mail: donna.shelton@ky.gov

## Office for Governmental Services Center

Academic Service Building 4W, Kentucky State University,
400 East Main Street, Frankfort, KY 40601
Fax: (502) 564-8076

Executive Director **(Vacant)** ........................ (502) 564-8170
Training and Employee Development Branch Manager
**Jeanne Olivas** ................................. (502) 564-8170

## Legal Services Office

Fax: (502) 564-0224

Executive Director **Lesley Bilby** .....................(502) 564-7430
Deputy Executive Director **Sharron Burton** ............ (502) 564-7430

## Public Protection Cabinet [PPC]

Capital Plaza Tower, 500 Mero Street, 5th Floor, Frankfort, KY 40601
Fax: (502) 564-3969   Internet: www.ppc.ky.gov

**Employees:** 646

■Secretary **David A. Dickerson** ...................... (502) 564-7760
E-mail: david.dickerson@ky.gov
Staff Assistant **Vicki Craycraft** ..................... (502) 564-7760
■Deputy Secretary and Small Business Ombudsman
**Gail Russell** .................................. (502) 564-7760
Policy Advisor **Heather Combs** ..................... (502) 564-7760
General Administration and Program Services Executive
Director **Ray Perry** ............................ (502) 564-7320
E-mail: ray.perry@ky.gov
Communications and Legislative Affairs Executive
Director **Doug Hogan** ........................... (502) 564-5525
E-mail: doug.hogan@ky.gov
Public Information Officer **Ricki Gardenhire** ........... (502) 564-5525
E-mail: ricki.gardenhire@ky.gov
Office of Legal Services Executive Director **Peter Ervin** . . . (502) 564-7760
Office of Legal Services Deputy Executive Director
**LaTasha Buckner** .............................. (502) 564-7760
Staff Attorney **Cannon G. Armstrong** ............... (502) 564-7760
Executive Secretary **Laura Gillis** ................... (502) 564-7760
E-mail: laura.gillis@ky.gov

## Department of Alcoholic Beverage Control [ABC]

1003 Twilight Trail, Frankfort, KY 40601-1442
Tel: (502) 564-4850  Fax: (502) 564-7479  E-mail: abc.info@ky.gov

Commissioner **LTC Steven Edwards, USA (Ret)** ........ (502) 564-4850
Executive Secretary **Amy Hislope** .................. (502) 782-1020

General Counsel **Steve Humphress** .................. (502) 564-4850
Enforcement Director **Ed Robinson** .................. (502) 564-4850
Distilled Spirits Administrator **Tony Dehner**........... (502) 564-4850
Malt Beverage Administrator **(Vacant)** ............... (502) 564-4850

## Department of Charitable Gaming [DCG]

132 Brighton Park Boulevard, Frankfort, KY 40601-3714
Tel: (502) 573-5528  Tel: (800) 729-5672 (Toll Free)  Fax: (502) 573-6625
Internet: http://dcg.ky.gov

Commissioner **Scott T. Jones** ...................... (502) 573-5528
Deputy Commissioner **Elizabeth Whitehouse** .......... (502) 573-5528
Administrative Specialist **Cassie Proctor** ........ (502) 573-5528 ext. 224
Executive Assistant **Morgan Miller** ................. (502) 573-5528
Network Analyst **(Vacant)** ......................... (502) 573-5528
Enforcement Director **Bryant Smith** ................. (502) 573-5528
Licensing Branch Director **(Vacant)** ................. (502) 573-5528
General Counsel **Noelle Bailey** ..................... (502) 573-5528
Licensing and Compliance Director **Greg Rankin** ........ (502) 573-5528

## Department of Financial Institutions [DFI]

1025 Capital Center Drive, Suite 200, Frankfort, KY 40601
Tel: (502) 573-3390  Fax: (502) 573-8787  E-mail: kfi@ky.gov

Commissioner **Charles A. Vice** ................. (502) 573-3390 ext. 227
E-mail: charles.vice@ky.gov
Education: Southern Mississippi BS
Executive Assistant to the Commissioner
**Christina M. Hayden** .......................... (502) 573-3390
Deputy Commissioner **Sarah Butler** ............ (502) 573-3390 ext. 246
E-mail: sarah.butler@ky.gov
Consumer Complaints Ombudsman
**Garry Wright** ............................ (502) 573-3390 ext. 226
Depository Institutions Division Director
**Sarah Butler** ............................ (502) 573-3390 ext. 246
E-mail: sarah.butler@ky.gov
Public Information Officer **Kelly May** ........... (502) 573-3390 ext. 252
E-mail: kelly.may@ky.gov
Public Information Officer **Jennifer Doom** ....... (502) 573-3390 ext. 228
E-mail: jennifer.doom@ky.gov
Securities Division Director **Shonita Bossier** .....(502) 573-3390 ext. 280
Applications and Administration Support Branch
Manager **Brian K. Raley** ................... (502) 573-3390 ext. 269
E-mail: brian.raley@ky.gov
General Counsel **Jessica R. Sharpe** ............ (502) 573-3390 ext. 233
Education: Florida 1997 BS; North Carolina 2003 JD
Nondepository Institutions Division Director
**Tammy Scruggs** ............................... (502) 573-3390

## Department of Housing, Buildings and Construction [DHBC]

101 Sea Hero Road, Suite 100, Frankfort, KY 40601-5412
Tel: (502) 573-0365  Fax: (502) 573-1057

■Commissioner **Steve Milby** ....................... (502) 573-0373
E-mail: steve.milby@ky.gov
Deputy Commissioner **(Vacant)** .................... (502) 573-0365
General Counsel **(Vacant)** ......................... (502) 573-0365
Building Codes Enforcement Division Director
**Duane Curry** .................................. (502) 573-0373
E-mail: duane.curry@ky.gov      Fax: (502) 573-1059
Heating, Ventilating and Air Conditioning Assistant
Director (Acting) **Roger Banks** ................... (502) 573-0395
E-mail: roger.banks@ky.gov      Fax: (502) 573-1401
Plumbing Division Director **David J. Moore** .......... (502) 573-0397
E-mail: davidj.moore@ky.gov      Fax: (502) 573-1058
State Fire Marshal **William Swope, Jr.** .............. (502) 573-0382
E-mail: william.swope@ky.gov      Fax: (502) 573-1004
Program Coordinator **Shawnna McMichael** .......... (502) 573-0365

## Department of Insurance

215 West Main, Frankfort, KY 40601
P.O. Box 517, Frankfort, KY 40602
Tel: (502) 564-3630  Fax: (502) 564-1453

■Commissioner **H. Brian Maynard** .................. (502) 564-3630

---

★ Elected Official   ■ Appointed by Governor   ● Appointed by Legislature   ▲ Appointed by Board or Commission   ◆ Appointed by State Supreme Court

Deputy Commissioner **Maggie Woods** . . . . . . . . . . . . . . . .(502) 564-3630
  E-mail: maggie.woods@ky.gov
Agent Licensing Director **Kendra Thompson** . . . . . . . . . . (502) 564-6004
General Counsel **Michael R. Wilson** . . . . . . . . . . . . . . . . .(502) 564-3630
Communications Director **Ronda Sloan** . . . . . . . . . . . . . . (502) 564-6098
  E-mail: ronda.sloan@ky.gov
Consumer Protection Division Director **Ryan Helfenbein** . . (502) 564-6034
Financial Standards and Exam Division Director
  **Sandra Batts** . . . . . . . . . . . . . . . . . . . . . . . . . . . . . . (502) 564-6082
Health and Life Division Director **Matt Lockett** . . . . . . . . . (502) 564-6088
  E-mail: matt.lockett@ky.gov
Insurance Fraud Investigations Division Director
  **Dwayne F. Depp** . . . . . . . . . . . . . . . . . . . . . . . . . . . . (502) 564-1461
Property and Casualty Division Director
  **Robert Adelberg** . . . . . . . . . . . . . . . . . . . . . . . . . . . . (502) 564-6046
Administrative Services **Tim C. Miller** . . . . . . . . . . . . . . . (502) 564-3630
  E-mail: timc.miller@ky.gov
Staff Assistant **D. J. Wasson** . . . . . . . . . . . . . . . . . . . . . .(502) 564-3630

## Tourism, Arts and Heritage Cabinet

Capital Plaza Tower, 500 Mero Street, 24th Floor, Frankfort, KY 40601
Tel: (502) 564-4270  Fax: (502) 564-1512

**Employees:** 1,451  **Fiscal Year:** 2015  **Budget:** $342,918,000

■ Secretary **Don Parkinson** . . . . . . . . . . . . . . . . . . . . . . . . .(502) 564-4270
Deputy Secretary **Lindy Casebier** . . . . . . . . . . . . . . . . . . . (502) 564-4270
  Education: Louisville ME
Deputy Secretary **Matt Sawyers** . . . . . . . . . . . . . . . . . . . . (502) 564-4270
  Executive Assistant **(Vacant)** . . . . . . . . . . . . . . . . . . . . . (502) 564-4270
Legal Affairs Executive Director **William R. Dexter** . . . . . . (502) 564-4270
                                            Fax: (502) 564-1079
Arts and Cultural Heritage Office and Deputy Secretary
  **Lindy Casebier** . . . . . . . . . . . . . . . . . . . . . . . . . . . . . (502) 564-4270
Adventure Tourism Executive Director **Elaine Wilson** . . . . . (502) 564-4270
Communications Executive Director
  **Garry Gupton** . . . . . . . . . . . . . . . . . . . (502) 564-4270 ext. 415
  E-mail: garry.gupton@ky.gov
Financial Affairs Executive Director **Tim Pollard** . . . . . . . . (502) 564-4270
Human Resources Executive Director **(Vacant)** . . . . . . . . . (502) 564-4270
Research Director **Laura Negron** . . . . . . . . . . . . . . . . . . . .(502) 564-4270
  E-mail: laurar.negron@ky.gov
Intergovernmental Relations **(Vacant)** . . . . . . . . . . . . . . . (502) 564-4270

## Fish and Wildlife Resources Department

Arnold Mitchell Building, One Sportsman's Lane, Frankfort, KY 40601
Tel: (502) 564-3400  Fax: (502) 564-0506

**Fiscal Year:** 2015  **Budget:** $153,514,000

Commissioner **Gregory K. Johnson** . . . . . . . . . . . . . . . . . .(502) 564-3400
  Education: Eastern Kentucky 1979 BS
Deputy Commissioner **Charles Bush** . . . . . . . . . . . . . . . . . (502) 564-3400
Deputy Commissioner **Dr. Karen Waldrop** . . . . . . . . . . . . . (502) 564-3400
Administrative Services Director/Chief of Staff
  **Charles Dooker** . . . . . . . . . . . . . . . . . . . . . . . . . . . . . (502) 564-3400
  E-mail: charles.dooker@ag.ky.gov
Engineering Division Director **Keith Parker** . . . . . . . . . . . .(502) 564-5160
Fisheries Division Director **Ron Brooks** . . . . . . . . . . . . . . . (502) 564-3400
Information and Education Division Director **Tim Slone** . . (502) 564-3400
  E-mail: tim.slone@ky.gov
Law Enforcement Division Director **Rodney Coffey** . . . . . . (502) 564-3400
Public Affairs Division Director **Brian V. Blank** . . (502) 564-3400 ext. 4428
Wildlife Division Director **(Vacant)** . . . . . . . . . . . . . . . . . .(502) 564-3400
Human Resources Branch Manager **Pat Barnard** . . . . . . . . (502) 564-3400

## Kentucky Department of Parks

Capital Plaza Tower, 500 Mero Street, 10th Floor, Frankfort, KY 40601
Tel: (502) 564-8110  Fax: (502) 564-9015

Commissioner **Donnie Holland** . . . . . . . . . . . . . . . (502) 564-2172 ext. 153
  E-mail: donnie.holland@ky.gov
Executive Assistant **Deborah Cobb** . . . . . . . . . . . (502) 564-2172 ext. 205
Deputy Commissioner **(Vacant)** . . . . . . . . . . . . . (502) 564-2172 ext. 300
Assistant Director, Resort Division **Kevin Main** . . . (502) 564-2172 ext. 256
  E-mail: kevin.main@ky.gov

Assistant Director, Resort Division
  **David Thacker** . . . . . . . . . . . . . . . . . . . . . (502) 564-2172 ext. 203
  E-mail: david.thacker@ky.gov
Facilities Management Director **Bill Novak** . . . . . . . . . . . . .(502) 564-2172
Financial Operations Director
  **Robert "Rob" Richards** . . . . . . . . . . . . . . . . (502) 564-2172 ext. 336
Food Service Director **Thomas "Tom" Brown** . . . (502) 564-2172 ext. 213
  E-mail: thomas.brown@ky.gov
Historic Sites Director **Ron Vanover** . . . . . . . . . . . (502) 564-2172 ext. 491
Human Resources Director **Laurie Googe** . . . . . . . (502) 564-2172 ext. 315
  E-mail: laurie.googe@ky.gov
Sales and Marketing Director **LaDonna Miller** . . . . (502) 564-2172 ext. 306
  E-mail: ladonna.miller@ky.gov
Purchasing Director **Jennifer Portmann** . . . . . . . . (502) 564-2172 ext. 320
  E-mail: jennifer.portmann@ky.gov
Park Rangers Division Director **(Vacant)** . . . . . . . . . . . . . . (502) 564-2172
Recreation Director **Diane Bonfert** . . . . . . . . . . . . (502) 564-2172 ext. 216
  E-mail: diane.bonfert@ky.gov
Resort Parks Director **(Vacant)** . . . . . . . . . . . . . . (502) 564-2172 ext. 239

## Kentucky Department of Tourism and Travel

Capital Plaza Tower, 500 Mero Street, 22nd Floor, Frankfort, KY 40601
Tel: (502) 564-4930  Fax: (502) 564-5695  Tel: (800) 225-8747

**Fiscal Year:** 2015  **Budget:** $3,209,000

Commissioner **Mike Mangeot** . . . . . . . . . . . . . . . . (502) 564-4930 ext. 142
Deputy Commissioner **Mona Juett** . . . . . . . . . . . . (502) 564-4930 ext. 146
Executive Secretary **Meghan Greenwell** . . . . . . . . (502) 564-4930 ext. 142
Marketing and Advertising Director
  **Mike Mangeot** . . . . . . . . . . . . . . . . . . . . . (502) 564-4930 ext. 142
Tourism Services Assistant Director
  **Kathy Yount** . . . . . . . . . . . . . . . . . . . . . . . (502) 564-4930 ext. 120
Cultural-Heritage Tourism Staff Assistant
  **Kimberly Clay** . . . . . . . . . . . . . . . . . . . . . . (502) 564-4930 ext. 119

## Kentucky Historical Society

100 West Broadway, Frankfort, KY 40601-1931
Tel: (502) 564-1792  Fax: (502) 564-4701

Executive Director **Kent Whitworth** . . . . . . . . . . . (502) 564-1792 ext. 4448
Deputy Director **Scott Alvey** . . . . . . . . . . . . . . . . (502) 564-1792 ext. 4498
Operations Director **Linda Redmon** . . . . . . . . . . . (502) 564-1792 ext. 4447
Historical Resources Director **Trevor Jones** . . . . . (502) 564-1792 ext. 4477
Learning Services Director **Scott Alvey** . . . . . . . . (502) 564-1792 ext. 4498
Marketing Communications Director
  **Laurel Harper** . . . . . . . . . . . . . . . . . . . . . . .(502) 564-1792 ext. 4489
  E-mail: laurel.harper@ky.gov
Research Experience Director **Louise Jones** . . . . (502) 564-1792 ext. 4407
Human Resources and Intern Administrator
  **Pam Brookman** . . . . . . . . . . . . . . . . . . . . . . (502) 564-1792 ext. 4409
Oral History Administrator **Allison Tracy** . . . . . . . . . . . . . .(502) 564-1792
  E-mail: allison.tracy@ky.gov
Professional Services Administrator
  **Stuart Sanders** . . . . . . . . . . . . . . . . . . . . . . (502) 564-1792 ext. 4420
Security and Planning Administrator
  **Corky Mohedano** . . . . . . . . . . . . . . . . . . . . .(502) 564-1792 ext. 4456
Visitor Services Manager **Phyllis Gilman** . . . . . . . (502) 564-1792 ext. 4422
  E-mail: phyllis.gilman@ky.gov
Historymobile and Museums-to-Go Program
  Coordinator **Kate Sowada** . . . . . . . . . . . . . . (502) 564-1792 ext. 4478
  E-mail: kate.sowada@ky.gov
Highway Markers Program Coordinator
  **Becky Riddle** . . . . . . . . . . . . . . . . . . . . . . . (502) 564-1792 ext. 4474
  E-mail: becky.riddle@ky.gov
Volunteer Coordinator **Samantha LaMar** . . . . . . . . . . . . . (502) 564-1792
  E-mail: samantha.lamar@ky.gov
"The Register" Editor **David Turpie** . . . . . . . . . . . (502) 564-1792 ext. 4435
  Education: U Memphis 2004 MA; Maine 2010 PhD

---

★ Elected Official    ■ Appointed by Governor    ● Appointed by Legislature    ▲ Appointed by Board or Commission    ◆ Appointed by State Supreme Court

EXECUTIVE BRANCH

# Kentucky Transportation Cabinet [KYTC]

Transportation Office Building, 200 Mero Street, Frankfort, KY 40622
Tel: (502) 564-4890  Fax: (502) 564-9540

**Employees:** 4,170

■Secretary **Greg Thomas** .......................... (502) 564-5102
 E-mail: greg.thomas@ky.gov
 Education: Tennessee 1984 BME
Deputy Secretary **(Vacant)** .......................... (502) 564-5102
Chief of Staff **Cindy James** ......................... (502) 564-5102
General Counsel **(Vacant)** .......................... (502) 564-7650
Audits Executive Director **(Vacant)** ............... (502) 564-6760
Civil Rights and Small Business Development Office
 Executive Director **Tyra Redus** ................ (502) 564-3601
Human Resource Management Office Executive Director
 **Carol Beth Martin** ............................... (502) 564-4610
Information Technology Executive Director
 **Heather Stout** .................................... (502) 564-8900
 E-mail: heather.stout@ky.gov
Inspector General Executive Director **Ben McKown** ...... (502) 564-0501
 E-mail: ben.mckown@ky.gov
Public Affairs Executive Director **Chuck Wolfe** ......... (502) 564-3419
 E-mail: chuck.wolfe@ky.gov        Fax: (502) 564-4809
Transportation Delivery Executive Director
 **Vickie Bourne** ................................... (502) 564-7433
Support Services Executive Director **Pat Grugin** ........ (502) 564-3040
 E-mail: pat.grugin@ky.gov

## Office of Budget and Fiscal Management

Transportation Cabinet Building, 200 Mero Street, Floor 6,
Frankfort, KY 40622
Tel: (502) 564-4550

Executive Director and Chief Financial Officer
 **Robin Brewer** .................................... (502) 564-4550
Accounts Division Director **Ronnie O'Nan** .......... (502) 564-7334
Purchases Division Director **Ben McCray** ............ (502) 564-4630

## Aviation Department

Commissioner **R. Winn Turney** ..................... (502) 564-4480

## Highways Department

Tel: (502) 564-3730

**Fiscal Year:** 2015  **Budget:** $2,973,512,000

State Highway Engineer **Patty Dunaway** .............. (502) 564-3730
 E-mail: patty.dunaway@ky.gov

## Rural and Municipal Aid Department

Commissioner **Don Pasley** .................. (502) 564-2060 ext. 3052

## Vehicle Regulation Department

Tel: (502) 564-1257

**Fiscal Year:** 2015  **Budget:** $52,248,000

Commissioner **John-Mark Hack** ............. (502) 564-7000 ext. 4269
 Education: Transylvania 1988 BA
Deputy Commissioner **Rick Taylor** ........... (502) 564-7000 ext. 4243
 E-mail: rick.taylor@ky.gov
Customer Service Division Director
 **Marty Greer** .................... (502) 564-7000 ext. 4256
 E-mail: marty.greer@ky.gov
Driver Licensing Division Director
 **Carolyn Brown** .................. (502) 564-7000 ext. 4222
 E-mail: carolyn.brown@ky.gov
Motor Carriers Division Director
 **Martin Mathews** ................. (502) 564-7000 ext. 4167
 E-mail: martin.mathews@ky.gov
Motor Vehicle Licensing Division Director **Paul Mauer** ... (502) 564-1257
 E-mail: paul.mauer@ky.gov

# Executive Branch Ethics Commission

Three Fountain Place, Frankfort, KY 40601
Tel: (502) 564-7954  Fax: (502) 564-2686  Internet: http://ethics.ky.gov

Chair **William David Denton** ...................... (502) 564-7954
 Education: Murray State Col 1964 BS; Kentucky 1969 JD
■Vice Chair **William G. Francis** .................... (502) 564-7954
Member **Martin E. Johnstone** ..................... (502) 564-7954
 Education: Western Kentucky 1971 BA; Louisville 1975 JD
■Member **Richard L. Masters** ..................... (502) 564-7954
Member **Lewis G. Paisley** ......................... (502) 564-7954
 Education: Georgetown; Kentucky JD
Executive Director (Interim)
 **Kathryn H. "Katie" Gabhart** .................. (502) 564-7954

# State Board of Accountancy

332 West Broadway, Suite 310, Louisville, KY 40202
Tel: (502) 595-3037  Fax: (502) 595-4500  E-mail: cpa@ky.gov
Internet: http://cpa.ky.gov

■Member **Margaret D. Combs** ..................... (502) 595-3037
 Term Expires: June 30, 2018
■Member **Kevin M. Doyle, CPA** ................... (502) 595-3037
 Term Expires: June 30, 2016
■Member **Joseph A. Hancock, CPA** ............... (502) 595-3037
 Term Expires: June 30, 2016
■Member **Jamie R. Laws, CPA** .................... (502) 595-3037
 Term Expires: June 30, 2017
■Member **Phillip M. Layne, CPA** .................. (502) 595-3037
 Term Expires: June 30, 2017
■Member **Lori Dawn Warden** ..................... (502) 595-3037
 Term Expires: June 30, 2018
■Citizen Member **Toni R. Carver Smith** ............ (502) 595-3037
 Note: Citizen Member
 Term Expires: June 30, 2016

# State Board of Elections

140 Walnut Street, Frankfort, KY 40601
Tel: (502) 573-7100  Fax: (502) 573-4369  Internet: www.elect.ky.gov

**Fiscal Year:** 2015  **Budget:** $19,889,000

Chairman **Alison Grimes** .......................... (502) 573-7100
 Affiliation: Secretary of State, Office of the Secretary of State,
 Commonwealth of Kentucky
 P.O. Box 718, Frankfort, KY 40601
 Education: Rhodes 2001 BS; Washington College of Law 2004 JD
■Member **Donald W. "Don" Blevins, Jr.** ............ (502) 573-7100
 Term Expires: September 15, 2018
 Education: Kentucky 1959 BS
Member **Albert Benjamin "Ben" Chandler III** ........ (502) 573-7100
 Term Expires: September 15, 2018
■Member **Joshua Branscum** ...................... (502) 573-7100
■Member **John W. Hampton** ...................... (502) 573-7100
 Term Expires: April 1, 2016
■Member **Stephen Huffman** ...................... (502) 573-7100
 Term Expires: September 15, 2018
■Member **George W. Russell** ..................... (502) 573-7100
 Term Expires: April 1, 2016
Executive Director **Maryellen Allen** ............... (502) 573-7100
 E-mail: maryellen.allen@ky.gov

# Office of the State Budget Director

Capitol Annex, 702 Capital Avenue, Suite 284, Frankfort, KY 40601
Tel: (502) 564-7300  Internet: www.osbd.ky.gov

**Fiscal Year:** 2015  **Budget:** $3,649,000

State Budget Director **John Chilton** ................ (502) 564-7300

---

★ Elected Official   ■ Appointed by Governor   ● Appointed by Legislature   ▲ Appointed by Board or Commission   ◆ Appointed by State Supreme Court

# Department for Local Government [DLG]

1024 Capital Center Drive, Suite 340, Frankfort, KY 40601
Tel: (502) 573-2382  Tel: (800) 346-5606 (Toll Free)  Fax: (502) 573-2939
Internet: www.dlg.ky.gov

**Fiscal Year:** 2015  **Budget:** $47,802,000

■Commissioner **Sandra K. "Sandy" Dunahoo** . . . . . . . . . . .(502) 573-2382
  E-mail: sandy.dunahoo@ky.gov
  Assistant to the Commissioner **Mary Palmer** . . . . . . . . . (800) 573-2382
Chief of Staff **Russell L. "Russ" Salsman** . . . . . . . . . . . .(502) 573-2382
Deputy Chief of Staff **(Vacant)** . . . . . . . . . . . . . . . . . . . . .(502) 573-2382
Staff Attorney **Darren Sammons** . . . . . . . . . . . . . . . . . . . .(502) 573-2382
Financial Management and Administration Executive
  Staff Advisor **Todd Kirby** . . . . . . . . . . . . . . . . . . . . . . . (800) 573-2382
    E-mail: todd.kirby@ky.gov
    Administration Branch Manager **Melinda Parrish** . . . . . .(800) 573-2382
      E-mail: melinda.parrish@ky.gov
Federal Grants Office Executive Director **(Vacant)** . . . . . . .(502) 573-2382
  Federal Grants Staff Assistant **Peggy Satterly** . . .(502) 573-2382 ext. 250
State Local Debt Officer/State Local Finance Officer
  **(Vacant)** . . . . . . . . . . . . . . . . . . . . . . . . . . . . . . . . . . (502) 573-2382

# Kentucky Infrastructure Authority

1024 Capital Center Drive, Suite 340, Frankfort, KY 40601
Tel: (502) 573-0260  Fax: (502) 573-0157  Internet: http://kia.ky.gov

**Fiscal Year:** 2015  **Budget:** $31,590,000

Executive Director **(Vacant)** . . . . . . . . . . . . . . . . . . . . . . .(502) 573-0260

# Kentucky Office of Homeland Security [KOHS]

200 Mero Street, Frankfort, KY 40622
Tel: (502) 564-2081  Fax: (502) 564-7764
Internet: http://homelandsecurity.ky.gov

■Executive Director **John Holiday** . . . . . . . . . . . . . . . . . . .(502) 564-2081
  E-mail: john.holiday@ky.gov

# Department of Military Affairs [DMA]

Boone National Guard Center, 100 Minuteman Parkway,
Frankfort, KY 40601
Fax: (502) 607-1271  Internet: dma.ky.gov

Adjutant General **BrigGen Stephen R. Hogan, ANG** . . . . .(502) 607-1558
  E-mail: stephen.hogan@ag.ky.gov
  Chief of Staff **COL Benjamin Adams, ARNG** . . . . . . . . .(502) 607-1494
Deputy Adjutant General (Army)
  **COL Charlie Jones, ARNG** . . . . . . . . . . . . . . . . . . . . . .(502) 607-1257
  Aviation Director **LtCol Mike Stevens, ANG** . . . . . . . . . .(502) 607-1471
  Information Management Director
    **LTC Todd Ewing, ARNG** . . . . . . . . . . . . . . . . . . . . . .(502) 607-1561
      E-mail: todd.ewing@ag.ky.gov
  Logistics and Operations Director
    **LTC Mike Ferguson, ARNG** . . . . . . . . . . . . . . . . . . . .(502) 607-1763
  Military Personnel Director **COL Mike Abel, ARNG** . . . .(502) 607-1265
  Facilities Management Officer
    **LTC Steven King, ARNG** . . . . . . . . . . . . . . . . . . . . . .(502) 607-1874
  Public Affairs Officer **LtCol Kirk Hilbrecht, ANG** . . . . . .(502) 607-1556
Management and Administration Office Executive
  Director **COL Mike Jones, USA (Ret)** . . . . . . . . . . . . . .(502) 607-1529
    E-mail: mike.jones@ky.gov
  Administrative Services Division Director
    **Steve Bullard** . . . . . . . . . . . . . . . . . . . . . . . . . . . . . .(502) 607-1738
      E-mail: steven.bullard@ag.ky.gov
  Bluegrass Station Division Director
    **BG Stephen D. Collins, ARNG** . . . . . . . . . . . . . . . . . .(859) 293-4212
                                                            Fax: (859) 293-4215
  Emergency Management Division Executive Director
    **Michael Dossett** . . . . . . . . . . . . . . . . . . . . . . . . . . . .(502) 607-1680
                                                            Fax: (502) 607-1251
  Facilities Division Director **Joseph Sanderson** . . . . . . . .(502) 607-1536
                                                            Fax: (502) 607-1270
  Kentucky Guard Youth Challenge Division Director
    **Patrick "Pat" Yewell** . . . . . . . . . . . . . . . . . . . . . . . .(502) 564-0494

Kentucky Community Crisis Response Board Executive
  Director **Debborah M. "Debra" Arnold** . . . . . . . . . . . .(502) 607-5781
  612-B Shelby Street, Frankfort, KY 40601        Fax: (502) 607-5780

# Kentucky Commission on Military Affairs [KCMA]

700 Capitol Avenue, Frankfort, KY 40601
Tel: (502) 564-2611  Fax: (502) 564-2853

■Chair **COL David E. Thompson, USA (Ret)** . . . . . . . . . . .(502) 564-2611
  Education: Central Michigan MA
■Vice Chair **MG Terry Lee Tucker, USA (Ret)** . . . .(502) 564-2611 ext. 302
■Member **Clarissa J. "T. C." Freeman** . . . . . . . . . .(502) 564-2611 ext. 302
■Member **Heather Renee French Henry** . . . . . . . . . . . . . . .(502) 564-9203
  E-mail: heather.henry@ag.ky.gov
  Education: Cincinnati 1997 BS, 2001 MA
■Member **Hugh A. Haydon** . . . . . . . . . . . . . . . . . .(502) 564-2611 ext. 302
  E-mail: hugh.haydon@ag.ky.gov
■Member **BrigGen Stephen R. Hogan, ANG** . . . . . . . . . . .(502) 607-1558
■Member **Richard Johnson** . . . . . . . . . . . . . . . . . .(502) 564-2611 ext. 302
  E-mail: richard.johnson@ag.ky.gov
■Member
  **MG Robert S. Silverthorn, Jr., USA (Ret)** . . . .(502) 564-2611 ext. 302
    E-mail: robert.silverthorn@ag.ky.gov
■Executive Director
  **COL David E. Thompson, USA (Ret)** . . . . . . . . . . . . . .(502) 564-2611
    E-mail: david.thompson@ky.gov

# Office of the Lieutenant Governor

700 Capital Avenue, Suite 142, Frankfort, KY 40601
Tel: (502) 564-2611  TTY: (502) 564-9551  Fax: (502) 564-2849
E-mail: feedback@mattbevin.com  Internet: ltgovernor.ky.gov

★Lieutenant Governor **Jenean Hampton** (R) . . . . . . . . . . . .(502) 564-2611
  Term Expires: December 2019
  Education: Wayne State U 1985 BIE; Rochester
  Career: Officer, Capt, United States Air Force, United States
  Department of the Air Force (1985-1992)
Chief of Staff **Stephen "Steve" Knipper** . . . . . . . . . . . . . .(502) 564-2611
Deputy Chief of Staff **Adrienne Southworth** . . . . . . . . . .(502) 564-2611

# Office of the Attorney General

700 Capitol Avenue, Suite 118, Frankfort, KY 40601
Tel: (502) 696-5300  Internet: ag.ky.gov

**Fiscal Year:** 2015  **Budget:** $41,186,000

★Attorney General **Andrew G. "Andy" Beshear** (D) . . . . . .(502) 696-5300
  Term Expires: January 2020
  Education: Vanderbilt 2000 BA; Virginia 2003 JD
  Career: Attorney, White & Case LLP (2003-2010)
Criminal Branch Deputy Attorney General
  **J. Michael Brown** . . . . . . . . . . . . . . . . . . . . . . . . . . . .(502) 696-5300
    Education: CCNY 1970 BA; Louisville 1979 JD
Civil Branch Deputy Attorney General
  **Mitchel T. Denham** . . . . . . . . . . . . . . . . . . . . . . . . . . .(502) 696-5300
Family Branch Deputy Attorney General
  **Maryellen B. Mynear** . . . . . . . . . . . . . . . . . . . . . . . . .(502) 696-5300
    E-mail: maryellen.mynear@ky.gov
Communications Director **Terry Sebastian**
  Deputy Communications Director
    **Crystal Pryor Staley** . . . . . . . . . . . . . . . . . . . . . . . . .(502) 696-5300

# Office of Civil and Environmental Law

State Capitol, 700 Capitol Avenue, Suite 118, Frankfort, KY 40601
Fax: (502) 564-2894

Executive Director **La Tasha Buckner** . . . . . . . . . . . . . . . .(502) 696-5300
Assistant Director **Ryan Halloran** . . . . . . . . . . . . . . . . . . .(502) 696-5300
Uninsured Employers' Fund Manager **James Carpenter** . .(502) 696-5321
  1024 Capitol Center Drive, Frankfort, KY 40601        Fax: (502) 573-8346

# Office of Consumer Protection

1024 Capital Center Drive, Frankfort, KY 40601
Tel: (888) 432-9257 (Consumer Protection)  Fax: (502) 573-8317

Executive Director **Todd Leatherman** . . . . . . . . . . . . . . . .(502) 696-5389

*(continued on next page)*

---

★ Elected Official    ■ Appointed by Governor    ● Appointed by Legislature    ▲ Appointed by Board or Commission    ◆ Appointed by State Supreme Court

EXECUTIVE BRANCH

**Office of Consumer Protection** *continued*

Cemetery and Funeral Home Branch Manager (Acting)
  **Kim Bellamy** ........................ (502) 696-5389
Compliance and Registration Branch Manager
  **Kim Bellamy** ........................ (502) 696-5389
Investigation and Litigation Branch Manager **(Vacant)** .... (502) 696-5389
Louisville Consumer Resource Branch Manager
  **Don W. Rodgers** ..................... (502) 429-7134
  310 Whittington Parkway, Suite 101,         Fax: (502) 429-7129
  Louisville, KY 40222
Mediation Branch Manager **Lori Farris** ............... (502) 696-5389

## Office of Criminal Appeals

1024 Capital Center Drive, Frankfort, KY 40601
Fax: (502) 696-5533

Executive Director **Vickie Wise** ...................... (502) 696-5342
Appellate Branch A Manager **Robert Long** ............. (502) 696-5342
Appellate Branch B Manager **Todd Ferguson** ........... (502) 696-5342
Appellate Branch C Manager **Kenneth Riggs** .......... (502) 696-5342

## Office of Victims' Advocacy

1024 Capital Center Drive, Frankfort, KY 40601
Fax: (502) 573-8315  Tel: (800) 372-2551 (Crime Victims' Information)
Director **Gretchen Hunt** .......................... (502) 696-5312

## Rate Intervention Office

1024 Capital Center Drive, Frankfort, KY 40601
Fax: (502) 573-8315

Director **Rebecca Goodman** ....................... (502) 696-5453
Assistant Director **(Vacant)** ....................... (502) 696-5453

## Department of Criminal Investigations [DCI]

1024 Capital Center Drive, Frankfort, KY 40601
Fax: (502) 573-8319

Commissioner **John Moberly** ....................... (502) 696-5367
Cyber Crime Branch Manager **William Baker** .......... (502) 696-5367
  E-mail: william.baker@ky.gov
Drug Investigations Branch Manager
  **Jennifer Shearer Carpenter** ..................... (502) 696-5367
Public Corruption and Special Investigations Manager
  **George Wilding** ................................ (502) 696-5367

## Administrative Services Division

700 Capitol Avenue, Suite 34, Frankfort, KY 40601
Fax: (502) 564-8735

Director **Holly McCoy-Johnson** ..................... (502) 696-5300
  E-mail: holly.mccoyjohnson@ag.ky.gov
Scheduling and Special Projects Director **Susan Rieber** ... (502) 696-5300
  E-mail: susan.rieber@ky.gov
Payroll Administrator/Benefits Coordinator
  **Kim McGaughey** ................................ (502) 696-5300
Personnel Administrator **Maureen Travers** ............. (502) 696-5300
Chief Financial Officer **Larry Clarke** ................. (502) 696-5300

## Medicaid Fraud and Abuse Control Division

1024 Capital Center Drive, Frankfort, KY 40601
Tel: (502) 696-5405  Fax: (502) 573-8316

Director **Michael Wright** .......................... (502) 696-5405
Fraud and Abuse Control Investigations Manager
  **(Vacant)** ...................................... (502) 696-5405
Litigation Branch Manager (Acting) **Michelle Rudovich** .. (502) 696-5405

## Special Prosecutions Division

1024 Capital Center Drive, Frankfort, KY 40601
Fax: (502) 573-1637  Tel: (800) 328-8683 (Election Fraud)
Director **Shawna Kincer** ........................... (502) 696-5337
Assistant Director **(Vacant)** ........................ (502) 696-5337

## Office of the Secretary of State

700 Capital Avenue, Suite 152, Frankfort, KY 40601
P.O. Box 718, Frankfort, KY 40601
Tel: (502) 564-3490  Fax: (502) 564-5687

★Secretary of State **Alison Grimes** (D) ................. (502) 564-3490
  Term Expires: January 2020
Assistant Secretary of State **Lindsay Hughes Thurston** ... (502) 564-3490
Administration and Elections Director **Mary Sue Helm** ... (502) 564-3490
  E-mail: marysue.helm@ky.gov
Communications Director **(Vacant)** ................... (502) 564-3490
Apostilles/Authentications and Trademarks
  **Johnna Ballinger** .............................. (502) 564-3490
Computer Division **Jeshua "Jesh" Caudle** ............. (502) 564-3490
  E-mail: jeshua.caudle@ky.gov
State Land Office **Kandie Adkinson** .................. (502) 564-3490
  E-mail: kandie.adkinson@ky.gov
Uniform Commercial Code Office **Michelle Mullins** ...... (502) 564-3490
Notary Commissions **(Vacant)** ...................... (502) 564-3490
Annual Reports **Donna Williams** .................... (502) 564-3490

## Office of the State Treasurer

1050 US Highway 127 South, Suite 100, Frankfort, KY 40601
Tel: (502) 564-4722  Fax: (502) 564-6545  E-mail: treasury.web@ky.gov
Internet: http://www.kytreasury.com/

**Fiscal Year:** 2015  **Budget:** $3,318,000

★State Treasurer **Allison Ball** (R) ..................... (502) 564-4722
  Term Expires: January 2020
Chief of Staff **Janet Cuthrell** ...................... (502) 564-4722
Communications Director **OJ Oleka** ................. (502) 564-4722
  E-mail: oj.oleka@ky.gov
Disbursements and Accounting Director **Dennis Paiva** ... (502) 564-4722
General Counsel **Noah Friend** ...................... (502) 564-4722

## Kentucky Lottery

1011 West Main Street, Louisville, KY 40202
Tel: (502) 560-1500  Fax: (502) 560-1533  Internet: www.kylottery.com

President and Chief Executive Officer
  **Arthur L. Gleason, Jr.** .......................... (502) 560-1551
  Education: John Carroll 1969 BSBA
Chief Financial Officer **Howard Kline** ................ (502) 560-1755
Chief Operating Officer **Margaret "Marty" Gibbs** ....... (502) 560-1552
Communications, Government and Public Relations Vice
  President **Chip Polston** ......................... (502) 560-1675
  E-mail: chip.polston@kylottery.com
  Education: Western Kentucky BA; Louisville ME
Security Vice President **Bill Hickerson** ............... (502) 560-1805
                                        Fax: (502) 560-1535
Legal Counsel **Mary Harville** ....................... (502) 560-1576

## Office of the Auditor of Public Accounts

209 Saint Clair Street, Frankfort, KY 40601-1817
Tel: (502) 564-5841  Internet: auditor.ky.gov

★Auditor of Public Accounts **Mike Harmon** (R) .......... (502) 564-5841
  Term Expires: January 2020
  Education: Eastern Kentucky BS
  Executive Assistant to the Auditor **Brian Darnell** ....... (502) 564-5841
  Assistant to the Auditor **Alta Renfro** ............... (502) 564-5841
Assistant State Auditor **Alice Wilson** ................. (502) 564-5841
Chief of Staff **Ginger Wills** ........................ (502) 564-5841
General Counsel **Sara Beth Gregory** ................. (502) 564-5841
  Education: Kentucky 2007 JD
  Executive Assistant to the Chief of Staff and General
    Counsel **Melissa Scott** ........................ (502) 564-5841
Technology and Special Audits Office Director
  **Libby Carlin, CPA** ............................. (502) 564-5841
Financial Audits Office Deputy Director **James Royse** .... (502) 564-5841
  Education: Kentucky BSAcc
Communications Director **Michael Goins** .............. (502) 564-5841
  E-mail: michael.goins@ky.gov

---

★ Elected Official   ■ Appointed by Governor   ● Appointed by Legislature   ▲ Appointed by Board or Commission   ◆ Appointed by State Supreme Court

Chief Operating Officer and Open Records Administrator
  **Gregory Giesler** . . . . . . . . . . . . . . . . . . . . . . . . . . . . . (502) 564-5841

# Kentucky Department of Agriculture [KDA]

111 Corporate Drive, Frankfort, KY 40601
Tel: (502) 564-4696  Fax: (502) 564-0046  TTY: (502) 564-2075
Internet: www.kyagr.com

**Fiscal Year:** 2015  **Budget:** $43,729,000

★ Commissioner **Ryan F. Quarles** (R) . . . . . . . . . . . . . . . . . . (502) 573-0450
  Term Expires: 2020
Deputy Commissioner **Steve Kelly** . . . . . . . . . . . . . . . . . (502) 564-4696
Chief of Staff **Keith Rogers** . . . . . . . . . . . . . . . . . . . . . . . .(502) 573-0450
  Education: Asbury Col 1991 BA

## Agricultural Marketing and Product Promotion Office

Executive Director **(Vacant)** . . . . . . . . . . . . . . . . . . . . . . . .(502) 564-4698
Deputy Executive Director **Tim Hughes** . . . . . . . . . . . . . . .(502) 564-4698
  E-mail: tim.hughes@ky.gov
  Education: Western Kentucky
Agriculture Education and Farmland Preservation
  Division Assistant Director **(Vacant)** . . . . . . . . . . . . . . . . (502) 564-4983
Agriculture Marketing and Agribusiness Recruitment
  Division Director **Ben Shaffar** . . . . . . . . . . . . . . . . . . . . . (502) 564-4696
Agritourism Division Director **Amelia Wilson** . . . . . . . . . .(502) 564-4696
Show and Fair Promotion Division Director
  **Chris Caudill** . . . . . . . . . . . . . . . . . . . . . . . . . . . . . . . . . (502) 564-4983
Value-Added Animal and Aquaculture Production Deputy
  Executive Director **(Vacant)** . . . . . . . . . . . . . . . . . . . . . . (502) 564-4983
Value-Added Plant Production Division Director (Acting)
  **Kristen Branscum** . . . . . . . . . . . . . . . . . . . . . . . . . . . . . .(502) 564-4696

## Consumer and Environmental Protection Office

Fax: (502) 573-0303

Executive Director **John Cook** . . . . . . . . . . . . . . . . . . . . . . .(502) 573-0282
Environmental Services Division Director **David Wayne** . . .(502) 573-0282
Food Distribution Division Director **Bill Wickliffe** . . . . . . . . (502) 573-0282
Regulation and Inspection Division Director
  **David Wayne** . . . . . . . . . . . . . . . . . . . . . . . . . . . . . . . . . (502) 573-0282

## State Veterinarian's Office

Fax: (502) 564-7852

State Veterinarian **Robert Stout** . . . . . . . . . . . . . . . . . . . . . (502) 564-3956
Deputy State Veterinarian **Dr. Bradley A. Keough** . . . . . . . .(502) 564-3956
Producer Services Division Director **David Hillard** . . . . . . . (502) 564-3956

## Strategic Planning and Administration Office

Fax: (502) 564-2133

Executive Director **Kem Delaney-Ellis** . . . . . . . . . . . . . . . . (502) 564-1133
Deputy Executive Director **Fred Nesler** . . . . . . . . . . . . . . . (502) 564-1133
  E-mail: fred.nesler@ky.gov
Information Technology Division Director
  **Kathy Harp-Willis** . . . . . . . . . . . . . . . . . . . . . . . . . . . . . (502) 564-1147
  E-mail: kathy.harp@ky.gov
Personnel and Budget Division Director **(Vacant)** . . . . . . . .(502) 564-1144

# Louisiana

Tel: (225) 342-6600 (State Operator)  Internet: www.louisiana.gov

**Number of U.S. Congressional Delegates:** 2 Senators; 6 Representatives  **Governor's Term:** 4 years
**Legislature Description:** 39 member Senate; 105 member House of Representatives; Term- Senate 4
years, House 4 years  **Next Election:** Governor November 2019; Legislature November 2019
**Number of Electoral Votes:** 8  **Official Name:** State of Louisiana (after Louis XIV of France)
**Nickname:** The Pelican State  **Motto:** Union, Justice and Confidence

**Population:** 4,670,724 (2015); Rank 25  **Fiscal Year:** 2014  **Budget:** $24,757,734,859

## Office of the Governor

P.O. Box 94004, Baton Rouge, LA 70804-9004
Tel: (225) 342-7015  Fax: (225) 342-7099

**John Bel Edwards**
Governor

Began Service: January 11, 2016
Term Expires: January 2020
Date of Birth: September 16, 1966
Education: West Point 1988 BS;
LSU Hebert Law 1999 JD
Home: Amite
Religion: Roman Catholic

★Governor **John Bel Edwards** (D) . . . . . . . . . . . . . . . . . . . (225) 342-7015
  Senior Special Assistant to the Governor
    **Alicia Williams** . . . . . . . . . . . . . . . . . . . . . . . . . . . (225) 342-7015
    E-mail: alicia.williams@la.gov
    Education: Grambling State 1983 BA
  Special Assistant to the Governor **Roderick Scott** . . . . . . (225) 342-7015
    E-mail: roderick.scott@la.gov
    Education: Southern U A&M
  Executive Assistant to the Governor **Roz Moore** . . . . . . . . (225) 342-7015
  Chief of Staff **Ben Nevers** . . . . . . . . . . . . . . . . . . . . . . . . (225) 342-7015
    Education: Louisiana Tech Col 1969 AS
  Deputy Chief of Staff for Communication, Legal, and
    Special Projects **Julie Baxter Payer** . . . . . . . . . . . . (225) 342-7015
  Deputy Chief of Staff for Intergovernmental Affairs
    **M. E. "Toye" Taylor** . . . . . . . . . . . . . . . . . . . . . . . . (225) 342-7015
    E-mail: toye.taylor@la.gov
  Deputy Chief of Staff for Programs and Planning
    **Johnny Anderson** . . . . . . . . . . . . . . . . . . . . . . . . . . (225) 342-7015
    E-mail: johnny.anderson@la.gov
    Education: Southern U (New Orleans) 1984 BS
  Communications Director **Richard Carbo** . . . . . . . . . . . . . . (225) 342-7015
    Education: LSU 2006 BA
  Digital Director **Micah Caswell** . . . . . . . . . . . . . . . . . . . (225) 342-7015
  Press Secretary **Shauna Sanford** . . . . . . . . . . . . . . . . . . . (225) 342-7015
    Education: Howard Col BS
  Constituent Services Director **Kim LaCour** . . . . . . . . . . . . (225) 342-7015
    E-mail: kim.lacour2@la.gov
  Legislative Affairs Director **Noble E. Ellington** . . . . . . . . (225) 342-7015
    E-mail: noble.ellington@la.gov
    Education: Louisiana Tech U BS
  Scheduling Director **Katie Kirkpatrick Justice** . . . . . . . . . (225) 342-7015
    E-mail: katie.justice@la.gov
  Executive Counsel **Matthew Block** . . . . . . . . . . . . . . . . . . (225) 342-7015
    E-mail: matthew.block@la.gov
    Deputy Executive Counsel **Emalie Boyce** . . . . . . . . . . . (225) 342-7015
  Special Counsel and Policy Director
    **Erin Monroe Wesley** . . . . . . . . . . . . . . . . . . . . . . . . (225) 342-7015
    E-mail: erin.monroewesley@la.gov
  Senior Policy Advisor **Richard Hartley** . . . . . . . . . . . . . . . (225) 342-7015
  Programs and Planning Coordinator **Bruce Parker** . . . . . . (225) 342-7015
    E-mail: bruce.parker@la.gov
  Director of Drug Policy **Chaunda Allen Mitchell** . . . . . . . (225) 342-7015
    E-mail: chaunda.mitchell@la.gov

## Governor's Office of Homeland Security and Emergency Preparedness [GOHSEP]

7667 Independence Boulevard, Baton Rouge, LA 70806
Tel: (225) 925-7500  Fax: (225) 925-7501

■Director **James Waskom** . . . . . . . . . . . . . . . . . . . . . . . . . (225) 925-7345
  E-mail: james.waskom@la.gov
Chief of Staff **William Rachal** . . . . . . . . . . . . . . . . . . . . . (225) 925-7345
Deputy Director for Grants and Administration
  **Christina Dayries** . . . . . . . . . . . . . . . . . . . . . . . . . (225) 358-5599
  E-mail: christina.dayries@la.gov
Deputy Director for Disaster Recovery **Mark S. Riley** . . . . . (225) 376-5493
Deputy Director for Preparedness, Response and
  Interoperability **Chris Guilbeaux** . . . . . . . . . . . . . . . . (225) 925-7333
  E-mail: christopher.guilbeaux@la.gov
Assistant Deputy Director for Grants and Administration
  **Sean Wyatt** . . . . . . . . . . . . . . . . . . . . . . . . . . . . . . (225) 925-1800
  E-mail: sean.wyatt@la.gov
Assistant Deputy Director for Hazard Mitigation
  **Casey Tingle** . . . . . . . . . . . . . . . . . . . . . . . . . . . . . (225) 389-2403
Assistant Deputy Director for Preparedness, Response
  and Interoperability **Kevin Breaux** . . . . . . . . . . . . . . . (225) 925-3506
Assistant Deputy Director for Public Assistance
  **Mark Debosier** . . . . . . . . . . . . . . . . . . . . . . . . . . . . (225) 338-6782
Executive Officer for Public Assistance **Lynne Browning** . . (225) 338-7342
Executive Counsel **Danielle Aymond** . . . . . . . . . . . . . . . . . (225) 925-7541
Executive Assistant **Toni Cyrus** . . . . . . . . . . . . . . . . . . . . (225) 925-7345

## Division of Administration

Claiborne Building, 1201 North Third Street, Suite 7-210,
Baton Rouge, LA 70802
P.O. Box 94095, Baton Rouge, LA 70804-9095
Tel: (225) 342-7000

**Employees:** 788  **Fiscal Year:** 2013-2014  **Budget:** $1,503,572,000

Commissioner **John L. "Jay" Dardenne** . . . . . . . . . . . . . . (225) 342-7000
  E-mail: doacommissioner@la.gov
  Education: LSU 1976 BA, 1979 JD
Deputy Commissioner **Barbara Goodson** . . . . . . . . . . . . . (225) 342-7000
  Education: LSU BS, MS
Chief Advisor **(Vacant)** . . . . . . . . . . . . . . . . . . . . . . . . . (225) 342-7000
Assistant Commissioner of Policy and Personnel
  **Randy Davis** . . . . . . . . . . . . . . . . . . . . . . . . . . . . . (225) 342-7000
Assistant Commissioner of Statewide Services
  **Desireé W. Honoré Thomas, CPA** . . . . . . . . . . . . . . . . (225) 342-7000
Executive Counsel **Richard McGimsey** . . . . . . . . . . . . . . . (225) 342-7154
Group Benefits Office Chief Executive Officer
  **Susan T. West** . . . . . . . . . . . . . . . . . . . . . . . . . . . . (225) 925-6625
Human Resources Director **Ronald Jackson** . . . . . . . . . . . (225) 342-6060
Policy and Communications Director **Jacques Berry** . . . . . (225) 342-7178
  E-mail: jacques.berry@la.gov
Risk Management Director **J.S. "Bud" Thompson** . . . . . . . (225) 342-8500
                                                   Fax: (225) 342-8473
State Buildings Office Director
  **William J. "Billy" Wilson** . . . . . . . . . . . . . . . . . . . . (225) 219-4800
  Education: LSU BArch                      Fax: (225) 219-4810
Legislative Affairs Director **(Vacant)** . . . . . . . . . . . . . . . (225) 342-7193
Confidential Assistant **Sue Israel** . . . . . . . . . . . . . . . . . . (225) 342-7000

## Office of Facility Planning and Control

Tel: (225) 342-0820  Fax: (225) 342-7624

Assistant Commissioner **Mark Moses**...................(225) 342-0820

## Office of Finance and Support Services

1201 North Third Street, Suite 6-180, Baton Rouge, LA 70802
Tel: (225) 342-0700  Fax: (225) 342-2606

Deputy Undersecretary **Marella Houghton** ............. (225) 342-5887
  Administrative Program Specialist **Bathsheba Rogers** ...(225) 342-2410
Payment Manager **Brenda Williams**................... (225) 342-5304
Executive Management Officer **Kerri Traxler** ........... (225) 342-5943
  E-mail: kerri.traxler@la.gov

## Office of Planning and Budget [OPB]

P.O. Box 94095, Baton Rouge, LA 70804-9094
Tel: (225) 342-7005  Fax: (225) 342-7220

State Budget Director **Barry Dusse**................... (225) 342-7005
Deputy Director **Ternisa Hutchinson** ................. (225) 342-7005
  E-mail: ternisa.hutchinson@la.gov

## Office of State Procurement

1201 North Third Street, Suite 2-160, Baton Rouge, LA 70802
Tel: (225) 342-8010  Fax: (225) 342-9756

State Procurement Director (Interim) **Paula B. Tregre** ..... (225) 219-4692
State Procurement Deputy Director **Paula B. Tregre** ..... (225) 342-3793
Agency Relations Assistant Director **Tom Ketterer** ....... (225) 342-4726
Vendor Relations and Legal Liaison Assistant Director
  **Karen Loftin**...................................(225) 342-8056
  Education: LSU 2005 JD
IT, Complex Services and Cooperative Contracts
  Assistant Director **Felicia Sonnier** ................. (225) 342-8029
Professional Contracts and RFPs Assistant Director
  **Pamela Bartfay Rice**............................. (225) 342-4700
Assistant Director **Tammy Toups** .................. (225) 342-8053
Travel Coordinator **Shelita Woods** ................. (225) 342-6322
Executive Staff Officer **Kara K. Allen** ................ (225) 342-8062
  E-mail: kara.allen@la.gov
Chief Analytics Officer **Jonathan Walker** .............. (225) 342-8010

## Office of Technology Services

1201 North Third Street, Suite 2-130, Baton Rouge, LA 70802
P.O. Box 94095, Baton Rouge, LA 70804-9095
Tel: (225) 342-7105  Tel: (225) 219-4994  Fax: (225) 219-9465
E-mail: cio@la.gov

Chief Information Officer **Richard "Dickie" Howze** ...... (225) 342-7105
  E-mail: cio@la.gov
  Executive Assistant **Yvette LaBauve** ................ (225) 342-7105
Deputy Chief Information Officer **Neal Underwood** ...... (225) 342-7105
  E-mail: neal.underwood@la.gov
Information Services Office Director **Michael Andresen** .. (225) 342-0900
  E-mail: michael.andresen@la.gov    Fax: (225) 342-0902
Telecommunications Office Director **Jane Patterson** ......(225) 342-7701
  E-mail: jane.patterson@la.gov

# Office of Financial Institutions

P.O. Box 94095, Baton Rouge, LA 70804-9095
Tel: (225) 925-4660  Fax: (225) 925-4548  E-mail: ofila@ofi.la.gov

**Employees:** 116  **Fiscal Year:** 2013-2014  **Budget:** $12,749,000

■Commissioner **John P. Ducrest, CPA, CFE, CEM** ........ (225) 925-4660
  P.O. Box 94094, Baton Rouge, LA 70804-9094
  E-mail: jducrest@ofi.state.la.us
  Education: Louisiana (Lafayette) 1984 BSBA
Securities Division Deputy Commissioner
  **Rhonda Reeves**................................. (225) 925-4660
Depository Institutions Chief Examiner
  **Sidney E. Seymour** .............................. (225) 925-4660
  E-mail: sseymour@ofi.state.la.us
Non-depository Institutions Chief Examiner
  **Darin Domingue** ............................... (225) 922-2596
  E-mail: ddomingue@ofi.la.gov

## Office of State Inspector General

602 North Fifth Street, Suite 621, Baton Rouge, LA 70802
Tel: (225) 342-4262  Fax: (225) 342-6761

**Fiscal Year:** 2013-2014  **Budget:** $1,783,031,000

■Inspector General **Stephen B. Street, Jr.**............... (225) 342-4262
  E-mail: stephen.street@la.gov
General Counsel **Joseph "Joe" Lotwick**.............. (225) 342-4262

# Louisiana Office of Student Financial Assistance [LOFSA]

602 North Fifth Street, Baton Rouge, LA 70802
P.O. Box 91202, Baton Rouge, LA 70806
Tel: (225) 219-1012  Fax: (225) 208-1496

**Fiscal Year:** 2013-2014  **Budget:** $344,000,000

Executive Director **Sujuan Boutté** ................... (225) 219-7295
  E-mail: sujuan.boutte@la.gov
Fiscal and Administrative Affairs Assistant Executive
  Director **Jack W. Hart**........................... (225) 219-7506
  E-mail: jack.hart@la.gov
Attorney **Robyn Lively**........................... (225) 219-7652
  E-mail: robyn.lively@la.gov
Human Resources Director **Stacy Oubre** ............... (225) 219-7661
Information Technology Director **Alice T. Brown**........ (225) 219-7624
  E-mail: alice.t.brown@la.gov
Public Information and Communications Director
  **Gus Wales** ..................................... (225) 219-7576
  E-mail: gus.wales@la.gov
Scholarship and Grant Division Director **Deborah Paul** ... (225) 219-7840
  E-mail: deborah.paul@la.gov
Start Saving Division Director **Carol Fulco**............. (225) 219-7705
Audit Manager **Kelvin Deloch** ...................... (225) 219-7681
Administrative Services Manager **Linda Roquemore** ..... (225) 219-7522
  E-mail: linda.roquemore@la.gov
Support Services Director and Fiscal Manager
  **Gayle Daigle** ................................... (225) 219-7516
  E-mail: gayle.daigle@la.gov
Field Outreach Services Director and Manager
  **Tireka Cobb**................................... (225) 219-0920

# Commission on Law Enforcement and Administration of Criminal Justice

P. O. Box 3133, New Orleans, LA 70821
Tel: (225) 342-1500

Chairman **Sid Gautreaux**...........................(225) 342-1500
  Affiliation: Sheriff, Office of the Sheriff, City of Baton Rouge and East
  Baton Rouge Parish, Louisiana
  8900 Jimmy Wedell Drive, Baton Rouge, LA 70807
Executive Director **Jim Craft** ........................ (225) 342-1500
  E-mail: jim.craft@lcle.la.gov

# Department of Children and Family Services

627 North Fourth Street, Baton Rouge, LA 70802
P.O. Box 3776, Baton Rouge, LA 70821
Tel: (225) 342-0286  Fax: (225) 342-8636

**Employees:** 3,726  **Fiscal Year:** 2013-2014  **Budget:** $769,165,816

■Secretary **Marketa Garner Walters** ................... (225) 342-7475
  627 North Fourth Street, 8th Floor, Baton Rouge, LA 70802-5343
  Education: Southern Mississippi
  Private Secretary **Melissa Horton** .................. (225) 342-6930
Audit and Compliance Services Director **Ben Foster**......(225) 342-4896
                                    Fax: (225) 342-9932
Communications Director **Catherine Heitman**...........(225) 342-9640
  Public Information Officer **Grace Weber**............. (225) 342-4908
  E-mail: grace.weber@la.gov
Emergency Preparedness Director **Ricky Montet** ........ (225) 342-1306
Executive Counsel **Terri Porche Ricks**................. (225) 342-1125
  Education: LSU 1991 BS; Tulane 1998 JD    Fax: (225) 342-9139

---

★ Elected Official    ■ Appointed by Governor    ● Appointed by Legislature    ▲ Appointed by Board or Commission    ◆ Appointed by State Supreme Court

## Division of Management and Finance

P.O. Box 3776, Baton Rouge, LA 70821

Undersecretary **Eric Horent** . . . . . . . . . . . . . . . . . . . . . . . . . . . (225) 342-1702
                                               Fax: (225) 342-8636
Deputy Undersecretary **Etta J. Harris** . . . . . . . . . . . . . . . . (225) 342-0805
                                               Fax: (225) 342-8636
Administrative Services Director **Marsha Woodcock** . . . . . (225) 342-4148
   E-mail: marsha.woodcock@la.gov        Fax: (225) 342-4220
Appeals Director **Doris Weston** . . . . . . . . . . . . . . . . . . . . . . :SS (225) 342-4120
                                               Fax: (225) 342-7797
Budget Director **Eddriene Sylvester** . . . . . . . . . . . . . . . . . . (225) 342-0442
Fiscal Services Director **Martina Stribling** . . . . . . . . . . . . . (225) 219-0536
Human Resources Director **Shelly Johnson** . . . . . . . . . . . . (225) 342-4310
                                               Fax: (225) 342-9833
Information Services Director **Barbara Hunter** . . . . . . . . . . (225) 342-2301
   E-mail: barbara.hunter@la.gov        Fax: (225) 342-8635

## Division of Operations

627 North Fourth Street, Baton Rouge, LA 70802-5343

Deputy Assistant Secretary **Sharon Tucker** . . . . . . . . . . . . . (225) 342-1102

## Division of Programs

627 North Fourth Street, Baton Rouge, LA 70802-5343
P.O. Box 94065, Baton Rouge, LA 70804
Tel: (225) 342-6482

■ Deputy Secretary of Child Welfare
   **Rhenda Hodnett, PhD, LCSW** . . . . . . . . . . . . . . . . . . . . (225) 342-9960
   E-mail: rhenda.hodnett@la.gov        Fax: (225) 342-8636
Deputy Assistant Secretary **Sammy Guillory** . . . . . . . . . . . (225) 342-3961
                                               Fax: (225) 219-9399
Disability Determination Services Division Executive
   Director **Chris Kirby** . . . . . . . . . . . . . . . . . . . . . . . . . . . . . (225) 342-2244
Child Support Enforcement Executive Director
   **Lisa Andry** . . . . . . . . . . . . . . . . . . . . . . . . . . . . . . . . . . . . . (225) 342-4780
   E-mail: lisa.andry@la.gov
Child Welfare Director **(Vacant)** . . . . . . . . . . . . . . . . . . . . . . (225) 342-6387
Economic Stability Executive Director **Kim Matherne** . . . . (225) 342-6482
                                               Fax: (225) 219-4363
Licensing Program Director **Angie Badeaux, LCSW** . . . . . (225) 342-9905
   E-mail: angie.badeaux@la.gov
Program Integrity and Improvement Executive Director
   **Guy Sylvester** . . . . . . . . . . . . . . . . . . . . . . . . . . . . . . . . . . (225) 342-9381
Fraud and Recovery Section Director **Jesse Wright** . . . . . . (225) 342-4267
Supplemental Nutrition Assistance Program Director
   **Allison Willeford** . . . . . . . . . . . . . . . . . . . . . . . . . . . . . . . . (225) 342-2530

## Department of Civil Service

P.O. Box 94111, Baton Rouge, LA 70804-9111
Tel: (225) 342-8272   TTY: (800) 846-5277   Fax: (225) 342-0966
Internet: www.civilservice.louisiana.gov

**Employees:** 213   **Fiscal Year:** 2013-2014   **Budget:** $25,199,563

▲ Director **Byron P. Decoteau, Jr.** . . . . . . . . . . . . . . . . . . . . . (225) 342-8272
   E-mail: byron.decoteau@la.gov
Deputy Director **Christopher Deer** . . . . . . . . . . . . . . . . . . . . (225) 342-8297
Chief of Staff **Toby Comeaux** . . . . . . . . . . . . . . . . . . . . . . . . (225) 342-8272
General Counsel **Adrienne Bordelon** . . . . . . . . . . . . . . . . . . (225) 342-8272
Administrative Law Division Director **Ann Wise** . . . . . . . . . (225) 342-1800
Compensation Division Chief **Brandy Malatesta** . . . . . . . . . (225) 342-8083
Ethics Code Division Chief **Kathleen Allen** . . . . . . . . . . . . . (225) 763-8777
   2415 Quail Drive, 3rd Floor, Baton Rouge, LA 70808
Management Information Systems Division Chief
   **Jackie Garrison** . . . . . . . . . . . . . . . . . . . . . . . . . . . . . . . . . (225) 342-8083
   E-mail: jackie.garrison@la.gov
Program Accountability Division Chief **Melinda Robert** . . . (225) 219-9437
Staffing Division Chief **Rainette Stephens** . . . . . . . . . . . . . (225) 219-9390
Policy and Project Adminstrator **Makayla Harris** . . . . . . . . (225) 342-8276
Public Information Officer **Lindsay Ruiz de Chavez** . . . . . . (225) 342-8272
   E-mail: lindsay.ruiz@la.gov

## Louisiana Economic Development [LED]

P.O. Box 94185, Baton Rouge, LA 70804-9185
Tel: (225) 342-3000   Fax: (225) 342-5389

**Employees:** 117   **Fiscal Year:** 2013-2014   **Budget:** $41,818,755

■ Secretary **Donald Pierson, Jr.** . . . . . . . . . . . . . . . . . . . . . . (225) 342-3000
   E-mail: pierson@la.gov
   Education: West Point BS
Deputy Secretary **(Vacant)** . . . . . . . . . . . . . . . . . . . . . . . . . . (225) 342-5478
Assistant Secretary **Quentin Messer** . . . . . . . . . . . . . . . . . . (225) 342-4851
Undersecretary **Anne G. Villa** . . . . . . . . . . . . . . . . . . . . . . . . (225) 342-5395
Deputy Undersecretary **Kathy Blankenship** . . . . . . . . . . . . (225) 342-9658
                                               Fax: (225) 342-5926
Business Development Senior Director **(Vacant)** . . . . . . . . . (225) 342-4319
Business Development Director **William Day** . . . . . . . . . . . . (225) 342-5256
                                               Fax: (225) 342-4058
Business Development Director **Joshua Fleig** . . . . . . . . . . . . (225) 342-6494
                                               Fax: (225) 342-5554
Business Development Director **Greg Trahan** . . . . . . . . . . . . (225) 342-1549
                                               Fax: (225) 342-3589
Business Development Director **(Vacant)** . . . . . . . . . . . . . . . (225) 342-0583
                                               Fax: (225) 342-9448
Business Intelligence Director **Larry Henson** . . . . . . . . . . . (225) 342-1135
Business Expansion and Retention Group Director
   **Kelsey Short** . . . . . . . . . . . . . . . . . . . . . . . . . . . . . . . . . . . (225) 342-5892
   Senior Project Manager **Shawn Welcome** . . . . . . . . . . . (225) 342-5379
Community Development Director
   **Lewis L. "Skip" Smart III** . . . . . . . . . . . . . . . . . . . . . . . (225) 342-4321
   Education: Colgate 1963 BS; LSU 1966 MBA     Fax: (225) 342-6820
Community Outreach Services Director
   **Patrick "Pat" Witty** . . . . . . . . . . . . . . . . . . . . . . . . . . . . (225) 342-9223
                                               Fax: (225) 342-6820
Digital Interactive Media Director **Thomas Tyler** . . . . . . . . (225) 342-3571
Entertainment Director **Chris Stelly** . . . . . . . . . . . . . . . . . . (225) 342-5555
                                               Fax: (225) 342-5554
Federal Programs Director **(Vacant)** . . . . . . . . . . . . . . . . . . . (225) 342-5443
Governmental Affairs and Federal Programs Director
   **Mandi Mitchell** . . . . . . . . . . . . . . . . . . . . . . . . . . . . . . . . . (225) 342-6499
Human Resources Director **Dawn Thibodeaux** . . . . . . . . . . (225) 342-3740
                                               Fax: (225) 342-5926
Live Performance and Music Director **Philip Mann** . . . . . . (225) 342-5521
                                               Fax: (225) 342-5554
Marketing and Communications Director **(Vacant)** . . . . . . . (225) 342-9005
                                               Fax: (225) 342-9390
Policy and Planning Director **Linda Regira** . . . . . . . . . . . . . (225) 342-5380
Small Business Services Director **John Matthews** . . . . . . . (225) 342-1181
                                               Fax: (225) 342-9390
State Economic Competitiveness Director
   **James Chappell** . . . . . . . . . . . . . . . . . . . . . . . . . . . . . . . . (225) 342-9448
Structuring and Valuation Director **Johan Salén** . . . . . . . . . (225) 342-5682
International Commerce Executive Director **Kathe Falls** . . . (225) 342-4323
Workforce Development Programs Executive Director
   **Jeff Lynn** . . . . . . . . . . . . . . . . . . . . . . . . . . . . . . . . . . . . . . (225) 342-0107
   E-mail: jeff.lynn@la.gov

## Department of Environmental Quality [DEQ]

602 North Fifth Street, Baton Rouge, LA 70802
P.O. Box 4301, Baton Rouge, LA 70821
Tel: (225) 219-3953   TTY: (800) 947-5277   Fax: (225) 219-3971
E-mail: webmasterdeq@la.gov   Internet: www.deq.louisiana.gov

**Employees:** 699   **Fiscal Year:** 2013-2014   **Budget:** $122,138,980

■ Secretary **Dr. Chuck Carr Brown** . . . . . . . . . . . . . . . . . . . . (225) 219-3953
   Education: Southern Mississippi BS; Southern U (New Orleans) MPA,
   PhD
   Confidential Assistant to the Secretary
   **Bijan Sharafkhani** . . . . . . . . . . . . . . . . . . . . . . . . . . . . . . (225) 219-3953
   Education: New Orleans BSCE, MSCE
■ Deputy Secretary **Denise Bennett** . . . . . . . . . . . . . . . . . . . . (225) 219-3953
   Education: Howard U BSChE; LSU MBA

---

★ Elected Official    ■ Appointed by Governor    ● Appointed by Legislature    ▲ Appointed by Board or Commission    ◆ Appointed by State Supreme Court

■Executive Counsel **Herman Robinson, CPM** . . . . . . . . . . . (225) 219-3985
  E-mail: herman.robinson@la.gov
  Education: Southern U A&M BA, JD
Press Secretary **Gregory Langley** . . . . . . . . . . . . . . . . . . (225) 219-3964
  Education: Tennessee BS
Criminal Investigations Director **Jeffrey T. Nolan** . . . . . . . . (225) 219-3939
  Education: LSU 1991 BS
Business, Community Outreach and Incentives
  Administrator **Jonathan McFarland** . . . . . . . . . . . . . . . (225) 219-3953
Ombudsman **Roger Ward** . . . . . . . . . . . . . . . . . . . . . . . . . . (225) 219-3985
  Fax: (225) 219-3971

## Office of Environmental Compliance
P.O. Box 4312, Baton Rouge, LA 70821-4312
Tel: (225) 219-3710  Fax: (225) 219-3708  E-mail: deqoec@la.gov

**Employees:** 373  **Fiscal Year:** 2013-2014  **Budget:** $39,480,668

■Assistant Secretary **Lourdes Iturralde** . . . . . . . . . . . . . . . . (225) 219-3710
  E-mail: lourdes.iturralde@la.gov
Assessment Division Administrator **Bryan Riche** . . . . . . . . (225) 219-3550
Enforcement Division Administrator **Celena Cage** . . . . . . . (225) 219-3715
Inspection Division Administrator **Tom Killeen** . . . . . . . . . (225) 219-3557
Underground Storage Tanks and Remediation Division
  Administrator **Gary Fulton** . . . . . . . . . . . . . . . . . . . . . . (225) 219-3715

## Office of Environmental Services
P.O. Box 4313, Baton Rouge, LA 70821-4313
Tel: (225) 219-3180  Fax: (225) 219-3309  E-mail: deqoes@la.gov

**Fiscal Year:** 2013-2014  **Budget:** $15,202,994

■Assistant Secretary **Elliott Vega** . . . . . . . . . . . . . . . . . . . . (225) 219-3180
  E-mail: elliott.vega@la.gov
Air Permits Division Administrator **Donald Trahan** . . . . . . . (225) 219-3181
Public Participation and Permit Support Services Division
  Administrator **Cheryl Nolan** . . . . . . . . . . . . . . . . . . . . . (225) 219-3181
  Education: Louisiana Col BS
Waste Permits Division Administrator **Estuardo Silva** . . . . . (225) 219-3070
  Education: LSU BS, MS  Fax: (225) 219-3474
Water Permits Division Administrator **Scott Gulliams** . . . . (225) 219-9371

## Office of Management and Finance
P.O. Box 4303, Baton Rouge, LA 70821-4303
Tel: (225) 219-3840  Fax: (225) 219-3846  E-mail: deqomf@la.gov

**Fiscal Year:** 2013-2014  **Budget:** $55,182,962

■Undersecretary **Karyn Andrews** . . . . . . . . . . . . . . . . . . . . (225) 219-3840
Procurement Director **(Vacant)** . . . . . . . . . . . . . . . . . . . . . (225) 219-3824
Financial Services Administrator **Theresa Chatelain** . . . . . . (225) 219-3863
  Fax: (225) 219-3867
Human Resources Director **Pamela Harrell** . . . . . . . . . . . . (225) 219-3840

## Department of Health and Hospitals [DHH]
P.O. Box 629, Baton Rouge, LA 70821-0629
Tel: (225) 342-9500  Fax: (225) 342-5568
Internet: www.dhh.louisiana.gov

**Employees:** 6,384  **Fiscal Year:** 2014-2015  **Budget:** $9,496,941,970

■Secretary **Dr. Rebekah E. Gee** . . . . . . . . . . . . . . . . . . . . . (225) 342-9500
  E-mail: rebekah.gee@la.gov
  Special Assistant to the Secretary **Chelsea Ardoin** . . . . . . (225) 342-9503
■Deputy Secretary **Michelle Alletto** . . . . . . . . . . . . . . . . . . (225) 342-7092
  E-mail: michelle.alletto@la.gov
Chief of Staff **Andrew Tuozzolo** . . . . . . . . . . . . . . . . . . . . (225) 342-2025
  E-mail: andrew.tuozzolo@la.gov
Medical Director and State Health Officer
  **Dr. Jimmy Guidry, MD** . . . . . . . . . . . . . . . . . . . . . . . . . (225) 342-3417
  Assistant State Health Officer **(Vacant)** . . . . . . . . . . . . . (504) 568-8198
Executive Counsel **Stephen Russo** . . . . . . . . . . . . . . . . . . (225) 342-1128
  E-mail: stephen.russo@la.gov  Fax: (225) 342-2232
Director of Legislative Relations **Tonya Joiner** . . . . . . . . . (225) 342-5274
  PO Box 3518, Baton Rouge, LA 70821
  E-mail: tonya.joiner@la.gov

Media and Communications Bureau Director
  **Robert L. Johannessen** . . . . . . . . . . . . . . . . . . . . . . . . (225) 342-7913
  E-mail: robert.johannessen@la.gov  Fax: (225) 342-3738
  Press Secretary **Robert L. Johannessen** . . . . . . . . . . . . (225) 342-5275
  E-mail: robert.johannessen@la.gov
Information Technology Director **Brad Coney** . . . . . . . . . . (225) 342-9258
  E-mail: brad.coney@la.gov
Chief Information Officer **(Vacant)** . . . . . . . . . . . . . . . . . . (225) 342-5643
Webmaster **W. Jerome Boyd** . . . . . . . . . . . . . . . . . . . . . . (225) 342-9957

## Bureau of Health Services Financing (Medicaid)
628 North Fourth Street, Baton Rouge, LA 70802
Tel: (888) 342-6207  Fax: (225) 342-9508

Medicaid Director **Jen Steele** . . . . . . . . . . . . . . . . . . . . . . (225) 342-9240
Medicaid Medical Director **(Vacant)** . . . . . . . . . . . . . . . . . (225) 342-5166
Deputy Medicaid Director for Eligibility Division
  **Diane Batts** . . . . . . . . . . . . . . . . . . . . . . . . . . . . . . . . (225) 342-2300
Deputy Medicaid Director for Policy, Waiver and
  Compliance Division **Lou Ann Owen** . . . . . . . . . . . . . . . (225) 342-1353
Deputy Medicaid Director for Medicaid Systems Division
  **Bill Perkins** . . . . . . . . . . . . . . . . . . . . . . . . . . . . . . . . (225) 342-8935
Deputy Medicaid Director and Chief Financial Officer
  **Amanda Joyner** . . . . . . . . . . . . . . . . . . . . . . . . . . . . . (225) 342-6043
Medicaid Quality and Reporting Section Chief
  **Mary Johnson** . . . . . . . . . . . . . . . . . . . . . . . . . . . . . . (225) 342-2300

## Office of Aging and Adult Services
Tel: (225) 219-0223
Assistant Secretary **Tara LeBlanc** . . . . . . . . . . . . . . . . . . (225) 219-0223
Deputy Assistant Secretary **Robin Wagner** . . . . . . . . . . . . (225) 219-0223

## Office of Behavioral Health [OBH]
Bienville Building, 628 North Fourth Street, Baton Rouge, LA 70802
P.O. Box 4049, Baton Rouge, LA 70821-4049
Tel: (225) 342-2540  Fax: (225) 342-5066

■Assistant Secretary **James E. Hussey** . . . . . . . . . . . . . . . . (225) 342-8916
  E-mail: james.hussey@la.gov
  Administrative Assistant **Leslie Deville-McDaniel** . . . . . . (225) 342-2540
Deputy Assistant Secretary for Administration **(Vacant)** . . . (225) 342-1868
Deputy Assistant Secretary for Adult, Child, and Family
  Operations **Janice Petersen** . . . . . . . . . . . . . . . . . . . . . (225) 342-9532
Deputy Assistant Secretary for Health Plan Management
  **Karen E. Stubbs** . . . . . . . . . . . . . . . . . . . . . . . . . . . . (225) 342-1562
  Education: Tulane; LSU Hebert Law JD
Adult Operations Director **(Vacant)** . . . . . . . . . . . . . . . . . (225) 342-4760
Fiscal Director **David McCants** . . . . . . . . . . . . . . . . . . . . (225) 342-2540
Medical Director **James E. Hussey** . . . . . . . . . . . . . . . . . . (225) 342-8916
Prevention Services Director **Leslie Brougham Freeman** . . (225) 342-2540
Regional Operations Director **(Vacant)** . . . . . . . . . . . . . . . (225) 342-2540

## Office for Citizens with Developmental Disabilities [OCDD]
628 North Fourth Street, Baton Rouge, LA 70802
Tel: (225) 342-0095  Fax: (225) 342-8823

**Fiscal Year:** 2013-2014  **Budget:** $157,665,000

Assistant Secretary **Mark A. Thomas** . . . . . . . . . . . . . . . . (225) 342-0095
  Education: LSU BA
  Administrative Assistant **Jackie Cobbs** . . . . . . . . . . . . . (225) 342-0095
Deputy Assistant Secretary for Community-Based
  Supports and Services **Julie Foster** . . . . . . . . . . . . . . . (225) 342-0095
Deputy Assistant Secretary for Support and Services
  Center and Resource Centers **Charles Ayles** . . . . . . . . . (225) 342-6822
Clinical Services Director **Brandi Kelly** . . . . . . . . . . . . . . . (225) 342-7912
Fiscal Director **Craig Gannuch** . . . . . . . . . . . . . . . . . . . . (225) 342-3418
Executive Management Officer **Tiffany Dickerson** . . . . . . . (225) 342-0095
  E-mail: tiffany.dickerson@la.gov

---

★ Elected Official  ■ Appointed by Governor  ● Appointed by Legislature  ▲ Appointed by Board or Commission  ◆ Appointed by State Supreme Court

EXECUTIVE BRANCH

## Office of Management and Finance

628 North Fourth Street, Baton Rouge, LA 70802

Undersecretary **Jeff Reynolds** . . . . . . . . . . . . . . . . . . . . . . (225) 342-6726
   E-mail: jeff.reynolds@la.gov            Fax: (225) 342-5568
   Education: Oklahoma State BSBA
Executive Officer **Timothy A. White** . . . . . . . . . . . . . . . . (225) 342-6726
   E-mail: timothy.white@la.gov
Health Education Authority Executive Director
   **Jacob C. Johnson** . . . . . . . . . . . . . . . . . . . . . . . . . . . . (504) 568-5835
   300 LaSalle Street, New Orleans, LA 70112
Administrative Review Director **Michael Distefano** . . . . . . (225) 342-6920
   E-mail: michael.distefa@la.gov
Health Standards Director **Cecile Castello** . . . . . . . . . . . . (225) 342-4997
                                      Fax: (225) 342-5073
Planning and Budget Director **Monique Cross** . . . . . . . . . (225) 342-4301
   E-mail: monique.cross@la.gov         Fax: (225) 342-8663
Fiscal Management Division Director **Pam Diez** . . . . . . . . (225) 342-9568

## Office of Public Health

628 North Fourth Street, Baton Rouge, LA 70802
Tel: (225) 342-8093 Fax: (225) 342-4848

Assistant Secretary (Interim) **Beth Scalco** . . . . . . . . . . . . (225) 342-6188
Administrative Assistant **Peggy Lantrip** . . . . . . . . . . . . . . (225) 342-6188
Deputy Assistant Secretary **Myra Lowe** . . . . . . . . . . . . . . (225) 342-8093
Community Preparedness Center Director **Doris Brown** . . . (225) 354-3500
Laboratory Services Division Director **Stephen Martin** . . . (225) 219-5200
   1209 Leesville Avenue, Baton Rouge, LA 70802     Fax: (225) 219-4903
Nutrition Services Chief **Monica Pierson-McDaniels** . . . . . (225) 342-8064
Chief Engineer **Amanda Laughlin** . . . . . . . . . . . . . . . . . . (225) 342-7499
Chief Financial Officer **Sheila Savoy** . . . . . . . . . . . . . . . . (225) 342-8483
Chief Sanitarian **Tenney Sibley** . . . . . . . . . . . . . . . . . . . . (225) 342-7550
Legislative Liaison and Community Affairs Director
   **Sundee Winder** . . . . . . . . . . . . . . . . . . . . . . . . . . . . (225) 342-8306
Health Promotion Director **Melissa R. Martin** . . . . . . . . . (225) 342-9361
Performance Improvement Director **Tammy Hall** . . . . . . . (225) 342-9826
Strategic Projects Director **Sundee Winder** . . . . . . . . . . . (225) 342-8306

## Department of Natural Resources [DNR]

P.O. Box 94396, Baton Rouge, LA 70804-9396
Tel: (225) 342-4500 TTY: (225) 342-8945

**Employees: 410 Fiscal Year: 2013-2014 Budget: $174,325,250**

■Secretary **Thomas F. "Tom" Harris** . . . . . . . . . . . . . . . . . (225) 342-2710
   E-mail: thomas.harris@la.gov         Fax: (225) 342-5861
   Education: LSU BS; Tulane MS
Public Information Director **Phyllis Darensbourg** . . . . . . . . (225) 342-8955
   E-mail: phyllis.darensbourg@la.gov     Fax: (225) 342-3442
Legal Division Director **Mark E. Falcon** . . . . . . . . . . . . . . (225) 342-2614
                                         Fax: (225) 342-2707

## Office of Coastal Management

P.O. Box 44487, Baton Rouge, LA 70804-4487

Assistant Secretary **Keith Lovell** . . . . . . . . . . . . . . . . . . . (225) 342-3583
Deputy Assistant Secretary **(Vacant)** . . . . . . . . . . . . . . . . (225) 342-6940
Interagency Affairs, Compliance and Field Services
   Division Administrator **Donald Haydel** . . . . . . . . . . . . (225) 342-8953
   E-mail: donald.haydel@la.gov
Permits Mitigation Support Division Administrator
   **Karl Morgan** . . . . . . . . . . . . . . . . . . . . . . . . . . . . . . (225) 342-6470
   E-mail: karl.morgan@la.gov

## Office of Conservation

P.O. Box 94275, Baton Rouge, LA 70804-9275

Commissioner **Richard P. Ieyoub** . . . . . . . . . . . . . . . . . . . (225) 342-5540
   Education: McNeese State 1968; LSU 1972 JD
Assistant Commissioner **Gary P. Ross** . . . . . . . . . . . . . . . (225) 342-5560
   E-mail: gary.ross@la.gov
Engineering Division-Administrative Director
   **R. Todd Keating** . . . . . . . . . . . . . . . . . . . . . . . . . . . . (225) 342-5507
   E-mail: todd.keating@la.gov
Engineering Division-Regulatory Director
   **J. Brent Campbell** . . . . . . . . . . . . . . . . . . . . . . . . . . . (225) 342-5519

Environmental Division Director **Gary Snellgrove** . . . . . . . (225) 342-7222
   E-mail: gary.snellgrove@la.gov
Geological Oil and Gas Division Director
   **David "Dave" Elfert** . . . . . . . . . . . . . . . . . . . . . . . . . . (225) 342-5523
   E-mail: david.elfert@la.gov
   Education: Nicholls State 1980 BS; Southern Mississippi 1983 MS
Injection and Mining Division Director **Stephen Lee** . . . . . (225) 342-5569
   E-mail: stephen.lee@la.gov
Pipeline Division Director **Steven Giambrone** . . . . . . . . . (225) 342-2989
   E-mail: steven.giambrone@la.gov

## Office of Mineral Resources

P.O. Box 2827, Baton Rouge, LA 70821-2827

Assistant Secretary **David Boulet** . . . . . . . . . . . . . . . . . . . (225) 342-4607
Deputy Assistant Secretary **Stacey Talley** . . . . . . . . . . . . . (225) 342-4615
   Education: Southeastern Louisiana 1986 BS, 1987 BS; LSU 1991 JD
Geologist Administrator **Victor M. Vaughn** . . . . . . . . . . . . (225) 342-7121
   Education: Southwestern Louisiana 1975 BS
Mineral Income Division Audit Director
   **Rachel Newman** . . . . . . . . . . . . . . . . . . . . . . . . . . . . (225) 342-4499
Petroleum Lands Director **Rick Heck** . . . . . . . . . . . . . . . . (225) 342-6122
   E-mail: rick.heck@la.gov
   Education: LSU 1971 BS, 1996 MBA

## Office of Management and Finance

617 North Third Street, Baton Rouge, LA 70802
P.O. Box 94396, Baton Rouge, LA 70804-9396
Tel: (225) 342-4540 Fax: (225) 342-4313

Undersecretary **Beverly P. Hodges** . . . . . . . . . . . . . . . . . . (225) 342-4540
Contracts and Grants Administrator **David Guidry** . . . . . . (225) 342-4502
Fiscal and Budget Director **Gwendolyn Thomas** . . . . . . . (225) 342-4840
Human Resource Manager **Mary F. Ginn, SPHR** . . . . . . . (225) 342-5467
                                         Fax: (225) 342-3402
Information Technology Manager (Interim)
   **Sara Harrison** . . . . . . . . . . . . . . . . . . . . . . . . . . . . . (225) 342-1473
                                         Fax: (225) 342-4471

## Department of Public Safety and Corrections

P.O. Box 94304, Baton Rouge, LA 70804-9304
504 Mayflower Street, Baton Rouge, LA 70802
Tel: (225) 342-6740 Fax: (225) 342-3095

■Secretary **James M. LeBlanc** . . . . . . . . . . . . . . . . . . . . . . (225) 342-6740
   E-mail: jleblanc@corrections.state.la.us
Deputy Assistant Secretary **Melissa Callahan** . . . . . . . . . . (225) 342-8131

## Corrections Services

Tel: (225) 342-8983 Internet: www.doc.la.gov

**Employees: 4,777 Fiscal Year: 2013-2014 Budget: $496,587,248**

Deputy Secretary **Genie Powers** . . . . . . . . . . . . . . . . . . . . (225) 342-6744
                                         Fax: (225) 342-3095
Undersecretary **Thomas C. Bickham III** . . . . . . . . . . . . . . (225) 342-6739
   E-mail: tbickham@corrections.state.la.us
Deputy Undersecretary **Elaine Leibenguth** . . . . . . . . . . . . (225) 342-7451
Medical and Mental Health Director **Dr. Raman Singh** . . . (225) 342-1320
                                         Fax: (225) 342-1329
Information Technology Director **Dawson Andrews** . . . . . . (225) 342-8782
   E-mail: dawson.andrews@doc.la.gov

## Public Safety Services

P.O. Box 66614, Baton Rouge, LA 70896
Tel: (225) 925-6006 Fax: (225) 925-3742

**Employees: 2,414 Fiscal Year: 2015-2016 Budget: $464,966,959**

■Deputy Secretary **Col. Michael D. Edmonson** . . . . . . . . . (225) 925-6118
   E-mail: deputy.secretary@la.gov
   Education: LSU

---

★ Elected Official     ■ Appointed by Governor     ● Appointed by Legislature     ▲ Appointed by Board or Commission     ◆ Appointed by State Supreme Court

## Fire Marshal's Office

8181 Independence Boulevard, Baton Rouge, LA 70806
Fax: (225) 925-4593

**Employees: 167  Fiscal Year: 2015-2016  Budget: $25,178,129**

■Fire Marshal **H. Butch Browning, Jr.** . . . . . . . . . . . . . . . . . .(225) 925-4911
  E-mail: butch.browning@la.gov

## Management and Finance Office

P.O. Box 66614, Baton Rouge, LA 70896
Tel: (225) 925-6032  Fax: (225) 925-4623

**Employees: 85  Fiscal Year: 2015-2016  Budget: $34,668,786**

Undersecretary **(Vacant)** . . . . . . . . . . . . . . . . . . . . . . . . . . . (225) 925-6032
Budget Director **Chad Felterman** . . . . . . . . . . . . . . . . . . . . (225) 925-1873
Chief Fiscal Officer **Scott Erwin** . . . . . . . . . . . . . . . . . . . . . (225) 925-4547
Human Resources Director **Ginger Krieg** . . . . . . . . . . . . . (225) 925-6067

## Office of Motor Vehicles [OMV]

P.O. Box 64886, Baton Rouge, LA 70896
Tel: (225) 925-6146  Fax: (225) 925-1838

**Employees: 503  Fiscal Year: 2015-2016  Budget: $52,946,490**

■Commissioner **Karen Gaudet St. Germain** . . . . . . . . . . . . (225) 925-4228

## State Police

P.O. Box 66614, Baton Rouge, LA 70896
Fax: (225) 925-3742  Internet: www.lsp.org

**Employees: 1,632  Fiscal Year: 2015-2016  Budget: $312,585,279**

■Superintendent **Col. Michael D. Edmonson** . . . . . . . . . . . . (225) 925-6118
  E-mail: deputy.secretary@la.gov
Assistant Superintendent and Chief of Staff
  **Lt. Col. Charles "Charlie" Dupuy** . . . . . . . . . . . . . . . . . (225) 922-0803
Criminal Investigations Deputy Superintendent
  **Lt. Col. Murphy Paul** . . . . . . . . . . . . . . . . . . . . . . . . . . . (225) 922-1467
Patrol Deputy Superintendent **Lt. Col. David Staton** . . . . . (225) 925-1980
Support Deputy Superintendent **Lt. Col. Adam White** . . . . (225) 925-6111

## Office of Juvenile Justice [OJJ]

P.O. Box 66458, Baton Rouge, LA 70896
Tel: (225) 287-7900  Fax: (225) 287-7969

■Deputy Secretary (Interim) **James Bueche** . . . . . . . . . . . . . (225) 287-7944
  E-mail: james.bueche@la.gov
Assistant Secretary **Sean C. Hamilton** . . . . . . . . . . . . . . . . (225) 287-7993
Undersecretary **Gearry Williams** . . . . . . . . . . . . . . . . . . . . (225) 287-7953
Deputy Undersecretary **Cassandra Washington** . . . . . . . . (225) 922-3060
Deputy Assistant Secretary **Elizabeth Touchet-Morgan** . . (225) 287-7622
General Counsel **Martha Morgan** . . . . . . . . . . . . . . . . . . . . (225) 287-7976
Chief of Operations **Ellyn Toney** . . . . . . . . . . . . . . . . . . . . (225) 287-7937
Communications Director **(Vacant)** . . . . . . . . . . . . . . . . . . . (225) 287-7898

## Department of Revenue

P.O. Box 201, Baton Rouge, LA 70821-0201
Tel: (225) 219-2700  TTY: (225) 219-2114  Fax: (225) 219-2708
Internet: www.revenue.louisiana.gov

**Employees: 689  Fiscal Year: 2013-2014  Budget: $82,244,671**

■Secretary **Kimberly Lewis Robinson** . . . . . . . . . . . . .(225) 219-2700 ext. 4
  Education: LSU 1993 BA, 1995 MPA, 1998 JD
■Deputy Secretary **Kevin Richard** . . . . . . . . . . . . . . . . . . . . (225) 219-2700
  E-mail: kevin.richard@la.gov
Undersecretary **Andrew Perilloux** . . . . . . . . . . . . . . . . . . . (225) 219-2700
  Charitable Gaming Office Director **Michael Legendre** . . . (225) 925-1835
  P.O. Box 98502, Baton Rouge, LA 70884-9502    Fax: (225) 925-7069
Criminal Investigation Service Director **Barry Kelly** . . . . . .(225) 219-2280
  617 North Third Street, Baton Rouge, LA 70802    Fax: (225) 219-2287
Controller **(Vacant)** . . . . . . . . . . . . . . . . . . . . . . . . . . . . . . . (225) 219-2300
                                                      Fax: (225) 219-2306
Human Resources Director **Sophia Pipsair** . . . . . . . . . . . . (225) 219-2020
                                                      Fax: (225) 219-2043
Internal Audit Director **Joyce Anderson** . . . . . . . . . . . . . . (225) 219-2750
                                                      Fax: (225) 219-2754
Legislative Liaison **Jane H. Smith** . . . . . . . . . . . . . . . . . . . (225) 219-2102
  E-mail: jane.smith@la.gov
  Education: Northwestern State BS, 1971 MEd

Press Secretary **Kizzy Payton** . . . . . . . . . . . . . . . . . . . . . . . (225) 219-2156
  Education: Southern U A&M 1999, 2003 MC    Fax: (225) 219-2771

# Department of Transportation and Development

1201 Capitol Access Road, Baton Rouge, LA 70802
P.O. Box 94245, Baton Rouge, LA 70804-9245
Tel: (225) 379-1100  Fax: (225) 379-1851  E-mail: dotd@la.gov

**Employees: 4,194**

■Secretary **Shawn D. Wilson** . . . . . . . . . . . . . . . . . . . . . . . . (225) 379-1200
  E-mail: shawn.wilson@la.gov
  Education: Louisiana (Lafayette) 1993 BA
  Confidential Assistant **Myles Brumfield** . . . . . . . . . . . . . (225) 379-2851
    Education: LSU
■Deputy Secretary **Eric Kalivoda** . . . . . . . . . . . . . . . . . . . . . (225) 379-1200
  E-mail: eric.kalivoda@la.gov
Executive Counsel **Cheryl Duvieilh** . . . . . . . . . . . . . . . . . . .(225) 379-1009
General Counsel **Brandon Brown** . . . . . . . . . . . . . . . . . . . . .(225) 242-4656
  E-mail: brandon.brown@la.gov    Fax: (225) 242-4690
Audit and Quality Control Director **Mark St. Cyr** . . . . . . . .(225) 379-1099
                                                      Fax: (225) 379-1731
Communications Director **Rodney Mallett** . . . . . . . . . . . . . (225) 379-1275
  E-mail: rodney.mallett@la.gov    Fax: (225) 379-1863
Compliance Programs Director **Stephanie Ducote** . . . . . . . (225) 379-1382
  E-mail: stephanie.ducote@la.gov    Fax: (225) 379-1865
Quality and Continuous Improvement Program (QCIP)
  Director **Denny Silvio** . . . . . . . . . . . . . . . . . . . . . . . . . . . (225) 379-1964
  E-mail: denny.silvio@la.gov    Fax: (225) 379-1865
Local Public Assistance Director **Ann Wills** . . . . . . . . . . . . (225) 379-2515
Legislative Liaison **Joshua Hollins** . . . . . . . . . . . . . . . . . . . (225) 379-1057
Louisiana Professional Engineers and Land Surveyors
  Board Executive Secretary **Donna Sentell** . . . . . . . . . . . .(225) 925-6291
  9643 Brookline Avenue, #121,    Fax: (225) 925-6292
  Baton Rouge, LA 70809-1433
Assistant to the Secretary for Policy **Chance McNeely** . . . .(225) 379-1089
  Education: LSU 2010 AB

## Office of Engineering

Fax: (225) 379-1861

Chief Engineer **Janice P. Williams** . . . . . . . . . . . . . . . . . . . (225) 379-1234
  Education: LSU 1985 BS
Deputy Chief Engineer **Edward Wedge** . . . . . . . . . . . . . . . (225) 379-1325
Contract Services Administrator **Masood Rasoulian** . . . . . .(225) 379-1471
  E-mail: masood.rasoulian@la.gov
Environmental Administrator **Noel Ardoin** . . . . . . . . . . . . . (225) 242-4502
  E-mail: noel.ardoin@la.gov    Fax: (225) 242-4500
  Education: LSU 1985 BS; Georgia Tech 1987 MS
Public Works and Water Resources Administrator
  **Christopher P. Knotts, PE** . . . . . . . . . . . . . . . . . . . . . . . (225) 379-3015
Traffic Engineering Division Administrator **Jody Colvin** . . .(225) 242-4635
Traffic Engineering Development Administrator
  **Joshua Harrouch** . . . . . . . . . . . . . . . . . . . . . . . . . . . . . . (225) 242-4640
                                                      Fax: (225) 242-4630
Traffic Engineering Management Administrator
  **Ryan Hoyt** . . . . . . . . . . . . . . . . . . . . . . . . . . . . . . . . . . . (225) 379-1370
Executive Management Officer **(Vacant)** . . . . . . . . . . . . . . . (225) 379-1284

## Management and Finance Office

Undersecretary **BG Barry D. Keeling, ARNG** . . . . . . . . . . . (225) 379-1270
  Education: Southeastern Oklahoma St BS; Army War Col MSS
Deputy Undersecretary **Donald Johnson** . . . . . . . . . . . . . . (225) 379-1010
  Education: Southern U A&M 1992 BS
Enterprise Support Services Director **Brad D. Doucet** . . . . .(225) 379-1624
                                                      Fax: (225) 379-1003
Human Resources Director **Susan S. Pellegrin** . . . . . . . . . . (225) 379-1259
                                                      Fax: (225) 379-1856
Information Technology Director **Tom Sands** . . . . . . . . . . . (225) 379-1666
  E-mail: tom.sands@la.gov    Fax: (225) 379-1850
Procurement Director **Charlotte Garrison** . . . . . . . . . . . . . (225) 379-1444
                                                      Fax: (225) 379-1862
Financial Services Administrator **Lesha Woods** . . . . . . . . . .(225) 379-1616
                                                      Fax: (225) 379-1759

*(continued on next page)*

---

★ Elected Official    ■ Appointed by Governor    ● Appointed by Legislature    ▲ Appointed by Board or Commission    ◆ Appointed by State Supreme Court

---

**Management and Finance Office** *continued*

Management and Budget Administrator **Susan Stockstill** . . (225) 379-1262
Fax: (225) 379-1264

## Operations Office
Assistant Secretary **Kirk Gallien** . . . . . . . . . . . . . . . . . . . . (225) 379-1836
Deputy Assistant Secretary **Vincent "Vince" Latino** . . . . . (225) 379-1553
Emergency Operations Chief **Richard Swan** . . . . . . . . . . . . (225) 379-1783
Maintenance Chief **David Miller** . . . . . . . . . . . . . . . . . . . . (225) 379-1552
Fax: (225) 379-1549
Loss Prevention Director **Haley Antee** . . . . . . . . . . . . . . . . (225) 242-4676
Fax: (225) 242-4679
Tolling Operations Program Director **Scott Rundell** . . . . . . (225) 379-1578
Fax: (225) 379-2521
ITS (Intelligent Traffic Systems) Administrator
**Stephen Glascock** . . . . . . . . . . . . . . . . . . . . . . . . . . . . (225) 379-2516
E-mail: stephen.glascock@la.gov          Fax: (225) 379-2521
Education: Texas A&M 1990 MS
Maintenance Management Administrator **Leslie Mix** . . . . . . (225) 379-1796
E-mail: leslie.mix@la.gov          Fax: (225) 379-1700
Education: LSU 1983 BS
Structures and Facilities Maintenance Administrator
**(Vacant)** . . . . . . . . . . . . . . . . . . . . . . . . . . . . . . . . . . . (225) 379-1552
Traffic Engineer and Operations Administrator
**Carl Courville** . . . . . . . . . . . . . . . . . . . . . . . . . . . . . . . (225) 935-0101
Fax: (225) 935-0262
District 2 Engineer Administrator **Chris Morvant** . . . . . . . . (504) 437-3102
P.O. Box 9180, Bridge City, LA 70096-9180          Fax: (504) 437-3260
E-mail: chris.morvant@la.gov
District 3 Engineer Administrator **William J. Oliver** . . . . . . (337) 262-6100
P.O. Box 3648, Lafayette, LA 70502-3648          Fax: (337) 262-6260
E-mail: bill.oliver@la.gov
District 4 Engineer Administrator **David North** . . . . . . . . . . (318) 549-8301
P.O. Box 38, Shreveport, LA 71161-0038          Fax: (318) 549-8463
E-mail: david.north@la.gov
District 5 Engineer Administrator **Marshall Hill** . . . . . . . . . (318) 342-0131
P.O. Box 4068, Monroe, LA 71211-4068          Fax: (318) 342-0260
E-mail: marshall.hill@la.gov
District 7 Engineer Administrator **Todd Landry** . . . . . . . . . (337) 437-9101
P.O. Box 1430, Lake Charles, LA 70602-1430          Fax: (337) 437-9260
E-mail: todd.landry@la.gov
Education: Southwestern Louisiana BSCE
District 8 Engineer Administrator **Murphy Ledoux** . . . . . . . (318) 561-5101
P.O. Box 5945, Alexandria, LA 71307-5945          Fax: (318) 561-5288
E-mail: murphy.ledoux@la.gov
District 58 Engineer Administrator **Kenneth Mason** . . . . . . (318) 412-3131
P.O. Box 110, Chase, LA 71324-0110          Fax: (318) 412-3260
E-mail: ken.mason@la.gov
District 61 Engineer Administrator **Chad Vosburg** . . . . . . . (225) 231-4100
P.O. Box 831, Baton Rouge, LA 70821-0831          Fax: (225) 231-4108
E-mail: chad.vosburg@la.gov
District 62 Engineer Administrator **Allison Schilling** . . . . (985) 375-0101
685 North Morrison Boulevard,          Fax: (985) 375-0260
Hammond, LA 70401
E-mail: allison.schilling@la.gov

## Office of Multimodal Programming
1201 Capitol Access Road, Baton Rouge, LA 70802
P.O. Box 94245, Baton Rouge, LA 70804-9245
Fax: (225) 242-4552
■Assistant Secretary **Dennis A. Decker** . . . . . . . . . . . . . . . (225) 379-1248
E-mail: dennis.decker@la.gov          Fax: (225) 379-1851
Data Collection and Management Systems Administrator
**Jason Chapman** . . . . . . . . . . . . . . . . . . . . . . . . . . . . . . (225) 242-4578
E-mail: jason.chapman@la.gov          Fax: (225) 242-4552
Highway Safety Administrator **Dan Magri** . . . . . . . . . . . . . (225) 379-1871
E-mail: dan.magri@la.gov          Fax: (225) 242-4552
Transportation Planning Administrator **(Vacant)** . . . . . . . . . (225) 379-1214
Fax: (225) 379-1807

## Intermodal Transportation Office
Fax: (225) 274-4110
Deputy Assistant Secretary **Phil Jones** . . . . . . . . . . . . . . . . (225) 379-3038
Fax: (225) 379-1394

Aviation Director **Bradley Brandt** . . . . . . . . . . . . . . . . . . . . (225) 379-3050
Fax: (225) 379-3072
Offshore Terminal Authority Executive Director
**Robert Adley** . . . . . . . . . . . . . . . . . . . . . . . . . . . . . . . . (225) 274-4139
Education: Louisiana Tech U AB
Marine and Rail Administrator **Sharon Balfour** . . . . . . . . . (225) 379-3035
E-mail: sharon.balfour@la.gov
Education: LSU BS
Public Transportation Administrator **Donna Lavigne** . . . . . . (225) 379-3060
E-mail: donna.lavigne@la.gov          Fax: (225) 379-3071
Port Priority Director **Randall Withers** . . . . . . . . . . . . . . . (225) 379-3065

## Department of Veterans Affairs
P.O. Box 94095, Baton Rouge, LA 70804-9095
Tel: (225) 219-5000  Tel: (877) 432-8982  Fax: (225) 219-5590

**Employees: 839  Fiscal Year: 2013-2014  Budget: $57,443,303**
■Secretary **COL Joey Strickland, USA (Ret)** . . . . . . . . . . . (225) 219-5000
Undersecretary **Homer Rodgers** . . . . . . . . . . . . . . . . . . . . (225) 219-5000
Deputy Chief of Staff **(Vacant)** . . . . . . . . . . . . . . . . . . . . (225) 219-5001
Benefits Deputy Assistant Secretary **Alfred Leger** . . . . . . . (225) 219-5000
Finance Deputy Undersecretary **Robert M. Hayes** . . . . . . . (225) 219-5000
Human Resources Director **Dustin Guy** . . . . . . . . . . . . . . . (225) 219-5000
Press Secretary **Robin Keller** . . . . . . . . . . . . . . . . . . . . . . (225) 219-5000
E-mail: robin.keller@la.gov

## Department of Wildlife and Fisheries
P.O. Box 98000, Baton Rouge, LA 70898-9000
Tel: (225) 765-2800  Fax: (225) 765-2871

**Employees: 773  Fiscal Year: 2013-2014  Budget: $198,485,865**
■Secretary **Charles J. "Charlie" Melancon** . . . . . . . . . . . . (225) 765-2623
Education: Southwestern Louisiana 1971 BS
Executive Assistant **Amy Cannizaro Burris** . . . . . . . . . . . (225) 765-2623
Management and Finance Undersecretary
**Bryan McClinton** . . . . . . . . . . . . . . . . . . . . . . . . . . . . (225) 765-2860
Fisheries Assistant Secretary **Patrick Banks** . . . . . . . . . . . (225) 765-2801
Fisheries Administrator **Scott Longman** . . . . . . . . . . . . (225) 765-2801
Wildlife Assistant Secretary **Randy Myers** . . . . . . . . . . . . (225) 765-2805
Enforcement Division Chief **Col. Joseph Broussard** . . . . . (225) 765-2989
Licensing Director **Michelle Rayburn** . . . . . . . . . . . . . . . . (225) 765-2881

## Louisiana Wildlife and Fisheries Commission
P.O. Box 98000, Baton Rouge, LA 70898-9000
Tel: (225) 765-2806  Fax: (225) 765-0948

■Chair **Bart R. Yakupzack** . . . . . . . . . . . . . . . . . . . . . . . . (337) 494-0694
Term Expires: April 30, 2019          Fax: (337) 494-0697
P.O. Box 1467, Lake Charles, LA 70602
E-mail: bartyak@graylawfirm.com
Education: LSU BS
■Vice-Chair **Chad J. Courville** . . . . . . . . . . . . . . . . . . . . . (337) 264-1695
Term Expires: March 19, 2021          Fax: (337) 264-9499
309 La Rue France, Suite 201, Lafayette, LA 70508
E-mail: ccourville@miami-corp.com
■Commissioner **Billy Broussard** . . . . . . . . . . . . . . . . . . . . (337) 652-4191
Term Expires: March 13, 2020          Fax: (337) 737-2395
27024 West Louisiana Highway 82, Kaplan, LA 70548
E-mail: bbillypb@kaplantel.net
■Commissioner **Julie M. Hebert** . . . . . . . . . . . . . . . . . . . . (504) 452-7433
P.O. Box 1528, Luling, LA 70070
E-mail: jhebert@coastalpermitting.net
Education: Indiana BS
■Commissioner **William D. "Bill" Hogan** . . . . . . . . . . . . . (318) 255-3733
Term Expires: December 20, 2016          Fax: (318) 232-7051
2317 Soyars Circle, Ruston, LA 71270
E-mail: bill@bankruston.com
■Commissioner **Telley S. Madina** . . . . . . . . . . . . . . . . . . . (504) 393-0037
Term Expires: January 7, 2022
5501 Wimbledon Court, New Orleans, LA 70131
E-mail: telleym@gmail.com
■Commissioner **Edwin "Pat" Manuel** . . . . . . . . . . . . . . . . (337) 457-0101
Term Expires: December 12, 2017          Fax: (337) 457-7401
P.O. Box 1046, Eunice, LA 70535
E-mail: patmanuel.wlf@gmail.com

---

★ Elected Official    ■ Appointed by Governor    ● Appointed by Legislature    ▲ Appointed by Board or Commission    ◆ Appointed by State Supreme Court

# Louisiana Workforce Commission

P.O. Box 94094, Baton Rouge, LA 70804-9094
Tel: (225) 342-3111  Fax: (225) 342-3778

**Employees:** 1,033  **Fiscal Year:** 2013-2014  **Budget:** $2,729,831,984

■Executive Director **Ava Dejoie** . . . . . . . . . . . . . . . . . . . . . .(225) 342-3111
 E-mail: adejoie@lwc.la.gov
 Education: Loyola U (New Orleans)
Deputy Executive Director and Chief of Staff
 **Cathy Wells** . . . . . . . . . . . . . . . . . . . . . . . . . . . . . . .(225) 342-3001
 Education: Southern Methodist BS
Executive Counsel **Rob Roux** . . . . . . . . . . . . . . . . . . . . . .(225) 342-3044
 E-mail: rroux@lwc.la.gov
 Education: LSU JD
Equal Opportunity and Compliance Division Director
 **Evella Quiett** . . . . . . . . . . . . . . . . . . . . . . . . . . . . . . .(225) 342-3075
 E-mail: equiett@lwc.la.gov
Communications Director **(Vacant)** . . . . . . . . . . . . . . . . . .(225) 342-3035
Press Secretary **Lori Cherry** . . . . . . . . . . . . . . . . . . . . . . .(225) 342-3035
 Education: Rhodes 1995 BA

# Louisiana Rehabilitation Services

950 North 22nd Street, Baton Rouge, LA 70802
Tel: (225) 219-2225  Fax: (225) 219-2942

Director **Mark Martin** . . . . . . . . . . . . . . . . . . . . . . . . . . . .(225) 219-2294
 Education: LSU BS; Southern U (New Orleans) MS
Assistant Director **Kenneth "Ken" York** . . . . . . . . . . . . . . .(225) 219-2225
Blind Services Executive Director **C. Kevin Monk** . . . . . . .(225) 219-2943
Community Rehabilitation Program and Employment
 Development Bureau Administrator **Chris Anthony** . . . . .(225) 219-2389
 E-mail: canthony@lwc.la.gov
Performance Planning and Program Services Bureau
 Administrator **Rosemary Yesso** . . . . . . . . . . . . . . . . . . .(225) 219-2405
Program Planning Resource Development Bureau
 Administrator **Teresa Milner** . . . . . . . . . . . . . . . . . . . . .(225) 219-2993
                                        Fax: (225) 219-4993
Randolph-Sheppard Business Enterprise Program
 Manager **Steven DeBruhl** . . . . . . . . . . . . . . . . . . . . . . .(504) 432-7824

# Office of Management and Finance

■Chief Financial Officer **Bennett J. Soulier** . . . . . . . . . . . .(225) 342-3110
 Education: Southwestern Louisiana 1986 BS
Administrative Services Director
 **Rachel Lewis Ghebreyesus** . . . . . . . . . . . . . . . . . . . . . .(225) 342-4528
 E-mail: rghebreyesus@lwc.la.gov
Human Resources Director **Sarah Ragona** . . . . . . . . . . . . .(225) 342-3055
 E-mail: sragona@lwc.la.gov
Fiscal Account Administrator **Wayne Knight** . . . . . . . . . . .(225) 342-3103

# Office of Occupational Information Services

Information Technology Director **Raj Jindal** . . . . . . . . . . . .(225) 342-3222
 E-mail: rjindal@lwc.la.gov
 Education: LSU MS
Research and Statistics Manager **(Vacant)** . . . . . . . . . . . . .(225) 342-3143

# Office of Unemployment Insurance Administration

■Director **Renita Ward Williams** . . . . . . . . . . . . . . . . . . . .(225) 342-9296
Deputy Director **John "Ricky" Masaracchia** . . . . . . . . . . .(225) 342-6001
Board of Review and Appeals Chief **Shaydra Guillory** . . . .(225) 342-5044
Unemployment Insurance Tax Chief **(Vacant)** . . . . . . . . . . .(225) 342-2990
Fraud and Overpayment Manager (Acting)
 **John "Ricky" Masaracchia** . . . . . . . . . . . . . . . . . . . . . .(225) 242-1338
Quality Controls Manager **Greg Gaspard** . . . . . . . . . . . . .(225) 922-0269
Unemployment Insurance Benefits Chief **Tana Perry** . . . . . .(225) 342-2833
Unemployment Insurance Chief of Project Management
 Office **Ashley Linder** . . . . . . . . . . . . . . . . . . . . . . . . . .(225) 219-0678

# Office of Workforce Development

1001 North 23rd Street, Baton Rouge, LA 70804-9094
P.O. Box 94094, Baton Rouge, LA 70804-9094
Fax: (225) 342-6447

■Director **Bryan T. Moore** . . . . . . . . . . . . . . . . . . . . . . . . .(225) 342-2679
 E-mail: bmoore@lwc.la.gov
 Community Services Block Grant Supervisor
 **Jonie Smith** . . . . . . . . . . . . . . . . . . . . . . . . . . . . . . .(225) 342-3292
 E-mail: jsmith3@lwc.la.gov
Customized Workforce Solutions Deputy Director
 **Kelly Ebey** . . . . . . . . . . . . . . . . . . . . . . . . . . . . . . . .(225) 342-2185
 E-mail: kebey@lwc.la.gov
Incumbent Worker Training Program Director
 **Kevin Joyce** . . . . . . . . . . . . . . . . . . . . . . . . . . . . . . .(225) 342-8981
 E-mail: kjoyce@lwc.la.gov
Job Training and Placement Deputy Director
 **Bryan T. Moore** . . . . . . . . . . . . . . . . . . . . . . . . . . . .(225) 342-2679
 E-mail: bmoore@lwc.la.gov
Labor Programs Manager **Debra LaRocca** . . . . . . . . . . . . .(225) 342-7690
 E-mail: dlarocca@lwc.la.gov
Rapid Response Program Compliance Office Manager
 **Sonya Williams** . . . . . . . . . . . . . . . . . . . . . . . . . . . . .(225) 342-2185
 E-mail: swilliams@lwc.la.gov

# Office of Workers' Compensation Administration

■Director **Sheral Kellar** . . . . . . . . . . . . . . . . . . . . . . . . . . .(225) 342-7561
 E-mail: skellar@lwc.la.gov
Deputy Director **Larry White** . . . . . . . . . . . . . . . . . . . . . . .(225) 342-7555
Hearings Division Chief Judge **(Vacant)** . . . . . . . . . . . . . . .(225) 342-7970
Second Injury Fund Director **Pauline Williams** . . . . . . . . .(225) 342-7868
Workplace Safety Manager **Steve Bowers** . . . . . . . . . . . . .(225) 342-4430
Occupational Safety and Health Administration (OSHA)
 Manager **Corey Gaines** . . . . . . . . . . . . . . . . . . . . . . . . .(225) 219-4216
Medical Services Manager **Jan Clary** . . . . . . . . . . . . . . . . .(225) 342-7587
Records Management Manager **Andre DeLafuente** . . . . . . .(225) 342-5662
Fraud Compliance Officer **Kaye Fournet** . . . . . . . . . . . . . .(225) 342-7558
 E-mail: kfournet@lwc.la.gov

# Office of the Lieutenant Governor

1051 North Third Street, Baton Rouge, LA 70802
P.O. Box 44243, Baton Rouge, LA 70804
Tel: (225) 342-7009  Fax: (225) 342-1949

★Lieutenant Governor **William H. "Billy" Nungesser** (R) . .(225) 342-7009
 Term Expires: January 2020
 E-mail: ltgov@crt.la.gov
 Career: Parish President, Office of the Parish President, Plaquemines
 Parish, Louisiana (2007-2014)
 Executive Secretary **Elizabeth Bordelon** . . . . . . . . . . . . .(225) 342-7009
Chief of Staff **Guy Laigast** . . . . . . . . . . . . . . . . . . . . . . . .(225) 342-7009
General Counsel **Julia George Moore** . . . . . . . . . . . . . . . .(225) 342-7009
Senior Advisor **Julie Samson** . . . . . . . . . . . . . . . . . . . . . . .(225) 342-7009
Deputy Secretary **Rennie J. Buras II** . . . . . . . . . . . . . . . . .(225) 342-7009
Internal Auditor **Cindy Summers** . . . . . . . . . . . . . . . . . . . .(225) 342-7009
Director of Boards and Commissions **(Vacant)** . . . . . . . . . .(225) 342-7009
Communications Director **(Vacant)** . . . . . . . . . . . . . . . . . . .(225) 342-7009

# Office of the Attorney General

1885 North Third Street, Baton Rouge, LA 70802
P.O. Box 94005, Baton Rouge, LA 70804
Tel: (225) 326-6709  Fax: (225) 326-6793

★Attorney General **Jeffrey M. "Jeff" Landry** (R) . . . . . . . .(225) 326-6705
 Term Expires: January 2020
 Education: Southwestern Louisiana 1999 BS;
 Southern U (New Orleans) (Attended);
 Loyola U (New Orleans) 2004 JD
 Career: U.S. Representative (R-LA, District 3), Office of Representative
 Jeff Landry, United States House of Representatives (2011-2013)
Chief Deputy Attorney General **Wilbur L. "Bill" Stiles** . . .(225) 326-6705
Director of Administrative Services Division
 **Michael Larisey** . . . . . . . . . . . . . . . . . . . . . . . . . . . . . .(225) 326-6705
 E-mail: lariseym@ag.louisiana.gov

*(continued on next page)*

---

★ Elected Official    ■ Appointed by Governor    ● Appointed by Legislature    ▲ Appointed by Board or Commission    ◆ Appointed by State Supreme Court

**Office of the Attorney General** *continued*

Director of Civil Division **Elizabeth Baker Murrill** . . . . . . . (225) 326-6000
  Education: LSU 1985 BA;                Fax: (225) 326-6097
  LSU Hebert Law 1991 JD; Pepperdine 2010
Director of Criminal Division **Brandon Fremin** . . . . . . . . . . (225) 326-6200
  Education: LSU Hebert Law JD          Fax: (225) 326-6297
Director of Gaming Division **Christopher Hebert** . . . . . . . . (225) 326-6500
  Education: LSU; Southern U Law JD     Fax: (225) 326-6599
Director of Investigation Division **Joseph Picone** . . . . . . . . (225) 326-6100
                                  Fax: (225) 326-6197
Director of Litigation Division **Sonia Mallett** . . . . . . . . . . (225) 326-6300
                                  Fax: (225) 326-6490
Director of Public Protection Division **Renée Free** . . . . . . . (225) 326-6438
  Education: McNeese State; Southern U Law JD   Fax: (225) 326-6497
Librarian **Mary Adams** . . . . . . . . . . . . . . . . . . . . . . . . . . . (225) 326-6400

## Alexandria Office - Litigation Division
429 Murray St., 4th Floor, Alexandria, LA 71301
Fax: (318) 487-5826
Office Chief **Victoria Murry** . . . . . . . . . . . . . . . . . . . . . . . (318) 487-5944

## Lafayette Office - Litigation Division
556 Jefferson Street, 4th Floor, Lafayette, LA 70501
Fax: (337) 262-1707
Office Chief **Owen Goudelocke** . . . . . . . . . . . . . . . . . . . . . (337) 262-1700

## New Orleans Office - Litigation Division
New Orleans Office, 400 Poydras Street, Suite 1600,
New Orleans, LA 70130
Tel: (504) 599-1200 Fax: (504) 599-1218
Office Chief **Stephen Babin** . . . . . . . . . . . . . . . . . . . . . . . (504) 599-1200

## Shreveport Office - Litigation Division
330 Marshall Street, Suite 777, Shreveport, LA 71101
Fax: (318) 676-5703
Office Chief **John Frederickson** . . . . . . . . . . . . . . . . . . . . (318) 676-5700

## Office of the Secretary of State
8585 Archives Avenue, Baton Rouge, LA 70809
Tel: (225) 922-2880 Fax: (225) 922-2003

**Employees: 752 Fiscal Year: 2015-2016 Budget: $82,902,649**

★Secretary of State **John Thomas "Tom" Schedler** (R) . . . (225) 922-2880
  Term Expires: January 2020
  Education: Louisiana (Lafayette) 1971 BS
  Career: State Senator (R-LA, District 11), Louisiana State Senate
  (1996-2008)
First Assistant Secretary of State **Kyle Ardoin** . . . . . . . . . . (225) 922-2880
Commissioner of Elections **Angie Rogers** . . . . . . . . . . . . . (225) 922-0900
Undersecretary of Management and Finance
  **Joe R. Salter** . . . . . . . . . . . . . . . . . . . . . . . . . . . . . . . (225) 922-2880
  Education: Northwestern State BS, MEd
Louisiana State Archivist **Florent Hardy, Jr., PhD** . . . . . . . (225) 922-1000
                                  Fax: (225) 922-0433
Commercial and Notary Division Director
  **Carla Bonaventure** . . . . . . . . . . . . . . . . . . . . . . . . . . . (225) 925-4716
Security and Elections Compliance Unit and Security
  Director **Jim McKenzie** . . . . . . . . . . . . . . . . . . . . . . . . (225) 362-5223
Human Resources Division Director **Ashley Gautreaux** . . . (225) 925-4696
Information Technology Division Director **Scott Mayers** . . (225) 922-0626
  E-mail: scott.mayers@sos.la.gov
Museums Division Director **Mary Durusau** . . . . . . . . . . . . (225) 219-6117
Accounting and Purchasing Division Director
  **Shanda Jones** . . . . . . . . . . . . . . . . . . . . . . . . . . . . . . (225) 922-1229
Press Secretary **Meg Casper** . . . . . . . . . . . . . . . . . . . . . . (225) 362-5086

## Louisiana Department of the Treasury
P.O. Box 44154, Baton Rouge, LA 70804
Tel: (225) 342-0010 Fax: (225) 342-0046
E-mail: comments@treasury.state.la.us Internet: www.latreasury.com

**Employees: 57 Fiscal Year: 2013-2014 Budget: $12,162,724**

★Treasurer **John Neely Kennedy** (R) . . . . . . . . . . . . . . . . . (225) 342-0431
  Term Expires: January 2020
  E-mail: jkennedy@treasury.state.la.us
  Education: Vanderbilt BA; Virginia 1971 JD; Oxford (UK) BCL
  Career: Secretary, Revenue Department, State of Louisiana (1996-1999)
  Confidential Assistant **Desie Mack** . . . . . . . . . . . . . . . . . (225) 342-0016
Deputy State Treasurer **Renee Ellender-Roberie** . . . . . . . . (225) 342-0010
First Assistant State Treasurer **Ron J. Henson** . . . . . . . . . . (225) 342-0055
  Education: Louisiana Tech U 1971 BS
  Policy and Research Director **Sharon Calcote** . . . . . . . . (225) 342-0006
    E-mail: scalcote@treasury.state.la.us
Chief Investment Officer **John J. Broussard** . . . . . . . . . . . (225) 342-0013
  E-mail: jbroussard@treasury.state.la.us
  Education: LSU 1991 MA
Executive Counsel **Thomas Enright** . . . . . . . . . . . . . . . . . . (225) 342-0040
  Education: LSU 1994 BA; LSU Hebert Law 1997 JD
Human Resources Director **Lynette Mack** . . . . . . . . . . . . . (225) 342-0030
  Education: Southern U (Shreveport) 1976 BS
Information Technology Director **Benjamin Morton** . . . . . . (225) 342-0239
  E-mail: bmorton@treasury.state.la.us
State Bond Commission Director **Lela M. Folse** . . . . . . . . (225) 342-0040
Unclaimed Property Director **Kathleen Lobell** . . . . . . . . . . (225) 219-9384
Communications Director **Michelle Millhollon** . . . . . . . . . (225) 342-0012
Internal Auditor **Donnie Ladatto** . . . . . . . . . . . . . . . . . . . (225) 342-0938

## Louisiana Department of Agriculture and Forestry [LDAF]
5825 Florida Boulevard, Suite 2000, Baton Rouge, LA 70806
P.O. Box 631, Baton Rouge, LA 70821-0631
Tel: (225) 922-1234 Fax: (225) 922-1253 Internet: www.ldaf.state.la.us

**Employees: 582 Fiscal Year: 2013-2014 Budget: $73,706,612**

★Commissioner **Michael G. "Mike" Strain, DVM** (R) . . . . . (225) 922-1234
  Term Expires: January 2020
  E-mail: commissioner@ldaf.la.gov
  Education: LSU BS, 1983 DVM
Deputy Commissioner **Brent Robbins, DVM** . . . . . . . . . . . (225) 922-1234
  Confidential Assistant **Fred Bass** . . . . . . . . . . . . . . . . . (225) 922-1234
Executive Counsel **Tabitha I. Gray** . . . . . . . . . . . . . . . . . . (225) 922-1234
  Education: Southern U A&M BS, JD
Press Secretary **Veronica Mosgrove** . . . . . . . . . . . . . . . . . (225) 922-1256
  Education: Loyola U (Chicago)
General Counsel **Lindsey Hunter** . . . . . . . . . . . . . . . . . . . . (225) 922-1234

## Louisiana Department of Insurance [LDI]
P.O. Box 94214, Baton Rouge, LA 70804-9214
Tel: (225) 342-5900 Tel: (800) 259-5300 (In State)
Tel: (800) 259-5301 (In State) Fax: (225) 342-8622
E-mail: public@ldi.la.gov Internet: www.ldi.la.gov

**Employees: 225 Fiscal Year: 2014-2015 Budget: $30,500,000**

★Insurance Commissioner **James J. "Jim" Donelon** (R) . . . (225) 342-5423
  Term Expires: January 2020
  Education: New Orleans 1967 BA; Loyola Law JD
Chief of Staff **Denise Brignac** . . . . . . . . . . . . . . . . . . . . . . (225) 342-5423
  Education: Southeastern Louisiana BA
Chief Deputy Commissioner **Denise Brignac** . . . . . . . . . . . (225) 342-5423
Consumer Advocacy and Diversity Deputy Commissioner
  **Ron C. Henderson III** . . . . . . . . . . . . . . . . . . . . . . . . . (225) 219-4775
  Education: Southern U (New Orleans) BS; Southern U Law JD
Financial Solvency Deputy Commissioner
  **Caroline Brock** . . . . . . . . . . . . . . . . . . . . . . . . . . . . . . (225) 342-1631
Chief Actuary **Rich Piazza** . . . . . . . . . . . . . . . . . . . . . . . . (225) 342-4690
Chief Examiner **Stewart Guerin** . . . . . . . . . . . . . . . . . . . . (225) 342-1631
Chief Examiner **Craig Gardner** . . . . . . . . . . . . . . . . . . . . . (225) 342-8391

---

★ Elected Official    ■ Appointed by Governor    ● Appointed by Legislature    ▲ Appointed by Board or Commission    ◆ Appointed by State Supreme Court

Consumer Services Deputy Commissioner **Jeffrey Zewe** . . (225) 219-0002
  Education: New Orleans BA; Loyola U (New Orleans) JD
Health Insurance Deputy Commissioner **Korey Harvey** . . . . (225) 342-1355
  Education: LSU BA, JD
Health Insurance Assistant Commissioner **Laura Bryan** . . (225) 219-9433
Licensing Deputy Commissioner **Barry Ward** . . . . . . . . . . . (225) 342-0814
  Licensing Assistant Commissioner **Michael Boutwell** . . . (225) 342-0800
Management and Finance Deputy Commissioner
  **Denise Brignac** . . . . . . . . . . . . . . . . . . . . . . . . . . . . . . . (225) 342-5423
  E-mail: dbrignac@ldi.la.gov
  Management and Finance Assistant Commissioner
    **Lance Herrin** . . . . . . . . . . . . . . . . . . . . . . . . . . . . . . . (225) 342-5347
    E-mail: lherrin@ldi.la.gov
  Fiscal Affairs Director **Penny Rodriguez** . . . . . . . . . . . . . (225) 342-5351
  Human Resources Division Director **Pamela Croxton** . . . (225) 342-5325
  Procurement Specialist **Shannon Gilchrist** . . . . . . . . . . . (225) 219-1701
Diversity Opportunity Assistant Commissioner
  **Patrick Bell** . . . . . . . . . . . . . . . . . . . . . . . . . . . . . . . . . (225) 342-8393
Property and Casualty Deputy Commissioner
  **Warren Byrd** . . . . . . . . . . . . . . . . . . . . . . . . . . . . . . . . . (225) 342-5203
  Insurance Fraud Assistant Commissioner **Trent Beach** . . . (225) 342-0073
Public Affairs Deputy Commissioner **Ileana Ledet** . . . . . . . (225) 342-4950
  Public Information Director **Judy Wright** . . . . . . . . . . . . (225) 342-1429
    E-mail: judy.wright@la.gov
Executive Counsel **Arlene D. Knighten** . . . . . . . . . . . . . . . (225) 342-4673
Fraud Director **Matthew Stewart** . . . . . . . . . . . . . . . . . . . (225) 342-4936
Health Care Commission Director **Crystal Campbell** . . . . . (225) 342-4311
Life and Annuity Director **Beth O'Quin** . . . . . . . . . . . . . . (225) 219-0633

# Military Department

Jackson Barracks, 6400 St. Claude Avenue, New Orleans, LA 70117
Tel: (504) 278-8357  Fax: (504) 278-8210

■Adjutant General **MG Glenn H. Curtis, ARNG** . . . . . . . . . (504) 278-8357
  E-mail: glenn.curtis@la.gov
  Education: LSU 1986 BS; Army War Col 2003 MS

# State Board of Elementary and Secondary Education [BESE]

P.O. Box 94064, Baton Rouge, LA 70804-9064
Tel: (225) 342-5840  Fax: (225) 342-5843  E-mail: sbese@la.gov
Internet: bese.louisiana.gov

★President
  **James D. "Jim" Garvey, Jr., CPA** (R-District 1) . . . . . . . (504) 836-6587
  One Galleria Boulevard, Suite 1400,           Fax: (504) 836-6565
  Metairie, LA 70001
  E-mail: james.garvey@la.gov
  Education: Loyola U (New Orleans) 1987 BBA, 1991 MBA, 1991 JD
★Vice President **Holly Boffy** (R-District 7) . . . . . . . . . . . . . (225) 342-5840
  E-mail: holly.boffy@la.gov
  Education: LSU BS, MEd, EdS
★Secretary-Treasurer **Kira Orange Jones** (D-District 2) . . . . (225) 342-5840
  E-mail: kira.orangejones@la.gov
  Affiliation: Executive Director and Senior Vice President, Greater New
    Orleans-Louisiana Delta Region, Teach For America, Inc.
  1055 St. Charles Avenue, Suite 600, New Orleans, LA 70130
  Education: Horace Mann (Riverdale, NY) 1996; Wesleyan U 2000 BA;
    Harvard MEd
★Member **Tony Davis** (R-District 4) . . . . . . . . . . . . . . . . . . (225) 342-5840
  Term Expires: 2020
  E-mail: tony.davis@la.gov
★Member **Kathy Edmonston** (R-District 6) . . . . . . . . . . . . . (225) 342-5840
  Term Expires: 2020
  E-mail: kathy.edmonston@la.gov
  Education: LSU
★Member **Gary L. Jones, PhD** (R-District 5) . . . . . . . . . . . . (225) 342-5840
  Term Expires: 2020
  E-mail: gary.jones@la.gov
★Member **Sandy Leblanc Holloway** (R-District 3) . . . . . . . . (225) 342-5840
  Term Expires: 2020
  E-mail: sandy.holloway@la.gov
★Member **Jada Lewis** (D-District 8) . . . . . . . . . . . . . . . . . . (225) 276-7776
  Term Expires: 2020
  E-mail: jada.lewis@la.gov
  Education: LSU BSChE

■Member **Thomas Roque** (At-Large) . . . . . . . . . . . . . . . . . . (318) 362-3058
■Member **Dr. Lurie Thomason, Jr.** (At-Large) . . . . . . . . . . (318) 362-3058
■Member **Doris Voitier** (At-Large) . . . . . . . . . . . . . . . . . . . (318) 362-3058
Executive Director **Shan N. Davis** . . . . . . . . . . . . . . . . . . . (225) 342-5840
  E-mail: shan.davis@la.gov

# Louisiana Department of Education [LDOE]

P.O. Box 94064, Baton Rouge, LA 70804-9064
Tel: (877) 453-2721

**Employees:** 552  **Fiscal Year:** 2013-2014  **Budget:** $5,162,751,518

▲State Superintendent **John C. White** . . . . . . . . . . . . . . . . . (225) 342-3974
  E-mail: johnwhite@la.gov
  Education: Virginia 1998 BA; NYU MPA
  Confidential Assistant **Vicky Thomas** . . . . . . . . . . . . . . . (225) 342-3607
Chief Operating Officer **Bridget Devlin** . . . . . . . . . . . . . . . (225) 342-3625
  E-mail: bridget.devlin@la.gov
Policy Director **Erin Bendily** . . . . . . . . . . . . . . . . . . . . . . (225) 342-3625
  E-mail: erin.bendily@la.gov
Communications Director **Barry Landry** . . . . . . . . . . . . . . (225) 342-3600
  E-mail: barry.landry@la.gov
General Counsel **Joan Hunt** . . . . . . . . . . . . . . . . . . . . . . . (225) 342-3754
Internal Audit Director **Dudley J. Garidel, Jr.** . . . . . . . . . . (225) 342-1518
Certification, Preparation and Policy Administrator
  **Blanche Adams** . . . . . . . . . . . . . . . . . . . . . . . . . . . . . . . (225) 342-6975
Children's Trust Fund Executive Director **(Vacant)** . . . . . . . (225) 342-2245
Child Development and Early Learning Program Director
  **(Vacant)** . . . . . . . . . . . . . . . . . . . . . . . . . . . . . . . . . . . . (225) 342-0694

## Office of Management and Finance

Tel: (877) 453-2721

Deputy Superintendent **Elizabeth "Beth" Scioneaux** . . . . . (225) 343-3617
  E-mail: beth.scioneaux@la.gov
Appropriation Control Division Director **(Vacant)** . . . . . . . (225) 342-3830
Education Finance Division Director **Charlotte Stevens** . . . (225) 343-4989
Planning, Analysis and Information Resources Division
  Director **(Vacant)** . . . . . . . . . . . . . . . . . . . . . . . . . . . . . (225) 342-0091
Information Technology Deputy Director
  **James McMahon** . . . . . . . . . . . . . . . . . . . . . . . . . . . . . . (225) 342-0092
  E-mail: james.mcmahon@la.gov            Tel: (225) 342-0101
Human Resources Director **Jason Hannaman** . . . . . . . . . . (225) 342-3774

## Office of Special School District

Building F, 2888 Brightside Lane, Baton Rouge, LA 70820
Tel: (225) 763-5515  Fax: (225) 763-5557

**Employees:** 140  **Fiscal Year:** 2013-2014  **Budget:** $13,538,331

Superintendent (Interim) **Monte Burke** . . . . . . . . . . . . . . . (225) 757-3200
Louisiana School for the Visually Impaired Director
  **Bobby Simpson** . . . . . . . . . . . . . . . . . . . . . . . . . . . . . . (225) 757-3482
  P.O. Box 4328, Baton Rouge, LA 70521-4328
  Education: LSU BS, MS
Louisiana School for the Deaf Director
  **Dr. Nancy Benham** . . . . . . . . . . . . . . . . . . . . . . . . . . . . (225) 757-3202
  P.O. Box 3074, Baton Rouge, LA 70821        Fax: (225) 757-3424
Louisiana Special Education Center Director
  **Richard Bushnell** . . . . . . . . . . . . . . . . . . . . . . . . . . . . . (318) 487-2223

---

★ Elected Official   ■ Appointed by Governor   ● Appointed by Legislature   ▲ Appointed by Board or Commission   ◆ Appointed by State Supreme Court

# Maine

Tel: (207) 264-9494 (State Information)

**Number of U.S. Congressional Delegates:** 2 Senators; 2 Representatives  **Governor's Term:** 4 years
**Legislature Description:** 35 member Senate; 151 member House of Representatives; Term - Senate 2 years, House 2 years  **Next Election:** Governor November 2018; Legislature November 2016
**Number of Electoral Votes:** 4  **Official Name:** State of Maine (after ancient French province)
**Nickname:** Pine Tree State  **Motto:** Dirigo (I direct)

**Population:** 1,329,328 (2015); Rank 42  **Fiscal Year:** 2013-2014  **Budget:** $8,238,867,000

## Office of the Governor

One State House Station, Augusta, ME 04333
Tel: (207) 287-3531  TTY: (207) 287-6548  Fax: (207) 287-1034

**Paul R. LePage**
Governor

Began Service: January 5, 2011
Term Expires: 2019
Date of Birth: October 9, 1948
Education: Husson 1971 BS; Maine 1975 MBA
Home: Waterville
Religion: Roman Catholic
Career: Consultant, LePage & Kasevich, Inc. (1983-1996); Council Member, City of Waterville, Maine (1997-2003); Mayor (R-ME), City of Waterville, Maine (2003-2011)

★Governor **Paul R. LePage** (R) . . . . . . . . . . . . . . . . . . . . . (207) 287-3531
  E-mail: governor@maine.gov
Chief of Staff **John McGough** . . . . . . . . . . . . . . . . . . . . . . (207) 287-3531
  Assistant to the Chief of Staff **Stephanie Ham** . . . . . . . . (207) 287-3531
    E-mail: stephanie.ham@maine.gov
Deputy Chief of Staff and Legislative Director
  **Kathleen Newman** . . . . . . . . . . . . . . . . . . . . . . . . . . . (207) 287-3531
    E-mail: kathleen.newman@maine.gov
Chief Legal Counsel **Avery Day** . . . . . . . . . . . . . . . . . . . . (207) 287-3531
Deputy Legal Counsel and Senior Policy Advisor
  **Hancock "Hank" Fenton** . . . . . . . . . . . . . . . . . . . . . . . (207) 287-3531
    E-mail: hancock.fenton@maine.gov
Economic Development Senior Policy Advisor
  **John Butera** . . . . . . . . . . . . . . . . . . . . . . . . . . . . . . . . (207) 287-3531
    E-mail: john.butera@maine.gov
    Education: Pennsylvania BA, MA
Constituency Services Director **Patricia A. Condon** . . . . . . (207) 287-3531
    E-mail: patricia.a.condon@maine.gov
Senior Health Policy Advisor **David Sorensen** . . . . . . . . . . (207) 287-3531
Senior Policy Advisor **Aaron Chadbourne** . . . . . . . . . . . . . (207) 287-3531
Senior Policy Advisor **Lance Libby** . . . . . . . . . . . . . . . . . . (207) 287-3531
Press Secretary **Adrienne Bennett** . . . . . . . . . . . . . . . . . . (207) 287-2531
    E-mail: adrienne.bennett@maine.gov
  Communications Director **Peter Steele** . . . . . . . . . . . . . (207) 287-5086
Boards and Commissions Special Assistant
  **Lindsey Oliver** . . . . . . . . . . . . . . . . . . . . . . . . . . . . . . (207) 287-3531
Scheduler **Nicole Desjardins** . . . . . . . . . . . . . . . . . . . . . . (207) 287-3531

## Department of Administrative and Financial Services [DAFS]

78 State House Station, Augusta, ME 04333-0078
Tel: (207) 624-7800  Fax: (207) 624-7804  TTY: (207) 287-4537
Internet: www.maine.gov/dafs

**Employees:** 1,385  **Fiscal Year:** 2015-2016  **Budget:** $384,539,000

■Commissioner **Richard W. Rosen** . . . . . . . . . . . . . . . . . . . (207) 624-7800
  E-mail: richard.rosen@maine.gov
  Administrative Assistant **Jennifer Merrow** . . . . . . . . . . . . (207) 624-7800
Deputy Commissioner of Finance **Michael J. Allen** . . . . . . . (207) 624-7827
  E-mail: michael.j.allen@maine.gov

Deputy Commissioner of Operations **David R. Lavway** . . . . (207) 624-7858
  E-mail: david.lavway@maine.gov
  Education: Maine BS
Associate Commissioner **Kimberly A. Smith** . . . . . . . . . . . (207) 624-7389
  E-mail: kimberly.a.smith@maine.gov

### State Controller's Office

14 State House Station, Augusta, ME 04333-0014
Tel: (207) 626-8420  Fax: (207) 626-8422  Internet: www.maine.gov/osc
State Controller (Acting) **Doug Cotnoir** . . . . . . . . . . . . . . (207) 626-8428
Accounting/Records Division Supervisor **Tammy Chase** . . . (207) 626-8420
Payroll/Pre-Audit Division Supervisor **Betty L. Everatt** . . . (207) 626-8442
Accounting and Budget Systems **Cathy J. Harrison** . . . . . . (207) 441-4632

### Alcoholic Beverages and Lottery Operations Bureau

8 State House Station, Augusta, ME 04333-0008
Tel: (207) 287-3721  Fax: (207) 287-6769
Internet: www.mainelottery.com
Director **Gregory Mineo** . . . . . . . . . . . . . . . . . . . . . . . . . (207) 287-3721
Merchandising Division Liquor Manager
  **Michael Boardman** . . . . . . . . . . . . . . . . . . . . . . . . . . . (207) 287-4614
Security and Production Manager **Clayton Smith** . . . . . . . . (207) 287-6759

### Budget Bureau

58 State House Station, Augusta, ME 04333-0058
State Budget Officer **Melissa Gott** . . . . . . . . . . . . . . . . . . (207) 624-7810

### General Services Bureau

Director **Ed Dahl** . . . . . . . . . . . . . . . . . . . . . . . . . . . . . . . (207) 624-7314
  E-mail: ed.dahl@maine.gov
Purchasing Division Director **Mark Lutte** . . . . . . . . . . . . . (207) 624-7335
  Central Services Director **Andy Giroux** . . . . . . . . . . . . . (207) 287-4593
Risk Management Division Director **David A. Fitts** . . . . . . . (207) 287-3352

### Human Resources Bureau

Director **Joyce A. Oreskovich** . . . . . . . . . . . . . . . . . . . . . (207) 624-7368
Employee Health Insurance Program Executive Director
  **Christine Brawn** . . . . . . . . . . . . . . . . . . . . . . . . . . . . . (207) 624-7361

### Office of Information Technology [OIT]

Chief Information Officer **Jim Smith** . . . . . . . . . . . . . . . . . (207) 624-7568
  E-mail: jim.smith@maine.gov
Chief Technology Officer **Greg A. McNeal** . . . . . . . . . . . . (207) 624-7568
  E-mail: greg.mcneal@maine.gov
Enterprise Security Officer **Kevin St. Thomas** . . . . . . . . . . (207) 624-9845
  E-mail: kevin.stthomas@maine.gov
Network Services Manager **Jon Richard** . . . . . . . . . . . . . . (207) 624-9861
  E-mail: jon.richard@maine.gov
Workforce Development Director **Kelly Samson-Rickert** . . (207) 624-9965
  E-mail: kelly.rickert@maine.gov
  Education: Westbrook; James Madison; Shenandoah MA, PhD

---

★ Elected Official    ■ Appointed by Governor    ● Appointed by Legislature    ▲ Appointed by Board or Commission    ◆ Appointed by State Supreme Court

EXECUTIVE BRANCH

## Maine Revenue Services

24 State House Station, Augusta, ME 04333-0024
Tel: (207) 626-8475  Fax: (207) 287-5855
Internet: www.maine.gov/revenue

State Tax Assessor **Jerome D. Gerard** . . . . . . . . . . . . . . . (207) 624-7854
Tax Policy Associate Commissioner **Michael J. Allen** . . . . . (207) 624-9570
  E-mail: michael.j.allen@maine.gov
Taxpayer Advocate **Bruce R. Livingston** . . . . . . . . . . . . . . (207) 624-9649
Chief Counsel **Nanette Ardry** . . . . . . . . . . . . . . . . . . (207) 624-9725
Appellate Division Director **Stanley W. Piecuch** . . . . . . . . (207) 624-9701
Compliance Division Director **Michael W. Fortin** . . . . . . . . (207) 624-9691
Income/Estate Tax Division Director
  **Heather O. Popadak** . . . . . . . . . . . . . . . . . . . . . . . (207) 624-9999
Property Tax Division Director **David P. Ledew** . . . . . . . . . (207) 624-5601
Sales, Fuel and Special Taxes Director
  **Peter B. Beaulieu** . . . . . . . . . . . . . . . . . . . . . . . . . (207) 624-9732

## Maine Department of Agriculture, Conservation and Forestry [MDACF]

Tel: (207) 287-3200  E-mail: dacf@maine.gov

**Fiscal Year:** 2014-2015  **Budget:** $57,936,000

Commissioner **Walter Whitcomb** . . . . . . . . . . . . . . . . . . . (207) 287-3419
  Assistant to Commissioner **Kathy Eastman** . . . . . . . . . . . (207) 287-3419
Deputy Commissioner **(Vacant)** . . . . . . . . . . . . . . . . . . . (207) 287-3200
Public Information Director **John C. Bott** . . . . . . . . . . . . . (207) 287-3156
  E-mail: john.c.bott@maine.gov

## Department of Corrections [DOC]

111 State House Station, Augusta, ME 04333
Tel: (207) 287-2711  Fax: (207) 287-4370  TTY: (207) 287-4472
Internet: www.maine.gov/corrections

**Employees:** 1,309  **Fiscal Year:** 2013-2014  **Budget:** $148,635,000

■Commissioner **Dr. Joseph Fitzpatrick** . . . . . . . . . . . . . . . (207) 287-4360
  E-mail: joseph.fitzpatrick@maine.gov
Associate Commissioner (Adults) **Rodney Bouffard** . . . . . . (207) 287-4384
Associate Commissioner (Juveniles) **Colin O'Neill** . . . . . . . (207) 287-4362
Deputy Commissioner (Legislative and Program Services)
  **Jody Breton** . . . . . . . . . . . . . . . . . . . . . . . . . . . . . (207) 287-4378
  E-mail: jody.breton@maine.gov
Classification Director **Scott McCaffery** . . . . . . . . . . . . . . (207) 287-4376
  Industries Director **Scott Reiff** . . . . . . . . . . . . . . . . . . (207) 287-4364
Juvenile Justice Advisory Group Director
  **Kathryn McGloin** . . . . . . . . . . . . . . . . . . . . . . . . . . (207) 287-1923
Budget and Fiscal Operations Division Director
  **Scott Ferguson** . . . . . . . . . . . . . . . . . . . . . . . . . . . (207) 592-3262
Operations Director **Gary LaPlante** . . . . . . . . . . . . . . . . (207) 287-2698
Personnel Division Director **Charlene Gamage** . . . . . . . . . (207) 287-4364

## Department of Defense, Veterans and Emergency Management [DVEM]

Camp Keyes, Augusta, ME 04333-0033
Tel: (207) 430-6000  Fax: (207) 626-4509
Internet: www.maine.gov/va/defense/dvs.htm

**Employees:** 201  **Fiscal Year:** 2013-2014  **Budget:** $226,294,000

■Commissioner **BrigGen Douglas Farnham, ANG** . . . . . . . . (207) 430-5158
Deputy Commissioner **Daniel Goodheart** . . . . . . . . . . . . . (207) 430-5161
Executive Officer **MAJ Paul A. Bosse, ARNG** . . . . . . . . . (207) 430-5950

## Bureau of Maine Veterans' Services

117 State House Station, Augusta, ME 04333
Tel: (207) 626-4464  Internet: www.maine.gov/dvem/bvs

Director **Adria Horn** . . . . . . . . . . . . . . . . . . . . . . . . . . (207) 626-4469
Togus Veterans Hospital Administration Claims Specialist
  **Maurice Lizotte** . . . . . . . . . . . . . . . . . . . . . . . . . . . (207) 623-5732

## Maine Emergency Management Agency [MEMA]

72 State House Station, Augusta, ME 04333
Fax: (207) 287-3180  Internet: www.maine.gov/mema

Director **Bruce Fitzgerald** . . . . . . . . . . . . . . . . . . . . . . (207) 624-4400
  Education: Maine BA

## Maine National Guard

33 State House Station, Augusta, ME 04333-0033
Fax: (207) 626-4509

■Adjutant General **BrigGen Douglas Farnham, ANG** . . . . . (207) 430-5158

## Maine Air National Guard

Tel: (207) 430-6121  Internet: www.mebngr.ang.af.mil/Default.cfm

Assistant Adjutant General
  **BrigGen Gerard Bolduc, ANG** . . . . . . . . . . . . . . . . . . (207) 430-6121
Judge Advocate General
  **LtCol Kenneth Wade Fredette, ANG** . . . . . . . . . . . . . . (207) 990-7604
  Education: Maine (Machias) BS; Southern Maine; Maine JD

## Maine Army National Guard

Internet: www.me.ngb.army.mil

Assistant Adjutant General
  **COL Michael Bouchard, ARNG** . . . . . . . . . . . . . . . . . . (207) 430-6000
  Education: Norwich 1985 BSCE; Troy State 1998 MPA;
  Army War Col 2006 MSS
Chief of Staff **COL Michael McLaughlin, ARNG** . . . . . . . . (207) 430-6000

## Department of Economic and Community Development [DECD]

59 State House Station, Augusta, ME 04333-0059
Tel: (207) 624-9800 ((Automated))
Tel: (888) 624-6345 (Tourist Information)  Fax: (207) 287-2861
E-mail: biz.growth@maine.gov

**Employees:** 32  **Fiscal Year:** 2013-2014  **Budget:** $45,175,000

■Commissioner **George Gervais** . . . . . . . . . . . . . . . . . . . (207) 624-9805
  E-mail: george.gervais@maine.gov
  Education: Maine BSBA
Deputy Commissioner **Denise Garland** . . . . . . . . . . . . . . (207) 624-7496
Film Office Director **Karen Carberry Warhola** . . . . . . . . . (207) 624-9828
  Education: Maine BA

## Maine Office of Tourism

59 State House Station, Augusta, ME 04333
Tel: (888) 624-6345  Tel: (207) 287-5711 (Automated Service)
Fax: (207) 287-8070  Internet: www.visitmaine.com

■Director **Carolann Ouellette** . . . . . . . . . . . . . . . . . . . . (207) 624-7483
  E-mail: carolann.ouellette@maine.gov
Administrative Assistant **Cheryl Breault** . . . . . . . . . . . . . (207) 624-7483

## Office of Community Development

Director **Deb Johnson** . . . . . . . . . . . . . . . . . . . . . . . . . (207) 624-7484
                                          Fax: (207) 287-8070

## Department of Education [DOE]

23 State House Station, Augusta, ME 04333-0023
Tel: (207) 624-6600  Fax: (207) 624-6700  Internet: www.maine.gov/doe

**Employees:** 164  **Fiscal Year:** 2014-2015  **Budget:** $1,408,970,000

■Commissioner **(Vacant)** . . . . . . . . . . . . . . . . . . . . . . . (207) 287-3531
Deputy Commissioner and Public Service Executive
  **William "Bill" Beardsley** . . . . . . . . . . . . . . . . . . . . . (207) 624-6620
  E-mail: william.beardsley@maine.gov
Deputy Commissioner **Suzan Beaudoin** . . . . . . . . . . . . . . (207) 624-6620
  E-mail: susan.beaudoin@maine.gov
Education in the Unorganized Territories Superintendent
  of Schools **Shelley B. Lane** . . . . . . . . . . . . . . . . . . . . (207) 624-6892
  E-mail: shelley.b.lane@maine.gov
Federal Liaison **Jaci Holmes** . . . . . . . . . . . . . . . . . . . . (207) 624-6669
  E-mail: jaci.holmes@maine.gov
Communications Director **Anne Gabbianelli** . . . . . . . . . . . (207) 624-6747
  E-mail: anne.gabbianelli@maine.gov

*(continued on next page)*

---

★ Elected Official   ■ Appointed by Governor   ● Appointed by Legislature   ▲ Appointed by Board or Commission   ◆ Appointed by State Supreme Court

**Department of Education** *continued*

Learning Technology Policy Director **Michael Muir** ...... (207) 624-6634
   E-mail: michael.muir@maine.gov
Chief Academic Officer **Rachelle Tome** ................ (207) 624-6705
   E-mail: rachelle.tome@maine.gov
High School Equivalency Test Administrator
   **Gail Senese** .................................... (207) 624-6752
   E-mail: gail.senese@maine.gov
School Finance and Operations Team Leader and Policy
   Director **(Vacant)** ................................ (207) 624-6790
Special Services Team Director **Jan Breton** ............. (207) 624-6676
   E-mail: janice.breton@maine.gov
Higher Education Support **Angel Loredo** ............... (207) 624-6607
Web Coordinator and Information Systems Support
   **Crystal Sullivan** ................................ (207) 624-6783
   E-mail: crystal.sullivan@maine.gov

## State Board of Education

23 State House Station, Augusta, ME 04333-0023
Tel: (207) 624-6616  Fax: (207) 624-6618

**Fiscal Year:** 2013-2014  **Budget:** $160,000

■Chair **Martha J. Harris** ............................... (207) 624-6616
   E-mail: mharrismsbe@yahoo.com
   Education: Northeastern JD
■Vice Chair **Alan R. Burton** ........................... (207) 624-6616
■Member **William "Bill" Beardsley** ................... (207) 624-6616
   E-mail: wbeardsley1@roadrunner.com
■Member **John Bird** ................................... (207) 624-6616
   Education: Bowdoin BA; George Washington MA
■Member **Nichi S. Farnham** ........................... (207) 624-6616
   E-mail: nichifarnham@gmail.com
■Member **Peter E. Geiger** ............................. (207) 624-6616
   E-mail: pgeiger@geiger.com
   Education: Villanova 1973 BS
■Member **Wilson G. Hess** ............................. (207) 624-6616
   Education: Baltimore 1973 BA; Maine 1974 MA
■Member **Jana Lapoint** ............................... (207) 624-6616
   E-mail: jana.f.lapoint@gmail.com
   Education: Bridgeport MEd
■Member **Heidi Sampson** ............................. (207) 624-6616
   E-mail: hsampson512@gmail.com
■Member **Jane Sexton** ................................ (207) 624-6616
   E-mail: knappjanes09@gmail.com
■Member **Ande Smith** ................................ (207) 624-6616
   E-mail: ande@maine.rr.com
■Student Member **Elise McKendry** ..................... (207) 624-6616
■Student Member **Noa Ann Sreden** .................... (207) 624-6616
   E-mail: noasreden@gmail.com
Assistant to the State Board **Mary Becker** ............. (207) 624-6616

## Department of Environmental Protection [DEP]

17 State House Station, Augusta, ME 04333-0017
Tel: (207) 287-7688  Fax: (207) 287-7826  Internet: www.maine.gov/dep

**Employees:** 390  **Fiscal Year:** 2013-2014  **Budget:** $67,966,000

■Commissioner **Paul Mercer** ........................... (207) 287-2812
Deputy Commissioner and Legislative Contact
   **Heather Parent** .................................. (207) 287-7830
Agency Web Director **Karl E. Wilkins** ................. (207) 287-2173
   E-mail: karl.e.wilkins@maine.gov
Assistance Director/Small Business Ombudsman
   **Julie M. Churchill** ............................... (207) 287-7881
   E-mail: julie.m.churchill@maine.gov
Communications and Education Director (Acting)
   **Karl E. Wilkins** ................................. (207) 592-2173
   E-mail: karl.e.wilkins@maine.gov
Procedures, Compliance, and Enforcement Director
   **Ron Mongeon** ................................... (207) 287-7740
Freedom of Access Contact **Andrea Lani** .............. (207) 287-5902
Innovation Director **Leslie Anderson** ................. (207) 287-7890
Policy Services Director (Acting) **Christina S. Zabierek** .. (207) 287-5219
Personnel Officer **Amanda Beckwith** .................. (207) 287-7578

■Environmental Protection Board Chair **Robert Foley** ...... (207) 287-7688

## Bureau of Air Quality

17 State House Station, Augusta, ME 04333
Tel: (207) 287-7688  Fax: (207) 287-7641

Director **Marc A. Cone** ............................... (207) 287-1932

## Bureau of Land and Water Quality

Tel: (207) 287-7688  Fax: (207) 287-7826
Internet: www.maine.gov/dep/blwq/

Director **Michael Kuhns** .............................. (207) 287-2827
Environmental Assessment (Water Resources) Division
   Director **Donald T. Witherill** ..................... (207) 215-9751
Water Quality Management Division Director
   **Brian W. Kavanah** ............................... (207) 287-7700
Watershed Management Division Director
   **Donald T. Witherill** ............................. (207) 215-9751
Enforcement Division Director **Michael "Mike" Mullen** .. (207) 446-1611
Sand and Salt Piles Program Manager **Erich Kluck** ....... (207) 592-2068

## Bureau of Remediation and Waste Management

Fax: (207) 287-7826  Internet: www.maine.gov/dep/rwm

Director **Melanie Loyzim** ............................. (207) 287-7890
   Education: Maine BS; Colorado MPA
Hazardous Waste Facilities Regulation, Licensing and
   Enforcement **Scott Whittier** ...................... (207) 287-7674
Oil Spill Contingency Planning/Training Director
   **Peter J. Blanchard** .............................. (207) 287-7190
Program Services Division Director **Mary R. James** ...... (207) 287-7758
Remediation Division Director **Victoria Eleftheriou** ...... (207) 287-6175
Solid Waste Management Director **Paula M. Clark** ....... (207) 287-7718
Underground Tank Program/Oil Spill Remediation
   **David E. "Dave" Burns** .......................... (207) 287-7166

## Department of Health and Human Services [DHHS]

211 State Street, Augusta, ME 04333
Tel: (207) 287-3707
Tel: (207) 626-8620 (Children/Adults Emergency Services)
Tel: (800) 452-1999 (Statewide Emergency Services; Child and Adult
Protective Services.)  Fax: (207) 287-3005  Internet: www.maine.gov/dhhs

**Employees:** 890  **Fiscal Year:** 2013-2014  **Budget:** $417,465,000

■Commissioner **Mary Mayhew** ......................... (207) 287-4223
   E-mail: mary.mayhew@maine.gov
   Administrative Assistant **Kathy Veilleux** ............. (207) 287-4223
Communications Director **John A. Martins** ............. (207) 287-3707
   E-mail: john.a.martins@maine.gov
Constituent Affairs Director **Scott Perkins** ............ (207) 287-3707
Contract Management Division Director **Karen Kalka** ..... (207) 287-5072
Facilities Management Director **Martha Kluzak** ......... (207) 287-5837
Legal Affairs Director **Kevin Wells** ................... (207) 287-3707
Legislative and Public Relations Senior Director
   **Nicholas "Nick" Adolphsen** ...................... (207) 287-4290
   E-mail: nick.adolphsen@maine.gov
Licensing and Regulatory Services Director
   **Kenneth J. "Ken" Albert III, RN** .................. (207) 287-9300
   E-mail: kenneth.albert@maine.gov
   Education: Southern Maine 1999 BSN; Maine 2003 JD
Media Relations and Policy Research Director
   **David Sorenson** ................................. (207) 287-3707
   E-mail: david.sorenson@maine.gov
Multicultural Affairs Director **Julia Trujillo Luergo** ....... (207) 287-4272
State Forensic Services Director **Ann LeBlanc** .......... (207) 624-4648

## Maine Center for Disease Control and Prevention

Tel: (207) 287-8016  Fax: (207) 287-9058

Director and Chief Operating Officer
   **Kenneth J. "Ken" Albert III, RN** .................. (207) 287-8016

---

★ Elected Official    ■ Appointed by Governor    ● Appointed by Legislature    ▲ Appointed by Board or Commission    ◆ Appointed by State Supreme Court

Chief Health Officer (Acting) **Dr. Christopher Pezzulo** . . . (207) 287-8016
Deputy Director **Christine Zukas** . . . . . . . . . . . . . . . . . . . . . (207) 287-8016
Health and Environmental Testing Laboratory Director
  **Ken Pote**. . . . . . . . . . . . . . . . . . . . . . . . . . . . . . . . . . . . . . .(207) 287-2727
Public Health Nursing Director
  **Theodore "Ted" Hensley**. . . . . . . . . . . . . . . . . . . . . . . . .(207) 287-8016
Public Health Systems Director **Kristine Perkins**. . . . . . . . (207) 287-8104
Environmental Health Division Director
  **Nancy Beardsley**. . . . . . . . . . . . . . . . . . . . . . . . . . . . . . . .(207) 287-5697
                         Fax: (207) 287-4172
Infectious Disease Division Director **Lori Wolanski**. . . . . . .(207) 287-6448
                         Fax: (207) 287-6868
Population Health Division Director **Debra Wigand** . . . . . . (207) 287-5387
Data, Research & Vital Statistics Office Director
  **Marty Henson**. . . . . . . . . . . . . . . . . . . . . . . . . . . . . . . . . . (207) 287-3771
  244 Water Street, Augusta, ME 04330     Fax: (207) 287-5470
  E-mail: marty.l.henson@maine.gov
State Epidemiologist **(Vacant)** . . . . . . . . . . . . . . . . . . . . . . . (207) 287-3960
State Toxicologist **Andrew E. "Andy" Smith** . . . . . . . . . . (207) 287-5189
Drinking Water Program Director **Roger Crouse**. . . . . . . . (207) 287-5684

## Financial Management Services Office

Tel: (207) 287-1921  Fax: (207) 287-3005

Deputy Commissioner for Finance
  **Alexander E. "Alec" Porteous** . . . . . . . . . . . . . . . . . . . . (207) 287-1921
  Education: Colby 2001 BA; Cornell 2007 MBA
  Administrative Assistant **Norma M. Tunks** . . . . . . . . . . . (207) 287-1921
Audit Director **Herb F. Downs** . . . . . . . . . . . . . . . . . . . . . . . (207) 287-2403
                         Fax: (207) 287-2601

## Office of MaineCare Services

Fax: (207) 287-2675

Director **Stefanie Nadeau** . . . . . . . . . . . . . . . . . . . . . . . . . . (207) 287-2674
  E-mail: stefanie.nadeau@maine.gov
Deputy Director and Health Information Technology
  Director **James F. Leonard**. . . . . . . . . . . . . . . . . . . . . . . . .(207) 287-4532
  E-mail: james.f.leonard@maine.gov
General Counsel **William P. Logan** . . . . . . . . . . . . . . . . . . . (207) 624-4083
  Education: Wake Forest BA; Maine JD
Administrative Services Director **(Vacant)** . . . . . . . . . . . . . (207) 287-3828
Contract Management Director **Stephen Turner** . . . . . . . . (207) 287-3828
Customer Service and Health Care Management Director
  **Beth Ketch**. . . . . . . . . . . . . . . . . . . . . . . . . . . . . . . . . . . . . (207) 287-4078
MaineCare Finance Director **Dimitri Michaud** . . . . . . . . . .(207) 624-4027
Program Management Director **(Vacant)**. . . . . . . . . . . . . . . (207) 287-3829
  CHIP (Children's Health Insurance Program) Director
  **Sam Senft**. . . . . . . . . . . . . . . . . . . . . . . . . . . . . . . . . . . . . .(207) 624-4053
                         Fax: (207) 287-9369
EPSDT Coordinator **Beth Pearce**. . . . . . . . . . . . . . . . . . . . . (207) 624-4006
                         Fax: (207) 287-8682
Value Based Purchasing Unit Director **Amy Dix**. . . . . . . . .(207) 624-6930

## Office of Quality Improvement

Director **Dr. Jay Yoe, PhD** . . . . . . . . . . . . . . . . . . . . . . . . . . (207) 624-7983
  Administrative Assistant **Stephen Hallee** . . . . . . . . . . . . (207) 624-7983

## Office of Aging and Disability Services [OADS]

Fax: (207) 287-9229

Director **Gary Wolcott** . . . . . . . . . . . . . . . . . . . . . . . . . . . . . (207) 287-9224
Care and Intervention Associate Director **Karen Mason** . . . (207) 287-9200
Central Operations and Support Associate Director
  **(Vacant)** . . . . . . . . . . . . . . . . . . . . . . . . . . . . . . . . . . . . . . (207) 287-9200
Community Living, Long Term Services, and Support
  Associate Director **Debra Halm** . . . . . . . . . . . . . . . . . . . (207) 287-9200

## Office of Child and Family Services [OCFS]

Fax: (207) 287-5282

Director **John Martin**. . . . . . . . . . . . . . . . . . . . . . . . . . . . . . . (207) 624-7900
Deputy Director **Grace Brace** . . . . . . . . . . . . . . . . . . . . . . . (207) 624-7900

Associate Director, Intervention and Coordination of Care
  **Mark Dalton**. . . . . . . . . . . . . . . . . . . . . . . . . . . . . . . . . . . .(207) 624-7900
Associate Director, Intervention and Care Management
  **Louise Boisvert**. . . . . . . . . . . . . . . . . . . . . . . . . . . . . . . . .(207) 287-3991
                         Fax: (207) 287-3993
Associate Director, Policy and Prevention
  **Angie Bellefleur** . . . . . . . . . . . . . . . . . . . . . . . . . . . . . . . . (207) 624-7900
  E-mail: angie.bellefleur@maine.gov
Accountability and Information Services **Bob Blanchard** . . (207) 624-7900
  E-mail: bob.blanchard@maine.gov
Medical Director **Lindsey Tweed** . . . . . . . . . . . . . . . . . . . . (207) 624-7900
Secretary **Bethanie Berube**. . . . . . . . . . . . . . . . . . . . . . . . . (207) 624-7900

## Office for Family Independence [OFI]

Tel: (207) 624-4162  Fax: (207) 287-3455

Director **Bethany Hamm** . . . . . . . . . . . . . . . . . . . . . . . . . . . .(207) 624-4100
Deputy Director **Michael Frey** . . . . . . . . . . . . . . . . . . . . . . . (207) 624-4100
Child Support Division Director **Jerry Joy** . . . . . . . . . . . . . . (207) 624-4100
  E-mail: jerry.joy@maine.gov
Disability Determination Services Director **Scott Mack** . . . (207) 377-9500
Management Information Systems and Quality Assurance
  Division Director **Anthony Pelotte** . . . . . . . . . . . . . . . . . (207) 287-3430
  E-mail: anthony.pelotte@maine.gov
ASPIRE (Additional Support for People for Retraining
  and Employment) Manager **Liz Ray** . . . . . . . . . . . . . . . (207) 287-4733
Food Supplement Program Manager **Karen L. Curtis**. . . . . (207) 287-7118
Policy and Programs Director **Bethany Hamm** . . . . . . . . . (207) 287-3931
Medical Program, Eligibility and Supplemental Security
  Income Manager **(Vacant)** . . . . . . . . . . . . . . . . . . . . . . . (207) 287-4076
TANF (Temporary Assistance for Needy Families)
  Manager **Dawn Mulcahey** . . . . . . . . . . . . . . . . . . . . . . . (207) 287-6426
  E-mail: dawn.mulcahey@maine.gov

# Department of Inland Fisheries and Wildlife [IFW]

41 State House Station, Augusta, ME 04333-0041
Tel: (207) 287-8000  TTY: (207) 287-4471  Fax: (207) 287-6395
E-mail: ifw.webmaster@maine.gov  Internet: www.maine.gov/ifw

**Employees:** 290  **Fiscal Year:** 2013-2014  **Budget:** $42,813,000

■Commissioner **Chandler E. Woodcock** . . . . . . . . . . . . . . . (207) 287-5202
  E-mail: chandler.woodcock@maine.gov
  Education: Maine (Farmington) BS
Deputy Commissioner **Andrea L. Erskine** . . . . . . . . . . . . . (207) 287-5201
Public Information Director **Bonnie Holding** . . . . . . . . . . . (207) 287-5248
  E-mail: bonnie.holding@maine.gov
Recreational Access and Landowner Relations
  Coordinator **Cpl Rick LaFlamme** . . . . . . . . . . . . . . . . . . (207) 287-5240

# Maine Department of Labor [MDOL]

54 State House Station, Augusta, ME 04333-0054
Tel: (207) 623-7900  TTY: (800) 794-1110  Fax: (207) 287-5292

**Employees:** 525  **Fiscal Year:** 2013-2014  **Budget:** $310,889,000

■Commissioner **Jeanne Paquette** . . . . . . . . . . . . . . . . . . . . . (207) 621-5095
  E-mail: jeanne.paquette@maine.gov
  Education: Dean AA; Kean U BAE
  Administrative Assistant **(Vacant)** . . . . . . . . . . . . . . . . . . . (207) 621-5095
Information Processing Director **Julie Rabinowitz** . . . . . . . (207) 621-5095
  E-mail: julie.rabinowitz@maine.gov
Legislative and Constituent Services Director
  **Jeanne St. Pierre** . . . . . . . . . . . . . . . . . . . . . . . . . . . . . . . (207) 623-7900

## Bureau of Employment Services

Tel: (207) 623-7981  Fax: (207) 287-5933
Internet: www.mainecareercenter.com

Director **Edward Upham** . . . . . . . . . . . . . . . . . . . . . . . . . . . .(207) 621-5097
  Education: Thomas Col (ME) BSBA
Field Services Deputy Director **Dawn Mealey** . . . . . . . . . . (207) 623-7981
  E-mail: dawn.mealey@maine.gov

---

★ Elected Official    ■ Appointed by Governor    ● Appointed by Legislature    ▲ Appointed by Board or Commission    ◆ Appointed by State Supreme Court

EXECUTIVE BRANCH

## Bureau of Labor Standards
Tel: (207) 623-7900  Fax: (207) 623-7938

Director **Pamela Megathlin** . . . . . . . . . . . . . . . . . . . . . . . (207) 623-7900
  E-mail: pamela.megathlin@maine.gov
Deputy Director **(Vacant)** . . . . . . . . . . . . . . . . . . . . . . . . (207) 623-7900
Research and Statistics Division Director **John L. Rioux** . . (207) 623-7900
  E-mail: john.l.rioux@maine.gov
Wage and Hour Labor Division Director **Verna Eldridge** . . (207) 623-7900
  E-mail: verna.eldridge@maine.gov

## Bureau of Rehabilitation Services
150 State House Station, Augusta, ME 04333-0150
Tel: (207) 623-7900  Fax: (207) 623-7938  TTY: (800) 698-4440
Internet: www.state.me.us/rehab

Director **Karen Fraser** . . . . . . . . . . . . . . . . . . . . . . . . . . (207) 623-7900

## Bureau of Unemployment Compensation
Director **Laura L. Boyett** . . . . . . . . . . . . . . . . . . . . . . . . (207) 621-5155
  E-mail: laura.l.boyett@maine.gov
Center for Workforce Research and Information Director
  **Christopher Boudreau** . . . . . . . . . . . . . . . . . . . . . . . (207) 623-7900
  E-mail: christopher.boudreau@maine.gov
Administrative Hearings Division Chief Hearings Officer
  **Elizabeth Wyman** . . . . . . . . . . . . . . . . . . . . . . . . . . (207) 621-5001
  E-mail: elizabeth.wyman@maine.gov    Fax: (207) 287-5949
  Education: Maine Law 1993 JD

## Department of Marine Resources [DMR]
21 State House Station, Augusta, ME 04333
Tel: (207) 624-6550  TTY: (207) 287-4474  Fax: (207) 624-6024

**Employees:** 163  **Fiscal Year:** 2013-2014  **Budget:** $20,281,000

■Commissioner **Patrick C. Keliher** . . . . . . . . . . . . . . . . . (207) 624-6553
  E-mail: patrick.keliher@maine.gov
  State Marine Policy Director **Deirdre Gilbert** . . . . . . . . . (207) 624-6576
    E-mail: deirdre.gilbert@maine.gov
    Education: Bowdoin 1995 AB; Maine 2002 MS
Deputy Commissioner **Meredith Mendelson** . . . . . . . . . . . (207) 624-6553
  E-mail: meredith.mendelson@maine.gov
Regulations & Information Officer **(Vacant)** . . . . . . . . . . . (207) 624-6573
Secretary Specialist **Amy Sinclair** . . . . . . . . . . . . . . . . . . (207) 624-6553

## Fisheries and Habitat Bureau
Director **Oliver N. Cox** . . . . . . . . . . . . . . . . . . . . . . . . . . (207) 941-4487

## Marine Patrol Bureau
Director **Col. John Cornish** . . . . . . . . . . . . . . . . . . . . . . . (207) 624-6581

## Resource Management Bureau
P.O. Box 8, W. Boothbay Harbor, ME 04575
Fax: (207) 633-9579

Director **Carl Wilson** . . . . . . . . . . . . . . . . . . . . . . . . . . . (207) 633-9525
  E-mail: carl.wilson@maine.gov
Biological Monitoring & Assessment Division Marine
  Scientist **David A. Libby** . . . . . . . . . . . . . . . . . . . . . . (207) 633-9532
  E-mail: david.a.libby@maine.gov
Education Division Director **Elaine P. Jones** . . . . . . . . . . . (207) 633-9580
  Education: Hood 1977 BS
Public Health Bureau Director **Kohl Kanwit** . . . . . . . . . . . (207) 633-9535

## Community Resource Development Division
21 State House Station, Augusta, ME 04333

Resource Management Coordinator **Sarah Cotnoir** . . . . . . . (207) 624-6596
Resource Management Coordinator **Trisha Cheney** . . . . . . . (207) 624-6554
Aquaculture Policy Development Specialist
  **Chris Vonderweidt** . . . . . . . . . . . . . . . . . . . . . . . . . (207) 624-6558
Communications Director **Jeff Nichols** . . . . . . . . . . . . . . . (207) 624-6569
  E-mail: jeff.nichols@maine.gov

## Department of Professional and Financial Regulation [PFR]
35 State House Station, Augusta, ME 04333
Tel: (207) 624-8500  TTY: (207) 624-8563  Fax: (207) 624-8590

**Employees:** 203  **Fiscal Year:** 2013-2014  **Budget:** $29,123,000

■Commissioner **Anne L. Head** . . . . . . . . . . . . . . . . . . . . . (207) 624-8511
  E-mail: anne.l.head@maine.gov
  Education: Ithaca 1972 BA; Catholic U 1974 MS;
  Columbus Law 1979 JD
Real Estate Commission Director **Karen Bivins** . . . . . . . . . (207) 624-8524
Administrative Services Division Director
  **Rachel H. Hendsbee** . . . . . . . . . . . . . . . . . . . . . . . . (207) 624-8503
  E-mail: rachel.h.hendsbee@maine.gov
Professional and Occupational Regulation Office Director
  **Anne L. Head** . . . . . . . . . . . . . . . . . . . . . . . . . . . . (207) 624-8511
Accountancy Board Administrator **Catherine M. Carroll** . . (207) 624-8605
  E-mail: catherine.m.carroll@maine.gov
Architects, Landscape, Interior Design Licensure Board
  Administrator **Karen Bivins** . . . . . . . . . . . . . . . . . . . (207) 624-8524
  Architects, Landscape, Interior Design Licensure Board
  Clerk **Kimberly J. Baker** . . . . . . . . . . . . . . . . . . . . . (207) 624-8522
    E-mail: kimberly.j.baker@maine.gov
Barber and Cosmetology Board Administrator
  **Geraldine L. Betts** . . . . . . . . . . . . . . . . . . . . . . . . . (207) 624-8625
Counseling Professionals Licensure Board Administrator
  **Torrey J. Gray** . . . . . . . . . . . . . . . . . . . . . . . . . . . . (207) 624-8603
  E-mail: torrey.j.gray@maine.gov
Dietetic Practices Licensure Board Administrator
  **Torrey J. Gray** . . . . . . . . . . . . . . . . . . . . . . . . . . . . (207) 624-8603
Electricians' Examining Board Administrator
  **Catherine M. Carroll** . . . . . . . . . . . . . . . . . . . . . . . (207) 624-8605
Funeral Services State Board Administrator
  **Torrey J. Gray** . . . . . . . . . . . . . . . . . . . . . . . . . . . . (207) 624-8603
Nursing Home Licensure Board Administrator
  **Torrey J. Gray** . . . . . . . . . . . . . . . . . . . . . . . . . . . . (207) 624-8603
Physical Therapy Examiners Board Administrator
  **Geraldine L. Betts** . . . . . . . . . . . . . . . . . . . . . . . . . (207) 624-8625
  E-mail: geraldine.l.betts@maine.gov
Podiatric Medicine Licensure Board Administrator
  **Torrey J. Gray** . . . . . . . . . . . . . . . . . . . . . . . . . . . . (207) 624-8603
Psychologists Examining State Board Administrator
  **Geraldine L. Betts** . . . . . . . . . . . . . . . . . . . . . . . . . (207) 624-8625
  E-mail: geraldine.l.betts@maine.gov
Respiratory Care Practitioners Board Administrator
  **Geraldine L. Betts** . . . . . . . . . . . . . . . . . . . . . . . . . (207) 624-8625
  E-mail: geraldine.l.betts@maine.gov
Securities Administrator **Judith M. "Judy" Shaw** . . . . . . . (207) 624-8551
  E-mail: judith.m.shaw@maine.gov
Speech Pathology & Audiology Examiners Board
  Administrator **Torrey J. Gray** . . . . . . . . . . . . . . . . . . (207) 624-8603
Veterinary Medicine State Board Administrator
  **Geraldine L. Betts** . . . . . . . . . . . . . . . . . . . . . . . . . (207) 624-8625
Auctioneers Licensure Board Clerk **Deborah A. Fales** . . . . (207) 624-8521
Charitable Solicitation Clerk **Jennifer M. Hawk** . . . . . . . . (207) 624-8617
Foresters Professional Licensure Board Clerk
  **Deborah A. Fales** . . . . . . . . . . . . . . . . . . . . . . . . . . (207) 624-8521
  E-mail: deborah.a.fales@maine.gov

## Bureau of Financial Institutions
■Superintendent **Lloyd P. LaFountain III** . . . . . . . . . . . . . . (207) 624-8570
  E-mail: lloyd.p.lafountainiii@maine.gov

## Bureau of Insurance
■Superintendent **Eric A. Cioppa** . . . . . . . . . . . . . . . . . . . (207) 624-8475
  E-mail: eric.a.cioppa@maine.gov
  Education: SUNY (Potsdam) BA; Clarkson U MBA
Deputy Superintendent **(Vacant)** . . . . . . . . . . . . . . . . . . . (207) 624-8475

---

★ Elected Official   ■ Appointed by Governor   ● Appointed by Legislature   ▲ Appointed by Board or Commission   ◆ Appointed by State Supreme Court

# Department of Public Safety [DPS]

104 State House Station, 45 Commerce Drive, Suite 1,
Augusta, ME 04333-0104
Tel: (207) 626-3800  TTY: (207) 287-3659  Fax: (207) 287-3042

**Employees:** 625  **Fiscal Year:** 2013-2014  **Budget:** $74,099,000

■Commissioner **John E. Morris** . . . . . . . . . . . . . . . . . . . . . . . (207) 626-3803
  E-mail: john.e.morris@maine.gov
Criminal Justice Academy Director **John B. Rogers** . . . . . . (207) 877-8000
  15 Oak Grove Drive, Vassalboro, ME 04989
  E-mail: john.rogers@maine.gov
Maine Drug Enforcement Director **Roy E. McKinney** . . . . . (207) 626-3850
  166 State House Station, Augusta, ME 04333-0166     Fax: (207) 287-3042
  E-mail: roy.e.mckinney@maine.gov
State Police Crime Lab Director **William Harwood** . . . . . . (207) 624-7101
  133 State House Station, Augusta, ME 04333-0133
Capitol Police Chief **Russell J. Gauvin** . . . . . . . . . . . . . . (207) 287-4357
  68 State House Station, Augusta, ME 04333-0068
■State Police Chief **Robert A. Williams** . . . . . . . . . . . . . . . (207) 624-7200
  42 State House Station, Augusta, ME 04333-0042
  E-mail: robert.a.williams@maine.gov
Fire Marshal **Joseph E. Thomas, Jr.** . . . . . . . . . . . . . . . . . (207) 626-3872
  State House Station, 52, Augusta, ME 04333-0052     Fax: (207) 287-6251
  E-mail: joseph.e.thomasjr@maine.gov
Public Information Officer **Stephen H. McCausland** . . . . . (207) 626-3811
  E-mail: stephen.mccausland@maine.gov

## Emergency Medical Services

152 State House Station, Augusta, ME 04330-0152
E-mail: maine.ems@maine.gov  Internet: www.maine.gov/dps/ems

Director **Jay R. Bradshaw** . . . . . . . . . . . . . . . . . . . . . . . . . (207) 626-3860

## Gambling Control Unit

45 Commerce Drive, Suite 3, Augusta, ME 04333-0087
Tel: (207) 626-3900

Director **Patrick J. Fleming** . . . . . . . . . . . . . . . . . . . . . . . . (207) 626-3900
  Education: Maine AA

## Highway Safety Bureau

164 State House Station, Augusta, ME 04333-0164
Tel: (207) 626-3840  Fax: (207) 287-3430
E-mail: lauren.v.stewart@maine.gov

Director **Lauren V. Stewart** . . . . . . . . . . . . . . . . . . . . . . . . (207) 626-3840
  E-mail: lauren.v.stewart@maine.gov

# Maine Department of Transportation [MaineDOT]

16 State House Station, Augusta, ME 04333-0016
Tel: (207) 624-3000  Fax: (207) 624-3001  TTY: (207) 287-3392
E-mail: mdot@maine.gov  Internet: www.state.me.us/mdot/

**Employees:** 1,954  **Fiscal Year:** 2013-2014  **Budget:** $980,000,000

■Commissioner **David Bernhardt** . . . . . . . . . . . . . . . . . . . . . (207) 624-3003
  E-mail: david.bernhardt@maine.gov
  Education: Maine AS, 1984 BS
Legal Services Chief Counsel **Toni Kemmerle** . . . . . . . . . . (207) 624-3020
  E-mail: toni.kemmerle@maine.gov     Fax: (207) 624-3021
Freight Transportation Office Director **Robert D. Elder** . . (207) 624-3560
                                              Fax: (207) 624-3561
Finance and Administration Bureau Director
  **Karen Doyle** . . . . . . . . . . . . . . . . . . . . . . . . . . . . . . . . (207) 624-3200
Press Secretary **Ted W. Talbot** . . . . . . . . . . . . . . . . . . . . . (207) 624-3030
  E-mail: ted.w.talbot@maine.gov
Legislative Liaison and Constituent Services **Nina Fisher** . . (207) 624-3002
  E-mail: nina.fisher@maine.gov

## Chief Engineer's Office

Chief Engineer **Joyce Noel Taylor** . . . . . . . . . . . . . . . . . . (207) 624-3011
Environmental Office Director **Judy Gates** . . . . . . . . . . . . (207) 624-3100
  E-mail: judy.gates@maine.gov
Agreement Coordination Officer **Debora Farrell** . . . . . . . . (207) 624-3324
  E-mail: debora.farrell@maine.gov

## Safety and Research Office

Director **Rhonda Fletcher** . . . . . . . . . . . . . . . . . . . . . . . . . (207) 624-3004
                                              Tel: (207) 453-7377
                                              (Fairfield Office)
Health and Safety Director **Janice Arsenault** . . . . . . . . . . (207) 624-3004
Transportation Research Division Director **Dale Peabody** . . (207) 624-3305
  E-mail: dale.peabody@maine.gov
Safety Office Director **Duane Brunell** . . . . . . . . . . . . . . . . (207) 624-3278

## Transportation Systems Planning Bureau

Tel: (207) 624-3300  Fax: (207) 624-3301

Director **Herb Thomson** . . . . . . . . . . . . . . . . . . . . . . . . . . (207) 624-3300
  E-mail: herb.thomson@maine.gov
Assistant Director **Scott Rollins** . . . . . . . . . . . . . . . . . . . . (207) 624-3300
  E-mail: scott.rollins@maine.gov
Community Services Division Director **Peter Coughlan** . . . (207) 624-3266
  E-mail: peter.coughlan@maine.gov
Plan and Program Development Director **Martin Rooney** . . (207) 624-3300
  E-mail: martin.rooney@maine.gov
Systems Management Division Director **Chip Getchell** . . . . (207) 624-3300
  E-mail: chip.getchell@maine.gov

## Deputy Commissioner's Office

Deputy Commissioner **(Vacant)** . . . . . . . . . . . . . . . . . . . . . (207) 624-3002

## Capitol Resource Management

Director **Karen Doyle** . . . . . . . . . . . . . . . . . . . . . . . . . . . . (207) 624-3200
                                              Fax: (207) 624-3201
Security and Employment Director **(Vacant)** . . . . . . . . . . . (207) 623-6701
                                              Fax: (207) 624-3201
Budget Director **Greg Goggin** . . . . . . . . . . . . . . . . . . . . . . (207) 624-7810
Financial and Program Management Director **(Vacant)** . . . (207) 624-3200

## Human Resources Bureau

Tel: (207) 624-3050  Fax: (207) 624-3051

Director **Rebecca Greene** . . . . . . . . . . . . . . . . . . . . . . . . . (207) 624-3050

## Maintenance and Operations Bureau

Tel: (207) 624-3600  Fax: (207) 624-3141

Director **Dale Doughty** . . . . . . . . . . . . . . . . . . . . . . . . . . . (207) 624-3600
Assistant Director **(Vacant)** . . . . . . . . . . . . . . . . . . . . . . . . (207) 624-3600
Bridge Maintenance Division Engineer **John Buxton** . . . . . (207) 624-3580
  E-mail: john.buxton@maine.gov     Fax: (207) 624-3581
Fleet Services Director **Donald Hutchins III** . . . . . . . . . . . (207) 287-2677
                                              Fax: (207) 287-2587
Fleet Services Assistant Director **Paul Picard** . . . . . . . . . . (207) 287-2677
Highway Maintenance Division Engineer **Brian T. Burne** . . (207) 624-3590
  E-mail: brian.burne@maine.gov
Traffic Engineering Division Engineer **Steve Landry** . . . . . (207) 624-3620
  E-mail: stephen.landry@maine.gov     Fax: (207) 624-3621

## Project Development Bureau

Tel: (207) 624-3400  Fax: (207) 624-3401

Director **William Pulver** . . . . . . . . . . . . . . . . . . . . . . . . . . (207) 624-3400
Assistant Director **Richard Crawford** . . . . . . . . . . . . . . . . (207) 624-3400
Property Office Director **Todd Pelletier** . . . . . . . . . . . . . . (207) 624-3400
Highway Program Manager **Brad Foley** . . . . . . . . . . . . . . (207) 624-3538
  E-mail: brad.foley@maine.gov     Fax: (207) 624-3481
Multi-Modal Program Manager **Jeff Tweedie** . . . . . . . . . . (207) 624-3420
  E-mail: jeff.tweedie@maine.gov
Urban and Federal Bridge Program Manager **(Vacant)** . . . (207) 624-3490
                                              Fax: (207) 624-3491

## Media and Graphics

Supervisor **Paul Giguere** . . . . . . . . . . . . . . . . . . . . . . . . . (207) 624-3227
  E-mail: paul.giguere@maine.gov
Librarian **Pam Shofner** . . . . . . . . . . . . . . . . . . . . . . . . . . (207) 624-3230
                                              Fax: (207) 624-3221
Mapping and Media Services **Kevin Riley** . . . . . . . . . . . . . (207) 624-3225
                                              Fax: (207) 624-3221
Webmaster **Kip Mitchell** . . . . . . . . . . . . . . . . . . . . . . . . . (207) 624-3030
  E-mail: kip.mitchell@maine.gov

---

★ Elected Official     ■ Appointed by Governor     ● Appointed by Legislature     ▲ Appointed by Board or Commission     ◆ Appointed by State Supreme Court

EXECUTIVE BRANCH

## Maine Arts Commission

25 State House Station, 193 State Street, Augusta, ME 04333-0025
Tel: (207) 287-2724  TTY: (877) 887-3878  Fax: (207) 287-2725
E-mail: mainearts.info@maine.gov  Internet: www.mainearts.com

**Employees:** 10  **Fiscal Year:** 2013-2014  **Budget:** $1,810,000

▲Director **Julie Richard** . . . . . . . . . . . . . . . . . . . . . . . . . . (207) 287-2710
  E-mail: julie.richard@maine.gov
Arts Education Director **Argy Nestor** . . . . . . . . . . . . . . . (207) 287-2713
Media Arts and Performing Arts Director **Kerstin Gilg** . . . . (207) 287-6719
Senior Grants Director **Kathy Shaw** . . . . . . . . . . . . . . . . (207) 287-2750
Special Programs Director **Kathleen Mundell** . . . . . . . . . . (207) 287-2724
Visual Arts Director **Julie Horn** . . . . . . . . . . . . . . . . . . . (207) 287-2790

## Maine Historic Preservation Commission

65 State House Station, 55 Capitol Street, Augusta, ME 04333-0065
Tel: (207) 287-2132  Fax: (207) 287-2335

**Employees:** 12  **Fiscal Year:** 2013-2014  **Budget:** $1,626,000

■Director and State Historic Preservation Officer
  **Kirk F. Mohney** . . . . . . . . . . . . . . . . . . . . . . . . . . (207) 287-2132
  E-mail: kirk.mohney@maine.gov

## Maine Public Employees Retirement System

46 State House Station, Augusta, ME 04333-0046
Tel: (207) 512-3100  Tel: (800) 451-9800  TTY: (207) 512-3102
Fax: (207) 512-3101

Executive Director **Sandra J. "Sandy" Matheson, CPA** . . (207) 512-3100
  Education: Northwestern BA; Washington State 1998 MBA
General Counsel **Michael J. Colleran** . . . . . . . . . . . . . . . (207) 512-3100
Deputy Executive Director **Rebecca Grant** . . . . . . . . . . . . (207) 512-3100

## Finance Authority of Maine [FAME]

5 Community Drive, Augusta, ME 04332-0949
P.O. Box 949, Augusta, ME 04332-0949
Tel: (207) 623-3263  Tel: (800) 228-3734  Fax: (207) 623-0095
TTY: (207) 626-2717  E-mail: info@famemaine.com
Internet: www.famemaine.com

**Fiscal Year:** 2013-2014  **Budget:** $16,013,000

■Chief Executive Officer **Bruce Wagner** . . . . . . . . . . . . . . (207) 623-3263
  E-mail: bruce.wagner@maine.gov
Chief Risk Officer **Carlos Mello** . . . . . . . . . . . . . . . . . . . (207) 623-3263
General Counsel **Chris Roney** . . . . . . . . . . . . . . (207) 623-3263 ext. 3520
  E-mail: chris.roney@maine.gov
Business Development and Marketing Director
  **Elizabeth Vanderweide** . . . . . . . . . . . . . . . . . . . . . . (207) 623-3263

## Maine Health and Higher Educational Facilities Authority [MHHEFA]

127 Community Drive, Augusta, ME 04330
P.O. Box 2268, Augusta, ME 04338
Tel: (207) 622-1958  Tel: (800) 821-1113 (Toll Free)  Fax: (207) 623-5359
Internet: www.mhhefa.com

Executive Director **Michael R. Goodwin** . . . . . . . . . . . . . . (207) 622-1958
Program Officer **Benson T. Caswell** . . . . . . . . . . . . . . . . . (207) 622-1958
  E-mail: btc@mhhefa.com
Program Assistant **Sharon L. Graham** . . . . . . . . . . . . . . . (207) 622-1958
Chief Financial Officer **David R. Delano** . . . . . . . . . . . . . . (207) 622-1958
Accounting Administrator **Gannet N. White** . . . . . . . . . . . (207) 622-1958

## Housing Authority

353 Water Street, Augusta, ME 04330-4633
Tel: (207) 626-4600  TTY: (800) 452-4603  Fax: (207) 626-4678
E-mail: frontdesk@mainehousing.org  Internet: www.mainehousing.org

**Fiscal Year:** 2013-2014  **Budget:** $12,395,000

■Director **John G. Gallagher** . . . . . . . . . . . . . . . . . . . . . . (207) 626-4682
  E-mail: jgallagher@mainehousing.org

Deputy Director **Margaret Bean** . . . . . . . . . . . . . . . . . . . . (207) 626-4613
  Education: Colby 1973 BA; Antioch U MM
Deputy Director **Peter Merrill** . . . . . . . . . . . . . . . . . . . . . (207) 626-4682
  Education: George Washington 1979 BA
Office Administrator **Jody Rollins** . . . . . . . . . . . . . . . . . . (207) 626-4682
Treasurer **Thomas "Tom" Cary** . . . . . . . . . . . . . . . . . . . . (207) 626-4657
  Education: SUNY (Buffalo) 1969 MBA
Chief Counsel **Linda Sears Uhl** . . . . . . . . . . . . . . . . . . . . (207) 626-4656
  E-mail: luhl@mainehousing.org
  Education: Hastings 1987 JD
Development Director **(Vacant)** . . . . . . . . . . . . . . . . . . . . (207) 626-4625
Energy and Housing Services Director **Dan Brennan** . . . (207) 624-4720
  Education: Maine 1988 BS
Homeownership Director **Craig Reynolds** . . . . . . . . . . . . . (207) 626-4627
Information Services Director **Jason Dupuy** . . . . . . . . . . . (207) 626-4676
  E-mail: jdupuy@mainehousing.org
Asset Management Director **Robert Conroy** . . . . . . . . . . . (207) 626-4624
  E-mail: bconroy@mainehousing.org
Human Resources Manager **Jane Whitley** . . . . . . . . . . . . (207) 626-4607
Public Information Manager **Deborah Turcotte** . . . . . . . . . (207) 626-4617
  E-mail: dturcotte@mainehousing.org
Communications and Planning Manager **Denise V. Lord** . . . (207) 624-5708
  E-mail: dlord@mainehousing.org
Controller **Darren Brown** . . . . . . . . . . . . . . . . . . . . . . . . (207) 626-4655
  Education: Rochester 1988 BS

## Governmental Ethics and Election Practices Commission

45 Memorial Circle, 2nd Floor, Augusta, ME 04332
135 State House Station, Augusta, ME 04333-0135
Tel: (207) 287-4179  Fax: (207) 287-6775  Internet: www.maine.gov/ethics
Internet: www.mainecampaignfinance.com (Campaign Finance
Information)

**Employees:** 6  **Fiscal Year:** 2013-2014  **Budget:** $2,449,000

■Chair **Margaret E. Matheson** . . . . . . . . . . . . . . . . . . . . . (207) 287-4179
  Education: Colby; Maine JD
■Member **André G. Duchette** . . . . . . . . . . . . . . . . . . . . . . (207) 287-4179
  Education: Middlebury BA; Maine JD
■Member **Michael T. Healy** . . . . . . . . . . . . . . . . . . . . . . . (207) 287-4179
  Education: Brown U 1964 AB; Boston U 1969 JD
■Member **William E. Lee III** . . . . . . . . . . . . . . . . . . . . . . . (207) 287-4179
■Member **Richard A. Nass** . . . . . . . . . . . . . . . . . . . . . . . . (207) 287-4179

## Commission Staff

Executive Director **Jonathan Wayne** . . . . . . . . . . . . . . . . (207) 287-4179

## Office of the Attorney General

Six State House Station, Augusta, ME 04333
Tel: (207) 626-8800  TTY: (207) 626-8865
E-mail: attorney.general@maine.gov

**Employees:** 300  **Fiscal Year:** 2015-2016  **Budget:** $37,447,000

●Attorney General **Janet T. Mills** . . . . . . . . . . . . . . . . . . . (207) 626-8800
  E-mail: janet.mills@maine.gov
  Career: State Representative (D-ME, District 89), Maine House of
  Representatives (2002-2008); Attorney General (D-ME), State of Maine
  (2009-2011)
Chief Deputy Attorney General **Linda M. Pistner** . . . . . . . . (207) 626-8800
Chief Medical Examiner
  **Mark A. Flomenbaum, MD, PhD** . . . . . . . . . . . . . . . . . (207) 624-7180
Administrative Services Division Chief
  **Kirsten LC Figueroa** . . . . . . . . . . . . . . . . . . . . . . . . . (207) 626-8800
  E-mail: kirsten.figueroa@maine.gov

## Office of the State Treasurer

Burton M. Cross Office Building, 111 Sewall Street, 3rd Floor,
Augusta, ME 04333-0039
Tel: (207) 624-7477  Tel: (888) 577-6690  Fax: (207) 287-2367

**Employees:** 15  **Fiscal Year:** 2013-2014  **Budget:** $147,251,000

●State Treasurer **Teresea M. "Terry" Hayes** . . . . . . . . . . . (207) 624-7477
  E-mail: terry.hayes@maine.gov
  Education: Bowdoin 1980 BA; Thomas Col (ME) 2014 MBA

---

★ Elected Official  ■ Appointed by Governor  ● Appointed by Legislature  ▲ Appointed by Board or Commission  ◆ Appointed by State Supreme Court

Deputy Treasurer **Kristi L. Carlow** . . . . . . . . . . . . . . . . . . . . . (207) 624-7468
Internal Operations Director **Tim Rodriguez** . . . . . . . . . . . . (207) 624-7460
Unclaimed Property Administrator **Tim Rodriguez** . . . . . . (207) 624-7460

# Office of the State Auditor

66 State House Station, Augusta, ME 04333-0066
Tel: (207) 624-6250  Fax: (207) 624-6273  Internet: www.state.me.us/audit

● State Auditor **Pola A. Buckley, CPA, CISA** . . . . . . . . . . . . (207) 624-6250
  E-mail: pola.buckley@maine.gov
Deputy State Auditor **Mary Gingrow-Shaw, CPA** . . . . . . . (207) 624-6260
Audit and Administration Director
  **Michael J. Poulin, CIA** . . . . . . . . . . . . . . . . . . . . . . . . . (207) 624-6266
  E-mail: michael.poulin@maine.gov
  Education: Thomas Col (ME) 1980 BS
Administrative Division Business Manager **(Vacant)** . . . . . . (207) 624-6267
Unorganized Territory Program Fiscal Administrator
  **Marica C. McInnis** . . . . . . . . . . . . . . . . . . . . . . . . . . . . . (207) 624-6263

# Department of the Secretary of State

Nash Building, 148 State House Station, 2nd Floor,
Augusta, ME 04333-0148
Tel: (207) 626-8400  Fax: (207) 287-8598
Tel: (207) 287-4476 (Maine Relay 711)  E-mail: sos.office@maine.gov
Internet: www.maine.gov/sos

**Employees:** 418  **Fiscal Year:** 2013-2014  **Budget:** $1,476,000

● Secretary of State **Matthew "Matt" Dunlap** . . . . . . . . . . . (207) 626-8400
  E-mail: matthew.dunlap@maine.gov
  Education: Maine 1987 BA, 1994 MA
  Career: State Representative, State Representative (D-ME), Maine
  House of Representatives (1996-2004); Secretary of State (D-ME),
  Department of the Secretary of State, State of Maine (2005-2011)
Chief Deputy Secretary of State **Barbara A. Redmond** . . . (207) 626-8400
  Education: Maine (Augusta) AS
Information Services Deputy Secretary of State
  **Donna E. Grant** . . . . . . . . . . . . . . . . . . . . . . . . . . . . . . . (207) 626-8400
  E-mail: donna.e.grant@maine.gov
Communications Director **Kristen Muszynski** . . . . . . . . . . (207) 626-8400
  E-mail: kristen.muszynski@maine.gov

## Corporations, Elections and Commissions Bureau

101 State House Station, Augusta, ME 04333-0101
Tel: (207) 624-7736  Fax: (207) 287-5874
Internet: www.maine.gov/sos/cec

Deputy Secretary of State **Julie Flynn** . . . . . . . . . . . . . . . . (207) 624-7736
  Education: Maine BA, MBA
Corporations Division Director **Cathy Beaudoin** . . . . . . . . (207) 624-7752
Elections Division Director **Melissa Packard** . . . . . . . . . . . (207) 624-7650

## Motor Vehicles Bureau

101 Hospital Street, 29 State House Station, Augusta, ME 04333-0029
Tel: (207) 624-9000  Fax: (207) 624-9013
Internet: www.maine.gov/sos/bmv

Deputy Secretary of State **Patty Morneault** . . . . . . . . . . . . (207) 624-9023
  E-mail: patty.morneault@maine.gov
Administrative Services Division Director
  **David Lachance** . . . . . . . . . . . . . . . . . . . . . . . . . . . . . . . (207) 624-9005
  E-mail: david.lachance@maine.gov
Driver License Services Division Director
  **Linda S. Grant** . . . . . . . . . . . . . . . . . . . . . . . . . . . . . . . . (207) 624-9124
Public Services Division Director **Jennifer Pease** . . . . . . . . (207) 624-9008
  E-mail: jennifer.pease@maine.gov
Vehicle Services Division Director **Garry Hinkley** . . . . . . . (207) 624-9055
                                                    Fax: (207) 624-9191
Legal Affairs, Adjudications and Hearings Director
  **Robert E. O'Connell, Jr.** . . . . . . . . . . . . . . . . . . . . . . . . (207) 624-9004
Motor Carrier Services Chief **Stephen Ashcroft** . . . . . . . . (207) 624-9056
  E-mail: stephen.ashcroft@maine.gov
Investigations Director **David W. Guilmette** . . . . (207) 624-9000 ext. 52144
  E-mail: david.w.guilmette@maine.gov              Fax: (207) 624-9258

# State Archives

Cultural Building, 84 State House Station, Augusta, ME 04333-0084
Tel: (207) 287-5790  Fax: (207) 287-5739
Internet: www.maine.gov/sos/arc

State Archivist **David Cheever** . . . . . . . . . . . . . . . . . . . . . . (207) 287-5790
Archives Services Division Director **David Cheever** . . . . . . (207) 287-5790
Records Management Services Division Director
  **Tammy Marks** . . . . . . . . . . . . . . . . . . . . . . . . . . . . . . . . (207) 287-5792

# Maine Public Utilities Commission [MPUC]

101 Second Street, Hallowell, ME 04347
18 State House Station, Augusta, ME 04333-0018
Tel: (207) 287-3831  Fax: (207) 287-1039  TTY: (800) 437-1220
E-mail: maine.puc@maine.gov

■ Chairman **Mark A. Vannoy** . . . . . . . . . . . . . . . . . . . . . . . (207) 287-3831
  E-mail: mark.vannoy@maine.gov
■ Commissioner **Carlisle "Carlie" McLean** . . . . . . . . . . . . . (207) 287-3831
  Education: Bates BS; Pace JD; Yale MEM
■ Commissioner **Bruce Williamson** . . . . . . . . . . . . . . . . . . . (207) 287-3831

---

★ Elected Official   ■ Appointed by Governor   ● Appointed by Legislature   ▲ Appointed by Board or Commission   ◆ Appointed by State Supreme Court

# Maryland

Tel: (410) 974-3901  Internet: www.maryland.gov

**Number of U.S. Congressional Delegates:** 2 Senators; 8 Representatives  **Governor's Term:** 4 years
**Legislature Description:** General Assembly - 47 member Senate; 141 member House of Delegates; Term - Senate 4 years; House 4 years  **Next Election:** Governor November 2018; Legislature November 2018
**Number of Electoral Votes:** 10  **Official Name:** State of Maryland (after Queen Henrietta Maria of England)  **Nickname:** Old Line State; Free State  **Motto:** Fatti Maschii, parole femine (Manly deeds, womanly words)

**Population:** 6,006,401 (2015); Rank 19  **Fiscal Year:** 2015  **Budget:** $38,729,000,000

## Office of the Governor

State Capitol, 100 State Circle, Annapolis, MD 21401
Tel: (410) 974-3901  Tel: (800) 811-8336 (In State)
Tel: (888) 372-8363 (Waste, Fraud and Abuse Hotline)
TTY: (800) 735-2258 (MD Relay)  Fax: (410) 974-3275

**Fiscal Year:** 2015  **Budget:** $11,442,000

**Lawrence J. "Larry" Hogan, Jr.**
Governor

Began Service: January 21, 2015
Term Expires: 2019
Date of Birth: May 25, 1956
Education: Florida State 1978 BA
Home: Edgewater
Career: Appointments Secretary, Office of Governor Bob Ehrlich, State of Maryland (2003-2007)

★Governor **Lawrence J. "Larry" Hogan, Jr.** (R) . . . . . . . . . (410) 974-3901
 Senior Advisor to the Governor
   **Martin G. "Marty" Madden** . . . . . . . . . . . . . . . . . . . (410) 260-3889
   E-mail: martin.madden@maryland.gov
   Education: Iona 1971 BA
 Senior Advisor to the Governor **Robert R. Neall** . . . . . . . (410) 974-3901
   Note: Effective July 1, 2016.
   Education: Maryland 1972 BA
 Senior Advisor and Board of Public Works Liaison
   **Mark Newgent** . . . . . . . . . . . . . . . . . . . . . . . . . . . . . . (410) 974-3066
   E-mail: mark.newgent@maryland.gov
 Senior Advisor for Emergency Management
   **Clay B. Stamp** . . . . . . . . . . . . . . . . . . . . . . . . . . . . . . . (410) 974-3901
   E-mail: clay.stamp@maryland.gov
 Special Advisor to the Governor
   **Keiffer Jackson Mitchell, Jr.** . . . . . . . . . . . . . . . . . . (410) 974-3336
   E-mail: keiffer.mitchell@maryland.gov
   Education: Emory 1990 BA; UDC 1994 JD
 Special Assistant **Kara M. Bowman** . . . . . . . . . . . . . . . (410) 974-5046
   E-mail: kara.bowman@maryland.gov
 Special Assistant **Alex Clark** . . . . . . . . . . . . . . . . . . . . (410) 974-5874
   E-mail: alex.clark@maryland.gov
 Special Assistant **Shawn C. Eum** . . . . . . . . . . . . . . . . . (410) 974-3805
   E-mail: shawn.eum@maryland.gov
 Chief of Staff **Craig A. Williams** . . . . . . . . . . . . . . . . . (410) 974-3591
   E-mail: craig.a.williams@maryland.gov
   Education: Bethany (WV) 1996 BA; Oklahoma 1999 MA, 2001 PhD
 Deputy Chief of Staff
   **Barbara Jeanne "Jeannie" Haddaway-Riccio** . . . . . . . . (410) 974-3901
   E-mail: jeannie.riccio@maryland.gov
   Education: Salisbury U 1999 BA
 Deputy Chief of Staff **Roy McGrath** . . . . . . . . . . . . . . . (410) 974-3921
   E-mail: roy.mcgrath@maryland.gov
 Deputy Chief of Staff **Christopher B. Shank** . . . . . . . . . . (410) 260-3952
   E-mail: christopher.shank@maryland.gov
   Education: Johns Hopkins 1994 BA; George Washington 1998 MA
 Executive Assistant **Amanda Allen** . . . . . . . . . . . . . . . (410) 974-5910
   E-mail: amanda.allen@maryland.gov
 Executive Assistant **Shannon Marino** . . . . . . . . . . . . . . (410) 260-3952
   E-mail: shannon.marino@maryland.gov

 Executive Assistant **(Vacant)** . . . . . . . . . . . . . . . . . . . . . . (410) 974-5019
 Director of Intergovernmental Affairs
   **Kristal Quarker Hartsfield** . . . . . . . . . . . . . . . . . . . (410) 974-5245
   E-mail: kristal.hartsfield@maryland.gov     Fax: (410) 974-5332
   Education: Alabama Birmingham 2004 BA; Troy U 2006 MPA
 Director of Public Affairs **(Vacant)** . . . . . . . . . . . . . . . . . (410) 260-3961
 Policy Director **Adam Dubitsky** . . . . . . . . . . . . . . . . . . (410) 974-2180
   E-mail: adam.dubitsky@maryland.gov
 Deputy Policy Director **(Vacant)** . . . . . . . . . . . . . . . . . . (410) 974-3901
 Executive Services Director **Wendy Hershey** . . . . . . . . . . (410) 974-3591
   E-mail: wendy.hershey@maryland.gov
 Communications Director **Matt Clark** . . . . . . . . . . . . . . . (410) 974-2316
   E-mail: matt.clark@maryland.gov
 Deputy Communications Director
   **Douglass V. "Doug" Mayer** . . . . . . . . . . . . . . . . . . . (410) 974-2439
   E-mail: douglass.mayer@maryland.gov
 Appointments Secretary **Dennis R. Schrader** . . . . . . . . . . (410) 974-2611
   E-mail: dennis.schrader@maryland.gov
   Education: Buffalo MILS
 Deputy Appointments Secretary **Chris Cavey** . . . . . . . . . . (410) 974-2611
   E-mail: chris.cavey@maryland.gov     Fax: (410) 974-2456
 Press Secretary **Shareese DeLeaver Churchill** . . . . . . . . . (410) 974-3901
   E-mail: shareese.churchill@maryland.gov
 Press Secretary **Erin Montgomery** . . . . . . . . . . . . . . . . . (410) 974-3824
   E-mail: erin.montgomery@maryland.gov
 Deputy Press Secretary **Hannah Marr** . . . . . . . . . . . . . . (410) 974-3901
   E-mail: hannah.marr@maryland.gov
 Chief Legislative Officer **Joseph M. Getty** . . . . . . . . . . . (410) 974-3336
   E-mail: joseph.getty@maryland.gov
   Education: Washington Col 1974 BA; George Washington 1980 MA; Maryland 1996 JD
 Deputy Legislative Officer **Chris Carroll** . . . . . . . . . . . . . (410) 974-3336
   E-mail: chris.carroll@maryland.gov
 Deputy Legislative Officer **Mathew J. Palmer** . . . . . . . . . (410) 974-3901
 Deputy Legislative Officer
   **Kathleen K. "Katie" Wunderlich, MPP** . . . . . . . . . . . . (410) 974-3103
   E-mail: katie.wunderlich@maryland.gov
   Education: DePaul BA; George Washington MPP
 Governor's Counsel **Bob Scholz** . . . . . . . . . . . . . . . . . . (410) 974-3005
   E-mail: robert.scholz@maryland.gov

## Grants Office

45 Calvert Street, Annapolis, MD 21401-1907
Tel: (410) 974-5090  E-mail: maryland.grants@maryland.gov
Internet: grants.maryland.gov

Director **Merril Oliver** . . . . . . . . . . . . . . . . . . . . . . . . . . . (410) 260-3910
   E-mail: merril.oliver@maryland.gov
   Education: Towson U BSBA
Deputy Director **(Vacant)** . . . . . . . . . . . . . . . . . . . . . . . . . (410) 260-3911
Research and Communications Manager **Susan E. Casey** . . (410) 260-3909
   E-mail: susan.casey@maryland.gov

## Office of Homeland Security

Fred L. Wineland Building, 16 Francis Street, Annapolis, MD 21401
Tel: (410) 974-2389

Director **Lt. Col. Walter F. "Pete" Landon** . . . . . . . . . . . . (410) 767-4511
   E-mail: dlgohs_gov@maryland.gov
   Executive Assistant **Linda Shapiro Bouchard** . . . . . . . . (410) 974-3901

---

★ Elected Official    ■ Appointed by Governor    ● Appointed by Legislature    ▲ Appointed by Board or Commission    ◆ Appointed by State Supreme Court

## Minority Affairs Office

Six Saint Paul Street, Suite 1502, Baltimore, MD 21202
Tel: (410) 767-8232  E-mail: info.goma@maryland.gov
Internet: goma.maryland.gov

Special Secretary **Jimmy Rhee** . . . . . . . . . . . . . . . . . (410) 767-8232
  Special Assistant **Pamela Gregory** . . . . . . . . . . . . . . (410) 767-8232
Deputy Special Secretary **Herbert Jordan III** . . . . . . . . . . (410) 767-8232
Communications Director **Alison Tavik** . . . . . . . . . . . . . (410) 767-8234
  E-mail: alison.tavik@maryland.gov
MBE Compliance Director **Janice Montague** . . . . . . . . (410) 767-5381
  MBE Compliance Manager **Chantal Kai-Lewis** . . . . . . . . (410) 767-8220
  MBE Compliance Manager **Lisa Sanford** . . . . . . . . . . . (410) 767-5690
  MBE Compliance Manager **Gerald Stinnett** . . . . . . . . . . (410) 767-3580
Policy and Legislative Affairs Director **James King, Jr.** . . . . (410) 767-4654
  E-mail: james.kingjr@maryland.gov
Small Business Outreach Manager **Eduardo Hayden** . . . . . (410) 767-0910

## Office of Performance Improvement

Jeffrey Building, 6 Saint Paul Street, 4th Floor, Baltimore, MD 21201
Tel: (410) 260-3945

Director **Luis A. Luna** . . . . . . . . . . . . . . . . . . . . . . . (410) 260-3945
  E-mail: luis.luna@maryland.gov
  Education: Maryland 1978 BA; Georgetown 1987 JD
Analyst **Charles P. "Pat" Pscherer** . . . . . . . . . . . . . . . (410) 260-3945
Analyst **Laura Bruner** . . . . . . . . . . . . . . . . . . . . . . . (410) 260-3945

## Washington Office

444 North Capitol Street, NW, Suite 311, Washington, DC 20001
Tel: (202) 624-1430  Fax: (202) 783-3061

Director of Federal Relations **Tiffany Waddell** . . . . . . . . . (202) 624-1430
  E-mail: tiffany.waddell@maryland.gov

## Volunteer Maryland

301 West Preston Street, 15th Floor, Baltimore, MD 21201
Tel: (410) 767-6203  Fax: (410) 767-6203  E-mail: volmd@erols.com
Internet: www.volunteermaryland.org

Director **Patrice Beverly** . . . . . . . . . . . . . . . . . . . . . . (410) 767-6231

## Office of the Lieutenant Governor

State House, 100 State Circle, Annapolis, MD 21401
Tel: (410) 974-2461  TTY: (410) 333-3098  Fax: (410) 974-5882
E-mail: lt.governor@gov.state.md.us

★Lieutenant Governor **Boyd Kevin Rutherford** (R) . . . . . . . (410) 974-2461
  Term Expires: January 2019
  E-mail: boyd.rutherford@maryland.gov
  Education: Howard U 1979 BA; USC 1990 MA, 1990 JD
Senior Advisor **Richard A. Tabuteau** . . . . . . . . . . . . . . (410) 974-2461
Special Assistant **Paul H. Beatty** . . . . . . . . . . . . . . . . (410) 974-2461
Executive Assistant **Diane O. Jennings** . . . . . . . . . . . . . (410) 974-2461

## Office of the Secretary of State

State House, 16 Francis Street, Annapolis, MD 21401
Tel: (410) 974-5521  Tel: (888) 874-0013
Tel: (800) 825-4510 (Charitable Organization Division)
Tel: (410) 974-5534 (Charitable Organization Information)
TTY: (800) 735-2258  Fax: (410) 974-5190
Fax: (410) 974-5527 (Charities)  E-mail: dlmdsos_sos@maryland.gov
Internet: www.marylandsos.gov

**Employees:** 24  **Fiscal Year:** 2015  **Budget:** $2,423,000

■Secretary of State **John Casper Wobensmith** . . . . . . . . . (410) 260-3894
  E-mail: john.wobensmith@maryland.gov
  Executive Assistant **Margaret A. Schnoor** . . . . . . . . . . (410) 260-3894
Assistant Attorney General **Josephine Yuzuik** . . . . . . . . . (410) 260-3855
Deputy Secretary of State **Luis E. Borunda** . . . . . . . . . . (410) 974-5521
  E-mail: luis.borunda@maryland.gov
Assistant Secretary for Charities and Legal Services
  **Kathleen M. Smith** . . . . . . . . . . . . . . . . . . . . . . (410) 974-5521
  E-mail: kathleen.smith1@maryland.gov
Deputy Secretary for Operations/Fiscal Officer
  **Frederick "Fred" Smalls** . . . . . . . . . . . . . . . . . . (410) 260-3853

Charities and Legal Services Administrator
  **Teresa Owens** . . . . . . . . . . . . . . . . . . . . . . . . (410) 260-3856
  Lead Charity Officer **Kimberly E. Smith** . . . . . . . . . . (410) 260-3864
    E-mail: kimberlye.smith@maryland.gov
  Notary Public Officer **Tanya T. Pinkney** . . . . . . . . . . (410) 974-5520
  Solicitors Administrator **Loraine Parks** . . . . . . . . . . . (410) 260-3857
    E-mail: loraine.parks@maryland.gov
  Charities and Notaries Investigator **Michael Schlein** . . . . (410) 260-3879
International and Intergovernmental Relations Director
  **Mary E. "Mendy" Nitsch** . . . . . . . . . . . . . . . . . . (410) 260-3865
  International and Intergovernmental Assistant
    Coordinator **Esther Yoo** . . . . . . . . . . . . . . . . . . (410) 260-3896
Cash Receipts and Procurement Officer **(Vacant)** . . . . . . . (410) 260-3852
Chief Information Officer **(Vacant)** . . . . . . . . . . . . . . . (410) 260-3869
Condominium and Trademark Officer **(Vacant)** . . . . . . . . (410) 974-5521
Notary Public Officer **Marquita Lewis** . . . . . . . . . . . . . (410) 260-3861
Service and Procurement Officer **Lanisha J. Hall** . . . . . . . (410) 260-3851
Webmaster **Tami Cathell** . . . . . . . . . . . . . . . . . . . . . (410) 260-3872
  E-mail: tcathell@sos.state.md.us

## Department of Aging

301 West Preston Street, Room 1007, Baltimore, MD 21201
Tel: (410) 767-1100  Fax: (410) 333-7943

**Employees:** 77  **Fiscal Year:** 2015  **Budget:** $51,374,000

■Secretary **Rona E. Kramer** . . . . . . . . . . . . . . . . . . . . (410) 767-1102
  E-mail: rona.kramer@maryland.gov
  Education: Maryland 1976 BA; Baltimore 1979 JD
Counsel **Jeffrey H. Myers** . . . . . . . . . . . . . . . . . . . . . (410) 767-1110
Chief of Staff **(Vacant)** . . . . . . . . . . . . . . . . . . . . . . (410) 767-5913
Senior Community Service Employment Program
  Manager **Deborah A. Wilburn** . . . . . . . . . . . . . . . . (410) 767-2160
  E-mail: deborah.wilburn@maryland.gov

## Maryland Department of Agriculture [MDA]

50 Harry S Truman Parkway, Annapolis, MD 21401
Tel: (410) 841-5700  TTY: (800) 735-2258 (MD Relay)
Tel: (800) 492-5590  Fax: (410) 841-5914  Fax: (410) 841-5894

**Employees:** 419  **Fiscal Year:** 2015  **Budget:** $80,285,000

■Secretary **Joseph "Joe" Bartenfelder** . . . . . . . . . . . . . (410) 841-5880
  E-mail: joe.bartenfelder@maryland.gov
  Education: Towson State U BSBA
  Emergency Preparedness and Response Coordinator
    **Daniel F. McMullen** . . . . . . . . . . . . . . . . . . . . (410) 841-5853
Deputy Secretary **James P. "Jim" Eichhorst** . . . . . . . . . (410) 841-5881
Chief of Staff **Kevin D. Conroy** . . . . . . . . . . . . . . . . . (410) 841-5916
  Education: Curry 2004 BA
Counsel **Craig A. Nielsen** . . . . . . . . . . . . . . . . . . . . . (410) 841-5883
Administrative Services Assistant Secretary
  **James P. Wallace** . . . . . . . . . . . . . . . . . . . . . . (410) 841-5855
  E-mail: james.wallace@maryland.gov
Communications Director **Julianne A. "Julie" Oberg** . . . . (410) 841-5888
  E-mail: julie.oberg@maryland.gov
Public Information Officer **Vanessa Orlando** . . . . . . . . . . (410) 841-5889
  E-mail: vanessa.orlando@maryland.gov

## Office of Marketing, Animal Industries and Consumer Services

Tel: (410) 841-5872  Fax: (410) 841-5999

Assistant Secretary **Steven A. "Steve" Connelly** . . . . . . . (410) 841-5782
  Education: Maryland BS
Animal Health Chief and State Veterinarian
  **Nancy Jo Chapman** . . . . . . . . . . . . . . . . . . . . . (410) 841-5810
Food Quality Assurance Chief **Deanna L. Baldwin** . . . . . . (410) 841-5769
                                        Fax: (410) 841-2750
Weights and Measures Chief **Kenneth Ramsburg** . . . . . . . (410) 841-5790
                                        Fax: (410) 841-2765

## Marketing Services

Chief **Mark S. Powell** . . . . . . . . . . . . . . . . . . . . . . . (410) 841-5775
                                        Fax: (410) 841-5987
International Marketing Chief **Theresa A. Brophy** . . . . . . . (410) 841-5770

---

★ Elected Official    ■ Appointed by Governor    ● Appointed by Legislature    ▲ Appointed by Board or Commission    ◆ Appointed by State Supreme Court

## Office of Plant Industries and Pest Management
Tel: (410) 841-5870

Assistant Secretary **Carol A. Holko** . . . . . . . . . . . . . . . . . . (410) 841-5734
                                               Fax: (410) 841-5734
State Chemist (Acting) **Thomas W. "Tom" Phillips** . . . . . . (410) 841-2721
Forest Health Program Manager **Robert Tatman** . . . . . . . . (410) 841-5922
Mosquito Control Program Chief (Acting)
  **Daniel J. Schamberger** . . . . . . . . . . . . . . . . . . . . . . . . (410) 841-5870
  E-mail: daniel.schamberger@maryland.gov
Pesticide Regulation Program Chief **Dennis W. Howard** . . (410) 841-5710
                                                Fax: (410) 841-2765
Plant Protection and Weed Management Program Chief
  **Kimberly A. Rice** . . . . . . . . . . . . . . . . . . . . . . . . . . . . (410) 841-5920
Turf and Seed Program Chief **Dale A. Morris** . . . . . . . . . . (410) 841-5960
  E-mail: dale.morris@maryland.gov

## Office of Resource Conservation
Assistant Secretary **Hans Schmidt** . . . . . . . . . . . . . . . . . . . (410) 841-5865
                                                Fax: (410) 841-5736
Conservation Grants Program Chief **Norman Astle** . . . . . . (410) 841-5864
  E-mail: norman.astle@maryland.gov       Fax: (410) 841-5950
Program Planning and Development Chief
  **Louise Lawrence** . . . . . . . . . . . . . . . . . . . . . . . . . . . . . (410) 841-5863
                                                Fax: (410) 841-5734
Nutrient Management Administrator **Dwight Dotterer** . . . . (410) 841-5959
  E-mail: dwight.dotterer@maryland.gov     Fax: (410) 841-5950
Resource Conservation Operations Administrator
  **Byron Petrauskas** . . . . . . . . . . . . . . . . . . . . . . . . . . . . (410) 841-5952
  E-mail: byron.petrauskas@maryland.gov

## Agricultural Land Preservation Foundation
Executive Director **Carol West** . . . . . . . . . . . . . . . . . . . . . (410) 841-5860

## State Department of Assessments and Taxation [SDAT]
301 West Preston Street, Room 808, Baltimore, MD 21201
Tel: (410) 767-1340  Tel: (410) 767-1330 (Charter Information)
TTY: (800) 735-2258  Fax: (410) 333-5873
E-mail: inquiry@dat.state.md.us  Internet: www.dat.state.md.us

**Employees:** 616  **Fiscal Year:** 2015  **Budget:** $130,130,000

■Director **Sean P. Powell** . . . . . . . . . . . . . . . . . . . . . . . . . . (410) 767-1184
  Special Assistant to the Director **Nruti Desai** . . . . . . . . (410) 767-4884
Deputy Director **Michael L. Higgs, Jr.** . . . . . . . . . . . . . . . (410) 767-1191
Counsel **Jeffrey Comen** . . . . . . . . . . . . . . . . . . . . . . . . . . . (410) 767-1280
Communications Director/Social Media Manager
  **Ashley Ricker** . . . . . . . . . . . . . . . . . . . . . . . . . . . . . . . (410) 767-1142
Public Information Officer **Ashley Ricker** . . . . . . . . . . . . . (410) 767-1142

## Department of Budget and Management [DBM]
45 Calvert Street, Annapolis, MD 21401-1907
Tel: (410) 260-7555  Tel: (800) 705-3493
TTY: (800) 735-2258 (Use MD Relay)  Fax: (410) 974-2585
E-mail: emaryland@maryland.gov  Internet: www.dbm.maryland.gov

**Employees:** 308  **Fiscal Year:** 2015  **Budget:** $35,524,000

■Secretary **David R. Brinkley** . . . . . . . . . . . . . . . . . . . . . . . (410) 260-7041
  E-mail: david.brinkley@maryland.gov
  Education: Maryland 1981 BA
Deputy Secretary **Marc L. Nicole** . . . . . . . . . . . . . . . . . . . (410) 260-7288
  Education: Western New England 1985 BA; Syracuse 1986 MPA
Chief of Staff **Kevin R. Igoe** . . . . . . . . . . . . . . . . . . . . . . . (410) 260-7026
Principal Counsel **Brent A. Bolea** . . . . . . . . . . . . . . . . . . . (410) 260-7202
Deputy Counsel **Michael S. Friedman** . . . . . . . . . . . . . . . (410) 767-1239
Government Relations Director **Barbara Wilkins** . . . . . . . . (410) 260-6371
Executive Director **Teresa Garraty** . . . . . . . . . . . . . . . . . . (410) 767-4534
Budget Analysis Executive Director **Jonathan D. Martin** . . (410) 260-7280

Finance and Administration Executive Director
  **Johnathan R. "John" West** . . . . . . . . . . . . . . . . . . . . . (410) 260-7059
  E-mail: john.west1@maryland.gov
Personnel Services and Benefits Executive Director
  **Cynthia "Cindy" Kollner** . . . . . . . . . . . . . . . . . . . . . . (410) 767-4716
  301 W. Preston Street, Baltimore, MD 21201
Procurement Policy and Administration Division Director
  **Mary M. Naramore** . . . . . . . . . . . . . . . . . . . . . . . . . . . (410) 260-7471
  E-mail: mary.naramore@maryland.gov
  Education: Central Florida BA, MAE
Central Collection Unit Director **Anthony Fugett** . . . . . . . . (410) 767-3046
Public Information Officer **Eric T. Shirk** . . . . . . . . . . . . . . (410) 260-7039

## Department of Commerce
401 East Pratt Street, Baltimore, MD 21202
Tel: (410) 767-6300  Tel: (800) 541-8549  Fax: (410) 333-6911
Internet: http://commerce.maryland.gov/

**Employees:** 226  **Fiscal Year:** 2016  **Budget:** $124,329,000

■Secretary **R. Michael "Mike" Gill** . . . . . . . . . . . . . . . . . . (410) 767-6301
  E-mail: mike.gill@maryland.gov
  Education: Towson U BBA
Executive Director **(Vacant)** . . . . . . . . . . . . . . . . . . . . . . . (410) 767-6301
Deputy Secretary and Chief Operating Officer
  **Benjamin H. Wu, Esq.** . . . . . . . . . . . . . . . . . . . . . . . . (410) 767-6302
  Education: NYU 1985 BA; Pittsburgh 1988 JD
Special Assistant Secretary **Brady Walker, JD** . . . . . . . . . . (410) 767-6440
Principal Counsel **Laila K. Atallah** . . . . . . . . . . . . . . . . . . (410) 767-6446
Marketing and Communications Managing Director
  **Allison S. Mayer** . . . . . . . . . . . . . . . . . . . . . . . . . . . . . (410) 767-6272
  E-mail: allison.mayer@maryland.gov
Marketing Director **Sherrie Diehl** . . . . . . . . . . . . . . . . . . . (410) 767-6835
Military and Federal Affairs Managing Director
  **J. Michael Hayes** . . . . . . . . . . . . . . . . . . . . . . . . . . . . (410) 767-2988
  E-mail: james.hayes@maryland.gov
Performance Measurement Director **Christine Rose** . . . . . . (410) 767-3383
Public Affairs Director **Karen Glenn-Hood** . . . . . . . . . . . . (410) 767-6318
  E-mail: karen.glennhood@maryland.gov
International Investment and Trade Managing Director
  **Signe J. Pringle** . . . . . . . . . . . . . . . . . . . . . . . . . . . . . . (410) 767-3542
  Education: Baltimore 2005 MPA
Internal Audits Chief Auditor **Maqsood Khan** . . . . . . . . . . (410) 767-2292

## Division of Business and Industry Sector Development
Tel: (410) 767-6870  Tel: (888) 246-6736  Fax: (410) 333-6792

**Employees:** 65  **Fiscal Year:** 2016  **Budget:** $73,975,000

Managing Director **Steven Pennington** . . . . . . . . . . . . . . . (410) 767-6662

## Division of Tourism, Film and the Arts
Tel: (410) 767-3400  Tel: (800) 543-1036 (Free Travel Kit Information)
Fax: (410) 333-6643

**Employees:** 40  **Fiscal Year:** 2016  **Budget:** $32,693,000

Managing Director **Elizabeth "Liz" Fitzsimmons** . . . . . . . (410) 767-6331
Deputy Assistant Secretary **William J. "Bill" Pencek, Jr.** . . (410) 767-6289
Film and Digital Media Director
  **John A. "Jack" Gerbes** . . . . . . . . . . . . . . . . . . . . . . . . (410) 767-6340
                                                Fax: (410) 333-0044
Maryland State Arts Council Executive Director
  **Theresa M. Colvin** . . . . . . . . . . . . . . . . . . . . . . . . . . . (410) 767-6412
  175 West Ostend Street, Suite E,      Fax: (410) 333-1062
  Baltimore, MD 21230
Sports Marketing Office Director **(Vacant)** . . . . . . . . . . . . (410) 223-4158
Tourism Development Executive Director
  **Elizabeth "Liz" Fitzsimmons** . . . . . . . . . . . . . . . . . . . (410) 767-6331

---

★ Elected Official    ■ Appointed by Governor    ● Appointed by Legislature    ▲ Appointed by Board or Commission    ◆ Appointed by State Supreme Court

# Department of Disabilities [MDOD]

217 East Redwood Street, Suite 1300, Baltimore, MD 21202
Tel: (410) 767-3660  Fax: (410) 333-6674
E-mail: mdod@mdod.state.md.us

**Employees:** 31  **Fiscal Year:** 2015  **Budget:** $12,879,000

■Secretary **Carol A. Beatty** . . . . . . . . . . . . . . . . . . . . . . . . . . (410) 767-3660
  E-mail: carol.beatty@maryland.gov
Deputy Secretary **William J. Frank**. . . . . . . . . . . . . . . . . . .(410) 767-3660
  Education: Mount St Mary's 1982 BA; Johns Hopkins 1992 MAS
Chief of Staff **John P. Brennan** . . . . . . . . . . . . . . . . . . . . . (410) 767-3640
Communications and Outreach Executive Director
  **Carrie McGraw** . . . . . . . . . . . . . . . . . . . . . . . . . . . . . . (410) 767-3654
  E-mail: carrie.mcgraw@maryland.gov
Community Living Policy Director **Jennifer Eastman** . . . . (410) 767-7901
Constituent Services Director **Nan Brittingham** . . . . . . . . . (410) 767-3948
Emergency Preparedness Director **Cecilia Warren** . . . . . . . (410) 767-3660
Employment Policy Director **Jade Ann Gingerich** . . . . . . . (410) 767-3651
  E-mail: jade.gingerich@maryland.gov
  Education: Yale 1990 MPhil, 1996 PhD
Health and Behavioral Health Policy Director
  **Anne Blackfield** . . . . . . . . . . . . . . . . . . . . . . . . . . . . . .(410) 767-3652
  E-mail: anne.blackfield@maryland.gov
Housing Policy Director **Patricia R. "Pat" Sylvester** . . . . . (410) 767-3640
Interagency Affairs and Education Policy Director
  **Anne Blackfield** . . . . . . . . . . . . . . . . . . . . . . . . . . . . . .(410) 767-3635
  E-mail: anne.blackfield@maryland.gov
Maryland Technology Assistance Program Executive
  Director **James D. McCarthy** . . . . . . . . . . . . . . . . . . . . (410) 554-9245
  E-mail: jmccarthy@mdtap.org
Research and Evaluation Director **Anne Blackfield** . . . . . . . (410) 767-3652
Transportation Policy Director **Thomas Curtis** . . . . . . . . . . .(410) 767-3629
  E-mail: thomas.curtis@maryland.gov
ADA Coordinator/Access Maryland **Cari Watrous** . . . . . . . .(410) 767-3616

# Department of the Environment [MDE]

1800 Washington Boulevard, Baltimore, MD 21230
Tel: (410) 537-3000  Tel: (800) 633-6101
Tel: (866) 633-4686 (Emergency Response [24 hours])
Fax: (410) 537-3888  TTY: (800) 735-2258
Internet: www.mde.state.md.us

**Employees:** 937  **Fiscal Year:** 2015  **Budget:** $379,064,000

■Secretary **Benjamin H. "Ben" Grumbles** . . . . . . . . . . . . . (410) 537-3084
  E-mail: ben.grumbles@maryland.gov
  Education: Wake Forest 1982 BA; Emory 1985 JD;
  George Washington 1991 LLM
Deputy Secretary for Operations **(Vacant)**. . . . . . . . . . . . . .(410) 537-3893
Deputy Secretary for Regulatory Programs and Policy
  **Horacio A. Tablada** . . . . . . . . . . . . . . . . . . . . . . . . . . . .(410) 537-3893

## Air and Radiation Management Administration

1800 Washington Boulevard, Baltimore, MD 21230
Tel: (410) 537-3255  Fax: (410) 537-3391

**Employees:** 171  **Fiscal Year:** 2015  **Budget:** $19,405,000

Director **George S. "Tad" Aburn, Jr.**. . . . . . . . . . . . . . . . . .(410) 537-3255
Deputy Director **Angelo J. Bianca** . . . . . . . . . . . . . . . . . . . .(410) 537-3260
Air Monitoring Program Manager **David Krask** . . . . . . . . . .(410) 537-3756
Air Quality Compliance Program Manager
  **B. Frank Courtright** . . . . . . . . . . . . . . . . . . . . . . . . . . . (410) 537-4225
Air Quality Policy, Planning and Regulation Development
  Program Manager **Brian J. Hug** . . . . . . . . . . . . . . . . . . (410) 537-4125
Mobile Source Control Program Manager
  **Marcia A. Ways**. . . . . . . . . . . . . . . . . . . . . . . . . . . . . . .(410) 537-3176
Radiological Health Program Manager
  **Roland G. Fletcher** . . . . . . . . . . . . . . . . . . . . . . . . . . . . (410) 537-3300

# Land Management Administration

1800 Washington Boulevard, Baltimore, MD 21230
Tel: (410) 537-3304

**Employees:** 237  **Fiscal Year:** 2015  **Budget:** $28,011,000

Director **Hilary Miller**. . . . . . . . . . . . . . . . . . . . . . . . . . . . . .(410) 537-3304
  E-mail: hilary.miller@maryland.gov
  Education: Maryland BS
Deputy Director **(Vacant)** . . . . . . . . . . . . . . . . . . . . . . . . . . .(410) 537-3304
Land Restoration Program Manager **James Carroll** . . . . . . .(410) 537-3437
Lead Poisoning Prevention Program Manager
  **Paula Montgomery** . . . . . . . . . . . . . . . . . . . . . . . . . . . (410) 537-3825
Mining Program Manager **Edmond "Ed" Larrimore** . . . . . (410) 537-3539
Oil Control Program Manager **Chris Ralston** . . . . . . . . . . . (410) 537-3442
Operational Services Program Manager **Cindy Keller** . . . . . (410) 537-3311
Solid Waste Program Manager **Edward A. Dexter** . . . . . . . . (410) 537-3318
Resource Management Program Manager **Hussain Alhija**. . (410) 537-3314

# Operational Services Administration

Tel: (410) 537-3429

**Fiscal Year:** 2015  **Budget:** $9,325,000

Director (Acting) **Thomas J. French** . . . . . . . . . . . . . . . . . (410) 537-3138
  E-mail: tom.french@maryland.gov
Deputy Director **Thomas J. French** . . . . . . . . . . . . . . . . . . (410) 537-3138
  E-mail: tom.french@maryland.gov
Human Resources Director **Michelle N. Romney** . . . . . . . . (410) 537-3100
Office of Financial Monitoring Director **Paul D. Kadin** . . . . (410) 537-3140
Office of Fiscal Services Director
  **William M. "Bill" Williams, Jr.**. . . . . . . . . . . . . . . . . (410) 537-3137
Office of Procurement Director **William Kamberger** . . . . . . (410) 537-3081
Chief Information Officer **James "Jim" Purvis** . . . . . . . . . (410) 537-3114
  E-mail: james.purvis@maryland.gov

# Science Services Administration

1800 Washington Boulevard, Baltimore, MD 21230
Tel: (410) 537-3572  Fax: (410) 537-3998

**Employees:** 84  **Fiscal Year:** 2015  **Budget:** $12,552,000

Director **Lee Currey** . . . . . . . . . . . . . . . . . . . . . . . . . . . . . . (410) 537-3818
  E-mail: lee.currey@maryland.gov
Deputy Director **Matthew Rowe** . . . . . . . . . . . . . . . . . . . . . (410) 537-3572
  E-mail: matthew.rowe@maryland.gov
Environmental Assessments and Standards Program
  Manager **John Backus** . . . . . . . . . . . . . . . . . . . . . . . . . (410) 537-3965
Field Services Program Manager **William Beatty** . . . . . . . . (443) 482-2702
Total Maximum Daily Load (TMDL) Program Manager
  **Dinorah Dalmasy** . . . . . . . . . . . . . . . . . . . . . . . . . . . . (410) 537-3699
Water Quality Protection and Restoration Program
  Manager **Jim George** . . . . . . . . . . . . . . . . . . . . . . . . . . (410) 537-3579

# Water Management Administration

1800 Washington Boulevard, Baltimore, MD 21230
Tel: (410) 537-3567  Fax: (410) 537-3874

**Employees:** 28

Director **Lynn Yerges Buhl** . . . . . . . . . . . . . . . . . . . . . . . . . (410) 537-3567
  Education: Virginia 1977 BA; Wake Forest 1981 JD
Assistant Director **Heather W. Barthel** . . . . . . . . . . . . . . . .(410) 537-3512
Compliance Program Manager (Acting) **Heather Nelson** . . (410) 537-3626
Sediment, Stormwater and Dam Safety Program Manager
  **Brian Clevenger** . . . . . . . . . . . . . . . . . . . . . . . . . . . . . (410) 537-3554
Wastewater Permits Program Manager
  **Edwal F. "Ed" Stone** . . . . . . . . . . . . . . . . . . . . . . . . . (410) 537-3599
Water Supply Program Manager **Saeid Kasraei** . . . . . . . . . (410) 537-3702
Operations Administrator **Pamela A. Wright** . . . . . . . . . . . (410) 537-3754
  E-mail: pamela.wright@maryland.gov
Chesapeake Bay Coordinator **Marya Levelev** . . . . . . . . . . . (410) 537-3720
Water Resources Planning Unit Head **Janice Outen** . . . . . . (410) 537-3860

---

★ Elected Official    ■ Appointed by Governor    ● Appointed by Legislature    ▲ Appointed by Board or Commission    ◆ Appointed by State Supreme Court

## Department of General Services [DGS]

301 West Preston Street, Room 1401, Baltimore, MD 21201
Tel: (410) 767-4960  Fax: (410) 333-5480
Internet: www.dgs.maryland.gov

**Employees:** 580  **Fiscal Year:** 2015  **Budget:** $93,205,000

■Secretary **C. Gail Bassette**...........................(410) 767-4960
  E-mail: gail.bassette@maryland.gov
Deputy Secretary **Nelson Reichart**....................(410) 767-4960
  E-mail: nelson.reichart@maryland.gov
Energy Deputy Secretary **A. Leigh Williams**...........(410) 767-4960
Principal Counsel **Turhan Robinson**...................(410) 767-4992
Communications Director **Therese Yewell**.............(410) 767-4285
  E-mail: therese.yewell@maryland.gov
Personnel Director **(Vacant)**.........................(410) 767-4985
Fiscal Services Division Chief **(Vacant)**..............(410) 767-4279

### Administrative Division

Assistant Secretary **Monique M. Anderson**...........(410) 767-4956
  E-mail: monique.anderson@maryland.gov
Capital Grants and Loans Director **Catherine J. Ensor**....(410) 767-4107
Fiscal Services Chief **Karen Tolley**..................(410) 767-4279
Human Resources Director (Acting) **Denise Estep**.......(410) 767-4988

### Facilities Operation and Maintenance Office

29 Saint John's Street, Annapolis, MD 21401
Tel: (410) 260-2981  Fax: (410) 974-2361

**Employees:** 207  **Fiscal Year:** 2015  **Budget:** $53,480,000

Director **Mark Mascarenhas**.........................(410) 260-2981
Annapolis Public Buildings and Grounds Superintendent
  **Mike Valenti**....................................(410) 260-2900
Baltimore Public Buildings and Grounds Superintendent
  **Daniel Campbell**.................................(410) 767-4426
  301 West Preston Street, Room 1311, Baltimore, MD 21201
Inner Harbor Complex Superintendent **Gary Gray**.......(410) 767-2275
Multi-Service Centers Superintendent **Barbara Bauman**...(410) 480-7990

### Facilities Planning, Design and Construction

301 West Preston Street, Room 1400, Baltimore, MD 21201
Tel: (410) 767-4214  Fax: (410) 767-1807

**Employees:** 81  **Fiscal Year:** 2015  **Budget:** $12,719,000

Assistant Secretary **Lauren Buckler**..................(410) 767-3174
  E-mail: lauren.buckler@maryland.gov
Construction Chief **Timothy W. Case**.................(410) 767-4360
Facilities Engineering Chief **James Keel**..............(410) 767-4263

### Procurement and Logistics Office

301 West Preston Street, Room M-6, Baltimore, MD 21201
Tel: (410) 767-7791  Fax: (410) 333-5986

**Employees:** 68  **Fiscal Year:** 2015  **Budget:** $6,973,000

Assistant Secretary **T. Suzette Moore**................(410) 767-7791
Minority Business Enterprise Program Director
  **Jack Howard**....................................(410) 767-6047
Procurement and Logistics Director (Acting)
  **David Bohannon**.................................(410) 767-4045
Board of Public Works Program Manager **Jane Bailey**....(410) 767-4307
  E-mail: jane.bailey@maryland.gov

### Real Estate Office

300 West Preston Street, Room 601, Baltimore, MD 21201
Tel: (410) 333-7144

**Employees:** 25

Assistant Secretary **Wendy Scott-Napier**..............(410) 767-4088
Land Acquisition and Disposal Chief **(Vacant)**..........(410) 767-4304
Lease Management & Procurement Chief **Robert Suit**....(410) 767-4328
Valuation and Appraisal Chief **William T. Beach**........(410) 767-4329

## Department of Health and Mental Hygiene [DHMH]

201 West Preston Street, Baltimore, MD 21201
6550 Reistertown Road, Baltimore, MD 21215 (Vital Records)
Tel: (410) 767-6500  Tel: (877) 463-3464
Tel: (410) 764-3038 (Vital Records)  Tel: (800) 832-3277 (Vital Records)
TTY: (800) 735-2258  Fax: (410) 767-6489
E-mail: dhmh.healthmd@maryland.gov

**Employees:** 6,737  **Fiscal Year:** 2015  **Budget:** $12,054,042,000

■Secretary **Van T. Mitchell**..........................(410) 767-4639
  E-mail: van.mitchell@maryland.gov
  Education: Campbell (Attended)
Chief of Staff **Shawn Cain**..........................(410) 767-0907
  E-mail: shawn.cain@maryland.gov
Health Workforce Associate Director **(Vacant)**..........(410) 764-4682
Principal Counsel **Kathleen A. Ellis**.................(410) 767-1861
Deputy Counsel **David S. Lapp**......................(410) 767-5292
Deputy Counsel **Kathleen A. Morse**.................(410) 767-1866

### Behavioral Health and Disabilities

Deputy Secretary **Gayle Jordan-Randolph**............(410) 767-3167
Chief of Staff **Shauna Donahue**.....................(410) 767-1909
Co-Occurring Substance Use and Mental Disorder
  Administrator **Lisa Hadley**.......................(410) 402-8446
  E-mail: lisa.hadley@maryland.gov
Forensic Services Clinical Director
  **Dr. Erik J. Roskes, MD**.........................(410) 724-3033
Resident Grievance System Director **Rhonda Callum**.....(410) 767-1051

### Health Care Financing

Tel: (410) 767-4139  Fax: (410) 333-7687

Deputy Secretary **Shannon M. McMahon**.............(410) 767-4139
  Education: Northeastern 1999 MPA
Chief of Staff **Erin McMullen**......................(410) 767-6373
  E-mail: erin.mcmullen@maryland.gov
  Education: American U

### Operations

**Fiscal Year:** 2015  **Budget:** $26,894,000

Deputy Secretary for Operations **(Vacant)**..............(410) 767-6505
Chief Administrative Officer **Lisa J. Ellis**............(410) 767-6510
  E-mail: lisa.ellis@maryland.gov
Chief of Staff **Yolanda Jiggetts**....................(410) 767-0136
Minority Business Enterprise Director **Janelle Robinson**..(410) 767-2206

### Public Health Services

Deputy Secretary **Howard M. Haft, MD, MMM, FACPE**..(410) 767-6525
Chief of Staff **Jennifer L. Newman Barnhart**..........(410) 767-6575
Anatomy Board Director **Ronn Wade**.................(410) 547-1222
Preparedness and Response Office Director
  **Sherry B. Adams, RN**...........................(410) 767-3541

## Maryland Health Care Commission [MHCC]

4160 Patterson Avenue, Baltimore, MD 21215
Tel: (410) 764-3460  Tel: (877) 245-1762  Fax: (410) 358-1236
E-mail: webmaster@mhcc.state.md.us  Internet: mhcc.maryland.gov

■Chair **Dr. Craig Tanio, MD**........................(410) 764-3565
Vice Chair **Frances B. Phillips, RN**.................(410) 764-3460
■Executive Director **Michael J. "Ben" Steffen**..........(410) 764-3565
  E-mail: ben.steffen@maryland.gov
  Education: American U 1981 MA

### Administration

Administration Director **Bridget Zombro**..............(410) 764-3558

### Legal Services

Assistant Attorney General **Siobhan Madison**.........(410) 764-3263
  Education: Mount St Mary's Sem 1997 BA; Cincinnati 2000 JD
Assistant Attorney General **Suellen Wideman**..........(410) 764-3326
  Education: Yale 1986 LLM

---

★ Elected Official　　■ Appointed by Governor　　● Appointed by Legislature　　▲ Appointed by Board or Commission　　◆ Appointed by State Supreme Court

EXECUTIVE BRANCH

## Center for Analysis and Information Systems
Director **Linda Bartnyska** . . . . . . . . . . . . . . . . . . . . . . (410) 764-3782
  E-mail: linda.bartnyska@maryland.gov
  Education: Johns Hopkins 1983 MHS
Special Projects Chief **Janet Ennis** . . . . . . . . . . . . . . . . . (410) 764-3779

## Center for Health Information Technology
Director **Paul David Sharp, PhD** . . . . . . . . . . . . . . . . . . (410) 764-3578
  Education: Western Maryland 1993 MA; Kennedy-Western 1998 PhD
Health Information Exchange Chief **Angela Evatt** . . . . . . . (410) 764-3574
  E-mail: angela.evatt@maryland.gov

## Center for Hospital Services
Director **Paul Parker** . . . . . . . . . . . . . . . . . . . . . . . . . . . (410) 764-3261

## Center for Quality Measurement and Reporting
Director **Theressa Lee** . . . . . . . . . . . . . . . . . . . . . . . . . . (410) 764-3328
HMO (Health Maintenance Organization) Quality and
  Performance Chief **(Vacant)** . . . . . . . . . . . . . . . . . . . . (410) 764-3483

## Department of Housing and Community Development [DHCD]
7800 Harkins Road, Lanham, MD 20706
Tel: (301) 429-7400  Tel: (800) 756-0119 (Customer Service Line)
TTY: (800) 735-2258 (Outside of Maryland)  Fax: (410) 514-7899
E-mail: webmaster@mdhousing.org  Internet: www.dhcd.state.md.us

**Employees:** 337  **Fiscal Year:** 2015  **Budget:** $364,738,000

■Secretary **Kenneth C. "Ken" Holt** . . . . . . . . . . . . . . . . (301) 429-7452
  E-mail: kenneth.holt@maryland.gov
Deputy Secretary **Ellington C. Churchill, Jr.** . . . . . . . . . . (301) 429-7452
Counsel **Anthony J. Mohan** . . . . . . . . . . . . . . . . . . . . . (301) 429-7477
  E-mail: mohan@mdhousing.org
Assistant Attorney General **Mark Petrauskas** . . . . . . . . . . (410) 514-7834
  E-mail: petrauskas@mdhousing.org
Chief Financial Officer **Sergei V. Kuzmenchuk** . . . . . . . . . (301) 429-7453
Business Process Improvement Director
  **Susan B. Traylor** . . . . . . . . . . . . . . . . . . . . . . . . . . . (301) 429-7582
  Business Process Improvement Deputy Director
    **Fereidoon Shahrokh** . . . . . . . . . . . . . . . . . . . . . . . (301) 429-7442
  Performance Business Office Chief **(Vacant)** . . . . . . . . . (301) 429-7438
Fair Practice Director **Gordon Outlaw** . . . . . . . . . . . . . . (410) 514-7019
Human Resources Office Director **Janice Ruth** . . . . . . . . . (410) 514-7021
  Legislative Affairs Director **J. Hunter Pickels** . . . . . . . . (410) 514-7015
    Education: Hampden-Sydney 2005 BA
Public Information Office Director **Michael White** . . . . . . . (410) 514-7704
  E-mail: michael.white@maryland.gov
Research Office Director **Asuntha Chiang-Smith** . . . . . . . . (410) 514-7004
  E-mail: chiangsmith@mdhousing.org

## Credit Assurance Division - Maryland Housing Fund
Tel: (410) 514-7325  Fax: (410) 514-7313

**Employees:** 48  **Fiscal Year:** 2015  **Budget:** $6,672,000

Director **Allen Cartwright** . . . . . . . . . . . . . . . . . . . . . . . (301) 429-7629
  Deputy Director **(Vacant)** . . . . . . . . . . . . . . . . . . . . . . (410) 514-7355
Asset Management Director **John MacLean** . . . . . . . . . . . (410) 429-7698
Codes Administration Director **Ed G. Landon** . . . . . . . . . (410) 514-7444
  Multi-Family Operations Director **(Vacant)** . . . . . . . . . . (301) 429-7698
  Single-Family Operations Director **Allen Cartwright** . . . . (301) 429-7629
Program Development Director **Jean Peterson** . . . . . . . . . (410) 514-7358
  E-mail: peterson@mdhousing.org

## Development Finance Division
Tel: (800) 756-0119  Internet: www.dhcd.state.md.us

**Employees:** 128  **Fiscal Year:** 2015  **Budget:** $288,458,000

Assistant Secretary **Tiffany P. Robinson, Esq.** . . . . . . . . . (301) 429-7796
  Special Assistant **Laura Bruner** . . . . . . . . . . . . . . . . . . (410) 514-7633
Deputy Director **Roy A. Westlund** . . . . . . . . . . . . . . . . . (410) 514-7411
Finance Director **(Vacant)** . . . . . . . . . . . . . . . . . . . . . . . (301) 429-7897
Housing Development Deputy Director **Jean Moreau** . . . . . (410) 514-7451

Multi-Family Programs Director **Elaine Cornick** . . . . . . . . (301) 429-7777
Multi-family Housing Deputy Director **Gregory Hare** . . . . . (410) 514-7487
Multi-family Housing Team Leader **(Vacant)** . . . . . . . . . . . (410) 514-7449
Single-Family Housing Director **Amy Shiman** . . . . . . . . . . (410) 514-7509
  Single-Family Housing Assistant Deputy Director
    **Maddy Ciulu** . . . . . . . . . . . . . . . . . . . . . . . . . . . . . (410) 514-7778
  Single-Family Housing Assistant Deputy Director
    **Shawn A. Kingston** . . . . . . . . . . . . . . . . . . . . . . . . (410) 514-7440
Weatherization/ Energy Construction Director
  **Joe Seehusen** . . . . . . . . . . . . . . . . . . . . . . . . . . . . . (410) 514-7071

## Finance and Administration Division
Tel: (410) 514-7100 (Administration)
Tel: (410) 514-7090 (Facilities and Fleet Management Services)
Fax: (410) 987-4676 (Administration)
Fax: (410) 514-7899 (Facilities and Fleet Management Services)

**Employees:** 44  **Fiscal Year:** 2015  **Budget:** $10,720,000

Director **Ruth Putnam** . . . . . . . . . . . . . . . . . . . . . . . . . . (301) 429-7583
  E-mail: ruth.putnam@maryland.gov
Deputy Director **Ruth Putnam** . . . . . . . . . . . . . . . . . . . . (301) 429-7582
Budget Director **Drusilla Pierce** . . . . . . . . . . . . . . . . . . . (301) 429-7564
Central Accounting Operations Director **Debbie Childers** . . (410) 514-7109
Facilities and Fleet Management Services Director
  **Deborah L. Tolson** . . . . . . . . . . . . . . . . . . . . . . . . . . (301) 429-7615
Insurance and Loan Accounting Director **Abdul Sylla** . . . . . (410) 429-7591
Systems, Analysis and Reporting Director
  **Anna Lisa Nelson** . . . . . . . . . . . . . . . . . . . . . . . . . . (301) 429-7565
Procurement Director **Jada J. Fletcher** . . . . . . . . . . . . . . . (301) 429-7570

## Information Technology Division
Tel: (410) 514-7182  Fax: (410) 987-4070

**Employees:** 16  **Fiscal Year:** 2015  **Budget:** $3,988,000

Chief Information Officer **Robert L. Dean** . . . . . . . . . . . . . (410) 429-7552
  E-mail: robert.dean@maryland.gov
Deputy Chief Information Officer **M. Sue McLean** . . . . . . . (410) 429-7553
  E-mail: sue.mclean@maryland.gov

## Neighborhood Revitalization Division
100 Community Place, Crownsville, MD 21032
Tel: (410) 209-5800 (Baltimore Office)
Tel: (410) 514-7288 (Crownsville Office)
Fax: (410) 685-8270 (Baltimore Office)
Fax: (410) 514-7925 (Crownsville Office)

**Employees:** 34  **Fiscal Year:** 2015  **Budget:** $47,791,000

Assistant Secretary/Director **Carol Anne Gilbert** . . . . . . . . (301) 429-7493
Deputy Director **Ronald D. Waters** . . . . . . . . . . . . . . . . . (301) 429-7494

## Community Programs Office
Community Development Block Grant Program Director
  **Cindy Stone** . . . . . . . . . . . . . . . . . . . . . . . . . . . . . . (301) 429-7519
  E-mail: cindy.stone@maryland.gov
Community Legacy and Sustainable Communities
  Programs Director **Kevin Baynes** . . . . . . . . . . . . . . . . (410) 209-5823
  E-mail: kevin.baynes@maryland.gov
Community Services Director **Reginald Stanfield** . . . . . . . . (301) 429-7522

## Project Development and Finance
Maryland Capital Access Program Director **Karen Ashby** . . (410) 514-7289
  E-mail: ashby@mdhousing.org

## Department of Human Resources [DHR]
311 West Saratoga Street, Baltimore, MD 21201
Tel: (800) 332-6347  TTY: (410) 767-7025  Fax: (410) 333-0099
Internet: www.dhr.state.md.us  E-mail: dhr-help@dhr.state.md.us

**Employees:** 6,529  **Fiscal Year:** 2015  **Budget:** $2,546,422,000

■Secretary **Sam Malhotra** . . . . . . . . . . . . . . . . . . . . . . . (410) 767-7109
  E-mail: sam.malhotra@maryland.gov
  Education: Maryland; Georgetown; Harvard MBA
Special Assistant to the Secretary **Samantha Blizzard** . . . . (410) 767-7365

*(continued on next page)*

---

★ Elected Official    ■ Appointed by Governor    ● Appointed by Legislature    ▲ Appointed by Board or Commission    ◆ Appointed by State Supreme Court

**Department of Human Resources** *continued*

Deputy Secretary for Operations **Gregory S. James** . . . . . . (410) 767-3950
  Education: Maryland BA; William & Mary JD
Deputy Secretary for Programs **Tracey Paliath** . . . . . . . . . . (410) 767-7109
Chief of Staff **Craig Eichler** . . . . . . . . . . . . . . . . . . . . . . . . . (410) 767-7616
Principal Counsel **David E. Beller** . . . . . . . . . . . . . . . . . . . . (410) 767-7726
Communications Director **Katherine Morris** . . . . . . . . . . . (410) 767-8944
Inspector General **William Johnson, Jr.** . . . . . . . . . . . . . . . (410) 767-7424
Chief Information Officer **Kenyatta Powers** . . . . . . . . . . . (410) 767-7893
  E-mail: kenyatta.powers@maryland.gov

## Operations Office

**Employees:** 195  **Fiscal Year:** 2015  **Budget:** $21,863,000

Administrative Operations Chief **Rainier C. Harvey** . . . . . . (410) 767-7699
  E-mail: rainier.harvey@maryland.gov
Deputy Chief **Curtis Murray** . . . . . . . . . . . . . . . . . . . . . . . . (410) 767-7699
Deputy Chief **Cynthia Smith** . . . . . . . . . . . . . . . . . . . . . . . (410) 767-7377
Personnel Director **Terry Chrapaty** . . . . . . . . . . . . . . . . . . (410) 767-8806

## Child Support Enforcement Administration

311 West Saratoga Street, Baltimore, MD 21201

**Employees:** 77  **Fiscal Year:** 2015  **Budget:** $40,754,000

Executive Director **Joseph J. DiPrimio** . . . . . . . . . . . . . . . (410) 767-7065
  E-mail: joseph.diprimio@maryland.gov
  Education: Widener JD

## Family Investment Administration

**Employees:** 245  **Fiscal Year:** 2015  **Budget:** $192,831,000

Executive Director **Rosemary Malone** . . . . . . . . . . . . . . . . (410) 767-7949

## Social Services Administration

**Employees:** 118  **Fiscal Year:** 2015  **Budget:** $22,769,000

Executive Director **(Vacant)** . . . . . . . . . . . . . . . . . . . . . . . . (410) 767-7216
Chief of Staff **(Vacant)** . . . . . . . . . . . . . . . . . . . . . . . . . . . . (410) 767-7754

## Department of Information Technology [DOIT]

45 Calvert Street, Annapolis, MD 21401-1907
300 - 301 West Preston Street, Baltimore, MD 21201
Tel: (410) 260-7778  Fax: (410) 974-5615

Secretary of Information Technology **David A. Garcia** . . . . (410) 260-4088
  E-mail: david.garcia@maryland.gov
  Education: Excelsior 1996 BS
Deputy Secretary **Luis Estrada** . . . . . . . . . . . . . . . . . . . . . . (410) 260-2994
  E-mail: luis.estrada@maryland.gov
Chief of Staff **Al Bullock** . . . . . . . . . . . . . . . . . . . . . . . . . . (410) 260-6256
Statewide Communications Interoperability Program
  Director **(Vacant)** . . . . . . . . . . . . . . . . . . . . . . . . . . . . . . (410) 260-7882
Statewide Cybersecurity Director **Chuck Ames** . . . . . . . . (410) 260-7593
Chief Operating Officer **Gregory J. "Greg" Urban** . . . . . . (410) 260-7279
  E-mail: greg@maryland.gov
Geographic Information Officer **Barney Krucoff** . . . . . . . . (410) 260-6351
  E-mail: barney.krucoff@maryland.gov
  Education: Vanderbilt 1986 BA; Georgia Tech 1991 MCP

## Department of Juvenile Services [DJS]

One Center Plaza, 120 West Fayette Street, Baltimore, MD 21201
Tel: (410) 230-3333  Fax: (410) 333-4197  TTY: (800) 735-2258
Internet: www.djs.state.md.us

**Employees:** 2,078  **Fiscal Year:** 2015  **Budget:** $286,480,000

■Secretary **Sam J. Abed** . . . . . . . . . . . . . . . . . . . . . . . . . . . (410) 230-3101
  E-mail: sam.abed@maryland.gov
Chief of Staff **Joseph "Jay" Cleary** . . . . . . . . . . . . . . . . . . (410) 230-3164
Operations Deputy Secretary **Linda McWilliams** . . . . . . . . (410) 230-3201
Support Services Deputy Secretary **Lynette Holmes** . . . . . . (410) 230-3116
Residential Services Executive Director **Wallis Norman** . . . (410) 230-3313

Principal Counsel **Karl Pothier** . . . . . . . . . . . . . . . . . . . . . . (410) 230-3135
  E-mail: karl.pothier@maryland.gov
Public Information Officer **Audra Harrison** . . . . . . . . . . . . (410) 230-3164
  Education: Penn State 1997 BA

## Department of Labor, Licensing and Regulation [DLLR]

500 North Calvert Street, Baltimore, MD 21202
Tel: (410) 230-6020  TTY: (800) 735-2258  Fax: (410) 333-0853
E-mail: mddllr@dllr.state.md.us  Internet: www.dllr.state.md.us

**Employees:** 1,628  **Fiscal Year:** 2015  **Budget:** $334,084,000

■Secretary **Kelly M. Schulz** . . . . . . . . . . . . . . . . . . . . . . . . (410) 230-6018
  E-mail: kelly.schulz@maryland.gov
  Education: Hood 2006 BA
Deputy Secretary **David McGlone** . . . . . . . . . . . . . . . . . . . (410) 230-6018
  E-mail: david.mcglone@maryland.gov
Chief of Staff **Kimberly M. Burns, Esq.** . . . . . . . . . . . . . . (410) 230-6070
  E-mail: kimberly.burns@maryland.gov
Special Assistant **(Vacant)** . . . . . . . . . . . . . . . . . . . . . . . . . (410) 230-6011
Budget and Fiscal Services Director **Barbara Kittrel** . . . . . . (410) 230-6049
  E-mail: barbara.kittrell@maryland.gov
General Services Director **Robert A. "Bob" Costa** . . . . . . (410) 767-2959
  1100 Eutaw Street, Room 612,    Fax: (410) 333-5175
  Baltimore, MD 21201
  E-mail: robert.costa@maryland.gov
Equal Opportunity Administrator
  **Jennifer Dashiell Reed** . . . . . . . . . . . . . . . . . . . . . . . . . (410) 230-6329
  1100 North Eutaw Street, Room 304,    Fax: (410) 333-3477
  Baltimore, MD 21201-2199
  E-mail: jreed@dllr.state.md.us

## Financial Regulation Division

Tel: (410) 230-6097  Fax: (410) 333-0475  E-mail: finreg@dllr.state.md.us

**Employees:** 86  **Fiscal Year:** 2015  **Budget:** $9,351,000

Commissioner **Gordon M. Cooley** . . . . . . . . . . . . . . . . . . . (410) 230-6361
  E-mail: gordon.cooley@maryland.gov
  Education: Randolph-Macon; Hood MA
Deputy Commissioner (Acting) **Teresa M. Louro** . . . . . . . . (410) 230-6022

## Labor and Industry Division

1100 North Eutaw Street, Baltimore, MD 21201-2199
Fax: (410) 767-2986  E-mail: dli@dllr.state.md.us

**Employees:** 191  **Fiscal Year:** 2015  **Budget:** $16,502,000

Commissioner **Thomas J. Meighen** . . . . . . . . . . . . . . . . . . (410) 767-2241
Deputy Commissioner **Craig D. Lowry** . . . . . . . . . . . . . . . (410) 767-2929
  E-mail: craig.lowry@maryland.gov
Occupational Safety and Health Assistant Commissioner
  **William E Dallas** . . . . . . . . . . . . . . . . . . . . . . . . . . . . . (410) 527-2065
Employment Standards and Classification Administrator
  **(Vacant)** . . . . . . . . . . . . . . . . . . . . . . . . . . . . . . . . . . . . (410) 767-2386
Safety Inspection Program Manager **Robert Gavel** . . . . . . . (410) 767-2178

## Occupational and Professional Licensing Division

Tel: (410) 230-6231  Fax: (410) 333-6314  Fax: (410) 962-8480
E-mail: op@dllr.state.md.us

**Employees:** 70  **Fiscal Year:** 2015  **Budget:** $10,244,000

Commissioner **Victoria L. Wilkins** . . . . . . . . . . . . . . . . . . . (410) 230-6225
  E-mail: victoria.wilkins@maryland.gov
Deputy Commissioner **John T. Papavasiliou** . . . . . . . . . . . (410) 230-6225

## Workforce Development and Adult Learning Division

1100 North Eutaw Street, Baltimore, MD 21201-2199
Tel: (410) 767-2999  Fax: (410) 333-5355

**Employees:** 426  **Fiscal Year:** 2015  **Budget:** $104,089,000

Assistant Secretary **James E. Rzepkowski** . . . . . . . . . . . . . (410) 767-2400
  E-mail: james.rzepkowski@maryland.gov
  Education: Maryland 1993 BA
Adult Education Director **Patricia H. Tyler** . . . . . . . . . . . . . (410) 767-1008
  E-mail: ptyler@dllr.state.md.us

---

★ Elected Official   ■ Appointed by Governor   ● Appointed by Legislature   ▲ Appointed by Board or Commission   ◆ Appointed by State Supreme Court

Performance and Workforce Information Office Director
**(Vacant)** . . . . . . . . . . . . . . . . . . . . . . . . . . . . . . . . . . . (410) 767-2250
GED (General Education Development) Administrator
**Molly Dugan** . . . . . . . . . . . . . . . . . . . . . . . . . . . . . . . . (410) 767-0069
E-mail: mdugan@dllr.state.md.us
Budget and Fiscal Manager **(Vacant)** . . . . . . . . . . . . . . . (410) 767-2822

## Unemployment Insurance Division
Assistant Secretary for Unemployment Insurance (Acting)
**Dennis C. Morton** . . . . . . . . . . . . . . . . . . . . . . . . . . . (410) 767-2488
E-mail: dennis.morton@maryland.gov

## Military Department [DMIL]
5th Regiment Armory, 29th Division Street, Baltimore, MD 21201-2288
Tel: (410) 576-6097  Fax: (410) 576-6079

**Employees:** 319  **Fiscal Year:** 2015  **Budget:** $81,522,000

■Adjutant General **MG Linda L. Singh, ARNG** . . . . . . . . . . (410) 576-6097
E-mail: linda.l.singh.mil@mail.mil
Assistant Adjutant General (Air)
**BrigGen Scott L. Kelly, ANG** . . . . . . . . . . . . . . . . . . . . (410) 234-3800
Education: Citadel 1983 BA
Assistant Adjutant General (Army)
**BG Timothy E. "Tim" Gowen, ARNG** . . . . . . . . . . . . . . (410) 576-6094
Senior Enlisted Advisor
**CSM Thomas B. Beyard, ARNG** . . . . . . . . . . . . . . . . . . (410) 576-6019
Chief of Staff **COL Adam R. Flasch, ARNG** . . . . . . . . . . (410) 576-6089
Public Affairs Director **COL Charles S. Kohler, ARNG** . . . (410) 576-6179
Legislative Liaison **Catherine Kelly** . . . . . . . . . . . . . . . . (410) 576-6163
E-mail: catherine.a.kelly26nfg@mail.mil
Director of Staff **Col Charles Blackiston, ANG** . . . . . . . (410) 234-3801
Chief Information Officer **LTC John Schott, ARNG** . . . . . (410) 702-9602
E-mail: john.a.schott2.mil@mail.mil

## Department of Natural Resources [DNR]
Tawes State Office Building, 580 Taylor Avenue, Annapolis, MD 21401
Tel: (410) 260-8021  Tel: (877) 620-8367
TTY: (800) 735-2258 (Use MD Relay)  Fax: (410) 260-8111
E-mail: customerservice@dnr.state.md.us  Internet: www.dnr.state.md.us

**Employees:** 1,295  **Fiscal Year:** 2015  **Budget:** $243,653,000

■Secretary **RADM Mark J. Belton, USN (Ret)** . . . . . . . . . . (410) 260-8101
Education: Naval Acad 1983; Regis U MBA
Deputy Secretary **Joanne M. Throwe** . . . . . . . . . . . . . . . (410) 260-8102
E-mail: joanne.throwe@maryland.gov
Communications Director **Stephen E. Schatz, Sr.** . . . . . . (410) 260-8004
E-mail: stephen.schatz@maryland.gov
Education: Catholic U 2002 BA
Principal Counsel **Jennifer Wazenski** . . . . . . . . . . . . . . . (410) 260-8350
E-mail: jwazenski@dnr.state.md.us

## Department of Planning [MDP]
301 West Preston Street, Room 1101, Baltimore, MD 21201-2365
Tel: (410) 767-4500  Fax: (410) 767-4480
Internet: www.planning.maryland.gov/

**Employees:** 145  **Fiscal Year:** 2015  **Budget:** $29,015,000

■Secretary **The Honorable David R. Craig** . . . . . . . . . . . . (410) 767-4510
E-mail: davidr.craig@maryland.gov
Education: Towson U BS; Morgan State
Deputy Secretary **Wendi W. Peters** . . . . . . . . . . . . . . . . (410) 767-4485
Education: Loyola Col (MD)
Operations Assistant Secretary **Robert S. McCord, JD** . . . . (410) 767-4544
Education: Baltimore JD; Loyola U (Maryland) MBA
Chief of Staff **Brandon P. Wright** . . . . . . . . . . . . . . . . . (410) 767-4964

## Maryland Historical Trust
100 Community Place, Crownsville, MD 21032-2023
Tel: (410) 514-7600  Fax: (410) 514-7678

Director/State Historic Preservation Officer
**Elizabeth A. Hughes** . . . . . . . . . . . . . . . . . . . . . . . . . (410) 514-7601

Planning, Education and Outreach Programs Manager
**Nell M. Ziehl** . . . . . . . . . . . . . . . . . . . . . . . . . . . . . . (410) 514-7625
E-mail: nell.ziehl@maryland.gov
Office of Preservation Services Chief **Michael K. Day** . . . . (410) 514-7629
Research and Survey Chief **Marcia M. Miller** . . . . . . . . . . (410) 514-7646
E-mail: marcia.miller@maryland.gov
Cultural Resource Information Manager **Gregory Brown** . . (410) 514-7660
E-mail: gregory.brown@maryland.gov
Jefferson Patterson Park and Museum Director
**Mark Thompson** . . . . . . . . . . . . . . . . . . . . . . . . . . . . (410) 586-8511
Maryland Archaeological Conservation Laboratory
Director **Patricia Samford** . . . . . . . . . . . . . . . . . . . . . . (410) 586-8551
Chief Archaeologist **Dennis C. Curry** . . . . . . . . . . . . . . . (410) 514-7664

## Planning Data and Analysis
Director **Stuart Sirota** . . . . . . . . . . . . . . . . . . . . . . . . . (410) 767-4460
Demographic Manager **Mark Goldstein** . . . . . . . . . . . . . (410) 767-4450
Property Mapping Section Manager **Gary Maragos** . . . . . . (410) 767-1218
E-mail: gary.maragos@maryland.gov
Redistricting, Planning and Analysis Manager **(Vacant)** . . . (410) 767-4450
State Data Center Manager **Jane Traynham** . . . . . . . . . . (410) 767-4450
E-mail: jane.traynham@maryland.gov
Smart Growth Policy Analysis Manager
**Joseph F. "Joe" Tassone** . . . . . . . . . . . . . . . . . . . . . . (410) 767-4562

## Planning Services Division
Planning Services Assistant Secretary **Stuart Sirota** . . . . . (410) 767-0901
Planning Coordination Director **Chuck Boyd** . . . . . . . . . . (410) 767-1401
Local Planning Manager **Peter G. Conrad** . . . . . . . . . . . . (410) 767-4553
Environmental Planning Director **Jason Dubow** . . . . . . . . (410) 767-3370
Infrastructure Policy Manager **Patricia "Pat" Goucher** . . . . (410) 767-4620
Lower Eastern Shore Regional Office Principal Planner
**Tracey Gordy** . . . . . . . . . . . . . . . . . . . . . . . . . . . . . . (410) 543-6904
Western Maryland Regional Office Principal Planner
**Bill Atkinson** . . . . . . . . . . . . . . . . . . . . . . . . . . . . . . (301) 777-2161
Appalachian Regional Commission Program Manager
**Bill Atkinson** . . . . . . . . . . . . . . . . . . . . . . . . . . . . . . (301) 777-2161

## Maryland State Clearinghouse for Intergovernmental Assistance
Assistant Secretary **Linda C. Janey** . . . . . . . . . . . . . . . . (410) 767-4488
Education: Morgan State 1973 BA, 1980 MA; Baltimore 1996 JD
Clearinghouse and Plan Review Section Manager
**Myra Barnes** . . . . . . . . . . . . . . . . . . . . . . . . . . . . . . (410) 767-4488

## Communication and Education Division
Communications and Education Director **(Vacant)** . . . . . . . (410) 767-4544
Public Information Officer **John G. Coleman, Jr.** . . . . . . . . (410) 767-4614
E-mail: johng.coleman@maryland.gov

## Department of Public Safety and Correctional Services [DPSCS]
300 East Joppa Road, Suite 1000, Towson, MD 21286-3020
Tel: (410) 339-5000  Tel: (877) 379-8636  TTY: (800) 735-2258
Fax: (410) 339-4240  Internet: www.dpscs.state.md.us

**Employees:** 11,046  **Fiscal Year:** 2015  **Budget:** $1,324,806,000

■Secretary **Lt. Col. Stephen T. Moyer** . . . . . . . . . . . . . . . (410) 339-5005
E-mail: smoyer@dpscs.state.md.us
Education: Towson U BA; Johns Hopkins MA
Executive Assistant **Anthony A. Gaskins** . . . . . . . . . . . . . (410) 339-5032
Deputy Secretary for Administration
**William G. Stewart** . . . . . . . . . . . . . . . . . . . . . . . . . . (410) 339-5050
E-mail: wgstewart@dpscs.state.md.us
Education: Princeton 1971 BA; Virginia 1973 MBA
Deputy Secretary for Operations **J. Michael Zeigler** . . . . . (410) 339-5050
E-mail: mzeigler@dpscs.state.md.us
Capital Programs Assistant Secretary
**David N. Bezanson** . . . . . . . . . . . . . . . . . . . . . . . . . . (410) 339-5068
E-mail: dbezanson@dpscs.state.md.us
Programs and Services Assistant Secretary **Rhea Harris** . . . (410) 339-5091
E-mail: rharris@dpscs.state.md.us

*(continued on next page)*

---

★ Elected Official  ■ Appointed by Governor  ● Appointed by Legislature  ▲ Appointed by Board or Commission  ◆ Appointed by State Supreme Court

EXECUTIVE BRANCH

**Department of Public Safety and Correctional Services** *continued*

Principal Counsel **Stuart M. Nathan** . . . . . . . . . . . . . . . . (410) 585-3070
  6776 Reisterstown Road, Suite 313,          Fax: (410) 764-5366
  Baltimore, MD 21215-2342
  E-mail: snathan@dpscs.state.md.us
Communications Director **Robert B. Thomas, Jr.** . . . . . . . . (410) 339-5009
  E-mail: rbthomas@dpscs.state.md.us
Professional Development and Training Division
  Executive Director **J. Michael Zeigler** . . . . . . . . . . . . . (410) 585-3820
  115 Sudbrook Lane, Suite 205 B, Pikesville, MD 21208-3878

## Capital Construction and Facilities Maintenance Division

6776 Reisterstown Road, Suite 201, Baltimore, MD 21215
Tel: (410) 585-3027  Fax: (410) 764-4434

Director **Katherine Z. Dixon** . . . . . . . . . . . . . . . . . . . . . (410) 585-3027
  E-mail: kzdixon@dpscs.state.md.us

## Correction Division

Commissioner **Wayne Webb** . . . . . . . . . . . . . . . . . . . . . . (410) 585-3301

## Equal Employment Opportunity Division

6776 Reisterstown Road, Suite 216, Baltimore, MD 21215
Tel: (410) 585-3005  Fax: (410) 318-8905

Director **Karen K. Shipley** . . . . . . . . . . . . . . . . . . . . . . . (410) 585-3005

## Human Resources Services Division

6776 Reisterstown Road, Suite 309, Baltimore, MD 21215
Tel: (410) 585-3408  Fax: (410) 764-4348
E-mail: hrsd@dpscs.state.md.us

Executive Director **Michael H. Stelmack** . . . . . . . . . . . . . (410) 585-3408

## Information Technology and Communications Division

6776 Reisterstown Road, Suite 209, Baltimore, MD 21215-2342
Tel: (410) 585-3106  Fax: (410) 746-4035

Chief Information Officer **Kevin Combs** . . . . . . . . . . . . . . (410) 585-3102
  E-mail: kcombs@dpscs.state.md.us
Deputy Chief Information Officer **Arthur C. Ray III** . . . . . . (410) 585-3100
  E-mail: aray3@dpscs.state.md.us
Chief Network Officer **(Vacant)** . . . . . . . . . . . . . . . . . . . (410) 585-2929

## Inmate Grievance Office

115 Sudbrook Lane, Suite 200, Pikesville, MD 21208-3878
Tel: (410) 585-3840  Fax: (410) 318-6015

**Employees: 7  Fiscal Year: 2015  Budget: $960,000**

Executive Director **Russell A. Neverdon, Sr.** . . . . . . . . . . (410) 339-5000

## Inmate Health Services

6776 Reisterstown Road, Suite 315, Baltimore, MD 21215
Fax: (410) 764-5112

Chief Executive Officer **(Vacant)** . . . . . . . . . . . . . . . . . . (443) 278-6076

## Internal Investigative Unit

P.O. Box 418, Savage, MD 20763
Tel: (410) 724-5720  Fax: (410) 724-2094

Director **Mark Carter** . . . . . . . . . . . . . . . . . . . . . . . . . . (410) 724-5720

## Legislative Affairs

300 East Joppa Road, Suite 1000, Towson, MD 21286
Tel: (410) 260-6070  Fax: (410) 339-4240

Director **Kevin Loeb** . . . . . . . . . . . . . . . . . . . . . . . . . . . (410) 260-6070
  E-mail: kloeb@dpscs.state.md.us
  Education: Lehigh 2006 BA

## Parole and Probation Division

6776 Reisterstown Road, Suite 305, Baltimore, MD 21215-2344
Tel: (410) 585-3500  Fax: (410) 764-4091

Director (Acting) **Joseph F. Clocker** . . . . . . . . . . . . . . . . (410) 585-3566

Central Operations Regional Executive Director
  **Walter Nolley** . . . . . . . . . . . . . . . . . . . . . . . . . . . . . (410) 209-4295
North Operations Regional Executive Director
  **Dale Maselli** . . . . . . . . . . . . . . . . . . . . . . . . . . . . . . (301) 600-3060
South Operations Regional Executive Director
  **David Dawkins** . . . . . . . . . . . . . . . . . . . . . . . . . . . . (301) 780-6847

## Office of the Inspector General

6776 Reisterstown Road, Suite 316, Baltimore, MD 21215
Tel: (410) 585-3240  Fax: (410) 764-4018

Inspector General **Joseph M. Perry** . . . . . . . . . . . . . . . . (410) 585-3240

## Office of Grants, Policy and Statistics

300 East Joppa Road, Suite 400B, Towson, MD 21286
Tel: (410) 339-5020  Fax: (410) 339-4227

Executive Director **Christina N. Lentz** . . . . . . . . . . . . . . . (410) 339-5020

## Office of Operation Division

6776 Reisterstown Road, Suite 310, Baltimore, MD 21215-2342
Tel: (410) 585-3300  Fax: (410) 764-4373

Director **Carlos Bivens** . . . . . . . . . . . . . . . . . . . . . . . . . (410) 585-3301
  E-mail: cbivens@dpscs.state.md.us

## Property Management Services Office

115 Sudbrook Lane, Suite 205, Pikesville, MD 21208
Fax: (410) 764-5283

Director **(Vacant)** . . . . . . . . . . . . . . . . . . . . . . . . . . . . . (410) 585-3850

## Procurement Services

300 East Joppa Road, Suite 1000, Towson, MD 21286
Tel: (410) 339-5018  Fax: (410) 339-4240
E-mail: procurement@dpscs.state.md.us

Director (Acting) **Rosetta R. Butler** . . . . . . . . . . . . . . . . (410) 339-5018

## Substance Abuse Treatment Services

6776 Reisterstown Road, Suite 210, Baltimore, MD 21215
Tel: (443) 768-3749  Fax: (410) 764-5150

Director **Sandi Davis-Hart** . . . . . . . . . . . . . . . . . . . . . . . (410) 585-3728
  E-mail: sjdavis-hart@dpscs.state.md.us

# Department of Transportation [MDOT]

7201 Corporate Center Drive, Hanover, MD 21076
Tel: (410) 865-1000  Fax: (410) 865-1338  TTY: (410) 865-1342
Tel: (888) 713-1414  Internet: www.mdot.state.md.us

**Employees: 8,819  Fiscal Year: 2015  Budget: $4,320,468,000**

■Secretary **Peter K. "Pete" Rahn** . . . . . . . . . . . . . . . . . . (410) 865-1001
  E-mail: secretary@mdot.state.md.us
  Executive Assistant to the Secretary **Vicki Savaliski** . . . . . (410) 865-1003
■Deputy Secretary **James F. "Jim" Ports, Jr.** . . . . . . . . . . (410) 865-1000
  Education: Comm Col Baltimore County 1990 AA
■Policy, Planning, and Enterprise Services Deputy
  Secretary **R. Earl Lewis, Jr.** . . . . . . . . . . . . . . . . . . . . (410) 865-1006
  E-mail: rlewis1@mdot.state.md.us
Operations Assistant Secretary **Kevin C. Reigrut** . . . . . . . . (410) 865-1125
  Education: Syracuse 1992 BS
Chief of Staff **Edward F. McDonald** . . . . . . . . . . . . . . . . (410) 865-1000
Senior Policy Analyst **Corey Stottlemyer** . . . . . . . . . . . . . (410) 865-1282
  E-mail: cstottlemyer@mdot.state.md.us
Audits Director **Brenda Cachuela** . . . . . . . . . . . . . . . . . (410) 865-1166
Equity and Diversity Director **Louis Jones** . . . . . . . . . . . . (410) 865-1156
Procurement Director **Michael C. Zimmerman** . . . . . . . . . (410) 865-1121
Strategic Customer Service Director **Diane Langhorne** . . . . (410) 865-1009
Human Resources Office Director **Judith Slater** . . . . . . . . (410) 865-1185
Legal Counsel Office Director
  **Cheryl A. Brown-Whitfield** . . . . . . . . . . . . . . . . . . . . (410) 865-1105
Minority Business Enterprise Office Director
  **Sabrina Bass** . . . . . . . . . . . . . . . . . . . . . . . . . . . . . . (410) 865-1240
Planning and Capital Programming Office Director
  **Heather R. Murphy** . . . . . . . . . . . . . . . . . . . . . . . . . (410) 865-1275
  E-mail: hmurphy@mdot.state.md.us

★ Elected Official   ■ Appointed by Governor   ● Appointed by Legislature   ▲ Appointed by Board or Commission   ◆ Appointed by State Supreme Court

Public Affairs Office Director **Erin C. Henson** . . . . . . . . . . (410) 865-1025
  E-mail: ehenson@mdot.state.md.us
Governmental Affairs Office Director
  **John G. Trueschler** . . . . . . . . . . . . . . . . . . . . . . . . . (410) 865-1090
  Education: West Virginia 1979 BS; Maryland 1991 JD
Transportation Technology Services Director
  **Ronald "Ron" Brothers** . . . . . . . . . . . . . . . . . . . . . . (410) 865-1040
Real Estate and Economic Development Office Director
  **Del T. Adams** . . . . . . . . . . . . . . . . . . . . . . . . . . . . . . (410) 865-1204
Fleet, Facilities and Administrative Services Manager
  **David Maier** . . . . . . . . . . . . . . . . . . . . . . . . . . . . . . . (410) 865-1139
  E-mail: dmaier@mdot.state.md.us

## Finance Office

Tel: (410) 865-1036  Fax: (410) 865-1032

Chief Financial Officer **David L. Fleming** . . . . . . . . . . . . . (410) 865-1036
Deputy Director **Steven P. Watson** . . . . . . . . . . . . . . . . . (410) 865-1037
Budget Assistant Director **Elizabeth Helmer** . . . . . . . . . . . (410) 865-1044
Accounting Manager **Brandie Karfonta** . . . . . . . . . . . . . . (410) 865-1045
Debt Manager **June Hornick** . . . . . . . . . . . . . . . . . . . . . (410) 865-1039
Financial Management Information Systems Manager
  **Karen Bohle** . . . . . . . . . . . . . . . . . . . . . . . . . . . . . . . (410) 865-1319
  E-mail: kbohle@mdot.state.md.us
Financial Planning Manager **Linda Williams** . . . . . . . . . . . (410) 865-1043

## Maryland Aviation Administration

Terminal Building, P.O. Box 8766, Third Floor, BWI Airport, MD 21240
Tel: (410) 859-7111  Fax: (410) 850-4729
Internet: www.marylandaviation.com

**Employees:** 497  **Fiscal Year:** 2016  **Budget:** $315,100,000

Executive Director/Chief Executive Officer
  **Ricky D. Smith, Sr.** . . . . . . . . . . . . . . . . . . . . . . . . . . (410) 859-7060
Chief of Staff **LTC Hazel L. Robinson, USA (Ret)** . . . . . . . (410) 859-7053
  Education: Howard U 1979 BA, 1986 MA
Counsel **Louisa H. Goldstein** . . . . . . . . . . . . . . . . . . . . (410) 859-7066
  E-mail: lgoldstein@bwiairport.com
Office of Parking and Transportation Director
  **Ralign T. Wells** . . . . . . . . . . . . . . . . . . . . . . . . . . . . . (410) 859-7125

## Maryland Port Administration

World Trade Center - Baltimore, 401 East Pratt Street,
Baltimore, MD 21202-3041
Tel: (410) 385-4400  Fax: (410) 333-3402
Internet: www.marylandports.com

**Employees:** 225  **Fiscal Year:** 2015  **Budget:** $201,689,000

■Executive Director **James J. White** . . . . . . . . . . . . . . . . (410) 385-4401
  E-mail: jjwhite@marylandports.com
  Chief of Staff **Christina Nichols** . . . . . . . . . . . . . . . . (410) 385-4400
                                                        Fax: (410) 385-4417
Deputy Executive Director **M. Kathleen Broadwater** . . . . . (410) 385-4405
Principal Counsel **Robert L. "Bob" Munroe** . . . . . . . . . . . (410) 385-4427
  E-mail: bmunroe@marylandports.com   Fax: (410) 333-4533
Communications Director **Richard M. Scher** . . . . . . . . . . . (410) 385-4483
  E-mail: rscher@marylandports.com    Fax: (410) 385-4485
Engineering Director **Mark Kreafle** . . . . . . . . . . . . . . . . (410) 385-4806
                                                        Fax: (410) 347-0783
Intermodal Trade Development Director **(Vacant)** . . . . . . . (410) 385-4464
                                                        Fax: (410) 333-1126
Finance Director and Chief Financial Officer
  **Wonza Spann-Nicholas** . . . . . . . . . . . . . . . . . . . . . . (410) 385-4560
                                                        Fax: (410) 347-0779
Maritime Commercial Management Director
  **Michael Miller** . . . . . . . . . . . . . . . . . . . . . . . . . . . . (410) 385-4747
Marketing Director **Richard Powers** . . . . . . . . . . . . . . . (410) 385-4731
                                                        Fax: (410) 333-3402
Operations Director **David Thomas** . . . . . . . . . . . . . . . . (410) 633-1043
                                                        Fax: (410) 633-3273
Security Director **David Espie** . . . . . . . . . . . . . . . . . . . (410) 633-1153
                                                        Fax: (410) 285-0891
Government Affairs, Business Relations and Safety,
  Environment and Risk Management Deputy Director
  **Bradley A. "Brad" Peganoff** . . . . . . . . . . . . . . . . . . . (410) 385-4761

Harbor Development Deputy Director **Chris Correale** . . . . . (410) 385-4465
                                                        Fax: (410) 347-0784
Planning Deputy Director **James Dwyer** . . . . . . . . . . . . . (410) 385-4469
                                                        Fax: (410) 385-4790

## Maryland Transit Administration [MTA]

William Donald Schaefer Tower, 6 Saint Paul Street,
Baltimore, MD 21202-1614
Tel: (410) 767-3943  Tel: (888) 218-2267  Fax: (410) 333-3279

**Employees:** 3,088  **Fiscal Year:** 2015  **Budget:** $1,201,294,000

Administrator and Chief Executive Officer
  **Paul W. Comfort** . . . . . . . . . . . . . . . . . . . . . . . . . . . (410) 767-3943
  E-mail: pcomfort@mta.maryland.gov
  Education: Maryland Baltimore County BA; Maryland Baltimore JD
Chief of Staff **James L. Knighton** . . . . . . . . . . . . . . . . . (410) 767-8769
Administrative Training Director **(Vacant)** . . . . . . . . . . . . (410) 767-3868
Bus Operations Director **Thomas Drozt** . . . . . . . . . . . . . (410) 454-7171
Communications and Marketing Senior Director
  **Ryan M. Nawrocki** . . . . . . . . . . . . . . . . . . . . . . . . . (410) 767-3932
  E-mail: rnawrocki@mta.maryland.gov
  Education: St Mary's Col (MD)
Chief Safety Director **Bernadette Fowlkes-Bridges** . . . . . . (410) 454-7145
Chief Information Officer/Information Technology
  Director (Acting) **Reid Kreider** . . . . . . . . . . . . . . . . . (410) 767-3890
  E-mail: rkreider@mta.maryland.gov
Customer Information Director **Chrys Wilson** . . . . . . . . . . (410) 767-8348
  Education: Cheyney 1973 BS, 1978 MS
Fair Practice Director **Bart Plano** . . . . . . . . . . . . . . . . . (410) 767-3934
Governmental Affairs Director
  **Col. Douglas "Doug" DeLeaver** . . . . . . . . . . . . . . . . (410) 767-0820
Human Resources Director **Robin Burgos** . . . . . . . . . . . . (410) 767-8365
Internal Audits Director **Channel Sumpter** . . . . . . . . . . . (410) 767-3747
Labor and Employee Relations Office Director
  **Brian K. Williams** . . . . . . . . . . . . . . . . . . . . . . . . . . (410) 767-3854
Light Rail Director **(Vacant)** . . . . . . . . . . . . . . . . . . . . . (410) 454-7662
Maryland Rail Commuter (MARC) Train and Commuter
  Bus Services Director **Erich Kolig** . . . . . . . . . . . . . . . (410) 454-7265
Metro Operations Deputy Director **Keith B. Jenkins** . . . . . (410) 454-7406
Mobility Operations Director **Carl Parr** . . . . . . . . . . . . . (410) 764-7434
Chief Performance Officer **Philip D. Sullivan** . . . . . . . . . . (410) 767-8760
Procurement Director **(Vacant)** . . . . . . . . . . . . . . . . . . . (410) 767-3763
Service Development Director
  **Thomas "Tom" Hewitt, Jr.** . . . . . . . . . . . . . . . . . . . . (410) 454-7257
Transit Development and Delivery Executive Director
  **Charles Lattuca** . . . . . . . . . . . . . . . . . . . . . . . . . . . (443) 451-3720
  E-mail: clattuca@mta.maryland.gov
Bus Transportation Deputy Director **(Vacant)** . . . . . . . . . (410) 454-7104
Deputy Administrator and Chief Administrative Officer
  **(Vacant)** . . . . . . . . . . . . . . . . . . . . . . . . . . . . . . . . . (410) 767-0029
Deputy Administrator and Chief Planning Engineering
  Officer **Suhair Alkhatib** . . . . . . . . . . . . . . . . . . . . . . (410) 767-3787
  E-mail: salkhatib@mta.maryland.gov
Deputy Executive Director Transit Development and
  Delivery **(Vacant)** . . . . . . . . . . . . . . . . . . . . . . . . . . (443) 451-3720
Media Relations Director **Sandy Arnette** . . . . . . . . . . . . . (410) 767-8367
Finance and Performance Management Director
  **Nancy Noonan** . . . . . . . . . . . . . . . . . . . . . . . . . . . . (410) 767-3796
Deputy Chief/Chief Engineer **(Vacant)** . . . . . . . . . . . . . . (410) 767-3806
Deputy Chief Statewide Network Officer **Pat Keller** . . . . . (410) 767-3889
  E-mail: pkeller@mta.maryland.gov
Deputy Chief Operating Officer of Core Operations
  **John Duncan** . . . . . . . . . . . . . . . . . . . . . . . . . . . . . . (410) 454-7724
MTA (Maryland Transit Administration) Chief of Police
  **John Gavrilis** . . . . . . . . . . . . . . . . . . . . . . . . . . . . . (410) 454-7529
Senior Deputy Administrator/ Chief Operating Officer
  **(Vacant)** . . . . . . . . . . . . . . . . . . . . . . . . . . . . . . . . . (410) 454-7033
Chief Counsel **T. Byron Smith, JD** . . . . . . . . . . . . . . . . . (410) 767-5833
  E-mail: bsmith10@mta.maryland.gov
  Education: North Carolina Central 1982 JD
Operations Compliance and Investigations Director
  **Thomas A. Burgess** . . . . . . . . . . . . . . . . . . . . . . . . . (410) 454-7122

---

★ Elected Official   ■ Appointed by Governor   ● Appointed by Legislature   ▲ Appointed by Board or Commission   ◆ Appointed by State Supreme Court

**EXECUTIVE BRANCH**

## Motor Vehicle Administration

6601 Ritchie Highway, NE, Glen Burnie, MD 21062
Tel: (410) 768-7000  Fax: (410) 424-3050  TTY: (800) 492-4575
Internet: www.marylandmva.com

**Employees:** 1,631  **Fiscal Year:** 2015  **Budget:** $215,507,000

Administrator **Christine E. Nizer** .................. (410) 768-7000
  Administrative Assistant **Gail G. Bartlebaugh** ......... (410) 787-7851
    E-mail: gbartlebaugh@marylandmva.com
Chief Deputy Administrator **Christine E. Nizer** .......... (410) 768-7830
    E-mail: cnizer@marylandmva.com
  Administrative Assistant **Regina A. Howard** .......... (410) 768-7282
    E-mail: rhoward@marylandmva.com
Chief Counsel **Damon Bell** ....................... (410) 768-7416
    E-mail: dbell1@mdot.state.md.us
Deputy Chief Counsel **Leight D. Collins** .............. (410) 768-7415
Assistant Attorney General **Donald Hoffman** .......... (410) 768-7414
    E-mail: donald.hoffman@mva.maryland.gov
Assistant Attorney General **Neil I. Jacobs** .......... (410) 768-7414
    E-mail: njacobs@mva.maryland.gov
Assistant Attorney General **Dore J. Lebowitz** .......... (410) 768-7414
    E-mail: dlebowitz@marylandmva.com
Central Operations and Safety Programs Deputy
  Administrator **Kim Nelson** ...................... (410) 787-7830
    E-mail: kim.nelson@mva.maryland.gov
Operations Deputy Administrator **(Vacant)** .............. (410) 424-3706

## State Highway Administration

707 North Calvert Street, Baltimore, MD 21202
Tel: (410) 545-0300  Tel: (800) 323-6742  Fax: (410) 209-5012
Internet: www.marylandroads.com

**Employees:** 3,071  **Fiscal Year:** 2015  **Budget:** $1,640,105,000

Administrator **Gregory C. "Greg" Johnson, PE** ........ (410) 545-0400
    E-mail: greg.johnson@michigan.gov
Deputy Administrator **Cheryl R.B. Hill** .............. (410) 545-0402
    E-mail: chill@sha.state.md.us
Deputy Administrator/Operations Chief Engineer
  **David J. "Dave" Coyne** ...................... (410) 545-0360
    E-mail: dcoyne@sha.state.md.us
Deputy Administrator/Planning and Engineering Chief
  Engineer **(Vacant)** .......................... (410) 545-0411
Chief Counsel **Edward S. Harris** .................. (410) 545-0050
    E-mail: EHarris@sha.state.md.us
Administration Director **Deborah E. Hammell** .......... (410) 545-0020
    E-mail: dhammel@sha.state.md.us
Chart Office Director **Mike J. Zezeski** .............. (410) 582-5605
  7491 Connelly Drive, Hanover, MD 21076
    E-mail: MZezeski@sha.state.md.us
Construction Director **Steve Marciszewski** ............ (443) 572-5235
    E-mail: smarciszewski@sha.state.md.us
Customer Relations and Information Director
  **Valerie Burnette Edgar** ...................... (410) 545-0301
Environmental Design Director **Sonal Sanghavi** ........ (410) 545-8640
Equal Opportunity Director **Wanda Dade** .............. (410) 545-0315
Finance Director **Lisa B. "Betty" Conners** ............ (410) 545-0030
Highway Development Director **Jason Ridgway** .......... (410) 545-8800
    E-mail: jridgeway@sha.state.md.us
Information Technology Director **James "Jim" Yarsky** ... (410) 545-8680
    E-mail: jyarsky@sha.state.md.us
Intercounty Connector Director **Mark Coblentz** ........ (301) 586-9267
Maintenance Director **Russell A. "Russ" Yurek** ........ (410) 582-5505
  7491 Connelley Drive, Hanover, MD 21076
    E-mail: RYurek@sha.state.md.us
Office of Structure Director **Earle S. Freedman** ........ (410) 545-8060
    E-mail: efreedman@sha.state.md.us
Planning and Preliminary Engineering Director
  **Gregory I. "Greg" Slater** .................... (410) 545-0412
    E-mail: gslater@sha.state.md.us
Policy and Research Director **Richard Y. Woo** .......... (410) 545-0340
    E-mail: rwoo@sha.state.md.us
Procurement and Contract Management Director
  **(Vacant)** .................................. (410) 545-0433
Real Estate Director **Gina Anthony** .................. (410) 545-2828
Technology and Materials Director **(Vacant)** ............ (443) 572-5037

Traffic and Safety Director **Cedric Ward** .............. (410) 787-5815
  7491 Connelly Drive, Hanover, MD 21076

## Maryland Transportation Authority

2310 Broening Highway, Suite 150, Baltimore, MD 21224
Tel: (410) 537-1000  Tel: (866) 713-1596
Tel: (888) 321-6824 (E-Z Pass Customer Service Center)
TTY: (877) 440-2950  Fax: (410) 537-1003
E-mail: mdta@mdtransportationauthority.com

■Executive Director **Milton Chaffee** ........... (410) 537-1001 ext. 71001
    E-mail: mchaffee1@marylandmva.com
    Education: Miami U (OH) 1975 BS
Deputy Executive Director **Deborah E. Sharpless** ....... (410) 537-1004
Chief Administrative Officer **Percy E. Dangerfield** ....... (410) 537-1031
    E-mail: pdangerfield@mdta.maryland.gov
    Education: Frostburg State U 1992 BS, 1996 MBA
Chief Financial Officer **Jaclyn D. Hartman** .... (410) 537-5748 ext. 75748
Principal Counsel **Kimberly A. Millender** ...... (410) 537-1007 ext. 71007
Banking and Investments Senior Director
  **Alison B. Williams** ................. (410) 537-5720 ext. 75720
Planning and Program Development Director
  **Dennis Simpson** ................. (410) 537-5650 ext. 75650
    E-mail: dsimpson@mdot.state.md.us
Construction Director **David "Dave" Ferrara** ... (410) 537-7882 ext. 77882
    E-mail: dferrara@mdta.state.md.us
Engineering Director **Dan Williams** .......... (410) 537-7824 ext. 77824
    E-mail: dwilliams1@mdta.maryland.gov
Information Technology Director
  **David Goldsborough** .............. (410) 537-1067 ext. 71067
    E-mail: dgoldsborough@mdta.maryland.gov
Operations Chief (Acting) **John J. O'Neill III** ........... (410) 537-1098
Easy Pass Deputy Director
  **Thomas H. Gugel** .................. (410) 537-1309 ext. 71309
Operations Deputy Director
  **John J. O'Neill III** ................. (410) 537-1098 ext. 71309
Operations Deputy Director **Michael E. Rice** .. (410) 537-5687 ext. 75687
Audit Office Director **Jody McCurley** ........ (410) 537-1093 ext. 71093
Communications Office Director
  **Cheryl M. Sparks** ................ (410) 537-1035 ext. 71035
    E-mail: csparks@mdta.state.md.us
MD Transportation Authority Police Chief
  **Michael Kundrat** ............................ (410) 537-7756
  Police Headquarters, 4330 Broening Highway, Baltimore, MD 21222
Facility Administrator **Gordon Garrettson** ..... (410) 537-8157 ext. 58157
  W. P. Lane Memorial Bridge, 850 Revell Highway,
  Annapolis, MD 21401
    E-mail: ggarrettson@mdot.state.md.us
Facility Administrator **Benjamin Gilmore** ...... (410) 537-7513 ext. 77513
    E-mail: bgilmore@mdta.state.md.us
Facility Administrator **Gary Jackson** .......... (301) 259-4871 ext. 76807
  Harry W. Nice Bridge, US Route 301 South, Newburg, MD 20664
  P.O. Box 8, Newburg, MD 20664-0008
    E-mail: gjackson@mdta.state.md.us
Facility Administrator **Richard Wolf** .......... (410) 537-7513 ext. 77513
    E-mail: rwolf@mdta.state.md.us
Facility Administrator and Intercounty
  Connector **Donald L. "Don" Smith** ...... (410) 537-6934 ext. 58157
  W. P. Lane Memorial Bridge, 850 Revell Highway,
  Annapolis, MD 21401
    E-mail: dsmith@mdot.state.md.us
Northern Region Administrator
  **John Lohmeyer** .................. (410) 537-1107 ext. 71107
    E-mail: jlohmeyer1@mdta.maryland.gov
Chief Engineer **(Vacant)** ...................... (410) 537-7825
Human Resources Director **(Vacant)** .............. (410) 767-8365

## Department of Veterans Affairs [MDVA]

The Wineland Building, 16 Francis Street, Annapolis, MD 21401
Tel: (410) 260-3838  Tel: (866) 793-1577  Fax: (410) 216-7928
E-mail: mdveteransinfo@maryland.gov  Internet: www.mdva.state.md.us

**Employees:** 76  **Fiscal Year:** 2015  **Budget:** $31,502,000

■Secretary **George W. Owings III** ................ (410) 260-3838
  Executive Assistant **Katharine S. "Katie" Sonntag** ..... (410) 260-3838

---

★ Elected Official  ■ Appointed by Governor  ● Appointed by Legislature  ▲ Appointed by Board or Commission  ◆ Appointed by State Supreme Court

Finance and Administration Director **Peter Pantzer**.......(410) 260-3867
Grant Administrator/Maryland Veterans Trust
**Mark Hendricks**....................................(410) 974-2399

## Outreach and Advocacy Program
Director **Dana Hendrickson**.........................(410) 260-3842
Education: Delaware

## Veterans Service and Benefits Program
Director **Phil Munley**................................(410) 230-4444

## Veterans Cemetery and Memorial Programs
Director **Chris Piscitelli**..........................(410) 923-6981
Fax: (410) 987-3920

## Health and Higher Educational Facilities Authority [MHHA]
401 East Pratt Street, Suite 1224, Baltimore, MD 21202
Tel: (410) 837-6220  Fax: (410) 685-1611
E-mail: webmaster@mhhefa.org  Internet: www.mhhefa.org
■Executive Director **Annette Anselmi**...........(410) 837-6220 ext. 101
E-mail: aanselmi@mhhefa.org
Assistant Executive Director **Ryan Ward**...............(410) 837-6220

## Maryland Lottery and Gaming Control Agency
Montgomery Park Business Center, 1800 Washington Boulevard,
Suite 330, Baltimore, MD 21230
Tel: (410) 230-8800  Fax: (410) 230-8728  TTY: (800) 735-2258
Internet: www.mdlottery.com
**Employees:** 317  **Fiscal Year:** 2015  **Budget:** $141,772,000
■Director **Gordon Medenica**.........................(410) 230-8790
E-mail: gordon.medenica@maryland.gov
Education: Harvard 1973 AB, 1979 MBA
Deputy Director and Chief Financial Officer **Gina Smith** . . (410) 230-8763
Regulatory Oversight Managing Director **John Mooney** . . . (410) 230-8948
Gaming Managing Director **Charles LaBoy** .............(410) 230-5588
Communications Director **Carole Everett** ..............(410) 230-8725
E-mail: carole.everett@maryland.gov
Managing Director and Chief Revenue Officer
**John A. Martin** ....................................(410) 230-8754
Policy and Planning Managing Director **Jaclyn Vincent** . . . (410) 230-8988
Chief Information Officer **Jeff Patchen** .............(410) 230-8947
E-mail: jeff.patchen@maryland.gov
Principal Counsel **Robert Fontaine**..................(410) 230-8780
Education: Maryland Law 1984 JD
Assistant Deputy Director, Chief Operating Officer
**Jim Nielsen** .....................................(410) 230-8823

## Lottery Gaming and Control Commission
Fax: (410) 230-8727
■Chairman **Kimberly Robertson Pannell, CPA**..........(410) 230-8790
■Vice Chairman **Diane Lee McGraw** ...................(410) 230-8790
■Member **F. Vernon Boozer, Esq.**....................(410) 230-8790
■Member **George L. Doestsch, Jr.**...................(410) 230-8790
■Member **Bert J. Hash, Jr.** ........................(410) 230-8790
■Member **John Morton III**...........................(410) 230-8790
Education: Harvard 1973 MBA
■Member **James J. Stakem** ..........................(410) 230-8790

## Maryland Energy Administration
60 West Street, Suite 300, Annapolis, MD 21401
Tel: (410) 260-7655  Tel: (800) 723-6374  Fax: (410) 974-2250
Internet: http://energy.maryland.gov/  E-mail: dlinfomea@maryland.gov
**Employees:** 30  **Fiscal Year:** 2015  **Budget:** $49,413,000
■Director **Mary Beth Tung, Esq.** ...................(410) 260-7655
E-mail: mary.tung@maryland.gov
Education: Maryland Law JD; Wright State PhD
Clean Energy Program Director **Chris Rice**............(410) 260-7544

Energy Efficiency Director **(Vacant)** .................(410) 260-7204
Finance and Administration Director **Ralph Scherini**....(410) 260-7184
Legislation and Communication Director **John Fiastro** ....(410) 260-7257
E-mail: john.fiastro@maryland.gov
Policy, Planning, Analysis Director **Ralph Scherini** .......(410) 260-7655
Chief of Staff **(Vacant)** .............................(410) 537-4000
Principal Counsel
**RADM Steven M. Talson, USNR (Ret)** .............(410) 260-7538
Assistant Attorney General **Sondra McLemore** .........(410) 260-7538
Assistant Attorney General **Christine Neiderer** .........(410) 260-7655
Assistant Attorney General
**RADM Steven M. Talson, USNR (Ret)** .............(410) 260-7538

## Maryland Insurance Administration [MIA]
200 Saint Paul Place, Suite 2700, Baltimore, MD 21202-2272
Tel: (410) 468-2000  Tel: (800) 492-6116  TTY: (800) 735-2258
Fax: (410) 468-2020  E-mail: insurance.mia@maryland.gov
Internet: www.insurance.maryland.gov
**Employees:** 266  **Fiscal Year:** 2015  **Budget:** $31,961,000
■Insurance Commissioner **Alfred W. Redmer, Jr.**........(410) 468-2090
Term Expires: May 31, 2019
E-mail: al.redmer@maryland.gov
Deputy Commissioner **Nancy S. Grodin** .............(410) 468-2009
Education: Goucher BA
Compliance and Enforcement Associate Commissioner
**Victoria R. August, Esq.** ........................(410) 468-2236
Education: Delaware BA; Baltimore JD
Consumer Education and Advocacy Associate
Commissioner **Joy Hatchette**......................(410) 468-2029
Examination and Audit Associate Commissioner
**Vincent P. O'Grady** .............................(410) 468-2122
Hearings Associate Commissioner
**Robert D. "Bob" Morrow, Jr.** ....................(410) 468-2018
Education: Washington Col BA; Widener JD
Insurance Fraud Division Associate Commissioner
**(Vacant)** .......................................(410) 468-3904
Life and Health Associate Commissioner **Brenda Wilson** . . (410) 468-2212
Property and Casualty Associate Commissioner
**Lynn Dickerson**.................................(410) 468-2321
Fax: (410) 468-2306
Chief Information Officer **Paula Keen** .................(410) 468-2059
E-mail: paula.keen@maryland.gov
Government Relations Director **Nancy Egan** ............(410) 468-2488
E-mail: nancy.egan@maryland.gov
Public Affairs Director **Tracy Imm** ...................(410) 468-2206
E-mail: tracy.imm@maryland.gov
Assistant Attorney General and Principal Counsel
**J. Van Lear Dorsey**.............................(410) 468-2023
Fax: (410) 468-2086
Chief Actuary **Sarah Li** .............................(410) 468-2042
Webmaster **Minu Sinha** ..............................(410) 468-2053
E-mail: minu.sinha@maryland.gov

## Ethics Commission
45 Calvert Street, Third Floor, Annapolis, MD 21401
Tel: (410) 260-7770  Tel: (877) 669-6085  Fax: (410) 260-7746
Internet: http://ethics.maryland.gov
▲Chairperson **Paul M. Vettori** .......................(410) 260-7770

## Health Services Cost Review Commission [HSCRC]
4160 Patterson Avenue, Baltimore, MD 21215
Tel: (410) 764-2605  Fax: (410) 358-6217  Internet: www.hscrc.state.md.us
■Chairman **Nelson J. Sabatini** .......................(410) 764-2605
■Vice Chairman **Herbert S. Wong, PhD** ...............(410) 764-2605
■Commissioner **Victoria W. Bayless**...................(410) 764-2605
■Commissioner **Dr. George H. Bone, MD** ..............(410) 764-2605
■Commissioner **John M. Colmers** .....................(410) 764-2605
Education: Johns Hopkins 1975 BA; North Carolina 1977 MPH;
Johns Hopkins 1983 ScD
■Commissioner **Dr. Stephen F. Jencks, MD, PhD, MPH** . . . (410) 764-2605

*(continued on next page)*

---

★ Elected Official     ■ Appointed by Governor     ● Appointed by Legislature     ▲ Appointed by Board or Commission     ◆ Appointed by State Supreme Court

**Health Services Cost Review Commission** *continued*

■ Commissioner **Jack C. Keane** . . . . . . . . . . . . . . . . . . . . (410) 764-2605

## Executive Staff

▲ Executive Director **Donna Kinzer** . . . . . . . . . . . . . . . . . (410) 764-2605
E-mail: donna.kinzer@maryland.gov
Education: Towson U 1984 BS

## Legal Department

Assistant Attorney General **Stanley Lustman** . . . . . . . . . . (410) 764-2575
E-mail: stan.lustman@maryland.gov
Assistant Attorney General **Leslie Schulman** . . . . . . . . . . (410) 764-2575
E-mail: leslie.schulman@maryland.gov

## Center for Center for Clinical and Financial Information

Payment Reform and Innovation Director **(Vacant)** . . . . . . (410) 764-2605
Policy Analysis Associate Director **Claudine Williams** . . . . (410) 764-5961
E-mail: claudine.williams@maryland.gov
Information Management and Program Administration
Chief **Oscar Ibarra** . . . . . . . . . . . . . . . . . . . . . . . . (410) 764-2566
E-mail: oscar.ibarra@maryland.gov
Advance Programmer Specialist **Kai-Ing Duh** . . . . . . . . . (410) 764-2605
E-mail: kai-ing.duh@maryland.gov
Program Manager **Amanda Vaughan** . . . . . . . . . . . . . . . . (410) 764-2605
E-mail: amanda.vaughan@maryland.gov
Programmer Analyst **Irene Cheng** . . . . . . . . . . . . . . . . . (410) 764-2605
E-mail: irene.cheng@maryland.gov

## Center for Engagement and Alignment

Administrative Officer III **Diann Miller** . . . . . . . . . . . . . . (410) 764-2605
E-mail: diann.miller@maryland.gov
Information Technology Associate Director **Xavier Colo** . . . (410) 764-2605
E-mail: xavier.colo@maryland.gov
IT Supervisor **Greg Reeves** . . . . . . . . . . . . . . . . . . . . . (410) 764-2605
E-mail: greg.reeves@maryland.gov
Computer Network Specialist **Osondu Elemuo** . . . . . . . . . (410) 764-2605
E-mail: osondu.elemuo@maryland.gov

## Center for Population Based Methodologies

Research and Methodology Deputy Director
**Sule Calikoglu Gerovich, PhD** . . . . . . . . . . . . . . . . . (410) 764-2673
E-mail: sule.gerovich@maryland.gov
Education: Bilkent U 2001 MA; Johns Hopkins 2003 MPP, 2008 PhD
Research and Methodology Associate Director
**Nduka "Andy" Udom** . . . . . . . . . . . . . . . . . . . . . . (410) 764-2584
E-mail: nduka.udom@maryland.gov
Education: Morgan State 1988 MA
Quality Initiative Associate Director **Dianne Feeney** . . . . . (410) 764-2605
Quality Analysis Chief **Noi Reid** . . . . . . . . . . . . . . . . . . (410) 764-2605
Performance Measurement Associate Director
**Alyson Schuster, PhD** . . . . . . . . . . . . . . . . . . . . . . (410) 764-5961
E-mail: alyson.schuster@maryland.gov
Health Policy Analyst **George Anyumba** . . . . . . . . . . . . . (410) 764-2605
Programmer Analyst **Robert Chen** . . . . . . . . . . . . . . . . . (410) 764-2605
E-mail: robert.chen@maryland.gov
Special Projects Chief **Denise Johnson** . . . . . . . . . . . . . . (410) 764-5961
E-mail: denise.johnson@maryland.gov

## Center for Revenue and Compliance

Hospital Rate Setting Deputy Director
**Gerard "Jerry" Schmith** . . . . . . . . . . . . . . . . . . . . . (410) 764-2578
Education: Baltimore 1977 BS
Rate Regulations Associate Director **Ellen Englert** . . . . . . (410) 764-2562
E-mail: ellen.englert@maryland.gov
Education: Towson State U 1976 BA
Hospital Rate Regulation Chief **Brian Morton** . . . . . . . . . (410) 764-2605
Audit and Compliance Associate Director
**Dennis Phelps** . . . . . . . . . . . . . . . . . . . . . . . . . . . (410) 764-2605
Audit and Compliance Chief
**Christopher "Chris" O'Brien** . . . . . . . . . . . . . . . . . . (410) 764-2579
E-mail: chris.obrien@maryland.gov
Audits and Compliance Assistant Chief **William Hoff** . . . (410) 764-2605
Audits and Compliance Assistant Chief
**Chris Konsowski** . . . . . . . . . . . . . . . . . . . . . . . . . (410) 764-2605

## Higher Education Commission [MHEC]

Six North Liberty Street, 10th Floor, Baltimore, MD 21201
Tel: (410) 767-3301  TTY: (800) 735-2258  Fax: (410) 332-0270
Internet: www.mhec.maryland.gov

**Employees:** 56  **Fiscal Year:** 2015  **Budget:** $466,024,000

■ Secretary **James D. Fielder, Jr., PhD** . . . . . . . . . . . . . . (410) 767-3312
E-mail: james.fielder@maryland.gov
Education: Maryland 1970 BS, 1972 MEd; Michigan State 1984 PhD
Chief of Staff **(Vacant)** . . . . . . . . . . . . . . . . . . . . . . . . (410) 767-3043

## Public Service Commission [PSC]

William Donald Schaefer Tower, Six Saint Paul Street, 16th Floor,
Baltimore, MD 21202-6806
Tel: (410) 767-8000  TTY: (800) 735-2258 (MD Relay)
Fax: (410) 333-6495  Internet: www.psc.state.md.us

**Employees:** 139  **Fiscal Year:** 2015  **Budget:** $37,887,000

■ Chairman **W. Kevin Hughes** . . . . . . . . . . . . . . . . . . . . (410) 767-8073
E-mail: kevin.hughes@maryland.gov
Education: Maryland BA; Harvard 1985 MPP; Maryland Law 1994 JD
■ Commissioner **Anne E. Hoskins, Esq.** . . . . . . . . . . . . . . (410) 767-8072
E-mail: anne.hoskins@maryland.gov
Education: Cornell 1984 BS; Princeton 1986 MPA; Harvard 1994 JD
■ Commissioner **Jeannette M. Mills** . . . . . . . . . . . . . . . . . (410) 767-8027
E-mail: jeannette.mills@maryland.gov
Education: Virginia Tech BS; Loyola Col (MD) MBA
■ Commissioner **Michael T "Mike" Richard** . . . . . . . . . . . (410) 767-8017
■ Commissioner **Harold D. Williams** . . . . . . . . . . . . . . . . (410) 767-8116
E-mail: haroldd.williams@maryland.gov
Education: Coppin State Col BS; Johns Hopkins MA

## Board of Contract Appeals

Six Saint Paul Street, Suite 601, Baltimore, MD 21202-1608
Tel: (410) 767-8228  Tel: (800) 827-1135  Fax: (410) 333-0890
E-mail: howe@msbca.state.md.us  Internet: www.msbca.state.md.us

**Employees:** 5  **Fiscal Year:** 2015  **Budget:** $669,000

■ Chairman **Michael J. Collins** . . . . . . . . . . . . . . . . . . . . (410) 767-8228
■ Member **Bethamy N. Beam** . . . . . . . . . . . . . . . . . . . . . (410) 767-8228
■ Member **Ann Marie Doory** . . . . . . . . . . . . . . . . . . . . . . (410) 767-8228
Education: Towson State U 1976 BA; Baltimore 1979 JD

## State Board of Education

200 West Baltimore Street, Baltimore, MD 21201
Tel: (410) 767-0467  Fax: (410) 333-2226
E-mail: stateboard.msde@maryland.gov

■ President **Guffrie M. Smith, Jr.** . . . . . . . . . . . . . . . . . . . (410) 767-0467
■ Vice President **Sylvester James Gates, Jr., PhD** . . . . . . . . (410) 767-0467
Education: MIT 1973 BSc, 1973 BSc, 1977 PhD
▲ Secretary/Treasurer (Interim) **Jack R. Smith, PhD** . . . . . . (410) 767-0462
Note: Until July 1, 2016
Education: Notre Dame PhD
■ Member **James H. DeGraffenreidt, Jr.** . . . . . . . . . . . . . . (410) 767-0467
Education: Yale 1974 BA; Columbia 1978 JD, 1978 MBA
■ Member **Linda Eberhart** . . . . . . . . . . . . . . . . . . . . . . . (410) 767-0467
■ Member **Chester E. Finn, Jr., EdD** . . . . . . . . . . . . . . . . . (410) 767-0467
■ Member **Michele Jenkins Guyton, PhD** . . . . . . . . . . . . . (410) 767-0467
■ Member **Laurie Halverson** . . . . . . . . . . . . . . . . . . . . . . (410) 767-0467
■ Member **Stephanie R. Iszard** . . . . . . . . . . . . . . . . . . . . (410) 767-0467
■ Member **Madhu Sidhu** . . . . . . . . . . . . . . . . . . . . . . . . (410) 767-0467
Education: Richard Stockton Col
■ Member **Andrew R. "Andy" Smarick** . . . . . . . . . . . . . . (410) 767-0467
■ Member **Laura Weeldreyer** . . . . . . . . . . . . . . . . . . . . . (410) 767-0467
■ Member **(Vacant)** . . . . . . . . . . . . . . . . . . . . . . . . . . . (410) 767-0467
■ Member **(Vacant)** . . . . . . . . . . . . . . . . . . . . . . . . . . . (410) 767-0467
■ Student Member **Quinn Wandalowski** . . . . . . . . . . . . . . (410) 767-0467
Executive Director **Miya T. Simpson, PhD** . . . . . . . . . . . . (410) 767-0467

# Maryland State Department of Education [MSDE]

Tel: (410) 767-0100  TTY: (410) 333-6442  Fax: (410) 333-2226

**Employees:** 1,446  **Fiscal Year:** 2015  **Budget:** $7,415,760,000

▲ State Superintendent of Schools (Acting)
**Jack R. Smith, PhD** .............................. (410) 767-0316
  Note: Until July 1, 2016.
  E-mail: jack.smith@maryland.gov
▲ State Superintendent of Schools (Acting)
**Karen B. Salmon, PhD**
  Note: Effective June 1, 2016.
  Education: Delaware BA; Maryland PhD
  Executive Assistant **Eileen E. "Betty" Mack, EdD** ..... (410) 767-0461
Chief of Staff **(Vacant)** ................................ (410) 767-0439
Principal Legal Counsel **Elizabeth Kameen** ............. (410) 576-6451
  200 Saint Paul Place, 19th Floor,           Fax: (410) 576-6309
  Baltimore, MD 21202
  E-mail: ekameen@oag.state.md.us
Department Coordination and National Legislation
  Director **Debra Lichter** ............................. (410) 767-0470
  E-mail: debra.lichter@maryland.gov
Governmental Relations Executive Director
  **Amanda Conn, Esq.** ................................ (410) 767-0469
State Board Executive Director **Miya T. Simpson, PhD** ... (410) 767-0467

## School Effectiveness Office

Fax: (410) 333-6033

Chief Performance Officer (Interim)
  **Karen B. Salmon, PhD** ............................ (410) 767-0464
  E-mail: karen.salmon@maryland.gov
Executive Assistant **Monica C. Bias** ................. (410) 767-0464
  E-mail: monica.bias@maryland.gov

## Deputy State Superintendent for Finance and Administration

Deputy State Superintendent for Finance and
  Administration and Chief Operating Officer
  **Kristy L. Michel** ................................... (410) 767-0011
  E-mail: kristy.michel@maryland.gov

# State Board of Elections

P.O. Box 6486, Annapolis, MD 21401-0486
Tel: (410) 269-2840  Tel: (800) 222-8683  TTY: (800) 735-2258
Fax: (410) 974-2019  E-mail: info.sbe@maryland.gov
Internet: www.elections.maryland.gov

**Employees:** 31  **Fiscal Year:** 2015  **Budget:** $17,452,000

■ Chairman **David J. McManus, Jr.** ................... (410) 269-2840
■ Vice Chairman **Patrick J. "P. J." Hogan** ............... (410) 269-2840
  Education: Indiana (PA) 1989 BS
■ Member **Kelley A. Howells** .......................... (410) 269-2840
■ Member **Michael R. Logan** .......................... (410) 269-2840
■ Member **Bobbie S. Mack** ............................ (410) 269-2840

## Administration

Administrator **Linda H. Lamone** ..................... (410) 269-2840
  E-mail: linda.lamone@maryland.gov
Deputy Administrator **Nikki Baines Charlson** .......... (410) 269-2843
  E-mail: nikki.charlson@maryland.gov

## Field Support Division

State Manager **Kimberly A. Meiklejohn** ............... (410) 269-2878
Regional Manager **Desvin Gabbidon** ................. (410) 269-2923
Regional Manager **Russell Hicks** ..................... (410) 269-2923
Regional Manager **Paula Paschall** .................... (410) 269-2923
Regional Manager **Duane Powell** ..................... (410) 269-2923
Regional Manager **Shafiq Satterfield** ................. (410) 269-2923
Regional Manager **John Speir** ....................... (410) 269-2923

# Office of the People's Counsel [OPC]

William Donald Schaefer Tower, Six Saint Paul Street, Suite 2102,
Baltimore, MD 21202
Tel: (410) 767-8150  Fax: (410) 333-3616
E-mail: dinfo_opc@maryland.gov  Internet: www.opc.state.md.us

**Employees:** 19

People's Counsel **Paula M. Carmody** ................. (410) 767-8150
  Education: McGill (Canada) BA; Antioch Law JD

# Office of the Public Defender [OPD]

Six Saint Paul Street, Suite 1400, Baltimore, MD 21202
Tel: (410) 767-8460  Tel: (877) 430-5187
TTY: (800) 735-2258 (Maryland Relay Service)  Fax: (410) 333-8496
E-mail: jsehorn@opd.state.md.us  Internet: www.opd.state.md.us

**Employees:** 925  **Fiscal Year:** 2015  **Budget:** $97,829,000

▲ Public Defender **Paul B. DeWolfe** ................... (410) 767-8479
  E-mail: pdewolfe@opd.state.md.us
Executive Associate **Janice Sehorn** .................. (410) 767-8479
Equal Employment Opportunity Officer **Lynn C. Bellamy** .. (410) 767-8463
Administrative Services Unit **Kathleen Mattis** .......... (410) 767-8481
  E-mail: kmattis@opd.state.md.us
Central Booking and Intake Facility
  **Mary-Denise Davis, JD** ............................ (410) 209-4465
Innocence Project **Michele Nethercott, Esq.** ........... (410) 223-3790
  E-mail: mnethercott@opd.state.md.us
Baltimore City (Eastern District) **Natascha Brown** ...... (410) 878-8605
Baltimore City (Southern District)
  **Donna Greenbeck-Marsh** ........................ (410) 878-8416
Baltimore City (Western District) **Maria McMahon** ...... (410) 878-8150
Baltimore City - Felony **Sonia Johnson** ........ (410) 333-4900 ext. 350
Baltimore City - Juvenile Court Division **Latricia Baker** ... (443) 263-6369

# Office of the State Prosecutor [OSP]

300 East Joppa Road, Suite 410, Towson, MD 21286
Tel: (410) 321-4067  Tel: (800) 695-4058  TTY: (800) 735-2258
Fax: (410) 321-3851  Internet: www.osp.maryland.gov

■ State Prosecutor **Emmet C. Davitt** ................... (410) 321-4067
  E-mail: emmet.davitt@maryland.gov
Office Administration Director **Genie Gunthrop** ........ (410) 321-4067
  E-mail: genie.gunthrop@maryland.gov
Deputy State Prosecutor **Thomas M. McDonough** ...... (410) 321-4067
Senior Assistant State Prosecutor **(Vacant)** ............. (410) 321-4067
Assistant State Prosecutor **Katherine D. Anthony** ....... (410) 321-4067
Chief Investigator **James I. Cabezas** ................. (410) 321-4067

# Maryland State Police [MSP]

1201 Reisterstown Road, Pikesville, MD 21208-3899
Tel: (410) 653-4200  TTY: (410) 486-0677  Fax: (410) 653-4269
E-mail: msp.media@maryland.gov  Internet: www.mdsp.org

**Employees:** 2,354  **Fiscal Year:** 2015  **Budget:** $361,941,000

■ Secretary **Col. William Pallozzi** .................... (410) 653-4219
  E-mail: msp.superintendent@maryland.gov
  Education: North Georgia 1988 BS
Criminal Investigation Bureau Chief (Acting)
  **Major David Ruel** ................................ (410) 653-4211
Field Operations Bureau Chief **Anthony Satchell** ....... (410) 653-4218
Support Services Bureau Chief **Laura L. Herman** ........ (410) 653-4212
Transportation Safety Commander
  **Major Norman "Bill" Dofflemyer** ................... (410) 579-5959

# State Fire Marshal

1201 Reisterstown Road, Pikesville, MD 21208-3899
Tel: (410) 653-8980  E-mail: msp.osfm@maryland.gov

■ State Fire Marshal **Brian Geraci** .................... (410) 653-8980
  E-mail: brian.geraci@maryland.gov
Chief Fire Protection Engineer **Larry Iseminger** ........ (410) 653-8980
Lower Eastern Shore Regional Chief Deputy Fire
  Marshal **Joseph Flanagan** ......................... (410) 713-3780
Northeast Regional Office Chief Deputy Fire Marshal
  **Matthews D. Steven** ............................. (410) 836-4844

*(continued on next page)*

---

★ Elected Official　　■ Appointed by Governor　　● Appointed by Legislature　　▲ Appointed by Board or Commission　　◆ Appointed by State Supreme Court

**State Fire Marshal** *continued*

Southern Regional Office Chief Deputy Fire Marshal
**Duane K. Svites** . . . . . . . . . . . . . . . . . . . . . . . . . (443) 550-6820
Upper Eastern Shore Regional Chief Deputy Fire
Marshal **Caryn L. McMahon** . . . . . . . . . . . . . . . (410) 822-7609 ext. 302
Western Regional Office Chief Deputy Fire Marshal
**Jason M. Mowbray** . . . . . . . . . . . . . . . . . . . . . . . . (301) 766-3888

# Office of the Attorney General

200 Saint Paul Place, Baltimore, MD 21202-2021
Tel: (410) 576-6300  E-mail: oag@oag.state.md.us

**Fiscal Year:** 2015  **Budget:** $34,277,000

★Attorney General **Brian E. Frosh** (D) . . . . . . . . . . . . . . . . . . (410) 576-6300
  Term Expires: January 2019
  Education: Wesleyan U 1968 BA; Columbia 1971 JD
  Career: Member, Joint Legislative Policy Committee, Joint Statutory
  Committees, Maryland General Assembly; Delegate, Maryland House
  of Delegates (1987-1995); State Senator (D-MD, District 16), Maryland
  Senate (1995-2015)
Chief Deputy Attorney General **Elizabeth F. Harris** . . . . . . (410) 576-7051
  Education: Richmond 1995; Maryland 1998 JD
Deputy Attorney General (Acting)
  **Donna Hill Staton, Esq.** . . . . . . . . . . . . . . . . . . . . . . . . . (410) 576-6962
Deputy Attorney General
  **Thiruvendran "Thiru" Vignarajah** . . . . . . . . . . . . . . (410) 576-6330
  Education: Yale 1998 BA; Harvard 2005 JD
Special Assistant to Attorney General **David Eppler** . . . . . . (410) 576-6345
Special Assistant and Senior Litigation Counsel
  **Joshua N. Auerbach** . . . . . . . . . . . . . . . . . . . . . . . . . . (410) 576-7299
Director of Communications and Policy Advisor
  **David Nitkin** . . . . . . . . . . . . . . . . . . . . . . . . . . . . . . (410) 576-6357
  E-mail: dnitkin@oag.state.md.us
Chief Counsel for Legislative Affairs and Civil Rights
  **Zenita Wickham-Hurley** . . . . . . . . . . . . . . . . . . . . . (410) 576-7939
  E-mail: zhurley@oag.state.md.us
  Education: NYU 2000 JD
  Deputy Director **Tiffany L. Jackson, Esq.** . . . . . . . . . . . . (410) 576-6584
Information Technology Director
  **Dustin Scott Beckmann** . . . . . . . . . . . . . . . . . . . . . . (410) 576-6487
  E-mail: sbeckmann@oag.state.md.us
Senior Advisor **(Vacant)** . . . . . . . . . . . . . . . . . . . . . . . . (410) 576-6300
Senior Counsel **John T. Willis** . . . . . . . . . . . . . . . . . . . . . (410) 576-6403

# Office of the State Treasurer

Louis L. Goldstein Treasury Building, 80 Calvert Street, Room 109,
Annapolis, MD 21401
Tel: (410) 260-7533  TTY: (800) 735-2258
Fax: (410) 974-3530  E-mail: treasurer@treasurer.state.md.us
Internet: www.treasurer.state.md.us

**Employees:** 57  **Fiscal Year:** 2015  **Budget:** $38,940,000

●State Treasurer **Nancy K. Kopp** . . . . . . . . . . . . . . . . . . . . . . (410) 260-7160
  E-mail: nkopp@treasurer.state.md.us
  Education: Wellesley 1965 BA; Chicago 1967 MA
  Career: State Representative (D-MD, District 16), Maryland House of
  Delegates (1975-2002)
Executive Assistant to Treasurer **Linda Pohuski** . . . . . . . . (410) 260-7160
                                                    Fax: (410) 260-6056
Chief Deputy Treasurer **Bernadette T. Benik** . . . . . . . . . . . (410) 260-7080
Deputy Treasurer for Financial Policy **Susanne Brogan** . . . (410) 260-6123
  Education: Washington Col BA; Maryland JD
Deputy Treasurer for Public Policy **Susanne Brogan** . . . . . (410) 260-7418

# Comptroller of Maryland

Louis L. Goldstein Treasury Building, 80 Calvert Street,
Annapolis, MD 21404-0466
P.O. Box 466, Annapolis, MD 21404-0466
Tel: (410) 260-7801  TTY: (410) 260-7157  Fax: (410) 974-3808
E-mail: taxhelp@comp.state.md.us  Internet: www.comp.state.md.us

**Employees:** 1,148  **Fiscal Year:** 2015  **Budget:** $121,213,000

★Comptroller **Peter V.R. Franchot** (D) . . . . . . . . . . . . . . . . . (410) 260-7801
  Term Expires: January 2019
  Education: Amherst 1973 BA; Northeastern 1978 JD
  Career: State Delegate (D-MD, District 20), Maryland House of
  Delegates (1987-2007)

# Board of Public Works [BPW]

Louis L. Goldstein Treasury Building, 80 Calvert Street, Room 117,
Annapolis, MD 21401
Tel: (410) 260-7335  Tel: (877) 591-7320  Fax: (410) 974-5240
E-mail: email.bpw@maryland.gov  Internet: www.bpw.maryland.gov

**Employees:** 9  **Fiscal Year:** 2015  **Budget:** $7,509,000

Member **Peter V.R. Franchot** . . . . . . . . . . . . . . . . . . . . . . . (410) 260-7801
  Affiliation: Comptroller, State of Maryland
  Louis L. Goldstein Treasury Building, 80 Calvert Street,
  Annapolis, MD 21404-0466
Member **Lawrence J. "Larry" Hogan, Jr.** . . . . . . . . . . . . . (410) 974-3901
  Affiliation: Governor, Office of the Governor, State of Maryland
  State Capitol, 100 State Circle, Annapolis, MD 21401
Member **Nancy K. Kopp** . . . . . . . . . . . . . . . . . . . . . . . . . . (410) 260-7160
  Affiliation: State Treasurer, Office of the State Treasurer, State of
  Maryland
  Louis L. Goldstein Treasury Building, 80 Calvert Street, Room 109,
  Annapolis, MD 21401

# Office of the Executive Secretary

Tel: (410) 260-7335  Fax: (410) 974-5240

▲Executive Secretary **Sheila C. McDonald** . . . . . . . . . . . . . (410) 260-7335
  E-mail: sheila.mcdonald@maryland.gov

---

★ Elected Official   ■ Appointed by Governor   ● Appointed by Legislature   ▲ Appointed by Board or Commission   ◆ Appointed by State Supreme Court

EXECUTIVE BRANCH

# Massachusetts

Tel: (671) 725-4000

**Number of U.S. Congressional Delegates:** 2 Senators; 9 Representatives **Governor's Term:** 4 years
**Legislature Description:** General Court- 40 member Senate; 160 House of Representatives; Term - Senate 2 years, House 2 years **Next Election:** Governor November 2018; Legislature November 2016
**Number of Electoral Votes:** 11 **Official Name:** Commonwealth of Massachusetts (Indian: large hill place)
**Nickname:** The Bay State, The Old Colony **Motto:** Ense petit placidam sub litertate quietem (By the sword we seek peace, but peace only under liberty)

**Population:** 6,794,422 (2015); Rank 15 **Fiscal Year:** 2015 **Budget:** $36,585,627,000

## Office of the Governor

State House, 24 Beacon Street, Room 280, Boston, MA 01233
Tel: (617) 725-4005 TTY: (617) 727-3666 Fax: (617) 727-9725
Internet: www.mass.gov/governor

**Employees:** 75 **Fiscal Year:** 2015 **Budget:** $6,010,000

**Charles D. "Charlie" Baker, Jr.**
Governor

Began Service: January 8, 2015
Term Expires: January 2019
Date of Birth: November 13, 1956
Education: Harvard 1979 AB; Northwestern 1986 MBA
Home: Swampscott

Career: Secretary, Executive Office of Health and Human Services, Commonwealth of Massachusetts (1992-1994); Secretary, Executive Office for Administration and Finance, Commonwealth of Massachusetts (1994-1998); Chief Executive Officer, Harvard Vanguard Medical Associates (1998-1999); President and Chief Executive Officer, Harvard Pilgrim Health Care, Inc. (1999-2009)

★ Governor **Charles D. "Charlie" Baker, Jr.** (R) . . . . . . . . . . (617) 725-4005
  E-mail: charlie.baker@state.ma.us
  Executive Assistant and Scheduling Director
    **Brianna Wehrs** . . . . . . . . . . . . . . . . . . . . . . . (617) 725-4005
    E-mail: brianna.wehrs@state.ma.us
  Senior Advisor **Tim Buckley** . . . . . . . . . . . . . . . . . . (617) 725-4025
    E-mail: timothy.buckley@state.ma.us
  Chief of Staff **Steven Kadish** . . . . . . . . . . . . . . . . . (617) 725-4005
    Education: Tufts 1978 BA; MIT 1982 MCP
  Deputy Chief of Staff **Michael Vallerelli** . . . . . . . . . . . (617) 725-4005
  Deputy Chief for Access and Opportunity **Jabes Rojas** . . . (617) 725-4005
  Deputy Chief for Cabinet Affairs **Joel Barrera** . . . . . (617) 725-4005
    Associate Chief for Cabinet Affairs **(Vacant)** . . . . . . . . . (617) 725-4005
  Associate Chief and Director of Strategic Operations
    **Adam Weikel** . . . . . . . . . . . . . . . . . . . . . . . (617) 725-4005
    E-mail: adam.weikel@state.ma.us
  Deputy Chief of Community Relations and Constituent
  Affairs **Mindy d'Arbeloff** . . . . . . . . . . . . . . . . . . (617) 725-4005
    E-mail: mindy.darbeloff@state.ma.us
  Community Affairs Director **Hodari Cail** . . . . . . . . . . . (617) 725-4005
    E-mail: hodari.cail@state.ma.us
  Associate Chief of Staff and Policy Director
    **Elizabeth K. Mahoney** . . . . . . . . . . . . . . . . . . (617) 725-4005
    E-mail: elizabeth.mahoney@state.ma.us
    Education: Harvard 2005
  Chief Legal Counsel **Lon F. Povich** . . . . . . . . . . . . . . (617) 725-4005
    E-mail: lon.povich@state.ma.us
    Deputy Chief Legal Counsel **Cathy Judd-Stein** . . . . . . . (617) 725-4005
    E-mail: cathy.juddstein@state.ma.us
    Education: Dartmouth 1982 AB; Harvard 1985 JD
  Chief Secretary **Carlo P. Basile** . . . . . . . . . . . . . . . (617) 725-4005
    E-mail: carlo.p.basile@state.ma.us

Director of Boards and Commissions
  **Edward Palleschi** . . . . . . . . . . . . . . . . . . . . . (617) 725-4005
  E-mail: ed.palleschi@state.ma.us
Communications Director **Tim Buckley** . . . . . . . . . . . (617) 725-4025
  E-mail: timothy.buckley@state.ma.us
Director of External Affairs **Thomas Dickens** . . . . . . . . (617) 725-4005
  E-mail: thomas.dickens@state.ma.us
Press Secretary **Elizabeth Guyton** . . . . . . . . . . . . . (617) 725-4005
  E-mail: elizabeth.guyton@state.ma.us
Digital Director **Ryan Boehm** . . . . . . . . . . . . . . . . (617) 725-4005
  E-mail: ryan.boehm@state.ma.us
Constituent Services Director **John Tapley** . . . . . . . . . (617) 725-4005
  E-mail: john.tapley@state.ma.us
Director of Operations **Dean Serpa** . . . . . . . . . . . . . (617) 725-4005
  E-mail: dean.serpa@state.ma.us
  Deputy Director of Operations **Scott Conway** . . . . . . . (617) 725-4005
  E-mail: scott.conway@state.ma.us
Director of Performance Management **Mark Fuller** . . . . . (617) 725-4005
Director of Personnel and Administration
  **Matt St. Hilaire** . . . . . . . . . . . . . . . . . . . . . (617) 725-4005
  E-mail: matt.sthilaire@state.ma.us
Legislative Affairs Director **Ryan Coleman** . . . . . . . . . (617) 725-4005
  E-mail: ryan.coleman@state.ma.us
  Deputy Legislative Affairs Director **Kaitlyn Sprague** . . . (617) 725-4005
Special Advisor for Technology and Innovation
  Competitiveness **Mark E. Nunnelly** . . . . . . . . . . . . (617) 725-4005
  E-mail: nunnellym@dor.state.ma.us
  Education: Centre 1980 AB; Harvard 1984 MBA

## Office of Federal-State Relations

444 North Capitol Street, NW, Suite 208, Washington, DC 20001
Tel: (202) 624-7713 Fax: (202) 624-7714

Director **Tiffany Watkins Ahern** . . . . . . . . . . . . . . (202) 624-7713
  E-mail: tiffany.watkinsahern@state.ma.us
  Education: Pennsylvania BA
Deputy Director **(Vacant)** . . . . . . . . . . . . . . . . . . (202) 624-7713

## Western Massachusetts Office

436 Dwight Street, Suite 300, Springfield, MA 01103
Tel: (413) 784-1200

Director **Ryan Chamberland** . . . . . . . . . . . . . . . . (413) 784-1200
  E-mail: ryan.chamberland@state.ma.us

## Governor's Council

★ Councilor **Michael J. Albano** (D-District 8) . . . . . . . (617) 725-4015 ext. 8
  Term Expires: 2017                          Tel: (413) 525-4438
  Education: Springfield (MA) 1974 BS;        Fax: (413) 525-4887
  American International 1976 MS; Hartford 1981 MPA
★ Councilor **Jennie L. Caissie** (R-District 7) . . . . . . . (617) 725-4015 ext. 7
  Term Expires: 2017                          Tel: (508) 765-0885
  53 Fort Hill Road, Oxford, MA 01540         Fax: (508) 765-0888
★ Councilor **Marilyn Petitto Devaney** (D-District 3) . . (617) 725-4015 ext. 3
  Term Expires: 2017                          Res: (617) 840-7689
  98 Westminster Ave., Watertown, MA 02472    Fax: (617) 727-6610
★ Councilor **Eileen Duff** (D-District 5) . . . . . . . . . . (617) 725-4015 ext. 5
  Term Expires: 2017                          Res: (978) 927-8700
  Eight Barberry Heights Road,                Fax: (617) 727-6610
  Gloucester, MA 01930

*(continued on next page)*

★ Elected Official   ■ Appointed by Governor   ● Appointed by Legislature   ▲ Appointed by Board or Commission   ◆ Appointed by State Supreme Court

EXECUTIVE BRANCH

**Governor's Council** *continued*

★Councilor **Joseph C. "Joe" Ferreira** (D-District 1). .(617) 725-4015 ext. 1
  Term Expires: 2017                              Fax: (508) 230-2510
  Seven Thomas Drive, Somerset, MA 02726

★Councilor **Christopher A. Iannella** (D-District 4) . . . (617) 725-4015 ext. 4
  Term Expires: 2017                              Tel: (617) 227-1538
  263 Pond Street, Boston, MA 02130                        (Business)
  Education: Boston Col 1974 BA; Suffolk 1977 JD    Fax: (617) 742-1424

★Councilor **Robert Jubinville** (D-District 2) . . . . . . . .(617) 725-4015 ext. 2
  Term Expires: 2017
  487 Adams Street, Milton, MA 02186

★Councilor **Terrence Kennedy** (D-District 6). . . . . . . .(617) 725-4015 ext. 6
  Term Expires: 2017                              Tel: (781) 387-9809
  Three Stafford Road, Lynnfield, MA 01940         Fax: (617) 727-6610
  Administrative Secretary **George F. Cronin, Jr.** . . . . . (617) 725-4015 ext. 0
    E-mail: george.cronin@gov.state.ma.us
    Education: Notre Dame 1959 BS

# Massachusetts Office of Information Technology

One Ashburton Place, Room 804, Boston, MA 02108-1518
Tel: (617) 626-4400  Fax: (617) 626-4459

**Employees:** 36  **Fiscal Year:** 2015  **Budget:** $5,903,000

Executive Director **Mark E. Nunnelly** . . . . . . . . . . . . . . . .(617) 626-4400
  Executive Assistant **Sue Adams** . . . . . . . . . . . . . . . . . . . .(617) 626-4664
Deputy Commonwealth Chief Information Officer
  **Karthik Viswanathan** . . . . . . . . . . . . . . . . . . . . . . . . . . . .(617) 626-4434
    E-mail: karthik.viswanathan@state.ma.us
Chief Application Officer **(Vacant)** . . . . . . . . . . . . . . . . . . .(617) 626-4549
Chief Operations Officer **Charles Desourdy** . . . . . . . . . . . (617) 626-4400
    E-mail: charles.desourdy@state.ma.us

# Executive Office for Administration and Finance [ANF]

373 State House, Room 373, Boston, MA 02133
Tel: (617) 727-2040  Fax: (617) 727-2779

■Secretary **Kristen Lepore** . . . . . . . . . . . . . . . . . . . . . . . . . .(617) 727-2040
    E-mail: kristen.lepore@state.ma.us
    Education: Suffolk MPA
Undersecretary **Rachel C. Madden** . . . . . . . . . . . . . . . . . . .(617) 727-2040
    E-mail: rachel.madden@state.ma.us
Assistant Secretary for Capital Finance
  **Jennifer F. Sullivan** . . . . . . . . . . . . . . . . . . . . . . . . . . . . . .(617) 727-2040
Chief of Staff and Communications Director
  **Dominick Ianno** . . . . . . . . . . . . . . . . . . . . . . . . . . . . . . . . .(617) 727-2040
    E-mail: dominick.ianno@state.ma.us
  Deputy Communications Director **Brendan Moss** . . . . . . (617) 352-6880
    E-mail: brendan.moss@state.ma.us
General Counsel **Robert "Bob" Ross** . . . . . . . . . . . . . . . . . .(617) 727-2040
    E-mail: bob.ross2@state.ma.us
Budget Director **Catharine Hornby** . . . . . . . . . . . . . . . . . . .(617) 727-2040
    Education: Northeastern 2010 JD

# Department of Revenue [DOR]

Tel: (617) 626-2201

**Employees:** 1,839  **Fiscal Year:** 2015  **Budget:** $1,169,897,000

Commissioner **Michael P. "Mike" Heffernan** . . . . . . . . . . .(617) 626-2201
    Education: Georgetown BA; NYU MBA; JFK School Govt MPA
Deputy Commissioner for Tax Administration
  **William R. Graham, Jr.** . . . . . . . . . . . . . . . . . . . . . . . . . . (617) 626-2201
Chief of Staff **Michael Rybicki** . . . . . . . . . . . . . . . . . . . . . .(617) 626-2201

## Administrative Affairs Division

100 Cambridge Street, 8th Floor, Boston, MA 02114
Tel: (617) 626-2130  Fax: (617) 626-2195

Deputy Commissioner **Breean Fortier** . . . . . . . . . . . . . . . . (617) 626-2246
Internal Affairs Director **Jim Reddington** . . . . . . . . . . . . . (617) 626-2135
Internal Audit Director **John Mogni** . . . . . . . . . . . . . . . . . .(617) 626-2172

## Audit Division

200 Arlington Street, Chelsea, MA 02150
Tel: (617) 887-6800  Fax: (617) 887-6760
Deputy Commissioner (Acting) **Stephen Moffatt** . . . . . . . . (617) 887-6800

## Child Support Enforcement Division

100 Cambridge Street, Boston, MA 02114
Tel: (800) 332-2733
Deputy Commissioner **Michele Cristello** . . . . . . . . . . . . . . .(617) 626-4211

## Information Services Organization Division

200 Arlington Street, Chelsea, MA 02150
Fax: (617) 887-5929

Secretariat and Chief Information Officer for
  Administration and Finance **Vincent Piccinni** . . . . . . . . .(617) 887-5451
    E-mail: vincent.piccinni@state.ma.us
Assistant Chief Information Officer **J. Michael Guerin** . . . .(617) 887-5626
    E-mail: guerinj@dor.state.ma.us

## Legal Division

Tel: (617) 626-3200
General Counsel **Kevin Brown** . . . . . . . . . . . . . . . . . . . . . . (617) 626-3200
Deputy General Counsel **Michael Fatale** . . . . . . . . . . . . . . (617) 626-3200

## Division of Local Services

Tel: (617) 626-2300
Senior Deputy Commissioner **Sean Cronin** . . . . . . . . . . . . (617) 626-2300
Accounts Director **Gerard D. Perry** . . . . . . . . . . . . . . . . . . (617) 626-2300
    E-mail: perryg@dor.state.ma.us
Local Assessments Bureau Chief **Joanne Graziano** . . . . . . (617) 626-2300
Municipal Data Management Technical Assistance
  Bureau Chief **Fredrick Kingsley** . . . . . . . . . . . . . . . . . . . .(617) 626-2300
    E-mail: kinglseyf@dor.state.ma.us
Municipal Finance Law Bureau Chief **Kathleen Colleary** . .(617) 626-2300

## Resolution Division

Deputy Commissioner (Interim) **Laurie McGrath** . . . . . . . .(617) 626-2201

## Taxpayer Service Division

200 Arlington Street, Chelsea, MA 02151
Tel: (800) 887-6367
Deputy Commissioner (Acting) **Charlene Hannaford** . . . . .(617) 887-6273

# Division of Capital Asset Management and Maintenance [DCAMM]

One Ashburton Place, Room 1505, Boston, MA 02108
Tel: (617) 727-4050  Fax: (617) 727-5363
E-mail: info.dcamm@state.ma.us  Internet: www.mass.gov/cam

**Employees:** 109  **Fiscal Year:** 2015  **Budget:** $22,101,000

Commissioner **Carol Gladstone** . . . . . . . . . . . . . . . . . . . . . (617) 727-4050
Finance and Administration Deputy Commissioner
  **Ronald N. Renaud** . . . . . . . . . . . . . . . . . . . . . . . . . . . . . .(617) 727-4050
    E-mail: ronald.renaud@state.ma.us
  Finance and Accounting Director **James D. Malary** . . . . .(617) 727-1100
Planning, Design and Construction Deputy Commissioner
  **Elizabeth Minnis** . . . . . . . . . . . . . . . . . . . . . . . . . . . . . . . .(617) 727-4050
Real Estate Management Services Deputy Commissioner
  **(Vacant)** . . . . . . . . . . . . . . . . . . . . . . . . . . . . . . . . . . . . . . .(617) 727-4050
State House Operations Superintendent **Tammy Kraus** . . . .(617) 727-1100
  State House, Room 1, Boston, MA 02133        Fax: (617) 727-7700
  State House Operations Director
    **Tyrone Lawless** . . . . . . . . . . . . . . . . . . . . . .(617) 727-1100 ext. 35522
    State House, Room 115, Boston, MA 02133    Fax: (617) 727-7700
Planning and Engineering Deputy Superintendent
  **Vincent Cirigliano** . . . . . . . . . . . . . . . . . . . . . .(617) 727-4030 ext. 214
  Operations Deputy Director **(Vacant)** . . . . . . . .(617) 727-1100 ext. 24133
Business Impact Services Director **(Vacant)** . . . . . . . . . . . (617) 727-4050
Security Director **(Vacant)** . . . . . . . . . . . . . . . . . . . . . . . . . (617) 727-1100
State House ADA Coordinator
  **Carl Richardson** . . . . . . . . . . . . . . . . . . . . . . .(617) 727-1100 ext. 35502
General Counsel **(Vacant)** . . . . . . . . . . . . . . . . . . . . . . . . . .(617) 727-4050

---

★ Elected Official   ■ Appointed by Governor   ● Appointed by Legislature   ▲ Appointed by Board or Commission   ◆ Appointed by State Supreme Court

EXECUTIVE BRANCH

## Human Resources Division

One Ashburton Place, Boston, MA 02108-1515
Tel: (617) 878-9700  Fax: (617) 727-1175

**Employees:** 56  **Fiscal Year:** 2015  **Budget:** $36,836,000

■Chief Human Resources Officer **Paul D. Dietl** . . . . . . . . . . (617) 878-9703
    E-mail: paul.d.dietl@state.ma.us
    Education: Hamline 1982 BA; Syracuse MBA
    Executive Assistant **Linda Clark** . . . . . . . . . . . . . . . . . . . (617) 878-9703
Deputy Chief Human Resources Officer **Renee Fullem** . . . . (617) 878-9887

## Operational Services Division

One Ashburton Place, Room 1017, Boston, MA 02108
Tel: (617) 720-3300  Fax: (617) 727-4527  TTY: (617) 727-2716

**Employees:** 84  **Fiscal Year:** 2015  **Budget:** $8,535,000

Operational Services Assistant Secretary and State
    Purchasing Agent **Gary Lambert** . . . . . . . . . . . . . . . . . . (617) 720-3183
Deputy State Purchasing Agent **Patricia A. Wynn** . . . . . . . (617) 720-3183

## Processing Division

200 Arlington Street, Chelsea, MA 02151

Director **Paula Potvin** . . . . . . . . . . . . . . . . . . . . . . . . . . . . (617) 887-5062
    E-mail: paula.potvin@state.ma.us

## Civil Service Commission

One Ashburton Place, Room 503, Boston, MA 02108
Tel: (617) 727-2293  Fax: (617) 727-7590
E-mail: cscwebmaster@mass.gov  Internet: www.mass.gov/csc

**Employees:** 4  **Fiscal Year:** 2015  **Budget:** $438,000

■Chairman **Christopher C. Bowman** . . . . . . . . . . . . . . . . . (617) 979-1902
    E-mail: christopher.bowman@state.ma.us
■Commissioner **Paul A. Camuso** . . . . . . . . . . . . . . . . . . . (617) 727-2293
■Commissioner **Cynthia A. Ittleman** . . . . . . . . . . . . . . . . (617) 979-1901
    E-mail: cynthia.a.ittleman@state.ma.us
    Education: Western New England JD
■Commissioner **Paul M. Stein** . . . . . . . . . . . . . . . . . . . . . . (617) 979-1904
    E-mail: paul.m.stein@state.ma.us
■Commissioner **Kevin M. Tivnan** . . . . . . . . . . . . (617) 727-2293 ext. 21903
    Education: New England Col BA; Anna Maria MA

## Group Insurance Commission

P.O. Box 8747, Boston, MA 02114-8747
Tel: (617) 727-2310  Fax: (617) 227-5181  Internet: www.mass.gov/gic

**Employees:** 54  **Fiscal Year:** 2015  **Budget:** $2,066,451,000

Executive Director (Interim) **Ray Campbell** . . . . . (617) 727-2310 ext. 7010
    Education: Bates BA; Suffolk JD
Executive Director **Dr. Roberta Herman, MD** . . . . . . . . . . (617) 727-2310
    Note: On March 23, 2016, Dr. Roberta Herman was named Executive
    Director of the Group Insurance Commission. Dr. Herman's start date
    has not yet been determined.
    Education: McGill (Canada) MD

## State Library of Massachusetts

State House, Room 341, Boston, MA 02133
Tel: (617) 727-5819  Fax: (617) 727-9730  Internet: www.mass.gov/lib

■State Librarian and Director **Elvernoy H. Johnson** . . . . . . (617) 727-5819
    E-mail: elvernoy.johnson@state.ma.us
    Education: UMass (Boston) BA; Simmons MLS;
    Emmanuel (MA) MEd
Head of Reference **Alix Quan** . . . . . . . . . . . . . . . . . . . . . . (617) 727-2403
Head of Special Collections
    **Elizabeth "Beth" Carroll-Horrocks** . . . . . . . . . . . . . . . . (617) 727-2595
Head of Technical Services **Judith Carlstrom** . . . . . . . . . . (617) 727-7456

## Executive Office of Education

One Ashburton Place, Room 1403, Boston, MA 02108
Tel: (617) 979-8340  Fax: (617) 727-0049

■Secretary **James A. "Jim" Peyser** . . . . . . . . . . . . . . . . . . (617) 979-8340
    E-mail: jim.peyser@state.ma.us
    Education: Colgate BA; Fletcher Law & Diplomacy MALD
Undersecretary and Chief Operating Officer **Ann Reale** . . . (617) 979-8340
    E-mail: ann.reale@state.ma.us

Assistant Secretary for Policy and Planning **Tom Moreau** . . (617) 979-8346
    E-mail: tom.moreau@state.ma.us
Chief Financial Officer **(Vacant)** . . . . . . . . . . . . . . . . . . . . (617) 979-8340
Budget Director **Meng You** . . . . . . . . . . . . . . . . . . . . . . . . (617) 979-8340
Human Resources Director **Patricia McCarthy** . . . . . . . . . . (617) 979-8340
Legislative Director **Blair Brown** . . . . . . . . . . . . . . . . . . . . (617) 979-8340
    E-mail: blair.brown@state.ma.us
Chief Information Officer **(Vacant)** . . . . . . . . . . . . . . . . . . (617) 979-8340
Senior Policy Advisor **(Vacant)** . . . . . . . . . . . . . . . . . . . . . (617) 979-8340
Policy Analyst **Maya Buki-Dabby** . . . . . . . . . . . . . . . . . . . (617) 979-8340
General Counsel **Katherine Lipper** . . . . . . . . . . . . . . . . . . (617) 979-8340
Communications Director **Laura Keehner Rigas** . . . . . . . . . (617) 979-8340
    E-mail: laura.rigas@state.ma.us
    Education: William & Mary BA; Harvard MPA

## Board of Early Education and Care

■Chair **Dr. Nonie K. Lesaux** . . . . . . . . . . . . . . . . . . . . . . . (617) 988-6600
    Education: Mount Allison U 1999 BA; British Columbia 2001 MA,
    2003 PhD
■Member **Joan H. Block** . . . . . . . . . . . . . . . . . . . . . . . . . . (617) 988-6600
■Member **J.D. Chesloff** . . . . . . . . . . . . . . . . . . . . . . . . . . . (617) 988-6600
    Affiliation: Director of Public Policy, Massachusetts Business
    Roundtable
    141 Tremont Street, Boston, MA 02111
■Member **Elizabeth Childs, MD, MPA** . . . . . . . . . . . . . . . (617) 988-6600
    Education: Mount Holyoke; Cincinnati; Harvard
■Member **Joan Wasser Gish, JD** . . . . . . . . . . . . . . . . . . . (617) 988-6600
    Education: Brown U BA; Columbia JD, MA
■Member **Kathleen "Katie" Joyce** . . . . . . . . . . . . . . . . . . (617) 988-6600
    Education: Boston Col 2002 BA; George Washington 2005 MPPA
■Member **James A. "Jim" Peyser** . . . . . . . . . . . . . . . . . . (617) 988-6600
    Affiliation: Secretary, Executive Office of Education, Commonwealth of
    Massachusetts
    One Ashburton Place, Room 1403, Boston, MA 02108
■Member **Sharon Scott-Chandler, Esq.** . . . . . . . . . . . . . . . (617) 988-6600
■Member **Marylou Sudders** . . . . . . . . . . . . . . . . . . . . . . . . (617) 988-6600
    E-mail: marylou.sudders@state.ma.us
    Affiliation: Secretary, Executive Office of Health and Human Services,
    Commonwealth of Massachusetts
    One Ashburton Place, Room 1109, Boston, MA 02108
■Member **Eleonora Villegas-Reimers, PhD** . . . . . . . . . . . . (617) 988-6600
■Member **Mary E. Walachy** . . . . . . . . . . . . . . . . . . . . . . . . (617) 988-6600

## Department of Early Education and Care [EEC]

51 Sleeper Street, Boston, MA 02210
Tel: (617) 988-6600  Fax: (617) 988-2451
E-mail: commissioners.office@massmail.state.ma.us

**Fiscal Year:** 2015  **Budget:** $537,624,000

Commissioner **Thomas L. "Tom" Weber** . . . . . . . . . . . . . (617) 988-6612
    Education: Col Holy Cross 1997 BA; Suffolk 2009 JD
Deputy Commissioner for Administration and Finance
    **William Concannon** . . . . . . . . . . . . . . . . . . . . . . . . . . . . (617) 988-6614
    E-mail: william.concannon@massmail.state.ma.us
Deputy Commissioner for Field and Legal Operations
    **Carmel Sullivan** . . . . . . . . . . . . . . . . . . . . . . . . . . . . . . (617) 988-6631
    Education: Col Holy Cross 1988 BA; Suffolk 1995 JD
Associate Commissioner for Accounting and Contracts
    **Sandra Fortier-Hollow** . . . . . . . . . . . . . . . . . . . . . . . . . (617) 988-6649
Associate Commissioner for Finance **Sean Reynolds** . . . . . (617) 988-6611
Associate Commissioner for Grants and Programming
    **Carol Nolan** . . . . . . . . . . . . . . . . . . . . . . . . . . . . . . . . . (617) 988-7816
    E-mail: carol.nolan@massmail.state.ma.us
Associate Commissioner for Program Quality Supports
    **Gwen Alexander** . . . . . . . . . . . . . . . . . . . . . . . . . . . . . . (617) 988-7812
Assistant Commissioner for Agency Operations
    **Sean Faherty** . . . . . . . . . . . . . . . . . . . . . . . . . . . . . . . . (617) 988-6648
    Education: Merrimack 2005 BA
Assistant Commissioner for Communication and External
    Affairs **Kathleen Hart** . . . . . . . . . . . . . . . . . . . . . . . . . . (617) 988-7819
    E-mail: kathleen.hart@massmail.state.ma.us
Audit Resolution Director **Alicia Wells** . . . . . . . . . . . . . . . (617) 988-6639
Human Resources Director **Sarah Harding** . . . . . . . . . . . . (617) 988-6604

---

★ Elected Official      ■ Appointed by Governor      ● Appointed by Legislature      ▲ Appointed by Board or Commission      ◆ Appointed by State Supreme Court

# Massachusetts Board of Elementary and Secondary Education

75 Pleasant Street, Malden, MA 02148-4906
Internet: www.doe.mass.edu/boe

■Chair **Paul L. Sagan** ....................................(781) 338-3000
  Affiliation: Executive in Residence and Partner, General Catalyst Partners
  20 University Road, 4th Floor, Cambridge, MA 02138
  Education: Northwestern

■Vice Chair **James O'S. Morton** ....................(781) 338-3000
  Education: Wisconsin BA; Northeastern JD

■Member **Katherine P. Craven** ......................(781) 338-3000
  Affiliation: Chief Administrative Officer, Babson College
  231 Forest Street, Babson Park, MA 02457
  Education: Boston Latin (Boston, MA); Harvard 1994 AB

■Member **Ed Doherty** ..................................(781) 338-3000
  E-mail: edoherty@doe.mass.edu

■Member **Dr. Roland Gerhard Fryer, Jr.** ........(781) 338-3000
  Affiliation: Henry Lee Professor of Economics, Department of Economics, Faculty of Arts and Sciences, Harvard University
  Littauer Center, 1805 Cambridge Street, Cambridge, MA 02138
  Education: Texas (Arlington) 1998 BA; Penn State 2002 PhD

■Member **Margaret A. McKenna** ....................(781) 338-3000
  Education: Emmanuel (MA) BA; Southern Methodist JD

■Member **Michael Moriarty** ..........................(781) 338-3000
  Education: Catholic U 1985 BA

■Member **Dr. Pendred Noyce** ........................(781) 338-3000
  Education: Harvard 1977 BA; Stanford 1983 MD

■Member **Mary Ann Stewart** ........................(781) 338-3000
  Education: UMass (Amherst) BS

▲Student Member **Donald Willyard** ................(781) 338-3000

▲Ex-Officio Member **Mitchell D. Chester** ........(781) 338-3000
  E-mail: mchester@state.ma.us
  Education: Connecticut BS; Harvard MEd, PhD

■Ex-Officio Member **James A. "Jim" Peyser** ....(781) 338-3000
  Affiliation: Secretary, Executive Office of Education, Commonwealth of Massachusetts
  One Ashburton Place, Room 1403, Boston, MA 02108

# Department of Elementary and Secondary Education

75 Pleasant Street, Malden, MA 02148-4906
Fax: (781) 338-3392  TTY: (800) 439-2370  Internet: www.doe.mass.edu

**Fiscal Year:** 2015  **Budget:** $4,970,662,000

▲Commissioner of Elementary and Secondary Education
  **Mitchell D. Chester** ................................(781) 338-3102
  E-mail: mchester@doe.mass.edu

Deputy Commissioner **Jeff Wulfson** ..............(781) 338-3600

Senior Associate Commissioner for Accountability, Partnerships and Technical Assistance
  **Russell Johnston** ..................................(781) 338-3525
  Education: DePaul; Boston Col 2004 PhD

Senior Associate Commissioner and General Counsel
  **Rhoda Schneider** ..................................(781) 338-3400
  E-mail: rschneider@doe.mass.edu
  Education: Wellesley 1970 BA; Boston U 1974 JD

Senior Associate Commissioner for School and District Improvement **Brooke Clenchy** ....................(781) 338-3813

Associate Commissioner for Charter Schools
  **Cliff Chuang** ........................................(781) 338-6500

Associate Commissioner for Educator Policy
  **Heather Peske** ......................................(781) 338-3560

Special Education State Director **Marcia Mittnacht** ......(781) 338-3388

Nutrition, Health and Safety Administrator (Acting)
  **Robert Leshin** ......................................(781) 338-6477

Chief of Staff **Helene Bettencourt** ..............(781) 338-3120

# Board of Higher Education

One Ashburton Place, Room 1401, Boston, MA 02108-1696
Tel: (617) 994-6950  Fax: (617) 727-6397
E-mail: webmaster@bhe.mass.edu  Internet: www.mass.edu

■Chairman **Christopher "Chris" Gabrieli** ........(617) 994-6950
  Education: Harvard 1981 AB

■Member **Dr. Sheila M. Harrity** ....................(617) 994-6950
  Education: Providence BA

■Member **Dr. Nancy Hoffman** ......................(617) 994-6950
  Affiliation: Youth Transitions Vice President, Jobs For The Future
  88 Broad Street, Boston, MA 02110
  Education: UC Berkeley BA, PhD

■Member **Thomas Hopcroft** ..........................(617) 994-6950

■Member **Donald R. Irving** ............................(617) 994-6950

■Member **Robert E Johnson, PhD** ..................(617) 994-6950

■Member **Jean-Daniel "J. D." LaRock** ............(617) 994-6950
  Education: Harvard 1993 BA; Georgetown 1997 JD; Harvard 2004 EdM

■Member **Dani Monroe** ................................(617) 994-6950
  Education: Cal State (Dominguez); Pepperdine

■Member **Dr. Fernando M. Reimers** ..............(617) 994-6950
  Education: U Central Venezuela; Harvard MEd, EdD

■Member **Henry M. Thomas III** ....................(617) 994-6950
  Affiliation: President and Chief Executive Officer, Urban League of Springfield, Inc.
  765 State Street, Springfield, MA 01109
  Education: American International AB, MS; Western New England JD

■Member **Paul F. Toner** ..............................(617) 994-6950
  Education: Boston U BA; UMass (Boston) MEd; Suffolk JD

■Student Member **Owen Wiggins** ..................(617) 994-6950

■Ex-Officio Member **James A. "Jim" Peyser** ....(617) 994-6950
  Affiliation: Secretary, Executive Office of Education, Commonwealth of Massachusetts
  One Ashburton Place, Room 1403, Boston, MA 02108

# Massachusetts Department of Higher Education [DHE]

One Ashburton Place, Room 1401, Boston, MA 02108
Tel: (617) 994-6950

**Fiscal Year:** 2015  **Budget:** $133,104,000

Commissioner **Dr. Carlos E. Santiago** ..........(617) 994-6901
  Education: Miami 1973 BA; Puerto Rico 1975 MA; Cornell 1979 MA, 1982 PhD

Executive Assistant to the Commissioner **Katty Mojica** ..(617) 994-6901

Administrative Assistant to the Commissioner
  **Bonnie Shapiro** ....................................(617) 994-6902

Senior Advisor to the Commissioner for P16 Access and Alignment Policy **Susan Lane** ................(617) 994-6930

Senior Deputy Commissioner for Access and Student Financial Assistance **Clantha McCurdy, PhD** ....(617) 391-6098

Deputy Commissioner of Administration and Finance
  **Sean Nelson** ........................................(617) 994-6918
  E-mail: snelson@bhe.mass.edu

Deputy Commissioner for Academic Affairs and Student Success **Patricia Marshall** ....................(617) 994-6939

Senior Associate Commissioner for Research and Planning **Jonathan Keller** ........................(617) 994-6941

Senior Associate Commissioner for Student Financial Assistance **Robert Brun** ............................(617) 391-6099

Associate Commissioner for Academic Affairs and Student Success **Winifred M. Hagan** ............(617) 994-6912
  E-mail: whagan@bhe.mass.edu

Associate Commissioner for Economic and Workforce Development **David Cedrone** ..................(617) 994-6904

Associate Commissioner for External Affairs **Katy Abel** ..(617) 994-6932

Assistant Commissioner for Access and Success Strategies **Cynthia K. Orellana** ................(617) 994-6908

Senior Director of Visual and Digital Communications
  **Sarah Mealey** ......................................(617) 994-6926
  E-mail: smealey@bhe.mass.edu

Director of Employee and Labor Relations
  **Michael Murray** ....................................(617) 994-6917

Director of Gaining Early Awareness and Readiness for Undergraduate Programs (GEAR UP) **Robert Dais** ..(617) 391-6075

Director of Learning Outcomes Assessment
  **Bonnie Orcutt** ......................................(617) 994-6915

Director for Veterans Education **George O'Connor** ......(617) 994-6948

Assistant Director for Regulatory and Veterans Affairs
  **Kristen Stone** ......................................(617) 994-6959

Veterans Education Program Specialist **Caitlyn Dean** ....(617) 994-6936

---

★ Elected Official   ■ Appointed by Governor   ● Appointed by Legislature   ▲ Appointed by Board or Commission   ◆ Appointed by State Supreme Court

Associate Director for Student Financial Assistance
**Kathleen Flanagan** ................................. (617) 391-6076
Associate Director of Workforce Development
**Christine Williams** ............................... (617) 994-6907
Academic Research Specialist **Franny Wood** ............ (617) 994-6920
Employee Relations Associate **(Vacant)** ............... (617) 994-6965
General Counsel **Constantia "Dena" Papanikolaou** ..... (617) 994-6947

## Executive Office of Elder Affairs

One Ashburton Place, 5th Floor, Suite 517, Boston, MA 02108
Tel: (617) 727-7750  Tel: (800) 243-4636  Fax: (617) 727-9368
TTY: (800) 872-0166  Internet: www.mass.gov/elders

■Secretary **Alice F. Bonner** ........................... (617) 222-7549
  E-mail: alice.bonner@state.ma.us
  Education: Cornell 1979 BS; UMass (Worcester) 2008 PhD
  Executive Assistant **Denise Bradley** ................. (617) 222-7549
General Counsel **Mathew Casey** ...................... (617) 222-7562
Assistant General Counsel **Siobhan Coyle** ............. (617) 222-7562
Director of Communications **Martha Waldron** .......... (617) 222-7458
  E-mail: martha.waldron@state.ma.us

## Executive Office of Energy and Environmental Affairs [EEA]

100 Cambridge Street, 9th Floor, Boston, MA 02114
Tel: (617) 626-1000  Fax: (617) 626-1181  Internet: www.mass.gov/eea

■Secretary **Matthew A. Beaton** ...................... (617) 626-1101
  E-mail: matthew.beaton@state.ma.us
Chief of Staff **Alexandra "Alex" Cahill** .............. (617) 626-1101
Undersecretary for Energy and Environmental Affairs
  **Ned Bartlett** ..................................... (617) 626-1000
  Assistant Secretary for Energy **(Vacant)** ............ (617) 626-1000
  Assistant Secretary for Environment **Dan Sieger** ...... (617) 626-1000
Communications Director **Peter Lorenz** ............... (617) 626-1809
  E-mail: peter.lorenz@state.ma.us
Chief Operating Officer **Michael Valanzola** ........... (617) 626-1165
General Counsel **Kate McKeever** ..................... (617) 626-4983
Conservation Services Division Director **Bob O'Connor** ... (617) 626-1170
Environmental Police Director **Col. James McGinn** ...... (617) 626-1650
  Education: Massachusetts Law JD
Human Resources Director **Cathy Grant** .............. (617) 626-1161

## Department of Agricultural Resources [DAR]

251 Causeway Street, Suite 500, Boston, MA 02114
Tel: (617) 626-1720  Fax: (617) 626-1850  Internet: www.mass.gov/agr

**Fiscal Year:** 2015  **Budget:** $20,596,000

■Commissioner **John I. Lebeaux** ..................... (617) 626-1701
  E-mail: john.lebeaux@state.ma.us
  Executive Assistant **Sheila Theodore** ............... (617) 626-1733
Assistant Commissioner **Jason Wentworth** ........... (617) 626-1715
Chief of Staff **Alisha Bouchard** ..................... (617) 626-1703
General Counsel **Tara Zadeh** ....................... (617) 626-1705
Human Resources Director **Mary Beth Burnand** ........ (617) 626-1710
Budget Director **Michael Rock** ..................... (617) 626-1716

## Department of Conservation and Recreation [DCR]

251 Causeway Street, Suites 600, Boston, MA 02114-2104
Tel: (617) 626-1250  Fax: (617) 626-1351
E-mail: mass.parks@state.ma.us  Internet: www.mass.gov/dcr

**Fiscal Year:** 2015  **Budget:** $79,872,000

■Commissioner **Leo Roy** ............................ (617) 626-4990
                                              Fax: (617) 626-4999
  Special Assistant to the Commissioner
    **Lauren Monahan** ............................... (617) 626-1309
Deputy Commissioner for Operations **Matthew Sisk** ..... (617) 626-4992
Chief of Staff **Stephen Doody** ...................... (617) 626-4998
Engineering Director **Norman J. Orrall** .............. (617) 626-1250

Finance and Administration Director (Acting)
  **Michael J. Abrahams** .............................. (617) 626-1456
  E-mail: michael.abrahams@state.ma.us
Governmental Affairs Director (Acting) **Sean Fierce** ...... (617) 626-1250
Human Resources Director **(Vacant)** .................. (617) 626-1250
Partnerships Director **(Vacant)** ..................... (617) 626-1250
General Counsel **Douglas Rice** ...................... (617) 626-1250
Planning and Resources Bureau Chief
  **Norman J. Orrall** .......................... (617) 626-1250 ext. 1340

### Division of State Parks and Recreation
State Parks Director **Priscilla E. Geigis** .............. (617) 626-4986
  E-mail: priscilla.geigis@state.ma.us
Deputy Director **Samantha Overton** .................. (617) 626-1250
  E-mail: samantha.overton@state.ma.us

### Division of Water Supply Protection
Director **Jonathan Yeo** ............................. (617) 626-1250

## Department of Energy Resources [DOER]

100 Cambridge Street, 10th Floor, Suite 1020, Boston, MA 02114
Tel: (617) 626-7300  Tel: (800) 351-0077 (Consumer Hotline)
Fax: (617) 727-0030  E-mail: doer.energy@state.ma.us

**Fiscal Year:** 2015  **Budget:** $3,856,000

Commissioner **Judith F. Judson** ..................... (617) 626-7351
  Education: Kettering Medical BSME; Harvard MBA
  Executive Assistant **Sharon Harris** ................. (617) 626-7332
Deputy Commissioner and Chief of Staff
  **Daniel Burgess** .................................. (617) 626-7385
  Education: Maine; Northeastern MPA
Deputy Commissioner for Energy Policy, Planning and
  Analysis **Joanne Morin** ........................... (617) 626-7319
  Education: New Hampshire 1978 BS; SUNY (Binghamton) 1981 MS
Energy Efficiency Division Director **Arah Schuur** ........ (617) 626-7313
Energy Markets Division Director **Farhad Aminpour** ..... (617) 626-7359
Green Communities Division Director **Daniel Knapik** ..... (617) 626-7358
Marketing and Stakeholder Engagement Director
  **(Vacant)** ...................................... (617) 626-7361
Renewable Energy Division Director **Michael Judge** ..... (617) 626-7368
Chief Financial Officer **Stephen A. White** ............. (617) 626-7389
Communication Director **Kevin O'Shea** ............... (617) 626-7362
  E-mail: kevin.o'shea@state.ma.us
Legal Counsel **Michael Altieri** ...................... (617) 626-1398

## Department of Environmental Protection [DEP]

One Winter Street, 2nd Floor, Boston, MA 02108
Tel: (617) 292-5500  Fax: (617) 574-6880

**Fiscal Year:** 2015-2016  **Budget:** $51,600,000

■Commissioner **Martin Suuberg** ..................... (617) 292-5856
  E-mail: martin.suuberg@state.ma.us
  Education: Brown U; Georgetown JD
Operations and Environmental Compliance Deputy
  Commissioner **Gary Moran** ........................ (617) 292-5775
Policy and Planning Deputy Commissioner
  **Bethany Card** ................................... (617) 292-5748
Administrative Services Assistant Commissioner
  **John Viola** ..................................... (617) 292-5581
  E-mail: john.viola@state.ma.us
General Counsel **Benjamin Ericson** ................... (617) 556-1121
Chief Financial Officer **Kristin Lacroix** ............... (617) 348-4062
Support Services Director **Chris Voss** ................ (617) 292-5524
                                              Fax: (617) 556-1049
Learning and Development Unit Director **Aprel McCabe** .. (617) 556-1171

## Department of Fish and Game [DFG]

251 Causeway Street, Suite 400, Boston, MA 02114-2152
Tel: (617) 626-1500  Fax: (617) 626-1505

**Fiscal Year:** 2015  **Budget:** $25,591,000

■Commissioner **George N. Peterson, Jr.** .............. (617) 626-1550
  E-mail: george.peterson@state.ma.us
Deputy Commissioner **Mary-Lee King** ................ (617) 626-1553

*(continued on next page)*

---

★ Elected Official    ■ Appointed by Governor    ● Appointed by Legislature    ▲ Appointed by Board or Commission    ◆ Appointed by State Supreme Court

**Department of Fish and Game** *continued*

General Counsel **Richard Lehan** . . . . . . . . . . . . . . . . . . . . . (617) 626-1552
  E-mail: richard.lehan@state.ma.us
Chief of Staff **Bob Greco** . . . . . . . . . . . . . . . . . . . . . . . . . . . . (617) 626-1556
Ecological Restoration Division Director **Tim Purinton** . . . (617) 626-1542
Fish and Wildlife Division Director **Jack Buckley** . . . . . . . . (617) 626-1570
Fishing and Boating Access Director **John P. Sheppard** . . . (617) 727-1843
Marine Fisheries Division Director **David E. Pierce** . . . . . . . (617) 626-1530
Chief Financial Officer **Brian Kelter** . . . . . . . . . . . . . . . . . . (617) 626-1555

## Department of Public Utilities [DPU]

One South Station, Boston, MA 02110
Tel: (617) 305-3500  Tel: (877) 886-5066 (Consumer Hotline)
Tel: (617) 737-2836 (Consumer Information)  Fax: (617) 345-9101
TTY: (800) 323-3298  Internet: www.mass.gov/dpu

**Fiscal Year:** 2015  **Budget:** $11,293,000

■Chairman **Angela O'Connor** . . . . . . . . . . . . . . . . . . . . . . . (617) 305-3653
  Education: UMass (Boston)
■Commissioner **Robert "Bob" Hayden** . . . . . . . . . . . . . . . (617) 305-3736
■Commissioner **Jolette A. Westbrook** . . . . . . . . . . . . . . . . (617) 305-3738
  E-mail: jolette.westbrook@state.ma.us
  Education: Russell Sage BS; Northeastern JD

## Massachusetts Environmental Policy Act (MEPA) Office

100 Cambridge Street, Suite 900, Boston, MA 02114
Tel: (617) 626-1031  Fax: (617) 626-1181

Director **Deirdre Buckley** . . . . . . . . . . . . . . . . . . . . . . . . . . (617) 626-1044
Assistant Director **(Vacant)** . . . . . . . . . . . . . . . . . . . . . . . . (617) 626-1130

## Office of Coastal Zone Management [CZM]

251 Causeway Street, Boston, MA 02114-2104
Tel: (617) 626-1200  Fax: (617) 626-1240  E-mail: czm@state.ma.us

Director **Bruce K. Carlisle** . . . . . . . . . . . . . . . . . . . . . . . . . (617) 626-1205

## Office of Technical Assistance and Technology

100 Cambridge Street, Suite 900, Boston, MA 02114
Tel: (617) 626-1060  Fax: (617) 626-1095  E-mail: maota@state.ma.us

Director **Rich Bizzozero** . . . . . . . . . . . . . . . . . . . . . . . . . . . (617) 626-1080
  Education: Vermont 1997 BA; UMass (Amherst)
Senior Engineer **Jim Cain** . . . . . . . . . . . . . . . . . . . . . . . . . . (617) 626-1081

## Executive Office of Health and Human Services [EOHHS]

One Ashburton Place, Room 1109, Boston, MA 02108
150 Mount Vernon Street, First Floor, Dorchester, MA 02125 (Vital Records)
Tel: (617) 573-1600  Tel: (617) 740-2600 (Vital Records)
Fax: (617) 573-1890  Internet: www.mass.gov/dph/rvrs (Vital Records)

■Secretary **Marylou Sudders** . . . . . . . . . . . . . . . . . . . . . . . (617) 573-1600
  E-mail: marylou.sudders@state.ma.us
  Chief of Staff **Leslie Darcy** . . . . . . . . . . . . . . . . . . . . . . (617) 573-1600
    E-mail: leslie.darcy@state.ma.us
    Education: Illinois 2003 BS; Boston U 2006 JD
Undersecretary of Health **Alice E. Moore** . . . . . . . . . . . . . (617) 573-1600
Undersecretary of Human Services **Patricia Mackin** . . . . (617) 573-1600
Assistant Secretary for Administration and Finance
  **Alda Rego** . . . . . . . . . . . . . . . . . . . . . . . . . . . . . . . . . . . . (617) 573-1600
  E-mail: alda.rego@state.ma.us
  Education: UMass (Dartmouth) BA
  Deputy Assistant Secretary for Children, Youth and
    Families **Robyn Kennedy** . . . . . . . . . . . . . . . . . . . . . . (617) 573-1600
    E-mail: robyn.kennedy@state.ma.us
Assistant Secretary for Communications and External
  Affairs **Sharon Torgerson** . . . . . . . . . . . . . . . . . . . . . . . (617) 573-1834
  E-mail: sharon.torgerson@state.ma.us
Director of Communications **Michelle Hillman** . . . . . . . . . (617) 573-1834
  E-mail: michelle.hillman@state.ma.us
  Education: Amherst BA

Assistant Secretary for Disability Policy and Programs
  **(Vacant)** . . . . . . . . . . . . . . . . . . . . . . . . . . . . . . . . . . . . . . . (617) 573-1600
Chief Financial Officer **Nick Dantzer** . . . . . . . . . . . . . . . . (617) 573-1600
  Education: Wayne State U; Northeastern MPA
  Budget Director **Monica McEnrue** . . . . . . . . . . . . . . . . (617) 573-1600
    Education: Vassar; Northeastern 2012 JD
General Counsel **Jesse M. Caplan** . . . . . . . . . . . . . . . . . . (617) 573-1600

## Office of the Child Advocate [OCA]

Tel: (617) 979-8360  Fax: (617) 979-8379
E-mail: childadvocate@state.ma.us

Child Advocate **Maria Z. Mossaides** . . . . . . . . . . . . . . . . (617) 979-8360
  E-mail: maria.mossaides@state.ma.us
Deputy Director and Counsel **(Vacant)** . . . . . . . . . . . . . . . (617) 979-8360

## Office of Medicaid [MassHealth]

One Ashburton Place, 11th Floor, Boston, MA 02108
Tel: (617) 573-1770  Fax: (617) 573-1894

■Assistant Secretary and Director of MassHealth
  **Daniel Tsai** . . . . . . . . . . . . . . . . . . . . . . . . . . . . . . . . . . . (617) 573-1770
  E-mail: daniel.tsai@state.ma.us
  Education: Harvard AB
Deputy Medicaid Director **Robin Callahan** . . . . . . . . . . . (617) 573-1745
                        Fax: (617) 573-1891

## Office of Refugees and Immigrants [ORI]

600 Washington Street, 4th Floor, Boston, MA 02111
Tel: (617) 727-7888  Fax: (617) 727-1822

■Executive Director **Mary Truong** . . . . . . . . . . . . . . . . . . . (617) 727-7888
  E-mail: mary.truong@state.ma.us
General Counsel **Vivie Hengst** . . . . . . . . . . . . . . . (617) 727-7888 ext. 306
Community Building Unit Director **Diane M. Randolph** . . (617) 727-7888
Family Independence Unit Director
  **Jennifer Schamel** . . . . . . . . . . . . . . . . . . . . . . (617) 727-7888 ext. 327
Chief Financial Officer **Didier Bertola** . . . . . . . . . . . . . . . (617) 727-7888

## Department of Children and Families [DCF]

600 Washington Street, Boston, MA 02111
Tel: (617) 748-2000  Fax: (617) 261-7435

**Fiscal Year:** 2015  **Budget:** $827,000,000

■Commissioner **Linda Spears** . . . . . . . . . . . . . . . . . . . . . . (617) 748-2325
  E-mail: linda.spears@state.ma.us
  Chief of Staff **Ryan Fitzgerald** . . . . . . . . . . . . . . . . . . . (617) 748-2260
Deputy Commissioner for Clinical Services and Program
  Operations **Danielle Ferrier** . . . . . . . . . . . . . . . . . . . . . (617) 748-2155
Deputy Commissioner for Field Operations (Acting)
  **Lian Hogan** . . . . . . . . . . . . . . . . . . . . . . . . . . . . . . . . . . (617) 748-2348
Assistant Commissioner for Continuous Quality
  Improvement **Ruben Ferreira** . . . . . . . . . . . . . . . . . . . (617) 748-2165
Assistant Commissioner for Policy and Practice
  Innovations **Amy Kershaw** . . . . . . . . . . . . . . . . . . . . . . (617) 748-2046
  E-mail: amy.kershaw@state.ma.us
General Counsel **Andrew Rome** . . . . . . . . . . . . . . . . . . . . (617) 748-2015
Children, Youth and Families and Human Resources
  Director **Rhett Cavicchi** . . . . . . . . . . . . . . . . . . . . . . . . (617) 348-5000
Legislative Director **Leah Robins** . . . . . . . . . . . . . . . . . . (617) 748-2000
  E-mail: leah.robins@state.ma.us
Ombudsman Office Director **Susan Cummings** . . . . . . . . (617) 748-2084
Public Affairs Director **Andrea Grossman** . . . . . . . . . . . . (617) 748-2252
  E-mail: andrea.grossman@state.ma.us
Strategic Planning Director **Andrea Bartolo** . . . . . . . . . . (617) 748-2000
Chief Financial Officer **David O'Callaghan** . . . . . . . . . . . (617) 748-2068
Chief Information Officer **Robert Brennan** . . . . . . . . . . . (617) 748-2000
  E-mail: robert.d.brennan@state.ma.us
Medical Director **Linda Sagor** . . . . . . . . . . . . . . . . . . . . . . (617) 573-1600

---

★ Elected Official   ■ Appointed by Governor   ● Appointed by Legislature   ▲ Appointed by Board or Commission   ◆ Appointed by State Supreme Court

# Department of Developmental Services

500 Harrison Avenue, Boston, MA 02118
Tel: (617) 727-5608  Fax: (617) 624-7575  E-mail: info@dmr.state.ma.us

**Fiscal Year:** 2015  **Budget:** $1,681,021,000

■Commissioner **Elin M. Howe** . . . . . . . . . . . . . . . . . . . .(617) 624-7723
  E-mail: elin.howe@state.ma.us         Fax: (617) 624-7577
  Education: SUNY (Albany) BA, MPA
  Executive Assistant **Bernadette Davis** . . . . . . . . . . . . . . .(617) 624-7723
                                  Fax: (617) 624-7577

Deputy Commissioner **Jane F. Ryder** . . . . . . . . . . . . . . . .(617) 624-7713
                                  Fax: (617) 624-7577

Deputy Assistant Commissioner **Victor Hernandez** . . . . . . .(617) 624-7577
                                  Fax: (617) 624-7572

Management and Finance Deputy Assistant
  Commissioner **Dana J. Roszkiewicz** . . . . . . . . . . . . . . . .(617) 624-7856
  Education: Boston U 1977 BA, 1980 JD

Field Operations Assistant Commissioner **Timothy Cahill** . . . . . . . . (617)
624-7754
                                  Fax: (617) 624-7572

Policy, Planning and Children's Services Assistant
  Commissioner **Janet L. George** . . . . . . . . . . . . . . . . . .(617) 624-7766
  E-mail: janet.george@state.ma.us        Fax: (617) 624-7578
  Education: Connecticut Col 1970 BA; Hartford 1973 MA;
  Boston U 1983 EdD

Quality Management Assistant Commissioner
  **Gail Grossman** . . . . . . . . . . . . . . . . . . . . . . . . . . . .(617) 624-7779
  Education: Brooklyn 1970 BA;       Fax: (617) 624-7578
  Case Western 1972 MSS

General Counsel **Marianne Meacham** . . . . . . . . . . . . . . . .(617) 624-7701
  Education: UMass (Amherst) 1984 BA;    Fax: (617) 624-7573
  Northeastern 1987 JD

Deputy General Counsel, Administration
  **Kathleen Gallagher** . . . . . . . . . . . . . . . . . . . . . . . .(617) 624-7719
  Education: Salem State Col 1983 BS;    Fax: (617) 624-7573
  New England 1989 JD

Deputy General Counsel, Field Operations
  **Jacquelyn Berman** . . . . . . . . . . . . . . . . . . . . . . . . .(617) 624-7708
  Education: UMass (Amherst) 1976 BA;    Fax: (617) 624-7573
  Northeastern 1993 JD

Chief Financial Officer **Thomas Simard** . . . . . . . . . . . . . .(617) 624-7747
  Education: West Point 1987 BS; Southern New Hampshire 1994 MBA;
  Harvard 2012 MPA

Accounting Director **E. Christopher Pacelli** . . . . . . . . . . . .(617) 624-7845
  Education: Southern Connecticut State U 1977 BS;
  Framingham State 1984 MA

Budget Director **Kimberly Egan** . . . . . . . . . . . . . . . . . . .(617) 624-7747

Contracts Director **Toni Gustus** . . . . . . . . . . . . . . . . . . .(617) 624-7856
  E-mail: toni.gustus@state.ma.us       Fax: (617) 624-7575

Engineering and Core Services Director **James Millins** . . . (617) 624-7750
                                  Fax: (617) 624-7576

Diversity, Equal Opportunity and Civil Rights Office
  Director **Lorraine Woodson** . . . . . . . . . . . . . . . . . . . .(617) 624-7530
                                  Fax: (617) 624-7577

Human Rights Office Director **Richard Santucci** . . . . . . . . .(617) 624-7738
  E-mail: rich.santucci@state.ma.us      Fax: (617) 624-7571

Office Manager **Karen E. Glass** . . . . . . . . . . . . . . . . . . .(617) 624-7800
  Education: Northeastern 1974 BS

# Department of Mental Health [DMH]

25 Staniford Street, Boston, MA 02114
Tel: (617) 626-8000

**Fiscal Year:** 2015  **Budget:** $1,723,029,000

■Commissioner **Joan Mikula** . . . . . . . . . . . . . . . . . . . . .(617) 626-8123
  E-mail: joan.mikula@state.ma.us
  Assistant to the Commissioner **Marianne Callinan** . . . . . .(617) 626-8123

Child/Adolescent Services Deputy Commissioner
  **(Vacant)** . . . . . . . . . . . . . . . . . . . . . . . . . . . . . . . .(617) 626-8086

Clinical and Professional Services Deputy Commissioner
  **Kathy Sanders, MD** . . . . . . . . . . . . . . . . . . . . . . . . .(617) 626-8059

Management and Budget Deputy Commissioner
  **Stephen "Steve" Barnard** . . . . . . . . . . . . . . . . . . . . .(617) 626-8305
  E-mail: stephen.barnard@state.ma.us

Mental Health Services Deputy Commissioner
  **Brooke Doyle** . . . . . . . . . . . . . . . . . . . . . . . . . . . . .(617) 626-8068

Administration and Finance Assistant Commissioner
  (Acting) **Karen Brady** . . . . . . . . . . . . . . . . . . . . . . .(617) 626-8042
  E-mail: karen.brady@state.ma.us

Forensic Mental Health Assistant Commissioner **(Vacant)** . .(617) 626-8071

General Counsel **Lester Blumberg** . . . . . . . . . . . . . . . . . .(617) 626-8233

# Department of Public Health [DPH]

250 Washington Street, 6th Floor, Boston, MA 02108-4619
Tel: (617) 624-6000  Fax: (617) 624-5206

**Fiscal Year:** 2015  **Budget:** $516,892,000

■Commissioner **Dr. Monica Bharel** . . . . . . . . . . . . . . . . . .(617) 624-5204
  E-mail: monica.bharel@state.ma.us
  Education: Harvard 2012 MSPH

Associate Commissioner **Lindsey Tucker** . . . . . . . . . . . . . .(617) 624-5200
  Education: Yale BA; Harvard MSc

Chief of Staff **Natalie Nguyen** . . . . . . . . . . . . . . . . . . . .(617) 624-5200

Chief Operating Officer **Eileen M. Sullivan** . . . . . . . . . . . .(617) 624-5257
  Education: Western Connecticut St 1984 BA; Shippensburg 1986 MS;
  UMass (Boston) 2005 MEd

General Counsel **Margret R. Cooke** . . . . . . . . . . . . . . . . .(617) 624-5220
  E-mail: margret.cooke@state.ma.us

Community Health and Prevention Bureau Director
  **Carlene Pavlos** . . . . . . . . . . . . . . . . . . . . . . . . . . . .(617) 624-6090

Emergency Preparedness Bureau Director **Mary E. Clark** . . .(617) 624-6088

Environmental Health Bureau Director (Interim)
  **Jan Sullivan** . . . . . . . . . . . . . . . . . . . . . . . . . . . . . .(617) 624-5757

Family Health and Nutrition Bureau Director
  **Ron Benham** . . . . . . . . . . . . . . . . . . . . . . . . . . . . . .(617) 624-6060

Health Care Safety and Quality Bureau Director (Acting)
  **Eric Sheehan** . . . . . . . . . . . . . . . . . . . . . . . . . . . . .(617) 753-8160

State Laboratory Sciences Director
  **Dr. Michael A. Pentella** . . . . . . . . . . . . . . . . . . . . . .(617) 983-6201
  305 South Street, Jamaica Plain, MA 02130   Fax: (617) 983-6210

Women, Infants and Children (WIC) Director
  **Judy Hause** . . . . . . . . . . . . . . . . . . . . . . . . . . . . . . .(617) 624-6100
  E-mail: judy.hause@state.ma.us

# Department of Transitional Assistance [DTA]

600 Washington Street, Boston, MA 02111
Tel: (617) 348-8400  Fax: (617) 348-8575  Internet: www.mass.gov/dta

**Fiscal Year:** 2015  **Budget:** $694,195,000

Commissioner **Jeff McCue** . . . . . . . . . . . . . . . . . . . . . . .(617) 348-8407
  Education: Merrimack BA; Suffolk MPA

Chief Operating Officer/Deputy Commissioner
  **Thomas G. Massimo** . . . . . . . . . . . . . . . . . . . . . . . .(617) 348-8436

Assistant Commissioner for Administration and Finance
  **Mary M. Sheehan** . . . . . . . . . . . . . . . . . . . . . . . . . .(617) 348-5974
  E-mail: mary.m.sheehan@state.ma.us

Assistant Commissioner for Change Management
  **Anne O'Sullivan** . . . . . . . . . . . . . . . . . . . . . . . . . . .(617) 348-5640

Assistant Commissioner for Management Information
  Systems **(Vacant)** . . . . . . . . . . . . . . . . . . . . . . . . . .(617) 348-5600

Assistant Commissioner for Program Integrity **(Vacant)** . . .(617) 348-5059

General Counsel **Nakisha Skinner** . . . . . . . . . . . . . . . . . .(617) 348-8472

Hearings Director **Colin Connor** . . . . . . . . . . . . . . . . . . .(617) 348-5064

Hearings Assistant Director **(Vacant)** . . . . . . . . . . . . . . . .(617) 348-5348

# Department of Veterans' Services [DVS]

600 Washington Street, 5th Floor, Boston, MA 02111
Tel: (617) 210-5480  Fax: (617) 210-5755
Internet: www.mass.gov/veterans

**Fiscal Year:** 2015  **Budget:** $87,961,000

■Secretary **Francisco Urena** . . . . . . . . . . . . . . . . . . . . . .(617) 210-5951
    E-mail: francisco.urena@state.ma.us

Chief of Staff **Mike Rigas** . . . . . . . . . . . . . . . . . . . . . . .(617) 210-5779

Chief Financial Officer **(Vacant)** . . . . . . . . . . . . . . . . . . .(617) 210-5905

General Counsel **Eric T. Donovan** . . . . . . . . . . . . . . . . . .(617) 210-5785

State Veterans' Cemeteries Director **Richard Bastien** . . . . .(413) 374-6334

Chelsea Soldiers Home Superintendent **Cheryl L. Poppe** . .(617) 884-5660
  91 Crest Avenue, Chelsea, MA 02150     Fax: (617) 884-1162

*(continued on next page)*

---

★ Elected Official   ■ Appointed by Governor   ● Appointed by Legislature   ▲ Appointed by Board or Commission   ◆ Appointed by State Supreme Court

**EXECUTIVE BRANCH**

**Department of Veterans' Services** *continued*

Holyoke Soldiers' Home Superintendent **Bennett Walsh** . . (413) 552-4700
110 Cherry Street, Holyoke, MA 01040
Communication Director **Joseph "Joe" Truschelli** . . . . . . . (617) 210-5761
E-mail: joseph.truschelli@state.ma.us

## Department of Youth Services [DYS]

600 Washington Street, Boston, MA 02111
Tel: (617) 727-7575  Fax: (617) 727-0696

**Fiscal Year:** 2015  **Budget:** $168,270,000

Commissioner **Peter J. Forbes** . . . . . . . . . . . . . . . . . . . . (617) 960-3304
E-mail: peter.j.forbes@state.ma.us
Deputy Commissioner of Administration and Finance
**Margaret Chow-Menzer** . . . . . . . . . . . . . . . . . . . . . (617) 960-3283
E-mail: margaret.chow-menzer@state.ma.us
Education: Rensselaer Poly BS; Albany Law JD
Deputy Commissioner for Operations and Support
Services **Ruth Rovezzi** . . . . . . . . . . . . . . . . . . . . . . . (617) 960-3301
Assistant Commissioner of Program Services
**Robert M. Turillo** . . . . . . . . . . . . . . . . . . . . . . . . . . . (617) 960-3268
E-mail: robert.m.turillo@state.ma.us
Chief Financial Officer **Gerry Wright** . . . . . . . . . . . . . . . (617) 960-3258
General Counsel **Cecely A. Reardon** . . . . . . . . . . . . . . . (617) 960-3330
E-mail: cecely.a.reardon@state.ma.us

## Massachusetts Rehabilitation Commission [MRC]

600 Washington Street, 2nd Floor, Boston, MA 02111
Tel: (617) 204-3600  Fax: (617) 727-1354  Internet: www.state.ma.us/mrc

**Fiscal Year:** 2015  **Budget:** $45,962,000

Commissioner **Adelaide "Nicky" Osborne** . . . . . . . . . . (617) 204-3600
Education: Nebraska BS; Boston Col MSW
Deputy Commissioner **Kasper M. Goshgarian** . . . . . . . . (617) 204-3600
Assistant Commissioner, Community Living Services
**Josh Mendelsohn** . . . . . . . . . . . . . . . . . . . . . . . . . . (617) 204-3600
Assistant Commissioner, Disability Determination
Services **Patricia Roda** . . . . . . . . . . . . . . . . . . . . . . . (617) 204-3600
Assistant Commissioner, Vocational Rehabilitation
Services **Joan Phillips** . . . . . . . . . . . . . . . . . . . . . . . (617) 204-3600
General Counsel **Richard Arcangeli** . . . . . . . . . . . . . . . (617) 727-1354
Chief Financial Officer (Interim) **Carol Foltz** . . . . . . . . . . (617) 204-3734
Chief Information Officer **(Vacant)** . . . . . . . . . . . . . . . . (617) 204-3600
Communications Director **Daniela Trammell** . . . . . . . . . . (617) 204-3824
E-mail: daniela.trammell@state.ma.us
Ombudsman **Mark Cowell** . . . . . . . . . . . . . . . . . . . . . . (617) 204-3670
Training Director **Ken Nicosia** . . . . . . . . . . . . . . . . . . . (617) 204-3600

## Executive Office of Housing and Economic Development [EOHED]

One Ashburton Place, Suite 2101, Boston, MA 02108-1518
Tel: (617) 788-3610

■Secretary **Jay Ash** . . . . . . . . . . . . . . . . . . . . . . . . . . . (617) 788-3610
E-mail: jay.ash@state.ma.us
Deputy Secretary **Carolyn Kirk** . . . . . . . . . . . . . . . . . . . (617) 788-3610
Chief of Staff **Aimee Ward** . . . . . . . . . . . . . . . . . . . . . (617) 788-3610
E-mail: aimee.ward@state.ma.us
General Counsel **Ricks P. Frazier** . . . . . . . . . . . . . . . . . (617) 788-3610
Assistant Secretary for Business Growth **Mike Kennealy** . . (617) 788-3610
Assistant Secretary of Innovation, Technology, and
Entrepreneurship **Katie Stebbins** . . . . . . . . . . . . . . . (617) 788-3610
Deputy Director of Policy and Communications
**Samantha Kaufman** . . . . . . . . . . . . . . . . . . . . . . . . . (617) 788-3610
E-mail: samantha.kaufman@state.ma.us

## Department of Housing and Community Development

100 Cambridge Street, Suite 300, Boston, MA 02114
Tel: (617) 573-1100  Fax: (617) 573-1120  Internet: www.mass.gov/dhcd

**Fiscal Year:** 2015  **Budget:** $520,520,000

■Undersecretary **Chrystal Kornegay** . . . . . . . . . . . . . . . . (617) 573-1100
E-mail: chrystal.kornegay@state.ma.us
Education: MIT 1997
Administrative Assistant **Jo-Ann Moriarty** . . . . . . . . . . (617) 573-1107
Policy Director **Charley Francis** . . . . . . . . . . . . . . . . . . (617) 573-1103
E-mail: charley.francis@state.ma.us
Chief Financial Officer **Jennifer Maddox** . . . . . . . . . . . . (617) 573-1252
Chief of Staff **(Vacant)** . . . . . . . . . . . . . . . . . . . . . . . (617) 573-1100
Chief Counsel **Roberta Rubin** . . . . . . . . . . . . . . . . . . . (617) 573-1501
E-mail: roberta.rubin@state.ma.us
Communications Specialist **(Vacant)** . . . . . . . . . . . . . . . (617) 573-1102

### Division of Community Services

Tel: (617) 573-1400  Fax: (617) 573-1460

Associate Director **Louis Martin** . . . . . . . . . . . . . . . . . . (617) 573-1401

### Division of Housing Development

Tel: (617) 573-1300  Fax: (617) 573-1330

Associate Director **Catherine Racer** . . . . . . . . . . . . . . . (617) 573-1322

### Division of Housing Stabilization

Tel: (617) 573-1370  Fax: (617) 573-1340

Associate Director **Ita Mullarkey** . . . . . . . . . . . . . . . . . (617) 573-1216

### Division of Public Housing and Rental Assistance

Tel: (617) 573-1150  Fax: (617) 573-1340

Associate Director **Sarah Glassman** . . . . . . . . . . . . . . . (617) 573-1215
Housing Development and Construction Bureau Director
**Amy Stitely** . . . . . . . . . . . . . . . . . . . . . . . . . . . . . . (617) 573-1156
Housing Management Bureau Director **Laura Taylor** . . . . . (617) 573-1289
Policy and Program Development Director
**Cate Mingoya** . . . . . . . . . . . . . . . . . . . . . . . . . . . . (617) 573-1190
E-mail: cate.mingoya@state.ma.us

## Office of Consumer Affairs and Business Regulation

10 Park Plaza, Suite 5170, Boston, MA 02116
Tel: (617) 973-8700  Tel: (617) 973-8787 (Consumer Information Line)
Tel: (888) 283-3757 (Consumer Information Line [In State])
TTY: (617) 973-8790  Fax: (617) 973-8799
E-mail: consumer@state.ma.us

■Undersecretary **John C. Chapman** . . . . . . . . . . . . . . . . (617) 973-8702
E-mail: john.chapman@state.ma.us
Education: Kenyon 1986 BA; Suffolk 1992 JD
Executive Assistant **Elaine Monge** . . . . . . . . . . . . . . . . (617) 973-8700
General Counsel and Chief of Staff **Gregory White** . . . . . (617) 973-8707
Communications Director **Christopher Goetcheus** . . . . . . (617) 973-8767
E-mail: chris.goetcheus@state.ma.us
Consumer Research and Programs Officer **(Vacant)** . . . . . (617) 973-8741
Chief Financial Officer **Gray Holmes** . . . . . . . . . . . . . . (617) 973-8770

### Division of Banks [DOB]

1000 Washington Street, 10th Floor, Boston, MA 02118-6400
Tel: (617) 956-1500
Tel: (800) 495-2265 (Consumer Information Line [In State])
Fax: (617) 956-1599  Internet: www.mass.gov/dob

**Fiscal Year:** 2015  **Budget:** $17,609,000

Commissioner **David J. Cotney** . . . . . . . . . . . . . . . (617) 956-1500 ext. 510
E-mail: david.cotney@state.ma.us
Education: Tufts 1989 BA; Harvard MPA; Boston U MBA
Special Assistant to the Commissioner **(Vacant)** . . . . . . . (617) 956-1510
Deputy Commissioner and General Counsel
**Merrily S. Gerrish** . . . . . . . . . . . . . . . . . . . . . . . . . (617) 956-1520
E-mail: merrily.gerrish@state.ma.us
Education: Connecticut Col BA; Boston U MBA; Suffolk JD

---

★ Elected Official     ■ Appointed by Governor     ● Appointed by Legislature     ▲ Appointed by Board or Commission     ◆ Appointed by State Supreme Court

Depository Institution Supervision and Outreach
Senior Deputy Commissioner **Jay P. Bienvenu** . . (617) 956-1500 ext. 535
E-mail: jay.bienvenu@state.ma.us
Education: Fitchburg State; UMass (Lowell) 1995 MBA

Non-Depository Institution Supervision Senior
Deputy Commissioner **Paul Gibson** . . . . . . . . . (617) 956-1500 ext. 536
E-mail: paul.gibson@state.ma.us
Education: Suffolk BABA

Community Reinvestment Act (CRA) and
Outreach Deputy Commissioner **Mayte Rivera** . . (617) 956-1500 ext. 557
E-mail: mayte.rivera@state.ma.us

Depository Institution Supervision Deputy
Commissioner **James Barrett** . . . . . . . . . . . . . . (617) 956-1500 ext. 401
E-mail: james.barrett@state.ma.us

Money Service Businesses and Consumer
Finance Deputy Commissioner **(Vacant)** . . . . . . . (617) 956-1500 ext. 549

Mortgage Supervision Deputy Commissioner **Kevin Cuff** . . (617) 956-1539
E-mail: kevin.cuff@state.ma.us

Chief Operating Officer **Mary L. Gallagher** . . . . . . . . . . . (617) 956-1513
Education: Harvard

Chief Risk Officer **Cynthia A. Begin** . . . . . . . . . . . (617) 956-1500 ext. 523
Education: Nichols BSBA; Suffolk JD

## Division of Insurance [DOI]

1000 Washington Street, Suite 810, Boston, MA 02118-6200
Tel: (617) 521-7794 Tel: (617) 521-7777 (Consumer Information Line)
Fax: (617) 521-7475 Internet: www.state.ma.us/doi

**Fiscal Year:** 2015 **Budget:** $12,705,000

■Insurance Commissioner **Daniel R. Judson** . . . . . . . . . . . . . (617) 521-7301
E-mail: daniel.judson@state.ma.us

First Deputy Commissioner **Gary Anderson** . . . . . . . . . . . . (617) 521-7308

Deputy Commissioner and General Counsel
**Rachel Davidson** . . . . . . . . . . . . . . . . . . . . . . . . . . . . . . . . (617) 521-1308

Deputy Commissioner of the Health Care Access Bureau
**Kevin Beagan** . . . . . . . . . . . . . . . . . . . . . . . . . . . . . . . . . (617) 521-7323

## Division of Professional Licensure [DPL]

1000 Washington Street, 7th Floor, Boston, MA 02118-6100
Tel: (617) 727-3074 Tel: (617) 727-7406 (Consumer Information)
Fax: (617) 727-2197 Internet: www.mass.gov/dpl

■Director **Charles Borstel** . . . . . . . . . . . . . . . . . . . . . . . . . . (617) 727-0026

Executive Assistant **Cheryl A. Yebba** . . . . . . . . . . . . . . . . (617) 727-4992

Chief of Staff **Neldy Jean-Francois** . . . . . . . . . . . . . . . . . . (617) 727-2108
E-mail: neldy.jean-francois@state.ma.us

Manager of Revenue and Fiscal Affairs
**Deborah M. Cassano** . . . . . . . . . . . . . . . . . . . . . . . . . . . . (617) 727-1219

Policy and Boards Deputy Director **Robert Fortes** . . . . . . . (617) 727-5369
E-mail: robert.fortes@state.ma.us

Allied Health Professions Board Executive Director
**Ana Garcia** . . . . . . . . . . . . . . . . . . . . . . . . . . . . . . . . . . . . (617) 727-1631

Allied Mental Health and Human Services Professionals
Board Executive Director **Erin M. Lebel** . . . . . . . . . . . . . (617) 727-4302

Architects Board Executive Director **Clinton W. Dick** . . . . . (617) 727-5970

Certification of Health Officers Board Executive Director
**Peter B. Kelly** . . . . . . . . . . . . . . . . . . . . . . . . . . . . . . . . . . (617) 727-3022
E-mail: peter.b.kelly@state.ma.us

Chiropractors Board Executive Director **Brian Bialas** . . . . . (617) 727-1807

Cosmetology and Barbering Board Executive Director
**Brian Bialas** . . . . . . . . . . . . . . . . . . . . . . . . . . . . . . . . . . . (617) 727-1807

Dietitians and Nutritionists Board Executive Director
**Brian Bialas** . . . . . . . . . . . . . . . . . . . . . . . . . . . . . . . . . . . (617) 727-1807

Dispensing Opticians Board Executive Director
**Michael E. Hawley** . . . . . . . . . . . . . . . . . . . . . . . . . . . . . . (617) 727-6524

Drinking Water and Supply Facilities Operators Board
Executive Director **Wayne E. Thomas** . . . . . . . . . . . . . . . (617) 727-6388

Electricians Board Executive Director **Robert Ferguson** . . . (617) 727-9931

Funeral Directors and Embalmers Board Executive
Director **Michael E. Hawley** . . . . . . . . . . . . . . . . . . . . . . . (617) 727-6524

Hearing Instrument Specialists Board Executive Director
**Michael E. Hawley** . . . . . . . . . . . . . . . . . . . . . . . . . . . . . . (617) 727-6524

Landscape Architects Board Executive Director
**Robert Ferguson** . . . . . . . . . . . . . . . . . . . . . . . . . . . . . . . (617) 727-9931

Massage Therapy Board Executive Director **Ana Garcia** . . . (617) 727-1631

Optometrists Board Executive Director
**Michael E. Hawley** . . . . . . . . . . . . . . . . . . . . . . . . . . . . . . (617) 727-6524

Plumbers and Gasfitters Board Executive Director
**Wayne E. Thomas** . . . . . . . . . . . . . . . . . . . . . . . . . . . . . . (617) 727-6388

Podiatrists Board Executive Director **Michael E. Hawley** . . (617) 727-1945

Private Occupational School Education Executive
Director **Clinton W. Dick** . . . . . . . . . . . . . . . . . . . . . . . . . (617) 727-5970

Professional Engineers and Land Surveyors Board
Executive Director **Clinton W. Dick** . . . . . . . . . . . . . . . . . (617) 727-5970

Psychologists Board Executive Director **Erin M. Lebel** . . . . (617) 727-4302

Public Accountants Board Executive Director
**Ana Garcia** . . . . . . . . . . . . . . . . . . . . . . . . . . . . . . . . . . . . (617) 727-1631

Real Estate Appraisers Board Executive Director
**Ann-Margarette Barry** . . . . . . . . . . . . . . . . . . . . . . . . . . . (617) 727-2214

Real Estate Brokers and Salespersons Board Executive
Director **Ann-Margarette Barry** . . . . . . . . . . . . . . . . . . . . (617) 727-2214

Sanitarians Board Executive Director **Peter B. Kelly** . . . . . . (617) 727-3022

Social Workers Board Executive Director **Erin M. Lebel** . . . (617) 727-4302

Speech - Language Pathologists and Audiologists Board
Executive Director **Michael E. Hawley** . . . . . . . . . . . . . . (617) 727-6524

Veterinarians Board Executive Director
**Ann-Margarette Barry** . . . . . . . . . . . . . . . . . . . . . . . . . . . (617) 727-2214

## Division of Standards

One Ashburton Place, Room 1115, Boston, MA 02108
Tel: (617) 727-3480 Fax: (617) 727-5705
Internet: www.state.ma.us/standards

**Fiscal Year:** 2015 **Budget:** $1,838,000

■Director **Charles H. Carroll** . . . . . . . . . . . . . . . . (617) 727-3480 ext. 21131
E-mail: charles.carroll@state.ma.us

## Department of Telecommunications and Cable

1000 Washington Street, Suite 820, Boston, MA 02118-6100
Tel: (617) 305-3580 Internet: http://www.mass.gov/dtc

**Fiscal Year:** 2015 **Budget:** $2,524,000

Commissioner **Karen Charles Peterson** . . . . . . . . . . . . . . . (617) 305-3580
Education: Suffolk 1993 BS
Special Assistant to the Commissioner **Andrea Nixon** . . . (617) 305-3580

Competition Division Director **Lindsay DeRoche** . . . . . . . . (617) 305-3580

Consumer Division Director **Joslyn Day** . . . . . . . . . . . . . . . (617) 305-3580

General Counsel **Sandra Merrick** . . . . . . . . . . . . . . . . . . . (617) 305-3580
Education: Boston U 1992 BA; Baruch Col 1996 MPA;
New England 2003 JD

## Massachusetts Office of Business Development [MOBD]

10 Park Plaza, Suite 3730, Boston, MA 02116
Tel: (617) 973-8600 Fax: (617) 973-8554

**Fiscal Year:** 2015 **Budget:**

Assistant Secretary of Business Development
**Nam Pham** . . . . . . . . . . . . . . . . . . . . . . . . . . . . . . . . . . . . (617) 973-8600
Education: Minnesota BS; JFK School Govt MPA

## Massachusetts Office of International Trade and Investment [MOITI]

10 Park Plaza, Suite 3730, Boston, MA 02116
Tel: (617) 973-8650 Fax: (617) 973-8554 E-mail: moiti@state.ma.us

Executive Director **Mark F. Sullivan** . . . . . . . . . . . . . . . . . (617) 830-5401
Education: St Michael's; Bentley Col MBA

## Massachusetts Office of Travel and Tourism [MOTT]

10 Park Plaza, Suite 4510, Boston, MA 02116
Tel: (617) 973-8500 Fax: (617) 973-8525
Internet: www.massvacation.com

Executive Director **Francois-Laurent Nivaud** . . . . . . . . . . . (617) 973-8500

★ Elected Official ■ Appointed by Governor ● Appointed by Legislature ▲ Appointed by Board or Commission ◆ Appointed by State Supreme Court

# Executive Office of Labor and Workforce Development [EOLWD]

John W. McCormack Building, One Ashburton Place, Boston, MA 02108
Tel: (617) 626-7122  Fax: (617) 727-1090

■Secretary **Ronald L. "Ron" Walker II** . . . . . . . . . . . . . . . . . (617) 626-7100
  E-mail: ronald.walker@state.ma.us
  Education: Prairie View A&M BBA
Undersecretary and Chief Operating Officer
  **Stephanie D. Neal-Johnson** . . . . . . . . . . . . . . . . . . (617) 626-7100
  Education: Columbia; Boston U JD
■Undersecretary of Workforce Development
  **Ronald G. Marlow** . . . . . . . . . . . . . . . . . . . . . . . . . (617) 626-7100
  E-mail: ronald.g.marlow@state.ma.us
Assistant Secretary for Program and Performance
  Management **Yashira Pepin** . . . . . . . . . . . . . . . . . . . (617) 626-7122
Communications Director **Colleen Quinn** . . . . . . . . . . . . . (617) 626-7121
  E-mail: colleen.quinn@state.ma.us
General Counsel **Michael Doheny** . . . . . . . . . . . . . . . . (617) 626-7100
  E-mail: michael.doheny@state.ma.us
  Education: Cornell 1988 BA; Suffolk 1999 JD
Legislative Director **Jessica Muradian** . . . . . . . . . . . . . . (617) 626-7100
  E-mail: jessica.muradian@state.ma.us
Board of Review Chairman **John A. "Jack" King, Esq.** . . . (617) 626-6420

## Massachusetts Workforce Investment Board

Fax: (617) 727-4404

Executive Director **Cheryl Scott** . . . . . . . . . . . . . . . . . . (617) 626-7112
  E-mail: cheryl.scott@state.ma.us

## Department of Career Services

Charles F. Hurley Building, 19 Staniford Street, First Floor,
Boston, MA 02114
Tel: (617) 626-5680

**Fiscal Year:** 2015  **Budget:** $14,629,000

Director **Alice Sweeney** . . . . . . . . . . . . . . . . . . . . . . . . (617) 626-5680
  E-mail: alice.sweeney@state.ma.us

## Department of Industrial Accidents [DIA]

One Congress Street, Suite 100, Boston, MA 02114-2017
Tel: (617) 727-4900  Fax: (617) 727-6477  Internet: www.mass.gov/dia

**Fiscal Year:** 2015  **Budget:** $18,120,000

Director **Linda Edmonds Turner** . . . . . . . . . . . . . . . . . . (617) 727-4900
Deputy Director and General Counsel
  **William "Bill" Tattan** . . . . . . . . . . . . . . . . . . . . . . . (617) 727-4900
Deputy Director **(Vacant)** . . . . . . . . . . . . . . . . . . . . . . . (617) 727-4900
Senior Judge **Omar Hernandez** . . . . . . . . . . . . . . . . . . . (617) 727-4900

## Department of Labor Relations [DLR]

Charles F. Hurley Building, 19 Straniford Street, Boston, MA 02114
Tel: (617) 626-6921  Fax: (617) 626-7157

**Fiscal Year:** 2015  **Budget:** $2,180,000

Director (Acting) **Edward B. Srednicki** . . . . . . . . . . . . . . (617) 626-7142
  E-mail: ed.srednicki@massmail.state.ma.us
Chief Counsel **Jane Gabriel** . . . . . . . . . . . . . . . . . . . . . (617) 626-7136
Executive Secretary **Edward B. Srednicki** . . . . . . . . . . . . (617) 626-7142

## Department of Labor Standards

Charles F. Hurley Building, 19 Staniford Street, Boston, MA 02114
Tel: (617) 626-6975  Fax: (617) 626-6944

**Fiscal Year:** 2015  **Budget:** $2,512,000

Director **William D. McKinney** . . . . . . . . . . . . . . . . . . . (617) 626-6975
  E-mail: william.mckinney@state.ma.us
  Education: Col Holy Cross; Babson
Deputy Director **(Vacant)** . . . . . . . . . . . . . . . . . . . . . . . (617) 626-5407
General Counsel **(Vacant)** . . . . . . . . . . . . . . . . . . . . . . . (617) 626-6952
Chief of Investigations, Enforcement, Asbestos and Lead
  Program **Brian Wong** . . . . . . . . . . . . . . . . . . . . . . . (617) 626-6975
Workplace Safety and Health Program Manager **(Vacant)** . . (617) 626-6975

# Department of Unemployment Assistance

Charles F. Hurley Building, 19 Staniford Street, 3rd Floor,
Boston, MA 02114
Tel: (617) 626-6600  Fax: (617) 727-0315  Internet: www.mass.gov/dua

Director **Robert T. Cunningham** . . . . . . . . . . . . . . . . . . (617) 626-6663
Chief Legal Counsel **David A. Guberman** . . . . . . . . . . . . (617) 626-7122
  E-mail: david.guberman2@state.ma.us

## Commonwealth Corporation

Schrafft Center, 529 Main Street, Suite 110, Boston, MA 02129
Tel: (617) 727-8158  Fax: (617) 242-7660  Internet: www.commcorp.org

■President and Chief Executive Officer **Nancy L. Snyder** . . . (617) 717-6910
  E-mail: nsnyder@commcorp.org
  Education: Boston U 1994 MBA

# Executive Office of Public Safety and Security [EOPSS]

One Ashburton Place, Room 2133, Boston, MA 02108
Tel: (617) 727-7775  TTY: (617) 727-6618  Fax: (617) 727-4764

■Secretary **Daniel J. Bennett** . . . . . . . . . . . . . . . . . . . . (617) 727-7775
  E-mail: daniel.bennett1@state.ma.us
Undersecretary of Criminal Justice **(Vacant)** . . . . . . . . . . (617) 727-7775
Undersecretary of Forensic Science and Technology and
  Chief Information Officer **Curtis M. Wood** . . . . . . . . . . (617) 727-7775
  E-mail: curtis.wood@state.ma.us
Undersecretary of Homeland Security **Patrick McMurray** . . (617) 727-7775
  E-mail: patrick.mcmurray@state.ma.us
  Education: American International MS
Undersecretary of Law Enforcement **Jennifer D. Queally** . . (617) 727-7775
Chief of Staff **Michelle Small** . . . . . . . . . . . . . . . . . . . (617) 727-7775
General Counsel **David Solet** . . . . . . . . . . . . . . (617) 727-7775 ext. 25522
Chief Fiscal Officer **Michelle Small** . . . . . . . . . . . . . . . . (617) 727-7775
Communications Director **Felix Browne** . . . . . . . (617) 727-7775 ext. 25542
  E-mail: felix.browne@state.ma.us
  Education: Georgetown

## Office of the Chief Medical Examiner [OCME]

720 Albany Street, Boston, MA 02118
Tel: (617) 267-6767  Fax: (617) 266-6763

**Employees:** 74  **Fiscal Year:** 2015  **Budget:** $10,874,000

■Chief Medical Examiner
  **Henry M. Nields, PhD, MD** . . . . . . . . . . . . . . . (617) 267-6767 ext. 187
  E-mail: henry.nields@state.ma.us                    Fax: (617) 266-6763

## Office of Grants and Research [OGR]

10 Park Plaza, Suite 3720, Boston, MA 02116
Tel: (617) 725-3301  Fax: (617) 725-0260

Executive Director **Arthur Kinsman** . . . . . . . . . . . . . . . . (617) 725-3301
  E-mail: art.kinsman@state.ma.us

## Department of Correction

50 Maple Street, Suite 3, Milford, MA 01757
Tel: (508) 422-3300  Fax: (508) 422-3385  Internet: www.state.ma.us/doc

**Employees:** 5,222  **Fiscal Year:** 2015  **Budget:** $586,584,000

■Commissioner **Carol Higgins O'Brien** . . . . . . . . . . . . . . (508) 422-3330
  E-mail: carol.higgins.obrien@massmail.state.ma.us
  Education: UMass (Lowell)
Deputy Commissioner of Administrative Services
  **Michael Grant** . . . . . . . . . . . . . . . . . . . . . . . . . . . (508) 422-3328
  E-mail: michael.grant@state.ma.us
Deputy Commissioner of Classification, Programs and
  Reentry Division **Katherine Chmiel** . . . . . . . . . . . . . . (508) 422-3301
Deputy Commissioner of Prisons **Thomas Dickhaut** . . . . . (978) 422-3346
                                                    Fax: (978) 422-3424
General Counsel **Nancy White** . . . . . . . . . . . . . (617) 727-3300 ext. 1124
Communication and Administrative Resolution Director
  **Christopher Fallon** . . . . . . . . . . . . . . . . . . . . . . . . (508) 422-3355
  E-mail: christopher.fallon@massmail.state.ma.us
Public Affairs Director **Darren Duarte** . . . . . . . . . . . . . . (508) 422-3317
  E-mail: darren.duarte@massmail.state.ma.us       Fax: (508) 422-3434

---

Investigations Chief **Patrick DePalo** . . . . . . . . . . . . . . . . . . . (508) 422-3363
E-mail: patrick.depalo@massmail.state.ma.us      Fax: (508) 422-3387
Legislative Director **John A. O'Malley** . . . . . . . . . . . . . . . . (508) 422-3319
E-mail: john.a.omalley@massmail.state.ma.us      Fax: (508) 422-3384

## Department of Criminal Justice Information Services [DCJIS]

200 Arlington Street, Suite 2200, Chelsea, MA 02150
Tel: (617) 660-4600  Fax: (617) 660-4613

**Employees:** 36  **Fiscal Year:** 2015  **Budget:** $4,677,000

Commissioner (Acting) **James F. Slater III** . . . . . . . . . . . (617) 660-4761
E-mail: james.slater@state.ma.us

## Department of Fire Services [DFS]

One State Road, Stow, MA 01775-1500
P.O. Box 1025, Stow, MA 01775
Tel: (978) 567-3100  Fax: (978) 567-3121

**Employees:** 70  **Fiscal Year:** 2015  **Budget:** $19,055,000

▲ State Fire Marshal **Peter Ostroskey** . . . . . . . . . . . . . . . . (978) 567-3112
E-mail: peter.ostroskey@state.ma.us
Deputy State Fire Marshal **(Vacant)** . . . . . . . . . . . . . . . . . (978) 567-3112
Administrative Services Director **Sheila Remondi** . . . . . . (978) 567-3149
E-mail: sheila.remondi@state.ma.us
Capital Asset Management Director **James DiRico** . . . . . . (978) 567-3161
Fire Safety Division Director **Paul Vigneau** . . . . . . . . . . . (978) 567-3301
Hazardous Materials Response Director **David Ladd** . . . . . (978) 567-3117
Operations Section Chief **David Clemons** . . . . . . . . . . . . . (978) 567-3179
Human Resources Director **Mary Travers** . . . . . . . . . . . . . (978) 567-3139
General Counsel **Steven Rourke** . . . . . . . . . . . . . . . . . . . . (978) 567-3182
Chief Fiscal Officer **Beth Hill** . . . . . . . . . . . . . . . . . . . . . (978) 567-3137
Public Information Officer **Jennifer Mieth** . . . . . . . . . . . . (978) 567-3381
E-mail: jennifer.mieth@state.ma.us
Executive Office Administrator **Kerry K. Weihn** . . . . . . . . (978) 567-3125

## Department of Public Safety [DPS]

One Ashburton Place, Room 1301, Boston, MA 02108
Tel: (617) 727-3200  Fax: (617) 248-0813  E-mail: DPSinfo@state.ma.us

**Employees:** 151  **Fiscal Year:** 2015  **Budget:** $17,211,250

■ Commissioner **Matthew E. Carlin** . . . . . . . . . . . . . . . . . (617) 727-3200
E-mail: matt.carlin@state.ma.us      Fax: (617) 727-5732
Chief of Staff and General Counsel **Beth McLaughlin** . . . . (617) 727-3200
Chief of Inspections-Buildings (Acting) **Felix Zemel** . . . . . (617) 727-3200
E-mail: felix.zemel@massmail.state.ma.us
Chief of Inspections-Elevators **Stephen Sampson** . . . . . . . (617) 727-3200
E-mail: stephen.sampson@massmail.state.ma.us
Chief of Inspections-Mechanical **Edward Kawa** . . . . . . . . (617) 727-3200
E-mail: edward.kawa@massmail.state.ma.us
Chief Financial Officer **Dana Clowes** . . . . . . . . . . . . . . . . (617) 727-3200
Administrative Services/Regulated Activities Director
**Guy Licciardi** . . . . . . . . . . . . . . . . . . . . . . . . . . . . . . (617) 727-3200
E-mail: guy.licciardi@state.ma.us
Human Resources Director **Penny O'Reilly** . . . . . . . . . . . . (617) 727-3200

## Department of State Police

470 Worcester Road, Framingham, MA 01702
Tel: (508) 820-2300  Fax: (617) 727-6874

**Fiscal Year:** 2016  **Budget:** $250,000,000

■ Superintendent **Col. Richard McKeon** . . . . . . . . . . . . . . (508) 820-2300
E-mail: richard.mckeon@state.ma.us      Fax: (617) 727-6874
Education: Framingham State; Anna Maria
Deputy Superintendent **Lt. Col. Francis P. Hughes** . . . . . . (508) 820-2300

## State 911 Department

151 Campanelli Drive, Suite A, Middleboro, MA 02346
Tel: (508) 828-2911  Fax: (508) 828-2585  E-mail: MASETB@state.ma.us

Executive Director **Frank Pozniak** . . . . . . . . . . . . (508) 828-2911 ext. 7215
Deputy Director **Normand Fournier** . . . . . . . . . . . . . . . . (508) 821-7209
Finance Director **Karen Robitaille** . . . . . . . . . . . . (508) 828-2911 ext. 7221
Programs Director **Monna Wallace** . . . . . . . . . . . . (508) 828-2911 ext. 7220
9-1-1 Systems Director **(Vacant)** . . . . . . . . . . . . . . . . . . . (508) 821-7209

General Counsel **Louise M. McCarthy** . . . . . . . . . . . . . . . (508) 821-7223

## Massachusetts National Guard

Two Randolph Road, Hanscom AFB, MA 01731-3001
Tel: (508) 233-6590

■ Adjutant General **MajGen Gary W. Keefe, ANG** . . . . . . . (508) 233-6552
Education: Norwich 1986 BS; Lesley U 1991 MS
Assistant Adjutant General (Air) **(Vacant)** . . . . . . . . . . . . (508) 233-6590
Assistant Adjutant General (Army)
**COL Richard F. Johnson, ARNG** . . . . . . . . . . . . . . . . (508) 233-6590
Command Sergeant Major
**CSM Carlos O. Ramos Rivera, ARNG** . . . . . . . . . . . (508) 233-6590
Public Affairs Director **LTC James Sahady, ARNG** . . . . . . (508) 233-6590

## Massachusetts Emergency Management Agency [MEMA]

400 Worcester Road, Framingham, MA 01702-5399
Tel: (508) 820-2000  Fax: (508) 820-2030  Internet: www.mass.gov/mema

**Employees:** 52  **Fiscal Year:** 2015  **Budget:** $7,352,000

■ Director **Kurt N. Schwartz** . . . . . . . . . . . . . . . . . . . . . . (508) 820-2010
E-mail: kurt.schwartz@state.ma.us      Fax: (508) 820-2015
Deputy Director **Christine H. Packard** . . . . . . . . . . . . . . . (508) 820-2056
Chief of Staff **Marybeth Groff** . . . . . . . . . . . . . . . . . . . . (508) 820-1435
E-mail: marybeth.groff@massmail.state.ma.us
Executive Assistant **Katy Bellemare** . . . . . . . . . . . . . . . . (508) 820-2014
Chief Administrative Officer **David Mahr** . . . . . . . . . . . . . (508) 820-2017
E-mail: david.mahr@state.ma.us
General Counsel **Ann McCarthy** . . . . . . . . . . . . . . . . . . . . (508) 820-1400
Human Resources Director **Debra Tata** . . . . . . . . . . . . . . . (508) 820-2060
Mitigation and Disaster Recovery Section Chief
**Scott MacLeod** . . . . . . . . . . . . . . . . . . . . . . . . . . . . . (508) 820-1445
Planning, Nuclear and Preparedness Section Chief
**John Giarrrusso** . . . . . . . . . . . . . . . . . . . . . . . . . . . . (508) 820-2040
Response and Field Services Section Chief
**Michael Russas** . . . . . . . . . . . . . . . . . . . . . . . . . . . . (508) 820-2018
Public Information Officer **Peter Judge** . . . . . . . . . . . . . . (508) 820-2002
E-mail: peter.judge@massmail.state.ma.us

## Parole Board

12 Mercer Road, Natick, MA 01760
Tel: (508) 650-4500  Fax: (508) 650-4599

**Fiscal Year:** 2015  **Budget:** $18,574,000

■ Chair **Paul M. Treseler** . . . . . . . . . . . . . . . . . . . . . . . . . (508) 650-4500
Education: Boston Col JD
■ Member **Dr. Charlene M. Bonner** . . . . . . . . . . . . . . . . . . (508) 650-4500
E-mail: charlene.bonner@state.ma.us
Education: St Anselm 1991 BA; Bridgewater State Col 1995 MEd
■ Member **Tonomey Coleman** . . . . . . . . . . . . . . . . . . . . . . (508) 650-4500
E-mail: tonomey.coleman@state.ma.us
Education: Delhi Tech 1984 AAS; Baruch Col 1989 BA;
Boston Col 1992 JD
■ Member **Sheila M. Dupre** . . . . . . . . . . . . . . . . . . . . . . . . (508) 650-4500
E-mail: sheila.dupre@state.ma.us
Education: Springfield (MA) BS
■ Member **Ina Howard-Hogan** . . . . . . . . . . . . . . . . . . . . . . (508) 650-4500
E-mail: ina.howard-hogan@state.ma.us
■ Member **Tina M. Hurley** . . . . . . . . . . . . . . . . . . . . . . . . (508) 650-4500
Term Expires: 2019
Education: Northeastern 1984 BS; UMass (Amherst) 1994 MS
■ Member **Lucy Soto-Abbe** . . . . . . . . . . . . . . . . . . . . . . . . (508) 650-4500
Term Expires: June 2017

## Massachusetts Department of Transportation Board

10 Park Plaza, Suite 3170, Boston, MA 02116
Tel: (857) 368-4636

■ Chair **Stephanie Pollack** . . . . . . . . . . . . . . . . . . . . . . . . (857) 368-4636
Education: MIT 1982 BS; Harvard 1985 JD
■ Member **Dominic L. Blue** . . . . . . . . . . . . . . . . . . . . . . . . (857) 368-4636
Education: Col Holy Cross BA; Boston Col MBA, JD
■ Member **Ruth Bonsignore** . . . . . . . . . . . . . . . . . . . . . . . (857) 368-4636
Education: UMass (Amherst) BSCE

*(continued on next page)*

EXECUTIVE BRANCH

---

★ Elected Official      ■ Appointed by Governor      ● Appointed by Legislature      ▲ Appointed by Board or Commission      ◆ Appointed by State Supreme Court

**Massachusetts Department of Transportation Board** *continued*

- Member **Lisa Calisle** . . . . . . . . . . . . . . . . . . . . . . . . . . . . (857) 368-4636
  Education: Boston Col BA
- Member **Russell Gittlen** . . . . . . . . . . . . . . . . . . . . . . . . . . (857) 368-4636
- Member **Dean Mazzarella** . . . . . . . . . . . . . . . . . . . . . . . . (857) 368-4636
- Member **Robert L. Moylan, Jr.** . . . . . . . . . . . . . . . . . . . . (857) 368-4636
- Member **Steve Poftak** . . . . . . . . . . . . . . . . . . . . . . . . . . . (857) 368-4636
  Education: Middlebury BA; Babson MBA
- Member **Joseph C. Sullivan** . . . . . . . . . . . . . . . . . . . . . . (857) 368-4636
  Affiliation: Mayor, Office of the Mayor, Town of Braintree, Massachusetts
  1 John F. Kennedy Memorial Drive, Braintree, MA 02184
  Education: UMass (Amherst) BA; JFK School Govt MPA
- Member **Betsy Taylor** . . . . . . . . . . . . . . . . . . . . . . . . . . . . (857) 368-4636
- Member **Monica Tibbitts-Nutt** . . . . . . . . . . . . . . . . . . . . (857) 368-4636
  Education: Southern Indiana BS

## Massachusetts Department of Transportation [MassDOT]

10 Park Plaza, Suite 3170, Boston, MA 02116
Tel: (857) 368-4636  Fax: (857) 368-0601  TTY: (857) 368-0655

**Fiscal Year:** 2015  **Budget:** $617,702,000

- Secretary and Chief Executive Officer
  **Stephanie Pollack** . . . . . . . . . . . . . . . . . . . . . . . . . (857) 368-8892
  E-mail: stephanie.pollack@state.ma.us
  Senior Advisor and Assistant to the Secretary **(Vacant)** . . (857) 368-4636
  Assistant Secretary and Chief of Staff **(Vacant)** . . . . . . . . (857) 368-4636
  Deputy Chief of Staff **Rob Garrett** . . . . . . . . . . . . . . . . (857) 368-4636
  Assistant Secretary for Performance Management and
  Innovation **Rachel Bain** . . . . . . . . . . . . . . . . . . . . . . (857) 368-4636
  E-mail: rachel.bain@state.ma.us
  Education: Maine 2002 BA, 2004 MPA
  Chief Diversity and Civil Rights Officer **(Vacant)** . . . . . . . (857) 368-4636
  Communications Director **(Vacant)** . . . . . . . . . . . . . . . . (857) 368-8908
  Assistant Secretary for Human Resources (Acting)
  **Jessie Saint Cyr** . . . . . . . . . . . . . . . . . . . . . . . . . . . (857) 368-8585
                                                    Fax: (857) 368-0601
  Labor Relations Director **Julian T. Tynes** . . . . . . . . . . . (857) 368-4636
  Education: UMass (Amherst); Eastern Nazarene;
  Western New England 1997 JD
  Legislative Director **(Vacant)** . . . . . . . . . . . . . . . . . . . . (857) 368-4636
  Real Estate and Asset Development Director
  **William Tuttle** . . . . . . . . . . . . . . . . . . . . . . . . . . . . (857) 368-4636
  General Counsel **(Vacant)** . . . . . . . . . . . . . . . . . . . . . . (857) 368-4636
  Chief Administrative Officer (Acting) **Michael Lee** . . . . . . (857) 368-4636
  Chief Financial Officer **Dana Levenson** . . . . . . . . . . . . (857) 368-9130
  Education: Brown U 1979 AB; NYU 1985 MBA
  Controller **Susan Bristol** . . . . . . . . . . . . . . . . . . . . . . (857) 368-9135
  Chief Information Officer **Gary Foster** . . . . . . . . . . . . . (857) 368-4636
  E-mail: gfoster@mbta.com

## Office of the Lieutenant Governor

State House, 24 Beacon Street, Boston, MA 01233
Tel: (617) 725-4000  Fax: (617) 727-9725
E-mail: ltgovoffice@state.ma.us

★ Lieutenant Governor **Karyn E. Polito** (R) . . . . . . . . . . . . . (617) 725-4000
  Term Expires: January 2019
  E-mail: karyn.polito@state.ma.us
  Education: Boston Col 1988 BS; New England 1991 JD
  Career: State Representative (R-MA, Worcester-11), Massachusetts
  House of Representatives (2001-2011)
  Executive Assistant **MaryAnne Smyth** . . . . . . . . . . . . . . (617) 725-4000

## Office of the Attorney General

One Ashburton Place, Boston, MA 02108
Tel: (617) 727-2200  TTY: (617) 727-4765  Fax: (617) 727-3251
E-mail: agoweb@state.ma.us  Internet: www.mass.gov/ago

**Employees:** 507  **Fiscal Year:** 2015  **Budget:** $42,205,000

★ Attorney General **Maura Healey** (D) . . . . . . . . . . . . . . . . (617) 727-2200
  Term Expires: January 2019
  Education: Harvard 1992 BA; Northeastern 1998 JD
  Career: Civil Rights Division Chief, Public Protection and Advocacy
  Bureau, Office of the Attorney General, Commonwealth of
  Massachusetts (2007-2012); Bureau Chief, Public Protection and
  Advocacy Bureau, Office of the Attorney General, Commonwealth of
  Massachusetts (2012-2013)
  First Assistant Attorney General
  **Christopher Barry-Smith** . . . . . . . . . . . . . . . . . . . . . . (617) 727-2200
  Deputy Attorney General **Joanna Lydgate** . . . . . . . . . . . . (617) 727-2200
  Education: UCLA 2010 JD
  Chief of Staff **Michael B. Firestone** . . . . . . . . . . . . . . . . (617) 727-2200
  Education: Harvard 2005
  General Counsel **Judy Zeprun Kalman** . . . . . . . . . . . . . . (617) 727-2200
  Chief Information Officer **Kevin Coluci** . . . . . . . . . . . . . . (617) 727-2200
  E-mail: kevin.coluci@state.ma.us
  Chief Legal Counsel **Richard Johnston** . . . . . . . . . . . . . . (617) 727-2200
  Director of Communications **Cyndi Roy Gonzalez** . . . . . . . (617) 727-2543
  E-mail: cyndi.roy.gonzalez@state.ma.us
  Education: Emerson 2004 BA

## Criminal Bureau

Tel: (617) 573-5330 (Insurance Fraud Tipline)
Bureau Chief **Kimberly West** . . . . . . . . . . . . . . . . . . . . . . (617) 727-2200
Deputy Bureau Chief **Dean A. Mazzone** . . . . . . . . . . . . . . (617) 727-2200
Appeals Division Chief **Randall Ravitz** . . . . . . . . . . . . . . . (617) 727-2200
Appeals Division Deputy Chief **Jessica V. Barnett** . . . . . . . (617) 727-2200
  Education: NYU 2001 JD
Enterprise, Major and Cyber Crimes Division Chief
  **Terrence Reidy** . . . . . . . . . . . . . . . . . . . . . . . . . . . . . (617) 727-2200
Cyber Crime Division Lab Director **Christopher Kelly** . . (617) 727-2200
Financial Investigations Division Director
  **Sallyann Nelligan** . . . . . . . . . . . . . . . . . . . . . . . . . . (617) 727-2200
  E-mail: sallyann.nelligan@state.ma.us
Gaming Enforcement Division Chief **Patrick Hanley** . . . . . (617) 573-5330
  Education: Brandeis; Northeastern 2003 JD
Human Trafficking Division Chief **Deb Bercovitch** . . . . . . (617) 573-5330
Victim Services Division Chief **Nikki Antonucci** . . . . . . . . (617) 727-2200
White Collar and Public Integrity Division Chief
  **David Andrews** . . . . . . . . . . . . . . . . . . . . . . . . . . . . (617) 727-2200
  Insurance and Unemployment Fraud Unit Director
  **April English** . . . . . . . . . . . . . . . . . . . . . . . . . . . . . (617) 727-2200
Boston State Police Unit Detective
  **Capt. Steve Fennessey** . . . . . . . . . . . . . . . . . . . . . . . (617) 727-2200
Child and Youth Protection Unit Director **Gail Garinger** . . . (617) 727-2200
  E-mail: gail.garinger@state.ma.us
  Education: Harvard 1972 JD

## Energy and Environment Bureau

Bureau Chief **Melissa Hoffer** . . . . . . . . . . . . . . . . . . . . . . (617) 727-2200
Deputy Bureau Chief **Rebecca Tepper** . . . . . . . . . . . . . . . (617) 727-2200
Energy and Telecommunications Division Chief
  **Rebecca Tepper** . . . . . . . . . . . . . . . . . . . . . . . . . . . . (617) 727-2200
  Energy and Telecommunications Deputy Division Chief
  **Nathan Forster** . . . . . . . . . . . . . . . . . . . . . . . . . . . . (617) 727-1047
Environmental Crimes Strike Force Division Chief
  **(Vacant)** . . . . . . . . . . . . . . . . . . . . . . . . . . . . . . . . (617) 727-2200
Environmental Protection Division Chief
  **Christophe Courchesne** . . . . . . . . . . . . . . . . . . . . . . . (617) 727-2200
  Education: Harvard JD
  Environmental Protection Deputy Division Chief
  **Betsy Harper** . . . . . . . . . . . . . . . . . . . . . . . . . . . . . (617) 727-2200

## Government Bureau

Bureau Chief **Robert E. "Robin" Toone, Jr.** . . . . . . . . . . . (617) 727-2200
  Education: Yale 1991 BA, 1995 JD
Deputy Bureau Chief **Juliana Rice** . . . . . . . . . . . . . . . . . (617) 727-2200

---

★ Elected Official  ■ Appointed by Governor  ● Appointed by Legislature  ▲ Appointed by Board or Commission  ◆ Appointed by State Supreme Court

Administrative Law Division Chief **William W. Porter** .... (617) 727-2200
Administrative Law Division Managing Attorney
  **Robert Quinan** ........................................ (617) 727-2200
Division of Open Government Director **(Vacant)** ........ (617) 727-2200
Municipal Law Unit Chief **Margaret Hurley** .... (508) 792-7600 ext. 4402
Trial Division Chief **Helene Kazanjian** .................(617) 727-2200
Trial Deputy Division Chief **James Sweeney** ........... (617) 727-2200
Trial Division Managing Attorney **Liza Tran** ............ (617) 727-2200

## Health Care and Fair Competition Bureau

Bureau Chief **Mary Beckman** ........................ (617) 727-2200
Deputy Bureau Chief **Mary Freeley** ................... (617) 727-2200
Antitrust Division Chief **William Matlack** ............. (617) 727-2200
False Claims Division Chief **Gillian Feiner** ............ (617) 727-2200
Health Care Division Chief **Karen Tseng** .............. (617) 727-2200
  Education: Harvard JD
Medicaid Fraud Division Chief **(Vacant)** ............... (617) 727-2200
  Medicaid Fraud Division Deputy Chief **Steve Hoffman** .. (617) 727-2200
  Medicaid Fraud Division Chief of Investigations
    **Kevin Ready** ....................................... (617) 727-2200
  Medicaid Fraud Division Managing Attorney
    **Lee Hettinger** ..................................... (617) 727-2200
  Medicaid Fraud Division Managing Attorney
    **Robert Patton** ..................................... (617) 727-2200
Non-Profit Organizations/Public Charities Division Chief
  **Courtney Aladro** .................................... (617) 727-2200
  E-mail: courtney.aladro@state.ma.us
  Non-Profit Organizations/Public Charities Deputy
    Division Chief **Nora Mann** ....................... (617) 727-2200
    E-mail: nora.mann@state.ma.us

## Public Protection and Advocacy Bureau

100 Cambridge Street, Boston, MA 02114
Bureau Chief **Jonathan Miller** ....................... (617) 727-2200
Civil Rights Division Chief **(Vacant)** ................... (617) 727-2200
Civil Rights Deputy Division Chief **Genevieve Nadeau** ... (617) 727-2200
  Education: Stanford JD
Consumer Advocacy Response Division Director
  **Laurin J. Mottle** .................................... (617) 727-2200
Consumer Protection Division Chief **Max Weinstein** ..... (617) 727-2200
  Consumer Protection Division Deputy Chief
    **Shennan Kavanagh** ............................... (617) 727-2200
    Education: Vermont; Suffolk JD
Fair Labor Division Chief **Cynthia Mark** ............. (617) 727-2200
  Fair Labor Division Deputy Chief **Lauren A. Goldman** .. (617) 727-2200
    Education: Suffolk JD
Insurance and Financial Services Division Chief
  **Glenn Kaplan** ...................................... (617) 727-2200
Insurance and Financial Services Deputy Chief
  **Monica Brookman** .................................. (617) 727-2200
Investigation Division Director **Kevin McCarthy** ........ (617) 727-2200

## Regional Offices

Central Massachusetts Office Regional Chief
  **Margaret Hurley** ................................... (508) 792-7600
  10 Mechanic Street, Suite 301,        TTY: (617) 727-4765
  Worcester, MA 01608                  Fax: (508) 795-1991
Southeastern Massachusetts Office Regional Chief
  **Stephen Marshalek** ................................ (508) 990-9700
  105 William Street, 1st Floor,        TTY: (617) 727-4765
  New Bedford, MA 02740-6527          Fax: (508) 997-8686
Western Massachusetts Office Regional Chief
  **Bart Hollander** .....................................(413) 784-1240
  1350 Main Street, 4th Floor,          TTY: (617) 727-4765
  Springfield, MA 01103-1629          Fax: (413) 784-1244
  Western Massachusetts Office Deputy Regional Chief
    **Amy Karangekis** .................................(413) 784-1240
    1350 Main Street, Springfield, MA 01103-1629  TTY: (617) 727-4765
                                        Fax: (413) 784-1244
Springfield State Police Detective Unit **Joseph Ballou** .... (413) 784-1240

# Office of the Comptroller

One Ashburton Place, Room 901, Boston, MA 02108
Tel: (617) 727-5000  Fax: (617) 727-2163  Internet: www.mass.gov/osc

**Employees:** 81  **Fiscal Year:** 2015  **Budget:** $518,753,000

■Comptroller **Thomas G. Shack III** .....................(617) 973-2315
  E-mail: thomas.shack@state.ma.us
  Education: American U 1995 MBA; New England Law 2000 JD
Deputy Comptroller and Chief Operating Officer
  **Jeffrey Shapiro** .................................... (617) 973-2622
Deputy Comptroller and Chief Information Officer
  **Christopher Guido** ................................. (617) 973-2695
Deputy Comptroller **Howard Merkowitz** ............... (617) 973-2602
  Education: Rochester 1979 BA; Oxford (UK) 1981 MA;
  Harvard 1986 MPP
Deputy Comptroller **Kathy Sheppard** .................. (617) 973-2666
Deputy Comptroller and General Counsel
  **Jenny Hedderman** ................................. (617) 973-2656
  Education: Connecticut Col BA; Albany Law JD

# Secretary of the Commonwealth

McCormack Building, One Ashburton Place, Room 1611,
Boston, MA 02108-1518
Tel: (617) 727-7030  Fax: (617) 742-4528

**Fiscal Year:** 2016  **Budget:** $40,000,070

★Secretary of the Commonwealth
  **William Francis Galvin** (D) ......................... (617) 727-7030
  Term Expires: January 16, 2019
  Education: Boston Col 1972 BS; Suffolk 1975 JD
  Career: State Representative (D-MA), Massachusetts House of
  Representatives (1974-1990)
Assistant Secretary of the Commonwealth,
  Legislative Director, and Director of Procurement
  **Michael A. Maresco** ................................(617) 727-2804
  E-mail: michael.maresco@sec.state.ma.us
Budget Director **Paul McCarthy** ...................... (617) 727-0556
Communications Director **Brian McNiff** ............... (617) 727-9180
Human Resources Director **Mary McCusker** ........... (617) 727-4918
Director of Operations **Daniel C. Wandell** ............. (617) 878-3010

## Elections Division

McCormack Building, One Ashburton Place, Room 1705,
Boston, MA 02108-1518
Tel: (617) 727-2828  Fax: (617) 742-3238

Director and Legal Counsel **Michelle K. Tassinari, Esq.** .... (617) 727-2828

## Publication and Regulations Division

State House, Room 116/117, Boston, MA 02133
Tel: (617) 727-2831  Fax: (617) 742-4822

Director **Steven Kfoury** .............................. (617) 727-9136
Citizen Information Service Director **Jeffrey Williams** .... (617) 727-7030
  E-mail: jeffrey.williams@sec.state.ma.us
State Bookstore Director **Steven Kfoury** .............. (617) 727-2834

## Public Records Division

McCormack Building, One Ashburton Place, Room 1719,
Boston, MA 02108-1518
Tel: (617) 727-2832  Fax: (617) 727-5914

Supervisor of Records **Shawn A. Williams, Esq.** ........ (617) 727-2832
Archivist **John D. Warner, Jr.** ....................... (617) 727-2816
Director of Massachusetts Archives, Assistant Archivist
  **J. Michael Comeau** ................................ (617) 727-2816
Commonwealth Museum Director **Stephen Kenney** ...... (617) 727-9268
Massachusetts Historical Commission Executive Director
  and State Archaeologist **Brona Simon** .............. (617) 727-8470
State Records Center Director **Brian Shea** ............ (617) 727-2470
State House Tours Director **Mary Rinehart-Stankiewicz** .. (617) 727-3676

---

★ Elected Official    ■Appointed by Governor    ●Appointed by Legislature    ▲ Appointed by Board or Commission    ◆ Appointed by State Supreme Court

## Registry of Deeds Division

One Ashburton Place, Room 1612, Boston, MA 02108-1512
Tel: (617) 878-3152  Fax: (617) 723-1372
E-mail: registry@sec.state.ma.us

Director **Paul McCarthy** . . . . . . . . . . . . . . . . . . . . . . . . . . . . .(617) 727-0556

## Securities Division

McCormack Building, One Ashburton Place, 17th Floor,
Boston, MA 02108-1518
Tel: (617) 727-3548  Fax: (617) 248-0177

First Deputy Secretary and Securities Director
  **Bryan Lantagne, Esq.** . . . . . . . . . . . . . . . . . . . . . . . . . . (617) 727-3548
Corporations Director and Chief Legal Counsel
  **Laurie Flynn** . . . . . . . . . . . . . . . . . . . . . . . . . . . . . . . . . .(617) 727-4919

## Office of the Inspector General

One Ashburton Place, Room 1311, Boston, MA 02108-1518
Tel: (617) 727-9140  Tel: (800) 322-1323 (Hotline)  Fax: (617) 723-2334
E-mail: ma-igo-general-mail@massmail.state.ms.us

**Fiscal Year:** 2015  **Budget:** $2,528,783

Inspector General **Glenn A. Cunha** . . . . . . . . . . . . . . . . . . . .(617) 727-9140
  Education: Boston Col 1984 BA; Bentley U 1989 MBA;
  Suffolk 1995 JD
Massachusetts Certified Public Purchasing Official
  Program Director **Joyce McEntee Emmett** . . . . . . . . . . .(617) 523-1205
  Executive Assistant **Nataliya Urciuoli** . . . . . . . . . . . . . . .(617) 722-8844

## Office of the State Auditor

State House, Room 230, Boston, MA 02133
Tel: (617) 727-2075  Fax: (617) 727-2383

**Fiscal Year:** 2016  **Budget:** $18,356,279

★ State Auditor **Suzanne M. Bump** (D) . . . . . . . . . . . . . . . .(617) 727-2075
  Term Expires: January 2019
  Education: Boston Col AB; Suffolk JD
  Career: Secretary, Executive Office of Labor and Workforce
  Development, Commonwealth of Massachusetts (2007-2009)
  Chief of Staff **Seth Andrea McCoy** . . . . . . . . . . . . . . . . .(617) 727-2075
Deputy Auditor for Administration and Finance
  **Pamela E. Lomax** . . . . . . . . . . . . . . . . . . . . . . . . . . . . . . .(617) 727-6200
  E-mail: pamela.lomax@sao.state.ma.us
Deputy Auditor for Audit Operations
  **Kenneth M. Woodland** . . . . . . . . . . . . . . . . . . . . . . . . . . (617) 727-6200
Deputy Auditor for Communications and External
  Relations **Alicia Curran** . . . . . . . . . . . . . . . . . . . . . . . . . .(857) 242-5306
  E-mail: alicia.bandy@sao.state.ma.us
Deputy Auditor and General Counsel
  **Timothy V. Dooling** . . . . . . . . . . . . . . . . . . . . . . . . . . . . .(617) 727-6200
Operations Director **Bernadette O'Malley** . . . . . . . . . . . . . .(617) 727-6200
Bureau of Special Investigations (BSI) Director
  **Alexandra Alland** . . . . . . . . . . . . . . . . . . . . . . . . . . . . . . .(617) 727-6771
Communications Manager **Michael Wessler** . . . . . . . . . . . .(617) 727-2075
  E-mail: michael.wessler@sao.state.ma.us
Division of Local Mandates (DLM) Director
  **Vincent McCarthy** . . . . . . . . . . . . . . . . . . . . . . . . . . . . . .(617) 727-0980

## Office of the Treasurer and Receiver General

State House, 24 Beacon Street, Room 227, Boston, MA 01233
Tel: (617) 367-6900  Internet: www.mass.gov/treasury

**Employees:** 561  **Fiscal Year:** 2016  **Budget:** $2,344,393,000

★ State Treasurer and Receiver General
  **Deborah B. Goldberg** (D) . . . . . . . . . . . . . . . . . . . . . . . .(617) 367-6900
  Term Expires: January 2019
  E-mail: dgoldberg@tre.state.ma.us
  Education: Boston Col 1983 JD; Harvard 1985 MBA
  Career: Selectman, Board of Selectman, Town of Brookline,
  Massachusetts (1998-2004)
Chief of Staff **David J. Falcone** . . . . . . . . . . . . . . . . . . . . . .(617) 367-6900
First Deputy Treasurer **James MacDonald** . . . . . . . . . . . . . .(617) 367-6900
  Education: Boston State Col

Deputy Treasurer **Maureen Godsey Valente** . . . . . . . . . . . .(617) 720-4466
  Education: UC Berkeley; George Washington MPA
Deputy Treasurer and Executive Director,
  Office of Economic Empowerment
  **Alayna Van Tassel** . . . . . . . . . . . . . . . . . . . . . . . .(617) 367-3900 ext. 460
Assistant Treasurer and Director, Unclaimed
  Property Division **Mark William Bracken** . . . . . .(617) 367-3900 ext. 421
Assistant Treasurer for Debt Management
  **Susan Perez** . . . . . . . . . . . . . . . . . . . . . . . . . . . .(617) 367-9333 ext. 816
  Education: Boston U 1989 BS
General Counsel **Sarah Kim** . . . . . . . . . . . . . . . . . .(617) 367-3900 ext. 233
Deputy General Counsel **Greg Polin** . . . . . . . . . . . .(617) 367-3900 ext. 532
Communications Director **Chandra Allard** . . . . . . .(617) 367-6900 ext. 620
  E-mail: callard@tre.state.ma.us
Human Resources Director **Swee Lin Wong** . . . . .(617) 367-3900 ext. 578

## Office of Campaign and Political Finance [OCPF]

One Ashburton Place, Room 411, Boston, MA 02108
Tel: (617) 979-8300  Fax: (617) 727-6549  E-mail: ocpf@cpf.state.ma.us

**Employees:** 17  **Fiscal Year:** 2015  **Budget:** $1,433,000

▲ Director **Michael J. Sullivan** . . . . . . . . . . . . . . . .(617) 979-8300 ext. 28303
  E-mail: msullivan@cpf.state.ma.us
General Counsel **Gregory Birne** . . . . . . . . . . . . . .(617) 979-8300 ext. 28304
Auditing Director **Patricia Jacobson** . . . . . . . . . .(617) 979-8300 ext. 28308
Communications and Public Education
  Director **Jason Tait** . . . . . . . . . . . . . . . . . . . . . .(617) 979-8300 ext. 28309
  E-mail: jtait@cpf.state.ma.us
Compliance Coordinator **Caroline Paras** . . . . . . .(617) 979-8300 ext. 28305
Chief Financial Officer **Margaret Muise** . . . . . . .(617) 979-8300 ext. 28306
Chief Information Officer **Albert Grimes** . . . . . . .(617) 979-8300 ext. 28319
  E-mail: albert.grimes@sec.state.ma.us

## MassHousing (Finance Agency)

One Beacon Street, Boston, MA 02108
Tel: (617) 854-1000  Fax: (617) 854-1029  TTY: (617) 854-1025
E-mail: webinfo@masshousing.com  Internet: www.masshousing.com

▲ Executive Director **Timothy C. Sullivan** . . . . . . . . . . . . . . .(617) 854-1258
  E-mail: tsullivan@masshousing.com
  Education: UMass (Boston) 1995 MS
Executive Director Emeritus **Thomas R. Gleason** . . . . . . . .(617) 854-1860
  Note: Until December 31, 2016.
  Education: Holy Cross Col 1976 BA
  Executive Secretary **Laurie Bennett** . . . . . . . . . . . . . . . . . .(617) 854-1886
Deputy Director **Karen E. Kelleher** . . . . . . . . . . . . . . . . . . .(617) 854-1850
Chief Financial Officer **Michael T. Fitzmaurice** . . . . . . . . . .(617) 854-1129
Chief Information Officer **Tyrone J. Reed** . . . . . . . . . . . . . .(617) 854-1746
  Education: Clark U BA; Boston U MBA
Communications Director **Eric Gedstad** . . . . . . . . . . . . . . . .(617) 854-1079
  E-mail: egedstad@masshousing.com
  Education: Boston U 1989 BS
General Counsel (Acting) **Beth M. Elliott** . . . . . . . . . . . . . .(617) 854-1273
  E-mail: belliott@masshousing.com
  Education: Michigan BA; Harvard JD
Government Affairs Director **Nancy M. McDonald** . . . . . . .(617) 854-1852
  Education: Stonehill 1990 BA
Managing Director of Administration **Francis P. Creedon** . .(617) 854-1890
  E-mail: fcreedon@masshousing.com
  Education: Cornell; Northeastern MPA
Managing Director of Government Affairs and
  Communications **Thomas J. Lyons** . . . . . . . . . . . . . . . . . .(617) 854-1075
Network and Computer Services Manager
  **Leo J. Saidnawey** . . . . . . . . . . . . . . . . . . . . . . . . . . . . . . .(617) 854-1731
  E-mail: lsaidnawey@masshousing.com      Fax: (617) 624-9400
Webmaster **Deepak Karamcheti** . . . . . . . . . . . . . . . . . . . . .(617) 854-1891
  Education: Penn State 1996 BA

---

★ Elected Official    ■ Appointed by Governor    ● Appointed by Legislature    ▲ Appointed by Board or Commission    ◆ Appointed by State Supreme Court

# Massachusetts Educational Financing Authority [MEFA]

160 Federal Street, 4th Floor, Boston, MA 02110
Tel: (800) 449-6332  Tel: (617) 261-9760  E-mail: info@mefa.org
Internet: www.mefa.org

■Executive Director **Thomas M. Graf** . . . . . . . . . . (617) 261-9760 ext. 4801
  E-mail: tgraf@mefa.org
  Education: Merrimack BS
Deputy Director **Elizabeth K. Fontaine** . . . . . . . . (617) 261-9760 ext. 4802
  Education: Assumption Col BA
Chief Financial Officer and Chief Operating
  Officer **James Leighton** . . . . . . . . . . . . . . . . . (617) 261-9760 ext. 4835
College Savings Programs Director
  **Anna Scimemi** . . . . . . . . . . . . . . . . . . . . . . . (617) 261-9760 ext. 4812
Marketing Director **Penny Hauck** . . . . . . . . . . . . (617) 261-9760 ext. 4840
Information Technology Director **Lori Seuch** . . . . (617) 261-9760 ext. 4806
  E-mail: lseuch@mefa.org
Programs and Operations Director
  **Francis Cavanaugh** . . . . . . . . . . . . . . . . . . . . (617) 261-9760 ext. 4810
  E-mail: francis.cavanaugh@state.ma.us
Board Secretary and Human Resource
  Administrator **(Vacant)** . . . . . . . . . . . . . . . . . . (617) 261-9760 ext. 4807

# Water Resources Authority

Charlestown Navy Yard, Building 39, 100 First Avenue, 3rd Floor,
Boston, MA 02129
Tel: (617) 242-6000  Fax: (617) 788-4893  TTY: (617) 788-4880
E-mail: mwralib@mwra.state.ma.us  Internet: www.mwra.com

■Chair **Matthew A. Beaton** . . . . . . . . . . . . . . . . . . . . . . . . . (617) 626-1100
  E-mail: matthew.beaton@state.ma.us
  Affiliation: Secretary, Executive Office of Energy and Environmental
  Affairs, Commonwealth of Massachusetts
  100 Cambridge Street, 9th Floor, Boston, MA 02114
Executive Director **Frederick A. Laskey** . . . . . . . . . . . . . . . (617) 788-1103
  Education: UMass (Boston) 1979 BA
General Counsel **Steven A. Remsberg** . . . . . . . . . . . . . . . (617) 788-1145
Chief Operating Officer **Michael J. Hornbrook** . . . . . . . . . . (617) 788-4359
  Education: UMass (Amherst) 1979 BS
Deputy Chief Operating Officer **John P. Vetere** . . . . . . . . . (617) 788-4366
Administration Director **Michele S. Gillen** . . . . . . . . . . . . . (617) 788-2042
  E-mail: michele.gillen@mwra.state.ma.us
  Education: Fordham BA; UMass (Boston) MS
Finance Director **Thomas J. Durkin** . . . . . . . . . . . . . . . . . (617) 788-4917
Planning Director **Stephen Estes-Smargiassi** . . . . . . . . . . (617) 788-1170
Public Affairs Director **Sean Navin** . . . . . . . . . . . . . . . . . . (617) 788-1112
Librarian and Records Manager **Elizabeth Steele** . . . . . . . . (617) 305-5584

# MassDevelopment

99 High Street, Boston, MA 02110
Tel: (617) 330-2000  Fax: (617) 330-2001
E-mail: marketingdepartment@massdevelopment.com
Internet: www.massdevelopment.com

President and Chief Executive Officer **Marty Jones** . . . . . . (617) 330-2000
Chief of Staff **Meg Delorier** . . . . . . . . . . . . . . . . . . . . . . . .(617) 330-2000
Executive Vice President, Finance and Chief Financial
  Officer **Simon R. Gerlin, CPA** . . . . . . . . . . . . . . . . . . . (617) 330-2000
  Education: Middlebury BA; Harvard MBA
Executive Vice President, Finance Programs
  **Laura Canter** . . . . . . . . . . . . . . . . . . . . . . . . . . . . . . . . (617) 330-2000
  Education: Emerson BS; Bentley Col MBA
Director of Defense Sector Initiatives **Anne Marie Dowd** . .(617) 330-2000
  E-mail: adowd@massdevelopment.com
  Education: Middlebury; Wisconsin JD
Director of Governmental Relations and Communications
  **Mark Sternman** . . . . . . . . . . . . . . . . . . . . . . . . . . . . . .(617) 330-2034
  E-mail: msternman@massdevelopment.com
  Education: Dartmouth BA; Columbia
Executive Vice President, Real Estate
  **Richard Henderson** . . . . . . . . . . . . . . . . . . . . . . . . . . . .(617) 330-2000
  Education: Williams; Edinburgh (Scotland) MPhil
Human Resources and Organizational Development
  Director **(Vacant)** . . . . . . . . . . . . . . . . . . . . . . . . . . . . . (617) 330-2000

General Counsel **Patricia DeAngelis** . . . . . . . . . . . . . . . . . (617) 330-2000
  Education: UMass (Amherst); U San Francisco JD
Communications Director **Kelsey Abbruzzese** . . . . . . . . . . (617) 330-2086
  E-mail: kabbruzzese@massdevelopment.com

# Ethics Commission

John W. McCormack Office Building, One Ashburton Place, Room 619,
Boston, MA 02108
Tel: (617) 371-9500  Tel: (888) 485-4766  Fax: (617) 723-5851
Internet: www.mass.gov/ethics

**Employees:** 22  **Fiscal Year:** 2015  **Budget:** $1,914,000

Chair **Barbara Dortch-Okara** . . . . . . . . . . . . . . . . . . . . . . .(617) 371-9500
  Education: Brandeis BA; Boston Col JD
Member **David A. Mills** . . . . . . . . . . . . . . . . . . . . . . . . . . . (617) 371-9500
  Education: Boston Col 1967 LLB
Member **Regina L. Quinlan** . . . . . . . . . . . . . . . . . . . . . . . (617) 371-9500
Member **Thomas J. Sartory** . . . . . . . . . . . . . . . . . . . . . . . (617) 371-9500
  Affiliation: Director/General Counsel, Goulston & Storrs
  400 Atlantic Avenue, Boston, MA 02110-3333
  Education: Loyola Marymount 1966 BA; Harvard 1969 JD
Member **William Trach** . . . . . . . . . . . . . . . . . . . . . . . . . . . (617) 371-9500
  Education: Harvard 2004 JD
Executive Director **Karen L. Nober** . . . . . . . . . . . . . . . . . . (617) 371-9516

---

★ Elected Official     ■ Appointed by Governor     ● Appointed by Legislature     ▲ Appointed by Board or Commission     ◆ Appointed by State Supreme Court

# Michigan

Tel: (517) 373-1837 (General Information Operator)  Internet: www.michigan.gov

**Number of U.S. Congressional Delegates:** 2 Senators; 14 Representatives  **Governor's Term:** 4 years
**Legislature Description:** 38 member Senate; 110 member House of Representatives; Term - Senate 4
years, House 2 years  **Next Election:** Governor November 2018; Legislature November 2016
**Number of Electoral Votes:** 16  **Official Name:** State of Michigan (Chippewa: great lake)
**Nickname:** The Wolverine State; Great Lake State  **Motto:** Si quaeris peninsulam amoenam circumspice (If
you seek a pleasant peninsula, look about you)

**Population:** 9,922,576 (2015); Rank 10  **Fiscal Year:** 2014  **Budget:** $48,924,068,000

## Office of the Governor

George W. Romney Building, Lansing, MI 48933
P.O. Box 30013, Lansing, MI 48909
Tel: (517) 373-3400  Fax: (517) 335-6863

**Fiscal Year:** 2014  **Budget:** $5,370,000

**Richard D. "Rick" Snyder**
Governor

Began Service: January 1, 2011
Term Expires: January 1, 2019
Date of Birth: August 19, 1958
Education: Michigan 1977 BS, 1979 MBA,
1982 JD
Career: Partner, Coopers & Lybrand LLP
(1988-1991); President and Chief Operating
Officer, Gateway, Inc. (1996-1997); Co-Founder,
President and Chief Executive Officer, Avalon
Capital Group, Inc. (1997-2000); Co-Founder,
Chairman and Chief Executive Officer, Ardesta,
LLC (2000-2005); Chairman, Board of Directors,
Gateway, Inc. (2005-2007)

★Governor **Richard D. "Rick" Snyder** (R) . . . . . . . . . . . . . . (517) 373-3400
  E-mail: rick.snyder@michigan.gov
Chief of Staff **Jarrod Agen** . . . . . . . . . . . . . . . . . . . . . . . . (517) 373-3400
Cabinet Secretary **Mike Zimmer** . . . . . . . . . . . . . . . . . . . . (517) 373-3400
  E-mail: zimmerm@michigan.gov
  Education: Michigan State; George Washington JD
Deputy Chief of Staff **Beth Emmitt** . . . . . . . . . . . . . . . . . (517) 373-3400
Administration Director **Marsha Quebbeman** . . . . . . . . . . . (517) 241-5190
  E-mail: quebbemanm@michigan.gov
Communications Director **Ari B. Adler** . . . . . . . . . . . . . . . (517) 373-3400
  Communications Manager **Josh David Paciorek** . . . . . . . (517) 373-3400
Chief Legal Counsel **Elizabeth "Beth" Clement** . . . . . . . . (517) 373-3400
Strategy Director **John J. Walsh** . . . . . . . . . . . . . . . . . . . (517) 373-3400
  Education: Michigan State 1984 BA; Wayne State U 1987 JD
  Strategy Deputy Director **Michael "Mike" Brownfield** . . (517) 373-3400
Scheduling Director **(Vacant)** . . . . . . . . . . . . . . . . . . . . . (517) 373-3400
  Assistant to the Director of Scheduling **Morgan Bedan** . . (517) 373-3400
Chief Adviser for Legislative Affairs
  **Richard "Dick" Posthumus** . . . . . . . . . . . . . . . . . . . . (517) 373-3400
  E-mail: posthumusd@michigan.gov
Senior Strategy Adviser **(Vacant)** . . . . . . . . . . . . . . . . . . . (517) 373-3400
Education Special Adviser (Interim) **Craig Ruff** . . . . . . . . . (517) 373-3400
Special Projects Manager **Meegan Holland** . . . . . . . . . . . . (517) 373-3400
Press Secretary **Anna Heaton** . . . . . . . . . . . . . . . . . . . . . (517) 373-3400
  Education: Western Michigan 2006 BA
Deputy Press Secretary **Laura Biehl** . . . . . . . . . . . . . . . . . (517) 373-3400
  Education: Michigan State 2007, 2011 MA
Deputy Press Secretary **Josh David Paciorek** . . . . . . . . . . (517) 373-3400

## Northern Michigan Office

234 W. Baraga Avenue, Marquette, MI 49855
Tel: (906) 228-2850  Fax: (906) 228-8347

Director **David "Dave" Nyberg** . . . . . . . . . . . . . . . . . (906) 228-2850
  E-mail: nybergd@michigan.gov
  Education: Michigan State 2004 BA, 2011 JD

## Washington Office

444 North Capitol Street, NW, Suite 411, Washington, DC 20001
Tel: (202) 624-5840  Fax: (202) 624-5841

Director **Bill McBride** . . . . . . . . . . . . . . . . . . . . . . . . . . . (202) 624-5840
  E-mail: mcbrideb@michigan.gov
Senior Federal Policy Representative **Rob Blackwell** . . . . . . (202) 624-5840
  Education: Michigan State BA
Senior Federal Policy Representative **Eric Brown** . . . . . . . . (202) 624-5840

## Office of the Lieutenant Governor

P.O. Box 30013, Lansing, MI 48909
Tel: (517) 373-6800  Fax: (517) 241-6863

★Lieutenant Governor **Brian Calley** (R) . . . . . . . . . . . . . . (517) 373-6800
  Term Expires: January 1, 2019
  E-mail: brian.calley@michigan.gov
  Education: Michigan State BS, MBA
  Career: State Representative, Michigan House of Representatives
  (2007-2011)
Chief of Staff **Nathaniel Forstner** . . . . . . . . . . . . . . . . . . . (517) 373-6800
Policy and Outreach Coordinator **(Vacant)** . . . . . . . . . . . . (517) 373-6800
Press Secretary **Anna Heaton** . . . . . . . . . . . . . . . . . . . . . (517) 373-6800

## Office of the Attorney General

P.O. Box 30212, Lansing, MI 48909
Tel: (517) 373-1113

**Employees:** 490  **Fiscal Year:** 2016  **Budget:** $92,100,000

★Attorney General **William D. "Bill" Schuette** (R) . . . . . . . (517) 373-1113
  Term Expires: January 1, 2019
  Education: Georgetown 1976 BSFS; U San Francisco 1979 JD
  Career: State Campaign Chair, Michigan Office, Romney for President,
  Inc. (2011-2012); Director, Board of Directors, NAAG Mission
  Foundation, National Association of Attorneys General (2011-2013)
Chief Deputy Attorney General **Carol L. Isaacs** . . . . . . . . . (517) 373-1115
Communications Director **Andrea Bitely** . . . . . . . . . . . . . . (517) 373-8060
Legislative Director **Alan Cropsey** . . . . . . . . . . . . . . . . . . (517) 373-8060
  E-mail: cropseya@michigan.gov
  Education: Bob Jones U BA; Thomas M Cooley JD
Public Affairs Director **John Sellek** . . . . . . . . . . . . . . . . . (517) 373-8060
Healthcare Fraud Division Director **David E. Tanay** . . . . . . (517) 241-6509
Senior Advisor **Rusty Hills** . . . . . . . . . . . . . . . . . . . . . . . (517) 373-8060
Chief Legal Counsel **Matthew Schneider** . . . . . . . . . . . . . (517) 241-8403
  Education: Michigan State 1996 BA; Michigan 2000 JD
■State Public Administrator **Michael E. Moody, Esq.** . . . . . . (517) 373-1123
  E-mail: moodym@michigan.gov
  Education: Michigan State 1990 BS; Detroit Mercy JD

## Office of the Auditor General

Victor Office Center, 201 North Washington Square, Suite 600,
Lansing, MI 48913
Tel: (517) 334-8050  Fax: (517) 334-8079  Internet: audgen.michigan.gov

●Auditor General **Doug Ringler** . . . . . . . . . . . . . . . . . . . . (517) 334-8050
  E-mail: dringler@audgen.michigan.gov
  Deputy Auditor General **Laura J. Hirst** . . . . . . . . . . . . . . (517) 334-8050
Administration Office Director **Paul J. Green** . . . . . . . . . . (517) 334-8050
  E-mail: pgreen@audgen.michigan.gov
Audit Operations Director **Laura J. Hirst** . . . . . . . . . . . . . (517) 334-8050

---

★ Elected Official    ■ Appointed by Governor    ● Appointed by Legislature    ▲ Appointed by Board or Commission    ◆ Appointed by State Supreme Court

Professional Practice Office Director **Craig M. Murray** .... (517) 334-8050
Chief Information Officer **Kimberly E. Jacobs** ......... (517) 334-8050
 E-mail: kjacobs@audgen.michigan.gov
State Relations Officer **Kelly C. Miller** ............... (517) 334-8050

# Department of Agriculture and Rural Development [MDA]

Constitution Hall, 525 West Allegan Street, Lansing, MI 48913
P.O. Box 30017, Lansing, MI 48909
Tel: (517) 284-5767 Fax: (517) 335-1423
E-mail: mda-info@michigan.gov Internet: www.michigan.gov/mdard

■Director **Jamie Clover Adams** ...................... (517) 284-5716
 E-mail: cloveradamsj@michigan.gov
 Education: Michigan 1985 BGS; Georgetown 1992 MPP
 Executive Assistant **Brenda Smith** ................... (517) 284-5716
Chief Deputy Director **Gordon Wenk** ................. (517) 284-5718
 Legislative Liaison **Matthew Blakely** ............... (517) 284-5720
 E-mail: blakelym1@michigan.gov
 Education: Aquinas Col BA; Central Michigan
Animal Industry Division Director **James Averill** ........ (517) 284-5680
Environmental Stewardship Division Director
 **James Johnson** ................................... (517) 284-5602
Food and Dairy Division Director **Kevin Besey** ......... (517) 284-5698
Human Resources Division Director
 **Tamara "Tammi" Eyer** .......................... (517) 284-5032
Laboratory Division Director **Craig VanBuren** .......... (517) 655-8202
Operational Services Division Director **David Bruce** ...... (517) 284-5743
 E-mail: bruced9@michigan.gov
Pesticide and Plant Pest Management Division Director
 **Gina Alessandri** ................................ (517) 284-5639
Food Emergency Planning and Response Manager
 **Dr. John D. Tilden** .............................. (517) 284-5711
State Statistician **Marlo D. Johnson** ................. (517) 324-5300
 E-mail: marlo.johnson@nass.usda.gov
 Education: Alcorn State 1993; Mississippi State 1994 MS
Emergency Management Coordinator **Brad Deacon** ...... (517) 284-5729

# Department of Civil Rights

Executive Office Building, 110 West Michigan, Suite 800,
Lansing, MI 48933
Tel: (517) 335-3165 TTY: (517) 241-1965 Fax: (517) 241-0546
E-mail: mdcr-info@michigan.gov Internet: www.michigan.gov/mdcr

**Employees: 122 Fiscal Year: 2014 Budget: $15,198,300**

▲Director **Agustin V. Arbulu** ....................... (517) 335-3164
 E-mail: arbulua@michigan.gov
 Assistant to the Director **Shawn Sanford** ............ (517) 335-3164
Civil Rights Operations Director **Lori Vinson** .......... (517) 241-3810
 E-mail: lori.vinson@michigan.gov
Communications Director **Vicki Levengood** ............ (517) 241-7978
 E-mail: levengoodv@michigan.gov
Public Affairs Director **Martha Gonzalez-Cortes** ........ (517) 335-3164
Michigan Women's Commission Executive Director
 **Susy Avery** .................................... (313) 456-3802
 E-mail: averys3@michigan.gov

# Michigan Department of Civil Service [MDCS]

400 South Pine Street, Lansing, MI 48909
P.O. Box 30002, Lansing, MI 48909
Tel: (517) 373-3030 TTY: (517) 335-0191 Fax: (517) 373-7609
E-mail: mdcs@michigan.gov Internet: www.michigan.gov/mdcs

▲State Personnel Director **Janine "Jan" Winters** ........ (517) 373-3020
 Human Resource Specialist **Keri Lardie** ............. (517) 241-6604
Deputy Director **Matthew Fedorchuk** ................ (517) 373-3020
General Counsel **John Gnodtke** ..................... (517) 373-3024
 E-mail: gnodtkej@michigan.gov
Audit and Compliance Director **Anne Harrington** ........ (517) 373-7704
Budget & Financial Services Director **Carol Vargovich** ... (517) 373-3168
Business Application Support Director **Susan Wilmore** ... (517) 335-5594
Compensation and HRTD Director **Amy Cahoon** ........ (517) 241-9586

Employee Benefits Director **Lauri Schmidt** ............ (517) 335-3068
Office Director **Matthew Wymans** ................... (517) 241-9091
 E-mail: wymansm@michigan.gov
Personal Services Review Director **Carla Gallagher** ...... (517) 241-7243
Technical Complaints Director **Katie Garner** ........... (517) 241-9093
Detroit Regional Office Director **Duane Lewis** ......... (313) 456-4404
 3042 West Grand Boulevard, Suite 4-400, Detroit, MI 48202

# Department of Corrections

P.O. Box 30003, Lansing, MI 48909
Tel: (517) 335-1426 TTY: (517) 373-0336
Fax: (517) 373-6883 E-mail: correctionsinfo@michigan.gov
Internet: www.michigan.gov/corrections

■Director **Heidi Washington** ....................... (517) 373-0720
 Executive Secretary **Sandy Simon** ................. (517) 241-7238
Legislative Liaison and Special Projects **Kyle Kaminski** ... (517) 373-0720
 E-mail: kaminskik@michigan.gov
Public Information Officer **Chris Gautz** ............... (517) 373-6391
 E-mail: gautzc@michigan.gov
 Education: Central Michigan 2004 BS
Health Care Services Bureau Administrator **Lia Gulick** .... (517) 241-0587
 E-mail: gulick1@michigan.gov

# Budget and Operations Administration

Budget and Operations Administration Deputy Director
 **Jeri-Ann Sherry** ................................ (517) 373-4568
 E-mail: sherryj@michigan.gov
Executive Assistant **Amy M. Droste** ................. (517) 373-4568
Automated Data Systems Services Manager **Jack Beeler** .. (517) 241-7698
 E-mail: beelerj@michigan.gov

# Correctional Facilities Administration

Deputy Director **Ken McKee** ....................... (517) 373-0287
 E-mail: mckeek@michigan.gov
Executive Assistant **Kathleen A. Kikendall** ............ (517) 335-1418
Administrative Assistant **Norma R. Killough** ........... (517) 373-0287

# Field Operations Administration

Deputy Director **Russell Marlan** .................... (517) 373-3184
 E-mail: marlanr@michigan.gov
Executive Assistant **Christine Navarro** ............... (517) 373-3184
Administrative Assistant **Greg Straub** ................ (517) 241-8868

# Department of Environmental Quality

P.O. Box 30473, Lansing, MI 48909-7973
Tel: (517) 373-7917
Tel: (800) 662-9278 (Environmental Assistance Center)
Fax: (517) 241-7401 Internet: www.michigan.gov/deq

■Director (Interim) **Keith Creagh** .................... (517) 284-6700
 E-mail: creaghk@michigan.gov
 Education: Michigan Tech 1974 BS
■Great Lakes Office Director **Jon Allan** ............... (517) 284-5035
 E-mail: allanj@michigan.gov
 Education: Michigan State BSc, MS
Human Resources Director **Tamara "Tammi" Eyer** ....... (517) 284-7973
 Fax: (517) 241-7433
Environmental Assistance Office Chief **Jack Schinderle** ... (517) 284-6852
Marketing, Education and Technology Chief **(Vacant)** ..... (517) 284-6065
Remediation and Redevelopment Division Chief
 **Robert Wagner** ................................. (517) 284-5087
 Fax: (517) 284-9581
Economic and Strategic Initiatives Deputy Director
 **Madhu Anderson** ............................... (517) 284-6702
Policy and Legislative Affairs Deputy Director
 **Maggie Pallone** ................................. (517) 284-6704
 E-mail: pallonem@michigan.gov
Communications Director (Interim) **Melanie L. Brown** .... (517) 284-6713

---

★ Elected Official ■ Appointed by Governor ● Appointed by Legislature ▲ Appointed by Board or Commission ◆ Appointed by State Supreme Court

# Department of Health and Human Services [MDHHS]

Internet: http://www.michigan.gov/mdhhs

■ Director **Nick Lyon** .................................. (517) 241-2787
  E-mail: lyonn2@michigan.gov
  Education: Yale 1990 BA
Child Support Director **Erin Frisch** .................... (517) 241-7460
  E-mail: frische@michigan.gov
Community Services Director **Paula Kaiser Van Dam** .... (517) 241-4040
Family Advocate Director **Seth Persky** ................. (517) 335-3969
  Education: Michigan 1992 BA, 1997 MSW
Legislative Services Director **Karla Ruest** ............. (517) 241-1939
  E-mail: ruestk@michigan.gov
  Executive Secretary **Nancy Grijalva** ................. (517) 335-0267
Legal Services and Policy Director **Mark Meyer** ........ (517) 373-2082
Chief Deputy Director **(Vacant)** ...................... (517) 373-3626
Aging Services Office Director **(Vacant)** .............. (517) 373-7876
Behavioral Health and Developmental Disabilities
  Administration Deputy Director **Lynda Zeller** ........ (517) 335-0196
Communications Manager **Bob Wheaton** ................. (517) 373-4287
  E-mail: wheatonb@michigan.gov
Health Information Technology Manager
  **Meghan Vanderstelt** ............................... (517) 241-2966
  E-mail: vansterltm@michigan.gov
External Relations Senior Deputy Director
  **Geralyn Lasher** ................................... (517) 241-2112
Inspector General and Deputy Director **Alan Kimichik** .... (517) 373-3657
Public Information Officer **Jennifer Smith** ............. (517) 241-2112
  E-mail: smithj32@michigan.gov

## Developmental Disabilities Council

201 Townsen Street, Lansing, MI 48913
Tel: (517) 335-3158  Fax: (517) 335-2751
E-mail: mdhhs-dd-council@michigan.gov

Chairperson **Kristen E. Columbus** ..................... (517) 335-3158
  Term Expires: September 30, 2019
Vice-Chairperson **Justin Caine** ....................... (517) 335-3158
  Term Expires: September 30, 2016
Member **Jill Barker** .................................. (517) 335-3158
  Term Expires: September 30, 2016
Member **Elmer L. Cerano** .............................. (517) 335-3158
  Term Expires: September 30, 2014
Member **Heidi A. DeVries** ............................. (517) 335-3158
  Term Expires: September 30, 2019
Member **Steven Johnson** ............................... (517) 335-3158
Member **Barbara LeRoy** ................................ (517) 335-3158
Member **Jeremiah Prusi** ............................... (517) 335-3158
  Term Expires: September 30, 2016
Member **Jane Reagan** .................................. (517) 335-3158
  Term Expires: September 30, 2016
Member **Deborah Rock** ................................. (517) 335-3158
  Term Expires: September 30, 2018
Member **Andrea Sargent** ............................... (517) 335-3158
  Term Expires: September 30, 2016
Member **Richard J. Suhrheinrich** ...................... (517) 335-3158
  Term Expires: September 30, 2016
Member **David Taylor** ................................. (517) 335-3158
  Term Expires: September 30, 2016
Member **David Verseput** ............................... (517) 335-3158
  Term Expires: September 30, 2016
Member **Deborah Wiese** ................................ (517) 335-3158
  Term Expires: September 30, 2016
Member **Marnie Wills** ................................. (517) 335-3158
  Term Expires: September 30, 2016
Member **Tammy Yeoman** ................................. (517) 335-3158
Member **(Vacant)** ..................................... (517) 335-3158

## Council Staff

Executive Director **Vendella M. Collins** .............. (517) 284-7292
Deputy Director **Yasmina Bouraoui** .................... (517) 284-7291
Executive Secretary **Sheila McCulloch** ................ (517) 284-7297
  E-mail: mccullochs@michigan.gov

Communications Representative **Meredith Smith** ........ (517) 284-7295
  E-mail: smithm10@michigan.gov

# Operations Administration Office

Lewis Cass Building, 320 South Walnut Street, Lansing, MI 48913
Tel: (517) 373-3740  Internet: www.michigan.gov/mdch

Operations Administration Senior Deputy Director
  **Farah Hanley** ..................................... (517) 241-6289
  E-mail: hanleyf@michigan.gov
Audit Office Director **Pam Myers** ..................... (517) 241-7599
Accounting Division Director **Paul McDonald** .......... (517) 241-5627
Budget Division Director **Cindy Masterson** ............ (517) 241-2409
Grants and Purchasing Division Director **Kristi Broessel** .. (517) 241-3770
  E-mail: broesselk@michigan.gov
Budget and Purchasing Bureau Director
  **Kimberly Stephen** ................................. (517) 241-2330
Finance Bureau Director **Steven Bendele** .............. (517) 335-5731
  E-mail: bendeles@michigan.gov

# Population Health and Community Services Administration

Capitol View Building, 201 Townsend Street, Sixth Floor,
Lansing, MI 48913

Deputy Director **Susan "Sue" Moran** ................... (517) 335-8024
  E-mail: morans@michigan.gov
Chronic Disease and Injury Control Director
  **Linda Scarpetta** .................................. (517) 335-8397
Family, Maternal & Child Health Director **Rashmi Travis** .. (517) 335-8922
WIC (Women, Infants and Children) Director **Stan Bien** .. (517) 335-8951
  320 South Walnut Street, Lansing, MI 48913
  E-mail: biens@michigan.gov
Children's Special Health Care Services Division
  Director **Lonnie Barnett** .......................... (517) 241-7186
Community Services Bureau Director
  **Paula Kaiser Van Dam** ............................. (517) 373-3740
Communicable Disease Division Director **Jim Collins** .... (517) 335-8165
Environmental Health Division Director **Linda Dykema** ... (517) 335-8350
Family and Community Health Division Director
  **Brenda Fink** ...................................... (517) 335-8863
Lifecourse Epidemiology and Genomics Division
  Director **Sarah Lyon-Callo** ........................ (517) 335-8806
Immunization Division Director
  **Robert W. "Bob" Swanson** .......................... (517) 335-8934
  Education: Michigan State BA, MA          Fax: (517) 335-9855
Disease Control, Prevention and Epidemiology Bureau
  Director **Corinne E. Miller** ....................... (517) 335-8900
Local Health and Administrative Deputy Director
  **Mikelle Robinson** ................................. (517) 335-8011
  E-mail: robinsonm18@michigan.gov
Vital Records and Health Statistics State Registrar
  **Glenn Copeland** ................................... (517) 335-8677
  E-mail: copelandg@michigan.gov     Fax: (517) 335-9513

# Aging and Adult Services Agency

The Chandler Plaza Building, 300 East Michigan Avenue, 3rd Floor,
Lansing, MI 48933
P.O. Box 30676, Lansing, MI 48909-8176
Tel: (517) 373-8230  TTY: (517) 373-4096  Fax: (517) 373-4092
Internet: www.michigan.gov/aasa

■ Executive Director **Kari Sederburg** .................. (517) 373-7876
  E-mail: sederburgk@michigan.gov
  Senior Executive Management Assistant **Carol Dye** .... (517) 373-8268
Deputy Director **Richard Kline** ....................... (517) 241-0988
  Executive Secretary **Annette Gamez** ................. (517) 241-4503
  E-mail: gameza@michigan.gov
Long Term Care Ombudsman Director **Sarah Slocum** .... (517) 335-0148
  Executive Secretary **(Vacant)** ..................... (517) 373-1560
Program and Partnership Development Division Director
  **Wendi Middleton** .................................. (517) 373-4071
Technical Assistance, Support, and Compliance (TASC)
  Division Director **Scott Wamsley** .................. (517) 241-0624

---

★ Elected Official    ■ Appointed by Governor    ● Appointed by Legislature    ▲ Appointed by Board or Commission    ◆ Appointed by State Supreme Court

Executive Secretary **Becky Payne**....................(517) 373-4548
E-mail: payner4@michigan.gov

# Behavioral Health and Developmental Disabilities Administration
Lewis Cass Building, 320 South Walnut Street, Lansing, MI 48913
Tel: (517) 373-3740

Deputy Director **Lynda Zeller**........................(517) 335-0196
Hospital Center and Forensic Mental Health Services
Director **Cynthia Kelly**...........................(517) 335-4076
Quality Management and Planning Director **(Vacant)**.....(517) 241-1822
Services to Children and Families Director **Sheri Falvay**...(517) 241-5767
Community Living Division Director **David Verseput**....(517) 373-8091
Program Development Consultation and Contracts
Division Director **Thomas Renwick**................(517) 241-5066
E-mail: renwickt@michigan.gov
Recipient Rights Division Director **John Sanford**........(517) 373-2319
Office of Recovery Oriented Systems of Care
**Deborah Hollis**................................(517) 335-6572
Autism Coordinator **Lisa Grost**......................(517) 241-5767

# Chief Medical Executive Health Administration
Capitol View Building, 201 Townsend, Seventh Floor, Lansing, MI 48913

Chief Medical Executive **Dr. Eden Wells, MD**..........(517) 335-9531
Public Health Preparedness Director **Jacqueline Scott**....(517) 335-8150
Chemistry and Toxicology Division Director **(Vacant)**.....(517) 335-9490
Infectious Disease Division Director **James Rudrik**......(517) 335-8063
Laboratories Bureau Director **Sandip Shah, PhD**........(517) 335-8063
3350 North Martin Lane King Jr. Boulevard, Lansing, MI 48906

# Medical Services Administration
400 South Pine, Lansing, MI 48913
Tel: (517) 373-3740

Director **Chris Priest**................................(517) 241-7882
Fax: (517) 335-5007
Customer Services Division Director **Dan Ridge**.........(517) 373-6561
Hospital and Clinic Reimbursement Division Director
**Sherri Gensterblum**.............................(517) 335-5331
Managed Care Plan Division Director
**Kimberly Hamilton**.............................(517) 241-7933
Medicaid Claims Payments Division Director
**John Spitzley**..................................(517) 335-8969
Program Policy Division Director **Jackie Prokop**.........(517) 335-5104
E-mail: prokopj@michigan.gov
Program Review Division Director **Shelia Embry**........(517) 335-5200
E-mail: embrys@michigan.gov
Third Party Liability Division Director
**Keelie Honsowitz**..............................(517) 373-8646
Medical Affairs Director **Debera Eggleston**............(517) 335-5181
Medicaid Operations and Actuarial Services Bureau
Director **Brian Keisling**.........................(517) 241-7192
Medicaid Care Management and Quality Assurance
Bureau Director **Kathy Stiffler**....................(517) 241-8055
E-mail: stifflerk@michigan.gov
Medical Policy and Health System Innovation Bureau
Director **Richard Miles**..........................(517) 241-7882
E-mail: milesr1@michigan.gov
Eligibility Policy Section Manager **Logan Dreasky**.......(517) 241-5414
Fax: (517) 241-8969

## Deputy Director's Office
Chief Deputy Director **Tim Becker**...................(517) 373-3626
Chief Financial Officer **Susan Kangas**..............(517) 373-7914
Accounting Director **(Vacant)**....................(517) 375-6008
Budget and Grants Management Director
**Amanda Bright McClanahan**....................(517) 371-9056
E-mail: brighta@michigan.gov
Contracts and Purchasing Director **Christine Sanches**...(517) 375-1161
Organization Services Director **Kurt Warner**...........(517) 373-7541
E-mail: warnerk5@michigan.gov

Technology and Project Services Bureau
Director **Teresa Spalding**...............(517) 335-1230 ext. 30940
E-mail: spaldingt@michigan.gov
CW Funding and Juvenile Programs Director
**Herman McCall**................................(517) 335-3489
Inspector General Office Director (Acting) **David Russell**..(517) 335-3899
Quality Assurance Director **Julie Horn Alexander**.......(517) 335-6188

# Bureau of Children and Adult Licensing
201 N. Washington Square, Lansing, MI 48933
Fax: (517) 335-6121

AFC/HFA Licensing and Child Care Licensing Director
**Jerry Hendrick**................................(517) 284-9730
Child Welfare Licensing Division Director **(Vacant)**......(517) 284-9740

# Children's Services Agency
Director **Steve Yager**..............................(517) 241-9859
E-mail: yagers@michigan.gov
Adult and Child Welfare Deputy Director **Stacie Bladen**..(517) 373-8626
Children's Protection Services and Family Preservation
Manager **Colin Parks**............................(517) 388-5125

# Field Operations Administration
Deputy Director **Terry Beurer**.......................(517) 373-3570
Field Operations and Cash Assistance Administration
Deputy Director **Sheryl D. Thompson**...............(517) 241-5168
E-mail: thompson2@michigan.gov
Office of Workforce Development and Training Director
**Stacie Gibson**.................................(517) 887-9444
Wayne County Operations Director
**Dwayne A. Haywood**...........................(313) 456-1025
3040 West Grand Boulevard, Cadillac Place, Suite 5-650,
Detroit, MI 48202-6040
Adult Services Administration **Bernell L. Wiggins**......(313) 937-4202
E-mail: wigginsb@michigan.gov
Financial Assistance Administration Director
**Patricia Smith**................................(313) 456-1024
E-mail: smithp10@michigan.gov

# Michigan Community Service Commission
235 South Grand Avenue, Suite 1108, Lansing, MI 48933
Fax: (517) 373-4977  Internet: www.michigan.gov/mcsc

Executive Director **Ginna Holmes**...................(517) 335-4295
E-mail: holmesv@michigan.gov

# Michigan Rehabilitation Services
P.O. Box 30010, Lansing, MI 48909
235 South Grand Avenue, 4th Floor, Lansing, MI 48933
Tel: (800) 605-6722  Fax: (517) 335-7277

Director **Suzanne Howell**..........................(517) 373-3390
E-mail: howells@michigan.gov

# Health Policy and Innovation Administration
Capitol View Building, 201 Townsend Street, Lansing, MI 48913

Deputy Director **Elizabeth Hertel**....................(517) 373-2559
E-mail: hertele@michigan.gov
EMS and Trauma Division Director **Kathy Wahl**.........(517) 241-3025
Education: Walden 2010 MSN
Health Policy and Access to Care Division Director
**(Vacant)**.....................................(517) 335-6169
Legal Affairs and FOIA Office Director **Matthew Rick**...(517) 241-0048
Legal and Policy Affairs Bureau Director **Kirk Krause**....(517) 373-2559
E-mail: krausek2@michigan.gov

★ Elected Official ■ Appointed by Governor ● Appointed by Legislature ▲ Appointed by Board or Commission ◆ Appointed by State Supreme Court

*State Yellow Book* © Leadership Directories, Inc. Summer 2016

EXECUTIVE BRANCH

## Department of Insurance and Financial Services [DIFS]

Mason Building, 530 W. Allegan Street, 7th Floor, Lansing, MI 48933
P.O. Box 30220, Lansing, MI 48909-7720
Tel: (517) 284-8800  Tel: (877) 999-6442  Fax: (517) 284-8837
E-mail: difs-Info@michigan.gov

■Director **Pat M. McPharlin** ........................ (517) 284-8661
   E-mail: mcpharlinp@michigan.gov
Chief Deputy Director **Teri Morante** ................. (517) 284-8671
  Administrative Assistant to the Director **Nancy Hill** ..... (517) 284-8658
                           Fax: (517) 284-8844
Budget Office Director **Penny Wright** ............... (517) 284-8734
Consumer Services Office Director **Cathy Kirby** ........ (517) 284-8734
Senior Deputy Director **Rhonda Fossitt** .............. (517) 284-8696
Senior Deputy Director **Judy Weaver** ................ (517) 284-8768
Chief of Staff **(Vacant)** ......................... (517) 373-9812
Office of Banking Director **Karen Lawson** ........... (517) 284-8687
                           Fax: (517) 335-0908
Office of Consumer Finance Director
  **Barbara J. Strefling** ......................... (517) 284-8611
   E-mail: streflingb@michigan.gov     Fax: (517) 373-6739
Office of Credit Unions Director **John Kolhoff** ...... (517) 284-8618
                           Fax: (517) 335-0908
Office of General Counsel Director **Randall Gregg** ...... (517) 335-5834
Office of Insurance Evaluation Director **Judy Weaver** .... (517) 284-8768
Office of Insurance Licensing and Market Conduct
  Director **Jean M. Boven** ...................... (517) 284-8625
Office of Insurance Rate and Forms Director
  **Rhonda Fossitt** ............................ (517) 284-8696
   E-mail: fossittr@michigan.gov
Administrative Assistant to the Deputy and Chief Deputy
  Director **Barb Elkins** ......................... (517) 284-8665
                           Fax: (517) 284-8844
Public Information Officer **Andrea Miller** ............. (517) 284-8668
   E-mail: millera16@michigan.gov

## Department of Licensing and Regulatory Affairs [LARA]

611 W. Ottawa Street, Lansing, MI 48909
Tel: (517) 373-1820

**Fiscal Year:** 2014  **Budget:** $502,918,700

■Director **Shelly Edgerton** ........................ (517) 373-3034
   E-mail: edgertons1@michigan.gov
  Administrative Assistant to the Director **Diane Burton** .. (517) 373-2729
Chief Deputy Director **(Vacant)** ................... (517) 373-1820
Deputy Director and Chief Financial Officer **Allan Pohl** ... (517) 373-3034
Deputy Director **Wanda Stokes** ................... (517) 373-3034
  Education: Michigan State BA; Detroit Mercy JD
Communications Office Director **Jason Moon** ........... (517) 373-9280
   E-mail: moonj@michigan.gov     Fax: (517) 241-1580
Policy and Legislative Affairs Director **Frank Waters** ..... (517) 241-4580
   E-mail: watersf@michigan.gov
Freedom of Information Coordinator **Stephani Fleming** ...(517) 373-0194
   E-mail: flemingS2@michigan.gov
Securities Division Deputy Commissioner **Diane Bissell** ...(517) 241-3034

## Human Resources Office

Tel: (517) 373-4769  Fax: (517) 373-6526

Director **Marie Lisle** ............................... (517) 373-4769
  Secretary to the Director **(Vacant)** ................ (517) 373-4769
Labor Relations Manager **Frank Russell** .............. (517) 373-6772
   E-mail: russellf@michigan.gov

## Finance and Administrative Services Office

P.O. Box 30004, Lansing, MI 48909
Fax: (517) 373-3621

Director (Acting) **LeAnn Droste** ................... (517) 373-3847
   E-mail: pohla1@michigan.gov
Budget Director **(Vacant)** ......................... (517) 373-0003

Financial Services Director **Shirley Callahan** ........... (517) 373-4915
Procurement Services Division Director **LeAnn Droste** .... (517) 373-3847
                          Fax: (517) 373-2927

## Office of Regulatory Reinvention

611 West Ottawa, Lansing, MI 48933
P.O. Box 30004, Lansing, MI 48909
Tel: (517) 335-8658  Fax: (517) 335-9512

Manager (Acting) **Adam Sandoval** .................. (517) 241-0861

## Bureau of Construction Codes

P.O. Box 30254, Lansing, MI 48909
Tel: (517) 241-9313  Fax: (517) 241-9308
Internet: www.michigan.gov/bcc

Director **Irvin Poke** ............................... (517) 241-9302
Deputy Director **Barbara Kunkel** ................... (517) 241-9302
Deputy Director **Keith Lambert** .................... (517) 241-9302
Administrative Services Office Director **(Vacant)** ........ (517) 241-9302
Management Services Office Director **(Vacant)** ......... (517) 241-9313
Land Survey and Remonumentation Division Director
  **(Vacant)** ................................. (517) 241-6321
Boiler Division Chief **Mark Moore** .................. (517) 241-9334
Electrical Division Chief **Dean Austin** ................ (517) 241-9320
Elevator Division Chief **Robert A. Babinski** ............ (517) 241-9337
Mechanical Division Chief **Kevin Kalakay** ............. (517) 241-9325
Plan Review and Building Division Chief
  **Stanley Skopek** ............................ (517) 241-9317
Plumbing Division Chief **Joe Madziar** ............... (517) 241-9330

## Bureau of Corporations, Securities Commercial Licensing

P.O. Box 30018, Lansing, MI 48909
Fax: (517) 241-0290  Internet: www.michigan.gov/bcs

Director **Alan J. Schefke** .......................... (517) 241-9223
Corporation Division Director **Jim Lotoszinski** .......... (517) 241-6470
Corporation Division Deputy Director **Julia Dale** ........ (517) 241-6470
Securities and Audit Director **Timothy Teague** ......... (517) 241-6470

## Bureau of Employment Relations

P.O. Box 02988, Detroit, MI 48202-2988
Tel: (313) 456-3510  Fax: (313) 456-3511  Internet: www.mi.gov/merc

Director **Ruthanne Okun** ......................... (313) 456-3519
   E-mail: okunr@michigan.gov
  Administrative Assistant **Nancy Pitt** ................ (313) 456-3517
   E-mail: pittn@michigan.gov
Staff Attorney **Lynn Morison** ...................... (313) 456-3516
   E-mail: morisonl@michigan.gov

## Bureau of Fire Services

525 West Allegan Street, 4th Floor, Lansing, MI 48933
P.O. Box 30700, Lansing, MI 48909
Tel: (517) 241-8847  Fax: (517) 335-4061

State Fire Marshal **Julie Secontine** .................. (517) 241-8847
  Education: Michigan State BA; Wayne State U JD

## Bureau of Professional Licensing

611 West Ottawa Street, 3rd Floor, Lansing, MI 48933-1070
P.O. Box 30670, Lansing, MI 48909-8170
Tel: (517) 373-8068  Fax: (517) 241-9416  E-mail: bplhelp@michigan.gov

Director **Kimberly H. Gaedeke** ..................... (517) 241-2649
Legal Affairs Division Director **Ann Ward-Fuchs** ........ (517) 373-8068
Licensing Division Director **Andrew Brisbo** ........... (517) 373-8068
Regulatory and Compliance Division Director
  **Joseph Campbell** ........................... (517) 373-4972
   E-mail: campbellj1@michigan.gov

---

★ Elected Official   ■ Appointed by Governor   ● Appointed by Legislature   ▲ Appointed by Board or Commission   ◆ Appointed by State Supreme Court

## Michigan Occupational Safety and Health Administration [MIOSHA]

State Secondary Complex, 7150 Harris Drive, Dimondale, MI 48821
P.O. Box 30643, Lansing, MI 48909-8143
Tel: (517) 284-7778  Fax: (517) 284-7775

Director (Acting) **Barton G. Pickelman** . . . . . . . . . . . . . . (517) 284-7777
  Executive Secretary **Kimberly Fedewa** . . . . . . . . . . . . . (517) 284-7777
Deputy Director **(Vacant)** . . . . . . . . . . . . . . . . . . . . . . . . (517) 322-1817
  Secretary **Kimberly Fedewa** . . . . . . . . . . . . . . . . . . . . (517) 636-4542

## Workers Compensation Agency

7150 Harris Drive, Dimondale, MI 48821
P.O. Box 30016, Lansing, MI 48909-7516
Tel: (888) 396-5041  Fax: (517) 322-6012  E-mail: wcinfo@michigan.gov
Internet: www.michigan.gov/wca

Director **Mark Long** . . . . . . . . . . . . . . . . . . . . . . . . . . . (517) 322-1106
  Secretary **(Vacant)** . . . . . . . . . . . . . . . . . . . . . . . . . . (517) 322-1106
Claims Processing Division Administrator **Ted Day** . . . . . . . (517) 322-5990
  E-mail: dayt@michigan.gov
Compliance and Employer Records Division
  Administrator **Cheryl Cornellier** . . . . . . . . . . . . . . . . . (517) 322-1195
  E-mail: cornellierc@michigan.gov          Fax: (517) 322-1990
Funds Administration Division Administrator **(Vacant)** . . . . (517) 636-6602
                                              Fax: (517) 636-6627
Health Care Services Division Administrator
  **Billie Newsom** . . . . . . . . . . . . . . . . . . . . . . . . . . . . . (313) 456-3659
  E-mail: newsomb@michigan.gov             Fax: (313) 456-3651
Self-Insured Programs Division Administrator
  **John Schrock** . . . . . . . . . . . . . . . . . . . . . . . . . . . . . . (517) 322-1868
  E-mail: schrockj@michigan.gov            Fax: (517) 322-5944
Contested Case Division Manager **(Vacant)** . . . . . . . . . . . . (517) 322-5996
Workers' Compensation Board of Magistrates
  Chairperson **Lisa Klaeren** . . . . . . . . . . . . . . . . . . . . . . (269) 544-4442
                                              Fax: (616) 447-2685

## Michigan Department of Natural Resources

P.O. Box 30028, Lansing, MI 48909
Tel: (517) 284-6367

■Director **Dr. William Bill Moritz** . . . . . . . . . . . . . . . . . (517) 284-6367
  E-mail: dnr-director@michigan.gov
Finance and Operations Chief **Sharon Schafer** . . . . . . . . . (517) 284-5958
Chief Administrative Officer **Mark Hoffman** . . . . . . . . . . . (517) 284-5810
  E-mail: hoffmanm@michigan.gov
Public Information Officer **Ed Golder** . . . . . . . . . . . . . . . (517) 284-5815
  E-mail: goldere@michigan.gov
Tribal Coordinator and Chief of Staff **Dennis Knapp** . . . . . (517) 243-1510
Legislative Liaison **Trevor VanDyke** . . . . . . . . . . . . . . . . (517) 284-5808
  E-mail: vandyket1@michigan.gov

## Department of Military and Veterans Affairs [DMVA]

3411 North MLK Jr. Boulevard, Lansing, MI 48906
Tel: (517) 481-8083  Fax: (517) 481-8125  E-mail: dma@state.mi.us
Internet: www.michigan.gov/dmva

■Director **MG Gregory J. Vadnais, ARNG** . . . . . . . . . . . . (517) 481-8083
  E-mail: gregory.j.vadnais.mil@mail.mil
Chief of Staff **COL Timothy "Tim" Houchlei, ARNG** . . . . (517) 481-8110
Facilities and Construction Office Director
  **COL Edward Hallenbeck, ARNG** . . . . . . . . . . . . . . . . (517) 481-7560
Public Affairs Office Director **William Humes** . . . . . . . . . . (517) 481-8140
State Operations Chief Financial Officer **Alfred Christian** . . (517) 481-7645
Legislative Liaison **Steve Kozera** . . . . . . . . . . . . . . . . . . (517) 481-8072
  E-mail: kozeras@michigan.gov

## Michigan National Guard

3411 North MLK Jr. Boulevard, Lansing, MI 48906
Fax: (517) 481-8125

■Adjutant General Director
  **MG Gregory J. Vadnais, ARNG** . . . . . . . . . . . . . . . . . (517) 481-8125
  E-mail: gregory.j.vadnais.mil@mail.mil

## Michigan Air National Guard

3411 North MLK Jr. Boulevard, Lansing, MI 48906
Fax: (517) 481-8279

Assistant Adjutant General
  **BrigGen Leonard Isabelle, ANG** . . . . . . . . . . . . . . . . . (517) 481-8083
  Education: Kettering 1984 BSEE; MIT 1985 MSEE

## Michigan Army National Guard

3411 North MLK Jr. Boulevard, Lansing, MI 48906
Fax: (517) 481-8125

Installations Assistant Adjutant General
  **BG Mike Stone, ARNG** . . . . . . . . . . . . . . . . . . . . . . . (517) 481-8080
Information Management Deputy Chief of Staff
  **COL Mark Tellier, ARNG** . . . . . . . . . . . . . . . . . . . . . (517) 481-8083

# Department of State

Richard H. Austin Building, 430 West Allegan Street, 4th Floor,
Lansing, MI 48918-8900
Tel: (888) 767-6424  TTY: (517) 322-1477  Fax: (517) 373-0727
Internet: www.michigan.gov/sos

**Employees:** 1,562  **Fiscal Year:** 2014  **Budget:** $209,723,000

★Secretary of State **Ruth Johnson** (R) . . . . . . . . . . . . . . . (517) 373-2511
  Term Expires: January 1, 2019
  E-mail: ruth.johnson@michigan.gov
Chief of Staff **Mike Senyko** . . . . . . . . . . . . . . . . . . . . . . (517) 373-2510
Communications Director **Gisgie Dávila Gendreau** . . . . . . (517) 373-2520
  E-mail: gendreaug@michigan.gov
Elections Bureau Director **Christopher Thomas** . . . . . . . . . (517) 373-2540
  Richard H. Austin Building, 430 West Allegan, 1st Floor,
  Lansing, MI 48918
External Affairs Director **Gary Koutsoubos** . . . . . . . . . . . (517) 335-4030
  E-mail: koutsoubos@michigan.gov
  Education: Central Michigan 2001 BA
Policy Initiatives Office Director **Kieran P. Marion** . . . . . . (517) 373-4422
  Education: Michigan State 1988 BA; Thomas M Cooley 2002 JD
Great Seal Office Supervisor **Robin Houston** . . . . . . . . . . (517) 373-2531

## Customer Services Administration

Secondary Complex, 7064 Crowner Drive, Lansing, MI 48918

Director **Michael Wartella** . . . . . . . . . . . . . . . . . . . . . . . (517) 322-3449
Customer Services Office Director **Mike Butcher** . . . . . . . . (517) 636-6339
Branch Office Services Bureau Director **Bill Strong** . . . . . . (517) 636-6383
Legal Services Bureau Director
  **William R. "Bill" Kordenbrock** . . . . . . . . . . . . . . . . . (517) 241-8322
  Education: Hope BA; Thomas M Cooley JD
Driver and Vehicle Records Division Director
  **Fred Bueter** . . . . . . . . . . . . . . . . . . . . . . . . . . . . . . . (517) 322-1934
  E-mail: bueterf@michigan.gov
Program Support and Development Director
  **Grace Ueberroth** . . . . . . . . . . . . . . . . . . . . . . . . . . . . (517) 373-3440

## Department Services Administration

Director **Rose Jarois** . . . . . . . . . . . . . . . . . . . . . . . . . . . (517) 373-3939
Information Security Bureau Director **Steven Stier** . . . . . . . (517) 335-0218
  E-mail: stiersl@michigan.gov

## Chief Legal Counsel Administration

Director **William R. "Bill" Kordenbrock** . . . . . . . . . . . . . (517) 241-3463

---

★ Elected Official    ■ Appointed by Governor    ● Appointed by Legislature    ▲ Appointed by Board or Commission    ◆ Appointed by State Supreme Court

# Department of State Police [MSP]
333 South Grand Avenue, Lansing, MI 48983
Tel: (517) 332-2521  Fax: (517) 241-0409
Internet: www.michigan.gov/msp
■ Director/Homeland Security Director
   **Col. Kriste Kibbey Etue** . . . . . . . . . . . . . . . . . . . . . . (517) 241-0403
   E-mail: etuek@michigan.gov

## Administrative Services Bureau
Fax: (517) 241-0409
Deputy Director **Shawn Sible** . . . . . . . . . . . . . . . . . . . . (517) 241-0407

## Michigan Commission on Law Enforcement Standards
106 West Allegan, Suite 600, Lansing, MI 48933
Fax: (517) 322-6439
Executive Director **David Harvey** . . . . . . . . . . . . . . . . . . (517) 322-1417

## Field Services Bureau
Fax: (517) 241-0409
Deputy Director **Lt. Col. Thomas W. Sands** . . . . . . . . . . (517) 241-0235

## State Services Bureau
Fax: (517) 241-0409
Deputy Director **Lt. Col. Richard Arnold** . . . . . . . . . . . . (517) 241-0132
   E-mail: arnoldr@michigan.gov
Budget Division Director **Sherri Irwin** . . . . . . . . . . . . . . (517) 241-1001
Criminal Justice Information Center Director
   **Dawn Brinningstaull** . . . . . . . . . . . . . . . . . . . . . . . (517) 241-0604
Criminal Justice Information Center Assistant Deputy
   Director **Katie Bower** . . . . . . . . . . . . . . . . . . . . . . . (517) 241-1661
Forensic Science Division Director
   **Capt. Gregoire Michaud** . . . . . . . . . . . . . . . . . . . . (517) 322-6100
   Education: Michigan State 1988 BSc, 2007 MM
Departmental Services Division Director **Sherri Irwin** . . . . . (517) 241-1001
   E-mail: irwins@michigan.gov
Highway Safety Planning Office Executive Director
   **Michael "Mike" Prince** . . . . . . . . . . . . . . . . . . . . . (517) 241-1512
   E-mail: princem@michigan.gov
Training Division Commanding Officer
   **Capt. Thomas Deasy** . . . . . . . . . . . . . . . . . . . . . . (517) 322-1500
Public Affairs Representative **Shanon Banner** . . . . . . . . . (517) 241-0995
   E-mail: banners@michigan.gov

# Department of Talent and Economic Development [TED]
Internet: www.michigan.gov/ted
■ Director **Steve Arwood** . . . . . . . . . . . . . . . . . . . . . . . (517) 373-3400
   Education: Michigan State
Communications Director **Ari B. Adler** . . . . . . . . . . . . . . (517) 373-3400

## Michigan Talent Investment Agency
Internet: www.michigan.gov/tia
■ Director **Stephanie Comai** . . . . . . . . . . . . . . . . . . . . . (517) 373-3400
   E-mail: stephanie.comai@michigan.gov

## Unemployment Insurance Agency
3024 West Grand Boulevard, Cadillac Place Suite 13-650,
Detroit, MI 48202-3196
Tel: (313) 456-2400  Fax: (313) 456-2424
Internet: www.michigan.gov/uia
Director **Sharon Moffett-Massey** . . . . . . . . . . . . . . . . . (313) 456-3275
   Secretary **Wannetta Joyce** . . . . . . . . . . . . . . . . . . . (313) 456-2411
Customer Service Director **(Vacant)** . . . . . . . . . . . . . . . (313) 456-4945
   Secretary **Gail Loving** . . . . . . . . . . . . . . . . . . . . . . (313) 456-2401
Physical Integrity Group Director **Anita M. Friday** . . . . . . (313) 456-3625
   Secretary **Annette Jones** . . . . . . . . . . . . . . . . . . . . (313) 456-3627
Trust Fund Office Director **Rodger M. Palm** . . . . . . . . . . (313) 456-2405
   Secretary **Christina Anthony** . . . . . . . . . . . . . . . . . . (313) 456-2415

# Workforce Development Agency
201 North Washington Square, Lansing, MI 48913
Director **Stephanie Beckhorn** . . . . . . . . . . . . . . . . . . (517) 335-5858
   Education: Michigan State       Fax: (517) 241-8217

# Department of Technology, Management and Budget [DTMB]
George W. Romney Building, 111 South Capitol Avenue,
Lansing, MI 48933
Tel: (517) 373-1004  Fax: (517) 373-7268  E-mail: dtmb@michigan.gov

**Employees:** 2,816  **Fiscal Year:** 2014  **Budget:** $811,731,000
■ Director **David B. Behen** . . . . . . . . . . . . . . . . . . . . . . (517) 373-1004
   E-mail: behend@michigan.gov
Public Information Officer **Caleb Buhs** . . . . . . . . . . . . . . (517) 241-7422
   E-mail: buhsc@michigan.gov
Executive Assistant **Chanda Donnan** . . . . . . . . . . . . . . (517) 373-3209
■ Chief Deputy Director **Brom Stibitz** . . . . . . . . . . . . . . . (517) 373-1004
   E-mail: stibitzb@michigan.gov
Legislative Liaison and Policy Advisor **Matt Sweeney** . . . . (517) 373-7505
   E-mail: sweeneym1@michigan.gov
Chief Information Officer **David B. Behen** . . . . . . . . . . . . (517) 373-1004
   E-mail: behend@michigan.gov

## Management
Customer Service Director **James McFarlane** . . . . . . . . . . (517) 241-1842
Financial Services Director **Mike Gilliland** . . . . . . . . . . . . (517) 335-3746
Human Resources Director **Susan King** . . . . . . . . . . . . . (517) 373-7717
Retirement Administration Senior Deputy Director
   **Kerrie Vandenbosch** . . . . . . . . . . . . . . . . . . . . . . (517) 322-6235
   E-mail: vandenboschk@michigan.gov

## Technology
IT Finance and Accounting Director **Leo LaPorte** . . . . . . . (517) 241-2000
   E-mail: leo.laporte@michigan.gov
Facilities and Business Services Administration Director
   **Michael Turnquist** . . . . . . . . . . . . . . . . . . . . . . . . (517) 284-7979
   E-mail: turnquistm@michigan.gov
Michigan Public Safety Communication System
   (MPSCS) Director **Brad Stoddard** . . . . . . . . . . . . . . (517) 336-6108
   E-mail: stoddardb@michigan.gov
Cybersecurity and Infrastructure Protection Chief
   Security Officer **Rodney Davenport** . . . . . . . . . . . . . (517) 241-4090
Infrastructure and Operations Director **Judy Odett** . . . . . . (517) 636-6504
   E-mail: odettj@michigan.gov
Shared Solutions Director **Eric Swanson** . . . . . . . . . . . . (517) 335-1338
   E-mail: swansone@michigan.gov
Telecom Division Director (Acting) **Greg Decamp** . . . . . . (517) 241-0257
Client Service Center Director **Jan Isaacs** . . . . . . . . . . . . (517) 335-1223
Budget Officer **Greg Decamp** . . . . . . . . . . . . . . . . . . . (517) 241-8540
Chief Technology Officer **Rod Davenport** . . . . . . . . . . . . (517) 241-5110
   E-mail: davenportr1@michigan.gov
Internal Auditor **John Juarez** . . . . . . . . . . . . . . . . . . . . (517) 241-2713

## State Budget Office
111 South Capitol Avenue, Lansing, MI 48913
Tel: (517) 373-7560  Fax: (517) 241-5428
E-mail: statebudgetoffice@michigan.gov
Internet: www.michigan.gov/budget
■ State Budget Director **John S. Roberts** . . . . . . . . . . . . . (517) 373-7560
   E-mail: john.roberts@michigan.gov
   Education: Michigan State
Deputy State Budget Director **Nancy Duncan** . . . . . . . . . (517) 373-0870
Budget Development Section **Megan Ramos** . . . . . . . . . . (517) 241-2668

## Office of the State Employer
400 South Pine Street, Lansing, MI 48909
P.O. Box 30026, Lansing, MI 48909
Tel: (517) 373-7400  E-mail: dtmb-ose@michigan.gov
Director **Marie L. Waalkes** . . . . . . . . . . . . . . . . . . . . . . (517) 373-7400
   Education: Michigan State BSCrimJ

---

★ Elected Official   ■ Appointed by Governor   ● Appointed by Legislature   ▲ Appointed by Board or Commission   ◆ Appointed by State Supreme Court

# Department of Transportation
P.O. Box 30005, Lansing, MI 48909
Tel: (517) 373-2090  Fax: (517) 373-0167
Internet: www.michigan.gov/mdot

■Director **Kirk T. Steudle, PE** . . . . . . . . . . . . . . . . . . (517) 373-2114
  E-mail: steudlek@michigan.gov
  Education: Lawrence Tech BS
  Chief Administrative Officer **Laura J. Mester, CPA** . . . . (517) 241-2674
    E-mail: mesterl@michigan.gov
  Governmental Affairs Office Legislative Office
    Administrator **Frank Raha** . . . . . . . . . . . . . . . . . . (517) 335-5507
    E-mail: rahaf@michigan.gov
  Human Resources Office Director **Todd White** . . . . . . . (517) 335-6538
  Business Development Director **Lisa Thompson** . . . . . . . (517) 373-2377
■Communications Director **Jeff Cranson** . . . . . . . . . . . . (517) 335-3084
  E-mail: cransonj@michigan.gov
  Chief Operations Officer **Mark A. VanPortfleet, PE** . . . . . (517) 373-4656

## Office of Aeronautic Services
Tel: (517) 335-9283  Fax: (517) 321-6422
Internet: www.michigan.gov/aero

Executive Administration Officer **Michael G. Trout** . . . . . . (517) 335-9568
Airports Division Administrator
  **Richard E. "Rick" Hammond** . . . . . . . . . . . . . . . . (517) 335-8472
  E-mail: hammondr@michigan.gov
Aviation Services Division Administrator **Pauline Misjak** . . (517) 335-9952
  E-mail: misjakp@michigan.gov

## Finance and Administration Bureau
Bureau Director **Myron G. Frierson, CPA** . . . . . . . . . . . (517) 373-2117
  E-mail: friersonm@michigan.gov
Contract Services Division Administrator
  **Demetrius Parker** . . . . . . . . . . . . . . . . . . . . . . (517) 373-4680
  E-mail: parkerd9@michigan.gov
Financial Operations Division Administrator
  **Edward A. Timpf, CPA** . . . . . . . . . . . . . . . . . . . . (517) 373-1527
  E-mail: timpfeE@michigan.gov

## Highway Delivery Bureau
Fax: (517) 335-2813

Bureau Director **Randel R. "Randy" VanPortfliet** . . . . . . (906) 786-1800
  E-mail: vanportflietr@michigan.gov
Construction & Field Services Division Engineer
  **Brenda J. O'Brien, PE** . . . . . . . . . . . . . . . . . . . (517) 322-1085
  E-mail: obrienb2@michigan.gov
Maintenance Division Engineer **(Vacant)** . . . . . . . . . . . (517) 322-3323
Safety and Security Administration Administrator
  **Eileen Phifer** . . . . . . . . . . . . . . . . . . . . . . . . (517) 373-1898
  E-mail: phifere@michigan.gov

## Highway Development Bureau
Director and Chief Engineer
  **Bradley "Brad" Wieferich, PE** . . . . . . . . . . . . . . . (517) 335-2345
  E-mail: wieferichb@michigan.gov
Design Division Engineer **Kristin Schuster** . . . . . . . . . . (517) 373-0030
  E-mail: schusterk@michigan.gov
Real Estate Division Officer **Matthew "Matt" Delong** . . . (517) 373-2200

## Passenger Transportation Bureau
Administrator **Sharon Edgar** . . . . . . . . . . . . . . . . . . (517) 373-0470

## Transportation Planning Bureau
Bureau Director **David Wresinski** . . . . . . . . . . . . . . . (517) 373-0343
Asset Management Division Administrator
  **William Tansil** . . . . . . . . . . . . . . . . . . . . . . . (517) 335-2639
  E-mail: tansilw@michigan.gov
Intermodal Policy Administrator **Polly Kent** . . . . . . . . . (517) 335-2905
  E-mail: kentp@michigan.gov
Statewide Transportation Planning Division Administrator
  **Denise Jackson** . . . . . . . . . . . . . . . . . . . . . . . (517) 335-2962
  E-mail: jacksond15@michigan.gov

# International Bridge Administration
934 Bridge Plaza, Sault Sainte Marie, MI 49783
Tel: (906) 635-5255  Fax: (906) 635-0540
General Manager **Phillip M. Becker, PE** . . . . . . . . (906) 635-5255 ext. 112

# Department of Treasury
Richard H. Austin Building, 430 West Allegan Street, Lansing, MI 48922
Tel: (517) 373-3200  TTY: (800) 649-3777
Fax: (517) 335-1785  E-mail: mistatetreasurer@michigan.gov
Internet: www.michigan.gov/treasury

**Employees: 2,530  Fiscal Year: 2014-2015  Budget: $1,945,052,000**

■State Treasurer **Naif A. "Nick" Khouri** . . . . . . . . . . . . (517) 373-3223
  E-mail: khourin@michigan.gov
  Education: Michigan BA; Michigan State MA
  Executive Assistant **Maureen Doyle** . . . . . . . . . . . . (517) 373-3223
Press Secretary **Terry Stanton** . . . . . . . . . . . . . . . . (517) 335-2167
  E-mail: stantont@michigan.gov
Budget and Information Technology Division **(Vacant)** . . . (517) 335-0965
                      Fax: (517) 373-6941
Capital Finance State Building Authority Director
  **(Vacant)** . . . . . . . . . . . . . . . . . . . . . . . . . . (517) 241-2432

## Chief Deputy Treasurer
Fax: (517) 373-4968
Chief Deputy Treasurer **Tom Saxton** . . . . . . . . . . . . . (517) 373-3223

## Financial and Administrative Services
Deputy Treasurer **Joseph Fielek** . . . . . . . . . . . . . . . (517) 373-3223
  E-mail: fielekj@michigan.gov         Fax: (517) 335-0997
Unclaimed Property Division Manager **(Vacant)** . . . . . . . (517) 636-5320
                      Fax: (517) 322-5986
Office of Accounting Services Administrator
  **Susan Nichols** . . . . . . . . . . . . . . . . . . . . . . . (517) 373-3165
                      Fax: (517) 335-0997
Office of Collections Administrator **Ann Good** . . . . . . . . (517) 636-5300
                      Fax: (517) 636-5215
Office of Departmental Services Administrator
  **Bruce Hanses** . . . . . . . . . . . . . . . . . . . . . . . (517) 636-6434
  E-mail: hansesb@michigan.gov     Fax: (517) 636-6826
Office of Financial Services Administrator
  **Andrew Boettcher** . . . . . . . . . . . . . . . . . . . . . (517) 636-0631
                      Fax: (517) 636-5401

## Office of Privacy and Security
Fax: (517) 636-4081
Administrator **Smruti Shah** . . . . . . . . . . . . . . . . . . . (517) 636-4084
                      Fax: (517) 636-5340

## Deputy Treasurer/Chief Operating Officer
Deputy Treasurer and Chief Investment Officer
  **Jon M. Braeutigam** . . . . . . . . . . . . . . . . . . . . . (517) 373-3140
  Education: Michigan State 1985, 1987 MBA

## Deputy Treasurer for Local Government Services
Deputy Treasurer **Wayne Workman** . . . . . . . . . . . . . . (517) 373-4415
Assessment and Certification Division Administrator
  **David A. Buick** . . . . . . . . . . . . . . . . . . . . . . . (517) 373-3269
  E-mail: buickd@michigan.gov     Fax: (517) 241-2621
Local Audit & Finance Division Administrator
  **Suzanne Schafer** . . . . . . . . . . . . . . . . . . . . . . (517) 373-3227
  E-mail: schafersk@michigan.gov   Fax: (517) 373-0633
Property Services Division Administrator
  **Larry Steckelberg** . . . . . . . . . . . . . . . . . . . . . (517) 241-3733
  E-mail: steckelbergl@michigan.gov

## Deputy Treasurer for State and Authority Finance
Deputy Treasurer **Thomas F. Saxton** . . . . . . . . . . . . . (517) 373-3223
                      Fax: (517) 241-2009

★ Elected Official  ■ Appointed by Governor  ● Appointed by Legislature  ▲ Appointed by Board or Commission  ◆ Appointed by State Supreme Court

## Deputy Treasurer for Tax Administration and Oversight

Deputy Treasurer **Gregory Gursky** . . . . . . . . . . . . . . . . . . . . (517) 373-3223
State Bureau Administrator **Jay Wortley** . . . . . . . . . . . . . . (517) 373-2158
                                                            Fax: (517) 335-3298
Tax Analysis Division Administrator **Howard Heideman** . . (517) 373-2697
    E-mail: heideman@michigan.gov                          Fax: (517) 335-3298

## State Board of Education

608 West Allegan, Lansing, MI 48933
P.O. Box 30008, Lansing, MI 48909
Tel: (517) 373-3900  Fax: (517) 335-4575
Internet: www.michigan.gov/sbe

★President **John C. Austin** (D) . . . . . . . . . . . . . . . . . . . . . . (517) 373-3900
    Term Expires: January 1, 2017
    E-mail: jcaustin@umich.edu
    Education: Swarthmore 1983 BA; Harvard 1990 MPA
★Vice President **Casandra E. Ulbrich** (D) . . . . . . . . . . . . . . .(517) 373-3900
    Term Expires: January 1, 2023
    E-mail: ulbrichc@michigan.gov
★Treasurer **Dr. Pamela Pugh** (D) . . . . . . . . . . . . . . . . . . . . .(517) 373-3900
    Term Expires: January 1, 2023
★Secretary **Michelle Fecteau** (D) . . . . . . . . . . . . . . . . . . . . (517) 373-3900
    Term Expires: January 1, 2021
    E-mail: mfecteau@aaupaft.org
    Education: Michigan State
★Board Member **Lupe Ramos-Montigny** (D) . . . . . . . . . . . . (517) 373-3900
    Term Expires: January 1, 2021
★Board Member **Kathleen Straus** (D) . . . . . . . . . . . . . . . . . (517) 373-3900
    Term Expires: January 1, 2017
    E-mail: strausk@michigan.gov
    Education: Hunter BA
★Board Member **Eileen Weiser** (D) . . . . . . . . . . . . . . . . . . . (517) 373-3900
    Term Expires: January 1, 2019
    E-mail: eileen_weiser@msn.com
    Education: Michigan State 1972 BM; Michigan 1975 MM
★Board Member **Richard Zeile** (R) . . . . . . . . . . . . . . . . . . . (517) 373-3900
    Term Expires: January 1, 2019
    E-mail: frzeile@juno.com
    Education: Valparaiso BA; Michigan MA; Concordia Theol Sem;
    Harvard; Wayne State U
State Board Executive **Marilyn Schneider** . . . . . . . . . . . . . (517) 373-3900

## Department of Education

Tel: (517) 373-3324  Fax: (517) 335-4565
Internet: www.michigan.gov/mde

▲State Superintendent **Brian J. Whiston** . . . . . . . . . . . . . . . (517) 241-0494
Special Assistant **Alisande Henry** . . . . . . . . . . . . . . . . . . . . (517) 241-2077
Legislative Liaison **Benjamin Williams** . . . . . . . . . . . . . . . (517) 241-1540
    E-mail: williamsb7@michigan.gov
Public and Governmental Affairs Director **Martin Ackley** . . (517) 241-4395
    E-mail: ackleym@michigan.gov

## Administration and School Support Services

Deputy Superintendent **Kyle Guerrant** . . . . . . . . . . . . . . . . (517) 241-0062
    E-mail: guerrantk@michigan.gov
Financial Management Office Director **Ann Dennis** . . . . . . . .(517) 373-1967
Human Resources Director **Joetta Parke** . . . . . . . . . . . . . . (517) 373-0794
School Support Services Director **Marla Moss** . . . . . . . . . . .(517) 373-4013
    E-mail: mossm1@michigan.gov
State Aid and School Finance Director
    **Daniel "Dan" Hanrahan** . . . . . . . . . . . . . . . . . . . . . . . . (517) 335-0521

## Library of Michigan

702 West Kalamazoo, Lansing, MI 48909-7507
P.O. Box 30007, Lansing, MI 48909
Tel: (517) 373-1580  TTY: (517) 373-1592
TTY: (517) 373-1300 (Reference)  Fax: (517) 373-5700
E-mail: librarian@michigan.gov

State Librarian **Randy Riley** . . . . . . . . . . . . . . . . . . . . . . . .(517) 373-5511
Collection Management Services Director **Don Todaro** . . . . (517) 373-2583

Commission for the Blind, Braille and Talking Book
    Library Director **Susan Chinault** . . . . . . . . . . . . . . . . . . (517) 373-5353
Michigan Newspaper Project Director **Kevin Driedger** . . . . (517) 373-9440

## Michigan Lottery

101 E. Hillsdale, Lansing, MI 48909
P.O. Box 30023, Lansing, MI 48909
Tel: (517) 335-5600  Fax: (517) 335-5644
E-mail: milottery@michigan.gov

■Commissioner **M. Scott Bowen** . . . . . . . . . . . . . . . . . . . . . (517) 335-5608
    E-mail: bowenm@michigan.gov
    Education: Michigan State 1987; Detroit 1990 JD
Public Relations Director **Jeffrey L. "Jeff" Holyfield** . . . . . (517) 335-5736
    E-mail: holyfieldj@michigan.gov

---

★ Elected Official    ■ Appointed by Governor    ● Appointed by Legislature    ▲ Appointed by Board or Commission    ◆ Appointed by State Supreme Court

# Minnesota

Tel: (651) 201-3400

**Number of U.S. Congressional Delegates:** 2 Senators; 8 Representatives  **Governor's Term:** 4 years
**Legislature Description:** 67 member Senate; 134 member House of Representatives; Term - Senate 4 years, House 2 years  **Next Election:** Governor November 2018; Legislature November 2016
**Number of Electoral Votes:** 10  **Official Name:** State of Minnesota (Sioux: sky-colored water)
**Nickname:** The North Star State, The Gopher State  **Motto:** L'Etoile du Nord (The Star of the North)

**Population:** 5,489,594 (2015); Rank 21  **Fiscal Year:** 2014-2015  **Budget:** $39,339,000,000

## Office of the Governor

Veterans Service Building, 20 West 12th Street, Room 116,
St. Paul, MN 55155
Tel: (651) 201-3400  Tel: (800) 657-3717  TTY: (651) 201-3460
Fax: (651) 797-1850

**Mark Dayton**
Governor

Began Service: January 3, 2011
Term Expires: January 2019
Date of Birth: January 26, 1947
Education: Yale 1969 BA
Home: Minneapolis
Religion: Presbyterian
Career: Legislative Assistant, Office of Senator Walter F. Mondale, United States Senate (1975-1976); Commissioner of Energy and Economic Development, State of Minnesota (1983-1986); State Auditor, State of Minnesota (1991-1995); U.S. Senator (DFL-MN), Office of Senator Mark Dayton, United States Senate (2001-2007)

★Governor **Mark Dayton** (DFL) ........................(651) 201-3400
  E-mail: mark.dayton@state.mn.us
Chief of Staff **Jaime Tincher** ........................(651) 201-3400
Deputy Chief of Staff **Katy Sen** ....................(651) 201-3420
Deputy Chief of Staff for Communications and Outreach
  **Bob Hume** ........................................(651) 201-3440
  E-mail: bob.hume@state.mn.us
Assistant Chief of Staff and General Counsel
  **Kimberly Slay Holmes** ...........................(651) 201-3409
  E-mail: kim.holmes@state.mn.us
Senior Advisor for Job Creation **Kathryn H. Tunheim** ....(651) 201-3400
  E-mail: kathy.tunheim@state.mn.us
  Affiliation: President and Chief Executive Officer, Tunheim Partners
  1100 Riverview Twr., 8009 34th Ave. S., Minneapolis, MN 55425
Senior Policy Advisor for Education **Shannon Patrick** ....(651) 201-3473
  E-mail: shannon.patrick@state.mn.us
Senior Policy Advisor **Joanna Dornfeld** ...............(651) 201-3423
  E-mail: joanna.dornfeld@state.mn.us
Policy Advisor **Lauren Gilchrist** ....................(651) 431-2189
  E-mail: lauren.gilchrist@state.mn.us
  Education: Wesleyan U 1999 BA; Minnesota 2007 MPH
Special Advisor **Allison Jones** ......................(651) 201-3422
  E-mail: allison.jones@state.mn.us
Senior Research Analyst **(Vacant)** ...................(651) 201-3427
Senior Aide **Sarah Hinde** ...........................(651) 201-3407
  E-mail: sarah.hinde@state.mn.us
Press Secretary **Matt Swenson** ......................(651) 201-3445
  E-mail: matt.swenson@state.mn.us
  Education: Gustavus Adolphus 2006 BA; Minnesota 2009 MPP
Senior Communications Advisor **Linden M. Zakula** ......(651) 201-3400
  Education: Gustavus Adolphus 2005 BA
Legislative Affairs Coordinator **Amy Hang** ...........(651) 201-3420
  E-mail: amy.hang@state.mn.us
Chief Inclusion Officer **James C. Burroughs II** .......(651) 201-3400

Policy Coordinator and Director of Federal Relations
  **Elizabeth Nordland Dressel** ......................(651) 201-3420
  E-mail: elizabeth.dressel@state.mn.us

## State Federal Affairs Office

1017 8th Street, NE, Washington, DC 20002
Tel: (202) 624-5308  Fax: (202) 624-5425
Director **William G. "Bill" Richard** .................(202) 236-3717
  E-mail: william.g.richard@verizon.net
  Education: St John's U (MN) 1964; Minnesota 1965

## Minnesota Department of Administration

200 Administration Building, 50 Sherburne Avenue, St. Paul, MN 55155
Tel: (651) 201-2555  Fax: (651) 297-7909  Internet: www.mn.gov/admin
■Commissioner **Matt Massman** ........................(651) 201-2555
  E-mail: matt.massman@state.mn.us
  Education: Hamline; Wisconsin MA
  Executive Assistant **Kathy Morgan** .................(651) 201-2556
Deputy Commissioner **Lenora A. Madigan** .............(651) 201-2563
  E-mail: lenora.madigan@state.mn.us
Property and Purchasing Assistant Commissioner
  **Alice Roberts-Davis** .............................(651) 201-2601
Developmental Disabilities Council Planning Director
  **Colleen A. Wieck** ................................(651) 296-9964
  Centennial Building, 658 Cedar Street, 3rd Floor, St. Paul, MN 55155
  E-mail: colleen.wieck@state.mn.us
STAR (System of Technology to Achieve Results)
  Program Manager **Kim Moccia** ......................(651) 201-2297
  E-mail: kim.moccia@state.mn.us
Chief Financial Officer **Micah Intermill** ............(651) 201-2537
  E-mail: micah.intermill@state.mn.us
Human Resources Director **(Vacant)** ..................(651) 201-8005

## Minnesota Department of Agriculture [MDA]

625 Robert Street North, St. Paul, MN 55155
Tel: (651) 201-6000  TTY: (800) 627-3529
Internet: www.mda.state.mn.us
■Commissioner **David J. "Dave" Frederickson**..........(651) 201-6219
  E-mail: dave.frederickson@state.mn.us
  Education: St Benedict BA
Deputy Commissioner **Jim Boerboom** ..................(651) 201-6395
Assistant Commissioner **Matthew J. Wohlman** .........(651) 201-6551
Assistant Commissioner and Department Counsel
  **(Vacant)** ........................................(651) 201-6480
Agricultural Marketing and Development Director
  **Mary Hanks** ......................................(651) 201-6277
Dairy and Food Inspection Director **Benjamin Miller** ....(651) 201-6670
Finance and Budget Director **Stephen Ernest** .........(651) 201-6580
Government Affairs Director **Whitney Place** ...........(651) 201-6480
Government Relations Director **Andrea Vaubel** .........(651) 201-6180
  E-mail: andrea.vaubel@state.mn.us
Human Resources Director **Mandy Papenguth** ..........(651) 201-6361
Laboratory Services Division Director **Gary Horvath** ....(651) 201-6563
Pesticide and Fertilizer Management Division Director
  (Interim) **Dan Stoddard** ..........................(651) 201-6291

*(continued on next page)*

★ Elected Official  ■ Appointed by Governor  ● Appointed by Legislature  ▲ Appointed by Board or Commission  ◆ Appointed by State Supreme Court

EXECUTIVE BRANCH

**Minnesota Department of Agriculture** *continued*

Plant Protection Division Director **Geir Friisoe** . . . . . . . . . . (651) 201-6174
Chief Information Officer **Tyrone Spratt** . . . . . . . . . . . . . . (651) 201-6347
  E-mail: tyrone.spratt@state.mn.us

# Minnesota Department of Commerce

85 Seventh Place East, Suite 500, St. Paul, MN 55101-2198
Tel: (651) 539-1500  Fax: (651) 539-1547
E-mail: general.commerce@state.mn.us

■Commissioner **Michael J. "Mike" Rothman** . . . . . . . . . . (651) 539-1441
  E-mail: mike.rothman@state.mn.us
  Education: Carleton 1984 BA; Minnesota 1988 JD
  Executive Assistant **Heidi Jo Retterath** . . . . . . . . . . . . . (651) 539-1445
Deputy Commissioner for Administration/Chief of Staff
  **Anne V. O'Connor** . . . . . . . . . . . . . . . . . . . . . . . . (651) 539-1442
  E-mail: anne.oconnor@state.mn.us
  Chief Financial Officer and Administrative Services
    Director **Tim Jahnke** . . . . . . . . . . . . . . . . . . . . . . (651) 539-1501
    E-mail: tim.jahnke@state.mn.us
  Chief Information Officer **Cindy Kevern** . . . . . . . . . . . . (651) 284-5630
    E-mail: cindy.kevern@state.mn.us
  Human Resources/Personnel Services Director
    **Colleen Hegstrom** . . . . . . . . . . . . . . . . . . . . . . . (651) 539-1502
Assistant Commissioner of Government and External
  Affairs **Peter Brickwedde** . . . . . . . . . . . . . . . . . . . . (651) 539-1443
  E-mail: peter.brickwedde@state.mn.us
General Counsel **Tamar N. Gronvall** . . . . . . . . . . . . . . . (651) 539-1450
  Education: Minnesota BA, JD
Licensing Director **Peter A. Bratsch** . . . . . . . . . . . . . . . (651) 539-1599
Media Relations Director **Ross Corson** . . . . . . . . . . . . . (651) 539-1463
  E-mail: ross.corson@state.mn.us
Securities Director **Brian Edstrom** . . . . . . . . . . . . . . . . (651) 539-1623

# Minnesota Department of Corrections [DOC]

1450 Energy Park Drive, Suite 200, St. Paul, MN 55108-5219
Tel: (651) 361-7200  TTY: (800) 627-3529  Fax: (651) 642-0223
Internet: www.doc.state.mn.us

■Commissioner **Thomas "Tom" Roy** . . . . . . . . . . . . . . . (651) 361-7226
  E-mail: tom.roy@state.mn.us
  Education: Minnesota 1974 BA
  Executive Aide **Miki Matte** . . . . . . . . . . . . . . . . . . . (651) 361-7227
Communications Director **Sarah Latuseck** . . . . . . . . . . . (651) 361-7229
  E-mail: sarah.latuseck@state.mn.us
Government Relations Director **Kathleen Lonergan** . . . . . . (651) 361-7219
  E-mail: kathleen.lonergan@state.mn.us
Planning and Performance Director **Deb Kerschner** . . . . . . (651) 361-7366
  E-mail: deb.kerschner@state.mn.us
Policy and Legal Services Director **Karen Robinson** . . . . . . (651) 361-7175
  E-mail: karen.robinson@state.mn.us

# Minnesota Department of Education [MDE]

1500 Highway 36 West, Roseville, MN 55113
Tel: (651) 582-8200  Fax: (651) 582-8202  Internet: education.state.mn.us

■Commissioner **Brenda Cassellius** . . . . . . . . . . . . . . . . (651) 582-8204
  E-mail: brenda.cassellius@state.mn.us        Fax: (651) 582-8724
  Education: Minnesota 1989 BA;
  U Social and Business Sciences 1995 MA; U Memphis 2007 EdD
  Assistant to the Commissioner **Maria Vincent** . . . . . . . . (651) 582-8206
Chief of Staff **Charlene Briner** . . . . . . . . . . . . . . . . . . (651) 582-1145
  E-mail: charlene.briner@state.mn.us        Fax: (651) 582-8730
School Board Administrators Director **Janet L. Mohr** . . . . . (651) 582-8796
State Board of Teaching Director **Erin Doan** . . . . . . . . . . (651) 582-8796
  E-mail: erin.doan@state.mn.us        Fax: (651) 582-8872
Academic Standards Director **Beth Aune** . . . . . . . . . . . . (651) 582-8795
  Community Education Services Learning Supervisor
    (Interim) **Michelle Kamenov** . . . . . . . . . . . . . . . . (651) 582-8330
Chief Financial Officer **Denise Anderson** . . . . . . . . . . . (651) 582-8560
Chief Information Officer **Matthew Porett** . . . . . . . . . . . (651) 582-8804
  E-mail: matthew.porett@state.mn.us
  Education: Albright BA; Lehigh MA

Communications Director **Josh Collins** . . . . . . . . . . . . . (651) 582-8205
  E-mail: josh.collins@state.mn.us
  Education: Macalester BA; Oregon
Government Relations Director **Adosh Unni** . . . . . . . . . . (651) 582-8292
  E-mail: adosh.unni@state.mn.us
  Education: Carleton; Minnesota JD
State Library Services Director **Jennifer R. Nelson** . . . . . . (651) 582-8791
  Faribault Library for the Blind Supervisor
    **Catherine A. Durivage** . . . . . . . . . . . . . . . . . . . (507) 333-6860

## Office of the Deputy Commissioner

Deputy Commissioner **Steve Dibb** . . . . . . . . . . . . . . . . (651) 582-8207
                                                      Fax: (651) 582-8693
Assessments Director **Jennifer Dugan** . . . . . . . . . . . . . (651) 582-8564
Human Resources Director **Andrea L. Turner** . . . . . . . . . (651) 582-8502
School Finance Director **Thomas R. "Tom" Melcher** . . . . . (651) 582-8828
  General Education Funding Supervisor
    **Teresa J. "Terri" Yetter** . . . . . . . . . . . . . . . . . . (651) 582-8868
    E-mail: terri.yetter@state.mn.us
  School Finance Manager **(Vacant)** . . . . . . . . . . . . . . (651) 582-8840
  Grant Services Supervisor **Pam Schneider** . . . . . . . . . . (651) 582-8292
    E-mail: pam.schneider@state.mn.us
    Grants Specialist **Debra Rose** . . . . . . . . . . . . . . . (651) 582-8853
    E-mail: debra.rose@state.mn.us
Information Technology Operations Manager **(Vacant)** . . . . (651) 582-8533
Procurement/Encumbrance Supervisor **(Vacant)** . . . . . . . (651) 582-1136

## Office of Early Learning

Tel: (651) 582-8200  E-mail: mde.els@state.mn.us
Director **Bobbie Burnham** . . . . . . . . . . . . . . . . . . . . (651) 582-8397
Deputy Director **(Vacant)** . . . . . . . . . . . . . . . . . . . . (651) 582-8414
Early Childhood Services Supervisor **(Vacant)** . . . . . . . . (651) 582-8422
Early Childhood Special Education **(Vacant)** . . . . . . . . . (651) 582-8473

## Office of Innovation

Assistant Commissioner **Hue Nguyen** . . . . . . . . . . . . . . (651) 582-8742
Charter Schools Director **Cynthia "Cindy" Murphy** . . . . . (651) 582-8217
Educator Licensing Director **Nels Onstad** . . . . . . . . . . . (651) 582-8807
  Education: Moorhead State BA, MA
Indian Education Director **Dennis W. Olson** . . . . . . . . . . (651) 582-8300

## Office of Student and School Success

Assistant Commissioner **Daron Korte** . . . . . . . . . . . . . . (651) 582-8215
Adult Basic Education Supervisor **Todd Wagner** . . . . . . . . (651) 582-8466
  GED (General Education Development) Administrator
    **(Vacant)** . . . . . . . . . . . . . . . . . . . . . . . . . . . (651) 582-8437
  GED (General Education Development) Records
    **Alice Smith** . . . . . . . . . . . . . . . . . . . . . . . . . (651) 582-8466
Compliance and Assistance Director **Marikay Litzau** . . . . . (651) 582-8247
  E-mail: marikay.litzau@state.mn.us
Nutrition, Health, and Youth Development Director
  **Monica Herrera** . . . . . . . . . . . . . . . . . . . . . . . . (651) 582-8453
  Food and Nutrition Services Deputy Director **(Vacant)** . . . (651) 582-8545
                                                      Fax: (651) 582-8497
Career and College Success Director **Paula Palmer** . . . . . . (651) 582-8737
  Child and Adult Care Food Compliance and Assistance
    Supervisor **(Vacant)** . . . . . . . . . . . . . . . . . . . . (651) 582-8775
  School Nutrition Programs Supervisor
    **Debra J. Lukkonen** . . . . . . . . . . . . . . . . . . . . . (651) 582-8228
School Support Director **Gregory B. Keith** . . . . . . . . . . . (651) 582-8655
  Professional Development Supervisor
    **Renee C. Ringold** . . . . . . . . . . . . . . . . . . . . . . (651) 582-8363
  Professional Development and Teacher Advancement
    Program Supervisor **(Vacant)** . . . . . . . . . . . . . . . (651) 582-8440
Student Support Director **John Moorse** . . . . . . . . . . . . . (651) 582-8649
Special Education Director **Robyn R. Widley** . . . . . . . . . . (651) 582-1143
  Education: North Dakota State EdS
  Special Education Interagency Partnerships Supervisor
    **(Vacant)** . . . . . . . . . . . . . . . . . . . . . . . . . . . (651) 582-1143
  Special Education Research, Practice and
    Implementation Supervisor **Eric Kloos** . . . . . . . . . . (651) 582-8268
    E-mail: eric.kloos@state.mn.us
  Special Education Workforce and Low-Incidence
    Supervisor **Joan Breslin-Larson** . . . . . . . . . . . . . . (651) 582-1599

---

★ Elected Official  ■ Appointed by Governor  ● Appointed by Legislature  ▲ Appointed by Board or Commission  ◆ Appointed by State Supreme Court

Maltreatment Supervisor **Jennifer Alexander** . . . . . . . . . (651) 582-8278
Turnaround Schools State Program Administrator
  **Lisa Grundstrom** . . . . . . . . . . . . . . . . . . . . . . . . . . . . . . (651) 582-8249
  E-mail: lisa.grundstrom@state.mn.us
Student Testing and Assessment Supervisor
  **Cheryl Alcaya** . . . . . . . . . . . . . . . . . . . . . . . . . . . . . . . . (651) 582-8419
Program Management Manager **Linda Sams** . . . . . . . . . (651) 582-8431
Psychometrician **(Vacant)** . . . . . . . . . . . . . . . . . . . . . . . . (651) 582-8340

# Minnesota Department of Employment and Economic Development [DEED]

First National Bank Building, 332 Minnesota Street, Suite E-200,
St. Paul, MN 55101-1351
Tel: (651) 259-7114  Tel: (800) 657-3858 (Outside Metro Area)
TTY: (651) 296-3900  Fax: (651) 215-4772
E-mail: deed.customerservice@state.mn.us  Internet: mn.gov/deed

■Commissioner **Shawntera M. Hardy** . . . . . . . . . . . . . . (651) 259-7119
  Education: Ohio State BS; SUNY (Buffalo) MURP
  Executive Assistant **Samantha Shalda** . . . . . . . . . . . . (651) 259-7112
Deputy Commissioner and Chief Operating Officer
  **Blake Chaffee** . . . . . . . . . . . . . . . . . . . . . . . . . . . . . . . (651) 259-7161
Deputy Commissioner for Economic Development
  **Kevin McKinnon** . . . . . . . . . . . . . . . . . . . . . . . . . . . . . (651) 259-7130
Deputy Commissioner for Workforce Development
  **Jeremy Hanson Willis** . . . . . . . . . . . . . . . . . . . . . . . . (651) 259-7116
  E-mail: jeremy.willis@state.mn.us
Broadband Development Office Executive Director
  **Danna MacKenzie** . . . . . . . . . . . . . . . . . . . . . . . . . . . . (651) 259-7114
  Education: Concordia U (MN)
Business Development Director **Jeffery D. Rossate** . . . . . . (651) 259-7493
Business Finance Director **Robert W. Isaacson** . . . . . . . . . (651) 259-7458
Communications Director **(Vacant)** . . . . . . . . . . . . . . . . . . (651) 259-7236
                                                Fax: (651) 215-3841
Community Finance Director **Meredith Udoibok** . . . . . . . . (651) 259-7114
Diversity and Equal Opportunity Director
  **Ann M. Feaman** . . . . . . . . . . . . . . . . . . . . . . . . . . . . . (651) 259-7097
Economic Analysis Director **(Vacant)** . . . . . . . . . . . . . . . (651) 259-7114
Human Resources Director **Dorcas Michaelson** . . . . . . . . (651) 259-7099
Unemployment Insurance Director
  **Richard "Rick" Caligiuri** . . . . . . . . . . . . . . . . . . . . . . (651) 259-7533
  E-mail: rick.caligiuri@state.mn.us
Labor Market Information Director **Steve Hine** . . . . . . . . (651) 259-7396
  E-mail: steve.hine@state.mn.us
Policy Director **Kim Babine** . . . . . . . . . . . . . . . . . . . . . . (651) 259-7677
  E-mail: kim.babine@state.mn.us
Strategic Business Projects Director **Richard W. Roy** . . . . . (651) 259-7544
Vocational Rehabilitation Services Director
  **Kimberley T. Peck** . . . . . . . . . . . . . . . . . . . . . . . . . . . (651) 259-7345
Workforce Development Division Director
  **Thomas Norman** . . . . . . . . . . . . . . . . . . . . . . . . . . . . . (651) 259-7563
                                                Fax: (651) 284-3307
Chief Financial Officer **Julie Freeman** . . . . . . . . . . . . . . (651) 259-1191
Chief Information Officer **Brian Allie** . . . . . . . . . . . . . . . (651) 259-7007
  E-mail: brian.allie@state.mn.us
Senior Librarian **(Vacant)** . . . . . . . . . . . . . . . . . . . . . . . (651) 259-7177
Performance Management Director **(Vacant)** . . . . . . . . . . (651) 259-7114

# Minnesota Department of Health [MDH]

Freeman Building, 625 Robert Street North, St. Paul, MN 55155
P.O. Box 64882, Saint Paul, MN 55164-0882
P.O. Box 64975, St. Paul, MN 55164-0975
Tel: (651) 201-5000 (General Information)
Tel: (651) 201-5970 (Vital Records)  TTY: (651) 201-5797
Fax: (651) 201-4986 (Executive Office)
Fax: (651) 201-5740 (Vital Records)
Fax: (651) 291-0101 (Vital Records, Credit Card Payments)

■Commissioner **Dr. Edward Ehlinger** . . . . . . . . . . . . . . . (651) 201-5810
  E-mail: ed.ehlinger@state.mn.us
  Education: Wisconsin 1968 BA, 1972 MD; North Carolina 1980 MSPH

Executive Aide **Sandy Pizzuti** . . . . . . . . . . . . . . . . . . . . (651) 201-5804
  E-mail: sandy.pizzuti@state.mn.us
Deputy Commissioner **Daniel "Dan" Pollock** . . . . . . . . . . (651) 201-4872
State Epidemiologist and Medical Director **Ruth Lynfield** . . (651) 201-5422
  Education: Cornell 1985 MD

## Health Improvement Bureau
Assistant Commissioner **Jeanne Ayers** . . . . . . . . . . . . . . . (651) 201-5540

## Community and Family Health Division
85 East Seventh Place, St. Paul, MN 55164-0882
P.O. Box 64882, St. Paul, MN 55164
Tel: (651) 201-3589

Director **Margaret "Maggie" Diebel** . . . . . . . . . . . . . . . . (651) 201-3594
Assistant Division Director **Janet Olstad** . . . . . . . . . . . . . (651) 201-3584
Children and Youth with Special Health Needs Section
  Manager **Barbara Dalbec** . . . . . . . . . . . . . . . . . . . . . . (651) 201-3758
  E-mail: barb.dalbec@state.mn.us
Maternal and Child Health Section Manager
  **Susan Castellano** . . . . . . . . . . . . . . . . . . . . . . . . . . . . (651) 201-3872
  E-mail: susan.castellano@state.mn.us
Women, Infants and Children (WIC)/Supplemental
  Nutrition Programs Section Manager **Betsy Clarke** . . . . . (651) 201-4403
  E-mail: betsy.clarke@state.mn.us

## Health Promotion and Chronic Disease Division
85 East Seventh Place, St. Paul, MN 55164-0882
P.O. Box 64882, St. Paul, MN 55164
Tel: (651) 201-3600

Director **Mary Manning** . . . . . . . . . . . . . . . . . . . . . . . . . (651) 201-3601
Health Promotion Center Section Manager
  **Donald B. "Don" Bishop** . . . . . . . . . . . . . . . . . . . . . . (651) 201-5402
Cancer Control Section Manager **Jonathan Slater** . . . . . . . (651) 201-5633
Chronic Disease and Environmental Epidemiology
  Section Manager **Alan Bender** . . . . . . . . . . . . . . . . . . (651) 201-5882
Sage Screening Program Section Manager
  **Shelly Madigan** . . . . . . . . . . . . . . . . . . . . . . . . . . . . . (651) 201-5161
  E-mail: shelly.madigan@state.mn.us

## Health Operations Bureau
Assistant Commissioner **Lee Ho** . . . . . . . . . . . . . . . . . . . (651) 201-5661
  E-mail: lee.ho@state.mn.us
Deputy Chief Operating Officer **Alyssa Haugen** . . . . . . . . (651) 201-5005
  Education: Minnesota (Duluth); Metropolitan State U

## Health Protection Bureau
Assistant Commissioner **Paul Allwood** . . . . . . . . . . . . . . . (651) 201-5711

## Environmental Health Division
625 North Robert Street, St. Paul, MN 55164
P.O. Box 64975, St. Paul, MN 55164-0975
Tel: (651) 201-4571

Director **Thomas "Tom" Hogan** . . . . . . . . . . . . . . . . . . . (651) 201-4675
Assistant Director **Dale Dorschner** . . . . . . . . . . . . . . . . . (651) 201-4603
Drinking Water Protection Manager **Randy Ellingboe** . . . . . (651) 201-4647
Environmental Surveillance and Assessment Manager
  **James Kelly** . . . . . . . . . . . . . . . . . . . . . . . . . . . . . . . (651) 201-4910
Food, Pools and Lodging Services Manager **Steven Diaz** . . (651) 201-3983
Indoor Environments and Radiation Manager
  **Mary B. Navara** . . . . . . . . . . . . . . . . . . . . . . . . . . . . . (651) 201-5826
Well Management Manager **Chris Elvrum** . . . . . . . . . . . . (651) 201-4598

## Infectious Disease Epidemiology, Prevention and Control Division [IDEPC]
625 North Robert Street, St. Paul, MN 55164
Tel: (651) 201-5414  Fax: (651) 201-5666

Director **Kristen R. Ehresmann, RN, MPH** . . . . . . . . . . . (651) 201-5507
Assistant Division Director **Emily J. Emerson** . . . . . . . . . (651) 201-5546
Medical Director **Aaron DeVries** . . . . . . . . . . . . . . . . . . (651) 201-5414
Epidemiology Program Manager **Richard Danila** . . . . . . . . (651) 201-5116
STD and HIV Section Manager **Krissie Guerard** . . . . . . . . (651) 201-4007

*(continued on next page)*

---

★ Elected Official  ■ Appointed by Governor  ● Appointed by Legislature  ▲ Appointed by Board or Commission  ◆ Appointed by State Supreme Court

**Health Protection Bureau** *continued*

Vaccine Preventable Disease Section Manager
**Margo Roddy** . . . . . . . . . . . . . . . . . . . . . . . (651) 201-5545

## Public Health Laboratory Division

601 Robert Street North, St. Paul, MN 55164
P.O. Box 64899, St. Paul, MN 55164-0899
Fax: (651) 201-5064

Director **Joanne Bartkus** . . . . . . . . . . . . . . . . . . . . . (651) 201-5256
Fax: (651) 201-5064
Assistant Director **(Vacant)** . . . . . . . . . . . . . . . . . . (651) 201-5583
Environmental Laboratory Accreditation Program Section
Manager **Joanne Bartkus** . . . . . . . . . . . . . . . . (651) 201-5256
Environmental Laboratory Section Manager
**Paul F. Moyer** . . . . . . . . . . . . . . . . . . . . . . . . (651) 201-5669
Fax: (651) 201-5301
Infectious Disease Laboratory Manager **Sara M. Vetter** . . . (651) 201-5255
Fax: (651) 201-5070
Newborn Screening Section Manager **Mark McCann** . . . . . (651) 201-5450

## Health Systems Bureau

Assistant Commissioner **Gilbert Acevedo** . . . . . . . . . . . . (651) 201-5811
E-mail: gilbert.acevedo@state.mn.us

# Minnesota Department of Human Rights [MDHR]

Freeman Building, 625 Robert Street North, St. Paul, MN 55155
Tel: (651) 539-1100  TTY: (651) 296-1283  Fax: (651) 296-9064
Internet: mn.gov/mdhr

■Commissioner **Kevin M. Lindsey** . . . . . . . . . . . . . . . (651) 539-1121
E-mail: kevin.lindsey@state.mn.us
Education: Iowa 1988 BA, 1991 JD
Assistant to the Commissioner and Administrative
Services Supervisor **Denise Romero-Zasada** . . . . . . . . (651) 539-1098
E-mail: denise.romero-zasada@state.mn.us
Deputy Commissioner **Rowzat Shipchandler** . . . . . . . . . (651) 539-1089
Communications Director **Christine Dufour** . . . . . . . . . . (651) 539-1118
E-mail: christine.dufour@state.mn.us
Legislative Liaison **Scott Beutel** . . . . . . . . . . . . . . . . (651) 539-1104
E-mail: scott.beutel@state.mn.us
Assistant Commissioner **(Vacant)** . . . . . . . . . . . . . . . . (651) 539-1125
Compliance Supervisor **Michael Allan Johnson** . . . . . . . (651) 539-1092
E-mail: michael.allan.johnson@state.mn.us
Enforcement Supervisor **Asuquo Ekpenyoung** . . . . . . . . (651) 539-1113
E-mail: asuquo.ekpenyoung@state.mn.us

# Minnesota Department of Human Services [DHS]

P.O. Box 64998, St. Paul, MN 55164
444 Lafayette Roads, St. Paul, MN 55155 (Mailroom)
Tel: (651) 431-2000  TTY: (800) 627-3529  Fax: (651) 431-7443
E-mail: dhs.webmaster@state.mn.us  Internet: www.dhs.state.mn.us

■Commissioner **Emily Johnson Piper** . . . . . . . . . . . . . . (651) 431-2907
E-mail: emily.piper@state.mn.us
Education: U St Thomas (MN) BS, JD
Assistant to the Commissioner **Joe Sathe** . . . . . . . . . . . (651) 431-2917
Executive Aide **Denise K. Flock** . . . . . . . . . . . . . . . (651) 431-2923
Deputy Commissioner **Charles E. "Chuck" Johnson** . . . . . (651) 431-5672
Executive Aide **Mari Konesky** . . . . . . . . . . . . . . . . (651) 431-2921
Chief of Staff **Luchelle Stevens** . . . . . . . . . . . . . . . (651) 431-2146

## Children and Family Services

Assistant Commissioner **James G. Koppel** . . . . . . . . . . . (651) 431-3835
Education: Mount Union 1973 BS; Howard Col 1977 MSW
Executive Assistant **Stephanie A. Ostwald** . . . . . . . . . . (651) 431-3830
Child Safety and Permanency Director **Jamie Sorenson** . . (651) 431-4655
Social Services Information System Director
**Thomas Kine** . . . . . . . . . . . . . . . . . . . . . . (651) 431-4745
E-mail: tom.kine@state.mn.us
Child Placement and Permanency Manager
**Edward L. McBrayer** . . . . . . . . . . . . . . . . . . (651) 431-4296

Child Support Enforcement Director
**Jeffrey J. Jorgenson** . . . . . . . . . . . . . . . . . . . (651) 431-4276
E-mail: jeffrey.j.jorgenson@state.mn.us
Community Partnerships and Child Care Services
Director **Cindi Yang** . . . . . . . . . . . . . . . . . . . (651) 431-3828
Community Living Supports Director **Jane Lawrenz** . . . . (651) 431-3844
Economic Assistance and Employment Supports Division
Director **Jovon Perry** . . . . . . . . . . . . . . . . . . . (651) 431-4006
Management Operations Division Director
**Ralph McQuarter** . . . . . . . . . . . . . . . . . . . . (651) 431-3858
E-mail: ralph.mcquarter@state.mn.us
Legislative Liaison **Nichole "Nikki" Farago** . . . . . . . (651) 431-2201
E-mail: nikki.farago@state.mn.us

## Community and Partner Relations

Assistant Commissioner **Anne M. Barry** . . . . . . . . . . . . (651) 431-3212
Education: St Catharine Col BA; Minnesota MPH; William Mitchell JD
Community Relations Director **Antonia M. Wilcoxon** . . . . (651) 431-3301
County Relations Director (Acting) **Anne M. Barry** . . . . (651) 431-3212
Chief Equity and Development Officer **Constance Tuck** . . . (651) 431-3037
Indian Policy Director **Vern LaPlante** . . . . . . . . . . . . (651) 431-2910

## Community Supports

Assistant Commissioner **(Vacant)** . . . . . . . . . . . . . . . (651) 431-2326
Executive Assistant **Linda Dahlquist** . . . . . . . . . . . . (651) 431-2324
Adult Mental Health Division Deputy Director
**Alice Nichols** . . . . . . . . . . . . . . . . . . . . . . (651) 431-2326
Alcohol and Drug Abuse Division Deputy Director
**Brian Zirbes** . . . . . . . . . . . . . . . . . . . . . . (651) 431-4928
Children's Mental Health Division Deputy Director
**Alice Nichols** . . . . . . . . . . . . . . . . . . . . . . (651) 431-2326
E-mail: alice.nichols@state.mn.us
Disability Services Director **Alexander "Alex" Bartolic** . . . (651) 431-2381
Deaf and Hard of Hearing Services Director
**David Rosenthal** . . . . . . . . . . . . . . . . . . . . (651) 431-2356
TTY: (651) 431-2356
Housing and Jensen Implementation Director
**Erin Sullivan Sutton** . . . . . . . . . . . . . . . . . . (651) 431-3849

## Continuing Care for Older Adults

Tel: (800) 333-2433 (Senior Link Age Line)
Assistant Commissioner **Loren Colman** . . . . . . . . . . . . (651) 431-2560
Executive Assistant **Darci J. Steffen** . . . . . . . . . . . . (651) 431-2598
Aging and Adult Services Director **Kari Benson** . . . . . . (651) 431-2566
Community Supports for Seniors Supervisor
**Lisa Rotegard** . . . . . . . . . . . . . . . . . . . . . (651) 431-2564
Operations and Contract Management Supervisor
**Margaret E. Bisek** . . . . . . . . . . . . . . . . . . . (651) 431-2576
Resource Development Supervisor **Rolf Hage** . . . . . . . . (651) 431-2594
Adult Protection Coordinator **Jennifer V. Kirchen** . . . . (651) 431-2546
Long-Term Care Ombudsman **Deb A. Holtz** . . . . . . . . (651) 431-2604
Community Services and Access Director
**Mary Alice Mowry** . . . . . . . . . . . . . . . . . . . (651) 431-2384
Intergovernmental and Management Operations Director
**Dan Allen Newman** . . . . . . . . . . . . . . . . . . . (651) 431-4897
HIV/AIDS and Management Operations Director
**Nicholas R. Metcalf** . . . . . . . . . . . . . . . . . . (651) 431-2403
Nursing Facility Rates and Policy Director
**Robert "Bob" Held** . . . . . . . . . . . . . . . . . . (651) 431-2261
Aging 2030 Director **LaRhae Knatterud** . . . . . . . . . . (651) 431-2606

## Health Care

Assistant Commissioner **Nathan Moracco** . . . . . . . . . . . (651) 431-5929
Administrative Assistant
**Christine M. "Chris" Wasieleski** . . . . . . . . . . . (651) 431-2182
Deputy Assistant Commissioner **Rachel Peterson** . . . . . . (651) 431-2702
Health Care Policy Director (Acting) **Jennifer Blanchard** . . . . . . . . (651) 431-3307
Health Care Eligibility and Access Director
**Karen Gibson** . . . . . . . . . . . . . . . . . . . . . (651) 431-2297
Divisionwide Services and Support Manager
**Larry Kontio** . . . . . . . . . . . . . . . . . . . . . (651) 431-2299
E-mail: larry.kontio@state.mn.us
MinnesotaCare Operations Manager **Pam Daniels** . . . . . . (651) 431-5814

---

★ Elected Official   ■ Appointed by Governor   ● Appointed by Legislature   ▲ Appointed by Board or Commission   ◆ Appointed by State Supreme Court

Special Needs Purchasing Manager
**Angela L. Urbanek** . . . . . . . . . . . . . . . . . . . . . . . (651) 431-2192
Payment Policy Manager **Liz Backe** . . . . . . . . . . . . . . . (651) 431-2532
Minnesota Health Care Programs Medical Director
**Jeff Schiff** . . . . . . . . . . . . . . . . . . . . . . . . . . . . . . (651) 431-3488
Member and Provider Services Director **(Vacant)** . . . . . . . . (651) 431-2703
Performance Measurement and Quality Improvement
Director **Karen Schirle** . . . . . . . . . . . . . . . . . . . . . (651) 431-2612
Health Program Quality Manager **Robert Lloyd** . . . . . . . . (651) 431-2613
Surveillance and Integrity Review Manager
**Jennifer Hasbargen** . . . . . . . . . . . . . . . . . . . . . . (651) 431-4356
Managed Care Ombudsman **Margaret Manderfield** . . . . . (651) 431-2657
Purchasing and Services Delivery Director
**Julie Marquardt** . . . . . . . . . . . . . . . . . . . . . . . . . (651) 431-2669
State Medicaid Director **Marie Zimmerman** . . . . . . . . . . . (651) 431-4233
Deputy Medicaid Director **Ann Berg** . . . . . . . . . . . . . . . (651) 431-2193

## Direct Care and Treatment
Deputy Commissioner **Nancy A. Johnston** . . . . . . . . . . . (651) 431-3684
Chief Administrative Officer **Michael West** . . . . . . . . . . . (651) 431-2766

## Policy and Operations
Chief Compliance Officer **Gregory Gray** . . . . . . . . . . . . . (651) 431-4266
  Appeals and Regulations Director **Darwin Lookingbill** . . (651) 431-3585
  Internal Audits Director **Gary L. Johnson** . . . . . . . . . (651) 431-3619
  Management and Policy Director **Nikki D. Thompson** . . . (651) 431-4248
Chief Financial Officer **Alexandra Kotze** . . . . . . . . . . . . (651) 431-2582
  Budget Director **Jayne Rankin** . . . . . . . . . . . . . . . . (651) 431-3432
  Financial Operations Director
  **Martin "Marty" Cammack** . . . . . . . . . . . . . . . . . . (651) 431-3742
  Reports and Forecasts Director **Shawn Welch** . . . . . . . . (651) 431-2939
Chief Information Officer **Scott Peterson** . . . . . . . . . . . . (651) 431-3315
  Information Technology Services Director
  **John Hoenigschmidt** . . . . . . . . . . . . . . . . . . . . . . (651) 431-3260
  E-mail: john.hoenigschmidt@state.mn.us
Communications Director **Terry Gunderson** . . . . . . . . . . . (651) 431-2912
  E-mail: terry.gunderson@state.mn.us
Human Resources and Management Services Director
**Connie L. Jones** . . . . . . . . . . . . . . . . . . . . . . . . . (651) 431-2999
  Management Services Director **Linda M. Nelson** . . . . . . . (651) 431-2205
  E-mail: linda.m.nelson@state.mn.us
Legislative Relations Director **Amy Dellwo** . . . . . . . . . . . (651) 431-5605
  E-mail: amy.dellwo@state.mn.us
Licensing Director **Laura Plummer Zrust** . . . . . . . . . . . . (651) 296-3024
Public Affairs Director **Kathryn A. Mintz** . . . . . . . . . . . (651) 431-5605
Inspector General **Jerry Kerber** . . . . . . . . . . . . . . . . . . (651) 431-6597
Management Operations Coordinator **Roger Ehresman** . . . (651) 431-2936
State Operated Services Chief Financial Officer
**Shirley Jacobson** . . . . . . . . . . . . . . . . . . . . . . . . (651) 431-3696

## Minnesota Department of Labor and Industry [DLI]
443 Lafayette Road North, St. Paul, MN 55155
Tel: (651) 284-5005  Fax: (651) 284-5720
E-mail: dli.communications@state.mn.us

■Commissioner **Kenneth Peterson** . . . . . . . . . . . . . . . . . (651) 284-5102
  E-mail: ken.peterson@state.mn.us
  Executive Secretary **Julie Klejewski** . . . . . . . . . . . . . . (651) 284-5113
  E-mail: julie.klejewski@state.mn.us
Deputy Commissioner **Jessica K. Looman** . . . . . . . . . . . (651) 284-5282
  E-mail: jessica.looman@state.mn.us
  Education: George Washington 1994 BA; Minnesota 2001 JD
Apprenticeship and Labor Standards Director
**John Aiken** . . . . . . . . . . . . . . . . . . . . . . . . . . . . . (651) 284-5070
  E-mail: john.aiken@state.mn.us
Communications Director **James Honerman** . . . . . . . . . . . (651) 284-5313
  E-mail: james.honerman@state.mn.us
Human Resources Director **Gail D. Krieg** . . . . . . . . . . . . (651) 284-5263
Chief Financial Officer **Doug Julin** . . . . . . . . . . . . . . . . (651) 284-5021
  E-mail: doug.julin@state.mn.us
Chief Information Officer **Cindy Kevern** . . . . . . . . . . . . . (651) 284-5630
  E-mail: cindy.kevern@state.mn.us

## Minnesota Department of Military Affairs [DMA]
20 12th Street, West, St. Paul, MN 55155-2004
Tel: (651) 282-4009  Fax: (651) 282-4541

■Adjutant General **MG Richard C. Nash, ARNG** . . . . . . . . (651) 268-8924
  Education: Mankato State 1972 BS; Army War Col 1998
Chief of Staff **BG Jon A. Jensen, ARNG** . . . . . . . . . . . . (651) 268-8927
Chief Information Officer
**COL Stefanie K. Horvath, ARNG** . . . . . . . . . . . . . . (651) 268-8888
  E-mail: stefanie.k.horvath.mil@mail.mil
Director of Communications **COL Kevin Olson, ARNG** . . . (651) 268-8855

## Minnesota National Guard
600 Cedar Street, Saint Paul, MN 55101
Tel: (651) 268-8919  Fax: (651) 282-4047
Internet: www.minnesotanationalguard.org

■Adjutant General **MG Richard C. Nash, ARNG** . . . . . . . . (651) 268-8924
  E-mail: eric.j.lewanski.mil@mail.mil
Senior Enlisted Advisor
**CSM Douglas J. Wortham, ARNG** . . . . . . . . . . . . . . (651) 268-8919

## Minnesota Army National Guard
20 West 12th Street, St. Paul, MN 55155
Tel: (651) 282-4046  Fax: (651) 282-4541

Assistant Adjutant General **BG Neal Loidolt, ARNG** . . . . . (651) 268-8921
  Education: Hamline 1992 JD

## Minnesota Air National Guard
Fax: (651) 282-4541

Assistant Adjutant General and Commander
**BrigGen David D. Hamlar, ANG** . . . . . . . . . . . . . . . (651) 268-8965
  Education: Tufts 1977 BSA; Howard U 1981 DDS;
  Ohio State 1989 MD
Chief of Staff **BrigGen Sandra Best, ANG** . . . . . . . . . . . (651) 268-8919
Vice Chief of Staff **Col James L. Wentzlass, ANG** . . . . . . (651) 268-8962

## Minnesota Department of Natural Resources [DNR]
500 Lafayette Road, St. Paul, MN 55155-4001
Tel: (651) 296-6157  Tel: (888) 646-6367  TTY: (651) 296-5484
Fax: (651) 297-3618  E-mail: info.dnr@state.mn.us
Internet: www.dnr.state.mn.us

■Commissioner **Thomas J. "Tom" Landwehr** . . . . . . . . . . (651) 259-5555
  E-mail: tom.landwehr@state.mn.us
  Education: Minnesota 1980 BS, 1986 MS, 2001 MBA
Deputy Commissioner **Dave Schad** . . . . . . . . . . . . . . . . (651) 259-5025
  E-mail: dave.schad@state.mn.us
Assistant Commissioner **Bob Meier** . . . . . . . . . . . . . . . . (651) 259-5024
  E-mail: bob.meier@state.mn.us
Assistant Commissioner **Barbara Naramore** . . . . . . . . . . . (651) 259-5033
  E-mail: barb.naramore@state.mn.us
Assistant Commissioner **Sarah Strommen** . . . . . . . . . . . . (651) 259-5021

## Minnesota Department of Public Safety [DPS]
Bremer Tower, 445 Minnesota Street, Suite 1000, St. Paul, MN 55101
Tel: (651) 201-7000  TTY: (651) 282-6555  Fax: (651) 297-5728

■Commissioner **Ramona L. Dohman** . . . . . . . . . . . . . . . . (651) 201-7160
  E-mail: mona.dohman@state.mn.us
  Education: Alexandria Tech 1982 AA; Metropolitan State U 1998 BA;
  U St Thomas (MN) 2003 MA
  Executive Aide to the Commissioner **Nancy Reissner** . . . (651) 201-7165
  E-mail: nancy.reissner@state.mn.us
Deputy Commissioner **Mark A. Dunaski** . . . . . . . . . . . . . (651) 201-7160
Assistant Commissioner **Cassandra O'Hern** . . . . . . . . . . . (651) 201-7160
Fire Marshal **Bruce West** Suite 145 . . . . . . . . . . . . . . . . (651) 201-7200
  E-mail: bruce.west@state.mn.us
Alcohol and Gambling Enforcement Division Director
**Michele Tuchner** Suite 222 . . . . . . . . . . . . . . . . . . . (651) 201-7529

*(continued on next page)*

---

★ Elected Official   ■ Appointed by Governor   ● Appointed by Legislature   ▲ Appointed by Board or Commission   ◆ Appointed by State Supreme Court

**EXECUTIVE BRANCH**

**Minnesota Department of Public Safety** *continued*

Driver and Vehicle Services Division Director
**Dawn M. Olson** Suite 195 . . . . . . . . . . . . . . . . . . . . . . . (651) 201-7815
E-mail: dawn.m.olson@state.mn.us

Emergency Communication Networks Division Director
**Jackie Mines** Suite 137 . . . . . . . . . . . . . . . . . . . . . .(651) 201-7550

Fiscal and Administrative Services Division Director
**Lawrence R. "Larry" Freund** Suite 125 . . . . . . . . . . . . . (651) 201-7050
E-mail: larry.freund@state.mn.us

Homeland Security and Emergency Management Division
Director **Joe Kelly** Suite 223 . . . . . . . . . . . . . . . . . . . .(651) 201-7405

Human Resources Division Director **Lowell Thompson**
Suite 135 . . . . . . . . . . . . . . . . . . . . . . . . . . . . . . . . . (651) 201-7382

Office of Justice Programs Director **Raeone Magnuson**
Suite 2300 . . . . . . . . . . . . . . . . . . . . . . . . . . . . . . . . (651) 201-7300
E-mail: raeone.magnuson@state.mn.us
Education: Iowa BA; Hamline

Traffic Safety Division Director **Donna Berger** Suite 150 . . (651) 201-7060
E-mail: donna.berger@state.mn.us

State Patrol Chief **Lt. Col. Matthew Langer** Suite 130 . . . .(651) 201-7100
E-mail: matthew.langer@state.mn.us

State Patrol - Capitol Security/Executive Protection
Division **Capt. Eric Roeske** . . . . . . . . . . . . . . . . . . (651) 201-6970

Criminal Apprehension Bureau Superintendent
**Drew Evans** . . . . . . . . . . . . . . . . . . . . . . . . . . . . . (651) 793-7000
1430 Maryland Avenue East, St. Paul, MN 55106      Fax: (651) 793-7001

Chief Information Officer **Paul Meekin** Suite 140 . . . . . . . (651) 201-7750
E-mail: paul.meekin@state.mn.us

Communications Office Director **Bruce Gordon** . . . . . . . . (651) 201-7171
E-mail: bruce.gordon@state.mn.us

Diversity and Internal Affairs Office Director
**(Vacant)** Suite 530 . . . . . . . . . . . . . . . . . . . . . . . . . (651) 201-7136
E-mail: dps.ia@state.mn.us

General Counsel/Rules Coordinator
**Joseph "Joe" Newton** . . . . . . . . . . . . . . . . . . . . . . . (651) 201-7170
E-mail: joseph.newton@state.mn.us

Legislative and Government Affairs Director
**Kathryn Weeks** . . . . . . . . . . . . . . . . . . . . . . . . . . . (651) 201-7169
E-mail: kathryn.weeks@state.mn.us

## Minnesota Department of Revenue

600 North Robert Street, St. Paul, MN 55146
Tel: (651) 556-3000  Tel: (800) 652-9094  Internet: www.taxes.state.mn.us

■Commissioner **Cynthia L. Bauerly** . . . . . . . . . . . . . . . . (651) 556-6003
E-mail: cynthia.bauerly@state.mn.us
Education: Concordia Col Moorhead MN 1993; Indiana 1998 MPA,
1998 JD

Deputy Commissioner **Ryan Church** . . . . . . . . . . . . . . . (651) 556-6006

Assistant Commissioner for Administration/Chief
Financial Officer **Peter Skwira** . . . . . . . . . . . . . . . . . (651) 556-4059
E-mail: peter.skwira@state.mn.us

Assistant Commissioner for Administrative Law and
Compliance **(Vacant)** . . . . . . . . . . . . . . . . . . . . . . . (651) 556-3000

Assistant Commissioner for Business Taxes **Jenny Starr** . . (651) 296-3403

Assistant Commissioner for Individual Income Tax
**Terri Steenblock** . . . . . . . . . . . . . . . . . . . . . . . . . . (651) 556-6366

Manager for Tax Policy **Paul Cumings** . . . . . . . . . . . . . .(651) 556-6205

Chief Information Officer **Greg Tschida** . . . . . . . . . . . . . .(651) 556-6207
E-mail: greg.tschida@state.mn.us

Internal Audit Manager **Mike Turner, CIA** . . . . . . . . . . . . (651) 556-6016
Education: Nebraska BAcc, MM

Internal Auditor **Fekade Cherinet** . . . . . . . . . . . . . . . . . (651) 556-6028
Education: Macalester 1986 BABA; Metropolitan State U 1998 MM

Appeals and Legal Services Division Director
**Terese Mitchell** . . . . . . . . . . . . . . . . . . . . . . . . . . . (651) 556-4075

Collection Division Director **Ron Schwagel** . . . . . . . . . . . (651) 556-6407

Communications Division Director **Libby Caulum** . . . . . . .(651) 556-6450
E-mail: libby.caulum@state.mn.us

Corporate Franchise Division Director **Jeff Vogt** . . . . . . . . (651) 556-6775

Criminal Investigation Division Director **Dan Anderson** . . .(651) 556-6652

Facilities Management Division Director
**Kathy Yzermans** . . . . . . . . . . . . . . . . . . . . . . . . . . . (651) 556-6003

Financial Management Division Director **Joshua Bunker** . .(651) 556-4059

Human Resources Management Division Director
**Kathy Zieminski** . . . . . . . . . . . . . . . . . . . . . . . . . . (651) 556-6660

Individual Income Tax and Withholding Division Director
**Cori Calhoun** . . . . . . . . . . . . . . . . . . . . . . . . . . . . (651) 556-6447

Information Systems Division Director **Don Friedlander** . . (651) 556-6261
E-mail: don.friedlander@state.mn.us

Information Systems Division Director
**Theodore "Ted" Trenzeluk** . . . . . . . . . . . . . . . . . . . (651) 556-6230
E-mail: ted.trenzeluk@state.mn.us

Property Tax Division Director **Cynthia Rowley** . . . . . . . . (651) 556-4814

Sales and Use Tax Division Director **Pam Evans** . . . . . . . (651) 556-6814

Special Taxes Division Director **Gina Amacher** . . . . . . . . (651) 556-6781

Tax Operations Division Director **Dan Getchel** . . . . . . . . (651) 556-4871

Tax Research Division Director **Paul Wilson** . . . . . . . . . .(651) 556-6138

Taxpayer Rights Advocate **Wende O'Brien** . . . . . . . . . . .(651) 556-6013

Media Relations Coordinator **Ryan Brown** . . . . . . . . . . . (651) 556-6397

## Minnesota Department of Transportation [MnDOT]

395 John Ireland Boulevard, St. Paul, MN 55155
Tel: (651) 296-3000
Tel: (800) 627-3529 (TTY/Voice/ASCII Relay Service)
Fax: (651) 366-4795  E-mail: info@dot.state.mn.us
Internet: www.dot.state.mn.us

■Commissioner **Charles A. "Charlie" Zelle** . . . . . . . . . . . (651) 366-4800
E-mail: charlie.zelle@state.mn.us
Education: Bates 1977 BA; Yale 1983 MBA

Deputy Commissioner and Chief Engineer
**Susan M. "Sue" Mulvihill** . . . . . . . . . . . . . . . . . . . .(651) 366-4800
E-mail: sue.mulvihill@state.mn.us

Deputy Commissioner, Chief Operating Officer and Chief
Financial Officer **Tracy Hatch** . . . . . . . . . . . . . . . . . (651) 366-4811

Assistant Commissioner **Sean Rahn** . . . . . . . . . . . . . . . (651) 366-4927

Audit Director **Daniel E. Kahnke** . . . . . . . . . . . . . . . (651) 366-4140
Fax: (651) 366-4155

Chief Counsel **Elizabeth M. Parker** . . . . . . . . . . . . . . . (651) 366-4841
E-mail: elizabeth.parker@state.mn.us

Chief of Staff **Eric Davis** . . . . . . . . . . . . . . . . . . . . . . (651) 366-3402

Communications Director **Kevin G. Gutknecht** . . . . . . . . (651) 366-4266
E-mail: kevin.gutknecht@state.mn.us      Fax: (651) 366-4275

Customer Relations Director **(Vacant)** . . . . . . . . . . . . . . (651) 366-3172

Government Affairs Director **Scott Peterson** . . . . . . . . . . (651) 366-4817
E-mail: scott.peterson@state.mn.us      Fax: (651) 366-4797

Ombudsman **Richard D. Davis** . . . . . . . . . . . . . . . . . . .(651) 366-3052

State Rail Director **Alene Tchourumoff** . . . . . . . . . . . . . (651) 296-3000

## Corporate Services Division

Division Director **Sue Stein** . . . . . . . . . . . . . . . . . . . . . (651) 366-4814

Administration Director **Robin Sylvester** . . . . . . . . . . . . (651) 366-4235
E-mail: robin.sylvester@state.mn.us
Education: Concordia Col Moorhead MN BA

Affirmative Action Office Coordinator
**Lynnette Marie Geschwind** . . . . . . . . . . . . . . . . . . . (651) 366-4717

Human Resources Director **Karin Van Dyck** . . . . . . . . . . (651) 366-3385
E-mail: karin.van.dyck@state.mn.us

Information and Technical Services Director **Jim Close** . . . (651) 366-4030
E-mail: jim.close@state.mn.us

## Engineering Services Division

Division Director **Nancy Daubenberger** . . . . . . . . . . . . . (651) 366-4826
E-mail: nancy.daubenberger@state.mn.us

Assistant Division Director **Amr Khalil Jabr** . . . . . . . . . .(651) 366-3303

State Bridge Engineer **Kevin Western** . . . . . . . . . . . . . . (651) 366-4506
Fax: (651) 366-4497

Construction and Innovative Contracting Director
**Thomas D. "Tom" Ravn** . . . . . . . . . . . . . . . . . . . . (651) 366-4228
E-mail: tom.ravn@state.mn.us      Fax: (651) 366-4248

Environmental Stewardship Office Director
**Lynn Clarkowski** . . . . . . . . . . . . . . . . . . . . . . . . . . (651) 366-3602
Fax: (651) 366-3603

Land Management Office Director **Bryan Dodds** . . . . . . . .(651) 366-3502
Fax: (651) 366-3450

Materials and Road Research Director **Glen Engstrom** . . . .(651) 366-5590
E-mail: glen.engstrom@state.mn.us      Fax: (651) 366-5461

---

★ Elected Official      ■ Appointed by Governor      ● Appointed by Legislature      ▲ Appointed by Board or Commission      ◆ Appointed by State Supreme Court

Summer 2016                              © Leadership Directories, Inc.                              *State Yellow Book*

Project Management and Technical Support Office
Director **Chris Roy** ............................... (651) 366-3183

## Modal Planning and Program Management Division

Division Director **Timothy A. "Tim" Henkel** .......... (651) 366-4829
E-mail: tim.henkel@state.mn.us
Aeronautics Office Director **Cassandra Isackson** ........ (651) 234-7210
Capital Programs and Performance Measures Office
Director **Mark Allen Gieseke** ...................... (651) 366-3770
E-mail: mark.gieseke@state.mn.us  Fax: (651) 366-3790
Freight and Commercial Vehicle Operations Office
Director **William D. "Bill" Gardner** ............... (651) 366-3665
E-mail: william.gardner@state.mn.us  Fax: (651) 366-3721
Statewide Multimodal Planning Office Director
**Mark A. Nelson** ................................ (651) 366-3794
E-mail: mark.a.nelson@state.mn.us
Transit Office Director **Michael A. "Mike" Schadauer** ... (651) 366-4161
Fax: (651) 366-4192
Transportation Data and Analysis Office Director
**(Vacant)** ..................................... (651) 366-3882
Fax: (651) 366-3886
Passenger Rail Office Director **Daniel "Dan" Krom** ...... (651) 366-3193

## Operations Division

Division Director **Michael A. Barnes** ................ (651) 366-4814
Assistant Division Director **(Vacant)** ............... (651) 366-4810
State Maintenance Engineer **Steven M. "Steve" Lund** .... (651) 366-3566
Fax: (651) 366-3555
District 1 Engineer **Duane Hill** (District 1 - Duluth) ...... (218) 725-2704
1123 Mesaba Avenue, Duluth, MN 55811  Fax: (218) 725-2800
E-mail: duane.hill@state.mn.us
District 2 Engineer **Craig Collison** (District 2 - Bemidji) .. (218) 755-6549
1991 Industrial Park Road, Baxter, MN 56425  Fax: (218) 755-6512
E-mail: craig.collison@state.mn.us
Education: North Dakota State
District 3 Engineer
**Daniel D. "Dan" Anderson** (District 3 - Brainerd) ..... (218) 828-5703
P.O. Box 490, Bemidji, MN 56619  Fax: (218) 828-5814
E-mail: daniel.d.anderson@state.mn.us
District 4 Engineer
**Jody Martinson** (District 4 - Detroit Lakes) .......... (218) 846-3603
1000 Highway 10 West, Detroit Lakes, MN 56501  Fax: (218) 847-1583
E-mail: jody.martinson@state.mn.us
District 6 Engineer
**Jeff Vlaminck** (District 6 - Rochester) ............... (507) 286-7501
2900 48th St., Northwest,  Fax: (507) 281-7780
Rochester, MN 55901-5848
E-mail: jeff.vlaminck@state.mn.us
District 7 Engineer **Greg B. Ous** (District 7 - Mankato) ... (507) 304-6101
501 S. Victory Dr., Mankato, MN 56001-5302  Fax: (507) 304-6109
E-mail: greg.ous@state.mn.us
District 8 Engineer **Jon Huseby** (District 8 - Wilmar) ..... (320) 231-5497
2505 Transportation Road, Willmar, MN 56201  Fax: (320) 214-6305
E-mail: jon.huseby@state.mn.us
Metropolitan District Engineer
**Scott McBride** (Metropolitan District) ............... (651) 234-7700
E-mail: scott.mcbride@state.mn.us  Fax: (651) 234-7708
Traffic, Safety and Technology Director **Sue Groth** ....... (651) 234-7004
Fax: (651) 234-7006

## State Aid for Local Transportation Division

Tel: (651) 366-6800  Fax: (651) 366-3801
Division Director **Mitch Rasmussen** ................. (651) 366-4831
E-mail: mitch.rasmussen@state.mn.us
Statewide Radio Communications Office Director
**Mukhtar A. Thakur** ............................. (651) 366-3800
E-mail: mukhtar.thakur@state.mn.us
State Aid Programs Engineer **Patti Jo Loken** ........... (651) 366-3803
E-mail: patti.loken@state.mn.us
State Aid for Local Transportation **Ted Schoenecker** ..... (651) 366-3804

## Minnesota Department of Veterans Affairs [MDVA]

Veterans Service Building, 20 West 12th Street, Suite 206,
St. Paul, MN 55155
Tel: (651) 296-2562  Fax: (651) 296-3954  Internet: mn.gov/mdva
■Commissioner **MG Larry W. Shellito, ARNG** .......... (651) 757-1555
E-mail: larry.shellito@state.mn.us
Education: Moorhead State 1972 BA, 1979 MS; Army War Col 1994;
Minnesota 1998 EdD
Chief of Staff **Michael S. McElhiney** ................ (651) 757-1530
Deputy Commissioner of Programs and Services
**Brad Lindsay** ................................. (651) 757-1582
Deputy Commissioner of Veterans Health Care (Acting)
**Andrew Burnside** .............................. (651) 539-2401
Communications Director **Anna Long** ................. (651) 757-1536
E-mail: anna.long@state.mn.us

## Minnesota Management and Budget [MMB]

400 Centennial Office Building, 658 Cedar Street, St. Paul, MN 55155
Tel: (651) 201-8000  TTY: (800) 627-3529  Fax: (651) 296-8685
E-mail: info.mmb@state.mn.us
■Commissioner **Myron L. Frans** ..................... (651) 201-8011
E-mail: myron.frans@state.mn.us  Fax: (651) 797-1300
Education: Washburn 1972 BA; Sam Houston State 1977 MA;
Kansas 1983 JD
Executive Assistant to the Commissioner
**Laury Anderson** .............................. (651) 201-8024
Deputy Commissioner **Eric C. Hallstrom** ............. (651) 201-8010
Education: Augustana (SD) 1998 BA; Iowa 2001 JD;
Georgetown 2004 LLM
Accounting Services Assistant Commissioner
**Cynthia "Cindy" Farrell** ....................... (651) 201-8012
Budget Services Assistant Commissioner/State Budget
Director **Margaret Kelly** ........................ (651) 201-8009
Education: Carleton BA; Hamline MPA
Debt Management and Treasury Assistant Commissioner
**(Vacant)** ..................................... (651) 201-8030
Employee Insurance/Enterprise Human Resources
Assistant Commissioner **Edwin K. Hudson** ........... (651) 259-3636
Labor Relations Assistant Commissioner/State Labor
Negotiator **(Vacant)** ........................... (651) 259-3740
Human Resource Management Director **Cathy Biffer** .... (651) 201-8005
Management Analysis Division Director
**Kristin F. Batson** ............................. (651) 259-3816
Chief Information Officer (Interim) **Bruce Yurrich** ....... (651) 259-3699
State Employee Assistance Program Director
**Edmund "Ned" Rousmaniere** ..................... (651) 259-3736
E-mail: ned.rousmaniere@state.mn.us
Legislative and Communications Director **John Pollard** ... (651) 201-8039
E-mail: john.pollard@state.mn.us
State Compensation Manager **(Vacant)** ............... (651) 201-8044
State Economist **Laura Kalambokidis** ................ (651) 201-8039
Statewide Affirmative Action Officer **Johnnie Burns** ..... (651) 259-3643
Webmaster **(Vacant)** ............................ (651) 259-3728

## Iron Range Resources and Rehabilitation Board [IRRRB]

Member **Tom Anzelc** .............................. (651) 296-4936
E-mail: rep.tom.anzelc@house.mn
Education: St Cloud State 1968 BS
Member **Thomas M. "Tom" Bakk** ................... (651) 296-8881
E-mail: sen.tom.bakk@senate.mn
Education: Minnesota (Duluth) BA
Member **Rob Ecklund** ............................ (651) 296-2190
4647 Highway 11, International Falls, MN 56649
E-mail: rep.rob.ecklund@house.mn
Member **Dale Lueck** ............................. (651) 297-9010
E-mail: rep.dale.lueck@house.mn
Member **Carly Melin** ............................ (651) 296-0172
E-mail: rep.carly.melin@house.mn
Education: Bemidji State BA; Hamline JD

*(continued on next page)*

---

★ Elected Official  ■ Appointed by Governor  ● Appointed by Legislature  ▲ Appointed by Board or Commission  ◆ Appointed by State Supreme Court

EXECUTIVE BRANCH

**Iron Range Resources and Rehabilitation Board** *continued*

Member **Jason Metsa** ................................. (651) 296-0170
  E-mail: rep.jason.metsa@house.mn
Member **Tom Saxhaug** ............................... (651) 296-4139
  E-mail: sen.tom.saxhaug@senate.mn
  Education: St Olaf 1970 BA
Member **Rod Skoe** .................................. (651) 296-4196
  E-mail: sen.rod.skoe@senate.mn
  Education: Augsburg BA
Member **David J. Tomassoni** ........................ (651) 296-8017
  E-mail: sen.david.tomassoni@senate.mn
  Education: Denver BA, BS

## Office of the Commissioner

Highway 53 South, P.O. Box 441, Eveleth, MN 55734
Tel: (218) 735-3047

■Commissioner **Mark Phillips** ....................... (218) 735-3014
  E-mail: mark.phillips@state.mn.us
  Education: Minnesota (Duluth) 1973 BABA
Executive Assistant **Laureen Hall** ................... (218) 735-3014
Deputy Commissioner **Mary Finnegan** ................ (218) 735-3054
Assistant Commissioner **(Vacant)** ................... (218) 735-3055
Legal Counsel **Al Becicka** .......................... (218) 735-3003
  E-mail: al.becicka@state.mn.us
Chief Operating Officer **Marianne Bouska** ............ (218) 735-3005
Executive Development Director **Steve Peterson** ....... (218) 735-3002

## Bureau of Mediation Services

1380 Energy Lane, Suite 2, St. Paul, MN 55108
Tel: (651) 649-5421  Fax: (651) 643-3013  TTY: (800) 627-3529

■Commissioner **Josh L. Tilsen** ..................... (651) 649-5436
  E-mail: josh.tilsen@state.mn.us
  Education: San Francisco State U 1974 BA
Deputy Commissioner **Todd L. Doncavage** ........... (651) 649-5431

## Office of Administrative Hearings

600 North Robert Street, St. Paul, MN 55101
P.O. Box 64620, Saint Paul, MN 55164-0620
Tel: (651) 361-7900  TTY: (651) 361-7878  Fax: (651) 539-0300
E-mail: admin.hearings@state.mn.us

■Chief Administrative Law Judge **Tammy L. Pust** ........ (651) 361-7830
  E-mail: tammy.pust@state.mn.us
  Education: Concordia Col Moorhead MN 1980 BA;
  Minnesota 1983 JD
Deputy Chief Administrative Law Judge **(Vacant)** ........ (651) 361-7856
Court Administrator **Donna E. Nelson** ................ (651) 361-7942

## MN.IT Services [OET]

Centennial Office Building, 658 Cedar Street, Suite 200,
St. Paul, MN 55155
Tel: (651) 201-1118

Commissioner and State Chief Information Officer
  **Thomas A. "Tom" Baden, Jr.** ..................... (651) 556-8029
  E-mail: thomas.baden@state.mn.us
Executive Aide **Jennifer Bell** ...................... (651) 201-1076
Deputy Commissioner and Chief Operating Officer
  **Jesse Oman** ..................................... (651) 556-8018
Assistant Commissioner and Chief Information Security
  Officer **Christopher "Chris" Buse** ................ (651) 201-1200
  E-mail: chris.buse@state.mn.us
Assistant Commissioner of Communications, Planning
  and Digital Technology Services **Jenna Covey** ....... (651) 201-1199
  Education: Minnesota St (Mankato) BA
Assistant Commissioner for Enterprise Operations
  Service Delivery **Thomas Schaeffer** ............... (651) 556-8001
  E-mail: thomas.schaeffer@state.mn.us
Chief Financial Officer **Tu Tong** ................... (651) 556-8028
Chief Technology Officer **Ed Valencia** .............. (651) 556-8029
  E-mail: ed.valencia@state.mn.us
Human Resources Director **Chad Thuet** .............. (651) 201-2281

Media Relations and Legislative Affairs Director
  **Jon Eichten** .................................... (651) 556-8027
  E-mail: jon.eichten@state.mn.us

## Minnesota Office of Higher Education

1450 Energy Park Drive, Suite 350, St. Paul, MN 55108-5227
Tel: (651) 259-3970  TTY: (800) 627-3529  Fax: (651) 642-0675
E-mail: info.ohe@state.mn.us  Internet: www.ohe.state.mn.us

■Commissioner **Lawrence J. "Larry" Pogemiller** ........ (651) 259-3900
  E-mail: larry.pogemiller@state.mn.us
  Education: Minnesota 1974 BS; Harvard 1988 MPA;
  Minnesota (Attended)
Deputy Commissioner **Diane O'Connor** ............... (651) 259-3922
Communications Director **Sandy Connolly** ............ (651) 259-3902
  E-mail: sandy.connolly@state.mn.us
Chief Financial Officer **Tim Geraghty** .............. (651) 259-3950
Audits General Manager **Robert Helgeson** ............ (651) 259-3997
Competitive Grants General Manager **Nancy Walters** ..... (651) 259-3907
Finance and Accountability Manager **Thomas Sanford** .... (651) 259-3960
Human Resources General Manager **Lynne Richard** ...... (651) 259-3941
Information Technology Services General Manager
  **Joseph E. Valasek** .............................. (651) 259-3945
  E-mail: joseph.valasek@state.mn.us
Outreach, Partnerships and Initiatives General Manager
  **Ashley Booker** .................................. (651) 259-3940
Registration and Licensing General Manager
  **Betsy Talbot** ................................... (651) 259-3975
State Financial Aid Programs General Manager
  **Ginny Dodds** .................................... (651) 355-0610
State Scholarships General Manager **Megan FitzGibbon** .. (651) 355-0606
Student Loans General Manager **Marilyn Kosir** ......... (651) 355-0600
Research and Policy Analyst **Alexandra Djurovich** ...... (651) 259-3962

## Minnesota Housing Finance Agency [MHFA]

400 Sibley Street, Room 300, St. Paul, MN 55101
Tel: (651) 296-7608  TTY: (651) 297-2361  Fax: (651) 296-8139
E-mail: mn.housing@state.mn.us  Internet: www.mnhousing.gov

■Commissioner **Mary Tingerthal** .................... (651) 296-5738
  E-mail: mary.tingerthal@state.mn.us
  Education: Minnesota 1974 BA; Stanford 1985 MSM
Deputy Commissioner **Barbara Sporlein** ............. (651) 297-3125
Executive Assistant **Becky Schack** .................. (651) 296-2172
Assistant Commissioner for Multifamily Division
  **Wesley J. Butler** ............................... (651) 296-3028
Assistant Commissioner for Policy and Community
  Development **Ryan P. Baumtrog** ................... (651) 296-9820
  E-mail: ryan.baumtrog@state.mn.us
Assistant Commissioner for Single Family Division
  **Kasey Kier** ..................................... (651) 297-3137
Communications Director **Megan Ryan** ............... (651) 297-3566
  E-mail: megan.ryan@state.mn.us
Community Development Director **Margaret Kaplan** ..... (651) 296-3617
Federal Liaison **Jessica Deegan** .................... (651) 297-3126
  E-mail: jessica.deegan@state.mn.us
Finance Director **Terry Schwartz** ................... (651) 296-5972
Planning, Research and Evaluation Director
  **John Patterson** ................................. (651) 296-0763
  E-mail: john.patterson@state.mn.us
Controller **Debbi Larson** .......................... (651) 296-8183
Chief Financial Officer **Kevin Carpenter** ............ (651) 297-4009
Chief Information Officer **Anthony "Tony" Peleska** ..... (651) 296-8189
  E-mail: tony.peleska@state.mn.us
Human Resources Director **Dan Boomhower** ........... (651) 296-4225
General Counsel **Thomas M. "Tom" O'Hern** .......... (651) 296-9796

---

★ Elected Official    ■ Appointed by Governor    ● Appointed by Legislature    ▲ Appointed by Board or Commission    ◆ Appointed by State Supreme Court

EXECUTIVE BRANCH

# Minnesota Pollution Control Agency [MPCA]

520 Lafayette Road, North, St. Paul, MN 55155-4194
Tel: (651) 296-6300  TTY: (651) 282-5332  Fax: (651) 296-7923
E-mail: webmaster@pca.state.mn.us  Internet: www.pca.state.mn.us

■ Commissioner **John Linc Stine** ........................ (651) 757-2014
    E-mail: john.stine@state.mn.us
Deputy Commissioner **Michelle Beeman** .............. (651) 757-2013
Assistant Commissioner **Rebecca Flood** ............... (651) 757-2022
Assistant Commissioner **Kirk Koudelka** ............... (651) 757-2241
Assistant Commissioner **David Thornton** .............. (651) 757-2018
Environmental Analysis and Outcomes Division Director
    **Shannon Lotthammer** ............................... (651) 757-2537
Industrial Division Director **Jeff Smith** ................. (651) 757-2735
Municipal Division Director **Mark Schmitt** ............. (651) 757-2698
Operations Division Director **Cathy Moeger** ........... (651) 757-2575
Resource Management and Assistance Division Director
    **David J. "Dave" Benke** ............................. (651) 757-2221
    E-mail: david.j.benke@state.mn.us
Remediation Division Director **Kathy Sather** ........... (651) 757-2691
Watershed Division Director **Glenn Skuta** .............. (651) 757-2730
Legislative Director **Greta Gauthier** ................... (651) 757-2031
    E-mail: greta.gauthier@state.mn.us

# Office of the Lieutenant Governor

Veterans Service Building, 20 West 12th Street, Room 116,
St. Paul, MN 55155
Tel: (651) 201-3400  Tel: (800) 657-3717  Fax: (651) 797-1850

★ Lieutenant Governor **Tina Flint Smith** (D) ............. (651) 201-3400
    Term Expires: January 2019
    E-mail: tina.smith@state.mn.us
    Career: Chief of Staff, Mayor R. T. Rybak, City of Minneapolis,
    Minnesota (2006-2009); Chief of Staff, Office of Governor Mark
    Dayton, State of Minnesota (2011-2014)

# Office of the Attorney General

1400 Bremer Tower, 445 Minnesota Street, St. Paul, MN 55101
Tel: (651) 296-3353  TTY: (651) 297-7206  Fax: (651) 297-4193
E-mail: consumer.ag@state.mn.us  Internet: www.ag.state.mn.us

★ Attorney General **Lori R. Swanson** (DFL) .............. (651) 296-6196
    Term Expires: January 2019
    Education: Wisconsin 1989 BA; William Mitchell 1995 JD
    Career: Deputy Attorney General, Office of the Attorney General, State
    of Minnesota (1999-2002); Solicitor General, Office of the Attorney
    General, State of Minnesota (2003-2006)
Solicitor General **Alan "Al" Gilbert** ................... (651) 757-1450
Agency Services Section Deputy Attorney General
    **Christie B. Eller** .................................... (651) 747-1440
Government Services Section Deputy Attorney General
    **David Voigt** ....................................... (651) 757-1350
    Education: Wisconsin 1989 BS; Minnesota 1994 JD
Legal Services Section Deputy Attorney General
    **Karen Olson** ...................................... (651) 757-1370
    Education: Minnesota 1986 BS; William Mitchell 1995 JD
Legal Operations Director **(Vacant)** ................... (651) 757-1111
Boards and Agencies Division Manager **Kelly Kemp** ...... (651) 757-1481
    E-mail: kelly.kemp@ag.state.mn.us
Charities and Civil Law Division Manager
    **Nathan "Nate" Brennaman** ....................... (651) 757-1415
    Education: Grinnell 1995 BA; Minnesota 2003 JD
Civil Litigation Division Manager **Alethea Huyser** ....... (651) 757-1226
Commerce and Utilities Division Manager
    **Julia Anderson** .................................... (651) 757-1202
    E-mail: julia.anderson@ag.state.mn.us
District Court Trial and Appellate Division Manager
    **Matthew "Matt" Frank** ............................ (651) 757-1448
Licensing Boards Division Manager **(Vacant)** ........... (651) 757-1404
Licensing Boards Legal Division Manager **(Vacant)** ...... (651) 757-1059
Medicaid Fraud Division Manager
    **Charles "Chuck" Roehrdanz** ...................... (651) 757-1299
Social Services Division Manager **Jacob Kraus** ......... (651) 757-1454
State Highway Division Manager **(Vacant)** ............. (651) 757-1330

State Resources Division Manager **Karen Olson** ........ (651) 757-1370
Schools and Revenue Division Manager **(Vacant)** ....... (651) 757-1455
Information Services Manager **Charles V. Ferguson** ...... (651) 355-0700
    E-mail: chuck.ferguson@ag.state.mn.us
Law Librarian **Anita M. Anderson** .................... (651) 757-1050

# Office of the Secretary of State

180 State Office Building,
100 Rev. Dr. Martin Luther King, Jr. Boulevard, St. Paul, MN 55155-1299
Tel: (651) 296-2803  TTY: (800) 627-3529  Fax: (651) 215-0682
E-mail: secretary.state@state.mn.us

★ Secretary of State **Steve Simon** (DFL) ................. (651) 296-2803
    Term Expires: January 2019
    Education: Tufts 1992 BA; Minnesota 1996 JD
    Career: State Representative (DFL-MN, District 44A), Minnesota
    House of Representatives (2005-2013); Assistant Minority Leader,
    Minnesota House of Representatives, Minnesota Legislature
    (2011-2013); State Representative (DFL-MN, District 46B), Minnesota
    House of Representatives (2013-2015)
Deputy Secretary of State **Ann Kaner-Roth** ........... (651) 296-2803
    E-mail: ann.kaner-roth@state.mn.us
    Education: Wisconsin 1990 BA; Boston U 1997 MSW
Chief of Staff **Jake Spano** ........................... (651) 296-2803
    Education: Hamline BA; Minnesota (Duluth) 2006 MAPL
Communications Director **Ryan Furlong** ............... (651) 296-2803
    E-mail: ryan.furlong@state.mn.us
    Education: USC BA

# Office of the State Auditor

525 Park Street, Suite 500, St. Paul, MN 55103
Tel: (651) 296-2551  TTY: (800) 627-3529  Fax: (651) 296-4755
E-mail: state.auditor@osa.state.mn.us

★ State Auditor **Rebecca Otto** (DFL) ................... (651) 296-2551
    Term Expires: January 2019
    Education: Macalester 1985 BA; Minnesota 1994 MEd
    Career: State Representative (R-MN, District 52B), Minnesota House of
    Representatives (2003-2004)
Deputy State Auditor and General Counsel
    **Ramona Advani** .................................... (651) 297-3673
Deputy State Auditor **Greg Hierlinger** ................ (651) 296-7003
    Education: St Cloud State 1975 BS
Director of Budget, Finance, and Technology
    **Matt Lindemann** ................................... (651) 296-7110
Director of Tax Increment Financing (TIF) **Jason Nord** ... (651) 296-7979
Pension Director **Rose Hennessy Allen** ............... (651) 296-5985
Communications Director **Jim Levi** ................... (651) 297-3683
    E-mail: jim.levi@osa.state.mn.us

---

★ Elected Official　■ Appointed by Governor　● Appointed by Legislature　▲ Appointed by Board or Commission　◆ Appointed by State Supreme Court

# Mississippi

Tel: (601) 359-3100 (State Operator)  Internet: www.mississippi.gov

**Number of U.S. Congressional Delegates:** 2 Senators; 4 Representatives  **Governor's Term:** 4 years
**Legislature Description:** 52 member Senate; 122 member House of Representatives; Term- Senate 4
years, House 4 years  **Next Election:** Governor November 2019; Legislature November 2019
**Number of Electoral Votes:** 6  **Official Name:** State of Mississippi (Choctaw: father of waters)
**Nickname:** The Magnolia State  **Motto:** Virtute et armis (By Valor and Arms)

**Population:** 2,992,333 (2015); Rank 32  **Fiscal Year:** 2014  **Budget:** $18,306,183,000

## Office of the Governor

P.O. Box 139, Jackson, MS 39205
Tel: (601) 359-3150  Fax: (601) 359-3741
E-mail: info@governorbryant.com

**Dewey Phillip "Phil" Bryant**
Governor

Began Service: January 9, 2012
Term Expires: January 2020
Date of Birth: December 9, 1954
Education: Southern Mississippi 1977 BA;
Mississippi Col 1988 MS
Religion: Methodist
Career: State Representative (R-MS), Mississippi
House of Representatives (1991-1996); State
Auditor, State of Mississippi (1996-2008);
Lieutenant Governor, State of Mississippi
(2008-2012)

★Governor **Dewey Phillip "Phil" Bryant** (R) . . . . . . . . . . . . (601) 359-3150
Chief of Staff **Joey Songy** . . . . . . . . . . . . . . . . . . . . . . . . . . . . (601) 359-3150
Chief Counsel **Robert G. "Bobby" Waites** . . . . . . . . . . . . . (601) 359-3150
  E-mail: bobby.waites@governor.ms.gov
Deputy Counsel **Drew Snyder** . . . . . . . . . . . . . . . . . . . . . . . . (601) 359-3150
  E-mail: drew.snyder@governor.ms.gov
Communications Director **Clay Chandler** . . . . . . . . . . . . . . (601) 359-3150
Senate Liaison and Policy Analyst
  **Robert Gene "Bobby" Morgan II** . . . . . . . . . . . . . . . . . . (601) 359-3150
  E-mail: bobby.morgan@governor.ms.gov
  Education: Mississippi 2009 AB; St John's Col (MD) (Attended)
Policy Analyst **Pierce Moore** . . . . . . . . . . . . . . . . . . . . . . . (601) 359-3150
  E-mail: pierce.moore@governor.ms.gov

## Office of the State Public Defender

Robert E. Lee Building, 239 North Lamar Street, Suite 601,
Jackson, MS 39201
PO Box 3510, Jackson, MS 39207-3510

State Defender **Leslie Lee, USAR (Ret)** . . . . . . . . . . . . . . . (601) 576-4290
  Education: Mississippi BS, JD

## Capital Defense Counsel Division

239 North Lamar Street, Jackson, MS 39201

Director **Andre de Gruy** . . . . . . . . . . . . . . . . . . . . . . . . . . . . (601) 576-2315

## Indigent Appeals Division

239 North Lamar Street, Jackson, MS 39201

Director **George Holmes** . . . . . . . . . . . . . . . . . . . . . . . . . . . (601) 576-4200

## Mississippi Department of Archives and History [MDAH]

P.O. Box 571, Jackson, MS 39205-0571
William F. Winter Archives and History Building, 200 North Street,
Jackson, MS 39201
Tel: (601) 576-6850  Fax: (601) 576-6975
E-mail: webadmin@mdah.state.ms.us  Internet: mdah.state.ms.us

**Employees:** 128  **Fiscal Year:** 2014  **Budget:** $15,062,000

▲Director **Katie Blount** . . . . . . . . . . . . . . . . . . . . . . . . . . . . . (601) 576-6850
  E-mail: kblount@mdah.state.ms.us
  Executive Assistant **Amanda Lyons** . . . . . . . . . . . . . . . . . (601) 576-6856
Information Systems Director **Torome Porter** . . . . . . . . . . (601) 576-6850
  E-mail: portert@mdah.state.ms.us
Personnel Director **Dianne Mattox** . . . . . . . . . . . . . . . . . . . (601) 576-6865
Public Information Director **Chris Goodwin** . . . . . . . . . . . (601) 576-6998
  E-mail: cgoodwin@mdah.state.ms.us
Finance Deputy Director **Robert Benson** . . . . . . . . . . . . . . (601) 576-6858
Archives and Records Services Division Director
  **Julia Marks Young** . . . . . . . . . . . . . . . . . . . . . . . . . . . . . (601) 576-6991
                                                Fax: (601) 576-6964
  Records Management Director **Bob Dent** . . . . . . . . . . . . (601) 576-6806
Local Government Records Office Director **Tim Barnard** . . (601) 576-6894
Historic Preservation Division Director **Jim Woodrick** . . . . (601) 576-6940
Museum Division Director **Lucy Allen** . . . . . . . . . . . . . . . . (601) 576-6926

## Department of Banking and Consumer Finance [DB&CF]

P. O. Box 12129, Jackson, MS 39236-2129
Tel: (601) 321-6901  Tel: (800) 844-2499  Fax: (601) 321-6933

**Employees:** 61  **Fiscal Year:** 2014  **Budget:** $7,489,000

■Commissioner **Charlotte N. Corley, CEM** . . . . . . . . . . . . . (601) 359-1031
  E-mail: charlotte.corley@dbcf.ms.gov
Deputy Commissioner **Rhoshunda Kelly** . . . . . . . . . . . . . . (601) 359-1031
  E-mail: rhoshunda.kelly@dbcf.ms.gov
Executive Assistant **Mary Elizabeth Brown** . . . . . . . . . . . . (601) 359-1031
Administrative Services and Finance Director
  **Richard Rogers** . . . . . . . . . . . . . . . . . . . . . . . . . . . . . . . . (601) 359-1031
  E-mail: richard.rogers@dbcf.ms.gov
Bank Supervision Director **Sam Hubbard** . . . . . . . . . . . . . (601) 359-1031
  E-mail: sam.hubbard@dbcf.ms.gov
Consumer Finance Director **Taft Webb** . . . . . . . . . . . . . . . (601) 359-1031
  E-mail: taft.webb@dbcf.ms.gov
Information Technology Systems Director **Paul Parrish** . . . . (601) 359-1031
  E-mail: paul.parrish@dbcf.ms.gov
Mortgage Director **Traci McCain** . . . . . . . . . . . . . . . . . . . . (601) 359-1031

## Mississippi Department of Corrections [MDOC]

723 North President, Jackson, MS 39202-3097
Tel: (601) 359-5600  Fax: (601) 359-5293  Internet: www.mdoc.state.ms.us

**Employees:** 2,865  **Fiscal Year:** 2014  **Budget:** $374,993,000

■Commissioner **Marshall Fisher** . . . . . . . . . . . . . . . . . . . . . . (601) 359-5297
  E-mail: mfisher@mdoc.state.ms.us
  Commissioner's Assistant **Belinda Scott** . . . . . . . . . . . . . (601) 359-5715
Chief of Staff **Pelicia Hall** . . . . . . . . . . . . . . . . . . . . . . . . . . (601) 359-5600

---

★ Elected Official     ■ Appointed by Governor     ● Appointed by Legislature     ▲ Appointed by Board or Commission     ◆ Appointed by State Supreme Court

Administration and Finance Deputy Commissioner
**Rick McCarty** . . . . . . . . . . . . . . . . . . . . . . . . . . . (601) 359-5297
  E-mail: rmccarty@mdoc.state.ms.us
Community Corrections Deputy Commissioner
**Christy Gutherz** . . . . . . . . . . . . . . . . . . . . . . . . . . (601) 359-5618
Institutions Deputy Commissioner **Jerry Williams** . . . . . . . . (601) 359-5610
Communications Director **Grace Simmons-Fisher** . . . . . . . (601) 359-5608
  E-mail: gfisher@mdoc.state.ms.us
Constituent Services Director **Kevin Jackson** . . . . . . . . . . . (601) 932-2880
Corrections Investigation Division Director **Sean Smith** . . . (601) 359-5715
  E-mail: ssmith@mdoc.state.ms.us
Victim Services Division Director **Dilworth Ricks** . . . . . . . (601) 359-5628
                                                    Fax: (601) 359-5719
Management Information Systems Director
**Audrey McAfee** . . . . . . . . . . . . . . . . . . . . . . . . . . (601) 359-5636
  E-mail: amcafee@mdoc.state.ms.us

## Mississippi State Penitentiary

P.O. Box 1057, Parchman, MS 38738
Fax: (662) 745-8912

Superintendent **Earnest Lee** . . . . . . . . . . . . . . . . . . . . . (662) 745-6611

## Mississippi Department of Employment Security [MDES]

1235 Echelon Parkway, Jackson, MS 39213
P.O. Box 1699, Jackson, MS 39215-1699
Tel: (601) 321-6000  Fax: (601) 321-6004  Internet: http://mdes.ms.gov

■Executive Director **Mark Henry** . . . . . . . . . . . . . . . . . . (601) 321-6000
  E-mail: mhenry@mdes.ms.gov
Deputy Executive Director and Chief Financial Officer
**Jackie Turner** . . . . . . . . . . . . . . . . . . . . . . . . . . . (601) 321-6000
Deputy Executive Director and Chief Operations Officer
**Dale Smith** . . . . . . . . . . . . . . . . . . . . . . . . . . . . . (601) 321-6000
  E-mail: dsmith@mdes.ms.gov
External and Strategic Affairs Director **Kathryn Stokes** . . . (601) 321-6000
  E-mail: kstokes@mdes.ms.gov

## Mississippi Department of Environmental Quality [MDEQ]

P.O. Box 2261, Jackson, MS 39225
Tel: (601) 961-5171  Fax: (601) 354-6965
E-mail: webmaster@deq.state.ms.us  Internet: www.deq.state.ms.us

**Employees:** 393  **Fiscal Year:** 2014  **Budget:** $159,102,000

■Executive Director **Gary Rikard, ARNG (Ret)** . . . . . . . . . . (601) 961-5171
  Education: Christian Brothers U BCE; Mississippi JD
Deputy Director **Alice T. Perry** . . . . . . . . . . . . . . . . . . (601) 961-5335
  Education: Mississippi State 1971 BA, 1974 MS
Accounting Director **Mona Varner** . . . . . . . . . . . . . . . . (601) 961-5572
Budget Director **Virginia "Ginny" Mizelle** . . . . . . . . . . . (601) 961-5381
Buildings and Property Director **Cathy Trotti** . . . . . . . . . . (601) 961-5223
Human Resources Director **Mandy Purvis** . . . . . . . . . . . . (601) 961-5171
Purchasing Director **Connie Wilson** . . . . . . . . . . . . . . . (601) 961-5370
Administrative Services Office Director **Terri Torrence** . . . . (601) 961-5012
  E-mail: terri_torrence@deq.state.ms.us
Information Technology Division Director **(Vacant)** . . . . . . . (601) 961-5039

## Office of Community Engagement

700 North State Street, Jackson, MS 39201
P.O. Box 2249, Jackson, MS 39225

Director **Melissa McGee-Collier** . . . . . . . . . . . . . . . . . (601) 961-5025

## Office of Geology

P.O. Box 2279, Jackson, MS 39225
Tel: (601) 961-5500  Fax: (601) 961-5521

Director **Michael B. E. Bograd** . . . . . . . . . . . . . . . . . . (601) 961-5528
  E-mail: michael_bograd@deq.state.ms.us
  Education: Mississippi State 1971 BS; Mississippi 2002 MS
Environmental Geology Division Director **John Marble** . . . (601) 354-6328
  Education: Mississippi State 1974 BS
Geospatial Resources Division Director
**Stephen "Steve" Champlin** . . . . . . . . . . . . . . . . . . . (601) 961-5506

Mining and Reclamation Division Director
**James Matheny** . . . . . . . . . . . . . . . . . . . . . . . . . . (601) 961-5527
  E-mail: james.matheny@deq.state.ms.us
Surface Geology Division Director **David T. Dockery** . . . . . (601) 961-5544
  Education: Mississippi State 1972 BS; Mississippi 1976 MS;
  Tulane 1991 PhD

## Office of Land and Water Resources

P.O. Box 2309, Jackson, MS 39225
Tel: (601) 961-5200  Fax: (601) 354-6938

Director **Kay Whittington** . . . . . . . . . . . . . . . . . . . . . (601) 961-5200
  Education: Alabama BS, MCE
Assistant Director **(Vacant)** . . . . . . . . . . . . . . . . . . . . (601) 961-5201

## Office of Pollution Control

P.O. Box 2261, Jackson, MS 39225
Fax: (601) 354-6612

Director **Richard Harrell** . . . . . . . . . . . . . . . . . . . . . . (601) 961-5100
Permitting Division Director **Harry Wilson** . . . . . . . . . . . (601) 961-5073
  E-mail: harry_wilson@deq.state.ms.us
Air Division Chief **Dallas S. Baker, PE** . . . . . . . . . . . . . (601) 961-5670
  Education: Mississippi 1993 BS, 1997 MS; Mississippi Col 2003 MS
Enforcement/Compliance Division Chief **Chris Sanders** . . . (601) 961-5682
  Education: Mississippi State 1995 BS
Groundwater Assessment and Remediation Division
  Chief **Trey Hess** . . . . . . . . . . . . . . . . . . . . . . . . . (601) 961-5221
Surface Water Division Chief **Mike Freiman** . . . . . . . . . . (601) 961-5102

## Department of Finance and Administration [DFA]

501 North West Street, Suite 1301, Jackson, MS 39201
P.O. Box 267, Jackson, MS 39201
Tel: (601) 359-3402  Fax: (601) 359-2405  Internet: www.dfa.ms.gov

**Employees:** 398  **Fiscal Year:** 2014  **Budget:** $33,595,000

■Executive Director and State Fiscal Officer
**Kevin J. Upchurch** . . . . . . . . . . . . . . . . . . . . . . . . . (601) 359-3402
  E-mail: kupchurch@dfa.state.ms.us
  Education: Anderson U BS
Deputy Director **Bennie Nutt** . . . . . . . . . . . . . . . . . . . (601) 359-3402
  E-mail: bnutt@dfa.state.ms.us
Deputy Director **Freddie "Flip" Phillips** . . . . . . . . . . . . . (601) 359-9435
  E-mail: fphillips@dfa.state.ms.us
Deputy Director **Rick Snowden** . . . . . . . . . . . . . . . . . . (601) 359-3031
  E-mail: rsnowden@dfa.state.ms.us
Deputy Director **Becky Thompson** . . . . . . . . . . . . . . . . (601) 359-1433
  E-mail: bthompson@dfa.state.ms.us
  Education: Arkansas 1976 BS
Human Resources Director **Karen Holloway** . . . . . . . . . . (601) 359-2514
Bond Advisory Office Director **Mark Valentine** . . . . . . . . (601) 359-5022
  E-mail: mark.valentine@dfa.ms.gov
Business Services Office Director **Catherine Willis** . . . . . . (601) 359-3905
  E-mail: willisc@dfa.state.ms.us
Insurance Office Director **Richard Self** . . . . . . . . . . . . . (601) 359-6797
Tort Claims Board Director **Lea Ann McElroy** . . . . . . . . . (601) 359-3627
Mississippi Management and Reporting System
  Administrator **Becky Thompson** . . . . . . . . . . . . . . . . (601) 359-1344
  E-mail: bthompson@dfa.state.ms.us
Public Information Officer **Chuck McIntosh** . . . . . . . . . . (601) 359-3402

## Financial Management, Budget, and Policy Office

Budget and Accounts Office Director **Reginald Welch** . . . . (601) 359-2011
Fiscal Management Office Director **Diane Langham** . . . . . . (601) 359-2061
  Education: Mississippi State MPA
Management Information Systems Office Director
**Arthur Bridges** . . . . . . . . . . . . . . . . . . . . . . . . . . (601) 359-3678
  E-mail: bridgea@dfa.state.ms.us
Purchasing Office Director **Monica Ritchie** . . . . . . . . . . . (601) 359-2007
Travel and Fleet Management Director **Wayne Cranford** . . (601) 359-2007

---

★ Elected Official   ■ Appointed by Governor   ● Appointed by Legislature   ▲ Appointed by Board or Commission   ◆ Appointed by State Supreme Court

**EXECUTIVE BRANCH**

## General Services and Support Services Office

Fax: (601) 359-2470

Building, Grounds and Real Property Director
**Glenn Kornbrek** . . . . . . . . . . . . . . . . . . . . . . . . . (601) 359-3894
Air Transport Services Office Director **Brandon Fons** . . . . (601) 939-3055
Capitol Facilities Office Director **Roe Grubbs** . . . . . . . . . . (601) 359-3645
Surplus Property Office Director **Missy Elmore** . . . . . . . . . (601) 939-2050
Budget and Fund Management Division Director
**Sandra P. Lohrisch** . . . . . . . . . . . . . . . . . . . . . . . . (601) 359-2011

## Mississippi Department of Human Services [MDHS]

P.O. Box 352, Jackson, MS 39205-0352
Tel: (601) 359-4457  Fax: (601) 359-4477  Internet: www.mdhs.ms.gov

**Employees:** 3,452  **Fiscal Year:** 2014  **Budget:** $149,145,000

■Executive Director **John Davis** . . . . . . . . . . . . . . . . . (601) 359-4457
  Education: Southern Mississippi BBA; Belhaven MS
  Executive Assistant **Beth Handelman** . . . . . . . . . . . . . (601) 359-4457
Deputy Executive Director **Mark Smith** . . . . . . . . . . . . . (601) 359-9669
Administrative Assistant **Carrie Annison** . . . . . . . . . . . . (601) 359-9669

### Administration

Deputy Director **Will Simpson** . . . . . . . . . . . . . . . . . (601) 359-4180
  E-mail: will.simpson@mdhs.ms.gov
  Administrative Assistant **Rebecca Gail Smith** . . . . . . . . (601) 359-4180
Budgets and Accounting Division Director **Earl Walker** . . . (601) 359-4690
Family Foundation and Support Division Director
**Walley Naylor** . . . . . . . . . . . . . . . . . . . . . . . . . . (601) 359-4102
Human Resources and Staff Development Division
Director **Daren Vandevender** . . . . . . . . . . . . . . . . . . (601) 359-4444
Management Information Services Division Director
**Mark Allen** . . . . . . . . . . . . . . . . . . . . . . . . . . . (601) 359-4600
  E-mail: mark.allen@mdhs.ms.gov
Program Integrity Division Director **Laura Griffin** . . . . . . (601) 359-4900
Youth Services Division Director **Jim Maccarone** . . . . . . . (601) 359-4972
  E-mail: james.maccarone@mdhs.ms.gov
Family and Children's Services Deputy Administrator
**Kim Schakelford** . . . . . . . . . . . . . . . . . . . . . . . . (601) 359-4458
  E-mail: kim.schackelford@mdhs.ms.gov

### Programs

Deputy Administrator **John Davis** . . . . . . . . . . . . . . . . (601) 359-9601
  Administrative Assistant **Margaret Frazier** . . . . . . . . . . (601) 359-4458
Aging and Adult Services Division Director
**Melinda Bertucci** . . . . . . . . . . . . . . . . . . . . . . . . (601) 359-4925
  750 North State Street, Jackson, MS 39202
Community Services Division Director **Tina Ruffin** . . . . . . (601) 359-4768
Early Childhood Care and Development Division Director
**Laura Dickson** . . . . . . . . . . . . . . . . . . . . . . . . . (601) 359-4555
  E-mail: laura.dickson@mdhs.ms.gov
Economic Assistance Division Director **Cathy Sykes** . . . . . (601) 359-4810
Family and Children's Services Division Director
**David A. Chandler** . . . . . . . . . . . . . . . . . . . . . . . (601) 359-4999
  E-mail: david.chandler@mdhs.ms.gov
  Education: Mississippi State BA, MA, PhD; Mississippi JD;
  Virginia LLM
Social Services Block Grant Division Director
**Leigh Washington** . . . . . . . . . . . . . . . . . . . . . . . (601) 359-4778

## Department of Marine Resources [DMR]

1141 Bayview Avenue, Suite 101, Biloxi, MS 39530
Tel: (228) 374-5000  Fax: (228) 374-5005

**Employees:** 135  **Fiscal Year:** 2014  **Budget:** $35,176,000

Executive Director **Jamie M. Miller** . . . . . . . . . . . . . . . (228) 374-5000
  E-mail: jamie.miller@dmr.ms.gov
  Education: Southern Mississippi 1996 AB
Deputy Director **(Vacant)** . . . . . . . . . . . . . . . . . . . . (228) 374-5000

## Department of Mental Health [DMH]

1101 Robert E. Lee Building, 239 North Lamar Street,
Jackson, MS 39201
Tel: (601) 359-1288  TTY: (601) 359-6230  Fax: (601) 359-6295

**Employees:** 7,500  **Fiscal Year:** 2014  **Budget:** $582,516,000

▲Executive Director **Diana S. Mikula** . . . . . . . . . . . . . (601) 359-1288
  E-mail: diana.mikula@dmh.state.ms.us
Developmental Disabilities Council Director
**Charles Hughes** . . . . . . . . . . . . . . . . . . . . . . . . (601) 359-1270
Public Information Director **Adam Moore** . . . . . . . . . . . (601) 359-1288
  E-mail: adam.moore@dmh.state.ms.us
Administration Bureau Director **Kenneth Leggett** . . . . . . . (601) 359-1288
  E-mail: kenneth.leggett@dmh.state.ms.us
Alcohol and Drug Services Bureau Director
**Mark Stovall** . . . . . . . . . . . . . . . . . . . . . . . . . . (601) 359-1288
Community Services Bureau Director **Jake Hutchins** . . . . . (601) 359-1288
Intellectual and Developmental Disabilities Bureau
Director **Renee Britt** . . . . . . . . . . . . . . . . . . . . . . (601) 359-1288
Mental Health Programs Bureau Director **Marc Lewis** . . . . (601) 359-1288
Outreach, Planning, and Development Bureau Director
**Wendy Bailey** . . . . . . . . . . . . . . . . . . . . . . . . . (601) 359-1288
Children and Youth Services Division Director
**Sandra Parks** . . . . . . . . . . . . . . . . . . . . . . . . . (601) 359-1288

## Department of Public Safety [DPS]

P.O. Box 958, Jackson, MS 39205
Tel: (601) 987-1212  Fax: (601) 987-1498  Internet: www.dps.state.ms.us

**Employees:** 1,030

■Commissioner **Albert Santa Cruz** . . . . . . . . . . . . . . . (601) 987-1490
  E-mail: commissioner@dps.ms.gov          Fax: (601) 987-1493
Administrative Operations Director **Lt. Col. Gale Mills** . . . (601) 987-1386
  E-mail: gmills@dps.ms.gov                Fax: (601) 987-1497
State Medical Examiner Office Director
**Dr. Mark LeVaughn** . . . . . . . . . . . . . . . . . . . . . . (601) 987-1600
Criminal Information Center Director **Lamond Wilson** . . . . (601) 933-2600
  E-mail: lwilson@dps.ms.gov
MIS (Management Information Systems) Director
**Clay Johnston** . . . . . . . . . . . . . . . . . . . . . . . . . (601) 933-2637
  E-mail: cjohnston@dps.ms.gov
Public Affairs Director **Warren Strain** . . . . . . . . . . . . . (601) 987-1390
Public Safety Planning Division Director (Interim)
**Capt. Donald McCain** . . . . . . . . . . . . . . . . . . . . . (601) 977-3700
  1025 Northpark Drive, Ridgeland, MS 39157    Fax: (601) 977-3701
  E-mail: dmccain@dps.ms.gov

### Highway Safety Patrol

**Employees:** 1,000  **Fiscal Year:** 2015  **Budget:** $62,898,000

■Director **Col. Donnell Berry** . . . . . . . . . . . . . . . . . . (601) 987-1495
  E-mail: donnellb@dps.ms.gov
Deputy Director **Lt. Col. Kevin Myers** . . . . . . . . . . . . . (601) 987-1495
Chief Inspector **Major Randy Ginn** . . . . . . . . . . . . . . . (662) 563-6405
  E-mail: rginn@dps.ms.gov
Chief Inspector **Major Jimmy O'Banner** . . . . . . . . . . . . (601) 420-6342
  E-mail: jo'banner@dps.ms.gov
Mississippi Bureau of Investigations (MBI) Assistant
Director **Lt. Col. Larry Waggoner** . . . . . . . . . . . . . . (601) 987-1573

### Driver Services Bureau

Driver Services Bureau Director **Major Chris Gillard** . . . . (601) 987-1206
  E-mail: cgillard@dps.ms.gov
Commercial Drivers License Division Director
**Major Chris Gillard** . . . . . . . . . . . . . . . . . . . . . . (601) 987-1200
  E-mail: cgillard@dps.ms.gov
Motor Carrier Safety Division Director
**Capt. Donald McCain** . . . . . . . . . . . . . . . . . . . . . (601) 987-1245
  E-mail: dmccain@dps.ms.gov
Highway Safety Issues Administrator **Shirley Thomas** . . . . (601) 987-1212
  E-mail: sthomas@dps.ms.gov

---

★ Elected Official    ■ Appointed by Governor    ● Appointed by Legislature    ▲ Appointed by Board or Commission    ◆ Appointed by State Supreme Court

# Homeland Security Office

P.O. Box 958, Jackson, MS 39205
Tel: (601) 346-1499  Fax: (601) 346-1521
E-mail: info@homelandsecurity.ms.gov
Internet: www.homelandsecurity.ms.gov

**Employees:** 22  **Fiscal Year:** 2014  **Budget:** $97,000

Director **Major Rusty Barnes** . . . . . . . . . . . . . . . . . . . . . . (601) 346-1500
   Education: Mississippi BPA

# Bureau of Narcotics

P.O. Box 7459, Jackson, MS 39282-7459
Tel: (601) 371-3600  Fax: (601) 354-7396

**Employees:** 169  **Fiscal Year:** 2014  **Budget:** $13,627,000

Director **Sam Owens** . . . . . . . . . . . . . . . . . . . . . . . . . . . . (601) 371-3623

# Crime Laboratory

**Employees:** 104  **Fiscal Year:** 2014  **Budget:** $9,974,000

Director **Sam Howell** . . . . . . . . . . . . . . . . . . . . . . . . . . . . (601) 987-1600

# Training Academy

3791 Highway 468, Pearl, MS 39208
Fax: (601) 933-2200

**Employees:** 25  **Fiscal Year:** 2014  **Budget:** $1,240,000

Director **Major Pat Cronin** . . . . . . . . . . . . . . . . . . . . . . . (601) 933-2130

# Mississippi Analysis and Information Center [MSAIC]

1 Mema Drive, Pearl, MS 39208
Tel: (601) 933-7200 (Tip Line)  Fax: (601) 933-7220
E-mail: msaic@mdps.state.ms.us

Director **Lamond Wilson** . . . . . . . . . . . . . . . . . . . . . . . . . (601) 933-2600

# Mississippi Department of Rehabilitation Services [MDRS]

P.O. Box 1698, Jackson, MS 39215-1698
Tel: (601) 853-5100  Fax: (601) 853-5205

**Employees:** 975

▲Executive Director **Chris M. Howard** . . . . . . . . . . . . . . . (601) 853-5203
   E-mail: choward@mdrs.ms.gov
Deputy Executive Director **(Vacant)** . . . . . . . . . . . . . . . . . (601) 853-5220
Chief of Staff **Billy Taylor** . . . . . . . . . . . . . . . . . . . . . . . . (601) 853-5100
Administration Security and Support Director
   **Tommy Browning** . . . . . . . . . . . . . . . . . . . . . . . . . . . (601) 853-5100
   E-mail: tbrowning@mdrs.ms.gov
Disability Determination Services Office Director
   **JoAnn Summers** . . . . . . . . . . . . . . . . . . . . . . . . . . . . (601) 853-5450
   P.O. Box 1271, Jackson, MS 39205
Human Resources Development Director **Katie Storr** . . . . . (601) 853-5260
Information Technology Director **Paula Brown** . . . . . . . . . . (601) 853-5141
   E-mail: pbrown@mdrs.ms.gov
Non-Vocational Programs Deputy Director **(Vacant)** . . . . . . (601) 853-5209
Special Disability Programs Office Director **Anita Naik** . . . (601) 853-5206
Vocational Rehabilitation Director **LaVonda Hart** . . . . . . . . (601) 853-5245
Vocational Rehabilitation for the Blind Office Director
   **Dorothy Young** . . . . . . . . . . . . . . . . . . . . . . . . . . . . . (601) 853-5300

# Department of Revenue [DOR]

P.O. Box 22828, Jackson, MS 39225-2828
Tel: (601) 923-7000  Fax: (601) 923-7423

**Employees:** 659  **Fiscal Year:** 2014  **Budget:** $59,097,000

■Commissioner **J. Ed Morgan** . . . . . . . . . . . . . . . . . . . . . . (601) 923-7400
   Note: Until June 30, 2016.
   E-mail: ed.morgan@dor.ms.gov
■Commissioner **Herb Frierson** . . . . . . . . . . . . . . . . . . . . . . (601) 923-7400
   Note: Effective July 1, 2016.
   Education: Mississippi State BS
Tax Policy and Economic Development Director
   **Ashley May** . . . . . . . . . . . . . . . . . . . . . . . . . . . . . . . . (601) 923-7440

Chairman, Board of Review **Ashley May** . . . . . . . . . . . . . . (601) 923-7440
   Affiliation: Tax Policy and Economic Development   Fax: (601) 923-7844
   Director, Department of Revenue, State of Mississippi
   P.O. Box 22828, Jackson, MS 39225-2828
Legal Counsel **Gary W. Stringer** . . . . . . . . . . . . . . . . . . . . (601) 923-7412
   Special Assistant to the Commissioner, Executive and
      Enforcement **Terry Smith** . . . . . . . . . . . . . . . . . . . . (601) 923-7400
Collection Activities Bureau Director **Wayne Ray** . . . . . . . (601) 923-7310
Communications Director **Kathy Waterbury** . . . . . . . . . . . (601) 923-7400
   E-mail: kathy.waterbury@dor.ms.gov
Human Resources Director **Lamar Wilson** . . . . . . . . . . . . . (601) 923-7750

## Agency Support

Associate Commissioner **Cynthia "Cindy" Wood** . . . . . . . (601) 923-7044
   E-mail: cindy.wood@dor.ms.gov
Information Technology Office Chief Information Officer
   **Jeff Bynum** . . . . . . . . . . . . . . . . . . . . . . . . . . . . . . . . (601) 923-7000
   E-mail: jeff.bynum@dor.ms.gov
Information Technology Office Chief Information Officer
   **Jennifer Summerlin** . . . . . . . . . . . . . . . . . . . . . . . . . (601) 923-7000
   E-mail: jennifer.summerlin@dor.ms.gov

# Alcoholic Beverage Control Office [ABC]

P.O. Box 540, Madison, MS 39110-0540
Tel: (601) 856-1301  Fax: (601) 856-1390

Director **James C. Eubanks** . . . . . . . . . . . . . . . . . . . . . . . (601) 856-1301
Enforcement Office Chief **Mark Hicks** . . . . . . . . . . . . . . . (601) 856-1320

# Business Taxes

Associate Commissioner **Meg Bartlett** . . . . . . . . . . . . . . . (601) 923-7305
Office Director **Lanell Strait** . . . . . . . . . . . . . . . . . . . . . . (601) 923-7305
Petroleum Tax Bureau Director **Glenn Boyette** . . . . . . . . . (601) 923-7150
Sales and Use Tax Bureau Director **Larry Allen** . . . . . . . . . (601) 923-7015

# Income and Property Taxes

Associate Commissioner **Jan Craig** . . . . . . . . . . . . . . . . . . (601) 923-7000
Registration Section Director **Pam Matthew** . . . . . . . . . . . (601) 923-7000
Income Office Director **Charmin Tillman** . . . . . . . . . . . . . (601) 923-7003
Foreign Audit Bureau Director **Melinda Lott** . . . . . . . . . . . (601) 923-7305
Income and Franchise Tax Bureau Director **Elisa Wells** . . . (601) 923-7040

# Mississippi Department of Wildlife, Fisheries and Parks [MDWFP]

1505 Eastover Drive, Jackson, MS 39211-6374
Tel: (601) 432-2400  Fax: (601) 432-2024  Internet: www.mdwfp.com

**Employees:** 540

Executive Director **Sam Polles, PhD** . . . . . . . . . . . . . . . . . (601) 432-2002
   E-mail: executive@mdwfp.state.ms.us
   Administrative Assistant **(Vacant)** . . . . . . . . . . . . . . . . . (601) 432-2400
Deputy Director **Robert Cook** . . . . . . . . . . . . . . . . . . . . . (601) 432-2002
Enforcement and Conservation Director **Larry Castle** . . . . (601) 432-2002
   E-mail: larryc@mdwfp.state.ms.us
   Director of Parks **Ramie Ford** . . . . . . . . . . . . . . . . . . . . (601) 432-2007
      E-mail: ramief@mdwfp.state.ms.us

## Administrative Services Division

Director **Michael Bolden** . . . . . . . . . . . . . . . . . . . . . . . . . (601) 432-2008
   E-mail: michaelb@mdwfp.state.ms.us

## Parks and Recreation Division

Operations Director **Paul Collins** . . . . . . . . . . . . . . . . . . . (601) 432-2231
   E-mail: paul.collins@mdwfp.state.ms.us
Facilities and Ground Development Director
   **Robert Neely** . . . . . . . . . . . . . . . . . . . . . . . . . . . . . . . (601) 432-2226
   E-mail: robertn@mdac.state.ms.us
Land and Water Grants Director **Jean Caraway** . . . . . . . . . (601) 432-2225
   E-mail: jean@mdwfp.state.ms.us

## Support Services Division

Accounting Director **Jennifer Head** . . . . . . . . . . . . . . . . . . (601) 432-2091
Fleet Services Director **Kelvin McCree** . . . . . . . . . . . . . . . (601) 432-2081
Information Systems Director **Curtis Thornhill** . . . . . . . . . (601) 432-2028
   E-mail: curtist@mdwfp.state.ms.us

*(continued on next page)*

---

★ Elected Official   ■ Appointed by Governor   ● Appointed by Legislature   ▲ Appointed by Board or Commission   ◆ Appointed by State Supreme Court

**Support Services Division** *continued*

Human Resources Director **Ivy Williams** . . . . . . . . . . . . . (601) 432-2138
  E-mail: Ivyw@mdac.ms.gov
License/Boat Registration Director **Jason Thompson** . . . . .(601) 432-2263
  E-mail: jasont@mdwfp.state.ms.us
Property Director **Brian Ferguson** . . . . . . . . . . . . . . . . . (601) 432-2155
Public Information Media Director **Jim Walker** . . . . . . . . . (601) 432-2249
  E-mail: jimw@mdwfp.state.ms.us
Purchasing Director **Brian Ferguson** . . . . . . . . . . . . . . . . (601) 432-2149
  E-mail: brianf@mdac.ms.gov

## Wildlife and Fisheries Division

Law Enforcement Chief **Steve Adcock** . . . . . . . . . . . . . . . (601) 432-2173
Law Enforcement Assistant Chief **Sammy Fisher** . . . . . . . (601) 432-2176
Freshwater Fisheries Director **Larry Pugh** . . . . . . . . . . . . (601) 432-2205
Natural Science Museum Director **Libby Hartfield** . . . . . . . (601) 578-6000
  2148 Riverside Drive, Jackson, MS 39202-1353     Fax: (601) 354-7227
Wildlife Management Director **Chad Dacus** . . . . . . . . . . . .(601) 432-2202
Hunter and Boat Education Administrator **Jerry Carter** . . . .(601) 432-2182

## State Board of Health

570 East Woodrow Wilson, Jackson, MS 39215-1700
Tel: (601) 576-7400

■Chairman **Lucius M. Lampton, FAAFP** . . . . . . . . . . . . . . (601) 576-7400
  Term Expires: June 30, 2019
■Vice Chairman **Dr. J. Edward Hill, FAAFP** . . . . . . . . . . . .(601) 576-7400
  Term Expires: June 30, 2021
  Education: Mississippi BS, MD
■Member **Dr. Ed D. "Tad" Barham** . . . . . . . . . . . . . . . . . (601) 576-7400
  Term Expires: June 30, 2017
  Education: Mississippi Col BS; George Washington MD
■Member **Elayne Hayes-Anthony, PhD** . . . . . . . . . . . . . . .(601) 576-7400
  Term Expires: June 30, 2019
■Member **Edward J. "Ed" Langton** . . . . . . . . . . . . . . . . . (601) 576-7400
  Term Expires: June 30, 2017
■Member **Robert J. "Bobby" Moody** . . . . . . . . . . . . . . . . (601) 576-7400
  Term Expires: June 30, 2019
■Member **Betty Jane "B.J." Phillips, DrPH** . . . . . . . . . . . .(601) 576-7400
  Term Expires: June 30, 2019
■Member **Sammie Ruth Rea, RN** . . . . . . . . . . . . . . . . . . (601) 576-7400
  Term Expires: June 30, 2021
■Member **Dwalia Sherree South** . . . . . . . . . . . . . . . . . . (601) 576-7400
  Term Expires: June 30, 2021
■Member **Wheeler Timothy "Tim" Timbs III** . . . . . . . . . . .(601) 576-7400
  Term Expires: June 30, 2017
■Member **Thad F. Waites, MD, FACC** . . . . . . . . . . . . . . . (601) 576-7400
  Term Expires: June 30, 2021

## Mississippi State Department of Health [MSDH]

570 East Woodrow Wilson, Jackson, MS 39215-1700
P.O. Box 1700, Jackson, MS 39215-1700 (Vital Records)
Tel: (601) 576-7400   Tel: (800) 489-7670 (Health Information)
Tel: (601) 206-8200 (Vital Records)   Internet: www.msdh.state.ms.us

**Fiscal Year:** 2014   **Budget:** $307,617,000

▲State Health Officer **Dr. Mary M. Currier, MD** . . . . . . . . . .(601) 576-7634
  E-mail: mary.currier@msdh.state.ms.us     Fax: (601) 576-7931
  Education: Rice 1978 BA; Mississippi Medical 1983
Communications Director **Liz Sharlot** . . . . . . . . . . . . . . . (601) 576-7667
                      Fax: (601) 576-7517
Internal Auditor **Sharon Nasianceno, CPA** . . . . . . . . . . . .(601) 576-7458
                      Fax: (601) 576-7805
Legal Counsel **Bob Fagan** . . . . . . . . . . . . . . . . . . . . . . . (601) 576-7847
                      Fax: (601) 576-7805

## Office of the State Epidemiologist

Tel: (601) 576-7725  Fax: (601) 576-7497

State Epidemiologist
  **Dr. Thomas E. Dobbs III, MD, MPH** . . . . . . . . . . . . . .(601) 576-7725
  Education: Emory MD; Alabama Birmingham MPH

## Office of Health Policy and Planning

Fax: (601) 576-7530

Health Policy and Planning Director **(Vacant)** . . . . . . . . . . (601) 576-7874
Planning Resources Chief **Keisi D. V. Ward** . . . . . . . . . . . (601) 576-7874
  E-mail: kward@msdh.state.ms.us
Primary Care Director **Rozella Harris** . . . . . . . . . . . . . . . .(601) 576-7216
                      Fax: (601) 576-7873

## Office of Health Administration

Tel: (601) 576-7635  Fax: (601) 576-7778

Senior Deputy and Chief Administrative Officer
  **Mitchell Adcock, CPA, CIA, CFE, CPM** . . . . . . . . . . . . (601) 576-7635
Finance and Accounts Director **Willie R. Thompson** . . . . . (601) 576-7542
Chief Information Systems Officer **(Vacant)** . . . . . . . . . . . (601) 576-8092
Public Health Pharmacy Director **Meg Pearson** . . . . . . . . .(601) 713-3457
                      Fax: (601) 364-2670
Field Services Director **Tim Darnell** . . . . . . . . . . . . . . . . . (601) 576-7951

## Office of Health Protection

Tel: (601) 576-7680  Fax: (601) 576-7270
Internet: www.msdh.state.ms.us/ohr

Director **James "Jim" Craig III** . . . . . . . . . . . . . . . . . . . (601) 576-7680
  Education: Southwestern Louisiana 1990 BS
Licensure Bureau Director **Vickey Berryman** . . . . . . . . . . .(601) 364-1100
  E-mail: vberryman@msdh.state.ms.us     Fax: (601) 364-5055
Emergency Medical Services Director **Alisa H. Williams** . . (601) 576-7380
  Education: Mississippi BS; Mississippi Medical

## Office of Health Services

Fax: (601) 576-7825

Director **Kathy G. Burk** . . . . . . . . . . . . . . . . . . . . . . . . . (601) 576-7472
Women's Health Division Director
  **Danielle Seale, LCSW** . . . . . . . . . . . . . . . . . . . . . . . (601) 576-7856
Domestic Violence Program Manager **Louisa Denson** . . . . (601) 576-7856
Early Intervention Program Manager **Susan Boone** . . . . . . (601) 576-7427
Family Planning Program Manager **Mary Reed** . . . . . . . . . (601) 576-7486
  E-mail: mreed@msdh.state.ms.us
Child and Adolescent Health Division Director
  **Beryl Polk, PhD** . . . . . . . . . . . . . . . . . . . . . . . . . . . .(601) 576-7464
  Education: Jackson State U EdD
  Adolescent Health Program Coordinator
    **Gwen Winters** . . . . . . . . . . . . . . . . . . . . . . . . . . . (601) 576-7464
    E-mail: gwen.winters@msdh.state.ms.us
Dental Services Division Director **Dionne Richardson** . . . . (601) 576-7500
Social Services **Danielle Seale, LCSW** . . . . . . . . . . . . . . . (601) 576-7477
Nutrition Services Division Director **(Vacant)** . . . . . . . . . . (601) 576-7941

## Division of Medicaid [DOM]

Sillers Building, 550 High Street, Suite 1000, Jackson, MS 39201
Tel: (601) 359-6050  Fax: (601) 359-6048

Executive Director **David J. Dzielak** . . . . . . . . . . . . . . . . . (601) 359-9562
  E-mail: david.dzielak@medicaid.ms.gov
Deputy Administrator for Communications
  **Erin Barham, APR** . . . . . . . . . . . . . . . . . . . . . . . . . . (601) 359-5773
  E-mail: erin.barham@medicaid.ms.gov
Deputy Administrator for Eligibility **Janis Bond** . . . . . . . . (601) 359-6050
                      Fax: (601) 987-3947

## Mississippi Emergency Management Agency [MEMA]

P.O. Box 5644, Pearl, MS 39288
Tel: (601) 933-6362  Fax: (601) 933-6800
E-mail: memainfo@mema.ms.gov  Internet: www.msema.org

**Fiscal Year:** 2014   **Budget:** $23,752,000

■Executive Director **COL Lee Smithson, ARNG** . . . . . . . . . (601) 933-6362
  Administrative Assistant **Stacy Purvis** . . . . . . . . . . . . . (601) 933-6362
Deputy Administrator **Ben Gaston** . . . . . . . . . . . . . . . . . (601) 933-6839
Deputy Administrator **Richard Wilson** . . . . . . . . . . . . . . . (601) 933-6882
Chief of Staff **Bill Brown** . . . . . . . . . . . . . . . . . . . . . . . . (601) 933-6635
Mitigation Office Director **Jana Henderson** . . . . . . . . . . . (601) 933-6884
Preparedness Office Director **Harrell Neal** . . . . . . . . . . . . (601) 933-6880

---

Radiological Emergency Preparedness Office Director
**David Huttie** . . . . . . . . . . . . . . . . . . . . . . . . . . . . . . . . . . . . (601) 933-6845
Support Services Office Director **Chris Fields** . . . . . . . . . . (601) 933-6883
Hazardous Materials Section Manager **Brian Maske** . . . . . . (601) 933-6362

# Ethics Commission

660 North Street, Suite 100-C, Jackson, MS 39202
P.O. Box 22746, Jackson, MS 39225-2746
Tel: (601) 359-1285  Fax: (601) 359-1292  E-mail: info@ethics.state.ms.us
Internet: www.ethics.state.ms.us

**Fiscal Year:** 2014  **Budget:** $621,000

▲Executive Director **Tom B. Hood** . . . . . . . . . . . . . . . . . . . . . (601) 359-1285
   E-mail: thood@ethics.state.ms.us

# Mississippi Forestry Commission [MFC]

660 North Street, Suite 300, Jackson, MS 39202
Tel: (601) 359-1386  Fax: (601) 359-1349

**Employees:** 457  **Fiscal Year:** 2014  **Budget:** $30,500,000

▲State Forester **Charlie W. Morgan** . . . . . . . . . . . . . . . . . . . . (601) 359-1386
   E-mail: cmorgan@mfc.state.ms.us

# Mississippi Gaming Commission [MGC]

620 North Street, Suite 200, Jackson, MS 39202
P.O. Box 23577, Jackson, MS 39225-3577
Tel: (601) 576-3800  Tel: (800) 504-7529 (Toll Free)  Fax: (601) 576-3929
E-mail: info@mgc.state.ms.us  Internet: www.mgc.state.ms.us

**Employees:** 125  **Fiscal Year:** 2014  **Budget:** $9,618,000

▲Executive Director **Allen Godfrey** . . . . . . . . . . . . . . . . . . . . (601) 576-3800
   E-mail: agodfrey@mgc.state.ms.us

# Library Commission

3881 Eastwood Drive, Jackson, MS 39211
Tel: (601) 432-4111  TTY: (601) 432-4493  Fax: (601) 432-4480
E-mail: mslib@mail.mlc.lib.ms.us  Internet: www.mlc.lib.ms.us

**Fiscal Year:** 2014  **Budget:** $13,814,000

Chair **Glenda Segars** . . . . . . . . . . . . . . . . . . . . . . . . . . . . . . (601) 432-4039
Commissioner **Celia C. Fisher** . . . . . . . . . . . . . . . . . . . . . . . (601) 432-4039
Commissioner **Jolee C. Hussey** . . . . . . . . . . . . . . . . . . . . . . (601) 432-4039
Commissioner **Ann Marsh** . . . . . . . . . . . . . . . . . . . . . . . . . . (601) 432-4039
Commissioner **Pamela Pridgen** . . . . . . . . . . . . . . . . . . . . . . (601) 432-4039
Executive Director **Susan Cassagne** . . . . . . . . . . . . . . . . . (601) 432-4038

# Mississippi Motor Vehicle Commission [MMVC]

1755 Lelia Drive, Suite 200, Jackson, MS 39216
P.O. Box 16873, Jackson, MS 39236-0873
Tel: (601) 987-3995  Fax: (601) 987-3997
E-mail: info@mmvc.state.ms.us  Internet: www.mmvc.state.ms.us

**Employees:** 3  **Fiscal Year:** 2014  **Budget:** $318,000

▲Executive Director **Chuck Nelms** . . . . . . . . . . . . . . . (601) 987-3995 ext. 4
   E-mail: nelms@mmvc.state.ms.us

# Soil and Water Conservation Commission

680 Monroe Street, Suite B, Jackson, MS 39202
TTY: (601) 354-7645  Fax: (601) 354-6628
Internet: www.mswcc.state.ms.us

**Employees:** 14  **Fiscal Year:** 2014  **Budget:** $1,980,000

▲Executive Director **Mark Gilbert** . . . . . . . . . . . . . . . . . . . . (601) 354-7645
   E-mail: mgilbert@mswcc.ms.gov

# Mississippi State Fair Commission

P.O. Box 892, Jackson, MS 39205
Tel: (601) 961-4000  Fax: (601) 354-6545

Executive Director **Rick Reno** . . . . . . . . . . . . . . . . . . . . . . . . (601) 961-4000

# Workers' Compensation Commission

P.O. Box 5300, Jackson, MS 39296-5300
Tel: (601) 987-4200  Fax: (601) 987-4220
Internet: www.mwcc.state.ms.us

**Employees:** 57  **Fiscal Year:** 2014  **Budget:** $5,649,000

■Chairman **Liles B. Williams** . . . . . . . . . . . . . . . . . . . . . . . . (601) 987-4258
■Commissioner
   **Elizabeth Ashley "Beth" Harkins Aldridge** . . . . . . . . . (601) 987-4270
■Commissioner **Tom Webb** . . . . . . . . . . . . . . . . . . . . . . . . . (601) 987-4270
▲Executive Director **Ray C. Minor** . . . . . . . . . . . . . . . . . . . . (601) 987-4204
   E-mail: rminor@mwcc.state.ms.us
   Education: Alcorn State 1978 BS

# Mississippi Development Authority [MDA]

Woolfolk Building, 501 North West Street, Jackson, MS 39201
Tel: (601) 359-3449  Fax: (601) 359-2832

**Employees:** 300  **Fiscal Year:** 2014  **Budget:** $266,180,000

■Executive Director **Glenn L. McCullough, Jr.** . . . . . . . . . . (601) 359-3449
   Education: Mississippi State 1977 BA
Deputy Director **Mike McGrevey** . . . . . . . . . . . . . . . . . . . . (601) 359-3449
Chief Administrative Officer **Manning McPhillips** . . . . . . (601) 359-3449
   E-mail: mmcphillips@mississippi.org
Chief Financial Officer **Jay McCarthy** . . . . . . . . . . . . . . . . (601) 359-3449
   Education: Mississippi Col 1986 BBA
Chief Marketing Officer **Pamela Weaver** . . . . . . . . . . . . . (601) 359-3449
Visit Mississippi Director **Daron Wilson** . . . . . . . . . . . . . (601) 359-3297
Asset Development Director **Joy Foy** . . . . . . . . . . . . . . . . (601) 359-3449
Community Services Director **Steve Hardin** . . . . . . . . . . . (601) 359-2366
Energy and Natural Resources Director (Interim)
   **Larissa Williams** . . . . . . . . . . . . . . . . . . . . . . . . . . . . . (601) 359-3449
Existing Industry and Business Director **Mickey Milligan** . . (601) 359-3593
Global Business Director (Interim) **Becky Thompson** . . . . (601) 359-3155
Minority and Small Business Development Division
   Director **Bob Covington** . . . . . . . . . . . . . . . . . . . . . . . . (601) 359-3448

# Appalachian Regional Commission Office

P. O. Box 1606, Tupelo, MS 38802

Director **Mike Armour** . . . . . . . . . . . . . . . . . . . . . . . . . . . . . (662) 842-3891

# Mississippi State Port Authority [MSPA]

2510 14th Street, Suite 1450, Gulfport, MS 39501
P.O. Box 40, Gulfport, MS 39502
Tel: (228) 865-4300  Fax: (228) 865-4335  Internet: www.shipmspa.com

Commissioner **Robert Knesal** . . . . . . . . . . . . . . . . . . . . . . . (228) 865-4300
   E-mail: rknesal@shipmspa.com
Commissioner **Jack Norris** . . . . . . . . . . . . . . . . . . . . . . . . . (228) 865-4300
   E-mail: jnorris@shipmspa.com
   Education: Mississippi BA
Commissioner **John K. Rester** . . . . . . . . . . . . . . . . . . . . . . (228) 865-4300
   E-mail: jrester@shipmspa.com
Commissioner **E. J. Roberts** . . . . . . . . . . . . . . . . . . . . . . . . (228) 865-4300
   E-mail: eroberts@shipmspa.com
Commissioner **James C. "Jim" Simpson, Jr.** . . . . . . . . . . . (228) 865-4300
   Education: Southern Mississippi BS;
   Washington College of Law 1979 JD
Executive Director and Chief Executive Officer
   **Jonathan Daniels** . . . . . . . . . . . . . . . . . . . . . . . . . . . . . (228) 865-4300

---

★ Elected Official   ■ Appointed by Governor   ● Appointed by Legislature   ▲ Appointed by Board or Commission   ◆ Appointed by State Supreme Court

EXECUTIVE BRANCH

# Mississippi Community College Board [MCCB]

3825 Ridgewood Road, Jackson, MS 39211
Tel: (601) 432-6518  Fax: (601) 432-6363  E-mail: info@mccb.edu

▲Executive Director **Andrea Mayfield** . . . . . . . . . . . . . . . . . (601) 432-6337
   E-mail: amayfield@mccb.edu

## Office of Adult Basic Education

Tel: (601) 432-6518

Adult Education and GED Testing Director
   **Eloise Richardson** . . . . . . . . . . . . . . . . . . . . . . . . . . (601) 432-6518
   E-mail: erichardson@mccb.edu
GED Specialist **Janice Young** . . . . . . . . . . . . . . . . . . . . . (601) 432-6518
   E-mail: jyoung@mccb.edu
Adult Education Program Specialist **Sandy Crist** . . . . . . . . (601) 432-6518
   E-mail: scrist@mccb.edu
GED Testing Program Specialist **Missy Saxton** . . . . . . . . . . (601) 432-6518
   E-mail: msaxton@mccb.edu

# State Board of Contractors

P.O. Box 320279, Jackson, MS 39232-0279
2679 Crane Ridge Drive, Suite C, Jackson, MS 39216
Tel: (800) 880-6161  Fax: (601) 354-6715  Internet: www.msboc.us

▲Executive Director **Stephanie Lee** . . . . . . . . . . . . . . . (601) 354-6161 ext. 112
   E-mail: stephanie@msboc.us

# Mississippi Board of Education

P.O. Box 771, Jackson, MS 39205
Fax: (601) 359-3242

**Fiscal Year:** 2014  **Budget:** $3,048,053,000

■Chair **Dr. John R. Kelly** (Supreme Court District 2) . . . . . . (601) 661-7308
   Term Expires: June 30, 2020
   Education: Alcorn State 1970; Wayne State U;
   Southern Mississippi PhD
■Vice Chair **Rosemary Aultman** (At-Large) . . . . . . . . . . . . . (601) 924-4830
   Term Expires: July 1, 2022
■Member **Buddy Bailey** (Supreme Court District 3) . . . . . . . (601) 825-5590
   Term Expires: June 30, 2023   Fax: (662) 844-3692
■Member **Kami Bumgarner** . . . . . . . . . . . . . . . . . . . . . . . . (601) 605-4171
   Note: Teacher Representative
   Term Expires: June 30, 2018
■Member **Dr. Jason S. Dean** (At-Large) . . . . . . . . . . . . . . . (601) 664-8858
   Term Expires: July 2024
   600 Crescent Boulevard, Suite B, Ridgeland, MS 39157
■Member **Karen Elam** (Supreme Court District 3) . . . . . . . . (662) 513-0705
   Term Expires: June 30, 2021
   Education: Purdue BA; Michigan State MS; Missouri PhD
■Member **Johnny Franklin** (Supreme Court District 1) . . . . . (601) 664-8363
   Term Expires: June 30, 2016
   Education: Mississippi Col BE, MEd
●Member **William Harold Jones** (At-Large) . . . . . . . . . . . . (601) 545-8324
   Term Expires: July 1, 2017   Fax: (601) 545-8389
■Member **Charles McClelland** (At-Large) . . . . . . . . . . . . . . (601) 991-2412
   Term Expires: July 1, 2019
   Education: Alcorn State 1964; Jackson State U MEd
▲Executive Secretary **Dr. Carey M. Wright** . . . . . . . . . . . . (601) 359-1750
   Note: State Superintendent of Education
   E-mail: cwright@mde.k12.ms.us
   Education: Maryland 1976 MEd, 1994 EdD

# Mississippi Department of Education [MDE]

Tel: (601) 359-3513  Fax: (601) 359-1728  Internet: www.mde.k12.ms.us

▲State Superintendent **Dr. Carey M. Wright** . . . . . . . . . . . . (601) 359-1750
   E-mail: cwright@mde.k12.ms.us

## Office of Communications and Legislative Services

Tel: (601) 359-1750

Deputy Superintendent **Washington Cole** . . . . . . . . . . . . . (601) 359-2038
   E-mail: wcole@mde.k12.ms.us
   Education: Jackson State U MEd

Communications Director **Patrice Guilfoyle** . . . . . . . . . . . . (601) 359-3515
Budget and Planning Bureau Director **Gracie Sanders** . . . . (601) 359-3923
   Education: Delta State MBA
Legislative Services Bureau Manager **Pete Smith** . . . . . . . (601) 359-3515
   E-mail: psmith@mde.k12.ms.us

## Office of Educational Accountability

Tel: (601) 359-5254  Fax: (601) 359-1748

Director **Todd Ivey** . . . . . . . . . . . . . . . . . . . . . . . . . . . (601) 359-2038
   Education: Mississippi State 1983 BA
Program Evaluations Director **(Vacant)** . . . . . . . . . . . . . . (601) 359-5539
Assistant Attorney General **Kathy Boteler** . . . . . . . . . . . . (601) 359-2038
   E-mail: kboteler@mde.k12.ms.us
School Financial Services Bureau Director
   **S. Melissa Barnes** . . . . . . . . . . . . . . . . . . . . . . . . . (601) 359-3294
Chief Information Officer **Robert "Bobby" Massey** . . . . . (601) 359-3487
   E-mail: bmassey@mde.k12.ms.us

## Office of Instructional Programs and Services

Tel: (601) 359-3768  Fax: (601) 359-3712

Deputy State Superintendent (Interim) **Kim S. Benton** . . . . (601) 359-3768
Special Education Office Associate Superintendent
   **Therrell Myers** . . . . . . . . . . . . . . . . . . . . . . . . . . . (601) 359-3498
Curriculum and Instruction Office Bureau Director
   **Nathan Oakley** . . . . . . . . . . . . . . . . . . . . . . . . . . . (601) 359-2586
Instructional Enhancement Director (Acting)
   **Trecina Green** . . . . . . . . . . . . . . . . . . . . . . . . . . . . (601) 359-3778
      Fax: (601) 359-1818
Student Assessment Office Bureau Director
   **James Mason** . . . . . . . . . . . . . . . . . . . . . . . . . . . . . (601) 359-3052

## Office of Vocational and Workforce Development

Tel: (601) 359-3090  Fax: (601) 359-3989

Associate State Superintendent **Jean Massey** . . . . . . . . . . (601) 359-3090
Compliance and Reporting Office Bureau Director
   **Mike Mulvihill** . . . . . . . . . . . . . . . . . . . . . . . . . . . (601) 359-3086
   Education: Mississippi MEd   Fax: (601) 359-6619
Instructional Development Bureau Director **Bill McGrew** . . (601) 359-3461
      Fax: (601) 359-3481
Student Organization Director **Sandra Parker** . . . . . . . . . . (601) 576-5007

## Office of Policy and Operations

P.O. Box 771, Jackson, MS 39205
Fax: (601) 359-2566

Deputy State Superintendent **Kim S. Benton** . . . . . . . . . . . (601) 359-3077
   E-mail: benton@mde.k12.ms.us
Business Services Associate Superintendent
   **Sonya M. Amis** . . . . . . . . . . . . . . . . . . . . . . . . . . . (601) 359-9714
   Education: Mississippi Col BA, BS
Accounting Bureau Director **James Hart** . . . . . . . . . . . . . (601) 359-3525
Face and Orderly Schools Director **Shane McNeill** . . . . . . (601) 359-1737
      Fax: (601) 576-1417
Healthy Schools Director **Scott Clements** . . . . . . . . . . . . . (601) 354-7017
   E-mail: sclements@mde.k12.ms.us
Procurement Bureau Director **Donna Hales** . . . . . . . . . . . (601) 359-2566

## Office of Quality Professionals and Special Schools

Tel: (601) 359-3631  Fax: (601) 359-1728

Deputy Superintendent **Daphne L. Buckley** . . . . . . . . . . . . (601) 359-3631
   Education: Mississippi 2002 PhD
▲School of the Arts Superintendent **Susan Hirsch** . . . . . . . (601) 823-1300
   110 South Jackson Street, Brookhaven, MS 39601   Fax: (601) 823-9257
   E-mail: shirsch@mde.k12.ms.us
▲School for the Blind Superintendent
   **Dr. Sandra G. Edwards** . . . . . . . . . . . . . . . . . . . . . . (601) 984-8061
   E-mail: sgedwards@mde.k12.ms.us   Fax: (601) 984-5563
▲School for the Deaf Superintendent
   **Dr. Sandra G. Edwards** . . . . . . . . . . . . . . . . . . . . . . (601) 984-8061
   1253 Eastover Drive, Jackson, MS 39211   TTY: (601) 984-3934
   E-mail: sgedwards@mde.k12.ms.us   Tel: (601) 984-8000
      Fax: (601) 984-5563
▲School for Mathematics and Science Superintendent
   **Charles Brown** . . . . . . . . . . . . . . . . . . . . . . . . . . . . (662) 329-7671
   E-mail: cbrown@msms.k12.ms.us   Fax: (662) 329-7467

---

★ Elected Official   ■ Appointed by Governor   ● Appointed by Legislature   ▲ Appointed by Board or Commission   ◆ Appointed by State Supreme Court

Mississippi Teacher Center Director **Cecily McNair**. . . . . . .(601) 359-3631
Educator Licensure Office Bureau Director **Cerissa Neal** . . (601) 359-3483
Fax: (601) 359-2778
Human Resources Office Bureau Manager
**Cassandra Moore**. . . . . . . . . . . . . . . . . . . . . . . . . . .(601) 576-2185
Fax: (601) 359-1748

## Office of School Improvement, Oversight and Recovery

Tel: (601) 359-1879  Fax: (601) 576-2180

Deputy Superintendent (Interim) **Larry Drawdy**. . . . . . . . .(601) 359-1879
E-mail: ldrawdy@mde.k12.ms.us
Accreditation Office Associate Superintendent
**Dr. Paula Vanderford** . . . . . . . . . . . . . . . . . . . . . . . . .(601) 359-3764
Fax: (601) 359-1979
Dropout Prevention Office Bureau Manager **Toni Kersh** . . . (601) 359-5743
E-mail: tkersh@mde.k12.ms.us
Fax: (601) 576-3504
Federal Programs Office Bureau Director
**Debbie B. Murphy**. . . . . . . . . . . . . . . . . . . . . . . . . . . .(601) 359-3499
E-mail: dmurphy@mde.k12.ms.us
Fax: (601) 359-2587
Safe and Orderly Schools Bureau Director
**Shane McNeill**. . . . . . . . . . . . . . . . . . . . . . . . . . . . . .(601) 359-1028
Information and Legislative Services Senior Assistant
**(Vacant)**. . . . . . . . . . . . . . . . . . . . . . . . . . . . . . . . . . .(601) 359-3515

## Information Technology Services Board

■Chairman **June Songy**. . . . . . . . . . . . . . . . . . . . . . . . . .(601) 432-8000
■Vice Chairman **D. Shane Loper** . . . . . . . . . . . . . . . . . . .(601) 432-8000
Education: Southern Mississippi; Troy State MBA
■Member **Rodney Pearson**. . . . . . . . . . . . . . . . . . . . . . . .(601) 432-8000
■Member **J. Keith Van Camp** . . . . . . . . . . . . . . . . . . . . . .(601) 432-8000
■Member **Thomas A. Wicker** . . . . . . . . . . . . . . . . . . . . . .(601) 432-8000

## Mississippi Department of Information Technology Services [ITS]

3771 Eastwood Drive, Jackson, MS 39211
Tel: (601) 432-8000  Fax: (601) 713-6380  Internet: www.its.ms.gov

**Employees: 151  Fiscal Year: 2015  Budget: $42,000,000**

▲Executive Director and Chief Information Officer
**Craig P. Orgeron**. . . . . . . . . . . . . . . . . . . . . . . . . . . . .(601) 432-8000
E-mail: craig.orgeron@its.ms.gov
Data Services Director **Laura Pentecost** . . . . . . . . . . . . . . (601) 432-8191
E-mail: laura.pentecost@its.ms.gov
Information Systems Services Director **Lynn Ainsworth** . . (601) 432-8150
E-mail: lynn.ainsworth@its.ms.gov
Security Services Director **Jay White**. . . . . . . . . . . . . . . . .(601) 432-8180
E-mail: jay.white@its.ms.gov
Chief Administration Officer **Michele Blocker**. . . . . . . . . .(601) 432-8111
E-mail: michele.blocker@its.ms.gov
Education: Mississippi State 1991 BS
Internal Services Director **David Johnson** . . . . . . . . . . . . .(601) 432-8126
E-mail: david.johnson@its.ms.gov
Chief Operations Officer **Roger Graves** . . . . . . . . . . . . . .(601) 432-8092
E-mail: roger.graves@its.ms.gov
Education: Mississippi Col 1991 BS
Telecommunication Services Director **Steven Walker**. . . . .(601) 432-8004

## Veterans Affairs Board

3466 Highway 80 East, Pearl, MS 39288-5947
P.O. Box 5947, Pearl, MS 39288-5947
Tel: (601) 576-4850  Fax: (601) 576-4868  E-mail: eclark@vab.ms.gov

**Employees: 552  Fiscal Year: 2014  Budget: $36,458,000**

▲Executive Director **Randy Reeves**. . . . . . . . . . . . . . . . . . .(601) 576-4850
E-mail: rreeves@vab.ms.gov

## Mississippi National Guard

P.O. Box 5027, Jackson, MS 39296-5027
Tel: (601) 313-6225  Fax: (601) 313-6251

■Adjutant General
**MG Augustus L. "Leon" Collins, ARNG** . . . . . . . . . . . (601) 313-6232
E-mail: augustus.l.collins.mil@mail.mil
Education: Mississippi 1982 BBA; Jackson State U 1993 MBA;
Army War Col 2000 MSS
Executive Assistant to the Adjutant General
**Timothy Prater**. . . . . . . . . . . . . . . . . . . . . . . . . . . . . .(601) 313-6225
Assistant Adjutant General, Army
**BG Jessie Roy Robinson, ARNG** . . . . . . . . . . . . . . . . . (601) 354-7555
Education: Southern Mississippi 1985 BS; Jackson State U 1998 MS
Assistant Adjutant General, Air
**MajGen William Hill, ANG** . . . . . . . . . . . . . . . . . . . . . (601) 313-6115
Command Sergeant Major **CSM John T. Raines, ARNG** . . (601) 313-6354
Command Chief Master Sergeant
**CMSgt Robbie Knight, ANG** . . . . . . . . . . . . . . . . . . . . (601) 214-6064
Chief Warrant Officer **CW5 Bobby Tanksley** . . . . . . . . . . .(601) 313-6185
Chief of Staff **BG Allen E. Brewer, ARNG** . . . . . . . . . . . .(601) 313-6225
Operations and Plans Deputy Chief of Staff
**COL David O. Smith, ARNG**. . . . . . . . . . . . . . . . . . . . .(601) 313-6311
Fax: (601) 313-6306
Senior Executive Secretary **Christie Cliburn** . . . . . . . . . . (601) 313-6231
Information Management Director
**COL Kevin Bullard, ARNG** . . . . . . . . . . . . . . . . . . . . .(601) 313-6225

## Office of the Lieutenant Governor

P.O. Box 1018, Jackson, MS 39215
Tel: (601) 359-3200  Fax: (601) 359-4054

★Lieutenant Governor **Tate Reeves, CFA** (R) . . . . . . . . . . . .(601) 359-3200
Term Expires: January 2020
E-mail: ltgov@senate.ms.gov
Education: Millsaps 1996 BA
Career: State Treasurer, State of Mississippi (2003-2012)
Executive Assistant and Scheduler **Barrie Nelson** . . . . . . . (601) 359-3200
E-mail: bnelson@senate.ms.gov
Communications Director **Laura Hipp**. . . . . . . . . . . . . . . .(601) 359-3200
E-mail: lhipp@senate.ms.gov
Legislative Affairs Director **Parks MacNabb** . . . . . . . . . . . (601) 359-3200
E-mail: pmacnabb@senate.ms.gov
Legislative Liaison **Kenny Ellis** . . . . . . . . . . . . . . . . . . . .(601) 359-3200
E-mail: kellis@senate.ms.gov
Policy Director **Lee Weiskopf** . . . . . . . . . . . . . . . . . . . . . .(601) 359-3200
Policy Advisor **Erika Berry**. . . . . . . . . . . . . . . . . . . . . . . .(601) 359-3200

## Office of the Secretary of State

P.O. Box 136, Jackson, MS 39205-0136
Tel: (601) 359-1350  Fax: (601) 359-1499
E-mail: administrator@sos.state.ms.us

**Employees: 111  Fiscal Year: 2015  Budget: $17,092,000**

★Secretary of State **C. Delbert Hosemann, Jr.** (R) . . . . . . . .(601) 359-6342
Term Expires: January 2020
E-mail: delbert.hosemann@sos.ms.gov
Education: Notre Dame 1969 BBA; Mississippi 1972 JD;
NYU 1973 ML
Career: United States Army Reserve, United States Department of the
Army, United States Department of Defense; Partner, Phelps Dunbar
LLP
Executive Assistant **Mona Enstrom** . . . . . . . . . . . . . . . . . (601) 359-6342
Chief of Staff **Douglas E. "Doug" Davis** . . . . . . . . . . . . . (601) 359-6339
Education: Mississippi Col (Attended)
Business Regulation and Enforcement Assistant Secretary
of State **Dave C. Scott** . . . . . . . . . . . . . . . . . . . . . . . . (601) 359-6747
Business Services Assistant Secretary of State **Tom Riley** . . (601) 359-1626
Charities Assistant Secretary of State **Tanya Webber** . . . . . (601) 359-1048
Education and Publications Assistant Secretary of State
**Lea Anne Brandon** . . . . . . . . . . . . . . . . . . . . . . . . . . (601) 359-6346
Elections Assistant Secretary of State **Kim Turner** . . . . . . . (601) 359-6340
Finance Assistant Secretary of State **Andria Matrick** . . . . . (601) 359-6596
Policy and Research Assistant Secretary of State
**1LT Preston Goff, ARNG** . . . . . . . . . . . . . . . . . . . . . . (601) 359-1621
Education: Southern Mississippi 2006 BA; Mississippi Col JD

*(continued on next page)*

★ Elected Official    ■ Appointed by Governor    ● Appointed by Legislature    ▲ Appointed by Board or Commission    ◆ Appointed by State Supreme Court

*State Yellow Book*    © Leadership Directories, Inc.    Summer 2016

**EXECUTIVE BRANCH**

**Office of the Secretary of State** *continued*

Public Lands Assistant Secretary of State
**Gerald McWhorter** . . . . . . . . . . . . . . . . . . (601) 359-6374
  E-mail: gerald.mcwhorter@sos.ms.gov
  Education: Mississippi State BA; Mississippi JD
Securities Assistant Secretary of State **Cheryn Netz** . . . . . (601) 359-1334
Chief Information Officer **Charlie Case** . . . . . . . . . . . . . (601) 359-1357
  E-mail: charlie.case@sos.ms.gov
Communications Director **(Vacant)** . . . . . . . . . . . . . . . . . . (601) 359-1350
Human Resources Director **Carla Thornhill** . . . . . . . . . . . (601) 359-5509
  Education: Mississippi Col BA, MSS
Legislative Director **Nathan Upchurch** . . . . . . . . . . . . . . . (601) 359-2975
  E-mail: nathan.upchurch@sos.ms.gov
External Marketing Assistant Secretary of State
**Sherri Bevis** . . . . . . . . . . . . . . . . . . . . . . . . . . (601) 359-1350

## Office of the Attorney General

P.O. Box 220, Jackson, MS 39205
Tel: (601) 359-3680  Fax: (601) 359-3441
E-mail: msago5@ago.state.ms.us  Internet: www.ago.state.ms.us

**Employees:** 289  **Fiscal Year:** 2014  **Budget:** $32,665,000

★Attorney General **James Matthew "Jim" Hood** (D) . . . . . (601) 359-3680
  Term Expires: January 2020
  E-mail: jhood@ago.state.ms.us
  Education: Mississippi 1988 JD
  Career: Assistant Attorney General, Office of the Attorney General,
  State of Mississippi; District Attorney, Third Judicial District,
  Mississippi Circuit Courts; Vice President, National Association of
  Attorneys General (2012-2013)
Executive Assistant **Delisa Jones** . . . . . . . . . . . . . . . . . . (601) 359-3692
Deputy Attorney General **Onetta Whitley** . . . . . . . . . . . . (601) 359-4208
Local Government and Opinions Deputy Attorney
General **Mike Lanford** . . . . . . . . . . . . . . . . . . . . . . (601) 359-9671
Civil Litigation Director **Harold Pizzetta** . . . . . . . . . . . . . (601) 359-3820
Medicaid Fraud Control Unit Director **Treasure Tyson** . . . . (601) 359-4711
Public Integrity Director **(Vacant)** . . . . . . . . . . . . . . . . . . (601) 359-4253
Chief Financial Officer **Robert Kersh** . . . . . . . . . . . . . . . . (601) 359-3956
  E-mail: rkersh@ago.state.ms.us
Chief of Staff **Geoffrey Morgan** . . . . . . . . . . . . . . . . . . (601) 359-3821
Public Information Officer **Melanie Web** . . . . . . . . . . . . . (601) 359-3680
  E-mail: mweb@ago.state.ms.us

## Office of the State Treasurer

P.O. Box 138, Jackson, MS 39205
Tel: (601) 359-3600  Fax: (601) 359-2001

★State Treasurer **Lynn Fitch** (R) . . . . . . . . . . . . . . . . . (601) 898-2410
  Term Expires: January 2020
  E-mail: lynn.fitch@treasury.ms.gov
  Education: Mississippi BS, 1985 JD
  Career: External Affairs and Support Services Deputy Executive
  Director, Department of Employment Security, State of Mississippi
  (2008-2009); Executive Director, Mississippi State Personnel Board,
  State of Mississippi (2009-2012)
External Affairs Deputy Treasurer **Laura Jackson** . . . . . . . (601) 359-3765
  Education: Mississippi Col BSBA, MBA
Internal Affairs Deputy Treasurer **Jesse Graham** . . . . . . . (601) 359-3843
Bond and Collateral Assistant State Treasurer
**Ricky Manning** . . . . . . . . . . . . . . . . . . . . . . . . (601) 359-3533
Investment and Cash Management Assistant State
Treasurer **Misti Munroe Preziosi** . . . . . . . . . . . . . . (601) 359-3536
College Savings Mississippi Director **Emelia Nordan** . . . . . (601) 359-5256
Information Technology Director **Russell Armstrong** . . . . . (601) 359-2169
  E-mail: rarmstrong@treasury.state.ms.us
Unclaimed Property Director **Tony Geiger** . . . . . . . . . . . . (601) 359-9258

## Office of the State Auditor

P.O. Box 956, Jackson, MS 39205-0956
Tel: (601) 576-2800  Fax: (601) 576-2650  E-mail: auditor@osa.ms.gov
Internet: www.osa.state.ms.us

★State Auditor **Stacey E. Pickering** (R) . . . . . . . . . . . . . (601) 576-2643
  Term Expires: January 2020
  E-mail: auditor@osa.ms.gov
  Career: State Senator (R-MO, District 42), Mississippi State Senate
  (2003-2007)
Deputy State Auditor, Financial and Compliance
**Patrick "Pat" Dendy, CPA** . . . . . . . . . . . . . . . . . . (601) 576-2645
Deputy State Auditor, Investigations **David R. Huggins** . . . (601) 576-2724
Chief of Staff **Bill Pope** . . . . . . . . . . . . . . . . . . . . . . (601) 576-2647
Budget Director **(Vacant)** . . . . . . . . . . . . . . . . . . . . . . (601) 576-2648
Communications Director **(Vacant)** . . . . . . . . . . . . . . . . . (601) 576-2623
County Audit Director **Joe McKnight** . . . . . . . . . . . . . . . (601) 576-2800
EDP Audit Director **David Ashly** . . . . . . . . . . . . . . . . . . (601) 576-2636
Education Audit Division Director **Tommy Vickers** . . . . . . (601) 576-2666
Financial and Compliance Audit Division Director
**Bill Doss, CPA** . . . . . . . . . . . . . . . . . . . . . . . . . (601) 576-2672
Fiscal Management Director **(Vacant)** . . . . . . . . . . . . . . . (601) 576-2648
Personnel Director **MarQuaita Lampkin** . . . . . . . . . . . . . (601) 576-2642
Information Technology Division Director **Jim Moore** . . . . (601) 576-2694
  E-mail: jim.moore@osa.ms.gov
Local Government Affairs Director **Brent Henderson** . . . . (601) 576-2639
Performance Audit Division Director **Sam Atkinson** . . . . . (601) 576-2655
Property Audit Division Director **Scott Rhodes** . . . . . . . . (601) 576-2712
Purchasing Director **Kathy Perkins** . . . . . . . . . . . . . . . . (601) 576-2649
State Agency Audit Director **Stephanie Palmertree** . . . . . (601) 576-2606
Technical Assistance Division Director **Tom Chain** . . . . . . (601) 576-2658
Payroll Administrator **MarQuaita Lampkin** . . . . . . . . . . . (601) 576-2642

## Mississippi Department of Agriculture and Commerce [MDAC]

P.O. Box 1609, Jackson, MS 39215-1609
Tel: (601) 359-1100  Fax: (601) 354-6290  Internet: www.mdac.state.ms.us

**Employees:** 187  **Fiscal Year:** 2014  **Budget:** $15,734,000

★Commissioner **Cindy Hyde-Smith** (R) . . . . . . . . . . . . . (601) 359-1100
  Term Expires: 2020
  E-mail: cindyhs@mdac.ms.gov
Deputy Commissioner **John Campbell** . . . . . . . . . . . . . . . (601) 359-1158
State Veterinarian **James Watson** . . . . . . . . . . . . . . . . . (601) 359-1170
  Education: Mississippi State 1982 DVM
Farmers Central Market Director **Frank Malta** . . . . . . . . . (601) 354-6573
Administration Bureau Director **Sara Davidson** . . . . . . . . (601) 359-1128
  E-mail: sara@mdac.ms.gov
Agricultural Theft Bureau Director **Barry Coward** . . . . . . (601) 359-1122
Marketing and International Trade Bureau Director
**Paige Manning** . . . . . . . . . . . . . . . . . . . . . . . . (601) 359-1158
Plant Industry Bureau Director **(Vacant)** . . . . . . . . . . . . (662) 325-3390
  P.O. Box 5207, Mississippi State, MS 39762
Regulatory Services Bureau Director **Julie McLemore** . . . . (601) 359-1111
  E-mail: julie@mdac.ms.gov
  Education: Mississippi 1991 BA, 1994 JD
Consumer Protection Division Director **Adam Choate** . . . . (601) 359-1148
Fruits and Vegetables/Organic Certification Division
Director **Kevin Riggin** . . . . . . . . . . . . . . . . . . . . (601) 359-1138
  E-mail: kevin@mdac.ms.gov
Information Technology Division Director
**Umesh Sanjanwala** . . . . . . . . . . . . . . . . . . . . . . (601) 359-1151
  E-mail: umesh@mdac.ms.gov
  Education: Mississippi Col 1983 BS; Mississippi State 1998 MS
Meat Inspection Division Director
**Dr. Richard A. Benton** . . . . . . . . . . . . . . . . . . . . (601) 359-1191
  E-mail: richardb@mdac.ms.gov
  Education: Mississippi State 1975 BS; Auburn 1979 DVM
Personnel Division Director **Samantha Hawkins** . . . . . . . . (601) 359-1152
Petroleum Products Inspection Division Director
**Jennifer B. Thompson** . . . . . . . . . . . . . . . . . . . . (601) 359-1101
  E-mail: jennifer@mdac.ms.gov
Seed Division Director **Fabian Watts** . . . . . . . . . . . . . . . (662) 325-3992
  P.O. Box 5207, Mississippi State, MS 39762
  Education: Mississippi State MS

---

★ Elected Official   ■ Appointed by Governor   ● Appointed by Legislature   ▲ Appointed by Board or Commission   ◆ Appointed by State Supreme Court

Weights and Measures Division Director **Brent Bowman** . . (601) 359-1149

# Mississippi Insurance Department [MID]

P.O. Box 79, Jackson, MS 39205-0079
Tel: (601) 359-3569  Fax: (601) 359-2474  Internet: www.mid.state.ms.us

**Employees: 135  Fiscal Year: 2014  Budget: $25,443,000**

★Insurance Commissioner and State Fire Marshal
  **Michael Jackson "Mike" Chaney** (R) . . . . . . . . . . . . . . (601) 359-3581
  Term Expires: January 2020
  E-mail: mike.chaney@mid.state.ms.us
  Education: Mississippi State 1996 BS
  Administrative Assistant **Mary Ellen Dillard** . . . . . . . . . . (601) 359-3581
Deputy Commissioner **Mark Haire** . . . . . . . . . . . . . . . . . (601) 359-3573
Administrative Services Director **Nancy Stuart** . . . . . . . . . (601) 359-3569
  E-mail: nancy.stuart@mid.ms.gov
Accounting Division Director **Tracey Gwin** . . . . . . . . . . . . (601) 359-2482
Consumer Services Division Director **Andy Case** . . . . . . . (601) 359-2453
Financial and Market Regulation Division Director
  **David Browning** . . . . . . . . . . . . . . . . . . . . . . . . . . . . . (601) 359-2127
  E-mail: david.browning@mid.state.ms.us
Management Information Systems Division Manager
  **Kevin Bauder** . . . . . . . . . . . . . . . . . . . . . . . . . . . . . . . (601) 359-9219
  E-mail: kevin.bauder@mid.ms.gov
Licensing Division Director **Wanda Magers** . . . . . . . . . . . (601) 359-1087
Life and Health Actuarial Director **Bob Williams** . . . . . . . (601) 359-2012
Liquefied Compressed Gas Division Director
  **Robert Pickering** . . . . . . . . . . . . . . . . . . . . . . . . . . . . . (601) 359-3569
Property and Casualty Rating Division Director
  **John Wells** . . . . . . . . . . . . . . . . . . . . . . . . . . . . . . . . . (601) 359-2676
  Education: Mississippi Col 1976 BS
Statutory Compliance **Nancy Cross** . . . . . . . . . . . . . . . . . (601) 359-3571
General Counsel **Kim Causey** . . . . . . . . . . . . . . . . . . . . . (601) 359-3569

# Mississippi Public Service Commission [MPSC]

P.O. Box 1174, Jackson, MS 39215-1174
Tel: (601) 961-5434  Fax: (601) 961-5469  Internet: www.psc.state.ms.us

**Fiscal Year: 2014  Budget: $5,428,000**

★Commissioner **Sam Britton** (D) . . . . . . . . . . . . . . . . . . . (601) 961-5434
  Term Expires: 2020
★Commissioner **Cecil C. Brown** (D) . . . . . . . . . . . . . . . . . (601) 961-5434
  Term Expires: 2020
★Commissioner **Brandon Presley** (D) . . . . . . . . . . . . . . . . (601) 961-5450
  Term Expires: 2020

# Mississippi Transportation Commission

401 North West Street, Jackson, MS 39201
Tel: (601) 359-7000  Fax: (601) 359-9860

★Commissioner **Dick Hall** (R-Central District) . . . . . . . . . . (601) 359-7035
  Term Expires: 2020      Fax: (601) 359-7051
  E-mail: dhall@mdot.ms.gov
  Education: Mississippi State 1960 BBA
★Commissioner **Tom King** (R-Southern District) . . . . . . . . . (601) 583-0859
  Term Expires: 2020      Fax: (601) 544-0227
  E-mail: tking@mdot.ms.gov
★Commissioner **Mike Tagert** (R-Northern District) . . . . . . . (662) 680-3323
  Term Expires: 2020
  E-mail: mtagert@mdot.ms.gov
  Education: Millsaps 1996 BS; Mississippi State 1998 MS

# Mississippi Department of Transportation [MDOT]

P.O. Box 1850, Jackson, MS 39215-1850
Tel: (601) 359-7074  Fax: (601) 359-7834  Internet: www.gomdot.com

**Employees: 3,300  Fiscal Year: 2014  Budget: $1,163,476,000**

▲Executive Director **Melinda McGrath** . . . . . . . . . . . . . . . . (601) 359-7002
  E-mail: mmcgrath@mdot.ms.gov

Deputy Executive Director/Administration **Lisa Hancock** . . (601) 359-9796
  E-mail: lhancock@mdot.ms.gov
Public Affairs Director **Jarrod Ravencraft** . . . . . . . . . . . . . (601) 359-7074
Civil Rights Office Director **Carolyn F. Bell** . . . . . . . . . . . (601) 359-7466
Audit Division Director **Diane P. Gavin** . . . . . . . . . . . . . . (601) 359-7499
Human Resources Division Director **John R. Head** . . . . . . (601) 359-7350
Legal Division Director **Roy M. Tipton** . . . . . . . . . . . . . . (601) 359-7600
State Aid Division Director **Carey Webb, PE** . . . . . . . . . . . (601) 359-7150
  E-mail: mail@osarc.state.ms.us    Fax: (601) 359-7141
  Education: Mississippi State BSCE
Chief Information Officer **Ben Cohen** . . . . . . . . . . . . . . . . (601) 359-7422
  E-mail: bcohen@mdot.ms.gov

## Office of Administrative Services
Central Services Division Director **Charlene Dear** . . . . . . . . (601) 359-9776
  E-mail: cdear@mdot.ms.gov
Asset Management Director **Julie Etheridge** . . . . . . . . . . . (601) 359-7892
Budget Division Director **Byron Flood** . . . . . . . . . . . . . . . (601) 359-7009
Financial Management Division Director **Alison Brown** . . . (601) 359-7361
Local Public Agency Division Director **Jeff Altman** . . . . . . (601) 359-7675
Procurement Division Director **Retha Gregory** . . . . . . . . . (601) 359-7445

## Office of Enforcement
Director **Willie Huff** . . . . . . . . . . . . . . . . . . . . . . . . . . . . (601) 359-1710
  E-mail: whuff@mdot.ms.gov
Permits Director **Tommy Thames** . . . . . . . . . . . . . . . . . . . (601) 359-1538

## Office of Highways
Deputy Executive Director/Chief Engineer
  **Mark McConnell** . . . . . . . . . . . . . . . . . . . . . . . . . . . . . (601) 359-7004
  E-mail: mmcconnell@mdot.ms.gov
Assistant Chief Engineer - Field Operations
  **Robert Wes Dean** . . . . . . . . . . . . . . . . . . . . . . . . . . . . (601) 359-7007
  E-mail: wdean@mdot.ms.gov
  Maintenance Division Director **Heath Patterson** . . . . . . . (601) 359-7113
    E-mail: hpatterson@mdot.ms.gov
  Traffic Engineering Division Director **James Sullivan** . . . (601) 359-1454
    E-mail: jssulivan@mdot.ms.gov
Assistant Chief Engineer - Operations **Randy Battey** . . . . . (601) 359-7007
  E-mail: rbattey@mdot.ms.gov
  State Construction Engineer **Richard Chisolm** . . . . . . . . (601) 359-7301
    E-mail: rchisolm@mdot.ms.gov
  Contract Administration Division Director **B. B. House** . . (601) 359-7730
    E-mail: BBHouse@mdot.ms.gov
  Materials Division Director **James Williams** . . . . . . . . . . (601) 359-1798
    E-mail: jwilliams@mdot.ms.gov
  Research Division Director **James Watkins** . . . . . . . . . . . (601) 359-7650
    E-mail: jwatkins@mdot.ms.gov
Assistant Chief Engineer - Preconstruction
  **Justin Walker** . . . . . . . . . . . . . . . . . . . . . . . . . . . . . . . (601) 359-7171
  E-mail: amood@mdot.ms.gov
  Bridge Design Division Director **(Vacant)** . . . . . . . . . . . (601) 359-7563
  Environmental/Location Division Director
    **Kim Thurman** . . . . . . . . . . . . . . . . . . . . . . . . . . . . . (601) 359-7921
    E-mail: kthurman@mdot.ms.gov
  Right-of-Way Division Administrator **Daniel B. Smith** . . (601) 359-7457
  Roadway Design Division Director **John Reese** . . . . . . . . (601) 359-7257
Consultant Services Director **Scot Ehrgott** . . . . . . . . . . . . (601) 359-7874
  E-mail: sehrgott@mdot.state.ms.us
Planning Division Engineer **Jeff Ely** . . . . . . . . . . . . . . . . (601) 359-7663
  E-mail: jely@mdot.ms.gov

## Office of Intermodal Planning
Director **Charles R. Carr** . . . . . . . . . . . . . . . . . . . . . . . . . (601) 359-7976
Aeronautics Division Director
  **Thomas M. "Tommy" Booth, Jr.** . . . . . . . . . . . . . . . . . (601) 359-7850
Freight, Rails, Ports, and Waterways Division Director
  **Robert "Robby" Burt** . . . . . . . . . . . . . . . . . . . . . . . . . (601) 359-7910
  E-mail: rburt@mdot.ms.gov
Public Transit Division Manager **Selena Standifer** . . . . . . . (601) 359-7781

★ Elected Official    ■ Appointed by Governor    ● Appointed by Legislature    ▲ Appointed by Board or Commission    ◆ Appointed by State Supreme Court

*State Yellow Book*    © Leadership Directories, Inc.    Summer 2016

EXECUTIVE BRANCH

# Missouri

Tel: (573) 751-2000 (State Operator)  Internet: www.mo.gov

**Number of U.S. Congressional Delegates:** 2 Senators; 8 Representatives  **Governor's Term:** 4 years
**Legislature Description:** General Assembly - 34 member Senate; 163 member House of Representatives;
Term - Senate 4 years, House 2 years  **Next Election:** Governor November 2016; Legislature November
2016  **Number of Electoral Votes:** 10  **Official Name:** State of Missouri (Algonquian: Canoe haven)
**Nickname:** The Show-Me State  **Motto:** Salus populi suprema lex esto (The welfare of the people shall be
the supreme law)

**Population:** 6,083,672 (2015); Rank 18  **Fiscal Year:** 2015  **Budget:** $24,105,198,000

## Office of the Governor

201 West Capitol Avenue, Jefferson City, MO 65101
P.O. Box 720, Jefferson City, MO 65102
Tel: (573) 751-3222  Fax: (573) 526-3291
E-mail: constituent.services@mo.gov

**Employees:** 30  **Fiscal Year:** 2015  **Budget:** $5,719,000

**Jeremiah W. "Jay" Nixon**
Governor

Began Service: January 12, 2009
Term Expires: January 2017
Date of Birth: February 13, 1956
Education: Missouri 1978 BA, 1981 JD
Religion: Methodist
Career: State Senator (D-MO, District 22),
Missouri Senate (1986-1992); Attorney General
(D-MO), State of Missouri (1993-2009)

★ Governor **Jeremiah W. "Jay" Nixon** (D) . . . . . . . . . . . . . (573) 751-3222
Chief of Staff **(Vacant)** . . . . . . . . . . . . . . . . . . . . . . . (573) 751-3222
   Assistant to the Chief of Staff **Kim Hoelscher** . . . . . . . . . (573) 751-3222
    E-mail: kim.hoelscher@mo.gov
Deputy Chief of Staff **Peter Lyskowski** . . . . . . . . . . . . . . . (573) 751-3222
   Education: Truman State; Missouri JD
Counsel to the Governor **Edward R. "Ted" Ardini, Jr.** . . . . . (573) 751-3222
   Education: Merrimack 1989 BA; New England 1992 JD
Deputy Counsel **Nick Heberle** . . . . . . . . . . . . . . . . . . . . (573) 751-3222
Boards and Commissions Director **A.J. Fox** . . . . . . . . . . . . (573) 751-3222
Communications Director **Channing Ansley** . . . . . . . . . . . (573) 751-3222
   Education: Columbia BA
   Press Secretary **Scott Holste** . . . . . . . . . . . . . . . . . (573) 751-3222
    E-mail: scott.holste@mo.gov
Constituent Service Director **(Vacant)** . . . . . . . . . . . . . . . (573) 751-3222
Legislative Director **Jason Zamkus** . . . . . . . . . . . . . . . . (573) 751-3222
   Education: Missouri BA, JD
Policy Director **Robert "Jeff" Harris** . . . . . . . . . . . . . . . (573) 751-5261
   E-mail: jeff.harris@mo.gov
   Education: Vanderbilt 1987 BA; Cornell 1991 JD
Senior Policy Advisor **Michael T. Nietzel** . . . . . . . . . . . . (573) 751-3222
   E-mail: mike.nietzel@mo.gov
   Education: Wheaton (IL) 1969 BA; Illinois 1972 MA, 1973 PhD
Senior Adviser **Andrea Spillars** . . . . . . . . . . . . . . . . . . (573) 751-3222
   E-mail: andrea.spillars@mo.gov
   Education: Central Missouri State; Missouri (Kansas City)
Media Coordinator **Seth Bundy** . . . . . . . . . . . . . . . . . . (573) 751-3222

## Kansas City Office

615 East Thirteenth Street, Suite 517, Kansas City, MO 64106
Fax: (816) 889-2315
Director **Lindsey Heeter** . . . . . . . . . . . . . . . . . . . . . . (816) 889-2337

## Saint Louis Office

111 North Seventh Street, Suite 929, St. Louis, MO 63101
Fax: (314) 340-7292
Director **Brian May** . . . . . . . . . . . . . . . . . . . . . . . . . (314) 340-6900
   E-mail: brian.may@sos.mo.gov

## Office of Administration

201 West Capitol Avenue, Room 125, Jefferson City, MO 65101
P.O. Box 809 A, Jefferson City, MO 65102
Tel: (573) 751-1851  TTY: (800) 735-2966  Fax: (573) 751-1212

**Employees:** 2,178  **Fiscal Year:** 2015  **Budget:** $276,282,000

■ Commissioner **Doug Nelson** . . . . . . . . . . . . . . . . . . . (573) 751-1851
   E-mail: doug.nelson@oa.mo.gov
Deputy Commissioner **Reneé Slusher** . . . . . . . . . . . . . . (573) 751-1851
   E-mail: renee.slusher@oa.mo.gov
General Counsel **Kristen Paulsmeyer** . . . . . . . . . . . . . . (573) 751-1851
Facilities Management, Design and Construction Division
   Director **Catherine F. "Cathy" Brown** . . . . . . . . . . . . (573) 751-1034
General Services Division Director **Mark S. Kaiser** . . . . . . . (573) 751-4656
   E-mail: mark.s.kaiser@oa.mo.gov
Information Technology Services Division Chief
   Information Officer (Interim) **Rich Kliethermes** . . . . . . . (573) 751-1851
Personnel Division Director **Nancy Johnston** . . . . . . . . . . (573) 751-3053
Purchasing, Materials Management Division Director
   **Karen Boeger** . . . . . . . . . . . . . . . . . . . . . . . . . . (573) 751-8900
                                                           Fax: (573) 526-5985
Child Advocate **Kelly Schultz** . . . . . . . . . . . . . . . . . . . (573) 526-8686
   E-mail: kelly.schultz@oa.mo.gov

## Health and Educational Facilities Authority

15450 South Outer Forty, Suite 230, Chesterfield, MO 63017
Fax: (636) 519-0792  Internet: www.mohefa.org

Executive Director **Michael J. Stanard** . . . . . . . . . . . . . . (636) 519-0700

## Missouri Department of Agriculture [MDA]

P.O. Box 630, Jefferson City, MO 65102
Tel: (573) 751-4211  Fax: (573) 751-1784  E-mail: aginfo@mda.mo.gov

■ Director **Richard Fordyce** . . . . . . . . . . . . . . . . . . . . . (573) 751-4211
   E-mail: richard.fordyce@mda.mo.gov
Deputy Director and Senior Policy Advisor **Loyd Wilson** . . (573) 751-5513
   E-mail: loyd.wilson@mda.mo.gov
Deputy Director and Executive Assistant **Christa Moody** . . (573) 522-1533
Administration and Budget Director **Robin Perso** . . . . . . . (573) 526-4892
   E-mail: robin.perso@mda.mo.gov
Agriculture Business Development Division Director
   **Ken Struemph** . . . . . . . . . . . . . . . . . . . . . . . . . . (573) 751-4762
                                                       Tel: (866) 466-8283
Animal Health Division Director and State Veterinarian
   **Linda Hickam** . . . . . . . . . . . . . . . . . . . . . . . . . . (573) 751-3377
   Education: Missouri DVM
Grain Inspection and Warehousing Division Director
   **Chris Klenklen** . . . . . . . . . . . . . . . . . . . . . . . . . (573) 751-5515
   E-mail: chris.klenklen@mda.mo.gov
Plant Industries Division Director **Judy Grundler** . . . . . . . (573) 751-2462
Weights and Measures Division Director
   **Ronald G. "Ron" Hayes** . . . . . . . . . . . . . . . . . . . . (573) 751-4316
Human Resources Director **Jennifer Hentges** . . . . . . . . . . (573) 751-1199
Legislative Affairs Director **Tony Benz** . . . . . . . . . . . . . (573) 526-2076
   E-mail: tony.benz@mda.mo.gov
General Counsel **Michael Warrick** . . . . . . . . . . . . . . . . . (573) 751-5617
   E-mail: michael.warrick@mda.mo.gov

---

★ Elected Official   ■ Appointed by Governor   ● Appointed by Legislature   ▲ Appointed by Board or Commission   ◆ Appointed by State Supreme Court

Strategic Initiative Advisor **Misti Preston** . . . . . . . . . . . . . (573) 522-9854

# Department of Corrections [DOC]
2729 Plaza Drive, Jefferson City, MO 65109
P.O. Box 236, Jefferson City, MO 65102
Tel: (573) 751-2389  TTY: (800) 735-2966  Fax: (573) 751-4099
Internet: www.doc.mo.gov

**Employees: 11,022  Fiscal Year: 2015  Budget: $682,207,000**
■Director **George Lombardi** . . . . . . . . . . . . . . . . . . . . . . . . (573) 526-6607
  Education: Central Missouri State BS, MS
Deputy Director **David Rost** . . . . . . . . . . . . . . . . . . . . . . (573) 526-6544
  Education: Central Missouri State BS; Missouri MPA
Adult Institutions Division Director **Dave Dormire** . . . . . . . (573) 526-6524
Offender Rehabilitation Services Division Director
  **Matt Sturm** . . . . . . . . . . . . . . . . . . . . . . . . . . . . . . . . . . (573) 526-6493
                                   Fax: (573) 526-8156
Human Services Division Director **Cari D. Collins** . . . . . . . . (573) 526-6472
  Education: Missouri 1999 BA; William & Mary 2002 JD
General Counsel **Rick Williams** . . . . . . . . . . . . . . . . . . . . . (573) 522-1634
Communications Director **David Owen** . . . . . . . . . . . . . . . (573) 522-1118
  E-mail: david.owen@doc.mo.gov

## Division of Probation and Parole
Chief State Supervisor **Julie Kempker** . . . . . . . . . . . . . . . . (573) 751-8488
Assistant Division Director **Peg McClure** . . . . . . . . . . . . . . (573) 751-8488
Board Operations Manager **Kelly Dills** . . . . . . . . . . . . . . . . (573) 751-8488

# Department of Economic Development [DED]
301 West High Street, Jefferson City, MO 65101
P.O. Box 1157, Jefferson City, MO 65102-1157
Tel: (573) 751-4962  Fax: (573) 526-7700  E-mail: ecodev@ded.mo.gov
Internet: http://ded.mo.gov

**Employees: 908  Fiscal Year: 2015  Budget: $220,793,000**
■Director **Michael Downing, CEcD** . . . . . . . . . . . . . . . . . (573) 751-4770
  Education: Arkansas State 1977 BBA; Missouri 1981 MPA
■Deputy Director **(Vacant)** . . . . . . . . . . . . . . . . . . . . . . . . (573) 751-4770
Legal Counsel **Nathan Nickolaus** . . . . . . . . . . . . . . . . . . . (573) 526-8216
Communications Director **Amy Susan** . . . . . . . . . . . . . . . . (573) 522-5058
  E-mail: amy.susan@ded.mo.gov
Financial Systems Director **Stacey Hirst** . . . . . . . . . . . . . . (573) 526-7863
Legislative Affairs and Strategic Initiatives Director
  **Sarah Nussbaum** . . . . . . . . . . . . . . . . . . . . . . . . . . . . . . (573) 526-8216
Personnel Systems Director **Rachel Potts** . . . . . . . . . . . . . . (573) 522-6102
Research and Planning Director **(Vacant)** . . . . . . . . . . . . . . (573) 751-1873
Budget and Planning Manager **Lynne Kempker** . . . . . . . . . (573) 751-3621
Community Development and Planning Specialist
  **Bill L. Ransdall** . . . . . . . . . . . . . . . . . . . . . . . . . . . . . . . (573) 526-1608
                                   Fax: (573) 522-9462

# Office of Public Counsel (Utility Regulations)
Governor Office Building, Suite 650, Jefferson City, MO 65102
P.O. Box 2230, Jefferson City, MO 65102
Fax: (573) 751-5562
Public Counsel (Acting) **Dustin Allison** . . . . . . . . . . . . . . . (573) 751-4857
  Education: Saint Louis U 1999 BA; George Washington 2002

# Office of the Military Advocate
■Military Advocate **Joseph L. Driskill** . . . . . . . . . . . . . . . . (573) 751-4962
  Term Expires: March 3, 2022

# Business and Community Services Division
301 West High Street, Room 720, Jefferson City, MO 65101
Director **Sallie Hemenway** . . . . . . . . . . . . . . . . . . . . . . . . (573) 751-8497

# Tourism Division
301 West High Street, Jefferson City, MO 65101
P.O. Box 1055, Jefferson City, MO 65102
Tel: (573) 751-4133  Fax: (573) 751-5160  E-mail: tourism@ded.mo.gov
Internet: www.visitmo.com
▲Director **Dan Lennon** . . . . . . . . . . . . . . . . . . . . . . . . . . . . (573) 751-3051
  E-mail: directormotourism@ded.mo.gov
Deputy Director of Administration **Barb Glover** . . . . . . . . . (573) 751-1912
  E-mail: barb.glover@ded.mo.gov
Research Administrator **Dee Ann McKinney** . . . . . . . . . . . (573) 526-1553
Communications Administrator **Kate Renfrow** . . . . . . . . . . (573) 522-9596
  E-mail: kate.renfrow@ded.mo.gov
International/Tour & Travel Contract Coordinator
  **Donna Cordle-Gray** . . . . . . . . . . . . . . . . . . . . . . . . . . (816) 444-0991
    1912 East Meyer Boulevard, Kansas City, MO 64132
Cooperative Marketing Officer **Megan Rogers** . . . . . . . . . (573) 751-3246
Webmaster **Barbara Brueggeman** . . . . . . . . . . . . . . . . . . (573) 522-5501

# Workforce Development Division
421 East Dunklin Street, Jefferson City, MO 65101
P.O. Box 1087, Jefferson City, MO 65102-1087
Fax: (573) 751-8162
Director **Julie Gibson** . . . . . . . . . . . . . . . . . . . . . . . . . . . . (573) 751-3349
  E-mail: julie.gibson@ded.mo.gov
  Education: South Alabama BA; New School MA
Employer Relations/Incentives Assistant Director
  **Amy Sublett** . . . . . . . . . . . . . . . . . . . . . . . . . . . . . . . . . (573) 526-8271
  E-mail: amy.sublett@ded.mo.gov
Field Operations Assistant Director **Mark Bauer** . . . . . . . . (573) 526-8256
Program Operations Assistant Director **Roger Baugher** . . . (573) 751-7897
  E-mail: roger.baugher@ded.mo.gov

# Housing Development Commission
3435 Broadway St, Kansas City, MO 64111
Tel: (816) 759-6600  Fax: (816) 759-6828
E-mail: information@mhdc.com  Internet: www.mhdc.com
Executive Director **Kip A. Stetzler** . . . . . . . . . . . . . . . . . . (816) 759-6676
  E-mail: kstetzler@mhdc.com

# Missouri Public Service Commission [PSC]
Governor Office Building, 200 Madison Street,
Jefferson City, MO 65101-0360
P.O. Box 360, Jefferson City, MO 65102-0360
Tel: (573) 751-3234  Fax: (573) 751-1847  E-mail: psc.info@psc.mo.gov
Internet: www.psc.mo.gov
■Chairman **Daniel Hall** . . . . . . . . . . . . . . . . . . . . . . . . . . . (573) 751-4221
  Term Expires: September 2019
  E-mail: daniel.hall@psc.mo.gov
■Commissioner **Maida J. Coleman** . . . . . . . . . . . . . . . . . . (573) 751-3234
  Term Expires: August 10, 2021
  Education: Lincoln U (MO) 1976 BA
■Commissioner **William P. "Bill" Kenney** . . . . . . . . . . . . . (573) 751-7508
  E-mail: william.kenney@psc.mo.gov
■Commissioner **Scott T. Rupp** . . . . . . . . . . . . . . . . . . . . . . (573) 751-1282
  E-mail: scott.rupp@psc.mo.gov
  Education: Missouri 1995 BA
■Commissioner **Stephen M. "Steve" Stoll** . . . . . . . . . . . . . (573) 751-4221
  E-mail: steve.stoll@psc.mo.gov
  Education: Missouri 1970 BA; Missouri (St Louis) 1979 MEd

# Missouri Development Finance Board
P.O. Box 567, Jefferson City, MO 65102
Fax: (573) 526-4418  E-mail: mdfb@ded.mo.gov
Executive Director **Robert V. "Bob" Miserez** . . . . . . . . . . (573) 751-8479

---

★ Elected Official   ■ Appointed by Governor   ● Appointed by Legislature   ▲ Appointed by Board or Commission   ◆ Appointed by State Supreme Court

EXECUTIVE BRANCH

## Department of Health and Senior Services [DHSS]

P.O. Box 570, Jefferson City, MO 65102
Tel: (573) 751-6400  Tel: (573) 751-6387 (Vital Records)
Fax: (573) 751-6010  E-mail: info@health.mo.gov

**Employees:** 1,785  **Fiscal Year:** 2015  **Budget:** $1,176,494,000

■Director (Acting) **Peter Lyskowski** . . . . . . . . . . . . . . . . . (573) 751-6001
Deputy Director **(Vacant)** . . . . . . . . . . . . . . . . . . . . . . (573) 751-6002

### Administration Division

Director **Bret Fischer** . . . . . . . . . . . . . . . . . . . . . . . (573) 751-6014
  E-mail: bret.fischer@health.mo.gov
Deputy Director **Patricia Bedell** . . . . . . . . . . . . . . . . (573) 751-6104
  E-mail: patricia.bedell@health.mo.gov

### Community and Public Health Division

930 Wildwood Drive, Jefferson City, MO 65102-0570
Tel: (573) 751-6080  Fax: (573) 526-5348

Director **Harold Kirbey** . . . . . . . . . . . . . . . . . . . . . . (573) 751-6080

### Regulation and Licensure Division

3418 Knipp Drive, Jefferson City, MO 65102
Tel: (573) 751-8535  Fax: (573) 522-1473

Director **Jeanne Serra** . . . . . . . . . . . . . . . . . . . . . . (573) 751-8535

### Senior and Disability Services Division

Director **Celesta Hartgraves** . . . . . . . . . . . . . . . . . . (573) 526-3626

## Department of Insurance, Financial Institutions and Professional Registration [DIFP]

301 West High Street, Suite 530, Jefferson City, MO 65101
Tel: (573) 751-4126  TTY: (573) 526-4536  Fax: (573) 751-1165
Internet: www.difp.mo.gov

**Employees:** 580  **Fiscal Year:** 2015  **Budget:** $34,658,000

■Insurance Director **John M. Huff** . . . . . . . . . . . . . . . (573) 751-4126
  E-mail: john.huff@difp.mo.gov
  Education: Southeast Missouri State BBA; Saint Louis U 1987 MBA; Washington U (MO) 1990 JD
  Special Assistant to the Director **Kim Gerlt** . . . . . . . . . (573) 751-4126
Deputy Director **James "Jim" McAdams** . . . . . . . . . . . . (573) 751-4126
Communications Director **Chris Cline** . . . . . . . . . . . . . (573) 751-4126
  E-mail: chris.cline@difp.mo.gov
  Education: Central Methodist Col
Administration and Technology Division Director
  **Grady Martin** . . . . . . . . . . . . . . . . . . . . . . . . (573) 522-6115
  E-mail: grady.martin@difp.mo.gov
Receivership Counsel/Supervisor **Tamara W. Kopp** . . . . . . . (573) 522-6115
  Education: Missouri 2006 JD
Chief of Investigations **Mary Johnson** . . . . . . . . . . . . . (573) 751-4126
  Education: Columbia Col (MO) BBA; William Woods MBA
Chief Industry Liaison **Angela Nelson** . . . . . . . . . . . . . (573) 751-2640

### Consumer Affairs Division

Tel: (800) 726-7390  Fax: (573) 526-4898
E-mail: consumeraffairs@insurance.mo.gov

Director **Carrie Couch** . . . . . . . . . . . . . . . . . . . . . . (573) 751-1922
Property and Casualty Section Manager
  **Jeana E. Thomas** . . . . . . . . . . . . . . . . . . . . . . (573) 751-2640

### Credit Unions Division

P.O. Box 1607, Jefferson City, MO 65102
Fax: (573) 751-6834  E-mail: cu@cu.mo.gov

Director **Ken Bonnot** . . . . . . . . . . . . . . . . . . . . . . . (573) 751-3419
Fiscal and Administrative Manager **Debbie Davis** . . . . . . . (573) 751-1669
  E-mail: debbie.davis@cu.mo.gov

### Finance Division

P.O. Box 716, Jefferson City, MO 65102
Tel: (573) 751-3242  Fax: (573) 751-9192  E-mail: finance@dof.mo.gov

Commissioner (Acting) **Debra J. Hardman** . . . . . . . . . . . (573) 751-2545
  E-mail: debra.hardman@dof.mo.gov
Deputy Commissioner (Acting) **Christie Kincannon** . . . . . . (573) 751-2545
Chief Counsel **Christie Kincannon** . . . . . . . . . . . . . . . (573) 751-4297
Chief Examiner **David A. "Dave" Doering** . . . . . . . . . . . (573) 751-4297
Consumer Credit Section Supervisor **Joseph L. Crider** . . . . (573) 751-3463
Supervisor of Mortgage Licensing **Mick Campbell** . . . . . . (573) 751-4243

### Company and Captive Regulation Division

Tel: (573) 526-4877  E-mail: insurancesolvency@insurance.mo.gov

Director **John Rehagen** . . . . . . . . . . . . . . . . . . . . . (573) 526-4877
Life and Health Actuary **William Leung, CPA** . . . . . . . . . (573) 526-4877
  E-mail: william.leung@insurance.mo.gov

### Insurance Market Regulation Division

Director **Angela Nelson** . . . . . . . . . . . . . . . . . . . . . (573) 751-4126
  E-mail: angela.nelson@insurance.mo.gov
Life and Health Section Manager **Mary Mealer** . . . . . . . . (573) 751-4126
Health Insurance Reforms Initiatives Manager
  **Molly L. White** . . . . . . . . . . . . . . . . . . . . . . . (573) 751-4126
  Education: Missouri MHA

### Professional Registration Division

P.O. Box 1335, Jefferson City, MO 65102-1335
Tel: (573) 751-0293  Fax: (573) 751-0878  E-mail: profreg@pr.mo.gov
Internet: www.pr.mo.gov

Director **Kathleen "Katie" Steele Danner** . . . . . . . . . . . (573) 751-1081

## Department of Labor and Industrial Relations [DLIR]

P.O. Box 504, Jefferson City, MO 65102-0504
Tel: (573) 751-3403  Fax: (573) 751-4135  E-mail: diroffice@labor.mo.gov

**Employees:** 823  **Fiscal Year:** 2015  **Budget:** $148,546,000

■Director **Ryan Glennon McKenna** . . . . . . . . . . . . . . . (573) 751-4091
  E-mail: ryan.mckenna@labor.mo.gov
  Education: Southwest Missouri State 1997 BEd
■Deputy Director **Ken Jacob** . . . . . . . . . . . . . . . . . . (573) 751-4091
  E-mail: ken.jacob@labor.mo.gov
Human Rights Commission Executive Director
  **Alisa Warren** . . . . . . . . . . . . . . . . . . . . . . . . (573) 751-3325
  P.O. Box 1129, Jefferson City, MO 65102-1129
  E-mail: mchr@labor.mo.gov
Employment Security Division Director **(Vacant)** . . . . . . . (573) 751-3215
  P.O. Box 59, Jefferson City, MO 65104-0059     Fax: (573) 751-4945
Labor Standards Division Director **John E. Lindsey** . . . . . . (573) 751-1422
  P.O. Box 449, Jefferson City, MO 65102-0449
  E-mail: laborstandards@labor.mo.gov
Workers' Compensation Division Director
  **John J. Hickey** . . . . . . . . . . . . . . . . . . . . . . . (573) 751-4231
  P.O. Box 58, Jefferson City, MO 65102-0058     Fax: (573) 751-2012

## Department of Natural Resources [DNR]

P.O. Box 176, Jefferson City, MO 65102
Tel: (573) 751-3443  Fax: (573) 751-7627  Internet: www.dnr.mo.gov

**Employees:** 1,756  **Fiscal Year:** 2015  **Budget:** $312,261,000

■Director **Sara Parker Pauley** . . . . . . . . . . . . . . . . . . (573) 522-6221
  Education: Missouri BJ, 1993 JD
  Secretary **Valerie Evers** . . . . . . . . . . . . . . . . . . . (573) 522-6221
Deputy Director **Todd Sampsell** . . . . . . . . . . . . . . . . (573) 751-4732
  Secretary **Jennifer Alexander** . . . . . . . . . . . . . . . . (573) 522-6221
Communications Director **Tom Bastian** . . . . . . . . . . . . . (573) 751-1010
General Counsel **Marty Miller** . . . . . . . . . . . . . . . . . . (573) 751-0323

---

★ Elected Official     ■ Appointed by Governor     ● Appointed by Legislature     ▲ Appointed by Board or Commission     ◆ Appointed by State Supreme Court

## Department of Public Safety [DPS]

P.O. Box 749, Jefferson City, MO 65102
Tel: (573) 751-4905  Fax: (573) 751-5399  E-mail: dpsinfo@dps.mo.gov

**Employees:** 5,007  **Fiscal Year:** 2015  **Budget:** $634,744,000

■Director **Lane Roberts, USAF (Ret)**...................(573) 751-4905
  E-mail: lane.roberts@dps.mo.gov
  Education: Liberty BS; William Woods MBA
  Executive Secretary **Darla Iven**......................(573) 751-5432
■Deputy Director **Stephen Sokoloff**..................(573) 751-4905
  E-mail: stephen.sokoloff@dps.mo.gov
  Education: Pace; Missouri JD
  General Counsel **Tracy McGinnis**.....................(573) 751-4905
  E-mail: tracy.mcginnis@dps.mo.gov

## Office of Homeland Security

1101 North Riverside Drive, Jefferson City, MO 65102
P.O. Box 749, Jefferson City, MO 65102
Tel: (573) 522-3007  Fax: (573) 751-5399
E-mail: homeland.security@dps.mo.gov

Homeland Security Coordinator **(Vacant)**..............(573) 522-3007
Grants and Training Administrator **Bruce Clemonds**......(573) 522-3007
  E-mail: bruce.clemonds@dps.mo.gov

## Alcohol and Tobacco Control Division

P.O. Box 837, Jefferson City, MO 65102

State Supervisor **Lafayette Lacy**....................(573) 751-2333
Enforcement Chief **Keith Hendrickson**................(573) 526-2772

## Fire Safety Division

P.O. Box 844, Jefferson City, MO 65102

Fire Marshal (Acting) **Greg Carrell**..................(573) 751-2930
  E-mail: greg.carrell@dps.mo.gov
Assistant Fire Marshal **(Vacant)**.....................(573) 751-2930
Boiler & Pressure Vessels Program Director
  **Joe Brockman**......................................(573) 751-8708
  E-mail: joe.brockman@dps.mo.gov
Fire Training Director **Kim Becker**...................(573) 751-2930
  E-mail: kim.becker@dps.mo.gov
Investigations & Fireworks Program Director Deputy
  Chief **Bill Zieres**.................................(573) 751-2930
  E-mail: bill.zieres@dps.mo.gov
Deputy Chief Elevator Inspector **Larry Watson**.........(573) 751-2930
  E-mail: larry.watson@dps.mo.gov

## Missouri National Guard

2302 Militia Drive, Jefferson City, MO 65101-1203
Fax: (573) 526-9929

■Adjutant General
  **MG Stephen L. "Steve" Danner, ARNG**............(573) 638-9710
  E-mail: steve.danner@dps.mo.gov
  Education: Missouri (Kansas City) 1977; Missouri 1980 JD;
  US Army Command; Army War Col 2004 MSS
  Chief of Staff **COL David L. Boyle, ARNG**...........(573) 638-9616
  Judge Advocate General's Corps
  **LTC John Keller, ARNG**............................(573) 526-9929
  Assistant Adjutant General (Air)
  **BrigGen Gregory Champagne, ANG**.............(573) 638-9710
  Assistant Adjutant General (Army)
  **BG Gregory Mason, ARNG**.........................(573) 638-9710

## State Emergency Management Agency

2302 Militia Drive, Jefferson City, MO 65101
P.O. Box 116, Jefferson City, MO 65102
Fax: (573) 634-7966

■Director **Ron Walker**...............................(573) 526-9101
  E-mail: ron.walker@dps.mo.gov
Deputy Director **Dawn Warren**.......................(573) 526-9103

## Gaming Commission

3417 Knipp Drive, Jefferson City, MO 65109
Fax: (573) 526-4084

■Executive Director **William K. Seibert**...............(573) 526-4080
  E-mail: william.seibert@dps.mo.gov

## Capitol Police

Truman State Office Building, Room 101, Jefferson City, MO 65102
Fax: (573) 526-3898  E-mail: mcpolice@dps.state.mo.us

Chief **Todd Hurt**....................................(573) 751-2764

## State Highway Patrol

P.O. Box 568, Jefferson City, MO 65102
Fax: (573) 751-9419

Superintendent **Col. J. Bret Johnson**.................(573) 751-3313
  Chief of Staff **Capt. Timothy "Tim" McDonald**......(573) 522-9816
Assistant Superintendent **Lt. Col. Sandra K. Karsten**.....(573) 751-3313

## Department of Revenue [DOR]

P.O. Box 311, Jefferson City, MO 65105-0311
Tel: (573) 751-4450  TTY: (800) 735-2966  Fax: (573) 751-7150
E-mail: dormail@dor.mo.gov

**Employees:** 1,122  **Fiscal Year:** 2015  **Budget:** $506,493,000

■Director **Nia Ray**..................................(573) 751-5671
  E-mail: nia.ray@dor.mo.gov
■Deputy Director **John R. Mollenkamp**.................(573) 751-2992
  E-mail: john.mollenkamp@dor.mo.gov
  Education: Missouri; Texas JD
  Motor Vehicle and Driver Licensing Division Director
  **Jackie L. Bemboom**...............................(573) 526-1827
  P.O. Box 629, Jefferson City, MO 65105-0629    Fax: (573) 526-4774
  E-mail: jackie.bemboom@dor.mo.gov
  Administration Division Director **Lynn Bexten**..........(573) 751-7429
  P.O. Box 87, Jefferson City, MO 65105-0087    Fax: (573) 522-2548
  E-mail: lynn.bexten@dor.mo.gov
  Legal Services Division Director and General Counsel
  (Acting) **Wood Miller**.............................(573) 751-4413
  P.O. Box 475, Jefferson City, MO 65105-0475    Fax: (573) 751-7151
  Taxation Division Director **Todd Iveson**..............(573) 751-3470
  P.O. Box 854, Jefferson City, MO 65105-0854    Fax: (573) 751-7273
  Legislative Director (Acting) **Casey Wasser**...........(573) 751-4450

## State Tax Commission [STC]

Harry S. Truman State Office Building, 301 West High Street, Room 840,
Jefferson City, MO 65101
P.O. Box 146, Jefferson City, MO 65102-0146
Tel: (573) 751-2414  Fax: (573) 751-1341  E-mail: stc@stc.mo.gov
Internet: www.stc.mo.gov

■Chairman **Bruce E. Davis**...........................(573) 751-2414
  Education: Westminster (MO)
■Commissioner **Victor Callahan**......................(573) 751-2414
■Commissioner **Randy B. Holman**.....................(573) 751-2414
  Education: Southeast Missouri State BSBA

## Department of Social Services [DSS]

221 West High Street, Jefferson City, MO 65102
P.O. Box 1527, Jefferson City, MO 65102
Tel: (573) 751-4815  TTY: (800) 735-2966  Fax: (573) 751-3203
Internet: www.dss.mo.gov

**Employees:** 7,158  **Fiscal Year:** 2015  **Budget:** $8,174,452,000

Director **Brian D. Kinkade**..........................(573) 751-4815
  Education: Missouri BSBA, MA
  Executive Assistant **Marla S. Lane**.................(573) 751-4815
Deputy Director **Jennifer Tidball**...................(573) 751-4815
Children's Division Director **Tim Decker**..............(573) 522-8024
  E-mail: tim.decker@dss.mo.gov
Family Support Division Director **Alyson Campbell**......(573) 751-4247
  E-mail: alyson.f.campbell@dss.mo.gov
Finance and Administrative Services Division Director
  **Patrick Luebbering**...............................(573) 751-7533
  E-mail: patrick.luebbering@dss.mo.gov

*(continued on next page)*

---

★ Elected Official    ■ Appointed by Governor    ● Appointed by Legislature    ▲ Appointed by Board or Commission    ◆ Appointed by State Supreme Court

**EXECUTIVE BRANCH**

**Department of Social Services** *continued*

Legal Services Division Director **Joel Anderson** . . . . . . . .(573) 751-2065
Missouri HealthNet Division Director **Dr. Joe Parks** . . . . . .(573) 751-6922
Youth Services Division Director (Acting) **Phyllis Becker** . .(573) 751-3324
   E-mail: phyllis.becker@dss.mo.gov
SNAP Program Manager **Kay E. Martello** . . . . . . . . . . . . (573) 751-4328

## Conservation Commission

2901 West Truman Boulevard, Jefferson City, MO 65102-0180
P.O. Box 180, Jefferson City, MO 65102
Tel: (573) 751-4115

■Chair **Marilynn J. Bradford** . . . . . . . . . . . . . . . . . . . . . .(573) 522-4115
   Term Expires: July 1, 2019
■Vice Chair **David W. Murphy** . . . . . . . . . . . . . . . . . . . . . .(573) 522-4115
   Term Expires: July 1, 2019
■Secretary **James T. Blair IV** . . . . . . . . . . . . . . . . . . . . . .(573) 522-4115
   Term Expires: June 1, 2017
■Commissioner **Don C. Bedell** . . . . . . . . . . . . . . . . . . . . (573) 522-4115
   Term Expires: July 1, 2021

## Missouri Department of Conservation [MDC]

Tel: (573) 751-4115  Fax: (573) 751-4467  E-mail: internet@mdc.mo.gov
Internet: http://mdc.mo.gov

**Employees:** 1,812  **Fiscal Year:** 2015  **Budget:** $142,281,000

▲Director **Bob Ziehmer** . . . . . . . . . . . . . . . . . . . . . . . . (573) 522-4115 ext. 3212
   E-mail: bob.ziehmer@mdc.mo.gov
Deputy Director **Jennifer Battson-Warren** . . . . . .(573) 522-4115 ext. 3216
Deputy Director **Tom Draper** . . . . . . . . . . . . . . . .(573) 522-4115 ext. 3217
Deputy Director **Aaron Jeffries** . . . . . . . . . . . . . . .(573) 522-4115 ext. 3146
   E-mail: aaron.jeffries@mdc.mo.gov
General Counsel **Jennifer Frazier** . . . . . . . . . . . . .(573) 522-4115 ext. 3210
   E-mail: jennifer.frazier@mdc.mo.gov
Internal Auditor **Lisa Wehmeyer** . . . . . . . . . . . . .(573) 522-4115 ext. 3522
Administrative Services Division Chief **Margie Mueller** . . .(573) 522-4115
Design and Development Division Chief
   **Jacob Careaga** . . . . . . . . . . . . . . . . . . . . . .(573) 522-4115 ext. 3757
Fisheries Division Chief **Brian Kennedy** . . . . . . . .(573) 522-4115 ext. 3599
Forestry Division Chief **Lisa Allen** . . . . . . . . . . . .(573) 522-4115 ext. 3120
Human Resources Division Chief
   **Tom Neubauer** . . . . . . . . . . . . . . . . . . . . . .(573) 522-4115 ext. 3230
Outreach and Education Division Chief
   **Joanie Straub** . . . . . . . . . . . . . . . . . . . . . . .(573) 522-4115 ext. 3235
   E-mail: joanie.straub@mdc.mo.gov
Private Land Services Division Chief **Bill White** . . . . . .(573) 522-4115 ext. 3163
Protection Division Chief **Larry Yamnitz** . . . . . . .(573) 522-4115 ext. 3254
   E-mail: larry.yamnitz@mdc.mo.gov
Resource Science Division Chief
   **Mike Hubbard** . . . . . . . . . . . . . . . . . . . . . . .(573) 522-4115 ext. 3168
Wildlife Division Chief **(Vacant)** . . . . . . . . . . . . . . . . . . .(573) 522-4115
Information Technology Services Chief
   **Douglas Fees** . . . . . . . . . . . . . . . . . . . . . . . .(573) 522-4115 ext. 3112
   E-mail: douglas.fees@mdc.mo.gov

## Missouri Highways and Transportation Commission

105 West Capitol Avenue, Jefferson City, MO 65101
P.O. Box 270, Jefferson City, MO 65102
Tel: (573) 751-2824  Fax: (573) 526-5419

■Chair **Gregg C. Smith** . . . . . . . . . . . . . . . . . . . . . . . . . .(573) 751-2824
   Term Expires: March 1, 2019
■Vice Chair **Stephen R. Miller** . . . . . . . . . . . . . . . . . . . .(573) 751-2824
   Term Expires: March 1, 2011
   Education: Notre Dame
■Member **John W. Briscoe** . . . . . . . . . . . . . . . . . . . . . .(573) 751-2824
   Term Expires: March 1, 2021
   Education: Westminster (MO) 1963 BA; Missouri 1966 JD
■Member **Mary E. Nelson** . . . . . . . . . . . . . . . . . . . . . . .(573) 751-2824
   Term Expires: March 1, 2017
   Education: Princeton 1977; Missouri 1980 JD

■Member **Michael B. Pace** . . . . . . . . . . . . . . . . . . . . . . . .(573) 751-2824
   Term Expires: March 1, 2019
■Member **Michael Thomas "Tom" Waters** . . . . . . . . . . . . .(573) 751-2824
   Term Expires: March 1, 2021
Secretary **Pam Harlan** . . . . . . . . . . . . . . . . . . . . . . . . . .(573) 751-2824

## Missouri Department of Transportation [MoDOT]

Tel: (573) 751-2551  Fax: (573) 526-4908  Internet: www.modot.org

**Employees:** 5,653  **Fiscal Year:** 2015  **Budget:** $1,973,005,000

▲Director **Patrick McKenna** . . . . . . . . . . . . . . . . . . . . . .(573) 751-2551
Chief Counsel **Richard Tiemeyer** . . . . . . . . . . . . . . . . . .(573) 751-7454
   E-mail: richard.tiemeyer@modot.mo.gov
Chief Engineer **Ed Hassinger, PE** . . . . . . . . . . . . . . . . . .(573) 751-2803
   E-mail: ed.hassinger@modot.mo.gov
   Education: Missouri 1983 BS
   Assistant Chief Engineer **Kathy Harvey** . . . . . . . . . . . .(573) 751-6602
Chief Financial Officer **Roberta Broeker** . . . . . . . . . . . .(573) 751-2803
Audits and Investigations Director **Bill Rogers** . . . . . . .(573) 751-7446
   E-mail: bill.rogers@modot.mo.gov
Equal Opportunity and Diversity Director **Rudy Nickens** . .(573) 526-5611
General Services Director **Debbie Rickard** . . . . . . . . . . . .(573) 751-1650
   E-mail: debbie.rickard@modot.mo.gov
Governmental Relations Director **Jay Wunderlich** . . . . . . .(573) 751-8273
   E-mail: jay.wunderlich@modot.mo.gov
Human Resources Director **Michaelene Knudsen** . . . . . . . .(573) 751-2804
Information Systems Director **Beth Ring** . . . . . . . . . . . . .(573) 751-1345
   E-mail: beth.ring@modot.mo.gov
Motor Carrier Services Director **Scott Marion** . . . . . . . . .(573) 526-4187
Multimodal Operations Director **Michelle Teel** . . . . . . . .(573) 522-5202
Customer Relations Director (Acting)
   **Sally Oxenhandler** . . . . . . . . . . . . . . . . . . . . . . . . . .(573) 526-4335
Financial Services Director **Brenda Morris** . . . . . . . . . . .(573) 526-8106
Risk and Benefits Management Director **Jeff Padgett** . . . . .(573) 751-4624
State Bridge Engineer **Dennis Heckman** . . . . . . . . . . . . .(573) 751-4676
State Construction & Materials Engineer **Dave Ahlvers** . . .(573) 751-3689
State Design Engineer **Eric Schroeter** . . . . . . . . . . . . . .(573) 526-8485
   E-mail: eric.schroeter@modot.mo.gov
State Maintenance Engineer **Becky Allmeroth** . . . . . . . . . .(573) 522-5301
State Traffic Engineer **Eileen Rackers** . . . . . . . . . . . . . .(573) 526-0117
External Civil Rights Director **Lester Woods** . . . . . . . . . .(573) 526-2978
Transportation Planning Director **Machelle Watkins** . . . . . .(573) 526-8058
   E-mail: machelle.watkins@modot.mo.gov

## Mental Health Commission

1706 East Elm Street, Box 687, Jefferson City, MO 65102
Tel: (573) 751-3070  Fax: (573) 526-7926
E-mail: mhcommission@dmh.mo.gov

■Chairman **Dennis H. Tesreau** . . . . . . . . . . . . . . . . . . . .(573) 751-3070
■Member **Kathleen A. "Kathy" Carter** . . . . . . . . . . . . . . .(573) 751-3070
   Education: Colorado (Denver); Missouri Southern State Col
■Member **Dr. Kenneth W. "Ken" Dobbins** . . . . . . . . . . . . .(573) 751-3070
   Education: Akron 1971 BS; Old Dominion 1979 MBA;
   Kent State 1987 PhD
■Member **Gary Duncan** . . . . . . . . . . . . . . . . . . . . . . . . .(573) 751-3070
   Term Expires: June 28, 2015
■Member **Dr. Stephen Huss** . . . . . . . . . . . . . . . . . . . . . .(573) 751-3070
   Term Expires: June 28, 2019
■Member **Steve Roling** . . . . . . . . . . . . . . . . . . . . . . . . .(573) 751-3070
■Member **Mary Patrick Siegfried** . . . . . . . . . . . . . . . . . .(573) 751-3070
   Term Expires: June 28, 2017
■Member **Neva G. Thurston** . . . . . . . . . . . . . . . . . . . . . .(573) 751-3070
■Member **Karl Wilson** . . . . . . . . . . . . . . . . . . . . . . . . . .(573) 751-3070
   Term Expires: June 28, 2018
Staff Liaison **Monica L. Hoy** . . . . . . . . . . . . . . . . . . . . .(573) 751-3070

---

★ Elected Official    ■ Appointed by Governor    ● Appointed by Legislature    ▲ Appointed by Board or Commission    ◆ Appointed by State Supreme Court

## Department of Mental Health [DMH]

1706 East Elm, Jefferson City, MO 65101
P.O. Box 687, Jefferson City, MO 65102
Tel: (573) 751-4122  Tel: (800) 364-9687  Fax: (573) 751-8224
E-mail: dmhmail@dmh.mo.gov  Internet: www.dmh.mo.gov

**Employees:** 7,445  **Fiscal Year:** 2015  **Budget:** $1,540,526,000

▲ Director **Mark Stringer** ............................... (573) 751-3070
   E-mail: mark.stringer@dmh.mo.gov
Deputy Director **(Vacant)** ........................... (573) 751-7033
General Counsel **Gail Vasterling** .................... (573) 751-4122
   Education: Missouri 1984 BSBA; Washington U (MO) 1990 JD
Chief Medical Officer for Children
   **Dr. Laine Young-Walker, MD** ................. (573) 751-4122
   E-mail: laine.youngwalker@dmh.mo.gov
Chief Medical Officer for Adults
   **Dr. Angeline Stanislaus, MD** ................. (573) 751-4122
Administration Services Director **(Vacant)** ............. (573) 751-8144
Developmental Disabilities Division Director
   **Valerie Huhn** ................................ (573) 751-8676
Human Resources Director **James Jackson** ............. (573) 751-8562
Psychiatric Facilities Director
   **Robert "Bob" Reitz, PhD** ...................... (573) 751-9482
   E-mail: robert.reitz@dmh.mo.gov
Public Affairs Director **Deborah Walker** ............... (573) 751-3070

## Coordinating Board for Higher Education [CBHE]

205 Jefferson Street, 11th Floor, Jefferson City, MO 65102-0480
P.O. Box 1469, Jefferson City, MO 65102
TTY: (800) 735-2966  Fax: (573) 751-6635  E-mail: info@dhe.mo.gov
Internet: www.dhe.mo.gov

■ Chair **Brian Fogle** .................................... (573) 751-2361
■ Vice Chair **Carolyn R. Mahoney** .................... (573) 751-2361
   Term Expires: July 27, 2018
   Education: Siena Col BS; Ohio State 1972 MS, 1984 PhD
■ Secretary **Douglas R. Kennedy** ..................... (573) 751-2361
   Term Expires: June 27, 2020
   Education: Missouri; U Memphis JD
■ Member **Samuel P. Murphey** ........................ (573) 751-2361
   Term Expires: June 27, 2020
■ Member **Elizabeth Green "Betty" Sims** ............... (573) 751-2361
   Term Expires: June 27, 2016
   Education: MICDS (St. Louis, MO) 1953
■ Member **Dr. John W. Siscel III** ...................... (573) 751-2361
   Term Expires: June 27, 2018
   Education: Missouri EdD
■ Member **Michael D. "Mike" Thomson** ................ (573) 751-2361
   Term Expires: June 27, 2016
■ Member **Dalton Wright** .............................. (573) 751-2361
   Education: Missouri

## Missouri Department of Higher Education [MDHE]

**Employees:** 79  **Fiscal Year:** 2015  **Budget:** $1,158,933,000

▲ Commissioner (Interim) **Leroy Wade** .................. (573) 751-2361
Deputy Commissioner **Leroy Wade** .................... (573) 751-2361
General Counsel **William Thornton** .................... (573) 751-2361
Academic Affairs Director **Rusty Monhollon** ........... (573) 751-2361
Financial Assistance and Outreach Director **Leroy Wade** .. (573) 751-2361
Information Technology Director **Dianne Prenger** ........ (573) 751-2361
   E-mail: dianne.prenger@dhe.mo.gov
Missouri Student Loan Group Director **Leanne Cardwell** .. (573) 751-2361
   E-mail: leanne.cardwell@dhe.mo.gov

## State Board of Education

205 Jefferson Street, Jefferson City, MO 65102-0480
P.O. Box 480, Jefferson City, MO 65102
Tel: (573) 751-4212  TTY: (800) 735-2966  Fax: (573) 751-8613

■ President **Peter F. Herschend** ...................... (573) 751-4212
   Education: Missouri BA

■ Vice President **Michael W. "Mike" Jones** ............ (573) 751-4212
   Education: Missouri (St Louis)
■ Member **Joseph L. Driskill** ......................... (573) 751-4212
■ Member **O. Victor Lenz, PhD** ....................... (573) 751-4212
   Term Expires: July 1, 2019
   Education: Central Methodist Col BA; Southern IL Edwardsville MS;
   Missouri (St Louis) PhD
■ Member **Dr. John A. Martin** ........................ (573) 751-4212
■ Member **Charles W. "Charlie" Shields** ............... (573) 751-4212
   Education: Missouri MBA
■ Member **Russell C. Still** ........................... (573) 751-4212
   Education: Michigan 1968 BA; Missouri 1976 JD
■ Member **Maynard Wallace** .......................... (573) 751-4212
   Term Expires: July 1, 2016
   Education: Southwest Missouri State 1966 BSEd, 1972 MAEd

## Department of Elementary and Secondary Education [DESE]

Tel: (573) 751-4212  TTY: (800) 735-2966  Fax: (573) 751-8613
E-mail: communications@dese.mo.gov

**Employees:** 1,693  **Fiscal Year:** 2015  **Budget:** $5,507,272,000

▲ Commissioner **Margaret M. Vandeven, PhD** ........... (573) 751-4446
   E-mail: margaret.vandeven@dese.mo.gov    Fax: (573) 751-1179
General Counsel **William "Bill" Thornton** .............. (573) 751-3527
   E-mail: counsel@dese.mo.gov

## Office of the Lieutenant Governor

State Capitol, Room 224, Jefferson City, MO 65101
Tel: (573) 751-4727  Fax: (573) 751-9422  Internet: www.ltgov.mo.gov

**Employees:** 6  **Fiscal Year:** 2015  **Budget:** $376,000

★ Lieutenant Governor **Peter D. Kinder** (R) .............. (573) 751-4727
   Term Expires: January 2017
   E-mail: ltgovinfo@ltgov.mo.gov
   Education: St Mary's U (TX) 1979 JD
   Career: President Pro Tem, Missouri Senate; State Senator (R-MO,
   District 27), Missouri Senate
Chief of Staff **Reid K. Forrester** ..................... (573) 751-4727
Administration Director **Laurie Dawson** ............... (573) 751-4727
   E-mail: laurie.dawson@ltgov.mo.gov
Communications Director **Jay Eastlick** ................ (573) 751-1088
Constituent Services Director **Willis Jones** ............ (573) 751-4727
   E-mail: willis.jones@ltgov.mo.gov
Policy Director and General Counsel **(Vacant)** .......... (573) 751-4727

## Office of the Secretary of State

P.O. Box 140252, Kansas City, MO 64114
P.O. Box 300026, St. Louis, MO 63130
Tel: (573) 751-4936  Fax: (573) 526-4903
Tel: (866) 223-6535 (Business Services)  Tel: (800) 669-8683 (Elections)
Tel: (800) 325-0131 (Library)  Tel: (800) 721-7996 (Securities)
E-mail: sosmain@sos.mo.gov

**Employees:** 270  **Fiscal Year:** 2015  **Budget:** $32,483,000

★ Secretary of State **Jason Kander** (D) .................. (573) 751-1880
   Term Expires: January 2017
   E-mail: jason.kander@sos.mo.gov
   Education: American U 2002 BA; Georgetown 2005 JD
   Career: State Representative (D-MO, District 44), Missouri House
   of Representatives (2009-2013); Committee on State Heritage
   Co-Chairman, National Association of Secretaries of State (2013-2014)
Chief of Staff **(Vacant)** .............................. (573) 751-4936
General Counsel **Barbara Wood** ....................... (573) 751-4936
Communications Director **(Vacant)** .................... (573) 522-1009
                      Fax: (573) 522-3082

## Office of the Executive Deputy Secretary of State

Executive Deputy Secretary of State **(Vacant)** .......... (573) 751-2418
Policy and Government Affairs Director **John Scott** ...... (573) 751-2567

---

★ Elected Official   ■ Appointed by Governor   ● Appointed by Legislature   ▲ Appointed by Board or Commission   ◆ Appointed by State Supreme Court

EXECUTIVE BRANCH

## Business Services Division

Internet: www.sos.mo.gov/business

Director **Jase Carter** ................................. (573) 751-3200
Commissions Officer **Sheila Heather** ................. (573) 751-2336

## Elections Division

Deputy Secretary of State for Elections **Julie A. Allen** .... (573) 526-1272

## Fiscal and Facilities Services Division

Internet: www.sos.mo.gov/adminsvcs.asp

Director **Val Heet** ................................. (573) 522-1813
E-mail: val.heet@sos.mo.gov

## Information Technology Division

Director **Julie A. Allen** ............................. (573) 751-8471
E-mail: julie.allen@sos.mo.gov

## Records Services Division

Archives Director/State Archivist **John Dougan** ........ (573) 751-4717
Local Records Director **John Dougan** ................ (573) 751-4717
Records Management Director **Nathan Troup** .......... (573) 751-4502

## Securities Division

Commissioner **Andrew Hartnett** ..................... (573) 751-4136
Fax: (573) 526-3124
Enforcement Assistant Commissioner **Mary Hosmer** ...... (573) 751-4704

## State Library

600 West Main Street, Jefferson City, MO 65101
P.O. Box 387, Jefferson City, MO 65102
Tel: (573) 522-4036  Fax: (573) 526-1142
Internet: www.sos.mo.gov/library

State Librarian **Barbara Reading** .................... (573) 526-4783
Tel: (800) 325-0131
ext. 2
Library Development Director **Debbie Musselman** ...... (573) 751-2679
Tel: (800) 325-0131
ext. 4
Reference Services Division Director **Waheedah Bilal** .... (573) 751-2862
WolfnerTalking Book and Braille Director **Donna Riegel** .. (573) 751-8720
Education: Delta State; Marquette; Wisconsin (Milwaukee) MLS;
Florida Atlantic MPA; Cal Southern DBA

## Office of the Attorney General

Supreme Court Building, Jefferson City, MO 65102
P.O. Box 899, Jefferson City, MO 65102
TTY: (800) 729-8668  Fax: (573) 751-0774

**Employees:** 439  **Fiscal Year:** 2015  **Budget:** $24,095,000

★ Attorney General **Chris Koster** (D) ................... (573) 751-3321
Term Expires: January 2017
E-mail: attorney.general@ago.mo.gov
Education: Missouri 1987 BA, 1991 JD;
Washington U (MO) 2002 MBA
Career: Majority Caucus Chairman, Missouri Senate; State Senator
(D-MO, District 31), Missouri Senate (2005-2009)
Chief Deputy Attorney General **Joseph Dandurand** ...... (573) 751-8828
Education: Central Missouri State BS; Missouri (Kansas City) JD
Chief of Staff **James Farnsworth** .................... (573) 751-3457
Deputy Chief of Staff **Rhonda Meyer** ................ (573) 751-4406
Counsel to the Attorney General **Joan Gummels** ........ (573) 751-8828
State Solicitor **James "Jim" Layton** .................. (573) 751-1800
Agriculture and Environment Division Chief Counsel
**Jack McManus** ................................. (573) 751-1622
E-mail: jack.mcmanus@ago.mo.gov
Consumer Protection Division Chief Counsel
**Joseph P. "Joe" Bindbeutel** ...................... (573) 751-8778
Public Safety Division Chief Counsel **Susan Boresi** ...... (573) 751-4418
E-mail: susan.boresi@ago.mo.gov
Criminal Appeals Division Director
**Shaun Mackelprang** ............................ (573) 751-0272
Financial Services Division Director **Greg Perry** ........ (573) 751-8819

Governmental Affairs Division Director
**Patricia Churchill** ............................. (573) 751-7543
Labor Division Director **Cara Harris** ................. (573) 751-0662
E-mail: cara.harris@ago.mo.gov
Litigation Division Director **Joel Poole** .............. (573) 751-8833
Medicaid Fraud Control Division Director
**Joanna Trachtenberg** ........................... (573) 751-8869
Prosecutions Services Office Director **Jason Lamb** ....... (573) 751-8763
Fiscal Officer **Arlene Boessen** ..................... (573) 751-7591
Personnel Officer **Kerry Kroll** ..................... (573) 751-8854
Information Technology Manager **Andrew Golightly** ..... (800) 729-8668
E-mail: andrew.golightly@ago.mo.gov

## Office of the State Treasurer

201 West Capitol Avenue, Room 229, Jefferson City, MO 65101
P.O. Box 210, Jefferson City, MO 65102
Tel: (573) 751-8533 (Main)  Tel: (573) 751-2411 (Capitol)
Fax: (573) 751-0343 (Main)  Fax: (573) 751-9443 (Capitol)
E-mail: info@treasurer.mo.gov  Internet: www.treasurer.mo.gov

**Employees:** 49  **Fiscal Year:** 2015  **Budget:** $46,009,000

★ State Treasurer **Clint Zweifel** (D) ................... (573) 751-8533
Term Expires: January 2017
E-mail: clint.zweifel@treasurer.mo.gov
Education: Missouri (St Louis) 1996 BA, 2001 MBA
Career: State Representative (D-MO, District 78), Missouri House of
Representatives (2003-2009)
Deputy State Treasurer **Angie Heffner Robyn** ........... (573) 751-4943
Education: Kansas; Missouri (Kansas City) 1993 JD
Deputy Chief of Staff **(Vacant)** .................... (573) 751-7595
Banking Director **Nicole Hackmann** ................. (573) 751-9002
E-mail: nicole.hackmann@treasurer.mo.gov
Communications Director **Meghan Lewis** ............. (573) 526-6024
E-mail: meghan.lewis@treasurer.mo.gov
Communications Coordinator **Spencer Girouard** ........ (573) 522-6274
E-mail: spencer.girouard@treasurer.mo.gov
Investments Director **Bruce Ring** ................... (573) 751-8530
Special Projects Coordinator **Nick Henderson** .......... (573) 751-5390
Unclaimed Property and General Services Director
**Scott Harper** ................................. (573) 751-2082
Executive Assistant **Debbie Schertzer** ............... (573) 522-1139
Legal Counsel **Sarah Swoboda** ..................... (573) 751-4910

## Office of the State Auditor

301 West High Street, Office 880, Jefferson City, MO 65102
P.O. Box 869, Jefferson City, MO 65102
Tel: (573) 751-0490  TTY: (800) 347-8597
Tel: (816) 889-3590 (Kansas City Office)
Tel: (417) 895-6515 (Springfield Office)
Tel: (314) 340-7575 (St. Louis Office)  Fax: (573) 751-6539
E-mail: moaudit@auditor.mo.gov  Internet: www.auditor.mo.gov

**Employees:** 108  **Fiscal Year:** 2015  **Budget:** $7,204,000

★ State Auditor **Nicole Galloway, CPA, CFE** (D) .......... (573) 751-4824
Term Expires: January 2019
Education: Missouri Science and Tech 2004 BAM;
Missouri 2008 MBA
Career: County Treasurer, County of Boone, Missouri
Deputy State Auditor **Keriann Wright, CPA** ............ (573) 751-4213
Chief of Staff **Michael Moorefield** .................. (573) 751-4213
Education: Missouri 2007 BA, 2011 MBA, 2011 JD
General Counsel **Paul Harper** ...................... (573) 751-4213
Local Government Audits Director **Regina Pruitt, CPA** .... (573) 751-5031
State Audit Director **Jon Halwes, CPA** ............... (573) 751-5029
Fiscal Officer **Carol Newgaard** .................... (573) 751-4213
Communications Director **Gena Terlizzi** .............. (573) 522-2358
E-mail: gena.terlizzi@auditor.mo.gov
Education: Southern Illinois 2004; Illinois (Springfield)
Public Information Officer **Rebecca Gorley** ............ (573) 751-5310
E-mail: rebecca.gorley@auditor.mo.gov

---

★ Elected Official    ■ Appointed by Governor    ● Appointed by Legislature    ▲ Appointed by Board or Commission    ◆ Appointed by State Supreme Court

# Montana

Tel: (406) 444-3111 (Governor)  Internet: www.mt.gov

**Number of U.S. Congressional Delegates:** 2 Senators; 1 Representatives  **Governor's Term:** 4 years
**Legislature Description:** 50 member Senate; 100 member House of Representatives; Term - Senate 4 years, House 2 years  **Next Election:** Governor November 2016; Legislature November 2016
**Number of Electoral Votes:** 3  **Official Name:** State of Montana (Latin: mountainous)
**Nickname:** The Treasure State  **Motto:** Oro y Plata (Gold and Silver)

**Population:** 1,032,949 (2015); Rank 44  **Fiscal Year:** 2014  **Budget:** $4,398,636,000

## Office of the Governor

Montana State Capitol Building, Montana State Capitol Building, Helena, MT 59620
P.O. Box 200801, Helena, MT 59620-0801
Tel: (406) 444-3111  Fax: (406) 444-5529

**Fiscal Year:** 2015  **Budget:** $12,243,000

**Steve Bullock**
Governor

Began Service: January 7, 2013
Term Expires: January 2017
Date of Birth: April 11, 1966
Education: Claremont McKenna 1988 BA; Columbia 1994 JD
Religion: Catholic
Career: Chief Legal Counsel, Office of the Secretary of State, State of Montana (1996-1997); Executive Assistant Attorney General, Department of Justice, State of Montana (1997-2001); Attorney, Steptoe & Johnson LLP (2001-2004); Attorney General (D-MT), Department of Justice, State of Montana (2009-2013)

★Governor **Steve Bullock** (D) ......................... (406) 444-3111
  E-mail: governor@mt.gov
  Executive Assistant and Scheduler **Brenda Carney** ......(406) 444-3111
Chief of Staff **Tracy Stone-Manning** ................... (406) 444-3111
  Education: Maryland BA; Montana 1990 MS
Deputy Chief of Staff **Ali Bovingdon** ................. (406) 444-3111
  E-mail: abovingdon@mt.gov
  Education: Montana 1995 BA, 1998 JD
Senior Policy Advisor **(Vacant)** ...................... (406) 444-3111
■Chief Legal Counsel **Andrew I. Huff, JD** .............. (406) 444-3111
  E-mail: ahuff@mt.gov
  Education: Harvard 1991 BA; Colorado 1999 JD
Communications Director **MAJ Tim Crowe, USA** ........(406) 444-9844
Deputy Communications Director **Ronja Abel** .......... (406) 444-9725
  E-mail: rabel@mt.gov
  Education: Carroll Col (MT) BBA
■Boards and Appointments Advisor **Stacey Otterstrom** ....(406) 444-3111
  E-mail: sotterstrom@mt.gov
  Education: Montana State 2005 BA; Montana 2011 MPA
Education Policy Advisor **Siri Smillie** ................(406) 444-3111
  E-mail: ssmillie@mt.gov
Health and Families Policy Advisor **Tara Veazey** ........(406) 444-3111
  E-mail: tveazey@mt.gov
Natural Resource Policy Advisor **Tim Baker** ........... (406) 444-3111
  E-mail: tbaker@mt.gov
Mental Health Ombudsman **Dennis Nyland** ............(406) 444-9669
  E-mail: govmhombudsman@mt.gov
Senior Advisor **Dave Parker** ..........................(406) 444-4930

## Budget and Program Planning Office

P.O. Box 200802, Helena, MT 59620-0802

**Employees:** 18  **Fiscal Year:** 2014  **Budget:** $1,583,000

Budget Director **Dan J. Villa** ......................... (406) 444-3616
  E-mail: dvilla@mt.gov

Deputy Director **Amy Sassano** ...................... (406) 444-0619

## Citizen's Advocate Office

State Capitol, Montana State Capitol Building, Room 232, Helena, MT 59620
Tel: (800) 332-2272 (Voice/TTY)

**Employees:** 2  **Fiscal Year:** 2014  **Budget:** $93,000

Citizen's Advocate **John Malia** ...................... (406) 444-3468
  E-mail: jmalia@mt.gov

## Economic Development Office

State Capitol, Room 234, Helena, MT 59601
P.O. Box 200801, Helena, MT 59620-0801
Tel: (406) 444-5634  Fax: (406) 444-3674  Internet: business.mt.gov

Chief Business Development Officer **John Rogers** ....... (406) 444-5634
  E-mail: jrogers@mt.gov
Small Business Ombudsman **Andy Shirtliff** ............. (406) 444-5472
Economic Development Specialist
  **Elizabeth L. "Liz" Ching** ........................ (406) 444-1355
Economic Development Specialist **Dan Lloyd** ...........(406) 444-1355
Promotions Manager **Davey Madison** ................. (406) 444-5634

## Department of Administration [DOA]

Sam W. Mitchell Building, Room 155, Helena, MT 59620
P.O. Box 200101, Helena, MT 59620-0102
Tel: (406) 444-2032  Fax: (406) 444-6194  Internet: www.doa.mt.gov

**Employees:** 149  **Fiscal Year:** 2015  **Budget:** $37,761,000

■Director **Sheila Hogan** ............................(406) 444-3033
  E-mail: shogan@mt.gov
Deputy Director and Chief Legal Counsel
  **Michael Manion** ................................. (406) 444-3310
Communications Director **Laura Smith** ................ (406) 444-3307
  E-mail: laurasmith@mt.gov
  Executive Assistant **Monica Abbott** .................(406) 444-2460
    E-mail: mabbott@mt.gov
Budget and Finance Bureau Chief **Mark Bruno** .......... (406) 444-4612
  E-mail: mbruno@mt.gov

## Architecture and Engineering Division

1520 East Sixth Avenue, Helena, MT 59601
P.O. Box 200103, Helena, MT 59620-0103
Fax: (406) 444-3399  Internet: www.architecture.mt.gov

**Employees:** 17  **Fiscal Year:** 2014  **Budget:** $1,828,000

Administrator **Thomas B. "Tom" O'Connell** ............(406) 444-3104
  E-mail: toconnell@mt.gov
Construction and Design Bureau Chief **James Whaley**....(406) 444-3106

## Banking and Financial Institutions Division

Fax: (406) 841-2930  Internet: www.banking.mt.gov

**Employees:** 37  **Fiscal Year:** 2014  **Budget:** $3,598,000

Commissioner **Melanie Hall** ..........................(406) 841-2920
  E-mail: mghall@mt.gov
Deputy Commissioner **Dave Novotny** .................. (406) 841-2938
  E-mail: dnovotny@mt.gov
Bank Analyst **James Darfler** ......................... (406) 841-2923
  E-mail: jdarfler@mt.gov

---

★ Elected Official   ■ Appointed by Governor   ● Appointed by Legislature   ▲ Appointed by Board or Commission   ◆ Appointed by State Supreme Court

EXECUTIVE BRANCH

## General Services Division
P.O. Box 200110, Helena, MT 59620-0110
Fax: (406) 444-3039

**Employees:** 11  **Fiscal Year:** 2014  **Budget:** $855,000

Administrator **Steve Baiamonte** . . . . . . . . . . . . . . . . . . . . . .(406) 444-3119
  E-mail: sbaiamonte@mt.gov
Print and Mail Services Bureau Chief **Ryan Bahnmiller** . . .(406) 444-0588
Mail Supervisor **Dennis McAlpin** . . . . . . . . . . . . . . . . . . . .(406) 444-4190
  E-mail: dmcalpin@mt.gov
Maintenance Supervisor **Tom Russ** . . . . . . . . . . . . . . . . . . .(406) 444-3120
Facilities Manager **Josh LaFromboise** . . . . . . . . . . . . . . . .(406) 444-3030
Contracting Officer **Garett Bacon** . . . . . . . . . . . . . . . . . . .(406) 444-3108

## State Financial Services Division
Mitchell Building, 125 North Roberts, Room 255, Helena, MT 59604
P.O. Box 200102, Helena, MT 59620-0102
Internet: www.accounting.mt.gov

**Fiscal Year:** 2014  **Budget:** $1,403,000

Administrator **Cheryl Grey** . . . . . . . . . . . . . . . . . . . . . . . . .(406) 444-7734
Local Government Services Bureau Section Supervisor
  **Kim Smith** . . . . . . . . . . . . . . . . . . . . . . . . . . . . . . . . . .(406) 444-9158
  E-mail: kims@mt.gov
State Accountant and Accounting Bureau Chief
  **Cody Pearce** . . . . . . . . . . . . . . . . . . . . . . . . . . . . . . . .(406) 444-3094
State Procurement Bureau Chief **Brad Sanders** . . . . . . . . .(406) 444-1459
Statewide Accounting Budgeting, and Human Resources
  System Bureau Chief **Matthew Pugh** . . . . . . . . . . . . . .(406) 444-3582

## State Human Resources Division
P.O. Box 200127, Helena, MT 59620-0127

**Employees:** 18  **Fiscal Year:** 2014  **Budget:** $1,501,000

Administrator **Anjenette Schafer** . . . . . . . . . . . . . . . . . . . .(406) 444-3885
Deputy Administrator **Dean Mack** . . . . . . . . . . . . . . . . . . .(406) 444-3894

## State Information Technology Services Division
P.O. Box 200113, Helena, MT 59620-0113
Tel: (406) 444-2700  Fax: (406) 444-2701

**Employees:** 7  **Fiscal Year:** 2014  **Budget:** $829,000

Chief Information Officer **Ron Baldwin** . . . . . . . . . . . . . . .(406) 444-2700
  E-mail: rbaldwin@mt.gov
Deputy Chief Information Officer and Chief Information
  Security Officer **Lynne Pizzini** . . . . . . . . . . . . . . . . . . .(406) 444-9127
  E-mail: lpizzini@mt.gov
Application Technology Services Bureau Chief
  **Audrey Hinman** . . . . . . . . . . . . . . . . . . . . . . . . . . . . . .(406) 444-1635
  E-mail: ahinman@mt.gov
Enterprise Services Bureau Chief **Irv Vavruska** . . . . . . . . . .(406) 444-6870
Enterprise Technology Systems Bureau Chief
  **Jerry Marks** . . . . . . . . . . . . . . . . . . . . . . . . . . . . . . . . .(406) 444-2576
  E-mail: jmarks@mt.gov
Financial Management Services Bureau Chief
  **Jenifer Alger** . . . . . . . . . . . . . . . . . . . . . . . . . . . . . . . .(406) 444-9841
Information Technology Services Bureau Chief
  **Dave Carlson** . . . . . . . . . . . . . . . . . . . . . . . . . . . . . . . .(406) 444-5763
  E-mail: davecarlson@mt.gov
Network Technology Services Bureau Chief
  **Kris Harrison** . . . . . . . . . . . . . . . . . . . . . . . . . . . . . . . .(406) 444-3344
Public Safety Services Bureau Chief **Quinn Ness** . . . . . . . .(406) 444-6134
  E-mail: qness@mt.gov

## Risk Management and Tort Defense Division
P.O. Box 200124, Helena, MT 59620-0124
Fax: (406) 444-2592

Administrator **Brett Dahl** . . . . . . . . . . . . . . . . . . . . . . . . . . .(406) 444-3687
Chief Defense Counsel **Bill Gianoulias** . . . . . . . . . . . . . . . .(406) 444-2438

## Montana Lottery
2525 North Montana Avenue, Helena, MT 59601-0598
Fax: (406) 444-5830  Internet: www.montanalottery.com

**Employees:** 32  **Fiscal Year:** 2014  **Budget:** $4,971,000

■Director **Angela Wong** . . . . . . . . . . . . . . . . . . . . . . . . . . . .(406) 444-5825
  E-mail: awong@mt.gov
Finance Director **Armond Sergeant** . . . . . . . . . . . . . . . . . .(406) 444-5813
Information Technology Services Director
  **Phil Charpentier** . . . . . . . . . . . . . . . . . . . . . . . . . . . . .(406) 444-5810
  E-mail: pcharpentier@mt.gov
Marketing and Sales Director **Jo Berg** . . . . . . . . . . . . . . . .(406) 444-5836
Security Director **John Tarr** . . . . . . . . . . . . . . . . . . . . . . . .(406) 444-5804
On-line Products/Creative Services Manager
  **Anne Charpentier** . . . . . . . . . . . . . . . . . . . . . . . . . . . .(406) 444-7090
  E-mail: acharpentier@mt.gov
Sales Manager **Marlene Teel** . . . . . . . . . . . . . . . . . . . . . . .(406) 444-5827
Instant Product Manager **Jay Boughn** . . . . . . . . . . . . . . . .(406) 444-5805
Administrative Supervisor **Denise Blankenship** . . . . . . . . . .(406) 444-5801
  E-mail: dblankenship@mt.gov

# Montana Department of Agriculture
P.O. Box 200201, Helena, MT 59620-0201
Tel: (406) 444-3144  Fax: (406) 444-5409  E-mail: agr@mt.gov
Internet: www.agr.mt.gov

**Employees:** 124  **Fiscal Year:** 2014  **Budget:** $35,396,000

■Director **Ron de Yong** . . . . . . . . . . . . . . . . . . . . . . . . . . . .(406) 444-3156
  E-mail: rdeyong@mt.gov
  Education: Montana State; Montana
  Executive Secretary **Sherry Rust** . . . . . . . . . . . . . . . . . .(406) 444-3156
Central Management Division Administrator
  **Libbi Lovshin** . . . . . . . . . . . . . . . . . . . . . . . . . . . . . . . .(406) 444-5408
Attorney **Cort Jensen** . . . . . . . . . . . . . . . . . . . . . . . . . . . .(406) 444-5402
Public Information Officer **Jayson O'Neill** . . . . . . . . . . . . . .(406) 444-3684
  E-mail: jaysononeill@mt.gov

## Agricultural Development Division
Administrator **Kimberly "Kim" Falcon** . . . . . . . . . . . . . . . .(406) 444-5406
Agricultural Marketing and Business Development
  Bureau Chief **Christy Clark** . . . . . . . . . . . . . . . . . . . . . .(406) 444-3571
State Grain Laboratory Bureau Chief **(Vacant)** . . . . . . . . . .(406) 444-9561
  P.O. Box 1397, Great Falls, MT 59403

## Agricultural Sciences Division
Administrator **Gregory H. Ames** . . . . . . . . . . . . . . . . . . . . .(406) 444-2945
  Education: Montana State 1978 BS; Montana 1990 MPA
Agricultural Services Bureau Chief **Donna Rise** . . . . . . . . . .(406) 444-9461
  Education: Montana State 1990 BS
Commodity Services Bureau Chief **Andy Gray** . . . . . . . . . .(406) 444-0512
Laboratory Bureau Chief **Heidi Hickes** . . . . . . . . . . . . . . . .(406) 994-3383
  McCall Hall, Montana State University, Bozeman, MT 59715
  Education: Montana State 1975 BS

# Department of Commerce
301 South Park Avenue, Helena, MT 59620-0513
P.O. Box 200501, Helena, MT 59620-0501
Tel: (406) 841-2700  TTY: (406) 841-2702  Fax: (406) 841-2701
Internet: www.commerce.mt.gov

■Director **Meg O'Leary** . . . . . . . . . . . . . . . . . . . . . . . . . . . .(406) 841-2700
  Education: Montana 1987 BABA
Deputy Director **Doug Mitchell** . . . . . . . . . . . . . . . . . . . . .(406) 841-2772
  Education: Stanford BEc
Chief Legal Counsel **G. Martin "Marty" Tuttle** . . . . . . . . . .(406) 841-2706
Facility Finance Authority Director **Michelle Barstad** . . . .(406) 444-0259
  2401 Colonial Drive, 3rd Floor, Helena, MT 59601-4980
  P.O. Box 200506, Helena, MT 59620-0506
Investments Board Executive Director **David Ewer** . . . . . . .(406) 444-1285
  2401 Colonial Drive, Helena, MT 59601-4980
  P.O. Box 200126, Helena, MT 59620-0126
  Education: Northeastern BA; JFK School Govt MCR
Census and Economic Information Center Administrative
  Officer **Mary Craigle** . . . . . . . . . . . . . . . . . . . . . . . . . . .(406) 841-2739
                                   Fax: (406) 841-2741
Webmaster **Larry Krause** . . . . . . . . . . . . . . . . . . . . . . . . . .(406) 841-2705

---

★ Elected Official    ■ Appointed by Governor    ● Appointed by Legislature    ▲ Appointed by Board or Commission    ◆ Appointed by State Supreme Court

# Montana Department of Corrections

5 South Last Chance Gulch, Helena, MT 59601
P.O. Box 201301, Helena, MT 59620-1301
Tel: (406) 444-3930  Fax: (406) 444-4920  Internet: www.cor.mt.gov

**Employees:** 1,310  **Fiscal Year:** 2014  **Budget:** $189,306,000

■Director **Mike Batista**..............................(406) 444-3930
   E-mail: mbatista@mt.gov
   Education: Eastern Washington 1982 BA
Deputy Director **Loraine Wodnik** ....................(406) 444-3930
   E-mail: lwodnik@mt.gov
   Education: Cal State (Dominguez) 1992 BBA; Montana 2007 MSPA
Executive Assistant **Sandy Jacke** .....................(406) 444-3911
Administrative Assistant **Travers Cox** .................(406) 444-3930
   E-mail: tcox2@mt.gov
Chief General Counsel **Colleen Ambrose** .............(406) 444-4152
Business Management Services Division Administrator
   **Pat Schlauch**......................................(406) 444-4939
   E-mail: pschlauch@mt.gov
Information Technology Division Administrator
   **John Daugherty** ..................................(406) 444-4469
   E-mail: jdaugherty@mt.gov
Probation and Parole Division Administrator
   **Kevin Olson**......................................(406) 444-9610
Youth Services Division Administrator **Cindy McKenzie** ..(406) 444-0851
   Applications Development Bureau Chief **Jason Nelson** ..(406) 444-0402
   E-mail: janelson@mt.gov
   Operations Bureau Chief **Jon Straughn** .............(406) 444-1706
   E-mail: jstraughn@mt.gov
   Statistics and Data Quality Bureau Chief
   **Mark Johnson** ...................................(406) 444-6719
   E-mail: mikjohnson@mt.gov
Montana Correctional Enterprises Administrator
   **Gayle Lambert**...........................(406) 846-1320 ext. 2373
Montana Women's Prison Warden **Joan Daly**...........(406) 247-5112
State Prison Warden **Leroy Kirkegard** .........(406) 846-1320 ext. 2200
Webmaster **Sarah Lyytinen** .........................(406) 444-4235

# Department of Environmental Quality [DEQ]

1520 East Sixth Avenue, Helena, MT 59601
P.O. Box 200901, Helena, MT 59620-0901
Tel: (406) 444-2544  TTY: (406) 444-9526  Fax: (406) 444-4386
Internet: www.deq.mt.gov

**Employees:** 385  **Fiscal Year:** 2014  **Budget:** $57,723,000

■Director **Tom Livers** ...............................(406) 444-2544
   E-mail: tlivers@mt.gov
Deputy Director **George Mathieus** ...................(406) 444-7432
Chief Legal Counsel **John North** ....................(406) 444-2018
Records and Information Manager **Joyce Wittenberg**.....(406) 444-6701
Human Resources Manager **Peggy MacEwen** ...........(406) 444-6717
Communications Director **Kristi Ponozzo**..............(406) 444-2667
   E-mail: kponozzo@mt.gov
Regulatory Affairs Coordinator **Bonnie Lovelace** ........(406) 444-1760

# Fish, Wildlife and Parks Department [FWP]

1420 East Sixth Avenue, Helena, MT 59620
P.O. Box 200701, Helena, MT 59620-0701
Tel: (406) 444-2535  TTY: (406) 444-1200  Fax: (406) 444-4952

**Employees:** 705  **Fiscal Year:** 2015  **Budget:** $156,624,000

■Director **M. Jeff Hagener** ..........................(406) 444-3186
   E-mail: jhagener@mt.gov
   Education: Montana 1976 BS, 1981 BS
Legal Counsel **Rebecca Dockter**.....................(406) 444-4047
   E-mail: rjakesdockter@mt.gov
Chief of Law Enforcement **Tom Flowers** ..............(406) 444-5657
   E-mail: tflowers@mt.gov
Chief of Operations **Mike Volesky** ...................(406) 444-4600
   E-mail: mvolesky@mt.gov

Communications and Education Division Administrator
   **Ron Aasheim**.....................................(406) 444-4038
   E-mail: raasheim@mt.gov
   Education: Montana State 1971 BSc, 1973 MS
Finance Division Administrator and Administrative
   Services Chief **Sue Daly** ...........................(406) 444-3751
   E-mail: sdaly@mt.gov
Fisheries Division Administrator **Bruce A. Rich** .........(406) 444-3183
   E-mail: brich@mt.gov
Parks Division Administrator **Chas Van Genderen** .......(406) 444-3750
   E-mail: cvangenderen@mt.gov
Wildlife Division Administrator **Ken McDonald** .........(406) 234-0900
   E-mail: Kmcdonald@mt.gov
Operations Chief **Paul Sihler** ........................(406) 444-3196
   E-mail: psihler@mt.gov
Human Resources **Kimberly Worthy**.................(406) 444-1298

# Department of Labor and Industry

P.O. Box 1728, Helena, MT 59624-1728
Tel: (406) 444-2840  TTY: (406) 444-0532  Fax: (406) 444-1419
Internet: www.dli.mt.gov

**Employees:** 752  **Fiscal Year:** 2015  **Budget:** $163,206,000

Commissioner **Pamela "Pam" Bucy**..................(406) 444-3299
   Education: Rocky Mt Col (MT) 1991 BA; Montana 1998 JD
Deputy Commissioner **(Vacant)** ......................(406) 444-1785
Communications Director **Jake Troyer** ................(406) 444-1674
Information Technology Director **George Parisot** ........(406) 444-4658
   E-mail: gparisot@mt.gov

# Department of Livestock

P.O. Box 202001, Helena, MT 59620
Fax: (406) 444-4316

**Employees:** 134  **Fiscal Year:** 2015  **Budget:** $21,677,000

▲Executive Officer to the Board of Livestock
   **Mike Honeycutt** ..................................(406) 444-9321
   E-mail: mhoneycutt@mt.gov
State Veterinarian/Animal Health Division Administrator
   **Martin Zuluski**...................................(406) 444-2043
Brands Enforcement Division Administrator **Leslie Doely** .........(406) 444-2045
   E-mail: ldoely@mt.gov       Fax: (406) 444-2877
Centralized Services Division Administrator
   **George H. Harris** .................................(406) 444-4994
Diagnostic Laboratory Division Administrator
   **Bill Layton**......................................(406) 994-4885
   P.O. Box 997, Bozeman, MT 59771   Fax: (406) 994-6344
Meat Inspection Bureau Chief **Gary Hamel** ............(406) 444-5293
                   Fax: (406) 444-1929
Milk and Egg Bureau Chief **Dan Turcotte** .............(406) 444-9761
Milk Control Bureau Chief **Chad Lee**..................(406) 444-4300
                    Fax: (406) 444-1432
Livestock Loss Board Executive Secretary
   **George Edwards**..................................(406) 855-6358
Human Resources Officer **Sheila Martin** ..............(406) 444-5684

# Department of Military Affairs

P.O. Box 4789, Fort Harrison, MT 59636-4789
1956 Mt. Majo Street, Fort Harrison, MT 59636
Tel: (406) 324-3010  Fax: (406) 324-4800
Internet: http://montanadma.org/

**Employees:** 199  **Fiscal Year:** 2015  **Budget:** $88,576,000

■Adjutant General
   **MG Matthew T. "Matt" Quinn, ARNG** ..............(406) 324-3010
   E-mail: matthew.quinn@us.army.mil
   Education: Montana State 1983 BSEE; Montana 2000 MSBA;
   Army War Col 2008 MSS
Joint Staff Chief **BG Jeff Ireland, ARNG** ..............(406) 324-3003
Joint Staff Vice Chief **Col J. Peter Hronek, ANG**........(406) 324-3015
   Education: North Dakota 1982 BS
Disaster and Emergency Services Division Administrator
   **Delila Bruno**.....................................(406) 324-4777

*(continued on next page)*

---

★ Elected Official   ■ Appointed by Governor   ● Appointed by Legislature   ▲ Appointed by Board or Commission   ◆ Appointed by State Supreme Court

**Department of Military Affairs** *continued*

Veterans Affairs Division Administrator
**Joseph S. Foster**.................................(406) 324-3741
Environmental Program Manager **John Wheeler**.........(406) 324-3080
  E-mail: jwheeler@precc.com
Military Support to Civilian Authority (**Vacant**).........(406) 324-3166
Public Affairs Officer **MAJ (P) Chris Lende**............(406) 324-3009

## Montana National Guard
Tel: (406) 324-3000

■Adjutant General
  **MG Matthew T. "Matt" Quinn, ARNG**..............(406) 324-3010
  E-mail: matthew.quinn@us.army.mil

## Montana Air National Guard
P.O. Box 4789, Fort Harrison, MT 59636-4789
1956 Mt. Majo Street, Fort Harrison, MT 59636
Tel: (406) 324-3018

Assistant Adjutant General **BrigGen Bryan Fox, ANG** ....(406) 324-3010
Chief of Staff (**Vacant**)............................(406) 324-3015

## Montana Army National Guard
P.O. Box 4789, Fort Harrison, MT 59636-4789
1956 Mt. Majo Street, Fort Harrison, MT 59636
Tel: (406) 324-3000

Land Component Commander
  **BG Robert A. "Bob" Sparing, ARNG**..............(406) 324-3010
Information Technology Director **Corey Halvorson**.......(406) 324-3000
  E-mail: corey.halvorson@ang.af.mil

## Department of Natural Resources and Conservation [DNRC]
1625 11th Avenue, Helena, MT 59620
P.O. Box 201601, Helena, MT 59620-1601
Tel: (406) 444-2074  TTY: (406) 444-2074  Fax: (406) 444-2684

**Employees:** 543  **Fiscal Year:** 2014  **Budget:** $891,375,000

■Director **John E. Tubbs**............................(406) 444-2074
  Education: Montana BS, MEcon
Deputy Director **Ray Beck**..........................(406) 444-6671
  E-mail: rbeck@mt.gov
Chief of Staff **Kerry Davant**.......................(406) 444-4942
Chief Legal Counsel **Danna Jackson**.................(406) 444-0503
Chief Information Officer **Kreh Germaine**.............(406) 444-0575
  E-mail: kgermaine@mt.gov
Chief Financial Officer **Patricia "Tricia" Greiberis**.......(406) 444-6734
Conservation and Resource Development Division
  Administrator **Mark Bostrom**......................(406) 444-9708
Forestry Division Administrator/State Forester
  **Robert "Bob" Harrington**.........................(406) 542-4301
  2705 Spurgin Road, Missoula, MT 59804    Fax: (406) 542-4217
Oil and Gas Conservation Board Administrator
  **Jim Halvorson**...................................(406) 656-0040
  E-mail: jhalvorson@mt.gov             Fax: (406) 655-6015
Trust Lands Management Division Administrator
  **Shawn Thomas**....................................(406) 444-4978
  E-mail: sthomas@mt.gov
Water Resource Division Administrator **Tim Davis**.......(406) 444-6605
  1424 Ninth Avenue, Helena, MT 59620    Fax: (406) 444-0533
  E-mail: tdavis@mt.gov
Reserved Water Rights Compact Commission Program
  Manager **Arne Wick**...............................(406) 444-5700

## Department of Public Health and Human Services [DPHHS]
P.O. Box 4210, Helena, MT 59620-4210
111 North Sanders, Room 301, Helena, MT 59601-4520
Tel: (406) 444-5622  Tel: (406) 444-4228 (Vital Records)
TTY: (406) 444-2590  Fax: (406) 444-1970
Fax: (406) 444-1803 (Vital Records)  Internet: www.dphhs.mt.gov

**Employees:** 2,953

■Director **Richard Opper**............................(406) 444-5622
  E-mail: ropper@mt.gov
  Education: Oklahoma State BS; Montana State 1979 MS
  Executive Assistant **Sheila Lopach**.................(406) 444-5623
    E-mail: slopach@mt.gov
Chief Legal Counsel **Frank Clinch**..................(406) 444-0207
Public Information Officer **Jon Ebelt**................(406) 444-0936
  E-mail: jebelt@mt.gov
Human Resources Director **Debra Sloat**...............(406) 444-3426
                                        Fax: (406) 444-0262
Supplemental Nutrition Assistance Program Manager
  **Melinda Cummings**................................(406) 444-5685
Women, Infants and Children (WIC) Director
  **Kate Girard**.....................................(406) 444-4747
  E-mail: kgirard@mt.gov                Fax: (406) 444-0239
Vital Records State Registrar **Karin Ferlicka**.........(406) 444-4250
  111 North Sanders, Room 6, Helena, MT 59604
Immunization Section Supervisor **Bekki Wehner**.........(406) 444-0065
                                        Fax: (406) 444-2920

## Operations Services Branch
Operations Services Manager **Marie Matthews**..........(406) 444-2754
Business and Financial Services Division Administrator
  **Becky Schlauch**..................................(406) 444-9407
                                        Fax: (406) 444-9763
Quality Assurance Division Administrator **Roy Kemp**.....(406) 444-5401
                                        Fax: (406) 444-3980
Technology Services Division Administrator
  **Stuart Fuller**...................................(406) 444-1232
  E-mail: sfuller@mt.gov
Chief Information Officer **Stuart Fuller**..............(406) 444-0928
  E-mail: sfuller@mt.gov

## Medicaid and Health Services Branch
Medicaid and Health Services Manager **Mary Dalton**.....(406) 444-4084
  Education: Montana State 1979 BS; Montana 1994 MA
Addictive and Mental Disorders Division Administrator
  **Glenda Oldenberg**................................(406) 444-3969
                                        Fax: (406) 444-4435
Health Resources Division Administrator
  **Duane Preshinger**................................(406) 444-4458
                                        Fax: (406) 444-1861
Senior and Long Term Care Division Administrator
  **Kelly Williams**..................................(406) 444-4174
  Education: Eastern Montana 1983 BS      Fax: (406) 444-7743
Aging Services Bureau Chief **Charles Rehbein**.........(406) 444-7788
                                        Fax: (406) 444-7743

## Economic Security Services Branch
Economic Security Services Manager
  **Robert "Bob" Runkel**.............................(406) 444-3470
Child and Family Services Division Administrator
  **Sarah Corbally**..................................(406) 841-2406
  E-mail: scorbally@mt.gov              Fax: (406) 841-2487
Child Support Enforcement Division Administrator
  **Chad Dexter**.....................................(406) 444-3338
  E-mail: cdexter@mt.gov                Fax: (406) 444-1370
Developmental Services Division Administrator
  **Jim Marks**.......................................(406) 444-9055
                                        Fax: (406) 444-0230
Human and Community Services Division Administrator
  **Jamie Palagi**....................................(406) 444-4154
                                        Fax: (406) 444-2547
Disability Transitions Programs Administrator
  **Jim Marks**.......................................(406) 444-2591
                                        Fax: (406) 444-3632

---

★ Elected Official   ■ Appointed by Governor   ● Appointed by Legislature   ▲ Appointed by Board or Commission   ◆ Appointed by State Supreme Court

## Public Health and Safety Division

Public Health and Safety Division Administrator
**Todd Harwell** . . . . . . . . . . . . . . . . . . . . . . . . . . . . . . . . . (406) 444-4141
Fax: (406) 444-6943

State Medical Officer
**Dr. Gregory S. Holzman, MD, MPH** . . . . . . . . . . . . . . . (406) 444-1286
Education: Michigan State 1988 BS; Florida Col 1995 MD;
Washington U (MO) 2002 MPH

## Quality Assurance Division

Program Compliance Bureau Chief **Michelle Truax** . . . . . . . (406) 444-4120
Quality Assurance Payment Error Rate Measurement
Supervisor **Jody Dalbec** . . . . . . . . . . . . . . . . . . . . . . . . . (406) 444-9365
Quality Control Supervisor **Steve Kranich** . . . . . . . . . . . . . (406) 444-9356
Surveillance and Utilization Review Supervisor
**Jennifer Tucker** . . . . . . . . . . . . . . . . . . . . . . . . . . . . . . . (406) 444-4586
Third Party Liability Supervisor **Olivia Roussan** . . . . . . . . (406) 444-6004
Recovery Audit Coordinator **Mike Murry** . . . . . . . . . . . . . (406) 444-4168

## Department of Revenue

Sam W. Mitchell Building, 125 North Roberts, Helena, MT 59604
P.O. Box 5805, Helena, MT 59604-5805
Tel: (406) 444-6900  TTY: (406) 444-2830  Fax: (406) 444-3696

**Employees: 679  Fiscal Year: 2015  Budget: $103,788,000**

■Director **Mike Kadas** . . . . . . . . . . . . . . . . . . . . . . . . . . . . (406) 444-1900
E-mail: mkadas@mt.gov
Education: Montana BA, MA
Deputy Director **Gene Walborn** . . . . . . . . . . . . . . . . . . . . (406) 444-0908
Taxpayer Assistance and Public Outreach Director
**Kristan Barbour** . . . . . . . . . . . . . . . . . . . . . . . . . . . . . . (406) 444-5845
E-mail: kbarbour@mt.gov
Tax Policy and Research Director **Ed Caplis** . . . . . . . . . . . . (406) 444-3531
Business and Income Taxes Administrator
**Lee Baerlocher** . . . . . . . . . . . . . . . . . . . . . . . . . . . . . . . (406) 444-3717
E-mail: lbaerlocher@mt.gov
Fiscal Administrator **Cindy Trimp** . . . . . . . . . . . . . . . . . . . (406) 444-6739
Human Resource Administrator **Charles Geary** . . . . . . . . . (406) 444-3965
Chief Information Officer **Tim Bottenfield** . . . . . . . . . . . . . (406) 444-9535
E-mail: tbottenfield@mt.gov
Liquor Control Administrator **Shauna Helfert** . . . . . . . . . . (406) 444-1464
Citizen Services and Resource Management Division
Administrator **Steve Austin** . . . . . . . . . . . . . . . . . . . . . . (406) 444-1479
Public Information Officer **Mary Ann Dunwell** . . . . . . . . . (406) 444-6700
E-mail: mdunwell@mt.gov

## Legal Services Office

Sam W. Mitchell Building, 125 North Roberts, Helena, MT 59604
P.O. Box 7701, Helena, MT 59604-7701

Chief Legal Counsel **Dan Whyte** . . . . . . . . . . . . . . . . . . . . (406) 444-3340
Chief Security Officer **Margaret Kauska** . . . . . . . . . . . . . . (406) 444-9535
Dispute Resolution Officer **Laura Cunningham** . . . . . . . . . (406) 444-3131
Dispute Resolution Officer **Joanna Wilson** . . . . . . . . . . . . (406) 444-3131

## Montana Department of Transportation [MDT]

2701 Prospect Avenue, Helena, MT 59620
P.O. Box 201001, Helena, MT 59620-1001
Tel: (406) 444-6200  TTY: (406) 444-7696  Fax: (406) 444-7643
E-mail: mdtwebadmin@mt.gov  Internet: www.mdt.mt.gov

**Employees: 2,129  Fiscal Year: 2015  Budget: $1,359,327,000**

■Director **Michael T. Tooley** . . . . . . . . . . . . . . . . . . . . . . . (406) 444-6201
E-mail: mitooley@mt.gov
Education: Grand Canyon 2007 BS
Deputy Director **Pat Wise** . . . . . . . . . . . . . . . . . . . . . . . . . (406) 444-7222
Education: Montana State 1979 BA
Human Resource Administrator **Keni Grose** . . . . . . . . . . . . (406) 444-6044
Administration Division Administrator **Larry Flynn** . . . . . . . (406) 444-9418
E-mail: lflynn@mt.gov
Aeronautics Division Administrator **Debbie Alke** . . . . . . . . . (406) 444-2506
Engineering Division Administrator **Dwane Kailey** . . . . . . . (406) 444-6414
E-mail: dkailey@mt.gov

Information Services Division Administrator
**Mike Bousliman** . . . . . . . . . . . . . . . . . . . . . . . . . . . . . . . (406) 444-7638
Maintenance Division Administrator **Jon Swartz** . . . . . . . . (406) 444-6158
Motor Carrier Services Division Administrator
**Duane Williams** . . . . . . . . . . . . . . . . . . . . . . . . . . . . . . . (406) 444-7312
Rail, Transit and Planning Administrator **Lynn Zanto** . . . . . (406) 444-3445
E-mail: lzanto@mt.gov
Legal Services Chief Counsel **(Vacant)** . . . . . . . . . . . . . . . . (406) 444-6302
Public Information Officer **Lori Ryan** . . . . . . . . . . . . . . . . . (406) 444-6821
E-mail: lryan@mt.gov

## Commissioner of Political Practices

1209 Eighth Avenue, Helena, MT 59620
P.O. Box 202401, Helena, MT 59620-2401
Tel: (406) 444-2942  Fax: (406) 444-1643
Internet: www.politicalpractices.mt.gov

■Commissioner **Jonathan Motl** . . . . . . . . . . . . . . . . . . . . . . (406) 444-2942
E-mail: jmotl@mt.gov
Program Supervisor **Mary Baker** . . . . . . . . . . . . . . . . . . . . (406) 444-2942
E-mail: mabaker@mt.gov

## Montana Public Service Commission [PSC]

P.O. Box 202601, Helena, MT 59620-2601
Tel: (406) 444-6199  TTY: (406) 444-4212
Tel: (800) 646-6150 (Utility Consumer Complaints)  Fax: (406) 444-7618
Internet: http://psc.mt.gov

★Chairman **Brad Johnson** (R-District 5) . . . . . . . . . . . . . . . (406) 444-6169
Term Expires: January 2019
Education: Illinois 1976 MS
★Vice Chairman **Travis Kavulla** (R-District 1) . . . . . . . . . . . (406) 444-6166
Term Expires: January 2019
E-mail: tkavulla@mt.gov
★Commissioner **Kirk Bushman** (R-District 2) . . . . . . . . . . . (406) 444-6165
Term Expires: January 2017
Education: Montana State BS
★Commissioner **Roger Koopman** (R-District 3) . . . . . . . . . . (406) 444-6168
Term Expires: January 2017
Education: Idaho BGS
★Commissioner **Bob Lake** (R-District 4) . . . . . . . . . . . . . . . (406) 444-6167
Term Expires: January 2017
Commission Secretary **Aleisha Solem** . . . . . . . . . . . . . . . . (406) 444-6175

## Board of Public Education

P.O. Box 200601 North 46 Last Chance Gulch, Helena, MT 59620
Tel: (406) 444-6576  Fax: (406) 444-0847  Internet: www.bpe.mt.gov

**Employees: 3  Fiscal Year: 2014  Budget: $377,000**

■Chair **Sharon Carroll** . . . . . . . . . . . . . . . . . . . . . . . . . . . . (406) 444-6576
Term Expires: February 1, 2019
E-mail: sharoncarrollbpe@gmail.com
■Vice Chairperson **Paul Andersen** . . . . . . . . . . . . . . . . . . . (406) 444-6576
Term Expires: February 1, 2020
E-mail: paul@bozemanscience.com
■Board Member **Jesse Barnhart** . . . . . . . . . . . . . . . . . . . . . (406) 444-6576
Term Expires: February 1, 2018
■Board Member **Mary Jo Bremner** . . . . . . . . . . . . . . . . . . . (406) 844-3282
Term Expires: February 1, 2021
■Board Member **Tammy Lacey** . . . . . . . . . . . . . . . . . . . . . . (406) 444-6576
Term Expires: February 1, 2023
E-mail: tammy_lacey@gfps.k12.mt.us
■Board Member **Darlene Schottle** . . . . . . . . . . . . . . . . . . . (406) 444-6576
Term Expires: February 1, 2022
■Board Member **Erin Williams** . . . . . . . . . . . . . . . . . . . . . . (406) 444-6576
Term Expires: February 1, 2017
E-mail: ewilliams@youthhomes.com
Education: Montana BA, MA
Student Representative Board Member **Molly Demarco** . . . (406) 444-6576
Term Expires: June 1, 2017
Executive Director **Pete Donovan** . . . . . . . . . . . . . . . . . . . (406) 444-0300
E-mail: pdonovan@mt.gov

---

★ Elected Official   ■ Appointed by Governor   ● Appointed by Legislature       ▲ Appointed by Board or Commission       ◆ Appointed by State Supreme Court

**EXECUTIVE BRANCH**

# State Library

1515 East Sixth Avenue, Helena, MT 59620
P.O. Box 201800, Helena, MT 59620-1800
Tel: (406) 444-3115  TTY: (406) 444-4799  Fax: (406) 444-0266
E-mail: msl@mt.gov  Internet: http://msl.mt.gov

▲ State Librarian **Jennie Stapp** . . . . . . . . . . . . . . . . . . . . . (406) 444-3116
  E-mail: jstapp2@mt.gov
Montana Talking Book Library Department Supervisor
  **Christie Briggs** . . . . . . . . . . . . . . . . . . . . . . . . . . . . . (406) 444-5399
Central Services Manager **Kris Schmitz** . . . . . . . . . . . . . . (406) 444-3117
  Education: Carroll Col (MT) 1985 BA
Digital Information Manager and Chief Information
  Officer **Evan Hammer** . . . . . . . . . . . . . . . . . . . . . . . . . (406) 444-5355
  E-mail: ehammer3@mt.gov
Communications and Marketing Coordinator
  **Sara Groves** . . . . . . . . . . . . . . . . . . . . . . . . . . . . . . . (406) 444-5357
  E-mail: sgroves@mt.gov
Continuing Education Coordinator **Jo Flick** . . . . . . . . . . . . (406) 431-1081
Webmaster **Tom Marino** . . . . . . . . . . . . . . . . . . . . . . . . . (406) 444-0243
  E-mail: tmarino@mt.gov
Statewide Library Resources Director **Sarah McHugh** . . . . (406) 444-9816

# Office of the Lieutenant Governor

Montana State Capitol Building, Room 207, Helena, MT 59620
Tel: (406) 444-3111  Tel: (406) 444-4648

★ Lieutenant Governor **Michael R. "Mike" Cooney** (D) . . . . (406) 444-3111
  Term Expires: January 2017
  E-mail: mcooney@mt.gov

# Office of the Secretary of State

State Capitol, 1301 East Sixth Avenue, Room 260, Helena, MT 59620
P.O. Box 202801, Helena, MT 59620-2801
Tel: (406) 444-2034  TTY: (406) 444-9068  Fax: (406) 444-3976
E-mail: sos@mt.gov

★ Secretary of State **Linda McCulloch** (D) . . . . . . . . . . . . . . (406) 444-4195
  Term Expires: January 2017
  Education: Montana 1982 BS, 1990 MS
  Career: Western Region Vice President, Executive Committee, National
  Association of Secretaries of State (2012-2013); Secretary, National
  Association of Secretaries of State (2011-2012); State Superintendent,
  Office of Public Instruction, State of Montana (2001-2009)
  Executive Assistant **Sue Tinsley** . . . . . . . . . . . . . . . . . (406) 444-4195
Chief Deputy Secretary of State and Chief of Staff
  **Eric Stern** . . . . . . . . . . . . . . . . . . . . . . . . . . . . . . . . . (406) 444-5359
Deputy Chief of Staff **Jane Demaray** . . . . . . . . . . . . . . . . (406) 444-2034
  E-mail: jdemaray@mt.gov
Chief Legal Counsel **Jorge Quintana** . . . . . . . . . . . . . . . . (406) 444-5375
Administrative Rules and Notary Services Deputy
  **Laura Vachowski** . . . . . . . . . . . . . . . . . . . . . . . . . . . . (406) 444-5596
Business Services Division Deputy **Tana Gormely** . . . . . . . (406) 444-2896
Elections and Government Services Deputy **Lisa Kimmet** . . (406) 444-5376
Records Management Deputy **Joe Defilippis** . . . . . . . . . . . (406) 444-9009
Communications Director **Blair Fjeseth** . . . . . . . . . . . . . . (406) 444-2807
  E-mail: bfjeseth@mt.gov
  Education: Carroll Col (MT) 2010
Information Services Manager **Mark Van Alstyne** . . . . . . . . (406) 444-4243
  E-mail: mvanalstyne@mt.gov
Chief Fiscal Officer **Brandi Pierson** . . . . . . . . . . . . . . . . . (406) 444-3334

# Office of the Commissioner of Securities and Insurance

840 Helena Avenue, Helena, MT 59601
Tel: (406) 444-2040  TTY: (406) 444-3246  Fax: (406) 444-3497

**Employees:** 88  **Fiscal Year:** 2014-2015  **Budget:** $20,118,000

★ Commissioner **Monica J. Lindeen** (D) . . . . . . . . . . . . . . . (406) 444-2040
  Term Expires: January 2017
  Education: Montana State (Billings) 1992 BSEd
Deputy Commissioner **Andrew Posewitz** . . . . . . . . . . . . . (406) 444-2006
  Executive Assistant to the Commissioner **Jodi Medlar** . . . (406) 444-2006
Chief Legal Counsel **Jesse Laslovich** . . . . . . . . . . . . . . . . (406) 444-5789
General Counsel **Christina Goe** . . . . . . . . . . . . . . . . . . . . (406) 444-1942

Centralized Services Division Administrator
  **Staci Litschauer** . . . . . . . . . . . . . . . . . . . . . . . . . . . . (406) 444-2041

## Insurance Division

Insurance Deputy Commissioner **Greg Dahl** . . . . . . . . . . . (406) 444-5438
Insurance Compliance Bureau Chief
  **Barbara van der Mars** . . . . . . . . . . . . . . . . . . . . . . . . (406) 444-9768
Insurance Examination Bureau Chief **Steve Matthews** . . . (406) 444-4372
Insurance Services Bureau Chief **Jeannie Keller** . . . . . . . . (406) 444-3897
Forms Licensing Bureau Chief **Richard Hersey** . . . . . . . . . (406) 444-3443

## Securities Division

Fax: (406) 444-5558

Securities Deputy Commissioner **Lynne Egan** . . . . . . . . . . (406) 444-4388
Senior Securities Analyst and Examiner **Mark Murray** . . . . (406) 444-6784

# Department of Justice [DOJ]

Justice Building, 215 North Sanders, Helena, MT 59620
P.O. Box 201401, Helena, MT 59620-1401
Tel: (406) 444-2026  TTY: (406) 444-9448  Fax: (406) 444-3549
E-mail: contactdoj@mt.gov

**Employees:** 764  **Fiscal Year:** 2014  **Budget:** $85,623,000

★ Attorney General **Timothy C. "Tim" Fox** (R) . . . . . . . . . . (406) 444-2026
  Term Expires: January 2017
  Education: Montana 1981 BA, 1987 JD
  Career: Special Assistant Attorney General and Acting Division
  Administrator, Department of Environmental Quality, State of Montana
  (1996-1999); Vice President and General Counsel, Mountain West
  Bank (1999-2003); Vice Chairman, Montana Republican Party,
  Republican National Committee (2009); Partner, Gough, Shanahan,
  Johnson & Waterman, PLLP (2001-2012)
  Executive Assistant **Julie James** . . . . . . . . . . . . . . . . . (406) 444-2026
Chief of Staff **Mike Milburn** . . . . . . . . . . . . . . . . . . . . . . (406) 444-2026
Chief Deputy Attorney General **Alan Joscelyn** . . . . . . . . . (406) 444-2026
Deputy Attorney General **Jon Bennion** . . . . . . . . . . . . . . . (406) 444-2026
  E-mail: jonbennion@mt.gov
Deputy Attorney General **Tommy Butler** . . . . . . . . . . . . . . (406) 444-2026
  E-mail: tommybutler@mt.gov
Solicitor General **Dale Schowengerdt** . . . . . . . . . . . . . . . . (406) 444-2026
Communications Director **John Barnes** . . . . . . . . . . . . . . . (406) 444-2026
  E-mail: johnbarnes@mt.gov
  Communications Officer **Anastasia Burton** . . . . . . . . . . . (406) 444-2026
    E-mail: aburton@mt.gov
Central Services Division Administrator
  **Christi Jacobsen** . . . . . . . . . . . . . . . . . . . . . . . . . . . . (406) 444-5842
Forensic Science Division Administrator **Philip Kinsey** . . . . (406) 329-1179
  2679 Palmer Street, Missoula, MT 59808
Gambling Control Division Administrator **Rick Ask** . . . . . . (406) 444-9132
Highway Patrol Division Administrator **Col. Tom Butler** . . (406) 444-3956
  Education: Montana State
Information Technology Services Division Administrator
  and Chief Information Officer **Joe Chapman** . . . . . . . . . (406) 444-2424
  E-mail: jchapman@mt.gov

# Office of Public Instruction [OPI]

P.O. Box 202501, Helena, MT 59620-2501
Tel: (406) 444-3095  TTY: (406) 444-0169  Fax: (406) 444-2893
Internet: www.opi.mt.gov

**Employees:** 166  **Fiscal Year:** 2015  **Budget:** $1,806,137,000

★ State Superintendent **Denise Juneau** (D) . . . . . . . . . . . . . (406) 444-5658
  Term Expires: January 2017
  E-mail: opisupt@mt.gov
  Education: Montana State 1993 BA; Harvard 1994 MA;
  Montana 2004 JD
  Executive Assistant **Billie LeDeau** . . . . . . . . . . . . . . . . . (406) 444-5658
Deputy Superintendent **Dennis Parman** . . . . . . . . . . . . . . (406) 444-5643
Chief of Staff **Madalyn Quinlan** . . . . . . . . . . . . . . . . . . . (406) 444-3168
Chief Legal Counsel **Ann Gilkey** . . . . . . . . . . . . . . . . . . . (406) 444-4402
  E-mail: agilkey@mt.gov
Community Learning Partnerships Policy Advisor
  **Deb Halliday** . . . . . . . . . . . . . . . . . . . . . . . . . . . . . . . (406) 444-3559
Public Information Officer **Emilie Ritter Saunders** . . . . . . . (406) 444-3160

---

★ Elected Official    ■ Appointed by Governor    ● Appointed by Legislature    ▲ Appointed by Board or Commission    ◆ Appointed by State Supreme Court

State Assessment Director **Judy Snow** . . . . . . . . . . . . . . . . . (406) 444-3656
Administrative Assistant **Amy A. Kruse** . . . . . . . . . . . . . . . (406) 444-5643
  E-mail: akruse@mt.gov

★ Elected Official    ■ Appointed by Governor    ● Appointed by Legislature    ▲ Appointed by Board or Commission    ◆ Appointed by State Supreme Court

*State Yellow Book*       © Leadership Directories, Inc.       Summer 2016

EXECUTIVE BRANCH

# Nebraska

Tel: (402) 471-2311 (State Operator)

**Number of U.S. Congressional Delegates:** 2 Senators; 3 Representatives  **Governor's Term:** 4 years
**Legislature Description:** Unicameral - 49 member Senate; Term - Senate 4 years
**Next Election:** Governor November 2018; Legislature November 2018  **Number of Electoral Votes:** 5
**Official Name:** State of Nebraska (Omaha: flat river)  **Nickname:** The Cornhusker State
**Motto:** Equality Before the Law

**Population:** 1,896,190 (2015); Rank 37  **Fiscal Year:** 2013-2014  **Budget:** $8,471,904,000

## Office of the Governor

State Capitol, 1445 K Street, Suite 2316, Lincoln, NE 68509-4848
P.O. Box 94848, Lincoln, NE 68509-4848
Tel: (402) 471-2244  Fax: (402) 471-6031  Internet: governor.nebraska.gov

**John Peter "Pete" Ricketts**
Governor

Began Service: January 8, 2015
Term Expires: 2019
Date of Birth: August 19, 1964
Education: Chicago 1986 AB, 1991 MBA
Home: Omaha
Religion: Catholic
Career: Chief Operating Officer, Ameritrade
Holding Corporation (1993-2005); Vice
Chairman, Ameritrade Holding Corporation
(2005-2006); Republican Candidate for U.S.
Senate, Nebraska Families for Pete Ricketts,
Nebraska (2006); Director, Board of Directors,
TD Ameritrade Holding Corporation (2007-2014)

★Governor **John Peter "Pete" Ricketts** (R) . . . . . . . . . . . . . (402) 471-2244
  E-mail: pete.ricketts@nebraska.gov
Chief of Staff **Matt Miltenberger** . . . . . . . . . . . . . . . . . . (402) 471-2244
  E-mail: matt.miltenberger@nebraska.gov
  Education: Nebraska JD
Human Resources Director **Sharon Rues Pettid** . . . . . . . . (402) 471-2244
  E-mail: sharon.pettid@nebraska.gov
Public Relations Director **Taylor Gage** . . . . . . . . . . . . . . (402) 471-1970
  E-mail: taylor.gage@nebraska.gov
Special Advisor to the Governor for External Affairs
  **Jessica Flanagain** . . . . . . . . . . . . . . . . . . . . . . . . . . . (402) 471-2244
Central Nebraska Representative **Brittany Hardin** . . . . . . . (308) 660-9111
  E-mail: brittany.hardin@nebraska.gov
  Education: Nebraska BA, BA
Western Nebraska Representative **Starr Lehl** . . . . . . . . . . . (308) 631-7780
  E-mail: starr.lehl@nebraska.gov

## Policy Research Office

State Capitol, Room 1319, Lincoln, NE 68509
P.O. Box 94601, Lincoln, NE 68509-4601
Tel: (402) 471-2414  Fax: (402) 471-2528
Director and General Counsel **Lauren Kintner** . . . . . . . . . . (402) 471-2414
  E-mail: lauren.kintner@nebraska.gov
Policy Advisor **Lauren Anthone** . . . . . . . . . . . . . . . . . . . (402) 471-2853
  E-mail: lauren.anthone@nebraska.gov
Policy Advisor **Cheryl Wolff** . . . . . . . . . . . . . . . . . . . . . (402) 471-2575
  E-mail: cheryl.wolff@nebraska.gov
Policy Advisor **(Vacant)** . . . . . . . . . . . . . . . . . . . . . . . . (402) 471-2576

## Homeland Security

Fax: (402) 471-6031
Director **Mike Foley** . . . . . . . . . . . . . . . . . . . . . . . . . . . (402) 471-2256
  Education: SUNY (Brockport) 1976 BS; Michigan State 1978 MBA

## Nebraska Energy Office

521 South 14th Street, Suite 300, Lincoln, NE 68509
Tel: (402) 471-2867  Fax: (402) 471-3064  Internet: www.neo.ne.gov
■Director **David Bracht** . . . . . . . . . . . . . . . . . . . . . . . . . (402) 471-2867
  E-mail: david.bracht@nebraska.gov
Public and Legislative Liaison **Danielle Jensen** . . . . . . . . . (402) 471-3360
  E-mail: danielle.jensen@nebraska.gov

## Nebraska State Fire Marshal's Office

246 South 14th Street, Lincoln, NE 68508-1804
Tel: (402) 471-2027  Tel: (888) 992-7766 (Arson Hotline)
Fax: (402) 471-3118
■State Fire Marshal **Jim Heine** . . . . . . . . . . . . . . . . . . . . (402) 471-2027
  E-mail: jim.heine@nebraska.gov
Assistant Fire Marshal **Don Fritz** . . . . . . . . . . . . . . . . . . (402) 471-9478
  E-mail: don.fritz@nebraska.gov
District "A" Chief Deputy Fire Marshal **Bob Sleight** . . . . . (402) 471-2590
  E-mail: bob.sleight@nebraska.gov
District "B" Chief Deputy Fire Marshal **Sean Lindgren** . . . (402) 395-2164
  438 West Market, Albion, NE 68620
  E-mail: sean.lindgren@nebraska.gov
Legal Counsel **Regina Shields** . . . . . . . . . . . . . . . . . . . . (402) 471-9477
Chief Investigator **Adam Matzner** . . . . . . . . . . . . . . . . . . (402) 471-9596
  E-mail: adam.matzner@nebraska.gov
Business Manager **Deb Hostetler** . . . . . . . . . . . . . . . . . . (402) 471-9479
  E-mail: deb.hostetler@nebraska.gov
Fuels Division Chief **Clark Conklin** . . . . . . . . . . . . . . . . . (402) 471-9467
  E-mail: clark.conklin@nebraska.gov
Plans Division Manager **Doug Hohbein** . . . . . . . . . . . . . . (402) 471-9474
  E-mail: doug.hohbein@nebraska.gov
Training Division Manager **Alan Joos** . . . . . . . . . . . . . . . (308) 385-6893
  3347 West Capital Ave, Grand Island, NE 68803-1334
  E-mail: alan.joos@nebraska.gov

## Department of Administrative Services [DAS]

State Capitol, Suite 1315, Lincoln, NE 68509-4664
Tel: (402) 471-2331  Fax: (402) 471-4157  Internet: www.das.state.ne.us
■Director **Byron Diamond** . . . . . . . . . . . . . . . . . . . . . . . (402) 471-2331
  E-mail: byron.diamond@nebraska.gov
  Administrative Assistant **Sarah Gibson** . . . . . . . . . . . . . (402) 471-2331
Deputy Director **Bo Botelho** . . . . . . . . . . . . . . . . . . . . . (402) 471-0972
  E-mail: bo.botelho@nebraska.gov
Accounting Division Administrator **Jerry Broz** . . . . . . . . . (402) 471-0600
Budget Division Administrator **Gerry A. Oligmueller** . . . . (402) 471-2529
  E-mail: gerry.oligmueller@nebraska.gov
Building Division Administrator **Rodney Anderson** . . . . . . (402) 471-2662
Employee Relations Division Administrator
  **William J. "Bill" Wood** . . . . . . . . . . . . . . . . . . . . . . . (402) 471-4106
Efficiency, Quality and Performance Improvement
  Administrator **Amy Archuleta** . . . . . . . . . . . . . . . . . . . (402) 471-0618
Benefits Division Administrator **Josh Stafursky** . . . . . . . . (402) 471-2832
Human Resources Division Administrator **Kellie Graham** . . (402) 471-4605
Materiel Division Administrator **Marilyn Bottrell** . . . . . . . (402) 471-6500
  E-mail: marilyn.bottrell@nebraska.gov
Personnel Division Director **Ruth Jones** . . . . . . . . . . . . . (402) 471-4439

---

★ Elected Official  ■ Appointed by Governor  ● Appointed by Legislature  ▲ Appointed by Board or Commission  ◆ Appointed by State Supreme Court

Transportation Services Bureau Administrator
**Steve Sulek** . . . . . . . . . . . . . . . . . . . . . . . . . . . . . . (402) 471-4134

AS 309 Task Force for Building Renewal Administrator
(Interim) **Ron Rehtus** . . . . . . . . . . . . . . . . . . . . . . . . (402) 471-3515

Risk Management Division Administrator
**Shereece Dendy** . . . . . . . . . . . . . . . . . . . . . . . . . . . (402) 471-4436

Chief Information Officer **Ed Toner** . . . . . . . . . . . . . . . .(402) 471-3560
Education: Texas A&M BS

Chief Labor Negotiator **William J. "Bill" Wood** . . . . . . . . (402) 471-4106

General Counsel **Bo Botelho** . . . . . . . . . . . . . . . . . . . . . (402) 471-4114

Central Services Administrator **Roger Wilson** . . . . . . . . . . (402) 471-4459
E-mail: roger.wilson@nebraska.gov

## Department of Aeronautics

P.O. Box 82088, Lincoln, NE 68501-2088
Tel: (402) 471-2371  Fax: (402) 471-2906
Internet: www.aero.nebraska.gov

■Director **Ronnie Mitchell** . . . . . . . . . . . . . . . . . . . . . . . (402) 471-7922
E-mail: ronnie.mitchell@nebraska.gov
Education: Evansville; Troy U
Administrative Secretary **Jan Keller** . . . . . . . . . . . . . . . . (402) 471-2371

Deputy Director **Andre Aman** . . . . . . . . . . . . . . . . . . . . . (402) 471-7938
Education: Chicago 1980 BA; Nebraska 1985 JD

Flight Operations and Aviation Services Division
Manager **David Morris** . . . . . . . . . . . . . . . . . . . . . . . . (402) 471-7932

Navigational Aids (NAVAIDS) Division Manager
**Marcy Meyer** . . . . . . . . . . . . . . . . . . . . . . . . . . . . . . .(308) 865-5696
5065 Airport Road, Kearney, NE 68847-3758

Planning and Programming Division Manager
**Anna Lannin** . . . . . . . . . . . . . . . . . . . . . . . . . . . . . . . (402) 471-7931

Project Management Division Manager **Russ Gasper** . . . . . (402) 471-7700

## Nebraska Department of Agriculture [NDA]

301 Centennial Mall South, Lincoln, NE 68508-4912
P.O. Box 94947, Lincoln, NE 68509-4947
Tel: (402) 471-2341  Tel: (800) 831-0550  Fax: (402) 471-6876
E-mail: agr.webmaster@nebraska.gov

■Director **Gregory A. "Greg" Ibach** . . . . . . . . . . . . . . . .(402) 471-2341
E-mail: greg.ibach@nebraska.gov
Education: Nebraska 1984 BS

Assistant Director **Mat Habrock** . . . . . . . . . . . . . . . . . . (402) 471-2341

Legal Counsel **Chris Shubert** . . . . . . . . . . . . . . . . . . . . . (402) 471-2341

State Veterinarian **Dennis Hughes, DVM** . . . . . . . . . . . . . (402) 471-2351
Fax: (402) 471-6893

Chief Administrator **Thomas L. Jensen** . . . . . . . . . . . . . . (402) 471-2341
E-mail: tom.jensen@nebraska.gov

Agriculture Laboratories Division Administrator
**Dirk Shoemaker** . . . . . . . . . . . . . . . . . . . . . . . . . . . . (402) 471-2176
E-mail: dirk.shoemaker@nebraska.gov          Fax: (402) 471-0091

Agriculture Promotion and Development Division
Administrator **(Vacant)** . . . . . . . . . . . . . . . . . . . . . . . (402) 471-4876

Farm Mediation Division Administrator **Karla Bahm** . . . . . (402) 471-3348
E-mail: karla.bahm@nebraska.gov          Fax: (402) 471-2759

Finance Division Administrator **Robert Storant** . . . . . . . . (402) 471-2341
E-mail: bob.storant@nebraska.gov

Foods and Dairies Division Administrator **Melva Ball** . . . . (402) 471-3422
E-mail: melva.ball@nebraska.gov          Fax: (402) 471-2759

Plant Industry Division Administrator
**Tammy Zimmerman** . . . . . . . . . . . . . . . . . . . . . . . . . (402) 471-2394
E-mail: tammy.zimmerman@nebraska.gov          Fax: (402) 471-6892

Potato Development Division Manager
**Steve K. Marquardt** . . . . . . . . . . . . . . . . . . . . . . . . .(308) 760-8182
PO Box 339, Alliance, NE 69301

Weights and Measures Division Administrator
**Ken Tichota** . . . . . . . . . . . . . . . . . . . . . . . . . . . . . . .(402) 471-3422
E-mail: ken.tichota@nebraska.gov          Fax: (402) 471-2759

Agriculture Statistician **Dean C. Groskurth** . . . . . . . . . . .(402) 437-5541
P.O. Box 81069, Lincoln, NE 68501          Fax: (402) 437-5547
E-mail: nass-ne@nass.usda.gov

## Nebraska Department of Banking and Finance [NDB&F]

1526 K Street, Suite 300, Lincoln, NE 68508-2732
P. O. Box 95006, Lincoln, NE 68509

■Director **Mark C. Quandahl** . . . . . . . . . . . . . . . . . . . . . (402) 471-2171
E-mail: mark.quandahl@nebraska.gov
Education: Nebraska 1984 BJ, 1987 JD

Deputy Director **Kelly Lammers** . . . . . . . . . . . . . . . . . . . (402) 471-2171
E-mail: kelly.lammers@nebraska.gov

General Counsel **Patricia A. Humlicek Herstein** . . . . . . . . (402) 471-2171
E-mail: patricia.herstein@nebraska.gov

Securities Bureau Assistant Director **Jack E. Herstein** . . . . (402) 471-3445
E-mail: jack.herstein@nebraska.gov

## Department of Correctional Services [DCS]

P.O. Box 94661, Lincoln, NE 68509-4661
TTY: (402) 479-5895  Fax: (402) 479-5623
Internet: www.corrections.state.ne.us/

■Director **Scott Frakes** . . . . . . . . . . . . . . . . . . . . . . . . .(402) 471-2654
E-mail: scott.frakes@nebraska.gov
Education: Evergreen State BA
Assistant to the Director **Traci Hanson** . . . . . . . . . . . . . (402) 471-2654

Deputy Director for Administrative Services
**Robin Spindler** . . . . . . . . . . . . . . . . . . . . . . . . . . . . (402) 471-2654
E-mail: robin.spindler@nebraska.gov

Deputy Director/Cornhusker State Industries
Administrator **John McGovern** . . . . . . . . . . . . . . . . . . . (402) 471-4597

Deputy Director for Institutions **Frank X. Hopkins** . . . . . . (402) 471-2654

Deputy Director for Programs and Community Services
**Larry Wayne** . . . . . . . . . . . . . . . . . . . . . . . . . . . . . . (402) 471-2654
E-mail: larry.wayne@nebraska.gov

General Counsel **(Vacant)** . . . . . . . . . . . . . . . . . . . . . . (402) 479-5735

Adult Parole Administrator **Cathy Gibson-Beltz** . . . . . . . . (402) 479-5771

Human Resources and Development Administrator
**Erinn Criner** . . . . . . . . . . . . . . . . . . . . . . . . . . . . . . (402) 479-5752

Material Administrator **Mary Carmichael** . . . . . . . . . . . . .(402) 479-5717

Planning/Research Administrator **Jeff Beaty** . . . . . . . . . . .(402) 479-5760
E-mail: jeff.beaty@nebraska.gov

Records Administrator **(Vacant)** . . . . . . . . . . . . . . . . . . .(402) 479-5750

Controller **Inga L. Hookstra** . . . . . . . . . . . . . . . . . . . . . (402) 471-2654

Facilities Engineering Manager **Doug Hanson** . . . . . . . . . .(402) 479-5742
E-mail: doug.hanson@nebraska.gov          Fax: (402) 479-5842

Federal Surplus Property Manager **Brad Frandsen** . . . . . . (402) 471-9169

Information Systems Manager
**Robert H. "Bob" Shanahan** . . . . . . . . . . . . . . . . . . . . (402) 479-5809
E-mail: bob.shanahan@nebraska.gov

Special Services Manager **(Vacant)** . . . . . . . . . . . . . . . . . (402) 479-5705
Fax: (402) 742-2334

Training and Development Manager **Ken Sturdy** . . . . . . . . (402) 471-1781
2320 North 57th Street, Lincoln, NE 65807          Fax: (402) 471-1787

Accommodations and Victim Services Coordinator
**Nikki Silva** . . . . . . . . . . . . . . . . . . . . . . . . . . . . . . . (402) 432-5182

Emergency Preparedness Coordinator
**Bradford "Brad" Hansen** . . . . . . . . . . . . . . . . . . . . . . (402) 479-5617

Grants Coordinator **Stephen "Steve" Weis** . . . . . . . . . . . .(402) 471-2654

Library Coordinator **Sam Shaw** . . . . . . . . . . . . . . . . . . . (402) 471-3161

Programs Coordinator **Layne A. Gissler** . . . . . . . . . . . . . (402) 479-5723
E-mail: layne.gissler@nebraska.gov

Safety/Sanitation Coordinator **Steve Vodicka** . . . . . . . . . .(402) 479-5778
Fax: (402) 479-5842

Legislative Coordinator and Public Information Officer
**Dawn Renee Smith** . . . . . . . . . . . . . . . . . . . . . . . . . . (402) 479-5713
E-mail: dawnrenee.smith@nebraska.gov

## Department of Economic Development [DED]

301 Centennial Mall South, Lincoln, NE 68508-4912
P.O. Box 94666, Lincoln, NE 68509-4666
Tel: (800) 426-6505  Fax: (402) 471-3778  Internet: www.neded.org

■Director **Courtney Dentlinger** . . . . . . . . . . . . . . . . . . . . (402) 471-5919

*(continued on next page)*

---

★ Elected Official     ■ Appointed by Governor     ● Appointed by Legislature     ▲ Appointed by Board or Commission     ◆ Appointed by State Supreme Court

EXECUTIVE BRANCH

**Department of Economic Development** *continued*

Assistant **Lori A. Cole** ............................... (402) 471-3746
Deputy Director **Lara Huskey** .................... (402) 471-3759
Marketing Director **Kate Ellingson** ........... (402) 471-3749
Business Development Division Director **Dan Curran** ..... (402) 471-6513
   Business Development Division Deputy Director
    **Eric Zeece** .......................................... (402) 471-3769
Public Information Officer **Sue Sitzmann** ............. (402) 471-3987
   E-mail: sue.sitzmann@nebraska.gov
Legislative Coordinator **Libby Elder** ................ (402) 471-3762
   E-mail: libby.elder@nebraska.gov

## Nebraska Department of Environmental Quality [NDEQ]

P.O. Box 98922, Lincoln, NE 68509-8922
Tel: (402) 471-2186  Fax: (402) 471-2909
E-mail: moreinfo@nebraska.gov  Internet: www.deq.ne.gov

■Director **Jim Macy** ................................. (402) 471-3383
   Education: Missouri BS, MEd
Administration Deputy Director (Interim)
   **Dennis Burling** ..................................... (402) 471-4235
Programs Deputy Director **Jay Ringenberg** ......... (402) 471-3372
Air Program Administrator **Shelley Schneider** ......... (402) 471-4299
Waste Program Administrator **David "Dave" Haldeman** .. (402) 471-4219
   Education: Nebraska BS
   Water Quality Division Associate Program Director
    **Marty Link** ........................................ (402) 471-4270
Field Services and Assistance Division Associate
   Program Director **Joe Francis** .................... (402) 471-6087
Agriculture Programs **Blake Onken** ................ (402) 471-2186
Legal Counsel **Annette Kovar** ..................... (402) 471-3194
Field Office Section Supervisor **Kevin Stoner** ......... (402) 471-4234
Public Information Officer **Brian McManus** ............. (402) 471-4223
   E-mail: brian.mcmanus@nebraska.gov
Training Coordinator **Carla Felix** .................. (402) 471-2923

## Department of Health and Human Services [DHHS]

301 Centennial Mall South, Lincoln, NE 68509
1033 O Street, Suite 130, Lincoln, NE 68508 (Vital Records)
Tel: (402) 471-3121  Tel: (402) 471-2871 (Vital Records)
Tel: (402) 471-6440 (Vitalchek for expedited service)
TTY: (402) 471-9570  Fax: (402) 471-9449
Fax: (402) 742-2388 (Vital Records)  E-mail: dhhs.helpline@nebraska.gov
Internet: www.dhhs.ne.gov

**Employees:** 5,624  **Fiscal Year:** 2014  **Budget:** $3,492,063,000

■Chief Executive Officer **Courtney N. Phillips** ........... (402) 471-9433
   P.O. Box 95026, Lincoln, NE 68509
   Education: LSU BS, MPA
Administrative Assistant **Bonnie Engel** ................ (402) 471-9433
Communications and Legislative Services Administrator
   **Kathie Osterman** ................................. (402) 471-9108
   E-mail: kathie.osterman@nebraska.gov
Legal and Regulatory Services Administrator
   **Brad Gianakos** .................................... (402) 471-4068
   E-mail: brad.gianakos@nebraska.gov

## Division of Behavioral Health

P.O. Box 95026, Lincoln, NE 68509
Fax: (402) 471-9449

**Employees:** 866

■Director **Sheri Dawson** .............................. (402) 471-8553
   E-mail: sheri.dawson@nebraska.gov
   Education: Nebraska Wesleyan BS
Administrative Assistant **Kelly Ostrander** .............. (402) 471-8553
Chief Clinical Officer **Dr. Todd Stull, MD** ............. (402) 471-3121

## Division of Children and Family Services

P.O. Box 95026, Lincoln, NE 68509-5026
Tel: (402) 471-9272  Fax: (402) 471-9449

**Employees:** 1,618

■Director **Doug Weinberg** ............................ (402) 471-1878
Administrative Assistant **Kim Krzycki** ................ (402) 471-1878
Food Distribution Deputy Director **Jill Schreck** ......... (402) 471-9243

## Division of Developmental Disabilities

P.O. Box 95026, Lincoln, NE 68509-5026
Fax: (402) 471-9449

**Employees:** 871

■Director **Courtney Miller** ........................... (402) 471-6038
   E-mail: courtney.miller@nebraska.gov
Administrative Assistant **Tyla Watson** ................ (402) 471-6038

## Division of Medicaid and Long Term Care

P.O. Box 95026, Lincoln, NE 68509-5026
Fax: (402) 471-9449

**Employees:** 568

■Director **Calder Lynch** .............................. (402) 471-2135
   E-mail: calder.lynch@nebraska.gov
   Administrative Assistant **Roxie Anderson** ............. (402) 471-2135

## Division of Operations

P.O. Box 95026, Lincoln, NE 68509-5026
Tel: (402) 471-1877  Fax: (402) 471-9449

**Employees:** 425

Chief Operating Officer **(Vacant)** ..................... (402) 471-1877
   Administrative Assistant **Sharon Kahm** ............... (402) 471-1877
DHHS System Advocate **Diana Duran** ................ (402) 471-6035

## Division of Public Health

P.O. Box 95026, Lincoln, NE 68509
Fax: (402) 471-9449

**Employees:** 460

■Director and Chief Medical Officer **(Vacant)** ........... (402) 471-8566
   Administrative Assistant **Karen Berry** ............... (402) 471-8566

## Division of Veterans' Homes

P.O. Box 95026, Lincoln, NE 68509
Fax: (402) 471-9499

**Employees:** 813

■Director **John A. Hilgert** ........................... (402) 471-6038
   E-mail: john.hilgert@nebraska.gov
   Education: Nebraska 1986 BBA; Creighton 1989 JD
Administrative Assistant **Lana Gilling-Weber** ........... (402) 471-0940

## Department of Insurance [DOI]

P.O. Box 82089, Lincoln, NE 68501-2089
Fax: (402) 471-4610  TTY: (800) 833-7352
Internet: www.doi.nebraska.gov/

■Director **Bruce R. Ramge** .......................... (402) 471-2201
   E-mail: bruce.ramge@nebraska.gov
   Education: Dana 1979; Nebraska (Omaha) 2008 MBA
Deputy Director and General Counsel
   **Christine "Christy" Neighbors** ...................... (402) 471-2201
Chief Examiner **Justin Schrader** ..................... (402) 471-2201
Casualty Actuary **Gordon Hay** ...................... (402) 471-2201
Administrative Services Administrator **Jay Mitchell** ...... (402) 471-2201
   E-mail: jay.mitchell@nebraska.gov
Consumer Affairs Administrator **Jane Francis** ........... (402) 471-2201
Licensing Administrator **Jason McCartney** ............. (402) 471-2201
Life and Health Administrator **Stephen King** .......... (402) 471-2201
   E-mail: stephen.e.king@nebraska.gov
Property and Casualty Administrator **Beverly Anderson** ... (402) 471-2201
   E-mail: beverly.anderson@nebraska.gov
Fraud Supervisor **Chuck Starr** ...................... (402) 471-2201
   E-mail: chuck.starr@nebraska.gov

---

★ Elected Official   ■ Appointed by Governor   ● Appointed by Legislature   ▲ Appointed by Board or Commission   ◆ Appointed by State Supreme Court

Market Regulation Chief **Bruce R. Ramge** . . . . . . . . . . . . . (402) 471-2201
Human Resources Officer **Kathy Vandenberg** . . . . . . . . . . (402) 471-2201
Public Information Officer **Peggy Jasa** . . . . . . . . . . . . . . . (402) 471-2201
  E-mail: peg.jasa@nebraska.gov

## Nebraska Department of Labor [NDOL]

P.O. Box 94600, Lincoln, NE 68509-4600
Tel: (402) 471-9000  Fax: (402) 471-2318  TTY: (800) 833-7352

■Commissioner **John Albin** . . . . . . . . . . . . . . . . . . . . . . . . (402) 471-3405
  E-mail: john.albin@nebraska.gov
Assistant to the Commissioner **Ann Tillery** . . . . . . . . . . . . .(402) 471-3405
Administrative Services Office Director
  **Terri Johnston Slone** . . . . . . . . . . . . . . . . . . . . . . . . . (402) 471-8358
  E-mail: terri.slone@nebraska.gov
General Counsel Office Director **Katie Thurber** . . . . . . . . . (402) 471-9912
  E-mail: katie.thurber@nebraska.gov
Chief Administrative Law Judge **Steven Chase** . . . . . . . . .(402) 471-9886
  E-mail: steven.chase@nebraska.gov
Human Resources Administrator **Dirk Hood** . . . . . . . . . . . . (402) 471-4957
  E-mail: dirk.hood@nebraska.gov
Employment and Training Office Director **Joan Modrell** . . (402) 471-9948
  E-mail: joan.modrell@nebraska.gov
Safety Standards Director **Chris Cantrell** . . . . . . . . . . . . . . (402) 471-4721
  E-mail: chris.cantrell@nebraska.gov
Controller **Kim Schreiner** . . . . . . . . . . . . . . . . . . . . . . . . .(402) 471-2492

## Nebraska Military Department

2433 Northwest 24th Street, Lincoln, NE 68524
Tel: (402) 309-8210  Fax: (402) 309-7147
E-mail: webmaster@ne.ngb.army.mil

■Adjutant General **MajGen Daryl Bohac, ANG** . . . . . . . . . (402) 309-8210
  Education: Nebraska 1987 BA, 1994 MA, 1994 PhD
Deputy Adjutant General **BG Rick Dahlman, ARNG** . . . . . (402) 309-8210

## Nebraska Emergency Management Agency [NEMA]

Director **MajGen Daryl Bohac, ANG** . . . . . . . . . . . . . . . . (402) 309-8210
Assistant Director **Bryan J. Tuma** . . . . . . . . . . . . . . . . . . . (402) 471-7410
  Education: Nebraska 1977 BS

## Nebraska National Guard

2433 Northwest 24th Street, Lincoln, NE 68524
Tel: (402) 309-8210  Fax: (402) 309-7147  Internet: www.neguard.com

■Adjutant General **MajGen Daryl Bohac, ANG** . . . . . . . . . (402) 309-8210

## Nebraska Air National Guard

2433 Northwest 24th Street, Lincoln, NE 68524
Tel: (402) 309-8210  Fax: (402) 309-7147
Internet: www.155arw.ang.af.mil

Assistant Adjutant General **(Vacant)** . . . . . . . . . . . . . . . . . (402) 309-8210
Chief of Staff **Col Wendy Johnson, ANG** . . . . . . . . . . . . .(402) 309-8210

## Nebraska Army National Guard

2433 Northwest 24th Street, Lincoln, NE 68524
Tel: (402) 309-8210  Fax: (402) 309-7147

Assistant Adjutant General **BG Rick Dahlman, ARNG** . . . . (402) 309-8210
Chief of Staff **COL Brett W. Andersen, ARNG** . . . . . . . . . (402) 309-8107
Information Management Director
  **LTC Gordon Bjorman, ARNG** . . . . . . . . . . . . . . . . . . . (402) 309-8210

## Department of Motor Vehicles [DMV]

P.O. Box 94789, Lincoln, NE 68509-4789
Tel: (402) 471-2281  Fax: (402) 471-3920  Internet: www.clickdmv.ne.gov

■Director **Rhonda Lahm** . . . . . . . . . . . . . . . . . . . . . . . . . . (402) 471-3900
  E-mail: rhonda.lahm@nebraska.gov
  Education: Nebraska Wesleyan BS; Doane MA
  Administrative Assistant **Veronica Lueders** . . . . . . . . . . (402) 471-2281
Deputy Director **Julie Maaske** . . . . . . . . . . . . . . . . . . . . . (402) 471-3900
  E-mail: julie.maaske@nebraska.gov

Driver Licensing Services Administrator **Sara O'Rourke** . . (402) 471-3861
  P.O. 94726, Lincoln, NE 68509
  E-mail: sara.orourke@nebraska.gov
Driver and Vehicle Services Administrator
  **Betty Johnson** . . . . . . . . . . . . . . . . . . . . . . . . . . . . . . (402) 471-3918
  P.O. Box 94789, Lincoln, NE 68509
  E-mail: betty.johnson@nebraska.gov
Financial Responsibility Administrator
  **Kathy Van Brocklin** . . . . . . . . . . . . . . . . . . . . . . . . . .(402) 471-3985
  P. O. 94877, Lincoln, NE 68509
Information Systems Administrator **Keith Dey** . . . . . . . . . . (402) 471-3906
  E-mail: keith.dey@nebraska.gov
Legal Administrator **Noelie Ackermann Sherdon** . . . . . . . (402) 471-9593
  P.O. Box 94699, Lincoln, NE 68509
Motor Carrier Services Administrator **Cathy Beedle** . . . . . (402) 471-4435
  P.O. Box 94729, Lincoln, NE 68509
  E-mail: cathy.beedle@nebraska.gov
Accounting and Finance Manager **Gary Ryken** . . . . . . . . . (402) 471-3902

## Department of Natural Resources [DNR]

301 Centennial Mall South, 4th Floor, Lincoln, NE 68509
P.O. Box 94676, Lincoln, NE 68509-4676
Tel: (402) 471-2363  Fax: (402) 471-2900  Internet: www.dnr.ne.gov

■Director **Jeff Fassett, PE** . . . . . . . . . . . . . . . . . . . . . . . . . (402) 471-2366
Deputy Director **(Vacant)** . . . . . . . . . . . . . . . . . . . . . . . . (402) 471-2363
Program Director **Jesse Bradley, PG** . . . . . . . . . . . . . . . . . (402) 471-0586
Business Manager **Jill Richters** . . . . . . . . . . . . . . . . . . . . . (402) 471-3944
Legal Counsel **LeRoy W. Sievers** . . . . . . . . . . . . . . . . . . . (402) 471-1113
  E-mail: leroy.sievers@nebraska.gov
Flood Plain, Dam Safety and Surveys Division Head
  **Shuhai Zheng** . . . . . . . . . . . . . . . . . . . . . . . . . . . . . . . (402) 471-3936
  E-mail: shuhai.zheng@nebraska.gov
Management Services Division Head **Rex Gittins** . . . . . . . . (402) 471-1767
  E-mail: rex.gittins@nebraska.gov
Programs Assistance Coordinator **Susan A. France** . . . . . .(402) 471-1684
  E-mail: susan.france@nebraska.gov
Permits and Registrations Division Manager
  **Mike Thompson** . . . . . . . . . . . . . . . . . . . . . . . . . . . . . (402) 471-0587
  E-mail: mike.thompson@nebraska.gov

## Department of Revenue

P.O. Box 94818, Lincoln, NE 68509-4818
Tel: (402) 471-2971
Tel: (800) 554-3835 (Motor Fuels Taxpayers Assistance)
Tel: (800) 742-7474 (Taxpayers Assistance [Nebraska and Iowa])
Fax: (402) 471-5608  TTY: (402) 471-5740
Internet: www.revenue.nebraska.gov

■Tax Commissioner **Tony Fulton** . . . . . . . . . . . . . . . . . . . . .(402) 471-8557
  Education: Nebraska 1997 BS
Compliance Division Director **Glen White** . . . . . . . . . . . . .(402) 471-5913
Operations and Administrative Services Director
  **Leonard J. "Len" Sloup** . . . . . . . . . . . . . . . . . . . . . . . (402) 471-5805
  E-mail: len.sloup@nebraska.gov
Legal Section Attorney **Karl Cochrane** . . . . . . . . . . . . . . . (402) 471-5924
Policy Section Attorney **James A. "Jim" Bogatz** . . . . . . . .(402) 471-5921
Human Resources Manager **Timothy A. "Tim" Young** . . . (402) 471-5611
Special Services Manager **Charles P. "Chuck" Long** . . . . . (402) 471-5624
Revenue Economist Manager **Hoa Phu Tran** . . . . . . . . . . . (402) 471-5896

## Property Assessment Division

P.O. Box 98919, Lincoln, NE 68509-8919
Tel: (402) 471-5724  Fax: (402) 471-5993

■Property Tax Administrator **Ruth Sorensen** . . . . . . . . . . . . (402) 471-5962
  E-mail: ruth.sorensen@nebraska.gov
  Education: Franklin Pierce Col 1992; Nebraska 1994 JD
Administrative Secretary **Cyndy Hermsen** . . . . . . . . . . . . . (402) 471-5724
Legal and Policy Division Attorney **Jon Cannon** . . . . . . . . (402) 471-5763
Measurement Division Manager **Dennis Donner** . . . . . . . . (402) 471-5986

★ Elected Official   ■ Appointed by Governor   ● Appointed by Legislature   ▲ Appointed by Board or Commission   ◆ Appointed by State Supreme Court

*State Yellow Book*   © Leadership Directories, Inc.   Summer 2016

**EXECUTIVE BRANCH**

## Nebraska Lottery and Charitable Gaming Divisions

1800 O Street, Suite 101, Lincoln, NE 68508
Tel: (402) 471-6100  TTY: (402) 471-2920  Fax: (402) 471-6108
Internet: www.nelottery.com

Director **James M. "Jim" Haynes** . . . . . . . . . . . . . . . . . . (402) 471-5630
Legal Counsel **Aaron Hendry** . . . . . . . . . . . . . . . . . . . . . . (402) 471-6145
Finance Manager **Dennis Nelson** . . . . . . . . . . . . . . . . . . (402) 471-6106
IT Supervisor **Shawn Fotinos** . . . . . . . . . . . . . . . . . . . . . (402) 471-6115
  E-mail: shawn.fotinos@nebraska.gov
IT App Developer/Senior **Eric McHargue** . . . . . . . . . . . . (402) 471-6117
  E-mail: eric.mchargue@nebraska.gov
IT Infranet Support Analyst/Senior **Barry Jelinek** . . . . . . . (402) 471-6118
  E-mail: barry.jelinek@nebraska.gov
Administration Manager **Bonnie Amgwert** . . . . . . . . . . . . (402) 471-6123
  E-mail: bonnie.amgwert@nebraska.gov
Lottery Accounts Manager **Dennis Knowles** . . . . . . . . . . (402) 471-6104
Investigations and Security Supervisor **Mike Olsen** . . . . . (402) 471-5948
Marketing and Communications Manager **Jill Marshall** . . . (402) 471-6122
  E-mail: jill.marshall@nebraska.gov
Products Manager **Mike Elwood** . . . . . . . . . . . . . . . . . . . (402) 471-6121
Revenue Agent Supervisor **Mike Haverman** . . . . . . . . . . . (402) 471-6119
Budget Officer **Kim Vu** . . . . . . . . . . . . . . . . . . . . . . . . . . . (402) 471-6116
Public Information Officer III **Tom Bash** . . . . . . . . . . . . . . (402) 471-6102
  E-mail: tom.bash@nebraska.gov
Public Information Officer III **Neil Watson** . . . . . . . . . . . . (402) 471-6120
  E-mail: neil.watson@nebraska.gov
Public Information Officer II **Danielle Beebe** . . . . . . . . . . (402) 471-6128
  E-mail: danielle.beebe@nebraska.gov
Attorney I **Nicholas Bussey** . . . . . . . . . . . . . . . . . . . . . . . (402) 471-5943
Revenue Section Manager **Gail Ross** . . . . . . . . . . . . . . . . (402) 471-5955
  E-mail: gail.ross@nebraska.gov

## Nebraska Department of Roads [NDOR]

1500 Highway 2, Lincoln, NE 68502
P.O. Box 94759, Lincoln, NE 68509-4759
Tel: (402) 471-4567  Fax: (402) 479-4325  TTY: (402) 479-3834

■Director - State Engineer **Kyle Schneweis** . . . . . . . . . . . . (402) 479-4615
  Administrative Assistant **Lori Larson** . . . . . . . . . . . . . . . . (402) 479-4701
  Administrative Assistant **Jill M. McAuliffe** . . . . . . . . . . . . (402) 479-4615
Deputy Director - Engineering **Khalil E. Jaber** . . . . . . . . . (402) 479-4671
  E-mail: khalil.jaber@nebraska.gov
Deputy Director - Operations **Mostafa Jamshidi** . . . . . . . . (402) 479-4671
Senior Auditor **Timothy C. "Tim" Baker, CICA** . . . . . . . . . (402) 479-4403
  E-mail: timothy.baker@nebraska.gov
Legal Counsel **(Vacant)** . . . . . . . . . . . . . . . . . . . . . . . . . . . (402) 479-4611
Librarian **Denise Matulka** . . . . . . . . . . . . . . . . . . . . . . . . . (402) 479-4316
                                                          Fax: (402) 479-3989
Webmaster **(Vacant)** . . . . . . . . . . . . . . . . . . . . . . . . . . . . . (402) 479-3662

## District Offices

District 1 Engineer, Lincoln
  **Thomas W. Goodbarn** . . . . . . . . . . . . . . . (402) 471-0850 ext. 1001
  E-mail: thomas.goodbarn@nebraska.gov
District 2 Engineer, Omaha
  **Timothy W. Weander** . . . . . . . . . . . . . . . . . (402) 595-2534 ext. 210
  E-mail: tim.weander@nebraska.gov
District 3 Engineer, Norfolk
  **Kevin G. Domogalla** . . . . . . . . . . . . . . . . . (402) 370-3470 ext. 104
  E-mail: kevin.domogalla@nebraska.gov
District 4 Engineer, Grand Island
  **Wesley W. Wahlgren** . . . . . . . . . . . . . . . . . (308) 385-6265 ext. 203
  E-mail: wes.wahlgren@nebraska.gov
District 5 Engineer, Gering
  **Douglas W. Hoevet** . . . . . . . . . . . . . . . . . . (308) 436-6587 ext. 5010
District 6 Engineer, North Platte **Gary D. Thayer** . . . . . . . (308) 535-8031
  E-mail: gary.thayer@nebraska.gov
District 7 Engineer, McCook **Kurt R. Vosburg** . . . . (308) 345-8490 ext. 701
  E-mail: kurt.vosburg@nebraska.gov
District 8 Engineer, Ainsworth **Mark A. Kovar** . . . . (402) 387-2471 ext. 203
  E-mail: mark.kovar@nebraska.gov

## Division Offices

Deputy Director **Mark J. Traynowicz** . . . . . . . . . . . . . . . . (402) 479-4701
  E-mail: mark.traynowicz@nebraska.gov
Government Affairs Manager **Andrew F. Cunningham** . . . (402) 479-4615
Business Technology Support Division Engineer
  **William B. Wehling** . . . . . . . . . . . . . . . . . . . . . . . . . . . (402) 479-3986
  E-mail: bill.wehling@nebraska.gov
Construction Division Engineer **Claude R. Oie** . . . . . . . . . (402) 479-4532
Materials and Research Division Engineer **Mick S. Syslo** . . (402) 479-4750
  E-mail: mick.syslo@nebraska.gov
Planning and Project Development Division Engineer
  **Michael H. Owen** . . . . . . . . . . . . . . . . . . . . . . . . . . . . . (402) 479-4795
  E-mail: michael.owen@nebraska.gov
Program Management Division Engineer **Amy Starr** . . . . . . (402) 479-4708
  E-mail: amy.starr@nebraska.gov
Rail and Public Transportation Division Engineer
  **Ryan Huff** . . . . . . . . . . . . . . . . . . . . . . . . . . . . . . . . . . . (402) 479-3797
  E-mail: ryan.huff@nebraska.gov
Roadway Design Division Engineer **James J. Knott** . . . . . . (402) 479-4601
  E-mail: jim.knott@nebraska.gov
Traffic Engineering Division Engineer **Daniel J. Waddle** . . (402) 479-4594
  E-mail: dan.waddle@nebraska.gov
Controller Division Finance Administrator
  **Marilyn Hayes** . . . . . . . . . . . . . . . . . . . . . . . . . . . . . . . (402) 479-4635
Human Resources Division Administrator
  **Susan E. Larson** . . . . . . . . . . . . . . . . . . . . . . . . . . . . . . (402) 479-3643
Communication Division Manager **Mary Jo Oie** . . . . . . . . (402) 479-4512
  E-mail: maryjo.oie@nebraska.gov
Operations Division Manager **Thomas B. Sands** . . . . . . . . (402) 479-4339
Right-of-Way Division Manager **Robert D. Frickel** . . . . . . . (402) 479-4460
  E-mail: bob.frickel@nebraska.gov

## Department of Veterans' Affairs

301 Centennial Mall South, 6th Floor, Lincoln, NE 68509-5083
Tel: (402) 471-2458  Fax: (402) 471-2491

■Director **John A. Hilgert** . . . . . . . . . . . . . . . . . . . . . . . . . (402) 471-2458
  E-mail: john.hilgert@nebraska.gov
  Administrative Secretary **Charlene Sheltraw** . . . . . . . . . (402) 471-2458
Deputy Director **John S. McNally** . . . . . . . . . . . . . . . . . . . (402) 471-2458
Business Manager **Gary Maixner** . . . . . . . . . . . . . . . . . . . (402) 471-2458
  E-mail: gary.maixner@nebraska.gov
Staff Assistant **Lisa Frederick** . . . . . . . . . . . . . . . . . . . . . (402) 471-2458

## State Cemetery Division

P.O. Box 718, Alliance, NE 69301
Tel: (308) 763-2958

Administrator **Clyde Allen Pannell** . . . . . . . . . . . . . . . . . . (308) 763-2958

## State Service Division

3800 Villiage Drive, Lincoln, NE 68501
P.O. Box 85816, Lincoln, NE 68501-5816
Tel: (402) 420-4021  Fax: (402) 471-7070

State Service Officer **Steve Burger** . . . . . . . . . . . . . . . . . . (402) 420-4021
State Service Officer **Michael Coatney** . . . . . . . . . . . . . . . (402) 420-4021
State Service Officer **Tom McDonough** . . . . . . . . . . . . . . . (402) 420-4021
State Service Officer **Garry Morgan** . . . . . . . . . . . . . . . . . (402) 420-4021
State Service Officer **Richard "Rick" Noyes** . . . . . . . . . . . (402) 421-4021
Office Supervisor **Kathy Gilmore** . . . . . . . . . . . . . . . . . . . (402) 420-4021
Secretary **Karen Solc** . . . . . . . . . . . . . . . . . . . . . . . . . . . . (402) 420-4021

## Nebraska Tourism Commission

Tel: (888) 444-1867

Director **Kathy McKillip** . . . . . . . . . . . . . . . . . . . . . . . . . . . (402) 471-1558
Note: On May 13, 2016, the Nebraska Tourism Commission suspended
Kathy McKillip.
Education: Nebraska Wesleyan; Peru State MS

---

★ Elected Official    ■ Appointed by Governor    ● Appointed by Legislature    ▲ Appointed by Board or Commission    ◆ Appointed by State Supreme Court

# Nebraska Game and Parks Commission

P.O. Box 30370, Lincoln, NE 68503-0370
2200 North 33rd Street, Lincoln, NE 68503
Tel: (402) 471-0641  Fax: (402) 471-5528
E-mail: ngpc.info@nebraska.gov
▲ Director **Jim Douglas** ............................. (402) 471-5539
  E-mail: jim.douglas@nebraska.gov

# Law Enforcement and Criminal Justice Commission

301 Centennial Mall South, Lincoln, NE 68508-4912
P.O. Box 94946, Lincoln, NE 68509-4946
Tel: (402) 471-2194  Fax: (402) 471-2837  Internet: www.ncc.state.ne.us
■ Executive Director **Darrell Fisher** ..................... (402) 471-3847
  E-mail: darrell.fisher@nebraska.gov

# Nebraska Library Commission

The Atrium, Suite 120, 1200 N Street, Lincoln, NE 68508-2020
Tel: (402) 471-2045  Fax: (402) 471-2083  TTY: (402) 471-4014
E-mail: nlc.ask@nebraska.gov
▲ Director **Rod G. Wagner** ........................... (402) 471-4001
  E-mail: rod.wagner@nebraska.gov

# Coordinating Commission for Postsecondary Education [CCPE]

140 North 8th Street, Suite 300, Lincoln, NE 68508
P.O. Box 95005, Lincoln, NE 68509-5005
Tel: (402) 471-2847  Fax: (402) 471-2886  Internet: www.ccpe.state.ne.us
▲ Executive Director **Dr. Michael Baumgartner** .......... (402) 471-0029
  E-mail: michael.baumgartner@nebraska.gov

# Tax Equalization and Review Commission

301 Centennial Mall South, Lincoln, NE 68509-4732
Tel: (402) 471-2842
■ Chair **Nancy J. Salmon** ............................ (402) 471-2842
  Term Expires: January 1, 2020
■ Vice Chair **Robert W. Hotz** ........................ (402) 471-2842
  Term Expires: January 1, 2022
  E-mail: rob.hotz@nebraska.gov
■ Commissioner **Steven Keetle** ...................... (402) 471-7693
  Term Expires: January 1, 2018
  E-mail: steve.keetle@nebraska.gov

# Board of Educational Lands and Funds

555 North Cotner Boulevard, Lincoln, NE 68505
Fax: (402) 471-3599
▲ Executive Secretary **Richard Endacott** ................ (402) 471-2014
  E-mail: richard.endacott@nebraska.gov

# Motor Vehicle Industry Licensing Board

Nebraska State Office Building, 301 Centennial Mall South,
1st Floor Northwest, Lincoln, NE 68509-4697
P. O. Box 94697, Lincoln, NE 68509-4697
Tel: (402) 471-2148  Fax: (402) 471-4563
Executive Director **William S. "Bill" Jackson** .......... (402) 471-2148
  E-mail: bill.jackson@nebraska.gov

# Board of Parole

P.O. Box 94754, Lincoln, NE 68509-4754
Fax: (402) 471-2453  Internet: www.parole.state.ne.us
■ Chair **Rosalyn Cotton** ............................. (402) 471-2156
  Term Expires: September 9, 2020
  E-mail: rcotton@nebraska.gov

# Nebraska State Board of Public Accountancy

1526 K Street, Lincoln, NE 68508-2732
P.O. Box 94725, Lincoln, NE 68509-4725
Tel: (402) 471-3595  Tel: (800) 564-6111 (In State)  Fax: (402) 471-4484
Internet: www.nbpa.ne.gov
▲ Executive Director **Daniel R. "Dan" Sweetwood** ........(402) 471-3595
  E-mail: dan.sweetwood@nebraska.gov
  Education: Nebraska 1994 MPA

# Nebraska Investment Council

941 O Street, Suite 500, Lincoln, NE 68508
Tel: (402) 471-2043  Fax: (402) 471-2498  Internet: www.nic.ne.gov
▲ State Investment Officer **Michael Walden-Newman** ...... (402) 471-2001
  E-mail: michael.waldennewman@nebraska.gov
Deputy State Investment Officer **Joseph P. Jurich** ........ (402) 471-2043

# Nebraska State Historical Society [NSHS]

1500 R Street, Lincoln, NE 68501
P.O. Box 82554, Lincoln, NE 68501-2554
Tel: (402) 471-3270  Fax: (402) 471-3100
Internet: www.nebraskahistory.org
▲ Director **Michael J. Smith** ..........................(402) 471-4745
  E-mail: michael.smith@nebraska.gov
Deputy Director **Lynne Ireland** ...................... (402) 471-4758
Conservation Division Associate Director **Deborah Long** .. (402) 595-1141
  G. R. Ford Conservation Center, 1326 South 32nd Street,
  Omaha, NE 68105
Collections Division Associate Director **Deb Arenz** ....... (402) 471-4759
Museum/Historic Sites Division Associate Director
  **Ann Billesbach** ................................. (402) 471-3499
Publications Division Associate Director **David Bristow** ... (402) 471-4748
  E-mail: david.bristow@nebraska.gov
State Historic Preservation Office Associate Director
  **L. Robert Puschendorf** ..........................(402) 471-4769
Facilities Officer **Charley McWilliams** ................. (402) 440-6380
Volunteer Services and Landmark Stores Manager
  **Deb McWilliams** ................................ (402) 471-4955
Executive Assistant and Membership Administrator
  **Lana Hatcher** .................................. (402) 471-3272

# Nebraska Public Employees Retirement Systems [NPERS]

P.O. Box 94816, Lincoln, NE 68509-4816
Tel: (402) 471-2053  Tel: (800) 245-5712  Fax: (402) 471-9493
▲ Director **Phyllis G. Chambers** .......................(402) 471-2053
  E-mail: phyllis.chambers@nebraska.gov
Deputy Director and Finance Manager **Randy Gerke** ..... (402) 471-2053
Administrative Assistant **Sheila Linder** ................ (402) 471-9482
Webmaster **John Winkelman** ........................ (402) 471-2053
  E-mail: john.winkelman@nebraska.gov

# State Library

P.O. Box 98931, Lincoln, NE 68509
Tel: (402) 471-3189  Fax: (402) 471-1011
E-mail: nsc.lawlibrary@nebraska.gov
◆ Librarian **Marie Wiechman** .........................(402) 471-3189
  E-mail: marie.wiechman@nebraska.gov

# State Patrol

P.O. Box 94907, Lincoln, NE 68509-4907
Tel: (402) 471-4545  Fax: (402) 479-4002
Internet: statepatrol.nebraska.gov/
■ Superintendent **Col. Bradley Rice** .................... (402) 479-4931
  E-mail: brad.rice@nebraska.gov
Assistant Superintendent
  **Lt. Col. Thomas "Tom" Schwarten** ................(402) 479-4931

*(continued on next page)*

★ Elected Official   ■ Appointed by Governor   ● Appointed by Legislature   ▲ Appointed by Board or Commission   ◆ Appointed by State Supreme Court

**EXECUTIVE BRANCH**

**State Patrol** *continued*

Administrative Services **Major Russell Stanczyk** . . . . . . . .(402) 471-4545
E-mail: russ.stanczyk@nebraska.gov
Field Services **Major Mike Gaudreault** . . . . . . . . . . . . . .(402) 471-4545
Investigative Services **Major Kyle Otte** . . . . . . . . . . . . . . .(402) 471-4545

## Office of the Lieutenant Governor

State Capitol, 1445 K Street, Suite 2311, Lincoln, NE 68509-4863
P.O. Box 94863, Lincoln, NE 68509-4863
Tel: (402) 471-2256  Fax: (402) 471-6031

★Lieutenant Governor **Mike Foley** (R) . . . . . . . . . . . . . . .(402) 471-2256
Term Expires: January 2019
E-mail: mike.foley@nebraska.gov

## Office of the Secretary of State

2300 State Capitol, P.O. Box 94608, Lincoln, NE 68509-4608
Tel: (402) 471-2554  Fax: (402) 471-3237
Tel: (888) 727-0007 (Election Fraud Unit)
E-mail: receptionist@nebraska.gov  Internet: www.sos.state.ne.us

★Secretary of State **John A. Gale** (R) . . . . . . . . . . . . . . . .(402) 471-1572
Term Expires: 2019
E-mail: john.gale@nebraska.gov
Education: Carleton 1962 BA; Chicago 1965 JD
Executive Assistant to the Secretary **Joni Sailors** . . . . . . .(402) 471-1572
Communications Director **Laura Strimple** . . . . . . . . . . . . .(402) 471-8408
E-mail: laura.strimple@nebraska.gov
International Relations Coordinator **Laura Strimple** . . . . . .(402) 471-8408
Business Services Manager **Ann Hinkle** . . . . . . . . . . . . . . .(402) 471-3921
P.O. Box 95104, Lincoln, NE 68509-5104
Deputy Secretary of State for Elections **Neal Erickson** . . . .(402) 471-4127
Deputy Secretary of State for Records Management
**Cathy Danahy** . . . . . . . . . . . . . . . . . . . . . . . . . . . . . . .(402) 471-2745
P.O. Box 94921, Lincoln, NE 68509-4921
Finance and Human Resources Division Deputy Secretary
of State **Suzie Hinzman** . . . . . . . . . . . . . . . . . . . . . . . .(402) 471-2384
Rules and Regulations Director **David Wilson** . . . . . . . . . .(402) 471-4071
Rules and Regulations Assistant **Bess Boesiger** . . . . . . . . .(402) 471-2385
IT Officer **Gavin Crowl** . . . . . . . . . . . . . . . . . . . . . . . . .(402) 471-8779
E-mail: gavin.crowl@nebraska.gov
IT Systems Analyst **Chad Sump** . . . . . . . . . . . . . . . . . . . .(402) 471-8779
E-mail: chad.sump@nebraska.gov
Network Administrator **Dale Arp** . . . . . . . . . . . . . . . . . . .(402) 471-6158
Notary Public Officer **Lynne Blacketer** . . . . . . . . . . . . . . .(402) 471-4094
Accountant **Burdette Schoen** . . . . . . . . . . . . . . . . . . . . .(402) 471-4082
Senior Filing Specialist **Jody Damian** . . . . . . . . . . . . . . . .(402) 471-4079

## Office of the Attorney General

2115 State Capitol, Lincoln, NE 68509
P. O. Box 98920, Lincoln, NE 98920
Tel: (402) 471-2682  Fax: (402) 471-3297
E-mail: ago.consumer@nebraska.gov  Internet: ago.nebraska.gov

**Employees:** 91

★Attorney General **Douglas J. "Doug" Peterson** (R) . . . . .(402) 471-2682
Term Expires: 2019
Education: Nebraska 1981 BS; Pepperdine 1985 JD
Career: Assistant Attorney General, Office of the Attorney General,
State of Nebraska (1988-1990)
Chief Deputy Attorney General **Dave Bydalek** . . . . . . . . . .(402) 471-2682
Chief of Staff **Joshua Shassere** . . . . . . . . . . . . . . . . . . . .(402) 471-2682
Communications Director **Suzanne Gage** . . . . . . . . . . . . .(402) 471-2682
E-mail: suzanne.gage@nebraska.gov

## Office of the State Treasurer

State Capitol, Room 2005, Lincoln, NE 68509
Tel: (402) 471-2455

★State Treasurer **Don Stenberg** (R) . . . . . . . . . . . . . . . . .(402) 471-2455
Term Expires: 2019
E-mail: don.stenberg@nebraska.gov
Education: Nebraska 1970 BA; Harvard 1974 JD, 1974 MBA
Career: Legal Counsel, Office of the Governor, State of Nebraska;
Attorney General, Office of the Attorney General, State of Nebraska
(1991-2003)

Assistant Treasurer for Child Support Payment Center
**Troy Reiners** . . . . . . . . . . . . . . . . . . . . . . . . . . . . . . . .(402) 471-8444
E-mail: troy.reiners@nebraska.gov
Assistant Treasurer for College Savings Plan **Rachel Biar** . .(402) 471-1088
Assistant Treasurer for Long Term Care Savings
**Rachel Biar** . . . . . . . . . . . . . . . . . . . . . . . . . . . . . . . . .(402) 471-1088
Assistant Treasurer for Treasury Management
**Char Scott** . . . . . . . . . . . . . . . . . . . . . . . . . . . . . . . . .(402) 471-4146
Assistant Treasurer for Unclaimed Property
**Meaghan Aguirre** . . . . . . . . . . . . . . . . . . . . . . . . . . . . .(402) 471-1089

## Office of the Auditor of Public Accounts

P.O. Box 98917, Lincoln, NE 68509-8917
Tel: (402) 471-2111  Fax: (402) 471-3301
Internet: www.auditors.nebraska.gov

★State Auditor **Charlie Janssen** (R) . . . . . . . . . . . . . . . . .(402) 471-2111
Term Expires: 2019
Education: Wayne State Col 1997 BS
Career: State Senator (I-NE, District 15), Nebraska Legislature
(2009-2014)

## Nebraska Public Service Commission

300 The Atrium, 1200 N Street, Lincoln, NE 68508-2020
P.O. Box 94927, Lincoln, NE 68509-4927
Tel: (402) 471-3101  Fax: (402) 471-0254  TTY: (402) 471-0213

★Chair **Frank E. Landis, Jr.** (R-First District) . . . . . . . . . .(402) 471-0229
E-mail: frank.landis@nebraska.gov        Fax: (402) 471-0233
Education: Nebraska BS, JD
★Commissioner **Rod Johnson** (R-Fourth District) . . . . . . . .(402) 471-0212
E-mail: rod.johnson@nebraska.gov        Fax: (402) 471-0233
Education: Nebraska Wesleyan BS
★Commissioner **Crystal Rhoades** (D-Second District) . . . . .(402) 471-0215
Fax: (402) 471-0233
★Commissioner **Tim Schram** (R-Third District) . . . . . . . . . .(402) 471-0218
E-mail: tim.schram@nebraska.gov        Fax: (402) 471-0233
Education: Nebraska BS
★Commissioner **Gerald L. Vap** (R-Fifth District) . . . . . . . . .(402) 471-0216
E-mail: jerry.vap@nebraska.gov        Fax: (402) 471-0233
Education: Nebraska BS

## State Board of Education

301 Centennial Mall South, Lincoln, NE 68508-4912
P.O. Box 94987, Lincoln, NE 68509-4987
TTY: (402) 471-2295  Fax: (402) 471-0117

★President **Rachel Wise** (District 3) . . . . . . . . . . . . . . . . . .(402) 471-5024
Term Expires: 2017
E-mail: rachel.wise@nebraska.gov
Education: Nebraska 1978 BS, 1982 MEd, 1999 PhD
★Vice President **Lillian "Lillie" Larsen** (D-District 1) . . . . . .(402) 669-6731
Term Expires: 2017
E-mail: john.sieler@nebraska.gov
Education: Kansas 1963 BS; Nebraska 1968 MEd
★Member **Glen Flint** (District 2) . . . . . . . . . . . . . . . . . . . .(402) 253-2809
Term Expires: 2017
E-mail: glen.flint@nebraska.gov
Education: Nebraska BS; Nebraska (Omaha) MBA
★Member **Patrick "Pat" McPherson** (District 8) . . . . . . . . .(402) 471-5024
Term Expires: 2019
★Member **Maureen Nickels** (District 6) . . . . . . . . . . . . . . .(308) 754-5574
Term Expires: 2017
★Member **Molly O'Holleran** (District 7) . . . . . . . . . . . . . . .(308) 532-8783
Term Expires: 2017
E-mail: molly.oholleran@gmail.com
Education: Nebraska 1976 BA
★Member **Patricia Timm** (District 5) . . . . . . . . . . . . . . . . .(402) 228-4054
Term Expires: 2017
E-mail: patriciatimm04@gmail.com
Education: Kearney State 1969 BA

---

★ Elected Official    ■ Appointed by Governor    ● Appointed by Legislature    ▲ Appointed by Board or Commission    ◆ Appointed by State Supreme Court

★ Member **John Witzel** (District 4) . . . . . . . . . . . . . . . . . . . . . (402) 597-1175
    Term Expires: 2017
    E-mail: john.witzel@nebraska.gov
    Education: Bellevue U BS; Ball State MA

## Nebraska Department of Education [NDE]

Tel: (402) 471-2295   TTY: (402) 471-2295   Fax: (402) 471-0117

▲ Commissioner **Matthew L. Blomstedt** . . . . . . . . . . . . . . . . (402) 471-5020
    E-mail: matt.blomstedt@nebraska.gov
    Education: Nebraska BA, MCP, PhD
Deputy Commissioner and Chief of Staff **Brian Halstead** . . (402) 471-0732
    E-mail: brian.halstead@nebraska.gov
Operations Deputy Commissioner **Dr. Scott Swisher** . . . . . (402) 471-4884
    Education: Iowa State BA; Nebraska (Omaha) MA; South Dakota EdD
School Improvement and Support Deputy Commissioner
    **Deborah A. Frison** . . . . . . . . . . . . . . . . . . . . . . . . . . . . . . (402) 471-4884
Curriculum, Instruction and Innovation Administrator
    **Donlynn Rice** . . . . . . . . . . . . . . . . . . . . . . . . . . . . . . . . . . (402) 471-3240
Professional Practices Commission Clerk **Kathi Vontz** . . . . (402) 471-2943
    E-mail: kathi.vontz@nebraska.gov
Public Information Officer **Betty VanDeventer** . . . . . . . . . . (402) 471-4537
    E-mail: betty.vandeventer@nebraska.gov
Web Specialist **Katie Bieber** . . . . . . . . . . . . . . . . . . . . . . . (402) 471-2697

## Nebraska Accountability and Disclosure Commission

P.O. Box 95086, Lincoln, NE 68509-5086
Fax: (402) 471-6599   Tel: (402) 471-2522   Internet: http://nadc.nol.org

Chair **Timothy Schulz** . . . . . . . . . . . . . . . . . . . . . . . . . . . . . (402) 471-2522
    Term Expires: June 30, 2017
Vice Chair **Sean Conway** . . . . . . . . . . . . . . . . . . . . . . . . . . (402) 471-2522
    Term Expires: June 30, 2018
Secretary **Andrew Loudon** . . . . . . . . . . . . . . . . . . . . . . . . . (402) 471-2522
    Term Expires: June 30, 2019
Commissioner **Jeffery Davis** . . . . . . . . . . . . . . . . . . . . . . . . (402) 471-2522
    Term Expires: June 30, 2021
Commissioner **Matthew M. Enenbach** . . . . . . . . . . . . . . . . (402) 471-2522
    Term Expires: June 30, 2021
Commissioner **Jeffery Peetz** . . . . . . . . . . . . . . . . . . . . . . . . (402) 471-2522
    Term Expires: June 30, 2021
Commissioner **R. Brad von Gillern** . . . . . . . . . . . . . . . . . . . (402) 471-2522
    Term Expires: June 30, 2016
Commissioner **James Ziebarth** . . . . . . . . . . . . . . . . . . . . . . (402) 471-2522
    Term Expires: June 30, 2021
Statutory Commission Member **John A. Gale** . . . . . . . . . . . (402) 471-2522
    Affiliation: Secretary of State, Office of the Secretary of State, State of
    Nebraska
    2300 State Capitol, P.O. Box 94608, Lincoln, NE 68509-4608

**EXECUTIVE BRANCH**

# Nevada

Tel: (775) 684-1000 (State Operator)   Internet: www.nv.gov

**Number of U.S. Congressional Delegates:** 2 Senators; 4 Representatives   **Governor's Term:** 4 years
**Legislature Description:** 21 member Senate; 42 member Assembly; Term - Senate 4 years, Assembly 2 years   **Next Election:** Governor November 2018; Legislature November 2016
**Number of Electoral Votes:** 6   **Official Name:** State of Nevada (Spanish: snow clad)
**Nickname:** The Silver State; The Sagebrush State   **Motto:** All for Our Country

**Population:** 2,890,845 (2015); Rank 35   **Fiscal Year:** 2014   **Budget:** $6,672,868,000

## Office of the Governor

Executive Chambers, 101 North Carson Street, Carson City, NV 89701
Grant Sawyer State Office Building, 555 East Washington, Suite 1500, Las Vegas, NV 89101
Tel: (775) 684-5670   Fax: (775) 684-5683
E-mail: govcontact@gov.nv.gov

**Fiscal Year:** 2014   **Budget:** $2,189,000

**Brian E. Sandoval**
Governor

Began Service: January 3, 2011
Term Expires: January 2019
Date of Birth: August 5, 1963
Education: Nevada (Reno) 1986 BA; Ohio State 1989 JD
Home: Reno
Religion: Roman Catholic
Career: Assembly Member (R-NV, Washoe-25), Nevada Assembly (1994-1998); Attorney General, State of Nevada (2003-2005); District Judge, United States District Court for the District of Nevada (2005-2009)

★Governor **Brian E. Sandoval** (R) . . . . . . . . . . . . . . . . . . . . (775) 684-5670
  Special Assistant to the Governor **Christina Davis** . . . . . . (775) 684-5670
    E-mail: cmdavis@gov.nv.gov
Chief of Staff **Michael J. "Mike" Willden** . . . . . . . . . . . . (775) 684-5670
  E-mail: mwillden@gov.nv.gov
  Education: Southern Utah BA
  Executive Assistant **Linda Fitzgerald** . . . . . . . . . . . . . . . (775) 684-5670
Communications Director **Mari St. Martin** . . . . . . . . . . . . (775) 684-5679
  E-mail: mstmartin@gov.nv.gov
Constituent Services Director **Shannon Litz** . . . . . . . . . . . (775) 684-5670
  E-mail: slitz@gov.nv.gov
Policy Director **Pam Robinson** . . . . . . . . . . . . . . . . . . . . . (775) 684-5670
  E-mail: probinson@gov.nv.gov
Southern Nevada Office Manager **Annalyn Bo Carrillo** . . . . (775) 684-5670
  E-mail: abcarrillo@gov.nv.gov
Chief Strategy Officer **Dale A.R. Erquiaga** . . . . . . . . . . . . . (775) 684-5670
  Education: Nevada (Reno) 1985 BA; Grand Canyon 2009 MS
Legislative Policy Analyst **Matthew Morris** . . . . . . . . . . . . (775) 684-5670
  E-mail: mmorris@gov.nv.gov
■Veterans Policy Analyst **Cesar O. Melgarejo** . . . . . . . . . . . (775) 684-5670
  E-mail: comelgarejo@gov.nv.gov
General Counsel **Joseph "Joe" Reynolds** . . . . . . . . . . . . . (775) 684-5670
  Education: Gonzaga JD
Boards and Commissions Officer **Nikki Haag** . . . . . . . . . . . (775) 684-5670
Public Information Officer **Mari St. Martin** . . . . . (775) 684-5670 ext. 7307
  E-mail: mstmartin@gov.nv.gov
Education Policy Advisor **Zachary Heit** . . . . . . . . . . . . . . . (775) 684-5670
  E-mail: zheit@gov.nv.gov

## Governors Finance Office

Office Director **James R. "Jim" Wells, CPA** . . . . . . . . . . . (775) 684-0222
Internal Audits Administrator **(Vacant)** . . . . . . . . . . . . . . . (775) 687-5280

## Emergency Management Office

2478 Fairview Drive, Carson City, NV 89701
Advisor **Caleb Cage** . . . . . . . . . . . . . . . . . . . . . . . . . . . . (775) 687-0300
  Education: West Point 2002

## Nevada State Office of Energy [NSOE]

755 North Roop Street, Suite 202, Carson City, NV 89701
Tel: (775) 687-1850   Fax: (775) 687-1869
Director **Angela Dykema** . . . . . . . . . . . . . . . . . . . . (775) 687-1850 ext. 7310
  E-mail: adykema@energy.nv.gov

## Washington Office

444 North Capitol Street, NW, Suite 209, Washington, DC 20001
Tel: (202) 624-5405   Fax: (202) 624-8181

**Fiscal Year:** 2014   **Budget:** $253,000

Director **Ryan McGinness** . . . . . . . . . . . . . . . . . . . . . . . . (202) 624-5426
  E-mail: ryan@nevadadc.org
Policy Advisor **Tyler Klimas** . . . . . . . . . . . . . . . . . . . . . . (202) 624-5406
  Education: UNLV BA

## Department of Administration

515 East Musser Street, Suite 300, Carson City, NV 89701
Tel: (775) 684-0299   Tel: (775) 684-1000 (State operator)
Fax: (775) 684-0298   E-mail: deptadmin@admin.nv.gov

**Fiscal Year:** 2014   **Budget:** $163,431,000

■Director **Patrick Cates** . . . . . . . . . . . . . . . . . . . . . . . . . . (775) 684-0299
  Education: Nevada (Reno) 1993 BA
  Deputy Director **Lee-Ann Easton** . . . . . . . . . . . . . . . . . (775) 684-0299
    E-mail: leaston@admin.nv.gov
Risk Management Administrator **Ana M. Andrews** . . . . . . . (775) 687-3192
Administrative Services Division Administrator
  **Evan Dale** . . . . . . . . . . . . . . . . . . . . . . . . . . . . . . . . (775) 684-0273
  E-mail: edale@admin.nv.gov
Fleet Services Division Administrator **Keith Wells** . . . . . . . (775) 684-1880
  E-mail: kdwells@admin.nv.gov
Purchasing Division Administrator **Jeff Haag** . . . . . . . . . . . (775) 684-0170
State Library and Archives Administrator **Jeff Kintop** . . . . (775) 684-3315
  100 North Stewart Street, Carson City, NV 89701   Fax: (775) 684-3311
Victims of Crime/Hearings Division Officer **Bryan Nix** . . . . (702) 486-2525
  E-mail: bnix@admin.nv.gov
  Education: UNLV 1978 BA, 1981 JD

## State Public Works Division

515 East Musser Street, Suite 102, Carson City, NV 89701
Fax: (775) 687-4142
Administrator **Gus Nunez** . . . . . . . . . . . . . . . . . . . . . . . . (775) 684-4141

## Division of Human Resource Management

100 North Stewart Street, Suite 200, Carson City, NV 89701-4204
Tel: (775) 684-0150   TTY: (800) 326-6888   Fax: (775) 684-0124
Internet: hr.nv.gov

**Fiscal Year:** 2014   **Budget:** $10,818,000

■Administrator **Peter Long** . . . . . . . . . . . . . . . . . . . . . . . . (775) 684-0101
  Executive Assistant **Tawny Polito** . . . . . . . . . . . . . . . . . (775) 684-0131
Compensation and Classification Division Deputy
  Administrator **Peter Long** . . . . . . . . . . . . . . . . . . . . . . (775) 684-0103

---

★ Elected Official   ■ Appointed by Governor   ● Appointed by Legislature   ▲ Appointed by Board or Commission   ◆ Appointed by State Supreme Court

Employee and Management Services Division Deputy
**Shelley Blotter, CPM** . . . . . . . . . . . . . . . . . . . . . (775) 684-0105
Education: Cal State (Chico) BSBA
Recruitment and Retention Services Division
Administrator **Peter Long** . . . . . . . . . . . . . . . . . . . (702) 486-5294
Equal Employment Opportunity Officer **Ron Grogan** . . . . . (702) 486-5294

## State Board of Agriculture

405 South 21st Street, Sparks, NV 89431-5557
Tel: (775) 353-3601 Fax: (775) 353-3661

■ Chair **Paul Anderson** . . . . . . . . . . . . . . . . . . . . . . . (775) 353-3601
■ Vice Chair **Boyd Spratling** . . . . . . . . . . . . . . . . . . . (775) 353-3601
Education: Washington State 1975 DVM
■ Member **Timothy Dufurrena** . . . . . . . . . . . . . . . . . . (775) 353-3601
■ Member **Charles Frey** . . . . . . . . . . . . . . . . . . . . . . . (775) 353-3601
■ Member **Ramona Morrison** . . . . . . . . . . . . . . . . . . . (775) 353-3601
■ Member **Brian Nakaguchi** . . . . . . . . . . . . . . . . . . . . (775) 353-3601
■ Member **Paul R. Noe** . . . . . . . . . . . . . . . . . . . . . . . . (775) 353-3601
Education: Georgetown 1990 JD
■ Member **Pete Paris** . . . . . . . . . . . . . . . . . . . . . . . . . (775) 353-3601
■ Member **Alan Perazzo** . . . . . . . . . . . . . . . . . . . . . . . (775) 353-3601
■ Member **Jim Snyder** . . . . . . . . . . . . . . . . . . . . . . . . (775) 353-3601
■ Member **David Stix, Jr.** . . . . . . . . . . . . . . . . . . . . . . (775) 353-3601

## Department of Agriculture

405 South 21st Street, Sparks, NV 89431-5557
Tel: (775) 353-3601 Fax: (775) 353-3638

**Fiscal Year:** 2014 **Budget:** $161,804,000

■ Director **James R. "Jim" Barbee** . . . . . . . . . . . . . . . (775) 353-3601
Education: UNLV 1999 BS
■ Deputy Director **Lynn C. Hettrick** . . . . . . . . . . . . . . (775) 353-3601
E-mail: lhettrick@agri.nv.gov
Animal Industry Division Administrator **Flint Wright** . . . . . (775) 353-3601
405 South 21st Street, Sparks, NV 89431
State Veterinarian **Dr. Julian Joesep Goicoechea, DVM** . . (775) 738-8076
Fax: (775) 688-1198
Animal Disease Laboratory Supervisor **Anette Rink** . . . . (775) 353-3601
Fax: (775) 688-1198
Consumer Equitability Division Administrator
**Bart O'Toole** . . . . . . . . . . . . . . . . . . . . . . . . . . . (775) 688-1166
Food and Nutrition Division Administrator
**Donnell Barton** . . . . . . . . . . . . . . . . . . . . . . . . . . (775) 353-3601
E-mail: dbarton@agri.nv.gov
Plant Industry Division Administrator **Robert Little** . . . . . (775) 353-3601
Nevada Beef Council Chairman **Lucy Rechel** . . . . . . . . . (877) 544-2335
PO Box 340310, Sacramento, CA 95843-0310 Fax: (916) 925-8155
Predatory Animal and Rodent Committee Chairman
**Pete Paris** . . . . . . . . . . . . . . . . . . . . . . . . . . . . . . (775) 353-3601
8775 Technology Way, Reno, NV 89521
State Grazing Board Chairman **Hank Vogler** . . . . . . . . . (775) 691-0404
Education: Nevada (Reno) BS
Junior Livestock Show Board President **Matt McKinney** . . (775) 853-6770
P.O. Box 8026, Reno, NV 89507
Executive Assistant **Jerri Conrad** . . . . . . . . . . . . . . . . (775) 353-3619
E-mail: jwilliams-conrad@agri.nv.gov

## Department of Business and Industry

1830 College Parkway, Suite 100, Carson City, NV 89706
555 East Washington Avenue, Suite 4900, Las Vegas, NV 89101
Tel: (775) 684-2999 Tel: (702) 486-2750 Fax: (702) 486-2758
E-mail: biinfo@dbi.state.nv.us

**Fiscal Year:** 2014 **Budget:** $174,035,000

■ Director **Bruce H. Breslow** . . . . . . . . . . . . . . . . . . . (775) 684-2999
E-mail: breslow@business.nv.gov
Education: Missouri 1977 BAJ
Financial Institutions Commissioner **George Burns** . . . . . (775) 486-4150
2785 E Desert Inn Road, Suite 180, Fax: (702) 486-4563
Las Vegas, NV 89121
Mortgage Lending Commissioner **James E. Westrin** . . . . . (702) 486-0780
7220 Bermuda Road, Suite A, Fax: (702) 486-0785
Las Vegas, NV 89119

Housing Division Administrator **C.J. Manthe** . . . . . . . . . (775) 687-2040
1535 Old Hot Springs Road, Suite 50, Fax: (775) 687-4040
Carson City, NV 89706
Manufactured Housing Administrator
**James "Jim" DeProsse** . . . . . . . . . . . . . . . . . . . . . (775) 684-2940
1535 Old Hot Springs Road, Suite 60, Fax: (775) 684-2949
Carson City, NV 89706
Education: Whittier 1977 BA
Injured Workers Attorney **Evan Beavers** . . . . . . . . . . . . (775) 684-7555
1000 East William Street, Suite 208, Fax: (775) 684-7575
Carson City, NV 89710

## Department of Conservation and Natural Resources [DCNR]

Bryan Building, 901 South Stewart Street, Suite 1003,
Carson City, NV 89701
Tel: (775) 684-2700 Fax: (775) 684-2715 Internet: www.dcnr.nv.gov

**Fiscal Year:** 2014 **Budget:** $107,671,000

■ Director **Leo Drozdoff** . . . . . . . . . . . . . . . . . . . . . . . (775) 684-2700
E-mail: ldrozdoff@dcnr.nv.gov
Deputy Director **Jim Lawrence** . . . . . . . . . . . . . . . . . . (775) 684-2700
Deputy Director **Kay Scherer** . . . . . . . . . . . . . . . . . . . (775) 684-2700
Public Information Officer **Jenny Ramella** . . . . . . . . . . . (775) 684-2704
E-mail: jramella@dcnr.nv.gov
Conservation Districts Program Manager **Tim Rubald** . . . . (775) 684-2760
State Lands Division Administrator **Charlie Donohue** . . . . (775) 684-2720
E-mail: cdonohue@lands.nv.gov
State Lands Division Deputy Administrator
**Elizabeth Kingsland** . . . . . . . . . . . . . . . . . . . . . . . (775) 684-2720
E-mail: ekingsland@lands.nv.gov
State Parks Division Administrator **Eric M. Johnson** . . . . . (775) 684-2770
State Parks Division Deputy Administrator
**Bob Mergell** . . . . . . . . . . . . . . . . . . . . . . . . . . . . (775) 684-2770
State Forester **Joe Freeland** . . . . . . . . . . . . . . . . . . . . (775) 684-2500
Deputy State Forester **Kacey KC** . . . . . . . . . . . . . . . . . (775) 684-2522
Deputy State Forester **Dave Prather** . . . . . . . . . . . . . . (775) 684-2500
Water Resources Division State Engineer **Jason King** . . . . (775) 684-2800
Historic Preservation Office Administrator
**Rebecca Palmer** Suite 5004 . . . . . . . . . . . . . . . . . . . (775) 684-3440
Fax: (775) 684-3442

## Division of Environmental Protection

901 South Stewart Street, Suite 4001, Carson City, NV 89701
Tel: (775) 687-9349 Fax: (775) 687-5856

Administrator **Dave Emme** . . . . . . . . . . . . . . . . . . . . . (775) 687-4670
E-mail: demme@ndep.nv.gov
Education: Montana; Nevada (Reno)

## Nevada Department of Corrections [NDOC]

P.O. Box 7011, Carson City, NV 89702
Tel: (775) 887-3249 Internet: www.doc.nv.gov

■ Director **James Dzurenda** . . . . . . . . . . . . . . . . . . . . (775) 887-3249
E-mail: jedzurenda@doc.nv.gov
Education: Southern Connecticut State U BS; New Haven MBA
Executive Assistant **Cynthia Keller** . . . . . . . . . . . . . . . (702) 486-9912
Medical Director **Romeo Aranas** . . . . . . . . . . . . . . . . . (775) 887-3392
Industrial Programs Deputy Director **Brian Connett** . . . . . (702) 486-9997
Operations North Deputy Director **(Vacant)** . . . . . . . . . . (702) 486-9912
Programs South Deputy Director **(Vacant)** . . . . . . . . . . . (702) 486-9990
Support Services Deputy Director **Scott Sisco** . . . . . . . . (775) 887-3203
Inspector General **Pamela Del Porto** . . . . . . . . . . . . . . (775) 887-3395
E-mail: pdelporto@doc.nv.gov
Family Services Chief **Ronda Larsen** . . . . . . . . . . . . . . (775) 887-3367
Fiscal Services Chief **John Borrowman** . . . . . . . . . . . . . (775) 887-3328
Inmate Services Administrator **Dawn Rosenberg** . . . . . . . (775) 887-3319
Offender Management Chief **Dwayne Deal** . . . . . . . . . . . (775) 887-3279
Plant Operations Chief **Kent Lefevre** . . . . . . . . . . . . . . (702) 486-9957
Purchasing Chief **Dawn Rosenberg** . . . . . . . . . . . . . . . (775) 887-3219
Human Resources Division Administrator
**Sharlet Gabriel** . . . . . . . . . . . . . . . . . . . . . . . . . . (702) 486-9944
MIS Chief IT Manager **(Vacant)** . . . . . . . . . . . . . . . . . (775) 887-3308

*(continued on next page)*

★ Elected Official    ■ Appointed by Governor    ● Appointed by Legislature    ▲ Appointed by Board or Commission    ◆ Appointed by State Supreme Court

**Nevada Department of Corrections** *continued*

Victim Services Officer **Traci Dory** . . . . . . . . . . . . . . . . . . (775) 887-3285
   E-mail: tdory@doc.nv.gov
                                      Fax: (775) 887-3167
Public Information Officer **Brooke Keast** . . . . . . . . . . . . . . (775) 887-3309
   E-mail: bkeast@doc.nv.gov

# Department of Employment, Training and Rehabilitation [DETR]

500 East Third Street, Carson City, NV 89713
Tel: (775) 684-3849  TTY: (775) 687-5353  Fax: (775) 684-3850
E-mail: detrinfo@nvdetr.org  Internet: www.nvdetr.org

■Director **Donald L. "Don" Soderberg** . . . . . . . . . . . . . . . . (702) 486-6637
   E-mail: dsoderberg@leg.state.nv.us
   Education: UNLV 1982 BA; San Diego 1988 JD
Deputy Director **Dennis Perea** . . . . . . . . . . . . . . . . . . . . . . . (775) 684-3849
   E-mail: dperea@leg.state.nv.us
Employment Security Division Administrator
   **Renee Olson, CPM** . . . . . . . . . . . . . . . . . . . . . . . . . . . . (775) 684-3849
   2800 East St. Louis Avenue, Las Vegas, NV 89104
   E-mail: rolson@leg.state.nv.us
   Education: Nevada (Reno) BS
Information Development and Processing Division
   Administrator **David "Dave" Haws** . . . . . . . . . . . . . . . . (775) 684-3849
   2800 East St. Louis Avenue, Las Vegas, NV 89104
   E-mail: dhaws@leg.state.nv.us
Rehabilitation Division Administrator
   **Shelley Rohr Hendren** . . . . . . . . . . . . . . . . . . . . . . . . . (775) 684-3849
   E-mail: shelley.hendren@leg.state.nv.us
   Education: Park U 1986 BA

# Department of Health and Human Services [DHHS]

4126 Technology Way, Suite 100, Carson City, NV 89706
Tel: (775) 684-4000  Fax: (775) 684-4010  E-mail: nvdhhs@dhhs.nv.gov
Internet: www.dhhs.nv.gov

■Director **Richard Whitley** . . . . . . . . . . . . . . . . . . . . . . . . . (775) 684-4000
   Education: Western Oregon U MCoun
Administrative Services Deputy Director **Deborah Harris** . . . (775) 684-4000
   E-mail: dharris@dhhs.nv.gov
Fiscal Services Deputy Director **Ellen Crecelius** . . . . . . . . . (775) 684-4000
Programs Deputy Director **Dena Schmidt** . . . . . . . . . . . . . (775) 684-4000
Public Information Officer **Chrystal C. Main** . . . . . . . . . . . (775) 684-4024

# State Public Defender's Office

Tel: (775) 687-1080  Fax: (775) 687-4993

**Fiscal Year:** 2014  **Budget:** $2,728,000

State Public Defender **Karin Kreizenbeck, JD** . . . . . . . . . . . (775) 684-1080
   Education: U Santa Clara JD
Chief Deputy Public Defender **Marcie E. Ryba** . . . . . . . . . (775) 684-1080
Chief Appellate Deputy **Sally DeSoto** . . . . . . . . . . . . . . . . (775) 684-1080
Chief Trial Deputy **William Murphy** . . . . . . . . . . . . . . . . . (775) 684-1080

# Aging and Disability Services Division

3416 Goni Road, Suite D-132, Carson City, NV 89706
Fax: (775) 687-0574  E-mail: adsd@adsd.nv.gov

Administrator **Jane Gruner** . . . . . . . . . . . . . . . . . . . . . . . . . (775) 687-4210

# Office of the Military

2460 Fairview Drive, Carson City, NV 89701-5502
Tel: (775) 887-7302  Fax: (775) 887-7315

**Employees:** 127  **Fiscal Year:** 2014  **Budget:** $17,545,000

■Adjutant General **BrigGen William R. Burks, ANG** . . . . . . (775) 887-7302
   E-mail: william.burks.1@ang.af.mil
   Education: Nevada (Reno) 1976 BA; National Defense U 2000 MS;
   Air Command Col 1996
Executive Officer to the Adjutant General
   **Nicholas Chabez** . . . . . . . . . . . . . . . . . . . . . . . . . . . . . (775) 887-7296
   E-mail: nicholas.chabez@us.army.mil
Executive Secretary **Samantha Perry** . . . . . . . . . . . . . . . . . (775) 887-7302
Senior Enlisted Leader **CSM Jared J. Kopacki, ARNG** . . . (775) 887-7302
Joint Staff Director **BG Zachary Doser, ARNG** . . . . . . . . . (775) 887-7302

Judge Advocate General **Scott Katherman** . . . . . . . . . . . . . (775) 887-8411
   E-mail: scott.katherman@leg.state.nv.us
Contracting and Small Business Officer **Dario Risoni** . . . . . (775) 887-7872
Public Affairs Officer **Mickey Kirschenbaum** . . . . . . . . . . (775) 887-7252
                                        Fax: (775) 887-7256

# Nevada National Guard

2460 Fairview Drive, Carson City, NV 89701-5502
Tel: (775) 887-7302  Fax: (775) 887-7315

■Adjutant General **BrigGen William R. Burks, ANG** . . . . . . (775) 887-7302
   E-mail: william.burks.1@ang.af.mil
State Command Sergeant Major
   **CSM Jared J. Kopacki, ARNG** . . . . . . . . . . . . . . . . . . (775) 887-7302

# Nevada Air National Guard

1776 National Guard Way, Reno, NV 89502
Tel: (775) 788-4515

Assistant Adjutant General
   **BrigGen Ondra L. Berry, ANG** . . . . . . . . . . . . . . . . . . (775) 788-4515
   Education: Evansville 1986 BA; Nevada (Reno) 1996 MPA
Commander **(Vacant)** . . . . . . . . . . . . . . . . . . . . . . . . . . . . (702) 521-2685
Chief of Staff **Col Glen Martel, ANG** . . . . . . . . . . . . . . . . (775) 887-7310
   Education: Nevada (Reno) BSCE, 2016 MBA

# Nevada Army National Guard

2460 Fairview Drive, Carson City, NV 89701-5502
Tel: (775) 887-7302

Commander **BG Michael Hanifan, ARNG** . . . . . . . . . . . . . (775) 887-7308
Chief of Staff **BG Zachary Doser, ARNG** . . . . . . . . . . . . . (775) 887-7308
Chief Information Officer **LTC Carsten Hall, ARNG** . . . . . . (775) 887-7261

# Department of Motor Vehicles [DMV]

555 Wright Way, Carson City, NV 89711-0900
Tel: (775) 684-4368  Tel: (877) 368-7828  Fax: (775) 684-4992
E-mail: info@dmv.nv.gov  Internet: www.dmvnv.com

**Fiscal Year:** 2014  **Budget:** $121,050,000

■Director **Terri Albertson** . . . . . . . . . . . . . . . . . . . . . . . . . . (775) 684-4549
   E-mail: talbertson@dmv.nv.gov
   Education: Fresno Pacific BA
   Executive Assistant **Charlene Peters** . . . . . . . . . . . . . . . (775) 684-4955
   Administrative Assistant **Tina Springer** . . . . . . . . . . . . . (775) 684-4549
Administrative Services Division Chief **Cyndie Munoz** . . . (775) 684-4501
   E-mail: cmunoz@dmv.nv.gov
   Administrative Assistant **(Vacant)** . . . . . . . . . . . . . . . . . (775) 684-4533
Central Services Administrator **Sean McDonald** . . . . . . . . . (775) 684-4934
   E-mail: smcdonald@dmv.nv.gov
   Administrative Assistant **Griselda Contreras-Madera** . . . (775) 684-4966
      E-mail: gmadera@dmv.nv.gov
Compliance Enforcement Administrator **Donnie Perry** . . . . (775) 684-4782
   E-mail: dperry@dmv.nv.gov
Field Services Administrator **Tonya Laney** . . . . . . . . . . . . . (775) 684-4791
   E-mail: tlaney@dmv.nv.gov
   Administrative Assistant **Aja Stewart-Hensley** . . . . . . . . (775) 684-4598
      E-mail: astewart-hensley@dmv.nv.gov
Motor Carrier Administrator **Wayne Seidel** . . . . . . . . . . . . (775) 684-4613
   E-mail: wseidel@dmv.nv.gov
Administrative Assistant **Anne Niebling** . . . . . . . . . . . . . . . (775) 684-4815
   E-mail: aniebling@dmv.nv.gov
Research and Development Administrator **Jude Hurin** . . . . (775) 684-4562
   E-mail: jhurin@dmv.nv.gov
   Administrative Assistant **Roxyanne Severance** . . . . . . . . (775) 684-4783
      E-mail: rseverance@dmv.nv.gov
Motor Vehicles Information Technology Administrator
   **Mark Froese** . . . . . . . . . . . . . . . . . . . . . . . . . . . . . . . . (775) 684-4578
   E-mail: mfroese@dmv.nv.gov
   Administrative Assistant **Kathlean Maskaly** . . . . . . . . . . (775) 684-4913

---

★ Elected Official   ■ Appointed by Governor   ● Appointed by Legislature   ▲ Appointed by Board or Commission   ◆ Appointed by State Supreme Court

## Department of Public Safety

555 Wright Way, Carson City, NV 89711-0900
Tel: (775) 684-4556  Fax: (775) 684-4809

**Fiscal Year:** 2014  **Budget:** $198,804,000

■Director **James "Jim" Wright** . . . . . . . . . . . . . . . . . . . (775) 684-4808
  E-mail: jwright@dps.state.nv.us
  Education: Col of the Desert AS; Cogswell Col BS
  Executive Assistant **Linda Herron** . . . . . . . . . . . . . . . . . . (775) 684-4556
Deputy Director **Jackie Muth** . . . . . . . . . . . . . . . . . . (775) 684-4556
Senior Deputy Attorney General **Mike Jensen** . . . . . . . . . . (775) 687-0394
State Fire Marshal **Peter "Pete" Mulvihill** . . . . . . . . . . . . (775) 684-7501
  Stewart Facility, 107 Jacobsen Way,    Fax: (775) 684-7507
  Carson City, NV 89710
  E-mail: pmulvihill@dps.state.nv.us
Administrative Services Division Chief
  **Sheri Brueggemann** . . . . . . . . . . . . . . . . . . . . . . . . (775) 684-4536
  E-mail: sbrueggemann@dps.state.nv.us
Capitol Police Division Chief **Jerome Tushbant** . . . . . . . . (775) 684-5700
                                   Fax: (775) 684-5701
General Services Division Chief **Julie Butler** . . . . . . . . . . (775) 684-6262
  E-mail: jbutler@dps.state.nv.us     Fax: (775) 684-4879
Highway Patrol Division Chief **Dennis Osborn** . . . . . . . . . (775) 687-5300
Investigation Division Chief **Patrick "Pat" Conmay** . . . . . . (775) 687-1600
  E-mail: pconmay@dps.state.nv.us     Fax: (775) 684-4879
Parole and Probation Division Chief **Natalie Wood** . . . . . (775) 684-2600
                                   Fax: (775) 684-2697
Traffic Safety Division Chief **Amy Davey** . . . . . . . . . . . . (775) 684-7476
                                   Fax: (775) 684-7482
Training Division Chief **Dean Buell** . . . . . . . . . . . . (775) 687-1610 ext. 223
  E-mail: dbuell@dps.state.nv.us     Fax: (775) 684-1613
Criminal Justice Assistance Chief **Charise Whitt** . . . . . . . . (775) 687-3700
Emergency Management/Homeland Security Chief
  **Caleb Cage** . . . . . . . . . . . . . . . . . . . . . . . (775) 687-0300
Public Information Officer **Davis Gibson** . . . . . . . . . . . . . (775) 434-9128
  E-mail: dgibson@dps.state.nv.us

## Tax Commission

1550 College Parkway, Suite 115, Carson City, NV 89706-7937
Tel: (775) 684-2100  Fax: (775) 684-2020

■Chairman **James C. DeVolld** . . . . . . . . . . . . . . . . . . (775) 684-2000
■Member **Dr. Ann Bersi** . . . . . . . . . . . . . . . . . . . . . . (775) 684-2000
  Education: San Diego State BA, MA; Connecticut PhD
■Member **George Kelesis** . . . . . . . . . . . . . . . . . . . . . (775) 684-2000
■Member **Francine J. Lipman** . . . . . . . . . . . . . . . . . . (775) 684-2000
■Member **John E. Marvel** . . . . . . . . . . . . . . . . . . . . . (775) 684-2000
  Education: Nevada (Reno) 1973 BS; McGeorge 1978 JD
■Member **Thomas R. Sheets** . . . . . . . . . . . . . . . . . . . (775) 684-2000
  Education: Ashland 1973 BS; Toledo 1975 JD
■Member **Craig M. Witt** . . . . . . . . . . . . . . . . . . . . . . (775) 684-2000
■Member **Anthony "Tony" Wren** . . . . . . . . . . . . . . . . . (775) 684-2000

## Department of Taxation

1550 College Parkway, Suite 115, Carson City, NV 89706-7937
Tel: (775) 684-2000  Fax: (775) 684-2020  Internet: http://tax.state.nv.us

**Fiscal Year:** 2014  **Budget:** $26,397,000

■Executive Director **Deonne Contine** . . . . . . . . . . . . . . . (775) 684-2060
  E-mail: contine@tax.state.nv.us
Chief Deputy Executive Director **Shellie Hughes** . . . . . . . (775) 684-2176
Deputy Executive Director **Jay Kvam** . . . . . . . . . . . . . . (775) 684-2154
Deputy Executive Director **Paulina Oliver** . . . . . . . . . . . (702) 486-2331
Deputy Executive Director **Terry Rubald** . . . . . . . . . . . . (775) 684-2095
  Education: Wyoming 1976 BS, 1998 MPA
Deputy Executive Director **Kannaiah Vadlakunta** . . . . . . . (775) 684-2167
Administrative Service Officer **Rick Gimlin** . . . . . . . . . . . (775) 684-2071
  E-mail: gimlin@tax.state.nv.us

## Department of Tourism and Cultural Affairs

401 North Carson Street, Suite B, Carson City, NV 89701
Tel: (775) 687-0621  Fax: (775) 687-6159  Internet: travelnevada.com

**Fiscal Year:** 2014  **Budget:** $31,012,000

■Director **Claudia Vecchio** . . . . . . . . . . . . . . . . . . . . . (775) 687-0621
  E-mail: cvecchio@travelnevada.com
  Education: BYU BA
Museums and History Administrator **Peter Barton** . . . . . . (775) 687-4340
  708 North Curry Street, Carson City, NV 89703    Fax: (775) 687-4333
  Education: SUNY (Albany) 1975 BS

## Department of Transportation

1263 South Stewart Street, Carson City, NV 89712
Tel: (775) 888-7000  Fax: (775) 888-7201  Internet: www.nevadadot.com

**Fiscal Year:** 2014  **Budget:** $38,007,000

■Director **Rudy Malfabon, PE** . . . . . . . . . . . . . . . . . . . (775) 888-7440
  E-mail: rmalfabon@dot.state.nv.us
  Education: Nevada (Reno) 1981 BSCE
  Executive Assistant **Holli Stocks** . . . . . . . . . . . . . . . . (775) 888-7440
Deputy Director North **Bill Hoffman** . . . . . . . . . . . . . . . (775) 888-7440
Deputy Director South **Tracy Larkin-Thomason** . . . . . . . . (702) 385-6506
Chief Counsel **Dennis Gallagher** . . . . . . . . . . . . . . . . . (775) 888-7420
  E-mail: dgallagher@ag.nv.gov
Administration Assistant Director **Robert Nellis** . . . . . . . . (775) 888-7440
  E-mail: rnellis@dot.state.nv.us
  Education: San José State 1991 BS; Regent U 1993 MA
Engineering Assistant Director **John Terry** . . . . . . . . . . . (775) 888-7440
  E-mail: jterry@dot.state.nv.us
Operations Assistant Director **Reid Kaiser** . . . . . . . . . . . (775) 888-7440
Planning Assistant Director **Sondra Rosenberg** . . . . . . . . (775) 888-7440
  E-mail: srosenberg@dot.state.nv.us
Safety Division Engineering Chief **Ken Mammen** . . . . . . . (775) 888-7335
  E-mail: kmammen@dot.state.nv.us
Traffic Division Engineering Chief **Denise Inda** . . . . . . . . (775) 888-7867
  E-mail: dinda@dot.state.nv.us
Design Division Chief and Road Design Engineer
  **Paul Frost** . . . . . . . . . . . . . . . . . . . . . . . . . . (775) 888-7490
  E-mail: pfrost@dot.state.nv.us
Bridge Division Engineer **Jessen Mortensen** . . . . . . . . . . (775) 888-7542
Chief Construction Division Engineer
  **Sharon Foerschler** . . . . . . . . . . . . . . . . . . . . . . . (775) 888-7065
Maintenance and Asset Management Division Engineer
  **Anita Bush** . . . . . . . . . . . . . . . . . . . . . . . . . . (775) 888-7856
  E-mail: abush@dot.state.nv.us
Materials Division Engineer **Darin Tedford** . . . . . . . . . . . (775) 888-7520
  E-mail: dtedford@dot.state.nv.us
Operations Analysis Division Engineer **Peter Aiyuk** . . . . . . (775) 888-7192
  E-mail: paiyuk@dot.state.nv.us
Transportation and Multi-Modal Planning Program
  Development **Mark Costa** . . . . . . . . . . . . . . . . . . . (775) 888-7120
Communications Manager **Sean Severs** . . . . . . . . . . . . . (775) 888-7278
  E-mail: ssever@dot.state.nv.us

## Department of Wildlife [NDOW]

1100 Valley Road, Reno, NV 89512
Tel: (775) 688-1500  Fax: (775) 688-1595  Internet: www.ndow.org

**Fiscal Year:** 2014  **Budget:** $38,007,000

■Director **Tony Wasley** . . . . . . . . . . . . . . . . . . . . . . . (775) 688-1500
  E-mail: twasley@ndow.org
  Education: Cal State (East Bay) BS; Idaho State MSc
  Executive Assistant to the Director **Suzanne Scourby** . . . (775) 688-1500
Deputy Director **Jack Robb** . . . . . . . . . . . . . . . . . . . . (775) 688-1500
Operations Deputy Director **Elizabeth "Liz" O'Brien** . . . . . (775) 688-1982
Conservation Education Division Chief **Teresa Moiola** . . . . (775) 688-1555
  E-mail: tmoiola@ndow.org
  Education: Nevada (Reno) 1998 BA
Fisheries Division Chief **Jon Sjoberg** . . . . . . . . . . . . . . . (775) 688-1569
Game Bureau Chief **Brian Wakeling** . . . . . . . . . . . . . . . (775) 688-1529
Habitat Division Chief **Allen Jenne** . . . . . . . . . . . . . . . . (775) 463-7816
  E-mail: ajenne@ndow.org
Law Enforcement Division Chief **Tyler Turnipseed** . . . . . . (775) 688-1549

*(continued on next page)*

---

★ Elected Official    ■ Appointed by Governor    ● Appointed by Legislature    ▲ Appointed by Board or Commission    ◆ Appointed by State Supreme Court

**Department of Wildlife** *continued*

Wildlife Diversity Division Chief **Jennifer Newmark**.....(775) 688-1996

# Agency for Nuclear Projects

1761 East College Parkway, Suite 118, Carson City, NV 89706
Tel: (775) 687-3744  Fax: (775) 687-5277  E-mail: nwpo@nuc.state.nv.us

■Executive Director **Robert J. "Bob" Halstead** .......... (775) 687-3744
  Education: Delaware BS; Wisconsin MS

# Department of Veterans Services [NOVS]

6880 S. McCarran Boulevard, Suite A., Reno, NV 89509
Tel: (866) 630-8387  Fax: (775) 688-1656

**Fiscal Year:** 2014  **Budget:** $21,997,000

■Director **COL Katherine Miller, USA (Ret)** ............ (775) 688-1653
  E-mail: kmiller@va.gov
■Deputy Director **(Vacant)** ......................... (702) 486-3828
  Benefits Deputy Director
  **RADM Kathleen M. Dussault, USN (Ret)** ....... (702) 486-3828
    Education: Virginia 1977 BA; National Defense U 1999 MS
  Wellness Deputy Director **Wendy Simons** ............. (775) 688-1653

# Commission on Postsecondary Education

8778 South Maryland Parkway, Suite 115, Las Vegas, NV 89123
Tel: (702) 486-7330  Fax: (702) 486-7340  Internet: www.cpe.state.nv.us

**Fiscal Year:** 2016  **Budget:** $406,000

■Chairman **Adriana F. Fralick, Esq.** ................... (702) 486-7330
  E-mail: afralick@leg.state.nv.us
  Education: Nevada (Reno) 1998; UNLV 2003 JD
■Vice Chairman **Ann Lynch**.......................... (702) 486-7330
  E-mail: alynch@leg.state.nv.us
■Commissioner **Larry Clark** ......................... (702) 486-7330
  E-mail: lclark@state.nv.us
■Commissioner **David Cook** ......................... (702) 486-7330
  E-mail: dcook@leg.state.nv.us
■Commissioner **Sharon L. Frederick** ................. (702) 486-7330
  E-mail: sfrederick@leg.state.nv.us
■Commissioner **Jill Greiner** ......................... (702) 486-7330
■Commissioner **B.J. North**........................... (702) 486-7330
  E-mail: bjnorth@leg.state.nv.us

## Staff
Administrator **Kelly Wuest** ......................... (702) 486-7330

# Public Utilities Commission of Nevada [PUCN]

1150 East William Street, Carson City, NV 89701-3109
Tel: (775) 684-6101  Fax: (775) 684-6110

**Fiscal Year:** 2014-2015  **Budget:** $13,123,000

■Chairman **Paul Thomsen**............................(775) 684-6107
  Education: UNLV BS; Nevada (Reno) MPA
■Commissioner **Alaina Burtenshaw, Esq.** .............(775) 684-6107
■Commissioner **David Noble**.........................(775) 684-6107
  Education: Pennsylvania; Loyola Law JD

# Nevada Commission on Tourism

401 North Carson Street, Carson City, NV 89701
Tel: (775) 687-4322  Fax: (775) 687-6779
E-mail: ncot@travelnevada.com  Internet: http://travelnevada.com

■Director **Claudia Vecchio**...........................(775) 687-4322
  E-mail: cvecchio@travelnevada.com

# Nevada Gaming Control Board

1919 College Park Way, Carson City, NV 89706
P.O. Box 8003, Carson City, NV 89702
Tel: (775) 684-7700  Fax: (775) 687-5817  Internet: gaming.state.nv.us

**Fiscal Year:** 2014  **Budget:** $60,097,000

■Chairman **A.G. Burnett** ............................ (775) 684-7740
Member **Terry Johnson** ............................. (775) 684-7740
Member **Shawn R. Reid** ............................. (775) 684-7740
▲Executive Secretary **Marie Bell** .................... (775) 684-7750

# State Board of Education

700 East Fifth Street, Carson City, NV 89701
Tel: (775) 687-9225  Fax: (775) 687-9202

■President **Elaine P. Wynn**...........................(702) 466-7705
  Term Expires: January 2017
  E-mail: kjohansen@doe.nv.gov
  Education: George Washington 1964 BA
★Vice President **Mark Newburn** (D-District 4) ......... (775) 687-9225
  Term Expires: January 4, 2017
  E-mail: mnewburn@doe.nv.gov
  Education: UNLV 1981 BS, 1983 MS
★Member **Felicia Ortiz** (District 3) ................... (775) 851-9059
  Term Expires: January 4, 2017
  E-mail: felicia.ortiz.nved@gmail.com
●Member **Freeman Holbrook** ....................... (775) 885-1454
  Term Expires: January 2017
  E-mail: fholbrook@washoeschools.net
●Member **Tonia Holmes-Sutton** ..................... (775) 885-1454
  Term Expires: January 2017
  E-mail: holmessutton@gmail.com
Member **Teri Jamin** ................................ (775) 687-9225
  Term Expires: January 1, 2017
  E-mail: booklover83153@aol.com
  Education: UC Riverside BS, BA; UCLA MA
Member **Dave Jensen** .............................. (702) 586-1742
  Term Expires: January 1, 2017
  E-mail: djensen@humboldt.k12.nv.us
Member **Allison Stephens** .......................... (775) 738-3278
  Term Expires: January 1, 2017
  E-mail: allison_stephens@nshe.nevada.edu
  Education: UNLV 2002 BS, 2004 MEd
■Member **Victor Wakefield** (District 1) ................ (775) 687-9225
  Term Expires: January 4, 2017
  E-mail: victor.wakefield.nved@gmail.com
★Member **Pat Hickey** (R) ............................ (775) 885-1454
  Term Expires: January 1, 2017
  Student Representative Member **Samantha Molisee** ......(702) 457-6568
  Term Expires: May 31, 2017
  E-mail: sam.molisee@gmail.com

# Department of Education

700 East Fifth Street, Carson City, NV 89701-5096
Tel: (775) 687-9200  Fax: (775) 687-9202  Internet: www.doe.nv.gov

**Fiscal Year:** 2014  **Budget:** $1,898,745,000

■Superintendent **Steve Canavero, PhD** ................ (775) 687-9200
  E-mail: scanavero@doe.nv.gov
Executive Assistant **Mayita Sanchez** ................. (775) 687-9217

## Administrative and Fiscal Services
Deputy Superintendent **Mindy Martini** ................(775) 687-9175
  E-mail: mmartini@doe.nv.gov
  Assistant to the Deputy Superintendent **Brett Barley** .... (775) 687-9224
Finance Director **Andrienne Monroe** ................. (775) 687-9234
Technology and Innovative Programs Director
  **Glenn Meyer** ................................... (775) 687-9126
  E-mail: gmeyer@doe.nv.gov
Safe and Respectful Learning Environment Office
  Director **Edward "Ed" Ableser** ................... (775) 687-5791
    Education: Arizona State 2000 BA

## Student Achievement
Deputy Superintendent **Brett Barley** .................. (775) 687-9224
Assessments, Program Accountability and Curriculum
  Director **Peter Zutz** ............................. (775) 687-9166

---

★ Elected Official   ■ Appointed by Governor   ● Appointed by Legislature   ▲ Appointed by Board or Commission   ◆ Appointed by State Supreme Court

Career, Technical and Adult Education Director
  **Mike Raponi** . . . . . . . . . . . . . . . . . . . . . . . . . . . (775) 687-7283
Family Engagement and Education Deputy
  Superintendent **Dena Durish** . . . . . . . . . . . . . . . . . (702) 486-6476
Public Information Officer **Gregory Bortolin** . . . . . . . . . . (775) 687-3201
  E-mail: gbortolin@doe.nv.gov

# Public Employees Retirement System

693 West Nye Lane, Carson City, NV 89703-1527
TTY: (775) 687-4200  Fax: (775) 687-5131  Internet: www.nvpers.org

**Fiscal Year:** 2016  **Budget:** $10,930,000

▲ Executive Officer **Tina Leiss** . . . . . . . . . . . . . . . . . . . (775) 687-4200
  E-mail: tleiss@nvpers.org
Investment Officer **Steve Edmundson** . . . . . . . . . . . . . . (775) 687-4200
  Chief Financial Officer **Lauren Larson** . . . . . . . . . . . . (775) 687-4200
Operations Officer **Cheryl Price** . . . . . . . . . . . . . . . . . . (775) 687-4200

# Office of the Lieutenant Governor

State Capitol Building, 101 North Carson Street, Suite 2,
Carson City, NV 89701
Tel: (775) 684-7111  Tel: (775) 684-7110  E-mail: ltgov@ltgov.nv.gov

**Fiscal Year:** 2014  **Budget:** $493,000

★ Lieutenant Governor **Mark Hutchison** (R) . . . . . . . . . . . . (775) 684-7111
  Term Expires: January 2019
  E-mail: mhutchison@ltgov.nv.gov
  Education: UNLV BA; J Reuben Clark Law JD
  Chief of Staff **Ryan Cherry** . . . . . . . . . . . . . . . . . . . . . (775) 684-7111

# Office of the Secretary of State

State Capitol Building, 101 North Carson Street, Suite 3,
Carson City, NV 89701
Tel: (775) 684-5708  Fax: (775) 684-5725  E-mail: sosmail@sos.nv.gov
Internet: www.nvsos.gov

★ Secretary of State **Barbara K. Cegavske** (R) . . . . . . . . . . (775) 684-5708
  Term Expires: January 2019
  Career: Minority Whip, Nevada Senate (2008-2011); Assistant Minority
  Floor Leader, Nevada Senate (2011-2013)
  Executive Assistant **Jennifer Russell** . . . . . . . . . . . . . . . (775) 684-5709
    Education: UC Santa Barbara
Chief Deputy Secretary of State **Scott Anderson** . . . . . . . . (775) 684-5708
Elections Deputy Secretary **Wayne Thorley** . . . . . . . . . . . (775) 684-5705
Operations Deputy Secretary **Cadence Matijevich** . . . . . . . (775) 684-5708
Southern Nevada Deputy Secretary **Gail Anderson** . . . . . . . (702) 486-2880
  Grant Sawyer Building, 555 East Washington Avenue, 5th Floor,
  Las Vegas, NV 89101
  Education: UNLV MEd
  Trademark Division Administrator **Jeffery Landerfelt** . . . (702) 486-2880
Commercial Recording Division Director
  **Jeffery Landerfelt** . . . . . . . . . . . . . . . . . . . . . . . . . . (775) 684-5708
Customer Service Division Administrator **Kaitlin Barker** . . (775) 684-5708
Notary Public Division Administrator **Sonja Prazak** . . . . . . (775) 684-5708
Securities Administrator **Diana J. Foley, Esq.** . . . . . . . . . . (702) 486-2440
  Grant Sawyer Building, 555 E. Washington Avenue, 5th Floor,
  Las Vegas, NV 89101
Public Information Officer **Kaitlin Barker** . . . . . . . . . . . . (702) 486-6982
  E-mail: sospio@sos.nv.gov

# Office of the Attorney General

100 North Carson Street, Carson City, NV 89701
Tel: (775) 684-1100  TTY: (775) 687-7353  Fax: (775) 684-1108
Internet: http://ag.nv.gov

**Employees:** 400  **Fiscal Year:** 2014  **Budget:** $131,789,000

★ Attorney General **Adam Paul Laxalt** (R) . . . . . . . . . . . . . (775) 684-1100
  Term Expires: January 2019
  Education: Georgetown 2001 BA, 2005 JD
  Career: Lieutenant Judge Advocate General Corps, Office of the Judge
  Advocate General, United States Department of the Navy (2005-2011)
First Assistant Attorney General **Wesley Duncan, JD** . . . . . (775) 684-1100
  Education: UC Berkeley 2003 AB; Ohio State 2006 JD
First Assistant Attorney General **Nicholas A. Trutanich** . . . (775) 684-1100
Solicitor General **Lawrence VanDyke** . . . . . . . . . . . . . . . (775) 684-1100

Communications Director (Acting) **Monica Moazez** . . . . . . (702) 486-0657
Information Technology Director **Catherine Krause** . . . . . . (775) 684-1100

# Office of the State Treasurer

State Capitol Building, 101 North Carson Street, Suite 4,
Carson City, NV 89701
Tel: (775) 684-5600  Fax: (775) 684-5781
E-mail: statetreasurer@nevadatreasurer.gov  Internet: nevadatreasurer.gov

**Fiscal Year:** 2014  **Budget:** $2,470,000

★ State Treasurer **Daniel Mark "Dan" Schwartz** (R) . . . . . . . (775) 684-5600
  Term Expires: January 2019
  Education: Princeton; Columbia MBA; Boston U JD
  Executive Assistant **Sandra "Sandy" Dombrowski** . . . . (775) 684-7109
Investments Deputy Treasurer **Kim Arnett** . . . . . . . . . . . . (775) 684-5600
Chief Deputy Treasurer **Tara Hagan** . . . . . . . . . . . . . . . . (775) 684-5753
Senior Deputy Treasurer **Linda J. English** . . . . . . . . . . . . (775) 684-5757
Senior Deputy Treasurer **Vincent "Budd" Milazzo** . . . . . . . (775) 684-5666

# Office of the Controller

State Capitol Building, 101 North Carson Street, Suite 5,
Carson City, NV 89701
Tel: (775) 684-5750  Fax: (775) 684-5696  Internet: www.controller.nv.gov

**Fiscal Year:** 2014  **Budget:** $5,095,000

★ State Controller **Ron Knecht** (R) . . . . . . . . . . . . . . . . . . (775) 684-5632
  Term Expires: January 2019
  Education: Illinois 1971 BA; Stanford 1989 MS;
  San Francisco Law 1995 JD
  Career: State Assembly Member (R-NV, District 40), Nevada State
  Assembly; Economist, Resource and Market Analysis Division, Public
  Utilities Commission of Nevada, State of Nevada (2001-2012)
Executive Assistant **Michelle Mann** . . . . . . . . . . . . . . . . . (775) 684-5632

---

★ Elected Official   ■ Appointed by Governor   ● Appointed by Legislature   ▲ Appointed by Board or Commission   ◆ Appointed by State Supreme Court

# New Hampshire

Tel: (603) 271-1110  Internet: www.nh.gov

**Number of U.S. Congressional Delegates:** 2 Senators; 2 Representatives  **Governor's Term:** 2 years
**Legislature Description:** General Court - 24 member Senate; 400 member House of Representatives; Term
- Senate 2 years, House 2 years  **Next Election:** Governor November 2016; Legislature November 2016
**Number of Electoral Votes:** 4  **Official Name:** State of New Hampshire (after Hampshire County,
England)  **Nickname:** The Granite State  **Motto:** Live Free or Die

**Population:** 1,330,608 (2015); Rank 41  **Fiscal Year:** 2014  **Budget:** $5,034,138,070

## Office of the Governor

107 North Main Street, Concord, NH 03301
Tel: (603) 271-2121

**Fiscal Year:** 2014  **Budget:** $1,436,250

**Margaret Wood "Maggie" Hassan**
Governor

Note: On October 5, 2015, Governor Maggie
Hassan announced she will not seek reelection to
the Office of the Governor in 2016.
Began Service: January 3, 2013
Term Expires: January 2017
Date of Birth: February 27, 1958
Education: Brown U 1980 BA;
Northeastern 1985 JD
Career: Attorney, Palmer & Dodge LLP
(1985-1992); Associate General Counsel, Brigham
and Women's Hospital (1993-1996); Partner,
Sullivan Weinstein & McQuay, P.C. (1996-2005);
Counsel, Pierce Atwood LLP (2007-2009); State
Senator (D-NH, District 23), New Hampshire
Senate (2005-2010)

★Governor **Margaret Wood "Maggie" Hassan** (D) . . . . . . . (603) 271-2121
  E-mail: margaret.hassan@nh.gov
  Executive Assistant **Amberlee Barbagallo** . . . . . . . . . . . . (603) 271-2121
  E-mail: amberlee.barbagallo@nh.gov
Chief of Staff **Pamela "Pam" Walsh** . . . . . . . . . . . . . . . . . (603) 271-2121
  E-mail: pamela.walsh@nh.gov
  Education: Northeastern 1996 BA
Deputy Chief of Staff **Jennifer Kuzma** . . . . . . . . . . . . . . . (603) 271-2121
Legal Counsel **Mary Ann Dempsey** . . . . . . . . . . . . . . . . . (603) 271-2121
  Education: Boston Col 1997 JD
Administration Director **Paxton M. Delano** . . . . . . . . . . . . (603) 271-2121
  E-mail: paxton.delano@nh.gov
Appointments Director and Liaison to the Executive
  Council **Catherine E. George** . . . . . . . . . . . . . . . . . . . . (603) 271-2121
  E-mail: catherine.george@nh.gov
Budget Director **Meridith Telus** . . . . . . . . . . . . . . . . . . . . (603) 271-1446
  E-mail: meredith.telus@nh.gov
Citizen Services Director **Benjamin G. Belanger** . . . . . . . . (603) 271-2121
  E-mail: benjamin.belanger@nh.gov
Communications Director **William Hinkle** . . . . . . . . . . . . . (603) 271-2121
  E-mail: william.hinkle@nh.gov
Press Secretary **(Vacant)** . . . . . . . . . . . . . . . . . . . . . . . . . (603) 271-2121
Legislative Director **(Vacant)** . . . . . . . . . . . . . . . . . . . . . . (603) 271-2121
Policy Director **Amy Kennedy** . . . . . . . . . . . . . . . . . . . . . . (603) 271-2121
  E-mail: amy.kennedy@nh.gov
  Education: Florida 2006 BA; North Florida 2011 MPA
  Policy Adviser **Kerry McHugh** . . . . . . . . . . . . . . . . . . . . (603) 271-2121
    E-mail: kerry.mchugh@nh.gov
  Policy Adviser **Brittany Weaver** . . . . . . . . . . . . . . . . . . . (603) 271-2121
    E-mail: brittany.weaver@nh.gov
Scheduling Director **Alexis J. Gipson** . . . . . . . . . . . . . . . (603) 271-2121
  E-mail: alexis.gipson@la.gov
Governor's Advisor on Addiction and Behavioral Health
  **James C. Vara** . . . . . . . . . . . . . . . . . . . . . . . . . . . . . . . (603) 271-2121
  E-mail: james.vara@nh.gov
  Education: Montclair State U; Rutgers JD

## New Hampshire Office of Energy and Planning

57 Regional Drive, Suite 3, Concord, NH 03301-8519
Tel: (603) 271-2155  TTY: (800) 735-2964  Fax: (603) 271-2615

**Fiscal Year:** 2014  **Budget:** $28,773,481

■Director **Meredith Hatfield** . . . . . . . . . . . . . . . . . . . . . . (603) 271-1755
  E-mail: meredith.hatfield@nh.gov
  Education: New Hampshire AAS; Wellesley 1994 BA;
  Vermont Law 1999 JD
Deputy Director **Richard A. Minard, Jr.** . . . . . . . . . . . . . . (603) 271-8341
Business Director **Jane Lemire** . . . . . . . . . . . . . . . . . . . . (603) 271-1098
Conservation Land Stewardship Program Director
  **Tracey L. Boisvert** . . . . . . . . . . . . . . . . . . . . . . . . . . . (603) 271-6809
Fiscal Manager **Barbara Shea** . . . . . . . . . . . . . . . . . . . . . (603) 271-6343
Grants and Compliance Officer **Wendy Gilman** . . . . . . . . . (603) 271-0596
Senior Planner **Jennifer Gilbert** . . . . . . . . . . . . . . . . . . . (603) 271-1755
  E-mail: jennifer.gilbert@nh.gov

## Office of the Attorney General

33 Capitol Street, Concord, NH 03301-6397
Tel: (603) 271-3658  TTY: (800) 735-2964  Fax: (603) 271-2110
E-mail: justice@doj.state.nh.us

**Employees:** 128

■Attorney General **Joseph A. Foster** . . . . . . . . . . . . . . . . (603) 271-1202
  E-mail: joseph.foster@doj.nh.gov
  Education: Tufts 1981 BA; George Washington 1984 JD
  Administrative Assistant **Pamela S. Murphy** . . . . . . . . . . (603) 271-1202
■Deputy Attorney General **Ann Rice** . . . . . . . . . . . . . . . . (603) 271-4900
  E-mail: ann.rice@doj.nh.gov
  Education: New England Col 1976 BS; New Hampshire 1988 JD
  Administrative Assistant **Jennifer Cawelti** . . . . . . . . . . . (603) 271-4900
Associate Attorney General **Anne M. Edwards** . . . . . . . . . (603) 271-1119
Homicide Unit Senior Assistant Attorney General
  **Jeffery Strelzin** . . . . . . . . . . . . . . . . . . . . . . . . . . . . . (603) 271-3671
  Education: Franklin Pierce Col 1991 JD; Keene State 1986 BS
Charitable Trusts Bureau Chief **Thomas J. Donovan** . . . . . (603) 271-3591
  Education: Harvard 1975 BA; Pennsylvania 1978 JD
Civil Bureau Chief and Associate Attorney General
  **Lisa M. English** . . . . . . . . . . . . . . . . . . . . . . . . . . . . . (603) 271-3658
  Education: SUNY (Potsdam) 1993 BA; Brandeis 2000 MA;
  Boston Col 2004 JD
Consumer Protection Bureau Chief and Senior Assistant
  Attorney General **James T. Boffetti** . . . . . . . . . . . . . . . (603) 271-3643
Criminal Justice Bureau Chief and Associate Attorney
  General **Jane E. Young** . . . . . . . . . . . . . . . . . . . . . . . (603) 271-3671
  Education: St Anselm 1986 BA; Franklin Pierce Col 1989 JD
Environmental Protection Bureau Chief and Senior
  Assistant Attorney General **K. Allen Brooks** . . . . . . . . . (603) 271-3679
Transportation and Construction Bureau Chief and Senior
  Assistant Attorney General **Karen Schlitzer** . . . . . . . . . (603) 271-3675
  E-mail: karen.schlitzer@doj.nh.gov
Chief Medical Examiner **Thomas A. Andrew** . . . . . . . . . . (603) 271-1235
  Education: Dayton 1978 BS; Cincinnati 1982 MD
Director of Administration **Kathleen Carr** . . . . . . . . . . . . (603) 271-1234
  E-mail: kathleen.carr@doj.nh.gov
Director of Medicaid Fraud Control Unit
  **Brooksley Belanger** . . . . . . . . . . . . . . . . . . . . . . . . . . (603) 271-7094

---

★ Elected Official     ■ Appointed by Governor     ● Appointed by Legislature     ▲ Appointed by Board or Commission     ◆ Appointed by State Supreme Court

# Office of the Secretary of State

State House, 107 North Main Street, Room 204, Concord, NH 03301
Tel: (603) 271-3242
Tel: (603) 271-3276 (Uniform Commercial Code Info.)
TTY: (603) 735-2964  Fax: (603) 271-6316
E-mail: elections@sos.state.nh.us  Internet: www.sos.nh.gov

**Employees:** 83  **Fiscal Year:** 2014  **Budget:** $7,975,014

● Secretary of State **William M. "Bill" Gardner** . . . . . . . . . . .(603) 271-3242
   E-mail: william.gardner@sos.nh.gov
Senior Deputy Secretary of State **Robert P. Ambrose** . . . . .(603) 271-3242
Deputy Secretary of State **David M. Scanlan** . . . . . . . . . . . .(603) 271-3242
Assistant Secretary of State **Karen Ladd** . . . . . . . . . . . . . . .(603) 271-3242
Assistant Secretary of State **Paula Penney** . . . . . . . . . . . . . .(603) 271-3242
Assistant Secretary of State **Anthony Stevens** . . . . . . . . . .(603) 271-8239

# Bureau of Securities Regulations

107 North Main Street, Suite 204, Concord, NH 03301
Tel: (603) 271-1463  Fax: (603) 271-7933  E-mail: securities@sos.nh.gov

Director **Barry Glennon, Jr.** . . . . . . . . . . . . . . . . . . . . . . . .(603) 271-1464
Deputy Director **Jeffrey D. Spill** . . . . . . . . . . . . . . . . . . . . .(603) 271-1464

# Office of the State Treasurer

State House Annex, 25 Capitol Street, Room 121,
Concord, NH 03301-6312
Tel: (603) 271-2621  Fax: (603) 271-3922

**Employees:** 22  **Fiscal Year:** 2014  **Budget:** $190,957,072

● State Treasurer **William F. "Bill" Dwyer** . . . . . . . . . . . . . .(603) 271-2621
   E-mail: bdwyer@treasury.state.nh.us
Chief Deputy State Treasurer **Rachel K. Miller** . . . . . . . . .(603) 271-2073
   Education: Oberlin 1986 BA; New Hampshire 1995 MBA
Deputy State Treasurer **Monica I. Mezzapelle** . . . . . . . . . . .(603) 271-2628
Assistant State Treasurer **Richard M. Bowen** . . . . . . . . . . .(603) 271-2331
Assistant State Treasurer **Sylvia J. Yeaton** . . . . . . . . . . . . .(603) 271-6623
Abandoned Property Director **Thomas P. McAnespie** . . . . .(603) 271-1499
Information Technology Manager **Brian Deschenes** . . . . . . .(603) 271-8413
   E-mail: bdeschenes@treasury.state.nh.us
Business Administrator **Linda Desmond** . . . . . . . . . . . . . . .(603) 271-1142

# Adjutant General's Department

One Minuteman Way, Concord, NH 03301-5607
Tel: (603) 225-1200  Tel: (603) 225-1360 (Business Administration)
TTY: (800) 735-2964  Fax: (603) 225-1257

**Employees:** 140  **Fiscal Year:** 2014  **Budget:** $20,581,249

■ Adjutant General **MajGen William N. Reddel III, ANG** . . .(603) 225-1200
   E-mail: william.n.reddel@us.army.mil
   Education: Nathaniel Hawthorne 1979 BA; Army War Col 2003
Deputy Adjutant General
   **COL Warren M. Perry, USA (Ret)** . . . . . . . . . . . . . . . . .(603) 225-1302
   Education: Maine 1986 BA; Louisiana Tech U MA;
   Western Kentucky MBA
Secretary and Administrative Assistant
   **Jacqueline "Jackie" Page** . . . . . . . . . . . . . . . . . . . . . . .(603) 225-1200
   Executive Officer **CPT Emily P. Riordan, ARNG** . . . . . . .(603) 225-1224
Chief of Staff **COL William T. Conway, ARNG** . . . . . . . . .(603) 225-1270

# New Hampshire National Guard

Four Pembroke Road, Concord, NH 03301-5652
Tel: (603) 228-1135  Internet: www.nh.ngb.army.mil

■ Adjutant General **MajGen William N. Reddel III, ANG** . . .(603) 225-1200
   E-mail: william.n.reddel@us.army.mil
Joint Staff Director **COL Todd Swass, ARNG** . . . . . . . . . .(603) 225-1336

# New Hampshire Air National Guard

Tel: (603) 430-2766  E-mail: usaf.nh.157-arw.mbx.arw-pa@mail.mil
Internet: www.157arw.ang.af.mil

Assistant Adjutant General and Commander
   **BrigGen Paul "Hutch" Hutchinson, ANG** . . . . . . . . . . .(603) 430-3563
   Education: UMass (Amherst) 1981 BS

# New Hampshire Army National Guard

Tel: (603) 228-1135  Tel: (877) 598-0665

Deputy Adjutant General **COL Thomas Spencer, ARNG** . .(603) 225-1302
Chief of Staff **COL William T. Conway, ARNG** . . . . . . . . .(603) 225-1270

# Department of Administrative Services

State House Annex, 25 Capitol Street, Concord, NH 03301
Tel: (603) 271-3201

**Employees:** 296

■ Commissioner **Vicki Quiram, PE** . . . . . . . . . . . . . . . . . . . .(603) 271-3201
   E-mail: vicki.quiram@nh.gov
Deputy Commissioner **Michael Connor** . . . . . . . . . . . . . . .(603) 271-6899
   E-mail: michael.connor@nh.gov
Financial Data Management Director **Charles Russell** . . . . .(603) 271-1500
Controller **Gerard J. Murphy** . . . . . . . . . . . . . . . . . . . . . . .(603) 271-1443
Personnel Division Director **Sara Willingham** . . . . . . . . . . .(603) 271-3261
                                                           Fax: (603) 271-1422
Personnel Division Deputy Director
   **Joseph Shoemaker** . . . . . . . . . . . . . . . . . . . . . . . . . . . .(603) 271-1420
Plant and Property Management Division Director
   **Lisa Pollard** . . . . . . . . . . . . . . . . . . . . . . . . . . . . . . . . .(603) 271-7272
   E-mail: lisa.pollard@nh.gov
Purchase and Property Bureau Administrator
   **Robert Stowell** . . . . . . . . . . . . . . . . . . . . . . . . . . . . . . .(603) 271-3606
   E-mail: robert.stowell@nh.gov          Fax: (603) 271-2700
Employee Relations Manager
   **Matthew "Matt" Newland** . . . . . . . . . . . . . . . . . . . . . . .(603) 271-3262
   E-mail: matthew.newland@nh.gov
   Education: New Hampshire Tech 1990 AS; New Hampshire BS

# Department of Agriculture, Markets and Food

P.O. Box 2042, Concord, NH 03302-2042
Tel: (603) 271-3551  TTY: (800) 735-2964  Fax: (603) 271-1109
Internet: www.agriculture.nh.gov

**Fiscal Year:** 2016  **Budget:** $6,071,167

■ Commissioner **Lorraine Stuart Merrill** . . . . . . . . . . . . . . .(603) 271-3551
   E-mail: lorraine.merrill@agr.nh.gov
   Education: New Hampshire 1973 BS
   Administrative Assistant **Beth Kiley** . . . . . . . . . . . . . . . .(603) 271-3687
Agricultural Development Director
   **Gail McWilliam Jellie** . . . . . . . . . . . . . . . . . . . . . . . . . .(603) 271-3551
Animal Industry State Veterinarian
   **Stephen K. Crawford** . . . . . . . . . . . . . . . . . . . . . . . . . .(603) 271-2404
Pesticide Control Director **David Rousseau** . . . . . . . . . . . .(603) 271-3550
Plant Industry Director **Piera Siegert** . . . . . . . . . . . . . . . .(603) 271-2561
Regulatory Services Director **Jennifer Z. Gornnert** . . . . . .(603) 271-7761
   E-mail: jennifer.gornnert@agr.nh.gov
Weights and Measures Director **Rebecca Malila** . . . . . . . . .(603) 271-3700

# New Hampshire Banking Department

53 Regional Drive, Suite 200, Concord, NH 03301
Tel: (603) 271-3561  TTY: (800) 735-2964  Fax: (603) 271-1090
E-mail: nhbd@banking.nh.gov  Internet: www.nh.gov/banking

■ Commissioner **Gerald H. "Jerry" Little** . . . . . . . . . . . . . .(603) 271-3561
   Note: Effective June 2, 2016.
   E-mail: commissioner@banking.nh.gov
   Education: New Hampshire 1977 BA
■ Deputy Commissioner **Ingrid E. White** . . . . . . . . . . . . . . .(603) 271-3561
   E-mail: ingrid.white@banking.nh.gov
Chief Bank Examiner **Todd A. Wells** . . . . . . . . . . . . . . . . .(603) 271-3561
   E-mail: todd.wells@banking.nh.gov
Consumer Credit Director **Raeleen Shutte** . . . . . . . . . . . . .(603) 271-3561
   Education: Walden BS; Wyoming
Legal Counsel **Emelia A. Galdieri** . . . . . . . . . . . . . . . . . . .(603) 271-3561
   E-mail: emelia.galdieri@banking.nh.gov

---

★ Elected Official   ■ Appointed by Governor   ● Appointed by Legislature      ▲ Appointed by Board or Commission      ◆ Appointed by State Supreme Court

# Department of Corrections [NHDOC]

P.O. Box 1806, Concord, NH 03302-1806
Tel: (603) 271-5600  Tel: (603) 271-5602 (Prison Information)
TTY: (603) 225-4033  Fax: (603) 271-5643  Internet: www.nh.gov/nhdoc

**Employees:** 897  **Fiscal Year:** 2014  **Budget:** $104,200,000

■Commissioner **William L. "Bill" Wrenn** . . . . . . . . . . . . . . .(603) 271-5603
  E-mail: wwrenn@nhdoc.state.nh.us
Assistant Commissioner **Helen Hanks** . . . . . . . . . . . . . . .(603) 271-5562
  Education: Brandeis MS
Medical and Forensic Services Director **Paula Mattis** . . . . .(603) 271-5563
Training Director **Chris Kench** . . . . . . . . . . . . . . . . . . . . . .(603) 528-9269
Administration Division Director **Doreen A. Wittenberg** . .(603) 271-5610
  E-mail: doreen.wittenberg@doc.nh.gov
Community Corrections and Programming Services
  Division Director **Kimberly MacKay** . . . . . . . . . . . . . . .(603) 271-5600
Field Services Division Director **Michael McAlister** . . . . . .(603) 271-5652
Information Technology Business Processing Manager
  **Linda Socha** . . . . . . . . . . . . . . . . . . . . . . . . . . . . . . . . .(603) 271-4926
  E-mail: linda.socha@doc.nh.gov
Warden, New Hampshire Correctional Facility
  for Women **Joanne Fortier** . . . . . . . . . . . . . . . . (603) 668-6137 ext. 301
  317 Mast Road, Goffstown, NH 03045
Warden, New Hampshire State Prison for Men
  **Michael A. Zenk** . . . . . . . . . . . . . . . . . . . . . . . . . . . .(603) 271-1801
  P.O. Box 14, Concord, NH 03301
Warden, Northern New Hampshire Correctional Facility
  **Michelle Goings** . . . . . . . . . . . . . . . . . . . . . . . . . . . . .(603) 752-2906
  138 East Milan Road, Berlin, NH 03570
Victim Services Coordinator **Amanda Breen** . . . . . . . . . . .(603) 271-1937
  E-mail: amanda.breen@nhdoc.state.nh.us

# Department of Cultural Resources

20 Park Street, Concord, NH 03301-6314
Tel: (603) 271-2540  TTY: (800) 735-2964
Fax: (603) 271-6826 (Administrative Offices)
Internet: www.nh.gov/nhculture

■Commissioner **Van McLeod** . . . . . . . . . . . . . . . . . . . . . . . . .(603) 271-2540
  E-mail: van.mcleod@dcr.nh.gov
Public Information Office **Shelly Angers** . . . . . . . . . . . . . .(603) 271-3136
  E-mail: shelly.angers@dcr.nh.gov

## Historical Resources Division

Tel: (603) 271-3483  Fax: (603) 271-3433  Internet: www.nh.gov/nhdhr

**Fiscal Year:** 2014  **Budget:** $1,024,165

Director **Elizabeth Muzzey** . . . . . . . . . . . . . . . . . . . . . . . . .(603) 271-8850

## Film and Digital Media Office

Tel: (603) 271-2220  Fax: (603) 271-3584  E-mail: film@nh.gov
Internet: www.nh.gov/film

Director **Matthew Newton** . . . . . . . . . . . . . . . . . . . . . . . . . .(603) 271-2220

## State Library

Tel: (603) 271-2144  Fax: (603) 271-6826  Internet: www.nh.gov/nhsl

**Fiscal Year:** 2014  **Budget:** $3,190,345

State Librarian **Michael York** . . . . . . . . . . . . . . . . . . . . . . .(603) 271-2397
  Administrator of Library Operations **Janet Eklund** . . . . .(603) 271-2393
Library Services to Persons with Disabilities Supervisor
  **Marilyn Stevenson** . . . . . . . . . . . . . . . . . . . . . . . . . . .(603) 271-1498
  117 Pleasant Street, Concord, NH 03301          Fax: (603) 271-8370
Reference and Information Services Supervisor
  **Donna Gilbreth** . . . . . . . . . . . . . . . . . . . . . . . . . . . . . .(603) 271-2060
  E-mail: nhslref@dcr.nh.gov          Fax: (603) 271-2205
  Education: Simmons 1977 MLS

# Department of Employment Security

45 South Fruit Street, Concord, NH 03301
Tel: (603) 224-3311  TTY: (800) 735-2964  Fax: (603) 228-4145

**Employees:** 343  **Fiscal Year:** 2014  **Budget:** $33,459,206

■Commissioner **George N. Copadis** . . . . . . . . . . . . . . . . . . .(603) 228-4000
  E-mail: george.n.copadis@nhes.nh.gov

Deputy Commissioner **Richard J. Lavers** . . . . . . . . . . . . . .(603) 228-4064
  E-mail: richard.j.lavers@nhes.nh.gov
General Counsel **Maria Dalterio** . . . . . . . . . . . . . . . . . . . . .(603) 228-4070
  E-mail: maria.dalterio@nhes.nh.gov
Economic and Labor Market Information Bureau Director
  **Bruce Demay** . . . . . . . . . . . . . . . . . . . . . . . . . . . . . . . .(603) 228-4126
  E-mail: bruce.demay@nhes.nh.gov
Employment Services Bureau and Operations Director
  **Pamela R. "Pam" Szacik** . . . . . . . . . . . . . . . . . . . . . .(603) 228-4051
Unemployment Compensation Bureau Director
  **Dianne M. Carpenter** . . . . . . . . . . . . . . . . . . . . . . . . .(603) 228-4031
  E-mail: dianne.m.carpenter@nhes.nh.gov

# Department of Environmental Services [DES]

29 Hazen Drive, Concord, NH 03301
Tel: (603) 271-3503  TTY: (800) 735-2964  Fax: (603) 271-2867
E-mail: pip@des.nh.gov

■Commissioner **Thomas S. "Tom" Burack** . . . . . . . . . . . . .(603) 271-2958
  E-mail: thomas.burack@des.nh.gov
  Education: Dartmouth 1982 BA; Virginia 1988 JD
  Administrative Assistant
    **Suzanne E. "Sue" Beauchesne** . . . . . . . . . . . . . . . . .(603) 271-3449
■Assistant Commissioner **Clark Freise** . . . . . . . . . . . . . . . .(603) 271-8806
  Education: Naval Acad BS; MIT MS; Harvard
■Chief Operating Officer **Susan Carlson** . . . . . . . . . . . . . . .(603) 271-1881
  E-mail: susan.carlson@des.nh.gov
■Air Resource Division Director **Craig Wright** . . . . . . . . . .(603) 271-6791
  E-mail: craig.wright@des.nh.gov
Waste Management Division Director
  **Michael J. Wimsatt, PG** . . . . . . . . . . . . . . . . . . . . . . . .(603) 271-1997
  E-mail: michael.wimsatt@des.nh.gov
Water Division Director **Eugene Forbes, PE, LEED AP** . . .(603) 271-3308
  E-mail: eugene.forbes@des.nh.gov
Public Information and Permitting Unit Administrator
  **Timothy Drew** . . . . . . . . . . . . . . . . . . . . . . . . . . . . . . .(603) 271-3306
  E-mail: timothy.drew@des.nh.gov

# New Hampshire Fish and Game Department

11 Hazen Drive, Concord, NH 03301
Tel: (603) 271-3211  TTY: (800) 735-2964  Fax: (603) 271-1438
E-mail: info@wildlife.state.nh.us  Internet: www.wildlife.state.nh.us

**Employees:** 192  **Fiscal Year:** 2014  **Budget:** $27,711,826

■Executive Director **Glenn Normandeau** . . . . . . . . . . . . . . .(603) 271-3511
  E-mail: glenn.normandeau@wildlife.nh.gov
  Administrative Assistant **Tanya L. Haskell** . . . . . . . . . . .(603) 271-3511
Business Division Chief **Kathy A. LaBonte** . . . . . . . . . . . . .(603) 271-2741
  E-mail: kathy.labonte@wildlife.nh.gov
Facilities and Land Division Chief **Richard Fink** . . . . . . . .(603) 271-1134
Inland Fisheries Division Chief **Jason M. Smith** . . . . . . . .(603) 271-2501
Law Enforcement Division Chief **Col. Kevin J. Jordan** . . .(603) 271-3127
Marine Fisheries Division Chief **Douglas E. Grout** . . . . . .(603) 868-1095
Public Affairs Division Chief **Jon Charpentier** . . . . . . . . .(603) 271-3211
  E-mail: jon.charpentier@wildlife.nh.gov
Wildlife Division Chief **Mark Ellingwood** . . . . . . . . . . . . .(603) 271-2461
Human Resources Administrator and ADA Coordinator
  **Thomas A. "Tom" Bourgault** . . . . . . . . . . . . . . . . . . .(603) 271-5824
Legislative/Rules Coordinator **Paul G. Sanderson** . . . . . .(603) 271-1136
  E-mail: paul.sanderson@wildlife.nh.gov
Licensing Supervisor **Susan L. "Sue" Perry** . . . . . . . . . . .(603) 271-6832

# Department of Health and Human Services [DHHS]

129 Pleasant Street, Concord, NH 03301-3857
Tel: (603) 271-9200  TTY: (800) 735-2964  Fax: (603) 271-4912
E-mail: dhhsfeedback@dhhs.state.nh.us  Internet: www.dhhs.state.nh.us

**Employees:** 3,253  **Fiscal Year:** 2014  **Budget:** $1,906,946,639

■Commissioner **Jeffrey A. Meyers** . . . . . . . . . . . . . . . . . . . .(603) 271-9200
  E-mail: jeffrey.meyers@dhhs.state.nh.us
  Education: George Washington 1978 BA; Georgetown 1989 JD

---

★ Elected Official   ■ Appointed by Governor   ● Appointed by Legislature   ▲ Appointed by Board or Commission   ◆ Appointed by State Supreme Court

Executive Assistant to the Commissioner
**Kathleen J. Henderson**..........................(603) 271-9445
Deputy Commissioner **Marilee Nihan**..................(603) 271-9409
  Administrative Assistant to the Deputy Commissioner
  **Trisha J. Carson**.................................(603) 271-5414
Associate Commissioner and Human Services Office
  Director **Mary Ann Cooney**.......................(603) 271-9444
   Education: St Anselm BN; New Hampshire Col MSN;
   New Hampshire 2008 MPH
  Administrative Assistant **Theresa Jones**.............(603) 271-9404
Associate Commissioner **Kathleen "Katie" Dunn**........(603) 271-9421
  Education: Boston U MPH
Chief Information Officer **Donna O'Leary**.............(603) 271-9469
Healthcare Policy Specialist **Deb Scheetz**.............(603) 271-9459

## Division of Behavioral Health [DBH]
Director **Katja Fox**..................................(603) 271-9200

## Division of Child Support Services
Tel: (603) 271-4745  Fax: (603) 271-4787

Director **Mary S. Weatherill**........................(603) 223-4822
  E-mail: mweather@dhhs.state.nh.us

## Division of Children, Youth and Families
Tel: (603) 271-4451  Fax: (603) 271-4455

Director **Lorraine Bartlett**..........................(603) 271-4440

## Juvenile Justice Services Division
Sununu Youth Services Center, 1056 North River Road,
Manchester, NH 03104-1998
Tel: (603) 625-5471  Fax: (603) 669-1203

Director **(Vacant)**.................................(603) 625-5471

## Division of Community Based Care Services
Tel: (603) 271-6410  Fax: (603) 271-4912

Associate Commissioner **(Vacant)**....................(603) 271-9520

## Division of Family Assistance
Tel: (603) 271-4238  Fax: (603) 271-4637

Director **Terry R. Smith**............................(603) 271-9281

## Division of Public Health Services
29 Hazen Drive, Concord, NH 03301-6527
Tel: (603) 271-4501  Fax: (603) 271-4827

Director (Acting) **Marcella J. Bobinsky**..............(603) 271-4501
State Laboratories Director **Christine Bean, MT (ASCP)**..(603) 271-4657
State Epidemiologist **Dr. Benjamin P. Chan**...........(603) 271-5325
Radiological Health Bureau Chief **Augustinus Ong**......(603) 271-4588
WIC (Women, Infants and Children) Nutrition Services
  Bureau Chief **Margaret Murphy**..................(603) 271-4546
  E-mail: mmurphy@dhhs.state.nh.us
Community and Public Health Development
  Administrator **Neil Twitchell**....................(603) 271-5194
Health Services Planning & Review Administrator
  **Cynthia Carrier**................................(603) 271-4606
Immunization Program Manager **Marcella J. Bobinsky**...(603) 271-4482
                 Fax: (603) 271-3850

## Office of Business Operations
Fax: (603) 271-4232

Chief Financial Officer **Steve Longer**................(603) 271-9291
Administrator **Adrian Wayland**.......................(603) 271-9293
  E-mail: adrian.wayland@dhhs.state.nh.us

## Office of Improvement and Integrity
Fax: (603) 271-7100

Administrator **Steve Longer**.........................(603) 271-9291

## Office of Medicaid Business and Policy
Tel: (603) 271-4344

Medicaid Director **Kathleen "Katie" Dunn**.............(603) 271-9421
  Assistant Medicaid Director **(Vacant)**.............(603) 271-9408
Dental Director **(Vacant)**...........................(603) 271-9251
Medicaid Medical Director **Doris Lotz**................(603) 271-9426
Planning and Research Administrator
  **Christine Shannon**.............................(603) 271-9424

## Office of Operations Support
Director **Mary P. Castelli**..........................(603) 271-9385

## Office of the Ombudsman
Tel: (603) 271-6941  Fax: (603) 271-4632

Ombudsman **Charles Weatherill**......................(603) 271-5573

## Department of Information Technology [DOIT]
27 Hazen Drive, Concord, NH 03301
Tel: (603) 223-5701  E-mail: oitweb@nh.gov  Internet: www.nh.gov/doit

**Employees: 369  Fiscal Year: 2014  Budget: $60,570,605**

Commissioner and Chief Information Officer
  **Denis Goulet**..................................(603) 223-5701
  E-mail: denis.goulet@doit.nh.gov
  Education: St Anselm 2005 BA

## New Hampshire Insurance Department
21 South Fruit Street, Suite 14, Concord, NH 03301
Tel: (603) 271-2261  Tel: (603) 271-7973  TTY: (800) 735-2964
Fax: (603) 271-1406  E-mail: requests@ins.nh.gov
Internet: www.nh.gov/insurance

**Employees: 81  Fiscal Year: 2014  Budget: $9,290,687**

■Commissioner **Roger A. Sevigny**....................(603) 271-7973
  Term Expires: June 9, 2018
  E-mail: roger.sevigny@ins.nh.gov
  Education: St Anselm 1964 BA
  Administrative Assistant **Sandra Barlow**.......(603) 271-7973 ext. 202
Deputy Commissioner **Alex Feldvebel**..........(603) 271-7973 ext. 248
  Education: John Carroll 1966 BS; Harvard 1984 JD
Operations Director **John R. Elias**..............(603) 271-7973 ext. 255
Chief Financial Examiner **Colin Wilkins**...............(603) 271-7973
License Supervisor **(Vacant)**..................(603) 271-7973 ext. 255
Director of Compliance and Consumer Services
  **Michael Wilkey**............................(603) 271-7973 ext. 330
Director of Financial Regulations **Douglas Bartlett**.......(603) 271-7973
Insurance Fraud Supervisor **John M. Gasaway**..........(603) 271-7973
General Counsel **Chiara Dolcino**.....................(603) 271-7973
  Education: Col of the Atlantic 1986 BA; Franklin Pierce Col 1989 JD
Enforcement and Compliance Counsel
  **Richard McCaffrey**.........................(603) 271-7973 ext. 236
Paralegal **Carolyn Petersen**.................(603) 271-7973 ext. 335
Paralegal **Sarah Prescott**..................(603) 271-7973 ext. 335
Fraud Attorney **John M. Gasaway**....................(603) 271-7973
  Health Care Policy Analyst **Tyler Brannen**.....(603) 271-7973 ext. 226
   Education: New Hampshire 1995 BS; Johns Hopkins 2001 MS
Chief Market Conduct Examiner **Edwin Pugsley**.........(603) 271-7973
Enforcement Examiner **Donald Belanger**.........(603) 271-7973 ext. 370
  Life, Accident and Health Benefits Appeals
   Consumer Services Officer **Keith Nyhan**.....(603) 271-7973 ext. 265
  Life Accident and Health Actuary **David Sky**...(603) 271-7973 ext. 239
   Education: Penn State 1992 MA; Bucknell 1983 BS
Property and Casualty Director **John R. Elias**....(603) 271-7973 ext. 375
  Property and Casualty Officer **Catherine Drew**..(603) 271-7973 ext. 203
  Property and Casualty Officer **Clara LaPointe**...(603) 271-7973 ext. 229
  Property and Casualty Actuary
  **Sally MacFadden**..........................(603) 271-7973 ext. 228

---

## New Hampshire Department of Labor [NHDOL]

State Office Park South, 95 Pleasant Street, Concord, NH 03301
Tel: (603) 271-3176  Fax: (603) 271-6149

**Employees:** 95  **Fiscal Year:** 2014  **Budget:** $7,844,392

■Commissioner **James W. "Jim" Craig** . . . . . . . . . . . . . . . . . (603) 271-3176
  E-mail: james.craig@dol.nh.gov
  Education: Keene State BA; USC MA; New Hampshire 1983 JD
  Administrative Assistant **Amanda Paveglio** . . . . . . . . . . . (603) 271-3176
    E-mail: amanda.paveglio@dol.nh.gov
Deputy Commissioner **Kathryn Barger** . . . . . . . . . . . . . . . (603) 271-3176
  E-mail: kathryn.barger@dol.nh.gov
Inspection Division Administrator **Michele Small** . . . . . . . (603) 271-3176
  E-mail: michele.small@dol.nh.gov
Workers' Compensation Division Director
  **Cynthia "C.J." Stone** . . . . . . . . . . . . . . . . . . . . . . . . . . . . (603) 271-3176
    E-mail: cindy.stone@dol.nh.gov

## Department of Resources and Economic Development [DRED]

172 Pembroke Road, Concord, NH 03301
Tel: (603) 271-2411  TTY: (800) 735-2964  Fax: (603) 271-2629
Internet: www.dred.state.nh.us

**Employees:** 208  **Fiscal Year:** 2014  **Budget:** $52,824,921

■Commissioner **Jeffrey Rose** . . . . . . . . . . . . . . . . . . . . . . . . (603) 271-2411
  E-mail: jeffrey.rose@dred.nh.gov
  Education: Marist 1995 BA
International Trade Administrator **Tina Kasim** . . . . . . . . . . . (603) 271-8444
                                                     Fax: (603) 271-6784
Economic Development Division Director
  **Carmen Lorentz** . . . . . . . . . . . . . . . . . . . . . . . . . . . . . . . . (603) 271-2591
                                                     Fax: (603) 271-6784
Forests and Lands Division Director **Brad W. Simpkins** . . . (603) 271-2214
                                                     Fax: (603) 271-6488
Parks and Recreation Division Director **Philip A. Bryce** . . . (603) 271-3556
  E-mail: phil.bryce@dred.nh.gov                     Fax: (603) 271-3553
  E-mail: nhparks@dred.nh.gov
  Education: Maine 1979; Plymouth State Col 1993 MBA
Travel and Tourism Development Division Director
  **Victoria Cimino** . . . . . . . . . . . . . . . . . . . . . . . . . . . . . . . . (603) 271-2665
                                                     Fax: (603) 271-6870

## Department of Revenue Administration [DRA]

Medical and Surgical Building, 109 Pleasant Street, Concord, NH 03301
P.O. Box 457, Concord, NH 03301-0637
Tel: (603) 230-5000  Tel: (603) 230-5001 (Forms Line)
TTY: (800) 735-2964  Fax: (603) 230-5945  Internet: www.revenue.nh.gov

**Employees:** 150  **Fiscal Year:** 2014  **Budget:** $16,965,062

■Commissioner **John T. Beardmore** . . . . . . . . . . . . . . . . . . (603) 230-5005
  E-mail: john.beardmore@dra.nh.gov
  Education: New Hampshire 2000 BA; UMass (Amherst) 2002 MPA
  Administrative Assistant **Vivian Provencher** . . . . . . . . . . (603) 230-5006
Assistant Commissioner **Lindsey M. Stepp** . . . . . . . . . . . . (603) 230-5020
  Education: Trinity Col (CT) BS
Revenue Counsel **Caroline Delaney** . . . . . . . . . . . . . . . . . (603) 230-5026
Audit Division Director **Kathleen Sher** . . . . . . . . . . . . . . . (603) 230-5030
Collection Division Director **Philip Lawrence** . . . . . . . . . . (603) 230-5900
  P.O. Box 454, Concord, NH 03302
Document Processing Division Director
  **Debra Bourbeau** . . . . . . . . . . . . . . . . . . . . . . . . . . . . . . . (603) 230-5000
  P.O. Box 637, Concord, NH 03302
Information Technology Director **Karen Sampson** . . . . . . . (603) 230-5996
  E-mail: karen.sampson@dra.nh.gov
Municipal and Property Division Director
  **Stephan Hamilton** . . . . . . . . . . . . . . . . . . . . . . . . . . . . . . (603) 230-5950
  P.O. Box 487, Concord, NH 03302
  Equalization Director **Linda Kennedy** . . . . . . . . . . . . . . . (603) 230-5950
  P.O. Box 487, Concord, NH 03302
Hearing Officer **Denise Daniel** . . . . . . . . . . . . . . . . . . . . . (603) 230-5002
  P.O. Box 1467, Concord, NH 03302

## Department of Safety [DOS]

33 Hazen Drive, Concord, NH 03305
Tel: (603) 271-2251  TTY: (800) 735-2964  Fax: (603) 271-3903

**Employees:** 1,120  **Fiscal Year:** 2014  **Budget:** $146,175,695

■Commissioner **John J. Barthelmes** . . . . . . . . . . . . . . . . . (603) 271-2791
  E-mail: john.barthelmes@dos.nh.gov
■Assistant Commissioner **Richard C. Bailey, Jr.** . . . . . . . . . (603) 271-2559
  E-mail: richard.c.baileyjr@dos.nh.gov
  Education: New Hampshire 1983 BS; Franklin Pierce Col 1993 JD
■Assistant Commissioner **Kevin P. O'Brien** . . . . . . . . . . . . . (603) 271-2559
  E-mail: kevin.obrien@dos.nh.gov
Chief of Policy and Planning **(Vacant)** . . . . . . . . . . . . . . . (603) 271-2559

### Division of Administration
Fax: (603) 271-4017

■Director **(Vacant)** . . . . . . . . . . . . . . . . . . . . . . . . . . . . . . . (603) 271-2589

### Division of Emergency Services and Communications
Director **Bruce Cheney** . . . . . . . . . . . . . . . . . . . . . . . . . . . (603) 271-6911

### Division of Fire Safety
Fiscal Year: 2014  Budget: $3,553,170

State Fire Marshal **J. William "Bill" Degnan** . . . . . . . . . . . (603) 223-4289
Deputy State Fire Marshal **Maxim F. Schultz** . . . . . . . . . . . (603) 223-4289

### Division of Fire Standards and Training and Emergency Medical Services
Richard M. Flynn Fire Academy, 222 Sheep Davis Road,
Concord, NH 03301-8523
Fax: (603) 271-1091

Fiscal Year: 2014  Budget: $6,437,430

■Director **Deborah A. Pendergast** . . . . . . . . . . . . . . . . . . . (603) 223-4220
  E-mail: deborah.a.pendergast@dos.nh.gov

### Division of Homeland Security and Emergency Management
Fax: (603) 271-1091

■Director **Perry Plummer** . . . . . . . . . . . . . . . . . . . . . . . . . . (603) 223-3637
  E-mail: perry.plummer@dos.nh.gov
Assistant Director **Jennifer Harper** . . . . . . . . . . . . . . . . . . (603) 271-2231
Field Services Section Chief **David E. Vaillancourt** . . . . . . (603) 223-3630
Operations Section Chief **Robert Christensen** . . . . . . . . . . (603) 271-6911
Planning Section Chief **Leigh A. Cheney** . . . . . . . . . . . . . . (603) 223-3639
Technological Hazards Section Chief **Diane L. Becker** . . . . (603) 223-3616
Administrative Assistant **Susan J. Parker** . . . . . . . . . . . . . . (603) 271-2231

### Division of Motor Vehicles [DMV]
23 Hazen Drive, Concord, NH 03305
Tel: (603) 227-4000

Fiscal Year: 2014  Budget: $15,330,493

■Director **Elizabeth A. Bielecki** . . . . . . . . . . . . . . . . . . . . . (603) 227-4050
  E-mail: elizabeth.bielecki@dos.nh.gov

### State Police
Tel: (603) 271-3636  Fax: (603) 271-1153

Fiscal Year: 2014  Budget: $39,948,117

■Director **Col. Robert L. Quinn** . . . . . . . . . . . . . . . . . . . . . (603) 271-3919
  E-mail: robert.quinn@dos.nh.gov
  Education: Merrimack 1983 BS

---

★ Elected Official   ■ Appointed by Governor   ● Appointed by Legislature   ▲ Appointed by Board or Commission   ◆ Appointed by State Supreme Court

## New Hampshire Department of Transportation [DOT]

P.O. Box 483, Concord, NH 03302
Tel: (603) 271-3734  Fax: (603) 271-3914

**Employees:** 1,650  **Fiscal Year:** 2014  **Budget:** $580,518,909

■Commissioner **Victoria Sheehan** . . . . . . . . . . . . . . . . . . . . (603) 271-1484
  E-mail: vsheehan@dot.state.nh.us
  Education: Edinburgh (Scotland) ME
■Assistant Commissioner and Chief Engineer
  **William J. Cass** . . . . . . . . . . . . . . . . . . . . . . . . . . . . . . . (603) 271-1484
  E-mail: bcass@dot.state.nh.us
■Deputy Commissioner
  **Christopher M. "Chris" Waszczuk, PE** . . . . . . . . . . . . . (603) 271-1484
  E-mail: cwaszczuk@dot.state.nh.us
Aeronautics, Rail and Transit Director **Patrick Herlihy** . . . . (603) 271-2468
Finance Director **Marie A. Mullen** . . . . . . . . . . . . . . . . . . . (603) 271-3466
■Operations Director **Dave Rodrigue** . . . . . . . . . . . . . . . . . (603) 271-1486
  E-mail: drodrigue@dot.state.nh.us
Policy and Administration Director **Fran Buczynski** . . . . . . (603) 271-1486
  E-mail: fbuczynski@dot.state.nh.us
■Project Development Director **Peter Stamnas** . . . . . . . . . . (603) 271-1484
  E-mail: pstamnas@dot.state.nh.us
  Project Development Assistant Director
  **William J. "Bill" Oldenburg** . . . . . . . . . . . . . . . . . . (603) 271-7419
Aeronautics Bureau Administrator **Tricia Lambert** . . . . . . . (603) 271-1674
Bridge Maintenance Bureau Administrator
  **Doug Gosling** . . . . . . . . . . . . . . . . . . . . . . . . . . . . . . . (603) 271-3667
Construction Bureau Administrator **Ted Kitsis** . . . . . . . . . . (603) 271-2571
Environment Bureau Administrator **Kevin Nyhan** . . . . . . . . (603) 271-1553
  E-mail: knyhan@dot.state.nh.us
Highway Design Bureau Administrator
  **James A. Marshall, PE** . . . . . . . . . . . . . . . . . . . . . . . . (603) 271-2171
Highway Maintenance Bureau Administrator
  **Caleb Dobbins** . . . . . . . . . . . . . . . . . . . . . . . . . . . . . . (603) 271-2693
Human Resources Bureau Administrator **Alexis Martin** . . . (603) 271-8313
Information Technology Services Bureau Administrator
  **Gail Hambleton** . . . . . . . . . . . . . . . . . . . . . . . . . . . . . (603) 271-1489
  E-mail: ghambleton@dot.state.nh.us
Materials and Research Bureau Administrator
  **Charles R. "Chuck" Dusseault** . . . . . . . . . . . . . . . . . (603) 271-3151
Office of Stewardship and Compliance Administrator
  **Shawn Byron** . . . . . . . . . . . . . . . . . . . . . . . . . . . . . . . (603) 271-4045
  E-mail: sbyron@dot.state.nh.us
Right-of-Way Bureau Administrator **Chuck Schmidt** . . . . . (603) 271-3222
Traffic Bureau Administrator **William Lambert** . . . . . . . . . (603) 271-2291
Transportation Planning and Community Assistance
  Bureau Administrator **William Watson** . . . . . . . . . . . . . (603) 271-3344
Turnpike Bureau Administrator **John Corcoran** . . . . . . . . . (603) 485-3806
  36 Hackett Hill Road, Hooksett, NH 03106
Bridge Design Division Administrator **(Vacant)** . . . . . . . . . (603) 271-2731
Public Rail and Transit Division Administrator
  **Shelley Winters** . . . . . . . . . . . . . . . . . . . . . . . . . . . . . (603) 271-2468
Internal Audit Supervisor **(Vacant)** . . . . . . . . . . . . . . . . . . (603) 271-6674

## New Hampshire Business Finance Authority [NHBFA]

Two Pillsbury Street, Suite 201, Concord, NH 03301-4954
Tel: (603) 415-0190  Fax: (603) 415-0194  Internet: www.nhbfa.com

▲Executive Director **Jack Donovan** . . . . . . . . . . . . . . . . . . . (603) 415-0190
  E-mail: jackd@nhbfa.com
  Administrative Assistant **Brenda Pelletier** . . . . . . . . . . . (603) 415-0190
▲Chief Financial Officer **Bill Rushforth** . . . . . . . . . . . . . . . (603) 415-0193
  E-mail: billr@nhbfa.com
Senior Credit Officer **Mike Donahue** . . . . . . . . . . . . . . . . . (603) 415-0192
Entrepreneurship Director **Elizabeth I. Gray** . . . . . . . . . . . (603) 856-8863

## New Hampshire Housing Finance Authority [NHHFA]

P.O. Box 5087, Manchester, NH 03108
Tel: (603) 472-8623  TTY: (603) 472-2089  Internet: www.nhhfa.org

▲Executive Director **Dean J. Christon** . . . . . . . . . . . . . . . . . (603) 310-9242
  E-mail: dchriston@nhhfa.org
  Education: St Anselm BA
  Executive Assistant **Colette Provencher** . . . . . . . . . . . . . (603) 310-9282
Administration and Human Resources Managing Director
  **Patricia Donahue** . . . . . . . . . . . . . . . . . . . . . . . . . . . . (603) 310-9206
  E-mail: pdonahue@nhhfa.org
Assisted Housing Division Managing Director
  **Dee Ann Pouliot** . . . . . . . . . . . . . . . . . . . . . . . . . . . . . (603) 310-9239
Finance and Accounting Managing Director and Chief
  Financial Officer **David B. Sargent** . . . . . . . . . . . . . . . (603) 310-9215
Home Ownership Division Managing Director
  **Ignatius MacLellan** . . . . . . . . . . . . . . . . . . . . . . . . . . . (603) 310-9270
Information Technology Division Managing Director
  **David Hebert** . . . . . . . . . . . . . . . . . . . . . . . . . . . . . . . (603) 310-9220
  E-mail: dhebert@nhhfa.org
Management and Development Division Managing
  Director **Christopher R. Miller** . . . . . . . . . . . . . . . . . . (603) 310-9213
Policy, Planning and Communications Managing Director
  **William Ray** . . . . . . . . . . . . . . . . . . . . . . . . . . . . . . . . (603) 310-9252
  E-mail: bray@nhhfa.org

## New Hampshire Retirement System [NHRS]

54 Regional Drive, Concord, NH 03301
Tel: (603) 410-3500  Tel: (877) 600-0158  TTY: (800) 735-2964
Fax: (603) 410-3501  Internet: www.nhrs.org

**Fiscal Year:** 2014  **Budget:** $7,269,050

Executive Director **George Lagos** . . . . . . . . . . . . . . . . . . . . (603) 410-3520
Finance Director **Jack W. Dianis** . . . . . . . . . . . . . . . . . . . . (603) 410-3656
Information Technology Director **Frank Clough** . . . . . . . . . . (603) 410-3500
  E-mail: frank.clough@nhrs.org
Investments Director **Lawrence A. Johansen** . . . . . . . . . . . (603) 410-3510
Member Services Director **Nancy Miller** . . . . . . . . . . . . . . . (603) 410-3552
Chief Legal Counsel **Timothy Crutchfield** . . . . . . . . . . . . . (603) 410-3526
Internal Auditor **Nancy Cone** . . . . . . . . . . . . . . . . . . . . . . . (603) 410-3598

## Commission for Human Rights

Two Industrial Park Drive, Concord, NH 03301
Tel: (603) 271-2767  Fax: (603) 271-6339
E-mail: humanrights@nhsa.state.nh.us  Internet: www.nh.gov/hrc

Chair **Paul J. Phillips, Esq.** . . . . . . . . . . . . . . . . . . . . . . . . (603) 271-2767
  Term Expires: January 1, 2018
Commissioner **Sarah Browning, Esq.** . . . . . . . . . . . . . . . . . (603) 271-2767
  Term Expires: November 1, 2016
Commissioner **David N. Cole, Esq.** . . . . . . . . . . . . . . . . . . . (603) 271-2767
  Term Expires: January 1, 2018
Commissioner **Harvey Keye** . . . . . . . . . . . . . . . . . . . . . . . . (603) 271-2767
  Term Expires: January 1, 2018
Commissioner **Sheryl L. Shirley, PhD** . . . . . . . . . . . . . . . . (603) 271-2767
  Term Expires: November 1, 2020
Commissioner **(Vacant)** . . . . . . . . . . . . . . . . . . . . . . . . . . . (603) 271-2767

## New Hampshire Lottery Commission

14 Integra Drive, Concord, NH 03301
Tel: (603) 271-3391  Fax: (603) 271-1160

Chairman **Debra Douglas** . . . . . . . . . . . . . . . . . . . . . . . . . . (603) 271-3391
Commissioner **David Gelinas** . . . . . . . . . . . . . . . . . . . . . . . (603) 271-3391
Commissioner **Paul Holloway** . . . . . . . . . . . . . . . . . . . . . . . (603) 271-3391

---

# Public Utilities Commission [PUC]

21 South Fruit Street, Suite 10, Concord, NH 03301-2429
Tel: (603) 271-2431 Fax: (603) 271-3878 E-mail: puc@puc.nh.gov
Internet: www.puc.nh.gov

**Employees:** 75 **Fiscal Year:** 2014 **Budget:** $34,394,420

■Chair **Martin P. Honigberg** . . . . . . . . . . . . . . . . . . . . . . . . (603) 271-2443
  Term Expires: June 30, 2019
  Education: Amherst 1981 BA; Vanderbilt 1985 JD
■Commissioner **Kathryn M. Bailey** . . . . . . . . . . . . . . . . . . . (603) 271-2431
  Term Expires: June 30, 2021
  Education: Union Col (NY) 1983 BSEE
■Commissioner **Robert R. "Bob" Scott** . . . . . . . . . . . . . . . (603) 271-2431
  Term Expires: July 1, 2017
  Education: Lehigh 1986 BS; Western New England (Attended)

# Judicial Council

25 Capitol Street, Room 424, Concord, NH 03301
Tel: (603) 271-3592 TTY: (800) 735-2964 Fax: (603) 271-1112

▲Executive Director **(Vacant)** . . . . . . . . . . . . . . . . . . . . . . . (603) 271-3592

# State Board of Education

101 Pleasant Street, Concord, NH 03301
Tel: (603) 271-3495 TTY: (800) 737-2964 Fax: (603) 271-1953

■Chairman **Tom Raffio, FLMI** (Fourth District) . . . . . . . . . (603) 223-1300
  Term Expires: January 31, 2017                    Res: (603) 715-2750
  57 Bow Bog Road, Bow, NH 03304                    Fax: (603) 223-1299
  E-mail: tomraffio@nedelta.com
■Member **Cindy C. Chagnon** (At-Large) . . . . . . . . . . . . . . . (603) 271-3495
  Term Expires: January 31, 2020
  12 Carriage Lane, Bedford, NH 03110
  E-mail: chags@comcast.net
■Member **Bill Duncan** (Third District) . . . . . . . . . . . . . . . . (603) 436-6306
  Term Expires: January 31, 2018
  12 Cranfield Street, New Castle, NH 03854
  E-mail: waduncan@gmail.com
■Member **Gary Groleau** (At-Large) . . . . . . . . . . . . . . . . . . (603) 271-3495
  Term Expires: January 31, 2019
  15 Carriage Lane, Laconia, NH 03246
  E-mail: ggroleau@nhbb.com
■Member **Helen G. Honorow** (Fifth District) . . . . . . . . . . . (603) 271-3144
  Term Expires: January 31, 2020                    Res: (603) 598-8433
  46 Raymond Street, Nashua, NH 03064
  E-mail: hhonorow@barrylawoffice.com
■Member **Gregory Odell** (First District) . . . . . . . . . . . . . . . (603) 271-3495
■Member **Emma L. Rous** (Second District) . . . . . . . . . . . . (603) 868-7030
  Term Expires: January 31, 2017
  50 Adams Point Road, Durham, NH 03824
  E-mail: rousemma@gmail.com
  Education: Mount Holyoke BA; Columbia MA

# New Hampshire Department of Education [NHDOE]

101 Pleasant Street, Concord, NH 03301
Tel: (603) 271-3494 TTY: (800) 735-2964 Fax: (603) 271-1953

**Employees:** 398 **Fiscal Year:** 2014 **Budget:** $1,345,773,622

■Commissioner **Virginia M. Barry** . . . . . . . . . . . . . . . . . . . (603) 271-3494
  E-mail: virginia.barry@doe.nh.gov
  Education: Florida State BS; Queens Col (NY) MS;
  Florida State 1979 PhD
Deputy Commissioner **Paul K. Leather** . . . . . . . . . . . . . . . (603) 271-7301
  Education: Georgetown; Keene State
State Director of Special Education **Santina Thibedeau** . . . (603) 271-6693
Business Management Administrator
  **Tammy Vaillancourt** . . . . . . . . . . . . . . . . . . . . . . . . . . (603) 271-3833
  E-mail: tammy.vaillancourt@doe.nh.gov
Programs Information Officer/Webmaster **Lori Kincaid** . . . . (603) 271-6646
  E-mail: lori.temple@doe.nh.gov
Administrative Assistant **Pat Butler** . . . . . . . . . . . . . . . . . (603) 271-3144

# Division of Adult Learning and Rehabilitation

21 South Fruit, Concord, NH 03301-2451
Tel: (603) 271-3471 Fax: (603) 271-7095

Director **Lisa K. Hatz** . . . . . . . . . . . . . . . . . . . . . . . . . . . . (603) 271-3802

Adult Basic Education Division Director
  **Arthur S. Ellison** . . . . . . . . . . . . . . . . . . . . . . . . . . . . . (603) 271-6698
  GED (General Education Development) Program
  Assistant **Barbara Crosby** . . . . . . . . . . . . . . . . . . . . . . (603) 271-6699
  E-mail: barbara.crosby@state.mn.us

## Division of Educational Improvement

Director **Heather Gage** . . . . . . . . . . . . . . . . . . . . . . . . . . . (603) 271-3870
Chapter I ESEA (Elementary and Secondary Education
  Act) Division Director **Dr. Mary Earick** . . . . . . . . . . . . (603) 271-3769
Foreign Languages and Bilingual Education Consultant
  **(Vacant)** . . . . . . . . . . . . . . . . . . . . . . . . . . . . . . . . . . . (603) 271-2772

## Division of Higher Education

Tel: (603) 271-0257 Fax: (603) 271-1953

■Director **Dr. Edward R. "Ed" MacKay** . . . . . . . . . . . . . . . (603) 271-0256
  E-mail: edward.mackay@doe.nh.gov
  Education: Bloomsburg BA; Lehigh MA; Vanderbilt EdD

## Division of Program Support

Director **Dr. Scott J. Mantie** . . . . . . . . . . . . . . . . . . . . . . . (603) 271-3844

# Executive Council

State House, 107 North Main Street, Room 207, Concord, NH 03301
Tel: (603) 271-3632 Tel: (800) 735-2964 Fax: (603) 271-3633
E-mail: gcweb@nh.gov

★Executive Councilor **Joseph D. Kenney** (R-District 1) . . . . (603) 271-3632
  Term Expires: 2017                    Res: (603) 581-8780
  P.O. Box 201, Union, NH 03887
  Education: New Hampshire
★Executive Councilor
  **Christopher C. Pappas** (D-District 4) . . . . . . . . . . . . . . (603) 271-3632
  Term Expires: 2017
  629 Kearney Circle, Manchester, NH 03104
★Executive Councilor
  **Christopher "Chris" Sununu** (R-District 3) . . . . . . . . . . (603) 271-3632
  Term Expires: 2017                    Res: (603) 969-1488
  71 Hemlock Court, Newfields, NH 03856
  Education: MIT BS
★Executive Councilor **Colin Van Ostern** (D-District 2) . . . . (603) 271-3632
  Term Expires: 2017                    Res: (603) 290-5848
  P.O. Box 193, Concord, NH 03301
  Education: George Washington 2000 BA
★Executive Councilor
  **David K. "Dave" Wheeler** (R-District 5) . . . . . . . . . . . . (603) 271-3632
  Term Expires: 2017                    Res: (603) 672-6062
  523 Mason Road, Milford, NH 03055
Executive Assistant **Joanne Ruel** . . . . . . . . . . . . . . . . . . . (603) 271-3632
  E-mail: jruel@nh.gov

---

★ Elected Official   ■ Appointed by Governor   ● Appointed by Legislature   ▲ Appointed by Board or Commission   ◆ Appointed by State Supreme Court

# New Jersey

Tel: (609) 292-2121 (New Jersey Information Center)  Internet: www.newjersey.gov

**Number of U.S. Congressional Delegates:** 2 Senators; 12 Representatives  **Governor's Term:** 4 years
**Legislature Description:** 40 member Senate; 80 member General Assembly; Term - Senate
4 years, Assembly 2 years  **Next Election:** Governor November 2017; Legislature November 2017
**Number of Electoral Votes:** 14  **Official Name:** State of New Jersey (after island of Jersey)
**Nickname:** The Garden State  **Motto:** Liberty and Prosperity

**Population:** 8,958,013 (2015); Rank 11  **Fiscal Year:** 2015  **Budget:** $21,150,816,000

## Office of the Governor

125 West State Street, Trenton, NJ 08608
P.O. Box 001, Trenton, NJ 08625
Tel: (609) 292-6000  TTY: (609) 777-1292  Fax: (609) 292-3454
Internet: www.state.nj.us/governor

**Fiscal Year:** 2015  **Budget:** $6,474,000

**Christopher J. "Chris" Christie**
Governor

Began Service: January 19, 2010
Term Expires: January 2018
Date of Birth: September 6, 1962
Education: Delaware 1984 BA;
Seton Hall 1987 JD
Religion: Roman Catholic
Career: Partner, Dughi, Hewit & Palatucci
(1987-2002); U.S. Attorney, New Jersey District,
Executive Office for United States Attorneys,
United States Department of Justice, George W.
Bush Administration (2002-2008)

★ Governor **Christopher J. "Chris" Christie** (R) . . . . . . . . . . (609) 292-6000
Chief of Staff **Amy Cradic** . . . . . . . . . . . . . . . . . . . . . . . . . . (609) 777-1265
    Education: Col New Jersey 1993 BA; NYU 2000 MA
Deputy Chief of Staff for Policy and Cabinet Liaison
**(Vacant)** . . . . . . . . . . . . . . . . . . . . . . . . . . . . . . . . . . . . . . . . (609) 777-1257
Director of Appointments **Matthew P. McDermott** . . . . . . . (609) 777-0251
    E-mail: matthew.mcdermott@gov.state.nj.us
Director of Budget **Beth Schermerhorn** . . . . . . . . . . . . . . . (609) 777-1257
    E-mail: beth.schermerhorn@gov.state.nj.us
Director of Constituent Relations **Jeanne Ashmore** . . . . . . (609) 777-2500
    E-mail: jeanne.ashmore@gov.state.nj.us
Director of Operations **Rosemary Iannacone** . . . . . . . . . . . (609) 777-1265
    E-mail: rosemary.iannacone@gov.state.nj.us
■ Chief Counsel **Thomas P. Scrivo** . . . . . . . . . . . . . . . . . . . . (609) 777-2450
    E-mail: thomas.scrivo@gov.state.nj.us
    Education: Fairfield 1985 BS; Seton Hall 1989 JD
Senior Deputy Chief Counsel **Scott A. Coffina** . . . . . . . . . (609) 777-2450
    E-mail: scott.coffina@gov.state.nj.us
    Education: Cornell BA; Pennsylvania 1992 JD
Senior Counsel **Dominick DiRocco** . . . . . . . . . . . . . . . . . . . (609) 777-2450
    E-mail: dominick.dirocco@gov.state.nj.us
Senior Counsel **Colin Newman** . . . . . . . . . . . . . . . . . . . . . . . (609) 777-2450
    E-mail: colin.newman@gov.state.nj.us
Senior Policy Advisor **(Vacant)** . . . . . . . . . . . . . . . . . . . . . . (609) 777-1257
Cybersecurity Advisor **David C. Weinstein** . . . . . . . . . . . . (609) 777-1257
    E-mail: david.weinstein@gov.state.nj.us
Education Policy Advisor **Marci D. Green** . . . . . . . . . . . . . (609) 633-7575
    E-mail: marci.green@gov.state.nj.us
Executive Director of Recovery and Rebuilding
**Terrence S. Brody** . . . . . . . . . . . . . . . . . . . . . . . . . . . . . . . . (609) 292-6000
    E-mail: terrence.brody@gov.state.nj.us
    Education: Scranton 2000; Rutgers (Newark) 2003 JD
■ Chief Ethics Officer **Heather V. Taylor** . . . . . . . . . . . . . . . (609) 777-2479
    E-mail: heather.taylor@gov.state.nj.us
Deputy Chief of Staff of Communications
**Jacqueline Halldow** . . . . . . . . . . . . . . . . . . . . . . . . . . . . . . . (609) 292-6000

Director of Community and Constituent Relations
**Vincent "Vinny" Napolitano** . . . . . . . . . . . . . . . . . . . . . (609) 777-2500
    E-mail: vincent.napolitano@gov.state.nj.us
    Education: Syracuse 2008 BA
Press Secretary **Brian Murray** . . . . . . . . . . . . . . . . . . . . . . . (609) 292-6000
Deputy Press Secretary **Lynne Richmond** . . . . . . . . . . . . . (609) 292-6000
    Education: Douglass 1985 BA
Deputy Press Secretary **Jeremy Rosen** . . . . . . . . . . . . . . . . (609) 292-6000

## Washington Office

444 North Capitol Street, NW, Suite 201, Washington, DC 20001
Tel: (202) 638-0631  Fax: (202) 638-2296

Director **Dona De Leon** . . . . . . . . . . . . . . . . . . . . . . (202) 638-0631 ext. 20
    E-mail: dona.deleon@gov.state.nj.us
Assistant Director **Suzanne "Sue" Tagliabue** . . . . . . . . . . (202) 638-0631
    E-mail: suzanne.tagliabue@gov.state.nj.us

## Department of Agriculture [NJDA]

John Fitch Plaza, Trenton, NJ 08625
P.O. Box 330, Trenton, NJ 08625
Tel: (609) 292-8896  Fax: (609) 292-3978
Internet: www.state.nj.us/agriculture

**Employees:** 209  **Fiscal Year:** 2015  **Budget:** $22,769,000

■ Secretary **Douglas H. "Doug" Fisher** . . . . . . . . . . . . . . . (609) 292-3976
    E-mail: douglas.fisher@ag.state.nj.us
    Education: Bryant Col BS
Assistant Secretary **Alfred "Al" Murray** . . . . . . . . . . . . . . (609) 292-5536
    Education: Susquehanna 1983 BS
Chief of Staff **Mary Tovar** . . . . . . . . . . . . . . . . . . . . . . . . . (609) 292-3976
    E-mail: mary.tovar@ag.state.nj.us
Chief Fiscal Officer **Louis A. Bruni, CPA** . . . . . . . . . . . . . (609) 292-6931
    Education: Trenton State 1983 BS
Policy Advisor **Jeff Beach** . . . . . . . . . . . . . . . . . . . . . . . . . . (609) 292-5531
    E-mail: jeffrey.beach@ag.state.nj.us
    Education: Temple 1986 BA
Legal Affairs **Judith I. "Judy" Gleason, Esq.** . . . . . . . . . (609) 984-0613
Legislative Affairs **Rob Vivian** . . . . . . . . . . . . . . . . . . . . . . (609) 282-8898
    E-mail: rob.vivian@ag.state.nj.us
Public Information Officer **Lynne Richmond** . . . . . . . . . . . (609) 633-2954
    E-mail: lynne.richmond@ag.state.nj.us

## Department of Banking and Insurance

20 West State Street, Trenton, NJ 08625
P.O. Box 325, Trenton, NJ 08625-0325
Tel: (609) 292-7272  Fax: (609) 292-3144
E-mail: inslic@dobi.nj.gov (Insurance Licensing)
E-mail: realestate@dobi.nj.gov (Real Estate Commission)
Internet: dobi.nj.gov

**Employees:** 515  **Fiscal Year:** 2016  **Budget:** $64,013,000

■ Commissioner (Acting) **Richard J. Badolato** . . . . . . . . . . . (609) 292-7272
    E-mail: commissioner@dobi.nj.gov
Chief of Staff **Aileen Egan** . . . . . . . . . . . . . . . . . . . . . . . . . (609) 633-7667
    E-mail: aileen.egan@dobi.nj.gov

*(continued on next page)*

---

★ Elected Official   ■ Appointed by Governor   ● Appointed by Legislature   ▲ Appointed by Board or Commission   ◆ Appointed by State Supreme Court

**Department of Banking and Insurance** *continued*

Administration Assistant Commissioner
  **John Walton** . . . . . . . . . . . . . . . . . . . . . . . . . . . . (609) 292-7272 ext. 50024
    E-mail: john.walton@dobi.nj.gov
Chief Technology Officer **Joseph Mingo** . . . . . . (609) 292-7272 ext. 50260
    E-mail: joseph.mingo@dobi.nj.gov
    Education: East Stroudsburg 1975 BS
Legislation and Regulation Director (Acting)
  **Denise M. Illes, Esq.** . . . . . . . . . . . . . . . . . . . . (609) 292-7272 ext. 50031

## Division of Banking

20 West State Street, Trenton, NJ 08608
P.O. Box 040, Trenton, NJ 08625
Tel: (609) 292-7272  Internet: dobi.nj.gov

Director **Patrick Mullen** . . . . . . . . . . . . . . . . . . (609) 292-7272 ext. 50111
    E-mail: patrick.mullen@dobi.nj.gov
Consumer Finance Division Assistant Director
  **Thomas Hunt** . . . . . . . . . . . . . . . . . . . . . . . . . . (609) 292-7272 ext. 50223
    E-mail: thomas.hunt@dobi.nj.gov
Depositories Assistant Director
  **Kevin McGrath** . . . . . . . . . . . . . . . . . . . . . . . . (609) 292-7272 ext. 50539

## Division of Insurance

Tel: (609) 292-7272  Fax: (609) 292-3144

Director **Peter L. Hartt** . . . . . . . . . . . . . . . . . . . (609) 292-7272 ext. 50009
Consumer Protection Services Assistant
  Commissioner **Gale P. Simon** . . . . . . . . . . . . . (609) 292-7272 ext. 50333
    Education: Trinity Col (CT) 1977 BS; Pennsylvania 1981 JD
Life and Health Assistant Commissioner
  **Brendan Peppard** . . . . . . . . . . . . . . . . . . . . . . (609) 292-7272 ext. 50122
Property and Casualty Operations Assistant
  Commissioner **William G. Rader** . . . . . . . . . . . (609) 292-7272 ext. 50359
    Education: Monmouth Col (NJ) 1979 BA
Solvency Regulation Assistant Commissioner
  **Steven Kerner** . . . . . . . . . . . . . . . . . . . . . . . . . (609) 292-7272 ext. 50205
    E-mail: steve.kerner@dobi.nj.gov

## Individual Health Coverage Program and Small Employer Health Benefits Program

Fax: (609) 633-2030

Executive Director **Ellen DeRosa** . . . . . . . . . . . . (609) 292-7272 ext. 50302

## Department of Children and Families [DCF]

50 East State Street, 2nd Floor, Trenton, NJ 08625-0700
Tel: (609) 888-7900  Internet: www.state.nj.us/dcf

**Employees:** 6,597  **Fiscal Year:** 2015  **Budget:** $1,113,502,000
■Commissioner **Allison M. Blake, LSW** . . . . . . . . . . . . . . . . . (609) 888-7900
    E-mail: dcf_commissioner@dcf.state.nj.us
    Education: Dayton 1984 BSW; Rutgers 1989 MSW;
    Fordham 2003 PhD
Assistant Commissioner **Lisa von Pier** . . . . . . . . . . . . . . . . (609) 888-7900
    E-mail: lisa.vonpier@dcf.state.nj.us
Deputy Commissioner **Joseph E. Ribsam, Jr., Esq.** . . . . . . (609) 888-7900
    E-mail: dcf_assistant_commissioner@dcf.state.nj.us
Chief of Staff **Suzanne Alvino** . . . . . . . . . . . . . . . . . . . . . . (609) 888-7900
    E-mail: dcf_chiefofstaff@dcf.state.nj.us
Administration and Legal Affairs Office Director
  **Laurie Hodian** . . . . . . . . . . . . . . . . . . . . . . . . . . . . . . . . . (609) 888-7900
    E-mail: dcf_ooa@dcf.state.nj.us
Communications and Public Affairs Office Director
  **Ernest Landante** . . . . . . . . . . . . . . . . . . . . . . . . . . . . . . . (609) 888-7900
    E-mail: communications@dcf.state.nj.us
Legal Affairs Office Director **Clinton Page** . . . . . . . . . . . . (609) 888-7900

## Department of Community Affairs [DCA]

101 South Broad Street, Trenton, NJ 08625
P.O. Box 800, Trenton, NJ 08625-0800
Tel: (609) 292-6420  TTY: (609) 278-0175  Fax: (609) 984-6696
E-mail: dca.feedback@dca.state.nj.us  Internet: www.nj.gov/dca

**Employees:** 900  **Fiscal Year:** 2015  **Budget:** $105,101,000
■Commissioner **Charles A. Richman** . . . . . . . . . . . . . . . . . . . (609) 292-6420
    E-mail: charles.richman@dca.state.nj.us
Assistant Commissioner **Laura Shea** . . . . . . . . . . . . . . . . . . (609) 292-0569
Chief of Staff **Joyce Paul** . . . . . . . . . . . . . . . . . . . . . . . . . . (609) 292-6420
Communications Director **Tammori Petty** . . . . . . . . . . . . . (609) 292-6055
    E-mail: tammori.petty@dca.state.nj.us
Communications Deputy Director **(Vacant)** . . . . . . . . . . . . . (609) 292-6055
Fiscal Affairs Director **Cynthia "Cindy" McDowell** . . . . . . (609) 292-6437
Human Resources Director **Jodi Evangelista** . . . . . . . . . . . (609) 292-6030
Information Technology Director **Linda Torres** . . . . . . . . . . (609) 943-5847
    E-mail: linda.torres@dca.state.nj.us
Legislative Affairs Director **(Vacant)** . . . . . . . . . . . . . . . . . (609) 633-3881
  Legal and Regulatory Affairs Director
    **Gabrielle Gallagher** . . . . . . . . . . . . . . . . . . . . . . . . . . (609) 292-4096
  Legal and Regulatory Affairs Assistant Director
    **(Vacant)** . . . . . . . . . . . . . . . . . . . . . . . . . . . . . . . . . . . (609) 943-4698
Local Planning Services Executive Director
  **Sean Thompson** . . . . . . . . . . . . . . . . . . . . . . . . . . . . . . (609) 292-1716
Strategic Communications Director **Lisa Ryan** . . . . . . . . . . (609) 292-6055
    E-mail: lisa.ryan@dca.state.nj.us
Webmaster **Amy Heath** . . . . . . . . . . . . . . . . . . . . . . . . . . . . (609) 294-1903
    E-mail: amy.heath@dca.state.nj.us

## Department of Corrections [DOC]

Whittlesey Road, Trenton, NJ 08625
P.O. Box 863, Trenton, NJ 08625-0863
Tel: (609) 292-4036  Fax: (609) 292-9083  E-mail: pubinfo@doc.nj.gov
Internet: www.state.nj.us/corrections

**Employees:** 8,131  **Fiscal Year:** 2015  **Budget:** $1,030,965
■Commissioner **Gary Lanigan** . . . . . . . . . . . . . . . . . . . . . . . (609) 292-4036
    E-mail: gary.lanigan@doc.state.nj.us
Chief of Staff **Judith Lang** . . . . . . . . . . . . . . . . . . (609) 292-4036 ext. 5660
Operations Assistant Commissioner **Bettie M. Norris** . . . . . (609) 292-4463
Administration Assistant Commissioner **Gary Alpert** . . . . . . (609) 826-5615
    E-mail: gary.alpert@doc.state.nj.us
Programs and Community Services Assistant
  Commissioner **Darcella Seesomes** . . . . . . . . . . (609) 292-4036 ext. 5629
    Education: Rutgers 1991 MSW
Information Technology Director
  **Satish Bhalerao** . . . . . . . . . . . . . . . . . . . . . . . . (609) 292-4036 ext. 5642
    E-mail: satish.bhalerao@doc.state.nj.us
Public Information Officer **Matthew Schuman** . . (609) 292-4036 ext. 5662
    E-mail: matthew.schuman@doc.nj.gov

## Bureau of State Use Industries [DEPTCOR]

Division Director **Kennedy O'Brien** . . . . . . . . . . . . . . . . . . . (609) 633-8100

## Department of Environmental Protection [DEP]

401 East State Street, Trenton, NJ 08625
P.O. Box 402, Trenton, NJ 08625-0402
Tel: (609) 292-2885  Fax: (609) 292-7995  Internet: www.state.nj.us/dep

**Employees:** 2,813  **Fiscal Year:** 2015-2016  **Budget:** $286,700,000
■Commissioner **Bob Martin** . . . . . . . . . . . . . . . . . . . . . . . . . (609) 292-2885
    E-mail: commissioner@dep.nj.gov
    Executive Secretary **Brenda Cook** . . . . . . . . . . . . . . . . (609) 777-4327
Deputy Commissioner **David L. "Dave" Glass** . . . . . . . . . . (609) 292-2885
  Chief Advisor to the Commissioner **Raymond Cantor** . . . (609) 292-2885
  Deputy Advisor to the Commissioner **Jane Engel** . . . . . . (609) 292-2885
Chief of Staff **Magdalena Padilla** . . . . . . . . . . . . . . . . . . . . (609) 292-2885
Deputy Chief of Staff and Legislative Liaison **John Gray** . . (609) 292-9954

---

Legal Affairs Office Director **Janis E. Hoagland** . . . . . . . . (609) 292-0716

## Office of Communications

Director **Angelene Taccini** . . . . . . . . . . . . . . . . . . . . . . (609) 984-1795
  E-mail: angelene.taccini@dep.nj.gov
Press Director **Bob Considine** . . . . . . . . . . . . . . . . . . . . . (609) 984-1795
  E-mail: bob.considine@dep.nj.gov
Legislative Affairs Director **John Hazen** . . . . . . . . . . . . . (609) 633-7698
  E-mail: john.hazen@dep.nj.gov
Constituent Services Office Manager **Kerry Kirk Pflugh** . . . (609) 633-7242
Local Government Assistance Coordinator
  **Cindy Randazzo** . . . . . . . . . . . . . . . . . . . . . . . . . . . (609) 633-7700
  E-mail: cindy.randazzo@dep.nj.gov
Strategic Communications Director **Bob Bostock** . . . . . . . . (609) 984-1795
  E-mail: bob.bostock@dep.nj.gov

## Compliance and Enforcement

P.O. Box 422, Trenton, NJ 08625-0422
Fax: (609) 292-1803

Assistant Commissioner **Ray Bukowski** . . . . . . . . . . . . . (609) 777-0122
Air and Hazardous Materials Director **Richelle Wormley** . . (609) 633-7288
  E-mail: richelle.wormley@dep.nj.gov
  Education: NJIT MS
Water and Land Use Enforcement Director
  **Marcedius T. Jameson** . . . . . . . . . . . . . . . . . . . . . . . (609) 984-2011
Coastal and Land Use Compliance Manager
  **Lawrence J. "Larry" Baier** . . . . . . . . . . . . . . . . . . . (609) 292-1240
Hazardous Waste Compliance and Enforcement Manager
  **Michael Hastry** . . . . . . . . . . . . . . . . . . . . . . . . . . . (609) 943-3019
                                Fax: (609) 292-3970
Solid Waste Compliance and Enforcement Manager
  **Tom Farrell** . . . . . . . . . . . . . . . . . . . . . . . . . . . . . . (609) 292-6305
                                Fax: (609) 292-4539

## Air Quality, Energy and Sustainability

401 East State Street, Trenton, NJ 08625
P.O. Box 423, Trenton, NJ 08625-0423
Tel: (609) 292-2795  Fax: (609) 777-1330  Internet: www.nj.gov/dep/er

Assistant Commissioner **John Giordano** . . . . . . . . . . . . . (609) 292-2795
Air Quality Division Director **Francis Steitz** . . . . . . . . . . (609) 984-1484
Environmental Safety and Health Division Director
  **Paul Baldauf** . . . . . . . . . . . . . . . . . . . . . . . . . . . . . (609) 633-7964
  E-mail: paul.baldauf@dep.nj.gov
Water Quality Division Director **Michele Putnam** . . . . . . . (609) 292-4543
Solid and Hazardous Waste Management Program
  Director **Mary Jo Aiello** . . . . . . . . . . . . . . . . . . . . . . (609) 984-3680

## Land Use Management

401 East State Street, 7th Floor, Trenton, NJ 08625
P.O. Box 402, Trenton, NJ 08625-0402
Tel: (609) 633-2201  Fax: (609) 633-0750

Assistant Commissioner **Ginger Kopkash** . . . . . . . . . . . . (609) 292-2178
Land Use Regulation Director **Diane Dow** . . . . . . . . . . . . (609) 984-3444
  E-mail: diane.dow@dep.nj.gov
Water Supply Assistant Director **Karen Fell** . . . . . . . . . . (609) 292-2957
New Jersey Geological Survey State Geologist (Acting)
  **Jeffrey Hoffman** . . . . . . . . . . . . . . . . . . . . . . . . . . . (609) 292-1185

## Management and Budget

440 East Strate Street, Trenton, NJ 08625
P.O. Box 420, Trenton, NJ 08625-0420
Fax: (609) 777-4395

Budget and Financial Operations Director
  **Adrienne Kreipke** . . . . . . . . . . . . . . . . . . . . . . . . . . (609) 292-9230
Human Resources Director **Robin Liebeskind** . . . . . . . . . . (609) 292-1899
Equal Opportunity and Public Contract Assistance Office
  Director **Melanie Armstrong** . . . . . . . . . . . . . . . . . . . (609) 984-9742
General Services and Systems Coordination Director
  **Juliet DelValle** . . . . . . . . . . . . . . . . . . . . . . . . . . . . (609) 292-1553
  E-mail: juliet.delvalle@dep.nj.gov
Occupational Health and Safety Manager **Amal Shah** . . . . (609) 292-1408

Information Resources Management Chief Information
  Officer **Peter Tenebruso** . . . . . . . . . . . . . . . . . . . . . . (609) 292-3211
  E-mail: peter.tenebruso@dep.nj.gov
Financial Operations Manager **(Vacant)** . . . . . . . . . . . . . . (609) 292-8046

## Natural and Historic Resources

501 East State Street, 3rd Floor, Trenton, NJ 08625
P.O. Box 404, Trenton, NJ 08625-0404
Fax: (609) 984-0836

Assistant Commissioner **Richard Boornazian** . . . . . . . . . . . (609) 292-3541
  E-mail: richard.boornazian@dep.nj.gov
Engineering and Construction Assistant Commissioner
  **Dave Rosenblatt** . . . . . . . . . . . . . . . . . . . . . . . . . . . (609) 292-9236
  E-mail: dave.rosenblatt@dep.nj.gov
Historic Preservation Office Administrator
  **Daniel D. "Dan" Saunders** . . . . . . . . . . . . . . . . . . . . (609) 984-0176
  E-mail: dan.saunders@dep.nj.gov
Leases Office Administrator **George Chidley** . . . . . . . . . . . (609) 633-7575
  E-mail: george.chidley@dep.nj.gov
Green Acres Program Deputy Administrator (Acting)
  **Martha Sapp** . . . . . . . . . . . . . . . . . . . . . . . . . . . . . . (609) 984-0058
  E-mail: martha.sapp@dep.nj.gov
Fish and Wildlife Division Director
  **David "Dave" Chanda** . . . . . . . . . . . . . . . . . . . . . . . . (609) 292-2965
  E-mail: david.chanda@dep.nj.gov
Forestry Deputy Director **John Sacco** . . . . . . . . . . . . . . . (609) 292-2938
  E-mail: john.sacco@dep.nj.gov
Parks and Forestry Division Director **Mark Texel** . . . . . . . (609) 292-2733

## Office of Science

P.O. Box 402, Trenton, NJ 08625-0402
401 East State Street, Trenton, NJ 08625
Fax: (609) 292-3268

Office of Science Manager **Gary Buchanan** . . . . . . . . . . . (609) 984-6070
Coastal Management Office Manager **Ruth Ehinger** . . . . . . (609) 633-2201

## Site Remediation

P.O. Box 420, Trenton, NJ 08625-0420
Fax: (609) 777-1914

Assistant Commissioner **Mark J. Pederson** . . . . . . . . . . . . (609) 292-1250
Division of Site Remediation Management Director
  **Kenneth "Ken" Kloo** . . . . . . . . . . . . . . . . . . . . . . . . (609) 292-1251
  E-mail: ken.kloo@dep.nj.gov
  Education: Seton Hall BS

## Department of Health [DOH]

Health and Agriculture Building, Trenton, NJ 08625
P.O. Box 360, Trenton, NJ 08625-0360
P.O. Box 370, Trenton, NJ 08625 (Vital Records)
Tel: (609) 292-7834  Tel: (609) 777-0092 (Superior Court)
Tel: (609) 292-4087 (Vital Records)
Tel: (877) 572-6342 (NIC USA eGovernment Services)
Fax: (609) 984-5474  Internet: www.state.nj.us/health/vital

**Employees:** 1,153  **Fiscal Year:** 2015  **Budget:** $354,936,000

■Commissioner (Acting) **Cathleen D. Bennett** . . . . . . . . . . (609) 292-7837
■Deputy Commissioner **Dr. Arturo Brito, MD, MPH** . . . . . (609) 292-7837
  E-mail: arturo.brito@doh.state.nj.us
Chief of Staff **Ruth Charbonneau** . . . . . . . . . . . . . . . . . . (609) 292-1447
Health Statistics Center Director **Abate Mammo, PhD** . . . . (609) 984-7508
  E-mail: abate.mammo@doh.state.nj.us
Human Resources Director **Loreta Sepulveda** . . . . . . . . . . (609) 633-0022
Information Technology Office Director **Sharon Eldridge** . . (609) 341-5006
  E-mail: sharon.eldridge@doh.state.nj.us
Legal and Regulatory Compliance Director **Joy L. Lindo** . . (609) 984-2177
  E-mail: joy.lindo@doh.state.nj.us
  Education: Seton Hall 2001 JD
Legislative Services Director **Victoria R. Brogan** . . . . . . . . (609) 633-3689
  E-mail: victoria.brogan@doh.state.nj.us
Minority Health Office Director **M. Carolyn Daniels** . . . . . (609) 292-6962
Policy and Strategic Planning Director
  **Cathleen D. Bennett** . . . . . . . . . . . . . . . . . . . . . . . . . (609) 633-3609
  E-mail: cathleen.bennett@doh.state.nj.us

*(continued on next page)*

---

**Department of Health** *continued*

Press Office/Public Information Office Director
**Donna Leusner** . . . . . . . . . . . . . . . . . . . . . . . . . . . . . (609) 984-7160
E-mail: donna.leusner@doh.state.nj.us
Affirmative Action Officer **Neela Sookdeo** . . . . . . . . . . . . (609) 292-7606
Education: Rutgers 2003 JD
Vital Statistics State Registrar **Vincent Arrisi** . . . . . . . . . . . (609) 292-4087
Education: Rutgers (Camden) 1979 BS; Seton Hall 1985 MBA;
Kean U 1992 MA; California Coast 2001 PsyD

## Health Care Quality and Access

Health Care Quality Assessment Director
**Emmanuel Noggoh** . . . . . . . . . . . . . . . . . . . . . . . . . . . (609) 984-7334
E-mail: emmanuel.noggoh@doh.state.nj.us

## Public Health Infrastructure Laboratories and Emergency Preparedness

Health and Agriculture Building, Trenton, NJ 08625-0360
P.O. Box 360, Trenton, NJ 08625-0360

Assistant Commissioner **Christopher Rinn** . . . . . . . . . . . . . . (609) 633-8350
E-mail: christopher.rinn@doh.state.nj.us
Local Public Health Office Director (Acting)
**Michael Lakat** . . . . . . . . . . . . . . . . . . . . . . . . . . . . . . . (609) 292-4993
Emergency Medical Services Program Manager (Acting)
**Nancy Kelly-Goodstein** . . . . . . . . . . . . . . . . . . . . . . . . (609) 633-7777
Education: Rutgers (Newark) 1979 BA
Emergency Preparedness Coordination Program Manager
**James Bruncati** . . . . . . . . . . . . . . . . . . . . . . . . . . . . . . (609) 633-2000
E-mail: james.bruncati@doh.state.nj.us

## Division of Management and Administration

Fax: (609) 633-0814

Director **Eric Anderson** . . . . . . . . . . . . . . . . . . . . . . . . . . (609) 292-6915
E-mail: eric.anderson@doh.state.nj.us
Budget Director **Eric Carlsson** . . . . . . . . . . . . . . . . . . . . . . (609) 292-7646
Fax: (609) 633-1683
Financial Services Director **(Vacant)** . . . . . . . . . . . . . . . . . (609) 633-1528
Fax: (609) 633-1362
Vital Statistics and Registration State Registrar
**Vincent Arrisi** . . . . . . . . . . . . . . . . . . . . . . . . . . . . . . . (609) 984-3445
Fax: (609) 292-4343

## Public Health Services

Deputy Commissioner **Dr. Arturo Brito, MD, MPH** . . . . . . . (609) 292-7836
Executive Assistant **Lisa Asare** . . . . . . . . . . . . . . . . . . . . (609) 292-7836
Medicinal Marijuana Program Director (Acting)
**James M. Baracia** . . . . . . . . . . . . . . . . . . . . . . . . . . . . (609) 292-0424

## Office of the State Epidemiologist

3635 Quakerbridge Road, Trenton, NJ 08619
P.O. Box 369, Trenton, NJ 08625
Fax: (609) 984-5474

State Epidemiologist **Christina G. Tan** . . . . . . . . . . . . . . . . (609) 826-5967
Cancer Epidemiology Services Director
**Antoinette M. "Nan" Stroup, PhD** . . . . . . . . . . . . . . . . . (609) 633-0500

## Office of Healthcare Financing

Executive Director **Brian O'Neill** . . . . . . . . . . . . . . . . . . . . (609) 633-9596

## Department of Human Services [DHS]

222 South Warren Street, Trenton, NJ 08625-0700
P.O. Box 700, Trenton, NJ 08625-0700
Tel: (609) 292-3717  TTY: (609) 292-9505
Tel: (609) 292-3703 (Public Affairs Office)  Fax: (609) 292-4556
Internet: www.state.nj.us/humanservices

**Employees:** 14,468  **Fiscal Year:** 2015  **Budget:** $6,150,840,000

■Commissioner (Acting) **Elizabeth "Beth" Connolly** . . . . . . (609) 292-3717
Note: On June 22, 2015, Governor Chris Christie nominated Elizabeth
Connolly as Commissioner of the Department of Human Services. Ms.
Connolly's nomination must be confirmed by the New Jersey State
Senate. She is currently acting in this position.
E-mail: elizabeth.connolly@dhs.state.nj.us
Chief of Staff **Christopher Bailey** . . . . . . . . . . . . . . . . . (609) 292-1626
Deputy Commissioner **Dawn Apgar, ACSW, LSW** . . . . . . . (609) 633-3844
Education: Bucknell BA; Rutgers MSW, PhD
Deputy Commissioner **Valerie J. Harr** . . . . . . . . . . . . . . . (609) 292-9265
Human Resources Assistant Commissioner
**Christina Mongon** . . . . . . . . . . . . . . . . . . . . . . . . . . . (609) 292-0202
Legal, Regulatory and Guardian Services Assistant
Commissioner **Bonny Fraser** . . . . . . . . . . . . . . . . . . . . (609) 777-2026
Public Affairs Assistant Commissioner **Nicole Brossoie** . . . (609) 292-3703
E-mail: nicole.brossoie@dhs.state.nj.us
Program Integrity and Accountability Director
**Lauri Woodward** . . . . . . . . . . . . . . . . . . . . . . . . . . . . (609) 292-1617
Information Systems Office Director **John Horoski** . . . . . . . (609) 292-5986
E-mail: john.horoski@dhs.state.nj.us
Budget and Finance Assistant **Christopher Bailey** . . . . . . . (609) 292-1626
Public Information Officer **Ellen Lovejoy** . . . . . . . . . . . . . (609) 292-3717
Public Information Officer **Pam Ronan** . . . . . . . . . . . . . . (609) 292-3717
E-mail: pam.ronan@dhs.state.nj.us

## Deaf and Hard of Hearing Division

P.O. Box 074, Trenton, NJ 08625
TTY: (609) 588-2648  Fax: (609) 588-2528

Director **Dr. David C. Alexander** . . . . . . . . . . . . . . . . . . . (609) 503-4862

## Developmental Disabilities Division

P.O. Box 726, Trenton, NJ 08625
Tel: (800) 832-9173  Fax: (609) 292-6610

Assistant Commissioner **Elizabeth "Liz" Shea** . . . . . . . . . . (800) 832-9173

## Disability Services Division

PO Box 705, Trenton, NJ 08625
Tel: (888) 285-3036  TTY: (609) 631-2450  Fax: (609) 631-4365

Director **Joseph Amoroso** . . . . . . . . . . . . . . . . . . . . . . . . (888) 285-3036

## Family Development Division

P.O. Box 716, Trenton, NJ 08625-0716
Tel: (609) 588-2401  Tel: (800) 792-9773  Fax: (609) 588-3369

Director **Natasha Johnson** . . . . . . . . . . . . . . . . . . . . . . . (609) 588-2401
Child Support Assistant Director **Patricia Risch** . . . . . . . . . (609) 631-2780
E-mail: patricia.risch@dhs.state.nj.us

## Medical Assistance and Health Services Division

Director **Meghan Davey** . . . . . . . . . . . . . . . . . . . . . . . . . (609) 588-2600
NJ FamilyCare Coordinator **Heidi J. Smith** . . . . . . . . . . . . (609) 588-3526
Fax: (609) 588-4643

## Mental Health and Addiction Services Division [DMHAS]

50 East State Street, Third Floor, Trenton, NJ 08625-0727
P.O. Box 727, Trenton, NJ 08625-0727
Tel: (609) 777-0702

Assistant Commissioner **Valerie Mielke** . . . . . . . . . . . . . . (609) 777-0702
Deputy Director **Lenore Velez-Rigney** . . . . . . . . . . . . . . . (609) 292-5760

---

★ Elected Official   ■ Appointed by Governor   ● Appointed by Legislature   ▲ Appointed by Board or Commission   ◆ Appointed by State Supreme Court

Summer 2016                              © Leadership Directories, Inc.                              *State Yellow Book*

# Department of Labor and Workforce Development [LWD]

P.O. Box 110, Trenton, NJ 08625-0110
Tel: (609) 292-2323  Fax: (609) 633-9271
E-mail: constituentrelations@dol.nj.gov  Internet: http://lwd.state.nj.us

**Employees:** 3,058  **Fiscal Year:** 2015  **Budget:** $921,454,000

■Commissioner **Harold J. "Hal" Wirths** . . . . . . . . . . . . . . . (609) 292-2323
  E-mail: hal.wirths@dol.nj.gov
Administrative Assistant **Janet M. Sliwinski** . . . . . . . . . . . . (609) 292-2975
Senior Policy Advisor **John C. Raue** . . . . . . . . . . . . . . . . (609) 984-3530
Senior Policy Advisor **Paul Yuen** . . . . . . . . . . . . . . . . . . . (609) 984-5487

## Chief of Staff's Office

Fax: (609) 984-2748

Chief of Staff **Gary Hasenbalg** . . . . . . . . . . . . . . . . . . . . (609) 984-1571
Senior Policy Advisor **Gary H. Altman** . . . . . . . . . . . . . . (609) 633-3820
Public Information Officer **Amanda Pisano** . . . . . . . . . . . . (609) 292-4503
  E-mail: amanda.pisano@dol.nj.gov
Human Resources and Labor Relations Executive
  Director **Mary Fitzgerald** . . . . . . . . . . . . . . . . . . . . . (609) 292-7003
Internal Audit Director **Gerald Calamia** . . . . . . . . . . . . . (609) 292-1885
Office of Diversity and Compliance Executive
  Administrator **Caroline Clarke** . . . . . . . . . . . . . . . . . . (609) 633-6500
Constituent Relations Coordinator **Cathy Mycoff** . . . . . . . . (609) 777-3200

## Finance and Accounting

Fax: (609) 633-9877

Assistant Commissioner and Chief Financial Officer
  **Robert F. Voorhees** . . . . . . . . . . . . . . . . . . . . . . . . . . (609) 292-9772
  E-mail: robert.voorhees@dol.nj.gov
  Executive Assistant **(Vacant)** . . . . . . . . . . . . . . . . . . . . (609) 984-7657
Finance and Accounting Director **(Vacant)** . . . . . . . . . . . . (609) 292-9290
Financial Systems and Support Director
  **Kathleen Bencivengo** . . . . . . . . . . . . . . . . . . . . . . . . (609) 292-8182

## Legal and Regulatory Services

Fax: (609) 292-8246

Executive Director **David Fish** . . . . . . . . . . . . . . . . . . . . (609) 777-2960
Legislative Affairs Director **Megan Fielder** . . . . . . . . . . . . (609) 292-1700
  E-mail: megan.fielder@dol.nj.gov
  Education: Lynchburg 2002 BA

## Information Technology

Information Technology Director and Chief Information
  Officer **Robert Schisler** . . . . . . . . . . . . . . . . . . . . . . . (609) 984-2254
  E-mail: robert.schisler@dol.nj.gov
Executive Assistant **Linda Chesko** . . . . . . . . . . . . . . . . . (609) 777-0493
  E-mail: linda.chesko@dol.nj.gov

## Deputy Commissioner's Office

Fax: (609) 633-9271

Deputy Commissioner **Aaron R. Fichtner, PhD** . . . . . . . . . (609) 292-1070
  E-mail: aaron.fichtner@dol.nj.gov

## Labor Standards and Safety Enforcement

Fax: (609) 695-1314

Assistant Commissioner **John Monahan** . . . . . . . . . . . . . . (609) 292-2313
  E-mail: john.monahan@dol.state.nj.us
  Executive Assistant **(Vacant)** . . . . . . . . . . . . . . . . . . . . (609) 777-0249
Public Safety and Occupational Safety and Health
  Director **Howard Black** . . . . . . . . . . . . . . . . . . . . . . . (609) 292-0501
Wage and Hour Compliance Director **Robert Gaines** . . . . . (609) 984-7356

## Income Security

Fax: (609) 984-3508

Assistant Commissioner **Ronald L. Marino** . . . . . . . . . . . . (609) 292-7586
  E-mail: ronald.marino@dol.state.nj.us
  Executive Assistant **Kevin Smith** . . . . . . . . . . . . . . . . . (609) 292-5359
Disability Determination Services Director **(Vacant)** . . . . . . (609) 777-1001
Employer Accounts Director **(Vacant)** . . . . . . . . . . . . . . . (609) 292-2810

Fraud Prevention and Risk Management Director
  **(Vacant)** . . . . . . . . . . . . . . . . . . . . . . . . . . . . . . . . . . (609) 984-3914
Temporary Disability Insurance Director
  **Christine Z. Madrid** . . . . . . . . . . . . . . . . . . . . . . . . . (609) 292-2680
Unemployment Insurance Director **Gregory Castellani** . . . . (609) 292-6073

## Office of Research and Information

Fax: (609) 777-3623

Assistant Commissioner **Jeffrey N. Stoller** . . . . . . . . . . . . (609) 292-2643
  E-mail: jeffrey.stoller@dol.nj.gov
  Executive Assistant **(Vacant)** . . . . . . . . . . . . . . . . . . . . (609) 292-5359
COEI (Center for Occupational Employment Information)
  Staff Director/Strategic Initiatives **Robert Grimmie** . . . . . (609) 292-8658
Labor Market and Demographic Research Director
  **Chester Chinsky** . . . . . . . . . . . . . . . . . . . . . . . . . . . . (609) 984-6925
Workforce Research and Analytics Principal Managing
  Analyst **David W. Ramsay** . . . . . . . . . . . . . . . . . . . . . (609) 292-0021

## Workforce Development

Fax: (609) 396-1685

Vocational Rehabilitation Services Director
  **Alice Hunnicutt** . . . . . . . . . . . . . . . . . . . . . . . . . . . . (609) 292-7318
Workforce Operations and Business Services Executive
  Director **Catherine Starghill** . . . . . . . . . . . . . . . . . . . (609) 292-5834
  E-mail: catherine.starghill@dol.state.nj.us  Fax: (609) 396-1685
Workforce Development and Economic Opportunity
  Executive Director **Patricia Moran** . . . . . . . . . . . . . . . (609) 984-3562
Workforce Portfolio and Contract Management Director
  **(Vacant)** . . . . . . . . . . . . . . . . . . . . . . . . . . . . . . . . . . (609) 984-2477

## Workers' Compensation

Fax: (609) 984-2515

Director/Chief Judge **Russell Wojtenko, Jr.** . . . . . . . . . . . . (609) 292-2414
  E-mail: russell.wojtenko@dol.nj.gov
  Executive Assistant **C. Gretchen McCall** . . . . . . . . . . . . (609) 341-2033
  E-mail: carol.mccall@dol.nj.gov
Special Compensation Funds Administrator
  **Larry J. Crider** . . . . . . . . . . . . . . . . . . . . . . . . . . . . . (609) 292-0165
Workers' Compensation Courts Administrator **(Vacant)** . . . . (609) 292-8802

# Department of Military and Veterans Affairs

101 Eggert Crossing Road, Lawrenceville, NJ 08648-2805
Tel: (609) 530-4600  TTY: (609) 530-6966  Fax: (609) 530-7100
Internet: www.state.nj.us/military

**Employees:** 1,487  **Fiscal Year:** 2015  **Budget:** $99,968,000

■Adjutant General **BrigGen Michael Cunniff, ANG** . . . . . . . (609) 530-6956
  E-mail: michael.cunniff@njdmava.state.nj.us
Director, Joint Staff **BG James Grant, ARNG** . . . . . . . . . . (609) 530-7033
Deputy Commissioner (Veterans Affairs)
  **Raymond Zawacki** . . . . . . . . . . . . . . . . . . . . . . . . . . (609) 530-7045
Government Relations **Terry Dearden** . . . . . . . . . . . . . . . (609) 530-6893
  E-mail: terry.dearden@njdmava.state.nj.us
Public Affairs Officer **CW2 Patrick Daugherty, ARNG** . . . (609) 530-6939
Information Technology Director **Dave Seneker** . . . . . . . . . (609) 530-4600

# Department of Transportation [NJDOT]

1035 Parkway Avenue, Trenton, NJ 08625
P.O. Box 600, Trenton, NJ 08625
Tel: (609) 530-2000  Fax: (609) 530-8294
E-mail: correspondenceunitdot@dot.nj.gov
Internet: www.state.nj.us/transportation

**Employees:** 3,125  **Fiscal Year:** 2015  **Budget:** $1,202,640,000

■Commissioner (Acting) **Richard T. "Rick" Hammer** . . . . . . (609) 530-3536
  E-mail: rick.hammer@dot.nj.gov
■Deputy Commissioner **Joseph D. Bertoni, PE** . . . . . . . . . . (609) 530-4314
  E-mail: joseph.bertoni@dot.nj.gov
  Education: Widener BSCE
Chief of Staff **(Vacant)** . . . . . . . . . . . . . . . . . . . . . . . . . (609) 530-2002

*(continued on next page)*

---

★ Elected Official   ■ Appointed by Governor   ● Appointed by Legislature   ▲ Appointed by Board or Commission   ◆ Appointed by State Supreme Court

**Department of Transportation** *continued*

Civil Rights and Affirmative Action Executive Director
**Linda Legge** . . . . . . . . . . . . . . . . . . . . . . . . . . . . . . (609) 530-3009
Inspector General **Johanna Barba Jones** . . . . . . . . . . . . (609) 530-3091
E-mail: johanna.jones@dot.nj.gov
Transportation Systems Management
**C. William Kingsland** . . . . . . . . . . . . . . . . . . . . . (609) 530-3971
1035 Parkway Avenue, Trenton, NJ 08625-0613
P.O. Box 613, Trenton, NJ 08625
Education: Bucknell BSCE
Traffic Operations Director **Salvatore Cowan** . . . . . . . . . (609) 530-4690

## Office of the Chief Financial Officer

Chief Financial Officer **Gary J. Brune** . . . . . . . . . . . . . . (609) 530-2046
Accounting and Auditing Director **Barbara DeLucia** . . . . . . (609) 530-2343
Budget Director **Deborah "Deb" Stevenson** . . . . . . . . . . (609) 530-2138
Information Technology Director **Gary Zayas** . . . . . . . . . . (609) 530-8192
E-mail: gary.zayas@dot.nj.gov
Procurement Director **Anthony F. "Tony" Genovese** . . . . . (609) 530-6355

## Administration

Assistant Commissioner **Jeanne Victor** . . . . . . . . . . . . . . (609) 530-5955
E-mail: jeanne.victor@dot.nj.gov
Education: Poly Inst New York BSCE; Rutgers (Newark) 1990 JD
Employee Relations Manager **Dianne Barretts** . . . . . . . . . . (609) 530-2953
Human Resources Director **Michele Shapiro** . . . . . . . . . . (609) 530-2755
Support Services Director **Deborah Hatzisavvas** . . . . . . . . (609) 530-2029
E-mail: debby.hatzisavvas@dot.nj.gov

## Capital Investment, Planning and Grant Administration

Director **Thomas "Tom" Wospil** . . . . . . . . . . . . . . . . . (609) 530-6113
Assistant Commissioner **David A. Kuhn** . . . . . . . . . . . . . (609) 530-3855
Environmental Resources Division Director **Elkins Green** . . (609) 530-8075
E-mail: elkins.green@dot.nj.gov
Local Aid and Economic Development Director
**Michael Russo** . . . . . . . . . . . . . . . . . . . . . . . . . . . (609) 530-3640
Multimodal Services Director **Nicole Minutola** . . . . . . . . . (609) 530-2852
Statewide Planning and Research Director
**Andrew Swords** . . . . . . . . . . . . . . . . . . . . . . . . . . (609) 530-2866
E-mail: andrew.swords@dot.nj.gov

## Capital Program Management

Assistant Commissioner **E. David Lambert III** . . . . . . . . . (609) 530-5704
Bridge Engineering and Infrastructure Management
Director **Nat B. Kasbekar** . . . . . . . . . . . . . . . . . . . . (609) 530-2733
Capital Program Support Division Director
**Richard G. Jaffe** . . . . . . . . . . . . . . . . . . . . . . . . . (609) 530-3007
Construction Services and Materials Director
**Dr. Snehal G. Patel, MD, FRCS (Eng)** . . . . . . . . . . . (609) 530-3811
Highway/Traffic Design Director **Robert Marshall** . . . . . . . (609) 530-2737
Project Management Director **Dana Hecht** . . . . . . . . . . . (609) 530-2191
Right of Way and Access Management Division Director
**Victor Akpu** . . . . . . . . . . . . . . . . . . . . . . . . . . . . (609) 530-2360

## Government and Community Relations

Assistant Commissioner **John M. Case** . . . . . . . . . . . . . (609) 530-3686
E-mail: john.case@dot.nj.gov
Education: Shippensburg
Community Relations Director **Scott Stephens** . . . . . . . . . (609) 530-4924

## Operations

Operations Executive Director **Ray Kauffman** . . . . . . . . . . (609) 530-2589
Assistant Commissioner **Andrew Tunnard** . . . . . . . . . . . (609) 530-2590
Education: Marywood U BA
Central Regional Director **Michael Davis** . . . . . . . . . . . . (732) 625-4340
North Regional Director **Christopher Tomlin** . . . . . . . . . . (973) 601-6601
200 Stierli Court, Mt. Arlington, NJ 07856-1322
South Regional Director **William Day** . . . . . . . . . . . . . . (856) 486-6600

## Department of Treasury

State House, P.O. Box 002, Trenton, NJ 08625
Tel: (609) 292-5031  Fax: (609) 292-6145
Internet: www.state.nj.us/treasury

**Employees:** 3,260  **Fiscal Year:** 2015  **Budget:** $976,886,000

■State Treasurer **Ford M. Scudder** . . . . . . . . . . . . . . . . (609) 292-6748
Education: Princeton BEc; Vanderbilt MBA
Deputy State Treasurer **Thomas Ness** . . . . . . . . . . . . . . (609) 984-2512
Assistant Deputy State Treasurer **Beth Schermerhorn** . . . . (609) 633-8185
Assistant State Treasurer **Roger Cohen** . . . . . . . . . . . . . (609) 984-9429
Associate Deputy State Treasurer
**Steven "Steve" Petrecca** . . . . . . . . . . . . . . . . . . . . (609) 292-8951
Chief of Staff **Jennifer Duffy** . . . . . . . . . . . . . . . . . . . (609) 633-6607
Deputy Chief of Staff **Matthew Murray** . . . . . . . . . . . . . (609) 984-6919
Chief Economist **Dr. James H. Wooster, PhD** . . . . . . . . (609) 826-4769
Education: Colgate 1969 BA; Amherst 1985 PhD
Communications Director **Joseph R. "Joe" Perone** . . . . . . (609) 633-6565
E-mail: joseph.perone@treas.nj.gov
Legislative Affairs Director **Matthew Spadaccini** . . . . . . . . (609) 984-3611

## Office of Administrative Law

P.O. Box 049, Trenton, NJ 08625-0049
Fax: (609) 689-4070  Internet: www.state.nj.us/oal

Director and Chief Administrative Law Judge (Acting)
**Laura Sanders** . . . . . . . . . . . . . . . . . . . . . . . . . . . (609) 689-4001
Deputy Director and Administrative Law Judge
**Lisa James-Beavers** . . . . . . . . . . . . . . . . . . . . . . . (609) 689-4042
Education: Rutgers 1985 BA; Villanova 1988 JD
Administration Chief **Patrick Mulligan** . . . . . . . . . . . . . . (609) 689-4003
E-mail: patrick.mulligan@oal.state.nj.us
Judicial Standards Manager **Sandra Desarno-Hlatky** . . . . . (609) 689-4010
Legal Research and Library Manager **Jennifer Campbell** . . (609) 689-4023
Public Information Officer **Patrick Mulligan** . . . . . . . . . . . (609) 689-4003
E-mail: patrick.mulligan@oal.state.nj.us
Administrative Law Judge **Robert Giordano** . . . . . . . . . . (973) 648-7136
33 Washington Street, Newark, NJ 07102       Fax: (973) 648-6058
Deputy Clerk **Kurt Schwartz** . . . . . . . . . . . . . . . . . . . (973) 648-7245
33 Washington Street, Newark, NJ 07102       Fax: (973) 648-6058

## Office of Information Technology [OIT]

P.O. Box 212, Trenton, NJ 08625-0212
Tel: (609) 292-2121  Fax: (609) 633-9100  Internet: www.state.nj.us/it

Chief of Staff **Sharon Pagano** . . . . . . . . . . . . . . . . . . . (609) 633-8028
E-mail: sharon.pagano@oit.state.nj.us
Administration Executive Director **Andrew Pratt** . . . . . . . . (609) 633-0110
E-mail: andrew.pratt@oit.state.nj.us
Chief Information Officer (Acting)
**Odysseus Marcopolus** . . . . . . . . . . . . . . . . . . . . . . (609) 777-5865
E-mail: odysseus.marcopolus@oit.state.nj.us
Deputy Chief Information Officer **(Vacant)** . . . . . . . . . . . (609) 984-4084
Chief Information Security Officer **(Vacant)** . . . . . . . . . . (609) 633-9120
Chief Operations Officer **Hagen Hottmann** . . . . . . . . . . . (609) 984-4082
Chief Technology Officer for Infrastructure and Support
Services **Hagen Hottmann** . . . . . . . . . . . . . . . . . . . (609) 633-0112
E-mail: hagen.hottmann@oit.state.nj.us
Deputy Chief Technology Officer
**Mary Lou Fels-Mycoff** . . . . . . . . . . . . . . . . . . . . . (609) 633-0040
E-mail: marylou.mycoff@oit.state.nj.us
Deputy Chief Technology Officer **David Hiznay** . . . . . . . . (609) 633-8925
E-mail: david.hiznay@oit.state.nj.us
Deputy Chief Technology Officer **Roy Roldan** . . . . . . . . . (609) 633-0071
E-mail: roy.roldan@oit.state.nj.us
Deputy Chief Technology Officer **Rehan Usman** . . . . . . . . (609) 633-8926
E-mail: rehan.usmani@oit.state.nj.us
Deputy Chief Technology Officer **(Vacant)** . . . . . . . . . . . (609) 633-0029
Configuration Management **Charles "Chuck" Gill** . . . . . . . (609) 633-8908
GIS Office Director **Andy Rowan** . . . . . . . . . . . . . . . . . (609) 633-0276
E-mail: andrew.rowan@oit.state.nj.us
Project Management Office Director **Kathleen Smith** . . . . . (609) 633-0118
E-mail: kathleen.smith@oit.state.nj.us
Emergency Telecommunication Services **Craig Reiner** . . . . (609) 777-3698

---

★ Elected Official    ■ Appointed by Governor    ● Appointed by Legislature    ▲ Appointed by Board or Commission    ◆ Appointed by State Supreme Court

# Office of Management and Budget

33 West State Street, Trenton, NJ 08625-0026
P.O. Box 221, Trenton, NJ 08625
Fax: (609) 633-8179

Director (Acting) **David Ridolfino** . . . . . . . . . . . . . . . . . . . . (609) 292-6746
Deputy Director **Mary Byrne** . . . . . . . . . . . . . . . . . . . . . . . . (609) 984-5230
Associate Director **Jacki Stevens** . . . . . . . . . . . . . . . . . . . . (609) 292-5066
Budget Assistant Director **Brian Francz** . . . . . . . . . . . . . . (609) 984-4271
Financial Management Assistant Director **Michael Griffin** . . . . . . . . . (609) 984-9611

# Office of the Public Defender

Hughes Justice Complex, 25 Market Street, 1st Floor N-Wing,
Trenton, NJ 08625
P.O. Box 850, Trenton, NJ 08625
Tel: (609) 292-7087 Fax: (609) 777-1795
Internet: www.state.nj.us/defender E-mail: thedefenders@opd.state.nj.us

■Public Defender **Joseph E. Krakora** . . . . . . . . . . . . . . . . . . (609) 292-7087
   E-mail: thedefenders@opd.state.nj.us
   Education: Princeton 1976 BA; Cornell 1983 JD
First Assistant Public Defender **Lorraine Augostini** . . . . . . (609) 341-4562
   Education: Trinity Col (CT) 1986 BA; Georgetown 1989 JD
Assistant Public Defender **Kevin Walker** . . . . . . . . . . . . . . . (609) 292-9736
Appellate Unit Deputy Public Defender
   **Matthew Astore** . . . . . . . . . . . . . . . . . . . . . . . . . . . . (973) 877-1200
Law Guardian Office Assistant Public Defender
   **Lorraine Augostini** . . . . . . . . . . . . . . . . . . . . . . . . . (609) 292-7087
Parental Representation Assistant Public Defender
   **Janice Anderson** . . . . . . . . . . . . . . . . . . . . . . . . . . . (609) 341-3832
Administration Director **Gerald Henry** . . . . . . . . . . . . . . . . (609) 292-7046
   E-mail: gerald.henry@opd.state.nj.us
Dispute Settlement Director **Eric R. Max** . . . . . . . . . . . . . (609) 292-1773
   Education: Vassar 1982 BA; Boston U 1986 JD
Investigations Director **Beth Kelly** . . . . . . . . . . . . . . . . . . . (609) 292-9089
Statewide Drug Court Director **Larry Bembry, Esq.** . . . . . . (609) 292-9350
Budget Operations Manager **Constance Willet, PhD** . . . . . (609) 292-7863
Mental Health and Guardianship Advocacy Division
   Director **Carl Herman** . . . . . . . . . . . . . . . . . . . . . . . . (609) 292-1780
Juvenile Defense Services **Carl Herman** . . . . . . . . . . . . . . (609) 292-7087

# Office of Public Finance

50 West State Street, Trenton, NJ 08625
Fax: (609) 777-1987

Director **James M. Petrino** . . . . . . . . . . . . . . . . . . . . . . . . . (609) 984-8229
Deputy Director **(Vacant)** . . . . . . . . . . . . . . . . . . . . . . . . . . (609) 633-6447

# Division of Administration

50 West State Street, 8th Floor, Trenton, NJ 08625
P.O. Box 211, Trenton, NJ 08625
Tel: (609) 633-2826 Fax: (609) 292-6160

Director (Acting) **Michael Tyger** . . . . . . . . . . . . . . . . . . . . . (609) 633-0813
Deputy Director **Michael Jonas** . . . . . . . . . . . . . . . . . . . . . (609) 984-4847
   E-mail: michael.jonas@treas.nj.gov
Affirmative Action Officer **Deirdre Webster Cobb** . . . . . . . (609) 984-7778
   E-mail: d.wcobb@treas.state.nj.us
Workforce Management Deputy Director **Doug Ianni** . . . . . (609) 292-5766

# Division of Purchase and Property

135 West Hanover Street, Third Floor, Trenton, NJ 08625
P.O. Box 209, Trenton, NJ 08625-0002
Tel: (609) 292-5473 Fax: (609) 984-4203

Director **Jignasa Desai-McCleary** . . . . . . . . . . . . . . . . . . . (609) 292-5473

# Division of Investment

50 W. State Street, Ninth Floor, Trenton, NJ 08608
P.O. Box 290, Trenton, NJ 08625-0290
Fax: (609) 984-4425

Director **Christopher McDonough** . . . . . . . . . . . . . . . . . . . (609) 292-5106
Deputy Director **Corey Amon** . . . . . . . . . . . . . . . . . . . . . . . (609) 292-8922
Assistant Director **(Vacant)** . . . . . . . . . . . . . . . . . . . . . . . . (609) 292-5152

Chief of Staff **Amanda Truppa** . . . . . . . . . . . . . . . . . . . . . . (609) 777-2945
Chief Trading Officer **(Vacant)** . . . . . . . . . . . . . . . . . . . . . . (609) 777-1333
Investment Officer **Brian Arena** . . . . . . . . . . . . . . . . . . . . . (609) 777-2946
   Note: Domestic Equities Portfolio
Investment Officer **(Vacant)** . . . . . . . . . . . . . . . . . . . . . . . . (609) 777-2942
Alternative Investments Co-Head
   **Samantha Rosenstock** . . . . . . . . . . . . . . . . . . . . . . . (609) 633-8657
   Note: Hedge Funds
Alternative Investments Co-Head **Jason MacDonald** . . . . . (609) 341-3243
Senior Portfolio Manager **Linda Brooks** . . . . . . . . . . . . . . . (609) 984-4187
   Note: Cash Management Fund
Director of Accounting **Ainsley A. Reynolds, CPA** . . . . . . . (609) 984-4189
Director of Operations and Compliance Manager
   **Susan Sarnowski** . . . . . . . . . . . . . . . . . . . . . . . . . . . (609) 292-8869

# State Investment Council

50 W. State Street, 9th Floor, Trenton, NJ 08608
P.O. Box 290, Trenton, NJ 08625-0290
Tel: (609) 292-5908

■Chairman **Brendan T. Byrne, Jr.** . . . . . . . . . . . . . . . . . . . (609) 292-5106
   E-mail: brendan.byrne@state.nj.us
   Education: Princeton 1949 BA; Harvard 1950 LLB
Vice Chairman **Adam Liebtag** . . . . . . . . . . . . . . . . . . . . . . . (609) 292-5106

# Division of Lottery

P.O. Box 041, Trenton, NJ 08625
Tel: (609) 599-5800 Fax: (609) 599-5935
E-mail: publicinfo@lottery.state.nj.us Internet: www.state.nj.us/lottery

Executive Director **Carole Hedinger** . . . . . . . . . . . . . . . . . . (609) 599-5900
   E-mail: carole.hedinger@lottery.state.nj.us
Deputy Executive Director **R. John Custodio** . . . . . . . . . . . (609) 599-5899
   E-mail: john.custodio@lottery.state.nj.us
New Jersey Lottery Commission Chairman
   **Thomas Tucci** . . . . . . . . . . . . . . . . . . . . . . . . . . . . . (609) 599-5900
Public Relations Manager **Judith Drucker** . . . . . . . . . . . . . (609) 826-7477
   E-mail: judith.drucker@lottery.state.nj.us

# Division of Pensions and Benefits

State Street Square Building, 50 West State Street, Eighth Floor,
Trenton, NJ 08625
P.O. Box 295, Trenton, NJ 08625-0295
Tel: (609) 292-7524 Fax: (609) 393-4606
E-mail: pensions.nj@treas.state.nj.us

Director (Acting) **Florence J. Sheppard** . . . . . . . . . . . . . . . (609) 292-3728
Deputy Director **David Pointer** . . . . . . . . . . . . . . . . . . . . . . (609) 633-7546
Finance Deputy Director **John D. Megariotis** . . . . . . . . . . . (609) 292-3674
Assistant Director of Benefits Operations and Client
   Services **Wendy Jamison** . . . . . . . . . . . . . . . . . . . . . (609) 943-4280
Assistant Director of Board of Trustees and Professional
   and Support Services **Susanne Culliton** . . . . . . . . . . . (609) 292-3501
Assistant Director of Client Services **MaryAnn Ryan** . . . . . (609) 984-3030
Assistant Director of Management Information Systems
   **Michael Weik** . . . . . . . . . . . . . . . . . . . . . . . . . . . . . (609) 292-6267

# Division of Property Management and Construction

33 West State Street, 9th Floor, Trenton, NJ 08625
P.O. Box 034, Trenton, NJ 08625-0034

Director **Steven M. Sutkin** . . . . . . . . . . . . . . . . . . . . . . . . . (609) 984-9701
                                             Fax: (609) 984-6185
Chief of Staff **Chris Chianese** . . . . . . . . . . . . . . . . . . . . . . . (609) 984-9701
Construction Deputy Director **Karen Smith** . . . . . . . . . . . . (609) 943-3365
   20 W. State St., 3rd Fl., Trenton, NJ 08625-0235   Fax: (609) 984-1750
   P.O. Box 235, Trenton, NJ 08625-0235
Contract Administration Deputy Director
   **Richard Flodmand** . . . . . . . . . . . . . . . . . . . . . . . . . . (609) 984-3629
   E-mail: richard.flodmand@treas.state.nj.us   Fax: (609) 984-8495
Property Management Deputy Director **Guy Bocage** . . . . . . (609) 292-5111
                                             Fax: (609) 984-8495

---

★ Elected Official   ■ Appointed by Governor   ● Appointed by Legislature   ▲ Appointed by Board or Commission   ◆ Appointed by State Supreme Court

## Division of Purchase and Property

33 West State Street, Trenton, NJ 08625
P.O. Box 039, Trenton, NJ 08625-0230
Tel: (609) 292-4886  Fax: (609) 984-2575
Internet: www.state.nj.us/treasury/purchase

Director **Jignasa Desai-McCleary** . . . . . . . . . . . . . . . . . . . (609) 292-4886
Chief Operations Officer **Andrew Michael Greaney** . . . . . . (609) 292-4927
 Fax: (609) 292-5899
Commodities and Distribution and Support Services
 Assistant Director **(Vacant)** . . . . . . . . . . . . . . . . . . . . . (609) 777-0206
Contract Compliance and Audit Unit Assistant Director
 **Amy Davis** . . . . . . . . . . . . . . . . . . . . . . . . . . . . . . . . . . (609) 292-2192
 Fax: (609) 292-5899
Healthcare Procurements, Risk Management and Staff
 Development Assistant Director **Philip Michaels** . . . . . . . (609) 633-0989
Professional and Environmental Services Assistant
 Director **Philip Michaels** . . . . . . . . . . . . . . . . . . . . . . . . (609) 292-6817
Strategic Sourcing and General Services Assistant
 Director **(Vacant)** . . . . . . . . . . . . . . . . . . . . . . . . . . . . . (609) 984-2084
Technology Procurements Assistant Director
 **Gregg Olivera** . . . . . . . . . . . . . . . . . . . . . . . . . . . . . . . (609) 292-1256

## Division of Rate Counsel

31 Clinton Street, 11th Floor, Newark, NJ 07102
P.O. Box 46005, Newark, NJ 07101
Tel: (973) 648-2690  Fax: (973) 648-2193
E-mail: njratepayer@rpa.state.nj.us  Internet: www.rpa.state.nj.us

Director **Stefanie A. Brand, Esq.** . . . . . . . . . . . . . . . . . . . (973) 648-2690
 Education: Columbia 1986
Litigation Manager **Brian Lipman** . . . . . . . . . . . . . . . . . . . (973) 648-2690
Chief of Staff **Kimberly Holmes** . . . . . . . . . . . . . . . . . . . . (973) 648-2690
 Education: Montclair State U 1988 AB; Seton Hall 1993 JD

## Division of Revenue and Enterprise Services

33 West State Street, Trenton, NJ 08625-0026
P.O. Box 628, Trenton, NJ 08646-0628
Fax: (609) 984-8460

Director **James J. Fruscione** . . . . . . . . . . . . . . . . . . . . . . . (609) 984-3997
Chief of Staff **Christopher Trappe** . . . . . . . . . . . . . . . . . . . (609) 633-7181
Business Services Bureau Assistant Director
 **Peter Lowicki** . . . . . . . . . . . . . . . . . . . . . . . . . . . . . . . . (609) 984-6209
Processing Bureau Assistant Director **Steve Crescenzi** . . . . (609) 292-5978
Technical Services Assistant Director **Steven Csogi** . . . . . . (609) 633-0558

## Division of Risk Management

P.O. Box 620, Trenton, NJ 08625
Tel: (609) 292-1850  Fax: (609) 292-2437

Director **William Mayo** . . . . . . . . . . . . . . . . . . . . . . . . . . . (609) 292-1850

## Division of Taxation

50 Barrack Street, Trenton, NJ 08695
P.O. Box 240, Trenton, NJ 08695
Fax: (609) 984-2061

Director (Acting) **John J. Ficara** . . . . . . . . . . . . . . . . . . . . (609) 292-5185
Office of Counsel Services Deputy Director
 **Denise Lambert-Harding** . . . . . . . . . . . . . . . . . . . . . . . . (609) 633-3723
 Fax: (609) 292-0647
Deputy Director **Dennis Shilling** . . . . . . . . . . . . . . . . . . . . (609) 292-5185
Business Audit Assistant Director **Michele Bartolomei** . . . (609) 292-0978
 Fax: (609) 633-6201
Compliance and Enforcement Assistant Director
 **Pete Rapetti** . . . . . . . . . . . . . . . . . . . . . . . . . . . . . . . . . (609) 633-8450
 Fax: (609) 292-9614
Local Property Administration Deputy Director
 **Patricia Wright** . . . . . . . . . . . . . . . . . . . . . . . . . . . . . . . (609) 292-8823
 E-mail: patricia.wright@treas.nj.gov  Fax: (609) 292-0411
Counsel Services Assistant Director **Sheri Silverstein** . . . . (609) 633-3723
Individual Audit and Audit Services Assistant Director
 **Michael Roach** . . . . . . . . . . . . . . . . . . . . . . . . . . . . . . . (609) 292-2163
 Fax: (609) 292-5470

Technical Services Assistant Director **Marita Sciarrotta** . . . (609) 633-6923
 Fax: (609) 292-3194
Audit Activity Deputy Director **Robert Conger** . . . . . . . . . (609) 777-3704
 Fax: (609) 292-0411
Criminal Investigations Special Agent in Charge
 **Charles Giblin** . . . . . . . . . . . . . . . . . . . . . . . . . . . . . . . (609) 588-5017
 Fax: (609) 588-2532

## Higher Education Student Assistance Authority [HESAA]

Four Quakerbridge Plaza, Trenton, NJ 08625
P.O. Box 540, Trenton, NJ 08625
Fax: (609) 588-3316  Internet: www.hesaa.org

■Executive Director **Gabrielle Charette, Esq.** . . . . . . . . . . . (609) 588-7113
Chief of Staff **Marcia A. Karrow** . . . . . . . . . . . . . (609) 588-3300 ext. 1212
 Education: Smith AB; Michigan MA; NYU MBA

## New Jersey Building Authority [NJBA]

292 W. State Street, Trenton, NJ 08625-0219
P.O. Box 219, Trenton, NJ 08625
Fax: (609) 948-4838  Internet: www.state.nj.us/njba

Chairman **John H. Fisher III** . . . . . . . . . . . . . . . . . . . . . . . (609) 943-4830
Executive Director **Raymond A. Arcario** . . . . . . . . . . . . . . (609) 943-4830

## Casino Control Commission

Arcade Building, Tennessee Avenue and Boardwalk,
Atlantic City, NJ 08401
Tel: (609) 441-3422  Fax: (609) 441-3329
E-mail: communications@ccc.state.nj.us  Internet: www.nj.gov/casinos

■Chairman and Chief Executive Officer
 **Matthew B. Levinson** . . . . . . . . . . . . . . . . . . . . . . . . . . (609) 441-3557
 E-mail: matthew.levinson@ccc.state.nj.us  Fax: (609) 441-7370
 Education: Villanova 2002
■Vice Chair **Sharon Anne Harrington** . . . . . . . . . . . . . . . . (609) 441-3748
 E-mail: sharon.harrington@ccc.state.nj.us  Fax: (609) 441-3752
■Commissioner **Alisa Cooper** . . . . . . . . . . . . . . . . . . . . . . (609) 441-3027
 E-mail: alisa.cooper@ccc.state.nj.us
General Counsel and Executive Secretary
 **Dianna W. Fauntleroy, Esq.** . . . . . . . . . . . . . . . . . . . . . (609) 441-3815
 Fax: (609) 441-7394

## Capital City Redevelopment Corporation

28 West State Street, 7th Floor, Trenton, NJ 08608
P.O. Box 203, Trenton, NJ 08625
Tel: (609) 984-5664  Fax: (609) 633-0815  Internet: www.state.nj.us/ccrc

Chair **Peter A. Inverso** . . . . . . . . . . . . . . . . . . . . . . . . . . . (609) 984-5664
 Education: Rider BS
Vice Chair **Gwendolyn L. Harris** . . . . . . . . . . . . . . . . . . . . (609) 984-5664
Member **Christopher Brashier** . . . . . . . . . . . . . . . . . . . . . . (609) 984-5664
Member **Richard E. "Rich" Constable III** . . . . . . . . . . . . . (609) 984-5664
 Education: Michigan; Pennsylvania 1997 JD, 1997 MGA
Member **Eric E. Jackson** . . . . . . . . . . . . . . . . . . . . . . . . . . (609) 984-5664
Member **Robert D. Prunetti** . . . . . . . . . . . . . . . . . . . . . . . (609) 984-5664
Member **Andrew P. Sidamon-Eristoff** . . . . . . . . . . . . . . . . (609) 984-5664
 Education: Princeton BA; Georgetown JD

## Office of the State Comptroller

20 West State Street, Trenton, NJ 08625
Tel: (609) 984-2888  Fax: (609) 292-2017

■State Comptroller **Philip James Degnan** . . . . . . . . . . . . . . (609) 984-2888
 Education: Davidson; Seton Hall JD

## Civil Service Commission

44 South Clinton Avenue, Trenton, NJ 08609
P.O. Box 317, Trenton, NJ 08625-0317
Tel: (609) 292-4145  Fax: (609) 984-1064
E-mail: cscinformation@csc.nj.gov

■Chair/Chief Executive Officer **Robert M. Czech** . . . . . . . . (609) 292-4145
 E-mail: robert.czech@csc.nj.gov

---

★ Elected Official  ■ Appointed by Governor  ● Appointed by Legislature  ▲ Appointed by Board or Commission  ◆ Appointed by State Supreme Court

# Office of the Secretary of Higher Education [NJHE]

20 West State Street, 4th Floor, Trenton, NJ 08608
P.O. Box 542, Trenton, NJ 08625-0542
Tel: (609) 292-4310  Fax: (609) 292-7225
E-mail: njhe.general@oshe.nj.gov
Internet: www.state.nj.us/highereducation

- Secretary **Rochelle Hendricks** . . . . . . . . . . . . . . . . . . (609) 292-4310
  E-mail: rochelle.hendricks@njhe.state.nj.us
Deputy Secretary **Gregg Edwards** . . . . . . . . . . . . . . . . . . (609) 292-8052

# New Jersey Turnpike Authority

P.O. Box 5042, Woodbridge, NJ 07095
Tel: (732) 750-5300  E-mail: info@turnpike.state.nj.us
Internet: www.state.nj.us/turnpike

- Chairman (Acting) **Richard T. "Rick" Hammer** . . . . . . . . (732) 750-5300
- Vice Chair **Ronald "Ron" Gravino** . . . . . . . . . . . . . . . . . (732) 750-5300
- Treasurer **Michael R. DuPont** . . . . . . . . . . . . . . . . . . . . (732) 750-5300
  E-mail: michael.dupont@nj.gov
- Commissioner **Daniel F. Becht, Esq.** . . . . . . . . . . . . . . . (732) 750-5300
- Commissioner **Ulises E. Diaz** . . . . . . . . . . . . . . . . . . . . (732) 750-5300
- Commissioner **John D. Minella** . . . . . . . . . . . . . . . . . . . (732) 750-5300
- Commissioner **Raymond M. Pocino** . . . . . . . . . . . . . . . . (732) 750-5300
- Commissioner **(Vacant)** . . . . . . . . . . . . . . . . . . . . . . . . . (732) 750-5300

# State Board of Education

River View Executive Plaza, Building 100, Trenton, NJ 08625
P.O. Box 500, Trenton, NJ 08625
Tel: (609) 292-0739  Fax: (609) 633-0267

- President **Mark W. Biedron** . . . . . . . . . . . . . . . . . . . . . . (609) 984-6024
- Vice President **Joseph Fisicaro** . . . . . . . . . . . . . . . . . . . (609) 984-6024
- Member **Arcelio Aponte** . . . . . . . . . . . . . . . . . . . . . . . . (609) 984-6024
  Education: Col New Jersey BS; Rutgers MA
- Member-Designate **David D. Blumenthal, PhD** . . . . . . . . (609) 984-6024
- Member **Ronald K. Butcher** . . . . . . . . . . . . . . . . . . . . . . (609) 984-6024
  Education: Western Michigan BS; Eastern Michigan MA;
  Michigan PhD
- Member **Jack A. Fornaro** . . . . . . . . . . . . . . . . . . . . . . . . (609) 984-6024
- Member **Edithe Fulton** . . . . . . . . . . . . . . . . . . . . . . . . . (609) 984-6024
- Member **Ernest P. LePore** . . . . . . . . . . . . . . . . . . . . . . . (609) 984-6024
  Education: UMass (Amherst) BA; Minnesota MA, PhD
- Member **Andrew J. Mulvihill** . . . . . . . . . . . . . . . . . . . . . (609) 984-6024
- Member **J. Peter Simon** . . . . . . . . . . . . . . . . . . . . . . . . . (609) 984-6024
  Education: Lafayette 1975 BA
- Member **Dorothy Strickland** . . . . . . . . . . . . . . . . . . . . . (609) 984-6024
- Member **(Vacant)** . . . . . . . . . . . . . . . . . . . . . . . . . . . . . (609) 984-6024
Director **Diane Shoener** . . . . . . . . . . . . . . . . . . . . . . . . (609) 984-6024

# Department of Education

Tel: (609) 292-4469  Fax: (609) 984-6756
Internet: www.state.nj.us/education

**Employees:** 1,032

- Commissioner **David C. Hespe** . . . . . . . . . . . . . . . . . . . . (609) 292-4450
  E-mail: dave.hespe@doe.state.nj.us
  Education: Rutgers BA; Rutgers (Newark) JD
  Chief of Staff **William Haldeman** . . . . . . . . . . . . . . . . . (609) 633-6681
Assistant Commissioner/Chief Legal Affairs and
  Operations Chief **Patricia Morgan** . . . . . . . . . . . . . . . (609) 341-3613
Chief Academic Officer **Kimberley Harrington** . . . . . . . . (609) 633-2766
                                                  Fax: (609) 292-4708
Deputy Commissioner/Chief Talent and Performance
  Officer **Peter Shulman** . . . . . . . . . . . . . . . . . . . . . . . (609) 292-2400
Field Services Division Assistant Commissioner
  **Robert Bumpus** . . . . . . . . . . . . . . . . . . . . . . . . . . . . (609) 292-4469
Learning Supports and Specialized Services Division
  Assistant Commissioner **Susan Martz** . . . . . . . . . . . . (609) 292-9899
Early Childhood Education Division Administrator
  **Ellen Wolock** . . . . . . . . . . . . . . . . . . . . . . . . . . . . . . (609) 777-2074
GED Administrator **Larry Breeden** . . . . . . . . . . . . . . . . (609) 341-3071
  E-mail: larry.breeden@doe.state.nj.us

Media Relations and Strategic Outreach Director
  **Valerie Francois** . . . . . . . . . . . . . . . . . . . . . . . . . . . (609) 292-1126

# School Ethics Commission

Fax: (609) 633-0279

Chairman **Robert Bender** . . . . . . . . . . . . . . . . . . . . . . . (609) 984-6941
  E-mail: robert.bender@state.nj.us
Executive Director (Acting) **Joanne Restivo** . . . . . . . . . . . (609) 984-6941

# Board of Public Utilities [BPU]

44 South Clinton Avenue, 9th Floor, Trenton, NJ 08625
Tel: (609) 777-3300  Fax: (973) 877-1168

- President **Richard S. Mroz** . . . . . . . . . . . . . . . . . . . . . . (609) 777-3310
  Education: Delaware 1983 BA; Villanova 1986 JD
- Commissioner **Upendra J. Chivukula** . . . . . . . . . . . . . . (609) 633-9837
  Education: New York City Col Tech MEE; Anna U (India) BEE
- Commissioner **Joseph L. Fiordaliso, Sr.** . . . . . . . . . . . . (609) 633-9842
  E-mail: joseph.fiordaliso@bpu.state.nj.us    Fax: (609) 292-3886
  Education: Montclair State U 1967 BA
- Commissioner **Mary-Anna Holden** . . . . . . . . . . . . . . . . (609) 633-9879
                                                  Fax: (609) 292-3886
- Commissioner **Dianne Solomon** . . . . . . . . . . . . . . . . . . (609) 777-3333
  Education: Rider U                          Fax: (973) 468-8514

# Board Staff

Executive Director **Paul E. Flanagan, Esq.** . . . . . . . . . . . (973) 648-2026
  Education: Fairfield 1971 BA;                Fax: (609) 292-1634
  Seton Hall 1975 MBA, 1980 JD

# Office of the Lieutenant Governor

125 West State Street, Trenton, NJ 08608
Tel: (609) 777-2581  Fax: (609) 777-1764

- ★ Lieutenant Governor
  **Kimberly M. "Kim" Guadagno** (R) . . . . . . . . . . . . . . . (609) 777-0884
  Term Expires: January 2018
  E-mail: lt.governor@nj.gov
  Education: Ursinus 1980 BA; Washington College of Law 1983 JD
Chief of Staff **Dennis R. Robinson** . . . . . . . . . . . . . . . . (609) 292-1166
  Education: Wesleyan U; Harvard MBA

# Department of Law and Public Safety

P.O. Box 080, Justice Complex, Trenton, NJ 08625
Tel: (609) 292-4925  Tel: (866) 713-8392 (Investigations)
Fax: (609) 292-3508  Internet: www.nj.gov/lps

**Employees:** 3,517

# Office of the Attorney General

P.O. Box 080, Justice Complex, Trenton, NJ 08625
Tel: (609) 292-4925  Fax: (609) 292-3508

- Attorney General (Acting) **Robert Lougy** . . . . . . . . . . . . (609) 292-4930
  Education: Penn State 1994; Columbia 2002 JD
Executive Assistant Attorney General
  **Deborah R. Edwards** . . . . . . . . . . . . . . . . . . . . . . . . (609) 292-3794
  Education: Pennsylvania 1985; Villanova 1988 JD
First Assistant Attorney **Robert Lougy** . . . . . . . . . . (973) 504-6320
Chief of Staff **Rebecca M. Ricigliano** . . . . . . . . . . . . . . (609) 292-9064
  Education: SUNY (Buffalo) 1996, 1999 JD
Deputy Chief of Staff **(Vacant)** . . . . . . . . . . . . . . . . . . . (609) 292-9064
Counsel to the Attorney General **(Vacant)** . . . . . . . . . . . (609) 292-8640
Assistant Attorney General **Ronald "Ron" Susswein** . . . . (609) 984-3978
  E-mail: ronald.susswein@lps.state.nj.us      Fax: (609) 984-0049
Attorney General Advocacy Institute Director
  **Daniel Dryzga** . . . . . . . . . . . . . . . . . . . . . . . . . . . . . (609) 633-1999
                                                  Fax: (609) 984-3974
Legislative Affairs Director **Stephan Finkel** . . . . . . . . . . (609) 984-9496
  E-mail: stephan.finkel@lps.state.nj.us
Public Information Director **Paul M. Loriquet** . . . . . . . . . (609) 292-4791
  E-mail: paul.loriquet@lps.state.nj.us        Fax: (609) 777-1529

---

★ Elected Official    ■ Appointed by Governor    ● Appointed by Legislature    ▲ Appointed by Board or Commission    ◆ Appointed by State Supreme Court

EXECUTIVE BRANCH

## Administration
P.O. Box 081, Trenton, NJ 08625
Fax: (609) 292-4299

Administrator **Jennifer Fradel** . . . . . . . . . . . . . . . . . . . . . . . . . (609) 292-9660
  E-mail: jennifer.fradel@lps.state.nj.us
Deputy Administrator **Peter Traum** . . . . . . . . . . . . . . . . . . (609) 341-5057
  E-mail: peter.traum@lps.state.nj.us
Budget and Grants Operation Director **(Vacant)** . . . . . . . . . (609) 633-0748
                                     Fax: (609) 341-3041
Financial Management Director **John Varga** . . . . . . . . . . . (609) 984-0633
                                       Fax: (609) 341-3041
Human Resource Management Director **Mirella Bednar** . . . (609) 292-9654
                                       Fax: (609) 341-3039
Information Technology Services Director (Acting)
  **Joy Fitoritt** . . . . . . . . . . . . . . . . . . . . . . . . . . . . . . . . . . (609) 984-2398
  E-mail: joy.fitoritt@state.nj.us       Fax: (609) 292-8268
Support Services Director **Stephen Mattson** . . . . . . . . . . . (609) 292-6061
                                       Fax: (609) 292-0279
Legal Affairs and Employee Relations Assistant Deputy
  Attorney General **Greg Stellneyer** . . . . . . . . . . . . . . . . (609) 984-6998
                                       Fax: (609) 984-9493

## Office of Equal Employment Opportunity
Deputy Director **Joanne Stipick** . . . . . . . . . . . . . . . . . . . . (609) 633-2345
P.O. Box 080, Trenton, NJ 08625-0080    Fax: (609) 633-2498

## Office of Homeland Security and Preparedness [OHSP]
Tel: (609) 584-4000  Fax: (609) 631-4914  E-mail: ohsp@ohsp.state.nj.us

■Director **Dr. Christopher Rodriguez, PhD** . . . . . . . . . . . . (609) 584-4078
  E-mail: crodriguez@njohsp.gov     Fax: (609) 631-4915
  Education: Notre Dame PhD
■Deputy Director **Steve Gutkin** . . . . . . . . . . . . . . . . . . . . (609) 584-4000
  E-mail: steven.gutkin@ohsp.state.nj.us
■Intelligence Director **Rosemary Martorana** . . . . . . . . . . (609) 584-4000
  E-mail: rmartorana@njohsp.gov
Policy and Planning Director **Eric Tysarczyk** . . . . . . . . . . (609) 584-4000
Chief Financial Officer **Randall Richardson** . . . . . . . . . . (609) 584-4000
Communications Director **Stephanie Raphael** . . . . . . . . . (609) 584-4000
  E-mail: sraphael@njohsp.gov
  Education: American U
Cyber Security Director **David C. Weinstein** . . . . . . . . . . (609) 584-4000
Chief of Staff **Dennis Quinn** . . . . . . . . . . . . . . . . . . . . . . (609) 584-4000
  Education: Seton Hall MA

## New Jersey Cybersecurity and Communications Integration Cell [NJCCIC]
1032 River Road, West Trenton, NJ 08628
Tel: (609) 963-6900  E-mail: njccic@cyber.nj.gov

Cyber Liaison Officer
  **Christopher "Chris" Kay** . . . . . . . . . . . . . . . . (609) 963-6900 ext. 6249

## Victims of Crime Compensation Office
50 Park Place, Newark, NJ 07102
Tel: (877) 658-2221  Fax: (973) 648-3937  Fax: (973) 648-7031
E-mail: njvictims@vccb.org

Director **Marsetta Lee** . . . . . . . . . . . . . . . . . . . . . . . . . . . (877) 658-2221
  Education: Temple JD
                                         Fax: (973) 648-3937

## State Police
P.O. Box 7068, West Trenton, NJ 08628-0068
Fax: (609) 882-6920

■Superintendent/Emergency
  Management State Office Director
  **Col. Joseph R. "Rick" Fuentes** . . . . . . . . . . (609) 882-2000 ext. 6500
  E-mail: joseph.fuentes@lps.state.nj.us    Fax: (609) 771-1496
  Education: Kean Col BS; John Jay Col MA; CUNY PhD
Homeland Security Deputy Superintendent
  **Lt. Col. Christian Schulz** . . . . . . . . . . . . . . . . . . . . . (609) 292-4925
Chief of Staff **Major Scott M. Ebner** . . . . . . . . . . . . . . . (609) 292-4925
Emergency Management Office Deputy State
  Director **Jeffrey Mottley** . . . . . . . . . . . . . . . . . (609) 882-2000 ext. 6500
                                         Fax: (609) 882-7118

## Alcoholic Beverage Control Division
140 East Front Street, Trenton, NJ 08625
P.O. Box 087, Trenton, NJ 08625-0087
Fax: (609) 633-6078  Internet: www.nj.gov/lps/abc

■Director **J. Wesley Geiselman** . . . . . . . . . . . . . . . . . . . . (609) 984-3230
  E-mail: wesley.geiselman@lps.state.nj.us
  Licensing Bureau Chief **Patti Valsac** . . . . . . . . . . . . . (609) 984-2736
                                       Fax: (609) 292-0691
Enforcement Assistant Attorney General
  **Kevin M. Schatz** . . . . . . . . . . . . . . . . . . . . . . . . . . . . (609) 984-1975
Counsel to the Director **(Vacant)** . . . . . . . . . . . . . . . . . . (609) 292-5296
Investigations Supervising Investigator **Kevin Barber** . . . . . (609) 984-1984
                                       Tel: (866) 713-8392
                                 (ABC Investigations)
                                       Fax: (609) 633-9150

## Civil Rights Division
Director **Craig Sashihara** . . . . . . . . . . . . . . . . . . . . . . . . . (973) 648-6262
  P.O. Box 080, Trenton, NJ 08625-0080    Fax: (609) 530-8880

## Consumer Affairs Division
124 Halsey Street, Newark, NJ 07102
P.O. Box 45027, Newark, NJ 07101
Tel: (973) 504-6200  Fax: (973) 648-3538

■Director (Acting) **Steve C. Lee** . . . . . . . . . . . . . . . . . . . . (973) 504-6534
  E-mail: lees@dca.lps.state.nj.us
  Education: Bowdoin 1999; Harvard 2003 JD
Deputy Director **Cindy K. Miller** . . . . . . . . . . . . . . . . . . . (973) 504-6200
Deputy Director **Howard Pine** . . . . . . . . . . . . . . . . . . . . . (973) 504-6319

## Criminal Justice Division
Justice Complex, Trenton, NJ 08625
P.O. Box 085, Trenton, NJ 08625-0085
Tel: (609) 984-6500  Fax: (609) 984-3974  Internet: www.njdcj.org

Director **Elie Honig, JD** . . . . . . . . . . . . . . . . . . . . . . . . . . (609) 984-0029
  Education: Rutgers 1997 BA; Harvard 2000 JD
Deputy Director **Christine Hoffman** . . . . . . . . . . . . . . . . (609) 984-0034
Deputy Director **Chris Romanyshyn** . . . . . . . . . . . . . . . . (609) 984-0020
Counsel to the Director **Michael Williams** . . . . . . . . . . . (609) 984-0034
Chief of Detectives **Paul Morris** . . . . . . . . . . . . . . . . . . . (609) 984-0020
Chief of Staff **E. Robbie Miller** . . . . . . . . . . . . . . . . . . . (609) 984-0048
Insurance Fraud Prosecutor (Acting) **Christopher Iu** . . . . . (609) 633-6978
  Education: Seton Hall 2003 JD
State Medical Examiner (Acting)
  **Dr. Andrew L. Falzon, MD** . . . . . . . . . . . . . . . . . . . . (609) 984-6500

## Gaming Enforcement Division
140 East Front Street, Trenton, NJ 08625
P.O. Box 047, Trenton, NJ 08625
Fax: (609) 633-7355  Internet: www.state.nj.us/lps/ge

■Director **David Rebuck** . . . . . . . . . . . . . . . . . . . . . . . . . . (609) 292-5113
  E-mail: david.rebuck@lps.state.nj.us    Fax: (609) 633-7355

## Highway Traffic Safety Division
P.O. Box 048, Trenton, NJ 08625-0048
Fax: (609) 633-9020  Internet: www.njsaferoads.com

■Director (Acting) **Gary Poedubicky** . . . . . . . . . . . . . . . . . (609) 633-9300
  E-mail: gary.poedubicky@lps.state.nj.us

## Law Division
Justice Complex, P.O. Box 112, Trenton, NJ 08625
Tel: (609) 984-3900  Tel: (973) 648-2500  Fax: (609) 777-3117

Director (Acting) **Michelle L. Miller** . . . . . . . . . . . . . . . . (609) 292-4965
  Education: Fairleigh Dickinson BA; Seton Hall JD   Fax: (609) 633-9738
                                         Fax: (609) 292-0690
Deputy Director **Kevin Jesperson** . . . . . . . . . . . . . . . . . . (609) 292-4965
                                         Fax: (609) 633-9738
                                         Fax: (609) 292-0690
Deputy Director **Sharon M. Joyce** . . . . . . . . . . . . . . . . . . (609) 292-4965
                                         Fax: (609) 633-9738
                                         Fax: (609) 292-0690
Counsel to the Director **John P. Bender** . . . . . . . . . . . . . . (609) 292-4965

---

★ Elected Official   ■ Appointed by Governor   ● Appointed by Legislature   ▲ Appointed by Board or Commission   ◆ Appointed by State Supreme Court

Deputy Counsel to the Director **Jean Reilley** . . . . . . . . . . . (609) 292-4965
Chief of Staff **Susan L. Olgiati** . . . . . . . . . . . . . . . . . . . . . . (609) 984-3900
Deputy Chief of Staff **Agnes Carson** . . . . . . . . . . . . . . . . . (609) 984-3900

## Election Law Enforcement Commission
P.O. Box 185, Trenton, NJ 08625-0185
Fax: (609) 777-1457
▲ Executive Director **Jeffrey M. Brindle** . . . . . . . . . . . . . . . . (609) 292-8700
  E-mail: jeffrey.brindle@elec.state.nj.us

## Juvenile Justice Commission
1001 Spruce Street, Suite 202, Trenton, NJ 08638
P.O. Box 107, Trenton, NJ 08625-0107
Fax: (609) 943-4611
■ Executive Director **Kevin M. Brown** . . . . . . . . . . . . . . . . . . . (609) 292-1400
  E-mail: kevin.m.brown@jjc.nj.gov

## Racing Commission
140 East Front Street, Trenton, NJ 08625
P.O. Box 088, Trenton, NJ 08625-0088
Fax: (609) 599-1785
■ Commissioner **Anthony T. Abbatiello** . . . . . . . . . . . . . . . . (609) 292-0613
  E-mail: anthony.abbatiello@lps.state.nj.us
■ Commissioner **Manny E. Aponte** . . . . . . . . . . . . . . . . . . . . (609) 292-0613
  E-mail: manny.aponte@lps.state.nj.us
■ Commissioner **Michael Arnone** . . . . . . . . . . . . . . . . . . . . . . (609) 292-0613
  E-mail: michael.arnone@lps.state.nj.us
■ Commissioner **Pamela J. Clyne** . . . . . . . . . . . . . . . . . . . . . (609) 292-0613
  E-mail: pamela.clyne@lps.state.nj.us
■ Commissioner **Peter J. Cofrancesco III** . . . . . . . . . . . . . . (732) 745-3366
  E-mail: peter.cofrancesco@lps.state.nj.us    Fax: (732) 745-4055
■ Commissioner **Anthony R. Copato** . . . . . . . . . . . . . . . . . . . (609) 292-0613
  E-mail: anthony.copato@lps.state.nj.us
■ Commissioner **Anthony DePaola** . . . . . . . . . . . . . . . . . . . . (609) 292-0613
  E-mail: anthony.depaola@lps.state.nj.us
■ Commissioner **Francis X. Keegan, Jr.** . . . . . . . . . . . . . . . . (609) 292-0613
  E-mail: francis.keegan@lps.state.nj.us
■ Commissioner **Peter Roselle** . . . . . . . . . . . . . . . . . . . . . . . (609) 292-0613
  E-mail: peter.roselle@lps.state.nj.us
▲ Executive Director **Frank Zanzuccki** . . . . . . . . . . . . . . . . . (609) 292-0613
  E-mail: frank.zanzuccki@lps.state.nj.us

## State Ethics Commission
P.O. Box 082, Trenton, NJ 08625
Fax: (609) 633-9252
▲ Executive Director **Susana Guerrero** . . . . . . . . . . . . . . . . (609) 292-1892
  E-mail: susana.guerrero@lps.state.nj.us

# Department of State
125 W. State Street, Trenton, NJ 08625-0300
P.O. Box 300, Trenton, NJ 08625
Tel: (609) 984-1900  Fax: (609) 777-1764  E-mail: feedback@sos.nj.gov
Internet: www.state.nj.us/state
■ Secretary of State **Kimberly M. "Kim" Guadagno** . . . . . . . (609) 777-2581
  Executive Assistant **Elizabeth Vouk** . . . . . . . . . . . . . . . . . (609) 777-0884
Assistant Secretary of the State **Kathleen M. Kisko** . . . . . . (609) 777-2579
Chief of Staff **Dennis R. Robinson** . . . . . . . . . . . . . . . . . . . (609) 292-1166
  Executive Assistant to the Chief of Staff **Carol Gant** . . . . (609) 777-2535
Communications Director **Suzanne Schwab** . . . . . . . . . . . . (609) 777-0830
  E-mail: suzanne.schwab@nj.gov

## Administration Division
225 W. State St., Trenton, NJ 08625-0459
P.O. Box 459, Trenton, NJ 08625
Fax: (609) 292-9897
Administrative Director **Bill Schaum** . . . . . . . . . . . . . . . . . . (609) 943-4993
  E-mail: bill.schaum@sos.nj.gov

## Archives Division
225 West State Street, Trenton, NJ 08625
P.O. Box 307, Trenton, NJ 08625
Tel: (609) 292-6260  Fax: (609) 292-9105
Director **Joseph Klett** . . . . . . . . . . . . . . . . . . . . . . . . . . . . . (609) 292-9507

## Elections Division
225 West State Street, 5th Floor, Trenton, NJ 08608
P.O. Box 304, Trenton, NJ 08625-0304
Tel: (609) 292-3760  TTY: (800) 292-0034
Tel: (877) 658-6837 (24 Hour Assistance)  Fax: (609) 777-1280
Internet: www.elections.nj.gov
Director **Robert F. "Bob" Giles** . . . . . . . . . . . . . . . . . . . . . (609) 292-4251
  E-mail: robert.giles@sos.nj.gov
Deputy Director **Michael DiSimoni** . . . . . . . . . . . . . . . . . . (609) 826-3946

## Travel and Tourism Division
P.O. Box 460, Trenton, NJ 08625
Tel: (609) 292-2470  Fax: (609) 633-7418
Executive Director (Acting) **Anthony Minick** . . . . . . . . . . . (609) 292-6963

## Faith Based Initiatives Office
225 W. State St., Trenton, NJ 08625-0459
P.O. Box 456, Trenton, NJ 08625
Tel: (609) 984-6952  Fax: (609) 633-7141
Director **Edward LaPorte** . . . . . . . . . . . . . . . . . . . . . . . . . . (609) 292-9808

---

★ Elected Official    ■ Appointed by Governor    ● Appointed by Legislature    ▲ Appointed by Board or Commission    ◆ Appointed by State Supreme Court

# New Mexico

Tel: (800) 825-6639 (State Information)  Internet: www.newmexico.gov

**Number of U.S. Congressional Delegates:** 2 Senators; 3 Representatives  **Governor's Term:** 4 years
**Legislature Description:** 42 member Senate; 70 member House of Representatives; Term - Senate 4 years, House 2 years  **Next Election:** Governor November 2018; Legislature November 2016
**Number of Electoral Votes:** 5  **Official Name:** State of New Mexico (name given to area by Spaniards)
**Nickname:** Land of Enchantment  **Motto:** Crescit Eundo (It grows as it goes)

**Population:** 2,085,109 (2015); Rank 36  **Fiscal Year:** 2015  **Budget:** $12,505,836,000

## Office of the Governor

State Capitol Building, 490 Old Santa Fe Trail, Room 400,
Santa Fe, NM 87501
Tel: (505) 476-2200  Fax: (505) 476-2226

**Susana Martinez**
Governor

Began Service: January 1, 2011
Term Expires: January 2019
Date of Birth: August 14, 1959
Education: Texas (El Paso) 1981 BA; Oklahoma 1986 JD
Home: Las Cruces
Religion: Catholic
Career: Assistant District Attorney, Third Judicial District, New Mexico (1986-1992); District Attorney, Third Judicial District, New Mexico (1997-2010)

★Governor **Susana Martinez** (R) . . . . . . . . . . . . . . . . . . . . . (505) 476-2200
    E-mail: susana.martinez2@state.nm.us
Chief of Staff **Keith J. Gardner** . . . . . . . . . . . . . . . . . . . . . (505) 476-2200
Deputy Chief of Staff **Scott Darnell** . . . . . . . . . . . . . . . . . (505) 476-2200
    Education: New Mexico
Deputy Chief of Staff **Jeremiah Ritchie** . . . . . . . . . . . . . . (505) 476-2200
    E-mail: jeremiah.ritchie@state.nm.us
General Counsel **Steven Blankinship** . . . . . . . . . . . . . . . . (505) 476-2200
    E-mail: steven.blankinship@state.nm.us
Assistant General Counsel **Matthew Stackpole** . . . . . . . . . (505) 476-2200
    E-mail: matthew.stackpole@state.nm.us
Communications Director **Christopher "Chris" Sanchez** . . (505) 819-1398
    E-mail: chrisj.sanchez3@state.nm.us
Operations Director **(Vacant)** . . . . . . . . . . . . . . . . . . . . . . . (505) 476-2200
Cabinet and Federal Affairs Director **James Ross** . . . . . . . . (505) 476-2200
    E-mail: james.ross@state.nm.us

## Office of the Lieutenant Governor

State Capitol Building, 490 Old Santa Fe Trail, Room 417,
Santa Fe, NM 87501
Tel: (505) 476-2250  Tel: (800) 432-4406  Fax: (505) 476-2257

★Lieutenant Governor **John A. Sanchez** (R) . . . . . . . . . . . . . (505) 476-2250
    Term Expires: 2019
    Career: State Representative (R-NM, District 15), New Mexico House of Representatives (2001-2003)
Chief of Staff **Mark Van Dyke** . . . . . . . . . . . . . . . . . . . . . . . (505) 476-2250
Policy Director and Legislative Liaison
    **Vincent A. Torres** . . . . . . . . . . . . . . . . . . . . . . . . . . . . . (505) 476-2250

## Office of the State Engineer

130 Concha Ortiz Y Pino Building, Santa Fe, NM 87504
P.O. Box 25102, Santa Fe, NM 87504-5102
Tel: (505) 827-6091  Fax: (505) 827-3806

**Employees:** 343  **Fiscal Year:** 2015  **Budget:** $39,852,000

■State Engineer **Tom Blaine** . . . . . . . . . . . . . . . . . . . . . . . . . (505) 827-6091
    E-mail: tom.blaine@state.nm.us
    Education: New Mexico State BSE

Assistant to the State Engineer **Kristina Eckhart** . . . . . . . . (505) 827-6091
Chief Counsel/Litigation and Adjudication Program
    Director **Gregory C. "Greg" Ridgley** . . . . . . . . . . . . . . . (505) 827-6174
    E-mail: greg.ridley@state.nm.us
    Education: Harvard; Hastings JD
Program Support Director **Curtis Eckhart** . . . . . . . . . . . . . . (505) 827-0536
    E-mail: curtis.eckhart@state.nm.us
Water Rights Director **John T. Romero, PE** . . . . . . . . . . . . . (505) 827-4187
    E-mail: john.romero2@state.nm.us
    Education: New Mexico State 1992 BS

## Aging and Long-Term Services Department

2550 Cerrillos Road, Santa Fe, NM 87505
Tel: (505) 476-4799  Fax: (505) 476-4836
Internet: www.nmaging.state.nm.us

**Employees:** 249  **Fiscal Year:** 2015  **Budget:** $62,237,000

■Secretary **Myles Copeland** . . . . . . . . . . . . . . . . . . . . . . . . . (505) 476-4590
    E-mail: myles.copeland@state.nm.us
Deputy Secretary **Kyky Knowles** . . . . . . . . . . . . . . . . . . . . (505) 476-4590

## Children, Youth and Families Department [CYFD]

P.O. Drawer 5160, Santa Fe, NM 87502-5160
Tel: (505) 827-7602  Fax: (505) 827-4053  Internet: www.cyfd.org

**Employees:** 2,224  **Fiscal Year:** 2015  **Budget:** $427,510,000

■Secretary **Monique Jacobson** . . . . . . . . . . . . . . . . . . . . . . (505) 827-7602
    E-mail: monique.jacobson@state.nm.us
    Education: Pennsylvania BSEc
Deputy Secretary **Jennifer Padgett** . . . . . . . . . . . . . . . . . . (505) 827-7602
General Counsel **Jennifer Saavedra** . . . . . . . . . . . . . . . . . . (505) 476-8599
Early Childhood Services Director **Steve Hendrix** . . . . . . . . (505) 827-7659
Juvenile Justice Director **Sandra Stewart** . . . . . . . . . . . . . . (505) 827-7629
    Child Development Office Bureau Chief
        **Alejandra Rebolledo-Rea** . . . . . . . . . . . . . . . . . . . . . (505) 827-7689
Protective Services Director **Jared Rounsville** . . . . . . . . . . . (505) 827-8400
    Protective Services Deputy Director **Anna Marie Luna** . . (505) 827-8400
    Protective Services Deputy Director **Yvette Sandoval** . . . (505) 827-8400
Chief of Staff **Helen Quintana** . . . . . . . . . . . . . . . . . . . . . . (505) 827-7694
Child Care Service Bureau Chief
    **Jeffrey H. "Jeff" Miles** . . . . . . . . . . . . . . . . . . . . . . . . . (505) 476-0453
Children's Behavioral Health Service and Community
    Services Bureau Director **Daphne Rood-Hopkins** . . . . . . (505) 827-4538
Data Processing Bureau Chief **(Vacant)** . . . . . . . . . . . . . . . (505) 841-2928
Family Nutrition Bureau Chief **Cesar Uriarte** . . . . . . . . . . . (505) 827-9968
Human Resources Manager **Lisa M. Fitting** . . . . . . . . . . . . (505) 827-7620
Staff Development Coordinator **Kathy Luker** . . . . . . . . . . . (505) 841-6658

---

★ Elected Official    ■ Appointed by Governor    ● Appointed by Legislature    ▲ Appointed by Board or Commission    ◆ Appointed by State Supreme Court

# New Mexico Corrections Department [NMCD]

P.O. Box 27116, Santa Fe, NM 87502-0116
Tel: (505) 827-8600  TTY: (505) 827-8696  Fax: (505) 827-8220
E-mail: corrections.secretary@state.nm.us  Internet: corrections.state.nm.us

**Employees:** 2,473  **Fiscal Year:** 2015  **Budget:** $313,463,000

■Secretary **Gregg Marcantel, USMC (Ret)** . . . . . . . . . . . . . (505) 827-8884
  E-mail: gregg.marcantel@state.nm.us
  Education: Chaminade BS; Leicester (UK) MS
  Executive Assistant **Laura Lovato** . . . . . . . . . . . . . . . . . (505) 827-8600
Chief of Staff **Mark Myers** . . . . . . . . . . . . . . . . . . . . . (505) 827-8631
  E-mail: mark.myers@state.nm.us       Fax: (505) 827-8634
Chief Deputy Secretary **Joe W. Booker, Jr.** . . . . . . . . . . . . (505) 827-8667
Administrative Support Deputy Secretary
  **Alexandria "Alex" Tomlin** . . . . . . . . . . . . . . . . . . . (505) 827-8667
General Counsel **James "Jim" Brewster** . . . . . . . . . . . . . (505) 827-8698
  E-mail: jim.brewster@state.nm.us
Administrative Services Director (Acting) **Paul Montoya** . . (505) 827-8632
  E-mail: paul.montoya@osa.state.nm.us       Fax: (505) 827-8634
Internal Audits and Standards Compliance Bureau Chief
  **(Vacant)** . . . . . . . . . . . . . . . . . . . . . . . . . . . . . . (505) 827-8633
Training (Corrections Academy) Director (Acting)
  **Michael Nunley** . . . . . . . . . . . . . . . . . . . . . . . . . . (505) 827-8905
  P.O. Box 5277, Santa Fe, NM 87502-5277       Fax: (505) 827-8904
Adult Prisons Division Director **Jerry Roark** . . . . . . . . . . . (505) 827-8767
                                                        Fax: (505) 827-8801
Corrections Industries Division Director (Acting)
  **Anna Martinez** . . . . . . . . . . . . . . . . . . . . . . . . . . (505) 827-8906
Probation and Parole Division Director **Rose Bobchak** . . . . (505) 827-8830
                                                        Fax: (505) 827-8679
Education Bureau Chief **(Vacant)** . . . . . . . . . . . . . . . . . (505) 891-4282
Recidivism Reduction Bureau Chief **Micaela Cadena** . . . . . (505) 827-8541
Chief Information Officer **Timothy N. Oakeley** . . . . . . . . . (505) 827-8713
  E-mail: timothy.oakeley@state.nm.us
Webmaster **Pam Smyth** . . . . . . . . . . . . . . . . . . . . . . . (505) 827-8796

# Office of the Public Defender

301 North Guadalupe, Suite 101, Santa Fe, NM 87501
Tel: (505) 476-0700  Fax: (505) 476-0777

**Employees:** 407  **Fiscal Year:** 2015  **Budget:** $45,209,000

■Chief Public Defender **(Vacant)** . . . . . . . . . . . . . . . . . (505) 476-0703
Assistant Chief Public Defender **Bennett J. Baur** . . . . . . . . (505) 476-0758
Appellate Public Defender **Sergio J. Viscoli** . . . . . . . . . . . (505) 476-0746
District Public Defender **(Vacant)** . . . . . . . . . . . . . . . . . (505) 476-0720
Human Resources Director **Barbara Auten** . . . . . . . . . . . . (505) 476-6486

# Department of Cultural Affairs [DCA]

Bataan Memorial Building, 407 Galisteo, Suite 260, Santa Fe, NM 87501
Tel: (505) 827-6364  Fax: (505) 827-7308
Internet: www.newmexicoculture.org

**Employees:** 541  **Fiscal Year:** 2015  **Budget:** $42,524,000

■Secretary **Veronica Gonzales** . . . . . . . . . . . . . . . . . . . (505) 827-6364
  E-mail: veronica.gonzales@state.nm.us
Deputy Cabinet Secretary **Michael Scott Delello** . . . . . . . . (505) 827-1128
  E-mail: michael.delello@state.nm.us
  Education: LSU BA
Farm and Ranch Heritage Museum Director
  **Mark Santiago** . . . . . . . . . . . . . . . . . . . . . . . . . . (575) 522-4100
  4100 Dripping Springs Road, Las Cruces, NM 88011
Museum of International Folk Art Director **Marsha Bol** . . . (505) 476-1200
  706 Camino Lejo, Santa Fe, NM 87505       Fax: (505) 476-1300
New Mexico Museum of Art Director **Mary Kershaw** . . . . . (505) 476-5073
  107 West Palace Avenue, Santa Fe, NM 87501   Fax: (505) 476-5076
Palace of the Governors/New Mexico History Museum
  Director **Andrew J. Wulf** . . . . . . . . . . . . . . . . . . . . (505) 476-5093
  105 West Palace Avenue, Santa Fe, NM 87501   Fax: (505) 476-5104
Administrative Services Division Director **Ron Lecero** . . . . (505) 476-2192
  E-mail: ron.lucero@state.nm.us
New Mexico Arts Director **Loie Fecteau** . . . . . . . . . . . . . (505) 827-6490
National Hispanic Cultural Center President and CEO
  **Rebecca Avitia** . . . . . . . . . . . . . . . . . . . . . . . . . . (505) 246-2261
  1701 Fourth St., SW, Albuquerque, NM 87102

Historic Preservation Division Director
  **Dr. Jeff Pappas, PhD** . . . . . . . . . . . . . . . . . . . . . . (505) 235-3968
  Education: BYU BA; Baylor MA; Arizona State PhD
Museum of Space History Division Director
  **Chris Orwoll** . . . . . . . . . . . . . . . . . . (505) 437-2840 ext. 41112
  P.O. Box 533, Alamogordo, NM 88311
  E-mail: chris.orwoll@state.nm.us
Natural History and Science Museum Division Director
  (Interim) **Gary Romero** . . . . . . . . . . . . . . . . . . . . . (505) 841-2800
  1801 Mountain Road NW, Albuquerque, NM 87104
Archaeological Studies Office Director **Eric Blinman** . . . . . (505) 827-6470
                                                        Fax: (505) 827-3904
State Librarian (Interim) **Michael Scott Delello** . . . . . . . . (505) 827-6354
  1209 Camino Carlos Rey, Santa Fe, NM 87507   Fax: (505) 476-9701

# New Mexico Economic Development Department [NMEDD]

Joseph Montoya Building, 1100 St. Francis Drive, Santa Fe, NM 87505
Tel: (505) 827-0300  Fax: (505) 827-0328  Internet: www.edd.state.nm.us

**Employees:** 52

■Secretary **Jon L. Barela** . . . . . . . . . . . . . . . . . . . . . . (505) 827-0305
  E-mail: jon.barela@state.nm.us
  Education: Georgetown BA, JD
Deputy Secretary **Barbara G. Brazil** . . . . . . . . . . . . . . . (505) 476-3747
Economic Development Division Director
  **Therese Varela** . . . . . . . . . . . . . . . . . . . . . . . . . . (505) 827-0323
                                                        Fax: (505) 827-0407
Administrative Services Director **Marilu Casillas** . . . . . . . . (505) 476-2192
  E-mail: marilu.casillas@state.nm.us       Fax: (505) 827-0211
Film Office Director **Nick Maniatis**
  Joseph M Montoya Building . . . . . . . . . . . . . . . . . . . (505) 476-5604
                                                        Fax: (505) 476-5601
Business Advocacy Office Director **Leslie Porter** . . . . . . . . (505) 827-0089
General Counsel **Wade Jackson** . . . . . . . . . . . . . . . . . . (505) 827-0328
  Education: New Mexico 2003 JD       Fax: (505) 827-0211
International Trade Office Director **Edward Herrera** . . . . . . (505) 827-0315

# Energy, Minerals and Natural Resources Department [EMNRD]

1220 St. Francis Drive, Santa Fe, NM 87505
Tel: (505) 476-3200  Fax: (505) 476-3320
Internet: www.emnrd.state.nm.us

**Employees:** 820  **Fiscal Year:** 2015  **Budget:** $63,512,000

■Secretary **F. David Martin** . . . . . . . . . . . . . . . . . . . . . (505) 476-3200
  E-mail: david.martin@state.nm.us
  Education: New Mexico Tech; Texas Tech
■Deputy Secretary **Brett F. Woods** . . . . . . . . . . . . . . . . (505) 476-3223
  Education: Sam Houston State BS; Pepperdine MA; Essex (UK) PhD
General Counsel **Bill Brancard** . . . . . . . . . . . . . . . . . . . (505) 476-3211
Communications Director **Beth Wojahn** . . . . . . . . . . . . . (505) 476-3226
  E-mail: beth.wojahn@state.nm.us

# Game and Fish Department

One Wildlife Way, Santa Fe, NM 87507
P.O. Box 25112, Santa Fe, NM 87504
Tel: (505) 476-8000  Tel: (800) 862-9310  TTY: (505) 476-8143
Fax: (505) 476-8124  Internet: www.wildlife.state.nm.us

**Employees:** 333

■Director **Alexandra Sandoval** . . . . . . . . . . . . . . . . . . . (505) 476-8070
  E-mail: alexandra.sandoval@state.nm.us
  Education: Colorado State BS; New Mexico Highlands MBA
Deputy Director **Daniel E. Brooks** . . . . . . . . . . . . . . . . . (505) 476-8008
Human Resource Chief **Angelica Ruiz** . . . . . . . . . . . . . . . (505) 476-8027
Administrative Services Division Chief **(Vacant)** . . . . . . . . (505) 476-8000
Conservation Services Division Chief **Matt Wunder** . . . . . . (505) 476-8101
Fisheries Management Division Chief **Mike Sloane** . . . . . . . (505) 476-8055
Information Systems Division Chief **Russell Verbosski** . . . . (505) 476-8016
Law Enforcement Division Chief **Robert Griego** . . . . . . . . (505) 476-8061
Law Enforcement Division Colonel **Donald Jaramillo** . . . . (505) 250-7563
Public Affairs Division Chief **(Vacant)** . . . . . . . . . . . . . . (505) 476-8013
Wildlife Management Division Chief **Cal Baca** . . . . . . . . . (505) 476-8038

★ Elected Official   ■ Appointed by Governor   ● Appointed by Legislature   ▲ Appointed by Board or Commission   ◆ Appointed by State Supreme Court

EXECUTIVE BRANCH

## State Game Commission

Tel: (505) 476-8000

■Chairman **Paul M. Kienzle III** . . . . . . . . . . . . . . . . . . . . . . (575) 523-9101
  P.O. Box 1292, Mesilla Park, NM 88047
  E-mail: paul@kienzlelaw.com

■Vice Chair **Bill Montoya** . . . . . . . . . . . . . . . . . . . . . . . . (505) 242-2533
  E-mail: billmontoya@hotmail.com

■Commissioner **Tom Arvas** . . . . . . . . . . . . . . . . . . . . . . . (505) 898-4884
  7905 Spain Road NE, Albuquerque, NM 87109
  E-mail: tomarvas@hotmail.com

■Commissioner **Robert Espinoza** . . . . . . . . . . . . . . . . . . . (505) 324-8208
  E-mail: robert_nmgf@live.com

■Commissioner **Ralph Ramos** . . . . . . . . . . . . . . . . . . . . . (505) 271-4550
  E-mail: ralphramos@comcast.net          Res: (575) 526-1314
                                          Fax: (505) 271-2472

■Commissioner **Bob Ricklefs** . . . . . . . . . . . . . . . . . . . . . (575) 376-1123
  E-mail: bob.ricklefs@gmail.com

■Commissioner **Elizabeth Ryan** . . . . . . . . . . . . . . . . . . . (505) 476-8000
  Education: Texas Tech JD

■Commissioner **Thomas R. "Dick" Salopek** . . . . . . . . . . . . (505) 476-8000
  975 Holcomb Road, Las Cruces, NM 88007    Fax: (575) 526-0867
  E-mail: dicksalopek@hotmail.com
  Education: New Mexico State BS

## New Mexico Environment Department [NMED]

1190 St. Francis Drive, Santa Fe, NM 87502-5469
P.O. Box 5469, Santa Fe, NM 87502
Tel: (505) 827-2855  Fax: (505) 827-2836
Internet: www.nmenv.state.nm.us

**Employees:** 670  **Fiscal Year:** 2015  **Budget:** $108,708,000

■Secretary **Ryan Flynn** . . . . . . . . . . . . . . . . . . . . . . . . . (505) 827-2855
  E-mail: ryan.flynn@state.nm.us
  Education: Harvard 2001 BA; James Rogers Law 2006 JD
  Executive Secretary **Jo Huntington** . . . . . . . . . . . . . . . (505) 827-2855
  General Counsel **Jeffrey M. Kendall** . . . . . . . . . . . . . . (505) 827-2750

■Deputy Secretary **Butch Tongate** . . . . . . . . . . . . . . . . . (505) 827-2855
  E-mail: butch.tongate@state.nm.us
  Public Information Officer and Policy Advisor
    **Rob Nikolewski** . . . . . . . . . . . . . . . . . . . . . . . . . . (505) 827-0314

## Administrative Services Division [ASD]

Tel: (505) 827-2855

Director **Stacy Lopez** . . . . . . . . . . . . . . . . . . . . . . . . . (505) 827-2144
Human Resources Bureau Chief **JC Borrego** . . . . . . . . . . (505) 827-9769
Chief Financial Officer **Marlene Cordova** . . . . . . . . . . . . (505) 476-3725
  Budget Bureau Chief **Barbara Maclellan** . . . . . . . . . . . (505) 827-0381
  Financial Services Bureau Chief **Manuelita Martinez** . . . (505) 476-3725
  Purchasing Bureau Chief **Ben Naranjo** . . . . . . . . . . . . . (505) 476-3689

## Environmental Health Division

Tel: (505) 827-2855  Fax: (505) 827-2836

Director (Acting) **Butch Tongate** . . . . . . . . . . . . . . . . . . (505) 827-2855
Executive Administrative Assistant **Theresa Macias** . . . . . (505) 827-2839
Constructions Programs Bureau Chief **Jim Chiasson** . . . . (505) 827-9570
Drinking Water Bureau Chief **Stephanie Stringer** . . . . . . (505) 476-8620
  525 Camino de los Marquez, Suite 4, Santa Fe, NM 87505

## Environmental Protection Division

Harold L. Runnels Building, 1190 St. Francis Drive, Suite N4050,
Santa Fe, NM 87502-5469
Tel: (505) 827-2109

Director **Michael Vonderheide** . . . . . . . . . . . . . . . . . . . (505) 827-2021

## Information Technology Division

Tel: (505) 827-0911

Chief Information Officer (Acting) **Mary Montoya** . . . . . . . (505) 476-3090
Network Services Bureau Director **Robert Levine** . . . . . . . (505) 827-2979

## Resource Protection Division

Tel: (505) 827-2855

Director (Acting) **Travis Kliphuis** . . . . . . . . . . . . . . . . . . (505) 827-1758

## Office of the Natural Resources Trustee

121 Tijeras Avenue, Albuquerque, NM 87102
Tel: (505) 231-8800  Fax: (505) 243-6644
E-mail: nmenv-onrtinfo@state.nm.us

Trustee **Ryan Flynn** . . . . . . . . . . . . . . . . . . . . . . . . . . (505) 243-8087
  E-mail: ryan.flynn@state.nm.us
Executive Director **Rebecca Neri Zagal** . . . . . . . . . . . . . (505) 243-8087
Environmental Scientist **William Fetner** . . . . . . . . . . . . . (505) 243-8087
Business Operations **Elysia C. Bunten** . . . . . . . . . . . . . . (505) 243-8087
  E-mail: elysia.martinez@state.nm.us

## Department of Finance and Administration

180 Bataan Memorial Building, Santa Fe, NM 87501
Tel: (505) 827-4985  Fax: (505) 827-4984

**Employees:** 156  **Fiscal Year:** 2015  **Budget:** $130,219,000

■Secretary **Tom Clifford** . . . . . . . . . . . . . . . . . . . . . . . . (505) 827-4985
  Note: Until May 27, 2016.
  E-mail: tom.clifford@state.nm.us
  Education: San José State 1979 BS; UC Berkeley 1980 MA;
  Berkeley Col 1984 PhD

■Secretary (Acting) **Dorothy "Duffy" Rodriguez** . . . . . . . . (505) 827-4985
  Note: Effective May 27, 2016.
  Deputy Secretary **Stephanie Schardin Clarke** . . . . . . . . (505) 827-3930
    E-mail: stephanie.schardin@state.nm.us
  Deputy Secretary **Dorothy "Duffy" Rodriguez** . . . . . . . . (505) 827-3881
    E-mail: duffy.rodriguez@state.nm.us
  Chief Legal Counsel (Acting) **Rebecca Jackson** . . . . . . . (505) 827-3639
  State Budget Division Director **(Vacant)** . . . . . . . . . . . . (505) 827-3640
    Budget Division, 407 Galisteo Street,     Fax: (505) 827-3861
    Santa Fe, NM 87501
  Administrative Services Division Director **(Vacant)** . . . . . (505) 827-4985
  Finance Board Division Director **Leila Burrows Kleats** . . . (505) 827-3930
  Financial Control Division Director
    **Ronald "Ron" Spilman** . . . . . . . . . . . . . . . . . . . . . (505) 827-3934
  Local Government Division Director **Wayne Sowell** . . . . . (505) 827-8053
    E-mail: wayne.sowell@state.nm.us

## General Services Department [GSD]

715 Alta Vista Street, Santa Fe, NM 87505
P.O. Box 6850, Santa Fe, NM 87502-0110
Tel: (505) 827-2000  Fax: (505) 827-2041

**Employees:** 325  **Fiscal Year:** 2015  **Budget:** $695,050,000

■Secretary **Ed Burckle** . . . . . . . . . . . . . . . . . . . . . . . . . (505) 827-2000
  E-mail: ed.burckle@state.nm.us
  Deputy Secretary **(Vacant)** . . . . . . . . . . . . . . . . . . . . (505) 827-2000
  General Counsel **Jay Hone** . . . . . . . . . . . . . . . . . . . . . (505) 827-2000
  Administrative Services Division Director **Zella Cox** . . . . . (505) 476-1857
    E-mail: zella.cox@state.nm.us
  Facilities Management Division Director
    **George Morgan** . . . . . . . . . . . . . . . . . . . . . . . . . . (505) 827-2141
  Risk Management Division Director **A.J. Forte** . . . . . . . . . (505) 827-0463
    Litigation Bureau Chief **(Vacant)** . . . . . . . . . . . . . . . (505) 827-2000
  State Purchasing Division Director **Lawrence Maxwell** . . . (505) 827-0472
  Transportation Services Division Deputy Director
    **James Chavez** . . . . . . . . . . . . . . . . . . . . . . . . . . . (505) 827-1958
  State Printing and Graphic Design Services Director
    **Robert Newlin** . . . . . . . . . . . . . . . . . . . . . . . . . . . (505) 476-1952
    E-mail: robert.newlin@state.nm.us
  Technology and Systems Support Bureau Chief
    **Karen Baltzley** . . . . . . . . . . . . . . . . . . . . . . . . . . (505) 827-2959
    E-mail: karen.baltzley@state.nm.us

---

★ Elected Official   ■ Appointed by Governor   ● Appointed by Legislature   ▲ Appointed by Board or Commission   ◆ Appointed by State Supreme Court

## State Personnel Office

2600 Cerrillos Road, Santa Fe, NM 87505
P.O. Box 26127, Santa Fe, NM 87505
Tel: (505) 476-7759  Fax: (505) 476-7832

■Director (Interim) **Justin Najaka**........................(505) 490-2414
  E-mail: justin.najaka@state.nm.us
Deputy Director **Nivia Thames**.......................(505) 629-7853
Compensation and Classification Director **Justin Najaka** .. (505) 490-2414

## Department of Health [DOH]

1190 South St. Francis Drive, Santa Fe, NM 87502
P.O. Box 25767, Santa Fe, NM 87125 (Vital Records)
Tel: (505) 827-2613  Tel: (505) 827-0121 (Vital Records)
Fax: (505) 827-2530  Internet: www.health.state.nm.us

**Employees:** 3,825  **Fiscal Year:** 2015  **Budget:** $540,019,000

■Cabinet Secretary **Lynn Gallagher** ...................(505) 827-2613
  E-mail: lynn.gallagher@state.nm.us
  Education: SUNY (Stony Brook) BA; Nova Southeastern JD
  Assistant to the Secretary **Marie Caisido** ..............(505) 827-2951
Deputy Secretary **Brad McGrath**.....................(505) 827-2613
  Administrative Assistant to the Deputy Secretaries
    **Antoinette Griego**.......................(505) 827-2613
  Administrative Assistant to the Deputy Secretaries
    **Regina Sena**...........................(505) 827-2613
Public Information Officer **Kenny C. Vigil** ............(505) 827-2613
  E-mail: kennyc.vigil@state.nm.us
General Counsel **Gabrielle Sanchez Sandoval** .........(505) 827-2997
  E-mail: gabrielle.sanchezsandoval@state.nm.us
Chief Information Officer **Terry Reusser** ..............(505) 660-6498
  E-mail: terry.reusser@state.nm.us
Chief Medical Officer **Dr. Steve Dorman** ..............(505) 827-2624
Applications Support Manager **Jenny Liu**..............(505) 827-2263

### Administrative Services Division

1190 St. Francis Drive, Suite S 3400, Santa Fe, NM 87502-5469
Fax: (505) 827-2530

Director **Leonard Tapia** ...........................(505) 827-2555
  E-mail: leonard.tapia@state.nm.us
Deputy Director **Kim Keahbone** ....................(505) 827-2525
  E-mail: kim.keahbone@state.nm.us
Budget Director **Shawnee Romo** ....................(505) 827-2581
Contracts Bureau Chief **(Vacant)** ....................(505) 827-2688
Grants Bureau Chief **(Vacant)** .......................(505) 827-2555
Human Resources Bureau Co-Chief **Elona Cruz** .........(505) 827-2735
Human Resources Bureau Co-Chief **Teresa Padilla**.......(505) 827-2735
Training Bureau Chief **Melissa Walker**................(505) 827-2832

### Developmental Disabilities Supports Division

Fax: (505) 476-8973

Director **Cathy Stevenson**..........................(505) 476-8974
Deputy Director **Marc Kolman** .......................(505) 490-0398
Community Programs Bureau Chief **Roberta Duran** ......(505) 476-8923
  E-mail: roberta.duran@state.nm.us
Metro Regional Office Program Manager
  **Kathleen Linnehan**........................(505) 841-6168
  5301 Central Avenue, NE, Suite 1700, Albuquerque, NM 87108
  E-mail: kathleen.linnehan@state.nm.us
Northeast Regional Office Program Manager
  **Charlene Cain** ............................(575) 758-5934
  224 Cruz Alta, Ste. B, Taos, NM 87571
  E-mail: charlene.cain@osa.state.nm.us
Northwest Regional Office Program Manager
  **Crystal Wright**............................(505) 476-2499
  2918 E. 66, Gallup, NM 87301
  E-mail: crystal.wright@state.nm.us
Southeast Regional Office Program Manager
  **Jessica Renteria** ..........................(575) 624-6100
  726B South Sunset Avenue, Roswell, NM 88201
Southwest Regional Office Program Manager
  **Scott Doan** ..............................(575) 528-5180
  1170 N. Solano Dr., Las Cruces, NM 88001-2369
  E-mail: scott.doan@state.nm.us

## Epidemiology and Response Division

1105 St. Francis Drive, Santa Fe, NM 87505 (Vital Records)
Tel: (505) 827-0121 (Vital Records)
State Epidemiologist **Michael Landen** ..............(505) 476-3575
Vital Records and Health Statistics Bureau Chief
  **Mark Kassouf** ...........................(505) 827-0121
  PO Box 25767, Albuquerque, NM 87125    Tel: (866) 534-0051

## Health Improvement Division

Tel: (505) 476-9093  Fax: (505) 476-9075

Director **Jack Evans**...............................(505) 476-9093
Deputy Director **Judith "Judy" Parks** ...............(505) 476-9098
Administrative Services Bureau Chief **(Vacant)** .........(505) 476-8925
Incident Management Bureau Chief **(Vacant)** ...........(505) 476-9015
Long Care Program Manager **Amber Espinosa Trujillo** ... (505) 476-9028
Quality Management Bureau Chief **Daniel Maxwell** ......(505) 841-5829

## Public Health Division

Tel: (505) 827-2389  Fax: (505) 827-2329

Director **(Vacant)** .................................(505) 827-2504
Deputy Director **Marcella Ortega** ...................(505) 827-2389
Chronic Disease Prevention and Control Bureau Chief
  **David Vigil** ..............................(505) 841-5836
Family Health Bureau Chief **Denita Richards** .........(505) 476-8901
Health Systems Bureau Chief **(Vacant)** ................(505) 476-3082
Infectious Diseases Bureau Chief **Jane Cotner** .........(505) 827-2412
Program Support **Joe Garcia**.......................(505) 827-2405

## Scientific Laboratory Division

1101 Camino De Salud, NE, Albuquerque, NM 87102
Fax: (505) 383-9011  Tel: (505) 383-9000  Internet: www.sld.state.nm.us

Director **David E. Mills** ...........................(505) 383-9000
Deputy Director **Twila Kunde** ......................(505) 383-9003
Biological Science Bureau Chief **Sharon Masters** .......(505) 383-9122
Chemistry Bureau Chief **Phillip Adams** ...............(505) 383-9023
Program Support Bureau Chief **Twila Kunde** ...........(505) 383-9009
  E-mail: twila.kunde@state.nm.us
Toxicology Bureau Chief **Rong-Jen Hwang** ............(505) 383-9086
  Education: Wayne State U PhD

## New Mexico Higher Education Department [NMHED]

2048 Galisteo Street, Santa Fe, NM 87505
Tel: (505) 476-8400  Tel: (800) 279-9777 (Financial Aid)
Fax: (505) 476-8454  Internet: www.hed.state.nm.us

**Employees:** 56  **Fiscal Year:** 2015  **Budget:** $117,051,000

■Cabinet Secretary **Barbara Damron, PhD, RN, FAAN** .... (505) 476-8404
  Education: Union Col (NE) BSN; Texas PhD
Deputy Secretary **Andrew Jacobson** .................(505) 383-2430
  E-mail: andrew.jacobson@state.nm.us
  Executive Assistant **Chandler Kahawai**..............(505) 476-8425
Chief Legal Counsel **David Mathews**.................(505) 476-8402

## Administrative Services Division

Director and Chief Financial Officer (Acting)
  **Kevin Romero**............................(505) 476-8413
  E-mail: kevin.romero1@state.nm.us
Human Resources Director/Assistant to the Secretary
  **Lawrence Quintana** .......................(505) 490-3932
Institutional Finance Director **Ronald "Ron" James** .....(505) 476-8434
  Senior Financial Coordinator **Liu Qi**................(505) 476-8403
  Capital Projects Coordinator **Ronald "Ron" James**.....(505) 476-8430
Financial Aid Program Coordinator **Mia Canelaria** .......(505) 476-8412
  Financial Aid Coordinator **Heather Romero** .........(505) 476-8410
Private and Proprietary Schools Division Administrator
  **(Vacant)** .................................(505) 476-8442

## Adult Basic Education Division

Adult Basic Education Director **Frances Bannowsky** .....(505) 476-8437
  Policy and Program Improvement Coordinator **(Vacant)** .. (505) 476-8429

*(continued on next page)*

---

★ Elected Official   ■Appointed by Governor   ●Appointed by Legislature   ▲Appointed by Board or Commission   ◆Appointed by State Supreme Court

**Adult Basic Education Division** *continued*

Business Manager **(Vacant)** . . . . . . . . . . . . . . . . . . . . . . . . .(505) 476-8421

## Information Technology Division

Director **Dan Koleski** . . . . . . . . . . . . . . . . . . . . . . . . . . . . . .(505) 476-8432
  E-mail: dan.koleski@state.nm.us

Systems Application Developer **Dan Koleski** . . . . . . . . . . . .(505) 476-8439

## Planning, Assessment and Evaluation Division

Planning and Research Director **Dina Advani** . . . . . . . . . . .(505) 476-8408

New Mexico GEAR UP Director (P-20 Policy and
  Program Analysis) **Patricia Brainard** . . . . . . . . . . . . . . . .(505) 476-8424

Policy Development and P-20 Programs Director
  **(Vacant)** . . . . . . . . . . . . . . . . . . . . . . . . . . . . . . . . . . . . . .(505) 476-8446

Administrative Assistant **(Vacant)** . . . . . . . . . . . . . . . . . . . .(505) 476-8400

## Department of Homeland Security and Emergency Management [DHSEM]

P.O. Box 27111, Santa Fe, NM 87502
13 Bataan Boulevard, Santa Fe, NM 87504
Tel: (505) 476-9600  Fax: (505) 476-9695  Internet: www.nmdhsem.org

Secretary **Col James "Jay" Mitchell, USAF (Ret)** . . . . . .(505) 476-0874
  E-mail: james.mitchell@osa.state.nm.us
  Education: Col Santa Fe BSBA; Embry-Riddle 1996 MAE

Executive Assistant **Danielle Gonzales** . . . . . . . . . . . . . . .(505) 476-0874

Deputy Secretary **Nicholas "Nick" Piatek** . . . . . . . . . . . . .(505) 476-0874

Legal Counsel **George F. Heidke** . . . . . . . . . . . . . . . . . . . .(505) 476-0867

Administrative Services Division Director **(Vacant)** . . . . . . .(505) 476-0873

Preparedness Bureau Chief **Susan Walker** . . . . . . . . . . . . .(505) 476-9640

Recovery and Response Bureau Chief **Valli Wasp** . . . . . . . .(505) 476-9677

Information Technology Staff Manager (Acting)
  **Robert McGee** . . . . . . . . . . . . . . . . . . . . . . . . . . . . . . . .(505) 476-9692

Chief Financial Officer **Peggy Martinez** . . . . . . . . . . . . . . .(505) 476-0631

Chief Information Officer **Robert McGee** . . . . . . . . . . . . . .(505) 476-0629
  E-mail: robert.mcgee@state.nm.us

Communications Officer **(Vacant)** . . . . . . . . . . . . . . . . . . . .(505) 476-9632

Public Information Officer **Estevan Lujan** . . . . . . . . . . . . . .(505) 827-1051

Fleet and Facility Coordinator **(Vacant)** . . . . . . . . . . . . . . .(505) 476-9621

## Human Services Department [HSD]

Pollon Plaza, 2009 South Pacheco, Third Floor, Santa Fe, NM 87504
P.O. Box 2348, Santa Fe, NM 87504-2348
Tel: (505) 827-7750  TTY: (800) 659-8331  Fax: (505) 827-6286
Internet: www.hsd.state.nm.us

**Employees:** 2,128  **Fiscal Year:** 2015  **Budget:** $6,291,656,000

■Secretary **Brent Earnest** . . . . . . . . . . . . . . . . . . . . . . . . . .(505) 827-7750
  E-mail: brent.earnest@state.nm.us
  Education: New Mexico BA; Maryland MPM

Deputy Secretary **(Vacant)** . . . . . . . . . . . . . . . . . . . . . . . . .(505) 827-7750
  Executive Assistant **Yolanda Ramoz** . . . . . . . . . . . . . . . .(505) 827-7758

General Counsel **Christopher Collins** . . . . . . . . . . . . . . . . .(505) 827-7701

Inspector General **Frank Sherman** . . . . . . . . . . . . . . . . . . .(505) 476-6213

Communications Director **Matt Kennicott** . . . . . . . . . . . . . .(505) 827-6236
  E-mail: matt.kennicott@state.nm.us

## Administrative Services Division

Internet: www.hsd.state.nm.us/asd  Tel: (505) 827-9445

Director **Danny Sandoval** . . . . . . . . . . . . . . . . . . . . . . . . . .(505) 827-9445
  E-mail: danny.sandoval@state.nm.us

Revenue and Compliance Deputy Director
  **Donna Sandoval** . . . . . . . . . . . . . . . . . . . . . . . . . . . . . . .(505) 827-9445
  E-mail: donna.sandoval@state.nm.us

Procurement and Budget Deputy Director **(Vacant)** . . . . . . .(505) 827-9445

General Services Bureau Chief **Gerald Charez** . . . . . . . . . .(505) 827-9433
  E-mail: geraldd.chavez@state.nm.us

Personnel Bureau Chief **Johnna Padilla** . . . . . . . . . . . . . . .(505) 476-6247

## Behavioral Health Services/Substance Abuse and Mental Health Division

Tel: (505) 476-9299  Fax: (505) 827-0097

Director **Wayne Lindstrom** . . . . . . . . . . . . . . . . . . . . . . . . .(505) 476-9299

Deputy Director **Leon Lopez** . . . . . . . . . . . . . . . . . . . . . . . .(505) 476-9261
  E-mail: leon.lopez@state.nm.us

Deputy Director **Karen Meador** . . . . . . . . . . . . . . . . . . . . . .(505) 476-9252
  E-mail: karen.meador@state.nm.us

Administrative Assistant **Deluvina Martinez** . . . . . . . . . . . .(505) 476-9299

## Child Support Enforcement Division

Director **Steven Smith** . . . . . . . . . . . . . . . . . . . . . . . . . . . . .(505) 476-7750
  E-mail: steven.smith@state.nm.us

Deputy Director **Betina McCracken Gonzales** . . . . . . . . . .(505) 476-7750

## Income Support Division

Director (Acting) **Marilyn Martinez** . . . . . . . . . . . . . . . . . . .(505) 827-7250

Central Office Operations Deputy Director
  **Laura Galindo** . . . . . . . . . . . . . . . . . . . . . . . . . . . . . . . . .(505) 827-7252

Field Operations Deputy Director **Vida Tapia-Sanchez** . . . .(505) 827-2696

Food and Nutrition Services Bureau Director **(Vacant)** . . . .(505) 841-2696

## Medical Assistance Division

Director **Nancy Smith-Leslie** . . . . . . . . . . . . . . . . . . . . . . . .(505) 827-3106
                                          Fax: (505) 827-3185

Finance Deputy Director **Matthew Onstott** . . . . . . . . . . . . .(505) 827-3120

Programs Deputy Director **Nancy Smith-Leslie** . . . . . . . . .(505) 827-3122

Systems Deputy Director **Russell Toal** . . . . . . . . . . . . . . . .(505) 827-1344
  E-mail: russell.toal@state.nm.us

Client Services Bureau Chief **Roy Burt** . . . . . . . . . . . . . . . .(505) 476-6801

Contract Administration Bureau Chief **Angela Martinez** . . .(505) 827-3131

Exempt Services and Programs Bureau Chief
  **Angela Medrano** . . . . . . . . . . . . . . . . . . . . . . . . . . . . . . .(505) 827-3164

Management Information Systems Bureau Chief
  **Linda Gonzales** . . . . . . . . . . . . . . . . . . . . . . . . . . . . . . .(505) 827-1327
  E-mail: linda.gonzales@state.nm.us

Quality Assurance Bureau Chief **(Vacant)** . . . . . . . . . . . . . .(505) 827-3161

## Indian Affairs Department [IAD]

Wendell Chino Building, 1220 South St. Francis Drive, 2nd Floor,
Santa Fe, NM 87505
Tel: (505) 476-1600  Fax: (505) 476-1601  Internet: www.iad.state.nm.us

**Employees:** 15  **Fiscal Year:** 2015  **Budget:** $2,950,000

■Secretary **Kelly K. Zunie** . . . . . . . . . . . . . . . . . . . . . . . . . .(505) 476-1600

Executive Assistant **Martina X. Garcia** . . . . . . . . . . . . . . . .(505) 476-1623

■Deputy Secretary **Suzette Shije** . . . . . . . . . . . . . . . . . . . . .(505) 476-1600
  E-mail: suzette.shije@state.nm.us

Chief Financial Officer **Joann Lapington** . . . . . . . . . . . . . . .(505) 476-1600

Accountant Auditor **Micah Clokey** . . . . . . . . . . . . . . . . . . .(505) 476-1600

Accountant Auditor **Audrey Gonzales** . . . . . . . . . . . . . . . . .(505) 476-1600

Infrastructure Manager **Laura Vanoni** . . . . . . . . . . . . . . . . .(505) 476-1600

Management Analyst **Heidi Todacheene** . . . . . . . . . . . . . . .(505) 476-1600

General Counsel **David Mann** . . . . . . . . . . . . . . . . . . . . . . .(505) 476-1600

Capital Outlay Coordinator **Marion Salvador** . . . . . . . . . . .(505) 476-1600
  E-mail: marion.salvador@state.nm.us

Public Relations Coordinator **Nicole Macias** . . . . . . . . . . . .(505) 476-1600

## Department of Information Technology [DoIT]

715 Alta Vista Street, Santa Fe, NM 87505
P.O. Box 22550, Santa Fe, NM 87502-2550
Tel: (505) 827-0000  Internet: www.doit.state.nm.us

**Employees:** 180  **Fiscal Year:** 2015  **Budget:** $62,129,000

■Secretary and Chief Information Officer **Darryl Ackley** . . . .(505) 827-2292
  E-mail: darryl.ackley@state.nm.us

Deputy Secretary for Enterprise Operations
  **Jacqueline Miller** . . . . . . . . . . . . . . . . . . . . . . . . . . . . . .(505) 827-0000

Administrative Services Division Director
  **Charles Martinez** . . . . . . . . . . . . . . . . . . . . . . . . . . . . . .(505) 827-0000
  E-mail: charles.martinez@osa.state.nm.us

---

★ Elected Official      ■ Appointed by Governor      ● Appointed by Legislature      ▲ Appointed by Board or Commission      ◆ Appointed by State Supreme Court

Project Oversight and Compliance Division Director
(Vacant) . . . . . . . . . . . . . . . . . . . . . . . . . . . . . . . . . . (505) 827-0000
Public Information Officer **Estevan Lujan** . . . . . . . . . . . . . (505) 827-1051
E-mail: estevan.lujan@state.nm.us
General Counsel **Maria Sanchez** . . . . . . . . . . . . . . . . . . . (505) 476-3761

## Public Education Department [PED]

Jerry Apodaca Education Building, 300 Don Gaspar Avenue,
Santa Fe, NM 87501-2786
Tel: (505) 827-5800 (Main Information Line) Fax: (505) 827-6520

**Employees:** 285

■Secretary **Hanna Skandera** . . . . . . . . . . . . . . . . . . . . . . (505) 827-6688
E-mail: hanna.skandera@state.nm.us
Assistant to Secretary of Education **Gloria Ruiz** . . . . . . . . (505) 827-6688
Indian Education Assistant Secretary **(Vacant)** . . . . . . . . . . (505) 827-6679
Policy and Programs Deputy Secretary **(Vacant)** . . . . . . . . . (505) 827-6655
Finance and Operations Deputy Secretary
**Paul J. Aguilar** . . . . . . . . . . . . . . . . . . . . . . . . . . . . . (505) 827-6519
Strategic Initiative Constituent Services Director
**Annjenette Torres** . . . . . . . . . . . . . . . . . . . . . . . . . . . (505) 795-3035
E-mail: annjenette.torres@state.nm.us
General Counsel Staff Manager **Daniel "Dan" Hill** . . . . . . . (505) 827-6641
Legislative Liaison **Kimberly Ulibarri** . . . . . . . . . . . . . . . (505) 827-4292
E-mail: kimberly.ulibarri@state.nm.us
Public Information Officer **Larry Behrens** . . . . . . . . . . . . . (505) 827-6661
E-mail: larry.behrens2@state.nm.us

### Accountability and Assessment Division
Director **(Vacant)** . . . . . . . . . . . . . . . . . . . . . . . . . . . . . (505) 827-7975
Assistant Director **(Vacant)** . . . . . . . . . . . . . . . . . . . . . . (505) 827-6528
Priority School Director **Debbie Montoya** . . . . . . . . . . . . (505) 827-6475

### Administrative Services Division
Division Director **Marian K. Rael** . . . . . . . . . . . . . . . . . . . (505) 827-6611
E-mail: marian.rael@state.nm.us
Capital Outlay Director **Antonio Ortiz** . . . . . . . . . . . . . . . (505) 827-3863
School Budget and Finance Analysis Bureau Chief
**Eileen Marrujo-Gallegos** . . . . . . . . . . . . . . . . . . . . . . (505) 827-6537
Accounts Bureau Chief **Daleen Martinez** . . . . . . . . . . . . . (505) 827-6645
Contracts **Elizabeth Montano** . . . . . . . . . . . . . . . . . . . . (505) 827-5892
Human Resources **Terese Vigil** . . . . . . . . . . . . . . . . . . . . (505) 827-6602

### Information Technology Division
Chief Information Officer **(Vacant)** . . . . . . . . . . . . . . . . . . (505) 827-4971

### Student Services and Transportation Division
Division Director **Antonio Ortiz** . . . . . . . . . . . . . . . . . . . (505) 827-3863
Federal Programs Director **Denise Koscielniak** . . . . . . . . . (505) 827-1458
Instructional Materials Director **Anthony Burns** . . . . . . . . (505) 827-6415
Student Health Director **Dean Hopper** . . . . . . . . . . . . . . (505) 222-4748
Student Nutrition Director **(Vacant)** . . . . . . . . . . . . . . . . (505) 827-1814

### Vocational Rehabilitation Division
Building D, 435 St. Michael's Drive, Santa Fe, NM 87505
Tel: (505) 954-8500 Fax: (505) 954-8562

Director **(Vacant)** . . . . . . . . . . . . . . . . . . . . . . . . . . . . . (505) 954-8511
Disability Determination Deputy Director **Daniel Roper** . . . (505) 798-0445
E-mail: daniel.roper@osa.state.nm.us
Program Development and Support Deputy Director
**Veronica DeLeon-Dowd** . . . . . . . . . . . . . . . . . . . . . . . (505) 954-8521
Rehabilitation Services Deputy Director **Ralph Vigil** . . . . . . (505) 954-8512

## Department of Public Safety [DPS]

P.O. Box 1628, Santa Fe, NM 87504-1628
Tel: (505) 827-9000 TTY: (505) 827-3413 Fax: (505) 827-9189
Internet: www.dps.nm.org

**Employees:** 1,274 **Fiscal Year:** 2015 **Budget:** $131,652,000

■Cabinet Secretary **Scott Weaver** . . . . . . . . . . . . . . . . . . (505) 827-3370
Education: Texas Tech BA
Executive Secretary **Michele Maxwell** . . . . . . . . . . . . . . (505) 827-9131

Statewide Law Enforcement Support Services Deputy
Secretary **Patrick M. Mooney** . . . . . . . . . . . . . . . . . . . (505) 827-9277
Administrative Services Division Director (Acting)
**Dianna DeJarnette** . . . . . . . . . . . . . . . . . . . . . . . . . . (505) 827-9035
E-mail: dianna.dejarnette@state.nm.us
Technical Support Division Director (Interim)
**Ronald "Ron" Burton** . . . . . . . . . . . . . . . . . . . . . . . . (505) 827-3353
E-mail: ronald.burton@state.nm.us
New Mexico Law Enforcement Academy Director
**Jack F. Jones** . . . . . . . . . . . . . . . . . . . . . . . . . . . . . . (505) 827-9610
Chief Information Officer **Ronald "Ron" Burton** . . . . . . . (505) 827-3353
E-mail: ronald.burton@state.nm.us

## New Mexico State Police [NMSP]

Tel: (505) 827-3394 Fax: (505) 827-3395

■Chief **Pete Kassetas** . . . . . . . . . . . . . . . . . . . . . . . . . . (505) 827-9219
E-mail: pete.kassetas@state.nm.us
Special Investigations Division Director
**Capt. Tim Johnson** . . . . . . . . . . . . . . . . . . . . . . . . . . (505) 827-9000
E-mail: tim.johnson@state.nm.us
Motor Transportation Police Division Chief
**Pete Kassetas** . . . . . . . . . . . . . . . . . . . . . . . . . . . . . . (505) 476-2457

## Regulation and Licensing Department [RLD]

2550 Cerrillos Road, Santa Fe, NM 87504
Tel: (505) 476-4500 Fax: (505) 476-4511 Internet: www.rld.state.nm.us

**Employees:** 316 **Fiscal Year:** 2015 **Budget:** $26,961,000

■Superintendent **Robert "Mike" Unthank** . . . . . . . . . . . . (505) 476-4508
E-mail: mike.unthank@state.nm.us
Education: Liberty
General Counsel **Claudia Armijo** . . . . . . . . . . . . . . . . . . (505) 476-4655
Deputy Superintendent **(Vacant)** . . . . . . . . . . . . . . . . . . (505) 476-4663
Administrative Services Division Director **Alexis Lotero** . . (505) 476-4800
E-mail: alexis.lotero@state.nm.us                    Fax: (505) 476-4520
■Alcohol and Gaming Division Director **Mary Kay Root** . . . (505) 476-4875
E-mail: marykay.root@state.nm.us
Boards and Commissions Executive Director
**Lori Wrobel** . . . . . . . . . . . . . . . . . . . . . . . . . . . . . . . (505) 476-4622
Construction Industries Division Director **Pat McMurray** . . (505) 476-4700
                                                       Fax: (505) 476-4685
Financial Institutions Division Director
**Cynthia Richards** . . . . . . . . . . . . . . . . . . . . . . . . . . . (505) 476-4885
E-mail: cynthia.richards@state.nm.us             Fax: (505) 476-4670
Manufactured Housing Division Director **Pat McMurray** . . (505) 476-4700
                                                       Fax: (505) 476-4702
Securities Division Director (Acting) **Alexis Lotero** . . . . . . (505) 476-4800
                                                       Fax: (505) 984-0617
Information Technology Director **David Martinez** . . . . . . . (505) 476-4540
E-mail: david.martinez@state.nm.us
Public Information Officer/Director of Communications
**Bernice Geiger** . . . . . . . . . . . . . . . . . . . . . . . . . . . . . (505) 228-8505
E-mail: bernice.geiger@state.nm.us

## Taxation and Revenue Department [TRD]

P.O. Box 630, Santa Fe, NM 87504-0630
Tel: (505) 827-0700 Fax: (505) 827-2505 E-mail: kathim@state.nm.us

**Employees:** 1,187 **Fiscal Year:** 2015 **Budget:** $92,492,000

■Secretary **Demesia Padilla** . . . . . . . . . . . . . . . . . . . . . . (505) 827-0341
E-mail: demesia.padilla@state.nm.us
Deputy Secretary **John Monforte** . . . . . . . . . . . . . . . . . . (505) 827-0341
Chief Information Officer **Mike Baca** . . . . . . . . . . . . . . . (505) 827-2292
E-mail: mike.baca@state.nm.us
Chief Legal Counsel **Brad O'Dell** . . . . . . . . . . . . . . . . . . (505) 827-0341

★ Elected Official     ■ Appointed by Governor     ● Appointed by Legislature     ▲ Appointed by Board or Commission     ◆ Appointed by State Supreme Court

# Tourism Department

491 Old Santa Fe Trail, Santa Fe, NM 87501
Tel: (800) 545-2070  TTY: (505) 827-0248  Fax: (505) 827-7402
Internet: www.newmexico.org

**Employees: 70  Fiscal Year: 2015  Budget: $16,453,000**

■Cabinet Secretary **Rebecca Latham** . . . . . . . . . . . . . . . . . (505) 827-7400
  E-mail: rebecca.latham@state.nm.us
Executive Assistant **Susan Kavanaugh** . . . . . . . . . . . . . . (505) 827-7469
  E-mail: susan.kavanaugh@state.nm.us
Administrative Services Director **Richard Pickering** . . . . . . (505) 827-7347
  E-mail: richard.pickering@state.nm.us
Public Information Officer **Jolene Mauer** . . . . . . . . . . . . . (505) 490-0241
  E-mail: jolene.mauer@state.nm.us
  Education: Iowa BA; LSU MA
New Mexico Magazine Editor in Chief
  **Stephen Bohannon** . . . . . . . . . . . . . . . . . . . . . . . . . . . (505) 827-6341
Media Relations Manager and Video Services Director
  **Dan Monaghan** . . . . . . . . . . . . . . . . . . . . . . . . . . . . (505) 231-2368
  E-mail: dan.monaghan@state.nm.us
Visitor and Information Center Manager **Toby Martinez** . . . (505) 670-0613
Communications Director **Heather Briganti** . . . . . . . . . . . (505) 578-7938

# Department of Veterans' Services [DVS]

Bataan Memorial Building, 407 Galisteo Street, Room 142,
Santa Fe, NM 87504
Tel: (866) 433-8387  Fax: (505) 827-6372

**Employees: 46  Fiscal Year: 2015  Budget: $3,678,000**

■Secretary **BG Jack R. Fox, USA (Ret)** . . . . . . . . . . . . . . (505) 827-6334
  E-mail: jackr.fox@state.nm.us
  Education: New Mexico State 1969 BA; Georgia State 1975 MEd;
  US Army Command
Deputy Secretary **Alan Martinez** . . . . . . . . . . . . . . . . . . (505) 827-6374
Executive Administrative Assistant **Melissa Castañeda** . . . (505) 827-6334
Fiduciary Program Manager **Carl Sutter** . . . . . . . . . . . . . (505) 827-6334

# Department of Workforce Solutions

P.O. Box 1928, Albuquerque, NM 87103
Tel: (505) 841-8450  Fax: (505) 841-8491

**Employees: 605  Fiscal Year: 2015  Budget: $66,094,000**

■Secretary **Celina Bussey** . . . . . . . . . . . . . . . . . . . . . . . (505) 841-8405
  E-mail: celina.bussey@state.nm.us
■Deputy Secretary **Joy Forehand** . . . . . . . . . . . . . . . . . . (505) 841-8405
  E-mail: joy.forehand@state.nm.us

## Administrative Services Division

Director **David Robbins** . . . . . . . . . . . . . . . . . . . . . . . . . (505) 841-8420
  E-mail: david.robbins@state.nm.us
Chief Financial Officer **David Robbins** . . . . . . . . . . . . . . . (505) 841-8572
Financial Management Bureau Chief & Deputy Chief
  Financial Officer (Acting) **David Robbins** . . . . . . . . . . . . (505) 841-8681
  E-mail: david.robbins@state.nm.us
General Services Bureau Chief **Kevin Quinn** . . . . . . . . . . . (505) 841-8507
  E-mail: kevin.quinn@state.nm.us
Human Resources Bureau Chief **(Vacant)** . . . . . . . . . . . . (505) 841-8458
Chief Information Officer **Suze Sue-ann Athens** . . . . . . . . (505) 841-8424
  E-mail: sueanne.athens@state.nm.us
Public Information Officer **Joy Forehand** . . . . . . . . . . . . . (505) 250-3926
  E-mail: joy.forehand@state.nm.us
Internal Security & Audit **(Vacant)** . . . . . . . . . . . . . . . . (505) 841-8426

## Labor Relations Division

Director **Jason Dean** . . . . . . . . . . . . . . . . . . . . . . . . . . . (505) 841-4411
  E-mail: jason.dean@state.nm.us
Unemployment Insurance and Employment Services
  Director **Roy Padilla** . . . . . . . . . . . . . . . . . . . . . . . . . . (505) 841-4505
  E-mail: roy.padilla@state.nm.us
Economic Research and Analysis Bureau Chief
  **Rachel Moskowitz** . . . . . . . . . . . . . . . . . . . . . . . . . . . (505) 222-4683
  E-mail: rachel.moskowitz@state.nm.us
Field Services Bureau Chief **Marcos Martinez** . . . . . . . . . (505) 841-8446
  E-mail: marcos.martinez@state.nm.us

Unemployment Insurance Bureau Chief **Jason Dean** . . . . . . (505) 841-8576
Appeal Tribunal Supervisor **(Vacant)** . . . . . . . . . . . . . . . (505) 841-8682
Supervising Bureau Chief, Human Rights **Jason Dean** . . . . (505) 827-6838
  E-mail: jason.dean@state.nm.us
Supervising Bureau Chief, Wage and Hour **Jason Dean** . . . (505) 841-4400
  E-mail: jason.dean@state.nm.us
State Apprenticeship Program Director **Katrina Vigil** . . . . . (505) 222-4674
  E-mail: katrina.vigil@state.nm.us

# New Mexico Bureau of Geology and Mineral Resources

801 Leroy Place, Socorro, NM 87801-4796
Tel: (575) 835-5490  Fax: (505) 835-6333

Director/State Geologist **Matthew J. Rhoades** . . . . . . . . . . (575) 835-7625
                                                    Fax: (575) 835-6333
Associate Director for Finance **Valentina Avramidi** . . . . . . (575) 835-5232
Laboratories Geochemist Assistant Director
  **Nelia Dunbar** . . . . . . . . . . . . . . . . . . . . . . . . . . . . . . (575) 835-5783
Senior Economic Geologist
  **Virginia "Ginger" McLemore** . . . . . . . . . . . . . . . . . . . (575) 835-5521
Senior Field Geologist **Steven M. Cather** . . . . . . . . . . . . . (575) 835-5153
Emeritus, Senior Field Geologist **Richard Chamberlin** . . . . (575) 835-5310
Emeritus, Senior Industrial Mineral Geologist
  **George S. Austin** . . . . . . . . . . . . . . . . . . . . . . . . . . . . (575) 835-5302
Principal Senior Petroleum Geologist **Ronald Broadhead** . . (575) 835-5202
Senior Principal Environmental Geologist **David Love** . . . . (575) 835-5146
Principal Senior Geologist **Paul W. Bauer** . . . . . . . . . . . . (575) 835-5106
Senior Field Geologist **Bruce Allen** . . . . . . . . . . . . . . . . . (505) 366-2531
Senior Field Geologist **Daniel J. Koning** . . . . . . . . . . . . . (575) 835-6950
Senior Field Geologist **Geoffrey C. Rawling** . . . . . . . . . . . (505) 366-2535
Special Projects Manager **Doug Bland** . . . . . . . . . . . . . . (505) 466-6696
ABQ Office Manager **Adam S. Read** . . . . . . . . . . . . . . . . (505) 366-2533
Senior Geophysicist and Field Geologist **Shari A. Kelley** . . (505) 412-9269
Geologist/Webmaster **Adam S. Read** . . . . . . . . . . . . . . . (505) 366-2533
  E-mail: adamread@nmbg.nmt.edu
Principal Senior Hydrogeologist **Peggy Johnson** . . . . . . . . (575) 835-5819
Hydrogeologist **Lewis Land** . . . . . . . . . . . . . . . . . . . . . . (575) 887-5508
Senior Mineralogist/Economic Geologist/Museum
  Director **Virgil Lueth** . . . . . . . . . . . . . . . . . . . . . . . . . (575) 835-5140
Senior Volcanologist/Geochronologist
  **William "Bill" McIntosh** . . . . . . . . . . . . . . . . . . . . . . . (575) 835-5324
  E-mail: mcintosh@nmt.edu
Administrative Services Coordinator **Connie Apache** . . . . . (575) 835-5302

# EXPO New Mexico

State Fair Grounds, 300 San Pedro NE, Albuquerque, NM 87108
P.O. Box 8546, Albuquerque, NM 87198
Tel: (505) 222-9700  Fax: (505) 266-7784  E-mail: expo.info@state.nm.us
Internet: www.exponm.com

■General Manager **Dan Mourning** . . . . . . . . . . . . . . . . . . (505) 222-9714
  E-mail: dan.mourning@state.nm.us
■Deputy Manager **Erin Thompson** . . . . . . . . . . . . . . . . . . (505) 222-9700
■Senior Manager **Sally Mayer** . . . . . . . . . . . . . . . . . . . . (505) 222-9700
  E-mail: sally.mayer@state.nm.us
Chief Financial Officer **Bill Nordin** . . . . . . . . . . . . . . . . . (505) 222-9741
Media and Marketing Director **Erin Thompson** . . . . . . . . . (505) 222-9700
  E-mail: erin.thompson@state.nm.us
Media and Marketing Officer **Oona Gonzales** . . . . . . . . . . (505) 222-9700
  E-mail: oona.gonzales@state.nm.us
Operations Manager **Kenneth "Ken" Salazar** . . . . . . . . . . (505) 222-9741

# New Mexico National Guard [NMNG]

47 Bataan Boulevard, Santa Fe, NM 87508
Tel: (505) 474-1200  Fax: (505) 474-1289  Internet: www.nm.ngb.army.mil

**Employees: 139**

■Adjutant General **BrigGen Andrew E. Salas, ANG** . . . . . . (505) 474-1210
  E-mail: andrew.salas@osa.state.nm.us        Fax: (505) 474-1355
Deputy Adjutant General **(Vacant)** . . . . . . . . . . . . . . . . . (505) 474-1520
Chief of Staff **COL Kenneth Nava, ARNG** . . . . . . . . . . . . (505) 474-1203
State Command Sergeant-Major
  **SMA Gregory Ivey, ARNG** . . . . . . . . . . . . . . . . . . . . . (505) 474-1205

---

★ Elected Official    ■ Appointed by Governor    ● Appointed by Legislature    ▲ Appointed by Board or Commission    ◆ Appointed by State Supreme Court

Information Technology Supervisor
  **CSM Brenda L. Mallary, ARNG** . . . . . . . . . . . . . . . . . (505) 474-1200

# Workers' Compensation Administration

2410 Centre Avenue, SE, Albuquerque, NM 87106
P.O. Box 27198, Albuquerque, NM 87125-7198
Tel: (505) 841-6000  Tel: (866) 967-5667 (Hotline)  TTY: (505) 841-6043
Fax: (505) 841-6840  E-mail: wcamail@state.nm.us

**Employees: 123**

■Director **Darin A. Childers** . . . . . . . . . . . . . . . . . . . . . . . . . .(505) 841-6007
  E-mail: darina.childers@state.nm.us
  Education: BYU BA
  Executive Assistant **Sabrina Bludworth** . . . . . . . . . . . . . . (505) 841-6007
  General Counsel **Rachel Bayless** . . . . . . . . . . . . . . . . . . . . .(505) 841-6085
  Executive Deputy Director **Dana G. Chavez** . . . . . . . . . . (505) 841-6000
  External Operations Deputy Director **Thomas E. Dow** . . . . (505) 841-6818
  Internal Operations Deputy Director **Dana G. Chavez** . . . . .(505) 841-6056
  Economic Research Bureau Chief
    **Richard Adu-Asamoah** . . . . . . . . . . . . . . . . . . . . . . . . .(505) 841-6044
  Public Information Officer **Diana Sandoval-Tapia** . . . . . . . .(505) 841-6004

# Public Records Commission

State Records Ctr. & Archives, 1205 Camino Carlos Rey,
Santa Fe, NM 87507
Tel: (505) 476-7900  Fax: (505) 476-7901
Internet: www.nmcpr.state.nm.us

**Employees: 46**

▲State Records Administrator **Linda M. Trujillo** . . . . . . . . . . (505) 476-7912
  E-mail: lindam.trujillo@state.nm.us
  Education: Seattle JD

# Transportation Commission

P.O. Box 1149, Santa Fe, NM 87504-1149
Tel: (505) 827-5258  Fax: (505) 827-5469

■Commissioner **Jackson Gibson** (District 6) . . . . . . . . . . . . . (505) 827-5258
  E-mail: jackson.gibson@state.nm.us
■Commissioner **Butch Mathews** (District 5) . . . . . . . . . . . . . (505) 827-5258
  E-mail: butch.mathews@state.nm.us
■Commissioner **Keith Mortensen** (District 3) . . . . . . . . . . . . (505) 827-5258
  E-mail: raschmeits@bacavalley.com
■Commissioner **Ronald L. Schmeits** (District 4) . . . . . . . . . .(505) 827-5258
  E-mail: raschmeits@bacavalley.com
■Commissioner **David Sepich** (District 2) . . . . . . . . . . . . . . .(505) 827-5258
  E-mail: david.sepich@osa.state.nm.us
■Commissioner **Kenneth White** (District 1) . . . . . . . . . . . . . .(505) 827-5258
  E-mail: kenneth.white@osa.state.nm.us

# Transportation Department

P.O. Box 1149, Santa Fe, NM 87504-1149
Tel: (505) 827-5100

**Employees: 2,434  Fiscal Year: 2015  Budget: $889,588,000**

■Secretary **Tom Church** . . . . . . . . . . . . . . . . . . . . . . . . . . . . (505) 827-5110
  E-mail: tom.church@state.nm.us
  General Counsel (Acting) **Lauren Hatch** . . . . . . . . . . . . . . . (505) 827-5124
  E-mail: lauren.hatch@osa.state.nm.us
  Inspector General **Jeff Canney** . . . . . . . . . . . . . . . . . . . . . . (505) 476-0900
  E-mail: jeff.canney@state.nm.us
  Community Relations Director **(Vacant)** . . . . . . . . . . . . . . . (505) 827-5134
  Equal Opportunity Program Bureau Chief **(Vacant)** . . . . . . .(505) 827-1775

## Business Support Office

Deputy Secretary **Lauren Hatch** . . . . . . . . . . . . . . . . . . . . . (505) 827-5695
  E-mail: lauren.hatch@osa.state.nm.us
Chief Financial Officer **(Vacant)** . . . . . . . . . . . . . . . . . . . . . (505) 827-5108
General Services Management Bureau Chief
  **Richard G. Chavez** . . . . . . . . . . . . . . . . . . . . . . . . . . . . .(505) 827-5256
  E-mail: richard.chavez@state.nm.us
Human Resource Management Bureau Chief
  **Gilbert Archuleta** . . . . . . . . . . . . . . . . . . . . . . . . . . . . . .(505) 827-5207
Information Systems Bureau Chief **Eva Campos** . . . . . . . . .(505) 827-3270
  E-mail: eva.campos@osa.state.nm.us

Procurement Bureau Chief **Richard Martinez** . . . . . . . . . .(505) 827-5125

# Highway Operations

Deputy Secretary **Anthony Lujan** . . . . . . . . . . . . . . . . . . . .(505) 827-5124
District 1 Engineer **Trent Doolittle** . . . . . . . . . . . . . . . . . . .(575) 544-6530
  2912 East Pine, Deming, NM 88030
  E-mail: trent.doolittle@state.nm.us
District 2 Engineer **Timothy Parker** . . . . . . . . . . . . . . . . . .(575) 637-7200
  P.O. Box 1457, Roswell, NM 88202-1457
  E-mail: timothy.parker@state.nm.us
District 3 Engineer (Acting) **Timothy Parker** . . . . . . . . . . .(505) 841-2700
  P.O. Box 91750, Albuquerque, NM 87199-1750
District 4 Engineer **David E. Trujillo, PE** . . . . . . . . . . . . . .(505) 454-3625
  Old US 85 South Grand Avenue, Las Vegas, NM 87701-0030
  E-mail: david.trujillo@state.nm.us
District 5 Engineer (Acting) **Paul Brasher** . . . . . . . . . . . . .(505) 476-4200
  P.O. Box 4127, Santa Fe, NM 87502-4127
  E-mail: paul.brasher@state.nm.us
District 6 Engineer **Larry Maynard** . . . . . . . . . . . . . . . . . . .(505) 285-3200
  P.O. Box 2159, Milan, NM 87021
  E-mail: larry.maynard@state.nm.us

# Office of Programs and Infrastructure

Deputy Secretary (Acting) **Anthony Lujan** . . . . . . . . . . . . .(505) 827-5171
  E-mail: anthony.lujan1@state.nm.us

# Mortgage Finance Authority

344 Fourth Street, SW, Albuquerque, NM 87102
Tel: (505) 843-6880  TTY: (800) 444-6880  Fax: (505) 243-3289
Internet: www.housingnm.org

Executive Director **Jay Czar** . . . . . . . . . . . . . . . . . . . . . . . . .(505) 767-2223
Finance and Administration Deputy Director
  **Gina Hickman** . . . . . . . . . . . . . . . . . . . . . . . . . . . . . . . .(505) 843-6880
  E-mail: ghickman@housingnm.org
Program Deputy Director **Izzy Hernandez** . . . . . . . . . . . . . .(505) 767-2250
  E-mail: ihernandez@housingnm.org
Communications Manager **Leann Kemp** . . . . . . . . . . . . . . .(505) 767-2254
  E-mail: lkemp@housingnm.org
Senior Policy and Program Advisor **Monica Abeita** . . . . . . (505) 767-2252
  E-mail: mabeita@housingnm.org

# State Investment Council

41 Plaza la Prensa, Santa Fe, NM 87507
Fax: (505) 424-2510  Internet: www.sic.state.nm.us

**Employees: 32  Fiscal Year: 2015  Budget: $50,100,000**

Chair **Susana Martinez** . . . . . . . . . . . . . . . . . . . . . . . . . . . . .(505) 476-9500
  Affiliation: Governor, Office of the Governor, State of New Mexico
  State Capitol Building, 490 Old Santa Fe Trail, Room 400,
  Santa Fe, NM 87501
●Vice Chair **Peter Bruce Frank** . . . . . . . . . . . . . . . . . . . . . . .(505) 476-2200
  Term Expires: 2020                           Res: (505) 955-0718
  E-mail: peter.frank.wh65@wharton.upenn.edu
  Education: Pennsylvania BSE, MSA
■Public Member **Linda Eitzen** . . . . . . . . . . . . . . . . . . . . . . . .(505) 476-9500
  Term Expires: 2016
●Public Member **Timothy Z. Jennings** . . . . . . . . . . . . . . . . .(505) 476-9500
  Term Expires: 2018
  Education: New Mexico State BA, BS
●Public Member **Harold W. Lavender, Jr.** . . . . . . . . . . . . . . .(505) 476-9500
  Term Expires: 2018
  Education: New Mexico 1969 BA, 1975 JD
●Public Member **Leonard Lee Rawson** . . . . . . . . . . . . . . . . .(505) 476-9500
  Term Expires: 2017
  Education: New Mexico State 1979 BA
■Public Member **Scott Smart** . . . . . . . . . . . . . . . . . . . . . . . . .(505) 476-9500
  Term Expires: 2016
●Public Member **John Young** . . . . . . . . . . . . . . . . . . . . . . . . .(505) 476-9500
  Term Expires: 2014
●Public Member **(Vacant)** . . . . . . . . . . . . . . . . . . . . . . . . . . . .(505) 476-9500
  Ex-Officio Member **Tom Clifford** . . . . . . . . . . . . . . . . . . . . .(505) 476-9500
  Affiliation: Secretary, Department of Finance and Administration, State
  of New Mexico (Note: Until May 27, 2016.)
  180 Bataan Memorial Building, Santa Fe, NM 87501

*(continued on next page)*

---

★ Elected Official   ■ Appointed by Governor   ● Appointed by Legislature   ▲ Appointed by Board or Commission   ◆ Appointed by State Supreme Court

**State Investment Council** *continued*

Ex-Officio Member **Aubrey Dunn** . . . . . . . . . . . . . . . . . . . . (505) 476-9500
  Affiliation: Commissioner of Public Lands, New Mexico State Land
  Office, State of New Mexico
  310 Old Santa Fe Trail, Santa Fe, NM 87504
Ex-Officio Member **Tim Eichenberg** . . . . . . . . . . . . . . . . . (505) 476-9500
  Affiliation: Treasurer, Office of the State Treasurer, State of New
  Mexico
  2055 South Pacheco Street, Suite 100, Santa Fe, NM 87505

# Public Employees Retirement Association

33 Plaza la Prensa, Santa Fe, NM 87507
P.O. Box 2123, Santa Fe, NM 87504-2123
Tel: (505) 476-9309  Fax: (505) 476-9401  Internet: www.pera.state.nm.us

**Employees: 53  Fiscal Year: 2015  Budget: $43,532,000**

Board Chair **Patricia French** . . . . . . . . . . . . . . . . . . . . . (505) 480-1335
▲ Executive Director **Wayne Propst** . . . . . . . . . . . . . . . . . (505) 476-9301
  E-mail: wayne.propst@state.nm.us
  Executive Assistant **Judy Olson** . . . . . . . . . . . . . . . . . . (505) 476-9305
    E-mail: judy.olson@state.nm.us

# Office of the Secretary of State

New Mexico State Capitol, 325 Don Gaspar, Suite 300,
Santa Fe, NM 87503
Tel: (505) 827-3600  Fax: (505) 827-8081  E-mail: nmsos@state.nm.us

★ Secretary of State **Brad D. Winter** (R) . . . . . . . . . . . . . . . (505) 827-3628
  Term Expires: January 2017
  Education: Oklahoma BA; New Mexico DEd
Deputy Secretary of State **Mary Quintana** . . . . . . . . . . . . (505) 827-3600
Chief of Staff **Ken Ortiz** . . . . . . . . . . . . . . . . . . . . . . . (505) 827-3600
  Education: New Mexico State 1993
Administrative Officer **Trish Winter** . . . . . . . . . . . . . . . . (505) 827-3628
  E-mail: trish.winter@state.nm.us
Business Services Division Administrator **Ken Ortiz** . . . . . . (505) 827-3600
                                                            Fax: (505) 827-3611
Elections Bureau Director (Interim) **Kari Fresquez** . . . . . . . (505) 827-3600
                                                            Fax: (505) 827-8403
Chief Financial Officer **Veronica Albin** . . . . . . . . . . . . . . (505) 827-3600
Chief Information Officer **Kari Fresquez** . . . . . . . . . . . . . (505) 827-3600
  E-mail: kari.fresquez@state.nm.us
  Deputy Chief Information Officer **Blezoo Varghese** . . . . (505) 827-3600
    E-mail: blezoo.varghese@state.nm.us
Public Information Officer **Ken Ortiz** . . . . . . . . . . . . . . . (505) 827-3600
  E-mail: kenneth.ortiz@state.nm.us
Webmaster **Angel Espinoza** . . . . . . . . . . . . . . . . . . . . . (505) 827-3600

# Office of the Attorney General

Villagra Building, 408 Galisteo Street, Santa Fe, NM 87501
P.O. Drawer 1508, Santa Fe, NM 87504-1508
Tel: (505) 827-6000  Fax: (505) 827-5826

**Employees: 203  Fiscal Year: 2015  Budget: $30,224,000**

★ Attorney General **Hector H. Balderas, CFE** (D) . . . . . . . . . (575) 770-7995
  Term Expires: 2019
  Education: New Mexico Highlands; New Mexico JD
  Career: Representative, New Mexico House of Representatives; State
  Auditor (D-NM), Office of the State Auditor Hector Balderas, State of
  New Mexico (2007-2015)
Chief of Staff **Carla Martinez** . . . . . . . . . . . . . . . . . . . . (505) 827-6000
Budget Director **Valerie J. Borrego** . . . . . . . . . . . . . . . . . (505) 827-6000
Contracts and Grants Administrator **Marie Estrada** . . . . . . (505) 827-6000
  Grant Writer **Nick Eckert** . . . . . . . . . . . . . . . . . . . . . (505) 827-6000
Executive Services Director **Michelle Garrett** . . . . . . . . . . (505) 827-6000
  E-mail: mgarrett@nmag.gov
Financial Manager **Tammy Herrera** . . . . . . . . . . . . . . . . . (505) 827-6000
Human Resources Director **Valerie Gallegos** . . . . . . . . . . . (505) 827-6000
  Human Resources Manager **Carla Smith** . . . . . . . . . . . (505) 827-6000
Information Technology Director **Scott Stokes** . . . . . . . . . . (505) 827-6000
  E-mail: sstokes@nmag.gov

# Medicaid Fraud Control Unit

111 Lomas Avenue, NW, Suite 300, Albuquerque, NM 87102
Fax: (800) 525-6519
Director **Patricia Tucker** . . . . . . . . . . . . . . . . . . . . . . . . (505) 222-9000

# Office of the State Treasurer

2055 South Pacheco Street, Suite 100, Santa Fe, NM 87505
P.O. Box 5135, Santa Fe, NM 87504-0608
Tel: (505) 955-1120  Fax: (505) 955-1195

**Employees: 40  Fiscal Year: 2015  Budget: $3,911,000**

★ Treasurer **Tim Eichenberg** (D) . . . . . . . . . . . . . . . . . . . (505) 710-1305
  Term Expires: January 2019
Investment Accounting Bureau Chief **Charmaine Cook** . . . (505) 955-1120
CMIA Coordinator **Michael Romero** . . . . . . . . . . . . . . . . (505) 955-1120
Staff Manager **Dominic Chavez** . . . . . . . . . . . . . . . . . . . (505) 955-1144

# Office of the State Auditor

2540 Camino Edward Ortiz, Santa Fe, NM 87507
Tel: (505) 476-3800  Fax: (505) 827-3512

★ State Auditor **Timothy M. Keller** (D) . . . . . . . . . . . . . . . (505) 216-6466
  Term Expires: January 2019
  Career: State Senator (D-NM, District 17), New Mexico Senate
  (2009-2015)
Deputy State Auditor **Sanjay Bhakta, CPA, CGFM, CFE** . . (505) 476-3800
Chief of Staff **Sunalei Stewart** . . . . . . . . . . . . . . . . . . . (505) 476-3800
  Education: Arizona 1999 BA; American U 2003 MA;
  Washington College of Law 2003 JD
Chief Government Accountability Officer and General
  Counsel **Sarita Nair** . . . . . . . . . . . . . . . . . . . . . . . . . (505) 476-3800
  Education: Wesleyan U 1995 BA; New Mexico 2000 MCRP, 2003 JD
Government Accountability Officer **(Vacant)** . . . . . . . . . . . (505) 476-3821

# New Mexico State Land Office

310 Old Santa Fe Trail, Santa Fe, NM 87504
P.O. Box 1148, Santa Fe, NM 87504-1148
Tel: (505) 827-5760  TTY: (800) 659-8331  Fax: (505) 827-5766
Internet: www.nmstatelands.org

**Employees: 165  Fiscal Year: 2015  Budget: $15,124,000**

★ Commissioner of Public Lands **Aubrey Dunn** (R) . . . . . . . (505) 827-5760
  Term Expires: January 2019
  E-mail: aubrey.dunn@osa.state.nm.us
Deputy Commissioner **(Vacant)** . . . . . . . . . . . . . . . . . . . (505) 827-5866
Beneficiary Relations Assistant Commissioner
  **Christina Cordova** . . . . . . . . . . . . . . . . . . . . . . . . . . (505) 827-3809
  E-mail: ccordova@slo.state.nm.us
Communications Assistant Commissioner **Karin Stangl** . . . (505) 827-5739
  E-mail: kstangl@slo.state.nm.us
Special Projects Assistant Commissioner **Ralph Gallegos** . . (505) 827-5764
  E-mail: rgallegos@slo.state.nm.us
Surface Resources Assistant Commissioner **Mike Anaya** . . . (505) 827-5866
  E-mail: mike.anaya@osa.state.nm.us
General Counsel **Harry Relkin** . . . . . . . . . . . . . . . . . . . . (505) 827-5713
  E-mail: hrelkin@slo.state.nm.us

## Administrative Management

Tel: (505) 827-5700

Administration/Operations Assistant Commissioner
  **L. Elaine Olah** . . . . . . . . . . . . . . . . . . . . . . . . . . . . (505) 827-5703
  E-mail: eolah@slo.state.nm.us
Records Management Division Director **Lucille Sisneros** . . (505) 827-5716
Accounting Manager **Margaret Sena** . . . . . . . . . . . . . . . . (505) 827-5705
Facility Management Manager **Steve Trujillo** . . . . . . . . . . (505) 827-5799
Human Resources Manager **Sandra D. Lopez** . . . . . . . . . . (505) 827-5755

## Commercial Resources

Tel: (505) 827-5733

Assistant Commissioner **Don Britt** . . . . . . . . . . . . . . . . . (505) 827-3809
  E-mail: dbritt@slo.state.nm.us
Division Director **Craig Johnson** . . . . . . . . . . . . . . . . . . (505) 827-5733
  E-mail: cjohnson@slo.state.nm.us
  Education: New Mexico BA, MBA

---

★ Elected Official   ■ Appointed by Governor   ● Appointed by Legislature   ▲ Appointed by Board or Commission   ◆ Appointed by State Supreme Court

Renewable Energy Division Director **Tom Leatherwood** . . (505) 827-1252
  E-mail: tleatherwood@slo.state.nm.us
Economic Development Representative
  **William Consuegra** . . . . . . . . . . . . . . . . . . . . . . . . . . . . (505) 827-5733
  Education: Trinity U BA; New Mexico 2008 JD

## Field Operations

Assistant Field Commissioner **John T. Romero, PE** . . . . . . (505) 827-5768
  E-mail: John.romero2@state.nm.us
Field Division Director **Jim Norwick** . . . . . . . . . . . . . . . . . . (505) 827-5739
  E-mail: jnorwick@slo.state.nm.us

## Oil, Gas and Mineral Resources
Tel: (505) 827-5744

Assistant Commissioner **(Vacant)** . . . . . . . . . . . . . . . . . . . . . (505) 827-5735
Royalty Management Division Director **Kurt McFall** . . . . . . (505) 827-5735
  E-mail: kmcfall@slo.state.nm.us

## New Mexico Department of Agriculture [NMDA]
MSC 3189, Box 30005, Las Cruces, NM 88003-8005
Tel: (575) 646-3007  Fax: (575) 646-8120  Internet: www.nmda.nmsu.edu

▲Secretary **Jeff M. Witte** . . . . . . . . . . . . . . . . . . . . . . . . . . . (575) 646-5063
  E-mail: jwitte@nmda.nmsu.edu
  E-mail: nmagsec@nmda.nmsu.edu
  Education: New Mexico State 1984 BS, 1985 MS
  Assistant to the Secretary **Summer Feind** . . . . . . . . . . . . (575) 646-5063
Deputy Director **Anthony J. Parra** . . . . . . . . . . . . . . . . . (575) 646-3007
  Executive Secretary **Amanda Romero** . . . . . . . . . . . . . . (575) 646-3007
Public Information Specialist **Katie Goetz** . . . . . . . . . . . . . (575) 646-2804
  E-mail: kgoetz@nmda.nmsu.edu
Industry and Agency Programs Director
  **Larry J. Dominguez** . . . . . . . . . . . . . . . . . . . . . . . . . . . (575) 646-8955
  E-mail: ldominguez@nmda.nmsu.edu
  Education: New Mexico State 1983 BS, 1985 MA
Agricultural and Environmental Services Division
  Director **Bonnie M. Rabe** . . . . . . . . . . . . . . . . . . . . . . . (575) 646-2220
  Education: New Mexico State 1987 BS
Agricultural Biosecurity Director **Kelly Hamilton** . . . . . . . . (575) 646-7243
Agricultural Programs and Resources Division Director
  **Julie Maitland** . . . . . . . . . . . . . . . . . . . . . . . . . . . . . . . (575) 646-2642
  E-mail: jmaitland@nmda.nmsu.edu
  Education: New Mexico State 1996 BA, 1998 MA
Dairy Division Director **Alfred Reeb** . . . . . . . . . . . . . . . . . (505) 841-9425
  Education: Penn State 1974 BS; New Mexico 2002 MA
Legislative Affairs Director **Jeff M. Witte** . . . . . . . . . . . . . (575) 646-5063
  E-mail: jwitte@nmda.nmsu.edu
Marketing and Development Division Director
  **David Lucero** . . . . . . . . . . . . . . . . . . . . . . . . . . . . . . . . (575) 646-4929
  Education: New Mexico State 1986 BS
Standards and Consumer Services Division Director
  **Joe E. Gomez** . . . . . . . . . . . . . . . . . . . . . . . . . . . . . . . . (575) 646-1616
  Education: New Mexico State 1983 BS, 1997 MA
Veterinarian Diagnostic Services Division Director
  **Dr. Tim Hanosh, DVM** . . . . . . . . . . . . . . . . . . . . . . . . . (505) 383-9299
  P.O. Box 4700, Albuquerque, NM 87196-4700

## New Mexico Public Regulation Commission [PRC]
1120 Paseo De Peralta, Santa Fe, NM 87501
P.O. Drawer 1269, Santa Fe, NM 87504-1269
Tel: (505) 827-4500  Internet: www.nmprc.state.nm.us

**Employees:** 162  **Fiscal Year:** 2015  **Budget:** $21,413,000

★Chair **Valerie L. Espinoza** (D-District 3) . . . . . . . . . . . . . (505) 827-4500
  Term Expires: January 1, 2017
  Education: Col Santa Fe 1997 BA
★Vice Chair **Karen Louise Montoya** (D-District 1) . . . . . . . (505) 827-4500
  Term Expires: January 1, 2017
★Commissioner **Sandy Jones** (D-District 5) . . . . . . . . . . . (505) 827-8020
  Term Expires: January 1, 2019

★Commissioner **Lynda M. Lovejoy** (D-District 4) . . . . . . . . (505) 827-4533
  Term Expires: January 1, 2019
  Education: Northern Arizona
★Commissioner **Patrick H. Lyons** (R-District 2) . . . . . . . . . . (505) 827-4531
  Term Expires: January 1, 2019
  Education: New Mexico State 1975 BS; Colorado State 1977 MS

---

★ Elected Official   ■ Appointed by Governor   ● Appointed by Legislature   ▲ Appointed by Board or Commission   ◆ Appointed by State Supreme Court

# New York

Tel: (518) 474-8390   Internet: www.ny.gov

**Number of U.S. Congressional Delegates:** 2 Senators; 27 Representatives **Governor's Term:** 4 years
**Legislature Description:** 63 member Senate; 150 member Assembly; Term -Senate 2 years,
Assembly 2 years **Next Election:** Governor November 2018; Legislature November 2016
**Number of Electoral Votes:** 29 **Official Name:** State of New York (after Duke of York, later James II)
**Nickname:** The Empire State **Motto:** Excelsior (Ever Upward)

**Population:** 19,795,791 (2015); Rank 4 **Fiscal Year:** 2014 **Budget:** $137,526,000,000

## Office of the Governor

State Capitol, Albany, NY 12224
Tel: (518) 474-8390

**Employees:** 136

**Andrew Mark Cuomo**
Governor

Began Service: January 1, 2011
Term Expires: January 2019
Date of Birth: December 6, 1957
Education: Fordham 1979 BA;
Albany Law 1982 JD
Home: Adirondack
Religion: Catholic
Career: Secretary, United States Department of
Housing and Urban Development, William
J. Clinton Administration (1997-2001);
Senior Executive, Island Capital Group LLC
(2003-2006); Attorney General (D-NY), Office of
Attorney General Andrew Cuomo, Department of
Law, State of New York (2007-2010)

★ Governor **Andrew Mark Cuomo** (D) . . . . . . . . . . . . . . . . . (518) 474-8390
Secretary to the Governor **William J. "Bill" Mulrow** . . . . . (518) 474-4246
   E-mail: bill.mulrow@exec.ny.gov
   Education: Yale BA; Harvard MPA
Counselor to the Governor **Linda A. Lacewell** . . . . . . . . . . . (518) 474-4623
   E-mail: linda.lacewell@exec.ny.gov
   Education: New Col South Florida BA; Miami 1988 JD
Executive Deputy Secretary to the Governor **(Vacant)** . . . . . (518) 486-3940
Chief of Staff **Melissa DeRosa** . . . . . . . . . . . . . . . . . . . . . . (518) 474-8390
   E-mail: melissa.derosa@exec.ny.gov
   Education: Cornell 2004 BS, 2009 MPA
Senior Policy Advisor for Economic Development
   **Tamara Dews** . . . . . . . . . . . . . . . . . . . . . . . . . . . . . . . (518) 474-8390
   E-mail: tamara.dews@exec.ny.gov
   Education: Mount Holyoke BA
Senior Policy Advisor for Labor and Workforce
   **Sherry Hwang Rodriguez** . . . . . . . . . . . . . . . . . . . . . . (518) 474-8390
   Education: Ohio State BS; Fordham JD
Education Policy Advisor **Daniel Fuller** . . . . . . . . . . . . . . . (518) 474-8390
   E-mail: daniel.fuller@exec.ny.gov
Special Advisor **Christine C. "Chris" Quinn** . . . . . . . . . . . (212) 681-4580
   Education: Trinity Col (CT) 1988 BA
Special Counselor for Interagency Initiatives
   **Richard "Rick" Cotton** . . . . . . . . . . . . . . . . . . . . . . . (518) 474-8494
   Education: Harvard 1965 AB; Yale 1969 LLB
Director of Policy **John Maggiore** . . . . . . . . . . . . . . . . . . . (518) 408-2576
   E-mail: john.maggiore@exec.ny.gov
   Education: Connecticut Col BA; Rutgers MA; JFK School Govt MPA
   Deputy Director of Policy **Barbara Williams** . . . . . . . . . . (518) 474-8390
   E-mail: barbara.williams@exec.ny.gov
Director of State Operations **James J. "Jim" Malatras** . . . (518) 486-9871
   Education: SUNY (Albany) BA, 2000 MA, 2008 PhD
   Deputy Director of State Operations for Administration
   **Matthew J. Millea** . . . . . . . . . . . . . . . . . . . . . . . . . . . (518) 474-8390
   E-mail: matthew.millea@exec.ny.gov
   Education: Siena Col BA; Columbia MPA

Deputy Director of State Operations for Policy
   **Andrew S. Kennedy** . . . . . . . . . . . . . . . . . . . . . . . . . . (518) 474-3478
   Note: On March 31, 2016, Andrew Kennedy was appointed President
   and Chief Executive Officer of the Center for Economic Growth,
   effective July 1, 2016. Mr. Kennedy's departure date from the Office
   of Governor Andrew Cuomo has not yet been determined.
   E-mail: andrew.kennedy@exec.ny.gov
   Education: Siena Col; SUNY (Albany) MPA
Deputy Director of State Operations for Programs
   **Joseph Rabito** . . . . . . . . . . . . . . . . . . . . . . . . . . . . . . (518) 474-8390
Agriculture and Markets Deputy Secretary
   **Patrick Hooker** . . . . . . . . . . . . . . . . . . . . . . . . . . . . . . (518) 486-9896
   E-mail: patrick.hooker@exec.ny.gov
   Agriculture and Markets Assistant Secretary **Liz Harris** . . (518) 486-9896
Civil Rights Deputy Secretary **Norma Ramos** . . . . . . . . . . (518) 474-8390
   E-mail: norma.ramos@exec.ny.gov
   Education: Fordham BA; Temple JD
Education Deputy Secretary **Jere Hochman** . . . . . . . . . . . . (518) 474-9883
   E-mail: jere.hochman@exec.ny.gov
   Education: Columbia BA, MEd, EdD
   Education Assistant Secretary **Jamie Frank** . . . . . . . . . . . (518) 474-9883
   E-mail: jamie.frank@exec.ny.gov
   Education: Rochester BA; Cornell MPA
Environment Deputy Secretary **(Vacant)** . . . . . . . . . . . . . . (518) 408-2552
   Environment Assistant Secretary **Kate Dineen** . . . . . . . . . (518) 408-2552
   E-mail: kate.dineen@exec.ny.gov
   Environment Assistant Secretary
   **Brenda Torres Barreto** . . . . . . . . . . . . . . . . . . . . . . . (518) 408-2552
   Education: Puerto Rico BS
   Environment Assistant Secretary **Peter Walke** . . . . . . . . . (518) 408-2552
   Education: Williams BA; Colorado (Colo Springs) MA
Energy Assistant Secretary **Kara M. Allen** . . . . . . . . . . . . (518) 474-8390
   E-mail: kara.allen@exec.ny.gov
   Education: Vanderbilt BS; Johns Hopkins MS
General Government and Financial Services Deputy
   Secretary **Brendan Fitzgerald** . . . . . . . . . . . . . . . . . . . (518) 408-2922
   E-mail: brendan.fitzgerald@exec.ny.gov
Health and Human Services Deputy Secretary
   **Paul E. Francis** . . . . . . . . . . . . . . . . . . . . . . . . . . . . . . (518) 408-2500
   E-mail: paul.francis@exec.ny.gov
   Education: Yale 1977 BA; NYU 1980 JD
   Health Assistant Secretary **Tracie M. Gardner** . . . . . . . . . (518) 408-2500
   E-mail: tracie.gardner@exec.ny.gov
   Education: Mount Holyoke BA
Labor Deputy Secretary **Elizabeth de Leon Bhargava** . . . . (518) 474-8390
   Education: SUNY (Binghamton) BA; SUNY Col (Buffalo) JD
Public Safety Deputy Secretary
   **Terence "Terry" O'Leary** . . . . . . . . . . . . . . . . . . . . . . (518) 474-8390
   Education: Loyola U (Maryland) BA; Seton Hall JD
Chief Digital Officer and Technology Deputy Secretary
   **(Vacant)** . . . . . . . . . . . . . . . . . . . . . . . . . . . . . . . . . . (518) 474-8390
Transportation Deputy Secretary **Ron Thaniel** . . . . . . . . . . (518) 408-2555
   Education: Morgan State BA; Hamline MPA
   Transportation Assistant Secretary **Sharif Kabir** . . . . . . . . (518) 474-0846
   E-mail: sharif.kabir@exec.ny.gov
   Education: Florida Atlantic BA; American U JD
Energy Policy and Finance Sub-Cabinet Chair
   **Richard L. Kauffman** . . . . . . . . . . . . . . . . . . . . . . . . . . (518) 474-8390
   E-mail: richard.kauffman@exec.ny.gov
   Education: Stanford 1979 BA; Yale 1983 MA

---

★ Elected Official    ■ Appointed by Governor    ● Appointed by Legislature    ▲ Appointed by Board or Commission    ◆ Appointed by State Supreme Court

Agency Redesign and Efficiency Deputy Director
**Derek Utter** . . . . . . . . . . . . . . . . . . . . . . . . . . . . . . .(212) 681-4580
Director of Constituency Affairs **David Contreras Turley** . .(518) 474-8390
E-mail: david.turley@exec.ny.gov
Deputy Director of Constituency Affairs
**Julissa Gutierrez, Esq.** . . . . . . . . . . . . . . . . . . . . . . . (518) 474-8390
E-mail: julissa.gutierrez@exec.ny.gov
Education: Delaware BA; Chicago MA
Assistant Director of Constituencies for Asian
American Affairs **Joanne Choi** . . . . . . . . . . . . . . . . . . (518) 474-8390
E-mail: joanne.choi@exec.ny.gov
Education: SUNY (Stony Brook) BA, MA
Director of Latino Affairs **Melissa R. Quesada** . . . . . . . . .(518) 474-8390
E-mail: melissa.quesada@exec.ny.gov
Education: SUNY (Binghamton) BA; Hofstra JD
Director of Legislative Affairs **(Vacant)** . . . . . . . . . . . . . . (518) 474-8337
Deputy Director of Legislative Affairs **Leslea Snyder** . . . (518) 474-8390
E-mail: leslea.snyder@exec.ny.gov
Director of Scheduling **Andrew Ball** . . . . . . . . . . . . . . . . (518) 474-8390
E-mail: andrew.ball@exec.ny.gov
Chief Diversity Officer **Rose Rodriguez** . . . . . . . . . . . . . .(212) 681-4580
Chief Risk Officer **Linda A. Lacewell** . . . . . . . . . . . . . . (518) 474-4623
E-mail: linda.lacewell@exec.ny.gov
Confidential Assistant to the Governor and Director of
Public Engagement **Quinn L. Staudt** . . . . . . . . . . . . . . (518) 474-8390
E-mail: quinn.staudt@exec.ny.gov
Special Assistant for Legislative Affairs
**Matthew Pennello** . . . . . . . . . . . . . . . . . . . . . . . . . . (518) 474-8390
E-mail: matthew.pennello@exec.ny.gov

## Office of Communications

Tel: (518) 474-8418

Director of Communications **James Allen** . . . . . . . . . . . . .(212) 681-4640
Education: SUNY (Albany) BA
Senior Deputy Communications Director
**Rich Azzopardi** . . . . . . . . . . . . . . . . . . . . . . . . . . . .(518) 474-8418

## Office of Counsel to the Governor

Counsel to the Governor **Alphonso B. David** . . . . . . . . . . .(518) 474-8343
E-mail: alphonso.david@exec.ny.gov
Education: Temple 2000 JD
First Assistant Counsel to the Governor **Sandi Toll** . . . . . . (518) 474-8434
E-mail: sandi.toll@exec.ny.gov
Education: Cornell BS; Loyola U (Chicago) JD

## Office of Intergovernmental Affairs

633 Third Avenue, New York, NY 10017

Deputy Secretary for Executive Operations
**Jill DesRosiers** . . . . . . . . . . . . . . . . . . . . . . . . . . . . .(518) 474-8390
Deputy Secretary for Legislative Affairs **Mark S. Weprin** . .(212) 681-4622
Education: SUNY (Albany) 1983 BA; Brooklyn Law 1992 JD
Assistant Secretary for Legislative Affairs
**Josh Rousseau** . . . . . . . . . . . . . . . . . . . . . . . . . . . . .(518) 474-8390
Education: SUNY (Plattsburgh) BS
Director of Intergovernmental Affairs **(Vacant)** . . . . . . . . .(518) 486-3940

## New York City Office

633 Third Avenue, New York, NY 10017
Tel: (212) 681-4580 Tel: (212) 681-4640 (Press Office)

■Community Affairs Director **(Vacant)** . . . . . . . . . . . . . . . .(212) 681-4622

## Washington Office

444 North Capitol Street, NW, Suite 301, Washington, DC 20001
Tel: (202) 434-7100 Fax: (202) 434-7110

■Director **Alexander Cochran** . . . . . . . . . . . . . . . . . . . . . .(202) 434-7100
E-mail: alexander.cochran@ny.gov
Education: Georgia JD

## Office of the Lieutenant Governor

State Capitol, Albany, NY 12224
Tel: (518) 402-2292

★Lieutenant Governor
**Kathleen Courtney "Kathy" Hochul** (D) . . . . . . . . . . . .(518) 402-2292
Term Expires: 2019
E-mail: kathy.hochul@ny.gov
Education: Syracuse 1980 BA; Columbus Law 1983 JD
Career: Councilwoman, Hamburg Town Board, Town of Hamburg, New
York (1994-2007); County Clerk, Office of the County Clerk, County
of Erie, New York (2007-2011); U.S. Representative (D-NY, District
26), Office of Representative Kathy Hochul, United States House of
Representatives (2011-2013)
Chief of Staff and Counsel **Jeff Pearlman** . . . . . . . . . . . . .(518) 402-2292
Education: SUNY (New Paltz) BA; Albany Law JD
Press Secretary **Chris White** . . . . . . . . . . . . . . . . . . . . . .(518) 402-2292

## New York State Department of State

One Commerce Plaza, 99 Washington Avenue, Albany, NY 12231-0001
Tel: (518) 474-4752 TTY: (518) 474-4203 Fax: (518) 474-4765
E-mail: info@dos.ny.gov

**Employees:** 515

■Secretary of State (Acting) **Rossana Rosado** . . . . . . . . . . .(518) 474-0050
Note: On February 3, 2016, Governor Andrew Cuomo nominated
Rossana Rosado to serve as Secretary of State. Rosado's nomination
must be confirmed by the New York State Senate. Rosado is currently
acting in this position.
Special Assistant **Helen Wilbard** . . . . . . . . . . . . . . . . . .(518) 474-0050
Special Counsel for Ethics, Risk and Compliance
**Matt Fernandez Konigsberg** . . . . . . . . . . . . . . . . . . .(518) 474-4752
Education: Wisconsin 2002 BA; Rutgers (Newark) 2007 JD
Executive Deputy Secretary of State **Tony Giardina** . . . . . .(518) 474-0050
Deputy Secretary of State for Business and Licensing
**Charles Fields** . . . . . . . . . . . . . . . . . . . . . . . . . . . . .(518) 473-2728
Deputy Secretary of State for Economic Opportunity
**Jorge Montalvo** . . . . . . . . . . . . . . . . . . . . . . . . . . . .(518) 474-0050
■Deputy Secretary of State for Local Government Services
**Dierdre K. "Dede" Scozzafava** . . . . . . . . . . . . . . . . . .(518) 473-3355
E-mail: localgov@dos.ny.gov
Education: Boston U 1982 BS; Clarkson U 1983 MBA
General Counsel **Linda Baldwin** . . . . . . . . . . . . . . . . . . . .(518) 474-6740
Public Information Officer **Laz Benitez** . . . . . . . . . . . . . . .(518) 474-4752
E-mail: laz.benitez@dos.ny.gov        Fax: (518) 474-4765
Cemeteries Division Director **Lewis Polishook** . . . . . . . . . .(212) 417-5713
123 William Street, New York, NY 10038-3804
Planning and Development Division Director
**Sandi Allen** . . . . . . . . . . . . . . . . . . . . . . . . . . . . . . .(518) 474-6000
Community Services Division Director **Veronica Cruz** . . . .(518) 474-5741
Corporations and State Records Division Director
**Sandra Tallman** . . . . . . . . . . . . . . . . . . . . . . . . . . . .(518) 473-2281
Uniform Commercial Code Division Director
**Sandra Tallman** . . . . . . . . . . . . . . . . . . . . . . . . . . . .(518) 473-2281
Administrative Rules Division Manager
**Maribeth St. Germain** . . . . . . . . . . . . . . . . . . . . . . . . .(518) 474-6957

## Administration and Management

Director **Judith Kenny** . . . . . . . . . . . . . . . . . . . . . . . . . . .(518) 474-0050
E-mail: judith.kenny@dos.ny.gov
Administrative Support Services Director
**Pamela Christopher** . . . . . . . . . . . . . . . . . . . . . . . . . .(518) 473-8221
E-mail: pamela.christopher@dos.ny.gov
Fiscal Management Director **LuAnn Hart** . . . . . . . . . . . . . .(518) 474-2754
Human Resource Management Director **Philip Kelly** . . . . . .(518) 474-2752
Affirmative Action Officer **Maria Herman** . . . . . . . . . . . . .(518) 474-6740
E-mail: maria.herman@dos.ny.gov

## Division of Consumer Protection

One Commerce Plaza, 99 Washington Avenue, Suite 640,
Albany, NY 12231-0001
Tel: (518) 474-8583 Tel: (800) 697-1220 Fax: (518) 486-3936
Division Director **Aiesha L. Battle** . . . . . . . . . . . . . . . . . . .(518) 474-2363

---

★ Elected Official   ■ Appointed by Governor   ● Appointed by Legislature   ▲ Appointed by Board or Commission   ◆ Appointed by State Supreme Court

# Office of the State Inspector General

Agency Building Two, Empire State Plaza, 16th Floor, Albany, NY 12203
Tel: (518) 474-1010  Fax: (518) 486-3745

■Inspector General **Catherine Leahy-Scott** . . . . . . . . . . . . . (212) 635-3150
    E-mail: inspector.general@ig.state.ny.us
    Education: Hofstra BA, 1988 JD
Executive Deputy Inspector General
    **Spencer B. Freedman** . . . . . . . . . . . . . . . . . . . . . . . . (518) 474-1010
Investigations Deputy Inspector General
    **Bernanrd Cosenza** . . . . . . . . . . . . . . . . . . . . . . . . . (212) 635-3150
Legal Deputy Inspector General **Jim Davis** . . . . . . . . . . . . (518) 474-1010
Legal Deputy Inspector General **Philip Foglia** . . . . . . . . . . (212) 635-3150
    Education: Pace 1980 JD
Chief of Staff and Counselor **Michael Clarke** . . . . . . . . . . . (212) 635-3150
    Education: Fordham 1985 BA; St John's U (NY) 1988 JD
Communications Director **John Milgrim** . . . . . . . . . . . . . . (518) 474-1010
    E-mail: john.milgrim@ig.ny.gov

# Office of the Medicaid Inspector General [OMIG]

800 North Pearl Street, 2nd Floor, Albany, NY 12204
Tel: (518) 473-3782  Fax: (518) 474-6773
E-mail: information@omig.ny.gov

■Medicaid Inspector General **Dennis Rosen** . . . . . . . . . . . . (518) 473-3782
    E-mail: dennis.rosen@omig.ny.gov
    Education: Brooklyn BA; Harvard 1972 JD
First Deputy Medicaid Inspector General
    **Thomas R. Meyer** . . . . . . . . . . . . . . . . . . . . . . . . . . (518) 473-3782
Executive Assistant **Diana Neeley** . . . . . . . . . . . . . . . . . . (518) 473-3782

# Department of Agriculture and Markets [NYSDAM]

10-B Airline Drive, Albany, NY 12235
Tel: (800) 554-4501  TTY: (518) 485-7784  Fax: (518) 457-3087
E-mail: info@agriculture.ny.gov

**Employees:** 511

■Commissioner **Richard A. Ball** . . . . . . . . . . . . . . . . . . . . (518) 457-8876
    E-mail: richard.ball@agriculture.ny.gov
    Secretary to the Commissioner **Laurie Levine** . . . . . . . . (518) 457-8876
First Deputy Commissioner **Jen McCormick** . . . . . . . . . . . (518) 457-2771
    Education: SUNY (Empire State) 1991 BA;
    SUNY (Albany) 2006 MPA
Deputy Commissioner **Phil Giltner** . . . . . . . . . . . . . . . . . (518) 457-2771
Deputy Commissioner **Maria Knirk** . . . . . . . . . . . . . . . . . (518) 457-2771
    Education: Ferris State MBA; Michigan State JD
Deputy Commissioner **Jackie Czub** . . . . . . . . . . . . . . . . . (518) 485-7728
    Education: Wesley Col (DE) BS
General Counsel **Scott Wyner** . . . . . . . . . . . . . . . . . . . . (518) 457-1059
    Education: Colgate BA; Michigan MA; Georgetown JD
Internal Control Officer **Joe Morrissey** . . . . . . . . . . . . . . . (518) 457-2771
Public Information Director **Jola Szubielski** . . . . . . . . . . . (518) 485-7728
    E-mail: jola.szubielski@agriculture.ny.gov
Director of Communications **(Vacant)** . . . . . . . . . . . . . . . . (518) 457-0889
Director of Intergovernmental Affairs **Geoff Palmer** . . . . . . (518) 457-2771
    E-mail: geoff.palmer@agriculture.ny.gov
Emergency Management Coordinator **Kelly Nilsson** . . . . . . (518) 457-2771

## Administration Programs

Fiscal Management Director **Lisa Brooks** . . . . . . . . . . . . . . (518) 457-2080
Human Resources Director **Mark Vanderpoel** . . . . . . . . . . (518) 457-3216
Information Systems Director **(Vacant)** . . . . . . . . . . . . . . . (518) 457-7368

## Animal and Dairy Services Program

Animal Industry Division Director **Dr. David Smith** . . . . . . (518) 457-3502
Dairy Services Division Director **Casey McCue** . . . . . . . . . (518) 457-1772
Milk Control Division Director **Casey McCue** . . . . . . . . . . (518) 457-1772

## Food Industry Services Program

Food Safety and Inspection Director **Stephen Stich** . . . . . . (518) 457-4492
    E-mail: stephen.stich@agriculture.ny.gov
    Education: SUNY (Morrisville)

---

Food Laboratory Director **Dr. Maria L. Ishida** . . . . . . . . . . (518) 457-4477
    E-mail: maria.ishida@agriculture.ny.gov

# Natural Resources and Environmental Programs

Agriculture Development Division Director **Kevin King** . . . (518) 457-7076
    E-mail: kevin.king@agriculture.ny.gov
Land and Water Resources Division Director
    **Michael Latham** . . . . . . . . . . . . . . . . . . . . . . . . . . . (518) 457-3738
                                                        Fax: (518) 457-3412
Plant Industry Division Director **Christopher Logue** . . . . . (518) 457-2087
    E-mail: christopher.logue@agriculture.ny.gov      Fax: (518) 457-1204
Weights and Measures Division Director **Mike Sikula** . . . . . (518) 457-3146
                                                        Fax: (518) 457-2552

# New York City Office

55 Hanson Place, 3rd Floor, Brooklyn, NY 11217
Fax: (718) 722-2836

Chief of Staff **Challey Comer** . . . . . . . . . . . . . . . . . . . . . (718) 722-2668
Food Inspection Chief **Robert Dondorf** . . . . . . . . . . . . . . (718) 722-2838
Kosher Law Enforcement Unit Director
    **Rabbi Aaron Metzger** . . . . . . . . . . . . . . . . . . . . . . . . (718) 722-2852

# Department of Civil Service

Empire State Plaza, Agency Building One, One Swan Street, (Core 1),
Albany, NY 12239
Tel: (518) 457-9375  Fax: (518) 473-2372  E-mail: pio@cs.state.ny.us

**Employees:** 408  **Fiscal Year:** 2014  **Budget:** $50,420,000

■President and Commissioner **(Vacant)** . . . . . . . . . . . . . . . (518) 457-3701
    Secretary to the Commissioner **Carol Light** . . . . . . . . . . (518) 473-5698
Executive Deputy Commissioner **Lola W. Brabham** . . . . . . (518) 473-5698
    Education: SUNY (Albany) BA, MPA
Administration Deputy Commissioner **Deirdre Taylor** . . . . . (518) 473-5694
    E-mail: deirdre.taylor@cs.state.ny.us
Operations Deputy Commissioner (Acting)
    **Deirdre Taylor** . . . . . . . . . . . . . . . . . . . . . . . . . . . . (518) 473-5694
General Counsel **Ilene Lees** . . . . . . . . . . . . . . . . . . . . . . (518) 473-2624
Commission Operations and Municipal Assistance
    **(Vacant)** . . . . . . . . . . . . . . . . . . . . . . . . . . . . . . . . (518) 473-6598
Financial Services Director (Acting) **Deirdre Taylor** . . . . . . (518) 473-5694
Internal Audit Director (Acting) **Deirdre Taylor** . . . . . . . . . (518) 473-5694
Public Information Director **Edward Walsh** . . . . . . . . . . . . (518) 457-9375
    E-mail: pio@cs.state.ny.us
Testing Services Director **Marcia Dudden** . . . . . . . . . . . . . (518) 486-4590
Workforce and Occupational Planning Director (Acting)
    **Deirdre Taylor** . . . . . . . . . . . . . . . . . . . . . . . . . . . . (518) 473-6411
                                                        Fax: (518) 473-5696
Classification and Compensation Division Director
    **Abner Jean-Pierre** . . . . . . . . . . . . . . . . . . . . . . . . . (518) 474-1011
                                                        Fax: (518) 474-0787
Affirmative Action Officer **(Vacant)** . . . . . . . . . . . . . . . . . (518) 473-2467
Employee Benefits Division Director **David J. Boland** . . . . (518) 473-1977
Employee Health Service Division Director
    **Maria C. Steinbach** . . . . . . . . . . . . . . . . . . . . . . . . . (518) 233-3112
    Education: SUNY (Albany) 1979 BS; Rensselaer Poly 1982 MBA
Information Resource Management Division Director
    **Frank Slade** . . . . . . . . . . . . . . . . . . . . . . . . . . . . . . (518) 473-7516
    E-mail: frank.slade@cs.state.ny.us
    Education: SUNY (Albany) 1981 BS, 1986 MBA
Staffing Services Division Director **Scott A. DeFruscio** . . . (518) 473-6437

# Department of Corrections and Community Supervision [DOCCS]

State Office Bldg. 2, 1220 Washington Avenue, Albany, NY 12226
97 Central Avenue, Albany, NY 12206
Tel: (518) 457-8126  Fax: (518) 457-7070

**Employees:** 29,000

■Commissioner (Acting) **Anthony J. Annucci** . . . . . . . . . . . (518) 457-8134
    E-mail: anthony.annucci@doccs.ny.gov
    Executive Assistant **(Vacant)** . . . . . . . . . . . . . . . . . . . (518) 457-1281
Deputy Commissioner and Counsel **Kevin Bruen** . . . . . . . (518) 457-4951
    E-mail: kevin.bruen@doccs.ny.gov

---

★ Elected Official    ■ Appointed by Governor    ● Appointed by Legislature    ▲ Appointed by Board or Commission    ◆ Appointed by State Supreme Court

Administrative Services Deputy Commissioner
**Daniel Martuscello III**............................(518) 457-8188
  E-mail: daniel.martuscello@doccs.ny.gov
Community Supervision Deputy Commissioner **(Vacant)** .. (518) 457-2540
Correctional Facilities Deputy Commissioner
**Joseph Bellnier**...................................(518) 457-8138
Correctional Industries and Accreditation Deputy
Commissioner **Osbourne A. McKay** .................(518) 485-2858
Health Services Deputy Commissioner and Chief Medical
Officer **Carl Koenigsmann**........................(518) 457-7072
Program Services Deputy Commissioner **Jeff McKoy** ..... (518) 457-5555
  E-mail: mckoy@doccs.ny.gov
Population Management Associate Commissioner
**Ann Marie McGrath**...............................(518) 457-7261
Sexual Abuse Prevention and Education Associate
Commissioner **Jason Effman**.......................(518) 457-4951
Associate Commissioner **Robert Kennedy**.............(518) 457-8126
Director of Public Information **Thomas Mailey**.........(518) 457-8182
  E-mail: thomas.mailey@doccs.ny.gov

# Department of Environmental Conservation [DEC]

625 Broadway, Albany, NY 12233-1010
Tel: (518) 402-8545  Fax: (518) 402-8541  Internet: www.dec.ny.gov

**Employees:** 3,003

■Commissioner (Acting) **Basil Seggos**..................(518) 402-8545
  Education: Trinity Col (CT) 1996; Pace 2001 JD
Executive Deputy Commissioner **Kenneth P. Lynch** ...... (518) 402-8560
  E-mail: kplynch@gw.dec.state.ny.us    Fax: (518) 402-9018
  Education: Yale 1984 BA; Syracuse 1988 JD
Special Assistant **(Vacant)** .........................(518) 402-8560
Assistant Secretary of Public Affairs **Emily DeSantis** ..... (518) 402-8560

## Office of Administration
Deputy Commissioner **Jeffrey Stefanko**................(518) 402-9401
  Education: Syracuse
Management and Budget Division Director
**Nancy Lussier**...................................(518) 402-9228
Operations Division Director **Mark Malinoski**..........(518) 402-9055
Office of Communication Services Director
**Harold Evans**....................................(518) 402-8046

## Office of Air Resources, Climate Change and Energy
Deputy Commissioner **Jared Snyder** ..................(518) 402-8549
Air Resources Division Director (Acting) **Steve Flint** ..... (518) 402-8452
Climate Change Office Director (Acting) **Lois New** ...... (518) 402-8448

## Office of Environmental Justice
Tel: (718) 482-4900  Fax: (518) 402-9018  E-mail: ej@gw.dec.state.ny.us
Director (Acting) **Lisa King** .........................(518) 402-8556

## Office of Natural Resources
Deputy Commissioner **Kathy Moser**...................(518) 402-8533
Fish, Wildlife and Marine Resources Division Director
**Patricia Riexinger**................................(518) 402-8924
Lands and Forests Division Director **Robert Davies** ...... (518) 402-9405

## Office of Public Protection and Regional Affairs
Fax: (518) 402-9016
Assistant Commissioner **Christian Ballantyne**..........(518) 402-8549
Environmental Permits Division Director **Jack Nasca** ..... (518) 402-9182
Forest Protection Division Director (Acting) **Eric Lahr** .... (518) 402-8839
Law Enforcement Division Director
**Joseph H. Schneider**.............................(518) 402-8829
Region 1 Regional Director **Carrie Meek Gallagher**......(631) 444-0345
  SUNY Stony Brook Campus, 50 Circle Road,   Fax: (631) 444-0349
  Building 40, Stony Brook, NY 11790-2356
  Education: Amherst BA; Maryland MS; Hofstra MBA
Region 2 Regional Director (Acting) **Steven Zahn** ....... (718) 482-4949
  One Hunter's Point Plaza, 47-40 - 21st Street,   Fax: (718) 482-4026
  Long Island City, NY 11101-5407

Region 3 Regional Director **Martin Brand**.............(845) 256-3033
  21 South Putt Corners Road, New Paltz, NY 12561   Fax: (845) 255-3042
Region 4 Regional Director **Keith Goertz** .............(518) 357-2068
  1130 North Westcott Road,   Fax: (518) 357-2398
  Schenectady, NY 12306-2014
Region 5 Regional Director **Robert Stegemann** ........(518) 897-1211
  Rt. 86, P.O. Box 296, Ray Brook, NY 12977-0296   Fax: (518) 897-1394
Region 6 Regional Director **Judith Drabicki** ...........(315) 785-2239
  317 Washington Street, Watertown, NY 13601-3787   Fax: (315) 785-2242
Region 7 Regional Director (Acting) **Joe Sluzar** ........(315) 426-7403
  615 Erie Boulevard West,   Fax: (315) 426-7408
  Syracuse, NY 13204-2400
Region 8 Regional Director **Paul D'Amato** .............(585) 226-5370
  6274 East Avon-Lima Road, Avon, NY 14414-9519   Fax: (585) 226-2830
Region 9 Regional Director **Abby Snyder** .............(716) 851-7200
  270 Michigan Ave., Buffalo, NY 14203-2999   Fax: (716) 851-7211

## Office of Remediation and Materials Management
Deputy Commissioner **Eugene Leff**...................(518) 402-2794
Environmental Remediation Division Director
**Robert W. Schick**................................(518) 402-9706
Materials Management Division Director (Acting)
**Bob Phaneuf**....................................(518) 402-8652
Mineral Resources Division Director (Acting)
**Kathy Sanford**...................................(518) 402-8076

## Office of Water Resources
Deputy Commissioner **James M. Tierney**..............(518) 402-2794
  Education: SUNY (Buffalo) 1988 JD
Water Division Director **Mark Klotz, PE**...............(518) 402-8233

# Department of Financial Services [DFS]

One State Street, New York, NY 10004-1511
Tel: (212) 709-3500

**Fiscal Year:** 2014  **Budget:** $552,196,823

■Superintendent (Acting) **Maria T. Vullo**................(212) 709-3501
  Note: On January 21, 2016, Governor Andrew Cuomo nominated
  Maria Vullo to serve as Superintendent of the Department of Financial
  Services. Vullo's nomination must be confirmed by the New York
  Senate. She is currently acting in this position.
  Education: Mount St Vincent 1984 BA; NYU 1987 JD, 2012 MPA
  Special Assistant to the Superintendent
  **Jennifer L. Smith**.............................(212) 709-3500
    Education: Lafayette BA; Columbia MA; Cardozo JD
Chief of Staff **(Vacant)** ............................(212) 709-1698
Executive Deputy Superintendent for Communications
and Strategy **Richard A. Loconte**...................(212) 709-1691
  E-mail: richard.loconte@dfs.ny.gov
  Education: Fordham BA; Brooklyn Law JD
Executive Deputy Superintendent for Enforcement
**Matthew L. Levine**...............................(212) 709-3500
  E-mail: matthew.levine@dfs.ny.gov
  Education: Lehigh BA; Columbia JD
Executive Deputy Superintendent for Financial Frauds
and Consumer Protection **Joy Feigenbaum** ........... (518) 474-6600
  Education: Rutgers BA; Pennsylvania 1980 JD
Executive Deputy Superintendent for Insurance
**Scott B. Fischer** ................................(212) 709-3500
  Education: Dickinson Col BA; NYU JD
Deputy Superintendent for Community and Regional
Banks Division **Ruth Adams** ......................(212) 709-1610
  E-mail: ruth.adams@dfs.ny.gov
Deputy Superintendent for Foreign and Wholesale Banks
Division **Jeffrey Raymond**.........................(212) 709-1568
  E-mail: jeffrey.raymond@dfs.ny.gov
Deputy Superintendent for Health **Troy Oechsner** ........ (518) 474-4567
  Education: SUNY (Plattsburgh) BA; SUNY (Buffalo) 1991 JD
Deputy Superintendent for Insurance **Laura Evangelista** .. (518) 474-4567
  Education: Trinity Col (CT) BA; Hofstra JD
  Insurance General Counsel **Martha A. Lees** ........... (212) 480-5282
    Education: Harvard AB, JD

*(continued on next page)*

---

★ Elected Official   ■ Appointed by Governor   ● Appointed by Legislature    ▲ Appointed by Board or Commission   ◆ Appointed by State Supreme Court

**Department of Financial Services** *continued*

Deputy Superintendent of Licensed Financial Services
Division **(Vacant)** . . . . . . . . . . . . . . . . . . . . . . . . . . . (212) 709-5500
Deputy Superintendent for Mortgage Banking Division
**Rholda Ricketts** . . . . . . . . . . . . . . . . . . . . . . . . . . . (212) 709-5540
Deputy Superintendent for Property **Stephen Doody** . . . . . (518) 474-6600
Deputy Superintendent for Public Affairs (Acting)
**Ron Klug** . . . . . . . . . . . . . . . . . . . . . . . . . . . . . . . . (212) 709-1691
Criminal Investigations Bureau Chief **Frank Orlando** . . . . . (212) 709-3540
E-mail: frank.orlando@dfs.ny.gov
Director of Administration **Chad Loshbaugh** . . . . . . . . . . (518) 474-6848
E-mail: chad.loshbaugh@dfs.ny.gov
General Counsel **Celeste L.M. Koeleveld** . . . . . . . . . . . . (212) 709-1640
Note: On March 29, 2016, Celeste Koeleveld was appointed General
Counsel of the Department of Financial Services. Koeleveld's start date
has not yet been determined.
Education: Harvard 1986 BA; Columbia 1989 JD
Special Counsel for Ethics, Risk and Compliance
**(Vacant)** . . . . . . . . . . . . . . . . . . . . . . . . . . . . . . . . (212) 709-3500
Taxes and Accounts Director **Mark Daigneault** . . . . . . . . . (518) 474-8567
Webmaster **Joel Obuchowski** . . . . . . . . . . . . . . . . . . . . (518) 473-7949

# New York State Department of Health [NYSDOH]

Mayor Erastus Corning II Tower, Empire State Plaza,
Albany, NY 12237-0001
P.O. Box 2602, Albany, NY 12220-2602 (Vital Records)
Tel: (518) 473-8600  Tel: (518) 474-3077 (Vital Records)
Tel: (212) 639-9675 (Vital Records [NYC])
Fax: (518) 473-7071  Fax: (518) 474-9168 (Vital Records)
E-mail: vr@health.ny.gov (Vital Records)  E-mail: nyhealth@health.ny.gov

**Employees:** 5,055

■Commissioner **Dr. Howard A. Zucker** . . . . . . . . . . . . . . (518) 474-2011
E-mail: howard.zucker@health.ny.gov
Education: McGill (Canada) BS; George Washington MD; Fordham JD;
Columbia LLM
Secretary **Jacqueline Silvia** . . . . . . . . . . . . . . . . . . . . (518) 474-2011
Executive Deputy Commissioner **Sally Dreslin** . . . . . . . . . (518) 473-2011
Education: Columbia 1994 BSN; Texas MA
First Deputy Commissioner **(Vacant)** . . . . . . . . . . . . . . . (518) 473-8600
School of Public Health Dean **Dr. Philip Nasca** . . . . . . . . (518) 402-0281
One University Place, Rensselaer, NY 12144      Fax: (518) 402-0329

## Administration Division

Deputy Commissioner **Michael Nazarko** . . . . . . . . . . . . . (518) 474-8565
E-mail: michael.nazarko@health.ny.gov
Deputy Director **Robert "Jake" LoCicero** . . . . . . . . . . . . (518) 474-8565
E-mail: rwl02@health.state.ny.us
Human Resources Director **Joyce Neznek** . . . . . . . . . . . (518) 473-3394
Fiscal Management Group Director **Marybeth Hefner** . . . . (518) 474-1208
Fiscal Management Group Deputy Director
**Edward M. Cahill** . . . . . . . . . . . . . . . . . . . . . . . . . . (518) 473-4263

## Division of Legal Affairs

Fax: (518) 473-2802
General Counsel **Richard J. Zahnleuter** . . . . . . . . . . . . . (518) 474-7553
E-mail: richard.zahnleuter@health.ny.gov
Education: SUNY Environmental BS; Albany Law JD
Deputy General Counsel **(Vacant)** . . . . . . . . . . . . . . . . . (518) 473-3818
Professional Medical Conduct Bureau Chief Counsel
**Henry Weintraub** . . . . . . . . . . . . . . . . . . . . . . . . . . (518) 417-4357
E-mail: henry.weintraub@health.ny.gov
Adjudication Bureau Director **James Horan** . . . . . . . . . . (518) 402-0748
Administrative Hearings Bureau Director **Mark Fleischer** . . (518) 473-1707
Health Facility Planning and Development Bureau
Director **Mark Furnish** . . . . . . . . . . . . . . . . . . . . . . . (518) 473-3303
House Counsel Bureau Director **Justin Pfeiffer** . . . . . . . . (518) 473-3233
Litigation Bureau Director **Michael G. Bass** . . . . . . . . . . (518) 473-4631
Regulatory Affairs Unit Administrative Assistant
**Katherine Ceroala** . . . . . . . . . . . . . . . . . . . . . . . . . . (518) 473-7488
E-mail: regsqna@health.ny.gov          Fax: (518) 473-2019

# Office of Health Insurance Programs [OHIP]

Deputy Commissioner and State Medicaid Director
**Jason A. Helgerson** . . . . . . . . . . . . . . . . . . . . . . . . (518) 474-3018
Education: American U 1993 BA;          Fax: (518) 486-6852
Chicago 1995 MPP
Deputy Director **Elizabeth J. Misa** . . . . . . . . . . . . . . . . (518) 474-8646
Education: SUNY (Albany) 1996 BA, 1999 MPA  Fax: (518) 486-4834
Chief Information Officer, OHIP Systems
**Chris Hall-Finney** . . . . . . . . . . . . . . . . . . . . . . . . . . (518) 649-4401
E-mail: chris.hall-finney@health.ny.gov
Administration and Contracts Bureau Director
**Dennis Wright** . . . . . . . . . . . . . . . . . . . . . . . . . . . . (518) 649-4274
E-mail: dennis.wright@health.ny.gov
Health Plan Contracting and Oversight Division Director
**Jonathan Bick** . . . . . . . . . . . . . . . . . . . . . . . . . . . . (518) 474-5737
Health Reform and Health Insurance Exchange
Integration Division Director **Judith Arnold** . . . . . . . . . . (518) 474-0180
Fax: (518) 474-3295

Quality and Patient Safety Office Director
**Patrick Roohan** . . . . . . . . . . . . . . . . . . . . . . . . . . . . (518) 473-2941
Fax: (518) 486-6098
Records Access Officer **James P. O'Hare** . . . . . . . . . . . (518) 474-8734

## Division of Long Term Care

Director **Mark Kissinger** . . . . . . . . . . . . . . . . . . . . . . . (518) 402-5673
Deputy Director **Becky Corso** . . . . . . . . . . . . . . . . . . . (518) 408-1833

## Office of Public Affairs

Director **James Plastiras** . . . . . . . . . . . . . . . . . . . . . . (518) 474-7354
Fax: (518) 473-7071
Deputy Director **Marci Natale** . . . . . . . . . . . . . . . . . . . (518) 474-7354
Fax: (518) 473-7071
Marketing and Creative Communications Bureau Director
**Mark F. Yanulavich** . . . . . . . . . . . . . . . . . . . . . . . . . (518) 474-8431
E-mail: mfy01@health.ny.gov

## Office of Public Health

Deputy Commissioner **Guthrie S. Birkhead, MD, MPH** . . . (518) 474-5073
Education: Princeton 1975 AB; Yale 1979 MD;
Johns Hopkins 1985 MPH
Deputy Director **Ellen Anderson** . . . . . . . . . . . . . . . . . . (518) 473-0771

# Department of Labor

State Office Building, 12, W. A. Harriman Campus, Albany, NY 12240
Tel: (518) 457-9000  Tel: (888) 469-7365  Fax: (518) 457-6908
E-mail: nysdol@labor.ny.gov  Internet: www.labor.ny.gov

**Employees:** 3,219  **Fiscal Year:** 2014  **Budget:** $6,363,788,456

■Commissioner (Acting) **Roberta Reardon** . . . . . . . . . . . (518) 457-2746
Note: On September 24, 2015, Governor Andrew Cuomo nominated
Roberta Reardon to be Commissioner of the Department of Labor.
Reardon's nomination must be confirmed by the New York Senate.
Reardon is currently acting in this position.
Education: Wyoming BA
Executive Deputy Commissioner **Mario Musolino** . . . . . . . (518) 457-4318
E-mail: mario.musolino@labor.ny.gov
Secretary to the Executive Deputy Commissioner
**(Vacant)** . . . . . . . . . . . . . . . . . . . . . . . . . . . . . . . . (518) 457-0380
Administration Deputy Commissioner and Chief
Financial Officer **Nathaalie M. Carey** . . . . . . . . . . . . . (518) 457-7994
Education: SUNY (Binghamton) MPA
Employment Security Deputy Commissioner **Mary Batch** . . (518) 457-5124
Workforce Development Deputy Commissioner
**Karen Coleman** . . . . . . . . . . . . . . . . . . . . . . . . . . . . (518) 485-6410
E-mail: karen.coleman@labor.ny.gov
Workforce Protection Deputy Commissioner
**James Rodgers** . . . . . . . . . . . . . . . . . . . . . . . . . . . . (518) 457-7350
E-mail: james.rodgers@labor.ny.gov
Intergovernmental Affairs and Federal Policy Associate
Commissioner (Acting) **James Rodgers** . . . . . . . . . . . . (518) 457-7350
E-mail: james.rodgers@labor.ny.gov
Special Counsel **(Vacant)** . . . . . . . . . . . . . . . . . . . . . . (518) 457-2746
Labor Statistics Chief **Bohdan Wynnyk** . . . . . . . . . . . . . (518) 457-7990

---

★ Elected Official   ■ Appointed by Governor   ● Appointed by Legislature   ▲ Appointed by Board or Commission   ◆ Appointed by State Supreme Court

Communications Director **Tiffany Portzer** . . . . . . . . . . . . (518) 457-5519
E-mail: tiffany.portzer@labor.ny.gov
Internal Audit Director **Rajni Chawla** . . . . . . . . . . . . . . . . . (518) 457-9016
Administrative Finance and Budget Director
**Kathleen Elfeldt** . . . . . . . . . . . . . . . . . . . . . . . . . . . . . . (518) 457-2647
E-mail: kathleen.elfeldt@labor.ny.gov
Equal Opportunity Development Director (Interim)
**Shawna McDaniel** . . . . . . . . . . . . . . . . . . . . . . . . . . . . (518) 457-1984
Labor Standards Division Director (Acting)
**Maura McMann** . . . . . . . . . . . . . . . . . . . . . . . . . . . . . . (518) 457-2460
Personnel Director **Carol Owsiany** . . . . . . . . . . . . . . . . . . (518) 457-1020
Public Works Division Director **Christopher Alund** . . . . . . (518) 485-5696
E-mail: christopher.alund@labor.ny.gov
Education: SUNY (Plattsburgh) 1980 BS
Safety and Health Division Director
**Eileen Franko, DrPH, MPH** . . . . . . . . . . . . . . . . . . . . . (518) 457-3518
Unemployment Insurance Division Director **Carl Boorn** . . . (518) 457-2878
Special Investigations Director **John Dormin** . . . . . . . . . . . (518) 457-7012
E-mail: john.dormin@labor.ny.gov

## Department of Motor Vehicles [DMV]

6 Empire State Plaza, Albany, NY 12228
Tel: (518) 474-0841 TTY: (800) 368-1186 Fax: (518) 473-1930
E-mail: nydmv@dmv.ny.gov

**Fiscal Year:** 2016-17 **Budget:** $302,333,000

■Commissioner **(Vacant)** . . . . . . . . . . . . . . . . . . . . . . . . . . (518) 474-0841
Executive Deputy Commissioner **Theresa L. Egan** . . . . . . . (518) 474-0846
E-mail: theresa.egan@dmv.ny.gov
Education: SUNY (Albany) BA; Albany Law JD
Governor's Traffic Safety Committee Assistant
Commissioner **Charles R. DeWeese** . . . . . . . . . . . . . . . (518) 474-0748
E-mail: chuck.deweese@dmv.ny.gov
Communications Assistant Commissioner **Joe Morrissey** . . (518) 473-7000
E-mail: joseph.morrissey@dmv.ny.gov
Governor's Traffic Safety Committee Operations Director
**James F. Allen** . . . . . . . . . . . . . . . . . . . . . . . . . . . . . . . (518) 474-7753

### Administration

Deputy Commissioner **Gregory J. Kline** . . . . . . . . . . . . . . . (518) 474-6876
E-mail: gregory.kline@dmv.ny.gov
Chief Financial Officer **Paul Gauthier** . . . . . . . . . . . . . . . . (518) 473-0990
Human Resource Management Director **Paul Gauthier** . . . . (518) 474-7602
Program Analysis **Mary Bidell** . . . . . . . . . . . . . . . . . . . . . (518) 474-7624
E-mail: mary.bidell@dmv.ny.gov

### Legal Services

Deputy Commissioner and Counsel **(Vacant)** . . . . . . . . . . . (518) 473-1965
Legal Affairs Director **Ida Traschen** . . . . . . . . . . . . . . . . . (518) 486-3131
E-mail: ida.traschen@dmv.ny.gov
Supervising Administrative Law Judge **Bushra Vahdat** . . . . (718) 539-8470
Legislative Liaison **Meg Murray** . . . . . . . . . . . . . . . . . . . . (518) 474-7726
E-mail: meg.murray@dmv.ny.gov

### Operations and Customer Service

Deputy Commissioner **Timothy Lennon** . . . . . . . . . . . . . . . (518) 474-0846
Central and Customer Service Operations Director
**Roseanne Kitchner** . . . . . . . . . . . . . . . . . . . . . . . . . . . (518) 402-4746
Customer Service and Field Operations Director
**Joseph Crisafulli** . . . . . . . . . . . . . . . . . . . . . . . . . . . . . (518) 473-7254
Education: SUNY (Albany) MPA
Field Operations Director **Cheryl Wasley** . . . . . . . . . . . . . (518) 473-7254

### Safety, Consumer Protection and Clean Air

Deputy Commissioner **Heriberto Barbot, Jr.** . . . . . . . . . . . (518) 402-4860
Education: Brooklyn BS; NYU JD
Driver and Vehicle Safety and Clean Air Director
**Jean Rosenthal** . . . . . . . . . . . . . . . . . . . . . . . . . . . . . . (518) 473-3347
Education: SUNY (Albany) BA
Field Investigations Director **Owen McShane** . . . . . . . . . . . (518) 474-8805
Education: York (PA) 1989 BS
Motor Carrier and Driver Safety Services Director
**Robin Long** . . . . . . . . . . . . . . . . . . . . . . . . . . . . . . . . . (518) 473-1828

## Department of Taxation and Finance

W. A. Harriman Campus, Albany, NY 12227
Tel: (518) 530-4444 Fax: (518) 435-2942

**Employees:** 4,368 **Fiscal Year:** 2013-2014 **Budget:** $464,074,400

■Commissioner **Jerry Boone** . . . . . . . . . . . . . . . . . . . . . . . (518) 530-4444
Education: Columbia BA; Boston Col JD
Executive Deputy Commissioner **Nonie Manion** . . . . . . . . (518) 530-4444
Internal Affairs Director **William Hamel** . . . . . . . . . . . . . . (518) 451-1566
E-mail: william.hamel@tax.ny.gov
Internal Audit and Quality Control Director
**James Brunt** . . . . . . . . . . . . . . . . . . . . . . . . . . . . . . . . . (518) 937-9459
E-mail: james.brunt@tax.ny.gov
Public Information Director **Geoffrey T. Gloak** . . . . . . . . . (518) 530-4692
E-mail: geoffrey.gloak@tax.ny.gov
Education: SUNY (Empire State) MA
Conciliation and Mediation Services Bureau Director
**Camille Siano Enders** . . . . . . . . . . . . . . . . . . . . . . . . . (518) 530-4628
Chief Information Officer **Nancy Mulholland** . . . . . . . . . . (518) 530-4444
Education: Vassar BA
Chief Risk Officer **Barry Ginsberg** . . . . . . . . . . . . . . . . . . (518) 530-5347
Special Counsel for Ethics, Risk and Compliance
**Michael Shollar** . . . . . . . . . . . . . . . . . . . . . . . . . . . . . . (518) 530-4444

## New York State Department of Transportation [NYSDOT]

50 Wolf Road, Albany, NY 12232
Tel: (518) 457-6195 Fax: (518) 457-5583

**Employees:** 8,708 **Fiscal Year:** 2014 **Budget:** $6,182,298,000

■Commissioner **Matthew J. Driscoll** . . . . . . . . . . . . . . . . . (518) 457-4422
Chief of Staff **Cathy Calhoun** . . . . . . . . . . . . . . . . . . . . . (518) 457-6195
Executive Deputy Commissioner and Chief Engineer
**Phillip Eng, PE** . . . . . . . . . . . . . . . . . . . . . . . . . . . . . . (518) 457-4430
Administrative Services Assistant Commissioner
**Ray LaMarco** . . . . . . . . . . . . . . . . . . . . . . . . . . . . . . . . (518) 457-3543
E-mail: raymond.lamarco@dot.ny.gov
Education: Nyack BS
Legal Affairs Division Assistant Commissioner and Chief
Counsel **David M. Cherubin** . . . . . . . . . . . . . . . . . . . . . (518) 457-2411
E-mail: david.cherubin@dot.ny.gov
Chief Operating Officer **Rosemary Powers** . . . . . . . . . . . . (518) 457-2470
Education: Suffolk BA; Harvard 2000 MPA
Civil Rights Division Director **Sondra Little** . . . . . . . . . . . (518) 457-1129
Public Information Officer (Acting) **Jennifer Post** . . . . . . . (518) 457-6400
Education: Chatham BS Fax: (518) 457-6506
Communications Office Director **Gary Holmes** . . . . . . . . . (518) 457-6400
E-mail: gary.holmes@dot.ny.gov
Operations and Asset Management Division Director
**Roderic Sechrist, PE** . . . . . . . . . . . . . . . . . . . . . . . . . . (518) 485-0887
Policy and Planning Division Director (Acting)
**Ronald L. "Ron" Epstein** . . . . . . . . . . . . . . . . . . . . . . . (518) 457-2320
E-mail: ron.epstein@dot.ny.gov
Education: SUNY (Cortland) BA; SUNY (Binghamton) MA
Chief Financial Officer and Finance Office Director
**Ronald L. "Ron" Epstein** . . . . . . . . . . . . . . . . . . . . . . . (518) 457-2320

## State Liquor Authority/Division of Alcoholic Beverage Control [SLA]

State Liquor Authority, 80 South Swan Street, Suite 900,
Albany, NY 12210
Tel: (518) 474-3114 TTY: (518) 474-9888 Fax: (518) 473-9565

■Chairman **Vincent Bradley** . . . . . . . . . . . . . . . . . . . . . . . (518) 473-6559
E-mail: vincent.bradley@sla.ny.gov
Education: Notre Dame BBA; SUNY (Buffalo) JD
Administrative Assistant **Kimberly Ciccone** . . . . . . . . . . . (518) 473-6559
■Commissioner **Kevin Kim** . . . . . . . . . . . . . . . . . . . . . . . . (212) 961-8300
317 Lenox Avenue, New York, NY 10027
E-mail: kevin.kim@sla.ny.gov
Education: Stanford BA, MA; Columbia JD
■Commissioner **(Vacant)** . . . . . . . . . . . . . . . . . . . . . . . . . . (518) 474-3114
Chief Executive Officer **Kerri J. O'Brien** . . . . . . . . . . . . . . (518) 473-0365
Licensing Deputy Commissioner **Jacqueline Held** . . . . . . . (518) 474-3114
Enforcement Director **Noel Colon** . . . . . . . . . . . . . . . . . . . (518) 474-3114

*(continued on next page)*

---

★ Elected Official ■ Appointed by Governor ● Appointed by Legislature ▲ Appointed by Board or Commission ◆ Appointed by State Supreme Court

**State Liquor Authority/Division of Alcoholic Beverage Control** *continued*

Information Technology Director **Michael Drake** . . . . . . . . (518) 474-3114
  E-mail: michael.drake@its.ny.gov

# Division of the Budget [DOB]

State Capitol, Albany, NY 12224-0341
Tel: (518) 474-2300  Fax: (518) 474-0132

■Director **Robert F. Mujica, Jr.** . . . . . . . . . . . . . . . . . . . (518) 474-2300
  E-mail: robert.mujica@budget.state.ny.us    Fax: (518) 402-2298
First Deputy Director **David Lara** . . . . . . . . . . . . . . . . (518) 402-4246
  Education: U Washington BS; Texas MPAff
Deputy Director **Sandra Beattie** . . . . . . . . . . . . . . . . . . (518) 474-6497
Chief Budget Examiner **Louis Raffaele** . . . . . . . . . . . (518) 474-4314
Chief Budget Examiner **Tom Wood** . . . . . . . . . . . . . . . (518) 474-2322
Communications Director **Morris Peters** . . . . . . . . . . . (518) 473-3885
  E-mail: morris.peters@budget.state.ny.us

# New York State Division of Criminal Justice Services [DCJS]

Alfred E. Smith Building, 80 South Swan Street, Albany, NY 12210
Tel: (518) 457-5837  Tel: (800) 262-3257

■Executive Deputy Commissioner
  **Michael C. "Mike" Green** . . . . . . . . . . . . . . . . . . . . . (518) 457-1260
  E-mail: michael.green@dcjs.ny.gov
  Education: Le Moyne 1983 BS; Western New England 1986 JD
First Deputy Commissioner **Mark Bonacquist** . . . . . . . . . . (518) 457-1260
Deputy Commissioner and Counsel **John Czajka** . . . . . . . (518) 457-4181
                                                     Fax: (518) 457-3089
Administration Office Deputy Commissioner **(Vacant)** . . . . (518) 457-6105
Criminal Justice Operations Office Deputy Commissioner
  **Joseph N. Morrissey** . . . . . . . . . . . . . . . . . . . . . . . . . (518) 485-2995
Justice Research and Performance Office Deputy
  Commissioner **Theresa Salo** . . . . . . . . . . . . . . . . . . . . (518) 457-7301
                                                     Fax: (518) 485-7715
Program Development and Funding Office Deputy
  Commissioner **Jeffrey Bender** . . . . . . . . . . . . . . . . . . (518) 457-8462
  E-mail: jeffrey.bender@dcjs.ny.gov
Public Safety Office Deputy Commissioner
  **Michael Wood** . . . . . . . . . . . . . . . . . . . . . . . . . . . . . (518) 457-2666
  E-mail: michael.wood@dcjs.ny.gov    Fax: (518) 485-7715
Public Information Director **Janine Kava** . . . . . . . . . . . . . . (518) 457-8828
  E-mail: janine.kava@dcjs.ny.gov
  Education: Boston U 1988 BS

# Office of Probation and Correctional Alternatives [OPCA]

Alfred E. Smith Office, 80 South Swan Street, Albany, NY 12210
Tel: (518) 485-2395  Fax: (518) 485-5140  E-mail: dpcaprog@dcjs.ny.gov

■Deputy Commissioner and Director
  **Robert M. Maccarone** . . . . . . . . . . . . . . . . . . . . . . . . (518) 485-7692
  E-mail: robert.maccarone@dcjs.ny.gov
  Education: Fordham BS, MA; JFK School Govt (Attended);
  Pace 1984 JD
Executive Deputy Director **John H. Adams** . . . . . . . . . . . . (518) 485-7692

# Division of Homeland Security and Emergency Services [DHSES]

State Office Campus, 1220 Washington Avenue, Suite 710,
Albany, NY 12242
633 Third Avenue, 32nd Floor, New York, NY 10017
Tel: (518) 402-2227 (Albany Office)
Tel: (212) 867-7060 (New York City Office)

■Commissioner **Col. John P. Melville** . . . . . . . . . . . . . . . (518) 242-5000
  E-mail: john.melville@dhses.ny.gov
  Education: SUNY (Cortland) BS; SUNY (Albany) MS
Executive Deputy Commissioner **(Vacant)** . . . . . . . . . . (518) 242-5085
Deputy Commissioner for Administration and Finance
  **(Vacant)** . . . . . . . . . . . . . . . . . . . . . . . . . . . . . . . . . . (518) 242-5000
■Deputy Commissioner for Special Projects
  **Andrew X. Feeney** . . . . . . . . . . . . . . . . . . . . . . . . . . (518) 242-5032
  E-mail: andrew.feeney@dhses.ny.gov

General Counsel **Frank G. Hoare** . . . . . . . . . . . . . . . . . . . (518) 242-5000
  Education: SUNY (Albany) 1982 BA; Albany Law 1985 JD
Intergovernmental Affairs Director **Lisa Black** . . . . . . . . . . (212) 867-7060
  Education: Col St Rose BA

# Division of Human Rights [DHR]

One Fordham Plaza, 4th Floor, Bronx, NY 10458
Tel: (718) 741-8400  TTY: (718) 741-8300  Fax: (718) 741-3214

■Commissioner **Helen Diane Foster** . . . . . . . . . . . . . . . . . (718) 741-8326
  E-mail: hfoster@dhr.ny.gov
  Special Counsel to the Commissioner
  **Joycelyn McGeachy-Kuls** . . . . . . . . . . . . . . . . . . . (718) 741-8400
■First Deputy Commissioner **Valerie P. Dent** . . . . . . . . . . . (718) 741-8330
  E-mail: vdent@dhr.ny.gov
  Education: Vanderbilt; Columbia JD
Finance Director **Chris Chirila** . . . . . . . . . . . . . . . . . . . . (718) 741-8360
  E-mail: cchirila@dhr.ny.gov
Deputy Commissioner for Enforcement **Melissa Franco** . . . (718) 741-8328
  E-mail: mfranco@dhr.ny.gov
  Education: South Florida BA; Fordham JD
Deputy Commissioner for Regional Affairs and Federal
  Programs **Gina Martinez** . . . . . . . . . . . . . . . . . . . . . . (718) 741-8334
  Education: SUNY (Binghamton) BA; St John's U (NY) JD
General Counsel **Caroline J. Downey** . . . . . . . . . . . . . . . (718) 741-8398
  E-mail: cdowney@dhr.ny.gov
  Education: Lake Erie; Antioch Law JD
Equal Opportunity and Diversity Officer **(Vacant)** . . . . . . . (718) 741-8309
Disability Rights Director **John Herrion** . . . . . . . . . . . . . . (718) 741-8332
  E-mail: jherrion@dhr.ny.gov
External Relations Director **(Vacant)** . . . . . . . . . . . . . . . . (718) 741-3223
Executive Assistant **Martin Munoz** . . . . . . . . . . . . . . . . . (718) 741-8326
  E-mail: mmunoz@dhr.ny.gov

# Division of Military and Naval Affairs [DMNA]

330 Old Niskayuna Road, Latham, NY 12110-2224
Tel: (518) 786-4500  Fax: (518) 786-4785

■Adjutant General **MajGen Anthony P. German, ANG** . . . . (518) 786-4502
  E-mail: anthony.p.german.mil@mail.mil
Assistant Adjutant General, Air
  **BrigGen Timothy J. Labarge, ANG** . . . . . . . . . . . . . . (518) 786-4317
  Education: St Lawrence 1983 BS
Assistant Adjutant General, Army
  **BG Raymond Shields, ARNG** . . . . . . . . . . . . . . . . . . (518) 756-4388
Army Chief of Staff **COL John C. Andonie, ARNG** . . . . . . (518) 786-4502
Senior Enlisted Advisor
  **CSM David A. Piwowarski, ARNG** . . . . . . . . . . . . . . (518) 786-4500
Director, Joint Staff **COL Patrick Center, ARNG** . . . . . . . . (518) 786-4501
Government Affairs Director **James M. Huelle** . . . . . . . . . . (518) 786-4580
  E-mail: james.m.huelle.mil@mail.mil
Public Affairs Director **Eric Durr** . . . . . . . . . . . . . . . . . . (518) 786-4581
Employee Assistance Program (EAP) Coordinator
  **Patricia Reihs** . . . . . . . . . . . . . . . . . . . . . . . . . . . . . (518) 389-4708
Special Assistant, State **Michael Friess** . . . . . . . . . . . . . . . (518) 786-4502
Information Technology Officer **James P. Freehart** . . . . . . . (518) 786-4690
  E-mail: james.p.freehart.mil@mail.mil

# Division of State Police

Building 22, 1220 Washington Avenue, Albany, NY 12226-2252
Tel: (518) 457-6811  TTY: (800) 342-4357  Fax: (518) 457-3207

■Superintendent **(Vacant)** . . . . . . . . . . . . . . . . . . . . . . . (518) 457-6721
■First Deputy Superintendent **Patricia M. Groeber** . . . . . . . (518) 457-6711
  E-mail: patricia.groeber@troopers.ny.gov
Deputy Superintendent **Steven Cumoletti** . . . . . . . . . . . . (518) 457-6811
                                                     Fax: (518) 457-3207
Employee Relations Deputy Superintendent
  **Francis P. Christensen** . . . . . . . . . . . . . . . . . . . . . . . (518) 457-3572
  E-mail: francis.christensen@troopers.ny.gov
Field Command Deputy Superintendent **Stephen Smith** . . (518) 457-5936
Internal Affairs Deputy Superintendent **Daniel R. Penny** . . (518) 457-6554
Chief Counsel **Thomas A. Capezza** . . . . . . . . . . . . . . . . . (518) 457-6137
  E-mail: thomas.capezza@troopers.ny.gov
  Education: Fordham 1993 JD

---

★ Elected Official    ■ Appointed by Governor    ● Appointed by Legislature    ▲ Appointed by Board or Commission    ◆ Appointed by State Supreme Court

## Division of Tax Appeals and Tax Appeals Tribunal

Agency Building One, Empire State Plaza, Albany, NY 12223
Tel: (518) 266-3000  Fax: (518) 271-0886  Fax: (518) 272-5178
E-mail: nysdota@dta.ny.gov  Internet: www.dta.ny.gov

■ President and Commissioner **Roberta Moseley Nero** . . . . . (518) 266-3050
   E-mail: roberta.nero@ny.gov
   Education: Russell Sage BA; Syracuse JD
■ Commissioner **Charles H. Nesbitt** . . . . . . . . . . . . . . . . . (518) 266-3050
   E-mail: charles.nesbitt@ny.gov
■ Commissioner **James H. Tully, Jr.** . . . . . . . . . . . . . . . . . (518) 266-3050
   E-mail: james.tully@ny.gov
   Education: Georgetown 1952 AB; New York Law JD
Secretary to the Commissioners **Sylvia S. Magin** . . . . . . . . (518) 266-3050
■ Secretary to the Tribunal **Jean A. McDonnell** . . . . . . . . . . (518) 266-3036
   E-mail: jean.mcdonnell@ny.gov
Supervising Administrative Law Judge **Daniel J. Ranalli** . . (518) 266-3000

## Division of Veterans' Affairs

Agency Building Two, 17th Floor, Albany, NY 12223
Tel: (518) 474-6114  Fax: (518) 473-0379
E-mail: dvainfo@veterans.ny.gov

■ Director **COL Eric J. Hesse, USA (Ret)** . . . . . . . . . . . . . . (518) 474-6114
   E-mail: eric.hesse@veterans.ny.gov
Executive Deputy Director **Joel Evans** . . . . . . . . . . . . . . . (518) 474-6114
Deputy Director **Jamal Othman** . . . . . . . . . . . . . . . . . . . (518) 474-6114
   Education: St Francis Col (NY) BA; Baruch Col MPA
General Counsel **Jonathan S. Fishbein** . . . . . . . . . . . . . . (518) 474-6114
   Education: Fairleigh Dickinson BS; Cardozo JD

## New York State Office for the Aging [NYSOFA]

Two Empire State Plaza, Albany, NY 12223-1251
Tel: (800) 342-9871  Fax: (518) 474-1398  Internet: www.aging.ny.gov
E-mail: nysofa@aging.ny.gov

■ Director (Acting) **Greg Olsen** . . . . . . . . . . . . . . . . . . . (518) 474-4425
   E-mail: greg.olsen@aging.ny.gov
Executive Deputy Director **Greg Olsen** . . . . . . . . . . . . . . (518) 474-4425
Deputy Director, Aging Network Operations Division
   **Jim DelBelso** . . . . . . . . . . . . . . . . . . . . . . . . . . . . . (518) 474-2631
   E-mail: jim.delbelso@aging.ny.gov
Deputy Director, Executive Division **John Cochran** . . . . . . (518) 474-7012
Deputy Director, Policy, Planning, Program and
   Outcomes Division **Laurie Pferr** . . . . . . . . . . . . . . . . . (518) 474-4425
   E-mail: laurie.pferr@aging.ny.gov
Public Information Officer **Reza Mizbani** . . . . . . . . . . . . . (518) 474-7181
   E-mail: reza.mizbani@aging.ny.gov

## Office of Alcoholism and Substance Abuse Services [OASAS]

1450 Western Avenue, Albany, NY 12203
Tel: (518) 473-3460  Fax: (518) 485-2335
E-mail: communications@oasas.ny.gov

■ Commissioner **Arlene González-Sánchez, MS, LMSW** . . . (518) 457-2061
   E-mail: arlene.gonzález-sánchez@oasas.ny.gov
   Education: Fordham MS; Hunter MSW
Executive Deputy Commissioner **Sean M. Byrne** . . . . . . . . (518) 485-2337
   Education: Syracuse, 1983 JD
Associate Commissioner for Fiscal Administration
   **P. David Sawicki** . . . . . . . . . . . . . . . . . . . . . . . . . . (518) 457-5312
Associate Commissioner for Outcome Management and
   System Information **William F. Hogan** . . . . . . . . . . . . . (518) 485-2322
Associate Commissioner for Prevention,
   Housing, and Management Services (Acting)
   **Mary Ann DiChristopher** . . . . . . . . . . . . . . . . . . . . . (518) 485-6022
   Education: Wisconsin
Associate Commissioner for Quality Assurance and
   Performance Improvement **Charles Monson** . . . . . . . . . (518) 485-2257
Associate Commissioner for Treatment and Practice
   Innovation **Steve Hanson** . . . . . . . . . . . . . . . . . . . . . (518) 457-7077
Chief Counsel **Robert A. Kent** . . . . . . . . . . . . . . . . . . . . (518) 485-2312

Human Resources Management Director **Erica Behan** . . . . . (518) 457-2963
Chief Information Officer **Laura Frost** . . . . . . . . . . . . . . . (518) 485-6457
   E-mail: laura.frost@oasas.ny.gov
Affirmative Action Officer **Nicole Watkins** . . . . . . . . . . . . (646) 728-4530
Public Information Officer **Susan A. Craig** . . . . . . . . . . . . (518) 457-8299
   E-mail: communications@oasas.ny.gov
Director of Government Affairs and Grants Management
   **Patricia Zuber-Wilson** . . . . . . . . . . . . . . . . . . . . . . . (518) 485-2332
   Education: Brown U
Medical Director (Acting) **Dr. Charles W. Morgan** . . . . . . . (585) 461-0410

## New York State Office of Information Technology Services

State Capitol, Empire State Plaza, Albany, NY 12220
P.O. Box 2062, Albany, NY 12220-0062
Tel: (518) 408-2140  Fax: (518) 402-2976

■ Chief Information Officer **Margaret "Maggie" Miller** . . . . (518) 408-2140
   E-mail: margaret.miller@its.ny.gov
   Education: Open U (UK) MBA
Executive Deputy Chief Information Officer
   **Mahesh Nattanmai** . . . . . . . . . . . . . . . . . . . . . . . . . (518) 408-2140
   E-mail: mahesh.nattanmai@its.ny.gov
Chief Counsel and Ethics Officer **(Vacant)** . . . . . . . . . . . . (518) 408-2140
Chief Data Officer **Barbara Cohn** . . . . . . . . . . . . . . . . . . (518) 408-2140
   E-mail: barbara.cohn@its.ny.gov
Chief Operations Officer **Raymond Rose** . . . . . . . . . . . . . (518) 408-2140
Chief Portfolio Officer **(Vacant)** . . . . . . . . . . . . . . . . . . . (518) 473-2658
Chief Technology Officer **Kishor Bagul** . . . . . . . . . . . . . . (518) 408-2140
   E-mail: kishor.bagul@its.ny.gov
Public Information Officer
   **Michelle Germain McDonald** . . . . . . . . . . . . . . . . . . . (518) 402-3899
   Education: SUNY (Albany) 1985 BA
Administration Director **Theresa Papa** . . . . . . . . . . . . . . . (518) 408-2140
   E-mail: theresa.papa@its.ny.gov

## Office of Children and Family Services [OCFS]

52 Washington Street, Rensselaer, NY 12144
Tel: (518) 473-7793  Fax: (518) 473-2570  E-mail: info@ocfs.ny.gov

■ Commissioner (Acting) **Sheila J. Poole** . . . . . . . . . . . . . . (518) 473-8437
   E-mail: sheila.poole@ocfs.ny.gov
   Administrative Assistant **(Vacant)** . . . . . . . . . . . . . . . . (518) 474-8437
Executive Deputy Commissioner **Sheila J. Poole** . . . . . . . . (518) 402-3108
   Executive Assistant **Erin Cassidy** . . . . . . . . . . . . . . . . . (518) 402-8400
   Executive Secretary **Nancy Degree** . . . . . . . . . . . . . . . . (518) 474-8437

## Division of Administration

Deputy Commissioner **(Vacant)** . . . . . . . . . . . . . . . . . . . . (518) 473-8453
   Audit and Quality Control Director **James Conway** . . . . (518) 486-6375
   Contract Management Director **Rich DiMezza** . . . . . . . . (518) 473-9161
   Contract Management Assistant Director **(Vacant)** . . . . . (518) 473-6001
Financial Management Associate Commissioner
   **Derek Holtzclaw** . . . . . . . . . . . . . . . . . . . . . . . . . . . (518) 486-7218
   Budget Management Director **Gabrielle R. Ares** . . . . . . . (518) 474-1361
   Financial Operations Director **Susan A. Costello** . . . . . . (518) 486-3848
   Grants Management Director **Dawn Rowan** . . . . . . . . . . (518) 473-0943
   Revenue and Rates Development Director **David Haase** . . (518) 486-6404
Human Resources Associate Commissioner
   **James Barron** . . . . . . . . . . . . . . . . . . . . . . . . . . . . . (518) 486-6942
   Human Resources Director **(Vacant)** . . . . . . . . . . . . . . (518) 402-3211
   Labor Relations Director **(Vacant)** . . . . . . . . . . . . . . . (518) 486-4240
   Personnel Director **Barbara Ruff** . . . . . . . . . . . . . . . . . (518) 402-3211
   Training Bureau Director **Pamela Kelly** . . . . . . . . . . . . (518) 474-9645
Management and Support Director **Stephanie Donato** . . . . (518) 402-3208
   E-mail: stephanie.donato@ocfs.ny.gov
   Capital Services Director **Raymond Farina** . . . . . . . . . . (518) 473-7325
   Management Services Director **(Vacant)** . . . . . . . . . . . . (518) 408-3343
   Emergency Preparedness Coordinator **Adrienne Clarke** . . (518) 486-5550

---

★ Elected Official   ■ Appointed by Governor   ● Appointed by Legislature   ▲ Appointed by Board or Commission   ◆ Appointed by State Supreme Court

## Division of Child Welfare and Community Services
Deputy Commissioner **Laura Vélez**......................(518) 474-3377
Bureau Program and Community Development Director
   **Lisa Gordon**..............................................(518) 474-1644
Close to Home Oversight and System Improvement
   Associate Commissioner **Nina Aledort**...............(212) 383-1833
   E-mail: nina.aledort@ocfs.ny.gov
Prevention, Permanency and Program Support Associate
   Commissioner **Renee Hallock**..........................(518) 402-3181
Special Populations Assistant Commissioner
   **Lisa Ghartey Ogundimu**...............................(518) 473-9447
New York State Adoption Services Director **(Vacant)**.....(518) 473-9406

## Division of Child Care Services
Deputy Commissioner **Janice Molnar**...................(518) 486-6247
Administrative Operations Director **Robert Korycinski**....(518) 474-9454
Assistant Deputy Counsel **Ed Watkins**.................(518) 473-7793

## Division of Communications
52 Washington Street, Rensselaer, NY 12144

External Affairs and Communications Assistant
   Commissioner **Jennifer Givner**........................(518) 402-3130
   E-mail: jennifer.givner@ocfs.ny.gov
Communications Assistant Director **Susan Steele**.......(518) 402-3130
   E-mail: susan.steele@ocfs.ny.gov
Public Information Officer **(Vacant)**....................(518) 486-3849
Translation Services and Special Projects
   **Mery Rosendorn**.......................................(518) 474-9514
   E-mail: mery.rosendorn@ocfs.ny.gov
Legislative Coordinator **Victoria Vattimo**..............(518) 402-3130
   E-mail: victoria.vattimo@ocfs.ny.gov

## Division of Juvenile Justice and Opportunities for Youth
Deputy Commissioner **Ines Nieves**.....................(518) 473-1786
   Executive Assistant **Matthew Carpenter**.............(518) 473-3725
Program Services Associate Commissioner (Acting)
   **Joseph "Joe" Tomassone**............................(518) 486-6766
   Behavioral Health Services Bureau Director
     **Iren Valentine**......................................(518) 408-4894
   Classification and Movement Bureau Manager
     **Kathleen Griffin**....................................(518) 473-8985
   Community Services Area Manager **Robert Ellis**.......(212) 961-4112
   Education Services Bureau Director
     **Timothy Bromirski**..................................(518) 473-4498
   Health Services Bureau Director
     **Michael D. Cohen, MD**.............................(518) 474-9560
   Juvenile Justice Entry Services Bureau Manager
     **Allison Campbell**...................................(518) 486-5513
   Technical Support Bureau Director **Jeff Evans**........(518) 486-4335
     E-mail: jeff.evans@ocfs.ny.gov
   Treatment Services Chief **Joseph "Joe" Tomassone**...(315) 423-1014
   Upstate Community Services Area Manager
     **Daniel "Dan" Maxwell**.............................(518) 486-4018
   ACA Accreditation Coordinator **Kurt Pfisterer**........(518) 474-0351
Facilities Management Associate Commissioner **(Vacant)**..(518) 473-4411
   Facility Manager **Daniel Comins**......................(315) 423-5159
   Facility Manager **Beverly "Bev" Sowersby**..........(607) 721-8177
   Facilities Fire Safety Supervisor **Dusty Deiter**.........(585) 238-8586
Program Support and Community Services Associate
   Commissioner **Tim Roche**............................(518) 473-1358
   Management and Program Support Bureau Director
     **Merle Brandwene**..................................(518) 486-7029
   Quality Assurance and Improvement Director
     **David Bach**.........................................(518) 486-5851
Chaplaincy Coordinator **Ntsiful-Amissah Kofi**.........(518) 474-9400
Youth in Transition Programs Bureau Director **(Vacant)**...(212) 961-4110

## Division of Legal Affairs
Deputy Commissioner and General Counsel
   **Suzanne Miles-Gustave**............................(518) 473-8418
   Education: SUNY (Buffalo) BA; Fordham 2002 JD

Deputy Counsel **Jill Swingruber-Sprotbery**............(518) 473-8418
Deputy Counsel **(Vacant)**.............................(518) 402-3294
Ombudsman **Viola I. Abbitt**...........................(518) 486-7082

## Office of Equal Opportunity and Diversity Development
Director **G. Bernett Marion, Sr.**.......................(518) 474-3715
Assistant Director **Betty Okrent**......................(518) 474-3715

## Office of Strategic Planning and Policy Development
Deputy Commissioner **Jeanne Milstein**................(518) 473-1776
Bureau of Research, Evaluation and Performance
   Analytics (BREPA) Director **Rebecca Colman**........(518) 474-9426
Policy Analysis Director **Jeanne Milstein**..............(518) 474-1327

## Office of Youth Development
Director **Matt Beck**...................................(518) 402-3296

## Regional Offices
Albany Regional Director (Acting) **Kerri Barber**.........(518) 486-7078
Buffalo Regional Director **Dana Whitcomb**.............(716) 847-3145
New York City Regional Director **Raymond Toomer**.....(212) 383-4718
Rochester Regional Director (Acting) **Karen Buck**.......(585) 238-8200
Spring Valley Regional Director **Yolanda Desarme**......(845) 708-2499
   11 Perlman Drive, Spring Valley, NY 10977
Syracuse Regional Director **Kelly Proctor-Leon**.........(315) 423-1200

## Office of General Services
Mayor Erastus Corning II Tower, Empire State Plaza, Albany, NY 12242
Tel: (518) 474-3899  Fax: (518) 486-9179

■Commissioner **Ro Ann Destito**.......................(518) 474-5991
   E-mail: roann.destito@ogs.ny.gov
   Education: Le Moyne 1977 BS
Executive Deputy Commissioner **Karen Tyler**..........(518) 473-6953
   Education: Russell Sage BS
Deputy Commissioner and Counsel **Bradley G. Allen**....(518) 474-5988
Chief Business Officer **Melissa Greenberg**.............(518) 408-7281
   Education: SUNY (Empire State) BS; SUNY (Albany) MS
Chief Financial Officer **Brian Matthews**................(518) 474-3899
Public Information Director **Heather R. Groll**...........(518) 474-5987
   E-mail: heather.groll@ogs.ny.gov

## Administration and Operations
Deputy Commissioner **Gail Hammond**.................(518) 473-8550
   E-mail: gail.hammond@ogs.ny.gov
Chief Procurement Officer **Susan Filburn**..............(518) 473-5294
Alternate Fueled Vehicle Program **Tom Osterhout**......(518) 473-6594
   E-mail: tom.osterhout@ogs.ny.gov
Central Printing and Copy Center **(Vacant)**............(518) 457-6593
Curatorial and Tour Services Director **Barbara Maggio**...(518) 473-7521
Human Resources Management Director
   **Dan Cunningham**....................................(518) 474-5995
   Education: Siena Col 1982 BA; Col St Rose 1984 MA
Risk-Insurance Management and Fleet Administration
   Director **Christian Jackstadt**.........................(518) 474-4725
Support Services Operations Director **Tom Osterhout**....(518) 402-5557
                                        Fax: (518) 474-0111
State and Federal Surplus Property Assistant Director
   **Michael Harris**.......................................(518) 457-1744
   E-mail: michael.harris@ogs.state.ny.us
Food Distribution and Warehousing Director
   **Annemarie Garceau**.................................(518) 474-5122
   E-mail: annemarie.garceau@ogs.state.ny.us
Mail and Freight Security **Arthur Hasson**..............(518) 486-2698

## Design and Construction Group
Fax: (518) 474-0341

Executive Director **Margaret Larkin**..................(518) 474-0337
Construction Division Director **(Vacant)**...............(518) 474-0333
Contract Administration Division Director
   **John D. Lewyckyj**....................................(518) 474-0201

---

★ Elected Official   ■ Appointed by Governor   ● Appointed by Legislature   ▲ Appointed by Board or Commission   ◆ Appointed by State Supreme Court

# Real Property Management and Facilities Group

Fax: (518) 474-1546

Deputy Director **James P. Sproat** . . . . . . . . . . . . . . . . . . . . (518) 474-4944
  Education: SUNY (Oswego) 1978 BA
Campus and Upstate Region Director **Louis Salerno** . . . . . . (518) 457-2290
Convention Center Marketing Director **Michael Snyder** . . . (518) 474-0538
  Education: Siena Col 1977 BA; Pace 1981 MS
Empire State Plaza Convention and Cultural Events
  Assistant Director **Heather Flynn** . . . . . . . . . . . . . . . . . . . (518) 474-0549
  Education: Southern Maine 1991 BFA
Food Services Director **Madeline Rizzo** . . . . . . . . . . . . . . . (518) 474-1606
Real Estate and Planning Development Group Director
  **(Vacant)** . . . . . . . . . . . . . . . . . . . . . . . . . . . . . . . . . . . . . (518) 474-4944
Real Estate Development Assistant Director
  **Jessica Gabriel** . . . . . . . . . . . . . . . . . . . . . . . . . . . . . . . . (518) 474-4944
Real Estate Planning Assistant Director **Leah Nicholson** . . (518) 474-4944
Real Property Management Group Executive Director
  **Eric S. McShane** . . . . . . . . . . . . . . . . . . . . . . . . . . . . . . . (518) 474-6057
Utilities Management Director **Robert Lobdell** . . . . . . . . . . (518) 474-3249
  E-mail: robert.lobdell@ogs.ny.gov
Capital Planning **Richard Stock** . . . . . . . . . . . . . . . . . . . . (518) 473-3927
Downstate Region Bureau Chief **Barbara Gray** . . . . . . . . . (518) 474-7963
Lease Construction and Compliance Bureau Chief
  **John Kravalis** . . . . . . . . . . . . . . . . . . . . . . . . . . . . . . . . . (518) 473-9887
Land Management Bureau Chief **Charles Scheifer** . . . . . . . (518) 474-2195
Parking Services Bureau Chief **Jeremy Disare** . . . . . . . . . . (518) 486-5437
  E-mail: jeremy.disare@ogs.ny.gov
Space Planning Bureau Chief **(Vacant)** . . . . . . . . . . . . . . . . (518) 473-9887
Upstate Region Bureau Chief **(Vacant)** . . . . . . . . . . . . . . . . (518) 486-1484
Downstate Region Manager **Kevin Cahill** . . . . . . . . . . . . . . (718) 923-4448
Empire State Plaza and Downtown Buildings Region
  Manager **Kevin O'Connor** . . . . . . . . . . . . . . . . . . . . . . . . (518) 474-8894

# Office of Mental Health [OMC]

44 Holland Avenue, Albany, NY 12229
Tel: (800) 597-8481  TTY: (518) 473-2714  Fax: (518) 474-2149

■Commissioner **Dr. Ann Marie T. Sullivan, MD** . . . . . . . . . (518) 474-4403
  Education: NYU 1970 BA, 1974 MD
Deputy Commissioner and Counsel **Joshua Pepper** . . . . . . (518) 474-1331
                                        Fax: (518) 473-7863
Consumer Affairs Director **John Allen** . . . . . . . . . . . . . . . . (518) 473-6579
                                        Fax: (518) 474-8998
Intergovernmental Relations Director
  **Leesa J. Rademacher** . . . . . . . . . . . . . . . . . . . . . . . . . . . (518) 474-4403
Medical Director **Lloyd I. Sederer, MD** . . . . . . . . . . . . . . . (518) 486-4302
  Education: SUNY (Albany) MD         Fax: (518) 474-8469
Public Information Director **Benjamin Rosen** . . . . . . . . . . . (518) 474-6540
  E-mail: benjamin.rosen@omh.ny.gov     Fax: (518) 473-3456

## Executive Deputy Commissioner's Office

Executive Deputy Commissioner
  **Martha Schaefer Hayes** . . . . . . . . . . . . . . . . . . . . . . . . . (518) 474-7056
                                          Fax: (518) 402-2361
Adult Services Division Senior Deputy Commissioner
  **Robert Myers, PhD** . . . . . . . . . . . . . . . . . . . . . . . . . . . . (518) 486-4327
                                          Fax: (518) 473-4690
Financial Management Office Deputy Commissioner
  **Emil Slane** . . . . . . . . . . . . . . . . . . . . . . . . . . . . . . . . . . . (518) 474-3631
                                          Fax: (518) 473-4690
Adult Services Division Senior Associate Commissioner
  **May Lum** . . . . . . . . . . . . . . . . . . . . . . . . . . . . . . . . . . . . (518) 474-4447
                                          Fax: (518) 473-7926
Integrated Community Services for Children and Family
  Associate Commissioner **Donna Bradbury** . . . . . . . . . . . (518) 473-6328
                                          Fax: (518) 473-4690
Forensic Services Division Associate Commissioner
  **Donna Hall** . . . . . . . . . . . . . . . . . . . . . . . . . . . . . . . . . . (518) 474-8207
                                          Fax: (518) 473-4926
Diversity Management Office Director
  **TeNeathia Wesolowski** . . . . . . . . . . . . . . . . . . . . . . . . . (518) 473-4144
                                          Fax: (518) 486-7988
Planning Director **Jeremy Darman** . . . . . . . . . . . . . . . . . . . (518) 474-4403
                                          Fax: (518) 473-4690

Evidence-Based Services and Implementation Science
  Director **Molly Finnerty, MD** . . . . . . . . . . . . . . . . . . . . . (212) 543-6180
                                          Fax: (212) 543-6220
Human Resources Management Center Director
  **J. Lynn Heath** . . . . . . . . . . . . . . . . . . . . . . . . . . . . . . . . (518) 474-0171
                                          Fax: (518) 402-4086
Internal Affairs Director **William McDermott** . . . . . . . . . . (518) 473-5940
Quality Management Office Deputy Commissioner
  **Christopher Tavella, PhD** . . . . . . . . . . . . . . . . . . . . . . . . (518) 474-6587
                                          Fax: (518) 474-8998
Central Field Office Director **Linda M. Nelson** . . . . . . . . . (315) 426-3930
  545 Cedar Street, Syracuse, NY 13210   Fax: (315) 426-3950
Hudson River Field Office **William Porter** . . . . . . . . . . . . . (845) 454-8229
  10 Ross Circle, Suite 5N, Poughkeepsie, NY 12601  Fax: (845) 454-8218
Long Island Field Office Director **Martha Carlin** . . . . . . . . (631) 761-2886
  998 Crooked Hill Road,             Fax: (631) 761-2820
  West Brentwood, NY 11717
New York City Field Office Director **Robert Moon** . . . . . . (212) 330-1650
  330 Fifth Avenue, Ninth Floor,      Fax: (212) 330-6359
  New York, NY 10001
Western New York Field Office Director
  **Christina Smith** . . . . . . . . . . . . . . . . . . . . . . . . . . . . . . . (716) 885-4219
  737 Delaware Avenue, Suite 200,     Fax: (716) 885-4096
  Buffalo, NY 14209

# Office for People With Developmental Disabilities [OPWDD]

44 Holland Avenue, Albany, NY 12229
Tel: (518) 473-1997  TTY: (518) 474-3694  Fax: (518) 473-1271

■Commissioner (Acting) **Kerry A. Delaney** . . . . . . . . . . . . . (518) 473-1997
  E-mail: kerry.a.delaney@opwdd.ny.gov
Executive Deputy Commissioner **Kerry A. Delaney** . . . . . . (518) 474-7700
Deputy Commissioner of Division of Enterprise Solutions
  **Kevin Valenchis** . . . . . . . . . . . . . . . . . . . . . . . . . . . . . . . (518) 408-2578
Deputy Commissioner of Division of Quality
  Improvement **Megan O'Connor-Hebert** . . . . . . . . . . . . . (518) 474-3625
Deputy Commissioner of Division of Person-Centered
  Supports **JoAnn Lamphere** . . . . . . . . . . . . . . . . . . . . . . . (518) 473-1997
Deputy Commissioner of Division of Service Delivery
  **Helene DeSanto** . . . . . . . . . . . . . . . . . . . . . . . . . . . . . . . (518) 474-9897
Deputy Commissioner of Division of Workforce and
  Talent Management **(Vacant)** . . . . . . . . . . . . . . . . . . . . . (518) 402-4315
Advocacy Services Director **Deborah Franchini** . . . . . . . . . (518) 473-1997
Communications Director **Jennifer O'Sullivan** . . . . . . . . . . (518) 473-1997
  E-mail: communications.office@opwdd.ny.gov
General Counsel **Roger Bearden** . . . . . . . . . . . . . . . . . . . . . (518) 474-7700
  E-mail: roger.bearden@ny.gov
  Education: Brown U; Harvard JD
Intergovernmental and Legislative Affairs Director
  **Greg Roberts** . . . . . . . . . . . . . . . . . . . . . . . . . . . . . . . . . (518) 474-1997
  E-mail: gregory.f.roberts@opwdd.ny.gov
Investigations and Internal Affairs Director
  **Marc A. Promutico** . . . . . . . . . . . . . . . . . . . . . . . . . . . . (518) 474-4376
  E-mail: marc.a.promutico@opwdd.ny.gov
Data Management Director **Laura D. Rosenthal** . . . . . . . . . (518) 473-1997
Audit Services Director **James Nellegar** . . . . . . . . . . . . . . . (518) 473-2100
Internal Controls Director **Mary E. Peck** . . . . . . . . . . . . . . (518) 486-6455

# Office of Parks, Recreation and Historic Preservation

Building 1, Empire State Plaza, Albany, NY 12238
Tel: (518) 474-0456  TTY: (518) 486-1899  Fax: (518) 486-2924
Internet: www.nysparks.com

■Commissioner **Rose H. Harvey** . . . . . . . . . . . . . . . . . . . . . (518) 474-0443
  E-mail: rose.harvey@oprhp.state.ny.us   Fax: (518) 474-1365
  Education: Colorado Col 1977 BA; Yale 1984 MES
Executive Deputy Commissioner
  **Andrew C. "Andy" Beers** . . . . . . . . . . . . . . . . . . . . . . . . (518) 473-5385
  Education: Colgate BA; Cornell 1987 MS  Fax: (518) 474-4492
Finance and Administration Deputy Commissioner
  **Melinda "Mindy" Scott** . . . . . . . . . . . . . . . . . . . . . . . . . (518) 474-0440
  E-mail: mindy.scott@parks.ny.gov     Fax: (518) 474-4492

*(continued on next page)*

---

★ Elected Official    ■ Appointed by Governor    ● Appointed by Legislature    ▲ Appointed by Board or Commission    ◆ Appointed by State Supreme Court

EXECUTIVE BRANCH

**Office of Parks, Recreation and Historic Preservation** *continued*

Historic Preservation Deputy Commissioner
**Ruth L. Pierpont** . . . . . . . . . . . . . . . . . . . . . . . . . . . . . . . . . (518) 474-5385
Fax: (518) 474-4492

Natural Resources Deputy Commissioner **Tom Alworth** . . . (518) 474-0414
E-mail: tom.alworth@parks.ny.gov      Fax: (518) 474-4492

Real Property and Legislature Affairs Deputy
Commissioner **Carol Clark** . . . . . . . . . . . . . . . . . . . . (518) 474-0440
Fax: (518) 474-4492

Agency Operations and Programs Director **Marc Talluto** . . . (518) 474-0440
E-mail: marc.talluto@parks.ny.gov

Regional Operations and Resource Development Director
**Christopher Pushkarsh** . . . . . . . . . . . . . . . . . . . . . . . (518) 474-0440

General Counsel **Paul J. Laudato** . . . . . . . . . . . . . . . . . . . (518) 474-0430
Fax: (518) 474-4492

Law Enforcement Director **David Herrick** . . . . . . . . . . . . . (518) 474-4029
Fax: (518) 408-1032

# Office of Temporary and Disability Assistance [OTDA]

40 North Pearl Street, Albany, NY 12243
Tel: (518) 473-1090   Fax: (518) 474-7870   E-mail: nyspio@otda.ny.gov

Commissioner **Samuel D. "Sam" Roberts** . . . . . . . . . . . . (518) 474-9475
Special Assistant to the Commissioner
**Donna M. Forino** . . . . . . . . . . . . . . . . . . . . . . . . . . . (518) 408-3847

Executive Deputy Commissioner **Michael Perrin** . . . . . . . . (518) 474-9475
Education: SUNY (Oswego) BA

Audit and Quality Improvement Bureau Director
**Kevin Kehmna** . . . . . . . . . . . . . . . . . . . . . . . . . . . . . (518) 473-6035

Budget, Finance and Data Management Director
**Nancy Maney** . . . . . . . . . . . . . . . . . . . . . . . . . . . . . . (518) 474-0183
E-mail: nancy.maney@otda.ny.gov

Budget Bureau Director **Elizabeth Dexter-Hinton** . . . . . . (518) 486-5163

Chief Accountant **Virginia Lattanzio** . . . . . . . . . . . . . . . (518) 474-2260

Data Management and Analysis Bureau Director
**David Dlugolecki** . . . . . . . . . . . . . . . . . . . . . . . . . . . (518) 474-1192

Administrative Hearings Director **Sam Spitzberg** . . . . . . . . (518) 473-9699

Equal Opportunity and Diversity Director
**Jessica Vaughn Tolle** . . . . . . . . . . . . . . . . . . . . . . . . (212) 961-8214

Intergovernmental Affairs Office Director **(Vacant)** . . . . . . . (518) 474-7420

Public Information Office Director **Kristi L. Berner** . . . . . . . (518) 474-9516
E-mail: nyspio@otda.ny.gov      Fax: (518) 486-6935

Special Counsel for Ethics, Risk and Compliance
**Kevin Hickey** . . . . . . . . . . . . . . . . . . . . . . . . . . . . . . (518) 473-1090
Education: SUNY (Albany) BS; Albany Law JD

# New York State Bridge Authority [NYSBA]

P.O. Box 1010, Highland, NY 12528
Tel: (845) 691-7245   Fax: (845) 691-3560   E-mail: info@nysba.net

■Chairman **Richard A. Gerentine** . . . . . . . . . . . . . . . . . . . (845) 691-7245
Education: Marist BBA

■Vice Chairman **Joseph Ramaglia** . . . . . . . . . . . . . . . . . . (845) 691-7245

■Member **Roderick O. Dressel** . . . . . . . . . . . . . . . . . . . . (845) 691-7245

■Member **Roger P. Higgins** . . . . . . . . . . . . . . . . . . . . . . (845) 691-7245

■Member **C. Vane Lashua** . . . . . . . . . . . . . . . . . . . . . . . (845) 691-7245
Education: Indiana BA; Western Kentucky MA

■Member **(Vacant)** . . . . . . . . . . . . . . . . . . . . . . . . . . . . (845) 691-7245

■Member **(Vacant)** . . . . . . . . . . . . . . . . . . . . . . . . . . . . (845) 691-7245

■Executive Director **Joseph Ruggiero** . . . . . . . . . . . . . . . (845) 691-7245
E-mail: jruggiero@nysba.ny.gov
Education: Dutchess Comm Col; SUNY (Utica/Rome) BS

Deputy Executive Director **Tara Sullivan** . . . . . . . . . . . . . (845) 691-7245

Chief of Staff **John Bellucci** . . . . . . . . . . . . . . . . . . . . . (845) 691-7245

Administration Services Director **Robert "Bob" Russo** . . . (845) 691-7245
E-mail: rrusso@nysba.ny.gov

Human Resources Director **Nancy Hritz-Seifts** . . . . . . . . (845) 691-7245

Information Technology Director
**Gregory J. "Greg" Herd** . . . . . . . . . . . . . . . . . . . . . (845) 691-7245
E-mail: gherd@nysba.ny.gov

Finance Director and Treasurer **Brian Bushek** . . . . . . . . . . (845) 691-7245

Chief Engineer **Jeffrey Wright** . . . . . . . . . . . . . . . . . . . . (845) 691-7245

Toll Collections Director and Bridge Operations Manager
**Wayne V. Ferguson** . . . . . . . . . . . . . . . . . . . . . . . . . (845) 691-7245

Contract Maintenance Manager **George Fong** . . . . . . . . . . (845) 691-7245

Maintenance Manager **Craig Gardner** . . . . . . . . . . . . . . . (845) 691-7245

# Dormitory Authority of the State of New York [DASNY]

515 Broadway, Albany, NY 12207-2964
Tel: (518) 257-3000   Fax: (518) 257-3100

■President and Chief Executive Officer **Gerrard P. Bushell** . . (518) 257-3180
E-mail: gbushell@dasny.org
Education: Columbia BA, MA, PhD

▲Vice President **Michael T. Corrigan** . . . . . . . . . . . . . . . . (518) 257-3192
E-mail: mcorriga@dasny.org
Education: SUNY (Plattsburgh) BS; UMass (Boston) MBA

Chief of Staff **Caroline V. Griffin** . . . . . . . . . . . . . . . . . (518) 257-3661
Education: Boston Col BA

▲Managing Director of Client Services and Solutions
**Caprice G. Spann** . . . . . . . . . . . . . . . . . . . . . . . . . . (518) 257-3386
E-mail: cspann@dasny.org

Managing Director of Construction **Stephen D. Curro** . . . . (518) 257-3271

Managing Director of Public Finance and Portfolio
Monitoring **Portia Lee** . . . . . . . . . . . . . . . . . . . . . . . (518) 257-3362

Chief Financial Officer and Treasurer
**Kimberly J. Nadeau** . . . . . . . . . . . . . . . . . . . . . . . . . (518) 257-3562
Education: Connecticut JD

General Counsel **Michael E. Cusack** . . . . . . . . . . . . . . . . (518) 257-3120

Internal Audit Director **Kathy D. Ebert** . . . . . . . . . . . . . . (518) 257-3696

Director of Communications and Marketing
**Freeman Klopott** . . . . . . . . . . . . . . . . . . . . . . . . . . . (518) 257-3747
E-mail: fklopott@dasny.org

# New York State Energy Research and Development Authority [NYSERDA]

17 Columbia Circle, Albany, NY 12203-6399
Tel: (518) 862-1090   Fax: (518) 862-1091   E-mail: info@nyserda.ny.gov

President and Chief Executive Officer
**John B. Rhodes** . . . . . . . . . . . . . . . . . . . . . . . . . . . . (518) 862-1090 ext. 3320
E-mail: john.rhodes@nyserda.ny.gov

Executive Assistant to the President
**Suzanne Baker** . . . . . . . . . . . . . . . . . . . . . . . . . . . . (518) 862-1090 ext. 3278

Chief of Staff **Sarah J. Osgood** . . . . . . . . . . . . . . . (518) 862-1090 ext. 3313

Technology and Strategic Planning Vice
President **Janet Joseph** . . . . . . . . . . . . . . . . . . . . . . (518) 862-1090 ext. 3296
E-mail: janet.joseph@nyserda.ny.gov

General Counsel and Secretary **Noah C. Shaw** . . (518) 862-1090 ext. 3100
Education: Brandeis 1998 BA; Northeastern 2002 JD

Treasurer and Internal Control Officer
**Jeffrey J. "Jeff" Pitkin** . . . . . . . . . . . . . . . . . . . . . . (518) 862-1090 ext. 3223

Consumer Services and Events Management
Director **Don G. LaVada** . . . . . . . . . . . . . . . . . . . . . (518) 862-1090 ext. 3428

Corporate Strategy and Planning Director
**Kevin C. Hale** . . . . . . . . . . . . . . . . . . . . . . . . . . . . (518) 862-1090 ext. 3266

Energy Analysis Program Director
**John G. Williams** . . . . . . . . . . . . . . . . . . . . . . . . . . (518) 862-1090 ext. 3333

Clean Energy Research and Market
Development Director **Mark R. Torpey** . . . . . . . . (518) 862-1090 ext. 3316

End-Use Application and Innovation Program
Director **(Vacant)** . . . . . . . . . . . . . . . . . . . . . . . . . . (518) 862-1090 ext. 3214

Residential Energy Services Program Director
**Karen E. Hamilton** . . . . . . . . . . . . . . . . . . . . . . . . . (518) 862-1090 ext. 3275

Renewable Thermal Director **Donovan Gordon** . . . . . . . . . (518) 862-1090
Education: St Francis Col (NY) BS; NYU MBA

West Valley Site Management Program Director
**Paul J. Bembia** . . . . . . . . . . . . . . . . . . . . . . . . . . . (716) 942-9960 ext. 4900
P.O. Box 191, West Valley, NY 14171-0191

Chief Operating Officer **David L. Margalit** . . . . . . (518) 862-1090 ext. 3233
Education: Delaware BS; Harvard MBA

Communications Director
**Katherine T. "Kate" Muller** . . . . . . . . . . . . . . . (518) 862-1090 ext. 3582
E-mail: kate.muller@nyserda.ny.gov

Government Affairs Director **Thomas Lynch** . . . . (518) 862-1090 ext. 3250

Internal Audit Director **Mark B. Mitchell** . . . . . . . (518) 862-1090 ext. 3289

---

★ Elected Official    ■ Appointed by Governor    ● Appointed by Legislature    ▲ Appointed by Board or Commission    ◆ Appointed by State Supreme Court

Marketing Director **Susan Moyer** . . . . . . . . . . . . (518) 862-1090 ext. 3420

# New York State Thruway Authority

200 Southern Boulevard, Albany, NY 12209
P.O. Box 189, Albany, NY 12201-0189
Tel: (518) 436-2900  TTY: (800) 253-6244  Fax: (518) 436-2899

■Chair **Joanne M. "Joanie" Mahoney** . . . . . . . . . . . . . . . . (518) 436-2900
  Education: Syracuse BA, JD
■Vice Chair **Donna J. Luh** . . . . . . . . . . . . . . . . . . . . . . . (518) 436-2900
  Education: Canisius BS, MS
■Board Member **Jose Holguin-Veras, PhD** . . . . . . . . . . . . (518) 436-2900
■Board Member **J. Donald Rice, Jr.** . . . . . . . . . . . . . . . . (518) 436-2900
  Education: Kettering BS; Harvard MBA
■Board Member **Richard N. Simberg** . . . . . . . . . . . . . . . (518) 436-2900
■Board Member **(Vacant)** . . . . . . . . . . . . . . . . . . . . . . . . (518) 436-2900
■Board Member **(Vacant)** . . . . . . . . . . . . . . . . . . . . . . . . (518) 436-2900
Executive Director and Chief Operating Officer (Interim)
  **Maria C. Lehman** . . . . . . . . . . . . . . . . . . . . . . . . . . (518) 436-2900
  E-mail: maria.lehman@thruway.ny.gov
  Education: SUNY Col (Buffalo) BSCE
Chief of Staff **Karen M. Hunter** . . . . . . . . . . . . . . . . . . (518) 436-2900
  E-mail: karen.hunter@thruway.ny.gov
  Education: Illinois BS
Chief Engineer **Catherine T. Sheridan, PE** . . . . . . . . . . . (518) 436-2900
  Education: Boston U; Columbia MS
Director of Media Relations and Communications
  **Dan Weiller** . . . . . . . . . . . . . . . . . . . . . . . . . . . . . . (518) 436-2983
  E-mail: dan.weiller@thruway.ny.gov
General Counsel **Gordon J. Cuffy** . . . . . . . . . . . . . . . . . (518) 436-2900
  E-mail: gordon.cuffy@thruway.ny.gov
  Education: Syracuse BA; Brooklyn Law JD

# Empire State Development Board of Directors

633 Third Avenue, New York, NY 10017
625 Broadway, Albany, NY 12233-1010
Tel: (212) 803-3100  Tel: (518) 292-5100

■Director **Peter Justus Beshar** . . . . . . . . . . . . . . . . . . . . (212) 803-3100
  Affiliation: Executive Vice President and General Counsel, Marsh &
  McLennan Companies, Inc.
  1166 Avenue of the Americas, New York, NY 10036-2774
  Education: Yale 1984 BA; Harvard 1989 JD
■Director **Derrick D. Cephas** . . . . . . . . . . . . . . . . . . . . . (212) 803-3100
  Education: Harvard 1975 AB, 1979 JD
■Director **Robert R. Dyson** . . . . . . . . . . . . . . . . . . . . . . (212) 803-3100
  Affiliation: Chairman and Chief Executive Officer, The
  Dyson-Kissner-Moran Corporation
  565 5th Avenue, 4th Floor, New York, NY 10017-2413
  Education: Marietta BA; Cornell 1974 MBA
■Director **Joyce L. Miller** . . . . . . . . . . . . . . . . . . . . . . . (212) 803-3100
■Director **Hilda Rosario Escher** . . . . . . . . . . . . . . . . . . . (212) 803-3100
■Director-Designate **Cesar A. Perales** . . . . . . . . . . . . . . (212) 803-3100
  Education: CCNY 1962 BA; Fordham 1965 JD
■Director **(Vacant)** . . . . . . . . . . . . . . . . . . . . . . . . . . . . (212) 803-3100
Ex-Officio Director **Maria T. Vullo** . . . . . . . . . . . . . . . . (212) 709-3501
  Affiliation: Superintendent (Acting), Department of Financial Services,
  State of New York (Note: On January 21, 2016, Governor Andrew
  Cuomo nominated Maria Vullo to serve as Superintendent of the
  Department of Financial Services. Vullo's nomination must be
  confirmed by the New York Senate. She is currently acting in this
  position.)
  One State Street, New York, NY 10004-1511
Ex-Officio Director **Howard Zemsky** . . . . . . . . . . . . . . . (212) 803-3700
  Affiliation: President and Chief Executive Officer, Empire State
  Development Corporation, State of New York
  633 Third Avenue, New York, NY 10017
  Education: Michigan State BA; Rochester MBA

# Empire State Development Corporation

633 Third Avenue, New York, NY 10017
Tel: (212) 803-3100  Fax: (212) 803-3175  E-mail: esd@esd.ny.gov

■President and Chief Executive Officer **Howard Zemsky** . . . (212) 803-3700
  E-mail: hzemsky@esd.ny.gov

Chief Operating Officer **Kevin Amien Younis** . . . . . . . . . . (212) 803-3100
  Education: SUNY (Cortland) BA; Dartmouth MPA
Chief of Staff **Lindsey C. Boylan** . . . . . . . . . . . . . . . . . . (212) 803-3100
  Education: Wellesley BA; Columbia MBA
Chief Financial Officer **(Vacant)** . . . . . . . . . . . . . . . . . . (212) 803-3510
General Counsel **Elizabeth "Liz" Fine** . . . . . . . . . . . . . . (212) 803-3750
  E-mail: efine@esd.ny.gov
  Education: Brown U BA; Georgetown LLM; NYU JD
Business Attraction and Expansion Executive Vice
  President **(Vacant)** . . . . . . . . . . . . . . . . . . . . . . . . . (212) 803-3100
Business Marketing Senior Vice President and Chief
  Marketing Officer **Harvey Cohen** . . . . . . . . . . . . . . . (518) 292-5375
Innovation and Broadband Executive Vice President
  **Jeffrey Nordhaus** . . . . . . . . . . . . . . . . . . . . . . . . . . (212) 803-3100
  Education: Harvard BA
Public Affairs and Strategic Initiatives Executive Vice
  President **Kay Sarlin Wright** . . . . . . . . . . . . . . . . . . . (212) 803-3740
  Education: Hobart & William Smith BA; Columbia MS
  Public Affairs Vice President **Gerardo "Jerry" Russo** . . (212) 803-3100
    Education: Pennsylvania BA; George Washington JD
Public Policy, Planning and Incentives Executive Vice
  President **(Vacant)** . . . . . . . . . . . . . . . . . . . . . . . . . (518) 292-5101
Real Estate Development and Subsidiaries Executive Vice
  President **Joseph "Joe" Chan** . . . . . . . . . . . . . . . . . . (212) 803-3730
  Education: NYU 1993 BA, 1998 MUP
Small Business Services and Community Economic
  Development Executive Vice President **(Vacant)** . . . . . . (212) 803-3237
State Marketing Strategy Executive Vice President
  **Richard Newman** . . . . . . . . . . . . . . . . . . . . . . . . . . (212) 803-3100
Administration Senior Vice President **Edward Hamilton** . . (518) 292-5907
  E-mail: ehamilton@esd.ny.gov
Regional Economic Development Senior Vice President
  **William B. "Sam" Hoyt III** . . . . . . . . . . . . . . . . . . . (716) 846-8250
  Education: SUNY (Buffalo) 1992 BA
Strategic Business Development Senior Vice President
  **Jeff Janiszewski** . . . . . . . . . . . . . . . . . . . . . . . . . . (518) 292-5201
  Education: SUNY (Albany) 1984 MBA
Construction and Design Vice President
  **Barbara Lampen** . . . . . . . . . . . . . . . . . . . . . . . . . . (212) 803-3100
Facilities Vice President **Rudy Rosefort** . . . . . . . . . . . . . (212) 803-3161
  E-mail: rrosefort@esd.ny.gov
Human Resources Vice President **Eileen Mason** . . . . . . . . (212) 803-3200
■International Trade and Investment Vice President
  **Claire McLeveighn** . . . . . . . . . . . . . . . . . . . . . . . . . (212) 803-3769
  E-mail: cmcleveighn@esd.ny.gov
  Education: Brown U BA; Columbia MPA
Director of Upstate Revitalization **Richard Tobe** . . . . . . . (518) 473-5076
Senior Advisor for Innovative Project Delivery
  **Karen J. Rae** . . . . . . . . . . . . . . . . . . . . . . . . . . . . . (212) 803-3100
  Education: East Stroudsburg BS

# Department of Economic Development

Tel: (212) 803-3100

**Employees:** 230

Commissioner **Howard Zemsky** . . . . . . . . . . . . . . . . . . . (212) 803-3700
Senior Advisor for Economic Policy **David Wright** . . . . . . (518) 292-5144

# Environmental Facilities Corporation

625 Broadway, 7th Floor, Albany, NY 12207-2997
Tel: (518) 402-6924  Fax: (518) 402-6954  E-mail: info@efc.ny.gov

President and Chief Executive Officer **Sabrina M. Ty** . . . . . (518) 402-6924
  Education: McGill (Canada) BA; Albany Law 1989 JD
General Counsel **Maureen A. Coleman** . . . . . . . . . . . . . . (518) 402-6924
  Education: Col St Rose BA; Brooklyn Law JD
  Executive Deputy Counsel **George N. Cholakis** . . . . . . . (518) 402-6924
    Education: Western New England JD; Thunderbird Global MIM
Controller and Director of Corporate Operations
  **Michael D. Malinoski** . . . . . . . . . . . . . . . . . . . . . . . (518) 402-6924
  Education: Siena Col BBA
Director of Engineering and Program Management
  **Timothy P. "Tim" Burns** . . . . . . . . . . . . . . . . . . . . . (518) 402-6924
  Education: SUNY Col (Buffalo) BSChE; CCNY ME
Director of Public Information **Linda Foglia** . . . . . . . . . . (518) 402-6924
  E-mail: press@efc.ny.gov

*(continued on next page)*

---

★ Elected Official  ■ Appointed by Governor  ● Appointed by Legislature  ▲ Appointed by Board or Commission  ◆ Appointed by State Supreme Court

EXECUTIVE BRANCH

**Environmental Facilities Corporation** *continued*

Deputy Director of Finance **(Vacant)** . . . . . . . . . . . . . . . . . (518) 402-7085

# Higher Education Services Corporation

99 Washington Avenue, Albany, NY 12255
Tel: (888) 697-4372  TTY: (800) 445-5234  Fax: (518) 474-5593
Internet: www.hesc.org

President (Acting) **Elsa Magee** . . . . . . . . . . . . . . . . . . . . . (518) 474-5592
Executive Vice President **Elsa Magee** . . . . . . . . . . . . . . . (518) 474-5775
Communications Senior Vice President **Kathy Crowder** . . . (518) 402-1448
  E-mail: kcrowder@hesc.ny.gov
Corporate Finance Senior Vice President and Chief
  Financial Officer **Warren Wallin** . . . . . . . . . . . . . . . . . (518) 486-7443
  E-mail: wwallin@hesc.ny.gov
Customer Relations Senior Vice President **John Austin** . . . (518) 473-0810
Information Technology Senior Vice President
  **Richard "Rich" Valenti** . . . . . . . . . . . . . . . . . . . . . . . (518) 474-7083
  E-mail: rvalenti@hesc.ny.gov
General Counsel **Thomas F. Brennan** . . . . . . . . . . . . . . . . (518) 473-1585
  Education: Oberlin 1983 BA; St John's U (NY) 1987 JD
Audit Division Director **Matthew "Matt" Downey** . . . . . . (518) 473-2523
Human Resources Management Bureau Director
  **Sue Stah-Cooper** . . . . . . . . . . . . . . . . . . . . . . . . . . . . (518) 474-0510

# State Commission of Correction

Alfred E. Smith State Office Building, 80 South Swan Street, 12th Floor,
Albany, NY 12210-8001
Tel: (518) 485-2346  Fax: (518) 485-2467  Internet: www.scoc.ny.gov

■Chairman **Thomas A. Beilein** . . . . . . . . . . . . . . . . . . . . . (518) 485-2330
■Member **Phyllis Harrison-Ross, MD** . . . . . . . . . . . . . . . . (518) 485-2330
■Member **Thomas J. Loughren** . . . . . . . . . . . . . . . . . . . . (518) 485-2346
  Education: McNeese State BS

# New York State Gaming Commission

One Broadway Center, Schenectady, NY 12305
P.O. Box 7500, Schenectady, NY 12301-7500
Tel: (518) 388-3415  Fax: (518) 388-3423  TTY: (518) 388-3584

Chair **(Vacant)** . . . . . . . . . . . . . . . . . . . . . . . . . . . . . . . . . (518) 388-3415
Commissioner **John A. Crotty** . . . . . . . . . . . . . . . . . . . . . (518) 388-3415
  Term Expires: January 31, 2017
  Affiliation: Founding Member, Workforce Housing Group
  5-14 51st Avenue, Long Island City, NY 11101
  Education: Rochester 1990 BA; Columbia 1996 MBA
Commissioner **Peter J. Moschetti, Jr.** . . . . . . . . . . . . . . . (518) 388-3415
  Term Expires: January 31, 2017
  Affiliation: Founding Partner, Anderson, Moschetti and Taffany
  26 Century Hill Drive, Suite 206, Latham, NY 12110
  Education: New Haven 1981; Albany Law 1984
Commissioner **John J. Poklemba** . . . . . . . . . . . . . . . . . . . (518) 388-3415
  Term Expires: January 21, 2020
  Education: Boston Col BA
Commissioner **Barry Sample** . . . . . . . . . . . . . . . . . . . . . . (518) 388-3415
  Term Expires: January 31, 2018
Commissioner **Todd R. Snyder** . . . . . . . . . . . . . . . . . . . . . (518) 388-3415
  Term Expires: January 31, 2016
  Affiliation: Managing Director, Rothschild Inc., N M Rothschild &
  Sons Limited
  1251 Avenue of the Americas, 33rd Floor, New York, NY 10020
  Education: Wesleyan U; Pennsylvania JD
■Director **Robert "Rob" Williams** . . . . . . . . . . . . . . . . . (518) 388-3400
  E-mail: robert.williams@gaming.ny.gov
New York Lottery Director **Gardner S. Gurney** . . . . . . . . . (518) 388-3406
  Education: Husson 1983 BA
General Counsel **Edmund Burns** . . . . . . . . . . . . . . . . . . . (518) 388-3408
Advertising Director **Dana Idema** . . . . . . . . . . . . . . . . . . (518) 388-3430
Audits and Investigations Director **(Vacant)** . . . . . . . . . . (518) 395-5400
Communications Director **Lee R. Park** . . . . . . . . . . . . . . . (518) 388-3415
Charitable Gaming Director **Stacy Harvey** . . . . . . (518) 395-5400 ext. 1407
Licensing Chief **Jeffrey Allen** . . . . . . . . . . . . . . . . . . . . . (518) 395-5400
Racing Officials Director **Brian Barry** . . . . . . . . . (518) 395-5400 ext. 1809

Horse Racing and Pari-Mutuel Wagering Director
  **Ronald. G. "Ron" Ochrym** . . . . . . . . . . . . . . . . . . . . (518) 395-5400
  Education: UNLV
Sales and Marketing Director **Daniel Martin** . . . . . . . . . . . (518) 388-3430

# Public Service Commission [PSC]

Three Empire State Plaza, Albany, NY 12223-1350
Tel: (518) 474-7080  TTY: (800) 662-1220  Fax: (518) 473-2838

**Employees: 494  Fiscal Year: 2013-2014  Budget: $86,142,000**

■Chair **Audrey Zibelman** . . . . . . . . . . . . . . . . . . . . . . . . . (518) 474-2532
  Term Expires: February 1, 2018
  E-mail: audrey.zibelman@dps.ny.gov
  Education: Penn State 1977 BA; Hamline 1983 JD
■Commissioner **Patricia L. Acampora** . . . . . . . . . . . . . . . (518) 474-2523
  Term Expires: February 1, 2015    Tel: (212) 417-3168
  E-mail: patricia.acampora@dps.ny.gov    (New York City)
■Commissioner **Diane X. Burman** . . . . . . . . . . . . . . . . . . (518) 408-1978
  Term Expires: February 1, 2018
  E-mail: diane.burman@dps.ny.gov
  Education: Molloy BA; Fordham JD
■Commissioner **Gregg C. Sayre** . . . . . . . . . . . . . . . . . . . (212) 408-1978
  Term Expires: February 1, 2018
  E-mail: gregg.sayre@dps.ny.gov
  Education: Grinnell; Harvard JD; RIT MS

# Office of the State Comptroller

110 State Street, 15th Floor, Albany, NY 12236
Tel: (518) 474-4044  Fax: (518) 473-5011  E-mail: press@osc.state.ny.us
Internet: www.osc.state.ny.us

★State Comptroller **Thomas P. "Tom" DiNapoli** (D) . . . . . . (518) 474-4040
  Term Expires: January 2019
  Education: Hofstra 1976 BA; New School 1988 MS
  Career: State Assembly Member (D-NY, District 16), New York State
  Assembly (1986-2006)
  Special Assistant for External Affairs
    **Darrel J. Aubertine** . . . . . . . . . . . . . . . . . . . . . . . . . (518) 474-4044
    E-mail: daubertine@osc.state.ny.us
First Deputy Comptroller **Alexander B. "Pete" Grannis** . . (518) 474-9025
  Education: Rutgers BS; Virginia JD
Chief of Staff **Shawn Thompson** . . . . . . . . . . . . . . . . . . . (518) 474-4044
Budget and Policy Analysis Deputy Comptroller
  **Robert Ward** . . . . . . . . . . . . . . . . . . . . . . . . . . . . . . . (518) 473-4333
  Education: Syracuse
Contracts and Expenditures Deputy Comptroller
  **Margaret Becker** . . . . . . . . . . . . . . . . . . . . . . . . . . . . (518) 402-4104
  E-mail: mnbecker@osc.state.ny.us
Diversity Deputy Comptroller **Nancy R. Hernandez** . . . . . (518) 473-1368
  Education: SUNY (Albany) BA, MPA
Human Resources and Administration Deputy
  Comptroller **Angela Dixon** . . . . . . . . . . . . . . . . . . . . (518) 474-5512
  E-mail: adixon@osc.state.ny.us
General Counsel **Nancy G. Groenwegen** . . . . . . . . . . . . . (518) 474-3444
Local Government and School Accountability Deputy
  Comptroller **Gabriel F. Deyo** . . . . . . . . . . . . . . . . . . . (518) 474-4037
  E-mail: gdeyo@osc.state.ny.us
Operations Executive Deputy Comptroller **John Traylor** . . . (518) 402-4103
Payroll, Accounting, and Revenue Services Deputy
  Comptroller **Chris Gorka** . . . . . . . . . . . . . . . . . . . . . . (518) 408-4149
State Government Accountability Executive Deputy
  Comptroller **Andrew A. "Andy" SanFilippo** . . . . . . . . (518) 474-4593
  E-mail: asanfilippo@osc.state.ny.us
  Education: SUNY (Brockport) 1973 BS
State Government Accountability Deputy Comptroller
  **H. Tina Kim** . . . . . . . . . . . . . . . . . . . . . . . . . . . . . . . . (518) 474-6048
Chief Information Officer and Deputy Comptroller
  **Robert Loomis** . . . . . . . . . . . . . . . . . . . . . . . . . . . . . (518) 486-4349
Intergovernmental Affairs Assistant Comptroller
  **Carlos Rodriguez** . . . . . . . . . . . . . . . . . . . . . . . . . . . (518) 402-3234
Communications Director **Jennifer Freeman** . . . . . . . . . . . (518) 474-2475
  E-mail: jfreeman@osc.state.ny.us
  Assistant Communications Director
    **Matthew Sweeney** . . . . . . . . . . . . . . . . . . . . . . . . . . (518) 474-4044
Inspector General **Stephen "Steve" Hamilton** . . . . . . . . . (518) 408-4906
Librarian **Rosemary A. Del Vecchio** . . . . . . . . . . . . . . . . (518) 473-5960

---

★ Elected Official    ■ Appointed by Governor    ● Appointed by Legislature    ▲ Appointed by Board or Commission    ◆ Appointed by State Supreme Court

EXECUTIVE BRANCH

## New York City Office

59 Maiden Lane, 29th Floor, New York, NY 10038

State Deputy Comptroller for New York City
**Kenneth Bleiwas** ................................. (212) 383-3900

## New York State and Local Retirement System [NYSLRS]

110 State Street, Albany, NY 12236
Tel: (518) 474-7736  Fax: (518) 402-4433

Executive Deputy Comptroller
**Colleen Crawford Gardner** .................... (518) 474-2600
  Education: Cornell BS
Pension Investment, Cash Management Chief Investment
  Officer and Deputy Comptroller **Vicki L. Fuller** ....... (518) 474-4003
  E-mail: vfuller@osc.state.ny.us
Retirement Services Division Deputy Comptroller
  **Melanie Whinnery** ............................ (518) 474-2600
  Education: Marist MPA
Benefit Information Services Director **Keith Zeto** ........ (518) 474-5728
  E-mail: kzeto@osc.state.ny.us

## Department of Law

State Capitol, Albany, NY 12224
120 Broadway, New York, NY 10271-0332
Tel: (518) 776-2000 (Albany)  Tel: (212) 416-8050 (New York)
TTY: (800) 788-9898 (New York)  Fax: (518) 473-9909 (Albany)
Fax: (212) 416-8942 (New York)

## Office of the Attorney General

State Capitol, Albany, NY 12224
120 Broadway, New York, NY 10271-0332
Tel: (518) 776-2000  Tel: (800) 771-7755  TTY: (800) 788-9898
Fax: (518) 915-7754

**Employees:** 2,032  **Fiscal Year:** 2014  **Budget:** $215,348,000

★Attorney General **Eric T. Schneiderman** (D) ........... (518) 776-2000
  Term Expires: January 2019
  Education: Amherst 1977 BA; Harvard 1982 JD
  Career: Deputy Minority Leader, New York Senate (2003-2006); State
  Senator (D-NY, District 31), New York State Senate (1999-2010)
  Chief of Staff **(Vacant)** ........................ (518) 776-2000
  Deputy Chief of Staff **Joshua Meltzer** .............. (518) 776-2000
Assistant Attorney General in Charge **John P. Amodeo** ... (518) 473-5525
  Education: New England JD
Chief Deputy Attorney General **Jason Brown III** ........ (212) 242-5301
  Education: Princeton 1981 BA; Harvard 1985 JD
Chief Deputy Attorney General **Janet Sabel** ............ (212) 242-5301
  Education: Harvard BA; NYU JD
First Deputy Attorney General of Affirmative Litigation
  **(Vacant)** ..................................... (212) 416-8450
Senior Enforcement Counsel and Special Advisor
  **Timothy "Tim" Wu** ............................. (212) 416-8160
  Education: McGill (Canada) 1995 BSc; Harvard 1998 JD
Senior Policy Advisor and Director of Legislative Affairs
  **Kate Powers** .................................. (518) 776-2000
Senior Advisor and Operations Director
  **Christina Harvey** .............................. (518) 776-2000
  Education: Sarah Lawrence BA; NYU MPA
Senior Adviser for Communications and Policy
  **Eric Soufer** ................................... (518) 776-2000
  E-mail: eric.soufer@ag.ny.gov
Chief Economist **Guy Ben-Ishai** .................... (212) 416-8050
  Education: UCLA BA; Hebrew U (Israel) PhD
Law Library Services Chief **Patricia Partello** .......... (518) 776-2000

## Administration

State Capitol, Albany, NY 12224

Chief Operating Officer **Shanti Nayak** ............... (518) 473-7900
  Education: Smith BA; Harvard MPP
Deputy Chief Operating Officer **Pauline Ross** ......... (518) 486-3991
  E-mail: pauline.ross@ag.ny.gov

Administrative Services and Facilities Director
  **Jennifer Gonroff** .............................. (518) 474-7906
  E-mail: jennifer.gonroff@ag.ny.gov
Budget and Fiscal Management Director
  **Michael Lefebvre** ............................. (518) 474-7699
Human Resources Director **Robert Pablo** ............. (518) 474-4848
Intergovernmental Affairs Director **Michael Meade** ...... (212) 416-6044
Legal Education Director **Michael McDermott** ......... (518) 473-5582
Chief Information Officer **Donna O'Leary** ............ (518) 474-9048
  E-mail: donna.oleary@ag.ny.gov

## Communications Department

State Capitol, Albany, NY 12224
120 Broadway, New York, NY 10271-0332
Tel: (518) 473-5525 (Albany Press Office)  Fax: (518) 402-2271
Tel: (212) 416-8060 (New York City Press Office)  Fax: (212) 416-6005

Communication Director **Damien J. Lavera** ........... (212) 416-8037
  E-mail: damien.lavera@ag.ny.gov
Deputy Communications Director **(Vacant)** ........... (212) 416-6179
Press Secretary **Matthew Mittenthal** ............... (212) 416-8015
Press Secretary (Spanish Language) **Fernando Aquino** .... (212) 416-8060
Senior Deputy Press Secretary **Nick Benson** .......... (212) 416-8060
Deputy Press Secretary **(Vacant)** .................. (212) 416-8060

## Appeals and Opinions Division

Office of the Attorney General, 120 Broadway,
New York, NY 10271-0332
Tel: (518) 776-2038 (Albany)  Tel: (212) 416-8020 (NYC)
Fax: (518) 473-4386 (Albany)  Fax: (212) 416-8962 (NYC)

Solicitor General **Barbara D. Underwood** ............. (212) 416-8016
  Education: Radcliffe 1966; Georgetown 1969 JD
Deputy Solicitor General **Andrew Bing** .............. (518) 776-2038
Deputy Solicitor General **Anisha S. Dasgupta** ........ (212) 416-8921
  Education: Yale 2006 JD
Deputy Solicitor General **Andrea Oser** .............. (518) 776-2046
Deputy Solicitor General **Steven C Wu** ............. (212) 416-6279
Deputy Solicitor General for Criminal Appeals
  **Nikki Kowalski** ............................... (212) 416-8370
Assistant Solicitor General **Andrew B. Ayers** ......... (518) 776-2024
  Education: Vassar 1998 BA; Georgetown 2005 JD
Assistant Solicitor General **Denise Hartman** .......... (518) 776-2040
Assistant Solicitor General, Opinions
  **Kathryn Sheingold** ............................ (518) 776-2049
Special Counsel **Cecilia Chang** .................... (212) 416-6312
  Education: Boalt Hall JD
Senior Counsel **Andrew Kent** ..................... (212) 416-8027

## Criminal Justice Division

Executive Deputy Attorney General for Criminal Justice
  **Kelly Donovan** ................................ (212) 416-8058
  Education: Boston Col; Columbus Law JD
Auto Insurance Fraud Unit Chief **Stephanie Swenton** .... (212) 416-8589
Criminal Enforcement and Financial Crimes Bureau
  Chief **Gary Fishman** ............................ (212) 416-8011
Public Integrity Bureau Chief **Daniel Cort** ........... (212) 416-8090
  Education: Drew; Georgetown JD

## Medicaid Fraud Control Unit

Tel: (212) 417-5300  Fax: (212) 417-5274

Deputy Attorney General in Charge/Director (Acting)
  **Amy Held** .................................... (212) 417-5250
Counsel **Jay Speers** ............................. (212) 417-5263
Chief Auditor **Thomasina Smith** ................... (212) 417-5124
Chief Investigator **Kenneth Morgan** ................ (212) 417-5431
Civil Enforcement Division Chief **Paul J. Mahoney** ...... (212) 417-5263

## Economic Justice Division

Executive Deputy Attorney General for Economic Justice
  **Manisha M. Sheth** ............................. (212) 416-8198
Antitrust Bureau Chief **Eric Stock** ................. (212) 416-8282
  Note: On April 4, 2016, Eric Stock announced he would be joining
  Gibson, Dunn, and Crutcher LLP. Mr. Stock's departure date from the
  Office of the Attorney General has not yet been determined.

*(continued on next page)*

---

★ Elected Official   ■ Appointed by Governor   ● Appointed by Legislature   ▲ Appointed by Board or Commission   ◆ Appointed by State Supreme Court

**EXECUTIVE BRANCH**

**Economic Justice Division** *continued*

Consumer Frauds and Protection Bureau Chief
**Jane Azia** . . . . . . . . . . . . . . . . . . . . . . . . . . . . . (212) 486-4519
Education: Northwestern 1973 JD; NYU 1977 JD

Internet Bureau Chief **Kathleen McGee** . . . . . . . . . . . . . . (212) 416-6494
Education: St Lawrence 1994 BA; Chicago 1995 MA;
Boston U 2001 JD

Investor Protection Bureau Chief **(Vacant)** . . . . . . . . . . . . . (212) 416-8225
Investor Protection Bureau Deputy Chief
**Katherine C. Milgram** . . . . . . . . . . . . . . . . . . . . . . (212) 416-6497

Real Estate Financing Bureau Chief **Erica Buckley** . . . . . . . (212) 416-8102
E-mail: erica.buckley@ag.ny.gov

Senior Enforcement Counsel **Steven Glassman** . . . . . . . . . (212) 416-8995
Education: MIT BS; Georgetown JD

## Investigations Division
Tel: (518) 776-2631

Chief Investigator **Dominick Zarrella** . . . . . . . . . . . . . . (518) 474-8686
Deputy Chief Investigator **John Reidy** . . . . . . . . . . . . . (518) 474-8686
Deputy Chief of Training and Firearms **Jonathan Wood** . . (518) 776-2525

## Regional Affairs Division
Executive Deputy Attorney General
**Martin J. "Marty" Mack** . . . . . . . . . . . . . . . . . . . . (315) 448-4800
Statler Towers, 107 Delaware Avenue,          Fax: (315) 448-4853
Buffalo, NY 14202-3473
Education: Cornell 1975 BS; SUNY (Cortland) MAT;
South Carolina JD

Assistant Attorney General in Charge **Gary Brown** . . . . . . . (914) 422-8731
101 East Post Road, White Plains, NY 10601-5008   Fax: (914) 422-8709

Assistant Attorney General in Charge **Debra Martin** . . . . . (585) 327-3220
144 Exchange Boulevard,                Fax: (585) 546-7514
Rochester, NY 14614-2176

Assistant Attorney General in Charge **Glenn Michaels** . . . . (518) 562-3288
43 Durkee Street, Plattsburgh, NY 12901-2942    Fax: (518) 562-3294

Assistant Attorney General in Charge **Michael J. Russo** . . (716) 853-8400
350 Main Street, Buffalo, NY 14202          Fax: (716) 853-8571

Assistant Attorney General in Charge **Valerie Singleton** . . (516) 248-3315
200 Old Country Road, Mineola, NY 11501-4241    Fax: (516) 747-6432

Assistant Attorney General in Charge **Ed J. Thompson** . . . (315) 448-4802
615 Erie Boulevard West,              Fax: (315) 448-4853
Syracuse, NY 13204-2465
Education: Albany Law JD

Assistant Attorney General in Charge **(Vacant)** . . . . . . . . . (845) 485-3910
One Civic Center Plaza, Poughkeepsie, NY 12601

## Social Justice Division
Executive Deputy Attorney General for Social Justice
**Alvin L. Bragg, Jr.** . . . . . . . . . . . . . . . . . . . . . . . . (212) 416-8501
Education: Harvard AB, JD

Charities Bureau Chief **James G. "Jim" Sheehan** . . . . . . . (212) 416-8490
Education: Swarthmore BA; Harvard JD

Civil Rights Bureau Chief **(Vacant)** . . . . . . . . . . . . . . . . (212) 416-8252

Environmental Protection Inspector General **Philip Bein** . . . (518) 474-7178
State Capitol, Albany, NY 12224-0341

Labor Bureau Chief **Terri Gerstein** . . . . . . . . . . . . . . . . (212) 416-8700

Tobacco Compliance Bureau Chief **Dana Biverman** . . . . . . (212) 416-6343

## State Counsel Division
State Capitol, Albany, NY 12224

Executive Deputy Attorney General **Kent T. Stauffer** . . . . . (212) 416-8525
Education: Amherst BA; Harvard JD, MPP

Deputy Attorney General (Albany) **Megan Levine** . . . . . . . (518) 473-8946

Deputy Attorney General (New York City)
**Arlene Smoler** . . . . . . . . . . . . . . . . . . . . . . . . . . . (212) 416-8972
120 Broadway, New York, NY 10271-0332

Civil Recoveries Bureau Chief **John Cremo** . . . . . . . . . . . (518) 474-7131

Claims Bureau Chief (Albany) **Eileen Bryant** . . . . . . . . . (518) 474-5209

Claims Bureau Chief (New York City) **Katharine Brooks** . . . . . . . . (212)
416-8514

Litigation Bureau Chief (Albany) **Jeffrey "Jeff" Dvorin** . . . (518) 473-7614

Litigation Bureau Chief (New York City) **Lisa Dell** . . . . . . . (212) 416-8618

---

Real Property Bureau Chief **Alison H. Crocker** . . . . . . . . . (518) 776-2726
Education: Skidmore BA; Texas JD

Sex Offender Management Bureau Chief (Albany and
New York City ) **Michael Connolly** . . . . . . . . . . . . . . . . (518) 402-2481

# New York State Education Department [NYSED]
89 Washington Avenue, Albany, NY 12234
Tel: (518) 474-5844  Fax: (518) 473-4909  Internet: www.nysed.gov

**Employees:** 2,806

▲Commissioner **MaryEllen Elia** . . . . . . . . . . . . . . . . . . . (518) 474-5844
Education: Buffalo 1973 MA; SUNY Col (Buffalo) 1983 MA
Assistant to the Commissioner **Anne Coonradt** . . . . . . . . (518) 473-1742

Senior Deputy Commissioner for Education Policy
**Johne Ebert** . . . . . . . . . . . . . . . . . . . . . . . . . . . . (518) 474-3862

General Counsel **Richard J. Trautwein** . . . . . . . . . . . . . . (518) 474-8864

## Operations and Management Services
Internet: www.oms.nysed.gov

Executive Deputy Commissioner **Elizabeth R. Berlin** . . . . . (518) 473-8381

Performance Improvement and Management Services
Deputy Commissioner **Sharon Cates-Williams** . . . . . . . . (518) 473-4706

Audit Services Director **Maria Guzman** . . . . . . . . . . . . . (518) 473-4516

Budget Coordination Director **Andrew Klippel** . . . . . . . . . (518) 486-1704

Communications Director **(Vacant)** . . . . . . . . . . . . . . . . (518) 474-1201

Diversity and Access Director **Steven M. Earle** . . . . . . . . (518) 474-1265
Education: Colby 1979

Education Finance Director **Brian Cechnicki** . . . . . . . . . . (518) 486-2422

Facilities and Business Services Director **Tom Casey** . . . . . (518) 474-7770

Fiscal Services Director **(Vacant)** . . . . . . . . . . . . . . . . . (518) 486-1704

Human Resources Management Director
**Annette Franchini** . . . . . . . . . . . . . . . . . . . . . . . . . (518) 474-5883
Application Development Assistant Director
**Lisa Barbagallo** . . . . . . . . . . . . . . . . . . . . . . . . . (518) 474-1538
E-mail: lbarbaga@mail.nysed.gov
Technical Services Assistant Director **Kenneth Mason** . . (518) 486-2342
E-mail: kmason@mail.nysed.gov

Governmental Relations and Special Projects Director
**Nicolas Storelli-Castro** . . . . . . . . . . . . . . . . . . . . . (518) 473-2831

Chief Financial Officer **Donald Juron** . . . . . . . . . . . . . . (518) 474-7751

Chief Information Officer **Benny Thottam** . . . . . . . . . . . . (518) 474-6261
E-mail: bthottam@mail.nysed.gov

External Affairs Chief **(Vacant)** . . . . . . . . . . . . . . . . . . (518) 474-1201

State Aid Chief **Andrea Hyary** . . . . . . . . . . . . . . . . . . (518) 473-8364

Grants Finance Coordinator **Margaret Zollo** . . . . . . . . . . (518) 474-4815
E-mail: mzollo@mail.nysed.gov

Federal Liaison **(Vacant)** . . . . . . . . . . . . . . . . . . . . . (518) 486-5644

Rate Setting Unit Coordinator **Susanne Bolling** . . . . . . . . (518) 474-3227

STAC (System to Track and Account for Children) and
Special Aids Unit Director **Steven Wright** . . . . . . . . . . (518) 474-7116

State Review Office Director **Justin Bates** . . . . . . . . . . . . (518) 485-9373

## Office of Adult Career and Continuing Education Services [ACCES]
89 Washington Avenue, Albany, NY 12234
Tel: (800) 222-5627

Deputy Commissioner **Kevin Smith** . . . . . . . . . . . . . . . . (518) 474-2714

Fiscal and Administrative Services Coordinator
**Harold "Hal" Matott** . . . . . . . . . . . . . . . . . . . . . . (518) 486-4038
E-mail: hmatott@mail.nysed.gov

Interagency, Legislative, Family and Community
Relations Coordinator **Michael Peluso** . . . . . . . . . . . . (518) 473-7213
E-mail: mpeluso@mail.nysed.gov

Adult Education Programs and Policy Director
**Mark A. Leinung** . . . . . . . . . . . . . . . . . . . . . . . . . (518) 486-6839
E-mail: rttt@mail.nysed.gov
Education: Upsala 1978; SUNY (Albany) 1980 MPA

---

★ Elected Official   ■ Appointed by Governor   ● Appointed by Legislature   ▲ Appointed by Board or Commission   ◆ Appointed by State Supreme Court

# Office of Cultural Education [OCE]

Cultural Education Center, One Madison Avenue, Room 10A46,
Albany, NY 12230
Tel: (518) 474-5976  Fax: (518) 474-2718  Internet: www.oce.nysed.gov

Deputy Commissioner **(Vacant)** . . . . . . . . . . . . . . . . . . . . . . . .(518) 474-5976

# Office of Higher Education

Education Building Addition, 89 Washington Avenue, Room 997,
Albany, NY 12234
Tel: (518) 486-3633  Fax: (518) 486-2254

Deputy Commissioner **John D'Agati** . . . . . . . . . . . . . . . . . . (518) 486-3633
Assistant Commissioner **(Vacant)** . . . . . . . . . . . . . . . . . . . . . (518) 473-8076
College and University Evaluation Coordinator
  **Leslie Templeman** . . . . . . . . . . . . . . . . . . . . . . . . . . . . . (518) 474-2593

# Office of K-16 Initiatives and Access Programs

Tel: (518) 474-3719  Fax: (518) 474-7468

Executive Director **Stanley S. Hansen, Jr.** . . . . . . . . . . . . . (518) 474-3719
Proprietary School Supervision Bureau Director
  **Carole Yates**. . . . . . . . . . . . . . . . . . . . . . . . . . . . . . . . . .(518) 474-3969

# Office of Teaching Initiatives

Tel: (518) 474-3901  Fax: (518) 474-6950

Director **Ann Jasinski** . . . . . . . . . . . . . . . . . . . . . . . . . . . . (518) 474-4661
School Personnel Review and Accountability Director
  **Deborah Marriott** . . . . . . . . . . . . . . . . . . . . . . . . . . . . . (518) 473-2998

# Office of P-12 Instructional Support

Education Building, Washington Avenue, Albany, NY 12234
Tel: (518) 474-3862  Fax: (518) 473-2056  Internet: www.emsc.nysed.gov

Deputy Commissioner **Angelica Infante** . . . . . . . . . . . . . . . .(518) 474-3862
Career and Technical Education Director **Eric Suhr** . . . . . . . (518) 486-1547
Charter Schools Director **(Vacant)** . . . . . . . . . . . . . . . . . . . (518) 474-1762
Student Support Services Director **Sharon L. Holder** . . . . . (518) 473-7123
Administrative Support Group Coordinator **(Vacant)** . . . . . . (518) 486-1544
Native American Education Coordinator **(Vacant)** . . . . . . . . (518) 474-0537
Supplemental Education Services Coordinator
  **Leon Hovish** . . . . . . . . . . . . . . . . . . . . . . . . . . . . . . . . . . (518) 473-0295

# Office of Accountability

55 Hanson Place, Brooklyn, NY 11217
Tel: (718) 722-2797  Fax: (718) 722-4559

Accountability Assistant Commissioner **Ira Schwartz** . . . . . (718) 722-2797
Accountability, Policy and Administration Supervisor
  **Lisa Long** . . . . . . . . . . . . . . . . . . . . . . . . . . . . . . . . . . . (718) 722-4533
  E-mail: llong@mail.nysed.gov
Intervention, Evaluation and Best Practices Coordinator
  **(Vacant)** . . . . . . . . . . . . . . . . . . . . . . . . . . . . . . . . . . . . . (718) 722-2784
Title I School and Community Services Coordinator
  **Maxine Meadows-Shuford** . . . . . . . . . . . . . . . . . . . .(518) 473-0295
  Education Building Annex, 89 Washington Avenue,     Fax: (518) 486-1762
  Room 320, Albany, NY 12234
District and School Review Director **Stephen Earley** . . . . . (718) 722-2796

# Office of School Operations

Tel: (518) 474-2238  Fax: (518) 402-5713

Assistant Commissioner **(Vacant)** . . . . . . . . . . . . . . . . . . . (518) 474-2238
Education Management Services/Nonpublic School
  Services Coordinator **Christina Coughlin** . . . . . . . . . . . . . (518) 474-6541
Facilities Planning Coordinator **Carl Thurnau**. . . . . . . . . . . .(518) 474-3906
Grants Management Services Coordinator
  **Maureen Lavare** . . . . . . . . . . . . . . . . . . . . . . . . . . . . . . (518) 474-3936
  E-mail: emscmsa@nysed.gov

# Office of Special Education

89 Washington Avenue, Room 309 EB, Albany, NY 12234
Tel: (518) 473-4818  E-mail: speced@mail.nysed.gov

Assistant Commissioner **(Vacant)** . . . . . . . . . . . . . . . . . . . (518) 473-4818
Special Education Policy and Professional Development
  Coordinator **Patricia J. Geary**. . . . . . . . . . . . . . . . . . . . . .(518) 473-2878
  E-mail: pgeary@mail.nysed.gov

Program Development and Support Services Supervisor
  **Noel Granger**. . . . . . . . . . . . . . . . . . . . . . . . . . . . . . . .(518) 486-7462
  E-mail: ngranger@mail.nysed.gov
Policy Development Supervisor **Joanne LaCrosse** . . . . . . . (518) 473-2878
  E-mail: jlacross@mail.nysed.gov
New York State School for the Blind
  Superintendent **Barbara J. Lemen** . . . . . . . . . . . . (585) 343-5384 ext. 205
  2A Richmond Avenue, Batavia, NY 14020
New York State School for the Deaf Superintendent
  **David Hubman** . . . . . . . . . . . . . . . . . . . . . . . . . . . . . . (315) 337-8400
  401 Turin St., Rome, NY 13440               TTY: (315) 337-8489

# Office of State Assessment [OSA]

Tel: (518) 474-5902  Fax: (518) 474-1989

Director **Steven E. Katz**. . . . . . . . . . . . . . . . . . . . . . . . . . .(518) 474-5099
Assistant Commissioner for Assessment, Standards and
  Curriculum **Peter J. Swerdzewski** . . . . . . . . . . . . . . . . . (518) 474-5902
  E-mail: pswerdze@mail.nysed.gov

# Office of P-12 School Services

Deputy Commissioner **(Vacant)** . . . . . . . . . . . . . . . . . . . . . .(518) 474-2238

# Office of the Professions

West Wing, 89 Washington Avenue, 2nd Floor, Albany, NY 12234
Tel: (518) 474-3817 ext. 470  Fax: (518) 474-3863
E-mail: opdep@mail.nysed.gov  Internet: www.op.nysed.gov

Deputy Commissioner **Douglas Lentivech** . . . . . . . (518) 474-3817 ext. 470

# Office of Professional Discipline

1411 Broadway, 10th Floor, New York, NY 10018
Tel: (212) 951-6400  Fax: (212) 951-6420

Executive Director **Louis J. Catone** . . . . . . . . . . . . (518) 474-3817 ext. 170
  E-mail: louis.catone@nysed.gov
Investigations Director **Donald Dawson** . . . . . . . . . . . . . . .(212) 951-6444
  E-mail: conduct@mail.nysed.gov
Legal Services Director **Andrew Tolkoff**. . . . . . . . . . . . . . .(212) 951-6550
Operations Director **Sarah Benson** . . . . . . . . . . . . . . . . . .(518) 486-1765
Prosecutions Director **George Ding**. . . . . . . . . . . . . . . . . .(212) 951-6419
  Education: Albany Law 1979 JD

# Office of Professional Licensing

North Wing, 89 Washington Avenue, 2nd Floor, Albany, NY 12234
Tel: (518) 474-3817 ext. 340  Fax: (518) 473-0578
E-mail: opdpls@mail.nysed.gov

Professional Licensing Services Director (Acting)
  **Susan Naccarato**. . . . . . . . . . . . . . . . . . . . . . . . . .(518) 474-3817 ext. 340
Comparative Education Director
  **William Murphy** . . . . . . . . . . . . . . . . . . . . . . . . . . (518) 474-3817 ext. 360
Professional Examinations Manager
  **Harrison Fisher** . . . . . . . . . . . . . . . . . . . . . . . . . . .(518) 474-3817 ext. 290

---

★ Elected Official     ■ Appointed by Governor     ● Appointed by Legislature     ▲ Appointed by Board or Commission     ◆ Appointed by State Supreme Court

EXECUTIVE BRANCH

# North Carolina

Tel: (919) 733-1110 (State Operator)

**Number of U.S. Congressional Delegates:** 2 Senators; 13 Representatives  **Governor's Term:** 4 years
**Legislature Description:** General Assembly - 50 member Senate; 120 member House of Representatives;
Term - Senate 2 years, House 2 years  **Next Election:** Governor November 2016; Legislature November
2016  **Number of Electoral Votes:** 15  **Official Name:** State of North Carolina (after Charles II of
England)  **Nickname:** The Tar Heel State; Old North State  **Motto:** Esse Quam Videri (To be rather than to
seem)

**Population:** 10,042,802 (2015); Rank 9  **Fiscal Year:** 2014-2015  **Budget:** $21,001,100,000

## Office of the Governor

20301 Mail Service Center, Raleigh, NC 27699-0301
116 West Jones Street, 1301 Mail Service Center, Raleigh, NC 27603
(Constituent Services Office)
Tel: (919) 814-2000  TTY: (919) 733-2391  Fax: (919) 733-2120
E-mail: governor.office@nc.gov

**Patrick Lloyd "Pat" McCrory**
Governor

Began Service: January 5, 2013
Term Expires: January 2017
Date of Birth: October 17, 1956
Education: Catawba 1978 BA
Religion: Christian
Career: President, Republican Mayors and Local
Officials; Manager of Business Relations, Duke
Energy Corporation; Mayor, City of Charlotte,
North Carolina (1995-2009)

★ Governor **Patrick Lloyd "Pat" McCrory** (R) . . . . . . . . . . . (919) 733-6001
  E-mail: pat.mccrory@nc.gov
  Executive Assistant **Mary Melissa "Lisa" Frazier** . . . . . . (919) 814-2105
Chief of Staff **Thomas A. Stith III** . . . . . . . . . . . . . . . . . . (919) 814-2111
  Education: North Carolina Central
Deputy Chief of Staff **John Baldwin** . . . . . . . . . . . . . . . . . (919) 814-2015
  Education: Wake Forest BA
Deputy Chief of Staff
  **James W. C. "Jimmy" Broughton** . . . . . . . . . . . . . . . . (919) 814-2000
  Education: Wake Forest 1990 BA
Chief Legal Counsel **Robert Clifton "Bob" Stephens** . . . . (919) 814-2025
  E-mail: bob.stephens@nc.gov
Boards and Commissions Director
  **Charles Kenneth "Chuck" Duckett** . . . . . . . . . . . . . . . (919) 814-2036
  Education: North Carolina 1982 BA
Communications Director **Joshua Nathanael Ellis** . . . . . . . (919) 733-3438
  E-mail: josh.ellis@nc.gov
  Education: North Carolina BA
Deputy Communications Director **(Vacant)** . . . . . . . . . . . (919) 733-4240
Press Secretary **(Vacant)** . . . . . . . . . . . . . . . . . . . . . . . . . (919) 733-5612
Community and Constituent Services Director
  **Judy Kay Jefferson** . . . . . . . . . . . . . . . . . . . . . . . . . . . (919) 814-2045
  E-mail: judy.jefferson@nc.gov
Senior Advisor on Jobs and the Economy **Tony Almeida** . . (919) 814-2112
  E-mail: tony.almeida@nc.gov
Advisor on Jobs and the Economy **Blannie Cheng** . . . . . . . (919) 814-2113
  E-mail: blannie.cheng@nc.gov
  Education: North Carolina JD
Senior Education Advisor **Catherine Lauterbach Truitt** . . . (919) 814-2000
  E-mail: catherine.truitt@nc.gov
Military Affairs Advisor
  **Col John A. Nicholson, USMC (Ret)** . . . . . . . . . . . . . . (919) 715-1444
  E-mail: john.nicholson@nc.gov
Legislative Liaison **Fred Franklin Steen II** . . . . . . . . . . . . (919) 814-2030
  E-mail: fred.steen@nc.gov
Scheduler **Meredith McCullen** . . . . . . . . . . . . . . . . . . . . . (919) 715-2427
  E-mail: meredith.mccullen@nc.gov

## Office of Federal Relations

444 North Capitol Street, NW, Suite 332, Washington, DC 20001
Fax: (202) 624-5836
Director **Virginia Hurt Johnson** . . . . . . . . . . . . . . . . . . . . (202) 624-5834
  E-mail: virginia.johnson@nc.gov
  Education: Duke 1981 BA; Wake Forest 1985 JD

## Eastern Office

O'Marks Building, 233 Middle Street, Suite 211, New Bern, NC 28563
Fax: (252) 514-4827
Director **Steven Preston "Steve" Keen** . . . . . . . . . . . . . . (919) 733-4240
  E-mail: steve.keen@nc.gov

## Piedmont Office

Charlotte-Mecklenburg Government Center, 600 East Fourth Street,
Charlotte, NC 28262
Fax: (704) 330-5287
Director **Bill "Billy" Constangy** . . . . . . . . . . . . . . . . . . . . (704) 330-5290
  E-mail: billy.constangy@nc.gov

## Western Office

300 Haywood Building, 46 Haywood Street, Suite 337,
Asheville, NC 28801-1512
Fax: (828) 251-6162
Director **Trudi Walend** . . . . . . . . . . . . . . . . . . . . . . . . . . . (828) 200-0742
  E-mail: trudi.walend@nc.gov

## Office of State Budget and Management [OSBM]

116 West Jones Street, 20320 Mail Service Center,
Raleigh, NC 27699-0320
Tel: (919) 807-4700  Fax: (919) 733-0640  Internet: www.osbm.state.nc.us

**Employees:** 63  **Fiscal Year:** 2014-2015  **Budget:** $8,081,000

■State Budget Director **Andrew Taube "Drew" Heath** . . . . (919) 807-2513
  E-mail: andrew.heath@osbm.nc.gov
  Executive Assistant to State Budget Director
  **Debbie Young** . . . . . . . . . . . . . . . . . . . . . . . . . . . . . . (919) 807-4716
Human Resources Director **(Vacant)** . . . . . . . . . . . . . . . . . (919) 807-4788
Special Projects Deputy Director **(Vacant)** . . . . . . . . . . . . (919) 807-4719
Chief Information Officer **(Vacant)** . . . . . . . . . . . . . . . . . . (919) 807-4753
Chief Operating Officer **Chloe Gossage** . . . . . . . . . . . . . . (919) 807-4771
Communications Manager **Melanie Jennings** . . . . . . . . . . . (919) 807-4725
  E-mail: melanie.jennings@osbm.nc.gov
Economic and Demographic Analysis Assistant State
  Budget Officer **Nathan Knuffman** . . . . . . . . . . . . . . . . (919) 807-4728
General Government Assistant State Budget Officer
  **Jay Drake** . . . . . . . . . . . . . . . . . . . . . . . . . . . . . . . . . (919) 807-4788
Health and Human Services Assistant State Budget
  Officer **Pam Kilpatrick** . . . . . . . . . . . . . . . . . . . . . . . . (919) 807-4722
Natural and Economic Resources, Transportation and JPS
  Assistant State Budget Officer **Mercidee Benton** . . . . . . (919) 807-4767
  Education: Shaw 1984 BS
Management Evaluation Assistant State Budget Officer
  and Internal Audit Director **Barbara Baldwin** . . . . . . . . (919) 807-4721
Statewide Analysis and Capital Assistant State Budget
  Officer **Donna Cox** . . . . . . . . . . . . . . . . . . . . . . . . . . . (919) 807-4746

---

★ Elected Official   ■ Appointed by Governor   ● Appointed by Legislature   ▲ Appointed by Board or Commission   ◆ Appointed by State Supreme Court

Strategic Management Assistant State Budget Officer
  **Erin Matteson** . . . . . . . . . . . . . . . . . . . . . . . . . . . . . (919) 807-4758
University, Community Colleges and Public Education
  Assistant State Budget Officer **(Vacant)** . . . . . . . . . . . . . (919) 807-4780
NC Government Efficiency and Reform (NCGEAR)
  Deputy Director **Joe Coletti** . . . . . . . . . . . . . . . . . . . . . (919) 807-4787

## Office of the State Controller [OSC]

1410 Mail Service Center, Raleigh, NC 27699-1410

Tel: (919) 707-0500  Fax: (919) 981-5567  Internet: www.osc.nc.gov

**Employees:** 190  **Fiscal Year:** 2014-2015  **Budget:** $23,628,000

■State Controller **Linda Morrison Combs** . . . . . . . . . . . . . . (919) 707-0500
  E-mail: linda.combs@osc.nc.gov
  Education: Appalachian State 1968 BA, 1978 MA;
  Virginia Tech 1985 PhD
Chief Deputy State Controller **Jim Dolan** . . . . . . . . . . . . . . (919) 707-0540
OSC BEACON Project Management Office Deputy
  Controller **Jim Tulenko** . . . . . . . . . . . . . . . . . . . . . . . . (919) 707-0505
State Accounting Deputy Controller **Anne Godwin** . . . . . . . (919) 707-0650
                                            Fax: (919) 981-5560
Business Services Manager **Robert Alford** . . . . . . . . . . . . . (919) 707-0768
                                            Fax: (919) 981-5553
Risk Mitigation Services Manager **Ben McLawhorn** . . . . . . (919) 707-0757
  Education: Appalachian State 1982 BSBA; Campbell 1987 MBA
Human Resources Director **Helen Dicken** . . . . . . . . . . . . . (919) 707-0482

## North Carolina Department of Administration [NCDOA]

116 West Jones Street, 1301 Mail Service Center, Suite 5106,
Raleigh, NC 27603
1301 Mail Service Center, Raleigh, NC 27699-1301
Tel: (919) 807-2425  Fax: (919) 733-9571  Internet: www.doa.nc.gov

**Employees:** 570  **Fiscal Year:** 2014  **Budget:** $197,000,000

■Secretary (Acting) **Kathryn Johnston** . . . . . . . . . . . . . . . (919) 807-2425
  E-mail: kathryn.johnston@doa.nc.gov
  Executive Assistant **Sheree Pratt** . . . . . . . . . . . . . . . . . . (919) 807-2425
Chief Operating Officer **Dee Jones** . . . . . . . . . . . . . . . . . (919) 807-2425
Human Resources Management Director
  **Christine "Chris" Midgette** . . . . . . . . . . . . . . . . . . . . . (919) 807-2319
                                            Fax: (919) 715-7669
Communications Director **Christopher F. "Chris" Mears** . . (919) 807-2340
  E-mail: chris.mears@doa.nc.gov          Fax: (919) 733-9571
Fiscal Management Office Director **Barbara Roper** . . . . . . . (919) 807-2444
  1306 Mail Service Center, Raleigh, NC 27699-1306

### Government Operations

Chief Policy Officer and Deputy Secretary
  **Speros J. Fleggas** . . . . . . . . . . . . . . . . . . . . . . . . . . . . . (919) 807-2425
  HUB (Historically Underutilized Businesses) Assistant
    to the Secretary **Dennis English** . . . . . . . . . . . . . . . . (919) 807-2330
    1336 Mail Service Center,            Fax: (919) 807-2335
    Raleigh, NC 27699-1336
State Construction Office Director **Greg Driver** . . . . . . . . . (919) 807-4100
  1307 Mail Service Center, 301 N. Wilmington Street,
  #450, Raleigh, NC 27699-1307
State Property Office Director **(Vacant)** . . . . . . . . . . . . . . . (919) 807-4650
  1321 Mail Service Center, Raleigh, NC 27699-1321
Facility Management Division Director
  **S. Tony Jordan, Jr.** . . . . . . . . . . . . . . . . . . . . . . . . . . . (919) 733-3855
  1313 Mail Service Center, 431 North Salisbury Street,
  Raleigh, NC 27699-1313
Mail Service Center Division Director **Retha Turner** . . . . . . (919) 733-2913
  3905 Reedy Creek Road, Raleigh, NC 27607    Fax: (919) 733-2838
  5901 Mail Service Center, Raleigh, NC 27699-5901
  E-mail: retha.turner@doa.nc.gov
Motor Fleet Management Division Director
  **Bill Buchanan** . . . . . . . . . . . . . . . . . . . . . . . . . . . . . . . (919) 733-6540
  1308 Mail Service Center, 1915 Blue Ridge Road,
  Raleigh, NC 26799-1308
  E-mail: bill.buchanan@doa.nc.gov
Purchase and Contract Division Director **Patti Bowers** . . . . (919) 807-4500
  1305 Mail Service Center, Raleigh, NC 27699-1305

Surplus Property Division Director **Mickey Sauls** . . . . . . . . (919) 854-2160
  1310 Mail Service Center, 6501 Chapel Hill Road,
  Raleigh, NC 27699-1310
  E-mail: mickey.sauls@doa.nc.gov

## Internal Services and Programs

Fax: (919) 733-9571

Deputy Secretary **Bill Bryan** . . . . . . . . . . . . . . . . . . . . . . . (919) 807-2425
  E-mail: bill.bryan@doa.nc.gov
Parking Systems Director **(Vacant)** . . . . . . . . . . . . . . . . . . (919) 807-4499
  1334 Mail Service Center, Raleigh, NC 27699-1334
Council for Women and Domestic Violence Commission
  Director **Gale Wilkins** . . . . . . . . . . . . . . . . . . . . . . . . . (919) 733-2455
  1320 Mail Service Center, Raleigh, NC 27699-1320
  E-mail: gale.wilkins@doa.nc.gov
Indian Affairs Commission Director
  **Gregory A. Richardson** . . . . . . . . . . . . . . . . . . . . . . . . (919) 807-4440
  1317 Mail Service Center, Raleigh, NC 27699-1317
  E-mail: Greg.Richardson@doa.nc.gov
Non-Public Education Director **David Mills** . . . . . . . . . . . . (919) 807-2412
  1309 Mail Service Center, Raleigh, NC 27699-1309
  E-mail: david.mills@doa.nc.gov
Youth Advocacy and Involvement Office Director
  **Stephanie Nantz** . . . . . . . . . . . . . . . . . . . . . . . . . . . . . (919) 807-4400
  1319 Mail Service Center, Raleigh, NC 27699-1319
Information Center Manager **Bob Zenkel** . . . . . . . . . . . . . (919) 807-2301
  1325 Mail Service Center, Raleigh, NC 27699-1325
  E-mail: bob.zenkel@doa.nc.gov

## North Carolina Department of Commerce

301 North Wilmington Street, Raleigh, NC 27601
Tel: (919) 733-4151  E-mail: info@nccommerce.com
Internet: www.nccommerce.com

**Employees:** 1,926  **Fiscal Year:** 2014-2015  **Budget:** $148,663,000

■Secretary **John Edward Skvarla** . . . . . . . . . . . . . . . . . . . . (919) 814-4608
  E-mail: john.skvarla@nccommerce.com
Assistant Secretary for Rural Economic Development
  **Dr. Patricia "Pat" Mitchell** . . . . . . . . . . . . . . . . . . . . (919) 715-7726
  Education: Berry BA; Georgia MPA, DPA
General Counsel **John Hoomani** . . . . . . . . . . . . . . . . . . . . (919) 715-5579
  Education: North Carolina State 1993 BA; Campbell 1997 JD
Chief Financial Officer **Shannon Hobby** . . . . . . . . . . . . . . (919) 715-5603
Chief Liaison Officer **Susan Fleetwood** . . . . . . . . . . . . . . . (919) 733-9304
Business Development and Services Executive Director
  **(Vacant)** . . . . . . . . . . . . . . . . . . . . . . . . . . . . . . . . . . . (919) 733-7193
                                            Fax: (919) 733-0110
Communications Director **Kim Genardo** . . . . . . . . . . . . . . (919) 733-3438
  E-mail: kim.genardo@nccommerce.com
  Education: Northwestern 1988 BA
Marketing Executive Director **David E. Rhoades** . . . . . . . . (919) 715-6556
Commerce Finance Division Director
  **Stewart Dickinson** . . . . . . . . . . . . . . . . . . . . . . . . . . . . (919) 715-6560
                                            Fax: (919) 715-5297
Information Services Division Director **Michael D. King** . . (919) 814-4688
  E-mail: mking@nccommerce.com
Personnel Division Director **Timothy D. "Tim" Mayes** . . . (919) 733-7243
Small Business Commissioner **Scott R. Daugherty** . . . . . . (919) 733-2104
Welcome Center Director **Wally Wazan** . . . . . . . . . . . . . . (919) 715-2098
Executive Director of Office of Science and Technology
  **John Hardin** . . . . . . . . . . . . . . . . . . . . . . . . . . . . . . . . (919) 715-0516
  E-mail: jhardin@nccommerce.com
Legislative Affairs Director **Ashley Jones** . . . . . . . . . . . . . (919) 715-2785
  E-mail: ashley.jones@nccommerce.com

### Division of Community Assistance [DCA]

100 East Six Forks Road, 2nd Floor, Raleigh, NC 27699
4313 Mail Services Center, Raleigh, NC 27699-4313
Tel: (919) 571-4900  Fax: (919) 571-4951

Director **Melody Adams** . . . . . . . . . . . . . . . . . . . . . . . . . (919) 571-4900
Administrative Officer **Patricia Bass** . . . . . . . . . . . (919) 571-4900 ext. 245
  E-mail: pbass@nccommerce.com

*(continued on next page)*

---

★ Elected Official    ■ Appointed by Governor    ● Appointed by Legislature    ▲ Appointed by Board or Commission    ◆ Appointed by State Supreme Court

**Division of Community Assistance** continued

Administrative Officer **Angela Williams** . . . . . . . . .(919) 571-4900 ext. 248
   E-mail: awilliams@nccommerce.com
Receptionist **Pecolia Harris** . . . . . . . . . . . . . . . . (919) 571-4900 ext. 221
   E-mail: pharris@nccommerce.com
Business Officer **Toni Moore** . . . . . . . . . . . . . . . . (919) 571-4900 ext. 250
Accounting Clerk **Lucrecia High** . . . . . . . . . . . . . (919) 571-4900 ext. 273
Appalachian Regional Commission Program
   Manager **Olivia Collier** . . . . . . . . . . . . . . . . . (919) 571-4900 ext. 222

## Division of Employment Security

P.O. Box 25903, Raleigh, NC 27611
Tel: (919) 707-1600  Fax: (919) 733-1129

Assistant Secretary (Interim) **W. T. Brinn** . . . . . . . . . . . . . . (919) 707-1010
   E-mail: assistantsecretary@nccommerce.com
Unemployment Insurance Director
   **Maurice Antwon Keith** . . . . . . . . . . . . . . . . . . . . . . (919) 707-1422
   E-mail: antwon.keith@nccommerce.com
Chief Legal Counsel (Acting) **Jason Kaus** . . . . . . . . . . . . . (919) 733-3098
   E-mail: jason.kaus@nccommerce.com
Finance Director **Kevin Carlson** . . . . . . . . . . . . . . . . . . . (919) 733-3098
Public Information Director **Chris Farr** . . . . . . . . . . . . . . . (919) 733-3098
   E-mail: chris.farr@nccommerce.com

## Division of Workforce Development

313 Chapanoke Road, Suite 120, Raleigh, NC 27603
4316 Mail Service Center, Raleigh, NC 27699
Tel: (919) 814-0400

Executive Director of Operations **Danny Giddens** . . . . . . . .(919) 814-0325
   E-mail: danny.giddens@nccommerce.com
   Executive Assistant **Belinda Boyette** . . . . . . . . . . . . (919) 814-0314
Administrative Services Director **Graham Watt** . . . . . . . . .(919) 814-0418
   E-mail: graham.watt@nccommerce.com
Employment Service Director **(Vacant)** . . . . . . . . . . . . . . . (919) 814-0445
Governance and Strategic Planning Director
   **Catherine Moga Bryant** . . . . . . . . . . . . . . . . . . . . . (919) 814-0318
   E-mail: catherine.mogabryant@nccommerce.com
Training Center Director **Gene Scott** . . . . . . . . . . . . . . . . (919) 814-0330
   E-mail: gene.scott@nccommerce.com

## Labor and Economic Analysis Division [LEAD]

301 North Wilmington Street, Raleigh, NC 27601
4325 Mail Service Center, Raleigh, NC 27699-4300
Tel: (919) 707-1500  Fax: (919) 715-6866
E-mail: esc.lmi.inquiries@nccommerce.com

Division Director (Acting) **Jacqueline "Jackie" Keener** . .(919) 707-1523
Federal/State Cooperative Programs Manager
   **Jacqueline "Jackie" Keener** . . . . . . . . . . . . . . . . . (919) 707-1523
Information Delivery Manager **Allan Sandoval** . . . . . . . . . .(919) 707-1575
   E-mail: allan.sandoval@nccommerce.com
Market Analysis and Strategy Manager **Jeff DeBellis** . . . . . (919) 707-1570
Workforce, Research, and Evaluation Manager
   **Dr. Elizabeth "Betty" McGrath** . . . . . . . . . . . . . . . . (919) 707-1506

## Department of Cultural Resources

109 East Jones Street, MSC 4601, Raleigh, NC 27699-4601
Tel: (919) 807-7300  Fax: (919) 733-1564

**Employees:** 663  **Fiscal Year:** 2014  **Budget:** $63,697,000

■Secretary **Susan W. Kluttz** . . . . . . . . . . . . . . . . . . . . . (919) 807-7250
   E-mail: susan.kluttz@ncdcr.gov
   Administrative Assistant **Jennifer McCrory Fontes** . . . . .(919) 807-7256
Chief Deputy Secretary **Karin Cochran** . . . . . . . . . . . . . . .(919) 807-7257
   E-mail: karin.cochran@ncdcr.gov
Deputy Secretary **Kevin Cherry** . . . . . . . . . . . . . . . . . . .(919) 807-7282
   Education: North Carolina 2010 PhD    Fax: (919) 733-8807
Director of Marketing and Communications **Cary Cox** . . . . (919) 807-7388
                               Fax: (919) 733-1620
   Public Relations Specialist **Fay Mitchell** . . . . . . . . . . . (919) 807-7389
   E-mail: fay.mitchell@ncdcr.gov
Historic Sites Division Director **Keith Hardison** . .(919) 733-7862 ext. 225
                               Fax: (919) 715-0678

History Museums Division Director
   **Kenneth B. "Ken" Howard** . . . . . . . . . . . . . . . . . . . .(919) 807-7878
                               Fax: (919) 733-8655
Human Resources Director **(Vacant)** . . . . . . . . . . . . . . . . (919) 807-7377
                               Fax: (919) 715-8724
Capital Projects Coordinator **Mark Cooney** . . . . . . . . . . . . (919) 807-7473
                               Fax: (919) 807-7499
Chief Information Officer **(Vacant)** . . . . . . . . . . . . . . . . . (919) 807-7294
Chief Financial Officer **Sarah Dozier** . . . . . . . . . . . . . . . (919) 807-7278
                               Fax: (919) 733-6993
Eastern Regional Office Administrator
   **Scott Power** . . . . . . . . . . . . . . . . . . . . .(252) 830-6580 ext. 226
   117 West Fifth Street, Greenville, NC 27858
Western Regional Office Supervisor **Jeff Futch** . . . . . . . . . (828) 296-7230
   176 Riceville Road, Asheville, NC 28805

## Archives and History

MSC 4610, Raleigh, NC 27699-4610
Tel: (919) 807-7280  Tel: (919) 807-7310 (State Archives Search Room)
Fax: (919) 733-8807  E-mail: archives@ncdcr.gov

State Archivist **Sarah Koonts** . . . . . . . . . . . . . . . . . . . . .(919) 807-7339
   E-mail: sarah.koonts@ncdcr.gov
Historical Publications Office Administrator
   **Donna Kelly** . . . . . . . . . . . . . . . . . . . . .(919) 733-7442 ext. 223
   120 West Lane Street, MSC 4622,     Fax: (919) 733-1439
   Raleigh, NC 27699-4622
   E-mail: donna.kelly@ncdcr.gov
State Historic Preservation Office Administrator
   **Ramona Murphy Bartos** . . . . . . . . . . . . . . . . . . . . .(919) 807-6583
   E-mail: ramona.bartos@ncdcr.gov     Fax: (919) 807-6599
State Archeologist **Steve Claggett** . . . . . . . . . . . . . . . . . .(919) 807-6551
                                 Fax: (919) 715-2671

## State Library

4640 Mail Service Center, Raleigh, NC 27699-4640
Tel: (919) 807-7450  Tel: (919) 807-7460 (Genealogy Desk)
Fax: (919) 733-8748

State Librarian **Caroline "Cal" Shepard** . . . . . . . . . . . . . . (919) 807-7410
Assistant State Librarian **Laura O'Donoghue** . . . . . . . . . . . (919) 807-7406
Library Development Chief **Jennifer Pratt** . . . . . . . . . . . . .(919) 807-7415
Director, Library for the Blind and Physically
   Handicapped **Carl Keehn** . . . . . . . . . . . . . . . . . . . .(919) 733-4376
   1841 Capital Boulevard, Raleigh, NC 27635   Tel: (888) 388-2460
                                 Fax: (919) 733-6910

## Department of Environment and Natural Resources [DENR]

1601 Mail Service Center, Raleigh, NC 27699-1601
Tel: (919) 707-8600
Tel: (919) 707-8100 (Environmental Assistance and Outreach)

**Employees:** 3,393  **Fiscal Year:** 2014-2015  **Budget:** $267,143,000

■Secretary **Donald van der Vaart** . . . . . . . . . . . . . . . . . .(919) 707-8622
   Education: Cambridge MChE
   Executive Assistant **Alice Miller** . . . . . . . . . . . . . . . . (919) 707-8625
Chief Deputy Secretary **John C. Evans** . . . . . . . . . . . . . . .(919) 707-8600
   E-mail: john.evans@ncdenr.gov
Environment Assistant Secretary **Mitch Gillespie** . . . . . . . .(919) 707-8619
   E-mail: mitch.gillespie@ncdenr.gov
   Executive Assistant **Cindy Hobbs** . . . . . . . . . . . . . . . .(919) 707-8601
Natural Resources Assistant Secretary **Brad Ives** . . . . . . . .(919) 707-8620
   E-mail: brad.ives@ncdenr.gov
   Executive Assistant **Cindy Hobbs** . . . . . . . . . . . . . . . .(919) 707-8601
Administrative Services Regional Offices Director
   **Joe Harwood** . . . . . . . . . . . . . . . . . . . . . . . . . . . . (919) 707-8645
   E-mail: joe.harwood@ncdenr.gov
Communications Director **Drew Elliott** . . . . . . . . . . . . . . . (919) 707-8626
   E-mail: drew.elliot@ncdenr.gov
Wildlife Resources Commission Director **Gordon Myers** . . .(919) 707-0010
   E-mail: gordon.myers@ncwildlife.org
Legislative and Intergovernmental Affairs Director
   **(Vacant)** . . . . . . . . . . . . . . . . . . . . . . . . . . . . . . . (919) 707-8618
General Counsel **Sam M. Hayes** . . . . . . . . . . . . . . . . . . .(919) 707-8616
   E-mail: sam.hayes@ncdenr.gov

---

★ Elected Official    ■ Appointed by Governor    ● Appointed by Legislature    ▲ Appointed by Board or Commission    ◆ Appointed by State Supreme Court

## Budget, Planning and Analysis
Tel: (919) 707-8510

Budget, Planning and Analysis Division Director
**Doug Lewis** . . . . . . . . . . . . . . . . . . . . . . . . . . (919) 707-8514
  E-mail: doug.lewis@ncdenr.gov
Chief Information Officer **Rex Wahley** . . . . . . . . . . . . . . . . (919) 707-8912
  E-mail: rex.wahley@ncdenr.gov
Personnel/Human Resources Division Director
**Ann E. Lasley** . . . . . . . . . . . . . . . . . . . . . . . . . . (919) 707-8304
Purchase and Services Division Director
**Michael G. Bryant** . . . . . . . . . . . . . . . . . . . . . . . (919) 707-8526
Controller **Jeannie Betts** . . . . . . . . . . . . . . . . . . . . . . . (919) 707-8566
  E-mail: jeannie.betts@ncdenr.gov

## Natural Resources
Ecosystem Enhancement Program Director
**Michael Ellison** . . . . . . . . . . . . . . . . . . . . . . . . . (919) 715-1412
  E-mail: michael.ellison@ncdenr.gov
Environmental Education Manager **Lisa Tolley** . . . . . . . . . . (919) 707-8125
North Carolina Aquariums Director
**David Griffin** . . . . . . . . . . . . . . . . . . . . . (919) 877-5500 ext. 222
  E-mail: david.griffin@ncaquariums.com
North Carolina Zoological Park Director
**David M. Jones** . . . . . . . . . . . . . . . . . . . . . . . . (336) 879-7101
  Route 4, Box 83, Asheboro, NC 27203
  E-mail: david.m.jones@nczoo.org
Marine Fisheries Division Director **Louis Daniel** . . . . . . . . (252) 808-8013
  3441 Arendell Street, Morehead City, NC 28557
  E-mail: louis.daniel@ncdenr.gov
Park and Recreation Division Director **Lewis R. Ledford** . . (919) 707-9333
  E-mail: lewis.ledford@ncdenr.gov

## Operations and Development
Air Quality Division Director **Shelia Holman** . . . . . . . . . . (919) 707-8430
Coastal Management Division Director **Braxton Davis** . . . . (252) 808-2808
  E-mail: braxton.davis@ncdenr.gov
Energy, Mineral and Land Resources Director
**Tracy Davis** . . . . . . . . . . . . . . . . . . . . . . . . . . . (919) 707-9201
  E-mail: tracy.davis@ncdenr.gov
Waste Management Division Director **Dexter Matthews** . . (919) 707-8238
  E-mail: dexter.matthews@ncdenr.gov
Water Resources and Quality Division Director
**Tom Reeder** . . . . . . . . . . . . . . . . . . . . . . . . . . . (919) 707-9027
  E-mail: tom.reeder@ncdenr.gov

## Department of Health and Human Services [DHHS]
2001 Mail Service Center, Raleigh, NC 27699-2001
Tel: (919) 855-4800  Internet: www.ncdhhs.gov

**Employees:** 16,093  **Fiscal Year:** 2014-2015  **Budget:** $19,014,237,000

■Secretary **Richard O. "Rick" Brajer** . . . . . . . . . . . . . . . (919) 855-4800
  E-mail: rick.brajer@dhhs.nc.gov
  Education: Purdue BS; Stanford MBS
Deputy Secretary of Health Services
**Dr. Randall Williams** . . . . . . . . . . . . . . . . . . . . . . (919) 855-4800
Deputy Secretary of Human Services **Sherry Bradsher** . . . (919) 855-4800
  Education: East Carolina MPA
Deputy Secretary of Mental Health, Developmental
Disabilities, and Substance Abuse
**Dale C. Armstrong, MBA, FACHE** . . . . . . . . . . . . . . . (919) 733-7011
Chief of Staff **Mark Payne** . . . . . . . . . . . . . . . . . . . . . (919) 855-4800
Chief Financial Officer **Rod Davis** . . . . . . . . . . . . . . . . . (919) 855-4800
  Education: North Carolina State 1976 BS;
  Appalachian State 1983 MBA
Chief Information Officer **Joseph A. "Joe" Cooper, Jr.** . . (919) 855-3060
  E-mail: joseph.cooper@dhhs.nc.gov
  Education: South Florida 1975 BA
Human Resources Division Director **Mark Gogal** . . . . . . . (919) 855-4900
Medical Assistance Division Director
**Dr. Robin Gary Cummings, MD** . . . . . . . . . . . . . . . . (919) 855-4100
  Education: North Carolina; Duke MD
Mental Health, Developmental Disabilities and Substance
Abuse Division Director (Acting) **Courtney Cantrell** . . . . (919) 855-4800

Office of Communications Director **Kendra Gerlach** . . . . . . (919) 855-4840
  E-mail: kendra.gerlach@dhhs.nc.gov
Office of Government Affairs Director **Adam Sholar** . . . . . (919) 855-4800
  E-mail: adam.sholar@dhhs.nc.gov
  Education: North Carolina 2008 JD
General Counsel **Emery Milliken** . . . . . . . . . . . . . . . . . . (919) 855-4890
Senior Policy Advisor **Margaret "Mardy" Peal** . . . . . . . . (919) 855-4800
  Education: East Carolina MA
Senior Policy Advisor **Matthew "Matt" McKillip** . . . . . . . (919) 855-4800

## Office of Rural Health and Community Care [ORHCC]
311 Ashe Avenue, Raleigh, NC 27606
Tel: (919) 527-6440  Fax: (919) 733-8300

Director **Chris Collins** . . . . . . . . . . . . . . . . . . . . . . . . (919) 527-6450
Program Manager, CHIPRA **(Vacant)** . . . . . . . . . . . . . . . (919) 527-6474
Program Manager, HealthNet **Anne Braswell** . . . . . . . . . . (919) 527-6449
Program Manager, Medical, Dental, and Psychiatric
Recruitment **Parcheul Harris** . . . . . . . . . . . . . . . . . . (919) 527-6468
Program Manager, Medication Assistance
**Ginny Klarman** . . . . . . . . . . . . . . . . . . . . . . . . . (919) 527-6457
Program Manager, North Carolina Farmworker Health
**Elizabeth Freeman-Lambar** . . . . . . . . . . . . . . . . . . (919) 527-6455
Program Manager, Rural Health Information Technology
**(Vacant)** . . . . . . . . . . . . . . . . . . . . . . . . . . . . . (919) 527-6470
Program Manager, Rural Hospital Assistance
**Jay Kennedy** . . . . . . . . . . . . . . . . . . . . . . . . . . . (919) 527-6467
Contracts Manager **Allison Owen** . . . . . . . . . . . . . . . . . (919) 527-6447
Human Resources and Communications Liaison
**Cindy Leighton** . . . . . . . . . . . . . . . . . . . . . . . . . (919) 527-6452
  E-mail: cindy.leighton@dhhs.nc.gov
Social Clinical Research Specialist **Stirling Cummings** . . . (919) 527-6486

## Aging, Disability and Long Term Care
Deputy Secretary for Human Services **Sherry Bradsher** . . . (919) 855-4800
Aging Division Director **(Vacant)** . . . . . . . . . . . . . . . . . (919) 855-3400
  2101 Mail Service Center, Raleigh, NC 27699-2101
Services for the Blind Division Director
**Donald E. Weaver** . . . . . . . . . . . . . . . . . . . . . . . (919) 733-9822
  Mail Service Center, 2601, Raleigh, NC 27699-2601
Services for the Deaf and the Hard of Hearing Division
Director **Jan Withers** . . . . . . . . . . . . . . . . . . . . . . (919) 874-2212
  2301 Mail Service Center, Raleigh, NC 27699-2301  TTY: (800) 851-6099
Vocational Rehabilitation Division Director **(Vacant)** . . . . . (919) 855-3500
  2801 Mail Service Center, Raleigh, NC 27699-2801

## Finance and Business Operations
Office of the Controller Director
**Laketha Marley Miller, CPA** . . . . . . . . . . . . . . . . . (919) 855-3700
  2019 Mail Service Center, Raleigh, NC 27699-2019
  E-mail: laketha.miller@dhhs.nc.gov
  Education: North Carolina State 1988 BAcc
Office of the Internal Auditor Director **Chet Spruill, CPA** . . (919) 855-3737
  E-mail: chet.spruill@dhhs.nc.gov
Budget and Analysis Division Director **Jim Slate** . . . . . . . . (919) 855-4850
Information Resource Management Division Director
**Karen Tomczak** . . . . . . . . . . . . . . . . . . . . . . . . . (919) 855-3000
  Mail Service Center, 2015, Raleigh, NC 27699-2015
  E-mail: karen.tomczak@dhhs.nc.gov

## Human Services and Education Policy
Child Development and Early Education Division
Director **Robert W. "Rob" Kindsvatter** . . . . . . . . . . . . (919) 527-6530
  Mail Service Center, 2201,    Fax: (919) 715-0976
  Raleigh, NC 27699-2201
Social Services Division Director **(Vacant)** . . . . . . . . . . . . (919) 733-3055
  Mail Service Center, 2401, Raleigh, NC 27699-2401

## Division of Medical Assistance [DMA]
Tel: (919) 855-4100

Medicaid Director **Dave Richard** . . . . . . . . . . . . . . . . . . (919) 855-4100
Chief Medical Officer **Dr. Nancy Henley, MD** . . . . . . . . . (919) 855-4263
Business Information Director **Steve W. Tedder** . . . . . . . . (919) 855-4100
Clinical Policy Director **Sandra "Sandy" Terrell** . . . . . . . (919) 855-4100

*(continued on next page)*

---

★ Elected Official    ■ Appointed by Governor    ● Appointed by Legislature    ▲ Appointed by Board or Commission    ◆ Appointed by State Supreme Court

**EXECUTIVE BRANCH**

**Division of Medical Assistance** *continued*

Finance Director **Trey Sutten** . . . . . . . . . . . . . . . . . . . . . .(919) 855-4100

## Division of Public Health

1931 Mail Service Center, Raleigh, NC 27699-1931
1903 Mail Service Center, Raleigh, NC 27699-1903 (Vital Records)
Tel: (919) 707-5000  Tel: (919) 733-3000 (Vital Records)
Fax: (919) 733-1511  Internet: www.ncpublichealth.com

**Employees:** 1,770  **Fiscal Year:** 2014-2015  **Budget:** $828,630,000

Division Director
 **RADM Penelope Slade-Sawyer, USPHS (Ret)** . . . . . . . .(919) 707-5000
State Health Director **(Vacant)** . . . . . . . . . . . . . . . . . . . .(919) 707-5000
Environmental Health Director **Larry Michael** . . . . . . . . . .(919) 707-5855
State Center for Health Statistics Director (Acting)
 **Dr. Eleanor Howell, RN** . . . . . . . . . . . . . . . . . . . . . . . .(919) 733-4728
 Education: Medical Col (GA) BSN; Alabama Birmingham MSN, PhD
State Laboratory Director **Dr. Scott J. Zimmerman** . . . . . .(919) 733-7834
Chief Medical Examiner
 **Deborah L. Radisch, MD, MPH** . . . . . . . . . . . . . . . . . .(919) 743-9000
 Education: Wake Forest MD; North Carolina MPH
Administrative Local and Community Support Section
 Chief **Danny Staley** . . . . . . . . . . . . . . . . . . . . . . . . . .(919) 707-5024
 E-mail: danny.staley@dhhs.nc.gov
Chronic Disease and Injury Section Chief
 **Dr. Ruth Petersen** . . . . . . . . . . . . . . . . . . . . . . . . . .(919) 707-5203
Epidemiology Chief **Dr. Megan Davies** . . . . . . . . . . . . . .(919) 733-3421
Minority Health and Health Disparities Office Director
 (Acting) **Belinda Pettiford** . . . . . . . . . . . . . . . . . . . .(919) 707-5700
Oral Health Section Chief (Acting)
 **Robert "Bob" Leddy, DDS** . . . . . . . . . . . . . . . . . . . . .(336) 294-4591
Women's and Children's Health Section Chief
 **Dr. Kevin J. Ryan, MD** . . . . . . . . . . . . . . . . . . . . . . . .(919) 707-5510
Immunization Program Manager **Wendy Holmes** . . . . . . . .(919) 707-5551
Cancer Prevention and Control Program Manager
 **Debi Nelson** . . . . . . . . . . . . . . . . . . . . . . . . . . . . . . .(919) 707-5300
 Education: Western Carolina MAEd
Family Planning and Reproductive Health Branch Chief
 **Sydney Atkinson** . . . . . . . . . . . . . . . . . . . . . . . . . . .(919) 707-5693
Forensic Tests for Alcohol Program Manager
 **Paul Glover** . . . . . . . . . . . . . . . . . . . . . . . . . . . . . . .(919) 707-5252
Aids Care Unit/Communicable Disease Branch
 **Mary Ann Chap** . . . . . . . . . . . . . . . . . . . . . . . . . . . .(919) 733-9526
Injury and Violence Prevention Program Head
 **Alan Dellapenna** . . . . . . . . . . . . . . . . . . . . . . . . . . .(919) 707-5441
Local Technical Assistance and Training Program
 Manager **Joy Reed, EdD, RN, FAAN** . . . . . . . . . . . . . . .(919) 707-5131
Occupational and Environmental Epidemiology Branch
 Head **Mina W. Shehee, PhD** . . . . . . . . . . . . . . . . . . . .(919) 707-5900
Tobacco Prevention and Control Program Manager
 **Sally Herndon** . . . . . . . . . . . . . . . . . . . . . . . . . . . . .(919) 707-5401
Director, Information Technology Services
 **Larry Forrister** . . . . . . . . . . . . . . . . . . . . . . . . . . . . .(919) 707-5170
 E-mail: larry.forrister@dhhs.nc.gov    Fax: (919) 870-4840
Bioterrorism Coordinator **Julie Casani** . . . . . . . . . . . . . .(919) 715-6734
Nutrition Services Branch Director **Josephine Cialone** . . .(919) 707-5800
 E-mail: josephine.cialone@dhhs.nc.gov    Fax: (919) 870-4818
Vital Records Director and State Registrar
 **Catherine Ryan** . . . . . . . . . . . . . . . . . . . . . . . . . . . .(919) 733-3526
 225 North McDowell Street, Raleigh, NC 27603-1382

## Division of Social Services

Tel: (919) 527-6335  Fax: (919) 334-1018

Division Director **Wayne Black** . . . . . . . . . . . . . . . . . . . .(919) 527-6335
 E-mail: wayne.black@dhhs.nc.gov

## Department of Information Technology [NC IT]

P.O. Box 17209, Raleigh, NC 27619-7209
Tel: (919) 754-6100  Fax: (919) 981-2548

■Secretary and State Chief Information Officer
 **Keith E. Werner** . . . . . . . . . . . . . . . . . . . . . . . . . . . .(919) 707-8917
 E-mail: keith.werner@nc.gov

Deputy State Chief Information Officer/Chief
 Administrative Officer/Chief Financial Officer
 **Kristen Culler** . . . . . . . . . . . . . . . . . . . . . . . . . . . . .(919) 754-6574
 E-mail: kristen.culler@nc.gov
Deputy State Chief Information Officer/Chief Services
 Officer **Tracy Doaks** . . . . . . . . . . . . . . . . . . . . . . . . .(919) 754-6574
 E-mail: tracy.doaks@nc.gov
Deputy State Chief Information Officer/Statewide
 Information Technology Division Director **(Vacant)** . . . . .(919) 707-8917
State Chief Information Risk Officer
 **Maria S. Thompson** . . . . . . . . . . . . . . . . . . . . . . . . . .(919) 754-6578
 E-mail: maria.s.thompson@nc.gov
Legislative Affairs Officer and Program Coordinator
 **Meghan Cook** . . . . . . . . . . . . . . . . . . . . . . . . . . . . . .(919) 754-6100
 E-mail: meghan.cook@nc.gov
General Counsel and Policy Director
 **Jeffrey "Jeff" Sural** . . . . . . . . . . . . . . . . . . . . . . . . . .(919) 715-0687
 E-mail: jeff.sural@nc.gov
Human Resources Director **Rob Barnes** . . . . . . . . . . . . . .(919) 754-6100
Public Affairs Director **Michelle C. Vaught** . . . . . . . . . . . .(919) 754-6291
 E-mail: michelle.vaught@nc.gov
 Education: Campbell 1994 BA

## Department of Military and Veteran Affairs

413 North Salisbury Street, Raleigh, NC 27603
4001 Mail Service Center, Raleigh, NC 27699-4001
Tel: (844) 624-8387  Fax: (919) 807-4260  Internet: milvets.nc.gov

■Secretary **MajGen Cornelius A. "Cornell" Wilson, Jr.,
 USMC (Ret)** . . . . . . . . . . . . . . . . . . . . . . . . . . . . . . .(844) 624-8387
 Education: South Carolina 1972 BSChem
Assistant Secretary
 **Ilario Gregory Pantano, USMC (Ret)** . . . . . . . . . . . . . .(844) 624-8387
 Education: NYU 1996 BA
Executive Assistant **Kelly Barretto** . . . . . . . . . . . . . . . . .(844) 624-8387
Executive Officer **MAJ Bobby Lumsden, ARNG** . . . . . . . . .(844) 624-8387

## Department of Public Safety

4201 Mail Service Center, Raleigh, NC 27699-4201
Tel: (919) 733-2126  Fax: (919) 715-8477

**Employees:** 22,688  **Fiscal Year:** 2014-2015  **Budget:** $1,988,715,000

■Secretary **Frank L. Perry** . . . . . . . . . . . . . . . . . . . . . . .(919) 733-2126
 E-mail: frank.perry@ncdps.gov
 Education: Wake Forest
Communications Director **Pamela Walker** . . . . . . . . . . . . .(919) 733-5027
 E-mail: pamela.walker@ncdps.gov
 Education: North Carolina Wilmington 1990 BA
Deputy Communications Director **Crystal Feldman** . . . . . .(919) 733-2126
 E-mail: crystal.feldman@nc.gov
 Education: Georgetown 2007 BA
Deputy Secretary and General Counsel **(Vacant)** . . . . . . . .(919) 733-2126
Controller's Office Director **(Vacant)** . . . . . . . . . . . . . . . .(919) 733-2126
Management Information Services
 **Bob Brinson, CISSP, CPA** . . . . . . . . . . . . . . . . . . . . . .(919) 716-3500
 2020 Yonkers Road, Raleigh, NC 27699-4222
 E-mail: bob.brinson@ncdps.gov
 Education: North Carolina State 1972 BS; North Carolina 1975 MBA
Personnel Director **David A. Shehden** . . . . . . . . . . . . . . .(919) 716-3700
 214 West Jones Street, Raleigh, NC 27699-4201
 Safety Office Director **Joseph "Joe" Simpson** . . . . . . . .(919) 716-3590
 2020 Yonkers Road, Raleigh, NC 27604
 Education: North Carolina State BA
 Central Engineering Director **Bill Stovall** . . . . . . . . . . . .(919) 716-3400
 2020 Yonkers Rd., Raleigh, NC 27604
 E-mail: bill.stovall@ncdps.gov
 Education: North Carolina State 1982 BS
Internal Audit Director **Tim Harrell** . . . . . . . . . . . . . . . . .(919) 733-2126
 430 N. Salisbury St., Raleigh, NC 27626-0540
Facility Management Director **Jerry Carroll** . . . . . . . . . . . .(919) 838-4000
Legislative Liaison **Ryan Combs** . . . . . . . . . . . . . . . . . . .(919) 733-2126
 E-mail: ryan.combs@ncdps.gov

★ Elected Official  ■ Appointed by Governor  ● Appointed by Legislature  ▲ Appointed by Board or Commission  ◆ Appointed by State Supreme Court

EXECUTIVE BRANCH

## Division of Adult Correction and Juvenile Justice [NCDOC]

512 North Salisbury Street, 4201 Mail Service Center,
Raleigh, NC 27699-4201
Tel: (919) 733-2126  E-mail: info@doc.state.nc.us

**Employees:** 22,589  **Fiscal Year:** 2014  **Budget:** $2,829,663,000

■Commissioner **W. David Guice** . . . . . . . . . . . . . . . . . . . . . . . (919) 733-2126
  E-mail: david.guice@ncdps.gov
Deputy Commissioner **William Lassiter** . . . . . . . . . . . . . . (919) 825-2719
  E-mail: william.lassiter@ncdps.gov
Deputy Commissioner **Timothy "Tim" Moose** . . . . . . . . . (919) 716-3700
  E-mail: tim.moose@ncdps.gov
  Education: North Carolina State 1983 BA
Deputy Commissioner **Joe Prater** . . . . . . . . . . . . . . . . . . . . (919) 733-2126
  E-mail: joe.prater@ncdps.gov
  Education: North Carolina State 1978 BA, 1980 MPA
  Staff Development and Training Director
    **Charles Walston** . . . . . . . . . . . . . . . . . . . . . . . . . . . . . (919) 367-7100
    2211 Schieffelin Road, Apex, NC 27699-4213
  Correction Enterprises Section Chief **Karen Brown** . . . . (919) 716-3600
    2020 Yonkers Rd., Raleigh, NC 27604
    Education: North Carolina BA; Meredith MBA
Community Supervision Director **Anne Precythe** . . . . . . . . (919) 716-3100
Juvenile Court Services Director **Michael Rieder** . . . . . . . (919) 733-3388
  E-mail: michael.rieder@ncdps.gov
Juvenile Facilities Director **Dave Hardesty** . . . . . . . . . . . . (919) 324-6425
  E-mail: dave.hardesty@ncdps.gov
PREA Director **Charlotte Willams** . . . . . . . . . . . . . . . . . . (919) 733-2126
Rehabilitative Programs and Support Services Director
  **Nicole Sullivan** . . . . . . . . . . . . . . . . . . . . . . . . . . . . . . . (919) 733-4080
Communications Officer **Keith Acree** . . . . . . . . . . . . . . . . (919) 733-5027
  Education: Greensboro 1991 BA
Communications Officer **Diana Kees** . . . . . . . . . . . . . . . . (919) 733-5027
  E-mail: diana.kees@ncdps.gov
Juvenile Community Programs Director **(Vacant)** . . . . . . . . (919) 733-3388

## Division of Law Enforcement

4701 Mail Service Center, Raleigh, NC 27699-4201
Tel: (919) 733-2126  Fax: (919) 715-8477

Operations Commissioner **Gregory K. Baker** . . . . . . . . . . . (919) 733-2126
  Education: Central Oklahoma BS
Communications Officer **Patty McQuillan** . . . . . . . . . . . . . (919) 733-5027
  E-mail: patty.mcquillan@ncdps.gov
  Education: South Carolina 1975 BA

## National Guard

1636 Gold Star Drive, Raleigh, NC 27607-6410
Internet: www.ncguard.com  Internet: www.nc.ngb.army.mil

Adjutant General **MG Gregory A. Lusk, ARNG** . . . . . . . . (919) 664-6000
  Education: North Carolina State BS; Army War Col MS
Chief Information Officer **LTC Matt Chytka, ARNG** . . . . . . (984) 664-6410

## State Bureau of Investigation

P.O. Box 29500, Raleigh, NC 27626
Tel: (919) 662-4500  Fax: (919) 662-4523

Director **Robert "Bob" Schurmeier, Jr.** . . . . . . . . . . . . . . (919) 662-4500
Deputy Director **Janie Pinkston Sutton** . . . . . . . . . . . . . . (919) 662-4500
  Education: UMass (Lowell) BA
Administrative Services Assistant Director
  **Robert Christopher Laws** . . . . . . . . . . . . . . . . . . . . . . (919) 733-2126
  E-mail: claws@ncdoj.gov
Field Operations Assistant Director **Brent Culbertson** . . . . (919) 733-2126
  Education: North Carolina Charlotte 1995 BS
Special Operations Assistant Director **Brian Neil** . . . . . . . . (919) 733-2126
  Education: Elon Col BA

## Department of Revenue [DOR]

501 North Wilmington Street, Raleigh, NC 27604
P.O. Box 25000, Raleigh, NC 27640-0640
Tel: (877) 252-3052  Fax: (919) 733-0023  Internet: www.dor.state.nc.us

**Employees:** 1,277  **Fiscal Year:** 2014-2015  **Budget:** $129,049,000

■Secretary **Jeffrey M. Epstein** . . . . . . . . . . . . . . . . . . . . . . (919) 814-1008
  E-mail: jeff.epstein@dornc.com
  Executive Assistant **Janice McDougald** . . . . . . . . . . . . . (919) 814-1006
Chief Financial Officer **Elizabeth Colcord** . . . . . . . . . . . . (919) 754-2519
Chief Operating Officer **(Vacant)** . . . . . . . . . . . . . . . . . . . (919) 814-1008
  Executive Assistant **Cheryl Benedetto** . . . . . . . . . . . . . . (919) 814-1008
Business Systems Assistant Secretary **Jerry Coble** . . . . . . . (919) 754-2277
Information and Technology Assistant Secretary
  **David Roseberry** . . . . . . . . . . . . . . . . . . . . . . . . . . . . . . (919) 754-2002
  E-mail: david.roseberry@dornc.com
Tax Administration Assistant Secretary
  **Jocelyn Andrews** . . . . . . . . . . . . . . . . . . . . . . . . . . . . . (919) 814-1112
Documents and Payments Processing Director
  **Cindy Mallard** . . . . . . . . . . . . . . . . . . . . . . . . . . . . . . . (919) 814-1300
Security Director **(Vacant)** . . . . . . . . . . . . . . . . . . . . . . . . . (919) 754-2395
Taxpayer Assistance Director **Kim Sabol** . . . . . . . . . . . . . . (919) 754-2529
Collection Division Director **Charlie H. Helms** . . . . . . . . . (919) 754-2537
Income Tax Division Director **Lennie Collins** . . . . . . . . . . (919) 814-1163
Examination Division Director **Alan Woodard** . . . . . . . . . . (919) 814-1030
Excise Tax Division Director **John Panza** . . . . . . . . . . . . . (919) 814-1100
Human Resources Division Director **Eric McKinney** . . . . . . (919) 814-1200
Local Government Division Director **David Baker** . . . . . . . . (919) 814-1129
Sales and Use Tax Division Director **Eric Wayne** . . . . . . . . (919) 814-1083
Tax Enforcement Division Director **(Vacant)** . . . . . . . . . . . (919) 707-7595

## North Carolina Department of Transportation [NCDOT]

Transportation Building, One S. Wilmington Street,
Raleigh, NC 27699-1501
Tel: (919) 707-2800  Tel: (877) 368-4968 (Customer Service)
Fax: (919) 733-9150

**Employees:** 11,791  **Fiscal Year:** 2014-2015  **Budget:** $6,708,248,000

■Secretary **Nicholas J. "Nick" Tennyson** . . . . . . . . . . . . . . (919) 707-2800
  E-mail: njtennyson@ncdot.gov
  Education: Duke BA; Pepperdine MA
  Executive Assistant **Vicki Stanley** . . . . . . . . . . . . . . . . . . (919) 707-2800
  Chief of Staff **Bobby Lewis** . . . . . . . . . . . . . . . . . . . . . . (919) 707-2800
Chief Deputy Secretary **(Vacant)** . . . . . . . . . . . . . . . . . . . . (919) 707-2800
Statewide Logistics Coordinator **(Vacant)** . . . . . . . . . . . . . (919) 707-2512
Communications Deputy Secretary **Mike Charbonneau** . . . (919) 707-2670
  E-mail: mcharbonneau@ncdot.com
General Counsel **Shelley Blake** . . . . . . . . . . . . . . . . . . . . . (919) 707-2800
  E-mail: sblake@ncdot.gov
Deputy Agency Counsel **Will A. Smith** . . . . . . . . . . . . . . . (919) 707-2800
  E-mail: wsmith@ncdot.gov
Special Deputy Attorney General **Beth McKay** . . . . . . . . . . (919) 707-4480
  E-mail: bmckay@ncdoj.gov
Inspector General **Mary Morton** . . . . . . . . . . . . . . . . . . . . (919) 707-4573
  E-mail: mjmorton1@ncdot.gov
Chief Information Officer **(Vacant)** . . . . . . . . . . . . . . . . . . (919) 707-2200
Governor's Highway Safety Program Director **Don Nail** . . . (919) 733-3083
  E-mail: dnail@ncdot.gov

## State Board of Transportation

1501 Mail Service Center, Raleigh, NC 27699-1501
Tel: (919) 707-2800  Fax: (919) 733-9150

■Chairman **Edward Curran** (At-Large) . . . . . . . . . . . . . . . . (704) 248-2070
  E-mail: elcurran1@ncdot.gov
■Vice-Chairman **Ferrell Blount** (At-Large) . . . . . . . . . . . . . (252) 758-7500
  E-mail: flblount@ncdot.gov
  Education: North Carolina 1972 BA
■Member **Jake Alexander** (Ninth Division) . . . . . . . . . . . . . (704) 637-7073
  E-mail: jfalexander@ncdot.gov
■Member **David L. Brown** (Thirteenth Division) . . . . . . . . . (828) 273-4877
  E-mail: dlevbrown@bellsouth.net

*(continued on next page)*

---

★ Elected Official    ■ Appointed by Governor    ● Appointed by Legislature    ▲ Appointed by Board or Commission    ◆ Appointed by State Supreme Court

**State Board of Transportation** *continued*

■ Member **Jim Crawford** (At-Large) . . . . . . . . . . . . . . (252) 492-0185
   E-mail: info@crawprop.com
■ Member **Walter "Jack" Debnam** (Fourteenth Division) . . . (828) 506-4709
   Term Expires: January 15, 2019
   E-mail: wjdebnam1@ncdot.gov
■ Member **Tracy Dodson** (Tenth Division) . . . . . . . . . . (704) 714-7694
   Term Expires: January 15, 2019
   E-mail: tfdodson@ncdot.gov
■ Member **Malcolm Fearing** (First Division) . . . . . . . . (252) 473-2208
   E-mail: mkfearing@ncdot.gov
■ Member **Sandra Fountain** (Third Division) . . . . . . . . . (910) 455-2977
   Term Expires: January 15, 2019
   E-mail: sgfountain@ncdot.gov
■ Member **H. Terry Hutchens, Sr.** (Sixth Division) . . . . . . . (910) 486-1493
   Term Expires: January 15, 2019
   E-mail: hthutchens@ncdot.gov
   Education: North Carolina State 1972 BA; Wake Forest 1974 MBA, 1977 JD
■ Member **John Lennon** (At-Large) . . . . . . . . . . . . . . . . . (910) 239-5895
   E-mail: jdlennon@ncdot.gov
■ Member **Cheryl McQueary** (Seventh Division) . . . . . . . . (336) 487-0000
   E-mail: clmcqueary@ncdot.gov
■ Member **Patrick Molamphy** (Eighth Division) . . . . . . . (910) 944-2344
   Term Expires: January 15, 2019
   E-mail: pdmolamphy@ncdot.gov
■ Member **Hugh R. Overholt** (Second Division) . . . . . . . . . (252) 672-5462
   E-mail: hoverholt@ncdot.gov
   Education: Arkansas 1955 AB, 1957 JD; National Defense U 1976
■ Member **James Palermo** (Eleventh Division) . . . . . . . . . . (336) 667-9111
   E-mail: jrpalermo@ncdot.gov
■ Member
   **Andrew M. Perkins, Jr.** (Ninth Division At-Large) . . . . . (336) 285-4551
   E-mail: perkins@ncat.edu
■ Member **Jeff Sheehan** (Fifth Division) . . . . . . . . . . . . . . (919) 461-8005
   E-mail: jbsheehan1@ncdot.gov
■ Member **Gus H. Tulloss** (Fourth Division) . . . . . . . . . . . . (252) 937-6913
   E-mail: ghtulloss@ncdot.gov
■ Member **Lou Wetmore** (Twelfth District) . . . . . . . . (828) 323-8777 ext. 214
   E-mail: lswetmore@ncdot.gov
   Board Secretary **Tereca W. Batts** . . . . . . . . . . . . . . . . . . . (919) 707-2820
   E-mail: twbatts@ncdot.gov

## Financial Management Division

Internet: www.ncdot.org/financial
Chief Financial Officer **David Tyeryar** . . . . . . . . . . . . . . . . (919) 707-4320
Accounting Operations Director **Kim Padfield** . . . . . . . . . . (919) 707-4290
Purchasing Director **(Vacant)** . . . . . . . . . . . . . . . . . . . . . . (919) 707-2623
Funds Administration Manager **Laurie P. Smith, CPA** . . . . . (919) 707-4322
   E-mail: lpsmith@ncdot.gov

## Highway Division

Transportation Building, One South Wilmington Street,
1536 Mail Service Center, Raleigh, NC 27699-1536
Fax: (919) 733-9428  Internet: www.ncdot.org/doh
■ Chief Engineer **Michael Holder** . . . . . . . . . . . . . . . . . . . (919) 707-2500
   E-mail: mholder@ncdot.gov
Deputy Chief Engineer **Jon Nance, PE** . . . . . . . . . . . . . . . (919) 707-2500
   E-mail: jnance@ncdot.gov
Field Operations Director **Ricky E. Greene, Jr., PE** . . . . . . (919) 707-2530
Preconstruction Director **Deborah M. Barbour, PE** . . . . . . (919) 707-2540
   E-mail: dbarbour@ncdot.gov
State Construction Engineer **Ron Hancock, PE** . . . . . . . . . (919) 707-2400
   E-mail: rhancock@ncdot.gov
   Materials and Tests Engineer **Chris Peoples** . . . . . . . . . . (919) 329-4000
      E-mail: cpeoples@ncdot.gov
   Pavement Management Engineer **Judith Corley-Lay** . . . . (919) 835-8201
      E-mail: jlay@ncdot.gov
   Roadside Environmental Engineer **Don G. Lee** . . . . . . . . (919) 733-2920
      E-mail: dlee@ncdot.gov
   State Intelligent Transportation System Operations
   Engineer **Meredith McDiarmid** . . . . . . . . . . . . . . . . . . (919) 825-2619
      E-mail: mmcdiarmid@ncdot.gov

State Asset Maintenance Engineer
   **Jennifer Brandenburg** . . . . . . . . . . . . . . . . . . . . . . . . (919) 733-3725
      E-mail: jbrandenburg@ncdot.gov
State Maintenance and Equipment Engineer
   **Scott Capps** . . . . . . . . . . . . . . . . . . . . (919) 733-2220 ext. 8000
Oversize and Overweight Permit Unit Director
   **Tammy C. Denning** . . . . . . . . . . . . . . . . . . . . . . . . (919) 733-4740
Right of Way Branch Manager **Tom Childrey** . . . . . . . . . (919) 707-4365
State Traffic Engineer **J. Kevin Lacy** . . . . . . . . . . . . . . . (919) 707-2550
   E-mail: jklacy@ncdot.gov
State Geotechnical Engineer **John Pilipchuk, PE** . . . . . . . (919) 250-6850
   E-mail: jpilipchuk@ncdot.gov
State Hydraulics Engineer **David Chang, PE** . . . . . . . . . . (919) 707-6700
   E-mail: dchang@ncdot.gov
State Location and Surveys Engineer **Charlie Brown** . . . . (919) 707-6800
   E-mail: charliebrown@ncdot.gov
State Photogrammetric Engineer **Keith Johnston, PE** . . . (919) 707-7090
   E-mail: kjohnston@ncdot.gov
State Roadway Design Engineer **Jay A. Bennett** . . . . . . . (919) 707-6200
   E-mail: jbennett@ncdot.gov
State Structure Engineer **Greg Perfetti** . . . . . . . . . . . . . (919) 707-6400
   E-mail: gperfetti@ncdot.gov
Operations Program Manager **Delbert Roddenberry** . . . . . (919) 707-2509
Transportation Engineering Associate (TEA) Program
   Manager **Helen Dickens** . . . . . . . . . . . . . . . . . . . . . (919) 707-6686
Safety and Risk Management Director
   **Robert K. "Bob" Andrews, Jr.** . . . . . . . . . . . . . . . . . (919) 707-4852
      E-mail: rkandrews@ncdot.gov

## Motor Vehicles Division [DMV]

1100 New Bern Avenue, Raleigh, NC 27697
Fax: (919) 733-0126
■ Commissioner **Kelly J. Thomas, USA (Ret)** . . . . . . . . . . (919) 861-3015
   3101 Mail Service Center, Raleigh, NC 27699-3101
   E-mail: kjthomas@ncdot.gov
   Education: Methodist Col 1981 BA; Army War Col 2001 MSS
   Executive Assistant **Beth Wise** . . . . . . . . . . . . . . . . . . (919) 861-3015
Deputy Commissioner **Randy Dishong** . . . . . . . . . . . . . . (919) 861-3024
Assistant Commissioner **Hope Mozingo** . . . . . . . . . . . . . (919) 861-3178
Deputy General Counsel **Ryan Boyce** . . . . . . . . . . . . . . . (919) 707-2800
Administrative Hearings Assistant Director
   **Jacob M. Joubert** . . . . . . . . . . . . . . . . . . . . . . . . . . (919) 861-3475
   3133 Mail Service Center, Raleigh, NC 27699-3133    Fax: (919) 861-3535
   E-mail: jmjoubert@ncdot.gov
Driver Services Assistant Director
   **Charlotte Boyd-Malette** . . . . . . . . . . . . . . . . . . . . . (919) 861-3195
Field Services Director **Portia Manley** . . . . . . . . . . . . . . (919) 861-3332
   Field Services Assistant Director **Paula Windley** . . . . . (919) 861-3331
   Field Services Deputy Director **James Semmens** . . . . . (919) 861-3812
   CDL Training Manager **Robbie Quinn** . . . . . . . . . . . . (919) 861-3258
Hearings Assistant Director **Dan Whittacre** . . . . . . . . . . (919) 861-3493
   3133 Mail Service Center, Raleigh, NC 27699-3133    Fax: (919) 861-3535
   E-mail: dwhittarce@ncdot.gov
Processing Services Hearings Director
   **Jeffrey R. Zimmerman** . . . . . . . . . . . . . . . . . . . . . . (919) 861-3167
   E-mail: jzimmerman1@ncdot.gov
School Bus and Traffic Safety Assistant Director
   **Rodney Coleman** . . . . . . . . . . . . . . . . . . . . . . . . . . (919) 861-3812
Training Director **Deanna Sevits** . . . . . . . . . . . . . . . . . . (919) 861-3042
   E-mail: dsevits@ncdot.gov
Traffic Records Assistant Director **Julian Council** . . . . . . (919) 861-3061
   3105 Mail Service Center, Raleigh, NC 27699-3105    Fax: (919) 715-9099
   E-mail: jhcouncil@ncdot.gov
License and Theft Bureau Director **Steven M. Watkins** . . . (919) 861-3144
   3125 Mail Services Center,    Fax: (919) 715-0169
   Raleigh, NC 27699-3125
   License and Theft Bureau Assistant Director
   **Jessica Locklear** . . . . . . . . . . . . . . . . . . . . . . . . . . . (919) 861-3177
   3125 Mail Services Center, Raleigh, NC 27699-3125
   License and Theft Bureau Assistant Director
   **Diego Santiago** . . . . . . . . . . . . . . . . . . . . . . . . . . . (919) 861-3144
   3125 Mail Services Center, Raleigh, NC 27699-3125
Communications Manager (Acting) **Marge Howell** . . . . . . (919) 861-3019
   E-mail: mhowell@ncdot.gov

---

★ Elected Official    ■ Appointed by Governor    ● Appointed by Legislature    ▲ Appointed by Board or Commission    ◆ Appointed by State Supreme Court

Marketing Officer **Laticia A. King** ................. (919) 861-3049
  E-mail: laking1@ncdot.gov
Facilities Administration Officer **Stephanie Mouzon** ..... (919) 861-3189
  3101 Mail Service Center, Raleigh, NC 27699-3101    Fax: (919) 715-4606

## Strategic Initiatives Division
Director **Bobby Lewis** ......................... (919) 707-2800
  E-mail: bobbylewis@ncdot.gov
Government Affairs and Policy Director **Mary Jernijen** ... (919) 707-2800
  E-mail: mjernijen@ncdot.gov
Interagency Director **Keith H. Weatherly** ......... (919) 707-2800
  E-mail: kweatherly@ncdot.gov
  Education: North Carolina BA
Environmental Program Supervisor **Jamie Shern** ........ (919) 707-2800
Program Analyst **Humberto Tasaico** ................ (919) 707-2800
  E-mail: htasaico@ncdot.gov

## Strategic Planning Division
Strategic Planning Office Director **Charles Edwards** ...... (919) 707-4740
Program Development Branch Manager
  **Calvin W. Leggett, PE** ...................... (919) 707-4611
  E-mail: cleggett@ncdot.gov
Transportation Planning Branch Manager
  **Patrick Norman** ........................... (919) 707-0901
  E-mail: pnorman@ncdot.gov
Education Initiatives Administrative Officer
  **Ashley Goolsby** ........................... (919) 508-1810
  E-mail: agoolsby@ncdot.gov
Strategic Initiatives Coordinator **Mike Bruff** ........... (919) 707-2800
Performance Metrics Management Engineer
  **Ehren Meister** ............................ (919) 707-2800
  E-mail: emeister@ncdot.gov
State Traffic Survey Engineer **Kent Taylor, PE** .......... (919) 771-2520

## Transit Division
Deputy Secretary **(Vacant)** ....................... (919) 707-2800

## Housing Finance Agency
3508 Bush Street, Raleigh, NC 27609
Tel: (919) 877-5700  Tel: (800) 393-0988  Fax: (919) 877-5701

▲Executive Director **A. Robert Kucab** ................ (919) 877-5600
  E-mail: arkucab@nchfa.com
  Education: Eastern Michigan BA; Wayne State U MA
Government Relations and Communications Director
  **(Vacant)** ................................ (919) 877-5606

## Ethics Commission
424 North Blount Street, Raleigh, NC 27601
1324 Mail Service Center, Raleigh, NC 27699-1324
Tel: (919) 715-2071  Fax: (919) 715-1644
E-mail: ethics.commission@doa.nc.gov
Internet: www.ethicscommission.nc.gov

■Chairman **George L. Wainwright, Jr.** ............... (919) 715-2071
  Term Expires: December 31, 2017
  E-mail: george.wainwright@doa.nc.gov
  Education: North Carolina 1966 BA; Wake Forest 1984 JD
■Vice Chair **Jane Flowers Finch** ................... (919) 715-2071
  Term Expires: December 31, 2015
  E-mail: jane.finch@doa.nc.gov
■Member **William P. Farthing, Jr.** ................. (704) 335-9014
  Term Expires: December 31, 2017
  E-mail: billfarthing@parkerpoe.com
  Education: North Carolina 1970 AB, 1974 JD
●Member **Tommy D. McKnight** ..................... (919) 715-2071
  Term Expires: December 31, 2018
  E-mail: tommy.mcknight@doa.nc.gov
●Member **Robert L. Moseley, Jr.** .................. (919) 715-2071
  Term Expires: December 31, 2016
●Member **Clarence G. "C.G." Newsome** ............. (919) 715-2071
  Term Expires: December 31, 2014
  E-mail: clarence.newsome@doa.nc.gov
  Education: Duke 1972 BA, 1975 MDiv, 1982 PhD
●Member **Patrick Roberts** ....................... (919) 715-2071
  Term Expires: December 31, 2019

## Commission Staff
Executive Director **Perry Y. Newson** ................ (919) 715-2071
  Administrative Assistant **Beth Carpenter** ........... (919) 715-2071
Assistant Director **Pamela "Pam" Cashwell** ........... (919) 715-2071
  Education: North Carolina BA, JD

## State Human Resources Commission [SHRC]
Tel: (919) 807-4850

Chairman **Susan B. Manning** ...................... (919) 807-4850
  Term Expires: June 30, 2017
Commissioner **Melvin L. "Mel" Asbury** ............. (919) 807-4850
  Term Expires: June 30, 2017
  Education: North Carolina Central; Purdue
Commissioner **Dan Barrett** ....................... (919) 807-4850
  Term Expires: June 30, 2017
Commissioner **Virgie DeVane-Hayes** ................ (919) 807-4850
  Term Expires: June 30, 2017
Commissioner **John K. Eller** ..................... (919) 807-4850
  Term Expires: June 30, 2017
Commissioner **Gloria Evans** ...................... (919) 807-4850
  Term Expires: June 30, 2017
Commissioner **Martin Falls** ...................... (919) 807-4850
  Term Expires: June 30, 2017
Commissioner **Kelly B. Sizemore** .................. (919) 807-4850
  Term Expires: June 30, 2017
Commissioner **Phillip Strach** ..................... (919) 807-4850
  Term Expires: June 30, 2017

## Commission Staff
Administrator **Delores Joyner** .................... (919) 807-4850

## North Carolina Utilities Commission [NCUC]
4325 Mail Service Center, Raleigh, NC 27699-4300
Tel: (919) 733-4249  Fax: (919) 733-7300

■Chairman **Edward S. "Ed" Finley, Jr.** ............. (919) 733-0829
  Term Expires: 2019
  E-mail: finley@ncuc.net
  Education: North Carolina
■Commissioner **Don M. Bailey** .................... (919) 733-0825
  Term Expires: 2017
  E-mail: dbailey@ncuc.net
■Commissioner **Bryan E. Beatty** .................. (919) 733-0825
  Term Expires: 2017
  E-mail: bbeatty@ncuc.net
  Education: SUNY (Stony Brook) 1980 BA; North Carolina 1987 JD
■Commissioner **ToNola Brown-Bland** ............... (919) 733-0825
  Term Expires: 2017
  E-mail: tbrownbland@ncuc.net
■Commissioner **Jerry C. Dockham** ................. (919) 733-4071
  Term Expires: 2019
  E-mail: jdockham@ncuc.net
  Education: Wake Forest 1972 BS
■Commissioner **Lyons Gray** ...................... (919) 733-4071
  E-mail: lgray@ncuc.net
■Commissioner **James G. "Jim" Patterson** .......... (919) 733-0829
  Term Expires: 2019
  E-mail: jpatterson@ncuc.net

## Public Staff-Utilities Commission
4326 Mail Service Center, Raleigh, NC 27699-4326
Internet: www.pubstaff.commerce.state.nc.us

■Executive Director **Christopher J. Ayers** ............. (919) 733-2435
  E-mail: chris.ayers@psncuc.nc.gov
  Education: North Carolina 2002 JD
Chief Legal Counsel **Antoinette Wike** ............... (919) 733-6110
  E-mail: antoinette.wike@psncuc.nc.gov
Accounting Division Director **Jim Hoard** ............. (919) 733-4279
  E-mail: jim.hoard@psncuc.nc.gov
Communications Division Director **John Garrison** ....... (919) 733-2810
  E-mail: john.garrison@psncuc.nc.gov
Consumer Services Division Director **Vickie Debnam** .... (919) 733-9277

*(continued on next page)*

---

★ Elected Official    ■ Appointed by Governor    ● Appointed by Legislature    ▲ Appointed by Board or Commission    ◆ Appointed by State Supreme Court

**North Carolina Utilities Commission** *continued*

Economic and Research Division Director
  **John "Bob" Hinton** ............................. (919) 733-2902
  E-mail: bob.hinton@psncuc.nc.gov
Electric Division Director **James McLawhorn** .......... (919) 733-2267
Natural Gas Division Director **Jeff Davis** ............. (919) 733-4326
Transportation Rates Division Director **Cynthia Smith** .... (919) 733-7766
  E-mail: cynthia.smith@psncuc.nc.gov
Water Division Director **David Furr** ................... (919) 733-5610
Budget Officer **Carl Goolsby** ........................ (919) 733-9682

## North Carolina State Education Assistance Authority

P.O. Box 14103, Research Triangle Park, NC 27709-4103
Tel: (919) 549-8614  Fax: (919) 549-8481
E-mail: information@ncseaa.edu  Internet: www.ncseaa.edu

▲Executive Director **Elizabeth V. McDuffie** .............. (919) 248-4642
  E-mail: emcduffie@ncseaa.edu
  Education: Meredith 2000 MBA
Administrative Services and Quality Control Director
  **Iona Duckworth** .................................. (919) 549-8614
  E-mail: duckworth@ncseaa.edu
Grants, Training and Outreach Director **(Vacant)** ......... (919) 248-4673
Guarantee Agency and Repayment Services Director
  **Wayne E. Johnson** ................................ (919) 248-4607
  Education: Wake Forest 1984 JD
Legal Affairs Director and General Counsel
  **Julia R. Hoke** ................................... (919) 248-4613
  E-mail: jhoke@ncseaa.edu
  Education: Wake Forest 1986 JD

## State Board of Education

Education Building, 301 North Wilmington Street,
6302 Mail Service Center, Raleigh, NC 27699-6302
Tel: (919) 807-3304  Fax: (919) 807-3198
E-mail: rgarland@dpi.state.nc.us

**Employees:** 1,163  **Fiscal Year:** 2014-2015  **Budget:** $11,571,287,000

■Chairman **William W. "Bill" Cobey, Jr.** (At-Large) ...... (828) 855-0283
  Term Expires: March 31, 2021
  E-mail: william.cobey@dpi.nc.gov
  Education: Emory 1962 BA; Wharton 1964 MBA;
  Pittsburgh 1968 MEd
■Vice Chairman **A.L. "Buddy" Collins** (Fifth District) ..... (336) 882-3800
  Term Expires: March 31, 2021
  E-mail: al.collins@dpi.nc.gov
■Member **Gregory Alcorn** (Seventh District) ............ (828) 264-1191
  Term Expires: March 2019
  E-mail: gregory.alcorn@dpi.nc.gov
■Member **Eric C. Davis** ............................. (252) 355-7299
  Term Expires: March 31, 2021
■Member **Kevin D. Howell** (Third District) ............. (919) 515-9340
  Term Expires: May 2015
  E-mail: kevin.howell@dpi.nc.gov
  Education: North Carolina State BA; North Carolina JD
■Member **Reginald Kenan** (Second District) ............ (910) 293-7801
  Term Expires: March 31, 2017
  E-mail: reginald.kenan@dpi.nc.gov
■Member **Wayne McDevitt** (Eighth District) ............ (828) 649-2144
  Term Expires: March 31, 2017
  E-mail: wayne.mcdevitt@dpi.nc.gov
  Education: North Carolina Asheville BS
■Member **Dr. Olivia Holmes Oxendine** (Fourth District) ... (800) 801-7983
  E-mail: olivia.oxendine@dpi.nc.gov
  Education: North Carolina Greensboro PhD
■Member **Rebecca H. Taylor** (First District) ........... (252) 355-7299
■Member **Patricia N. "Tricia" Willoughby** (At-Large) ..... (919) 715-3535
  Term Expires: March 31, 2017
  E-mail: patricia.willoughby@dpi.nc.gov
  Education: North Carolina AB; Meredith MA
Ex-Officio Member **Janet Cowell** ..................... (919) 807-3304
  Affiliation: State Treasurer, Department of State Treasurer, State of
  North Carolina
  325 North Salisbury Street, Raleigh, NC 27603-1385

Ex-Officio Member **Dan Forest** ....................... (919) 807-3304
  E-mail: dan.forest@dpi.nc.gov
  Affiliation: Lieutenant Governor, Office of the Lieutenant Governor,
  State of North Carolina
  310 North Blount Street, 20401 Mail Service Center,
  Raleigh, NC 27699-0401
  Education: North Carolina Charlotte 1993 BA, MAArch
Board Secretary **June St. Clair Atkinson** ............... (919) 807-3432
  Education: Radford BS; Virginia Tech MEd; North Carolina State EdD
Local Board Member Advisor **Christine Fitch** ........... (919) 807-3404
  E-mail: drclfedd@yahoo.com
Superintendent Advisor **Rodney Shotwell** .............. (919) 807-3441
  E-mail: rshotwell@rock.k12.nc.us
Principal Advisor **Steve Lassiter** ..................... (919) 807-3304
  E-mail: lassits@pitt.k12.nc.us
Teacher Advisor **James E. Ford** ...................... (919) 807-3304
  E-mail: jamesefordnctoy@gmail.com
Teacher Advisor **Keana Triplett** ...................... (919) 807-3304
  E-mail: keanatriplettnctoy@gmail.com
Student Advisor **Yates McConnell** .................... (919) 807-3304
Student Advisor **Grace Russell** ...................... (919) 807-3304

### Board Staff
Executive Director **J. Martez Hill** .................... (919) 807-3404
  Executive Assistant **Janice Hedgepeth** .............. (919) 807-3404
  Executive Assistant **Loretta Peace-Bunch** ........... (919) 807-3403
Assistant Executive Director **Betsy West** .............. (919) 807-3405
Legal Advisor **Katie G. Cornetto** .................... (919) 807-3406
  E-mail: katie.cornetto@dpi.state.nc.us
  Education: North Carolina 1994 BA; North Carolina Central 2001 JD
Legislative Liaison **Zane Stilwell** .................... (919) 807-4068
  E-mail: zane.stilwell@dpi.state.nc.us

## Public Instruction Department

301 North Wilmington Street, Raleigh, NC 27601-2825
Tel: (919) 807-3300  Fax: (919) 807-3445
Internet: www.ncpublicschools.org

★Superintendent of Public Instruction
  **June St. Clair Atkinson** (D) ...................... (919) 807-3430
  E-mail: june.atkinson@dpi.nc.gov
Deputy State Superintendent **Dr. Rebecca Garland** ...... (919) 807-3435
  E-mail: rebecca.garland@dpi.nc.gov
Human Resources Director **Lou Ann Phillips** ........... (919) 807-3395
Communication and Information Services Division
  Director **Vanessa Jeter** .......................... (919) 807-3450
  E-mail: vanessa.jeter@dpi.nc.gov
Early College High School Initiative Director
  **Joyce Chaffers Loveless** ......................... (919) 277-3761
Office of Early Learning Executive Director
  **John Pruette** ................................... (919) 807-3424
Virtual Public School Executive Director **Eliz Colbert** ..... (919) 513-8550

## State Board of Elections [SBE]

441 North Harrington Street, Raleigh, NC 27603
P.O. Box 27255, Raleigh, NC 27611-7255
Tel: (919) 733-7173  Fax: (919) 715-0135
E-mail: elections.sboe@ncsbe.gov  Internet: www.sboe.state.nc.us

**Employees:** 51

■Chair **Joshua B. Howard** ........................... (919) 733-7173
■Secretary **Rhonda K. Amoroso** ..................... (919) 733-7173
■Member **Maja Kricker** ............................. (919) 733-7173
■Member **Joshua Dale Malcolm** ...................... (919) 733-7173
  Education: North Carolina Pembroke 1992; North Carolina Central
■Member **(Vacant)** ................................. (919) 733-7173

### Administration
Executive Director **Kimberly Westbrook "Kim" Strach** ... (919) 733-7173
Agency Counsel **George McCue** ...................... (919) 733-7173
General Counsel **Joshua Lawson** ..................... (919) 733-7173
  Education: UCLA BA; George Washington MPS; North Carolina JD;
  Duke 2013 LLM
Public Information Officer **Jackie Hyland** .............. (919) 733-7173
  Education: St John's U (NY)

---

★ Elected Official   ■ Appointed by Governor   ● Appointed by Legislature   ▲ Appointed by Board or Commission   ◆ Appointed by State Supreme Court

# North Carolina Education Lottery

2100 Yonkers Road, Raleigh, NC 27604
Tel: (919) 301-3300  Fax: (919) 715-8825
Internet: www.nc-educationlottery.org
Executive Director **Alice Garland** . . . . . . . . . . . . . . . . . . . . (919) 301-3600
    Fax: (919) 715-8825
Finance, Administration, and Security Deputy Executive
  Director **William T. "Bill" Jourdain** . . . . . . . . . . . . . (919) 301-3603
    E-mail: bjourdain@lotterync.net    Fax: (919) 715-8831
Brand Management and Communications Deputy
  Executive Director **Frank Suarez** . . . . . . . . . . . . . . . . . (919) 301-3609
    E-mail: fsuarez@lotterync.net    Fax: (919) 715-8833
MIS and Gaming Systems Deputy Executive Director
  **George Walker** . . . . . . . . . . . . . . . . . . . . . . . . . . . . . (919) 301-3610
    E-mail: gwalker@lotterync.net    Fax: (919) 715-8831
Sales Deputy Executive Director **Terri Avery** . . . . . . . . . . . (919) 301-3611
    Fax: (919) 715-8826
Government Affairs Director **Jaime Fuquay** . . . . . . . . . . (919) 301-3602
    Fax: (919) 715-8825

# North Carolina Lottery Commission

■ Chair **Keith Ballentine** . . . . . . . . . . . . . . . . . . . . . . . . . (919) 301-3300
  Term Expires: August 31, 2017
● Member **Douglas Baker** . . . . . . . . . . . . . . . . . . . . . . . . . (919) 301-3300
  Term Expires: August 31, 2018
■ Member **Courtney Crowder** . . . . . . . . . . . . . . . . . . . . . . . (919) 301-3300
  Term Expires: August 31, 2017
● Member **Abraham J. Daoud** . . . . . . . . . . . . . . . . . . . . . . (919) 301-3300
  Term Expires: August 31, 2018
● Member **Amy B. Ellis** . . . . . . . . . . . . . . . . . . . . . . . . . . (919) 301-3300
  Term Expires: August 31, 2018
■ Member **David F. Kirby** . . . . . . . . . . . . . . . . . . . . . . . . . (919) 301-3300
  Term Expires: August 31, 2016
■ Member **Chris Shew** . . . . . . . . . . . . . . . . . . . . . . . . . . . (919) 301-3300
  Term Expires: August 31, 2016
● Member **Jody Tyson** . . . . . . . . . . . . . . . . . . . . . . . . . . . (919) 301-3300
  Term Expires: August 31, 2017
■ Member **Alice Graham Underhill** . . . . . . . . . . . . . . . . . . (919) 301-3300
  Term Expires: August 31, 2016

# Office of the Lieutenant Governor

310 North Blount Street, 20401 Mail Service Center,
Raleigh, NC 27699-0401
Tel: (919) 733-7350  Fax: (919) 733-6595
★ Lieutenant Governor **Dan Forest** (R) . . . . . . . . . . . . . . . . (919) 733-7350
  Term Expires: January 2017
  E-mail: ltgov@nc.gov
Chief of Staff **Harold C. "Hal" Weatherman III** . . . . . . . . (919) 733-7350
  Education: Wake Forest 1991 BA; Wheaton (IL) 1993 MA
External Relations Manager **Rebekah Bradley** . . . . . . . . . . (919) 733-7350
General Counsel and Policy Director
  **David Stevenson Walker** . . . . . . . . . . . . . . . . . . . . . . (919) 733-7350
Operations Director and Press Secretary
  **Jamey Falkenbury** . . . . . . . . . . . . . . . . . . . . . . . . . . (919) 733-7350
  E-mail: jamey.falkenbury@nc.gov
  Education: Elon U 2007 AB; Citadel 2009 MBA

# Office of the State Auditor

2 South Salisbury Street, 20601 Mail Service Center,
Raleigh, NC 27699-0601
Tel: (919) 807-7500  Tel: (800) 730-8477  Fax: (919) 807-7600
Internet: www.ncauditor.net

**Employees:** 139  **Fiscal Year:** 2014  **Budget:** $16,951,000

★ State Auditor **Beth A. Wood, CPA** (D) . . . . . . . . . . . . . . . (919) 807-7526
  Term Expires: January 2017
Chief Deputy State Auditor **J. Wesley Ray, Jr.** . . . . . . . . . . (919) 807-7665
  Education: North Carolina 1975 BA
Deputy State Auditor **Linda Hollar, CPA** . . . . . . . . . . . . . . (919) 807-7565
Deputy State Auditor **Kent McLamb** . . . . . . . . . . . . . . . . . (919) 807-7652
Chief Financial Officer **Cynthia "Cindy" Gilliam** . . . . . . . . (919) 807-7553
Chief Information Officer **Hunter Robinson** . . . . . . . . . . . (919) 807-7566
  E-mail: hunter_robinson@ncauditor.net

General Counsel **Timothy J. "Tim" Hoegemeyer** . . . . . . . (919) 807-7670
External Affairs Director **Bill Holmes** . . . . . . . . . . . . . . . . (919) 807-7513
  E-mail: bill_holmes@ncauditor.net
Financial Related Unit Director **Bill Styres** . . . . . . . . . . . . (919) 807-7580
Information Systems Audit Director **Michael Burch** . . . . . . (919) 807-7677
  E-mail: michael_burch@ncauditor.net
Investigative Audit Director **David King** . . . . . . . . . . . . . . (919) 807-7606

# North Carolina Department of Agriculture and Consumer Services [NCDA&CS]

1001 Mail Service Center, Raleigh, NC 27699
2 West Edenton Street, Raleigh, NC 27601
Tel: (919) 707-3021  Fax: (919) 733-1141  E-mail: agweb@ncmail.net

**Employees:** 1,915  **Fiscal Year:** 2014-2015  **Budget:** $176,203,000

★ Commissioner **Steve Troxler** (R) . . . . . . . . . . . . . . . . . . . (919) 707-3000
  Term Expires: January 2017
  E-mail: steve.troxler@ncagr.gov
  Education: North Carolina State 1974 BS
Webmaster **Matt Ryan** . . . . . . . . . . . . . . . . . . . . . . . . . . . (919) 707-3089

# North Carolina Department of Insurance [NCDOI]

430 North Salisbury Street, Raleigh, NC 27603
1201 Mail Service Center, Raleigh, NC 27699-1201
Tel: (919) 807-6000  Fax: (919) 733-0085  Internet: www.ncdoi.com

**Employees:** 403  **Fiscal Year:** 2014  **Budget:** $59,686,000

★ Insurance Commissioner **Wayne Goodwin** (D) . . . . . . . . . (919) 807-6000
  Term Expires: January 2017
  E-mail: wayne.goodwin@ncdoi.gov
  Education: North Carolina 1989 BA, 1992 JD
  Executive Assistant **Teresa Berry** . . . . . . . . . . . . . . . . (919) 807-6003
Chief Deputy Commissioner **Louis Belo** . . . . . . . . . . . . . . (919) 807-6866
  Education: North Carolina Wilmington 1988 BS
  Executive Assistant **Trista Nance** . . . . . . . . . . . . . . . . (919) 807-6866
Assistant Commissioner **Mark Edwards** . . . . . . . . . . . . . . (919) 807-6866
  Executive Assistant **Trista Nance** . . . . . . . . . . . . . . . . (919) 807-6866
Public Information Director **Kerry Hall** . . . . . . . . . . . . . . . (919) 807-6011
  E-mail: kerry.hall@ncdoi.gov
Legislative Fiscal Services Liaison **Ben Popkin** . . . . . . . . . (919) 807-6004
  E-mail: ben.popkin@ncdoi.gov
  Special Assistant to Commissioner **Kelly Smith** . . . . . . . (919) 807-6753

## Administrative Services

General Counsel **Stewart Johnson** . . . . . . . . . . . . . . . . . . (919) 807-6651
Chief Legislative Counsel **(Vacant)** . . . . . . . . . . . . . . . . . . (919) 807-6008
Controller **Bennie Aiken** . . . . . . . . . . . . . . . . . . . . . . . . . (919) 807-6026
  Education: South Carolina 1979 BS
Personnel Officer **Ronnie Condrey** . . . . . . . . . . . . . . . . . . (919) 807-6045
Information Systems Officer **Rob Main** . . . . . . . . . . . . . . . (919) 807-6118
  E-mail: rob.main@ncdoi.gov

## Alternative Markets Division

Dobbs Building, 430 North Salisbury Street, Raleigh, NC 27603
1203 Mail Service Center, Raleigh, NC 27699-1203
Tel: (919) 807-6140  Internet: www.ncdoi.com
Senior Deputy Commissioner **Raymond Martinez** . . . . . . . (919) 807-6144
Deputy Commissioner **Debra Walker, CPA** . . . . . . . . . . . . (919) 807-6165

## Company Services

1203 Mail Service Center, Raleigh, NC 27699-1203
Senior Deputy Commissioner and Receivership Office
  **Raymond Martinez** . . . . . . . . . . . . . . . . . . . . . . . . . . (919) 807-6144
  430 North Salisbury Street, Raleigh, NC 27603
Financial Analysis and Financial Evaluation Deputy
  Commissioner **Tony Riddick** . . . . . . . . . . . . . . . . . . . (919) 807-6602
Actuarial Services Division Chief Actuary **Kevin Conley** . . (919) 807-6649
Financial Examinations Chief Financial Examiner
  **Monique Smith** . . . . . . . . . . . . . . . . . . . . . . . . . . . . (919) 807-6605

*(continued on next page)*

---

★ Elected Official   ■ Appointed by Governor   ● Appointed by Legislature   ▲ Appointed by Board or Commission   ◆ Appointed by State Supreme Court

**Company Services** *continued*

Company Admissions Officer **Anne Morgan** . . . . . . . . . . . (919) 807-6603
Market Regulations Deputy Commissioner
  **Tracy Miller Biehn** . . . . . . . . . . . . . . . . . . . . . . . . . . . (919) 807-6882
  11 South Boylan Avenue, Raleigh, NC 27603-1839

## Consumer Assistance Group

Senior Deputy Commissioner **Carla Obiol** . . . . . . . . . . . . (919) 807-6019
SHIIP (Seniors' Health Insurance Information Program)
  Deputy Commissioner **R. Van Braxton** . . . . . . . . . . . . . . (919) 814-9935
  11 South Boylan Avenue, Raleigh, NC 27603-1839
  E-mail: van.braxton@ncdoi.gov
Health Insurance Smart North Carolina **Susan Nestor** . . . . (919) 814-9911
Consumer Services Deputy Commissioner **Kathy Shortt** . . (919) 807-9878

## Producers, Fraud, and Products Group

Senior Deputy Commissioner **Angela Ford** . . . . . . . . . . . . (919) 807-6756
Agent Services Deputy Commissioner **Rebecca Shigley** . . (919) 814-9836
Investigations Deputy Commissioner **Shane Guyant** . . . . . (919) 807-6841
Life and Health Deputy Commissioner **Ted Hamby** . . . . . . (919) 807-6055
Property and Casualty Deputy Commissioner **Bob Mack** . . (919) 807-6076

## State Fire Marshal's Office

322 Chapanoke Road, Raleigh, NC 27603-3400
1202 Mail Service Center, Raleigh, NC 27699-1202
Tel: (919) 661-5880  Internet: www.ncdoi.com/osfm

Senior Deputy Commissioner and Assistant State
  Fire Marshal **Rick McIntyre** . . . . . . . . . . . . . . . . . (919) 661-5880 ext. 216
Engineering and Codes Division Deputy
  Commissioner **Chris Noles** . . . . . . . . . . . . . . . . . (919) 661-5880 ext. 260
Manufactured Building Deputy Commissioner
  **Joe Sadler** . . . . . . . . . . . . . . . . . . . . . . . . . . . . (919) 661-5880 ext. 265
Research and Program Development Deputy
  Director **Rob Roegner** . . . . . . . . . . . . . . . . . . . . (919) 661-5880 ext. 313
Injury Prevention and Safe Kids Deputy Director
  **Meg Lanston** . . . . . . . . . . . . . . . . . . . . . . . . . . (919) 661-5880 ext. 325
Risk Management Division Deputy Director
  **Bryan Heckle** . . . . . . . . . . . . . . . . . . . . . . . . . . . . . . . (919) 661-5880
Fire and Rescue Commission Deputy Director
  **Wayne Bailey** . . . . . . . . . . . . . . . . . . . . . . . . . . (919) 661-5880 ext. 216
Administration and Finance Supervisor
  **Kim Williams** . . . . . . . . . . . . . . . . . . . . . . . . . . (919) 661-5880 ext. 216
  E-mail: kim.williams@ncdoi.gov

# Department of Justice [DOJ]

9001 Mail Service Center, Raleigh, NC 27699-9001
Tel: (919) 716-6400  Fax: (919) 716-6750  E-mail: ncago@ncdoj.gov

**Fiscal Year:** 2014-2015  **Budget:** $81,563,000

## Office of the Attorney General

9001 Mail Service Center, Raleigh, NC 27699-9001
Tel: (919) 716-6400  Fax: (919) 716-6750

**Employees:** 946

★Attorney General **Roy A. Cooper** (D) . . . . . . . . . . . . . . . (919) 716-6400
  Term Expires: January 2017
  E-mail: roy.cooper@nc.gov
  Education: North Carolina 1979 BA, 1982 JD
Chief Deputy Attorney General **Grayson G. Kelley** . . . . . . (919) 716-6400
Consumer Protection Division Senior Deputy Attorney
  General **Kevin Anderson** . . . . . . . . . . . . . . . . . . . . . . (919) 716-6000
Chief of Staff **Kristi Hyman** . . . . . . . . . . . . . . . . . . . . . (919) 716-6400
Solicitor General **John Maddrey** . . . . . . . . . . . . . . . . . . (919) 716-6400

# North Carolina Department of Labor [NCDOL]

Labor Building, Four W. Edenton Street, Raleigh, NC 27601-1020
1101 Mail Service Center, Raleigh, NC 27699-1101
Tel: (919) 733-7166  Tel: (800) 625-2267  Fax: (919) 733-6197
Internet: www.nclabor.com

**Employees:** 355  **Fiscal Year:** 2014-2015  **Budget:** $33,222,000

★Commissioner **Cherie Killian Berry** (R) . . . . . . . . . . . . . . (919) 733-7166
  Term Expires: January 2017
  E-mail: cherie.berry@labor.nc.gov
  Executive Assistant **Joyce Bulluck** . . . . . . . . . . . . . . . . (919) 733-7166
  E-mail: joyce.bulluck@labor.nc.gov
Chief of Staff **Art Britt** . . . . . . . . . . . . . . . . . . . . . . . . . (919) 733-0370
  E-mail: art.britt@labor.nc.gov
  Education: Campbell BA
Administration and Governmental Affairs Director
  **Jennifer Haigwood** . . . . . . . . . . . . . . . . . . . . . . . . . . (919) 733-0365
  E-mail: jennifer.haigwood@labor.nc.gov
Communications Director **Dolores Quesenberry** . . . . . . . . (919) 733-0348
  E-mail: dolores.quesenberry@labor.nc.gov
Budget and Management Division Director **Jack Brinson** . . (919) 733-7426
  E-mail: jack.brinson@labor.nc.gov
Human Resources Division Director **Renathe Cotten** . . . . . (919) 733-6943
Research and Information Technology Division Director
  **Tina Morris-Anderson** . . . . . . . . . . . . . . . . . . . . . . . . (919) 715-7415
  E-mail: tina.morris-anderson@labor.nc.gov
Publications and Mailroom Bureau Chief **Mike Daniels** . . . (919) 733-0341
  E-mail: mike.daniels@labor.nc.gov

## Legal Affairs and Research

General Counsel **Jane Ammons Gilchrist** . . . . . . . . . . . . . (919) 733-0368
  E-mail: jane.gilchrist@labor.nc.gov
Deputy General Counsel **Britne Becker** . . . . . . . . . . . . . . (919) 733-0368
  E-mail: britne.becker@labor.nc.gov

## Occupational Safety and Health

Deputy Commissioner **Allen McNeely** . . . . . . . . . . . . . . . (919) 807-2860
  Education: Appalachian State 1974 BA
Assistant Deputy Commissioner **Kevin Beauregard** . . . . . . (919) 807-2863
  Education: Maryland 1987 BS
Agricultural Safety and Health Bureau Chief
  **Regina Cullen** . . . . . . . . . . . . . . . . . . . . . . . . . . . . . (919) 807-2923
Consultative Services Bureau Chief **Kevin O'Barr** . . . . . . . (919) 807-2905
Education, Training & Technical Assistance Bureau Chief
  **Wanda Lagoe** . . . . . . . . . . . . . . . . . . . . . . . . . . . . . (919) 807-2875
Librarian **Nick Vincelli** . . . . . . . . . . . . . . . . . . . . . . . . . (919) 807-2850
Planning, Statistics and Information Management Bureau
  Chief **Anne Weaver** . . . . . . . . . . . . . . . . . . . . . . . . . (919) 807-2950
  E-mail: anne.weaver@labor.nc.gov
Safety and Health Compliance Eastern Bureau Chief
  **Nicole Brown** . . . . . . . . . . . . . . . . . . . . . . . . . . . . . (919) 779-8512
Safety and Health Compliance Western Bureau Chief
  **Robby Jones** . . . . . . . . . . . . . . . . . . . . . . . . . . . . . (704) 665-4341
  E-mail: robby.jones@labor.nc.gov        Fax: (704) 665-4342
State Plan Coordinator **Steve Sykes** . . . . . . . . . . . . . . . . (919) 807-2900
  Education: Pfeiffer Col 1974 BA

## Occupational Safety and Health Review Commission

222 West Person Street, Raleigh, NC 27601

■Chairman **Oscar A. Keller, Jr.** . . . . . . . . . . . . . . . . . . . . (919) 733-3589
  E-mail: oscar.keller@nc.gov
■Member **Arlene Edwards, CSP** . . . . . . . . . . . . . . . . . . . (919) 733-3589
  Term Expires: September 26, 2019
  E-mail: arlene.edwards@nc.gov
  Education: North Carolina Asheville
■Member **Dr. Richard G. Pearson** . . . . . . . . . . . . . . . . . . (919) 733-3589
  E-mail: richard.pearson@nc.gov

---

★ Elected Official    ■ Appointed by Governor    ● Appointed by Legislature    ▲ Appointed by Board or Commission    ◆ Appointed by State Supreme Court

## Standards and Inspections

111 Hillsborough Street, Hillsborough, NC 27601

Deputy Commissioner **Phil Hooper** . . . . . . . . . . . . . . . . . . . .(919) 807-2787
    E-mail: phil.hooper@labor.nc.gov
Boiler Safety Bureau Chief **Cliff Dautrich** . . . . . . . . . . . . . (919) 807-2774
    E-mail: cliff.dautrich@labor.nc.gov
Elevator and Amusement Device Bureau Chief
    **Tom Chambers** . . . . . . . . . . . . . . . . . . . . . . . . . . . . . . . . (919) 807-2770
Mine and Quarry Bureau Chief **William Gerringer** . . . . . . . (919) 807-2838
    E-mail: william.gerringer@labor.nc.gov
Employment Discrimination Administrator
    **Tiffany Lathan** . . . . . . . . . . . . . . . . . . . . . . . . . . . . . . . . .(919) 807-2826
    E-mail: tiffany.lathan@labor.nc.gov
Wage and Hour Administrator **Christine Ryan** . . . . . . . . . . .(919) 807-2801
    E-mail: christine.ryan@labor.nc.gov

## Department of the Secretary of State

P.O. Box 29622, Raleigh, NC 27626-0622
Tel: (919) 807-2000  Fax: (919) 807-2010  Internet: www.sosnc.com

**Employees:** 183  **Fiscal Year:** 2014-2015  **Budget:** $11,601,000

★ Secretary of State **Elaine Folk Marshall** (D) . . . . . . . . . . . (919) 807-2008
    Term Expires: January 2017
    E-mail: emarshal@sosnc.com
    Education: Maryland 1968 BS; Campbell 1981 JD
    Executive Assistant **Jennell Baughman** . . . . . . . . . . . . . (919) 807-2008
Chief Deputy Secretary of State **Rodney Maddox** . . . . . . . .(919) 807-2005
Deputy Secretary of State **Haley H. Haynes** . . . . . . . . . . . .(919) 807-2005
Information Technology Deputy Secretary of State
    **B. Dwayne Beamon** . . . . . . . . . . . . . . . . . . . . . . . . . . . .(919) 807-2195
    E-mail: dbeamon@sosnc.com
Certification and Filing Director **Tina Wagstaff** . . . . . . . . .(919) 807-2121
Communications Director **George Jeter** . . . . . . . . . . . . . . . (919) 807-2155
    E-mail: gjeter@sosnc.com
Land Records Management Director **Tom Morgan** . . . . . . . (919) 807-2268
Securities Director **David S. "Dave" Massey** . . . . . . . . . . .(919) 733-3924
                                                    Fax: (919) 821-0818
Charitable Solicitation Licensing Division Director
    **(Vacant)** . . . . . . . . . . . . . . . . . . . . . . . . . . . . . . . . . . . . . (919) 807-2214
Corporation Division Director **Cheri Myers** . . . . . . . . . . . . (919) 807-2225
Lobbying Compliance Division Director **Joal Broun** . . . . . .(919) 807-2172
LAN (Local Area Network) Administrator
    **Steven Kornegay** . . . . . . . . . . . . . . . . . . . . . . . . . . . . . . (919) 807-2200
    E-mail: skornegay@sosnc.com
Chief Fiscal Officer **Thomas Clark** . . . . . . . . . . . . . . . . . . . (919) 807-2012
General Counsel **Ann Wall** . . . . . . . . . . . . . . . . . . . . . . . . . .(919) 807-2230
Trademarks Registration Supervisor **Deborah Butler** . . . . . (919) 807-2162
Service of Process Agent **David Parrish** . . . . . . . . . . . . . . . (919) 807-2201
Webmaster **Pat Halcomb** . . . . . . . . . . . . . . . . . . . . . . . . . . .(919) 807-2191
    E-mail: pholcomb@sosnc.com

## Department of State Treasurer

325 North Salisbury Street, Raleigh, NC 27603-1385
Tel: (919) 508-5176  Fax: (919) 508-5167  Internet: www.nctreasurer.com

**Employees:** 354  **Fiscal Year:** 2014-2015  **Budget:** $51,646,000

★ State Treasurer **Janet Cowell** (D) . . . . . . . . . . . . . . . . . . . .(919) 508-5176
    Term Expires: January 2017
    E-mail: janet.cowell@nctreasurer.com
    Special Assistant to the Treasurer **(Vacant)** . . . . . . . . . . .(919) 508-5166
Chief of Staff **Melissa Waller** . . . . . . . . . . . . . . . . . . . . . . .(919) 508-5176
Real Estate Director **Alison Garcia** . . . . . . . . . . . . . . . . . . .(919) 508-5176
Retirement Systems Director **Steve Toole** . . . . . . . . . . . . . .(919) 508-5377
Financial Operations Deputy State Treasurer
    **Fran Lawrence** . . . . . . . . . . . . . . . . . . . . . . . . . . . . . . . . (919) 508-5953
State and Local Government Finance Deputy Treasurer
    **Greg Gaskins** . . . . . . . . . . . . . . . . . . . . . . . . . . . . . . . . . .(919) 807-2351
    E-mail: greg.gaskins@nctreasurer.com
Unclaimed Property Administrator **Brenda Williams** . . . . . (919) 508-5929
General Counsel and Senior Policy Advisor
    **Andrew Holton** . . . . . . . . . . . . . . . . . . . . . . . . . . . . . . . .(919) 508-5176
    E-mail: andrew.holton@nctreasurer.com

Deputy General Counsel **Blake Thomas** . . . . . . . . . . . . . . . .(919) 508-1024
    E-mail: blake.thomas@nctreasurer.com
Communications Manager and Deputy Treasurer
    **Schorr Johnson** . . . . . . . . . . . . . . . . . . . . . . . . . . . . . . . .(919) 807-3072
    E-mail: schorr.johnson@nctreasurer.com
    Education: North Carolina 1999 BA
State Investment Officer **Kevin SigRist** . . . . . . . . . . . . . . . .(919) 807-3101
Legislative Liaison **Anthony Solari** . . . . . . . . . . . . . . . . . . .(919) 508-5176
    E-mail: anthony.solari@nctreasurer.com

★ Elected Official    ■ Appointed by Governor    ● Appointed by Legislature    ▲ Appointed by Board or Commission    ◆ Appointed by State Supreme Court

*State Yellow Book*    © Leadership Directories, Inc.    Summer 2016

# North Dakota

Tel: (701) 328-2000  Internet: www.nd.gov

**Number of U.S. Congressional Delegates:** 2 Senators; 1 Representatives  **Governor's Term:** 4 years
**Legislature Description:** Legislative Assembly - 47 member Senate; 94 member House of Representatives;
Term - Senate 4 years, House 4 years  **Next Election:** Governor November 2016; Legislature November
2016  **Number of Electoral Votes:** 3  **Official Name:** State of North Dakota (Sioux: allies)
**Nickname:** Peace Garden State  **Motto:** Liberty and Union, Now and Forever, One and Inseparable

**Population:** 756,927 (2015); Rank 47  **Fiscal Year:** 2013-2015  **Budget:** $13,745,000,000

## Office of the Governor

State Capitol, 600 East Boulevard Avenue, Department 101,
Bismarck, ND 58505-0001
Tel: (701) 328-2200  Fax: (701) 328-2205

**John S. "Jack" Dalrymple III**
Governor

Note: On August 24, 2015, Governor John
Dalrymple announced he will not seek reelection
in 2016.
Began Service: December 7, 2010
Term Expires: December 2016
Date of Birth: October 16, 1948
Education: Yale 1970 BA
Home: Casselton
Religion: Presbyterian
Career: State Representative, North Dakota House
of Representatives (1985-2000); Lieutenant
Governor, State of North Dakota (2000-2010)

★Governor **John S. "Jack" Dalrymple III** (R) . . . . . . . . . . . (701) 328-2200
    E-mail: governor@nd.gov
Chief of Staff **Ron Rauschenberger** . . . . . . . . . . . . . . . . . (701) 328-2222
Legal Counsel **Bonnie Storbakken** . . . . . . . . . . . . . . . . . . (701) 328-2200
    E-mail: bstorbakken@nd.gov
    Education: North Dakota 2004 JD
Senior Policy Advisor **Kayla Kleven** . . . . . . . . . . . . . . . . . (701) 328-2229
    E-mail: kmeffertz@nd.gov
Senior Policy Advisor **Jody Link** . . . . . . . . . . . . . . . . . . . . (701) 328-2200
    E-mail: jlink@nd.gov
Senior Policy Advisor **Andrea Travnicek** . . . . . . . . . . . . . (701) 328-2200
    E-mail: atravnicek@nd.gov
Board Appointments Advisor **Rose Laning** . . . . . . . . . . . . (701) 328-2200
    E-mail: rlaning@nd.gov
Communications Director and Policy Advisor **Jeff Zent** . . . (701) 328-2200
    E-mail: jlzent@nd.gov
Health and Human Services Advisor **Tami Ternes** . . . . . . . . (701) 328-2200
    E-mail: tlternes@nd.gov
Research Analyst **Jason Nisbet** . . . . . . . . . . . . . . . . . . . . . (701) 328-2201
    E-mail: jnisbet@nd.gov
Constituent Services **Shelly Haugen** . . . . . . . . . . . . . . . . . (701) 328-2200
Scheduler **Rachael Nelson** . . . . . . . . . . . . . . . . . . . . . . . . (701) 328-2200
    E-mail: rachnelson@nd.gov

## Washington Office

500 New Jersey Avenue, NW, Suite 400, Washington, DC 20001
Tel: (202) 715-1256  Fax: (202) 478-0811

Washington Representative **Krista Carman** . . . . . . . . . . . . . (202) 715-1256
    E-mail: kristacarman@mac.com
    E-mail: kc@carmancommunications.com
    Education: Mary Washington Col BA

## Office of the Lieutenant Governor

State Capitol, 600 East Boulevard Avenue, Department 101,
Bismarck, ND 58505-0001
TTY: (800) 366-6888  Fax: (701) 328-1880  E-mail: governor@nd.gov

★Lieutenant Governor **Drew Howard Wrigley** (R) . . . . . . . . (701) 328-2200
    Term Expires: December 2016
    E-mail: dhwrigley@nd.gov
    Education: North Dakota BA; Washington College of Law 1991 JD
    Career: Deputy Chief of Staff, Office of the Governor, State of North
    Dakota (1999-2001); U.S. Attorney, North Dakota District, Executive
    Office for United States Attorneys, United States Department of
    Justice, George W. Bush Administration (2001-2009)
Assistant to Lieutenant Governor/Scheduler
    **Lyndsay Witt** . . . . . . . . . . . . . . . . . . . . . . . . . . . . . . . . . (701) 328-2200
    E-mail: lwitt@nd.gov

## Office of Management and Budget [OMB]

Department 110, 600 East Boulevard Avenue, Bismarck, ND 58505-0400
Tel: (701) 328-2680  Fax: (701) 328-3230  E-mail: omb@nd.gov
Internet: www.nd.gov/omb

■Director **Pam Sharp** . . . . . . . . . . . . . . . . . . . . . . . . . . . . . (701) 328-4606
    E-mail: psharp@nd.gov
    Administrative Assistant **Lori Anderson** . . . . . . . . . . . . . (701) 328-4904
Central Services Division Director **Sherry Neas** . . . . . . . . . (701) 328-1726
    E-mail: sneas@nd.gov
Facility Management Division Director **John Boyle** . . . . . . (701) 328-4002
Fiscal Management Division Director **Sheila Peterson** . . . . (701) 328-4905
Human Resource Management Services Division Director
    **Ken Purdy** . . . . . . . . . . . . . . . . . . . . . . . . . . . . . . . . . . (701) 328-4735
Risk Management Division Director **Tag Anderson** . . . . . . (701) 328-7580
Webmaster **Lori Anderson** . . . . . . . . . . . . . . . . . . . . . . . . (701) 328-4904

## Department of Commerce

1600 East Century Avenue, Suite 2, Bismarck, ND 58503
P.O. Box 2057, Bismarck, ND 58502
Tel: (701) 328-5300  Fax: (701) 328-5320  E-mail: commerce@nd.gov
Internet: www.ndcommerce.com

**Employees:** 69  **Fiscal Year:** 2013-2015  **Budget:** $139,820,000

■Commissioner **Alan Anderson** . . . . . . . . . . . . . . . . . . . . . (701) 328-5312
    E-mail: alranderson@nd.gov
    Education: North Dakota BS; Utah MBA
Office Manager **LaVonne Stair** . . . . . . . . . . . . . . . . . . . . . (701) 328-5317

## Community Services Division

1600 East Century Avenue, Suite 2, Bismarck, ND 58503
P.O. Box 2057, Bismarck, ND 58502
Tel: (701) 328-5300  Fax: (701) 328-2308  E-mail: dcs@nd.gov

■Director **Bonnie Malo** . . . . . . . . . . . . . . . . . . . . . . . . . . . (701) 328-2476
    E-mail: bmalo@nd.gov
    Community Development Block Grant Program Manager
    **Bonnie Malo** . . . . . . . . . . . . . . . . . . . . . . . . . . . . . . . . . (701) 328-2476
Self Sufficiency Program Administrator **Tran Doan** . . . . . . (701) 328-2290
Home Program Manager **Bonnie Malo** . . . . . . . . . . . . . . . (701) 328-2476
    E-mail: bmalo@nd.gov

★ Elected Official    ■ Appointed by Governor    ● Appointed by Legislature    ▲ Appointed by Board or Commission    ◆ Appointed by State Supreme Court

## Economic Development and Finance Division

Tel: (701) 328-5300  TTY: (800) 366-6888  Fax: (701) 328-5320
E-mail: ndedf@nd.gov

- Director **Paul Lucy** .................................... (701) 328-5388
  E-mail: plucy@nd.gov
North Dakota Development Fund Chief Executive Officer
  **Dean Reese** ..................................... (701) 328-5334
Business Development Associate Project Manager
  **Laura Willard** ................................... (701) 328-5337
Research Manager **Leigh Ann Huether** ............... (701) 328-5336
  E-mail: lhuether@nd.gov
Manufacturing Extension Partnership Director
  **Randy Schwartz** .................................. (701) 328-5471

## Tourism Division

Tel: (701) 328-2525  Tel: (800) 435-5663  Fax: (701) 328-4878
E-mail: tourism@nd.gov  Internet: www.ndtourism.com

- Director **Sara Otte Coleman** ........................ (701) 328-2525
  E-mail: socoleman@nd.gov

## Workforce Development Division

Tel: (701) 328-5300  Fax: (701) 328-5320
Internet: www.ndcommerce.com

- Director **Wayde Sick** ................................ (701) 328-5345
  E-mail: wsick@nd.gov

## Department of Corrections and Rehabilitation [DOCR]

3100 Railroad Avenue, Bismarck, ND 58501-5011
P.O. Box 1898, Bismarck, ND 58502-1898
Tel: (701) 328-6390  TTY: (800) 366-6888  Fax: (701) 328-6651
E-mail: mlinster@nd.gov  Internet: www.nd.gov/docr

**Fiscal Year:** 2013-2015  **Budget:** $217,051,000

- Director **Leann K. Bertsch** ................... (701) 328-6390 ext. 1
  E-mail: lebertsc@nd.gov
  Education: North Dakota State 1988 BS; North Dakota 1991 JD
Rough Rider Industries Director **Rick L. Gardner** ........ (701) 328-6161
                                                Fax: (701) 328-6164
James River Correctional Center Warden **Chad Pringle** .... (701) 253-3660
                                                Fax: (701) 253-3666
Juvenile Services Division Director **Lisa Bjergaard** ....... (701) 328-6674
Missouri River Correctional Center Deputy Warden
  **Joseph Joyce** ................................... (701) 328-9696
                                                Fax: (701) 328-9690
North Dakota State Penitentiary Warden **Colby Braun** .... (701) 328-6100
                                                Fax: (701) 328-6640
Youth Correctional Center Director **Tim Tausend** ........ (701) 667-1400
  701 - 16th Avenue, SW, Mandan, ND 58554     Fax: (701) 667-1414
Adult Interstate Compact Administrator **Amy Vorachek** ... (701) 328-6198
Deputy Juvenile Compact Director **Lea Quam** ........... (701) 328-3936
Information Systems Director **David Huhncke** ........... (701) 328-6361
  E-mail: dhuhncke@nd.gov
  Computer Network Specialist **John Arbach** ........... (701) 328-6230
  E-mail: jdarbach@nd.gov
  Computer Network Specialist **Myles Noon** ............ (701) 328-6364
  E-mail: mnoon@nd.gov
  Computer Network Specialist **Joshua Stewart** ......... (701) 328-6660
  E-mail: jwstewart@nd.gov
Warden of Transitional Facilities **James Sayler** ......... (701) 328-6789

## North Dakota Department of Emergency Services [NDDES]

P.O. Box 5511, Bismarck, ND 58506-5511
Tel: (701) 328-8100  Fax: (701) 333-2017

- Adjutant General **BG Alan S. Dohrmann, ARNG** ........ (701) 333-2001
Emergency Management Director and Homeland Security
  Coordinator **Greg Wilz** ............................ (701) 328-8249
                                                Fax: (701) 328-8181
Radio Communications Operations Director
  **Michael "Mike" Lynk** .............................. (701) 328-8100

## North Dakota National Guard

P.O. Box 5511, Bismarck, ND 58506-5511
Tel: (701) 328-8100  Fax: (701) 333-2017
Internet: www.guard.bismarck.nd.us

- Adjutant General **BG Alan S. Dohrmann, ARNG** ........ (701) 333-2002
Deputy Adjutant General **(Vacant)** ................... (701) 333-2300
  Fraine Barracks, Building 30, Bismarck, ND 58506
State Command Sergeant Major
  **CSM Bradley Heim, ARNG** .......................... (701) 333-3009
  4200 E. Divide Ave., Bismarck, ND 58506-5511    Fax: (701) 333-3011
Chief Information Officer **LTC Ray Knutson, ARNG** ..... (701) 328-8100
  E-mail: ray.knutson.mil@mail.mil

## North Dakota Air National Guard

P.O. Box 5511, Bismarck, ND 58506-5511
Tel: (701) 333-2000  Fax: (701) 333-2017
Internet: www.guard.bismarck.nd.us/air

Assistant Adjutant General **BrigGen Ron Solberg, ANG** .. (701) 333-2020
  Fraine Barracks, Building 30, Bismarck, ND 58506-5511

## North Dakota Army National Guard

P.O. Box 5511, Bismarck, ND 58506-5511
Tel: (701) 333-2000  Fax: (701) 333-2017
Internet: www.guard.bismarck.nd.us/army

Assistant Adjutant General **(Vacant)** ................. (701) 333-3432

## Department of Financial Institutions [DFI]

2000 Schafer Street, Suite G, Bismarck, ND 58501-1204
Tel: (701) 328-9933  Fax: (701) 328-0290  E-mail: dfi@nd.gov
Internet: www.nd.gov/dfi

**Employees:** 29  **Fiscal Year:** 2013-2015  **Budget:** $7,580,000

- Commissioner **Robert J. Entringer, CEM** ............. (701) 328-9933
  E-mail: rentring@nd.gov
  Education: U Mary 1979 BS
Assistant Commissioner **Aaron K. Webb** .............. (701) 328-9935
  E-mail: aaronwebb@nd.gov
Banks Chief Examiner **I. Lise Kruse** ................. (701) 328-9938
  E-mail: lkruse@nd.gov
Credit Unions Chief Examiner **Corey Krebs** ........... (701) 328-9937
Administration Director **Joan M. Becker** ............. (701) 328-9958
  E-mail: jmbecker@nd.gov
  Education: Valley City State 1977 BS

## Game and Fish Department

100 North Bismarck Expressway, Bismarck, ND 58501-5095
Tel: (701) 328-6300  Fax: (701) 328-6352  E-mail: ndgf@nd.gov
Internet: www.gf.nd.gov

**Employees:** 158  **Fiscal Year:** 2013-2015  **Budget:** $67,554,000

- Director **Terry Steinwand** .......................... (701) 328-6313
  E-mail: tsteinwa@nd.gov
  Education: North Dakota 1980 BS, 1982 MS
Deputy Director **Scott Peterson** ..................... (701) 328-6350
Administrative Services Chief **Kim Kary** .............. (701) 328-6605
  E-mail: kkary@nd.gov
Conservation and Communication Division Chief
  **Greg Link** ...................................... (701) 328-6331
  E-mail: glink@nd.gov
Enforcement Division Chief **Robert Timian** ........... (701) 328-6324
Fisheries Division Chief **Greg Power** ................. (701) 328-6323
Wildlife Division Chief **Jeb Williams** ................ (701) 328-6386

---

★ Elected Official   ■ Appointed by Governor   ● Appointed by Legislature   ▲ Appointed by Board or Commission   ◆ Appointed by State Supreme Court

# Department of Health

State Capitol, 600 East Boulevard Avenue, Bismarck, ND 58505-0200
Tel: (701) 328-2372  Tel: (701) 328-2360 (Vital Records)
Fax: (701) 328-4727  Fax: (701) 328-1850 (Vital Records)
E-mail: vitalrec@nd.gov (Vital Records)  Internet: www.ndhealth.gov
Internet: ndhealth.gov/vital (Vital Records)

**Employees:** 340  **Fiscal Year:** 2013-2015  **Budget:** $185,570,000

■State Health Officer **Terry L. Dwelle, MD** . . . . . . . . . . . . . (701) 328-2372
  E-mail: tdwelle@nd.gov
  Education: Saint Louis U MD; Tulane MA
■Deputy State Health Officer **Arvy Smith, CPA** . . . . . . . . . . (701) 328-2372
  E-mail: asmith@nd.gov
  Education: Moorhead State 1981 BA
  Accounting Division Director **Brenda Weisz** . . . . . . . . . . (701) 328-2392
  Personnel Division Director **Dirk Wilke** . . . . . . . . . . . . (701) 328-2392
  Vital Records Division Director **Darin J. Meschke**
  Dept. 301 . . . . . . . . . . . . . . . . . . . . . . . . . . . . . (701) 328-2360

## Community Health Section

Chief **(Vacant)** . . . . . . . . . . . . . . . . . . . . . . . . . . . . . . (701) 328-2493

## Emergency Preparedness and Response Section

Internet: www.ndhealth.gov/EPR

Emergency Medical Services and Trauma Division
  Director **Thomas Nehring** . . . . . . . . . . . . . . . . . . . . . (701) 328-2388

## Environmental Health Section

918 East Divide Avenue, Bismarck, ND 58501-1947
Tel: (701) 328-5150  Fax: (701) 328-5200
Internet: www.ndhealth.gov/EHS

Chief **L. David Glatt** . . . . . . . . . . . . . . . . . . . . . . . . . . (701) 328-5150
General Counsel **Margaret Olson** . . . . . . . . . . . . . . . . . . (701) 328-3640
  E-mail: maiolson@nd.gov
Air Quality Division Director **Terry O'Clair** . . . . . . . . . . . (701) 328-5188
Municipal Facilities Division Director **Wayne Kern** . . . . . . (701) 328-5211
Waste Management Division Director **Scott Radig** . . . . . . (701) 328-5166
Water Quality Division Director **Karl Rockeman** . . . . . . . . (701) 328-5210
Laboratory Services Director **Myra Kosse** . . . . . . . . . . . (701) 328-6272
  2635 East Main, Bismarck, ND 58501
  P.O. Box 5520, Bismarck, ND 58506-5520
Webmaster **Allen Johnson** . . . . . . . . . . . . . . . . . . . . . . (701) 328-5155
  E-mail: ajohnson@nd.gov

## Health Resources Section

Internet: www.ndhealth.gov

Chief **Darleen Bartz** . . . . . . . . . . . . . . . . . . . . . . . . . . (701) 328-2352
Food and Lodging Division Director **Kenan Bullinger** . . . . (701) 328-1291
  E-mail: kbulling@nd.gov
Health Facilities Division Director **Bruce Pritschet** . . . . . . (701) 328-2352

## Medical Services Section

Internet: ndhealth.gov/ms

Disease Control Division Director **Kirby Kruger** . . . . . . . . (701) 328-2378

# Department of Human Services [DHS]

State Capitol - Judicial Wing, 600 East Boulevard Avenue,
Department 325, Bismarck, ND 58505
Tel: (701) 328-2310  Tel: (800) 472-2622 (Toll Free)  Fax: (701) 328-2359
E-mail: dhseo@nd.gov  Internet: www.nd.gov/dhs

**Fiscal Year:** 2013-2015  **Budget:** $2,949,453,000

■Executive Director **Maggie Anderson** . . . . . . . . . . . . . . . (701) 328-2538
  E-mail: manderson@nd.gov
  Education: North Dakota State BS; U Mary MA
  Administrative Staff Officer **Cheryl Fitzgerald** . . . . . . . . (701) 328-2538
Chief Financial Officer **Deb McDermott** . . . . . . . . . . . . . (701) 328-1980
Human Resource Director **Marcie Wuitschick** . . . . . . . . . (701) 328-1290
Information Technology Services Director
  **Jennifer Witham** . . . . . . . . . . . . . . . . . . . . . . . . . . (701) 328-2570
  E-mail: jwitham@nd.gov

Medical Director **Dr. Andrew J. McLean** . . . . . . . . . . . . . (701) 253-3650
  Education: North Dakota BS, MD          Fax: (701) 253-3999
Legal Advisory Unit Attorney **Julie Leer** . . . . . . . . . . . . . (701) 328-2311
Public Information Specialist **LuWanna Lawrence** . . . . . . (701) 328-2310
  E-mail: lklawrence@nd.gov
Public Information Specialist **Heather Steffl** . . . . . . . . . . (701) 328-2310
  E-mail: hsteffl@nd.gov

## Economic Assistance

Economic Assistance Policy Director **Carol Cartledge** . . . . (701) 328-2332
Low-Income Energy Assistance Program Unit Director
  **Carol Cartledge** . . . . . . . . . . . . . . . . . . . . . . . . . . (701) 328-2332
Supplemental Nutrition Assistance Program Director
  **Arlene Dura** . . . . . . . . . . . . . . . . . . . . . . . . . . . . (701) 328-2064
Quality Control Unit Director **Brenda Holzworth** . . . . . . . (701) 328-4007
Child Support Division Director **Jim Fleming** . . . . . . . . . . (701) 328-3582
  E-mail: jfleming@nd.gov
Medical Services Division Director **(Vacant)** . . . . . . . . . . . (701) 328-1603
                               Fax: (701) 328-1544
Public Assistance Division Director **Carol Cartledge** . . . . . (701) 328-2332
State Children's Health Insurance Program (SCHIP)
  Program Administrator **Jodi M. Hulm** . . . . . . . . . . . . . (701) 328-2323

## Program and Policy

Developmental Disabilities Director **Tina Bay** . . . . . . . . . . (701) 328-8966
Aging Services Division Director **Cindy Marihart** . . . . . . . (701) 328-4601
Children and Family Services Division Director
  **Shari Doe** . . . . . . . . . . . . . . . . . . . . . . . . . . . . . . (701) 328-2316
Mental Health/Substance Abuse Division Director
  **JoAnne Hoesel** . . . . . . . . . . . . . . . . . . . . . . . . . . . (701) 328-8920
Vocational Rehabilitation Division Director
  **Russell Cusack** . . . . . . . . . . . . . . . . . . . . . . . . . . (701) 328-8926
Grafton Development Center Superintendent
  **Alex Schweitzer** . . . . . . . . . . . . . . . . . . . . . . . . . . (701) 352-4200
  701 West Sixth Street, Grafton, ND 58237-1399      Fax: (701) 352-4376
Jamestown State Hospital Superintendent
  **Alex Schweitzer** . . . . . . . . . . . . . . . . . . . . . . . . . . (701) 253-3650
  2605 Circle Drive, Jamestown, ND 58401-6905      Fax: (701) 253-3999
  P.O. Box 476, Jamestown, ND 58402-0476
North Dakota State Hospital Medical Director **(Vacant)** . . . (701) 253-3650
  2605 Circle Dr., Jamestown, ND 58401-6905
  P.O. Box 476, Jamestown, ND 58402-0476

# Information Technology Department [ITD]

State Capitol, 600 East Boulevard Avenue, Department 112,
Bismarck, ND 58505-0100
Tel: (701) 328-3190  Fax: (701) 328-3000  E-mail: itd@nd.gov
Internet: www.state.nd.us/itd

**Employees:** 328  **Fiscal Year:** 2013-2015  **Budget:** $170,929,000

■Chief Information Officer **Mike Ressler, CPA, CCP** . . . . . . (701) 328-3193
  E-mail: mressler@nd.gov
  Education: U Mary BS
  Administrative Assistant **Darlene Wolfgram** . . . . . . . . . (701) 328-3190
Director of Operations and Deputy Chief Information
  Officer **Dan Sipes, CPA, CISA** . . . . . . . . . . . . . . . . . (701) 328-3190
  E-mail: dsipes@nd.gov
  Education: U Mary BS

# North Dakota Department of Labor and Human Rights

State Capitol, Department 406, 600 East Boulevard Avenue,
Bismarck, ND 58505-0340
Tel: (701) 328-2660  Tel: (800) 582-8032 (In State)  TTY: (800) 366-6888
Fax: (701) 328-2031  E-mail: humanrights@nd.gov  E-mail: labor@nd.gov
Internet: www.nd.gov/labor

■Commissioner **Troy Thomas Seibel** . . . . . . . . . . . . . . . . (701) 328-2660
  E-mail: ttseibel@nd.gov
  Education: North Dakota 1999 BA; Denver 2002 JD
  Administrative Assistant **Mary Lauf** . . . . . . . . . . . . . . . (701) 328-2660
Human Rights Director **Kathy Kulesa** . . . . . . . . . . . . . . . (701) 328-2660
  E-mail: kkulesa@nd.gov

---

★ Elected Official    ■ Appointed by Governor    ● Appointed by Legislature    ▲ Appointed by Board or Commission    ◆ Appointed by State Supreme Court

Compliance Investigator **Dustin Assel** . . . . . . . . . . . . . . . . (701) 328-2660
E-mail: djassel@nd.gov
Compliance Investigator **Chad Best** . . . . . . . . . . . . . . . . . (701) 328-2660
E-mail: cjbest@nd.gov
Compliance Investigator **Sheena Cole** . . . . . . . . . . . . . . . (701) 328-2660
E-mail: scole@nd.gov
Compliance Investigator **Brenda Halvorson** . . . . . . . . . . . .(701) 328-2660
E-mail: bjhalvor@nd.gov
Compliance Investigator **Marcus Roehrich** . . . . . . . . . . . . .(701) 328-2660
E-mail: mroehrich@nd.gov
Compliance Investigator **Vicki Slavik** . . . . . . . . . . . . . . . (701) 328-2660
E-mail: vslavik@nd.gov
Compliance Investigator **Kiersten Sneddon** . . . . . . . . . . . .(701) 328-2660
E-mail: ksneddon@nd.gov
Compliance Investigator **Milena Stojkovic** . . . . . . . . . . . . .(701) 328-2660
E-mail: mstojkov@nd.gov
Compliance Investigator **Connie Todd** . . . . . . . . . . . . . . . (701) 328-2660
E-mail: cctodd@nd.gov
Business Manager **Loni Grothier** . . . . . . . . . . . . . . . . . . .(701) 328-2660
E-mail: lgrothier@nd.gov
Administrative Assistant **Sarah Metzger** . . . . . . . . . . . . . . (701) 328-2660

## Parks and Recreation Department

1600 East Century Avenue, Suite 3, Bismarck, ND 58503-0649
Tel: (701) 328-5357  TTY: (800) 366-6888  Fax: (701) 328-5363
E-mail: parkrec@nd.gov  Internet: www.parkrec.nd.gov

**Employees:** 55  **Fiscal Year:** 2013-2015  **Budget:** $31,868,000

■Director **Mark Zimmerman** . . . . . . . . . . . . . . . . . . . . . .(701) 328-5357
E-mail: markzimmerman@nd.gov
Business Manager **Renae L. Gall** . . . . . . . . . . . . . . . . . . .(701) 328-5357
E-mail: rengall@nd.gov
Education: Minot State 2003 BAS
Computer and Network Specialist **Eric Godel** . . . . . . . . . . .(701) 328-5357
E-mail: egodel@nd.gov
Public Information Officer **Gordon Weixel** . . . . . . . . . . . . (701) 328-5357
E-mail: gweixel@nd.gov
Field Manager **Brad Pozarnsky** . . . . . . . . . . . . . . . . . . . (701) 263-4054
Lake Metigoshe State Park, Bottineau, ND 58318       Fax: (701) 263-4648
E-mail: bpozarnsky@nd.gov
Education: North Dakota State 1975 BS
Field Operations Assistant **Karen Assel** . . . . . . . . . . . . . (701) 328-5357
Education: North Dakota 1980 BA

## Securities Department

State Capitol, 600 East Boulevard Avenue, 5th Floor, Department 414,
Bismarck, ND 58505-0510
Tel: (701) 328-2910  Fax: (701) 328-2946  E-mail: ndsecurities@nd.gov
Internet: www.nd.gov/securities

**Employees:** 9  **Fiscal Year:** 2013-2015  **Budget:** $2,298,000

■Commissioner **Karen Tyler** . . . . . . . . . . . . . . . . . . . . . .(701) 328-2910
E-mail: ktyler@nd.gov
Registration Examiner/Administrative Officer
**Jacqui Ferderer** . . . . . . . . . . . . . . . . . . . . . . . . . . (701) 328-2987
Investor Education Coordinator **Lauren Strinden** . . . . . . . . (701) 328-4698
Education: Florida Atlantic 1993 MURP
Chief Examiner **Harold P. Kocher** . . . . . . . . . . . . . . . . . .(701) 328-4703
Franchise Examiner/Budget Analyst **Diane Lillis** . . . . . . . . .(701) 328-4712
Attorney **Michael F. Daley** . . . . . . . . . . . . . . . . . . . . . .(701) 328-4701
Investigations and Examinations Supervisor
**Kelly Mathias** . . . . . . . . . . . . . . . . . . . . . . . . . . . . (701) 328-2929
Investigator/Examiner **Rachel Rice** . . . . . . . . . . . . . . . . . (701) 352-4592
E-mail: rarice@nd.gov
Investigator **Douglas W. Smith** . . . . . . . . . . . . . . . . . . . .(701) 328-2926
E-mail: dwsmith@nd.gov

## North Dakota Department of Transportation [NDDOT]

608 East Boulevard Avenue, Bismarck, ND 58505-0700
Tel: (701) 328-2500  TTY: (701) 328-4156  Fax: (701) 328-0310
E-mail: dot@nd.gov  Internet: www.dot.nd.gov

**Employees:** 1,079  **Fiscal Year:** 2013-2015  **Budget:** $3,384,800,000

■Director **Grant Levi** . . . . . . . . . . . . . . . . . . . . . . . . . . (701) 328-2581
E-mail: glevi@nd.gov
Education: North Dakota State BS
Communication Director **Peggy L. Anderson** . . . . . . . . . . . (701) 328-4322
E-mail: peganderson@nd.gov

### Business Support
Deputy Director **Darcy Rosendahl** . . . . . . . . . . . . . . . . . (701) 328-2639
E-mail: drosendahl@nd.gov
Financial Management Division Director
**Shannon Sauer** . . . . . . . . . . . . . . . . . . . . . . . . . . . .(701) 328-2630
Human Resources Division Director **Michael Sandal** . . . . . (701) 328-4365
Education: Bemidji State 1980 BS; U Mary 1996 MM
Information Technology Division Director
**Russ Buchholz** . . . . . . . . . . . . . . . . . . . . . . . . . . . (701) 328-2561
E-mail: rjbuchholz@nd.gov
State Fleet Services Director **Robin Rehborg** . . . . . . . . . . .(701) 328-2543
Fax: (701) 328-4623

### Driver and Vehicle Services
Deputy Director **Mark Nelson** . . . . . . . . . . . . . . . . . . . . .(701) 328-2727
Drivers License Division Director **Glenn Jackson** . . . . . . . .(701) 328-4792
E-mail: gjackson@nd.gov       Fax: (701) 328-2435
Motor Vehicle Division Director **Linda Sitz** . . . . . . . . . . . .(701) 328-1986
E-mail: ldsitz@nd.gov       Fax: (701) 328-1487

### Engineering
Deputy Director **Ron Henke** . . . . . . . . . . . . . . . . . . . . . (701) 328-2584
E-mail: rhenke@nd.gov
Operations Director **Wayde Swenson** . . . . . . . . . . . . . . . (701) 328-4408
Construction Services Division Director **Cal Gendreau** . . . .(701) 328-2563
Fax: (701) 328-4928
Legal Division Director **Paul Seado** . . . . . . . . . . . . . . . . .(701) 328-2625
Maintenance Division Director **Brad Darr** . . . . . . . . . . . . .(701) 328-4443
E-mail: bdarr@nd.gov       Fax: (701) 328-4623
Safety Division Director **Karin Mongeon** . . . . . . . . . . . . . (701) 328-4559
E-mail: kamongeon@nd.gov

## North Dakota Housing Finance Agency [NDHFA]

2624 Vermont Avenue, Bismarck, ND 58504
P.O. Box 1535, Bismarck, ND 58502
Tel: (701) 328-8080  Tel: (800) 292-8621  TTY: (800) 366-6888
Fax: (701) 328-8090  E-mail: info@ndhfa.org  Internet: www.ndhfa.org

▲Executive Director **Jolene Kline** . . . . . . . . . . . . . . . . . . (701) 328-8072
E-mail: jkline@nd.gov
Chief Financial Officer **Patrick J. "Pat" Nagel** . . . . . . . . . (701) 328-8081
Homeownership Programs Director **Dave Flohr** . . . . . . . . . (701) 328-8060
Planning and Housing Development Director
**Jennifer Henderson** . . . . . . . . . . . . . . . . . . . . . . . . (701) 328-8072
Property Management Director **Wayne Glaser** . . . . . . . . . .(701) 328-8070
Business Manager **Delores Hummel** . . . . . . . . . . . . . . . . (701) 328-8055
E-mail: dhummel@nd.gov
Public Information Specialist **Sarah L. Mudder** . . . . . . . . . (701) 328-8056
Public Affairs Director **Max Wetz** . . . . . . . . . . . . . . . . . .(701) 328-8098
E-mail: mwetz@nd.gov

★ Elected Official  ■ Appointed by Governor  ● Appointed by Legislature  ▲ Appointed by Board or Commission  ◆ Appointed by State Supreme Court

*State Yellow Book*       © Leadership Directories, Inc.       Summer 2016

# North Dakota Industrial Commission [NDIC]

State Capitol, 14th Floor, 600 East Boulevard Avenue, Department 405, Bismarck, ND 58505-0840
Tel: (701) 328-3722  TTY: (800) 366-6888  Fax: (701) 328-2820
Internet: www.nd.gov/ndic

**Employees:** 93  **Fiscal Year:** 2013-2015  **Budget:** $63,468,000

Chairman **John S. "Jack" Dalrymple III** . . . . . . . . . . . . . . (701) 328-3722
  Affiliation: Governor, Office of the Governor, State of North Dakota
  (Note: On August 24, 2015, Governor John Dalrymple announced he will not seek reelection in 2016.)
  State Capitol, 600 East Boulevard Avenue, Department 101, Bismarck, ND 58505-0001
Member **Doug Charles Goehring** . . . . . . . . . . . . . . . . . (701) 328-3722
  Term Expires: December 31, 2018
  Affiliation: Commissioner, Department of Agriculture, State of North Dakota
  State Capitol, Department 602, 600 East Boulevard Avenue, Bismarck, ND 58505-0001
Member **Wayne Stenehjem** . . . . . . . . . . . . . . . . . . . . . (701) 328-3722
  Term Expires: December 31, 2018
  Affiliation: Attorney General, Office of the Attorney General, State of North Dakota
  State Capitol, 600 East Boulevard Avenue, 1st Floor, Department 125, Bismarck, ND 58505-0040
  Education: North Dakota 1974 BS, 1977 JD
▲Executive Director **Karlene K. Fine** . . . . . . . . . . . . . . .(701) 328-3722
  E-mail: kfine@nd.gov

# Department of Mineral Resources

600 East Boulevard Avenue, Department 405, Bismarck, ND 58505-0001
Tel: (701) 328-8020  Fax: (701) 328-2820

Director **Lynn D. Helms** . . . . . . . . . . . . . . . . . . . . . . . . (701) 328-8020
  Fax: (701) 328-2820

# State Water Commission [SWC]

Department 770, 900 East Boulevard Avenue, Bismarck, ND 58505-0850
Tel: (701) 328-2750  TTY: (800) 366-6888  Fax: (701) 328-3696
E-mail: swc@nd.gov  Internet: www.swc.state.nd.us

**Employees:** 90  **Fiscal Year:** 2013-2015  **Budget:** $859,046,000

▲State Engineer and Secretary **Todd Sando** . . . . . . . . . . . . . (701) 328-4940
  E-mail: tsando@nd.gov

# Administrative Committee on Veterans Affairs [ACOVA]

■Chairman **Dean Overby** . . . . . . . . . . . . . . . . . . . . . (701) 671-1509
  Term Expires: June 30, 2016    Res: (701) 642-1684
  E-mail: doverby@nd.gov
■Secretary **James "Jim" Verwey** . . . . . . . . . . . . . . . .(701) 845-8511
  Term Expires: June 30, 2016    Res: (701) 845-1229
  E-mail: jverwey@bektel.com
■Member **Richard Belling** . . . . . . . . . . . . . . . . . . . . (701) 282-5809
  Term Expires: June 30, 2017
  E-mail: bellwhop@hotmail.com
■Member **Roy Fillion** . . . . . . . . . . . . . . . . . . . . . . . (701) 775-5357
  Term Expires: June 30, 2018
  E-mail: roylinda@gra.midco.net
■Member **Emery Fisher** . . . . . . . . . . . . . . . . . . . . . .(701) 662-2609
  Term Expires: June 30, 2017
  E-mail: grandmafish62@yahoo.com
■Member **Kenneth Hasby** . . . . . . . . . . . . . . . . . . . . .(701) 627-4294
  Term Expires: June 30, 2017
  E-mail: kaje91@hotmail.com
■Member **Jim Haukedahl** . . . . . . . . . . . . . . . . . . . . .(701) 866-6191
  Term Expires: June 30, 2016    Res: (701) 280-0924
  E-mail: jhaukedahl67@gmail.com
■Member **Dave Hilleren**
  Term Expires: June 30, 2017
  E-mail: dhilleren@gmail.com
■Member **Trish Hodny** . . . . . . . . . . . . . . . . . . . . . . .(701) 777-6265
  Term Expires: June 30, 2016
  E-mail: hodnylaw@yahoo.com

■Member **Myron Langehaug** . . . . . . . . . . . . . . . . . . . . . . . (701) 228-2511
  Term Expires: June 30, 2017
  E-mail: mailman@utma.com
■Member **Marlys Morgenstern** . . . . . . . . . . . . . . . . . . . . . .(701) 328-2416
  Term Expires: June 30, 2017
■Member **Bill Peschel**
  Term Expires: June 30, 2018
  E-mail: billpeschel@gmail.com
■Member **Carroll Quam** . . . . . . . . . . . . . . . . . . . . . . . . . (701) 899-2011
  Term Expires: June 30, 2016    Res: (701) 642-5448
  E-mail: cquam@nd.gov
■Member **Marlin Schneider** . . . . . . . . . . . . . . . . . . . . . . . (701) 222-6698
  Term Expires: June 30, 2015    Res: (701) 221-9501
  E-mail: marlin@bis.midco.net
■Member **Hal Weninger** . . . . . . . . . . . . . . . . . . . . . . . . . (701) 770-0594
  Term Expires: June 30, 2015    Res: (701) 627-4699
  E-mail: halweninger@ymail.com
Ex-Officio Member **Cheri L. Giesen** . . . . . . . . . . . . . . . . . .(701) 328-2836
  Affiliation: Executive Director, Job Service North Dakota, State of North Dakota
  P.O. Box 5507, Bismarck, ND 58506-5507
  Education: U Mary BS, MB
Ex-Officio Member **Lavonne Liversage, FACHE** . . . . . . . . .(701) 328-2836
  Affiliation: Healthcare Center Director, Fargo VA Health Care System, VISN 23 - VA Midwest Health Care Network, United States Department of Veterans Affairs
  2101 Elm Street, Fargo, ND 58102
Ex-Officio Member **BG Alan S. Dohrmann, ARNG** . . . . . .(701) 333-2004
Ex-Officio Member **Lonnie Wangen** . . . . . . . . . . . . . . . .(701) 239-7165
  Affiliation: Commissioner, Department of Veterans Affairs, State of North Dakota
  4201 38th Street SW, Suite 104, Fargo, ND 58106

# Department of Veterans Affairs

4201 38th Street SW, Suite 104, Fargo, ND 58106
P.O. Box 9003, Fargo, ND 58106
Tel: (701) 239-7165  Tel: (866) 634-8387  Fax: (701) 239-7166

**Fiscal Year:** 2013-2015  **Budget:** $1,716,000

▲Commissioner **Lonnie Wangen** . . . . . . . . . . . . . . . . . . . . .(701) 239-7165
  E-mail: lwangen@nd.gov
  Administrative Assistant **Cathy Halgunseth** . . . . . . . . . . .(701) 239-7165

# State Board for Career and Technical Education

Chairperson **Brian Duchscherer** . . . . . . . . . . . . . . . . . . . . . (701) 652-3136
Vice Chairperson **Debby Marshall** . . . . . . . . . . . . . . . . . . . .(701) 537-5414
Member **Kirsten Baesler** . . . . . . . . . . . . . . . . . . . . . . . . . .(701) 328-4572
  Education: Bismarck State AA;    Fax: (701) 328-2461
  Minot State 2001 BSEd; Valley City State 2009 MEd
Member **Cheri L. Giesen** . . . . . . . . . . . . . . . . . . . . . . . . . .(701) 328-3030
  Affiliation: Executive Director, Job Service North Dakota, State of North Dakota
  P.O. Box 5507, Bismarck, ND 58506-5507
Member **Jeffery Lind** . . . . . . . . . . . . . . . . . . . . . . . . . . . . (701) 751-6500
Member **Sonia Meehl** . . . . . . . . . . . . . . . . . . . . . . . . . . . .(701) 753-7431
Member **Val Moritz** . . . . . . . . . . . . . . . . . . . . . . . . . . . . . (701) 845-2769
Member **David Richter** . . . . . . . . . . . . . . . . . . . . . . . . . . . (701) 774-4263
  Fax: (701) 845-4590
Member **Dr. Mark Haggerott** . . . . . . . . . . . . . . . . . . . . . . .(701) 328-2974

# Department of Career and Technical Education [CTE]

State Capitol, 600 East Boulevard Avenue, 15th Floor, Department 270, Bismarck, ND 58505-0610
Tel: (701) 328-3180  Fax: (701) 328-1255  E-mail: cte@nd.gov
Internet: www.nd.gov/cte

▲State Director/Executive Officer **Wayne Kutzer** . . . . . . . . . .(701) 328-2259
  E-mail: wkutzer@nd.gov
  Education: North Dakota BS, MS
Assistant State Director **Mark Wagner** . . . . . . . . . . . . . . .(701) 328-2711
  Administrative Staff Officer III **Brenda J. Schuler** . . . . . .(701) 328-3181
  E-mail: bschuler@nd.gov

---

★ Elected Official   ■ Appointed by Governor   ● Appointed by Legislature   ▲ Appointed by Board or Commission   ◆ Appointed by State Supreme Court

# Board of University and School Lands

Member **Kirsten Baesler** . . . . . . . . . . . . . . . . . . . . . . . . . . . . (701) 328-2800
Affiliation: State Superintendent, Department of Public Instruction,
State of North Dakota
600 East Boulevard Avenue, Department 201,
Bismarck, ND 58505-0440

Member **John S. "Jack" Dalrymple III** . . . . . . . . . . . . . . (701) 328-2800
Affiliation: Governor, Office of the Governor, State of North Dakota
(Note: On August 24, 2015, Governor John Dalrymple announced he
will not seek reelection in 2016.)
State Capitol, 600 East Boulevard Avenue, Department 101,
Bismarck, ND 58505-0001

Member **Alvin A. "Al" Jaeger** . . . . . . . . . . . . . . . . . . . . . . . (701) 328-2800
Affiliation: Secretary of State, Office of the Secretary of State, State of
North Dakota
State Capitol, 600 East Boulevard Avenue, Dept 108,
Bismarck, ND 58505-0500
Education: Dickinson State U 1966 BS

Member **Kelly L. Schmidt** . . . . . . . . . . . . . . . . . . . . . . . . . . . (701) 328-2800
Affiliation: State Treasurer, Office of the State Treasurer, State of North
Dakota
State Capitol, 600 East Boulevard Avenue, Department 120, 3rd Floor,
Bismarck, ND 58505-0600
Education: Kellogg 2005

Member **Wayne Stenehjem** . . . . . . . . . . . . . . . . . . . . . . . . (701) 328-2800
Affiliation: Attorney General, Office of the Attorney General, State of
North Dakota
State Capitol, 600 East Boulevard Avenue, 1st Floor, Department 125,
Bismarck, ND 58505-0040

# Department of Trust Lands

1707 North Ninth Street, Bismarck, ND 58501
P.O. Box 5523, Bismarck, ND 58506-5523
Tel: (701) 328-2800  Fax: (701) 328-3650  E-mail: InfoLandDept@nd.gov

**Employees:** 31

▲Commissioner **Lance D. Gaebe** . . . . . . . . . . . . . . . . . . . . . . (701) 328-2807
E-mail: lancegaebe@nd.gov

Operations Deputy Commissioner **Linda Fisher** . . . . . . . . . (701) 328-2806
E-mail: llfisher@nd.gov

Investment Division Director **Jeff Engleson** . . . . . . . . . . . . (701) 328-1921
E-mail: jengleso@nd.gov
Education: North Dakota 1981 BSBA

Minerals Management Division Director **Drew Combs** . . . . (701) 328-1909

Revenue Compliance Division Director **Taylor K. Lee** . . . . . (701) 328-1925
E-mail: tklee@nd.gov

Surface Management Division Director **Mike Humann** . . . . (701) 328-1917
E-mail: mhumann@nd.gov

Unclaimed Property Administrator **Susan Dollinger** . . . . . . (701) 328-1944
E-mail: sdollinger@nd.gov

Energy Impact Assistant Director **Rick Owens** . . . . . . . . . (701) 328-1948
E-mail: rwowings@nd.gov

Claims Processor **Suzie Entzel** . . . . . . . . . . . . . . . . . . . . . . (701) 328-2805
E-mail: sentzel@nd.gov

Account Budget Specialist **Peggy Gudvangen** . . . . . . . . . . (701) 328-1913
E-mail: pjgudvangen@nd.gov

Account Budget Specialist **(Vacant)** . . . . . . . . . . . . . . . . . . (701) 328-1951

# Energy Development Impact Office

1707 North Ninth Street, Bismarck, ND 58501

▲Director **Lance D. Gaebe** . . . . . . . . . . . . . . . . . . . . . . . . . . (701) 328-2800
E-mail: lancegaebe@nd.gov

# Highway Patrol

State Capitol - Judicial Wing, 600 East Boulevard Avenue, Dept. 504,
Bismarck, ND 58505-0240
Tel: (701) 328-2455  TTY: (800) 366-6888  Fax: (701) 328-1717
E-mail: ndhpinfo@nd.gov  Internet: www.nd.gov/ndhp

**Fiscal Year:** 2015-2017  **Budget:** $59,719,000

■Superintendent **Col. Michael T. Gerhart, Jr.** . . . . . . . . . . . (701) 328-2455
E-mail: mtgerhart@nd.gov
Education: Dickinson State U 1991 BS

Administrative Services Commander
**Capt. Aaron Hummel** . . . . . . . . . . . . . . . . . . . . . . . . . . . . (701) 328-2455
E-mail: arhummel@nd.gov

Chief of Staff **Major Brandon J. Solberg** . . . . . . . . . . . . . (701) 328-2455
E-mail: bjsolberg@nd.gov

Security Director **Sgt Steve L. Johnson** . . . . . . . . . . . . . . (701) 328-2455
E-mail: sljohnson@nd.gov

Training Director **Lt. Daniel Haugen** . . . . . . . . . . . . . . . . . (701) 328-9969
E-mail: dhaugen@nd.gov

Support Services Director **Capt. Norman C. Ruud** . . . . . . . (701) 328-2455
E-mail: ncruud@nd.gov

Safety and Education Officer **Lt. Thomas Iverson** . . . . . . . (701) 328-2455
E-mail: tiverson@nd.gov

Motor Carrier Operations **Capt. Eldon P. Mehrer** . . . . . . . . (701) 328-5124

# State Historical Society

North Dakota Heritage Center, 612 East Boulevard Avenue,
Bismarck, ND 58505-0830
Tel: (701) 328-2666  TTY: (800) 366-6888  Fax: (701) 328-3710
E-mail: histsoc@state.nd.us

**Employees:** 78  **Fiscal Year:** 2015-2017  **Budget:** $28,751,000

▲Director **Claudia Berg** . . . . . . . . . . . . . . . . . . . . . . . . . . . . (701) 328-2667
E-mail: cberg@nd.gov
Education: North Dakota 1974 BA, 1978 MFA

Assistant Director **David C. Skalsky** . . . . . . . . . . . . . . . . . . (701) 328-2666
Education: Minot State 1989 BS

Communication, Marketing and Education Director
**Kimberly Jondahl** . . . . . . . . . . . . . . . . . . . . . . . . . . . . . . (701) 328-1476
E-mail: kjondahl@nd.gov

Historic Preservation Division Director
**Fern E. Swenson** . . . . . . . . . . . . . . . . . . . . . . . . . . . . . . (701) 328-2672
Education: St Cloud State 1976 BA; Oklahoma 1986 MA

State Archives Director **Ann Jenks** . . . . . . . . . . . . . . . . . . (701) 328-2668

Museum Division Director (Interim) **Len C. Thorson** . . . . . (701) 328-2124

Security Supervisor **Duane Edwards** . . . . . . . . . . . . . . . . . (701) 328-3564

Visitor Services Coordinator **Toni Reinbold** . . . . . . . . . . . . (701) 328-4187

Administrative Officer **Ronald Phil Warner** . . . . . . . . . . . . (701) 328-2666
E-mail: rwarner@nd.gov
Education: Minot State 1969 BS; North Dakota 1986 MA

# Workforce Safety and Insurance [WSI]

1600 East Century Avenue, Suite 1, Bismarck, ND 58506
P.O. Box 5585, Bismarck, ND 58506
Tel: (701) 328-3800  Tel: (800) 243-3331 (Fraud & Safety Hotline)
Tel: (800) 777-5033 (Helpline)  TTY: (701) 328-3786
Fax: (701) 328-3820  Internet: www.WorkforceSafety.com

**Fiscal Year:** 2013-2015  **Budget:** $63,323,000

■Executive Director and Chief Executive Officer
**Bryan R. Klipfel, SPHR** . . . . . . . . . . . . . . . . . . . . . . . . . (701) 328-3856
E-mail: bklipfel@nd.gov
Education: North Dakota 1975 BPA

Executive Secretary **Mary Marthaller** . . . . . . . . . . . . . . . . (701) 328-3856

Deputy Director and Public Affairs Officer
**Clare A. Carlson** . . . . . . . . . . . . . . . . . . . . . . . . . . . . . . . (701) 328-3856
Education: North Dakota State BS; U Mary MM

General Counsel **Jodi Bjornson** . . . . . . . . . . . . . . . . . . . . . (701) 328-6023

Chief Operating Officer **John Halvorson** . . . . . . . . . . . . . . (701) 328-6016
E-mail: jhalvorson@nd.gov

Claims Director **Kim Ehli** . . . . . . . . . . . . . . . . . . . . . . . . . . (701) 328-3836

Information Technology Director **Timothy Schenfisch** . . . . (701) 328-5945
E-mail: tschenfisch@nd.gov

Medical Services Director **(Vacant)** . . . . . . . . . . . . . . . . . . (701) 328-5961

Pharmacy Director **Harvey Hanel** . . . . . . . . . . . . . . . . . . . (701) 328-7222

Quality Assurance Director **Michele Blumhagen** . . . . . . . . (701) 328-3781
E-mail: mblumhagen@nd.gov

Safety and Loss Prevention Director **Nick Jolliffe** . . . . . . . (701) 328-3850

Employer Services Chief **Barry Schumacher** . . . . . . . . . . . (701) 328-3815
E-mail: baschumacher@nd.gov

Injury Services Chief **Tim Wahlin** . . . . . . . . . . . . . . . . . . . (701) 328-7201

Customer Service Manager **Carla Usselman** . . . . . . . . . . . (701) 328-3777

Decision Review Office **Cade Jorgenson** . . . . . . . . . . . . . . (701) 328-9904

Facility Director **Curt W. Zimmerman** . . . . . . . . . . . . . . . . (701) 328-3795

Finance Director **Cindy Ternes** . . . . . . . . . . . . . . . . . . . . . (701) 328-3837

Human Resources Officer **Mary Selzler** . . . . . . . . . . . . . . (701) 328-3851

Internal Audit Director **Micole Kvas** . . . . . . . . . . . . . . . . . (701) 328-3824

*(continued on next page)*

---

★ Elected Official    ■ Appointed by Governor    ● Appointed by Legislature    ▲ Appointed by Board or Commission    ◆ Appointed by State Supreme Court

**Workforce Safety and Insurance** *continued*

Office Services Director **Denise Bachler** . . . . . . . . . . . . . . (701) 328-3834
Return-to-Work Director **Robin Halvorson** . . . . . . . . . . . (701) 328-3826
    E-mail: rhalvorson@nd.gov
Special Investigations Unit Director **Rob Forward** . . . . . . . (701) 328-3875

## North Dakota Public Employees Retirement System [NDPERS]

400 East Broadway, Suite 505, Bismarck, ND 58502-1657
P.O. Box 1657, Bismarck, ND 58502-1657
Tel: (701) 328-3900  Tel: (800) 803-7377  Fax: (701) 328-3920
E-mail: ndpers-info@nd.gov  Internet: www.nd.gov/ndpers

**Employees:** 33  **Fiscal Year:** 2013-2015  **Budget:** $7,651,000

▲ Executive Director **J. Sparb Collins, CEBS** . . . . . . . . . . . . (701) 328-3900
    E-mail: scollins@nd.gov
Chief Operating Officer **Sharon Schiermeister** . . . . . . . . . (701) 328-3902
    E-mail: sschierm@nd.gov
Administrative Services Manager **Cheryl Stockert** . . . . . . . (701) 328-3903
    E-mail: cstocker@nd.gov
Benefits Programs Manager **Kathy M. Allen** . . . . . . . . . . . (701) 328-3918

## Forest Service

307 First Street East, Bottineau, ND 58318-1100
Tel: (701) 228-5422  Fax: (701) 228-5448  E-mail: forest@nd.gov

State Forester **Larry A. Kotchman** . . . . . . . . . . . . . . . . . (701) 228-5422
Administration Team Leader **Brenda Johnson** . . . . . . . . . . (701) 228-5486
    E-mail: brenda.johnson@ndsu.edu
Forestry and Fire Management Team Leader
    **Thomas Claeys** . . . . . . . . . . . . . . . . . . . . . . . . . . . . (701) 328-9945
Nursery and State Forests Team Leader **Michael Kangas** . . (701) 231-5936
Fire Manager **Ryan Melin** . . . . . . . . . . . . . . . . . . . . . . . (701) 328-9985
Information & Education Coordinator **Glenda Fauske** . . . . (701) 228-5446

## Office of the Secretary of State

State Capitol, 600 East Boulevard Avenue, Dept 108,
Bismarck, ND 58505-0500
Tel: (701) 328-2900  Tel: (800) 352-0867  Fax: (701) 328-2992
E-mail: sos@nd.gov  Internet: www.nd.gov/sos

**Fiscal Year:** 2013-2015  **Budget:** $12,491,000

★ Secretary of State **Alvin A. "Al" Jaeger** (R) . . . . . . . . . . . (701) 328-2900
    Term Expires: January 2019
    E-mail: sos@nd.gov
Deputy Secretary of State **James "Jim" Silrum** . . . . . . . . (701) 328-2900
Business Services Director **Leann Meccowan** . . . . . . . . . . (701) 328-4284
Central Indexing (UCC) Unit Lead **Lori Feldman** . . . . . . . (701) 328-3662
Operational Management Director **Lori Feldman** . . . . . . . (701) 328-3665
Lobbyist Registration Director **Lori Feldman** . . . . . . . . . . (701) 328-3665
    E-mail: sosadlic@nd.gov
Notary Licensing Director **Beth Herzog** . . . . . . . . . . . . . (701) 328-2901
Elections Unit Lead **Lee Ann Oliver** . . . . . . . . . . . . . . . . (701) 328-4146

## Office of the Attorney General

State Capitol, 600 East Boulevard Avenue, 1st Floor, Department 125,
Bismarck, ND 58505-0040
Tel: (701) 328-2210  TTY: (800) 366-6888  Fax: (701) 328-2226
Internet: www.ag.state.nd.us

**Employees:** 213  **Fiscal Year:** 2013-2015  **Budget:** $83,834,000

★ Attorney General **Wayne Stenehjem** (R) . . . . . . . . . . . . . (701) 328-2210
    Term Expires: January 2019
    E-mail: wstenehjem@nd.gov
Solicitor General **Douglas A. Bahr** . . . . . . . . . . . . . . . . . (701) 328-3640
    500 N. Ninth St., Bismarck, ND 58501      Fax: (701) 328-4300
    Education: BYU 1987 BS; South Dakota 1990 JD
Chief Deputy **Thomas L. Trenbeath** . . . . . . . . . . . . . . . . (701) 328-2210
    Education: North Dakota BA, BS, JD
Consumer Protection and Antitrust Division Director
    **Parrell D. Grossman** . . . . . . . . . . . . . . . . . . . (701) 328-3404
    Education: Minot State 1978 BS;      Fax: (701) 328-5568
    North Dakota 1989 JD

Criminal and Regulatory Division Director
    **Jonathan Byers** . . . . . . . . . . . . . . . . . . . . . . . . . .(701) 328-4848
    Education: North Dakota 1988 JD      Fax: (701) 328-3535
Finance and Administration Division Director **Kathy Roll** . . (701) 328-2210
    E-mail: kroll@nd.gov
    Education: U Mary 1980 BS
Gaming Division Director **Deborah McDaniel** . . . . . . . . . .(701) 328-4848
    Fax: (701) 328-3535
Information Technology Division Director **Cher Thomas** . . (701) 328-5500
    E-mail: cthomas@nd.gov
Lottery Division Director **Randall Miller** . . . . . . . . . . . . . (701) 328-1574
Natural Resources and Indian Affairs Division Director
    **Matthew "Matt" Sagsveen** . . . . . . . . . . . . . . . . . . . (701) 328-2210
    500 N. Ninth St., Bismarck, ND 58501      Fax: (701) 328-4300
State and Local Government Division Director
    **Mary Kae Kelsch** . . . . . . . . . . . . . . . . . . . . . . . . . .(701) 328-2210

## Bureau of Criminal Investigation

P.O. Box 1054, Bismarck, ND 58502-1054
Fax: (701) 328-5510

Director **Dallas Carlson** . . . . . . . . . . . . . . . . . . . . . . . . (701) 328-5500

## Crime Laboratory Division

Fax: (701) 328-6145

Director **Hope Olson** . . . . . . . . . . . . . . . . . . . . . . . . . . . (701) 328-6159
    Education: North Dakota 1990 MS, 1998 MPA;
    St Cloud State 1985 BS

## State Fire Marshal's Office

P.O. Box 1054, Bismarck, ND 58502-1054
Fax: (701) 328-5510

Fire Marshal **Ray Lambert** . . . . . . . . . . . . . . . . . . . . . . .(701) 328-5555
    E-mail: rlambert@nd.gov

## Office of the State Treasurer

State Capitol, 600 East Boulevard Avenue, Department 120, 3rd Floor,
Bismarck, ND 58505-0600
Tel: (701) 328-2643  Fax: (701) 328-3002  E-mail: treasurer@nd.gov
Internet: www.nd.gov/treasurer

**Employees:** 8  **Fiscal Year:** 2015-2017  **Budget:** $249,542,000

★ State Treasurer **Kelly L. Schmidt** (R) . . . . . . . . . . . . . . . (701) 328-2643
    Term Expires: January 2017
Deputy State Treasurer **Sheri Haugen-Hoffart** . . . . . . . . . (701) 328-2643
    Executive Assistant **Karla Brent** . . . . . . . . . . . . . . . . (701) 328-2643

## Office of the State Auditor

State Capitol, 600 East Boulevard Avenue, 3rd Floor, Department 117,
Bismarck, ND 58505-0060
Tel: (701) 328-2241  Fax: (701) 328-1406  E-mail: ndsao@nd.gov
Internet: www.nd.gov/auditor

**Employees:** 53  **Fiscal Year:** 2013-2015  **Budget:** $11,613,000

★ State Auditor **Robert R. "Bob" Peterson** (R) . . . . . . . . . . (701) 328-2241
    Term Expires: January 2017
    E-mail: rpeterso@nd.gov
    Education: North Dakota 1974 BA
    Career: Accounting and Budget Specialist, Land Department, State of
    North Dakota (1978-1996)
Director **Edwin J. Nagel, Jr., CPA** . . . . . . . . . . . . . . . . . . (701) 328-2241
    Education: U Mary 1978 BA
College and University Audit Manager
    **Robyn Hoffmann, CPA** . . . . . . . . . . . . . . . . . . . . . . . (701) 239-7291
Information Systems Audit Manager
    **Donald LaFleur, CISA, CPA** . . . . . . . . . . . . . . . . . . . (701) 328-4744
    E-mail: dlafleur@nd.gov
    Education: Minot State 1992 BS
Local Government Audit Manager **Dave Mix, CPA** . . . . . . . (701) 239-7252
Performance Audit Manager **Jason Wahl, CPA** . . . . . . . . . . (701) 328-2594
Royalty Audit Manager **Dennis Roller, CPA** . . . . . . . . . . .(701) 250-4682
State Agency Audit Manager **Cindi Pedersen, CPA** . . . . . . (701) 328-4743
State Agency Audit Manager **Paul Welk, CPA** . . . . . . . . . . (701) 328-2320
Technical Specialist **Ron Tolstad** . . . . . . . . . . . . . . . . . . (701) 328-2243
    E-mail: rtolstad@nd.gov

---

★ Elected Official   ■ Appointed by Governor   ● Appointed by Legislature   ▲ Appointed by Board or Commission   ◆ Appointed by State Supreme Court

# Office of the State Tax Commissioner

State Capitol, 600 East Boulevard Avenue, Bismarck, ND 58505-0599
Tel: (701) 328-7088  TTY: (800) 366-6888  Fax: (701) 328-3700
E-mail: taxinfo@nd.gov  Internet: www.nd.gov/tax

**Employees:** 134  **Fiscal Year:** 2013-2015  **Budget:** $57,180,000

★ State Tax Commissioner **Ryan Rauschenberger** (R) . . . . . . (701) 328-7088
   Term Expires: January 2019
   E-mail: rarauschenberger@nd.gov
   Education: North Dakota BACCY, MBA
Deputy Commissioner **Joe Morrissette** . . . . . . . . . . . . . . (701) 328-7088
Tax Administration Director **Myles Vosberg** . . . . . . . . . . . (701) 328-3471
Associate Director of Tax Administration
   **Nathan Bergman** . . . . . . . . . . . . . . . . . . . . . . . . . . . (701) 328-3345
Associate Director of Tax Administration **Matt Peyerl** . . . . (701) 328-2706
Chief Auditor/Sales Tax Supervisor **Darrell Engen** . . . . . . . (701) 239-7232
Information Management and Technology Director
   **Lucas Asche** . . . . . . . . . . . . . . . . . . . . . . . . . . . . . . (701) 328-3129
   E-mail: lwasche@nd.gov
Legal Division Director **Donnita Wald** . . . . . . . . . . . . . . . (701) 328-2777
Property Tax Assessments Division Director
   **Linda Leadbetter** . . . . . . . . . . . . . . . . . . . . . . . . . . . (701) 328-3128
Corporate Income Tax Supervisor **Doug Coyle** . . . . . . . . . (701) 328-3164
Estate Tax Supervisor **Kevin Schatz** . . . . . . . . . . . . . . . . (701) 328-3657
Motor Fuels and Miscellaneous Tax Supervisor
   **Kevin Schatz** . . . . . . . . . . . . . . . . . . . . . . . . . . . . . . (701) 328-3657
Oil & Gas Gross Production Tax Supervisor
   **Kevin Schatz** . . . . . . . . . . . . . . . . . . . . . . . . . . . . . . (701) 328-3657
Sales Tax Compliance Supervisor **Blane Braunberger** . . . . (701) 328-3011
Research & Statistics Analyst **Kathryn Strombeck** . . . . . . (701) 328-3402
Utility Tax Appraiser **Linda Leadbetter** . . . . . . . . . . . . . . (701) 328-3128

# Department of Agriculture

State Capitol, Department 602, 600 East Boulevard Avenue,
Bismarck, ND 58505-0001
Tel: (701) 328-2231  Tel: (800) 242-7535 (Toll Free)  Fax: (701) 328-4567
E-mail: ndda@nd.gov  Internet: www.agdepartment.com

**Employees:** 77  **Fiscal Year:** 2013-2015  **Budget:** $25,274,000

★ Commissioner **Doug Charles Goehring** (R) . . . . . . . . . . . (701) 328-4754
   Term Expires: January 2019
   E-mail: goehring@nd.gov
   Assistant to the Commissioner **Jody Reinke** . . . . . . . . . (701) 328-4754
Deputy Commissioner **Tom Bodine** . . . . . . . . . . . . . . . . . (701) 328-2231
State Entomologist **(Vacant)** . . . . . . . . . . . . . . . . . . . . . (701) 328-4765
State Veterinarian **Dr. Susan Keller** . . . . . . . . . . . . . . . . . (701) 328-2655
   Education: Kansas State 1981 BS, 1985 DVM
Administrative Services Director **Ken Junkert** . . . . . . . . . . (701) 328-4756
   E-mail: kjunkert@nd.gov
   Education: U Mary 1990 BS
Marketing and Information Director **Dana Hager** . . . . . . . . (701) 328-4763
Livestock Development Director **Shaun Quissell** . . . . . . . . (701) 328-4761
Pesticide, Feed and Fertilizer Director **(Vacant)** . . . . . . . . (701) 328-1505
Plant Industries Director (Acting)
   **Charles Elhard**
Public Information Specialist **Michelle Mielke** . . . . . . . . . . (701) 328-2233
   E-mail: mmielke@nd.gov

# Insurance Department

State Capitol, 600 East Boulevard Avenue, Fifth Floor, Department 401,
Bismarck, ND 58505-0320
Tel: (701) 328-2400  Tel: (800) 247-0560 (Toll-Free)
TTY: (800) 366-6888  Fax: (701) 328-4880  E-mail: insurance@nd.gov
Internet: www.nd.gov/ndins

**Fiscal Year:** 2013-2015  **Budget:** $26,377,000

★ Insurance Commissioner **Adam W. Hamm** (R) . . . . . . . . . (701) 328-2440
   Education: Sam Houston State BSCrimJ; North Dakota 1998 JD
Deputy Commissioner **Rebecca Ternes** . . . . . . . . . . . . . . (701) 328-2440
   Education: Minnesota St (Moorhead) 1990 BS;
   North Dakota 1996 MBA
Executive Assistant **Marcy Ost** . . . . . . . . . . . . . . . . . . . . (701) 328-2856

Chief Examiner **Edward Moody** . . . . . . . . . . . . . . . . . . . . (701) 328-9608
General Counsel **Jeffrey Ubben** . . . . . . . . . . . . . . . . . . . (701) 328-2440
Consumer Assistance Division Director
   **David Zimmerman** . . . . . . . . . . . . . . . . . . . . . . . . . . (701) 328-9611
Product Filing Division Director **Chrystal Bartuska** . . . . . . (701) 328-2441
Special Funds Division Director **Jeff Bitz** . . . . . . . . . . . . . (701) 328-9606
   Education: North Dakota 1984 BA

# Department of Public Instruction [DPI]

600 East Boulevard Avenue, Department 201, Bismarck, ND 58505-0440
Tel: (701) 328-2260  TTY: (701) 328-4920  Fax: (701) 328-2461
Internet: www.dpi.state.nd.us

**Fiscal Year:** 2013-2015  **Budget:** $2,160,610,000

★ State Superintendent **Kirsten Baesler** (R) . . . . . . . . . . . . (701) 391-4572
   Term Expires: 2017
Deputy Superintendent **Robert J. "Bob" Christman** . . . . . (701) 328-1240
   Executive Assistant **Lynette Norbeck** . . . . . . . . . . . . . (701) 328-4572
Education and Community Support Assistant
   Superintendent **Robert Marthaller** . . . . . . . . . . . . . . . . (701) 328-2267
Assessment Director **Greg Gallagher** . . . . . . . . . . . . . . . . (701) 328-1838
Child Nutrition and Food Distribution Director
   **Linda Schloer** . . . . . . . . . . . . . . . . . . . . . . . . . . . . . . (701) 328-4565
Safe and Healthy Schools and Adult Education Director
   **Valerie Fischer** . . . . . . . . . . . . . . . . . . . . . . . . . . . . . (701) 328-4138
Fiscal Management Director **Stephanie Gullickson** . . . . . . (701) 328-2176
Human Resources Assistant Director **Addy Schmaltz** . . . . (701) 328-3298
Indian Education Director **Lucy Fredericks** . . . . . . . . . . . . (701) 328-1718
Information, Communications, and Research Director
   **Dale Wetzel** . . . . . . . . . . . . . . . . . . . . . . . . . . . . . . . (701) 328-2247
   E-mail: dwetzel@nd.gov
Management Information Systems Director
   **Frank "Steve" Snow** . . . . . . . . . . . . . . . . . . . . . . . . (701) 328-2189
   E-mail: fsnow@nd.gov
Teacher and School Effectiveness Director
   **Sherry Houdek** . . . . . . . . . . . . . . . . . . . . . . . . . . . . . (701) 328-2755
School Finance Director **Jerry Coleman** . . . . . . . . . . . . . . (701) 328-4051
Special Education Director **Gerry Teevens** . . . . . . . . . . . . . (701) 328-2277
Title I Director **Laurie Matzke** . . . . . . . . . . . . . . . . . . . . . (701) 328-2284
Webmaster **Roxie Dietrich** . . . . . . . . . . . . . . . . . . . . . . . (701) 328-3231
   E-mail: rdietrich@nd.gov

# North Dakota Public Service Commission [PSC]

State Capitol, 600 East Boulevard Avenue, Department 408,
Bismarck, ND 58505-0480
Tel: (701) 328-2400  TTY: (800) 366-6888  Fax: (701) 328-2410
E-mail: ndpsc@nd.gov

**Employees:** 44  **Fiscal Year:** 2013-2015  **Budget:** $20,479,000

★ Chairman **Brian P. Kalk** (R) . . . . . . . . . . . . . . . . . . . . . . (701) 328-4195
   Term Expires: 2020
   Education: Campbell 1991 BA; North Dakota State 2001 MS,
   2006 PhD
★ Commissioner **Randel "Randy" Christmann** (R) . . . . . . . . (701) 328-2400
   Term Expires: 2018
   Education: North Dakota State 1982 BSBA
★ Commissioner **Julie Fedorchak** (R) . . . . . . . . . . . . . . . . . (701) 328-2400
   Term Expires: 2016
   E-mail: jfedorchak@nd.gov
   Education: North Dakota 1991 BA

---

★ Elected Official    ■ Appointed by Governor    ● Appointed by Legislature    ▲ Appointed by Board or Commission    ◆ Appointed by State Supreme Court

# Ohio

Tel: (614) 466-3357 (State Information)  Internet: www.ohio.gov

**Number of U.S. Congressional Delegates:** 2 Senators; 16 Representatives  **Governor's Term:** 4 years
**Legislature Description:** General Assembly - 33 member Senate; 99 member House of Representatives;
Term - Senate 4 years, House 2 years  **Next Election:** Governor November 2018; Legislature
November 2016  **Number of Electoral Votes:** 18  **Official Name:** State of Ohio (Indian: great)
**Nickname:** The Buckeye State  **Motto:** With God, all things are possible

**Population:** 11,613,423 (2015); Rank 7  **Employees:** 79,472  **Fiscal Year:** 2015
**Budget:** $67,166,762,000,000

## Office of the Governor

Vern Riffe Center, 77 South High Street, 30th Floor,
Columbus, OH 43215-6123
Tel: (614) 466-3555  Tel: (614) 644-4357  Fax: (614) 466-9354

**Employees:** 34

**John Richard Kasich**
Governor

Began Service: January 10, 2011
Term Expires: January 2019
Date of Birth: May 13, 1952
Education: Ohio State 1974 BA
Religion: Christian
Career: U.S. Representative (R-OH), Office of
Representative John R. Kasich, United States
House of Representatives (1983-2001); Chair,
Committee on the Budget, United States House
of Representatives (1995-2000); Managing
Director, Investment Banking Group, Lehman
Brothers Holdings Inc. (2001-2008); Associate,
Schottenstein Stores Corporation (2008-2010)

★Governor **John Richard Kasich** (R) . . . . . . . . . . . . . . . . (614) 466-3555
Chief of Staff **Wayne T. Struble** . . . . . . . . . . . . . . . . . (614) 466-3555
  E-mail: wayne.struble@governor.ohio.gov
Deputy Chief of Staff **Scott Milburn** . . . . . . . . . . . . . . (614) 466-3555
  Education: Ohio 1991 BA
Communications Director **Jim Lynch** . . . . . . . . . . . . . . (614) 466-5585
  E-mail: jim.lynch@governor.ohio.gov
Press Secretary **Joseph "Joe" Andrews** . . . . . . . . . . . . (330) 760-7582
  E-mail: joseph.andrews@governor.ohio.gov
Deputy Press Secretary **(Vacant)** . . . . . . . . . . . . . . . . . (330) 760-7582
Boards and Commissions Director **Megan Fitzmartin** . . . . (614) 995-1860
  E-mail: megan.fitzmartin@governor.ohio.gov
Faith Based and Community Initiatives Director
  **Kim Hettel** . . . . . . . . . . . . . . . . . . . . . . . . . . . . . (614) 644-0842
  E-mail: kim.hettel@governor.ohio.gov
Legislative Affairs Director **Merle Madrid** . . . . . . . . . . . (614) 644-0924
  E-mail: merle.madrid@governor.ohio.gov
Public Liaison Director **(Vacant)** . . . . . . . . . . . . . . . . . (614) 644-0924
Chief Legal Counsel **Mike Grodhaus** . . . . . . . . . . . . . . (614) 644-0825
  E-mail: michael.grodhaus@governor.ohio.gov.
Senior Advisor to the Governor **(Vacant)** . . . . . . . . . . . (614) 466-3555
Cabinet Secretary **Kim Kutschbach** . . . . . . . . . . . . . . . (614) 644-0809
  E-mail: kim.kutschbach@governor.ohio.gov
Assistant Policy Director **R. David Frash III** . . . . . . . . . . (614) 466-3555
Education Policy Advisor **Jana Fornario** . . . . . . . . . . . . (614) 466-3555
  E-mail: jana.fornario@governor.ohio.gov

## Policy Office

Policy Director **Benjamin "Ben" Kanzeg** . . . . . . . . . . . . (614) 644-0839

## Department of Administrative Services [DAS]

30 East Broad Street, 40th Floor, Columbus, OH 43215-3414
Tel: (614) 466-6511  TTY: (800) 750-0750  Fax: (614) 644-8151
Internet: http://das.ohio.gov

**Fiscal Year:** 2015  **Budget:** $164,388,000

■Director **Robert "Bob" Blair** . . . . . . . . . . . . . . . . . . . (614) 466-6511
  E-mail: robert.blair@das.state.oh.us
Chief of Staff **(Vacant)** . . . . . . . . . . . . . . . . . . . . . . . (614) 752-8258
Chief of Performance and Results **Randall F. Howard** . . . . (614) 466-6511
  E-mail: randall.howard@das.state.oh.us
Executive Assistant **Jackie Murray** . . . . . . . . . . . . . . . . (614) 466-6511
  E-mail: jackie.murray@das.state.oh.us

## Office of Collective Bargaining [OCB]

1602 W. Broad Street, Columbus, OH 43223
Tel: (614) 466-0570  Fax: (614) 644-0121

Deputy Director (Interim) **Kristen Rankin** . . . . . . . . . . . . (614) 466-3317

## Administrative Support Division

Communications Deputy Director **Thomas "Tom" Hoyt** . . (614) 644-8953
  E-mail: thomas.hoyt@das.ohio.gov
Employee Services Administrator **Marissa Walter** . . . . . . . (614) 466-2136
  E-mail: marissa.walter@das.state.oh.us
Deputy Chief of Staff **Patrick Smith** . . . . . . . . . . . . . . . (614) 995-0936
  E-mail: patrick.smith@das.ohio.gov
Chief Financial Officer **Jennifer Leymaster** . . . . . . . . . . . (614) 644-9653
Chief Legal Counsel **Paul Russell** . . . . . . . . . . . . . . . . . (614) 644-1773

## Equal Opportunity Division

4200 Surface Road, 18th Floor, Columbus, OH 43228-3414
Tel: (614) 466-8380  Fax: (614) 728-5628  Internet: das.ohio.gov/Eod

Deputy Director **Gregory L. "Greg" Williams** . . . . . . . . . (614) 466-8380
  E-mail: gregory.williams@das.ohio.gov
  Education: Akron 2005 BA; Ohio State 2010 JD

## General Services Division

4200 Surface Road, Columbus, OH 43228-4459
Tel: (614) 752-0003  Fax: (614) 466-1040  Internet: das.ohio.gov/gsd

Deputy Director **Erik Yassenoff** . . . . . . . . . . . . . . . . . . (614) 466-4459
Chief Procurement Officer **Kelly Sanders** . . . . . . . . . . . . (614) 752-5259
Asset Management State Program Manager
  **Fred Zabonik** . . . . . . . . . . . . . . . . . . . . . . . . . . . . (614) 752-0076
Fleet Management Administrator **William Simon** . . . . . . . (614) 644-3309
Real Estate Administrator **Marcey Earley-Jeter** . . . . . . . . (614) 466-7319
Risk Management Administrator **Bobbi Miller** . . . . . . . . . (614) 752-0486
State and Federal Surplus Manager **Amy Rice** . . . . . . . . . (614) 466-6585
State Printing Administrator **Charles Stang** . . . . . . . . . . . (614) 644-6355
State Chief Facilities Officer **Peter A.J. Gunnell** . . . . . . . . (614) 732-0455

## Human Resources Division

30 East Broad Street, 27th Floor, Columbus, OH 43215-3414
Tel: (614) 466-3455  Fax: (614) 728-2785  Internet: http://das.ohio.gov/hrd

Chief of Staff **Stephanie Loucka** . . . . . . . . . . . . . . . . . (614) 466-3463
Deputy Director (Interim) **Steven Gray** . . . . . . . . . . . . . (614) 466-0131

---

★ Elected Official  ■ Appointed by Governor  ● Appointed by Legislature  ▲ Appointed by Board or Commission  ◆ Appointed by State Supreme Court

## Office of Information Technology

■Chief Information Officer and Assistant Director
**Stuart R. "Stu" Davis** . . . . . . . . . . . . . . . . . . . . . (614) 644-6446
  E-mail: stu.davis@oit.ohio.gov
Information Technology Services Administrator
**Katrina Flory** . . . . . . . . . . . . . . . . . . . . . . . . . . . (614) 466-6446
  E-mail: katrina.flory@oit.ohio.gov

## Infrastructure Services Division

1320 Arthur E. Adams Drive, Columbus, OH 43221-3595
Tel: (614) 752-7320 Fax: (614) 644-2133

Chief Operating Officer **Spencer Wood** . . . . . . . . . . . . . . . (614) 752-7320
  E-mail: spencer.wood@dot.state.oh.us

## Department of Aging [ODA]

246 North High Street, First Floor, Columbus, OH 43215
Tel: (614) 466-5500 TTY: (614) 466-6191 Fax: (614) 466-5741
E-mail: odamail@age.ohio.gov

**Fiscal Year:** 2015 **Budget:** $15,254,000

■Director **Bonnie Kantor Burman** . . . . . . . . . . . . . . . (614) 466-1055
  E-mail: bkburman@age.ohio.gov
Assistant Director **Julie Trackler** . . . . . . . . . . . . . . . (614) 721-8682
General Counsel **Jennifer Stires** . . . . . . . . . . . . . . . (614) 721-8637
  E-mail: jstires@age.ohio..gov
Communications and Government Outreach Division
  Chief **John Ratliff** . . . . . . . . . . . . . . . . . . . . . . . (614) 466-9614
  E-mail: jratliff@age.ohio.gov
Community Living Division Chief **Matt Hobbs** . . . . . . . . . (614) 752-9168
Elder Rights Division Chief **Beverley E. Laubert** . . . . . . . (614) 644-7922
Fiscal Division Chief **Kevin Flanagan** . . . . . . . . . . . (614) 752-9184
  Education: Wright State 1986 MS; Capital U 1983 BA
Information Systems Division Chief **David Saunders** . . . . . (614) 764-4798
  E-mail: dsaunders@age.ohio.gov
Human Resources Division Chief **Helena Carter** . . . . . . . . (614) 728-5086
Strategic Partnerships Chief **Marcus Molea** . . . . . . . . . . . (614) 752-9167
  E-mail: mmolea@age.ohio.gov
Webmaster **John Ratliff** . . . . . . . . . . . . . . . . . . . . . (614) 466-9614
  E-mail: jratliff@age.ohio.gov

## Department of Agriculture

8995 East Main Street, Reynoldsburg, OH 43068
Tel: (614) 728-6200 TTY: (800) 750-0750 Fax: (614) 466-6124
E-mail: administration@agri.ohio.gov

■Director **David T. Daniels** . . . . . . . . . . . . . . . . . . . (614) 466-2732
  E-mail: david.daniels@agri.ohio.gov
  Program Administrator **Connie Ellis** . . . . . . . . . . . . . (614) 466-2732
    E-mail: ellis@agri.ohio.gov.
Assistant Director **Howard F. Wise** . . . . . . . . . . . . . . (614) 728-4828
  Program Administrator **Celia Beaman** . . . . . . . . . . . (614) 466-2732
    E-mail: beaman@agri.ohio.gov
Deputy Director **Janelle Mead** . . . . . . . . . . . . . . . . . (614) 387-0911
  Education: Ohio State BA
Deputy Director **Jared Parko** . . . . . . . . . . . . . . . . . . . (614) 728-6200
Deputy Director **John M. Schlichter** . . . . . . . . . . . . . . (614) 644-5812
Chief Legal Counsel **Julie Phillips** . . . . . . . . . . . . . . (614) 728-6204
Communications Director **Erica Hawkins** . . . . . . . . . . . (614) 752-9817
  E-mail: ehawkins@agri.ohio.gov
  Public Information Officer **Ashley McDonald** . . . . . . . . (614) 752-9817
    E-mail: ashley.mcdonald@agri.ohio.gov.
  Publications Editor **Susan Showalter** . . . . . . . . . . . . (614) 752-9817
    E-mail: susan.showalter@agri.ohio.gov
Chief Information Officer **Steve Swayne** . . . . . . . . . . . (614) 728-6233
  E-mail: sswayne@agri.ohio.gov
Human Resources Administrator **Traci Orahood** . . . . . . . . (614) 466-5339
Legislative Liaison **George McNab** . . . . . . . . . . . . . . (614) 728-4213
  E-mail: george.mcnab@agri.ohio.gov
Legislative Liaison **Erin Dillon** . . . . . . . . . . . . . . . . (614) 752-4505
  E-mail: erin.honnold@agri.ohio.gov
Chief Financial Officer **Cathy Dodson** . . . . . . . . . . . . (614) 466-4597
Equal Employment Opportunity/Training Officer (Acting)
  **Traci Orahood** . . . . . . . . . . . . . . . . . . . . . . . . . (614) 466-0211
Personnel Officer **Linda Roberts** . . . . . . . . . . . . . . . (614) 752-9819

Public Information Officer **Brett Gates** . . . . . . . . . . . . . (614) 752-9712
  E-mail: bgates@agri.ohio.gov

## Amusement Ride Safety Division

Fax: (614) 728-6416

Amusement Ride Safety Supervisor **Gary Hill** . . . . . . . . . . (614) 728-6280
Amusement Ride Safety Assistant Supervisor
  **Mike Vartorella** . . . . . . . . . . . . . . . . . . . . . . . . (614) 728-6280
    E-mail: mvartorella@agri.ohio.gov

## Animal Industry Division

8995 East Main Street, Reynoldsburg, OH 43068-3399
Tel: (614) 728-6220 Fax: (614) 728-6310 E-mail: animal@agri.ohio.gov

State Veterinarian **Dr. Tony Forshey** . . . . . . . . . . . . . (614) 728-6220
Administrative Assistant **Cindy Bodie** . . . . . . . . . . . . . (614) 728-6220

## Consumer Protection Laboratories Division

Fax: (614) 728-6322

Chief **Dr. Beverly Byrum** . . . . . . . . . . . . . . . . . . . . (614) 728-6230
Purchasing Agent **Charles Bentley** . . . . . . . . . . . . . . (614) 728-2461

## Dairy Division

Fax: (614) 728-2652

Chief **Roger Tedrick** . . . . . . . . . . . . . . . . . . . . . . . (614) 466-5550
Assistant Chief **Brian Wise** . . . . . . . . . . . . . . . . . . . (614) 466-5550
Customer Service Assistant **Angie Smith** . . . . . . . . . . . (614) 466-5550

## Enforcement Division

Fax: (614) 728-6328

Chief **Gary Hill** . . . . . . . . . . . . . . . . . . . . . . . . . . (614) 728-6240
  E-mail: hill@agri.ohio.gov
Administrative Professional **Linda Loveridge** . . . . . . . . . . (614) 728-6240

## Food Safety Division

Fax: (614) 644-0720

Chief **Terri Gerhardt** . . . . . . . . . . . . . . . . . . . . . . (614) 728-6250
Assistant Chief **Jodie M. Taylor** . . . . . . . . . . . . . . . . (614) 728-6250
Program Administrator **Debra Strait** . . . . . . . . . . . . . . (614) 728-6250

## Markets Division

Tel: (614) 752-9814 Fax: (614) 644-5017

Chief **Janelle Mead** . . . . . . . . . . . . . . . . . . . . . . . (614) 387-0911
Ohio Proud Coordinator **Lori Panda** . . . . . . . . . . . . . . (614) 466-8798
                                                          Tel: (800) 467-7683

## Meat Inspection Division

Tel: (614) 728-6260 Fax: (614) 728-6434

Chief **Dr. Nick Wagner** . . . . . . . . . . . . . . . . . . . . . (614) 728-6357
Assistant Chief **Dr. Rayan Powell** . . . . . . . . . . . . . . . (614) 728-6357

## Plant Health Division

Fax: (614) 466-9754

Chief **Matt Beal** . . . . . . . . . . . . . . . . . . . . . . . . . (614) 728-6270
  Education: Ohio State 1982 BS
Assistant Chief **Dan Kenny** . . . . . . . . . . . . . . . . . . . (614) 728-6270
Administrative Professional **Kelly Boubary** . . . . . . . . . . (614) 728-6270
Grain, Feed, Seed Section **David Simmons** . . . . . . . . . . (614) 728-6410
  Education: Ohio State 1987 BS
Gypsy Moth Section **David Adkins** . . . . . . . . . . . . . . (614) 728-6270
Pesticide Fertilizer Section **Jim Belt** . . . . . . . . . . . . . (614) 728-6987
Plant Pest/Apiary Section **Dan Kenny** . . . . . . . . . . . . . (614) 728-6400

## Soil and Water Conservation Division

Chief **Kirk Hines** . . . . . . . . . . . . . . . . . . . . . . . . . (614) 265-6617
  Education: Ohio State BE

## Weights and Measures Division

Fax: (614) 728-6424

Chief **Fran Elson-Houston** . . . . . . . . . . . . . . . . . . . (614) 728-6290

---

★ Elected Official   ■ Appointed by Governor   ● Appointed by Legislature        ▲ Appointed by Board or Commission   ◆ Appointed by State Supreme Court

## Farmland Preservation Office

Executive Director **(Vacant)** ........................... (614) 728-4203
Program Administrator **Jody Bowen** ................. (614) 728-6210

## Livestock Environmental Permitting Program

Fax: (614) 728-6335

Chief **Kevin Elder** ...................................... (614) 387-0469
Program Administrator **Nancy Cunningham** ............ (614) 728-6356

## Department of Commerce

Vern Riffe Center, 77 South High Street, 23rd Floor,
Columbus, OH 43215-6123
Tel: (614) 466-3636  Fax: (614) 644-8292
E-mail: webadmin@com.state.oh.us  Internet: www.com.ohio.gov

**Employees:** 979  **Fiscal Year:** 2015  **Budget:** $185,898,000

■Director **Jacqueline T. "Jackie" Williams** .............. (614) 466-3636
   E-mail: jacqueline.williams@com.state.oh.us
   Education: Miami U (OH) MS
Assistant Director **Matt Close** .......................... (614) 466-7063
Communications Director **Carry Francis** ................. (614) 644-7115
   E-mail: carry.francis@com.state.oh.us
Chief Legal Counsel **Kelly Kuffman** .................... (614) 644-7063
Human Resources Chief **Sandra Kellam** ............... (614) 644-7177
Securities Commissioner **Andrea Seidt** ............... (614) 644-7063
                                          Fax: (614) 466-3316
Financial Institutions Superintendent **Charles J. Dolezal** ... (614) 728-8400
   E-mail: charles.dolezal@dfi.com.state.oh.us
Industrial Compliance Superintendent (Interim)
   **Shannon Hines** ...................................... (614) 644-2223
Liquor Control Superintendent **Bruce D. Stevenson** ...... (614) 644-2360
                                        Fax: (614) 644-2480
Unclaimed Funds Superintendent **Yaw Obeng** .......... (614) 466-4433
■State Fire Marshal **Larry L. Flowers** ................ (614) 752-8200
   E-mail: larry.flowers@com.ohio.gov
Building Appeals Executive Secretary **Susan Steer** ...... (614) 644-2223
Building Standards Executive Secretary
   **Regina Hanshaw** ................................... (614) 644-2613
Ohio Construction Industry Examining Board
   Administrator **Carol Ross** .......................... (614) 644-3495
Chief Financial Officer **David E. Hannan, Jr.** ......... (614) 466-3636
Chief Information Officer **Teresa Philbrick** ............. (614) 466-3636

## Real Estate and Professional Licensing Division

77 South High Street, Columbus, OH 43215-6123
Tel: (614) 466-4100  Fax: (614) 644-0584  E-mail: repld@com.state.oh.us
Internet: www.com.ohio.gov/real

Superintendent **Anne M. Petit** .......................... (614) 644-9734
   Administrative Assistant **Tyler Fehrman** ........... (614) 644-9734

## Development Services Agency

P.O. Box 1001, Columbus, OH 43215-1001
Tel: (614) 466-2480  Tel: (800) 848-1300  Fax: (614) 644-5167

**Employees:** 361  **Fiscal Year:** 2015  **Budget:** $1,197,457,000

■Director **David Goodman** ............................. (614) 466-3379
   E-mail: david.goodman@development.ohio.gov
   Education: Miami U (OH) BA; Case Western JD
   Executive Assistant **Amy Jarvis** .................... (614) 466-3379
   Executive Assistant **Wende Jourdan** ............... (614) 644-6474
Chief of Staff **Andrew Pusateri** ...................... (614) 644-8630
   Minority Business Enterprise Division Director
   **(Vacant)** ........................................... (614) 466-2625
Assistant Director **Matt Peters** ...................... (614) 644-0571
Business Services Division Director **Daryl P. Hennessy** ... (614) 466-3379
Chief Legal Counsel **John Stock** ..................... (614) 466-5017
Chief Financial Officer **Kenyatta A. Chandler** .......... (614) 466-5355

■Governor's Office of Appalachia Director
   **Jason H. Wilson** .................................... (614) 752-9227
   141 College Lane, Poland, OH 44514
   E-mail: jason.wilson@development.ohio.gov
   Education: Ohio State BA; Wheeling Jesuit MBA
Chief Human Resources Officer **Susan Boothe** ........ (614) 466-2072
Communications Deputy Director **Todd Walker** ....... (614) 466-2609
   E-mail: todd.walker@development.ohio.gov
Community Development Division Deputy Director
   **Sadicka White** ..................................... (614) 466-4394
   Education: Ohio Northern 1971 BA; Dayton 1977 MS
Strategic Business Investment Division Director
   **Christopher "Chris" Long** .......................... (614) 466-5656
Export Assistance Assistant Deputy Chief
   **Wesley "Wes" Aubihl** ............................. (614) 644-9759
Technological Innovation Division Deputy Chief
   **Norman Chagnon** .................................. (614) 466-3887
   E-mail: norm.chagnon@development.ohio.gov
Tourism Deputy Chief **Mary Cusick** ................... (614) 466-8844
Community Services Division Chief **Sadicka White** ...... (614) 466-2480

## Department of Developmental Disabilities [DODD]

30 East Broad Street, Columbus, OH 43215
Tel: (800) 617-6733  Fax: (614) 644-5013

**Employees:** 2,402  **Fiscal Year:** 2015  **Budget:** $2,549,522,000

■Director **John L. Martin** .............................. (614) 466-0129
   E-mail: john.martin@dodd.ohio.gov
   Administrative Assistant **Cathy Hutzel** ............. (614) 466-0129
Legislative Affairs and Communications Deputy Director
   **Zachary Haughawout** ............................. (614) 752-4676
   E-mail: zach.haughawout@dodd.ohio.gov
Policy and Strategic Direction Deputy Director
   **Teresa Kobelt** ..................................... (614) 644-6309
Fiscal Administration Deputy Director **Kim Mowery** ..... (614) 466-3081
Human Resources Deputy Director **Antoinette Wallace** ... (614) 466-2508
Information Technology Services Deputy Director
   **Michelle Burk** ..................................... (614) 466-2201
   E-mail: michelle.burk@dodd.ohio.gov
Legal and Oversight Deputy Director **Kate Haller** ........ (614) 466-5216
Medicaid Development and Administration Deputy
   Director **Lori Horvath** .............................. (614) 752-2484
   E-mail: lori.horvath@dodd.ohio.gov
State-Operated Services and Supports Deputy Director
   **Ginnie Whisman** ................................... (740) 393-6228

## Department of Health [ODH]

246 North High Street, Columbus, OH 43215
P.O. Box 15098, Columbus, OH 43215-0098 (Vital Records)
Tel: (614) 466-3543  Tel: (614) 466-2531 (Vital Records)
E-mail: vitalstat@odh.ohio.gov (Vital Records)
Internet: www.odh.ohio.gov

**Employees:** 1,244  **Fiscal Year:** 2015  **Budget:** $667,285,000

■Director **Richard A. "Rick" Hodges** ................. (614) 466-2253
   E-mail: director@odh.ohio.gov
   Education: Oberlin BA
   Executive Assistant **(Vacant)** ...................... (614) 466-2253
Chief of Staff **Julie Walburn** ......................... (614) 466-3543
Chief General Counsel **Lance Himes** ................. (614) 466-4882
   E-mail: lance.himes@odh.ohio.gov
   Education: Wittenberg BB; Cincinnati JD
Medical Director **Dr. Mary DiOrio** ................... (614) 466-3543
   Education: Notre Dame; Ohio State MD
Assistant Counsel/Privacy Officer **Socrates H. Tuch** ... (614) 466-4882
   E-mail: socrates.tuch@odh.ohio.gov
Government Affairs Assistant Director **Jessica Cruz** ...... (614) 728-9166
Chief Administrative Officer **(Vacant)** ................. (614) 644-7756
Vital Statistics State Registrar **Judith B. "Judy" Nagy** ... (614) 466-0538
   Education: Ohio State 1989 BSBA, 1994 BS

---

★ Elected Official   ■ Appointed by Governor   ● Appointed by Legislature   ▲ Appointed by Board or Commission   ◆ Appointed by State Supreme Court

## Office of Financial Affairs

Tel: (614) 466-1863

Chief **(Vacant)** . . . . . . . . . . . . . . . . . . . . . . . . . . . . . . (614) 466-3543
Accounting Unit Chief **Tamara Harrison** . . . . . . (614) 466-3543 ext. 26363
Administrative Services Unit Chief
  **Quanta Brown** . . . . . . . . . . . . . . . . . . . . . (614) 466-3543 ext. 44632
  E-mail: quanta.brown@odh.ohio.gov
Grants Management Unit Chief **Karen Tinsley** . . (614) 466-3543 ext. 47546
  E-mail: karen.tinsley@odh.ohio.gov
Purchasing and Mail Unit Chief
  **Paul Maragos** . . . . . . . . . . . . . . . . . . . . . . (614) 466-3543 ext. 46213

## Office of Management Information Systems

Chief **Nathan Huskey** . . . . . . . . . . . . . . . . . . . . . . (614) 466-3225
  E-mail: nathan.huskey@odh.ohio.gov
Network and Administration Chief **(Vacant)** . . . . . . . . . . . (614) 466-3225
State Registrar **Judith B. "Judy" Nagy** . . . . . . . . . . . . . (614) 466-2531

## Office of Communications

Fax: (614) 644-8208

Director **Russ Kennedy** . . . . . . . . . . . . . . . . . . . . . . (614) 644-8562
  E-mail: russ.kennedy@odh.ohio.gov
Web Manager **Russell Satori** . . . . . . . . . . . . . . . . . . . (614) 644-0176

## Office of Health Assurance and Licensing

Chief **David Holston** . . . . . . . . . . . . . . . . . . . . . . . (614) 466-7857
Community Health Care Chief **Drema Phelps** . . . . . . . . . . (614) 995-7466
Licensure Operations Bureau Chief **Debra Walsh** . . . . . . . (614) 466-4704
  E-mail: debra.walsh@odh.ohio.gov
Long Term Care Bureau Chief **Lea A. Blair** . . . . . . . . . . (614) 752-9524
Regulatory Enforcement Bureau Chief **Brian Dean** . . . . . . (614) 644-6220
  E-mail: brian.dean@odh.ohio.gov
Environmental Health and Radiation Protection Bureau
  Chief **Gene Phillips** . . . . . . . . . . . . . . . . . . . . . . . (614) 644-8480

## Office of Health Improvement and Wellness

Tel: (614) 466-4718

Chief **Shancie Jenkins** . . . . . . . . . . . . . . . . . . . . . . (614) 466-4718
                                                           Fax: (614) 728-9163
Maternal and Child Health Bureau Chief (Interim)
  **Theresa Seagraves** . . . . . . . . . . . . . . . . . . . . . . . (614) 466-5332
Health Promotion Bureau Chief **Heather Reed** . . . . . . . . . (614) 466-8933
Health Services Bureau Chief **Michele Frizzell** . . . . . . . . (614) 644-8006
  Education: Ohio State 1977 BS; Dayton 1990 MBA    Fax: (614) 564-2470

## Division of Prevention and Health Promotion

246 North High Street, Columbus, OH 43215
Tel: (614) 466-0302

Environmental Health Bureau Chief **(Vacant)** . . . . . . . . . . (614) 466-1390
Health Promotion and Risk Reduction Bureau Chief
  **(Vacant)** . . . . . . . . . . . . . . . . . . . . . . . . . . . . . (614) 466-2144
Infectious Disease Control Bureau Chief
  **Sietske De-Fijter** . . . . . . . . . . . . . . . . . (614) 995-5599 ext. 60239
Laboratory Bureau Chief **Rose Marie Gearhart** . . . . . . . . (614) 644-4632
Radiation Protection Bureau Chief
  **Michael Snee** . . . . . . . . . . . . . . . . . . . . . (614) 466-3543 ext. 42732

## Department of Insurance [ODI]

50 West Town Street, 3rd Floor, Suite 300, Columbus, OH 43215-1067
Tel: (614) 644-2658  Fax: (614) 644-3743

**Employees:** 252

■Director **Mary Taylor, CPA** . . . . . . . . . . . . . . . . . . . (614) 728-1003
  E-mail: mary.taylor@insurance.ohio.gov
  Education: Akron 1989 BS, 1998 MA
Deputy Director **Jillian Froment** . . . . . . . . . . . . . . . . (614) 728-1059

Health Policy and Product Coordination Assistant
  Director **Carrie Haughawout** . . . . . . . . . . . . . . . . . . (614) 387-0411
  E-mail: carrie.haughawout@insurance.ohio.gov
Communications Chief **Leslie Minnich** . . . . . . . . . . . . . (614) 728-1292
  E-mail: leslie.minnich@insurance.ohio.gov
Ohio Senior Health Insurance and Information Program
  Chief **Christina "Chris" Reeg** . . . . . . . . . . . . . . . . . (614) 644-3464
  Education: Ohio Dominican U BBA
Fraud and Enforcement and Assistant Director
  **Michelle Rafeld** . . . . . . . . . . . . . . . . . . . . . . . . . (614) 728-1009
Licensing Chief **Karen Vourvopoulos** . . . . . . . . . . . . . . (614) 728-1249
Market Conduct Chief **Angela Dingus** . . . . . . . . . . . . . . (614) 644-2663
Legislative Liaison **Allison Conklin** . . . . . . . . . . . . . . (614) 644-2475
  E-mail: allison.conklin@insurance.ohio.gov
  Education: Wittenberg
Chief Administrative Officer and Director of Consumer
  Relations **Tynesia Dorsey** . . . . . . . . . . . . . . . . . . . (614) 728-1111
Regulatory Compliance Director **Todd Oberholtzer** . . . . . . (614) 387-1459

## Department of Job and Family Services [ODJFS]

30 East Broad Street, 32nd Floor, Columbus, OH 43215-3414
Tel: (614) 466-2100  Internet: www.jfs.ohio.gov

**Employees:** 3,724  **Fiscal Year:** 2015  **Budget:** $3,099,681,000

■Director **Cynthia C. Dungey** . . . . . . . . . . . . . . . . . . (614) 466-6283
  E-mail: cynthia.dungey@jfs.ohio.gov
  Executive Assistant **Susan "Sue" Burns** . . . . . . . . . . . (614) 466-6283
Assistant Director **Michael McCreight** . . . . . . . . . . . . . (614) 466-6283
Chief Operating Officer **Jayme Brown** . . . . . . . . . . . . . (614) 466-6283
Employment Services Assistant Director **Bruce Madson** . . (614) 466-6283
  Executive Assistant **Joyce Richardson** . . . . . . . . . . . (614) 466-6283

## Office of the Chief Inspector

Tel: (614) 466-3015  Tel: (800) 260-5627 (Emergency Line)
Fax: (614) 466-0207

Deputy Director **Robert L. Ferguson** . . . . . . . . . . . . . . (614) 387-0553
  Administrative Assistant **Jody Nichols** . . . . . . . . . . . . (614) 466-3015
Security Manager **Steve D. Jones** . . . . . . . . . . . . . . . (614) 466-9272
  4020 East 5th Avenue, Columbus, OH 43219    Fax: (614) 728-7294
Investigations Manager **Steven Johnson** . . . . . . . . . . . . (614) 752-3757

## Office of Child Support

50 West Town Street, Columbus, OH 43215
Tel: (800) 686-1556 (Customer Inquiries Consumer Hotline)
Fax: (614) 995-7159

Deputy Director **Jeffrey M. "Jeff" Aldridge** . . . . . . . . . . (614) 728-5193
  E-mail: jeffrey.aldridge@jfs.ohio.gov
Information Services Chief **Patrick D. Stricker** . . . . . . . . (614) 752-2638
  E-mail: pat.stricker@jfs.ohio.gov
Outreach and Grants Management Deputy Director
  **Athena Riley** . . . . . . . . . . . . . . . . . . . . . . . . . . (614) 752-2649
Program Services Administrator **David Fleischman** . . . . . . (614) 752-2644
  E-mail: david.fleischman@jfs.ohio.gov
Fiscal and Monitoring Chief **Eric Mency** . . . . . . . . . . . . (614) 644-9512

## Office of Media Relations

30 East Broad Street, 32nd Floor, Columbus, OH 43215
Tel: (614) 466-6650  TTY: (614) 752-3951  Fax: (614) 466-0292

Deputy Director **Angela Terez** . . . . . . . . . . . . . . . . . . (614) 466-8390
Legislation Deputy Director **Daniel J. Fitzpatrick** . . . . . . . (614) 644-0801
  E-mail: daniel.fitzpatrick@jfs.ohio.gov

## Office of Families and Children

50 West Town Street, Sixth Floor, Suite 400, Columbus, OH 43215-5222
Tel: (614) 466-4815  Fax: (614) 752-7193

Deputy Director **Jennifer R. Justice** . . . . . . . . . . . . . . (614) 466-1213
Fiscal Accountability Program Assistant Deputy Director
  **Daniel Shook** . . . . . . . . . . . . . . . . . . . . . . . . . . (614) 752-0619
Office of Family Assistance Deputy Director
  **Kara Bertke Wente** . . . . . . . . . . . . . . . . . . . . . . . (614) 466-4815

*(continued on next page)*

---

★ Elected Official    ■ Appointed by Governor    ● Appointed by Legislature    ▲ Appointed by Board or Commission    ◆ Appointed by State Supreme Court

**Office of Families and Children** *continued*

Child Care and Early Child Development Deputy
Director **Alicia Leatherman** . . . . . . . . . . . . . . . . . . . . . (614) 752-2196
E-mail: alicia.leatherman@jfs.ohio.gov
Automated Systems Bureau Chief **Kevin Bullock** . . . . . . . . (513) 551-1940
E-mail: kevin.bullock@jfs.ohio.gov
Child Care and Development Bureau Chief
**Michelle Albast** . . . . . . . . . . . . . . . . . . . . . . . . . . . (614) 752-0582
Protection Services Child/Adult Bureau Chief
**Lisa M. Wiltshire** . . . . . . . . . . . . . . . . . . . . . . . . . (614) 752-0655
Administrative Assistant **Joanna Valentine** . . . . . . . . . . . . (614) 466-1213

## Office of Employee and Business Services

30 East Broad Street, 30th Floor, Columbus, OH 43215-3414
Tel: (614) 466-4503  Fax: (614) 644-1208

Deputy Director **Tiffany Richardson** . . . . . . . . . . . . . . . . . (614) 466-5456
Business Operations Manager **Jeffrey A. Hissem** . . . . . . (614) 728-2315
Employee Services Assistant Deputy Director **(Vacant)** . . . . (614) 466-4503
Employee and Organizational Development Program
Administrator **Anita L. Jennings** . . . . . . . . . . . . . . . . . . (614) 466-8409
30 East Broad Street, 32nd Floor,          Fax: (614) 728-5858
Columbus, OH 43215-0421

## Office of Fiscal and Monitoring Services

30 East Broad Street, 37th Floor, Columbus, OH 43215-3414
Tel: (614) 466-9195  Fax: (614) 995-5004  E-mail: fiscal@odjfs.state.oh.us

Chief Fiscal Officer **Eric Mency** . . . . . . . . . . . . . . . . . . . (614) 644-9512
Administrative Assistant **Sharon Fletcher** . . . . . . . . . . . . . (614) 728-8490
Assistant Deputy Director **Thomas Holsinger** . . . . . . . . . . (614) 466-9200
Assistant Deputy Director **Eric Zhang** . . . . . . . . . . . . . . . (614) 752-3149
Accounting Bureau Chief **Yvonne Gore** . . . . . . . . . . . . . . (614) 466-9596
Fax: (614) 466-1376
Budget and Cost Management Fiscal Officer
**Kurtis Wingo** . . . . . . . . . . . . . . . . . . . . . . . . . . . . . (614) 644-5220
Fax: (614) 995-5400

## Office of Information Services

Air Center, 4200 East Fifth Avenue, Columbus, OH 43219
Tel: (614) 466-2303  Fax: (614) 752-6815

Chief Information Officer **(Vacant)** . . . . . . . . . . . . . . . . . . (614) 466-2303
Information Technology Portfolio Management Chief
**(Vacant)** . . . . . . . . . . . . . . . . . . . . . . . . . . . . . . . . (614) 387-8607
Application Development Assistant Deputy Director
**Sylvan Wilson** . . . . . . . . . . . . . . . . . . . . . . . . . . . . . (614) 466-2303
E-mail: sylvan.wilson@jfs.ohio.gov

## Office of Legal and Acquisition Services

30 East Broad Street, 31st Floor, Columbus, OH 43215-3414
Tel: (614) 466-4605  TTY: (614) 728-2985  Fax: (614) 752-8298
E-mail: legal@odjfs.state.oh.us

Deputy Director and Chief Legal Counsel
**Lewis C. George** . . . . . . . . . . . . . . . . . . . . . . . . . . . (614) 466-1988
State Hearings Chief **Judith L. Cicatiello** . . . . . . . . . . . . . (614) 644-6905
Administrative Assistant **Julie R. Malfe** . . . . . . . . . . . . . . (614) 466-4605

## Office of Unemployment Compensation

4020 East Fifth Avenue, Columbus, OH 43219
Tel: (614) 446-5492  Fax: (614) 466-6873

Deputy Director **Julie A. Smith** . . . . . . . . . . . . . . . . . . . . (614) 466-5492
Benefits and Technology Assistant Deputy Director
**Marge Benton** . . . . . . . . . . . . . . . . . . . . . . . . . . . . . (614) 466-3657
E-mail: jeff.long@jfs.ohio.gov
Tax and Employer Services Assistant Deputy Director
**Marcia Macon-Bruce** . . . . . . . . . . . . . . . . . . . . . . . . (614) 644-3109

Tax and Integrity Assistant Deputy Director
**Kimberly Lind** . . . . . . . . . . . . . . . . . . . . . . . . . . . . . (614) 644-3610
Program Administrator II **(Vacant)** . . . . . . . . . . . . . . . . . (614) 466-5492

## Office of Workforce Development

4020 East Fifth Avenue, Columbus, OH 43219
Tel: (614) 752-3091  Fax: (614) 995-1298  Internet: www.jfs.ohio.gov/owd
E-mail: workforce@jfs.ohio.gov

Deputy Director **John B. Weber** . . . . . . . . . . . . . . . . . . . (614) 466-9494
Program Management Assistant Deputy Director
**Alice Worrell** . . . . . . . . . . . . . . . . . . . . . . . . . . . . . . (614) 752-3091
Labor Market Information Chief **Coretta Pettway** . . . . . . (614) 466-9820
Veterans Services Program Administrator
**Ryan J. Thompson** . . . . . . . . . . . . . . . . . . . . . . . . . . (614) 644-0978
Areas Covered: West District.

## Department of Medicaid

50 West Town Street, Suite 400, Columbus, OH 43215
Tel: (800) 324-8680  Internet: medicaid.ohio.gov

Medicaid Director **John B. McCarthy** . . . . . . . . . . . . . . . (614) 466-4443
Education: Indiana 1994 BA, 1994 MPA
Chief Financial Officer **(Vacant)** . . . . . . . . . . . . . . . . . . . (614) 644-0140
Chief Policy Officer **(Vacant)** . . . . . . . . . . . . . . . . . . . . . (614) 752-3634
Chief Strategic Officer **(Vacant)** . . . . . . . . . . . . . . . . . . . (614) 466-4443
Chief of Staff **Jennifer D. Demory** . . . . . . . . . . . . . . . . . (614) 466-0140
Community Access Policy Chief **(Vacant)** . . . . . . . . . . . . (614) 644-7130
30 East Broad Street, Columbus, OH 43215          Fax: (614) 644-9358
Health Plan Policy and Management Bureau Chief
**(Vacant)** . . . . . . . . . . . . . . . . . . . . . . . . . . . . . . . . (614) 752-4766
Longterm Care Services and Support Chief **(Vacant)** . . . . . (614) 752-3633
Fax: (614) 387-7661
Communications Director **Sam Rossi** . . . . . . . . . . . . . . . (614) 752-3747
Managed Care Bureau Chief **Patrick Stephan** . . . . . . . . . (614) 752-2660
Tel: (614) 752-3842
Program Integrity Director **John Maynard** . . . . . . . . . . . . (614) 752-2799

## Department of Mental Health and Addiction Services [MHAS]

30 East Broad Street, 8th Floor, Columbus, OH 43215-3430
Tel: (614) 466-2596  TTY: (614) 752-9696  Fax: (614) 752-9453
Internet: mha.ohio.gov

**Employees:** 2,679  **Fiscal Year:** 2015  **Budget:** $661,747,000

■Director **Tracy J. Plouck** . . . . . . . . . . . . . . . . . . . . . . . (614) 466-2337
E-mail: tracy.plouck@mh.ohio.gov
Legislative Liaison and Public Affairs
**Melissa A. "Missy" Craddock** . . . . . . . . . . . . . . . . . . (614) 644-6791
E-mail: melissa.craddock@mh.ohio.gov
Administrative Assistant **Nicole Marx** . . . . . . . . . . . . . . . . (614) 466-2337
Chief Legal Counsel **Michaela Peterson** . . . . . . . . . . . . . (614) 728-5682
Quality and Planning Deputy Director **Sanford Starr** . . . . . (614) 644-8316
Education: Ohio State 1977 BS, 1980 MSW
Prevention Services Division Chief **(Vacant)** . . . . . . . . . . . (614) 752-8356
Communications Chief **Trudy Sharp** . . . . . . . . . . . . . . . . (614) 644-6518
E-mail: trudy.sharp@mh.ohio.gov
Chief Fiscal Officer **Daniel Schreiber** . . . . . . . . . . . . . . . (614) 644-8219

## Department of Natural Resources [ODNR]

2045 Morse Road, Columbus, OH 43229-6693
Tel: (614) 265-6565  TTY: (800) 750-0750  Fax: (614) 261-9601
E-mail: dnrmail@dnr.state.oh.us

**Employees:** 2,660  **Fiscal Year:** 2015  **Budget:** $325,298,000

■Director **James J. "Jim" Zehringer** . . . . . . . . . . . . . . . . (614) 265-6879
E-mail: james.zehringer@dnr.state.oh.us
Assistant Director **Eric Harrell** . . . . . . . . . . . . . . . . . . . . (614) 265-6789
E-mail: eric.c.harrell@das.ohio.gov
Chief Legal Counsel **Michael "Mike" Williams** . . . . . . . . (614) 265-6882
E-mail: michael.williams@dnr.state.oh.us

---

★ Elected Official   ■ Appointed by Governor   ● Appointed by Legislature   ▲ Appointed by Board or Commission   ◆ Appointed by State Supreme Court

Deputy Director **Andy Ware** . . . . . . . . . . . . . . . . . . . . . . . (614) 265-6877
　E-mail: andy.ware@dnr.state.oh.us
Budget and Finance Chief **Tom Johnston** . . . . . . . . . . . . . (614) 265-6801
Communications Chief **Bethany McCorkle** . . . . . . . . . . . . (614) 265-6873
　E-mail: bethany.mccorkle@dnr.state.oh.us
Human Resources Chief **Michael Luers** . . . . . . . . . . . . . . (614) 265-6879
Information Technology Office Chief (Acting)
　**Donovan Powers** . . . . . . . . . . . . . . . . . . . . . . . . . . . . (614) 265-6844
　E-mail: donovan.powers@dnr.state.oh.us
Legislative Services Office Chief **Brittney Colvin** . . . . . . . (614) 265-7989
　E-mail: brittney.colvin@dnr.state.oh.us
Engineering Division Chief **Hung Thai** . . . . . . . . . . . . . . . (614) 265-6714
　E-mail: hung.thai@dnr.state.oh.us
Forestry Division Chief **Bob Boyles** . . . . . . . . . . . . . . . . . (614) 265-6699
Geological Survey Chief **Tom Serenko** . . . . . . . . . . . . . . .(614) 265-6598
Mineral Resources Management Chief **Lanny Erdos** . . . . . . (614) 265-7072
Natural Areas and Preserves Division Chief
　**Gary Obermiller** . . . . . . . . . . . . . . . . . . . . . . . . . . . . (614) 265-6475
Parks and Recreation Division Chief **Gary Obermiller** . . . . (614) 265-6475
　E-mail: gary.obermiller@dnr.state.oh.us
Soil and Water Resources Division Chief **Michael Bailey** . . (614) 265-6618
　Education: Ohio State BA, MA
Watercraft Division Chief **Mike Miller** . . . . . . . . . . . . . . . (614) 265-6475
Wildlife Division Chief **Scott Zody** . . . . . . . . . . . . . . . . . (614) 265-6311
　E-mail: scott.zody@dnr.state.oh.us
　Education: Ashland 1988 BS
Coastal Management Office Chief **Scudder Mackey** . . . . . . (419) 626-7982
Law Enforcement Coordinator **(Vacant)** . . . . . . . . . . . . . . (614) 265-7067
External Auditor **Emily A. Hay, CPA** . . . . . . . . . . . . . . . . (614) 265-6675
　Education: Ohio State 1996 BSBA
Webmaster **Shaun Casbarro** . . . . . . . . . . . . . . . . . . . . . . (614) 265-6863
　E-mail: shaun.casbarro@dnr.state.oh.us

# Department of Public Safety [ODPS]

1970 West Broad Street, Columbus, OH 43223
P.O. Box 182081, Columbus, OH 43223
Tel: (614) 466-2550　Fax: (614) 466-0433
Internet: www.publicsafety.ohio.gov

**Employees: 3,708　Fiscal Year: 2015　Budget: $693,977,000**

■Director **John Born** . . . . . . . . . . . . . . . . . . . . . . . . . . . . (614) 466-3383
　E-mail: john.born@dvs.ohio.gov
Assistant Director **Joseph Montgomery** . . . . . . . . . . . . . . (614) 466-3383
　E-mail: jmontgomery@dps.state.oh.us
Chief of Staff **Mark Gibson** . . . . . . . . . . . . . . . . . . . . . . . (614) 466-3383
　Program Administrator **Melva Dodd** . . . . . . . . . . . . . . . (614) 752-4569
　Project Manager **Jeff Grayson** . . . . . . . . . . . . . . . . . . . (614) 387-3171
　Program Administrator **Frances Huggins** . . . . . . . . . . . . (614) 387-1454
Communications Director **Joseph "Joe" Andrews** . . . . . . (614) 466-6178
　E-mail: jandrews@dps.ohio.gov　　　　　Fax: (614) 752-8410
　Assistant Communications Director **Kristen Castle** . . . . (614) 728-4623
　E-mail: kcastle@dps.ohio.gov　　　　　　Fax: (614) 752-8410
Chief Legal Counsel **Heather Frient** . . . . . . . . . . . . . . . . . (614) 466-7014
Legislative Liaison **Andrew Bowsher** . . . . . . . . . . . . . . . (614) 752-0422
　E-mail: abowsher@dps.state.oh.us　　　　Fax: (614) 752-6063
Legislative Liaison **Alex Lapso** . . . . . . . . . . . . . . . . . . . . (614) 752-0422
　E-mail: alapso@dps.state.oh.us　　　　　Fax: (614) 752-6063

## Administration

Tel: (614) 466-6973

Director **(Vacant)** . . . . . . . . . . . . . . . . . . . . . . . . . . . . . . (614) 466-6973
　　　　　　　　　　　　　　　　　　　　　　　Fax: (614) 995-5153
Human Resources and Labor Relations Administrator
　**(Vacant)** . . . . . . . . . . . . . . . . . . . . . . . . . . . . . . . . . . . (614) 466-4570
　　　　　　　　　　　　　　　　　　　　　　　Fax: (614) 752-9842
Chief Information Officer **Brent Rawlins** . . . . . . . . . . . . . . (614) 644-4430
　E-mail: brawlins@dps.state.oh.us
EEO (Equal Employment Opportunity) Safety and Health
　Coordinator **Toby Ferguson** . . . . . . . . . . . . . . . . . . . . (614) 466-7651

# Office of Criminal Justice Services

1970 West Broad Street, Columbus, OH 43223
Tel: (614) 466-7782　Tel: (888) 448-4842　Fax: (614) 466-5061
E-mail: webmaster@ocjs.state.oh.us　Internet: www.ocjs.ohio.gov

■Director **Karhlton Moore** . . . . . . . . . . . . . . . . . . . . . . . . .(614) 466-7782
　E-mail: kmoore@dps.state.oh.us
Chief Policy Advisor **Carol Ellensohn** . . . . . . . . . . . . . . . (614) 466-1830
　E-mail: cellensohn@dps.state.oh.us
Assistant Policy Advisor **(Vacant)** . . . . . . . . . . . . . . . . . . (614) 466-0286
Driver Training Program Coordinator **Valerie Walb** . . . . . . (614) 466-3250

# Emergency Management Agency

2855 West Dublin-Granville Road, Columbus, OH 43235-2206
Tel: (614) 889-7150　Fax: (614) 889-7183
E-mail: ohioema@dps.state.oh.us　Internet: www.ema.ohio.gov

Executive Director **Sima Merick** . . . . . . . . . . . . . . . . . . . . (614) 889-7152
Assistant Director **Lt. Col. Dan Kolcum** . . . . . . . . . . . . . .(614) 799-3675
Preparation Branch Chief **Andrew Elder** . . . . . . . . . . . . . . (614) 889-7178
Technology Support Branch Chief **(Vacant)** . . . . . . . . . . . . (614) 889-7155
Communications Branch Chief **Dave Ford** . . . . . . . . . . . . . (614) 889-7154
　E-mail: rdford@dps.ohio.gov
Data Management Branch Chief **(Vacant)** . . . . . . . . . . . . . (614) 889-7157
Logistics Plan Branch Chief **Phil Johnson** . . . . . . . . . . . . .(614) 799-3838
Mitigation Branch Chief **Steve Ferryman** . . . . . . . . . . . . . (614) 799-3539
Recovery Branch Chief **Laura Adcock** . . . . . . . . . . . . . . . (614) 799-3539
Plans Branch Chief **(Vacant)** . . . . . . . . . . . . . . . . . . . . . . (614) 799-3688
Radiological Branch Chief **Mike Bear** . . . . . . . . . . . . . . . .(614) 799-3915
Readiness and Response Branch Chief
　**James Dwertman** . . . . . . . . . . . . . . . . . . . . . . . . . . . . .(614) 799-3692
Public Information Officer **Jay Carey** . . . . . . . . . . . . . . . . (614) 799-3695

# Emergency Medical Services

P.O. Box 182073, Columbus, OH 43218-2073
Tel: (800) 233-0785　Fax: (614) 466-9461　Internet: ems.ohio.gov

Executive Director **Melvin House** . . . . . . . . . . . . . . . . . . . (614) 995-4752
　　　　　　　　　　　　　　　　　　　　　　　Fax: (614) 995-7012

# Investigative Unit Division

1970 West Broad Street, Columbus, OH 43223-1102

Executive Director **Gary Allen** . . . . . . . . . . . . . . . . . . . . . (614) 644-2415
　E-mail: gallen@dps.state.oh.us　　　　　Fax: (614) 644-2463
Deputy Director **Jeremy Landis** . . . . . . . . . . . . . . . . . . . . (614) 644-2533
　E-mail: jlandis@dps.state.oh.us

# Bureau of Motor Vehicles

P.O. Box 16520, Columbus, OH 43216-6520
Tel: (614) 752-7500　Fax: (614) 752-7972　Internet: www.bmv.ohio.gov

Registrar **Don Petit** . . . . . . . . . . . . . . . . . . . . . . . . . . . . . (614) 387-3000
　E-mail: dpetit@dps.state.oh.us
Assistant Registrar **Anne Dean** . . . . . . . . . . . . . . . . . . . . (614) 387-3000

# Ohio State Highway Patrol [OSHP]

P.O. Box 182074, Columbus, OH 43218-2074
Tel: (614) 466-2660　Fax: (614) 644-9749
Internet: www.statepatrol.ohio.gov

Superintendent **Col Paul Pride** . . . . . . . . . . . . . . . . . . . . .(614) 466-2990
　Education: Ohio State AS
Administration Assistant Superintendent
　**Lt. Col. Kevin Teaford** . . . . . . . . . . . . . . . . . . . . . . . . (614) 466-2990
Operations Assistant Superintendent
　**Lt. Col. George Williams** . . . . . . . . . . . . . . . . . . . . . .(614) 466-2990
Public Information Officer **Craig Cvetan** . . . . . . . . . . . . . . (614) 466-2660
　E-mail: ccvetan@dps.state.oh.us

# Homeland Security

1970 West Broad Street, Columbus, OH 43223-1102
P.O. Box 182081, Columbus, OH 43218-2081
Tel: (614) 387-6171

Executive Director **Capt. Rick Zwayer** . . . . . . . . . . . . . . . (614) 644-1002
　Education: Naval Postgrad 2014　　　　　Fax: (614) 752-2419

---

★ Elected Official　　■ Appointed by Governor　　● Appointed by Legislature　　▲ Appointed by Board or Commission　　◆ Appointed by State Supreme Court

# Department of Rehabilitation and Correction [DRC]

770 West Broad Street, Columbus, OH 43222
Tel: (614) 752-1153 Fax: (614) 752-1086 Internet: www.drc.ohio.gov

**Employees:** 11,986 **Fiscal Year:** 2015 **Budget:** $1,627,633,000

■Director **Gary C. Mohr** . . . . . . . . . . . . . . . . . . . . . . . . . . . . (614) 752-1153
   E-mail: gary.mohr@odrc.state.oh.us
Operations Managing Director **Edwin Voorhies** . . . . . . . . (614) 752-1162
Administration Deputy Director **Kevin Stockdale** . . . . . . . (614) 752-0283
   E-mail: kevin.stockdale@odrc.state.oh.us
   Education: Ohio State 2004 BA, 2007 MPA
Human Resources Deputy Director **Kim Rowe** . . . . . . . . . . (614) 752-1795
Chief Inspector **Roger Wilson** . . . . . . . . . . . . . . . . . . . . . (614) 752-1765
   E-mail: roger.wilson@odrc.state.oh.us
Communications Chief **Joellen Smith** . . . . . . . . . . . . . . . . (614) 752-1150
   E-mail: joellen.smith@odrc.state.oh.us
Legal Counsel Chief **Stephen Gray** . . . . . . . . . . . . . . . . . . (614) 752-1765
   E-mail: stephen.gray@odrc.state.oh.us
Information and Technology Services Bureau Chief
   **Vinko Kucinic** . . . . . . . . . . . . . . . . . . . . . . . . . . . . . . . . (614) 752-1313
   E-mail: vinko.kucinic@odrc.state.oh.us

## Parole and Community Services

Court and Community Managing Director
   **Cynthia Mausser** . . . . . . . . . . . . . . . . . . . . . . . . . . . . . (614) 752-1235

## Office of Enterprise Development

Administrator **William A. "Will" Eleby** . . . . . . . . . . . . . . . (614) 752-1419
   E-mail: william.eleby@odrc.state.oh.us

# Department of Taxation

30 East Broad Street, Columbus, OH 43215
4485 Northland Ridge Boulevard, Columbus, OH 43229
Tel: (614) 466-0093 (General Information)
Tel: (614) 466-2166 (Tax Commissioner's Office) TTY: (800) 750-0750
Fax: (614) 466-6401

**Employees:** 1,240 **Fiscal Year:** 2015 **Budget:** $1,897,144,000

■Tax Commissioner **Joseph W. "Joe" Testa** . . . . . . . . . . . (614) 466-2166
   E-mail: joseph.testa@tax.state.oh.us
   Education: Central Florida BA; Ohio State
Chief Counsel **Matthew H. Chafin** . . . . . . . . . . . . . . . . . . (614) 466-2166
Deputy Chief Counsel **(Vacant)** . . . . . . . . . . . . . . . . . . . . (614) 466-2166
Compliance/Audit Deputy Tax Commissioner
   **Marjorie A. Kruse** . . . . . . . . . . . . . . . . . . . . . . . . . . . . (614) 466-2166
Enforcement and Tax Equalization Deputy Tax
   Commissioner **Stanley Dixon** . . . . . . . . . . . . . . . . . . . . (614) 466-2166
Information Technology Deputy Tax Commissioner
   **Mark Walker** . . . . . . . . . . . . . . . . . . . . . . . . . . . . . . . . (614) 387-1800
   E-mail: mark.walker@tax.state.oh.us
Policy/Budget Deputy Tax Commissioner **Nicholas Cipiti** . . (614) 466-2166
Communications Director **Gary Gudmundson** . . . . . . . . . (614) 466-0099
   E-mail: gary.gudmundson@tax.state.oh.us
Audit Executive Administrator
   **Joseph "Joe" Hammond** . . . . . . . . . . . . . . . . . . . . . . . (614) 387-1802
Appeals Management Executive Administrator
   **Margaret Brewer** . . . . . . . . . . . . . . . . . . . . . . . . . . . . (614) 466-6750
   E-mail: margaret.brewer@tax.state.oh.us
Excise and Energy - Personal Property - CAT Executive
   Administrator **Sarah O'Leary** . . . . . . . . . . . . . . . . . . . . (614) 387-0124
Human Resources Executive Administrator **Steven Gray** . . (614) 466-3020
Processing Center Executive Administrator **Ron Pottorf** . . . (614) 466-2425
Real Estate Executive Administrator **Shelley Wilson** . . . . . (614) 466-5744
Taxpayer Appeals Executive Administrator
   **Charles Rhilinger** . . . . . . . . . . . . . . . . . . . . . . . . . . . . (614) 466-6750
Taxpayer Services/Compliance Executive Administrator
   **Ron Pottorf** . . . . . . . . . . . . . . . . . . . . . . . . . . . . . . . . (614) 466-2425
   E-mail: ron.pottorf@tax.state.oh.us
Bankruptcy Administrator **Rebecca L. Daum** . . . . . . . . . . (614) 752-6864
   E-mail: rebecca.daum@tax.state.oh.us
Business/Tax Administrator (Acting) **Alan Moore** . . . . . . . (614) 466-1614
Commercial Activity Tax (CAT) Administrator
   **Jennifer McFarland** . . . . . . . . . . . . . . . . . . . . . . . . . . (614) 466-8667

Compliance Administrator **David Peck** . . . . . . . . . . . . . . . (614) 752-9909
Discovery Unit Administrator **David Peck** . . . . . . . . . . . . . (614) 752-9909
Enforcement Administrator **Rick Shirk** . . . . . . . . . . . . . . . (614) 466-6939
   E-mail: rick.shirk@tax.state.oh.us
Energy Tax Administrator **Will Ditto** . . . . . . . . . . . . . . . . . (614) 466-8613
Excise Tax Administrator **Will Ditto** . . . . . . . . . . . . . . . . . (614) 466-8613
   E-mail: will.ditto@tax.state.oh.us
Income and School District Tax Administrator
   **Deborah D. Smith** . . . . . . . . . . . . . . . . . . . . . . . . . . . (614) 387-0224
Legislation Administrator **Tim Lynch** . . . . . . . . . . . . . . . . (614) 466-5461
   E-mail: tim.lynch@tax.state.oh.us
Revenue Accounting Administrator
   **Michael "Mike" O'Leary** . . . . . . . . . . . . . . . . . . . . . . . (614) 466-7150
Sales and Use Tax Administrator **Jennifer McFarland** . . . . (614) 466-8667
Tax Analysis Administrator **Gregory Siegfried** . . . . . . . . . (614) 466-0098
   E-mail: gregory.siegfried@tax.state.oh.us
Tax Policy/Analysis Executive **Gregory Siegfried** . . . . . . . (614) 752-7412
Taxpayer Services Administrator **Brenda McDonald** . . . . . (614) 466-8145
Fiscal Services Executive Director
   **Michael "Mike" O'Leary** . . . . . . . . . . . . . . . . . . . . . . . (614) 466-6405
ISD (Information Services Division) Chief Information
   Officer **Mark Walker** . . . . . . . . . . . . . . . . . . . . . . . . . . (614) 995-0365
   E-mail: mark.walker@tax.state.oh.us
Forms and Purchasing Administrative Officer
   **Terry Wadlington** . . . . . . . . . . . . . . . . . . . . . . . . . . . . (614) 466-5164
Problem Resolution Officer **Einon Plummer** . . . . . . . . . . . (614) 466-0832
Facilities Management **Donald Cox** . . . . . . . . . . . . . . . . . (614) 466-5287
Records Management **Sandy Weimer** . . . . . . . . . . . . . . . (614) 466-5348
Internal Auditor **Bradford P. Arnold** . . . . . . . . . . . . . . . . (614) 466-3953
Organizational Development Administrator
   **Stacey Savarise** . . . . . . . . . . . . . . . . . . . . . . . . . . . . . (614) 466-7683

# Department of Transportation [ODOT]

1980 West Broad Street, Columbus, OH 43223
Tel: (614) 466-7170 TTY: (614) 466-3174 Fax: (614) 644-8662
Internet: www.dot.state.oh.us

**Employees:** 5,883 **Fiscal Year:** 2015 **Budget:** $1,878,028,000

■Director **Jerry Wray** . . . . . . . . . . . . . . . . . . . . . . . . . . . . . (614) 466-2335
   E-mail: jerry.wray@dot.state.oh.us

## Business and Human Resources

Business and Human Resources Assistant Director
   **David Coyle** . . . . . . . . . . . . . . . . . . . . . . . . . . . . . . . . . (614) 466-8990

## Facilities Services Division

1980 West Broad Street, Columbus, OH 43223
Assistant Director **David Coyle** . . . . . . . . . . . . . . . . . . . . (614) 387-5178
   E-mail: david.coyle@dot.state.oh.us
Facilities Management Office Administrator
   **Stephen "Steve" Masters** . . . . . . . . . . . . . . . . . . . . . . (614) 752-0415
Equipment Management Administration
   **Stephen "Steve" Masters** . . . . . . . . . . . . . . . . . . . . . . (614) 752-0415
   1620 W. Broad Street, Columbus, OH 43215
   E-mail: stephen.masters@dot.state.oh.us

## Finance Division

Deputy Director **Rich Winning** . . . . . . . . . . . . . . . . . . . . . (614) 644-5424
Accounting Office Administrator **Jim Snyder** . . . . . . . . . . (614) 752-6699
Budget and Statistics Office Administrator **Jana Cassidy** . . (614) 644-7892
Payroll and Federal Accounting Office Administrator
   **(Vacant)** . . . . . . . . . . . . . . . . . . . . . . . . . . . . . . . . . . . (614) 644-6395

## Human Resources Division

Deputy Director **Anne Fornshell** . . . . . . . . . . . . . . . . . . . . (614) 466-8992
Labor Relations Office Administrator **Anne Fornshell** . . . . (614) 466-6113
Personnel Administrator **Mike Bussa** . . . . . . . . . . . . . . . . (614) 466-4692
Training Office Administrator **(Vacant)** . . . . . . . . . . . . . . . (614) 351-2895

## Information Technology Division

Deputy Director **Bill Taylor** . . . . . . . . . . . . . . . . . . . . . . . (614) 466-3553
   E-mail: bill.taylor@dot.state.oh.us

---

★ Elected Official   ■ Appointed by Governor   ● Appointed by Legislature   ▲ Appointed by Board or Commission   ◆ Appointed by State Supreme Court

Application Services Office Administrator **Charles Ash** . . . (614) 466-7007
E-mail: charles.ash@dot.state.oh.us

## Planning Division
Tel: (614) 466-7493

Planning Deputy Director **Jennifer Townley** . . . . . . . . . . . (614) 466-7493
Administrative Assistant **Lisa Hall** . . . . . . . . . . . . . . . . . . . (614) 644-0273

## Field Operations
Field Operations Assistant Director
**Michael C. Flynn, PE** . . . . . . . . . . . . . . . . . . . . . . . . . . . (614) 466-8991

## Transportation Policy
Transportation Policy and Chief Engineer Assistant
Director **James A. Barna, PE** . . . . . . . . . . . . . . . . . . . . (614) 466-8990
E-mail: james.barna@dot.state.oh.us

## Engineering Division
Materials Management Office Administrator
**Lisa Zigmund** . . . . . . . . . . . . . . . . . . . . . . . . . . . . . . . . . . (614) 275-1351
1600 W. Broad St., Columbus, OH 43215
E-mail: lisa.zigmund@dot.state.oh.us
Structural Engineering Office Administrator **Tim Keller** . . . (614) 466-3893
E-mail: tim.keller@dot.state.oh.us

## Policy and Legislative Services
Legislative Services Office Deputy Director
**Andrew Bremer** . . . . . . . . . . . . . . . . . . . . . . . . . . . . . . . . (614) 466-8480
E-mail: andrew.bremer@dot.state.oh.us
Legislative Liaison **Johann Klein** . . . . . . . . . . . . . . . . . . . . (614) 466-7440
E-mail: johann.klein@dot.state.oh.us

## Chief Legal Counsel
Chief Legal Counsel **Patrick Piccininni** . . . . . . . . . . . . . . . (614) 466-3664
E-mail: patrick.piccininni@dot.state.oh.us
Administrative Assistant **Tricia Mobley** . . . . . . . . . . . . . . . (614) 466-2728

## Operations Division
Deputy Director **Sanja Simpson** . . . . . . . . . . . . . . . . . . . . . (614) 752-9970
Roadway Administrator **Dave Holstein** . . . . . . . . . . . . . . . (614) 644-8137

## Department of Veterans Services
77 South High Street, 7th Floor, Columbus, OH 43215-6123
Tel: (614) 644-0898  Fax: (614) 728-9498

**Employees:** 875

■Director **COL Rodney "Chip" Tansill, USA (Ret)** . . . . . . . (614) 644-0898
Education: Fairmont State U 1986 BA; Army War Col 2011 MSS
■Assistant Director **Mark Cappone** . . . . . . . . . . . . . . . . . . . (614) 644-0898
E-mail: jason.dominguez@dvs.ohio.gov
State Approving Agency for Veterans Education and
Training Director **Robert Breeckner** . . . . . . . . . . . . . . . . (614) 466-9287
E-mail: robert.breeckner@dvs.ohio.gov

## Department of Youth Services [DYS]
30 West Spring Street, Columbus, OH 43215-2256
Tel: (614) 466-4314  Fax: (614) 387-2606  Internet: www.dys.ohio.gov

**Employees:** 1,426  **Fiscal Year:** 2015  **Budget:** $247,160,000

■Director **Harvey J. Reed** . . . . . . . . . . . . . . . . . . . . . . . . . . (614) 466-8783
E-mail: harvey.reed@dys.ohio.gov
Assistant Director **Linda S. Janes** . . . . . . . . . . . . . . . . . . . (614) 752-7620
Education: Ohio State
Chief Inspector **Monica Ellis** . . . . . . . . . . . . . . . . . . . . . . (614) 466-3576
Chief Legislative Liaison **Kyle Petty** . . . . . . . . . . . . . . . . . (614) 466-8657
E-mail: kyle.petty@dys.ohio.gov

## Finance and Planning Division
Internet: www.dys.ohio.gov

Deputy Director **Heath McCoy** . . . . . . . . . . . . . . . . . . . . . . (614) 466-4841
Management Information Systems Chief **(Vacant)** . . . . . . . (614) 644-6198

Construction, Maintenance and Renovation Administrator
**Vincent Corcoran** . . . . . . . . . . . . . . . . . . . . . . . . . . . . . . . (614) 752-9391

## Human Resources Division
Bureau Chief **Rochelle Jones** . . . . . . . . . . . . . . . . . . . . . . . (614) 644-8886
E-mail: rochelle.jones@dys.ohio.gov

## Legal Services Division
Chief Legal Counsel **Dustin Calhoun** . . . . . . . . . . . . . . . . . (614) 644-8968

## Facilities Program and Operations
Deputy Director **Ginine Trim** . . . . . . . . . . . . . . . . . . . . . . . (614) 644-7640

## Parole, Release and Re-entry Integrated Services
Bureau Chief **Steve Curl** . . . . . . . . . . . . . . . . . . . . . . . . . . . (614) 752-7620

## Environmental Protection Agency
P.O. Box 1049, Columbus, OH 43216-1049
Tel: (614) 644-3020  TTY: (614) 644-2110  Fax: (614) 644-3184
E-mail: web.requests@epa.ohio.gov  Internet: www.epa.ohio.gov

**Employees:** 1,100

■Director **Craig W. Butler** . . . . . . . . . . . . . . . . . . . . . . . . . . (614) 644-2782
E-mail: craig.butler@epa.ohio.gov
Education: Mansfield BA; Ohio 1997 MS
Assistant Director **Jim Canepa** . . . . . . . . . . . . . . . . . . . . . . (614) 644-2782
Assistant Director **Laura Factor** . . . . . . . . . . . . . . . . . . . . . (614) 644-2782
Education: Duke 1987 BA
Business Relations Deputy Director **Laurie Stevenson** . . . . (614) 644-2782
Communication Deputy Director **Heidi Griesmer** . . . . . . . . (614) 644-2782
E-mail: heidi.griesmer@epa.ohio.gov
Legal Counsel Chief **Cynthia "Cindy" Hafner** . . . . . . . . . (614) 644-2782
Education: Heidelberg BS; Kent State MS; Cincinnati 1986 JD
Water Resources Deputy Director **Karl Gebhardt** . . . . . . . . (614) 644-2782
Education: Franklin U 1979 BS; Ohio State 1997 MA
Air Pollution Control Division Chief **Robert Hodanbosi** . . (614) 644-2270
Education: Cleveland State 1977 MS          Fax: (614) 644-3681
Drinking and Ground Waters Division Chief **Mike Baker** . . (614) 644-2752
Education: Ohio State 1983 BS
Environmental and Financial Assistance Division Chief
**(Vacant)** . . . . . . . . . . . . . . . . . . . . . . . . . . . . . . . . . . . . . (614) 644-2798
Environmental Response and Revitalization Division
Chief **Peter Whitehouse** . . . . . . . . . . . . . . . . . . . . . . . . . (614) 644-2924
Environmental Services Division Chief **Nik Dzamov** . . . . . (614) 644-4247
8955 East Main Street, Reynoldsburg, OH 43068     Fax: (614) 644-4272
Materials and Waste Management Division Chief
**Terrie TerMeer** . . . . . . . . . . . . . . . . . . . . . . . . . . . . . . . . (614) 644-2621
Surface Water Division Chief **Tiffani Kavalec** . . . . . . . . . . (614) 644-2001
Compliance Assistance and Pollution Prevention Chief
**(Vacant)** . . . . . . . . . . . . . . . . . . . . . . . . . . . . . . . . . . . . . (614) 644-3469
Employee Services Chief **Karen Haight** . . . . . . . . . . . . . . . (614) 644-2100
Education: Capital U 1987 JD
Fiscal Chief **Chris Geyer** . . . . . . . . . . . . . . . . . . . . . . . . . . (614) 644-2339
Education: Ohio State 1992 MS
Information Technology Services Chief **Rick Magni** . . . . . . (614) 644-2990
E-mail: richard.magni@epa.ohio.gov
Operations and Facilities Chief **Satch Dzamov** . . . . . . . . . (614) 644-2089
Public Interest Center Chief **Heidi Griesmer** . . . . . . . . . . . (614) 644-2782
E-mail: heidi.griesmer@epa.ohio.gov          Fax: (614) 644-2737
Environmental Education Office Chief **Carolyn Watkins** . . (614) 644-2873
Education: North Carolina 1982 MS
Webmaster **Cathryn Allen** . . . . . . . . . . . . . . . . . . . . . . . . . (614) 644-2160
E-mail: web.requests@epa.ohio.gov
Education: Ohio State 1992 BS

---

★ Elected Official     ■ Appointed by Governor     ● Appointed by Legislature     ▲ Appointed by Board or Commission     ◆ Appointed by State Supreme Court

**EXECUTIVE BRANCH**

# Bureau of Workers' Compensation [BWC]

30 West Spring Street, Columbus, OH 43215-2256
Tel: (614) 644-6292  Tel: (800) 644-6292  Fax: (877) 520-6446
Internet: www.bwc.ohio.gov

**Employees:** 1,881

■Administrator and Chief Executive Officer
  **Sarah D. Morrison** . . . . . . . . . . . . . . . . . . . . . . . . . . . . (614) 466-5223
Employer Services Chief **Kevin Abrams** . . . . . . . . . . . . . (614) 466-1100
  E-mail: kevin.a.13@bwc.state.oh.us
Chief Health and Medical Officer **John Annarino** . . . . . . . . (614) 752-5984
Chief Medical Officer **Dr. Stephen T. Woods, MD** . . . . . . (614) 644-7458
Chief of Medical Operations **Deborah Kroninger** . . . . . . . . (614) 644-6292
Medical Services Chief **Freddie L. Johnson** . . . . . . . . . . . . (614) 728-8075
Chief Actuarial Officer **Christopher Carlson** . . . . . . . . . . . (614) 466-1926
Chief Fiscal and Planning Officer
  **Barbara "Barb" Ingram** . . . . . . . . . . . . . . . . . . . . . . (614) 466-1241
Chief Human Resources Officer **Toni Brokaw** . . . . . . . . . . (614) 644-8735
Chief Information Officer (Interim) **Dylan Scott** . . . . . . . . (614) 644-6292
Chief of Internal Audit **David Kooser** . . . . . . . . . . . . . . . . (614) 644-6292
Chief Investments Officer **Bruce Dunn** . . . . . . . . . . . . . . . (614) 466-0088
Chief Legal Officer (Interim) **Tom Sico** . . . . . . . . . . . . . . . (614) 728-4634
Chief Operating Officer **Dale Hamilton** . . . . . . . . . . . . . . . (614) 728-2804
Legislative Liaison **(Vacant)** . . . . . . . . . . . . . . . . . . . . . . . (614) 728-6197
Operational Policy, Analytics and Compliance Chief
  **Dr. Rick Percy** . . . . . . . . . . . . . . . . . . . . . . . . . . . . . (614) 728-8890
  E-mail: r.richard.p.1@bwc.state.oh.us
Chief of Communications **(Vacant)** . . . . . . . . . . . . . . . . . . (614) 644-6292
  Communications Director **William "Bill" Teets** . . . . . . . . (614) 728-8045
    E-mail: william.t.12@bwc.state.oh.us

# Office of the Adjutant General

2825 West Dublin Granville Road, Columbus, OH 43235-2789
Tel: (614) 336-6000  Fax: (614) 336-7074  E-mail: tag@oh.ngb.army.mil

**Fiscal Year:** 2015  **Budget:** $55,864,000

■Adjutant General **MajGen Mark E. Bartman, ANG** . . . . . . (614) 336-7070
  E-mail: mark.bartman@mail.mil
  Education: Ohio State 1982 BS; Boston U 1992 MSME;
  Air Command Col 1996; Air War Col 1999
Director of Communications **James A. Sims II** . . (614) 336-7126 ext. 7126
  E-mail: james.a.sims20.nfg@mail.mil

# Ohio National Guard

2825 West Dublin Granville Road, Columbus, OH 43235-2789
Tel: (614) 336-6000  Internet: http://ong.ohio.gov

■Adjutant General **MajGen Mark E. Bartman, ANG** . . . . . . (614) 336-7070
  E-mail: mark.bartman@mail.mil

# Ohio Air National Guard

2825 West Dublin Granville Road, Columbus, OH 43235-2789
Tel: (614) 336-7324  Internet: www.oh.ang.af.mil

Assistant Adjutant General for Air
  **Col Gregory N. Schnulo, ANG** . . . . . . . . . . . . (614) 336-7075 ext. 7075

# Ohio Army National Guard

2825 West Dublin Granville Road, Columbus, OH 43235-2789
Tel: (614) 336-6000

Assistant Adjutant General for Army
  **MG John C. Harris, Jr., ARNG** . . . . . . . . . . . . . . . . . (614) 336-7073
Information Technology Deputy Director **Rich Kerwood** . . (614) 336-7213

# Office of Budget and Management

30 East Broad Street, 34th Floor, Columbus, OH 43215-3457
Tel: (614) 466-4034  Fax: (614) 466-3813  E-mail: obm@obm.state.oh.us

**Employees:** 217  **Fiscal Year:** 2015  **Budget:** $27,600,000

■Director **Timothy S. "Tim" Keen** . . . . . . . . . . . . . . . . . . (614) 466-4034
  E-mail: timothy.keen@obm.ohio.gov
  Education: UMass (Amherst) BA; Rutgers MA

Assistant Director **Kurt Kauffman** . . . . . . . . . . . . . . . . . . (614) 466-4034
  Education: Indiana 1993 MPA
Policy Administrator **Christine Morrison** . . . . . . . . . . . . . (614) 728-8778
  E-mail: christine.morrison@obm.ohio.gov
Controlling Board President **Christine Morrison** . . . . . . . . (614) 728-8778

# Office of the Ohio Consumers' Counsel

10 West Broad Street, 18th Floor, Columbus, OH 43215
Tel: (614) 466-8574  Fax: (614) 466-9475  Internet: www.occ.ohio.gov
E-mail: occ@occ.state.oh.us

**Employees:** 36

Consumers' Counsel **Bruce Weston** . . . . . . . . . . . . . . . . . . (614) 466-9555

# Office of the Public Defender

The Midland Building, 250 East Broad Street, Suite 1400,
Columbus, OH 43215
Fax: (614) 644-9972

**Employees:** 131  **Fiscal Year:** 2015  **Budget:** $80,747,000

▲State Public Defender **Timothy "Tim" Young** . . . . . . . . . . (614) 466-5394
  E-mail: tim.young@opd.ohio.gov
  Education: Dayton 1988 BA, 1992 JD
Assistant Director **Elizabeth R. Miller** . . . . . . . . . . . . . . . (614) 466-5394
  Program Administrator **Terri L. Wilson** . . . . . . . . . . . . . (614) 466-5394

# Civil Rights Commission

30 East Broad Street, 5th Floor, Columbus, OH 43215-3414
Tel: (614) 466-2785  Tel: (888) 278-7101  TTY: (614) 752-2391
Fax: (614) 644-8776

**Employees:** 78  **Fiscal Year:** 2015  **Budget:** $6,903,000

▲Executive Director **G. Michael Payton** . . . . . . . . . . . . . . . (614) 466-2785
  E-mail: michael.payton@civ.ohio.gov
  Education: Ohio State BA, JD
Chief Legal Counsel **Stephanie Demers** . . . . . . . . . . . . . . (614) 466-6255
Operations Director **Keith P. McNeil** . . . . . . . . . . . . . . . . . (614) 466-6103
  E-mail: keith.mcneil@civ.ohio.gov
  Education: Akron BA, JD
Public Affairs and Civic Engagement Director
  **Mary Turocy** . . . . . . . . . . . . . . . . . . . . . . . . . . . . . . . (614) 466-2785
  Education: London School Econ (UK) MS

# Ohio Ethics Commission

William Green Building, 30 West Spring Street, L3, Columbus, OH 43215
Tel: (614) 466-7090  Fax: (614) 466-8368

**Employees:** 19  **Fiscal Year:** 2015  **Budget:** $2,023,000

■Chair **Merom Brachman** . . . . . . . . . . . . . . . . . . . . . . . . . (614) 466-7090
  Term Expires: January 1, 2019
  E-mail: merom.brachman@ethics.ohio.gov
■Vice Chair **Michael A. Flack** . . . . . . . . . . . . . . . . . . . . . . (614) 466-7090
  Term Expires: January 1, 2017
  E-mail: michael.flack@ethics.ohio.gov
  Education: Ohio Wesleyan BA; Harvard MBA
■Commissioner **Bruce Bailey** . . . . . . . . . . . . . . . . . . . . . . . (614) 466-7090
  Term Expires: January 1, 2018
  E-mail: bruce.bailey@ethics.ohio.gov
■Commissioner **Megan C. Kelley** . . . . . . . . . . . . . . . . . . . . (614) 466-7090
  Term Expires: January 1, 2022
■Commissioner **Elizabeth E. Tracy** . . . . . . . . . . . . . . . . . . (614) 466-7090
  Term Expires: January 1, 2020
  E-mail: elizabeth.tracy@ethics.ohio.gov
■Commissioner **Mark A. Vander Laan** . . . . . . . . . . . . . . . . (614) 466-7090
  Education: Hope 1970 AB; Michigan 1972 JD
▲Executive Director **Paul M. Nick** . . . . . . . . . . . . . . . . . . . (614) 466-7090
  E-mail: paul.nick@ethics.ohio.gov
  Education: Illinois 1987 BA; Ohio State 1990 JD

---

★ Elected Official   ■ Appointed by Governor   ● Appointed by Legislature   ▲ Appointed by Board or Commission   ◆ Appointed by State Supreme Court

---

## Public Utilities Commission of Ohio [PUCO]

180 East Broad Street, Columbus, OH 43215-3793
Tel: (614) 466-3016  TTY: (800) 686-1570  Fax: (614) 644-9546
Internet: www.puco.ohio.gov

**Employees:** 355

■ Chairman **Asim Z. Haque** . . . . . . . . . . . . . . . . . . . . . . . . . (614) 466-3016
  Term Expires: April 2021
  E-mail: asim.haque@puc.state.oh.us
  Education: Case Western BA; Ohio State JD
■ Commissioner **Thomas W. Johnson** . . . . . . . . . . . . . . . (614) 466-3204
  Term Expires: April 10, 2019                   Fax: (614) 995-3690
  E-mail: thomas.johnson@puc.state.oh.us
  Education: Muskingum Col BA
■ Commissioner **Lynn C. Slaby** . . . . . . . . . . . . . . . . . . . . . (614) 466-3038
  Term Expires: April 10, 2017
  E-mail: lynn.slaby@puc.state.oh.us
  Education: Akron 1967 BS, 1972 JD
■ Commissioner **M. Beth Trombold** . . . . . . . . . . . . . . . . (614) 466-3905
  Term Expires: April 10, 2018
  E-mail: beth.trombold@puc.state.oh.us
■ Commissioner **(Vacant)** . . . . . . . . . . . . . . . . . . . . . . . . . . (614) 466-3016

### Office of the Chief of Staff
▲ Chief of Staff **Jason Rafeld** . . . . . . . . . . . . . . . . . . . . . . . (614) 466-0122
  E-mail: jason.rafeld@puc.state.oh.us
Business Resources Director **Susan Patterson** . . . . . . . . . (614) 466-3307

## Ohio State Racing Commission

Vern Riffe Center, 77 South High Street, 18th Floor,
Columbus, OH 43215-6108
Tel: (614) 466-2757  Fax: (614) 466-1900
Internet: www.racing.ohio.gov/commission.stm

■ Chairman **Robert K. Schmitz** . . . . . . . . . . . . . . . . . . . . . (614) 466-2757
  Term Expires: March 31, 2019
  E-mail: robert.schmitz@rc.state.oh.us
■ Member **Thomas Todd Book** . . . . . . . . . . . . . . . . . . . . . . (614) 466-2757
  Term Expires: March 31, 2019
  Education: Western Michigan 1990 BA; William & Mary 1993 JD
■ Member **Gary G. Koch** . . . . . . . . . . . . . . . . . . . . . . . . . . . (614) 466-2757
  Term Expires: March 31, 2019
  E-mail: gary.koch@rc.state.oh.us
  Education: Ohio State 1967 BA
■ Member **Mark Munroe** . . . . . . . . . . . . . . . . . . . . . . . . . . . (330) 482-6498
  Term Expires: March 31, 2017
  E-mail: mark.munroe@rc.state.oh.us
■ Member **Thomas R. Winters** . . . . . . . . . . . . . . . . . . . . . (614) 466-2757
  Term Expires: March 31, 2017
  E-mail: thomas.winters@rc.state.oh.us
Executive Director **William "Bill" Crawford** . . . . . . . . . . (614) 466-2758

## Turnpike Commission

682 Prospect Street, Berea, OH 44017
Tel: (440) 234-2081  Fax: (440) 234-4618
E-mail: customerservice@ohioturnpike.org
Internet: www.ohioturnpike.org

▲ Executive Director **Randy Cole** . . . . . . . . . . . . . . (440) 234-2081 ext. 1002
  E-mail: randy.cole@obm.state.oh.us
Chief Engineer **Anthony "Tony" Yacobucci** . . . . (440) 234-2081 ext. 1201
  E-mail: tony.yacobucci@ohioturnpike.org       Fax: (440) 234-7273
Deputy Executive Director and Chief Financial
  Officer /Comptroller **Martin S. Seekely, CPA** . . (440) 234-2081 ext. 1131
  Education: John Carroll BS                     Fax: (440) 234-0232
Marketing and Communications Director
  **Adam L. Greenslade** . . . . . . . . . . . . . . . . . . . . .(440) 234-2081 ext. 1011
  E-mail: adam.greenslade@ohioturnpike.org      Fax: (440) 234-3881
  Education: Ohio State BA
Safety Services Manager **Ed Miller** . . . . . . . . . . . . (440) 234-2081 ext. 1231
                                                Fax: (440) 234-2282

General Counsel and Chief Legal Officer
  **Jennifer Stueber** . . . . . . . . . . . . . . . . . . . . . . . . .(440) 234-2081 ext. 1021
                                                Fax: (440) 234-7392

Government Affairs Director
  **Adam L. Greenslade** . . . . . . . . . . . . . . . . . . . . . .(440) 234-2081 ext. 1011
                                                Fax: (440) 234-4618

## Public Employees Retirement System

277 East Town Street, Columbus, OH 43215
Tel: (800) 222-7377  Fax: (614) 222-2917

▲ Executive Director **Karen Carraher** . . . . . . . . . . . . . . . . . . (614) 222-0011
  E-mail: kcarraher@opers.org

## Office of the Lieutenant Governor

Vern Riffe Center, 77 South High Street, 30th Floor,
Columbus, OH 43215
Tel: (614) 644-0935

★ Lieutenant Governor **Mary Taylor, CPA** (R) . . . . . . . . . . . . (614) 644-0935
  Term Expires: 2019
Chief of Staff **Chris Brock** . . . . . . . . . . . . . . . . . . . . . . . . . . (614) 644-9570
Communication Director **Todd Walker** . . . . . . . . . . . . . . . . (614) 644-0927
  E-mail: todd.walker@development.ohio.gov

## Office of the Secretary of State

180 East Broad Street, 16th Floor, Columbus, OH 43215-3793
Tel: (614) 466-2655  Fax: (614) 644-0649  Tel: (877) 767-6446

**Employees:** 145  **Fiscal Year:** 2015  **Budget:** $21,009,000

★ Secretary of State **Jon A. Husted** (R) . . . . . . . . . . . . . . . . .(614) 728-2981
  Term Expires: 2019
  Education: Dayton BS, MA
  Career: State Senator (R-OH, District 6), Ohio Senate (2009-2011)
Assistant Secretary of State and Chief of Staff Elections
  Director **Matthew "Matt" Damschroder** . . . . . . . . . . . .(614) 995-5221
Deputy Assistant Secretary of State Chief Legal Counsel
  **Jack Christopher** . . . . . . . . . . . . . . . . . . . . . . . . . . . . . . .(614) 728-5639
  E-mail: jchristopher@ohiosecretaryofstate.gov
Business Services Director **Allison Desantis** . . . . . . . . . . . (614) 728-6855
Deputy Chief of Staff and Legislative Services Director
  **Peter Craig Forbes** . . . . . . . . . . . . . . . . . . . . . . . . . . . . . (614) 466-6698
  E-mail: pforbes@ohiosecretaryofstate.gov
Security Director **Doug Miller** . . . . . . . . . . . . . . . . . . . . . . . (614) 466-0064

## Office of the Attorney General

30 East Broad Street, 17th Floor, Columbus, OH 43215-0421
Tel: (614) 466-4320  Fax: (614) 466-5087

**Employees:** 1,700  **Fiscal Year:** 2015  **Budget:** $264,944,000

★ Attorney General **Richard Michael "Mike" DeWine** (R) . . (614) 466-4320
  Term Expires: 2019
  Education: Miami U (OH) 1969 BS; Ohio Northern 1972 JD
  Career: U.S. Senator (R-OH), Office of Senator Michael DeWine,
  United States Senate (1995-2007)
First Assistant Attorney General **Mary Mertz** . . . . . . . . . .(614) 728-2318
Law Enforcement Deputy Attorney General
  **Stephen Schumaker** . . . . . . . . . . . . . . . . . . . . . . . . . . . (614) 728-1171
Chief Counsel **Sheryl Maxfield** . . . . . . . . . . . . . . . . . . . . . .(614) 466-1653
Solicitor General **Eric C. Murphy, JD** . . . . . . . . . . . . . . . . (614) 728-7510
  Education: Miami U (OH) 2001; Chicago 2005 JD
Chief Information Officer **Ervan D. Rodgers** . . . . . . . . . . . (614) 466-5272
  E-mail: ervan.rodgers@ohioattorneygeneral.gov
Chief Operating Officer **Kimberly Murnieks** . . . . . . . . . . . (614) 728-4941
Communications Director **Lisa Hackley** . . . . . . . . . . . . . . . (614) 466-3840
Senior Advisor and Policy and Public Affairs Director
  **Ann O'Donnell** . . . . . . . . . . . . . . . . . . . . . . . . . . . . . . . . (614) 728-7275

## Office of the State Treasurer

30 East Broad Street, 9th Floor, Columbus, OH 43215-0421
Tel: (614) 466-2160  TTY: (800) 228-1102  Fax: (614) 644-7313

**Employees:** 117  **Fiscal Year:** 2015  **Budget:** $40,827,000

★ State Treasurer **Josh Mandel** (R) . . . . . . . . . . . . . . . . . . . . (614) 466-2160
  Term Expires: 2019
  E-mail: josh.mandel@tos.ohio.gov
  Education: Ohio State 2000 BS; Case Western 2003 JD

*(continued on next page)*

---

★ Elected Official  ■ Appointed by Governor  ● Appointed by Legislature     ▲ Appointed by Board or Commission     ◆ Appointed by State Supreme Court

EXECUTIVE BRANCH

**Office of the State Treasurer** *continued*

Deputy Treasurer **Seth Metcalf** . . . . . . . . . . . . . . . . . . . . . (614) 466-2191
    Education: Ohio State; Cornell JD
Chief of Staff **Kevin Benacci** . . . . . . . . . . . . . . . . . . . . . . . (614) 466-2160
Chief Operating Officer **Jennifer E. Day** . . . . . . . . . . . . (614) 387-2834
    Education: Kentucky 1983 BA; Salmon P Chase 1991 JD
General Counsel **Meredith Rockwell** . . . . . . . . . . . . . . . . (614) 644-0169
Deputy Press Secretary **Amanda R. Merritt** . . . . . . . . . . . (614) 466-2160

# Office of the Auditor of State

88 East Broad Street, 5th Floor, Columbus, OH 43215
Tel: (800) 282-0370  Fax: (614) 466-4490

**Employees:** 811  **Fiscal Year:** 2015  **Budget:** $72,453,000

★ Auditor of State **Dave Yost** (R) . . . . . . . . . . . . . . . . . . . (800) 282-0370
    Term Expires: 2019
    Education: Ohio State BS; Capital U 1991 JD
    Executive Assistant **Andrea Tawney** . . . . . . . . . . . . . . . (614) 466-4460
Chief Deputy Auditor **Robert Hinkle** . . . . . . . . . . . . . . . (614) 728-7108
Chief of Staff **Brenda L. Rinehart** . . . . . . . . . . . . . . . . . (614) 387-6294
    Education: Ohio; Capital U JD
Deputy Chief of Staff **Tony Tanner** . . . . . . . . . . . . . . . . . (614) 728-7189
Chief Legal Counsel **Mark Altier** . . . . . . . . . . . . . . . . . . (614) 728-7116
Medicaid/Contract Audit Section Director
    **Kristi Erlewine** . . . . . . . . . . . . . . . . . . . . . . . . . . . . . . . (614) 728-7245
Senior Policy Advisor **Bill Owen** . . . . . . . . . . . . . . . . . . . (614) 466-1873
External Affairs Senior Policy Advisor **Carrie Bartunek** . . . (800) 282-0370
Press Secretary/Public Affairs Director **Brittany Halpin** . . . (614) 728-7198
    E-mail: press@ohioauditor.gov              Fax: (614) 466-6228
Communication Director **Benjamin J. "Ben" Marrison** . . . (800) 282-0370

# State Board of Education

25 South Front Street, Mailstop 703, Columbus, OH 43215-4183
Tel: (877) 644-6338  Fax: (614) 728-4781

**Fiscal Year:** 2015  **Budget:** $10,077,927,000

■ President **Thomas W. Gunlock** (At-Large) . . . . . . . . . . . . (937) 291-6318
    Term Expires: December 31, 2018
    10050 Innovation Drive, Suite 100, Dayton, OH 45453
    E-mail: tom.gunlock@education.ohio.gov
    Education: Miami U (OH) BS; Ball State MA
■ Vice President **Tess Elshoff** (At-Large) . . . . . . . . . . . . . . (614) 466-4838
    05768 Southland Road, New Knoxville, OH 45871     Tel: (419) 753-2583
    E-mail: tess.elshoff@education.ohio.gov
■ Member **Melanie P. Bolender** (At-Large) . . . . . . . . . . . . . (740) 501-0749
    Term Expires: June 31, 2016
    1486 Park Road, Mount Vernon, OH 43050
    E-mail: melanie.bolender@education.ohio.gov
★ Member **Pat Bruns** (D-Fourth District) . . . . . . . . . . . . . . (513) 310-8953
    Term Expires: December 31, 2018
    E-mail: pat.bruns@education.ohio.gov
★ Member **Michael L. Collins** (Sixth District) . . . . . . . . . . . (614) 299-8596
    Term Expires: December 31, 2016
    6169 Sugar Maple, Westerville, OH 43082
    E-mail: michael.collins@education.ohio.gov
    Education: Miami U (OH) BS; Ball State MA
★ Member **Stephanie Dodd** (D-Ninth District) . . . . . . . . . . . (740) 629-1333
    Term Expires: December 31, 2016
    6169 Sugar Maple, Westerville, OH 43082
    E-mail: stephanie.dodd@education.ohio.gov
■ Member **Joseph L. Farmer** (At-Large) . . . . . . . . . . . . . . . (614) 466-4838
    Term Expires: December 31, 2018     Tel: (740) 862-8649
    1775 West Market Street, Baltimore, OH 43105
    E-mail: joe.farmer@education.ohio.gov
■ Member **Cathye Flory** (At-Large) . . . . . . . . . . . . . . . . . . (740) 603-6365
    13735 Old McArthur Road, Logan, OH 43138
    E-mail: cathye.flory@education.ohio.gov
★ Member **Sarah Fowler** (R-Seventh District) . . . . . . . . . . . (614) 466-4838
    Term Expires: December 31, 2018
    E-mail: sarah.fowler@education.ohio.gov
★ Member **Nancy P. Hollister** (R-Eighth District) . . . . . . . . (877) 644-6338
    Term Expires: December 31, 2018

★ Member **Ann E. Jacobs** (R-First District) . . . . . . . . . . . . (614) 466-4838
    Term Expires: December 31, 2016     Tel: (419) 229-9800
    558 West Spring Street, Lima, OH 45801
    E-mail: ann.jacobs@education.ohio.gov
    Affiliation: Attorney, Jacobs Law Offices
■ Member **C. Todd Jones** (At-Large) . . . . . . . . . . . . . . . . . (614) 466-4838
    Term Expires: December 31, 2016     Tel: (614) 228-2196
    5957 Carters Grove, New Albany, OH 43054
    E-mail: todd.jones@education.ohio.gov
    Affiliation: President and General Counsel, Association of Independent
    Colleges and Universities of Ohio
    Huntington Center, 41 South High Street, Suite 2424,
    Columbus, OH 43125
    Education: Denver BSBA, JD; Georgetown 1996 LLM
★ Member **Kathleen A. McGervey** (R-Second District) . . . . . (614) 466-4838
    Term Expires: December 31, 2018
    2643 Joseph Street, Avon, OH 44011
    E-mail: kathleen.mcgervey@education.ohio.gov
★ Member **Mary Rose Oakar** (D-Eleventh District) . . . . . . . (614) 466-4838
    Term Expires: December 31, 2016     Tel: (216) 631-2260
    E-mail: maryrose.oakar@education.ohio.gov
★ Member **Roslyn Painter-Goffi** (D-Fifth District) . . . . . . . . (877) 644-6338
    Term Expires: December 31, 2018
■ Member **Frank Pettigrew, Jr.** (At-Large) . . . . . . . . . . . . . (740) 497-7873
    Term Expires: December 31, 2016
■ Member **Ronald W. "Ron" Rudduck** (Tenth District) . . . . (877) 644-6338
    Term Expires: December 31, 2018
    E-mail: ron.rudduck@education.ohio.gov
■ Member **Rebecca Vazquez-Skillings** (At-Large) . . . . . . . . (614) 259-3815
    Term Expires: December 31, 2016
    E-mail: rebecca.vazquez-skillings@education.ohio.gov
★ Member **A.J. Wagner** (D-Third District) . . . . . . . . . . . . . (937) 307-2261
    Term Expires: December 31, 2018
    E-mail: a.j.wagner@education.ohio.gov
    Education: Dayton 1977 JD
Director **Dr. Richard A. Ross** . . . . . . . . . . . . . . . . . . . . . (614) 466-4838
    E-mail: richard.ross@education.ohio.gov

# Department of Education [ODE]

Tel: (877) 644-6338  Fax: (614) 387-0964

**Employees:** 552

▲ Superintendent of Public Instruction **Paolo DeMaria** . . . . . (877) 644-6338
    Program Administrator III **Carolyn Jones** . . . . . . . . . . . (614) 995-1985
Chief Research Officer **(Vacant)** . . . . . . . . . . . . . . . . . . . (614) 752-8729
Chief of Staff **Jimmy Sheppard** . . . . . . . . . . . . . . . . . . . (614) 387-0954
Chief Legal Counsel **Diane Lease** . . . . . . . . . . . . . . . . . . (614) 466-4705
Accountability and Teaching Profession Division
    Associate Superintendent **Lonny Rivera, EdD** . . . . . . . . (614) 752-9059
Learning and School Choice Division Associate
    Superintendent **Jennifer Felker** . . . . . . . . . . . . . . . . . . (614) 387-2256
Press Secretary **Kim Norris** . . . . . . . . . . . . . . . . . . . . . . . (614) 728-5959

## Operations

Communications and Outreach Executive Director
    **Kim Norris** . . . . . . . . . . . . . . . . . . . . . . . . . . . . . . . . . (614) 387-0146
    E-mail: kimberly.norris@education.ohio.gov
Human Resources Executive Director **Pamela King** . . . . . . (614) 466-3763
Information Technology Office Chief Information Officer
    **Beth Juillerat** . . . . . . . . . . . . . . . . . . . . . . . . . . . . . . . (614) 466-7000
    E-mail: beth.juillerat@education.ohio.gov

## Center for Accountability and Continuous Improvement

Senior Executive Director **Christopher "Chris" Woolard** . . (614) 387-7570
Federal Programs Director **Jeremy Marks** . . . . . . . . . . . . . (614) 466-4161
    E-mail: jeremy.marks@education.ohio.gov

## Center for Curriculum and Assessment

Senior Executive Director **Stephanie Siddens** . . . . . . . . . (614) 995-9974
Curriculum and Instruction Director **Jim Wright** . . . . . . . . (614) 466-3224
Career-Technical Education Director **(Vacant)** . . . . . . . . . . (614) 466-3430

## Office for Exceptional Children

Exceptional Children Executive Director **Sue Zake** . . . . . . . (614) 466-2650

---

★ Elected Official   ■ Appointed by Governor   ● Appointed by Legislature   ▲ Appointed by Board or Commission   ◆ Appointed by State Supreme Court

Early Learning and School Readiness Director
 **Wendy Grove** . . . . . . . . . . . . . . . . . . . . . . . . . . . . . . . . (614) 466-0224

## Center for Student Support and Education Options

Senior Executive Director **Steve Gratz** . . . . . . . . . . . . . . . . (614) 466-4235
Budget and School Funding Office Director
 **Aaron Rausch** . . . . . . . . . . . . . . . . . . . . . . . . . . . . . . . . (614) 995-9936
Community Schools Director **Joni Hoffman** . . . . . . . . . . . (614) 466-7058
Finance Program Services Director **(Vacant)** . . . . . . . . . . . (614) 466-5736
Nonpublic Educational Options Director **Sue Cosmo** . . . . . (614) 387-2154
Pupil Transportation Associate Director **(Vacant)** . . . . . . . . (614) 466-4230

## Center for the Teaching Profession

Senior Executive Director **Julia Simmerer** . . . . . . . . . . . . . (614) 466-9501
Educator Effectiveness Director **Carolyn Everidge-Frey** . . . (614) 752-8996
Educator Equity Director **Matthew Lutz** . . . . . . . . . . . . . . . (614) 752-1473
Educator Licensure Director **(Vacant)** . . . . . . . . . . . . . . . . . (877) 644-6338
Professional Conduct Director **Lori Kelly** . . . . . . . . . . . . . . (614) 466-5638

---

★ Elected Official ■ Appointed by Governor ● Appointed by Legislature ▲ Appointed by Board or Commission ◆ Appointed by State Supreme Court

EXECUTIVE BRANCH

# Oklahoma

Tel: (405) 521-2011  Internet: www.ok.gov

**Number of U.S. Congressional Delegates:** 2 Senators; 5 Representatives  **Governor's Term:** 4 years
**Legislature Description:** 48 member Senate; 101 member House of Representatives; Term - Senate 4
years, House 2 years  **Next Election:** Governor November 2018; Legislature November 2016
**Number of Electoral Votes:** 7  **Official Name:** State of Oklahoma (Choctaw: red people)
**Nickname:** The Sooner State  **Motto:** Labor omnia vincit (Labor conquers all things)

**Population:** 3,911,338 (2015); Rank 28  **Fiscal Year:** 2014  **Budget:** $7,114,129,653

## Office of the Governor

2300 North Lincoln Boulevard, Suite 212, Oklahoma City, OK 73105
Tel: (405) 521-2342  Fax: (405) 521-3353

**Employees:** 29  **Fiscal Year:** 2014  **Budget:** $2,172,900

**Mary Fallin**
Governor

Began Service: January 10, 2011
Term Expires: January 2019
Date of Birth: December 9, 1954
Education: Oklahoma State 1977 BS
Home: Oklahoma City
Religion: Christian
Career: State Representative (R-OK, District 85),
Oklahoma House of Representatives (1990-1994);
Lieutenant Governor (R-OK), State of Oklahoma
(1994-2006); U.S. Representative (R-OK, District
5), Office of Representative Mary Fallin, United
States House of Representatives (2007-2011)

★Governor **Mary Fallin** (R) . . . . . . . . . . . . . . . . . . . . . . . . . . . (405) 521-2342
  E-mail: mary.fallin@gov.ok.gov
  E-mail: governor@gov.ok.gov
Chief of Staff **Denise Northrup** . . . . . . . . . . . . . . . . . . . . . . (405) 521-2342
General Counsel **(Vacant)** . . . . . . . . . . . . . . . . . . . . . . . . . . . (405) 521-2342
Secretary of Commerce and Tourism
  **Deborah "Deby" Snodgrass** . . . . . . . . . . . . . . . . . . . . . . (405) 815-5306
  E-mail: deby_snodgrass@okcommerce.gov
Secretary of Education and Workforce Development
  **Natalie Sue Shirley** . . . . . . . . . . . . . . . . . . . . . . . . . . . . (405) 743-5444
  Education: Oklahoma State 1979; Oklahoma 1982 JD
Secretary of Energy and Environment
  **COL Michael J. Teague, USA (Ret)** . . . . . . . . . . . . . . . . (405) 530-8995
  Education: Norwich BSCE
Secretary of Finance, Administration and Information
  Technology **Preston L. Doerflinger** . . . . . . . . . . . . . . . . (405) 521-2141
  E-mail: preston.doerflinger@omes.ok.gov
  Education: Southern Nazarene BS
Secretary of Health and Human Services
  **Terry L. Cline, PhD** . . . . . . . . . . . . . . . . . . . . . . . . . . . . (405) 271-4200
  E-mail: terryc@health.ok.gov
  Education: Oklahoma 1980 BS; Oklahoma State MS, PhD
Secretary of Safety and Security
  **Michael C. "Mike" Thompson** . . . . . . . . . . . . . . . . . . . (405) 521-2342
  E-mail: mthompson@dps.state.ok.us
Secretary of Science and Technology
  **Dr. Stephen W. McKeever** . . . . . . . . . . . . . . . . . . . . . . (405) 521-2342
  Education: U Col North Wales 1972 BS, 1973 MS, 1975 PhD
Secretary of Transportation **Gary Ridley** . . . . . . . . . . . . . . (405) 522-1800
  Education: Oklahoma State 1960 BS                    Tel: (405) 521-2342
Secretary of Veterans Affairs
  **MG Myles L. Deering, ARNG** . . . . . . . . . . . . . . . . . . . . (405) 521-3684
  Education: Oklahoma 1990 BBA; Oklahoma State 1996 MS;
  Army War Col 2000 MSS
Communications Director **Michael McNutt** . . . . . . . . . . . . . (405) 521-2342
  E-mail: michael.mcnutt@gov.ok.gov
Deputy Communications Director **Jay Marks** . . . . . . . . . . . (405) 521-2342
  E-mail: jay.marks@gov.ok.gov
  Education: Oklahoma State

Policy Director **Katie Gumerson Altshuler** . . . . . . . . . . . . . (405) 521-2342
  E-mail: katie.altshuler@gov.ok.gov
  Education: Sweet Briar 1997 BA
  Policy Deputy Director **Jake Yunker** . . . . . . . . . . . . . . . . (405) 521-2342
  E-mail: jake.yunker@gov.ok.gov
Small Business Advocate **Todd Lamb** . . . . . . . . . . . . . . . . . (405) 521-2342
  Education: Oklahoma BS; Oklahoma City 2005 JD
Special Adviser on Child Welfare and Pinnacle Plan
  Implementation **Tom Bates** . . . . . . . . . . . . . . . . . . . . . . (405) 521-2342
  Education: Oklahoma City, JD
Special Adviser on Economic Development
  **Robert W. Sullivan, Jr.** . . . . . . . . . . . . . . . . . . . . . . . . . (405) 521-2342
Native American Liaison **Chris Benge** . . . . . . . . . . . . . . . . (405) 521-3912
  Education: Oklahoma State 2007 BAA
Veterans Affairs Liaison
  **MajGen LaRita A. "Rita" Aragon, ANG (Ret)** . . . . . . . . (405) 521-2342
  Education: Central State 1970 BS, 1979 MA; Air Command Col 1995;
  Air War Col 1998

## Office of the Secretary of Energy and Environment

204 North Robinson, Suite 1010, Oklahoma City, OK 73102
Tel: (405) 522-7099  E-mail: ee@ee.ok.gov

■Secretary **COL Michael J. Teague, USA (Ret)** . . . . . . . . . . (405) 522-7099
  E-mail: michael.teague@ee.ok.gov
Deputy Secretary of Energy **Tom Robins** . . . . . . . . . . . . . . (405) 522-7099
  Education: Utah State BA; George Washington MA
Deputy Secretary of Environment **Tyler Powell** . . . . . . . . . (405) 522-7099
Legislative Affairs Director **Carly Cordell** . . . . . . . . . . . . . (405) 522-7099
  E-mail: carly.cordell@ee.ok.gov
Stakeholder Engagements Director **(Vacant)** . . . . . . . . . . . (405) 522-7099
Environmental Grants Manager **Gayle N. Bartholomew** . . (405) 522-7099
Administrative Director **Jodi McKee** . . . . . . . . . . . . . . . . . (405) 522-7099

## Office of the Secretary of State

101 State Capitol, 2300 North Lincoln Boulevard,
Oklahoma City, OK 73105-4897
Tel: (405) 521-3912  Fax: (405) 521-2031

**Employees:** 33  **Fiscal Year:** 2014  **Budget:** $14,442,570

■Secretary of State **Chris Benge** . . . . . . . . . . . . . . . . . . . . . (405) 521-3912
  E-mail: chris.benge@sos.ok.gov
  Executive Assistant **Merrill Williamson** . . . . . . . . . . . . . . (405) 521-6434
Assistant Secretary of State **Tod Wall** . . . . . . . . . . . . . . . . (405) 521-3912
  Education: Central Oklahoma 1994 BBA
Administrative Rules Division Director **Peggy Coe** . . . . . . . (405) 521-4911
  Education: Central Oklahoma 1987 BA            Fax: (405) 522-3555
Agricultural Liens Central Filing Division Director
  **Peggy Coe** . . . . . . . . . . . . . . . . . . . . . . . . . . . . . . . . . . (405) 521-4911
                                                   Fax: (405) 522-3555
Business Division Director **Tamra Laxson** . . . . . . . . . . . . . (405) 521-3912
Information Systems Division Director **Tod Wall** . . . . . . . . (405) 521-3912
  E-mail: tod.wall@sos.ok.gov
Chief International Protocol Officer **Chris Morriss** . . . . . . . (405) 521-3912
  Education: Rowan U 1982 BS               Fax: (405) 522-3555
Administrative Assistant I **Amy Canton** . . . . . . . . . . . . . . . (405) 522-4565

---

★ Elected Official   ■ Appointed by Governor   ● Appointed by Legislature   ▲ Appointed by Board or Commission   ◆ Appointed by State Supreme Court

# Office of the Oklahoma State Fire Marshal

2401 Northwest 23rd Street, Suite 4, Oklahoma City, OK 73107
Tel: (405) 522-5005  TTY: (800) 722-0353  Fax: (405) 522-5028

**Employees:** 21  **Fiscal Year:** 2014  **Budget:** $1,796,764

▲ State Fire Marshal **Robert Doke** . . . . . . . . . . . . . . . . . . . . . (405) 522-5011
    E-mail: robert.doke@fire.ok.gov
▲ Assistant State Fire Marshal **Sam Schafnitt** . . . . . . . . . . . . (405) 522-5010

# Oklahoma Department of Agriculture, Food and Forestry [ODAFF]

2800 North Lincoln Boulevard, Oklahoma City, OK 73105-4210
P.O. Box 528804, Oklahoma City, OK 73152-8804
Tel: (405) 521-3864  Fax: (405) 521-4912

**Employees:** 395

■ Cabinet Secretary and Commissioner
    **James "Jim" Reese** . . . . . . . . . . . . . . . . . . . . . . . . (405) 522-5719
    E-mail: jim.reese@ag.ok.gov
    Education: Northern Oklahoma AA; Oklahoma State BS
    Executive Assistant **Kandi Batts** . . . . . . . . . . . . . . . . . . . . (405) 522-5488
Deputy Commissioner **Betty Thompson** . . . . . . . . . . . . . . (405) 522-6105
General Counsel **Teena Gunter, Esq.** . . . . . . . . . . . . . . . . . (405) 522-5997
Agricultural Environmental Management Services
    Director **Jeremy Seiger** . . . . . . . . . . . . . . . . . . . . . . . . (405) 522-4659
Communications/Administrative Director **Bryan Painter** . . . (405) 521-6479
    E-mail: bryan.painter@ag.ok.gov
State Veterinarian/Animal Industry Services Director
    **Dr. Rod Hall** . . . . . . . . . . . . . . . . . . . . . . . . . . . . . . . . (405) 522-0270
Agricultural Statistical Services Division Director
    **Wilbert C. "Wil" Hundl, Jr.** . . . . . . . . . . . . . . . . . . . . (405) 522-5404
    E-mail: wil_hundl@nass.usda.gov
Consumer Protection Services Division Director
    **Kenny Naylor** . . . . . . . . . . . . . . . . . . . . . . . . . . . . . . . (405) 522-5879
Food Safety Division Director **Stanley A. Stromberg** . . . . (405) 522-6113
Laboratory Services Division Director **Tanna Kilpatrick** . . . (405) 522-5432
Market Development Services Division Director
    **Jamey Allen** . . . . . . . . . . . . . . . . . . . . . . . . . . . . . . . . (405) 522-4676
Public Information Division Director **Blayne Arthur** . . . . . . (405) 522-5600
    E-mail: blayne.arthur@ag.ok.gov
Wildlife Services Division Director **Kevin R. Grant** . . . . . . (405) 521-4039
State Forester **George Geissler** . . . . . . . . . . . . . . . . . . . . . (405) 522-6158

# Oklahoma State Banking Department [OSBD]

2900 North Lincoln Boulevard, Oklahoma City, OK 73105
Tel: (405) 521-2782  Fax: (405) 522-2993
Dist: (918) 295-3649 (Tulsa Office)  Dist: (918) 893-6405 (Tulsa Office)

**Employees:** 41

■ Commissioner **Mick Thompson** . . . . . . . . . . . . . . . . . . . . (405) 521-2782
    E-mail: mick.thompson@banking.ok.gov
    Education: Southeastern Oklahoma St 1969 BS;
    Northeastern State 1971 MBA
Deputy Commissioner **Dudley Gilbert** . . . . . . . . . . . . . . . . (405) 521-2782
    E-mail: dudley.gilbert@banking.ok.gov
Chief of Staff **Regina Rainey** . . . . . . . . . . . . . . . . . . . . . . (405) 521-2782
    E-mail: regina.rainey@banking.ok.gov
Assistant Deputy Commissioner **Wayne Arbuthnot** . . . . . . (405) 521-2782
Assistant Deputy Commissioner **Harold A. Reel** . . . . . . . . (405) 521-2782
    E-mail: tony.reel@banking.ok.gov
Director of Administration **Rhonda Bruno** . . . . . . . . . . . . . (405) 521-2782
    E-mail: rhonda.bruno@banking.ok.gov
Administrative Assistant **Angela Morris** . . . . . . . . . . . . . . . (405) 521-2782

# Oklahoma Department of Career and Technology Education [CareerTech]

1500 West Seventh Avenue, Stillwater, OK 74074-4364
Tel: (405) 377-2000  Fax: (405) 743-6809  TTY: (405) 743-6816

**Employees:** 260

▲ Director **Marcie Mack** . . . . . . . . . . . . . . . . . . . . . . . . . . (405) 743-5430
    E-mail: marcie.mack@careertech.ok.gov
    Education: Oklahoma State BS, PhD
    Assistant to the Director **Sharon Schonthaler** . . . . . . . . (405) 743-5445
Deputy State Director/Chief Operating Officer **(Vacant)** . . . (405) 743-5430
Associate State Director for Curriculum, Assessment, and
    Digital Delivery **Kimberly Sadler** . . . . . . . . . . . . . . . . (405) 743-5410
Associate State Director for Educational Services
    (Interim) **Becki Foster** . . . . . . . . . . . . . . . . . . . . . . . . (405) 743-5432
Associate State Director for Partnerships, Workforce
    Recovery and Customize Services **Joe Robinson** . . . . . (405) 743-5198
Associate State Director for Research, STEM, Innovative
    and Federal Programs **Becki Foster** . . . . . . . . . . . . . . . (405) 743-5432
    E-mail: becki.foster@careertech.ok.gov
Chief Financial Officer **Jim Aulgur** . . . . . . . . . . . . . . . . . . (405) 743-5500

# Oklahoma Department of Commerce

900 North Stiles, Oklahoma City, OK 73104-3234
Tel: (405) 815-6552  Fax: (405) 815-5199  Internet: www.okcommerce.gov

**Employees:** 133

■ Executive Director **Deborah "Deby" Snodgrass** . . . . . . . . (405) 815-5306
    E-mail: deby.snodgrass@okcommerce.gov
    Assistant to the Executive Director **Janet Craven** . . . . . . (405) 815-5347
Chief of Staff **Jamie Herrera** . . . . . . . . . . . . . . . . . . . . . . (405) 815-5153
Deputy Director and Legal Counsel **Don Hackler** . . . . . . . (405) 815-5359
    Education: Oklahoma State BSBA; Oklahoma 1984 JD;
    Southern Nazarene 1988 MS
Human Resources and Organizational Development
    Director **LaRonda Molina** . . . . . . . . . . . . . . . . . . . . . . (405) 815-5247
National Recruiting Deputy Director
    **Charles Kimbrough** . . . . . . . . . . . . . . . . . . . . . . . . . . (405) 815-5361
Community Development Office Director **Vaughn Clark** . . . (405) 815-5370
Main Street Center Director **Linda Barnett** . . . . . . . . . . . . (405) 650-0739
Research and Economic Analysis Director **Jon Chiappe** . . . (405) 815-5210
Administrative Services Division Director **Stacie Willis** . . . (405) 815-5302
    E-mail: stacie.willis@okcommerce.gov

# Oklahoma Development Finance Authority

9220 North Kelly Avenue, Oklahoma City, OK 73131
Tel: (405) 842-1145  Fax: (405) 848-3314
E-mail: partner@okfinance.com

▲ Chairman **G. Bridger "Bridge" Cox** . . . . . . . . . . . . . . . . (405) 842-1145
    Affiliation: Chairman and President, Citizens Bank & Trust Co.
    P.O. Box 1689, Ardmore, OK 73402-1689
    Education: Oklahoma; Stonier
Chief Executive Officer/President **Michael Davis** . . . . . . . . (405) 842-1145
Senior Vice President **Jeremy Stoner** . . . . . . . . . . . . . . . . . (405) 842-1145

# Oklahoma Department of Corrections [DOC]

P.O. Box 11400, Oklahoma City, OK 73136-0400
Tel: (405) 425-2500  Fax: (405) 425-2886  Internet: www.ok.gov/doc

**Employees:** 4,264  **Fiscal Year:** 2014  **Budget:** $463,731,068

▲ Director (Interim) **Joe M. Allbaugh** . . . . . . . . . . . . . . . . (405) 425-2506
    E-mail: director@doc.state.ok.us
    Education: Oklahoma State 1975 BA
    Special Assistant to the Director **Lance Hetmer** . . . . . . . (405) 425-2505
    Executive Assistant **Kimberley Owen** . . . . . . . . . . . . . . (405) 425-2500
Administrative Operations Associate Director **Tina Hicks** . . (405) 425-2722
    E-mail: tina.hicks@doc.state.ok.us
    Community Sentencing Administrator
    **Becky Lawmaster** . . . . . . . . . . . . . . . . . . . . . . . . . . . (405) 523-3076
    E-mail: becky.lawmaster@doc.state.ok.us
    Health Services Division Manager **Clint Castleberry** . . . . (405) 962-6084

*(continued on next page)*

---

★ Elected Official   ■ Appointed by Governor   ● Appointed by Legislature   ▲ Appointed by Board or Commission   ◆ Appointed by State Supreme Court

**Oklahoma Department of Corrections** *continued*

Chief Medical Officer **(Vacant)** . . . . . . . . . . . . . . . . . . .(405) 962-6155
   2901 North Classen Boulevard, Suite 100,     Fax: (405) 962-6147
   Oklahoma City, OK 73106

Field Operations Associate Director
   **Edward L. "Ed" Evans** . . . . . . . . . . . . . . . . . . .(405) 425-2550

Community Corrections Division Manager (Acting)
   **Anthony Rowell** . . . . . . . . . . . . . . . . . . . . . . .(405) 523-3075

Field Support Division Manager **Laura Pitman** . . . . . . . .(405) 962-6100

East Institutions Division Manager **David Parker** . . . . . . (918) 426-6116
   122 E. Carl Albert Pkwy., McAlester, OK 74501

West Institutions Division Manager **Greg Williams** . . . . .(405) 425-7516

Communications Director **Terri Watkins** . . . . . . . . . . . . . .(405) 425-2565
   E-mail: terri.watkins@doc.state.ok.us

Public Information Officer **(Vacant)** . . . . . . . . . . . . . . .(405) 425-2520

Legislative Liaison **Marilyn Davidson** . . . . . . . . . . . . . . .(405) 425-2505

General Counsel **David Cincotta** . . . . . . . . . . . . . . . . . .(405) 425-2515

Inspector General **Johnny Blevins** . . . . . . . . . . . . . . . . . .(405) 425-2567
   E-mail: johnny.blevins@doc.state.ok.us

# Oklahoma Department of Emergency Management [OEM]

P.O. Box 53365, Oklahoma City, OK 73152-3365
Tel: (405) 521-2481  Fax: (405) 521-4053

**Employees:** 28

■Director **Albert Ashwood** . . . . . . . . . . . . . . . . . . . . . .(405) 521-2481
   E-mail: albert.ashwood@oem.ok.gov
   Education: Central Oklahoma 1989 BA

Deputy Director **Michelann Ooten** . . . . . . . . . . . . . . . .(405) 521-2481

Chief Financial Officer **Sandra Jackson** . . . . . . . . . . . . .(405) 521-2481

Grants Management Chief **Bonnie McKelvey** . . . . . . . . . .(405) 521-2481

Public Information Officer **Keli Cain** . . . . . . . . . . . . . . .(405) 521-2481
   E-mail: keli.cain@oem.ok.gov

# Oklahoma Department of Environmental Quality [DEQ]

707 North Robinson, Oklahoma City, OK 73101-1677
P.O. Box 1677, Oklahoma City, OK 73101
Tel: (405) 702-0100  Tel: (800) 522-0206 (Complaints Hotline)
Tel: (800) 869-1400 (Customer Assistance Hotline)  Fax: (405) 702-7101
Internet: www.deq.state.ok.us

**Employees:** 516

▲Executive Director **Scott Thompson** . . . . . . . . . . . . . . . .(405) 702-7100
   E-mail: scott.thompson@deq.ok.gov

Deputy Executive Director **Jimmy D. Givens** . . . . . . . . . .(405) 702-7100

General Counsel **Martha Penisten** . . . . . . . . . . . . . . . . .(405) 702-7100
   E-mail: martha.penisten@deq.ok.gov

Air Quality Division Director **Eddie Terrill** . . . . . . . . . . . .(405) 702-4100

Environmental Complaints and Local Services Division
   Director **Gary Collins** . . . . . . . . . . . . . . . . . . . . . . .(405) 702-6100

Land Protection Division Director **Kelly Dixon** . . . . . . . . . .(405) 702-5100

State Environmental Laboratory Services Division
   Director **Chris Armstrong** . . . . . . . . . . . . . . . . . . . .(405) 702-1000

Water Quality Division Director **Shellie Chard-McClary** . .(405) 702-8100

External Affairs Director **Lloyd Kirk** . . . . . . . . . . . . . . . .(405) 702-5100

Public Information Manager **Erin Hatfield** . . . . . . . . . . . .(405) 702-7100
   E-mail: erin.hatfield@deq.ok.gov

# Oklahoma State Department of Health [OSDH]

1000 N.E. 10th Street, Oklahoma City, OK 73117-1207
P.O. Box 53551, Oklahoma City, OK 73152 (Vital Records)
Tel: (405) 271-5600  Tel: (405) 271-4040 (Vital Records)
Fax: (405) 271-3431  E-mail: webmaster@health.ok.gov

**Employees:** 2,400

■Commissioner **Terry L. Cline, PhD** . . . . . . . . . . . . . . . .(405) 271-4200
   E-mail: terryc@health.ok.gov

Senior Deputy Commissioner **Julie Cox-Kain** . . . . . . . . . .(405) 271-5600
   Education: Oklahoma BA, MPA

General Counsel **Donald Maisch** . . . . . . . . . . . . . . . . . . .(405) 271-6017

Communications Office Director **Tony D. Sellars** . . . . . . . .(405) 271-5601
   E-mail: tonys@health.ok.gov

Minority Health Director **Linda Thomas** . . . . . . . . . . . . . .(405) 271-1337

Center for the Advancement of Wellness Director
   **Stephanie U'Ren** . . . . . . . . . . . . . . . . . . . . . . . . .(405) 271-3619

Center for Health Innovation and Effectiveness
   Director **Joseph Fairbanks** . . . . . . . . . . . . . . .(405) 271-9444 ext. 56309
   E-mail: joef@health.ok.gov

Partnerships for Health Improvement Director
   **James Allen** . . . . . . . . . . . . . . . . . . . . . . . . . . .(405) 271-6127

Chief Financial Officer **(Vacant)** . . . . . . . . . . . . . . . . . .(405) 271-5600

Chief Operating Officer **Deborah Nichols** . . . . . . . . . . . .(405) 271-4200

Controller (Interim) **Mike Truitt** . . . . . . . . . . . . . . . . . . .(405) 271-4042

Continuation of Operations Director **John McCarty** . . . . .(405) 271-3781

Accounting Services Chief **Mike Truitt** . . . . . . . . . . . . . .(405) 271-4042

Building Management and Internal Services Chief
   (Interim) **Rocky McElvany** . . . . . . . . . . . . . . . . . .(405) 271-1777

Human Resources Office Chief **Jacqueline Petit** . . . . . . . .(405) 271-4171

Procurement Chief (Interim) **Ashley Hillemeyer** . . . . . . . .(405) 271-4043

## Community and Family Health Services

Deputy Commissioner **Tina Johnson, RN** . . . . . . . . . . . . .(405) 271-5585

Assistant Deputy Commissioner **Neil Hann, CHES** . . . . . .(405) 271-5585

Child Guidance Service Director **Beth Martin** . . . . . . . . . .(405) 271-4477

Dental Health Service Director **Jana Winfree, DDS** . . . . . .(405) 271-5502

Family Support and Prevention Service Director
   **Annette Jacobi** . . . . . . . . . . . . . . . . . . . . . . . . .(405) 271-7611

Maternal and Child Health Service Director
   **Joyce Marshall** . . . . . . . . . . . . . . . . . . . . . . . . .(405) 271-4480
   E-mail: joycem@health.ok.gov

Nursing Service Director **Tina Johnson, RN** . . . . . . . . . . .(405) 271-5183

Record Evaluation and Support Director **Michael Ewald** . .(405) 271-5585

SoonerStart Service Director **John Corpolongo** . . . . . . . . .(405) 271-6617

WIC (Women, Infants and Children) Services Director
   **Terry Bryce** . . . . . . . . . . . . . . . . . . . . . . . . . . .(405) 271-4676
   E-mail: terryb@health.ok.gov

## Prevention and Preparedness Services

Deputy Commissioner **Toni Frioux** . . . . . . . . . . . . . . . . .(405) 271-3272

State Epidemiologist **Kristy Bradley** . . . . . . . . . . . . . . . .(405) 271-4060
   Education: Oklahoma 1996 MPH; Iowa State DVM

Acute Disease Service Director **Lauri Smithee** . . . . . . . . .(405) 271-4060

Chronic Disease Service Director **Jon Lowry, MPH** . . . . . .(405) 271-4072

Emergency Preparedness and Response Service Director
   **Scott Sproat** . . . . . . . . . . . . . . . . . . . . . . . . . . .(405) 271-0900

HIV/STD Service Director **Jan Fox** . . . . . . . . . . . . . . . . .(405) 271-4636

Immunization Service Director **Lori Linstead** . . . . . . . . . .(405) 271-4073

Injury Prevention Service Director **Sheryll Brown** . . . . . . .(405) 271-3430

Public Health Laboratory Service Director
   **S. Terence "Terry" Dunn** . . . . . . . . . . . . . . . . . . . .(405) 271-5070

Screening and Special Services Director **Sharon Vaz** . . . . .(405) 271-6617

## Protective Health Services

Tel: (405) 271-6868  Fax: (405) 271-3442

Deputy Commissioner **Henry "Hank" Hartsell** . . . . . . . . .(405) 271-5288

Consumer Health Services Director **Lynnette Jordan** . . . . .(405) 271-5243

Health Resources Development Service Director
   **James Joslin** . . . . . . . . . . . . . . . . . . . . . . . . . . .(405) 271-6868
                         Fax: (405) 271-7360

Long Term Care Services Director **Michael Cook** . . . . . . .(405) 271-6868
                         Fax: (405) 271-2206

Medical Facilities Services Director **Lee Martin** . . . . . . . .(405) 271-4027

Quality Improvement and Evaluation Service Director
   **Nancy Atkinson** . . . . . . . . . . . . . . . . . . . . . . . . .(405) 271-5278

---

★ Elected Official   ■ Appointed by Governor   ● Appointed by Legislature   ▲ Appointed by Board or Commission   ◆ Appointed by State Supreme Court

# Oklahoma Department of Human Services [OKDHS]

P.O. Box 25352, Oklahoma City, OK 73125
Tel: (405) 521-3646  TTY: (405) 521-2778  Fax: (405) 522-3146

**Employees:** 7,185

▲ Director **Edward Lake** . . . . . . . . . . . . . . . . . . . . . . (405) 521-3646
  E-mail: ed.lake@okdhs.org
  Education: East Tennessee State BS; North Carolina MSW
  Executive Assistant **Daphne Mosley** . . . . . . . . . . . . . . (405) 521-3646
Chief of Staff **Lee Anne Bruce Boone** . . . . . . . . . . . . . . (405) 521-3646
  Education: Carson-Newman BA; Tennessee JD
General Counsel **Ronald Baze** . . . . . . . . . . . . . . . . . . (405) 521-3638
Civil Rights Administrator **William Drapala** . . . . . . . . . . (405) 521-3529
Inspector General Office Division Administrator
  **Tony Bryan** . . . . . . . . . . . . . . . . . . . . . . . . . . . . (405) 522-5888
Client Advocacy General **Kathryn Brewer** . . . . . . . . . . . (405) 525-4850
Human Resources Management Director (Acting)
  **Lee Anne Bruce Boone** . . . . . . . . . . . . . . . . . . . . (405) 521-3646
Planning, Research and Statistics Office Director
  **Connie Schlittler** . . . . . . . . . . . . . . . . . . . . . . . (405) 521-3552
Intergovernmental Relations and Policy Office
  Coordinator **Renee Banks** . . . . . . . . . . . . . . . . . . (405) 521-6392
  E-mail: renee.banks@okdhs.org

## Adult and Family Services

Director **James "Jim" Struby** . . . . . . . . . . . . . . . . . . (405) 521-3076
  Education: Trinity U 1976 BA
Child Care Services Director **Lesli Blazer** . . . . . . . . . . . (405) 521-3561

## Child Welfare Services

Fax: (405) 521-4373
Director **Jami Ledoux** . . . . . . . . . . . . . . . . . . . . . . . (405) 521-3777

## Communications and Community Relations

Director **Sheree Powell** . . . . . . . . . . . . . . . . . . . . . . (405) 521-3027
  E-mail: sheree.powell@okdhs.org
Communications Coordinator **Sheree Powell** . . . . . . . . . (405) 521-3027
  E-mail: sheree.powell@okdhs.org
Community and Faith Engagement Administrator
  **Karen Jacobs** . . . . . . . . . . . . . . . . . . . . . . . . . . (405) 522-2528
  Education: Central Oklahoma 1999 BA
Information and Referral Office Coordinator
  **Cynthia Kinkade** . . . . . . . . . . . . . . . . . . . . . . . . (405) 521-3646
  E-mail: Cynthia.Kinkade@okdhs.org

## Community Living and Support Services

Director **Mark Lawton Jones** . . . . . . . . . . . . . . . . . . (405) 521-6395
  Education: Oklahoma 1977 BA, 1980 JD
Aging Services Director **Lance Robertson** . . . . . . . . . . . (405) 521-2281
Child Support Services Director (Interim)
  **Jim Hutchinson** . . . . . . . . . . . . . . . . . . . . . . . . (405) 522-2273
  E-mail: jim.hutchinson@okdhs.org
Developmental Disabilities Services Director
  **Marie Moore** . . . . . . . . . . . . . . . . . . . . . . . . . . (405) 521-6267

## Finance and Administration

Director **David Ligon** . . . . . . . . . . . . . . . . . . . . . . . (405) 521-3557
Support Services Director **Kelly Kappelman** . . . . . . . . . . (405) 521-3095
  E-mail: kelly.kappelman@okdhs.org
Office of Business Quality Director **Mark Robison** . . . . . . (405) 525-4861

# Oklahoma Department of Libraries [ODL]

200 NE 18th Street, Oklahoma City, OK 73105-3298
Tel: (405) 521-2502  Fax: (405) 525-7804  Internet: www.odl.state.ok.us

**Employees:** 46

▲ Director **Susan McVey** . . . . . . . . . . . . . . . . . . . . . (405) 522-3173
  E-mail: susan.mcvey@libraries.ok.gov
  Education: Oklahoma 1973 BA; Texas 1975 MLS;
  Oklahoma 1983 MPA

Deputy Director **Vicki Sullivan** . . . . . . . . . . . . . . . . . (405) 522-3215
  Education: Oklahoma 1973 BS, 1974 MLS; Oklahoma State 1977 MA
Archives and Records Administrator **Jan Davis** . . . . . . . . (405) 522-3191
Library Resources Administrator **Kitty Pittman** . . . . . . . . (405) 522-3192
  E-mail: kitty.pittman@libraries.ok.gov
  Education: Oklahoma 1974 BA, 1976 MLS
Library Development Office Administrator **Vicki Mohr** . . . . (405) 522-3293
  Education: Oklahoma 1973 BA, 1975 MLS
Public Information Office Administrator **Bill Young** . . . . . . (405) 522-3562
  E-mail: bill.young@libraries.ok.gov
  Education: Oklahoma 1980 BA
Senior Legal Reference Librarian **Christine Chen** . . . . . . . (405) 522-3212

# Oklahoma Department of Mental Health and Substance Abuse Services [ODMHSAS]

P.O. Box 53277, Oklahoma City, OK 73152-3277
Tel: (405) 522-3908  TTY: (405) 522-3851  Fax: (405) 522-3650

**Employees:** 1,729

▲ Commissioner **Terri White** . . . . . . . . . . . . . . . . . . (405) 522-3877
  E-mail: tlwhite@odmhsas.org
  Education: Oklahoma 1997 BASW, 1998 MSW
Chief Operating Officer **Durand Crosby** . . . . . . . . . . . . (405) 522-3877
Deputy Commissioner of Treatment and Recovery
  Services **Carrie Slatton-Hodges** . . . . . . . . . . . . . . . (405) 522-3877
  Executive Assistant **Angie Patterson** . . . . . . . . . . . . (405) 522-3877
Decision Support Services **Mark Reynolds** . . . . . . . . . . (405) 522-3813
Financial Services Director **Rich Edwards** . . . . . . . . . . . (405) 522-3900
Human Resources Management and Development
  Director **Ellen Buettner** . . . . . . . . . . . . . . . . . . . (405) 522-3902
Information and Network Services Director
  **Kevin Marble** . . . . . . . . . . . . . . . . . . . . . . . . . (405) 522-3801
  E-mail: kmarble@odmhsas.org
Provider Certification Director **Stephanie Gay** . . . . . . . . (405) 522-3800
  E-mail: sgay@odmhsas.org
Consumer Advocate General **Joseph Mickey** . . . . . . . . . (405) 573-6605
Inspector General **Jason Maddox** . . . . . . . . . . . . . . . (405) 522-4058
Public Information Director **Jeffrey Dismukes** . . . . . . . . (405) 522-3907
  E-mail: jdismukes@odmhsas.org

## General Counsel's Office

Tel: (405) 522-3871
General Counsel **Dewayne Moore** . . . . . . . . . . . . . . . (405) 522-3871
  E-mail: dmoore@odmhsas.org
Risk Management Coordinator **Tom Ferguson** . . . . . . . . (405) 522-3830

# Oklahoma Military Department

3501 Military Circle, Oklahoma City, OK 73111-4398
Tel: (405) 228-5000  Fax: (405) 228-5524

**Employees:** 350

■ Adjutant General **MG Robbie L. Asher, ARNG** . . . . . . . (405) 228-5201
  E-mail: robbie.asher@ok.gov
  Education: Oklahoma 1985 BBA; Oklahoma State 1994 MS
Assistant Adjutant General for Air
  **BrigGen Gregory Ferguson, ANG** . . . . . . . . . . . . . (405) 228-5000
  Education: Oklahoma 1983 BS; Oklahoma State 2007 MS
Assistant Adjutant General for Army
  **BG Hopper T. Smith, ARNG** . . . . . . . . . . . . . . . . (405) 228-5000
Chief of the Joint Staff **COL Jon M. Harrison, ARNG** . . . . (405) 228-5200
Aviation Deputy Chief of Staff **(Vacant)** . . . . . . . . . . . (405) 228-5606
Engineering Deputy Chief of Staff
  **LTC Mark Clifton, ARNG** . . . . . . . . . . . . . . . . . . (405) 228-5577
Plans, Operations and Training Deputy Chief of Staff
  **COL Bobby Yandell, ARNG** . . . . . . . . . . . . . . . . . (405) 228-5208
  E-mail: bobby.yandell@ok.gov
Personnel and Administration Deputy Chief of Staff
  **COL Cynthia Tinkham, ARNG** . . . . . . . . . . . . . . . (405) 228-5098
Director, J6 **LTC Tommy Mancino, ARNG** . . . . . . . . . . (405) 228-5660
Director of Manpower and Personnel
  **COL Tracy Spencer, ARNG** . . . . . . . . . . . . . . . . . (405) 228-5383
Public Affairs Officer **COL Max Moss, ARNG** . . . . . . . . (405) 228-5158

*(continued on next page)*

EXECUTIVE BRANCH

**Oklahoma Military Department** *continued*

USPFO (US Property and Fiscal Officer) for Oklahoma
 **COL Curtis D. Arnold, ARNG** . . . . . . . . . . . . . . . . . . . . . . (405) 228-5280
Command Chief Warrant Officer
 **CW5 Christopher A. Rau, ARNG** . . . . . . . . . . . . . . . . . (405) 228-5000
Command Sergeant Major **CSM Tony F. Riggs, ARNG** . . . . (405) 228-5000

# Oklahoma Department of Mines [ODOM]

2915 North Classen Boulevard, Suite 213, Oklahoma City, OK 73106
Tel: (405) 427-3859  Fax: (405) 427-9646

**Employees:** 31

▲Director **Mary Ann Pritchard** . . . . . . . . . . . . . . . . . . . . . . . (405) 427-3859
 E-mail: mary.pritchard@mines.ok.gov
Deputy Director **Doug Schooley** . . . . . . . . . . . . . . . . . . . . . (405) 427-3859
Coal Administrator **Rhonda Dossett** . . . . . . . . . . . . . . . . . (918) 485-3999
 29858 East 690 Road, Wagoner, OK 74467
 E-mail: rhonda.dossett@mines.ok.gov
Minerals Administrator **Richard Shore** . . . . . . . . . . . . . . . (405) 427-3859
 E-mail: richard.shore@mines.ok.gov

# Oklahoma Department of Public Safety [DPS]

P.O. Box 11415, Oklahoma City, OK 73136
Tel: (405) 425-2424  Fax: (405) 419-2050
E-mail: comment@dps.state.ok.us  Internet: www.dps.state.ok.us

**Employees:** 1,458

■Commissioner **Michael C. "Mike" Thompson** . . . . . . . . . (405) 425-2001
 E-mail: mike.thompson@dps.ok.gov
Assistant Commissioner **Gerald Davidson** . . . . . . . . . . . . (405) 425-2002
General Counsel **Stephen Krise** . . . . . . . . . . . . . . . . . . . . (405) 425-2148
Comptroller **Stevi Vinson** . . . . . . . . . . . . . . . . . . . . . . . . (405) 425-2951
Commercial Driver License Administrator
 **Tamara Shepherd** . . . . . . . . . . . . . . . . . . . . . . . . . . . . . (405) 425-2015
Department Services Administrator **George Randolph** . . . . (405) 425-2940
 E-mail: george.randolph@dps.ok.gov
Driver Compliance Unit Director **Douglas Young** . . . . . . . (405) 425-2148
 E-mail: douglas.young@dps.ok.gov
Driver License Services Director **Jeff Hankins** . . . . . . . . . (405) 425-7745
 E-mail: jeff.hankins@dps.ok.gov
Finance Division Director **Cynthia C. Hughes** . . . . . . . . . . (405) 425-7009
Human Resources Director **Tanara Lang** . . . . . . . . . . . . . (405) 425-2163
Oklahoma Highway Safety Office Director **Toby Taylor** . . . (405) 523-1584
 E-mail: toby.taylor@dps.ok.gov
Public Affairs Office Director **Capt. Paul Timmons** . . . . . . (405) 425-7709
 E-mail: paul.timmons@dps.ok.gov
Record Management Division Director **Virgil Bonham** . . . . (405) 425-2047
Telecommunications Division Director **Gene Thaxton** . . . . (405) 425-2340
Highway Patrol Chief **Ricky G. Adams** . . . . . . . . . . . . . . . (405) 425-2003
Legislative Services Manager **Chris Sherman** . . . . . . . . . . (405) 425-7394
 E-mail: thomas.sherman@dps.ok.gov
Legislative Liaison **Randy Rogers** . . . . . . . . . . . . . . . . . . (405) 425-2761
 E-mail: randy.rogers@dps.ok.gov

# Oklahoma Office of Homeland Security [OKOHS]

P.O. Box 11415, Oklahoma City, OK 73111
Tel: (405) 425-7296  Fax: (405) 425-7295  E-mail: info@okohs.ok.gov

■Director **Kim Edd Carter** . . . . . . . . . . . . . . . . . . . . . . . . (405) 425-7296
 E-mail: kim.carter@okohs.ok.gov
 Education: Oklahoma State BA, MS

# Oklahoma Department of Rehabilitation Services [DRS]

3535 NW 58th Street, Suite 500, Oklahoma City, OK 73112-4815
Tel: (405) 951-3400  Tel: (800) 845-8476  TTY: (405) 951-3400
Fax: (405) 951-3529  E-mail: info@okdrs.gov  Internet: www.okdrs.gov

**Employees:** 934

▲Director (Interim) **Noel Tyler** . . . . . . . . . . . . . . . . . . . . . (405) 951-3400

Executive Secretary **Linda Santin** . . . . . . . . . . . . . . . . . . (405) 951-3490
Chief of Staff **Cheryl Gray** . . . . . . . . . . . . . . . . . . . . . . . (405) 951-3400
Disability Determination Division Administrator
 **Noel Tyler** . . . . . . . . . . . . . . . . . . . . . . . . . . . . . . . . . . (405) 419-2507
  Fax: (405) 419-2785
Visual Services Division Administrator **Douglas Boone** . . . (405) 951-3485
Vocational Rehabilitation Division Administrator
 **Mark Kinnison** . . . . . . . . . . . . . . . . . . . . . . . . . . . . . . (405) 951-3491
Chief Fiscal Officer **Kevin Statham** . . . . . . . . . . . . . . . . . (405) 951-3418
Public Information Manager **Jody Harlin** . . . . . . . . . . . . . (405) 951-3497
 E-mail: jharlin@okdrs.gov

# Oklahoma School for the Blind

3300 Gibson Street, Muskogee, OK 74403
Tel: (918) 781-8200  Fax: (918) 682-8300

Superintendent **Christine Boone** . . . . . . . . . . . . . . . . . . . (918) 781-8200

# Oklahoma School for the Deaf

1100 East Oklahoma Avenue, Sulphur, OK 73086-3108
Tel: (888) 685-3323  Fax: (580) 622-4950

Superintendent **KaAnn Varner** . . . . . . . . . . . . . . . . . . . . (580) 622-4908
 Education: Montevallo

# Oklahoma Department of Transportation [ODOT]

200 NE 21st Street, Oklahoma City, OK 73105
Tel: (405) 522-8000  Fax: (405) 521-2524  E-mail: odotinfo@odot.org

**Employees:** 2,323

■Director **J. Michael Patterson** . . . . . . . . . . . . . . . . . . . . (405) 522-1800
 E-mail: mpatterson@odot.org  Fax: (405) 522-1805
 Education: Central Oklahoma 1976 BS, 1993 MBA
 Executive Assistant **Tammy Nowakowski** . . . . . . . . . . . (405) 522-1801
Deputy Director **Tim Gatz** . . . . . . . . . . . . . . . . . . . . . . . (405) 521-6000
 Education: Oklahoma State 1989 BLA
Chief Engineer **Casey Shell, PE** . . . . . . . . . . . . . . . . . . . (405) 521-2688
 Education: Arkansas 1986 BCE
General Counsel **Norman Hill** . . . . . . . . . . . . . . . . . . . . . (405) 521-2630
 E-mail: nhill@odot.org
 Education: Oklahoma 1971 BBA, 1975 JD

## Transportation Commission

■Chairman **Gregory M. "Greg" Love** (District 4) . . . . . . . . (405) 521-2631
 10601 North Pennsylvania Avenue,  Dist: (405) 302-6644
 Oklahoma City, OK 73120
 E-mail: gregl@loves.com
 Affiliation: Co-Chief Executive Officer, Love's Travel Stops & Country
 Stores, Inc.
 10601 North Pennsylvania Avenue, Oklahoma City, OK 73120
 Education: Trinity U 1984
■Vice Chairman **J. David Burrage** (District 2) . . . . . . . . . . (580) 889-7357
 P.O. Box 960, Atoka, OK 74525-0960
 E-mail: davidburrage@firstbank-ok.com
■Secretary **C. Todd Huckabay** (District 5) . . . . . . . . . . . . (405) 521-2631
 P.O. Box 348, Snyder, OK 73566  Dist: (580) 569-4347
 E-mail: thuckabay@bankofthewichitas.com
 Affiliation: President and Chief Executive Officer, Bank of the Wichitas
 623 E Street, Snyder, OK 73566
■Commissioner **Bobby J. Alexander** (District 6) . . . . . . . . . (405) 521-2631
 P.O. Box 1570, Woodward, OK 73802  Dist: (580) 254-3232
 E-mail: babby@powerrig.net
 Affiliation: Owner and Operator, Power Rig
■Commissioner **Bradley Warren Burgess** (District 7) . . . . . (405) 521-2631
 21 Northwest 44th Street, Suite 201,  Dist: (580) 355-8920
 Lawton, OK 73505
 E-mail: brad@burgess-hightower.com
 Affiliation: Managing Partner, Burgess, Burgess, Burgess & Hightower
 21 NW 44th Street, Suite 201, Lawton, OK 73505
 Education: Cameron 1980 BA; Oklahoma 1983 JD
■Commissioner **John Fidler** (District 1) . . . . . . . . . . . . . . . (405) 521-2631
 P.O. Box 1117, Okmulgee, OK 74447-1117  Dist: (918) 756-7993
 E-mail: jfidler@citizenssecurity.com
 Affiliation: Executive Vice President, Citizens Security Bank
 14821 South Memorial, Bixby, OK 74008

---

★ Elected Official   ■ Appointed by Governor   ● Appointed by Legislature   ▲ Appointed by Board or Commission   ◆ Appointed by State Supreme Court

EXECUTIVE BRANCH

■Commissioner
**Danny Blaine "Dan" Overland** (District 3) . . . . . . . . . . (405) 521-2631
P.O. Box 66, Earlsboro, OK 74840        Dist: (405) 997-5201
E-mail: dan@goptc.net
Affiliation: Senior Vice President, Pottawatomie Telephone Company
300 West Main Street, Earlsboro, OK 74840-8903

■Commissioner **Peter J. Regan** (District 8) . . . . . . . . . . . . . (405) 521-2631
4124 South Rockford, Suite 201, Tulsa, OK 74105        Dist: (918) 293-3921
E-mail: pete@devonshirelaw.com
Affiliation: Executive Director, Domestic Energy Producers Alliance
PO Box 18359, Oklahoma City, OK 73154

## Capital Programs

Director of Capital Programs **Dawn Sullivan, PE** . . . . . . . . (405) 522-6000
E-mail: dsullivan@odot.org
Education: Oklahoma BS

Project Management Division Manager **Ray Sanders** . . . . . (405) 522-7600
E-mail: rsanders@odot.org

Local Government Division Engineer **Shannon Sheffert** . . (405) 521-2553

Facilities Management Division Manager **Rick Johnson** . . . (405) 522-6000
Education: Southern Nazarene

Rail Programs Division Manager **Craig Moody** . . . . . . . . . (405) 522-6000

Strategic Asset and Performance Management Division
Engineer **David Ooten, PE** . . . . . . . . . . . . . . . . . . . . (405) 521-2704
E-mail: dooten@odot.org
Education: Oklahoma State BS

Tribal Coordinator **Rhonda Sair** . . . . . . . . . . . . . . . . . . (405) 522-6000

## Engineering
Fax: (405) 522-6994

Director of Engineering **Tim Tegeler, PE** . . . . . . . . . . . . (405) 521-6916
E-mail: ttegeler@odot.org
Education: Iowa State BS

Bridge Division Engineer **Steve Jacobi** . . . . . . . . . . . . . . (405) 521-2606
E-mail: sjacobi@odot.org

Chief Traffic Engineer **Harold Smart** . . . . . . . . . . . . . . . (405) 521-2861

Environmental Programs Division Engineer **(Vacant)** . . . . . (405) 521-2927

Legal Division Manager **Morris Bell** . . . . . . . . . . . . . . . . (405) 521-2681
Education: Oklahoma 1977 JD

Right of Way and Utilities Division Manager **(Vacant)** . . . . (405) 521-2661

Roadway Design Division Engineer **Caleb Austin** . . . . . . . . (405) 521-2695
E-mail: caustin@odot.org
Education: Oklahoma State BSCE

Survey Division Manager **Leroy Tackett** . . . . . . . . . . . . . . (405) 521-2621
E-mail: ltackett@odot.org

## Finance and Administration
Fax: (405) 522-5957

Director of Finance and Administration **Russell Hulin** . . . . (405) 522-8000
E-mail: rhulin@odot.org

Comptroller Division **Chelley Hilmes** . . . . . . . . . . . . . . . (405) 521-2591

Human Resources Division **Brian Kirtley** . . . . . . . . . . . . . (405) 521-2541

Media and Public Affairs Director **Terri Angier** . . . . . . . . (405) 521-6004
Education: Oklahoma 1989 BA, MA

Programs Division **Sam Adkins** . . . . . . . . . . . . . . . . . . . (405) 521-2521
E-mail: sadkins@odot.org

Training Division **Scott Lange** . . . . . . . . . . . . . . . . . . . (405) 521-4141

Purchasing Branch **Jennifer Mason, CPO** . . . . . . . . . . . . (405) 522-6792

## Operations
Fax: (405) 521-4253

Director of Operations **Paul D. Green, PE** . . . . . . . . . . . . (405) 521-4675
E-mail: pdgreen@odot.org
Education: Oklahoma State 1996

Assistant Director of Operations **George Raymond, PE** . . . (405) 521-4884
Education: Oklahoma BS

Construction Division Engineer **John Leonard, PE** . . . . . . (405) 521-2561
E-mail: jleonard@odot.org

Maintenance Division Engineer **Brad Mirth** . . . . . . . . . . . (405) 521-2557
E-mail: bmirth@odot.org

Materials and Research Division Engineer
**Scott Seiter, PE** . . . . . . . . . . . . . . . . . . . . . . . . . . . (405) 521-2677
E-mail: sseiter@odot.org

Office Engineer **Anthony Delce, PE** . . . . . . . . . . . . . . . . (405) 521-2625
E-mail: adelce@odot.org

# Oklahoma Department of Veterans Affairs [ODVA]
P.O. Box 53067, Oklahoma City, OK 73152
Tel: (405) 521-3684  Fax: (405) 521-6533

**Employees:** 1,915

▲Executive Director **MG Myles L. Deering, ARNG** . . . . . . . (405) 521-3684
E-mail: mdeering@odva.state.ok.us
Assistant to the Executive Director
**MajGen LaRita A. "Rita" Aragon, ANG (Ret)** . . . . . . (405) 521-4626

Deputy Director **Doug Elliott** . . . . . . . . . . . . . . . . . . . (405) 521-3684

Human Resources Director **Susan McClure** . . . . . . . . . . . (405) 521-3091

Chief Financial Officer **Shantha Varahan** . . . . . . . . . . . . (405) 522-6722

Construction Program Administrator **Dorita Herd** . . . . . . . (405) 521-3157

Public Information Office **Shane Faulkner** . . . . . . . . . . . . (405) 521-6099

State Veterans Homes Director **Terry Wilkerson** . . . . . . . . (405) 521-6212

Veterans Education and Training Director **Beki Miller** . . . . . (405) 522-5303

Legislative Liaison **Nicole Miller** . . . . . . . . . . . . . . . . . . (405) 521-2044
E-mail: nrmiller@odva.state.ok.us

## War Veterans Commission
P.O. Box 53067, Oklahoma City, OK 73152
Tel: (405) 521-3684  Fax: (405) 521-6533

■Chair **Jerletta M. Halford-Pandos** . . . . . . . . . . . . . . . . (405) 521-3684

■Vice-Chair **John Carter** . . . . . . . . . . . . . . . . . . . . . . . (405) 521-3684

■Secretary **Eric Tuck** . . . . . . . . . . . . . . . . . . . . . . . . . . (405) 521-3684
Affiliation: Contract Specialist, Eastern Oklahoma VA Health Care
System, VISN 16 - South Central VA Healthcare Network, United
States Department of Veterans Affairs
1011 Honor Heights Drive, Muskogee, OK 74401

■Commissioner **Robert A. "Robbie" Clark** . . . . . . . . . . . . (405) 521-3684

■Commissioner **Rebecca McGary** . . . . . . . . . . . . . . . . . . (405) 521-3684

■Commissioner **Ivenhoe "Tom" Richey** . . . . . . . . . . . . . (405) 521-3684

■Commissioner **Everett "Lloyd" Smithson** . . . . . . . . . . . . (405) 521-3684

■Commissioner **Larry Van Schuyver** . . . . . . . . . . . . . . . . (405) 521-3684

■Commissioner **Robert L. Willis** . . . . . . . . . . . . . . . . . . (405) 521-3684

# Oklahoma Securities Commission
204 North Robinson, Suite 400, Oklahoma City, OK 73102
Tel: (405) 280-7700  Fax: (405) 280-7742

■Chair **Nancy Hyde** . . . . . . . . . . . . . . . . . . . . . . . . . . (405) 280-7700

■Vice Chair **Charles E. Newton** . . . . . . . . . . . . . . . . . . . (405) 280-7700

■Member **P. David Newsome, Jr.** . . . . . . . . . . . . . . . . . . (405) 280-7700

■Member **Robert M. Neville** . . . . . . . . . . . . . . . . . . . . . (405) 280-7700

■Ex-Officio **Mick Thompson** . . . . . . . . . . . . . . . . . . . . . (405) 280-7700

# Oklahoma Department of Securities
204 North Robinson, Suite 400, Oklahoma City, OK 73102
Tel: (405) 280-7700  Fax: (405) 280-7742
E-mail: general@securities.ok.gov  Internet: www.securities.ok.gov

**Employees:** 26

Administrator **Irving L. Faught** . . . . . . . . . . . . . . (405) 280-7700 ext. 7706
Education: Oklahoma 1962 BA; Virginia 1965 JD

Deputy Administrator **Melanie Hall** . . . . . . . . . . . . . . . . (405) 280-7707

# Oklahoma Tourism and Recreation Commission
900 North Stiles, Oklahoma City, OK 73104-3234
Tel: (405) 230-8300

■Chair **Todd Lamb** . . . . . . . . . . . . . . . . . . . . . . . . . . (405) 230-8301

■Member **Gean B. Atkinson** . . . . . . . . . . . . . . . . . . . . . (405) 230-8301
Affiliation: President, Atkinson Advertising Associates, Inc.
2200 Northwest 50th Street, Suite 280, Oklahoma City, OK 73112
Education: Central Oklahoma BA, MA

■Member **Robyn Batson** . . . . . . . . . . . . . . . . . . . . . . . (405) 230-8301

■Member **Rick Henry** . . . . . . . . . . . . . . . . . . . . . . . . . (405) 230-8301
Affiliation: Council Member, Office of the Mayor and City Council,
City of Altus, Oklahoma
509 South Main Street, Altus, OK 73521

■Member **Grant Humphreys** . . . . . . . . . . . . . . . . . . . . (405) 230-8301
Education: Baylor

*(continued on next page)*

---

★ Elected Official        ■ Appointed by Governor        ● Appointed by Legislature        ▲ Appointed by Board or Commission        ◆ Appointed by State Supreme Court

**EXECUTIVE BRANCH**

**Oklahoma Tourism and Recreation Commission** *continued*

■ Member **Xavier Neira** . . . . . . . . . . . . . . . . . . . . . . . . . . . (405) 230-8301
■ Member **Chuck Perry** . . . . . . . . . . . . . . . . . . . . . . . . . . . (405) 230-8301
■ Member **Rhonda Roush** . . . . . . . . . . . . . . . . . . . . . . . . . (405) 230-8301
■ Member **Mike Wilt** . . . . . . . . . . . . . . . . . . . . . . . . . . . . . (405) 230-8301
   Education: John Brown 1986 BS

# Oklahoma Tourism and Recreation Department

900 North Stiles, Oklahoma City, OK 73104-3234
P.O. Box 52002, Oklahoma City, OK 73152-2002
Tel: (405) 230-8300  Fax: (405) 230-8600
E-mail: information@travelok.com  Internet: www.travelok.com

**Employees:** 580

■ Executive Director **Dick Dutton** . . . . . . . . . . . . . . . . . . . . (405) 230-8414
   E-mail: dick.dutton@travelok.com
Chief Financial Officer and Administrative Division
   Director **Zettie Farrow** . . . . . . . . . . . . . . . . . . . . . . . . (405) 230-8331
   E-mail: zettie.farrow@travelok.com
State Parks, Resorts and Golf Division Director
   **Kris Marek** . . . . . . . . . . . . . . . . . . . . . . . . . . . . . . . . . . (405) 230-8476
Travel Promotion Division Director **Jennifer Mullins** . . . . . (405) 230-8301

# Oklahoma Wildlife Conservation Commission

1801 North Lincoln Boulevard, Oklahoma City, OK 73105

■ Member **Ed Abel** (District 5) . . . . . . . . . . . . . . . . . . . . . . . (405) 522-6279
   Education: Oklahoma 1963 BA, 1966 JD
■ Member **Bill K. Brewster** (District 3) . . . . . . . . . . . . . . . (405) 522-6279
   Affiliation: Chairman, Capitol Hill Consulting Group
   499 South Capitol Street, SW, Suite 608, Washington, DC 20003
   Education: Southwestern Oklahoma St BS
■ Member **Leigh Gaddis** (District 4) . . . . . . . . . . . . . . . . . (405) 522-6279
   Education: East Central U
■ Member **John D. Groendyke** (District 8) . . . . . . . . . . . . . (405) 522-6279
   Education: Oklahoma State BSBA; Oklahoma
■ Member **Robert S. Hughes II** (District 1) . . . . . . . . . . . . . (405) 522-6279
   Education: Oklahoma State 1983 BS
■ Member **Bruce R. Mabrey** (District 2) . . . . . . . . . . . . . . . (405) 522-6279
   Education: Northeastern Oklahoma State U
■ Member **Danny Robbins** (District 7) . . . . . . . . . . . . . . . . (405) 522-6279
■ Member **John P. Zelbst** (District 6) . . . . . . . . . . . . . . . . . (405) 522-6279

# Oklahoma Department of Wildlife Conservation [ODWC]

P.O. Box 53465, Oklahoma City, OK 73152
1801 North Lincoln Boulevard, Oklahoma City, OK 73105
Tel: (405) 521-3851  TTY: (800) 522-8506  Fax: (405) 521-6535
Internet: www.wildlifedepartment.com

▲ Director **Richard T. Hatcher** . . . . . . . . . . . . . . . . . . . . . . (405) 522-6279
   E-mail: richard.hatcher@odwc.ok.gov
   Education: Trinity Col (DC) 1975 BS; Oklahoma State 1979 MS
   Executive Assistant **Rhonda Hurst** . . . . . . . . . . . . . . . . (405) 522-6279
      E-mail: rhonda.hurst@odwc.ok.gov
Operations Assistant Director **Wade Free** . . . . . . . . . . . . . (405) 521-4660
   Administrative Assistant **Becky Rouner** . . . . . . . . . . . . . (405) 521-4660
   E-mail: becky.rouner@odwc.ok.gov          Fax: (405) 521-6505
Administration and Finance Assistant Director
   **Melinda Sturgess-Streich** . . . . . . . . . . . . . . . . . . . . . . (405) 521-6685
   E-mail: melinda.streich@odwc.ok.gov
   Education: Oklahoma State 1982 BS
Fisheries Division Chief **Barry Bolton** . . . . . . . . . . . . . . . . (405) 521-3721
Information and Education Division Chief
   **Nels Rodefeld** . . . . . . . . . . . . . . . . . . . . . . . . . . . . . . (405) 521-3856
   E-mail: nels.rodefeld@odwc.ok.gov
   Education: Wisconsin BS
Law Enforcement Division Chief **Robert Fleenor** . . . . . . . . (405) 521-3719
Wildlife Division Chief **Alan Peoples** . . . . . . . . . . . . . . . . . (405) 521-2739
   Education: Oklahoma State 1988 BS, 1990 MS
Employee Services (Property) Supervisor **Johnny Hill** . . . . . (405) 521-4600

Licensing Section Supervisor **Mike Chrisman** . . . . . . . . . . . (405) 521-3852
   E-mail: mike.chrisman@odwc.ok.gov
Hunter Safety Education Coordinator **Lance Meek** . . . . . . . (405) 522-4572
   E-mail: lance.meek@odwc.ok.gov
Webmaster **Jeff Robertson** . . . . . . . . . . . . . . . . . . . . . . . . (405) 521-2085
   E-mail: jeff.robertson@odwc.ok.gov

# Office of Juvenile Affairs

3812 North Santa Fe Avenue, Suite 400, Oklahoma City, OK 73118
P.O. Box 268812, Oklahoma City, OK 73126-8812
Tel: (405) 530-2800  Fax: (405) 530-2890

**Employees:** 712

▲ Executive Director **Steven L. Buck** . . . . . . . . . . . . . . . . . . (405) 530-2806
   E-mail: steven.buck@oja.ok.gov
Chief of Staff **(Vacant)** . . . . . . . . . . . . . . . . . . . . . . . . . . . (405) 530-2832
General Counsel **Dorothy Brown** . . . . . . . . . . . . . . . . . . . . (405) 530-2813
   E-mail: dorothy.brown@oja.ok.gov
Advocate General **Donna Glandon** . . . . . . . . . . . . . . . . . . (405) 530-2939
Public Integrity Director **Travis Kirkpatrick** . . . . . . . . . . . . (405) 530-2921
   State Advisory Group Director **Dennis Gober** . . . . . . . . (405) 530-2838
      E-mail: dennis.gober@oja.ok.gov
Parole Administrator **Cathy McLean** . . . . . . . . . . . . . . . . . (405) 530-2877
Government Relations Director **J'Lynn Hartman** . . . . . . . . (405) 530-2866
   E-mail: jlynn.hartman@oja.ok.gov
Chief Psychologist **Ryan Jones** . . . . . . . . . . . . . . . . . . . . . (405) 530-2824
Chaplain **(Vacant)** . . . . . . . . . . . . . . . . . . . . . . . . . . . . . . (405) 530-2830
Communications Director **Paula Christiansen** . . . . . . . . . . (405) 530-2814
   E-mail: paula.christiansen@oja.ok.gov
Chief of Programs **Janelle Bretten** . . . . . . . . . . . . . . . . . . (405) 530-2867

# Community Based Youth Services Division

Director **Dennis Gober** . . . . . . . . . . . . . . . . . . . . . . . . . . . (405) 530-2838
   E-mail: dennis.gober@oja.ok.gov
Assistant Division Director **Anna Kelly** . . . . . . . . . . . . . . . (405) 530-2804
   E-mail: anna.kelly@oja.ok.gov
Federal Grants Supervisor **Anna Kelly** . . . . . . . . . . . . . . . (405) 530-2804

# Financial Services Division

Tel: (405) 530-2996  Fax: (405) 530-2946

Director **Kevin Clagg** . . . . . . . . . . . . . . . . . . . . . . . . . . . . (405) 530-2986
Assistant Division Administrator **Elda Walker** . . . . . . . . . . (405) 530-2988
Procurement and Contracts Administrator
   **Jeanette Wedington-Wagner** . . . . . . . . . . . . . . . . . . . . (405) 530-2805

# Institutional Services Division

Tel: (405) 530-2881  Fax: (405) 530-2912

Director **Robert Morey** . . . . . . . . . . . . . . . . . . . . . . . . . . . (405) 530-2820
Deputy Director **Carol Miller** . . . . . . . . . . . . . . . . . . . . . . (405) 530-2888
Program Manager **Warren Field** . . . . . . . . . . . . . . . . . . . . (405) 530-2871
Central Oklahoma Juvenile Center Superintendent
   **Jerry Fry** . . . . . . . . . . . . . . . . . . . . . . . . . . . . . . . . . . . (405) 598-4118
   700 S. Ninth St., Tecumseh, OK 74873-4636
Southwest Oklahoma Juvenile Center Superintendent
   **Marc Norvell** . . . . . . . . . . . . . . . . . . . . . . . . . . . . . . . (580) 397-2105
   P.O. Box 99, Manitou, OK 73555-0099

# Juvenile Services Division

Tel: (405) 530-2860  Fax: (405) 530-2892

Director **Jim Goble** . . . . . . . . . . . . . . . . . . . . . . . . . . . . . . (405) 530-2848
Assistant Division Director **Shelley Waller** . . . . . . . . . . . . . (405) 530-2837
District 1 Supervisor **Jerry Skinner** . . . . . . . . . . . . . . . . . (580) 323-4076
   422 Avant, Clinton, OK 73601
District 2 Supervisor **Linda Rothe** . . . . . . . . . . . . . . . . . . (918) 323-0022
   442104 East 250 Road, Vinita, OK 74301
District 3 Supervisor **Jennifer Thatcher** . . . . . . . . . . . . . . (405) 523-4629
   3700 North Classen Boulevard, Suite C-15,
   Oklahoma City, OK 73118-5904
District 4 Supervisor **Blaine Bowers** . . . . . . . . . . . . . . . . (918) 581-2211
   444 South Houston, Suite 301, Tulsa, OK 74127

---

★ Elected Official     ■ Appointed by Governor     ● Appointed by Legislature     ▲ Appointed by Board or Commission     ◆ Appointed by State Supreme Court

District 5 Supervisor **Ron Coplan** . . . . . . . . . . . . . . . . . . . . (918) 683-9160
    444 Court Street, Muskogee, OK 74401
District 6 Supervisor **Greg Delaney** . . . . . . . . . . . . . . . . . (580) 355-7466
    715 SW 11th, Suite 2, Lawton, OK 73501
District 7 Supervisor **Allen Miller** . . . . . . . . . . . . . . . . . . . (580) 224-0141
    333 West Main, Suite 250, Ardmore, OK 73401
District 8 Supervisor **William Coggburn** . . . . . . . . . . . . . (580) 298-5568
    205 Southwest Second Street, Antlers, OK 74523

## Support Services Division

Tel: (405) 530-2870  Fax: (405) 530-2967

Director **Jeff Gifford** . . . . . . . . . . . . . . . . . . . . . . . . . . . . . . . . (405) 530-2875
    E-mail: jeff.gifford@oja.ok.gov
Human Resources Administrator **Paula Tillison** . . . . . . . . . (405) 530-2949
Information Technology Director and Chief Information
    Officer **Len Morris** . . . . . . . . . . . . . . . . . . . . . . . . . . . . . . (405) 530-2844
    E-mail: len.morris@oja.ok.gov
Operations Supervisor **James Eakins** . . . . . . . . . . . . . . . . . (405) 530-2884
    E-mail: james.eakins@oja.ok.gov
Research and Program Development Administrator
    **(Vacant)** . . . . . . . . . . . . . . . . . . . . . . . . . . . . . . . . . . . . . . . . (405) 530-2898

## Office of Management and Enterprise Services

2300 North Lincoln Boulevard, Room 122,
Oklahoma City, OK 73105-4801
Tel: (405) 521-2141  Fax: (405) 521-3902

■Director **Preston L. Doerflinger** . . . . . . . . . . . . . . . . . . . . (405) 521-2141
    E-mail: preston.doerflinger@omes.ok.gov
    Executive Assistant **Susan Perry** . . . . . . . . . . . . . . . . . . . (405) 521-6175
Human Capital Management Administrator
    **Lucinda Meltabarger** . . . . . . . . . . . . . . . . . . . . . . . . . . . . (405) 521-6301
    Education: Oklahoma City BBA, MBA
Budget and Policy Deputy Director **Brandy Manek** . . . . . . . (405) 521-3786
■Chief Information Officer **James "Bo" Reese** . . . . . . . . . . . (405) 522-6175
    E-mail: bo.reese.@omes.ok.gov
State Comptroller **Lynne Bajema** . . . . . . . . . . . . . . . . . . . . (405) 521-6162
Human Resources Director **Carrie Towery** . . . . . . . . . . . . . (405) 522-0264
    Education: Central Oklahoma 2003 BBA;
    Oklahoma Christian 2011 MBA

## Human Capital Management Division

2101 North Lincoln Boulevard, G-80, Oklahoma City, OK 73105-4904
Tel: (405) 521-2177  Fax: (405) 524-6942  E-mail: opm-mail@opm.ok.gov
Internet: www.opm.ok.gov

■Administrator **Lucinda Meltabarger** . . . . . . . . . . . . . . . . . (405) 521-2177
    Executive Assistant **Anita Rhea** . . . . . . . . . . . . . . . . . . . . (405) 521-2177
General Counsel **Matt Stewart** . . . . . . . . . . . . . . . . . . . . . . (405) 522-1736
Talent Management Director **Jacob "Jake" Smith** . . . . . . . . (405) 522-0422
Training and Development Director **Lisa Fortier** . . . . . . . . . (405) 521-6345

## Division of Capital Assets Management [DCAM]

2401 N. Lincoln Boulevard, Room 206, Oklahoma City, OK 73105
P.O. Box 53218, Oklahoma City, OK 73152-3218
Tel: (405) 521-2124  Fax: (405) 521-6403  Internet: www.ok.gov/dcs

■Administrator **Dan Ross** . . . . . . . . . . . . . . . . . . . . . . . . . . . . (405) 521-2124
    E-mail: dan.ross@omes.ok.gov
Executive Assistant **Tammy Knoch** . . . . . . . . . . . . . . . . . . . (405) 521-2124
Zoning Commission Administrator **Ben Davis** . . . . . . . . . . . (405) 521-3678
Assistant Administrator **(Vacant)** . . . . . . . . . . . . . . . . . . . . (405) 521-2124
Facilities Management Department Director
    **Mark Sauchuk** . . . . . . . . . . . . . . . . . . . . . . . . . . . . . . . . . (405) 522-0084
Printing Department Director **Jon Paulk** . . . . . . . . . . . . . . . (405) 425-2714
Risk Management Department Director **Gene Lidyard** . . . . (405) 521-6051
Fleet Management Division Director **Terry Zuniga** . . . . . . . (405) 521-2206
Purchasing Division Director **Serris Barger** . . . . . . . . . . . . (405) 521-2115
Human Resources Coordinator **Kristin Elsenbeck** . . . . . . . (405) 521-6030
Property Distribution Administrator **Roger Stone** . . . . . . . (405) 521-2354
Financial Officer **Kelly Wilson** . . . . . . . . . . . . . . . . . . . . . . . (405) 521-1160

## Oklahoma Housing Finance Agency [OKFA]

100 NW 63rd, Suite 200, Oklahoma City, OK 73116
P.O. Box 26720, Oklahoma City, OK 73126
Tel: (405) 848-1144  TTY: (405) 848-7471  Fax: (405) 840-1109
Internet: www.ohfa.org

▲Executive Director **Dennis Shockley** . . . . . . . . . . . . . . . . . (405) 419-8276
    E-mail: dennis.shockley@ohfa.org
    Education: Louisiana Tech U 1970 BA; Pittsburg State 1973 MA;
    Kansas State 1986 PhD
Communications Director **Holley Mangham** . . . . . . . . . . . . (405) 419-8222
    E-mail: holley.mangham@ohfa.org
    Education: Central Oklahoma 1996 BA
Information Technology Director **Nelson Morgan** . . . . . . . . (405) 419-8205
    E-mail: nelson.morgan@ohfa.org
    Education: Central Oklahoma 1977 BBA
Personnel Director **Linda Sargent** . . . . . . . . . . . . . . . . . . . . (405) 419-8291
    Education: Central Oklahoma 1971 BS, 1981 MS, 1985 MS
Finance Team Leader **Eldon Overstreet** . . . . . . . . . (405) 419-8209 ext. 209
    Education: Oklahoma State 1970 BSA; Tulsa 1989 JD
Housing Development Team Leader **Darrell Beavers** . . . . . . (405) 419-8261
Rental Assistance Team Leader **Deborah Jenkins** . . . . . . . . (405) 419-8290
    Education: Central Oklahoma 1995 BA

## Oklahoma Educational Television Authority [OETA]

7403 North Kelley, Box 14190, Oklahoma City, OK 73113
Tel: (405) 848-8501  Fax: (405) 841-9282

**Employees:** 49  **Fiscal Year:** 2014  **Budget:** $3,822,000

▲Executive Director **Dan Schiedel** . . . . . . . . . . . . . . . . . . . . (405) 848-8501
    E-mail: dschiedel@oeta.tv
Vice President of Communications **Cassie Gage** . . . . . . . . . (405) 848-8501
    E-mail: cgage@oeta.tv
Vice President of Operations **Janette Thornbrue** . . . . . . . . (405) 848-8501
Vice President of Programming **Holly Emig** . . . . . . . . . . . . (405) 848-8501
Vice President of Technology **Mark Norman** . . . . . . . . . . . . (405) 848-8501
    E-mail: mnorman@oeta.tv

## Grand River Dam Authority [GRDA]

226 West Dwain Willis Avenue, Vinita, OK 74301
P.O. Box 409, Vinita, OK 74301-0409
Tel: (918) 256-5545  Fax: (918) 256-5289  Internet: www.grda.com

**Employees:** 512

▲Chief Executive Officer **Daniel S. "Dan" Sullivan** . . . . . . . (918) 256-5545
    E-mail: dsullivan@grda.com
    Education: Northeastern State 1985 BS; Tulsa 1988 JD
    Secretary to the General Manager **Sheila Allen** . . . . . . . . (918) 256-5545
Assistant General Manager and Law Enforcement and
    Homeland Security Chief **Brian Edwards** . . . . . . . . . . . . (918) 782-4726
    Education: Langston 1995 BS; Oklahoma City 2003 MBA
Assistant General Manager of Ecosystems and Lake
    Management **Darrell Townsend** . . . . . . . . . . . . . . . . . . . (918) 782-4726
    E-mail: dtownsend@grda.com
Assistant General Manager of Engineering, System
    Operations and Reliability **Mike Herron** . . . . . . . . . . . . (918) 610-9716
                                                    Fax: (918) 825-9416
Assistant General Manager of Fuel and Generation
    Projects **Charles J. Barney** . . . . . . . . . . . . . . . . . . . . . . (918) 476-5840
Assistant General Manager of Human Resources
    **John Goodwin** . . . . . . . . . . . . . . . . . . . . . . . . . . . . . . . . . (918) 256-5545
    Education: Arizona BS
Assistant General Manager of Hydroelectric Projects
    **Steven R. Jacoby** . . . . . . . . . . . . . . . . . . . . . . . . . . . . . . (918) 256-5545
    Education: Oklahoma State BS, MBA
Transmission Superintendent **Michael Waddell** . . . . . . . . . (918) 825-0280
General Counsel **Ellen Edwards** . . . . . . . . . . . . . . . . . . . . . (918) 256-5545
    Education: Colorado Col BS; Oklahoma JD
Chief Financial Officer and Treasurer
    **Carolyn Dougherty** . . . . . . . . . . . . . . . . . . . (918) 256-5545 ext. 4409
Chief Operating Officer **Tim Brown** . . . . . . . . . . . . . . . . . . (918) 256-5545
    Education: Maine BSME; Auburn (Attended)

*(continued on next page)*

---

★ Elected Official    ■ Appointed by Governor    ● Appointed by Legislature    ▲ Appointed by Board or Commission    ◆ Appointed by State Supreme Court

**EXECUTIVE BRANCH**

**Grand River Dam Authority** *continued*

Support Properties and Programs Director
  Holly M. Moore . . . . . . . . . . . . . . . . . . . . . . . . (918) 256-5545 ext. 40707

# Oklahoma Health Care Authority [OHCA]

4345 North Lincoln Boulevard, Oklahoma City, OK 73105
Tel: (405) 522-7300  Fax: (405) 522-7187  Internet: www.okhca.org

**Employees:** 489

Chief Executive Officer **Joel "Nico" Gomez** . . . . . . . . . . .(405) 522-7300
  Education: Oklahoma 1995 BA; Southern Nazarene MBA
Deputy Chief Executive Officer **Garth L. Splinter, MD** . . . (405) 522-7382
Chief of Federal and State Policy **Tywanda Cox** . . . . . . . . (405) 522-7153
Chief Financial Officer **Carrie Evans** . . . . . . . . . . . . . . . . (405) 522-7359
Chief Operations Officer **Lisa Gifford** . . . . . . . . . . . . . . . . (405) 522-7424
Chief of Legal Services **Nicole Nantois** . . . . . . . . . . . . . . (405) 522-7431
State Medicaid Director **Becky Pasternik-Ikard** . . . . . . . . .(405) 522-7208

# Alcoholic Beverage Laws Enforcement Commission [ABLE]

3812 North Santa Fe Avenue, Suite 200, Oklahoma City, OK 73118
Tel: (405) 521-3484  Fax: (405) 521-6578

**Employees:** 37

■Chairman **Bryan Close** . . . . . . . . . . . . . . . . . . . . . . . . . . (405) 521-3484
■Vice Chairman **Harry "Trey" Kouri III** . . . . . . . . . . . . . . (405) 521-3484
■Commissioner **Joseph Forrest** . . . . . . . . . . . . . . . . . . . . (405) 521-3484
  Term Expires: June 23, 2020
■Commissioner **Devin S. Graves** . . . . . . . . . . . . . . . . . . . (405) 521-3484
■Commissioner **Robert Heidlage, Jr.** . . . . . . . . . . . . . . . . (405) 521-3484
  Term Expires: June 23, 2020
■Commissioner **James Maisano** . . . . . . . . . . . . . . . . . . . .(405) 521-3484
  Term Expires: June 23, 2019
■Commissioner **Clarence Warner** . . . . . . . . . . . . . . . . . . (405) 521-3484
▲Director **A. Keith Burt** . . . . . . . . . . . . . . . . . . . . . . . . . . (405) 521-3484
  E-mail: keith.burt@able.ok.gov

# Oklahoma Conservation Commission

2800 North Lincoln Boulevard, Room 160,
Oklahoma City, OK 73105-4210
Tel: (405) 521-2384  Fax: (405) 521-6686

**Employees:** 60

▲Executive Director **Trey Lam** . . . . . . . . . . . . . . . . . . . . . (405) 521-2384
  E-mail: trey.lam@conservation.ok.gov
  Education: Yale
  Executive Secretary **Kim Tweed** . . . . . . . . . . . . . . . . . . (405) 521-4826
Assistant Director **Lisa Knauf Owen** . . . . . . . . . . . . . . . . (405) 521-6797
  E-mail: lisa.knauf@conservation.ok.gov
  Education: Austin State 1986 BS; Tennessee 1989 MS
Abandoned Mine Land Reclamation Program Director
  **Robert W. Toole** . . . . . . . . . . . . . . . . . . . . . . . . . . . . . (405) 521-4818
  E-mail: robert.toole@conservation.ok.gov
  Education: Oklahoma State 1975 BS
Conservation Programs Director **Tammy Sawatzky** . . . . . . (405) 521-4823
  E-mail: tammy.sawatzky@conservation.ok.gov
Geographic Information and Technical Services Director
  **Mike Sharp** . . . . . . . . . . . . . . . . . . . . . . . . . . . . . . . . (405) 521-4813
  E-mail: mike.sharp@conservation.ok.gov
  Education: Oklahoma State 1970 BS, 1977 PhD
Water Quality Director **Shanon Phillips** . . . . . . . . . . . . . (405) 522-4728
  E-mail: shanon.phillips@conservation.ok.gov
General Counsel **Janet Stewart** . . . . . . . . . . . . . . . . . . . . (405) 742-1240
Public Information Officer **(Vacant)** . . . . . . . . . . . . . . . . (405) 437-9171

# Oklahoma Commission on Consumer Credit

3613 Northwest 56th Street, Suite 240, Oklahoma City, OK 73112
Tel: (405) 521-3653  Tel: (800) 448-4904 (Consumer line)
Fax: (405) 521-6740

Chairman **Bob Moses** . . . . . . . . . . . . . . . . . . . . . . . . . . (405) 521-3653
  Term Expires: January 1, 2020
Vice Chairman **Joe Wilbanks** . . . . . . . . . . . . . . . . . . . . . (405) 521-3653
  Term Expires: February 15, 2020
Commissioner **Suzy Barnes** . . . . . . . . . . . . . . . . . . . . . . (405) 521-3653
  Term Expires: January 1, 2018
Commissioner **Jerry Douglas** . . . . . . . . . . . . . . . . . . . . . (405) 521-3653
  Term Expires: February 15, 2018
Commissioner **Rick Harper** . . . . . . . . . . . . . . . . . . . . . . (405) 521-3653
  Term Expires: January 1, 2019
Commissioner **Armando Rosell** . . . . . . . . . . . . . . . . . . . (405) 521-3653
  Term Expires: January 1, 2017
Commissioner **Craig Stanley** . . . . . . . . . . . . . . . . . . . . . (405) 521-3653
  Term Expires: February 15, 2019
Commissioner **Spencer Stanley** . . . . . . . . . . . . . . . . . . . (405) 521-3653
  Term Expires: January 1, 2016
Commissioner **Kent Carter** . . . . . . . . . . . . . . . . . . . . . . (405) 521-3653
  Term Expires: January 1, 2020
State Banking Commissioner **Mick Thompson** . . . . . . . . . (405) 521-3653

# Oklahoma Department of Consumer Credit [OKDOCC]

3613 Northwest 56th Street, Oklahoma City, OK 73112
Tel: (405) 521-3653  Tel: (800) 448-4904  Fax: (405) 521-6740

**Employees:** 27

▲Administrator **Scott Lesher** . . . . . . . . . . . . . . . . . . . . . .(405) 521-3907
  E-mail: slesher@okdocc.ok.gov
Deputy Administrator **Ruben Tornini** . . . . . . . . . . . . . . . (405) 521-3653
General Counsel **Roy John Martin** . . . . . . . . . . . . . . . . . (405) 521-3653
Chief of Staff **Lindsie Lundy** . . . . . . . . . . . . . . . . . . . . . (405) 521-3653
Licensing Director **Meredith Fazendin** . . . . . . . . . . . . . . (405) 521-3653
Chief Examiner **Drew S'Renco** . . . . . . . . . . . . . . . . . . . . (405) 521-3653

# Oklahoma Employment Security Commission [OESC]

2401 North Lincoln Boulevard, Suite 504, WRB,
Oklahoma City, OK 73105
P.O. Box 52003, Oklahoma City, OK 73152-2003
Tel: (405) 557-7100  TTY: (405) 557-7531  Fax: (405) 557-7174

**Employees:** 644

▲Executive Director **Richard McPherson** . . . . . . . . . . . . . (405) 557-7201
  E-mail: richard.mcpherson@oesc.state.ok.us
Deputy Director **Teresa Keller** . . . . . . . . . . . . . . . . . . . . (405) 557-7237
  E-mail: teresa.keller@oesc.state.ok.us
General Counsel **John Miley** . . . . . . . . . . . . . . . . . . . . . (405) 557-7146
  E-mail: john.miley@oesc.state.ok.us
Economic Research and Analysis Director **Lynn Gray** . . . . (405) 557-7221
Chief Financial Officer and Administrative Services
  Division Director **Riley Shaull** . . . . . . . . . . . . . . . . . . (405) 557-7210
  E-mail: riley.shaull@oesc.state.ok.us
Appellate Division Director **Clyde Stevens** . . . . . . . . . . . (405) 601-3311
  P.O. Box 53345, Oklahoma City, OK 73152-3345
  2800 NW 36th Street, Suite 102, Oklahoma City, OK 73112
  E-mail: clyde.stevens@oesc.state.ok.us
Customer Service Division Director **Lisa Graven** . . . . . . . .(405) 557-7121
  E-mail: lisa.graven@oesc.state.ok.us
Internal Audit Division Director **Anna Johnson** . . . . . . . . (405) 557-5487
  E-mail: anna.johnson@oesc.state.ok.us
Support and Compliance Division Director
  **Shalonda Sanders** . . . . . . . . . . . . . . . . . . . . . . . . . . (405) 557-7219
  E-mail: shalonda.sanders@oesc.state.ok.us
Targeted Populations Division Director **Jon Eller** . . . . . . . .(405) 557-7193
Public Information Officer **(Vacant)** . . . . . . . . . . . . . . . . (405) 557-5469
Civil Rights Administrator **Emma Woodford** . . . . . . . . . . (405) 557-7235
  E-mail: emma.woodford@oesc.state.ok.us

★ Elected Official   ■ Appointed by Governor   ● Appointed by Legislature   ▲ Appointed by Board or Commission   ◆ Appointed by State Supreme Court

# Oklahoma Ethics Commission [OEC]

2300 North Lincoln Boulevard, B-5, Oklahoma City, OK 73105-4812
Tel: (405) 521-3451  Fax: (405) 521-4905

**Employees:** 7

Chair **Cathy Lee Stocker** (3rd Congressional Dist. Rep.). . (405) 521-3451
  Note: Appointed by the Attorney General
  Term Expires: July 2017
  Education: Oklahoma JD

●Vice Chair
  **John C. Hawkins** (2nd Congressional Dist. Rep.) . . . . . . (405) 521-3451
  Term Expires: July 2019

●Commissioner
  **Karen L. Long** (1st Congressional Dist. Rep.) . . . . . . . . . (405) 521-3451
  Term Expires: July 2019
  Affiliation: Partner, Rosenstein, Fist & Ringold
  Park Centre, 525 South Main, Suite 700, Tulsa, OK 74103
  Education: William & Mary 1975 BA; Oklahoma City 1978 JD

■Commissioner
  **Jo Pettigrew** (5th Congressional Dist. Rep.) . . . . . . . . . . (405) 521-3451
  Term Expires: July 2017
  Education: Southern Methodist; North Texas State;
  Oklahoma State DEd

◆Commissioner **(Vacant)** (4th Congressional Dist. Rep.) . . . . (405) 521-3451

Executive Director **Lee Slater** . . . . . . . . . . . . . . . . . . . . (405) 521-3451
  Note: Until June 30, 2016.

Executive Director **Ashley Kemp** . . . . . . . . . . . . . . . . . . . . (405) 521-3451
  Note: Effective July 1, 2016.

Deputy Director **Ashley Kemp** . . . . . . . . . . . . . . . . . . . . . (405) 521-3451
  Note: Until June 30, 2016.

# Oklahoma Bureau of Narcotics and Dangerous Drugs Commission

419 N.E. 38th Terrace, Oklahoma City, OK 73105
Tel: (405) 521-2885  Tel: (800) 522-8031  Fax: (405) 524-7619
Fax: (405) 530-3789

■Chair **Layne Subera** . . . . . . . . . . . . . . . . . . . . . . . . . . . . (405) 530-3122
  Term Expires: December 31, 2020
  E-mail: lsubera@obn.state.ok.us

■Vice-Chair **Gretchen Zumwalt-Smith** . . . . . . . . . . . . . . . . (405) 530-3122
  E-mail: gsmith@obn.state.ok.us

■Commission Member **Phillip "Phil" Cole** . . . . . . . . . . . . . . (405) 530-3122
  E-mail: pcole@obn.state.ok.us

■Commission Member **Greg Mashburn** . . . . . . . . . . . . . . . . (405) 530-3122
  Term Expires: December 31, 2019
  E-mail: gmashburn@obn.state.ok.us
  Affiliation: District Attorney, Office of the District Attorney, County of
  Cleveland, Oklahoma
  201 South Jones Avenue, Suite 300, Norman, OK 73069
  Education: Harding 1995; Oklahoma 1998 JD

■Commission Member **Jan Miller** . . . . . . . . . . . . . . . . . . . (405) 530-3122
  Term Expires: December 31, 2016
  E-mail: jamiller@obn.state.ok.us

■Commission Member **Larry Rhodes** . . . . . . . . . . . . . . . . . (405) 530-3122
  E-mail: lrhodes@obn.state.ok.us

■Commission Member **(Vacant)** . . . . . . . . . . . . . . . . . . . . . (405) 530-3122

# Oklahoma Bureau of Narcotics and Dangerous Drugs [OBNDD]

**Employees:** 139

▲Director **John Scully** . . . . . . . . . . . . . . . . . . . . . . . . . . . (405) 521-2885
  Executive Assistant **Misty Chandler** . . . . . . . . . . . . . . . . (405) 521-2885
Fiscal Services Director **Anita Smart** . . . . . . . . . . . . . . . . . (405) 521-2885
Diversion Chief Agent **Mark Stewart** . . . . . . . . . . . . . . . . (405) 521-2885
Enforcement Chief Agent - East **Bob Cook** . . . . . . . . . . . (405) 521-2885
Enforcement Chief Agent - West **Mel Woodrow** . . . . . . . . (405) 521-2885
Human Trafficking Chief Agent **Cindy Cunningham** . . . . . (405) 521-2885
Public Information Officer **Mark Woodward** . . . . . . . . . . . (405) 521-2885
  E-mail: mwoodward@obn.state.ok.us

# Oklahoma Real Estate Commission [OREC]

1915 North Stiles Avenue, Suite 200, Oklahoma City, OK 73105-4919
Tel: (405) 521-3387  Tel: (866) 521-3389  Fax: (405) 521-2189
E-mail: help@orec.ok.gov

**Employees:** 15

■Chairman **Rodger Erker** (District 1) . . . . . . . . . . . . . . . . . (405) 522-9161
  Term Expires: June 30, 2017
  E-mail: rodger.erker@ok.gov

■Vice Chairman **Julie Tetsworth** (District 1) . . . . . . . . . . . . (405) 522-9162
  Term Expires: June 30, 2016
  E-mail: julie.tetsworth@ok.gov

■Commissioner **Mike Cassidy** (District 5) . . . . . . . . . . . . . . (405) 522-9167
  Term Expires: June 30, 2017
  E-mail: mike.cassidy@ok.gov

■Commissioner **John Mosley** (District 4) . . . . . . . . . . . . . . (405) 522-9163
  Term Expires: June 30, 2016
  E-mail: john.mosley@ok.gov

■Commissioner **Steven Oliver** (District 2) . . . . . . . . . . . . . (405) 522-9164
  Term Expires: June 30, 2018
  E-mail: steve.oliver@ok.gov

■Commissioner **Stephen A. Sherman** (District 5) . . . . . . . . (405) 522-9168
  Term Expires: June 30, 2017
  E-mail: stephen.sherman@ok.gov

■Commissioner **Theresa Stewart Smith** (District 4) . . . . . . (405) 522-9165
  Term Expires: June 30, 2018
  E-mail: theresa.stewartsmith@ok.gov

Executive Director **Charla J. Slabotsky** . . . . . . . . . . . . . . . (405) 521-3387

# Oklahoma Tax Commission

2501 North Lincoln Boulevard, Oklahoma City, OK 73194
Tel: (405) 521-3160  Fax: (405) 521-3826
E-mail: helpmaster@oktax.state.ok.us

**Employees:** 714

■Chairman **Steve Burrage, CPA** . . . . . . . . . . . . . . . . . . . . (405) 521-3114
  Education: Oklahoma 1975 BBA

■Vice Chairman **Dawn Cash** . . . . . . . . . . . . . . . . . . . . . . . (405) 521-2134
  E-mail: dawnc@oktax.state.ok.us
  Education: Oklahoma BA; Tulsa JD

■Secretary **Thomas E. Kemp, Jr.** . . . . . . . . . . . . . . . . . . . (405) 521-3115
  E-mail: tkemp@oktax.state.ok.us

Executive Director **Tony Mastin** . . . . . . . . . . . . . . . . . . . . (405) 521-3214
  Education: Central Oklahoma; Oklahoma City JD

Controller and Management Services **(Vacant)** . . . . . . . . . . (405) 521-2967
General Counsel **Doug Allen** . . . . . . . . . . . . . . . . . . . . . . (405) 521-3141
Counsel to Commissioners **(Vacant)** . . . . . . . . . . . . . . . . . (405) 521-3213
Economist **Reece Womack** . . . . . . . . . . . . . . . . . . . . . . . (405) 521-4309
Account Maintenance Division Director **Jerry Statton** . . . . (405) 521-4271
Ad Valorem Tax Division Director **Joe Hapgood** . . . . . . . . (405) 521-3178
Central Processing Division Director **Fredda Puckett** . . . . . (405) 521-3176
Communications Division Director **Paula Ross** . . . . . . . . . . (405) 521-3637
  E-mail: paular@oktax.state.ok.us
Compliance Division Director **Jim Fourcade** . . . . . . . . . . . (405) 521-3251
Human Resources Division Director **Kanda Woods** . . . . . . (405) 521-3750
Information Technology Division Director **(Vacant)** . . . . . . . (405) 521-3732
Motor Vehicle Division Director **Russ Nordstrom** . . . . . . . (405) 521-2519
  E-mail: russn@oktax.state.ok.us
Tax Policy and Research Division Director **Rick Miller** . . . . (405) 521-3123
Taxpayer Assistance Division Director
  **Joanne Kurjan Cook** . . . . . . . . . . . . . . . . . . . . . . . . . . (405) 522-4328
Commerce and Industry Administrator **(Vacant)** . . . . . . . . . (405) 521-4325

# Oklahoma State Election Board

P.O. Box 53156, Oklahoma City, OK 73152-3156
Tel: (405) 521-2391  TTY: (405) 521-3028  Fax: (405) 521-6457
E-mail: info@elections.ok.gov  Internet: www.elections.state.ok.us

**Employees:** 19

■Chairman **Steve Curry** . . . . . . . . . . . . . . . . . . . . . . . . . . (405) 521-2391
  Term Expires: March 15, 2019

■Vice Chairman **Tom Montgomery** . . . . . . . . . . . . . . . . . . (405) 521-2391
  Term Expires: March 15, 2019

*(continued on next page)*

---

★ Elected Official   ■ Appointed by Governor   ● Appointed by Legislature   ▲ Appointed by Board or Commission   ◆ Appointed by State Supreme Court

**EXECUTIVE BRANCH**

**Oklahoma State Election Board** *continued*

■ Member **Tim Mauldin** ............................. (405) 521-2391
   Term Expires: March 15, 2019
● Secretary **Paul Ziriax** ............................. (405) 521-2391
   Assistant Secretary **Pam Slater** ..................... (405) 521-2391

## Pardon and Parole Board

120 North Robinson, 900 West, Oklahoma City, OK 73102
Tel: (405) 521-6600 Fax: (405) 602-6437

**Employees:** 32

■ Chair **Vanessa Price** ............................... (405) 521-6600
   Term Expires: January 12, 2019
■ Vice Chair **Patricia L. "Pattye" High** ............... (405) 521-6600
   Term Expires: January 12, 2019
   Education: Oklahoma JD
   Member **Thomas Gillert** ............................ (405) 521-6600
   Note: Appointed by State Court of Criminal Appeals.
   Term Expires: January 12, 2019
◆ Member **William E. Latimer** ...................... (405) 521-6600
   Term Expires: January 12, 2019
■ Member **Robert "Brett" Macy** ..................... (405) 521-6600
   Term Expires: January 12, 2019
   Education: Central Oklahoma
▲ Executive Director **DeLynn Fudge** ................. (405) 521-6600
   E-mail: delynn.fudge@ppb.state.ok.us

## Oklahoma Public Employees Retirement System [OPERS]

P.O. Box 53007, Oklahoma City, OK 73152-3007
Tel: (405) 858-6737 Tel: (800) 733-9008 Fax: (405) 848-5967
Internet: www.opers.ok.gov

**Employees:** 52

▲ Executive Director **Joseph A. Fox** .................... (405) 858-6701
   E-mail: jfox@opers.ok.gov
   Executive Assistant **Tahrae Patton** .................. (405) 858-6707
Chief Financial Officer and Finance Director
   **Susan Reed** ...................................... (405) 858-6704
   E-mail: sreed@opers.ok.gov
General Counsel **Dessa Baker-Inman** ................. (405) 858-6703
   Education: Duke 2004 JD
Information Technology Director **Paul Thompson** ....... (405) 858-6763
   E-mail: pthompson@opers.ok.gov
Member Services Director **Patrick W. Lane** ........... (405) 858-6720
   E-mail: plane@opers.ok.gov
Defined Contribution Plans Director **Ray Pool** .......... (405) 858-6710
   E-mail: rpool@opers.ok.gov
Communications Manager **Stephanie White** ............ (405) 858-6768
   E-mail: swhite@opers.ok.gov

## Office of the Lieutenant Governor

2300 North Lincoln Boulevard, Oklahoma City, OK 73105-4812
Tel: (405) 521-2161 Fax: (405) 522-8694

**Fiscal Year:** 2014 **Budget:** $506,591

★ Lieutenant Governor **Todd Lamb** (R) ................. (405) 521-2161
   Term Expires: 2019
   E-mail: ltgov@gov.ok.gov
Chief of Staff **Keith Beall** .......................... (405) 521-2161
Communications Director (Acting) **Keith Beall** .......... (405) 521-2161
   E-mail: keith.beall@ltgov.ok.gov
Director of Constituent Services **Madison Hobson** ....... (405) 521-2161
Director of Scheduling and Special Projects **Pat Thrower** .. (405) 521-2161

## Office of the Attorney General

313 Northeast 21st Street, Oklahoma City, OK 73105
Tel: (405) 521-3921 Fax: (405) 521-6246 Tel: (918) 581-2885 (Tulsa)

**Employees:** 163

★ Attorney General **E. Scott Pruitt** (R) ................. (405) 521-3921
   Term Expires: 2019
   Education: Georgetown 1990 BA; Tulsa 1993 JD
   Career: State Senator (R-OK, District 36), Oklahoma State Senate
   (1998-2006)

Chief of Staff **(Vacant)** ............................ (405) 521-3921
First Assistant Attorney General
   **Michael J. "Mike" Hunter** ........................ (405) 521-3921
   Education: Oklahoma State 1978 BA; Oklahoma 1982 JD
Senior Assistant Attorney General **(Vacant)** ............. (405) 521-3921
Solicitor General **Patrick Wyrick** .................... (405) 521-3921
   Education: Oklahoma 2007 JD
Communications Director **Lincoln Ferguson** ........... (405) 522-2924
   E-mail: lincoln.ferguson@oag.ok.gov
   Press Secretary **Will Gattenby** ..................... (405) 522-4391
   E-mail: will.gattenby@oag.ok.gov
Public Policy Director **Jonathan "Johnny" Moyer** ...... (405) 521-3921
   Public Policy Coordinator **Emily Shipley** ............ (405) 521-3921
Criminal Appeals Division Chief **Jennifer Miller** ........ (405) 521-3921
General Counsel Section Chief **Jan Preslar** ............ (405) 521-3921
Litigation Section Chief **Kindanne Jones** ............. (405) 521-3921
Medicaid Fraud Control Unit Chief **Mykel Fry** ........ (405) 521-3921
   Education: Southwestern Oklahoma St BBA; Oklahoma City JD
Multicounty Grand Jury Unit Chief **Megan Tilly** ....... (405) 521-3921
   Education: Washington and Lee; Oklahoma JD
Public Protection Unit Chief **Julie Bays** .............. (405) 521-3921
   Education: Oklahoma 1995 BA, 1998 JD
Public Utilities Unit Chief **Dara Derryberry** ........... (405) 521-3921
   E-mail: dara.derryberry@oag.ok.gov
Victim Services Unit Chief **Lesley March** ............. (405) 521-3921
Worker's Compensation, Insurance, and Social Security
   Fraud Unit Chief **George Burnett** .................. (405) 522-3921
   Education: Oklahoma State 1981; Oklahoma 1987 JD
Address Confidentiality Program Director **(Vacant)** ..... (405) 557-1700
   E-mail: acp@oag.ok.gov      Tel: (866) 227-7784
                                      (In State)
                          Fax: (405) 557-1770

## Office of the State Treasurer

2300 North Lincoln Boulevard, Room 217,
Oklahoma City, OK 73105-4812
Tel: (405) 521-3191 Fax: (405) 521-4994
E-mail: okla.treas@treasurer.ok.gov

**Employees:** 46

★ State Treasurer **Ken A. Miller** (R) ................... (405) 521-4526
   Term Expires: January 14, 2019
   E-mail: ken.miller@treasurer.ok.gov
   Education: Lipscomb U 1989 BA; Pepperdine 1993 MBA;
   Oklahoma PhD
   Career: State Representative (R-OK, District 81), Oklahoma House of
   Representatives (2005-2010)
   Executive Assistant **Carrie Bowen** .................. (405) 521-4526
Chief Deputy Treasurer **Susan Nicewander** ........... (405) 522-4214
   Education: Oklahoma State 1976 BS
Communications and Program Administration Deputy
   Treasurer **Tim Allen** .............................. (405) 522-4212
   E-mail: tim.allen@treasurer.ok.gov
   Education: Oklahoma State 1982 BS
Government Affairs Deputy Treasurer **Andrew Messer** ... (405) 521-4504
Banking Services Manager **Diedre O'Neil** ............. (405) 522-4216
Portfolio Accounting and Reporting Director
   **Sherian Kerlin** .................................. (405) 522-4221
Unclaimed Property Director **Kathy Janes** ............. (405) 522-6743
   Education: Tulsa 1986 BS
Chief Investment Officer **Lisa Murray** ............... (405) 522-4211
   E-mail: lisa.murray@treasurer.ok.gov
Internal Auditor **Craig Sanger** ...................... (405) 522-6745

## Office of the State Auditor and Inspector

2300 North Lincoln Boulevard, Suite 100,
Oklahoma City, OK 73105-4812
Tel: (405) 521-3495 Fax: (405) 521-3426

**Employees:** 123

★ State Auditor and Inspector
   **Gary A. Jones, CPA, CFE** (R) ..................... (405) 521-3495
   Term Expires: 2019
   Education: Cameron 1978 BS

---

★ Elected Official    ■ Appointed by Governor    ● Appointed by Legislature    ▲ Appointed by Board or Commission    ◆ Appointed by State Supreme Court

Deputy State Auditor for Local Government Services
**Cindy Byrd, CPA** ................................. (580) 332-3845
Education: East Central U 1997 BS
Deputy State Auditor for State Agencies and Special
Audits **Lisa Hodges, CFE, CGFM** ................. (405) 522-6443
Education: Oklahoma State 1981
Financial Services Director/Chief Financial Officer
**Lisa Hodges, CFE, CGFM** ....................... (405) 521-2299
E-mail: lhodges@sai.ok.gov
Information Technology Audit and Support Director
**Sheila Adkins** .................................. (405) 522-6448
E-mail: sadkins@sai.ok.gov
Performance Audit Division Director **(Vacant)** .......... (405) 522-6445
Specialized Audit Division Director **Mark Hudson, CPA** .. (405) 522-6481
Education: East Central U BSAcc
State Agency Audit Division Director **Shelly Fleming** .... (405) 522-6417
Training and Public Information Director **Trey Davis** ...... (405) 521-3390
E-mail: tdavis@sai.ok.gov
Quality Assurance Director **Cindy Wheeler, CPA** ........ (405) 522-6425
Education: Central Oklahoma 1990 BSAcc;
Oklahoma Christian 2002 MBA

# Oklahoma State Department of Education

2500 North Lincoln Boulevard, Oklahoma City, OK 73105-4599
Tel: (405) 521-3308  Fax: (405) 521-6205

**Employees:** 289

★Superintendent of Public Instruction **Joy Hofmeister** (R) .. (405) 521-3301
Term Expires: 2019
E-mail: joy.hofmeister@sde.ok.gov
Education: Texas Christian BEd
Executive Assistant **Tonya Pogue** .................... (405) 521-3301
Chief of Staff **LTC Lance Nelson, ARNG (Ret)** ......... (405) 521-4516
E-mail: lance.nelson@sde.ok.gov
Education: American Military U MBA
Deputy State Superintendent of Academic Affairs
**Cindy Koss** ..................................... (405) 522-6369
Deputy State Superintendent for Educator Effectiveness
and Policy Research **Robyn Miller** .................. (405) 521-3332
General Counsel **David L. Kinney** ................... (405) 521-4352
E-mail: david.kinney@sde.ok.gov
Education: Oklahoma JD
Director of Government Affairs **Carolyn Thompson** ..... (405) 522-3520
Chief of Communications **Phil Bacharach** ............. (405) 521-4894
E-mail: phil.bacharach@sde.ok.gov
Executive Director of Human Resource Development
**Joni Younts** .................................... (405) 521-3977

# State Board of Education

2500 North Lincoln Boulevard, Oklahoma City, OK 73105-4599
Tel: (405) 521-3308  Fax: (405) 521-6205

Chair **Joy Hofmeister** .............................. (405) 521-3301
Affiliation: Superintendent of Public Instruction, Oklahoma State
Department of Education, State of Oklahoma
2500 North Lincoln Boulevard, Oklahoma City, OK 73105-4599
■Member **MG Leo J. "Lee" Baxter, USA (Ret)**
(4th Congressional Dist. Rep.) ..................... (405) 521-3308
Education: North Dakota State BA; Central Michigan MS;
Army War Col
■Member
**William E. Flanagan** (2nd Congressional Dist. Rep.) .... (405) 521-3308
Education: Southeastern Oklahoma St 1975
■Member **Cathryn Franks** (3rd Congressional Dist. Rep.) .. (405) 521-3308
Education: Oklahoma State BS; George Washington MEd
■Member
**Daniel G. Keating** (1st Congressional Dist. Rep.) ...... (405) 521-3308
Affiliation: President, Summit Consolidated Group
1350 South Boulder Avenue, Third Floor, Tulsa, OK 74119
Education: Tulsa BA; Oklahoma MBA
■Member
**William S. "Bill" Price** (5th Congressional Dist. Rep.) .. (405) 521-3308
Education: Georgetown 1970 BSFS; Oklahoma 1973 JD
■Member **Robert J. "Bob" Ross** (At-Large) ............. (405) 521-3308
Education: Washington and Lee BSBA; Oklahoma JD

Chief Executive Secretary **(Vacant)** ................... (405) 521-4906

# Oklahoma Insurance Department [OID]

P.O. Box 53408, Oklahoma City, OK 73152-3408
Five Corporate Plaza, 3625 Northwest 56th Street, Suite 100,
Oklahoma City, OK 73112
Tel: (405) 521-2828  Tel: (800) 522-0071 (In State)  Fax: (405) 521-6635
E-mail: feedback@oid.ok.gov

**Employees:** 126

★Commissioner **John D. Doak** (R) .................... (405) 521-2828
Term Expires: 2019
Finance Deputy Commissioner **Joel Sander** ........... (405) 521-2991
Government Affairs, Public Policy and Communications
Deputy Commissioner **William Combs** .............. (405) 522-8398
Health Insurance Deputy Commissioner **Mike Rhoads** .... (405) 521-2828
Chief Actuary **Frank Stone** ......................... (405) 521-2668
Communications Director **Kelly Dexter** ................ (405) 522-0683
E-mail: kelly.dexter@oid.ok.gov
General Counsel **Gordon Amini** ...................... (405) 521-6628
Information Technology Manager **Michael Pavlik** ....... (405) 522-4616
E-mail: michael.pavlik@oid.ok.gov

# Oklahoma Department of Labor [ODOL]

3017 North Stiles, Suite 100, Oklahoma City, OK 73105
Tel: (405) 521-6100  Fax: (405) 521-6018  Internet: www.labor.ok.gov

**Employees:** 76

★Commissioner **Melissa McLawhorn Houston** (R) ....... (405) 521-6110
E-mail: melissa.houston@labor.ok.gov
Education: Oklahoma JD
Executive Assistant to the Commissioner
**Brittoni Lantz** .................................. (405) 521-6110
Finance and Human Resources Director **Lia Tepker** ...... (405) 521-6933
General Counsel **Don A. Schooler** .................... (405) 521-6181
E-mail: don.schooler@labor.ok.gov
Employment Standards Division Director **Curtis Towery** .. (405) 521-6600
E-mail: curtis.towery@labor.ok.gov    Fax: (405) 521-6017
Safety and Health Director **Diana Jones** .............. (405) 521-6137
Fax: (405) 521-6020
Safety Standards and Licensing Director
**James "Jim" Buck** ............................... (405) 521-6111
E-mail: james.buck@labor.ok.gov
Communications Director and Legislative Liaison
**(Vacant)** ....................................... (405) 521-6102

# Oklahoma Corporation Commission [OCC]

Jim Thorpe Building, P.O. Box 52000, Oklahoma City, OK 73152-2000
Tel: (405) 521-2211  TTY: (405) 521-3513  Fax: (405) 522-1623
E-mail: webmaster@occemail.com  Internet: www.occ.state.ok.us

**Employees:** 424

★Chairman **Bob Anthony** (R) ......................... (405) 521-2261
Term Expires: 2019
Education: Pennsylvania 1970 BS;
London School Econ (UK) 1971 MS; Yale 1973 MA;
Harvard 1977 MPA
★Vice Chairman **Dana L. Murphy** (R) ................. (405) 521-2267
Term Expires: 2017
★Commissioner **Todd Hiett** (R) ....................... (405) 521-2211
Term Expires: 2019
Education: Oklahoma State 1989 BS

★ Elected Official    ■ Appointed by Governor    ● Appointed by Legislature    ▲ Appointed by Board or Commission    ◆ Appointed by State Supreme Court

EXECUTIVE BRANCH

# Oregon

Tel: (503) 378-3111 (State Information)  Internet: www.oregon.gov

**Number of U.S. Congressional Delegates:** 2 Senators; 5 Representatives  **Governor's Term:** 4 years
**Legislature Description:** Legislative Assembly - 30 member Senate; 60 member House of Representatives;
Term - Senate 4 years, House 2 years  **Next Election:** Governor November 2016; Legislature November
2016  **Number of Electoral Votes:** 7  **Official Name:** State of Oregon (Algonquian: beautiful water)
**Nickname:** The Beaver State  **Motto:** She Flies With Her Own Wings

**Population:** 4,028,977 (2015); Rank 27  **Fiscal Year:** 2013-2015  **Budget:** $137,207,000,000

## Office of the Governor

State Capitol Building, 900 Court Street, NE, Salem, OR 97301-4047
Tel: (503) 378-4582  Fax: (503) 378-4307
Internet: www.governor.oregon.gov

**Kate Brown**
Governor

Began Service: February 18, 2015
Term Expires: 2017
Date of Birth: June 21, 1960
Education: Colorado 1981 BA;
Lewis & Clark 1985 JD
Career: State Representative (D-OK, District 13),
Oregon House of Representatives (1991-1997);
State Senator (D-OR, District 21), Oregon State
Senate (1997-2009); Secretary of State, Office of
Secretary of State Kate Brown, State of Oregon
(2009-2015)

★Governor **Kate Brown** (D)...................(503) 378-4582
  Governor's Assistant and Scheduler **Jan Murdock**......(503) 378-3111
    E-mail: jan.murdock@state.or.us
  Executive Assistant **Kevin Frazier**...................(503) 378-3111
Chief of Staff **Kristen Leonard**......................(503) 378-1565
  Education: Arizona BA
  Executive Assistant to the Chief of Staff **Grace Roth**....(503) 373-1565
    E-mail: grace.roth@state.or.us
Equity and Community Engagement Director
  **Serena Wesley**....................................(503) 378-4582
  Equity Policy Coordinator **Robin Johnson**..........(503) 373-1686
    E-mail: robin.johnson@state.or.us
    Education: Portland State BS, MSc
Legislative Office Director **Ivo Martin Trummer**........(503) 378-6548
  Legislative Office Deputy Director **Kate Sinner**.......(503) 378-6548
  Policy and Legislative Office Assistant **Stacey Hall**.....(503) 378-6548
General Counsel **Benjamin Souede, JD**..............(503) 378-8636
  E-mail: ben.souede@state.or.us
  Executive Assistant to the General Counsel
  **Jen Andrew**.....................................(503) 378-6246
  Deputy General Counsel **Misha A. Isaak**.............(503) 378-3014
    E-mail: misha.isaak@state.or.us
    Education: Pennsylvania 2008 JD
Senior Policy Advisor **Gina Zejdlik**...................(503) 378-4582
  E-mail: gina.zejdlik@state.or.us
  Education: U Washington BA; Notre Dame 2005 JD
Energy Policy Advisor **Ruchi Sadhir**.................(503) 986-6523
Communications Director **Kristen Grainger**............(503) 378-8197
  E-mail: kristen.grainger@state.or.us
  Press Secretary **Bryan Hockaday**..................(503) 378-5965
  Press Secretary **Melissa Navas**...................(503) 378-5965
    E-mail: melissa.navas@state.or.us
  Press Secretary **Chris Pair**......................(503) 378-5965
    E-mail: chris.pair@state.or.us
Executive Appointments Director **Mary Rae Moller**......(503) 373-1558
  E-mail: mary.moller@state.or.us
  Education: Portland State 2002 BA
  Executive Appointments Assistant **Judge Kemp**.......(503) 378-2317

Operations Director **Shelby Campos**..................(503) 986-6520
  E-mail: shelby.campos@state.or.us
  Assistant to the Operations Director and General
    Counsel **Sheril Arroyo**.........................(503) 373-1686
    E-mail: sheril.arroyo@state.or.us

## Washington Office

Hall of the States, 444 North Capitol Street, NW, Suite 134,
Washington, DC 20001
Tel: (202) 508-3850  Fax: (202) 624-7785

Federal Relations Director **Drew Johnston**............(202) 508-3847
  E-mail: drew.johnston@oregon.gov

## Office of the Long-Term Care Ombudsman

3855 Wolverine NE, Suite 6, Salem, OR 97305-1251
Tel: (800) 522-2602 (In State)  Fax: (503) 373-0852
TTY: (888) 926-6600  TTY: (503) 378-5847
E-mail: ltco.contact@ltco.state.or.us

■Director **Fred Steele**..............................(503) 378-6533

## Office of Rural Health [ORH]

Tel: (503) 494-4450  Fax: (503) 494-4798  E-mail: ruralweb@ohsu.edu

Director **Scott Ekblad**.............................(503) 494-4450

## Department of Administrative Services [DAS]

155 Cottage Street, NE, U30, Salem, OR 97301-3972
Tel: (503) 378-3104  TTY: (503) 373-3737  Fax: (503) 373-7643
E-mail: oregon.info@state.or.us  Internet: www.oregon.gov/das

■Director and Chief Operating Officer (Interim)
  **George M. Naughton**.............................(503) 373-0914
    Education: Oregon State BA; Seattle JD
Deputy Director **(Vacant)**..........................(503) 378-2168
Chief Financial Officer **George M. Naughton**..........(503) 378-5460
  E-mail: george.m.naughton@das.state.or.us
Chief Human Resources Officer **Madilyn Zike**..........(503) 378-3020
Communications Strategist **Matthew "Matt" Shelby**.....(503) 378-3118
  E-mail: matthew.shelby@oregon.gov
Executive Assistant **Richelle Borden**.................(503) 378-5967

## Office of Economic Analysis

State Economist **Mark McMullen**.....................(503) 378-3455
  Education: Pomona BEc; Pennsylvania MA

## Enterprise Asset Management Division

1225 Ferry Street, Suite U100, Salem, OR 97301-4281
Tel: (503) 378-2865  Fax: (503) 373-7210

Administrator **Shannon Ryan**.......................(503) 428-3362
  E-mail: shannon.ryan@oregon.gov

## Enterprise Technology Services

Tel: (503) 378-2176  Fax: (503) 378-2736  E-mail: sdc.info@state.or.us

Chief Information Officer **Alex Pettit**................(503) 378-2128
  E-mail: alex.pettit@oregon.gov
  Education: Wisconsin (Parkside) BBA; Loyola U (Chicago) MA

---

★ Elected Official     ■ Appointed by Governor     ● Appointed by Legislature     ▲ Appointed by Board or Commission     ◆ Appointed by State Supreme Court

Administrator (Interim) **John Koreski** . . . . . . . . . . . . . . . . (503) 378-2176
Deputy Administrator **(Vacant)** . . . . . . . . . . . . . . . . . . . . (503) 378-2176

## Statewide Internal Audits
155 Cottage Street, NE, U20, Salem, OR 97301-3972
Tel: (503) 378-3076
Chief Audit Executive **Zachary Gehringer** . . . . . . . . . . . . (503) 378-3076

## Oregon Department of Agriculture [ODA]
635 Capitol Street, NE, Salem, OR 97301-2532
Tel: (503) 986-4550  Fax: (503) 986-4750  TTY: (503) 986-4762
E-mail: info@oda.state.or.us  Internet: oregon.gov/ODA

■Director **Katy Coba** . . . . . . . . . . . . . . . . . . . . . . . . . . . (503) 986-4552
 E-mail: kcoba@oda.state.or.us
 Executive Assistant **Sherry A. Kudna** . . . . . . . . . . . . . (503) 986-4619
 Special Assistant **Stephanie Page** . . . . . . . . . . . . . . . . (503) 986-4550
Deputy Director **Lisa R. Hanson** . . . . . . . . . . . . . . . . . . (503) 986-4552
 Assistant Director **Lauren L. Henderson** . . . . . . . . . . . (503) 986-4580
 Market Access and Certification Programs Director
  **Lindsay Eng** . . . . . . . . . . . . . . . . . . . . . . . . . . . . . (503) 986-4620
 Market Access and Certification Programs Marketing
  Director **Gary B. Roth** . . . . . . . . . . . . . . . . . . . . . . (503) 872-6600
 Food Safety and Animal Health Programs Director
  **(Vacant)** . . . . . . . . . . . . . . . . . . . . . . . . . . . . . . . . (503) 986-4727
 Food Safety and Animal Health Programs State
  Veterinarian **Brad LeaMaster** . . . . . . . . . . . . . . . . (503) 986-4760
  E-mail: bleamaster@oda.state.or.us
 Internal Service and Consumer Protection Programs
  Director **Jason M. Barber** . . . . . . . . . . . . . . . . . . . . (503) 986-4767
  E-mail: jbarber@oda.state.or.us
 Natural Resource Programs Director **Ray Jaindl** . . . . . . (503) 986-4713
 Plant Programs Director **Dan Hilburn** . . . . . . . . . . . . (503) 986-4663
Communications Director **Bruce A. Pokarney** . . . . . . . . (503) 986-4559
 E-mail: bpokarney@oda.state.or.us
Publications Coordinator **Liz Beeles** . . . . . . . . . . . . . . . (503) 986-4560
 E-mail: ebeeles@oda.state.or.us

## Oregon Department of Aviation [ODA]
3040 25th Street, SE, Salem, OR 97302-1125
Tel: (503) 378-4880  Fax: (503) 373-1688
E-mail: aviation.mail@state.or.us  Internet: www.aviation.state.or.us

■Director **Mitch T. Swecker** . . . . . . . . . . . . . . . . . . . . . (503) 378-2340
 E-mail: mitch.t.swecker@aviation.state.or.us
State Airports Manager **Matthew D. Maass** . . . . . . . . . . (503) 378-2523
 State Airports Maintenance Coordinator
  **Dueford E. "Adam" Adams** . . . . . . . . . . . . . . . . . . (503) 378-2531
Planning and Projects Manager **Heather Peck** . . . . . . . . (503) 378-3168
Aviation Planner **Jeff Caines** . . . . . . . . . . . . . . . . . . . . (503) 378-2529
Business Manager **Joy Howard** . . . . . . . . . . . . . . . . . . . (503) 378-4881
 Fiscal Analyst **Kristen R. Forest** . . . . . . . . . . . . . . . . (503) 378-2522
 Fiscal Analyst **Nohemi Ramos** . . . . . . . . . . . . . . . . . (503) 378-4881
Accounting Technician **Rita F. Rogerson** . . . . . . . . . . . . (503) 378-5480
Airport Operations Specialist **Donald E. Hankwitz** . . . . . (503) 378-4176
Airport Operations Specialist **John P. Wilson** . . . . . . . . (503) 378-2521
Administrative Assistant **Roger Sponseller** . . . . . . . . . . (503) 378-2211

## Department of Consumer and Business Services [DCBS]
350 Winter Street, NE, Salem, OR 97301-3878
P.O. Box 14480, Salem, OR 97309-0405
Tel: (503) 378-4100  Tel: (800) 452-0288 (Injured Workers' Hotline)
Tel: (800) 927-1271 (Ombudsman for Injured Workers)
Tel: (503) 947-7984 (Insurance Consumer Services)
Tel: (800) 922-2689 (Occupational Safety & Health Message Line)
Fax: (503) 378-6444  E-mail: info@oregon.gov
Internet: www.oregon.gov/dcbs

■Director **Patrick Allen** . . . . . . . . . . . . . . . . . . . . . . . . (503) 947-7872
 E-mail: dcbs.director@oregon.gov
 E-mail: patrick.allen@oregon.gov
 Education: Oregon State 1985 BSE

Deputy Director **Jean M. Straight** . . . . . . . . . . . . . . . . . (503) 947-7872
 E-mail: jean.m.straight@oregon.gov
 Public Information and Communications
  **Lisa Morawski** . . . . . . . . . . . . . . . . . . . . . . . . . . . (503) 947-7873
  E-mail: lisa.m.morawski@oregon.gov
 Senior Policy Advisor **Theresa Van Winkle** . . . . . . . . . . (503) 947-7867
 Building Codes Division Administrator **Mark Long** . . . . . (503) 378-4133
 Finance and Corporate Securities Division
  Administrator **David C. Tatman** . . . . . . . . . . . . . . . (503) 378-4140
 Central Services Division Administrator
  **Nancy J. Boysen** . . . . . . . . . . . . . . . . . . . . . . . . . (503) 947-7077
 Chief Information Officer **Sandy C. Wheeler** . . . . . . . . (503) 947-7323
  E-mail: sandy.c.wheeler@oregon.gov
 Insurance Commissioner **Laura N. Cali** . . . . . . . . . . . . (503) 947-7980
 Occupational Safety and Health Administration
  (OR-OSHA) Division Administrator **Michael Wood** . . . . (503) 378-3272
 Workers' Compensation Division Administrator **(Vacant)** . . (503) 947-7500
 Injured Workers' Ombudsman **Jennifer R. Flood** . . . . . . . (503) 378-3351
 Workers' Compensation Small Business Ombudsman
  **David "Dave" Waki** . . . . . . . . . . . . . . . . . . . . . . . (503) 378-4209

## Department of Corrections [DOC]
2575 Center Street, NE, Salem, OR 97301-4667
Tel: (503) 945-0927  Fax: (503) 945-1034  E-mail: doc.info@state.or.us

■Director **Colette S. Peters** . . . . . . . . . . . . . . . . . . . . . . (503) 945-0927
 E-mail: colette.s.peters@doc.state.or.us
 Education: St Benedict BA; Colorado MCJ
 Executive Assistant **Annola DeJong** . . . . . . . . . . . . . . (503) 945-0927
Deputy Director **Kim Brockamp** . . . . . . . . . . . . . . . . . . (503) 945-0927
General Services Assistant Director **Daryl Borello** . . . . . . (503) 945-0990
 E-mail: daryl.r.borello@doc.state.or.us
Human Resources Assistant Director
 **Christine M. Popoff** . . . . . . . . . . . . . . . . . . . . . . . . (503) 945-5278
Operations Assistant Director **Michael F. Gower** . . . . . . (503) 945-0950
Inspector General **Leonard Williamson** . . . . . . . . . . . . (503) 945-9043
 E-mail: leonard.w.williamson@doc.state.or.us
Community Corrections Assistant Director
 **Jeremiah Stromberg** . . . . . . . . . . . . . . . . . . . . . . . . (503) 945-9062
Oregon Corrections Enterprises Administrator **Ken Jeske** . . (503) 945-2802
Planning and Budget Administrator **Steve C. Robbins** . . . . (503) 945-9006
 E-mail: steve.c.robbins@doc.state.or.us
Communications Manager **Elizabeth A. Craig** . . . . . . . . (503) 945-0930
 E-mail: elizabeth.a.craig@doc.state.or.us
Community Development Manager **(Vacant)** . . . . . (503) 373-1572 ext. 7105
Facilities Services Administrator **Troy Bowser** . . . . . . . . (503) 934-1060
Information Technology Administrator and Chief
 Information Officer **Bettina Davis** . . . . . . . . . . . . . . . (503) 373-2128
 E-mail: bettina.m.davis@doc.state.or.us

## Oregon Employment Department [OED]
875 Union Street, NE, Salem, OR 97311
Tel: (503) 947-1394  Tel: (800) 237-3710  Fax: (503) 947-1472
E-mail: oed_ui_info@oregon.gov  Internet: www.employment.oregon.gov

■Director **Lisa Nisenfeld** . . . . . . . . . . . . . . . . . . . . . . . (503) 947-1477
 Term Expires: September 30, 2017
Deputy Director **Salvador Llerenas** . . . . . . . . . . . . . . . . (503) 947-1476
 Executive Assistant **Audrey D. Povis** . . . . . . . . . . . . . (503) 947-1474
  E-mail: audrey.d.povis@oregon.gov
Business and Employment Services Assistant Director
 **James "Jim" Pfarrer** . . . . . . . . . . . . . . . . . . . . . . . (503) 947-1655
 E-mail: james.f.pfarrer@oregon.gov
Unemployment Insurance Assistant Director
 **David K. Gerstenfeld** . . . . . . . . . . . . . . . . . . . . . . . (503) 947-1330
US Veterans Employment Service Director
 **Tonja M. Pardo** . . . . . . . . . . . . . . . . . . . . . . . . . . . (503) 947-1490
Chief Financial Officer **Michael T. "Mike" Smith** . . . . . . (503) 947-1213
Communications and Legislative Manager
 **Andrea Fogue** . . . . . . . . . . . . . . . . . . . . . . . . . . . . (503) 947-1301
 E-mail: andrea.j.fogue@oregon.gov
Chief Administrative Law Judge **Gary L. Tyler** . . . . . . . . (503) 947-1516
Human Resources Manager **Tasha L. Petersen** . . . . . . . . (503) 947-1319

*(continued on next page)*

---

★ Elected Official   ■ Appointed by Governor   ● Appointed by Legislature   ▲ Appointed by Board or Commission   ◆ Appointed by State Supreme Court

**Oregon Employment Department** *continued*

Research and Economic Services Administrator
**Graham J. Slater** .................................. (503) 947-1212
 E-mail: graham.j.slater@oregon.gov
Unemployment Insurance Program Manager
**Jason M. Barbee** ................................. (503) 947-1656
Unemployment Insurance Tax Deputy Administrator
**Isabel M. Joslen** ................................. (503) 947-1696
Farmworker Services Monitor Advocate
**Fernando Gutierrez** ............................. (503) 947-1996
 E-mail: fernando.gutierrez@state.or.us

## Employment Appeals Board [EAB]

875 Union Street, NE, Salem, OR 97311
Tel: (503) 378-2077  Fax: (503) 378-2129
Internet: www.oregon.gov/employ/eab

■Chairperson **Susan Rossiter** ...................... (503) 378-2077
■Member **Sara Cromwell** ......................... (503) 378-2077
■Member **(Vacant)** ............................... (503) 378-2077
Staff Attorney **Glenn M. Feest** .................... (503) 378-2077
 E-mail: glenn.m.feest@state.or.us
Staff Attorney **Sarah Gove** ........................ (503) 378-2077
 E-mail: sarah.gove@state.or.us
Staff Attorney **Duncan P. Hettle** ................. (503) 378-2077
 E-mail: duncan.p.hettle@state.or.us
Staff Attorney **Denise L. Jarrard** ................. (503) 378-2077
 E-mail: denise.l.jarrard@state.or.us

## Oregon Department of Energy [ODOE]

625 Marion Street, NE, Salem, OR 97301-3737
Tel: (503) 378-4040  Tel: (800) 221-8035 (Toll Free)
Fax: (503) 373-7806  E-mail: energy.in.internet@odoe.state.or.us
Internet: www.oregon.gov/energy

■Director **Michael Kaplan** ......................... (503) 373-7563
 E-mail: mike.kaplan@state.or.us
Deputy Director **(Vacant)** ......................... (503) 378-4040
Legislative Coordinator **Robin Freeman** ......... (503) 378-2293
 E-mail: robin.freeman@state.or.us

## Department of Environmental Quality [DEQ]

811 SW Sixth Avenue, Portland, OR 97204-1390
Tel: (503) 229-5696  Fax: (503) 229-6124
E-mail: deq.info@deq.state.or.us  Internet: www.oregon.gov/deq

▲Director **Peter D. Shepherd** ..................... (503) 229-5332
Deputy Director **Joni Hammond** .................. (503) 229-5332

### Central Services Division

Tel: (503) 229-5696  Fax: (503) 229-6124
E-mail: deq.info@deq.state.or.us

Administrator **Kerri Nelson** ....................... (503) 229-5045
 E-mail: kerri.nelson@state.or.us
Health and Safety Lead **Todd F. Brown** ......... (503) 229-6160
Human Resources Manager **Susan Korn** ......... (503) 229-5389

### Environmental Solutions Division

Tel: (503) 229-5696  Fax: (503) 229-6977
E-mail: deq.info@deq.state.or.us

Administrator **Wendy Wiles** ...................... (503) 229-6834
 Education: Oregon State BS; Oregon 1987 MS

### Operations Division

Tel: (503) 229-5696  Fax: (503) 229-6124
E-mail: deq.info@deq.state.or.us

Operations Administrator **Lydia Emer** ........... (503) 229-6411

## Laboratory Environmental Assessment Program [LEAP]

Tel: (503) 693-5700  Fax: (503) 693-4999
E-mail: deq.info@deq.state.or.us

Administrator **Brian Boling** ....................... (503) 693-5705

## Department of Geology and Mineral Industries [DOGAMI]

State Office Building, 800 NE Oregon Street, Mailbox 28, Suite 965,
Portland, OR 97232
Tel: (971) 673-1555  Fax: (971) 673-1562

▲State Geologist and Director **Brad Avy** ........... (971) 673-1542
 E-mail: brad.avy@state.or.us
Assistant Director (Interim) **Holly Mercer, RN** ..... (971) 673-1548
Communications Director **Alison "Ali" Hansen** ..... (971) 673-0628
 E-mail: ali.hansen@state.or.us
Minerals and Land Assistant Director **Richard Riggs** ..... (971) 673-1555
                                                      Fax: (541) 967-2075
Chief Scientist and Geologic Mapping Section Leader
 **(Vacant)** ...................................... (971) 673-1555
Mineral Resources Geologist **Clark Niewendorp** ......... (971) 673-1540
Geohazard Section Leader **Yumei Wang** ............ (971) 673-1551
Agency Accountant **(Vacant)** ..................... (971) 673-1549
Regional Geologist **Thomas J. Wiley** ............. (541) 673-0229

### Baker City Field Office

1995 3rd Street, Baker City, OR 97814
Regional Geologist **Jason McClaughry** ............. (541) 523-3133

### Newport Field Office

313 SW Second, Suite D, Newport, OR 97365
Fax: (541) 265-5241
Resident Geologist **Jonathan Allan** ................ (541) 574-6658

## Department of Human Services [DHS]

Human Services Building, 500 Summer Street, NE,
Salem, OR 97301-1097
P.O. Box 14050, Portland, OR 97293 (Vital Records)
Tel: (503) 945-5944  Tel: (971) 673-1190 (Vital Records)
TTY: (503) 945-6214  Fax: (503) 378-2897
Fax: (503) 234-8417 (Vital Records)  E-mail: dhs.info@state.or.us
Director **Clyde Saiki** .............................. (503) 945-7001
 Education: Oregon State BS
 Executive Assistant to the Director **Karrie Pitrof** ........ (503) 945-7001
Chief Audit Officer **Dave M. Lyda** ................ (503) 945-6700
Chief Financial Officer **Eric L. Moore** ............ (503) 884-4701
Governor's Advocacy Office Administrator
 **Naomi R. Steenson** ............................ (503) 945-6904
Legislative and Client Relations Director **(Vacant)** ..... (503) 945-5944
Tribal Relations Liaison **Nadja Jones** ............. (503) 945-7034

## Aging and People with Disabilities Division [APD]

Tel: (503) 945-5811  Tel: (800) 282-8096  TTY: (503) 945-5933
Fax: (503) 373-7823
Director **Michael R. "Mike" McCormick** ............ (503) 945-5811
Deputy Director **Ashley B. Cottingham** ........... (503) 945-5811
 Education: Oregon 2001 BA; Vermont 2006 JD
Chief Operating Officer **Patricia E. Baxter** ....... (503) 945-6478
Federal Resource Reporting and Financial Eligibility
 Administrator **(Vacant)** ......................... (503) 947-1180

## Budget, Planning and Analysis

Forecasting and Research Analysis Administrator
 **Betsy A. Jensvold** ............................. (503) 884-4975
Children, Adults and Families Program and
 Policy-Budget Administrator **(Vacant)** ............ (503) 947-5458
AMH Budget Administrator **Silke Blaine** ......... (503) 945-6198
Research Analyst/Administrative Support
 **Katie L. Brown** ................................ (503) 947-5185

---

★ Elected Official   ■ Appointed by Governor   ● Appointed by Legislature   ▲ Appointed by Board or Commission   ◆ Appointed by State Supreme Court

Summer 2016                    © Leadership Directories, Inc.                    *State Yellow Book*

## Children, Adults and Families Division [CAF]

Tel: (503) 945-7001  TTY: (503) 945-5896  Fax: (503) 581-6198

Assistant Director **(Vacant)** . . . . . . . . . . . . . . . . . . . . . . . . (503) 945-5600
Field Services Deputy Assistant Director **(Vacant)** . . . . . . . (503) 945-7001
Policy and Program Deputy Assistant Director **(Vacant)** . . . (503) 945-7001
Vocational Rehabilitation Director **Trina M. Lee** . . . . . . . . . (503) 945-6201
　Vocational Rehabilitation Deputy Director **Dan Haun** . . . . (503) 945-7001
Self Sufficiency Programs Manager **Belit Burke** . . . . . . . . . (503) 947-5389
Program Performance and Reporting Office Administrator
　**Angela Long** . . . . . . . . . . . . . . . . . . . . . . . . . . . . . . . . . . . (503) 945-6170
Safety and Permanency for Children Office Administrator
　**Nancy Keeling** . . . . . . . . . . . . . . . . . . . . . . . . . . . . . . . . . . (503) 945-6627

## Operations

Fax: (503) 378-5577

Chief Operating Officer **Jim Scherzinger** . . . . . . . . . . . . . (503) 947-2320
　Assistant to the Chief Operating Officer **Jason Nunev** . . (503) 947-2463
Payment Accuracy and Recovery Office Administrator
　**Chuck Hibner, CPA** . . . . . . . . . . . . . . . . . . . . . . . . . . . . . (503) 378-3584
　Provider Audit Unit Manager **Fritz Jenkins** . . . . . . . . . . . (503) 378-8113

## Department of Land Conservation and Development [DLCD]

635 Capitol Street, NE, Suite 150, Salem, OR 97301-2540
Tel: (503) 373-0050  TTY: (800) 735-2900  Fax: (503) 378-5518

▲Director **Jim Rue** . . . . . . . . . . . . . . . . . . . . . . . . . . (503) 373-0050 ext. 223
　E-mail: jim.rue@state.or.us
　Executive Assistant **Amie Abbott** . . . . . . . . . . . . (503) 373-0050 ext. 271
Deputy Director **Caroline MacLaren** . . . . . . . . . . . . (503) 373-0050 ext. 280
Ocean and Coastal Manager **Patty Snow** . . . . . . . . (503) 373-0050 ext. 281
　E-mail: patty.snow@state.or.us
Community Services Division Manager
　**Rob Hallyburton** . . . . . . . . . . . . . . . . . . . . . . . . (503) 373-0050 ext. 239
　E-mail: rob.hallyburton@state.or.us
Operations Service Division Manager
　**Teddy Leland** . . . . . . . . . . . . . . . . . . . . . . . . . . . (503) 373-0050 ext. 237
　E-mail: teddy.leland@state.or.us
Planning Services Division Manager
　**Matthew Crall** . . . . . . . . . . . . . . . . . . . . . . . . . . (503) 373-0050 ext. 272
　E-mail: matthew.crall@state.or.us
Central Representative **Scott Edelman** . . . . . . . . . . . . . . . (541) 325-6927
　Bend Field Office, 888 Northwest Hill Street,　　Fax: (541) 318-8361
　Suite 2, Bend, OR 97701
　E-mail: scott.edelman@state.or.us
Central and Southeastern Regional Representative
　**Jon Jinings** . . . . . . . . . . . . . . . . . . . . . . . . . . . . . . . . . . . (541) 318-2890
　Bend Field Office, 888 Northwest Hill Street,　　Fax: (541) 318-8361
　Suite 2, Bend, OR 97701
　E-mail: jon.jinings@state.or.us
Metro Regional Representative **Anne Debbaut** . . . . . . . . . (503) 725-2182
　Portland Field Office, 1600 Southwest Fourth Avenue, Suite 109,
　Portland, OR 97201
　E-mail: anne.debbaut@state.or.us
Metro Regional Representative **Jennifer Donnelly** . . . . . . . (503) 725-2183
　Portland Field Office, 1600 Southwest Fourth Avenue, Suite 109,
　Portland, OR 97201
　E-mail: jennifer.donnelly@state.or.us
North Coast Regional Representative **Matt Spangler** . . . . . (541) 574-1095
　Coastal Field Office, 810 Southwest Alder Street, Unit B,
　Newport, OR 97201
　E-mail: matt.spangler@state.or.us
Northeastern Regional Representative **Grant S. Young** . . . . (541) 962-3982
　La Grand Field Office, EOU Badgely Hall, Room 233A,
　La Grande, OR 97880
　E-mail: grant.s.young@state.or.us
South Coast Regional Representative **Dave Perry** . . . . . . . . (541) 563-2056
　Coastal Field Office, 810 Southwest Alder Street,　　Fax: (541) 574-1584
　Unit B, Newport, OR 97201
　E-mail: dave.perry@state.or.us
Southern Regional Representative **Ed W. Moore** . . . . . . . . (541) 239-9453
　720 East Thirteenth Avenue, Suite 304, Eugene, OR 97401
　E-mail: ed.w.moore@state.or.us

Principal Marine Scientist **Paul Klarin** . . . . . . . . . . (503) 373-0050 ext. 249
　635 Capitol Street, NE, Salem, OR 97301-2532
　E-mail: paul.klarin@state.or.us

## Oregon Military Department

1776 Militia Way SE, Salem, OR 97309-5047
P.O. Box 14350, Salem, OR 97309
Tel: (503) 584-3980  Fax: (503) 584-3962

■Adjutant General **MG Michael E. Stencel, ANG** . . . . . . . . (503) 584-3991
　E-mail: michael.e.stencel@ang.af.mil
　Executive Assistant **Ullyssa Althaus** . . . . . . . . . . . . . . . . (503) 584-3991
Oregon State Defense Force Commander **(Vacant)** . . . . . . . (503) 584-3884
Deputy Director of State Affairs **Dave Stuckey** . . . . . . . . . (503) 584-3884
Public Affairs Officer
　**MAJ Stephen S. "Steve" Bomar, ARNG** . . . . . . . . . . . . (503) 584-3885
Homeland Security Advisor to the Governor **(Vacant)** . . . . . (503) 584-3980

## Oregon National Guard

■Adjutant General **MG Michael E. Stencel, ANG** . . . . . . . . (503) 584-3991
　E-mail: michael.e.stencel@ang.af.mil
Chief of the Joint Staff **(Vacant)** . . . . . . . . . . . . . . . . . . . . (503) 584-3639
Deputy Chief of Staff, Information Management
　**MAJ Gary Nash, ARNG** . . . . . . . . . . . . . . . . . . . . . . . . . . (503) 584-3820

## Oregon Air National Guard

Assistant Adjutant General (Air)
　**Col Jeffrey M. Silver, ANG** . . . . . . . . . . . . . . . . . . . . . . (503) 584-3646
Commander **(Vacant)** . . . . . . . . . . . . . . . . . . . . . . . . . . . . . (503) 584-3646

## Oregon Army National Guard

Assistant Adjutant General (Army)
　**BG Steven Russell Beach, ARNG** . . . . . . . . . . . . . . . . . (503) 584-3980

## Office of Emergency Management

P. O. Box 14370, Salem, OR 97309-5062
Tel: (503) 378-2911  Fax: (503) 373-7833  TTY: (503) 373-7857

Director **Andrew Phelps** . . . . . . . . . . . . . . . . (503) 378-2911 ext. 22292
Deputy Director **Laurie J. Holien** . . . . . . . . . . . (503) 378-2911 ext. 22225
Mitigation and Recovery Services Section
　Manager **Clint Fella** . . . . . . . . . . . . . . . . . . . (503) 378-2911 ext. 22227
Operations and Preparedness Section Manager
　**Matt Marheine** . . . . . . . . . . . . . . . . . . . . . . . (503) 378-2911 ext. 22239
Technology and Response Services Section
　Manager **Mark Tennyson** . . . . . . . . . . . . . . . . (503) 378-2911 ext. 22265
　E-mail: mark.tennyson@state.or.us

## Oregon Parks and Recreation Department [OPRD]

725 Summer Street, NE, Suite C, Salem, OR 97301-1266
Tel: (503) 986-0707  Fax: (503) 986-0796
Internet: www.oregonstateparks.org

▲Director **Lisa L. Sumption** . . . . . . . . . . . . . . . . . . . . . . . . (503) 986-0660
　E-mail: lisa.vanlaanen@oregon.gov
　Assistant to the Director and Commission
　　**Jennifer Busey** . . . . . . . . . . . . . . . . . . . . . . . . . . . . . . (503) 986-0719
Deputy Director **M. G. Devereux** . . . . . . . . . . . . . . . . . . . . (503) 986-0707
　E-mail: mg.devereux@oregon.gov
Internal Services Director **Larry Warren** . . . . . . . . . . . . . . . (503) 986-0072
　E-mail: larry.warren@oregon.gov
Heritage Programs Assistant Director **Chrissy Curran** . . . . . (503) 986-0677
Operations Assistant Director **Scott Nebeker** . . . . . . . . . . . (503) 986-0707
　E-mail: scott.nebeker@oregon.gov
Media Contact **Chris Havel** . . . . . . . . . . . . . . . . . . . . . . . . (503) 986-0722
Webmaster **Beth Wilson** . . . . . . . . . . . . . . . . . . . . . . . . . . (503) 986-0666
　E-mail: beth.wilson@oregon.gov

---

★ Elected Official　　■ Appointed by Governor　　● Appointed by Legislature　　▲ Appointed by Board or Commission　　◆ Appointed by State Supreme Court

## Oregon State Fair and Exposition Center [OSFEC]

2330 17th Street Northeast, Salem, OR 97301
Tel: (971) 701-6573  Fax: (503) 947-3206
Internet: www.oregonstatefair.org

Director and Chief Executive Officer **Mike Paluszak** . . . . . . (971) 701-6573

## Department of Public Safety Standards and Training [DPSST]

4190 Aumsville Highway, Salem, OR 97317
Tel: (503) 378-2100  Fax: (503) 378-3306  Internet: www.oregon.gov/dpsst

■Director **Eriks Gabliks** . . . . . . . . . . . . . . . . . . . . . . . . . (503) 378-2332
  E-mail: eriks.gabliks@state.or.us
  Executive Assistant **Theresa Janda** . . . . . . . . . . . . . . . . (503) 378-1553
Human Resources Director **Brian Henson** . . . . . . . . . . . . (503) 378-2243
Training Director **Todd Anderson** . . . . . . . . . . . . . . . . . . (503) 378-3312
Business Services Division Director **Denver Peterson** . . . . (503) 378-2245
Facilities and Technology Division Director
  **Brian Henson** . . . . . . . . . . . . . . . . . . . . . . . . . . . . . . . (503) 378-2888
  E-mail: brian.henson@state.or.us
Information Services Operations Manager
  **Denver Peterson** . . . . . . . . . . . . . . . . . . . . . . . . . . . . (503) 378-2245
Business Systems Analyst **Marsha Morin** . . . . . . . . . . . . . (503) 378-2155
  E-mail: marsha.morin@state.or.us
User Support Specialist **Cary Smith** . . . . . . . . . . . . . . . . (503) 378-2419

## Department of Revenue

Revenue Building, 955 Center Street, NE, Salem, OR 97301
Tel: (503) 378-4988  Fax: (503) 945-8738  Internet: www.oregon.gov/dor

■Director (Interim) **Kristine M. "Kris" Kautz** . . . . . . . . . . . (503) 945-8214
  E-mail: directors.office@oregon.gov
Deputy Director **(Vacant)** . . . . . . . . . . . . . . . . . . . . . . . . (503) 378-4988
Administrative Services Division Administrator
  **Shawn N. Waite** . . . . . . . . . . . . . . . . . . . . . . . . . . . . . (503) 798-7852
  E-mail: shawn.waite@oregon.gov
Business Tax Division Administrator **Jack H. Ogami** . . . . . (503) 945-8400
Personal Tax and Compliance Division Administrator
  **JoAnn M. Martin** . . . . . . . . . . . . . . . . . . . . . . . . . . . . (503) 945-8539
Property Tax Division Administrator **Gary D. Humphrey** . . (503) 779-6521
Webmaster **Amy Velez** . . . . . . . . . . . . . . . . . . . . . . . . . . (503) 945-8563
  E-mail: amy.velez@dor.state.or.us              Tel: (503) 378-4988

## Department of State Lands [DSL]

775 Summer Street, NE, Suite 100, Salem, OR 97301-1279
Tel: (503) 986-5200  Fax: (503) 378-4844

▲Director **Jim Paul** . . . . . . . . . . . . . . . . . . . . . . . . . . . . . (503) 986-5224
  E-mail: jim.paul@state.or.us
  Executive Assistant **Lorna Stafford** . . . . . . . . . . . . . . . . (503) 986-5224
Finance and Administration Assistant Director
  **Cynthia "Cyndi" Wickham** . . . . . . . . . . . . . . . . . . . . . (503) 986-5227
  E-mail: cyndi.wickham@dsl.state.or.us
Land Management Division Assistant Director **Jim Paul** . . . (503) 986-5279
Wetlands and Waterways Conservation Division Assistant
  Director **Bill Ryan** . . . . . . . . . . . . . . . . . . . . . . . . . . . . (503) 986-5259
Fiscal Manager **Vena McCoy** . . . . . . . . . . . . . . . . . . . . . (503) 986-5283
Public Information Manager **Julie Curtis** . . . . . . . . . . . . . (503) 986-5298
  E-mail: julie.curtis@dsl.state.or.us
Senior Policy and Legislative Analyst **Chris Castelli** . . . . . (503) 986-5280
  E-mail: chris.castelli@state.or.us

## Department of Oregon State Police [OSP]

255 Capitol Street, NE, 4th Floor, Salem, OR 97310
Tel: (503) 378-3720  Fax: (503) 378-8282  TTY: (800) 735-2900
E-mail: askosp@osp.state.or.us  Internet: www.oregon.gov/osp

■Superintendent **Richard "Rich" Evans** . . . . . . . . . . . . . . (503) 934-0234
  E-mail: revans@osp.state.or.us
Deputy Superintendent **Pat Ashmore** . . . . . . . . . (503) 378-3720 ext. 40275
Chief Financial Officer **Kailean Kneeland** . . . . . (503) 378-3720 ext. 40193

Administrative Services Division Director **Rick Willis** . . . (503) 934-0225
  E-mail: rick.willis@state.or.us
  Education: USC 1974 BA
Criminal Investigative Division Director
  **Capt. Terri Davie** . . . . . . . . . . . . . . . . . . . . . . . . . . . (503) 934-0313
Fish and Wildlife Division Director
  **Capt. Jeff Samuels** . . . . . . . . . . . . . . . . (503) 378-3720 ext. 40221
Forensic Services Division Director
  **Capt. Ted Phillips** . . . . . . . . . . . . . . . . . (503) 378-3720 ext. 40238
Lottery Division Director **Lt. Glenn Chastain** . . . . . . . . (503) 540-1406
Gaming and Employee Services Director
  **Major Joel E. Lujan** . . . . . . . . . . . . . . . . . . . . . . . . . (503) 378-3720
  E-mail: jlujan@osp.state.or.us
Oregon State Medical Examiner Division Director
  **Karen Gunson** . . . . . . . . . . . . . . . . . . . . . . . . . . . . . (503) 451-2200
  13309 SE 84th Avenue, Suite 100, Clackamas, OR 97015
Criminal Justice Information Services Director
  **Patricia "Tricia" Whitfield** . . . . . . . . . . . . . . . . . . . . (503) 378-3070
  E-mail: patricia.whitfield@state.or.us
Public Safety Services Section
  **Major Mike Bloom** . . . . . . . . . . . . . . . . . (503) 378-3720 ext. 40261
Patrol Services Division Captain
  **Capt. David Anderson** . . . . . . . . . . . . . . . (503) 378-3720 ext. 40268
Law Enforcement Data Systems (LEDS)/Information
  Management Division **(Vacant)** . . . . . . . . . . . . . . . . . (503) 378-3055
Professional Standards Office Commanding Officer
  **Capt. Eric Davenport** . . . . . . . . . . . . . . . . . . . . . . . . (503) 378-3720

## Office of the State Fire Marshal

State Fire Marshal **James "Jim" Walker** . . . . . . . . . . . . . (503) 373-1540
  4760 Portland Road, NE, Salem, OR 97305
  E-mail: jim.walker@state.or.us
Deputy Fire Marshal **Sean Condon** . . . . . . . . . . . . . . . . (503) 373-1540
  4760 Portland Road, NE, Salem, OR 97305
  E-mail: sean.condon@state.or.us

## Oregon Department of Transportation [ODOT]

355 Capitol Street Northeast, Mail Stop 11, Salem, OR 97301
Tel: (503) 986-3289  Fax: (503) 986-3432  Internet: www.oregon.gov/odot

■Director **Matthew Garrett** . . . . . . . . . . . . . . . . . . . . . . . (503) 986-3452
  E-mail: matthew.l.garrett@odot.state.or.us
Communications Division Administrator
  **Thomas "Tom" Fuller** . . . . . . . . . . . . . . . . . . . . . . . . (503) 986-3455
  E-mail: thomas.fuller@odot.state.or.us

### Central Services Division

Fax: (503) 986-4060

Deputy Director **(Vacant)** . . . . . . . . . . . . . . . . . . . . . . . . (503) 986-4399
Civil Rights Manager **Michael A. Cobb** . . . . . . . . . . . . . (503) 986-5753
                                                       Fax: (503) 986-6382
Chief Human Resources Officer **Jane S. Lee** . . . . . . . . . . (503) 986-4057
                                                       Fax: (503) 986-2630
Chief Information Systems Officer **Kurtis Danka** . . . . . . . (503) 986-4400
  555 - 13th Street, Salem, OR 97310-4166       Fax: (503) 986-4072
  E-mail: kurtis.danka@odot.state.or.us
Chief Internal Audit Officer **Marlene V. Hartinger** . . . . . . (503) 986-3291
                                                       Fax: (503) 986-4177

### Driver and Motor Vehicle Services Division

1905 Lana Avenue, NE, Salem, OR 97314
Fax: (503) 945-5254

Administrator **Thomas M. "Tom" McClellan** . . . . . . . . . . (503) 945-5100
Customer Service Administrator **Diane L. Reeves** . . . . . . . (503) 986-3289
  E-mail: diane.l.reeves@odot.state.or.us
Field Services Administrator **Stefanie Coons** . . . . . . . . . . (503) 986-3289
Processing Services Administrator **Mark Cadotte** . . . . . . . (503) 986-3289
Program Services Administrator **Lana Tribbey** . . . . . . . . . (503) 986-3289

### Highway Division

Fax: (503) 986-3432
Administrator **Paul R. Mather** . . . . . . . . . . . . . . . . . . . . . (503) 986-3500

★ Elected Official   ■ Appointed by Governor   ● Appointed by Legislature   ▲ Appointed by Board or Commission   ◆ Appointed by State Supreme Court

Summer 2016                    © Leadership Directories, Inc.                    *State Yellow Book*

Technical Services Manager/Chief Engineer
 **Thomas J. "Tom" Lauer** . . . . . . . . . . . . . . . . . . . . . . . . . (503) 986-4412
  E-mail: thomas.j.lauer@odot.state.or.us   Fax: (503) 986-4469
Region I Manager **(Vacant)** . . . . . . . . . . . . . . . . . . . . . . . (503) 731-8256
  123 NW Flanders, Portland, OR 97209-4012   Fax: (503) 731-8259
Region II Manager **Sonny P. Chickering** . . . . . . . . . . . . . (503) 986-2631
  Building B, 455 Airport Road, SE,   Fax: (503) 986-2630
  Salem, OR 97301-5395
Region III Manager **Frank H. Reading** . . . . . . . . . . . . . . . (541) 957-3507
  3500 NW Stewart Parkway, Roseburg, OR 97470-1687
Region IV Manager **Robert W. "Bob" Bryant** . . . . . . . . . (541) 388-6184
  63055 North Hwy. 97, Bend, OR 97701-5765   Fax: (541) 388-6231
Region V Manager **Monte Grove** . . . . . . . . . . . . . . . . . . . . (541) 963-3177
  3012 Island Avenue, La Grande, OR 97850-9497   Fax: (541) 963-9079
Statewide Maintenance Engineer
 **Lucinda M. "Luci" Moore** . . . . . . . . . . . . . . . . . . . . . . . (503) 986-3005
  800 Airport Rd., SE, Salem, OR 97301-4798
  E-mail: lucinda.m.moore@odot.state.or.us

## Motor Carrier Transportation Division
550 Capitol Street, NE, Salem, OR 97301-2530
Fax: (503) 373-1940
Administrator **Gregg DalPonte** . . . . . . . . . . . . . . . . . . . . . (503) 378-6351
Field Motor Carrier Services Manager **Edward Scrivner** . . (503) 378-6071
Investigations & Safety Manager **David J. McKane** . . . . . . (503) 373-0884
  E-mail: david.j.mckane@odot.state.or.us
Salem Motor Carrier Services Manager **Ric Listella** . . . . . . (503) 378-6653
Audit Manager **Gayle Green** . . . . . . . . . . . . . . . . . . . . . . . (503) 378-6656

## Public Transit Division
Mill Creek Building, 555 - 13th Street, NE, Salem, OR 97301-4179
Administrator **Howard A. "Hal" Gard** . . . . . . . . . . . . . . . (503) 986-4077

## Rail Division
Mill Creek Building, 555 - 13th Street, NE, Salem, OR 97301-4179
Administrator **Howard A. "Hal" Gard** . . . . . . . . . . . . . . . (503) 986-4077
  E-mail: howard.a.gard@state.or.us

## Transportation Development Division
Mill Creek Building, Suite 2, 555 - 13th Street, NE,
Salem, OR 97301-1333
Tel: (503) 986-3421  Fax: (503) 986-4173
Administrator **Jerri L. Bohard** . . . . . . . . . . . . . . . . . . . . . (503) 986-3435
Planning Section Manager **Erik M. Havig** . . . . . . . . . . . . . (503) 986-4127
  E-mail: erik.m.havig@odot.state.or.us
Transportation Data Section Manager **Dave Ringeisen** . . . . (503) 986-4171

## Transportation Safety Division
235 Union Street, NE, Salem, OR 97301-1054
Administrator **Troy E. Costales** . . . . . . . . . . . . . . . . . . . . (503) 986-4190

## Oregon Department of Veterans' Affairs [ODVA]
700 Summer Street, NE, Salem, OR 97301-1285
Tel: (503) 373-2000  Fax: (503) 373-2362  TTY: (503) 373-2217
E-mail: odvainformation@odva.state.or.us  Internet: www.oregondva.gov
■Director **Cameron Smith** . . . . . . . . . . . . . . . . . . . . . . . . . (503) 373-2388
  E-mail: cameron.smith@state.or.us
  Education: Carleton BA
  Special Assistant to the Director **Tracy Ann Gill** . . . . . . . (503) 373-2383
Deputy Director **Edward Van Dyke** . . . . . . . . . . . . . . . . . (503) 373-2387
Financial Services Administrator and Chief Financial
  Officer **Bruce Shriver** . . . . . . . . . . . . . . . . . . . . . . . . . . (503) 373-2268
Veterans Services Division Administrator
 **Mitchell Sparks** . . . . . . . . . . . . . . . . . . . . . . . . . . . . . . (503) 373-2327
  E-mail: mitchel.sparks@state.or.us
Veterans' Home Admissions and Liaison Officer
 **Dallas Swafford** . . . . . . . . . . . . . . . . . . . . . . . . . . . . . . (541) 296-7152
  700 Veterans' Drive, The Dalles, OR 97058
Veterans' Home Admissions and Liaison Officer
 **Jeremy Woodall** . . . . . . . . . . . . . . . . . . . . . . . . . . . . . . (541) 497-7265
  600 North Fifth Street, Lebanon, OR 97355

Facility and Construction Manager **John Osborn** . . . . . . . . (503) 373-2023
Human Resources Manager **Julie Owens** . . . . . . . . . . . . . . (503) 373-2381
  E-mail: julie.owens@odva.state.or.us
Public Information Services Manager **Nicole Hoeft** . . . . . . . (503) 373-2386
  E-mail: nicole.hoeft@state.or.us

## Oregon Housing and Community Services [OHCS]
725 Summer Street, NE, Suite B, Salem, OR 97301-1266
Tel: (503) 986-2000  Fax: (503) 986-6752  TTY: (503) 986-2100
E-mail: info@hcs.state.or.us

**Employees:** 120
■Director **Margaret Shepard Van Vliet** . . . . . . . . . . . . . . . (503) 986-2005
  Note: Until May 31, 2016.
  E-mail: margaret.vanvliet@hcs.state.or.us
■Director (Interim) **Claire Seguin** . . . . . . . . . . . . . . . . . . . (503) 986-2000
  Note: Effective June 1, 2016.
  Executive Assistant **Katherine Silva** . . . . . . . . . . . . . . . . (503) 986-2000
Administrative Services Section Manager
 **Sandy McDonnell** . . . . . . . . . . . . . . . . . . . . . . . . . . . . (503) 986-2012
  E-mail: sandy.mcdonnell@hcs.state.or.us
Human Resources Section Manager **Rebecca Gray** . . . . . . . (503) 986-2098
Regional Advisor to the Department - East and Central
  Region **Kim Travis** . . . . . . . . . . . . . . . . . . . . . . . . . . . . (503) 428-3843
  Central Oregon Regional Solutions Office, 650 SW Columbia St.,
  Millpoint Building 7100, Bend, OR 97702
  E-mail: kim.travis@hcs.state.or.us
Regional Advisor to the Department - Metro Region
  (Acting) **Margaret Shepard Van Vliet** . . . . . . . . . . . . . . (971) 673-7184
Regional Advisor to the Department - Metro and
  Northwest Region **Vince Chiotti** . . . . . . . . . . . . . . . . . . (503) 725-2184
  1600 Southwest Fourth Avenue, Portland, OR 97201
Regional Advisor to the Department - Mid-Williamette
  Region **Karen Clearwater** . . . . . . . . . . . . . . . . . . . . . . . (503) 986-2044
  Southern Valley Regional Solutions Center, 720 East Thirteenth
  Avenue, Thompson Center, Suite 304, Eugene, OR 97401
Regional Advisor to the Department - Southwest Region
 **Karen Chase** . . . . . . . . . . . . . . . . . . . . . . . . . . . . . . . . (503) 400-2787
  SW Oregon Regional Solutions Center, 100 E Main Street,
  Medford, OR 97501

## Chief Financial Office
Chief Financial Officer **Caleb Yant** . . . . . . . . . . . . . . . . . . (503) 986-2000
  Executive Assistant **Leigha Carver** . . . . . . . . . . . . . . . . . (503) 986-2000
Internal Auditor **(Vacant)** . . . . . . . . . . . . . . . . . . . . . . . . . (503) 986-2000
Budget Officer **Linda Morter** . . . . . . . . . . . . . . . . . . . . . . (503) 986-2000
Finance Section Manager **Sandra Flickinger** . . . . . . . . . . . (503) 986-2000
  Grants and Monitoring Unit Leader **Carol Wagner** . . . . . . (503) 986-2121
Information Services Division Administrator
 **William A. Carpenter** . . . . . . . . . . . . . . . . . . . . . . . . . . (503) 986-2128

## Housing Finance Division
Assistant Director **Julie Cody** . . . . . . . . . . . . . . . . . . . . . . (503) 986-2000
  E-mail: julie.cody@hcs.state.or.us
  Executive Assistant **Greg Current** . . . . . . . . . . . . . . . . . . (503) 986-2000
Asset Management and Compliance Section Manager
 **Ryan Miller** . . . . . . . . . . . . . . . . . . . . . . . . . . . . . . . . . (503) 986-2028
  Lead Compliance Officer and Technology Advisor
 **Jennifer Marchand** . . . . . . . . . . . . . . . . . . . . . . . . . . . (503) 986-6748
  E-mail: jennifer.marchand@hcs.state.or.us
Debt Management Section Manager **Robert Larson** . . . . . . (503) 986-2058
Multi-Family Programs Section Manager **Heather Pate** . . . (503) 986-6757
  E-mail: heather.pate@hcs.state.or.us
Single Family Programs Section Manager **Kim Freeman** . . (503) 986-2000

## Housing Stabilization Division
Assistant Director **Claire Seguin** . . . . . . . . . . . . . . . . . . . . (503) 986-2000
  Note: Until May 31, 2016.
  Executive Assistant **Jo L. Bell** . . . . . . . . . . . . . . . . . . . . (503) 986-2000
Energy Services Policy and Program Analyst
 **Tim Zimmer** . . . . . . . . . . . . . . . . . . . . . . . . . . . . . . . . (503) 986-2067
Homeless Services Lead Policy Program Specialist
 **Marilyn Miller** . . . . . . . . . . . . . . . . . . . . . . . . . . . . . . (503) 986-2000

*(continued on next page)*

EXECUTIVE BRANCH

**Housing Stabilization Division** *continued*

HUD Contract Administration Section Manager
  **Rhonda Crawford** . . . . . . . . . . . . . . . . . . . . . . . . . . . (503) 986-2149

## Public Affairs Division
Assistant Director **Rem Nivens** . . . . . . . . . . . . . . . . . . . . (503) 986-2000
Executive Assistant **Samantha Gamelgaard** . . . . . . . . . . . (503) 986-2000

## Real Estate Agency
1177 Center Street, NE, Salem, OR 97301-2505
Tel: (503) 378-4770  Fax: (503) 378-2491  E-mail: orea.info@state.or.us
Internet: www.rea.state.or.us

■Commissioner **Gene Bentley** . . . . . . . . . . . . . . . . . . . . . . . (503) 378-4770
  E-mail: gene.bentley@state.or.us
Deputy Commissioner **Dean Owens** . . . . . . . . . . . . . . . . . (503) 378-4407

## Oregon Commission for the Blind
535 Southeast 12th Avenue, Portland, OR 97214-2488
Tel: (971) 673-1588  Fax: (971) 234-7468  E-mail: ocbmail@state.or.us

Executive Director **Dacia Johnson** . . . . . . . . . . . (971) 673-1588 ext. 31590
  Education: Portland State 1998 MS
Chief Financial Officer **Gail Stevens** . . . . . . . . . (971) 673-1588 ext. 31600
  E-mail: gail.stevens@state.or.us
Business Enterprises Program Director
  **Eric Morris** . . . . . . . . . . . . . . . . . . . . . . . . . (971) 673-1588 ext. 31607
Rehabilitation Services Program Director
  **Angel Hale** . . . . . . . . . . . . . . . . . . . . . . . . . (971) 673-1588 ext. 31611
Orientation and Career Center Director
  **Richard Turner** . . . . . . . . . . . . . . . . . . . . . . (971) 673-1588 ext. 31615

## Oregon Business Development Commission
■Chair **Kanth Gopalpur** . . . . . . . . . . . . . . . . . . . . . . . . . . (503) 986-0123
  Term Expires: June 2017
■Member **Jessica Gomez** . . . . . . . . . . . . . . . . . . . . . . . . . (503) 986-0123
  Term Expires: June 2019
■Member **Nkenge Leian Harmon Johnson** . . . . . . . . . . . . . (503) 986-0123
  Term Expires: June 2016
  Education: Florida A&M 1999 BSBA; Howard U 2002 JD
■Member **Keith Leavitt** . . . . . . . . . . . . . . . . . . . . . . . . . . . (503) 986-0123
  Term Expires: June 2019
■Member **Win McCormack** . . . . . . . . . . . . . . . . . . . . . . . . (503) 986-0123
  Term Expires: April 2016
  Education: Harvard AB; Oregon MFA
■Member **Gregory Semler** . . . . . . . . . . . . . . . . . . . . . . . . (503) 986-0123
  Term Expires: June 2017
■Member **Fred Warner, Jr.** . . . . . . . . . . . . . . . . . . . . . . . . (503) 986-0123
  Term Expires: September 2017
■Ex Officio Member **Elizabeth "Betsy" Johnson** . . . . . . . . . (503) 986-0123
  Education: Carleton 1973 BA; Lewis & Clark 1977 JD
■Ex Officio Member **Tobias J. Read** . . . . . . . . . . . . . . . . . (503) 986-0123
  Affiliation: Representative (District 27), Oregon House of
  Representatives
  State Capitol, 900 Court Street, NE, Room H-390, Salem, OR 97301
  Education: Willamette 1997 AB; U Washington 2003 MBA

## Oregon Business Development Department [Business Oregon]
775 Summer Street, NE, Suite 200, Salem, OR 97301-1280
Tel: (503) 986-0123  Tel: (866) 467-3466  Fax: (503) 581-5115

■Director **Chris Harder** . . . . . . . . . . . . . . . . . . . . . . . . . . (503) 986-0110
  Education: U Puget Sound BBA; North Carolina MPA, MCRP
Deputy Director **Lynn Schoessler** . . . . . . . . . . . . . . . . . . . (503) 986-0110
Arts Commission Director **Brian Rogers** . . . . . . . . . . . . . . (503) 986-0087
Infrastructure Finance Authority Executive Director
  **Lynn Schoessler** . . . . . . . . . . . . . . . . . . . . . . . . . . . . (503) 986-0110
Infrastructure Finance Authority Program/Regional
  Services Division Manager **Chris Cummings** . . . . . . . . (503) 986-0158
Chief Financial Officer **Amanda Beitel** . . . . . . . . . . . . . . . (503) 986-0018
Employee Services Manager **Pua Sequeira** . . . . . . . . . . . . (503) 986-0148
Information Systems Manager **Jared Cornman** . . . . . . . . . (503) 986-0024
  E-mail: jared.cornman@biz.state.or.us

Oregon Cultural Trust Manager **Aili Schreiner** . . . . . . . . . (503) 986-0089
Research and Policy Assistant Director
  **Karen Wilde Goddin** . . . . . . . . . . . . . . . . . . . . . . . . (503) 229-6054
  E-mail: karen.goddin@biz.state.or.us
Research and Policy Analyst **Marc Zolton** . . . . . . . . . . . . . (503) 229-5634
Policy and Strategic Services Division Administrator
  **Lisa M. Ansell** . . . . . . . . . . . . . . . . . . . . . . . . . . . . . (503) 986-0037
Branding and Marketing Manager **Nathan Buehler** . . . . . . (503) 229-5225
Business Services Section Manager **John Saris** . . . . . . . . . (503) 986-0163
Government Affairs Manager **Ivo Martin Trummer** . . . . . . (503) 229-5226
Recruitment Services Manager **Samantha Julian** . . . . . . . . (503) 986-0134
Small Business Officer **Gabriel Silva** . . . . . . . . . . . . . . . . (503) 986-0161

## Oregon Fish and Wildlife Commission
4034 Fairview Industrial Drive Southeast, Salem, OR 97302
Tel: (503) 947-6044  E-mail: odfw.commission@state.or.us

■Chair **Michael Finley** . . . . . . . . . . . . . . . . . . . . . . . . . . . (503) 947-6044
■Member **Laura Anderson** (Fifth Congressional) . . . . . . . . (503) 947-6044
■Member **Jason A. Atkinson** (Second Congressional) . . . . . (503) 947-6044
  Education: Southern Oregon 1992 BS; Willamette 1997 MBA
■Member **Robert "Bob" Webber** (Fourth Congressional) . . (503) 947-6044
■Member **Gregory J. Wolley** (Third Congressional) . . . . . . (503) 947-6044
  Term Expires: May 31, 2016
  Education: UC Berkeley BA; Southern Oregon U MS
■Eastern Oregon Member **Holly Akenson** . . . . . . . . . . . . . (503) 947-6044
  Education: Eastern Oregon BS; Idaho MS
■Eastern Oregon Member **Bruce Buckmaster** . . . . . . . . . . (503) 947-6044

## Oregon Department of Fish and Wildlife [ODFW]
Tel: (503) 947-6002 (Auto-Attendent)  TTY: (503) 947-6339
E-mail: odfw.info@state.or.us  Internet: www.dfw.state.or.us

▲Director **Curt Melcher** . . . . . . . . . . . . . . . . . . . . . . . . . . (503) 947-6044
  E-mail: curt.melcher@state.or.us              Fax: (503) 947-6042
  Executive Assistant to the Director **Michelle Tate** . . . . . (503) 947-6033
Administration Deputy Director (Interim) **Bill Herber** . . . . . (503) 947-6044
  E-mail: bill.herber@state.or.us
  Executive Support Specialist **Lisa Evans** . . . . . . . . . . . (503) 947-6034
Fish and Wildlife Programs Deputy Director
  **Shannon M. Hurn** . . . . . . . . . . . . . . . . . . . . . . . . . . (503) 947-6044
Fish Division Administrator **Ed Bowles** . . . . . . . . (503) 947-6201 ext. 6206
                                               Fax: (503) 947-6202
Human Resources Division Administrator **Roxie Burns** . . . . (503) 947-6059
Information and Education Division Administrator
  (Interim) **Richard J. "Rick" Hargrave** . . . . . . . . . . . . . (503) 947-6010
  E-mail: richard.j.hargrave@state.or.us
Wildlife Division Administrator **Ron E. Anglin** . . (503) 947-6301 ext. 6312
                                               Fax: (503) 947-6330
Chief Information Officer **Doug A. Juergensen** . . . . . . . . . (503) 947-6261
  E-mail: douglas.juergensen@state.or.us        Fax: (503) 947-6246

## Oregon Government Ethics Commission [OGEC]
3218 Pringle Road, SE, Suite 220, Salem, OR 97302-1544
Tel: (503) 378-5105  Fax: (503) 373-1456  E-mail: ogec.mail@oregon.gov
Internet: www.oregon.gov/ogec

●Chair **Charles Tauman** . . . . . . . . . . . . . . . . . . . . . . . . . . (503) 378-5105
  Term Expires: December 12, 2016
■Vice-Chair **Jan Hooper** . . . . . . . . . . . . . . . . . . . . . . . . . (503) 378-5105
  Term Expires: June 25, 2018
■Commissioner **Marilyn Cover** . . . . . . . . . . . . . . . . . . . . (503) 378-5105
  Term Expires: April 30, 2017
●Commissioner **Daniel Golden** . . . . . . . . . . . . . . . . . . . . . (503) 378-5105
  Term Expires: May 31, 2018
●Commissioner **Alison Kean** . . . . . . . . . . . . . . . . . . . . . . (503) 378-5105
  Term Expires: February 16, 2020
●Commissioner **Mary F. Kremer** . . . . . . . . . . . . . . . . . . . (503) 378-5105
  Term Expires: March 12, 2017
■Commissioner **Kenneth Montoya** . . . . . . . . . . . . . . . . . . (503) 378-5105
  Term Expires: June 30, 2017

---

★ Elected Official   ■ Appointed by Governor   ● Appointed by Legislature   ▲ Appointed by Board or Commission   ◆ Appointed by State Supreme Court

## Commission Staff

▲ Executive Director **Ronald A. Bersin** . . . . . . . . . . . . . . . . (503) 378-5108
E-mail: ron.a.bersin@oregon.gov

## Oregon Liquor Control Commission [OLCC]

9079 SE McLoughlin Boulevard, Portland, OR 97222-7355
Tel: (503) 872-5000  Fax: (503) 872-5266  Internet: www.oregon.gov/olcc

■ Chair **Rob Patridge** . . . . . . . . . . . . . . . . . . . . . . . . . . (541) 210-8280
E-mail: rob.patridge@state.or.us
Education: Willamette 1990 BS, 1993 JD
■ Commissioner **Michael E. Harper, Sr.** . . . . . . . . . . . . . (503) 349-8733
E-mail: meharpersr@comcast.net
■ Commissioner **Marvin D. Révoal** . . . . . . . . . . . . . . . . (541) 341-3478
E-mail: mrevoal@pacificbenefitplanners.com    Fax: (541) 434-1109
■ Commissioner **Robert "Bob" Rice** . . . . . . . . . . . . . . . (503) 319-6791
E-mail: rarice1946@msn.com
■ Commissioner **Pamela Weatherspoon** . . . . . . . . . . . . (503) 415-5421
E-mail: paweathe@lhs.org

## Commission Staff

▲ Executive Director **Steven Marks** . . . . . . . . . . . . . . . . . (503) 872-5062
E-mail: steven.marks@state.or.us

## Public Utility Commission of Oregon [PUC]

201 High Street Southeast, Suite 100, Salem, OR 97301
P.O. Box 1088, Salem, OR 97308-1088
Tel: (503) 373-7394  Fax: (503) 378-5505  TTY: (800) 648-3458
E-mail: puc.commission@state.or.us  Internet: www.puc.state.or.us/

■ Chairman **Susan K. Ackerman** . . . . . . . . . . . . . . . . . . . (503) 378-6611
E-mail: susan.ackerman@state.or.us
■ Commissioner **Stephen "Steve" Bloom** . . . . . . . . . . . . (503) 378-6611
E-mail: stephen.bloom@state.or.us
■ Commissioner **John F. Savage** . . . . . . . . . . . . . . . . . . . (503) 378-6611
E-mail: john.f.savage@state.or.us
Education: Oregon State BS, MS
Commission Secretary **Becky Beier** . . . . . . . . . . . . . . . . (503) 373-1571
E-mail: becky.beier@state.or.us

## State Board of Education

Public Service Building, 255 Capitol Street, NE, Salem, OR 97310-0203
Tel: (503) 947-5600  Fax: (503) 378-5156
E-mail: stateboard.members@state.or.us

■ Chair **Miranda Summer** (1st Congressional Dist. Rep.) . . . (503) 947-5637
Term Expires: March 14, 2017
Education: Regis U BA; Oregon JD
■ Vice Chair **Charles R. Martinez, Jr.**
(4th Congressional Dist. Rep.) . . . . . . . . . . . . . . . . . . (503) 947-5801
Term Expires: June 30, 2017
Education: Pitzer 1991; California Psychology
■ Second Vice Chair **Angela Bowen** (At-Large) . . . . . . . . (503) 947-5801
Term Expires: June 30, 2016
Education: Southern Oregon U BS; Oregon MAED
■ Member
**Jerome E. Colonna** (2nd Congressional Dist. Rep.) . . . . (503) 947-5637
Term Expires: June 30, 2018
■ Member
**Samuel D. Henry** (3rd Congressional Dist. Rep.) . . . . . . (503) 947-5801
Term Expires: June 30, 2016
Education: DC Teachers Col; Teachers Col Columbia U
■ Member **Anthony Veliz** (5th Congressional Dist. Rep.) . . . (541) 389-9843
Term Expires: March 14, 2017
Education: Portland State BA; Rhode Island MA
■ Ex-Officio Member **Jeanne Atkins** . . . . . . . . . . . . . . . . (541) 389-9843
Education: U Washington 1971 BA; Oregon 1978 JD
■ Ex-Officio Member **Ted Wheeler** . . . . . . . . . . . . . . . . . (541) 389-9843
Education: Stanford BA; Columbia MBA; Harvard MPP
Executive Officer **Emily Nazarov** . . . . . . . . . . . . . . . . . (503) 947-5637

## Oregon Department of Education [ODE]

Tel: (503) 947-5600  Fax: (503) 378-5156  Internet: www.ode.state.or.us

Deputy Superintendent **Dr. Salam Noor** . . . . . . . . . . . . . . (503) 947-5740
Executive Assistant **Lauren Slyh** . . . . . . . . . . . . . . . . . . (503) 947-5740
Office of Assessment and Accountability Assistant
Superintendent (Interim) **Derek Brown** . . . . . . . . . . . . (503) 947-5663
Office of Education Equity Assistant Superintendent
**David Bautista** . . . . . . . . . . . . . . . . . . . . . . . . . . . . (503) 947-5750
Office of Finance and Administration Assistant
Superintendent **Richard W. "Rick" Crager** . . . . . . . . . . (503) 947-5658
E-mail: rick.crager@state.or.us
Office of Student Services Assistant Superintendent
**Sarah Drinkwater** . . . . . . . . . . . . . . . . . . . . . . . . . . (503) 947-5702
Office of Research and Data Analysis Deputy
Superintendent **Brian Reeder** . . . . . . . . . . . . . . . . . . (503) 947-5670
E-mail: brian.reeder@state.or.us
Communications Director **Crystal Greene** . . . . . . . . . . . . (503) 947-5650
Chief Information Officer **Ben Tate** . . . . . . . . . . . . . . . . (503) 947-5708
E-mail: ben.tate@state.or.us
Early Learning Division Director **Megan Irwin** . . . . . . . . . (503) 373-0071
Education: Arizona State BA
Youth Development Division Director **Iris Bell** . . . . . . . . . (503) 378-6250
E-mail: iris.bell@state.or.us

## Higher Education Coordinating Commission [HECC]

Tel: (503) 378-3111

Chair **Neil Bryant** . . . . . . . . . . . . . . . . . . . . . . . . . . . . (503) 378-3111
Vice Chair **David Rives** . . . . . . . . . . . . . . . . . . . . . . . . (503) 378-3111
Member **Terry L. Cross, MSW, ACSW, LCSW** . . . . . . . . . (503) 378-3111
Member **Betty Duvall** . . . . . . . . . . . . . . . . . . . . . . . . . (503) 378-3111
Member **Timothy J. Nesbitt** . . . . . . . . . . . . . . . . . . . . . (503) 378-3111
Member **Ramon Ramirez** . . . . . . . . . . . . . . . . . . . . . . . (503) 378-3111
Member **Dr. Larry D. Roper** . . . . . . . . . . . . . . . . . . . . . (503) 378-3111
Education: Heidelberg 1975; Bowling Green State; Maryland 1988 PhD
Member **Carmen Rubio** . . . . . . . . . . . . . . . . . . . . . . . . (503) 378-3111
Member **Duncan Wyse** . . . . . . . . . . . . . . . . . . . . . . . . (503) 378-3111
Education: Pomona; Stanford MBA
Member (Non-Voting) **Lee Ayers-Preboski** . . . . . . . . . . . (503) 378-3111
Member (Non-Voting) **Rob Fullmer** . . . . . . . . . . . . . . . . (503) 378-3111
Member (Non-Voting) **Frank Goulard** . . . . . . . . . . . . . . (503) 378-3111
Member (Non-Voting) **Claire McMorris** . . . . . . . . . . . . . (503) 378-3111
Member (Non-Voting) **(Vacant)** . . . . . . . . . . . . . . . . . . . (503) 378-3111
Executive Director **Ben Cannon** . . . . . . . . . . . . . . . . . . (503) 378-3072
Education: Washington U (MO) BA; Oxford (UK)
Chief of Staff **Cheryl L. Myers** . . . . . . . . . . . . . . . . . . . (503) 378-3111

## Department of Community Colleges and Workforce Development [CCWD]

Public Service Building, 255 Capitol Street, NE, Salem, OR 97310
Tel: (503) 947-2401  Fax: (503) 378-3365  Internet: www.oregon.gov/ccwd

▲ Deputy Commissioner **Krissa Caldwell** . . . . . . . . . . . . . (503) 947-2401
Executive Support **Anna Gonzalez** . . . . . . . . . . . . . . . . . (503) 947-2405

## Employment Relations Board [ERB]

528 Cottage Street, NE, Suite 400, Salem, OR 97301-3807
Tel: (503) 378-3807  Fax: (503) 373-0021
E-mail: emprel.board@oregon.gov  Internet: www.oregon.gov/erb

■ Chair **Kathryn A. Logan** . . . . . . . . . . . . . . . . . . . . . . . (503) 378-3807
E-mail: kathryn.logan@oregon.gov
■ Member **Adam L. Rhynard** . . . . . . . . . . . . . . . . . . . . . (503) 378-3807
E-mail: adam.rhynard@oregon.gov
■ Member **Jason M. Weyand** . . . . . . . . . . . . . . . . . . . . . (503) 378-3807
E-mail: jason.weyand@oregon.gov

## Board Staff

Office Administrator **Juril Stover** . . . . . . . . . . . . . . . . . . (503) 378-8610
Board Secretary **April Bathurst** . . . . . . . . . . . . . . . . . . . (503) 378-3808

---

★ Elected Official    ■ Appointed by Governor    ● Appointed by Legislature    ▲ Appointed by Board or Commission    ◆ Appointed by State Supreme Court

## Board of Forestry

Chairman **Thomas J. "Tom" Imeson** . . . . . . . . . . . . . . (503) 945-7200
   Term Expires: December 14, 2016
   Education: Johns Hopkins BS
Member **Sybil Ackerman** . . . . . . . . . . . . . . . . . . . . . . . (503) 945-7200
   Term Expires: June 30, 2018
Member **Nils Christoffersen** . . . . . . . . . . . . . . . . . . . . (503) 945-7200
   Term Expires: February 29, 2016
Member **Tom A. Insko** . . . . . . . . . . . . . . . . . . . . . . . . . (503) 945-7200
   Term Expires: February 29, 2016
   Education: Eastern Oregon; William & Mary MBA
Member **Mike Rose** . . . . . . . . . . . . . . . . . . . . . . . . . . . (503) 945-7200
   Term Expires: December 14, 2016
Member **Gary Springer** . . . . . . . . . . . . . . . . . . . . . . . . (503) 945-7200
   Term Expires: April 30, 2018
Member **Cindy Deacon Williams** . . . . . . . . . . . . . . . . (503) 945-7200
   Term Expires: February 29, 2016

## Oregon Department of Forestry [ODF]

2600 State Street, Salem, OR 97310
Tel: (503) 945-7200  Fax: (503) 945-7212

▲State Forester **Doug S. Decker** . . . . . . . . . . . . . . . . (503) 945-7211
   E-mail: doug.s.decker@oregon.gov
Deputy State Forester **Nancy Hirsch** . . . . . . . . . . . . (503) 945-7205
Administrative Services Division Chief
  **Satish Upadhyay** . . . . . . . . . . . . . . . . . . . . . . . . (503) 945-7203
   E-mail: satish.upadhyay@oregon.gov
Private Forests Division Chief **Peter Daugherty** . . . . . . . . . (503) 945-7482
State Forests Division Chief **Liz Dent** . . . . . . . . . . . . (503) 945-7351
Fire Protection Division Chief **Doug Grafe** . . . . . . . . . . . (503) 945-7204
Public Affairs Program Director **Ken W. Armstrong** . . . . . . (503) 945-7420
   E-mail: ken.w.armstrong@oregon.gov

## Medical Board

1500 SW First Avenue, Suite 620, Portland, OR 97201-5847
Tel: (971) 673-2700  Fax: (971) 673-2670  E-mail: omb.info@state.or.us
Internet: www.oregon.gov/omb

▲Executive Director **Kathleen Haley** . . . . . . . . . . . . . (971) 673-2700
   E-mail: kathleen.haley@state.or.us

## Oregon State Board of Nursing [OSBN]

17938 SW Upper Boones Ferry Road, Portland, OR 97224-7012
Tel: (971) 673-0685  Fax: (971) 673-0684
E-mail: oregon.bn.info@state.or.us  Internet: www.oregon.gov/OSBN

▲Executive Director **Ruby Jason, MSN, RN** . . . . . . . . . . . (971) 673-0685
   E-mail: ruby.jason@state.or.us

## Board of Parole and Post-Prison Supervision

2575 Center Street NE, Suite 100, Salem, OR 97301-4621
Tel: (503) 945-0900  Fax: (503) 373-7558

■Chairperson **Kristin Winges-Yanez** . . . . . . . . . . . . . (503) 945-0900
■Board Member **Sid Thompson** . . . . . . . . . . . . . . . . . (503) 945-0900
■Board Member **Michael Wu** . . . . . . . . . . . . . . . . . . . (503) 945-0900
Executive Director **Brenda K. Carney** . . . . . . . . . . . . (503) 945-0919

## Oregon Board of Pharmacy

800 NE Oregon Street, Suite 150, Portland, OR 97232-2162
Tel: (971) 673-0001  Fax: (971) 673-0002
E-mail: pharmacy.board@state.or.us

■President **Roberto Linares, RPh** . . . . . . . . . . . . . . . (971) 673-0001
   Term Expires: June 30, 2016
■Vice President **Kate James** . . . . . . . . . . . . . . . . . . . (971) 673-0001
   Term Expires: June 30, 2018
■Member **Heather Anderson** . . . . . . . . . . . . . . . . . . . (971) 673-0001
   Term Expires: March 31, 2017
■Member **Christine Chute** . . . . . . . . . . . . . . . . . . . . . (971) 673-0001
   Term Expires: September 30, 2018
■Member **Brad Fujisaki, RPh** . . . . . . . . . . . . . . . . . . . (971) 673-0001
   Term Expires: June 30, 2016

■Member **Penny Reher, RPh** . . . . . . . . . . . . . . . . . . . (971) 673-0001
   Term Expires: June 30, 2019
■Member **Ken Wells, RPh** . . . . . . . . . . . . . . . . . . . . . (971) 673-0001
   Term Expires: June 30, 2017

## Public Employees Retirement System [PERS]

P.O. Box 23700, Tigard, OR 97281-3700
Tel: (503) 598-7377  Fax: (503) 598-1218  Internet: www.oregon.gov/pers

Director **Steve P. Rodeman** . . . . . . . . . . . . . . . . . . . (503) 598-7377
  Executive Assistant **Joli A. Whitney** . . . . . . . . . . . (503) 603-7621
Deputy Director **(Vacant)** . . . . . . . . . . . . . . . . . . . . . (503) 598-7377
Chairman **John Thomas** . . . . . . . . . . . . . . . . . . . . . . (503) 603-7575

## State Library

250 Winter Street, NE, Salem, OR 97301-3950
Tel: (503) 378-4243  Fax: (503) 585-8059  Internet: www.oregon.gov/OSL

▲State Librarian **MaryKay Dahlgreen** . . . . . . . . . . . . (503) 378-4367
   E-mail: marykay.dahlgreen@state.or.us
  Executive Assistant **Jessica Rondema** . . . . . . . . . . (503) 378-2464
Program Manager **Margie Harrison** . . . . . . . . . . . . . (503) 378-5030
   E-mail: margie.harrison@state.or.us
Program Manager **Susan B. Westin** . . . . . . . . . . . . . (503) 378-5435
   E-mail: susan.b.westin@state.or.us
Federal Programs Coordinator **Ann Reed** . . . . . . . . . (503) 378-5027
   E-mail: ann.reed@state.or.us

## Office of the Secretary of State

136 State Capitol, Salem, OR 97310
Tel: (503) 986-1523  Fax: (503) 986-1616  E-mail: oregon.sos@state.or.us
Internet: sos.oregon.gov

★Secretary of State **Jeanne Atkins** (D) . . . . . . . . . . . (503) 986-1523
  Personal Assistant and Scheduler **Laura Hutchings** . . . . . (503) 986-1523
   E-mail: laura.hutchings@state.or.us
  Special Assistant to the Secretary **Laura Terrill** . . . . . (503) 986-1523
Deputy Secretary of State **Robert Taylor** . . . . . . . . . . (503) 986-1523
   Education: Brown U 1999; Willamette 2004 JD
Legislative Director **Rachele Altman** . . . . . . . . . . . . . (503) 986-1500
   Education: Pomona BA; George Washington JD
Press Secretary **Tony Green** . . . . . . . . . . . . . . . . . . . (503) 507-0082
   E-mail: tony.green@state.or.us

## Archives Division

800 Summer Street, NE, Salem, OR 97310
Tel: (503) 373-0701  Fax: (503) 373-0953

State Archivist **Mary Beth Herkert** . . . . . . . . . . . . . . (503) 373-0701

## Audits Division

500 Public Service Building, 255 Capitol Street, NE, Salem, OR 97310
Tel: (503) 986-2255  Fax: (503) 378-6767

Director **Gary Blackmer** . . . . . . . . . . . . . . . . . . . . . . (503) 986-2355

## Business Services Division

180 Public Service Building, 255 Capitol Street, NE, Salem, OR 97310

Director **Jeff Morgan** . . . . . . . . . . . . . . . . . . . . . . . . (503) 986-2239
   E-mail: jeffry.morgan@state.or.us
Chief Accountant **Kevin Herburger** . . . . . . . . . . . . . . (503) 986-2240

## Corporation Division

151 Public Service Building, 255 Capitol Street, NE, Salem, OR 97301
Tel: (503) 986-2200

Director **Peter Threlkel** . . . . . . . . . . . . . . . . . . . . . . . (503) 986-2205
   E-mail: peter.threlkel@state.or.us

## Elections Division

255 Capitol Street, NE, Salem, OR 97310
Tel: (503) 986-1518

Director **James R. "Jim" Williams** . . . . . . . . . . . . . . (503) 986-1518

---

★ Elected Official    ■ Appointed by Governor    ● Appointed by Legislature    ▲ Appointed by Board or Commission    ◆ Appointed by State Supreme Court

Candidate and Campaign Services Deputy Director
**Brenda Bayes** . . . . . . . . . . . . . . . . . . . . . . . . . . . . . . (503) 986-2312
Voter Registration and Voting Services Deputy Director
**Codi Trudell** . . . . . . . . . . . . . . . . . . . . . . . . . . . . . . . (503) 986-0523

## Human Resources Division

143 State Capitol, Salem, OR 97310

Director **Jackie Steffens** . . . . . . . . . . . . . . . . . . . . . . . (503) 986-2168

## Information Systems Division

103 Public Service Building, 255 Capitol Street, NE, Salem, OR 97310

Director **Chris Molin** . . . . . . . . . . . . . . . . . . . . . . . . . . (503) 986-0521
E-mail: chris.molin@state.or.us
Education: Maryland AA, BS

## Office of the State Treasurer

159 State Capitol, 900 Court Street, NE, Salem, OR 97301-3896
Tel: (503) 378-4329  Fax: (503) 373-7051
E-mail: oregon.treasurer@state.or.us  Internet: www.ost.state.or.us

★ State Treasurer **Ted Wheeler** (D) . . . . . . . . . . . . . . . . . (503) 378-4329
Term Expires: 2017
E-mail: oregon.treasurer@state.or.us
Deputy State Treasurer **Darren Bond** . . . . . . . . . . . . . . (503) 378-4000
Education: Oregon 1984 BA
Communications Director **James Sinks** . . . . . . . . . . . . . (503) 378-4329
E-mail: james.sinks@state.or.us
Policy Director **Kristin Dennis** . . . . . . . . . . . . . . . . . . . (503) 378-4329
E-mail: kristin.dennis@ost.state.or.us
Debt Management Division Director
**Laura Lockwood-McCall** . . . . . . . . . . . . . . . . . . . . . . . (503) 378-4930
Education: Cal State (Fresno) 1983 BA; Harvard 1985 MPP
Finance Division Director **Cora R. Parker** . . . . . . . . . . . . (503) 378-4633
Information Systems Division Director
**Nancy O'Halloran** . . . . . . . . . . . . . . . . . . . . . . . . . . . (503) 378-4059
E-mail: nancy.ohalloran@ost.state.or.us
Human Resources Manager **Kristin Stewart** . . . . . . . . . . . (503) 378-2336
Education: George Fox Col 2002 BA
Chief Investment Officer **John D. Skjervem** . . . . . . . . . . . (503) 378-4111
Education: UC Berkeley 1984 BA; Chicago 1991 MBA

## Department of Justice [DOJ]

Justice Building, 1162 Court Street, NE, Salem, OR 97301-4096
Tel: (503) 378-4400  Fax: (503) 378-4017  Internet: www.doj.state.or.us

## Office of the Attorney General

Justice Building, 1162 Court Street, NE, Salem, OR 97301-4096
Tel: (503) 378-4400  Fax: (503) 378-4017

**Employees:** 1,285

★ Attorney General **Ellen F. Rosenblum** (D) . . . . . . . . . . . . (503) 378-4400
Term Expires: 2017
Education: Oregon 1975 JD
Career: Judge, Chambers of Judge Ellen F. Rosenblum, Oregon Court
of Appeals (2005-2011)
Assistant to the Attorney General **Jennifer Busey** . . . . . . (503) 378-4400
Deputy Attorney General **Mary H. Williams** . . . . . . . . . . (503) 378-4400
Education: Lewis & Clark JD
Assistant to the Deputy Attorney General
**Chrystal M. Bader** . . . . . . . . . . . . . . . . . . . . . . . . . . (503) 378-4400
Communications Director **Kristina Edmunson** . . . . . . . . . (503) 378-6002
E-mail: kristina.edmunson@doj.state.or.us
Government Transparency Counsel **Michael Kron** . . . . . . . (503) 378-6002
Education: Oregon 1998 BA; NYU 2001 MA; Columbia 2004 JD
Legislative Coordinator **Aaron D. Knott** . . . . . . . . . . . . . (503) 378-6002
E-mail: aaron.d.knott@doj.state.or.us
Solicitor General **Anna Joyce** . . . . . . . . . . . . . . . . . . . (503) 378-4402
Education: Oregon 1996 BA, 2001 JD
Deputy Solicitor General **Michael Casper** . . . . . . . . . . . . (503) 378-4402
Criminal Justice Division Chief Counsel and Assistant
Attorney General **Darin E. Tweedt** . . . . . . . . . . . . . . . (503) 378-6347
General Counsel Division Chief and Assistant Attorney
General **Steve Wolf** . . . . . . . . . . . . . . . . . . . . . . . . . (503) 947-4540
Trial Division Chief Counsel **Cheryl Pellegrini** . . . . . . . . (503) 947-4700

Child Support Division Administrator
**Kate Cooper Richardson** . . . . . . . . . . . . . . . . . . . . . . . (503) 986-6087
E-mail: kate.richardson@state.or.us
Education: Oregon 1987 JD
Civil Enforcement Division Administrative Counsel
**Frederick M. Boss** . . . . . . . . . . . . . . . . . . . . . . . . . . . (503) 947-4333

## Bureau of Labor and Industries [BOLI]

State Office Building, 800 NE Oregon Street, Suite 1045,
Portland, OR 97232
Tel: (971) 673-0761  Fax: (971) 673-0762  TTY: (503) 731-4106
Internet: www.oregon.gov/boli

★ Commissioner **Brad Avakian** (D) . . . . . . . . . . . . . . . . . (971) 673-0781
Term Expires: 2019
E-mail: brad.avakian@state.or.us
Education: Lewis & Clark JD
Deputy Commissioner **Christine N. Hammond** . . . . . . . . . (971) 673-0785
E-mail: christie.n.hammond@state.or.us
Apprenticeship and Training Division Administrator
**Stephen "Steve" Simms** . . . . . . . . . . . . . . . . . . . . . . . (971) 673-0777
E-mail: steve.simms@state.or.us
Civil Rights Division Administrator **Amy K. Klare** . . . . . . . (971) 673-0792
E-mail: amy.k.klare@state.or.us
Wage and Hour Division Administrator **Gerhard Taeubel** . . (971) 673-0837
E-mail: gerhard.taeubel@state.or.us
Business Services Unit Manager **Terry D. Bonebrake** . . . . . (971) 673-0812
E-mail: Terry.D.Bonebrake@state.or.us
Legal Policy Advisor **Marcia L. Ohlemiller** . . . . . . . . . . . (971) 673-0784
E-mail: marcia.l.ohlemiller@state.or.us
Administrative Prosecution Unit Manager **Jenn Gaddis** . . . (971) 673-0822
E-mail: jenn.gaddis@state.or.us

---

★ Elected Official    ■ Appointed by Governor    ● Appointed by Legislature    ▲ Appointed by Board or Commission    ◆ Appointed by State Supreme Court

# Pennsylvania

Tel: (717) 787-2500 (Governor) Internet: www.pa.gov

**Number of U.S. Congressional Delegates:** 2 Senators; 18 Representatives **Governor's Term:** 4 years
**Legislature Description:** General Assembly - 50 member Senate; 203 member House of Representatives;
Term - Senate 4 years, House 2 years **Next Election:** Governor November 2018; Legislature
November 2016 **Number of Electoral Votes:** 20 **Official Name:** Commonwealth of Pennsylvania
(Sylvania: woodland. Named by Charles II, in honor of William Penn's father, an English admiral)
**Nickname:** The Keystone State **Motto:** Virtue, Liberty and Independence

**Population:** 12,802,503 (2015); Rank 6 **Fiscal Year:** 2015 **Budget:** $35,186,248,000

## Office of the Governor

225 Main Capitol Building, 501 North 3rd Street, Harrisburg, PA 17120
Tel: (717) 787-2500 Fax: (717) 772-8284 Internet: www.governor.pa.gov
**Fiscal Year:** 2015 **Budget:** $6,503,000

**Thomas W. "Tom" Wolf**
Governor

Began Service: January 20, 2015
Term Expires: 2019
Date of Birth: November 17, 1948
Education: Dartmouth 1972 BA;
U London 1978 MPhil; MIT 1981 PhD
Home: York
Career: Secretary, Revenue Department,
Commonwealth of Pennsylvania (2007-2008);
Chairman and Chief Executive Officer, The Wolf
Organization, Inc.

★Governor **Thomas W. "Tom" Wolf** (D) . . . . . . . . . . . . . . (717) 787-2500
 E-mail: governor@pa.gov
Executive Deputy Chief of Staff **Mike Brunelle** . . . . . . . . . (717) 787-2500
 E-mail: mbrunelle@pa.gov
Government Affairs and Outreach Director
 **Mark W. Smith** . . . . . . . . . . . . . . . . . . . . . . . . . . . (717) 787-2500
Special Assistant to the Governor **Yesenia Bane** . . . . . . . . (717) 787-2500
 E-mail: ybane@pa.gov
Special Assistant to the Governor **Elena Cross** . . . . . . . . . (717) 787-2500
 E-mail: elcross@pa.gov
Special Assistant to the Governor **(Vacant)** . . . . . . . . . . . (717) 787-2500
Chief of Staff **Mary Isenhour** . . . . . . . . . . . . . . . . . . . (717) 787-2500
 E-mail: misenhou@pa.gov

## Governor's Office of General Counsel

333 Market Street, 17th Floor, Harrisburg, PA 17101
Tel: (717) 783-6563 Fax: (717) 787-1788

General Counsel **Denise J. Smyler** . . . . . . . . . . . . . . . . . . (717) 787-2500
 E-mail: dsmyler@pa.gov
Deputy General Counsel **Rodney R. Akers** . . . . . . . . . . . . . (717) 783-6563
Deputy General Counsel **Linda C. Barrett** . . . . . . . . . . . . . (717) 783-6563
 Education: Syracuse BA; Notre Dame JD
Deputy General Counsel **Sean M. Concannon** . . . . . . . . . . (717) 783-6563
Deputy General Counsel **Ann Gingrich Cornick** . . . . . . . . (717) 783-6563
Deputy General Counsel **Jessica A. Diaz** . . . . . . . . . . . . . (717) 783-6563
Deputy General Counsel **Thomas P. Howell** . . . . . . . . . . . (717) 783-6563
Deputy General Counsel **John K. Lavelle** . . . . . . . . . . . . . (717) 783-6563
Deputy General Counsel **Marisa G.Z. Lehr** . . . . . . . . . . . . (717) 783-6563
Deputy General Counsel
 **H. Geoffrey "Geoff" Moulton, Jr.** . . . . . . . . . . . . . . (717) 783-6563
 Education: Amherst 1980 BA; Columbia 1984 JD
Deputy General Counsel **Erin J. Osevala** . . . . . . . . . . . . . (717) 783-6563
 Education: West Chester 2001 BS; Widener 2004 JD
Deputy General Counsel **Tyrone Powell** . . . . . . . . . . . . . . (717) 783-6563
Deputy General Counsel **Gregory T. Thall** . . . . . . . . . . . . (717) 783-6563

## Governor's Office of Homeland Security

1800 Elmerton Avenue, Harrisburg, PA 17110-9758
Tel: (717) 346-4460 Fax: (717) 214-1298

Director **Marcus L. Brown** . . . . . . . . . . . . . . . . . . . . . . . (717) 214-1290
Deputy Director **Ronald "Ron" Stanko III** . . . . . . . . . . . . (717) 346-4460

## Governor's Office of Policy and Planning

238 Main Capitol Building, Harrisburg, PA 17120
Fax: (717) 787-4590

Secretary **Sarah Galbally** . . . . . . . . . . . . . . . . . . . . . . . (717) 787-2500
 Education: Pennsylvania BA; Villanova

## Governor's Office of Press and Communications

308 Main Capitol Building, Harrisburg, PA 17120
Tel: (717) 783-1116

Communications Director **Mark C. Nicastre** . . . . . . . . . . . (717) 783-1116
 E-mail: mnicastre@pa.gov
 Education: Johns Hopkins 2006 BA, MA
Press Secretary **Jeffrey Sheridan** . . . . . . . . . . . . . . . . . . (717) 783-1116
 E-mail: jsheridan@pa.gov
Deputy Press Secretary **Megan Healey** . . . . . . . . . . . . . . . (717) 783-1116
 E-mail: mhealey@pa.gov

## Office of Administration [OA]

207 Finance Building, Harrisburg, PA 17120
Tel: (717) 787-9945 Fax: (717) 783-4374

Secretary **Sharon Minnich** . . . . . . . . . . . . . . . . . . . . . . . (717) 787-9945
 E-mail: ra-govofficeofadmin@pa.gov
 Education: Albright BA; Pennsylvania 1995 MGA
Human Resources Director
 **Christopher J. "Chris" O'Neal** . . . . . . . . . . . . . . . . . (717) 346-9347
 E-mail: coneal@pa.gov
Human Resources and Management Deputy Secretary
 **James A. Honchar** . . . . . . . . . . . . . . . . . . . . . . . . . (717) 787-8191
 E-mail: jhonchar@pa.gov  Fax: (717) 783-4429
 Education: Pittsburgh BA; St Francis U MA
■Deputy Secretary for Information Technology and Chief
 Information Officer **John MacMillan** . . . . . . . . . . . . . (717) 787-8191
 E-mail: jmacmillan@pa.gov  Fax: (717) 783-4429
 JNET (Justice Network) Executive Director **(Vacant)** . . . . (717) 772-1460
         Fax: (717) 783-6955

## Administrative Services Office

508 E-Floor, Main Capitol Building, Harrisburg, PA 17120

Administrative Services Director **Paula J. Wilcox** . . . . . . . . (717) 787-5330
 E-mail: pawilcox@pa.gov

## Office of the Budget

Tel: (717) 787-2542 Fax: (717) 787-3368

Secretary **Randy Albright** . . . . . . . . . . . . . . . . . . . . . . . (717) 787-4472
 E-mail: raalbright@pa.gov
 Special Assistant to the Secretary **Natalie Sabadish** . . . . (717) 787-4472

---

★ Elected Official  ■ Appointed by Governor  ● Appointed by Legislature  ▲ Appointed by Board or Commission  ◆ Appointed by State Supreme Court

Special Assistant to the Secretary **Jen Swails**..........(717) 787-2542

Executive Deputy Secretary **Brenda Warburton**.........(717) 787-2542

# Office of Inspector General

555 Walnut Street, Harrisburg, PA 17101

Tel: (717) 787-6835  Fax: (717) 787-7923  E-mail: pafraud@state.pa.us

Internet: www.oig.state.pa.us

■ Inspector General **Grayling G. Williams**..............(717) 772-5606
  E-mail: graywillia@pa.us
  Education: New Haven 1977 BSLE; Johns Hopkins MM

■ Deputy Inspector General **David P. Todd**................(717) 787-6835

■ Chief Counsel **Robert T. DaTorre**.....................(717) 787-6835
  E-mail: rdatorre@pa.gov
  Education: Florida 1998 BABA; Miami 2001 JD

# Department of Aging

555 Walnut Street, Fifth Floor, Harrisburg, PA 17101-1919

Tel: (717) 783-1550  Fax: (717) 783-6842  Internet: www.aging.state.pa.us

**Employees:** 102

■ Secretary **Teresa Osborne**.........................(717) 783-1550
  E-mail: tosborne@pa.gov
  Education: Marywood U BSW

Deputy Secretary **David Gingerich**....................(717) 772-4646

Chief Counsel **Neeka Jones**..........................(717) 783-6128

Press Secretary **Kirstin D. Snow**.....................(717) 787-3368
  E-mail: ksnow@pa.gov

Advocacy, Protection and Education Bureau Director
  **(Vacant)**.......................................(717) 783-8975

Operations and Management Office Director
  **Kelly O'Donnell**................................(717) 783-7373

Pharmaceutical Assistance Bureau Director
  **Thomas Snedden**.................................(717) 787-7313

Council on Aging Executive Director **Donna Reinaker**....(717) 787-4644

Legislative Liaison **Dwayne Heckert**..................(717) 783-0508
  E-mail: dwheckert@pa.gov

# Department of Agriculture [PDA]

2301 North Cameron Street, Harrisburg, PA 17110

Tel: (717) 787-4737  Fax: (717) 772-2780

Internet: www.agriculture.state.pa.us

**Employees:** 592  **Fiscal Year:** 2015  **Budget:** $163,256,000

■ Secretary **Russell C. Redding**......................(717) 772-2853
  E-mail: rredding@pa.gov

Executive Assistant **Caryn Earl**.....................(717) 346-9643

Chief Counsel **D. Holbrook Duer**.....................(717) 705-6021

Legislative Liaison **Charles Quinnan**................(717) 772-2854
  E-mail: cquinnan@pa.gov

Press Secretary **Brandi Hunter-Davenport**.............(717) 787-5085

Policy Director **Erin Smith**.........................(717) 772-4365

## Administration

Fax: (717) 783-9709

Executive Deputy Secretary **Michael Smith**.............(717) 787-5789
  E-mail: mfsmith@pa.gov
  Education: Indiana (PA) 2002 BA, 2005 MPA; Penn State 2013 PhD

Human Resources Director **Deborah Laughman**........(717) 787-1065

Agricultural Statistics Services Director
  **King Whetstone**.................................(717) 783-8462

Chief Information Officer **Cheryl L. Cook**.............(717) 705-8897
  E-mail: chercook@pa.gov
  Education: Lebanon Valley; Dickinson Law JD

## Regional Administration Office

Administration Services Director **Mary Bender**.........(717) 346-0438
  E-mail: mabender@pa.gov

## Animal Health and Food Safety

Deputy Secretary **Gregory Hostetter**.................(717) 705-8895

Dog Law Enforcement Bureau Director
  **Kristen Donmoyer**...............................(717) 705-8896

Food Safety and Laboratory Services Bureau Director
  **Lydia Johnson**..................................(717) 787-4315

Animal Health and Diagnostic Services Bureau Director
  and State Veterinarian **Dr. Craig E. Shultz**...........(717) 783-2200
  Education: Cornell 1973 BS, 1976 DVM

## Market Development

Deputy Secretary **Hannah Smith-Brubaker**.............(717) 787-4626

Bureau Director **Lela Reichart**......................(717) 783-8462

Farmland Preservation Bureau Director
  **Douglas Wolfgang**...............................(717) 783-3167

Food Distribution Bureau Director **Joseph Quattrocchi**...(717) 787-2940

Farm Show Executive Director **Sharon Altland**.........(717) 787-5373

## Plant Industry and Consumer Protection

Deputy Secretary **Fred Strathmeyer, Jr.**..............(717) 214-3758

Harness Racing Executive Secretary **George Crawford**...(717) 787-5196
  E-mail: gcrawford@pa.gov

Horse Racing Executive Secretary (Acting)
  **Walter Remmert**.................................(717) 787-1942

Horse Racing Commission Chief Operating Officer
  **(Vacant)**.......................................(717) 787-1942

Equine Toxicology & Research Laboratory Director
  (Acting) **Mary Robinson**.........................(610) 436-3501
  West Chester University, West Chester, PA 19382

Plant Industry Bureau Director **John Breitsman**.........(717) 772-5215

Ride and Measurement Standards Bureau Director
  **Walter Remmert**.................................(717) 787-9089

# Department of Banking and Securities [DOBS]

17 North Second Street, Suite 1300, Harrisburg, PA 17101-2290

Tel: (717) 787-2665  Tel: (800) 722-2657 (Consumer Complaints)

TTY: (800) 679-5070  Fax: (717) 214-0808

**Employees:** 233

■ Secretary **Robin L. Wiessmann**......................(717) 787-6991
  E-mail: rwiessmann@pa.gov
  Education: Lafayette; Rutgers (Camden) JD

Chief Counsel **Leo Pandeladis**.......................(717) 787-1471
  E-mail: lepandelad@pa.gov

  Senior Legislative Director **Paul H. Wentzel, Jr.**.......(717) 787-2112
  E-mail: pwentzel@pa.gov

Executive Deputy Secretary **Victoria A. Reider**.........(717) 783-2255
  Education: Mercyhurst; Dickinson Law JD

Depository Institutions Deputy Secretary
  **Wendy S. Spicher**...............................(717) 787-5783

Nondepository Institutions Deputy Secretary **(Vacant)**.....(717) 346-9353

Financial Services for Consumers and Business Deputy
  Secretary **Brian LaForme**........................(717) 787-6828

Securities Deputy Secretary **Joseph Minisi**............(717) 783-4186

Policy Director **John Raymond**.......................(717) 787-4129

# Department of Community and Economic Development [DCED]

Commonwealth Keystone Building, 400 North Street, 4th Floor,
Harrisburg, PA 17120-0225

Tel: (717) 787-3003  Fax: (717) 787-6866  Internet: www.newpa.com

**Employees:** 310  **Fiscal Year:** 2015  **Budget:** $270,478,000

■ Secretary **Dennis M. Davin**.........................(717) 787-3003
  E-mail: ddavin@pa.gov

Executive Secretary **Kara Ruby**......................(717) 787-3003

Executive Deputy Secretary **Neil Weaver**..............(717) 787-3003

Chief of Staff **(Vacant)**............................(717) 787-3003

Business Financing Deputy Secretary
  **Scott Dunkelberger**.............................(717) 787-7120
  Education: Shippensburg 1984 BS, 1985 MA

Community Affairs and Development Deputy Secretary
  **(Vacant)**.......................................(717) 787-3003

Energy and Advanced Manufacturing Deputy Secretary
  **(Vacant)**.......................................(717) 787-3003

International Business Development Deputy Secretary
  **(Vacant)**.......................................(717) 787-3003

Marketing, Tourism and Film Deputy Secretary
  **Carrie Fischer Lepore**..........................(717) 783-3003

*(continued on next page)*

---

★ Elected Official  ■ Appointed by Governor  ● Appointed by Legislature    ▲ Appointed by Board or Commission    ◆ Appointed by State Supreme Court

**Department of Community and Economic Development** *continued*

Office of Technology and Innovation Deputy Secretary
**Sheri Collins** . . . . . . . . . . . . . . . . . . . . . . . . . . . . . (717) 787-3003
  E-mail: shcollins@pa.gov
Chief Counsel **Arthur F. "Art" McNulty** . . . . . . . . . . . . (717) 783-8452
Marketing Executive Director **(Vacant)** . . . . . . . . . . . . . (717) 787-3003
Governor's Action Team Director **Brent Vernon** . . . . . . (717) 720-1331
Legislative Affairs Director **Barry Wickes** . . . . . . . . . . . (717) 787-3003
  E-mail: bwickes@pa.gov
  Education: Westminster (PA) 1977 BA; Pittsburgh 1979 MPA
Policy Director **Steven D'Ettorre** . . . . . . . . . . . . . . . . . (717) 787-3003
Budget Division Director **Bruce Karper** . . . . . . . . . . . . . (717) 720-1399
Chief Financial Officer **Kevin Rowland** . . . . . . . . . . . . . (717) 720-7423
Center for Private Financing Office Director
  **Stephen Drizos** . . . . . . . . . . . . . . . . . . . . . . . . . . . . (717) 783-1109
Community Development Deputy Secretary **(Vacant)** . . . . . (717) 720-7407
Communications Director **Lyndsay Kensinger** . . . . . . . . . (717) 787-3003

# Department of Conservation and Natural Resources [DCNR]

Rachel Carson State Office Building, 400 Market Street, 7th Floor,
Harrisburg, PA 17105-8767
P.O. Box 8767, Harrisburg, PA 17105-8767
Tel: (717) 787-2869  TTY: (800) 654-5984  Fax: (717) 705-2832
E-mail: askdcnr@state.pa.us  Internet: www.dcnr.state.pa.us

**Employees:** 1,403  **Fiscal Year:** 2014-2015  **Budget:** $340,958,000

■Secretary **Cynthia Adams "Cindy" Dunn** . . . . . . . . . . . . (717) 772-9084
  Education: Shippensburg MS
Chief Counsel **Audrey Feinman Miner** . . . . . . . . . . . . . . (717) 772-4171
Senior Advisor to the Secretary **Gretchen A. Leslie** . . . . . (717) 772-9101
  E-mail: gleslie@pa.gov
Legislation and Advisory Councils Director
  **Joseph P. "Joe" Graci** . . . . . . . . . . . . . . . . . . . . . . . (717) 772-9306
Senior Policy Analyst **Sara J. Nicholas** . . . . . . . . . . . . . (717) 772-9306
  E-mail: snicholas@pa.gov
Education, Communications and Partnership Office
  Director **Christina Novak** . . . . . . . . . . . . . . . . . . . . . (717) 772-9101
  E-mail: cnovak@pa.gov
Legislative Liaison **Jennie Shade** . . . . . . . . . . . . . . . . . (717) 787-9306
  E-mail: jeshade@pa.gov

## Administration

Deputy Secretary **Michael A. Walsh** . . . . . . . . . . . . . . . (717) 772-9100
  E-mail: micwalsh@pa.gov
Special Assistant **(Vacant)** . . . . . . . . . . . . . . . . . . . . . . (717) 787-7398

## Conservation and Technical Services

Deputy Secretary **Nathan Flood** . . . . . . . . . . . . . . . . . . . (717) 787-7398

# Department of Corrections [DOC]

1920 Technology Parkway, Mechanicsburg, PA 17050
Tel: (717) 728-2573  Fax: (717) 728-4178  Internet: www.cor.pa.gov

**Employees:** 15,000  **Fiscal Year:** 2014-2015  **Budget:** $2,059,500,000

■Secretary **John E. Wetzel** . . . . . . . . . . . . . . . . . . . . . . (717) 728-4109
  E-mail: ra-contactdoc@pa.gov
  Education: Bloomsburg BA; Penn State (Attended)
Executive Deputy Secretary **Shirley R. Moore Smeal** . . . . (717) 728-4110
  Education: Edinboro BBA
Administrative Services Deputy Secretary (Acting)
  **Christopher H. Oppman** . . . . . . . . . . . . . . . . . . . . . . . (717) 728-4122
  E-mail: ra-contactdoc@pa.gov
Central Region Deputy Secretary **Tabb Bickell** . . . . . . . . (717) 728-4122
Eastern Region Deputy Secretary **Michael Wenerowicz** . . . (717) 728-4122
Western Region Deputy Secretary **Steven Glunt** . . . . . . . . (717) 728-4123
Chief Counsel **Theron Perez** . . . . . . . . . . . . . . . . . . . . . (717) 728-4029
  E-mail: tperez@pa.gov
Administration Bureau Director **Harry Jones** . . . . . . . . . . (717) 728-4037
  E-mail: hjones@pa.gov
Community Corrections Bureau Director (Acting)
  **Luis Resto** . . . . . . . . . . . . . . . . . . . . . . . . . . . . . . . . (717) 728-4060
Correction Education Bureau Director **Steven Davy** . . . . . (717) 728-2007

Correctional Industries Bureau Director
  **Anthony "Tony" Miller** . . . . . . . . . . . . . . . . . . . . . . (717) 425-7292
Health Care Services Bureau Director (Acting)
  **Andrea Norris** . . . . . . . . . . . . . . . . . . . . . . . . . . . . . (717) 728-5309
Human Resources Bureau Director **Ty Stanton** . . . . . . . . (717) 728-2009
Information Technology Bureau Director **Dustin Rhoads** . . (717) 728-0342
  E-mail: durhoads@pa.gov
  Education: Shippensburg BSCrimJ
  Applications Division Director **Lisa Mosier** . . . . . . . . . . (717) 728-5363
  E-mail: lmosier@pa.gov
Treatment Services Bureau Director (Acting)
  **Tracy Smith** . . . . . . . . . . . . . . . . . . . . . . . . . . . . . . (717) 728-2000
Operations Bureau Director **Marcel Tassin** . . . . . . . . . . . (717) 728-0375
Staff Development and Training Bureau Director
  **Michael Dooley** . . . . . . . . . . . . . . . . . . . . . . . . . . . (717) 367-9070
  1451 North Market Street, Elizabethtown, PA 17022-1299
Equal Employment Opportunity Office Director
  **Raphael K. Chieke** . . . . . . . . . . . . . . . . . . . . . . . . . . (717) 728-2570
Special Investigations and Intelligence Office Director
  **James C. Barnacle** . . . . . . . . . . . . . . . . . . . . . . . . . . (717) 728-2033
  E-mail: jbarnacle@pa.gov
■Policy and Grant Office Director **Diana Woodside** . . . . . (717) 728-4119
  E-mail: dwoodside@pa.gov
Mental Health Advocate Office Director **Lynn Patrone** . . . (717) 728-2573
Press Secretary **Susan McNaughton** . . . . . . . . . . . . . . . . (717) 728-4025
Legislative Liaison **Andrew Barnes** . . . . . . . . . . . . . . . . (717) 728-4030
  E-mail: abarnes@pa.gov
Planning, Research and Statistics Director
  **Kristopher Bucklen** . . . . . . . . . . . . . . . . . . . . . . . . . (717) 728-4051
  E-mail: kbucklen@pa.gov
Population Management Director **William Nicklow** . . . . . . (717) 728-2817
Webmaster **Susan McNaughton** . . . . . . . . . . . . . . . . . . . (717) 728-4025

# Department of Environmental Protection [DEP]

P.O. Box 2063, Harrisburg, PA 17105-2063
Tel: (717) 783-2300  TTY: (800) 654-5984  Fax: (717) 783-8926
E-mail: raepdepinfo@state.pa.us  Internet: www.depweb.state.pa.us

**Employees:** 2,511  **Fiscal Year:** 2015  **Budget:** $148,824,000

■Secretary (Acting) **Patrick McDonnell** . . . . . . . . . . . . . . (717) 787-2814
Executive Deputy Secretary **John Stefanko** . . . . . . . . . . . (717) 772-1856
Environmental Emergency Response Coordinator
  **Brian Moore** . . . . . . . . . . . . . . . . . . . . . . . . . . . . . . (717) 787-5715
Program Integration Office Director **Ann Roda** . . . . . . . . (717) 772-1856

## Active and Abandoned Mine Operations Office

Fax: (717) 772-3336
Deputy Secretary **(Vacant)** . . . . . . . . . . . . . . . . . . . . . . (717) 783-9958
Abandoned Mine Reclamation Bureau Director
  **Eric Cavazza** . . . . . . . . . . . . . . . . . . . . . . . . . . . . . . (717) 783-2267
District Mining Operations Bureau Director
  **William Plassio** . . . . . . . . . . . . . . . . . . . . . . . . . . . . (724) 925-5500
Mine Safety Bureau Director **(Vacant)** . . . . . . . . . . . . . . (724) 439-7469

## Administration and Management Office

Fax: (717) 705-4890
■Administration Management Executive Deputy Secretary
  **Darrin Bodner** . . . . . . . . . . . . . . . . . . . . . . . . . . . . . (717) 787-7116
Fiscal Management Bureau Director **Tina Sutton** . . . . . . . (717) 787-1319
Human Resources Bureau Director **Jason Swarthout** . . . . . (717) 783-6220
Office Systems Director **Sally Langianese** . . . . . . . . . . . . (717) 787-4190

## Bureau of Information Technology

Fax: (717) 783-0546
Chief Information Officer **Sean Crager** . . . . . . . . . . . . . . (717) 772-5909
  E-mail: scrager@pa.gov

## Chief Counsel's Office

Chief Counsel **Alexandra Chiaruttini, Esq.** . . . . . . . . . . . (717) 787-4449
Deputy Chief Counsel **James Bohan** . . . . . . . . . . . . . . . . (717) 787-4449
Investigations Bureau Director **Doreen Harr** . . . . . . . . . . (717) 787-0453

---

★ Elected Official   ■ Appointed by Governor   ● Appointed by Legislature   ▲ Appointed by Board or Commission   ◆ Appointed by State Supreme Court

Regulatory Counsel Bureau Director **Kim Childe** . . . . . . . . (717) 787-7060
Administrative Officer **April Hain** . . . . . . . . . . . . . . . . . . . . . (717) 783-2300
  E-mail: ahain@pa.gov

## Communications Office
Director **Julie Lalo** . . . . . . . . . . . . . . . . . . . . . . . . . . . . . . . . . (717) 787-1323
  E-mail: jlalo@pa.gov
Press Secretary **Neil Shader** . . . . . . . . . . . . . . . . . . . . . . . . . (717) 783-2300
  E-mail: nshader@pa.gov

## Legislative Affairs
Director **Sarah L. Clark, Esq.** . . . . . . . . . . . . . . . . . . . . . . . . (717) 783-8303

## Field Operations Office
Fax: (717) 772-3314

Deputy Secretary **Dana K. Aunkst, PE** . . . . . . . . . . . . . . . . (717) 772-1856
  Education: Penn State BSChE

## Oil and Gas Office
Deputy Secretary **Scott Perry** . . . . . . . . . . . . . . . . . . . . . . . (717) 783-9438

## Policy Office
Director (Acting) **Jessica Shirley** . . . . . . . . . . . . . . . . . . . . . (717) 783-8727
Regulatory Coordinator **Laura Edinger** . . . . . . . . . . . . . . . . (717) 783-8727

## Waste, Air, Radiation and Remediation
Deputy Secretary **Kenneth Reisinger** . . . . . . . . . . . . . . . . . (717) 772-2725
Air Quality Bureau Director **Joyce Epps** . . . . . . . . . . . . . . . (717) 787-9702
Radiation Protection Bureau Director **David Allard** . . . . . . . (717) 787-2480
Waste Management Bureau Director **(Vacant)** . . . . . . . . . . (717) 783-2388

## Water Programs Office
Fax: (717) 772-5996

Deputy Secretary **(Vacant)** . . . . . . . . . . . . . . . . . . . . . . . . . . (717) 783-4693
Point and Non-Point Source Management
  **Lee McDonnell** . . . . . . . . . . . . . . . . . . . . . . . . . . . . . . . . . (717) 787-5017
Waterways Engineering and Wetlands Bureau Director
  **Ramez Ziahed** . . . . . . . . . . . . . . . . . . . . . . . . . . . . . . . . . (717) 787-3411
Interstate Waters Office Manager **Dana K. Aunkst, PE** . . . . (717) 772-5633

## Department of General Services [DGS]
515 North Office Building, Harrisburg, PA 17125
P.O. Box 1365, Harrisburg, PA 17125
Tel: (717) 787-5996  TTY: (800) 342-8040  Fax: (717) 772-2026
Internet: www.dgs.state.pa.us

**Employees:** 1,003  **Fiscal Year:** 2012-2103  **Budget:** $117,590,000

■Secretary **Curtis "Curt" Topper** . . . . . . . . . . . . . . . . . . . . (717) 787-5996
  E-mail: gs-secretary@pa.gov
  Education: Brown U BA; Carnegie Mellon MPP
  Executive Assistant **Tracy Wright** . . . . . . . . . . . . . . . . . . . (717) 346-4040
Chief of Staff **Matthew Bembenick** . . . . . . . . . . . . . . . . . . (717) 787-5996
Deputy Secretary for Administration **Beverly A. Hudson** . . (717) 783-8874
  E-mail: bhudson@pa.gov
  Education: Susquehanna; Johns Hopkins
Chief Counsel **Charles E. "Chuck" Anderson** . . . . . . . . . (717) 787-5599
                                                  Fax: (717) 787-9138
Press Secretary **Troy Thompson** . . . . . . . . . . . . . . . . . . . . . (717) 787-3197
  E-mail: tthompson@pa.gov
Legislative Liaison **Stephen Rudman** . . . . . . . . . . . . . . . . . (717) 787-4004
  E-mail: srudman@pa.gov
Special Assistant **Matthew Kaminske** . . . . . . . . . . . . . . . . . (717) 787-5996
  E-mail: mkaminske@pa.gov

## Administration
E-mail: gs-procure@pa.gov
■Deputy Secretary **Beverly A. Hudson** . . . . . . . . . . . . . . . . (717) 787-5996
  E-mail: bhudson@pa.gov
  Administrative Assistant **Tracy Wright** . . . . . . . . . . . . . . . (717) 787-5296
Financial and Management Services Bureau Director
  **Vicky ChiChi** . . . . . . . . . . . . . . . . . . . . . . . . . . . . . . . . . . (717) 787-5051

Commonwealth Media Services Director
  **Suzanne Chubb** . . . . . . . . . . . . . . . . . . . . . . . . . . . . . . . (717) 787-9779
                                            Fax: (717) 783-5139
Human Resources Director **Patrick Striggle** . . . . . . . . . . . . (717) 787-6846
Risk and Insurance Management Bureau Director
  **Kenneth Love** . . . . . . . . . . . . . . . . . . . . . . . . . . . . . . . . . (717) 787-2492

## Property and Asset Management
■Deputy Secretary **Julien Gaudion** . . . . . . . . . . . . . . . . . . . (717) 783-5028
  E-mail: jugaudion@pa.gov         Fax: (717) 772-5317
Executive Assistant **Kathleen Harrison** . . . . . . . . . . . . . . . . (717) 783-5029
Police and Safety Superintendent
  **Joseph M. "Joe" Jacob** . . . . . . . . . . . . . . . . . . . . . . . . . (717) 787-9013
  E-mail: jjacob@pa.gov            Fax: (717) 787-8637
  Police and Safety Deputy Superintendent **Kevin Brown** . . (717) 787-9013
  E-mail: kbrown@pa.gov          Fax: (717) 787-8637
Facilities Management Bureau Director **Jason Snyder** . . . . (717) 787-5341
                                            Fax: (717) 772-5317
Maintenance Management Bureau Director
  **David Szobocsan** . . . . . . . . . . . . . . . . . . . . . . . . . . . . . . (717) 787-5412
Property Administration Bureau Director **Mary Masland** . . (717) 787-5240
                                            Fax: (717) 772-5717
Real Estate Bureau Director **Elizabeth Woods** . . . . . . . . . . (717) 787-4394
                                            Fax: (717) 783-0570
Special Events Office Director **Lori Sherlock** . . . . . . . . . . . (717) 783-9100
                                            Fax: (717) 705-2897
Vehicle Management Bureau Director
  **James "Jim" Fiore** . . . . . . . . . . . . . . . . . . . . . . . . . . . . . . (717) 787-3162
  E-mail: jafiore@pa.gov           Fax: (717) 787-0276

## Public Works
■Deputy Secretary **Elizabeth O'Reilly** . . . . . . . . . . . . . . . . . (717) 787-7095
  E-mail: loreilly@pa.gov          Fax: (717) 783-3473
Construction Bureau Director **Daniel Weinzierl** . . . . . . . . . (717) 787-6330
Engineering and Architecture Bureau Director
  **Gary Taylor** . . . . . . . . . . . . . . . . . . . . . . . . . . . . . . . . . . . (717) 787-6200
Professional Selections & Administrative Services Bureau
  Director **(Vacant)** . . . . . . . . . . . . . . . . . . . . . . . . . . . . . . . (717) 787-7856

## Department of Health
Health and Welfare Building, Eighth Floor West, Harrisburg, PA 17120
P.O. Box 1528, New Castle, PA 16103 (Vital Records)
Tel: (877) 724-3258  Tel: (724) 656-3100 (Vital Records)
TTY: (717) 783-6514  Fax: (717) 772-6959
E-mail: webmaster@health.state.pa.us  Internet: www.health.pa.gov/
Internet: www.health.state.pa.us/vitalrecords/ (Vital Records)

**Employees:** 1,323  **Fiscal Year:** 2015  **Budget:** $202,244,000

■Secretary **Dr. Karen Murphy** . . . . . . . . . . . . . . . . . . . . . . . (717) 787-6436
  E-mail: kamurphy@pa.gov
  Education: Scranton 1990 BS; Marywood U 2001 MBA;
  Temple 2007 PhD
  Executive Secretary **Tabbitha Bosack** . . . . . . . . . . . . . . . . (717) 547-3100
General Counsel **Alison Taylor** . . . . . . . . . . . . . . . . . . . . . . (717) 783-2500
  E-mail: altaylor@pa.gov
Communications Office Director **Amy Worden** . . . . . . . . . . (717) 787-1783
  E-mail: aworden@pa.gov
Legislative Affairs Office Director **Neil Malady** . . . . . . . . . (717) 783-3985
  E-mail: nmalady@pa.gov
Policy Office Director **Lawrence "Larry" Clark** . . . . . . . . (717) 705-6925

## Administration
Deputy Secretary **Terri Matio** . . . . . . . . . . . . . . . . . . . . . . . (717) 787-6325
Administrative and Financial Services Bureau Director
  **Lori Stubbs** . . . . . . . . . . . . . . . . . . . . . . . . . . . . . . . . . . . (717) 787-6325
Information Technology Bureau Director **Patrick Keating** . . (717) 787-7521
  E-mail: pakeating@pa.gov
Health Statistics and Registries Bureau Director
  **Lana Adams** . . . . . . . . . . . . . . . . . . . . . . . . . . . . . . . . . . (717) 783-2548
  101 South Mercer Street, New Castle, PA 16103

## Health Planning and Assessment
Deputy Secretary (Acting) **Richard Gibbons** . . . . . . . . . . . (717) 783-8804
  E-mail: rigibbons@pa.gov
Infectious Disease Division Director **Atmaram Nambiar** . . (717) 787-3350

*(continued on next page)*

---

★ Elected Official   ■ Appointed by Governor   ● Appointed by Legislature   ▲ Appointed by Board or Commission   ◆ Appointed by State Supreme Court

**EXECUTIVE BRANCH**

**Health Planning and Assessment** *continued*

Community Health Bureau Director **Doug Koszalka** . . . . . . (717) 787-4366

Emergency Medical Services Bureau Director
**Richard Gibbons** . . . . . . . . . . . . . . . . . . . . . . . . . . . . . . . . (717) 787-8740

Public Health Preparedness Office Director
**Andrew Pickett** . . . . . . . . . . . . . . . . . . . . . . . . . . . . . . . . . (717) 346-0640

## Health Promotions and Disease Prevention

Deputy Secretary **Dr. Loren K. Robinson, MD** . . . . . . . . . (717) 787-9857
Education: Spelman BA; Duke MD

Health Promotion/Risk Reduction Bureau Director
**Tomas J. Aguilar** . . . . . . . . . . . . . . . . . . . . . . . . . . . . . . . (717) 787-6214

Communicable Diseases Bureau Director
**Robin Rothermel** . . . . . . . . . . . . . . . . . . . . . . . . . . . . . . (717) 787-5681
Fax: (717) 705-5513

Family Health Bureau Director **Carolyn Cass** . . . . . . . . . . . (717) 547-3385

Women, Infants and Children (WIC) Division Director
**William Cramer** . . . . . . . . . . . . . . . . . . . . . . . . . . . . . . . (717) 783-1289
E-mail: wcramer@pa.gov                        Fax: (717) 705-0462

## Quality Assurance

Deputy Secretary **Christine Filipovich** . . . . . . . . . . . . . . . (717) 783-1078
Executive Assistant **Amy Stum** . . . . . . . . . . . . . . . . . . . . . (717) 783-1078

Community Program Licensure and Certification Bureau
Director **Susan Coble** . . . . . . . . . . . . . . . . . . . . . . . . . . . (717) 736-7361

Facility Licensure and Certification Bureau Director
**Ann Chronister** . . . . . . . . . . . . . . . . . . . . . . . . . . . . . . . (717) 787-8015

## Office of the Physician General

■Physician General **Dr. Rachel Levine, MD** . . . . . . . . . . . . (717) 787-6436
E-mail: ralevine@pa.gov

Community Epidemiology Division Director
**Gene Weinberg** . . . . . . . . . . . . . . . . . . . . . . . . . . . . . . . (717) 787-3350

Epidemiology Bureau Director **Dr. Sharon Watkins** . . . . . . (717) 787-3350
E-mail: swatkins@pa.gov

Environmental Health Epidemiology Division Director
(Acting) **Farhad Ahmed** . . . . . . . . . . . . . . . . . . . . . . . . . (717) 787-3350

## Laboratories Bureau

Laboratories Bureau Director (Interim)
**Dr. Michael A. Husson, MD** . . . . . . . . . . . . . . . . . . . . . . (610) 450-2104

Assistant Bureau Director **Dr. James Lute** . . . . . . . . . . . . . (610) 450-2104

## Chemistry and Toxicology Division

Director **Jennifer Okraska** . . . . . . . . . . . . . . . . . . . . . . . . . (484) 870-6405
Toxicology Section Supervisor **David Fardig** . . . . . . . . . . . (484) 870-6384
Administrative Support **Teresa Sagwitz** . . . . . . . . . . . . . . . (484) 870-6436

## Clinical Microbiology Division

Director **Lisa Dettinger** . . . . . . . . . . . . . . . . . . . . . . . . . . . (610) 450-3464

## Laboratory Improvement Division

Director **Debra Tyler** . . . . . . . . . . . . . . . . . . . . . . . . . . . . . (484) 870-6418

## Health Innovation

Executive Secretary **Denise Williams** . . . . . . . . . . . . . . . . (717) 547-3102

Health Planning Bureau Director **Robert Richardson** . . . . . (717) 772-5298
E-mail: roberricha@pa.gov

Deputy Secretary/Health Innovation Office Director
**Lauren Hughes** . . . . . . . . . . . . . . . . . . . . . . . . . . . . . . . . (717) 547-3102

Managed Care Bureau Director **William Wiegmann** . . . . . . (717) 787-5193
Health Research Office Director **Sirisha Reddy** . . . . . . . . . (717) 547-3102

## Insurance Department

1326 Strawberry Square, Harrisburg, PA 17120
Tel: (717) 787-7000  TTY: (717) 783-3898  Fax: (717) 787-8585

**Employees:** 273  **Fiscal Year:** 2015  **Budget:** $447,372,000

■Insurance Commissioner **Teresa D. Miller** . . . . . . . . . . . . (717) 787-7000
E-mail: termiller@pa.gov
Education: Pacific Lutheran 1996 BA; Willamette 2002 JD

Corporate and Financial Regulation Deputy
Commissioner **Joe DiMemmo** . . . . . . . . . . . . . . . . . . . . . (717) 783-2142
E-mail: jdimemmo@pa.gov                        Fax: (717) 787-8557
Education: Penn State 1978 BS

Liquidation, Rehabilitations and Special Funds Deputy
Commissioner **Laura Slaymaker** . . . . . . . . . . . . . . . . . . . . (717) 787-6009
Fax: (717) 783-9326

Market Regulation Deputy Commissioner
**Christopher "Chris" Monahan** . . . . . . . . . . . . . . . . . . . . (717) 783-2627
Fax: (717) 772-4334

Product Regulation and Administration Deputy
Commissioner **Seth Mendelsohn** . . . . . . . . . . . . . . . . . . . (717) 783-5079
Fax: (717) 787-8555

Chief Counsel (Acting) **Amy Daubert** . . . . . . . . . . . . . . . . (717) 787-2567
Fax: (717) 772-1969

Administration Bureau Director **Mark Lersch** . . . . . . . . . . . (717) 787-4298
E-mail: mlersch@pa.gov                        Fax: (717) 705-3873

Human Resources Director **Donna Fleischauer** . . . . . . . . . (717) 787-4298
Fax: (717) 705-3873

Office Management Chief **Joe Korman** . . . . . . . . . . . . . . . (717) 787-4429
E-mail: jkorman@pa.gov                        Fax: (717) 705-3873

Legislative Affairs Director **Kristen Erway** . . . . . . . . . . . . (717) 783-2005
E-mail: krerway@pa.gov                        Fax: (717) 772-1969
Education: Lebanon Valley 2006 BA

Policy Director **Glenda Ebersole** . . . . . . . . . . . . . . . . . . . (717) 787-2734
Fax: (717) 772-1969

Administrative Hearing Office Chief Hearing Officer
**James A. Johnson** . . . . . . . . . . . . . . . . . . . . . . . . . . . . . (717) 783-2126
Education: Penn State 1978 BA; Pittsburgh 1983 JD  Fax: (717) 787-8781

Press Secretary **Ronald G. Ruman** . . . . . . . . . . . . . . . . . . (717) 787-3289
E-mail: roruman@pa.gov                        Fax: (717) 775-1969

## Department of Labor and Industry

651 Boas Street, Harrisburg, PA 17121
Tel: (717) 787-5279  Fax: (717) 787-8826  Internet: www.dli.pa.gov

**Employees:** 5,898  **Fiscal Year:** 2013-2014  **Budget:** $58,898,000

■Secretary **Kathy M. Manderino** . . . . . . . . . . . . . . . . . . . (717) 705-2630
E-mail: kmanderino@pa.gov
Education: Penn State 1980 BS; Temple 1989 JD

■Chief Counsel **Marsha Sajer** . . . . . . . . . . . . . . . . . . . . . . (717) 787-4186

■Legislative Affairs Office Director
**Michael "Mike" Stefan** . . . . . . . . . . . . . . . . . . . . . . . . . (717) 787-5087

Press Secretary **Sara Goulet** . . . . . . . . . . . . . . . . . . . . . . (717) 787-7530
E-mail: sgoulet@pa.gov

## Administration

Deputy Secretary **Chris Dwyer** . . . . . . . . . . . . . . . . . . . . . (717) 787-8667
E-mail: chrisdwyer@pa.gov

Citizen Service Office (PENNSERVE) Executive Director
**Patricia "Pat" Schwartz** . . . . . . . . . . . . . . . . . . . . . . . . . (717) 772-5430
E-mail: pschwartz@pa.gov

Equal Opportunity Office Director **James Kayer** . . . . . . . . (717) 772-9197

Administrative Services Bureau Director
**Nathan Bortner** . . . . . . . . . . . . . . . . . . . . . . . . . . . . . . . (717) 783-0332
E-mail: nbortner@pa.gov

Human Resources Bureau Director **Mark Grab** . . . . . . . . . (717) 783-4838

## Compensation and Insurance

Deputy Secretary **Michael Vovokes** . . . . . . . . . . . . . . . . . (717) 787-5082
E-mail: mvovokes@pa.gov

State Workers' Insurance Fund Director **(Vacant)** . . . . . . . . (570) 963-4601

Disability Determination Bureau Director **Steve Rollins** . . . (717) 425-7904

Workers' Compensation Bureau Director (Acting)
**Michael Vovokes** . . . . . . . . . . . . . . . . . . . . . . . . . . . . . . (717) 783-5421
E-mail: mvovokes@pa.gov

## Deaf and Hard of Hearing Office

1521 North Sixth Street, Harrisburg, PA 17102
Tel: (717) 783-4912 (Voice/TTY)  Tel: (800) 233-3008 (Voice/TTY)
Fax: (717) 783-4913

Director **Sharon Behun** . . . . . . . . . . . . . . . . . . . . . . . . . . . (717) 783-4912
Education: Bloomsburg BS

## Information Technology

Executive Director and Chief Information Officer
**David Naisby** . . . . . . . . . . . . . . . . . . . . . . . . . . . . . . . . . (717) 705-6494
E-mail: dnaisby@pa.gov

---

★ Elected Official   ■ Appointed by Governor   ● Appointed by Legislature   ▲ Appointed by Board or Commission   ◆ Appointed by State Supreme Court

Business Application Development Bureau Director
**David Andrews** . . . . . . . . . . . . . . . . . . . . . . . . . (717) 783-5811
E-mail: daandrews@pa.gov
Enterprise Services and Solutions Director **(Vacant)** . . . . . . (717) 772-8628
Infrastructure and Operations Bureau Director
**John Malinoski** . . . . . . . . . . . . . . . . . . . . . . . . (717) 346-4220
E-mail: jmalinoski@pa.gov

## Safety and Labor - Management Relations
Deputy Secretary **Sean Ramaley** . . . . . . . . . . . . . . . . (717) 787-8665
Labor Law Compliance Bureau Director **Peter Getzie** . . . . (717) 787-3681
Mediation Bureau Director **William D. Gross** . . . . . . . . . (717) 787-2803
E-mail: wigross@pa.gov
Occupational and Industrial Safety Bureau Director
**Jennifer Berrier** . . . . . . . . . . . . . . . . . . . . . . . . (717) 783-6304

## Special Programs
Pennsylvania Labor Relations Board Secretary
**Larry Cheskawich** . . . . . . . . . . . . . . . . . . . . . . . (717) 783-6018
E-mail: jekreider@pa.gov
Veterans' Employment & Training Service (USDOL)
State Director **(Vacant)** . . . . . . . . . . . . . . . . . . . . (717) 787-5835
Unemployment Compensation Appeals System
Administrator **Randall Brandes** . . . . . . . . . . . . . . . . (717) 787-5122
E-mail: rbrandes@pa.gov

## Unemployment Compensation Program
Deputy Secretary **Kevin Cicak** . . . . . . . . . . . . . . . . . (717) 787-3907
Unemployment Compensation Appeals Board of Review
Director **Randall Brandes** . . . . . . . . . . . . . . . . . . (717) 787-2953
E-mail: rbrandes@pa.gov
Unemployment Compensation Benefits Office Director
**(Vacant)** . . . . . . . . . . . . . . . . . . . . . . . . . . . (717) 772-8811
Unemployment Compensation Tax Services Office
Director **(Vacant)** . . . . . . . . . . . . . . . . . . . . . . (717) 787-2097
Social Security for Public Employees State Administrator
**(Vacant)** . . . . . . . . . . . . . . . . . . . . . . . . . . . (717) 214-1003

## Vocational Rehabilitation
Executive Director **David De Notaris** . . . . . . . . . . . . . (717) 787-7312
E-mail: ddenotaris@pa.gov
Education: East Stroudsburg BA; Montclair State U MA
Deputy Executive Director **(Vacant)** . . . . . . . . . . . . . (717) 783-8187
Blindness and Visual Services Bureau Director
**Joe Strechay** . . . . . . . . . . . . . . . . . . . . . . . . . (717) 783-3784
Central Operations Bureau Director **Ryan Hyde** . . . . . . . (717) 783-6382
Rehabilitation Center Operations Bureau Director
(Acting) **Jill Moriconi** . . . . . . . . . . . . . . . . . . . (814) 254-0400
727 Goucher Street, Johnstown, PA 15905
Vocational Rehabilitation Services Director
**Denise Verchimak** . . . . . . . . . . . . . . . . . . . . . . (717) 772-3511
E-mail: dverchimak@pa.gov

## Workforce Development
■Deputy Secretary **(Vacant)** . . . . . . . . . . . . . . . . . (717) 787-0805
Workforce Information and Analysis Center Director
**Keith Bailey** . . . . . . . . . . . . . . . . . . . . . . . . . (717) 787-3266
Workforce Development Partnership Bureau Director
**(Vacant)** . . . . . . . . . . . . . . . . . . . . . . . . . . . (717) 214-4827

## Department of Military and Veterans Affairs [DMVA]
Building S-O-47, Ft. Indiantown Gap, Annville, PA 17003-5002
Tel: (717) 861-2000  Fax: (717) 861-8481  Internet: www.dmva.state.pa.us

**Employees:** 2,226  **Fiscal Year:** 2015  **Budget:** $425,789,000

■Adjutant General **MG James R. Joseph, ARNG** . . . . . . (717) 861-2000
Note: On leave of absence
E-mail: james.r.joseph.mil@mail.mil
■Adjutant General (Acting)
**BrigGen Anthony J. Carrelli, ANG** . . . . . . . . . . . . (717) 861-2000
E-mail: anthony.carrelli@ang.af.mil
Education: Air Force Acad 1985 BS; Embry-Riddle 1995 MS;
Air Command Col 2001; Air War Col 2005

Deputy Adjutant General (Veterans Affairs)
**BG Jerry G. Beck, Jr., ARNG (Ret)** . . . . . . . . . . . . (717) 861-8902
Education: Millersville 1975 BA; Penn State 1995 MEd;
Capella U 2011 PhD
Chief of Staff **COL Mark J. Schindler, ARNG** . . . . . . . (717) 861-2000
Operations and Training Deputy Chief of Staff
**COL Marc Ferraro, ARNG** . . . . . . . . . . . . . . . . . (717) 861-8504
Fax: (717) 861-8313
Facilities and Engineering Deputy **Mark A. Austin** . . . . . (717) 861-8580
Education: Penn State BS; Southern Methodist MS

## Pennsylvania Air National Guard
Fort Indiantown Gap, Annville, PA 17003
Tel: (717) 861-8552  Fax: (717) 861-8314
Deputy Adjutant General
**BrigGen Anthony J. Carrelli, ANG** . . . . . . . . . . . . (717) 861-8550

## Pennsylvania Army National Guard
Building S-0-47, Fort Indiantown Gap, Annville, PA 17003
Tel: (717) 861-2000
Deputy Adjutant General **(Vacant)** . . . . . . . . . . . . . (717) 861-2000
Information Technology Director **Timothy "Tim" Irvin** . . . (717) 861-8229
E-mail: timothy.irvin.mil@mail.mil

## Department of Human Services [DHS]
Box 2675, Harrisburg, PA 17105
Tel: (717) 787-2600  Fax: (717) 772-2062
E-mail: dpw_content_webmaster@pa.gov  Internet: www.dpw.state.pa.us

**Employees:** 16,722  **Fiscal Year:** 2015  **Budget:** $11,718,626,000

■Secretary **Theodore "Ted" Dallas** . . . . . . . . . . . . . (717) 787-2600
E-mail: tdallas@pa.gov
Education: Temple MBA
Special Assistant to the Secretary
**Lisa M. Watson, Esq.** . . . . . . . . . . . . . . . . . . . (717) 787-9883
Executive Secretary/Scheduler **Michele Messinger** . . . . . (717) 787-2600
Executive Deputy Secretary **Brendan Harris** . . . . . . . . . (717) 787-2600
Administration Deputy Secretary **Jay Bausch** . . . . . . . . (717) 787-3422
E-mail: jbausch@pa.gov
Children, Youth and Families Deputy Secretary
**Cathy Utz** . . . . . . . . . . . . . . . . . . . . . . . . . . . (717) 787-4756
Income Maintenance Deputy Secretary **Lourdes Padilla** . . . (717) 783-3063
Child Support Enforcement Bureau Director **(Vacant)** . . . (717) 783-9659
Medical Assistance Deputy Secretary **Leesa M. Allen** . . . (717) 787-1870
Fax: (717) 787-4639
Mental Health and Substance Abuse Office Deputy
Secretary **Dennis Marion** . . . . . . . . . . . . . . . . . . (717) 787-6443
Chief Information Officer **Sandy Patterson** . . . . . . . . . (717) 772-7101
E-mail: spatterson@pa.gov
Comptroller **Anna Maria Kiehl, CPA** . . . . . . . . . . . . . (717) 787-6496
Education: Penn State BBA
General Counsel **Doris Leisch** . . . . . . . . . . . . . . . . (717) 783-2800
Press Secretary **Kathaleen Gillis** . . . . . . . . . . . . . . . (717) 787-4592
E-mail: kgillis@pa.gov

## Pennsylvania Department of Revenue
Strawberry Square, 11th Floor, Harrisburg, PA 17128
Tel: (717) 787-8201  TTY: (800) 447-3020
Internet: www.revenue.state.pa.us

**Employees:** 2,001  **Fiscal Year:** 2015  **Budget:** $1,091,466,000

■Secretary **Eileen Healy McNulty** . . . . . . . . . . . . . . (717) 783-3680
E-mail: emcnulty@pa.gov
Education: Michigan State BA
Chief Counsel **Jeffrey S. Snavely** . . . . . . . . . . . . . . (717) 787-1440
Press Office Secretary **Kevin Hensil** . . . . . . . . . . . . . (717) 787-6960
E-mail: khensil@pa.gov
Legislative Affairs Office Director **Kristin Crawford** . . . . (717) 787-1007
Enforcement, Planning, Analysis and Discovery Bureau
Director **Kevin Milligan** . . . . . . . . . . . . . . . . . . (717) 783-5571
Education: Messiah 1980 BA; Carnegie Mellon 1982 MSPA
■Lottery Executive Director **Drew Svitko** . . . . . . . . . . (717) 702-8009
E-mail: dsvitko@legis.state.pa.us
Taxpayers' Rights Advocate **Marva Patterson** . . . . . . . . (717) 772-9347

★ Elected Official   ■ Appointed by Governor   ● Appointed by Legislature   ▲ Appointed by Board or Commission   ◆ Appointed by State Supreme Court

*State Yellow Book*   © Leadership Directories, Inc.   Summer 2016

## Administration

Deputy Secretary **Christin Heidingsfelder** . . . . . . . . . . . . . (717) 783-3691
  E-mail: cheidingsfelder@pa.gov
Administrative Services Director **Pamela McGranaghan** . . (717) 787-8293
  E-mail: pmcgranagh@pa.gov
Budget Director **Melody Rhine** . . . . . . . . . . . . . . . . . . . . . (717) 787-6737
Human Resources Director **Linda Miller** . . . . . . . . . . . . . . (717) 787-7315

## Compliance and Collections

Deputy Secretary **Suzanne "Sue" Leighton, CPA** . . . . . . . (717) 783-3690
Collections and Taxpayer Services Director
  **Thomas Scott** . . . . . . . . . . . . . . . . . . . . . . . . . . . . . . . (717) 787-6611
Compliance Director **Sean Washington** . . . . . . . . . . . . . . (717) 787-3847
Criminal Tax Investigations Director **Anthony Beccone** . . . (717) 783-9681
Pass Through Business Office Director **Karen Sutsko** . . . . . (717) 346-0018

## Information Technology

Turnpike Industrial Park, 2850 Turnpike Drive, Middletown, PA 17057
Tel: (717) 787-2300  Fax: (717) 986-4767
Chief Information Officer **Ronald Wilt** . . . . . . . . . . . . . . . . (717) 772-1731
  E-mail: rwilt@pa.gov
Imaging and Document Management Director
  **Bernard "Bernie" Stakem** . . . . . . . . . . . . . . . . . . . . . (717) 787-8117
  E-mail: bstakem@state.pa.us
Information Systems Director **Mike Dailey** . . . . . . . . . . . . . (717) 787-2300

## Tax Policy

Deputy Secretary **C. Daniel Hassell** . . . . . . . . . . . . . . . . . (717) 787-4099
  Education: Carnegie Mellon MS
Board of Appeals Chairman **Lauren A. Zaccarelli** . . . . . . . (717) 787-4916
Audits Director **Jason Weimer, CPA** . . . . . . . . . . . . . . . . . (717) 783-1731
Research Director **Amy Gill** . . . . . . . . . . . . . . . . . . . . . . . (717) 787-6300

## Taxation

Deputy Secretary **John Kaschak** . . . . . . . . . . . . . . . . . . . . (717) 783-3685
Business Trust Fund Taxes Director **Matt DeFrank** . . . . . . . (717) 783-5470
Corporation Taxes Director **Thomas Bordner** . . . . . . . . . . . (717) 787-8211
Individual Taxes Director **Meggan Swisher** . . . . . . . . . . . . (717) 787-8346
Motor Fuel Taxes Director **James Dehnert** . . . . . . . . . . . . . (717) 783-9191
Taxpayer Services and Information Center Director
  **Don Bianchi** . . . . . . . . . . . . . . . . . . . . . . . . . . . . . . . . (717) 787-4573

## Pennsylvania Department of State

302 North Office Building, Harrisburg, PA 17120
Tel: (717) 787-6458  Fax: (717) 787-1734
E-mail: press@pados.dos.state.pa.us  Internet: www.dos.state.pa.us

**Fiscal Year:** 2015  **Budget:** $88,071,000

■Secretary of the Commonwealth **Pedro A. Cortés** . . . . . . . . (717) 787-8727
  E-mail: pcortes@state.pa.us
  Education: UMass (Amherst) BA; Penn State MPA;
  Dickinson Law 1999 JD
  Special Assistant to the Secretary of the
    Commonwealth **Melissa Frey** . . . . . . . . . . . . . . . . . . (717) 705-5552
Deputy Secretary for Elections and Administration
  **Marian K Schneider** . . . . . . . . . . . . . . . . . . . . . . . . . . (717) 787-3796
  Education: Pennsylvania BA; George Washington JD
Bureau of Management Information Systems Chief
  Information Officer **F. William Finnerty, Jr.** . . . . . . . . . . (717) 787-8727
  E-mail: ffinnerty@state.pa.us
  Education: Mansfield BSEd; Shippensburg MS
Chief Counsel **Timothy E. Gates** . . . . . . . . . . . . . . . . . . . . (717) 783-0736
Communications and Press Office Director
  **Adriana Arvizo** . . . . . . . . . . . . . . . . . . . . . . . . . . . . . . (717) 783-1621
                     Fax: (717) 772-4175
  E-mail: aarvizo@state.pa.us
Human Resource Director **Patrick Striggle** . . . . . . . . . . . . . (717) 787-6604
  North Office Bldg., 306, Harrisburg, PA 17120    Fax: (717) 783-0630
Legislative Affairs Office Director **Patty Dillon** . . . . . . . . . (717) 783-5279
  E-mail: pdillon@state.pa.us
Policy Office Director **Leigh Chapman** . . . . . . . . . . . . . . . . (717) 787-8727
Press Secretary **Wanda Murren** . . . . . . . . . . . . . . . . . . . . . (717) 783-1621
  E-mail: wmurren@state.pa.us

State Athletic Commission Executive Director **Greg Sirb** . . (717) 787-5720
  2601 North 3rd Street, Harrisburg, PA 17101    Fax: (717) 783-0824
  E-mail: gsirb@state.pa.us
  Education: Edinboro BA; Penn State 1985 MPA
Charitable Corporation Bureau Director **Frank Miranda** . . . (717) 783-1720
                     Fax: (717) 783-6014
Finance and Operations Bureau Director
  **Justin R. Cowan** . . . . . . . . . . . . . . . . . . . . . . . . . . . . . (717) 783-1775
                     Fax: (717) 783-2724

## Pennsylvania Department of Transportation [PennDOT]

400 North Street, Harrisburg, PA 17120
Tel: (717) 787-2838
Tel: (800) 932-4600 (Motor Vehicle/Driver License Info)
TTY: (800) 228-0676  Fax: (717) 787-1738
E-mail: ra-penndotexecutiveoffices@state.pa.us
Internet: www.dot.state.pa.us

**Employees:** 11,880  **Fiscal Year:** 2015  **Budget:** $8,135,883,000

■Secretary **Leslie S. Richards** . . . . . . . . . . . . . . . . . . . . . . (717) 787-5574
  E-mail: ra-penndotexecutiveoffices@pa.gov
  Education: Brown U
Chief Counsel **William Cressler** . . . . . . . . . . . . . . . . . . . . (717) 787-5473
  E-mail: wcressler@pa.gov
Chief Information Officer **Phil Tomassini** . . . . . . . . . . . . . . (717) 783-8428
  E-mail: ptomassini@pa.gov
Legislative Affairs Office Director **Cindy Cashman** . . . . . . (717) 787-5144
  E-mail: ccashman@state.pa.us
Policy Director **Roger J. Cohen** . . . . . . . . . . . . . . . . . . . . . (717) 787-0787
  Education: Teachers Col Columbia U 1974 BA
Press Secretary **Rich A. Kirkpatrick** . . . . . . . . . . . . . . . . . (717) 783-8800
  E-mail: rikirkpatr@pa.gov

## Administration

P.O. Box 3447, Harrisburg, PA 17105-3447
Tel: (717) 787-5628
Deputy Secretary **Suzanne H. Itzko** . . . . . . . . . . . . . . . . . . (717) 787-5628
  E-mail: sitzko@pa.gov
  Education: George Washington BA; Pennsylvania 1997 MGA
  Special Assistant **Erica Dutton** . . . . . . . . . . . . . . . . . . . (717) 705-1216
Equal Opportunity Bureau Director **Jocelyn Harper** . . . . . . (717) 787-5891
Fiscal Management Bureau Director **David L. Margolis** . . . (717) 787-5705
Human Resource Bureau Director **Christopher Norris** . . . . (717) 783-3803
Office Services Bureau Director **Diane Chamberlin** . . . . . . (717) 787-4050
  E-mail: dchamberli@pa.gov
Welcome Centers, Tourism Services Manager
  **Tiffany Brown** . . . . . . . . . . . . . . . . . . . . . . . . . . . . . . . (717) 783-3506

## Aviation

Commonwealth Keystone Building, 6th Floor, Harrisburg, PA 17120
Director **Anthony McCloskey** . . . . . . . . . . . . . . . . . . . . . . (717) 705-1200
Business Management and Administration Division Chief
  **David Bratina** . . . . . . . . . . . . . . . . . . . . . . . . . . . . . . . (717) 705-1230
  E-mail: djbratina@pa.gov

## Driver and Vehicle Services

Riverfront Office Center, 1101 South Front Street, Fourth Floor,
Harrisburg, PA 17104
Tel: (717) 787-3928  Fax: (717) 705-1046
Deputy Secretary **Kurt J. Myers** . . . . . . . . . . . . . . . . . . . . . (717) 787-3928
  Education: Kenyon BA
Driver Licensing Bureau Director **Kara Templeton** . . . . . . . (717) 787-4701
Motor Vehicles Bureau Director **Anita Wasko** . . . . . . . . . . (717) 787-2171
  E-mail: awasko@state.pa.us
Bureau of Services Director **Doug Haines** . . . . . . . . . . . . . . (717) 783-5923
  E-mail: dohaines@pa.gov
Information and Fiscal Services Office Director
  **David Rotigel** . . . . . . . . . . . . . . . . . . . . . . . . . . . . . . . . (717) 787-7713
  E-mail: drotigel@pa.gov
Risk Management Office Director **Brent Lawson** . . . . . . . . (717) 787-7740

## Highway Administration

P.O. Box 3541, Harrisburg, PA 17105-3541
Tel: (717) 787-6875

Deputy Secretary **R. Scott Christie, PE** . . . . . . . . . . . . . (717) 787-6875
Project Delivery Bureau Director **Brian Thompson, PE** . . . (717) 787-3310
Maintenance and Operations Bureau Director
  **Richard Roman** . . . . . . . . . . . . . . . . . . . . . . . . . . . (717) 787-6899
  Special Assistant **Christine Reilly** . . . . . . . . . . . . . . . . . (717) 787-9512

## Multimodal Transportation

P.O. Box 3347, Harrisburg, PA 17105-3347
Tel: (717) 787-8197

Deputy Secretary **Toby L. Fauver** . . . . . . . . . . . . . . . . . (717) 787-8197
  Special Assistant **Susan Heimberger** . . . . . . . . . . . . . . (717) 783-1941
Public Transportation Bureau Director **Danielle Spila** . . . . . (717) 783-8025
PennPorts Office Director (Acting)
  **Jennie Granger, AICP** . . . . . . . . . . . . . . . . . . . . . . . (717) 720-7448

## Planning

P.O. Box 3643, Harrisburg, PA 17105-3643
Tel: (717) 787-3154

Deputy Secretary **James D. Ritzman** . . . . . . . . . . . . . . . (717) 787-3154
  E-mail: jritzman@state.pa.us
  Education: Geneva BS
Planning and Research Bureau Director
  **Laine Heltebridle** . . . . . . . . . . . . . . . . . . . . . . . . . . (717) 787-5796
Program Development and Management Center Director
  **Larry Shifflet** . . . . . . . . . . . . . . . . . . . . . . . . . . . . (717) 787-2862
  E-mail: lshifflet@state.pa.us
Strategic Management Assistant **Doug Zimmerman** . . . . . . (717) 783-9776

## Pennsylvania Emergency Management Agency [PEMA]

2605 Interstate Drive, Harrisburg, PA 17110
Tel: (717) 651-2007  Fax: (717) 651-2040  Internet: www.pema.pa.gov

■Director **Richard D. Flinn, Jr.** . . . . . . . . . . . . . . . . . . . (717) 651-2007
  E-mail: rfinn@pa.gov
  Education: Penn State BS; Pennsylvania
Executive Deputy Director **Jeffrey Thomas** . . . . . . . . . . . (717) 651-2007
Administrative Deputy Director **Rita Rellick** . . . . . . . . . . . (717) 651-2186
  E-mail: rrellick@pa.gov
Operations Deputy Director **Martyn "Marty" Nevil** . . . . . . (717) 651-2214
9-1-1 Deputy Director **Robert F. Mateff, Sr.** . . . . . . . . . . (717) 651-2288
  Education: DeSales U BA       Fax: (717) 651-2282
State Fire Commissioner **Timothy J. Solobay** . . . . . . . . . . (717) 651-2201
  E-mail: tsolobay@pa.gov
  Education: California U (PA) 1984 BS; California Coast 1990 BS
Communications Director **Ruth Miller** . . . . . . . . . . . . . . . (717) 651-2009
  E-mail: ruthmiller@pa.gov
Chief Counsel **Nicole Bordonaro, Esq.** . . . . . . . . . . . . . . (717) 651-2010

## Pennsylvania Higher Education Assistance Agency [American Education Services]

1200 North Seventh Street, Harrisburg, PA 17102-1444
Tel: (717) 720-2575  Fax: (717) 720-3902  Internet: www.pheaa.org

▲President/Chief Executive Officer **James L. Preston** . . . . . . (717) 720-2575
  E-mail: jpreston@pheaa.org
  Executive Secretary **Lisa Gipe** . . . . . . . . . . . . . . . . . . (717) 720-2575
Senior Vice President and Program Director of FedLoan
  Servicing **Dan Weigle** . . . . . . . . . . . . . . . . . . . . . . . (717) 720-2029
  E-mail: dweigle@pheaa.org
Senior Vice President of Client Relations, Loan
  Operations, and Client Contractual Testing
  **Stephanie Martella** . . . . . . . . . . . . . . . . . . . . . . . . . (717) 720-3450
  Education: Albright BS; Duquesne MS
Senior Vice President of Public Affairs
  **Nathaniel Hench** . . . . . . . . . . . . . . . . . . . . . . . . . . (717) 720-2511
  E-mail: nhench@pheaa.org
Senior Vice President and Chief Financial Officer
  **James H. Steeley** . . . . . . . . . . . . . . . . . . . . . . . . . . (717) 270-2555

Senior Vice President and Chief Information Officer
  **Brian Lecher** . . . . . . . . . . . . . . . . . . . . . . . . . . . . . (717) 720-2615
  E-mail: blecher@pheaa.org
Senior Vice President, Chief Legal and Compliance
  Officer **Jason Swartley** . . . . . . . . . . . . . . . . . . . . . . . (717) 720-3610
  E-mail: jswartle@pheaa.org
Senior Vice President and Federal Relations Director
  **Scott E. Miller** . . . . . . . . . . . . . . . . . . . . . . . . . . . . (202) 955-0055
  1850 M Street, NW, Suite 920, Washington, DC 20036
  E-mail: smiller1@pheaa.org
Public and Media Relations Director **Keith New** . . . . . . . . (717) 720-2938
  E-mail: knew@pheaa.org

## Pennsylvania Housing Finance Agency [PHFA]

211 North Front Street, Harrisburg, PA 17101
P.O. Box 8029, Harrisburg, PA 17105-8029
Tel: (717) 780-3800  TTY: (800) 346-3597  Fax: (717) 780-4026
Internet: www.phfa.org

▲Executive Director and Chief Executive Officer
  **Brian A. Hudson, Sr., CPA, CTP** . . . . . . . . . . . . . . . (717) 780-3911
  E-mail: bhudson@phfa.org
  Education: Penn State 1977 BA
  Executive Assistant **Carrie Barnes** . . . . . . . . . . . . . . . . (717) 780-3911
Communications Manager **Scott D. Elliott** . . . . . . . . . . . . (717) 780-3800
  E-mail: selliott@pa.gov
  Education: Kutztown; U Washington 1991 MA
Chief Counsel **Rebecca L. Peace** . . . . . . . . . . . . . . . . . (717) 780-3846
Finance Director **Joseph Knopic** . . . . . . . . . . . . . . . . . . (717) 780-3837
Homeownership Programs Director **Kathryn W. Newton** . . (717) 780-3872
Information Technology Director **Kimberly A. Boal** . . . . . . (717) 780-3850
  E-mail: kboal@pa.gov
Strategic Planning and Policy Director **Bryce Maretzki** . . . . (717) 780-3912
  E-mail: bmaretzki@legis.state.pa.us

## Pennsylvania Public Utility Commission [PUC]

P.O. Box 3265, Harrisburg, PA 17105-3265
TTY: (800) 692-7380  Internet: www.puc.pa.gov

■Chairman **Gladys M. Brown** . . . . . . . . . . . . . . . . . . . . (717) 787-1031
  Term Expires: April 1, 2018       Fax: (717) 783-0698
  E-mail: gmb@pa.gov
  Education: Pittsburgh JD
■Vice Chairman **Andrew G. Place** . . . . . . . . . . . . . . . . . (717) 783-1197
  Term Expires: April 1, 2020
  E-mail: aplace@pa.gov
  Education: Pittsburgh BS; Carnegie Mellon MSPPM
■Commissioner **John F. Coleman, Jr.** . . . . . . . . . . . . . . . (717) 772-0692
  Term Expires: April 1, 2017      Fax: (717) 787-5620
  E-mail: jfc@pa.gov
■Commissioner **Robert F. Powelson** . . . . . . . . . . . . . . . . (717) 705-6767
  Term Expires: April 1, 2019      Fax: (717) 783-8698
  E-mail: rfp@pa.gov
  Education: St Joseph's U BA; Pennsylvania 2003 MGA
■Commissioner **David W. Sweet** . . . . . . . . . . . . . . . . . . (717) 783-1763
  E-mail: dasweet@pa.gov
  Education: Pennsylvania 1970 BA; Chicago 1971 MA;
  Dickinson Col 1981 JD

## Office of the Executive Director

Executive Director **Jan H. Freeman** . . . . . . . . . . . . . . . . (717) 787-1035
  E-mail: janfreeman@pa.gov

## Board of Game Commissioners

2001 Elmerton Avenue, Harrisburg, PA 17110-9797
Tel: (717) 787-4250  Fax: (717) 772-2411  E-mail: info@pgc.state.pa.us
Internet: www.pgc.state.pa.us

■President **Brian H. Hoover** (District 8) . . . . . . . . . . . . . . (717) 787-3633
  Term Expires: 2020
■Vice President **Tim Layton** (District 4) . . . . . . . . . . . . . . (717) 787-3633
  Term Expires: 2021
■Secretary **Charles E. Fox** (District 5) . . . . . . . . . . . . . . . (717) 787-3633
  Term Expires: October 15, 2020
  Education: Lycoming BA; Mansfield MA

*(continued on next page)*

---

★ Elected Official    ■ Appointed by Governor    ● Appointed by Legislature    ▲ Appointed by Board or Commission    ◆ Appointed by State Supreme Court

**EXECUTIVE BRANCH**

**Board of Game Commissioners** *continued*

■Commissioner **James R. Daley** (District 1) . . . . . . . . . . . . (717) 787-3633
　Term Expires: 2018
■Commissioner **David J. Putnam** (District 3) . . . . . . . . . . . (717) 787-3633
　Term Expires: 2017
■Commissioner **Robert Schlemmer** (District 2) . . . . . . . . . (717) 787-3633
　Term Expires: 2017
■Commissioner **Ronald A. Weaner** (District 6) . . . . . . . . . . (717) 787-3633
　Term Expires: 2016
　Education: Penn State
■Commissioner **(Vacant)** (District 7) . . . . . . . . . . . . . . . . . . (717) 787-3633

## Executive Office

▲Executive Director **R. "Matt" Hough** . . . . . . . . . . . . . . . . (717) 705-6540
　E-mail: rhough@pa.gov
　Education: West Virginia 1980 BS
North Central Regional Director **Barry Zaffuto** . . . . . . . . . (570) 398-4744
Northeast Regional Director **Daniel Figured** . . . . . . . . . . . (570) 675-1143
Northwest Regional Director **Keith Harbaugh** . . . . . . . . . . (814) 432-3188
Southcentral Regional Director **Bradley J. Myers** . . . . . . . (814) 643-1831
Southeast Regional Director **Bruce Metz** . . . . . . . . . . . . . (610) 926-3136
Southwest Regional Director **Pat Anderson** . . . . . . . . . . . . (724) 238-9523
　Education: Edinboro 1972 BS

## Board of Probation and Parole

1101 South Front Street, Suite 5100, Harrisburg, PA 17104-2517
Tel: (717) 787-5699  TTY: (717) 772-3521  Fax: (717) 705-1774
Internet: www.pbpp.state.pa.us

■Chairman **Leo L. Dunn** . . . . . . . . . . . . . . . . . . . . . . . . . . .(717) 787-5100
　Education: Penn State 1987 BS; Widener 2007 JD
■Member **Edward L. Burke** . . . . . . . . . . . . . . . . . . . . . . . . (717) 787-5699
　Education: Penn State 1981 BS
■Member **Leslie M. Grey** . . . . . . . . . . . . . . . . . . . . . . . . . (717) 787-5699
　Education: Duquesne 1986 JD
■Member **Lydia Kirkland** . . . . . . . . . . . . . . . . . . . . . . . . . (717) 787-5699
　Education: Howard U 1974 BS, 1977 JD
■Member **Craig R. McKay** . . . . . . . . . . . . . . . . . . . . . . . . (717) 787-5699
■Member **Michael C. Potteiger** . . . . . . . . . . . . . . . . . . . . (717) 787-5699
■Member **(Vacant)** . . . . . . . . . . . . . . . . . . . . . . . . . . . . . . (717) 787-5699
■Victim Advocate **Jennifer Storm** . . . . . . . . . . . . . . . . . . (717) 214-2256
　E-mail: jstorm@pa.gov
　Education: Penn State 2002 BA
Board Secretary **Kimberly Barkley** . . . . . . . . . . . . . . . . . (717) 787-5699
Chief Counsel (Acting) **Alan Robinson** . . . . . . . . . . . . . . (717) 787-8126
Communications Director **Sherry Tate** . . . . . . . . . . . . . . (717) 231-4411
　E-mail: shtate@pa.gov
Policy and Legislative Affairs Director **Mark Koch** . . . . . . (717) 787-6208
　E-mail: mkoch@pa.gov
Administrative Services Office Director **Richard Dash** . . . . (717) 787-0306
　E-mail: rdash@pa.gov
Interstate Parole Services Director **Kay Longenberger** . . . . (717) 787-5699
Interstate Probation Services Director
　**Margaret Thompson** . . . . . . . . . . . . . . . . . . . . . . . . . (717) 787-5699
Training Division Director **Gregory Young** . . . . . . . . . . . . (717) 783-7045
Sexual Offenders Assessment Board Executive Director
　**Meghan M. Dade** . . . . . . . . . . . . . . . . . . . . . . . . . . . (717) 787-5430
Central Services Bureau Director **Ryan Smith** . . . (717) 787-5699 ext. 1109
Human Resources Bureau Director **Jennifer A. Goetz** . . . . (717) 787-5699
Probation Services Bureau Director **William McDevitt** . . . . (717) 787-7461
Field Probation and Parole Supervision Deputy Executive
　Director **Daniel D. McIntyre** . . . . . . . . . . . . . . . . . . . . (717) 787-5699

## State Board of Education

333 Market Street, First Floor, Harrisburg, PA 17126-0333
Tel: (717) 787-3787  Fax: (717) 787-7306

■Chairperson **Larry A. Wittig** . . . . . . . . . . . . . . . . . . . . . (717) 787-3787
　Education: Drexel 1975 MBA
Ex-Officio Member **Gilbert R. Griffiths** . . . . . . . . . . . . . . (717) 787-3787
Executive Director **Karen Molchanow** . . . . . . . . . . . . . . . (717) 346-9449
　E-mail: kamolchano@pa.gov
Chief Executive Officer **Pedro A. Rivera** . . . . . . . . . . . . . (717) 783-9780
Administrative Officer **Stephanie Jones** . . . . . . . . . . . . . . (717) 787-3787

## Basic Education Council

■Chairperson **James E. Barker** . . . . . . . . . . . . . . . . . . . . . (717) 787-3787
■Member **Carol Aichele** . . . . . . . . . . . . . . . . . . . . . . . . . . (717) 787-3787
　Education: Cornell 1971 AB
■Member **Jay Badams** . . . . . . . . . . . . . . . . . . . . . . . . . . . (717) 787-3787
■Member **Kirk Hallett** . . . . . . . . . . . . . . . . . . . . . . . . . . . (717) 787-3787
■Member **The Honorable Maureen E. Lally-Green** . . . . . . . (717) 787-3787
　Education: Duquesne 1971 BA, 1974 JD
■Member **Mollie O'Connell Phillips** . . . . . . . . . . . . . . . . . (717) 787-3787
■Member **James R. Roebuck, Jr.** . . . . . . . . . . . . . . . . . . . (717) 787-3787
　Affiliation: Representative (District 188), Pennsylvania House of
　Representatives
　4712 Baltimore Avenue, Philadelphia, PA 19143
　Education: Virginia Union 1966 BA; Virginia 1969 MA, 1977 PhD
■Member **Colleen Sheehan** . . . . . . . . . . . . . . . . . . . . . . . (717) 787-3787
　E-mail: colleen.sheehan@villanova.edu
　Education: Eisenhower Col 1977 BA
　Member **Lloyd K. Smucker** . . . . . . . . . . . . . . . . . . . . . . (717) 787-3787
　Education: Lebanon Valley; Franklin & Marshall
■Member **Karen Farmer White** . . . . . . . . . . . . . . . . . . . . (717) 787-3787
■Senior Student Member **Joshita Varshney** . . . . . . . . . . . (717) 787-3787
　Term Expires: May 2017
■Junior Student Member **Shirlann Harmon** . . . . . . . . . . . (717) 787-3787
　Note: Effective July 2016

## Higher Education Council

■Chairperson **James Grandon** . . . . . . . . . . . . . . . . . . . . . (717) 787-3787
■Member **James R. Agras** . . . . . . . . . . . . . . . . . . . . . . . . (717) 787-3787
　Term Expires: 2020
■Member **Nicole Carnicella** . . . . . . . . . . . . . . . . . . . . . . (717) 787-3787
　Term Expires: 2018
■Member **Andrew E. Dinniman** . . . . . . . . . . . . . . . . . . . . (717) 787-3787
　E-mail: andy@pasenate.com
　Education: Connecticut 1966 BA; Maryland 1969 MA;
　Penn State 1978 EdD
■Member **Sandra Dungee Glenn** . . . . . . . . . . . . . . . . . . . (717) 787-3787
　Term Expires: 2015
　Education: Penn State 1978 BS
■Member **Dr. Pamela J. Gunter-Smith** . . . . . . . . . . . . . . . (717) 787-3787
　Term Expires: 2020
　Education: Spelman BS; Emory PhD
■Member **Jonathan Peri** . . . . . . . . . . . . . . . . . . . . . . . . . (717) 787-3787
■Member **Stanley E. "Stan" Saylor** . . . . . . . . . . . . . . . . . (717) 787-3787
■Member **Craig Snider** . . . . . . . . . . . . . . . . . . . . . . . . . . (717) 787-3787
■Member **A. Lee Williams** . . . . . . . . . . . . . . . . . . . . . . . . (717) 787-3787
■Senior Student Member **Lavinia Soliman** . . . . . . . . . . . . (717) 787-3787
　Term Expires: 2017
■Junior Student Member **Andrew Ahr** . . . . . . . . . . . . . . . (717) 787-3787
　Note: Effective July 2016

## State Police

1800 Elmerton Avenue, Harrisburg, PA 17110-9758
Tel: (717) 787-5558  Fax: (717) 787-2948  Internet: www.psp.state.pa.us

■Commissioner **Col. Tyree C. Blocker** . . . . . . . . . . . . . . . (717) 787-5558
Executive Officer **Capt. Richard T. Ferrara** . . . . . . . . . . . (717) 772-6928
Chief Counsel **Joanna N. Reynolds** . . . . . . . . . . . . . . . . (717) 783-5568
Municipal Police Officer's Education and
　Training Commission Executive Director
　**Major Adam M. Kisthardt** . . . . . . . . . . . . . . . . . . . . . (717) 346-7749

## Administration

■Administration and Professional Responsibility Deputy
　Commissioner **Lisa Christie** . . . . . . . . . . . . . . . . . . . . (717) 346-9122
Equal Employment Opportunity Office Director
　**Capt. Wendell B. Morris** . . . . . . . . . . . . . . . . . . . . . . (717) 787-7220
　E-mail: wmorris@pa.gov
Human Resources Bureau Director **Kim Studenroth** . . . . . (717) 783-5533
Training and Education Bureau Director
　**William P. White** . . . . . . . . . . . . . . . . . . . . . . . . . . . (717) 533-9111
　175 East Hershey Park Drive, Hershey, PA 17033

## Operations

■Deputy Commissioner (Acting)
　**Major William A. Horgas** . . . . . . . . . . . . . . . . . . . . . . (717) 787-7219

---

★ Elected Official　　■ Appointed by Governor　　● Appointed by Legislature　　▲ Appointed by Board or Commission　　◆ Appointed by State Supreme Court

Criminal Investigation Bureau Director
**Major David e. Ralph** . . . . . . . . . . . . . . . . . . . . . . . . . . . . (717) 783-5524
Emergency and Special Operations Bureau Director
**Major Keith A. Stone** . . . . . . . . . . . . . . . . . . . . . . . . . . . (717) 508-0035
171 East Hershey Park Drive, Hershey, PA 17033-0444
P.O. Box 444, Hershey, PA 17033-0444
Liquor Control Enforcement Bureau Director
**Major Thomas P. Butler** . . . . . . . . . . . . . . . . . . . . . . . . . (717) 540-7410
3655 Vartan Way, Harrisburg, PA 17110
Patrol Bureau Director **Major Edward Hoke** . . . . . . . . . . . (717) 772-1823

## Staff

■Deputy Commissioner **Stephen A. Bucar** . . . . . . . . . . . . . (717) 783-5567
E-mail: sbucar@pa.gov
Forensic Services Bureau Director **Marshall A. Martin** . . . . (717) 783-5548
E-mail: mmartin@pa.gov
Records and Identification Bureau Director (Acting)
**Major Scott C. Price** . . . . . . . . . . . . . . . . . . . . . . . . . . . . . (717) 783-5588
Research and Development Bureau Director
**Capt. Patrick D. Brinkley** . . . . . . . . . . . . . . . . . . . . . . . . . (717) 783-5536
Staff Services Bureau Director **Marc Infantino** . . . . . . . . . (717) 783-5483
E-mail: minfantino@state.pa.us
Communication and Information Technology Bureau
Director **Michael C. Shevlin** . . . . . . . . . . . . . . . . . . . . . . (717) 787-8596
E-mail: mshevlin@pa.gov
Communication Bureau Director
**Major Diane M. Stackhouse** . . . . . . . . . . . . . . . . . . . . . . . (717) 787-8596
E-mail: distackhou@pa.gov

## Office of the Lieutenant Governor

200 Capitol Building, 501 North 3rd Street, Harrisburg, PA 17120
Tel: (717) 787-3300  Fax: (717) 787-0150
Internet: www.ltgovernor.state.pa.us

★Lieutenant Governor **Michael J. "Mike" Stack III** (D) . . . . (717) 787-2500
Term Expires: 2019
E-mail: mstack@pa.gov
Education: LaSalle Extension U 1987 BA; Villanova 1992 JD
Career: Senator, Pennsylvania Senate (2012-2015)
Chief of Staff **Matt Franchak** . . . . . . . . . . . . . . . . . . . . . . . (717) 214-3681
Special Assistant **Anthony Costa** . . . . . . . . . . . . . . . . . . . . (717) 798-5826
Special Assistant **Juvencio Gonzalez** . . . . . . . . . . . . . . . . . (717) 798-4863
Special Assistant **Dylan McGarry** . . . . . . . . . . . . . . . . . . . (717) 787-5956
Press Secretary **Gary Tuma** . . . . . . . . . . . . . . . . . . . . . . . . . (717) 787-2088
E-mail: gtuma@pa.gov
Executive Assistant **Eric Pettis** . . . . . . . . . . . . . . . . . . . . . . (717) 787-3300

## Office of the Attorney General

Strawberry Square, 16th Floor, Harrisburg, PA 17120
Tel: (717) 787-3391  Fax: (717) 787-8242

★Attorney General **Kathleen Granahan Kane** (D) . . . . . . . (717) 787-3391
Term Expires: 2017
Education: Scranton 1988 BS; Temple 1993 JD
First Deputy Attorney General **Bruce Beemer** . . . . . . . . . . . (717) 787-3391
Deputy Attorney General **Thomas P. Cummings III** . . . . . . (570) 963-4913
Solicitor General **Bruce L. Castor, Jr.** . . . . . . . . . . . . . . . . (717) 787-3391
Education: Lafayette 1983 AB; Washington and Lee 1986 JD
Chief of Staff (Acting) **Jonathan A. Duecker** . . . . . . . . . . . (717) 787-3391
Education: Wisconsin JD
Government Affairs (Acting) **Alyssa L. Weinhold** . . . . . . . (717) 783-3085
Communications Director **(Vacant)** . . . . . . . . . . . . . . . . . . . (717) 787-5211
Deputy Press Secretary **Jeffrey A. Johnson** . . . . . . . . . . . . (717) 787-5211
Deputy Press Secretary **Cathryn Hinesley** . . . . . . . . . . . . . (717) 787-5211
E-mail: chinesley@legis.state.pa.us
Civil Law Division Executive Deputy Attorney General
**Robert A. Mulle** . . . . . . . . . . . . . . . . . . . . . . . . . . . . . . . . . (717) 787-1100
Criminal Law Division Executive Deputy Attorney
General **Lawrence Cherba** . . . . . . . . . . . . . . . . . . . . . . . . . (717) 787-2100
Public Protection Division Executive Deputy Attorney
General **James A. Donahue III** . . . . . . . . . . . . . . . . . . . . . . (717) 787-9716
Education and Outreach Director **Renee George Martin** . . (717) 787-3391
Management Services Director **Shari L. McGraw** . . . . . . . . (717) 787-4499

Charitable Trusts and Organization Section Chief
**Mark Pacella** . . . . . . . . . . . . . . . . . . . . . . . . . . . . . . . . . . . . (717) 787-9716
Education: Pittsburgh 1981 BA; Antioch Law 1984 JD
Consumer Advocate (Acting) **Tanya McCloskey** . . . . . . . . (717) 783-5048
Webmaster **Abhisek Vikram** . . . . . . . . . . . . . . . . . . . . . . . (717) 705-7301
E-mail: avikram@attorneygeneral.gov
Communications Advisor **Charles "Chuck" Ardo** . . . . . . . (717) 787-5211
E-mail: charlesardo@attorneygeneral.gov
Education: Ohio State

## Department of the Auditor General

229 Finance Building, Harrisburg, PA 17120-0018
Tel: (717) 787-2543  Fax: (717) 783-4407
E-mail: auditorgen@auditorgen.state.pa.us
Internet: www.auditorgen.state.pa.us

**Fiscal Year:** 2015  **Budget:** $320,469,000

★Auditor General **Eugene A. DePasquale, JD** (D) . . . . . . . . (717) 787-2543
Term Expires: January 2017
Education: Wooster BA; Pittsburgh MA; Widener JD
Chief of Staff **Elizabeth Gerloff "Liz" Wagenseller** . . . . . (717) 787-2543
E-mail: lwagenseller@auditorgen.state.pa.us
Administration Deputy Auditor General and Human
Resources Director **Martin Rowan** . . . . . . . . . . . . . . . . . . (717) 787-2543
E-mail: mrowan@auditorgen.state.pa.us
Audits Deputy Auditor General **John Lori** . . . . . . . . . . . . . (717) 705-4126
External Affairs Deputy Auditor General
**Elizabeth Gerloff "Liz" Wagenseller** . . . . . . . . . . . . . . . (717) 787-2543
Budget and Finance Office Director **Jennifer Boger** . . . . . . (717) 787-3636
Chief Counsel **Victoria "Vicci" Madden** . . . . . . . . . . . . . . (717) 787-4546
Communications Director **Barry Ciccocioppo** . . . . . . . . . . (717) 787-1381
E-mail: bciccocioppo@auditorgen.state.pa.us
Press Secretary **Susan Woods** . . . . . . . . . . . . . . . . . . . . . . . (717) 787-1381

## Department of Education

333 Market Street, Harrisburg, PA 17126
Tel: (717) 783-6788  TTY: (717) 783-8445  Fax: (717) 783-4517
Fax: (717) 787-7222  Internet: www.pde.state.pa.us

**Employees:** 534  **Fiscal Year:** 2015  **Budget:** $15,816,408,000

■Secretary **Pedro A. Rivera** . . . . . . . . . . . . . . . . . . . . . . . . . (717) 783-9780
E-mail: privera@pa.gov
Executive Deputy Secretary **Dr. David Volkman** . . . . . . . . (717) 783-9780
Chief Counsel **Gregory G. Schwab** . . . . . . . . . . . . . . . . . . . (717) 787-5500
Education: Catholic U 2001 BA; Maryland Law 2004 JD
Press Secretary **Nicole Reigelman** . . . . . . . . . . . . . . . . . . . (717) 705-8642
E-mail: nreigelman@pa.gov
Government Relations Director **Angela Fitterer** . . . . . . . . . (717) 787-7575
Policy Director **Beth Olanoff** . . . . . . . . . . . . . . . . . . . . . . . (717) 783-6828
E-mail: bolanoff@pa.gov

## Administration Office

Deputy Secretary **Deborah A. Reeves** . . . . . . . . . . . . . . . . . (717) 772-4789
Budget and Fiscal Management Director
**Danielle Mariano** . . . . . . . . . . . . . . . . . . . . . . . . . . . . . . . . (717) 787-7808
Human Resources Bureau Director **Diana Hershey** . . . . . . (717) 787-4417
Chief Information Officer **Kim Ebert** . . . . . . . . . . . . . . . . . (717) 346-3291
E-mail: kwebert1@alum.villanova.edu
Management Services Bureau Director **Eric Chubb** . . . . . . . (717) 783-9791
E-mail: echubb@state.pa.us
Education Technology Director **(Vacant)** . . . . . . . . . . . . . . . (717) 346-3291

## Commonwealth Libraries

Tel: (717) 787-2646  Internet: www.statelibrary.state.pa.us

Deputy Secretary/State Librarian **Glenn Miller** . . . . . . . . . . (717) 783-2466
Library Development Information Technology Advisor
**Brian Dawson** . . . . . . . . . . . . . . . . . . . . . . . . . . . . . . . . . . (717) 214-4047
State Library Bureau Director **Alice Lubrecht** . . . . . . . . . . . (717) 783-5968
Division Advisory and Outreach Services Chief **(Vacant)** . . (717) 783-5737

★ Elected Official   ■ Appointed by Governor   ● Appointed by Legislature   ▲ Appointed by Board or Commission   ◆ Appointed by State Supreme Court

## Office of Child Development and Early Learning [OCDEL]

333 Market Street, Harrisburg, PA 17126
Tel: (717) 346-9320

**Note:** The Office of Child Development and Early Learning is jointly overseen by the Department of Public Welfare and the Department of Education. The office is located within the Department of Education.

Deputy Secretary **Michelle Figlar** . . . . . . . . . . . . . . . . . . . . (717) 346-9320

## Office of Elementary/Secondary Education

Deputy Secretary **Matthew Stem** . . . . . . . . . . . . . . . . . . . . (717) 787-2127
Career and Technical Education Bureau Director
  **Lee Burket** . . . . . . . . . . . . . . . . . . . . . . . . . . . . . . . . . . . . (717) 787-5530
Teaching and Learning Bureau Director **(Vacant)** . . . . . . . . (717) 787-8913

## School Leadership and Teacher Quality

Director **Wilfredo Del Pilar** . . . . . . . . . . . . . . . . . . . . . . . . (717) 772-4737
  E-mail: widelpilar@pa.gov
  Education: Chapman 1995 BA; Cal State (Dominguez) 2007 MEd; Penn State 2013 PhD

## Treasury Department

129 Finance Building, Harrisburg, PA 17120-0018
Tel: (717) 787-2465  Tel: (800) 222-2046 (Bureau of Unclaimed Property)
Tel: (800) 440-4000 (Pennsylvania 529 College Savings Program)

**Fiscal Year:** 2014-2015  **Budget:** $1,146,936,000

★State Treasurer **Timothy A. "Tim" Reese** . . . . . . . . . . . . . (717) 787-2465
  Term Expires: January 17, 2017
  E-mail: treasurerreese@patreasury.gov
  Education: Temple 1987 AS, 1990 BS
Chief of Staff **Charlotte McKines** . . . . . . . . . . . . . . . . . . . . (717) 787-2465
  E-mail: cmckines@patreasury.gov
Deputy Chief of Staff **(Vacant)** . . . . . . . . . . . . . . . . . . . . . . (717) 787-2465
Chief Investment Officer **Sandy Leopold** . . . . . . . . . . . . . . (717) 787-2465
Communications Director **Scott Sloat** . . . . . . . . . . . . . . . . (717) 787-2465
  E-mail: ssloat@patreasury.gov
Chief Counsel **Christopher B. Craig, Esq.** . . . . . . . . . . . . . (717) 787-2465
Chief Administrative Officer **Mark Lavelle** . . . . . . . . . . . . . (717) 783-6098
  E-mail: mdlavelle@patreasury.gov
Chief Information Officer **PN Narayanan, PMP** . . . . . . . . . (717) 787-8726
  E-mail: pn@patreasury.gov
External Affairs Deputy State Treasurer
  **Doug K. Rohanna** . . . . . . . . . . . . . . . . . . . . . . . . . . . . . . (717) 787-2991
  Education: Waynesburg Col BBA
Fiscal Operations Deputy State Treasurer and Senior
  Advisor for Policy **Keith Welks, Esq.** . . . . . . . . . . . . . . . . (717) 772-1830

## Pennsylvania Turnpike Commission [PTC]

P.O. Box 67676, Harrisburg, PA 17106-7676
Tel: (717) 939-9551  TTY: (800) 331-3414  Fax: (717) 986-9649
E-mail: ptccustsrv@paturnpike.com  Internet: www.paturnpike.com

■Chairman **Sean F. Logan** . . . . . . . . . . . . . . . . . . . . . . . . . (717) 939-9551
  Education: Pittsburgh 1993 BA                    Fax: (717) 986-9686
■Vice Chairman **William K. Lieberman** . . . . . . . . . . . . . . . (717) 939-9551
  E-mail: wliebm@paturnpike.com                   Fax: (717) 939-9686
■Secretary and Treasurer **Pasquale T. Deon, Sr.** . . . . . . . . (717) 939-9551
  E-mail: pdeon@paturnpike.com                    Fax: (717) 986-9686
■Commissioner **Barry T. Drew, Esq.** . . . . . . . . . . . . . . . . . (717) 939-9551
  Education: Western New England JD
■Commissioner **Leslie S. Richards** . . . . . . . . . . . . . . . . . . (717) 986-9681
                                                   Fax: (717) 986-8768
■Commissioner **(Vacant)** . . . . . . . . . . . . . . . . . . . . . . . . . (717) 939-9551
                                                   Fax: (717) 986-8768
Chief Executive Officer **Mark Compton** . . . . . . . . . . . . . . (717) 939-9551
  E-mail: mcompton@paturnpike.com                 Fax: (717) 986-9653

▲Inspector General **Ray A. Morrow** . . . . . . . . . . . . . . . . . . (717) 939-9551
  E-mail: ramorrow@pa.gov
Director of Policy and External Affairs **Stacia Ritter** . . . . . (717) 939-9551
                                                   Fax: (717) 986-9686

---

★ Elected Official  ■ Appointed by Governor  ● Appointed by Legislature  ▲ Appointed by Board or Commission  ◆ Appointed by State Supreme Court

# Puerto Rico

Tel: (787) 721-7000 (Governor)

**Number of U.S. Congressional Delegates:** 1 nonvoting Resident Commissioner at Large
**Governor's Term:** 4 years  **Legislature Description:** Legislative Assembly - 27 member Senate; 51 member House of Representatives; Term - Senate 4 years, House 4 years  **Next Election:** Governor November 2016; Legislature November 8, 2016  **Official Name:** Commonwealth of Puerto Rico
**Nickname:** Island of Enchantment  **Motto:** Joannes Est Nomen Ejus (John Is His Name)

**Population:** 3,474,182 (2015)

## Office of the Governor

P.O. Box 9020082, San Juan, PR 00902-0082
Tel: (787) 721-7000  Fax: (787) 721-5072

**Alejandro Javier García Padilla**
Governor

Note: On December 14, 2015, Governor Alejandro García Padilla announced he will not seek reelection to the Office of the Governor in 2016.
Began Service: January 2, 2013
Term Expires: January 2017
Date of Birth: August 3, 1971
Education: Puerto Rico BA; Inter American JD
Religion: Catholic
Career: Secretary, Consumer Affairs Department, Office of the Governor, Commonwealth of Puerto Rico (2005-2007); State Senator (PDP-PR, At-Large), Puerto Rico Senate (2009-2013)

★ Governor **Alejandro Javier García Padilla** (PDP) . . . . . . . (787) 725-7234
Chief of Staff **Victor Suárez Meléndez** . . . . . . . . . . . . . . . (787) 721-7000
  Education: Puerto Rico BChE, MEM;
  Pontifical Catholic (Puerto Rico) JD
■ Secretary for Public Affairs
  **Jesus Manuel González Ortiz** . . . . . . . . . . . . . . . . . . . . (787) 721-7000
Communications Director **Jose Javier Diaz** . . . . . (787) 721-7000 ext. 2410

## Puerto Rico Federal Affairs Administration [PRFAA]

1100 17th Street, NW, Suite 800, Washington, DC 20036
Tel: (202) 778-0710  Fax: (202) 778-0721  E-mail: info@prfaa.pr.gov

Executive Director **Juan E. Hernández** . . . . . . . . . . . . . . . (202) 778-0710
  E-mail: info@prfaa.pr.gov
Legislative Affairs Director **Patrick Cavanagh** . . . . . . . . . . (202) 778-0710
Intergovernmental Affairs Director **Ricard Alfaro** . . . . . . . . (202) 778-0710
Senior Community Officer **Reyes Rodriguez** . . . . . . . . . . . (212) 252-7300
  135 West 50th Street, 22nd Floor,                Fax: (212) 726-9957
  New York, NY 10020

## Office of Management and Budget [OMB]

P.O. Box 9023228, San Juan, PR 00902-3228
Tel: (787) 725-9420  Fax: (787) 722-0299

■ Director **Luis Cruz** . . . . . . . . . . . . . . . . . . . . . . . . . . . . (787) 725-9420
  E-mail: lfcruz@ogp.pr.gov

## Agriculture Department

P.O. Box 10163, San Juan, PR 00908-1163
Fax: (787) 723-8512  Internet: www.agricultura.gobierno.pr

■ Secretary **Myrna Comas Pagán** . . . . . . . . . . . . . . . . . . . . (787) 722-0291
  E-mail: mcomas@agricultura.pr.gov

## Consumer Affairs Department

P.O. Box 41059, San Juan, PR 00940-1059
Fax: (787) 726-5707  Internet: www.daco.gobierno.pr

■ Secretary **Nery Adames Soto** . . . . . . . . . . . . . . . . . . . . . (787) 722-7555
  E-mail: nadames@daco.gobierno.pr

## Corrections and Rehabilitation Department

P.O. Box 71308, San Juan, PR 00936
Fax: (787) 792-7677

■ Secretary **José Negrón Fernandez** . . . . . . . . . . . (787) 273-6464 ext. 5909

## Economic Development and Commerce Department

P.O. Box 362350, San Juan, PR 00936-2350
Internet: www.pridco.com

■ Secretary **Alberto Bacó Bagué** . . . . . . . . . . . . . (787) 765-2900 ext. 2113
  E-mail: secretario@ddec.pr.gov              Fax: (787) 753-4094
  Education: Puerto Rico 1979 BBA, 1984 JD
■ Industrial Development Company Executive
  Director **Antonio Medina Comas** . . . . . . . . . . . (787) 758-4747 ext. 4700
  E-mail: antonio.medina@pridco.pr.gov            Fax: (787) 764-1415
  Education: Rensselaer Poly BS, ME; Pennsylvania 1999 MBA
■ Tourism Company Executive Director
  **Ingrid Rivera Rocafort** . . . . . . . . . . . . . . . . . . (787) 721-2400 ext. 2005
  P.O. Box 902-3960, San Juan, PR 00902-3960        Fax: (787) 722-6238
  E-mail: ingrid.rivera@tourism.pr.gov
Trade Company Executive Director **Francisco Chévere** . . . (787) 294-0101
  P.O. Box 195009, Hato Rey, PR 00918
  Education: Georgetown; Pennsylvania JD

## Puerto Rico Tourism Company

Edif. La Princesa #2, Paseo La Princesa, Old San Juan, PR 00902
PO Box 9023960, San Juan, PR 00902-3960
Tel: (787) 721-2898  Fax: (787) 722-6238
Internet: www.gotopuertorico.com

Executive Director **Ingrid Rivera Rocafort** . . . . . . . . . . . . (787) 721-2898

## Education Department

P.O. Box 190759, San Juan, PR 00919-0759
Fax: (787) 250-0275  Internet: www.de.gobierno.pr

■ Secretary **Rafael Román-Melendez** . . . . . . . . . . . . . . . . . (787) 759-2000
                                              Fax: (787) 281-0999
GED Administrator **Luis Ruiz** . . . . . . . . . . . . . . . . . . . . . (787) 773-4881
  E-mail: ruiz_l@de.gobierno.pr              Tel: (787) 773-4880
                                              Tel: (787) 773-4884

## Department of the Family

P.O. Box 11398, San Juan, PR 00910-1398
Fax: (787) 294-0732

■ Secretary **Idalia Colón Rondón** . . . . . . . . . . . . . . . . . . . (787) 294-4900
  Education: Puerto Rico 1999 BA
Socioeconomic Development of the Family,
  Director **Marta Elsa Fernandez** . . . . . . . . . . . . (787) 289-7600 ext. 2700
  E-mail: mefernandez@adsef.pr.gov              Tel: (787) 289-7645

*(continued on next page)*

---

★ Elected Official    ■ Appointed by Governor    ● Appointed by Legislature    ▲ Appointed by Board or Commission    ◆ Appointed by State Supreme Court

EXECUTIVE BRANCH

**Department of the Family** *continued*

Administration for Child Support, Director
**Rosabelle Padín Batista** . . . . . . . . . . . . . . . . . . . . . . . . (787) 294-4900
   E-mail: rosabelle.batista@pr.gov
Administration for the Care and Development of
Children, Director **Olga Bernardy** . . . . . . . . . . . . . . . . (787) 294-4900
   E-mail: obernardy@acuden.pr.gov

# Health Department
P.O. Box 70184, San Juan, PR 00936-8184
P.O. Box 11854, Fernandez Juncos Station, San Juan, PR 00910 (Vital Records)
Tel: (787) 765-2929 (Vital Records)  Fax: (787) 274-3307
Internet: www.salud.gov.pr

■Secretary (Interim) **Dr. Ana Rius, MD** . . . . . . . . .(787) 765-2929 ext. 3376
   E-mail: ana.rius@pr.gov
Medicaid Executive Director **Ricardo Colon-Padilla** . . . . . .(787) 765-2929
   E-mail: ricolon@salud.pr.gov
Demographic Registry Director
**Wanda C. Llovet Diaz** . . . . . . . . . . . . . . . . .(787) 767-9120 ext. 2402
   171 Quisqueya Street, San Juan, PR 00910        Tel: (787) 767-9120
   P.O. Box 11854, San Juan, PR 00917                            ext. 2406
                                                            Tel: (787) 767-9120
                                                                       ext. 2415
                                                             Fax: (787) 753-5003
Medicaid Program Operational Director **(Vacant)** . . . . . . . .(787) 765-2929

# Housing Department
P.O. Box 21365, San Juan, PR 00928-1365
Fax: (787) 758-9263  Internet: www.vivienda.gobierno.pr

■Secretary **Alberto Lastra Power** . . . . . . . . . . . . . . (787) 274-2527 ext. 6403
   E-mail: alberto.power@pr.gov
   Education: Cornell 1993 BARC
■Public Housing Administrator
**Gabriel Lopez Arrieta** . . . . . . . . . . . . . . . . . . . .(787) 274-2527 ext. 6403
   E-mail: gabriel.arrieta@pr.gov
   Education: Puerto Rico 2008 MBA

# Justice Department
P.O. Box 909192, San Juan, PR 00902-9192
Fax: (787) 724-4770  E-mail: webmail@justicia.pr.gov
Internet: www.justicia.gobierno.pr

■Attorney General **César R. Miranda** . . . . . . . . . . (787) 721-2900 ext. 2747
   E-mail: cmiranda@justicia.pr.gov
Director **Obdulio Melendez Ramos, JD** . . . . . . (787) 721-2900 ext. 2747

# Labor and Human Resources Department
Prudencio Rivera Martinez Building, 505 Avenue Mu-01noz Rivera,
21st Floor, Hato Rey, PR 00918
P.O. Box 195540, Hato Rey, PR 00919-5540
Fax: (787) 753-9550

■Secretary **Vance Thomas** . . . . . . . . . . . . . . . . . . . . . . .(787) 754-2119
   E-mail: vthomas@trabajo.pr.gov              Tel: (787) 754-2120
                                                            Fax: (787) 753-9550

# Natural and Environmental Resources Department
P.O. Box 366147, San Juan, PR 00936
Fax: (787) 999-2303  Internet: www.drna.gobierno.pr
■Secretary **Carmen R. Guerrero Pérez** . . . . . . . . . . . . . . . (787) 999-2200

# Police of Puerto Rico
P.O. Box 70166, San Juan, PR 00936-8166
Fax: (787) 781-0080
■Superintendent **Col. Jose Caldero Lopez** . . . . . . . . . . . . . .(787) 792-0002
   E-mail: jlopez@cmpr.pr.gov

# Recreation and Sports Department
P.O. Box 9023207, San Juan, PR 00902-3207
Fax: (787) 721-8318
■Secretary **Ramón Enrique Orta Rodríguez** . . . . . . . . . . . .(787) 721-8259
   E-mail: secretario@drd.gobierno.pr

# State Department
P.O. Box 9023271, San Juan, PR 00902-3271
Fax: (787) 722-2684  Internet: www.estado.gobierno.pr
■Secretary of State **Dr. David Enrique Bernier Rivera** . . . . .(787) 722-2121
   E-mail: secretario@estado.gobierno.pr
   Education: U Puerto Rico BS; Puerto Rico MD

# Transportation and Public Works Department
P.O. Box 41269, San Juan, PR 00940-1269
Fax: (787) 728-8963  Internet: www.dtop.gov.pr
■Secretary **Miguel Torres-Diaz** . . . . . . . . . . . . . . . . . . . . . (787) 725-7112
   E-mail: migueltorres@dtop.gov.pr              Tel: (787) 729-8714
   Education: Poly U Puerto Rico 1996 BSCE, 2003 MScE

# Highways and Transportation Authority
Executive Director **Javier E. Ramos Hernandez** . . . . . . . .(787) 721-7000

# Treasury Department
P.O. Box 9024140, San Juan, PR 00902-4140
Fax: (787) 724-4037  Internet: http://hacienda.gobierno.pr
■Secretary **Juan C. Zaragoza Gómez** . . . . . . . . . . . . . . . . . (787) 722-0216
   E-mail: jzaragoza@hacienda.pr.gov

# Emergency Management Agency
P.O. Box 194140, San Juan, PR 00919-4140
Fax: (787) 775-1202  Internet: www.manejodeemergencias.pr.gov
■Executive Director **Angel Crespo Ortiz** . . . . . . . (787) 724-0124 ext. 40075
                                                            Tel: (787) 354-4815

# Office of the Financial Institutions Commissioner
P.O. Box 11855, San Juan, PR 00910-3855
Fax: (787) 723-3131
■Commissioner **Rafael Blanco, Esq.** . . . . . . . . . . . . . . . . . . .(787) 723-8004
   E-mail: rblanco@ocif.gobierno.pr

# Environmental Quality Board
P.O. Box 11488, San Juan, PR 00910-1488
Fax: (787) 767-4861
**Employees:** 497
■Chairman **Weldin Fernando Ortiz Franco** . . . . . . . . . . . . .(787) 767-8056
   E-mail: weldinortiz@jca.gobierno.pr

# Planning Board
P.O. Box 41119, San Juan, PR 00940-1119
Fax: (787) 268-6858  Internet: www.jp.gobierno.pr
■President **Luis Garcia Pelatti** . . . . . . . . . . . . . . . .(787) 723-6200 ext. 4693
   E-mail: garcia_l@jp.pr.gov
   Education: Puerto Rico BA, MEc

# Government Development Bank [GDB]
P.O. Box 42001, San Juan, PR 00940-2001
Fax: (787) 721-1443  Internet: www.gdb-pur.com
■President **Melba Acosta Febo** . . . . . . . . . . . . . . . . . . . . . . .(787) 722-3760
   E-mail: melba.acosta@bgfpr.com
Senior Advisor to the President **(Vacant)** . . . . . . . . . . . . . . . (787) 721-7000

# National Guard
P.O. Box 9023786, San Juan, PR 00902-3786
Fax: (787) 723-6360
■Adjutant General **Martha Carcaña Cross** . . . . . . . . . . . . . .(787) 289-1400

---

★ Elected Official    ■ Appointed by Governor    ● Appointed by Legislature    ▲ Appointed by Board or Commission    ◆ Appointed by State Supreme Court

# Rhode Island

Tel: (401) 222-2000 (Governnment Information Line)  Internet: www.ri.gov

**Number of U.S. Congressional Delegates:** 2 Senators; 2 Representatives  **Governor's Term:** 4 years
**Legislature Description:** General Assembly - 38 member Senate; 75 member House of Representatives;
Term - Senate 2 years, House 2 years  **Next Election:** Governor November 2018; Legislature November
2016  **Number of Electoral Votes:** 4  **Official Name:** State of Rhode Island and Providence Plantations
(red island - for its red clay)  **Nickname:** Little Rhody; Ocean State  **Motto:** Hope

**Population:** 1,056,298 (2015); Rank 43  **Fiscal Year:** 2015  **Budget:** $8,540,000,000

## Office of the Governor

82 Smith Street, Providence, RI 02903-1196
Tel: (401) 222-2080  E-mail: governor@governor.ri.gov

**Fiscal Year:** 2015  **Budget:** $4,402,000

**Gina Marie Raimondo**
Governor

Began Service: January 6, 2015
Term Expires: January 2019
Date of Birth: May 17, 1971
Education: Harvard; Oxford (UK) PhD;
Yale 1998 JD
Home: Providence
Career: Chair, Refunding Bond Authority, State
of Rhode Island; General Treasurer, Office of
the General Treasurer Gina Raimondo, State of
Rhode Island (2011-2015)

★Governor **Gina Marie Raimondo** (D) . . . . . . . . . . . . . . . . . (401) 222-2080
   E-mail: gina.raimondo@governor.ri.gov
Chief of Staff **Stephen Neuman, JD** . . . . . . . . . . . . . . . (401) 222-2080
   E-mail: stephen.neuman@governor.ri.gov
   Education: Missouri (St Louis) BA; Washington U (MO) JD
   Special Assistant to the Chief of Staff
   **Miellette McFarlane** . . . . . . . . . . . . . . . . . . . (401) 222-2080
      E-mail: miellette.mcfarlane@governor.ri.gov
Deputy Chief of Staff **Eric Beane** . . . . . . . . . . . . . . . . . (401) 222-2080
   E-mail: eric.beane@governor.ri.gov
Deputy Chief of Staff **Kevin Gallagher** . . . . . . . . . . . . . (401) 222-2080
   E-mail: kevin.gallagher@governor.ri.gov
Deputy Chief of Staff **Lisa Vura-Weis** . . . . . . . . . . . . . (401) 222-2080
   E-mail: lisavuraweis@governor.ri.gov
Special Assistant to the Governor **Ronald DeSiderato** . . . . (401) 222-2080
   E-mail: ronald.desiderato@governor.ri.gov
Special Assistant to the Governor **Jason Natareno** . . . . . . (401) 222-2080
   E-mail: jason.natareno@governor.ri.gov
Appointments Director **Meredith Curren** . . . . . . . . . . . . (401) 222-2080
   E-mail: meredith.curren@governor.ri.gov
   Education: Smith BA; Columbia MBA
Legislative Director **R. David Cruise** . . . . . . . . . . . . . . (401) 222-2080
   E-mail: david.cruise@governor.ri.gov
Office Director **Matthew J. "Matt" Bucci** . . . . . . . . . . . (401) 222-2080
   E-mail: matthew.bucci@governor.ri.gov
   Education: Quinnipiac 2005 BA
Principal Project Manager/Administrative Assistant
   **Dana Wilson** . . . . . . . . . . . . . . . . . . . . . . . (401) 222-2080
   E-mail: dana.wilson@governor.ri.gov
Scheduler **Kelly Harris** . . . . . . . . . . . . . . . . . . . . . (401) 222-2080
   E-mail: kelly.harris@governor.ri.gov
Administrative Assistant **Rebecca Castriotta** . . . . . . . . . . (401) 222-2080
   E-mail: rebecca.castriotta@governor.ri.gov
Office Manager **Jennifer Fondeur** . . . . . . . . . . . . . . . (401) 222-2080
   E-mail: jennifer.fonduer@governor.ri.gov
Constituent Services Associate **Matthew Golderese** . . . . . . (401) 222-2080
   E-mail: matthew.golderese@governor.ri.gov
Public Engagement Director **Gabriel F. Amo, Jr.** . . . . . . . (401) 222-2080
   E-mail: gabe.amo@governor.ri.gov

Policy Advisor **Keshav Poddar** . . . . . . . . . . . . . . . . . . (401) 222-2080
   E-mail: keshav.poddar@governor.ri.gov
Special Counsel **Andrea Iannazzi** . . . . . . . . . . . . . . . . (401) 222-2080
   E-mail: andrea.iannazzi@governor.ri.gov
Constituent Services Director **Brad Inman** . . . . . . . . . . . (401) 222-2080
   E-mail: brad.inman@governor.ri.gov
Policy Analyst **Hannah Abelow** . . . . . . . . . . . . . . . . . (401) 222-2080
   E-mail: hannah.abelow@governor.ri.gov
Appointments Special Assistant **Catherine Gering** . . . . . . (401) 222-2080
   E-mail: catherine.gering@governor.ri.gov
Protocol Manager **Julia Gutierrez** . . . . . . . . . . . . . . . (401) 222-2080
   E-mail: julia.gutierrez@governor.ri.gov
Deputy Counsel **Amy Moses** . . . . . . . . . . . . . . . . . . (401) 222-2080
   E-mail: amy.moses@governor.ri.gov
Deputy Counsel **Eileen Cheng** . . . . . . . . . . . . . . . . . (401) 222-2080
   E-mail: eileen.cheng@governor.ri.gov
Legal Administrative Assistant **Judith Greene** . . . . . . . . . (401) 222-2080
   E-mail: judith.green@governor.ri.gov
Deputy Legislative Director **Steve Kavanagh** . . . . . . . . . (401) 222-2080
   E-mail: steve.kavanagh@governor.ri.gov
Legislative Aide **Neil Hytinen** . . . . . . . . . . . . . . . . . . (401) 222-2080
   E-mail: neil.hytinen@governor.ri.gov
Outreach Manager **David Allard** . . . . . . . . . . . . . . . . (401) 222-2080
   E-mail: david.allard@governor.ri.gov
Outreach Manager **Norman Birenbaum** . . . . . . . . . . . . (401) 222-2080
   E-mail: norman.birenbaum@governor.ri.gov
Executive Counsel **Claire Richards** . . . . . . . . . . . . . . . (401) 222-2080
   E-mail: claire.richards@governor.ri.gov
Education Policy Advisor **Heather Hudson** . . . . . . . . . . . (401) 222-2080
   E-mail: heather.hudson@governor.ri.gov
   Education: Colorado 2012 MA
Small Business Liaison **Donald J. Lally, Jr.** . . . . . . . . . . (401) 222-2080
   Education: Rhode Island 1977 BA; New England 1980 JD
Constituent Services Associate **Emmanuel Traub** . . . . . . . (401) 222-2080
   E-mail: emmanuel.traub@governor.ri.gov
Communications Director **Joy Fox** . . . . . . . . . . . . . . . (401) 222-2080
   E-mail: joy.fox@governor.ri.gov
   Education: Rhode Island Col 1999 BA
   Communications Deputy Director
   **Ashley Gingerella O'Shea** . . . . . . . . . . . . . . . (401) 222-2080
      E-mail: ashley.oshea@governor.ri.gov
Communications Associate **Catherine Rolfe** . . . . . . . . . . (401) 222-2080
   E-mail: catherine.rolfe@governor.ri.gov
Press Secretary **Marie E. Aberger** . . . . . . . . . . . . . . . (401) 222-8290
   E-mail: marie.aberger@governor.ri.gov
   Education: Duke 2010
Deputy Press Secretary **Katie O'Hanlon** . . . . . . . . . . . . (401) 222-2080
   E-mail: katie.ohanlon@governor.ri.gov

## Department of Administration [DOA]

One Capitol Hill, Providence, RI 02908-5890
Tel: (401) 222-2280  Fax: (401) 222-6436  Internet: www.doa.state.ri.us

**Employees:** 712  **Fiscal Year:** 2015  **Budget:** $415,449,000

■Director **Michael DiBiase** . . . . . . . . . . . . . . . . . . . . . (401) 222-2280
   E-mail: michael.dibiase@doa.ri.gov    Fax: (401) 222-6436
   Education: Pennsylvania 1983 JD
Deputy Director **Mark A. Dingley** . . . . . . . . . . . . . . . (401) 222-2280
   E-mail: mark.a.dingle@doa.ri.gov

*(continued on next page)*

★ Elected Official    ■ Appointed by Governor    ● Appointed by Legislature    ▲ Appointed by Board or Commission    ◆ Appointed by State Supreme Court

**EXECUTIVE BRANCH**

**Department of Administration** *continued*

Capital Asset Management and Maintenance Division
Director **Carole Cornelison** . . . . . . . . . . . . . . . . . . . . . (401) 222-1930
  E-mail: carole.cornelison@doa.ri.gov
Statewide Planning Chief **Parag Agrawal** . . . . . . . . . . . . (401) 222-5772
  E-mail: parag.agrawal@doa.ri.gov
Comprehensive Planning and Consistency Review
  Supervising Planner **Kevin Nelson** . . . . . . . . . . . . . . . (401) 222-5781
  E-mail: kevin.nelson@doa.ri.gov
Policy Director **Allison Rogers** . . . . . . . . . . . . . . . . . . . (401) 222-2280
Performance-Management Initiative Director
  **Brian M. Daniels** . . . . . . . . . . . . . . . . . . . . . . . . . . . . (401) 574-9202
  E-mail: brian.daniels@omb.ri.gov
  Education: Duke BA; Yale MBA
RI Film and TV Office Director
  **Steven "Steve" Feinberg** . . . . . . . . . . . . . . . . . . . . . . (401) 222-3456

## Accounts and Control
Internet: controller.doa.state.ri.us
State Controller **Marc A. Leonetti** . . . . . . . . . . . . . . . . (401) 222-2271
  E-mail: marc.leonetti@doa.ri.gov

## Human Resources Office
■Administrator **Deborah A. Dawson** . . . . . . . . . . . . . . . (401) 222-2160
  E-mail: deborah.dawson@doa.ri.gov
Deputy Administrator **(Vacant)** . . . . . . . . . . . . . . . . . . . (401) 222-8233

## Library and Information Services Office
Tel: (401) 574-9300 Fax: (401) 574-9320 Internet: www.olis.state.ri.us
Library Development Director **Donna Longo DiMichele** . . (401) 574-9302
State Data Coordinator **Lauren Miklovic** . . . . . . . . . . . . (401) 574-9314

## Office of Management and Budget
One Capitol Hill, Fourth Floor, Providence, RI 02908
Tel: (401) 574-8430 Fax: (401) 222-6436 Internet: www.omb.ri.gov
■Director **Jonathan Womer** . . . . . . . . . . . . . . . . . . . . . . (401) 222-2280
  E-mail: jonathan.womer@omb.ri.gov
  Education: Duke BA; Michigan 1997 MPP, 2000 MS
Strategic Management Chief **(Vacant)** . . . . . . . . . . . . . . (401) 574-8422

## Office of Diversity, Equity, and Opportunity
Associate Director **Cheryl Burrell** . . . . . . . . . . . . . . . . . (401) 222-6397
  Education: Bryan Col

## Workers' Compensation Office
■Administrator **Paula M. Cofone** . . . . . . . . . . . . . . . . . (401) 574-8515
  E-mail: paula.cofone@doa.ri.gov

## Audits Bureau
Chief **Dorothy Z. Pascale, CPA** . . . . . . . . . . . . . . . . . . (401) 222-1217

## Central Procurement, Materials and Information Management Division
■Associate Director/Purchasing Agent **Nancy McIntyre** . . . . (401) 574-8100
  E-mail: nancy.mcintyre@doa.ri.gov

## Facilities Management Division
■Associate Director **Marco Schiappa** . . . . . . . . . . . . . . (401) 222-6200
  E-mail: marco.schiappa@doa.ri.gov
Capitol Police Chief **Joseph Little** . . . . . . . . . . . . . . . . (401) 222-6905
                                            Fax: (401) 222-1090

## Information Technology Division
Chief Information Officer **Thom Guertin** . . . . . . . . . . . . (401) 574-9220
  Administrative Assistant **Carol Ciotola** . . . . . . . . . . . . (401) 222-4444
  E-mail: carol.ciotola@doa.ri.gov
Assistant Director of Information Technology **Alan Dias** . . . (401) 222-2000
  E-mail: alan.dias@doa.ri.gov
Assistant Director of Information Technology
  **Linda Nelson** . . . . . . . . . . . . . . . . . . . . . . . . . . . . . . (401) 222-2000
  E-mail: linda.nelson@doa.ri.gov

Assistant Director of Information Technology **Phil Silva** . . . (401) 222-2000
  E-mail: phil.silva@doa.ri.gov
Library Services Chief **Karen Mellor** . . . . . . . . . . . . . . . (401) 574-9304

# Department of Business Regulation [DBR]
John O. Pastore Complex Building 68 and 69, 1511 Pontiac Avenue, Cranston, RI 02920
Tel: (401) 462-9500 Fax: (401) 462-9532 Internet: www.dbr.ri.gov

**Employees:** 87 **Fiscal Year:** 2015 **Budget:** $12,676,000
■Director **Sidney "Macky" McCleary** . . . . . . . . . . . . . . . (401) 462-9552
  E-mail: macky.mccleary@dbr.ri.gov          Fax: (401) 462-9532
  Education: Yale BA, MA
Chief of Legal Services **Pamela J. Toro** . . . . . . . . . . . . . (401) 462-9556
                                            Fax: (401) 462-9536
Banking and Insurance Superintendent
  **Elizabeth Kelleher Dwyer** . . . . . . . . . . . . . . . . . . . . . (401) 462-9503
                                            Fax: (401) 462-9602
Securities Division Deputy Director **Maria D'Alessandro** . . (401) 462-9527
                                            Fax: (401) 462-9645
Accountancy Board Administrator **Dawne Broadfield** . . . . (401) 462-9516
  E-mail: dawne.broadfield@dbr.ri.gov          Fax: (401) 462-9632

# Department of Corrections
40 Howard Avenue, Cranston, RI 02920
Tel: (401) 462-1000 Tel: (401) 462-2261 (Bail Information)
Tel: (401) 462-3900 (Records and Identification) TTY: (401) 462-5180
Fax: (401) 462-2630 Internet: www.doc.ri.gov

**Employees:** 1,381 **Fiscal Year:** 2015 **Budget:** $201,390,000
■Director **Ashbel T. Wall II** . . . . . . . . . . . . . . . . . . . . . . (401) 462-2611
  E-mail: at.wall@doc.ri.gov
  Education: Yale 1975 BA, 1980 JD
Programming Services Officer **Susan Lamkins** . . . . . . . . . (401) 462-2905
Chief Inspector **Robert Catlow** . . . . . . . . . . . . . . . . . . . (401) 462-2551
  E-mail: robert.catlow@doc.ri.gov          Fax: (401) 462-1888
  E-mail: doc.inspector@doc.ri.gov
Chief Legal Counsel **Kathleen Kelly, Esq.** . . . . . . . . . . . (401) 462-2622
  E-mail: kathleen.kelly@doc.ri.gov          Fax: (401) 462-2583
  E-mail: doc.legal@doc.ri.gov
Information and Public Relations Chief
  **Jhompy R. "J.R." Ventura** . . . . . . . . . . . . . . . . . . . . . (401) 462-2609
  E-mail: jhomphy.ventura@doc.ri.gov

## Administration Division
Assistant Director **Patricia Coyne-Fague** . . . . . . . . . . . . (401) 462-3950
  E-mail: patricia.coynefague@doc.ri.gov          Fax: (401) 462-3953
Financial Resources Associate Director **Joanne M. Hill** . . . (401) 462-2617
  Education: Pittsburgh 1991 MPFM          Fax: (401) 462-3953
  Financial Management Administrator **Brenda Brodeur** . . (401) 462-1954
  E-mail: brenda.brodeur@doc.ri.gov          Fax: (401) 462-3953
Management Information Systems Associate Director
  **Michelle Lanciaux** . . . . . . . . . . . . . . . . . . . . . . . . . . . (401) 462-3902
  10 Garvey Road, Cranston, RI 02920          Fax: (401) 462-1709
  E-mail: michelle.lanciaux@doc.ri.gov
  Technical Support Manager **Ramon Fernandez** . . . . . . . . (401) 462-3975
    E-mail: rfernandez@doit.ri.gov          Fax: (401) 462-1709
  Technical Support Specialist **Joseph Cataldo** . . . . . . . . . (401) 462-1697
    E-mail: joe.cataldo@doc.ri.gov
  Technical Support Specialist II **David Wilson** . . . . . . . . . (401) 462-3972
    E-mail: davew@doc.ri.gov
  Technical Support Specialist III **(Vacant)** . . . . . . . . . . . . (401) 462-3929
  Information Aide **Mary Jane Langlais** . . . . . . . . . . . . . . (401) 462-3910
    E-mail: maryjane.langlais@doc.ri.gov
  Programmer Analyst II **Ronald Belanger** . . . . . . . . . . . . (401) 462-3909
    E-mail: ron.belanger@doc.ri.gov
  Programmer Analyst II **Deborah Farnsworth** . . . . . . . . . (401) 462-3908
    E-mail: deborah.farnsworth@doc.ri.gov
  Programmer Analyst II **David Hollinsworth** . . . . . . . . . . (401) 462-0338
    E-mail: david.hollinsworth@doc.ri.gov
  Programmer Analyst III **Alex Frisman** . . . . . . . . . . . . . . (401) 462-3907
    E-mail: alex.frisman@doc.ri.gov
  Programmer Analyst III **Igor Nakhamkin** . . . . . . . . . . . . (401) 462-3902
    E-mail: igor.nakhamkin@doc.ri.gov

---

★ Elected Official  ■ Appointed by Governor  ● Appointed by Legislature  ▲ Appointed by Board or Commission  ◆ Appointed by State Supreme Court

Planning and Research Associate Director
**Jeffrey D. Renzi**.....................................(401) 462-0373
  E-mail: jeff.renzi@doc.ri.gov          Fax: (401) 462-1507
Human Resources Administrator **Lois Hayes**............(401) 462-3250
  Education: Providence 1978 BS          Fax: (401) 462-2685
Physical Resources Unit Administrator
**Terrence McNamara**................................(401) 462-4023
  E-mail: terrence.mcnamara@doc.ri.gov   Fax: (401) 462-5287
Policy Unit Chief/Program Development
**Jayne DelSesto**....................................(401) 462-3533
  E-mail: jayne.delsesto@doc.ri.gov      Fax: (401) 462-5197
Recruitment and Training Chief **Paul M. Kennedy**.......(401) 462-2697
                                       Fax: (401) 462-5126
Inmate Accounts Business Management Officer (Acting)
**Susan Vani**.......................................(401) 462-5293
  E-mail: susan.vani@doc.ri.gov          Fax: (401) 462-3342

## Adult Correctional Institutions

Institutions and Operations Assistant Director
**James Weeden**.....................................(401) 462-5163
                                       Fax: (401) 462-0077
Correctional Industries Associate Director
**Joseph J. Flaherty**...............................(401) 462-1444
                                       Fax: (401) 462-2135
Facilities and Maintenance Associate Director
**Anthony Feole**....................................(401) 462-3066
                                       Fax: (401) 462-1465
Food Services Associate Director **John Rogers**.........(401) 462-5142
                                       Fax: (401) 462-1811
Special Investigations Unit Administrative Investigator
**Lynda Aul**........................................(401) 462-5108
  E-mail: lynda.aul@doc.ri.gov           Fax: (401) 462-1975
Central Office Warden **Donna Collins**.................(401) 462-5347
                                       Fax: (401) 462-0077
High Security Center Warden **Matthew Kettle**..........(401) 462-2636
  P.O. Box 8200, Cranston, RI 02920      Fax: (401) 462-1112
High Security Center Deputy Warden
**Joseph Jankowski**.................................(401) 462-2125
  P.O. Box 8200, Cranston, RI 02920      Fax: (401) 462-1112
Intake Service Center Warden **Nelson Lefebvre**........(401) 462-3801
  P.O. Box 8249, Cranston, RI 02920      Fax: (401) 462-1404
Intake Service Center Deputy Warden
**Wayne S. Salisbury**...............................(401) 462-3802
                                       Fax: (401) 462-1404
Intake Service Center Deputy Warden (Acting)
**Kathleen Lyons**...................................(401) 462-1410
                                       Fax: (401) 462-1404
Maximum Security Warden **Matthew Kettle**.............(401) 462-2636
  P.O. Box 8273, Cranston, RI 02920      Fax: (401) 462-2526
Maximum Security Deputy Warden **Jeffrey "Jeff" Aceto**..(401) 462-1639
                                       Fax: (401) 462-2526
John J. Moran Medium Security Warden
**Sergio Desousarosa**...............................(401) 462-3700
  P.O. Box 8274, Cranston, RI 02920      Fax: (401) 462-1161
  Education: Rhode Island Col 2009 ABS
John J. Moran Medium Security Facility Deputy Warden
**Rui Diniz**........................................(401) 462-2515
                                       Fax: (401) 462-1161
John J. Moran Medium Security Facility Deputy Warden
**Kerri McCaughey**..................................(401) 462-3703
                                       Fax: (401) 462-1161
Minimum Security Warden **James Vierra**...............(401) 462-1234
  P.O. Box 8212, Cranston, RI 02920      Fax: (401) 462-2161
Minimum Security Deputy Warden **Silma-del Langley**....(401) 462-2947
                                       Fax: (401) 462-2161
Minimum Security Deputy Warden **Anthony Grassini**....(401) 462-2570
                                       Fax: (401) 462-2161
Women's Facilities Warden **Carole Dwyer**..............(401) 462-2364
                                       Fax: (401) 462-2030
Women's Facilities Deputy Warden **Lynn Corry**.........(401) 462-3127
                                       Fax: (401) 462-2327

## Rehabilitative Services Division

Assistant Director **Barry Weiner**.....................(401) 462-2676
                                       Fax: (401) 462-1964

Medical Program Director **Jennifer Clarke**............(401) 462-1115
                                       Fax: (401) 462-2000
Mental Health Services Clinical Director **Louis Cerbo**....(401) 462-0432
                                       Fax: (401) 462-3222
  Health Care Services Associate Director
**Joseph R. Marocco**................................(401) 462-3792
                                       Fax: (401) 462-3222
Classification Associate Director **Joseph A. DiNitto**......(401) 462-2288
                                       Fax: (401) 462-3973
Special Education Director **Ralph Oreck**..............(401) 462-2507
                                       Fax: (401) 462-2509

## Adult Probation and Parole

Associate Director of Community Corrections
**Shelley Cortese**..................................(401) 462-1620
                                       Fax: (401) 462-0375
Probation and Parole Assistant Administrator
**Lisa Blanchette**..................................(401) 462-1619
                                       Fax: (401) 462-0375

## Parole Board

Varley Building, 1 Regan Court, Cranston, RI 02920
Tel: (401) 462-0900  Fax: (401) 462-0915
Fax: (401) 462-0916 (Sex Offender Community Notification Unit)
Internet: www.paroleboard.ri.gov

Chairperson **Laura Pisaturo**.........................(401) 462-0841
  Education: Suffolk JD

## Rhode Island Department of Education [RIDE]

255 Westminster Street, Providence, RI 02903
Tel: (401) 222-8700  TTY: (800) 745-6575

Employees: 355  Fiscal Year: 2015  Budget: $2,303,761,000

■Commissioner **Ken Wagner**..........................(401) 222-8700
  E-mail: ken.wagner@ride.ri.gov
  Education: Hofstra PhD
  Special Assistant to the Commissioner and Liaison to
    the Board of Education **Angela Teixeira**...........(401) 222-8435
Deputy Commissioner **David V. Abbott**................(401) 222-4275
Chief Legal Counsel **George Muksian**.................(401) 222-8933
Chief of Staff **Kimberly Bright**.....................(401) 222-8700
Post-Secondary Education Commissioner
**James E. "Jim" Purcell**...........................(401) 736-1147
  Education: Auburn BSPA; Montevallo MEd; Alabama EdD
Finance and Management Department Associate
  Commissioner **Susan LaPanne**......................(401) 736-1147
  E-mail: slapanne@ribghe.org
Policy and Planning Department Associate Commissioner
**Deborah Grossman-Garber**..........................(401) 736-1147
Accelerating School Performance Chief
**Stephen Osborn**...................................(401) 222-8485
Educator Excellence and Instructional Effectiveness Chief
**Mary Ann Snider**..................................(401) 222-8492
Fiscal Integrity and Effectiveness Chief
**Andrea Castaneda**.................................(401) 222-4645
Educator Quality Director **Lisa Foehr**...............(401) 222-8809
  E-mail: lisa.foehr@ride.ri.gov
Finance and Administration Director **Mark Dunham**......(401) 222-4648
  E-mail: mark.dunham@ride.ri.gov
Multiple Pathways Director **Sharon Lee**..............(401) 222-8484
Network and Information Systems Director
**Edward A. "Ed" Giroux**............................(401) 222-8965
  E-mail: edward.giroux@ride.ri.gov
GED Administrator **Philip Less**......................(401) 222-8949
  E-mail: philip.less@ride.ri.gov
General Counsel **Ronald Cavallaro**...................(401) 456-6006
  E-mail: rcavallaro@ribghe.org
Legislative Affairs Special Assistant **Andy Andrade**......(401) 222-8476
  E-mail: andy.andrade@ride.ri.gov

★ Elected Official   ■ Appointed by Governor   ● Appointed by Legislature   ▲ Appointed by Board or Commission   ◆ Appointed by State Supreme Court

# Department of Environmental Management [DEM]

235 Promenade Street, Suite 425, Providence, RI 02908
Tel: (401) 222-2771  Tel: (401) 222-3070 (24 Hour Hotline)
Fax: (401) 222-6802  Internet: dem.ri.gov

**Employees:** 399  **Fiscal Year:** 2016  **Budget:** $79,470,000

■Director **Janet Coit**....................(401) 222-4700 ext. 2409
  E-mail: janet.coit@dem.ri.gov
  Assistant to the Director **Rayna Maguire**......(401) 222-2409 ext. 2409
  Programming Services Officer
    **Joseph Masino**........................(401) 222-4700 ext. 2038
  Legal Services Executive Counsel **Mary Kay** ....(401) 222-6607 ext. 2304
  Communications Director **Gail Mastrati**........(401) 222-4700 ext. 2402
    E-mail: gail.mastrati@dem.ri.gov
  Administrative Adjudication Division Chief **David Kerins**..(401) 222-1357
  Environmental Response Administrator
    **James Ball**.........................(401) 222-4700 ext. 7129

## Environmental Protection Bureau

Environmental Protection Associate Director
  **Terrence Gray**.....................(401) 222-4700 ext. 7100
Water Resources Assistant Director
  **Alicia Good**.....................(401) 222-3961 ext. 7200
Compliance and Inspections Office Chief
  **David Chopy**.....................(401) 222-1360 ext. 7400
Technical and Customer Assistance Office Chief
  **Ronald Gagnon**.................(401) 222-6822 ext. 7500
Air Resources Chief **Douglas McVay**.........(401) 222-2808 ext. 7011
Groundwater and Wetland Protection Chief
  **Brian M. Moore, PE**.............(401) 222-6820 ext. 7700
Surface Water Protection Chief **Angelo Liberti**..(401) 222-3961 ext. 7225
Waste Management Chief **Leo Hellested**.......(401) 222-2797 ext. 7502

## Natural Resources Bureau

Fax: (401) 222-3162

Associate Director **Larry Mouradjian**..........(401) 222-4700 ext. 2414
  E-mail: larry.mouradjian@dem.ri.gov
Natural Resources Assistant Director
  **Catherine "Cathy" Sparks** .......(401) 222-4700 ext. 2301
  1037 Hartford Pike, N. Smithfield, RI 02857    Fax: (401) 222-6802
Agriculture and Resource Marketing Chief
  **Ken Ayars**.....................(401) 222-2781 ext. 4500
Enforcement Chief **Dean Hoxie**.................(401) 222-2284
Forest Environment Deputy Chief
  **Bruce Payton**...................(401) 222-2445 ext. 2056
                                       Fax: (401) 568-2045
Parks and Recreational Services Chief **Robert Paquette**...(401) 667-6200
  1100 Tower Hill Road, North Kingstown, RI 02852    Fax: (401) 667-3970
  E-mail: robert.paquette@dem.ri.gov

## Policy and Administration Bureau

Assistant Director **Terrence Maguire**..........(401) 222-4700 ext. 4902
  E-mail: Terrence.Maguire@dem.ri.gov
Planning and Development Division Chief
  **Lisa Primiano**...................(401) 222-2776 ext. 4307
  E-mail: lisa.primiano@dem.ri.gov
Financial Management Administrator
  **Lynne Keller**....................(401) 222-6825 ext. 4901
  E-mail: lynne.keller@dem.ri.gov
MIS (Management Information Systems)
  Coordinator **Warren Angell**.............(401) 222-4700 ext. 2424
  E-mail: warren.angell@dem.ri.gov

# Department of Human Services

57 Howard Avenue, Cranston, RI 02920
Tel: (401) 462-5300  TTY: (401) 462-3363  Fax: (401) 462-3677
E-mail: dhs.contact@dhs.ri.gov

■Director **Melba Depeña**.........................(401) 462-2121
  E-mail: melba.depena@dhs.ri.gov
Deputy Director **Corinne Calise Russo** ...............(401) 462-2121
  Education: Rhode Island MSW
  Executive Assistant **Tamika Jean**...................(401) 462-2121

Executive Legal Counsel **Deborah Barclay** ............(401) 462-2326
  E-mail: dbarclay@dhs.ri.gov
Community Relations Liaison Officer **Maritza Perez**......(401) 462-6251
  E-mail: mperez@dhs.ri.gov
Long Term Care Services Administrator **Tom Conlon** ....(401) 462-1871

## Child Support Services Division

77 Dorrance Street, Providence, RI 02903

Associate Director **Sharon A. Santilli** ...............(401) 458-4400
  E-mail: ssantilli@dhs.ri.gov

## Division of Elderly Affairs [DEA]

Hazard Building, 74 West Road, Cranston, RI 02920
Tel: (401) 462-3000  Fax: (401) 462-0503

■Director **Charles J. "Charlie" Fogarty**.............(401) 462-0501
  E-mail: cfogarty@dea.ri.gov
  Education: Providence BA; Rhode Island MPA
  Assistant Director **Paula Parker**.....................(401) 462-0530

## Economic Support Division

Associate Director **Lissa DiMauro**...................(401) 462-2121
Employment and Training Administrator **(Vacant)**........(401) 462-2423
Food Stamp Program Administrator **Christine Ruggieri** ...(401) 462-0993
                                                        Tel: (401) 462-2121
                                                        Fax: (401) 432-1846
Rehabilitation Services Office Administrator
  **Ronald Racine**.....................(401) 421-7005
  40 Fountain Street, Providence, RI 02903
Services for the Blind and Visually Impaired Deputy
  Administrator **(Vacant)**.....................(401) 222-2300
  40 Fountain St., Providence, RI 02903

## Management Services - Administration Division

Financial Management Associate Director **Maureen Wu**....(401) 462-0574
Collections Unit Assistant Administrator
  **Christine Messier**.....................(401) 415-8300

## Management Services - Operations Division

Associate Director **Deborah B. Buffi, Esq.**.............(401) 462-2424
Field Operations Management Administrator
  **Denise Tatro**.....................(401) 462-3019
Specialized Services Administrator **Tom Conlon** .........(401) 462-2651
Staff Development Assistant Administrator (Acting)
  **Christine Ruggieri**.....................(401) 462-2255
Region 1 - Regional Manager **Maria Volpe** .............(401) 222-7000
  206 Elmwood Ave., Providence, RI 02903
Region 2 - Regional Manager **Denise Tatro** ............(401) 729-5400
  24 Commerce Street, Pawtucket, RI 02860
Region 3 - Regional Manager **David Celeste** ...........(401) 267-1030
  4808 Tower Hill Road, G1, Wakefield, RI 02879

## Veterans' Affairs Division

Director **LCDR Kasim Yarn, USN (Ret)** ...............(401) 462-5300
Administrator **Kim Ripoli** ...........................(401) 253-8000
Veterans' Home Medical Services Assistant
  Administrator **Rick Baccus** .....................(401) 253-8000

## Office of the Veterans' Cemetery

Veterans' Cemetery Director **Jonathan Scott Rascoe** ....(401) 268-3088
  301 South County Trail, Exeter, RI 02822

# Department of Labor and Training [DLT]

1511 Pontiac Avenue, Cranston, RI 02920-4407
Tel: (401) 462-8000  TTY: (401) 462-8006  Fax: (401) 462-8872
Internet: www.dlt.ri.gov

**Employees:** 470  **Fiscal Year:** 2015  **Budget:** $429,214,000

■Director **Scott R. Jensen**..........................(401) 462-8875
  E-mail: scott.jensen@dlt.ri.gov

Deputy Director **Lisa C. D'Agostino** . . . . . . . . . . . . . . . . . (401) 462-8584
  E-mail: lisa.dagostino@dlt.ri.gov
  Education: Rhode Island 1980 BS
Business Affairs Assistant Director **Diane Gagne** . . . . . . . . (401) 462-8147
  E-mail: diane.gagne@dlt.ri.gov
Information Technology Division Administrator
  **Robert Genest** . . . . . . . . . . . . . . . . . . . . . . . . . . . . . . . . (401) 462-8012
  E-mail: robert.genest@dlt.ri.gov
  Education: Central Conn State U BS; Rensselaer Poly MS
Labor Market Information Administrator **Donna Murray** . . (401) 462-8751
  E-mail: donna.murray@dlt.ri.gov
Labor Market Information Assistant Director
  **Donna Murray** . . . . . . . . . . . . . . . . . . . . . . . . . . . . . . . . (401) 462-8767
  E-mail: donna.murray@dlt.ri.gov
Chief Public Affairs Officer **Michael J. Healey** . . . . . . . . . (401) 462-8090
  E-mail: michael.healey@dlt.ri.gov
Human Resources Administrator **Kathleen M. Lanphear** . . (401) 222-6880
Executive Counsel **Sean Fonts** . . . . . . . . . . . . . . . . . . . . . (401) 462-8892

## Income Support Division

Income Support Assistant Director
  **Robert "Bob" Langlais** . . . . . . . . . . . . . . . . . . . . . . . . (401) 462-8767
  Education: Rhode Island Col 1976 BA
Interstate and Federal/Military Claims Manager **(Vacant)** . . (401) 462-8662
TDI Customer Service Manager **Kathy McCaughey** . . . . . . (401) 462-8428
TDI Medical Update Manager **Kathy McCaughey** . . . . . . . (401) 462-8142
Temporary Disability Insurance Administrator
  **Fernanda Casimiro** . . . . . . . . . . . . . . . . . . . . . . . . . . . (401) 462-8543
  E-mail: fern.casimiro@dlt.ri.gov
UI and TDI Fraud Unit Manager **Sarah Palmieri** . . . . . . . . (401) 462-8662
Unemployment Insurance Service Center Principal
  Manager **Jason Bliss Wohlers** . . . . . . . . . . . . . . . . . . . . (401) 462-8403
  E-mail: jason.wohlers@dlt.ri.gov
Unemployment Insurance Administrator
  **Rosemarie Lemoine** . . . . . . . . . . . . . . . . . . . . . . . . . . (401) 462-8628
Non-monetary Determinations Chief **Jessica Videira** . . . . . (401) 462-8662
  E-mail: jessica.videira@dlt.ri.gov
Police and Fire Relief Coordinator **Rachel Brawn** . . . . . . . (401) 462-8643

## Workers' Compensation Division

P.O. Box 20190, Cranston, RI 02920

Assistant Director **Matt Carey** . . . . . . . . . . . . . . . . . . . . . . (401) 462-8127
  Education: Rhode Island 1984 BA, 1986 MS
Chief Investigator **Julie Tamuleviz** . . . . . . . . . . . . . . . . . . (401) 462-8122

## Workforce Development Division

Building 73, 1511 Pontiac Avenue, Third Floor, Cranston, RI 02920-4407

Workforce Development Services Assistant Director
  **Susan Chomka** . . . . . . . . . . . . . . . . . . . . . . . . . . . . . . . (401) 462-8712
Labor and Training Programs Administrator **(Vacant)** . . . . . (401) 462-8842
Employment and Training Program Administrator
  **(Vacant)** . . . . . . . . . . . . . . . . . . . . . . . . . . . . . . . . . . . . (401) 462-8712
Labor and Training Business Services Chief **(Vacant)** . . . . . (401) 462-8724
State Workforce Investment Office Administrator
  **(Vacant)** . . . . . . . . . . . . . . . . . . . . . . . . . . . . . . . . . . . . (401) 462-8812
Statewide Youth Services Chief **(Vacant)** . . . . . . . . . . . . . (401) 462-8813

## Workforce Regulation and Safety Division

Building 70, 1511 Pontiac Avenue, Second Floor,
Cranston, RI 02920-4407

Workforce Regulation/Safety Assistant Director **(Vacant)** . . (401) 462-8538

## Labor Standards Unit

Building 70, 1511 Pontiac Avenue, Second Floor,
Cranston, RI 02920-4407

Chief Labor Standards Examiner **Helen Gage** . . . . . . . . . . . (401) 462-8545
  E-mail: helen.gage@dlt.ri.gov

## Occupational Safety Unit and Health Review Board

Building 70, 1511 Pontiac Avenue, Second Floor, Cranston, RI 02920

Occupational Safety and Health Code Commission Chair
  **Robin Melfi Coia** . . . . . . . . . . . . . . . . . . . . . . . . . . . . . (401) 462-8570

Occupational Safety and Health Review Board Chair
  **Jerome Squatrito** . . . . . . . . . . . . . . . . . . . . . . . . . . . . . (401) 462-8570
Employment and Training Administrator **John Shaw** . . . . . (401) 462-8570
Weights and Measures (Mercantile Unit) Supervising
  Metrologist **(Vacant)** . . . . . . . . . . . . . . . . . . . . . . . . . . (401) 462-8554

## Prevailing Wage Unit

Prevailing Wage Chief Investigator **Lisa Tirocchi** . . . . . . . . (401) 462-8539
  E-mail: lisa.tirocchi@dlt.ri.gov

## Professional Regulation Unit

Building 70, 1511 Pontiac Avenue, Second Floor, Cranston, RI 02920

Labor and Training Administrator **(Vacant)** . . . . . . . . . . . . (401) 462-8538
■Electrician Examiners Board Chair **William O. Lepore** . . . . (401) 462-8580
Hoisting Engineers Examining Board Chair
  **David Burnham** . . . . . . . . . . . . . . . . . . . . . . . . . . . . . . (401) 462-8580
■Labor and Payment of Debts Appeals Board Chair
  **Joseph Contarino** . . . . . . . . . . . . . . . . . . . . . . . . . . . . (401) 462-8580
■Mechanical Board Chair **Stanley Davies** . . . . . . . . . . . . . (401) 462-8580
Plumbers Examiners Board Chair **Michael St. Martin** . . . . (401) 462-8580
Rhode Island Apprenticeship Council Chair
  **William Holmes** . . . . . . . . . . . . . . . . . . . . . . . . . . . . . . (401) 462-8580
Safety Awareness Board Chair **Joseph Sabitoni** . . . . . . . . . (401) 462-8541
■Telecommunication Systems Examination and Licensing
  Contractors, Technicians and Installers Board Chair
  **William McGowan** . . . . . . . . . . . . . . . . . . . . . . . . . . . . (401) 462-8580
Apprenticeship Training Programs Supervisor
  **Bernard E. Treml III** . . . . . . . . . . . . . . . . . . . . . . . . . . (401) 462-8536
  E-mail: bernard.treml@dlt.ri.gov
Senior Chief Mechanical Investigator **Nick ReNown** . . . . . . (401) 462-8535
Chief Electrical Investigator **Glenn Dusablon** . . . . . . . . . . (401) 462-8571
Chief Elevator Investigator **Sean Nolan** . . . . . . . . . . . . . . (401) 462-8579
Chief Hoisting Engineer Investigator
  **David M. Rodrigues** . . . . . . . . . . . . . . . . . . . . . . . . . . (401) 462-8554
Chief Plumbing Investigator **Patrick Luther** . . . . . . . . . . . (401) 462-8525
Chief Telecommunications Investigator **Robert Gaj** . . . . . . . (401) 462-8533

## Governor's Workforce Board

Building 72, 1511 Pontiac Avenue, Cranston, RI 02920-4407

■Chair **Constance A. Howes, FACHE** . . . . . . . . . . . . . . . . (401) 462-8860
  Education: Kenyon; Virginia
Executive Director **Rick Brooks** . . . . . . . . . . . . . . . . . . . . (401) 462-8584
  E-mail: rick.brooks@dlt.ri.gov

## Labor Relations Board

Building 73, 1511 Pontiac Avenue, Second Floor, Cranston, RI 02920

■Chairman **Walter J. Lanni** . . . . . . . . . . . . . . . . . . . . . . . (401) 462-8545
  E-mail: LRB@dlt.ri.gov
Administrator **Robyn H. Golden** . . . . . . . . . . . . . . . . . . . (401) 462-8771
  E-mail: robyn.golden@dlt.ri.gov
  Education: Rhode Island 1975 BA

## Board of Review

Building 74, West Road, First Floor, Cranston, RI 02920-4407
E-mail: bor@dlt.state.ri.us  Internet: www.dlt.ri.gov/bor/

Chair **Christopher M. "Chris" Fierro** . . . . . . . . . . . . . . . . . (401) 462-9400
  E-mail: christopher.fierro@dlt.ri.gov
  Education: UMass (Amherst) 2002 BA, 2004 MS

# Department of Public Safety [RISP]

311 Danielson Pike, North Scituate, RI 02857
Tel: (401) 444-1000  TTY: (401) 444-1144  Fax: (401) 444-1105
E-mail: risp@risp.dps.ri.gov  Internet: www.dps.ri.gov

**Employees:** 634  **Fiscal Year:** 2015  **Budget:** $117,205,000

■Superintendent and Commissioner **Steven G. O'Donnell** . . (401) 444-1120
  E-mail: odonnell@risp.dps.ri.gov
  Education: New Haven 1982 BS; Salve Regina U MS
  Executive Assistant **Barbara J. Laird** . . . . . . . . . . . . . . . . (401) 444-1120
Chief Administrative Officer
  **MAJ Robert S. Wall, ARNG** . . . . . . . . . . . . . . . . . . . . . (401) 444-1004
Deputy Superintendent/Field Operations Chief
  **Todd E. Catlow, CPA, CFE** . . . . . . . . . . . . . . . . . . . . . . (401) 444-1002
  Education: Bryant U BSCrimJ

*(continued on next page)*

---

★ Elected Official    ■ Appointed by Governor    ● Appointed by Legislature        ▲ Appointed by Board or Commission        ◆ Appointed by State Supreme Court

**EXECUTIVE BRANCH**

### Department of Public Safety *continued*
Chief Sheriff **David M. DeCesare** . . . . . . . . . . . . . . . . . . (401) 757-3115
   Education: Roger Williams 2002 BS

## Division of the State Fire Marshal
1951 Smith Street, North Providence, RI 02911
Fax: (401) 415-8608  Internet: www.fire-marshal.ri.gov

**Employees:** 36

■Fire Marshal **John E. "Jack" Chartier** . . . . . . . . . . . . . . (401) 383-7717
   E-mail: john.chartier@sfm.dps.ri.gov
   Executive Assistant **Elizabeth "Beth" Forshee** . . . . . . . (401) 383-7717
Chief Deputy Fire Marshal **James Gumbley** . . . . . . . . . . (401) 383-7068

## Department of Revenue
One Capitol Hill, Providence, RI 02908
Tel: (401) 574-8822  Internet: www.dor.ri.gov

**Employees:** 489  **Fiscal Year:** 2015  **Budget:** $449,018,000

■Director **Robert S. "Rob" Hull** . . . . . . . . . . . . . . . . . . . . (401) 574-8999
   Education: Virginia 1986 BA; Harvard 1991 MBA
■Deputy Director **Heather L. Martino, Esq.** . . . . . . . . . . . . (401) 574-8997
   Education: Boston U JD
Head of Legal Services **Marilyn Shannon McConaghy** . . . (401) 574-8822
Chief Financial Officer **Janet Cole** . . . . . . . . . . . . . . . . . (401) 574-8822
Chief of Information and Public Relations **Paul Grimaldi** . . (401) 574-8822

### Lottery Division
1425 Pontiac Avenue, Cranston, RI 02920
TTY: (800) 745-5555  Tel: (401) 463-6500  Fax: (401) 463-5669
Internet: www.rilot.com

Director **Gerald S. "Gerry" Aubin** . . . . . . . . . . . . . . . . . (401) 463-6500
   E-mail: gaubin@rilot.ri.gov
Deputy Director **Margaret "Peg" Rose** . . . . . . . . . . . . . . (401) 463-6500
   E-mail: prose@rilot.ri.gov
Casino Operations and Compliance Manager
   **Keith J. Tucker** . . . . . . . . . . . . . . . . . . . . . . . . . . . . . (401) 463-6500

### Division of Motor Vehicles [DMV]
Forand Building, 600 New London Avenue, Cranston, RI 02905
Tel: (401) 462-4368  Fax: (401) 462-5784
■Administrator **Walter R. Craddock** . . . . . . . . . . . . . . . . . (401) 462-5705

### Taxation Division
Tel: (401) 574-8829  Fax: (401) 574-8917  Internet: www.tax.ri.gov
Tax Administrator **(Vacant)** . . . . . . . . . . . . . . . . . . . . . . . (401) 574-8922
Revenue Services/Taxation Associate Director **(Vacant)** . . . (401) 574-8922
Compliance and Collection Chief **Jacques Moreau** . . . . . . (401) 574-8892
E-Government Chief **Susan Galvin** . . . . . . . . . . . . . . . . . (401) 574-8769
Examiner Chief **Michael Canole** . . . . . . . . . . . . . . . . . . . (401) 574-8729
Office Audit/Discovery Chief **Steven Cobb** . . . . . . . . . . . (401) 574-8734
Personal Income Tax Chief **Leo Lebeus** . . . . . . . . . . . . . (401) 574-8231
Tax Processing Service Chief **Susan Galvin** . . . . . . . . . . (401) 574-8754
Corporation Tax Chief Revenue Agent **Marlen Bautista** . . . (401) 574-8806
Employer Tax Chief Revenue Agent **Phillip D'Ambra** . . . . (401) 574-8700
Estate and Gift Tax Chief Revenue Agent
   **Meaghan Kelly** . . . . . . . . . . . . . . . . . . . . . . . . . . . . . (401) 574-8852
Research and Taxpayer Assistance Chief Revenue Agent
   **Patrick Gengarella** . . . . . . . . . . . . . . . . . . . . . . . . . . (401) 222-1040
Sales Tax Chief Revenue Agent **Donald Englert** . . . . . . . . (401) 574-8762

## Department of Transportation [RIDOT]
Two Capitol Hill, Providence, RI 02903-1124
Tel: (401) 222-2481  Fax: (401) 222-2086  TTY: (401) 222-4971

**Employees:** 773  **Fiscal Year:** 2015  **Budget:** $415,640,000

■Director **Peter Alviti** . . . . . . . . . . . . . . . . . . . . . . . . . . (401) 222-2481
   E-mail: peter.alviti@dot.ri.gov
   Assistant to the Director **Diane Bestwick** . . . . . (401) 222-2481 ext. 4001
Chief of Staff **Celia J. Blue** . . . . . . . . . . . . . . . . . . . . . . (401) 222-2481
   Education: Worcester State Col BS; Anna Maria MBA
Deputy Director and Chief Operating Officer
   **Peter Garino** . . . . . . . . . . . . . . . . . . . . . . . . . . . . . . (401) 222-2481

Deputy Director **(Vacant)** . . . . . . . . . . . . . . . . . . . . . . . (401) 222-5826
Executive Counsel **Lisa M. Martinelli, Esq.** . . . . . . . . . . . (401) 222-6510
   E-mail: lisa.martinelli@dot.ri.gov
Chief Public Affairs Officer **Rosamaria "Rose" Jones** . . . (401) 222-1362
Human Resources Administrator **Paul E. Pysz** . . . . . . . . . (401) 222-2572

### Administration Division
Assistant Director **(Vacant)** . . . . . . . . . . . . . . . . . . . . . . (401) 222-2495
Contracts and Specifications Administrator
   **Vanessa Crum, Esq.** . . . . . . . . . . . . . . . . . . . . . . . . (401) 222-2495
   E-mail: vanessa.crum@dot.ri.gov
Business and Community Resources **(Vacant)** . . . . . . . . . (401) 222-3260

### Financial Management
Chief Financial Officer (Acting) **Loren Doyle** . . . . (401) 222-6590 ext. 4535
Management Information Chief
   **Thomas "Tom" Lewandowski** . . . . . . . . . . . . (401) 222-6590 ext. 4535
   E-mail: thomas.lewandowski@dot.ri.gov

### Highway and Bridge Maintenance
Highway and Bridge Maintenance Operations
   Administrator **Joseph Baker, PE** . . . . . . . . . . . (401) 222-2378 ext. 4800
   E-mail: joseph.baker@dot.ri.gov
Traffic Research Civil Engineer Chief
   **Joseph A. Bucci, PE** . . . . . . . . . . . . . . . . . . (401) 222-4010 ext. 4211
   E-mail: jbucci@dot.ri.gov
Fleet Management Officer **Louis DiStefano** . . . . . (401) 222-2468 ext. 4325

### Infrastructure Development
Chief Engineer **Kazem Farhoumand, PE** . . . . . . . . . . . . . (401) 222-2492
   E-mail: kazem.farhoumand@dot.ri.gov
Construction Management Deputy Chief
   Engineer **Frank Corrao III, PE** . . . . . . . . . . . (401) 222-2468 ext. 4202
   E-mail: frank.corrao@dot.ri.gov
Bridge Engineer **David Fish, PE** . . . . . . . . . . . . (401) 222-2053 ext. 4022
   E-mail: david.fish@dot.ri.gov
Design Deputy Chief Engineer **(Vacant)** . . . . . . . (401) 222-2023 ext. 4023
Managing Engineer/Materials **Mark E. Felag, PE** . . . . . . . (401) 222-2524
   E-mail: mfelag@dot.ri.gov
Research and Technology Engineer **Colin A. Franco, PE** . . (401) 222-3030
   E-mail: cfranco@dot.ri.gov
Road Engineer **Vincent Palumbo, PE** . . . . . . . . . (401) 222-2023 ext. 4049
   E-mail: vpalumbo@dot.ri.gov
Traffic Engineer **Robert Rocchio, PE** . . . . . . . . . (401) 222-2694 ext. 4206
   E-mail: robert.rocchio@dot.ri.gov
Planning and Finance Chief
   **Robert A. Shawver, PE** . . . . . . . . . . . . . . . . (401) 222-6940 ext. 4224
Program Development Chief
   **Stephen A. Devine** . . . . . . . . . . . . . . . . . . . (401) 222-4203 ext. 4063
Senior Audit Manager **Andrea Butola** . . . . . . . . . . . . . . . (401) 222-2297
Survey Manager **Michael Gaston, PLS** . . . . . . . . . . . . . . (401) 222-6835
   E-mail: michael.gaston@dot.ri.gov
Traffic Management Center Manager **J Michael Wreh** . . . . (401) 222-3005

### Project Management Division
Administrator **(Vacant)** . . . . . . . . . . . . . . . . . . . . . . . . . (401) 222-2481
Chief Operating Officer **(Vacant)** . . . . . . . . . . . . . . . . . . (401) 222-2481

## Executive Office Health and Human Services
Hazard Building, 74 West Road, Cranston, RI 02920
Tel: (401) 462-7290  Fax: (401) 462-3677

**Employees:** 169  **Fiscal Year:** 2015  **Budget:** $2,334,650,000

■Secretary **Elizabeth H. Roberts** . . . . . . . . . . . . . . . . . . . (401) 462-5274
   E-mail: elizabeth.roberts@ltgov.ri.gov
   Education: Brown U 1978 BA; Boston U 1984 MBA
   Executive Assistant to the Secretary
   **Christine O'Connor** . . . . . . . . . . . . . . . . . . . . . . . . . (401) 462-5274
Administration Deputy Secretary **Wayne Hannon** . . . . . . . (401) 462-5274
Deputy Secretary/General Counsel **Jennifer L. Wood** . . . . (401) 462-5274
Legal Services Administrator **Deborah "Deb" George** . . . . (401) 462-3575
                                         Fax: (401) 462-6338

---

★ Elected Official   ■ Appointed by Governor   ● Appointed by Legislature   ▲ Appointed by Board or Commission   ◆ Appointed by State Supreme Court

Medicaid Director **Anya Rader Wallack**..................(401) 462-3575
  Education: Vermont 1988 BA; Brandeis 2007 PhD
Management Services Associate Director **Robert Farley** ...(401) 462-7290
Communications Director **Michael "Mike" Raia**.........(401) 462-1834
Communications Deputy Director **Sophie O'Connell**.....(401) 462-0854

## Department of Behavioral Healthcare, Developmental Disabilities and Hospitals [BHDDH]

14 Harrington Road, Cranston, RI 02920
Tel: (401) 462-3201  Fax: (401) 462-3204

**Employees:** 1,383  **Fiscal Year:** 2015  **Budget:** $375,124,000

■Director **Maria Montanaro**.........................(401) 462-2339
  E-mail: maria.montanaro@bhddh.ri.gov
■Deputy Director **Rebecca Boss**......................(401) 462-0917
  E-mail: rebecca.boss@bhddh.ri.gov
Operations and Policy Executive Director **(Vacant)**.......(401) 462-0917
Developmental Disabilities Associate Director
  **Charles Williams**................................(401) 462-6032
Policy Implementation Director **Michelle Brophy**........(401) 462-2770
  Education: Rhode Island Col 1993 BSW
Facilities and Program Standards and Licensure
  Administrator **Heather Daglieri**....................(401) 462-0581
Administrative Officer **Connie Cirelli**................(401) 462-2339
  E-mail: connie.cirelli@bhddh.ri.gov
Chief Financial Officer **Chris Feisthamel**.............(401) 462-3100
Eleanor Slater Hospital Chief Executive Officer **(Vacant)** ..(401) 462-2339

## Department of Children, Youth and Families [DCYF]

101 Friendship Street, Providence, RI 02903
Tel: (401) 528-3502  Tel: (800) 742-4453 (Child Abuse Hotline)
Fax: (401) 528-3590

**Employees:** 666  **Fiscal Year:** 2015  **Budget:** $221,570,000

■Director **(Vacant)** ...................................(401) 528-3590
Deputy Director (Acting) **Christy E. Healey**...........(401) 528-3549
Chief of Staff **Abby Swienton**.......................(401) 528-3889
Chief Legal Counsel **Kevin Aucoin**...................(401) 528-3570
Chief Financial Officer **David Alves**..................(401) 528-3630
  Education: Assumption Col 2006 BA; Bryant U 2008 MBA
Chief Strategy Officer **Jamia McDonald**...............(401) 528-3540
  Education: John Marshall JD
Child Welfare Institute Director **Tonya Glantz**.........(401) 456-4626
  610 Mount Pleasant Avenue, Providence, RI 02908    Fax: (401) 456-4628
Permanency Associate Director **Susan Lindberg**........(401) 528-3756
East Bay Area Regional Director **Paula Fontaine**........(401) 254-7010
  530 Wood Street, Bristol, RI 02809
Northern/Northwestern Rhode Island Area Regional
  Director **Dorn Dougan**............................(401) 721-2505
Providence Area Regional Director **Joan Harmon**.......(401) 528-3745
  101 Friendship Street, Providence, RI 02908
Southern Rhode Island Area Regional Director
  **Debbie Souza**..................................(401) 294-5350
  650 Ten Rod Road, North Kingstown, RI 02852
Licensing Administrator **Laura Kiesler**................(401) 428-3605
Management Information Systems Administrator
  **David Allenson**.................................(401) 528-3858
  E-mail: david.allenson@dcyf.ri.gov
Data and Evaluation Administrator **Colleen Caron**......(401) 528-3720
Juvenile Corrections Executive Director **Kevin Mckenna** ..(401) 462-1085
Juvenile Probation Assistant Administrator (Acting)
  **Jessica Nash**...................................(401) 528-3520

## Department of Health

Cannon Building, Three Capitol Hill, Providence, RI 02908-5097
Tel: (401) 222-2232  Tel: (401) 222-2812 (Divorce Records)
Tel: (401) 222-2812 (Vital Records)  TTY: (401) 222-2506
Fax: (401) 222-6548

■Director **Dr. Nicole Alexander-Scott**.................(401) 222-2232
  E-mail: nicole.alexander-scott@ri.gov
  Education: Cornell BS; SUNY (Syracuse) MD; Brown U MPH
Deputy Director **Leonard B. Green**...................(401) 222-7841

Chief of Staff **Steven Boudreau**......................(401) 222-2232
Public Health Communications Center Lead
  **Andrea Bagnall-Degos**..........................(401) 222-3998
  E-mail: andrea.bagnall-degos@health.ri.gov
  Education: New Hampshire 1992 BA; Tulane 1996 MPH
Women, Infants and Children (WIC) Program Chief
  **Ann Barone**....................................(401) 222-4604
  E-mail: ann.barone@health.ri.gov    Fax: (401) 222-1442

## Office of the Auditor General [OAG]

86 Weybosset Street, 2nd Floor, Providence, RI 02903-2800
Fax: (401) 222-2111

●Auditor General **Dennis E. Hoyle, CPA**...............(401) 222-2435
  E-mail: dennis.hoyle@oag.ri.gov
  Education: Providence BS, MBA
Assistant Auditor General **(Vacant)**...................(401) 222-2435

## Office of the Adjutant General

645 New London Avenue, Cranston, RI 02920-3097
Tel: (401) 275-4102  Fax: (401) 275-4338

■Adjutant General **COL Christopher P. Callahan, ARNG**...(401) 275-4102
  E-mail: christopher.p.callahan4.mil@mail.mil
  Education: Army War Col MSS
  Confidential Secretary/Office Manager **Tonia Kaplan** ....(401) 275-4102
Air National Guard Assistant Adjutant General
  **BrigGen Matthew J. Dzialo, ANG**.................(401) 275-4118
Army National Guard Assistant Adjutant General
  **BG David Medeiros, ARNG**.......................(401) 275-4102
Information Management Director
  **LTC Michael "Mike" Tetreault, USA, ARNG** ....(401) 275-4140
  E-mail: mike.tetreault@us.army.mil
Plans, Operations and Training Officer
  **Col James M Vartanian, ANG**....................(401) 275-4396
    Fax: (401) 275-4332
Webmaster **MSG James A. Loffler, ARNG**............(401) 275-4152
  E-mail: james.loffler@us.army.mil
Joint Staff Director **(Vacant)**........................(401) 275-4102

## Office of the Public Defender

160 Pine Street, Providence, RI 02903
Tel: (401) 222-1511  Fax: (401) 222-3287

**Employees:** 93  **Fiscal Year:** 2015  **Budget:** $10,902,000

■Public Defender **Mary McElroy**.....................(401) 222-1511
  E-mail: mmcelroy@ripd.org
  Education: Providence; Suffolk 1992 JD
Deputy Public Defender **Matthew Toro**................(401) 222-1511

## Emergency Management Agency [RIEMA]

645 New London Avenue, Cranston, RI 02920-3003
Tel: (401) 946-9996  TTY: (401) 751-7635  Fax: (401) 944-1891
Internet: www.riema.ri.gov

■Director **Peter T. Gaynor**..........................(401) 946-9996
  E-mail: peter.gaynor@ema.ri.gov
Communications Coordinator **Joseph Swift**............(401) 462-7150
Chief Financial Officer **Catherine King Avila**...........(401) 462-7107
  Education: Providence 1983 BA; New England 1987 JD
Grants Manager **Mike Hogan**........................(401) 462-7063
External Affairs Officer **Armand J. Randolph**..........(401) 462-7183
Legal Counsel **Anita Flax**...........................(401) 462-7010
Operations Section Chief **(Vacant)**...................(401) 462-7335
Planning and Mitigation Branch Manager
  **Michelle Burnett**...............................(401) 462-7048

---

★ Elected Official    ■ Appointed by Governor    ● Appointed by Legislature    ▲ Appointed by Board or Commission    ◆ Appointed by State Supreme Court

**EXECUTIVE BRANCH**

## Division of Higher Education Assistance [RIHEAA]

560 Jefferson Boulevard, Warwick, RI 02886
Tel: (401) 736-1100  TTY: (401) 734-9481  Fax: (401) 732-3541
E-mail: info@riheaa.org  Internet: www.riheaa.org

**Employees:** 10  **Fiscal Year:** 2015  **Budget:** $15,191,000

Commissioner **James E. "Jim" Purcell** . . . . . . . . . . . . . . . (401) 736-1100
 E-mail: jim.purcell@ribghe.org
▲Postsecondary Education Deputy Director
 **Gail E. Mance-Rios** . . . . . . . . . . . . . . . . . . . . . . . . . . . . (401) 736-1100
 E-mail: gmrios@riheaa.org

## Rhode Island Turnpike and Bridge Authority [RITBA]

P.O. Box 437, Jamestown, RI 02835-0437
Tel: (401) 423-0800  Fax: (401) 423-0830

▲Executive Director **Earl J. "Buddy" Croft III** . . . . . . . . . (401) 423-0800
 E-mail: buddy@ritba.org
 Education: Providence BA
 Executive Assistant **MaryAnn Durgin** . . . . . . . . . . . . . . . (401) 423-0800

## Rhode Island Board of Elections

50 Branch Avenue, Providence, RI 02904-2790
Tel: (401) 222-2345  Fax: (401) 222-3135
E-mail: boe.elections@elections.ri.gov

**Employees:** 11  **Fiscal Year:** 2015  **Budget:** $4,656,000

Chairman **William West** . . . . . . . . . . . . . . . . . . . . . . . . . . (401) 222-2345
Executive Director **Robert Kando** . . . . . . . . . . . . . . . . . . . (401) 222-2345
 E-mail: robert.kando@elections.ri.gov

## Rhode Island Commerce Corporation [RIEDC]

315 Iron Horse Way, Suite 101, Providence, RI 02908
Tel: (401) 278-9100  Fax: (401) 273-8270  E-mail: info@commerceri.com
Internet: www.commerceri.com

■Secretary **Stefan Pryor** . . . . . . . . . . . . . . . . . . . . . . . . . (401) 278-9100
 E-mail: stefan.pryor@commerceri.com
 Education: Yale 1993 BA, 2006 JD
 Assistant to the Commerce Secretary **Kayla S. Rosen** . . . (401) 222-6951
 E-mail: kayla.rosen@commerci.com
 Education: Brown U 2014
■Chief of Staff **Wade Gibson** . . . . . . . . . . . . . . . . . (401) 278-9100 ext. 130
 E-mail: wade.gibson@governor.ri.gov
 Education: Princeton 2006 AB; Yale 2011 JD
Chief Financial Officer **Lisa Lasky** . . . . . . . . . . . . . . . . . . (401) 278-9100
Chief Marketing Officer **(Vacant)** . . . . . . . . . . . . . . . . . . . (401) 278-9100
President **Darin Early** . . . . . . . . . . . . . . . . . . . . . . . . . . . (401) 278-9100
Community and Government Relations Deputy
 Director **(Vacant)** . . . . . . . . . . . . . . . . . . (401) 278-9100 ext. 130
Tourism Executive **Mark Brodeur** . . . . . . . . . . . . . . . . . . (401) 278-9100
Senior Economic Development Advisor **Daniel Jennings** . . (401) 278-9100
 Education: NYU BA; Columbia MS
Senior Economic Development Advisor
 **Marcel A. Valois** . . . . . . . . . . . . . . . . . . . . . . . . . . . . . (401) 278-9100
 Education: Rhode Island 1973 BA, 1975 MA
Human Resources Manager **Jeanine Lucia** . . . . . . . (401) 278-9100 ext. 121

## Rhode Island Health and Educational Building Corporation [RIHEBC]

170 Westminster Street, 12th Floor, Providence, RI 02903
Fax: (401) 421-3910  Internet: www.rihebc.com

Executive Director **Robert E. Donovan** . . . . . . . . . . . . . . . (401) 831-3770

## Office of the Lieutenant Governor

82 Smith Street, Providence, RI 02903-1105
Tel: (401) 222-2371  Fax: (401) 222-2012

**Fiscal Year:** 2015  **Budget:** $972,000

★Lieutenant Governor **Daniel J. "Dan" McKee** (D) . . . . . . . (401) 222-2000
 Term Expires: January 2019
 E-mail: daniel.mckee@ltgov.ri.gov
 Education: Assumption Col 1973 BSEd; Harvard 2005 MPA
Chief of Staff **Anthony J. Silva** . . . . . . . . . . . . . . . . . . . . (401) 222-2000
 E-mail: anthony.silva@ltgov.ri.gov
 Education: Bryant Col BS; Salve Regina U MS

## Office of the Secretary of State

82 Smith Street, Providence, RI 02903-1120
Tel: (401) 222-2357  Fax: (401) 222-1356

★Secretary of State **Nellie M. Gorbea** (D) . . . . . . . . . . . . . (401) 222-2357
 Term Expires: January 2019
 Education: Princeton
 Career: Administration Director, Office of the Secretary of State, State
 of Rhode Island; Deputy Secretary of State/Administration Director,
 Office of the Secretary of State, State of Rhode Island
Chief of Staff **Gonzalo Cuervo** . . . . . . . . . . . . . . . . . . . . . (401) 222-2357
 E-mail: gcuervo@sos.ri.gov
Communications Director **Nicole Lagace** . . . . . . . . . . . . . . (401) 222-4293
 E-mail: nlagace@sos.ri.gov
Corporations Director **Maureen Ewing** . . . . . . . . . . . . . . . (401) 222-3040
 148 West River Street, Providence, RI 02904
Human Resources Director **(Vacant)** . . . . . . . . . . . . . . . . (401) 222-2357
Elections Director **Rob Basler Rock** . . . . . . . . . . . . . . . . . (401) 222-2340
 148 West River Street, Providence, RI 02904
 E-mail: elections@sos.ri.gov
 Education: Rhode Island 2014 MPA
Finance and Personnel Director **(Vacant)** . . . . . . . . . . . . . (401) 222-2357
Public Information Director **Stacy DiCola** . . . . . . . . . . . . . (401) 222-3983
 E-mail: sdicola@sos.ri.gov
State Archives and Public Records Administrator
 **R. Gwenn Stearn** . . . . . . . . . . . . . . . . . . . . . . . . . . . . . (401) 222-2353
 337 Westminster Street, Providence, RI 02903
State Librarian **Thomas R. "Tom" Evans** . . . . . . . . . . . . . (401) 222-2473
 State House, Rm. 208, Providence, RI 02903

## Office of the Attorney General

150 South Main Street, Providence, RI 02903
Tel: (401) 274-4400  Fax: (401) 222-2725

**Employees:** 236  **Fiscal Year:** 2015  **Budget:** $30,937,000

★Attorney General **Peter F. Kilmartin** (D) . . . . . . . . . . . . . (401) 274-4400
 Term Expires: January 2019
 Education: Roger Williams 1988 BS, 1998 JD
 Career: State Representative (D-RI, District 61), Rhode Island House of
 Representatives (1990-2010)
Deputy Attorney General **Gerald J. Coyne** . . . . . . . . . . . . . (401) 274-4400
Assistant Attorney General **(Vacant)** . . . . . . . . . . . . . . . . (401) 274-4400
Chief of Staff **Ernest "Ernie" Carlucci** . . . . . . . . (401) 274-4400 ext. 2357
Executive Assistant **Monica Nason** . . . . . . . . . . . (401) 274-4400 ext. 2338
Information Technology Director **Joseph Rodrigues** . . . . . (401) 274-4400
 E-mail: jrodrigues@riag.ri.gov

## Criminal Investigation Bureau

Chief **William Karalis** . . . . . . . . . . . . . . . . . . . . . (401) 274-4400 ext. 2244

## Office of the General Treasurer

82 Smith Street, Room 102, Providence, RI 02903
Tel: (401) 222-2397  Fax: (401) 222-6140
E-mail: generaltreasurer@treasury.ri.gov  Internet: www.treasury.ri.gov/

★General Treasurer **Seth Magaziner** (D) . . . . . . . . . . . . . . (401) 222-2397
 Term Expires: January 2019
Chief of Staff **Jeff Padwa** . . . . . . . . . . . . . . . . . . . . . . . . (401) 222-2397
General Counsel and Deputy Treasurer **(Vacant)** . . . . . . . . (401) 222-2397
Operations Chief Operating Officer **Patrick Marr** . . . . . . . . (401) 222-2397
Communication Director **David Ortiz** . . . . . . . . . . . . . . . . (401) 222-2397

---

★ Elected Official   ■ Appointed by Governor   ● Appointed by Legislature   ▲ Appointed by Board or Commission   ◆ Appointed by State Supreme Court

# South Carolina

Tel: (803) 896-0000 (Directory of State Government Listing)  Internet: www.sc.gov

**Number of U.S. Congressional Delegates:** 2 Senators; 7 Representatives  **Governor's Term:** 4 years
**Legislature Description:** General Assembly - 46 member Senate; 124 member House of Representatives;
Term - Senate 4 years, House 2 years  **Next Election:** Governor November 2018; Legislature November
2016  **Number of Electoral Votes:** 9  **Official Name:** State of South Carolina (after Charles II of England)
**Nickname:** The Palmetto State  **Motto:** Animis opibusque parati (Prepared in mind and resources); Dum
spiro spero (While I breathe, I hope)

**Population:** 4,896,146 (2015); Rank 23  **Fiscal Year:** 2015  **Budget:** $24,313,624,000

## Office of the Governor

1205 Pendleton Street, Columbia, SC 29201
Tel: (803) 734-2100  Fax: (803) 734-5167

**Fiscal Year:** 2013-2014  **Budget:** $1,924,000

**Nimrata Randhawa "Nikki" Haley**
Governor

Began Service: January 12, 2011
Term Expires: January 2019
Date of Birth: January 20, 1972
Education: Clemson 1994 BSAcc
Home: Columbia
Religion: Methodist
Career: Director, Board of Directors, Lexington
County Chamber of Commerce (2003-2006);
State Representative (R-SC, District 87), South
Carolina House of Representatives (2005-2010)

★ Governor **Nimrata Randhawa "Nikki" Haley** (R) . . . . . . (803) 734-2100
Chief of Staff **Swati Patel** . . . . . . . . . . . . . . . . . . . . . . . . (803) 734-2100
Deputy Chief of Staff (Budget and Policy)
  **Joshua "Josh" Baker** . . . . . . . . . . . . . . . . . . . . . . . . . . (803) 734-2100
  E-mail: joshbaker@gov.sc.gov
Deputy Chief of Staff (Cabinet) **Austin Smith** . . . . . . . . . . (803) 734-2100
  E-mail: austinsmith@gov.sc.gov
  Education: South Carolina 2004 BA; South Carolina State 2009 JD
Deputy Chief of Staff (Operations)
  **Katherine Haltiwanger** . . . . . . . . . . . . . . . . . . . . . . . (803) 734-2100
Chief Legal Counsel **Holly Gillespie Pisarik** . . . . . . . . . . . (803) 734-2100
  E-mail: hollypisarik@gov.sc.gov
  Education: South Carolina 2007 JD
Legislative Affairs Director **Katherine Veldran** . . . . . . . . . (803) 734-2100
  E-mail: katherineveldran@gov.sc.gov
Deputy Chief of Staff (Communications and External
  Affairs) **Rob Godfrey** . . . . . . . . . . . . . . . . . . . . . . . . . . (803) 734-2100
  E-mail: robgodfrey@gov.sc.gov
  Education: North Carolina 2003 BA
Press Secretary **Chaney Adams** . . . . . . . . . . . . . . . . . . (803) 734-2100
  E-mail: chaneyadams@gov.sc.gov

## Department of Administration

Wade Hampton Building, 1200 Senate Street, Suite 460,
Columbia, SC 29201
P.O. Box 2825, Columbia, SC 29211
Tel: (803) 734-8120  Tel: (803) 734-9260
E-mail: information@admin.sc.gov

Executive Director **Marcia S. Adams** . . . . . . . . . . . . . . . . (803) 734-9260
Chief of Staff **Paul Koch** . . . . . . . . . . . . . . . . . . . . . . . . . (803) 734-9260
Policy and Public Affairs Director **Lindsey Kremlick** . . . . . (803) 896-0695

## Department of Agriculture

P.O. Box 11280, Columbia, SC 29211-1280
Tel: (803) 734-2190  Fax: (803) 734-2192

**Employees:** 104  **Fiscal Year:** 2015  **Budget:** $15,904,000

★ Commissioner **Hugh E. Weathers** (R) . . . . . . . . . . . . . . . (803) 734-2190
  Term Expires: 2019
  E-mail: hweathe@scda.sc.gov
  Education: South Carolina BS
  Executive Assistant **Stefanie Kitchen** . . . . . . . . . . . . . . (803) 734-2190
  Administrative Coordinator **Cindy Thompson** . . . . . . . . (803) 734-2179
Agricultural Services Division Assistant Commissioner
  **Martin Eubanks** . . . . . . . . . . . . . . . . . . . . . . . . . . . . . (803) 734-2221
Public Information Director **Stephanie Sox** . . . . . . . . . . . (803) 734-2196
  E-mail: ssox@scda.sc.gov

## Department of Alcohol and Other Drug Abuse Services [DAODAS]

2414 Bull Street, Columbia, SC 29201
P.O. Box 8268, Columbia, SC 29202
Tel: (803) 896-5555  Fax: (803) 896-5557
Internet: www.daodas.state.sc.us

**Employees:** 46

■ Director **Bob Toomey** . . . . . . . . . . . . . . . . . . . . . . . . . . . (803) 896-5555
  E-mail: btoomey@daodas.sc.gov
  Administrative Coordinator **Taineshia Brooks** . . . . . . . . (803) 896-4282
Project Manager **(Vacant)** . . . . . . . . . . . . . . . . . . . . . . . . (803) 896-1561

## Department of Archives and History

8301 Parklane Road, Columbia, SC 29223-4905
Tel: (803) 896-6100  Fax: (803) 896-6198

**Employees:** 29  **Fiscal Year:** 2015  **Budget:** $4,734,000

▲ Director **W. Eric Emerson, PhD** . . . . . . . . . . . . . . . . . . (803) 896-6185
  E-mail: eemerson@scdah.state.sc.us     Tel: (803) 896-6186
▲ Deputy Director **Brenda C. House** . . . . . . . . . . . . . . . . . (803) 896-6160
Historical Services Director **Elizabeth Johnson** . . . . . . . . (803) 896-6168
                      Fax: (803) 896-6167
Archival Director **Steve Tuttle** . . . . . . . . . . . . . . . . . . . . . (803) 896-6204
Records Management Director **Richard Harris** . . . . . . . . . (803) 896-6123
                      Fax: (803) 896-6138

## Department of Commerce

1201 Main Street, Suite 1600, Columbia, SC 29201
Tel: (803) 737-0400  Fax: (803) 737-0894
Internet: www.sccommerce.com

**Employees:** 67  **Fiscal Year:** 2014-2015  **Budget:** $84,978,000

■ Secretary **Robert M. "Bobby" Hitt III** . . . . . . . . . . . . . . (803) 737-0400
  E-mail: bhitt@sccommerce.com
  Executive Assistant **Vicki S. Wooten** . . . . . . . . . . . . . . (803) 737-0400
Deputy Secretary **Jennifer E. Noel** . . . . . . . . . . . . . . . . . (803) 737-0400
  E-mail: jnoel@sccommerce.com
  Education: Oklahoma
General Counsel **Karen Blair Manning** . . . . . . . . . . . . . . (803) 737-0400

*(continued on next page)*

---

★ Elected Official    ■ Appointed by Governor    ● Appointed by Legislature    ▲ Appointed by Board or Commission    ◆ Appointed by State Supreme Court

EXECUTIVE BRANCH

**Department of Commerce** *continued*

Economic Development Coordinating Council/Grant and
Incentives Director **Daniel Young** .........(803) 737-0400
External Affairs Director **Michael McInerney** ..........(803) 737-0400
Global Business Development Director
**P. Nelson Lindsay** ...................(803) 737-0400
Education: Wofford; South Carolina MPA
Marketing and Communications Director
**Adrienne Sairwell** ...................(803) 737-0400
Small Business and Rural Development Director
**Maceo Nance** .......................(803) 737-0400
ARC Program Manager **Jill Francisco** ................(803) 734-0568
Chief Financial Officer **Chris Huffman** .............(803) 737-0400
Palmetto Railways President and Chief Executive Officer
**Jeffrey McWhorter** ...................(843) 727-2067
540 E. Bay Street, Charleston, SC 29403       Fax: (843) 727-2005

# Department of Consumer Affairs

P.O. Box 5757, Columbia, SC 29250
Tel: (803) 734-4200  Fax: (803) 734-4299  Internet: www.consumer.sc.gov

**Employees:** 42  **Fiscal Year:** 2015  **Budget:** $3,368,000

▲Administrator **Carri Grube Lybarker** ..................(803) 734-4233
E-mail: clybarker@scconsumer.gov
Education: Winthrop; South Carolina JD
Director of Procurement and Accounting
**Latitia Trezevant** ....................(803) 734-0366
E-mail: ltrezevant@scconsumer.gov
Consumer Advocate **Carri Grube Lybarker** ...........(803) 734-4233
Consumers Services Director **Donna Backwinkel** .......(803) 734-4214
Senior Communications Coordinator **Juliana Harris** ......(803) 734-4296
E-mail: jharris@scconsumer.gov
Procurement Manager **Latitia Trezevant** ...............(803) 734-0366
E-mail: ltrezevant@scconsumer.gov

# Department of Corrections [SCDC]

P.O. Box 21787, Columbia, SC 29221-1787
Tel: (803) 896-8500  Fax: (803) 896-3972
E-mail: corrections.info@doc.state.sc.us  Internet: www.doc.sc.gov

**Employees:** 5,621  **Fiscal Year:** 2015  **Budget:** $450,019,000

■Director **Bryan P. Stirling** ...........................(803) 896-8555
E-mail: stirling.bryan@doc.sc.gov
Education: South Carolina 1991 BA, 1996 JD
Executive Assistant **Maria Leggins** .................(803) 896-8555
Internal Communications Director **Clark Newsome** ......(803) 896-8578
Policy Development Director **Sandra Bowie** ...........(803) 896-2385
E-mail: bowie.sandra@doc.state.sc.us
Communications Deputy Director **Stephanie Givens** .....(803) 896-8578
E-mail: givens.stephanie@doc.sc.gov

# Department of Disabilities and Special Needs [DDSN]

3440 Harden Street Extension, Columbia, SC 29203
P.O. Box 4706, Columbia, SC 29240
Tel: (803) 898-9600  Tel: (888) 376-4636  TTY: (803) 898-9600
Fax: (803) 898-9656  E-mail: ddsn@ddsn.sc.gov

**Employees:** 106  **Fiscal Year:** 2015  **Budget:** $670,888,000

▲State Director **Beverly A.H. Buscemi, PhD** ............(803) 898-9769
E-mail: bbuscemi@ddsn.sc.gov
Administrative Assistant to the State Director
**Sandra Delaney** .....................(803) 898-9769
General Counsel **Tana Vanderbilt** ....................(803) 898-9683
Government and Community Relations Director
**Lois Park Mole** ......................(803) 898-9743
E-mail: lpmole@ddsn.sc.gov
Human Resources Director **Deirdre Blake-Sayers** .......(803) 898-9612
Internal Audit Director **Kevin Yacobi** ...............(803) 898-9690

## Administration Division

Associate Deputy State Director **Thomas P. Waring** ......(803) 898-9769
E-mail: twaring@ddsn.sc.gov

Budget Director **Lisa B. Weeks** ......................(803) 898-9699
Cost Analysis Director **Chuck Norman** ...............(803) 898-9626
Division of Information Technology Director
**David Foshee** .......................(803) 898-9781
E-mail: dfoshee@ddsn.sc.gov
Finance Director **Martin Taylor** ....................(803) 898-9626
Supply and Services Director **(Vacant)** ...............(803) 898-9750

## Policy Office

Associate State Director **Susan Kreh Beck** ............(803) 898-9686
Autism Division Director **Daniel Davis** ...............(803) 898-9609
Consumer Assessment Division Director
**Belle Mead Cooper** ...................(803) 935-6715
Head and Spinal Cord Injuries Division Director
**Linda S. Veldheer** ...................(803) 898-9798
Intellectual Disability and Related Division Director
**Janet Priest** ........................(803) 898-9620
Quality Management Division Director **Ann Dalton** .....(803) 898-9813

## Operations Office

Associate State Director **David Goodell** ...............(803) 898-9686
Education: Kansas 1985 MA
District I Director **John King** .......................(864) 938-3497
P.O. Box 239, Clinton, SC 29325
District II Director **Rufus Britt** ....................(843) 832-5567
9995 Jamison Road, Summerville, SC 29485
Coastal Regional Facility Administrator **Becky Hill** ......(843) 821-5802
9995 Jamison Road, Summerville, SC 29485
Midlands Regional Facility Administrator **Nancy Hall** ....(803) 935-7502
8301 Farrow Road, Columbia, SC 29203
Pee Dee Regional Facility Administrator **John Hitchman** ..(843) 664-2656
714 National Cemetery Road, Florence, SC 29506
Whitten Center Facility Administrator **Wes Leonard** ......(864) 938-3422
P.O. Box 239, Clinton, SC 29325

# Department of Education

1429 Senate Street, Room 1006, Columbia, SC 29201
Tel: (803) 734-8500  Fax: (803) 734-3389  Internet: www.ed.sc.gov

**Employees:** 720  **Fiscal Year:** 2015  **Budget:** $4,209,976,000

★State Superintendent **Molly M. Spearman** (R)..........(803) 727-9282
Term Expires: 2019
P.O. Box 54, Newberry, SC 29108
Education: George Washington MA; South Carolina EdS
Chief Operating Officer **Elizabeth "Betsy" Carpenter** ...(803) 734-3224
Divisions of Federal, State, and Community Resources
Deputy Superintendent **Karla Hawkins** ..............(803) 737-3150
Legal Division Deputy Superintendent
**Cathy L. Hazelwood** ..................(803) 734-8218
Education: South Carolina 1991 JD
General Counsel **Margaret Hazel** ....................(803) 734-2746
Public Information Office Director
**Sandeep "Dino" Teppara** ..............(803) 734-8043
E-mail: dteppara@ed.sc.gov
Education: Nebraska 1997 BA; Indiana 2000 JD

## Accountability Division

Deputy Superintendent **Karla Hawkins** ...............(803) 734-8105
Adult Education Director **David Stout** ................(803) 734-8348
Assessment Office Director **Elizabeth Jones** ...........(803) 734-8295
Career and Technology Education Director
**Susan C. Flanagan** ...................(803) 734-8412
Data Management and Analysis Director **Daniel Ralyea** ...(803) 734-8086
E-mail: dralyea@ed.sc.gov                Fax: (803) 734-8661
Federal and State Accountability Director **Roy Stehle** .....(803) 734-8118
E-mail: rstehle@ed.sc.gov
Special Educations Services Office Director **John Payne** ..(803) 734-8224
Fax: (803) 734-4605
Student Intervention Director **Sabrina Moore** ..........(803) 734-8433
E-mail: smoore@ed.sc.gov                Fax: (803) 734-5281
Virtual Education Director **Bradley Mitchell** ...........(803) 734-7169
E-mail: bmitchell@ed.sc.gov              Fax: (803) 734-8029

---

★ Elected Official   ■ Appointed by Governor   ● Appointed by Legislature   ▲ Appointed by Board or Commission   ◆ Appointed by State Supreme Court

## Chief Financial Office

Chief Financial Officer **Melanie Jinnette**................(803) 734-3605
Internal Technology Director **Don Cantrell**..............(803) 734-3287
    E-mail: dcantrell@ed.sc.gov
Employee Relations Manager **Michael E. Addison**.......(803) 734-8461
Chief Procurement Officer **Shelly Bezanson Kelly, Esq.**...(803) 734-8248
Audits Manager **Melissa Myers**......................(803) 734-8453

## Innovation and Effectiveness Division

Deputy Superintendent **Sheila Quinn**.................(803) 737-3150
Public School Choice and Innovation Director **(Vacant)**...(803) 734-3698
                                            Fax: (803) 734-3247
School Facilities Office Director **Delisa Clark**..........(803) 734-4837
    3710 Landmark Drive, 2nd Floor, Room 1114, Columbia, SC 29204
Transportation Office Director **Tim Camp**..............(803) 734-8248
Nutrition Programs Office Director
    **Juanita Bowens Seabrook, RD, SNS**..............(803) 734-8205
Grants Manager **(Vacant)**...........................(803) 734-5810
Educator Certification Coordinator **Marcia Berry**........(803) 896-0307

# Department of Employment and Workforce [SCDEW]

1550 Gadsden Street, Columbia, SC 29201
P.O. Box 995, Columbia, SC 29202
Tel: (803) 737-2400  TTY: (800) 206-8035  Fax: (803) 737-2642

**Employees:** 755  **Fiscal Year:** 2015  **Budget:** $181,622,000

■Director **Cheryl M. Stanton**.......................(803) 737-2617
    E-mail: cstanton@dew.sc.gov                Tel: (803) 737-2400
    Education: Williams 1994 BA; Chicago 1997 JD
Chief of Staff **Darrell T. Scott**......................(803) 737-0366
    Education: Clemson 2002 BA
General Counsel **Susan M. Boone**...................(803) 737-2176
    E-mail: sboone@dew.sc.gov
Support and Operations Assistant Executive Director
    **Martha Stephenson**..........................(803) 737-0108
    E-mail: mstephenson@dew.sc.gov
Unemployment Insurance Assistant Executive Director
    **Jamie Suber**................................(803) 737-3552
Communications and Marketing Director **Robert Bouyea**..(803) 737-2623
    E-mail: rbouyea@dew.sc.gov
Communications and Marketing Deputy Director
    **Dorothy Weaver**.............................(803) 737-2400
    E-mail: dweaver@dew.sc.gov
    Education: South Carolina MMC
Government Affairs Director **Sally Foster**.............(803) 737-0089
Workforce and Economic Development Assistant
    Executive Director **(Vacant)**.....................(803) 737-2628

# Department of Health and Environmental Control [DHEC]

2600 Bull Street, Columbia, SC 29201
Tel: (803) 898-3432  Tel: (803) 898-3630 (Vital Records)
Fax: (803) 898-3323  Internet: www.scdhec.gov

**Employees:** 3,739

▲Agency Director **Catherine Edwards Heigel**...........(803) 898-0124
    E-mail: catherine.heigel@dhec.sc.gov
    Education: South Carolina 1992 BA; Ohio State 1995 JD
Executive Assistant **Teresa Higgins**..................(803) 898-0124
    Education: South Carolina 1983 BA
Legislative Affairs Senior Director
    **David E. Wilson, PE**.........................(803) 898-3300
    E-mail: david.wilson@dhec.sc.gov
Communications Director **Jennifer Read**..............(803) 898-9518
                                            Fax: (803) 898-3887
Freedom of Information Center Director **Karla Mew**.....(803) 898-3882
                                            Fax: (803) 898-3816
Environmental Affairs Director **Myra Reece**............(803) 898-3136
Public Health Director **Lisa Davis**....................(803) 898-0298
General Counsel **W. Marshall Taylor, Jr.**...............(803) 898-3350
                                            Fax: (803) 898-3367
Webmaster **Melissa Palmer**........................(803) 898-3726

## Deputy Director of Administration

Chief Operating Officer **Kevin J. Guion**...............(803) 898-3380
Affirmative Action and Equal Employment Opportunity
    Office Director **Quentin P. Chavis**.................(803) 898-3310
Public Health Preparedness Office Director
    **Michael A. "Mike" Elieff**......................(803) 898-0748
    Education: Upper Iowa 1997 BPA
Staff Development and Training Manager **Donna Rowe**...(803) 896-5456
                                            Fax: (803) 896-0603
Drug Control Bureau Director **Lisa A. Thomson**........(803) 896-1959

## Environmental Quality Control

Fax: (803) 896-8941

Director **Myra Reece**.............................(803) 898-3136
    Special Assistant to the Director **Robin Stephens**......(803) 898-3137

## Health Regulations

1777 St. Julian Place, Columbia, SC 29204
Tel: (803) 545-4200  Fax: (803) 545-4579

Deputy Director **Shelly Bezanson Kelly, Esq.**...........(803) 545-4178
Certification Bureau Chief **MaryJo Roué**..............(803) 545-4293
    Education: Marywood U 1988 BA          Fax: (803) 545-4563
Health Facilities and Construction Division Director
    **William "Bill" McCallum**.......................(803) 545-4211
Radiological Health Bureau Chief **Aaron Gant**.........(803) 545-4420
                                            Fax: (803) 545-4412
    Electronic Products Division Director **Charles Ditmer**...(803) 545-4437
                                            Fax: (803) 545-4412
    Radioactive Materials, License and Compliance
        Division Director **James K. "Jim" Peterson**........(803) 545-4407
                                            Fax: (803) 545-4412

# Ocean and Coastal Resource Management

1362 MacMillan Avenue, Suite 400, Charleston, SC 29405
Tel: (843) 953-0200  Fax: (843) 953-0201

Deputy Commissioner **Sara Bazemore**.................(843) 953-0200

# Department of Health and Human Services [DHHS]

1801 Main Street, Columbia, SC 29201
P.O. Box 8206, Columbia, SC 29202
Tel: (803) 898-2500  Fax: (803) 255-8235  E-mail: askus@scdhhs.gov

**Employees:** 507

■Director **Christian L. Soura**.......................(803) 898-2580
    E-mail: christian.soura@scdhhs.gov
    Education: Penn State BA; Illinois MA
    Executive Assistant **Jan Polatty**...................(803) 898-2504
    E-mail: polattyj@scdhhs.gov
Compliance and Performance Review Bureau Chief
    **Kathleen Snider**............................(803) 898-8881
    E-mail: sniderk@scdhhs.gov
    Administrative Assistant **Cyndi Myers**...............(803) 898-8881
General Counsel Deputy Director **Byron R. Roberts**......(803) 898-2796
    E-mail: byron.roberts@scdhhs.gov
    Administrative Coordinator **Marie A. Brown**..........(803) 898-2796

## Finance and Administration Office

Deputy Director **Adriana Day**......................(803) 898-7145
    E-mail: adriana.day@scdhhs.gov
Administrative Coordinator **Lesley King**..............(803) 898-7145
Human Resources Director **Tonya M. Chambers**........(803) 898-2670
Administrative Services Program Director **Mike Cannon**..(803) 898-2508
    E-mail: cannonm@scdhhs.gov
Planning and Budget Director **(Vacant)**...............(803) 898-1084
Reimbursement Methodology and Policy Program
    Director **Jeffrey A. Saxon**......................(803) 898-1022

---

★ Elected Official   ■ Appointed by Governor   ● Appointed by Legislature   ▲ Appointed by Board or Commission   ◆ Appointed by State Supreme Court

## Information Management Office

Chief Information Officer Deputy Director **Jim Coursey** . . (803) 898-1167
  Education: Illinois 1992 BA
  Program Coordinator **Tamara McDaniel** . . . . . . . . . . . . . (803) 898-2502
    E-mail: tamara.mcdaniel@scdhhs.gov
Information Technology Services Program Director
  **Rod Davis** . . . . . . . . . . . . . . . . . . . . . . . . . . . . . . . . . (803) 898-2787
    E-mail: davisr@scdhhs.gov

## Medicaid Eligibility and Beneficiary Services

Deputy Director **Beth Hutto** . . . . . . . . . . . . . . . . . . . . . (803) 898-1035
                                                Fax: (803) 255-8235
  Administrative Coordinator **Libby Powers** . . . . . . . . . . . . (803) 898-1035
    E-mail: libby.powers@scdhhs.gov
Eligibility Processing Program Director **Michael Jones** . . . (803) 898-3985
Public Information Director **Kim Cox** . . . . . . . . . . . . . . . . (803) 898-4439
    E-mail: coxkim@scdhhs.gov
Chief of Staff **Bryan G. Kost** . . . . . . . . . . . . . . . . . . . . . (803) 898-2865
    E-mail: kostbr@scdhhs.gov

## Health Programs

Deputy Director **Deirdra T. Singleton** . . . . . . . . . . . . . . (803) 898-3202
Office of Manager Care Program Director
  **Jennifer Campbell** . . . . . . . . . . . . . . . . . . . . . . . . . . . (803) 898-0178
Long Term Care and Behavioral Health Services Deputy
  Director **Peter Liggett** . . . . . . . . . . . . . . . . . . . . . . . . . (803) 898-0178

## Department of Insurance [DOI]

1201 Main Street, Suite 1000, Columbia, SC 29201
P.O. Box 100105, Columbia, SC 29202-3105
Tel: (803) 737-6227  TTY: (803) 737-5769  Fax: (803) 737-6159
Internet: www.doi.sc.gov

**Employees: 94  Fiscal Year: 2015  Budget: $18,680,000**

■Director **Raymond G. "Ray" Farmer** . . . . . . . . . . . . . . . (803) 737-6805
    E-mail: ray.farmer@doi.sc.gov
  Executive Assistant **Casey Clyburn** . . . . . . . . . . . . . . . (803) 737-6805
    Education: South Carolina 2009 BS
  Public Information Officer **Ann S. Roberson** . . . . . . . . . (803) 737-6207
    Education: South Carolina 1982 BA
General Counsel **Julia Barton** . . . . . . . . . . . . . . . . . . . . (803) 737-6207
Administration Division Deputy Director **Ben Duncan** . . . . (803) 737-6343
    E-mail: bduncan@doi.sc.gov
    Education: Benedict 1984 BS; South Carolina 1998 MPA
Financial Services Division Deputy Director **Lee Hill** . . . . . (803) 737-6199
Legal and Legislative and External Division Deputy
  Director **Gwendolyn "Gwen" Fuller-McGriff** . . . . . . . . (803) 737-6153
    Education: South Carolina State 1988 BA; Tennessee JD
Market and Consumer Services Deputy Director
  **Kendall Buchanan** . . . . . . . . . . . . . . . . . . . . . . . . . . . (803) 737-6143

## Department of Juvenile Justice

P.O. Box 21069, Columbia, SC 29211-1069
Tel: (803) 896-9749  Fax: (803) 896-9767  Internet: www.state.sc.us/djj

**Employees: 1,746  Fiscal Year: 2015  Budget: $123,343,000**

■Director **Sylvia Murray** . . . . . . . . . . . . . . . . . . . . . . . . (803) 896-5940
    E-mail: slmurr@scdjj.net
General Counsel **Elizabeth Hill** . . . . . . . . . . . . . . . . . . . (803) 896-7553
    E-mail: eahill@scdjj.net
Inspector General **Ray Cavanagh** . . . . . . . . . . . . . . . . . (803) 896-9502
    E-mail: rmcava@scdjj.net
Educational Services Superintendent **James Quinn** . . . . . . (803) 896-9110
Administrative Services Deputy Director
  **Robin E. Owens** . . . . . . . . . . . . . . . . . . . . . . . . . . . . (803) 896-9744
Community Services Deputy Director **Angie Rita** . . . . . . . (803) 896-9113
Rehabilitative Services Deputy Director **(Vacant)** . . . . . . . (803) 896-9105
Public Affairs Director **Eric L. Rousey** . . . . . . . . . . . . . . (803) 896-9765

## Department of Labor, Licensing and Regulation [LLR]

P.O. Box 11329, Columbia, SC 29211-1329
Tel: (803) 896-4300  Fax: (803) 896-4393
E-mail: contact.pharmacy@llr.sc.gov  Internet: www.llr.sc.gov

**Employees: 364  Fiscal Year: 2015  Budget: $41,048,000**

■Director **Richele Taylor** . . . . . . . . . . . . . . . . . . . . . . . . (803) 896-4300
    Education: North Carolina; South Carolina JD
  Executive Assistant **Stephanie Collier** . . . . . . . . . . . . . . (803) 896-4390
General Counsel **Melina Mann** . . . . . . . . . . . . . . . . . . . . (803) 896-4483
    E-mail: melina.mann@llr.sc.gov
Communications Director **Lesia Kudelka** . . . . . . . . . . . . . (803) 896-4376

## Fire and Life Safety Division

141 Monticello Trail, Columbia, SC 29203
Tel: (803) 896-9800

Deputy Director and State Fire Marshal **Bert Polk** . . . . . . . (803) 896-9800
    E-mail: bert.polk@llr.sc.gov

## Labor Division

Elevator and Amusement Rides Administrator
  **Duane Scott** . . . . . . . . . . . . . . . . . . . . . . . . . . . . . . . (803) 896-7630
    E-mail: duane.scott@llr.sc.gov
Mediation for Organized Labor Administrator **(Vacant)** . . . . (803) 896-4390
Occupational Safety and Health Administrator
  **Dottie Ison** . . . . . . . . . . . . . . . . . . . . . . . . . . . . . . . . (803) 896-7665
Occupational Safety and Health Administration (OSHA)
  Voluntary Program Manager **Harvey Jessup** . . . . . . . . . (803) 896-7744
    E-mail: harvey.jessup@llr.sc.gov

## Office of the State Fire Marshal

Liquefied Petroleum Gas Fire Marshal **Bert Polk** . . . . . . . . (803) 896-9802
Pyrotechnics Fire Marshall **Bert Polk** . . . . . . . . . . . . . . . (803) 896-9807

## Department of Mental Health

2414 Bull Street, Columbia, SC 29202
P.O. Box 485, Columbia, SC 29202
Tel: (803) 898-8581  TTY: (803) 798-4936  Fax: (803) 898-8316
E-mail: scdmh@yahoo.com  Internet: www.scdmh.org

**Employees: 5,560**

▲Director **John H. Magill** . . . . . . . . . . . . . . . . . . . . . . . . (803) 898-8319
    E-mail: john.magill@nc.gov
General Counsel **Allan Powell** . . . . . . . . . . . . . . . . . . . . (803) 898-8557
Children, Adolescents and Their Families Director
  **Louise Johnson** . . . . . . . . . . . . . . . . . . . . . . . . . . . . (803) 898-8350
    E-mail: louise.johnson@sc.gov
Financial Services Director **David A. Schaefer** . . . . . . . . . (803) 898-8511
Human Resource Services Director **Eleanor Odom** . . . . . . (803) 898-8611
Internal Audit Director **Valarie M. Perkins** . . . . . . . . . . . . (803) 898-8322
Medical Director **Robert L. Bank, MD** . . . . . . . . . . . . . . (803) 898-8339
  Assistant to Medical Director **(Vacant)** . . . . . . . . . . . . . (803) 898-8571
Administrative Services Deputy Director
  **Mark W. Binkley** . . . . . . . . . . . . . . . . . . . . . . . . . . . . (803) 898-8392
    E-mail: mark.binkley@sc.gov
Community Mental Health Services Deputy Director
  **Geoff Mason** . . . . . . . . . . . . . . . . . . . . . . . . . . . . . . . (803) 898-8348
Agency Disaster Response Manager **William L. Wells** . . . . (803) 898-8571

## Department of Motor Vehicles

Building C, 10311 Wilson Boulevard, Blythewood, SC 29016
P.O. Box 1498, Blythewood, SC 29016
Tel: (803) 896-5000  E-mail: help@scdmvonline.com
Internet: www.scdmvonline.com

**Fiscal Year: 2015  Budget: $84,945,000**

Director **COL Kevin A. Shwedo, USA (Ret)** . . . . . . . . . . . (803) 896-8925
    Note: On detail
    E-mail: kevin.shwedo@scdmv.net
    Education: Valley Forge Military 1976; North Carolina 1978 BSB;
    Shippensburg MPA

★ Elected Official    ■ Appointed by Governor    ● Appointed by Legislature    ▲ Appointed by Board or Commission    ◆ Appointed by State Supreme Court

Summer 2016                    © Leadership Directories, Inc.                    *State Yellow Book*

Director (Acting) **COL John F. Laganelli, USA** . . . . . . . . . (803) 896-5000
  Education: Daniel Webster 1983 BS; Army War Col 2009 MSS
Chief of Staff and Director of Operations
  **COL John F. Laganelli, USA** . . . . . . . . . . . . . . . . . . . . . (803) 896-5000
Director of Administration **Patricia "Trish" Blake** . . . . . . . (803) 896-5000
  E-mail: trish.blake@scdmv.net
  Education: Clemson BSAcc
Director of Customer Service Delivery **Mike Newman** . . . . (803) 896-5000
  Education: Embry-Riddle 1998 MS
Director of Procedures and Compliance **Annie L. Phelps** . . (803) 896-9675
  E-mail: annie.phelps@scdmv.net
General Counsel **Frank L Valenta, Jr.** . . . . . . . . . . . . . . . . . (803) 896-5000
  E-mail: frank.valenta@scdmv.net
Inspector General **Karl McClary** . . . . . . . . . . . . . . . . . . . . . (803) 896-5000

# Department of Natural Resources [SCDNR]

P.O. Box 167, Columbia, SC 29202
Fax: (803) 734-9809  Internet: www.dnr.sc.gov

**Employees:** 569

Chairman **D. Glenn McFadden** (Fifth Congressional) . . . . . (803) 487-7600
  Term Expires: July 1, 2018
  E-mail: mcfaddeng@dnr.sc.gov
Vice Chairman **Cary L. Chastain** (Sixth Congressional) . . . (843) 442-0609
  Term Expires: July 1, 2016            Fax: (843) 577-0400
  E-mail: chastainc@dnr.sc.gov
Board Member
  **Michael E. Hutchins** (Second Congressional) . . . . . . . . . (803) 359-0414
  Term Expires: July 1, 2017            Fax: (843) 359-2171
Board Member
  **Robert R. "Randy" Lowe** (Seventh Congressional) . . . . . (843) 393-6127
  Term Expires: July 1, 2014            Fax: (843) 395-0468
  E-mail: lower@dnr.sc.gov
Board Member
  **Norman F. Pulliam** (Fourth Congressional) . . . . . . . . . . (864) 583-6964
  Term Expires: July 1, 2016            Fax: (864) 573-7191
  E-mail: norman@pulliaminvestment.com
Board Member
  **Elizabeth Hood Willis** (First Congressional) . . . . . . . . . . (843) 789-1778
  Term Expires: July 1, 2018            Fax: (843) 720-8355
Board Member **Larry L. Yonce** (Third Congressional) . . . . . (803) 734-4007
  Term Expires: July 1, 2014
▲ Director **Col. Alvin A. Taylor** . . . . . . . . . . . . . . . . . . . . . . (803) 734-4007
  E-mail: taylora@dnr.sc.gov
  Special Assistant to the Director
    **D. Breck Carmichael, Jr.** . . . . . . . . . . . . . . . . . . . . . . (803) 734-3941
    E-mail: carmichaelb@dnr.sc.gov
  Executive Assistant **Rose M. Scheibler** . . . . . . . . . . . . . . (803) 734-4007
Chief of Staff **(Vacant)** . . . . . . . . . . . . . . . . . . . . . . . . . . . (803) 734-3672
Chief Counsel **Shannon Bobertz** . . . . . . . . . . . . . . . . . . . . (803) 734-4006
  E-mail: bobertzs@dnr.sc.gov
  Education: Cornell 1997 BA; South Carolina 2002 JD
Chief Information Security Officer **Bill O'Neal** . . . . . . . . . . (803) 734-9556
Audit Services Director **Angela Williams Cassella** . . . . . . (803) 734-3948
Environmental Programs Director **Bob Perry** . . . . . . . . . . . (803) 734-3766
  E-mail: perryb@dnr.sc.gov
Human Resources Director **Terri J. McGee** . . . . . . . . . . . . (803) 734-4400
  E-mail: mcgeet@dnr.sc.gov
Legislative Services Director **Capt. Mike Sabaka** . . . . . . . (803) 734-4048
  E-mail: sabakam@dnr.sc.gov

## Land, Water and Conservation Division

Rembert C. Dennis Building, Columbia, SC 29202
P.O. Box 167, Columbia, SC 29202

Deputy Director **Joseph Kenneth Rentiers, Jr.** . . . . . . . . . (803) 734-9035
  E-mail: rentiersk@dnr.sc.gov
  Education: Col Charleston BA; South Carolina JD
Assistant Deputy Director **(Vacant)** . . . . . . . . . . . . . . . . . . (803) 734-9114
Conservation Districts Coordinator **Marc Cribb** . . . . . . . . . (803) 734-6367
  E-mail: cribbm@dnr.sc.gov
Flood Insurance Director **Maria Cox Lamm** . . . . . . . . . . . . (803) 734-9493
Habitat Protection Director
  **Joseph Kenneth Rentiers, Jr.** . . . . . . . . . . . . . . . . . . . . (803) 734-9035
  E-mail: rentiersk@dnr.sc.gov

State Geologist **William "Bill" Clendenin** . . . . . . . . . . . . . (803) 896-7702
  Five Geology Rd., Columbia, SC 29210

### State Climatology Office
Director **Hope Mizzell** . . . . . . . . . . . . . . . . . . . . . . . . . . . . (803) 734-9568

## Law Enforcement Division
Deputy Director **Col. Chisolm Frampton** . . . . . . . . . . . . . (803) 734-4004
Assistant Deputy Director **(Vacant)** . . . . . . . . . . . . . . . . . (803) 734-4016
Law Enforcement Staff Operations **Major Mark Carey** . . . . (803) 734-4017
Law Enforcement Staff Operations **Capt. Lee Ellis** . . . . . . (803) 734-0022
  E-mail: ellisl@dnr.sc.gov
Law Enforcement Statewide Field Operations
  **Col. Chisolm Frampton** . . . . . . . . . . . . . . . . . . . . . . . . (843) 734-4004
Law Enforcement Statewide Field Operations
  **Major Jamie Landrum** . . . . . . . . . . . . . . . . . . . . . . . . . (803) 734-3607
Law Enforcement Statewide Field Operations
  **Major William Poole** . . . . . . . . . . . . . . . . . . . . . . . . . . (803) 734-3607

## Marine Resources Division
P.O. Box 12559, Charleston, SC 29422

Deputy Director **Robert H. Boyles, Jr.** . . . . . . . . . . . . . . . (843) 953-9304
  E-mail: boylesr@dnr.sc.gov
Assistant Deputy Director **David Whitaker** . . . . . . . . . . . . (843) 953-9392
  E-mail: whitakerd@dnr.sc.gov
Budget and Finance Director **Chantal Rice** . . . . . . . . . . . . (843) 953-9043
Coastal Reserves and Outreach Director **Phil Maier** . . . . . (843) 953-9001
  E-mail: maierp@dnr.sc.gov
Fisheries Management Office Director **Mel Bell** . . . . . . . . . (843) 953-9007
Marine Resources Research Institute Director
  **Dr. Mike Denson** . . . . . . . . . . . . . . . . . . . . . . . . . . . . . (843) 953-9819
  E-mail: densonm@dnr.sc.gov

## Wildlife and Freshwater Fisheries Division
Deputy Director **Emily P. Cope** . . . . . . . . . . . . . . . . . . . . . (803) 734-3889
  E-mail: copee@dnr.sc.gov
Assistant Deputy Director **Ken Prosser** . . . . . . . . . . . . . . . (803) 734-3914
  E-mail: prosserk@dnr.sc.gov
Wildlife Regional Operations Chief **Billy Dukes, Jr.** . . . . . . (803) 734-3939
  E-mail: dukesb@dnr.sc.gov
Wildlife Management/Statewide Projects, Research and
  Survey **Derrell Shipes** . . . . . . . . . . . . . . . . . . . . . . . . . (803) 734-3938
  E-mail: shipesd@dnr.sc.gov
Fisheries Chief **Ross Self** . . . . . . . . . . . . . . . . . . . . . . . . . (803) 734-3808
  E-mail: selfr@dnr.sc.gov
Fisheries Assistant Chief **Lynn Quattro** . . . . . . . . . . . . . . . (803) 734-3912
  E-mail: quattrol@dnr.sc.gov

## Office of Support Services
Deputy Director **Derrick Meggie** . . . . . . . . . . . . . . . . . . . . (803) 734-9911
  E-mail: meggied@dnr.sc.gov
Assistant Deputy Director **Scott Speares** . . . . . . . . . . . . . (803) 734-3624
  E-mail: spearess@dnr.sc.gov
Natural Resource Information Management & Analysis
  Director **Mark Litz** . . . . . . . . . . . . . . . . . . . . . . . . . . . . (803) 734-9494
  E-mail: litzm@dnr.sc.gov
Boat Titling and Registration Manager(Charleston)
  **Tony Reed** . . . . . . . . . . . . . . . . . . . . . . . . . . . . . . . . . . (843) 953-9301
  E-mail: reedt@dnr.sc.gov
Boat Titling and Registration Manager(Columbia)
  **Bryan Kyzer** . . . . . . . . . . . . . . . . . . . . . . . . . . . . . . . . (803) 734-3857
Customer Services Manager **Bryan Kyzer** . . . . . . . . . . . . . (803) 734-4585
Finance and Business Services Manager **Valerie Duncan** . . (803) 734-3984
Media Services Manager **Brett Witt** . . . . . . . . . . . . . . . . . . (803) 734-4133
  E-mail: wittb@dnr.sc.gov
Purchasing Manager **(Vacant)** . . . . . . . . . . . . . . . . . . . . . . (803) 734-3984
Graphics and Publications Supervisor **Brittany Caldwell** . . (803) 734-2510
  E-mail: caldwellb@dnr.sc.gov
Camp Wildwood Coordinator **Dan DuPre** . . . . . . . . . . . . . (803) 734-3954
  E-mail: dupred@dnr.sc.gov
Magazine Editor **(Vacant)** . . . . . . . . . . . . . . . . . . . . . . . . . (803) 734-3859

★ Elected Official   ■ Appointed by Governor   ● Appointed by Legislature   ▲ Appointed by Board or Commission   ◆ Appointed by State Supreme Court

EXECUTIVE BRANCH

# Department of Parks, Recreation and Tourism

1205 Pendleton Street, Columbia, SC 29201
Tel: (803) 734-0168  Fax: (803) 734-1409  Internet: http://www.scprt.com/

**Employees: 70  Fiscal Year: 2015  Budget: $93,844,000**

■Director **Duane N. Parrish** . . . . . . . . . . . . . . . . . . . . . . . . . . (803) 734-0166
  E-mail: dparrish@scprt.com
Chief of Staff **Amy Duffy** . . . . . . . . . . . . . . . . . . . . . . . . . . . (803) 734-3272
  E-mail: aduffy@scprt.com
Executive Assistant **Victoria Lewis** . . . . . . . . . . . . . . . . . (803) 734-0166
                                           Fax: (803) 734-1409
Communications Director **Dawn Dawson-House** . . . . . . . . (803) 734-1370
  Education: South Carolina 1985 BJ
Corporate Affairs Director **(Vacant)** . . . . . . . . . . . . . . . . . . (803) 734-1368
Finance Director **Yvette Sistare** . . . . . . . . . . . . . . . . . . . . . (803) 734-1759
Sales and Marketing Director **Beverly Shelley** . . . . . . . . . . (803) 734-0126
  E-mail: bshelley@scprt.com
State Park Director **Phil Gaines** . . . . . . . . . . . . . . . . . . . . . (803) 734-0345
  E-mail: pgaines@scprt.com
Technical Services Director **David Elwart** . . . . . . . . . . . . . (803) 734-0184
  E-mail: delwart@scprt.com
Tourism and Recreation Development Director **(Vacant)** . . . (803) 734-0148

# Department of Probation, Parole and Pardon Services [DPPPS]

2221 Devine Street, Suite 600, Columbia, SC 29205
P.O. Box 50666, Columbia, SC 29250
Tel: (803) 734-9220  Fax: (803) 734-9440  Internet: www.dppps.sc.gov

**Employees: 632  Fiscal Year: 2015  Budget: $57,565,000**

■Director **Jerry B. Adger** . . . . . . . . . . . . . . . . . . . . . . . . . . . (803) 734-9278
  E-mail: jerry.adger@ppp.sc.gov
Audit Director **Lisa Hawkins** . . . . . . . . . . . . . . . . . . . . . . . . (803) 734-9143
Hearing Parole Board Support Director **Larry Patton** . . . . . (803) 734-3295
Public Information Director **Peter A. O'Boyle** . . . . . . . . . . . (803) 734-9367
  E-mail: peter.oboyle@ppp.sc.gov
Staff Development & Training Director **Melissa Ray** . . . . . (803) 734-9220
Victim Services Director **Debora "Debbie" Curtis** . . . . . . . (803) 734-9274
Chief Legal Counsel **Matthew Buchanan** . . . . . . . . . . . . . (803) 734-9220
Attorney **Thomas Evans** . . . . . . . . . . . . . . . . . . . . . . . . . . . (803) 734-0048

## Administrative Services Division

Deputy Director **Sonya Bookard** . . . . . . . . . . . . . . . . . . . . . (803) 734-9244
  E-mail: sonya.bookard@ppp.sc.gov
Fiscal Management Director **Cheryl Thompson** . . . . . . . . . (803) 734-9244
Executive Programs Office Director **Jodi Gallman** . . . . . . . (803) 734-9220
  E-mail: jodi.gallman@ppp.sc.gov

## Field Operations Division

Deputy Director **Michael Nichols** . . . . . . . . . . . . . . . . . . . . (803) 734-9281
Field Operations Support Programs Director
  **Rebecca Raybon** . . . . . . . . . . . . . . . . . . . . . . . . . . . . . (803) 734-9281
Compact Administrator **Victoria Jakes** . . . . . . . . . . . . . . . (803) 734-9228
Ignition Interlock System Director **Ruth Ann Cartwright** . . . . . . . . (803) 734-0019

# Department of Public Safety

10311 Wilson Boulevard, Blythewood, SC 29016
P.O. Box 1993, Blythewood, SC 29016
Tel: (803) 896-9000

**Employees: 755  Fiscal Year: 2015  Budget: $160,664,000**

■Director **Leroy Smith** . . . . . . . . . . . . . . . . . . . . . . . . . . . . . (803) 896-7979
  E-mail: leroysmith@scdps.gov
  Administrative Coordinator **Bonnie Brooks** . . . . . . . . . . . (803) 896-7979
    E-mail: bonniebrooks@scdps.gov
General Counsel **Warren Ganjehsani** . . . . . . . . . . . . . . . . . (803) 896-8750
Human Resources Office Director **Tosha Autry** . . . . . . . . . (803) 896-7943
Professional Responsibility Office Chief Inspector
  **Kenneth Phelps** . . . . . . . . . . . . . . . . . . . . . . . . . . . . . . (803) 896-8247
  E-mail: kennethphelps@scdps.gov

Information Technology Administrator **Michael Orecchio** . . (803) 896-8145
  E-mail: michaelorecchio@scdps.gov
Chief Financial Officer **Paul Lewis** . . . . . . . . . . . . . . . . . . . (803) 896-8355

## Office of Communications

Public Information Director **Sherri Iacobelli** . . . . . . . . . . . . (803) 896-8409
  E-mail: sherriiacobelli@scdps.gov

## Office of Highway Safety and Justice Programs

Building C, 10311 Wilson Boulevard, Blythewood, SC 29016
Tel: (803) 896-9950

Justice Programs/Highway Safety Office Director
  **Phil Riley** . . . . . . . . . . . . . . . . . . . . . . . . . . . . . . . . . . . (803) 896-9970
  E-mail: philriley@scdps.gov
Assistant Director **Ed Harmon, PhD** . . . . . . . . . . . . . . . . . (803) 896-9971
Public Affairs Manager **(Vacant)** . . . . . . . . . . . . . . . . . . . . (803) 896-9402

## Highway Patrol

Highway Patrol Division Commander
  **Col. Michael Oliver** . . . . . . . . . . . . . . . . . . . . . . . . . . . . (803) 896-8228
Public Information Officer **Sgt Bob Beres** . . . . . . . . . . . . . (803) 896-8164
  E-mail: rberes@scdps.gov

## State Transport Police

Tel: (803) 896-5500  Fax: (803) 896-5526

State Transport Police Deputy Director **Leroy Taylor** . . . . . . (803) 896-5513

## Bureau of Protective Services

Tel: (803) 896-5442  Fax: (803) 737-7729

Bureau Administrator and Chief of Police
  **Zackary "Zack" Wise** . . . . . . . . . . . . . . . . . . . . . . . . . . (803) 896-5442
Assistant Chief **Major John D. Hancock** . . . . . . . . . . . . . . (803) 896-5442

# Department of Revenue [SCDOR]

P.O. Box 125, Columbia, SC 29214
Tel: (803) 898-5000  TTY: (803) 898-5656  Fax: (803) 898-5822
Internet: dor.sc.gov

**Employees: 789  Fiscal Year: 2014-2015  Budget: $81,363,000**

■Director **Rick Reames III** . . . . . . . . . . . . . . . . . . . . . . . . . . (803) 898-5148
  E-mail: rick.reames@dor.sc.gov
Communications Director **Ashley Thomas** . . . . . . . . . . . . . (803) 898-5773
  E-mail: ashley.thomas@dor.sc.gov
Chief Information Security Officer
  **Michael "Mike" Sayles** . . . . . . . . . . . . . . . . . . . . . . . . . (803) 898-5501
  E-mail: mike.sayles@dor.sc.gov
Field Operations Deputy Director **Mont Alexander** . . . . . . (803) 898-5950
Internal Audit Director **Kimberley "Kim" Tudor** . . . . . . . . (803) 898-5051
Administrative Services Deputy Director
  **Laura Watts, CIA, CPA** . . . . . . . . . . . . . . . . . . . . . . . . . (803) 898-5038
  E-mail: laura.watts@dor.sc.gov
Government and Communication Services Deputy
  Director **Meredith Cleland** . . . . . . . . . . . . . . . . . . . . . . (803) 898-5402
  E-mail: meredith.cleland@dor.sc.gov
Taxpayers and Business Services Deputy Director
  **Sherrie McTeer** . . . . . . . . . . . . . . . . . . . . . . . . . . . . . . (803) 896-1912
Chief Financial Officer **Laura Watts, CIA, CPA** . . . . . . . . . (803) 898-5038
Human Resources Development and Planning Office
  Administrator **Nancy Wilson** . . . . . . . . . . . . . . . . . . . . (803) 898-5453
  E-mail: nancy.wilson@dor.sc.gov
  Education: Presbyterian Col 1971 BA, MEd; South Carolina 1980 PhD
General Counsel **Joe S. Dusenberry, Jr.** . . . . . . . . . . . . . . (803) 898-5035
General Counsel **Milton Kimpson** . . . . . . . . . . . . . . . . . . . (803) 898-5131

---

★ Elected Official     ■ Appointed by Governor     ● Appointed by Legislature     ▲ Appointed by Board or Commission     ◆ Appointed by State Supreme Court

# Department of Social Services

P.O. Box 1520, Columbia, SC 29202-1520
Tel: (803) 898-1390  TTY: (800) 311-7219  TTY: (803) 898-7272 (Local)
Fax: (803) 898-7277

**Employees:** 4,139  **Fiscal Year:** 2015  **Budget:** $692,184,000

■Director **Susan Alford** . . . . . . . . . . . . . . . . . . . . . . . . . . . (803) 898-7601
E-mail: susan.alford@dss.sc.gov
Chief of Staff **Joan Meachum** . . . . . . . . . . . . . . . . . . . . . (803) 898-1805
Administrative Coordinator **Linda Stillinger** . . . . . . . . . . (803) 898-1390

# Department of Transportation [SCDOT]

955 Park Street, Columbia, SC 29201-3959
Tel: (803) 737-2314  TTY: (803) 737-3870  Internet: www.dot.state.sc.us

**Employees:** 888  **Fiscal Year:** 2015  **Budget:** $1,627,325,000

■Transportation Secretary **Christy A. Hall, PE, C.P.M.** . . . . . . (803) 737-1302
E-mail: christyhall@scdps.gov
Education: Clemson BCE

## Office of the Chief Financial Officer

Tel: (803) 737-1243

Chief Financial Officer **Kace Smith** . . . . . . . . . . . . . . . . . (803) 737-1240
Deputy Secretary for Finance and Procurement
**Brian W. Keys** . . . . . . . . . . . . . . . . . . . . . . . . . . . . . . (803) 737-1240
Communications Director **Pete Poore** . . . . . . . . . . . . . . . . (803) 737-1270
Public Involvement Coordinator **Vivian M. Patterson** . . . . . (803) 737-1444
Business Development and Special Programs Deputy
Director **Arlene Prince** . . . . . . . . . . . . . . . . . . . . . . . . (803) 737-1717
E-mail: princeaf@scdot.org
Human Resource Services Director
**Mary Gail Monts Chamblee** . . . . . . . . . . . . . . . . . . . (803) 737-1321
Information Technology Services Director **Doug Harper** . . . (803) 737-1640
E-mail: harperds@scdot.org
Office of Contract Assurance Director **J. Darrin Player** . . . . (803) 737-1472
E-mail: playerjd@scdot.org
Procurement Director **Sherry D. Barton** . . . . . . . . . . . . . . (803) 737-1474
Chief Legal Counsel **Linda C. MacDonald** . . . . . . . . . . . . (803) 737-1347
E-mail: mcdonaldlc@scdot.org

## Engineering Division

Deputy Secretary for Engineering (Acting)
**Leland Colvin, PE** . . . . . . . . . . . . . . . . . . . . . . . . . . . (803) 737-7900
Chief Engineer for Location and Design **(Vacant)** . . . . . . . . (803) 737-5028
Chief Engineer for Operations **Leland Colvin, PE** . . . . . . . (803) 737-7900
Construction Director **Todd Steagall, PE** . . . . . . . . . . . . . (803) 737-1308
Maintenance Director **Jim Feda, PE** . . . . . . . . . . . . . . . . . (803) 737-1290
E-mail: fedajj@scdot.org
Preconstruction Director **Ladd Gibson** . . . . . . . . . . . . . . (803) 737-1350
Traffic Engineering Director **Anthony "Tony" Fallaw** . . . . (803) 737-1462
District 1 Engineering Administrator **Bryan L. Jones, PE** . . (803) 737-6660
1400 Shop Road, Columbia, SC 29201
E-mail: jonesbl@scdot.org
District 2 Engineering Administrator
**Kevin McLaughlin, PE** . . . . . . . . . . . . . . . . . . . . . . . . (864) 227-6971
510 West Alexander Avenue, Greenwood, SC 29646
District 3 Engineering Administrator
**Stephanie Amell-Jackson** . . . . . . . . . . . . . . . . . . . . . . (864) 241-1010
P.O. Box 6608, Greenville, SC 29606
E-mail: jacksonas@scdot.org
District 4 Engineering Administrator **John McCarter, PE** . . (803) 377-4155
P.O. Box 130, Chester, SC 29706
E-mail: mccarterjm@scdot.org
District 5 Engineering Administrator **Kyle Berry** . . . . . . . . (843) 661-4710
E-mail: berrywk@scdot.org
District 6 Engineering Administrator **Robert Clark** . . . . . . . (843) 740-1665
6355 Fain Street, North Charleston, SC 29406
E-mail: clarkrt@scdot.org
District 7 Engineering Administrator **Jo Ann Woodrum** . . (803) 531-6850
P.O. Box 1086, Orangeburg, SC 29116
E-mail: woodrumjh@scdot.org

## Intermodal Planning Division

Deputy Secretary **Ron Patton, PE** . . . . . . . . . . . . . . . . . . (803) 737-1446

# South Carolina Department of Transportation Commission

■Chairman **James Michael "Mike" Wooten** (District 7) . . . (843) 692-3200
E-mail: wootenjm@scdot.org
■Vice-Chairman **John N. Hardee** (District 2) . . . . . . . . . . . (803) 737-2314
E-mail: hardeejn@scdot.org
Commissioner
**David E. "Gene" Branham, Sr.** (District 5) . . . . . . . . . . (803) 995-2874
P.O. Box 12407, Rock Hill, SC 29731
E-mail: branhamde@scdot.org
■Commissioner **Ben H. Davis, Jr.** (District 3) . . . . . . . . . . (864) 882-2441
E-mail: davisbh@scdot.org
■Commissioner **Samuel B. Glover** (District 6) . . . . . . . . . . (803) 737-2314
Education: South Carolina State BA, MA
■Commissioner **G. Clifton Parker** (At-Large) . . . . . . . . . . . (803) 936-6015
E-mail: parkergc@scdot.org
■Commissioner **Robert D. "Robby" Robbins** (District 1) . . (803) 995-2875
E-mail: robbinsrd@scdot.org
■Commissioner
**Woodrow W. "Woody" Willard, Jr.** (District 4) . . . . . . (864) 542-7949

# South Carolina Vocational Rehabilitation Department [SCVRD]

1410 Boston Avenue, West Columbia, SC 29170
P.O. Box 15, Columbia, SC 29170
Tel: (803) 896-6500  TTY: (803) 896-6559  Fax: (803) 896-6525
E-mail: scvrhr@infoave.net

▲Commissioner **Neal Getsinger** . . . . . . . . . . . . . . . . . . . . (803) 896-6500
E-mail: neal.getsinger@sc.gov
Assistant Commissioner **Rick Elam** . . . . . . . . . . . . . . . . . (803) 896-6503
Assistant Commissioner **Mark Wade** . . . . . . . . . . . . . . . . (803) 896-6500
Disability Determination Services Director
**Shirley Jarrett** . . . . . . . . . . . . . . . . . . . . . . . . . . . . . . (803) 896-6400
Human Resources Director **Eric S. Moore** . . . . . . . . . . . . . (803) 896-6551
Staff Development and Training Director
**Belinda Langton** . . . . . . . . . . . . . . . . . . . . . . . . . . . . (803) 896-6533
Job Recruiter **Cathy Smith** . . . . . . . . . . . . . . . . . . . . . . . (803) 896-6553

## Administrative Services

Data Processing Director **Jerold Rolin** . . . . . . . . . . . . . . . (803) 896-6800
E-mail: jerold.rolin@sc.gov
Finance Director **Denise Koon** . . . . . . . . . . . . . . . . . . . . . (803) 896-6600
Internal Audit and Inventory Director
**John Sandifer, CPMR** . . . . . . . . . . . . . . . . . . . . . . . . . (803) 896-6614
Procurement Services Director **Todd Blake** . . . . . . . . . . . . (803) 896-6520

# State Law Enforcement Division [SLED]

4400 Broad River Road, Columbia, SC 29210
P.O. Box 21398, Columbia, SC 29221
Tel: (803) 737-9000  Fax: (803) 896-7588

■Chief **Mark A. Keel** . . . . . . . . . . . . . . . . . . . . . . . . . . . (803) 896-7001
E-mail: mkeel@sled.sc.gov
Education: South Carolina JD
Assistant Chief **Major Paul Grant** . . . . . . . . . . . . . . . . . . (803) 896-7002
Administration Director **Don Royal** . . . . . . . . . . . . . . . . . (803) 896-7425
E-mail: droyal@sled.sc.gov
Human Resources Director **Teresa C. Kitchens** . . . . . . . . . (803) 896-7168
Forensic Services Program Manager
**Major C. Todd Hughey, PhD** . . . . . . . . . . . . . . . . . . . (803) 896-7068
Education: Wofford 1986 BS; South Carolina 1995 PhB
Major Investigations **Major Roger Owens** . . . . . . . . . . . . (803) 737-9000
Arson Law Enforcement Officer **Major Dave Tafaoa** . . . . . (803) 896-7273
Executive Protection Law Enforcement Officer
**Jack Proffitt** . . . . . . . . . . . . . . . . . . . . . . . . . . . . . . . (803) 896-7578
Freedom of Information Law Enforcement Officer
**Thom Berry** . . . . . . . . . . . . . . . . . . . . . . . . . . . . . . . . (803) 896-7156

*(continued on next page)*

★ Elected Official    ■ Appointed by Governor    ● Appointed by Legislature    ▲ Appointed by Board or Commission    ◆ Appointed by State Supreme Court

**State Law Enforcement Division** *continued*

Regulatory Services Law Enforcement Officer
  **Lt. Derick Horton** ................................ (803) 896-7029
    E-mail: dhorton@sc.gov
Homeland Security Grants Coordinator
  **Major Richard Hunton** ......................... (803) 896-6389
Public Information Coordinator and Legislative Liaison
  **Kathryn Richardson** ............................. (803) 737-9000
    E-mail: krichardson@sled.sc.gov
Procurement Manager **Wendy Threlkeld** ............... (803) 896-7004

## Office of Regulatory Staff

1401 Main Street, Suite 900, Columbia, SC 29201
Tel: (803) 737-0800  Fax: (803) 737-0801
Internet: www.regulatorystaff.sc.gov

Executive Director **C. Dukes Scott** ................... (803) 737-0805
    E-mail: cdscott@regstaff.sc.gov
    Education: Clemson BS; South Carolina JD
Deputy Executive Director **Nanette S. Edwards** ......... (803) 737-0575
    E-mail: nsedwar@regstaff.sc.gov
General Counsel **Florence Belser** ..................... (803) 737-0853
    E-mail: fbelser@regstaff.sc.gov
    Education: Col Charleston BS; South Carolina JD
Information Services Director **Florence N. Gailey** ....... (803) 737-0807
    E-mail: fgailey@regstaff.sc.gov
    Education: South Carolina BS, MPA

## Higher Education Commission

1122 Lady Street, Suite 300, Columbia, SC 29201
Tel: (803) 737-2260  Fax: (803) 737-2297  Internet: www.che.sc.gov

**Employees:** 40  **Fiscal Year:** 2015  **Budget:** $77,496,000

▲Executive Director (Interim) **Gary Glenn** .............. (803) 737-2155
    E-mail: gglenn@che.sc.gov
Executive Assistant **Beth Rogers** .................... (803) 737-2275

## Education Assistance Authority

P.O. Box 102425, Columbia, SC 29224
Tel: (803) 798-7960  Fax: (803) 612-5045
Internet: www.scstudentloan.org

▲President **Charles "Chuck" Sanders** ................. (803) 798-7960
    E-mail: csanders@scstudentloan.org
Senior Vice President **Anne-Harvin Gavin** ............. (803) 798-7960
    E-mail: a.gavin@scmanet.org

## Jobs - Economic Development Authority

1201 Main Street, Suite 1600, Columbia, SC 29201
Tel: (803) 737-0268  Fax: (803) 737-0628
E-mail: generalinfo@sceda.com

**Employees:** 2

▲Executive Director **Harry A. Huntley, CPA** .............. (803) 737-0627
    E-mail: hhuntley@scjeda.com
    Education: South Carolina 1977 BS, 1982 MBA
Executive Assistant/Office Manager **Claudia Miller** ..... (803) 737-0284

## Santee Cooper (South Carolina Public Service Authority)

One Riverwood Drive, Moncks Corner, SC 29461
Tel: (843) 761-8000  Internet: www.santeecooper.com

▲President and Chief Executive Officer **Lonnie N. Carter** ... (843) 761-7024
    E-mail: lncarter@santeecooper.com
    Education: Citadel BSBA, MBA
Senior Vice President and Chief Financial Officer
  **Jeff D. Armfield** ................................ (843) 761-4066
    Education: Citadel 1977 BS, 1988 MBA
Senior Vice President and General Counsel
  **J. Michael Baxley** .............................. (843) 761-4092

Senior Vice President, Power Delivery
  **Arnold R. Singleton** ............................ (843) 761-8000
    E-mail: arsingle@santeecooper.com
Executive Vice President, Competitive Markets and
  Generation **Marc Tye** ............................ (843) 761-8000
    E-mail: mrtye@santeecooper.com
Executive Vice President, Corporate Services
  **Pamela Williams** ............................... (843) 761-4129
    E-mail: pamela.williams@santeecooper.com
Vice President, Fuels Strategy **Jane Hood** ............. (843) 761-8000
    Education: Clemson BS; Citadel MBA
Vice President, Generating Stations **Thomas B. Curtis** .... (843) 761-8000
Vice President, Government and Community Relations
  **Richard S. Kizer** ............................... (843) 761-8000
Vice President, Human Resource Management
  **Laura Varn** ..................................... (843) 761-4133
    E-mail: lgvarn@santeecooper.com
General Auditor **Kenneth Lott** ....................... (843) 761-5113
Corporate Communications Manager **Mollie Gore** ........ (843) 761-7093

## State Housing Finance and Development Authority

300-C Outlet Pointe Boulevard, Columbia, SC 29210
Tel: (803) 896-9001  TTY: (803) 896-8831  Fax: (803) 896-8826

**Employees:** 141  **Fiscal Year:** 2015  **Budget:** $182,072,000

▲Executive Director **Valarie M. Williams** ............... (803) 896-9005
    E-mail: valarie.williams@schousing.com
    Administrative Assistant **Bonita Shropshire** .......... (803) 896-9005
Development Director **Laura Nicholson** ............... (803) 896-9190
Investor Services Director **Kim Spires** ............... (803) 896-9479
Administration and Finance Deputy Director
  **Richard Hutto** .................................. (803) 896-8664
Programs Deputy Director **Ed Knight** ................ (803) 896-8686
    E-mail: ed.knight@schousing.com
Webmaster **Todd Sipos** ............................. (803) 896-9164
Marketing and Communications Manager
  **Clayton Ingram** ................................ (803) 896-9520
    E-mail: clayton.ingram@schousing.com
Neighborhood Stabilization Program Manager
  **Jennifer Cogan** ................................ (803) 896-9824
    E-mail: jennifer.cogan@schousing.com
Home Program Manager **Leanne Johnson** ............. (803) 896-9248
    E-mail: leanne.johnson@schousing.com
Underwriting Manager **Jeff Maddox** .................. (803) 896-9197

## State Board of Education

1429 Senate Street, Room 1002, Columbia, SC 29201
Tel: (803) 734-8392  Fax: (803) 734-3389  E-mail: rkerley@ed.sc.gov

■Chair **Michael R. Brenan** ........................... (803) 251-1440
    Note: Serves at will of the Governor
    E-mail: mbrenan@bbandt.com
●Chair-Elect **Dr. Ivan Randolph** (Circuit 8) ............. (864) 378-2567
    Term Expires: December 31, 2017
    E-mail: sirandolph53@gmail.com
●Member **Dr. Samuel Alston** (Circuit 1) ................ (803) 874-3454
    Term Expires: January 31, 2017
    E-mail: sc29135@windstream.net
●Member **Sharon Bynum** (Circuit 16) ................. (803) 548-5066
    Term Expires: December 31, 2018
●Member **Dr. Traci Young Cooper, EdD** (Circuit 5) ....... (803) 231-6842
    Term Expires: December 31, 2016
    E-mail: cooper4kids@gmail.com
    Education: Georgetown BA; South Carolina MA;
    South Carolina State PhD
●Member
  **Dr. Rhonda Yvonne Edwards** (Circuit 14)
    Term Expires: December 31, 2016
    E-mail: doctored50@gmail.com
●Member **Tom Ewart** (Circuit 12) ..................... (843) 319-2669
    Term Expires: December 31, 2017
    E-mail: tewart@firstreliance.com
●Member **Dr. Janice Murray Gamble** (Circuit 3) ........ (803) 428-6852
    Term Expires: December 31, 2019
    E-mail: harrytlc2000@yahoo.com

---

★ Elected Official   ■ Appointed by Governor   ● Appointed by Legislature   ▲ Appointed by Board or Commission   ◆ Appointed by State Supreme Court

- ●Member **Jane P. Harmon** (Circuit 7) . . . . . . . . . . . . . . . . . .(803) 734-8392
  Term Expires: December 31, 2018
- ●Member **Del-Gratia Jones** (Circuit 2) . . . . . . . . . . . . . . (734) 516-2582
  Term Expires: December 31, 2019
- ●Member **Richard S. Kizer** (Circuit 9) . . . . . . . . . . . . . . . . (803) 734-8392
  Term Expires: December 31, 2016
- ●Member **Jeff Kubu** (Circuit 10)
  Term Expires: December 31, 2016
- ●Member **Gerald Reeves** (Circuit 4)
  Term Expires: December 31, 2018
- ●Member **Tom Shortt** (Circuit 15) . . . . . . . . . . . . . . . . . . . (843) 833-2170
  Term Expires: December 31, 2015
  E-mail: tshortt@istation.com
- ●Member **James Stroman** (Circuit 6) . . . . . . . . . . . . . . . . (803) 385-6120
  Term Expires: December 31, 2017
  E-mail: stro@truvista.net
- ●Member **Danny Varat** (Circuit 13) . . . . . . . . . . . . . . . . . . (864) 787-4150
  Term Expires: December 31, 2015
  E-mail: dannyvarat@att.net
- ●Member **Dr. Sharon Wall** (Circuit 11) . . . . . . . . . . . . . . (803) 275-7207
  Term Expires: December 31, 2018
  Secretary and Administrative Coordinator
  **LaTonia Halloway** . . . . . . . . . . . . . . . . . . . . . . . . . . . (803) 734-8225
  E-mail: thalloway@ed.sc.gov
  General Counsel **Kathy Hazelwood** . . . . . . . . . . . . . . . . . . (803) 734-8783

## Financial Institutions Board

P.O. Box 11778, Columbia, SC 29211
Tel: (803) 734-2016  Fax: (803) 734-2013

**Employees:** 45  **Fiscal Year:** 2015  **Budget:** $4,284,000

Chairman **Curtis M. Loftis, Jr.** . . . . . . . . . . . . . . . . . . . . . (803) 734-2020
  E-mail: state.treasurer@sto.sc.gov
  Education: South Carolina 1981 BA
  Assistant to the Chairman **Tony Kester** . . . . . . . . . . . . . . (803) 734-2699

### Bank Examining Division

1205 Pendleton Street, Suite 305, Columbia, SC 29201

Commissioner of Banking **Louie A. Jacobs** . . . . . . . . . . . .(803) 734-2001
  E-mail: louie.jacobs@banking.sc.gov
Assistant Commissioner of Banking **Kathy L. Bickham** . . . (803) 734-2001
  E-mail: kathy.bickham@banking.sc.gov

### Consumer Finance Division

Tel: (803) 734-2020  Fax: (803) 734-2025

Commissioner of Consumer Finance **Ron Bodvake** . . . . . . . (803) 734-2020
Assistant Commissioner of Consumer Finance
  **James "Jim" Copeland** . . . . . . . . . . . . . . . . . . . . . . . .(803) 734-2020
  E-mail: jim.copeland@bofi.sc.gov
Assistant Commissioner of Consumer Finance
  **Carl Jeffcoat** . . . . . . . . . . . . . . . . . . . . . . . . . . . . . . . . (803) 734-2020
  E-mail: carl.jeffcoat@bofi.sc.gov

## South Carolina Transportation Infrastructure Bank

955 Park Street, Columbia, SC 29201-3959
Tel: (803) 737-2875  Fax: (803) 737-2014

State Infrastructure Bank Director **Debra Rountree** . . . . . . (803) 312-5674

## Office of the Lieutenant Governor

P.O. Box 142, Columbia, SC 29202
Tel: (803) 734-2080  Fax: (803) 734-2082
E-mail: ltgovernor@scstatehouse.gov  Internet: www.ltgov.sc.gov

**Fiscal Year:** 2015  **Budget:** $47,648,000

★Lieutenant Governor **Henry Dargan McMaster** (R) . . . . . . (803) 724-2169
  Term Expires: 2019
  Education: South Carolina 1969 BA, 1973 JD
  Career: Attorney General, Office of Attorney General Henry McMaster,
  State of South Carolina (2002-2011)
Chief of Staff **Mark W. Plowden** . . . . . . . . . . . . . . . . . . . (803) 734-2080
Deputy Chief of Staff for Administration **Leigh LeMoine** . .(803) 734-2080
  E-mail: leighlemoine@scstatehouse.gov

Deputy Chief of Staff for External Affairs
  **Kristy Quattrone** . . . . . . . . . . . . . . . . . . . . . . . . . . . . . (803) 734-2080
Chief Legal Counsel **Andy Fiffick IV** . . . . . . . . . . . . . . . . (803) 734-2080
Deputy Chief of Staff for Policy and Research
  **Jason Brown** . . . . . . . . . . . . . . . . . . . . . . . . . . . . . . . . (803) 734-2080

## Office of the Secretary of State

Edgar Brown Building, 1205 Pendleton Street, Suite 525,
Columbia, SC 29201
Tel: (803) 734-2170  Internet: www.scsos.com

**Employees:** 29  **Fiscal Year:** 2015  **Budget:** $2,546,000

★Secretary of State **Mark Hammond** (R) . . . . . . . . . . . . . . (803) 734-2156
  Term Expires: January 2019            Fax: (803) 734-1661
  E-mail: mhammond@sos.sc.gov
  Education: Newberry 1986 BA; Clemson 1988 MEd
  Career: Criminal Investigator, Office of 7th Circuit Solicitor, Seventh
  Judicial Circuit, South Carolina Circuit Courts (1991-1996); Clerk of
  Court, Office of Clerk of Court, County of Spartanburg, South Carolina
  (1997-2003)
  Executive Assistant, Trademarks Coordinator and
    Media Relations Director **Renee S. Daggerhart** . . . . . . (803) 734-0629
    E-mail: rdaggerhart@sos.sc.gov
Deputy Secretary of State and Chief Legal Counsel
  **Melissa Wheeler Dunlap** . . . . . . . . . . . . . . . . . . . . . . .(803) 734-2157
General Counsel **Shannon Wiley** . . . . . . . . . . . . . . . . . . . (803) 734-0246
Notaries, Boards and Commissions Director
  **Tracy Sharpe** . . . . . . . . . . . . . . . . . . . . . . . . . . . . . . . .(803) 734-6045
                                        Fax: (803) 734-1610
Business Filings Division Director **Jody Steigerwalt** . . . . . (803) 734-2345
                                        Fax: (803) 734-2164
Charities Division Director **Kimberly Wickersham** . . . . . . .(803) 734-1796
                                        Fax: (803) 734-1604
Investigator **Doug Renew** . . . . . . . . . . . . . . . . . . . . . . . . (803) 734-1728
Service of Process and Cable Franchising Coordinator
  **Allyson Green** . . . . . . . . . . . . . . . . . . . . . . . . . . . . . . .(803) 734-0367
  E-mail: agreen@sos.sc.gov

## Office of the Attorney General

P.O. Box 11549, Columbia, SC 29211
Rembert Dennis Building, 1000 Assembly Street, Room 519,
Columbia, SC 29201
Tel: (803) 734-3970  E-mail: info@scattorneygeneral.com

**Employees:** 200

★Attorney General **Alan McCrory Wilson** (R) . . . . . . . . . . . (803) 734-3970
  Term Expires: January 2019
  Education: Francis Marion 1996; South Carolina 2002 JD
  Career: Assistant Attorney General, Office of the Attorney General,
  State of South Carolina
Chief Deputy Attorney General **John W. McIntosh** . . . . . . (803) 734-5089
Chief of Staff **Barry Bernstein** . . . . . . . . . . . . . . . . . . . . .(803) 734-3970
Government Relations Director **Adam Piper** . . . . . . . . . . . (803) 734-3970
Solicitor General and Head of Opinions **Robert Cook** . . . . .(803) 734-3970
Deputy Solicitor General **J. Emory Smith, Jr.** . . . . . . . . . . (803) 734-3970
Securities Deputy Attorney General **Stephen Lynch** . . . . . . (803) 734-9916
                                        Fax: (803) 734-3677
Communications Director **(Vacant)** . . . . . . . . . . . . . . . . . .(803) 734-3970
Finance Division Director **Kim Buckley** . . . . . . . . . . . . . . (803) 734-3726
Administration Division Director **Tammie Hall Wilson** . . . .(803) 734-3970
  E-mail: twilson@scag.gov
Capital and Collateral Litigation Section Director
  **Don Zelenka** . . . . . . . . . . . . . . . . . . . . . . . . . . . . . . . (803) 734-6305
Criminal Appeals Director **Ben Aplin** . . . . . . . . . . . . . . . .(803) 734-3727
Government and Civil Litigation Division Director
  **Stephen Lynch** . . . . . . . . . . . . . . . . . . . . . . . . . . . . . . (803) 734-3680
Information Technology Director **Andrew Blais** . . . . . . . . . .(803) 734-3746
  E-mail: ablais@scag.gov
Insurance Fraud Section Director **Melissa Manning** . . . . . . (803) 737-6424
Medicaid Provider Fraud Section Director
  **Charles William "Bill" Gambrell** . . . . . . . . . . . . . . . . . (803) 734-3970
Medicaid Recipient Fraud Section Director
  **Camille E. Guthrie** . . . . . . . . . . . . . . . . . . . . . . . . . . . (803) 734-3970

*(continued on next page)*

★ Elected Official   ■ Appointed by Governor   ● Appointed by Legislature   ▲ Appointed by Board or Commission   ◆ Appointed by State Supreme Court

*State Yellow Book*                    © Leadership Directories, Inc.                    Summer 2016

**Office of the Attorney General** *continued*

Post Conviction Relief Section Director
  Johanna C. Valenzuela . . . . . . . . . . . . . . . . . . . . (803) 734-3737
    Education: South Carolina 2010 JD
Human Resources Manager **Katie Elliott** . . . . . . . . . . . . (803) 734-3152

# Office of the State Treasurer

P.O. Box 11778, Columbia, SC 29211
Wade Hampton Building, 1200 Senate Street, Columbia, SC 29201
Tel: (803) 734-2101  Fax: (803) 734-2690  E-mail: treasurer@sto.sc.gov

**Fiscal Year:** 2016  **Budget:** $7,885,000

★Treasurer **Curtis M. Loftis, Jr.** (R) . . . . . . . . . . . . . . . . (803) 734-2101
    Term Expires: January 2019
Deputy State Treasurer **Cynthia Dannels** . . . . . . . . . . . . . (803) 734-2101
Deputy State Treasurer **Tonia Morris** . . . . . . . . . . . . . . . (803) 734-2101
Chief of Staff **Clarissa T. Adams** . . . . . . . . . . . . . . . . (803) 734-5063
Accounting and Banking Services Senior Assistant State
  Treasurer **Paul Jarvis** . . . . . . . . . . . . . . . . . . . . . (803) 734-2101
Administration Senior Assistant State Treasurer
  **Paul J. Ham** . . . . . . . . . . . . . . . . . . . . . . . . . . (803) 734-2101
    E-mail: paul.ham@sto.sc.gov
Debt Management Senior Assistant State Treasurer
  **Kevin D. Kibler** . . . . . . . . . . . . . . . . . . . . . . . . (803) 734-2101
Investments Senior Assistant State Treasurer
  **J. West Summers** . . . . . . . . . . . . . . . . . . . . . . . . (803) 734-2101
    Education: Wofford 1984 BA
Information Technology Director **Chuck Fallaw** . . . . . . . . . (803) 734-2101
    E-mail: chuck.fallaw@sto.sc.gov

# Office of the Comptroller General

305 Wade Hampton Building, 1200 Senate Street, Columbia, SC 29201
Tel: (803) 734-2121  Fax: (803) 734-1765  E-mail: cgoffice@cg.sc.gov
Internet: www.cg.sc.gov

**Employees:** 32  **Fiscal Year:** 2015-2016  **Budget:** $2,966,000

★Comptroller General **Richard A. Eckstrom, CPA** (R) . . . . . (803) 734-2121
    Term Expires: January 2019
    E-mail: reckstrom@cg.sc.gov
    Education: South Carolina 1970 BS, 1977 MBA, 1978 MAcc
    Career: State Treasurer, Office of the State Treasurer, State of South
    Carolina (1995-1999)
Chief of Staff **William E. Gunn** . . . . . . . . . . . . . . . . . (803) 734-2121
Administrative Services Senior Assistant Comptroller
  General **Joy D. Stagg** . . . . . . . . . . . . . . . . . . . . . (803) 734-2588
    E-mail: jstagg@cg.sc.gov
Legislative Liaison Assistant Comptroller General
  **William E. Gunn** . . . . . . . . . . . . . . . . . . . . . . . . (803) 734-2121
    E-mail: egunn@cg.sc.gov
Operations Director **John Barfield** . . . . . . . . . . . . . . . (803) 734-2132
Statewide Accounting Services Director **Anjali Griffin** . . . . (803) 734-2609
Statewide Financial Reporting Division Director
  **David Starkey** . . . . . . . . . . . . . . . . . . . . . . . . . (803) 734-2542
Statewide Payroll Assistant Comptroller General
  **Ronald Head** . . . . . . . . . . . . . . . . . . . . . . . . . . (803) 734-2347
Information Technology Director **Scott Houston** . . . . . . . . (803) 734-2568
    E-mail: shouston@cg.sc.gov

# Office of the Adjutant General

One National Guard Road, Columbia, SC 29201
Tel: (803) 299-4200

**Fiscal Year:** 2015  **Budget:** $58,457,000

★Adjutant General
  **MG Robert E. "Bob" Livingston, Jr., ARNG** (R) . . . . . . (803) 299-4032
    Term Expires: January 2019
    Education: Hampden-Sydney 1978 BS; Georgia Tech 1980 BEE,
    1981 MSEE; South Carolina 1988 MBA; Army War Col 2001 MS
Deputy Adjutant General **BG Roy V. McCarty, ARNG** . . . . (803) 299-4215
    E-mail: roy.v.mccarty.mil@mail.mil
  Chief of Staff **COL Ronald Taylor, ARNG** . . . . . . . . . . (803) 299-1461
  Chief of Staff (Air) **BrigGen Scott Lambe, ANG** . . . . . . (803) 299-4032
  Assistant Chief of Staff
    **LTC Marion A. Bulwinkle III, ARNG** . . . . . . . . . . . . (803) 299-4032

Public Affairs Director
  **LTC Cynthia "Cindi" King, ARNG** . . . . . . . . . . . . . . (803) 299-4327
    E-mail: cynthia.m.king4.mil@mail.mil

# South Carolina Education Lottery

1333 Main Street, 4th Floor, Columbia, SC 29201-1488
P.O. Box 11949, Columbia, SC 29211-1949
Tel: (803) 737-2002  Fax: (803) 737-2893
E-mail: questions@sceducationlottery.com
Internet: www.sceducationlottery.com

●Chairman **Timothy E. "Tim" Madden** . . . . . . . . . . . . . (803) 737-2002
    Education: Wofford 1985 BA; South Carolina 1988 JD
●Vice Chairman **Dr. Edward Keith** . . . . . . . . . . . . . . . (803) 737-2002
●Secretary **Sam Litchfield** . . . . . . . . . . . . . . . . . . . (803) 737-2002
    E-mail: sam.litchfield@sclot.com
●Treasurer **Nancy Cannon** . . . . . . . . . . . . . . . . . . . (803) 737-2002
■Member **Karen Ballentine** . . . . . . . . . . . . . . . . . . . (803) 737-2002
    E-mail: karen.ballentine@sclot.com
●Member **Thomas O. DeLoach, JD** . . . . . . . . . . . . . . . (803) 737-2002
■Member **H. B. "Buck" Limehouse, Jr.** . . . . . . . . . . . . (803) 737-2002
    Education: Citadel 1960 BA
●Member **Otis Morris, Jr.** . . . . . . . . . . . . . . . . . . . . (803) 737-2002
    E-mail: otis.morris@sclot.com
●Member **Keith D. Munson** . . . . . . . . . . . . . . . . . . . (803) 737-2002
    E-mail: keith.munson@sclot.com
■Member **Michael "Mickey" Renner** . . . . . . . . . . . . . . (803) 737-2002
Executive Director **Paula Harper Bethea** . . . . . . . . . . . (803) 737-2002
    Education: South Carolina 1975 BA
Chief Financial Officer **Joseph Boyle** . . . . . . . . . . . . . (803) 737-2002
Audit Services Director **Bethany A. Parler** . . . . . . . . . . (803) 737-2002
Human Resources Director **Claire Jones** . . . . . . . . . . . . (803) 737-2002
Information Technology Systems Director **Del Collins** . . . . (803) 737-2002
    E-mail: del.collins@sclot.com
Investigations and Security Director **J. Craig Perry** . . . . . (803) 737-2002
Legal Services Director **William Hogan Brown** . . . . . . . . (803) 737-2002
Marketing and Product Development Director
  **Jay Johnson** . . . . . . . . . . . . . . . . . . . . . . . . . . (803) 737-2002
Sales and Retailer Relations Director **Ann Scott** . . . . . . . (803) 737-2002
Chief Operating Officer **Anthony S. Cooper** . . . . . . . . . (803) 737-2002

---

★ Elected Official    ■ Appointed by Governor    ● Appointed by Legislature    ▲ Appointed by Board or Commission    ◆ Appointed by State Supreme Court

# South Dakota

Tel: (605) 773-3011 (State Information/Switchboard)

**Number of U.S. Congressional Delegates:** 2 Senators; 1 Representative **Governor's Term:** 4 years
**Legislature Description:** 35 member Senate; 70 member House of Representatives; Term - Senate 2 years; House 2 years **Next Election:** Governor November 2018; Legislature November 2016
**Number of Electoral Votes:** 3 **Official Name:** State of South Dakota (Sioux: allies)
**Nickname:** The Mount Rushmore State **Motto:** Under God the People Rule

**Population:** 858,469 (2015); Rank 46 **Fiscal Year:** 2014 **Budget:** $3,851,635,000

## Office of the Governor

500 East Capitol Avenue, Pierre, SD 57501
Tel: (605) 773-3212 Fax: (605) 773-4711

**Fiscal Year:** 2015 **Budget:** $2,217,000

**Dennis M. Daugaard**
Governor

Began Service: January 8, 2011
Term Expires: January 2019
Date of Birth: June 11, 1953
Education: South Dakota 1975 BS;
Northwestern 1978 JD
Home: Sioux Falls
Religion: Lutheran
Career: State Senator (R-SD, District 9), South
Dakota Senate (1997-2003); Lieutenant Governor
(R-SD), State of South Dakota (2003-2011)

★Governor **Dennis M. Daugaard** (R) . . . . . . . . . . . . . . . . . (605) 773-3212
Chief of Staff **Tonnis H. "Tony" Venhuizen** . . . . . . . . . . . (605) 773-3212
  Education: South Dakota State BS
General Counsel **Jim Seward** . . . . . . . . . . . . . . . . . . . . . . . (605) 773-3661
  E-mail: jim.seward@state.sd.us
Deputy General Counsel **A.J. Franken** . . . . . . . . . . . . . . . (605) 773-3661
  Education: Augusta BA; South Dakota JD
Executive Assistant **Kris Erickson** . . . . . . . . . . . . . . . . . . . (605) 773-3212
Executive Assistant **Monica Harding** . . . . . . . . . . . . . . . . (605) 773-3662
  E-mail: monica.harding@state.sd.us
Executive Assistant **Morgan Ness** . . . . . . . . . . . . . . . . . . . (605) 773-3212
Administrative Assistant **Judy Swartz** . . . . . . . . . . . . . . . . (605) 773-3661
Senior Advisor **Kim Malsam-Rysdon** . . . . . . . . . . . . . . . . (605) 773-3212
  E-mail: kim.malsam-rysdon@state.sd.us
  Education: South Dakota BA; Wisconsin MSW
Policy Advisor **Liza Clark** . . . . . . . . . . . . . . . . . . . . . . . . . . (605) 773-3212
  E-mail: liza.clark@state.sd.us
Policy Advisor **Matt Konenkamp** . . . . . . . . . . . . . . . . . . . (605) 773-3212
  E-mail: matt.konenkamp@state.sd.us
  Education: South Dakota 2002 JD
Policy Advisor **Hunter Roberts** . . . . . . . . . . . . . . . . . . . . . (605) 773-3212
  E-mail: hunter.roberts@state.sd.us
Deputy Policy Advisor **Kelsey Smith** . . . . . . . . . . . . . . . . (605) 773-5689
  E-mail: kelsey.webb@state.sd.us
Deputy Policy Advisor **Patrick Weber** . . . . . . . . . . . . . . . (605) 773-3212
  E-mail: patrick.weber@state.sd.us
  Education: South Dakota State BS; South Dakota JD
Policy Analyst **Grace Kessler** . . . . . . . . . . . . . . . . . . . . . . (605) 773-3212
  E-mail: grace.kessler@state.sd.us
Legislative Director **(Vacant)** . . . . . . . . . . . . . . . . . . . . . . . (605) 773-3212
Communications Director **Kelsey Pritchard** . . . . . . . . . . . (605) 773-3661
  E-mail: kelsey.pritchard@state.sd.us
Communications Assistant Director **(Vacant)** . . . . . . . . . . (605) 773-3212
Constituent Services Director **Sadie Stevens** . . . . . . . . . . . (605) 773-3212
  E-mail: sadie.stevens@state.sd.us
  Education: American U 2014
Policy and Operations Director **Nathan Sanderson** . . . . . . (605) 773-3212
  E-mail: nathan.sanderson@state.sd.us
Scheduler **Doreen Kayser** . . . . . . . . . . . . . . . . . . . . . . . . . (605) 773-3212
  E-mail: doreen.kayser@state.sd.us

State Demographer **(Vacant)** . . . . . . . . . . . . . . . . . . . . . . . . (605) 688-4901
  South Dakota State University Census Data Center, Scobey 202, Box
  504, Brookings, SD 57007-1296
Fiscal Officer **Travis Dovre** . . . . . . . . . . . . . . . . . . . . . . . . . (605) 773-3212

## Governor's Office of Economic Development

711 East Wells Avenue, Pierre, SD 57501-3369
Tel: (605) 773-3301 TTY: (800) 877-1113 Fax: (605) 773-3256
E-mail: goedinfo@goed.state.sd.us Internet: www.sdreadytowork.com

**Fiscal Year:** 2015 **Budget:** $65,982,000

Commissioner **J. Pat Costello** . . . . . . . . . . . . . . . . . . . . . . (605) 773-3301
Deputy Commissioner **Aaron Scheibe** . . . . . . . . . . . . . . . (605) 773-3256
Administrative Services Director **Karen Watson** . . . . . . . . (605) 773-5032
Business Development Director **Steve Watson** . . . . . . . . . . (605) 367-4518
Finance Director **Cassie Stoeser** . . . . . . . . . . . . . . . . . . . . (605) 773-3301
  Education: Black Hills State 2009        Tel: (800) 872-6190
Media and Public Relations Director
  **Mary Lehecka Nelson** . . . . . . . . . . . . . . . . . . . . . . . . . (605) 773-3301
                                           Tel: (800) 872-6190
Research Director **Mary Cerney** . . . . . . . . . . . . . . . . . . . . (605) 773-3301
  E-mail: mary.cerney@state.sd.us       Tel: (800) 872-6190
State Energy Development Director **(Vacant)** . . . . . . . . . . (605) 773-3301
Community Development Block Grant Program Specialist
  **Paul Mehlhaff** . . . . . . . . . . . . . . . . . . . . . . . . . . . . . . . (605) 773-5032

## Department of Agriculture [DOA]

Joe Foss Building, 523 East Capitol Avenue, Pierre, SD 57501-3182
Tel: (605) 773-3375 Fax: (605) 773-5926 E-mail: agmail@state.sd.us

**Employees:** 201 **Fiscal Year:** 2015 **Budget:** $45,120,000

■Secretary (Interim) **Dr. Dustin Oedekoven, DVM** . . . . . . . . (605) 773-5425
  E-mail: agmail@state.sd.us
  Executive Assistant **Judy Larson** . . . . . . . . . . . . . . . . . . (605) 773-5425
Deputy Secretary **Kyle Holt** . . . . . . . . . . . . . . . . . . . . . . . (605) 773-5425
General Counsel **Taya Runyan** . . . . . . . . . . . . . . . . . . . . . . (605) 773-5425
Public Affairs Manager **Jody Heemstra** . . . . . . . . . . . . . . . (605) 773-4073
Fiscal Officer **Chris Petersen** . . . . . . . . . . . . . . . . . . . . . . . (605) 773-3396
Personnel Officer **Jeff Wilson** . . . . . . . . . . . . . . . . . . . . . . (605) 773-6946
Accountant **Jennifer Schrempp** . . . . . . . . . . . . . . . . . . . . . (605) 773-5378
Accountant **Stephanie Lyons** . . . . . . . . . . . . . . . . . . . . . . (605) 773-5914
Policy Advisor **Dani Hanson** . . . . . . . . . . . . . . . . . . . . . . . (605) 773-5425
Special Project Coordinator and Communications
  Assistant **Jodi Bechard** . . . . . . . . . . . . . . . . . . . . . . . . . (605) 773-3375

## Agricultural Development Division

Director **Paul Kostboth** . . . . . . . . . . . . . . . . . . . . . . . . . . . (605) 773-5436
  Finance Program Specialist **(Vacant)** . . . . . . . . . . . . . . . (605) 773-5436
Central Regional Specialist **David Skaggs** . . . . . . . . . . . . . (605) 773-5436
Northeast Regional Specialist **(Vacant)** . . . . . . . . . . . . . . . (605) 626-3272
Southeast Regional Specialist **(Vacant)** . . . . . . . . . . . . . . . (605) 773-5436
West Regional Specialist **Bob Weyrich** . . . . . . . . . . . . . . . (605) 431-8002
Loan Administrator **Terri Labrie** . . . . . . . . . . . . . . . . . . . . (605) 773-5436

## Agricultural Services Division

Director **Brandon Beshears** . . . . . . . . . . . . . . . . . . . . . . . . (605) 773-4432
                                         Fax: (605) 773-3481

★ Elected Official    ■ Appointed by Governor    ● Appointed by Legislature    ▲ Appointed by Board or Commission    ◆ Appointed by State Supreme Court

## Resource Conservation and Forestry Division

Director and State Forester **William "Bill" Smith** . . . . . . . . (605) 773-3623
  Education: Michigan State; Kansas State MS          Fax: (605) 773-4003
Conservation and Urban Community Forest Supervisor
  **Greg Josten** . . . . . . . . . . . . . . . . . . . . . . . . . . . . . . . . . . . (605) 773-3623
Forest Health Program Supervisor **Greg Josten** . . . . . . . . . (605) 394-2395
  E-mail: greg.josten@state.sd.us
Prairie and Urban Forestry Specialist **(Vacant)** . . . . . . . . . . (605) 773-3623

## Wildland Fire Suppression Division [WFS]

3305 West South Street, Rapid City, SD 57702
Director **Jay Esperance** . . . . . . . . . . . . . . . . . . . . . . . . . . . . (605) 393-8011
                                                  Fax: (605) 393-8044
Deputy Director **Steve Hasenohrl** . . . . . . . . . . . . . . . . . . . . (605) 393-8011
  E-mail: steve.hasenohrl@state.sd.us
Chief Fire Management Officer **Jim Strain** . . . . . . . . . . . . . (605) 393-8011
Rural Fire Assistance Specialist **Jim Burk** . . . . . . . . . . . . . (605) 369-4471

## Department of Corrections [DOC]

3200 East Highway 34, 500 East Capitol Avenue, Pierre, SD 57501-5070
Tel: (605) 773-3478  Fax: (605) 773-3194
E-mail: docinternetinfo@state.sd.us  Internet: http://doc.sd.gov

**Employees:** 869 **Fiscal Year:** 2016 **Budget:** $117,648,000

■Secretary **Denny Kaemingk** . . . . . . . . . . . . . . . . . . . . . . . . (605) 773-3478
  E-mail: denny.kaemingk@state.sd.us
  Executive Assistant **Karen Webber-Boyer** . . . . . . . . . . . . (605) 773-3478
Deputy Secretary **Laurie Feiler** . . . . . . . . . . . . . . . . . . . . . (605) 773-3478
Juvenile Services Director **Doug Herrmann** . . . . . . . . . . . . (605) 394-1617
Operations Director **Candy Snyder** . . . . . . . . . . . . . . . . . . . (605) 773-3478
Research and Grants Director **Kevin McLain** . . . . . . . . . . . (605) 773-3478
  E-mail: kevin.mclain@state.sd.us
Community Service Director **Darwin Weeldreyer** . . . . . . . . (605) 773-3478

## Department of Education

800 Governors Drive, Pierre, SD 57501-2294
Tel: (605) 773-3134  Fax: (605) 773-6139

**Employees:** 128 **Fiscal Year:** 2015 **Budget:** $604,086,000

■Secretary **Melody Schopp** . . . . . . . . . . . . . . . . . . . . . . . . . (605) 773-5669
  E-mail: melody.schopp@state.sd.us
  Executive Assistant **Betty Leidholt** . . . . . . . . . . . . . . . . . (605) 773-5669
Deputy Secretary **Mary Stadick Smith** . . . . . . . . . . . . . . . (605) 773-7228
Assessment and Accountability Director
  **Abby Javurek-Humig** . . . . . . . . . . . . . . . . . . . . . . . . . . . (605) 773-4708
Curriculum, Career and Technical Education Director
  **Tiffany Sanderson** . . . . . . . . . . . . . . . . . . . . . . . . . . . . . (605) 773-7006
Child and Adult Nutrition Services Director
  **Sandra Kangas** . . . . . . . . . . . . . . . . . . . . . . . . . . . . . . . . (605) 773-3413
Finance and Management Director **Tamara Darnall** . . . . . . . (605) 773-3248
  E-mail: tamara.darnall@state.sd.us
Head Start State Collaboration Director **(Vacant)** . . . . . . . . (605) 773-4640
Learning and Instruction Director **Becky Nelson** . . . . . . . . (605) 773-4681
Special Education Director **Linda Turner** . . . . . . . . . . . . . . (605) 773-3327
Delivery Unit Head **Steve Fiechtner** . . . . . . . . . . . . . . . . . (605) 773-4774
Data Management Administrator **Judy Merriman** . . . . . . . . (605) 773-3248
  E-mail: judy.merriman@state.sd.us
Grants Management Administrator **Rob Huffman** . . . . . . . . (605) 773-3248
  E-mail: robyn.huffman@state.sd.us
Title I Program Administrator **Shannon Malone** . . . . . . . . . (605) 773-6400

## State Library

800 Governors Drive, Pierre, SD 57501-2294
Tel: (800) 423-6665  Fax: (605) 773-6962  E-mail: library@state.sd.us
State Librarian **Daria Bossman** . . . . . . . . . . . . . . . . . . . . . . (605) 773-3131
Deputy State Librarian and State Data Coordinator
  **(Vacant)** . . . . . . . . . . . . . . . . . . . . . . . . . . . . . . . . . . . . . (605) 773-3131
Public Services Director **(Vacant)** . . . . . . . . . . . . . . . . . . . . (605) 773-5051

## South Dakota Board of Education

800 Governors Drive, Pierre, SD 57501-2294
Tel: (605) 773-3426  Fax: (605) 773-6139

■President **Donald A. "Don" Kirkegaard** . . . . . . . . . . . . . . . (605) 232-6285
  Term Expires: December 31, 2018
  E-mail: don.kirkegaard@k12.sd.us
■Vice President **Terry Sabers** . . . . . . . . . . . . . . . . . . . . . . . (605) 996-3983
  Term Expires: December 31, 2015
  E-mail: terry.sabers@k12.sd.us
■Member **Susan Aguilar** . . . . . . . . . . . . . . . . . . . . . . . . . . . (605) 773-3426
  Term Expires: December 31, 2019
■Member **Kelly Duncan** . . . . . . . . . . . . . . . . . . . . . . . . . . . . (605) 339-2952
  Term Expires: December 31, 2016
  Education: South Dakota 1983 BBEd, 2003 PhD
■Member **Glenna N. Fouberg** . . . . . . . . . . . . . . . . . . . . . . . . (605) 229-1310
  Term Expires: December 31, 2017
  E-mail: gfouberg@abe.midco.net
  Education: Northern State 1963 BS; South Dakota State 1968 MEd
■Member **Scott Herman** . . . . . . . . . . . . . . . . . . . . . . . . . . . . (605) 773-5669
  Term Expires: December 31, 2016
■Member **Marilyn Hoyt** . . . . . . . . . . . . . . . . . . . . . . . . . . . . (605) 353-2060
  Term Expires: December 31, 2017
  E-mail: mhoyt@santel.net
  Education: South Dakota BSBA
■Member **Dr. Julie Mathiesen** . . . . . . . . . . . . . . . . . . . . . . . (605) 489-2026
  Term Expires: December 31, 2016
  E-mail: jmathiesen@tie.net
  Education: Pepperdine 2008 EdD
■Member **Deb Shephard** . . . . . . . . . . . . . . . . . . . . . . . . . . . (605) 342-5066
  Term Expires: December 31, 2018

## Department of Environment and Natural Resources [DENR]

Joe Foss Building, 523 East Capitol Avenue, Pierre, SD 57501-3181
Tel: (605) 773-3151  Fax: (605) 773-6035
E-mail: denrinternet@state.sd.us

**Employees:** 181 **Fiscal Year:** 2015 **Budget:** $18,840,000

■Secretary **Steven M. Pirner, PE** . . . . . . . . . . . . . . . . . . . . (605) 773-5559
  E-mail: steve.pirner@state.sd.us
  Education: South Dakota Mines BA, MS
  Executive Assistant **Vicki Murray** . . . . . . . . . . . . . . . . . . (605) 773-5559
  E-mail: vicki.murray@state.sd.us

## Environmental Services Division

Fax: (605) 773-5286  E-mail: denrinternet@state.sd.us
Director **Tim Tollefsrud** . . . . . . . . . . . . . . . . . . . . . . . . . . . (605) 773-3153
  Education: South Dakota Mines BS

## Financial and Technical Assistance Division

Fax: (605) 773-4068  E-mail: denrinternet@state.sd.us
Director **Jim Feeney** . . . . . . . . . . . . . . . . . . . . . . . . . . . . . . (605) 773-4216

## Department of Game, Fish and Parks [GFP]

Joe Foss Building, 523 East Capitol Avenue, Pierre, SD 57501-3182
Tel: (605) 773-3387  Fax: (605) 773-6245

**Employees:** 566 **Fiscal Year:** 2015 **Budget:** $74,404,000

■Secretary **Kelly R. Hepler** . . . . . . . . . . . . . . . . . . . . . . . . . (605) 773-3718
  E-mail: kelly.hepler@state.sd.us          Fax: (605) 773-6245
  Education: St Cloud State 1974 BA; Montana State 1978 BS
  Executive Secretary **Rachel Comes** . . . . . . . . . . . . . . . . . (605) 773-3718
    E-mail: rachel.comes@state.sd.us
Parks and Recreation Director **Doug Hofer** . . . . . . . . . . . . . (605) 773-3391
  E-mail: doug.hofer@state.sd.us
  Education: South Dakota State 1972 BS
Wildlife Division Director **Tony Leif** . . . . . . . . . . . . . . . . . . (605) 773-3387
  E-mail: tony.leif@state.sd.us
Attorney **Richard Neill** . . . . . . . . . . . . . . . . . . . . . . . . . . . . (605) 773-2750
  E-mail: richard.neill@state.sd.us

---

★ Elected Official     ■ Appointed by Governor     ● Appointed by Legislature     ▲ Appointed by Board or Commission     ◆ Appointed by State Supreme Court

# Department of Health

600 East Capitol Avenue, Pierre, SD 57501-2536
Tel: (605) 773-3361  Tel: (605) 773-4961 (Vital Records)
Fax: (605) 773-5683  Internet: www.doh.sd.gov
Internet: http://doh.sd.gov/records/ (Vital Records)

**Employees:** 419

- Secretary **Kim Malsam-Rysdon** . . . . . . . . . . . . . . . . . . (605) 773-3361
  Executive Secretary **Colleen Kozel** . . . . . . . . . . . . . . . . (605) 773-3361
Financial Management Director **Kari Williams** . . . . . . . . . (605) 773-3361
Administration Division Director **Joan Adam** . . . . . . . . . . (605) 773-3361
  E-mail: joan.adam@state.sd.us
Health and Medical Services Division Director
  **Colleen Winter** . . . . . . . . . . . . . . . . . . . . . . . . . . . (605) 773-3737
  615 East Fourth Street, Pierre, SD 57501-1700  Fax: (605) 773-5942
Health System Development and Regulation Division
  Director **Tom Martinec** . . . . . . . . . . . . . . . . . . . . . . . (605) 773-3361
  E-mail: tom.martinec@state.sd.us
State Epidemiologist **Lon Kightlinger** . . . . . . . . . . . . . . . (605) 773-3737
  Education: Augustana (SD) 1977 BA;  Fax: (605) 773-5509
  Tulane 1984 MSPH; North Carolina 1993 PhD
Women, Infants and Children (WIC) Director
  **Rhonda Buntrock** . . . . . . . . . . . . . . . . . . . . . . . . . . . (605) 773-3361
  E-mail: rhonda.buntrock@state.sd.us  Fax: (605) 775-5683

## State Health Laboratory

615 East Fourth Street, Pierre, SD 57501-1700
Tel: (605) 773-3368  Fax: (605) 773-6129

Director **Timothy "Tim" Southern, PhD** . . . . . . . . . . . . . (605) 773-3368
  Education: East Tennessee State PhD

# Department of Human Services [DHS]

Hillsview Plaza, East Highway 34, 500 East Capitol Avenue,
Pierre, SD 57501-5070
Tel: (605) 773-5990  TTY: (605) 773-5990  Fax: (605) 773-5483
E-mail: infodhs@state.sd.us  Internet: www.state.sd.us/dhs

**Employees:** 528  **Fiscal Year:** 2015  **Budget:** $174,598,000

- Secretary **Gloria Pearson** . . . . . . . . . . . . . . . . . . . . . . . (605) 773-5990
  E-mail: gloria.pearson@state.sd.us
  Education: South Dakota BASc; Northern State MSEd
  Executive Assistant **Marilyn Hanson** . . . . . . . . . . . . . . . (605) 773-5948
Developmental Disabilities Division Director **Dan Lusk** . . . (605) 773-3438
Rehabilitation Services Division Director **Eric Weiss** . . . . . (605) 773-3195
Service to the Blind and Visually Impaired Division
  Director **Gaye Mattke** . . . . . . . . . . . . . . . . . . . . . . . . (605) 773-5114
Disability Determination Services Vocational
  Rehabilitation Manager **Joanna Fischer** . . . . . . . . . . . . . (605) 367-5499

## South Dakota Developmental Center

17267 West Third Street, Redfield, SD 57469-1001
Fax: (605) 472-4216

Director (Interim) **Barb Abeln** . . . . . . . . . . . . . . . . . . . . (605) 472-4214

# Department of Labor and Regulation [SDDOL]

Kneip Building, 700 Governors Drive, Pierre, SD 57501-2291
Tel: (605) 773-3101  Fax: (605) 773-6184

**Employees:** 444  **Fiscal Year:** 2015  **Budget:** $41,737,000

- Secretary **Marcia Hultman** . . . . . . . . . . . . . . . . . . . . . . (605) 773-3101
  E-mail: marcia.hultman@state.sd.us
Deputy Secretary **Tom Hart** . . . . . . . . . . . . . . . . . . . . . . (605) 773-3101
Workforce Planning, Policy and Public Affairs Director
  **Dawn Dovre** . . . . . . . . . . . . . . . . . . . . . . . . . . . . . . . (605) 773-3101
Retirement System Director **Robert A. "Rob" Wylie** . . . . . (605) 773-3731
GED Administrator **Barb Unruh** . . . . . . . . . . . . . . . . . . . (605) 773-5017
  E-mail: barb.unruh@state.sd.us
Senior Staff Attorney **Aaron Arnold** . . . . . . . . . . . . . . . . (605) 773-3090

## Administrative Services Division

P.O. Box 4730, Aberdeen, SD 57402-4730
700 Governors Drive, Pierre, SD 57501-2291
Tel: (605) 773-3101  Fax: (605) 626-2322

Director **Emily Ward** . . . . . . . . . . . . . . . . . . . . . . . . . . . (605) 773-3101
  E-mail: emily.ward@state.sd.us
Labor Market Information Center Administrator
  **Bernie Moran** . . . . . . . . . . . . . . . . . . . . . . . . . . . . . . (605) 626-2314
  E-mail: bernie.moran@state.sd.us  Fax: (605) 626-2322

## Banking Division

1601 North Harrison Avenue, Suite 1, Pierre, SD 57501
Tel: (605) 773-3421  Fax: (866) 326-7504  E-mail: banking@state.sd.us

Banking Division Director **Bret Afdahl** . . . . . . . . . . . . . . . (605) 773-3421
  E-mail: bret.afdahl@state.sd.us
Deputy Director-Banking **John Crompton** . . . . . . . . . . . . (605) 773-3421
  E-mail: john.crompton@state.sd.us
Deputy Director-Trust **Scott Kelly** . . . . . . . . . . . . . . . . . . (605) 773-3421
  E-mail: scott.kelly@state.sd.us
Division Counsel **Brock Jensen** . . . . . . . . . . . . . . . . . . . . (605) 773-3421
Policy Analyst **Jean Blow** . . . . . . . . . . . . . . . . . . . . . . . . (605) 773-3421

## Employment Services Division

Division Director **Andy Szilvasi** . . . . . . . . . . . . . . . . . . . . (605) 773-3101
  E-mail: andrew.szilvasi@state.sd.us

## Equal Opportunity to Services Division

Equal Opportunity Officer **Andy Szilvasi** . . . . . . . . . . . . . (605) 773-3101
Equal Opportunity Officer for Unemployment Insurance
  **Dawn Williams** . . . . . . . . . . . . . . . . . . . . . . . . . . . . . (605) 626-2312
Equal Opportunity Officer for Workforce Investment Act
  **Deb Halling** . . . . . . . . . . . . . . . . . . . . . . . . . . . . . . . (605) 773-3101

## Field Operations Division

Field Operations Division Director
  **Michael L. "Mike" Ryan** . . . . . . . . . . . . . . . . . . . . . . (605) 773-3101
  E-mail: mike.ryan@state.sd.us

## Insurance Division

Division of Insurance, 124 S. Euclid Avenue, 2nd Floor, Pierre, SD 57501
Tel: (605) 773-3563  E-mail: insurance@state.sd.us

Insurance Division Director **Larry Deiter** . . . . . . . . . . . . . (605) 773-4104

## Labor and Management Division

Kneip Building, 700 Governors Drive, Pierre, SD 57501-2291
Tel: (605) 773-3681

Labor and Management Division Director **James Marsh** . . (605) 773-3681
  E-mail: james.marsh@state.sd.us

## Securities Division

445 East Capitol Avenue, Pierre, SD 57501-3185
Tel: (605) 773-4823  Fax: (605) 773-5953

Securities Division Director **Michael Youngberg** . . . . . . . . (605) 773-4823

## Unemployment Insurance Division

P.O. Box 4730, Aberdeen, SD 57402-4730

Unemployment Insurance Division Director
  **Pauline Heier** . . . . . . . . . . . . . . . . . . . . . . . . . . . . . . (605) 626-2452

## Workforce Training Division

Kneip Building, 700 Governors Drive, Pierre, SD 57501-2291

Workforce Training Division Director **Bill McEntaffer** . . . . (605) 773-5017
  E-mail: bill.mcentaffer@state.sd.us

# Department of the Military [MVA]

2823 West Main, Rapid City, SD 57702-8170
Tel: (605) 737-6702  Fax: (605) 737-6677

**Employees:** 104

- Secretary **MG Timothy A. "Tim" Reisch, ARNG** . . . . . . . (605) 737-6702
  E-mail: timothy.a.reisch2.mil@mail.mil
  Program Analyst **Reggan Labore** . . . . . . . . . . . . . . . . . . (605) 737-6702

*(continued on next page)*

---

★ Elected Official  ■ Appointed by Governor  ● Appointed by Legislature  ▲ Appointed by Board or Commission  ◆ Appointed by State Supreme Court

**Department of the Military** *continued*

Air Staff Director **Col Russell M. Limke, ANG**. . . . . . . . . . (605) 737-6704
  Education: Augustana (SD) BA
Chief of Staff **COL William J. "Bill" Freidel, ARNG**. . . . . (605) 737-6702
Education Program Manager **Shane Oliver**. . . . . . . . . . . . (605) 773-3648
  E-mail: shane.olivier@state.sd.us

## Michael Fitzmaurice Veterans Home

2500 Minnekahta Avenue, Hot Springs, SD 57747-1199
Fax: (605) 745-5547

Superintendent **Bradley Richardson**. . . . . . . . . . (605) 745-5127 ext. 111
Operations Director **Randall Meyers**. . . . . . . . . . . (605) 745-5127 ext. 220

## South Dakota National Guard

2823 West Main, Rapid City, SD 57702-8170
Tel: (605) 737-6702  Fax: (605) 737-6677

■Adjutant General
  **MG Timothy A. "Tim" Reisch, ARNG**. . . . . . . . . . . . (605) 737-6702
  E-mail: timothy.a.reisch2.mil@mail.mil
Freedom of Information Act Officer
  **MAJ Jason Campbell, ARNG**. . . . . . . . . . . . . . . . . . . (605) 737-6769
Small Business Officer **(Vacant)**. . . . . . . . . . . . . . . . . . . . (605) 737-6740

## South Dakota Air National Guard

1201 West Algonquin Street, Sioux Falls, SD 57104-0264
Tel: (605) 988-5700  Internet: www.sdsiou.ang.af.mil

Assistant Adjutant General **(Vacant)**. . . . . . . . . . . . . . . . . (605) 988-5801

## South Dakota Army National Guard

2823 West Main, Rapid City, SD 57702-8170
Tel: (605) 737-6702

Assistant Adjutant General **BG Kevin R. Griese, ARNG**. . . (605) 737-6702
Chief Information Officer
  **LTC Theodore L. "Ted" Bartunek, ARNG**. . . . . . . . . . . (605) 737-6676
  E-mail: theodore.l.bartunek.mil@mail.mil

## Department of Public Safety [DPS]

118 West Capitol Avenue, Pierre, SD 57501
Tel: (605) 773-3178  Tel: (800) 877-1113 (Relay Service)
Fax: (605) 773-3018  E-mail: DPSInfo@state.sd.us

**Employees:** 394  **Fiscal Year:** 2015  **Budget:** $52,010,000

■Secretary **Trevor Jones**. . . . . . . . . . . . . . . . . . . . . . . . . . (605) 773-3178
  E-mail: trevor.jones@state.sd.us
  Administrative Assistant **Dawn Hill**. . . . . . . . . . . . . . . (605) 773-3178
Fire Marshal **Paul Merriman**. . . . . . . . . . . . . . . . . . . . . . (605) 773-3562
  E-mail: paul.merriman@state.sd.us
Accident Records Director **Lee Axdahl**. . . . . . . . . . . . . . . (605) 773-3868
Driver Licensing Program Director **Jane Schrank**. . . . . . . . (605) 773-6883
  E-mail: jane.schrank@state.sd.us
Highway Safety Office Director **Lee Axdahl**. . . . . . . . . . . (605) 773-4949
State Inspection Program Director **Lori Jacobson**. . . . . . . . (605) 773-3697
  E-mail: lori.jacobson@state.sd.us
Emergency Management Division Director **Tina Titze**. . . . . (605) 773-3231
Administration and Grants Management Division Director
  **Angela Lemieux**. . . . . . . . . . . . . . . . . . . . . . . . . . . . . (605) 773-3178
  E-mail: angela.lemieux@state.sd.us
Legal and Regulatory Services Division Director
  **Jenna Howell**. . . . . . . . . . . . . . . . . . . . . . . . . . . . . . . (605) 773-3178
Highway Patrol Superintendent **Craig Price**. . . . . . . . . . . (605) 773-3105
Highway Patrol Major **Rick Miller**. . . . . . . . . . . . . . . . . . (605) 773-3105
Highway Patrol Major **Dana Svendsen**. . . . . . . . . . . . . . . (605) 773-3105
State Radio Dispatch **Lt. Jason Husby**. . . . . . . . . . . . . . . (605) 773-8483

## Office of Homeland Security

118 West Capitol Avenue, Pierre, SD 57501
Tel: (605) 773-3450  Fax: (605) 773-6631

Director **Stefan Pluta**. . . . . . . . . . . . . . . . . . . . . . . . . . . . (605) 773-3450

## Department of Revenue [DRR]

Anderson Building, 445 East Capitol Avenue, Pierre, SD 57501-3185
Tel: (605) 773-3311  TTY: (800) 829-9188  Fax: (605) 773-5129
Internet: www.state.sd.us/drr

**Employees:** 237  **Fiscal Year:** 2015  **Budget:** $68,665,000

■Secretary **Andy Gerlach**. . . . . . . . . . . . . . . . . . . . . . . . . (605) 773-5131
  E-mail: andy.gerlach@state.sd.us
  Education: Northern State (Attended); South Dakota 1993 MBA
Deputy Secretary **David Wiest**. . . . . . . . . . . . . . . . . . . . . (605) 773-5131
Chief Legal Counsel **Andy Fergel**. . . . . . . . . . . . . . . . . . (605) 773-3311
Special Projects Director **Jon Harms**. . . . . . . . . . . . . . . . . (605) 773-3311
Audit Division Director **(Vacant)**. . . . . . . . . . . . . . . . . . . . (605) 773-3311
Business Tax Division Director
  **Douglas "Doug" Schinkel**. . . . . . . . . . . . . . . . . . . . . . (605) 773-3414
                                          Fax: (605) 773-6729
Motor Vehicle Division Director **Lisa Wire**. . . . . . . . . . . . (605) 773-3541
  E-mail: motorv@state.sd.us
Property Taxes and Special Taxes Division Director
  **Michael Houdyshell**. . . . . . . . . . . . . . . . . . . . . . . . . . (605) 773-3311
Administrative Services Director **Toni Richardson**. . . . . . . (605) 773-5137
  E-mail: toni.richardson@state.sd.us

## South Dakota Commission on Gaming

221 West Capitol Avenue, Suite 101, Pierre, SD 57501
Tel: (605) 773-6050  Tel: (605) 578-3074  Fax: (605) 773-6053
Fax: (605) 578-2263  E-mail: gaminginfo@state.sd.us

▲Executive Secretary **Larry B. Eliason**. . . . . . . . . . . . . . . (605) 773-6050
  E-mail: larry.eliason@state.sd.us
Deputy Executive Secretary **Craig Sparrow**. . . . . . . . . . . . (605) 773-6050
  E-mail: craig.sparrow@state.sd.us

## South Dakota Lottery

P.O. Box 7107, Pierre, SD 57501
South Dakota Lottery Dolly Reed Building, 711 East Wells Avenue,
Pierre, SD 57501-3369
Tel: (605) 773-5770  Fax: (605) 773-5786  E-mail: lottery@state.sd.us
Internet: www.sdlottery.org

Executive Director **Norman Lingle**. . . . . . . . . . . . . . . . . . (605) 773-5770
  Education: South Dakota State BS

## Department of Social Services [DSS]

Kneip Building, 700 Governors Drive, Pierre, SD 57501-2291
Tel: (605) 773-3165  Fax: (605) 773-4855  E-mail: dssinfo@state.sd.us
Internet: www.dss.sd.gov

**Employees:** 1,652

■Secretary **Lynne Valenti**. . . . . . . . . . . . . . . . . . . . . . . . . (605) 773-3165
  E-mail: lynne.valenti@state.sd.us
  Education: South Dakota; New England
  Executive Assistant **Olivia Waggoner**. . . . . . . . . . . . . . (605) 773-3165
Deputy Secretary **Amy Iverson-Pollreisz**. . . . . . . . . . . . . . (605) 773-3165
Deputy Secretary **Brenda Tidball-Zeltinger**. . . . . . . . . . . . (605) 773-3165
Constituent Services Director **Justin Pierson**. . . . . . . . . . . (605) 773-3165
  Constituent Liaison **Valerie Kelly**. . . . . . . . . . . . . . . . (800) 597-1603
Communications Director **Tia Kafka**. . . . . . . . . . . . . . . . . (605) 773-3165
Management Information Statistician **(Vacant)**. . . . . . . . . . (605) 773-3165
Chief Financial Officer (Acting)
  **Brenda Tidball-Zeltinger**. . . . . . . . . . . . . . . . . . . . . . (605) 773-3165
Deputy Financial Officer **Doug Dix**. . . . . . . . . . . . . . . . . (605) 773-3165
Deputy Financial Officer **Laura Schaeffer**. . . . . . . . . . . . . (605) 773-3165
  Accounting and Financial Reporting Administrator
  **Bill Regynski**. . . . . . . . . . . . . . . . . . . . . . . . . . . . . . . (605) 773-3586
  Provider Reimbursement and Audits Administrator
  **Greg Evans**. . . . . . . . . . . . . . . . . . . . . . . . . . . . . . . . (605) 773-3643
  Electronic Benefits Transfer Administrator
  **Sandra Vanneman**. . . . . . . . . . . . . . . . . . . . . . . . . . . (605) 773-6527
Prevention Program Manager **Gilbert "Gib" Sudbeck**. . . . . (605) 773-3123

---

★ Elected Official    ■ Appointed by Governor    ● Appointed by Legislature    ▲ Appointed by Board or Commission    ◆ Appointed by State Supreme Court

EXECUTIVE BRANCH

# Department of Tourism

Tel: (605) 773-3301   Internet: www.sdvisit.com

**Fiscal Year:** 2015   **Budget:** $15,171,000

■Secretary **James D. "Jim" Hagen** . . . . . . . . . . . . . . . . . . (605) 773-3301
E-mail: james.hagen@state.sd.us

Executive Assistant **Harla Jessop** . . . . . . . . . . . . . . . . . (605) 773-3301
E-mail: harla.jessop@state.sd.us

# Department of Transportation [SDDOT]

Becker Hansen Building, 700 East Broadway Avenue,
Pierre, SD 57501-2586
Tel: (605) 773-3265   Fax: (605) 773-3921

**Employees:** 980   **Fiscal Year:** 2015   **Budget:** $559,037,000

■Secretary **Darin Bergquist** . . . . . . . . . . . . . . . . . . . . . . (605) 773-5105
E-mail: darin.bergquist@state.sd.us
Education: Jamestown Col BBA; South Dakota JD

Deputy Secretary **Joel Jundt** . . . . . . . . . . . . . . . . . . . . . (605) 773-3265

Finance and Management Division Director **Kellie Beck** . . . (605) 773-4863
E-mail: kellie.beck@state.sd.us

Operations Division Director **Greg Fuller** . . . . . . . . . . . . . (605) 773-5155

Planning and Engineering Director
**Michael "Mike" Behm** . . . . . . . . . . . . . . . . . . . . . . . (605) 773-3265
E-mail: michael.behm@state.sd.us

Communications Manager **Kristi Sandal** . . . . . . . . . . . . . (605) 773-3265
E-mail: kristi.sandal@state.sd.us

# Department of Tribal Relations

Capitol Lake Plaza, 711 East Wells Avenue, Suite 250,
Pierre, SD 57501-3369
Tel: (605) 773-3415   Fax: (605) 773-6592   Internet: www.state.sd.us/oia
Internet: www.sdtribalrelations.com

**Employees:** 5   **Fiscal Year:** 2015   **Budget:** $421,000

■Secretary **Steve Emery** . . . . . . . . . . . . . . . . . . . . . . . . (605) 773-3415
E-mail: steve.emery@state.sd.us

# Department of Veterans Affairs

2525 W. Main Street, Suite #4, Rapid City, SD 57702

Secretary **Larry Zimmerman** . . . . . . . . . . . . . . . . . . . . . (605) 773-5046

Deputy Secretary **Aaron Pollard** . . . . . . . . . . . . . . . . . . (605) 333-6869
Fax: (605) 333-5386

# Administrative Office

425 E. Capitol Avenue, Pierre, SD 57501

Program Manager **Steve Oliva** . . . . . . . . . . . . . . . . . . . . (605) 773-8180

Public Information Officer **Audry Rickets** . . . . . . . . . . . . (605) 773-8242

Executive Secretary **Jeri Smith** . . . . . . . . . . . . . . . . . . . (605) 773-3269

Finance Director **Connie Hohn** . . . . . . . . . . . . . . . . . . . (605) 773-4984

# Veterans Affairs Claims Office

P.O. Box 5046, Sioux Falls, SD 57117-5046

Program Manager II **Heather M. Bullerman** . . . . . . . . . . . (605) 333-6869

Program Manager I **Donald Thomson** . . . . . . . . . . . . . . . (605) 333-6869

# Bureau of Administration [BOA]

500 East Capitol Avenue, Pierre, SD 57501-5070
Tel: (605) 773-3688   Fax: (605) 773-3887   Internet: http://boa.sd.gov/

■Commissioner **Jeff Holden** . . . . . . . . . . . . . . . . . . . . . . (605) 773-3688
E-mail: jeff.holden@state.sd.us

Deputy Commissioner **(Vacant)** . . . . . . . . . . . . . . . . . . . (605) 773-3688
Administrative Assistant **Tammy Florentz** . . . . . . . . . . . (605) 773-3688

Buildings and Grounds Director **Rollie Isaacson** . . . . . . . . (605) 773-3344

Central Duplicating Services Director **Eric Feiler** . . . . . . . (605) 773-5870
E-mail: eric.feiler@state.sd.us

Central Mail Services Director **Roger Getz** . . . . . . . . . . . (605) 773-3767
E-mail: roger.getz@state.sd.us

Central Supply Services Director **Lennis Axdahl** . . . . . . . . (605) 773-4935

Federal Surplus Property Director **Kaelene Borkowski** . . . . (605) 353-7150

Fleet and Travel Management Director **John DeLoache** . . . (605) 773-3162

Records Management Director **Dana Hoffer** . . . . . . . . . . . (605) 773-3589

Space (Lease) Management Director **Kevin Fridley** . . . . . . . (605) 773-3688

Procurement Management Office Director **Steven Berg** . . . (605) 773-3405

Risk Management Office Director **Craig Ambach** . . . . . . . . (605) 773-5879

State Property Management Office Director
**Lennis Axdahl** . . . . . . . . . . . . . . . . . . . . . . . . . . . . (605) 773-4935

Sustainability Coordinator **(Vacant)** . . . . . . . . . . . . . . . . (605) 773-3688

State Engineer **Kristi Honeywell** . . . . . . . . . . . . . . . . . . (605) 773-3466

Chief Hearing Examiner **Catherine Duenwald** . . . . . . . . . . (605) 773-6811

General Counsel **(Vacant)** . . . . . . . . . . . . . . . . . . . . . . . (605) 773-3688

# Bureau of Finance and Management [BFM]

State Capitol, 500 East Capitol Avenue, Room 217,
Pierre, SD 57501-5070
Tel: (605) 773-3411   Fax: (605) 773-4711   E-mail: bfminfo@state.sd.us

■Chief Financial Officer **Jason Dilges** . . . . . . . . . . . . . . . (605) 773-3411
E-mail: jason.dilges@state.sd.us
Education: South Dakota 1994 BS, 1995 MBA

Executive Assistant **Barb Nincehelser** . . . . . . . . . . . . . . (605) 773-3411

Accounting Analysis Director **Keith Senger** . . . . . . . . . . . (605) 773-3411

Financial Systems Director **Colin Keeler** . . . . . . . . . . . . . (605) 773-3411
Education: South Dakota State 1986 BS

Internal Compliance Coordinator **Ronald "Ron" Wire** . . . . (605) 773-3411
Education: Dakota Wesleyan 1973 BA

# Bureau of Information and Telecommunication [BIT]

Kneip Building, 700 Governors Drive, Pierre, SD 57501
Fax: (605) 773-6040   E-mail: webmaster@state.sd.us

■Commissioner **David Zolnowsky** . . . . . . . . . . . . . . . . . . (605) 773-4165
E-mail: david.zolnowsky@state.sd.us

■Deputy Commissioner **Jim Edman** . . . . . . . . . . . . . . . . . (605) 773-4861
E-mail: jim.edman@state.sd.us

## Development Division

Director **Deanne Booth** . . . . . . . . . . . . . . . . . . . . . . . . . (605) 773-4018
E-mail: deanne.booth@state.sd.us

Manager (Team 1) **Francis Taft** . . . . . . . . . . . . . . . . . . . (605) 773-4585
E-mail: frenchy.taft@state.sd.us

Manager (Team 2) **Mark Cichos** . . . . . . . . . . . . . . . . . . . (605) 773-4642
E-mail: mark.cichos@state.sd.us

Manager (Team 3) **Monty Gloe** . . . . . . . . . . . . . . . . . . . (605) 773-3792

Manager (Team 4) **(Vacant)** . . . . . . . . . . . . . . . . . . . . . . (605) 773-3984

Manager (Team 5) **Bruce Kinder** . . . . . . . . . . . . . . . . . . (605) 626-7614
E-mail: bruce.kinder@state.sd.us

Manager (Team 6) **Lonnie Stoltenburg** . . . . . . . . . . . . . . (605) 773-5464
E-mail: lonnie.stoltenburg@state.sd.us

## Telecommunications

Internet: www.state.sd.us/bit

Director **Dennis "Denny" Nincehelser** . . . . . . . . . . . . . . (605) 773-4264
E-mail: dennis.nincehelser@state.sd.us

Engineering Manager **Jeff Pierce** . . . . . . . . . . . . . . . . . . (605) 773-4347
E-mail: jeff.pierce@state.sd.us

Network Technologies Manager **Pat Snow** . . . . . . . . . . . . (605) 773-4861

Support Services Administrator **Deb DuFour** . . . . . . . . . . (605) 773-6334
E-mail: deb.dufour@state.sd.us

## Public Broadcasting Division

Tel: (605) 677-5861   Fax: (605) 677-5010   Internet: www.sdpb.org

Executive Director **Julie Overgaard** . . . . . . . . . . . . . . . . (605) 677-6419
Education: South Dakota State 1989 BA

Assistant Director **Larry Rohrer** . . . . . . . . . . . . . . . . . . (605) 677-6442
Education: Sioux Falls 1998 BA

Education and Outreach Director **Ken Osborne** . . . . . . . . . (605) 677-6454
E-mail: kent.osborne@state.sd.us

Public Radio Director **(Vacant)** . . . . . . . . . . . . . . . . . . . (605) 677-8814

*(continued on next page)*

---

★ Elected Official    ■ Appointed by Governor    ● Appointed by Legislature    ▲ Appointed by Board or Commission    ◆ Appointed by State Supreme Court

EXECUTIVE BRANCH

**Public Broadcasting Division** *continued*

Engineering Manager **Severn Ashes** . . . . . . . . . . . . . . . . . . . (605) 473-5643
TV Program and Operations Manager **Bob Bosse** . . . . . . . . (605) 677-6267
   Education: South Dakota 1988 BA
Marketing Manager **Fritz Miller** . . . . . . . . . . . . . . . . . . . . . (605) 677-6455

# Bureau of Human Resources

State Capitol, 500 East Capitol Avenue, Pierre, SD 57501-5070
Tel: (605) 773-3148 Fax: (605) 773-4344 E-mail: bhrinfo@state.sd.us

■Commissioner **Laurie R. Gill** . . . . . . . . . . . . . . . . . . . . . . . (605) 773-4918
   Executive Assistant **Erin Flynn** . . . . . . . . . . . . . . . . . . . . (605) 773-4918

# South Dakota Health and Educational Facilities Authority [SDHEFA]

330 South Poplar, Suite 102, Pierre, SD 57501
P.O. Box 846, Pierre, SD 57501
Tel: (605) 224-9200 Fax: (605) 224-7177 Internet: www.sdhefa.com

▲Executive Director **Donald A. "Don" Templeton** . . . . . . . . (605) 224-9200
   E-mail: don.templeton@sdhefa.com
Assistant Director **Dustin Christopherson** . . . . . . . . . . . . . (605) 224-9200

# South Dakota Housing Development Authority [SDHDA]

3060 East Elizabeth Street, Pierre, SD 57501
P.O. Box 1237, Pierre, SD 57501-1237
Tel: (605) 773-3181 Fax: (605) 773-5154 E-mail: info@sdhda.org
Internet: www.sdhda.org

■Executive Director **Mark Lauseng, CPA** . . . . . . . . . . . . . . . (605) 773-3181
   E-mail: mark@sdhda.org
   Education: Northern State
   Executive Assistant **Sheila Ricketts** . . . . . . . . . . . . . . . . (605) 773-7603
Finance Director **Todd Hight** . . . . . . . . . . . . . . . . . . . . . . . (605) 773-5665
Homeownership Director **Brent Adney** . . . . . . . . . . . . . . . . (605) 773-5157
Housing Development Director **Lorraine Polak** . . . . . . . . . . (605) 773-3108
Rental Housing Management Director **Vona Johnson** . . . . (605) 773-4567
Research and Marketing Director **Amanda Weisgram** . . . . (605) 773-4568
   E-mail: amanda@sdhda.org
Single Family Development Director **Mike Harsma** . . . . . . . (605) 773-5236

# Animal Industry Board [AIB]

411 South Fort Street, Pierre, SD 57501
Tel: (605) 773-3321 Fax: (605) 773-5459 E-mail: aibmail@state.sd.us

▲State Veterinarian **Dr. Dustin Oedekoven, DVM** . . . . . . . . (605) 773-3321
   E-mail: dustin.oedekoven@state.sd.us
Assistant State Veterinarian **Mendel Miller, DVM** . . . . . . . (605) 773-3321
Business Manager **Teresa J. "Terry" Johnson** . . . . . . . . . . (605) 773-3321
   Education: Sioux Falls 1984 BA

# South Dakota Public Utilities Commission [PUC]

500 East Capitol Avenue, First Floor, Pierre, SD 57501-5007
Tel: (605) 773-3201

★Chair **Chris Nelson** (R) . . . . . . . . . . . . . . . . . . . . . . . . . . . (605) 773-3201
   Term Expires: 2017
   Education: South Dakota State 1987 BS
★Vice Chair **Kristie Fiegen** (R) . . . . . . . . . . . . . . . . . . . . . . (605) 773-3201
   Term Expires: 2019
★Commissioner **Gary Hanson** (R) . . . . . . . . . . . . . . . . . . . . (605) 773-3201
   Term Expires: 2021

# Office of the Lieutenant Governor

State Capitol, 500 East Capitol Avenue, Room A215,
Pierre, SD 57501-5007
Tel: (605) 773-3661

★Lieutenant Governor **Matthew "Matt" Michels** (R) . . . . . . (605) 773-3661
   Term Expires: January 2019
   E-mail: matt.michels@state.sd.us
   Education: South Dakota 1980 BSN, 1982 BS, 1985 JD
   Career: State Representative (R-SD, District 18), South Dakota House
   of Representatives (1998-2006); Speaker of the House, South Dakota
   House of Representatives (2003-2006); Veterans Affairs Secretary,
   Department of the Military and Veterans Affairs, State of South Dakota
   (2011-2013)

# Office of the Secretary of State

500 East Capitol Avenue, Pierre, SD 57501-5070
Tel: (605) 773-3537 Fax: (605) 773-6580 E-mail: sdsos@state.sd.us

**Employees:** 15 **Fiscal Year:** 2015 **Budget:** $2,725,000

★Secretary of State **Shantel Krebs** (R) . . . . . . . . . . . . . . . . (605) 773-3537
   Term Expires: January 2019
   Career: State Representative (R-SD, District 10), South Dakota House
   of Representatives (2005-2011); State Senator (R-SD, District 10),
   South Dakota Senate (2011-2015)
Administrative Services Deputy Secretary of State
   **Teresa Bray** . . . . . . . . . . . . . . . . . . . . . . . . . . . . . . . . . (605) 773-3537
Business Services Deputy Secretary of State
   **Thomas J. "Tom" Deadrick** . . . . . . . . . . . . . . . . . . . . . (605) 773-3537
Elections Deputy Secretary of State **Kea Warne** . . . . . . . . . (605) 773-3537

# Office of the Attorney General

1302 East Highway 14, Pierre, SD 57501-8501
Tel: (605) 773-3215 Fax: (605) 773-4106 E-mail: atghelp@state.sd.us

**Employees:** 175

★Attorney General **Martin J. "Marty" Jackley** (R) . . . . . . . . (605) 773-3215
   Term Expires: January 2019       Fax: (605) 773-4106
   E-mail: marty.jackley@state.sd.us
   Education: South Dakota Mines 1992 BSEE; South Dakota 1995 JD
   Career: U.S. Attorney, South Dakota District, Executive Office for
   United States Attorneys, United States Department of Justice, George
   W. Bush Administration (2006-2009)
   Administrative Assistant **Debbie Dougherty** . . . . . . . . . . (605) 773-3215
   Administrative Assistant **Lynell Erickson** . . . . . . . . . . . . (605) 773-3215
Chief Deputy **Charles McGuigan** . . . . . . . . . . . . . . . . . . . . (605) 773-3215
   Education: South Dakota 1988 BA; Montana 1991 JD
Appellate Director **Sherri Wald** . . . . . . . . . . . . . . . . . . . . . (605) 773-3215
Charitable Donations Director **(Vacant)** . . . . . . . . . . . . . . . (605) 773-4400
Consumer Protection Director **Jody Swanson** . . . . . . . . . . (605) 773-4400
   Consumer Protection Deputy Director **(Vacant)** . . . . . . . . (605) 773-4400
Criminal Investigation Division Director
   **Bryan Gortmaker** . . . . . . . . . . . . . . . . . . . . . . . . . . . . . (605) 773-3331
   Education: Augustana (SD)
Litigation Director **Robert Mayer** . . . . . . . . . . . . . . . . . . . . (605) 773-3215
Medicaid Fraud Unit Director **Paul Cremer** . . . . . . . . . . . . (605) 773-4102
Press Secretary **Sara Rabern** . . . . . . . . . . . . . . . . . . . . . . (605) 773-3215
   E-mail: sara.rabern@state.sd.us
Webmaster **Jamie Freestone** . . . . . . . . . . . . . . . . . . . . . . . (605) 773-3215
   E-mail: jamie.freestone@state.sd.us

# Office of the State Treasurer

State Capitol, 500 East Capitol Avenue, Suite 212, Pierre, SD 57501-5007
Tel: (605) 773-3378 Fax: (605) 773-3115

**Fiscal Year:** 2015 **Budget:** $28,488,000

★State Treasurer **Richard L. "Rich" Sattgast** (R) . . . . . . . . . (605) 773-3378
   Term Expires: January 2019
   E-mail: rich.sattgast@state.sd.us
   Education: Black Hills State BS
   Career: State Auditor (R-SD), State of South Dakota (2002-2010)
Deputy Director **Rik Drewes** . . . . . . . . . . . . . . . . . . . . . . . . (605) 773-3378
   E-mail: rik.drewes@state.sd.us
   Education: Northern State BA

★ Elected Official ■ Appointed by Governor ● Appointed by Legislature ▲ Appointed by Board or Commission ◆ Appointed by State Supreme Court

EXECUTIVE BRANCH

# Office of the State Auditor

500 East Capitol Avenue, Pierre, SD 57501-5007
Tel: (605) 773-3341  Fax: (605) 773-5929  E-mail: sdauditor@state.sd.us

**Fiscal Year:** 2015  **Budget:** $1,256,000

★ State Auditor **Steve Barnett** (R) . . . . . . . . . . . . . . . . . . . . . (605) 773-3341
  Term Expires: January 2019
  Education: South Dakota
  Career: Coalitions Director, South Dakota Republican Party (2002);
  Constituent Services Representative (R-SD), Aberdeen Office, Office of
  Senator John Thune, United States Senate (2009-2010)
  Administrative Assistant **Laura Lentsch** . . . . . . . . . . . . . (605) 773-3341
Deputy State Auditor **Jason Lutz** . . . . . . . . . . . . . . . . . . . . (605) 773-3341
Accounting Manager **Robert Swanson** . . . . . . . . . . . . . . . (605) 773-4468
Contract Manager **Robert Swanson** . . . . . . . . . . . . . . . . . (605) 773-4468
Payroll Manager **Judy Flagstad** . . . . . . . . . . . . . . . . . . . . (605) 773-3342
State Social Security-IRS Administrator
  **Amanda Schmitgen** . . . . . . . . . . . . . . . . . . . . . . . . . . . . (605) 773-6926
Auditor Supervisor **Dennis Keith** . . . . . . . . . . . . . . . . . . (605) 773-3144

# Office of School and Public Lands

State Capitol, 500 East Capitol Avenue, Room 108,
Pierre, SD 57501-5070
Tel: (605) 773-3303  Fax: (605) 773-5520
Internet: www.sdpubliclands.com

★ Commissioner **Ryan Brunner** (R) . . . . . . . . . . . . . . . . . . . (605) 773-3303
  Term Expires: January 2019
Deputy Commissioner **Mike Lauritsen** . . . . . . . . . . . . . . . (605) 773-3303
Land Agent **Mike Cornelison** . . . . . . . . . . . . . . . . . . . . . . (605) 773-4172
Oil, Gas, and Minerals Agent **Michael J. Mehlhaff** . . . . . . (605) 773-4171
Investment Officer **Renee Knapp** . . . . . . . . . . . . . . . . . . . (605) 773-3303
Secretary **Claudia Cepak** . . . . . . . . . . . . . . . . . . . . . . . . . (605) 773-3303

---

★ Elected Official   ■ Appointed by Governor   ● Appointed by Legislature   ▲ Appointed by Board or Commission   ◆ Appointed by State Supreme Court

# Tennessee

Tel: (615) 741-2001 (State Information)

**Number of U.S. Congressional Delegates:** 2 Senators; 9 Representatives **Governor's Term:** 4 years
**Legislature Description:** General Assembly - 33 member Senate; 99 member House of Representatives;
Term - Senate 4 years, House 2 years **Next Election:** Governor November 2018; Legislature November
2016 **Number of Electoral Votes:** 11 **Official Name:** State of Tennessee (name of a group of Cherokee
villages) **Nickname:** The Volunteer State **Motto:** Agriculture and Commerce

**Population:** 6,600,299 (2015); Rank 17 **Fiscal Year:** 2014-2015 **Budget:** $32,600,000,000

## Office of the Governor

State Capitol, 600 Charlotte Avenue, First Floor, Nashville, TN 37243
Tel: (615) 741-2001  TTY: (615) 741-0435  Fax: (615) 532-9711

**William Edward "Bill" Haslam**
Governor

Began Service: January 15, 2011
Term Expires: January 2019
Date of Birth: August 23, 1958
Education: Emory 1980 BA
Home: Knoxville
Religion: Presbyterian
Career: President, Pilot Oil Corp.; Chief
Executive Officer, SAKS Direct, Saks
Incorporated; Mayor, Mayor, City of Knoxville,
Tennessee (2003-2011)

★Governor **William Edward "Bill" Haslam** (R) . . . . . . . . . (615) 741-2001
  E-mail: bill.haslam@tn.gov
  Chief of Staff and Deputy to the Governor
    **James M. "Jim" Henry** . . . . . . . . . . . . . . . . . . (615) 741-2001
General Counsel **Dwight E. Tarwater** . . . . . . . . . . . . . . . (615) 741-3761
  E-mail: dwight.tarwater@tn.gov
  Education: Tennessee, JD
Communications Director **David Smith** . . . . . . . . . . . . . (615) 253-7726
  E-mail: david.smith@tn.gov
  Deputy Communications Director **Laura Herzog** . . . . . . . (615) 253-7726
    E-mail: laura.herzog@tn.gov
    Education: Tennessee 2001 BA
  Press Secretary **Jennifer Donnals** . . . . . . . . . . . . . . (615) 253-1390
    E-mail: jennifer.donnals@tn.gov
Senior Advisor **Leslie K. Hafner** . . . . . . . . . . . . . . . . (615) 741-2001
  E-mail: leslie.hafner@tn.gov
  Education: Mid Tennessee State 1992 BS
Special Advisor for Higher Education **Mike Krause** . . . . . . (615) 741-2001
  E-mail: mike.krause@tn.gov
Special Assistant to the Governor for Strategy and Policy
  Director **Will Cromer** . . . . . . . . . . . . . . . . . . . . . . . (615) 253-7726
    E-mail: will.cromer@tn.gov

## Department of Agriculture

440 Hogan Road, Nashville, TN 37220-9029
P.O. Box 40627, Nashville, TN 37204
Tel: (615) 837-5103  Fax: (615) 837-5333  E-mail: tn.agriculture@tn.gov
Internet: www.tennessee.gov/agriculture

■Commissioner **Jai Templeton** . . . . . . . . . . . . . . . . . . . (615) 837-5103
  E-mail: jai.templeton@tn.gov
  Executive Assistant to the Commissioner
    **Joyce Jackson** . . . . . . . . . . . . . . . . . . . . . . . . . (615) 837-5100
Deputy Commissioner **(Vacant)** . . . . . . . . . . . . . . . . . . (615) 837-5103
  Administrative Assistant **Eileen Beard** . . . . . . . . . . . . . (615) 837-5103
Administration and Grants Assistant Commissioner
  **Larry Maxwell** . . . . . . . . . . . . . . . . . . . . . . . . . . (615) 837-5111
  E-mail: larry.maxwell@tn.gov
Consumer and Industry Services Assistant Commissioner
  **Jimmy Hopper** . . . . . . . . . . . . . . . . . . . . . . . . . . (615) 837-5152
  E-mail: jimmy.hopper@tn.gov
                        Fax: (615) 837-5335

Market Development Assistant Commissioner **Ed Harlan** . . (615) 837-5165
                        Fax: (615) 837-5194
Policy and Legislation Assistant Commissioner
  **Carol Coley McDonald** . . . . . . . . . . . . . . . . . . . . (615) 837-5172
  E-mail: carol.mcdonald@tn.gov
Public Affairs Assistant Commissioner **Corinne Gould** . . . . (615) 837-5207
  E-mail: corinne.gould@tn.gov
Agriculture Statistics Director **Debra K. Kenerson** . . . . . . (615) 781-5300
  E-mail: debra_kenerson@nass.usda.gov
Program Operations Director **Randy F. Jennings** . . . . . . . . (615) 837-5150
  Education: Mid Tennessee State BS; Tennessee State BS
Human Resources Director **Liz Sneed** . . . . . . . . . . . . . . . (615) 837-5115
General Counsel **Theresa Denton** . . . . . . . . . . . . . . . . . (615) 837-5280
Information Systems Director **Eric Whisler** . . . . . . . . . . . (615) 837-5401
  E-mail: eric.whisler@tn.gov

### Forestry Division

Ellington Ag Center, 440 Hogan Road, Nashville, TN 37220-9029
Tel: (615) 837-5520

Assistant Commissioner and State Forester **Jere Jeter** . . . . (615) 837-5435
                        Fax: (615) 837-5003
  Administrative Assistant **Lisa Jones** . . . . . . . . . . . . . . . (615) 837-5411
Assistant State Forester **David Arnold** . . . . . . . . . . . . . . (615) 837-5426
  Administrative Assistant **(Vacant)** . . . . . . . . . . . . . . . (615) 837-5421
Assistant State Forester **David Todd** . . . . . . . . . . . . . . . (615) 837-5539
  Administrative Assistant **Debra Dawson** . . . . . . . . . . . . (615) 837-5540

## Department of Children's Services [DCS]

Cordell Hull Building, 436 Sixth Avenue North,
Seventh, Eighth, and Ninth Floors, Nashville, TN 37243-1290
Tel: (615) 741-9701  Fax: (615) 532-8079  E-mail: elspecops@state.tn.us
Internet: www.state.tn.us/youth

■Commissioner **Bonnie Hommrich** . . . . . . . . . . . . . . . . . (615) 741-9701
  E-mail: bonnie.hommrich@tn.gov
  Executive Administrative Assistant to the Commissioner
    **Jeannie Vogel** . . . . . . . . . . . . . . . . . . . . . . . . . (615) 741-7250
Chief of Staff **(Vacant)** . . . . . . . . . . . . . . . . . . (865) 544-3825 ext. 264
                        Fax: (865) 546-8507
General Counsel **Doug Dimond** . . . . . . . . . . . . . . . . . . (615) 741-7326
  E-mail: douglas.e.dimond@tn.gov      Fax: (615) 532-2348
  Deputy General Counsel **Elizabeth Cambrom** . . . . . . . . (615) 532-5554
                        Fax: (615) 532-2348
Child Health Deputy Commissioner
  **Dr. Tom Cheetham, MD** . . . . . . . . . . . . . . . . . . . . (615) 741-9699
  E-mail: tom.cheetham@tn.gov
Child Programs Deputy Commissioner **(Vacant)** . . . . . . . . (615) 532-3591
                        Fax: (615) 253-7868
Quality Control Assistant Commissioner **Debbie Miller** . . . (615) 253-1112
                        Fax: (615) 253-5216
Centralized Permanency Services Director **Cheri Stewart** . . (615) 532-5618
                        Fax: (615) 253-5422
Children's Services Program (TennCare) Director
  **(Vacant)** . . . . . . . . . . . . . . . . . . . . . . . . . . . . . (615) 253-4506
                        Fax: (615) 253-5216
Communications Director **Rob Johnson** . . . . . . . . . . . . . (615) 253-8467
                        Fax: (615) 253-5596

---

★ Elected Official    ■Appointed by Governor    ●Appointed by Legislature    ▲Appointed by Board or Commission    ◆Appointed by State Supreme Court

Continuous Quality Improvement Director
**Anthony Neese** . . . . . . . . . . . . . . . . . . . . . . . . . . . (615) 253-1112
Fax: (615) 253-5216
Investigation Director **Richard Osgood** . . . . . . . . . . . . . . (615) 741-9190
Fax: (615) 255-6309
Legislative and Constituent Services Program Director
**Tammy Feldman** . . . . . . . . . . . . . . . . . . . . . . . . . . (615) 532-3111
E-mail: tammy.feldman@tn.gov          Fax: (615) 532-2348
Legislative and Constituent Services Program Manager
**Kristi Timmerman** . . . . . . . . . . . . . . . . . . . . . . . . (615) 741-9711
E-mail: kristy.timmerman@tn.gov       Fax: (615) 532-5729
Program Accountability Review Director **Carter Overton** . . (615) 253-0061
Fax: (615) 244-1723
Residential Licensing Director
**Mark Anderson** . . . . . . . . . . . . . . . . . . . . (865) 594-2836 (Knoxville)
Tel: (615) 532-5598
(Nashville)
Fax: (615) 244-1723
Special Investigations Unit Director **Irma Buchanan** . . . . . (615) 253-0058
E-mail: irma.buchanan@tn.gov          Fax: (615) 253-0060
Systems Development and Enhancement Director
**(Vacant)** . . . . . . . . . . . . . . . . . . . . . . . . . . . . . (615) 741-9699
Information Systems Chief Information Officer (Acting)
**Joe Huertas** . . . . . . . . . . . . . . . . . . . . . . . . . . . (615) 532-2455
E-mail: joe.huertas@tn.gov            Fax: (615) 532-9411
Interstate Compact of Placement for Children Deputy
Compact Administrator **Cheri Stewart** . . . . . . . . . . . (615) 532-5618
E-mail: cheri.stewart@tn.gov          Fax: (615) 253-5422
Performance Improvement Program (PIP) and Policy
Manager **Daphne Billingsley** . . . . . . . . . . . . . . . . . (615) 532-5539
E-mail: daphne.billingsley@tn.gov     Fax: (615) 251-9532
Records and Information Management Manager
**Chuck Brown** . . . . . . . . . . . . . . . . . . . . . . . . . . (615) 253-5989
E-mail: chuck.brown@tn.gov            Fax: (615) 253-5975
Administrative Judge **Tara Moore** . . . . . . . . . . . . . . . . (615) 741-1110
Fax: (615) 741-4518
Legislative Liaison **Zack Blair** . . . . . . . . . . . . . . . . . . (615) 532-4801
E-mail: zack.blair@tn.gov             Fax: (615) 532-2348
Risk Management **Richard Osgood** . . . . . . . . . . . . . . . . (615) 741-9190
Fax: (615) 255-6309

# Tennessee Department of Commerce and Insurance [TDCI]

Davy Crockett Tower, 500 James Robertson Parkway,
Nashville, TN 37243-1141
Tel: (615) 741-6007  Fax: (615) 532-6934
E-mail: ask.tdci@mail.state.tn.us  Internet: www.state.tn.us/commerce

■Commissioner **Julie Mix McPeak** . . . . . . . . . . . . . . . . . (615) 741-6007
E-mail: julie.mcpeak@tn.gov
Education: Kentucky 1990; Louisville 1994 JD
Administrative Assistant **Denise Lewis** . . . . . . . . . . . . . (615) 741-6007
Deputy Commissioner **Bill Giannini** . . . . . . . . . . . . . . . (615) 741-3449
Deputy Commissioner **Chlora Lindley-Myers** . . . . . . . . . (615) 741-6007
Deputy Commissioner **Gary West** . . . . . . . . . . . . . . . . (615) 532-5747
Communications Director **Kevin Walters** . . . . . . . . . . . . (615) 741-6007
Internal Audit Director **John G. Williams** . . . . . . . . . . . (615) 253-5736
General Counsel **Lorrie Brouse** . . . . . . . . . . . . . . . . . (615) 741-2199
Legislative Liaison **Denise Lawrence** . . . . . . . . . . . . . . (615) 741-6007
E-mail: denise.lawrence@tn.gov
Legislative Liaison **Marybeth Gribble** . . . . . . . . . . . . . (615) 741-6007
E-mail: marybeth.gribble@tn.gov

## Administration Division

Fax: (615) 532-0729
Information Systems Director **Paul Hartbarger** . . . . . . . . (615) 532-5259
E-mail: paul.hartbarger@tn.gov
Personnel Director **Shannon Tolbert** . . . . . . . . . . . . . . (615) 741-0481
E-mail: shannon.tolbert@tn.gov
Chief Fiscal Officer **Robert Lee Wright** . . . . . . . . . . . . (615) 741-2705

## Consumer Affairs Division

Fax: (615) 532-4994  E-mail: dca@mail.state.tn.us
Internet: www.state.tn.us/consumer
Director **(Vacant)** . . . . . . . . . . . . . . . . . . . . . . . . . (615) 741-4737

## Fire Prevention Division

Fax: (615) 741-1583
Deputy Commissioner **Gary L. West** . . . . . . . . . . . . . . (615) 741-2981
Fire Services and Codes Enforcement Academy
Executive Director **Roger C. Hawks** . . . . . . . . . . . . (931) 294-4111
2161 Unionvill-Deason Road, Bell Buckle, TN 37020
E-mail: roger.c.hawks@tn.gov
Arson Investigation Director
**Glenn N. "Andy" Anderson** . . . . . . . . . . . . . . . . . (615) 532-0355
Codes Enforcement Director
**Christopher "Chris" Bainbridge** . . . . . . . . . . . . . . (615) 741-7190
Contract Inspection Services Director **Gary Farley** . . . . . . (615) 741-7170
Permits and Licenses Administrator
**Deann Demonbreun** . . . . . . . . . . . . . . . . . . . . . (615) 741-7823
Programs and Policy Director **Peyton Bullen** . . . . . . . . . (615) 532-7840
E-mail: peyton.bullen@tn.gov

## Insurance Division

Fax: (615) 532-2788
Assistant Commissioner **Michael Humphreys** . . . . . . . . . (615) 741-2176
Agent Licensing Director **Brenda Sechler** . . . . . . . . . . . (615) 741-2693
Captives Section Director **Michael A. Corbett** . . . . . . . . (615) 741-6253
Education: Mississippi; Emory MBA
Consumer Insurance Services Director **Vickie Trice** . . . . . . (615) 741-2218
Fraud Investigations Section Director
**Frank Borger-Gilligan** . . . . . . . . . . . . . . . . . . . . (615) 532-2375
Insurance Analysis Director **Mark Jaquish** . . . . . . . . . . (615) 741-1692
Life and Health Actuarial Director **Brian Hoffmeister** . . . . (615) 741-2825
Property and Casualty Rating Manager **John E. Duncan** . . (615) 532-0693
Workers' Compensation Unit Manager **Mike Shinnick** . . . . (615) 741-0472
Self-Insurance/Surplus Lines Chief Analyst **(Vacant)** . . . . . (615) 741-6007
Chief Examiner **Joy Little** . . . . . . . . . . . . . . . . . . . (615) 741-1869
E-mail: joy.little@tn.gov

## Regulatory Boards Division

Fax: (615) 741-6470
Assistant Commissioner **Brian McCormack** . . . . . . . . . . (615) 741-3449

## Real Estate Commission

Real Estate Commission Director **Eve Maxwell** . . . . . . . . (615) 741-2273

## Securities Division

Fax: (615) 532-8375
Assistant Commissioner **Daphne D. Smith** . . . . . . . . . . (615) 741-2947
Broker-Dealer Agent/Investment Adviser Chief
**Steven Patterson** . . . . . . . . . . . . . . . . . . . . . . . (615) 532-2693
Enforcement Assistant Director **Carmen Jones** . . . . . . . . (615) 532-3945
Registration Assistant Director **Judith Poynter** . . . . . . . . (615) 532-2693

## TennCare Oversight Division

Fax: (615) 532-8872
Assistant Commissioner **Lisa Jordan** . . . . . . . . . . . . . (615) 741-2677

## Fire Fighting Commission

Director **Randy Fox** . . . . . . . . . . . . . . . . . . . . . . . (615) 741-1788

## Emergency Communications Board

Director **Curtis Sutton** . . . . . . . . . . . . . . . . . . . . . (615) 253-2164

## Tennessee Law Enforcement and Training Academy [TLETA]

3025 Lebanon Pike, Nashville, TN 37214
Tel: (615) 741-4448  Fax: (615) 741-3366
E-mail: law.enforcement@tn.gov  Internet: www.tn.gov/let
Executive Director **Brian Grisham** . . . . . . . . . . . . . . . (615) 741-2980
Education: Mid Tennessee State 1984 BS; Nashville 1989 JD

*(continued on next page)*

★ Elected Official   ■ Appointed by Governor   ● Appointed by Legislature   ▲ Appointed by Board or Commission   ◆ Appointed by State Supreme Court

**EXECUTIVE BRANCH**

**Tennessee Law Enforcement and Training Academy** *continued*

Assistant Director **Ray Farris** . . . . . . . . . . . . . . . . . . . . . . . (615) 741-4448
Assistant Director **Sam Reed** . . . . . . . . . . . . . . . . . . . . . . . (615) 741-4448
  Education: Mid Tennessee State 1983 BS, 1992 MS
Supervisor of Training **Mark Hall** . . . . . . . . . . . . . . . . . . . (615) 741-4448
  E-mail: mark.hall@tn.gov
Chief Post Investigator **(Vacant)** . . . . . . . . . . . . . . . . . . . . (615) 741-4448
Post Investigator **Stan Murphy** . . . . . . . . . . . . . . . . . . . . . (615) 741-4448
  E-mail: stan.murphy@tn.gov
Administrative Services Assistant II **Dean Lewis** . . . . . . . . (615) 741-4448
Administrative Services Assistant II **Kim Moss** . . . . . . . . . (615) 741-4448
Administrative Secretary **(Vacant)** . . . . . . . . . . . . . . . . . . . (615) 741-4448

## Peace Officer Standards and Training Commission [P.O.S.T.]

3025 Lebanon Pike, Nashville, TN 37214
Tel: (615) 741-4461  Fax: (615) 532-0502
E-mail: law.enforcement@tn.gov

Member **Rita B. Baker** . . . . . . . . . . . . . . . . . . . . . . . . . . . . (615) 741-4461
●Member **Mike Bell** . . . . . . . . . . . . . . . . . . . . . . . . . . . . . . (615) 741-4461
●Member **David Richard Bennett** . . . . . . . . . . . . . . . . . . . (615) 741-4461
  E-mail: david.bennett@tncourts.gov
Member **Brent Cherry** . . . . . . . . . . . . . . . . . . . . . . . . . . . . (615) 741-4461
■Member **Gerald Fanion, Jr.** . . . . . . . . . . . . . . . . . . . . . . . (615) 741-4461
  E-mail: gerald.fanion@tncourts.gov
Member **Carl Jenkins** . . . . . . . . . . . . . . . . . . . . . . . . . . . . . (615) 741-4461
■Member **Franklin Lax** . . . . . . . . . . . . . . . . . . . . . . . . . . . (615) 741-4461
  E-mail: franklin.lax@tncourts.gov
■Member **Jeffery C. Lewis** . . . . . . . . . . . . . . . . . . . . . . . . . (615) 741-4461
  E-mail: jeffery.lewis@tncourts.gov
Member **Robert M. Rhodes** . . . . . . . . . . . . . . . . . . . . . . . . (615) 741-4461
■Member **Kim Wallace** . . . . . . . . . . . . . . . . . . . . . . . . . . . (615) 741-4461
  E-mail: kwallace@dovertn.com
Member **James R. Wheeler** . . . . . . . . . . . . . . . . . . . . . . . . (615) 741-4461
■Member **Bobby Williamson** . . . . . . . . . . . . . . . . . . . . . . . (615) 741-4461
  E-mail: bobby.williamson@tncourts.gov
■Member **Ric Wilson** . . . . . . . . . . . . . . . . . . . . . . . . . . . . . (615) 741-4461
  E-mail: ric.wilson@tncourts.gov

### Commission Staff

Executive Secretary **Brian Grisham** . . . . . . . . . . . . . . . . . . (615) 741-4461
  Affiliation: Executive Director, Tennessee Law Enforcement and
  Training Academy, State of Tennessee
  3025 Lebanon Pike, Nashville, TN 37214
Executive Assistant **Kelly Morgan** . . . . . . . . . . . . . . . . . . . (615) 741-4461
Staff Member **Stan Murphy** . . . . . . . . . . . . . . . . . . . . . . . . (615) 741-4461
  Affiliation: Post Investigator, Tennessee Law Enforcement and Training
  Academy, State of Tennessee
  3025 Lebanon Pike, Nashville, TN 37214
Staff Member **(Vacant)** . . . . . . . . . . . . . . . . . . . . . . . . . . . (615) 741-4461

## Tennessee Corrections Institute [TCI]

Davy Crockett Tower, 500 James Robertson Parkway,
Nashville, TN 37243-1141
Tel: (615) 741-3816  Fax: (615) 532-2333  Internet: www.tn.gov/tci

Executive Director **Beth Ashe** . . . . . . . . . . . . . . . . . . . . . . . (615) 741-3816
  E-mail: beth.ashe@tn.gov
Deputy Director **William Wall** . . . . . . . . . . . . . . . . . . . . . . (615) 741-3816

## Tennessee Department of Correction [TDOC]

Rachel Jackson Building, 320 Sixth Avenue North, 6th Floor,
Nashville, TN 37243-0465
Tel: (615) 741-1000  TTY: (615) 532-4423
Internet: www.state.tn.us/correction

■Commissioner **Derrick Schofield** . . . . . . . . . . . . . . (615) 741-1000 ext. 8139
  E-mail: derrick.schofield@tn.gov
  Assistant to the Commissioner
    **James "Jim" Thrasher** . . . . . . . . . . . . . . . . (615) 741-1000 ext. 8146
  Executive Secretary **Pat Crockett** . . . . . . . . . . . . (615) 741-1000 ext. 8140
Chief of Staff **Chuck Taylor** . . . . . . . . . . . . . . . . . . (615) 741-1000 ext. 8248
  Assistant to the Deputy Commissioner **Emily Gibson** . . . (615) 741-1000
    Education: Mid Tennessee State 1998 BA, 2002 MA

Executive Secretary **Miranda Merkle** . . . . . . . . . . . . . . . . . (615) 741-1000
Administrative Services Deputy Commissioner
  **Emily Gibson** . . . . . . . . . . . . . . . . . . . . . . . . . . . . . . . (615) 741-1000
  E-mail: emily.gibson@tn.gov
  Executive Secretary **Rebecca "Becky" Johns** . . . . . . . . . (615) 741-1000
Facilities Construction Specialist **Roger Shaw** . . . (615) 741-1000 ext. 8103
Engineering Director
  **Thomas "Tom" Robinson** . . . . . . . . . . . . . . (615) 741-1000 ext. 8101
  E-mail: thomas.robinson@tn.gov
Food Services Director **Jane Amonett** . . . . . . . . . (615) 741-1000 ext. 8156
Clinical Services Director **Dr. Marina Cadreche** . . . . . . . . (615) 253-8157
Internal Audit and Accreditation Director
  **Kristy Carroll-Grimes** . . . . . . . . . . . . . . . . (615) 741-1000 ext. 8188
Medical Director **Dr. Kenneth Williams** . . . . . . . (615) 741-1000 ext. 8210
Mental Health Director **Mark Simpson** . . . . . . . . (615) 741-1000 ext. 8163
Human Resources Director **Lisa Patton** . . . . . . . . (615) 741-1000 ext. 8018
Planning and Research Director (Acting)
  **Tanya Washington** . . . . . . . . . . . . . . . . . . . (615) 741-1000 ext. 8153
  E-mail: tanya.washington@tn.gov
General Counsel **Debra Inglis** . . . . . . . . . . . . . . . (615) 741-3087 ext. 8147
  E-mail: debbie.inglis@tn.gov
Internal Affairs Director **Terence Davis** . . . . . . . . . . . . . . . (615) 741-7144

## Budget/Fiscal Section

Chief Financial Officer **Wes Landers** . . . . . . . . . . (615) 741-1000 ext. 8141
  E-mail: wes.landers@tn.gov
  Administrative Assistant **Carolyn Fiedler** . . . . . (615) 741-1000 ext. 8142
  Executive Secretary **Diane Speyerer** . . . . . . . . . (615) 741-1000 ext. 8095
Budget/Fiscal Director **Lisa C. Parks** . . . . . . . . . (615) 741-1000 ext. 8096
Central Maintenance Director (Acting)
  **Dennis Hayes** . . . . . . . . . . . . . . . . . . . . . . . (615) 741-1000 ext. 8102
  E-mail: dennis.hayes@tn.gov
Contracts Administration Director
  **William M. Anderson** . . . . . . . . . . . . . . . . . (615) 741-1000 ext. 8104
  E-mail: william.m.anderson@tn.gov
Management Information Services Director
  **Mary Moewe** . . . . . . . . . . . . . . . . . . . . . . . . . . . . . . . (615) 741-1000
  E-mail: mary.moewe@tn.gov
Purchasing Director **Terry C. Anderson** . . . . . . . . . . . . . . . (423) 260-6118
Judicial Cost Accountant
  **Judith "Judy" Lambert** . . . . . . . . . . . . . . . . (615) 741-1000 ext. 8108

## Operations Division

Deputy Commissioner **Jason Woodall** . . . . . . . . . (615) 741-1000 ext. 8172
  Executive Secretary **Kathrine Elam** . . . . . . . . . (615) 741-1000 ext. 8172
Classification Director **Brandon Maloney** . . . . . . (615) 741-1000 ext. 8180
Community Work Projects Director **(Vacant)** . . . . (615) 741-1000 ext. 8173
Security Threat Groups Director **Korey Cooper** . . . . . . . . . (615) 741-7144

## Rehabilitation Division

Tel: (615) 741-1000

Rehabilitative Services Division Assistant
  Commissioner (Acting) **Dr. Marina Cadreche** . . (615) 741-1000 ext. 8260
Education Director **Rhonda Whitt** . . . . . . . . . . . . (615) 741-1000 ext. 8162
Prerelease Programs Director
  **Cleatrice McTorry** . . . . . . . . . . . . . . . . . . . (615) 741-1000 ext. 8128
  E-mail: cleatrice.mctorry@tn.gov
Religious Services Director
  **Deborah Thompson** . . . . . . . . . . . . . . . . . . (615) 741-1000 ext. 8161
  E-mail: deborah.thompson@tn.gov
Substance Abuse Director
  **Michelle R. Hergert** . . . . . . . . . . . . . . . . . . (615) 741-1000 ext. 8195
Volunteer Services Director
  **Deborah Thompson** . . . . . . . . . . . . . . . . . . (615) 741-1000 ext. 8161

## Department of Economic and Community Development [TNECD]

Tennessee Tower, 312 Rosa L. Parks Avenue, 11th Floor,
Nashville, TN 37243-1102
Tel: (615) 741-1888  Fax: (615) 741-7306

■Commissioner **Randy Boyd** . . . . . . . . . . . . . . . . . . . . . . . (615) 741-1888
  Education: Tennessee 1979 BA; Oklahoma State 1988 MLA

---

★ Elected Official   ■ Appointed by Governor   ● Appointed by Legislature   ▲ Appointed by Board or Commission   ◆ Appointed by State Supreme Court

Executive Assistant and Scheduler **Betsy VanDam** . . . . . . (615) 741-8915
  E-mail: betsy.vandam@tn.gov
Chief of Staff **Ted Townsend** . . . . . . . . . . . . . . . . . . . . . (615) 532-9060
Assistant Commissioner for Rural Development
  **Amy New** . . . . . . . . . . . . . . . . . . . . . . . . . . . . . . . . . (615) 253-1948
Assistant Commissioner for Strategy **(Vacant)** . . . . . . . . . . (615) 770-1163
Human Resources Director **Leslie Hathaway** . . . . . . . . . . . . (615) 741-1888
Internal Audit Director **Judy Tribble** . . . . . . . . . . . . . . . . . (615) 253-1760
Senior Advisor for Fiscal Policy **(Vacant)** . . . . . . . . . . . . . (615) 532-1284
Senior Advisor for Grant Program **Philip Trauernicht** . . . . . (615) 253-1903
  E-mail: philip.trauernicht@tn.gov

## Administration

Assistant Commissioner **Paula Davis** . . . . . . . . . . . . . . . . . (615) 532-3886
  E-mail: paula.davis@tn.gov
  Education: Tennessee
Budget and Fiscal Policy Director **Jessica Johnson** . . . . . . (615) 532-1289
Information Technology Director **Gary Jenkins** . . . . . . . . . . (615) 532-1906
  E-mail: gary.jenkins@tn.gov
Research and Planning Director **Sally Haar** . . . . . . . . . . . . (615) 532-1912
Webmaster **Sama Bahjat** . . . . . . . . . . . . . . . . . . . . . . . . . (615) 532-8002
  E-mail: sama.bahjat@tn.gov

## Business Development

Fax: (615) 741-5829

Assistant Commissioner **W. Allen Borden** . . . . . . . . . . . . . (615) 532-9821
Global Project Manager **(Vacant)** . . . . . . . . . . . . . . . . . . . (615) 532-8895
Regional Director (Eastern Tennessee) **Gary Human** . . . . . . (865) 210-1333
  E-mail: gary.human@tn.gov
Regional Director (Greater Memphis) **Gwyn R. Fisher** . . . . (901) 208-9920
  E-mail: gwyn.fisher@tn.gov
Regional Director (Northeastern Tennessee)
  **Iliff McMahan, Jr.** . . . . . . . . . . . . . . . . . . . . . . . . . . . (423) 290-1520
  E-mail: iliff.mcmahan@tn.gov
Regional Director (Northern Middle Tennessee)
  **Reggie Mudd** . . . . . . . . . . . . . . . . . . . . . . . . . . . . . . . (615) 532-8898
  E-mail: reggie.mudd@tn.gov
Regional Director (Northwestern Tennessee)
  **Blake Swaggart** . . . . . . . . . . . . . . . . . . . . . . . . . . . . . (731) 437-9443
  E-mail: blake.swaggart@tn.gov
Regional Director (Southeastern Tennessee) **Sam Wills** . . . . (423) 254-4275
  E-mail: sam.wills@tn.gov
Regional Director (Southern Middle Tennessee)
  **Clay Banks** . . . . . . . . . . . . . . . . . . . . . . . . . . . . . . . . (731) 803-9301
  E-mail: clay.banks@tn.gov
Regional Director (Southwestern Tennessee)
  **Tracey Exum** . . . . . . . . . . . . . . . . . . . . . . . . . . . . . . . (731) 414-4463
  E-mail: tracey.exum@tn.gov
Regional Director (Upper Cumberland) **Rebecca Smith** . . . (931) 252-8088
  E-mail: rebecca.smith@tn.gov
Statistical Research Specialist **Rob Settles** . . . . . . . . . . . . (615) 532-9047
Statewide Director, Appalachian Regional Commission
  **W. Allen Borden** . . . . . . . . . . . . . . . . . . . . . . . . . . . . (615) 624-2185

## Communications and Marketing

Fax: (615) 253-6443  Internet: www.tnecd.gov

Assistant Commissioner **Clint Brewer** . . . . . . . . . . . . . . . . (615) 741-1888
  E-mail: clint.brewer@tn.gov
Communications Director **Laura Elkins** . . . . . . . . . . . . . . . (615) 532-1910
  E-mail: laura.elkins@tn.gov
Communications Deputy Director **Erin Holt** . . . . . . . . . . . . (615) 741-8548
  E-mail: erin.holt@tn.gov

## Tennessee Department of Education [TDOE]

Andrew Johnson Tower, 710 James Robertson Parkway, 11th Floor,
Nashville, TN 37243-0375
Tel: (615) 741-5158  Fax: (615) 532-4791

■Commissioner **Dr. Candice McQueen** . . . . . . . . . . . . . . . (615) 741-5158
  E-mail: candice.mcqueen@tn.gov
  Education: Lipscomb U BA; Vanderbilt; Texas PhD
  Executive Administrative Assistant **Janice Mann** . . . . . . (615) 741-8457

Deputy Commissioner **Dr. Kathleen Airhart** . . . . . . . . . . . (615) 741-5158
Career and Technical Education Assistant Commissioner
  **Danielle Mezera** . . . . . . . . . . . . . . . . . . . . . . . . . . . . (615) 253-2114
    Fax: (615) 532-9412
Data and Research Assistant Commissioner **Erin O'Hara** . . . (615) 253-8854
Legislative and Policy Assistant Commissioner
  **Stephen M. Smith** . . . . . . . . . . . . . . . . . . . . . . . . . . . (615) 741-1111
  E-mail: stephen.m.smith@tn.gov
Federal Programs Director **Eve Carney** . . . . . . . . . . . . . . . (615) 532-6245
    Fax: (615) 532-5706
Post-Secondary Coordination and Alignment Executive
  Director **Emily Carter** . . . . . . . . . . . . . . . . . . . . . . . . (615) 532-2841
Teachers and Leaders Assistant Commissioner **(Vacant)** . . . (615) 253-8856
Special Populations Assistant Commissioner
  **Joey Hassell** . . . . . . . . . . . . . . . . . . . . . . . . . . . . . . (615) 253-2112
    Fax: (615) 253-4989
Leadership Effectiveness Executive Director
  **Paul Fleming** . . . . . . . . . . . . . . . . . . . . . . . . . . . . . . (615) 532-6276
    Fax: (615) 532-8312
Information Technology Executive Director
  **Richard Charlesworth** . . . . . . . . . . . . . . . . . . . . . . . . (615) 532-2818
  E-mail: richard.charlesworth@tn.gov    Fax: (615) 532-5303
Budget Director **John Sharp** . . . . . . . . . . . . . . . . . . . . . . (615) 532-1658
Communications Director **Ashley M. Ball** . . . . . . . . . . . . . (615) 532-6260
  E-mail: ashley.m.ball@tn.gov
Safe and Supportive Schools Office Director **Pat Conner** . . (615) 741-3248
Human Resources Director **Vickie Hall** . . . . . . . . . . . . . . . (615) 532-6188
    Fax: (615) 741-6236
Internal Audit Director **Chris Steppee** . . . . . . . . . . . . . . . (615) 532-6224
    Fax: (615) 532-7860
Quality and Integrity Director **Karen Daniels** . . . . . . . . . . (615) 532-1254
Operations and Planning Director
  **Deborah Boshears-Davis** . . . . . . . . . . . . . . . . . . . . . . (615) 532-1681
  E-mail: deborah.davis@tn.gov    Fax: (615) 532-3268
School Nutrition Services Executive Director
  **Sarah C. White** . . . . . . . . . . . . . . . . . . . . . . . . . . . . . (615) 532-0362
LEA and SFA Support **Phyllis M. Hodges, SNS** . . . . . . . . (615) 532-4742
  1240 Foster Avenue, Nashville, TN 37243
Analytic Strategy Executive Director **Amy Wooten** . . . . . . (615) 741-7857
Licensure Operations Director **(Vacant)** . . . . . . . . . . . . . . (615) 532-4885
    Fax: (615) 532-1448
Student Success Executive Director
  **Casey Haugner-Wrenn** . . . . . . . . . . . . . . . . . . . . . . . . (615) 532-4879
    Fax: (615) 532-8226
General Counsel **Christy Ballard** . . . . . . . . . . . . . . . . . . . (615) 741-2921
  E-mail: christy.ballard@tn.gov

## Tennessee Department of Environment and Conservation [TDEC]

312 Rosa L. Parks Avenue, Nashville, TN 37243-1102
Tel: (615) 532-0109
Tel: (888) 891-8332 (Environment Assistance Centers [Statewide])
Fax: (615) 532-0120  Internet: www.tn.gov/environment

■Commissioner **Robert J. "Bob" Martineau, Jr.** . . . . . . . . (615) 532-0106
  E-mail: bob.martineau@tn.gov
  Education: St John's U (MN) 1980 BA; Cincinnati 1983 JD
  Administrative Assistant **Kelley Clemons** . . . . . . . . . . . (615) 532-0106
Assistant Commissioner for External Affairs
  **David Owenby** . . . . . . . . . . . . . . . . . . . . . . . . . . . . . (615) 532-1531
  Communications Director **Kelly Brockman** . . . . . . . . . . (615) 253-1916
    E-mail: kelly.brockman@tn.gov
General Counsel **Joe Sanders** . . . . . . . . . . . . . . . . . . . . . (615) 532-0131
Emergency Services Director **Brenda Apple** . . . . . . . . . . . (615) 253-5914
Internal Audit Director **Vince Haymon** . . . . . . . . . . . . . . . (615) 532-0510
Legislative Liaison **Jenny Howard** . . . . . . . . . . . . . . . . . . (615) 532-8685
  E-mail: jenny.howard@tn.gov

## Bureau of Environment

Deputy Commissioner **Shari Meghreblian** . . . . . . . . . . . . . (615) 532-0102
Senior Advisor **Chuck Head** . . . . . . . . . . . . . . . . . . . . . . (615) 532-0998
  Administrative Assistant **Carolyn MacWilliams** . . . . . . . (615) 532-0102
Air Pollution Control Director **Michelle Owenby** . . . . . . . . (615) 532-0554
Sustainable Practices Director **Lori Munkeboe** . . . . . . . . . (615) 532-0705
Geology Director **Ron Zurawski** . . . . . . . . . . . . . . . . . . . (615) 532-1502

*(continued on next page)*

---

★ Elected Official    ■ Appointed by Governor    ● Appointed by Legislature    ▲ Appointed by Board or Commission    ◆ Appointed by State Supreme Court

EXECUTIVE BRANCH

**Bureau of Environment** *continued*

Parks Bureau Archaeology Director
**Mike C. Moore** . . . . . . . . . . . . . . . . . . . . . . . . . . .(615) 741-1588 ext. 109
 5103 Edmonson Pike, Nashville, TN 37211-5129
 E-mail: mike.c.moore@tn.gov
Radiological Health Director **Debra Shults** . . . . . . . . . . . . (615) 532-0364
Remediation Director **Steve Goins** . . . . . . . . . . . . . . . . . . (615) 532-0900
 Remediation Deputy Director **Chris Thompson** . . . . . . . . (615) 532-0911
  Education: Clemson
Solid Waste Management Director **Patrick Flood** . . . . . . . .(615) 532-0780
Underground Storage Tanks Director **Stan Boyd** . . . . . . . .(615) 532-0945
Water Resources Director **Tisha Calabrese-Benton** . . . . . .(615) 532-0191
West Tennessee River Basin Authority Director
**David Salyers** . . . . . . . . . . . . . . . . . . . . . . . . . . . . . . (731) 784-8173
 3628 East End Drive, Humboldt, TN 38343

## Administrative Services

Assistant Commissioner **Tom Eck** . . . . . . . . . . . . . . . . . . . (615) 532-0103
Administrative Assistant **Kim Ridings** . . . . . . . . . . . . . . . .(615) 532-0290
Facilities Management Director **David Benton** . . . . . . . . . .(615) 532-0118
Human Resources Director **Selena Cunningham** . . . . . . . .(615) 532-0098
Information Systems Director **Ken Bernhardt** . . . . . . . . . . (615) 532-0265
 E-mail: ken.bernhardt@tn.gov

## State Parks and Conservation

Deputy Commissioner **Brock Hill** . . . . . . . . . . . . . . . . . . .(615) 532-0696
 E-mail: brock.hill@tn.gov
Senior Advisor to the Deputy Commissioner
**Anne Marshall** . . . . . . . . . . . . . . . . . . . . . . . . . . . . . .(423) 854-5471
 E-mail: anne.marshall@tn.gov
Historical Commission Director
**Patrick McIntyre** . . . . . . . . . . . . . . . . . . . . . . . . (615) 532-1550 ext. 101
Recreation Educational Services Director **Gerald Parish** . . .(615) 532-1370

# Department of Finance and Administration [F&A]

State Capitol, First Floor, Nashville, TN 37243-0285
Tel: (615) 741-2401  Fax: (615) 741-9872

■Commissioner **Larry B. Martin** . . . . . . . . . . . . . . . . . . . . (615) 741-2401
 E-mail: larry.martin@tn.gov
 Education: Tennessee BS
Deputy Commissioner **Eugene Neubert** . . . . . . . . . . . . . . .(615) 741-0300
 E-mail: eugene.neubert@tn.gov
Legal Counsel **Martha Nichols** . . . . . . . . . . . . . . . . . . . . .(615) 532-9618
 Tennessee Tower, 312 Rosa L. Parks Avenue, 21st Floor,
 Nashville, TN 37243

## Accounts Division

Tennessee Tower, 312 Eighth Avenue North, 21st Floor,
Nashville, TN 37243

Chief of Accounts **Mikel Mike Corricelli** . . . . . . . . . . . . . (615) 741-2382
Payroll Director **Susan V. Walker** . . . . . . . . . . . . . . . . . . .(615) 741-9766

## Administration Division

Tennessee Tower, 312 Rosa L. Parks Avenue, 21st Floor,
Nashville, TN 37243

Director **Robert "Buddy" Lea** . . . . . . . . . . . . . . . . . . . . . .(615) 741-6049
 E-mail: buddy.lea@tn.gov
Office of Internal Audit Director **Thad DelConte** . . . . . . . .(615) 532-7098
Human Resource Director **Renee Jackson** . . . . . . . . . . . . .(615) 741-3478

## Benefits Administration Division

Tennessee Tower, 312 Rosa L. Parks Avenue, 13th and 26th Floors,
Nashville, TN 37243

Director **Laurie Lee** . . . . . . . . . . . . . . . . . . . . . . . . . . . . . .(615) 253-2861

## Budget Division

Tennessee Tower, 312 Rosa L. Parks Avenue, 16th Floor,
Nashville, TN 37243

Director **David Thurman** . . . . . . . . . . . . . . . . . . . . . . . . . .(615) 741-4806

## Enterprise Resource Planning Division

Tennessee Tower, 312 Rosa L. Parks Avenue, 19th Floor,
Nashville, TN 37243

Director **Sandy Graf** . . . . . . . . . . . . . . . . . . . . . . . . . . . . . .(615) 253-2978

## Information Resources Office

Tennessee Tower, 312 Eighth Avenue North, 16th Floor,
Nashville, TN 37243
Fax: (615) 532-0471

Chief Information Officer **Mark Bengel** . . . . . . . . . . . . . . .(615) 741-7951
Deputy Chief Information Officer **Jamie Etheridge** . . . . . .(615) 741-7358
 E-mail: jamie.etheridge@tn.gov

## TennCare Office of the Inspector General

P.O. Box 282368, Nashville, TN 37228
Tel: (800) 433-3982

Inspector General **Manny Tyndall** . . . . . . . . . . . . . . . . . . .(615) 687-7201

## TennCare Bureau

310 Great Circle Road, Nashville, TN 37243
Tel: (800) 342-3145

TennCare Bureau Deputy Commissioner
**Darin J. Gordon** . . . . . . . . . . . . . . . . . . . . . . . . . . . (615) 507-6444
 Note: Until June 30, 2016.                 Fax: (615) 253-5607
TennCare Bureau Deputy Commissioner
**Wendy Long, MD** . . . . . . . . . . . . . . . . . . . . . . . . . . .(615) 507-6444
 Note: Effective July 1, 2016.
 Education: Ohio State, MD; South Carolina MPH
Assistant Commissioner and Long Term Care Chief
**Patti Killingsworth** . . . . . . . . . . . . . . . . . . . . . . . . . (615) 507-6468
Assistant Commissioner and Chief Financial Officer
**Casey Dungan** . . . . . . . . . . . . . . . . . . . . . . . . . . . . .(615) 507-6347
Managed Care Operations Director **Keith Gaither** . . . . . . .(615) 507-6454
Member Services Director **Tracy Purcell** . . . . . . . . . . . . . .(615) 507-6994
Pharmacy Director **James R. "Rusty" Hailey** . . . . . . . . . . (615) 507-6415
Chief Medical Officer **Vaughn Frigon** . . . . . . . . . . . . . . . (615) 507-6440
Chief Operations Officer **Mike Cole** . . . . . . . . . . . . . . . . .(615) 507-6476
Chief of Staff **Wendy Long, MD** . . . . . . . . . . . . . . . . . . . .(615) 507-6444
 Note: Until June 30, 2016.
Program Integrity Chief **Dennis Garvey** . . . . . . . . . . . . . .(615) 507-6386
Public Information Officer **Kelly Gunderson** . . . . . . . . . . .(615) 507-6450
 E-mail: kelly.gunderson@tn.gov

# Tennessee Department of Financial Institutions [TDFI]

414 Union Street, Suite 1000, Nashville, TN 37219
Tel: (615) 741-2236  Fax: (615) 741-2883

■Commissioner **Greg Gonzales** . . . . . . . . . . . . . . . . . . . . .(615) 741-5603
 E-mail: greg.gonzales@tn.gov              Fax: (615) 253-6306
 Education: Tennessee Tech; Tennessee JD
Deputy Commissioner and General Counsel
**Tina G. Miller** . . . . . . . . . . . . . . . . . . . . . . . . . . . . . (615) 532-1030
 E-mail: tina.g.miller@tn.gov              Fax: (615) 253-6306
Bank Division Assistant Commissioner **Tod K. Trulove** . . . .(615) 741-5604
 E-mail: tod.trulove@tn.gov                Fax: (615) 532-3721
 Education: Mid Tennessee State BSBA
Compliance Division Assistant Commissioner
**Mike Igney** . . . . . . . . . . . . . . . . . . . . . . . . . . . . . . . (615) 741-1020
 E-mail: mike.igney@tn.gov                 Fax: (615) 532-1018
Credit Union Division Assistant Commissioner
**Tina G. Miller** . . . . . . . . . . . . . . . . . . . . . . . . . . . . . (615) 741-2236
                                           Fax: (615) 253-3787

# Department of General Services

William R. Snodgrass - TN Tower, 312 Rosa L. Parks Avenue, 24th Floor,
Nashville, TN 37243-0530
Tel: (615) 741-9263  Fax: (615) 532-8594
E-mail: general.services@tn.gov

■Commissioner **Robert E. "Bob" Oglesby** . . . . . . . . . . . . .(615) 741-2081
 E-mail: bob.oglesby@tn.gov
 Education: Tennessee

---

★ Elected Official   ■ Appointed by Governor   ● Appointed by Legislature    ▲ Appointed by Board or Commission   ◆ Appointed by State Supreme Court

Executive Administrative Assistant to the Commissioner
(Interim) **Marsha Shelton** . . . . . . . . . . . . . . . . . . . . . . (615) 741-2081
Deputy Commissioner **Reen L. Baskin** . . . . . . . . . . . . . . . (615) 253-7816
Deputy Commissioner **Thomas W. Chester** . . . . . . . . . . . (615) 253-7816
Chief Procurement Officer **Mike Perry** . . . . . . . . . . . . . . (615) 741-3625
Office of Financial Management Director **Ron Plumb** . . . . . (615) 532-7272
Human Resources Division Director **Vincent Barnes** . . . . . (615) 741-1379
Facilities Administration Director **Kevin Powell** . . . . . . . . (615) 741-5973
  6500 Centennial Boulevard, Nashville, TN 37243
Legislative Affairs Director **Kelly K. Smith** . . . . . . . . . . . (615) 741-1299
Motor Vehicle Management Director **Bob Williams** . . . . . . (615) 741-9263
  E-mail: bob.williams@tn.gov
Postal Services Director **Phillip O. "Phil" Page** . . . . . . . . (615) 741-8358
Printing and Media Services Director **Tammy Golden** . . . . (615) 741-4198
  B-8 Andrew Jackson Building, 501 Deaderick Street,
  Nashville, TN 37219

## State of Tennessee Real Estate Asset Management [STREAM]
Tel: (615) 741-9263  Fax: (615) 532-8594

Deputy Commissioner **John Hull** . . . . . . . . . . . . . . . . . . . (615) 253-7816
General Counsel **Thaddeus E. Watkins** . . . . . . . . . . . . . . (615) 741-5922
Information Technology Director **Brad Taylor** . . . . . . . . . . (615) 741-1889
  E-mail: brad.taylor@tn.gov
Internal Audit Director **Debi Moss** . . . . . . . . . . . . . . . . . (615) 741-0068
Services Contracting Coordinator **(Vacant)** . . . . . . . . . . . (615) 741-1298

## Department of Health
Andrew Johnson Tower, 710 James Robertson Parkway,
Nashville, TN 37243-0375
Tel: (615) 741-3111  Tel: (615) 532-2679 (Vital Records)
Fax: (615) 741-2491  Fax: (615) 741-9860 (Vital Records)
Internet: www.tennessee.gov/health

■Commissioner **Dr. John J. Dreyzehner, MD, MPH** . . . . . . (615) 741-9409
  E-mail: john.dreyzehner@tn.gov
  Education: Illinois 1985 BS; Illinois (Chicago) 1989 MD;
  Utah 1997 MPH
Executive Assistant **Tammy Stanton** . . . . . . . . . . . . . . . . (615) 741-9409
Deputy Commissioner **Bruce Behringer** . . . . . . . . . . . . . . (615) 741-3111
Deputy Commissioner for Population Health
  **Dr. Michael D. Warren, MD** . . . . . . . . . . . . . . . . . . . . (615) 741-3111
  Education: Wake Forest; East Carolina MD; Vanderbilt MPH
Assistant Commissioner, Legislative Services
  **Valerie Nagonshiner** . . . . . . . . . . . . . . . . . . . . . . . . (615) 741-3111
  E-mail: valerie.nagoshiner@tn.gov
Policy, Planning and Assessment Director
  **Lori Ferranti, PhD, MSN, MBA** . . . . . . . . . . . . . . . . . (615) 253-6814
  E-mail: lori.ferranti@tn.gov
General Counsel **Jane Young** 5th Floor . . . . . . . . . . . . . (615) 532-7663
  E-mail: jane.young@tn.gov
Health Policy Advisor **Rosalind Kurita** . . . . . . . . . . . . . . (615) 741-9411
  Education: Arkansas BA
Health Policy Advisor **Eric Harkness** . . . . . . . . . . . . . . . (615) 770-6806
Communications & Media Relations Director
  **Woody McMillin** . . . . . . . . . . . . . . . . . . . . . . . . . . . (615) 741-3446
  E-mail: woody.mcmillin@tn.gov
Laboratory Services Director
  **Richard Steece, PhD, D(ABMM)** . . . . . . . . . . . . . . . . (615) 262-6300
  630 Hart Lane, Nashville, TN 37243
Compliance Division Director **Mike Gaines, CPA** . . . . . . . (615) 741-1733
  Andrew Johnson Tower, 710 James Robertson Parkway, 5th Floor,
  Nashville, TN 37243
Human Resources Director **Wendy Barrickman** . . . . . . . . (615) 532-6574
                                             Fax: (615) 532-9952
Information Technology Services Director
  **Mike Newman** . . . . . . . . . . . . . . . . . . . . . . . . . . . . (615) 253-5417
  E-mail: mike.newman@tn.gov
Minority Health Division Director
  **Tené Hamilton Franklin** . . . . . . . . . . . . . . . . . . . . . . (615) 741-9443
Quality Improvement Division Director **(Vacant)** . . . . . . . (615) 532-9223
Legislative Liaison **Valerie Nagonshiner** . . . . . . . . . . . . (615) 741-3111
Chief Medical Officer **David Reagan, MD** . . . . . . . . . . . . (615) 741-3111

## Division of Administrative Services
Andrew Johnson Tower, 710 James Robertson Parkway, Fifth Floor,
Nashville, TN 37243
Tel: (615) 741-3151  Fax: (615) 253-1998

Assistant Commissioner **(Vacant)** . . . . . . . . . . . . . . . . . (615) 741-9398
Budget and Financial Management Director
  **Wayne Pierson** . . . . . . . . . . . . . . . . . . . . . . . . . . . . (615) 532-7148
Contract Review Director **(Vacant)** . . . . . . . . . . . . . . . . (615) 741-1614
Facilities Management Director **Peggy S. Wilson** . . . . . . . (615) 532-5326
  Education: Southern Mississippi 1960 BS
Procurement Director **Karen Olive** . . . . . . . . . . . . . . . . . (615) 532-9986
Fiscal Management Director **Valerie Oliver** . . . . . . . . . . . (615) 532-7121

## Division of Community Health Services
Tel: (615) 253-3407  Fax: (615) 532-2286

Assistant Commissioner **Leslie Humphreys** . . . . . . . . . . . (615) 741-4139
Dental Services Director **Veran Fairrow, DDS** . . . . . . . . . (615) 741-8618
Deputy Assistant Commissioner of Community Health
  Services **Rick Long** . . . . . . . . . . . . . . . . . . . . . . . . . (615) 532-1957
  E-mail: richard.long@tn.gov

## Division of Family Health and Wellness
Director **(Vacant)** . . . . . . . . . . . . . . . . . . . . . . . . . . . . (615) 741-0310
Deputy Director **Melissa Blair** . . . . . . . . . . . . . . . . . . . . (615) 532-7772
  E-mail: melissa.blair@tn.gov

## Division of Health Licensure and Regulation
665 Mainstream Drive, Nashville, TN 37243
Tel: (615) 741-8402  Fax: (615) 741-5542

Assistant Commissioner **Michelle Long** . . . . . . . . . . . . . (615) 741-6257
  E-mail: michelle.j.long@tn.gov
  Education: Northwestern BA; Tennessee (Chattanooga) JD
Emergency Medical Services Director **Donna G. Tidwell** . . (615) 741-4521
  E-mail: donna.g.tidwell@tn.gov
Health Care Facilities Director **Vincent Davis** . . . . . . . . . (615) 741-7532
Health Related Boards Director **Rosemarie Otto** . . . . . . . (615) 741-4540
  E-mail: rosemarie.otto@tn.gov
Investigations Director **Denise Moran, JD** . . . . . . . . . . . (615) 532-3425
  E-mail: denise.moran@tn.gov

## Communicable and Environmental Diseases and Emergency Preparedness [CEDEP]
710 James Robertson Parkway, Nashville, TN 37243-0375
Tel: (615) 741-7247  Fax: (615) 741-3857

State Epidemiologist and Division Director
  **Timothy F. Jones, MD** . . . . . . . . . . . . . . . . . . . . . . . (615) 532-7561
Emergency Services Preparedness Director
  **Paul Petersen, PhD** . . . . . . . . . . . . . . . . . . . . . . . . . (615) 741-8529
General Environmental Health Director **Hugh Atkins** . . . . . (615) 741-7206

## Department of Human Resources [HR]
505 Deaderick Street, First Floor, Nashville, TN 37243-1402
Tel: (615) 741-2958  Fax: (615) 741-7880

■Commissioner **Rebecca R. Hunter, SPHR** . . . . . . . . . . . (615) 741-2958
  E-mail: rebecca.hunter@tn.gov
  Education: Tennessee (Chattanooga) 1979 BSBA
Deputy Commissioner and General Counsel
  **Danielle Barnes** . . . . . . . . . . . . . . . . . . . . . . . . . . . (615) 253-8967
Assistant Commissioner and Chief Learning Officer
  **Trish Holliday** . . . . . . . . . . . . . . . . . . . . . . . . . . . . (615) 741-4126
Assistant Commissioner, Human Resources Consulting
  Services **Lisa Spencer, SPHR, IPMA-CP** . . . . . . . . . . . (615) 532-3224
Assistant Commissioner, Operations **Terence Donaldson** . . (615) 532-2958
Fiscal Director **Cindy Hobbs** . . . . . . . . . . . . . . . . . . . . . (615) 741-6199
  E-mail: cindy.hobbs@tn.gov
Employee Relations Division Director **(Vacant)** . . . . . . . . (615) 741-2799
Records Management Division Director **Steve Brown** . . . . . (615) 741-0668

★ Elected Official    ■ Appointed by Governor    ● Appointed by Legislature    ▲ Appointed by Board or Commission    ◆ Appointed by State Supreme Court

*State Yellow Book*    © Leadership Directories, Inc.    Summer 2016

## Technical Services

Deputy Commissioner **Stephanie Penney** . . . . . . . . . . . . (615) 741-0585
Recruiting Management Division Director
**Sharon Moidja** . . . . . . . . . . . . . . . . . . . . . . . . . . . . (615) 741-4841
Classification/Compensation Division Director
**Ritchie Worrell** . . . . . . . . . . . . . . . . . . . . . . . . . . . . (615) 741-5561
Technical Services Division Director **Sheila Marchman** . . . (615) 741-2087

## Department of Human Services [DHS]

400 Deaderick Street, 15th Floor, Nashville, TN 37243-1403
Tel: (615) 313-4700 TTY: (800) 270-1349 Fax: (615) 741-4165

■Commissioner **Raquel Hatter** . . . . . . . . . . . . . . . . . . . (615) 313-4700
E-mail: raquel.hatter@tn.gov
Education: Michigan BS; Eastern Michigan MSW;
Nova Southeastern EdD
Executive Administrative Assistant **Sandy Troope** . . . . . . (615) 313-4700
Deputy Commissioner **Shalonda Cawthon** . . . . . . . . . . . (615) 313-4700
Appeals and Hearings Assistant Commissioner
**Barbara Broersma** . . . . . . . . . . . . . . . . . . . . . . . . . (615) 313-6689
General Counsel/Assistant Commissioner **Bill Russell** . . . . (615) 313-4731
Human Resources and Professional Development
Assistant Commissioner **Gena Lewis** . . . . . . . . . . . . . (615) 313-4783
Quality Improvements and Strategic Solutions Assistant
Commissioner **Petrina Jones-Jezz** . . . . . . . . . . . . . . . (615) 770-6936
Inspector General **Patricia Reinhard** . . . . . . . . . . . . . . (615) 313-5382
Communications Director **(Vacant)** . . . . . . . . . . . . . . . (615) 313-4707

## Community and Social Services

Assistant Commissioner **Pat Wade** . . . . . . . . . . . . . . . (615) 741-7418
Adult Protective Services Director **(Vacant)** . . . . . . . . . . (615) 313-4784
Child and Adult Care Food Program Director **(Vacant)** . . . . (615) 313-4893
Child Care Services Director **(Vacant)** . . . . . . . . . . . . . (615) 313-4770
Community Services Programs Director **Leslie Schenk** . . . (615) 313-5768

## Family Assistance and Child Support Services

Assistant Commissioner (Interim) **Patricia Stubblefield** . . . (615) 313-4595
E-mail: patricia.stubblefield@tn.gov
Child Support Operations Director **Charles Bryson** . . . . . . (615) 313-4880
E-mail: charles.bryson@tn.gov
Child Support Fiscal Director **Richard Paige** . . . . . . . . . . (615) 313-5348
E-mail: richard.paige@tn.gov
Child Support Centralized Services Director
**Pamela Harney** . . . . . . . . . . . . . . . . . . . . . . . . . . (615) 313-2282
E-mail: pamela.c.harney@tn.gov
ACCENT Child Support Systems Support Program
Director **Tracy Bell** . . . . . . . . . . . . . . . . . . . . . . . . (615) 313-6690
E-mail: tracy.bell@tn.gov
Child Support Customer Service and Administration
Director **Patricia Hymer** . . . . . . . . . . . . . . . . . . . . . (615) 313-4712
E-mail: patricia.hymer@tn.gov
Families First (TANF) Director (Interim)
**Jenny Chapman** . . . . . . . . . . . . . . . . . . . . . . . . . . (615) 547-5040
Family Assistance Director **(Vacant)** . . . . . . . . . . . . . . (615) 313-5652
Food Stamp Policy Director **Lisa Cowell** . . . . . . . . . . . (615) 741-5934
Medicaid Eligibility/TennCare Policy Director
**Marcia Garner** . . . . . . . . . . . . . . . . . . . . . . . . . . . (615) 313-5465

## Finance and Administration

Finance and Administration Deputy Commissioner
**Basil Dosunmu** . . . . . . . . . . . . . . . . . . . . . . . . . . (615) 313-4715
E-mail: basil.dosunmu@tn.gov
Fiscal Services Director **Steven Tydings** . . . . . . . . . . . (615) 313-5391
Information Technology Director **Manohar Arumbur** . . . . . (615) 313-5619
E-mail: manohar.arumbur@tn.gov

## Rehabilitation Services

Assistant Commissioner **Cherrell Campbell-Street** . . . . . . (615) 313-4714
Deaf and Hard of Hearing Council Executive Director
**Thom Roberts** . . . . . . . . . . . . . . . . . . . . . . . . . . . (615) 313-4913
Blind and Visually Impaired/Deaf and Hard of Hearing
Services Director **Patti Bell-Norris** . . . . . . . . . . . . . . (615) 313-4921
Disability Determination Director **(Vacant)** . . . . . . . . . . (615) 743-7584

Vocational Rehabilitation Services Assistant Director
**Yovancha Lewis-Brown** . . . . . . . . . . . . . . . . . . . . . (615) 313-5004
Tennessee Rehabilitation Center Superintendent
**Karen Carothers** . . . . . . . . . . . . . . . . . . (615) 459-6811 ext. 159

## Intellectual and Developmental Disabilities Department

Citizens Plaza, 400 Deaderick Street, Nashville, TN 37243-1403
Tel: (615) 532-6530 TTY: (866) 249-0711 Fax: (615) 532-9940

■Commissioner **Debra "Debbie" Payne** . . . . . . . . . . . . . (615) 532-5970
E-mail: debbie.payne@tn.gov
Education: Mid Tennessee State BS
Fiscal and Administration Deputy Commissioner
**Lance D. Iverson** . . . . . . . . . . . . . . . . . . . . . . . . . (615) 253-6710
E-mail: lance.d.iverson@tn.gov                Fax: (615) 253-6713
Program Operations Deputy Commissioner **Jordan Allen** . . (615) 253-6879
Assistant Commissioner and General Counsel
**Theresa C. Sloan** . . . . . . . . . . . . . . . . . . . . . . . . . (615) 253-8731
Policy and Innovation Assistant Commissioner
**Courtney Kelly** . . . . . . . . . . . . . . . . . . . . . . . . . . (615) 532-5450
Quality Management Assistant Commissioner
**Pat Nichols** . . . . . . . . . . . . . . . . . . . . . . . . . . . . (615) 532-6548
Behavioral Services Director **Bruce Davis, PhD** . . . . . . . (615) 532-1610
Civil Rights Office Director **Brenda Clark** . . . . . . . . . . . (615) 253-5516
Communications Director **Cara Kumari** . . . . . . . . . . . . (615) 253-2236
Constituent Services Director **Susan Moss** . . . . . . . . . . (615) 253-4632
Grier Appeals Director **Jon Hamrick** . . . . . . . . . . . . . . (615) 253-8734
Health Services Office Director **Dr. Tom Cheetham, MD** . . (615) 253-6711
Human Resources Director **Ronnie E. Rogers-Sirten** . . . . (615) 532-6535
                                                Fax: (615) 532-6790
Incident Management Director **Kenneth Binion** . . . . . . . . (615) 532-2896
Investigations Director **Angela Friedenreich** . . . . . . . . . (615) 532-3060
Policy Director **Jeanine C. Miller, MD, PhD** . . . . . . . . . (615) 253-8370
Protection from Harm Director **Fredrick Zimmermann** . . . (615) 253-8406
Risk Management Office Director **Lee Vestal** . . . . . . . . . (615) 253-8733
Staff and Provider Development Director **Sandra Wise** . . . (615) 741-6159
Quality Management Deputy Director **Joe Kirkpatrick** . . . . (615) 741-6673
Chief Administrative Officer **Benita Chapman** . . . . . . . . (615) 532-6535
                                                Fax: (615) 532-6790
Chief Information Officer **Russell Nicoll** . . . . . . . . . . . . (615) 741-6632
E-mail: russell.nicoll@tn.gov
Public Information Officer **Matthew Parriott** . . . . . . . . . . (615) 770-1010
E-mail: matthew.parriott@tn.gov                Fax: (615) 532-9940
Web Developer **John McLearran** . . . . . . . . . . . . . . . . (615) 770-1002

## Tennessee Department of Labor and Workforce Development [TDLWD]

220 French Landing Drive, Nashville, TN 37243
Tel: (615) 741-6642 Fax: (615) 253-8903 TTY: (615) 532-2879

■Commissioner **Burns Phillips** . . . . . . . . . . . . . . . . . . (615) 741-6642
E-mail: burns.phillips@tn.gov
Education: Mid Tennessee State BA, MA; Nashville 1978 JD
Deputy Commissioner **Dustin Swayne** . . . . . . . . . . . . . (615) 741-6642
E-mail: dustin.swayne@tn.gov
Education: Murray State U 2003 BS; Nashville 2008 JD
General Counsel **Stephanie Mitchell** . . . . . . . . . . . . . . (615) 741-6642
E-mail: stephanie.mitchell@tn.gov
Communications, Constituent, and Government Relations
Director **Melinda Williams** . . . . . . . . . . . . . . . . . . . (615) 741-2257
E-mail: melinda.williams@tn.gov
Internal Audit Division Director **Chris Risher** . . . . . . . . . (615) 741-6278
Fiscal Services Administrator **Mickey Butler** . . . . . . . . . (615) 532-3628
E-mail: mickey.butler@tn.gov
Human Resources Administrator **Fred Gaston** . . . . . . . . (615) 741-2551
E-mail: fred.gaston@tn.gov

## Employment Security

Fax: (615) 253-5091

Administrator **Linda J. Davis** . . . . . . . . . . . . . . . . . . . (615) 253-4809
E-mail: linda.davis@tn.gov

---

★ Elected Official     ■ Appointed by Governor     ● Appointed by Legislature     ▲ Appointed by Board or Commission     ◆ Appointed by State Supreme Court

## Occupational Safety and Health
Fax: (615) 741-3325
Administrator **Steve Hawkins** . . . . . . . . . . . . . . . . . . . . .(615) 741-2793
Assistant Administrator **James "Jim" Flanagan** . . . . . . . .(615) 741-2793

## Workers' Compensation
Fax: (615) 532-1468
Administrator **Abbie Hudgens** . . . . . . . . . . . . . . . . . . . . .(615) 741-2395
E-mail: abbie.hudgens@tn.gov
Education: U Memphis; Tennessee MPA
Assistant Administrator **Jeff Francis** . . . . . . . . . . . . . . . . .(615) 253-6269
E-mail: jeff.francis@tn.gov

## Workforce Regulation and Compliance
Fax: (615) 741-2741
Administrator **Kim Y. Jefferson** . . . . . . . . . . . . . . . . . . . . .(615) 253-2741
E-mail: kim.y.jefferson@tn.gov

## Workforce Services
Tel: (615) 741-1031  Fax: (615) 741-3003
Administrator **Sterling Van Der Spuy** . . . . . . . . . . . . . . . .(615) 741-1031
E-mail: sterling.vanderspuy@tn.gov

## Tennessee Department of Mental Health and Substance Abuse Services
Andrew Jackson Building, 500 Deaderick Street, Sixth Floor,
Nashville, TN 37242-1099
Tel: (615) 532-6500  Fax: (615) 532-6514  Internet: www.tn.gov/mental
■Commissioner **E. Douglas "Doug" Varney** . . . . . . . . . . .(615) 532-6500
E-mail: doug.varney@tn.gov
Deputy Commissioner **Marie Williams, LCSW** . . . . . . . . .(615) 532-6500
Administrative Services Assistant Commissioner
**Bob Micinski** . . . . . . . . . . . . . . . . . . . . . . . . . . . . .(615) 532-6670
E-mail: bob.micinski@tn.gov
Hospital Services, Regional Mental Health Institutes
Assistant Commissioner **John Arredondo** . . . . . . . . . . . .(615) 532-6515
Mental Health Services Assistant Commissioner
**Sejal West** . . . . . . . . . . . . . . . . . . . . . . . . . . . . . . .(615) 253-3049
Planning, Research and Forensics Assistant
Commissioner **Marthagem Whitlock** . . . . . . . . . . . . . .(615) 532-6744
Substance Abuse Services Assistant Commissioner
**Rod Bragg** . . . . . . . . . . . . . . . . . . . . . . . . . . . . . . .(615) 741-8518
Human Resources Office Director **Vickie Graham** . . . . . .(615) 532-8206
General Counsel **Zack Griffith** . . . . . . . . . . . . . . . . . . . . .(615) 532-6518
Licensure and Review Director **Cynthia Tyler** . . . . . . . . .(615) 532-6586
Education: Millsaps 1980 BA; Mississippi Col 1986 JD
Medical Director **Dr. Howard Burley** . . . . . . . . . . . . . . . .(615) 532-6564
Education: Howard U 1979 BS; Meharry Medical 1985 MD
Communications Office Director **Mike Machak** . . . . . . . . .(615) 532-6597
Controller **Michael Walden** . . . . . . . . . . . . . . . . . . . . . . .(615) 770-0464

## Tennessee Military Department
Houston Barracks, 3041 Sidco Drive, Nashville, TN 37204-1502
Tel: (615) 313-3001  Fax: (615) 313-3100  Internet: www.tnmilitary.org
■Adjutant General **MG Terry M. "Max" Haston, ARNG** . . .(615) 313-3001
E-mail: terry.m.haston.mil@mail.mil
Assistant Adjutant General (Air)
**BrigGen Donald L. Johnson, ANG** . . . . . . . . . . . . . . .(615) 313-3012
Assistant Adjutant General (Army)
**BG Tommy H. Baker, ARNG** . . . . . . . . . . . . . . . . . . .(615) 313-3002
Senior Enlisted Leader **CSM Terry J. Scott, ARNG** . . . . . .(615) 313-3046
Chief of the Joint Staff **COL Darrell Darnbush, ARNG** . . .(615) 313-3019
Chief of Staff, Army **COL William E. Wynns, ARNG** . . . .(615) 313-3007
Director of Staff, Air **Col William D. Dockery, ANG** . . . .(615) 313-3018
Aviation Deputy Chief of Staff
**LTC Steven E. Reese, ARNG** . . . . . . . . . . . . . . . . . . .(615) 355-3735
Human Resources Deputy Chief of Staff
**COL Kenneth H. Jones, ARNG** . . . . . . . . . . . . . . . . . .(615) 313-3025
Information Management Deputy Chief of Staff
**LtCol George R. Haynes, ANG** . . . . . . . . . . . . . . . . . .(615) 313-3053
E-mail: george.r.hayes.mil@mail.mil

Logistics Deputy Chief of Staff
**LTC Thomas W. VonWeisenstein, ARNG** . . . . . . . . . .(615) 313-0528
Personnel Deputy Chief of Staff
**COL Joseph M. Lyles, ARNG** . . . . . . . . . . . . . . . . . . .(615) 313-3125
Plans, Operations and Training Deputy Chief of Staff
**COL Jimmy L. Cole, ARNG** . . . . . . . . . . . . . . . . . . . .(615) 313-3071
E-mail: jimmy.l.cole6.mil@mail.mil
Inspector General **(Vacant)** . . . . . . . . . . . . . . . . . . . . . . . .(615) 313-3068
Director of Strategic Plans (J-5) **(Vacant)** . . . . . . . . . . . . .(615) 313-0936
Joint Public Affairs Director
**MAJ Randy D. Harris, ARNG (Ret)** . . . . . . . . . . . . . . .(615) 313-0662
US Property and Fiscal Office Director
**COL Patricia M. "Patty" Jones, ARNG** . . . . . . . . . . . . .(615) 313-2625
Staff Judge Advocate **LTC Brett Rypma, ARNG** . . . . . . . .(615) 313-0659

## Tennessee Emergency Management Agency [TEMA]
Tel: (615) 741-0001  Internet: www.tnema.org
Director **David W. Purkey** . . . . . . . . . . . . . . . . . . . . . . . .(615) 741-9987
Note: Until June 14, 2016.
Director **Patrick Sheehan** . . . . . . . . . . . . . . . . . . . . . . . .(615) 741-9987
Note: Effective June 15, 2016.
Executive Assistant **Stephanie Favors** . . . . . . . . . . . . . .(615) 741-9987
Assistant Director for Response **Charlie Bryant** . . . . . . . .(615) 741-9108
Public Information Officer **Jeremy Heidt** . . . . . . . . . . . . .(615) 741-0482

## Department of Revenue
Andrew Jackson Building, 500 Deaderick Street,
Nashville, TN 37242-1099
Tel: (615) 253-0600  Fax: (615) 741-0682  E-mail: tn.revenue@tn.gov
■Commissioner **Richard H. Roberts** . . . . . . . . . . . . . . . . .(615) 741-2461
E-mail: richard.roberts@tn.gov
Deputy Commissioner **David Gerregano** . . . . . . . . . . . . .(615) 741-2461
Assistant Commissioner and General Counsel
**Kristin Husat** . . . . . . . . . . . . . . . . . . . . . . . . . . . . . .(615) 741-2348
E-mail: kristin.husat@tn.gov
Revenue Assistant Commissioner **John Duncan** . . . . . . . .(615) 253-7331
E-mail: john.duncan@tn.gov
Communications Director **Kelly Cortesi** . . . . . . . . . . . . . .(615) 770-6942
E-mail: kelly.cortesi@tn.gov
Human Resources Division Director
**Abigail "Abby" Sparks** . . . . . . . . . . . . . . . . . . . . . . .(615) 741-2828
Internal Audit Division Director **Melvin Jones** . . . . . . . . .(615) 741-3436
Special Investigations Division Director **Tommy Sneed** . . .(615) 365-6208
Administrative Hearing Officer **Bernadette Welch** . . . . . . .(615) 741-3810
Chief Financial Officer **Amanda McGraw** . . . . . . . . . . . .(615) 253-8950

## Support Services
Fiscal Services Division Director **(Vacant)** . . . . . . . . . . . . .(615) 253-0600
Chief Information Officer **Anthony "Tony" Starnes** . . . . . .(615) 741-2411
E-mail: anthony.starnes@tn.gov
Processing Division Director **Yvonne Holbert** . . . . . . . . . .(615) 741-2505
Research Division Director **Kirk Johnson** . . . . . . . . . . . . .(615) 741-2446
Tax Enforcement Division Director
**Wilbur "Buddy" Hooks** . . . . . . . . . . . . . . . . . . . . . . .(615) 741-7071

## Tax Administration
Audit Administration Assistant Commissioner
**Stacy Gibson** . . . . . . . . . . . . . . . . . . . . . . . . . . . . . .(615) 741-8499
Taxpayer Services Division Director **Kathy Smith** . . . . . . .(615) 741-7384
Vehicle Services Director **Allison Raymer** . . . . . . . . . . . . .(615) 532-5072
E-mail: allison.raymer@tn.gov

## Department of Safety and Homeland Security
312 Rosa L. Parks Avenue, Nashville, TN 37243-1102
Tel: (615) 251-5166  TTY: (615) 532-2281  Fax: (615) 253-2091
E-mail: email.safety@tn.gov
■Commissioner **William L. "Bill" Gibbons** . . . . . . . . . . . .(615) 251-5128
E-mail: bill.gibbons@tn.gov
Executive Administrative Assistant **Doris Davis** . . . . . . . .(615) 251-5128

*(continued on next page)*

★ Elected Official   ■ Appointed by Governor   ● Appointed by Legislature   ▲ Appointed by Board or Commission   ◆ Appointed by State Supreme Court

EXECUTIVE BRANCH

EXECUTIVE BRANCH

**Department of Safety and Homeland Security** *continued*

Assistant Commissioner **Larry Godwin** . . . . . . . . . . . . . . (615) 251-8594
  E-mail: larry.godwin@tn.gov
Executive Administrative Assistant **Mary Walker** . . . . . . . (615) 251-1626
Chief of Staff **David McGriff** . . . . . . . . . . . . . . . . . . . . . (615) 251-5166
Driver Services Assistant Commissioner **Lori Bullard** . . . . . (615) 251-5310
  E-mail: lori.bullard@tn.gov
  Education: U Memphis BA; Union U MAED
Homeland Security Advisor and Assistant Commissioner
  **David W. Purkey** . . . . . . . . . . . . . . . . . . . . . . . . . (615) 251-7825
  E-mail: david.purkey@tn.gov
Highway Patrol Colonel and Chief **Col. Tracy Trott** . . . . . . (615) 251-5175
General Counsel **Roger Hutto** . . . . . . . . . . . . . . . . . . . . (615) 251-5255
Legislative Liaison **Kevin Crawford** . . . . . . . . . . . . . . . . (615) 251-5199
  E-mail: kevin.crawford@tn.gov
Legislative Liaison **Chris Gobble** . . . . . . . . . . . . . . . . . . (615) 251-5199
  E-mail: chris.gobble@tn.gov
Communications Director **(Vacant)** . . . . . . . . . . . . . . . . (615) 509-3154
Driver Services Director **Michael Hogan** . . . . . . . . . . . . . (615) 251-5140
  E-mail: michael.hogan@tn.gov
Human Resources Director **Kerri Balthrop** . . . . . . . . . . . . (615) 251-5203
Research, Planning and Development Director
  **Michael McAlister** . . . . . . . . . . . . . . . . . . . . . . . . (615) 687-2400
  E-mail: michael.mcalister@tn.gov
Technology Systems Director **Paul Battenfield** . . . . . . . . . (615) 251-5268
  E-mail: paul.battenfield@tn.gov
Capitol Security Division Director **Capt. Mark Proctor** . . . (615) 741-7965
Criminal Investigations Division Director
  **Major Stacy Williams** . . . . . . . . . . . . . . . . . . . . . . (615) 251-5185
Inspectional Services Bureau Director **Victor Donoho** . . . . (615) 251-5228
  E-mail: vic.donoho@tn.gov
Safety Education Division Director **Capt. Tony Barham** . . . (615) 687-2327
Training Center Division Director **Capt. Robert Bighem** . . (615) 232-2901
  275 Stewarts Ferry Pike, Nashville, TN 37214
  E-mail: robert.bighem@tn.gov
  Handgun Permits Officer **Lisa Knight** . . . . . . . . . . . . (615) 251-5330
    E-mail: lisa.knight@tn.gov
Special Operations Officer **Capt. Robert Eckerman** . . . . . . (615) 741-5660
  E-mail: robert.eckerman@tn.gov

## Office of Homeland Security

312 Rosa L. Parks Avenue, Nashville, TN 37243-1102
Tel: (615) 532-7825   Fax: (615) 253-5379

■Assistant Commissioner **David W. Purkey** . . . . . . . . . . . . (615) 532-7825
  E-mail: david.purkey@tn.gov
Deputy Director **Rick Shipkowski** . . . . . . . . . . . . . . . . . (615) 532-7825
  Executive Assistant **Stephanie Hamby** . . . . . . . . . . . . (615) 532-7825
Technology Plans Division State Coordinator and Oak
  Ridge National Laboratory Liaison **Dave Lannom** . . . . . . (615) 532-7825
  E-mail: lannomwdjr@ornl.gov
Training Division State Coordinator **Brice Allen** . . . . . . . . (615) 532-7825
Information Sharing, Law Enforcement and Investigative
  Support State Coordinator **James Cotter** . . . . . . . . . . . (615) 532-7825

## Department of Tourist Development

312 Rosa L. Parks Avenue, 13th Floor, Nashville, TN 37243
Tel: (615) 741-2159   Tel: (615) 741-2159 (Vacation Travel Info.)
Tel: (800) 462-8366 (Vacation Travel Info.)   Fax: (615) 741-7225
E-mail: tourdev@tn.gov   Internet: www.state.tn.us/tourdev

■Commissioner **Kevin Triplett** . . . . . . . . . . . . . . . . . . . (615) 741-9001
  E-mail: kevin.triplett@tn.gov
  Education: East Tennessee State
  Executive Assistant to the Commissioner **Patricia Gray** . . (615) 741-9016
Assistant Commissioner **John Carr** . . . . . . . . . . . . . . . . . (615) 741-9023
Sales and Marketing Assistant Commissioner **(Vacant)** . . . . (615) 532-7853
Welcome Centers Assistant Commissioner
  **Pete Rosenboro** . . . . . . . . . . . . . . . . . . . . . . . . . . (615) 741-9035
Legislative Liaison **Lee Curtis** . . . . . . . . . . . . . . . . . . . (615) 741-9045
  E-mail: lee.curtis@tn.gov
Public Information Officer and Public Relations Director
  **Cindy Dupree** . . . . . . . . . . . . . . . . . . . . . . . . . . . (615) 741-9010
  E-mail: cindy.dupree@tn.gov

# Tennessee Department of Transportation [TDOT]

700 James K. Polk Building, Nashville, TN 37243-1402
Tel: (615) 741-3011 (State Information)   TTY: (615) 532-1603
Fax: (615) 741-2508   E-mail: tdot.comments@tn.gov
Internet: www.tdot.state.tn.us

■Commissioner **John Schroer** . . . . . . . . . . . . . . . . . . . . (615) 741-2848
  E-mail: john.schroer@tn.gov
  Education: Indiana BA; Tennessee MBA
Deputy Commissioner and Chief of Staff **Lyndsay Botts** . . (615) 741-2848
  E-mail: lyndsay.botts@tn.gov
  Community Relations Office Director **B. J. Doughty** . . . . (615) 741-7736
  Special Assistant/Legislative Services Manager
    **Matt Barnes** . . . . . . . . . . . . . . . . . . . . . . . . . . (615) 532-3565
    E-mail: matt.barnes@tn.gov
Assistant Commissioner, Operational Efficiency
  **Ralph Comer** . . . . . . . . . . . . . . . . . . . . . . . . . . . (615) 741-4838
  E-mail: ralph.comer@tn.gov
Strategic Planning Office Director **Patsy Mimms** . . . . . . . (615) 532-3507
  E-mail: patsy.mimms@tn.gov
Aeronautics Division Director **Bill Orellana** . . . . . . . . . . . (615) 741-3208
Legal Office Director **John Reinbold** . . . . . . . . . . . . . . . (615) 741-2941

## Administration

Deputy Commissioner/Chief Financial Officer
  **Joe Galbato** . . . . . . . . . . . . . . . . . . . . . . . . . . . . (615) 741-2848
  E-mail: joe.galbato@tn.gov
Assistant Bureau Chief/Human Resources Office Director
  **Delaine Linville** . . . . . . . . . . . . . . . . . . . . . . . . . . (615) 741-3461
Central Services Office Director **Bob Alwine** . . . . . . . . . . (615) 741-7750
  E-mail: bob.alwine@tn.gov
Finance Office Director **Jennifer Herstek** . . . . . . . . . . . . (615) 741-2261
Governor's Highway Safety Office Director
  **Kendell Poole** . . . . . . . . . . . . . . . . . . . . . . . . . . (615) 741-2589
  E-mail: kendell.poole@tn.gov
Information Technology Office Director **Joe Kirk** . . . . . . . (615) 741-0601
  E-mail: joe.kirk@tn.gov
Internal Audit Office Director **Mel Marcella** . . . . . . . . . . (615) 741-1651
Civil Rights Office Director **Deborah Luter** . . . . . . . . . . . (615) 741-3681
  E-mail: deborah.luter@tn.gov

## Bureau of Engineering

Deputy Commissioner/Chief Engineer **Paul Degges** . . . . . . (615) 741-0791
  E-mail: paul.degges@tn.gov
Program Development Director **Jim M. Moore** . . . . . . . . . (615) 741-3301
  E-mail: jim.m.moore@tn.gov
Bid Analysis and Estimating Office Director
  **Wayburn Crabtree** . . . . . . . . . . . . . . . . . . . . . . . . (615) 253-2901
Project Management Division Director
  **Danielle Hagewood** . . . . . . . . . . . . . . . . . . . . . . . (615) 253-2520
Strategic Transportation Investments Division Director
  **Steve Allen** . . . . . . . . . . . . . . . . . . . . . . . . . . . . (615) 741-2208

## Design

Assistant Chief Engineer **Jeff C. Jones** . . . . . . . . . . . . . . (615) 741-2831
Roadway Design Division Director **Jennifer Lloyd** . . . . . . . (615) 741-2221
  E-mail: jennifer.lloyd@tn.gov
Right of Way Division Director **Jeff Hoge** . . . . . . . . . . . . (615) 741-3196
  E-mail: jeff.hoge@tn.gov
Structures Division Director **Wayne Seger** . . . . . . . . . . . . (615) 741-3351
  E-mail: wayne.seger@tn.gov

## Environment and Planning

Deputy Commissioner **Toks Omishakin** . . . . . . . . . . . . . . (615) 741-5376
  Education: Jackson State U MURP
Environmental Division Director **Jim Ozment** . . . . . . . . . . (615) 741-5373
  E-mail: jim.ozment@tn.gov
Long Range Planning Division Director **Tanisha Hall** . . . . . (615) 741-3421
  E-mail: tanisha.hall@tn.gov
Office of Community Transportation Director **(Vacant)** . . . . (615) 741-3011
Multimodal Transportation Division Director
  **Liza Joffrion** . . . . . . . . . . . . . . . . . . . . . . . . . . . (615) 741-2781

---

★ Elected Official   ■ Appointed by Governor   ● Appointed by Legislature   ▲ Appointed by Board or Commission   ◆ Appointed by State Supreme Court

## Operations

Assistant Chief Engineer **Charles "Chuck" Rychen** . . . . . . (615) 741-2342
Construction Division Director **Will Reid** . . . . . . . . . . (615) 741-2414
Maintenance Division Director **Jerry Hatcher** . . . . . . . . . (615) 741-2027
Materials and Tests Division Director **Brian Egan** . . . . . . . (615) 350-4101
  6601 Centennial Boulevard, Nashville, TN 37243-0360
  E-mail: brian.egan@tn.gov
Traffic Operations Director **Brad Freeze** . . . . . . . . . . . . (615) 741-5017

## Regional Offices

Region 1 Transportation Director **Steve Borden** . . . . . . . . (865) 594-2400
  7345 Region Lane, Knoxville, TN 37914
Region 2 Transportation Director **Ray Rucker** . . . . . . . . (423) 892-3430
  P.O. Box 22368, Chattanooga, TN 37422-2368
Region 3 Transportation Director **David Layhew** . . . . . . . (615) 350-4300
  6601 Centennial Boulevard, Nashville, TN 37243-0360
Region 4 Transportation Director **Jason Baker** . . . . . . . . (731) 935-0194
  300 Benchmark Place, Jackson, TN 38301

## Department of Veterans Affairs

312 Rosa L. Parks Avenue, Floor 13, Nashville, TN 37243
Tel: (615) 741-2931  Fax: (615) 741-5056  E-mail: tn.veterans@tn.gov

■Commissioner **COL Many-Bears Grinder, ARNG** . . . . . . . (615) 741-2931
  E-mail: many-bears.grinder@tn.gov
  Education: Army War Col MSS; Tennessee MSHRM
  Executive Assistant **Anna Holmbraker** . . . . . . . . . . . . . (615) 741-1959
Deputy Commissioner **CSM Mark A. Breece, ARNG** . . . . . (615) 741-2931
Assistant Commissioner of Outreach and
  Communications **Yvette Martinez** . . . . . . . . . . . . . . . . (615) 741-2931
  E-mail: yvette.martinez@tn.gov
Assistant Commissioner **CSM John Denek, ARNG** . . . . . . (731) 423-6569
Assistant Commissioner **Lorenza Wills** . . . . . . . . . . . . . (865) 594-9421
Director of Claims Division **Travis Murphy** . . . . . . . . . . . (615) 695-6385

## Tennessee Housing Development Agency [THDA]

502 Deaderick Street, Third Floor, Nashville, TN 37243
Tel: (615) 815-2200  Fax: (615) 564-2700  Internet: www.thda.org

▲Executive Director **Ralph M. Perrey** . . . . . . . . . . . . . . . (615) 815-2015
  E-mail: rperrey@thda.org
Chief Financial Officer **Trent Ridley** . . . . . . . . . . . . . . (615) 815-2012
Chief Legal Counsel **Lynn Miller** . . . . . . . . . . . . . . . . (615) 815-2028
  E-mail: lmiller@thda.org
Chief Strategy Officer **Lorrie Shearon** . . . . . . . . . . . . . (615) 815-2013
  E-mail: lshearon@thda.org
Controller **Joe W. Brown** . . . . . . . . . . . . . . . . . . . . (615) 815-2050
Information Technology Director **Nicole Lucas** . . . . . . . . . (615) 815-2250
  E-mail: nlucas@thda.org
Internal Audit Director **Gathelyn Oliver** . . . . . . . . . . . . (615) 815-2132
  Education: Mid Tennessee State 1985 BBA; Vanderbilt 1999 MBA
Public Affairs Director **Patricia M. Smith** . . . . . . . . . . . (615) 815-2185
Research and Planning Director **Bettie Teasley** . . . . . . . . (615) 815-2125
  E-mail: bteasley@thda.org
Multifamily Programs Division Senior Director
  **Cheryl Jett** . . . . . . . . . . . . . . . . . . . . . . . . . . . . (615) 815-2186
  E-mail: cjett@thda.org
Single Family Programs Division Senior Director
  **Lindsay Hall** . . . . . . . . . . . . . . . . . . . . . . . . . . . (615) 815-2100
  E-mail: lhall@thda.org
Community Programs Division Director **Don Watt** . . . . . . . (615) 815-2032
  E-mail: dwatt@thda.org
Finance Director **Wayne Beard** . . . . . . . . . . . . . . . . . (615) 815-2157
Housing Choice Voucher Programs Division Director
  **Jada Lattimore** . . . . . . . . . . . . . . . . . . . . . . . . . . (615) 815-2163
  E-mail: jlattimore@thda.org
Operations Director **Debra Murray** . . . . . . . . . . . . . . . (615) 815-2053
Program Compliance Director **Gwen Coffey** . . . . . . . . . . (615) 815-2219

## Tennessee Wildlife Resources Agency [TWRA]

P.O. Box 40747, Nashville, TN 37204
Tel: (615) 781-6500  Fax: (615) 741-4606  Internet: www.tnwildlife.org

▲Executive Director **Ed Carter** . . . . . . . . . . . . . . . . . . (615) 781-6552
  E-mail: ed.carter@tn.gov
  Education: Tennessee 1971 BS
Assistant Director, Field Operations **Bobby Wilson** . . . . . . (615) 781-6557
Assistant Director, Staff Operations **Barry Sumners** . . . . . (615) 781-6555
  Education: Memphis State 1993 MS
Attorney **Sheryl Holtam** . . . . . . . . . . . . . . . . . . . . . (615) 781-6607
  E-mail: sheryl.holtam@tn.gov
  Education: Cumberland 1988 JD
Administrative Services Division Chief
  **Ken W. Tarkington, Jr.** . . . . . . . . . . . . . . . . . . . . . (615) 781-6512
  E-mail: ken.tarkington@tn.gov
  Education: Mid Tennessee State 1970 BS
Boating and Law Enforcement Division Chief
  **Darren Rider** . . . . . . . . . . . . . . . . . . . . . . . . . . . (615) 781-6580
  E-mail: darren.rider@tn.gov
Engineering Division Chief **Dwight Hensley** . . . . . . . . . . (615) 781-6547
Fish Management Division Chief **Frank Fiss** . . . . . . . . . . (615) 781-6578
Human Resources Division Chief **Rick S. Pharris** . . . . . . . (615) 781-6594
Information and Education Division Chief **Don King** . . . . . . (615) 781-6502
  E-mail: don.king@tn.gov
Information Technology Division Chief **Michael May** . . . . . (615) 781-6639
  E-mail: michael.may@tn.gov
Wildlife Management Division Chief **Mark Gudlin** . . . . . . . (615) 781-6614
Legislation and Policy **Chris Richardson** . . . . . . . . . . . . (615) 781-6016
  E-mail: chris.richardson@tn.gov

## Tennessee Bureau of Investigation

901 R.S. Gass Boulevard, Nashville, TN 37216
Tel: (615) 744-4000  TTY: (615) 744-4001  Fax: (615) 744-4500
Internet: www.tbi.state.tn.us

■Director **Mark R. Gwyn** . . . . . . . . . . . . . . . . . . . . . (615) 744-4100
  E-mail: mark.gwyn@tn.gov
  Executive Administrative Assistant **Melany Martin** . . . . . (615) 744-4100
Deputy Director **Jeff Puckett** . . . . . . . . . . . . . . . . . . (615) 744-4042
  Administrative Services Assistant III **Karen Lankford** . . . (615) 744-4042
Personnel Director **Pamela Busby** . . . . . . . . . . . . . . . (615) 744-4118
Drug Investigation Division Assistant Director
  **T. J. Jordan** . . . . . . . . . . . . . . . . . . . . . . . . . . . (615) 744-4252
Forensic Services Assistant Director **Dan Royse** . . . . . . . (615) 744-4518
Tennessee Crime Information Center Information
  Systems Director **Brad Truitt** . . . . . . . . . . . . . . . . . (615) 744-4008
Criminal Intelligence Unit Special-Agent-in-Charge
  **Jerri Siegrist** . . . . . . . . . . . . . . . . . . . . . . . . . . . (615) 744-4332
  Cookeville Office Special-Agent-in-Charge
  **Dennis Daniels** . . . . . . . . . . . . . . . . . . . . . . . . . (931) 526-5041
East Tennessee Criminal Investigation Unit Assistant
  Special-Agent-in-Charge **Josh Melton** . . . . . . . . . . . . (423) 634-3044
  6040 Century Oaks Drive, Chattanooga, TN 37416
East Tennessee Drug Investigation Unit
  Special-Agent-in-Charge **Richard Brogan** . . . . . . . . . . (423) 634-3044
  6040 Century Oaks Drive, Chattanooga, TN 37416
Medicaid Fraud Control Unit Special-Agent-in-Charge
  **Norman Tidwell** . . . . . . . . . . . . . . . . . . . . . . . . . (615) 744-4322
Middle Tennessee Criminal Investigation Unit
  Special-Agent-in-Charge **Jason Locke** . . . . . . . . . . . . (615) 744-4354
Upper East Tennessee Criminal Investigation Unit
  Special-Agent-in-Charge **Dewayne Johnson** . . . . . . . . (865) 549-7800
  1791 Neals Commerce Lane, Knoxville, TN 37914
Upper East Tennessee Drug Investigation Unit
  Special-Agent-in-Charge **Jim Williams** . . . . . . . . . . . (865) 549-7800
  1791 Neals Commerce Lane, Knoxville, TN 37914
  Tri-Cities Office Assistant Special-Agent-in-Charge
  **Chris Wilhoit** . . . . . . . . . . . . . . . . . . . . . . . . . . (423) 434-6424
    2001 Waters Edge Road, Johnson City, TN 37604
West Tennessee Criminal Investigation Unit
  Special-Agent-in-Charge **John Simmons** . . . . . . . . . . (731) 984-6600
  121 Executive Drive, Jackson, TN 38301

*(continued on next page)*

---

★ Elected Official   ■ Appointed by Governor   ● Appointed by Legislature   ▲ Appointed by Board or Commission   ◆ Appointed by State Supreme Court

**Tennessee Bureau of Investigation** *continued*

West Tennessee Drug Investigation Unit
Special-Agent-in-Charge **Jay Barnes** . . . . . . . . . . . . . . . . (731) 984-6600
121 Executive Drive, Jackson, TN 38301
Memphis Office Assistant Special-Agent-in-Charge
**Mark Lewis** . . . . . . . . . . . . . . . . . . . . . . . . . . . . . . . . . . . (901) 379-3400
6325 Haley Road, Memphis, TN 38134
Drug Enforcement Coordinator Special-Agent-in-Charge
**Thomas Farmer** . . . . . . . . . . . . . . . . . . . . . . . . . . . . . . . . . (423) 752-1479
Fingerprint Identification Specialist Supervisor
**Deborah Gordon** . . . . . . . . . . . . . . . . . . . . . . . . . . . . . . . . (615) 744-4211
Tennessee Instant Check Unit Manager **Sandi Duncan** . . . . (615) 744-4205
Chief Information Officer **Mark Hackney** . . . . . . . . . . . . . . (615) 744-4000
E-mail: mark.hackney@tn.gov

## Commission on Aging and Disability

Andrew Jackson Building, 502 Deaderick Street, Ninth Floor,
Nashville, TN 37243
Tel: (615) 741-2056  TTY: (800) 848-0299  Fax: (615) 741-3309

■Chairman **Clinton M. Lewis** . . . . . . . . . . . . . . . . . . . . . . . (615) 430-9868
Note: Urban Area of Greater Nashville District
Term Expires: September 30, 2016
■Vice Chairman **Ludell Neill Coffey** . . . . . . . . . . . . . . . . . (865) 577-9426
Note: Urban Area, East Tennessee Representative
Term Expires: September 30, 2016
■Executive Committee Member **William E. Gentner III** . . . . (615) 741-2056
Note: South Central Tennessee Representative
Term Expires: September 30, 2018
■Executive Committee Member **Dr. Rose Rubin** . . . . . . . . . . (615) 253-4423
Note: West Tennessee Representative
Term Expires: September 30, 2016
E-mail: rmrubin@memphis.edu
■Executive Committee Member **Margot Seay** . . . . . . . . . . . . (615) 741-2056
Note: East Tennessee Representative
Term Expires: September 30, 2018
Executive Director **Jim Shulman** . . . . . . . . . . . . . . . . . . . . (615) 532-4543

## Tennessee Alcoholic Beverage Commission [TABC]

226 Capitol Boulevard Building, Suite 300, Nashville, TN 37243-0755
Tel: (615) 741-1602  Fax: (615) 741-0847
Internet: www.tennessee.gov/abc

■Chairman **Mary McDaniel** . . . . . . . . . . . . . . . . . . . . . . . . . (615) 741-1602
E-mail: mary.mcdaniel@tn.gov
Executive Director **Keith Bell** . . . . . . . . . . . . . . . . . . . . . . . (615) 741-1602

## Tennessee Higher Education Commission [THEC]

Parkway Towers, 404 James Robertson Parkway, Suite 1900,
Nashville, TN 37243-0830
Tel: (615) 741-3605  Fax: (615) 741-6230  Internet: www.tn.gov/thec

Chair **Evan Cope** (4th Congressional Dist. Rep.) . . . . . . . . . (615) 893-5522
Term Expires: June 30, 2018
Education: Rhodes 1998 BA; U Memphis 2001 JD
Vice Chair **Sharon Hayes** (8th Congressional Dist. Rep.) . . (901) 634-4257
Vice Chair **Keith Wilson** (5th Congressional Dist. Rep.) . . . (423) 392-1314
Secretary
**A. C. Wharton, Jr.** (9th Congressional Dist. Rep.) . . . . . (615) 576-6000
Term Expires: June 30, 2017
Education: Tennessee State 1962 BA; Mississippi 1971 JD
Member **Tré Hargett** . . . . . . . . . . . . . . . . . . . . . . . . . . . . . (615) 741-2819
Affiliation: Secretary of State, Tennessee Department of State, State of
Tennessee
State Capitol, First Floor, Nashville, TN 37243-0305
Education: Memphis State 1991 BBA, 1992 MBA
Member **Jon Kinsey** (3rd Congressional Dist. Rep.) . . . . . . (423) 266-4323
Member **Pam Koban** (1st Congressional Dist. Rep.) . . . . . . (731) 388-3046
Member
**William "Bill" Lee** (7th Congressional Dist. Rep.) . . . . . . (615) 567-1000

Member **David H. Lillard, Jr.** . . . . . . . . . . . . . . . . . . . . . . . (615) 741-2956
Affiliation: State Treasurer, Tennessee Department of Treasury, State of
Tennessee
State Capitol, First Floor, Nashville, TN 37243-0225
Education: U Memphis AB, JD; Florida 1983 MLT
Member **Pam Martin** (6th Congressional Dist. Rep.) . . . . . (615) 238-6311
Member **Mintha Roach** (2nd Congressional Dist. Rep.) . . . (865) 673-6735
Member **Justin P. Wilson** . . . . . . . . . . . . . . . . . . . . . . . . . (615) 741-2501
Affiliation: Comptroller, Office of the Comptroller of the Treasury,
State of Tennessee
State Capitol, Nashville, TN 37243-0260
Education: Stanford; Vanderbilt JD; NYU 1974 ML
Student Member **Robert Fisher** . . . . . . . . . . . . . . . . . . . . . (931) 542-7943
Student Member **Alex Martin** . . . . . . . . . . . . . . . . . . . . . . (615) 963-1305
■Executive Director (Interim) **Russ Deaton** . . . . . . . . . . . . (615) 532-3860
E-mail: russ.deaton@tn.gov
Education: Vanderbilt 1998 BE; Tennessee 1999 MS
Executive Secretary **Lovella Carter** . . . . . . . . . . . . . . . . . (615) 741-7562
Academic Affairs Associate Executive Director
**Betty Dandridge-Johnson** . . . . . . . . . . . . . . . . . . . . . . . . (615) 741-7573
Fiscal Affairs Associate Executive Director **Russ Deaton** . . (615) 532-3860
Fiscal Affairs Assistant Executive Director
**O. W. Higley, Jr.** . . . . . . . . . . . . . . . . . . . . . . . . . . . . . . . (615) 532-9846
Education: Tennessee 1971 BS
Gear Up Associate Executive Director **Troy Grant** . . . . . . . (615) 532-0423
Legal and Regulatory Affairs Associate Executive
Director **Scott Sloan** . . . . . . . . . . . . . . . . . . . . . . . . . . . . (615) 741-7571
Policy, Planning and Research Associate Executive
Director **David L. Wright** . . . . . . . . . . . . . . . . . . . . . . . . (615) 532-3862
Education: Florida State MS
Veterans Education Assistant Executive Director
**Tom Morrison** . . . . . . . . . . . . . . . . . . . . . . . . . . . . . . . . . (615) 741-7569
Education: Old Dominion 1993 MSEd
Facilities Analysis and Fiscal Policy Director
**Crystal Collins** . . . . . . . . . . . . . . . . . . . . . . . . . . . . . . . . (615) 741-7578
Postsecondary Authorization Director
**Stephanie Bellard-Chase** . . . . . . . . . . . . . . . . . . . . . . . . (615) 532-7495
Education: Tennessee State 2001 PhD
Student Information Systems Director
**Anamika Mazumdar** . . . . . . . . . . . . . . . . . . . . . . . . . . . . . (615) 741-7566
E-mail: anamika.mazumdar@tn.gov

## Human Rights Commission

312 Rosa L. Parks Avenue, 23rd Floor, Nashville, TN 37243-1102
Tel: (800) 251-3589  Fax: (615) 532-2197

■Commissioner **Eric Crafton** . . . . . . . . . . . . . . . . . . . . . . . (615) 741-5825
Term Expires: June 30, 2017
Education: Vanderbilt; Keio (Japan)
■Commissioner **Chrystal Cross Horne** . . . . . . . . . . . . . . . . (615) 741-5825
Term Expires: June 30, 2018
■Commissioner **Annazette Houston** . . . . . . . . . . . . . . . . . . (615) 741-5825
Term Expires: June 30, 2019
■Commissioner **Bill Martin** . . . . . . . . . . . . . . . . . . . . . . . . (615) 741-5825
Term Expires: June 30, 2021
■Commissioner **Rieta Selberg** . . . . . . . . . . . . . . . . . . . . . . (615) 741-5825
Term Expires: June 30, 2017
■Commissioner **Julius Sloss** . . . . . . . . . . . . . . . . . . . . . . . (615) 741-5825
Term Expires: June 30, 2021
■Commissioner **Rev. Ralph White** . . . . . . . . . . . . . . . . . . . (615) 741-5825
Term Expires: June 30, 2019
■Commissioner **(Vacant)** . . . . . . . . . . . . . . . . . . . . . . . . . . (615) 741-5825
■Commissioner **(Vacant)** . . . . . . . . . . . . . . . . . . . . . . . . . . (615) 741-5825

### Commission Staff

▲Executive Director **Beverly L. Watts** . . . . . . . . . . . . . . . . (615) 253-1608
E-mail: beverly.watts@tn.gov
Education: Tennessee State 1969 BS; Southern Illinois 1973 MS

## Tennessee Regulatory Authority [TRA]

460 James Robertson Parkway, Nashville, TN 37243-0505
Tel: (615) 741-3125  Tel: (800) 342-8359 (Toll Free)
TTY: (888) 276-0677  Fax: (615) 741-5015

■Chair **Herbert H. "Herb" Hilliard** . . . . . . . . . . . . . . . . . . (615) 741-3125
E-mail: herb.hillard@tn.gov

---

★ Elected Official  ■ Appointed by Governor  ● Appointed by Legislature  ▲ Appointed by Board or Commission  ◆ Appointed by State Supreme Court

■Vice Chairman **David Jones** . . . . . . . . . . . . . . . . . . . . . . . . (615) 741-3125
    E-mail: david.jones@tn.gov
    Education: Tennessee BA; Houston MBA
■Director **James "Jim" Allison** . . . . . . . . . . . . . . . . . . . . (615) 741-3125
    E-mail: jim.allison@tn.gov
●Director **Robin Bennett** . . . . . . . . . . . . . . . . . . . . . . . . . (615) 741-3125
■Director **Kenneth C. Hill** . . . . . . . . . . . . . . . . . . . . . . . . . (615) 741-4648
■Executive Director **Earl Taylor** . . . . . . . . . . . . . . . . . . . (615) 741-0917
    E-mail: earl.taylor@tn.gov
    Education: Tennessee BA; U Memphis JD
General Counsel **Jean A. Stone** . . . . . . . . . . . . . . (615) 741-2904 ext. 170
    E-mail: jean.a.stone@tn.gov
Consumer Services Division Chief **Lisa Cooper** . . . (615) 741-2904 ext. 150
Economic Analysis and Policy Division Chief
    **Jerry Kettles** . . . . . . . . . . . . . . . . . . . . . . . . . (615) 741-2904 ext. 153
Gas Pipeline Safety Division Chief
    **Annette Ponds** . . . . . . . . . . . . . . . . . . . . . . . (615) 741-2904 ext. 184
    E-mail: annette.ponds@tn.gov
Information Technology Division Chief
    **Tracy Stinson** . . . . . . . . . . . . . . . . . . . . . . . . (615) 741-2904 ext. 112
    E-mail: tracy.stinson@tn.gov
    Education: Trevecca Nazarene Col 2001 BA
Utility Division Chief **David Foster** . . . . . . . . . . . (615) 741-2904 ext. 188

## State Board of Education

Andrew Johnson Tower, 710 James Robertson Parkway, First Floor,
Nashville, TN 37243-1050
Tel: (615) 741-2966  Fax: (615) 741-0371
E-mail: education.comments@tn.gov

■Chairman **B. Fielding Rolston** (First Congressional) . . . . . (615) 741-2966
    Term Expires: 2018
    E-mail: frolston@ecu.org
    Education: Virginia Tech 1964 BS; American U 1968 MBA
■Vice Chair **Carolyn Pearre** (Fifth Congressional) . . . . . . . (615) 741-2966
    Term Expires: 2020
    E-mail: cpearre@comcast.net
    Education: Tennessee BS, MS
■Member **Allison Chancey** (Third Congressional) . . . . . . . . (615) 741-2966
    Term Expires: 2018
    E-mail: ahc1478@yahoo.com
    Education: Tennessee (Chattanooga) BS; Lincoln Memorial MS
■Member **Mike Edwards** (Second Congressional) . . . . . . . . (615) 741-2966
    Term Expires: 2016
    E-mail: medwards@knoxvillechamber.com
    Education: Tennessee BS
■Member **Lillian Hartgrove** (Sixth Congressional) . . . . . . . (615) 741-2966
    Term Expires: 2019
    3631 Burton Cove Road, Cookeville, TN 38506-6132
    E-mail: lhartgrove@highlandsoftn.com
    Education: Mississippi State BA
■Member **Cato Johnson** (Eighth Congressional) . . . . . . . . . (615) 741-2966
    Term Expires: 2019
    9155 Hillman Way Drive, Memphis, TN 38134
    E-mail: cato.johnson@mlh.org
    Education: Memphis State BS, MS
■Member **Lonnie Roberts** (Fourth Congressional) . . . . . . . . (615) 741-2966
    Term Expires: 2016
    E-mail: lroberts@trh.com
    Education: Jacksonville State BS
■Member
    **Dr. William E. "Bill" Troutt** (Ninth Congressional) . . . . (615) 741-2966
    Term Expires: 2020
    E-mail: teresa.sloyan@gmail.com
    Education: Union U 1971 BA; Louisville 1972 MA;
    Vanderbilt 1978 PhD
■Member **Wendy Tucker** (Seventh Congressional) . . . . . . . . (615) 741-2966
    Term Expires: 2019
    2819 Polo Club Road, Nashville, TN 37221-4345
    E-mail: tuckerwing@gmail.com
    Education: Tulane BA, JD
■Student Member **(Vacant)** . . . . . . . . . . . . . . . . . . . . . . . . (615) 741-2966
Ex-officio Member (Non-voting) (Interim) **Russ Deaton** . . (615) 741-3605
    Affiliation: Executive Director (Interim), Tennessee Higher Education
    Commission, State of Tennessee
    Parkway Towers, 404 James Robertson Parkway, Suite 1900,
    Nashville, TN 37243-0830

### Board Staff
Executive Director **Sara Heyburn** . . . . . . . . . . . . . . . . . . (615) 741-2966

## Board of Parole [BOP]
404 James Robertson Parkway, Suite 1300, Nashville, TN 37243-0850
Tel: (615) 741-1150  Fax: (615) 532-8581  E-mail: bop.webmail@tn.gov

■Chairman **Richard Montgomery** . . . . . . . . . . . . . . . . . . . (615) 741-1150
    E-mail: richard.montgomery@tn.gov
    Education: Tennessee BS
■Member **Patsy Bruce** . . . . . . . . . . . . . . . . . . . . . . . . . . . (615) 741-1150
    E-mail: patsy.bruce@tn.gov
■Member **Ronnie Cole** . . . . . . . . . . . . . . . . . . . . . . . . . . . (731) 288-6041
    E-mail: ronnie.cole@tn.gov
■Member **Gary M. Faulcon** . . . . . . . . . . . . . . . . . . . . . . . (615) 741-1150
    E-mail: gary.faulcon@tn.gov
■Member **Tim Gobble** . . . . . . . . . . . . . . . . . . . . . . . . . . . (423) 559-5096
    E-mail: tim.gobble@tn.gov
    Education: David Lipscomb U 1986 BS
■Member **Gay Gregson** . . . . . . . . . . . . . . . . . . . . . . . . . . (731) 423-2511
    E-mail: gay.greyson@tn.gov
■Member **Barrett Rich** . . . . . . . . . . . . . . . . . . . . . . . . . . . (615) 741-1150
    Term Expires: December 31, 2019

### Board Staff
Executive Director **David Liner** . . . . . . . . . . . . . . . . . . . . (615) 741-9941

## Tennessee Education Lottery Corporation
One Century Place, 26 Century Boulevard, Suite 200,
Nashville, TN 37214
P.O. Box 291869, Nashville, TN 37229-1869
Tel: (615) 324-6500  Internet: www.tnlottery.com

■Chairman **(Vacant)** . . . . . . . . . . . . . . . . . . . . . . . . . . . . . (615) 324-6500
■Vice Chair **(Vacant)** . . . . . . . . . . . . . . . . . . . . . . . . . . . . (615) 324-6500
■Member **William Carver** . . . . . . . . . . . . . . . . . . . . . . . . . (615) 324-6500
    Term Expires: June 30, 2018
■Member **Craig Powers** . . . . . . . . . . . . . . . . . . . . . . . . . . (615) 324-6500
    Affiliation: Manager, Natural Gas Construction and Maintenance
    Division, Memphis Light, Gas and Water Division, City of Memphis,
    Tennessee
    220 South Main Street, Memphis, TN 38103
    Education: Tennessee (Chattanooga) BSME
■Member **Pearl Shaw** . . . . . . . . . . . . . . . . . . . . . . . . . . . . (615) 324-6500
■Member **Thomas White** . . . . . . . . . . . . . . . . . . . . . . . . . (615) 324-6500
Chief Executive Officer **Rebecca Paul Hargrove** . . . . . . . . (615) 324-6500
Chief Operating Officer and General Counsel
    **Wanda Young Wilson** . . . . . . . . . . . . . . . . . . . . . . . . (615) 324-6500
Advertising and Marketing Executive Vice President
    **Lou Ann Russell** . . . . . . . . . . . . . . . . . . . . . . . . . . . . (615) 324-6500
Sales Executive Vice President **Sidney Chambers** . . . . . . . (615) 324-6500
Sales Vice President **Edward Bradley** . . . . . . . . . . . . . . . (615) 324-6500
Chief Financial and Information Systems Officer
    **Andy Davis** . . . . . . . . . . . . . . . . . . . . . . . . . . . . . . . (615) 324-6500
    E-mail: andy.davis@tnlottery.com
    Information Systems Vice President **David Kan** . . . . . . . (615) 324-6500
    E-mail: david.kan@tnlottery.com
Corporate Affairs Vice President **(Vacant)** . . . . . . . . . . . . (615) 324-6500
Financial Management Vice President **Vicki Updike** . . . . . . (615) 324-6500
Human Resources Vice President **Amy Bush** . . . . . . . . . . (615) 324-6500
Internal Controls Vice President **Khristie Stoecklein** . . . . . (615) 324-6500
Legal Affairs Vice President **Andrew Morin** . . . . . . . . . . . (615) 324-6500
Legal Compliance Vice President **Alonda McCutcheon** . . . (615) 324-6500
Security Vice President **David Jennings** . . . . . . . . . . . . . . (615) 324-6500

---

★ Elected Official   ■ Appointed by Governor   ● Appointed by Legislature   ▲ Appointed by Board or Commission   ◆ Appointed by State Supreme Court

# Office of the Lieutenant Governor

Legislative Plaza, Suite One, Nashville, TN 37243-0202
Tel: (615) 741-4524  Fax: (615) 253-0197

Lieutenant Governor **Ronald Lynn "Ron" Ramsey** . . . . . . (615) 741-4524
  Note: On March 16, 2016, Lieutenant Governor Ron Ramsey
  announced he would not run for reelection to his seat in the Tennessee
  Senate in 2016.
  Education: East Tennessee State 1978 BS
  Career: State Representative (R-TN, District 1), Tennessee House of
  Representatives (1992-1997)
  Executive Assistant **Pamela "Pam" George** . . . . . . . . . . (615) 741-4524
Chief of Staff **Lance Frizzell** . . . . . . . . . . . . . . . . . . . . . . . . (615) 741-4524
Deputy Chief of Staff **Jordan Young** . . . . . . . . . . . . . . . . . (615) 741-4524
Communications Officer **Adam Kleinheider** . . . . . . . . . . . (615) 741-4524
  E-mail: adam.kleinheider@capitol.tn.gov
Scheduler/ Executive Assistant **Debbie Rankin** . . . . . . . . . (615) 741-4524
  E-mail: debbie.rankin@capitol.tn.gov

# Office of the Attorney General and Reporter

P.O. Box 20207, Nashville, TN 37202
Tel: (615) 741-3491  Fax: (615) 741-2009
Internet: www.tn.gov/attorneygeneral

**Employees:** 320

◆Attorney General **Herbert H. Slatery III** . . . . . . . . . . . . . . (615) 741-3491
  Term Expires: 2022
  E-mail: herbert.slatery@tn.gov
  Education: Virginia 1974 BA; Tennessee 1980 JD
Chief Deputy Attorney General **Lucy Honey Haynes** . . . . . (615) 532-2580
Solicitor General **Andrée Sophia Blumstein** . . . . . . . . . . . (615) 741-3492
Associate Attorney General **Bill Young** . . . . . . . . . . . . . . . . (615) 741-3226
  Education: Vanderbilt 1977 BA, 1981 JD
Associate Solicitor General **Joseph F. Whalen** . . . . . . . . . (615) 741-3499
Chief of Staff **Leigh Ann Apple Jones** . . . . . . . . . . . . . . . . (615) 741-2162
Administrative Division Deputy Attorney General
  **Ruth Thompson** . . . . . . . . . . . . . . . . . . . . . . . . . . . . . . (615) 253-4509
Bankruptcy Division Deputy Attorney General
  **Kathryn Celauro** . . . . . . . . . . . . . . . . . . . . . . . . . . . . . . (615) 741-2868
    Fax: (615) 741-3334
Civil Litigation and State Services Division Deputy
  Attorney General **Kevin Steiling** . . . . . . . . . . . . . . . . . . (615) 741-2370
    Fax: (615) 741-7327
Civil Rights and Claims Division Deputy Attorney
  General **Dawn Jordan** . . . . . . . . . . . . . . . . . . . . . . . . . . (615) 741-7401
    Fax: (615) 532-2541
Consumer Advocate and Protection Division Deputy
  Attorney General **Cynthia E. Kinser** . . . . . . . . . . . . . . . (615) 741-6422
    Fax: (615) 532-2910
Criminal Justice Division Deputy Attorney General
  **Amy Tarkington** . . . . . . . . . . . . . . . . . . . . . . . . . . . . . . . (615) 741-2216
    Fax: (615) 532-7791
Environmental Division Deputy Attorney General
  **Barry Turner** . . . . . . . . . . . . . . . . . . . . . . . . . . . . . . . . . (615) 532-2586
    Fax: (615) 741-8724
Financial Division Deputy Attorney General
  **C. Scott Jackson** . . . . . . . . . . . . . . . . . . . . . . . . . . . . . . (615) 741-3756
  E-mail: scott.jackson@ag.tn.gov
    Fax: (615) 532-8223
General Civil Division Deputy Attorney General
  **Martha Campbell** . . . . . . . . . . . . . . . . . . . . . . . . . . . . . . (615) 741-6420
    Fax: (615) 532-5683
Health Care Division Deputy Attorney General
  **Linda Ross** . . . . . . . . . . . . . . . . . . . . . . . . . . . . . . . . . . . (615) 741-1771
    Fax: (615) 532-1120
Law Enforcement and Special Prosecutions Division
  Deputy Attorney General **Jennifer L. Smith** . . . . . . . . . . (615) 741-3487
  E-mail: jennifer.smith@ag.tn.gov
    Fax: (615) 532-4892
Medicaid Fraud and Integrity Division Deputy Attorney
  General **Leslie Ann Bridges** . . . . . . . . . . . . . . . . . . . . . . (615) 741-4710
    Fax: (615) 532-4892
Public Interest Division Deputy Attorney General
  **Janet M. Kleinfelter** . . . . . . . . . . . . . . . . . . . . . . . . . . . (615) 741-7403
    Fax: (615) 532-6951

Real Property and Transportation Division Deputy
  Attorney General **Larry Teague** . . . . . . . . . . . . . . . . . . . (615) 741-3493
  E-mail: larry.teague@ag.tn.gov
    Fax: (615) 741-8151
Tax Division Deputy Attorney General **Larry Lewis** . . . . . . (615) 741-2968
    Fax: (615) 532-2571
Tobacco Enforcement Division Deputy Attorney General
  **John H. Sinclair** . . . . . . . . . . . . . . . . . . . . . . . . . . . . . . (615) 741-1376
    Fax: (615) 741-3284
Special Litigation Division, Special Counsel **Steve Hart** . . . (615) 741-3505
    Fax: (615) 532-6951

# Office of the Comptroller of the Treasury

State Capitol, Nashville, TN 37243-0260
James K. Polk Building, 505 Deaderick Street, 17th Floor,
Nashville, TN 37243-1402
Fax: (615) 741-7328

●Comptroller **Justin P. Wilson** . . . . . . . . . . . . . . . . . . . . . . (615) 741-2501
  Term Expires: 2017
  E-mail: justin.wilson@cot.tn.gov
Chief of Staff **Jason E. Mumpower** . . . . . . . . . . . . . . . . . (615) 741-2501
  Education: King BA
Deputy Chief of Staff **Lauren Plunk** . . . . . . . . . . . . . . . . . (615) 401-7903
  E-mail: lauren.plunk@cot.tn.gov
  Executive Secretary **Terry Baxter** . . . . . . . . . . . . . . . . . (615) 741-2501
  Executive Secretary **Bettye Stanton** . . . . . . . . . . . . . . . (615) 741-2501
Public Finance Assistant to the Comptroller
  **Ann Butterworth** . . . . . . . . . . . . . . . . . . . . . . . . . . . . . (615) 401-7910
  Education: Duke 1978 AB; Vanderbilt 1981 JD        Fax: (615) 741-1551
General Counsel **Stephanie Maxwell** . . . . . . . . . . . . . . . . (615) 401-7786
    Fax: (615) 532-7776
Deputy General Counsel **(Vacant)** . . . . . . . . . . . . . . . . . . . (615) 401-7786
Open Records Counsel **Ann Butterworth** . . . . . . . . . . . . . (615) 401-7891
    Fax: (615) 784-1551
Local Government Audit Director **Jim Arnette** . . . . . . . . . . (615) 401-7841
    Fax: (615) 741-6216
Management Services Director
  **Melinda K. Parton, CGFM** . . . . . . . . . . . . . . . . . . . . . . (615) 401-7720
  E-mail: melinda.parton@cot.tn.gov        Fax: (615) 532-2224
Property Assessments Director **Donald "Don" Osborne** . . (615) 401-7737
    Fax: (615) 741-3888
Property Assessments, Local Government, and GIS/
  Mapping Director **Susan Gullette** . . . . . . . . . . . . . . . . . (615) 401-7737
    Fax: (615) 741-3888
Research and Education Accountability Director
  **Phillip "Phil" Doss** . . . . . . . . . . . . . . . . . . . . . . . . . . . . (615) 401-7866
    Fax: (615) 532-9237
State Assessed Properties Director **(Vacant)** . . . . . . . . . . . (615) 741-0140
State Audit Director
  **Deborah Vaughan Loveless, CGFM, CPA** . . . . . . . . . . . (615) 401-7897
    Fax: (615) 532-2765
State and Local Finance Director **Sandi Thompson** . . . . . . (615) 401-7872
    Fax: (615) 741-5986
Small Business Advocate **Richard Wilson** . . . . . . . . . . . . . (615) 401-7806
    Fax: (615) 741-1551
Higher Education Resource Officer
  **Nneka Norman-Gordon** . . . . . . . . . . . . . . . . . . . . . . . . (855) 440-4376
Legislative Policy Coordinator **(Vacant)** . . . . . . . . . . . . . . (615) 401-7744
Legislative Research Coordinator **Linda Penny** . . . . . . . . . (615) 401-7744
  E-mail: linda.penny@cot.tn.gov

# State Board of Equalization

W.R. Snodgrass TN Tower, 312 Rosa L. Parks Avenue, 9th Floor,
Nashville, TN 37243-1102
Tel: (615) 401-7883  Fax: (615) 253-4847  E-mail: sb.web@cot.tn.gov

Executive Secretary **Kelsie E. Jones** . . . . . . . . . . . . . . . . . (615) 741-0162
  E-mail: kelsie.jones@cot.tn.gov
Executive Program Manager **Karen B. Hale, CGFM** . . . . . . (615) 401-7742
  E-mail: karen.b.hale@cot.tn.gov

---

★ Elected Official   ■ Appointed by Governor   ● Appointed by Legislature   ▲ Appointed by Board or Commission   ◆ Appointed by State Supreme Court

EXECUTIVE BRANCH

# Tennessee Department of State

State Capitol, First Floor, Nashville, TN 37243-0305
Fax: (615) 532-9547  Internet: www.state.tn.us/sos

● Secretary of State **Tré Hargett** . . . . . . . . . . . . . . . . . . . . . . . (615) 741-2819
  Term Expires: 2017
  E-mail: tre.hargett@tn.gov
  Executive Assistant **Antoinette "Tawnie" Mathieu** . . . . . (615) 741-2819
Chief of Staff **Jonathan Rummel** . . . . . . . . . . . . . . . . . . . . (615) 741-2819
General Counsel **Mary Beth Thomas** . . . . . . . . . . . . . . . . . (615) 741-2819
Administrative Procedures Division Director
  **Richard Collier** . . . . . . . . . . . . . . . . . . . . . . . . . . . . (615) 741-0518
  E-mail: richard.collier@tn.gov
  Education: Florida State 1975 BS; Vanderbilt 1978 JD, 1990 MDiv
Charitable Solicitations Division Director
  **Brent Culberson** . . . . . . . . . . . . . . . . . . . . . . . . . . . (615) 741-2555
Publications Division Director **Cody York** . . . . . . . . . . . . . (615) 741-2650
Business Services Division Director **Nathan Burton** . . . . . . (615) 741-0584
Uniform Commercial Code Assistant Director
  **Kevin Rayburn** . . . . . . . . . . . . . . . . . . . . . . . . . . . . (615) 741-3276
State Election Coordinator **Mark Goins** . . . . . . . . . . . . . . (615) 741-7956

## Fiscal and Administrative Services Division

Director **Rose Case** . . . . . . . . . . . . . . . . . . . . . . . . . . . . (615) 741-2683
  E-mail: rose.case@tn.gov
Assistant Fiscal Director **Barbara Deharde** . . . . . . . . . . . . (615) 741-2683
  E-mail: barbara.deharde@tn.gov

## Information Systems Division

Director **Joni Kies** . . . . . . . . . . . . . . . . . . . . . . . . . . . . . (615) 532-8467
  E-mail: joni.kies@tn.gov

## Personnel and Development Division

Director **Margaret Bahou** . . . . . . . . . . . . . . . . . . . . . . . . (615) 741-7411

## State Library and Archives Division

403 Seventh Avenue North, Nashville, TN 37243-0312
Fax: (615) 741-6471

State Librarian and Archivist **Charles A. Sherrill** . . . . . . . . (615) 741-7996
  Education: Case Western MA
Assistant State Librarian for Administration
  **Ashley Bowers** . . . . . . . . . . . . . . . . . . . . . . . . . . . . (615) 741-7996
  E-mail: ashley.bowers@tn.gov
Archival Technical Services Director **Cathi Carmack** . . . . . (615) 253-3468
Blind and Physically Handicapped Library Director
  **Maria Sochor** . . . . . . . . . . . . . . . . . . . . . . . . . . . . . (615) 741-3915
Preservation Services Director **Jami Awalt** . . . . . . . . . . . . (615) 741-2997
Public Services Director **Gordon Belt** . . . . . . . . . . . . . . . . (615) 741-2764
Regional Libraries Director **Lynette Sloan** . . . . . . . . . . . . . (615) 532-4629
Network Services Coordinator **Lisa Walker** . . . . . . . . . . . . (615) 532-4894
  E-mail: lisa.walker@tn.gov
State Data Coordinator **Cecilie Maynor** . . . . . . . . . . . . . . (615) 532-4601
  E-mail: cecilie.maynor@tn.gov

## State Election Commission

Snodgrass Tower, 312 Rosa L. Parks Avenue, 7th Floor,
Nashville, TN 37243-1102
Tel: (615) 741-7956

● Member **Donna Barrett** . . . . . . . . . . . . . . . . . . . . . . . . (615) 741-7956
● Member **Judy Blackburn** . . . . . . . . . . . . . . . . . . . . . . . (615) 741-7956
● Member **Greg Ducklett** . . . . . . . . . . . . . . . . . . . . . . . . (615) 741-7956
● Member **James "Tommy" Head** . . . . . . . . . . . . . . . . . . . (615) 741-7956
  Education: Austin Peay State 1967 BS
● Member **Jimmy Wallace** . . . . . . . . . . . . . . . . . . . . . . . . (615) 741-7956
● Member **Tom Wheeler** . . . . . . . . . . . . . . . . . . . . . . . . . (615) 741-7956
● Member **Kent Younce** . . . . . . . . . . . . . . . . . . . . . . . . . (615) 741-7956

# Tennessee Department of Treasury

State Capitol, First Floor, Nashville, TN 37243-0225
Tel: (615) 741-2956  Fax: (615) 253-1591
Internet: www.treasury.state.tn.us

● State Treasurer **David H. Lillard, Jr.** . . . . . . . . . . . . . . . . (615) 741-2956
  Term Expires: 2017
  E-mail: david.lillard@tn.gov
  Executive Assistant to the Treasurer
    **Heather Sczepczenski** . . . . . . . . . . . . . . . . . . . . . . (615) 741-2956
  Staff Assistant to the Treasurer **Cynthia Todd** . . . . . . . . . (615) 741-8091
  Chief of Staff **Joy Harris** . . . . . . . . . . . . . . . . . . . . . . (615) 741-2956
  Assistant Treasurer, Legal and Compliance
    **Christy Allen** . . . . . . . . . . . . . . . . . . . . . . . . . . . (615) 253-3853
Information Systems and Support Services Deputy
  Treasurer **Rick Dubray** . . . . . . . . . . . . . . . . . . . . . . (615) 253-5764
  E-mail: rick.dubray@tn.gov
Program Services Deputy Treasurer **Steve Curry** . . . . . . . . (615) 532-8045
Accounting Director **Kim Morrow** . . . . . . . . . . . . . . . . . . (615) 532-3840
Cash Management Director **Tim McClure** . . . . . . . . . . . . . (615) 532-1166
Claims Administration Director **Rodney Escobar** . . . . . . . . (615) 741-2734
Consolidated Retirement Director **Jill Bachus** . . . . . . . . . . (615) 741-7063
Deferred Compensation Manager **Kaci Lantz** . . . . . . . . . . (615) 532-2347
Fiscal Services Director **Kerry Hartley** . . . . . . . . . . . . . . . (615) 532-8552
Information Systems Director **(Vacant)** . . . . . . . . . . . . . . . (615) 532-8035
Internal Audit Director **Andrew Furlong** . . . . . . . . . . . . . . (615) 253-2018
Chief Investment Officer **Michael Brakebill** . . . . . . . . . . . (615) 532-1157
Old Age and Survivors Insurance Manager
  **Mary E. Griffin** . . . . . . . . . . . . . . . . . . . . . . . . . . . (615) 741-7902
Personnel Director **Greg Cason** . . . . . . . . . . . . . . . . . . . . (615) 741-2956
Risk Management Director **Rodney Escobar** . . . . . . . . . . . (615) 741-9957
Unclaimed Property Director **John Gabriel** . . . . . . . . . . . . (615) 741-6499
BEST (Baccalaureate Education System Trust) Manager
  **Lakesha Page** . . . . . . . . . . . . . . . . . . . . . . . . . . . . (615) 532-5888
Webmaster **Roxanna Pierce** . . . . . . . . . . . . . . . . . . . . . (615) 532-1282

---

★ Elected Official   ■ Appointed by Governor   ● Appointed by Legislature   ▲ Appointed by Board or Commission   ◆ Appointed by State Supreme Court

# Texas

Tel: (512) 463-2000  Internet: www.texas.gov

**Number of U.S. Congressional Delegates:** 2 Senators; 36 Representatives  **Governor's Term:** 4 years
**Legislature Description:** 31 member Senate; 150 member House of Representatives; Term - Senate 4 years,
House 2 years  **Next Election:** Governor November 2018; Legislature November 2016  **Number of
Electoral Votes:** 38  **Official Name:** State of Texas (Indian: friend)  **Nickname:** Lone Star State
**Motto:** Friendship

**Population:** 27,469,114 (2015); Rank 2  **Fiscal Year:** 2014-2015  **Budget:** $200,421,100,000

## Office of the Governor

1100 San Jacinto Boulevard, Austin, TX 78701
P.O. Box 12428, Austin, TX 78711
Tel: (512) 463-2000
Tel: (800) 843-5789 (Information & Referral Hotline)
TTY: (512) 463-5746  Tel: (800) 475-3165 (Information & Referral)
Fax: (512) 463-1849

**Greg Abbott**
Governor

Began Service: January 20, 2015
Term Expires: January 2019
Date of Birth: November 13, 1957
Education: Texas 1981 BBA; Vanderbilt 1984 JD
Home: Austin
Career: Attorney, Butler & Binion L.L.P.
(1984-1992); Trial Judge, 129th District, Texas
(1993-1995); Justice, Supreme Court of Texas
(1996-2001); Attorney General (R-TX), Office of
Attorney General Greg Abbott, State of Texas
(2002-2015)

★ Governor **Greg Abbott** (R) . . . . . . . . . . . . . . . . . . . . . . . . (512) 463-2000
  E-mail: greg.abbott@gov.texas.gov
Chief of Staff **Daniel Hodge** . . . . . . . . . . . . . . . . . . . . . . . . (512) 463-2000
  Education: Texas 2004 JD
Deputy Chief of Staff **Robert Allen** . . . . . . . . . . . . . . . . . . (512) 463-2000
Deputy Chief of Staff **Reed Clay** . . . . . . . . . . . . . . . . . . . . (512) 463-2000
  Education: Wake Forest 2001 BA; Duke 2005 JD
General Counsel **James D. Blacklock** . . . . . . . . . . . . . . . . (512) 463-2000
  Education: Yale 2005 JD
Senior Advisor **(Vacant)** . . . . . . . . . . . . . . . . . . . . . . . . . . . (512) 463-2000
Appointments Director **David Whitley** . . . . . . . . . . . . . . . . (512) 463-1828
  E-mail: david.whitley@gov.texas.gov
  Deputy Appointments Director **Sarah Gouak** . . . . . . . . . (512) 463-1828
    E-mail: sarah.gouak@gov.texas.gov
    Education: Texas Tech
Communications Director **Matt Hirsch** . . . . . . . . . . . . . . . . (512) 463-2000
  E-mail: matt.hirsch@gov.texas.gov
Press Secretary **John Wittman** . . . . . . . . . . . . . . . . . . . . . (512) 463-2000
  E-mail: john.wittman@gov.texas.gov
Legislative Director **Jay Dyer** . . . . . . . . . . . . . . . . . . . . . . (512) 463-1830
  E-mail: jay.dyer@gov.texas.gov
  Education: Texas 1995 BA, 1998 JD
  Deputy Legislative Director **Ashley Morgan** . . . . . . . . . . (512) 463-1830
    E-mail: ashley.morgan@gov.texas.gov
    Education: Austin State 1998 BA; Texas 2007 JD
Outreach Director **Ben Taylor** . . . . . . . . . . . . . . . . . . . . . . (512) 463-1826
  E-mail: ben.taylor@gov.texas.gov
Scheduling and Advance Director **Kimberly C. Snyder** . . . . (512) 463-2000
  E-mail: kim.snyder@gov.texas.gov
Special Assistant to the Governor **Erin Hodges** . . . . . . . . . (512) 463-1762
  E-mail: erin.hodges@gov.texas.gov

## Office of the First Lady

P.O. Box 12428, Austin, TX 78711
Tel: (512) 475-2324  Fax: (512) 475-2598

First Lady **Cecilia Abbott** . . . . . . . . . . . . . . . . . . . . . . . . . (512) 475-2324
  Education: U St Thomas (TX)

## Administration

Director **Jordan Hale** . . . . . . . . . . . . . . . . . . . . . . . . . . . . . (512) 463-1776
  E-mail: jordan.hale@gov.texas.gov
Constituent Communication Director
  **Gregory S. Davidson** . . . . . . . . . . . . . . . . . . . . . . . . . . (512) 463-1800
  E-mail: greg.davidson@gov.texas.gov
Human Resources Director **Maggie Freeman** . . . . . . . . . . (512) 463-5873
Information Technology Director **Jeffrey Smith** . . . . . . . . (512) 463-2000
  E-mail: jeffrey.smith@gov.texas.gov

## Budget and Policy

1100 San Jacinto Boulevard, Austin, TX 78701
Tel: (512) 463-1778  Fax: (512) 463-1975

Director of Budget and Policy **Drew DeBerry** . . . . . . . . . . (512) 463-1778
  Education: Texas Tech BS
Budget Director **Ky Ash** . . . . . . . . . . . . . . . . . . . . . . . . . . . (512) 463-1778
  E-mail: ky.ash@gov.texas.gov
Deputy Budget Director **(Vacant)** . . . . . . . . . . . . . . . . . . . (512) 463-1778
Policy Director **Constance Allison** . . . . . . . . . . . . . . . . . . (512) 463-1778
  E-mail: constance.allison@gov.texas.gov
Senior Policy Advisor **Elizabeth "Libby" Elliott** . . . . . . . . (512) 463-1778
  E-mail: libby.elliott@gov.texas.gov
Education Advisor **Candice Woodruff** . . . . . . . . . . . . . . . . (512) 463-1778
  E-mail: candice.woodruff@gov.texas.gov
Health and Human Services Advisor **Kara Crawford** . . . . . (512) 463-1778
  Note: Until May 31, 2016.
  E-mail: kara.crawford@gov.texas.gov
  Education: Texas State (San Marcos) MPA
Legal and Judicial Advisor **Mike Goldman** . . . . . . . . . . . . (512) 463-1778
  E-mail: mike.goldman@gov.texas.gov
Natural Resources Advisor **Ryan Vise** . . . . . . . . . . . . . . . . (512) 463-1778
  E-mail: ryan.vise@gov.texas.gov
Natural Resources Advisor **(Vacant)** . . . . . . . . . . . . . . . . . (512) 463-5856
Public Education Advisor **Julie Shields** . . . . . . . . . . . . . . . (512) 463-1778
  E-mail: julie.shields@gov.texas.gov
Public Safety Advisor **Seth Christensen** . . . . . . . . . . . . . . (512) 463-1778
  E-mail: seth.christensen@gov.texas.gov

## Criminal Justice

Tel: (512) 463-1919  Tel: (800) 252-8477 (Crime Stoppers Hotline)
Fax: (512) 475-2440

Director **C. Camille Cain** . . . . . . . . . . . . . . . . . . . . . . . . . . (512) 463-1919
  E-mail: camille.cain@gov.texas.gov
Deputy Director **(Vacant)** . . . . . . . . . . . . . . . . . . . . . . . . . (512) 463-1919
Crime Stoppers Director **Elaine Williams** . . . . . . . . . . . . . (512) 463-1919
Juvenile Justice Program Manager **(Vacant)** . . . . . . . . . . . (512) 463-1919

---

★ Elected Official     ■ Appointed by Governor     ● Appointed by Legislature     ▲ Appointed by Board or Commission     ◆ Appointed by State Supreme Court

# Economic Development and Tourism Division

P.O. Box 12428, Austin, TX 78711
1100 San Jacinto Boulevard, Austin, TX 78701
Tel: (512) 936-0100  Fax: (512) 936-0303

Executive Director **Bryan Daniel** . . . . . . . . . . . . . . . . . . . . . (512) 936-0100
 E-mail: bryan.daniel@gov.texas.gov
 Education: Texas Tech BS, MS
Deputy Director **Mary York** . . . . . . . . . . . . . . . . . . . . . (512) 936-0100
Business Development Director **Jose Romano** . . . . . . . . . (512) 936-0250
Texas Economic Development Bank Director
 **Terry Zrubek** . . . . . . . . . . . . . . . . . . . . . . . . . . . . . . . (512) 936-0528
Texas Military Preparedness Commission Director
 **Keith Graf** . . . . . . . . . . . . . . . . . . . . . . . . . . . . . . . . (512) 475-0487
Texas Tourism Director **Brad Smyth** . . . . . . . . . . . . . . . . . (512) 936-0209

# Texas Office of State - Federal Relations

10 G Street NE, Suite 650, Washington, DC 20002
Tel: (202) 638-3927  Fax: (202) 628-1943  Internet: www.osfr.state.tx.us

■Executive Director **Jerry Strickland** . . . . . . . . . . . . . . . (202) 434-0218
 E-mail: jerry.strickland@gov.texas.gov
Federal Liaison, Health **Theresa Vawter** . . . . . . . . . . . . . (202) 434-0207
 E-mail: theresa.vawter@hhsc.state.tx.us
 Education: Villanova 2005 BA
Federal Liaison, Transportation **Melanie A. Alvord** . . . . . . (202) 434-0209
 E-mail: melanie.alvord@txdot.gov
 Education: Virginia 1989 BA
Federal Liaison, Transportation **Melissa Meyer** . . . . . . . . (202) 434-0214
 E-mail: melissa.meyer@txdot.gov
Federal Liaison, Workforce **Allison Robertson** . . . . . . . . . (202) 434-0210
 E-mail: allison.slayton@twc.state.tx.us
Legislative Liaison **(Vacant)** . . . . . . . . . . . . . . . . . . . . . (512) 936-2600

# Adjutant General's Department [AGD]

West 35th Street, Austin, TX 78763
P.O. Box 5218, Austin, TX 78763-5218
Tel: (512) 782-5001  TTY: (800) 735-2988  Fax: (512) 782-5578
E-mail: ng.tx.txarng.mbx.pao@mail.mil

**Employees:** 626  **Fiscal Year:** 2014  **Budget:** $75,162,212

■Adjutant General **MajGen John F. Nichols, ANG** . . . . . . . (512) 782-5006
 Term Expires: February 1, 2018
 Education: Air Force Acad 1979 BS; Army War Col 1999
Chief of Staff to the Adjutant General
 **COL Gregory Chaney, ARNG** . . . . . . . . . . . . . . . . . . (512) 782-5022
Public Affairs Officer **LTC Travis Walters, ARNG** . . . . . . . (512) 782-5620
Construction and Facilities Management Office Director
 **COL Tracy R. Norris, ARNG** . . . . . . . . . . . . . . . . . . (512) 782-5646
 P.O. Box 5218, Austin, TX 78763    Fax: (512) 782-5141
Senior Enlisted Advisor **CSM Mark A. Weedon, ARNG** . . (512) 782-5001

# Texas Military Forces

West 35th Street, Austin, TX 78763
P.O. Box 5218, Austin, TX 78763
Tel: (512) 782-5006

■Adjutant General **MajGen John F. Nichols, ANG** . . . . . . . (512) 782-5006
Deputy Adjutant General for Air
 **BrigGen Dawn Ferrell, ANG** . . . . . . . . . . . . . . . . . . (512) 782-5007
 Education: Midwestern State; North Texas
Deputy Adjutant General for Army
 **MG William "Len" Smith, ARNG** . . . . . . . . . . . . . . (512) 782-5027
 Education: Southwest Texas State BA; Touro U International MBA;
 Army War Col
Director, Command and Control Communications and
 Computers (J6) **Brian S. Attaway** . . . . . . . . . . . . . . (512) 782-6946
 E-mail: brian.attaway@us.army.mil

# Texas Air National Guard

West 35th Street, Austin, TX 78763
Tel: (512) 782-5001

Commander **BrigGen David McMinn, ANG** . . . . . . . . . . . (512) 782-5007
 Education: Clemson 1985

Senior Enlisted Advisor
 **CMSgt Marlon K. Nation, ANG** . . . . . . . . . . . . . . . . (512) 782-5001
 Education: Texas Southern 1990 BA

# Texas Army National Guard

P.O. Box 5218, Austin, TX 78763-5218
Tel: (512) 782-5027

Commander **MG William "Len" Smith, ARNG** . . . . . . . . (512) 782-5027
Senior Enlisted Advisor **CSM John Hoxie, ARNG** . . . . . . (512) 782-5027
Commander, 36th Infantry Division
 **BG Lester Simpson, ARNG** . . . . . . . . . . . . . . . . . . (512) 782-5049
Contracting Officer **Carol Koenig** . . . . . . . . . . . . . . . . . (512) 782-5529
Public Affairs Officer **LTC Travis Walters, ARNG** . . . . . . . (512) 782-5620
 E-mail: ng.tx.xarng.mbx.pao@mail.mil

# Texas State Guard [TXSG]

2200 West 35th Street, Austin, TX 78763-5218
Tel: (512) 782-5101

■Commander **BG Gerald "Jake" Betty, ARNG** . . . . . . . . . (512) 782-5101
Senior Enlisted Advisor
 **SgtMaj Bryan Becknel, USMCR** . . . . . . . . . . . . . . . . (512) 782-5101

# Texas Department of Agriculture [TDA]

P.O. Box 12847, Austin, TX 78711-2847
1700 North Congress Avenue, 11th Floor, Austin, TX 78701
Tel: (512) 463-7476  Fax: (800) 831-3884  TTY: (800) 735-2989

**Employees:** 704

★Commissioner **Sid Miller** (R) . . . . . . . . . . . . . . . . . . . (512) 463-7567
 Term Expires: 2019
 Education: Tarleton State 1978 BA
 Career: State Representative (R-TX, District 59), Texas House of
 Representatives (2001-2013)
Deputy Commissioner **Jason Fearneyhough** . . . . . . . . . . (512) 463-7567
 Education: Wyoming BA
Assistant Commissioner for Enforcement, Consumer
 Protection and Border Security **Terry Keel** . . . . . . . . . . (512) 463-7476
 Education: Texas 1980 BA; Houston 1983 JD
Assistant Commissioner for Legislative Affairs and
 External Relations **Walt Roberts** . . . . . . . . . . . . . . . . (512) 463-7476
Assistant Commissioner for Water and Rural Affairs
 **Dan Hunter** . . . . . . . . . . . . . . . . . . . . . . . . . . . . . . (512) 463-7476
 Education: Texas Tech; Tarleton State

## Agency Administration Division

Director **Bertha Serna** . . . . . . . . . . . . . . . . . . . . . . . . (512) 463-1402
 E-mail: bertha.serna@texasagriculture.gov
Administrator for Human Resources **Cynthia Mendoza** . . . (512) 463-7423
Chief Applications Development Officer **Greg Berglund** . . (512) 463-6051
Chief of Operational Support **Michael Clark** . . . . . . . . . (512) 463-7488
Coordinator for Licensing Operations Officer **(Vacant)** . . . (512) 463-4701
Manager for Information Resources Operations Officer
 **Greg Berglund** . . . . . . . . . . . . . . . . . . . . . . . . . . . . (512) 463-6051
 E-mail: greg.berglund@texasagriculture.gov

## Agriculture and Consumer Protection Division

Chief Administrator **David Kostroun** . . . . . . . . . . . . . . . (512) 463-0012
 E-mail: david.kostroun@texasagriculture.gov
Agriculture Protection and Certification Administrator
 **Randy Rivera** . . . . . . . . . . . . . . . . . . . . . . . . . . . . . (512) 463-7717
Consumer Protection Administrator **Stephen Pahl** . . . . . . (512) 463-6514
Aquaculture, Eggs, Weights and Measures Coordinator
 **Christopher Drews** . . . . . . . . . . . . . . . . . . . . . . . . . (512) 463-7401
 E-mail: christopher.drews@texasagriculture.gov
Biosecurity and Agriculture Resource Management
 Coordinator **Awinash Bhatkar** . . . . . . . . . . . . . . . . . (512) 463-5025
 E-mail: awinash.bhatkar@texasagriculture.gov
Co-ops, Grain Warehouse, HMPC and Piece Rate
 Coordinator **Thomas R. "Rick" Garza** . . . . . . . . . . . . (512) 936-2430
 E-mail: rick.garza@texasagriculture.gov

*(continued on next page)*

---

★ Elected Official   ■ Appointed by Governor   ● Appointed by Legislature   ▲ Appointed by Board or Commission   ◆ Appointed by State Supreme Court

**Agriculture and Consumer Protection Division** *continued*

Metrology, Licensed Services and Inspection Companies
Coordinator **Harvey Fischer** . . . . . . . . . . . . . . . . . . . (979) 542-3231
1258 County Road, #226, Giddings, TX 78942
E-mail: harvey.fischer@texasagriculture.gov

Organic Certification Coordinator **Mary Ellen Holliman** . . . (512) 936-4178
E-mail: mary.holliman@texasagriculture.gov

Pest Management and Citrus Programs Coordinator
**Robert Crocker** . . . . . . . . . . . . . . . . . . . . . . . . . (512) 463-6332
E-mail: robert.crocker@texasagriculture.gov

Regulatory Programs Branch Chief **Joe Benavides** . . . . . . . (512) 463-5706
E-mail: joe.benavides@texasagriculture.gov

Seed Quality Coordinator **Jeff Claxton** . . . . . . . . . . . . . . . (979) 542-3691
P.O. Box 629, Giddings, TX 78942
E-mail: jeffery.claxton@texasagriculture.gov

## Communications Division
Director **(Vacant)** . . . . . . . . . . . . . . . . . . . . . . . . . (512) 463-7664

## Financial Services Division
Chief Financial Officer **Diana Warner** . . . . . . . . . . . . . . (512) 463-3640
Education: Austin State 1974 BBA

Administrator for Licensing and Emergency Management
**Chris Sims** . . . . . . . . . . . . . . . . . . . . . . . . . . . . . (512) 463-7476
E-mail: chris.sims@texasagriculture.gov
Education: Texas Tech 1994, 1996 MPA

## Food and Nutrition Division
Tel: (877) 839-6325  E-mail: squaremeals@texasagriculture.gov
Assistant Commissioner **Angela Olige** . . . . . . . . . . . . . (512) 463-8583
Administrator **Tracy Mueck** . . . . . . . . . . . . . . . . . . . . (512) 936-6723
Business Operations Director **Robin O. Roark** . . . . . . . . . (512) 463-3910
Policy and Nutrition Director **Beth Thorson** . . . . . . . . . . (512) 463-2164

## Internal Audit Division
Director **Nicole Campbell** . . . . . . . . . . . . . . . . . . . . . (512) 463-8251

## Legal Affairs and General Counsel Division
General Counsel **Tim Kleinschmidt** . . . . . . . . . . . . . . . . (512) 463-4075
Education: Texas A&I 1978 BS; Baylor 1981 JD

Lead Deputy General Counsel **Stephen Dillon** . . . . . . . . . (512) 463-4075
Education: Texas; Houston JD

Deputy General Counsel **Martina Barrera** . . . . . . . . . . . . (512) 475-3617
E-mail: martina.barrera@texasagriculture.gov

Deputy General Counsel **Susan Maldonado** . . . . . . . . . . (512) 463-7528
Ethics Officer **(Vacant)** . . . . . . . . . . . . . . . . . . . . . . (512) 463-7528

## Marketing and Promotion Division
Trade and Business Chief Administrator **(Vacant)** . . . . . . . (512) 463-9195
Marketing and International Trade Administrator
**Mary York** . . . . . . . . . . . . . . . . . . . . . . . . . . . . . (512) 463-8289

Commodity Reporting and Livestock Pens Director
**Jon Garza** . . . . . . . . . . . . . . . . . . . . . . . . . . . . . (512) 463-6098

Horticulture and Forestry State Marketing Coordinator
**Richard De Los Santos** . . . . . . . . . . . . . . . . . . . . . (512) 463-7472
E-mail: richard.delossantos@texasagriculture.gov

Livestock Marketing Coordinator **Amanda Lyles** . . . . . . . (512) 463-7560
Marketing Campaigns State Coordinator (Acting)
**Mary York** . . . . . . . . . . . . . . . . . . . . . . . . . . . . . (512) 463-8289

## Office of Rural Affairs
Tel: (877) 428-7848
Administrator **Rick Rhodes** . . . . . . . . . . . . . . . . . . . . (512) 463-7577
Community Development Block Grant State Coordinator
**Becky Dempsey** . . . . . . . . . . . . . . . . . . . . . . . . . (512) 463-6612
State Office of Rural Health Director **Brad Denton** . . . . . . (512) 463-6121

# Texas Department of Housing and Community Affairs Governing Board
221 East 11th Street, Austin, TX 78701
P.O. Box 13941, Austin, TX 78711
Tel: (512) 475-3800  TTY: (800) 725-2989  Fax: (512) 469-9606
E-mail: info@tdhca.state.tx.us

■Chair **J. Paul Oxer** . . . . . . . . . . . . . . . . . . . . . . . . (832) 532-7852
Term Expires: January 31, 2017
Five Baileys Place Court, Sugar Land, TX 77479
Affiliation: Managing Director, McDaniell, Hunter and Prince Inc.
Education: Georgia Tech 1973 BCE; Texas (Arlington) 1983

■Vice Chair **Dr. Juan Sanchez Muñoz** . . . . . . . . . . . . . (806) 742-2025
Term Expires: March 31, 2017                    Fax: (806) 742-2138
P.O. Box 42005, Lubbock, TX 79409-2005
Affiliation: Senior Vice President, Institutional Diversity, Equity and
Community Engagement, Texas Tech University
P.O. Box 42013, Lubbock, TX 79409-2013
Education: UC Santa Barbara 1990 BA;
Cal State (Los Angeles) 1994 MA; UCLA 2001 PhD

■Member **Tolbert Chisum** . . . . . . . . . . . . . . . . . . . . . (214) 768-2839
Education: Sam Houston State

■Member **Leslie Bingham Escareño** . . . . . . . . . . . . . . . (956) 698-5800
Term Expires: January 31, 2019                  Fax: (956) 698-5747
1040 West Jefferson, Brownsville, TX 78520
Education: Mississippi; Texas Pan American MBA

■Member **Thomas H. "Tom" Gann** . . . . . . . . . . . . . . . (936) 633-2622
Term Expires: January 31, 2019                  Fax: (936) 632-9676
2808 South John Redditt Drive, Lufkin, TX 75904
Education: Baylor BBA, MBA

■Member **JB Goodwin** . . . . . . . . . . . . . . . . . . . . . . . (214) 768-2839
Term Expires: January 31, 2019
Education: Texas

# Texas Department of Housing and Community Affairs [TDHCA]
Tel: (512) 475-3800  Fax: (512) 469-9606  Internet: www.tdhca.state.tx.us

**Employees:** 277  **Fiscal Year:** 2015  **Budget:** $233,067,147

▲Executive Director **Timothy K. "Tim" Irvine** . . . . . . . . . (512) 475-3296
E-mail: tim.irvine@tdhca.state.tx.us
Education: Claremont McKenna 1971 BA

Chief of Staff **(Vacant)** . . . . . . . . . . . . . . . . . . . . . . (512) 475-2213
Deputy Executive Director for Housing Programs
**Tom Gouris** . . . . . . . . . . . . . . . . . . . . . . . . . . . . (512) 475-1470
Asset Management Director **Raquel Morales** . . . . . . . . . (512) 475-2109
E-mail: raquel.morales@tdhca.state.tx.us
Bond Finance Director **Monica Galuski** . . . . . . . . . . . . (512) 936-9268
Program Services Director **(Vacant)** . . . . . . . . . . . . . . (512) 475-3033
Real Estate Analysis Director **Brent Stewart** . . . . . . . . . (512) 475-2973
E-mail: brent.stewart@tdhca.state.tx.us

Deputy Executive Director of Single Family, Community
Affairs and Metrics **Brooke Boston** . . . . . . . . . . . . . . (512) 475-1762
Community Affairs Director **Michael De Young** . . . . . . . . (512) 475-2125
Single Family Operations and Services Director
**Homero Cabello** . . . . . . . . . . . . . . . . . . . . . . . . . (512) 475-2118
HOME Program Director **Jennifer Molinari** . . . . . . . . . . (512) 475-2224
E-mail: jennifer.molinari@tdhca.state.tx.us
Information Systems Director **Curtis Howe** . . . . . . . . . . (512) 475-1740
E-mail: curtis.howe@tdhca.state.tx.us
Neighborhood Stabilization Program Director
**Marni Holloway** . . . . . . . . . . . . . . . . . . . . . . . . . (512) 475-3726
E-mail: marni.holloway@tdhca.state.tx.us
Texas Homeownership Program Director
**Cathy Gutierrez** . . . . . . . . . . . . . . . . . . . . . . . . . (512) 475-0277
Compliance Chief **Patricia Murphy** . . . . . . . . . . . . . . . (512) 475-3140
Multifamily Compliance Director **Stephanie Naquin** . . . (512) 475-2330
E-mail: stephanie.naquin@tdhca.state.tx.us
External Affairs Chief **Michael Lyttle** . . . . . . . . . . . . . (512) 475-4542
Housing Resource Center Director **Elizabeth Yevich** . . . . (512) 463-7961
General Counsel **Beau Eccles** . . . . . . . . . . . . . . . . . . (512) 475-3932
E-mail: beau.eccles@tdhca.state.tx.us
Education: Texas Tech 1995 JD
Human Resources Director **Gina Esteves** . . . . . . . . . . . (512) 475-3943
Internal Audit Director **Mark Scott** . . . . . . . . . . . . . . . (512) 475-3813
Multifamily Finance Director **Marni Holloway** . . . . . . . . (512) 475-3344

---

★ Elected Official    ■ Appointed by Governor    ● Appointed by Legislature    ▲ Appointed by Board or Commission    ◆ Appointed by State Supreme Court

Chief Financial Officer **David Cervantes** . . . . . . . . . . . . . . (512) 475-3875
 Financial Administration Director **Ernie Palacios** . . . . . . . (512) 475-3354
Public Information Officer **Gordon Anderson** . . . . . . . . . . (512) 475-4743
 E-mail: gordon.anderson@tdhca.state.tx.us
Webmaster **Victor Martinez** . . . . . . . . . . . . . . . . . . . . . . . (512) 475-1238
Executive Director of Manufactured Housing **Joe Garcia** . . (512) 475-4999

# Texas Department of Information Resources [DIR]

William P. Clements Building, 300 West 15th Street, Suite 1300,
Austin, TX 78701
Tel: (512) 475-4700  Fax: (512) 475-4759  E-mail: dirinfo@dir.texas.gov

**Employees: 186  Fiscal Year: 2016-2017  Budget: $700,679,628**

▲Executive Director **Stacey Napier** . . . . . . . . . . . . . . . . . . . . (512) 475-4700
 Education: LSU 1995 BA; Southern Methodist 1998 JD
 Executive Assistant **Chandra Thompson** . . . . . . . . . . . . (512) 936-7577
Deputy Executive Director and State Chief Information
 Officer **Todd Kimbriel** . . . . . . . . . . . . . . . . . . . . . . . . . (512) 475-4700
 E-mail: todd.kimbriel@dir.texas.gov
 Education: Syracuse BS
Director of Digital Government/Information Resources
 Manager **Janet Gilmore** . . . . . . . . . . . . . . . . . . . . . . . . . (512) 463-8447
 E-mail: janet.gilmore@dir.texas.gov
Director of Internal Audit **Lissette Nadal-Hogan** . . . . . . . . (512) 936-2029
 Education: Puerto Rico BSBA
Chief Financial Officer **Nick Villalpando** . . . . . . . . . . . . . . (512) 936-2167
Chief Information Security Officer
 **Edward "Eddie" Block** . . . . . . . . . . . . . . . . . . . . . . . . . (512) 463-8807
 E-mail: eddie.block@dir.texas.gov
Chief Operations Officer **Dale Richardson** . . . . . . . . . . . . . (512) 463-7370
 Education: Texas; Southern Methodist MBA
Chief Technology Officer **John Hoffman** . . . . . . . . . . . . . . (512) 936-2501
 E-mail: john.hoffman@dir.texas.gov
 Education: Missouri BS
General Counsel **Martin Zelinsky** . . . . . . . . . . . . . . . . . . . (512) 463-9884
State Cybersecurity Coordinator **Edward "Eddie" Block** . . (512) 463-8807
Statewide Data Coordinator **Ed Kelly** . . . . . . . . . . . . . . . . (512) 463-1811
 E-mail: ed.kelly@dir.texas.gov
Director of Public Affairs **Robert Armstrong** . . . . . . . . . . (512) 936-9851
 E-mail: robert.armstrong@dir.texas.gov
 Education: Texas Christian BBA; Texas JD

# Texas Department of Insurance [TDI]

333 Guadalupe Street, Austin, TX 78701
P.O. Box 149104, Austin, TX 78714
Tel: (800) 578-4677  TTY: (512) 322-4238  Fax: (512) 490-1045
E-mail: pio@tdi.texas.gov  Internet: www.tdi.texas.gov

**Employees: 1,626  Fiscal Year: 2014  Budget: $121,285,495**

■Insurance Commissioner **David Mattax** . . . . . . . . . . . . . . (512) 676-6020
 E-mail: david.mattax@tdi.texas.gov
 Education: Texas 1983 JD
 Executive Assistant **Laverne Chase** . . . . . . . . . . . . . . . . (512) 676-6022
Administrative Operations Deputy Commissioner
 **Patricia David** . . . . . . . . . . . . . . . . . . . . . . . . . . . . . . . (512) 676-6025
 E-mail: patricia.david@tdi.texas.gov
Compliance Deputy Commissioner **Mark Einfalt** . . . . . . . . (512) 676-6210
 Education: UC Santa Barbara; Texas MPA, JD
Financial Regulation Deputy Commissioner **Doug Slape** . . (512) 676-6416
Legal and Regulatory Services Deputy Commissioner
 **Stanton Strickland** . . . . . . . . . . . . . . . . . . . . . . . . . . . (512) 676-6545
Public Affairs Deputy Commissioner
 **Stephanie Goodman** . . . . . . . . . . . . . . . . . . . . . . . . . . (512) 676-6590
Regulatory Policy Deputy Commissioner **Cassie Brown** . . . (512) 676-6610
Consumer Protection Senior Associate Commissioner
 **Melissa Hield** . . . . . . . . . . . . . . . . . . . . . . . . . . . . . . . . (512) 676-6213
Enforcement Senior Associate Commissioner
 **Sandra Nicolas** . . . . . . . . . . . . . . . . . . . . . . . . . . . . . . (512) 676-6326
Insurance Fraud Associate Commissioner and Chief
 Investigator **Christopher Davis** . . . . . . . . . . . . . . . . . . (512) 676-6295
 Life and Health Division Deputy Commissioner and
  Chief Actuary **Jan Graeber** . . . . . . . . . . . . . . . . . . . (512) 676-6889
General Counsel and Chief Clerk **Norma Garcia** . . . . . . . . (512) 676-6586
 Education: Southern Methodist; Texas JD

Chief Financial Officer **Nancy Clark** . . . . . . . . . . . . . . . . . (512) 676-6166
 Fax: (512) 463-6203
Government Relations Director **Melissa Hamilton** . . . . . . . (512) 676-6605
 Education: Texas 2004 JD
Human Resources Director **Patty David** . . . . . . . . . . . . . . (512) 676-6101
Internal Audit Director **Greg Royal** . . . . . . . . . . . . . . . . . . (512) 676-6200
Information Technology Services Director **Amy Lugo** . . . . . (512) 676-6031
 E-mail: amy.lugo@tdi.texas.gov
Marketing and Communications Director
 **Leslie Leal-Gauna** . . . . . . . . . . . . . . . . . . . . . . . . . . . (512) 676-6598
Procurement and General Services Director
 **Mike Powers** . . . . . . . . . . . . . . . . . . . . . . . . . . . . . . . . (512) 676-6125
 E-mail: mike.powers@tdi.texas.gov         Fax: (512) 322-2272
Public Information Office Director **Ben Gonzalez** . . . . . . . . (512) 676-6593
 E-mail: ben.gonzalez@tdi.texas.gov

## Division of Workers' Compensation

7551 Metro Center Drive, Austin, TX 78744
Tel: (512) 804-4000  Fax: (512) 804-4001

■Commissioner **Ryan Brannan** . . . . . . . . . . . . . . . . . . . . . (512) 804-4400
 Term Expires: February 1, 2017
 E-mail: ryan.brannan@tdi.texas.gov
 Education: Southern Methodist BA; Oklahoma JD;
 Southern Methodist MBA
 Special Advisor **Amy Lee** . . . . . . . . . . . . . . . . . . . . . . . (512) 804-4410
Executive Deputy Commissioner for Health Care
 Management and System Monitoring **Matthew Zurek** . . . (512) 804-4870
Deputy Commissioner of Claims and Customer Services
 **Kathy McMaster** . . . . . . . . . . . . . . . . . . . . . . . . . . . . (512) 804-4125
Deputy Commissioner of Hearings **Kerry Sullivan** . . . . . . (512) 804-4015
 Education: Texas 1985 JD
Director of External Relations **Kristen Harmon** . . . . . . . . . (512) 804-4405
Chief Deputy **Barbara Salyers** . . . . . . . . . . . . . . . . . . . . . (512) 804-4409
 E-mail: barbara.salyers@tdi.texas.gov
General Counsel **Nicholas Canaday** . . . . . . . . . . . . . . . . . (512) 804-4422
Assistant General Counsel, Subsequent Injury Fund
 **Marisa Lopez Wagley** . . . . . . . . . . . . . . . . . . . . . . . . . (512) 804-4739
Medical Advisor **Dr. David G. Davis, MD** . . . . . . . . . . . . . (512) 804-4415
 E-mail: david.davis@tdi.texas.gov
Enforcement Manager **Toya Lutz** . . . . . . . . . . . . . . . . . . . (512) 804-4294
Public Information Officer **John Greeley** . . . . . . . . . . . . . . (512) 305-7132
 E-mail: john.greeley@tdi.texas.gov

## State Fire Marshal's Office

333 Guadalupe Street, Austin, TX 78701
P.O. Box 149221, Austin, TX 78714-9221
Tel: (512) 676-6800  Fax: (512) 490-1063
E-mail: fire.marshall@tdi.texas.gov

State Fire Marshal **Chris Connealy** . . . . . . . . . . . . . . . . . . (512) 676-6800
 Education: Western Illinois BA; Grand Canyon MA

## State Office of Administrative Hearings [SOAH]

300 West 15th Street, Suite 504, Austin, TX 78701
P.O. Box 13025, Austin, TX 78711-3025
Tel: (512) 475-4993  Fax: (512) 475-4994  Internet: www.soah.state.tx.us

**Employees: 115  Fiscal Year: 2014  Budget: $9,674,576**

■Chief Administrative Law Judge **Lesli Ginn** . . . . . . . . . . . (512) 475-4993
 E-mail: lesli.ginn@soah.state.tx.us
 Education: Texas State (San Marcos) BS; Houston JD
 Executive Assistant **Norma Lopez** . . . . . . . . . . . . . . . . . (512) 475-1276
Chief Financial Officer **Kimberly "Kim" Dudish** . . . . . . . . (512) 463-8575
General Counsel **Tom Walston** . . . . . . . . . . . . . . . . . . . . . (512) 936-0711
Administrative License Revocation Team Leader and
 Field Office Coordinator **John Beeler** . . . . . . . . . . . . . . (512) 463-7510
Alternative Dispute Resolution Team Leader
 **Howard Seitzman** . . . . . . . . . . . . . . . . . . . . . . . . . . . . (512) 936-0721
Economic Team Leader **Gary W. Elkins** . . . . . . . . . . . . . . (512) 305-9384
Licensing and Enforcement Team Leader
 **Suzanne Marshall** . . . . . . . . . . . . . . . . . . . . . . . . . . . (512) 475-1173
Natural Resources Team Leader **William Newchurch** . . . . . (512) 936-0716
 E-mail: bill.newchurch@soah.state.tx.us
Tax Team Leader **Victor J. Simonds** . . . . . . . . . . . . . . . . . (512) 936-0709

*(continued on next page)*

---

★ Elected Official   ■ Appointed by Governor   ● Appointed by Legislature   ▲ Appointed by Board or Commission   ◆ Appointed by State Supreme Court

EXECUTIVE BRANCH

**State Office of Administrative Hearings** *continued*

Utilities Team Leader **Lilo Pomerleau** . . . . . . . . . . . . . . . . (512) 936-0720
   E-mail: lilo.pomerleau@soah.state.tx.us
Docketing Supervisor **Susan Gage** . . . . . . . . . . . . . . . . . . . (512) 936-0735
Human Resources Supervisor **Pamela "Pam" Wood** . . . . . (512) 305-9386
Docketing and Support Staff Manager (Austin)
   **Susan Gage** . . . . . . . . . . . . . . . . . . . . . . . . . . . . . . . . . . (512) 936-0735
Information Resources Manager **Anthony "Tony" Gray** . . . (512) 463-1541
   E-mail: tony.gray@soah.state.tx.us
Direct Hearings Support Assistant **Tommy Broyles** . . . . . . (512) 936-0713

## State Office of Risk Management [SORM]

300 West 15th Street, Sixth Floor, Austin, TX 78711
P.O. Box 13777, Austin, TX 78711-3777
Tel: (512) 475-1440  Fax: (512) 472-0234  Internet: www.sorm.state.tx.us

**Employees:** 122  **Fiscal Year:** 2014  **Budget:** $52,240,761

▲Executive Director **Stephen S. Vollbrecht** . . . . . . . . . . . . . (512) 936-1515
   E-mail: stephen.vollbrecht@sorm.state.tx.us
   Education: Texas Tech 1998 JD
Deputy Executive Director **L. Todd Holt** . . . . . . . . . . . . . . (512) 936-1515
   Education: Texas Tech
Internal Operations Division Chief and Chief Financial
   Officer **Stuart B. Cargile** . . . . . . . . . . . . . . . . . . . . . . . (512) 936-1523
Legal Services Division Chief **Deea L. Western** . . . . . . . . . (512) 936-1503
   Education: Arkansas State; Arkansas JD
Strategic Programs Division Chief **Angela English** . . . . . . . (512) 936-2939
Training Coordinator **Michelle Hammett** . . . . . . . . . . . . . . (512) 936-1537

## Office of Public Utility Counsel [OPC]

1701 North Congress Avenue, Suite 9-180, Austin, TX 78701
P.O. Box 12397, Austin, TX 78711-2397
Tel: (512) 936-7500  Fax: (512) 936-7525

**Employees:** 26  **Fiscal Year:** 2014  **Budget:** $2,153,383

■Public Counsel **Tonya Baer** . . . . . . . . . . . . . . . . . . . . . . . . (512) 936-7500
   Term Expires: February 1, 2017
   Education: South Dakota BSBA, 2000 JD
   Special Assistant **Marie Boren** . . . . . . . . . . . . . . . . . . . . (512) 936-7500
      E-mail: marie.boren@opuc.texas.gov

## Texas Education Agency [TEA]

1701 North Congress Avenue, Austin, TX 78701-1494
Tel: (512) 463-9734  Fax: (512) 463-9838  Internet: www.tea.texas.gov

**Employees:** 804  **Fiscal Year:** 2014  **Budget:** $25,843,734,042

■Commissioner **Michael "Mike" Morath** . . . . . . . . . . . . . . (512) 463-8985
   Education: George Washington BBA
   State Board of Education Support Director
      **Renee Jackson** . . . . . . . . . . . . . . . . . . . . . . . . . . . . . . (512) 463-9007
■Chief Deputy Commissioner
   **Lizzette Gonzalez Reynolds** . . . . . . . . . . . . . . . . . . . . . (512) 463-8629
   E-mail: lizzette.reynolds@tea.texas.gov
   Education: Southwestern 1987 BA
Chief Information Officer **Melody Parrish** . . . . . . . . . . . . . (512) 463-9229
   E-mail: melody.parrish@tea.texas.gov
General Counsel **Von W. Byer** . . . . . . . . . . . . . . . . . . . . . . (512) 463-9720
   E-mail: von.byer@tea.texas.gov
Governance Director **Ron Rowell** . . . . . . . . . . . . . . . . . . . (512) 475-3697
   E-mail: ron.rowell@tea.texas.gov
Internal Auditor **Bill Wilson** . . . . . . . . . . . . . . . . . . . . . . . (512) 463-9846
Rule Making Director **Cristina DeLaFuente-Valadez** . . . . . (512) 475-1497
   E-mail: cristina.delafuente-valadez@tea.texas.gov

### State Board of Education

Tel: (512) 463-9007  Fax: (512) 936-4319
E-mail: sboesupport@tea.texas.gov

★Chair **Donna Bahorich** (R-Sixth District) . . . . . . . . . . . . . (832) 303-9091
   Term Expires: January 1, 2017
   P.O. Box 79842, Houston, TX 77279
   Education: Virginia Tech BS; Liberty 1990 MA

★Vice Chair **Thomas Ratliff** (R-Ninth District) . . . . . . . . . . (903) 717-1190
   Term Expires: January 1, 2017
   P.O. Box 232, Mt. Pleasant, TX 75456
   E-mail: thomas@thomasratliff.com
   Affiliation: Associate, Ratliff Company
   500 West 13th Street, Austin, TX 78701
   Education: Texas Tech 1989 BBA; Texas 1994 MPA
★Secretary **Ruben Cortez, Jr.** (D-Second District) . . . . . . . . (956) 639-9171
   Term Expires: January 1, 2019
   1875 Los Angeles Court, Brownsville, TX 78521
★Member **Lawrence Alvin Allen, Jr.** (D-Fourth District) . . . (713) 203-1355
   Term Expires: January 1, 2019        Fax: (713) 556-7243
   3717 Cork Drive, Houston, TX 77047
   Education: Prairie View A&M BS, MS
★Member **Erika Beltran** (D-Thirteenth District) . . . . . . . . . . (650) 269-8544
   Term Expires: January 1, 2019
   P.O. Box 17196, Fort Worth, TX 76102
   E-mail: ebeltransboe@gmail.com
★Member **David Bradley** (R-Seventh District) . . . . . . . . . . . (409) 835-3808
   Term Expires: January 1, 2019
   2165 North Street, Beaumont, TX 77701
★Member **Barbara Cargill** (R-Eighth District) . . . . . . . . . . . (512) 463-9007
   Term Expires: January 1, 2017
   1701 North Congress Avenue, Austin, TX 78701
   Education: Baylor BEd; Texas Woman's MSEd
★Member **Martha M. Dominguéz** (D-First District) . . . . . . . (915) 373-3563
   Term Expires: January 1, 2017
   1771 Billy Casper, El Paso, TX 79936
   Education: Texas (El Paso) BBA; Austin State MEd;
   New Mexico State PhD
★Member **Patricia "Pat" Hardy** (R-Eleventh District) . . . . . (817) 598-2968
   Term Expires: January 1, 2019        Fax: (817) 598-2833
   900 North Elm, Weatherford, TX 76086
   Education: Howard Payne BA; North Texas MEd
★Member **Tom Maynard** (R-Tenth District) . . . . . . . . . . . . . (512) 763-2801
   Term Expires: January 1, 2017        Tel: (512) 532-9517
   P.O. Box 625, Georgetown, TX 76527
   Affiliation: Executive Director, Texas Future Farmers of America
   Association
   314 East 12th Street, Austin, TX 78701
   Education: Texas Tech 1986 BS
★Member **Sue Melton-Malone** (R-Fourteenth District) . . . . . (254) 749-0415
   Term Expires: January 1, 2019
   101 Brewster, Waco, TX 76706
   E-mail: smelton51@gmail.com
   Education: Baylor BS
★Member **Ken Mercer** (R-Fifth District) . . . . . . . . . . . . . . . (512) 463-9007
   Term Expires: January 1, 2017
   P.O. Box 781301, San Antonio, TX 78278-1301
   Education: Texas BA; Texas (San Antonio) BBA;
   St Mary's U (TX) MBA
★Member **Geraldine "Tincy" Miller** (R-Twelfth District) . . . (972) 419-4000
   Term Expires: January 1, 2019        Fax: (214) 522-8560
   1100 Providence Tower West, 5001 Spring Valley Road,
   Dallas, TX 75244
   E-mail: tincymiller35@gmail.com
   Education: Southern Methodist BS; Texas A&M (Commerce) MS
★Member **Marisa B. Perez** (D-Third District) . . . . . . . . . . . . (210) 317-4651
   Term Expires: January 1, 2019
   P.O. Box 276406, San Antonio, TX 78227
   E-mail: marisa.perez@tea.texas.gov
   Education: Texas BA
★Member **Marty Rowley** (R-Fifteenth District) . . . . . . . . . . . (806) 374-4600
   Term Expires: January 1, 2017        Fax: (806) 373-3454
   P.O. Box 2129, Amarillo, TX 79105
   E-mail: marty@martyrowley.com
   Education: Eastern New Mexico 1979 BSBA; Texas Tech 1982 JD
Senior Executive Assistant **Renee Jackson** . . . . . . . . . . . . . (512) 463-9007

### Academics

Deputy Commissioner of Academics **Penny Schwinn** . . . . (512) 463-9734
   Education: UC Berkeley 2004 BA; Johns Hopkins 2006 MAT

### Educator Support

Deputy Commissioner of Educator Support
   **Martin Winchester** . . . . . . . . . . . . . . . . . . . . . . . . . . . . (512) 463-9734

---

★ Elected Official   ■ Appointed by Governor   ● Appointed by Legislature   ▲ Appointed by Board or Commission   ◆ Appointed by State Supreme Court

## Finance
Tel: (512) 463-9437

Deputy Commissioner of Finance **Kara Belew** . . . . . . . . . . . (512) 463-7038
Education: Texas 2004 JD
  Chief Technology Officer **Lara Coffer** . . . . . . . . . . . . . . . (512) 463-9229
    E-mail: lara.coffer@tea.texas.gov
  Student Data Systems **Sharon Gaston** . . . . . . . . . . . . . . . (512) 463-9229
    E-mail: sharon.gaston@tea.texas.gov
  Statewide Education Data Systems/Public Education
  Information Management System (PEIMS)
    **Melody Parrish** . . . . . . . . . . . . . . . . . . . . . . . . . . . . (512) 463-9229
    E-mail: melody.parrish@tea.texas.gov

## Governance
Deputy Commissioner of Governance **A.J. Crabill** . . . . . . . . (512) 936-1533

## Operations
Deputy Commissioner of Operations
  **Megan Aghazadian** . . . . . . . . . . . . . . . . . . . . . . . . . . . . . (512) 463-8880
  Governmental Relations Director **Julie Kopycinski** . . . . . (512) 463-9682
    E-mail: julie.kopycinski@tea.texas.gov

## Texas Municipal Power Agency [TMPA]

P.O. Box 7000, Bryan, TX 77805
Tel: (936) 873-1100  Fax: (936) 873-1183  Internet: www.texasmpa.org

General Manager **Bob Kahn** . . . . . . . . . . . . . . . . . . . . . . . . . (936) 873-1144
  Education: Ohio 1975 BA; Dayton 1978 JD
Chief Financial Officer **Russell Huff** . . . . . . . . . . . . . . . . . . (936) 873-1100
  Education: Texas A&M 1988 BBA
Plant Manager **Craig York** . . . . . . . . . . . . . . . . . . . . . . . . . (936) 873-1100
Regulatory and Security Manager **Jan Horbaczewski** . . . . (936) 873-1144
  Education: Durham (UK) 1972 BSc, 1976 PhD
Facilities Coordinator **Gary Teston** . . . . . . . . . . . . . . . . . . (936) 873-1100

## Bureau of Economic Geology [BEG]

University of Texas at Austin, University Station Box X,
Austin, TX 78713-8924
Tel: (512) 471-1534  Fax: (512) 471-0140
E-mail: begmail@beg.utexas.edu  Internet: www.beg.utexas.edu

Director **Scott W. Tinker, PhD** . . . . . . . . . . . . . . . . . . . . . . . (512) 471-1534
  Education: Trinity U 1982 BS; Michigan 1985 MS;
  Colorado 1996 PhD

## Texas Alcoholic Beverage Commission [TABC]

P.O. Box 13127, Austin, TX 78711
Tel: (512) 206-3333  TTY: (800) 735-2989 (Relay Texas)
Fax: (512) 206-3203  E-mail: questions@tabc.texas.gov
Internet: www.tabc.state.tx.us

**Employees: 639  Fiscal Year: 2016-2017  Budget: $100,000,000**

■Chairman **José Cuevas, Jr.** . . . . . . . . . . . . . . . . . . . . . . . . (512) 206-3217
  Term Expires: November 15, 2015
  E-mail: jose.cuevas@tabc.texas.gov
■Commissioner **Ida Clement Steen** . . . . . . . . . . . . . . . . . . . (512) 206-3217
  Term Expires: November 15, 2019
  E-mail: ida.steen@tabc.texas.gov
  Affiliation: Director, Board of Directors, Cullen/Frost Bankers, Inc.
  100 West Houston Street, San Antonio, TX 78205
  Profession: Private Investor
■Commissioner **Steve M. Weinberg, MD, JD** . . . . . . . . . . . (512) 206-3217
  E-mail: steve.weinberg@tabc.texas.gov
▲Executive Director **Sherry Cook** . . . . . . . . . . . . . . . . . . . . (512) 206-3217
  E-mail: sherry.cook@tabc.texas.gov
  Education: Texas State (San Marcos) BAAS

## Credit Union Commission

914 East Anderson Lane, Austin, TX 78752-1699
Fax: (512) 832-0278  E-mail: info@cud.texas.gov

■Chair **Manuel Cavazos** . . . . . . . . . . . . . . . . . . . . . . . . . . . . (512) 837-9236

■Member **Beckie Stockstill Cobb** . . . . . . . . . . . . . . . . . . . . (512) 837-9236
  Term Expires: February 15, 2021
■Member **Yusuf Elias Farran** . . . . . . . . . . . . . . . . . . . . . . . . (512) 837-9236
  Term Expires: February 15, 2021
  Education: Texas (El Paso) BSME, MS
■Member **Steven Gilman** . . . . . . . . . . . . . . . . . . . . . . . . . . . (512) 837-9236
  Term Expires: February 15, 2021
  Education: Cal State (Chico) BSBA
■Member **Sherri Merket** . . . . . . . . . . . . . . . . . . . . . . . . . . . . (512) 837-9236
■Member **Allyson "Missy" Morrow** . . . . . . . . . . . . . . . . . . . (512) 837-9236
■Member **Barbara "Kay" Stewart** . . . . . . . . . . . . . . . . . . . . (512) 837-9236
■Member **Gary Tuma** . . . . . . . . . . . . . . . . . . . . . . . . . . . . . . (512) 837-9236
■Member **Vik Vad** . . . . . . . . . . . . . . . . . . . . . . . . . . . . . . . . . (512) 837-9236

## Credit Union Department [TCUD]
**Employees: 24**

Commissioner **Harold E. Feeney** . . . . . . . . . . . . . . . . . . . . . (512) 837-9236
Deputy Commissioner **Robert W. Etheridge** . . . . . . . . . . . (512) 837-9236
Assistant Commissioner and General Counsel
  **Shari Shivers** . . . . . . . . . . . . . . . . . . . . . . . . . . . . . . . . . (512) 837-9236
    E-mail: shari.shivers@cud.texas.gov
Staff Services Officer **Linda M. Clevlen** . . . . . . . . . . . . . . . (512) 837-9236

## Texas Commission on Environmental Quality [TCEQ]

12100 Park 35 Circle, Austin, TX 78753
P.O. Box 13087, Austin, TX 78711-3087
Tel: (512) 239-1000  E-mail: commissr@tceq.texas.gov

**Employees: 2,767  Fiscal Year: 2015  Budget: $368,000,000**

■Chairman **Bryan W. Shaw, PhD, PE** . . . . . . . . . . . . . . . . . (512) 239-5500
  Term Expires: August 31, 2013
  E-mail: bryan.shaw@tceq.texas.gov
  Education: Texas A&M 1988 BS, 1990 MS; Illinois 1994 PhD
  Senior Advisor to the Commission **Marshall Coover** . . . . (512) 239-5527
  Assistant **Grace Bledsoe** . . . . . . . . . . . . . . . . . . . . . . . . . (512) 239-5519
■Commissioner **Toby Baker** . . . . . . . . . . . . . . . . . . . . . . . . . (512) 239-5515
  Term Expires: August 31, 2017
  E-mail: toby.baker@tceq.texas.gov
  Education: Texas A&M, MPA
  Executive Assistant and Counsel **Stephen Tatum** . . . . . . (512) 239-5537
  Assistant **Cristina Tejeda** . . . . . . . . . . . . . . . . . . . . . . . . (512) 239-5512
■Commissioner **Jonathan K. "Jon" Niermann** . . . . . . . . . . (512) 239-5505
  Term Expires: August 31, 2021
  Education: Oregon 2001 JD
  Executive Assistant and Counsel **Jim Rizk** . . . . . . . . . . . (512) 239-5535
  Assistant **Susie Smith** . . . . . . . . . . . . . . . . . . . . . . . . . . . (512) 239-5531
General Counsel **Tucker Royall** . . . . . . . . . . . . . . . . . . . . . . (512) 239-5525
  Special Assistant **Melissa Chao** . . . . . . . . . . . . . . . . . . . (512) 239-5234
Public Interest Counsel **Vic McWherter** . . . . . . . . . . . . . . . (512) 239-6363
                                        Fax: (512) 239-6377
Chief Auditor **Carlos Contreras** . . . . . . . . . . . . . . . . . . . . . (512) 239-0780
                                        Fax: (512) 239-3333
Chief Clerk **Bridget C. Bohac** . . . . . . . . . . . . . . . . . . . . . . . (512) 239-3300
                                        Fax: (512) 239-3311

## Executive Director's Office
Tel: (512) 239-3900  Fax: (512) 239-3939  E-mail: execdir@tceq.texas.gov

Executive Director **Richard A. Hyde, PE** . . . . . . . . . . . . . . . (512) 239-3900
  E-mail: richard.hyde@tceq.texas.gov
  Education: Texas A&M BS; Texas State (San Marcos) BS, MEd
  Special Assistant **Lori Wilson** . . . . . . . . . . . . . . . . . . . . . (512) 239-1635
  Executive Assistant **Barbara Robinson** . . . . . . . . . . . . . . (512) 239-1279
Deputy Executive Director **Stephanie Bergeron Perdue** . . (512) 239-3900
  E-mail: stephanie.bergeron_perdue@tceq.texas.gov
  Education: South Texas 1995 JD
  Special Assistant **Emily Lindley** . . . . . . . . . . . . . . . . . . . (512) 239-4086
  Technical Advisor **Minor Hibbs, PE** . . . . . . . . . . . . . . . . (512) 239-6590
Agency Communications Division Director
  **Terry Clawson** . . . . . . . . . . . . . . . . . . . . . . . . . . . . . . . . (512) 239-5544
    E-mail: ac@tceq.texas.gov             Fax: (512) 239-5010
    E-mail: terry.clawson@tceq.texas.gov

*(continued on next page)*

---

★ Elected Official  ■Appointed by Governor  ●Appointed by Legislature  ▲Appointed by Board or Commission  ◆Appointed by State Supreme Court

EXECUTIVE BRANCH

**Executive Director's Office** *continued*

Environmental Assistance Division Director
  **Brian Christian** . . . . . . . . . . . . . . . . . . . . . . . . . (512) 239-5007
      Fax: (512) 239-5678
Intergovernmental Relations Division Director
  **Mark Harmon** . . . . . . . . . . . . . . . . . . . . . . . . . . (512) 239-5022
      E-mail: mark.harmon@tceq.texas.gov    Fax: (512) 239-3335
Toxicology Division Director **Michael Honeycutt, PhD** . . . (512) 239-1793
      Fax: (512) 239-1794
Take Care of Texas Program Director **John Bentley** . . . . . . (512) 239-6786

## Administrative Services Office

Tel: (512) 239-0590  Fax: (512) 239-0596  E-mail: admin@tceq.texas.gov

Deputy Director **John Racanelli** . . . . . . . . . . . . . . . . . . . (512) 239-0590
      E-mail: john.racanelli@tceq.texas.gov
  Administrative Assistant **Tabitha Martin** . . . . . . . . . . . . . (512) 239-2935
Budget and Planning Division Director
  **Elizabeth Sifuentez** . . . . . . . . . . . . . . . . . . . . . . . (512) 239-4713
      E-mail: elizabeth.sifuentez@tceq.texas.gov    Fax: (512) 239-0222
Chief Financial Officer **Liz Day** . . . . . . . . . . . . . . . . . . . (512) 239-0299
      Fax: (512) 239-0664
Financial Administration Division Director
  **Greg Yturralde** . . . . . . . . . . . . . . . . . . . . . . . . . . (512) 239-1952
      E-mail: greg.yturralde@tceq.texas.gov    Fax: (512) 239-0371
Human Resources and Staff Development Division
  Director **Melissa Applegate, PHR** . . . . . . . . . . . . . . . (512) 239-5890
      Fax: (512) 239-5700
Information Resources Division Director **Greg Rogers** . . . . (512) 239-4782
      E-mail: greg.rogers@tceq.texas.gov    Fax: (512) 239-0888

## Compliance and Enforcement Office

Tel: (512) 239-5100  Fax: (512) 239-4390  E-mail: oce@tceq.texas.gov

Deputy Director **Ramiro Garcia, Jr.** . . . . . . . . . . . . . . . . (512) 239-5100
  Executive Assistant **Monica Aplin** . . . . . . . . . . . . . . . (512) 239-0640
Critical Infrastructure Division Director **Kelly Cook** . . . . . . (512) 239-0044
      Fax: (512) 239-1781
Enforcement Division Director **Bryan H. Sinclair** . . . . . . . (512) 239-2171
      Fax: (512) 239-4562
Monitoring Division Director **Cory Chism** . . . . . . . . . . . . (512) 239-0539
      Fax: (512) 239-0867
  Field Operations Border and Permian Basin Area
    Director **David A. Ramirez** . . . . . . . . . . . . . . . . . (956) 425-6010
        Fax: (956) 412-5059
  Field Operations Central Texas Area Director
    **Susan Jablonski, PE** . . . . . . . . . . . . . . . . . . . . . (512) 239-6731
  Field Operations Coastal and East Texas Area Director
    **Kelly Keel Linden** . . . . . . . . . . . . . . . . . . . . . . . (512) 239-3607
  Field Operations North Central and West Texas Area
    Director **Randy J. Ammons** . . . . . . . . . . . . . . . . . (806) 796-7092
        Fax: (806) 796-7107

## Legal Services Office

Tel: (512) 239-0600  Fax: (512) 239-0606
E-mail: olsadmin@tceq.texas.gov

Deputy Director **Caroline Sweeney** . . . . . . . . . . . . . . . . (512) 239-0665
  Education: South Texas 1993 JD
  Executive Assistant **Jackie Heinemann** . . . . . . . . . . . . (512) 239-0229
Environmental Law Division Director **Robert Martinez** . . . (512) 239-0681
General Law Division Director **David Timberger** . . . . . . . . (512) 239-2584
Litigation Division Director **Kathleen Decker** . . . . . . . . . . (512) 239-3424
      Fax: (512) 239-3434

## Office of Air

Tel: (512) 239-2104  Fax: (512) 239-3341

Deputy Director **Steve Hagle, PE** . . . . . . . . . . . . . . . . . (512) 239-2104
  Executive Assistant **Keisha Townsend** . . . . . . . . . . . . (512) 239-6520
Air Permits Division Director
  **Michael P. "Mike" Wilson, PE** . . . . . . . . . . . . . . . . (512) 239-1924
Air Quality Division Director **David Brymer** . . . . . . . . . . . (512) 239-1725
      Fax: (512) 239-6188

## Office of Waste

Tel: (512) 239-2300  Fax: (512) 239-0659

Deputy Director **Brent Wade** . . . . . . . . . . . . . . . . . . . . (512) 239-6566

Executive Assistant **Rachel Kradjel** . . . . . . . . . . . . . . . . (512) 239-0609
Permitting and Registration Support Division Director
  **Jaya Zyman** . . . . . . . . . . . . . . . . . . . . . . . . . . . (512) 239-2012
Radioactive Materials Division Director
  **Charles Maguire** . . . . . . . . . . . . . . . . . . . . . . . . (512) 239-5308
      E-mail: charles.maguire@tceq.texas.gov
Remediation Division Director **Beth Seaton** . . . . . . . . . . . (512) 239-2526
      Fax: (512) 239-6400
Waste Permits Division Director **Earl Lott** . . . . . . . . . . . . (512) 239-2047

## Office of Water

Tel: (512) 239-6696  Fax: (512) 239-5737

Deputy Director **L'Oreal W. Stepney, PE** . . . . . . . . . . . . (512) 239-1321
  Executive Assistant **Shannon Harris** . . . . . . . . . . . . . (512) 239-5735
Water Availability Division Director **Kim Wilson** . . . . . . . . (512) 239-4691
      Tel: (512) 239-2214
Water Quality Division Director **David W. Galindo** . . . . . . . (512) 239-0951
      Tel: (512) 239-4430
Water Quality Planning Division Director **Kelly Holligan** . . (512) 239-2369
      Fax: (512) 239-4732
Water Supply Division Director **Linda Brookins** . . . . . . . . (512) 239-4625
      Fax: (512) 239-2214

# Texas Ethics Commission [TEC]

201 East 14th Street, 10th Floor, Austin, TX 78701
P.O. Box 12070, Austin, TX 78711-2070
Tel: (512) 463-5800  TTY: (800) 735-2989  Fax: (512) 463-5777
Internet: www.ethics.state.tx.us

● Chair **Ambassador Charles G. "Chase" Untermeyer** . . . (512) 463-5800
    Term Expires: November 19, 2017
    Education: Harvard 1968 BA
■ Vice Chair **Tom Harrison** . . . . . . . . . . . . . . . . . . . . . (512) 463-5800
  Commissioner **Hugh C. Akin** . . . . . . . . . . . . . . . . . . . (512) 463-5800
    Note: Appointed by the Lieutenant Governor.
    Term Expires: November 19, 2017
■ Commissioner **James "Jim" Clancy, Jr.** . . . . . . . . . . . . (512) 463-5800
    Term Expires: November 19, 2017
    Affiliation: Attorney and Partner, Branscomb P.C.
    802 North Carancahua, Suite 1900, Corpus Christi, TX 78470
    Education: West Point 1986 BS; Texas 1995 JD
  Commissioner **Wilhelmina Delco** . . . . . . . . . . . . . . . . (512) 463-5800
    Note: Appointed by the Lieutenant Governor.
    Term Expires: November 19, 2015
● Commissioner **Paul William Hobby** . . . . . . . . . . . . . . (512) 463-5800
    Term Expires: November 19, 2015
    Education: Virginia BA; Texas
■ Commissioner **Robert "Bob" Long** . . . . . . . . . . . . . . . (512) 463-5800
    Term Expires: November 19, 2015
    Education: Texas A&M
■ Commissioner **Thomas "Tom" Ramsay, ANG** . . . . . . . . (512) 463-5800
    Term Expires: November 19, 2017
    Education: Southern Methodist

# Texas Facilities Commission

P.O. Box 13047, Austin, TX 78711-3047
Tel: (512) 463-3446  Fax: (512) 463-7966
E-mail: openrecords@tfc.state.tx.us  Internet: www.tfc.state.tx.us

**Employees: 415  Fiscal Year: 2014  Budget: $91,702,069**

■ Chairman **Robert D. Thomas** . . . . . . . . . . . . . . . . . . (512) 463-3446
    Term Expires: January 31, 2021
    Education: Loyola U (New Orleans) 1990; Texas 1993 JD, 2000 MBA
■ Vice Chairman **Michael "Mike" Novak** . . . . . . . . . . . . (512) 463-3446
    Term Expires: January 31, 2019
■ Commissioner **William D. Darby** . . . . . . . . . . . . . . . . (512) 463-3446
    Education: Angelo State BBA; South Texas JD
■ Commissioner **Patti Jones** . . . . . . . . . . . . . . . . . . . . (512) 463-3446
    Term Expires: January 31, 2021
    Affiliation: Commissioner, Commissioners' Court, County of Lubbock,
    Texas
    904 Broadway, Room 101, Lubbock, TX 79401
  Commissioner **Jack W. Perry** . . . . . . . . . . . . . . . . . . . (512) 463-3446
    Note: Appointed by the Lieutenant Governor
    Term Expires: January 31, 2019

---

★ Elected Official    ■ Appointed by Governor    ● Appointed by Legislature    ▲ Appointed by Board or Commission    ◆ Appointed by State Supreme Court

■Commissioner **Betty Reinbeck** . . . . . . . . . . . . . . . . . . . . . (512) 463-3446
Term Expires: January 31, 2017
Affiliation: Executive Director, Economic Development Corporation,
City of Tomball, Texas
14011 Park Drive, Tomball, TX 77377-0820
Education: Sam Houston State BABA

# Finance Commission of Texas

State Finance Commission Building, 2601 North Lamar Boulevard,
Suite 201, Austin, TX 78705
Tel: (512) 936-6222  Fax: (512) 475-1505
E-mail: finance.commission@sml.texas.gov

■Chair **Stacy G. London, CMC** . . . . . . . . . . . . . . . . . . . . . (512) 936-6222
Term Expires: February 1, 2020
Education: Texas; Houston MBA
■Vice Chair **H. J. "Jay" Shands III** . . . . . . . . . . . . . . . . . . (512) 936-6222
Term Expires: February 1, 2018
Affiliation: President and Chief Executive Officer, First Bank & Trust
East Texas
104 North Temple Drive, Diboll, TX 75941
Education: Texas
■Member **Robert "Bob" Borochoff** . . . . . . . . . . . . . . . . . . (512) 936-6222
Term Expires: February 1, 2022
■Member **Hector J. Cerna** . . . . . . . . . . . . . . . . . . . . . . . . . (512) 936-6222
Term Expires: February 1, 2020
Affiliation: President and Chief Executive Officer, International Bank of
Commerce, Eagle Pass, International Bank of Commerce
2395 East Main Street, Eagle Pass, TX 78852
Education: Texas BBA
■Member **Margaret "Molly" Curl** . . . . . . . . . . . . . . . . . . . (512) 936-6222
Term Expires: February 1, 2022
Education: John Carroll BS
■Member **Phillip Holt** . . . . . . . . . . . . . . . . . . . . . . . . . . . . (512) 936-6222
Term Expires: February 1, 2022
Education: Texas (Permian Basin) BS
■Member **Victor Leal** . . . . . . . . . . . . . . . . . . . . . . . . . . . . . (512) 936-6222
Term Expires: February 1, 2018
■Member **William Lucas** . . . . . . . . . . . . . . . . . . . . . . . . . . (512) 936-6222
Term Expires: February 1, 2018
■Member **Lori B. McCool** . . . . . . . . . . . . . . . . . . . . . . . . . (512) 936-6222
Term Expires: February 1, 2020
Affiliation: Principal, WoodWay Associate LLC
4900 Woodway Drive, Houston, TX 77056
Education: North Texas; Texas Tech; Baylor JD
■Member **Matt Moore** . . . . . . . . . . . . . . . . . . . . . . . . . . . . (512) 936-6222
Term Expires: February 1, 2022
Education: Texas A&M BBA
■Member **Paul Plunket** . . . . . . . . . . . . . . . . . . . . . . . . . . . (512) 936-6222
Term Expires: February 1, 2020
Education: Texas; Houston
Executive Director **Charles G. Cooper** . . . . . . . . . . . . . . . (512) 475-1325
Education: Baylor BBA

# Texas Department of Banking

State Finance Commission Building, 2601 North Lamar Boulevard,
Austin, TX 78705-4294
Tel: (512) 475-1300  Fax: (512) 475-1313

▲Banking Commissioner **Charles G. Cooper** . . . . . . . . . . . . (512) 475-1325
E-mail: charles.cooper@dob.texas.gov
Executive Assistant **Anne Benites** . . . . . . . . . . . . . . . . . . (512) 475-1325
Deputy Commissioner **Robert "Bob" Bacon** . . . . . . . . . . . (512) 475-1302
E-mail: bob.bacon@dob.texas.gov
Deputy Commissioner **Stephanie Newberg** . . . . . . . . . . . (512) 475-1332
E-mail: stephanie.newberg@dob.texas.gov
General Counsel **Catherine Reyer** . . . . . . . . . . . . . . . . . . (512) 475-1327
E-mail: catherine.reyer@dob.texas.gov
Bank and Trust Supervision Division Director
**W. Kurt Purdom** . . . . . . . . . . . . . . . . . . . . . . . . . . . . (512) 475-1333
E-mail: kurt.purdom@dob.texas.gov
Corporate Activities Division Director **Dan Frasier** . . . . . . . (512) 475-1322
Special Audits Division Director **Russell Reese** . . . . . . . . . (512) 475-1324
Strategic Support Division Director **Wendy Rodriguez** . . . . (512) 475-1320
E-mail: wendy.rodriguez@dob.texas.gov
Human Resources Manager **Lori Wright** . . . . . . . . . . . . . . (512) 475-1345

# Texas Department of Savings and Mortgage Lending [SML]

State Finance Commission Bldg., 2601 North Lamar Boulevard,
Suite 201, Austin, TX 78705
Tel: (512) 475-1350  Fax: (512) 475-1505  E-mail: smlinfo@sml.texas.gov
Internet: www.sml.texas.gov

Commissioner **Caroline C. Jones** . . . . . . . . . . . . . . . . . . . (512) 475-1352
Education: Tulane; St Mary's U (TX) JD
Administration and Finance Director **Antonia Antov** . . . . . (512) 475-1350
E-mail: aantov@sml.texas.gov
Licensing Director **Steven O'Shields** . . . . . . . . . . . . . . . . (512) 475-1350
General Counsel **Ernest Garcia** . . . . . . . . . . . . . . . . . . . . (512) 475-1350

# Texas Commission on Fire Protection [TCFP]

P.O. Box 2286, Austin, TX 78768-2286
Tel: (512) 936-3838  Fax: (512) 936-3808  E-mail: info@tcfp.texas.gov

**Employees:** 31  **Fiscal Year:** 2014  **Budget:** $1,946,059

■Presiding Officer **Robert Moore** . . . . . . . . . . . . . . . . . . . (512) 936-3838
Term Expires: February 1, 2021
■Assistant Presiding Officer **Joseph A. "Jody" Gonzalez** . . (512) 936-3838
Term Expires: February 1, 2019
Affiliation: Chief Fire Marshal/Emergency Management Coordinator,
Department of Emergency Services, County of Denton, Texas
9060 Teasley Lane, Denton, TX 76210-4010
Education: Southwest Texas State BA
■Secretary **John Kelly Gillette III** . . . . . . . . . . . . . . . . . . . (512) 936-3838
Term Expires: February 1, 2017
Education: Oklahoma State BA
■Member **Tommy Anderson** . . . . . . . . . . . . . . . . . . . . . . . (512) 936-3838
Term Expires: February 1, 2021
E-mail: tommy.anderson@tcfp.texas.gov
■Member **Elroy Carson** . . . . . . . . . . . . . . . . . . . . . . . . . . . (512) 936-3838
Term Expires: February 1, 2017
Affiliation: Insurance Agent, State Farm Mutual Automobile Insurance
Company
3602 Slide Road, Suite B7, Lubbock, TX 79414-2532
Education: Dallas Baptist BAcc
■Member **Carlos Cortez, Jr.** . . . . . . . . . . . . . . . . . . . . . . . (512) 936-3838
Term Expires: February 1, 2021
E-mail: carlos.cortez@tcfp.texas.gov
■Member **Kelly Doster** . . . . . . . . . . . . . . . . . . . . . . . . . . . (512) 936-3838
Term Expires: February 1, 2021
E-mail: kelly.doster@tcfp.texas.gov
Education: Louisiana Tech U BS
■Member **Pat Ekiss** . . . . . . . . . . . . . . . . . . . . . . . . . . . . . . (512) 936-3838
Term Expires: February 1, 2017
Education: Weatherford AA
■Member **Mike Jones** . . . . . . . . . . . . . . . . . . . . . . . . . . . . (512) 936-3838
Term Expires: February 1, 2017
E-mail: mike.jones@tcfp.texas.gov
■Member **John T. McMakin** . . . . . . . . . . . . . . . . . . . . . . . (512) 936-3838
Term Expires: February 1, 2019
Education: Texas (Attended)
■Member **Leonardo "Lenny" Perez** . . . . . . . . . . . . . . . . . . (512) 936-3838
Term Expires: February 1, 2019
E-mail: lenny.perez@tcfp.texas.gov
Education: Texas Southmost AA
■Member **Steven C. Tull** . . . . . . . . . . . . . . . . . . . . . . . . . . (512) 936-3838
Term Expires: February 1, 2021
■Member **Tivy Whitlock** . . . . . . . . . . . . . . . . . . . . . . . . . . (512) 936-3838
Term Expires: February 1, 2019
Education: Southwestern 1991 BA

## Commission Staff

▲Executive Director **Timothy Rutland** . . . . . . . . . . . . . . . . (512) 936-3812
E-mail: timothy.rutland@tcfp.texas.gov

---

★ Elected Official   ■ Appointed by Governor   ● Appointed by Legislature   ▲ Appointed by Board or Commission   ◆ Appointed by State Supreme Court

# Health and Human Services Commission [HHSC]

P.O. Box 13247, Austin, TX 78711-3247
Brown-Healty Building, 4900 North Lamar Boulevard, Austin, TX 78751
Tel: (512) 424-6500  TTY: (888) 425-6889  Fax: (512) 491-1967
E-mail: contact@hhsc.state.tx.us  Internet: www.hhsc.state.tx.us

**Fiscal Year:** 2014  **Budget:** $24,021,656,279

■Executive Commissioner **Chris Traylor** . . . . . . . . . . . . . . . (512) 424-6603
    Note: Until May 31, 2016.
    E-mail: chris.traylor@hhsc.state.tx.us
    Education: Texas Tech
■Executive Commissioner **Charles Smith** . . . . . . . . . . . . . . .(512) 424-6500
    Note: Effective June 1, 2016.
    E-mail: charles.smith@hhsc.state.tx.us
    Education: Texas Tech 1988 BA
    Assistant to the Executive Commissioner
      **Sandra Medel Reyes** . . . . . . . . . . . . . . . . . . . . . . . . . . (512) 424-6535
■Chief Deputy Executive Commissioner **Charles Smith** . . . . (512) 424-6502
    Note: Until May 31, 2016.
    E-mail: charles.smith@hhsc.state.tx.us
■Chief Deputy Executive Commissioner **Cecile Young** . . . . . (512) 424-6500
    Note: Effective June 1, 2016.
    E-mail: cecile.young@hhsc.state.tx.us
Chief Counsel **Karen Ray** . . . . . . . . . . . . . . . . . . . . . . . . . . .(512) 424-6614
Chief Ethics Officer **David A. Reisman** . . . . . . . . . . . . . . . (512) 424-6500
    E-mail: david.reisman@hhsc.state.tx.us
    Education: Wesleyan Col BA; Kentucky MPA, JD
Chief Operating Officer **Heather Griffith-Peterson** . . . . . . .(512) 424-6500
    Note: Effective June 1, 2016.
    Education: SUNY (Plattsburgh) BS
State Refugee Coordinator **Cecile Young** . . . . . . . . . . . . . (512) 424-6500
General Counsel **Carey E. Smith** . . . . . . . . . . . . . . . . . . . . (512) 424-6894
    Education: Austin State BA; Utah 1982 JD
Communications Director **Enrique Marquez** . . . . . . . . . . . (512) 424-6951
    E-mail: enrique.marquez@hhsc.state.tx.us
    Press Officer **Bryan Black** . . . . . . . . . . . . . . . . . . . . . . (512) 424-6951
      E-mail: bryan.black@hhsc.state.tx.us
      Education: Cal State (Fullerton)

## Health and Human Services Council

Tel: (512) 424-6603

■Chairman **Dr. Ben G. "Benny" Raimer, MD** . . . . . . . . . . .(512) 424-6603
    Term Expires: February 1, 2015
    Affiliation: Senior Vice President, Health Policy and Legislative Affairs,
    University of Texas Medical Branch at Galveston
    301 University Boulevard, Galveston, TX 77555-0144
    Education: East Texas Baptist; Texas (Galveston) MD
■Vice-Chair **Dr. Maryann Choi, MD, CMD** . . . . . . . . . . . . . (512) 424-6603
    Term Expires: February 1, 2017
    Affiliation: Geriatric Clinical Services Director, SunStar Geriatrics
    Healthcare
    501 South Austin Avenue, Georgetown, TX 78626
    Education: Texas A&M MPH; Hofstra MS
■Member **James "Richard" Barajas** . . . . . . . . . . . . . . . . . . (512) 424-6603
    Term Expires: February 1, 2019
    Education: Texas Wesleyan U
■Member **Sharon Swift Butterworth** . . . . . . . . . . . . . . . . . (512) 424-6603
    Term Expires: February 1, 2017
■Member **Antonio Falcon, MD** . . . . . . . . . . . . . . . . . . . . . .(512) 424-6603
    Term Expires: February 1, 2017
    Education: Baylor; Baylor Col Medicine MD
■Member **Manson B. Johnson** . . . . . . . . . . . . . . . . . . . . . . .(512) 424-6603
    Term Expires: February 1, 2015
    Affiliation: Pastor, Holman Street Baptist Church
    3422B Holman Street, Houston, TX 77004
    Education: Texas Southern
■Member **Leon J. Leach** . . . . . . . . . . . . . . . . . . . . . . . . . . . (512) 424-6603
    Term Expires: February 1, 2019
    Education: Rutgers; Widener MBA; Southwestern Baptist
■Member **Thomas Craig Wheat** . . . . . . . . . . . . . . . . . . . . . .(512) 424-6603
    Term Expires: February 1, 2019
    Education: Texas Tech
■Member **Teresa Durkin "Terry" Wilkinson** . . . . . . . . . . . . (512) 424-6603
    Term Expires: February 1, 2015
■Member **(Vacant)** . . . . . . . . . . . . . . . . . . . . . . . . . . . . . . . (512) 424-6603

# Department of Assistive and Rehabilitative Services [DARS]

4800 North Lamar Boulevard, Austin, TX 78756
Tel: (512) 424-4060  Tel: (800) 628-5115  TTY: (866) 581-9328
Internet: www.dars.state.tx.us

**Employees:** 3,210  **Fiscal Year:** 2014  **Budget:** $630,211,370

■Commissioner **Veronda L. Durden** . . . . . . . . . . . . . . . . . . .(512) 377-0600
    E-mail: veronda.durden@dars.state.tx.us
    Education: Northwestern BEd; Southwest Texas State MHA
    Executive Assistant **Tammy Miller** . . . . . . . . . . . . . . . . (512) 377-0601
Deputy Commissioner **David Hagerla** . . . . . . . . . . . . . . . . (512) 377-0614
    E-mail: david.hagerla@dars.state.tx.us
    Education: Auburn; Texas
Chief Financial Officer (Interim) **Ellen Baker** . . . . . . . . . . .(512) 377-0659
    Education: Texas A&M 1981 BBA
Chief Operating Officer **Daniel Bravo** . . . . . . . . . . . . . . . . (512) 377-0605
    Education: Texas
Internal Audit Director **Karin Hill** . . . . . . . . . . . . . . . . . . . (512) 424-4021
Legal Services Director **Sylvia Hardman-Dingle** . . . . . . . . (512) 424-4055

# Department of Aging and Disability Services [DADS]

701 West 51st Street, Austin, TX 78751
P.O. Box 149030, Mail Code W623, Austin, TX 78714
Tel: (512) 438-3011  TTY: (888) 425-6889  Fax: (512) 438-3884
Internet: www.dads.state.tx.us

**Employees:** 17,548  **Fiscal Year:** 2014  **Budget:** $6,598,215,222

■Commissioner **Jon Weizenbaum** . . . . . . . . . . . . . . . . . . . . (512) 438-3030
    E-mail: jon.weizenbaum@dads.state.tx.us
    Education: Texas, MSW
Internal Audit Director (Interim)
    **Charlotte Schneemann** . . . . . . . . . . . . . . . . . . . . . . . . . (512) 438-5638

# Department of Family and Protective Services [DFPS]

701 West 51st Street,, M.C. E-654, Austin, TX 78751
P.O. Box 149030, Austin, TX 78714-9030
Tel: (512) 438-4800  Fax: (512) 339-5880  Internet: www.dfps.state.tx.us

**Employees:** 12,252  **Fiscal Year:** 2014  **Budget:** $1,505,659,660

▲Commissioner **Henry "Hank" Whitman** . . . . . . . . . . . . . . (512) 438-4870
    Education: Southwest Texas State BS;
    Texas A&M (Corpus Christi) MPA
Deputy Commissioner **Kathleen "Katie" Olse** . . . . . . . . . . (512) 438-4800
    Education: Indiana
    Center for Consumer and External Affairs Director
      **Lesley Guthrie** . . . . . . . . . . . . . . . . . . . . . . . . . . . . . (512) 438-3318
    Center for Policy, Innovation and Program Coordination
      Director **Peter J. Hajmasy** . . . . . . . . . . . . . . . . . . . . . (512) 438-4124
      E-mail: peter.hajmasy@dfps.state.tx.us
Associate Commissioner **(Vacant)** . . . . . . . . . . . . . . . . . . . (512) 438-4800
General Counsel **Trevor Woodruff** . . . . . . . . . . . . . . . . . . . (512) 438-2910
Media Relations Manager **Patrick Crimmins** . . . . . . . . . . . (512) 438-3112
Consumer Affairs Manager **José Martinez** . . . . . . . . . . . . . (512) 929-6739

# Department of State Health Services [DSHS]

1100 West 49th Street, Austin, TX 78756
P.O. Box 12040, Austin, TX 78711-2040 (Vital Records)
P.O. Box 149347, Austin, TX 78714-9347
Tel: (512) 776-7111  Fax: (512) 776-7477
Fax: (512) 776-7711 (Vital Records)  Internet: www.dshs.state.tx.us

**Employees:** 12,321  **Fiscal Year:** 2014  **Budget:** $3,276,274,931

■Commissioner **Dr. John Hellerstedt, MD** . . . . . . . . . . . . . . (512) 776-7363
Associate Commissioner **Kirk Cole** . . . . . . . . . . . . . . . . . . .(512) 776-7375
Behavioral Health Medical Director
    **Lisa Cornelius, MD, MPH** . . . . . . . . . . . . . . . . . . . . . . .(512) 206-5936
Internal Audit Director **Thomas Martinec** . . . . . . . . . . . . . . (512) 776-7375
State Epidemiologist **Linda Gaul, PhD, MPH** . . . . . . . . . . .(512) 776-7375

---

## Texas Historical Commission [THC]

P.O. Box 12276, Austin, TX 78711-2276
1511 Colorado, Austin, TX 78701
Tel: (512) 463-6100 Fax: (512) 463-8222 E-mail: thc@thc.state.tx.us
Internet: www.thc.state.tx.us

**Employees:** 190 **Fiscal Year:** 2014 **Budget:** $25,131,968

■Chair **John L. Nau III**..........................(512) 463-6100
 Term Expires: February 1, 2021
 Affiliation: President and Chief Executive Officer, Silver Eagle
 Distributors, LP
 7777 Washington Avenue, Houston, TX 77007
 Education: Virginia 1968 BA
■Vice Chair **John Crain**..........................(512) 463-6100
 Term Expires: February 1, 2019
■Commissioner **Earl Broussard, Jr.**..............(512) 463-6100
 Term Expires: February 1, 2017
 Affiliation: Founder and President, TBG Partners
 Building 2, 901 South MoPac, Suite 350, Austin, TX 78746
 Education: LSU BA; Harvard MA
■Commissioner **Thomas M. Hatfield**...............(512) 463-6100
 Term Expires: February 1, 2017
 Education: Trinity U BS; Texas MA, PhD
■Commissioner **Wallace B. Jefferson**.............(512) 463-6100
 Term Expires: February 1, 2019
 Affiliation: Attorney, Alexander Dubose Jefferson & Townsend LLP
 515 Congress Avenue, Suite 2350, Austin, TX 78701
 Education: Michigan State 1985; Texas 1988 JD
■Commissioner **Tom Perini**......................(512) 463-6100
 Term Expires: February 1, 2017
■Commissioner **Gilbert E. Peterson**.............(512) 463-6100
 Term Expires: February 1, 2019
■Commissioner **Judy Richardson**.................(512) 463-6100
 Term Expires: February 1, 2017
■Commissioner **Robert K. Shepard**...............(512) 463-6100
 Term Expires: February 1, 2017
■Commissioner **Daisy Sloan White**...............(512) 463-6100
 Term Expires: February 1, 2017
■Commissioner **(Vacant)**.......................(512) 463-6100
■Commissioner **(Vacant)**.......................(512) 463-6100
■Commissioner **(Vacant)**.......................(512) 463-6100
▲Executive Director **Mark Wolfe**................(512) 936-4323
 E-mail: mark.wolfe@thc.state.tx.us

## Texas Commission on Jail Standards

300 West 15th Street, Suite 503, Austin, TX 78701
P.O. Box 12985, Austin, TX 78711
Tel: (512) 463-5505 Fax: (512) 463-3185 E-mail: info@tcjs.state.tx.us
Internet: www.tcjs.state.tx.us

**Employees:** 19 **Fiscal Year:** 2014 **Budget:** $910,490

■Chair **(Vacant)**..............................(512) 463-5505
■Vice Chair **Stanley Egger**.....................(512) 463-5505
 Term Expires: January 31, 2017
■Secretary **Dr. Michael M. Seale, MD**...........(512) 463-5505
 Term Expires: January 31, 2017
■Commissioner **Irene Armendariz**................(512) 463-5505
 Term Expires: January 31, 2015
 Affiliation: Network Development and Strategy Vice President, Superior
 HealthPlan
 2100 South IH 35, Suite 202, Austin, TX 78704
 Education: U Phoenix BS
■Commissioner **Allan Cain**......................(512) 463-5505
 Term Expires: January 31, 2017
 Education: Sam Houston State
■Commissioner **Jerry W. Lowry**..................(512) 463-5505
 Term Expires: January 31, 2019
■Commissioner **Larry S. May**....................(512) 463-5505
 Term Expires: January 31, 2019
■Commissioner **Gary Painter**....................(512) 463-5505
 Term Expires: January 31, 2015
 Education: Sul Ross State BS
■Commissioner **Dennis Wilson**...................(512) 463-5505
 Term Expires: January 31, 2015
 Education: Navarro
Executive Director **Brandon Wood**...............(512) 463-8236

## Texas Commission on Law Enforcement

6330 East Highway 290, Suite 200, Austin, TX 78723
Tel: (512) 936-7700 Fax: (512) 936-7714 Internet: www.tcole.texas.gov

■Presiding Officer **Joel Richardson**............(512) 936-7700
 Education: West Texas State 1992
Executive Director **Kim Vickers**................(512) 936-7712
 E-mail: kim.vickers@tcole.texas.gov
Agency Operations Director **John Helenberg**.....(512) 936-7768
 E-mail: john.helenberg@tcole.texas.gov
Chief Financial Officer **Brian Roth**............(512) 936-7725
General Counsel **John Beauchamp**................(512) 936-7746

## Texas Commission of Licensing and Regulation

E.O. Thompson State Ofc. Bldg., 920 Colorado, Austin, TX 78701
P.O. Box 12157, Austin, TX 78711
Tel: (512) 463-6599 Fax: (512) 475-2874

■Chairman **Mike Arismendez**.....................(512) 463-3173
 Term Expires: February 1, 2015
 Education: Texas Tech BBA
■Commissioner **Thomas F. Butler**................(512) 463-3173
 Term Expires: February 1, 2019
 Education: Houston BBA
■Commissioner **Helen Callier**...................(512) 463-3173
 Term Expires: February 1, 2021
 Education: Prairie View A&M BS
■Commissioner **Rick Figueroa**...................(512) 463-3173
 Term Expires: February 1, 2021
 Education: Texas A&M BBA, MS
■Commissioner **Catherine Rodewald**..............(512) 463-3173
 Term Expires: February 1, 2017
 Education: Northwood
■Commissioner **Ravi Shah, CBO**..................(512) 463-3173
 Term Expires: February 1, 2017
 Affiliation: Director, Development Services, City of Carrollton, Texas
 1945 East Jackson Road, Carrollton, TX 75006
 Education: Texas (Arlington)
■Commissioner **Deborah A. Yurco**................(512) 463-3173
 Term Expires: February 1, 2019

## Texas Department of Licensing and Regulation [TDLR]

P.O. Box 12157, Austin, TX 78711
Tel: (512) 463-6599 Fax: (512) 475-2871
E-mail: prosecutions@tldr.texas.gov

**Employees:** 382 **Fiscal Year:** 2014 **Budget:** $24,168,465

▲Executive Director **William H. Kuntz, Jr.**.....(512) 463-3173
 E-mail: executive.director@tdlr.texas.gov
 Education: LSU 1971 BBA; New Orleans 1974 MBA
Deputy Executive Director **Brian Francis**.......(512) 475-4765
 Education: Southwest Texas State 1987 BBA; St Edward's 1993 MBA
Assistant Deputy Executive Director **(Vacant)**..(512) 463-7182
 Executive Assistant **Tamala Fletcher**..........(512) 475-4765
 Executive Assistant **Christina Guzman**.........(512) 475-0583
 Executive Assistant **Kay Mahan**................(512) 463-3173
General Counsel **Brad Bowman**...................(512) 463-3306
 E-mail: brad.bowman@tdlr.texas.gov
 Education: Texas A&M 1992 BS; Houston 1995 JD
 Assistant General Counsel **Charles Johnson**....(512) 463-3306
  E-mail: charles.johnson@tdlr.texas.gov
 Assistant General Counsel **Lynn Latombe**.......(512) 475-2108
  E-mail: lynn.latombe@tdlr.texas.gov
 Assistant General Counsel **Pamela Legate**......(512) 463-7352
  E-mail: pamela.legate@tdlr.texas.gov
 Assistant General Counsel **Della Lindquist**....(512) 463-0589
  E-mail: della@tdlr.texas.gov
 Assistant General Counsel **Wendy Pellow**.......(512) 463-3306
  E-mail: wendy.pellow@tdlr.texas.gov
Enforcement Director **Christina Kaiser**.........(512) 539-5611
 Education: Texas 1989 BS, 1993 JD

*(continued on next page)*

---

★ Elected Official   ■ Appointed by Governor   ● Appointed by Legislature   ▲ Appointed by Board or Commission   ◆ Appointed by State Supreme Court

**Texas Department of Licensing and Regulation** *continued*

Compliance Director **George Ferrie** . . . . . . . . . . . . . . . . . (512) 475-4817
  Education: Texas 1983 BA
Communications, Education and Examination Director
  **Ray Pizarro** . . . . . . . . . . . . . . . . . . . . . . . . . . . . . . . . (512) 463-4190
Information Services Director **Simon Skedd** . . . . . . . . . . (512) 463-2923
  E-mail: simon.skedd@tdlr.texas.gov
Information Systems Development Director **(Vacant)** . . . . . (512) 463-3572
Licensing Director **Dede McEachern** . . . . . . . . . . . . . . . (512) 475-2896
Financial Management Director **Jerry Daniels** . . . . . . . . . . (512) 463-2924
Government Relations Officer **Michael A. Kelley** . . . . . . . (512) 463-7574
  E-mail: michael.kelley@tdlr.texas.gov
Public Information Officer **Susan Stanford** . . . . . . . . . . . (512) 463-3208
  E-mail: susan.stanford@tdlr.texas.gov

# Texas Lottery Commission

611 East Sixth Street, Austin, TX 78701
P.O. Box 16630, Austin, TX 78761-6630
Tel: (512) 344-5000  Fax: (512) 478-3682
E-mail: customer.service@lottery.state.tx.us  Internet: www.txlottery.org

**Employees:** 326.5  **Fiscal Year:** 2014  **Budget:** $208,316,335

■Chairman **J. Winston Krause** . . . . . . . . . . . . . . . . . . . . (512) 344-5000
  Term Expires: February 1, 2019
  Education: Texas 1977 BBA; Southern Methodist 1982 JD
■Commissioner **Carmen Arrieta-Candelaria** . . . . . . . . . . . (512) 344-5000
  Term Expires: February 1, 2017
  Education: New Mexico State 1988 BAcc, 2004 MBA
■Commissioner **Peggy A. Heeg** . . . . . . . . . . . . . . . . . . . . (512) 344-5000
  Term Expires: February 1, 2019
  Education: Louisville 1983 BA, 1986 JD
■Commissioner **Doug Lowe** . . . . . . . . . . . . . . . . . . . . . . (512) 344-5000
  Term Expires: February 1, 2017
  Education: Houston BS, JD
■Commissioner **Robert Rivera** . . . . . . . . . . . . . . . . . . . . (512) 344-5000
  Term Expires: February 1, 2021
  Affiliation: Council Member, Office of the Mayor and City Council,
  City of Arlington, Texas
  P.O. Box 90231, Arlington, TX 76004-0231
  Education: Texas (Arlington) BA
▲Executive Director **Gary Grief** . . . . . . . . . . . . . . . . . . . . (512) 344-5160
  E-mail: gary.grief@lottery.state.tx.us
  Education: Texas (Permian Basin) 1987 BBA

# Texas Parks and Wildlife Commission

4200 Smith School Road, Austin, TX 78744
Tel: (512) 389-4802  TTY: (512) 389-8915  Fax: (512) 389-4814

■Chairman **T. Dan Friedkin** . . . . . . . . . . . . . . . . . . . . . . (512) 389-4802
  Term Expires: February 1, 2017           Fax: (713) 580-5220
  1375 Enclave Parkway, Houston, TX 77077
  Education: Georgetown BSBA; Rice MBA
■Vice-Chairman **Ralph H. Duggins** . . . . . . . . . . . . . . . . . (512) 389-4802
  Term Expires: February 1, 2019           Fax: (817) 877-2807
  600 West Sixth, Suite 300, Fort Worth, TX 76102
■Member **Anna B. Galo** . . . . . . . . . . . . . . . . . . . . . . . . . (512) 389-4802
  Term Expires: February 1, 2019           Fax: (956) 796-9911
  1202 East Del Mar Boulevard, Suite 3, Laredo, TX 78041
  Education: St Mary's U (TX) BA
■Member **Bill Jones** . . . . . . . . . . . . . . . . . . . . . . . . . . . . (512) 389-4802
  Term Expires: February 1, 2017           Fax: (512) 469-6306
  100 Congress Avenue, Suite 2000, Austin, TX 78701
  Affiliation: Attorney and Owner, Jones Law Firm
  917 Franklin Street, Suite 600, Houston, TX 77002-1741
  Education: Texas A&M 1981 BBA; Baylor 1985 JD
■Member **Jeanne W. Latimer** . . . . . . . . . . . . . . . . . . . . . (512) 389-4802
  Term Expires: February 1, 2021           Fax: (210) 249-2161
  7801 Broadway, Suite 100, San Antonio, TX 78209
■Member **James H. "Jim" Lee** . . . . . . . . . . . . . . . . . . . . (512) 389-4802
  Term Expires: February 1, 2019           Fax: (713) 552-1441
  1330 Post Oak Boulevard, Suite 1550, Houston, TX 77056
  Affiliation: President, JHL Capital Holdings, LLC
  Education: Texas 1988 BBA, 1992 MBA

■Member **S. Reed Morian** . . . . . . . . . . . . . . . . . . . . . . . . (512) 389-4802
  Term Expires: February 1, 2021           Fax: (713) 863-8202
  300 Jackson Hill, Houston, TX 77007
  Affiliation: Chairman, President and Chief Executive Officer, Officers
  and Management, DX Service Company, Inc.
  8901 Telephone Road, Houston, TX 77061
■Member **Richard "Dick" Scott** . . . . . . . . . . . . . . . . . . . (512) 389-4802
  Term Expires: February 1, 2017           Fax: (713) 453-2756
  P.O. Box 2489, Wimberley, TX 78676
  Education: Lamar
■Member **Kelcy L. Warren** . . . . . . . . . . . . . . . . . . . . . . . (512) 389-4802
  Term Expires: February 1, 2021           Fax: (214) 981-0701
  8111 Westchester, #700, Dallas, TX 75225
  Affiliation: Chairman and Chief Executive Officer, Energy Transfer
  Equity, L.P.
  3738 Oak Lawn Avenue, Dallas, TX 75219

# Texas Parks and Wildlife Department [TPWD]

4200 Smith School Road, Austin, TX 78744
Tel: (512) 389-4802  TTY: (512) 389-8450  Fax: (512) 389-4814
Internet: www.tpwd.state.tx.us

**Employees:** 3,042  **Fiscal Year:** 2016  **Budget:** $436,721,976

Executive Director **Carter Smith** . . . . . . . . . . . . . . . . . . . (512) 389-4802
Deputy Executive Director of Natural Resources
  **Ross Melinchuk** . . . . . . . . . . . . . . . . . . . . . . . . . . . (512) 389-4868
  E-mail: ross.melinchuk@tpwd.texas.gov
Deputy Executive Director of Policy & Administration
  **Dawn Heikkila** . . . . . . . . . . . . . . . . . . . . . . . . . . . (512) 389-4727
  E-mail: dawn.heikkila@tpwd.texas.gov
Chief Financial Officer and Administrative Resources
  Division Director **Michael J. "Mike" Jensen** . . . . . . . . . (512) 389-4803
  E-mail: mike.jensen@tpwd.texas.gov
General Counsel **Ann Bright** . . . . . . . . . . . . . . . . . . . . . (512) 389-4804
Coastal Fisheries Director **Robin Riechers** . . . . . . . . . . . . (512) 389-4636
Communications Director **Josh Havens** . . . . . . . . . . . . . . (512) 389-4557
  E-mail: josh.havens@tpwd.texas.gov
  Education: Texas 2004 BA
Human Resources Director **Kent B. White** . . . . . . . . . . . . (512) 389-4808
  Education: New Mexico State 1988 BBA; Embry-Riddle 1997 MAS
Information Technology Director **George Rios** . . . . . . . . . . (512) 389-8066
  E-mail: george.rios@tpwd.texas.gov
Infrastructure Director **Jessica Davisson** . . . . . . . . . . . . . (512) 389-4741
Inland Fisheries Director **Craig Bonds** . . . . . . . . . . . . . . . (512) 389-4643
Intergovernmental Affairs Director **Harold Stone** . . . . . . . (512) 463-0840
Internal Affairs Director **Jonathan Gray** . . . . . . . . . . . . . (512) 389-4440
Internal Auditor **Cynthia "Cindy" Hancock, CIA, CFE** . . . (512) 389-4422
Law Enforcement Director **Col. Craig Hunter** . . . . . . . . . (512) 389-4845
Outreach and Education Director **Nancy Herron** . . . . . . . (512) 389-4362
  E-mail: nancy.herron@tpwd.texas.gov
State Parks Director **Brent Leisure** . . . . . . . . . . . . . . . . . (512) 389-4866
Wildlife Director **Clayton Wolf** . . . . . . . . . . . . . . . . . . . (512) 389-8092
Chief Diversity and Inclusion Officer **David Buggs** . . . . . . (512) 389-8595

# Texas Public Safety Commission

5805 North Lamar Boulevard, Austin, TX 78752
Box 4087, Austin, TX 78773-0110
Tel: (512) 424-2000  Fax: (512) 424-5708

■Chair **A. Cynthia "Cindy" Leon** . . . . . . . . . . . . . . . . . . (512) 424-7770
  Term Expires: January 1, 2016
  Education: Austin Col BA; Colorado MPA
■Commissioner **Manny Flores, Jr.** . . . . . . . . . . . . . . . . . . (512) 424-7770
  Term Expires: December 31, 2017
  Affiliation: Chief Executive Officer and Managing Partner, LatinWorks
  206 East 9th Street, Austin, TX 78701
  Education: Texas (San Antonio) BA
■Commissioner **Faith S. Johnson** . . . . . . . . . . . . . . . . . . (512) 424-7770
  Term Expires: December 31, 2015
  Education: Texas Southern JD
■Commissioner **Steven P. Mach** . . . . . . . . . . . . . . . . . . . (512) 424-7770
  Term Expires: December 31, 2019
■Commissioner **Randy Watson** . . . . . . . . . . . . . . . . . . . . (512) 424-7770
  Term Expires: January 1, 2018

---

★ Elected Official    ■ Appointed by Governor    ● Appointed by Legislature    ▲ Appointed by Board or Commission    ◆ Appointed by State Supreme Court

EXECUTIVE BRANCH

# Texas Department of Public Safety [DPS]

Tel: (512) 424-2000  E-mail: webmaster@dps.texas.gov

**Employees:** 9,165  **Fiscal Year:** 2014  **Budget:** $1,400,769,379

■Director **Steven C. "Steve" McCraw** . . . . . . . . . . . . . . (512) 424-7771
   E-mail: steven.mccraw@dps.texas.gov
   Education: West Texas State, MA
   Executive Assistant **Sophie Yanez** . . . . . . . . . . . . . . . (512) 424-7771
Deputy Director for Homeland Security and Services
   **Robert S. "Duke" Bodisch** . . . . . . . . . . . . . . . . . . (512) 424-2368
   Education: Houston 1978 BS
Deputy Director for Law Enforcement Operations
   **Col. David Baker** . . . . . . . . . . . . . . . . . . . . . . . . . . (512) 424-7774
   E-mail: david.baker@dps.texas.gov
Chief Auditor **Catherine A. Melvin, CIA, CPA** . . . . . . . . (512) 424-2158
Public Information Office Director **Katherine Cesinger** . . . (512) 424-2011
   E-mail: katherine.cesinger@dps.texas.gov
   Education: LSU 2004 BA
Emergency Management Chief **W. Nim Kidd** . . . . . . . . . . . (512) 424-2443
Administration Assistant Director **Amanda Arriaga** . . . . . . (512) 424-7772
   E-mail: amanda.arriaga@dps.texas.gov
Law Enforcement Support Assistant Director
   **Skylor Hearn** . . . . . . . . . . . . . . . . . . . . . . . . . . . . . (512) 424-7901
Criminal Investigations Assistant Director
   **Thomas Ruocco** . . . . . . . . . . . . . . . . . . . . . . . . . . . (512) 424-2130
   Education: St John's U (NY) BSCrimJ
Driver License Assistant Director **Joe Peters** . . . . . . . . . . (512) 424-5232
   E-mail: joe.peters@dps.texas.gov
Information Technology Assistant Director **Jon Percy** . . . . . (512) 424-2775
   E-mail: jon.percy@dps.texas.gov
Intelligence and Counter Terrorism Assistant Director
   **John Jones** . . . . . . . . . . . . . . . . . . . . . . . . . . . . . . . (512) 424-2000
Regulatory Licensing Assistant Director **RenEarl Bowie** . . . (512) 424-2320
   E-mail: renearl.bowie@dps.texas.gov
Texas Rangers Assistant Director **Randy Prince** . . . . . . . . (512) 424-7659
Statewide Communications Interoperability Coordinator
   **Todd Early** . . . . . . . . . . . . . . . . . . . . . . . . . . . . . . . (512) 424-2121
General Counsel **Phillip Adkins** . . . . . . . . . . . . . . . . . . . (512) 424-2891
   E-mail: phillip.adkins@dps.texas.gov
Inspector General **Rhonda Fleming** . . . . . . . . . . . . . . . . (512) 424-2000

# Public Utility Commission of Texas [PUCT]

William B. Travis Building, 1701 North Congress Avenue,
Austin, TX 78701
P.O. Box 13326, Austin, TX 78711-3326
Tel: (512) 936-7000  Tel: (888) 782-8477  Tel: (512) 936-7120 (Hot Line)
TTY: (512) 936-7136  Fax: (512) 936-7003  E-mail: web@puc.texas.gov
Internet: www.puc.texas.gov

**Employees:** 181  **Fiscal Year:** 2014  **Budget:** $626,456,755

■Chairman **Donna L. Nelson** . . . . . . . . . . . . . . . . . . . . . (512) 936-7015
   E-mail: donna.nelson@puc.texas.gov             Fax: (512) 936-7018
   Education: Black Hills State; Texas Tech 1986 JD
   Advisor **Laura Kennedy** . . . . . . . . . . . . . . . . . . . . . . (512) 936-7026
      E-mail: laura.kennedy@puc.texas.gov
■Commissioner **Kenneth W. Anderson, Jr.** . . . . . . . . . . . . (512) 936-7005
   Term Expires: September 1, 2017               Fax: (512) 936-7008
   E-mail: kenneth.anderson@puc.texas.gov
   Education: Georgetown; Southern Methodist 1981 JD
   Advisor **Rich Wakeland** . . . . . . . . . . . . . . . . . . . . . . (512) 936-7006
      E-mail: rich.wakeland@puc.texas.gov
■Commissioner **Brandy Marty Marquez** . . . . . . . . . . . . . . (512) 936-7025
   E-mail: brandy.marty@puc.texas.gov           Fax: (512) 936-7028
   Education: Texas BA; St Mary's U (TX) 2008 JD
   Advisor **David Smeltzer** . . . . . . . . . . . . . . . . . . . . . . (512) 936-7247
      E-mail: david.smeltzer@puc.texas.gov

# Texas Racing Commission [TXRC]

8505 Cross Park, Suite 110, Austin, TX 78754-4552
P.O. Box 12080, Austin, TX 78711
Tel: (512) 833-6699  Fax: (512) 833-6907  E-mail: info@txrc.texas.gov
Internet: www.txrc.texas.gov

**Employees:** 51  **Fiscal Year:** 2016  **Budget:** $7,681,200

■Chairman **Rolando B. Pablos** . . . . . . . . . . . . . . . . . . . . (512) 833-6699
   Term Expires: February 1, 2021
   Education: St Mary's U (TX) 1992; Texas (San Antonio) 1994 MBA;
   Houston 1996 MS; St Mary's U (TX) 1998 JD
■Vice Chairman **Ronald F. Ederer** . . . . . . . . . . . . . . . . . . (512) 833-6699
   Term Expires: February 1, 2019
■Commissioner **Gary P. Aber, DVM** . . . . . . . . . . . . . . . . (512) 833-6699
   Term Expires: February 1, 2021
■Commissioner **Gloria Hicks** . . . . . . . . . . . . . . . . . . . . . (512) 833-6699
   Term Expires: February 1, 2017
■Commissioner **Margaret Martin** . . . . . . . . . . . . . . . . . . . (512) 833-6699
   Term Expires: February 1, 2021
   Education: Laredo State
■Commissioner **Robert Schmidt, MD** . . . . . . . . . . . . . . . . (512) 833-6699
   Term Expires: February 1, 2017
   Education: Williams; Virginia MD
■Commissioner **John Thomas Steen III, CFA** . . . . . . . . . . (512) 833-6699
   Term Expires: February 1, 2019
   Education: Vanderbilt; Wharton MBA; Pennsylvania MA
Ex-Officio Commissioner **Glenn Hegar** . . . . . . . . . . . . . . (512) 833-6699
   Affiliation: Comptroller, Office of the Comptroller of Public Accounts,
   State of Texas
   Lyndon B. Johnson State Office Building, 111 East 17th Street,
   Austin, TX 78774
   Education: Texas A&M 1993 BA; St Mary's U (TX) 1997 MA,
   1997 JD; Arkansas 1998 LLM
Ex-Officio Commissioner **A. Cynthia "Cindy" Leon** . . . . . (512) 833-6699
   Affiliation: Chair, Texas Public Safety Commission, State of Texas
   5805 North Lamar Boulevard, Austin, TX 78752
▲Executive Director **Chuck Trout** . . . . . . . . . . . . . . . . . . (512) 833-6699
   E-mail: chuck.trout@txrc.texas.gov

# Railroad Commission of Texas [RRC]

P.O. Box 12967, Austin, TX 78711-2967
Tel: (877) 228-5740  TTY: (512) 463-6710  Fax: (512) 463-7161
Internet: www.rrc.state.tx.us

**Employees:** 807  **Fiscal Year:** 2014  **Budget:** $79,725,345

★Chairman **David J. Porter, CPA** (R) . . . . . . . . . . . . . . . . (512) 463-7131
   Term Expires: 2017
   Education: Harding 1977 BAcc
★Commissioner **Christi L. Craddick** (R) . . . . . . . . . . . . . . (512) 463-7140
   Term Expires: 2019
   Education: Texas BA; Texas (Brownsville) 1995 JD
★Commissioner **Ryan Sitton** (R) . . . . . . . . . . . . . . . . . . . (512) 463-7144
   Term Expires: 2021
   Education: Texas A&M
▲Commission Secretary **Kathy Way** . . . . . . . . . . . . . . . . . (512) 463-7865
   E-mail: kathy.way@rrc.state.tx.us

# Texas State Library and Archives Commission [TSLAC]

1201 Brazos Street, Austin, TX 78701
P.O. Box 12927, Austin, TX 78711-2927
Tel: (512) 463-5455  Fax: (512) 463-5436  E-mail: info@tsl.texas.gov
E-mail: commission@tsl.texas.gov  Internet: www.tsl.texas.gov

**Employees:** 164  **Fiscal Year:** 2015  **Budget:** $28,600,000

■Chair **Michael C. Waters** . . . . . . . . . . . . . . . . . . . . . . . (512) 463-5460
   Term Expires: September 28, 2019
   E-mail: commission@tsl.texas.gov
   Education: Lamar; Pittsburgh MHA
■Commissioner **Sharon T. Carr** . . . . . . . . . . . . . . . . . . . . (512) 463-5460
   Term Expires: September 28, 2017
   E-mail: commission@tsl.texas.gov
   Affiliation: Library Learning Resources Administrator, El Paso
   Independent School District
   6531 Boeing Drive, El Paso, TX 79925
   Education: North Texas MLS

*(continued on next page)*

★ Elected Official   ■ Appointed by Governor   ● Appointed by Legislature   ▲ Appointed by Board or Commission   ◆ Appointed by State Supreme Court

EXECUTIVE BRANCH

**Texas State Library and Archives Commission** *continued*

■ Commissioner **Dr. F. Lynwood Givens, PhD** . . . . . . . . . . . (512) 463-5460
  Term Expires: September 28, 2017
  E-mail: commission@tsl.texas.gov
  Education: Midwestern State; Texas MS, PhD

■ Commissioner **Larry G. Holt** . . . . . . . . . . . . . . . . . . . . . . (512) 463-5460
  Term Expires: September 28, 2021
  E-mail: commission@tsl.texas.gov
  Education: Baylor JD; Southern Methodist ML

■ Commissioner **Romanita Matta-Barrera** . . . . . . . . . . . . . (512) 463-5460
  Term Expires: September 28, 2021
  E-mail: commission@tsl.texas.gov

■ Commissioner **Wm. Scott McAfee** . . . . . . . . . . . . . . . . . (512) 463-5460
  Term Expires: September 28, 2019
  E-mail: commission@tsl.texas.gov
  Education: St Edward's; Southwest Texas State MBA

■ Commissioner **Martha Wong** . . . . . . . . . . . . . . . . . . . . (713) 622-7888
  Term Expires: September 28, 2021
  15 Greenway Plaza, Unit 16F, Houston, TX 77045
  E-mail: commission@tsl.texas.gov
  Education: Texas BS; Houston MEd, EdD

▲ Director and Librarian **Mark Smith** . . . . . . . . . . . . . . . . (512) 463-6856
  E-mail: msmith@tsl.texas.gov

# Texas Transportation Commission

125 East 11th Street, Austin, TX 78701-2483
Tel: (512) 305-9509  Fax: (512) 475-3072

■ Chairman **Tryon D. Lewis** . . . . . . . . . . . . . . . . . . . . . . . . (512) 305-9509
  Term Expires: February 1, 2021
  Education: Texas BA; Baylor 1973 JD

■ Commissioner **Jeff Austin III** . . . . . . . . . . . . . . . . . . . . . . (512) 305-9509
  Term Expires: February 1, 2019
  E-mail: jeff.austin@txdot.gov
  Education: Texas, MBA

■ Commissioner **J. Bruce Bugg** . . . . . . . . . . . . . . . . . . . . . . (512) 305-9509
  Term Expires: February 1, 2021

■ Commissioner **Jeff Moseley** . . . . . . . . . . . . . . . . . . . . . . . (512) 305-9509
  Term Expires: February 1, 2017
  E-mail: jeff.moseley@txdot.gov

■ Commissioner **Victor T. Vandergriff** . . . . . . . . . . . . . . . (512) 305-9509
  Term Expires: February 1, 2019
  E-mail: victor.vandergriff@txdot.gov
  Education: USC; Southern Methodist JD

# Texas Department of Transportation [TXDOT]

Tel: (512) 463-8585  Fax: (512) 463-9896  Internet: www.txdot.gov

**Employees:** 12,087  **Fiscal Year:** 2014  **Budget:** $11,092,157,085

▲ Executive Director **James M. Bass** . . . . . . . . . . . . . . . . . (512) 305-9501
  E-mail: james.bass@txdot.gov
  Education: Texas

Executive Secretary **Cassandra Mata** . . . . . . . . . . . . . . (512) 305-9515

Deputy Executive Director **Marc Williams** . . . . . . . . . . . . (512) 463-0151
  E-mail: marc.williams@txdot.gov

Director of Communications and Customer Service
  **Bob Kaufman** . . . . . . . . . . . . . . . . . . . . . . . . . . . . . . (512) 305-9503
  E-mail: bob.kaufman@txdot.gov

Director of Strategy and Innovation **Darran Anderson** . . . . (512) 305-9508
  E-mail: darran.anderson@txdot.gov
  Education: Texas

Chief of Staff **Rich McMonagle** . . . . . . . . . . . . . . . . . . . (512) 305-9502
  E-mail: rich.mcmonagle@txdot.gov
  Education: Notre Dame BSCE

Chief Audit and Compliance Officer **Benito Ybarra** . . . . . . (512) 463-8654

Chief Engineer **Bill Hale, PE** . . . . . . . . . . . . . . . . . . . . . (512) 305-9505
  E-mail: bill.hale@txdot.gov
  Education: Texas (Arlington) 1983 BSCE, 1989 MSCE

Chief Financial Officer **Brian Ragland** . . . . . . . . . . . . . . . (512) 305-9512
  Education: Austin State 1990 BBA; Southwest Texas State 1999 MBA

District Operations Director **Randy Hopmann, PE** . . . . . . . (512) 463-8585
  Education: Texas A&M 1984

Engineering and Safety Operations Director
  **Mark Marek, PE** . . . . . . . . . . . . . . . . . . . . . . . . . . . . (512) 463-8585
  Education: Texas 1981; Southwest Texas State 1986 MBA

Federal Affairs Director **Andrea Lofye** . . . . . . . . . . . . . . . (512) 463-6397
  E-mail: andrea.lofye@txdot.gov

Government Affairs Director **Jerry Haddican** . . . . . . . . . . (512) 936-7584
  Education: Texas BS; Florida 1995 JD

Human Resources Director **David McMillan** . . . . . . . . . . . (512) 486-5304
  Education: Houston

Innovative Financing and Debt Management Director
  **Benjamin H. Asher** . . . . . . . . . . . . . . . . . . . . . . . . . (512) 463-8611

Local Government Projects Director **David Millikan, PE** . . . (512) 416-2122

Rail Director **Erik Steavens** . . . . . . . . . . . . . . . . . . . . . . (512) 486-5230

Strategic Projects Director **Katherine D. Nees, PE** . . . . . . (512) 936-0965

Aviation Division Director **David S. Fulton** . . . . . . . . . . . (512) 416-4500
                                                          Fax: (512) 416-4510

Bridge Division Director **Gregg Freeby** . . . . . . . . . . . . . . (512) 416-2183

Civil Rights Division Director **Michael D. Bryant** . . . . . . . (512) 416-4700
  Education: Texas JD

Communications Division Director **Jess Blackburn** . . . . . . (512) 475-1388
  Education: Texas Tech

Compliance Division Director **Kristin Alexander** . . . . . . . (512) 465-7509
  Education: Texas BBA; St Edward's MBA

Construction Division Director **Tracy Cain** . . . . . . . . . . . (512) 416-2559
  Education: Texas 1996 BSCE          Fax: (512) 416-2539

Contracts and Purchasing Division Director
  **Janice Mullenix** . . . . . . . . . . . . . . . . . . . . . . . . . . . (512) 305-9508
  Education: Princeton 1976 BA; Georgetown 1979 JD

Design Division Director **Rene Garcia, PE** . . . . . . . . . . . . (512) 416-2197
  Education: Texas 1983

Environmental Affairs Division Director **Carlos Swonke** . . (512) 416-2734

Finance Division Director **Brian Ragland** . . . . . . . . . . . . . (512) 486-5555

General Services Division Director **Glenn Hagler** . . . . . . . (512) 302-2401
  E-mail: glenn.hagler@txdot.gov

Information Technology Division Director **Tim Jennings** . . (512) 305-9527
  E-mail: tim.jennings@txdot.gov

Internal Audit Division Director **Craig Otto** . . . . . . . . . . . (512) 463-8654

Maintenance Division Director **C. Michael Lee, PE** . . . . . . (512) 416-3034
  Education: Texas A&M 1988

Occupational Safety Division Director **Jerral Wyer** . . . . . . (512) 416-3385

Professional Engineering Procurement Services Division
  Director **Martin Rodin** . . . . . . . . . . . . . . . . . . . . . . (512) 416-2037

Public Transportation Division Director **Eric Gleason** . . . . (512) 374-5231

Right-of-Way Division Director **Gus Cannon** . . . . . . . . . . (512) 416-2852
  Education: Texas A&M (Kingsville) 1973

Strategic Contract Management Division Director
  **Frank P. Holzmann** . . . . . . . . . . . . . . . . . . . . . . . . . (512) 936-0965

Strategic Planning Division Director **Kent Marquardt** . . . . (512) 436-8588

Toll Operations Director **Richard Nelson** . . . . . . . . . . . . . (512) 874-9000
  Education: Rollins

Traffic Operations Division Director **Carol Rawson, PE** . . . (512) 416-3200

Transportation Planning and Programming Division
  Director (Interim) **Lauren Garduño, PE** . . . . . . . . . . . (512) 486-5003
  E-mail: lauren.garduno@txdot.gov
  Education: Texas Tech 1987 BCE; Abilene Christian 1991 MS;
  Texas A&M 1994 MCE

Travel Information Division Director **Joan Henderson** . . . . (512) 486-5900

Contract Services Office Director (Interim)
  **Kenneth Stuart** . . . . . . . . . . . . . . . . . . . . . . . . . . . . (512) 375-5120
  E-mail: kenneth.stuart@txdot.gov

General Counsel Division Director **Jeff Graham** . . . . . . . . (512) 463-8630
  Education: Washington U (MO) 2000 JD

Public Involvement Office Director **Jefferson Grimes** . . . . (512) 475-3097

Research Office Director **Dana Glover** . . . . . . . . . . . . . . . (512) 416-4730
  E-mail: dana.glover@txdot.gov

State Legislative Affairs Director **Trent Thomas** . . . . . . . . (512) 463-8622
  E-mail: trent.thomas@txdot.gov
  Education: Tarleton State

---

★ Elected Official    ■ Appointed by Governor    ● Appointed by Legislature    ▲ Appointed by Board or Commission    ◆ Appointed by State Supreme Court

# Texas Veterans Commission [TVC]

Stephen F. Austin Building, 1700 North Congress Avenue, 8th Floor,
Suite 800, Austin, TX 78701
P.O. Box 12277, Austin, TX 78711
Tel: (512) 463-6564  Fax: (512) 475-2395
E-mail: executiveoffice@tvc.texas.gov  Internet: www.tvc.state.tx.us

**Employees:** 383  **Fiscal Year:** 2014  **Budget:** $27,001,967

■Chair **Major Eliseo "Al" Cantu, Jr., USA (Ret)** . . . . . . . . . (512) 463-6564
  Term Expires: December 31, 2019
■Vice Chair **James H. "Jim" Scott, USAF (Ret)** . . . . . . . . (512) 463-6564
  Term Expires: December 31, 2015
■Secretary **Jake Ellzey** . . . . . . . . . . . . . . . . . . . . . . . . . . . (512) 463-6564
  Term Expires: December 31, 2017
■Member **Richard A. McLeon IV, USA (Ret)** . . . . . . . . . . . (512) 463-6564
  Term Expires: December 31, 2017
  Education: Texas A&M BS; Sul Ross State MBA
■Member **Daniel P. Moran, USMC (Ret)** . . . . . . . . . . . . . . (512) 463-6564
  Term Expires: December 31, 2019
  Education: Texas A&M BA

# Texas Workforce Commission [TWC]

101 East 15th Street, Austin, TX 78778-0001
Tel: (512) 463-2222  TTY: (800) 735-2989  Fax: (512) 936-0772
E-mail: customers@twc.state.tx.us

**Employees:** 2,931  **Fiscal Year:** 2016  **Budget:** $1,206,651,915

■Chairman and Commissioner (Public) **Andres Alcantar** . . . (512) 463-3030
  Term Expires: February 1, 2019
  Education: Texas Tech, MPA
  Executive Assistant **Billie Menchaca** . . . . . . . . . . . . . . . (512) 463-3030
■Commissioner (Employers) **Ruth Ruggero Hughs** . . . . . . . (512) 463-2800
  Term Expires: February 1, 2019
  E-mail: employerinfo@twc.state.tx.us
  Education: Texas; Rutgers JD
  Executive Assistant **Lisa Reid** . . . . . . . . . . . . . . . . . . . . (512) 463-2800
■Commissioner (Labor) **Julian Alvarez** . . . . . . . . . . . . . . . (512) 463-2829
  Term Expires: February 1, 2017
  E-mail: laborinfo@twc.state.tx.us
  Education: Texas A&M (Kingsville) BS
  Executive Assistant **Alicia Barrientos** . . . . . . . . . . . . . . (512) 463-2874

# Texas Board of Criminal Justice [TBCJ]

P.O. Box 13084, Austin, TX 78711
Tel: (512) 475-3250  Fax: (512) 305-9398  E-mail: tbcj@tdcj.texas.gov

■Chairman **Dale Wainwright** . . . . . . . . . . . . . . . . . . . . . . . (512) 475-3250
  Term Expires: February 1, 2021
  Affiliation: Managing Partner, Austin, TX Office, Bracewell LLP
  111 Congress Avenue, Suite 2300, Austin, TX 78701-4061
  Education: Howard U 1983 BA; Chicago 1988 JD
■Vice-Chairman **R. Terrell McCombs** . . . . . . . . . . . . . . . . . (512) 475-3250
  Term Expires: February 1, 2019
  Education: Houston BS; George Washington MBA
■Secretary **Leopoldo R. "Leo" Vasquez III** . . . . . . . . . . . . (512) 475-3250
  Term Expires: February 1, 2017
  Education: Yale BA; Columbia MBA
■Member **Thomas G. Fordyce** . . . . . . . . . . . . . . . . . . . . . . (512) 475-3250
  Term Expires: February 1, 2021
■Member **John "Eric" Gambrell** . . . . . . . . . . . . . . . . . . . . (512) 475-3250
  Term Expires: February 1, 2019
  Education: Texas A&M BA; Texas JD
■Member **Lawrence "Larry" Gist** . . . . . . . . . . . . . . . . . . . (512) 475-3250
  Term Expires: February 1, 2017
  Affiliation: Presiding Judge, Chambers of Presiding Judge Larry Gist,
  Second Administrative Judicial Region, Texas District Courts
  215 Franklin, Beaumont, TX 77701
  Education: Notre Dame; Texas JD
■Member **Pastor Larry Don Miles** . . . . . . . . . . . . . . . . . . . (512) 475-3250
  Term Expires: February 1, 2017
■Member **Derrelynn Perryman** . . . . . . . . . . . . . . . . . . . . . (512) 475-3250
  Term Expires: February 1, 2021
■Member **Thomas P. Wingate** . . . . . . . . . . . . . . . . . . . . . . (512) 475-3250
  Term Expires: February 1, 2019
  Education: Texas JD

Internal Audit Director **Christopher Cirrito** . . . . . . . . . . . . (936) 437-7100
  Two Financial Plaza, Suite 130,              Fax: (936) 437-2821
  Huntsville, TX 77340
State Counsel for Offenders Director **Rudolph Brothers** . . (936) 437-5203
  P.O. Box 4005, Huntsville, TX 77342-4005      Fax: (936) 437-5293
Inspector General **Bruce Toney** . . . . . . . . . . . . . . . . . . . . . (512) 671-2480
  4616 West Howard Lane, Suite 250,            Fax: (512) 671-2135
  Austin, TX 78728
PREA Ombudsman **Lynne Sharp** . . . . . . . . . . . . . . . . . . . . (936) 437-2133
  P.O. Box 99, Huntsville, TX 77342-0099       Fax: (936) 437-6981
Windham School District Superintendent
  **Dr. Clint Carpenter** . . . . . . . . . . . . . . . . . . . . . . . . . . . (936) 291-5303
  P.O. Box 40, Huntsville, TX 77342-0040       Fax: (936) 436-4031

# Texas Department of Criminal Justice [TDCJ]

P.O. Box 99, Huntsville, TX 77342-0099
Tel: (936) 295-6371  Fax: (936) 437-2123
E-mail: questions@tdcj.texas.gov  Internet: www.tdcj.texas.gov

**Employees:** 39,467  **Fiscal Year:** 2014-2015  **Budget:** $6,365,313,768

▲Executive Director **Brad Livingston** . . . . . . . . . . . . . . . . . (936) 437-2101
  E-mail: exec.director@tdcj.texas.gov
Deputy Executive Director **Bryan Collier** . . . . . . . . . . . . . . (936) 437-6251

## Executive Administrative Services

Tel: (936) 437-6391  Fax: (936) 437-2125

Chief of Staff **Jeff Baldwin** . . . . . . . . . . . . . . . . . . . . . . . . (512) 463-9776
                                                 Fax: (512) 936-2169
Public Information Office Director **Jason Clark** . . . . . . . . . . (936) 437-6052
  E-mail: jason.clark@tdcj.texas.gov           Fax: (936) 437-6055

# Texas Higher Education Coordinating Board [THECB]

1200 East Anderson Lane, Austin, TX 78752
P.O. Box 12788, Austin, TX 78711
Tel: (512) 427-6104  Fax: (512) 427-6127
E-mail: board.member@thecb.state.tx.us  Internet: www.thecb.state.tx.us

**Employees:** 280

■Chair **Robert W. "Bobby" Jenkins** . . . . . . . . . . . . . . . . . . (512) 427-6104
  Affiliation: President, ABC Home & Commercial Services
  9359 Interstate Highway 35 North, Austin, TX 78753
  Education: Texas A&M
■Vice Chair **Stuart West Stedman** . . . . . . . . . . . . . . . . . . . (512) 427-6104
  Term Expires: August 31, 2021
  Education: Texas 1979 BA, 1985 MBA, 1985 JD
■Secretary **David D. Teuscher, MD** . . . . . . . . . . . . . . . . . . (512) 427-6104
  Term Expires: August 31, 2017
  Affiliation: Orthopedic Surgeon and Partner, Beaumont Bone and Joint
  Institute
  3650 Laurel Street, Beaumont, TX 77707
  Education: Illinois; Texas (San Antonio) MD
■Member **Arcilia C. Acosta** . . . . . . . . . . . . . . . . . . . . . . . . (512) 427-6104
  Term Expires: August 31, 2019
  Affiliation: President and Chief Executive Officer, CARCON Industries
  & Construction, LLC
  8908 Ambassador Row, Dallas, TX 75247
■Member **S. Javaid Anwar** . . . . . . . . . . . . . . . . . . . . . . . . (512) 427-6104
  Term Expires: August 31, 2021
  Education: Wyoming
■Member **Dr. Fred Farias III** . . . . . . . . . . . . . . . . . . . . . . . (512) 427-6104
  Term Expires: August 31, 2019
  Education: Texas 1980; Southern Col Optometry 1987 DO
■Member **Ricky A. Raven** . . . . . . . . . . . . . . . . . . . . . . . . . (512) 427-6104
  Term Expires: August 31, 2021
  Education: Houston 1983 BS, 1986 JD
■Member **Wanda "Janelle" Shepard** . . . . . . . . . . . . . . . . . (512) 427-6104
  Term Expires: August 31, 2017
■Member **John T. Steen, Jr.** . . . . . . . . . . . . . . . . . . . . . . . . (512) 427-6104
  Term Expires: August 31, 2019
  Education: Princeton 1971 BA; Texas 1974 JD
■Student Representative **Christina Delgado** . . . . . . . . . . . . (512) 427-6104
  Term Expires: May 31, 2016

*(continued on next page)*

---

★ Elected Official   ■ Appointed by Governor   ● Appointed by Legislature   ▲ Appointed by Board or Commission   ◆ Appointed by State Supreme Court

EXECUTIVE BRANCH

**Texas Higher Education Coordinating Board** *continued*

■Student Representative **Haley Rader DeLaGarza** . . . . . . . . (512) 427-6104
   Note: Effective June 1, 2016.
   Term Expires: May 31, 2017

# Texas Juvenile Justice Department Board

■Chair **Scott W. Fisher** . . . . . . . . . . . . . . . . . . . . . . . . . . (512) 490-7004
   Term Expires: February 1, 2019
   E-mail: scott.fisher@tjjd.texas.gov
■Member **John A. Brieden III** . . . . . . . . . . . . . . . . . . . . . (512) 490-7004
   Term Expires: February 1, 2017
   E-mail: john.brieden@tjjd.texas.gov
■Member **Carol Bush** . . . . . . . . . . . . . . . . . . . . . . . . . . . (512) 490-7004
   Term Expires: February 1, 2019
   E-mail: carol.bush@tjjd.texas.gov
   Affiliation: County Judge, Office of the County Judge, County of Ellis,
   Texas
   Ellis County Courthouse, 101 West Main Street,
   Waxahachie, TX 75165
■Member **Rebecca A. "Becky" Gregory** . . . . . . . . . . . . . (512) 490-7004
   Term Expires: February 1, 2017
   E-mail: becky.gregory@tjjd.texas.gov
   Education: Dallas BA; St Mary's U (TX) JD
■Member **Jane Anderson King** . . . . . . . . . . . . . . . . . . . . (512) 490-7004
   Term Expires: February 1, 2017
   E-mail: jane.king@tjjd.texas.gov
■Member **David "Scott" Matthew** . . . . . . . . . . . . . . . . . (512) 490-7004
   Term Expires: February 1, 2017
   E-mail: scott.matthew@tjjd.texas.gov
■Member **Mary Lou Mendoza** . . . . . . . . . . . . . . . . . . . . (512) 490-7004
   Term Expires: February 1, 2019
   E-mail: marylou.mendoza@tjjd.texas.gov
■Member **Rene Olvera** . . . . . . . . . . . . . . . . . . . . . . . . . . (512) 490-7004
   Term Expires: February 1, 2017
   E-mail: rene.olvera@tjjd.texas.gov
■Member **Laura Parker** . . . . . . . . . . . . . . . . . . . . . . . . . . (512) 490-7004
   Term Expires: February 1, 2015
   E-mail: laura.parker@tjjd.texas.gov
■Member **Riley Shaw** . . . . . . . . . . . . . . . . . . . . . . . . . . . (512) 490-7004
   Term Expires: February 1, 2017
   E-mail: riley.shaw@tjjd.texas.gov
   Affiliation: Juvenile Chief, Office of the Criminal District Attorney,
   County of Tarrant, Texas
   401 West Belknap Street, Fort Worth, TX 76196-0201
■Member **Jimmy Smith** . . . . . . . . . . . . . . . . . . . . . . . . . (512) 490-7004
   Term Expires: February 1, 2015
   E-mail: jimmy.smith@tjjd.texas.gov
■Member **Calvin W. Stephens** . . . . . . . . . . . . . . . . . . . . (512) 490-7004
   Term Expires: February 1, 2015
   E-mail: calvin.stephens@tjjd.texas.gov
   Education: Houston 1972; Southern Methodist MBA
■Member **(Vacant)** . . . . . . . . . . . . . . . . . . . . . . . . . . . . . (512) 490-7004
■Member **(Vacant)** . . . . . . . . . . . . . . . . . . . . . . . . . . . . . (512) 490-7004

## Texas Juvenile Justice Department [TJJD]

Building H, 11209 Metric Boulevard, Austin, TX 78758
P.O. Box 12757, Austin, TX 78711-2757
Tel: (512) 490-7130  Fax: (512) 490-7717

**Employees: 2,855**

▲Executive Director **David Reilly** . . . . . . . . . . . . . . . . . . (512) 490-7004
   E-mail: david.reilly@tjjd.texas.gov
   Education: St Mary's U (TX) BA; Our Lady of Lake 1970 MSW
   Executive Assistant to the Executive Director
      **Jeannette Cantu** . . . . . . . . . . . . . . . . . . . . . . . . . . (512) 490-7004
Chief of Staff **Chelsea Buchholtz** . . . . . . . . . . . . . . . . . (512) 490-7779
General Counsel **Jill Mata** . . . . . . . . . . . . . . . . . . . . . . (512) 490-7103
   E-mail: jill.mata@tjjd.texas.gov
   Education: Trinity U BA; St Mary's U (TX) JD
Senior Director of Education Services **Luther Taliaferro** . . . (512) 490-7423
   Education: Texas (Tyler) BS; Texas A&M (Commerce) MS
Senior Director of Probation and Community Services
   **James Williams** . . . . . . . . . . . . . . . . . . . . . . . . . . . (512) 490-7991
   Education: Howard Payne

Senior Director of State Programs and Facilities
   **Teresa Stroud** . . . . . . . . . . . . . . . . . . . . . . . . . . . . (512) 490-7312
   Education: East Texas Baptist 1988 BA; Austin State 1995 MS
Senior Director of Training and Organizational
   Development **(Vacant)** . . . . . . . . . . . . . . . . . . . . . . (512) 490-7672
Director of Human Resources **Royce R. Myers** . . . . . . . . (512) 490-7673
   Education: Texas
Director of Monitoring and Inspections **Terri Dollar** . . . (512) 490-7747
   Education: Oklahoma State 1988 BS
Director of Operational Analysis and Facility Support
   **Chip Walters** . . . . . . . . . . . . . . . . . . . . . . . . . . . . . (512) 490-7130
Director of Training **Kristy Almager** . . . . . . . . . . . . . . (512) 490-7130
   Education: St Edward's 2000 MA
Director of Youth Placement and Program Development
   **Rebecca Walters** . . . . . . . . . . . . . . . . . . . . . . . . . . (512) 490-7130
   Education: Cornell 1990 BS; Texas 1992 MSW
Medical Director **Dr. Tushar Desai** . . . . . . . . . . . . . . . . (512) 490-7130
Chief Financial Officer **Mike Meyer** . . . . . . . . . . . . . . . (512) 490-7657
Chief Information Officer **Elaine Mays** . . . . . . . . . . . . . (512) 490-7102
   E-mail: elaine.mays@tjjd.texas.gov
Chief Internal Auditor **Eleazar Garcia** . . . . . . . . . . . . . (512) 490-7190
   Education: Texas BBA
Chief Inspector General **Roland D. Luna** . . . . . . . . . . . . (512) 490-7130
   Education: Sam Houston State BBA; Texas State (San Marcos) MA
■Independent Ombudsman **Debbie Unruh** . . . . . . . . . . . (512) 490-7993
   Term Expires: February 1, 2015
   E-mail: debbie.unruh@tjjd.texas.gov
   Education: Wayland Baptist
Communications Director **Jim Hurley** . . . . . . . . . . . . . . (512) 490-7016
   E-mail: jim.hurley@tjjd.texas.gov
   Education: Texas
Governmental Relations Director **Carolyn Beck** . . . . . . . (512) 490-7035
   E-mail: carolyn.beck@tjjd.texas.gov
   Education: Texas BA, MPA

## Texas State Securities Board

Rusk Building, 208 East 10th Street, Room 610, Austin, TX 78701
P.O. Box 13167, Austin, TX 78711-3167
Tel: (512) 305-8300  Fax: (512) 305-8336  Internet: www.ssb.state.tx.us

**Employees: 95  Fiscal Year: 2014  Budget: $6,986,591**

■Chair **Beth Ann Blackwood** . . . . . . . . . . . . . . . . . . . . (512) 305-8300
■Member **David Appleby** . . . . . . . . . . . . . . . . . . . . . . . (512) 305-8300
■Member **E Wally Kinney** . . . . . . . . . . . . . . . . . . . . . . (512) 305-8300
■Member **Miguel Romano, Jr.** . . . . . . . . . . . . . . . . . . . (512) 305-8300
   Term Expires: January 20, 2021
   Education: Florida State BA; Florida MIB
■Member **Alan Waldrop** . . . . . . . . . . . . . . . . . . . . . . . . (512) 305-8300
   Education: Texas 1984 BA, 1987 JD
Commissioner **John R. Morgan** . . . . . . . . . . . . . . . . . . (512) 305-8306

## Texas Water Development Board [TWDB]

1700 North Congress Avenue, Austin, TX 78711
P.O. Box 13231, Austin, TX 78711
Tel: (512) 463-7847  TTY: (800) 735-2989  Fax: (512) 475-2053
E-mail: customer_service@twdb.texas.gov  Internet: www.twdb.texas.gov

**Employees: 325  Fiscal Year: 2016-2017  Budget: $290,000,000**

■Chair **Bech K. Bruun** . . . . . . . . . . . . . . . . . . . . . . . . . (512) 463-7847
   Term Expires: February 1, 2019
   Education: Texas BBA, JD
■Board Member **Kathleen Thea Jackson** . . . . . . . . . . . . (512) 463-7847
   Term Expires: February 1, 2017
   Education: North Carolina State
■Board Member **Peter M. Lake** . . . . . . . . . . . . . . . . . . . (512) 463-7847
   Term Expires: February 1, 2021
   Education: Chicago BA; Stanford MBA

## Board Staff

▲Executive Administrator **Jeff Walker** . . . . . . . . . . . . . . (512) 463-7847
   E-mail: jeff.walker@twdb.texas.gov
Chief Financial Officer **Cindy Demers, CPA** . . . . . . . . . (512) 463-7854
   Education: St Edward's BA, MBA
General Counsel **Les Trobman** . . . . . . . . . . . . . . . . . . . (512) 475-1673

---

★ Elected Official     ■ Appointed by Governor     ● Appointed by Legislature          ▲ Appointed by Board or Commission     ◆ Appointed by State Supreme Court

Operations and Administration Deputy Executive
Administrator **Edna Jackson** . . . . . . . . . . . . . . . . . . . . (512) 463-8482
E-mail: edna.jackson@twdb.texas.gov
Texas Natural Resources Information Systems Deputy
Executive Administrator **Richard Wade** . . . . . . . . . . . . (512) 463-4010
Water Science and Conservation Deputy Executive
Administrator **Robert E. Mace** . . . . . . . . . . . . . . . . . . (512) 463-8043
Education: New Mexico Tech BS, MS; Texas PhD
Water Supply and Infrastructure Deputy Executive
Administrator **(Vacant)** . . . . . . . . . . . . . . . . . . . . . . . . (512) 936-9748
Internal Audit Director **Nicole Campbell** . . . . . . . . . . . . (512) 463-7978

# Office of the Lieutenant Governor

P.O. Box 12068, Austin, TX 78711
Tel: (512) 463-0001  Fax: (512) 936-0677  Internet: www.ltgov.state.tx.us

★Lieutenant Governor **Dan Patrick** (R) . . . . . . . . . . . . . . . (512) 463-0001
Term Expires: January 2019
E-mail: dan.patrick@ltgov.state.tx.us
Education: Maryland Baltimore County BA
Career: State Senator (R-TX, District 7), Texas State Senate
(2007-2015)
Chief of Staff **Logan Spence** . . . . . . . . . . . . . . . . . . . . (512) 463-0001
General Counsel **Darrell D. Dávila** . . . . . . . . . . . . . . . . (512) 463-0295
Education: Texas A&M; Texas JD
Communications Director **Keith Elkins** . . . . . . . . . . . . . (512) 463-0715
E-mail: keith.elkins@ltgov.state.tx.us
External Affairs Director **(Vacant)** . . . . . . . . . . . . . . . . . (512) 463-0001
Policy Director **Kate McGrath** . . . . . . . . . . . . . . . . . . . (512) 463-2525
Research Director **Travis L. Richmond** . . . . . . . . . . . . . (512) 463-0001
Education: Texas 2002 BJ; North Texas 2007 BA
Legislative Coordinator **Colby Beuck** . . . . . . . . . . . . . . (512) 463-4088
E-mail: colby.beuck@ltgov.state.tx.us
Policy Coordinator **John Gibbs** . . . . . . . . . . . . . . . . . . (512) 463-0001
Budget Analyst **Joaquin Guadarrama** . . . . . . . . . . . . . . (512) 463-0001
Senior Advisor **(Vacant)** . . . . . . . . . . . . . . . . . . . . . . . (512) 463-2998
Business and Commerce Policy Advisor **John Gibbs** . . . . (512) 463-0001
Criminal Justice Policy Advisor **Lauren Fleming** . . . . . . . (512) 463-0001
Education and Higher Education Policy Advisor
**Marian Wallace** . . . . . . . . . . . . . . . . . . . . . . . . . . . (512) 463-0001
General Government Policy Advisor
**Suzanne Mackowiak** . . . . . . . . . . . . . . . . . . . . . . . (512) 463-0001
Health and Human Services Policy Advisor
**Jessica Olson** . . . . . . . . . . . . . . . . . . . . . . . . . . . . (512) 463-0001
E-mail: jessica.olson@ltgov.state.tx.us
Intergovernmental Relations Policy Advisor **Julie Frank** . . . (512) 463-0001
Natural Resources Policy Advisor **Deb Mamula** . . . . . . . (512) 463-0001
Tax Advisor **Carolyn Merchan Seagert** . . . . . . . . . . . . . (512) 463-0001
Transportation Policy Advisor **Aaron Kocian** . . . . . . . . . (512) 463-0001
E-mail: aaron.kocian@ltgov.state.tx.us
Budget Director **Mike Morrissey** . . . . . . . . . . . . . . . . . (512) 463-0001
Education: Oklahoma 1981 BA; Arkansas 1985 JD
Parliamentarian **Karina Casari Davis** . . . . . . . . . . . . . . . (512) 463-0248

# Office of the Attorney General

300 West 15th Street, Austin, TX 78701
Tel: (512) 463-2100  TTY: (800) 252-8011  Fax: (512) 463-2050

**Fiscal Year:** 2016  **Budget:** $599,483,480

★Attorney General **Ken Paxton** (R) . . . . . . . . . . . . . . . . . (512) 463-2100
Term Expires: December 31, 2018
Education: Baylor 1985 BA, 1986 MBA; Virginia 1991 JD
Career: Legal Counsel, J. C. Penney Company, Inc. (1995-2002); State
Representative (R-TX, District 70), Texas House of Representatives
(2003-2013); State Senator (R-TX, District 8), Texas State Senate
(2013-2015)
Chief of Staff **Katherine Minter "Missy" Cary** . . . . . . . . (512) 463-2100
Education: St Mary's U (TX) 1990 JD
Deputy Chief of Staff **Steve Roddy** . . . . . . . . . . . . . . . (512) 463-2100
Education: Baylor 1985
Senior Advisor to the Attorney General **Ben Williams** . . . (512) 463-2100
Education: Texas (Dallas) MS
Senior Counsel to the Attorney General **Prerak Shah** . . . (512) 463-2100
Education: Chicago 2010 JD

First Assistant Attorney General **Jeff Mateer, Esq.** . . . . . . (512) 463-2100
Education: Dickinson Col 1987 BA; Southern Methodist 1990 JD
Deputy First Assistant Attorney General **Brantley Starr** . . . (512) 463-2100
Education: Abilene Christian; Texas JD
Deputy Attorney General for Administration **(Vacant)** . . . . (512) 936-2714
Deputy Attorney General for Child Support
**Mara Friesen** . . . . . . . . . . . . . . . . . . . . . . . . . . . . (512) 460-6000
E-mail: mara.friesen@texasattorneygeneral.gov
Deputy Attorney General for Civil Litigation **Jim Davis** . . . (512) 463-2191
Education: Texas 1996 BA; Harvard 1999 JD
Deputy Attorney General for Criminal Justice
**Adrienne McFarland** . . . . . . . . . . . . . . . . . . . . . . . (512) 463-2191
Education: Texas A&M 1988 BS; South Texas 1991 JD
Deputy Attorney General for Legal Counsel **(Vacant)** . . . . (512) 463-2191
Associate Deputy for General and Legal Counsel
**Amanda Crawford** . . . . . . . . . . . . . . . . . . . . . . . . (512) 936-6736
Education: Houston 1999 JD
Crime Victims Services Division Chief **Gene McCleskey** . . (512) 936-1200
Environmental Protection Division Chief
**Priscilla M. Hubenak** . . . . . . . . . . . . . . . . . . . . . . . (512) 463-2012
Education: St Edward's BS; Houston JD
Financial Litigation and Charitable Trusts Division Chief
**(Vacant)** . . . . . . . . . . . . . . . . . . . . . . . . . . . . . . . (512) 463-2018
General Litigation Division Chief **Angela Colmenero** . . . . (512) 463-2120
Education: Texas; Notre Dame JD
Tax Division Chief **Robert O'Keefe** . . . . . . . . . . . . . . . (512) 463-2002
Education: South Texas 1974 JD
Solicitor General **Scott A. Keller** . . . . . . . . . . . . . . . . . (512) 936-2191
Education: Texas 2007 JD
Chief Information Officer **Rudy Montoya** . . . . . . . . . . . . (512) 936-1323
E-mail: rudy.montoya@texasattorneygeneral.gov
Education: Texas A&M 1989
Director of Communications **Marc Rylander** . . . . . . . . . . (512) 463-2191
E-mail: marc.rylander@texasattorneygeneral.gov
Director of Government Relations and Strategic
Initiatives **Steve Pier** . . . . . . . . . . . . . . . . . . . . . . (512) 463-2191
Director of Law Enforcement **David Maxwell** . . . . . . . . . (512) 463-2191
Director of Scheduling **Katie Lawhon** . . . . . . . . . . . . . . (512) 936-1874
E-mail: katie.lawhon@texasattorneygeneral.gov
Education: Mississippi

# Medicaid Fraud Control Unit

P.O. Box 12307, Austin, TX 78711
Tel: (512) 463-2011  E-mail: mfcu@texasattorneygeneral.gov

# Office of the Secretary of State

State Capitol, P.O. Box 12697, Austin, TX 78711
Tel: (512) 463-5770  Fax: (512) 475-2761  Internet: www.sos.state.tx.us

**Employees:** 203  **Fiscal Year:** 2014  **Budget:** $37,760,982

■Secretary of State **Carlos H. Cascos, CPA, CGFM** . . . . . . (512) 463-5770
E-mail: secretary@sos.texas.gov
Deputy Secretary of State **Coby Shorter III** . . . . . . . . . . (512) 463-5770
Assistant Secretary of State for Mexican and Border
Affairs **Avdiel Huerta** . . . . . . . . . . . . . . . . . . . . . . (512) 463-5770
General Counsel **Lindsey Wolf** . . . . . . . . . . . . . . . . . . (512) 463-5770
Communications Director **Alicia Pierce** . . . . . . . . . . . . . (512) 463-6116
Administrative Services Division Director
**Vincent Houston** . . . . . . . . . . . . . . . . . . . . . . . . . (512) 463-5593
E-mail: vhouston@sos.texas.gov
Business and Public Filings Division Director
**Carmen Flores** . . . . . . . . . . . . . . . . . . . . . . . . . . (512) 463-5588
Business and Commercial Filings Section Director
**Mike Powell** . . . . . . . . . . . . . . . . . . . . . . . . . . (512) 463-9856
Information Technology Division Director **Scott Brandt** . . . (512) 463-5640
E-mail: sbrandt@sos.texas.gov
Financial Management Section Director **Louis Ng** . . . . . . . (512) 463-5594
Government Filings Section Director **Robert Sumners** . . . . (512) 463-5562
International Protocol Director **Cammy Jones** . . . . . . . . . (512) 463-5268
International Protocol and Communications Deputy
Director **Mari Bergman** . . . . . . . . . . . . . . . . . . . . (512) 463-5994
E-mail: mbergman@sos.texas.gov
Executive Assistant and Scheduler **Linda Payne** . . . . . . . (512) 463-5702
E-mail: lpayne@sos.texas.gov

★ Elected Official   ■ Appointed by Governor   ● Appointed by Legislature   ▲ Appointed by Board or Commission   ◆ Appointed by State Supreme Court

# State Auditor's Office [SAO]

Robert E. Johnson Building, 1501 North Congress Avenue, 4th Floor,
Austin, TX 78701
P.O. Box 12067, Austin, TX 78711-2067
Tel: (512) 936-9500  Fax: (512) 936-9400  E-mail: auditor@sao.state.tx.us
Internet: www.sao.state.tx.us

- State Auditor **(Vacant)** . . . . . . . . . . . . . . . . . . . . (512) 936-9500
  First Assistant State Auditor **Lisa Collier** . . . . . . . . . . . . . (512) 936-9448
  Assistant State Auditor and Audit Manager **Kelly Linder** . . (512) 936-9327
  Assistant State Auditor, Audit Manager and Quality
  Control Team **(Vacant)** . . . . . . . . . . . . (512) 936-9450
  Chief of Staff, General Counsel, and Risk Manager
  **Anita D'Souza** . . . . . . . . . . . . . . . . . . . . (512) 936-9340
  Audit Manager **Verma Elliott** . . . . . . . . . . . . . (512) 936-9611
  Audit Manager **Angelica Ramirez** . . . . . . . . . . . . . (512) 936-9602
  Audit Manager **James Timberlake** . . . . . . . . . . . . (512) 936-9672
  Audit Manager **John Young** . . . . . . . . . . . . . (512) 936-9577
  Business Services Director **Lisa Collier** . . . . . . . . . . (512) 936-9448
  Fax: (512) 936-9420
  Human Resources **Barry Holcomb** . . . . . . . . . . . . (512) 936-9773
  Information Systems Support and User Network Services
  **Jon Knippa** . . . . . . . . . . . . . . . . . . (512) 936-9757
  E-mail: jknippa@sao.state.tx.us
  Legislative Coordination and Risk Assessment
  **Kelly Linder** . . . . . . . . . . . . . . . . . (512) 936-9327
  E-mail: klinder@sao.state.tx.us
  Professional Development **Jo Dale Guzman** . . . . . . . . (512) 936-9460
  State Classification Team **John Young** . . . . . . . . . . . (512) 936-9577

# Office of the Comptroller of Public Accounts

Lyndon B. Johnson State Office Building, 111 East 17th Street,
Austin, TX 78774
P.O. Box 13528, Austin, TX 78711-3528
Tel: (512) 463-4600  Tel: (800) 252-5555  Fax: (512) 475-0352
Internet: www.comptroller.texas.gov  Internet: thetexaseconomy.org

**Employees:** 2,819  **Fiscal Year:** 2016  **Budget:** $312,870,461

- ★ Comptroller **Glenn Hegar** (R) . . . . . . . . . . . . . . (512) 463-4444
  Term Expires: January 2019
  Executive Assistant **Kimberley Buzard** . . . . . . . (512) 463-3991
  Deputy Comptroller and Chief Clerk **Mike Reissig** . . . . (512) 463-4260
  Education: Texas Lutheran BA
  Chief of Staff **Lisa Craven** . . . . . . . . . . . . . (512) 463-3920
  Associate Deputy Comptroller for Fiscal Matters
  **Phillip Ashley** . . . . . . . . . . . . . . . . . (512) 463-4275
  Education: Baylor BBA, MBA
  Associate Deputy Comptroller for Operations and
  Support **Robert Wood** . . . . . . . . . . . . . . (512) 463-3973
  Education: Texas A&M 1985
  Associate Deputy Comptroller for Tax **Karey W. Barton** . . (512) 463-3895
  Education: Texas A&M 1984 BS
  Chief Revenue Estimator **Tom Currah** . . . . . . . . . (512) 936-2568
  Senior Advisor for Fiscal Research **John Heleman** . . . . . (512) 475-0042
  E-mail: john.heleman@cpa.texas.gov
  Legislative Affairs Director **Brooke Paup** . . . . . . . . (512) 463-7252
  E-mail: brooke.paup@cpa.texas.gov
  Education: Texas A&M 2001; Texas Tech 2005 JD
  Educational Opportunities and Investments Director
  **Linda Fernandez** . . . . . . . . . . . . . . . . (512) 463-4863
  E-mail: linda.fernandez@cpa.texas.gov
  Fiscal Management Director **Rob Coleman** . . . . . . . . (512) 463-7630
  Property Tax Assistance Division Director **Mike Esparza** . . (512) 475-0288
  Education: Notre Dame 1983; Texas 1988 JD
  Texas Procurement and Support Services (TPASS)
  Director **Chuks Amajor** . . . . . . . . . . . . . (512) 463-8476
  Treasury Operations Director **Tom Smelker** . . . . . . . (512) 463-1698

# Texas General Land Office [GLO]

1700 North Congress Avenue, Austin, TX 78701
P.O. Box 12873, Austin, TX 78711-2873
Tel: (512) 463-5001  Tel: (800) 998-4456  TTY: (512) 463-5330
Fax: (512) 475-1558  Internet: www.glo.texas.gov

**Employees:** 658  **Fiscal Year:** 2014  **Budget:** $866,698,512

- ★ Texas Land Commissioner **George Prescott Bush** (R) . . . . (512) 463-5001
  Term Expires: January 2019
  E-mail: gpb@glo.texas.gov
  Education: Rice 1998; Texas 2003 JD
  Director of Executive Administration **Sandra Ortiz** . . . . . . . (512) 936-1912
  E-mail: sandra.ortiz@glo.texas.gov
  Executive Assistant **Suzanne Nelson** . . . . . . . . . . . . (512) 463-2785
  Chief Clerk/Deputy Land Commissioner **Anne Idsal** . . . . . (512) 936-1925
  E-mail: anne.idsal@glo.texas.gov
  Education: Baylor JD
  Chief Investments Officer **Rusty Martin** . . . . . . . . . . . (512) 463-5120
  E-mail: rusty.martin@glo.texas.gov
  Director of Communications **Bryan Preston** . . . . . . . . . (512) 936-0719
  Deputy Director of Compliance and Ethics
  **Christopher Burnett** . . . . . . . . . . . . . (512) 936-2307
  Education: Colorado 1982 BA; St Mary's U (TX) 1997 JD
  Deputy Director of Governmental Relations **Don Forse** . . (512) 936-3572
  E-mail: don.forse@glo.texas.gov
  Chief Auditor **Tracey Hall** . . . . . . . . . . . . . . . (512) 463-6078
  E-mail: tracey.hall@glo.texas.gov
  Litigation Chief Counsel **Marc Barenblat** . . . . . . . . . (512) 305-9121
  Director of Open Government **Hadassah Schloss** . . . . . . (512) 463-9072
  Deputy Director of Energy **Robert Hatter** . . . . . . . . . (512) 475-1542
  E-mail: robert.hatter@glo.texas.gov
  Deputy Director of Oil Spill Prevention and Response
  **Greg Pollock** . . . . . . . . . . . . . . . . (512) 463-5329
  Senior Deputy Director of Asset Enhancement
  **Brian Carter** . . . . . . . . . . . . . . . . (512) 936-0902
  E-mail: brian.carter@glo.texas.gov
  Senior Deputy Director of Coastal Protection
  **MajGen Kenneth W. Wisian, ANG** . . . . . . . (512) 463-5087
  Education: Texas; Centenary (LA) MS; Army War Col MSS;
  Air Command Col; Southern Methodist PhD
  Deputy Director of Archives and Records **Mark Lambert** . . (512) 463-5260
  E-mail: mark.lambert@glo.texas.gov
  Deputy Director of Coastal Resources **David Green** . . . . (512) 463-9971
  Deputy Director of Community Development and
  Revitalization **Pete Phillips** . . . . . . . . . . . . (512) 475-5015
  Chief Financial Officer **Kenny McLeskey** . . . . . . . . . (512) 475-0686
  Chief Information Officer **Cory Wilburn** . . . . . . . . . (512) 463-5084
  E-mail: cory.wilburn@glo.texas.gov
  Deputy Director of Human Resources **Kalani Hawks** . . . . (512) 463-6293
  General Counsel **Mark Havens** . . . . . . . . . . . . (512) 936-4441
  E-mail: mark.havens@glo.texas.gov
  Deputy General Counsel **Jeff Gordon** . . . . . . . . . . (512) 463-7205
  Special Counsel **Hector Valle** . . . . . . . . . . . . (512) 463-5331
  Deputy Director of Public Affairs **J.R. Hernandez** . . . . . (512) 463-5035
  Press Secretary **Brittany Eck** . . . . . . . . . . . . (512) 463-5708
  Education: Texas A&M 2000 BS
  Webmaster **Bob Michaels** . . . . . . . . . . . . . (512) 936-8119
  E-mail: webmaster@glo.texas.gov

# Veterans Land Board

P.O. Box 12873, Austin, TX 78711
Tel: (512) 463-5060  Internet: www.texasveterans.com

Chairman **George Prescott Bush** . . . . . . . . . . . (512) 463-5001
- ■ Member **Andrew J. Cobos** . . . . . . . . . . . . (512) 463-5001
  Term Expires: December 2018
  Education: West Point BS; Houston JD, MBA
- ■ Member **Alan L. Johnson** . . . . . . . . . . . . (512) 463-5001
  Term Expires: December 29, 2016
  Education: Texas A&I

---

★ Elected Official  ■ Appointed by Governor  ● Appointed by Legislature  ▲ Appointed by Board or Commission  ◆ Appointed by State Supreme Court

# Utah

Tel: (801) 538-3000 (State Information)   Internet: www.utah.gov

**Number of U.S. Congressional Delegates:** 2 Senators; 4 Representatives   **Governor's Term:** 4 years
**Legislature Description:** 29 member Senate; 75 member House of Representatives; Term - Senate 4 years,
House 2 years   **Next Election:** Governor November 2016; Legislature November 2016   **Number of**
**Electoral Votes:** 6   **Official Name:** State of Utah (Navajo: upper)   **Nickname:** The Beehive State
**Motto:** Industry

**Population:** 2,995,919 (2015); Rank 31   **Fiscal Year:** 2015   **Budget:** $13,518,345,120

## Office of the Governor

350 North State Street, Suite 200, Salt Lake City, UT 84114
P.O. Box 142220, Salt Lake City, UT 84114-2220
Tel: (801) 538-1000   Tel: (800) 705-2464   Fax: (801) 538-1528
Internet: www.utah.gov/governor

**Gary Richard Herbert**
Governor

Began Service: August 11, 2009
Term Expires: January 2017
Date of Birth: May 7, 1947
Religion: Latter-Day Saints (LDS)
Career: Commissioner, County Commission,
County of Utah, Utah (1990-2004); Lieutenant
Governor, Office of Lieutenant Governor Gary
Herbert, State of Utah (2005-2009)

★ Governor **Gary Richard Herbert** (R) . . . . . . . . . . . . . . . (801) 538-1000
   E-mail: gherbert@utah.gov          Fax: (801) 538-1557
   Executive Assistant and Scheduler **Fran Stultz** . . . . . . . . (801) 538-1680
     E-mail: fstultz@utah.gov
Chief of Staff **Justin Harding** . . . . . . . . . . . . . . . . . . . . (801) 538-1000
   Education: Southern Utah 2000 BS
Deputy Chief of Staff **Michael "Mike" Mower** . . . . . . . . . (801) 538-1924
   Education: Utah 1993 JD
Communications Director **Jon Cox** . . . . . . . . . . . . . . . . . (801) 538-1503
   E-mail: joncox@utah.gov
   Public Information Officer **Kirsten Rappleye** . . . . . . . . . (801) 538-1509
     E-mail: rappleye@utah.gov
     Education: Utah State
   Communications Specialist **Caroline Slater** . . . . . . . . . . . (801) 538-1017
     E-mail: cslater@utah.gov
General Counsel **Jacey Skinner** . . . . . . . . . . . . . . . . . . . . (801) 538-1000
   E-mail: jskinner@utah.gov
   Education: Utah State; J Reuben Clark Law JD
Boards and Commissions Director **Cherilyn Bradford** . . . . . (801) 538-1525
   E-mail: cbradford@utah.gov
Constituent Services Director **Austin Cox** . . . . . . . . . . . . . (801) 538-1288
   E-mail: austincox@utah.gov
Correspondence and Declarations Director
   **Katriina Adair** . . . . . . . . . . . . . . . . . . . . . . . . . . . . . (801) 538-1514
     E-mail: kadair@utah.gov
Policy Director **Cody Stewart** . . . . . . . . . . . . . . . . . . . . (801) 538-1574
   E-mail: codystewart@utah.gov
   Education: Utah State BA; Johns Hopkins MBA, 2008 MA
   Criminal Justice Policy Advisor
   **Ronald B. "Ron" Gordon** . . . . . . . . . . . . . . . . . . . . (801) 538-1432
     E-mail: rbgordon@utah.gov
     Education: BYU BS; Utah JD
Economic Development Senior Adviser **Val Hale** . . . . . . . (801) 538-1000
   E-mail: vhale@utah.gov
   Education: BYU MA
Education Advisor **Tami W. Pyfer** . . . . . . . . . . . . . . . . . (801) 538-7512
   E-mail: tpyfer@utah.gov
   Education: Utah State
Energy Policy Advisor **Dr. Laura S. Nelson** . . . . . . . . . . . (801) 419-2787
   E-mail: lnelson@utah.gov
   Education: Utah PhD

Legislative Affairs and Rural Advisor **Ben Onofrio** . . . . . (801) 538-1000
   E-mail: bonofrio@utah.gov
Senior Environmental Advisor **Alan Matheson, Jr.** . . . . . . (801) 536-4404
   E-mail: amatheson@utah.gov
   Education: Stanford 1985 AB; UCLA 1989 JD
State and Federal Relations Director **Wesley G. Smith** . . . . (801) 538-1329
   E-mail: wesleysmith@utah.gov
   Education: BYU; George Washington JD

## Governor's Office of Economic Development

60 East South Temple, 3rd Floor, Salt Lake City, UT 84111
Tel: (801) 538-8680   Fax: (801) 538-8888

**Fiscal Year:** 2015   **Budget:** $71,415,400

■ Executive Director **Val Hale** . . . . . . . . . . . . . . . . . . . . . . (801) 538-8769
   E-mail: vhale@utah.gov
Deputy Director **Theresa A. Foxley** . . . . . . . . . . . . . . . . (801) 538-8850
Communications Director **Aimee Edwards** . . . . . . . . . . . . (801) 538-8811
   E-mail: edwards@utah.gov
   Education: Weber State

## Governor's Office of Management and Budget [GOMB]

Utah State Capitol, Suite 150, Salt Lake City, UT 84114
P.O. Box 132210, Salt Lake City, UT 84114-2210
Tel: (801) 538-1027   Fax: (801) 538-1547

Director **Kristen Cox** . . . . . . . . . . . . . . . . . . . . . . . . . . . (801) 538-1705
   E-mail: kristencox@utah.gov
   Education: BYU BS
   Administrative Coordinator **Lorie Davis** . . . . . . . . . . . . . (801) 526-9685
     E-mail: lorie@utah.gov
Budget Director and Chief Economist **Phillip V. Dean** . . . . (801) 538-1714
Performance Measures Director **Rick Little** . . . . . . . . . . . . (801) 538-1516
State Planning Coordinator **Evan Curtis** . . . . . . . . . . . . . . (801) 538-1427
   Education: Utah State BA, MS

## Department of Administrative Services [DAS]

3120 State Office Building, Salt Lake City, UT 84114
Tel: (801) 538-3010   TTY: (801) 538-3340   Fax: (801) 538-3844

**Employees:** 151   **Fiscal Year:** 2015   **Budget:** $51,935,854

■ Executive Director **Kimberly K. Hood** . . . . . . . . . . . . . . . (801) 538-1056
   E-mail: khood@utah.gov
   Education: Utah BSEc, MEcon
Executive Deputy Director **Kenneth A. Hansen** . . . . . . . . (801) 538-3777
   E-mail: khansen@utah.gov
Administrative Rules Director (Acting)
   **Patricia Smith-Mansfield** . . . . . . . . . . . . . . . . . . . . . (801) 538-3777
     E-mail: pmansfie@utah.gov
Archives Director **Patricia Smith-Mansfield** . . . . . . . . . . . (801) 531-3850
   E-mail: pmansfie@utah.gov
Facilities Construction and Management Director
   **Eric Tholen** . . . . . . . . . . . . . . . . . . . . . . . . . . . . . . . (801) 538-3261
Chief Financial Officer **John Reidhead** . . . . . . . . . . . . . . (801) 538-3095
Fleet Operations Director **Jeff Mottishaw** . . . . . . . . . . . . . (801) 538-3601
Purchasing and General Services Director **Kent Beers** . . . . (801) 538-3143
   E-mail: kbeers@utah.gov

*(continued on next page)*

---

★ Elected Official    ■ Appointed by Governor    ● Appointed by Legislature    ▲ Appointed by Board or Commission    ◆ Appointed by State Supreme Court

**Department of Administrative Services** *continued*

Research Consultant **Jake Njord** . . . . . . . . . . . . . . . . . . . . . . (801) 538-1551
Risk Management Director **Tani Pack Downing** . . . . . . . . (801) 538-9598
Director of Operations **Marilee Richins** . . . . . . . . . . . . . . (801) 538-3215

## Utah Department of Agriculture and Food [UDAF]

P.O. Box 146500, Salt Lake City, UT 84114-6500
Tel: (801) 538-7100  TTY: (801) 538-7100  Fax: (801) 538-7126
Internet: www.ag.utah.gov

**Employees:** 205  **Fiscal Year:** 2015  **Budget:** $29,875,782

■Commissioner **LuAnn Adams** . . . . . . . . . . . . . . . . . . . . . . . (801) 815-3314
    E-mail: luannadams@utah.gov
Deputy Commissioner **Scott Ericson** . . . . . . . . . . . . . . . (801) 538-7102
    Administrative Assistant **Kathleen Mathews** . . . . . . . . . . (801) 538-7103
    Public Information Officer **Larry Lewis** . . . . . . . . . . . . . . (801) 538-7104
        E-mail: larrylewis@utah.gov
        Education: San Diego State 1975 AB
    Homeland Security Director **Thayne Mickelson** . . . . . . . . (801) 538-7121
Administrative Services Division Director
    **Stephen Ogilvie** . . . . . . . . . . . . . . . . . . . . . . . . . . . (801) 538-7110
        E-mail: stephenogilvie@utah.gov
Animal Industry Division Director and State Veterinarian
    **Cody James** . . . . . . . . . . . . . . . . . . . . . . . . . . . . . (801) 538-7166
Marketing Division Director **Wayne Bradshaw** . . . . . . . . . (801) 538-7108
Plant Industry Division Director **Rob Hougaard** . . . . . . . . (801) 538-7180
Regulatory Services Division Director **Travis Waller** . . . . . . (801) 538-7150
    E-mail: twaller@utah.gov
State Chemist **Weston Judd** . . . . . . . . . . . . . . . . . . . . . . (801) 538-7128
Geographic Information System (GIS) Coordinator
    **Anne M. Johnson** . . . . . . . . . . . . . . . . . . . . . . . . . (801) 538-9904
        E-mail: annejohnson@utah.gov

## Utah Department of Alcoholic Beverage Control [DABC]

1625 South 900 West, Salt Lake City, UT 84104
Tel: (801) 977-6800  Fax: (801) 977-6888  E-mail: hotline@utah.gov

**Employees:** 552  **Fiscal Year:** 2015  **Budget:** $244,833,405

▲Executive Director **Salvador D. "Sal" Petilos** . . . . . . . . . . . (801) 977-6800
    E-mail: spetilos@utah.gov                    Fax: (801) 977-6889
    Education: Rutgers; Fordham 1986 JD
    Administrative Assistant and Public Information Officer
        **Vickie Ashby** . . . . . . . . . . . . . . . . . . . . . . . . . . . . (801) 977-6800
            E-mail: vickieashby@utah.gov
Deputy Director **Cade Meier** . . . . . . . . . . . . . . . . . . . . . . (801) 977-6800
    Education: Utah BS, MBA
Alcohol Education Director **Doug Murakami** . . . . . . . . . . . (801) 977-6800
Compliance and Licensing Enforcement Director
    **Nina McDermott** . . . . . . . . . . . . . . . . . . . . . . . . . . (801) 977-6800
Finance Director **Man Diep** . . . . . . . . . . . . . . . . . . . . . . . (801) 977-6830
Purchasing Director **(Vacant)** . . . . . . . . . . . . . . . . . . . . . (801) 977-6800
Information Technology Manager **Chris Christensen** . . . . . (801) 977-6833
    E-mail: chrischristensen@utah.gov
Human Resources Specialist **Michelle Imperiale** . . . . . . . . (801) 530-6954
    Human Resources Analyst **Tami Hart** . . . . . . . . . . . . . . (801) 977-6800
        E-mail: tamihart@utah.gov
    Training Coordinator **Andrew Hofeling** . . . . . . . . . . . . . (801) 977-6800

### Alcoholic Beverage Control Commission

■Chair **John T. Nielsen** . . . . . . . . . . . . . . . . . . . . . . . . . . (801) 977-6800
    Term Expires: March 1, 2017
■Member **Olivia Vela Agraz** . . . . . . . . . . . . . . . . . . . . . . . (801) 977-6800
    Term Expires: July 1, 2016
■Member **Steven B. Bateman** . . . . . . . . . . . . . . . . . . . . . . (801) 977-6800
    Term Expires: July 1, 2017
■Member **S. Neal Berube** . . . . . . . . . . . . . . . . . . . . . . . . . (801) 977-6800
    Term Expires: July 1, 2019
■Member **Kathleen McConkie Collinwood** . . . . . . . . . . . . . (801) 977-6800
    Term Expires: July 1, 2018
■Member **Amanda Smith** . . . . . . . . . . . . . . . . . . . . . . . . . (801) 977-6800
    Term Expires: July 1, 2019
    Education: Utah 1989 BS; Gonzaga 1993 JD

■Member **Jeff Wright** . . . . . . . . . . . . . . . . . . . . . . . . . . . . (801) 977-6800
    Term Expires: July 1, 2017

## Utah Department of Commerce

Box 146701, Salt Lake City, UT 84114-6701
Tel: (801) 530-6701  Fax: (801) 530-6446  TTY: (801) 530-6917
Internet: www.commerce.utah.gov

**Employees:** 253  **Fiscal Year:** 2015  **Budget:** $29,740,375

■Executive Director **Francine A. Giani** . . . . . . . . . . . . . . . . . (801) 530-6431
    E-mail: fgiani@utah.gov
    Education: Hunter 1981 BComm; BYU 1991 MPA
    Executive Assistant **Julie Price** . . . . . . . . . . . . . . . . . . . (801) 530-6431
Deputy Director **Thomas "Tom" Brady** . . . . . . . . . . . . . . . (801) 530-6431
Public Information Officer **Jennifer Bolton** . . . . . . . . . . . . (801) 530-6646
    E-mail: jenniferbolton@utah.gov

### Division of Consumer Protection

Tel: (801) 530-6601  Fax: (801) 530-6001
E-mail: consumerprotection@utah.gov

Director **Daniel O'Bannon** . . . . . . . . . . . . . . . . . . . . . . . (801) 530-6601

### Division of Corporations and Uniform Commercial Code

160 East 300 South, Salt Lake City, UT 84111
Tel: (801) 530-4849  Fax: (801) 530-6438
Internet: www.corporations.utah.gov

Director **Kathy Berg** . . . . . . . . . . . . . . . . . . . . . . . . . . . (801) 530-6024

### Division of Occupational and Professional Licensing [DOPL]

Tel: (801) 530-6628  Tel: (866) 275-3675  Fax: (801) 530-6511

Director **Mark B. Steinagel** . . . . . . . . . . . . . . . . . . . . . . . (801) 530-6292

### Division of Public Utilities

160 East 300 South, 4th Floor, Salt Lake City, UT 84111
Tel: (801) 530-7622  Fax: (801) 530-6512

Director **Chris Parker** . . . . . . . . . . . . . . . . . . . . . . . . . . . (801) 530-6659
    E-mail: chrisparker@utah.gov
    Education: J Reuben Clark Law 2002 JD

### Division of Real Estate [DRE]

Heber M. Wells Building, 160 East 300 South, 2nd Floor,
Salt Lake City, UT 84111
P.O. Box 146711, Salt Lake City, UT 84114-6711
Tel: (801) 530-6747  Fax: (801) 526-4387  E-mail: realestate@utah.gov

Director **Jonathan C. Stewart** . . . . . . . . . . . . . . . . . . . . . (801) 530-6612
    Education: Utah BS, 2011 MPA
Education and Licensing Director **Mark Fagergren** . . . . . . . (801) 536-7967
Chief Investigator **Jeffery Nielsen** . . . . . . . . . . . . . . . . . . (801) 530-6127
Hearing Officer and Records Manager **Justin Barney** . . . . . (801) 530-6603
Timeshare and Subdivision Specialist **Craig Livingston** . . . (801) 530-6328
Office Specialist **Jill Ellis** . . . . . . . . . . . . . . . . . . . . . . . . (801) 530-6747

### Division of Securities

160 East 300 South, 2nd Floor, Salt Lake City, UT 84111
Tel: (801) 530-6600  Fax: (801) 530-6980  E-mail: securities@utah.gov

Director **Keith Woodwell** . . . . . . . . . . . . . . . . . . . . . . . . (801) 530-6606

## Utah Department of Corrections [UDC]

14717 South Minuteman Drive, Draper, UT 84020
Tel: (801) 545-5525  Fax: (801) 523-7473
Internet: www.corrections.utah.gov

**Employees:** 2,266  **Fiscal Year:** 2015  **Budget:** $266,937,800

■Executive Director **Rollin E. Cook** . . . . . . . . . . . . . . . . . . . (801) 545-5515
    E-mail: rollincook@utah.gov
    Education: Columbia Col (MO) 1999 AA, 1999 AS, 2000 BA;
    U Phoenix 2007 MBA
Deputy Director **Mike Haddon** . . . . . . . . . . . . . . . . . . . . . (801) 545-5913

---

★ Elected Official    ■ Appointed by Governor    ● Appointed by Legislature    ▲ Appointed by Board or Commission    ◆ Appointed by State Supreme Court

Executive Assistant **Mindy Usher** . . . . . . . . . . . . . . . . . (801) 545-5513
Deputy Director **London Stromberg** . . . . . . . . . . . . . . . (801) 545-5537
Adult Probation and Parole Director **James Hudspeth** . . . .(801) 545-5901
Finance Director **Robert P. Bond, CGFM** . . . . . . . . . . . . .(801) 545-5612
                                        Fax: (801) 545-5724
Information Technology Director **Brad Franchina** . . . . . . . (801) 545-5508
   E-mail: bfranchina@utah.gov
Institutional Operations Division Director **Jerry Pope** . . . . .(801) 545-5710
   Education: U Phoenix 2008 BS
Institutional Programming Division Director
   **Victor Kersey** . . . . . . . . . . . . . . . . . . . . . . . . . . . .(801) 545-5525
   Education: Maryland
Special Projects Coordinator **Steve Turley** . . . . . . . . . . . . (801) 545-5633
Public Information Officer **Brooke Adams** . . . . . . . . . . . . .(801) 545-5536
   E-mail: brookeadams@utah.gov

# Utah Department of Environmental Quality [DEQ]

195 North 1950 West, Salt Lake City, UT 84116-4840
Tel: (801) 536-4400  TTY: (801) 536-4414  Fax: (801) 536-4457
E-mail: deqinfo@deq.state.ut.us  Internet: www.deq.utah.gov

**Employees:** 385  **Fiscal Year:** 2015  **Budget:** $60,285,089,000

■Executive Director **Alan Matheson, Jr.** . . . . . . . . . . . . . . (801) 536-4404
   E-mail: amatheson@utah.gov
Deputy Director **Brad T. Johnson** . . . . . . . . . . . . . . . . . . (801) 536-4403
Communications Director **Donna Spangler** . . . . . . . . . . . . (801) 536-4400
   E-mail: dspangler@utah.gov
Business Compliance Assistant **Paul Harding** . . . . . . . . . (801) 536-4108
Legislative and Government Affairs Director **Scott Baird** . . (801) 536-4400
   E-mail: scottbaird@utah.gov
   Education: BYU BS; Syracuse MPA, JD
Support Services Division Director **Craig Silotti** . . . . . . . . (801) 536-4414
   E-mail: csilotti@utah.gov
Human Resource Manager **Dana Powers** . . . . . . . . . . . . . (801) 536-4412

## Division of Air Quality

150 North 1950 West, Salt Lake City, UT 84116
Tel: (801) 536-4000  Fax: (801) 536-4099

Director **Bryce Bird** . . . . . . . . . . . . . . . . . . . . . . . . . . . .(801) 536-4000
                                   Fax: (801) 536-0085
Deputy Director **Brock LeBaron** . . . . . . . . . . . . . . . . . . . (801) 536-4006
   Education: Utah State BS
Air Monitoring Manager **Bowen "Bo" Call** . . . . . . . . . . . . (801) 887-0762
Compliance Branch Manager **Rusty Ruby** . . . . . . . . . . . . (801) 536-4133
Permitting Branch Manager **Regg Olsen** . . . . . . . . . . . . . (801) 536-4165
Planning Branch Manager **Dave McNeill** . . . . . . . . . . . . . (801) 536-4064
Records Officer **Teri Weiss** . . . . . . . . . . . . . . . . . . . . . . . (801) 536-4183

## Division of Drinking Water

150 North 1950 West, Salt Lake City, UT 84116
Tel: (801) 536-4200  Fax: (801) 536-4211
Internet: www.drinkingwater.utah.gov

Director **Kenneth H. "Ken" Bousfield** . . . . . . . . . . . . . . . (801) 536-4200
Administrative Services Program Manager
   **Kate Johnson** . . . . . . . . . . . . . . . . . . . . . . . . . . . . (801) 536-4206
   E-mail: katej@utah.gov
Construction Assistant Program Manager
   **Michael Grange** . . . . . . . . . . . . . . . . . . . . . . . . . . (801) 536-0069
Engineering Program Manager **Ying-Ying Macauley** . . . . . .(801) 536-4188
Field Services Program Manager **Kim Dyches** . . . . . . . . . (801) 536-4202
Rules Section Program Manager **Patti Fauver** . . . . . . . . . (801) 536-4196

## Division of Environmental Response and Remediation

Building Two, 168 North 1950 West, 1st Floor,
Salt Lake City, UT 84116-4840
Tel: (801) 536-4100  Fax: (801) 359-8853
Internet: www.environmentalresponse.utah.gov

Director **Brent H. Everett** . . . . . . . . . . . . . . . . . . . . . . . (801) 536-4171
Superfund Branch Manager **Duane Mortensen** . . . . . . . . . (801) 536-4172

Underground Storage Tanks Branch Manager
   **Therron Blatter** . . . . . . . . . . . . . . . . . . . . . . . . . . . (801) 536-4100

# Division of Waste Management and Radiation Control

195 North 1950 West, 2nd Floor, Salt Lake City, UT 84116
P.O. Box 144880, Salt Lake City, UT 84114-4880
Tel: (801) 536-0200  Fax: (801) 536-0222

Director **Scott T. Anderson** . . . . . . . . . . . . . . . . . . . . . . (801) 536-0201
Deputy Director **Rusty Lundberg** . . . . . . . . . . . . . . . . . . (801) 536-4485
Corrective Action Manager **Brad Maulding** . . . . . . . . . . . (801) 536-0205
Hazardous Waste Manager **Deborah Ng** . . . . . . . . . . . . . (801) 536-0218
Hazardous Waste Manager **Don Verbica** . . . . . . . . . . . . . (801) 536-0206
Low Level Uranium Mill Compliance Section Manager
   **Phil Goble** . . . . . . . . . . . . . . . . . . . . . . . . . . . . . . (801) 536-4044
Planning and Tech Support Manager **Ralph Bohn** . . . . . . . (801) 536-0212
Solid Waste Landfills and Used Tires Manager
   **Allan Moore** . . . . . . . . . . . . . . . . . . . . . . . . . . . . . (801) 536-0211
Records Officer **Jerry Rogers** . . . . . . . . . . . . . . . . . . . . . (801) 536-0228

# Division of Water Quality

195 North 1950 West, Salt Lake City, UT 84116
P.O. Box 144870, Salt Lake City, UT 84114-4870
Tel: (801) 536-4300  Fax: (801) 536-4301

Director **Walter "Walt" Baker** . . . . . . . . . . . . . . . . . . . . . (801) 536-4312
Engineering, Groundwater, and UPDES Branch Assistant
   Director **Leah Ann Lamb** . . . . . . . . . . . . . . . . . . . . . (801) 536-4318

# Department of Financial Institutions [DFI]

324 South State Street, Suite 201, Salt Lake City, UT 84111
P.O. Box 146800, Salt Lake City, UT 84114-6800
Tel: (801) 538-8830  Fax: (801) 538-8894  Internet: www.dfi.utah.gov

**Employees:** 53  **Fiscal Year:** 2015  **Budget:** $6,794,927

■Commissioner **G. Edward "Ed" Leary, USNR (Ret)** . . . . . (801) 538-8761
   E-mail: eleary@utah.gov
   Education: Utah BS, MBA
Deputy Commissioner **Paul Allred** . . . . . . . . . . . . . . . . . . (801) 538-8837
   E-mail: pallred@utah.gov
Chief Examiner **Darryle Rude** . . . . . . . . . . . . . . . . . . . . . (801) 538-8836
   E-mail: drude@utah.gov
Finance Director **Michael Jones** . . . . . . . . . . . . . . . . . . . (801) 538-8839
Banks Supervisor **Tom Bay** . . . . . . . . . . . . . . . . . . . . . . (801) 538-8835
   E-mail: tbay@utah.gov
Consumer Credit and Compliance Supervisor **Eva Rees** . . . (801) 538-8834
   E-mail: erees@utah.gov
Credit Unions Supervisor **Riley Bergstedt** . . . . . . . . . . . . (801) 538-8840
   E-mail: rbergstedt@utah.gov
Holding Companies Supervisor **Andrea Staheli** . . . . . . . . . (801) 538-8776
   E-mail: astaheli@utah.gov
Industrial Banks Supervisor **Shaun Berrett** . . . . . . . . . . . (801) 538-8841
   E-mail: shaunberrett@utah.gov
Money Service Businesses and Trust Supervisor
   **Paul Cline** . . . . . . . . . . . . . . . . . . . . . . . . . . . . . . (801) 538-8842
   E-mail: pcline@utah.gov
Office Specialist **Irene Walisky** . . . . . . . . . . . . . . . . . . . . (801) 538-8832

# Utah Department of Health [UDOH]

288 North 1460 West, Salt Lake City, UT 84116-0700
P.O. Box 141000, Salt Lake City, UT 84114-1000 (Vital Records)
Tel: (801) 538-6111  Tel: (801) 538-6105 (Vital Records)
TTY: (801) 538-6622  Fax: (801) 538-6306
Fax: (801) 538-7012 (Vital Records)
E-mail: vrequest@utah.gov (Vital Records)  Internet: www.health.utah.gov
Internet: www.health.utah.gov/vitalrecords (Vital Records)

**Employees:** 967  **Fiscal Year:** 2015  **Budget:** $2,766,013,425

■Executive Director **Joseph K. Miner, MD, MSPH** . . . . . . . (801) 538-6111
   E-mail: joeminer@utah.gov
   Education: BYU 1971 BS; Utah 1974 MD, 1983 MS
   Administrative Assistant **Angie Stefaniak** . . . . . . . . . . . (801) 538-6179

*(continued on next page)*

★ Elected Official    ■ Appointed by Governor    ● Appointed by Legislature    ▲ Appointed by Board or Commission    ◆ Appointed by State Supreme Court

**EXECUTIVE BRANCH**

**Utah Department of Health** *continued*

Deputy Director and State Health Information
  Technology Coordinator **Robert T. Rolfs, MD, MPH** . . . . (801) 538-6386
  Education: Notre Dame 1976 BS; Northwestern 1980 MD;
  U Washington 1998 MPH
Fiscal Operations Office Director **Shari Watkins** . . . . . . . . (801) 538-6601
Human Resource Management Director
  **Cassandra Opheikens** . . . . . . . . . . . . . . . . . . . . . . . . . . (801) 538-7062
Information Technology Director **Greg Mead** . . . . . . . . . . . (801) 538-6368
  E-mail: gmead@utah.gov
General Services Manager **Janeill Allen** . . . . . . . . . . . . . . (801) 538-9310
Public Information Officer **Tom Hudachko** . . . . . . . . . . . . . (801) 538-6232
  E-mail: thudachko@utah.gov
Travel and Conference Coordinator **(Vacant)** . . . . . . . . . . (801) 538-9169

## Office of the State Medical Examiner

48 Medical Drive, Salt Lake City, UT 84113
Tel: (801) 584-8410  Fax: (801) 584-8435
■Chief Medical Examiner **Todd C. Grey** . . . . . . . . . . . . . . . (801) 584-8410
  E-mail: toddgrey@utah.gov
  Education: Yale 1976 BA; Dartmouth 1980 MD
Deputy Chief Medical Examiner **Edward A. Leis, MD** . . . . (801) 584-8410
Assistant Medical Examiner **Dr. Erik D. Christensen** . . . . . (801) 584-8425

## Division of Disease Control and Prevention

288 North 1460 West, Salt Lake City, UT 84116
P.O. Box 142102, Salt Lake City, UT 84114-2102
Tel: (801) 538-6129  Fax: (801) 538-6036
Director **Jennifer Brown** . . . . . . . . . . . . . . . . . . . . . . . . . . (801) 538-6131
State Epidemiologist **Dr. Allyn Nakashima, MD** . . . . . . . . (801) 538-6246
  Education: Utah, MD
Deputy State Epidemiologist **(Vacant)** . . . . . . . . . . . . . . . (801) 538-6191
Epidemiology Bureau Director **Christie Chesler** . . . . . . . . . (801) 538-9465
Health Promotion Bureau Director
  **Heather Borski, MPH, CHES** . . . . . . . . . . . . . . . . . . . . . (801) 538-9998
Unified State Laboratories Director **Robyn Atkinson** . . . . . (801) 965-2424
  Chemical and Environmental Services Bureau Director
    **Bret Van Ausdall** . . . . . . . . . . . . . . . . . . . . . . . . . . . . (801) 965-2470
  Forensic Toxicology Bureau Director **Gambrelli Layco** . . (801) 965-2400
  Laboratory Improvement Bureau Director **Brent Curtis** . . (801) 965-2530
  Microbiology Bureau Director **(Vacant)** . . . . . . . . . . . . . (801) 965-2550
  Microbiology, Bioterrorism and Molecular Biology
    Section Chief **(Vacant)** . . . . . . . . . . . . . . . . . . . . . . . . (801) 965-2560

## Division of Family Health and Preparedness

P.O. Box 142002, Salt Lake City, UT 84114-2002
Tel: (801) 273-6601  Fax: (801) 273-4150
Director **Marc E. Babitz, MD** . . . . . . . . . . . . . . . . . . . . . . (801) 273-6601
Emergency Medical Services and Preparedness Director
  **Paul R. Patrick** . . . . . . . . . . . . . . . . . . . . . . . . . . . . . . . (801) 273-6604
Health Facility Licensing, Certification and Resident
  Assessment Director **Joel Hoffman** . . . . . . . . . . . . . . . . (801) 538-6529
  E-mail: jhoffman@utah.gov
Maternal and Child Health Director **Lynne Nilson** . . . . . . . (801) 538-9963
Oral Health Programs Director **Kim Michelson, DDS** . . . . . (801) 538-9177
  E-mail: kmichelson@utah.gov
  Education: Weber State BS; Creighton 1987 DDS
WIC (Women, Infants and Children) Services Director
  **Chris Furner** . . . . . . . . . . . . . . . . . . . . . . . . . . . . . . . . . (801) 538-6199
  E-mail: cfurner@utah.gov
Child Development Bureau Director **Teresa Whiting** . . . . . (801) 538-9084
Children with Special Health Care Needs Bureau
  Director **Noel Taxin** . . . . . . . . . . . . . . . . . . . . . . . . . . . (801) 584-8529
Primary Care Bureau Director **Steve K. Ipsen** . . . . . . . . . . (801) 273-6637
Hearing, Speech and Vision Services Manager
  **Stephanie McVicar** . . . . . . . . . . . . . . . . . . . . . . . . . . . . (801) 584-8215
Financial Resources Director **Curtis Burk** . . . . . . . . . . . . . (801) 538-6911
Indian Health Liaison/Health Policy Consultant
  **Melissa Zito** . . . . . . . . . . . . . . . . . . . . . . . . . . . . . . . . . (801) 273-6644

## Division of Medicaid and Health Financing

P.O. Box 143101, Salt Lake City, UT 84114-3101
Tel: (801) 538-6417  Fax: (801) 538-6478
Deputy Director (Interim) **Nathan Checketts** . . . . . . . . . . (801) 538-6689
Assistant Division Director **Emma Chacon** . . . . . . . . . . . . (801) 538-6577
Assistant Division Director **Nathan Checketts** . . . . . . . . . (801) 538-6043
Authorization and Community Based Services Bureau
  Director **Tonya Hales** . . . . . . . . . . . . . . . . . . . . . . . . . . (801) 538-9136
Coverage and Reimbursement Policy Bureau Director
  **John Curless** . . . . . . . . . . . . . . . . . . . . . . . . . . . . . . . . (801) 538-6149
Eligibility Policy Bureau Director **Jeff Nelson** . . . . . . . . . . (801) 538-6471
  E-mail: jeffnelson@utah.gov
Financial Services Bureau Director **Rick Platt** . . . . . . . . . . (801) 538-7015
Managed Health Care Bureau Director **Julie Ewing** . . . . . . (801) 538-9125
  E-mail: julieewing@utah.gov
Medicaid Operations Bureau Director **David Lewis** . . . . . . . (801) 538-6586
Privacy Officer **Blake Anderson** . . . . . . . . . . . . . . . . . . . . (801) 538-9925
Security Officer **Nicole Neilan** . . . . . . . . . . . . . . . . . . . . . (801) 538-6453

# Utah Department of Heritage and Arts [DHA]

300 South Rio Grande Street, Salt Lake City, UT 84101
Tel: (801) 245-7202  Fax: (801) 245-4727
Internet: www.heritage.utah.gov

**Employees:** 125  **Fiscal Year:** 2015  **Budget:** $24,089,178

■Executive Director **Julie Fisher** . . . . . . . . . . . . . . . . . . . . (801) 245-7202
  E-mail: jwfisher@utah.gov
  Education: Indiana 1980 BA
  Executive Assistant **Marjorie Moore** . . . . . . . . . . . . . . . . (801) 245-7202
Deputy Director **Brian Somers** . . . . . . . . . . . . . . . . . . . . . (801) 245-7204
Communications Director **Josh Loftin** . . . . . . . . . . . . . . . . (801) 245-7205
  E-mail: jloftin@utah.gov
Community Services Director **LaDawn Stoddard** . . . . . . . . (801) 245-7223
                                                        Fax: (801) 355-3081
Chief Financial Officer **Jill Flygare** . . . . . . . . . . . . . . . . . . (801) 245-7206

## Office of Multicultural Affairs

300 South Rio Grande Street, Salt Lake City, UT 84101
Tel: (801) 245-7210  Fax: (801) 521-4727
Director **Claudia Nakano** . . . . . . . . . . . . . . . . . . . . . . . . . (801) 245-7211

## Division of Arts and Museums

617 East South Temple, Salt Lake City, UT 84102
Tel: (801) 236-7555  Fax: (801) 236-7556
Director **Gay Cookson** . . . . . . . . . . . . . . . . . . . . . . . . . . . (801) 236-7551

## Division of Indian Affairs

250 North 1950 West, Suite A, Salt Lake City, UT 84116
Fax: (801) 715-6767
■Director **Shirlee Silversmith** . . . . . . . . . . . . . . . . . . . . . (801) 715-6701
  E-mail: ssilversmith@utah.gov
  Education: BYU BS; Arizona State MEd

## History Division

300 Rio Grande, Salt Lake City, UT 84101
Tel: (801) 245-7225  Fax: (801) 533-3503
Director **Brad Westwood** . . . . . . . . . . . . . . . . . . . . . . . . . (801) 245-7248

## State Library

250 North 1950 West, Suite A, Salt Lake City, UT 84116
Tel: (801) 715-6777  Fax: (801) 715-6767
■Director **Donna Jones Morris** . . . . . . . . . . . . . . . . . . . . . (801) 715-6770
  E-mail: dmorris@utah.gov
Assistant Director **Kari May** . . . . . . . . . . . . . . . . . . . . . . . (801) 715-6776
Multistate Center Director **David Valentine** . . . . . . . . . . . . (801) 715-6783
Administrative Services Manager **Ron Van Harten** . . . . . . . (801) 715-6756
Financial Manager **Paul Kroff** . . . . . . . . . . . . . . . . . . . . . . (801) 715-6771
Library for the Blind Program Manager **Lisa Nelson** . . . . . (801) 715-6720
  E-mail: lfnelson@utah.gov

---

★ Elected Official   ■ Appointed by Governor   ● Appointed by Legislature   ▲ Appointed by Board or Commission   ◆ Appointed by State Supreme Court

State Data Coordinator **Kristen Stehel** . . . . . . . . . . . . . . . . . (801) 715-6753

# Department of Human Resource Management [DHRM]

State Office Building, Suite 2120, Salt Lake City, UT 84114
Tel: (801) 538-3025  TTY: (801) 538-3696  Fax: (801) 538-3081
Internet: www.dhrm.utah.gov

**Employees: 135  Fiscal Year: 2015  Budget: $2,237,394**

■Executive Director **Debbie Cragun** . . . . . . . . . . . . . . . . . . . (801) 538-3185
   E-mail: dcragun@utah.gov
   Education: U Phoenix 2003 BS, 2005 MA
   Administrative Assistant **Angela Kula** . . . . . . . . . . . . . . (801) 538-3080
Deputy Director **Wendy Peterson** . . . . . . . . . . . . . . . . . . . . (801) 538-3075
Information/Technology Division Director **Scott Wolford** . . (801) 538-3132
   E-mail: swolford@utah.gov

# Utah Department of Human Services [DHS]

195 North 1950 West, Salt Lake City, UT 84116
Tel: (801) 538-4171  TTY: (801) 538-4187  Fax: (801) 538-4016
E-mail: dirdhs@utah.gov  Internet: www.dhs.utah.gov

**Employees: 3,945  Fiscal Year: 2015  Budget: $736,754,700**

■Executive Director **Ann S. Williamson** . . . . . . . . . . . . . . . . (801) 538-3998
   E-mail: annwilliamson@utah.gov
   Education: Wofford 1995 BA; LSU 1998 MSSW
   Executive Assistant **Mary Carole Blackburn** . . . . . . . . . . (801) 538-3998
Deputy Director **Mark Brasher** . . . . . . . . . . . . . . . . . . . . . (801) 538-3998
Deputy Director **Lana Stohl** . . . . . . . . . . . . . . . . . . . . . . . (801) 538-3998
   Education: Utah MBA
Aging and Adult Services Division Director
   **Nels Holmgren** . . . . . . . . . . . . . . . . . . . . . . . . . . . . (801) 538-3921
Child and Family Services Division Director **Brent Platt** . . (801) 538-4021
Juvenile Justice Services Director **Susan Burke** . . . . . . . . . (801) 538-4098
Recovery Services Director **Liesa Stockdale** . . . . . . . . . . . (801) 536-8500
   515 E. 100 South, Salt Lake City, UT 84012
   E-mail: lcorbri2@utah.gov
Services for People with Disabilities Director
   **Paul T. Smith** . . . . . . . . . . . . . . . . . . . . . . . . . . . . . (801) 538-4200
Substance Abuse and Mental Health Director
   **Douglas P. Thomas** . . . . . . . . . . . . . . . . . . . . . . . . . (801) 538-4139
Administrative Hearings Office Director **Sonia Sweeney** . . (801) 538-3900
Webmaster **Rich Rayl** . . . . . . . . . . . . . . . . . . . . . . . . . . . (801) 538-4673
   E-mail: rrayl@utah.gov
Chief Financial Officer **Jennifer Evans** . . . . . . . . . . . . . . . (801) 538-4107
Licensing Director **Diane Moore** . . . . . . . . . . . . . . . . . . . (801) 538-9897
   Education: BYU MPA
Public Guardian **Shannon Alvey** . . . . . . . . . . . . . . . . . . . (801) 538-8255

# Utah Insurance Department

State Office Building, Room 3110, Salt Lake City, UT 84114
Tel: (801) 538-3800  Fax: (801) 538-3829
Internet: www.insurance.utah.gov

**Employees: 92  Fiscal Year: 2015  Budget: $12,046,190**

■Commissioner **Todd E. Kiser** . . . . . . . . . . . . . . . . . . . . . . (801) 538-3804
   E-mail: tkiser@utah.gov
   Executive Assistant **Jill White** . . . . . . . . . . . . . . . . . . . (801) 538-3804
Deputy Commissioner **Brett J. Barratt** . . . . . . . . . . . . . . . (801) 538-3870
Assistant Commissioner **Tanji Northrup** . . . . . . . . . . . . . . (801) 538-1801
Chief Insurance Examiner **Jacob W. "Jake" Garn** . . . . . . . (801) 538-3811
Administration Division Director **Patrick Lee** . . . . . . . . . . (801) 538-3778
   E-mail: pwlee@utah.gov
Captive Insurers Division Director **David J. Snowball** . . . . (801) 537-9047
   Education: BYU BA
Fraud Division Director **Armand Glick** . . . . . . . . . . . . . . . (801) 531-5388
Life and Health Insurance Division Director
   **Nancy Askerlund** . . . . . . . . . . . . . . . . . . . . . . . . . . . (801) 537-9293
Market Conduct Division Director
   **Suzette Green-Wright** . . . . . . . . . . . . . . . . . . . . . . . (801) 538-9674
Producer Licensing Services Division Director
   **Randy Overstreet** . . . . . . . . . . . . . . . . . . . . . . . . . . (801) 538-3645

Property and Casualty Division Director
   **Tracy Klausmeier** . . . . . . . . . . . . . . . . . . . . . . . . . . . (801) 538-3869
Information Specialist **Steve Gooch** . . . . . . . . . . . . . . . . . (801) 538-8669
   E-mail: sgooch@utah.gov

# Utah Department of Natural Resources [DNR]

1594 West North Temple, Suite 3710, Salt Lake City, UT 84116-3154
P.O. Box 145610, Salt Lake City, UT 84114-5610
Tel: (801) 538-7200  TTY: (801) 538-7458  Fax: (801) 538-7315
E-mail: help@nrdomain.nris  Internet: www.nr.utah.gov

**Employees: 1,238  Fiscal Year: 2015  Budget: $187,501,967**

■Executive Director **Michael R. "Mike" Styler** . . . . . . . . . . (801) 538-7201
   E-mail: mikestyler@utah.gov
   Education: BYU BSAg, BBEd
   Executive Assistant **Kaelyn Anfinsen** . . . . . . . . . . . . . . (801) 538-7201
Deputy Director **Darin G. Bird** . . . . . . . . . . . . . . . . . . . . (801) 538-7201
Deputy Director **Robyn Pearson** . . . . . . . . . . . . . . . . . . . (801) 538-7201
Finance Director **Dennis Carver** . . . . . . . . . . . . . . . . . . . (801) 538-7307
   E-mail: denniscarver@utah.gov

## Forestry, Fire and State Lands Division

1594 West North Temple, Suite 3520, Salt Lake City, UT 84116-3154
P.O. Box 145703, Salt Lake City, UT 84114-5703
Tel: (801) 538-5555  Fax: (801) 533-4111

State Forester and Director **Brian Cottam** . . . . . . . . . . . . . (801) 538-5504
   Administrative Assistant **Whitney Norton** . . . . . . . . . . . (801) 538-5418

## Oil, Gas and Mining Division

1594 West North Temple, Suite 1210, Salt Lake City, UT 84116-3154
P.O. Box 145801, Salt Lake City, UT 84114-5801
Tel: (801) 538-5340  Fax: (801) 359-3940

Director **John Baza** . . . . . . . . . . . . . . . . . . . . . . . . . . . . (801) 538-5334
Mining Associate Director **Dana Dean** . . . . . . . . . . . . . . . (801) 538-5320
Public Information Officer **Hollie Brown** . . . . . . . . . . . . . (801) 538-5324
   E-mail: holliebrown@utah.gov
Administrative Assistant **Sheri Sasaki** . . . . . . . . . . . . . . . (801) 538-5448

## Parks and Recreation Division

1594 West North Temple, Suite 116, Salt Lake City, UT 84116-3154
P.O. Box 146001, Salt Lake City, UT 84114-6001
Tel: (801) 538-7220  Fax: (801) 538-7378

Director **Fred Hayes** . . . . . . . . . . . . . . . . . . . . . . . . . . . (801) 538-7220
   E-mail: fredhayes@utah.gov
Administrative Secretary **Wendy Wack** . . . . . . . . . . . . . . (801) 538-7418

## Water Resources Division

1594 West North Temple, Suite 310, Salt Lake City, UT 84116-3154
P.O. Box 146201, Salt Lake City, UT 84114-6201
Tel: (801) 538-7230  Fax: (801) 538-7279  Internet: www.water.utah.gov

Director **Eric Millis** . . . . . . . . . . . . . . . . . . . . . . . . . . . . (801) 538-7230
   E-mail: ericmillis@utah.gov
   Education: BYU BS, MS
Administrative Secretary **Barbara Allen** . . . . . . . . . . . . . . (801) 538-7230

## Water Rights Division

1594 West North Temple, Suite 220, Salt Lake City, UT 84116-3154
P.O. Box 146300, Salt Lake City, UT 84114-6300
Tel: (801) 538-7240  Fax: (801) 538-7467
Internet: www.waterrights.utah.gov

■State Engineer and Director **Kent L. Jones, PE** . . . . . . . . . (801) 538-7240
   E-mail: kentljones@utah.gov
   Education: Utah State 1975 BSCE
Administrative Secretary **Marianne Burbidge** . . . . . . . . . . (801) 538-7370

## Wildlife Resources Division

1594 West North Temple, Suite 2110, Salt Lake City, UT 84116-3154
P.O. Box 146301, Salt Lake City, UT 84114-6301
Tel: (801) 538-4700  Fax: (801) 538-4709

Director **Greg Sheehan** . . . . . . . . . . . . . . . . . . . . . . . . . . (801) 538-4702

---

★ Elected Official   ■ Appointed by Governor   ● Appointed by Legislature   ▲ Appointed by Board or Commission   ◆ Appointed by State Supreme Court

## Utah Geological Survey

1594 West North Temple, Suite 3110, Salt Lake City, UT 84116-3154
P.O. Box 146100, Salt Lake City, UT 84114-6100
Tel: (801) 537-3300  Fax: (801) 537-3400

State Geologist and Director **Richard "Rick" Allis** . . . . . . . (801) 537-3305
Deputy Director **(Vacant)** . . . . . . . . . . . . . . . . . . . . . . . . . (801) 537-3313
Financial Manager **Jodi Patters** . . . . . . . . . . . . . . . . . . . . .(801) 537-3310
Administrative Secretary **Dianne Davis** . . . . . . . . . . . . . . .(801) 537-3305

## Utah Department of Public Safety

4501 South 2700 West, Salt Lake City, UT 84119
Tel: (800) 222-0038  TTY: (801) 965-4461  Fax: (801) 965-4608

**Employees:** 1,278  **Fiscal Year:** 2015  **Budget:** $169,447,032

■Commissioner **Keith Squires** . . . . . . . . . . . . . . . . . . . . . . . (801) 965-4062
  E-mail: ksquires@utah.gov
  Education: Columbia Col (MO); Naval Postgrad 2009 MA
  Executive Assistant **Emily Smith** . . . . . . . . . . . . . . . . . . . (801) 965-4062
  E-mail: emsmith@utah.gov
Deputy Commissioner **Nannette Rolfe** . . . . . . . . . . . . . . . (801) 965-4118
  Executive Assistant **Emily Smith** . . . . . . . . . . . . . . . . . . . (801) 965-4062
State Fire Marshal **Coy Porter** . . . . . . . . . . . . . . . . . . . . . . (801) 284-6358
  5272 South College Drive, Suite 302, Murray, UT 84123
  State Bureau of Investigation Deputy Director
    **Major Brian Redd** . . . . . . . . . . . . . . . . . . . . . . . . . . . . (801) 532-2168
    E-mail: bredd@utah.gov                       Fax: (801) 579-4414
Administrative Services Division Director **Joe Brown** . . . . (801) 965-4476
  E-mail: jbrown@utah.gov
Driver License Division Director **Christopher Caras** . . . . . .(801) 965-4469
  E-mail: ccaras@utah.gov
Highway Safety Division Director **Kristy Rigby** . . . . . . . . . (801) 366-6040
  E-mail: krigby@utah.gov
Management Information Services Division Director
  **Mike Sadler** . . . . . . . . . . . . . . . . . . . . . . . . . . . . . . . . . .(801) 965-4822
  E-mail: msadler@utah.gov
Peace Officer Standards and Training Division Director
  **Scott Stephenson** . . . . . . . . . . . . . . . . . . . . . . . . . . . . . (801) 256-2322
  E-mail: sstephen@utah.gov

## Department of Technology Services [DTS]

One State Office Building, Sixth Floor, Salt Lake City, UT 84114
Tel: (801) 537-9000  Fax: (801) 538-3622

**Employees:** 750  **Fiscal Year:** 2015  **Budget:** $2,911,131,000

Chief Information Officer and Executive Director
  **Michael S. Hussey** . . . . . . . . . . . . . . . . . . . . . . . . . . . . (801) 538-3298
  E-mail: mhussey@utah.gov
  Assistant to the Chief Information Officer **Jenni Griffin** . .(801) 538-3298
Chief Information Security Officer **Phil Bates** . . . . . . . . . . (801) 538-3298
Chief Operating Officer **Kenneth G. "Ken" Petersen** . . . . (801) 538-3298
Chief Technical Architect **Anthony Booyse** . . . . . . . . . . . . (801) 538-1072
  E-mail: abooyse@utah.gov
Chief Technology Officer **David G. "Dave" Fletcher** . . . . . (801) 538-3476
  E-mail: dfletcher@utah.gov
Finance Director **Dan Frei** . . . . . . . . . . . . . . . . . . . . . . . . (801) 538-3459
Public Information Officer **Stephanie Weteling** . . . . . . . . . (801) 538-3284
  E-mail: stweiss@utah.gov

## Utah Department of Veterans and Military Affairs

550 Foothill Boulevard, Suite 105, Salt Lake City, UT 84113
Tel: (801) 326-2372  Fax: (801) 326-2369  E-mail: veterans@utah.gov

**Employees:** 14

Executive Director **Gary R. Harter** . . . . . . . . . . . . . . . . . . (801) 326-2372
  E-mail: gharter@utah.gov
  Education: Pittsburgh 1980 BS; National Defense U MS
Deputy Director **Dennis McFall** . . . . . . . . . . . . . . . . . . . . (801) 584-1914
Director of Military Affairs **Ted Frederick** . . . . . . . . . . . . (801) 326-2433
  Education: West Point BS; Harvard MBA
State Approving Agency for Veterans Education Director
  **Berni Davis** . . . . . . . . . . . . . . . . . . . . . . . . . . . . . . . . . (801) 584-1973

Veterans Nursing Home Director **Jeff B. Hanson** . . . . . . . . (801) 326-2372
Financial Analyst **Raitos Archuleta** . . . . . . . . . . . . . . . . . . (801) 326-2372
  E-mail: rarchule@utah.gov
State Veterans Cemetery Coordinator **Arnold Warner** . . . . . (801) 326-2372
Veteran Service Officer **Monica Mann** . . . . . . . . . . . . . . . . (801) 326-2372

## Department of Workforce Services [DWS]

140 East 300 South, Salt Lake City, UT 84111
P.O. Box 45249, Salt Lake City, UT 84145-0249
Tel: (801) 526-9675  Fax: (801) 526-9211
E-mail: dwscontactus@utah.gov

■Executive Director **Jon Pierpont** . . . . . . . . . . . . . . . . . . . (801) 526-9210
  E-mail: jpierpo@utah.gov
Deputy Director **Casey Cameron** . . . . . . . . . . . . . . . . . . . (801) 526-9832
  E-mail: caseycameron@utah.gov
Deputy Director **Greg Paras** . . . . . . . . . . . . . . . . . . . . . . (801) 526-9313
  E-mail: gregparas@utah.gov
Administrative Support Director **Nathan Harrison** . . . . . . . (801) 526-9402
  E-mail: nharrison@utah.gov
Information Technologies Director **Mark Schultz** . . . . . . . . (801) 580-5311
  E-mail: mschultz@utah.gov
Workforce Research and Analysis Director **Carrie Mayne** . .(801) 526-9721
  E-mail: cjmayne@utah.gov
Unemployment Insurance Director **Michelle Beebe** . . . . . . .(801) 526-9410
Communications Director **Nate McDonald** . . . . . . . . . . . . (801) 694-0294
  E-mail: nmcdonald@utah.gov
Public Information Officer **Christina Davis** . . . . . . . . . . . . (801) 638-8280
  E-mail: christinadavis@utah.gov
Public Information Officer **Bethany Hyatt** . . . . . . . . . . . . . (801) 315-1208
  E-mail: bethanyhyatt@utah.gov
Public Information Officer **Britnee Johnston** . . . . . . . . . . (385) 495-0060
  E-mail: bjohnston@utah.gov

## Utah Labor Commission

160 East 300 South, Third Floor, Salt Lake City, UT 84111
P.O. Box 146600, Salt Lake City, UT 84114-6600
Tel: (801) 530-6800  Fax: (801) 530-6390  E-mail: laborcom@utah.gov

**Employees:** 118  **Fiscal Year:** 2015  **Budget:** $12,985,459

■Commissioner **Sheryl M. "Sherrie" Hayashi** . . . . . . . . . . (801) 530-6848
  E-mail: shayashi@utah.gov
  Education: Utah, JD
Deputy Commissioner and Chief Legal Counsel
  **Jaceson Maughan** . . . . . . . . . . . . . . . . . . . . . . . . . . . . (801) 530-6036
  E-mail: jacesonmaughan@utah.gov
Antidiscrimination and Labor Director
  **Alison Adams-Perlac** . . . . . . . . . . . . . . . . . . . . . . . . . . (801) 530-6921
                                              Fax: (801) 530-7609
Adjudication Division Director and Administrative Law
  Judge **Heather Gunnarson** . . . . . . . . . . . . . . . . . . . . . . (801) 536-7928
  E-mail: hgunnarson@utah.gov            Fax: (801) 530-6333
Boiler and Elevator Safety Division Director
  **Pete C. Hackford** . . . . . . . . . . . . . . . . . . . . . . . . . . . . . (801) 530-7605
                                              Fax: (801) 530-6871
Industrial Accidents Division Director **Ronald Dressler** . . . (801) 530-6841
                                              Fax: (801) 530-6804
Employers' Reinsurance Fund Administrator
  **Ronald Dressler** . . . . . . . . . . . . . . . . . . . . . . . . . . . . . (801) 530-6841
                                              Fax: (801) 530-6804
Utah Occupational Safety and Health Administrator
  **Chris Hill** . . . . . . . . . . . . . . . . . . . . . . . . . . . . . . . . . . (801) 530-6901
  E-mail: chill@utah.gov                  Fax: (801) 530-7606
Public Information Officer **Jacob Barnhart** . . . . . . . . . . . . (801) 530-6918
  E-mail: jbarnhart@utah.gov

---

★ Elected Official   ■ Appointed by Governor   ● Appointed by Legislature   ▲ Appointed by Board or Commission   ◆ Appointed by State Supreme Court

## Public Service Commission of Utah

Heber M. Wells Building, 160 East 300 South, 4th Floor,
Salt Lake City, UT 84111
P.O. Box 45585, Salt Lake City, UT 84145-0585
Tel: (801) 530-6716  Tel: (866) 772-8824  Fax: (801) 530-6796
E-mail: psc@utah.gov  Internet: www.psc.utah.gov

**Employees:** 22  **Fiscal Year:** 2015  **Budget:** $13,977,685

■Chair **Thad LeVar** . . . . . . . . . . . . . . . . . . . . . . . . . . . . (801) 530-6716
  Term Expires: March 1, 2021
  E-mail: tlevar@utah.gov
■Commissioner **David Clark** . . . . . . . . . . . . . . . . . . . . . . (801) 530-6716
  Term Expires: March 1, 2019
  E-mail: drexclark@utah.gov
■Commissioner **Jordan A. White** . . . . . . . . . . . . . . . . . . (801) 530-6716
  Term Expires: March 1, 2017
  E-mail: jordanwhite@utah.gov

### Commission Staff

▲Commission Administrator **Gary Widerburg** . . . . . . . . . . . (801) 530-6713
  E-mail: gwiderburg@utah.gov
▲Executive Staff Director **Carol Revelt** . . . . . . . . . . . . . . . . (801) 530-6711
  E-mail: crevelt@utah.gov

## Utah State Tax Commission

210 North 1950 West, Salt Lake City, UT 84134
Tel: (801) 297-2200  TTY: (801) 297-2020  Fax: (801) 297-7574
E-mail: taxmaster@utah.gov  Internet: http://tax.utah.gov
Internet: www.incometax.utah.gov (Income Tax Guide)

**Employees:** 748  **Fiscal Year:** 2015  **Budget:** $84,842,000

■Chair **John L. Valentine** . . . . . . . . . . . . . . . . . . . . . . . . (801) 297-3901
  Education: BYU 1973 BS; J Reuben Clark Law 1976 JD
■Commissioner **Michael J. Cragun** . . . . . . . . . . . . . . . . . . (801) 297-3901
  E-mail: mcragun@utah.gov
  Education: BYU 1991 BA; Lewis & Clark 1993 JD
■Commissioner **Robert Pero** . . . . . . . . . . . . . . . . . . . . . . . (801) 297-3800
  E-mail: rpero@utah.gov
■Commissioner **Rebecca L. Rockwell** . . . . . . . . . . . . . . . . (801) 297-3901
  Term Expires: June 30, 2019
▲Executive Director **Barry C. Conover** . . . . . . . . . . . . . . . . (801) 297-3820
  E-mail: bconover@utah.gov
  Education: BYU 1972 BS

## Utah Transportation Commission

4501 South 2700 West, Salt Lake City, UT 84119-5998
P.O. Box 141255, Salt Lake City, UT 84114
Tel: (801) 965-4000  Fax: (801) 965-4338

■Chairman **(Vacant)** . . . . . . . . . . . . . . . . . . . . . . . . . . . . (801) 745-2200
■Commissioner **Wayne K. Barlow** . . . . . . . . . . . . . . . . . . (435) 753-1635
  170 East 1700 South, Providence, UT 84332
  E-mail: waynebarlow@utah.gov
  Education: Utah State BS
■Commissioner **Meghan Zanolli Holbrook** . . . . . . . . . . . . (801) 844-7908
  775 North Hilltop Road, Salt Lake City, UT 84103
  E-mail: mholbrook@utah.gov
■Commissioner **Dannie R. McConkie**
  616 West 1000 North, Unit A, Bountiful, UT 84087
  E-mail: dmcconkie@utah.gov
■Commissioner **Gayle F. McKeachnie** . . . . . . . . . . . . . . . . (435) 789-4908
  2575 West Highway 40, Vernal, UT 84078
  E-mail: gaylemckeachnie@utah.gov
  Education: Southern Utah BA; Utah JD
■Commissioner **J. Kent Millington** . . . . . . . . . . . . . . . . . . (801) 763-8426
  5006 Country Club Drive, Highland, UT 84003-9010
  E-mail: kmillington@utah.gov
■Commissioner **Naghi Zeenati** . . . . . . . . . . . . . . . . . . . . (435) 623-2222
  164 West 700 South, St. George, UT 84770
  E-mail: nzeenati@utah.gov
  Education: Texas (Arlington) BS, MS

## Utah Department of Transportation [UDOT]

4501 South 2700 West, Salt Lake City, UT 84119-5998
P.O. Box 141245, Salt Lake City, UT 84114
Tel: (801) 965-4000  Fax: (801) 965-4338  Internet: www.udot.utah.gov

**Employees:** 1,735  **Fiscal Year:** 2015  **Budget:** $297,828,335

■Executive Director **Carlos Braceras, PE** . . . . . . . . . . . . . . (801) 965-4027
  E-mail: cbraceras@utah.gov
  Administrative Assistant **Diane Josie** . . . . . . . . . . . . . . . (801) 965-4027
Deputy Director **Shane Marshall** . . . . . . . . . . . . . . . . . . (801) 965-4030
  Education: BYU BSCE
Legal Counsel **James Palmer** . . . . . . . . . . . . . . . . . . . . . (801) 965-4197
  E-mail: jimpalmer@utah.gov
Legal Counsel **Renee Spooner** . . . . . . . . . . . . . . . . . . . . (801) 965-4168
  E-mail: rspooner@utah.gov
Aeronautics Director **Patrick Morley** . . . . . . . . . . . . . . . . (801) 231-4418
Communications Director **Joseph Walker** . . . . . . . . . . . . . (801) 965-4088
  E-mail: josephwalker@utah.gov
Fiscal Audit Director **Jimmy Holfeltz** . . . . . . . . . . . . . . . (801) 965-4819
Human Resources Director **Carlos Rodriguez** . . . . . . . . . . (801) 965-4051
Motor Carrier Director **Chad Sheppick** . . . . . . . . . . . . . . (801) 965-4156
Operations Director **Jason Davis** . . . . . . . . . . . . . . . . . . . (801) 965-4895
  Education: Utah State 1994
Policy and Legislative Services Director **Linda Toy Hull** . . . (801) 965-4253
  E-mail: lhull@utah.gov
Project Development Director **Randy Park** . . . . . . . . . . . . . (801) 965-4022
  Education: Utah State 1976 BS, 1978 MS
Right-of-Way Director **Lyle McMillan** . . . . . . . . . . . . . . . (801) 965-4331
Comptroller **Becky Bradshaw** . . . . . . . . . . . . . . . . . . . . . (801) 965-4358
Construction, Materials and Civil Rights Engineering
  Manager **Rob Wight** . . . . . . . . . . . . . . . . . . . . . . . . . . (801) 965-4869
  E-mail: rwight@utah.gov
Maintenance Engineering Director **Kevin Griffin** . . . . . . . . (801) 965-4120
  E-mail: kgriffin@utah.gov
Traffic and Safety Engineer **Robert Miles** . . . . . . . . . . . . . (801) 965-4273
  Chief Railroad Engineer **Eric Cheng** . . . . . . . . . . . . . . . (801) 965-4284
Program Development Director **Nathan Lee** . . . . . . . . . . . (801) 965-4082
  E-mail: nlee@utah.gov

## State Board of Education

250 East 500 South, Salt Lake City, UT 84111
P.O. Box 144200, Salt Lake City, UT 84114-4200
Tel: (801) 538-7500  TTY: (801) 538-7876  Fax: (801) 538-7768
Internet: www.schools.utah.gov/board

★Chair **David L. Crandall** (District 10) . . . . . . . . . . . . . . . (801) 232-0795
  Term Expires: January 2017
  13464 Saddle Ridge Drive, Draper, UT 84020
  E-mail: crandall@xmission.com
  Education: Utah BSME, MSME
★First Vice Chair **David L. Thomas** (R-District 4) . . . . . . . . (801) 479-7479
  Term Expires: January 2017
  7875 South 2250 East, South Weber, UT 84405
  E-mail: dthomas@summitcounty.org
  Education: BYU BS; William & Mary JD
★Second Vice Chair
  **Jennifer A. Johnson, CFA** (District 8) . . . . . . . . . . . . . . (801) 742-1616
  Term Expires: January 2017
  802 Winchester Street, Suite 100, Murray, UT 84107
  E-mail: jj@jenniferajohnson.com
  Education: BYU BS, MBA
★Member **Dixie Allen** (D-District 12) . . . . . . . . . . . . . . . . (435) 790-6673
  Term Expires: January 2017
  218 West 5250 North, Vernal, UT 84078
  E-mail: dixieleeallen@gmail.com
  Education: Utah State 1980 BEd; Utah 1987 MEd
★Member **Laura Collier Belnap** (District 5) . . . . . . . . . . . . (801) 699-7588
  Term Expires: January 2019
  845 East 1500 South, Bountiful, UT 84010
  E-mail: lbelnap@utahonline.org
★Member **Leslie B. Castle** (District 7) . . . . . . . . . . . . . . . . (801) 581-9752
  Term Expires: January 2017
  2465 St. Mary's Drive, Salt Lake City, UT 84108
  E-mail: lesliebrookscastle@gmail.com
  Education: BYU BN; Utah MAA

*(continued on next page)*

---

★ Elected Official  ■ Appointed by Governor  ● Appointed by Legislature  ▲ Appointed by Board or Commission  ◆ Appointed by State Supreme Court

EXECUTIVE BRANCH

**State Board of Education** *continued*

★Member **Barbara W. Corry** (District 15)..............(435) 586-3050
   Term Expires: January 2017
   1022 Cedar Knolls, Cedar City, UT 84720
   E-mail: barbara.corry@schools.utah.gov
   Education: Southern Utah BA

★Member **Brittney Cummins** (District 6)..............(801) 969-5712
   Term Expires: January 2019
   4601 Poseidon Drive, West Valley City, UT 84120
   E-mail: b4cummins@gmail.com
   Education: BYU BS

★Member **Linda B. Hansen** (District 3)................(801) 966-5492
   Term Expires: January 2019
   5149 Village Wood Drive, West Valley City, UT 84120
   E-mail: linda.hansen@schools.utah.gov

★Member **Mark A. Huntsman** (District 14)............(435) 979-4301
   Term Expires: January 2019
   435 South 700 East, Fillmore, UT 84631
   E-mail: mhuntsman@sunrise-eng.com

★Member **Stan Lockhart** (District 13)................(801) 368-2166
   Term Expires: January 2017
   1413 South 1710 East, Provo, UT 84606
   E-mail: stanlockhartutah@gmail.com

★Member **Jefferson Moss** (District 11)..............(801) 916-7386
   Term Expires: January 2017
   1668 Aspen Circle, Saratoga Springs, UT 84045
   E-mail: jeffersonrmoss@gmail.com
   Education: BYU 2002 BA, MBA

★Member **Spencer Stokes** (District 2)................(801) 923-4908
   Term Expires: January 2019
   4259 Skyline Drive, Ogden, UT 88403
   E-mail: utahboard2@gmail.com

★Member **Terryl Warner** (District 1)..................(435) 512-5241
   Term Expires: January 2017
   623 Anderson Avenue, Hyrum, UT 84319
   E-mail: terryl.warner6@gmail.com
   Education: USC BA

★Member **Joel D. Wright** (District 9)................(801) 426-2120
   Term Expires: January 2019
   E-mail: joel.wright.uted@gmail.com
   Education: BYU 1996 BA; NYU 1999 JD

Secretary to the Board **Lorraine Austin**...............(801) 538-7517

## Utah State Office of Education

P.O. Box 144200, Salt Lake City, UT 84114-4200
Tel: (801) 538-7500  TTY: (801) 538-7876  Fax: (801) 538-7521
Internet: www.schools.utah.gov

**Fiscal Year:** 2015 **Budget:** $3,913,285,503

▲State Superintendent of Public Instruction (Interim)
  **Sydnee Dickson**.....................................(801) 538-7510
   E-mail: sydnee.dickson@schools.utah.gov
Charter Schools Director **Marlies Burns**................(801) 538-7817
Law and Policy Advisor **Ben Rasmussen**..............(801) 538-7835
Associate Superintendent for Data, Assessment and
  Accountability **Rich Nye**...........................(801) 538-7500

### Business and Operations

Tel: (801) 538-7500

Deputy Superintendent **Scott Jones**..................(801) 538-7514
   E-mail: scott.jones@schools.utah.gov
Child Nutrition Director **Kathleen Britton**.............(801) 538-7513
   E-mail: kathleen.britton@schools.utah.gov
Human Resources Director **Dave Rodemack**...........(801) 538-7652
Internal Accounting Director **Brian Ipson**.............(801) 538-7621
Public Relations Director **Mark Peterson**.............(801) 538-7635
   E-mail: mark.peterson@schools.utah.gov
School Children's Trust Director **Tim Donaldson**.......(801) 538-7709
School Finance Director **Natalie Grange**..............(801) 538-7668

### Instructional Services

Deputy Superintendent (Interim) **Sydnee Dickson**........(801) 538-7515
   E-mail: sydnee.dickson@schools.utah.gov
Career, Technical and Adult Education Director
  **Thalea Longhurst**.................................(801) 538-7852
Educational Equity Coordinator **Richard Gomez**.........(801) 538-7643

Elementary and Secondary Education Act and Special
  Programs Director **Ann White**......................(801) 538-7827
   E-mail: ann.white@schools.utah.gov
Teaching and Learning Director **Diana Suddreth**.......(801) 538-7739
  Education Technology Services Coordinator
   **Kathleen Webb**..................................(801) 538-7736

### Student Services and Federal Programs

Associate Superintendent (**Vacant**)....................(801) 538-7550
Assessment Director **Jo Ellen Shaeffer**..............(801) 538-7811
   E-mail: joellen.shaeffer@schools.utah.gov
Information Technology Director **Jerry Winkler**.........(801) 538-7842
Special Education Director **Glenna Gallo**..............(801) 538-7757
   E-mail: glenna.gallo@schools.utah.gov
Data and Statistics Quality Manager **Aaron Brough**......(801) 538-7922
   E-mail: aaron.brough@schools.utah.gov

## Utah State Office of Rehabilitation [USOR]

Tel: (801) 538-7536  Fax: (801) 538-7522  Internet: www.usor.utah.gov

Executive Director **Darin Brush**.......................(801) 538-7530

## Utah Schools for the Deaf and the Blind [USDB]

742 Harrison Boulevard, Ogden, UT 84404
Tel: (801) 629-4700

Superintendent **Joel Coleman**.........................(801) 629-4700
   E-mail: joelc@usdb.org
   Education: BYU MPA

## Utah National Guard

12953 South Minuteman Drive, Draper, UT 84020
Tel: (801) 432-4400  Fax: (801) 432-4677

**Employees:** 221 **Fiscal Year:** 2015 **Budget:** $74,412,944

■Adjutant General **MG Jefferson S. Burton, ARNG**......(801) 432-4402
   E-mail: jefferson.s.burton.mil@mail.mil
   Education: SUNY (Albany) 1986 BS; U Phoenix 2001 MA;
   Army War Col 2006 MS
  Administrative Assistant **Patti Griffith**.............(801) 432-4402
Assistant Adjutant General (Air)
  **BrigGen David R. Fountain, ANG**.................(801) 245-2459
Assistant Adjutant General (Army)
  **BG Dallen Atack, ARNG**..........................(801) 432-4268
Director of Joint Staff
  **BrigGen Kenneth L. Gammon, ANG**..............(801) 432-4194
   Education: Weber State 1991 BS; Air Command Col 1998;
   Air War Col 2001
Joint Forces Headquarters Chief of Staff
  **COL Milada A. Copeland, ARNG**..................(801) 432-4403
151st Air Refueling Wing Commander
  **Col Darwin L. Craig, ANG**........................(801) 245-2307
Command Sergeant Major
  **CSM Michael M. Miller, ARNG**....................(801) 432-4410
Financial Manager **COL Lawrence A. Schmidt, ARNG**...(801) 432-4087
Public Affairs/Freedom of Information Act Officer
  **LTC Steven A. Fairbourn, ARNG**..................(801) 432-4407
   E-mail: steven.a.fairbourn.mil@mail.mil
Deputy Chief of Staff, Information Technology
  **COL Gordon D. Behunin, ARNG**..................(801) 432-4110
   E-mail: gordon.d.behunin.mil@mail.mil

## Office of the Lieutenant Governor

Utah State Capitol, Suite 220, Salt Lake City, UT 84114
Tel: (801) 538-1041  Fax: (801) 538-1133  Internet: www.lg.utah.gov

★Lieutenant Governor **Spencer J. Cox** (R)..............(801) 538-1048
   Term Expires: January 2017
   E-mail: spencercox@utah.gov
   Education: Snow AA; Utah State BA; Washington and Lee 2000 JD
   Career: State Representative (R-UT, District 58), Utah House of
   Representatives (2013)
Chief Deputy and Director of Elections **Mark Thomas**....(801) 538-1494
  Deputy Director of Elections **Justin Lee**.............(801) 538-1129
Office Administrator **Spencer Hadley**.................(801) 538-1513
   E-mail: spencerhadley@utah.gov

---

★ Elected Official   ■ Appointed by Governor   ● Appointed by Legislature   ▲ Appointed by Board or Commission   ◆ Appointed by State Supreme Court

# Office of the Attorney General

350 North State Street, Suite 230, Salt Lake City, UT 84114
P.O. Box 142320, Salt Lake City, UT 84114-2320
Tel: (801) 366-0260  Tel: (801) 538-9600  Fax: (801) 538-1121

**Employees:** 430  **Fiscal Year:** 2015  **Budget:** $59,342,147

★ Attorney General **Sean D. Reyes** (R) . . . . . . . . . . . . . . . . (801) 366-0260
   Term Expires: January 2017
   Education: BYU 1994 BA; Boalt Hall 1997 JD
   Career: Attorney, Litigation Department, Parsons Behle & Latimer
Chief Civil Deputy Attorney General **Bridget Romano** . . . (801) 366-0260
   Education: Utah 1994 JD
Chief Criminal Deputy Attorney General
   **Spencer Austin** . . . . . . . . . . . . . . . . . . . . . . . . . . . . . . (801) 281-1201
   Education: Utah BS, JD
Chief of Staff **Missy Larsen** . . . . . . . . . . . . . . . . . . . . . . (801) 366-0260
   Education: Utah BS
Chief Federal Deputy and General Counsel
   **Parker Douglas** . . . . . . . . . . . . . . . . . . . . . . . . . . . . . . (801) 366-0260
   Education: Pitzer BA; Utah JD
Solicitor General **Tyler R. Green** . . . . . . . . . . . . . . . . . . (801) 366-0179
   Education: Utah BS, JD
Law Office Administrator and Budget Director
   **Werner Haidenthaller** . . . . . . . . . . . . . . . . . . . . . . . . . (801) 366-0555
Child and Family Support Division Chief
   **John H. Bowen** . . . . . . . . . . . . . . . . . . . . . . . . . . . . . . (801) 536-8300
   E-mail: jbowen@utah.gov
   Education: Utah 1993 JD
Child Protection Division Chief **David Carlson** . . . . . . . . . (801) 366-0251
   E-mail: dcarlson@utah.gov
Children's Justice Division Chief **Craig Barlow** . . . . . . . . . (801) 538-1941
   E-mail: crbarlow@utah.gov
   Education: Utah 1977 JD
Commercial Enforcement Division Chief
   **Blaine Ferguson** . . . . . . . . . . . . . . . . . . . . . . . . . . . . . (801) 366-0310
Criminal Appeals Division Chief **(Vacant)** . . . . . . . . . . . . (801) 366-0180
Criminal Justice Division Chief **Scott Reed** . . . . . . . . . . . (801) 281-1240
Education and Health Division Chief **David Jones** . . . . . . . (801) 366-0270
   E-mail: djones@utah.gov
Environment Division Chief **Craig Anderson** . . . . . . . . . . (801) 536-0286
   195 North 1950 West, Salt Lake City, UT 84116
Litigation Division Chief **Steve Walkenhorst** . . . . . . . . . . (801) 366-0127
   Education: J Reuben Clark Law 1978 JD
Natural Resources Division Chief **Norman K. Johnson** . . . (801) 538-7444
   E-mail: njohnson@utah.gov
   Education: Utah 1979 BA, 1982 JD
State Agency Counsel Division Chief **Susan Eisenman** . . . (801) 538-4128
Tax and Revenue Division Chief **John McCarrey** . . . . . . . . (801) 366-0375
   Education: J Reuben Clark Law 1990 JD
Medicaid Fraud Control Unit Director **Robert E. Steed** . . . (801) 281-1258
Director of Communications **Daniel Burton** . . . . . . . . . . . (801) 386-6830
   E-mail: danburton@utah.gov
   Press Secretary **Camille Anderson** . . . . . . . . . . . . . . . (801) 538-9600
     E-mail: camilleanderson@utah.gov
     Education: Syracuse BA
Investigations Director **(Vacant)** . . . . . . . . . . . . . . . . . . . (801) 281-1207
Information Technology Section Director **Chris Earl** . . . . . . (801) 366-0220
   E-mail: cearl@utah.gov

# Office of the State Auditor

Utah State Capitol Complex, State Office Building, Suite E310,
Salt Lake City, UT 84114
P.O. Box 142310, Salt Lake City, UT 84114-2310
Tel: (801) 538-1025

**Employees:** 46  **Fiscal Year:** 2015  **Budget:** $6,309,500

★ State Auditor **John Dougall** (R) . . . . . . . . . . . . . . . . . . . (801) 538-1025
   Term Expires: January 2017
   Education: BYU BSEE, MSEE, MBA
   Career: State Representative (R-UT, District 27), Utah House of
   Representatives (2003-2013)
   Administrative Assistant **Maria Fandl** . . . . . . . . . . . . . . (801) 538-1361
Financial Audit Director **Hollie Andrus** . . . . . . . . . . . . . . (801) 808-0467
Financial Audit Director **Van Christensen** . . . . . . . . . . . . (801) 808-0698
Financial Audit Director **Jon Johnson** . . . . . . . . . . . . . . . (801) 808-0658

Performance Audit Director **Dave Pulsipher** . . . . . . . . . . . (801) 866-8504

# Office of the State Treasurer

Utah State Capitol Complex, 350 North State Street, #180,
Salt Lake City, UT 84114
Tel: (801) 538-1042  TTY: (801) 538-1042  Fax: (801) 538-1465

**Employees:** 26  **Fiscal Year:** 2015  **Budget:** $3,096,066

★ State Treasurer **David Damschen** (R) . . . . . . . . . . . . . . . (801) 538-1042
   Term Expires: January 2017
   E-mail: ddamschen@utah.gov
   Executive Secretary **Kathy Tenhoeve Wilkey** . . . . . . . . (801) 538-1468
Chief Deputy Treasurer **(Vacant)** . . . . . . . . . . . . . . . . . . . (801) 538-1042
Deputy Treasurer and Unclaimed Property Office
   Administrator **Dennis Johnston** . . . . . . . . . . . . . . . . . (801) 715-3300
   168 North 1950 West, Suite 102, Salt Lake City, UT 84116-4840
Investment Officer **Christine Brandt** . . . . . . . . . . . . . . . . (801) 538-1042
   E-mail: cbrandt@utah.gov

# Utah Housing Corporation

2479 South Lake Park Boulevard, West Valley City, UT 84120
Tel: (801) 902-8200  E-mail: info@utahhousingcorp.org

▲ President and Chief Executive Officer
   **Grant S. Whitaker** . . . . . . . . . . . . . . . . . . . . . . . . . . . (801) 902-8200
   E-mail: gwhitaker@uthc.org
Senior Vice President and Chief Financial Officer
   **Cleon P. Butterfield** . . . . . . . . . . . . . . . . . . . . . . . . . . (801) 902-8200
Senior Vice President and Chief Operating Officer
   **Jonathan A. Hanks** . . . . . . . . . . . . . . . . . . . . . . . . . . . (801) 902-8200

# Utah Retirement System

540 East Second South, Salt Lake City, UT 84102
Tel: (801) 366-7700  Fax: (801) 366-7734

▲ Executive Director **Daniel D. Andersen** . . . . . . . . . . . . . . (801) 366-7309
   E-mail: dan.andersen@urs.org     Fax: (801) 328-7343
Deputy Executive Director **Todd W. Rupp, CPA** . . . . . . . . (801) 366-7364
                        Fax: (801) 328-7364
Defined Contribution Plans Saving Director
   **Craige D. Stone** . . . . . . . . . . . . . . . . . . . . . . . . . . . . (801) 366-7412
                        Fax: (801) 328-7412
Education and Marketing Director **Joel Sheppard** . . . . . . . (801) 366-3940
                        Fax: (801) 328-3940
Finance Director **Kim Kellersberger, CGFM** . . . . . . . . . . . (801) 366-7457
                        Fax: (801) 328-7457
Internal Audit Director **Steven M. West, CPA, CFE** . . . . . . (801) 366-7356
                        Fax: (801) 328-7356
Records Management Director **Matthew Judd** . . . . . . . . . . (801) 366-7386
                        Fax: (801) 328-7386
Retirement Director **Judy Lund** . . . . . . . . . . . . . . . . . . . . (801) 366-7770
                        Fax: (801) 328-7733
Shared Services Director **Jeff J. Allen** . . . . . . . . . . . . . . . (801) 366-7351
   Education: Utah BS               Fax: (801) 328-7351
Chief Information Officer **Kendall Rima** . . . . . . . . . . . . . . (801) 366-7766
   E-mail: kendall.rima@urs.org     Fax: (801) 245-7766
Chief Investment Officer **Bruce H. Cundick, CFA, CPA** . . . (801) 366-7330
                        Fax: (801) 328-7330
General Counsel **Dee Larsen** . . . . . . . . . . . . . . . . . . . . . . (801) 366-3937
                        Fax: (801) 328-3937

---

★ Elected Official   ■ Appointed by Governor   ● Appointed by Legislature   ▲ Appointed by Board or Commission   ◆ Appointed by State Supreme Court

# Vermont

Tel: (802) 828-1110 (State Information)  Internet: www.vermont.gov

**Number of U.S. Congressional Delegates:** 2 Senators; 1 Representative  **Governor's Term:** 2 years
**Legislature Description:** General Assembly - 30 member Senate; 150 member House of Representatives;
Term - Senate 2 years, House 2 years  **Next Election:** Governor November 2016; Legislature November
2016  **Number of Electoral Votes:** 3  **Official Name:** State of Vermont (French: green mountain)
**Nickname:** Green Mountain State  **Motto:** Freedom and Unity

**Population:** 626,042 (2015); Rank 50  **Fiscal Year:** 2014  **Budget:** $7,075,527,000

## Office of the Governor

Pavilion Office Building, 109 State Street, Fifth Floor,
Montpelier, VT 05609-0101
Tel: (802) 828-3333  Fax: (802) 828-3339

**Peter E. Shumlin**
Governor

Note: Governor Peter Shumlin announced he will
not seek reelection in 2016.
Began Service: January 6, 2011
Term Expires: 2017
Date of Birth: March 24, 1956
Education: Wesleyan Col 1979 BA
Home: Putney
Career: Representative (D-VT), Vermont House of
Representatives (1990-1993); Senator (D-VT),
Vermont Senate (1993-2002); Senator (D-VT),
Vermont Senate (2007-2011)

★Governor **Peter E. Shumlin** (D) . . . . . . . . . . . . . . . . . . . . (802) 828-3333
Chief of Staff **Darren M. Springer** . . . . . . . . . . . . . . . . (802) 828-3333
  Education: Florida Atlantic BA; Vermont Law MEL, JD
Chief Legal Counsel **Sarah E. B. London** . . . . . . . . . . . . . (802) 828-3333
  Education: Dartmouth; Northeastern JD
Civil and Military Affairs Secretary **Susan Allen-Picone** . . (802) 828-3333
  E-mail: susan.allen@state.vt.us
Special Assistant to the Governor (Press) **Scott Coriell** . . . . (802) 828-3333
  E-mail: scott.coriell@state.vt.us
  Education: Middlebury 2007 BA
Special Assistant to the Governor for Health Care
  **Robin Lunge** . . . . . . . . . . . . . . . . . . . . . . . . . . . . . . . (802) 828-3333
Senior Advisor to the Governor and Chief of Health Care
  Reform **Lawrence Miller** . . . . . . . . . . . . . . . . . . . . . . . (802) 828-3333
Intergovernmental Affairs Director and Policy Advisor
  **James Pepper** . . . . . . . . . . . . . . . . . . . . . . . . . . . . . . (802) 828-3333
Special Projects Director and Policy Advisor **Laura Gray** . . (802) 828-3333
Legislative Liaison **Jahala Dudley** . . . . . . . . . . . . . . . . . . (802) 828-3333

## Office of the Defender General [ODG]

6 Baldwin Street, 4th Floor, Montpelier, VT 05633-3301
Tel: (802) 828-3168  Fax: (802) 828-3163
■Defender General **Matthew F. Valerio** . . . . . . . . . . . . . . . (802) 828-3168
  E-mail: matthew.valerio@vermont.gov
  Education: St Michael's 1985 BA; Western New England 1988 JD
Administrative Services Manager **Lora A. Evans** . . . . . . . . (802) 828-3168
  E-mail: lora.evans@vermont.gov

## Office of Veterans Affairs

118 State Street, Montpelier, VT 05620-4401
Tel: (802) 828-3379  Fax: (802) 828-5932
Director **Robert E. Burke** . . . . . . . . . . . . . . . . . . . . . . . . (802) 828-3379

## Agency of Administration

Pavilion Office Building, 109 State Street, Montpelier, VT 05609
Tel: (802) 828-3322  Fax: (802) 828-3320  Internet: www.adm.state.vt.us

**Employees:** 827  **Fiscal Year:** 2015  **Budget:** $95,524,000
■Secretary **Justin G. Johnson** . . . . . . . . . . . . . . . . . . . . . (802) 828-3322
  E-mail: justin.johnson@state.vt.us
Deputy Secretary **Michael Clasen** . . . . . . . . . . . . . . . . . . (802) 828-3322
  E-mail: michael.clasen@state.vt.us
  Education: Iowa 1984 BA
Chief Performance Officer **Susan Zeller** . . . . . . . . . . . . . . (802) 828-3322

## Finance and Management Department

Internet: www.finance.state.vt.us
■Commissioner **Andrew "Andy" Pallito** . . . . . . . . . . . . . . (802) 828-2376
Deputy Commissioner and Financial Operations Director
  **Bradley "Brad" Ferland** . . . . . . . . . . . . . . . . . . . . . . (802) 828-3322
  E-mail: brad.ferland@state.vt.us
Budget and Management Operations Director
  **Emily Byrne** . . . . . . . . . . . . . . . . . . . . . . . . . . . . . . (802) 828-6446
  E-mail: emily.byrne@state.vt.us

## Human Resources Department

110 State Street, Montpelier, VT 05620-3001
■Commissioner **Maribeth Spellman** . . . . . . . . . . . . . . . . (802) 828-3491
  E-mail: maribeth.spellman@state.vt.us
■Deputy Commissioner **Tom Cheney** . . . . . . . . . . . . . . . . (802) 828-3491
  E-mail: tom.cheney@state.vt.us
Labor Relations Division Director **John Berard** . . . . . . . . . (802) 828-3642

## Information and Innovation Department

Tel: (802) 828-4141  Fax: (802) 828-3398  Internet: http://dii.vermont.gov
■Commissioner and State Chief Information Officer
  **Richard Boes** . . . . . . . . . . . . . . . . . . . . . . . . . . . . . . (802) 828-4141
  E-mail: richard.boes@state.vt.us
Deputy Commissioner **Darwin Thompson** . . . . . . . . . . . . (802) 828-1142
  E-mail: darwin.thompson@state.vt.us

## Libraries Department

109 State Street, Montpelier, VT 05609-0601
Tel: (802) 828-3261  Fax: (802) 828-2199
State Librarian **Martha Reid** . . . . . . . . . . . . . . . . . . . . . (802) 828-3265
  Assistant State Librarian **(Vacant)** . . . . . . . . . . . . . . . . (802) 828-2714
Information Technology Librarian **Sheila Kearns** . . . . . . . . (802) 828-6952
  E-mail: sheila.kearns@vermont.gov
Budget and Fiscal Officer **Paul Rousseau** . . . . . . . . . . . . (802) 828-0681

## State Buildings and General Services Department

Two Governor Aiken Avenue, Montpelier, VT 05633-5801
Drawer 33, Montpelier, VT 05633-5801
Internet: www.bgs.state.vt.us
■Commissioner **Michael J. Obuchowski** . . . . . . . . . . . . . (802) 828-3519
  E-mail: mike.obuchowski@state.vt.us
Security Programs Director **Peter Danles** . . . . . . . . . . . . . (802) 828-1423

---

★ Elected Official     ■ Appointed by Governor     ● Appointed by Legislature     ▲ Appointed by Board or Commission     ◆ Appointed by State Supreme Court

Central Support Service Director
**William H. "Bill" Laferriere** . . . . . . . . . . . . . . . . . . . . . . . . (802) 828-1115

## Tax Department

133 State Street, Montpelier, VT 05633
E-mail: vttaxdept@tax.state.vt.us  Internet: www.state.vt.us/tax

■Commissioner **Mary N. Peterson** . . . . . . . . . . . . . . . . . . . . (802) 828-3763
  E-mail: mary.peterson@state.vt.us
Deputy Tax Commissioner **Gregg A. Mousley** . . . . . . . . . (802) 828-3763
Compliance Division Director **Valerie Rickert** . . . . . . . . . . (802) 828-2821
Property Valuation and Review Division Director
  **Douglas Farnham** . . . . . . . . . . . . . . . . . . . . . . . . . . . . . . . (802) 828-5867
Taxpayer Services Division Director **Sharon Acasy** . . . . . . (802) 828-2535

## Vermont Agency of Agriculture, Food and Markets [VAAFM]

116 State Street, Montpelier, VT 05620-2901
Tel: (802) 828-2430  Fax: (802) 828-2361
Internet: www.vermontagriculture.com

**Employees: 95  Fiscal Year: 2015  Budget: $17,698,000**

■Secretary **Charles R. "Chuck" Ross, Jr.** . . . . . . . . . . . . . . (802) 828-5667
  E-mail: chuck.ross@state.vt.us
■Deputy Secretary **Jolinda H. LaClair** . . . . . . . . . . . . . . . . (802) 828-5667
  E-mail: jolinda.laclair@state.vt.us
■Deputy Secretary and Director of Agricultural
  Development **Diane Bothfeld** . . . . . . . . . . . . . . . . . . . . . . (802) 828-5667
  E-mail: diane.bothfeld@state.vt.us
Food Safety and Consumer Protection Division Director
  **Dr. Kristin Haas** . . . . . . . . . . . . . . . . . . . . . . . . . . . . . . . . (802) 828-2426
Agriculture Resource Management and Environment
  Stewardship Division Director **James "Jim" Leland** . . . . (802) 828-3478
  Consumer Protection Chief **Henry Marckres** . . . . . . . . . . (802) 828-2436
  Dairy Industries Chief **Dan Scruton** . . . . . . . . . . . . . . . . (802) 828-2433
  Meat Inspection Chief **Randy Quenneville** . . . . . . . . . . . (802) 828-2426
Laboratories Director **Guy Roberts** . . . . . . . . . . . . . . . . . . (802) 585-4441
  Laboratories Supervisor **John Jaworski** . . . . . . . . . . . . . (802) 828-2430
    UVM, Hills Building, 103 South Main Street, Waterbury, VT 05676
    Education: Castleton State 1979 BA; Northeastern 1981 MS
State Veterinarian **Dr. Kristin Haas** . . . . . . . . . . . . . . . . . . (802) 828-2426
  Assistant State Veterinarian **Katherine McNamara** . . . . . (802) 828-2426
  Assistant State Veterinarian **Shelley Mehlenbacher** . . . . (802) 828-2421

## Agency of Commerce and Community Development [ACCD]

One National Life Drive, Montpelier, VT 05620-0501
Tel: (802) 828-3211  Fax: (802) 828-3383

**Employees: 91  Fiscal Year: 2015  Budget: $33,629,000**

■Secretary **Patricia "Pat" Moulton** . . . . . . . . . . . . . . . . . . (802) 828-5204
  E-mail: pat.moulton@state.vt.us
■Deputy Secretary **Lucy R. Leriche** . . . . . . . . . . . . . . . . . . (802) 828-5204
  E-mail: lucy.leriche@state.vt.us
General Counsel **John W. Kessler** . . . . . . . . . . . . . . . . . . . (802) 828-5202
Administrative Services Division Director
  **Katheran "Kathy" Thayer** . . . . . . . . . . . . . . . . . . . . . . . . (802) 828-5205
  E-mail: kathy.thayer@state.vt.us

## Economic Development Department

Fax: (802) 828-3258  Internet: www.thinkvermont.com
Commissioner **Lisa Gosselin** . . . . . . . . . . . . . . . . . . . . . . . (802) 828-3258

## Housing and Community Development Department

One National Life Drive, Montpelier, VT 05620-0501
Tel: (802) 828-3258

Commissioner **Noelle Mackay** . . . . . . . . . . . . . . . . . . . . . . (802) 828-3080
  E-mail: noelle.mackay@state.vt.us
Deputy Commissioner **(Vacant)** . . . . . . . . . . . . . . . . . . . . . (802) 828-5208
State Historic Preservation Officer **Laura Trieschmann** . . . (802) 828-3222
                                     Fax: (802) 828-3206

## Tourism and Marketing Department

One National Life Drive, Montpelier, VT 05620-0501
Fax: (802) 828-3233

■Commissioner **Megan M. Smith** . . . . . . . . . . . . . . . . . . . . (802) 828-3649
  E-mail: megan.smith@state.vt.us
■Deputy Commissioner **Steve Cook** . . . . . . . . . . . . . . . . . . (802) 522-2896
  E-mail: steve.cook@state.vt.us

## Vermont Housing Finance Agency [VHFA]

164 Saint Paul Street, Burlington, VT 05041
P. O. Box 405, Burlington, VT 05402
Tel: (802) 864-5743  Fax: (802) 864-8081  E-mail: home@vhfa.org
Internet: www.vhfa.org

Executive Director **Sarah E. Carpenter** . . . . . . . . . . . . . . . (802) 652-3421
  E-mail: scarpenter@vhfa.org            Fax: (802) 864-8746
  Education: Vermont BS; Harvard 1982 MPA
Administration and Policy Director **Maura Collins** . . . . . . . (802) 652-3463
  E-mail: mcollins@vhfa.org              Fax: (802) 864-8746
Development Director **Joseph Erdelyi** . . . . . . . . . . . . . . . . (802) 652-3432
Homeownership Programs Director **Jacklyn R. Santerre** . . (802) 652-3446
  E-mail: jsanterre@vhfa.org            Fax: (802) 863-5422
Homeownership Operations Coordinator **Veronica Devos** . . (802) 652-3456
                                       Fax: (802) 863-5422
Multifamily Programs Director **Sam Falzome** . . . . . . . . . . (802) 652-3435
Multifamily Programs Assistant Director
  **Kimberly A. Roy** . . . . . . . . . . . . . . . . . . . . . . . . . . . . . . . (802) 652-3433
Multifamily Management Officer **Kathy Curley** . . . . . . . . . (802) 652-3457
  E-mail: kcurley@vhfa.org              Fax: (802) 864-5746
Program Operations Chief **David S. Adams** . . . . . . . . . . . . (802) 652-3478
  E-mail: dadams@vhfa.org             Fax: (802) 864-5746
Communications Coordinator **Leslie Black-Plumeau** . . . . . (802) 652-3429
  E-mail: lblack-plumeau@vhfa.org
Chief Financial Officer **Tom Connors** . . . . . . . . . . . . . . . . (802) 652-3436
                                       Fax: (802) 864-5746
Bond Financing and Investments Manager
  **Michelle Baird** . . . . . . . . . . . . . . . . . . . . . . . . . . . . . . . . . (802) 652-3405
Finance Operations Manager **Lisa Clark** . . . . . . . . . . . . . . (802) 652-3430
                                       Fax: (802) 863-5422
General Counsel **George Demas** . . . . . . . . . . . . . . . . . . . . (802) 652-3459
  E-mail: gdemas@vhfa.org             Fax: (802) 864-5746

## Agency of Human Services [AHS]

State Complex, 103 South Main Street, Waterbury, VT 05671
Tel: (802) 241-0440  Fax: (802) 241-2979

**Employees: 3,540  Fiscal Year: 2015  Budget: $3,733,262,000**

■Secretary **Hal Cohen** . . . . . . . . . . . . . . . . . . . . . . . . . . . . (802) 241-0440
  E-mail: hal.cohen@state.vt.us
Deputy Secretary **Paul Dragon** . . . . . . . . . . . . . . . . . . . . . (802) 241-0430
  Administrative Assistant **Katie Whitney** . . . . . . . . . . . . . (802) 871-3252
Rate Setting Division Director **Kathleen Denette** . . . . . . . . (802) 652-6528
Chief Information Officer **Darin Prail** . . . . . . . . . . . . . . . . (802) 828-3887
  E-mail: darin.prail@ahs.state.vt.us
Health Care Operations Director **Stephanie Beck** . . . . . . . . (802) 871-3265
Special Projects Coordinator **Susan J. Bartlett** . . . . . . . . . (802) 241-2220
  Education: Vermont 1968 BA; Johnson State 1976 MA

## Department for Children and Families [DCF]

State Complex, 103 South Main Street, Waterbury, VT 05671-5920
Tel: (802) 871-3385  Fax: (802) 769-2064

■Commissioner **Ken Schatz** . . . . . . . . . . . . . . . . . . . . . . . . (802) 871-3385
  E-mail: ken.schatz@state.vt.us
  Education: Vermont 1977 BS; Cornell JD
  Executive Staff Assistant to the Commissioner
    **Luciana Diruocco** . . . . . . . . . . . . . . . . . . . . . . . . . . . . . (802) 871-3385
Child Development Division Deputy Commissioner
  **Reeva Murphy** . . . . . . . . . . . . . . . . . . . . . . . . . . . . . . . . . (802) 769-6028
Family Services Division Deputy Commissioner
  **Cynthia "Cindy" Walcott** . . . . . . . . . . . . . . . . . . . . . . . . (802) 769-6399
Economic Services Deputy Commissioner **Sean Brown** . . . (802) 769-6457

*(continued on next page)*

---

★ Elected Official    ■ Appointed by Governor    ● Appointed by Legislature    ▲ Appointed by Board or Commission    ◆ Appointed by State Supreme Court

**Department for Children and Families** *continued*

Operations Chief **Pamela P. "Pam" Dalley** . . . . . . . . . . (802) 769-1686
Health Access Eligibility Unit Director
  **Michele M. Betit** . . . . . . . . . . . . . . . . . . . . . . . . (802) 769-6500
   E-mail: michele.betit@state.vt.us
Fraud and Prevention Chief **Donna Hosking** . . . . . (802) 769-2776
Child Protection Director **Karen Shea** . . . . . . . . . . . . . (802) 769-2053
Disability Determination Services Director
  **Trudy M. Lyon-Hart** . . . . . . . . . . . . . . . . . . . . . . (802) 241-2475
Computer Services Division Director **Laurie D. Sabens** . . . (802) 828-4615
   E-mail: laurie.sabens@state.vt.us
Economic Opportunity Office Administrator
  **Sarah Phillips** . . . . . . . . . . . . . . . . . . . . . . . . . . . . (802) 871-3398
Child Support Services Office Director **Jeffrey P. Cohen** . . (802) 769-2128
   E-mail: jeff.cohen@state.vt.us
Food and Nutrition Program Director **Pat Duda** . . . . . . . . (802) 769-6439
  Workforce Development Director **Doreen Marquis** . . . . . (802) 871-3397
General Counsel **Leslie Wisdom** . . . . . . . . . . . . . . . . . (802) 828-2106

# Vermont Department of Corrections

426 Industrial Avenue, Williston, VT 05495
Tel: (802) 241-2442  Fax: (802) 241-0020

■Commissioner **Lisa M. Menard** . . . . . . . . . . . . . . . . . (802) 241-2442
   E-mail: lisa.menard@vermont.gov
Deputy Commissioner **Cheryl Elovirta** . . . . . . . . . . . (802) 241-2442
Financial Director **Matthew D'Agostino** . . . . . . . . . . . (802) 951-5008
Correctional Facilities Director **Mike Touchette** . . . . . . . . (802) 951-5010
Field Services Executive **Dale Crook** . . . . . . . . . . . . . (802) 241-2247
Programs Services Executive **Kim Bushey** . . . . . . . . . . . (802) 951-5012
  Finance and Personnel Assistant Director **(Vacant)** . . . . . . (802) 564-4300

# Disabilities, Aging, and Independent Living Department

HC 2 South, 280 State Drive, Waterbury, VT 05671-2020
Tel: (802) 241-2401  Internet: http://dail.vermont.gov

Commissioner **Monica Caserta Hutt** . . . . . . . . . . . . . . (802) 871-3350
   E-mail: monica.hutt@state.vt.us
Deputy Commissioner **Camille George** . . . . . . . . . . . . . (802) 871-3350
Business Office Director **William R. "Bill" Kelly** . . . . . . . .(802) 871-3208
Blind and Visually Impaired Division Director
  **Fred Jones** . . . . . . . . . . . . . . . . . . . . . . . . . . . . . . (802) 871-3038
Licensing and Protection Division Director
  **Clayton Clark** . . . . . . . . . . . . . . . . . . . . . . . . . . . (802) 871-3317
Vocational Rehabilitation Division Director
  **Diane Dalmasse** . . . . . . . . . . . . . . . . . . . . . . . . . (802) 871-3068
                       Fax: (802) 241-3359

# Health Department

P.O. Box 70, Burlington, VT 05402
Tel: (802) 863-7200  Tel: (802) 863-7275 (Vital Records)
Fax: (802) 863-7425  Internet: www.healthvermont.gov

■Commissioner **Dr. Harry L. Chen, MD** . . . . . . . . . . . . . (802) 863-7280
   E-mail: harry.chen@ahs.state.vt.us
   Education: Oregon Health MD
Alcohol & Drug Abuse Programs Deputy Commissioner
  **Barbara Cimaglio** . . . . . . . . . . . . . . . . . . . . . . . . (802) 651-1258
Public Health Deputy Commissioner **Tracy Dolan** . . . . . . . (802) 863-7281
Board Medical Practical Director **David K. Herlihy** . . . . . . (802) 863-7320
Health Promotion Disease Prevention Director **Julie Arel** . . (802) 863-7269
Health Surveillance Director **Heidi Klein** . . . . . . . . . . . (802) 863-7300
Maternal Child Health Director **Dr. Breena Holmes** . . . . . . (802) 863-7347
Public Health Laboratory Director **Mary J. Celotti** . . . . . (802) 863-7570
Public Health Preparedness Director **Christopher Bell** . . . . (802) 863-7230
  Education: Ohio State 2009 MPH, 2009 MA
Children with Special Health Needs Division Director
  **Carol Hassler** . . . . . . . . . . . . . . . . . . . . . . . . . . . (802) 863-7338
Emergency Medical Services Division Director
  **Christopher Bell** . . . . . . . . . . . . . . . . . . . . . . . . . (802) 863-7263

# Board of Medical Practice

108 Cherry Street, Burlington, VT 05401
P.O. Box 70, Burlington, VT 05402
Tel: (802) 657-4220  Fax: (802) 657-4227
E-mail: medicalboard@vermont.gov  Internet: healthvermont.gov

Chair **William K. Hoser, PA-C** . . . . . . . . . . . . . . . . . . (802) 657-4220
Vice Chair **Robert G. Hayward** . . . . . . . . . . . . . . . . . (802) 657-4220
Secretary **Richard Bernstein** . . . . . . . . . . . . . . . . . . . (802) 657-4220
Executive Director **David K. Herlihy** . . . . . . . . . . . . . . (802) 657-4221

# Mental Health Department

P.O. Box 70, Burlington, VT 05402
Tel: (802) 652-2601  Fax: (802) 652-2005

Mental Health Commissioner **Frank Reed** . . . . . . . . . . . (802) 828-3808
Mental Health Deputy Commissioner **Melissa Bailey** . . . . . (802) 828-3808
Financial Services Division Director **Heidi Hall** . . . . . . . . (802) 828-3808
Legal Services Division Director **Dena Monahan** . . . . . . . (802) 657-4094

# Department of Vermont Health Access [DVHA]

312 Hurricane Lane, Williston, VT 05495
Tel: (802) 879-5900  Fax: (802) 879-5651

Commissioner **Steven M. Costantino** . . . . . . . . . . . . . . (802) 879-5901
   E-mail: steven.costantino@state.vt.us    Fax: (802) 879-5962
   Education: Providence 1979 BA
Deputy Commissioner **Tom Boyd** . . . . . . . . . . . . . . . . (802) 879-5901
                       Fax: (802) 879-5962
Health Services and Managed Care Deputy
  Commissioner **Aaron French** . . . . . . . . . . . . . . . . (802) 879-5906
                       Fax: (802) 879-5962
Policy Fiscal and Support Services Deputy Commissioner
  **Lori Collins** . . . . . . . . . . . . . . . . . . . . . . . . . . . . (802) 879-5901
                       Fax: (802) 879-5962
Chief Medical Officer
  **Dr. Thomas "Tom" Simpatico, MD** . . . . . . . . . . . . . (802) 879-5955
                       Fax: (802) 879-5963
Policy Director **Selina Hickman** . . . . . . . . . . . . . . . . . (802) 879-5939
   E-mail: selina.hickman@state.vt.us

# Developmental Disabilities Council

State Complex, 103 South Main Street, Room 117N,
Waterbury, VT 05676

President **John Hall** . . . . . . . . . . . . . . . . . . . . . . . . . (802) 828-1310
Executive Director **Karen Swartz** . . . . . . . . . . . . . . . . (802) 828-1310

# Vermont Housing and Conservation Board

Tel: (802) 828-3250  Fax: (802) 828-3203  E-mail: info@vhcb.org

Chair **Neil Mickenberg** . . . . . . . . . . . . . . . . . . . . . . . (802) 828-3250
Vice Chair **Emily E. Wadhams** . . . . . . . . . . . . . . . . . . (802) 828-3250
  Education: Vermont BA, MS
Member **Sarah E. Carpenter** . . . . . . . . . . . . . . . . . . . (802) 828-3250
Member **Hal Cohen** . . . . . . . . . . . . . . . . . . . . . . . . . (802) 828-3250
Member **Joshua Laughlin** . . . . . . . . . . . . . . . . . . . . . (802) 828-3250
Member **Deborah L. "Deb" Markowitz** . . . . . . . . . . . . . (802) 828-3250
  Education: Vermont 1983 BA; Georgetown 1987 JD
Member **David Marvin** . . . . . . . . . . . . . . . . . . . . . . . (802) 828-3250
Member **Bill Roper** . . . . . . . . . . . . . . . . . . . . . . . . . (802) 828-3250
Member **Charles R. "Chuck" Ross, Jr.** . . . . . . . . . . . . . (802) 828-3250
Member **Hannah Sessions** . . . . . . . . . . . . . . . . . . . . (802) 828-3250
Member **Tom Yahn** . . . . . . . . . . . . . . . . . . . . . . . . . (802) 828-3250

## Board Staff

Executive Director **Gus Seelig** . . . . . . . . . . . . . . . . . . (802) 828-3250
Administrative Officer **Larry Miles** . . . . . . . . . . . . . . . (802) 828-5072
Communications Director **Pam Boyd** . . . . . . . . . . . . . . (802) 828-5075
Policy and Special Projects Director **Jennifer Hollar** . . . . . (802) 828-5865
Grants Coordinator **Marcy Christian** . . . . . . . . . . . . . . (802) 828-5070
Information Systems Manager **Dan Herman** . . . . . . . . . . (802) 828-2432
Office Manager **Laurie Graves** . . . . . . . . . . . . . . . . . . (802) 828-5063

---

★ Elected Official   ■ Appointed by Governor   ● Appointed by Legislature   ▲ Appointed by Board or Commission   ◆ Appointed by State Supreme Court

# Agency of Natural Resources [ANR]

State Complex, 103 South Main Street, Waterbury, VT 05676
Tel: (802) 828-1294  Fax: (802) 828-1250  Internet: www.anr.state.vt.us

**Employees:** 618  **Fiscal Year:** 2015  **Budget:** $109,883,000

- Secretary **Deborah L. "Deb" Markowitz** . . . . . . . . . . . . . .(802) 828-1294
  E-mail: deb.markowitz@state.vt.us
  Deputy Secretary **(Vacant)** . . . . . . . . . . . . . . . . . . . . . . (802) 828-1294
  General Counsel **Jon Groveman** . . . . . . . . . . . . . . . . . . . .(802) 828-1294
  E-mail: jon.groveman@state.vt.us
  Human Resources Manager **Barbara Morway** . . . . . . . . . . (802) 249-4470
  Management Services Division Director
  **Steven Chadwick** . . . . . . . . . . . . . . . . . . . . . . . . . . . .(802) 828-1294
  E-mail: steve.chadwick@state.vt.us
  Senior Planner and Policy Analyst
  **William "Billy" Coster** . . . . . . . . . . . . . . . . . . . . . . .(802) 595-0900
  E-mail: billy.coster@state.vt.us

# Environmental Conservation Department

Tel: (802) 828-1556  Fax: (802) 828-1541

- Commissioner **Alyssa Schuren** . . . . . . . . . . . . . . . . . . . . .(802) 828-1556
- Deputy Commissioner **(Vacant)** . . . . . . . . . . . . . . . . . . . .(802) 828-1556
  Administration Director **Joanna Pallito** . . . . . . . . . . . . . . (802) 828-1556
  Air Quality Division Director **Elaine O'Grady** . . . . . . . . . .(802) 828-1556
  Facilities Engineering Division Director **Eric Blatt** . . . . . . .(802) 828-1556
  Drinking Water and Ground Water Protection Division
  Director **Christine "Chris" Thompson** . . . . . . . . . . . . . .(802) 828-1556
  Operations and Compliance Division Director
  **Julie Hackbarth** . . . . . . . . . . . . . . . . . . . . . . . . . . . . .(802) 828-1556
  E-mail: julie.hackbarth@state.vt.us
  Waste Management Division Director
  **Charles "Chuck" Schwer** . . . . . . . . . . . . . . . . . . . . . . (802) 249-5324
  Watershed Management Division Director
  **Pete LaFlamme** . . . . . . . . . . . . . . . . . . . . . . . . . . . . .(802) 828-1556
  State Geologist **Laurence "Larry" Becker** . . . . . . . . . . . . .(802) 828-1556
  Senior Counsel for Government Affairs **Rebecca Ellis** . . . .(802) 828-1556
  Education: Harvard 1986 BA; Princeton MPA; Georgetown JD

# Fish and Wildlife Department

Dewey Building, One National Life Drive, Montpelier, VT 05620-3702
Tel: (802) 828-1000  Fax: (802) 828-1250

- Commissioner **Louis Porter** . . . . . . . . . . . . . . . . . . . . . . .(802) 828-1294
  E-mail: louis.porter@state.vt.us
- Special Assistant to the Fish and Wildlife Commissioner
  **Kimberly Royar** . . . . . . . . . . . . . . . . . . . . . . . . . . . . .(802) 828-1000
  Chief Warden **(Vacant)** . . . . . . . . . . . . . . . . . . . . . . . . .(802) 828-1000
  Financial Manager **Steven "Steve" Gomez** . . . . . . . . . . . (802) 828-1000
  Financial Officer **Elizabeth Stratton** . . . . . . . . . . . . . . . (802) 828-1000
  Financial Officer **Ryan Leam** . . . . . . . . . . . . . . . . . . . . (802) 828-1000
  Grants Administrator **Ryan Leamy** . . . . . . . . . . . . . . . . .(802) 828-1000
  Operations Director **(Vacant)** . . . . . . . . . . . . . . . . . . . . .(802) 828-1000
  Counsel **Catherine Gjessing** . . . . . . . . . . . . . . . . . . . . .(802) 828-1000
  Public Relations Director **Susan Warner** . . . . . . . . . . . . .(802) 828-1000
  Fisheries Director **Eric Palmer** . . . . . . . . . . . . . . . . . . . .(802) 828-1000
  Wildlife Director **Mark Scott** . . . . . . . . . . . . . . . . . . . . .(802) 828-1000

# Forests, Parks and Recreation Department [FPR]

Tel: (802) 828-1534  Fax: (802) 828-1399

- Commissioner **Michael Snyder** . . . . . . . . . . . . . . . . . . . .(802) 828-1534
  E-mail: michael.snyder@state.vt.us
  Forests Division Director **Steven Sinclair** . . . . . . . . . . . . (802) 828-1534
  Lands Division Director **Michael Fraysier** . . . . . . . . . . . . (802) 828-1534
  Parks Division Director **Craig Whipple** . . . . . . . . . . . . . . (802) 828-1534

# Vermont Agency of Transportation [VTrans]

One National Life Drive, Montpelier, VT 05633-5001
Tel: (802) 828-2657  TTY: (800) 253-0191  Fax: (802) 828-3522
Internet: www.aot.state.vt.us

**Employees:** 1,250  **Fiscal Year:** 2015  **Budget:** $616,232,000

- Secretary **Chris Cole** . . . . . . . . . . . . . . . . . . . . . . . . . . .(802) 828-2657
- Deputy Secretary **Richard Tetreault** . . . . . . . . . . . . . . . . .(802) 828-2657
  E-mail: richard.tetreault@state.vt.us
  Assistant Attorney General **John Dunleavy** . . . . . . . . . . . .(802) 828-2784
  E-mail: john.dunleavy@state.vt.us
  Administrative Assistant **Jo Maguire** . . . . . . . . . . . . . . . .(802) 828-2657
  Finance and Administration Division Director
  **Faith Brown** . . . . . . . . . . . . . . . . . . . . . . . . . . . . . . .(802) 828-2667
  E-mail: faith.brown@state.vt.us          Fax: (802) 828-3522
  Operations Division Director **Scott Rogers** . . . . . . . . . . . .(802) 828-2709
  Policy, Planning and Intermodal Development Division
  Director **(Vacant)** . . . . . . . . . . . . . . . . . . . . . . . . . . . .(802) 828-1647
  Program Development Division Director **(Vacant)** . . . . . . . .(802) 828-2663

# Motor Vehicles Department

120 State Street, Montpelier, VT 05603-0001
Tel: (802) 828-2000  Fax: (802) 828-2170

- Commissioner **Robert D. Ide** . . . . . . . . . . . . . . . . . . . . . .(802) 828-2011
  E-mail: robert.ide@state.vt.us
  Education: Danville School (Danville, VT); Vermont Tech;
  Vermont 1974 BS
  Enforcement and Safety Director **Glendon Button** . . . . . . .(802) 828-2156
  E-mail: glen.button@state.vt.us
  Operations Director **Michael "Mike" Smith** . . . . . . . . . . .(802) 828-2066

# Department of Financial Regulation [DFR]

89 Main Street, Montpelier, VT 05620-3101
Tel: (802) 828-3301  Fax: (802) 828-3306

**Employees:** 101  **Fiscal Year:** 2016  **Budget:** $14,897,000

- Commissioner **Susan L. Donegan** . . . . . . . . . . . . . . . . . .(802) 828-3301
  Note: Until June 30, 2016.
  E-mail: susan.donegan@vermont.gov
  Education: Vermont Law JD; Boston U LLM
  Banking Deputy Commissioner **Cynthia Stuart** . . . . . . . . . (802) 828-4874
  E-mail: cynthia.stuart@vermont.gov
  Captive Insurance Deputy Commissioner **David Provost** . . . (802) 828-0287
  Insurance Deputy Commissioner **Kaj Samsom** . . . . . . . . . (802) 828-4842
  Securities Deputy Commissioner **Michael Pieciak** . . . . . . . (802) 828-4874
  Education: Union Col (NY) BA; Miami JD          Fax: (802) 828-2896
  Administrative Services Director **David Cameron** . . . . . . . .(802) 828-2379
  E-mail: david.cameron@vermont.gov
  Public Information Programs Chief **Dale Schaft** . . . . . . . . . (802) 828-4872
  E-mail: dale.schaft@vermont.gov

# Vermont Department of Labor [VDOL]

Five Green Mountain Drive, Montpelier, VT 05601
P.O. Box 488, Montpelier, VT 05601-0488
Tel: (802) 828-4000  Fax: (802) 828-4181

**Employees:** 290  **Fiscal Year:** 2015  **Budget:** $30,246,000

- Commissioner **Anne M. "Annie" Noonan** . . . . . . . . . . . . .(802) 828-4301
  E-mail: annie.noonan@state.vt.us
  Deputy Commissioner **Maureen Tivnan** . . . . . . . . . . . . . .(802) 828-4100
  E-mail: maureen.tivnan@state.vt.us
  General Counsel **Dirk Anderson** . . . . . . . . . . . . . . . . . . .(802) 828-4391
  E-mail: dirk.anderson@state.vt.us
  Administration Director **Tom R. Tomasi** . . . . . . . . . . . . . .(802) 828-4376
  E-mail: tom.tomasi@state.vt.us
  Workers' Compensation and Safety Director
  **J. Stephen "Steve" Monahan** . . . . . . . . . . . . . . . . . . . .(802) 828-2138
  E-mail: stephen.monahan@state.vt.us
  Workforce Development Director **Rose Lucenti** . . . . . . . . . (802) 828-4151
  E-mail: rose.lucenti@state.vt.us

---

★ Elected Official    ■ Appointed by Governor    ● Appointed by Legislature        ▲ Appointed by Board or Commission        ◆ Appointed by State Supreme Court

## Department of Public Safety

State Complex, 103 South Main Street, Waterbury, VT 05671
Tel: (802) 244-8727  Fax: (802) 241-5551  Internet: www.dps.state.vt.us

**Employees:** 594  **Fiscal Year:** 2015  **Budget:** $108,714,000

■Commissioner **Keith W. Flynn**.......................(802) 244-8718
E-mail: kflynn@dps.state.vt.us
Deputy Commissioner **Joseph Flynn** .................(802) 241-5488
Forensic Laboratory Director **Trisha Conti** ..............(802) 244-8788
E-mail: tconti@dps.state.vt.us
State Police Director **Matthew Birmingham** ............(802) 875-2112
Emergency Management Office Director
**Christopher Herrick** .........................(802) 244-8721
Crime Information Center Director **Jeffrey Wallin** ........(802) 241-5220
E-mail: jwallin@dps.state.vt.us
Criminal Division Commander **Glenn Hall** ..............(802) 334-8881
Field Force Division Commander **Walter Goodell** ........(802) 334-8881
E-mail: wgoodell@dps.state.vt.us
Administrative Officer **Joanne Chadwick** ..............(802) 241-5496
E-mail: joanne.chadwick@state.vt.us
Communications System Manager **Terry Lavalley** ........(802) 241-5215
Information Technology Manager **Dean Hamel** ..........(802) 241-5483
E-mail: dean.hamel@state.vt.us

### Fire Safety Division

1311 US Route 302 Berlin, Suite 600, Barre, VT 05641-2351
Tel: (802) 479-7561  Tel: (800) 640-2106  Fax: (802) 479-7562

Fire Safety Director **Michael Desrochers**...............(802) 479-7572
Deputy Director **Joseph Benard** ......................(802) 479-7566
Chief Hazardous Materials Response Team Coordinator
**Todd Cosgrove** .............................(802) 479-7586
E-mail: todd.cosgrove@vermont.gov

## Department of Public Service [DPS]

112 State Street, Montpelier, VT 05620-2601
Tel: (802) 828-2811  TTY: (800) 734-8390  Fax: (802) 828-2342
E-mail: vtdps@psd.state.vt.us

**Employees:** 49  **Fiscal Year:** 2015  **Budget:** $10,296,000

■Commissioner **Christopher "Chris" Recchia**..........(802) 828-4071
Special Assistant to the Commissioner
**Michelle Hughes** ...........................(802) 828-4071
Deputy Commissioner **Jon Copans**...................(802) 828-3088

### Consumer Affairs and Public Information Division

112 State Street, Drawer 20, Montpelier, VT 05620-2601
Tel: (802) 828-2811  Fax: (802) 828-2342

Director **Autumn Barnett**...........................(802) 828-4009

### Engineering Division

112 State Street, Drawer 20, Montpelier, VT 05620-2701
Tel: (802) 828-2811  Fax: (802) 828-2342

Director **Bill Jordan** ...............................(802) 828-4038

### Finance and Economics Division

112 State Street, Montpelier, VT 05620-2601
Tel: (802) 828-2811  Fax: (802) 828-2342

Director **Ronald Behrns**............................(802) 828-2325

### Public Advocacy Division

112 State Street, Drawer 20, Montpelier, VT 05620-2601
Tel: (802) 828-2811  Fax: (802) 828-2342

Director **Geoff Commons** ..........................(802) 828-4010

### Telecommunications Division

112 State Street, Drawer 20, Montpelier, VT 05620-2701
Tel: (802) 828-2811  Fax: (802) 828-2342

Director **James Porter**.............................(802) 828-4003

## Lottery Commission

1311 US Route 302, Suite 100, Barre, VT 05641-2399
Tel: (802) 479-5686  Fax: (802) 479-4294  E-mail: staff@vtlottery.com
Internet: www.vtlottery.com

■Executive Director **Gregory Smith** ...................(802) 476-0100
E-mail: gregory.smith@state.vt.us
Administrative Assistant **Mary Stridsberg** ...........(802) 476-0105
Agent and Customer Response Representative
**Frances McAvoy** ............................(802) 476-0108
Director of Security **Michael Ferrant** ................(802) 479-8596
Marketing and Sales Director **Jeff Cavender** ...........(802) 476-0103
Business Manager **Mary Cassani** ....................(802) 476-0109
Marketing and Sales Supervisor **Carney Daniels** ........(802) 476-0111
Web Marketing/Game Coordinator **Courtney Bridges**.....(802) 476-0102
Information Technology II **Ellen Pulsifer** ..............(802) 476-0107
E-mail: ellen@vtlottery.com

## Vermont Economic Development Authority [VEDA]

58 East State Street, Suite 5, Montpelier, VT 05602-3044
Tel: (802) 828-5627  Fax: (802) 828-5474  Internet: www.veda.org

▲Chief Executive Officer **Rosalea W. "Jo" Bradley** .......(802) 828-5627
E-mail: jbradley@veda.org
Education: Johnson State 1971 BA; Boston U 1981 MBA
Chief Operating Officer **Steven J. Greenfield** ..........(802) 828-5459
Education: Vermont 1969 BBA; Tuck School 1971 MBA
Office Manager **Carol J. Brown** .....................(802) 828-5465
Chief Financial Officer **David E. Carter** ...............(802) 828-5470
Education: Champlain 1996 BA

## Vermont Public Power Supply Authority [VPPSA]

5195 Waterbury-Stowe Road, Waterbury Center, VT 05677
Tel: (802) 244-7678  Fax: (802) 244-6889  Internet: www.vppsa.com

▲General Manager **David Mullett** ..............(802) 244-7678 ext. 227
Information Systems Manager
**Kenneth St. Amour** ...............(802) 244-7678 ext. 233
E-mail: kstamour@vppsa.com
Education: Vermont BS, MBA

## State Board of Education

State Office Building, 120 State Street, Montpelier, VT 05620-2501
Tel: (802) 828-3135  Fax: (802) 828-3140

■Chair **Stephan Morse** ..............................(802) 365-4255
Term Expires: 2017
E-mail: stephan.a.morse@vermont.gov
■Vice Chair **Sean-Marie Oller**.......................(802) 447-7827
Term Expires: 2017                           Fax: (802) 447-7827
E-mail: sean-marie.oller@vermont.gov
■Member **Rebecca Holcombe**......................(802) 828-3135
E-mail: rebecca.holcombe@vermont.gov      Fax: (802) 828-3140
Affiliation: Secretary, Education Department, State Board of Education, State of Vermont
State Office Building, 120 State Street, Montpelier, VT 05620-2501
■Member **Krista Huling** ............................(802) 652-7000
Term Expires: 2015                           Res: (802) 644-8433
E-mail: krista.huling@vermont.gov
■Member **Bonnie Johnson-Aten** .....................(802) 864-8486
Term Expires: 2018                           Fax: (802) 656-0855
E-mail: bonnie.johnson-aten@vermont.gov
Education: Union Inst U MAED
■Member **William J. "Bill" Mathis, PhD** .............(802) 383-0058
Term Expires: 2015                           Res: (802) 247-6720
E-mail: william.mathis@vermont.gov          Fax: (802) 247-8501
■Member **Philip "Peter" Peltz** ......................(802) 472-6524
Term Expires: 2015
E-mail: philip.peltz@vermont.gov
■Member **Mark Perrin**
Term Expires: 2019                           Fax: (802) 464-5903
E-mail: mark.perrin@vermont.gov
■Member **Stacy Weinberger** .........................(802) 229-4441
Term Expires: 2019                           Res: (802) 869-6495
Fax: (802) 223-4689

■ Student Member **Rainbow Chen** . . . . . . . . . . . . . . . . . . . . . (802) 426-3213
   Term Expires: 2017
   E-mail: rainbow.chen@vermont.gov
■ Student Member **Dylan McAllister** . . . . . . . . . . . . . . . . . . (802) 472-6511
   Term Expires: 2016
   E-mail: dylan.mcallister@vermont.gov

## Education Department
Tel: (802) 479-1030  Fax: (802) 479-1835

■ Secretary **Rebecca Holcombe** . . . . . . . . . . . . . . . . . . . . . . . (802) 479-1030
   E-mail: rebecca.holcombe@state.vt.us
Executive Assistant **Maureen Gaidys** . . . . . . . . . . . . . . . . (802) 479-1030
General Counsel **Greg Glennon** . . . . . . . . . . . . . . . . . . . . . (802) 479-1030
   E-mail: greg.glennon@state.vt.us
Communications Director **Gillian Guest "Jill" Remick** . . . (802) 479-1030
   E-mail: jill.remick@state.vt.us
   Web Manager **Stephanie Brackin** . . . . . . . . . . . . . . . . (802) 479-1030
   E-mail: stephanie.brackin@state.vt.us
Human Resources Coordinator **Mary Hannigan** . . . . . . . . . (802) 479-1030
State Board of Education Liaison **Perry Thompson** . . . . . . (802) 479-1030
   E-mail: perry.thompson@state.vt.us

## Finance and Administration Division
Deputy Commissioner and Chief Financial Officer
   **William "Bill" Talbott** . . . . . . . . . . . . . . . . . . . . . . . . . . (802) 479-1030
Business Office Finance Director **Kathy Flanagan** . . . . . . . (802) 479-1030
Special Education Finance Director **Nicole Tousignant** . . . (802) 479-1030
   E-mail: nicole.tousignant@state.vt.us
Information Technology Manager **Brian Townsend** . . . . . . . (802) 479-1030
   E-mail: brian.townsend@state.vt.us

## Transformation and Innovation Division
Deputy Commissioner **(Vacant)** . . . . . . . . . . . . . . . . . . . . . . (802) 479-1030
Integrated Learning Support Director (High School and
   Adult) **Tom Alderman** . . . . . . . . . . . . . . . . . . . . . . . . . . (802) 479-1030
Integrated Learning Support Director (Pre-K through
   Middle) **Karin Edwards** . . . . . . . . . . . . . . . . . . . . . . . . (802) 479-1030
Educator Quality Director **Deborah Price** . . . . . . . . . . . . . (802) 479-1030
General Supervision and Monitoring Director
   **Deb Quackenbush** . . . . . . . . . . . . . . . . . . . . . . . . . . . . . (802) 479-1030

## Public Service Board [PSB]
112 State Street, Fourth Floor, Montpelier, VT 05620-2701
Tel: (802) 828-2358  TTY: (800) 253-0191  Fax: (802) 828-3351
E-mail: psb.clerk@vermont.gov

■ Chairman **James Volz** . . . . . . . . . . . . . . . . . . . . . . . . . . . . (802) 828-2358
   Term Expires: February 28, 2017
   Education: Boston U 1978 BA; Franklin Pierce Col 1981 JD
■ Member **Margaret Cheney** . . . . . . . . . . . . . . . . . . . . . . . . . (802) 828-2358
   Term Expires: February 28, 2019
   Education: Harvard 1974 AB
■ Member **Sarah Hofmann** . . . . . . . . . . . . . . . . . . . . . . . . . . (802) 828-2358
   Term Expires: February 28, 2021

## Commission Staff
Tel: (802) 828-2358  Fax: (802) 828-3351

Clerk of the Board **Judith Whitney** . . . . . . . . . . . . . . . . . (802) 828-2358
   E-mail: psb.clerk@vermont.gov

## Vermont National Guard
Office of the Adjutant General, 789 Vermont National Guard Road,
Colchester, VT 05446-3099
Tel: (802) 338-3124  Fax: (802) 654-3982  Internet: www.vtguard.com

● Adjutant General **MajGen Steven A. Cray, ANG** . . . . . . . (802) 338-3124
   E-mail: steven.a.cray.mil@mail.mil
Deputy Adjutant General
   **BrigGen Michael Heston, ANG** . . . . . . . . . . . . . . . . . . (802) 338-3124
Director of Joint Staff **BG Mark Lovejoy, ARNG** . . . . . . . . (802) 338-3125
Military Support Director **LTC Randall K. Gates, ARNG** . . (802) 338-3342
State Public Affairs Officer (Air Force)
   **Capt Dyana K. Allen, ANG** . . . . . . . . . . . . . . . . . . . . . (802) 338-3324
State Public Affairs Officer (Army)
   **MAJ Chris Gookin, ARNG** . . . . . . . . . . . . . . . . . . . . . . (802) 338-3324

Chief Information Officer
   **CW4 Jim Woodworth, ARNG** . . . . . . . . . . . . . . . . . . . . (802) 338-3341
   E-mail: james.m.woodworth3.mil@mail.mil

## Office of the Lieutenant Governor
115 State Street, Montpelier, VT 05633
Tel: (802) 828-2226  Fax: (802) 828-3198

★ Lieutenant Governor **Philip B. "Phil" Scott** (R) . . . . . . . . (802) 828-2226
   Term Expires: 2017
   E-mail: phil.scott@vermont.gov
   Education: Vermont 1980 BS
   Career: State Senator, Vermont Senate (2000-2011)
Chief of Staff **Rachel Feldman** . . . . . . . . . . . . . . . . . . . . . (802) 828-2226

## Office of the Secretary of State
128 State Street, Montpelier, VT 05633
Tel: (802) 828-2363

★ Secretary of State **James C. "Jim" Condos** (D) . . . . . . . . (802) 828-2148
   Term Expires: January 11, 2017
   Education: Vermont 1974 BS
   Career: State Senator (D-VT, Chittenden), Vermont Senate (2001-2009)
Deputy Secretary of State
   **Christopher D. "Chris" Winters** . . . . . . . . . . . . . . . . . (802) 828-2148
Corporations and Administrative Services Director
   **Marlene Betit** . . . . . . . . . . . . . . . . . . . . . . . . . . . . . . . . (802) 828-2386
   E-mail: marlene.betit@sec.state.vt.us          Fax: (802) 828-2496
Elections and Campaign Finance Division Director
   **Will Senning** . . . . . . . . . . . . . . . . . . . . . . . . . . . . . . . . (802) 828-0175
                                                         Fax: (802) 828-5171
State Archivist **Tanya Marshall** . . . . . . . . . . . . . . . . . . . . (802) 828-3700
                                                         Fax: (802) 828-1135

## Office of the Attorney General
Pavilion Office Building, 109 State Street, Montpelier, VT 05609-1001
Tel: (802) 828-3171  Tel: (802) 656-3183 (Consumer Assistance)
TTY: (802) 828-3665  Fax: (802) 828-2154  Fax: (802) 828-1500
E-mail: atginfo@atg.state.vt.us  Internet: www.atg.state.vt.us

**Employees:** 80

★ Attorney General **William H. Sorrell** (D) . . . . . . . . . . . . . . (802) 828-3173
   Term Expires: 2017
   E-mail: bsorrell@atg.state.vt.us
   Education: Notre Dame 1970 AB; Cornell 1974 JD
   Career: Secretary of Administration, State of Vermont (1992-1997)
Deputy Attorney General **Susanne Young** . . . . . . . . . . . . . (802) 828-3173
   Education: Vermont BA, JD
Chief Assistant Attorney General **William E. Griffin** . . . . . . (802) 828-5500
Civil Rights Division Assistant Attorney General
   **Julio A. Thompson** . . . . . . . . . . . . . . . . . . . . . . . . . . . (802) 828-5519
Transportation Division Assistant Attorney General
   **John Dunleavy** . . . . . . . . . . . . . . . . . . . . . . . . . . . . . . (802) 828-3430
   Administration Bldg., Montpelier, VT 05633-5001
Medicaid Fraud Director **Jason Turner** . . . . . . . . . . . . . . . (802) 828-5521
Civil Law Division Chief **Megan Shafritz** . . . . . . . . . . . . . (802) 828-3176
Criminal Division Chief **John Treadwell** . . . . . . . . . . . . . . (802) 828-5512
Environmental Division Chief **Scot L. Kline** . . . . . . . . . . . (802) 828-3186
Human Services Division Chief **Linda A. Purdy** . . . . . . . . (802) 769-2160
   103 South Main Street, Waterbury, VT 05671-0701
Public Protection Division Chief **Wendy Morgan** . . . . . . . . (802) 828-5507
General Counsel and Administrative Law Director
   **Michael Duane** . . . . . . . . . . . . . . . . . . . . . . . . . . . . . . . (802) 828-5531
Technology Manager **Jay Bailey** . . . . . . . . . . . . . . . . . . . . (802) 828-3171
   E-mail: jbailey@atg.state.vt.us

## Office of the Treasurer
109 State Street, 4th Floor, Montpelier, VT 05609-6200
Tel: (802) 828-2301  Fax: (802) 828-2772
Internet: www.vermonttreasurer.gov

★ State Treasurer **Elizabeth A. "Beth" Pearce** (D) . . . . . . . . (802) 828-1452
   Term Expires: 2017
   E-mail: treasurers.office@state.vt.us
   Education: New Hampshire BA
   Career: Deputy Treasurer, Office of the Treasurer, State of Vermont

*(continued on next page)*

---

★ Elected Official   ■ Appointed by Governor   ● Appointed by Legislature   ▲ Appointed by Board or Commission   ◆ Appointed by State Supreme Court

EXECUTIVE BRANCH

**Office of the Treasurer** *continued*

Executive Assistant **Timothy Lueders-Dumont** . . . . . . . . (802) 828-1451
Deputy Treasurer **Stephen Wisloski** . . . . . . . . . . . . . . . . . . (802) 828-1452
Information Technology Systems Director **Ram Verma** . . . . (802) 828-2498
 E-mail: ram.verma@state.vt.us
 Education: Siena Col 1985 BS
Investments Director **Matthew Considine** . . . . . . . . . . . . . (802) 828-3668
Retirement Operations Director **Laurie P. Lanphear** . . . . . (802) 828-5897
Treasury Operations Director **John Booth** . . . . . . . . . . . . . (802) 828-1258
Unclaimed Property Director **Albert LaPerle** . . . . . . . . . . . (802) 828-2318
Webmaster **Ram Verma** . . . . . . . . . . . . . . . . . . . . . . . . . . (802) 828-2498

# Office of the State Auditor

132 State Street, Montpelier, VT 05633
Tel: (802) 828-2281  Tel: (877) 290-1400  Fax: (802) 828-2198
E-mail: auditor@state.vt.us

★ Auditor of Accounts **Douglas R. Hoffer** (D) . . . . . . . . . . . (802) 828-2281
 Term Expires: 2017
 Education: Williams 1985 BA; SUNY (Buffalo State Col) 1988 JD
Deputy Auditor of Accounts **Susan Mesner** . . . . . . . . . . . (802) 828-1094
 Education: Vermont BA; Rensselaer Poly MS

---

★ Elected Official  ■ Appointed by Governor  ● Appointed by Legislature  ▲ Appointed by Board or Commission  ◆ Appointed by State Supreme Court

# Virgin Islands

Internet: www.usvi.net

**Number of U.S. Congressional Delegates:** 1 Nonvoting Delegate  **Governor's Term:** 4 years
**Legislature Description:** Unicameral - 15 member Senate; Term - 2 years  **Next Election:** Governor
November 2018; Legislature November 2016  **Official Name:** The Virgin Islands of the United States
**Nickname:** St. John; St. Croix; St. Thomas

**Population:** 104,170 (2014)  **Fiscal Year:** 2014  **Budget:** $761,200,000

## Office of the Governor

21-22 Kongens Gade, St. Thomas, VI 00802
Tel: (340) 774-0001 (St. Thomas and Water Island Office)
Tel: (340) 773-1404 (St. Croix Office)
Tel: (340) 776-8484 (St. John Office)

**Kenneth E. Mapp**
Governor

Began Service: January 5, 2015
Term Expires: 2019
Education: U Virgin Islands;
JFK School Govt 1999 MPA

Career: State Senator, Virgin Islands Legislature;
Lieutenant Governor, Office of the Lieutenant
Governor, Virgin Islands of the United States
(1995-1999)

★Governor **Kenneth E. Mapp** (I) . . . . . . . . . . . . . . . . . . . . . . (340) 774-0001
Chief of Staff **Randy Knight** . . . . . . . . . . . . . . . . . . . . . . . . (340) 775-6277
Deputy Chief of Staff **Rochelle Todman** . . . . . . . . . . . . . . (340) 775-6277
Communications Director **Kimberly Jones** . . . . . . . . . . . . . (340) 775-6277
Chief Legal Counsel **Emile Henderson III** . . . . . . . . . . . . . (340) 775-6277
Chief Economist and Financial Adviser
   **Simon Jones-Hendrickson** . . . . . . . . . . . . . . . . . . . . . . . (340) 775-6277
Senior Policy Adviser **Franklin Johnson** . . . . . . . . . . . . . . (340) 775-6277
Senior Policy Adviser **Juel T. R. Molloy** . . . . . . . . . . . . . . (340) 775-6277
St. Croix Administrator **Stephanie Williams** . . . . . . . . . . . (340) 773-1404
St. John Administrator **Camille Parris** . . . . . . . . . . . . . . . . (340) 776-8484

## Washington Office

444 North Capitol Street, NW, Suite 298, Washington, DC 20001
Fax: (202) 624-3594

Director **Steven Steele** . . . . . . . . . . . . . . . . . . . . . . . . . . . . (202) 624-3590
   E-mail: ssteele@sso.org

## Office of the Lieutenant Governor

18 Kongens Gade, St. Thomas, VI 00802
Internet: www.ltg.gov.vi

★Lieutenant Governor **Osbert Potter** (I) . . . . . . . . . . . . . . . (340) 715-6277
   Term Expires: 2019
   E-mail: osbert.potter@lgo.vi.gov
   Education: Col Virgin Islands 1978 BA
   Career: State Senator, Virgin Islands Legislature (1992-1996);
   Commissioner, Licensing and Consumer Affairs Department, Virgin
   Islands of the United States (1997-1998)

## Office of the Attorney General

GERS Building, 3438 Kronprindsens Gade, 2nd Floor,
St. Thomas, VI 00802
Fax: (340) 774-9710  E-mail: justice@usvi.org

**Employees:** 170

■Attorney General **Claude E. Walker** . . . . . . . . . . . . (340) 774-5666 ext. 107
   E-mail: claude.walker@viwapa.vi
■Solicitor General **Bernard VanSluytman** . . . . . . . . . . . . . . (340) 774-5666
   E-mail: bernard.vansluytman@viwapa.vi
   Education: Howard U 1973 JD

## Office of the Adjutant General

4031 La Grande Princesse, Lot 1B - Christiansted,
St. Croix, VI 00820-4353
Fax: (340) 712-7782

Adjutant General **Deborah Howell** . . . . . . . . . . . . . . . . . . . (340) 712-7711
Chief of Staff **COL Linda Cills, ARNG** . . . . . . . . . . . . . . . . (340) 712-7711

## Office of the Inspector General

75 Kronprindsens Gade, St. Thomas, VI 00802
Fax: (340) 774-6431

Inspector General
   **Steven G. Van Beverhoudt, CFE, CGFM** . . . . . . . . . . . (340) 774-3388
   Term Expires: 2016
   Education: Col Virgin Islands BA

## Agriculture Department

7944 Estate Dorothea, St. Thomas, VI 00802
Fax: (340) 774-1823  E-mail: agriculture@usvi.org
Internet: www.usvi.org/agriculture

Commissioner **Louis E. Petersen, Jr., PhD** . . . . . . . . . . . . . (340) 774-5182
Deputy Commissioner **Errol Chichester** . . . . . . . . . . . . . . . (340) 778-0997
Assistant Commissioner **Luther Renee** . . . . . . . . . . . . . . . . (340) 778-0997

## Education Department

1834 Kongens Gade Street, St. Thomas, VI 00802
Fax: (340) 779-7153  E-mail: education@usvi.org  Internet: www.doe.vi

Commissioner **Sharon McCollum** . . . . . . . . . . . . . . . . . . . . (340) 776-5687
   E-mail: dgregory@doe.vi
GED Administrator **Eduardo Corneiro** . . . . . . . . . . . . . . . . (340) 776-3484
   E-mail: eduardo.corneiro@viwapa.vi

## Finance Department

2314 Kronprindsens Gade, St. Thomas, VI 00802
Fax: (340) 776-4028  Internet: www.usvi.org/finance

Commissioner **Valdamier Collens** . . . . . . . . . . . . . . . . . . . . (340) 774-4750
Executive Assistant Commissioner **(Vacant)** . . . . . . . . . . . . (340) 773-1105

## Health Department

1303 Hospital Ground, Suite 10, St. Thomas, VI 00802-6722
Tel: (340) 774-7477  Fax: (340) 777-4001

Commissioner **Michelle S. Davis** . . . . . . . . . . . . . . . . . . . . . (340) 774-0117
Assistant Medical Director **Marc Jerome** . . . . . . . . . . . . . . . (340) 773-6551

## Human Services Department

3011 Golden Rock, Christiansted, VI 00820
Fax: (340) 774-3466  E-mail: humanservices@usvi.org

Commissioner **Vivian Ebbesen-Fludd** . . . . . . . . . . . . . . . . . (340) 773-2980
Assistant Commissioner **Carla Benjamin** . . . . . . . . . . . . . . . (340) 773-2980
Assistant Commissioner **Michal Rhymer-Brown** . . . . . . . . . (340) 773-2980

## Labor Department

2203 Church Street, St. Croix, VI 00820-4612
Fax: (340) 773-0094  Internet: www.vidol.org

Commissioner **Albert Bryan, Jr.** . . . . . . . . . . . . . . . (340) 773-1994 ext. 232

*(continued on next page)*

---

★ Elected Official    ■ Appointed by Governor    ● Appointed by Legislature    ▲ Appointed by Board or Commission    ◆ Appointed by State Supreme Court

**Labor Department** *continued*

Assistant Commissioner **Arah Lockhart** . . . . . . . . . . . . . . . (340) 776-3700
  E-mail: aclockhart@vidol.gov
Deputy Commissioner **(Vacant)** . . . . . . . . . . . . . . . . . . . . . (340) 777-1202

## Licensing and Consumer Affairs Department [DCLA]

Property and Procurement Building, Number One, Sub Base, Room 205,
St. Thomas, VI 00802
Fax: (340) 776-8303  E-mail: dlca@usvi.org  Internet: www.dlca.gov.vi

Commissioner **Devin Carrington** . . . . . . . . . . . . . . . . . . . . (340) 774-3130
  E-mail: devin.carrington@viwapa.vi

## Planning and Natural Resources Department [DPNR]

Cyril E. King Airport Terminal Building, 2nd Floor,
St. Thomas, VI 00802
Tel: (340) 774-3320  Fax: (340) 775-5706  Internet: dpnr.vi.gov

Commissioner **Dawn Henry** . . . . . . . . . . . . . . . . . . . . . . . . (340) 774-3320
Assistant Commissioner **(Vacant)** . . . . . . . . . . . . . . . . . . . (340) 774-3320
Chief Financial Officer **Daisy May Millin** . . . . . . . . . . . . . (340) 774-3320

## Police Department

Alexander A. Farrelly Center, Second Floor, St. Thomas, VI 00802
Fax: (340) 715-5517  E-mail: police@usvi.org

Commissioner **Delroy Richards** . . . . . . . . . . . . . . . . . . . . . (340) 774-2310
  E-mail: delroy.richards@vipd.gov.vi
Deputy Commissioner **Giselle C. Richardson Jones** . . . . . (340) 712-6018

## Property and Procurement Department

Building Number 1, 3rd Floor Sub Base, St. Thomas, VI 00802
Fax: (340) 777-9587  E-mail: pnp@usvi.org  Internet: http://dpp.vi.gov/

Commissioner **Randolph Bennett** . . . . . . . . . . . . . . . . . . . . (340) 774-0828
  Education: Liberty 2015 MA
Assistant Commissioner **Herbert Grigg** . . . . . . . . . . . . . . . (340) 773-1561

## Public Works Department

Sub Base, No. 8, St. Thomas, VI 00802
Fax: (340) 774-5869  E-mail: publicworks@usvi.org
Internet: www.usvi.org/publicworks

Commissioner **Gustav James** . . . . . . . . . . . . . . . . . . . . . . . (340) 776-4844
Assistant Commissioner **Roberto Cintron** . . . . . . . . . . . . . (340) 773-1290

## Sports, Parks and Recreation Department

3000 LBJ Gardens, S, St. Croix, VI 00820
Fax: (340) 774-4600

Commissioner **Pedro Cruz** . . . . . . . . . . . . . . . . . . . . . . . . . (340) 774-0255

## Tourism Department

P.O. Box 6400, St. Thomas, VI 00804
Fax: (340) 774-4390

Commissioner **Beverly Nicholson Doty** . . . . . . . . . . . . . . . (340) 774-8784
Deputy Commissioner **(Vacant)** . . . . . . . . . . . . . . . . . . . . . (340) 774-8784

## Collective Bargaining Office

5001 Chandlers Wharf, Suite 5, St. Croix, VI 00820
Tel: (340) 713-0735  Fax: (340) 713-0757

Director **Valdemar Hill, Jr.** . . . . . . . . . . . . . . . . . . . . . . . . (340) 774-6450
  E-mail: valdemar.hill@ocb.vi.gov

## Energy Office

4101 Estate Mars Hill, Frederiksted, St. Croix, VI 00840-4474
Tel: (340) 713-8436  Fax: (340) 772-0063  E-mail: vieo0441@viaccess.net
Internet: www.vienergy.org

Director **Karl Knight** . . . . . . . . . . . . . . . . . . . . . . . . . . . . . (340) 773-8436
  Education: Morgan State BS

## Management and Budget Office

Emancipation Garden Station, Number 41 Norre Gade, 2nd Floor,
St. Thomas, VI 00802
Fax: (340) 776-0069  E-mail: omb@usvi.org  Internet: www.vi.gov/omb

Director **Nellon Bowry** . . . . . . . . . . . . . . . . . . . . . . . . . . . (340) 774-0750

## Emergency Management Agency [VITEMA]

AQ Building, 2C Estate Contant, St. Thomas, VI 00802
Fax: (340) 774-1491

State Director **Elton Lewis** . . . . . . . . . . . . . . . . . . . . . . . . (340) 774-2244
                                                     Fax: (340) 774-1491

## Fire Services

15 Crown Bay Fill, St. Thomas, VI 00802
Fax: (340) 774-4630

Director **Capt. Clifford Joseph** . . . . . . . . . . . . . . . . . . . . . (340) 773-8050
Assistant Director **Darryl George** . . . . . . . . . . . . . . . . . . . (340) 773-8050

## Bureau of Information Technology

King Cross Street, Sutie 2164, St. Croix, VI 00820
Government Development Bank Building, 1050 Norre Gade 5, Suite 5,
St. Thomas, VI 00802
Tel: (340) 713-0354 (St. Croix Branch)
Tel: (340) 774-1013 (St. Thomas Branch)
Fax: (340) 719-1623 (St. Croix Branch)
Fax: (340) 774-1490 (St. Thomas Branch)

Director **Rueben Molloy** . . . . . . . . . . . . . . . . . . . . . . . . . . (340) 774-1013
  E-mail: reuben.molloy@vi.gov

## Corrections Bureau

Tel: (340) 773-0295

■ Director **Rick Mullgrav** . . . . . . . . . . . . . . . . . . . . . . . . . (340) 773-0295
  E-mail: rick.mullgrav@doj.vi.gov

## Economic Research Bureau

1050 Norre Gade 5, St. Thomas, VI 00802
Fax: (340) 776-7953  Internet: www.usviber.org

Director **Wharton Berger** . . . . . . . . . . . . . . . . . . . . . . . (340) 714-1700 ext. 248

## Internal Revenue Bureau

9601 Estate Thomas, St. Thomas, VI 00802
Tel: (340) 715-1040  Fax: (340) 714-9345  Internet: www.usvi.org/irb

Director **Marvin Pickering** . . . . . . . . . . . . . . . . . . . . . . . . (340) 715-1040

## Motor Vehicle Bureau

Patrick Sweeney yPolice Headquarters, RR2 Kingshill,
St. Croix, VI 00850
Tel: (340) 778-2211  Fax: (340) 713-0855

Director **Lawrence Olive** . . . . . . . . . . . . . . . . . . . . . . . . . (340) 713-4268

## Casino Control Commission

Five Orange Grove, Christiansted, St. Croix, VI 00820
Fax: (340) 773-3136

Chairman **Violet Ann Golden** . . . . . . . . . . . . . . . . . . . . . . (340) 773-3616

---

★ Elected Official     ■ Appointed by Governor     ● Appointed by Legislature     ▲ Appointed by Board or Commission     ◆ Appointed by State Supreme Court

# Law Enforcement Planning Commission
8172 Sub Base, Suite 3, St. Thomas, VI 00802
Fax: (340) 776-3317
Director **Victor Browne** . . . . . . . . . . . . . . . . . . . . . (340) 774-6400 ext. 211
 E-mail: vbrowne@irb.gov.vi

# Personnel Division
GERS Complex, 3438 Kronprindsens Gade, Third Floor,
St. Thomas, VI 00802
Fax: (340) 714-5040
Director **Milton Potter** . . . . . . . . . . . . . . . . . . . . . . . . . (340) 774-8588

# Economic Development Authority
1050 Norre Gade, Room 5, St. Thomas, VI 00802
P.O. Box 305038, St. Thomas, VI 00803
Fax: (340) 773-7701 Internet: www.usvieda.org
Chief Executive Officer **Percival Clouden** . . . . . . . . . . . (340) 773-6499
Assistant Chief Executive Officer **Jennifer Nygent-Hill** . . . (340) 773-6499

# Housing Finance Authority
Frenchtown Plaza, 3202 Demarara 3, Suite 200, St. Thomas, VI 00802
Fax: (340) 775-7913
Executive Director **Adrienne L. Williams** . . . . . . . . . . . . . (340) 774-4481

# Port Authority
P.O. Box 301707, St. Thomas, VI 00803-1707
Fax: (340) 774-0025
Executive Director **Carlton "Ital" Dowe** . . . . . . . . . . . . . (340) 774-1629

# Water and Power Authority
P.O. Box 1450, St. Thomas, VI 00804
Fax: (340) 774-3422
Executive Director and Chief Executive Officer **(Vacant)** . . (340) 774-3552

# Veterans Affairs
1013 Estate Richmond, St. Croix, VI 00820-4349
Fax: (340) 692-9563 E-mail: veterans@usvi.org
Internet: www.usvi.org/veterans
Director **Morris D. Moorehead** . . . . . . . . . . . . . . . . . . . . (340) 773-6663

# Virgin Islands Housing Authority Board
Commissioner **Luis R. Ayala, Jr.** . . . . . . . . . . . . . . . . . . . (340) 777-8442
Commissioner **George Blackhall** . . . . . . . . . . . . . . . . . . . (340) 777-8442
Commissioner **Daphne Edwards** . . . . . . . . . . . . . . . . . . . (340) 777-8442
Commissioner **Colette Jones** . . . . . . . . . . . . . . . . . . . . . (340) 777-8442
Commissioner **Noreen Michael** . . . . . . . . . . . . . . . . . . . (340) 777-8442
Commissioner **Luis Sylvester** . . . . . . . . . . . . . . . . . . . . . (340) 777-8442
 E-mail: luis.sylvester@go.vi.gov
Ex-Officio **Vivian Ebbesen-Fludd** . . . . . . . . . . . . . . . . . . (340) 777-8442
 E-mail: vivian.ebbesen-fludd@dhs.vi.gov
 Affiliation: Commissioner, Human Services Department, Virgin Islands
 of the United States
 3011 Golden Rock, Christiansted, VI 00820
Ex-Officio **Robert Graham, CPM** . . . . . . . . . . . . . . . . . . . (340) 777-8442
 Affiliation: Executive Director, Virgin Islands Housing Authority,
 Virgin Islands of the United States
 P.O. Box 7668, St. Thomas, VI 00801
Ex-Officio **Adrienne L. Williams** . . . . . . . . . . . . . . . . . . (340) 777-8442
 Affiliation: Executive Director, Housing Finance Authority, Virgin
 Islands of the United States
 Frenchtown Plaza, 3202 Demarara 3, Suite 200, St. Thomas, VI 00802

# Virgin Islands Housing Authority [VIHA]
P.O. Box 7668, St. Thomas, VI 00801
Fax: (340) 775-0832
Executive Director **Robert Graham, CPM** . . . . . . . . . . . . . (340) 777-8442
 E-mail: rgraham@vihousing.org

# Virgin Islands Lottery
Barbel Plaza, South Eight-A Ross Estate, St. Thomas, VI 00802
Fax: (340) 776-4730
Executive Director **Conrad E. "Ricky" Francois II** . . . . . . . (340) 774-2502
 Education: Lincoln U (PA) 1972 BA; Tulane 1978 MBA

---

★ Elected Official ■ Appointed by Governor ● Appointed by Legislature ▲ Appointed by Board or Commission ◆ Appointed by State Supreme Court

# Virginia

Tel: (804) 786-0000 (State Operator)  Internet: www.virginia.gov

**Number of U.S. Congressional Delegates:** 2 Senators; 11 Representatives  **Governor's Term:** 4 years
**Legislature Description:** General Assembly - 40 member Senate; 100 member House of Delegates; Term -
Senate 4 years, House 2 years  **Next Election:** Governor November 2017; Legislature November 2017
**Number of Electoral Votes:** 13  **Official Name:** Commonwealth of Virginia (after Elizabeth I, Virgin
Queen of England)  **Nickname:** The Old Dominion  **Motto:** Sic Semper Tyrannis (Thus always to tyrants)

**Population:** 8,382,993 (2015); Rank 12  **Fiscal Year:** 2015  **Budget:** $46,832,371,000

## Office of the Governor

P.O. Box 1475, Richmond, VA 23218
Tel: (804) 786-2211  Internet: governor.virginia.gov

**Terence Richard "Terry" McAuliffe**
Governor

Began Service: January 11, 2014
Term Expires: January 2018
Date of Birth: February 9, 1957
Education: Catholic U 1979;
Georgetown 1984 JD
Religion: Catholic
Career: Co-Chair, Presidential Inaugural
Committee (1997); Chairman, Democratic
National Committee (2001-2005); Chairman,
Hillary Clinton for President (2007-2008)

★Governor **Terence Richard "Terry" McAuliffe** (D) . . . . . . . (804) 786-2211
  E-mail: terence.mcauliffe@governor.virginia.gov
  Confidential Assistant to the Governor **Yael Belkind** . . . . .(804) 786-4273
    E-mail: yael.belkind@governor.virginia.gov
    Education: Tufts BA
Chief of Staff **Paul J. Reagan** . . . . . . . . . . . . . . . . . . . . . . . . .(804) 786-2211
  Education: William & Mary 1982 BA; George Mason 1991 JD
  Confidential Assistant to the Chief of Staff
  **Kim Steinhoff** . . . . . . . . . . . . . . . . . . . . . . . . . . . . . . . . . . (804) 225-4810
    E-mail: kim.steinhoff@governor.virginia.gov
Deputy Chief of Staff **Suzette P. Denslow** . . . . . . . . . . . . . (804) 225-4810
  Education: VCU BS; Virginia MPA
Special Assistant **Michelle R. Kirby** . . . . . . . . . . . . . . . . . . (804) 786-2211
  Education: VCU BA
Special Assistant **David Elliot Meyer** . . . . . . . . . . . . . . . . . (804) 786-2211
  Education: Randolph-Macon 2015 BA
Legislative Director **(Vacant)** . . . . . . . . . . . . . . . . . . . . . . . (804) 786-2211
Counsel to the Governor **Carlos L. Hopkins** . . . . . . . . . . . .(804) 786-2211
  E-mail: carlos.hopkins@governor.virginia.gov
Policy Director **Anna Healy James** . . . . . . . . . . . . . . . . . . (804) 663-7871
  E-mail: anna.james@governor.virginia.gov
  Education: Virginia Tech 2002 BS; VCU 2010 MBA
  Deputy Policy Director **Erik Johnston** . . . . . . . . . . . . . . .(804) 692-2559
    Education: Mary Washington Col BA; Virginia Tech MPA
  Special Assistant for Policy
  **Kathleen L. "Khaki" LaRiviere** . . . . . . . . . . . . . . . . . . (804) 786-2211
    Education: William & Mary BA; Virginia Tech MPA
Senior Legislative Advisor **Robert H. "Bob" Brink** . . . . . . .(804) 692-2590
  E-mail: robert.brink@governor.virginia.gov
  Education: Monmouth Col (IL) 1969 BA; William & Mary 1978 JD
Senior Policy Advisor **Jennie P. O'Holleran** . . . . . . . . . . . .(804) 692-2566
  E-mail: jennie.oholleran@governor.virginia.gov
  Education: Virginia; George Washington MPA
Deputy Counsel to the Governor and Policy Advisor
  **Tracy Retchin** . . . . . . . . . . . . . . . . . . . . . . . . . . . . . . . . . .(804) 786-2211
    E-mail: tracy.retchin@governor.virginia.gov
    Education: UCLA BA; Georgetown JD
Deputy Counsel **Noah Sullivan** . . . . . . . . . . . . . . . . . . . . . . (804) 663-7875
  E-mail: noah.sullivan@governor.virginia.gov
  Education: Virginia BA

Director for Constituent Services **Irma Palmer** . . . . . . . . . .(804) 786-2211
  E-mail: irma.palmer@governor.virginia.gov
  Education: Virginia BA, 2015 MPP
  Special Assistant for Constituent Services **Ian Ceraolo** . . (804) 786-2211
    E-mail: ian.ceraolo@governor.virginia.gov
    Education: Florida State BA, BEc
  Special Assistant for Constituent Services **Darryl Holt** . . . (804) 786-2211
    E-mail: darryl.holt@governor.virginia.gov
Director of Scheduling and Advance
  **Carrie Henderson Caumont** . . . . . . . . . . . . . . . . . . . . . . . (804) 692-0139
  E-mail: carrie.caumont@governor.virginia.gov
  Education: James Madison 2003 BA
  Deputy Director of Scheduling **Ryan O'Toole** . . . . . . . . . (804) 786-2211
    E-mail: ryan.otoole@governor.virginia.gov
    Education: Fordham BA
Communications Director **Brian Coy** . . . . . . . . . . . . . . . . . . (804) 225-4260
  E-mail: brian.coy@governor.virginia.gov
  Education: James Madison 2006 BA
  Deputy Communications Director **Christina Nuckols** . . . .(804) 786-9135
    E-mail: christina.nuckols@governor.virginia.gov
    Education: Randolph-Macon; Ohio MC
  Assistant Communications Director **Sam Coleman** . . . . . (804) 786-2211
Press Secretary **Brian Coy** . . . . . . . . . . . . . . . . . . . . . . . . . (804) 786-2211
  E-mail: brian.coy@governor.virginia.gov
Press Special Assistant **(Vacant)** . . . . . . . . . . . . . . . . . . . . . (804) 971-8513
Traveling Press Secretary **(Vacant)** . . . . . . . . . . . . . . . . . . (804) 786-2211
Executive Director of the Mansion **Kaci Easley** . . . . . . . . . (804) 786-2211
  E-mail: kaci.easley@governor.virginia.gov
  Education: Hampton BA
  Deputy Director of the Mansion **Stacy Ellis** . . . . . . . . . . (804) 786-2211

## Office of the Inspector General

Internet: www.osig.virginia.gov  Tel: (804) 625-3255
■State Inspector General **June W. Jennings** . . . . . . . . . . . . (804) 786-2211
  E-mail: june.jennings@osig.virginia.gov

## Office of the Secretary of the Commonwealth

Patrick Henry Building, 1111 East Broad Street, 4th Floor,
Richmond, VA 23219
P.O. Box 2454, Richmond, VA 23218
Tel: (804) 786-2441  Fax: (804) 371-0017
E-mail: soc@governor.virginia.gov
Internet: www.commonwealth.virginia.gov

■Secretary of the Commonwealth
  **Kelly Thomasson Mercer** . . . . . . . . . . . . . . . . . . . . . . . . (804) 786-2441
  E-mail: kelly.thomasson@governor.virginia.gov
  ■Executive Assistant to the Secretary of the
  Commonwealth **Denise Burch** . . . . . . . . . . . . . . . . . . . . (804) 786-2441
    E-mail: denise.burch@governor.virginia.gov
■Deputy Secretary of the Commonwealth **(Vacant)** . . . . . . . (804) 786-2441
Authentications Division Director **Jennifer Crown** . . . . . . . (804) 786-2441
Boards and Appointments Director **Lana Westfall** . . . . . . . (804) 786-2441
  E-mail: lana.westfall@governor.virginia.gov
Conflict of Interest Director **Margaret D. Sacks** . . . . . . . . . (804) 786-2441
  Education: Richmond BA; George Washington MPP
Extraditions Director **Patricia B. "Patty" Tucker** . . . . . . . . .(804) 786-2441
Lobbyist Registration Director **Christopher Frink** . . . . . . . .(804) 786-2441
Notary Division Director **Jennifer Crown** . . . . . . . . . . . . . (804) 786-2441

---

★ Elected Official  ■ Appointed by Governor  ● Appointed by Legislature  ▲ Appointed by Board or Commission  ◆ Appointed by State Supreme Court

Restoration of Rights Director **Anne Forsythe**..........(804) 786-2441
  Clemency/Pardons Specialist **Jennifer Crown**..........(804) 786-2441
Service of Process Director (Interim) **Kari Ellis**..........(804) 786-2441

# Administration Secretariat
Patrick Henry Building, 1111 East Broad Street, Fourth Floor,
Richmond, VA 23219
P.O. Box 1475, Richmond, VA 23218
Tel: (804) 786-1201  Fax: (804) 692-2466
E-mail: administration@governor.state.va.us
Internet: www.administration.virginia.gov

**Employees: 893  Fiscal Year: 2015  Budget: $2,498,574,000**

■Secretary **Nancy Rodrigues**...........................(804) 786-1201
  E-mail: nancy.rodrigues@governor.virginia.gov
  Education: Rutgers BS
  Confidential Assistant **Kyle Rosner**...................(804) 786-1201
    Education: Radford 2015 BA
■Deputy Secretary **Felix Sarfo-Kantanka, Jr.**............(804) 786-1201
  Education: Methodist U; VCU 2001 MPA
Executive Assistant **Charlotte Hurd**...................(804) 786-1201

# Department of General Services
Washington Building, 1100 Bank Street, Suite 420, Richmond, VA 23219
Tel: (804) 786-3311  Fax: (804) 371-8305  Internet: www.dgs.virginia.gov

■Director **Christopher L. Beschler**.....................(804) 786-3311
  E-mail: richard.sliwoski@dgs.virginia.gov
  Education: Connecticut BSME, MBA
Deputy Director **Joseph F. "Joe" Damico**..............(804) 371-7724
  E-mail: joe.damico@dgs.virginia.gov
  Education: James Madison 1976 BS, 1977 MBA
Controller **Bryan W. Wagner**..........................(804) 786-7925
Fleet Management Director **Michael Bisogno**...........(804) 367-6526
  2400 W. Leigh St., Richmond, VA 23220
Human Resources Director **Katherine "Kitty" Kennedy**..(804) 786-3221
Information Systems Services Director
  **Maurion Edwards**....................................(804) 786-1819
  E-mail: maurion.edwards@dgs.virginia.gov    Fax: (804) 371-6527
Internal Audit Manager **Annette Grier**.................(804) 786-4361
Communications Director **Dena Potter**.................(804) 371-8359
  E-mail: dena.potter@dgs.virginia.gov
Graphic Communications Office Director
  **Paris Ashton-Bressler**..............................(804) 371-8359
  E-mail: paris.ashton@dgs.virginia.gov

## Consolidated Laboratory Services Division [DCLS]
600 North Fifth Street, Richmond, VA 23219
Fax: (804) 371-7973

Director **Tom York**.............................(804) 648-4480 ext. 151
Deputy Director **Dr. Denise Toney**.............(804) 648-4480 ext. 282

## Engineering and Buildings Division
Fax: (804) 371-7934  Internet: www.dgs.virginia.gov/deb

Director **Ed Gully**....................................(804) 225-3870
Capital Outlay Bureau Director **William Michael Coppa**..(804) 786-4398
Facilities Management Bureau Director
  **Thomas "Tom" George**..............................(804) 786-1821
  203 Governor St., Richmond, VA 23219
Parking Services Administrator **Sheila Erickson**.........(804) 786-8413
  203 Governor St., Rm. 102, Richmond, VA 23219

## Purchases and Supply Division
P.O. Box 1199, Richmond, VA 23218-1199
Tel: (804) 786-3842  Fax: (804) 225-3707  Internet: www.dgs.virginia.gov

Director **Ron Bell**....................................(804) 786-3846
                                              Fax: (804) 371-7877

## Real Estate Services Division
1100 Bank Street, Third Floor, Richmond, VA 23219
Tel: (804) 225-3764  Fax: (804) 225-4673

Director **Holly Law Eve**..............................(804) 371-4327

# Human Resource Management Department
James Monroe Building, 101 North 14th Street, 12th Floor,
Richmond, VA 23219
Tel: (804) 225-2131  Fax: (804) 371-7401
Internet: www.dhrm.virginia.gov

■Director **Sara Redding Wilson**.......................(804) 225-2237
  E-mail: sara.wilson@dhrm.virginia.gov
  Receptionist/Office Assistant **Kathryn Brooks**.........(804) 225-2131
■Chief Deputy Director **(Vacant)**......................(804) 225-4198
Agency Human Resources Services Director
  **Rueyenne White**....................................(804) 225-3465
Equal Employment Services Director
  **George E. Gardner, Jr.**............................(804) 225-2136
Health Benefits Programs Director
  **Eugene "Gene" Raney**..............................(804) 371-7932
  E-mail: gene.raney@dhrm.virginia.gov
Ombudsman **Sharon Finn**.............................(804) 371-6210
                                              Fax: (804) 371-0231
Information Technology Director **Belchior Mira**.........(804) 225-2203
  E-mail: belchior.mira@dhrm.virginia.gov
Workers' Compensation Director
  **Frances Kristie McClaren**..........................(804) 786-0362

# Office of Employment Dispute Resolution
101 North 14th Street, Richmond, VA 23219
Tel: (804) 786-7994  Tel: (888) 232-3842  Fax: (804) 786-0100
E-mail: administrator@edr.virginia.gov

■Director **Christopher Grab**..........................(804) 786-7994
  E-mail: chris.grab@dhrm.virginia.gov
Hearing Officer **Carl Wilson Schmidt**.................(804) 225-2973
  E-mail: carl.schmidt@dhrm.virginia.gov
  Administrative and Program Specialist
  **Marsha C. Heath**..................................(804) 225-2973
  E-mail: marsha.heath@dhrm.virginia.gov
Webmaster **Michelle Thompson**.......................(804) 225-4005
  E-mail: michele.thompson@vdot.virginia.gov

# Compensation Board
102 Governor Street, Suite 120, Richmond, VA 23219
Tel: (804) 786-0786  Fax: (804) 371-0235  Internet: www.scb.virginia.gov

■Chairman **Susan R. Swecker**.........................(804) 786-0786
  Education: Mary Baldwin; Washington and Lee
Executive Secretary **Robyn M. de Socio**..............(804) 225-3439
  E-mail: robyn.desocio@scb.virginia.gov
  Education: VCU BS, MS
Customer Service Manager **Charlene M. Rollins**........(804) 225-3321
Fiscal Officer **Linda B. Gutshall**.....................(804) 225-3428

# Department of Elections
Washington Building, 1100 Bank Street, First Floor, Richmond, VA 23219
Tel: (800) 552-9745  TTY: (800) 260-3466  Fax: (804) 371-0194

■Commissioner **Edgardo Cortés**.......................(804) 864-8901
  Education: Cornell; George Washington MPM
Deputy Commissioner **Elizabeth Howard**..............(800) 552-9745
  E-mail: elizabeth.howard@dgs.virginia.gov
  Education: Tennessee BAcc; William & Mary JD

# State Board of Elections
Internet: www.sbe.virginia.gov

■Chairman **James B. Alcorn**..........................(800) 552-9745
■Vice Chair **Clara Belle Wheeler**.....................(800) 552-9745
■Secretary **Singleton B. McAllister**..................(804) 864-8903
  Education: Maryland 1975 BA; Howard U 1984 JD

---

★ Elected Official    ■ Appointed by Governor    ● Appointed by Legislature    ▲ Appointed by Board or Commission    ◆ Appointed by State Supreme Court

# Agriculture and Forestry Secretariat

1111 East Broad Street, Richmond, VA 23219
P.O. Box 1475, Richmond, VA 23218
Tel: (804) 692-2511  Fax: (804) 692-2466
Internet: www.ag-forestry.virginia.gov

**Employees:** 789  **Fiscal Year:** 2015  **Budget:** $95,471,000

■Secretary **Todd Patterson Haymore** . . . . . . . . . . . . . . . . . (804) 692-2511
   E-mail: todd.haymore@governor.virginia.gov
■Deputy Secretary **Samuel Thurston Towell** . . . . . . . . . . . (804) 692-2511
   E-mail: sam.towell@governor.virginia.gov
   Education: MIT BSME; Virginia JD
■Assistant Secretary **Cassidy Rasnick** . . . . . . . . . . . . . . . (804) 692-2511
   E-mail: cassidy.rasnick@governor.virginia.gov
   Education: James Madison 2007 BA
   Special Assistant **Meghan Hobbs** . . . . . . . . . . . . . . . . . (804) 692-2511

# Agriculture and Consumer Services Department [VDACS]

102 Governor Street, Richmond, VA 23219
P.O. Box 1163, Richmond, VA 23218
Tel: (804) 786-3501  TTY: (800) 828-1120  Fax: (804) 371-2945
E-mail: webmaster@vdacs.virginia.gov  Internet: www.vdacs.virginia.gov

■Commissioner **Sandra J. Adams** . . . . . . . . . . . . . . . . . . (804) 786-3501
   E-mail: sandra.adams@vdacs.virginia.gov
   Education: Mary Washington Col BA
   Deputy Commissioner **Charles Green** . . . . . . . . . . . . . . . (804) 786-3501
   Administrative and Financial Services Director
   **Jennifer S. Cavedo** . . . . . . . . . . . . . . . . . . . . . . . . . (804) 786-7161
      E-mail: jennifer.cavedo@vdacs.virginia.gov
   Animal & Food Industry Services Director
   **Richard L Wilkes** . . . . . . . . . . . . . . . . . . . . . . . . . . (804) 692-0601
   Consumer Protection Director **Andres Alvarez** . . . . . . . . (804) 225-3821
   Information Systems Director **Cathy Nott** . . . . . . . . . . . . (804) 786-1338
      E-mail: catherine.nott@vdacs.virginia.gov
   International Marketing Director **Keith B. Long** . . . . . . . . (804) 371-8990
   Marketing Division Director (Acting) **E. L. Knicely** . . . . . . (804) 786-3530
■Milk Commission Administrator **Crafton O. Wilkes** . . . . . . (804) 786-2013
   E-mail: crafton.wilkes@vdacs.virginia.gov
   Education: Virginia Tech BS, MS
   Webmaster **Maurcine Dalton** . . . . . . . . . . . . . . . . . . . (804) 371-8578

## Office of Charitable Gaming

102 Governor Street, Terrace Level, Richmond, VA 23219-3523
Tel: (804) 371-0495

Program Manager **Michael Menefee** . . . . . . . . . . . . . . . . (804) 371-0495

## Department of Forestry

900 Natural Resources Drive, Suite 800, Charlottesville, VA 22903
Tel: (434) 977-6555  Fax: (434) 296-2369  Internet: www.dof.virginia.gov

■State Forester **Bettina Ring, CF** . . . . . . . . . . . . . . . . . . (434) 977-6555
   E-mail: bettina.ring@dof.virginia.gov
   Administrative Staff Specialist **Mary Weaver** . . . . . . . . . (434) 220-9045
   Deputy State Forester **Robert W. Farrell** . . . . . . . . . . . . (434) 977-6555
   State Wildland Fire Chief **John Miller** . . . . . . . . . . . . . . (434) 977-6555

# Commerce and Trade Secretariat

Patrick Henry Building, 1111 East Broad Street, Richmond, VA 23219
P.O. Box 1475, Richmond, VA 23218
Tel: (804) 225-4522  Fax: (804) 371-0250

■Secretary **Maurice A. Jones** . . . . . . . . . . . . . . . . . . . . (804) 225-4522
   Education: Hampden-Sydney 1986 BA; Oxford (UK) 1988 MPhil;
   Virginia 1992 JD
   Executive Assistant **Meggie Lareau** . . . . . . . . . . . . . . . (804) 225-4518
      Education: Richmond BA
   Special Assistant **George Stewart** . . . . . . . . . . . . . . . . (804) 225-4520
      Education: Vanderbilt BEc
   Advisor for Infrastructure and Development
   **Benjamin "Hayes" Framme** . . . . . . . . . . . . . . . . . . . . (804) 225-4517
      Education: Col Charleston BA; DePaul MBA
■Advisor for Workforce Development **Elizabeth Creamer** . . (804) 692-2563
   E-mail: elizabeth.creamer@governor.virginia.gov

■Special Advisor for Rural Partnerships **Mary Rae Carter** . . (804) 225-4316
   E-mail: maryrae.carter@governor.virginia.gov
   Education: Averett U BS
   Communications and External Affairs Manager
   **Kelly Spraker** . . . . . . . . . . . . . . . . . . . . . . . . . . . . (804) 225-4522
      E-mail: kelly.spraker@governor.virginia.gov

# Department of Housing and Community Development [DHCD]

Main Street Centre, 600 East Main Street, Suite 300,
Richmond, VA 23218
Tel: (804) 371-7000  Fax: (804) 371-7090
Internet: www.dhcd.virginia.gov

■Director **William C. "Bill" Shelton** . . . . . . . . . . . . . . . . (804) 371-7002
   E-mail: director@dhcd.virginia.gov
   Administrative Assistant **Jennifer Kibe** . . . . . . . . . . . . . (804) 371-7002
■Principal Deputy Director **(Vacant)** . . . . . . . . . . . . . . . . (804) 371-7011
   Administration Division Deputy Director
   **Alvin D. Williams** . . . . . . . . . . . . . . . . . . . . . . . . . (804) 371-7020
      E-mail: al.williams@dhcd.virginia.gov
   Building and Fire Regulations Division Deputy Director
   **Cindy L. Davis** . . . . . . . . . . . . . . . . . . . . . . . . . . . (804) 371-7150
   Community Development Division Deputy Director
   **Lisa Atkinson** . . . . . . . . . . . . . . . . . . . . . . . . . . . . (804) 371-7030
   Housing Division Deputy Director **Chris Thompson** . . . . . (804) 371-7101
   Local Government Policy Manager **Zachary Robbins** . . . . . (804) 786-6508

# Department of Labor and Industry

Powers-Taylor Building, 13 South 13th Street, Richmond, VA 23219-4101
Tel: (804) 371-2327  TTY: (804) 786-2376  Fax: (804) 371-6524
Internet: www.doli.virginia.gov

■Commissioner **Carlton Ray Davenport** . . . . . . . . . . . . . (804) 786-9878
   E-mail: william.burge@doli.virginia.gov
   Education: Antioch U BA; UMass (Amherst) MS
   Assistant Commissioner **(Vacant)** . . . . . . . . . . . . . . . . . (804) 371-2327
   Human Resource Director **Holly Clary** . . . . . . . . . . . . . . (804) 225-4684
      E-mail: holly.clary@doli.virginia.gov
   Administrative Staff Assistant **(Vacant)** . . . . . . . . . . . . . (804) 371-2327

## Administration and Finance

Fax: (804) 786-9877

Administration and Finance Director **Nancy M. Sanders** . . (804) 371-7414
   E-mail: nancy.sanders@doli.virginia.gov
General Services Director **(Vacant)** . . . . . . . . . . . . . . . . . (804) 786-4267
Planning and Policy Specialist **Reba D. O'Connor** . . . . . . . (804) 371-2631
   E-mail: reba.oconnor@doli.virginia.gov
Management Information Services Director and
   Information Security Director **Michael L. MacEwen** . . . . (804) 371-0537
   E-mail: mike.macewen@doli.virginia.gov

## Virginia Occupational Safety and Health

Fax: (804) 786-2391

Occupational Safety and Health Program Director
   **James Garrett** . . . . . . . . . . . . . . . . . . . . . . . . . . . . (804) 786-7776
      E-mail: james.garrett@doli.virginia.gov
Legal Support Office Director **Jay W. Withrow** . . . . . . . . . (804) 786-9873
   E-mail: jay.withrow@doli.virginia.gov
Cooperative Programs Division Director
   **Sharon H. Sykes** . . . . . . . . . . . . . . . . . . . . . . . . . . (804) 786-9931
Occupational Health Compliance Division Director
   **Ronald L. Graham** . . . . . . . . . . . . . . . . . . . . . . . . . (804) 786-0574
   Occupational Safety and Health Consultation Service
      Manager **Warren Rice** . . . . . . . . . . . . . . . . . . . . . (804) 786-6613
   Occupational Safety and Health Voluntary Protection
      Programs Coordinator **(Vacant)** . . . . . . . . . . . . . . . (540) 562-3580
   Occupational Safety and Health Training Officer (Acting)
   **Warren Rice** . . . . . . . . . . . . . . . . . . . . . . . . . . . . . (804) 786-6613

## State Program Operations

Fax: (804) 371-2324

Boiler & Pressure Vessel Division Director **Ed Hilton** . . . . . (804) 786-3262
Registered Apprenticeship Program Director
   **Beverly G. Donati** . . . . . . . . . . . . . . . . . . . . . . . . . (804) 225-4362
      E-mail: bev.donati@doli.virginia.gov

---

★ Elected Official   ■Appointed by Governor   ●Appointed by Legislature   ▲Appointed by Board or Commission   ◆Appointed by State Supreme Court

State Labor & Employment Law Program Director
**Wendy Inge** . . . . . . . . . . . . . . . . . . . . . . . . . . . . (804) 786-3224
E-mail: wendy.inge@doli.virginia.gov

## Department of Mines, Minerals and Energy [DMME]

Washington Building, 1100 Bank Street, 8th Floor, Richmond, VA 23219
Tel: (804) 692-3200  TTY: (800) 828-1120  Fax: (804) 692-3237
E-mail: DmmeInfo@dmme.virginia.gov  Internet: www.dmme.virginia.gov

■Director **John W. Warren** . . . . . . . . . . . . . . . . . . . (804) 692-3206
E-mail: john.warren@dmme.virginia.gov
Deputy Director **Bradley C. "Butch" Lambert** . . . . . . . . (276) 523-8145
P.O. Drawer 900, Big Stone Gap, VA 24219
E-mail: butch.lambert@dmme.virginia.gov
Education: Lincoln Memorial 1997 BS
Energy Division Director **Al Christopher** . . . . . . . . . . . . . . (804) 692-3216
Gas and Oil Division Director **Rick W. Cooper** . . . . . . . . . (276) 415-9700
135 Highland Drive, Lebanon, VA 24266
Mined Land Reclamation Division Director
**Randy R. Casey** . . . . . . . . . . . . . . . . . . . . . . . . (276) 523-8286
P.O. Drawer 900, Big Stone Gap, VA 24219
Mineral Mining Division Director **Phillip Skorupa** . . . . . . . (434) 951-6312
900 Natural Resources Drive, Charlottesville, VA 22903
Geology and Mineral Resources Division Chief and State
Geologist **David B. Spears** . . . . . . . . . . . . . . . . . . . (434) 951-6350
900 Natural Resources Drive, Suite 500, Charlottesville, VA 22903
Mines Division Chief **Randy Moore** . . . . . . . . . . . . . . . . . (276) 523-8226
P.O. Drawer 900, Big Stone Gap, VA 24219
Education: Virginia 1980 BSBA
Program Support Manager **Michael A. Skiffington** . . . . . . (804) 692-3212
Public Relations Manager **Tarah Kesterson** . . . . . . . . . . . (276) 523-8146
E-mail: tarah.kesterson@dmme.virginia.gov
Energy Policy Special Advisor **Chris McDonald** . . . . . . . . (804) 692-3201
Education: Vanderbilt BA; Washington and Lee JD

## Department of Professional and Occupational Regulation

Perimeter Center, 9960 Mayland Drive, Suite 400,
Henrico, VA 23233-1463
Tel: (804) 367-8500  Fax: (804) 527-4408
E-mail: dpor@dpor.virginia.gov  Internet: www.dpor.virginia.gov

■Director **Jay Wayne DeBoer** . . . . . . . . . . . . . . . . . . (804) 367-8519
E-mail: jay.deboer@dpor.virginia.gov
Education: William & Mary 1975 AB, 1979 JD
Compliance and Investigations Deputy Director
**Nick A. Christner** . . . . . . . . . . . . . . . . . . . . . . . (804) 367-8504
Education: St Leo Col 1997 BS
Licensing and Regulations Deputy Director
**Nick A. Christner** . . . . . . . . . . . . . . . . . . . . . . . (804) 367-8504
E-mail: nick.christner@dpor.virginia.gov
Communications, Legislation, and Consumer Education
Director **Mary C. Broz-Vaughn** . . . . . . . . . . . . . . . . . (804) 367-9142
E-mail: mary.broz@dpor.virginia.gov
Education: Virginia 1996 BA
Examinations and Education Director **Bill Murray** . . . . . . . (804) 367-8554
E-mail: bill.murray@dpor.virginia.gov
Fair Housing Director **Lizbeth T. "Liz" Hayes** . . . . . . . . . (804) 367-8530
Human Resources Director **Linda Bell** . . . . . . . . . . . . . (804) 367-8517
Information Technology Director **Jeanne H. Branch** . . . . . . (804) 367-2720
E-mail: jeanne.branch@dpor.virginia.gov
Education: Howard U 1973 BS; Rutgers 1980 MBA
Quality Process/Performance Measures **(Vacant)** . . . . . . . (804) 367-2681

## Department of Small Business and Supplier Diversity

Bank of America Building, 1111 East Main Street, Suite 300,
Richmond, VA 23219
Tel: (804) 786-6585  Fax: (804) 786-6585

Agency Director **Tracey Jeter** . . . . . . . . . . . . . . . . . . (804) 371-6228
Director of Operations **Angela Chiang** . . . . . . . . . . . . . (804) 786-6585
Business Information Center Counselor (Acting)
**Tongela Wright** . . . . . . . . . . . . . . . . . . . . . . . . . (804) 371-8230

Advisor for Small Business Development
**Susan Y. "Syd" Dorsey** . . . . . . . . . . . . . . . . . . . . . (804) 371-0125
Education: Virginia 1982 BS, 1987 MBA
Advisor for Social Entrepreneurism and Innovation
**Lawrence D. "Larry" Wilder, Jr.** . . . . . . . . . . . . . . . . (804) 786-5560
Education: Virginia BA, JD; USC MBA

## Education Secretariat

Patrick Henry Building, 1111 East Broad Street, 4th Floor,
Richmond, VA 23219
P.O. Box 1475, Richmond, VA 23218
Tel: (804) 786-1151  Fax: (804) 371-0154

**Employees:** 56,897  **Fiscal Year:** 2015  **Budget:** $17,211,235,000

■Secretary **Anne Holton** . . . . . . . . . . . . . . . . . . . . . (804) 786-1151
E-mail: anne.holton@governor.virginia.gov
Education: Princeton 1980 AB; Harvard 1983 JD
Confidential Assistant **Laura Jennings** . . . . . . . . . . . . (804) 786-1151
Special Assistant **Eric Von Steigleder** . . . . . . . . . . . . (804) 786-1151
Education: U Mary Washington BA; VCU MJ
Deputy Secretary **Holly M. Coy** . . . . . . . . . . . . . . . . (804) 786-1151
E-mail: holly.coy@governor.virginia.gov
Education: Virginia 2007 BA; American U 2010 MS
Deputy Secretary **Dietra Y. Trent** . . . . . . . . . . . . . . . (804) 775-2314
E-mail: deitra_trent@warner.senate.gov          Tel: (804) 786-1151
Education: Hampton BA; VCU MPA, DPA

## Education Department

James Monroe Building, 101 North 14th Street,
Richmond, VA 23219-3665
P.O. Box 2120, Richmond, VA 23218-2120
Tel: (804) 225-2020  TTY: (804) 371-0655  Fax: (804) 371-2099
Internet: www.doe.virginia.gov

■Superintendent of Public Instruction
**Dr. Steven R. Staples** . . . . . . . . . . . . . . . . . . . . . (804) 225-2023
E-mail: steven.staples@doe.virginia.gov
Chief Deputy Superintendent of Public Instruction
**(Vacant)** . . . . . . . . . . . . . . . . . . . . . . . . . . . . (804) 225-2979
Assessment and Reporting Assistant Superintendent
**Shelley Loving-Ryder** . . . . . . . . . . . . . . . . . . . . . (804) 225-2102
Deputy Superintendent of Financial Operations
**Kent Dickey** . . . . . . . . . . . . . . . . . . . . . . . . . . (804) 225-2025
Instruction Assistant Superintendent
**Dr. John W. "Billy" Haun** . . . . . . . . . . . . . . . . . . . (804) 225-2034
Policy and Public Affairs Assistant Superintendent
**Dr. Cynthia Cave** . . . . . . . . . . . . . . . . . . . . . . . (804) 225-2092
E-mail: cynthia.cave@doe.virginia.gov
Special Education and Student Services Assistant
Superintendent **John Eisenberg** . . . . . . . . . . . . . . . . (804) 786-8079
Teacher Education/Professional Licensure Assistant
Superintendent **Patricia S. "Patty" Pitts** . . . . . . . . . . (804) 371-2522
Technology Assistant Superintendent **(Vacant)** . . . . . . . . (804) 225-2757
Architectural Consultant/Building Principal
**ViJay Ramnarain** . . . . . . . . . . . . . . . . . . . . . . . (804) 225-2035
E-mail: vijay.ramnarain@doe.virginia.gov      Fax: (804) 225-2831
Humanities and Early Childhood Office Director
**Christine Harris** . . . . . . . . . . . . . . . . . . . . . . . (804) 371-7578
Board Liaison **Melissa Luchau** . . . . . . . . . . . . . . . . . (804) 225-2924
E-mail: melissa.luchau@doe.virginia.gov
Human Resources Officer **Rebecca Marable** . . . . . . . . . . (804) 225-2021
School Nutrition Programs Director
**Catherine Digilio-Grimes, SNS** . . . . . . . . . . . . . . . . (804) 225-2074

## Commission on Higher Education Board Appointments

State Capitol, 1111 East Broad Street, Richmond, VA 23219
Tel: (804) 786-2211

■Member **Eva Teig Hardy** . . . . . . . . . . . . . . . . . . . . (804) 786-2211
Education: Hood 1965; American U MPA
■Member **Joni L. Ivey** . . . . . . . . . . . . . . . . . . . . . (804) 786-2211
Education: Norfolk State
■Member **Leonard W. Sandridge, Jr.** . . . . . . . . . . . . . . (804) 786-2211
Education: Richmond 1964; Virginia 1974

*(continued on next page)*

---

★ Elected Official   ■ Appointed by Governor   ● Appointed by Legislature   ▲ Appointed by Board or Commission   ◆ Appointed by State Supreme Court

**EXECUTIVE BRANCH**

**Commission on Higher Education Board Appointments** *continued*

- Member **Dr. Charles W. Steger** . . . . . . . . . . . . . . . . (804) 786-2211
  Education: Virginia Tech 1969 BA, 1972 MS, 1978 PhD
- Member **Jeffrey B. "Jeff" Trammell** . . . . . . . . . . . . . (804) 786-2211
  Affiliation: President, Trammell and Company
  1501 M Street, NW, Suite 200, Washington, DC 20006
  Education: William & Mary 1973 BA; Florida State 1977 JD
- Ex-Officio Member **Janet Vestal Kelly** . . . . . . . . . . . . . (804) 786-2211
- Ex-Officio Member **Javaid Siddiqi** . . . . . . . . . . . . . . . (804) 786-2211
  Education: VCU; Virginia State MA; VCU DEd

## State Council of Higher Education

James Monroe Building, 101 North 14th Street, Ninth Floor,
Richmond, VA 23219
Tel: (804) 225-2600  Fax: (804) 371-7911  Internet: www.schev.edu

Chair **G. Gilmer Minor III** . . . . . . . . . . . . . . . . . . . . . (804) 225-2600
  Term Expires: June 30, 2017
  Education: VMI 1963 BA; Colgate Darden 1966 MBA
Vice Chair **W. Heywood Fralin** . . . . . . . . . . . . . . . . . . (804) 225-2600
  Term Expires: June 30, 2017
Secretary **Marjorie M. "Marge" Connelly** . . . . . . . . . . . (804) 225-2600
  Term Expires: June 30, 2018
  Education: Delaware BA
Member **Gilbert T. Bland** . . . . . . . . . . . . . . . . . . . . . . (804) 225-2600
  Term Expires: June 30, 2016
Member **Stephen D. Haner** . . . . . . . . . . . . . . . . . . . . . (804) 225-2600
  Term Expires: June 30, 2015
Member **Henry D. Light** . . . . . . . . . . . . . . . . . . . . . . . (804) 225-2600
  Term Expires: June 30, 2018
  Education: Rensselaer Poly 1962; Virginia 1969
Member **H. Eugene "Gene" Lockhart, Jr.** . . . . . . . . . . . . (804) 225-2600
  Term Expires: June 30, 2016
  Education: Virginia 1972 BS, 1974 MBA
Member **Pamela R. Moran** . . . . . . . . . . . . . . . . . . . . . (804) 225-2600
  Term Expires: June 30, 2017
Member **Bill Murray** . . . . . . . . . . . . . . . . . . . . . . . . . (804) 225-2600
  Term Expires: June 30, 2018
Member **Gary Nakamoto** . . . . . . . . . . . . . . . . . . . . . . (804) 225-2600
  Term Expires: June 30, 2016
Member **Carlyle Ramsey** . . . . . . . . . . . . . . . . . . . . . . (804) 225-2600
  Term Expires: June 30, 2017
Member **Minnis E. Ridenour** . . . . . . . . . . . . . . . . . . . . (804) 225-2600
  Term Expires: June 30, 2019
  Education: Tennessee 1969 BS, 1972 MS
Member **Katharine M. Webb** . . . . . . . . . . . . . . . . . . . . (804) 225-2600
  Term Expires: June 30, 2019
  Education: Sweet Briar AB; VCU MSW
Ex-Officio Member **Daniel C. "Dan" Gundersen** . . . . . . . (804) 225-2600
  Education: Hope 1982 BA; Pennsylvania 1988 MGA

### Executive Staff

Executive Director **Peter A. Blake** . . . . . . . . . . . . . . . . (804) 225-2601
Budget and Finance Director **(Vacant)** . . . . . . . . . . . . . (804) 225-2600
Executive and Council Affairs Director **Lee Ann Rung** . . (804) 225-2602
  E-mail: leeannrung@schev.edu
Academic Affairs and Planning Director
  **Joseph De Filippo** . . . . . . . . . . . . . . . . . . . . . . . . (804) 225-2629
  E-mail: joedefilippo@schev.edu
Finance Policy Director **R. Dan Hix** . . . . . . . . . . . . . . . (804) 225-3188
  E-mail: danhix@schev.edu
Government Relations and Communications Director
  **(Vacant)** . . . . . . . . . . . . . . . . . . . . . . . . . . . . . . (804) 225-2627
Policy Research and Data Warehousing Director
  **Tod Massa** . . . . . . . . . . . . . . . . . . . . . . . . . . . . (804) 225-3147
  E-mail: todmassa@schev.edu
Policy Studies Director **Alan Edwards** . . . . . . . . . . . . . (804) 225-3189

## Library of Virginia

800 East Broad Street, Richmond, VA 23219-8000
Tel: (804) 692-3500  Fax: (804) 692-3594  Internet: www.lva.virginia.gov

▲ Librarian **Sandra Gioia Treadway** . . . . . . . . . . . . . . . (804) 692-3535
  E-mail: sandra.treadway@lva.virginia.gov
  Education: Manhattanville 1971 BA; Virginia 1972 MA, 1978 PhD
Executive Assistant **Jean Strohm** . . . . . . . . . . . . . . . . (804) 692-3535

Deputy of Administration **Connie Warne** . . . . . . . . . . . . (804) 692-3811
  E-mail: connie.warne@lva.virginia.gov
Deputy of Collections and Programs **John Metz** . . . . . . . (804) 692-3607
  E-mail: john.metz@lva.virginia.gov
Information Technology Services Division Director
  **Paul J. Casalaspi** . . . . . . . . . . . . . . . . . . . . . . . . (804) 692-3756
  E-mail: paul.casalaspi@lva.virginia.gov
  Education: Lafayette 1984 BSEE; Richmond 1992 MBA
Library Development and Networking Division Director
  **Amy Bridge** . . . . . . . . . . . . . . . . . . . . . . . . . . . . (804) 692-3762
Records and Government Services Division Director
  **Barbara Teague** . . . . . . . . . . . . . . . . . . . . . . . . . (804) 692-3739
  Education: Kentucky BA; Virginia MPA
Public Services and Outreach Division Director
  **Gregg Kimball** . . . . . . . . . . . . . . . . . . . . . . . . . . (804) 692-3722
Public Information Officer **Janice M. Hathcock** . . . . . . . (804) 692-3592
  E-mail: jan.hathcock@lva.virginia.gov
  Education: Mary Washington Col 1972 BA

## Board of Education

James Monroe Building, 101 North 14th Street, Richmond, VA 23219
Tel: (804) 225-2540  Fax: (804) 225-2524  E-mail: boe@doe.virginia.gov
Internet: www.doe.virginia.gov/boe/index.shtml

- President **Dr. Billy K. Cannaday, Jr.** . . . . . . . . . . . . . . (804) 225-2540
  Term Expires: June 30, 2019
  Education: Virginia Tech 1972 BA; Hampton 1980 MA;
  Virginia Tech 1990 PhD
- Vice President **Joan E. Wodiska** . . . . . . . . . . . . . . . . . (804) 225-2540
  Term Expires: January 29, 2017
  E-mail: Joan.Wodiska@doe.virginia.gov
  Education: Concordia Col Moorhead MN BA; George Washington MA
- Member **Diane T. Atkinson** . . . . . . . . . . . . . . . . . . . . (804) 225-2540
  Term Expires: January 29, 2020
- Member **Dr. Oktay Baysal** . . . . . . . . . . . . . . . . . . . . . (804) 225-2540
  Term Expires: January 29, 2017
  Education: Istanbul Tech 1977 BS; U Birmingham (UK) 1978 MS;
  LSU 1982 PhD
- Member **Wes J. Bellamy** . . . . . . . . . . . . . . . . . . . . . . (804) 225-2540
  Term Expires: June 30, 2020
- Member **James H. Dillard II** . . . . . . . . . . . . . . . . . . . . (804) 225-2540
  Term Expires: January 29, 2018
  Education: William & Mary BA; American U 1972 MA
- Member **Daniel A. "Dan" Gecker** . . . . . . . . . . . . . . . . (804) 225-2540
  Term Expires: January 29, 2020
  Education: Princeton 1978 BA; William & Mary 1982 JD
- Member **Elizabeth Vickrey Lodal** . . . . . . . . . . . . . . . . (804) 225-2540
  Term Expires: January 29, 2019
- Member **Sal Romero, Jr.** . . . . . . . . . . . . . . . . . . . . . . (804) 225-2540
  Term Expires: January 29, 2018
  Education: James Madison; Shenandoah
- Member **(Vacant)** . . . . . . . . . . . . . . . . . . . . . . . . . . (804) 225-2540
  Term Expires: June 30, 2019
Board Secretary **Marian F. Morris** . . . . . . . . . . . . . . . . (804) 225-2540
Executive Assistant **Melissa Luchau** . . . . . . . . . . . . . . (804) 225-2924

## Finance Secretariat

Patrick Henry Building, 1111 East Broad Street, 3rd Floor,
Richmond, VA 23219
P.O. Box 1475, Richmond, VA 23218
Tel: (804) 786-1148  TTY: (804) 786-7765  Fax: (804) 692-0676
Internet: www.finance.virginia.gov

**Employees:** 1,278  **Fiscal Year:** 2015  **Budget:** $2,686,422,000

- Secretary **Richard D. "Ric" Brown** . . . . . . . . . . . . . . . (804) 786-1148
  E-mail: ric.brown@governor.virginia.gov
  Education: William & Mary 1968 BA; Richmond 1971 MA
  Executive Assistant **Connie Biggs** . . . . . . . . . . . . . . (804) 786-1148
- Deputy Secretary **Gina Burgin** . . . . . . . . . . . . . . . . . . (804) 786-1148
- Deputy Secretary **R. Neil Miller** . . . . . . . . . . . . . . . . . (804) 786-1148
  E-mail: neil.miller@governor.virginia.gov
  Education: Florida BSBA; Villanova 2000 JD; Georgetown 2001 LLM

---

★ Elected Official   ■ Appointed by Governor   ● Appointed by Legislature   ▲ Appointed by Board or Commission   ◆ Appointed by State Supreme Court

## Department of Accounts

James Monroe Building, 101 North 14th Street, 2nd Floor,
Richmond, VA 23219
P.O. Box 1971, Richmond, VA 23218
Tel: (804) 225-3038  Fax: (804) 786-3356  Internet: www.doa.virginia.gov

■ Comptroller **David A. Von Moll, CPA, CGFM** . . . . . . . . . . (804) 225-2109
  E-mail: david.vonmoll@doa.virginia.gov
  Education: Old Dominion 1978 BS; VCU 1985 MBA

## Department of Planning and Budget [DPB]

Patrick Henry Building, 1111 East Broad Street, Room 5040,
Richmond, VA 23219
Tel: (804) 786-7455  TTY: (804) 786-7574  Fax: (804) 225-3291
E-mail: dpbwebmaster@dpb.virginia.gov

■ Director **Daniel S. "Dan" Timberlake** . . . . . . . . . . . . . . . . (804) 786-7700
  E-mail: dan.timberlake@dpb.virginia.gov
  Education: William & Mary 1984 BA

## Department of Taxation

Main Street Center, 600 East Main Street, 23rd Floor,
Richmond, VA 23218
P.O. Box 2475, Richmond, VA 23218-2475
Tel: (804) 786-3587  Fax: (804) 786-3536  Internet: www.tax.virginia.gov

■ Commissioner **Craig M. Burns** . . . . . . . . . . . . . . . . . . . . . (804) 786-3332
  E-mail: craig.burns@tax.virginia.gov
  Education: SUNY (Cortland) BA; Syracuse MPA
Deputy Commissioner **Linda D. Foster** . . . . . . . . . . . . . . . . (804) 786-1716
Compliance Assistant Commissioner **Richard Dotson** . . . . . (804) 786-2126
General Legal and Technical Services Assistant
  Commissioner **Lawrence E. Durbin** . . . . . . . . . . . . . . . (804) 786-3337
Customer Services Office Assistant Commissioner
  **Tom Edicola** . . . . . . . . . . . . . . . . . . . . . . . . . . . . . . . . (804) 404-4190
Tax Policy Assistant Commissioner **William White** . . . . . . . (804) 371-2293
Tax Processing Operations Assistant Commissioner
  **Patti Higgins** . . . . . . . . . . . . . . . . . . . . . . . . . . . . . . . (804) 367-8157
Chief Administrative Officer **Joy Yeh** . . . . . . . . . . . . . . . . . (804) 786-3492
  E-mail: joy.yeh@tax.virginia.gov
Chief Technology Officer **Sharon L. Kitchens** . . . . . . . . . . (804) 786-2001
  E-mail: sharon.kitchens@tax.virginia.gov
Public Relations Manager **Joel Davison** . . . . . . . . . . . . . . . (804) 786-3507
  E-mail: joel.davison@tax.virginia.gov

## Department of the Treasury

James Monroe Building, 101 North 14th Street, Richmond, VA 23219
Tel: (804) 225-2142  Fax: (804) 225-3187  Internet: www.trs.virginia.gov

■ State Treasurer **Manju S. Ganeriwala** . . . . . . . . . . . . . . . (804) 225-2142
  E-mail: manju.ganeriwala@trs.virginia.gov
  Education: Bombay U (India) 1975 BCom; Texas 1981 MBA
Deputy State Treasurer **Brandy E. Mikell** . . . . . . . . . . . . . (804) 225-2142
Debt Management Director **Janet A. Aylor** . . . . . . . . . . . . . (804) 371-6006
  Education: William & Mary BA, MBA
Employee Relations Director **Stephanie Asbell** . . . . . . . . . (804) 225-3758
Financial Policy Director **Harold E. Moore** . . . . . . . . . . . . (804) 371-6013
  E-mail: harold.moore@trs.virginia.gov
Internal Audit Director **(Vacant)** . . . . . . . . . . . . . . . . . . . . (804) 225-2142
Risk Management Director **Don W. LeMond** . . . . . . . . . . . . (804) 225-4620
  Education: Lincoln U (MO) BA; Maryland MA
Treasury Operations Director **Kristin A. Reiter** . . . . . . . . . (804) 225-3240
  Education: Virginia Tech 1979 BS
Unclaimed Property Division Director
  **Vicki D. Bridgeman** . . . . . . . . . . . . . . . . . . . . . . . . . . (804) 225-2393
  Education: VCU 1980 BS
Cash Management and Investments **Tim Wilhide** . . . . . . . . (804) 225-3168

## Health and Human Resources Secretariat

Patrick Henry Building, 1111 East Broad Street, Suite 4001,
Richmond, VA 23219
P.O. Box 1475, Richmond, VA 23218
Tel: (804) 786-7765  Fax: (804) 786-3389
E-mail: shhr@governor.virginia.gov  Internet: www.hhr.virginia.gov

**Employees:** 16,612  **Fiscal Year:** 2015  **Budget:** $12,862,757,000

■ Secretary **William A. "Bill" Hazel, Jr., MD** . . . . . . . . . . . (804) 692-2571
  E-mail: bill.hazel@governor.virginia.gov
  Education: Princeton 1978 BS; Duke 1983 MD
  Executive Assistant **M. Elaina Schramm** . . . . . . . . . . . . (804) 786-2599
■ Deputy Secretary **K. Joseph "Joe" Flores** . . . . . . . . . . . (804) 786-7765
  E-mail: joseph.flores@governor.virginia.gov
  Education: Texas A&M; Carnegie Mellon MS
■ Deputy Secretary **Pamela Kestner** . . . . . . . . . . . . . . . . . (804) 786-7765
  Education: Emory & Henry BA; VCU MSW
■ Children's Health and Education Assistant Secretary
  **(Vacant)** . . . . . . . . . . . . . . . . . . . . . . . . . . . . . . . . . . . (804) 786-7765
Special Assistant **Jonathan Mathews, ANG** . . . . . . . . . . . (804) 786-7765
  Education: VCU 2010 BS
Communications Advisor **(Vacant)** . . . . . . . . . . . . . . . . . . (804) 786-7765

## Department for the Blind and Vision Impaired

397 Azalea Avenue, Richmond, VA 23227
Tel: (804) 371-3140  Tel: (800) 622-2155  Fax: (804) 371-3351
Internet: www.vdbvi.org

■ Commissioner **Raymond E. Hopkins** . . . . . . . . . . . . . . . . (804) 371-3145
  E-mail: ray.hopkins@dbvi.virginia.gov
Administration Deputy Commissioner **Wallica Gaines** . . . . (804) 371-3591
  E-mail: wallica.gaines@dbvi.virginia.gov
Enterprise Deputy Commissioner **Matt Koch** . . . . . . . . . . (804) 371-3110
Services Deputy Commissioner **Dr. Rick L. Mitchell** . . . . . (804) 371-3146

## Department for the Deaf and Hard of Hearing

Ratcliff Building, 1602 Rolling Hills Drive, Suite 203,
Richmond, VA 23229-5012
Tel: (804) 662-9502 (Voice/TTY)
Tel: (800) 552-7917 (Voice/TTY Virginia & DC Metro area)
Fax: (804) 662-9718  E-mail: frontdsk@vddhh.virginia.gov
Internet: www.vddhh.org

■ Director **Ronald L. Lanier** . . . . . . . . . . . . . . . . . . . . . . . . (804) 662-9502
  E-mail: ronald.lanier@vddhh.virginia.gov
  Education: VCU 1975 BS
Business Manager **Primrose Coffey** . . . . . . . . . . . . . . . . . (804) 662-9702
Interpreter Program Manager **Leslie H. Prince** . . . . . . . . . (804) 662-9703
  Interpreter Services Coordinator **Pamala Dorman** . . . . . (804) 662-9703
Outreach and Program Manager **Gary Talley** . . . . . . . . . . (804) 325-1289
  Outreach Specialist, Central Area **Sherry Ross** . . . . . . . (804) 662-9701
Policy Manager **Leslie H. Prince** . . . . . . . . . . . . . . . . . . . (804) 662-9703
Technology Program Specialist **Christine C. Ruderson** . . . . (804) 662-9710
  E-mail: christine.ruderson@vddhh.virginia.gov
Quality Assurance Screening Specialist **Elaine S. Ziehl** . . . (804) 662-9705
Relay and Technology Programs Manager
  **Clayton E. Bowen** . . . . . . . . . . . . . . . . . . . . . . . . . . . (804) 662-9704
Virginia Relay Channel Manager **(Vacant)** . . . . . . . . . . . . (804) 662-9502

## Department of Health [VDH]

109 Governor's Street, Richmond, VA 23219
2001 Maywill Street, Richmond, VA 23230
Tel: (804) 662-6200 (Vital Records)  Internet: www.vdh.virginia.gov

■ State Health Commissioner (Interim)
  **Dr. Marissa Levine, MD, MPH** . . . . . . . . . . . . . . . . . . . (804) 864-7009
  E-mail: marissa.levine@vdh.virginia.gov       Fax: (804) 864-7022
  Education: Rochester; Albert Einstein Medical MD;
  Johns Hopkins MPH
Deputy Commissioner for Administration **Joan Martin** . . . . (804) 864-7169
  E-mail: joan.martin@vdh.virginia.gov

*(continued on next page)*

---

★ Elected Official  ■ Appointed by Governor  ● Appointed by Legislature  ▲ Appointed by Board or Commission  ◆ Appointed by State Supreme Court

**Department of Health** *continued*

Communications Director **Maribeth Brewster** . . . . . . . . . . (804) 864-7008
    Fax: (804) 864-8239

Government and Regulatory Affairs Director
  **Joseph "Joe" Hilbert** . . . . . . . . . . . . . . . . . . . . . . . (804) 864-7006
Internal Audit Director **Richard P. Corrigan** . . . . . . . . . . . . (804) 864-7450
Vital Records Division Director **Janet Rainey** . . . . . . . . . (804) 662-6245
Special Policy Advisor **Carole Pratt** . . . . . . . . . . . . . . (804) 662-6200
    Education: Virginia Tech BS; Medical Col (VA) DDS

## Office of the Deputy Commissioner for Community Health Services

Deputy Commissioner for Community Health Services
  **Robert W. Hicks** . . . . . . . . . . . . . . . . . . . . . . . . . . . (804) 864-7003
    Administrative Staff Assistant **Julie Seppelt** . . . . . . . . . . (804) 864-7003
Public Health Nursing Director **Joanne Wakeham** . . . . . . (804) 864-7017
Healthcare Reimbursement Manager **Lisa Park** . . . . . . . . . . (804) 864-7018

## Office of Drinking Water

Director **John Aulbach** . . . . . . . . . . . . . . . . . . . . . . . . (804) 864-7500
Technical Services Division Director **Susan Douglas** . . . . . (804) 864-7500
Financial and Construction Assistant Program Director
  **Steve Pellei** . . . . . . . . . . . . . . . . . . . . . . . . . . . . . (804) 864-7489
Enforcement and Compliance Division Director
  **Robert Payne** . . . . . . . . . . . . . . . . . . . . . . . . . . . . . (804) 864-7498
Technology Transfer Director **Mark Anderson** . . . . . . . . . . (804) 864-7514
    E-mail: markc.anderson@vdh.virginia.gov
Abingdon Field Office Director **Richard Puckett** . . . . . . (276) 676-5650
    454 East Main Street, Abingdon, VA 24210
Culpeper Field Office Director **Hugh Eggborn** . . . . . . . . (540) 829-7340
    400 South Main Street, Second Floor,      Fax: (540) 829-7337
    Culpeper, VA 22701
Danville Field Office Director **Mitchell Childrey** . . . . . . . . (434) 836-8416
    211 Nor Dan Drive, Suite 1040,          Fax: (434) 836-8424
    Danville, VA 24540
East Central Field Office Director **Bennett Ragnauth** . . . . (804) 674-2880
    300 Turner Road, Richmond, VA 23225     Fax: (804) 674-2815
Lexington Field Office Director **Doug M. Caldwell** . . . . . . (540) 463-7136
    131 Walker Street, Lexington, VA 24450   Fax: (540) 463-3892
Southeast Virginia Field Office Director **Daniel Horne** . . . . (757) 683-2000
    803 Southampton Avenue, Room 2058,      Fax: (757) 683-2007
    Norfolk, VA 23510

## Office of Environmental Health Services

Environmental Services Director **Allen Knapp** . . . . . . . . . . (804) 864-7456
    Fax: (804) 864-7475
Shellfish Sanitation Division Director
  **Robert Croonenberghs** . . . . . . . . . . . . . . . . . . . . . . (804) 864-7477

## Office of Epidemiology

Tel: (804) 864-8141  Fax: (804) 864-8213
E-mail: epi-comments@vdh.virginia.gov

Director and State Epidemiologist
  **Laurie Forlano, DO, MPH** . . . . . . . . . . . . . . . . . . . . (804) 864-8141
Deputy Director and Deputy State Epidemiologist
  **(Vacant)** . . . . . . . . . . . . . . . . . . . . . . . . . . . . . . . (804) 864-8141
Administrative Deputy (Acting) **Kimberly Boehme** . . . . . . (804) 864-8141
    E-mail: kimberly.boehme@vdh.virginia.gov

## Office of Family Health Services [OFHS]

Director **Lilian Peake, MD, MPH** . . . . . . . . . . . . . . . . (804) 864-7651

## Office of the Chief Deputy for Public Health and Preparedness

Chief Deputy Commissioner for Public Health and
  Preparedness **(Vacant)** . . . . . . . . . . . . . . . . . . . . . . (804) 864-7025
    Fax: (804) 864-7029
Licensure and Certification Office Director **Erik Bodin** . . . . (804) 367-2102
Emergency Medical Services Director **Gary Brown** . . . . . . (804) 888-9100
Long Term Care Division Director **(Vacant)** . . . . . . . . . . . (804) 367-2100
Acute Care Division Director **Frederick Kyle** . . . . . . . . . . (804) 367-2114
    Fax: (804) 527-4504

## Chief Medical Examiner's Office

400 East Jackson Street, Richmond, VA 23219
Tel: (804) 786-3174  Fax: (804) 371-8595

Chief Medical Examiner **William T. Gormley** . . . . . . . . . . (804) 786-1034
    Executive Secretary **Beth A. Plutro** . . . . . . . . . . . . . . (804) 786-3174
Chief Administrative Officer **Arkuie Williams** . . . . . . . . . . (804) 786-3174
    E-mail: arkuie.williams@vdh.virginia.gov

## Department of Health Professions [DHP]

Perimeter Center, 9960 Mayland Drive, Suite 300,
Henrico, VA 23233-1463
Tel: (804) 367-4400  Fax: (804) 527-4475  Internet: www.dhp.virginia.gov

■Director **David E. Brown** . . . . . . . . . . . . . . . . . . . . . . (804) 367-4648
    E-mail: david.brown@dhp.virginia.gov
    Education: Virginia 1977
    Assistant to the Director **Laura Z. Rothrock** . . . . . . . . . (804) 367-4649
■Chief Deputy Director **Lisa Hanh** . . . . . . . . . . . . . . . . (804) 367-4542
    E-mail: lisa.hanh@dhp.virginia.gov
    Education: Maryland BA; VCU MPA

## Medical Assistance Services Department

600 East Broad Street, Suite 1300, Richmond, VA 23219
Tel: (804) 786-7933  TTY: (800) 343-0634  Fax: (804) 371-4981
Internet: www.dmas.virginia.gov

■Director **Cynthia B. "Cindi" Jones** . . . . . . . . . . . . . . . (804) 786-8099
    E-mail: cindi.jones@dmas.virginia.gov        Fax: (804) 371-4981
    Education: Virginia Tech BS, MS
    Executive Assistant **Ashley Hazelton** . . . . . . . . . . . . . (804) 786-8099
        E-mail: ashley.hazelton@dmas.virginia.gov
Chief Deputy Director **Linda Naplo** . . . . . . . . . . . . . . . (804) 786-8099
Administration Deputy Director **Suzanne Gore** . . . . . . . . (804) 786-8099
    E-mail: suzanne.gore@dmas.virginia.gov
Complex Care Services Deputy Director **Karen Kimsey** . . . (804) 786-3206
    E-mail: karen.kimsey@dmas.virginia.gov
Finance Deputy Director **Scott Crawford** . . . . . . . . . . . . (804) 786-8099
    E-mail: scott.crawford@dmas.virginia.gov
Programs Deputy Director **Cheryl J. Roberts** . . . . . . . . . (804) 786-8099
    E-mail: cheryl.roberts@dmas.virginia.gov
Long-Term Care Division Director **Terry Smith** . . . . . . . . (804) 786-3206
    E-mail: terry.smith@dmas.virginia.gov

## Medical Assistance Services Board

Chair **Dr. Karen Rheuban, MD** . . . . . . . . . . . . . . . . . . (804) 786-8099
    Term Expires: March 7, 2020
Member **Mirza Z. Baig** . . . . . . . . . . . . . . . . . . . . . . . (804) 786-8099
Member **Cara L. Coleman** . . . . . . . . . . . . . . . . . . . . . (804) 786-8099
    Term Expires: March 7, 2020
Member **Michael H. Cook** . . . . . . . . . . . . . . . . . . . . . (804) 786-8099
    Term Expires: March 7, 2019
Member **Alexis Y. Edwards** . . . . . . . . . . . . . . . . . . . . (804) 786-8099
    Term Expires: March 7, 2019
Member **Rebecca E. Gwilt** . . . . . . . . . . . . . . . . . . . . . (804) 786-8099
    Term Expires: March 7, 2020
Member **Maureen Sue Hollowell** . . . . . . . . . . . . . . . . . (804) 786-8099
Member **Maria D. Jankowski** . . . . . . . . . . . . . . . . . . . (804) 786-8099
    Term Expires: March 7, 2017
Member **Peter R. Kongstvedt** . . . . . . . . . . . . . . . . . . . (804) 786-8099
Member **McKinley L. Price** . . . . . . . . . . . . . . . . . . . . . (804) 786-8099
Member **Marcia Wright Yeskoo** . . . . . . . . . . . . . . . . . . (804) 786-8099
    Term Expires: March 7, 2017
Member **Dr. Erica L. Wynn, MD** . . . . . . . . . . . . . . . . . (804) 786-8099
    Term Expires: March 7, 2017
Board Liaison and Media Spokesperson
  **Mamie V. White** . . . . . . . . . . . . . . . . . . . . . . . . . . (804) 786-8096
    Education: Virginia State BS

## Department of Behavioral Health and Developmental Services [DBHDS]

Jefferson Building, 1220 Bank Street, Richmond, VA 23219
P.O. Box 1797, Richmond, VA 23218
Tel: (804) 786-3921  Tel: (800) 451-5544  TTY: (804) 371-8977
Fax: (804) 371-6638

■Commissioner **Jack Barber** . . . . . . . . . . . . . . . . . . . . (804) 786-3921

---

★ Elected Official   ■ Appointed by Governor   ● Appointed by Legislature   ▲ Appointed by Board or Commission   ◆ Appointed by State Supreme Court

Chief Deputy Commissioner (Interim)
  **Kathy Drumwright** . . . . . . . . . . . . . . . . . . . . . . . . (804) 786-3921
Behavioral Health Services Assistant Commissioner
  **Daniel Herr** . . . . . . . . . . . . . . . . . . . . . . . . . . . . . . (804) 371-0828
Communications Assistant Commissioner **(Vacant)** . . . . . . . (804) 786-9048
  Fax: (804) 371-2308
Developmental Services Assistant Commissioner
  **Connie Cochran** . . . . . . . . . . . . . . . . . . . . . . . . . . (804) 786-0580
Human Resources Director **(Vacant)** . . . . . . . . . . . . . . . (804) 786-5859
  Fax: (804) 786-4146
Information Technology Services Director **Joseph Bass** . . . (804) 786-1552
  E-mail: joseph.bass@dbhds.virginia.gov     Fax: (804) 786-2029
Internal Audit Director **Randy Sherrod** . . . . . . . . . . . . . (804) 786-5839
  Fax: (804) 692-0059
Licensing Director (Acting) **Cleopatra Booker** . . . . . . . . (804) 786-3475
Planning and Development Director **(Vacant)** . . . . . . . . . (804) 786-7357
  Fax: (804) 371-0092

## Office of the Inspector General [OIG]
Inspector General **June W. Jennings** . . . . . . . . . . . . . . . (804) 692-0276

## Community Services
Quality Management and Development Assistant
  Commissioner **Dee Keenan** . . . . . . . . . . . . . . . . . . . . (804) 225-3857

## Facility Management
Fax: (804) 786-8623

Human Rights Director **Deb Lochart** . . . . . . . . . . . . . . . (804) 786-0032
  E-mail: deb.lochart@dbhds.virginia.gov     Fax: (804) 371-2308
Licensing Deputy Director **Chandra Braggs** . . . . . . . . . . (804) 786-3475
  Fax: (804) 692-0066
Risk Management Director **Marion Greenfield** . . . . . . . . (804) 225-3396
  Fax: (804) 371-6638

## Finance and Administration
Fax: (804) 786-3827

Assistant Commissioner, Finance and Administration
  **Don Darr** . . . . . . . . . . . . . . . . . . . . . . . . . . . . . . . . (804) 786-1131
  E-mail: don.darr@dbhds.virginia.gov
Administrative Services Office Director **Chris Foca** . . . . . . (804) 371-2433
  E-mail: chris.foca@dbhds.virginia.gov
Budget and Financial Reporting Office Director
  **Kenneth "Ken" Gunn** . . . . . . . . . . . . . . . . . . . . . . . (804) 786-1555
Cost Accounting and Reimbursement Office Director
  **Florence Wells** . . . . . . . . . . . . . . . . . . . . . . . . . . . . (804) 663-7260
  Fax: (804) 692-0069
Fiscal and Grants Management Office Director
  **Philippe Peter** . . . . . . . . . . . . . . . . . . . . . . . . . . . . (804) 371-0361
Budget Development and Analysis Director
  **Andrew Diefenthaler** . . . . . . . . . . . . . . . . . . . . . . . (804) 786-9889

## Aging and Rehabilitative Services Department
8004 Franklin Farms Drive, Henrico, VA 23229
Tel: (804) 662-7000  Fax: (804) 662-9532

■Commissioner **James A. Rothrock** . . . . . . . . . . . . . . . . (804) 662-7010
  E-mail: james.rothrock@dars.virginia.gov
  Education: VCU 1977 MS
  Special Assistant **(Vacant)** . . . . . . . . . . . . . . . . . . . . (804) 662-7000
■Deputy Commissioner **(Vacant)** . . . . . . . . . . . . . . . . . (804) 662-9312
Chief Operations Officer **Ernest F. Steidle** . . . . . . . . . . . (804) 662-7010
  Education: Virginia 1992 PhD

## Social Services Department
801 East Main Street, Richmond, VA 23219
Fax: (804) 726-7015  Internet: www.dss.virginia.gov

■Commissioner (Interim) **Margaret Ross Schultze** . . . . . . (804) 726-7011
  E-mail: commissioner@dss.virginia.gov
  Executive Secretary to the Commissioner
  **Moniko Coleman** . . . . . . . . . . . . . . . . . . . . . . . . . . (804) 726-7011
■Chief Deputy Commissioner **J. R. Simpson, USN (Ret)** . . (804) 726-7204
  E-mail: j.r.simpson@dss.virginia.gov
  Education: Georgia MBA

Child Support Enforcement Deputy Commissioner
  **Craig Burshem** . . . . . . . . . . . . . . . . . . . . . . . . . . . . (800) 257-9986
  E-mail: craig.burshem@dss.virginia.gov
Public Affairs Director **Necole Simmonds** . . . . . . . . . . . (804) 726-7105
Benefit Programs Division Director
  **Thomas Steinhauser** . . . . . . . . . . . . . . . . . . . . . . . . (804) 726-7362

## Natural Resources Secretariat
Patrick Henry Building, 1111 East Broad Street,
Richmond, VA 23219-1922
P.O. Box 1475, Richmond, VA 23218
Tel: (804) 786-0044  E-mail: natural.resources@governor.virginia.gov
Internet: www.naturalresources.virginia.gov

**Employees: 2,175  Fiscal Year: 2015  Budget: $395,885,000**

■Secretary **Molly Joseph Ward** . . . . . . . . . . . . . . . . . . . (804) 786-0044
  Education: Virginia 1983 BA; William & Mary 1987 JD
■Deputy Secretary **Angela Navarro** . . . . . . . . . . . . . . . . (804) 786-0044
  Education: Florida; Georgetown JD
■Deputy Secretary for the Chesapeake Bay
  **Russell W. Baxter** . . . . . . . . . . . . . . . . . . . . . . . . . . (804) 786-0044
■Executive Assistant to the Secretary **Rachel Levy** . . . . . . (804) 786-0044
  Education: UC Davis BA

## Conservation and Recreation Department
600 East Main Street, Floor 24, Richmond, VA 23219
Tel: (804) 786-6124  Fax: (804) 786-6141  Internet: www.dcr.virginia.gov

■Director **Clyde E. Cristman** . . . . . . . . . . . . . . . . . . . . (804) 786-2123
  E-mail: clyde.cristman@dcr.virginia.gov
■Operations Deputy Director **Joe Elton** . . . . . . . . . . . . . (804) 786-2123
Policy Director **Lisa M. McGee** . . . . . . . . . . . . . . . . . . (804) 786-2123
Board and FOIA Services Liaison **Michael R. Fletcher** . . . (804) 786-8445
  E-mail: michael.fletcher@dcr.virginia.gov

### Administration Division
Fax: (804) 371-0799

Director **Rochelle Altholz** . . . . . . . . . . . . . . . . . . . . . . (804) 371-7483

### Dam Safety and Floodplain Management Division
Fax: (804) 371-2630  Internet: www.dcr.virginia.gov/sw/damsafty

Director **Robert Bennett** . . . . . . . . . . . . . . . . . . . . . . . (804) 786-3914
  E-mail: robert.bennett@dcr.virginia.gov
Deputy Director **David C. Dowling** . . . . . . . . . . . . . . . . (804) 786-2291
  E-mail: david.dowling@dcr.virginia.gov

### Finance Division
Fax: (804) 371-4919

Comptroller **Sharon Partee** . . . . . . . . . . . . . . . . . . . . . (804) 786-6142

### Natural Heritage Division
Fax: (804) 371-2674  Internet: www.dcr.virginia.gov/dnh

Director **Thomas L. Smith** . . . . . . . . . . . . . . . . . . . . . . (804) 786-4554
  E-mail: tom.smith@dcr.virginia.gov
Natural Area Protection Manager **(Vacant)** . . . . . . . . . . . (804) 371-6205

### Planning and Recreation Resources Division
Fax: (804) 371-7899  Internet: www.dcr.virginia.gov/lanm_sum

Director **Danette Poole** . . . . . . . . . . . . . . . . . . . . . . . . (804) 786-1119

### State Parks Division
Fax: (804) 786-9294  Internet: www.dcr.virginia.gov/parks

Director **Craig Seaver** . . . . . . . . . . . . . . . . . . . . . . . . . (804) 786-4377
  E-mail: craig.seaver@dcr.virginia.gov

## Environmental Quality Department [DEQ]
629 East Main Street, Richmond, VA 23219
P.O. Box 1105, Richmond, VA 23218
Tel: (804) 698-4000  TTY: (804) 698-4021
Internet: www.deq.virginia.gov

■Director **David K. Paylor** . . . . . . . . . . . . . . . . . . . . . . (804) 698-4020
  E-mail: david.paylor@deq.virginia.gov
  Education: Duke BS; Oregon State MS

*(continued on next page)*

---

★ Elected Official    ■ Appointed by Governor    ● Appointed by Legislature    ▲ Appointed by Board or Commission    ◆ Appointed by State Supreme Court

EXECUTIVE BRANCH

**Environmental Quality Department** *continued*

Air Program Director **Michael Dowd** . . . . . . . . . . . . . . . . (804) 698-4284
  E-mail: michael.dowd@deq.virginia.gov
Enforcement Director **Jefferson Reynolds** . . . . . . . . . . . . (804) 698-4376
Environmental Enhancement Director **Sharon Baxter** . . . . . (804) 698-4344
Operations Director **James Golden** . . . . . . . . . . . . . . . . . (804) 698-4220
Training Director **Kevin Vaughan** . . . . . . . . . . . . . . . . . . (804) 698-4470
Land Protection Program Director **Justin Williams** . . . . . . . (804) 698-4079
Water Permitting Director **Melanie D. Davenport** . . . . . . . (804) 698-4038

## Department of Game and Inland Fisheries

7870 Willa Park Drive, Henrico, VA 23228
TTY: (804) 367-1000  Fax: (804) 367-0405  E-mail: dgifweb@virginia.gov
Internet: www.dgif.virginia.gov

▲Executive Director **Robert W. "Bob" Duncan** . . . . . . . . . . (804) 367-9231
  E-mail: bob.duncan@dgif.virginia.gov
  Education: Tennessee 1971 BS, 1974 MS
  Executive Advisor to the Director **Gary F. Martel** . . . . . . . (804) 367-1004
    Education: Virginia Tech 1976 MS
  Staff Assistant **Angele Goff** . . . . . . . . . . . . . . . . . . . . (804) 367-9231
Law Enforcement Director **Col. Ron Henry** . . . . . . . . . . . . (804) 367-0171
  Law Enforcement Training Manager **Jeff McCuistion** . . . (804) 367-0419
Personnel Director **William Brenzovich** . . . . . . . . . . . . . . (804) 367-0849
Wildlife Resources Deputy Director **Robert Ellis** . . . . . . . . (804) 367-6878
Bureau of Wildlife Resources Director
  **David K. Whitehurst** . . . . . . . . . . . . . . . . . . . . . . . . (804) 367-4335
  Education: North Carolina State 1976 MS
Director of Agency Outreach **Robert Lee Walker** . . . . . . . . (804) 912-6121
Director of Infrastructure **(Vacant)** . . . . . . . . . . . . . . . . . (804) 367-1295
Boating Laws Administrator **Tom Guess** . . . . . . . . . . . . . (804) 367-8693
Boat Registration and Titling Section Manager
  **Dorita K. Adams** . . . . . . . . . . . . . . . . . . . . . . . . . . (804) 367-1339

## Department of Historic Resources

2801 Kensington Avenue, Richmond, VA 23221
Tel: (804) 367-2323  TTY: (804) 367-2386  Fax: (804) 367-2391

■Director **Julie Langan** . . . . . . . . . . . . . . . . . . . . . . . . (804) 482-6087
  E-mail: julie.langan@dhr.virginia.gov
■Deputy Director **Stephanie Bishop Williams** . . . . . . . . . . (804) 367-2323
  Education: Col Charleston 1994; North Carolina State 2004
  Administrative Staff Specialist **(Vacant)** . . . . . . . . . . . . (804) 367-2323
  Administrative Director **Jennifer Mayton** . . . . . . . . . . . . (804) 862-6408
    E-mail: jennifer.mayton@dhr.virginia.gov
Community Services Division Director **David Edwards** . . . (540) 868-7030
Policy and Planning Deputy Director **(Vacant)** . . . . . . . . . (804) 482-6083
Northern Regional Office Director **David Edwards** . . . . . . . (540) 868-7030
    Fax: (540) 868-7588
Tidewater Regional Office Director
  **Pamela A. "Pam" Schenian** . . . . . . . . . . . . . . . . . . . (757) 886-2818
  14415 Old Courthouse Way, Second Floor,    Fax: (757) 396-6712
  Newport News, VA 23608
Resource Information and Services Director
  **Julie Langan** . . . . . . . . . . . . . . . . . . . . . . (804) 482-6087 ext. 115
  Publications/Public Affairs Specialist **Randall Jones** . . . . (540) 578-3031
    E-mail: randy.jones@dhr.virginia.gov
Archivist **Quatro Hubbard** . . . . . . . . . . . . . . . . . . . . . . (804) 482-6102

## Marine Resources Commission

2600 Washington Avenue, Third Floor, Newport News, VA 23607
Tel: (757) 247-2200
Tel: (800) 541-4646 (Information & Emergency Hotline)
TTY: (757) 247-2292  Fax: (757) 247-2020
Internet: www.mrc.virginia.gov

■Commissioner **John M.R. Bull** . . . . . . . . . . . . . . . . . . . (757) 247-2205
  E-mail: john.bull@mrc.virginia.gov
  Administrative Staff Assistant **Michele Guilford** . . . . . . . (757) 247-2206
Administration and Finance Division Chief
  **Jane B. McCroskey** . . . . . . . . . . . . . . . . . . . . . . . . . (757) 247-2215
  E-mail: jane.mccroskey@mrc.virginia.gov
  Senior Administrative Manager **Erik J. Barth** . . . . . . . . . (757) 247-2262
    E-mail: erik.barth@mrc.virginia.gov
Fisheries Management Division Chief **Rob O'Reilly** . . . . . . (757) 247-2236

Habitat Management Division Chief **Tony Watkinson** . . . . . (757) 247-2250
Law Enforcement Division Chief **Richard Lauderman** . . . . . (757) 247-2278
Conservation and Replenishment Department Head
  **James A. Wesson** . . . . . . . . . . . . . . . . . . . . . . . . . . (757) 247-2121
  E-mail: jim.wesson@mrc.virginia.gov
Plans and Statistics Department Head **Joseph Cimino** . . . . (757) 247-2237
  E-mail: joseph.cimino@mrc.virginia.gov
Engineering and Surveying (Eastern District) Chief
  Engineer **George H. Badger** . . . . . . . . . . . . . . . . . . . (757) 414-0710
Engineering and Surveying (Western District) Chief
  Engineer **Robert B. Stagg** . . . . . . . . . . . . . . . . . . . . (757) 247-2009
  Note: Western District
Social Media and Public Relations Director
  **Laurie Naismith** . . . . . . . . . . . . . . . . . . . . . . . . . . . (757) 247-2269
  Education: Old Dominion

## Virginia Museum of Natural History

21 Starling Avenue, Martinsville, VA 24112
Tel: (276) 634-4141  Fax: (276) 634-4199  Internet: www.vmnh.net
E-mail: information@vmnh.virginia.gov

▲Director **Joe B. Keiper** . . . . . . . . . . . . . . . . (276) 634-4141 ext. 4150
  E-mail: joe.keiper@vmnh.virginia.gov
  Education: Bloomfield BS; Slippery Rock U MS; Kent State PhD
  Executive Assistant **Cindy Gray** . . . . . . . . . . . . . . . . . (276) 634-4150
Deputy Director **Ryan Barber** . . . . . . . . . . . . . . . . . . . . (276) 634-4163
Administration and Services Director
  **Gloria Niblett, VCO** . . . . . . . . . . . . . . . . . . . . . . . . (276) 634-4153
  E-mail: gloria.niblett@vmnh.virginia.gov
  Education: Averett U 1994
Marketing and Public Relations Manager **Zachary Ryder** . . (276) 634-4165
  E-mail: zachary.ryder@vmnh.virginia.gov

# Public Safety and Homeland Security Secretariat

Patrick Henry Building, 1111 East Broad Street, Richmond, VA 23219
P.O. Box 1475, Richmond, VA 23218
Tel: (804) 786-5351  Fax: (804) 371-6381
E-mail: sops-cs@governor.virginia.gov
Internet: www.publicsafety.virginia.gov

**Employees:** 20,232  **Fiscal Year:** 2015  **Budget:** $2,735,430,000

■Secretary **Brian J. Moran** . . . . . . . . . . . . . . . . . . . . . . (804) 786-5351
  E-mail: brian.moran@governor.virginia.gov
  Education: UMass (Amherst) 1982 BA; Columbus Law 1988 JD
  Executive Assistant to the Secretary **Delaney Perdue** . . . (804) 786-8032
    Education: Virginia Tech BA
■Assistant Secretary **Nicky Zamostny** . . . . . . . . . . . . . . (804) 786-5351
■Deputy Secretary **Curtis Brown** . . . . . . . . . . . . . . . . . . (804) 786-5351
  Education: Radford BS; Virginia Tech MPA; VCU MA
■Deputy Secretary **Victoria Cochran** . . . . . . . . . . . . . . . (804) 786-5351
Office Manager/Confidential Assistant **(Vacant)** . . . . . . . . (804) 786-5351
Policy Assistant **Asif Bhavnagri** . . . . . . . . . . . . . . . . . . (804) 786-5351
Critical Infrastructure Coordinator **Mike Landefeld** . . . . . . (804) 371-2602
Interoperability Program Manager **Brandon Smith** . . . . . . . (804) 663-7766
  Interoperability Project Coordinator **Suzanne Trachy** . . . (804) 225-3826
  Interoperability Project Assistant **Priscilla Wilinski** . . . . . (804) 692-2514
BRAC Coordinator **(Vacant)** . . . . . . . . . . . . . . . . . . . . . (804) 225-4521

## Alcoholic Beverage Control Board

2901 Hermitage Road, Richmond, VA 23220
Box 27491, Richmond, VA 23261
Tel: (804) 213-4400  Fax: (804) 213-4411
Internet: www.publicsafety.state.va.us/abc.html
Internet: www.abc.virginia.gov

■Chairman **Jeffrey L. Painter** . . . . . . . . . . . . . . . . . . . . (804) 213-4404
  E-mail: jeffrey.painter@abc.virginia.gov
  Education: Emory & Henry
■Commissioner **Henry L. Marsh III** . . . . . . . . . . . . . . . . . (804) 213-4403
  Education: Virginia Union AB; Howard U LLB
■Commissioner **Judith G. "Judy" Napier** . . . . . . . . . . . . . (804) 213-4403
  E-mail: judy.napier@abc.virginia.gov

---

★ Elected Official   ■ Appointed by Governor   ● Appointed by Legislature   ▲ Appointed by Board or Commission   ◆ Appointed by State Supreme Court

Chief Operating Officer and Secretary to the Board
**Travis G. Hill** . . . . . . . . . . . . . . . . . . . . . . . . . . . . . . . (804) 367-6606
  Education: North Carolina 2000 BA, 2003 JD

## Alcoholic Beverage Control Department

2901 Hermitage Road, Richmond, VA 23220
Tel: (804) 213-4400

Deputy Secretary to the Board
**S. Christopher "Chris" Curtis** . . . . . . . . . . . . . . . . . . (804) 325-8470
Deputy Director, Enforcement Administration
**Francis J. Monahan** . . . . . . . . . . . . . . . . . . . . . . . . . (804) 213-4564
  E-mail: francis.monahan@abc.virginia.gov
Director, Enforcement Bureau **Shawn Walker** . . . . . . . . . . (804) 213-4569
Audit Director **John W. Wszelaki, CIA, CRMA** . . . . . . . (804) 213-4646
Special Policy Advisor for Law Enforcement
**Ryant L. Washington** . . . . . . . . . . . . . . . . . . . . . . . . (804) 213-4400
  E-mail: ryant.l.washington@abc.virginia.gov
  Education: National Col; Piedmont Virginia Comm Col (Attended)

## Virginia Department of Corrections [VADOC]

6900 Atmore Drive, Richmond, VA 23225
Tel: (804) 674-3000  Fax: (804) 674-3509
Internet: http://vadoc.virginia.gov

■Director **Harold W. Clarke** . . . . . . . . . . . . . . . . . . . . . (804) 674-3119
  E-mail: director.clarke@vadoc.virginia.gov
  Education: Doane 1974 BA
Administration Deputy Director **N. H. "Cookie" Scott** . . . . (804) 674-3221
  E-mail: nh.scott@vadoc.virginia.gov
  Education: Longwood U BA
Corrections Operations Chief **David Robinson** . . . . . . . . . (804) 674-3010
Human Resources Director **Joe Walters** . . . . . . . . . . . . . . (804) 674-3507
Chief Technology Officer **Rick A. Davis** . . . . . . . . . . . . . (804) 674-3423
  E-mail: rick.davis@vadoc.virginia.gov
■Superintendent of Correctional Education **Chris Colville** . . . (804) 887-8058
  E-mail: chris.colville@vadoc.virginia.gov

## Department of Criminal Justice Services

1100 Bank Street, Richmond, VA 23219
Tel: (804) 786-4000

■Director **Francine C. "Fran" Ecker** . . . . . . . . . . . . . . . . (804) 786-8718
  E-mail: fran.ecker@dcjs.virginia.gov
  Education: Temple 1978 BSW, 1981 EdM
■Deputy Director **Andrew "Drew" Molloy** . . . . . . . . . . . . (804) 786-7840
  E-mail: andrew.molloy@dcjs.virginia.gov
Administration Division Director **John Colligan, Jr.** . . . . . . (804) 786-4961
  E-mail: john.colligan@dcjs.virginia.gov
Law Enforcement and Security Services Division
  Director **Teresa P. Gooch** . . . . . . . . . . . . . . . . . . . . . (804) 786-8730
  E-mail: teresa.gooch@dcjs.virginia.gov
  Education: Guilford Col BA
Programs and Services Division Director **Bruce Cruser** . . . (804) 225-4564
  E-mail: bruce.cruser@dcjs.virginia.gov
Policy Advisor **Thomas Okuda Fitzpatrick** . . . . . . . . . . . . (804) 786-2211

## Department of Emergency Management

10501 Trade Court, Chesterfield, VA 23236
Fax: (804) 897-6506

■State Coordinator **Jeffrey D. Stern, CEM** . . . . . . . . . . . . (804) 897-6501
  E-mail: jeffrey.stern@vdem.virginia.gov
  Education: William & Mary BA; American U MPA; Virginia Tech
■Chief Deputy State Coordinator **(Vacant)** . . . . . . . . . . . . (804) 897-6501
Deputy State Coordinator **Brett Burdick** . . . . . . . . . . . . . (804) 897-6501
  Education: VCU MS
Preparedness Director **Ted Costin** . . . . . . . . . . . . . . . . . (804) 897-9770
Technological Hazards Director **Gregory "Greg" Britt** . . . . (804) 897-9950
Training and Exercises Director **Susan Mongold** . . . . . . . . (804) 897-9980
Chief Technology Officer (Acting) **Rex Pyle** . . . . . . . . . . . (804) 897-9747
  E-mail: rex.pyle@vdem.virginia.gov

## Department of Fire Programs

1005 Technology Park Drive, Glen Allen, VA 23059-4500
Tel: (804) 371-0220  Fax: (804) 371-3444  Internet: www.vafire.com

■Executive Director **Melvin D. Carter** . . . . . . . . . . . . . . . (804) 371-0220
  E-mail: melvin.carter@vdfp.virginia.gov
  Executive Administrative Assistant **Marketta Kelley** . . . . . (804) 249-1962
Training and Operations Branch Chief **Tim Hansbrough** . . (804) 249-1990
  E-mail: tim.hansbrough@vdfp.virginia.gov       Fax: (804) 371-3444
Training and Technical Services Branch Chief
  **Don Hansen** . . . . . . . . . . . . . . . . . . . . . . . . . . . . . (804) 249-1986
  E-mail: don.hansen@vdfp.virginia.gov
Marketing and Communications Manager **Mark Buff** . . . . . (804) 249-1965
  E-mail: mark.buff@vdfp.virginia.gov
Deputy Executive Director **Brook Pittinger** . . . . . . . . . . . (804) 249-1961
  E-mail: brook.pittinger@vdfp.virginia.gov
Webmaster **Diana Attuso** . . . . . . . . . . . . . . . . . . . . . . (804) 249-1985
Policy Analyst **Erin B. Rice** . . . . . . . . . . . . . . . . . . . . . (757) 727-4700

## Department of Forensic Science

700 North Fifth Street, Richmond, VA 23219
Tel: (804) 786-2281  Fax: (804) 786-6857  Internet: www.dfs.virginia.gov

■Director **Linda C. Jackson** . . . . . . . . . . . . . . . . . . . . . (804) 786-2281
  E-mail: linda.jackson@dfs.virginia.gov
Chief Deputy Director **Katya Herndon** . . . . . . . . . . . . . . (804) 786-2281
  Education: Guilford Col 1991 BS; Richmond 1995 JD
Deputy Director **David Barron** . . . . . . . . . . . . . . . . . . . (804) 786-2281
Technical Services Director **Alka Lohmann** . . . . . . . . . . . (804) 786-2281

## Department of Juvenile Justice

700 Centre Building,, Seventh & Franklin Street, Fourth Floor,
Richmond, VA 23219
P.O. Box 1110, Richmond, VA 23219
Tel: (804) 371-0700  Fax: (804) 371-0773  Internet: www.djj.virginia.gov

■Director **Andrew K. Block, Jr.** . . . . . . . . . . . . . . . . . . . (804) 371-0704
  E-mail: andrew.block@dce.virginia.gov
  Education: Yale 1987; Northwestern 1994 JD
  Assistant to the Director **Deborah Hayes** . . . . . . . . . . . (804) 588-3403
■Chief Deputy Director **Lionel F. Jackson, Jr.** . . . . . . . . . . (804) 371-0704
  E-mail: lionel.jackson@dce.virginia.gov
Administration and Finance Deputy Director
  **Daryl W. Francis** . . . . . . . . . . . . . . . . . . . . . . . . . . (804) 371-0705
  E-mail: daryl.francis@dce.virginia.gov
Operations Deputy Director **Ralph Thomas** . . . . . . . . . . . (804) 371-0706
                                         Fax: (804) 786-1461
Deputy Superintendent for School Operations
  **Belinda Friday** . . . . . . . . . . . . . . . . . . . . . . . . . . . (804) 225-3328
Policy Analyst **Courtney Warren** . . . . . . . . . . . . . . . . . . (804) 371-0700

## Military Affairs Department

5901 Beulah Road, Sandston, VA 23150
Tel: (804) 236-7880  Fax: (804) 236-7901

■Adjutant General
  **MG Timothy Paschal "Tim" Williams, ARNG** . . . . . . . . (804) 236-7880
  Education: Virginia Tech; Webster; Army War Col
Chief of Staff **Col James W. Ring, ANG** . . . . . . . . . . . . . (804) 236-7880
Deputy Chief of Staff **LTC Allysa A. Kropp, ARNG** . . . . . (434) 298-6390
  316 Fort Picket, Blackstone, VA 23824

## Virginia National Guard (TAG)

Tel: (804) 236-7880  Fax: (804) 236-7901

■Adjutant General
  **MG Timothy Paschal "Tim" Williams, ARNG** . . . . . . . . (804) 236-7880

## Virginia Army National Guard (Land Component Commander)

Virginia Army National Guard, Building 316, Fort Pickett,
Blackstone, VA 23824-6316
Fax: (434) 298-6338

Land Component Commander
  **BG Blake C. Ortner, ARNG** . . . . . . . . . . . . . . . . . . . (434) 298-6101
Information Management Director
  **LTC Lesley E. Kipling, ARNG** . . . . . . . . . . . . . . . . . . (804) 236-7880
  E-mail: lesley.e.kipling.mil@mail.mil

---

★ Elected Official   ■ Appointed by Governor   ● Appointed by Legislature   ▲ Appointed by Board or Commission   ◆ Appointed by State Supreme Court

EXECUTIVE BRANCH

## Virginia Air National Guard
100 Falcon Road, Sandston, VA 23150-2526
Tel: (804) 236-6000

Assistant Adjutant General
  **BrigGen Zane R. Johnson, ANG** . . . . . . . . . . . . . . . . . (434) 298-6101

## State Police Department
P.O. Box 27472, Richmond, VA 23261-7472
Tel: (804) 674-2000  Fax: (804) 674-2132

■Superintendent **Col. W. Steven Flaherty** . . . . . . . . . . . . . (804) 674-2087
  E-mail: supt@vsp.virginia.gov
  Education: Excelsior 2002 BS
Deputy Superintendent **Lt. Col. Robert B. Northern** . . . . . . (804) 674-2100
  Education: Emory & Henry 1979 BS
Administration Director **Lt. Col. Robert G. Kemmler** . . . . (804) 674-2122
  E-mail: robert.kemmler@vsp.virginia.gov
Criminal Investigations Director
  **Lt. Col. Rick A. Jenkins** . . . . . . . . . . . . . . . . . . . . . . . . . (804) 674-2133
Field Operations Director **Lt. Col. George Daniels** . . . . . . . (804) 674-2088

## Virginia Parole Board
6900 Atmore Drive, Richmond, VA 23225-5644
Fax: (804) 674-3284

■Chairman **Karen Brown** . . . . . . . . . . . . . . . . . . . . . . . . . . (804) 674-3081
  Education: Hampton 1977 BA; George Mason 1991 JD
■Vice Chairman **Algie T. Howell, Jr., USAF (Ret)** . . . . . . . (804) 674-3081
  Education: Norfolk State 1967 BS; Hampton 1973 MA
■Member **Rev. A. Lincoln James** . . . . . . . . . . . . . . . . . . . . (804) 674-3081
  Education: North Park Col; Virginia Union MDiv
■Member **Sherman P. Lea** . . . . . . . . . . . . . . . . . . . . . . . . . (804) 674-3081
■Member **Minor Stone** . . . . . . . . . . . . . . . . . . . . . . . . . . . (804) 674-3081

## Technology Secretariat
1111 East Broad Street, Richmond, VA 23219
Tel: (804) 786-9579  Fax: (804) 786-9584
E-mail: technology@governor.virginia.gov
Internet: www.technology.virginia.gov

**Employees:** 299  **Fiscal Year:** 2015  **Budget:** $391,149,000

■Secretary of Technology **Karen R. Jackson** . . . . . . . . . . . . (804) 786-9579
  E-mail: karen.jackson@governor.virginia.gov
  Education: Christopher Newport; William & Mary MBA
■Deputy Secretary **Anthony W. Fung** . . . . . . . . . . . . . . . . (804) 786-9579
  Education: Pittsburgh BS
Assistant Secretary of Technology and Senior Policy
  Advisor **(Vacant)** . . . . . . . . . . . . . . . . . . . . . . . . . . . . . . (804) 786-9579

## Center for Innovative Technology [CIT]
CIT Tower, Suite 600, 2214 Rock Hill Road, Herndon, VA 20170
Tel: (703) 689-3000  Fax: (703) 689-3041  Internet: www.cit.org

▲President and Chief Executive Officer **Ed Albrigo** . . . . . . . (703) 689-3040
Consulting Services Vice President **Paul McGowan** . . . . . . (703) 689-3070
                                                          Fax: (804) 371-3621
CIT Entrepreneur Vice President and GAP Fund Manager
  **Tom Weithman** . . . . . . . . . . . . . . . . . . . . . . . . . . . . . . . (703) 689-3060
  Education: Notre Dame BA; Michigan State MBA;    Fax: (703) 689-3051
  Harvard
CIT Research and Development Vice President
  **Nancy Vorona** . . . . . . . . . . . . . . . . . . . . . . . . . . . . . . . (703) 689-3043
  Education: North Carolina BA;           Fax: (703) 464-1720
  Thunderbird International MIM
CIT Broadband Vice President (Interim) **Sandie Terry** . . . . (804) 786-9579
Government and Public Affairs Vice President
  **Henry "Hap" Connors** . . . . . . . . . . . . . . . . . . . . . . . . . (703) 689-3048
                                                          Fax: (703) 464-1716
Chief Financial Officer **Linda E. Gentry, CPA** . . . . . . . . . . (703) 689-3035
  E-mail: linda.gentry@cit.org            Fax: (703) 464-1706
  Education: George Washington 1984 BS; William & Mary MBA
Chief Technology Officer **David Ihrie** . . . . . . . . . . . . . . . . (703) 689-3037
  E-mail: david.ihrie@cit.org             Fax: (703) 464-1707
MACH 37 Managing Partner **Rick Gordon** . . . . . . . . . . . . (703) 689-3000
MACH 37 General Partner **Robert Stratton** . . . . . . . . . . . . (703) 689-3000
MACH 37 General Partner **Dan Woolley** . . . . . . . . . . . . . . (703) 689-3000

## Virginia Information Technologies Agency [VITA]
11751 Meadowville Lane, Chester, VA 23836
Tel: (804) 416-6100  E-mail: vccc@vita.virginia.gov
Internet: www.vita.virginia.gov

■Chief Information Officer **Nelson Moe** . . . . . . . . . . . . . . . (804) 416-6004
  E-mail: nelson.moe@vita.virginia.gov
  Education: Naval Acad BS; Catholic U 1994 MSE
Deputy Chief Information Officer **(Vacant)** . . . . . . . . . . . . (804) 343-9003
Chief Information Security Officer/VITA Security
  Director **Michael Watson** . . . . . . . . . . . . . . . . . . . . . . . . (804) 416-6013
  E-mail: michael.watson@vita.virginia.gov
  Education: James Madison BS; Pennsylvania MS
Administration and Finance Director **Dana Smith** . . . . . . . (804) 416-6009
  E-mail: dana.smith@vita.virginia.gov
Customer Service Project Management Organization
  Director **(Vacant)** . . . . . . . . . . . . . . . . . . . . . . . . . . . . . (804) 416-6126
Human Resource Management Services Director
  **Susan E. "Susie" Witter** . . . . . . . . . . . . . . . . . . . . . . . . (804) 416-6011
Internal Audit Director **Sheila Alves** . . . . . . . . . . . . . . . . (804) 416-6100
Internal Technology and Portfolio Management Director
  **Debbie Dodson** . . . . . . . . . . . . . . . . . . . . . . . . . . . . . . (804) 416-6016
  E-mail: debbie.dodson@vita.virginia.gov
Legal and Legislative Services Director **(Vacant)** . . . . . . . . (804) 416-6100
Service Management and Delivery Director
  **Judy Marchand** . . . . . . . . . . . . . . . . . . . . . . . . . . . . . . (804) 416-6015
Enterprise Applications Director and Chief Applications
  Officer **Peggy Feldmann** . . . . . . . . . . . . . . . . . . . . . . . . (804) 416-6100
  E-mail: peggy.feldmann@vita.virginia.gov

## Transportation Secretariat
Patrick Henry Building, 1111 East Broad Street, 3rd Floor,
Richmond, VA 23219
P.O. Box 1475, Richmond, VA 23218
Tel: (804) 786-8032  Fax: (804) 786-6683
E-mail: transportation1@governor.virginia.gov
Internet: www.transportation.virginia.gov

**Employees:** 9,784  **Fiscal Year:** 2015  **Budget:** $5,761,206,000

■Secretary **Aubrey L. Layne, Jr.** . . . . . . . . . . . . . . . . . . . . (804) 786-8032
  E-mail: aubrey.layne@governor.virginia.gov
  Special Assistant to the Secretary **Georgia Esposito** . . . . (804) 786-8032
■Deputy Secretary **Nicholas "Nick" Donohue** . . . . . . . . . . (804) 786-8032
  E-mail: nick.donohue@governor.virginia.gov
■Deputy Secretary **Grindly R. Johnson** . . . . . . . . . . . . . . . (804) 786-8032
  E-mail: grindly.johnson@governor.virginia.gov
■Assistant Secretary **Taylor O'Sullivan** . . . . . . . . . . . . . . . (804) 786-8032

## Aviation Department
5702 Gulfstream Road, Richmond, VA 23250-2422
Tel: (804) 236-3624  Fax: (804) 236-3635  Internet: www.doav.virginia.gov

■Director **Randall P. Burdette** . . . . . . . . . . . . . . . . . (804) 236-3625 ext. 108
  E-mail: randall.burdette@doav.virginia.gov
Finance and Administration Director
  **Roger L. Bowling** . . . . . . . . . . . . . . . . . . . . . . . (804) 236-3628 ext. 117
  E-mail: roger.bowling@doav.virginia.gov
Office Manager/Administrative Assistant
  **(Vacant)** . . . . . . . . . . . . . . . . . . . . . . . . . . . . . (804) 236-3626 ext. 102
Webmaster **Betty Wilson** . . . . . . . . . . . . . . . . . . . . (804) 236-3624 ext. 107

## Department of Motor Vehicles
P.O. Box 27412, Richmond, VA 23269
Tel: (804) 497-7100  Fax: (804) 367-2296  Internet: www.dmvnow.com

■Commissioner **Richard D. "Rick" Holcomb** . . . . . . . . . . . (804) 367-6606
  E-mail: richard.holcomb@dmv.virginia.gov
  Education: Richmond JD
Deputy Commissioner **George Bishop IV** . . . . . . . . . . . . . (804) 497-7100
  E-mail: george.bishop@dmv.virginia.gov
  Education: Virginia 1985 BA
Deputy Commissioner **Dave Burhop** . . . . . . . . . . . . . . . . (804) 367-0672
Deputy Commissioner **David A. Mitchell** . . . . . . . . . . . . . (804) 367-6604
  E-mail: david.mitchell@dmv.virginia.gov

---

★ Elected Official   ■ Appointed by Governor   ● Appointed by Legislature   ▲ Appointed by Board or Commission   ◆ Appointed by State Supreme Court

Assistant Commissioner for Communications
**Pam Goheen** . . . . . . . . . . . . . . . . . . . . . . . . . . . . . . . . . . . (804) 367-1519
  E-mail: pam.goheen@dmv.virginia.gov
Assistant Commissioner for Driver, Vehicle, and Data
  Management Services **Karen Grim** . . . . . . . . . . . . . . . (804) 367-6606
  E-mail: karen.grim@dmv.virginia.gov    Fax: (804) 367-4336
Assistant Commissioner for Law Enforcement
**Joseph Hill** . . . . . . . . . . . . . . . . . . . . . . . . . . . . . . . . . . . .(804) 367-1579
  E-mail: joseph.hill@dmv.virginia.gov
Human Resources Director **Jeannie Thorpe** . . . . . . . . . . . (804) 367-6079
Highway Safety Director **John Saunders** . . . . . . . . . . . . . .(804) 497-7100
  E-mail: john.saunders@dmv.virginia.gov

## Department of Rail and Public Transportation [DRPT]

600 East Main Street, Suite 2102, Richmond, VA 23219
Tel: (804) 786-4440 Fax: (804) 225-3752

■Director **Jennifer L. Mitchell** . . . . . . . . . . . . . . . . . . . . . .(804) 371-4866
  E-mail: jennifer.mitchell@drpt.virginia.gov
  Executive Assistant **Sarah Jackson** . . . . . . . . . . . . . . . . (804) 371-4866
Deputy Director **Cheryl Openshaw** . . . . . . . . . . . . . . . . . . (804) 371-4866
Chief Financial Officer **William S. "Steve" Pittard** . . . . . . (804) 786-5756
Chief of Infrastructure Initiatives and Strategic
  Partnerships **(Vacant)** . . . . . . . . . . . . . . . . . . . . . . . . . . (804) 786-3963
Director of Policy, Communications, and Legislative
  Affairs **Christopher S. "Chris" Smith** . . . . . . . . . . . . . (804) 786-3963
Planning and Mobility Programs Administrator (Acting)
  **Chris Arabia** . . . . . . . . . . . . . . . . . . . . . . . . . . . . . . . .(804) 786-1059
Public Transportation Programs Administrator
  **Terry Brown** . . . . . . . . . . . . . . . . . . . . . . . . . . . . . . . . . (804) 786-1722
Rail Transit Safety Programs Administrator
  **Sharmila Samarasinghe** . . . . . . . . . . . . . . . . . . . . . . . (703) 259-3248
Rail Transportation Programs Administrator
  **Jeremy Latimer** . . . . . . . . . . . . . . . . . . . . . . . . . . . . . . (804) 225-4016
Rail Transportation Chief **Peter Burrus** . . . . . . . . . . . . . . . (804) 225-4016
  Education: Wooster BA; Marshall MBA
Engineering and Project Oversight Director
  **Jacob "Jake" Craig** . . . . . . . . . . . . . . . . . . . . . . . . . . . (804) 929-4893
Northern Virginia Transit Programs Director
  **Todd Horsley** . . . . . . . . . . . . . . . . . . . . . . . . . . . . . . . . (804) 929-4893

## Department of Transportation [VDOT]

1401 East Broad Street, Suite 311, Richmond, VA 23219
Tel: (804) 786-2801 Fax: (804) 786-2940 Internet: www.virginiadot.org

■Commissioner **Charles A. Kilpatrick, PE** . . . . . . . . . . . . . (804) 786-2801
  E-mail: charlie.kilpatrick@vdot.virginia.gov
■Chief Deputy Commissioner **Quintin D. Elliott, PE** . . . . . . (804) 786-2701
  E-mail: quintin.elliott@vdot.virginia.gov
Chief Engineer **Garrett W. Moore** . . . . . . . . . . . . . . . . . . . (804) 786-4798
  E-mail: garrett.moore@vdot.virginia.gov
Deputy Chief Engineer **Mohammad Mirshahi** . . . . . . . . . (804) 786-1476
  E-mail: m.mirshahi@vdot.virginia.gov
Chief Financial Officer **John W. Lawson** . . . . . . . . . . . . . . (804) 786-2707
  E-mail: john.lawson@vdot.virginia.gov
Chief of Policy **Richard L. Walton** . . . . . . . . . . . . . . . . . . (804) 786-2703
Public Affairs Director **Tamara Rollison** . . . . . . . . . . . . . . (804) 786-2715
  E-mail: tamara.rollison@vdot.virginia.gov
Technology, Research and Innovation Chief **Jose Gomez** . . (434) 293-1936
  E-mail: jose.gomez@vdot.virginia.gov

## Veteran and Defense Affairs Secretariat

Patrick Henry Building, 1111 East Broad Street, Third Floor,
Richmond, VA 23219
P.O. Box 1475, Richmond, VA 23218
Tel: (804) 225-3826 Fax: (804) 225-3882

Secretary of Veterans Affairs and Homeland Security
  **ADM John C. Harvey, Jr., USN (Ret)** . . . . . . . . . . . . . . (804) 225-3826
  E-mail: john.harvey@governor.virginia.gov
  Education: Naval Acad 1973 BS; Harvard 1988 MPA
Deputy Secretary of Veterans Affairs and Homeland
  Security **COL Jaime Areizaga-Soto, ARNG** . . . . . . . . . .(804) 225-3826
  Education: Georgetown BS; Stanford 1994 MA, 1994 JD

## Veterans Services Department

Pocahontas Building, West Wing, 900 East Main Street, Sixth Floor,
Richmond, VA 23219
Fax: (804) 786-0302 Internet: www.dvs.virginia.gov

■Commissioner **(Vacant)** . . . . . . . . . . . . . . . . . . . . . . . . . . (804) 786-0286
■Deputy Commissioner **Cathy Wilson** . . . . . . . . . . . . . . . . (804) 371-8431
  E-mail: catherine.wilson@dvs.virginia.gov
■Director of Policy and Planning **Steve Combs** . . . . . . . . . (804) 786-0294
  E-mail: steven.combs@dvs.virginia.gov
Virginia Veterans Care Center Administrator
  **Bill VanThiel** . . . . . . . . . . . . . . . . . . . . . . . . . . . . . . . . (540) 982-2860
  4550 Shenandoah Avenue, Northwest,    Fax: (540) 982-8667
  Roanoke, VA 24017-0334
  E-mail: bill.vanthiel@dvs.virginia.gov
Virginia Veterans Cemetery Director **Dan Kemano** . . . . . . . (757) 255-7217
  Albert G. Hortion, Jr. Memorial Veterans Cemetery, 5310 Milners
  Road, Suffolk, VA 23434

## Virginia War Memorial

621 South Belvidere Street, Richmond, VA 23220-6504
Tel: (804) 786-2060 Fax: (804) 786-6652
Internet: www.vawarmemorial.org

Executive Director **Jon C. Hatfield** . . . . . . . . . . . . . . . . . . (804) 786-2060
  Note: Until June 15, 2016.
Executive Director
  **LTC John C. Mountcastle, USA (Ret)** . . . . . . . . . . . . . . (804) 786-2060
  Note: Effective June 16, 2016.
  Education: VMI; Duke PhD

## Virginia Retirement System

1200 East Main Street, Richmond, VA 23219
P.O. Box 2500, Richmond, VA 23218-2500
Tel: (804) 289-5919 Fax: (804) 786-1541 E-mail: vrs@state.va.us
Internet: www.varetire.org

▲Director **Patricia S. Bishop** . . . . . . . . . . . . . . . . . . . . . . . (888) 827-3847
  E-mail: pbishop@vrs.state.va.us
Controller **Kathy Quiriconi** . . . . . . . . . . . . . . . . . . . . . . . . (888) 827-3847
Customer Relationships Deputy Director **(Vacant)** . . . . . . . (888) 827-3847
Internal Audit Director **Frank Berry** . . . . . . . . . . . . . . . . . . (888) 827-3847
Internal Equity Director **John T. "JT" Grier, CFA** . . . . . . . (804) 344-3171
Public Relations Director **Jeanne Chenault** . . . . . . . . . . . . (888) 827-3847
  E-mail: jchenault@vrs.state.va.us
Real Estate Investments Director **Field Griffith** . . . . . . . . . (804) 697-6676
  Education: Beloit; U Washington 1983 MBA
Policy, Planning and Compliance Division Director
  **Cindy Comer** . . . . . . . . . . . . . . . . . . . . . . . . . . . . . . . . (888) 827-3847
Internal Asset Management Managing Director
  **Charles W. Grant** . . . . . . . . . . . . . . . . . . . . . . . . . . . . . (888) 827-3847
Chief Customer Programs Officer **Shanta Harris** . . . . . . . . (888) 827-3847
Chief Customer Support Officer **Deardrian Carver** . . . . . . . (888) 827-3847
Chief Financial Officer **Barry Faison** . . . . . . . . . . . . . . . . . (888) 827-3847
Human Resources Director **Ken Robertson** . . . . . . . . . . . . (888) 827-3847
Chief Investment Officer **Ronald D. Schmitz** . . . . . . . . . . . (888) 827-3847
  E-mail: rschmitz@vrs.state.va.us
  Education: Western Illinois 1975 BB; Northwest Col 1981 MBA
Chief Technology and Security Officer
  **L. Farley Beaton, Jr.** . . . . . . . . . . . . . . . . . . . . . . . . . . . (888) 827-3847
  E-mail: fbeaton@vrs.state.va.us
Webmaster **John Hewitt** . . . . . . . . . . . . . . . . . . . . . . . . . . (888) 827-3847

## Office of the Lieutenant Governor

102 Governor Street, Richmond, VA 23219-3523
P.O. Box 1195, Richmond, VA 23218
Tel: (804) 786-2078 Fax: (804) 786-7514 Internet: ltgov.virginia.gov

★Lieutenant Governor **Ralph S. Northam** (D) . . . . . . . . . . . (804) 786-2078
  Term Expires: January 2018
  E-mail: ltgov@ltgov.virginia.gov
  Education: VMI BS; Eastern Virginia Medical 1984 MD
  Career: State Senator (D-VA, District 6), Virginia Senate (2008-2014)
Chief of Staff **Clark Mercer** . . . . . . . . . . . . . . . . . . . . . . . . (804) 786-2078
  Education: Yale 2002 BA; George Washington 2005 MPP

*(continued on next page)*

---

★ Elected Official    ■ Appointed by Governor    ● Appointed by Legislature     ▲ Appointed by Board or Commission    ◆ Appointed by State Supreme Court

EXECUTIVE BRANCH

**Office of the Lieutenant Governor** *continued*

Constituent Services and Scheduling Director
  **Ellen Nicholas** . . . . . . . . . . . . . . . . . . . . . . . . . . . . . . . . . . (804) 786-2078
    E-mail: ellen.nicholas@ltgov.virginia.gov
Policy Director **Alexsis Rodgers** . . . . . . . . . . . . . . . . . . . . (804) 786-2078

# Office of the Attorney General
900 East Main Street, Richmond, VA 23219
Tel: (804) 786-2071   Internet: oag.state.va.us

★Attorney General **Mark R. Herring** (D) . . . . . . . . . . . . . . . (804) 786-2071
    Term Expires: January 2018
    Education: Virginia 1983 BA, 1986 MA; Richmond 1990 JD
    Career: President, The Herring Law Firm PC; State Senator (D-VA,
    District 33), Virginia Senate (2006-2014)
    Confidential Assistant to the Attorney General
      **Jonathan Ward** . . . . . . . . . . . . . . . . . . . . . . . . . . . . . . (804) 786-2071
        Education: VCU
    Special Assistant to the Attorney General
      **Brittany Anderson** . . . . . . . . . . . . . . . . . . . . . . . . . . . (804) 786-2071
        Education: Virginia Tech 2010 BA
Chief Deputy Attorney General **Cynthia Hudson** . . . . . . . . (804) 786-2071
Deputy Attorney General **Jeffrey M. Bourne** . . . . . . . . . . . (804) 786-2071
    Education: William & Mary 1999 BA
Deputy Attorney General **Linda Bryant, USAR** . . . . . . . . . (804) 786-2071
    E-mail: lbryant@oag.state.va.us
    Education: Virginia BA; William & Mary JD
Deputy Attorney General **John W. Daniel II** . . . . . . . . . . . (804) 786-2071
Deputy Attorney General **Rhodes B. Ritenour** . . . . . . . . . (804) 786-2071
    Education: Virginia 2000 BA, 2005 JD
Deputy Attorney General for Health, Education, and
    Social Services **Cynthia V. Bailey** . . . . . . . . . . . . . . . . (804) 786-2071
    Education: Richmond JD
Chief of Staff **Kevin O'Holleran** . . . . . . . . . . . . . . . . . . . . (804) 786-2071
Solicitor General **Stuart A. Raphael** . . . . . . . . . . . . . . . . . (804) 786-2071
    Education: Harvard 1986 BA; Virginia 1989 JD
    Deputy Solicitor General **Trevor S. Cox** . . . . . . . . . . . . . (804) 786-2071
        Education: Harvard; Cambridge (UK); Harvard JD
Opinions Counsel **G. Timothy Oksman** . . . . . . . . . . . . . . . (804) 786-2071
    Education: Virginia JD
Director of Administration **Leigh Archer** . . . . . . . . . . . . . . (804) 786-2071
    E-mail: larcher@oag.state.va.us
    Education: Richmond JD
Director of Communication **Michael K. Kelly** . . . . . . . . . . (804) 786-5874
    E-mail: mkelly@oag.state.va.us
Director of Human Resources **Tonya E. Woodson, PHR** . . (804) 786-2071
    Education: James Madison
Director of Information Systems **Nicole Monroe** . . . . . . . . (804) 786-2071
    E-mail: nmonroe@oag.state.va.us
    Education: Spelman; Strayer U
Director of Scheduling **Emily Bowles** . . . . . . . . . . . . . . . . (804) 786-2071
    E-mail: ebowles@oag.state.va.us
    Education: Virginia

---

★ Elected Official     ■ Appointed by Governor     ● Appointed by Legislature     ▲ Appointed by Board or Commission     ◆ Appointed by State Supreme Court

# Washington

Tel: (360) 753-5000 (State Information)

**Number of U.S. Congressional Delegates:** 2 Senators; 10 Representatives **Governor's Term:** 4 years
**Legislature Description:** 49 member Senate; 98 member House of Representatives, Term - Senate 4 years, House 2 years **Next Election:** Governor November 2016; Legislature November 2016
**Number of Electoral Votes:** 12 **Official Name:** State of Washington (after George Washington)
**Nickname:** The Evergreen State **Motto:** Alki (By and by)

**Population:** 7,170,351 (2015); Rank 13 **Fiscal Year:** 2013-2015 **Budget:** $74,813,000,000

## Office of the Governor

416 Sid Snyder Avenue, SW, Suite 200, Olympia, WA 98504
P.O. Box 40002, Olympia, WA 98504-0002
Tel: (360) 902-4111  Fax: (360) 753-4110

**Employees:** 45

**Jay Robert Inslee**
Governor

Began Service: January 16, 2013
Term Expires: January 2017
Date of Birth: February 9, 1951
Education: U Washington 1972 BA; Willamette 1976 JD
Home: Bainbridge Island
Religion: Christian
Career: State Representative (D-WA), Washington House of Representatives (1989-1993); U.S. Representative (D-WA, District 1), Office of Representative Jay Inslee, United States House of Representatives (1993-1995); Regional Director, Region X, United States Department of Health and Human Services, William J. Clinton Administration (1997-1998); U.S. Representative (D-WA, District 1), Office of Representative Jay Inslee, United States House of Representatives (1999-2012)

★Governor **Jay Robert Inslee** (D) . . . . . . . . . . . . . . . . . . . . . (360) 902-4111
  Executive Assistant **Lisa Van der Lugt** . . . . . . . . . . . . . . (360) 902-4111
    E-mail: lisa.vanderlugt@gov.wa.gov
Chief of Staff **David Postman** . . . . . . . . . . . . . . . . . . . . . . . (360) 902-4111
Deputy Chief of Staff **Kelly Wicker** . . . . . . . . . . . . . . . . . . (360) 902-4112
  E-mail: kelly.wicker@gov.wa.gov
General Counsel **Nicholas Brown** . . . . . . . . . . . . . . . . . . . . (360) 902-4118
  E-mail: nicholas.brown@gov.wa.gov
  Education: Morehouse Col 1999 BA; Harvard 2002 JD
Executive Director of Communications **Jaime Smith** . . . . . (360) 902-4136
  E-mail: jaime.smith@gov.wa.gov
  Media Relations Director **(Vacant)** . . . . . . . . . . . . . . . . . (360) 902-4136
Executive Director of External Relations **Aisling Kerins** . . . (360) 902-4105
  E-mail: aisling.kerins@gov.wa.gov
Executive Policy Director
  **Matthew M. "Matt" Steuerwalt** . . . . . . . . . . . . . . . . . (360) 902-0645
  E-mail: matt.steuerwalt@gov.wa.gov
  Education: UC San Diego BA; U Washington 1997 MPA
Legislative Affairs Director **Miguel Pérez-Gibson** . . . . . . . (360) 902-4105
  E-mail: miguel.perezgibson@gov.wa.gov
Higher Education Policy Advisor **(Vacant)** . . . . . . . . . . . . . (360) 902-0667
Senior Education Policy Advisor **Marcie Maxwell** . . . . . . . (360) 902-0667

## Governor's Office of Indian Affairs

210 Eleventh Avenue, SW, Suite 415, P.O. Box 40909, Olympia, WA 98504-0909
Fax: (360) 902-8829  E-mail: goia@goia.wa.gov
Internet: www.goia.wa.gov/

**Employees:** 3 **Fiscal Year:** 2013-2015 **Budget:** $502,000

Executive Director **Craig Bill** . . . . . . . . . . . . . . . . . . . . . . . (360) 902-8827
  E-mail: craig.bill@goia.wa.gov
Communications Research Analyst **Rebecca George** . . . . . (360) 902-8828
  E-mail: rgeorge@goia.wa.gov
Executive Assistant **Mystique Hurtado** . . . . . . . . . . . . . . . (360) 902-8825

## Board of Industrial Insurance Appeals [BIAA]

2430 Chandler Court Southwest, Olympia, WA 98504
P.O. Box 42401, Olympia, WA 98504-2401
Tel: (360) 753-6823  Fax: (360) 586-5611  Internet: www.biia.wa.gov

**Employees:** 150 **Fiscal Year:** 2013-2015 **Budget:** $39,609,000

■Chairperson **David E. Threedy** . . . . . . . . . . . . . . . . . . . . . (360) 753-6824
  Education: Illinois 1977 BA; U Puget Sound 1982 JD
  Confidential Secretary **Jay Raish** . . . . . . . . . . . . . . . . . . (360) 753-6824
    Education: UCLA 1992 BA
  Executive Secretary **Scott Timmons** . . . . . . . . . . . . . . . . (360) 753-6824
Information Technology Manager **Gretchen Zatarain** . . . . . (360) 753-6823
  E-mail: zatarain@biia.wa.gov

## Washington State Board of Accountancy [WBOA]

P.O. Box 9131, Olympia, WA 98507-9131
Tel: (360) 753-2586  TTY: (800) 833-6388
Fax: (360) 664-9190  E-mail: customerservice@cpaboard.wa.gov
Internet: www.cpaboard.wa.gov

**Employees:** 10 **Fiscal Year:** 2013-2015 **Budget:** $2,709,000

■Chair **Thomas G. Neill** . . . . . . . . . . . . . . . . . . . . . . . . . . . (360) 753-2586
  Term Expires: June 9, 2017
■Vice Chair **Elizabeth Deak Masnari** . . . . . . . . . . . . . . . . . (360) 753-2586
  Term Expires: June 9, 2016
■Secretary **James R. "Jim" Ladd, CPA** . . . . . . . . . . . . . . . . (360) 753-2586
  Term Expires: June 9, 2018
●Member **Donald F. Aubrey, CPA** . . . . . . . . . . . . . . . . . . . . (360) 753-2585
  Term Expires: June 9, 2016
■Member **Lauren C. Jassny** . . . . . . . . . . . . . . . . . . . . . . . . (360) 753-2586
  Term Expires: June 9, 2016
■Member **Edwin G. Jolicoeur, CPA, CFE** . . . . . . . . . . . . . . (360) 753-2586
  Term Expires: June 9, 2016
■Member **Emily Rollins** . . . . . . . . . . . . . . . . . . . . . . . . . . . (360) 753-2586
  Term Expires: June 9, 2018
■Member **Karen Saunders** . . . . . . . . . . . . . . . . . . . . . . . . . (360) 753-2586
  Term Expires: June 9, 2016
■Member **Favian Valencia** . . . . . . . . . . . . . . . . . . . . . . . . . (360) 753-2586
  Term Expires: June 9, 2017

### Board Staff
■Executive Director **Charles Satterlund, CPA, CIA** . . . . . . . (360) 586-0785
  E-mail: charless@cpaboard.wa.gov

*(continued on next page)*

---

★ Elected Official    ■ Appointed by Governor    ● Appointed by Legislature    ▲ Appointed by Board or Commission    ◆ Appointed by State Supreme Court

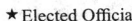

EXECUTIVE BRANCH

**Board Staff** *continued*

Deputy Director **Jennifer Sciba** . . . . . . . . . . . . . . . . . . (360) 586-0952
    E-mail: jennifers@cpaboard.wa.gov
Chief Information Officer **Michelle Tuscher**. . . . . . . . . . .(360) 753-2586
    E-mail: michellet@cpaboard.wa.gov
    Data and Systems Administrator **Tia Landry** . . . . . . . . . (360) 664-9194
      E-mail: tial@cpaboard.wa.gov
Lead Investigator **Taylor Shahon** . . . . . . . . . . . . . . . . . (360) 664-9194
Management Analyst **Lori Mickelson** . . . . . . . . . . . . . . . (360) 586-0784
Communications Specialist **Anthony Manfre** . . . . . . . . . .(360) 586-1026
    E-mail: anthonym@cpaboard.wa.gov
Enforcement Administrator **Kelly Wulfekuhle** . . . . . (360) 753-2586
Confidential Records Manager **Kirsten Donovan** . . . . . . . .(360) 664-9191

## Office of the Education Ombudsman

Northgate Executive Center, Building B, 155 NE 100th Street, Suite 210, Seattle, WA 98125-8012

Director-Ombudsman **Stacy Gillett**. . . . . . . . . . . . . . . . .(360) 725-0154
    E-mail: stacy.gillett@gov.wa.gov

## Office of the Family and Children's Ombudsman

6720 Fort Dent Way, Suite 240, Mail Stop TT-99, Tukwila, WA 98188

Director-Ombudsman **Patrick Dowd** . . . . . . . . . . . . . . . (206) 439-3870
    E-mail: patrick.dowd@governor.wa.gov      Fax: (206) 439-3877

## Washington DC Office

444 North Capitol Street, NW, Suite 411, Washington, DC 20001
Fax: (202) 624-5841

Director **Sam Ricketts** . . . . . . . . . . . . . . . . . . . . . . . . .(202) 624-3691
    E-mail: sam.ricketts@gov.wa.gov

## Clemency and Pardons Board

Tel: (360) 902-4111

■Chair **Jennifer J. Rancourt** . . . . . . . . . . . . . . . . . . . . .(360) 902-4111
■Vice Chair **James A. McDevitt** . . . . . . . . . . . . . . . . . . .(360) 902-4111
    Education: U Washington 1965 BA; Gonzaga 1974 JD, 1975 MBA
■Member **Raul Almeida** . . . . . . . . . . . . . . . . . . . . . . . . .(360) 902-4111
■Member **Cheryl Terry** . . . . . . . . . . . . . . . . . . . . . . . . .(360) 902-4111
■Member **(Vacant)** . . . . . . . . . . . . . . . . . . . . . . . . . . . .(360) 902-4111

## Results Washington

210 Eleventh Avenue, SW, Olympia, WA 98504-0909
Tel: (360) 902-0591  E-mail: results@gov.wa.gov

Director **Wendy Korthuis-Smith** . . . . . . . . . . . . . . . . . .(360) 902-0591
    E-mail: wendy.korthuis-smith@gov.wa.gov
    Administrative Assistant **Max Brown** . . . . . . . . . . . . . .(360) 902-0591
Engagements Manager **Tami Johnson** . . . . . . . . . . . . . . (360) 902-3055
    E-mail: tami.johnson@gov.wa.gov
Events and Engagements Coordinator **Heidi Loveall** . . . . . (360) 725-5159
    E-mail: heidi.loveall@gov.wa.gov
Performance Audit Liaison **Tammy Firkins** . . . . . . . . . . .(360) 902-3069
Senior Performance Advisor **Jon Cooper** . . . . . . . . . . . .(360) 902-9809
Senior Performance Advisor **Jessica Dang** . . . . . . . . . . . .(360) 902-7934
Senior Performance Advisor **KayLyne Newell** . . . . . . . . . (360) 902-0849
Senior Performance Advisor **Pam Pannkuk** . . . . . . . . . . .(360) 902-0424
Senior Performance Advisor **Tristan Wise** . . . . . . . . . . . (360) 902-0538
Enterprise Lean Consultant **Hollie Jensen** . . . . . . . . . . . (360) 902-9817
Enterprise Lean Consultant **Todd MacDonald** . . . . . . . . . (360) 902-4107

## Washington State Department of Agriculture [WSDA]

P.O. Box 42560, Olympia, WA 98504-2560
Tel: (360) 902-1800  TTY: (360) 902-1996  Fax: (360) 902-2092
Internet: www.agr.wa.gov

**Employees: 729  Fiscal Year: 2013-2015  Budget: $63,067,000**

■Director **Derek Sandison** . . . . . . . . . . . . . . . . . . . . . . .(360) 902-1887
    E-mail: dsandison@agr.wa.gov
    Executive Assistant **Megan Finkenbinder** . . . . . . . . . . .(360) 902-1887
Special Assistant **(Vacant)** . . . . . . . . . . . . . . . . . . . . . .(360) 902-2177

Deputy Director **Kirk Robinson** . . . . . . . . . . . . . . . . . . .(360) 902-1888
    Executive Assistant **Debbie Hacker** . . . . . . . . . . . . . . (360) 902-1801
Chief of Staff **(Vacant)** . . . . . . . . . . . . . . . . . . . . . . . .(360) 725-3898
Senior Counsel and Assistant Attorney General
    **Kristen Mitchell**. . . . . . . . . . . . . . . . . . . . . . . . . . .(360) 753-6215
Animal Services Assistant Director **Lynn Briscoe** . . .(360) 902-1800
Commodity Inspection Division Assistant Director
    **Brad Avy**. . . . . . . . . . . . . . . . . . . . . . . . . . . . . . . .(360) 902-1827
    E-mail: bavy@agr.wa.gov
Food Safety and Consumer Services Division Assistant
    Director **Kirk Robinson** . . . . . . . . . . . . . . . . . . . . . .(360) 902-1888
Pesticide Management Division Assistant Director
    **Ted Maxwell** . . . . . . . . . . . . . . . . . . . . . . . . . . . . (360) 902-2011
Plant Protection Division Assistant Director **Brad White** . . .(360) 902-1907
Information Technology Program Director **(Vacant)** . . . . . .(360) 725-3898
State Veterinarian **Dr. Joe Baker** . . . . . . . . . . . . . . . . . (360) 902-1881
Chief Financial Officer **Mark Johnson** . . . . . . . . . . . . . .(360) 902-1989
Policy Director **Larry Sheahan** . . . . . . . . . . . . . . . . . . .(360) 902-1918
    Education: Washington State 1982 BA; Willamette 1985 JD
Policy Assistant **Patrick Capper** . . . . . . . . . . . . . . . . . . (360) 902-2083
Policy Assistant **Steve Fuller** . . . . . . . . . . . . . . . . . . . .(360) 902-1945
Webmaster **Tim Valdez** . . . . . . . . . . . . . . . . . . . . . . . .(360) 725-5507
    E-mail: webmaster@agr.wa.gov

## Department of Commerce

1011 Plum Street Southeast, Olympia, WA 98504
P.O. Box 42525, Olympia, WA 98504-2525
Tel: (360) 725-4000  TTY: (360) 586-4224  Fax: (360) 586-8440

**Employees: 298  Fiscal Year: 2013-2015  Budget: $514,491,000**

■Director **Brian N. Bonlender** . . . . . . . . . . . . . . . . . . . .(360) 725-4000
    E-mail: brian.bonlender@commerce.wa.gov
Deputy Director **Connie Robins** . . . . . . . . . . . . . . . . . . (360) 725-2662
Communications Director **Barbara Dunn** . . . . . . . . . . . .(360) 725-4000
    E-mail: barbara.dunn@commerce.wa.gov
Economic Development Director, Information and
    Communication Technology **Dr. Joseph Williams** . . . . . (360) 725-4000
    Education: UC Berkeley 1978 BA; Wisconsin 1980 MA;
    Texas 1982 MBA, 1987 PhD
Administrative Services Assistant Director
    **Kendrick Stewart** . . . . . . . . . . . . . . . . . . . . . . . . . .(360) 725-2662
    E-mail: kendrick.stewart@commerce.wa.gov
Community Services and Housing Assistant Director
    **Diane Klontz** . . . . . . . . . . . . . . . . . . . . . . . . . . . . .(360) 725-2910
Energy Division Assistant Director **Michael Furze** . . . . . . .(360) 725-4000
    Executive Assistant **Karisa Sherwood** . . . . . . . . . . . . (360) 725-4021
External Relations Division Assistant Director
    **Nick Demerice** . . . . . . . . . . . . . . . . . . . . . . . . . . .(360) 725-4010
Local Government Division Assistant Director
    **Mark Barkley** . . . . . . . . . . . . . . . . . . . . . . . . . . . .(360) 725-4000
    Education: Seattle BA; Central Michigan MPA
Office of Aerospace Director **John Thornquist** . . . . . . . . (360) 725-4000
    Education: Arizona State BME; U Washington MBA
Office of Economic Development and Competitiveness
    Assistant Director **Chris Green** . . . . . . . . . . . . . . . . . .(360) 725-4000
Bioenergy Coordinator **Peter Moulton** . . . . . . . . . . . . . .(360) 725-3116

## Department of Corrections [DOC]

Edna Lucille Goodrich Building, 7345 Linderson Way SW,
Tumwater, WA 98501
P.O. Box 41101, Olympia, WA 98504-1100
Tel: (360) 725-8213  Fax: (360) 664-4056  Internet: www.doc.wa.gov

**Employees: 7,942  Fiscal Year: 2013-2015  Budget: $1,668,388,000**

■Secretary (Acting) **Richard L. "Dick" Morgan** . . . . . . . . .(360) 725-8810
    Confidential Secretary **Courtney Grubb** . . . . . . . . . . . .(360) 725-8810
Administrative Services Assistant Secretary
    **Marcos Rodriguez** . . . . . . . . . . . . . . . . . . . . . . . . .(360) 725-8416
    E-mail: marcos.rodriguez@doc.wa.gov
Community Corrections Assistant Secretary
    **Anmarie Aylward** . . . . . . . . . . . . . . . . . . . . . . . . . .(360) 725-8787
Health Services Assistant Secretary **Kevin Bovenkamp** . . .(360) 725-8729
Senior Assistant Attorney General, Corrections Division
    Chief **Timothy N. "Tim" Lang** . . . . . . . . . . . . . . . . . (360) 586-1445
    E-mail: timothy.lang@atg.wa.gov

---

★ Elected Official   ■ Appointed by Governor   ● Appointed by Legislature   ▲ Appointed by Board or Commission   ◆ Appointed by State Supreme Court

Communications Director **Stephen Gehrke** . . . . . . . . . . . . (360) 725-8817
  E-mail: stephen.gehrke@doc.wa.gov
Risk Management Director **Kathy Gastreich** . . . . . . . . . . . (360) 725-8587
Prisons Assistant Secretary **Stephen Sinclair** . . . . . . . . . . (360) 725-8226
Offender Change Division Director **Amy Seidlitz** . . . . . . . . (360) 725-8689
  E-mail: amy.seidlitz@doc.wa.gov

## Indeterminate Sentence Review Board [ISRB]

4317 Sixth Avenue, SE, Olympia, WA 98504-0907
P.O. Box 40907, Olympia, WA 98504-0907
Tel: (360) 407-2400  Fax: (360) 493-9287  E-mail: isrb@doc1.wa.gov

**Employees:** 14

■Chair **Kecia Rongen** . . . . . . . . . . . . . . . . . . . . . . . . . . . . . (360) 407-2400
Administrative Assistant **Robin L. Riley** . . . . . . . . . . . . . . (360) 407-2415

## Department of Ecology

P.O. Box 47600, Olympia, WA 98504-7600
Tel: (360) 407-6000  Fax: (360) 407-6989
TTY: (800) 833-6388 (Statewide)  Internet: www.ecy.wa.gov

**Employees:** 1,586  **Fiscal Year:** 2013-2015  **Budget:** $464,932,000

Director **Maia Bellon** . . . . . . . . . . . . . . . . . . . . . . . . . . . . . (360) 407-7001
  E-mail: maib461@ecy.wa.gov
  Executive Secretary **Teri North** . . . . . . . . . . . . . . . . . . . (360) 407-7009
Deputy Director **Polly Zehm** . . . . . . . . . . . . . . . . . . . . . . . (360) 407-7011
Legislative and Governmental Relations Director
  **Denise Clifford** . . . . . . . . . . . . . . . . . . . . . . . . . . . . . . (360) 407-7003
  E-mail: decl461@ecy.wa.gov
Central Region Office Director (Acting) **James Rovard** . . . (509) 457-7120
  15 West Yakima Avenue, Suite 200, Yakima, WA 98902-3387
Eastern Region Office Director **Grant Pheifer** . . . . . . . . . . (509) 329-3516
  N. 4601 Monroe, Suite 202, Spokane, WA 99205-1295
Northwest Region Office Director **Josh Baldi** . . . . . . . . . . (425) 649-7010
  3190 160th Avenue, SE, Bellevue, WA 98008-5452
Southwest Region Office Director **Sally Toteff** . . . . . . . . . (360) 407-6307
  300 Desmond Drive, Lacey, WA 98503    Fax: (360) 407-6305

### Programs

Air Program Manager **Stuart Clark** . . . . . . . . . . . . . . . . . . (360) 407-6880
Environmental Assessments Program Manager
  **Carol Smith** . . . . . . . . . . . . . . . . . . . . . . . . . . . . . . . . (360) 407-6699
Hazardous Waste and Toxics Reduction Program
  Manager **Darin Rice** . . . . . . . . . . . . . . . . . . . . . . . . . . (360) 407-6702
Nuclear Waste Program Manager **Jane A. Hedges** . . . . . . . (509) 372-7905
  Education: Washington State BS
Shorelands and Environmental Assistance Program
  Manager **Gordon White** . . . . . . . . . . . . . . . . . . . . . . . . (360) 407-6977
Solid Waste and Financial Assistance Manager
  **Laurie Davies** . . . . . . . . . . . . . . . . . . . . . . . . . . . . . . . (360) 407-6103
Spill Prevention, Preparedness and Response Program
  Manager **Dale Jensen** . . . . . . . . . . . . . . . . . . . . . . . . . (360) 407-7450
Toxics Cleanup Program Manager **Jim Pendowski** . . . . . . . (360) 407-7177
Water Quality Program Manager **Heather Bartlett** . . . . . . . (360) 407-6405
Water Resources Program Manager **Tom Loranger** . . . . . . (360) 407-6602
Building Services and Facilities Manager **Steve Fry** . . . . . . (360) 407-6018
                                 Fax: (360) 407-6137
Librarian **Donna Seegmueller** . . . . . . . . . . . . . . . . . . . . . (360) 407-6150

## Department of Early Learning [DEL]

1110 Jefferson Street Southeast, Olympia, WA 98504
P.O. Box 40970, Olympia, WA 98504-0970
Tel: (360) 725-4665  Tel: (866) 482-4325 (Toll Free)  Fax: (360) 413-3482
Internet: www.del.wa.gov

■Director **Ross Hunter** . . . . . . . . . . . . . . . . . . . . . . . . . . . (360) 725-4584
  E-mail: ross.hunter@del.wa.gov
  Education: Yale 1983 BS
Deputy Director **Heather Moss** . . . . . . . . . . . . . . . . . . . . (360) 725-4932
  E-mail: heather.moss@del.wa.gov

## Employment Security Department

P.O. Box 9046, Olympia, WA 98507-9046
Tel: (360) 902-9500  Fax: (360) 902-9383  Internet: www.esd.wa.gov

**Employees:** 1,635  **Fiscal Year:** 2013-2015  **Budget:** $686,093,000

■Commissioner **Dale Peinecke** . . . . . . . . . . . . . . . . . . . . . (360) 902-9301
  E-mail: dpeinecke@esd.wa.gov
  Education: Carnegie Mellon BABA; Oregon State BS
Deputy Director **Lisa Marsh** . . . . . . . . . . . . . . . . . . . . . . . (360) 902-9304
  E-mail: lmarsh@esd.wa.gov
Assistant Attorney General **Eric Peterson** . . . . . . . . . . . . . (360) 587-4211
  E-mail: epeterson@esd.wa.gov
Budget Performance and Research Division Assistant
  Commissioner (Acting) **Sandy Triggs** . . . . . . . . . . . . . . (360) 902-9423
  E-mail: striggs@esd.wa.gov
Human Resource Services Division Assistant
  Commissioner **Ron Marshall** . . . . . . . . . . . . . . . . . . . . (360) 725-9401
  E-mail: rmarshall@esd.wa.gov
Information Technology Services Division Assistant
  Commissioner **Renee Linder** . . . . . . . . . . . . . . . . . . . . (360) 407-4646
  E-mail: rlinder@esd.wa.gov
Unemployment Insurance Division Assistant
  Commissioner **Neil Gorrell** . . . . . . . . . . . . . . . . . . . . . (360) 902-9334
Workforce and Career Development Division Assistant
  Commissioner **Sandy Miller** . . . . . . . . . . . . . . . . . . . . (360) 407-4906
  E-mail: smiller@esd.wa.gov
Communications Director **Janelle Guthrie** . . . . . . . . . . . . . (360) 902-9289
  E-mail: jguthrie@esd.wa.gov
Government Relations Director **Cathy Hoover** . . . . . . . . . . (360) 902-9407
  E-mail: choover@esd.wa.gov

## Department of Enterprise Services

1500 Jefferson Street, SE, Olympia, WA 98504
P.O. Box 42445, Olympia, WA 98504-2445
Tel: (360) 407-9211

Director **Christopher "Chris" Liu** . . . . . . . . . . . . . . . . . . . (360) 407-9211
  E-mail: christopher.liu@des.wa.gov
  Education: Hawaii (West Oahu) BS
Deputy Director **Bob Covington** . . . . . . . . . . . . . . . . . . . . (360) 407-9203
  E-mail: bob.covington@des.wa.gov
  Confidential Secretary **Kennly Asato** . . . . . . . . . . . . . . (360) 407-9211
    E-mail: kennly.asato@des.wa.gov
Deputy Director **Lynne McGuire** . . . . . . . . . . . . . . . . . . . . (360) 407-9211
  E-mail: lynne.mcguire@des.wa.gov
  Executive Assistant **Betty Loy** . . . . . . . . . . . . . . . . . . . (360) 407-9211
    E-mail: betty.loy@des.wa.gov
Communications Director **Curt Hart** . . . . . . . . . . . . . . . . . (360) 407-9211
  E-mail: curt.hart@des.wa.gov
Facilities Director **Bonnie Scheel** . . . . . . . . . . . . . . . . . . . (360) 570-5034
Finance Director **Annette Meyer** . . . . . . . . . . . . . . . . . . . (360) 407-9222
Government Relations Director **Arlen Harris** . . . . . . . . . . . (360) 407-9211
Human Resource Director **Jeff Canaan** . . . . . . . . . . . . . . . (360) 407-9214
Business Resources Services Assistant Director
  **Phil Grigg** . . . . . . . . . . . . . . . . . . . . . . . . . . . . . . . . . . (360) 407-2211
  E-mail: phil.grigg@des.wa.gov

## Department of Financial Institutions [DFI]

P.O. Box 41200, Olympia, WA 98504-1200
Tel: (360) 902-8700  TTY: (360) 664-8126  Fax: (360) 586-5068
Internet: www.dfi.wa.gov

**Employees:** 192

■Director **Scott Jarvis** . . . . . . . . . . . . . . . . . . . . . . . . . . . . (360) 902-8707
  E-mail: confsec@dfi.wa.gov
  Confidential Secretary **Susan K. Putzier** . . . . . . . . . . . . (360) 902-8764
Deputy Director and Administration Division Director
  **Gloria Papiez** . . . . . . . . . . . . . . . . . . . . . . . . . . . . . . . (360) 902-8820
  E-mail: gloria.papiez@dfi.wa.gov
Banks Division Director **Richard M. Riccobono** . . . . . . . . (360) 902-8704
  E-mail: banks@dfi.wa.gov         Fax: (360) 753-6070
  Education: SUNY (Albany); Western New England JD
Consumer Services Division Director **Charles Clark** . . . . . . (360) 902-0511
                             Fax: (360) 664-2258

*(continued on next page)*

---

★ Elected Official   ■ Appointed by Governor   ● Appointed by Legislature   ▲ Appointed by Board or Commission   ◆ Appointed by State Supreme Court

EXECUTIVE BRANCH

**Department of Financial Institutions** *continued*

Credit Unions Division Director **Linda Jekel** . . . . . . . . . . . (360) 902-8778
Fax: (360) 704-6901

Securities Division Director **William "Bill" Beatty** . . . . . . . (360) 902-8824
P.O. Box 9033, Olympia, WA 98507-9033      Fax: (360) 902-0524

# Department of Health [DOH]

101 Israel Road, SE, Tumwater, WA 98501
P.O. Box 9709, Olympia, WA 98507-9709 (Vital Records)
P.O. Box 47890, Olympia, WA 98504-7890
Tel: (360) 236-4501
Tel: (800) 525-0127 (Health Consumer Assistance Line [In State])
Tel: (360) 236-4053 (Health Consumer Assistance Line [Out of State])
Tel: (360) 236-4300 (Vital Records)  Fax: (360) 586-7424
Internet: www.doh.wa.gov

**Employees:** 1,534  **Fiscal Year:** 2013-2015  **Budget:** $964,338,000

■Secretary **John M. Wiesman** . . . . . . . . . . . . . . . . . . . . (360) 236-4030
E-mail: secretary@doh.wa.gov
Education: Lawrence U 1983 BA; Yale 1987 MPH;
North Carolina 2012 DrPH
Deputy Secretary **Jessica Todorovich** . . . . . . . . . . . . . . (360) 236-4030
Health Systems Quality Assurance Assistant Secretary
**Martin Mueller** . . . . . . . . . . . . . . . . . . . . . . . . . . (360) 236-4601
Communications Office Director **Joby Winans** . . . . . . . . . (360) 236-4077
E-mail: joby.winans@doh.wa.gov
Policy, Legislative and Constituent Relations Office
Director **Drew Bouton** . . . . . . . . . . . . . . . . . . . . . . (360) 236-4048
Partnership, Planning, and Performance Office Director
**Karen Jensen** . . . . . . . . . . . . . . . . . . . . . . . . . . . (360) 236-4062
Chief Human Resources Officer **(Vacant)** . . . . . . . . . . . . (360) 236-4406
Chief Technology and Information Officer **Don Peck** . . . . . .(360) 236-3105
E-mail: don.peck@doh.wa.gov
State Health Officer **Kathy Lofty** . . . . . . . . . . . . . . . . . (360) 236-4018

## Disease Control and Health Statistics Division

Epidemiology, Health Statistics and Public Health
Laboratories Assistant Secretary **Jennifer Tebaldi** . . . . . . (360) 236-4204
PO Box 47811, Olympia, WA 98504-7811
Deputy Assistant Secretary **Pamela Lovinger** . . . . . . . . . . (360) 236-4205
E-mail: pamela.lovinger@doh.wa.gov
Organizational Performance Development and Policy
Director **Angi Miller** . . . . . . . . . . . . . . . . . . . . . . . (360) 236-4225

## Environmental Health Division

Environmental Health Assistant Secretary
**Maryanne Guichard** . . . . . . . . . . . . . . . . . . . . . . . (360) 236-3050
Chief Administrator **Peggy Johnson** . . . . . . . . . . . . . . . (360) 236-3053
Information Management Director **David Jennings** . . . . . .(360) 236-4576
Environmental Epidemiology Manager **Glen Patrick** . . . . . (360) 236-3177

## Prevention and Community Health Division

Prevention and Community Health Assistant Secretary
**Allene Mares** . . . . . . . . . . . . . . . . . . . . . . . . . . . .(360) 236-3723
Deputy Assistant Secretary **Jennifer McNamara** . . . . . . . .(360) 236-3713
E-mail: jennifer.mcnamara@doh.wa.gov

# Department of Labor and Industries [L&I]

P.O. Box 44000, Olympia, WA 98504-4000
Tel: (360) 902-5800  TTY: (360) 902-5889  Fax: (360) 902-4202
Internet: www.lni.wa.gov

**Employees:** 2,746  **Fiscal Year:** 2013-2015  **Budget:** $653,472,000

■Director **Joel Sacks** . . . . . . . . . . . . . . . . . . . . . . . . . (360) 902-4203
E-mail: joel.sacks@lni.wa.gov
Education: Haverford 1991 BA; Syracuse 1994 MPA
Deputy Director **Ernie LaPalm** . . . . . . . . . . . . . . . . . . .(360) 902-9140
E-mail: lapa235@lni.wa.gov
Executive Assistant **Lisa Rodriguez** . . . . . . . . . . . . . . . . (360) 902-4204
E-mail: decl235@lni.wa.gov

Senior Assistant Attorney General **Steve Reinmuth** . . . . . . (360) 586-7730
E-mail: steve.reinmuth@lni.wa.gov
Internal Audit Director **Dan Johnston** . . . . . . . . . . . . . . . (360) 902-5584
Operations Deputy Director, Financial Management
**Randi Warick** . . . . . . . . . . . . . . . . . . . . . . . . . . . (360) 902-4214
E-mail: ware235@lni.wa.gov
Administrative Services Assistant Director
**Christine Freed** . . . . . . . . . . . . . . . . . . . . . . . . . (360) 902-6961
E-mail: frch235@lni.wa.gov
Communications Assistant Director **Kim Contris** . . . . . . . . (360) 902-5417
E-mail: conq235@lni.wa.gov
Field Services and Public Safety Assistant Director
**Jose Rodriguez** . . . . . . . . . . . . . . . . . . . . . . . . . . (360) 902-6348
E-mail: rodr235@lni.wa.gov
Human Resources Assistant Director **(Vacant)** . . . . . . . . . (360) 902-5800
Information Services Division Assistant Director
**Bob Lanouette** . . . . . . . . . . . . . . . . . . . . . . . . . . (360) 902-5964
E-mail: lano235@lni.wa.gov
Insurance Services Division Assistant Director
**Vickie Kennedy** . . . . . . . . . . . . . . . . . . . . . . . . . (360) 902-4209
E-mail: kene235@lni.wa.gov
Safety and Health Services Division Assistant Director
**Anne Soiza** . . . . . . . . . . . . . . . . . . . . . . . . . . . . (360) 902-4805
Lean Transformation Office Director
**Roy Plaeger-Brockway** . . . . . . . . . . . . . . . . . . . . . (360) 902-5800
E-mail: plae235@lni.wa.gov
Budget Manager **Roger Wilson** . . . . . . . . . . . . . . . . . . . (360) 902-6998
Fraud Prevention and Labor Standards Manager
**Elizabeth "Liz" Smith** . . . . . . . . . . . . . . . . . . . . . . (360) 902-5933
E-mail: elizabeth.smith@lni.wa.gov
Web Technical Manager **Brian Criss** . . . . . . . . . . . . . . . . (360) 902-4648
E-mail: cric235@lni.wa.gov
Legislative and Government Affairs Liaison
**Tammy Fellin** . . . . . . . . . . . . . . . . . . . . . . . . . . . (360) 902-6805
E-mail: fel4235@lni.wa.gov
Librarian **Lisa Engvall** . . . . . . . . . . . . . . . . . . . . . . . . (360) 902-5498

# Department of Licensing [DOL]

Highways-Licenses Building, Olympia, WA 98504
Tel: (360) 902-3600  TTY: (360) 664-0116  Fax: (360) 902-4042

**Employees:** 1,232  **Fiscal Year:** 2013-2015  **Budget:** $295,772,000

■Director **Pat A. Kohler** . . . . . . . . . . . . . . . . . . . . . . . . (360) 902-3933
E-mail: doldirector@dol.wa.gov
Deputy Director **Teresa Berntsen** . . . . . . . . . . . . . . . . . . (360) 902-0191
Administrative Services Division Assistant Director
**Tami Dohrman** . . . . . . . . . . . . . . . . . . . . . . . . . . (360) 902-4044
E-mail: tdohrman@dol.wa.gov
Business and Professions Division Assistant Director
**Kathleen Drew** . . . . . . . . . . . . . . . . . . . . . . . . . . (360) 664-1452
Education: Ohio 1981 BA
Customer Relations Division Assistant Director
**Chuck Simchuk** . . . . . . . . . . . . . . . . . . . . . . . . . . (360) 902-3820
Programs and Services Division Assistant Director
**Julie Knittle** . . . . . . . . . . . . . . . . . . . . . . . . . . . . (360) 902-3850
E-mail: jknittle@dol.wa.gov
Communications and Education Director **Brad Benfield** . . . (360) 902-3611
Human Resources Director **Laurie Milligan** . . . . . . . . . . . . (360) 902-3605
Policy and Legislative Director **Tony Sermonti** . . . . . . . . . (360) 902-3609
Chief Information Officer **Ann Bruner** . . . . . . . . . . . . . . . (360) 660-6601
E-mail: abruner@dol.wa.gov

# Washington Military Department

Camp Murray, TA-20, Camp Murray, WA 98430-5000
Tel: (253) 512-8000  Fax: (253) 512-8497
E-mail: pao@washingtonguard.org  Internet: http://mil.wa.gov

**Employees:** 314  **Fiscal Year:** 2015-2017  **Budget:** $250,836,000

■Adjutant General/Homeland Security Advisor
**MG Bret D. Daugherty, ARNG** . . . . . . . . . . . . . . . . . (253) 512-8201
E-mail: bret.daugherty@mil.wa.gov
Education: Seattle 1980 BA
Confidential Secretary **Catherine "Cathy" Senn** . . . . . . . (253) 512-8201
Department Deputy Director **BG Wallace Turner, ARNG** . . (253) 512-8202

---

★ Elected Official   ■ Appointed by Governor   ● Appointed by Legislature   ▲ Appointed by Board or Commission   ◆ Appointed by State Supreme Court

Communications Director **Karina Shagren**..............(253) 512-8222
E-mail: karina.shagren@mil.wa.gov
Education: Washington State
Information Services **CPT Joseph Siemandel, ARNG**....(253) 512-8481
E-mail: pao@washingtonguard.org

## Emergency Management Division
Camp Murray, Building 20, Tacoma, WA 98430-5122
TTY: (800) 562-6108  Fax: (253) 512-7207  Internet: http://emd.wa.gov
Director **Robert Ezelle**.............................(253) 512-7001
Deputy Director **Kurt Hardin**.....................(253) 512-7002
E-mail: kurt.hardin@mil.wa.gov
Public Information Officer **Mark Stewart**............(253) 512-7703
E-mail: mark.stewart@mil.wa.gov

## Washington National Guard Joint Force Headquarters
Washington National Guard Building 1, Camp Murray, WA 98430-5000
Tel: (253) 512-8000  Fax: (253) 512-8497  E-mail: wamil@mil.wa.gov
Internet: http://washingtonguard.org
Joint Chief of Staff **Col Gent Welsh, ANG**...........(253) 512-8203

## Washington Air National Guard
Washington Air National Guard, Building 118, Camp Murray, Tacoma, WA 98430-5016
Tel: (253) 512-3354  Fax: (253) 512-3350  E-mail: wamil@mil.wa.gov
Internet: washingtonairguard.org
Assistant Adjutant General **BrigGen John Tuohy, ANG**...(253) 512-3354
Air Director of Staff **Col Anne Maziar, ANG**..........(253) 512-3353

## Washington Army National Guard
Washington Army National Guard, Building 1, Camp Murray, 1 Militia Drive, Tacoma, WA 98430-5000
Tel: (253) 512-8202  Fax: (253) 512-8497  E-mail: wamil@mil.wa.gov
Internet: washingtonarmyguard.org
Assistant Adjutant General **BG Wallace Turner, ARNG**...(253) 512-8202
Army Chief of Staff **COL Jeff Sabatine, ARNG**.........(253) 512-8204

## Department of Retirement Systems [DRS]
6835 Capitol Boulevard, Tumwater, WA 98501
P.O. Box 48380, Olympia, WA 98504-8380
Tel: (360) 664-7000  Tel: (800) 547-6657  TTY: (360) 586-5450
Fax: (360) 753-3166  E-mail: recep@drs.wa.gov
Internet: www.drs.wa.gov

**Employees:** 230  **Fiscal Year:** 2013-2015  **Budget:** $53,000,000
■Director **Marcie Frost**............................(360) 664-7312
E-mail: marcief@drs.wa.gov
Deputy Director **(Vacant)**.........................(360) 664-7724
Executive Assistant **Wilma Eby**...................(360) 664-7311
Administrative Services Assistant Director **Mike Ricchio**..(360) 664-7227
Information Services Assistant Director **Rose Bossio**.....(360) 664-7286
E-mail: roseb@drs.wa.gov
Policy and Strategic Initiatives Assistant Director
**Shawn Merchant**................................(360) 664-7303
Retirement Services Assistant Director **Dave Nelsen**......(360) 664-7304
Human Resources Manager **Chris Greenwalt**.........(360) 664-7065
Legal and Legislative Services Manager **Jacob White**....(360) 664-7304
E-mail: jacobw@drs.wa.gov
Communications Officer **David Brine**................(360) 664-7097
E-mail: davidb@drs.wa.gov

## Department of Revenue
P.O. Box 47454, Olympia, WA 98504-7454
Tel: (800) 647-7706  TTY: (800) 647-7706  Fax: (360) 534-1606

**Employees:** 1,145  **Fiscal Year:** 2013-2015  **Budget:** $251,333,000
■Director **Vikki Smith**............................(360) 534-1600
E-mail: vikkis@dor.wa.gov
Executive Assistant **Denise Ertman**...............(360) 534-1618
Deputy Director (Acting) **Marcus Glasper**..........(360) 534-1605

Administrative Services Senior Assistant Director
**Marcus Glasper**................................(360) 534-1615
E-mail: marcusg@dor.wa.gov
Research and Fiscal Analysis Division Assistant Director
**Kathy Oline**...................................(360) 534-1534
Tax Policy Senior Assistant Director **Gil Brewer**.........(360) 534-1601
Senior Assistant Attorney General **Cameron Comfort**....(360) 664-9429
Appeals Division Assistant Director **Mary Barrett**.......(360) 534-1343
Audit Division Assistant Director **John Ryser**..........(360) 725-7518
Compliance Division Assistant Director **Nicole Ross**.....(360) 725-7301
Human Resources Assistant Director **Katie Gerard**.......(360) 725-7499
Information Services Assistant Division Director
**David Sorrel**..................................(360) 596-3792
E-mail: davidso@dor.wa.gov
Interpretations and Technical Advice Assistant Director
**Alan Lynn**....................................(360) 534-1505
Legislation and Policy Division Assistant Director
**Drew Shirk**...................................(360) 534-1547
E-mail: drews@dor.wa.gov
Operations Senior Assistant Director **Janetta Taylor**.....(360) 534-1603
Special Programs Division Assistant Director
**Stuart Thronson**..............................(360) 534-1300
Taxpayer Account Administration Division Assistant
Director **Debra Conn**...........................(360) 902-7045
Taxpayer Services Division Assistant Director
**Janet Shimaburkuro**...........................(360) 705-6602
Webmaster **Jenny Smith**..........................(360) 596-3760

## Department of Services for the Blind [DSB]
4565 Seventh Avenue, Lacey, WA 98503
P.O. Box 40933, Olympia, WA 98504-0933
Tel: (360) 725-3830  Tel: (800) 552-7103  TTY: (360) 586-6437
Fax: (360) 407-0679  Internet: www.dsb.wa.gov

**Employees:** 90  **Fiscal Year:** 2013-2015  **Budget:** $24,000,000
■Executive Director **LouOma Durand**.................(360) 725-3830
E-mail: louoma.durand@dsb.wa.gov
Business Services Assistant Director **(Vacant)**..........(360) 725-3840
Executive Assistant **Kristina Cox**...................(360) 725-3836

## Programs
3411 South Alaska Street, Seattle, WA 98118-1631
Fax: (206) 721-4103
Assistant Director for Customer Service
**Michael MacKillop**.............................(206) 906-5520

## Department of Social and Health Services [DSHS]
P.O. Box 45010, Olympia, WA 98504-5010
Tel: (360) 902-8400  TTY: (360) 902-8000  Fax: (360) 902-7848
Internet: www.dshs.wa.gov

■Secretary (Acting) **Patricia Lashway**................(360) 902-7829
Executive Assistant **Eci Ameh**....................(360) 902-8400
Administration and External Relations Assistant
Secretary **Patricia Lashway**.....................(360) 902-7812
P.O. Box 45115, Olympia, WA 98504-5115
E-mail: patricia.lashway@dshs.wa.gov
Deaf and Hard of Hearing Office Director **Eric Raff**......(360) 902-8000
P.O. Box 45300, Olympia, WA 98504-5300
Diversity and Inclusion Senior Director (Interim)
**Colleen Yamaguchi**............................(360) 902-8400
Human Resources Senior Director
**David L. "Dave" Stewart, IPMA-CP**..............(360) 725-5844
P.O. Box 45023, Olympia, WA 98504-5023
Indian Policy Office Senior Director **(Vacant)**..........(360) 902-7816
P.O. Box 45105, Olympia, WA 98504-5105
Policy and External Relations Senior Director
**Dana Phelps**..................................(360) 902-8400
Assistant Attorney General and General Counsel
**Rochelle Tillett**...............................(360) 902-8400
Chief Financial Officer **Kathy Marshall**.............(360) 902-8181
P.O. Box 45013, Olympia, WA 98504-5020

*(continued on next page)*

★ Elected Official  ■ Appointed by Governor  ● Appointed by Legislature  ▲ Appointed by Board or Commission  ◆ Appointed by State Supreme Court

*State Yellow Book*  © Leadership Directories, Inc.  Summer 2016

EXECUTIVE BRANCH

**Department of Social and Health Services** *continued*

Chief Information Officer **Sue Langen** . . . . . . . . . . . . . . . (360) 902-7714
P.O. Box 45880, Olympia, WA 98504-5880      Fax: (360) 902-7848
E-mail: sue.langen@dshs.wa.gov
Food Assistance Programs Manager **Vicki Baxter** . . . . . . . (360) 725-4613

# Washington State Department of Transportation [WSDOT]

P.O. Box 47300, Olympia, WA 98504-7300
Tel: (360) 705-7000   TTY: (800) 468-8392   Internet: www.wsdot.wa.gov

■ Secretary (Acting) **Roger Millar** . . . . . . . . . . . . . . . . (360) 705-7054
                                                 Fax: (360) 705-6800
Chief Counsel **Bryce Brown** . . . . . . . . . . . . . . . . . . . (360) 753-4960
E-mail: bryceb@atg.wa.gov
Audit Office Director **Steve McKerney** . . . . . . . . . . . . . (360) 705-7004
Equal Opportunity Office Director (Interim)
**Kara Larsen** . . . . . . . . . . . . . . . . . . . . . . . . . . . . (360) 705-7090
Deputy Secretary and Chief Operating Officer
**Campbell M. "Cam" Gilmour** . . . . . . . . . . . . . . . . (360) 705-7027
Education: Oregon State 1971 BS; Idaho 1972 MS    Fax: (360) 705-6800
■ Deputy Secretary **Roger Millar** . . . . . . . . . . . . . . . . . (360) 705-7054
Federal Liaison Director **Allison Camden** . . . . . . . . . . . (360) 705-7024
                                                 Fax: (360) 705-6800
Tribal Liaison **Megan Cotton** . . . . . . . . . . . . . . . . . . . (360) 705-7025
E-mail: cottonm@wsdot.wa.gov
Purchasing and Materials Manager
**David A. "Dave" Davis, CPPO** . . . . . . . . . . . . . . . . (360) 570-6711
                                                 Fax: (360) 570-6725

## Community of Economic Development

Assistant Secretary **Amy Scarton** . . . . . . . . . . . . . . . . (360) 705-7000
E-mail: scartoa@wsdot.wa.gov
Aviation Division Director **Tristin Atkins** . . . . . . . . . . . . (360) 651-6300
3704 172nd Street, NE, Suite K2, Arlington, WA 98223
Freight Systems Director **Barbara Ivanov** . . . . . . . . . . . (360) 705-7931
Highways and Local Programs Director
**Kathleen B. Davis** . . . . . . . . . . . . . . . . . . . . . . . . (360) 705-7871
E-mail: davisk@wsdot.wa.gov
Public Transportation Division Director **Brian Lagerberg** . . (360) 705-7878
State Rail and Marine Office Director **Ron Pate** . . . . . . . . (360) 705-6903

## Engineering and Regional Operations

Assistant Secretary/Chief Engineer **Linea Laird** . . . . . . . . (360) 705-7032
E-mail: lairdl@wsdot.wa.gov             Fax: (360) 705-6800
Equipment and Facilities Administrator **Yvonne Medina** . . (360) 705-7890
Motor Carrier Services Administrator **Anne Ford** . . . . . . . (360) 704-7341
Maintenance Operations Director/State Maintenance
Engineer **Chris Christopher** . . . . . . . . . . . . . . . . . . (360) 705-7851
Traffic Operations Director/State Traffic Engineer
**John Nisbet** . . . . . . . . . . . . . . . . . . . . . . . . . . . . (360) 705-7800
Safety and Health Manager **Kathy Dawley** . . . . . . . . . . . (360) 705-7808
Eastern Region Administrator **Keith Metcalf** . . . . . . . . . (509) 324-6010
2714 N. Mayfair Street, Spokane, WA 99207-2090
North Central Region Administrator **Dan Sarles** . . . . . . . (509) 667-3001
1551 North Wenatchee Avenue, Wenatchee, WA 98801-1156
P.O. Box 98, Wenatchee, WA 98807-0098
Northwest Region Administrator **Lorena Eng** . . . . . . . . . (206) 440-4706
15700 Dayton Avenue, North, Shoreline, WA 98133-5910
P.O. Box 330310, Seattle, WA 98133-9710
Olympic Region Administrator **Kevin Dayton** . . . . . . . . . (360) 357-2605
P.O. Box 47440, Olympia, WA 98504-7440
South Central Region Administrator **Don Whitehouse** . . . . (509) 577-1620
2809 Rudkin Rd., Union Gap, P.O. Box 12560,
Yakima, WA 98909-2560
Southwest Region Administrator **Don Wagner** . . . . . . . . (360) 905-2001
11018 NE 51st Circle, S-15, Vancouver, WA 98682-6686
P.O. Box 1709, Vancouver, WA 98668-1709

## Environmental and Engineering Programs

Bridges and Structures Engineer **Tom Baker** . . . . . . . . . (360) 705-7207
E-mail: bakert@wsdot.wa.gov
Consultant Services Engineer **Marylou Nebergall** . . . . . . (360) 705-7458
State Construction Engineer **Jeff Carpenter** . . . . . . . . . . (360) 705-7821

State Design Engineer **Pasco Bakotich III** . . . . . . . . . . . (360) 705-7231
E-mail: bakotip@wsdot.wa.gov
State Materials Engineer **(Vacant)** . . . . . . . . . . . . . . . . (360) 709-5401
Environmental Services Director **Megan White** . . . . . . . . (360) 705-7480
E-mail: whitem@wsdot.wa.gov
Research Director **Leni Oman** . . . . . . . . . . . . . . . . . . . (360) 705-7974
E-mail: omanl@wsdot.wa.gov
Real Estate Services Director **Terry Meara** . . . . . . . . . . . (360) 705-7324
Division Services Manager **Laura Sanborn** . . . . . . . . . . . (360) 705-7113
E-mail: sanborl@wsdot.wa.gov

## Strategic Enterprise and Employment Services

Assistant Secretary **Katy Taylor** . . . . . . . . . . . . . . . . . (360) 705-7773
                                                 Fax: (360) 705-6800
Communications Director **Lars Erickson** . . . . . . . . . . . . (360) 705-7075
E-mail: lars.erickson@wsdot.wa.gov     Fax: (360) 705-6800
Enterprise Risk Management Director **John Milton** . . . . . . (360) 704-6363
Government Relations Director **Allison Camden** . . . . . . . . (360) 705-7024
E-mail: camdena@wsdot.wa.gov
Human Resources Director (Acting) **Jeff Pelton** . . . . . . . . (360) 705-7920
Information Technology Director **Grant Rodeheaver** . . . . . (360) 705-7601
E-mail: rodeheg@wsdot.wa.gov

## Washington State Ferries

2901 Third Avenue, Suite 500, Seattle, WA 98121
Tel: (206) 515-3400   Internet: wsdot.wa.gov/ferries

Assistant Secretary **Lynne Griffith** . . . . . . . . . . . . . . . . (206) 515-3401
2911 2nd Avenue, Seattle, WA 98121
Ferry Operations and Construction Deputy Chief
**George Capacci** . . . . . . . . . . . . . . . . . . . . . . . . . (206) 515-3401
Education: US Coast Guard Acad BS; George Washington MPA

## Strategic Planning and Finance

Tel: (360) 705-7151   Fax: (360) 705-6813
Chief Financial Officer **Amy Arnis** . . . . . . . . . . . . . . . . (360) 705-7525
                                                 Fax: (360) 705-6886
Accounting Services Chief **Jennifer Dahl** . . . . . . . . . . . . (360) 705-7337
Budget Services Chief **Doug Vaughn** . . . . . . . . . . . . . . (360) 705-7401
Project Control and Reporting Director **Jay Alexander** . . . . (360) 705-7121
Public and Private Partnerships Director (Interim)
**Tonia Buell** . . . . . . . . . . . . . . . . . . . . . . . . . . . . (360) 705-7039
E-mail: buellt@wsdot.wa.gov
Strategic Planning Division Director **Kerri Woehler** . . . . . . (360) 705-7958
E-mail: woehlek@wsdot.wa.gov
Geographic Services Manager **Alan Smith** . . . . . . . . . . . (360) 596-8925

# Washington Department of Veterans Affairs [WDVA]

1102 Quince Street, SE, Olympia, WA 98504
P.O. Box 41150, Olympia, WA 98504-1150
Tel: (360) 725-2200   TTY: (360) 725-2199   Fax: (360) 725-2197
E-mail: heidia@dva.wa.gov   Internet: www.dva.wa.gov

**Employees:** 700   **Fiscal Year:** 2013-2015   **Budget:** $132,001,000

■ Director **Lourdes E. "Alfie" Alvarado-Ramos** . . . . . . . . . (360) 725-2167
E-mail: alfie@dva.wa.gov
Executive Assistant **Liza Narcisso** . . . . . . . . . . . . . . . . (360) 725-2167
Deputy Director **Gary Condra** . . . . . . . . . . . . . . . . . . . (360) 725-2167
Education: Tennessee BA; Baylor MA
Chief Financial Officer **Erwin Vidallon** . . . . . . . . . . . . . . (360) 725-2200

## Soldiers' Home and Colony

1301 Orting Kapowsin Highway, Orting, WA 98360
P.O. Box 199, Orting, WA 98360
Tel: (360) 893-4500   Fax: (360) 893-4590

Superintendent (Acting) **William "Willy" Slysarski** . . . . . . (360) 893-4501

## Veterans' Home

1141 Beach Drive, Port Orchard, WA 98378
Tel: (360) 895-4700   Fax: (360) 895-4719

Superintendent (Acting) **Dax Dowling** . . . . . . . . . . . . . . (360) 895-4700

---

★ Elected Official    ■ Appointed by Governor    ● Appointed by Legislature    ▲ Appointed by Board or Commission    ◆ Appointed by State Supreme Court

## Office of Financial Management [OFM]

302 Sid Snyder Avenue Southwest, Olympia, WA 98501
P.O. Box 43113, Olympia, WA 98504-3113
Tel: (360) 902-0555  Fax: (360) 664-2832
E-mail: ofm.administration@ofm.wa.gov  Internet: www.ofm.wa.gov

■Director **David Schumacher** . . . . . . . . . . . . . . . . . . . . . . . . . . . (360) 902-0555
  E-mail: david.schumacher@ofm.wa.gov
  Education: U Washington 1986 BA, 1990 BA
  Executive Assistant **Liz Mattos** . . . . . . . . . . . . . . . . . . . . (360) 902-0526
Deputy Director **Tracy Guerin** . . . . . . . . . . . . . . . . . . . . . . . . (360) 902-0545
  Executive Assistant **Pam Phillips** . . . . . . . . . . . . . . . . . . . (360) 902-0536
Budget Division Assistant Director **Jim Crawford** . . . . . . . (360) 902-0565
Forecasting Assistant Director **Marc Baldwin** . . . . . . . . . . (360) 902-0590
  Executive Assistant **Rachel Hughes** . . . . . . . . . . . . . . . . . (360) 902-3092
Communications Assistant Director **Ralph Thomas** . . . . . . (360) 902-7607
  E-mail: ralph.thomas@ofm.wa.gov
Executive Policy Director
  **Matthew M. "Matt" Steuerwalt** . . . . . . . . . . . . . . . . . . (360) 902-0645
  E-mail: matt.steuerwalt@gov.wa.gov
  Executive Assistant **Mary Anderson** . . . . . . . . . . . . . . . . (360) 902-0667
Accounting Assistant Director **Brian Pinney** . . . . . . . . . . . (360) 725-0185
Accounting Assistant **Anwar Wilson** . . . . . . . . . . . . . . . . . (360) 725-0184

## Office of the Chief Information Officer [OCIO]

P.O. Box 43113, Olympia, WA 98504

State Chief Information Officer **Michael Cockrill** . . . . . . . . (360) 902-7325
  E-mail: michael.cockrill@ofm.wa.gov
Executive Assistant **Angela Knight** . . . . . . . . . . . . . . . . . . (360) 902-7310
Deputy Chief Information Officer **Michael DeAngelo** . . . . . (360) 902-0965
  E-mail: michael.deangelo@ofm.wa.gov
Senior Policy Advisor **William "Bill" Schrier** . . . . . . . . . . . (360) 902-3574

## State Human Resources Office

P.O. Box 47500, Olympia, WA 98504-7500
Tel: (360) 407-4105

**Employees: 70**

Assistant Director **Franklin Plaistowe** . . . . . . . . . . . . . . . . (360) 407-4104
  Executive Assistant **Leslie McGuire** . . . . . . . . . . . . . . . . . (360) 407-4105

## Office of Minority and Women's Business Enterprises [OMWBE]

210 11th Avenue Southwest, Suite 401, P.O. Box 41160,
Olympia, WA 98504-1160
Seattle District Office, 2401 Fourth Avenue, Suite 450, Seattle, WA 98121
Tel: (360) 664-9750  Fax: (360) 586-7079  Dist: (206) 553-7356 (Seattle)

■Director **Teresa Berntsen** . . . . . . . . . . . . . . . . . . . . . . . . . . (360) 664-9757
  E-mail: tberntsen@dol.wa.gov
  Executive Assistant **Tammi Hazlitt** . . . . . . . . . . . . . . . . . . (360) 664-9755
Certification and Compliance Assistant Director
  **Sarah Erdmann** . . . . . . . . . . . . . . . . . . . . . . . . . . . . . . . . (360) 664-9771
Communications and External Relations Assistant
  Director **Lawrence Coleman** . . . . . . . . . . . . . . . . . . . . . . (360) 664-9750
Policy Assistant Director **Mark Kifowit** . . . . . . . . . . . . . . . (360) 664-9750

## Recreation and Conservation Office

1111 Washington Street SE, Olympia, WA 98501
P.O. Box 40917, Olympia, WA 98504-0917
Tel: (360) 902-3000  Fax: (360) 902-3026

■Director **Kaleen Cottingham** . . . . . . . . . . . . . . . . . . . . . . . (360) 902-3003
  E-mail: kaleen.cottingham@rco.wa.gov
Deputy Director **Scott Robinson** . . . . . . . . . . . . . . . . . . . . . (360) 902-0207
Communications Manager **Susan Zemek** . . . . . . . . . . . . . . (360) 902-3081
  E-mail: susan.zemek@rco.wa.gov
Executive Assistant **Leslie Frank** . . . . . . . . . . . . . . . . . . . . (360) 902-0220
Administrative Assistant **Rachel LeBaron Anderson** . . . . . (360) 725-3932
Receptionist **Kathleen Barkis** . . . . . . . . . . . . . . . . . . . . . . (360) 902-3000

## Washington State Conservation Commission

300 Desmond Drive, Lacey, WA 98503
P.O. Box 47721, Olympia, WA 98504-7721
Tel: (360) 407-6200  Fax: (360) 407-6215  Internet: www.scc.wa.gov

**Employees: 18  Fiscal Year: 2013-2015  Budget: $16,893,000**

Chair **Lynn Brown** . . . . . . . . . . . . . . . . . . . . . . . . . . . . . . . . (360) 407-6200
Vice Chair **Jim Kropf** . . . . . . . . . . . . . . . . . . . . . . . . . . . . . . (360) 407-6200
  Education: Washington State BS, MS
Commissioner **Lynn Bahrych** . . . . . . . . . . . . . . . . . . . . . . . (360) 407-6200
Commissioner **Perry Beale** . . . . . . . . . . . . . . . . . . . . . . . . . (360) 407-6200
Commissioner **Larry Cochrane** . . . . . . . . . . . . . . . . . . . . . . (360) 407-6200
Commissioner **Mark Craven** . . . . . . . . . . . . . . . . . . . . . . . . (360) 407-6200
Commissioner **Dr. Dean Longrie, PhD** . . . . . . . . . . . . . . . . (360) 407-6200
Commissioner **Kelly Susewind** . . . . . . . . . . . . . . . . . . . . . . (360) 407-6200
Commissioner **Todd Welker** . . . . . . . . . . . . . . . . . . . . . . . . (360) 407-6200
Commissioner **Daryl Williams** . . . . . . . . . . . . . . . . . . . . . . (360) 407-6200

### Commission Staff

Executive Director **Mark A. Clark** . . . . . . . . . . . . . . . . . . . . (360) 407-6201
  E-mail: mark.clark@scc.wa.gov
  Education: Washington State 1978 BS
Director of Policy and Intergovernmental Relations
  **Ron Shultz** . . . . . . . . . . . . . . . . . . . . . . . . . . . . . . . . . . . (360) 407-7507
Fiscal Analyst **Melissa Livingston** . . . . . . . . . . . . . . . . . . . (360) 407-7617
Fiscal Analyst **(Vacant)** . . . . . . . . . . . . . . . . . . . . . . . . . . . (360) 407-6205
Executive Assistant **Lori Gonzalez** . . . . . . . . . . . . . . . . . . . (360) 407-6200
Administrative Assistant **Alicia Johnson** . . . . . . . . . . . . . . (360) 407-6200

## Fish and Wildlife Commission

Tel: (360) 902-2267  Fax: (360) 902-2448
E-mail: commission@dfw.wa.gov

■Chair **Dr. Bradley F. "Brad" Smith** . . . . . . . . . . . . . . . . . . (360) 902-2267
  Term Expires: December 31, 2020
  Education: Western Michigan BA, MA; Michigan PhD
■Vice Chair **Larry Carpenter** . . . . . . . . . . . . . . . . . . . . . . . . (360) 902-2267
  Term Expires: December 31, 2016
■Member **Jay Holzmiller** . . . . . . . . . . . . . . . . . . . . . . . . . . . (360) 902-2267
  Term Expires: December 31, 2019
■Member **Jay Kehne** . . . . . . . . . . . . . . . . . . . . . . . . . . . . . . (360) 902-2267
  Term Expires: December 31, 2016
■Member **Robert "Bob" Kehoe** . . . . . . . . . . . . . . . . . . . . . . (360) 902-2267
  Term Expires: December 31, 2020
■Member **Conrad Mahnken** . . . . . . . . . . . . . . . . . . . . . . . . (360) 902-2267
  Term Expires: December 31, 2016
■Member **Miranda Wecker** . . . . . . . . . . . . . . . . . . . . . . . . . (360) 902-2267
  Term Expires: December 31, 2018
Executive Assistant **Tami Lininger** . . . . . . . . . . . . . . . . . . . (360) 902-2267

## Washington Fish and Wildlife Department [WDFW]

600 Capitol Way, North, Olympia, WA 98501-1091
Tel: (360) 902-2200  TTY: (360) 902-2207  Fax: (360) 902-2947
Internet: http://wdfw.wa.gov

**Employees: 1,729  Fiscal Year: 2013-2015  Budget: $370,237,000**

▲Director **James "Jim" Unsworth** . . . . . . . . . . . . . . . . . . . (360) 902-2720
  Education: Idaho BS; Montana State MS; Idaho DF
Deputy Director **Joseph "Joe" Stohr** . . . . . . . . . . . . . . . . (360) 902-2650
Public Affairs Director **Bruce Botka** . . . . . . . . . . . . . . . . . (360) 902-2262
  E-mail: bruce.botka@dfw.wa.gov
Enforcement Assistant Chief **Steven Crown** . . . . . . . . . . . (360) 902-2373
Financial Services Assistant Director **David Giglio** . . . . . . . (360) 902-8128
Fish Program Assistant Director **Jim Scott** . . . . . . . . . . . . (360) 902-2736
Habitat Program Assistant Director **Lisa Veneroso** . . . . . . . (360) 902-2836
Wildlife Management Assistant Director
  **Nathan Pamplin** . . . . . . . . . . . . . . . . . . . . . . . . . . . . . . . (360) 902-2693
Legal Services Senior Assistant Attorney General
  **Joe Shorin** . . . . . . . . . . . . . . . . . . . . . . . . . . . . . . . . . . . (360) 753-2496
Region 1 (Eastern Region) Director **Steve Pozzanghera** . . (509) 892-7852
  2315 North Discovery Place, Spokane, WA 99216-1566

*(continued on next page)*

---

★ Elected Official  ■ Appointed by Governor  ● Appointed by Legislature  ▲ Appointed by Board or Commission  ◆ Appointed by State Supreme Court

---

EXECUTIVE BRANCH

**Washington Fish and Wildlife Department** *continued*

Region 2 (North Central Region) Director
**James S. Brown** . . . . . . . . . . . . . . . . . . . . (509) 754-4624 ext. 219
1550 Alder St., NW, Ephrata, WA 98823-9699

Region 3 (South Central Region) Director
**Michael "Mike" Livingston** . . . . . . . . . . . . . . . . . . . (509) 454-2201
1701 S. 24th Ave., Yakima, WA 98902-5720

Region 4 (North Puget Sound Region) Director
**Bob Everitt** . . . . . . . . . . . . . . . . . . . (425) 775-1311 ext. 118
16018 Mill Creek Blvd., Mill Creek, WA 98012-1296

Region 5 (Southwest Region) Director
**Guy Norman** . . . . . . . . . . . . . . . . . . . (360) 696-6211 ext. 6704
2108 Grand Blvd., Vancouver, WA 98663-1299

Region 6 (Coastal Region) Director
**Michele Culver** . . . . . . . . . . . . . . . . . (360) 249-4628 ext. 1211
48 Devonshire Road, Montesano, WA 98563

## Washington State Gambling Commission [WSGC]

P.O. Box 42400, Olympia, WA 98504-2400
Tel: (360) 486-3440  Tel: (800) 345-2529  TTY: (360) 486-3637
Fax: (360) 486-3623  Fax: (360) 486-3629
E-mail: publicaffairs@wsgc.wa.gov  Internet: www.wsgc.wa.gov

**Employees: 139**

■Chair **Chris Stearns** . . . . . . . . . . . . . . . . . . . (360) 486-3453
Term Expires: June 30, 2021

■Vice Chair **Bud Sizemore** . . . . . . . . . . . . . . . . (360) 486-3453
Term Expires: June 30, 2020

■Commissioner **Kelsey Gray** . . . . . . . . . . . . . . . (360) 486-3453
Term Expires: June 30, 2017

■Commissioner **Julia Patterson** . . . . . . . . . . . . . (360) 486-3453
Education: Washington State BS; U Washington BA

■Commissioner **Edward C. Troyer** . . . . . . . . . . . . (360) 486-3453
Term Expires: June 30, 2020

■Commissioner **(Vacant)** . . . . . . . . . . . . . . . . . . (360) 486-3453

Ex-Officio **Bruce Chandler** . . . . . . . . . . . . . . . . . (360) 486-3453
Affiliation: Representative (District 15), Washington House of
Representatives
P.O. Box 40600, Olympia, WA 98504-0600

Ex-Officio **Steve Conway** . . . . . . . . . . . . . . . . . . (360) 486-3453
Affiliation: Senator (District 29), Washington State Senate
P. O. Box 40429, Olympia, WA 98504
Education: Portland 1966 BS; Oregon 1969 MS, 1979 PhD

Ex-Officio **Mike Hewitt** . . . . . . . . . . . . . . . . . . . (360) 486-3453
Affiliation: Senator (District 16), Washington State Senate
P. O. Box 40416, Olympia, WA 98504

Ex-Officio **Christopher Hurst** . . . . . . . . . . . . . . . (360) 486-3453
Affiliation: Representative (District 31), Washington House of
Representatives
John L. O'Brien Building, Room 320, Olympia, WA 98504

▲Director **David "Dave" Trujillo** . . . . . . . . . . . . . (360) 486-3446
E-mail: dave.trujillo@wsgc.wa.gov

Executive Assistant (Acting) **Michelle Rancour** . . . . . . . . (360) 486-3623

Deputy Director **Amy Hunter** . . . . . . . . . . . . . . . . (360) 486-3463
Education: Kansas State BA; Seattle JD

Field Operations Assistant Director **Mark Harris** . . . . . . . . (360) 486-3579

Licensing Operations Assistant Director (Acting)
**Tina Griffin** . . . . . . . . . . . . . . . . . . . . . . . . . (360) 486-3546

Tribal and Technical Gaming Unit Assistant Director
**Julie Lies** . . . . . . . . . . . . . . . . . . . . . . . . . (360) 486-3586
Fax: (360) 486-3634

Business Operations Division Administrator
**Judy Pittelkau** . . . . . . . . . . . . . . . . . . . . . . (360) 486-3449
Fax: (360) 486-3628

Communications and Legal Division Administrator
**(Vacant)** . . . . . . . . . . . . . . . . . . . . . . . . . . (360) 486-3440

Human Resources and Training Administrator
**Lisa Benavidez** . . . . . . . . . . . . . . . . . . . . . . (360) 486-3456
Fax: (360) 486-3624

Information Technology Administrator **Tom Means** . . . . . . (360) 486-3480
E-mail: tom.means@wsgc.wa.gov  Fax: (360) 486-3627

## Washington Horse Racing Commission [WHRC]

6326 Martin Way, Suite 209, Olympia, WA 98516-5578
Tel: (360) 459-6462  Fax: (360) 459-6461  E-mail: whrc@whrc.state.wa.us
Internet: www.whrc.wa.gov

**Employees:** 10  **Fiscal Year:** 2013-2015  **Budget:** $5,540,000

■Chair **Jeff Colliton** . . . . . . . . . . . . . . . . . . . . (360) 459-6462
▲Executive Secretary **Douglas L. Moore** . . . . . . . . . . (360) 459-6462

## Housing Finance Commission

1000 Second Avenue, Suite 2700, Seattle, WA 98104-1046
Tel: (206) 464-7139  Tel: (800) 767-4663 (In State)  Fax: (206) 587-5113
E-mail: askus@wshfc.org  Internet: www.wshfc.org

■Chair **Karen Miller** . . . . . . . . . . . . . . . . . . . . (206) 464-7139
■Member **Beth Baum** . . . . . . . . . . . . . . . . . . . (206) 464-7139
Member **Brian N. Bonlender** . . . . . . . . . . . . . . . (206) 464-7139
■Member **Ellen Evans** . . . . . . . . . . . . . . . . . . . (206) 464-7139
■Member **Diane Klontz** . . . . . . . . . . . . . . . . . . (206) 464-7139
■Member **Ken A. Larsen** . . . . . . . . . . . . . . . . . . (206) 464-7139
■Member **Wendy L. Lawrence** . . . . . . . . . . . . . . (206) 464-7139
■Member **Steven Moss** . . . . . . . . . . . . . . . . . . (206) 464-7139
■Member **Randy Robinson** . . . . . . . . . . . . . . . . (206) 464-7139
Education: Whitman BA
■Member **Gabe Spencer** . . . . . . . . . . . . . . . . . . (206) 464-7139
■Member **Pam Tietz** . . . . . . . . . . . . . . . . . . . (206) 464-7139
■Member **(Vacant)** . . . . . . . . . . . . . . . . . . . . (206) 464-7139
■Ex-Officio Member **James Leonard "Jim" McIntire** . . . . (206) 464-7139
Education: Macalester 1976 BA; Michigan 1978 MPP;
U Washington 1993 PhD

## Executive Management

▲Executive Director **Kim Herman** . . . . . . . . . . . . . (206) 287-4419
E-mail: kim.herman@wshfc.org
Education: Washington State 1967 BA

Deputy Director **Paul Edwards** . . . . . . . . . . . . . . (206) 287-4462

Finance and Information Technology Director
**Robert Cook** . . . . . . . . . . . . . . . . . . . . . . . (206) 287-4432
E-mail: askusfin@wshfc.org
Education: Missouri 1978 BSBA; Northern Illinois 1990 MBA

Homeownership Director **Lisa DeBrock** . . . . . . . . . . (206) 287-4414

Asset Management and Compliance Director
**Paul Fitzgerald** . . . . . . . . . . . . . . . . . . . . . (206) 464-7139

Multifamily Housing and Community Director
**Lisa Vatske** . . . . . . . . . . . . . . . . . . . . . . . (206) 287-4467

## Washington State Human Rights Commission [WSHRC]

711 South Capitol Way, Suite 402, Olympia, WA 98504-2490
P.O. Box 42490, Olympia, WA 98504-2490
Tel: (360) 753-6770  Tel: (800) 233-3247  TTY: (800) 300-7525
Fax: (360) 586-2282  Internet: www.hum.wa.gov

**Employees:** 26  **Fiscal Year:** 2013-2015  **Budget:** $6,286,000

■Commission Chair **Charlene Strong** . . . . . . . . . . . (360) 753-6770
Term Expires: June 2017

■Commissioner **Clarence Henderson** . . . . . . . . . . . (360) 753-6770
Term Expires: June 2017
Education: Norfolk State 1999 BA; Regent U 2004 JD

■Commissioner **Skylee Sahlstrom** . . . . . . . . . . . . (360) 753-6770
■Commissioner **Lenore Three Stars** . . . . . . . . . . . (360) 753-6770
Term Expires: June 2018

▲Executive Director **Sharon Ortiz** . . . . . . . . . . . . (360) 753-2558
E-mail: sharon.ortiz@hum.wa.gov

Commission Clerk **Laura Skinner** . . . . . . . . . . . . (360) 753-4876 ext. 108
E-mail: lskinner@hum.wa.gov

---

★ Elected Official     ■Appointed by Governor     ●Appointed by Legislature     ▲ Appointed by Board or Commission     ◆ Appointed by State Supreme Court

EXECUTIVE BRANCH

## State Parks and Recreation Commission

1111 Israel Road, Olympia, WA 98504-2650
P.O. Box 42650, Olympia, WA 98504-2650
Tel: (360) 902-8500 Fax: (360) 753-1594 E-mail: infocent@parks.wa.gov
Internet: www.parks.wa.gov

**Employees:** 582 **Fiscal Year:** 2013-2015 **Budget:** $127,252,000

▲ Director **Don Hoch** ................................. (360) 902-8501
  E-mail: don.hoch@parks.wa.gov
Administration, Finance and Technology Director
  **Shelly Hagen** ...................................... (360) 902-8500
  E-mail: shelly.hagen@parks.wa.gov
Human Resources Director **Becky Daniels** .............. (360) 902-8500
Planning and Development Assistant Director
  **Peter Herzog** ...................................... (360) 902-8642
  E-mail: peter.herzog@parks.wa.gov
Parks Operations Assistant Director **Mike Sternback** ..... (360) 902-8660
  E-mail: mike.sternback@parks.wa.gov
Public Affairs Director **Virginia Painter** ................ (360) 902-8562
  E-mail: virginia.painter@parks.wa.gov
Public Affairs Specialist **Linda Bernett** ................ (360) 902-8561
  E-mail: linda.burnett@parks.wa.gov
Health and Safety Program Manager **Greg Yi** ........... (360) 902-8558
  E-mail: greg.yi@parks.wa.gov

## Traffic Safety Commission

621 8th Avenue, SE, Suite 409, Olympia, WA 98501
P.O. Box 40944, Olympia, WA 98504-0944
Tel: (360) 753-6197 Fax: (360) 586-6489 E-mail: sysop@wtsc.wa.gov
Internet: www.wtsc.wa.gov

Director **Darrin Grondel** ............................. (360) 725-9899
  E-mail: dgrondel@wtsc.wa.gov

## Washington Utilities and Transportation Commission [UTC]

1300 South Evergreen Park Drive, SW, Olympia, WA 98504-7250
P.O. Box 47250, Olympia, WA 98504-7250
Tel: (360) 664-1160 TTY: (360) 586-8203 Fax: (360) 586-1150
E-mail: info@utc.wa.gov

**Employees:** 140 **Fiscal Year:** 2013-2015 **Budget:** $46,196,000

Chairman **David W. "Dave" Danner** ................. (360) 664-1173
  E-mail: ddanner@utc.wa.gov
Commissioner **Philip B. Jones** ...................... (360) 664-1169
  E-mail: pjones@utc.wa.gov
Commissioner **Ann Rendahl** ......................... (360) 664-1171
  E-mail: arendahl@utc.wa.gov

## Health Care Authority [HCA]

626 Eighth Avenue Southeast, Olympia, WA 98501
P.O. Box 45502, Olympia, WA 98504-5502
Tel: (360) 725-1040 Internet: www.hca.wa.gov

**Employees:** 1,004 **Fiscal Year:** 2013-2015 **Budget:** $11,489,455,000

■ Director **Dorothy Frost Teeter** ..................... (360) 725-1040
  E-mail: dorothy.teeter@hca.wa.gov
Executive Secretary **Tamarra Paradee** ............... (360) 725-1040
Chief Medical Officer **Dr. Daniel Lesser** ............. (360) 725-1612
Deputy Chief Medical Officer **Charissa Fotinos, MD** ..... (360) 725-9822
Policy, Planning, and Performance Director
  **Nathan Johnson** ................................. (360) 725-0857
Chief Communication Officer **Amy Plondin** ........... (360) 725-1915
  E-mail: amy.plondin@hca.wa.gov
Chief Data Officer **(Vacant)** ........................ (360) 725-1146
Chief Financial Officer **Thuy Hua-Ly** ................ (360) 725-1855
Chief Information Officer **Adam Aaseby** ............. (360) 725-1241
  E-mail: adam.aaseby@hca.wa.gov
Chief Operations Officer **Susan Lucas** ............... (360) 725-1703
Deputy State HIT Coordinator **Melodie Olsen** ......... (360) 725-1983
Children's Health Insurance Program (CHIP) Director
  **Mary Wood** ..................................... (360) 725-1416
  E-mail: mary.wood@hca.wa.gov

Eligibility Policy and Service Delivery Director
  **Mary Wood** ..................................... (360) 725-1416
  E-mail: mary.wood@hca.wa.gov
Healthcare Services Director **Preston W. Cody** ......... (360) 725-1786
Human Resources Director **Jody Costello** ............. (360) 725-1937
Medicaid Director **MaryAnne Lindeblad** .............. (360) 725-1550
  E-mail: maryanne.lindeblad@hca.wa.gov
  Education: Eastern Washington BSN; U Washington MSPH
Program and Payment Integrity Director **Cathie Ott** ...... (360) 725-2116
Legal and Administrative Services Director
  **Annette Schuffenhauer** .......................... (360) 725-1254
  E-mail: annette.schuffenhauer@hca.wa.gov
Public Employee Benefits Board Program Director
  **Lou McDermott** ................................. (360) 725-0891
Public Employee Benefits Board Program Deputy
  Division Director **Mary Fliss** ..................... (360) 725-0822
Prescription Drug Program Manager **Duane Thurman** .... (206) 521-2036
Office of Legislative Affairs and Analysis Administrator
  **Dennis Martin** .................................. (360) 725-9808
  E-mail: dennis.martin@hca.wa.gov
Office of Tribal Affairs Administrator **Jessie Dean** ....... (360) 725-1649

## Washington Student Achievement Council [WSAC]

917 Lakeridge Way SW, Olympia, WA 98502
P.O. Box 43430, Olympia, WA 98504-3430
Tel: (360) 753-7800 Fax: (360) 753-7808 E-mail: info@hecb.wa.gov

■ Member **Marty Brown** .............................. (360) 753-7800
  Education: Iowa 1974 BGS; Puget Sound Col 1979 JD
■ Member **Jeffrey "Jeff" Charbonneau, NBCT** .......... (360) 753-7800
■ Member **Maud Daudon** ............................. (360) 753-7800
■ Member **Paul Francis** .............................. (360) 753-7800
■ Member **Ray Lawton** ............................... (360) 753-7800
■ Member **Karen Lee** ................................ (360) 753-7800
■ Member **Dr. Gil Mendoza** .......................... (360) 753-7800
  E-mail: gil.mendoza@k12.wa.us
■ Member **Rai Nauman Mumtaz** ...................... (360) 753-7800
  Education: U Washington BA, BS
■ Member **Susana Reyes** ............................. (360) 753-7800

### Executive Staff

Executive Director **Gene Sharrat** .................... (360) 753-7810
  Education: Washington State BA; Pacific Lutheran MA;
  Washington State PhD
Executive Secretary **Kristin Ritter** .................. (360) 753-7810
Academic Affairs Director **Randy Spaulding** ........... (360) 753-7823
Guaranteed Education Tuition Director **Betty Lochner** .... (360) 753-7871
Policy Planning and Research Associate Director
  **Jim West** ....................................... (360) 753-7890
Public Relations and Communications Director
  **Aaron Wyatt** .................................... (360) 704-4169
  E-mail: aaronw@wsac.wa.gov
Student Financial Assistance Associate Director
  **Jeffrey Powell** .................................. (360) 704-4150

## Washington State Investment Board [WSIB]

2100 Evergreen Park Drive, SW, Suite 100, Olympia, WA 98504-0916
P.O. Box 40916, Olympia, WA 98504-0916
Tel: (360) 956-4600 Fax: (360) 956-4785 E-mail: recep@sib.wa.gov
Internet: www.sib.wa.gov

▲ Executive Director **Theresa Whitmarsh** ............... (360) 956-4710
  E-mail: twhitmarsh@sib.wa.gov
  Education: Seattle Pacific 1978 BA; Pacific Lutheran 2000 MBA
Executive Assistant **Kristi Haines** .................. (360) 956-4612
Institutional Relations Director **Liz Mendizabal** ......... (360) 956-4616
  Education: Evergreen State 1974 BA
Chief Investment Officer **Gary Bruebaker, CFA** ......... (360) 956-4620
  Education: Oregon State 1978 BS; Oregon 1997 MBA
Chief Operating Officer **Victor A. Moore** ............. (360) 956-4713

---

★ Elected Official   ■ Appointed by Governor   ● Appointed by Legislature   ▲ Appointed by Board or Commission   ◆ Appointed by State Supreme Court

EXECUTIVE BRANCH

# Washington State Liquor Control Board [WSLCB]

3000 Pacific Avenue, SE, Olympia, WA 98504
P.O. Box 43075, Olympia, WA 98504-3075
Tel: (360) 664-1600  TTY: (360) 586-4727  Fax: (360) 664-9689
E-mail: wslcb@liq.wa.gov  Internet: www.liq.wa.gov

**Employees:** 267

■ Chair **Jane Rushford** . . . . . . . . . . . . . . . . . . . . . . . . . (360) 664-1600
  Term Expires: January 15, 2021          Fax: (360) 586-3190
■ Board Member **Russell D. "Russ" Hauge** . . . . . . . . . . . . (360) 664-1713
  Term Expires: January 15, 2017
  Education: U Washington 1980 BA; Oregon 1983 JD
■ Board Member **Ruthann Kurose** . . . . . . . . . . . . . . . . . . (360) 664-1715
  Term Expires: January 15, 2018
■ Board Member **(Vacant)** . . . . . . . . . . . . . . . . . . . . . . . (360) 664-1713
  Director **Rick J. Garza** . . . . . . . . . . . . . . . . . . . . . . . (360) 664-1703
    E-mail: rjg@liq.wa.gov
  Deputy Director **Rand Simmons** . . . . . . . . . . . . . . . . . (360) 664-1650
    E-mail: rls@liq.wa.gov
  Communications Director **Brian Smith** . . . . . . . . . . . . . (360) 664-1774
    E-mail: besmi@liq.wa.gov
  Enforcement and Education Division Chief
    **Justin Nordhorn** . . . . . . . . . . . . . . . . . . . . . . . . . (360) 664-1726
    E-mail: jtn@liq.wa.gov
  Financial Services Director **Michael Kashmar** . . . . . . . . . . (360) 664-1671
  Human Resources Director **Clarice Nnanabu** . . . . . . . . . . (360) 664-1642
  Chief Information Officer **Heidi Geathers** . . . . . . . . . . . . (360) 664-1696
    E-mail: heg@liq.wa.gov

# Board of Tax Appeals [BTA]

910 Fifth Avenue SE, Olympia, WA 98504
P.O. Box 40915, Olympia, WA 98504-0915
Tel: (360) 753-5446  Tel: (866) 788-5446  TTY: (360) 753-5446
Fax: (360) 586-9020  E-mail: bta@bta.state.wa.us

**Employees:** 11  **Fiscal Year:** 2013-2015  **Budget:** $2,407,000

■ Chairman **Marta B. Powell** . . . . . . . . . . . . . . . . . . . . . (360) 753-5446
  Education: Agnes Scott 1974 BA; North Carolina 1978 MA;
  Columbia 1981 PhD; U Washington 1995 JD
■ Vice Chairman **Mark J. Maxwell** . . . . . . . . . . . . . . . . . (360) 753-5446
  Education: Washington State MBA
■ Member **Carol A. Lien** . . . . . . . . . . . . . . . . . . . . . . . . (360) 753-5446
  Education: Washington State BA

## Executive Staff

▲ Executive Director **Kate Adams** . . . . . . . . . . . . . . . . . (360) 586-4909
  E-mail: kadams@bta.state.wa.us
  Clerk of the Board **Marilyn R. First** . . . . . . . . . . . . . . . (360) 753-5446

# Workforce Training and Education Coordinating Board

P.O. Box 43105, Olympia, WA 98504-3105
Tel: (360) 709-4600  Fax: (360) 586-5862  E-mail: workforce@wtb.wa.gov
Internet: www.wtb.wa.gov

**Employees:** 25  **Fiscal Year:** 2013-2015  **Budget:** $59,503,000

■ Executive Director **Eleni Papadakis** . . . . . . . . . . . . . . . (360) 709-4600
  E-mail: eleni.papadakis@wtb.wa.gov
  Deputy Director **Dave Pavelchek** . . . . . . . . . . . . . . . . . (360) 709-4600
  Executive Assistant **Erica Hansen** . . . . . . . . . . . . . . . . (360) 709-4608
  Operations Manager **Patrick Woods** . . . . . . . . . . . . . . . (360) 709-4622

# Washington State Patrol

P.O. Box 42600, Olympia, WA 98504-2600
TTY: (800) 888-8384  Fax: (360) 753-2492
E-mail: webmaster@wsp.wa.gov

Chief **John R. Batiste** . . . . . . . . . . . . . . . . . . . . . . . . (360) 753-6540
  Education: City U (WA) BS
Deputy Chief **Curt Hattell** . . . . . . . . . . . . . . . . . . . . . (360) 753-6540

# Office of the State Fire Marshal

P.O. Box 42600, Olympia, WA 98504-2600
Tel: (360) 596-3900  Fax: (360) 596-3939  E-mail: firemarsh@wsp.wa.gov
State Fire Marshal **Charles M. Duffy** . . . . . . . . . . . . . . . (360) 596-3902
Prevention Division Assistant State Fire Marshal
  **Chuck LeBlanc** . . . . . . . . . . . . . . . . . . . . . . . . . . (360) 596-3903
  E-mail: charles.leblanc@wsp.wa.gov
Fire Training Academy Administrator **Lt. Dan Atchison** . . . (425) 453-3000

# Washington State Lottery

814 East Fourth Avenue, Olympia, WA 98506
P.O. Box 43000, Olympia, WA 98504-3000
Tel: (360) 664-4720  TTY: (360) 586-0933  Fax: (360) 586-1039
E-mail: director's_office@walottery.com  Internet: www.walottery.com

**Employees:** 180

■ Chair **Valoria Loveland** . . . . . . . . . . . . . . . . . . . . . . . (360) 664-4800
  E-mail: vloveland@walottery.com
■ Commissioner **Peter Bogdanoff** . . . . . . . . . . . . . . . . . (360) 664-4800
  E-mail: pbogdanoff@walottery.com
■ Commissioner **Fred Finn** . . . . . . . . . . . . . . . . . . . . . . (360) 664-4800
  E-mail: ffinn@walottery.com
■ Commissioner **Judy Guenther** . . . . . . . . . . . . . . . . . . (360) 664-4800
  E-mail: jguenther@walottery.com
■ Director **Harold William "Bill" Hanson** . . . . . . . . . . . . (360) 664-4800
  E-mail: bhanson@walottery.com
  Deputy Director **Jim Warick** . . . . . . . . . . . . . . . . . . . (360) 664-4807
  Finance and Administration Director **Beckie Foster** . . . . . . (360) 664-4798
    E-mail: bfoster@walottery.com          Fax: (360) 586-6586
  Human Resources Director **Debbie Robinson** . . . . . . . . . (360) 664-4814
                                          Fax: (360) 664-4817
  Information Services Director **Crystal Fischer** . . . . . . . . . (360) 664-4720
    E-mail: cfischer@walottery.com
  Legal Services Director **Jana Jones** . . . . . . . . . . . . . . . (360) 664-4833
                                          Fax: (360) 664-2630
  Sales and Marketing Director **Kurt Geisreiter** . . . . . . . . . (360) 664-4735
                                          Fax: (360) 586-2234
    Assistant Marketing Director **Randy Warick** . . . . . . . . . (360) 664-4730
                                          Fax: (360) 586-2234
  Security Director **Len Brudvik** . . . . . . . . . . . . . . . . . . (360) 664-4742
                                          Fax: (360) 753-2467
  Research and Development Manager **Stephen Wade** . . . . . (360) 664-4803

# Office of Privacy and Data Protection

Tel: (360) 902-0555

Chief Privacy Officer **Alexander D. "Alex" Alben** . . . . . . . (360) 902-0965
  E-mail: alex.alben@ocio.wa.gov
  Education: Stanford 1980 AB, 1984 JD

# Office of the Lieutenant Governor

220 Legislative Building, 416 Sid Snyder Avenue, SW,
Olympia, WA 98504
P.O. Box 40400, Olympia, WA 98504-0400
Tel: (360) 786-7700  Fax: (360) 786-7749  E-mail: ltgov@leg.wa.gov
Internet: www.ltgov.wa.gov

**Employees:** 7  **Fiscal Year:** 2013-2015  **Budget:** $1,408,000

★ Lieutenant Governor **Bradley Scott "Brad" Owen** (D) . . . (360) 786-7700
  Term Expires: January 2017
  E-mail: brad.owen@leg.wa.gov
  Education: Walla Walla Col LittD
  Career: State Representative Bradley Owen (D-WA), Washington House
  of Representatives (1976-1979); State Senator Bradley Owen (D-WA),
  Washington House of Representatives (1983-1986)
  Office Director **Ken Camp** . . . . . . . . . . . . . . . . . . . . . (360) 786-7714
    Education: USC 1998 BA
  Communications Director **Brian Dirks** . . . . . . . . . . . . . . (360) 786-7707
    E-mail: brian.dirks@leg.wa.gov
    Education: Washington State BA
  International Relations/Economic Development Director
    **Brent Pendleton** . . . . . . . . . . . . . . . . . . . . . . . . . (360) 786-7786
  Executive Assistant **Blaire Stewart** . . . . . . . . . . . . . . . (360) 786-7746
  Administrative Assistant **Jennifer Way** . . . . . . . . . . . . . (360) 786-7700

---

★ Elected Official  ■ Appointed by Governor  ● Appointed by Legislature  ▲ Appointed by Board or Commission  ◆ Appointed by State Supreme Court

# Office of the Secretary of State

416 Sid Snyder Avenue, SW, Olympia, WA 98504
PO Box 40220, Olympia, WA 98504-0220
Tel: (360) 902-4151 Tel: (360) 725-0377 (Corporations Information)
TTY: (800) 422-8683 Fax: (360) 586-5629 E-mail: mail@sos.wa.gov

**Employees:** 234 **Fiscal Year:** 2013-2015 **Budget:** $64,923,000

★Secretary of State **Kim Wyman, CERA** (R) . . . . . . . . . . . . (360) 902-4499
  Term Expires: January 2017
  Education: Cal State (Long Beach) 1995 BS; Troy State 1990 MPA
  Career: County Auditor, Office of the County Auditor, County of
  Thurston, Washington (2001-2013)
Assistant Secretary of State **Mark Neary** . . . . . . . . . . . . . . (360) 902-4186
Deputy Secretary of State **Greg Lane** . . . . . . . . . . . . . (360) 902-4151
Communications Director **David "Dave" Ammons** . . . . . . .(360) 902-4140
  E-mail: dave.ammons@sos.wa.gov
Deputy Communications Director **Brian Zylstra** . . . . . . . . (360) 902-4173
  E-mail: brian.zylstra@sos.wa.gov
Director of Legislative Policy and Governmental
  Relations **Katie Blinn**. . . . . . . . . . . . . . . . . . . . . . . . .(360) 902-4168
  E-mail: katie.blinn@sos.wa.gov
State Archivist **Steve Excell** . . . . . . . . . . . . . . . . . . . . . (360) 586-2664
Corporations/Charities Division Director **Pam Floyd** . . . . . .(360) 725-0310
Corporations/Charities Deputy Director **Dan Speigle** . . . . .(360) 725-0311
State Elections Director **Lori Augino**. . . . . . . . . . . . . . . .(360) 725-5771
  Deputy Director of Elections **Allyson Ruppenthal**. . . . . .(360) 725-5781
State Librarian **Rand Simmons**. . . . . . . . . . . . . . . . . . . . .(360) 570-5585
Assistant for Facilities and Protocol **Patrick McDonald**. . . .(360) 902-4148
Special Programs Director **Stephanie Horn** . . . . . . . . . . . .(360) 902-4193

# Office of the Attorney General

1125 Washington Street, SE, Olympia, WA 98504
P.O. Box 40100, Olympia, WA 98504-0100
Tel: (360) 753-6200 TTY: (800) 276-9883 Fax: (360) 664-0228
E-mail: emailago@atg.wa.gov

★Attorney General **Robert W. "Bob" Ferguson** (D) . . . . . .(360) 753-6200
  Term Expires: January 2017
  Education: U Washington 1989 BA; NYU 1995 JD
  Career: Executive Director, King County Democrats (1991-1992);
  Litigation Associate, Preston Gates & Ellis LLP; Council Member,
  Office of the Metropolitan County Council, County of King,
  Washington (2004-2013)
Deputy Chief of Staff **Mamie Marcuss** . . . . . . . . . . . . . . (360) 586-0729
Chief Deputy Attorney General **David M. Horn** . . . . . . . . .(360) 664-2476
  Education: Whitman 1980 BA; Harvard 1983 JD
Deputy Attorney General **Christina Beusch**. . . . . . . . . . . .(360) 586-3801
Deputy Attorney General **Rob Costello** . . . . . . . . . . . . . . (360) 664-2961
Deputy Attorney General **Paige Deitrich** . . . . . . . . . . . . . (206) 464-6293
Deputy Attorney General **Darwin Roberts**. . . . . . . . . . . . .(206) 389-3881
Deputy Attorney General **Erica Uhl**. . . . . . . . . . . . . . . . . (360) 586-2563
Solicitor General **Noah Guzzo Purcell** . . . . . . . . . . . . . . .(360) 753-6200
  Education: U Washington; Harvard 2007 JD
Communications Director **Peter Lavallee** . . . . . . . . . . . . . (360) 586-0725
  E-mail: peterl@atg.wa.gov

# Office of the State Treasurer

416 Sid Snyder Avenue, SW, Olympia, WA 98504
P.O. Box 40200, Olympia, WA 98504-0200
Tel: (360) 902-9000 Fax: (360) 902-9037 E-mail: watreas@tre.wa.gov
Internet: www.tre.wa.gov

**Employees:** 64 **Fiscal Year:** 2013-2015 **Budget:** $15,525,000

★State Treasurer **James Leonard "Jim" McIntire** (D) . . . . .(360) 902-9001
  Term Expires: January 2017
  E-mail: james.mcintire@tre.wa.gov
  Executive Assistant **Andrew Smith** . . . . . . . . . . . . . . . .(360) 902-9023
Assistant State Treasurer **Wolfgang Opitz** . . . . . . . . . . . .(360) 902-9002
Debt Management Deputy Treasurer **Ellen Evans** . . . . . . .(360) 902-9007
                                      Fax: (360) 902-9045
Investments Deputy Treasurer **Doug Extine** . . . . . . . . . . .(360) 902-9012
                                      Fax: (360) 902-9044
Operations Deputy Treasurer **Shad Pruitt**. . . . . . . . . . . . .(360) 902-8904
Accounting Services Director **Megan Dietz** . . . . . . . . . . . .(360) 902-8903

Budget and Fiscal Director **Dan Mason** . . . . . . . . . . . . . . (360) 902-9000
                                      Fax: (360) 902-9045
Cash Management Director **Sue Penley** . . . . . . . . . . . . . . (360) 902-8914
Communications Director **Andrew Smith** . . . . . . . . . . . . . (360) 902-9023
  E-mail: andrew.smith@tre.wa.gov
Community and External Affairs Director **Regina Stark** . . .(360) 902-9003

# Office of the State Auditor

302 Sid Snyder Avenue SW, Olympia, WA 98504
P.O. Box 40021, Olympia, WA 98504
Tel: (360) 902-0370 Fax: (360) 753-0646

**Employees:** 380 **Fiscal Year:** 2015-2017 **Budget:** $61,156,000

★State Auditor **Troy Kelley** (D) . . . . . . . . . . . . . . . . . . . . (360) 902-0370
  Term Expires: January 2017
  Career: State Representative (D-WA, District 28), Washington House of
  Representatives (2007-2013)
Deputy State Auditor **Jan Jutte, CPA, CGFM** . . . . . . . . . . (360) 902-0360
Chief of Staff **(Vacant)** . . . . . . . . . . . . . . . . . . . . . . . . . .(360) 902-0900

# Office of Superintendent of Public Instruction [OSPI]

600 Washington Street, SE, Olympia, WA 98504
P.O. Box 47200, Olympia, WA 98504-7200
Tel: (360) 725-6000 TTY: (360) 664-3631 Fax: (360) 753-6712
Internet: www.k12.wa.us

★State Superintendent of Public Instruction
  **Randolf "Randy" Dorn** (D). . . . . . . . . . . . . . . . . . . . .(360) 725-6000
  Term Expires: January 2017
  Administrative Assistant **Karen Conway** . . . . . . . . . . . .(360) 725-6000
  Executive Assistant **Roni Pettit**. . . . . . . . . . . . . . . . . .(360) 725-6000

# Office of the Chief of Staff

Fax: (360) 753-6712

Chief of Staff **Ken Kanikeberg** . . . . . . . . . . . . . . . . . . . .(360) 725-6115
Agency Support Manager **Dodie Richter** . . . . . . . . . . . . . (360) 725-6194
  E-mail: dodie.richter@k12.wa.us        Fax: (360) 664-0372

# Communications

Communications Media Manager **Nathan Olson** . . . . . . . . .(360) 725-6015
Communication Specialist **Kristen Jaudon** . . . . . . . . . . . .(360) 725-6032
  E-mail: kristen.jaudon@k12.wa.us

# K-12 Education

Deputy Superintendent **Gil Mandoza** . . . . . . . . . . . . . . . .(360) 725-6343

# State Board of Education

Old Capitol Building, 600 SE Washington Street, Room 253,
Olympia, WA 98504
P.O. Box 47206, Olympia, WA 98504-7206
Tel: (360) 725-6025 Fax: (360) 586-2357 E-mail: sbe@k12.wa.us
Internet: www.sbe.wa.gov

■Chair **Isabel Munoz-Colon** . . . . . . . . . . . . . . . . . . . . . .(360) 725-6025
  Term Expires: January 30, 2018
■Member **Janis Avery** . . . . . . . . . . . . . . . . . . . . . . . . . .(360) 725-6025
  Term Expires: January 30, 2019
■Member **Mona H. Bailey** . . . . . . . . . . . . . . . . . . . . . . . (360) 725-6025
  Term Expires: January 30, 2017
  Education: Florida A&M 1954 BS; Oregon State MS
■Member **Jeffrey C. Estes** . . . . . . . . . . . . . . . . . . . . . . . (360) 725-6025
  Term Expires: January 30, 2018
  E-mail: jeff.estes@pnnl.gov
  Affiliation: Director, Office of Science, Technology, Engineering &
  Math (STEM) Education, Pacific Northwest National Laboratory,
  United States Department of Energy
  902 Battelle Boulevard, Richland, WA 99352
  Education: Western Washington 1982 MEd
■Member **Bob Hughes** (Region 4) . . . . . . . . . . . . . . . . . .(360) 725-6025
  Term Expires: January 30, 2017
  E-mail: sbe.hughes@k12.wa.us
■Member **Holly Koon** . . . . . . . . . . . . . . . . . . . . . . . . . . .(360) 725-6025
  Term Expires: January 30, 2018
  E-mail: holly.sbe@gmail.com

*(continued on next page)*

★ Elected Official   ■ Appointed by Governor   ● Appointed by Legislature   ▲ Appointed by Board or Commission   ◆ Appointed by State Supreme Court

**EXECUTIVE BRANCH**

**State Board of Education** *continued*

Member **Kevin Laverty** (Region 3) . . . . . . . . . . . . . . . . . (360) 725-6025
  Term Expires: January 30, 2016
  E-mail: sbe.laverty@k12.wa.us
Member **Peter Maier, PhD** . . . . . . . . . . . . . . . . . . . . . . (360) 725-6025
  Term Expires: January 30, 2018
■Member **Tre Maxie** (Region 5) . . . . . . . . . . . . . . . . . . (360) 725-6025
  Term Expires: January 30, 2017
  E-mail: sbe.maxie@k12.wa.us
Member **Cynthia "Cindy" McMullen** (Region 1) . . . . . . . (360) 725-6025
  Term Expires: January 30, 2016
  E-mail: sbe.mcmullen@k12.wa.us
Member **Dan Plung** (Region 2) . . . . . . . . . . . . . . . . . . . (360) 725-6025
  Term Expires: January 30, 2018
  E-mail: sbe.frank@k12.wa.us
■Member **Dr. Deborah J. Wilds, PhD** . . . . . . . . . . . . . . (360) 725-6025
  Term Expires: January 30, 2017
Private School Representative Member **Judy Jennings** . . . . (360) 725-6025
  Term Expires: January 30, 2016
Student Representative Member **Baxter Hershman** . . . . . . . (360) 752-6025
  Term Expires: May 2017
  E-mail: marachilds@gmail.com
Student Representative Member **Madaleine Osmun** . . . . . . (360) 725-6025
  E-mail: sbe@k12.wa.us
Ex-Officio Member **Randolf "Randy" Dorn** . . . . . . . . . . . (360) 725-6000
  Affiliation: State Superintendent of Public Instruction, Office of
  Superintendent of Public Instruction, State of Washington
  P.O. Box 47200, Olympia, WA 98504-7200

## Executive Staff

Executive Director **Ben Rarick** . . . . . . . . . . . . . . . . . . . (360) 725-6025
  Executive Assistant **Denise Ross** . . . . . . . . . . . . . . . . (360) 725-6027
Research Director **Linda Drake** . . . . . . . . . . . . . . . . . . (360) 725-6028
  E-mail: linda.drake@k12.wa.us
Basic Education Oversight Director **Jack Archer** . . . . . . . . (360) 725-6035
  E-mail: jack.archer@k12.wa.us
Senior Policy Analyst **Andrew Parr** . . . . . . . . . . . . . . . . (360) 725-6063
Senior Research Analyst **Julia Suliman** . . . . . . . . . . . . . . (360) 725-6029
Special Assistant **Parker Teed** . . . . . . . . . . . . . . . . . . . (360) 725-6047

## Office of the Insurance Commissioner

Olympia Office, 302 Sid Snyder Avenue SW, Suite 200,
Olympia, WA 98504
Tumwater Office, 5000 Capitol Boulevard, Tumwater, WA 98501
P.O. Box 40255, Olympia, WA 98504-0255
Tel: (360) 725-7000  Tel: (800) 562-6900 (Consumer Hotline)
TTY: (360) 586-0241  Fax: (360) 586-3535
E-mail: insurance@oic.wa.gov  Internet: www.insurance.wa.gov

**Employees:** 217  **Fiscal Year:** 2013-2015  **Budget:** $55,126,000

★Insurance Commissioner **Mike Kreidler** (D) . . . . . . . . . . . . (360) 725-7000
  Term Expires: January 1, 2017
  E-mail: mikek@oic.wa.gov
  Education: UCLA MPH; Pacific U OD
  Executive Assistant **Sue Hedrick** . . . . . . . . . . . . . . . . (360) 725-7103
    Education: Western Washington 1982 BA
Chief Deputy Commissioner **Jim Odiorne** . . . . . . . . . . . . (360) 725-7104
  Education: Texas; Baylor JD
Consumer Protection Deputy Commissioner **John Hamje** . . (360) 725-7263
Company Supervision Deputy Commissioner
  **Doug Hartz** . . . . . . . . . . . . . . . . . . . . . . . . . . . . . . (360) 725-7212
  Consumer Advocacy Manager **Mary Childers** . . . . . . . . (360) 725-7084
Legal Affairs Deputy Commissioner
  **AnnaLisa Gellermann** . . . . . . . . . . . . . . . . . . . . . . . (360) 725-7047
Operations Deputy Commissioner (Acting)
  **Stacey Warick** . . . . . . . . . . . . . . . . . . . . . . . . . . . . (360) 725-7030
Policy and Legislative Affairs Deputy Commissioner
  **Jason Siems** . . . . . . . . . . . . . . . . . . . . . . . . . . . . . (360) 725-7038
  E-mail: jasons@oic.wa.gov
Public Affairs Deputy Commissioner **Steve Valandra** . . . . . (360) 725-7052
  E-mail: steveva@oic.wa.gov
Rates and Forms Deputy Commissioner **Molly Nollette** . . . (360) 725-7114

Healthcare Consumer Access Manager
  **Jennifer Kreitler** . . . . . . . . . . . . . . . . . . . . . . . . . . . (360) 725-7127
Health Care and Disability Manager
  **Andrea Philhower** . . . . . . . . . . . . . . . . . . . . . . . . . . (360) 725-7119
Property and Casualty and Life and Annuities Manager
  **Alan Hudina** . . . . . . . . . . . . . . . . . . . . . . . . . . . . . (360) 725-7126
Chief Financial Examiner **Pat McNaughton** . . . . . . . . . . . (360) 464-6624
  810 3rd Avenue, Suite 650, Seattle, WA 98104
Legislative Liaison **Lonnie Johns-Brown** . . . . . . . . . . . . . (360) 725-7101
  E-mail: lonniej@oic.wa.gov
  Special Investigations Unit (Anti-Fraud) Director
    **Mark Couey** . . . . . . . . . . . . . . . . . . . . . . . . . . . . (360) 586-2565

## Department of Natural Resources [DNR]

P.O. Box 47001, Olympia, WA 98504-7001
Tel: (360) 902-1000  TTY: (360) 902-1125  Fax: (360) 902-1775

**Employees:** 1,498  **Fiscal Year:** 2013-2015  **Budget:** $304,787,000

★Commissioner of Public Lands **Peter J. Goldmark** (D) . . . (360) 902-1004
  Term Expires: January 2017
  E-mail: cpl@dnr.wa.gov
  Education: Haverford; UC Berkeley 1971 PhD
  Career: Regent, Washington State University (1996-2000)
  Commissioner's Assistant **Kelli Parks** . . . . . . . . . . . . . (360) 902-1001
Budget Director **Lisa Largent** . . . . . . . . . . . . . . . . . . . (360) 902-1093
  E-mail: lisa.largent@dnr.wa.gov
Communications and Outreach Director **Sandra Kaiser** . . . (360) 902-1023
  E-mail: sandra.kaiser@dnr.wa.gov
Policy and Governmental Relations Director **(Vacant)** . . . . (360) 902-1028
Aquatic Division Manager **Kristin Swenddal** . . . . . . . . . . (360) 902-1124
Asset and Property Management Division Manager
  **Jeb Werman** . . . . . . . . . . . . . . . . . . . . . . . . . . . . . (360) 902-1702
Engineering and General Services Division Manager
  **Bill Frare** . . . . . . . . . . . . . . . . . . . . . . . . . . . . . . . (360) 902-1199
Financial Management Division Manager
  **Brian Richardson** . . . . . . . . . . . . . . . . . . . . . . . . . . (360) 902-1251
Forest Practices Division Manager **Chris Hanlon-Meyer** . . . (360) 902-1398
Forest Resources and Conservation Division Manager
  **Angus Brodie** . . . . . . . . . . . . . . . . . . . . . . . . . . . . (360) 902-1370
Geology and Earth Resources Division Manager
  **David "Dave" Norman** . . . . . . . . . . . . . . . . . . . . . . . (360) 902-1439
Human Resources Division Manager **Phil Wilson** . . . . . . . (360) 902-1652
Information Technology Division Manager
  **Steven Young** . . . . . . . . . . . . . . . . . . . . . . . . . . . . (360) 902-1555
  E-mail: steven.young@dnr.wa.gov
Resource Protection Division Manager **Albert Kassel** . . . . . (360) 902-1317
Tribal Relations Manager **Joenne McGerr** . . . . . . . . . . . . (360) 902-1012
  E-mail: joenne.mcgerr@dnr.wa.gov
Department Supervisor **Lenny Young** . . . . . . . . . . . . . . . (360) 902-1000
  E-mail: lenny.young@dnr.wa.gov
Aquatics and Agency Resources Deputy Supervisor
  **Megan Huffy** . . . . . . . . . . . . . . . . . . . . . . . . . . . . . (360) 902-1034
  E-mail: megan.huffy@dnr.wa.gov
Regulatory Programs Deputy Supervisor **Mary Verner** . . . . (360) 902-1684
  E-mail: mary.verner@dnr.wa.gov
Legislative and External Affairs Director **Jon Noski** . . . . . . (360) 902-1593
Internal Audit Manager **Ben Hainline** . . . . . . . . . . . . . . . (360) 902-1040

## Regional Operations

Northeast (Colville) Region Manager **Loren Torgerson** . . . (509) 684-7474
Northwest (Sedro Woolley) Region Manager **Jean Fike** . . . (360) 856-3500
Olympic (Forks) Region Manager **Sue Trettevik** . . . . . . . . (360) 374-2808
Pacific (Cascade) Region Manager **Eric Wisch** . . . . . . . . . (360) 575-5002
Southeast (Ellensburg) Region Manager **Todd Welker** . . . . (509) 925-0954
South Puget Sound (Enumclaw) Region Manager
  **Art Tasker** . . . . . . . . . . . . . . . . . . . . . . . . . . . . . . . (360) 802-7038

---

★ Elected Official   ■ Appointed by Governor   ● Appointed by Legislature   ▲ Appointed by Board or Commission   ◆ Appointed by State Supreme Court

# West Virginia

Tel: (304) 558-3456 (State Operator)  Internet: www.wv.gov

**Number of U.S. Congressional Delegates:** 2 Senators; 3 Representatives  **Governor's Term:** 4 years
**Legislature Description:** 34 member Senate; 100 member House of Delegates; Term - Senate 4
years; House 2 years  **Next Election:** Governor November 2016; Legislature November 2016
**Number of Electoral Votes:** 5  **Official Name:** State of West Virginia  **Nickname:** The Mountain State
**Motto:** Montani Semper Liberi (Mountaineers are always free)

**Population:** 1,844,128 (2015); Rank 38  **Employees:** 41,884  **Fiscal Year:** 2014  **Budget:** $22,719,748,613

## Office of the Governor

State Capitol Building, 1900 Kanawha Boulevard East,
Charleston, WV 25305
Tel: (304) 558-2000  Tel: (888) 438-2731  TTY: (304) 342-7386
Fax: (304) 558-2722  E-mail: governor@wvgov.org

**Employees:** 57  **Fiscal Year:** 2014  **Budget:** $44,221,721

**Earl Ray Tomblin**
Governor

Began Service: November 16, 2010
Term Expires: January 2017
Date of Birth: March 15, 1952
Education: West Virginia 1974 BS;
Marshall 1975 MBA; Charleston (Attended)
Home: Chapmanville
Religion: Presbyterian
Career: State Representative (D-WV), West
Virginia House of Delegates (1975-1980);
Senator, West Virginia Senate (1981-2011);
Acting Governor, State of West Virginia (2011)

★Governor **Earl Ray Tomblin** (D) . . . . . . . . . . . . . . . . . . . . . (304) 558-2000
  E-mail: governor@wv.gov
  Governor's Executive Aide **Rebecca L. "Becky" Neal** . . (304) 558-2000
    E-mail: rebecca.l.neal@wv.gov
Chief of Staff **Charles O. Lorensen** . . . . . . . . . . . . . . . . . (304) 558-2000
  Education: West Virginia 1986 JD; NYU 2001 LLM
General Counsel **Peter G. Markham** . . . . . . . . . . . . . . . . . (304) 558-2000
  E-mail: peter.g.markham@wv.gov
  Education: Virginia Tech 2000 BA; West Virginia 2003 JD
  Deputy General Counsel **Mark A. Imbrogno** . . . . . . . . . (304) 558-2000
    E-mail: mark.a.imbrogno@wv.gov
  Deputy General Counsel **Brittany L. Vascik** . . . . . . . . . (304) 558-2000
    E-mail: brittany.l.vascik@wv.gov
Communications Director **Chris Stadelman** . . . . . . . . . . . . (304) 558-2000
  E-mail: christopher.p.stadelman@wv.gov
  Education: Marshall
  Press Secretary **Shayna S. Varner** . . . . . . . . . . . . . . . . . (304) 558-2000
    E-mail: shayna.s.varner@wv.gov
Advance and Scheduling Director **Sherrie L. Stone** . . . . . . (304) 558-2000
  E-mail: sherrie.l.stone@wv.gov
Constituent Services Director **Patricia A. Burdette** . . . . . . (304) 558-2000
  E-mail: patricia.a.burdette@wv.gov
Intergovernmental Affairs Director **Robby Queen** . . . . . . . (304) 558-2000
  E-mail: robert.e.queen@wv.gov
Legislative Director **Joseph D. Garcia** . . . . . . . . . . . . . . . (304) 558-2000
  E-mail: joseph.d.garcia@wv.gov
  Education: West Virginia 2005 BA, 2009 JD
Policy Director **Lawrence J. "Larry" Malone** . . . . . . . . . . (304) 558-2000
  E-mail: lawrence.j.malone@wv.gov
Senior Advisor **(Vacant)** . . . . . . . . . . . . . . . . . . . . . . . . . . (304) 558-2000

## Department of Administration

State Capitol Complex, Building One, 1900 Kanwaha Boulevard, East,
Room E-119, Charleston, WV 25305-0120
Tel: (304) 558-4331  Fax: (304) 558-2999

**Employees:** 916  **Fiscal Year:** 2014  **Budget:** $4,397,759,058

■Secretary (Acting) **Mary Jane Pickens** . . . . . . . . . . . . . . . (304) 558-4331
  E-mail: maryjane.pickens@wv.gov
  Education: West Virginia 1982 BA; Ohio Northern 1985 JD
  Executive Assistant to the Secretary **Carol J. Nichols** . . . (304) 558-4331
Deputy Secretary **Gale Y. Given** . . . . . . . . . . . . . . . . . . . . (304) 558-8101
  E-mail: gale.y.given@wv.gov
  Education: Marshall BS, MBA
Assistant Secretary and Chief Financial Officer
  **Susannah Carpenter** . . . . . . . . . . . . . . . . . . . . . . . . . . (304) 558-4331
  Education: Virginia Tech
General Counsel **Robert P. Paulson** . . . . . . . . . . . . . . . . . (304) 558-4331
  Deputy General Counsel and Legislative Liaison
    **Jennelle Jones** . . . . . . . . . . . . . . . . . . . . . . . . . . . . (304) 558-5466
    Education: West Virginia JD
Communications Director **Diane M. Holley-Brown** . . . . . . . (304) 558-0661
  E-mail: diane.m.holley@wv.gov
General Services Division Director **Gregory L. Melton** . . . (304) 558-1808
  Building 1, MB-60, 1900 Kanawha Boulevard, East,
  Charleston, WV 25305-0120
  E-mail: gregory.l.melton@wv.gov
Purchasing Division Director **David R. Tincher** . . . . . . . . . (304) 558-2538
  2019 Washington St., East, Charleston, WV 25305-0130
Executive Coordinator/Legislative Liaison **(Vacant)** . . . . . . (304) 558-3392
ADA Coordinator **Kim P. Nuckles** . . . . . . . . . . . (304) 558-4331 ext. 57004
  Education: West Virginia 2001 JD

## Department of Commerce

Building 6, 1900 Kanawha Boulevard East, Room 553,
Charleston, WV 25305
Tel: (304) 558-2234  Fax: (304) 558-1189

**Employees:** 1,912  **Fiscal Year:** 2014  **Budget:** $238,993,927

■Secretary **J. Keith Burdette** . . . . . . . . . . . . . . . . . . . . . . (304) 558-2234
  Executive Assistant **Debbie A. Browning** . . . . (304) 558-2234 ext. 52006
  Administrative Assistant **Patricia J. White** . . . (304) 558-2234 ext. 52034
■Deputy Secretary **Amy Shuler Goodwin** . . . . . . . . . . . . . (304) 558-2200
  E-mail: amy.s.goodwin@wv.gov
  Education: West Virginia BA
Deputy Secretary and General Counsel
  **Joshua L. Jarrell** . . . . . . . . . . . . . . . . . . . . (304) 558-2234 ext. 52008
  Education: West Virginia 2009 JD
Marketing and Communications Director
  **Chelsea A. Ruby** . . . . . . . . . . . . . . . . . . . . . . . . . . . (304) 957-9364
  90 MacCorkle Avenue SW, South Charleston, WV 25303
  E-mail: chelsea.a.ruby@wv.gov

## Division of Energy

State Capitol Complex, Building 6, 1900 Kanawha Boulevard East,
Room 645, Charleston, WV 25305
Tel: (304) 558-2234  Fax: (304) 558-0362

Director **Jeff F. Herholdt, Jr.** . . . . . . . . . . . . . . . . . . . . . . (304) 558-2234

---

★ Elected Official  ■ Appointed by Governor  ● Appointed by Legislature  ▲ Appointed by Board or Commission  ◆ Appointed by State Supreme Court

## Division of Forestry

Guthrie Agriculture Center, 1900 Kanawha Boulevard East,
Charleston, WV 25305-0180
Seven Players Club Drive, Suite 2, Charleston, WV 25311-1626
Tel: (304) 558-2788  Fax: (304) 558-0143

■ Director **Charles R. "Randy" Dye** .................... (304) 558-3446
   E-mail: c.randy.dye@wv.gov
   Education: West Virginia BS
Deputy State Forester **Gregory W. Cook** .............. (304) 558-2788

## Division of Labor

State Capitol Complex, Building Six, 1900 Kanawha Boulevard, East,
Room B-749, Charleston, WV 25305
Tel: (304) 558-7890  Fax: (304) 558-2273

■ Commissioner (Acting) **John R. Junkins** ............. (304) 558-7890
   E-mail: john.r.junkins@wv.gov
   Assistant to the Commissioner
   **Derek H. Coleman** .................... (304) 558-7890 ext. 58024
Deputy Commissioner (Acting)
   **Mitchell E. "Mitch" Woodrum** ........... (304) 558-7890 ext. 58041
General Counsel **Elizabeth G. Farber** ................ (304) 558-7890
   E-mail: elizabeth.g.farber@wv.gov
Consumer Safety Director
   **Melissa A. Richardson** .................. (304) 558-7890 ext. 58031
Manufactured Housing and Licensing Director
   (Acting) **Victor L. Zamora** .............. (304) 558-7890 ext. 58041
                                              Fax: (304) 558-2174
Occupational Safety and Health Administration (OSHA)
   Director **Carla J. Campbell** ..................... (304) 558-7890
Safety and Boiler Director **Carla J. Campbell** ........... (304) 558-7890
                                              Fax: (304) 558-2415
Wage and Hour Director **Frank Jordan** .............. (304) 558-7890
   E-mail: william.f.jordan@wv.gov
                                              Fax: (304) 558-3797
   Wage and Hour Assistant Director **(Vacant)** ... (304) 722-7890 ext. 58014
                                              Fax: (304) 558-3797
   Weights and Measures Director **Victor L. Zamora** ........(304) 722-0602
   E-mail: victor.l.zamora@wv.gov                 Fax: (304) 722-0605

## Division of Natural Resources

Building 74, 324 4th Avenue, South Charleston, WV 25303-1224
Tel: (304) 558-2754  Fax: (304) 558-2768

■ Director **Robert A. Fala** ........................... (304) 558-2754
   Education: Penn State
Deputy Director **Emily J. Fleming** ................... (304) 558-2754
   Education: West Virginia 1979 BS
Administration Chief **Verena M. Mullins** .............. (304) 558-3315
   E-mail: verena.m.mullins@wv.gov
Law Enforcement Chief **Col. Jerry B. Jenkins** .......... (304) 558-2784
   E-mail: jerry.b.jenkins@wv.gov
   Education: West Virginia BS
Parks and Recreation Chief **Samuel A. England** ......... (304) 558-2764
   E-mail: samuel.a.england@wv.gov
   Education: West Virginia MBA
Wildlife Resources Chief **Paul R. Johansen** ............ (304) 558-2771
   E-mail: paul.r.johansen@wv.gov
   Education: UMass (Amherst) BS; Virginia Tech MS
Land and Streams Office Supervisor **Joe T. Scarberry** .... (304) 558-3225
   E-mail: joe.t.scarberry@wv.gov
Public Information Officer **Hoy R. Murphy** ............. (304) 957-9365
   E-mail: hoy.r.murphy@wv.gov
   Education: West Virginia 1976 BS

## Division of Tourism

90 MacCorkle Avenue SW, South Charleston, WV 25303
Tel: (304) 558-2200  Fax: (304) 746-0010  Internet: www.gotowv.com

■ Commissioner **Amy Shuler Goodwin** ................ (304) 558-2200
   E-mail: amy.s.goodwin@wv.gov
   Assistant to the Commissioner **Valerie E. Amick** ....... (304) 957-9355
Deputy Commissioner **Loarie H. Butcher** .............. (304) 957-9314
Matching Advertising Partnership Program (MAPP)
   Director **Anna M. Plantz** ...................... (304) 957-9325
Director of Special Projects and Strategic Initiatives
   **Tina L. Stinson** ............................. (304) 957-9338

Welcome Centers Director **Vicki L. Vaughan** ........... (304) 957-9225
West Virginia Film Office Director **Pamela J. Haynes** .... (304) 957-9382

## Division of Workforce West Virginia

112 California Avenue, Charleston, WV 25305-0112
Tel: (304) 558-7024  Fax: (304) 558-3512  Internet: www.workforcewv.org

Executive Director (Acting) **Russell L. Fry** ............. (304) 558-7024
Federal Programs Deputy Executive Director
   **Valerie V. Comer** .......................... (304) 558-7024
   E-mail: valerie.v.comer@wv.gov
Fiscal and Administrative Management Director **(Vacant)** .. (304) 558-2631
Field Operations Director **Claudia D. George** ........... (304) 558-1138
Research, Information and Analysis Division Director
   **Jeffrey A. "Jeff" Green** ..................... (304) 558-2660
   E-mail: jeffrey.a.green@wv.gov
Unemployment Compensation Division Director
   **Beth Carenbauer** ........................... (304) 558-2624

## Unemployment Compensation Board of Review

1321 Plaza East, Charleston, WV 25301
Tel: (304) 558-2636  Fax: (304) 558-1363

Chair **Jack Canfield** ................................ (304) 558-2636
Member **Gino Colombo** ............................ (304) 558-2636
Member **Les Facemyer** ............................. (304) 558-2636
Chief Administrative Law Judge **Truman L. Sayre** ....... (304) 558-2636
   E-mail: truman.l.sayre@wv.gov
Deputy Chief Administrative Law Judge **Larry J. Conrad** .. (304) 558-2636

## West Virginia Development Office

State Capitol Complex, Building Six, 1900 Kanawha Boulevard, East,
Room 553, Charleston, WV 25305-0311
Tel: (304) 558-2234  Fax: (304) 558-1189

Executive Director **J. Keith Burdette** ................. (304) 558-2234

## Business and Industrial Development Division

State Capitol Complex, Building Six, 1900 Kanawha Boulevard, East,
Room 504, Charleston, WV 25305-0311
Tel: (304) 558-2234

Director **Kristopher N. Hopkins** ..................... (304) 558-2234
   Education: Harvard; Charleston MBA

## Community Development Division

State Capitol Complex, Building Six, 1900 Kanawha Boulevard, East,
Room 553, Charleston, WV 25305-0311
Tel: (304) 558-2234  Fax: (304) 558-2246

Director **Mary Jo Thompson** ............... (304) 558-2234 ext. 52307
   Education: Fairmont State Col 1994 BA
Local Capacity Development Manager
   **Monica D. Miller** ................... (304) 558-2234 ext. 52020
Project Development Manager
   **Kelly A. Workman** .................. (304) 558-2234 ext. 52077
Infrastructure Bond and Special Grants
   Coordinator **Debra Legg** .............. (304) 558-2234 ext. 52036

## International Development Division

State Capitol Complex, Building Six, 1900 Kanawha Boulevard, East,
Room 517, Charleston, WV 25305-0311
Tel: (304) 558-2234

Executive Director **Stephen E. Spence** ....... (304) 558-2234 ext. 52067
European Office Director **Angela Mascia** ............... (304) 558-2234
Japan Office Director **(Vacant)** ...................... (304) 558-2234

## Economic Development Authority

NorthGate Business Park, 160 Association Drive, Charleston, WV 25311
Tel: (304) 558-3650  Fax: (304) 558-0206

▲ Executive Director **David A. Warner** ................. (304) 558-3650
   E-mail: david.a.warner@wv.gov

---

★ Elected Official     ■ Appointed by Governor     ● Appointed by Legislature     ▲ Appointed by Board or Commission     ◆ Appointed by State Supreme Court

## Small Business Development Center

State Capitol Complex, Building Six, 1900 Kanawha Boulevard, East,
Room 652, Charleston, WV 25305-0311
Tel: (304) 558-2960  Fax: (304) 558-0127  Internet: www.sbdcwv.org

Director **Kristina J. Oliver** . . . . . . . . . . . . . . . . . . (304) 558-2960 ext. 52090
Deputy Director **Debra K. Martin** . . . . . . . . . . . . . . . . . . . . . (304) 957-2042

## Office of Miners' Health Safety and Training

Seven Players Club Drive, Suite 2, Charleston, WV 25311-1626
Tel: (304) 558-1425  Fax: (304) 558-1282  E-mail: mineinfo@wv.gov
Internet: www.wvminesafety.org

■Director **Eugene E. White** . . . . . . . . . . . . . . . . . . . . . . . . . (304) 558-1425
  E-mail: eugene.e.white@wv.gov

## Geological and Economic Survey

1 Mont Chateau Road, Morgantown, WV 26508-8079
Tel: (304) 594-2331  Fax: (304) 594-2575  E-mail: info@geosrv.wvnet.edu
Internet: www.wvgs.wvnet.edu

■Director/State Geologist **Michael E. Hohn** . . . . . . . . . . . . . (304) 594-2331
  E-mail: hohn@geosrv.wvnet.edu
  Education: Birmingham 1972 BS; Indiana 1975 MA, 1976 PhD
Deputy Director for Finance and Administration
  **John D. May** . . . . . . . . . . . . . . . . . . . . . . . . . . . . . . . . . (304) 594-2331
  E-mail: may@geosrv.wvnet.edu
  Education: West Virginia 1989 MBA

## Department of Education and the Arts

State Capitol Complex, Building Five, 1900 Kanawha Boulevard, East,
Room 205, Charleston, WV 25305
Tel: (304) 558-2440  Fax: (304) 558-1311
Internet: www.edandarts.wv.gov

**Employees:** 956  **Fiscal Year:** 2014  **Budget:** $116,481,581

■Cabinet Secretary **Kathleen Huffman "Kay" Goodwin** . . . (304) 558-2440
  E-mail: kay.h.goodwin@wv.gov
  Education: West Virginia 1963 BFA, 1968 MFA
  Special Assistant **Tiffany Davis Redman** . . . . . (304) 558-2440 ext. 54417
    Education: West Liberty State 1993 BS; West Virginia 1997 JD
Deputy Cabinet Secretary **Martha B. McKee** . . . . . . . . . . . (304) 558-2440
Chief Financial Officer **Brett E. Sansom** . . . . . . (304) 356-2060 ext. 54402
  Education: Marshall BBA
Partnerships to Assure Student Success Director
  **Jack D. Wiseman** . . . . . . . . . . . . . . . . . . . . . . . . . . . . . (304) 558-2440
Special Projects Coordinator **Beth F. Hughes** . . . . . . . . . . . (304) 558-2440

## Division of Culture and History

Tel: (304) 558-0220  Fax: (304) 558-2779  Internet: www.wvculture.org

■Commissioner **Randall Reid-Smith** . . . . . . . . . . . . . . . . . . (304) 558-0220
  Executive Assistant **Eric B. Aluise** . . . . . . . . . . . (304) 558-0220 ext. 113
Deputy Commissioner **Caryn Gresham** . . . . . . . . . (304) 558-0220 ext. 120
Administration Director **Susan G. Chapman** . . . . . (304) 558-0220 ext. 119
  E-mail: sue.g.chapman@wv.gov
Archives and History Director
  **Joseph N. "Joe" Geiger** . . . . . . . . . . . . . . . . . (304) 558-0230 ext. 165
Arts Director **Renée Margocee** . . . . . . . . . . . . . . (304) 558-0240 ext. 145
Historic Preservation Director **Susan M. Pierce** . . . (304) 558-0240 ext. 158
Museum Director **Charles W. Morris III** . . . . . . . . (304) 558-0220 ext. 704

## Division of Rehabilitation Services

P.O. Box 50890, Charleston, WV 25305-0890
Tel: (304) 356-2060  Fax: (304) 558-1421  Internet: www.wvdrs.org

■Director **Donna L. Ashworth** . . . . . . . . . . . . . . (304) 356-2094 ext. 55043
  E-mail: donna.l.ashworth@wv.gov
  Executive Secretary **Karen D. Shuck** . . . . . . . . . . . . . . . . (304) 356-2060
Disability Determination Services Assistant Director
  **Kathleen Jordan** . . . . . . . . . . . . . . . . . . . . . . . . . . . . . (304) 353-4253
Field Services Assistant Director **Marijane K. Waldron** . . . (304) 356-2098
Program Development Assistant Director
  **Michael K. Meadows** . . . . . . . . . . . . . . . . . . . . . . . . . . (304) 356-2362

State and Federal Relations Senior Manager
  **Tracy J. Carr** . . . . . . . . . . . . . . . . . . . . . . . . . . . . . . . . (304) 356-2061
  E-mail: tracy.j.carr@wv.gov

## Educational Broadcasting Authority

600 Capitol Street, Charleston, WV 25301
Tel: (304) 556-4900  Fax: (304) 556-4980  Internet: wvpublic.org

Executive Director **Scott Finn** . . . . . . . . . . . . . . . . . . . . . . (304) 556-4900
  Administrative Assistant **Belinda McCallister** . . . . . . . . . (304) 556-4931
Development Director **Marilyn Divita** . . . . . . . . . . . . . . . . (304) 556-4900
Engineering Director **Dave McClanahan** . . . . . . . . . . . . . . (304) 556-4900
Finance Director **Tammy Treadway** . . . . . . . . . . . . . . . . . (304) 556-4900
Human Resource Manager **Jan Johnson** . . . . . . . . . . . . . . (304) 556-4900
Marketing Director **Shawn Patterson** . . . . . . . . . . . . . . . . (304) 556-4900
News and Public Affairs Director **Jesse Wright** . . . . . . . . . (304) 284-1473
  E-mail: jwright2@wvpublic.org
  Education: West Virginia BJ
Programming and Operations Director **Craig Lanham** . . . . . (304) 556-4900
Radio Operations Director **Kristi George** . . . . . . . . . . . . . (304) 556-4900
Television Production Director **Chuck Roberts** . . . . . . . . . . (304) 556-4900
Underwriting Director **Jane Siers Wright** . . . . . . . . . . . . . (304) 556-4900

## Center for Professional Development [CPD]

208 Hale Street, Charleston, WV 25301
Tel: (304) 558-0539  Fax: (304) 558-0989  E-mail: info@wvcpd.org
Internet: www.wvcpd.org

Chief Executive Officer **Dr. Dixie M. Billheimer** . . . . . . . . (304) 558-0539
  Education: Marshall BASecEd, 2007 DEd
Chief Operating Officer **Lorrie A. Smith** . . . . . . . . . . . . . (304) 558-0539
Advanced Placement Program Director **Karen R. Linville** . . (304) 558-0539
Communications Director **Christy B. Day** . . . . . . . . . . . . . (304) 558-0539
  E-mail: christy.b.day@wv.gov
Principal Programs Director **Emily Papadopoulos** . . . . . . . (304) 558-0539
The Teacher Academy and Mentoring Program Director
  **Carla Y. Warren** . . . . . . . . . . . . . . . . . . . . . . . . . . . . . (304) 558-0539

## Department of Environmental Protection

601 57th Street, Southeast, Charleston, WV 25304-2345
Tel: (304) 926-0440  Fax: (304) 926-0447

**Employees:** 951  **Fiscal Year:** 2014  **Budget:** $246,447,878

■Secretary **Randy C. Huffman** . . . . . . . . . . . . . . . (304) 926-0499 ext. 1546
  E-mail: randy.c.huffman@wv.gov
  Education: West Virginia Tech BS
  Executive Assistant to the Secretary
    **Thomas L. "Tom" Clarke** . . . . . . . . . . . . . . . . . . . . (304) 926-0440
    E-mail: thomas.l.clarke@wv.gov
Deputy Secretary **Scott G. Mandirola** . . . . . . . . (304) 926-0499 ext. 1058
                                                      Fax: (304) 926-0482
  Chief Information Technology Officer
    **Neil A.M. Chakrabarty** . . . . . . . . . . . . . . . (304) 926-0499 ext. 1626
    E-mail: neil.a.m.chakrabarty@wv.gov
General Counsel **Kristin A. Boggs** . . . . . . . . . . . (304) 926-0499 ext. 1548
Human Resources Director **Chad J. Bailey** . . . . . . (304) 926-0499 ext. 1554
Air Quality Division Director
  **William F. Durham** . . . . . . . . . . . . . . . . . . . (304) 926-0499 ext. 1238
Land Restoration Division Director
  **Patricia A. Hickman** . . . . . . . . . . . . . . . . . . (304) 926-0499 ext. 1263
  Land Restoration Assistant Director **(Vacant)** . . . . . . . . . (304) 924-6211
Mining and Reclamation Division Director
  **Harold D. Ward** . . . . . . . . . . . . . . . . . . . . . . . . . . . . (304) 926-0499
Water and Waste Management Division Director
  (Acting) **Scott G. Mandirola** . . . . . . . . . . . . . (304) 926-0499 ext. 1058
  State Revolving Fund and
    Management Services Engineer Chief
    **Katheryn Emery-Fultineer** . . . . . . . . . . . . . (304) 926-0499 ext. 1596
    E-mail: katheryn.d.emery@wv.gov
Special Reclamation Office Assistant Director
  **Michael P. Sheehan** . . . . . . . . . . . . . . . . . . . . . . . . . . (304) 457-3219

*(continued on next page)*

**Department of Environmental Protection** *continued*

Abandoned Mine Lands and Reclamation Office
Chief **Robert Rice** . . . . . . . . . . . . . . . . . . . . . . . . . . . . (304) 926-0499 ext. 1476
E-mail: robert.rice@wv.gov
Business and Technology Office Chief
**Melinda S. Campbell** . . . . . . . . . . . . . . . . . . . . . . (304) 926-0499 ext. 1701
E-mail: melinda.s.campbell@wv.gov
Explosives and Blasting Office Chief
**David L. Vande Linde** . . . . . . . . . . . . . . . . . . . . . . . . . . . . (304) 926-0464
Legal Services Office Chief **(Vacant)** . . . . . . . . . . . . . . . . . (304) 926-0460
Oil and Gas Office Chief **James A. Martin** . . . . . (304) 926-0499 ext. 1654
Chief Inspector **Jeremy W. Bandy** . . . . . . . . . . . (304) 926-0488 ext. 1279
Chief Communications Officer **Kelley J. Gillenwater** . . . . . (304) 926-0440
E-mail: kelley.j.gillenwater@wv.gov
Environmental Ombudsman **Terry L. Polen** . . . . . . (304) 926-0499 ext. 1381

## Air Quality Board

601 57th Street, Southeast, Charleston, WV 25304-2345
Tel: (304) 926-0445  Fax: (304) 926-0486  Internet: www.wvaqb.org

■Chair **J. Michael Koon** . . . . . . . . . . . . . . . . . . . . . . . . . . . (304) 926-0445
Education: West Virginia 1973 BA, 1977 MS
■Vice Chair **R. Thomas Hansen, PhD** . . . . . . . . . . . . . . . . . (304) 926-0445
Education: Montana 1967 BSChem; West Virginia 1969 PhD
■Member **Jon Blair Hunter** . . . . . . . . . . . . . . . . . . . . . . . . . (304) 926-0445
■Member **Stanley B. Mills** . . . . . . . . . . . . . . . . . . . . . . . . . . (304) 926-0445
■Member **Robert C. Orndoff** . . . . . . . . . . . . . . . . . . . . . . . . (304) 926-0445
Education: Millersville
■Ex-Officio **Walt Helmick** . . . . . . . . . . . . . . . . . . . . . . . . . . (304) 926-0445
E-mail: whelmick@wvda.us
Affiliation: Commissioner, Department of Agriculture, State of West
Virginia
State Capitol Complex, Building One, 1900 Kanawha Boulevard, East,
Room M-28, Charleston, WV 25305-0170
Education: West Virginia Tech 1993 BA
■Ex-Officio **Walter M. Ivey** . . . . . . . . . . . . . . . . . . . . . . . . . (304) 558-2971
Affiliation: Director (Interim), Office of Environmental Health Services,
Department of Health and Human Services, State of West Virginia
One Davis Square, Suite 200, Charleston, WV 25301
Clerk of the Board **Jackie D. Shultz** . . . . . . . . . . (304) 926-0499 ext. 1683
E-mail: jackie.d.schultz@wv.gov

## Environmental Quality Board

601 57th Street Southeast, Charleston, WV 25304
Tel: (304) 926-0445  Fax: (304) 926-0486  Internet: www.wveqb.org

■Chair **Edward M. Snyder, PhD** . . . . . . . . . . . . . . . . . . . . . (304) 926-0445
Education: Eastern Washington 1973 MS; Illinois 1984 PhD
■Vice Chair **D. Scott Simonton, PhD, PE** . . . . . . . . . . . . . . . (304) 926-0445
Education: West Virginia Tech 1991 BS; Marshall 1997 MS;
New Mexico 2002 PhD
■Member **B. Mitchel Blake, Jr., PhD** . . . . . . . . . . . . . . . . . . (304) 926-0445
■Member **William H. Gillespie** . . . . . . . . . . . . . . . . . . . . . . (304) 926-0445
■Member **Charles C. Somerville, PhD** . . . . . . . . . . . . . . . . . (304) 926-0445
Attorney **Nicholas T. Dalton** . . . . . . . . . . . . . . . (304) 926-0445 ext. 1684
Administrative Secretary **Kathy C. Coleman** . . . . (304) 926-0445 ext. 1682
Clerk of the Board **Jackie D. Shultz** . . . . . . . . . . (304) 926-0445 ext. 1683
E-mail: jackie.d.schultz@wv.gov

## Solid Waste Management Board [SWMB]

601 57th Street, S.E., Charleston, WV 25304
Tel: (304) 926-0448  Fax: (304) 926-0472
Internet: www.state.wv.us/swmb

■Chair **Mallie Combs** . . . . . . . . . . . . . . . . . . . . . . . . . . . . . (304) 926-0448
■Vice Chair **Roger Bryant** . . . . . . . . . . . . . . . . . . . . . . . . . (304) 926-0448
■Member **Tim Blankenship** . . . . . . . . . . . . . . . . . . . . . . . . (304) 926-0448
■Member **Alice Jo Buzzard** . . . . . . . . . . . . . . . . . . . . . . . . (304) 926-0448
■Member **Steve Pilato** . . . . . . . . . . . . . . . . . . . . . . . . . . . . (304) 926-0448
Member - Ex Officio **Karen L. Bowling, FNP, FACHE** . . . . (304) 558-0684
Affiliation: Cabinet Secretary, Department of Health and Human
Resources, State of West Virginia
350 Capitol Street, Charleston, WV 25301 (Vital Records)
Education: Bluefield State 1977 AS; West Virginia 1983 BSN,
1990 MS

Member - Ex Officio **Randy C. Huffman** . . . . . . . . . . . . . . (304) 926-0448
Affiliation: Secretary, Department of Environmental Protection, State of
West Virginia
601 57th Street, Southeast, Charleston, WV 25304-2345
▲Director **Mark D. Holstine** . . . . . . . . . . . . . . . . . . . . . . . . (304) 926-0448
E-mail: mark.d.holstine@wv.gov

## Surface Mine Board

601 57th Street Southeast, Charleston, WV 25304
Tel: (304) 926-0445 ext. 1685  Fax: (304) 926-0486

■Chair **James Smith** . . . . . . . . . . . . . . . . . . . . . . . . . . . . . . (304) 926-0449
■Vice Chair **Ed Grafton** . . . . . . . . . . . . . . . . . . . . . . . . . . . (304) 926-0449
■Member **Ronald "Ron" Crites** . . . . . . . . . . . . . . . . . . . . . (304) 926-0449
■Member **Jon Blair Hunter** . . . . . . . . . . . . . . . . . . . . . . . . . (304) 926-0449
■Member **Charles K. Meadows II** . . . . . . . . . . . . . . . . . . . . (304) 926-0449
■Member **Don Michael** . . . . . . . . . . . . . . . . . . . . . . . . . . . . (304) 926-0449
■Member **Henry Rauch** . . . . . . . . . . . . . . . . . . . . . . . . . . . (304) 926-0449
Education: Penn State PhD
■Member **Mark Schuerger** . . . . . . . . . . . . . . . . . . . . . . . . . (304) 926-0449
▲Clerk **Fran C. Ryan** . . . . . . . . . . . . . . . . . . . . . (304) 926-0449 ext. 1685
E-mail: fran.c.ryan@wv.gov

## Department of Health and Human Resources [DHHR]

One Davis Square, Suite 100 East, Charleston, WV 25301
350 Capitol Street, Charleston, WV 25301 (Vital Records)
Tel: (304) 558-0684  Tel: (304) 558-2931 (Vital Records)
Fax: (304) 558-1130  Fax: (304) 558-8001 (Vital Records)
Internet: www.wvdhhr.org
Internet: www.wvdhhr.org/bph/hsc/vital (Vital Records)

**Employees:** 6,407  **Fiscal Year:** 2014  **Budget:** $8,134,361,315

■Cabinet Secretary **Karen L. Bowling, FNP, FACHE** . . . . . . (304) 558-9147
E-mail: dhhrsecretary@wv.gov
Executive Assistant **Judy L. Payne** . . . . . . . . . . . . . . . . . (304) 558-9147
State and Federal Policy Coordination Deputy Secretary
**Molly M. Jordan** . . . . . . . . . . . . . . . . . . . . . . . . . . . . . . (304) 558-0399
E-mail: molly.m.jordan@wv.gov
Executive Secretary **Ruth F. Kemp** . . . . . . . . . . . . . . . . . (304) 558-1245
General Counsel **Karen Villanueva-Matkovich** . . . . . . . . . (304) 558-0741
Education: Penn State 1990 BA; Rutgers JD; Johns Hopkins 2009 MS
Communications Director **Allison Adler** . . . . . . . . . . . . . . (304) 558-7899
Education: West Virginia State Col 1991 BA; West Virginia 2000 MA
Health Resources Development Director **(Vacant)** . . . . . . . (304) 356-5405
James Tiger Morton - Catastrophic Illness Commission
Executive Director **Regina C. "Genie" Hupp**
Room 523 . . . . . . . . . . . . . . . . . . . . . . . . . . . . . . . . . . . . . (304) 558-6073

## Administration

One Davis Square, Suite 300, Charleston, WV 25301
Deputy Secretary for Administration **Warren D. Keefer** . . . (304) 558-1184
E-mail: warren.d.keefer@wv.gov
Chief Operational Officer **Greg C. Nicholson**
Suite 100 West . . . . . . . . . . . . . . . . . . . . . . . . . . . . . . . . . (304) 558-3217
Human Resources Director **Harold D. Clifton** . . . . . . . . . (304) 558-8291

## Finance

One Davis Square, Suite 300, Charleston, WV 25301
Tel: (304) 558-5208

Chief Budget Officer **Starlah A. Wilcox** . . . . . . . . . . . . . . (304) 558-2814
Chief Financial Officer **Tara L. Buckner** . . . . . . . . . . . . . . (304) 558-9138
Accountability and Management Reporting Office
Director **Jeffrey L. "Jeff" Bush** . . . . . . . . . . . . . . . . . . . (304) 558-2587

## Management Information Services Office

One Davis Square, Suite 200, Charleston, WV 25301
Tel: (304) 558-9145  Fax: (304) 558-1097

Chief Technology Officer **Darlene F. Thomas** . . . . . . . . . . (304) 558-9145
E-mail: darlene.f.thomas@wv.gov

---

★ Elected Official   ■ Appointed by Governor   ● Appointed by Legislature   ▲ Appointed by Board or Commission   ◆ Appointed by State Supreme Court

## Office of the Inspector General [OIG]

State Capitol Complex, Room 817-B, Building 6, Charleston, WV 25305
Tel: (304) 558-2278  Fax: (304) 558-1992  E-mail: dhhroig@wv.gov

Inspector General **M. Katherine Lawson** . . . . . . . . . . . . . . . (304) 558-2278
  E-mail: kathy.m.lawson@wv.gov
Deputy Inspector General **Sheila R. Lee** . . . . . . . . . . . . . . (304) 558-2278
  E-mail: sheila.r.lee@wv.gov
General Counsel **April L. Robertson** . . . . . . . . . . . . . . . . . (304) 558-1117
  E-mail: april.l.robertson@wv.gov
Board of Review Chairman **Cheryl A. Henson** . . . . . . . . . (304) 558-2134
  E-mail: cheryl.a.henson@wv.gov
Investigations and Fraud Management Director
  **Christopher G. "Chris" Nelson** . . . . . . . . . . . . . . (304) 558-1970
  E-mail: christopher.g.nelson@wv.gov
Medicaid Fraud Control Unit Director **Trina C. Crowder** . . (304) 558-1858
  408 Leon Sullivan Way, Charleston, WV 25301
  E-mail: trina.c.crowder@wv.gov
Quality Control Director **Retha L. Lilly** . . . . . . . . . . . . . . . (304) 558-0630
Olmstead Coordinator **Vanessa K. VanGilder** . . . . . . . . . . (304) 558-3287

## Office of Health Facility Licensure and Certification [OHFLAC]

408 Leon Sullivan Way, Charleston, WV 25301
Fax: (304) 558-2515

Director **Jolynn Marra** . . . . . . . . . . . . . . . . . . . . . . . . . . . . (304) 558-0050
  E-mail: jolynn.marra@wv.gov
  Education: West Virginia BSBA

## Health Care Authority

100 Dee Drive, Charleston, WV 25301
Tel: (304) 558-7000  Fax: (304) 558-7001

■Chairman **James L. "Jim" Pitrolo** . . . . . . . . . . . . . (304) 558-7000 ext. 214
  E-mail: jpitrolo@hcawv.org
▲Executive Director **Jennifer J. Meeks** . . . . . . . . . . (304) 558-7000 ext. 208
  E-mail: jennifer.j.meeks@wv.gov
Chief Privacy Officer
  **Sallie H. Milam, JD, CIPP, CIPP/G** . . . . . . . . . . (304) 558-7000 ext. 254

## Developmental Disabilities Council

110 Stockton Street, Charleston, WV 25312
Tel: (304) 558-0416  Fax: (304) 558-0941

Director **Steven A. "Steve" Wiseman** . . . . . . . . . . . . . . . (304) 558-0416

## Bureau for Behavioral Health and Health Facilities

350 Capitol Street, Room 350, Charleston, WV 25301-3702
Tel: (304) 356-4811  Fax: (304) 558-1008

Commissioner **Victoria L. "Vickie" Jones** . . . . . . . . . . . . . (304) 356-4538
Administration Deputy Commissioner **Damon E. Iarossi** . . (304) 356-4832
  E-mail: damon.e.iarossi@wv.gov
Operations Deputy Commissioner **Shevona R. Lusk** . . . . . . (304) 356-4813
Programs Deputy Commissioner **Kimberly A. Walsh** . . . . . (304) 356-4792

## Bureau for Child Support Enforcement [BCSE]

350 Capitol Street, Room 147, Charleston, WV 25301-3703
Tel: (304) 356-4762  Fax: (304) 558-1121

Commissioner **Garrett M. Jacobs** . . . . . . . . . . . . . . . . . . . (304) 356-4707
  E-mail: garrett.m.jacobs@wv.gov
  Education: West Virginia 1988 BSBA, 1991 JD
Deputy Commissioner **David M. Welker** . . . . . . . . . . . . . (304) 822-6900
  E-mail: david.m.welker@wv.gov
Finance and Administration Deputy Commissioner
  **Hal Pendell** . . . . . . . . . . . . . . . . . . . . . . . . . . . . . . (304) 356-4726
  E-mail: hall.m.pendell@wv.gov
  Education: Tennessee BSBA; LaSalle Col (Canada) BBL, MS
General Counsel **Heidi L. Talmage** . . . . . . . . . . . . . . . . . . (304) 558-4737

## Bureau for Children and Families [BCF]

350 Capitol Street, Room 730, Charleston, WV 25301-3711
Tel: (304) 558-0628  Fax: (304) 558-4194  Internet: www.wvdhhr.org/bcf

Commissioner **Nancy N. Exline** . . . . . . . . . . . . . . . . . . . . (304) 356-4543
  E-mail: nancy.n.exline@wv.gov
Operations Deputy Commissioner **Linda J. Adkins** . . . . . . . (304) 356-4543
Programs Deputy Commissioner **Sue C. Hage** . . . . . . . . . . (304) 356-4527
  E-mail: sue.c.hage@wv.gov
Children and Adult Services Director
  **Jane B. McCallister** . . . . . . . . . . . . . . . . . . . . . . . (304) 356-4575
  E-mail: jane.b.mccallister@wv.gov
Early Care and Education Director **Janie M. Cole** . . . . . . . (304) 356-4598
Family Assistance Director **Betty Jo Scarberry** . . . . . . . . . (304) 356-4615
  E-mail: betty.jo.scarberry@wv.gov
Grants and Contracts Director **Melisa J. Green** . . . . . . . . . (304) 558-4549
  E-mail: melisa.j.green@wv.gov
Training Director **Susan M. Richards** . . . . . . . . . . . . . . . . (304) 356-4648
Community Services Manager **Paula J. Taylor** . . (304) 368-4420 ext. 79230
  9083 Middletown Mall, Fairmont, WV 26554
  Education: West Virginia 2005 MSW

## Bureau for Medical Services

350 Capitol Street, Room 251, Charleston, WV 25301-3706
Tel: (304) 558-1700  Fax: (304) 558-1451

Commissioner (Acting) **Cynthia E. Beane** . . . . . . . . . . . . . (304) 558-1700
Deputy Commissioner for Finance and Administration
  **Tony Atkins** . . . . . . . . . . . . . . . . . . . . . . . . . . . . . . (304) 356-5050
Deputy Commissioner for Operations Management
  **(Vacant)** . . . . . . . . . . . . . . . . . . . . . . . . . . . . . . . . . (304) 558-1700
Deputy Commissioner for Policy Coordination (Acting)
  **Sarah K. Young** . . . . . . . . . . . . . . . . . . . . . . . . . . . (304) 558-1700
Legal and Regulatory Services Director **Ryan Sims** . . . . . . (304) 558-4931

## Bureau for Public Health

350 Capitol Street, Room 702, Charleston, WV 25301-3712
Tel: (304) 558-2971  Fax: (304) 558-1035

Commissioner and State Health Officer
  **Rahul Gupta, MD, MPH, FACP** . . . . . . . . . . . . . . . (304) 558-2971
Administration Deputy Commissioner **Chuck E. Thayer** . . . (304) 558-2971
  E-mail: chuck.e.thayer@wv.gov
  Education: West Virginia 1994 MS
Health Improvement Deputy Commissioner
  **Anne A. Williams** . . . . . . . . . . . . . . . . . . . . . . . . . . (304) 356-4135
Health Protection Deputy Commissioner
  **Barbara S. Taylor** . . . . . . . . . . . . . . . . . . . . . . . . . (304) 558-2971
  E-mail: barb.s.taylor@wv.gov
Public Health Regulations Director **Brian Skinner** . . . . . . . (304) 356-4122
Public Information Officer **Toby D. Wagoner** . . . . . . . . . . (304) 356-4042
  E-mail: toby.d.wagoner@wv.gov
Chief Financial Officer **Tim J. Whitener** . . . . . . . . . . . . . . (304) 356-4085

## Office of the Chief Medical Examiner [OCME]

619 Virginia Street, West, Charleston, WV 25302
Tel: (304) 558-6920

Chief Medical Examiner **Allen R. Mock** . . . . . . . . (304) 558-6920 ext. 4001
First Deputy Chief Medical Examiner **(Vacant)** . . . . . . . . . (304) 558-6920
Chief Toxicologist **James C. Kraner, PhD** . . . . . . (304) 558-6920 ext. 4007

## Office of Community Health Systems and Health Promotion [OCHS]

350 Capitol Street, Room 515, Charleston, WV 25301-3716
Tel: (304) 356-4193  Fax: (304) 558-8740

Director **Joe Barker** . . . . . . . . . . . . . . . . . . . . . . . . . . . . . (304) 356-4249
Associate Director **Bruce Adkins** . . . . . . . . . . . . . . . . . . . (304) 356-4222

## Office of Emergency Medical Services

350 Capitol Street, Room 425, Charleston, WV 25301
Tel: (304) 558-3956  Fax: (304) 558-8379  Internet: www.wvoems.org

Director (Interim) **Melissa J. Kinnaird** . . . . . . . . . . . . . . . (304) 558-3956
Medical Director **Michael R. Mills** . . . . . . . . . . . . . . . . . . (304) 558-3956

---

★ Elected Official   ■ Appointed by Governor   ● Appointed by Legislature   ▲ Appointed by Board or Commission   ◆ Appointed by State Supreme Court

## Office of Environmental Health Services [OEHS]

One Davis Square, Suite 200, Charleston, WV 25301
Tel: (304) 558-2981  Fax: (304) 558-1291  Internet: www.wvdhhr.org/oehs

Director (Interim) **Walter M. Ivey** . . . . . . . . . . . . . . . . . . . (304) 356-4258

Environmental Engineering Division Director
  **Bill Toomey** . . . . . . . . . . . . . . . . . . . . . . . . . . . . . (304) 356-4298
  Fax: (304) 558-0289

  Infrastructure and Capacity Development Manager
    **Robert W. "Bob" DeCrease** . . . . . . . . . . . . . . . . . . (304) 356-4301

Public Health Sanitation Division Director
  **Brad J. Cochran, RS** . . . . . . . . . . . . . . . . . . . . . . . (304) 356-4286
  Fax: (304) 558-1071

Radiation, Toxics and Indoor Air Division Assistant
  Director **Tony Turner** . . . . . . . . . . . . . . . . . . . . . . . (304) 558-6716
  Fax: (304) 558-1289

## Office of Epidemiology and Prevention Services [OEPS]

350 Capitol Street, Room 206, Charleston, WV 25301-3715
Tel: (304) 558-5358  Fax: (304) 558-1553

State Epidemiologist **Loretta E. Haddy** . . . . . . . . . . . . . . (304) 356-4053
  Education: Marshall BA, MA; Ohio State MS; Capella U PhD

Cancer Epidemiology Division Director
  **Shawn O. Farley** . . . . . . . . . . . . . . . . . . . . . . . . . . . (304) 356-4953

Epidemiologic Informatics and Evaluation Division
  Director **Anil S. Nair** . . . . . . . . . . . . . . . . . . . . . . . . (304) 356-5067

Immunization Services Division Director
  **Jeffrey J. "Jeff" Neccuzi** . . . . . . . . . . . . . . . . . . . . . (304) 558-2188

Infectious Disease Epidemiology Division Director
  **Danae "Dee" Bixler** . . . . . . . . . . . . . . . . . . . . . . . . (304) 356-4024

Sexually Transmitted Diseases, HIV and Hepatitis
  Division Director **Susan Hall** . . . . . . . . . . . . . . . . . . . (304) 558-2195

Tuberculosis Elimination Division Director
  **Carmen Priddy** . . . . . . . . . . . . . . . . . . . . . . . . . . . . (304) 558-3669

## Office of Laboratory Services [OLS]

167 11th Avenue, South Charleston, WV 25303
Tel: (304) 558-3530  Fax: (304) 558-2006

Director **(Vacant)** . . . . . . . . . . . . . . . . . . . . . (304) 558-3530 ext. 2110

Clinical Laboratory Services Associate Director
  **Sharon L. Cibrik** . . . . . . . . . . . . . . . . . (304) 558-3530 ext. 2106

Environmental Health Services Laboratory
  Director **Thomas L. "Tom" Ong** . . . . . . . . . . . (304) 558-3530 ext. 2710

## Office of Maternal, Child and Family Health [OMCFH]

350 Capitol Street, Room 427, Charleston, WV 25301-3714
Tel: (304) 558-5388  Fax: (304) 558-2866

Director (Interim) **Christina R. Mullins** . . . . . . . . . . . . . . (304) 558-5388
  E-mail: christina.r.mullins@wv.gov

Children with Special Health Care Needs Director
  **Mekell L. Golden** . . . . . . . . . . . . . . . . . . . . . . . . . . (304) 558-5388

Infant, Child and Adolescent Health Director
  **James E. "Jim" Jeffries** . . . . . . . . . . . . . . . . . . . . . (304) 558-5388
  E-mail: james.e.jeffries@wv.gov

Oral Health Dental Director **Dr. Jason M. Roush** . . . . . . . . (304) 558-5388

Perinatal and Women's Services Director
  **Denise A. Smith** . . . . . . . . . . . . . . . . . . . . . . . . . . . (304) 558-5388

## Office of Nutrition Services [ONS]

350 Capitol Street, Room 519, Charleston, WV 25301-3717
Tel: (304) 558-0030  Fax: (304) 558-1541

Director **Cynthia M. Pillo** . . . . . . . . . . . . . . . . . . . . . . . (304) 356-4495
  E-mail: cindy.m.pillo@wv.gov

## Center for Local Health

350 Capitol Street, Room 515, Charleston, WV 25301
Tel: (304) 558-8870  Fax: (304) 558-1437

Director **Amy D. Atkins** . . . . . . . . . . . . . . . . . . . . . . . . (304) 558-8870

Deputy Director **Rebecca A. Schmidt** . . . . . . . . . . . . . . . (304) 558-8870

Public Health Administrative Coordinator
  **Linda F. Lipscomb** . . . . . . . . . . . . . . . . . . . . . . . . . (304) 558-8870
  E-mail: linda.f.lipscomb@wv.gov

Public Health Financial Coordinator **Lisa M. Thompson** . . (304) 558-8870

Public Health Nursing Coordinator **Judy P. McGill, RN** . . . (304) 558-8870

## Center for Threat Preparedness

505 Capitol Street, Suite 200, Charleston, WV 25301
Tel: (304) 558-6900  Fax: (304) 558-0464
Internet: www.dhhr.wv.gov/healthprep

Director **Jerry Rhodes** . . . . . . . . . . . . . . . . . . . (304) 558-6900 ext. 2007

## Health Statistics Center

350 Capitol Street, Room 165, Charleston, WV 25301
Tel: (304) 558-9100  Fax: (304) 558-1787

Director **Dan M. Christy** . . . . . . . . . . . . . . . . . . . . . . . . (304) 356-4186

State Registrar and Assistant Director
  **Gary L. Thompson** . . . . . . . . . . . . . . . . . . . . . . . . . (304) 558-2931
  Fax: (304) 558-1051

Statistical Services Manager **Matthew Wickert** . . . . . . . . . (304) 356-4175

# Department of Military Affairs and Public Safety [DMAPS]

State Capitol Complex, Building 1, 1900 Kanawha Boulevard, East,
Room 400W, Charleston, WV 25305-0120
Tel: (304) 558-2930  Fax: (304) 558-6221

**Employees:** 5,993  **Fiscal Year:** 2014  **Budget:** $637,039,980

■Secretary **Joseph C. Thornton** . . . . . . . . . . . . . . . . . . . (304) 558-2930
  E-mail: joseph.c.thornton@wv.gov
  Education: Marshall BA, MA
  Executive Assistant **Hannah M. Cunningham** . . . . . . . . . (304) 558-2930

Deputy Secretary **Jim E. Rubenstein** . . . . . . . . . . . . . . . (304) 558-2036
  Education: Fairmont State Col BA

Deputy Secretary for Legislative Affairs
  **Christine F. Morris** . . . . . . . . . . . . . . . . . . . . . . . . . (304) 558-2930
  E-mail: christine.f.morris@wv.gov

Assistant Secretary/Communications Director
  **Lawrence C. Messina** . . . . . . . . . . . . . . . . . . . . . . . (304) 558-2930
  E-mail: lawrence.c.messina@wv.gov

Administrative Services Manager I **Kelly S. Reese** . . . . . . . (304) 558-2930
  E-mail: kelly.s.reese@wv.gov
  Executive Secretary **Stephanie R. Tiller** . . . . . . . . . . . . (304) 558-2930

Chief Financial Officer **Michael W. Cutlip** . . . . . . . . . . . . (304) 558-2930

## Adjutant General's Office

1703 Coonskin Drive, Charleston, WV 25311-1085
Tel: (304) 561-6318  Fax: (304) 561-6327

■Adjutant General **MG James A. Hoyer, ARNG** . . . . . . . . . (304) 561-6317
  E-mail: james.a.hoyer.mil@mail.mil
  Education: Charleston 1983 BS; West Virginia Grad 1987 MS;
  Army War Col 2004 MSS
  Joint Staff Director **BG Harrison B. Gilliam, ARNG** . . . . (304) 561-6316

Assistant Adjutant General (Air)
  **BrigGen Timothy L. Frye, ANG** . . . . . . . . . . . . . . . . . (304) 341-6113

Assistant Adjutant General/Commander (Army)
  **BG Charles R. Veit, ARNG** . . . . . . . . . . . . . . . . . . . . (304) 561-6761

Air Staff Director **Col Michael O. Cadle, ANG** . . . . . . . . . (304) 341-6111

Communications and Cyber Programs Director
  **LtCol Jody Ogle, ANG** . . . . . . . . . . . . . . . . . . . . . . . (304) 561-6318
  E-mail: jody.ogle@ang.af.mil

Commander, Joint Task Force Homeland Defense
  **BG Russell A. Crane, ARNG** . . . . . . . . . . . . . . . . . . . (304) 561-6356

Joint Chief of Staff **BG Paige P. Hunter, ARNG** . . . . . . . . (304) 561-6631

Chief of Staff (Army) **COL William Crane, ARNG** . . . . . . . (304) 561-6436

Webmaster **Greg Wright** . . . . . . . . . . . . . . . . . . . . . . . (304) 561-6312

## State Fire Marshal's Office

1207 Quarrier Street, Suite 202, Charleston, WV 25301
Fax: (304) 558-2537

▲State Fire Marshal **Kenneth E. Tyree** . . . . . . . . . . . . . . . (304) 558-2191
  E-mail: kenneth.e.tyree@wv.gov

Chief Deputy State Fire Marshal **Bob Sharp** . . . . . . . . . . . (304) 558-2930

---

★ Elected Official     ■ Appointed by Governor     ● Appointed by Legislature     ▲ Appointed by Board or Commission     ◆ Appointed by State Supreme Court

Deputy State Fire Marshal for Inspections
**Clarence J. Leake** ................................. (304) 558-2191
Deputy State Fire Marshal for Investigation
**Jason D. Baltic** ...................... (304) 558-2191 ext. 53221

## Division of Corrections
Building 84, 1409 Greenbrier Street, Suite 230, Charleston, WV 25311
Tel: (304) 558-2036  Fax: (304) 558-5367
■Commissioner **Jim E. Rubenstein** ................... (304) 558-2036
  E-mail: james.e.rubenstein@wv.gov
Deputy Commissioner **Mike V. Coleman** .............. (304) 558-2036
Assistant Commissioner **Loita C. Butcher** ............. (304) 558-2036
Assistant Commissioner **Paul E. Simmons** ............. (304) 558-2036
Chief of Staff **Brad T. Douglas** ..................... (304) 558-2036
  E-mail: brad.t.douglas@wv.gov
  Education: West Virginia State U; Marshall
Administration Director **Patti J. Withrow** ............. (304) 558-2036
  E-mail: patti.j.withrow@wv.gov          Fax: (304) 558-8048
Classification Director **Rita M. Albury** ................ (304) 558-2036
                                         Fax: (304) 558-5934
Correctional Industries Director **Eddie N. Long** ......... (304) 558-6054
Corrections Investigation Director **Denver L. Rosier** ..... (304) 636-0222
                                         Fax: (304) 636-0010
Corrections Program Manager **Anthony W. Carrico** ..... (304) 558-2036
  Education: West Virginia
Human Resources Director **Katherine N. "Kathy" Hess** .. (304) 558-2036
                                         Fax: (304) 558-4878
Internal Auditor **David Phillips** ..................... (304) 558-2036
                                         Fax: (304) 558-1495
Parole Services Director **Robert B. Arnold** ............ (304) 558-2036
                                         Fax: (304) 558-1495
Programs Director **Jennifer M. Ballard** ............... (304) 558-2036
  E-mail: jennifer.m.ballard@wv.gov
Records and Interstate Compact Administrator and
  Coordinator **Diann Skiles** ...................... (304) 558-2036
Research and Technology Director **Debbie Richmond** .... (304) 558-2036
  E-mail: debbie.d.richmond@wv.gov        Fax: (304) 558-5934
Security Director **Steven R. Caudill** .................. (304) 221-2213

## Division of Homeland Security and Emergency Management
Tel: (304) 558-5380  Fax: (304) 344-4538

**Employees:** 50
■Director **James J. "Jimmy" Gianato** ................. (304) 558-5380
  E-mail: jimmy.j.gianato@wv.gov
Administration Director **Tom L. Dingess** .............. (304) 558-5380
  E-mail: tommy.l.dingess@wv.gov
Mitigation and Recovery Director **Albert M. Lisko, Jr.** ..... (304) 558-5380
Operations Director **Paul S. Howard** ................. (304) 558-5380
General Counsel **John A. Hoyer** ..................... (304) 746-2471
Public Information Officer **Timothy T. Rock** ............ (304) 558-5380
  E-mail: timothy.t.rock@wv.gov

## Division of Justice and Community Services
1204 Kanawha Boulevard, Charleston, WV 25301
Tel: (304) 558-8814  Fax: (304) 558-0391
Director **W. Rick Staton** ................... (304) 558-8814 ext. 53335
  E-mail: rick.w.staton@wv.gov
  Education: West Virginia 1980 BA, 1984 JD
Chief Deputy Director **Jeffrey D. Estep** ....... (304) 558-8814 ext. 53324
  E-mail: jeff.d.estep@wv.gov
Deputy Director **Leslie S. Boggess** ........... (304) 558-8814 ext. 53330
  E-mail: leslie.s.boggess@wv.gov
Director, Office of Research and Strategic
  Planning (Acting) **Douglas H. Spence** ....... (304) 558-8814 ext. 53317
  E-mail: douglas.h.spence@wv.gov

## Division of Juvenile Services
1200 Quarrier Street, 2nd Floor, Charleston, WV 25301
Tel: (304) 558-9800  Fax: (304) 558-2965
Internet: www.wvdjs.state.wv.us
■Director **Stephanie J. Bond** ...................... (304) 558-9800
  E-mail: stephanie.j.bond@wv.gov
Deputy Director **Denny E. Dodson** ................... (304) 558-9800
  E-mail: denny.e.dodson@wv.gov

## Division of Protective Services
Tel: (304) 558-9911  Fax: (304) 558-5604
Director **Kevin J. Foreman** ........................ (304) 558-9911
Deputy Director **Lt. Col. Jack C. Chambers** ........... (304) 558-9911

## West Virginia State Police
725 Jefferson Road, South Charleston, WV 25309
Tel: (304) 746-2100  Fax: (304) 746-2246
■Superintendent **Col. Carl Robert "Jay" Smithers** ....... (304) 746-2115
  E-mail: jay.smithers@wvsp.gov
  Education: West Virginia BA; Marshall MS
Deputy Superintendent **Lt. Col. Timothy D. Bradley** ..... (304) 746-2115
Field Services Chief **Anthony L. Cummings** ............ (304) 746-2115
Staff Services Chief **Major W. J. Scott** ............... (304) 746-2115
Special Operations Chief **Ronald D. Arthur** ............ (304) 766-5875
Forensic Lab Director **(Vacant)** ..................... (304) 746-2273

## Regional Jail and Correctional Facility Authority
1325 Virginia Street, East, Charleston, WV 25301
Tel: (304) 558-2110
Executive Director **David A. Farmer** .................. (304) 558-2110
Deputy Executive Director **Lori Lynch** ................ (304) 558-2110

## Parole Board
1356 Hansford Street, Suite B, Charleston, WV 25301
Tel: (304) 558-6366  Fax: (304) 558-5678
■Chair **Benita F. Murphy** .......................... (304) 558-6366
  E-mail: benita.f.murphy@wv.gov
■Member **Carol Bowen Greene** ..................... (304) 558-6366
  E-mail: carol.b.greene@wv.gov
  Education: Marshall
■Member **Christie L. Love** .......................... (304) 558-6366
  E-mail: christie.l.love@wv.gov
■Member **Michael J. McCarthy** ...................... (304) 558-6366
  E-mail: michael.j.mccarthy@wv.gov
■Member **David Clay Nohe** ......................... (304) 558-6366
  E-mail: david.c.nohe@wv.gov
■Member **Peggy J. Pope** ........................... (304) 558-6366
  E-mail: peggy.j.pope@wv.gov
■Member **Brenda J. Stucky** ......................... (304) 558-6366
  E-mail: brenda.j.stucky@wv.gov
■Member **Stephen T. Svokas** ........................ (304) 558-6366
  E-mail: stephen.t.svokas@wv.gov
■Member **Michael J. Trupo** ......................... (304) 558-6366
  E-mail: michael.j.trupo@wv.gov
Executive Secretary **Michelle L. Jones** ................ (304) 558-6366

## Department of Revenue
State Capitol Building, 1900 Kanawha Boulevard, East, Room 300-W, Charleston, WV 25305
Tel: (304) 558-1017  Fax: (304) 558-2324

**Employees:** 1,011  **Fiscal Year:** 2014  **Budget:** $2,140,849,006
■Secretary **Robert S. "Bob" Kiss** .................... (304) 558-0755
  E-mail: robert.s.kiss@wv.gov
  Education: Ohio State 1979 BA, JD
  Executive Assistant **Audrey C. Pennington** .......... (304) 558-0755
Deputy Secretary **Robert John Doyle** ................ (304) 558-1017
  Education: Shepherd U 1966 BS
Deputy Secretary **Mark B. Muchow** .................. (304) 558-8730
  State Capitol Building, 1900 Kanawha Boulevard East, Room 417-W, Charleston, WV 25305

*(continued on next page)*

---

★ Elected Official    ■ Appointed by Governor    ● Appointed by Legislature    ▲ Appointed by Board or Commission    ◆ Appointed by State Supreme Court

**Department of Revenue** continued

General Counsel **Doug Buffington** . . . . . . . . . . . . . . . . . (304) 558-3356
    Executive Secretary to the General Counsel
        **Kathy A. Torlone** . . . . . . . . . . . . . . . . . . . . . . (304) 558-3356
Communications Director **Lalena D. Price** . . . . . . . . . . . (304) 558-1017
    E-mail: lalena.d.price@wv.gov

## Alcohol Beverage Control Administration

900 Pennsylvania Avenue, 4th Floor, Charleston, WV 25302
Tel: (304) 356-5500  Fax: (304) 558-0081

■Commissioner **Ronald M. Moats** . . . . . . . . . . . . . . . . . (304) 356-5501
    E-mail: ronald.m.moats@wv.gov
    Education: Fairmont State U 1981 BS
    Executive Secretary **Jane Ann Reed** . . . . . . . . . . . . . (304) 356-5501
Deputy Commissioner **(Vacant)** . . . . . . . . . . . . . . . . . . (304) 356-5504
Comptroller **Julia M. Jones** . . . . . . . . . . . . . . . . . . . . . (304) 356-5510
                                                        Fax: (304) 957-0365
Enforcement Director **Thomas G. Valencia** . . . . . . . . . . . (304) 356-5526
Human Resources Director **Lisa B. Wensil** . . . . . . . . . . . (304) 356-5551
                                                        Fax: (304) 957-0307
Information Technology Director **Randy L. Haynes** . . . . . (304) 356-5531
    E-mail: randy.l.haynes@wv.gov          Fax: (304) 957-0197
Beer Administrator **Cindy J. Clark** . . . . . . . . . . . . . . . . (304) 356-5520
                                                        Fax: (304) 957-0303
Spirits and Wine Administrator
    **Kimberly D. "Kim" Hayes** . . . . . . . . . . . . . . . . . . (304) 536-5562
                                                        Fax: (304) 957-0350
Warehouse Manager **Ed L. Hart** . . . . . . . . . . . . . . . . . (304) 356-5570
                                                        Fax: (304) 759-0755
Licensing and Education **Shawn E. Smith** . . . . . . . . . . . (304) 356-5525
                                                        Fax: (304) 957-0306

## Lottery Commission

P.O. Box 2067, Charleston, WV 25327-2067
900 Pennsylvania Avenue, Charleston, WV 25302
Tel: (304) 558-0500  Fax: (304) 558-3321  E-mail: mail@wvlottery.com

■Director (Acting) **John A. Myers** . . . . . . . . . . . . . (304) 558-0500 ext. 311
    E-mail: jmyers@wvlottery.com
    Education: Ohio State

## Municipal Bond Commission

900 Pennsylvania Avenue, Suite 1117, Charleston, WV 25302
Tel: (304) 558-3971  Fax: (304) 558-1280

Executive Director **Sara L. Rogers** . . . . . . . . . . . . . . . . (304) 558-3971

## State Tax Department

Revenue Center, 1001 Lee Street, East, Charleston, WV 25301
Fax: (304) 558-8999

■Commissioner **Mark W. Matkovich** . . . . . . . . . . . . . . . (304) 558-0751
    E-mail: mark.w.matkovich@wv.gov
    Education: Albright BS; New Hampshire 1992 JD
    Executive Assistant **Alicia Elam** . . . . . . . . . . . . . . . . (304) 558-0751
        1001 Lee Street East, Charleston, WV 25301
Deputy Tax Commissioner **Gilbert W. Brewster** . . . . . . . (304) 558-8351
Assistant Commissioner of Operations
    **Danny W. Morgan** . . . . . . . . . . . . . . . . . . . . . . . . (304) 558-3834
General Counsel and Legal Division Director
    **Mark S. Morton** . . . . . . . . . . . . . . . . . . . . . . . . . (304) 558-8594
Account Administration Division Director
    **Matthew R. Irby** . . . . . . . . . . . . . . . . . . . . . . . . . (304) 558-8700
    E-mail: matthew.r.irby@wv.gov
Auditing Division Director **Dana K. Angell** . . . . . . . . . . . (304) 558-8553
Compliance Director **Thomas A. Moore** . . . . . . . . . . . . . (304) 558-8751
Criminal Investigations Division Director (Acting)
    **Randy M. Young** . . . . . . . . . . . . . . . . . . . . . . . . . (304) 558-8516
    Criminal Investigations Division Assistant Director
        (Acting) **Victor G. Bonnett** . . . . . . . . . . . . . . . (304) 558-8510
Information Technology Division Director
    **Kwasi Toombs** . . . . . . . . . . . . . . . . . . . . . . . . . . (304) 558-8850
        1206 Quarrier Street, Charleston, WV 25301
Property Tax Division Director **Jeffrey A. Amburgey** . . . . (304) 558-3940
    1124 Smith Street, East, Charleston, WV 25301

Research and Development Division Director (Acting)
    **Mark B. Muchow** . . . . . . . . . . . . . . . . . . . . . . . . (304) 558-8730
    State Capitol Building, 1900 Kanawha Boulevard, East, Room W-417,
    Charleston, WV 25305
Taxpayer Services Division Director
    **Mary-Margaret Chandler** . . . . . . . . . . . . . . . . . . . (304) 558-2051

## West Virginia Offices of the Insurance Commissioner [WVOIC]

Al Summers Building, 1124 Smith Street, Charleston, WV 25301
P.O. Box 50540, Charleston, WV 25305-0540
Tel: (304) 558-3386  Fax: (304) 558-0412  Internet: www.wvinsurance.gov

■Insurance Commissioner **Michael D. "Mike" Riley** . . . . . . (304) 558-3354
    E-mail: michael.riley@wv.gov
    Education: Marshall BBA, MBA
Deputy Commissioner **(Vacant)** . . . . . . . . . . . . . (304) 558-6279 ext. 1105
Finance Assistant Commissioner **Melinda Kiss** . . . . . . . . (304) 558-5091
                                                        Fax: (304) 558-5586
Regulation Assistant Commissioner **Tonya Gillespie** . . . . . (304) 558-2100
                                                        Fax: (304) 558-1365
Special Projects Assistant Commissioner **(Vacant)** . . . . . . (304) 558-3707
                                                        Fax: (304) 558-8037
Agents Licensing and Education Director
    **Elizabeth G. Webb** . . . . . . . . . . . . . . . . . . . . . . . (304) 558-0610
                                                        Fax: (304) 558-4966
Consumer Advocacy Director **Dennis Garrison** . . . . . . . . (304) 558-3864
                                                        Fax: (304) 558-2381
Information Systems Director **Mike Farren** . . . . . . . . . . . (304) 558-2293
    E-mail: mike.farren@wv.gov              Fax: (304) 558-4089
Legal Division Director/General Counsel
    **Andrew Pauley** . . . . . . . . . . . . . . . . . . . . . . . . . (304) 558-0401
                                                        Fax: (304) 558-1362
Access West Virginia Division Director **(Vacant)** . . . . . . . (304) 558-8264
                                                        Fax: (304) 558-3085
Claims Management Division Director
    **Samantha L. Chase** . . . . . . . . . . . . . . . . . (304) 558-1966 ext. 1236
                                                        Fax: (304) 558-8948
Consumer Services Division Director **Dena Wildman** . . . . . (304) 558-3386
                                                        Fax: (304) 558-4965
Employer Coverage Division Director **Deborah Tincher** . . . (304) 558-6279
    E-mail: deborah.tincher@wv.gov          Fax: (304) 558-5586
Financial Accounting Division Director **Melinda Kiss** . . . . . (304) 558-6279
                                                        Fax: (304) 558-5586
Financial Conditions Division Director/Chief Examiner
    **Leah Cooper** . . . . . . . . . . . . . . . . . . . . . . . . . . . (304) 558-2100
                                                        Fax: (304) 558-1365
Office of Inspector General Division Director
    **Dennis R. Rinehart** . . . . . . . . . . . . . . . . . . . . . . (304) 558-9065
                                                        Fax: (304) 558-5239
Rates and Forms Division Director **William Adamson** . . . . (304) 558-2094
                                                        Fax: (304) 558-1610
Receivables Management Division Director **Tina Clark** . . . . (304) 558-1200
                                                        Fax: (304) 558-0671
Administrative Services Manager **Debra Hughes** . . . . . . . . (304) 558-6279
    E-mail: debbie.hughes@wv.gov            Fax: (304) 558-4967
Document and Imaging Services **Mike Farren** . . . . . . . . . (304) 558-2293
                                                        Fax: (304) 558-4089
Offices of Judges - Chief Administrative Law Judge
    **Rebecca Roush** . . . . . . . . . . . . . . . . . . . . . . . . . (304) 558-1686
                                                        Fax: (304) 558-1021
Board of Review Chairperson **James Gray** . . . . . . . . . . . (304) 558-5230
                                                        Fax: (304) 558-1322
Public Relations Specialist **(Vacant)** . . . . . . . . . . . . . . . (304) 558-3029

## Division of Financial Institutions

900 Pennsylvania Avenue, Suite 306, Charleston, WV 25302
Tel: (304) 558-2294  Fax: (304) 558-0442  Internet: www.dfi.wv.gov

■Commissioner (Acting) **Dawn E. Holstein** . . . . . . . . . . . (304) 558-2294
    E-mail: dholstein@wvdob.org
Legal Director **Robert J. Lamont** . . . . . . . . . . . . . . . . . (304) 558-2294
    E-mail: blamont@wvdob.org

---

★ Elected Official     ■ Appointed by Governor     ● Appointed by Legislature     ▲ Appointed by Board or Commission     ◆ Appointed by State Supreme Court

## Office of Tax Appeals

1012 Kanawha Boulevard, East, Suite 300, Charleston, WV 25301
Tel: (304) 558-1666  Fax: (304) 558-1670  E-mail: wvota@wv.gov
Internet: www.wvota.gov

Chief Administrative Law Judge **Heather G. Harlan** . . . . . . (304) 558-1666

## State Budget Office

State Capitol Building One, 1900 Kanawha Boulevard, East,
Room 310-W, Charleston, WV 25305
Tel: (304) 558-0040  Fax: (304) 558-1588

State Budget Office Director **Mike P. McKown, CPA** . . . . . .(304) 558-0040

## Department of Transportation [WVDOT]

State Capitol Complex, Building Five, 1900 Kanawha Boulevard, East,
Room A-109, Charleston, WV 25305-0430
Tel: (304) 558-0444  TTY: (800) 724-6991  Fax: (304) 558-1004
E-mail: dot.secretary@wv.gov

**Employees:** 6,138  **Fiscal Year:** 2014  **Budget:** $1,213,240,148

■Secretary **Paul Mattox, Jr.** . . . . . . . . . . . . . . . . . . . . . . . . . (304) 558-0444
  E-mail: dot.secretary@wv.gov
  Executive Secretary **Karen N. Zamow** . . . . . . . . . . . . . . . (304) 558-0444
  Engineering Advisor **Jimmy D. Wriston** . . . . . . . . . . . . . (304) 647-7450
  Deputy Secretary **Harry L. Bergstrom** . . . . . . . . . . . . . . . (304) 558-0444
    Education: West Virginia 1975 BBA
  Deputy Secretary of Finance and Administration
    **Keith E. Chapman** . . . . . . . . . . . . . . . . . . . . . . . . . . . . . (304) 558-2811
                                                Fax: (304) 558-4076
  Assistant Deputy Secretary **Marvin G. Murphy** . . . . . . . . (304) 473-5500
  Communications Director **Brent H. Walker** . . . . . . . . . . . . (304) 558-0103
    E-mail: brent.h.walker@wv.gov
  Equal Employment Opportunity Director
    **Drema L. Smith** . . . . . . . . . . . . . . . . . . . . . . . . . . . . . . . (304) 558-3931

## Highways Division

Building Five, 1900 Kanawha Boulevard, East, Room A-110,
Charleston, WV 25305
Tel: (304) 558-3505

■Commissioner **Paul Mattox, Jr.** . . . . . . . . . . . . . . . . . . . . . (304) 558-3505
  E-mail: dot.secretary@wv.gov
  Deputy Commissioner **Harry L. Bergstrom** . . . . . . . . . . . (304) 558-3505
    E-mail: harry.l.bergstrom@wv.gov
  Assistant Commissioner **John R. McBrayer** . . . . . . . . . . . (304) 558-2530
    E-mail: john.r.mcbrayer@wv.gov
  State Highway Engineer **Gregory L. "Greg" Bailey** . . . . . . (304) 558-2804
    E-mail: gregory.l.bailey@wv.gov
  Construction Deputy State Highway Engineer (Acting)
    **Stephen Todd Rumbaugh** . . . . . . . . . . . . . . . . . . . . . . . (304) 558-6266
    E-mail: stephen.t.rumbaugh@wv.gov
  Development Deputy State Highway Engineer (Acting)
    **Stephen Todd Rumbaugh** . . . . . . . . . . . . . . . . . . . . . . . (304) 558-0191
    E-mail: stephen.t.rumbaugh@wv.gov
  Operations Deputy State Highway Engineer
    **Ronald G. Smith** . . . . . . . . . . . . . . . . . . . . . . . . . . . . . . (304) 558-6264
    E-mail: ronald.g.smith@wv.gov
  Equipment Director **Marvin G. Murphy** . . . . . . . . . . . . . . (304) 473-5500
    E-mail: marvin.murphy@wv.gov
  Finance Director **James B. "Jim" Hash** . . . . . . . . . . . . . . (304) 558-9411
    E-mail: jim.b.hash@wv.gov
  Human Resources Director **Kathleen C. Dempsey** . . . . . . . (304) 558-3111
  Information Systems Services Director
    **Kimber Lee Asseff** . . . . . . . . . . . . . . . . . . . . . . . . . . . . (304) 558-9408
    E-mail: kimber.l.asseff@wv.gov
  Legal Director **Michael J. Folio** . . . . . . . . . . . . . . . . . . . . (304) 558-2823
    E-mail: michael.j.folio@wv.gov
  Office Services Director **Ameche L. Watson** . . . . . . . . . . . (304) 558-9216
    E-mail: ameche.l.watson@wv.gov
  Program Planning and Administration Director
    **Ryland W. Musick, PE** . . . . . . . . . . . . . . . . . . . . . . . . . (304) 558-3113
    E-mail: ryland.w.musick@wv.gov
  Right-of-Way Director **David A. Neil** . . . . . . . . . . . . . . . . (304) 558-2822

Traffic Engineering Director **Cindy L. Cramer** . . . . . . . . . . (304) 558-3063
  E-mail: cindy.l.cramer@wv.gov
Contract Administration Division Director
  **Jason M. Boyd, PE** . . . . . . . . . . . . . . . . . . . . . . . . . . . . . (304) 558-3304
  E-mail: jason.m.boyd@wv.gov
Engineering Division Director **R.J. Scites** . . . . . . . . . . . . . (304) 558-9722
  E-mail: r.j.scites@wv.gov
Maintenance Division Director **W. Kyle Stollings** . . . . . . . (304) 558-2901
  E-mail: w.kyle.stollings@wv.gov
Materials Control, Soil & Testing Division Director
  **Ron L. Stanevich** . . . . . . . . . . . . . . . . . . . . . . . . . . . . . . (304) 558-9892
  E-mail: ronald.l.stanevich@wv.gov

## Motor Vehicles Division [DMV]

State Capitol Complex, Building Three, 1800 Kanawha Boulevard, East,
Room 319, Charleston, WV 25317
Tel: (304) 558-3900  Fax: (304) 558-1987

■Commissioner **Patricia S. Reed** . . . . . . . . . . . . . . . . . . . . . (304) 558-2723
  E-mail: patricia.s.reed@wv.gov
  E-mail: dot.dmvcommissioner@wv.gov
Deputy Commissioner **(Vacant)** . . . . . . . . . . . . . . . . . . . . . (304) 558-2723
  Executive Assistant to the Commissioner
    **Esther L. Miller** . . . . . . . . . . . . . . . . . . . . . . . . . . . . . . (304) 558-2723
    E-mail: esther.l.miller@wv.gov
Legal Counsel **Jill C. Dunn** . . . . . . . . . . . . . . . . . . . . . . . . . (304) 558-3611
  E-mail: jill.c.dunn@wv.gov
Driver Services Director **David H. Bolyard** . . . . . . . . . . . . (304) 558-3913
  E-mail: david.h.bolyard@wv.gov
Field Services Director **Donald Pete Lake** . . . . . . . . . . . . . (304) 558-1040
  E-mail: d.pate.lake@wv.gov
Management Services Director **Jerry L. Conrad** . . . . . . . . . (304) 926-3842
  E-mail: jerry.l.conrad@wv.gov
Motor Vehicles Division Information Services Director
  **Wilbur L. Thaxton** . . . . . . . . . . . . . . . . . . . . . . . . . . . . . (304) 558-3900
  E-mail: wilbur.l.thaxton@wv.gov
Titles and Registration Director **Michael L. Maggard** . . . . (304) 558-5309
  E-mail: michael.l.maggard@wv.gov
■Vehicle Services, IRP, and Dealers Director
  **Michael L. Maggard** . . . . . . . . . . . . . . . . . . . . . . . . . . . . (304) 558-5309
  E-mail: michael.l.maggard@wv.gov

## Public Transit Division

State Capitol Complex, Building Five, 1900 Kanawha Boulevard, East,
Room 906, Charleston, WV 25305
Fax: (304) 558-0174

Director **William C. Robinson** . . . . . . . . . . . . . . . . . . . . . . (304) 558-0428

## Public Port Authority

State Capitol Complex, Building Five, 1900 Kanawha Boulevard, East,
Room 503, Charleston, WV 25305

▲Director **Charles Neal Vance** . . . . . . . . . . . . . . . . . . . . . . (304) 558-0330
  E-mail: charles.n.vance@wv.gov
Executive Secretary **Barbara Bosley** . . . . . . . . . . . . . . . . . (304) 558-0330

## State Rail Authority

P.O. Box 470, Moorefield, WV 26836

▲Executive Director **Cindy K. Butler** . . . . . . . . . . . . (304) 538-2305 ext. 223
  E-mail: cindy.k.butler@wv.gov

## West Virginia Parkways Authority

3310 Piedmont Road, Charleston, WV 25311
Tel: (304) 926-1900  Fax: (304) 926-1909

General Manager **Gregory C. Barr** . . . . . . . . . . . . . . . . . . . (304) 926-1900
  Education: Marshall 1974 BBA
Director of Maintenance Engineering **Ron Hamilton** . . . . . . (304) 929-1900
  374 George Street, Beckley, WV 25801
  E-mail: rhamilton@wvturnpike.com

★ Elected Official   ■ Appointed by Governor   ● Appointed by Legislature   ▲ Appointed by Board or Commission   ◆ Appointed by State Supreme Court

*State Yellow Book*          © Leadership Directories, Inc.          Summer 2016

EXECUTIVE BRANCH

## Department of Veterans Assistance

1514-B Kanawha Boulevard, East, Charleston, WV 25311
Tel: (304) 558-3661 Fax: (304) 558-3662 E-mail: wvdva@state.wv.us

**Employees:** 292 **Fiscal Year:** 2014 **Budget:** $20,741,719

■Cabinet Secretary **(Vacant)**...........................(304) 558-3661
  Chief Administrative Officer **Stacy E. Brown**..........(304) 558-3661
Deputy Cabinet Secretary **Billy Wayne Bailey, Jr.**........(304) 558-3661
  Education: Morris Harvey Col (Attended); Marshall (Attended)
Donel C. Kinnard Memorial State Veterans Cemetery
  Administrator **Larissa M. Wines**......................(304) 746-0026
West Virginia Veterans Home Administrator
  **Thomas L. McBride**..................................(304) 736-1027
                         Fax: (304) 736-1093
West Virginia Veterans Nursing Facility Administrator
  **Kevin B. Crickard**..................................(304) 626-1600
Operations Manager **Mike C. Lyons**....................(304) 558-3661
Public Affairs Coordinator **Randy W. Coleman**.........(304) 558-3661

## Higher Education Policy Commission

1018 Kanawha Boulevard, East, Suite 700, Charleston, WV 25301
Tel: (304) 558-2101 Fax: (304) 558-5719 Internet: www.wvhepc.com

▲Chancellor **Dr. Paul L. Hill, PhD**.....................(304) 558-0699
  E-mail: chancellor.hill@wvhepc.edu
  Education: Marshall BS, MS; Louisville 1983 PhD
Academic Affairs Vice Chancellor
  **Dr. Corley Dennison**......................(304) 558-0261 ext. 237
  Education: James Madison 1976 BA;
  Northwest Missouri State 1984 MA; West Virginia 1992 EdD
Administration Executive Vice Chancellor
  **Matthew R. "Matt" Turner**................(304) 558-4016 ext. 230
  E-mail: matt.turner@wvhepc.edu
  Education: Marshall
Finance Vice Chancellor **Dr. Edward Magee**.....(304) 558-0281 ext. 335
Health Sciences Vice Chancellor
  **Dr. Robert B. Walker, MD**..........................(304) 558-0530
  E-mail: robert.walker@wvhepc.edu
Human Resources Vice Chancellor **Patricia "Trish" Clay**..(304) 558-2104
Policy and Planning Vice Chancellor **Dr. Neal Holly**......(304) 558-1112
  E-mail: neal.holly@wvhepc.edu
Student Affairs Vice Chancellor **Dr. Adam S. Green**.....(304) 558-0655
General Counsel **Bruce Walker**............(304) 558-2102 ext. 221
  Education: Michigan State BA; Washington and Lee JD
Financial Aid Senior Director **Brian Weingart**....(304) 558-4618 ext. 234
  Education: Alderson-Broaddus BA; West Virginia MA
Science and Research Director **Dr. Jan R. Taylor**..(304) 558-4128 ext. 286
Statewide Academic Initiatives Director
  **Dr. Keri Ferro**..........................(304) 558-0261 ext. 240
Student and Educational Services Director
  **Daniel Crockett**....................................(304) 558-0655
  Education: Marshall BA; West Virginia Grad MA
Veterans Education and Training Programs Director
  **L.G. Corder**........................................(304) 558-0263

## Public Service Commission of West Virginia

201 Brooks Street, Charleston, WV 25301
P.O. Box 812, Charleston, WV 25323
Tel: (304) 340-0300 Tel: (800) 344-5113 Fax: (304) 340-0325
Internet: www.psc.state.wv.us

■Chairman **Michael A. "Mike" Albert**................(304) 340-0306
  Term Expires: June 30, 2019
  E-mail: malbert@psc.state.wv.us
  Education: West Virginia 1965 BBA, 1972 JD
■Commissioner **Brooks F. McCabe, Jr.**...............(304) 340-0303
  Term Expires: June 30, 2021
  Education: Vermont 1970 BS, 1972 MEd; West Virginia 1975 EdD
■Commissioner **Kara Cunningham Williams**...........(304) 340-0307
  Term Expires: June 30, 2017
  Education: Washington and Lee BA; Harvard JD

## West Virginia Real Estate Commission [WVREC]

300 Capitol Street, Suite 400, Charleston, WV 25301
Tel: (304) 558-3555 Fax: (304) 558-6442 E-mail: wvrec@wv.gov
Internet: www.wvrec.org

**Employees:** 12 **Fiscal Year:** 2014 **Budget:** $577,738,000

■Chairman **Cheryl L. Dawson**.........................(304) 720-1201
                         Fax: (304) 344-5352
■Vice Chairman **Kathryn L. Martin**....................(304) 296-1533
                         Fax: (304) 296-1897
■Secretary **Kathy J. Zaferatos**.......................(304) 254-0972
                         Fax: (304) 254-0991
■Member **Joe L. Ellison**..............................(304) 558-3555
■Member **Densil L. Nibert**...........................(304) 876-2418
                         Fax: (304) 876-8772
▲Executive Director **Jerry A. Forren**..................(304) 558-3555
  E-mail: jerry.a.forren@wv.gov

## West Virginia Board of Education

State Capitol Complex, Building 6, 1900 Kanawha Boulevard, East,
Room 351, Charleston, WV 25305-0330
Tel: (304) 558-3660 Fax: (304) 558-0198 E-mail: vharris@k12.wv.us

■President **Michael I. Green**..........................(304) 558-3660
  Term Expires: November 2018
  Education: Boston U BA; Johns Hopkins MS
■Vice President **Lloyd G. Jackson II**..................(304) 558-3660
  Term Expires: November 2020
  Education: West Virginia 1974, 1977 JD
■Secretary **Tina H. Combs**...........................(304) 558-3660
  Term Expires: November 2016
  Education: Mountain State BS
■Member **Thomas W. Campbell**.......................(304) 558-3660
  Term Expires: November 2021
  Education: West Virginia 1983 BSBA
■Member **Beverly E. Kingery**.........................(304) 558-3660
  Term Expires: November 4, 2022
■Member **Gayle Conelly Manchin**.....................(304) 558-3660
  Term Expires: November 2015
  Education: West Virginia BA, MA
■Member **Scott Rotruck**.............................(304) 558-3660
  Affiliation: Director of Energy and Transportation Services,
  Governmental Affairs Practice Group, Spilman Thomas & Battle,
  PLLC
  48 Donley Street, Morgantown, WV 26501
■Member **William M. "Bill" White**...................(304) 558-3660
  Term Expires: November 2019
  Education: Bluefield Col BS; Fielding DEd
■Member **Dr. James S. Wilson**.......................(304) 558-3660
  Term Expires: November 4, 2023
  Education: West Virginia DDS
Ex Officio Member **Dr. Paul L. Hill, PhD**..............(304) 558-2101
  Affiliation: Chancellor, Higher Education Policy Commission, State of
  West Virginia
  1018 Kanawha Boulevard, East, Suite 700, Charleston, WV 25301
Ex Officio Member **Michael J. Martirano, EdD**.........(304) 558-2681
  Affiliation: State Superintendent of Schools, West Virginia Department
  of Education, West Virginia Board of Education, State of West Virginia
  Building 6, 1900 Kanawha Boulevard, East, Charleston, WV 25305
  Education: Maryland 1981 BS; Nova Southeastern 1994 EdD
Ex Officio Member **Dr. Sarah Armstrong Tucker**......(304) 558-0265
  Affiliation: Chancellor, Community and Technical College System of
  West Virginia, State of West Virginia
  1018 Kanawha Boulevard, East, Suite 700, Charleston, WV 25301

## West Virginia Department of Education [WVDE]

Building 6, 1900 Kanawha Boulevard, East, Charleston, WV 25305
Tel: (304) 558-2681 TTY: (304) 558-2696 ext. 200 Fax: (304) 558-0048

**Employees:** 566 **Fiscal Year:** 2014 **Budget:** $2,459,968,876

▲State Superintendent of Schools
  **Michael J. Martirano, EdD**.........................(304) 558-2681
  E-mail: superintendent@wvde.state.wv.us
  Administrative Assistant **Darcel Vermillion**...........(304) 558-2681

---

★ Elected Official   ■ Appointed by Governor   ● Appointed by Legislature   ▲ Appointed by Board or Commission   ◆ Appointed by State Supreme Court

Chief of Staff **Jill Newman** . . . . . . . . . . . . . . . . . . . . . . . . . (304) 558-3762
  E-mail: jill.newman@k12.wv.us
Deputy Superintendent **Cynthia Daniel** . . . . . . . . . . . . . . . . (304) 558-3762
Chief Academic Officer **Clayton Burch** . . . . . . . . . . . . . . . (304) 558-9994
Chief Accountability and Performance Officer
  **Michele Blatt** . . . . . . . . . . . . . . . . . . . . . . . . . . . . . . . . . (304) 558-3199
Chief Career and Technical Education Officer
  **Dr. Kathy J. D'Antoni** . . . . . . . . . . . . . . . . . . . . . . . . . . (304) 558-2346
    Education: West Virginia PhD
    GED (General Education Development) Assistant
    Director **Debra Kimbler** . . . . . . . . . . . . . . . . . . . . . . . . (304) 558-6315
      E-mail: dkimbler@k12.wv.us
Chief Operations Officer **Joe Panetta** . . . . . . . . . . . . . . . . . (304) 558-2691
Chief Technology Officer **Sterling Beane, Jr.** . . . . . . . . . . . (304) 558-3705
  E-mail: sbeane@k12.wv.us

# Office of the Attorney General

State Capitol Complex, Building 1, Room E-26, Charleston, WV 25305
Tel: (304) 558-2021  Fax: (304) 558-1040

**Employees:** 197  **Fiscal Year:** 2014  **Budget:** $14,199,197

★ Attorney General **Patrick Morrisey** (R) . . . . . . . . . . . . . . . . (304) 558-2021
  Term Expires: January 2017
  Education: Rutgers 1989 BA, 1992 JD
  Career: Deputy Staff Director and Chief Health Counsel, Committee
  on Energy and Commerce, United States House of Representatives
  (2003-2004); Partner, Washington, DC Office, Sidley Austin LLP
  (2004-2010)
  Administrative Assistant **Vicki L. Pendell** . . . . . . . . . . . . (304) 558-2021
Senior Deputy Attorney General and Chief Operating
  Officer **Anthony P. Martin** . . . . . . . . . . . . . . . . . . . . . . . (304) 558-2021
Senior Deputy Attorney General **James R. "Bob" Leslie** . . (304) 558-0546
  E-mail: james.r.leslie@wvago.gov
Deputy Attorney General **Chris S. Dodrill** . . . . . . . . . . . . . (304) 558-2021
  Education: Naval Acad 2001 BS; Duke 2008 JD
Assistant Attorney General **Katlyn M. Miller** . . . . . . . . . . . (304) 558-2021
  Education: Vanderbilt 2014 JD
Solicitor General **Elbert Lin** . . . . . . . . . . . . . . . . . . . . . . . . (304) 558-2021
  Education: Yale BA, 2003 JD
Tax, Revenue and Transportation Senior Deputy Attorney
  General **Katherine A. Schultz** . . . . . . . . . . . . . . . . . . . . (304) 558-2522
  E-mail: kas@wvago.gov             Fax: (304) 558-2525
  Education: West Virginia 1985 JD
Administrative and Education Deputy Attorney General
  **Kelli D. Talbott** . . . . . . . . . . . . . . . . . . . . . . . . . . . . . . . (304) 558-2021
  State Capitol, 1900 Kanawha Boulevard, East,   Fax: (304) 558-0140
  Room 26-E, Charleston, WV 25305-0220
  E-mail: kdt@wvago.gov
  Education: West Virginia 1988 JD
Appellate Division Deputy Attorney General
  **Laura J. Young** . . . . . . . . . . . . . . . . . . . . . . . . . . . . . . . . (304) 558-5830
Civil Rights Division Deputy Attorney General
  **Ann L. Haight** . . . . . . . . . . . . . . . . . . . . . . . . . . . . . . . . (304) 558-0546
  812 Quarrier Street, 2nd Floor,      Fax: (304) 558-0649
  Charleston, WV 25301-2617
Consumer Protection/Antitrust Division Deputy Attorney
  General **Ann L. Haight** . . . . . . . . . . . . . . . . . . . . . . . . . . (304) 558-8986
  812 Quarrier Street, 1st Floor,      Fax: (304) 558-0184
  Charleston, WV 25301-2617
Natural Resources Division Assistant Attorney General
  **Will Valentino** . . . . . . . . . . . . . . . . . . . . . . . . . . . . . . . . (304) 558-2021
  E-mail: william.r.valentino@wvago.gov   Fax: (304) 558-0140
Press Secretary **Curtis M. Johnson** . . . . . . . . . . . . . . . . . . (304) 558-2021
  E-mail: curtis.m.johnson@wvago.gov
Deputy Press Secretary **Erin D. Timony** . . . . . . . . . . . . . . (304) 558-2021
  E-mail: erin.d.timony@wvago.gov
  Education: Mississippi
Chief Financial Officer **Jamion A. Wolford** . . . . . . . . . . . . (304) 558-2021

# Office of the Secretary of State

State Capitol Complex, Building One, 1900 Kanawha Boulevard, East,
Suite 157K, Charleston, WV 25305-0770
Tel: (304) 558-6000  Fax: (304) 558-0900  E-mail: wvsos@wvsos.com

**Employees:** 62  **Fiscal Year:** 2014  **Budget:** $7,247,139

★ Secretary of State **Natalie E. Tennant** (D) . . . . . . . . . . . . . (304) 558-6000
  Term Expires: January 2017
  Education: West Virginia 1991 BA, 2000
Deputy Secretary of State **Sheryl Webb** . . . . . . . . . . . . . . . (304) 558-6000
Chief Counsel **E. Ashley Summitt** . . . . . . . . . . . . . . . . . . . (304) 558-6000
Chief Financial Officer **John Sandoro** . . . . . . . . . . . . . . . . (304) 558-6000
Chief Information Officer **Beth Ann Surber** . . . . . . . . . . . . (304) 558-6000
  E-mail: bsurber@wvsos.com
Business and Licensing Director **Penney Barker** . . . . . . . . (304) 558-8000
Communications Director **Briana Wilson** . . . . . . . . . . . . . . (304) 558-6000
  E-mail: bwilson@wvsos.com
Elections Director **Layna Brown** . . . . . . . . . . . . . . . . . . . . . (304) 558-6000
Legislative Director **David Nichols** . . . . . . . . . . . . . . . . . . . (304) 558-6000
  E-mail: dnichols@wvsos.com
Policy Director **Justin Williams** . . . . . . . . . . . . . . . . . . . . . (304) 558-6000

# Office of the State Treasurer

State Capitol Building, 1900 Kanawha Boulevard, East, Room E-145,
Charleston, WV 25305
Tel: (304) 558-5000  Tel: (800) 422-7498  TTY: (304) 340-1598
Fax: (304) 558-4097  E-mail: webmaster@wvsto.com

**Employees:** 131  **Fiscal Year:** 2014  **Budget:** $285,061,205

★ State Treasurer **John D. Perdue** (D) . . . . . . . . . . . . . . . . . . (304) 558-5000
  Term Expires: January 2017
  E-mail: john.perdue@wvsto.com
  Education: West Virginia 1972 BS
Assistant State Treasurer **Josh Daniel Stowers** . . . . . . . . . . (304) 558-5000
  Education: Concord Col BS; Marshall MA
Deputy Treasurer of Administration **Bryan W. Archer** . . . . (304) 341-0713
  E-mail: bryan.archer@wvsto.com
  Education: Charleston
Deputy Treasurer of Cash Management **Misty Price** . . . . . . (304) 341-1570
  Education: Marshall BSBA
Deputy Treasurer of College Savings **Tazuer Smith** . . . . . . (304) 340-5025
  Education: West Virginia JD
Deputy Treasurer of Communications **Gina Joynes** . . . . . . (304) 341-0758
  E-mail: gina.joynes@wvsto.com
Deputy Treasurer of Local Government **Pat Jack** . . . . . . . . (304) 254-2944
  Education: Shepherd U BA
Deputy Treasurer of Purchasing **Shelly Murray** . . . . . . . . . (304) 341-7089
  Education: West Virginia State Col BS
Deputy Treasurer of Records Management and Security
  **Mike Comer** . . . . . . . . . . . . . . . . . . . . . . . . . . . . . . . . . . (304) 340-5021
Deputy Treasurer of Unclaimed Property
  **Carolyn Atkinson** . . . . . . . . . . . . . . . . . . . . . . . . . . . . . (304) 341-0703
  Education: Wake Forest BA; Capital U JD
General Counsel **Diana Stout** . . . . . . . . . . . . . . . . . . . . . . . (304) 341-7081

# Office of the State Auditor

1900 Kanawha Boulevard, East, Room W-100, Charleston, WV 25305
Tel: (304) 558-2251  TTY: (877) 982-9148  Fax: (304) 558-5200
Internet: www.wvsao.gov

**Employees:** 195  **Fiscal Year:** 2014  **Budget:** $35,450,864

★ State Auditor **Lisa Hopkins** . . . . . . . . . . . . . . . . . . . . . . . . (304) 558-2261
  Term Expires: January 2017
  Education: Barnard; Boston U JD
  Career: General Counsel and Deputy Commissioner of Securities,
  Office of the State Auditor, State of West Virginia (2001-2016)
Senior Deputy State Auditor **Russell Rollyson** . . . . . . . . . . (304) 558-2261
General Counsel and Deputy Securities Commissioner
  **(Vacant)** . . . . . . . . . . . . . . . . . . . . . . . . . . . . . . . . . . . . . (304) 558-2261
  Executive Assistant to the Auditor **Andrea Bower** . . . . . (304) 558-2261
Chief Inspector Division Deputy State Auditor
  **Stuart Stickel** . . . . . . . . . . . . . . . . . . . . . . . . . . . . . . . . . (304) 558-2261
County Collections Deputy State Auditor **(Vacant)** . . . . . . . (304) 558-2261
Financial Services Deputy State Auditor **Mike Sizemore** . . (304) 558-2261

*(continued on next page)*

---

★ Elected Official   ■ Appointed by Governor   ● Appointed by Legislature   ▲ Appointed by Board or Commission   ◆ Appointed by State Supreme Court

EXECUTIVE BRANCH

**Office of the State Auditor** *continued*

Local Government Services Deputy State
  Auditor **Ora Ash** . . . . . . . . . . . . . . . . . . . . . . . . . (304) 627-2415 ext. 5114
Purchasing Card Deputy State Auditor **Amy Lewis** . . . . . . . (304) 558-2261
Controller **Charles Perdue** . . . . . . . . . . . . . . . . . . . . . . . . . (304) 558-2261
Accounting Division Director (Acting) **Pam Selbe** . . . . . . . (304) 558-2261
Human Resources Administrator (Acting) **Julia Gray** . . . . . (304) 558-2261
Information Services Chief Information Officer
  **David H. Williams** . . . . . . . . . . . . . . . . . . . . . . . . . . . (304) 558-2261
    E-mail: dh.williams@wvsao.gov
  Information Technology Operations Director
    **Michael "Mike" Barker** . . . . . . . . . . . . . . . . . . . . . . (304) 558-2261
      E-mail: mike.barker@wvsao.gov
Communications Director **Justin Southern** . . . . . (304) 558-2251 ext. 2132
    E-mail: justin.southern@wvsao.gov

# Department of Agriculture

State Capitol Complex, Building One, 1900 Kanawha Boulevard, East,
Room M-28, Charleston, WV 25305-0170
Tel: (304) 558-3200  Fax: (304) 558-0451

**Employees:** 338  **Fiscal Year:** 2014  **Budget:** $30,789,613

★ Commissioner **Walt Helmick** (D) . . . . . . . . . . . . . . . . . . . . (304) 558-3200
    Term Expires: January 2017
    E-mail: whelmick@wvda.us
Chief of Staff **Christopher T. Ferro** . . . . . . . . . . . . . . . . . . (304) 558-3200
    E-mail: cferro@wvda.us
Senior Manager **Robert C. "Bob" Tabb** . . . . . . . . . . . . . . . (304) 558-3200
  Senior Executive Assistant **Robin L. Gothard** . . . . . . . . . (304) 558-3200
  Executive Assistant **Jennifer Keaton** . . . . . . . . . . . . . . . . (304) 558-3200
  Executive Assistant **Jodee Martin** . . . . . . . . . . . . . . . . . . (304) 558-3200
Investigator **Ron Adkins** . . . . . . . . . . . . . . . . . . . . . . . . . . (304) 558-2214
    E-mail: radkins@wvda.us
West Virginia Conservation Agency Executive Director
  **Brian Farkas** . . . . . . . . . . . . . . . . . . . . . . . . . . . . . . . . (304) 558-2204
Administrative Services Division Director
  **Sandra Gillispie** . . . . . . . . . . . . . . . . . . . . . . . . . . . . . (304) 558-2222
    E-mail: sgillispie@wvda.us
State Veterinarian and Animal Health Division Director
  **Jewell Plumley, DVM** . . . . . . . . . . . . . . . . . . . . . . . . . . (304) 538-2397
                                                          Fax: (304) 538-8133
Communications Division Director **Butch Antolini** . . . . . . . (304) 558-3708
    E-mail: bantolini@wvda.us                             Fax: (304) 558-3131
  Communications Division Assistant Director
    **Beth Southern** . . . . . . . . . . . . . . . . . . . . . . . . . . . . . (304) 558-3708
      E-mail: bsouthern@wvda.us                           Fax: (304) 558-3131
Information Technology Division Director **Jon Adkins** . . . . (304) 558-3200
    E-mail: jadkins@wvda.us
Marketing and Development Division Director
  **Jean F. Smith** . . . . . . . . . . . . . . . . . . . . . . . . . . . . . . . (304) 558-2210
Meat and Poultry Inspection Division Director
  **Robert Pitts, DVM** . . . . . . . . . . . . . . . . . . . . . . . . . . . (304) 558-2206
    E-mail: rpitts@wvda.us
Plant Industries Division Director **Eric W. Ewing** . . . . . . . . (304) 558-2212
    E-mail: eewing@wvda.us
Regulatory and Environmental Affairs Division Director
  **Herma Johnson** . . . . . . . . . . . . . . . . . . . . . . . . . . . . . . (304) 558-2226
    E-mail: hjohnson@wvda.us
US-WV Agriculture Statistics State Statistician
  **Charmaine Wilson** . . . . . . . . . . . . . . . . . . . . . . . . . . . . (304) 345-5958

---

★ Elected Official    ■ Appointed by Governor    ● Appointed by Legislature    ▲ Appointed by Board or Commission    ◆ Appointed by State Supreme Court

# Wisconsin

Tel: (608) 266-1212 (State Information)   Internet: www.wisconsin.gov

**Number of U.S. Congressional Delegates:** 2 Senators; 8 Representatives   **Governor's Term:** 4 years
**Legislature Description:** 33 member Senate; 99 member Assembly; Term - Senate 4 years, House 2 years
**Next Election:** Governor November 2018; Legislature November 2016   **Number of Electoral Votes:** 10
**Official Name:** State of Wisconsin (Chippewa: gathering of the waters)   **Nickname:** The Badger State
**Motto:** Forward

**Population:** 5,771,337 (2015); Rank 20   **Fiscal Year:** 2015   **Budget:** $35,937,816,000

## Office of the Governor

State Capitol, 115 East Capitol, Madison, WI 53702
Tel: (608) 266-1212   Fax: (608) 267-8983

**Scott K. Walker**
Governor

Began Service: January 3, 2011
Term Expires: 2019
Date of Birth: November 2, 1967
Education: Marquette 1990 (Attended)
Religion: Baptist
Career: State Assembly Member (R-WI, District 14), Wisconsin State Assembly (1993-2002); County Executive, County of Milwaukee, Wisconsin (2002-2010)

★ Governor **Scott K. Walker** (R) . . . . . . . . . . . . . . . . . . . . . (608) 266-1212
E-mail: govgeneral@wisconsin.gov
Chief of Staff **Rich Zipperer** . . . . . . . . . . . . . . . . . . . . . . (608) 266-1212
Deputy Chief of Staff for Budget, Legislative, and
Intergovernmental Affairs **Cindy Polzin** . . . . . . . . . . . . . . (608) 266-1212
Deputy Chief of Staff for Communications
**Jack Jablonski** . . . . . . . . . . . . . . . . . . . . . . . . . . . . . . (608) 266-1212
Deputy Chief of Staff for Operations
**Matthew S. "Matt" Moroney** . . . . . . . . . . . . . . . . . . . . (608) 266-1212
Education: Loras 1991 BA; Iowa 1994 JD
Chief Legal Counsel **Katie Ignatowski** . . . . . . . . . . . . . . . (608) 266-1212
Deputy Legal Counsel **(Vacant)** . . . . . . . . . . . . . . . . . . . . (608) 267-3672
Assistant Legal Counsel **David Rabe** . . . . . . . . . . . . . . . . . (608) 267-3672
E-mail: karley.downing@wisconsin.gov
Deputy Communications Director and Press Secretary
**Tom Evenson** . . . . . . . . . . . . . . . . . . . . . . . . . . . . . . . (608) 266-1212
External Communications Director **(Vacant)** . . . . . . . . . . . . (608) 266-1212
Senior Legislative Director **(Vacant)** . . . . . . . . . . . . . . . . . (608) 266-1212
Senior Policy Advisor **Eileen Schoenfeldt** . . . . . . . . . . . . . (608) 267-3672
E-mail: eileen.schoenfeldt@wisconsin.gov
Policy Advisor **Patrick Hughes** . . . . . . . . . . . . . . . . . . . . (608) 266-1212
Senior Advisor **(Vacant)** . . . . . . . . . . . . . . . . . . . . . . . . . (608) 267-3672
Health Reform Policy Advisor **John Hoelter** . . . . . . . . . . . (608) 266-2157
Press Spokesperson **Laurel Patrick** . . . . . . . . . . . . . . . . . . (608) 267-7303
Special Assistant **Scott Matejov** . . . . . . . . . . . . . . . . . . . . (608) 267-3672
E-mail: scott.matejov@wisconsin.gov
Education: Wisconsin (Green Bay) 2003 BA

## Milwaukee Office

819 North Sixth Street, Room 560, Milwaukee, WI 53203
Fax: (414) 227-4500   Tel: (414) 227-4344

Director **Madeline Henry** . . . . . . . . . . . . . . . . . . . . . . . . (608) 266-1212
E-mail: madeline.henry@wisconsin.gov

## Washington Office

444 North Capitol Street, NW, Suite 613, Washington, DC 20001
Fax: (202) 624-5871

Federal Relations Director **Kyle Roskam** . . . . . . . . . . . . . . (202) 624-5870
E-mail: kyle.roskam@wisconsin.gov
Education: U St Thomas (MN)

## Office of the Commissioner of Insurance [OCI]

125 South Webster Street, Madison, WI 53703-3474
Tel: (608) 266-3585   Tel: (800) 236-8517   TTY: (608) 266-3586
Fax: (608) 266-9935   Internet: http://oci.wi.gov

■ Insurance Commissioner **Ted Nickel** . . . . . . . . . . . . . . . . . (608) 267-3782
E-mail: ted.nickel@wisconsin.gov
Education: Valparaiso BSBA
Executive Staff Assistant **Kathleen Beadles** . . . . . . . . . . . (608) 267-3782
Deputy Commissioner **Daniel "Dan" Schwartzer** . . . . . . . . (608) 267-1233
Education: Cardinal Stritch U BSBA
Executive Staff Assistant **Jill Kelly** . . . . . . . . . . . . . . . . . (608) 267-1233
Funds and Program Management Insurance Administrator
**(Vacant)** . . . . . . . . . . . . . . . . . . . . . . . . . . . . . . . . . . (608) 264-8113
Regulation and Enforcement Division Administrator
**Cari Lee** . . . . . . . . . . . . . . . . . . . . . . . . . . . . . . . . . (608) 267-4384
E-mail: cari.lee@wisconsin.gov
General Counsel **(Vacant)** . . . . . . . . . . . . . . . . . . . . . . . . (608) 266-7726
Legislative Liaison and Public Information Officer
**J. P. Wieske** . . . . . . . . . . . . . . . . . . . . . . . . . . . . . . . (608) 267-1233
E-mail: jp.wieske@wisconsin.gov
Education: Carroll Col (WI)
Financial Analysis and Examinations Bureau Director
**Rebecca "Becky" Easland** . . . . . . . . . . . . . . . . . . . . . (608) 261-8562
Market Regulation Bureau Director **(Vacant)** . . . . . . . . . . . (608) 266-8885
Policy Advisor **Jason Levine** . . . . . . . . . . . . . . . . . . . . . . (608) 267-7911
Webmaster **Marcia Elliott** . . . . . . . . . . . . . . . . . . . . . . . (608) 267-4396
E-mail: marcia.elliott@wisconsin.gov

## Office of State Employment Relations [OSER]

101 East Wilson Street, 4th Floor, Madison, WI 53702-0004
P.O. Box 7855, Madison, WI 53707-7855
Fax: (608) 267-1020   E-mail: derssec@oser.state.wi.us
Internet: http://oser.state.wi.us

**Employees:** 50   **Fiscal Year:** 2014   **Budget:** $6,108,000

■ Director **Gregory L. "Greg" Gracz** . . . . . . . . . . . . . . . . . . (608) 266-9820
E-mail: greg.gracz@wisconsin.gov
Education: Marquette 1970 BA; Milwaukee Tech 1970 AA
Deputy Director **(Vacant)** . . . . . . . . . . . . . . . . . . . . . . . . (608) 266-9820
Executive Assistant **Dominga "Dee" Surillo** . . . . . . . . . . (608) 266-9820
Chief Legal Counsel **Danielle L. Carne** . . . . . . . . . . . . . . . (608) 266-0047
Affirmative Action and Workforce Planning Division
Administrator **Jeanette Johnson** . . . . . . . . . . . . . . . . . . (608) 266-3017
Compensation and Labor Relations Division
Administrator **Kathy Kopp** . . . . . . . . . . . . . . . . . . . . . . (608) 266-0711
E-mail: kathy.kopp@wisconsin.gov
Merit Recruitment and Selection Division Administrator
**(Vacant)** . . . . . . . . . . . . . . . . . . . . . . . . . . . . . . . . . . (608) 266-1212

---

★ Elected Official    ■ Appointed by Governor    ● Appointed by Legislature    ▲ Appointed by Board or Commission    ◆ Appointed by State Supreme Court

EXECUTIVE BRANCH

## Department of Administration [DOA]

101 East Wilson Street, First Floor, Madison, WI 53702
P.O. Box 7864, Madison, WI 53707-7864
Tel: (608) 266-2309  Fax: (608) 264-9500  Internet: www.doa.state.wi.us

**Employees:** 1,014  **Fiscal Year:** 2015  **Budget:** $935,195,000

■Secretary **Scott A. Neitzel** .........................(608) 266-1741
  E-mail: scott.neitzel@wisconsin.gov
■Deputy Secretary **Cate Zeuske** ...................(608) 266-1741
  E-mail: cate.zeuske@wisconsin.gov
Assistant Deputy Secretary **John Hogan** ..............(608) 266-2309
Administrative Services Division Administrator
  **James Langdon** ...............................(608) 267-1001
  E-mail: james.langdon@wisconsin.gov
Capitol Police Division Administrator **David Erwin** .......(608) 266-7546
Enterprise Operations Division Administrator
  **Helen McCain** ...............................(608) 266-0779
  E-mail: helen.mccain@wisconsin.gov
Enterprise Technology Division Administrator and Chief
  Information Officer **David Cagigal** ..................(608) 264-9502
  Education: DePaul BS, MBA                Fax: (608) 267-0626
Executive Budget and Finance Division Administrator
  **Michael Heifetz** ..............................(608) 266-1035
Gaming Division Administrator **Steve Knudson** .........(608) 270-2560
  2005 West Beltline Highway, Suite 201, Madison, WI 53713-2314
  P.O. Box 8979, Madison, WI 53708-8979
  E-mail: steven.knudson@wisconsin.gov
Hearings and Appeals Division Administrator
  **Brian Hayes** .................................(608) 266-8007
  5005 University Avenue, Suite 201, Madison, WI 53705-5400
  P.O. Box 7875, Madison, WI 53707-7875
  E-mail: brian.hayes@wisconsin.gov
Intergovernment Relations Division Administrator
  **Ed Eberle** ...................................(608) 267-1824
  E-mail: ed.eberle@wisconsin.gov
State Facilities Development Division Administrator
  **Summer Strand** ..............................(608) 266-1031
  E-mail: summer.strand@wisconsin.gov
Communications Director **Cullen Werwie** ............(608) 266-7326

## Claims Board

101 East Wilson Street, Tenth Floor, Madison, WI 53702
Tel: (608) 264-9595  Fax: (608) 267-3842

Chairman **Corey Finkelmeyer** ......................(608) 264-9595
Secretary **Greg Murray**...........................(608) 264-9595
●Member **Mary Czaja**.............................(608) 264-9595
  Education: Wisconsin (River Falls) 1986 BS
●Member **Luther S. Olsen** ........................(608) 264-9595
  Education: Wisconsin 1973 BS
■Member **(Vacant)** ..............................(608) 264-9595
Staff Assistant **Patricia Reardon** ..................(608) 264-9595
  E-mail: Patricia.Reardon@wisconsin.gov

## Public Records Board

4622 University Avenue, Room 10A, Madison, WI 53702
Fax: (608) 266-5050

■Chair **Matthew Blessing**.........................(715) 267-6224
  E-mail: matthew.blessing@wisconsinhistory.org
■Vice-Chair **Sandra E. Broady-Rudd, CRM** ............(608) 429-2368
  E-mail: sandra.broadyrudd@wisconsin.gov
■Secretary **Carl Buesing** .........................(920) 912-5766
  E-mail: bues513@sbcglobal.net
Member **Paul Ferguson** ..........................(608) 264-9464
■Member **Anne Sappenfield**.......................(608) 259-9807
  E-mail: anne.sappenfield@legis.wisconsin.gov
■Member **Melissa Schmidt** ........................(608) 266-0922
  E-mail: melissa.schmidt@legis.state.wi.us
■Member **Peter Sorce** ...........................(262) 253-0561
  E-mail: ps9444@aol.com
■Member **(Vacant)** ..............................(608) 516-3746
Executive Secretary **Harold Coltharp** ................(608) 266-2770

## Building Commission

P.O. Box 7866, Madison, WI 53707
Tel: (608) 266-1855  TTY: (608) 267-9629  Fax: (608) 267-2710

Chair **Scott K. Walker** ...........................(608) 266-1212
  Affiliation: Governor, Office of the Governor, State of Wisconsin
  State Capitol, 115 East Capitol, Madison, WI 53702
▲Secretary **Summer Strand** ........................(608) 266-2731
Recording Secretary **Ruby Martin**...................(608) 266-1855

## Department of Agriculture, Trade and Consumer Protection [DATCP]

P.O. Box 8911, Madison, WI 53708-8911
Tel: (608) 224-5012  TTY: (608) 224-5058  Fax: (608) 224-5034
Internet: datcp.state.wi.us

**Employees:** 630  **Fiscal Year:** 2015  **Budget:** $97,074,000

■Secretary **Ben Brancel** ..........................(608) 224-5015
  E-mail: ben.brancel@wisconsin.gov
  Education: Wisconsin BS
Deputy Secretary **Jeff Lyon** .......................(608) 224-5035
Assistant Deputy Secretary **Sandra "Sandy" Chalmers** ..(608) 224-5035
  Education: Wisconsin BA; Nebraska MM
  Executive Assistant **Kelly Markor** .................(608) 224-5035
Agricultural Development Division Administrator
  **Daniel Smith** .................................(608) 224-5142
Agricultural Resource Management Division
  Administrator **John Petty** ........................(608) 224-4567
Animal Health Division Administrator **Dr. Paul McGraw** ..(608) 224-4880
Food Safety Division Administrator
  **Dr. Steven "Steve" Ingham** .....................(608) 224-4701
Management Services Division Administrator
  **Michelle Wachter** .............................(608) 224-4740
  E-mail: michelle.wachter@wi.gov
Trade and Consumer Protection Division Administrator
  **Frank J. Frassetto**.............................(608) 224-4920
  Education: Wisconsin (Oshkosh) 1984 BS
Executive Staff Assistant **Kelly Longfield** .............(608) 224-5015
Webmaster **Raechelle Cline** .......................(608) 224-4782

## Department of Children and Families [DCF]

201 East Washington Avenue, 2nd Floor, Madison, WI 53703
P.O. Box 8916, Madison, WI 53708-8916
Tel: (608) 267-3905  Fax: (608) 266-6836  E-mail: dcfweb@wisconsin.gov
Internet: dcf.wisconsin.gov

■Secretary **Eloise Anderson** .......................(608) 266-8684
  E-mail: eloise.anderson@wisconsin.gov
■Deputy Secretary **Ronald "Ron" Hunt**................(608) 267-8684
  E-mail: ron.hunt@wisconsin.gov
Assistant Deputy Secretary **Sara Buschman** ...........(608) 267-8684
Early Care and Education Division Administrator
  **Judy Norman-Nunnery** .........................(608) 267-8790
Management Services Division Administrator
  **Robert Nikolay** ...............................(608) 266-2687
  E-mail: robert.nikolay@wisconsin.gov
Family and Economic Security Division Administrator
  **Kris Randal** ..................................(608) 266-8718
  E-mail: kris.randal@wisconsin.gov
Safety and Permanence Division Administrator
  **Fredi-Ellen Bove** ..............................(608) 266-8710
  E-mail: frediellen.bove@wisconsin.gov
Communications Director **Joe Scialfa** ................(608) 266-8684
  E-mail: joe.scialfa@wisconsin.gov
Chief Legal Counsel **Randall Keys** ..................(608) 266-8684
  E-mail: randall.keys@wisconsin.gov

---

★ Elected Official    ■ Appointed by Governor    ● Appointed by Legislature    ▲ Appointed by Board or Commission    ◆ Appointed by State Supreme Court

# Department of Corrections [DOC]

3099 East Washington Avenue, Madison, WI 53704
P.O. Box 7925, Madison, WI 53707-7925
Tel: (608) 240-5000  TTY: (608) 240-3760  Fax: (608) 240-3305
E-mail: docweb@wisconsin.gov  Internet: www.wi-doc.com

**Employees:** 10,287  **Fiscal Year:** 2014  **Budget:** $1,296,401,000

■Secretary **Jon Litscher** .................................(608) 240-5055
Deputy Secretary **Deirdre A. Morgan** ...................(608) 240-5055
Assistant Deputy Secretary **Col Scott Legwold** .........(608) 240-5055
Legal Counsel **Kathryn Anderson** ......................(608) 240-5049
   E-mail: kathryn.anderson@wisconsin.gov
Communications Director **Joy Staab** ...................(608) 240-5060
   E-mail: joy.staab@wi.gov
Victim Services and Programs Office Director
   **Stephanie Hove** ...................................(608) 240-5880
   E-mail: stephanie.hove@wisconsin.gov   Fax: (608) 240-3353
Detention Facilities Office Director **Kristi Dietz** .........(608) 240-5052
Legislative Liaison **Melissa B. Roberts** ...............(608) 240-5056
   E-mail: melissa.b.roberts@wisconsin.gov

## Parole Commission

P.O. Box 7960, Madison, WI 53707-7960
Tel: (608) 240-7280  Fax: (608) 240-7299
E-mail: parole.comm@wisconsin.gov

■Chair **Dean F. Stensberg** ..........................(608) 240-7280
Member **Douglas D. Drankiewicz** ....................(608) 240-7280
Member **Danielle M. LaCost** .........................(608) 240-7280
Member **Steven Landreman** ..........................(608) 240-7280

# Department of Financial Institutions [DFI]

201 West Washington Avenue, Suite 500, Madison, WI 53703
P.O. Box 8861, Madison, WI 53708-8861
Tel: (608) 264-9555  TTY: (608) 266-8818  Fax: (608) 261-7200
Internet: www.wdfi.org

**Employees:** 141  **Fiscal Year:** 2015  **Budget:** $18,381,000

■Secretary **Lon E. Roberts** ..........................(608) 267-1709
   E-mail: lon.roberts@dfi.wisconsin.gov
   Education: Wisconsin (Stevens Point) BS; Wisconsin JD
Deputy Secretary **Jay Risch** ........................(608) 267-1719
Assistant Deputy Secretary **Alex Ignatowski** ...........(608) 267-1718
Chief Legal Counsel **Chris Green** .....................(608) 264-7800
Communications Director **George Althoff** .............(608) 261-4504
   E-mail: dficommunications@wisconsin.gov
Executive Staff Assistant **Deidre Taylor** ...............(608) 267-1709

## Administrative Services and Technology Division

P.O. Box 7876, Madison, WI 53707-7876
Tel: (608) 266-1622  Fax: (608) 261-7200

Administrator **Mike Trepanier** .......................(608) 267-1707

## Banking Division

P.O. Box 7876, Madison, WI 53707-7876
Fax: (608) 267-6889

Administrator (Acting) **Cheryll Olson-Collins** ...........(608) 261-7578

## Corporate and Consumer Services Division

P.O. Box 7846, Madison, WI 53707-7846
Tel: (608) 261-7577  Fax: (608) 267-6813

Administrator **George Petak** ........................(608) 261-7577
   E-mail: george.petak@dfi.wisconsin.gov

## Credit Unions Office

P.O. Box 14137, Madison, WI 53714-0137
Tel: (608) 261-9543  Fax: (608) 267-0479

Director **Kim Santos** ...............................(608) 266-8893
   Administrative Assistant **Cindy Zaemisch** .............(608) 267-2020

## Securities Division

201 West Washington Avenue, Fourth Floor, Suite 300,
Madison, WI 53703
P.O. Box 1768, Madison, WI 53701-1768
Tel: (608) 266-1064  Fax: (608) 264-7979

Administrator (Acting) **Chris Green** ..................(608) 266-3432
   Operations Program Associate **Cheryl Casas** ..........(608) 266-8279

# Department of Health Services [DHS]

P.O. Box 7850, Madison, WI 53707-7850
P.O. Box 309, Madison, WI 53701-0309 (Vital Records)
Tel: (608) 266-1865  Tel: (608) 266-1371 (Vital Records)
TTY: (608) 266-3683  Fax: (608) 266-7882
E-mail: dhsvitalrecords@wisconsin.gov (Vital Records)
Internet: http://dhs.wisconsin.gov
Internet: http://dhs.wisconsin.gov/vitalrecords (Vital Records)

**Employees:** 6,172  **Fiscal Year:** 2015  **Budget:** $10,430,855,000

■Secretary **Mary "Kitty" Rhoades** ...................(608) 266-9622
   E-mail: kitty.rhoades@wi.gov
   Education: Wisconsin (River Falls) 1973 BS; Illinois State 1978 MA
■Deputy Secretary **Thomas Engels** ...................(608) 266-9622
   E-mail: thomas.engels@wi.gov
Assistant Deputy Secretary **Laura Riske** ...............(608) 266-9622
   E-mail: laura.riske@wi.gov
Communications Director **Stephanie Smiley** ...........(608) 266-5862
   E-mail: stephanie.smiley@wi.gov
Legislative Liaison **(Vacant)** .........................(608) 266-3262
Chief Legal Counsel **Sandram "Sandy" Rowe** .........(608) 266-9622
   E-mail: sandram.rowe@dhs.wisconsin.gov

## Enterprise Services Division

Tel: (608) 266-8445  Fax: (608) 267-6749

Administrator **Cheryl K. Johnson** ....................(608) 266-5869
   E-mail: cherylk.johnson@dhs.wisconsin.gov
Deputy Administrator **Amy McDowell** ................(608) 266-8445
   E-mail: amy.mcdowell@dhs.wisconsin.gov
Area Administration Director **William Hanna** ..........(608) 261-8342
   E-mail: william.hanna@dhs.wisconsin.gov
Information and Technology Systems Director and Chief
   Information Officer **Matt Dedrick** ...................(608) 266-6837
   E-mail: matta.dedrick@wisconsin.gov
Affirmative Action/Civil Rights Officer **David Lopez** .....(608) 266-3465

## Health Care Access and Accountability Division

Administrator **Kevin Moore** ..........................(608) 266-9466
   E-mail: kevin.moore@dhs.wisconsin.gov   Fax: (608) 266-6786
Deputy Administrator **Marlia Mattke** .................(608) 266-8922
Associate Administrator **(Vacant)** .....................(608) 266-0203
Disability Determination Supervisor **Sally Fitzer** .........(608) 266-1865
   E-mail: sally.fitzer@dhs.wisconsin.gov
Benefits Management Bureau Director
   **Rachel Currans-Henry** .............................(608) 261-7838
Enrollment, Policy, and Systems Bureau Director
   **Shawn Smith** .....................................(608) 266-1935

## Long Term Care Division

Tel: (608) 266-2000  TTY: (608) 266-7376  Fax: (608) 266-2579

Administrator **Brian Shoup** ..........................(608) 266-0554
Deputy Administrator **Beth Wroblewski** ...............(608) 261-5987
Family Care Expansion Director **Margaret Kristan** .......(608) 266-5156
Deaf and Hard of Hearing Office Director **Currie Molke** ...(608) 266-5267
Central Wisconsin Center Director **Jan Holling** ..........(608) 301-9229
   317 Knutson Drive, Madison, WI 53704-1197
Northern Wisconsin Center Director
   **Jacqueline Neurohr** ...............................(715) 723-5542
   2820 East Park Avenue, Chippewa Falls, WI 54729
   P.O. Box 340, Chippewa Falls, WI 54729-0340
Southern Wisconsin Center Director
   **Jim Henkes** ...........................(262) 878-2411 ext. 2211
Aging and Long Term Care Bureau Director
   **Currie Molke** .....................................(608) 266-5267

*(continued on next page)*

---

★ Elected Official   ■ Appointed by Governor   ● Appointed by Legislature   ▲ Appointed by Board or Commission   ◆ Appointed by State Supreme Court

**Long Term Care Division** *continued*

Blind and Visually Impaired Bureau Director **(Vacant)** .... (608) 266-2000
Developmental Disabilities Council Program Assistant
  **Denise Cox** . . . . . . . . . . . . . . . . . . . . . . . . . . . . . . (608) 266-0547
Managed Care Director **Margaret Kristan** . . . . . . . . . . . . . (608) 261-7807

## Mental Health and Substance Abuse Services Division

Tel: (608) 266-2000  Fax: (608) 266-2579

Administrator **Linda Harris** . . . . . . . . . . . . . . . . . . . . (608) 267-7909
Deputy Administrator **Patrick Cork** . . . . . . . . . . . . . . . . (608) 267-8929
Sand Ridge Secure Treatment Center Director
  **Deborah "Deb" McCulloch** . . . . . . . . . . . . . . . . . . (608) 847-1720
  1111 North Road, Mauston, WI 53948
Wisconsin Resource Center Director **Byran Bartow** . . . . . . (920) 426-4310
Mendota Mental Health Institute Director
  **Gregory Van Rybroek** . . . . . . . . . . . . . . . . . . . . . . . (608) 301-1000
Winnebago Mental Health Institute Director
  **Tom Speech** . . . . . . . . . . . . . . . . . . . . . . . . . . . . . . (920) 237-2802
Mental Health and Secure Treatment Service Planning
  Manager **Glenn Larson** . . . . . . . . . . . . . . . . . . . . . . (608) 266-2715
Prevention, Treatment, and Recovery Bureau Director
  **Joyce Allen** . . . . . . . . . . . . . . . . . . . . . . . . . . . . . . (608) 266-2717
Alien Clients' Rights Office Supervisor **James Yeadon** . . . (608) 266-5525
Community Forensics Supervisor **Glenn Larson** . . . . . . . . (608) 266-2862

## Public Health Division

Tel: (608) 266-9780  Fax: (608) 267-2832

Administrator **Karen McKeown** . . . . . . . . . . . . . . . . . . (608) 266-9780
Deputy Administrator **Charles Warzecha** . . . . . . . . . . . . . (608) 266-9780
Communicable Diseases and Preparedness Director
  **Diane Christen** . . . . . . . . . . . . . . . . . . . . . . . . . . . (608) 266-1251
Health Informatics Director **Oskar Anderson** . . . . . . . . . . (608) 267-7279
Community Health Promotion Director **Susan Uttech** . . . . (608) 267-3561
Environmental and Occupational Health Director
  **(Vacant)** . . . . . . . . . . . . . . . . . . . . . . . . . . . . . . . . (608) 264-9880
Policy and Practice Alignment Director **(Vacant)** . . . . . . . . (608) 266-1347
Operations Office Director **Donna Moore** . . . . . . . . . . . . (608) 261-9434

## Policy Initiatives and Budget Office

Tel: (608) 266-3816  Fax: (608) 267-0358

Director **Andy Forsaith** . . . . . . . . . . . . . . . . . . . . . . . (608) 266-7684
  E-mail: andy.forsaith@wi.gov
Budget Director **Andy Forsaith** . . . . . . . . . . . . . . . . . . (608) 266-7684
  E-mail: andy.forsaith@wi.gov

## Department of Military Affairs [DMA]

2400 Wright Street, Madison, WI 53704
P.O. Box 8111, Madison, WI 53708-2572
Tel: (608) 242-3000  Fax: (608) 242-3111
Internet: www.homelandsecurity.wi.gov

**Employees:** 428  **Fiscal Year:** 2015  **Budget:** $104,666,000

■Adjutant General **MajGen Donald P. Dunbar, ANG** . . . . . . (608) 242-3001
  E-mail: donald.dunbar@wisconsin.gov
Deputy Adjutant General (Air Force)
  **BrigGen Gary L. Ebben, ANG** . . . . . . . . . . . . . . . . . . (608) 242-3020
Deputy Adjutant General (Army)
  **BG Mark Anderson, ARNG** . . . . . . . . . . . . . . . . . . . . (608) 242-3010
■Wisconsin Emergency Management Administrator
  **Brian Satula** . . . . . . . . . . . . . . . . . . . . . . . . . . . . . (608) 242-3232
  E-mail: brian.satula@wisconsin.gov
  Education: Concordia U (CA) BA
  Deputy Director of Emergency Police Services
  **Todd Nehls** . . . . . . . . . . . . . . . . . . . . . . . . . . . . . . (608) 444-0003
Executive Assistant **Col Michael T. Hinman, ANG** . . . . . (608) 242-3009
  Education: Idaho 1986 BA
Information Management Director
  **LTC Jeffrey Alston, ARNG** . . . . . . . . . . . . . . . . . . . . (608) 242-3650
  E-mail: jeff.alston@us.army.mil
Legislative Liaison
  **LTC Jacqueline "Jackie" Guthrie, ARNG (Ret)** . . . . . . . (608) 242-3026

## Department of Natural Resources [DNR]

101 South Webster Street, Madison, WI 53703
P.O. Box 7921, Madison, WI 53707-7924
Tel: (608) 266-2621  TTY: (608) 267-6897  Fax: (608) 261-7921

**Employees:** 2,682  **Fiscal Year:** 2015  **Budget:** $574,855,000

■Secretary **Cathy Stepp** . . . . . . . . . . . . . . . . . . . . . . . (608) 267-7556
  E-mail: cathy.stepp@wisconsin.gov
Deputy Secretary **Kurt Thiede** . . . . . . . . . . . . . . . . . . (608) 264-6266
  E-mail: kurt.thiede@wisconsin.gov
Assistant Deputy Secretary **(Vacant)** . . . . . . . . . . . . . . . (608) 266-5375
Legislative Liaison **Timothy Gary** . . . . . . . . . . . . . . . . . (608) 266-2120
  E-mail: timothy.gary@wisconsin.gov
Legal Services Bureau Director **Tim Andryk** . . . . . . . . . . (608) 264-9228
  E-mail: tim.andryk@wisconsin.gov
Management and Budget Bureau Director
  **Joseph Polasek** . . . . . . . . . . . . . . . . . . . . . . . . . . . (608) 266-2794
  E-mail: joseph.polasekjr@wisconsin.gov
Business Support and Sustainability Director
  **Mark Aquino** . . . . . . . . . . . . . . . . . . . . . . . . . . . . . (608) 275-3262

## Air and Waste Division

Administrator **Patrick "Pat" Stevens** . . . . . . . . . . . . . . . (608) 264-9210
  E-mail: patrick.stevens@wisconsin.gov
Deputy Administrator **Bart Sponseller** . . . . . . . . . . . . . . (608) 275-3262
  E-mail: bart.sponseller@wisconsin.gov
Air Management Bureau Director **Andy Stewart** . . . . . . . . (608) 264-8884
Remediation and Redevelopment Bureau Director
  **Darsi Foss** . . . . . . . . . . . . . . . . . . . . . . . . . . . . . . (608) 267-6713
  E-mail: darsi.foss@wisconsin.gov
Waste Management Bureau Director **Ann Coakley** . . . . . . . (608) 516-2492

## Customer and Employee Services Division

Administrator **Diane Brookbank** . . . . . . . . . . . . . . . . . . (608) 266-2241
  E-mail: diane.brookbank@wisconsin.gov
Communications Director **William "Bill" Cosh** . . . . . . . . . (608) 267-2773
  E-mail: william.cosh@wisconsin.gov
Community Financial Assistance Bureau Director
  **Mary Rose Teves** . . . . . . . . . . . . . . . . . . . . . . . . . . (608) 267-7683
Customer Service and Licensing Bureau Director
  **(Vacant)** . . . . . . . . . . . . . . . . . . . . . . . . . . . . . . . . (608) 267-7799
Finance Bureau Director **(Vacant)** . . . . . . . . . . . . . . . . . (608) 266-2621
Human Resources Bureau Director **Amber Passno** . . . . . . . (608) 266-6999
Technology Services Bureau Director **Debra Hanrahan** . . . (608) 261-4399
  E-mail: debra.hanrahan@wisconsin.gov

## Enforcement and Science Division

Law Enforcement Bureau Director **Todd Schaller** . . . . . . . (608) 267-2774
Science Services Bureau Director
  **John R. "Jack" Sullivan** . . . . . . . . . . . . . . . . . . . . . (608) 267-9753
  E-mail: johnr.sullivan@wisconsin.gov
  Education: Wisconsin (Oshkosh) 1976 BS; Wisconsin 1979 MS

## Forestry Division

Administrator **Paul DeLong** . . . . . . . . . . . . . . . . . . . . . (608) 264-9224
  Education: Wisconsin (Stevens Point) 1985 BS; Michigan 1988 MS
Deputy Administrator **Darrell Zastrow** . . . . . . . . . . . . . . (608) 266-0290

## Land Division

Fax: (608) 266-6983

Administrator **(Vacant)** . . . . . . . . . . . . . . . . . . . . . . . . (608) 266-5833
Deputy Administrator **Sanjay Olson** . . . . . . . . . . . . . . . (608) 261-6453
Endangered Resources Bureau Director **Erin Crain** . . . . . . (608) 267-7479
Facilities and Lands Bureau Director **Steven Miller** . . . . . (608) 266-5782
  Education: Utah State 1971 BS; Oklahoma State 1973 MS
Parks and Recreation Bureau Director
  **Daniel "Dan" Schuller** . . . . . . . . . . . . . . . . . . . . . . (608) 266-2185
  E-mail: daniel.schuller@wisconsin.gov
Wildlife Management Bureau Director
  **Thomas "Tom" Hauge** . . . . . . . . . . . . . . . . . . . . . . (608) 266-2193
  E-mail: tom.hauge@wisconsin.gov
  Education: Wisconsin 1975 BS, 1979 MS

---

★ Elected Official    ■ Appointed by Governor    ● Appointed by Legislature    ▲ Appointed by Board or Commission    ◆ Appointed by State Supreme Court

## Water Division

Fax: (608) 266-6983

Administrator **Russell "Russ" Rasmussen** . . . . . . . . . . . . . (608) 267-7651
    E-mail: russell.rasmussen@wisconsin.gov
Deputy Administrator **(Vacant)** . . . . . . . . . . . . . . . . . . . . (608) 266-2621
Water Quality Director **Susan Sylvester** . . . . . . . . . . . . . . (608) 266-1099
Watershed Management Bureau Director
    **Pamela "Pam" Biersach** . . . . . . . . . . . . . . . . . . . . . . (608) 261-8447
    E-mail: pamela.biersach@wisconsin.gov
Drinking Water and Groundwater Bureau Director
    **Jill Jonas** . . . . . . . . . . . . . . . . . . . . . . . . . . . . . . . . . (608) 267-7545
    E-mail: jill.jonas@wisconsin.gov
    Education: Wisconsin (Platteville) 1977 BS;
    Wisconsin (Stevens Point) 1990 MS
Fisheries Management and Habitat Protection Bureau
    Director **Justine Hasz** . . . . . . . . . . . . . . . . . . . . . . . . . (608) 266-1099
    E-mail: justine.hasz@wisconsin.gov
Fisheries Management and Habitat Protection Bureau
    Warmwater Lakes and Regulations Specialist
    **Joe Hennessy** . . . . . . . . . . . . . . . . . . . . . . . . . . . . . . (608) 267-9427
    101 South Webster Street, Madison, WI 53707-7921

## Department of Revenue

P.O. Box 8933, Madison, WI 53708-8933
Tel: (608) 266-2772  TTY: (800) 947-3529  Fax: (608) 266-5718
Internet: www.revenue.wi.gov

**Employees:** 1,090  **Fiscal Year:** 2015  **Budget:** $186,989,000

■Secretary **Richard G. Chandler** . . . . . . . . . . . . . . . . . . . . (608) 266-6466
    E-mail: richard.chandler@dor.state.wi.us
Deputy Secretary **(Vacant)** . . . . . . . . . . . . . . . . . . . . . . . (608) 266-6466
    Executive Assistant **Jennifer Western** . . . . . . . . . . . . . (608) 266-6466
Enterprise Services Division Administrator **Jon Reneau** . . . (608) 264-8175
    E-mail: jon.reneau@revenue.wi.gov
    Education: Colorado 1978 BA; Wisconsin 1981 MPA
Income, Sales and Excise Tax Division Administrator
    **Diane L. Hardt** . . . . . . . . . . . . . . . . . . . . . . . . . . . . . (608) 261-5116
Lottery Division Administrator **Patricia Lashore** . . . . . . . . (608) 266-2772
Research and Policy Division Administrator **(Vacant)** . . . . . (608) 267-8973
Technology Services Division Administrator
    **Richard "Rick" Offenbecher** . . . . . . . . . . . . . . . . . . . (608) 266-9751
    E-mail: richard.offenbecher@wisconsin.gov
■State and Local Finance Division Administrator
    **Claude Lois** . . . . . . . . . . . . . . . . . . . . . . . . . . . . . . . (608) 266-0939
    E-mail: claude.lois@revenue.wi.gov
Chief Legal Counsel **Dana J. Erlandsen** . . . . . . . . . . . . . . (608) 266-3974
Communications Director **Stephanie Marquis** . . . . . . . . . . (608) 266-2300
Legislative Advisor **Nate Ristow** . . . . . . . . . . . . . . . . . . . (608) 266-6466
    E-mail: nate.ristow@revenue.wi.gov
Holder Reporting Director **Erin Egan** . . . . . . . . . . . . . . . . (608) 264-6997

## Department of Safety and Professional Services [DSPS]

1400 East Washington Avenue, Room 112, Madison, WI 53703-8935
P.O. Box 8935, Madison, WI 53708-8935
Tel: (608) 266-2112  TTY: (608) 267-2416  Fax: (608) 267-0644

**Employees:** 284  **Fiscal Year:** 2015  **Budget:** $51,899,000

■Secretary **Dave Ross** . . . . . . . . . . . . . . . . . . . . . . . . . . . (608) 266-8608
    E-mail: dave.ross@wisconsin.gov
    Education: Wisconsin (Superior) 1974 BS
Deputy Secretary **Jonathan B. Barry** . . . . . . . . . . . . . . . . (608) 267-2435
Assistant Deputy Secretary **Eric Esser** . . . . . . . . . . . . . . . (608) 266-2112
    E-mail: eric.esser@wisconsin.gov
Chief Legal Counsel **Michael Berndt** . . . . . . . . . . . . . . . . (608) 267-2914
    E-mail: michael.berndt@wisconsin.gov
Executive Director, Policy and Development
    **Thomas "Tom" Ryan** . . . . . . . . . . . . . . . . . . . . . . . . (608) 261-2378
Executive Director, Policy and Development
    **Dan Williams** . . . . . . . . . . . . . . . . . . . . . . . . . . . . . . (608) 267-7223
Industry Services Division Administrator **Jeff Weingand** . . (608) 266-2112
    E-mail: jeffrey.weigand@wisconsin.gov
Legal Services and Compliance Administrator
    **Al Rohmeyer** . . . . . . . . . . . . . . . . . . . . . . . . . . . . . . (608) 266-8419

Management Services Division Administrator
    **Angela "Angie" Herl** . . . . . . . . . . . . . . . . . . . . . . . . . (608) 261-0462
    E-mail: angie.hellenbrand@wisconsin.gov
Policy and Development Division Administrator
    **Greg Gasber** . . . . . . . . . . . . . . . . . . . . . . . . . . . . . . . (608) 266-8419
    E-mail: greg.gasper@wisconsin.gov
Professional Credential Processing Division Administrator
    **Kirsten Reader** . . . . . . . . . . . . . . . . . . . . . . . . . . . . . (608) 261-4466
    E-mail: kirsten.reader@wisconsin.gov

## Department of Tourism

P.O. Box 8690, Madison, WI 53708-8690
Tel: (608) 266-2161  Tel: (800) 432-8747  Fax: (608) 266-3403
E-mail: tourinfo@travelwisconsin.com  Internet: www.travelwisconsin.com

**Employees:** 35  **Fiscal Year:** 2015  **Budget:** $17,875,000

■Secretary **Stephanie Klett** . . . . . . . . . . . . . . . . . . . . . . . (608) 266-2345
    E-mail: sklett@travelwisconsin.com
    Education: Beloit
Deputy Secretary **Sarah Klavas** . . . . . . . . . . . . . . . . . . . . (608) 266-3750
Communications Director **Lisa Marshall** . . . . . . . . . . . . . . (608) 267-3773
    E-mail: lmarshall@travelwisconsin.com

## Wisconsin Department of Transportation [WisDOT]

P.O. Box 7910, Madison, WI 53707-7910
Tel: (608) 266-1113  Fax: (608) 266-9912
E-mail: sec.exec@dot.state.wi.us  Internet: www.dot.state.wi.us

**Employees:** 3,549  **Fiscal Year:** 2015  **Budget:** $3,016,552,000

■Secretary **Mark Gottlieb** . . . . . . . . . . . . . . . . . . . . . . . . (608) 266-1114
    E-mail: mark.gottlieb@dot.wi.gov
    Education: Wisconsin (Milwaukee) 1981 BS, 1984 ME
■Deputy Secretary **Michael Berg** . . . . . . . . . . . . . . . . . . . (608) 266-1114
    E-mail: mike.berg@dot.wi.gov
    Assistant Deputy Secretary **Tom Rhatican** . . . . . . . . . . (608) 266-2743
General Counsel **Rebecca Roeker** . . . . . . . . . . . . . . . . . . . (608) 266-8928
    E-mail: rebecca.roeker@dot.wi.gov
Public Affairs Office Director **Peg Schmitt** . . . . . . . . . . . . (608) 266-5599
Business Management Division Administrator
    **Denise Solie** . . . . . . . . . . . . . . . . . . . . . . . . . . . . . . . (608) 266-2090
    E-mail: denise.solie@dot.wi.gov
Motor Vehicles Division Administrator
    **Patrick A. Fernan** . . . . . . . . . . . . . . . . . . . . . . . . . . . (608) 266-7079
    E-mail: patrick.fernan@dot.wi.gov
Policy, Budget, and Finance Division Administrator
    **Paul Hammer** . . . . . . . . . . . . . . . . . . . . . . . . . . . . . . (608) 261-8616
Transportation Investment Management Division
    Administrator **Aileen Switzer** . . . . . . . . . . . . . . . . . . . (608) 266-5791
Transportation System Development Division
    Administrator **Daniel Grasser** . . . . . . . . . . . . . . . . . . . (608) 267-6885
State Patrol Superintendent **Stephen Gilbert Fitzgerald** . . . (608) 267-7102

## Department of Workforce Development [DWD]

201 East Washington Avenue, Madison, WI 53703
P.O. Box 7946, Madison, WI 53707
Tel: (608) 266-3131  TTY: (608) 267-0477  Fax: (608) 266-1784

**Employees:** 1,677  **Fiscal Year:** 2015  **Budget:** $370,608,000

■Secretary **Ray Allen** . . . . . . . . . . . . . . . . . . . . . . . . . . . (608) 267-1410
    E-mail: ray.allen@dwd.wisconsin.gov
    Education: Wisconsin BJ
Deputy Secretary **Georgia Maxwell** . . . . . . . . . . . . . . . . . (608) 267-9692
    E-mail: georgia.maxwell@dwd.wisconsin.gov
Assistant Deputy Secretary **Dave Anderson** . . . . . . . . . . . (608) 266-0786
    E-mail: davidg.anderson@dwd.wisconsin.gov
Legal Counsel **Karl Dahlen** . . . . . . . . . . . . . . . . . . . . . . . (608) 266-9427
    E-mail: karl.dahlen@dwd.wi.gov
Communications Director **John A. Dipko** . . . . . . . . . . . . . . (608) 266-6753

---

★ Elected Official    ■ Appointed by Governor    ● Appointed by Legislature        ▲ Appointed by Board or Commission    ◆ Appointed by State Supreme Court

EXECUTIVE BRANCH

# Labor and Industry Review Commission

P.O. Box 8126, Madison, WI 53708-8126
Tel: (608) 266-9850  Fax: (608) 267-4409
E-mail: lirc@dwd.wisconsin.gov

■Chairperson **Laurie McCallum** ........................ (608) 266-9850
■Commissioner **David Falstad** ........................ (608) 266-9850
  Term Expires: March 1, 2015
  Education: Wisconsin BS, JD
■Commissioner **C. William "Bill" Jordahl** ........... (608) 266-9850
  Education: Pomona 1979 BA; Wisconsin 1995 JD
General Counsel **Tracey Schwalbe** .................. (608) 266-7728
  E-mail: tracey.schwalbe@dwd.wisconsin.gov
Business Manager **Morgan Dixon** ................... (608) 266-7560
  E-mail: morgan.dixon@dwd.wisconsin.gov

## Administrative Services Division

Fax: (608) 267-7952  Internet: http://dwd.wisconsin.gov/asd
Administrator **Robert A. Rodriguez** ............... (608) 261-4599
  E-mail: robert.rodriguez@dwd.wisconsin.gov
Deputy Administrator **Lynda Hanold** ............. (608) 261-2138
  E-mail: lynda.hanold@dwd.wisconsin.gov
BITS (Bureau of Information Technology) Director
  **Daniel "Dan" McCarthy** ....................... (608) 264-8800
  E-mail: daniel.mccarthy@dwd.wisconsin.gov
General Services Bureau Director **Margaret McGrath** .... (608) 266-1777
  E-mail: margaret.mcgrath@dwd.wisconsin.gov
Human Resources Director **Steve Laesch** ............. (608) 266-1092
Affirmative Action Officer **Amanda Jorgenson** ........ (608) 267-4411
Chief Financial Officer **Tami Moe** .................. (608) 261-4582

## Employment and Training Division

Tel: (608) 266-0327  Fax: (608) 261-8506
Internet: http://dwd.wisconsin.gov/det
Administrator **Scott Jansen** ....................... (608) 266-0327
  E-mail: scott.jansen@dwd.wisconsin.gov
  Education: Chicago 1980 BS
Deputy Administrator **Bruce Palzkill** ............... (608) 266-3623
  E-mail: bruce.palzkill@dwd.wisconsin.gov
Apprenticeship Standards Bureau Director
  **Karen Morgan** ................................ (608) 266-3133
  E-mail: karen.morgan@dwd.wisconsin.gov   Fax: (608) 266-0766
Job Service Bureau Director **Dave Shaw** ............ (608) 741-3561
  E-mail: daved.shaw@dwd.wisconsin.gov   Fax: (608) 267-0330
Program Management and Special Populations Director
  **Juan José López** .............................. (608) 266-0002
  E-mail: juanjose.lopez@dwd.wisconsin.gov
Veterans Services Director **Gary Meyer** ............. (608) 267-7277
Workforce Information and Technical Support Bureau
  Director **Dennis Winters** ...................... (608) 267-3262
  E-mail: dennis.winters@dwd.wisconsin.gov
Workforce Training Bureau Director **Phil Koenig** ........ (608) 267-7277
  E-mail: phil.koenig@dwd.wisconsin.gov

## Equal Rights Division

Fax: (608) 267-4592
Administrator **James J. "Jim" Chiolino** ............ (608) 266-3345
  E-mail: jim.chiolino@dwd.wisconsin.gov
Deputy Administrator **James J. "Jim" Chiolino** ........ (608) 266-3345
  E-mail: jim.chiolino@dwd.wisconsin.gov
Civil Rights Bureau Director **Larry Jakubowski** ........ (414) 227-4376
  E-mail: larry.jakubowski@dwd.wisconsin.gov
Labor Standards Bureau Director
  **James J. "Jim" Chiolino** ....................... (608) 266-3345
  E-mail: jim.chiolino@dwd.wisconsin.gov
Office Manager **Morgan Dixon** ..................... (608) 266-7560

## Unemployment Insurance Division

Fax: (608) 267-0593
Administrator **Joseph W. "Joe" Handrick** ............. (608) 266-0946
Deputy Administrator **Ben Peirce** .................. (608) 266-3635
Benefit Operations Bureau Director **Lutfi Shahrani** ....... (608) 266-8211
Legal Affairs Bureau Director **Janell Knutson** .......... (608) 267-1639

Tax and Accounting Bureau Director
  **Thomas "Tom" McHugh** ........................ (608) 266-3130

## Vocational Rehabilitation Division

P.O. Box 7852, Madison, WI 53707-7852
201 East Washington Avenue, Madison, WI 53702
Tel: (608) 261-0050  Fax: (608) 266-1133
Internet: http://dwd.wisconsin.gov/dvr

Administrator **Delora Newton** ..................... (608) 261-4576
  E-mail: delora.newton@dwd.wisconsin.gov
Deputy Administrator **Enid Glenn** .................. (608) 261-0073
  E-mail: enid.glenn@dwd.wisconsin.gov
Consumer Services Bureau Director **Meredith Dressel** .... (608) 261-0075
Management Services Bureau Director **Enid Glenn** ..... (608) 261-0073
  E-mail: enid.glenn@dwd.wisconsin.gov
Program Development Section Director **Lorie Lange** ...... (608) 261-0049
Special Projects Coordinator **JoAnna Richard** .......... (608) 261-0074

## Worker's Compensation Division

Fax: (608) 266-1340
Administrator **BJ Dernbach** ....................... (608) 267-4415
Deputy Administrator **Brian Krueger** ............... (608) 267-4415
Claims Management Bureau Director **Tracy Aiello** ........ (608) 267-9407
Insurance Programs Bureau Director **Joseph Moreth** ..... (608) 267-4415
Legal Services Bureau Director **Jim O'Malley** .......... (608) 266-3131

## Office of Skills Development [OSD]

Tel: (608) 266-3131
Director **Scott Jansen** ............................ (608) 266-3131
Grant Specialist **Sandra Hiebert** .................. (608) 266-3131
Grant Specialist **Meghan Sprager** ................. (608) 266-3131
Policy Analyst **Shelly Harkins** .................... (608) 266-3131
Policy Analyst **Jayne Wanless** .................... (608) 266-3131

# Employment Relations Commission

4868 High Crossing Boulevard, Madison, WI 53704-7403
Tel: (608) 243-2424  Fax: (608) 243-2433  E-mail: werc@werc.state.wi.us
Internet: http://werc.wi.gov

**Employees:** 10  **Fiscal Year:** 2015  **Budget:** $1,505,000

■Chairman **James R. Scott** ......................... (608) 243-2431
  E-mail: james.scott@wisconsin.gov
  Education: Wisconsin 1996 BS; Marquette 1969 JD
■Commissioner **James J. Daley** ..................... (608) 243-2432
  E-mail: james.daley@wisconsin.gov
■Commissioner **Rodney G. Pasch** ................... (608) 243-2430
  E-mail: rodney.pasch@wisconsin.gov
Chief Legal Counsel **Peter G. Davis** ................ (608) 243-2421
  E-mail: peterg.davis@wisconsin.gov
  Education: Wisconsin 1975 JD
Paralegal **Dawn Clark** ............................ (608) 243-2434
  E-mail: dawn.clark@wisconsin.gov
Office Manager **Carol Lynch** ...................... (608) 243-2427
Staff Attorney **William C. Houlihan** ............... (608) 243-2422
Staff Attorney **Raleigh Jones** .................... (608) 243-2426
Staff Attorney **Lauri A. Millot** ................... (715) 362-0370
Staff Attorney **Karl R. Hanson** ................... (608) 243-2436

# Public Service Commission of Wisconsin [PSC]

610 North Whitney Way, Madison, WI 53705-2729
P.O. Box 7854, Madison, WI 57307-7854
Tel: (888) 816-3831 (In State)  Tel: (608) 266-5481 (Out of State)
TTY: (800) 251-8345 (In State)  TTY: (608) 267-1479 (Out of State)
Tel: (800) 225-7729 (Consumer Affairs, In State)
Tel: (608) 266-2001 (Consumer Affairs, Out of State)
Fax: (608) 266-3957  Fax: (608) 266-1401 (Commissioners)
E-mail: pscrecordsmail@wisconsin.gov

**Employees:** 149  **Fiscal Year:** 2015  **Budget:** $24,668,000

■Chair **Ellen E. Nowak** ........................... (608) 267-7899
  E-mail: ellen.nowak@wisconsin.gov
  Education: Wisconsin (Milwaukee) BS; Marquette JD

---

★ Elected Official　■ Appointed by Governor　● Appointed by Legislature　▲ Appointed by Board or Commission　◆ Appointed by State Supreme Court

■Commissioner **Michael D. "Mike" Huebsch** . . . . . . . . . . . . (608) 267-7898
  E-mail: mike.huebsch@wisconsin.gov
  Education: Oral Roberts (Attended)

■Commissioner **Phil Montgomery** . . . . . . . . . . . . . . . . . . . . (608) 267-7898
  E-mail: phil.montgomery@wisconsin.gov
  Education: Houston (Downtown) 1988 BS

## Commissioner's Office
Tel: (608) 267-7898

■Executive Staff Assistant to the Chairperson **Bob Seitz** . . . . (608) 267-7899
  E-mail: bob.seitz@wisconsin.gov

Executive Staff Assistant to Commissioner Huebsch
  **Krystal Jones** . . . . . . . . . . . . . . . . . . . . . . . . . . . . . . . . . . . (608) 267-7898
  E-mail: krystal.jones@wisconsin.gov

Executive Staff Assistant to Commissioner Nowak
  **Sandra J. Paske** . . . . . . . . . . . . . . . . . . . . . . . . . . . . . . . . (608) 267-7899
  E-mail: sandra.paske@wisconsin.gov

Executive Assistant **Delanie Breuer** . . . . . . . . . . . . . . . . . . (608) 267-7899
  E-mail: delanie.breuer@wisconsin.gov

Executive Assistant **Teresa Hatchell** . . . . . . . . . . . . . . . . . (608) 267-7898
  E-mail: teri.hatchell@wisconsin.gov

Secretary to the Commission **Sandra J. Paske** . . . . . . . . . (608) 266-1265
  E-mail: sandra.paske@wisconsin.gov

Chief Legal Counsel **Cynthia Smith** . . . . . . . . . . . . . . . . . (608) 266-1264
  E-mail: cynthia.smith@wisconsin.gov

Communications Director **Nathan Conrad** . . . . . . . . . . . . . (608) 266-9600
  E-mail: nathan.conrad@wisconsin.gov

Administrative Law Judge **Michael Newmark** . . . . . . . . . . (608) 261-8522

## Business and Communications Services Division
Tel: (608) 261-8524

Division Administrator **Sarah Klein** . . . . . . . . . . . . . . . . . . (608) 266-3587
  E-mail: sarah.klein@wisconsin.gov

Assistant Administrator **(Vacant)** . . . . . . . . . . . . . . . . . . . . (608) 266-6744

## Gas and Energy Division
Tel: (608) 266-5481

Administrator **Jeffrey Ripp** . . . . . . . . . . . . . . . . . . . . . . . . . (608) 267-9813
  E-mail: jeffrey.ripp@wisconsin.gov

Deputy Administrator **(Vacant)** . . . . . . . . . . . . . . . . . . . . . . (608) 267-9813

## Regional Energy Markets Division
Administrator **Janet Wheeler** . . . . . . . . . . . . . . . . . . . . . . . (608) 266-2655
  E-mail: janet.wheeler@wisconsin.gov

Assistant Administrator **Randel Pilo** . . . . . . . . . . . . . . . . . (608) 266-3165
  E-mail: randel.pilo@wisconsin.gov

## Water, Compliance, and Consumer Affairs Division
Tel: (608) 266-3767

Administrator **Jeffrey "Jeff" Stone** . . . . . . . . . . . . . . . . . . (608) 267-7829
  E-mail: jeff.stone@wisconsin.gov
  Education: Washburn 1983 BA

## Tax Appeals Commission
5005 University Avenue, Suite 110, Madison, WI 53705

■Commissioner **Lorna Hemp Boll** . . . . . . . . . . . . . . . . . . . . (608) 266-1391
  Term Expires: March 1, 2017

■Commissioner **David D. Wilmoth** . . . . . . . . . . . . . . . . . . . (608) 266-1391
  Term Expires: March 1, 2019
  Education: Wisconsin 1978 BA; Marquette 1981 JD

■Commissioner **David Coon** . . . . . . . . . . . . . . . . . . . . . . . . (608) 266-1391

Legal Assistant **Nancy Batz** . . . . . . . . . . . . . . . . . . . . . . . . (608) 266-1391

Webmaster **Nancy Batz** . . . . . . . . . . . . . . . . . . . . . . . . . . . (608) 266-1391

## Housing and Economic Development Authority [WHEDA]
P.O. Box 1728, Madison, WI 53701-1728
201 West Washington Avenue, Suite 700, Madison, WI 53701
Tel: (608) 266-7884  TTY: (800) 943-9430  Fax: (608) 267-1099
E-mail: info@wheda.com  Internet: www.wheda.com

■Executive Director **Wyman Winston** . . . . . . . . . . . . . . . . . (608) 266-2893
  E-mail: wyman.winston@wheda.com

■Deputy Executive Director/Chief Operating Officer
  **Brian Schimming** . . . . . . . . . . . . . . . . . . . . . . . . . . . . . . (608) 267-2307
  E-mail: brian.schimming@wheda.com

Assistant Deputy Director **Mary Ann McCoshen** . . . . . . . . (608) 267-5200
  E-mail: mary_ann.mccoshen@wheda.com

  Executive Secretary **Maureen Brunker** . . . . . . . . . . . . . . (608) 266-7354

General Counsel **Matt Fortney** . . . . . . . . . . . . . . . . . . . . . (608) 267-0535

Business Development Director **Farshad Maltes** . . . . . . . . (608) 266-2027

Commercial Lending Director **Sean O'Brien** . . . . . . . . . . . (608) 267-1453

Human Resources and Administration Director
  **Mark Emmrich** . . . . . . . . . . . . . . . . . . . . . . . . . . . . . . . . (608) 267-2921
  E-mail: mark.emmrich@wheda.com

Information Technology Director **Dan Zadra** . . . . . . . . . . . (608) 266-3183
  E-mail: dan.zadra@wheda.com

Marketing and Communications Director
  **Brenda Marquardt** . . . . . . . . . . . . . . . . . . . . . . . . . . . . . (608) 266-8655

Risk Compliance Director **Jennifer Harrington** . . . . . . . . . (608) 266-6622

Single Family Housing Director **David Rouse** . . . . . . . . . . (608) 266-2184

Chief Financial Officer **Laura Morris** . . . . . . . . . . . . . . . . . (608) 266-1640

## Educational Communications Board
3319 West Beltline Highway, Madison, WI 53713-4296
Tel: (608) 264-9600  TTY: (608) 264-9710  Fax: (608) 264-9664
E-mail: ecbwebmaster@ecb.org  Internet: www.ecb.org

**Employees: 56  Fiscal Year: 2015  Budget: $19,920,000**

Executive Director **Gene Purcell** . . . . . . . . . . . . . . . . . . . . (608) 264-9666

Deputy Director **Marta Bechtol** . . . . . . . . . . . . . . . . . . . . . (608) 264-9733

Finance Management Supervisor **Aimee Wierzba** . . . . . . . (608) 264-9668

Public Radio Director **Mike Crane** . . . . . . . . . . . . . . . . . . . (608) 265-3378

Public Television Director **(Vacant)** . . . . . . . . . . . . . . . . . . (608) 263-1232

Delivery Division Administrator **Terry Baun** . . . . . . . . . . . (608) 264-9746

Education Division Administrator **(Vacant)** . . . . . . . . . . . . (608) 264-9733

## Employee Trust Funds Board
Tel: (605) 266-3285  Fax: (608) 267-4549

Chair **Wayne Koessl** . . . . . . . . . . . . . . . . . . . . . . . . . . . . . (608) 266-3285
  Term Expires: May 1, 2015

Vice Chair **John David** . . . . . . . . . . . . . . . . . . . . . . . . . . . . (608) 266-3285
  Term Expires: May 1, 2015

Secretary **Robert Niendorf** . . . . . . . . . . . . . . . . . . . . . . . . (608) 266-3285
  Term Expires: May 1, 2017

Member **William Ford** . . . . . . . . . . . . . . . . . . . . . . . . . . . . (608) 266-3285
  Term Expires: May 1, 2015

Member **Kimberly Hall** . . . . . . . . . . . . . . . . . . . . . . . . . . . . (608) 266-3285
  Term Expires: May 1, 2015

Member **Michael Langyel** . . . . . . . . . . . . . . . . . . . . . . . . . (608) 266-3285
  Term Expires: May 1, 2017

Member **Leilani Paul** . . . . . . . . . . . . . . . . . . . . . . . . . . . . . (608) 266-3285

Member **Roberta Rasmus** . . . . . . . . . . . . . . . . . . . . . . . . . (608) 266-3285
  Term Expires: May 1, 2017

Member **Victor Shier** . . . . . . . . . . . . . . . . . . . . . . . . . . . . . (608) 266-3285
  Term Expires: May 1, 2017

Member **Mary Von Ruden** . . . . . . . . . . . . . . . . . . . . . . . . . (608) 266-3285
  Term Expires: May 1, 2017

Member **David Wiltgen** . . . . . . . . . . . . . . . . . . . . . . . . . . . (608) 266-3285
  Term Expires: May 1, 2015

Ex Officio Member **Stacey Rolston** . . . . . . . . . . . . . . . . . . (608) 266-3285

■Ex Officio Member **Robert F. "Bob" Ziegelbauer** . . . . . . . (608) 266-3285
  Education: Notre Dame 1973 BBA; Wharton 1975 MBA

★ Elected Official   ■ Appointed by Governor   ● Appointed by Legislature   ▲ Appointed by Board or Commission   ◆ Appointed by State Supreme Court

EXECUTIVE BRANCH

## Department of Employee Trust Funds [ETF]

801 West Badger Road, Madison, WI 53713
P.O. Box 7931, Madison, WI 53707-7931
Tel: (608) 266-3285  Tel: (877) 533-5020  TTY: (608) 266-0676
Fax: (608) 267-4549  Internet: www.etf.wi.gov

**Employees:** 262  **Fiscal Year:** 2015  **Budget:** $42,854,000

▲Secretary **Robert J. "Bob" Conlin** . . . . . . . . . . . . . . . . . . (608) 266-0301
  E-mail: bob.conlin@etf.state.wi.us
Deputy Secretary **(Vacant)** . . . . . . . . . . . . . . . . . . . . . . (608) 266-3641
Communications and Legislation Director **Mark Lamkins** . . (608) 266-3641
  E-mail: mark.lamkins@etf.wi.gov
Legislative Liaison **Tarna Hunter** . . . . . . . . . . . . . . . . . (608) 266-3285
  E-mail: tarna.hunter@etf.state.wi.us
Internal Audit Director **John Vincent** . . . . . . . . . . . . . . . (608) 266-3951
Chief Information Officer **Dana Perry** . . . . . . . . . . . . . . . (608) 264-6943
  E-mail: dana.perry@etf.state.wi.us
Insurance Services Division Administrator **Lisa Ellinger** . . . (608) 266-0207
Management Services Division Administrator
  **Pamela Henning** . . . . . . . . . . . . . . . . . . . . . . . . . . (608) 267-2929
  E-mail: pamela.henning@etf.state.wi.us
Retirement Services Division Administrator
  **Matthew Stohr** . . . . . . . . . . . . . . . . . . . . . . . . . . . (608) 266-1210
  Retirement Services Deputy Administrator
  **Ann Boudreau** . . . . . . . . . . . . . . . . . . . . . . . . . . . (608) 266-1210
Chief Trust Finance Officer/Controller
  **Robert "Bob" Willett** . . . . . . . . . . . . . . . . . . . . . . . (608) 266-0904
Librarian **(Vacant)** . . . . . . . . . . . . . . . . . . . . . . . . . . (608) 267-2926
Enterprise Initiative Office Director **Bob Martin** . . . . . . . . (608) 267-9036
Policy, Privacy, and Compliance Director **Steve Hurley** . . . (608) 266-3285

## Government Accountability Board [GAB]

212 East Washington Avenue, 3rd Floor, Madison, WI 53703
P.O. Box 7984, Madison, WI 53707
Tel: (608) 266-8005  Fax: (608) 267-0500  E-mail: gab@wi.gov
Internet: http://gab.wi.gov

**Note:** On December 16, 2015, Governor Scott Walker announced the closure of the Government Accountability Board, effective June 30, 2016. The board will be replaced by two separate commissions to oversee the administration of elections and ethics.

■Chair **Judge Victor Manian** . . . . . . . . . . . . . . . . . . . . (608) 266-8005
  Term Expires: June 30, 2016
■Vice Chair **Judge Harold V. Froehlich** . . . . . . . . . . . . . (608) 266-8005
■Member **John Franke** . . . . . . . . . . . . . . . . . . . . . . . . (608) 266-8005
  Term Expires: May 1, 2020
  Education: Wesleyan U 1973; Wisconsin 1976 JD
■Member **Edward E. Leineweber** . . . . . . . . . . . . . . . . . . (608) 266-8005
  Term Expires: June 30, 2016
■Member **Judge Gerald Nichol** . . . . . . . . . . . . . . . . . . . (608) 266-8005
■Member **Judge Timothy Vocke** . . . . . . . . . . . . . . . . . . (608) 266-8005
  Education: Kansas; Wisconsin JD
▲Director and General Counsel **Kevin J. Kennedy** . . . . . . . (608) 266-8005
  Note: Until June 29, 2016.
  E-mail: kevin.kennedy@wisconsin.gov

## Administrative Division

Chief Administrative Officer **Sharrie Hauge** . . . . . . . . . . . (608) 266-8005
  E-mail: sharrie.hauge@wi.gov
Accountant **(Vacant)** . . . . . . . . . . . . . . . . . . . . . . . . . (608) 261-2010
Public Information Officer **Reid Magney** . . . . . . . . . . . . . (608) 267-7887
  E-mail: reid.magney@wi.gov
Staff Counsel **Nathan Judnic** . . . . . . . . . . . . . . . . . . . . (608) 266-0136
Staff Counsel **(Vacant)** . . . . . . . . . . . . . . . . . . . . . . . . (608) 266-2094
Office Operations Associate **Tony Bridges** . . . . . . . . . . . . (608) 266-8005

## Elections Division

Fax: (608) 267-0500
Administrator **Michael "Mike" Haas** . . . . . . . . . . . . . . . (608) 266-0136
Elections Supervisor **Ross Hein** . . . . . . . . . . . . . . . . . . (608) 267-3666
Lead Elections Specialist **Diane Lowe** . . . . . . . . . . . . . . (608) 266-3276

Elections Specialist **Marianne Griffin** . . . . . . . . . . . . . . . (608) 266-3061
Elections Specialist **Mai Choua Thao** . . . . . . . . . . . . . . . (608) 267-7891
Elections Specialist **Jennifer Webb** . . . . . . . . . . . . . . . . (608) 261-2030
Public Outreach Coordinator and Elections Specialist
  **Meagan Wolfe** . . . . . . . . . . . . . . . . . . . . . . . . . . . (608) 266-8175
Elections Specialist - Help America Vote Act (HAVA)
  Compliance **David Buerger** . . . . . . . . . . . . . . . . . . . (608) 267-0951
Elections Specialist - Voting Equipment Certification
  Coordinator **(Vacant)** . . . . . . . . . . . . . . . . . . . . . . . (608) 267-0714

## Ethics Division

Fax: (608) 264-9319  E-mail: gabethics@wi.gov
Administrator **Jonathan Becker** . . . . . . . . . . . . . . . . . . (608) 267-0647
Lead Campaign Finance Auditor **Richard Bohringer** . . . . . (608) 267-7735
Campaign Finance Auditor/Ethics Specialist **(Vacant)** . . . . (608) 266-8005
Campaign Finance Auditor/Ethics Specialist
  **Adam Harvell** . . . . . . . . . . . . . . . . . . . . . . . . . . . (608) 267-9252
Campaign Finance Auditor/Ethics Specialist **(Vacant)** . . . . (608) 267-7804
Ethics and Lobbying Program Support **Molly Nagappala** . . (608) 261-2014

## State of Wisconsin Investment Board [SWIB]

P.O. Box 7842, Madison, WI 53707
Tel: (608) 266-2381  Fax: (608) 266-2436  E-mail: info@swib.state.wi.us
Internet: www.swib.state.wi.us

**Employees:** 145  **Fiscal Year:** 2014  **Budget:** $41,643,000

▲Executive Director **Michael Williamson** . . . . . . . . . . . . . (608) 266-9451
  E-mail: michael.williamson@swib.state.wi.us
  Education: North Carolina BA, MA
Analytics and Fund Management Managing Director
  **Ron Mensink** . . . . . . . . . . . . . . . . . . . . . . . . . . . . (608) 266-2381
Private Markets Managing Director **Charles Carpenter** . . . (608) 266-2381
Chief Financial Officer **Lori Wersal** . . . . . . . . . . . . . . . . (608) 266-2831
Chief Human Resources Officer **Jennifer Schmeiser** . . . . . (608) 266-2381
Chief Investment Officer **David Villa** . . . . . . . . . . . . . . . (608) 266-2381
Chief Legal Officer **Rochelle H. Klaskin** . . . . . . . . . . . . (608) 266-2381
  Education: North Carolina BA; Chicago-Kent JD
Chief Operating Officer **Cindy Klimke-Armatoski** . . . . . . (608) 267-0221
Strategic Planning and Transformation Director
  **Elizabeth Fadell** . . . . . . . . . . . . . . . . . . . . . . . . . . (608) 266-2381

## Wisconsin State Public Defender Board

Chair **Daniel M. Berkos** . . . . . . . . . . . . . . . . . . . . . . . (608) 266-0087

## Office of the State Public Defender [SPD]

P.O. Box 7923, Madison, WI 53707-7923
Tel: (608) 266-0087  Fax: (608) 267-0584  Internet: www.wispd.org

**Employees:** 579  **Fiscal Year:** 2015  **Budget:** $84,201,000

▲State Public Defender **Kelli S. Thompson** . . . . . . . . . . . . (608) 266-0087
  E-mail: thompsonk@opd.wi.gov
Deputy Public Defender **L. Michael Tobin** . . . . . . . . . . . . (608) 266-5480
Budget Director **Anna Oehler** . . . . . . . . . . . . . . . . . . . . (608) 267-0311
Appellate Division Director **Jeremy Perri** . . . . . . . . . . . . (414) 227-4975
Assigned Counsel Division Director **Kathleen Pakes** . . . . . (608) 261-8856
Communications Director **Randy Kraft** . . . . . . . . . . . . . . (608) 267-3587
Trial Division Director **Jennifer Bias** . . . . . . . . . . . . . . . (608) 227-4028
Deputy Trial Division Director **Jennifer Bias** . . . . . . . . . . (414) 227-4028
Legal Counsel **Devon Lee** . . . . . . . . . . . . . . . . . . . . . . (608) 261-0633
Training Director **Gina Pruski** . . . . . . . . . . . . . . . . . . . (608) 266-6782
Legislative Liaison **Adam Plotkin** . . . . . . . . . . . . . . . . . (608) 264-8572
  E-mail: plotkina@opd.wi.gov
Chief Information Officer **Cynthia "Cindy" Archer** . . . . . . (608) 261-0636
  E-mail: archerc@opd.wi.gov

## Board of Veterans Affairs

Tel: (608) 266-1315
■Chair **John F. Townsend** . . . . . . . . . . . . . . . . . . . . . . . (608) 266-1315
  Term Expires: May 1, 2017
  Education: Wayne State U 1960 BS, 1967 MBA

---

★ Elected Official    ■ Appointed by Governor    ● Appointed by Legislature    ▲ Appointed by Board or Commission    ◆ Appointed by State Supreme Court

■Vice Chair **John Gaedke** . . . . . . . . . . . . . . . . . . . . . . . (608) 266-1315
  Term Expires: May 1, 2019
■Secretary **Daniel Bohlin** . . . . . . . . . . . . . . . . . . . . . . (608) 266-1315
  Term Expires: May 1, 2017
■Member **Cathy J. Gorst** . . . . . . . . . . . . . . . . . . . . . . . (608) 266-1315
  Term Expires: May 1, 2017
■Member **Carl Krueger** . . . . . . . . . . . . . . . . . . . . . . . . . (608) 266-1315
  Term Expires: May 1, 2015
■Member **Larry Kutschma** . . . . . . . . . . . . . . . . . . . . . . (608) 266-1315
  Term Expires: May 1, 2019
■Member **Leigh Neville-Neil** . . . . . . . . . . . . . . . . . . . . (608) 266-1315
  Term Expires: May 1, 2017
■Member **Kevin Nicholson** . . . . . . . . . . . . . . . . . . . . . . (608) 266-1315
  Term Expires: May 1, 2017
■Member **Alan Richards** . . . . . . . . . . . . . . . . . . . . . . . . (608) 266-1315
  Term Expires: May 1, 2017

## Wisconsin Department of Veterans Affairs [WDVA]

P.O. Box 7843, Madison, WI 53707
Tel: (608) 266-1311  Fax: (608) 267-0403
E-mail: wisvets@dva.wisconsin.gov

**Employees:** 1,332  **Fiscal Year:** 2015  **Budget:** $137,763,000

■Secretary **COL John A. Scocos, USAR** . . . . . . . . . . . . . . . (608) 266-1315
  E-mail: john.scocos@dva.wisconsin.gov
  Education: Mankato State 1978 BS; Touro 2001 MBA
Deputy Secretary **Michael Trepanier** . . . . . . . . . . . . . . . . . (608) 266-0784
  Education: Wisconsin BA, JD
Management Services Division Administrator
  **Kelli Kaalele** . . . . . . . . . . . . . . . . . . . . . . . . . . . (608) 267-7207
  E-mail: kelli.kaalele@dva.wisconsin.gov
Veterans Benefits Division Administrator **James Bond** . . . . (608) 266-7916
  E-mail: james.bond@dva.wisconsin.gov
Veterans Homes Division Administrator
  **Randall M. Nitschke** . . . . . . . . . . . . . . . . . . . . . . . (262) 878-6752
  E-mail: randy.nitschke@dva.wisconsin.gov
  Education: Wisconsin (Milwaukee) BA; William & Mary MEd
Veterans Services Division Administrator **Ken Grant** . . . . . . (608) 267-7207
  E-mail: ken.grant@dva.wisconsin.gov

## Office of the Lieutenant Governor

19 East State Capitol, Madison, WI 53702
Tel: (608) 266-3516  Fax: (608) 267-3571  E-mail: ltgov@wisconsin.gov

★Lieutenant Governor **Rebecca Kleefisch** (R) . . . . . . . . . . . (608) 266-3516
  Term Expires: 2019
  E-mail: rebecca.kleefisch@wisconsin.gov
  Education: Wisconsin 1997 BA
  Career: Anchor, Channel 12 News This Morning, WISN-TV
Chief of Staff **Daniel R. Suhr** . . . . . . . . . . . . . . . . . . . . . (608) 266-3516
  Education: Marquette 2006 BA, 2008 JD; Georgetown 2011 LLM
Communications Manager **Tierney Gill** . . . . . . . . . . . . . . . (608) 261-3516
  E-mail: tierney.gill@wisconsin.gov

## Office of the Secretary of State

State Capitol, B41 West, Madison, WI 53702
P.O. Box 7848, Madison, WI 53707-7848
Tel: (608) 266-8888  Fax: (608) 266-3159  Internet: www.sos.state.wi.us

**Employees:** 2  **Fiscal Year:** 2015  **Budget:** $514,000

★Secretary of State **Douglas La Follette** (D) . . . . . . . . . . . (608) 266-8888
  Term Expires: 2019
  E-mail: doug.lafollette@wisconsin.gov
  Education: Marietta BS; Stanford MS; Columbia 1967 PhD
  Career: State Senator (D-WI), Wisconsin State Senate (1972-1974)
Deputy Secretary of State **(Vacant)** . . . . . . . . . . . . . . . . . (608) 266-8888
Government Records Supervisor **Ann Bloczynski** . . . . . . . . (608) 266-5503

## Office of the State Treasurer

State Capitol, B41 West, Madison, WI 53701
P.O. Box 2114, Madison, WI 53707
Tel: (608) 266-1714  Fax: (608) 266-2647
E-mail: treasury@ost.state.wi.us

**Employees:** 1

★Treasurer **Matt Adamczyk** (R) . . . . . . . . . . . . . . . . . . . . (608) 266-1714
  Term Expires: 2019
  Education: Wisconsin 2000 BA

## Department of Justice

P.O. Box 7857, Madison, WI 53707
Tel: (608) 266-1221  Fax: (608) 267-2779  Internet: www.doj.state.wi.us

## Office of the Attorney General

P.O. Box 7857, Madison, WI 53707
Fax: (608) 267-2779

**Employees:** 666  **Fiscal Year:** 2015  **Budget:** $124,136,000

★Attorney General **Brad Schimel** (R) . . . . . . . . . . . . . . . . (608) 266-1221
  Term Expires: 2019
  Education: Wisconsin 1990 JD; Wisconsin (Milwaukee) 1987 BA
Deputy Attorney General **Andrew C. "Andy" Cook** . . . . . . (608) 266-1221
  Education: Wisconsin (Eau Claire) BS; John Marshall JD
Crime Victims Services Director **Jill Karofsky** . . . . . . . . . . (608) 264-9497
Criminal Investigation Division Administrator
  **David Matthews** . . . . . . . . . . . . . . . . . . . . . . . . . (608) 266-1671
  E-mail: matthewsds@doj.state.wi.us
Law Enforcement Services Division Administrator
  **Brian O'Keefe** . . . . . . . . . . . . . . . . . . . . . . . . . . (608) 266-5710
Legal Services Division Administrator **David Meany** . . . . . (262) 955-8981
Management Services Division Administrator
  **Bonnie L. Cyganek** . . . . . . . . . . . . . . . . . . . . . . . (608) 266-5710
  E-mail: cyganekbl@doj.state.wi.us
Senior Attorney **Paul Connell** . . . . . . . . . . . . . . . . . . . . (262) 955-8981
Chief Information Officer **Igor Steinberg** . . . . . . . . . . . . . (608) 266-1221
Communications Director **Annie E. Schwartz** . . . . . . . . . . (262) 955-8981
  E-mail: schwartzae@doj.state.wi.us
Government Affairs Director **Mike Austin** . . . . . . . . . . . . . (262) 955-8981

## Department of Public Instruction

P.O. Box 7841, Madison, WI 53707-7841
Tel: (608) 266-3390  Tel: (800) 441-4563  Internet: www.dpi.wi.gov

**Employees:** 634  **Fiscal Year:** 2015  **Budget:** $6,402,759,000

★State Superintendent **Anthony "Tony" Evers** (D) . . . . . . . (608) 266-1771
  Term Expires: 2017                          Fax: (608) 266-5188
  E-mail: dpistatesuperintendent@dpi.wi.gov
  Education: Wisconsin 1986 PhD
  Chief of Staff **Jessica Justman** . . . . . . . . . . . . . . . . . (608) 266-8009
Deputy State Superintendent
  **Michael "Mike" Thompson** . . . . . . . . . . . . . . . . . . (608) 266-1771
Chief Legal Counsel **Janet Jenkins** . . . . . . . . . . . . . . . . . (608) 266-9332
  E-mail: janet.jenkins@dpi.wi.gov
Communications Officer **Thomas "Tom" McCarthy** . . . . . . (608) 266-3559
  E-mail: thomas.mccarthy@dpi.wi.gov

---

★ Elected Official  ■ Appointed by Governor  ● Appointed by Legislature  ▲ Appointed by Board or Commission  ◆ Appointed by State Supreme Court

EXECUTIVE BRANCH

# Wyoming

Tel: (307) 777-7220   Internet: www.wyoming.gov

**Number of U.S. Congressional Delegates:** 2 Senators; 1 Representatives  **Governor's Term:** 4 years
**Legislature Description:** 30 member Senate; 60 member House of Representatives; Term - Senate 4
years, House 2 years   **Next Election:** Governor November 2018; Legislature November 2016
**Number of Electoral Votes:** 3   **Official Name:** State of Wyoming (Delaware: end of the plains)
**Nickname:** The Equality State; The Cowboy State   **Motto:** Equal Rights

**Population:** 586,107 (2015); Rank 51   **Fiscal Year:** 2014   **Budget:** $7,600,000,000

## Office of the Governor

State Capitol, 200 West 24th Street, Cheyenne, WY 82002-0010
Tel: (307) 777-7434   TTY: (307) 777-7860   Fax: (307) 632-3909

**Employees:** 46   **Fiscal Year:** 2015   **Budget:** $33,566,000

**Matthew Hansen "Matt" Mead**
Governor

Began Service: January 3, 2011
Term Expires: 2019
Date of Birth: March 11, 1962
Education: Trinity U 1984 BA;
Wyoming 1987 JD
Career: Deputy County Attorney, County
Attorney's Office, County of Campbell, Wyoming
(1987-1990); Assistant U.S. Attorney and Special
Assistant U.S. Attorney, Wyoming District, United
States Department of Justice (1991-1995);
U.S. Attorney, Wyoming District, Executive
Office for United States Attorneys, United
States Department of Justice, George W. Bush
Administration (2001-2007)

★Governor **Matthew Hansen "Matt" Mead** (R) . . . . . . . . (307) 777-7434
Special Counsel to the Governor **Richard Barrett** . . . . . . . . (307) 777-7434
  E-mail: richard.barrett@wyo.gov
Executive Assistant **Melissa Martinez** . . . . . . . . . . . . . . . (307) 777-7434
  E-mail: melissa.martinez@wyo.gov
Chief of Staff **Kari Gray** . . . . . . . . . . . . . . . . . . . . . . . . . . (307) 777-7434
Deputy Chief of Staff **Tony Young** . . . . . . . . . . . . . . . . . . (307) 777-7434
  E-mail: tony.young@wyo.gov
General Counsel **Carol A. Statkus** . . . . . . . . . . . . . . . . . . (307) 777-7434
  E-mail: carol.statkus@wyo.gov
Communication Director **David Bush** . . . . . . . . . . . . . . . . (307) 777-7437
  E-mail: david.bush@wyo.gov
  Education: Wyoming
Policy Director **Mary Kay Hill** . . . . . . . . . . . . . . . . . . . . . . (307) 777-8006
  E-mail: mary.hill@wyo.gov
Natural Resources Policy Director **Jerimiah Rieman** . . . . . (307) 777-8006
  E-mail: jerimiah.rieman@wyo.gov
Policy Advisor **Matt Fry** . . . . . . . . . . . . . . . . . . . . . . . . . . . (307) 777-8006
Energy Policy Advisor **Rob Hurless** . . . . . . . . . . . . . . . . . (307) 777-8006
  E-mail: rob.hurless@wyo.gov
  Education: Montana State BS, BA; Stanford MA; Harvard MBA
Health Care Policy Advisor **(Vacant)** . . . . . . . . . . . . . . . . . (307) 777-8006
Health Issues Policy Advisor **(Vacant)** . . . . . . . . . . . . . . . . (307) 777-8006
Wildlife and Endangered Species Policy Advisor
  **David Willms** . . . . . . . . . . . . . . . . . . . . . . . . . . . . . . . . . (307) 777-8006
  E-mail: david.willms@wyo.gov
Scheduler **Ruth Critchfield** . . . . . . . . . . . . . . . . . . . . . . . . (307) 777-7434
  E-mail: ruth.critchfield@wyo.gov
Boards and Commissions Coordinator **Vicki Bowsher** . . . . (307) 777-7434
  E-mail: vicki.bowsher@wyo.gov
Military Liaison **Gary Hartman** . . . . . . . . . . . . . . . . . . . . . (307) 777-8006
  E-mail: gary.hartman@wyo.gov

## Office of Homeland Security [WOHS]

Herschler Building, 122 West 25th Street, First Floor East,
Cheyenne, WY 82002
Tel: (307) 777-4663   Fax: (307) 635-6017   TTY: (800) 877-9965
Internet: wyohomelandsecurity.state.wy.us
Director **Guy E. Cameron** . . . . . . . . . . . . . . . . . . . . . . . . . (307) 777-4663
  E-mail: guy.cameron@wyo.gov
Deputy Director **Larry Majerus** . . . . . . . . . . . . . . . . . . . . . (307) 777-4663
  Education: Wyoming BA
Operations Unit Chief **Kim Lee** . . . . . . . . . . . . . . . . . . . . . (307) 777-4903
  E-mail: kim.lee@wyo.gov
Security Unit Chief **Larry Green** . . . . . . . . . . . . . . . . . . . . . (307) 777-4908
Public Information Officer **Kelly Ruiz** . . . . . . . . . . . . . . . . . (307) 777-4919

## Office of the Attorney General

2320 Capitol Avenue, Cheyenne, WY 82002
Tel: (307) 777-7841   Fax: (307) 777-6869
E-mail: ag.webmaster@wyo.gov

**Employees:** 243

■Attorney General **Peter K. Michael** . . . . . . . . . . . . . . . . . (307) 777-7841
  E-mail: peter.michael@wyo.gov
  Education: Yale 1978 BA; Wyoming JD
  Supervisor/Manager **Judy Mitchell** . . . . . . . . . . . . . . . . (307) 777-7650
Chief Deputy Attorney General **John G. Knepper, Jr.** . . . . . (307) 777-7841
  Education: Michigan 2001 JD
Special Assistant Attorney General **Jay Jerde** . . . . . . . . . . (307) 777-7841
  E-mail: jay.jerde@wyo.gov
Crime Laboratory Director **John Jolley** . . . . . . . . . . . . . . . (307) 777-7181
Civil Division Director **Ryan Schelhaas** . . . . . . . . . . . . . . . (307) 777-7876
Criminal Division Director **David Delicath** . . . . . . . . . . . . . (307) 777-7977
                                                          Fax: (307) 777-5034
Criminal Investigation Division Director
  **Steve Woodson** . . . . . . . . . . . . . . . . . . . . . . . . . . . . . . (307) 777-7181
Human Services Division Deputy **Misha Westby** . . . . . . . . (307) 777-8638
Litigation Division Deputy **John D. Rossetti** . . . . . . . . . . . (307) 777-6886
Victim Services Division Director
  **Cara Boyle Chambers** . . . . . . . . . . . . . . . . . . . . . . . . . (307) 777-6515
Water Resources Division Deputy **James Kaste** . . . . . . . . (307) 777-6946

## Peace Officers Standards and Training Commission

2320 Capitol Avenue, Cheyenne, WY 82002
860 Stillwater Road, Suite 100, West Sacramento, CA 95605
Fax: (307) 638-9706   Internet: ag.wyo.gov
Director **Len DeClercq** . . . . . . . . . . . . . . . . . . . . . . . . . . . (307) 777-7718
  Education: Wyoming 1982 BAA

## Law Enforcement Academy

1556 Riverbend Drive, Douglas, WY 82633
Fax: (307) 358-9603   Internet: www.wleacademy.com
Director **Dave Harris** . . . . . . . . . . . . . . . . . . . . . . . . . . . . (307) 358-3617

---

★ Elected Official   ■ Appointed by Governor   ● Appointed by Legislature   ▲ Appointed by Board or Commission   ◆ Appointed by State Supreme Court

## Medicaid Fraud Control Unit
2320 Capitol Avenue, Cheyenne, WY 82002
Fax: (307) 777-5094

Director **Melissa R. Theriault** . . . . . . . . . . . . . . . . . . . . . . . (307) 777-3444
 Education: Roosevelt BFA; Wyoming 2007 JD

## Department of Administration and Information
Emerson Building, 2001 Capitol Avenue, Cheyenne, WY 82002
Tel: (307) 777-7011

**Employees:** 238

■Director **Dean Fausset** . . . . . . . . . . . . . . . . . . . . . . . . . . . . . (307) 777-7201
 E-mail: dean.fausset@wyo.gov
Deputy Director **Russell Noel** . . . . . . . . . . . . . . . . . . . . . . . (307) 777-7201
 E-mail: russell.noel@wyo.gov
Budget Division Administrator **Kevin Hibbard** . . . . . . . . . . (307) 777-6045
Economic Analysis Division Administrator
 **Kevin Hibbard** . . . . . . . . . . . . . . . . . . . . . . . . . . . . . . . . . (307) 777-7504
General Services Division Administrator **Russell Noel** . . . . (307) 777-7767
Human Resources Division Administrator **(Vacant)** . . . . . . . (307) 777-6722
Purchasing Section Manager **Lori Galles** . . . . . . . . . . . . . . . (307) 777-7253

## State Library
2800 Central Avenue, Cheyenne, WY 82002

State Librarian (Interim) **Jamie Markus** . . . . . . . . . . . . . . . (307) 777-5914
Fiscal Services Program Manager **Melanie Reedy** . . . . . . . . (307) 777-5917
 E-mail: melanie.reedy@wyo.gov
Publications and Marketing Program Manager
 **Cary Dunlap** . . . . . . . . . . . . . . . . . . . . . . . . . . . . . . . . . . . (307) 777-6338
 E-mail: cary.dunlap1@wyo.gov
Wyoming Library Database (WYLD) Network
 Development Program Manager **Brian Greene** . . . . . . . . (307) 777-6339
 E-mail: brian.greene@wyo.gov

## Department of Agriculture [WDA]
2219 Carey Avenue, Cheyenne, WY 82002-0100
Tel: (307) 777-7321  Fax: (307) 777-6593  E-mail: wda1@state.wy.us
Internet: wyagric.state.wy.us

**Employees:** 83

■Director **Douglas Miyamoto** . . . . . . . . . . . . . . . . . . . . . . . . (307) 777-6569
 E-mail: doug.miyamoto@wyo.gov
 Education: Wyoming
 Executive Assistant **Pam Bell** . . . . . . . . . . . . . . . . . . . . . . (307) 777-6569
Deputy Director **Stacia Berry** . . . . . . . . . . . . . . . . . . . . . . . (307) 777-6591
Administrative Services Manager **Julie Cook** . . . . . . . . . . . (307) 777-6575
 E-mail: julie.cook@wyo.gov
Analytical Services Manager **Teresa Jarvis** . . . . . . . . . . . . . (307) 742-2984
 E-mail: teresa.jarvis@wyo.gov                Fax: (307) 742-2156
Consumer Health Services Manager **Dean Finkenbinder** . . . (307) 777-6587
Natural Resources Manager **Chris Wichmann** . . . . . . . . . . (307) 777-6579
Technical Services Manager **Hank Uhden** . . . . . . . . . . . . . . (307) 777-6574
Public Information Officer **Derek Grant** . . . . . . . . . . . . . . . (307) 777-7180

## Department of Audit
Herschler Building, 122 West 25th Street, Third Floor East,
Cheyenne, WY 82002
Tel: (307) 777-6605  TTY: (307) 777-7230  Fax: (307) 777-5341
Internet: http://audit.wyo.gov

■Director **Jeffrey C. "Jeff" Vogel, CEM** . . . . . . . . . . . . . . . (307) 777-6605
 E-mail: jeff.vogel@wyo.gov
Administration Division Administrator **Dennis Grenier** . . . (307) 777-6600
 Education: Wyoming 1976 BS

## Banking Division
Herschler Building, 122 West 25th Street, 3rd Floor East,
Cheyenne, WY 82002
Tel: (307) 777-7797  Fax: (307) 777-3555

Banking Division Commissioner **Albert L. Forkner** . . . . . . . (307) 777-7797
 E-mail: albert.forkner@wyo.gov
Attorney **Cecil Alice Johnstone** . . . . . . . . . . . . . . . . . . . . . (307) 777-7797

Executive Assistant **Christina Straw** . . . . . . . . . . . . . . . . . . (307) 777-5611
 E-mail: christina.straw@wyo.gov

## Excise Tax Division
Herschler Building, 122 West 25th Street, 3rd Floor East,
Cheyenne, WY 82002
Tel: (307) 777-7307  Fax: (307) 777-5642

Excise Tax Division Administrator **Rick Scheer** . . . . . . . . . (307) 777-5209
Administrative Assistant **Debbie Rodekohr** . . . . . . . . . . . . (307) 777-7307

## Public Funds Division
Tel: (307) 777-7798  Fax: (307) 777-5341

Public Funds Division Administrator **Pamela Robinson** . . . (307) 777-7798
 Education: Wyoming 1979 BS
Senior Office Support Specialist
 **Mary Ann Schwalbendorf** . . . . . . . . . . . . . . . . . . . . . . . (307) 777-7799
IT Security Auditor **Brett Bates** . . . . . . . . . . . . . . . . . . . . . (307) 777-7686
Supervising Auditor **Norm Bratton** . . . . . . . . . . . . . . . . . . (307) 777-5459

## Mineral Audit
Mineral Audit Division Administrator **Steven Dilsaver** . . . . (307) 777-6663
 Education: Nebraska 1988 BS
Office Assistant **Emma Cain** . . . . . . . . . . . . . . . . . . . . . . . . (307) 777-6605

## Department of Corrections [DOC]
1934 Wyott Drive, Suite 100, Cheyenne, WY 82002
Tel: (307) 777-7208  Fax: (307) 777-7846

**Employees:** 1,281

■Director **Robert O. "Bob" Lampert** . . . . . . . . . . . . . . . . . . (307) 777-7208
 E-mail: bob.lampert@wyo.gov
 Education: Sam Houston State BS, MBA; Houston JD
Deputy Director **Steve Lindly** . . . . . . . . . . . . . . . . . . . . . . . (307) 777-7208
Central Services Division Administrator **Jeffie Wiggins** . . . (307) 777-7208
 E-mail: jeffie.wiggins@wyo.gov
Field Services Division Administrator **Dawn Sides** . . . . . . . (307) 777-7208
 E-mail: dawn.sides@wyo.gov
Prison Division Administrator **Dan Shannon** . . . . . . . . . . . . (307) 777-7208
Human Resources Manager **Brenda Reedy** . . . . . . . . . . . . . (307) 777-7208
Public Information Officer **Mark Horan** . . . . . . . . . . . . . . . (307) 777-5889
 E-mail: mark.horan@wyo.gov

## Department of Enterprise Technology Services
Emerson Building, 2001 Capitol Avenue, Room 237,
Cheyenne, WY 82002
Tel: (307) 777-5840  Fax: (307) 777-3696  E-mail: cio@wyo.gov

■State Chief Information Officer **Flint Waters** . . . . . . . . . . . (307) 777-5840
 E-mail: flint.waters@wyo.gov
State Deputy Chief Information Officer **Meredith Bickell** . . (307) 777-5840
 E-mail: meredith.bickell@wyo.gov
Office Manager **Leah Stewart** . . . . . . . . . . . . . . . . . . . . . . . (307) 777-5840

## Department of Environmental Quality [DEQ]
Herschler Building, 122 West 25th Street, Fourth Floor,
Cheyenne, WY 82002
Tel: (307) 777-7937  Fax: (307) 777-7682

**Employees:** 264

■Director **Todd T. Parfitt** . . . . . . . . . . . . . . . . . . . . . . (307) 777-7937 ext. 5
 Executive Secretary **Connie Osborne** . . . . . . . . . . . . . . . (307) 777-5593
Abandoned Mine Land Division Administrator
 **Alan Edwards** . . . . . . . . . . . . . . . . . . . . . . . . . . . . . . . . . (307) 777-7062
                                                Fax: (307) 777-5973
Air Quality Division Administrator **Nancy Vehr** . . . . . . . . . (307) 777-3746
                                                Fax: (307) 777-5616
Industrial Siting Division Administrator **Brian Lovett** . . . . . (307) 777-7555
Land Quality Division Administrator **Kyle J. Wendtland** . . (307) 777-7046
                                                Fax: (307) 777-5864
Management Services Division Administrator
 **James S. Uzzell** . . . . . . . . . . . . . . . . . . . . . . . . . . . . . . . . (307) 777-7198

*(continued on next page)*

---

★ Elected Official    ■ Appointed by Governor    ● Appointed by Legislature    ▲ Appointed by Board or Commission    ◆ Appointed by State Supreme Court

EXECUTIVE BRANCH

**Department of Environmental Quality** *continued*

Solid and Hazardous Waste Division Administrator
**Brian Lovett** . . . . . . . . . . . . . . . . . . . . . . . . . . . . . . . . . .(307) 777-7753
Fax: (307) 777-5973
Water Quality Division Administrator **Kevin Frederick** . . . .(307) 777-7072
Fax: (307) 777-5973

## Department of Family Services [DFS]
Hathaway Building, 2300 Capitol Avenue, Third Floor,
Cheyenne, WY 82002-0490
Tel: (307) 777-7561  Fax: (307) 777-7747  E-mail: jbensl@wyo.gov
Internet: dfsweb.state.wy.us
■Director **Steve Corsi** . . . . . . . . . . . . . . . . . . . . . . . . . . . . . (307) 777-7564
E-mail: steve.corsi@wyo.gov
   Executive Assistant **Nicki Romero** . . . . . . . . . . . . . . . . .(307) 777-6597
   Executive Assistant **Codee Augustin** . . . . . . . . . . . . . . . .(307) 777-6597
Child Support Enforcement Program Administrator
   **Kristie Langley** . . . . . . . . . . . . . . . . . . . . . . . . . . . . . . (307) 777-6068
   E-mail: kristie.langley@wyo.gov
Homeless Services Program Administrator **Brenda Lyttle** . .(307) 777-6948
   Education: Drake 1995 BA; Wyoming 1999 JD
Economic Assistance Division Administrator **(Vacant)** . . . .(307) 777-5846
Family Assistance Division Program Administrator
   **Roxanne O'Connor** . . . . . . . . . . . . . . . . . . . . . . . . . . .(307) 777-6101
Financial Services Division Administrator **Nick Baird** . . . .(307) 777-5468
Social Services Division Administrator **Marty Nelson** . . . .(307) 777-7091
Low Income Energy Assistance Program Manager
   **Brenda Ilg** . . . . . . . . . . . . . . . . . . . . . . . . . . . . . . . . . (307) 777-6346

## Department of Fire Prevention and Electrical Safety
320 W. 25th Street, 3rd Floor, Cheyenne, WY 82001
Tel: (307) 777-7288  Fax: (307) 777-7119  Internet: wsfm.wyo.gov
■Director and State Fire Marshal **Lanny Applegate** . . . . . . .(307) 777-7288
   E-mail: lanny.applegate@wyo.gov
Chief Electrical Inspector **Jonathan "Jon" Vosters** . . . . . .(307) 777-7288
Fax: (307) 777-7119
Assistant State Fire Marshal **Mark Young** . . . . . . . . . . . . . .(307) 777-7288
Training Manager **Ian Kraft** . . . . . . . . . . . . . . . . . . . . . . . . (307) 777-7288

## Wyoming Game and Fish Department
5400 Bishop Boulevard, Cheyenne, WY 82006
Tel: (307) 777-4600  TTY: (307) 777-4647  Fax: (307) 777-4699
Internet: wgfd.wyo.gov
■Director **Scott Talbott** . . . . . . . . . . . . . . . . . . . . . . . . . . . (307) 777-4501
   E-mail: scott.talbott@wyo.gov
   Executive Assistant **Sheridan Todd** . . . . . . . . . . . . . . . . .(307) 777-4632
Deputy Director **John Kennedy** . . . . . . . . . . . . . . . . . . . . . .(307) 777-4501
Fiscal Division Chief **Jean Cole** . . . . . . . . . . . . . . . . . . . . . (307) 777-4516
Fish Division Chief **Mark Fowden** . . . . . . . . . . . . . . . . . . . .(307) 777-4559
Services Division Chief **Scot Kofron** . . . . . . . . . . . . . . . . . .(307) 777-4591
Wildlife Division Chief **COL Brian Nesvik, ARNG** . . . . . . .(307) 777-4579
   Education: Wyoming 1994 BS

## Game and Fish Commission
President **T. Carrie Little** (District 4) . . . . . . . . . . . . . . . . . .(307) 777-4600
   Term Expires: March 1, 2017
Vice President **Keith Culver** (District 6) . . . . . . . . . . . . . . . .(307) 777-4600
   Term Expires: March 1, 2019
Commissioner **Mark Anselmi** (District 2) . . . . . . . . . . . . . .(307) 777-4600
   Term Expires: March 1, 2019
Commissioner **Patrick J. Crank** (District 1) . . . . . . . . . . . .(307) 777-4600
   Term Expires: March 1, 2021
   Education: Wyoming 1982 BS, 1985 JD
Commissioner **Richard Klouda** (District 7) . . . . . . . . . . . . .(307) 777-4600
   Term Expires: March 1, 2017
Commissioner **Charles C. Price** (District 3) . . . . . . . . . . . .(307) 777-4600
   Term Expires: March 1, 2017
Commissioner **David Rael** (District 5) . . . . . . . . . . . . . . . . .(307) 777-4600
   Term Expires: March 1, 2021

## Wyoming Department of Health [WDH]
401 Hathaway Building, 2300 Capitol Avenue, Cheyenne, WY 82002
Tel: (307) 777-7656  Tel: (307) 777-7264 (Vital Records)
Fax: (307) 777-7439  E-mail: wdh@wyo.gov

**Employees:** 1,346
■Director **Thomas O. "Tom" Forslund** . . . . . . . . . . . . . . . .(307) 777-7656
   E-mail: tom.forslund@wyo.gov
   Education: Iowa 1973 BA; Missouri 1977 MPA
Deputy Director **Korin Schmidt** . . . . . . . . . . . . . . . . . . . . .(307) 777-5759
Chief Financial Officer **Eric McVicker** . . . . . . . . . . . . . . . .(307) 777-8205
Fax: (307) 777-5896
State Children's Health Insurance Program (SCHIP)
   Director **Susie Scott** . . . . . . . . . . . . . . . . . . . . . . . . . . .(307) 777-6228
   E-mail: susie.scott@wyo.gov        Fax: (307) 777-7085

## Wyoming Insurance Department
106 East 6th Avenue, Cheyenne, WY 82002-0440
Tel: (307) 777-7401  Fax: (307) 777-2446  E-mail: wyinsdep@wyo.gov
■Insurance Commissioner **Paul Thomas "Tom" Glause** . . .(307) 777-6887
   E-mail: tom.glause@wyo.gov
   Human Resources **Cheryl Fiechtner** . . . . . . . . . . . . . . . .(307) 777-6887
Deputy Insurance Commissioner **Jeff Rude** . . . . . . . . . . . .(307) 777-6896
Chief Examiner **Linda Johnson** . . . . . . . . . . . . . . . . . . . . . (307) 777-5619
Licensing Supervisor **Renee Austin** . . . . . . . . . . . . . . . . . .(307) 777-7344
   E-mail: renee.austin@wyo.gov
Consumer Affairs Specialist **Ruth Case** . . . . . . . . . . . . . . .(307) 777-7402
Consumer Affairs Specialist **Nancy Olsen** . . . . . . . . . . . . .(307) 777-7402
Life and Health Insurance Standards Consultant
   **Brittany Buss** . . . . . . . . . . . . . . . . . . . . . . . . . . . . . . .(307) 777-2447
Life and Health Insurance Standards Consultant
   **Jonathan Staniforth** . . . . . . . . . . . . . . . . . . . . . . . . . .(307) 777-6888
Property and Casualty Insurance Standards Consultant
   **D'Anna Feurt** . . . . . . . . . . . . . . . . . . . . . . . . . . . . . . .(307) 777-7336
Property and Casualty Insurance Standards Consultant
   **Donna Stewart** . . . . . . . . . . . . . . . . . . . . . . . . . . . . . .(307) 777-7308
Webmaster **Peter Greff** . . . . . . . . . . . . . . . . . . . . . . . . . . . (307) 777-2448
   E-mail: peter.greff@wyo.gov

## Wyoming Military Department
5410 Bishop Boulevard, Cheyenne, WY 82009-3320
Tel: (307) 772-5234  Fax: (307) 772-5010

**Employees:** 230
■Adjutant General **MG K. Luke Reiner, ARNG** . . . . . . . . . .(307) 772-5234
   E-mail: luke.reiner@us.army.mil
   Education: Nebraska 1986 BS
Assistant Adjutant General (Air)
   **BrigGen Stephen E. "Steve" Rader, ANG** . . . . . . . . . .(307) 772-5292
   Education: Southern Illinois 1983 AAS, 1992 BS
Assistant Adjutant General (Army)
   **COL Tammy J. Maas, ARNG** . . . . . . . . . . . . . . . . . . .(307) 772-5028
Agency Deputy Director **Douglas C. "Doug" Shope** . . . . .(307) 777-8100
94th Troop Command Commander
   **LTC Shane Crofts, ARNG** . . . . . . . . . . . . . . . . . . . . . .(307) 772-5302
115th Fires Brigade Commander
   **LTC Greg Phipps, ARNG** . . . . . . . . . . . . . . . . . . . . . .(307) 772-5928
2-300 Field Artillery Battalion Commander
   **LTC Jim Cudney, ARNG** . . . . . . . . . . . . . . . . . . . . . . .(307) 772-5873
153rd Airlift Wing Commander **Col Paul Lyman, ANG** . . .(307) 772-6153
Commander (153rd Maintenance Group)
   **Col Pete Linde, ANG** . . . . . . . . . . . . . . . . . . . . . . . . .(307) 772-6314
Commander (153rd Mission Support Group)
   **Col Shelley R. Campbell, ANG** . . . . . . . . . . . . . . . . . .(307) 772-6186
Commander (153rd Operations Group)
   **Col Justin Walrath, ANG** . . . . . . . . . . . . . . . . . . . . . .(307) 772-6212
Army Chief of Staff **LtCol Steve Alkire, ANG** . . . . . . . . . .(307) 772-5028
Deputy Chief of Staff, Operations **John Papile** . . . . . . . . .(307) 772-5264
Joint Staff Director **BG Greg Porter, ARNG** . . . . . . . . . . .(307) 772-5292
State Public Affairs Officer **Deidre Forster** . . . . . . . . . . . .(307) 772-5235
Human Resources Officer **(Vacant)** . . . . . . . . . . . . . . . . . .(307) 772-5134
US Property and Fiscal Officer
   **COL Tim Sheppard, USA** . . . . . . . . . . . . . . . . . . . . . .(307) 772-5271
Staff Director **COL James P. "Pat" Moffett, ANG** . . . . . . .(307) 772-5444

---

★ Elected Official   ■ Appointed by Governor   ● Appointed by Legislature      ▲ Appointed by Board or Commission      ◆ Appointed by State Supreme Court

Chief Information Officer **James M. "Mike" Jones** . . . . . . (307) 772-5234

## Veterans' Commission
WY Army National Guard Armory, 5905 Cy Avenue, Room 101, Casper, WY 82604
E-mail: wvac@bresnan.net

▲Chairman **Linda Allegeier** . . . . . . . . . . . . . . . . . . . . . . . . . . . (307) 467-5327
Director **Larry Barttelbort** . . . . . . . . . . . . . . . . . . . . . . . . . . . (307) 777-8151
Veterans' Service Officer **Robert Stall** . . . . . . . . . . . . . . . (307) 777-8153

## Wyoming Department of Revenue
Herschler Building, 122 West 25th Street, Second Floor West, Cheyenne, WY 82002-0110
Tel: (307) 777-7961  Fax: (307) 777-7722  E-mail: DOR@wyo.gov
Internet: revenue.state.wy.us

■Director **Daniel W. "Dan" Noble** . . . . . . . . . . . . . . . . . . . (307) 777-5287
   E-mail: dan.noble@wyo.gov
   Education: Wyoming (Attended)
Administrative Services Division Administrator
   **Christie Yurek** . . . . . . . . . . . . . . . . . . . . . . . . . . . . . . . . (307) 777-5275
   E-mail: christie.yurek@wyo.gov
Excise Tax Division Administrator **Kim E. Lovett** . . . . . . . . (307) 777-5220
Liquor Division Administrator **Greg Cook** . . . . . . . . . . . . . (307) 777-6448
   122 West 25th Street, 2-W, Cheyenne, WY 82002
Mineral Tax Division Administrator **Craig Grenvik** . . . . . . . (307) 777-5237
Property Tax Division Administrator **Brenda Arnold** . . . . . . (307) 777-5235
Human Resources Director **Pam Glick** . . . . . . . . . . . . . . . . (307) 777-7962

## Wyoming State Parks and Cultural Resources [SPCR]
2301 Central Avenue, Cheyenne, WY 82002
Tel: (307) 777-6303  Fax: (307) 777-6005  Internet: wyospcr.state.wy.us
E-mail: spcr@state.wy.us

**Employees:** 167

■Director **Milward Simpson** . . . . . . . . . . . . . . . . . . . . . . . . . . (307) 777-6303
   E-mail: milward.simpson@wyo.gov
   Education: Wyoming BA; Colorado (Denver) MHum

## Administrative Services
Human Resource Supervisor **Stacy Sprengeler** . . . . . . . . . (307) 777-7010
Information Technology Manager **Eric Schooley** . . . . . . . . (307) 777-6315
   E-mail: eric.schooley@wyo.gov
Public Information Officer **Gary Schoene** . . . . . . . . . . . . . (307) 777-7014
   E-mail: gary.schoene@wyo.gov

## Cultural Resources Division
Administrator **Sara Needles** . . . . . . . . . . . . . . . . . . . . . . . . (307) 777-7637
   Administrative Assistant **Christie Christensen** . . . . . . . . . (307) 777-7496

## Archives and Records Management Unit
Archives/Museum/Records Program Manager
   **Mike Strom** . . . . . . . . . . . . . . . . . . . . . . . . . . . . . . . . . . (307) 777-7020
Arts Program Manager **Michael Lange** . . . . . . . . . . . . . . . (307) 777-7723
   E-mail: michael.lange@wyo.gov
   Education: Wyoming 2005 BA, 2008 MPA
Museum Director **Mark Brammer** . . . . . . . . . . . . . . . . . . . . (307) 777-8021
State Archaeologist **Greg Pierce** . . . . . . . . . . . . . . . . . . . . (307) 766-5564
State Historic Preservation Officer **Mary Hopkins** . . . . . . . (307) 777-6311
Museum Program Manager **(Vacant)** . . . . . . . . . . . . . . . . . (307) 777-7022

## State Parks and Historic Sites Division
E-mail: sphs@state.wy.us

**Employees:** 172

Administrator **Domenic Bravo** . . . . . . . . . . . . . . . . . . . . . . (307) 777-6324
Chief of Field Support **Darin Westby** . . . . . . . . . . . . . . . . . (307) 777-6697
   E-mail: darin.westby@wyo.gov
Chief of Operations **William Westerfield** . . . . . . . . . . . . . (307) 777-6318
   E-mail: bill.westerfield@wyo.gov

Trails Program Manager **Ron McKinney** . . . . . . . . . . . . . . . (307) 332-5036
   E-mail: ron.mckinney@wyo.gov

## Wyoming Department of Transportation [WYDOT]
5300 Bishop Boulevard, Cheyenne, WY 82009-3340
Tel: (307) 777-4375  Fax: (307) 777-4163

**Employees:** 1,951

■Director **Bill Panos** . . . . . . . . . . . . . . . . . . . . . . . . . . . . . . . (307) 777-4484
   E-mail: bill.panos@wyo.gov
Legal Representative **Mike Kahler** . . . . . . . . . . . . . . . . . . . (307) 777-7196
Chief Engineer **Gregg Fredrick** . . . . . . . . . . . . . . . . . . . . . (307) 777-4484
   E-mail: gregg.fredrick@wyo.gov
Construction Engineer **Andy Long** . . . . . . . . . . . . . . . . . . . (307) 777-4425
   E-mail: andy.long@wyo.gov
Equipment Engineer **Bernie Kushnir** . . . . . . . . . . . . . . . . . (307) 777-4061
   E-mail: bernie.kushnir@wyo.gov
Maintenance Engineer **Kent Ketterling** . . . . . . . . . . . . . . . (307) 777-4051
Internal Review Services Program Manager
   **Kristin Burkart** . . . . . . . . . . . . . . . . . . . . . . . . . . . . . . . (307) 777-4797
Public Affairs Manager **Doug McGee** . . . . . . . . . . . . . . . . (307) 777-4010
Strategic Performance Improvement Manager
   **Janet Farrar** . . . . . . . . . . . . . . . . . . . . . . . . . . . . . . . . (307) 777-4780
Commission Secretary/Legislative Liaison **Sandra Scott** . . (307) 777-4007
Field Operations **Mark Eisenhart** . . . . . . . . . . . . . . . . . . . (307) 777-4459

## Aeronautics Division
200 East Eighth Avenue, Cheyenne, WY 82001
Fax: (307) 637-7352

Administrator **Dennis Byrne** . . . . . . . . . . . . . . . . . . . . . . . . (307) 777-3952
Commission Secretary **Katie Pfister** . . . . . . . . . . . . . . . . . (307) 777-3952
Flight Operations Manager and Chief Pilot **Tory Meisel** . . . (307) 777-3952

## Engineering and Planning Division
Assistant Chief Engineer **Keith Fulton** . . . . . . . . . . . . . . . (307) 777-4484
   E-mail: keith.fulton@wyo.gov
Contracts & Estimates Engineer **Ken Spear** . . . . . . . . . . . (307) 777-4487
   E-mail: ken.spear@wyo.gov
State Bridge Engineer **Michael Menghini** . . . . . . . . . . . . . (307) 777-4043
   E-mail: michael.menghini@wyo.gov
State Highway Development Engineer **Tony Laird** . . . . . . . . (307) 777-4134
   E-mail: tony.laird@wyo.gov
State Materials Engineer **Greg Milburn** . . . . . . . . . . . . . . . (307) 777-4070
   E-mail: greg.milburn@wyo.gov
State Planning Engineer **Martin Kidner** . . . . . . . . . . . . . . . (307) 777-4411
Transportation Programming Engineer **Tim McDowell** . . . . (307) 777-4177
   E-mail: tim.mcdowell@wyo.gov
Chief Engineering Geologist **Jim Coffin** . . . . . . . . . . . . . . (307) 777-4205
State Right-of-Way Program Manager **Kevin Lebeda** . . . . . (307) 777-4116
   E-mail: kevin.lebeda@wyo.gov
Local Government Coordinator **Taylor Rossetti** . . . . . . . . . (307) 777-4438
   E-mail: taylor.rossetti@wyo.gov

## Highway Patrol Division
Patrol Administrator **Col. Kebin Haller** . . . . . . . . . . . . . . . (307) 777-4301
   E-mail: kebin.haller@wyo.gov
Field Operations Commander **Major Keith Groeneweg** . . . (307) 777-4307
Operations Commander **Lt. Col. Shannon Ratliff** . . . . . . . (307) 777-4302
Support Services Commander **Major Perry Jones** . . . . . . . (307) 777-4318
   E-mail: perry.jones@wyo.gov
Commercial Carrier Officer **Capt. Scot Montgomery** . . . . (307) 777-4312
   E-mail: scot.montgomery@wyo.gov

## Operations Division
Operations Assistant Chief Engineer **Ken Shultz** . . . . . . . . (307) 777-4484
State Highway Safety Engineer **Matt Carlson** . . . . . . . . . . (307) 777-4450
   E-mail: matt.carlson@wyo.gov
State Traffic Engineer **Joel Meena** . . . . . . . . . . . . . . . . . . (307) 777-4374
   E-mail: joel.meena@wyo.gov
Enterprise Technology Manager **D. Michael Bush** . . . . . . . (307) 777-4100
   E-mail: michael.bush@wyo.gov
Facilities Management **Ray Vigil** . . . . . . . . . . . . . . . . . . . . (307) 777-4105
   E-mail: raymond.vigil@wyo.gov

*(continued on next page)*

---

★ Elected Official   ■ Appointed by Governor   ● Appointed by Legislature   ▲ Appointed by Board or Commission   ◆ Appointed by State Supreme Court

**Operations Division** *continued*

Information Technology Program Manager
**James "Rusty" England** . . . . . . . . . . . . . . . . . . . . . . . (307) 777-4421
E-mail: rusty.england@wyo.gov
Management Services Manager **John Davis** . . . . . . . . . . . (307) 777-4158
E-mail: john.davis@wyo.gov
Procurement Services Program Manager **Hans Hehr** . . . . . . (307) 777-4106
E-mail: hans.hehr@wyo.gov
Telecommunications Program Manager **Robert Wilson** . . . . (307) 777-4440
E-mail: robert.wilson4@wyo.gov
Financial Services Administrator **David Stearns** . . . . . . . . (307) 777-4024

## Support Services Division

Administrator **Tom Loftin** . . . . . . . . . . . . . . . . . . . . . . . . (307) 777-4484
E-mail: tom.loftin@wyo.gov
Compliance and Investigation Program Manager
**Bob Stauffacher** . . . . . . . . . . . . . . . . . . . . . . . . . . . . . (307) 777-3849
E-mail: bob.stauffacher@wyo.gov
Driver Services Manager **Debbie Trojovsky** . . . . . . . . . . . (307) 777-4866
Fuel Tax Administration Program Manager
**Wayne Hassinger** . . . . . . . . . . . . . . . . . . . . . . . . . . . . (307) 777-3909
E-mail: wayne.hassinger@wyo.gov
Human Resources Program Manager **Lon Pfau** . . . . . . . . . (307) 777-4103
E-mail: lonny.pfau@wyo.gov
Motor Vehicle Services Manager **Debbie Lopez** . . . . . . . . . (307) 777-4714
E-mail: deborah.lopez@wyo.gov
Office Services Program Manager **Tim Tyler** . . . . . . . . . . . (307) 777-4380
E-mail: timothy.tyler@wyo.gov
Training Services Program Manager **Jim Boyd** . . . . . . . . . . (307) 777-4792
Civil Rights Coordinator **Lisa Fresquez** . . . . . . . . . . . . . . (307) 777-4457
Budget Supervisor **Rodney Freier** . . . . . . . . . . . . . . . . . . (307) 777-4174
Employee Safety Officer **Ron Chavez** . . . . . . . . . . . . . . . . (307) 777-4460

## District Offices

District 1 Engineer **Pat Persson** . . . . . . . . . . . . . . . . . . . (307) 745-2100
3411 South 3rd Street, Laramie, WY 82070
District 2 Engineer **Lowell Fleenor** . . . . . . . . . . . . . . . . . (307) 473-3200
900 Bryan Stock Trail, Casper, WY 82601
District 3 Engineer **Keith Compton** . . . . . . . . . . . . . . . . . (307) 352-3031
3200 Elk Street, Rock Springs, WY 82901
E-mail: keith.compton@wyo.gov
District 4 Engineer **Mark Gillett** . . . . . . . . . . . . . . . . . . . (307) 674-2300
10 East Brundage Lane, Sheridan, WY 82801
E-mail: mark.gillett@wyo.gov
District 5 Engineer **Shelby Carlson** . . . . . . . . . . . . . . . . . (307) 568-3400
218 West C, Basin, WY 82410
E-mail: shelby.carlson@wyo.gov

# Department of Workforce Services

Herschler Building, 122 West 25th Street, 2 East, Cheyenne, WY 82002
Tel: (307) 777-8650  Fax: (307) 777-5857
E-mail: workforceservices@state.wy.us
Internet: www.wyomingworkforce.org

■Director **John Cox** . . . . . . . . . . . . . . . . . . . . . . . . . . . . . (307) 777-8728
E-mail: john.cox@wyo.gov
Deputy Director **Lisa M. Osvold** . . . . . . . . . . . . . . . . . . . (307) 777-8728
E-mail: lisa.osvold@wyo.gov
Standards and Compliance Administrator **John Ysebaert** . . (307) 777-7671
E-mail: john.ysebaert@wyo.gov
Mine Inspections and Safety Division Administrator
**Terry Adcock** . . . . . . . . . . . . . . . . . . . . . . . . . . . . . . . (307) 362-5222
P.O. Box 1094, Rock Springs, WY 82902

# Office of the State Engineer

Herschler Building, 122 West 25th Street, Fourth Floor East,
Cheyenne, WY 82002-0370
Tel: (307) 777-6150  Fax: (307) 777-5451  Internet: seo.wyo.gov

■State Engineer **Patrick T. Tyrrell, PE** . . . . . . . . . . . . . . . (307) 777-6150
E-mail: patrick.tyrrell@wyo.gov
Executive Assistant **Susan Jenkins** . . . . . . . . . . . . . . . . . (307) 777-6150
Safety of Dams Engineer **Nathan Graves, PE** . . . . . . . . . . (307) 777-3500
E-mail: nathan.graves@wyo.gov

Safety of Dams Engineer **Mike Hand, PE** . . . . . . . . . . . . . (307) 777-6153
E-mail: mike.hand@wyo.gov
Interstate Streams Administrator **Sue Lowry** . . . . . . . . . . . (307) 777-5927
Support Services Administrator **Martin Zimmerman** . . . . . . (307) 777-5956
Board of Control Division Administrator
**Cheryl Verplancke** . . . . . . . . . . . . . . . . . . . . . . . . . . . . (307) 777-6177
Ground Water Division Administrator
**Lisa Lindemann, PG** . . . . . . . . . . . . . . . . . . . . . . . . . . (307) 777-5063
Surface Water and Engineering Division Administrator
**Rick Deuell, PE** . . . . . . . . . . . . . . . . . . . . . . . . . . . . . . (307) 777-6168
Human Resource Officer III **Loretta E. Green** . . . . . . . . . . (307) 777-6143

# Office of the Public Defender

Rogers Building, 316 West 22nd Street, Cheyenne, WY 82002
Fax: (307) 777-8742  Internet: http://wyodefender.state.wy.us

**Employees:** 73

■State Public Defender **Diane M. Lozano** . . . . . . . . . . . . . . (307) 777-7519
E-mail: diane.lozano@wyo.gov
■Deputy State Public Defender **Ryan Roden** . . . . . . . . . . . (307) 777-7519
E-mail: ryan.roden@wyo.gov
■Chief Appellate Counsel **Tina Olson** . . . . . . . . . . . . . . . . (307) 777-3451
E-mail: tina.olson@wyo.gov
Chief Trial Counsel **Kerri Johnson** . . . . . . . . . . . . . . . . . . (307) 261-2162

# Office of Administrative Hearings [OAH]

Wyoming Financial Center, 2020 Carey Avenue, Fifth Floor,
Cheyenne, WY 82002-0270
Tel: (307) 777-6660  Fax: (307) 777-5269  Internet: http://oah.state.wy.us

■Director **Deborah Baumer** . . . . . . . . . . . . . . . . . . . . . . . . (307) 777-6660
E-mail: deborah.baumer@wyo.gov
Education: Northern Colorado BA; Wyoming JD
Office Manager **Jana R. Reutlinger** . . . . . . . . . . . . . . . . . . (307) 777-6834
E-mail: jana.reutlinger1@wyo.gov

# Office of State Lands and Investments

Herschler Building, 122 West 25th Street, Third Floor West,
Cheyenne, WY 82002-0600
Tel: (307) 777-7331  Fax: (307) 777-5400  E-mail: slfmail@wyo.gov
Internet: http://lands.state.wy.us

■Director **Bridget Hill** . . . . . . . . . . . . . . . . . . . . . . . . . . . . (307) 777-6629
E-mail: bridget.hill@wyo.gov
Education: Wyoming 2002 JD
Deputy Director **Susan Child** . . . . . . . . . . . . . . . . . . . . . . (307) 777-3428
Executive Assistant **Machá Ledet** . . . . . . . . . . . . . . . . . . (307) 777-6629
State Forester **Bill Crapser** . . . . . . . . . . . . . . . . . . . . . . . (307) 777-5644
Administrative Services Division Assistant Director
**Amanda Sewell** . . . . . . . . . . . . . . . . . . . . . . . . . . . . . . (307) 777-7028
E-mail: amanda.sewell@wyo.gov
Field Services Division Assistant Director
**Benjamin "Ben" Bump** . . . . . . . . . . . . . . . . . . . . . . . . . (307) 777-6545
Trust Land Management Division Assistant Director
**Jason Crowder** . . . . . . . . . . . . . . . . . . . . . . . . . . . . . . . (307) 777-6639
Royalty Compliance Supervisor **Billie Hunter** . . . . . . . . . . (307) 777-6641

# Wyoming Public Service Commission

Hansen Building, 2515 Warren Avenue, Suite 300, Cheyenne, WY 82002
Tel: (307) 777-7427  Fax: (307) 777-5700  E-mail: dcrock@state.wy.us
Internet: http://psc.state.wy.us

■Chair **Alan B. Minier** . . . . . . . . . . . . . . . . . . . . . . . . . . . (307) 777-5725
E-mail: al.minier@wyo.gov
Education: Yale 1970 BA
■Deputy Chair **Bill Russell** . . . . . . . . . . . . . . . . . . . . . . . . (307) 777-5746
Education: Wyoming JD
■Commissioner **Kara Brighton** . . . . . . . . . . . . . . . . . . . . . (307) 777-5746

★ Elected Official    ■ Appointed by Governor    ● Appointed by Legislature    ▲ Appointed by Board or Commission    ◆ Appointed by State Supreme Court

Summer 2016 | © Leadership Directories, Inc. | *State Yellow Book*

## State Building Commission

700 West 21st Street, Cheyenne, WY 82002-0060
Tel: (307) 777-8660  Fax: (307) 777-6273

Chairman **Matthew Hansen "Matt" Mead** . . . . . . . . . . . . (307) 777-7434
Commissioner **Jillian Balow** . . . . . . . . . . . . . . . . . . . . . . . . . (307) 777-7675
  Term Expires: January 2019
  Education: Wyoming BA; Regis U MEd
Commissioner **Cynthia I. Cloud, CPA** . . . . . . . . . . . . . . . . (307) 777-7831
  Term Expires: January 2019
Commissioner **Mark Gordon** . . . . . . . . . . . . . . . . . . . . . . . . (307) 777-7408
  Term Expires: January 2019
  Education: Middlebury 1979 BA
Commissioner **Edward F. "Ed" Murray III** . . . . . . . . . . . . . (307) 777-7378
  Term Expires: January 2019
  Education: Wyoming JD
Secretary of the Commission **Mel Muldrow** . . . . . . . . . . . . (307) 777-8660

## Wyoming Retirement System

6101 Yellowstone Road, 5th Floor West, Suite 500, Cheyenne, WY 82002
Tel: (307) 777-7691  Fax: (307) 777-5995  Internet: retirement.wyo.gov

▲Executive Director **Ruth Ryerson** . . . . . . . . . . . . . . . . . . . . (307) 777-7691
  E-mail: ruth.ryerson@wyo.gov
Deputy Director **David "Dave" Swindell** . . . . . . . . . . . . . . . (307) 777-7691
Deferred Compensation Manager **Polly Scott** . . . . . . . . . . . (307) 777-7691
Chief Investment Officer **Sam Masoudi** . . . . . . . . . . . . . . . . (307) 777-7691

## Office of the Secretary of State

2020 Carey Avenue, Suites 600 and 700, Cheyenne, WY 82002-0020
Tel: (307) 777-7378  Fax: (307) 777-6217  E-mail: secofstate@wyo.gov

★Secretary of State **Edward F. "Ed" Murray III** (R) . . . . . . . . (307) 777-7378
  Term Expires: February 2019
Deputy Secretary of State **Karen L. Wheeler** . . . . . . . . . . . . (307) 777-5333
  E-mail: secofstate@wyo.gov
Administrative Support Director **Thomas Cowan** . . . . . . . . (307) 777-5348
  E-mail: sosadminservices@wyo.gov          Tel: (307) 777-5339
Business Division Director **Jeri Melsness** . . . . . . . . . . . . . . (307) 777-7311
  E-mail: business@wyo.gov                   Fax: (307) 777-5339
Compliance Division Director **Kelly Janes** . . . . . . . . . . . . . (307) 777-7370
                                             Fax: (307) 777-7640
State Elections Director **Kai Schon** . . . . . . . . . . . . . . . . . . . (307) 777-5860
Technology Director **Andrea Byrne** . . . . . . . . . . . . . . . . . . . (307) 777-5953
                                             Fax: (307) 777-7640

## Office of the Treasurer

State Capitol, 200 West 24th Street, Cheyenne, WY 82002
Tel: (307) 777-7408  Fax: (307) 777-3731

★State Treasurer **Mark Gordon** (R) . . . . . . . . . . . . . . . . . . . (307) 777-7408
  Term Expires: 2019
  E-mail: mark.gordon@wyo.gov
Deputy Treasurer **Patricia O'Brien Arp** . . . . . . . . . . . . . . . (307) 777-7408
Chief Accountant **(Vacant)** . . . . . . . . . . . . . . . . . . . . . . . . . (307) 777-7171
Chief Investments Officer **Patrick Fleming** . . . . . . . . . . . . . (307) 777-7779
General Counsel **Betsy Anderson** . . . . . . . . . . . . . . . . . . . . (307) 777-5395
Administrative Accountant **Jeanne Hartman** . . . . . . . . . . . (307) 777-8602
  E-mail: jeanne.hartman1@wyo.gov
Information Technology Director **Mitchell Haden** . . . . . . . . (307) 777-6540
  E-mail: mitchell.haden@wyo.gov
Executive Assistant **Kathy Ramsey** . . . . . . . . . . . . . . . . . . . (307) 777-2991
  E-mail: kathy.ramsey@wyo.gov
Human Resources Professional **Deebs Sullivan** . . . . . . . . . (307) 777-2417

## Office of the State Auditor

200 West 24th Street, Cheyenne, WY 82002-0010
Tel: (307) 777-7831  Fax: (307) 777-6983

★State Auditor **Cynthia I. Cloud, CPA** (R) . . . . . . . . . . . . . . (307) 777-7831
  Term Expires: 2019
  Executive Assistant **Caitlin Argyle** . . . . . . . . . . . . . . . . . (307) 777-7831
Deputy State Auditor **Sandy Urbanek** . . . . . . . . . . . . . . . . (307) 777-7831

## Wyoming Department of Education [WDE]

Hathaway Building, 2300 Capitol Avenue, 2nd Floor,
Cheyenne, WY 82002-2060
Tel: (307) 777-7690  TTY: (307) 777-7744  Fax: (307) 777-6234
E-mail: info@educ.state.wy.us

★Superintendent of Public Instruction **Jillian Balow** (R) . . . . (307) 777-7675
  Term Expires: 2019
  Executive Assistant **Rita Watson** . . . . . . . . . . . . . . . . . . . (307) 777-7675
Deputy Superintendent **Dicky Shanor** . . . . . . . . . . . . . . . . (307) 777-2061
Chief Academic Officer **Brent Bacon** . . . . . . . . . . . . . . . . . (307) 777-6132
Chief Operations Officer **Dianne Bailey** . . . . . . . . . . . . . . . (307) 777-7720
  E-mail: dianne.bailey@wyo.gov
Chief Policy Officer **Brent Young** . . . . . . . . . . . . . . . . . . . . (307) 777-2059
  Education: Wyoming BA
Communications Division **Kari Eakins** . . . . . . . . . . . . . . . . (307) 777-2053
  E-mail: kari.eakins@wyo.gov
Special Programs Division Director **Lisa Weigel** . . . . . . . . . (307) 777-2871
Accountability Division Director **Julie Magee** . . . . . . . . . . . (307) 777-8740
School Support Division Director **Rob Bryant** . . . . . . . . . . . (307) 777-7708
Assessment Supervisor **Deb Lindsey** . . . . . . . . . . . . . . . . . (307) 777-8753

## State Board of Education

Hathaway Building, 2300 Capitol Avenue, Second Floor,
Cheyenne, WY 82002-0050
Tel: (307) 777-6503  Tel: (307) 777-7675  Fax: (307) 777-6234

■Chairman **Pete Gosar** (Second Appointment District) . . . . . (307) 777-6503
  Education: Wyoming 1992 BA
■Vice Chair **Kathy Coon** (Fourth Appointment District) . . . . (307) 777-6503
  E-mail: kathy.coon@wyoboards.gov
■Treasurer **Ken Rathbun** (Sixth Appointment District) . . . . . (307) 777-6503
  E-mail: ken.rathbun@wyoboards.gov
■Member **Sue Belish** (Fourth Appointment District) . . . . . . . (307) 777-6503
■Member **Nate Breen** (First Appointment District) . . . . . . . . (307) 777-7675
■Member **Hugh Hageman** . . . . . . . . . . . . . . . . . . . . . . . . . . (307) 777-6503
■Member **Scott Ratliff** (Seventh Appointment District) . . . . . (307) 777-6503
■Member **Kathryn L. Sessions** . . . . . . . . . . . . . . . . . . . . . . . (307) 777-6503
  E-mail: kathryn.sessions@wyoboards.gov
  Education: Utah State BA, MA
■Member **Walter Wilcox** . . . . . . . . . . . . . . . . . . . . . . . . . . . (307) 777-6503
  E-mail: walt.wilcox@wyoboards.gov
■Member **Belenda Willson** (Fifth Appointment District) . . . (307) 777-6503
  E-mail: belenda.willson@wyoboards.gov
■Member **(Vacant)** (Third Appointment District) . . . . . . . . . (307) 777-6503
Attorney **Mackenzie Williams** . . . . . . . . . . . . . . . . . . . . . . (307) 777-8781
Board Executive Secretary **Chelsie Oaks** . . . . . . . . . . . . . . (307) 777-6213
  E-mail: chelsie.bailey@wyo.gov
Webmaster **(Vacant)** . . . . . . . . . . . . . . . . . . . . . . . . . . . . . . (307) 777-6386

★ Elected Official   ■ Appointed by Governor   ● Appointed by Legislature   ▲ Appointed by Board or Commission   ◆ Appointed by State Supreme Court

*State Yellow Book*          © Leadership Directories, Inc.          Summer 2016

# Legislative Branch

# Alabama Legislature

State House, 11 South Union Street, Montgomery, AL 36130
Tel: (334) 242-7800  Internet: www.legislature.state.al.us

# Alabama State Senate

State House, 11 South Union Street, Montgomery, AL 36130
Tel: (334) 242-7800  Fax: (334) 242-8819

President of the Senate **Kay Ivey** (R).................(334) 242-7900
  Education: Auburn 1967 BS
President Pro Tem **Del Marsh** (R)...................(334) 242-7877
  Education: Auburn BA
Majority Leader **Greg Reed** (R) ......................(334) 242-7894
  Education: Alabama BSB
Majority Whip **Dr. Gerald O. Dial** (R) ..............(334) 242-7874
  Education: Livingston BS; Jacksonville State EdD
Minority Leader **Quinton T. Ross, Jr.** (D) ...........(334) 242-7880
  Education: Alabama State BS, MA
Secretary of the Senate **David Patrick Harris** ...........(334) 242-7803

## Senators

**Party Affiliation Statistics:** Republicans: 27, Democrats: 7,
Independents: 1

Senator **Greg Albritton** (R-District 22) Suite 735 ........ (334) 242-7843
  Counties Represented: Baldwin (part), Choctaw (part), Clarke (part),
  Conecuh (part), Escambia, Mobile (part), Monroe (part), Washington
  Term Expires: 2018
  E-mail: galbritton@att.net
  Committees: Agriculture, Conservation and Forestry; Constitution,
  Ethics and Elections; Local Legislation Mobile County; Transportation
  and Energy
  Education: Weber State BS; Jones Law JD

Senator **Gerald Allen** (R-District 21) .................. (334) 242-7889
  Counties Represented: Hale (part), Pickens,     Res: (205) 556-5310
  Tuscaloosa (part)
  Term Expires: 2018
  P.O. Box 70007, Tuscaloosa, AL 35407
  E-mail: gerald.allen@alsenate.gov
  Committees: Confirmations; Finance and Taxation Education;
  Transportation and Energy
  Education: Alabama BS

Senator **Billy Beasley** (D-District 28) ................. (334) 242-7868
  Counties Represented: Barbour, Bullock, Henry, Lee     Dist: (334) 775-7711
  (part), Macon, Russell (part)
  Term Expires: 2018
  P.O. Box 606, Clayton, AL 36016
  E-mail: billy.beasley@alhouse.org
  Committees: Agriculture, Conservation and Forestry; Finance and
  Taxation General Fund; Health and Human Services; Rules
  Education: Auburn 1962 BS

Senator **Slade Blackwell** (R-District 15)...............(334) 242-7851
  Counties Represented: Jefferson (part), Shelby (part)     Dist: (205) 396-1144
  Term Expires: 2018
  2501 20th Place South, Suite 225, Birmingham, AL 35223
  E-mail: sb@sladeblackwell.com
  Committees: Banking and Insurance; Confirmations; Finance and
  Taxation Education; Health and Human Services; Local Legislation
  Jefferson County; Local Legislation Shelby County
  Education: Montevallo 1991 BA

Senator **Dick L. Brewbaker** (R-District 25) ............. (334) 242-7895
  Counties Represented: Elmore (part), Montgomery (part)
  Term Expires: 2018
  P. O. Box 230088, Montgomery, AL 36123
  E-mail: dick.brewbaker@alsenate.gov
  Committees: Confirmations; Constitution, Ethics and Elections;
  Education and Youth Affairs; Governmental Affairs; Rules
  Education: Vanderbilt 1983 BA

Senator **Paul Bussman** (R-District 4) ................. (334) 242-7855
  Counties Represented: Cullman, Lawrence (part),     Dist: (256) 734-1700
  Winston (part)
  Term Expires: 2018
  1625 Main Avenue, SW, Cullman, AL 35055
  E-mail: p_bussman@bellsouth.net
  Committees: Agriculture, Conservation and Forestry; Banking and
  Insurance; Education and Youth Affairs; Finance and Taxation
  Education; Governmental Affairs; Health and Human Services
  Education: Troy State BS; Alabama DDS

Senator **Clyde Chambliss** (R-District 30) Suite 733 ...... (334) 242-7883
  Counties Represented: Autauga (part), Chilton (part), Coosa, Elmore
  (part), Tallapoosa (part)
  Term Expires: 2018
  E-mail: clyde.chambliss@alsenate.gov
  Committees: Agriculture, Conservation and Forestry; County and
  Municipal Government; Finance and Taxation General Fund; Fiscal
  Responsibility and Economic Development; Transportation and Energy

Senator **Linda Coleman** (D-District 20) ...............(334) 242-7864
  Counties Represented: Jefferson (part)     Res: (205) 798-1045
  Term Expires: 2018     Fax: (205) 353-8417
  926 Chinchona Drive, Birmingham, AL 35214
  E-mail: linda.coleman@alsenate.gov
  Committees: Banking and Insurance; Constitution, Ethics and Elections;
  Governmental Affairs; Health and Human Services; Judiciary; Local
  Legislation Jefferson County; Transportation and Energy
  Education: Alabama A&M BS; Alabama Birmingham MA

Senator **Dr. Gerald O. Dial** (R-District 13) ..............(334) 242-7874
  Counties Represented: Chambers, Cherokee (part),     Dist: (256) 396-5600
  Clay, Cleburne, Lee (part), Randolph     Res: (334) 242-5626
  Term Expires: 2018
  P.O. Box 248, Lineville, AL 36266
  E-mail: gerald_dial@yahoo.com
  Committees: Finance and Taxation Education; Health and Human
  Services; Rules; Transportation and Energy; Veterans and Military
  Affairs

Senator **Priscilla Dunn** (D-District 19) .................(334) 242-7793
  Counties Represented: Jefferson (part)     Res: (205) 426-3795
  Term Expires: 2018     Fax: (334) 353-9625
  460 Carriage Hills Drive, Bessemer, AL 35022
  E-mail: priscilla.dunn@alsenate.gov
  Committees: County and Municipal Government; Finance and Taxation
  General Fund; Fiscal Responsibility and Economic Development;
  Governmental Affairs; Local Legislation Jefferson County
  Education: Alabama State BS; Montevallo MA

Senator **Vivian Davis Figures** (D-District 33) ...........(334) 242-7871
  Counties Represented: Mobile (part)     Dist: (251) 208-5480
  Term Expires: 2018     Fax: (251) 208-5492
  104 South Lawrence Street, Mobile, AL 36602
  E-mail: vivian.figures@alsenate.gov
  Committees: Confirmations; Education and Youth Affairs; Finance and
  Taxation Education; Judiciary; Local Legislation Mobile County; Rules
  Education: New Haven 1980 BS; Jones Law

Senator **Rusty Glover** (R-District 34) .................(334) 242-7886
  Counties Represented: Mobile (part)     Dist: (251) 649-7380
  Term Expires: 2018     Fax: (334) 353-3970
  P.O. Box 2175, Semmes, AL 36575
  E-mail: rusty.glover@alsenate.gov
  Committees: Agriculture, Conservation and Forestry; Confirmations;
  Finance and Taxation Education; Governmental Affairs; Local
  Legislation Mobile County; Rules
  Education: South Alabama BS, MEd, MA

Senator **Bill Hightower** (R-District 35)................(334) 242-7882
  Counties Represented: Mobile (part)
  Term Expires: 2018
  104 South Lawrence Street, Mobile, AL 36602
  E-mail: bill.hightower@alsenate.gov
  Committees: Banking and Insurance; Constitution, Ethics and Elections;
  County and Municipal Government; Fiscal Responsibility and
  Economic Development; Local Legislation Mobile County; Rules

Senator **Jimmy W. Holley** (R-District 31) Room 732 ..... (334) 242-7845
  Counties Represented: Coffee, Covington, Dale (part), Houston (part)
  Term Expires: 2018
  E-mail: jimmy.holley@alsenate.org
  Committees: Finance and Taxation Education; Governmental Affairs;
  Rules; Transportation and Energy; Veterans and Military Affairs
  Education: East Tennessee State BS, MA

Senator **Bill Holtzclaw** (R-District 2) .................(334) 242-7854
  Counties Represented: Limestone (part), Madison (part)
  Term Expires: 2018
  P.O. Box 1801, Madison, AL 35758
  E-mail: bill.holtzclaw@alsenate.gov
  Committees: Banking and Insurance; County and Municipal
  Government; Finance and Taxation General Fund; Local Legislation
  Madison County; Transportation and Energy; Veterans and Military
  Affairs
  Education: Athens State BS

*(continued on next page)*

LEGISLATIVE BRANCH

**Senators** *continued*

Senator **Steve Livingston** (R-District 8) Room 731 ...... (334) 242-7858
Counties Represented: DeKalb, Jackson, Madison (part)
Term Expires: 2018
E-mail: steve.livingston@alsenate.gov
Committees: Agriculture, Conservation and Forestry; Finance and Taxation General Fund; Fiscal Responsibility and Economic Development; Local Legislation Madison County; Transportation and Energy; Veterans and Military Affairs

Senator **Del Marsh** (R-District 12) ................... (334) 242-7877
Counties Represented: Calhoun, St. Clair (part)    Dist: (256) 237-8647
Term Expires: 2018    Fax: (256) 237-1579
PO Drawer 3265, Anniston, AL 36202
E-mail: del.marsh@alsenate.gov
Committees: Tourism and Marketing

Senator **Jim McClendon** (R-District 11) Suite 729 ....... (334) 242-7898
Counties Represented: Shelby (part), St. Clair (part), Talladega (part)
Term Expires: 2018
E-mail: jimmcc@windstream.net
Committees: Education and Youth Affairs; Fiscal Responsibility and Economic Development; Health and Human Services; Local Legislation Shelby County; Rules; Transportation and Energy
Education: Birmingham-Southern BS; Houston OD

Senator **Tim Melson** (R-District 1) Suite 735 ............(334) 242-7888
Counties Represented: Colbert (part), Lauderdale
Term Expires: 2018
Committees: Agriculture, Conservation and Forestry; Constitution, Ethics and Elections; County and Municipal Government; Finance and Taxation General Fund; Health and Human Services; Local Legislation Madison County

Senator **Arthur Orr** (R-District 3) ................... (334) 242-7891
Counties Represented: Limestone (part), Madison    Dist: (256) 260-2147
(part), Morgan
Term Expires: 2018
P.O. Box 305, Decatur, AL 35602
E-mail: arthur.orr@alsenate.gov
Committees: Confirmations; Finance and Taxation Education; Finance and Taxation General Fund; Fiscal Responsibility and Economic Development; Governmental Affairs; Judiciary; Local Legislation Madison County; Rules; Transportation and Energy
Education: Wake Forest BA; Alabama JD

Senator **Lee "Trip" Pittman** (R-District 32) ............(334) 242-7897
Counties Represented: Baldwin (part)    Dist: (251) 621-0535
Term Expires: 2018
P.O. Box 1812, Daphne, AL 36526
E-mail: trip.pittman@alsenate.gov
Committees: Banking and Insurance; Constitution, Ethics and Elections; County and Municipal Government; Education and Youth Affairs; Finance and Taxation Education; Finance and Taxation General Fund; Fiscal Responsibility and Economic Development; Rules; Tourism and Marketing
Education: Alabama BS

Senator **Greg Reed** (R-District 5) ................... (334) 242-7894
Counties Represented: Jefferson (part), Tuscaloosa (part), Walker, Winston (part)
Term Expires: 2018
800 Highway 78 East, Suite 200, Jasper, AL 35502
E-mail: greg.reed@alsenate.gov
Committees: Banking and Insurance; Fiscal Responsibility and Economic Development; Health and Human Services; Judiciary; Local Legislation Jefferson County; Rules; Transportation and Energy

Senator **Quinton T. Ross, Jr.** (D-District 26) Suite 735 ....(334) 242-7880
Counties Represented: Montgomery (part)    Fax: (334) 353-8417
Term Expires: 2018
P.O. Box 6183, Montgomery, AL 36106
E-mail: quinton.ross@alsenate.gov
Committees: Banking and Insurance; Confirmations; County and Municipal Government; Education and Youth Affairs; Finance and Taxation Education; Transportation and Energy; Veterans and Military Affairs

Senator **Henry "Hank" Sanders** (D-District 23) .........(334) 242-7860
Counties Represented: Autauga (part), Clarke (part),    Dist: (334) 526-4531
Conecuh (part), Dallas, Lowndes, Marengo (part), Monroe (part), Perry (part), Wilcox
Term Expires: 2018
1 Union Street, PO Box 1290, Selma, AL 36702
E-mail: hank.sanders@alsenate.gov
Committees: Banking and Insurance; Education and Youth Affairs; Finance and Taxation Education; Transportation and Energy
Education: Talladega BA; Harvard 1970 JD

Senator **Paul Sanford** (R-District 7) ................... (334) 242-7867
Counties Represented: Madison (part)    Dist: (256) 539-5441
Term Expires: 2018
726 Madison Street, Huntsville, AL 35801
E-mail: paul.sanford@alsenate.gov
Committees: Agriculture, Conservation and Forestry; Banking and Insurance; County and Municipal Government; Finance and Taxation General Fund; Fiscal Responsibility and Economic Development; Governmental Affairs; Local Legislation Madison County; Rules
Education: Culinary Institute of America

Senator **Clay Scofield** (R-District 9) ................... (334) 242-7876
Counties Represented: Blount (part), Madison    Dist: (256) 582-0619
(part), Marshall
Term Expires: 2018
412-A Gunter Avenue, Guntersville, AL 35976
E-mail: clay.scofield@alsenate.gov
Committees: Agriculture, Conservation and Forestry; Confirmations; County and Municipal Government; Fiscal Responsibility and Economic Development; Governmental Affairs; Local Legislation Madison County; Rules; Transportation and Energy
Education: Auburn BS

Senator **Shay Shelnutt** (R-District 17) Suite 735 ....... (334) 242-7794
Counties Represented: Blount (part), Jefferson (part), St. Clair (part), Talladega (part)
Term Expires: 2018
E-mail: shay.sd17@gmail.com
Committees: Banking and Insurance; Confirmations; Education and Youth Affairs; Governmental Affairs; Local Legislation Jefferson County

Senator **Bobby Singleton** (D-District 24) Suite 735 ...... (334) 242-7935
Counties Represented: Bibb (part), Choctaw (part),    Fax: (334) 353-8417
Greene, Hale (part), Marengo (part), Perry (part), Sumter, Tuscaloosa (part)
Term Expires: 2018
E-mail: bsingle164@yahoo.com
Committees: Agriculture, Conservation and Forestry; Finance and Taxation General Fund; Fiscal Responsibility and Economic Development; Tourism and Marketing
Education: Alabama State BS; Miles Col JD

Senator **Harri Anne Smith** (I-District 29) ..............(334) 242-7879
Counties Represented: Dale (part), Geneva, Houston    Fax: (334) 242-7901
(part)
Term Expires: 2018
P.O. Box 483, Slocomb, AL 36375
E-mail: has@harrianne.com
Committees: Agriculture, Conservation and Forestry; County and Municipal Government; Finance and Taxation Education; Health and Human Services; Veterans and Military Affairs
Education: Troy State BS

Senator **Rodger Mell Smitherman** (D-District 18) ....... (334) 242-7870
Counties Represented: Jefferson (part)    Dist: (205) 322-0012
Term Expires: 2018    Fax: (205) 324-2000
2029 Second Avenue North, Birmingham, AL 35203
E-mail: rodger.smitherman@alsenate.gov
Committees: Confirmations; Constitution, Ethics and Elections; Finance and Taxation Education; Fiscal Responsibility and Economic Development; Judiciary; Local Legislation Jefferson County; Rules
Education: Montevallo BBA; Miles Col JD

Senator **Larry Stutts** (R-District 6) Suite 735 ............(334) 242-7862
Counties Represented: Colbert (part), Fayette, Franklin, Lamar, Lawrence (part), Marion, Winston (part)
Term Expires: 2018
E-mail: larry.stutts@alsenate.gov
Committees: Agriculture, Conservation and Forestry; Finance and Taxation General Fund; Fiscal Responsibility and Economic Development; Health and Human Services; Judiciary

Senator **J. T. "Jabo" Waggoner** (R-District 16) .........(334) 242-7892
Counties Represented: Jefferson (part), Shelby (part)    Fax: (205) 242-2278
Term Expires: 2018
P.O. Box 660609, Vestavia Hills, AL 35266-0609
E-mail: jabo.waggoner@alsenate.gov
Committees: Banking and Insurance; Confirmations; County and Municipal Government; Finance and Taxation Education; Finance and Taxation General Fund; Health and Human Services; Local Legislation Jefferson County; Local Legislation Shelby County; Rules
Education: Birmingham-Southern BA; Birmingham JD

Senator **Cam Ward** (R-District 14) . . . . . . . . . . . . . . . . . . . (334) 242-7873
Counties Represented: Bibb (part), Chilton (part),    Dist: (205) 620-6610
Jefferson (part), Shelby (part)
Term Expires: 2018
PO Box 1749, Alabaster, AL 35007
E-mail: camjulward@aol.com
Committees: Confirmations; Finance and Taxation General Fund;
Fiscal Responsibility and Economic Development; Health and Human
Services; Judiciary; Local Legislation Jefferson County; Local
Legislation Shelby County
Education: Troy State 1993 BS; Cumberland 1996 JD

Senator **Tom Whatley** (R-District 27) . . . . . . . . . . . . . . . . . (334) 242-7865
Counties Represented: Lee (part), Russell (part),    Fax: (334) 826-7700
Tallapoosa (part)
Term Expires: 2018
337 East Magnolia Drive, Auburn, AL 36830
E-mail: tom.whatley@alsenate.gov
Committees: Agriculture, Conservation and Forestry; Banking and
Insurance; Confirmations; Finance and Taxation Education; Health and
Human Services; Judiciary; Transportation and Energy; Veterans and
Military Affairs
Education: Jones Law JD

Senator **Phil W. Williams** (R-District 10) . . . . . . . . . . . . . . (334) 242-7857
Counties Represented: Cherokee (part), Etowah
Term Expires: 2018
P. O. Box 7024, Rainbow City, AL 35906
E-mail: philw.williams@alsenate.gov
Committees: Constitution, Ethics and Elections; Education Policy;
Fiscal Responsibility and Economic Development; Judiciary; Veterans
and Military Affairs
Education: South Alabama 1988 BS; Birmingham 2003 JD

# Senate Standing Committees
## Agriculture, Conservation and Forestry
**Majority Members** | **Minority Members**
Tom Whatley (R-27) *Chairperson* — Billy Beasley (D-28)
Greg Albritton (R-22) — Bobby Singleton (D-24)
*Vice Chairperson*
Paul Bussman (R-4)
Clyde Chambliss (R-30)
Rusty Glover (R-34)
Steve Livingston (R-8)
Tim Melson (R-1)
Paul Sanford (R-7)
Clay Scofield (R-9)
Larry Stutts (R-6)

**Members**
Harri Anne Smith (I-29)

## Banking and Insurance
**Majority Members** | **Minority Members**
Slade Blackwell (R-15) *Chairperson* — Linda Coleman (D-20)
Bill Hightower (R-35) — Quinton T. Ross, Jr. (D-26)
*Vice Chairperson* — Henry "Hank" Sanders (D-23)
Paul Bussman (R-4)
Bill Holtzclaw (R-2)
Lee "Trip" Pittman (R-32)
Greg Reed (R-5)
Paul Sanford (R-7)
Shay Shelnutt (R-17)
J. T. "Jabo" Waggoner (R-16)
Tom Whatley (R-27)

## Confirmations
**Majority Members** | **Minority Members**
Clay Scofield (R-9) *Chairperson* — Vivian Davis Figures (D-33)
J. T. "Jabo" Waggoner (R-16) — Quinton T. Ross, Jr. (D-26)
*Vice Chairperson* — Rodger Mell Smitherman (D-18)
Gerald Allen (R-21)
Slade Blackwell (R-15)
Dick L. Brewbaker (R-25)
Rusty Glover (R-34)
Arthur Orr (R-3)
Shay Shelnutt (R-17)
Cam Ward (R-14)
Tom Whatley (R-27)

## Constitution, Ethics and Elections
**Majority Members** | **Minority Members**
Bill Hightower (R-35) *Chairperson* — Linda Coleman (D-20)
Greg Albritton (R-22) — Rodger Mell Smitherman (D-18)
Dick L. Brewbaker (R-25)
Tim Melson (R-1)
Lee "Trip" Pittman (R-32)
Phil W. Williams (R-10)

## County and Municipal Government
**Majority Members** | **Minority Members**
Paul Sanford (R-7) *Chairperson* — Priscilla Dunn (D-19)
Clyde Chambliss (R-30) — Quinton T. Ross, Jr. (D-26)
Bill Hightower (R-35)
Bill Holtzclaw (R-2)
Tim Melson (R-1)
Lee "Trip" Pittman (R-32)
Clay Scofield (R-9)
J. T. "Jabo" Waggoner (R-16)

**Members**
Harri Anne Smith (I-29)

## Education and Youth Affairs
**Majority Members** | **Minority Members**
Dick L. Brewbaker (R-25) — Quinton T. Ross, Jr. (D-26)
*Chairperson* — *Vice Chairperson*
Paul Bussman (R-4) — Vivian Davis Figures (D-33)
Jim McClendon (R-11) — Henry "Hank" Sanders (D-23)
Lee "Trip" Pittman (R-32)
Shay Shelnutt (R-17)

## Finance and Taxation Education
**Majority Members** | **Minority Members**
Lee "Trip" Pittman (R-32) — Vivian Davis Figures (D-33)
*Chairperson* — Quinton T. Ross, Jr. (D-26)
Rusty Glover (R-34) — Henry "Hank" Sanders (D-23)
*Vice Chairperson* — Rodger Mell Smitherman (D-18)
Gerald Allen (R-21)
Slade Blackwell (R-15)
Paul Bussman (R-4)
Dr. Gerald O. Dial (R-13)
Jimmy W. Holley (R-31)
Arthur Orr (R-3)
J. T. "Jabo" Waggoner (R-16)
Tom Whatley (R-27)

**Members**
Harri Anne Smith (I-29)

## Finance and Taxation General Fund
**Majority Members** | **Minority Members**
Arthur Orr (R-3) *Chairperson* — Billy Beasley (D-28)
Clyde Chambliss (R-30) — Priscilla Dunn (D-19)
Bill Holtzclaw (R-2) — Bobby Singleton (D-24)
Steve Livingston (R-8)
Tim Melson (R-1)
Lee "Trip" Pittman (R-32)
Paul Sanford (R-7)
Larry Stutts (R-6)
J. T. "Jabo" Waggoner (R-16)
Cam Ward (R-14)

## Fiscal Responsibility and Economic Development
**Majority Members** | **Minority Members**
Phil W. Williams (R-10) — Priscilla Dunn (D-19)
*Chairperson* — Bobby Singleton (D-24)
Cam Ward (R-14) *Vice Chairperson* — Rodger Mell Smitherman (D-18)
Clyde Chambliss (R-30)
Bill Hightower (R-35)
Steve Livingston (R-8)
Jim McClendon (R-11)
Arthur Orr (R-3)
Lee "Trip" Pittman (R-32)
Greg Reed (R-5)
Paul Sanford (R-7)
Clay Scofield (R-9)
Larry Stutts (R-6)

## Governmental Affairs

| Majority Members | Minority Members |
|---|---|
| Jimmy W. Holley (R-31) *Chairperson* | Linda Coleman (D-20) |
| Dick L. Brewbaker (R-25) | Priscilla Dunn (D-19) |
| Paul Bussman (R-4) | |
| Rusty Glover (R-34) | |
| Arthur Orr (R-3) | |
| Paul Sanford (R-7) | |
| Clay Scofield (R-9) | |
| Shay Shelnutt (R-17) | |
| Phil Williams (R-6) | |

## Health and Human Services

| Majority Members | Minority Members |
|---|---|
| Dr. Gerald O. Dial (R-13) *Chairperson* | Billy Beasley (D-28) |
| Jim McClendon (R-11) *Vice Chairperson* | Linda Coleman (D-20) |
| Greg Reed (R-5) *Deputy Chairperson* | |
| Slade Blackwell (R-15) | |
| Paul Bussman (R-4) | |
| Tim Melson (R-1) | |
| Larry Stutts (R-6) | |
| J. T. "Jabo" Waggoner (R-16) | |
| Cam Ward (R-14) | |
| Tom Whatley (R-27) | |

**Members**
Harri Anne Smith (I-29)

## Judiciary

| Majority Members | Minority Members |
|---|---|
| Cam Ward (R-14) *Chairperson* | Linda Coleman (D-20) |
| Phil W. Williams (R-10) *Vice Chairperson* | Vivian Davis Figures (D-33) |
| Arthur Orr (R-3) | Rodger Mell Smitherman (D-18) |
| Greg Reed (R-5) | |
| Larry Stutts (R-6) | |
| Tom Whatley (R-27) | |

## Local Legislation Jefferson County

| Majority Members | Minority Members |
|---|---|
| J. T. "Jabo" Waggoner (R-16) *Chairperson* | Linda Coleman (D-20) |
| Slade Blackwell (R-15) | Priscilla Dunn (D-19) |
| Greg Reed (R-5) | Rodger Mell Smitherman (D-18) |
| Shay Shelnutt (R-17) | |
| Cam Ward (R-14) | |

## Local Legislation Madison County

**Majority Members**
Paul Sanford (R-7) *Chairperson*
Bill Holtzclaw (R-2)
Steve Livingston (R-8)
Tim Melson (R-1)
Arthur Orr (R-3)
Clay Scofield (R-9)

## Local Legislation Mobile County

| Majority Members | Minority Members |
|---|---|
| Rusty Glover (R-34) *Chairperson* | Vivian Davis Figures (D-33) |
| Greg Albritton (R-22) | |
| Bill Hightower (R-35) | |

## Local Legislation Shelby County

**Majority Members**
Cam Ward (R-14) *Chairperson*
Slade Blackwell (R-15)
Jim McClendon (R-11)
J. T. "Jabo" Waggoner (R-16)

## Rules

| Majority Members | Minority Members |
|---|---|
| J. T. "Jabo" Waggoner (R-16) *Chairperson* | Billy Beasley (D-28) |
| Dick L. Brewbaker (R-25) | Vivian Davis Figures (D-33) |
| Dr. Gerald O. Dial (R-13) | Rodger Mell Smitherman (D-18) |
| Rusty Glover (R-34) | |
| Bill Hightower (R-35) | |
| Jimmy W. Holley (R-31) | |
| Jim McClendon (R-11) | |
| Arthur Orr (R-3) | |
| Lee "Trip" Pittman (R-32) | |
| Greg Reed (R-5) | |
| Paul Sanford (R-7) | |
| Clay Scofield (R-9) | |

## Tourism and Marketing

| Majority Members | Minority Members |
|---|---|
| Del Marsh (R-12) *Chairperson* | Bobby Singleton (D-24) *Vice Chairperson* |
| Lee "Trip" Pittman (R-32) | |

## Transportation and Energy

| Majority Members | Minority Members |
|---|---|
| Gerald Allen (R-21) *Chairperson* | Linda Coleman (D-20) |
| Greg Albritton (R-22) | Quinton T. Ross, Jr. (D-26) |
| Clyde Chambliss (R-30) | Henry "Hank" Sanders (D-23) |
| Dr. Gerald O. Dial (R-13) | |
| Jimmy W. Holley (R-31) | |
| Bill Holtzclaw (R-2) | |
| Steve Livingston (R-8) | |
| Jim McClendon (R-11) | |
| Arthur Orr (R-3) | |
| Greg Reed (R-5) | |
| Clay Scofield (R-9) | |
| Tom Whatley (R-27) | |

## Veterans and Military Affairs

| Majority Members | Minority Members |
|---|---|
| Bill Holtzclaw (R-2) *Chairperson* | Quinton T. Ross, Jr. (D-26) |
| Dr. Gerald O. Dial (R-13) | |
| Jimmy W. Holley (R-31) | |
| Steve Livingston (R-8) | |
| Tom Whatley (R-27) | |
| Phil W. Williams (R-10) | |

**Members**
Harri Anne Smith (I-29) *Vice Chairperson*

# Alabama House of Representatives

State House, 11 South Union Street, Montgomery, AL 36130
Tel: (334) 242-7600  Fax: (334) 242-2488

Speaker of the House **Mike Hubbard** (R) . . . . . . . . . . . . . . (334) 242-7668
  Education: Georgia 1983 BA
Speaker Pro Tem **Victor Gaston** (R) . . . . . . . . . . . . . . . . . (334) 242-7664
  Education: Southern Mississippi 1965 BS; South Alabama MS; Auburn EdD
Majority Leader **Micky Hammon** (R) . . . . . . . . . . . . . . . . . (334) 242-7709
Minority Leader **Craig Ford** (D) . . . . . . . . . . . . . . . . . . . . (334) 242-7690
  Education: Auburn 1991 BS
Clerk of the House **Jeff Woodard** . . . . . . . . . . . . . . . . . . . (334) 242-7609
  Education: Auburn 1975 BA

## Representatives

**Party Affiliation Statistics:** Republicans: 72, Democrats: 33

Representative **Will Ainsworth** (R-District 27)
  Suite 524-B . . . . . . . . . . . . . . . . . . . . . . . . . . . . . . . . . . . . (334) 242-7609
  Counties Represented: Blount (part), DeKalb (part), Marshall (part)
  Term Expires: 2018
  E-mail: will.ainsworth@alhouse.gov
  Committees: Agriculture and Forestry; Transportation, Utilities and Infrastructure

Representative **Louise Alexander** (D-District 56)
  Suite 537-B . . . . . . . . . . . . . . . . . . . . . . . . . . . . . . . . . . . . (334) 242-7609
  Counties Represented: Jefferson (part)
  Term Expires: 2018
  E-mail: louise.alexander@alhouse.gov
  Committees: Commerce and Small Business; Insurance; Local Legislation

LEGISLATIVE BRANCH

Representative **Alan Baker** (R-District 66) . . . . . . . . . . . . . (334) 242-7720
Counties Represented: Baldwin (part), Escambia
(part)
Term Expires: 2018
P.O. Box 975, Brewton, AL 36427
E-mail: staterep@co.escambia.al.us
Committees: Baldwin County Legislation; Ethics and Campaign
Finance; Local Legislation; Technology and Research; Ways and Means
Education
Education: Auburn 1978 BS
　　Dist: (251) 867-0244
　　Res: (251) 867-6514
　　Fax: (251) 867-8600

Representative **Mike Ball** (R-District 10) . . . . . . . . . . . . . . (334) 242-7683
Counties Represented: Madison (part)
Term Expires: 2018
P.O. Box 6302, Huntsville, AL 35824
E-mail: mikeball@knology.net
Committees: Ethics and Campaign Finance; Judiciary; Madison County
Legislation
Education: Jefferson State Comm Col 1982 AS; Athens State BS
　　Dist: (256) 539-5441
　　Res: (256) 772-8730

Representative **George C. Bandy** (D-District 83) . . . . . . . . (334) 242-7721
Counties Represented: Lee (part), Russell (part)
Term Expires: 2018
1307-A Glenn Circle, Opelika, AL 36801
E-mail: george.bandy@alhouse.gov
Committees: Lee County Legislation; State Government;
Transportation, Utilities and Infrastructure
Education: Morehouse Col BA
　　Res: (334) 749-0051

Representative **Paul Beckman** (R-District 88) . . . . . . . . . . (334) 242-7499
Counties Represented: Autauga (part), Elmore (part)
Term Expires: 2018
P.O. Box 680155, Prattville, AL 36068
E-mail: paulbeckmanjr@yahoo.com
Committees: Constitutions, Campaigns and Elections; Judiciary
Education: Florida State 1978 BS; Jones Law 1988 JD
　　Dist: (334) 323-5918
　　Res: (334) 361-0977

Representative **Elaine Beech** (D-District 65) . . . . . . . . . . . (334) 242-7702
Counties Represented: Choctaw (part), Clarke (part),
Marengo (part), Washington (part)
Term Expires: 2018
P.O. Box 1256, Chatom, AL 36518
E-mail: elaine_h_beech@yahoo.com
Committees: Health; Rules; Ways and Means General Fund
Education: Auburn 1983 BS
　　Res: (251) 847-2604

Representative **Marcel Black** (D-District 3) . . . . . . . . . . . . (334) 242-7686
Counties Represented: Colbert (part), Lauderdale
(part), Lawrence (part)
Term Expires: 2018
210 North Main Street, Tuscumbia, AL 35674
E-mail: marcel.black@alhouse.org
Committees: Ethics and Campaign Finance; Financial Services;
Judiciary
Education: Alabama 1972 BA, 1975 JD
　　Dist: (256) 383-2435
　　Res: (256) 381-5277

Representative **Chris Blackshear** (R-District 80) . . . . . . . . (334) 242-7600
Counties Represented: Lee (part), Russell (part)
Term Expires: 2018
E-mail: chris.blackshear@alhouse.gov
Committees: County and Municipal Government

Representative **Alan C. Boothe** (R-District 89) . . . . . . . . . (334) 242-7710
Counties Represented: Dale (part), Pike
Term Expires: 2018
P.O. Box 561, Troy, AL 36081
E-mail: alan.boothe@alhouse.gov
Committees: Internal Affairs; State Government; Ways and Means
Education
Education: Troy State 1973 BS, 1975 MS
　　Dist: (334) 670-3897

Representative **Barbara Bigsby Boyd** (D-District 32) . . . . . (334) 242-7692
Counties Represented: Calhoun (part), Talladega
(part)
Term Expires: 2018
2222 McDaniel Avenue, Anniston, AL 36202
E-mail: barbara.boyd@alhouse.gov
Committees: Children and Senior Advocacy; County and Municipal
Government; Rules; State Government
Education: Miles Col 1960 BA; Alabama 1976 MA, 1989 EdD
　　Dist: (256) 741-8683
　　Res: (256) 236-7423
　　Fax: (256) 741-8686

Representative **Napoleon Bracy, Jr.** (D-District 98)
Room 540-A . . . . . . . . . . . . . . . . . . . . . . . . . . . . . . . . . (334) 242-7756
Counties Represented: Mobile (part)
Term Expires: 2018
E-mail: napoleon.bracy@alhouse.gov
Committees: Mobile County Legislation; Transportation, Utilities and
Infrastructure; Ways and Means General Fund
Education: Dillard 2000 BA

Representative **Koven L. Brown** (R-District 40) . . . . . . . . . (334) 353-1778
Counties Represented: Calhoun (part)
Term Expires: 2018
1304 6th Avenue, NE, Jacksonville, AL 36265
322 Nisbet Street NW, Jacksonville, AL 36265
E-mail: klbrown@cableone.net
Committees: Agriculture and Forestry; Children and Senior Advocacy;
Economic Development and Tourism
　　Dist: (256) 435-7042
　　Res: (256) 435-9437
　　Fax: (256) 435-2702

Representative **James E. Buskey** (D-District 99) . . . . . . . . (334) 242-7757
Counties Represented: Mobile (part)
Term Expires: 2018
2207 Barretts Lane, Mobile, AL 36617
104 South Lawrence Street, Mobile, AL 36617
E-mail: james.buskey@alhouse.gov
Committees: County and Municipal Government; Mobile County
Legislation; Rules; Ways and Means Education
Education: Alabama BS; North Carolina MAT; Colorado EdS
　　Dist: (251) 208-5480
　　Res: (251) 457-7928
　　Fax: (251) 208-5492

Representative **Mack Butler** (R-District 30) . . . . . . . . . . . . (334) 242-7446
Counties Represented: Etowah (part), St. Clair (part)
Term Expires: 2018
PO Box 7184, Rainbow City, AL 35906
E-mail: mack.butler@alhouse.gov
Committees: Education Policy; Financial Services; State Government
Education: Gadsden State Comm Col 1983 AS

Representative **Jim Carns** (R-District 48) . . . . . . . . . . . . . . (334) 242-7609
Counties Represented: Jefferson (part), Shelby (part)
Term Expires: 2018
P.O. Box 43797, Birmingham, AL 35243
E-mail: jwcarns@yahoo.com
Committees: Children and Senior Advocacy; Commerce and Small
Business; County and Municipal Government; Shelby County
Legislation
Education: Alabama 1962 BS
　　Res: (205) 967-3571
　　Fax: (205) 967-1840

Representative **Donnie Chesteen** (R-District 87) . . . . . . . . (334) 242-7742
Counties Represented: Geneva, Houston (part)
Term Expires: 2018
P.O. Box 39, Geneva, AL 36340
306 Goose Hollow Road, Geneva, AL 36340
E-mail: dchesteen@panhandle.rr.com
Committees: Agriculture and Forestry; Ways and Means Education
Education: Troy U 1975 BS
　　Dist: (334) 449-1040
　　Res: (334) 684-2196

Representative **Adline C. Clarke** (D-District 97) . . . . . . . . . (334) 242-7609
Counties Represented: Mobile (part)
Term Expires: 2018
856 Canal Street, Mobile, AL 36602
E-mail: adline.clarke@alhouse.gov
Committees: Commerce and Small Business; Constitutions, Campaigns
and Elections; County and Municipal Government; Mobile County
Legislation
Education: Spring Hill BA

Representative **Steve Clouse** (R-District 93) . . . . . . . . . . . . (334) 242-7717
Counties Represented: Dale (part), Houston (part)
Term Expires: 2018
P.O. Box 818, Ozark, AL 36361-0818
E-mail: steve.clouse@alhouse.gov
Committees: Military and Veterans Affairs; Ways and Means General
Fund
Affiliation: Owner, Clouse Marketing Company
Education: Alabama BA
　　Dist: (334) 774-9122
　　Res: (334) 774-7384

Representative **Merika Coleman-Evans** (D-District 57) . . . (334) 242-7755
Counties Represented: Jefferson (part)
Term Expires: 2018
P.O. Box 28888, Birmingham, AL 35228
E-mail: merika.coleman@alhouse.gov
Committees: Financial Services; Judiciary
Education: Alabama Birmingham 1995 BA, 1997 MPA
　　Dist: (205) 325-5308

Representative **Terri Collins** (R-District 8) . . . . . . . . . . . . . (334) 242-7693
Counties Represented: Morgan (part)
Term Expires: 2018
2128 6th Avenue, Suite 504, Decatur, AL 35601
E-mail: terri.collins@alhouse.gov
Committees: Education Policy; Ways and Means Education
　　Dist: (256) 260-2146
　　Fax: (256) 260-2144

Representative **Danny F. Crawford** (R-District 5) . . . . . . . . (334) 242-7600
Counties Represented: Limestone (part)
Term Expires: 2018
E-mail: danny.crawford@alhouse.gov
Committees: County and Municipal Government; Health
Education: Auburn MS

*(continued on next page)*

**Representatives** *continued*

Representative **Anthony Daniels** (D-District 53)
Suite 522-F . . . . . . . . . . . . . . . . . . . . . . . . . . . . . . . (334) 242-7609
Counties Represented: Madison (part)
Term Expires: 2018
E-mail: anthony.daniels@alhouse.gov
Committees: Commerce and Small Business; Insurance; Madison County Legislation

Representative **Randy Davis** (R-District 96) . . . . . . . . . . . . (334) 242-7724
Counties Represented: Baldwin (part), Mobile (part)   Dist: (251) 442-2552
Term Expires: 2018   Dist: (251) 990-4615
6590 Thompson Lane, Daphne, AL 36526   Res: (251) 621-0814
E-mail: randalldavis14@gmail.com   Fax: (251) 442-2526
Committees: Agriculture and Forestry; Baldwin County Legislation; Constitutions, Campaigns and Elections; Mobile County Legislation; Rules
Education: Southern Mississippi 1974 BMEd, 1976 MMEd; Alabama State 1998 EdS

Representative **Dickie Drake** (R-District 45) . . . . . . . . . . . . (334) 242-7600
Counties Represented: Jefferson (part), Shelby (part)   Fax: (205) 699-3670
Term Expires: 2018
7049 Briarwood Land, Leeds, AL 35094
E-mail: ddrake1080@aol.com
Committees: Judiciary; Military and Veterans Affairs; Public Safety and Homeland Security; Shelby County Legislation

Representative **Barbara Drummond** (D-District 103)
Suite 536-C . . . . . . . . . . . . . . . . . . . . . . . . . . . . . . . (334) 242-7609
Counties Represented: Mobile (part)
Term Expires: 2018
E-mail: drummondbarbara@att.net
Committees: Children and Senior Advocacy; Education Policy; Mobile County Legislation; Transportation, Utilities and Infrastructure

Representative **Christopher J. England** (D-District 70) . . . (334) 242-7703
Counties Represented: Tuscaloosa (part)   Dist: (205) 248-5140
Term Expires: 2018
1681 Ozier Drive, Tuscaloosa, AL 35405
P.O. Box 2089, Tuscaloosa, AL 35403
E-mail: cengland1@hotmail.com
Committees: Jefferson County Legislation; Judiciary; Public Safety and Homeland Security; Tuscaloosa County Legislation
Education: Howard U 1999 BA; Alabama 2002 JD

Representative **Allen Farley** (R-District 15) . . . . . . . . . . . . (334) 242-7767
Counties Represented: Jefferson (part), Shelby (part)   Res: (205) 477-5617
Term Expires: 2018
P.O. Box 516, Mc Calla, AL 35111
E-mail: allenfarley@bellsouth.net
Committees: Children and Senior Advocacy; Judiciary; Public Safety and Homeland Security; Shelby County Legislation

Representative **David L. Faulkner, Jr.** (R-District 46)
Suite 522-B . . . . . . . . . . . . . . . . . . . . . . . . . . . . . . . (334) 242-7609
Counties Represented: Jefferson (part)
Term Expires: 2018
E-mail: david.faulkner@alhouse.gov
Committees: Financial Services; Insurance; Judiciary

Representative **Teddy Joe Faust, Sr.** (R-District 94) . . . . . . (334) 242-7699
Counties Represented: Baldwin (part)   Dist: (251) 990-4615
Term Expires: 2018   Res: (251) 928-5445
20452 Beecher Street, Fairhope, AL 36532   Fax: (251) 990-4616
E-mail: jfaust@co.baldwin.al.us
Committees: Agriculture and Forestry; Baldwin County Legislation; County and Municipal Government; Transportation, Utilities and Infrastructure

Representative **Bob Fincher** (R-District 37) Suite 538-A . . . (334) 242-7609
Counties Represented: Chambers (part), Cleburne (part), Randolph
Term Expires: 2018
E-mail: rsfincher77@gmail.com
Committees: Agriculture and Forestry; Constitutions, Campaigns and Elections; Education Policy

Representative **Craig Ford** (D-District 28) . . . . . . . . . . . . . (334) 242-7690
Counties Represented: Etowah (part)   Dist: (256) 413-7611
Term Expires: 2018   Res: (256) 547-2727
P.O. Box 8208, Gadsden, AL 35902
E-mail: craig.ford@alhouse.gov
Committees: Commerce and Small Business; Ways and Means Education

Representative **Grover Berry Forte** (D-District 84) . . . . . . (334) 242-7553
Counties Represented: Barbour, Bullock, Russell   Dist: (334) 616-1272
(part)   Res: (334) 687-9985
Term Expires: 2018
620 Davis Avenue, Eufaula, AL 36027
E-mail: berry.forte@alhouse.gov
Committees: Economic Development and Tourism; Ethics and Campaign Finance

Representative **Matthew David Fridy** (R-District 73)
Suite 403-E . . . . . . . . . . . . . . . . . . . . . . . . . . . . . . . (334) 242-7609
Counties Represented: Shelby (part)
Term Expires: 2018
E-mail: mdfridy@gmail.com
Committees: Health; Judiciary; Shelby County Legislation
Education: Cumberland 2001 JD

Representative **J. Daniel Garrett** (R-District 44)
Suite 538-B . . . . . . . . . . . . . . . . . . . . . . . . . . . . . . . (334) 242-7609
Counties Represented: Jefferson (part)
Term Expires: 2018
E-mail: jdaniel.garrett@yahoo.com
Committees: Commerce and Small Business; Ways and Means Education
Education: Alabama 1980 BS, 1981

Representative **Victor Gaston** (R-District 100) . . . . . . . . . . (334) 242-7664
Counties Represented: Mobile (part)   Res: (251) 639-2555
Term Expires: 2018
1136 Hillcrest Crossing West, Mobile, AL 36695
E-mail: victor.gaston@alhouse.gov
Committees: Mobile County Legislation; Rules; Transportation, Utilities and Infrastructure; Ways and Means General Fund

Representative
**Juandalynn "Lee Lee" Givan** (D-District 60) . . . . . . . . (334) 242-7684
Counties Represented: Jefferson (part)   Dist: (205) 929-1467
Term Expires: 2018   Res: (205) 798-8310
63 Greenleaf Drive, Birmingham, AL 35214   Fax: (205) 929-1453
P.O. Box 13803, Birmingham, AL 35202
E-mail: 3007j@att.net
Committees: Constitutions, Campaigns and Elections; Judiciary
Education: Miles Col BA, JD

Representative **Lynn Greer** (R-District 2) Room 527-A . . . . (334) 242-7576
Counties Represented: Lauderdale (part), Limestone (part)
Term Expires: 2018
E-mail: lynn.greer@alhouse.gov
Committees: Rules; Transportation, Utilities and Infrastructure; Ways and Means General Fund
Education: Auburn BS

Representative **Dexter Grimsley** (D-District 85) . . . . . . . . . (334) 242-7740
Counties Represented: Henry, Houston (part)   Res: (334) 889-0602
Term Expires: 2018
168 Res Drive, Newville, AL 36353
E-mail: wlmdex@hotmail.com
Committees: Agriculture and Forestry; Children and Senior Advocacy; Transportation, Utilities and Infrastructure
Education: Northwestern State 1993 BS

Representative **Laura Hall** (D-District 19) . . . . . . . . . . . . . (334) 242-7688
Counties Represented: Madison (part)   Res: (256) 859-2234
Term Expires: 2018   Dist: (256) 539-5441
726 Madison Street, Huntsville, AL 35810   Fax: (256) 539-5444
P.O. Box 3367, Huntsville, AL 35810
E-mail: laura.hall@alhouse.org
Committees: Health; Internal Affairs; Madison County Legislation; Ways and Means General Fund
Education: Morris Col 1965 BS; Ohio State 1973 MA; Alabama A&M CAES

Representative **Micky Hammon** (R-District 4) . . . . . . . . . . (334) 242-7709
Counties Represented: Limestone (part), Morgan   Dist: (256) 260-2146
(part)   Fax: (256) 260-2144
Term Expires: 2018
2128 6th Avenue SE, Suite 504, Decatur, AL 35601
E-mail: micky.hammon@alhouse.gov
Committees: Commerce and Small Business; Economic Development and Tourism; Internal Affairs

Representative
**James T. "Tommy" Hanes, Jr.** (R-District 23)
Suite 527-D . . . . . . . . . . . . . . . . . . . . . . . . . . . . . . . (334) 242-7609
Counties Represented: DeKalb (part), Jackson (part)
Term Expires: 2018
E-mail: jhanes55@gmail.com
Committees: Agriculture and Forestry; Economic Development and Tourism; Public Safety and Homeland Security

Representative **Corey Harbison** (R-District 12) . . . . . . . . . (334) 242-7609
  Counties Represented: Cullman (part)
  Term Expires: 2018
  E-mail: corey.harbison@alhouse.gov
  Committees: Boards, Agencies and Commissions; Constitutions,
  Campaigns and Elections; Economic Development and Tourism

Representative **Alan Harper** (R-District 61) . . . . . . . . . . . . (334) 242-7732
  Counties Represented: Greene (part), Pickens (part),    Dist: (205) 391-7885
  Tuscaloosa (part)
  Term Expires: 2018
  419 Memorial Parkway East, Aliceville, AL 35442
  P.O. Box 403, Aliceville, AL 35442
  E-mail: salanharper@gmail.com
  Committees: Constitutions, Campaigns and Elections; Economic
  Development and Tourism; Jefferson County Legislation; Rules;
  Technology and Research; Tuscaloosa County Legislation
  Education: Alabama 1986 BS

Representative **Ed Henry** (R-District 9) . . . . . . . . . . . . . . . (334) 242-7736
  Counties Represented: Cullman (part), Marshall    Dist: (256) 260-2146
  (part), Morgan (part)    Fax: (256) 260-2144
  Term Expires: 2018
  2128 6th Avenue. SE, Suite 504, Decatur, AL 35601
  E-mail: ed.henry@alhouse.gov
  Committees: Education Policy; State Government; Ways and Means
  Education

Representative **Jim Hill** (R-District 50) Suite 526-B . . . . . . (334) 242-7609
  Counties Represented: St. Clair (part)
  Term Expires: 2018
  E-mail: jim.hill@alhouse.gov
  Committees: Ethics and Campaign Finance; Judiciary

Representative **Mike Hill** (R-District 41) . . . . . . . . . . . . . . (334) 242-7715
  Counties Represented: Shelby (part)    Dist: (205) 620-6610
  Term Expires: 2018    Res: (205) 669-6264
  114 Arlington Avenue, Columbiana, AL 35051    Fax: (205) 669-4125
  21325 Highway 25, Columbiana, AL 35051
  1134 County Services Drive, Pelham, AL 35124
  E-mail: mhillcolum@aol.com
  Committees: Financial Services; Insurance; Internal Affairs; Shelby
  County Legislation
  Education: Auburn 1972 BS; LSU; Oklahoma State

Representative **Alvin A. Holmes** (D-District 78) . . . . . . . . (334) 242-7706
  Counties Represented: Montgomery (part)    Dist: (334) 264-7807
  Term Expires: 2018    Res: (334) 281-8637
  P.O. Box 6064, Montgomery, AL 36106
  E-mail: alvin.holmes@alhouse.org
  Committees: Montgomery County Legislation
  Education: Atlanta; Alabama; Alabama State; Pennsylvania

Representative **Mike Holmes** (R-District 31)
  Room 527-A . . . . . . . . . . . . . . . . . . . . . . . . . . . . . . . . (334) 242-7215
  Counties Represented: Autauga (part), Elmore (part)    Dist: (334) 224-1347
  Term Expires: 2018
  67 Cabin Road, Wetumpka, AL 36093
  E-mail: mike.holmes@alhouse.gov
  Committees: Boards, Agencies and Commissions; Ways and Means
  General Fund

Representative **Ralph A. Howard** (D-District 72) . . . . . . . . (334) 242-7759
  Counties Represented: Bibb (part), Greene (part),    Dist: (334) 624-1887
  Hale, Marengo (part), Perry (part), Sumter (part)
  Term Expires: 2018
  700 M.W. Rollins Lane, Greensboro, AL 36744
  E-mail: ralph.howard@alhouse.gov
  Committees: Local Legislation; Military and Veterans Affairs; State
  Government
  Education: Alabama BA

Representative **Mike Hubbard** (R-District 79) . . . . . . . . . . (334) 242-7668
  Counties Represented: Lee (part)    Dist: (334) 826-9946
  Term Expires: 2018    Res: (334) 821-9706
  P.O. Box 950, Auburn, AL 36831-0950    Fax: (334) 826-9151
  E-mail: mike.hubbard@alhouse.gov
  Committees: Lee County Legislation

Representative **Steve Hurst** (R-District 35) . . . . . . . . . . . . (334) 353-9215
  Counties Represented: Calhoun (part), Clay (part),    Res: (256) 761-1935
  Coosa (part), Talladega (part)
  Term Expires: 2018
  155 Quail Run Road, Munford, AL 36268
  E-mail: steve.hurst@alhouse.gov
  Committees: Boards, Agencies and Commissions; County and
  Municipal Government

Representative **Reed Ingram** (R-District 75) Suite 531 . . . . (334) 242-7609
  Counties Represented: Elmore (part), Montgomery (part)
  Term Expires: 2018
  E-mail: reedingram75@gmail.com
  Committees: Agriculture and Forestry; County and Municipal
  Government; Financial Services; Montgomery County Legislation

Representative **Thomas E. Jackson** (D-District 68) . . . . . . (334) 242-7738
  Counties Represented: Baldwin (part), Clarke (part),    Dist: (334) 246-3597
  Conecuh (part), Marengo (part), Monroe (part),    Res: (334) 636-0094
  Washington (part)
  Term Expires: 2018
  P.O. Box 656, Thomasville, AL 36784-0656
  E-mail: thomas.jackson@alhouse.gov
  Committees: Ethics and Campaign Finance; Public Safety and
  Homeland Security; Technology and Research
  Education: Knoxville 1972 BS; Alabama State 1977 MA

Representative **Ken Johnson** (R-District 7) . . . . . . . . . . . . (334) 242-7754
  Counties Represented: Franklin (part), Lawrence    Dist: (256) 974-5175
  (part), Morgan (part), Winston (part)    Res: (256) 974-5468
  Term Expires: 2018
  12001 Highway 157, Suite 6, Moulton, AL 35650
  E-mail: kenjohnsonrep@gmail.com
  Committees: Financial Services; Insurance; Ways and Means General
  Fund

Representative
  **Ronald G. "Ron" Johnson** (R-District 33) . . . . . . . . . . (334) 242-7777
  Counties Represented: Clay (part), Coosa (part),    Res: (256) 249-9489
  Talladega (part)
  Term Expires: 2018
  3770 Sylacauga-Fayette Highway, Sylacauga, AL 35151
  E-mail: ronald.johnson@alhouse.org
  Committees: Economic Development and Tourism; Health; Rules
  Education: Florida State 1965 BS; Auburn PharmD

Representative **Mike Jones, Jr.** (R-District 92) . . . . . . . . . (334) 242-7739
  Counties Represented: Coffee (part), Covington,    Res: (334) 222-4367
  Escambia (part)
  Term Expires: 2018
  486 Sutton Road, Andalusia, AL 36420
  P.O. Box 957, Andalusia, AL 36420
  E-mail: mljatty@andycable.com
  Committees: Judiciary
  Education: Birmingham-Southern 1989 BS; Alabama JD

Representative **John F. Knight, Jr.** (D-District 77) . . . . . . . (334) 242-7512
  Counties Represented: Montgomery (part)    Dist: (334) 229-4286
  Term Expires: 2018    Res: (334) 834-7445
  P.O. Box 6300, Montgomery, AL 36106
  E-mail: john.knight@alhouse.gov
  E-mail: jknight@alasu.edu
  Committees: Health; Internal Affairs; Montgomery County Legislation;
  Ways and Means General Fund
  Education: Alabama State BS

Representative **Kelvin J. Lawrence** (D-District 69)
  Suite 536-A . . . . . . . . . . . . . . . . . . . . . . . . . . . . . . . . (334) 242-7609
  Counties Represented: Autauga (part), Lowndes, Montgomery (part),
  Wilcox
  Term Expires: 2018
  E-mail: kelvinj73@gmail.com
  Committees: Boards, Agencies and Commissions; Economic
  Development and Tourism

Representative **Nathaniel Ledbetter** (R-District 24)
  Suite 522-D . . . . . . . . . . . . . . . . . . . . . . . . . . . . . . . . (334) 242-7609
  Counties Represented: DeKalb (part)
  Term Expires: 2018
  E-mail: nathaniel.ledbetter@alhouse.gov
  Committees: Children and Senior Advocacy; Commerce and Small
  Business; Transportation, Utilities and Infrastructure

Representative **Paul Lee** (R-District 86) . . . . . . . . . . . . . . . (334) 242-7675
  Counties Represented: Houston (part)    Res: (334) 792-9682
  Term Expires: 2018    Fax: (334) 793-5232
  2319 Eddins Road, Dothan, AL 36301
  E-mail: pwlee@graceba.net
  Committees: Health; Rules; Ways and Means General Fund

Representative **Richard J. Lindsey** (D-District 39) . . . . . . . (334) 242-7713
  Counties Represented: Calhoun (part), Cherokee,    Res: (256) 475-3415
  Cleburne (part), DeKalb (part)    Fax: (256) 475-6438
  Term Expires: 2018
  14160 County Road 22, Centre, AL 35960
  E-mail: richard.lindsey@alhouse.gov
  Committees: Agriculture and Forestry; Constitutions, Campaigns and
  Elections; Economic Development and Tourism; Internal Affairs
  Education: Jacksonville State BS

*(continued on next page)*

**Representatives** *continued*

Representative
**James M. "Jimmy" Martin** (R-District 42) Suite 404 . . (334) 242-7609
Counties Represented: Autauga (part), Chilton (part)
Term Expires: 2018
E-mail: jimmy.martin@alhouse.gov
Committees: Commerce and Small Business; Financial Services;
Insurance
Education: John A Gupton BS

Representative **Artis "A.J." McCampbell** (D-District 71) . . (334) 242-7747
Counties Represented: Choctaw (part), Greene    Dist: (334) 295-5634
(part), Marengo (part), Pickens (part), Sumter    Dist: (334) 652-6531
(part), Tuscaloosa (part)    Res: (334) 289-5465
Term Expires: 2018
P.O. Box 487, Demopolis, AL 36732
E-mail: aj.mccampbell@alhouse.gov
Committees: Agriculture and Forestry; Insurance; Jefferson County
Legislation; Tuscaloosa County Legislation
Education: Alabama 1976 BA

Representative **Thad McClammy** (D-District 76) . . . . . . . . (334) 242-7780
Counties Represented: Montgomery (part)    Dist: (334) 224-1769
Term Expires: 2018    Res: (334) 264-6767
858 West South Boulevard, Montgomery, AL 36105    Fax: (334) 284-5769
E-mail: thad.mcclammy@alhouse.gov
Committees: Financial Services; Judiciary; Military and Veterans
Affairs; Montgomery County Legislation
Education: Auburn BS, MS

Representative **Mac McCutcheon** (R-District 25) . . . . . . . . (334) 242-7705
Counties Represented: Limestone (part), Madison    Dist: (256) 539-5441
(part)    Fax: (256) 539-5444
Term Expires: 2018
726 Madison Street, Huntsville, AL 35801
P.O. Box 370, Capshaw, AL 35742
E-mail: c.mac.mccutcheon@gmail.com
Committees: Madison County Legislation; Rules
Education: Trinity U BS

Representative
**Stephen A. "Steve" McMillan** (R-District 95) . . . . . . . . (334) 242-7723
Counties Represented: Baldwin (part)    Res: (251) 948-5575
Term Expires: 2018
P.O. Box 776, Bay Minette, AL 36507
E-mail: bcld07@gmail.com
Committees: Baldwin County Legislation; County and Municipal
Government; Internal Affairs; Technology and Research; Ways and
Means Education
Education: Auburn 1964 BA

Representative **Darrio Melton** (D-District 67) . . . . . . . . . . . (334) 242-7540
Counties Represented: Dallas, Perry (part)    Res: (334) 874-2569
Term Expires: 2018    Fax: (334) 874-2571
P.O. Box 346, Selma, AL 36702
E-mail: darriomelton@gmail.com
Committees: Boards, Agencies and Commissions; Economic
Development and Tourism; State Government
Education: Alabama Birmingham BS; Emory MDiv

Representative
**Michael J. "Mike" Millican** (R-District 17) . . . . . . . . . . (334) 242-7354
Counties Represented: Lamar (part), Marion,    Res: (205) 921-3214
Winston (part)    Fax: (334) 353-3350
Term Expires: 2018
995 Country Estates Drive, Hamilton, AL 35570
E-mail: mike.millican@alhouse.gov
Committees: Health; Ways and Means General Fund
Affiliation: Instructor, Bevil Community College
Education: Athens State BS

Representative **Arnold Mooney** (R-District 43)
Suite 538-D . . . . . . . . . . . . . . . . . . . . . . . . . . . . . . . . . . . . (334) 242-7609
Counties Represented: Jefferson (part), Shelby (part)
Term Expires: 2018
E-mail: arnold.mooney@alhouse.gov
Committees: Health; Shelby County Legislation; Ways and Means
General Fund

Representative **Barry Moore** (R-District 91) . . . . . . . . . . . . (334) 242-7773
Counties Represented: Coffee (part)    Res: (334) 348-2402
Term Expires: 2018    Fax: (334) 343-0436
561 County Road 623, Enterprise, AL 36330
502 Windsor Trace, Enterprise, AL 36330
E-mail: barry@barrymooreindustries.com
Committees: Commerce and Small Business; Education Policy; Military
and Veterans Affairs; Rules

Representative **Mary Moore** (D-District 59) . . . . . . . . . . . . (334) 242-7608
Counties Represented: Jefferson (part)    Res: (205) 322-0254
Term Expires: 2018    Fax: (205) 322-4097
1622 - 36th Avenue North, Birmingham, AL 35207
E-mail: mamoor48@bellsouth.net
Committees: Local Legislation; Public Safety and Homeland Security;
Technology and Research
Education: Tuskegee BS; Alabama A&M MBA;
Alabama Birmingham CAS

Representative **Johnny Mack Morrow** (D-District 18) . . . . (334) 242-7698
Counties Represented: Colbert (part), Franklin    Res: (256) 356-8043
(part), Lauderdale (part)
Term Expires: 2018
1895 Highway 28, Red Bay, AL 35582
E-mail: johnny.morrow@alhouse.org
Committees: Boards, Agencies and Commissions; Local Legislation
Education: Mississippi State BS; Samford MBA

Representative **Becky Nordgren** (R-District 29) . . . . . . . . . (334) 353-9032
Counties Represented: Calhoun (part), DeKalb    Res: (256) 546-1378
(part), Etowah (part)    Fax: (256) 240-7216
Term Expires: 2018
101 Cook Street, Gadsden, AL 35904
930 Keith Avenue, Anniston, AL 36207
E-mail: becky.nordgren@alhouse.gov
Committees: Economic Development and Tourism; Health; State
Government

Representative **James "Jim" Patterson** (R-District 21) . . . (334) 242-7531
Counties Represented: Madison (part)    Dist: (256) 975-7990
Term Expires: 2018
P.O. Box 286, Meridianville, AL 35759
E-mail: jimpattersonhd21@gmail.com
Committees: Education Policy; Health; Madison County Legislation

Representative **Phillip Pettus** (R-District 1) Suite 524-C . . . (334) 242-7609
Counties Represented: Lauderdale (part)
Term Expires: 2018
E-mail: phillip.pettus@alhouse.gov
Committees: Judiciary; Military and Veterans Affairs; Transportation,
Utilities and Infrastructure

Representative **Dimitri Polizos** (R-District 74)
Room 522-C . . . . . . . . . . . . . . . . . . . . . . . . . . . . . . . . . . . (334) 242-7609
Counties Represented: Montgomery (part)
Term Expires: 2018
E-mail: dimitri.polizos@alhouse.gov
Committees: Commerce and Small Business; Constitutions, Campaigns
and Elections; Ethics and Campaign Finance; Montgomery County
Legislation

Representative **Bill E. Poole** (R-District 63) . . . . . . . . . . . . (334) 242-7624
Counties Represented: Tuscaloosa (part)    Dist: (205) 752-8338
Term Expires: 2018    Fax: (205) 752-1283
1927 7th Street, Tuscaloosa, AL 35401
E-mail: poole@gpr-law.com
Committees: Jefferson County Legislation; Tuscaloosa County
Legislation; Ways and Means Education

Representative **Chris Pringle** (R-District 101)
Suite 427-M . . . . . . . . . . . . . . . . . . . . . . . . . . . . . . . . . . . (334) 242-7609
Counties Represented: Mobile (part)
Term Expires: 2018
E-mail: chrispringle@southerntimberlands.com
Committees: Constitutions, Campaigns and Elections; Education Policy;
Internal Affairs; Mobile County Legislation; State Government

Representative **Kerry Rich** (R-District 26) . . . . . . . . . . . . . (334) 242-7538
Counties Represented: DeKalb (part), Marshall    Tel: (256) 505-0885
(part)    Dist: (256) 582-0619
Term Expires: 2018    Res: (256) 894-7872
1301 North Carlisle Street, Albertville, AL 35951
E-mail: kerryrich@bellsouth.net
Committees: Education Policy; Ethics and Campaign Finance; Rules

Representative **Oliver Robinson** (D-District 58) . . . . . . . . . (334) 242-7769
Counties Represented: Jefferson (part)    Res: (205) 849-6765
Term Expires: 2018
9640 Eastpoint Circle, Birmingham, AL 35217
E-mail: oliver.robinson@alhouse.gov
Committees: Education Policy; Financial Services; Military and
Veterans Affairs
Education: Alabama Birmingham BS

Representative **John W. Rogers, Jr.** (D-District 52) . . . . . . (334) 242-7761
Counties Represented: Jefferson (part)    Dist: (205) 934-0364
Term Expires: 2018    Res: (205) 925-3522
1424 18th Street SW, Birmingham, AL 35211
E-mail: john.rogers@alhouse.org
Committees: State Government; Ways and Means Education
Education: Tennessee State BS; Alabama Birmingham AA;
Alabama MS

Representative **Connie Rowe** (R-District 13) Suite 538-C . . (334) 242-7609
Counties Represented: Blount (part), Walker (part)
Term Expires: 2018
E-mail: connie.rowe@alhouse.gov
Committees: Judiciary; Public Safety and Homeland Security

Representative **Howard Sanderford** (R-District 20) . . . . . . (334) 242-4368
Counties Represented: Madison (part)          Dist: (256) 533-1989
Term Expires: 2018                            Res: (256) 881-8390
908 Tannahill Drive SE, Huntsville, AL 35802-1971
E-mail: howard.sanderford@alhouse.gov
Committees: Boards, Agencies and Commissions; Constitutions,
Campaigns and Elections; Internal Affairs; Madison County
Legislation; Technology and Research
Affiliation: President, Computer Leasing Company, Inc.
Education: Mississippi State 1957 BS

Representative
**Roderick Hampton "Rod" Scott** (D-District 55) . . . . . . (334) 242-7752
Counties Represented: Jefferson (part)        Dist: (205) 929-1534
Term Expires: 2018                            Res: (205) 781-1322
657 Maple Street, Fairfield, AL 35064
E-mail: rod.scott@alhouse.gov
Committees: Education Policy; Technology and Research; Ways and
Means Education
Education: Yale 1980 BA; Tuck School MBA

Representative **Chris Sells** (R-District 90) Suite 526-E . . . . (334) 242-7609
Counties Represented: Butler, Coffee (part), Conecuh (part), Crenshaw,
Montgomery (part)
Term Expires: 2018
E-mail: csea@centurytel.net
Committees: Transportation, Utilities and Infrastructure; Ways and
Means General Fund

Representative **David Sessions** (R-District 105) . . . . . . . . (334) 242-0947
Counties Represented: Mobile (part)           Res: (251) 865-4275
Term Expires: 2018                            Fax: (251) 865-9565
13000 Hugh Fort Road, Grand Bay, AL 36541
E-mail: d.r.sessions@att.net
Committees: Agriculture and Forestry; Ethics and Campaign Finance;
Mobile County Legislation

Representative **Randall Shedd** (R-District 11) . . . . . . . . . . (334) 242-7330
Counties Represented: Blount (part), Cullman (part),    Res: (256) 796-5870
Marshall (part), Morgan (part)
Term Expires: 2018
1461 Welcome Road, Cullman, AL 35058
E-mail: randall.shedd@alhouse.gov
Committees: Children and Senior Advocacy; Financial Services; Local
Legislation
Education: Wallace State

Representative **Harry Shiver** (R-District 64) . . . . . . . . . . . . (334) 242-7745
Counties Represented: Baldwin (part), Monroe    Dist: (251) 937-0240
(part)                                          Fax: (251) 580-1645
Term Expires: 2018
46007 Sunset Drive, Bay Minette, AL 36507
E-mail: harryshiver@aol.com
Committees: Baldwin County Legislation; Local Legislation; Public
Safety and Homeland Security; State Government

Representative **Kyle South** (R-District 16) Suite 427-G . . . . (334) 242-7609
Counties Represented: Fayette, Jefferson (part), Lamar (part),
Tuscaloosa (part)
Term Expires: 2018
E-mail: ksouth@watvc.com
Committees: Jefferson County Legislation; Local Legislation; State
Government; Transportation, Utilities and Infrastructure; Tuscaloosa
County Legislation

Representative **David Standridge** (R-District 34) . . . . . . . . (334) 242-7475
Counties Represented: Blount (part), Marshall (part)    Dist: (205) 543-0647
Term Expires: 2018
11 South Union Street, Suite 524-D, Montgomery, AL 36130-3550
E-mail: david.standridge@alhouse.gov
Committees: Boards, Agencies and Commissions; Local Legislation
Education: Wallace State AS; Athens State BS

Representative **Patricia Todd** (D-District 54) . . . . . . . . . . . (334) 242-7718
Counties Represented: Jefferson (part)        Dist: (205) 324-9822
Term Expires: 2018                            Res: (205) 599-2856
3520 7th Avenue South, Birmingham, AL 35222
1320 58th Street South, Birmingham, AL 35222
E-mail: reptodd@gmail.com
Committees: Education Policy; Ways and Means Education
Education: Kentucky BA; Alabama Birmingham MPA

Representative
**Benjamin "Allen" Treadaway** (R-District 51) . . . . . . . . (334) 242-7685
Counties Represented: Jefferson (part)        Dist: (205) 254-1720
Term Expires: 2018                            Res: (205) 566-6835
P.O. Box 126, Morris, AL 35116
E-mail: bsketa@aol.com
Committees: County and Municipal Government; Military and Veterans
Affairs; Public Safety and Homeland Security

Representative **Mark Tuggle** (R-District 81) . . . . . . . . . . . . (334) 242-7219
Counties Represented: Chilton (part), Coosa (part),    Res: (256) 329-3352
Tallapoosa (part)
Term Expires: 2018
110 Calhoun Street, Suite 108, Alexander City, AL 35010
E-mail: tughd81@gmail.com
Committees: Internal Affairs; State Government; Ways and Means
Education

Representative **Tim Wadsworth** (R-District 14)
Suite 528-D . . . . . . . . . . . . . . . . . . . . . . . . . . . . . . . . . .(334) 242-7609
Counties Represented: Jefferson (part), Walker (part), Winston (part)
Term Expires: 2018
E-mail: wadsworth@centurytel.net
Committees: Children and Senior Advocacy; Jefferson County
Legislation; Local Legislation; Technology and Research; Tuscaloosa
County Legislation

Representative **Pebblin W. Warren** (D-District 82) . . . . . . (334) 242-7734
Counties Represented: Lee (part), Macon,      Dist: (334) 280-4469
Tallapoosa (part)                             Res: (334) 727-9127
Term Expires: 2018                            Fax: (334) 727-2213
P.O. Box 1328, Tuskegee Institute, AL 36087
E-mail: tiger9127@bellsouth.net
Committees: Health; Lee County Legislation; Rules; Ways and Means
General Fund
Education: Tuskegee 1974 BS, 1986 EdM

Representative **April Weaver** (R-District 49)
Room 522-B . . . . . . . . . . . . . . . . . . . . . . . . . . . . . . . . . .(334) 242-7731
Counties Represented: Bibb (part), Chilton (part), Shelby (part)
Term Expires: 2018
E-mail: april.weaver@alhouse.gov
Committees: Health; Internal Affairs; Shelby County Legislation; State
Government

Representative **Isaac Whorton** (R-District 38)
Suite 427-C . . . . . . . . . . . . . . . . . . . . . . . . . . . . . . . . . .(334) 242-7609
Counties Represented: Chambers (part), Lee (part)
Term Expires: 2018
E-mail: isaac.whorton@alhouse.gov
Committees: Boards, Agencies and Commissions; Lee County
Legislation; Local Legislation; Public Safety and Homeland Security

Representative **Ritchie Whorton** (R-District 22)
Suite 526-C . . . . . . . . . . . . . . . . . . . . . . . . . . . . . . . . . .(334) 242-7609
Counties Represented: Jackson (part), Madison (part)
Term Expires: 2018
E-mail: ritchiewhorton@gmail.com
Committees: Commerce and Small Business; Economic Development
and Tourism; Ethics and Campaign Finance; Madison County
Legislation

Representative **J. M. "Margie" Wilcox** (R-District 104) . . . (334) 242-7609
Counties Represented: Mobile (part)
Term Expires: 2018
E-mail: j.m.wilcox@alhouse.gov
Committees: Children and Senior Advocacy; Economic Development
and Tourism; Mobile County Legislation; Transportation, Utilities and
Infrastructure

Representative **Jack Williams** (R-District 47) . . . . . . . . . . . (334) 242-7779
Counties Represented: Jefferson (part)        Dist: (205) 414-7539
Term Expires: 2018                            Res: (205) 979-7901
2501 Glendmere Place, Vestavia Hills, AL 35216    Fax: (205) 414-7531
E-mail: jack@jackwilliams.org
Committees: Commerce and Small Business; Insurance
Education: Southeastern Bible BA

Representative **Jack W. Williams** (R-District 102)
Suite 524-F . . . . . . . . . . . . . . . . . . . . . . . . . . . . . . . . . .(334) 242-7609
Counties Represented: Mobile (part)
Term Expires: 2018
E-mail: jackwilliams55@icloud.com
Committees: Agriculture and Forestry; County and Municipal
Government; Health; Mobile County Legislation

*(continued on next page)*

**LEGISLATIVE BRANCH**

**LEGISLATIVE BRANCH**

Representatives *continued*

Representative **Phil Williams** (R-District 6) . . . . . . . . . . . (334) 242-7704
Counties Represented: Limestone (part), Madison    Res: (256) 489-5471
(part)
Term Expires: 2018
2185 Old Monrovia Road, Huntsville, AL 35806
E-mail: philhouse44@gmail.com
Committees: Governmental Affairs; Madison County Legislation;
Technology and Research; Ways and Means Education
Education: Alabama Huntsville BA

Representative **Rich Wingo** (R-District 62) Suite 522-D . . . (334) 242-7609
Counties Represented: Tuscaloosa (part)
Term Expires: 2018
E-mail: rich@blackwaterresources.com
Committees: Financial Services; Insurance; Jefferson County
Legislation; Tuscaloosa County Legislation; Ways and Means General
Fund

Representative **Randy Wood** (R-District 36) . . . . . . . . . . . (334) 242-7700
Counties Represented: Calhoun (part), St. Clair    Dist: (256) 237-8114
(part), Talladega (part)                           Res: (256) 820-6700
Term Expires: 2018                                 Fax: (256) 236-7379
4422 Sprague Avenue, Anniston, AL 36206
P.O. Box 4432, Anniston, AL 36204
E-mail: randy.wood@alhouse.gov
Committees: Military and Veterans Affairs; Public Safety and
Homeland Security; State Government

# House Standing Committees
## Agriculture and Forestry

**Majority Members**
David Sessions (R-105)
  *Chairperson*
Donnie Chesteen (R-87) *Vice Chair*
Will Ainsworth (R-27)
Koven L. Brown (R-40)
Randy Davis (R-96)
Teddy Joe Faust, Sr. (R-94)
Bob Fincher (R-37)
James T. "Tommy" Hanes, Jr.
  (R-23)
Reed Ingram (R-75)
Jack W. Williams (R-102)

**Minority Members**
Richard J. Lindsey (D-39)
  *Ranking Minority Member*
Dexter Grimsley (D-85)
Artis "A.J." McCampbell (D-71)

## Baldwin County Legislation

**Majority Members**
Randy Davis (R-96) *Chair*
Harry Shiver (R-64) *Vice Chair*
Alan Baker (R-66)
Teddy Joe Faust, Sr. (R-94)
Stephen A. "Steve" McMillan (R-95)

## Boards, Agencies and Commissions

**Majority Members**
Howard Sanderford (R-20) *Chair*
Mike Holmes (R-31)
  *Vice Chairperson*
Corey Harbison (R-12)
Steve Hurst (R-35)
David Standridge (R-34)
Isaac Whorton (R-38)

**Minority Members**
Johnny Mack Morrow (D-18)
  *Ranking Minority Member*
Kelvin J. Lawrence (D-69)
Darrio Melton (D-67)

## Children and Senior Advocacy

**Majority Members**
Koven L. Brown (R-40) *Chair*
Randall Shedd (R-11) *Vice Chair*
Jim Carns (R-48)
Allen Farley (R-15)
Nathaniel Ledbetter (R-24)
Tim Wadsworth (R-14)
J. M. "Margie" Wilcox (R-104)

**Minority Members**
Barbara Bigsby Boyd (D-32)
  *Ranking Minority Member*
Barbara Drummond (D-103)
Dexter Grimsley (D-85)

# Commerce and Small Business

**Majority Members**
Jack Williams (R-47) *Chairperson*
Dimitri Polizos (R-74)
  *Vice Chairperson*
Jim Carns (R-48)
J. Daniel Garrett (R-44)
Micky Hammon (R-4)
Nathaniel Ledbetter (R-24)
James M. "Jimmy" Martin (R-42)
Barry Moore (R-91)
Ritchie Whorton (R-22)

**Minority Members**
Craig Ford (D-28)
  *Ranking Minority Member*
Louise Alexander (D-56)
Adline C. Clarke (D-97)
Anthony Daniels (D-53)

# Constitutions, Campaigns and Elections

**Majority Members**
Randy Davis (R-96) *Chairperson*
Paul Beckman (R-88)
  *Vice Chairperson*
Bob Fincher (R-37)
Corey Harbison (R-12)
Alan Harper (R-61)
Chris Pringle (R-101)
Dimitri Polizos (R-74)
Howard Sanderford (R-20)

**Minority Members**
Richard J. Lindsey (D-39)
  *Ranking Minority Member*
Adline C. Clarke (D-97)
Juandalynn "Lee Lee" Givan (D-60)

# County and Municipal Government

**Majority Members**
Stephen A. "Steve"
  McMillan (R-95)
  *Chair*
Chris Blackshear (R-80)
Jim Carns (R-48)
Danny F. Crawford (R-5)
Teddy Joe Faust, Sr. (R-94)
Steve Hurst (R-35)
Reed Ingram (R-75)
Benjamin "Allen" Treadaway (R-51)
Jack W. Williams (R-102)

**Minority Members**
James E. Buskey (D-99)
  *Ranking Minority Member*
Barbara Bigsby Boyd (D-32)
Adline C. Clarke (D-97)

# Economic Development and Tourism

**Majority Members**
Alan Harper (R-61) *Chairperson*
Becky Nordgren (R-29)
  *Vice Chairperson*
Koven L. Brown (R-40)
Micky Hammon (R-4)
Corey Harbison (R-12)
James T. "Tommy" Hanes, Jr.
  (R-23)
Ronald G. "Ron" Johnson (R-33)
Ritchie Whorton (R-22)
J. M. "Margie" Wilcox (R-104)

**Minority Members**
Richard J. Lindsey (D-39)
  *Ranking Minority Member*
Grover Berry Forte (D-84)
Kelvin J. Lawrence (D-69)
Darrio Melton (D-67)

# Education Policy

**Majority Members**
Terri Collins (R-8) *Chairperson*
Kerry Rich (R-26)
  *Vice Chairperson*
Mack Butler (R-30)
Bob Fincher (R-37)
Ed Henry (R-9)
Barry Moore (R-91)
James "Jim" Patterson (R-21)
Chris Pringle (R-101)
Phil W. Williams (R-10)

**Minority Members**
Oliver Robinson (D-58)
  *Ranking Minority Member*
Barbara Drummond (D-103)
Roderick Hampton "Rod" Scott
  (D-55)
Patricia Todd (D-54)

# Ethics and Campaign Finance

**Majority Members**
Mike Ball (R-10) *Chairperson*
Alan Baker (R-66)
Jim Hill (R-50)
Dimitri Polizos (R-74)
Kerry Rich (R-26)
David Sessions (R-105)
Ritchie Whorton (R-22)

**Minority Members**
Thomas E. Jackson (D-68)
  *Ranking Minority Member*
Marcel Black (D-3)
Grover Berry Forte (D-84)

## Financial Services

| Majority Members | Minority Members |
|---|---|
| Ken Johnson (R-7) *Vice Chairperson* | Marcel Black (D-3) *Ranking Minority Member* |
| Mack Butler (R-30) | Merika Coleman-Evans (D-57) |
| David L. Faulkner, Jr. (R-46) | Thad McClammy (D-76) |
| Mike Hill (R-41) | Oliver Robinson (D-58) |
| Reed Ingram (R-75) | |
| James M. "Jimmy" Martin (R-42) | |
| Randall Shedd (R-11) | |
| Rich Wingo (R-62) | |

## Health

| Majority Members | Minority Members |
|---|---|
| April Weaver (R-49) *Chairperson* | John F. Knight, Jr. (D-77) *Ranking Minority Member* |
| Michael J. "Mike" Millican (R-17) *Vice Chairperson* | Elaine Beech (D-65) |
| Danny F. Crawford (R-5) | Laura Hall (D-19) |
| Matthew David Fridy (R-73) | Pebblin W. Warren (D-82) |
| Ronald G. "Ron" Johnson (R-33) | |
| Paul Lee (R-86) | |
| Arnold Mooney (R-43) | |
| Becky Nordgren (R-29) | |
| James "Jim" Patterson (R-21) | |
| Jack W. Williams (R-102) | |

## Insurance

| Majority Members | Minority Members |
|---|---|
| Mike Hill (R-41) *Chairperson* | Artis "A.J." McCampbell (D-71) *Ranking Minority Member* |
| Ken Johnson (R-7) *Vice Chairperson* | Louise Alexander (D-56) |
| David L. Faulkner, Jr. (R-46) | Anthony Daniels (D-53) |
| James M. "Jimmy" Martin (R-42) | |
| Jack Williams (R-47) | |
| Rich Wingo (R-62) | |

## Internal Affairs

| Majority Members | Minority Members |
|---|---|
| Alan C. Boothe (R-89) *Chairperson* | Laura Hall (D-19) *Ranking Minority Member* |
| Micky Hammon (R-4) *Vice Chairperson* | John F. Knight, Jr. (D-77) |
| Mike Hill (R-41) | Richard J. Lindsey (D-39) |
| Stephen A. "Steve" McMillan (R-95) | |
| Chris Pringle (R-101) | |
| Howard Sanderford (R-20) | |
| Mark Tuggle (R-81) | |
| April Weaver (R-49) | |

## Jefferson County Legislation

| Majority Members | Minority Members |
|---|---|
| Bill E. Poole (R-63) *Chairperson* | Christopher J. England (D-70) *Vice Chairperson* |
| Alan Harper (R-61) | Artis "A.J." McCampbell (D-71) |
| Kyle South (R-16) | |
| Tim Wadsworth (R-14) | |
| Rich Wingo (R-62) | |

## Judiciary

| Majority Members | Minority Members |
|---|---|
| Mike Jones, Jr. (R-92) *Chairperson* | Thad McClammy (D-76) *Ranking Minority Member* |
| Jim Hill (R-50) *Vice Chairperson* | Marcel Black (D-3) |
| Mike Ball (R-10) | Merika Coleman-Evans (D-57) |
| Paul Beckman (R-88) | Christopher J. England (D-70) |
| Dickie Drake (R-45) | Juandalynn "Lee Lee" Givan (D-60) |
| Allen Farley (R-15) | |
| David L. Faulkner, Jr. (R-46) | |
| Matthew David Fridy (R-73) | |
| Phillip Pettus (R-1) | |
| Connie Rowe (R-13) | |

## Lee County Legislation

| Majority Members | Minority Members |
|---|---|
| Mike Hubbard (R-79) | George C. Bandy (D-83) *Chairperson* |
| Isaac Whorton (R-38) | Pebblin W. Warren (D-82) |

## Local Legislation

| Majority Members | Minority Members |
|---|---|
| Alan Baker (R-66) *Chairperson* | Johnny Mack Morrow (D-18) *Ranking Minority Member* |
| Kyle South (R-16) *Vice Chairperson* | Louise Alexander (D-56) |
| Randall Shedd (R-11) | Ralph A. Howard (D-72) |
| Harry Shiver (R-64) | Mary Moore (D-59) |
| David Standridge (R-34) | |
| Tim Wadsworth (R-14) | |
| Isaac Whorton (R-38) | |

## Madison County Legislation

| Majority Members | Minority Members |
|---|---|
| Mike Ball (R-10) *Chairperson* | Laura Hall (D-19) *Vice Chairperson* |
| Mac McCutcheon (R-25) | Anthony Daniels (D-53) |
| James "Jim" Patterson (R-21) | |
| Howard Sanderford (R-20) | |
| Phil Williams (R-6) | |
| Ritchie Whorton (R-22) | |

## Military and Veterans Affairs

| Majority Members | Minority Members |
|---|---|
| Barry Moore (R-91) *Chairperson* | Thad McClammy (D-76) *Ranking Minority Member* |
| Dickie Drake (R-45) *Vice Chairperson* | Ralph A. Howard (D-72) |
| Steve Clouse (R-93) | Oliver Robinson (D-58) |
| Phillip Pettus (R-1) | |
| Benjamin "Allen" Treadaway (R-51) | |
| Randy Wood (R-36) | |

## Mobile County Legislation

| Majority Members | Minority Members |
|---|---|
| David Sessions (R-105) *Chairperson* | James E. Buskey (D-99) *Vice Chairperson* |
| Randy Davis (R-96) | Napoleon Bracy, Jr. (D-98) |
| Victor Gaston (R-100) | Adline C. Clarke (D-97) |
| Chris Pringle (R-101) | Barbara Drummond (D-103) |
| J. M. "Margie" Wilcox (R-104) | |
| Jack W. Williams (R-102) | |

## Montgomery County Legislation

| Majority Members | Minority Members |
|---|---|
| Reed Ingram (R-75) | Alvin A. Holmes (D-78) *Chairperson* |
| Dimitri Polizos (R-74) | John F. Knight, Jr. (D-77) |
| | Thad McClammy (D-76) |

## Public Safety and Homeland Security

| Majority Members | Minority Members |
|---|---|
| Randy Wood (R-36) *Chairperson* | Thomas E. Jackson (D-68) *Ranking Minority Member* |
| Allen Farley (R-15) *Vice Chairperson* | Christopher J. England (D-70) |
| Dickie Drake (R-45) | Mary Moore (D-59) |
| James T. "Tommy" Hanes, Jr. (R-23) | |
| Connie Rowe (R-13) | |
| Harry Shiver (R-64) | |
| Benjamin "Allen" Treadaway (R-51) | |
| Isaac Whorton (R-38) | |

## Rules

| Majority Members | Minority Members |
|---|---|
| Mac McCutcheon (R-25) *Chairperson* | James E. Buskey (D-99) *Ranking Minority Member* |
| Ronald G. "Ron" Johnson (R-33) *Vice Chairperson* | Elaine Beech (D-65) |
| Randy Davis (R-96) | Barbara Bigsby Boyd (D-32) |
| Victor Gaston (R-100) | Pebblin W. Warren (D-82) |
| Lynn Greer (R-2) | |
| Alan Harper (R-61) | |
| Paul Lee (R-86) | |
| Barry Moore (R-91) | |
| Kerry Rich (R-26) | |

**LEGISLATIVE BRANCH**

## Shelby County Legislation

**Majority Members**
April Weaver (R-49) *Chairperson*
Matthew David Fridy (R-73) *Vice Chairperson*
Jim Carns (R-48)
Dickie Drake (R-45)
Allen Farley (R-15)
Mike Hill (R-41)
Arnold Mooney (R-43)

## State Government

**Majority Members**
Mark Tuggle (R-81) *Chairperson*
Chris Pringle (R-101)
  *Vice Chairperson*
Alan C. Boothe (R-89)
Mack Butler (R-30)
Ed Henry (R-9)
Becky Nordgren (R-29)
Harry Shiver (R-64)
Kyle South (R-16)
April Weaver (R-49)
Randy Wood (R-36)

**Minority Members**
Barbara Bigsby Boyd (D-32)
  *Ranking Minority Member*
George C. Bandy (D-83)
Ralph A. Howard (D-72)
Darrio Melton (D-67)
John W. Rogers, Jr. (D-52)

## Technology and Research

**Majority Members**
Phil Williams (R-6) *Chairperson*
Howard Sanderford (R-20)
  *Vice Chairperson*
Alan Baker (R-66)
Alan Harper (R-61)
Stephen A. "Steve" McMillan
  (R-95)
Tim Wadsworth (R-14)

**Minority Members**
Thomas E. Jackson (D-68)
  *Ranking Minority Member*
Mary Moore (D-59)
Roderick Hampton "Rod" Scott
  (D-55)

## Transportation, Utilities and Infrastructure

**Majority Members**
Lynn Greer (R-2) *Chairperson*
Teddy Joe Faust, Sr. (R-94)
  *Vice Chairperson*
Will Ainsworth (R-27)
Victor Gaston (R-100)
Nathaniel Ledbetter (R-24)
Phillip Pettus (R-1)
Chris Sells (R-90)
Kyle South (R-16)
J. M. "Margie" Wilcox (R-104)

**Minority Members**
George C. Bandy (D-83)
  *Ranking Minority Member*
Napoleon Bracy, Jr. (D-98)
Barbara Drummond (D-103)
Dexter Grimsley (D-85)

## Tuscaloosa County Legislation

**Majority Members**
Bill E. Poole (R-63) *Chairperson*
Alan Harper (R-61)
Kyle South (R-16)
Tim Wadsworth (R-14)
Rich Wingo (R-62)

**Minority Members**
Christopher J. England (D-70)
  *Vice Chairperson*
Artis "A.J." McCampbell (D-71)

## Ways and Means Education

**Majority Members**
Bill E. Poole (R-63) *Chairperson*
Stephen A. "Steve"
  McMillan (R-95)
  *Vice Chairperson*
Alan Baker (R-66)
Alan C. Boothe (R-89)
Donnie Chesteen (R-87)
Terri Collins (R-8)
J. Daniel Garrett (R-44)
Ed Henry (R-9)
Mark Tuggle (R-81)
Phil Williams (R-6)

**Minority Members**
James E. Buskey (D-99)
  *Ranking Minority Member*
Craig Ford (D-28)
John W. Rogers, Jr. (D-52)
Roderick Hampton "Rod" Scott
  (D-55)
Patricia Todd (D-54)

## Ways and Means General Fund

**Majority Members**
Steve Clouse (R-93) *Chairperson*
Ken Johnson (R-7)
  *Vice Chairperson*
Victor Gaston (R-100)
Lynn Greer (R-2)
Mike Holmes (R-31)
Paul Lee (R-86)
Michael J. "Mike" Millican (R-17)
Arnold Mooney (R-43)
Chris Sells (R-90)
Rich Wingo (R-62)

**Minority Members**
Laura Hall (D-19)
  *Ranking Minority Member*
Elaine Beech (D-65)
Napoleon Bracy, Jr. (D-98)
John F. Knight, Jr. (D-77)
Pebblin W. Warren (D-82)

# Alaska State Legislature

State Capitol, Juneau, AK 99801-1182
Tel: (907) 465-4648  TTY: (907) 465-4980  Fax: (907) 465-2864
E-mail: lio.juneau@akleg.gov  Internet: www.akleg.gov

## Alaska Senate

Tel: (907) 465-6600  Fax: (907) 465-2832
President of the Senate **Kevin Meyer** (R) . . . . . . . . . . . . . . (907) 465-4945
  Education: Nebraska 1978 BS; New Mexico 1982 MPA;
  Alaska Pacific 1992 MBA
Majority Leader **John B. Coghill, Jr.** (R) . . . . . . . . . . . . . (907) 465-3719
Minority Leader **Berta Gardner** (D) . . . . . . . . . . . . . . . . . (907) 465-4930
  Education: UC Riverside 1977 BA
Secretary of the Senate **Liz Clark** . . . . . . . . . . . . . . . . . . . (907) 465-3701
  E-mail: liz.clark@akleg.gov
  E-mail: senate_secretary@legis.state.ak.us
Sergeant-at-Arms **Grace Ellsworth** . . . . . . . . . . . . . . . . . (907) 465-4987

## Senators

**Party Affiliation Statistics:** Republicans: 14, Democrats: 6
Senator **Clark "Click" Bishop** (R-District C) . . . . . . . . . . . (907) 465-2327
  Counties Represented: Big Delta, Buffalo          Dist: (907) 465-8161
  Soapstone, Chena Ridge, Chickaloon, College       Fax: (907) 465-5241
  (part), Delta Junction, Deltana, Ester (part), Eureka  Dist: (907) 465-8163
  Roadhouse, Farm Loop (part), Fishhook (part), Fort Greely, Glacier
  View, Glennallen, Goldstream (part), Harding-Birch Lakes, Lake
  Louise, Lakes (part), Mendeltna, Nelchina, Paxson (part), Salcha (part),
  South Van Horn (part), Sutton-Alpine, Tanaina (part), Tolsona, Valdez,
  Whitestone, Willow Creek
  Term Expires: 2019
  1292 Sadler Way, Suite 308, Fairbanks, AK 99701
  E-mail: senator.click.bishop@akleg.gov
  Committees: Armed Services; Community and Regional Affairs;
  Energy; Finance; Legislative Budget and Audit; Transportation
Senator **John B. Coghill, Jr.** (R-District A) . . . . . . . . . . . . (907) 465-3719
  Counties Represented: Badger (part), College (part),  Res: (907) 488-1546
  Eielson AFB, Farmers Loop, Fox, Goldstream         Fax: (907) 465-3258
  (part), Moose Creek, North Pole, Pleasant Valley,  Res: (907) 488-4271
  Salcha (part), Steele Creek (part), Two Rivers
  Term Expires: 2017
  301 Santa Claus Lane, North Pole, AK 99705
  E-mail: senator.john.coghill@akleg.gov
  Committees: Armed Services; Judiciary; Legislative Council;
  Resources; Rules; State Affairs
Senator **Mia Costello** (R-District K) . . . . . . . . . . . . . . . . . (907) 465-4968
  Counties Represented: Anchorage Municipality       Fax: (907) 465-2040
  (part)
  Term Expires: 2019
  E-mail: senator.mia.costello@akleg.gov
  Committees: Administrative Regulation Review; Judiciary; Labor and
  Commerce; Resources
  Education: Harvard 1990 BA
Senator **Mike J. Dunleavy** (R-District E) . . . . . . . . . . . . . (907) 465-6600
  Counties Represented: Big Lake, Knik-Fairview      Dist: (907) 376-3370
  (part), Lakes (part), Meadow Lakes (part), Point   Fax: (907) 465-3805
  MacKenzie, Susitna (part), Tanaina (part), Wasilla  Dist: (907) 376-3157
  (part)
  Term Expires: 2019
  600 East Railroad Avenue, Wasilla, AK 99654
  E-mail: sen.mike.dunleavy@akleg.gov
  Committees: Education; Finance; Transportation
  Education: Col Misericordia 1983 BA; Alaska (Fairbanks) 1992 MEd
Senator **Dennis Egan** (D-District Q) . . . . . . . . . . . . . . . . . (907) 465-4947
  Counties Represented: Angoon, Coffman Cove,        Fax: (907) 465-2108
  Covenant Life, Craig, Edna Bay, Elfin Cove, Game Creek, Haines,
  Hollis, Hoonah, Hydaburg, Hyder, Kake, Kasaan, Ketchikan, Klawock,
  Klukwan, Loring, Lutak, Metlakatla, Mosquito Lake, Mud Bay, Naukati
  Bay, Pelican, Point Baker, Port Alexander, Port Protection, Saxman,
  Sitka City and Borough, Thorne Bay, Whale Pass, Whitestone Logging
  Camp, Wrangell City and Borough
  Term Expires: 2019
  E-mail: senator.dennis.egan@akleg.gov
  Committees: Community and Regional Affairs; Energy; Select
  Committee on Legislative Ethics; Transportation

Senator **Johnny Ellis** (D-District I) . . . . . . . . . . . . . . . . . (907) 465-3704
  Counties Represented: Anchorage Municipality       Dist: (907) 269-0169
  (part)                                             Fax: (907) 465-2529
  Term Expires: 2017                                 Dist: (907) 269-0172
  716 West 4th Avenue, Anchorage, AK 99501-2133
  E-mail: senator.johnny.ellis@akleg.gov
  Committees: Health and Social Services; Labor and Commerce
  Education: Claremont McKenna 1982 BA
Senator **Berta Gardner** (D-District I) . . . . . . . . . . . . . . . . (907) 465-4930
  Counties Represented: Anchorage Municipality       Dist: (907) 269-0174
  (part)                                             Fax: (907) 465-3834
  Term Expires: 2019                                 Dist: (907) 269-0177
  716 West 4th Avenue, Suite 340, Anchorage, AK 99501-2133
  E-mail: senator.berta.gardner@akleg.gov
  Committees: Administrative Regulation Review; Education; Rules;
  Select Committee on Legislative Ethics; World Trade
Senator **Catherine Giessel, ANP, FAANP** (R-District N) . . (907) 465-4843
  Counties Represented: Anchorage Municipality       Dist: (907) 269-0181
  (part), Bear Creek, Cooper Landing, Crown Point,   Fax: (907) 269-0184
  Hope, Lowell Point, Moose Pass, Nikiski, Point Possession, Primrose,
  Ridgeway (part), Salamatof, Seward, Sterling, Sunrise
  Term Expires: 2019
  716 West 4th Avenue, Anchorage, AK 99501-2133
  E-mail: senator.gathy.giessel@akleg.gov
  Committees: Arctic Policy; Education; Health and Social Services;
  Labor and Commerce; Legislative Budget and Audit; Resources
Senator **Lyman F. Hoffman** (D-District S) Room 518 . . . . (907) 465-4453
  Counties Represented: Adak, Akutan, Alakanuk,      Fax: (907) 465-4523
  Anderson, Atka, Attu Station, Bethel, Cantwell, Chevak, Chignik,
  Chignik Lagoon, Chignik Lake, Clark's Point, Cold Bay, Eek, Egegik,
  Emmonak, Ester (part), False Pass, Ferry, Four Mile Road, Goldstream
  (part), Goodnews Bay, Grayling, Healy, Hooper Bay, Ivanof Bay, King
  Cove, Kotlik, Lake Minchumina, Manley Hot Springs, Marshall,
  McGrath, McKinley Park, Mekoryuk, Minto, Mountain Village, Nelson
  Lagoon, Nenana, Nikolai, Nikolski, Nunam Iqua, Perryville, Pilot Point,
  Pilot Station, Pitkas Point, Platinum, Port Heiden, Portage Creek,
  Quinhagak, Ruby, Sand Point, Scammon Bay, St. George, St. Mary's,
  St. Paul, Takotna, Tanana, Togiak, Twin Hills, Ugashik, Unalaska
  Term Expires: 2019
  E-mail: senator.lyman.hoffman@akleg.gov
  Committees: Arctic Policy; Community and Regional Affairs; Energy;
  Finance; Legislative Budget and Audit; Legislative Council; World
  Trade
Senator **Charles R. "Charlie" Huggins, USA (Ret)**
  (R-District E) . . . . . . . . . . . . . . . . . . . . . . . . . . . . . . . . (907) 465-3878
  Counties Represented: Big Lake, Knik-Fairview      Dist: (907) 376-4866
  (part), Lakes (part), Meadow Lakes (part), Point   Fax: (907) 465-3265
  MacKenzie, Susitna (part), Tanaina (part), Wasilla  Dist: (907) 373-4724
  (part)
  Term Expires: 2017
  600 East Railroad Avenue, Wasilla, AK 99654
  E-mail: senator.charlie.huggins@akleg.gov
  Committees: Education; Legislative Council; Rules; State Affairs;
  World Trade
  Education: Florida State 1969 BA; Webster 1980 MA
Senator **Pete Kelly** (R-District A) . . . . . . . . . . . . . . . . . . (907) 465-3709
  Counties Represented: Badger (part), College (part),  Dist: (907) 451-4347
  Eielson AFB, Farmers Loop, Fox, Goldstream         Fax: (907) 465-4714
  (part), Moose Creek, North Pole, Pleasant Valley,  Dist: (907) 451-4348
  Salcha (part), Steele Creek (part), Two Rivers
  Term Expires: 2019
  1292 Sadler Way, Fairbanks, AK 99701
  E-mail: senator.pete.kelly@akleg.gov
  Committees: Armed Services; Finance; Health and Social Services;
  Rules
  Education: Liberty 1996 BBA
Senator **Anna I. MacKinnon** (R-District G) . . . . . . . . . . . (907) 465-3777
  Counties Represented: Anchorage Municipality       Dist: (907) 694-8944
  (part)                                             Fax: (907) 465-2819
  Term Expires: 2019                                 Dist: (907) 694-1015
  12641 Old Glenn Highway, Eagle River, AK 99577
  E-mail: senator.anna.mackinnon@akleg.gov
  Committees: Armed Services; Community and Regional Affairs;
  Finance; Legislative Budget and Audit; Legislative Council
Senator **Lesil L. McGuire** (R-District K) . . . . . . . . . . . . . (907) 465-2995
  Counties Represented: Anchorage Municipality       Dist: (907) 269-0250
  (part)                                             Fax: (907) 465-6592
  Term Expires: 2017                                 Dist: (907) 269-0249
  716 West 4th Avenue, Anchorage, AK 99501-2133
  E-mail: senator.lesil.mcguire@akleg.gov
  Committees: Administrative Regulation Review; Arctic Policy;
  Judiciary; State Affairs; World Trade
  Education: Willamette 1993 BA, 1998 JD

*(continued on next page)*

**Senators** *continued*

Senator **Kevin Meyer** (R-District M) . . . . . . . . . . . . . . . . . . (907) 465-4945
Counties Represented: Anchorage Municipality    Dist: (907) 269-0199
(part)    Fax: (907) 465-3476
Term Expires: 2019    Dist: (907) 269-0197
716 West 4th Avenue, Anchorage, AK 99501-2133
E-mail: senator.kevin.meyer@akleg.gov
Committees: Labor and Commerce; Legislative Council; Rules; World
Trade

Senator **Peter A. Micciche** (R-District O) . . . . . . . . . . . . . . (907) 465-2828
Counties Represented: Anchor Point, Clam Gulch,    Dist: (907) 283-7996
Cohoe, Diamond Ridge, Fox River, Fritz Creek,    Fax: (907) 465-4779
Funny River, Halibut Cove, Happy Valley, Homer,    Dist: (907) 283-3075
Kachemak, Kalifornsky, Kasilof, Kenai, Nikolaevsk, Ninilchik,
Ridgeway (part), Seldovia, Seldovia Village, Soldotna
Term Expires: 2019
145 Main Street Loop, Suite 217, Kenai, AK 99611
E-mail: senator.peter.micciche@akleg.gov
Committees: Energy; Finance; Judiciary; Legislative Council;
Resources; Select Committee on Legislative Ethics; Transportation;
World Trade
Education: Alaska Pacific 2004 BA

Senator **Donald "Donny" Olson** (D-District T) . . . . . . . . . (907) 465-3707
Counties Represented: Alatna, Alcan Border,    Dist: (907) 269-0254
Allakaket, Ambler, Anaktuvuk Pass, Arctic Village,    Fax: (907) 465-4821
Atqasuk, Barrow, Beaver, Bettles, Birch Creek,    Dist: (907) 269-2031
Brevig Mission, Buckland, Central, Chalkyitsik, Chicken, Chisana,
Chistochina, Chitina, Circle, Coldfoot, Copper Center, Deering,
Diomede, Dot Lake, Dot Lake Village, Dry Creek, Eagle, Eagle
Village, Elim, Evansville, Fort Yukon, Gakona, Galena, Gambell,
Golovin, Gulkana, Healy Lake, Hughes, Huslia, Kaktovik, Kaltag,
Kenny Lake, Kiana, Kivalina, Kobuk, Kotzebue, Koyuk, Koyukuk,
Livengood, McCarthy, Mentasta Lake, Nabesna, New Allakaket,
Noatak, Nome, Noorvik, Northway, Northway Junction, Northway
Village, Nuiqsut, Nulato, Paxson (part), Point Hope, Point Lay, Port
Clarence, Prudhoe Bay, Rampart, Red Dog Mine, Savoonga, Selawik,
Shaktoolik, Shishmaref, Shungnak, Silver Springs, Slana, St. Michael,
Stebbins, Stevens Village, Tanacross, Tazlina, Teller, Tetlin, Tok,
Unalakleet, Venetie, Wainwright, Wales, White Mountain, Wiseman
Term Expires: 2019
716 West 4th Avenue, Suite 560, Anchorage, AK 99501-2133
E-mail: senator.donny.plson@akleg.gov
Committees: Arctic Policy; Finance
Education: Minnesota (Duluth) BA; Oral Roberts MD

Senator **Bert Stedman** (R-District Q) . . . . . . . . . . . . . . . . . . (907) 465-3873
Counties Represented: Angoon, Coffman Cove,    Dist: (907) 225-8088
Covenant Life, Craig, Edna Bay, Elfin Cove,    Fax: (907) 465-3922
Game Creek, Haines, Hollis, Hoonah, Hydaburg,    Dist: (907) 225-0713
Hyder, Kake, Kasaan, Ketchikan, Klawock, Klukwan, Loring, Lutak,
Metlakatla, Mosquito Lake, Mud Bay, Naukati Bay, Pelican,
Point Baker, Port Alexander, Port Protection, Saxman, Sitka City
and Borough, Thorne Bay, Whale Pass, Whitestone Logging Camp,
Wrangell City and Borough
Term Expires: 2017
1900 First Avenue, Suite 310, Ketchikan, AK 99901
E-mail: senator.bert.stedman@akleg.gov
Committees: Community and Regional Affairs; Energy; Health
and Social Services; Legislative Budget and Audit; Resources;
Transportation
Education: Oregon 1985 BS

Senator **Gary Lee Stevens, USA** (R-District P) . . . . . . . . . (907) 465-4925
Counties Represented: Excursion Inlet, Gustavus,    Dist: (907) 486-4925
Hobart Bay, Juneau City and Borough, Kupreanof,    Fax: (907) 465-3517
Petersburg, Skagway Municipality, Tenakee Springs    Dist: (907) 486-5264
Term Expires: 2019
305 Center Avenue, Kodiak, AK 99615
E-mail: senator.gary.stevens@akleg.gov
Committees: Arctic Policy; Education; Labor and Commerce;
Legislative Council; Select Committee on Legislative Ethics; World
Trade
Education: Linfield 1963 BA; Oregon 1965 MFA, 1984 PhD

Senator **Bill Stoltze** (R-District F) . . . . . . . . . . . . . . . . . . . (907) 465-4958
Counties Represented: Anchorage Municipality    Fax: (907) 465-4928
(part), Butte, Farm Loop (part), Gateway (part), Knik River,
Knik-Fairview (part), Lazy Mountain
Term Expires: 2019
E-mail: senator.bill.stoltze@akleg.gov
Committees: Health and Social Services; Resources; State Affairs
Education: Alaska (Fairbanks) 1984 BA

Senator **Bill Wielechowski** (D-District G) . . . . . . . . . . . . . (907) 465-2435
Counties Represented: Anchorage Municipality    Dist: (907) 269-0120
(part)    Fax: (907) 465-6615
Term Expires: 2017    Dist: (907) 269-0122
716 West 4th Avenue, Anchorage, AK 99501-2133
E-mail: senator.bill.wielechowski@akleg.gov
Committees: Armed Services; Judiciary; Resources; State Affairs
Education: Seton Hall 1989 BS, 1992 JD

# Senate Standing Committees

## Community and Regional Affairs
State Capitol, Room 105, Juneau, AK 99801-1182

| **Majority Members** | **Minority Members** |
|---|---|
| Clark "Click" Bishop (R-C) *Chair* | Dennis Egan (D-Q) |
| Bert Stedman (R-Q) *Vice Chair* | Lyman F. Hoffman (D-S) |
| Anna I. MacKinnon (R-G) | |

## Education
State Capitol, Room 105, Juneau, AK 99801-1182

| **Majority Members** | **Minority Members** |
|---|---|
| Mike J. Dunleavy (R-E) *Chair* | Berta Gardner (D-I) |
| Charles R. "Charlie" Huggins (R-E) *Vice Chair* | |
| Catherine Giessel (R-N) | |
| Gary Lee Stevens (R-P) | |

## Finance
State Capitol, Room 532, Juneau, AK 99801-1182

| **Majority Members** | **Minority Members** |
|---|---|
| Pete Kelly (R-A) *Co-Chair* | Lyman F. Hoffman (D-S) |
| Anna I. MacKinnon (R-G) *Co-Chair* | Donald "Donny" Olson (D-T) |
| Peter A. Micciche (R-O) *Vice Chair* | |
| Clark "Click" Bishop (R-C) | |
| Mike J. Dunleavy (R-E) | |

## Health and Social Services
State Capitol, Room 205, Juneau, AK 99801-1182

| **Majority Members** | **Minority Members** |
|---|---|
| Bert Stedman (R-Q) *Chair* | Johnny Ellis (D-I) |
| Catherine Giessel (R-N) *Vice Chair* | |
| Pete Kelly (R-A) | |
| Bill Stoltze (R-F) | |

## Judiciary
State Capitol, Room 105, Juneau, AK 99801-1182

| **Majority Members** | **Minority Members** |
|---|---|
| Lesil L. McGuire (R-K) *Chair* | Bill Wielechowski (D-G) |
| John B. Coghill, Jr. (R-A) *Vice Chair* | |
| Mia Costello (R-K) | |
| Peter A. Micciche (R-O) | |

## Labor and Commerce
State Capitol, Room 105, Juneau, AK 99801-1182

| **Majority Members** | **Minority Members** |
|---|---|
| Mia Costello (R-K) *Chair* | Johnny Ellis (D-I) |
| Catherine Giessel (R-N) *Vice Chair* | |
| Kevin Meyer (R-M) | |
| Gary Lee Stevens (R-P) | |

## Resources
State Capitol, Room 205, Juneau, AK 99801-1182

| **Majority Members** | **Minority Members** |
|---|---|
| Catherine Giessel (R-N) *Chair* | Bill Wielechowski (D-G) |
| Mia Costello (R-K) *Vice Chair* | |
| John B. Coghill, Jr. (R-A) | |
| Peter A. Micciche (R-O) | |
| Bert Stedman (R-Q) | |
| Bill Stoltze (R-F) | |

# Rules

State Capitol, Room 203, Juneau, AK 99801-1182

| **Majority Members** | **Minority Members** |
|---|---|
| Charles R. "Charlie" Huggins (R-E) | Berta Gardner (D-I) |
| *Chair* | |
| John B. Coghill, Jr. (R-A) | |
| *Vice Chair* | |
| Pete Kelly (R-A) | |
| Kevin Meyer (R-M) | |

# State Affairs

State Capitol, Room 205, Juneau, AK 99801-1182

| **Majority Members** | **Minority Members** |
|---|---|
| Bill Stoltze (R-F) *Chair* | Bill Wielechowski (D-G) |
| John B. Coghill, Jr. (R-A) | |
| *Vice Chair* | |
| Charles R. "Charlie" Huggins (R-E) | |
| Lesil L. McGuire (R-K) | |

# Transportation

State Capitol, Room 205, Juneau, AK 99801-1182

| **Majority Members** | **Minority Members** |
|---|---|
| Peter A. Micciche (R-O) *Chair* | Dennis Egan (D-Q) |
| Clark "Click" Bishop (R-C) | |
| *Vice Chair* | |
| Mike J. Dunleavy (R-E) | |
| Bert Stedman (R-Q) | |

# Alaska House of Representatives

Tel: (907) 465-3725  Fax: (907) 465-5334

Speaker of the House **Charles M. "Mike" Chenault** (R) . . (907) 465-3779
Majority Leader **Charisse E. Millett** (R) . . . . . . . . . . . . . . (907) 465-3879
Majority Whip **Bob Herron** (D) . . . . . . . . . . . . . . . . . . . . . (907) 465-4942
Minority Leader **Chris S. Tuck** (D) . . . . . . . . . . . . . . . . . . (907) 465-2095
Minority Whip **Sam Kito III** (D) . . . . . . . . . . . . . . . . . . . . (907) 465-4766
  Education: Alaska BSCE
Chief Clerk **Crys Jones** . . . . . . . . . . . . . . . . . . . . . . . . . . . (907) 465-3725
  E-mail: crystaline.jones@akleg.gov
Sergeant-at-Arms **Micaela Bradner** . . . . . . . . . . . . . . . . . . (907) 465-3869
  E-mail: micaela.bradner@akleg.gov

# Representatives

**Party Affiliation Statistics:** Republicans: 23, Democrats: 16,
Independents: 1

Representative
**Charles M. "Mike" Chenault** (R-District 29) . . . . . . . . . (907) 465-3779
Counties Represented: Kalifornsky (part), Kenai,     Dist: (907) 283-7223
Ridgeway (part), Soldotna     Fax: (907) 465-2833
Term Expires: 2017     Dist: (907) 283-7184
145 Main Street Loop, Kenai, AK 99611
E-mail: rep.mike.chenault@akleg.gov
Committees: Labor and Commerce; Legislative Council; Rules

Representative
**Matthew W. "Matt" Claman** (D-District 21) . . . . . . . . (907) 465-4919
Counties Represented: Anchorage Municipality     Fax: (907) 465-2137
(part)
Term Expires: 2017
E-mail: rep.matt.claman@akleg.gov
Committees: Energy; Judiciary; Transportation
Education: Colorado Col BA; Texas JD

Representative **Jim Colver** (R-District 9) . . . . . . . . . . . . . (907) 465-4859
Counties Represented: Knik-Fairview (part), Lakes     Fax: (907) 465-3799
(part), Meadow Lakes (part), Tanaina (part), Wasilla (part)
Term Expires: 2017
E-mail: rep.jim.colver@akleg.gov
Committees: Administrative Regulation Review; Education; Energy;
Labor and Commerce; Military and Veterans' Affairs

Representative **Harriet Drummond** (D-District 18) . . . . . . . (907) 465-3875
Counties Represented: Anchorage Municipality     Fax: (907) 465-4588
(part)
Term Expires: 2017
716 West 4th Avenue, Anchorage, AK 99501-2133
E-mail: rep.harriet.drummond@akleg.gov
Committees: Community and Regional Affairs; Education
Education: Cornell 1974 BS

Representative **Bryce Edgmon** (D-District 37) . . . . . . . . . . (907) 465-4451
Counties Represented: Adak, Akutan, Atka, Attu     Dist: (907) 269-0275
Station, Bethel, Chignik, Chignik Lagoon, Chignik     Fax: (907) 465-3445
Lake, Clark's Point, Cold Bay, Eek, Egegik, False     Dist: (907) 269-0274
Pass, Goodnews Bay, Ivanof Bay, King Cove, Mekoryuk, Nelson
Lagoon, Nikolski, Perryville, Pilot Point, Platinum, Port Heiden,
Portage Creek, Quinhagak, Sand Point, St. George, St. Paul, Togiak,
Twin Hills, Ugashik, Unalaska
Note: Democrat Bryce Edgmon caucused with the Republican majority
during the 2016 legislative session.
Term Expires: 2017
716 West 4th Avenue, Anchorage, AK 99501-2133
E-mail: rep.bryce.edgmon@akleg.gov
Committees: Finance
Education: Alaska BBA

Representative **Neal Foster** (D-District 39) . . . . . . . . . . . . (907) 465-3789
Counties Represented: Alatna, Alcan Border,     Dist: (907) 443-5036
Allakaket, Arctic Village, Beaver, Bettles, Birch     Fax: (907) 465-3242
Creek, Brevig Mission, Central, Chalkyitsik,     Dist: (907) 443-2162
Chicken, Chisana, Chistochina, Chitina, Circle, Coldfoot, Copper
Center, Diomede, Dot Lake, Dot Lake Village, Dry Creek, Eagle, Eagle
Village, Elim, Evansville, Fort Yukon, Gakona, Galena, Gambell,
Golovin, Gulkana, Healy Lake, Hughes, Huslia, Kaltag, Kenny Lake,
Koyuk, Koyukuk, Livengood, McCarthy, Mentasta Lake, Nabesna, New
Allakaket, Nome, Northway, Northway Junction, Northway Village,
Nulato, Paxson (part), Port Clarence, Rampart, Savoonga, Shaktoolik,
Shishmaref, Silver Springs, Slana, St. Michael, Stebbins, Stevens
Village, Tanacross, Tazlina, Teller, Tetlin, Tok, Unalakleet, Venetie,
Wales, White Mountain, Wiseman
Note: Democrat Neal Foster caucused with the Republican majority
during the 2016 legislative session.
Term Expires: 2017
103 East Front Street, Nome, AK 99762
E-mail: rep.neal.foster@akleg.gov
Committees: Fisheries; Health and Social Services; Judiciary;
Transportation
Education: Stanford 1994 BA; Alaska 1997 BBA

Representative **Les S. Gara** (D-District 20) . . . . . . . . . . . . . (907) 465-2647
Counties Represented: Anchorage Municipality     Dist: (907) 269-0106
(part)     Fax: (907) 465-3518
Term Expires: 2017     Dist: (907) 269-0109
716 West 4th Avenue, Anchorage, AK 99501-2133
E-mail: rep.les.gara@akleg.gov
Committees: Finance
Education: Boston U 1985 BA; Harvard 1988 JD

Representative **Lynn Gattis** (R-District 7) . . . . . . . . . . . . . . (907) 465-4833
Counties Represented: Chase, Fishhook (part),     Dist: (907) 373-6285
Houston, Lakes (part), Meadow Lakes (part),     Fax: (907) 465-4586
Petersville, Skwentna, Susitna (part), Susitna North,     Dist: (907) 373-6286
Talkeetna, Tanaina (part), Trapper Creek, Willow
Term Expires: 2017
600 East Railroad Avenue, Wasilla, AK 99654
E-mail: rep.lynn.gattis@akleg.gov
Committees: Finance

Representative **David Guttenberg** (D-District 4) . . . . . . . . (907) 465-4457
Counties Represented: College (part), Fairbanks     Dist: (907) 456-8172
(part), South Van Horn (part)     Fax: (907) 465-3519
Term Expires: 2017     Dist: (907) 456-2490
1292 Sadler Way, Fairbanks, AK 99701
E-mail: rep.david.guttenberg@akleg.gov
Committees: Finance

Representative **Mike Hawker, CPA** (R-District 28) . . . . . . . (907) 465-4949
Counties Represented: Bear Creek, Cooper Landing,     Dist: (907) 269-0244
Crown Point, Hope, Lowell Point, Moose Pass,     Fax: (907) 465-4979
Nikiski, Point Possession, Primrose, Ridgeway     Dist: (907) 269-0248
(part), Salamatof, Seward, Sterling, Sunrise
Term Expires: 2017
716 West 4th Avenue, Anchorage, AK 99501-2133
E-mail: rep.mike.hawker@akleg.gov
Committees: Administrative Regulation Review; Finance; Legislative
Budget and Audit; Legislative Council; Resources; Rules
Education: Northern Iowa 1979 BA

*(continued on next page)*

**Representatives** *continued*

Representative **Bob Herron** (D-District 38) . . . . . . . . . . . . . (907) 465-4942
Counties Represented: Alakanuk, Anderson,     Dist: (907) 543-5898
Cantwell, Chevak, Emmonak, Ester (part), Ferry,     Fax: (907) 465-4589
Four Mile Road, Goldstream, Grayling, Healy,     Dist: (907) 543-5892
Hooper Bay, Kotlik, Lake Minchumina, Manley Hot Springs, Marshall,
McGrath, McKinley Park, Minto, Mountain Village, Nenana, Nikolai,
Nunam Iqua, Pilot Station, Pitkas Point, Ruby, Scammon Bay, St.
Mary's, Takotna, Tanana
Note: Democrat Bob Herron caucused with the Republican majority
during the 2016 legislative session.
Term Expires: 2017
P.O. Box 886, Bethel, AK 99559
E-mail: rep.bob.herron@akleg.gov
Committees: Economic Development, Tourism, and Arctic Policy;
Fisheries; Legislative Council; Military and Veterans' Affairs;
Resources; Rules

Representative **Shelley Hughes** (R-District 11) . . . . . . . . . (907) 465-3743
Counties Represented: Anchorage Municipality     Dist: (907) 376-3725
(part), Butte, Farm Loop (part), Gateway (part),     Fax: (907) 465-2381
Knik River, Knik-Fairview (part), Lazy Mountain     Dist: (907) 376-4768
Term Expires: 2017
600 East Railroad Avenue, Wasilla, AK 99654
E-mail: rep.shelley.hughes@akleg.gov
Committees: Community and Regional Affairs; Labor and Commerce;
Military and Veterans' Affairs; Transportation
Education: Alaska 2002 BA

Representative **Craig W. Johnson** (R-District 24) . . . . . . . . (907) 465-4993
Counties Represented: Anchorage Municipality     Dist: (907) 269-0200
(part)     Fax: (907) 465-3872
Term Expires: 2017     Dist: (907) 269-0204
716 West 4th Avenue, Anchorage, AK 99501-2133
E-mail: rep.craig.johnson@akleg.gov
Committees: Economic Development, Tourism, and Arctic Policy;
Fisheries; Legislative Council; Resources; Rules

Representative
**Andrew L. "Andy" Josephson** (D-District 17) . . . . . . . . (907) 465-4939
Counties Represented: Anchorage Municipality     Dist: (907) 269-0265
(part)     Fax: (907) 465-2418
Term Expires: 2017     Dist: (907) 269-0264
716 West 4th Avenue, Anchorage, AK 99501-2133
E-mail: rep.andy.josephson@akleg.gov
Committees: Labor and Commerce; Resources; Select Committee on
Legislative Ethics

Representative **Scott J. Kawasaki** (D-District 1) . . . . . . . . (907) 465-3466
Counties Represented: Badger (part), Eielson     Dist: (907) 456-7423
AFB, Moose Creek, North Pole, Salcha (part)     Fax: (907) 465-2937
Term Expires: 2017     Dist: (907) 451-9293
1292 Sadler Way, Fairbanks, AK 99701
E-mail: rep.scott.kawasaki@akleg.gov
Committees: Finance
Education: Alaska (Fairbanks) 1999 BSChem

Representative **Wes Keller** (R-District 10) . . . . . . . . . . . . . (907) 465-2186
Counties Represented: Big Lake, Knik-Fairview     Dist: (907) 373-1842
(part), Meadow Lakes (part), Point MacKenzie,     Fax: (907) 465-3818
Susitna (part)     Dist: (907) 373-4729
Term Expires: 2017
600 East Railroad Avenue, Wasilla, AK 99654
E-mail: rep.wes.keller@akleg.gov
Committees: Armed Services; Education; Judiciary; State Affairs
Education: Wisconsin (Superior) 1986 BS

Representative **Sam Kito III** (D-District 33) . . . . . . . . . . . . (907) 465-4766
Counties Represented: Coffman Cove, Edna Bay,     Fax: (907) 465-4748
Hollis, Hyder, Ketchikan, Loring, Naukati Bay, Point Baker, Port
Protection, Saxman, Thorne Bay, Whale Pass, Wrangell City and
Borough
Term Expires: 2017
E-mail: rep.sam.kito.iii@akleg.gov
Committees: Labor and Commerce; Legislative Budget and Audit;
Legislative Council

Representative
**Jonathan Kreiss-Tomkins** (D-District 35) . . . . . . . . . . (907) 465-3732
Counties Represented: Akhiok, Aleneva, Chenega,     Fax: (907) 465-2652
Chiniak, Cordova, Karluk, Kodiak, Kodiak Station, Larsen Bay, Old
Harbor, Ouzinkie, Port Lions, Tatitlek, Whittier, Womens Bay, Yakutat
City and Borough
Term Expires: 2017
Juneau, AK 99801
E-mail: rep.jonathan.kreiss-tomkins@akleg.gov
Committees: Fisheries; Judiciary; Rules; State Affairs
Education: Yale 2012

Representative **Gabrielle LeDoux** (R-District 15) . . . . . . . . .(907) 465-4998
Counties Represented: Anchorage Municipality     Fax: (907) 465-4419
(part)
Term Expires: 2017
716 West 4th Avenue, Anchorage, AK 99501-2133
E-mail: rep.gabrielle.ledoux@akleg.gov
Committees: Armed Services; Judiciary; Labor and Commerce;
Military and Veterans' Affairs
Education: UC Berkeley 1970 BA; Boalt Hall 1973 JD

Representative **Bob Lynn, USAF (Ret)** (R-District 26) . . . . (907) 465-4931
Counties Represented: Anchorage Municipality     Dist: (907) 269-0205
(part)     Fax: (907) 465-4316
Term Expires: 2017     Dist: (907) 269-0207
716 West 4th Avenue, Anchorage, AK 99501-2133
E-mail: rep.bob.lynn@akleg.gov
Committees: Armed Services; Judiciary; Military and Veterans' Affairs;
State Affairs
Education: Arizona BA; Cal State (Long Beach) MA

Representative **Charisse E. Millett** (R-District 25) . . . . . . . . (907) 465-3879
Counties Represented: Anchorage Municipality     Dist: (907) 269-0222
(part)     Fax: (907) 465-2069
Term Expires: 2017     Dist: (907) 269-0223
716 West 4th Avenue, Anchorage, AK 99501-2133
E-mail: rep.charisse.millett@akleg.gov
Committees: Economic Development, Tourism, and Arctic Policy;
Fisheries; Judiciary; Legislative Council; Select Committee on
Legislative Ethics; Transportation

Representative **Cathy Engstrom Muñoz** (R-District 34) . . . (907) 465-3744
Counties Represented: Angoon, Covenant Life,     Fax: (907) 465-2273
Craig, Elfin Cove, Game Creek, Haines, Hoonah, Hydaburg, Kake,
Kasaan, Klawock, Klukwan, Lutak, Metlakatla, Mosquito Lake, Mud
Bay, Pelican, Port Alexander, Sitka City and Borough, Whitestone
Logging Camp
Term Expires: 2017
E-mail: rep.cathy.munoz@akleg.gov
Committees: Finance
Education: U Pacific BA

Representative
**Benjamin P. "Ben" Nageak** (D-District 40) . . . . . . . . . . (907) 465-3473
Counties Represented: Ambler, Anaktuvuk Pass,     Fax: (907) 465-2827
Atqasuk, Barrow, Buckland, Deering, Kaktovik, Kiana, Kivalina,
Kobuk, Kotzebue, Noatak, Noorvik, Nuiqsut, Point Hope, Point Lay,
Prudhoe Bay, Red Dog Mine, Selawik, Shungnak, Wainwright
Note: Democrat Ben Nageak caucused with the Republican majority
during the 2016 legislative session.
Term Expires: 2017
State Capitol, Room 428, Juneau, AK 99801
E-mail: rep.benjamin.nageak@akleg.gov
Committees: Community and Regional Affairs; Energy; Resources;
Transportation

Representative **Mark A. Neuman** (R-District 8) . . . . . . . . . . (907) 465-2679
Counties Represented: Farm Loop (part), Fishhook     Dist: (907) 376-2679
(part), Gateway (part), Knik-Fairview (part), Lakes     Fax: (907) 465-4822
(part), Palmer, Wasilla (part)     Dist: (907) 373-4745
Term Expires: 2017
600 East Railroad Avenue, Wasilla, AK 99654
E-mail: rep.mark.neuman@akleg.gov
Committees: Finance; Legislative Budget and Audit; Legislative
Council

Representative **Kurt E. Olson** (R-District 30) . . . . . . . . . . . . (907) 465-2693
Counties Represented: Anchor Point, Clam Gulch,     Dist: (907) 283-2690
Cohoe, Diamond Ridge, Fox River, Fritz Creek,     Fax: (907) 465-3835
Funny River, Halibut Cove, Happy Valley, Homer,     Dist: (907) 283-2763
Kachemak, Kalifornsky (part), Kasilof, Nikolaevsk, Ninilchik, Seldovia,
Seldovia Village
Term Expires: 2017
145 Main Street Loop, Kenai, AK 99611
E-mail: rep.kurt.olson@akleg.gov
Committees: Labor and Commerce; Legislative Budget and Audit;
Resources; Rules
Education: Cal State (Long Beach) 1977 BA

Representative **Daniel H. Ortiz** (I-District 36) . . . . . . . . . . (907) 465-3824
Counties Represented: Akiachak, Akiak, Aleknagik,    Fax: (907) 465-3175
Aniak, Anvik, Atmautluak, Beluga, Chefornak, Chuathbaluk, Crooked
Creek, Dillingham, Ekwok, Flat, Holy Cross, Igiugig, Iliamna,
Kasigluk, King Salmon, Kipnuk, Kokhanok, Koliganek, Kongiganak,
Kwethluk, Kwigillingok, Levelock, Lime Village, Lower Kalskag,
Manokotak, Mertarvik, Naknek, Nanwalek, Napakiak, Napaskiak, New
Stuyahok, Newhalen, Newtok, Nightmute, Nondalton, Nunapitchuk,
Oscarville, Pedro Bay, Pope-Vannoy Landing, Port Alsworth, Port
Graham, Red Devil, Russian Mission, Shageluk, Sleetmute, South
Naknek, Stony River, Toksook Bay, Tuluksak, Tuntutuliak, Tununak,
Tyonek, Upper Kalskag
Note: Representative Daniel Ortiz caucused with the Democratic Party
during the 2016 legislative session.
Term Expires: 2017
E-mail: rep.dan.ortiz@akleg.gov
Committees: Community and Regional Affairs; Economic
Development, Tourism, and Arctic Policy; Fisheries; Transportation

Representative **Lance Pruitt** (R-District 27) . . . . . . . . . . . (907) 465-3438
Counties Represented: Anchorage Municipality    Dist: (907) 269-0100
(part)    Fax: (907) 465-4565
Term Expires: 2017    Dist: (907) 269-0105
716 West 4th Avenue, Anchorage, AK 99501-2133
E-mail: rep.lance.pruitt@akleg.gov
Committees: Finance; Legislative Budget and Audit

Representative **Lora Reinbold** (R-District 14) . . . . . . . . . . (907) 465-3822
Counties Represented: Anchorage Municipality    Dist: (907) 622-8950
(part)    Fax: (907) 465-3756
Term Expires: 2017    Dist: (907) 694-1015
12641 Old Glenn Highway, Eagle River, AK 99577
E-mail: rep.lora.reinbold@akleg.gov
Committees: Community and Regional Affairs
Education: Alaska (Attended); Oral Roberts 1987 BSBA

Representative **Dan Saddler** (R-District 13) . . . . . . . . . . . . (907) 465-3783
Counties Represented: Anchorage Municipality    Dist: (907) 622-3783
(part)    Fax: (907) 465-2293
Term Expires: 2017    Dist: (907) 622-3784
10928 Eagle River Road, Eagle River, AK 99577
E-mail: rep.dan.saddler@akleg.gov
Committees: Armed Services; Finance
Education: Miami U (OH) 1983 BA; Ohio State 1987 MA

Representative **Paul Seaton** (R-District 31) . . . . . . . . . . . . (907) 465-2689
Counties Represented: Juneau City and Borough    Dist: (907) 235-2921
(part)    Fax: (907) 465-3472
Term Expires: 2017    Dist: (907) 235-4008
345 West Sterling Highway, Homer, AK 99603
E-mail: rep.paul.seaton@akleg.gov
Committees: Community and Regional Affairs; Education; Health and
Social Services; Resources
Education: Alaska (Fairbanks) 1968 BS, 1969 MAT;
San Diego State 1972 MS

Representative **Ivy Spohnholz** (D-District 16) . . . . . . . . . . (907) 465-4940
Counties Represented: Anchorage Municipality    Fax: (907) 465-3766
(part)
Term Expires: 2017
E-mail: rep.ivy.spohnholz@akleg.gov
Committees: Education; Military and Veterans' Affairs; State Affairs
Education: U Washington 1997 BA, 2014 MPA

Representative **Louise B. Stutes** (R-District 32) . . . . . . . . (907) 465-2487
Counties Represented: Excursion Inlet, Gustavus,    Fax: (907) 465-4956
Hobart Bay, Juneau City and Borough (part), Kupreanof, Petersburg,
Skagway Municipality, Tenakee Springs
Term Expires: 2017
E-mail: rep.louise.stutes@akleg.gov
Committees: Economic Development, Tourism, and Arctic Policy;
Fisheries; Health and Social Services; State Affairs; Transportation

Representative **David Talerico** (R-District 6) . . . . . . . . . . . . (907) 465-4527
Counties Represented: Big Delta, Buffalo    Fax: (907) 465-2197
Soapstone, Chickaloon, Delta Junction, Deltana, Eureka Roadhouse,
Farm Loop (part), Fishhook (part), Fort Greely, Glacier View,
Glennallen, Lake Louise, Lakes (part), Mendeltna, Nelchina, Paxson
(part), Sutton-Alpine, Tanaina (part), Tolsona, Valdez, Whitestone,
Willow Creek
Term Expires: 2017
E-mail: rep.david.talerico@akleg.gov
Committees: Education; Energy; Health and Social Services;
Resources; State Affairs

Representative **Geran Tarr** (D-District 19) . . . . . . . . . . . . . (907) 465-3424
Counties Represented: Anchorage Municipality    Dist: (907) 269-0144
(part)    Fax: (907) 465-3793
Term Expires: 2017    Dist: (907) 269-0148
716 West 4th Avenue, Anchorage, AK 99501-2133
E-mail: rep.geran.tarr@akleg.gov
Committees: Armed Services; Health and Social Services; Resources

Representative **Steve M. Thompson** (R-District 2) . . . . . . . (907) 465-3004
Counties Represented: Badger (part), College    Dist: (907) 452-1088
(part), Farmers Loop, Fox, Goldstream (part),    Fax: (907) 465-2070
Pleasant Valley, Steele Creek (part), Two Rivers    Dist: (907) 452-1146
Term Expires: 2017
1292 Sadler Way, Fairbanks, AK 99701
E-mail: rep.steve.thompson@akleg.gov
Committees: Finance; Legislative Budget and Audit; Legislative
Council

Representative **Cathy Tilton** (R-District 12) . . . . . . . . . . . . (907) 465-2199
Counties Represented: Anchorage Municipality    Fax: (907) 465-4587
(part)
Term Expires: 2017
E-mail: rep.cathy.tilton@akleg.gov
Committees: Community and Regional Affairs; Economic
Development, Tourism, and Arctic Policy; Energy; Labor and
Commerce

Representative **Chris S. Tuck** (D-District 23) . . . . . . . . . . . (907) 465-2095
Counties Represented: Anchorage Municipality    Dist: (907) 269-0240
(part)    Fax: (907) 465-3810
Term Expires: 2017    Dist: (907) 269-0242
716 West 4th Avenue, Anchorage, AK 99501-2133
E-mail: rep.chris.tuck@akleg.gov
Committees: Military and Veterans' Affairs; Rules; Select Committee
on Legislative Ethics

Representative **Liz Vazquez** (R-District 22) . . . . . . . . . . . . (907) 465-3892
Counties Represented: Anchorage Municipality    Fax: (907) 465-6595
(part)
Term Expires: 2017
E-mail: rep.liz.vazquez@akleg.gov
Committees: Education; Energy; Health and Social Services; Select
Committee on Legislative Ethics; State Affairs

Representative **Tammie Wilson** (R-District 3) . . . . . . . . . . . (907) 465-4797
Counties Represented: Badger (part), Fairbanks    Dist: (907) 488-0857
(part), Steele Creek (part)    Fax: (907) 465-3884
Term Expires: 2017    Dist: (907) 488-4271
301 Santa Claus Lane, North Pole, AK 99705
E-mail: rep.tammie.wilson@akleg.gov
Committees: Finance
Education: Illinois State 1983 BS

Representative **Adam Wool** (D-District 5) . . . . . . . . . . . . . (907) 465-4976
Counties Represented: Chena Ridge, College (part),    Fax: (907) 465-3883
Ester (part), Goldstream (part), Harding-Birch Lakes, Salcha (part),
South Van Horn (part)
Term Expires: 2017
E-mail: rep.adam.wool@akleg.gov
Committees: Administrative Regulation Review; Economic
Development, Tourism, and Arctic Policy; Energy; Health and Social
Services

# House Standing Committees
## Community and Regional Affairs

**Majority Members**    **Minority Members**
Cathy Tilton (R-12) *Chair*    Harriet Drummond (D-18)
Paul Seaton (R-31) *Vice Chair*    Daniel H. Ortiz (I-36)
Shelley Hughes (R-11)
Benjamin P. "Ben" Nageak (D-40)
Lora Reinbold (R-14)

## Education

**Majority Members**    **Minority Members**
Wes Keller (R-10) *Chair*    Harriet Drummond (D-18)
Liz Vazquez (R-22) *Vice Chair*    Ivy Spohnholz (D-16)
Jim Colver (R-9)
Paul Seaton (R-31)
David Talerico (R-6)

## Finance

**Majority Members**
Mark A. Neuman (R-8) *Co-Chair*
Steve M. Thompson (R-2) *Co-Chair*
Dan Saddler (R-13) *Vice Chair*
Bryce Edgmon (D-37)
Lynn Gattis (R-7)
Cathy Engstrom Muñoz (R-34)
Lance Pruitt (R-27)
Tammie Wilson (R-3)
Mike Hawker (R-28) *Alternate*

**Minority Members**
Les S. Gara (D-20)
David Guttenberg (D-4)
Scott J. Kawasaki (D-1)

## Health and Social Services

**Majority Members**
Paul Seaton (R-31) *Chair*
Liz Vazquez (R-22) *Vice Chair*
Louise B. Stutes (R-32)
David Talerico (R-6)
Neal Foster (D-39)

**Minority Members**
Geran Tarr (D-19)
Adam Wool (D-5)

## Judiciary

**Majority Members**
Gabrielle LeDoux (R-15) *Chair*
Wes Keller (R-10) *Vice Chair*
Bob Lynn (R-26)
Charisse E. Millett (R-25)
Neal Foster (D-39)

**Minority Members**
Matthew W. "Matt" Claman (D-21)
Jonathan Kreiss-Tomkins (D-35)

## Labor and Commerce

**Majority Members**
Kurt E. Olson (R-30) *Chair*
Shelley Hughes (R-11) *Vice Chair*
Jim Colver (R-9)
Gabrielle LeDoux (R-15)
Cathy Tilton (R-12)
Charles M. "Mike" Chenault (R-29)
 *Alternate*

**Minority Members**
Andrew L. "Andy" Josephson
 (D-17)
Sam Kito III (D-33)

## Resources

**Majority Members**
Benjamin P. "Ben" Nageak (D-40)
 *Co-Chair*
David Talerico (R-6) *Co-Chair*
Mike Hawker (R-28) *Vice Chair*
Bob Herron (D-38)
Craig W. Johnson (R-24)
Kurt E. Olson (R-30)
Paul Seaton (R-31)

**Minority Members**
Andrew L. "Andy" Josephson
 (D-17)
Geran Tarr (D-19)

## Rules

**Majority Members**
Craig W. Johnson (R-24) *Chair*
Kurt E. Olson (R-30) *Vice Chair*
Charles M. "Mike" Chenault (R-29)
Mike Hawker (R-28)
Bob Herron (D-38)

**Minority Members**
Jonathan Kreiss-Tomkins (D-35)
Chris S. Tuck (D-23)

## State Affairs

**Majority Members**
Bob Lynn (R-26) *Chair*
Wes Keller (R-10) *Vice Chair*
Louise B. Stutes (R-32)
David Talerico (R-6)
Liz Vazquez (R-22)

**Minority Members**
Jonathan Kreiss-Tomkins (D-35)
Ivy Spohnholz (D-16)

## Transportation

**Majority Members**
Neal Foster (D-39) *Co-Chair*
Shelley Hughes (R-11) *Co-Chair*
Charisse E. Millett (R-25)
Benjamin P. "Ben" Nageak (D-40)
Louise B. Stutes (R-32)

**Minority Members**
Matthew W. "Matt" Claman (D-21)
Daniel H. Ortiz (I-36)

# American Samoa Legislature

American Samoa Government, Pago Pago, AS 96799
Tel: (684) 633-1781  Fax: (684) 633-1681

## American Samoa Senate

Tel: (684) 633-4565

President of the Senate **Gaoteote Palaie Tofau** (I) . . . . . . . (684) 633-4565
President Pro Tem **Nuanuaolefeagaiga Sao Luaga** (I) . . . (684) 633-4656
Secretary of the Senate **Leo'o Va'a Ma'o** . . . . . . . . . . . . . (684) 633-5866
Sergeant-at-Arms **Vaifale Akeli Alosio** . . . . . . . . . . . . . . . (684) 633-1621

## Senators

Senator **Mata'utia Lui Afonotele** (I-District 5) . . . . . . . . . (684) 633-5853
 Committees: Agriculture; Communication/Fisheries; Economic
 Development and Ways and Means; Government Operations; Hospital
 and Public Health; Judiciary; Parks and Recreation; Public Safety and
 Homeland Security; Public Works; Retirement; Samoan Affairs; Senate
 House Rules, Marine and Wildlife

Senator **Avegalio P. Aigamaua** (I-District 11) . . . . . . . . . . (684) 633-4568
 Committees: Agriculture; Budget and Appropriations;
 Communication/Fisheries; Economic Development and Ways and
 Means; Education; Government Operations; Hospital and Public Health;
 Parks and Recreation; Public Works; Retirement; Samoan Affairs;
 Transportation, Ports and Airport

Senator **Leatualevao S. Asifoa** (I-District 9) . . . . . . . . . . . (684) 633-4654
 Committees: Agriculture; Budget and Appropriations; Economic
 Development and Ways and Means; Energy Power and Water; Human
 Resources and Human Social Services; Public Safety and Homeland
 Security; Public Works; Retirement; Senate House Rules, Marine and
 Wildlife; Transportation, Ports and Airport

Senator **Fuiava Avaloa** (I-District 4) . . . . . . . . . . . . . . . . . (684) 633-5668
 Committees: Budget and Appropriations; Communication/Fisheries;
 Economic Development and Ways and Means; Education; Energy
 Power and Water; Government Operations; Hospital and Public Health;
 Human Resources and Human Social Services; Judiciary; Retirement;
 Transportation, Ports and Airport

Senator **Tuiasina Siolosega Esera** (I-District 10) . . . . . . . . (684) 633-5757
 Committees: Communication/Fisheries; Education; Energy Power and
 Water; Government Operations; Hospital and Public Health; Human
 Resources and Human Social Services; Judiciary; Parks and Recreation;
 Public Safety and Homeland Security; Retirement; Senate House Rules,
 Marine and Wildlife; Transportation, Ports and Airport

Senator **Alo Fa'au'uga** (I-District 7) . . . . . . . . . . . . . . . . . (684) 633-4553
 Committees: Budget and Appropriations; Economic Development
 and Ways and Means; Education; Government Operations; Human
 Resources and Human Social Services; Parks and Recreation; Public
 Safety and Homeland Security; Public Works; Retirement; Senate
 House Rules, Marine and Wildlife

Senator **Gaea Perefoti Failautusi** (I-District 8) . . . . . . . . . (684) 633-4057
 Committees: Human Resources and Human Social Services; Judiciary;
 Public Safety and Homeland Security; Retirement; Transportation, Ports
 and Airport

Senator **Tuaolo M. E. Fruean** (I-District 6) . . . . . . . . . . . . (684) 633-4947
 Committees: Budget and Appropriations; Energy Power and Water;
 Hospital and Public Health; Human Resources and Human Social
 Services; Judiciary; Samoan Affairs

Senator **Soliai Tuipine Fuimaono** (I-District 7) . . . . . . . . . (684) 633-5854
 Committees: Agriculture; Communication/Fisheries; Education; Energy
 Power and Water; Hospital and Public Health; Judiciary; Samoan
 Affairs

Senator **Magalei Logovi'i** (I-District 8) . . . . . . . . . . . . . . . (684) 633-5553
 Committees: Agriculture; Budget and Appropriations; Economic
 Development and Ways and Means; Energy Power and Water; Hospital
 and Public Health; Human Resources and Human Social Services;
 Retirement

Senator **Tialavea Misiualapa** (I-District 5) . . . . . . . . . . . . (684) 633-4869
 Committees: Agriculture; Communication/Fisheries; Judiciary; Samoan
 Affairs

Senator **Afoa Moega Lutu** (I-District 6) . . . . . . . . . . . . . . (684) 633-4759
 Committees: Agriculture; Communication/Fisheries; Parks and
 Recreation; Samoan Affairs; Transportation, Ports and Airport
 Education: Hawaii 1971 BA; Valparaiso 1974 JD

Senator **Uti Petelo** (I-District 6) . . . . . . . . . . . . . . . . . . . . (684) 633-5359

Senator **Nuanuaolefeagaiga Sao Luaga** (I-District 1) . . . . (684) 633-4656
 Counties Represented: Hawaii
 Committees: Human Resources and Human Social Services; Public
 Works; Retirement; Senate House Rules, Marine and Wildlife;
 Transportation, Ports and Airport

Senator **Gaoteote Palaie Tofau** (I-District 3) . . . . . . . . . . . (684) 633-4565
Senator **Galea'i Moali'itele Tu'ufuli** (I-District 1) . . . . . . . . (684) 633-5453
  Counties Represented: Hawaii
  Committees: Budget and Appropriations; Economic Development and
  Ways and Means; Energy Power and Water; Government Operations;
  Public Safety and Homeland Security; Retirement
Senator **Faletagoa'i I. Tuiolemotu** (I-District 12) . . . . . . . (684) 633-4457
  Committees: Communication/Fisheries; Education; Government
  Operations; Judiciary; Parks and Recreation; Public Safety and
  Homeland Security; Public Works; Retirement; Samoan Affairs; Senate
  House Rules, Marine and Wildlife
Senator **Laolagi Fonoti Savali Vaeao** (I-District 2) . . . . . . (684) 633-5663
  Committees: Budget and Appropriations; Economic Development and
  Ways and Means; Education; Energy Power and Water; Government
  Operations; Human Resources and Human Social Services; Parks and
  Recreation; Public Safety and Homeland Security; Public Works;
  Retirement; Senate House Rules, Marine and Wildlife

## Senate Standing Committees
Tel: (684) 633-5866

### Agriculture
**Members**
Leatualevao S. Asifoa (I-9) *Chairman*
Mata'utia Lui Afonotele (I-5) *Vice Chairman*
Avegalio P. Aigamaua (I-11)
Soliai Tuipine Fuimaono (I-7)
Magalei Logovi'i (I-8)
Afoa Moega Lutu (I-6)
Tialavea Misiualapa (I-5)

### Budget and Appropriations
**Members**
Laolagi Fonoti Savali Vaeao (I-2) *Chairman*
Magalei Logovi'i (I-8) *Vice Chairman*
Avegalio P. Aigamaua (I-11)
Leatualevao S. Asifoa (I-9)
Fuiava Avaloa (I-4)
Alo Fa'au'uga (I-7)
Tuaolo M. E. Fruean (I-6)
Galea'i Moali'itele Tu'ufuli (I-1)

### Communication/Fisheries
**Members**
Afoa Moega Lutu (I-6) *Chairman*
Faletagoa'i I. Tuiolemotu (I-12) *Vice Chairman*
Mata'utia Lui Afonotele (I-5)
Avegalio P. Aigamaua (I-11)
Fuiava Avaloa (I-4)
Tuiasina Siolosega Esera (I-10)
Soliai Tuipine Fuimaono (I-7)
Tialavea Misiualapa (I-5)

### Economic Development and Ways and Means
**Members**
Fuiava Avaloa (I-4) *Chairman*
Alo Fa'au'uga (I-7) *Vice Chairman*
Mata'utia Lui Afonotele (I-5)
Avegalio P. Aigamaua (I-11)
Leatualevao S. Asifoa (I-9)
Magalei Logovi'i (I-8)
Galea'i Moali'itele Tu'ufuli (I-1)
Laolagi Fonoti Savali Vaeao (I-2)

### Education
**Members**
Laolagi Fonoti Savali Vaeao (I-2) *Vice Chairman*
Avegalio P. Aigamaua (I-11)
Fuiava Avaloa (I-4)
Tuiasina Siolosega Esera (I-10)
Alo Fa'au'uga (I-7)
Soliai Tuipine Fuimaono (I-7)
Faletagoa'i I. Tuiolemotu (I-12)

### Energy Power and Water
**Members**
Tuiasina Siolosega Esera (I-10) *Chairman*
Tuaolo M. E. Fruean (I-6) *Vice Chairman*
Fuiava Avaloa (I-4)
Leatualevao S. Asifoa (I-9)
Soliai Tuipine Fuimaono (I-7)
Magalei Logovi'i (I-8)
Galea'i Moali'itele Tu'ufuli (I-1)
Laolagi Fonoti Savali Vaeao (I-2)

### Government Operations
**Members**
Galea'i Moali'itele Tu'ufuli (I-1) *Chairman*
Tuiasina Siolosega Esera (I-10) *Vice Chairman*
Mata'utia Lui Afonotele (I-5)
Avegalio P. Aigamaua (I-11)
Fuiava Avaloa (I-4)
Alo Fa'au'uga (I-7)
Faletagoa'i I. Tuiolemotu (I-12)
Laolagi Fonoti Savali Vaeao (I-2)

### Hospital and Public Health
**Members**
Tuaolo M. E. Fruean (I-6) *Chairman*
Fuiava Avaloa (I-4) *Vice Chairman*
Mata'utia Lui Afonotele (I-5)
Avegalio P. Aigamaua (I-11)
Tuiasina Siolosega Esera (I-10)
Soliai Tuipine Fuimaono (I-7)
Magalei Logovi'i (I-8)

### Human Resources and Human Social Services
**Members**
Magalei Logovi'i (I-8) *Chairman*
Gaea Perefoti Failautusi (I-8) *Vice Chairman*
Leatualevao S. Asifoa (I-9)
Fuiava Avaloa (I-4)
Tuiasina Siolosega Esera (I-10)
Alo Fa'au'uga (I-7)
Tuaolo M. E. Fruean (I-6)
Nuanuaolefeagaiga Sao Luaga (I-1)
Laolagi Fonoti Savali Vaeao (I-2)

### Judiciary
**Members**
Soliai Tuipine Fuimaono (I-7) *Chairman*
Tuiasina Siolosega Esera (I-10) *Vice Chairman*
Mata'utia Lui Afonotele (I-5)
Fuiava Avaloa (I-4)
Gaea Perefoti Failautusi (I-8)
Tuaolo M. E. Fruean (I-6)
Tialavea Misiualapa (I-5)
Faletagoa'i I. Tuiolemotu (I-12)

### Parks and Recreation
**Members**
Mata'utia Lui Afonotele (I-5) *Chairman*
Avegalio P. Aigamaua (I-11) *Vice Chairman*
Tuiasina Siolosega Esera (I-10)
Alo Fa'au'uga (I-7)
Afoa Moega Lutu (I-6)
Faletagoa'i I. Tuiolemotu (I-12)
Laolagi Fonoti Savali Vaeao (I-2)

### Public Safety and Homeland Security
**Members**
Faletagoa'i I. Tuiolemotu (I-12) *Chairman*
Galea'i Moali'itele Tu'ufuli (I-1) *Vice Chairman*
Mata'utia Lui Afonotele (I-5)
Leatualevao S. Asifoa (I-9)
Tuiasina Siolosega Esera (I-10)
Alo Fa'au'uga (I-7)
Gaea Perefoti Failautusi (I-8)
Laolagi Fonoti Savali Vaeao (I-2)

**LEGISLATIVE BRANCH**

LEGISLATIVE BRANCH

## Public Works
### Members
Alo Fa'au'uga (I-7) *Chairman*
Nuanuaolefeagaiga Sao Luaga (I-1) *Vice Chairman*
Mata'utia Lui Afonotele (I-5)
Avegalio P. Aigamaua (I-11)
Leatualevao S. Asifoa (I-9)
Faletagoa'i I. Tuiolemotu (I-12)
Laolagi Fonoti Savali Vaeao (I-2)

## Retirement
### Members
Avegalio P. Aigamaua (I-11) *Chairman*
Leatualevao S. Asifoa (I-9) *Vice Chairman*
Mata'utia Lui Afonotele (I-5)
Fuiava Avaloa (I-4)
Tuiasina Siolosega Esera (I-10)
Alo Fa'au'uga (I-7)
Gaea Perefoti Failautusi (I-8)
Magalei Logovi'i (I-8)
Nuanuaolefeagaiga Sao Luaga (I-1)
Galea'i Moali'itele Tu'ufuli (I-1)
Faletagoa'i I. Tuiolemotu (I-12)
Laolagi Fonoti Savali Vaeao (I-2)

## Samoan Affairs
### Members
Tialavea Misiualapa (I-5) *Chairman*
Soliai Tuipine Fuimaono (I-7) *Vice Chairman*
Mata'utia Lui Afonotele (I-5)
Avegalio P. Aigamaua (I-11)
Tuaolo M. E. Fruean (I-6)
Afoa Moega Lutu (I-6)
Faletagoa'i I. Tuiolemotu (I-12)

## Senate House Rules, Marine and Wildlife
### Members
Nuanuaolefeagaiga Sao Luaga (I-1) *Chairman*
Laolagi Fonoti Savali Vaeao (I-2) *Vice Chairman*
Mata'utia Lui Afonotele (I-5)
Leatualevao S. Asifoa (I-9)
Tuiasina Siolosega Esera (I-10)
Alo Fa'au'uga (I-7)
Faletagoa'i I. Tuiolemotu (I-12)

## Transportation, Ports and Airport
### Members
Gaea Perefoti Failautusi (I-8) *Chairman*
Avegalio P. Aigamaua (I-11)
Leatualevao S. Asifoa (I-9)
Fuiava Avaloa (I-4)
Tuiasina Siolosega Esera (I-10)
Afoa Moega Lutu (I-6)
Nuanuaolefeagaiga Sao Luaga (I-1)

# American Samoa House of Representatives
Tel: (684) 633-1781  Fax: (684) 633-1681

Speaker of the House **Savali Talavou Ale** (I) . . . . . (684) 633-5763 ext. 222
Chief Clerk of the House **Fialupe F. Lutu** . . . . . . . . (684) 633-5763 ext. 224
  E-mail: houseclerk.flutu@samoatelco.com

## Representatives
Representative **Savali Talavou Ale** (I-District 14) . . . . . (684) 633-5763 ext. 222
  Counties Represented: Lealataua
  Term Expires: January 3, 2017
  E-mail: savali.ale@gmail.com

Representative
**Faimealelei Anthony Fue Allen** (I-District 11) . . (684) 633-5763 ext. 244
  Counties Represented: Maoputasi #5
  Term Expires: January 3, 2017
  E-mail: anthonyallen_644@yahoo.com
  Committees: Budget and Appropriations; Department of
  Education/Scholarships; Government Operations; House Rules

Representative
**Vailoata Eteuati Amituana'i** (I-District 7) . . . . . (684) 633-5763 ext. 233
  Counties Represented: Aitulagi
  Term Expires: January 3, 2017
  E-mail: talofa04@yahoo.com
  Committees: American Samoa Power Authority/Territorial Energy
  Offices; Budget and Appropriations; Communications; Department of
  Commerce and Economic Development Committee; Department of
  Education/Scholarships; Department of Public Works; House Rules;
  Local Government, Territorial Administration on Aging (TAOA), and
  Election; Retirement

Representative **Atalina Asifoa** (I-District 17) . . . . . (684) 633-5762 ext. 230
  Counties Represented: Leasina
  Term Expires: January 3, 2017
  E-mail: asifoaatalina@yahoo.com
  Committees: Communications; Department of Commerce and
  Economic Development Committee; Department of Homeland Security;
  Health Committee; Human and Social Services/Youth and Women's
  Affairs; Legal Affairs/Judiciary

Representative **Toeaina F. Autele** (I-District 2) . . . . (684) 633-5763 ext. 240
  Counties Represented: Manu'a (part)
  Term Expires: January 3, 2017
  E-mail: toeainaf@gmail.com
  Committees: Agriculture/Marine and Wildlife and Forestry; Department
  of Commerce and Economic Development Committee; Department of
  Public Works; Legal Affairs/Judiciary

Representative
**Vesi Talalelei Fautanu** (I-District 1) . . . . . . . . . (684) 633-5763 ext. 236
  Counties Represented: Hawaii, Manu'a (part)
  Term Expires: January 3, 2017
  E-mail: tj_fautanu@yahoo.com
  Committees: Agriculture/Marine and Wildlife and Forestry;
  Department of Education/Scholarships; Department of Homeland
  Security; Department of Parks and Recreation; Department of Port
  Administration/Transportation; Health Committee; Human and Social
  Services/Youth and Women's Affairs; Legal Affairs/Judiciary;
  Retirement

Representative **Fetu Fetui, Jr.** (I-District 1) . . . . . . (684) 633-5763 ext. 245
  Counties Represented: Hawaii, Manu'a (part)    Res: (684) 699-4479
  Term Expires: January 3, 2017
  Committees: American Samoa Power Authority/Territorial Energy
  Offices; Budget and Appropriations; House Rules

Representative
**Alexander Eli Jennings** (I-District SI) . . . . . . . . (684) 633-5763 ext. 234
  Term Expires: January 3, 2017
  E-mail: rep.alexanderjennings@gmail.com
  Committees: Agriculture/Marine and Wildlife and Forestry;
  Department of Parks and Recreation; Department of Port
  Administration/Transportation

Representative **Puletuimalo Dick "Puletu"**
**Koko** (I-District 13) . . . . . . . . . . . . . . . . . . . . . . . (684) 633-5763 ext. 249
  Counties Represented: Fofo
  Term Expires: January 3, 2017
  Committees: Agriculture/Marine and Wildlife and Forestry; American
  Samoa Power Authority/Territorial Energy Offices; Department of Parks
  and Recreation; Department of Port Administration/Transportation;
  Department of Public Safety; House Rules; Local Government,
  Territorial Administration on Aging (TAOA), and Election; Retirement

Representative
**Meauta Lauoi Mageo** (I-District 9) . . . . . . . . . . (684) 633-5763 ext. 235
  Counties Represented: Maoputasi #3
  Term Expires: January 3, 2017
  E-mail: utamageo@yahoo.com
  Committees: Budget and Appropriations; Department of
  Education/Scholarships; Department of Homeland Security; Department
  of Parks and Recreation; Government Operations; Health Committee;
  Retirement; Ways and Means

Representative
**Mulinu'u Vae'iaitu Filo Maluia** (I-District 12) . . (684) 633-5763 ext. 241
  Counties Represented: Itu'au
  Term Expires: January 3, 2017
  E-mail: mulinuumaluia@yahoo.com
  Committees: Agriculture/Marine and Wildlife and Forestry; Department
  of Homeland Security; Department of Public Works; Human and
  Social Services/Youth and Women's Affairs; Legal Affairs/Judiciary;
  Local Government, Territorial Administration on Aging (TAOA), and
  Election; Retirement; Ways and Means

Representative **Legae'e F. Mauga** (I-District 3) . . . (684) 633-5763 ext. 228
  Counties Represented: Vaifanua
  Term Expires: January 3, 2017
  Committees: Communications; Department of Public Works; Ways and
  Means

Representative
**Matagi David Sialega Mauga** (I-District 6) . . . . (684) 633-5763 ext. 248
Counties Represented: Sua #2
Term Expires: January 3, 2017
E-mail: david.mauga@yahoo.com
Committees: Budget and Appropriations; Department of Commerce
and Economic Development Committee; Department of Parks and
Recreation; Department of Public Safety; Government Operations;
Ways and Means

Representative **Vaetasi Tuumolimoli Saena
"Tuua" Moliga** (I-District 10) . . . . . . . . . . . . . . . (684) 633-5763 ext. 246
Counties Represented: Maoputasi #4
Term Expires: January 3, 2017
E-mail: tmoliga25@yahoo.com
Committees: Agriculture/Marine and Wildlife and Forestry;
American Samoa Power Authority/Territorial Energy Offices;
Department of Education/Scholarships; Department of Port
Administration/Transportation; Government Operations; House Rules;
Local Government, Territorial Administration on Aging (TAOA), and
Election; Retirement

Representative **Larry Sanitoa** (I-District 15) . . . . . . (684) 633-5763 ext. 227
Counties Represented: Maopu (Tualauta)
Term Expires: January 3, 2017
E-mail: lsanitoa@blueskynet.as
Committees: Budget and Appropriations; Department of
Commerce and Economic Development Committee; Department
of Education/Scholarships; Human and Social Services/Youth and
Women's Affairs; Local Government, Territorial Administration on
Aging (TAOA), and Election; Retirement

Representative **Vui Florence Vaili Tuaumu
Saulo** (I-District 15) . . . . . . . . . . . . . . . . . . . . . . . (684) 633-5763 ext. 231
Counties Represented: Maopu (Tualauta)
Term Expires: January 3, 2017
E-mail: tualauta15@yahoo.com
Committees: American Samoa Power Authority/Territorial Energy
Offices; Budget and Appropriations; Communications; Department of
Public Safety; Department of Public Works; Health Committee; House
Rules; Human and Social Services/Youth and Women's Affairs; Legal
Affairs/Judiciary

Representative
**Maugaoalii Le'apai Sipa Anoa'i** (I-District 8) . . (684) 633-5763 ext. 247
Counties Represented: Maoputasi #2
Term Expires: January 3, 2017
E-mail: fagatogovalu@yahoo.com
Committees: American Samoa Power Authority/Territorial Energy
Offices; Budget and Appropriations; Department of Commerce and
Economic Development Committee; Department of Parks and
Recreation; Department of Public Safety; Department of Public Works;
Government Operations; House Rules

Representative
**Talaimatai Elisara Sua** (I-District 4) . . . . . . . . . (684) 633-5763 ext. 243
Counties Represented: Saole
Term Expires: January 3, 2017
E-mail: talaimataisua15@yahoo.com
Committees: Agriculture/Marine and Wildlife and Forestry;
Budget and Appropriations; Communications; Department of
Education/Scholarships; Department of Homeland Security; Department
of Port Administration/Transportation; Department of Public Safety;
Health Committee; House Rules; Local Government, Territorial
Administration on Aging (TAOA), and Election; Retirement; Ways and
Means

Representative
**Puleleiite Li'amatua Tufele, Jr.** (I-District 5) . . . (684) 633-5763 ext. 242
Counties Represented: Sua #1
Term Expires: January 3, 2017
Committees: Communications; Department of Commerce and
Economic Development Committee; Department of Port
Administration/Transportation; Department of Public Safety;
Government Operations; House Rules; Human and Social
Services/Youth and Women's Affairs; Ways and Means

Representative
**Manumau Wayne Wilson** (I-District 12) . . . . . . (684) 633-5763 ext. 239
Counties Represented: Itu'au
Term Expires: January 3, 2017
E-mail: musuiaiga@hotmail.com
Committees: American Samoa Power Authority/Territorial
Energy Offices; Communications; Department of Homeland
Security; Department of Parks and Recreation; Department of Port
Administration/Transportation; Department of Public Safety;
Government Operations; Health Committee; Legal Affairs/Judiciary;
Local Government, Territorial Administration on Aging (TAOA), and
Election; Retirement; Ways and Means

Representative **Timusa Lam Yuen** (I-District 16) . . (684) 633-5763 ext. 229
Counties Represented: Tualatai
Term Expires: January 3, 2017
E-mail: tclamyuen@yahoo.com
Committees: Budget and Appropriations; Department of Commerce
and Economic Development Committee; Department of Homeland
Security; Department of Public Works; Government Operations; Health
Committee; Human and Social Services/Youth and Women's Affairs;
Legal Affairs/Judiciary; Retirement

# House Standing Committees
P.O. Box 485, Pago Pago, AS 96799
Tel: (684) 633-5763  Fax: (684) 633-1681

## Agriculture/Marine and Wildlife and Forestry
**Members**
Alexander Eli Jennings (I-SI) *Chairman*
Mulinu'u Vae'iaitu Filo Maluia (I-12) *Vice Chairman*
Toeaina F. Autele (I-2)
Vesi Talalelei Fautanu (I-1)
Puletuimalo Dick "Puletu" Koko (I-13)
Vaetasi Tuumolimoli Saena "Tuua" Moliga (I-10)
Talaimatai Elisara Sua (I-4)

## American Samoa Power Authority/ Territorial Energy Offices
Tel: (684) 633-5763  Fax: (684) 633-1681

**Members**
Puletuimalo Dick "Puletu" Koko (I-13) *Chairman*
Manumau Wayne Wilson (I-12) *Vice Chairman*
Vailoata Eteuati Amituana'i (I-7)
Fetu Fetui, Jr. (I-1)
Vaetasi Tuumolimoli Saena "Tuua" Moliga (I-10)
Vui Florence Vaili Tuaumu Saulo (I-15)
Maugaoalii Le'apai Sipa Anoa'i (I-8)

## Budget and Appropriations
Tel: (684) 633-5763  Fax: (684) 633-1681

**Members**
Timusa Lam Yuen (I-16) *Chairman*
Faimealelei Anthony Fue Allen (I-11) *Vice Chairman*
Vailoata Eteuati Amituana'i (I-7)
Fetu Fetui, Jr. (I-1)
Meauta Lauoi Mageo (I-9)
Matagi David Sialega Mauga (I-6)
Vui Florence Vaili Tuaumu Saulo (I-15)
Maugaoalii Le'apai Sipa Anoa'i (I-8)
Talaimatai Elisara Sua (I-4)
Larry Sanitoa (I-15)

## Communications
**Members**
Puleleiite Li'amatua Tufele, Jr. (I-5) *Chairman*
Vailoata Eteuati Amituana'i (I-7) *Vice Chairman*
Atalina Asifoa (I-17)
Legae'e F. Mauga (I-3)
Vui Florence Vaili Tuaumu Saulo (I-15)
Talaimatai Elisara Sua (I-4)
Manumau Wayne Wilson (I-12)

## Department of Commerce and Economic Development Committee
Tel: (684) 633-5763  Fax: (684) 633-1681

**Members**
Larry Sanitoa (I-15) *Chairman*
Timusa Lam Yuen (I-16) *Vice Chairman*
Vailoata Eteuati Amituana'i (I-7)
Atalina Asifoa (I-17)
Toeaina F. Autele (I-2)
Matagi David Sialega Mauga (I-6)
Maugaoalii Le'apai Sipa Anoa'i (I-8)
Puleleiite Li'amatua Tufele, Jr. (I-5)

## Department of Education/Scholarships
Tel: (684) 633-5763  Fax: (684) 633-1681

**Members**
Vaetasi Tuumolimoli Saena "Tuua" Moliga (I-10) *Chairman*
Meauta Lauoi Mageo (I-9) *Vice Chairman*
Faimealelei Anthony Fue Allen (I-11)
Vailoata Eteuati Amituana'i (I-7)
Vesi Talalelei Fautanu (I-1)
Larry Sanitoa (I-15)
Talaimatai Elisara Sua (I-4)

## Government Operations
Tel: (684) 633-5763  Fax: (684) 633-1681

**Members**
Faimealelei Anthony Fue Allen (I-11) *Chairman*
Maugaoalii Le'apai Sipa Anoa'i (I-8) *Vice Chairman*
Meauta Lauoi Mageo (I-9)
Matagi David Sialega Mauga (I-6)
Vaetasi Tuumolimoli Saena "Tuua" Moliga (I-10)
Puleleiite Li'amatua Tufele, Jr. (I-5)
Manumau Wayne Wilson (I-12)
Timusa Lam Yuen (I-16)

## Health Committee
Tel: (684) 633-5763  Fax: (684) 633-1681

**Members**
Vesi Talalelei Fautanu (I-1) *Chairman*
Atalina Asifoa (I-17) *Vice Chairman*
Meauta Lauoi Mageo (I-9)
Vui Florence Vaili Tuaumu Saulo (I-15)
Talaimatai Elisara Sua (I-4)
Manumau Wayne Wilson (I-12)
Timusa Lam Yuen (I-16)

## Department of Homeland Security
**Members**
Meauta Lauoi Mageo (I-9) *Chairman*
Manumau Wayne Wilson (I-12) *Vice Chairman*
Atalina Asifoa (I-17)
Vesi Talalelei Fautanu (I-1)
Mulinu'u Vae'iaitu Filo Maluia (I-12)
Talaimatai Elisara Sua (I-4)
Timusa Lam Yuen (I-16)

## House Rules
Tel: (684) 633-5763  Fax: (684) 633-1681

**Members**
Fetu Fetui, Jr. (I-1) *Chairman*
Vaetasi Tuumolimoli Saena "Tuua" Moliga (I-10) *Vice Chairman*
Faimealelei Anthony Fue Allen (I-11)
Vailoata Eteuati Amituana'i (I-7)
Puletuimalo Dick "Puletu" Koko (I-13)
Vui Florence Vaili Tuaumu Saulo (I-15)
Maugaoalii Le'apai Sipa Anoa'i (I-8)
Talaimatai Elisara Sua (I-4)
Puleleiite Li'amatua Tufele, Jr. (I-5)

## Human and Social Services/Youth and Women's Affairs
**Members**
Atalina Asifoa (I-17) *Chairman*
Larry Sanitoa (I-15) *Vice Chairman*
Vesi Talalelei Fautanu (I-1)
Mulinu'u Vae'iaitu Filo Maluia (I-12)
Vui Florence Vaili Tuaumu Saulo (I-15)
Puleleiite Li'amatua Tufele, Jr. (I-5)
Timusa Lam Yuen (I-16)

## Legal Affairs/Judiciary
Tel: (684) 633-5763  Fax: (684) 633-1681

**Members**
Vui Florence Vaili Tuaumu Saulo (I-15) *Chairman*
Toeaina F. Autele (I-2) *Vice Chairman*
Atalina Asifoa (I-17)
Vesi Talalelei Fautanu (I-1)
Mulinu'u Vae'iaitu Filo Maluia (I-12)
Manumau Wayne Wilson (I-12)
Timusa Lam Yuen (I-16)

## Local Government, Territorial Administration on Aging (TAOA), and Election
Tel: (684) 633-5763  Fax: (684) 633-1681

**Members**
Mulinu'u Vae'iaitu Filo Maluia (I-12) *Chairman*
Puletuimalo Dick "Puletu" Koko (I-13) *Vice Chairman*
Vailoata Eteuati Amituana'i (I-7)
Vaetasi Tuumolimoli Saena "Tuua" Moliga (I-10)
Larry Sanitoa (I-15)
Talaimatai Elisara Sua (I-4)
Manumau Wayne Wilson (I-12)

## Department of Parks and Recreation
**Members**
Matagi David Sialega Mauga (I-6) *Chairman*
Alexander Eli Jennings (I-SI) *Vice Chairman*
Vesi Talalelei Fautanu (I-1)
Puletuimalo Dick "Puletu" Koko (I-13)
Meauta Lauoi Mageo (I-9)
Maugaoalii Le'apai Sipa Anoa'i (I-8)
Manumau Wayne Wilson (I-12)

## Department of Port Administration/ Transportation
Tel: (684) 633-5763  Fax: (684) 633-1681

**Members**
Talaimatai Elisara Sua (I-4) *Chairman*
Vesi Talalelei Fautanu (I-1) *Vice Chairman*
Alexander Eli Jennings (I-SI)
Puletuimalo Dick "Puletu" Koko (I-13)
Vaetasi Tuumolimoli Saena "Tuua" Moliga (I-10)
Puleleiite Li'amatua Tufele, Jr. (I-5)
Manumau Wayne Wilson (I-12)

## Department of Public Safety
Tel: (684) 633-5763  Fax: (684) 633-1681

**Members**
Manumau Wayne Wilson (I-12) *Chairman*
Matagi David Sialega Mauga (I-6) *Vice Chairman*
Puletuimalo Dick "Puletu" Koko (I-13)
Vui Florence Vaili Tuaumu Saulo (I-15)
Maugaoalii Le'apai Sipa Anoa'i (I-8)
Talaimatai Elisara Sua (I-4)
Puleleiite Li'amatua Tufele, Jr. (I-5)

## Department of Public Works
Tel: (684) 633-5763  Fax: (684) 633-1681

**Members**
Maugaoalii Le'apai Sipa Anoa'i (I-8) *Chairman*
Vui Florence Vaili Tuaumu Saulo (I-15) *Vice Chairman*
Vailoata Eteuati Amituana'i (I-7)
Toeaina F. Autele (I-2)
Mulinu'u Vae'iaitu Filo Maluia (I-12)
Legae'e F. Mauga (I-3)
Timusa Lam Yuen (I-16)

## Retirement

**Members**

Vailoata Eteuati Amituana'i (I-7) *Chairman*
Talaimatai Elisara Sua (I-4) *Vice Chairman*
Vesi Talalelei Fautanu (I-1)
Puletuimalo Dick "Puletu" Koko (I-13)
Meauta Lauoi Mageo (I-9)
Mulinu'u Vae'iaitu Filo Maluia (I-12)
Vaetasi Tuumolimoli Saena "Tuua" Moliga (I-10)
Larry Sanitoa (I-15)
Manumau Wayne Wilson (I-12)
Timusa Lam Yuen (I-16)

## Ways and Means

Tel: (684) 633-5763  Fax: (684) 633-1681

**Members**

Legae'e F. Mauga (I-3) *Chairman*
Puleleiite Li'amatua Tufele, Jr. (I-5)
Meauta Lauoi Mageo (I-9)
Matagi David Sialega Mauga (I-6)
Mulinu'u Vae'iaitu Filo Maluia (I-12)
Talaimatai Elisara Sua (I-4)
Manumau Wayne Wilson (I-12)

# Arizona Legislature

Tel: (602) 542-4900  Tel: (800) 352-8404 (In State)  TTY: (800) 367-8939

## Arizona State Senate

Capitol Complex, 1700 West Washington Street, Phoenix, AZ 85007-2890
Tel: (602) 926-3559  Fax: (602) 926-3429  Internet: www.azsenate.gov

President of the Senate **Andy Biggs** (R) . . . . . . . . . . . . . . . (602) 926-4371
  Education: BYU BA; Arizona State MA; Arizona JD
President Pro Tem **Sylvia Allen** (R) . . . . . . . . . . . . . . . . . . (602) 926-5409
Majority Leader **Steve B. Yarbrough** (R) . . . . . . . . . . . . . . (602) 926-5863
  Education: Arizona State 1968 BS, 1971 JD
Majority Whip **Gail Griffin** (R) . . . . . . . . . . . . . . . . . . . . . (602) 926-5895
Minority Leader **Katie Hobbs** (D) . . . . . . . . . . . . . . . . . . . (602) 926-5325
  Education: Northern Arizona 1992 BA; Arizona State 1995 MSW
Assistant Minority Leader **Steve Farley** (D) . . . . . . . . . . . (602) 926-3022
  Education: Williams 1985 BA
Minority Whip
  **Guadalupe Chavira "Lupe" Contreras** (D) . . . . . . . . . . (602) 926-5284
Minority Whip **Martin J. Quezada** (D) . . . . . . . . . . . . . . . (602) 926-5911
Secretary of the Senate **Charmion Billington** . . . . . . . . . . (602) 926-4231
  E-mail: cbillington@azleg.gov
Sergeant-at-Arms **Joe Kubacki** . . . . . . . . . . . . . . . . . . . . . (602) 542-5969
  E-mail: jkubacki@azleg.gov

## Senators

**Party Affiliation Statistics:** Republicans: 18, Democrats: 12

Senator **Sylvia Allen** (R-District 6) . . . . . . . . . . . . . . . . . . (602) 926-5409
  Counties Represented: Coconino (part), Gila (part),      Fax: (602) 417-3105
  Navajo (part), Yavapai (part)
  Term Expires: 2017
  E-mail: sallen@azleg.gov
  Committees: Appropriations; Education; Government; Rural Affairs and
  Environment; Water and Energy
Senator **Nancy K. Barto** (R-District 15) Room 307 . . . . . . . (602) 926-5766
  Counties Represented: Maricopa (part)      Fax: (602) 926-3261
  Term Expires: 2017
  E-mail: nbarto@azleg.gov
  Committees: Federalism, Mandates and Fiscal Responsibility; Health
  and Human Services; Judiciary
Senator **Carlyle W. Begay** (R-District 7) Room 315 . . . . . . (602) 926-5862
  Counties Represented: Apache, Coconino (part),      Fax: (602) 417-3099
  Gila (part), Graham (part), Mohave (part), Navajo (part), Pinal (part)
  Term Expires: 2017
  E-mail: cbegay@azleg.gov
  Committees: Education; Financial Institutions; Transportation; Water
  and Energy
  Education: Arizona 2003 BS
Senator **Andy Biggs** (R-District 12) Room 205 . . . . . . . . . . (602) 926-4371
  Counties Represented: Maricopa (part), Pinal (part)      Fax: (602) 417-3248
  Term Expires: 2017
  E-mail: abiggs@azleg.gov
  Committees: Joint Capital Review; Joint Legislative Council; Rules
Senator **David T. Bradley** (D-District 10) Room 313 . . . . . . (602) 926-5262
  Counties Represented: Pima (part)      Fax: (602) 926-3429
  Term Expires: 2017
  E-mail: dbradley@azleg.gov
  Committees: Education; Federalism, Mandates and Fiscal
  Responsibility; Health and Human Services; Water and Energy
  Education: Maryland 1977 BS; Old Dominion 1979 MSEd;
  U Phoenix 1996 MBA
Senator **Judy M. Burges** (R-District 22) Room 302 . . . . . . (602) 926-5861
  Counties Represented: Maricopa (part)      Fax: (602) 926-3104
  Term Expires: 2017
  E-mail: jburges@azleg.gov
  Committees: Federalism, Mandates and Fiscal Responsibility;
  Government; Public Safety, Military and Technology; Transportation;
  Water and Energy
  Education: Yavapai 1984 AA; U Phoenix 1993 BA, 1996 MBA
Senator **Olivia Cajero Bedford** (D-District 3) Room 314 . . (602) 926-5835
  Counties Represented: Pima (part)      Fax: (602) 417-3262
  Term Expires: 2017
  E-mail: ocajerobedford@azleg.gov
  Committees: Appropriations; Commerce and Workforce Development;
  Federalism, Mandates and Fiscal Responsibility; Rules
  Education: Arizona

*(continued on next page)*

**Senators** *continued*

Senator
**Guadalupe Chavira "Lupe" Contreras** (D-District 19)
Room 313 . . . . . . . . . . . . . . . . . . . . . . . . . . . . . . (602) 926-5284
Counties Represented: Maricopa (part)         Fax: (602) 417-3106
Term Expires: 2017
E-mail: lcontreras@azleg.gov
Committees: Government; Judiciary; Public Safety, Military and
Technology; State Debt and Budget Reform

Senator **Andrea Dalessandro, CPA** (D-District 2)
Room 312 . . . . . . . . . . . . . . . . . . . . . . . . . . . . . . (602) 926-5342
Counties Represented: Pima (part)         Fax: (602) 417-3169
Term Expires: 2017
E-mail: adalessandro@azleg.gov
Committees: Financial Institutions; Judiciary; Rural Affairs and
Environment
Education: Jersey City State 1970 BA; New Jersey City U 1975 MA;
Rutgers (Newark) 1981 MBA

Senator **Jeff Dial** (R-District 18) Room 304 . . . . . . . . . . . . (602) 926-5550
Counties Represented: Maricopa (part)         Fax: (602) 417-3120
Term Expires: 2017
E-mail: jdial@azleg.gov
Committees: Commerce and Workforce Development; Education; State
Debt and Budget Reform; Transportation
Education: Arizona State 2004 BA

Senator **Susan "Sue" Donahue** (R-District 5)
Room 304 . . . . . . . . . . . . . . . . . . . . . . . . . . . . . . (602) 926-4138
Counties Represented: Mohave (part)         Fax: (602) 417-3067
Term Expires: 2017
E-mail: sdonahue@azleg.gov
Committees: Financial Institutions; Public Safety, Military and
Technology; State Debt and Budget Reform

Senator **Adam Driggs** (R-District 28) Room 309 . . . . . . . . (602) 926-3016
Counties Represented: Maricopa (part)         Fax: (602) 417-3007
Term Expires: 2017
E-mail: adriggs@azleg.gov
Committees: Financial Institutions; Judiciary; Natural Resources
Education: BYU 1990 BA; Arizona State 1993 JD

Senator **Steve Farley** (D-District 9) Room 213 . . . . . . . . . (602) 926-3022
Counties Represented: Pima (part)         Fax: (602) 926-3128
Term Expires: 2017
E-mail: sfarley@azleg.gov
Committees: Appropriations; Finance; Financial Institutions; Joint
Legislative Council

Senator
**David Christian "Dave" Farnsworth** (R-District 16)
Room 304 . . . . . . . . . . . . . . . . . . . . . . . . . . . . . . (602) 926-3020
Counties Represented: Maricopa (part), Pinal (part)         Fax: (602) 417-3119
Term Expires: 2017
E-mail: dfarnsworth@azleg.gov
Committees: Commerce and Workforce Development; Federalism,
Mandates and Fiscal Responsibility; Financial Institutions; Natural
Resources
Education: Mesa Comm Col 1979 AA

Senator **Gail Griffin** (R-District 14) Room 212 . . . . . . . . . . . (602) 926-5895
Counties Represented: Cochise, Graham (part),         Fax: (602) 926-3025
Greenlee, Pima (part)
Term Expires: 2017
E-mail: ggriffin@azleg.gov
Committees: Financial Institutions; Rules; Rural Affairs and
Environment; Water and Energy

Senator **Katie Hobbs** (D-District 24) Room 213 . . . . . . . . . (602) 926-5325
Counties Represented: Maricopa (part)         Fax: (602) 417-3149
Term Expires: 2017
E-mail: khobbs@azleg.gov
Committees: Appropriations; Health and Human Services; Rules

Senator **John Kavanagh** (R-District 23) Room 303A . . . . . (602) 926-5170
Counties Represented: Maricopa (part)         Fax: (602) 417-3108
Term Expires: 2017
E-mail: jkavanagh@azleg.gov
Committees: Appropriations; Government; Public Safety, Military and
Technology; State Debt and Budget Reform
Education: NYU 1973 AB; Rutgers (Newark) 1995 PhD;
St John's U (NY) 1978 MA

Senator **Debbie Lesko** (R-District 21) Room 302 . . . . . . . . (602) 926-5413
Counties Represented: Maricopa (part)         Fax: (602) 417-3109
Term Expires: 2017
E-mail: dlesko@azleg.gov
Committees: Finance; Health and Human Services; State Debt and
Budget Reform; Water and Energy
Education: Wisconsin BBA

Senator **Barbara McGuire** (D-District 8) Room 314 . . . . . . (602) 926-5836
Counties Represented: Gila (part), Pinal (part)         Fax: (602) 926-3131
Term Expires: 2017
E-mail: bmcguire@azleg.gov
Committees: Natural Resources; Public Safety, Military and
Technology; Rural Affairs and Environment
Education: Central Arizona (Attended)

Senator **Robert Meza** (D-District 30) Room 311 . . . . . . . . (602) 926-3425
Counties Represented: Maricopa (part)         Fax: (602) 926-3114
Term Expires: 2017
E-mail: rmeza@azleg.gov
Committees: Commerce and Workforce Development; Government;
Natural Resources
Education: Arizona State, JD

Senator **Catherine H. Miranda** (D-District 27) . . . . . . . . . (602) 926-4893
Counties Represented: Maricopa (part)         Fax: (602) 417-3116
Term Expires: 2017
E-mail: cmiranda@azleg.gov
Committees: Commerce and Workforce Development; Natural
Resources; Transportation
Education: Northern Arizona 2000 BAE, 2004 MAEd

Senator **Lynne Pancrazi** (D-District 4) Room 213 . . . . . . . . (602) 926-3004
Counties Represented: Maricopa (part), Pima (part),         Fax: (602) 926-3179
Pinal (part), Yuma (part)
Term Expires: 2017
E-mail: lpancrazi@azleg.gov
Committees: Finance; Health and Human Services; Water and Energy
Education: Point Loma BA; Northern Arizona MA

Senator **Steve Pierce** (R-District 1) Room 301 . . . . . . . . . (602) 926-5584
Counties Represented: Maricopa (part), Yavapai         Fax: (602) 417-3101
(part)
Term Expires: 2017
E-mail: spierce@azleg.gov
Committees: Joint Legislative Council; Judiciary; Natural Resources;
Transportation

Senator **Martin J. Quezada** (D-District 29) Room 313 . . . . (602) 926-5911
Counties Represented: Maricopa (part)         Fax: (602) 417-3113
Term Expires: 2017
E-mail: mquezada@azleg.gov
Committees: Government; Judiciary; Rules

Senator **Andrew C. Sherwood** (D-District 26) . . . . . . . . . (602) 926-3028
Counties Represented: Maricopa (part)         Fax: (602) 417-3038
Term Expires: 2017
E-mail: asherwood@azleg.gov
Committees: Federalism, Mandates and Fiscal Responsibility; Financial
Institutions; State Debt and Budget Reform; Transportation

Senator **Don Shooter** (R-District 13) Room 200 . . . . . . . . (602) 926-4139
Counties Represented: Maricopa (part), Yavapai         Fax: (602) 926-3024
(part), Yuma (part)
Term Expires: 2017
E-mail: dshooter@azleg.gov
Committees: Appropriations; Joint Capital Review; Natural Resources;
Rural Affairs and Environment

Senator **Steve Smith** (R-District 11) Room 303 . . . . . . . . . (602) 926-5685
Counties Represented: Pima (part), Pinal (part)         Fax: (602) 417-3167
Term Expires: 2017
E-mail: stsmith@azleg.gov
Committees: Commerce and Workforce Development; Education;
Federalism, Mandates and Fiscal Responsibility; Government; Public
Safety, Military and Technology

Senator **Bob Worsley** (R-District 25) Room 310 . . . . . . . . (602) 926-5760
Counties Represented: Maricopa (part)         Fax: (602) 417-3091
Term Expires: 2017
E-mail: bworsley@azleg.gov
Committees: Commerce and Workforce Development; Judiciary;
Transportation
Education: BYU 1980 BAcc

Senator **Steve B. Yarbrough** (R-District 17) Room 309 . . . (602) 926-5863
Counties Represented: Maricopa (part)         Fax: (602) 417-3121
Term Expires: 2017
E-mail: syarbrough@azleg.gov
Committees: Finance; Financial Institutions; Joint Legislative Council;
Rules

Senator **Kimberly Yee** (R-District 20) Room 300 . . . . . . . . (602) 926-3024
Counties Represented: Maricopa (part)         Fax: (602) 417-3110
Term Expires: 2017
E-mail: kyee@azleg.gov
Committees: Commerce and Workforce Development; Education;
Finance; Health and Human Services
Education: Pepperdine BA; Arizona State MA

# Senate Standing Committees

## Appropriations

| Majority Members | Minority Members |
|---|---|
| Don Shooter (R-13) *Chair* | Olivia Cajero Bedford (D-3) |
| John Kavanagh (R-23) *Vice Chair* | Steve Farley (D-9) |
| Sylvia Allen (R-6) | Katie Hobbs (D-24) |

## Commerce and Workforce Development

| Majority Members | Minority Members |
|---|---|
| Kimberly Yee (R-20) *Chair* | Olivia Cajero Bedford (D-3) |
| Steve Smith (R-11) *Vice Chair* | Robert Meza (D-30) |
| Jeff Dial (R-18) | Catherine H. Miranda (D-27) |
| David Christian "Dave" Farnsworth (R-16) | |
| Bob Worsley (R-25) | |

## Education

| Majority Members | Minority Members |
|---|---|
| Sylvia Allen (R-6) *Chair* | David T. Bradley (D-10) |
| Kimberly Yee (R-20) *Vice Chair* | |
| Carlyle W. Begay (R-7) | |
| Jeff Dial (R-18) | |
| Steve Smith (R-11) | |

## Federalism, Mandates and Fiscal Responsibility

| Majority Members | Minority Members |
|---|---|
| Judy M. Burges (R-22) *Chair* | David T. Bradley (D-10) |
| David Christian "Dave" Farnsworth (R-16) *Vice Chair* | Olivia Cajero Bedford (D-3) |
| Nancy K. Barto (R-15) | Andrew C. Sherwood (D-26) |
| Steve Smith (R-11) | |

## Financial Institutions

| Majority Members | Minority Members |
|---|---|
| David Christian "Dave" Farnsworth (R-16) *Chair* | Andrea Dalessandro (D-2) |
| Steve B. Yarbrough (R-17) *Vice Chair* | Steve Farley (D-9) |
| Carlyle W. Begay (R-7) | Andrew C. Sherwood (D-26) |
| Susan "Sue" Donahue (R-5) | |
| Adam Driggs (R-28) | |
| Gail Griffin (R-14) | |

## Finance

| Majority Members | Minority Members |
|---|---|
| Debbie Lesko (R-21) *Chair* | Steve Farley (D-9) |
| Steve B. Yarbrough (R-17) *Vice Chair* | Lynne Pancrazi (D-4) |
| Kimberly Yee (R-20) | |

## Government

| Majority Members | Minority Members |
|---|---|
| John Kavanagh (R-23) *Chair* | Guadalupe Chavira "Lupe" Contreras (D-19) |
| Sylvia Allen (R-6) *Vice Chair* | Robert Meza (D-30) |
| Judy M. Burges (R-22) | Martin J. Quezada (D-29) |
| Steve Smith (R-11) | |

## Health and Human Services

| Majority Members | Minority Members |
|---|---|
| Nancy K. Barto (R-15) *Chair* | David T. Bradley (D-10) |
| Debbie Lesko (R-21) | Katie Hobbs (D-24) |
| Kimberly Yee (R-20) | Lynne Pancrazi (D-4) |

## Judiciary

| Majority Members | Minority Members |
|---|---|
| Adam Driggs (R-28) *Chair* | Guadalupe Chavira "Lupe" Contreras (D-19) |
| Nancy K. Barto (R-15) *Vice Chair* | Andrea Dalessandro (D-2) |
| Steve Pierce (R-1) | Martin J. Quezada (D-29) |
| Bob Worsley (R-25) | |

## Natural Resources

| Majority Members | Minority Members |
|---|---|
| Steve Pierce (R-1) *Chair* | Barbara McGuire (D-8) |
| Don Shooter (R-13) *Vice Chair* | Robert Meza (D-30) |
| Adam Driggs (R-28) | Catherine H. Miranda (D-27) |
| David Christian "Dave" Farnsworth (R-16) | |

## Public Safety, Military and Technology

| Majority Members | Minority Members |
|---|---|
| Steve Smith (R-11) *Chair* | Guadalupe Chavira "Lupe" Contreras (D-19) |
| John Kavanagh (R-23) *Vice Chair* | Barbara McGuire (D-8) |
| Judy M. Burges (R-22) | |
| Susan "Sue" Donahue (R-5) | |

## Rules

| Majority Members | Minority Members |
|---|---|
| Andy Biggs (R-12) *Chair* | Olivia Cajero Bedford (D-3) |
| Steve B. Yarbrough (R-17) *Vice Chair* | Katie Hobbs (D-24) |
| Gail Griffin (R-14) | Martin J. Quezada (D-29) |

## Rural Affairs and Environment

| Majority Members | Minority Members |
|---|---|
| Sylvia Allen (R-6) *Chair* | Andrea Dalessandro (D-2) |
| Gail Griffin (R-14) *Vice Chair* | Barbara McGuire (D-8) |
| Don Shooter (R-13) | |

## State Debt and Budget Reform

| Majority Members | Minority Members |
|---|---|
| Jeff Dial (R-18) *Chair* | Guadalupe Chavira "Lupe" Contreras (D-19) |
| Debbie Lesko (R-21) *Vice Chair* | Andrew C. Sherwood (D-26) |
| Susan "Sue" Donahue (R-5) | |
| John Kavanagh (R-23) | |

## Transportation

| Majority Members | Minority Members |
|---|---|
| Bob Worsley (R-25) *Chair* | Catherine H. Miranda (D-27) |
| Judy M. Burges (R-22) *Vice Chair* | Andrew C. Sherwood (D-26) |
| Carlyle W. Begay (R-7) | |
| Jeff Dial (R-18) | |
| Steve Pierce (R-1) | |

## Water and Energy

| Majority Members | Minority Members |
|---|---|
| Gail Griffin (R-14) *Chair* | David T. Bradley (D-10) |
| Sylvia Allen (R-6) *Vice Chair* | Lynne Pancrazi (D-4) |
| Carlyle W. Begay (R-7) | |
| Judy M. Burges (R-22) | |
| Debbie Lesko (R-21) | |

# Arizona House of Representatives

Capitol Complex, 1700 West Washington Street, Phoenix, AZ 85007-2890
Tel: (602) 926-4221  TTY: (602) 926-6241  Internet: www.azhouse.gov

Speaker of the House **David M. Gowan, Sr.** (R) . . . . . . . . . (602) 926-3312
  Education: Arizona BA
Speaker Pro Tem **Bob Robson** (R) . . . . . . . . . . . . . . . . . . . (602) 926-5549
Majority Leader **Steve B. Montenegro** (R) . . . . . . . . . . . . (602) 926-5955
  Education: Arizona State 2004 BS
Majority Whip **David Livingston** (R) . . . . . . . . . . . . . . . . . (602) 926-4178
  Education: Arizona State 1988 BS
Minority Leader **Eric Meyer** (D) . . . . . . . . . . . . . . . . . . . . (602) 926-3037
  Education: USC BS; Arizona MD
Assistant Minority Leader **Bruce Wheeler** (D) . . . . . . . . . . (602) 926-3300
Minority Whip **Rebecca Rios** (D) . . . . . . . . . . . . . . . . . . . (602) 926-3073
  Education: Central Arizona 1987 AA; Arizona State 1989 BS, 2003 MS
Chief Clerk of the House **Cheryl Laube** . . . . . . . . . . . . . . (602) 926-3032

**LEGISLATIVE BRANCH**

# Representatives

**Party Affiliation Statistics:** Republicans: 36, Democrats: 24

Representative
**John Christopher Ackerley** (R-District 2) Room 127 . . . (602) 926-3077
Counties Represented: Pima (part)        Fax: (602) 417-3277
Term Expires: 2017
E-mail: jackerley@azleg.gov
Committees: Children and Family Affairs; Government and Higher
Education; Transportation and Infrastructure
Education: Northern Arizona 1999 BS

Representative **John M. Allen** (R-District 15) Room 131 . . (602) 926-4916
Counties Represented: Maricopa (part)        Fax: (602) 417-3150
Term Expires: 2017
E-mail: jallen@azleg.gov
Committees: Appropriations; Banking and Financial Services; Children
and Family Affairs
Education: Arizona State

Representative **Lela Alston** (D-District 24) Room 330 . . . . . (602) 926-5829
Counties Represented: Maricopa (part)        Fax: (602) 417-3115
Term Expires: 2017
E-mail: lalston@azleg.gov
Committees: Appropriations; County and Municipal Affairs; Joint
Capital Review
Education: Arizona 1967 BA; Arizona State 1971 MS

Representative **Richard C. Andrade** (D-District 29)
Room 125 . . . . . . . . . . . . . . . . . . . . . . . . . . . . . . . (602) 926-3130
Counties Represented: Maricopa (part)        Fax: (602) 417-3292
Term Expires: 2017
E-mail: randrade@azleg.gov
Committees: Military Affairs and Public Safety; Transportation and
Infrastructure

Representative **Brenda Barton** (R-District 6) Room 114 . . . (602) 926-4129
Counties Represented: Coconino (part), Gila (part),        Fax: (602) 417-3010
Navajo (part), Yavapai (part)
Term Expires: 2017
E-mail: bbarton@azleg.gov
Committees: Agriculture, Water and Lands; Energy, Environment and
Natural Resources; Rural and Economic Development
Education: Eastern Arizona (Attended)

Representative **Jennifer D. Benally** (D-District 7) . . . . . . . . (602) 926-3079
Counties Represented: Apache, Coconino (part),        Fax: (602) 417-3278
Gila (part), Graham (part), Mohave (part), Navajo (part), Pinal (part)
Term Expires: 2017
E-mail: jbenally@azleg.gov
Committees: Agriculture, Water and Lands; Rural and Economic
Development

Representative **Reginald Bolding, Jr.** (D-District 27)
Room 116 . . . . . . . . . . . . . . . . . . . . . . . . . . . . . . . (602) 926-3132
Counties Represented: Maricopa (part)        Fax: (602) 417-3274
Term Expires: 2017
E-mail: rbolding@azleg.gov
Committees: County and Municipal Affairs; Education

Representative **Sonny Borrelli** (R-District 5) Room 113 . . . (602) 926-5051
Counties Represented: Mohave (part)        Fax: (602) 417-3153
Term Expires: 2017
E-mail: sborrelli@azleg.gov
Committees: Judiciary; Military Affairs and Public Safety;
Transportation and Infrastructure

Representative
**Russell Wesley "Rusty" Bowers** (R-District 25)
Room 309 . . . . . . . . . . . . . . . . . . . . . . . . . . . . . . . (602) 926-3128
Counties Represented: Maricopa (part)        Fax: (602) 417-3290
Term Expires: 2017
E-mail: rbowers@azleg.gov
Committees: Appropriations; Energy, Environment and Natural
Resources; Rural and Economic Development

Representative **Paul Boyer** (R-District 20) Room 129 . . . . . (602) 926-4173
Counties Represented: Maricopa (part)        Fax: (602) 417-3153
Term Expires: 2017
E-mail: pboyer@azleg.gov
Committees: County and Municipal Affairs; Education; Health
Education: Arizona State W 2003 BA, 2011 MA

Representative **Kate Brophy McGee** (R-District 28)
Room 304 . . . . . . . . . . . . . . . . . . . . . . . . . . . . . . . (602) 926-4486
Counties Represented: Maricopa (part)        Fax: (602) 417-3170
Term Expires: 2017
E-mail: kbrophymcgee@azleg.gov
Committees: Banking and Financial Services; Children and Family
Affairs
Education: Arizona 1977 BA

Representative **Noel Campbell** (R-District 1) Room 345 . . (602) 926-3124
Counties Represented: Maricopa (part), Yavapai        Fax: (602) 417-3287
(part)
Term Expires: 2017
E-mail: ncampbell@azleg.gov
Committees: Federalism and States' Rights; Military Affairs and Public
Safety; Transportation and Infrastructure

Representative **Mark A. Cardenas** (D-District 19)
Room 334 . . . . . . . . . . . . . . . . . . . . . . . . . . . . . . . (602) 926-3014
Counties Represented: Maricopa (part)        Fax: (602) 417-3048
Term Expires: 2017
E-mail: mcardenas@azleg.gov
Committees: Appropriations; Military Affairs and Public Safety

Representative **Dr. Heather Carter, EdD** (R-District 15)
Room 303 . . . . . . . . . . . . . . . . . . . . . . . . . . . . . . . (602) 926-5503
Counties Represented: Maricopa (part)        Fax: (602) 417-3107
Term Expires: 2017
E-mail: hcarter@azleg.gov
Committees: Elections; Energy, Environment and Natural Resources;
Health
Education: Arizona State 1992 BS; Arizona State W 2001 MEd;
Northern Arizona 2006 EdD

Representative **Ken Clark** (D-District 24) . . . . . . . . . . . . . . (602) 926-3108
Counties Represented: Maricopa (part)        Fax: (602) 417-3285
Term Expires: 2017
E-mail: kenclark@azleg.gov
Committees: Elections; Energy, Environment and Natural Resources

Representative **Regina Cobb** (R-District 5) Room 335 . . . . (602) 926-3126
Counties Represented: Mohave (part)        Fax: (602) 417-3289
Term Expires: 2017
E-mail: rcobb@azleg.gov
Committees: Agriculture, Water and Lands; Children and Family
Affairs; Health

Representative **Doug Coleman** (R-District 16)
Room 306 . . . . . . . . . . . . . . . . . . . . . . . . . . . . . . . (602) 926-3160
Counties Represented: Maricopa (part), Pinal (part)        Fax: (602) 417-3151
Term Expires: 2017
E-mail: dcoleman@azleg.gov
Committees: County and Municipal Affairs; Education; Insurance
Education: Arizona State 1981 BA; Northern Arizona 1989 MA

Representative **Diego Espinoza** (D-District 19) . . . . . . . . . (602) 926-3134
Counties Represented: Maricopa (part)        Fax: (602) 417-3273
Term Expires: 2017
E-mail: despinoza@azleg.gov
Committees: Banking and Financial Services; Commerce

Representative **Karen Fann** (R-District 1) Room 316 . . . . . . (602) 926-5874
Counties Represented: Maricopa (part), Yavapai        Fax: (602) 417-3001
(part)
Term Expires: 2017
E-mail: kfann@azleg.gov
Committees: Agriculture, Water and Lands; County and Municipal
Affairs; Insurance; Transportation and Infrastructure

Representative
**Edwin W. "Eddie" Farnsworth** (R-District 12)
Room 224 . . . . . . . . . . . . . . . . . . . . . . . . . . . . . . . (602) 926-5735
Counties Represented: Maricopa (part), Pinal (part)        Fax: (602) 417-3122
Term Expires: 2017
E-mail: efarnsworth@azleg.gov
Committees: Banking and Financial Services; Judiciary; Military
Affairs and Public Safety
Education: Arizona 1988 BA; George Washington 1991 MBA, 1991 JD

Representative **Charlene R. Fernandez** (D-District 4)
Room 126 . . . . . . . . . . . . . . . . . . . . . . . . . . . . . . . (602) 926-3098
Counties Represented: Maricopa (part), Pima (part),        Fax: (602) 417-3281
Pinal (part), Yuma (part)
Term Expires: 2017
E-mail: cfernandez@azleg.gov
Committees: Transportation and Infrastructure
Education: Northern Arizona 1993 BS

Representative **Mark Finchem** (R-District 11) . . . . . . . . . . (602) 926-3122
Counties Represented: Pima (part), Pinal (part)        Fax: (602) 417-3286
Term Expires: 2017
E-mail: mfinchem@azleg.gov
Committees: Energy, Environment and Natural Resources; Federalism
and States' Rights; Military Affairs and Public Safety

Representative **Randall Friese** (D-District 9) . . . . . . . . . . . (602) 926-3138
Counties Represented: Pima (part)        Fax: (602) 417-3272
Term Expires: 2017
E-mail: rfriese@azleg.gov
Committees: Government and Higher Education; Health; Judiciary

Representative **Rosanna Gabaldón** (D-District 2)
Room 117 . . . . . . . . . . . . . . . . . . . . . . . . . . . . . . (602) 926-3424
Counties Represented: Pima (part)        Fax: (602) 417-3129
Term Expires: 2017
E-mail: rgabaldon@azleg.gov
Committees: Agriculture, Water and Lands; Banking and Financial
Services; County and Municipal Affairs

Representative **Sally Ann Gonzales** (D-District 3)
Room 331 . . . . . . . . . . . . . . . . . . . . . . . . . . . . . . (602) 926-3278
Counties Represented: Pima (part)        Fax: (602) 417-3127
Term Expires: 2017
E-mail: sgonzales@azleg.gov
Committees: Children and Family Affairs; Rural and Economic
Development
Education: Arizona State 1985 BAElEd; Arizona 1994 MA

Representative **David M. Gowan, Sr.** (R-District 14)
Room 223 . . . . . . . . . . . . . . . . . . . . . . . . . . . . . . (602) 926-3312
Counties Represented: Cochise, Graham (part),    Fax: (602) 417-3130
Greenlee, Pima (part)
Term Expires: 2017
E-mail: dgowan@azleg.gov
Committees: Rules

Representative **Rick Gray** (R-District 21) Room 224 . . . . . . (602) 926-5993
Counties Represented: Maricopa (part)        Fax: (602) 471-3225
Term Expires: 2017
E-mail: rgray@azleg.gov
Committees: Appropriations; County and Municipal Affairs;
Transportation and Infrastructure

Representative **Albert Hale** (D-District 7) Room 129 . . . . . (602) 926-4323
Counties Represented: Apache, Coconino (part),    Fax: (602) 926-3160
Gila (part), Graham (part), Mohave (part), Navajo (part), Pinal (part)
Term Expires: 2017
E-mail: ahale@azleg.gov
Committees: Joint Legislative Council; Judiciary; Rules
Education: Arizona State 1973 BS; New Mexico 1977 JD

Representative **Anthony Kern** (R-District 20) Room 341 . . (602) 926-3102
Counties Represented: Maricopa (part)        Fax: (602) 417-3282
Term Expires: 2017
E-mail: akern@azleg.gov
Committees: Judiciary; Military Affairs and Public Safety; Ways and
Means

Representative **Matthew Kopec** (D-District 9) . . . . . . . . . . (602) 926-3032
Counties Represented: Pima (part)
Term Expires: 2017
E-mail: mkopec@azleg.gov
Committees: Energy, Environment and Natural Resources;
Transportation and Infrastructure

Representative **Jonathan Larkin** (D-District 30)
Room 318 . . . . . . . . . . . . . . . . . . . . . . . . . . . . . . (602) 926-5058
Counties Represented: Maricopa (part)        Fax: (602) 417-3015
Term Expires: 2017
E-mail: jlarkin@azleg.gov
Committees: Elections; Government and Higher Education; Insurance

Representative **Jay Lawrence** (R-District 23) Room 339 . . (602) 926-3095
Counties Represented: Maricopa (part)        Fax: (602) 417-3280
Term Expires: 2017
E-mail: jlawrence@azleg.gov
Committees: Commerce; Education; Health

Representative **Vince Leach** (R-District 11) Room 342 . . . . (602) 926-3106
Counties Represented: Pima (part), Pinal (part)    Fax: (602) 417-3284
Term Expires: 2017
E-mail: vleach@azleg.gov
Committees: Appropriations; Energy, Environment and Natural
Resources; Rural and Economic Development
Education: Wisconsin (Stevens Point) BS

Representative **David Livingston** (R-District 22)
Room 207 . . . . . . . . . . . . . . . . . . . . . . . . . . . . . . (602) 926-4178
Counties Represented: Maricopa (part)        Fax: (602) 417-3154
Term Expires: 2017
E-mail: dlivingston@azleg.gov
Committees: Insurance

Representative **Phil Lovas** (R-District 22) Room 110 . . . . . (602) 926-3297
Counties Represented: Maricopa (part)        Fax: (602) 417-3004
Term Expires: 2017
E-mail: plovas@azleg.gov
Committees: Children and Family Affairs; Government and Higher
Education; Insurance

Representative **Stefanie Mach** (D-District 10) Room 329 . . (602) 926-3398
Counties Represented: Pima (part)        Fax: (602) 417-3126
Term Expires: 2017
E-mail: smach@azleg.gov
Committees: Appropriations; Commerce; Military Affairs and Public
Safety
Education: Wisconsin (Stevens Point) BA; Brown U 2011 MPP

Representative **Debbie McCune-Davis** (D-District 30)
Room 333 . . . . . . . . . . . . . . . . . . . . . . . . . . . . . . (602) 926-4485
Counties Represented: Maricopa (part)        Fax: (602) 417-3014
Term Expires: 2017
E-mail: ddavis@azleg.gov
Committees: Banking and Financial Services; Insurance
Education: Arizona State 1975 BA

Representative **Juan Jose Mendez** (D-District 26)
Room 120 . . . . . . . . . . . . . . . . . . . . . . . . . . . . . . (602) 926-4124
Counties Represented: Maricopa (part)        Fax: (602) 417-3017
Term Expires: 2017
E-mail: jmendez@azleg.gov
Committees: Children and Family Affairs; Rural and Economic
Development
Education: Phoenix Col 2006 AA; Arizona State 2008 BA

Representative
**Javan D. "J. D." Mesnard** (R-District 17) Room 308 . . . (602) 926-4481
Counties Represented: Maricopa (part)        Fax: (602) 417-3152
Term Expires: 2017
E-mail: jmesnard@azleg.gov
Committees: Elections; Judiciary; Ways and Means
Education: Arizona State 2002 BA; U Phoenix 2006 MA;
Keller Grad School 2006 MA

Representative **Eric Meyer** (D-District 28) Room 320 . . . . . (602) 926-3037
Counties Represented: Maricopa (part)        Fax: (602) 417-3111
Term Expires: 2017
E-mail: emeyer@azleg.gov
Committees: Health

Representative **Darin Mitchell** (R-District 13) Room 313 . . (602) 926-5894
Counties Represented: Maricopa (part), Yavapai    Fax: (602) 417-3012
(part), Yuma (part)
Term Expires: 2017
E-mail: dmitchell@azleg.gov
Committees: Agriculture, Water and Lands; Federalism and States'
Rights; Ways and Means
Education: Arizona State BS

Representative **Steve B. Montenegro** (R-District 13)
Room 208 . . . . . . . . . . . . . . . . . . . . . . . . . . . . . . (602) 926-5955
Counties Represented: Maricopa (part), Yavapai    Fax: (602) 417-3168
(part), Yuma (part)
Term Expires: 2017
E-mail: smontenegro@azleg.gov
Committees: Agriculture, Water and Lands; Rules

Representative **Jill Norgaard** (R-District 18) Room 128 . . . (602) 926-3140
Counties Represented: Maricopa (part)        Fax: (602) 417-3265
Term Expires: 2017
E-mail: jnorgaard@azleg.gov
Committees: Banking and Financial Services; Commerce; Education

Representative **Justin D. Olson** (R-District 25)
Room 204 . . . . . . . . . . . . . . . . . . . . . . . . . . . . . . (602) 926-5288
Counties Represented: Maricopa (part)        Tel: (602) 417-3161
Term Expires: 2017
E-mail: jolson@azleg.gov
Committees: Appropriations; Government and Higher Education; Joint
Capital Review; Ways and Means
Education: Arizona State BS

Representative **Lisa Otondo** (D-District 4) Room 123 . . . . . (602) 926-3002
Counties Represented: Maricopa (part), Pima (part),    Fax: (602) 417-3124
Pinal (part), Yuma (part)
Term Expires: 2017
E-mail: lotondo@azleg.gov
Committees: Agriculture, Water and Lands; Education; Insurance
Education: Monterey Inst BA, MPA

Representative **Warren H. Petersen** (R-District 12)
Room 312 . . . . . . . . . . . . . . . . . . . . . . . . . . . . . . (602) 926-4136
Counties Represented: Maricopa (part), Pinal (part)    Fax: (602) 417-3222
Term Expires: 2017
E-mail: wpetersen@azleg.gov
Committees: Appropriations; Commerce; Government and Higher
Education

Representative **Celeste Plumlee** (D-District 26) . . . . . . . . . (602) 926-3032
Counties Represented: Maricopa (part)
Term Expires: 2017
E-mail: cplumlee@azleg.gov
Committees: Commerce; County and Municipal Affairs

*(continued on next page)*

**LEGISLATIVE BRANCH**

**Representatives** *continued*

Representative **Frank Pratt** (R-District 8) Room 223 . . . . . . (602) 926-5761
  Counties Represented: Gila (part), Pinal (part)    Fax: (602) 417-3023
  Term Expires: 2017
  E-mail: fpratt@azleg.gov
  Committees: Energy, Environment and Natural Resources; Military
  Affairs and Public Safety; Rural and Economic Development

Representative **Rebecca Rios** (D-District 27) Room 322 . . . (602) 926-3073
  Counties Represented: Maricopa (part)    Fax: (602) 417-3288
  Term Expires: 2017
  E-mail: rrios@azleg.gov
  Committees: Children and Family Affairs; Federalism and States'
  Rights

Representative **Tony Rivero** (R-District 21) Room 344 . . . . (602) 926-3104
  Counties Represented: Maricopa (part)    Fax: (602) 417-3283
  Term Expires: 2017
  E-mail: trivero@azleg.gov
  Committees: Appropriations; Commerce; County and Municipal Affairs

Representative **Bob Robson** (R-District 18) Room 222 . . . . (602) 926-5549
  Counties Represented: Maricopa (part)    Fax: (602) 417-3157
  Term Expires: 2017
  E-mail: brobson@azleg.gov
  Committees: Insurance; Rules

Representative **Macario Saldate IV** (D-District 3)
  Room 332 . . . . . . . . . . . . . . . . . . . . . . . . . . . . . . . (602) 926-4171
  Counties Represented: Pima (part)    Fax: (602) 417-3162
  Term Expires: 2017
  E-mail: msaldate@azleg.gov
  Committees: Energy, Environment and Natural Resources; Government
  and Higher Education

Representative **Thomas "T.J." Shope** (R-District 8)
  Room 112 . . . . . . . . . . . . . . . . . . . . . . . . . . . . . . . (602) 926-3012
  Counties Represented: Gila (part), Pinal (part)    Fax: (602) 417-3123
  Term Expires: 2017
  E-mail: tshope@azleg.gov
  Committees: Agriculture, Water and Lands; Commerce; Rural and
  Economic Development

Representative **David W. Stevens** (R-District 14)
  Room 205 . . . . . . . . . . . . . . . . . . . . . . . . . . . . . . . (602) 926-4321
  Counties Represented: Cochise, Graham (part),    Fax: (602) 417-3146
  Greenlee, Pima (part)
  Term Expires: 2017
  E-mail: dstevens@azleg.gov
  Committees: Appropriations; Rules; Transportation and Infrastructure

Representative **Bob Thorpe** (R-District 6) Room 130 . . . . . (602) 926-5219
  Counties Represented: Coconino (part), Gila (part),    Fax: (602) 417-3118
  Navajo (part), Yavapai (part)
  Term Expires: 2017
  E-mail: bthorpe@azleg.gov
  Committees: Education; Federalism and States' Rights; Government
  and Higher Education; Rules

Representative **Kelly Townsend** (R-District 16)
  Room 302 . . . . . . . . . . . . . . . . . . . . . . . . . . . . . . . (602) 926-4467
  Counties Represented: Maricopa (part), Pinal (part)    Fax: (602) 417-3018
  Term Expires: 2017
  E-mail: ktownsend@azleg.gov
  Committees: Children and Family Affairs; Federalism and States'
  Rights; Government and Higher Education

Representative **Michelle B. Ugenti-Rita** (R-District 23)
  Room 111 . . . . . . . . . . . . . . . . . . . . . . . . . . . . . . . (602) 926-4480
  Counties Represented: Maricopa (part)    Tel: (602) 417-3155
  Term Expires: 2017
  E-mail: mugenti@azleg.gov
  Committees: Appropriations; Elections; Ways and Means

Representative **Ceci Velásquez** (D-District 29)
  Room 124 . . . . . . . . . . . . . . . . . . . . . . . . . . . . . . . (602) 926-3144
  Counties Represented: Maricopa (part)    Fax: (602) 417-3245
  Term Expires: 2017
  E-mail: cvelasquez@azleg.gov
  Committees: Federalism and States' Rights; Rules

Representative **Jeff Weninger** (R-District 17) Room 338 . . (602) 926-3092
  Counties Represented: Maricopa (part)    Fax: (602) 417-3279
  Term Expires: 2017
  E-mail: jweninger@azleg.gov
  Committees: Banking and Financial Services; Elections; Ways and
  Means

Representative **Bruce Wheeler** (D-District 10) Room 321 . . (602) 926-3300
  Counties Represented: Pima (part)    Fax: (602) 417-3028
  Term Expires: 2017
  E-mail: bwheeler@azleg.gov
  Committees: Federalism and States' Rights; Rules; Ways and Means

# House Standing Committees

## Agriculture, Water and Lands

| Majority Members | Minority Members |
|---|---|
| Brenda Barton (R-6) *Chair* | Jennifer D. Benally (D-7) |
| Darin Mitchell (R-13) *Vice Chair* | Rosanna Gabaldón (D-2) |
| Regina Cobb (R-5) | Lisa Otondo (D-4) |
| Karen Fann (R-1) | |
| Steve B. Montenegro (R-13) | |
| Thomas "T.J." Shope (R-8) | |

## Appropriations

| Majority Members | Minority Members |
|---|---|
| Justin D. Olson (R-25) *Chair* | Lela Alston (D-24) |
| Vince Leach (R-11) *Vice Chair* | Mark A. Cardenas (D-19) |
| John M. Allen (R-15) | Stefanie Mach (D-10) |
| Russell Wesley "Rusty" Bowers (R-25) | |
| Rick Gray (R-21) | |
| Warren H. Petersen (R-12) | |
| Tony Rivero (R-21) | |
| David W. Stevens (R-14) | |
| Michelle B. Ugenti-Rita (R-23) | |

## Banking and Financial Services

| Majority Members | Minority Members |
|---|---|
| Kate Brophy McGee (R-28) *Chair* | Diego Espinoza (D-19) |
| Jeff Weninger (R-17) *Vice Chair* | Rosanna Gabaldón (D-2) |
| John M. Allen (R-15) | Debbie McCune-Davis (D-30) |
| Edwin W. "Eddie" Farnsworth (R-12) | |
| Jill Norgaard (R-18) | |

## Children and Family Affairs

| Majority Members | Minority Members |
|---|---|
| John M. Allen (R-15) *Chair* | Sally Ann Gonzales (D-3) |
| Kate Brophy McGee (R-28) *Vice Chair* | Juan Jose Mendez (D-26) |
| John Christopher Ackerley (R-2) | Rebecca Rios (D-27) |
| Regina Cobb (R-5) | |
| Phil Lovas (R-22) | |
| Kelly Townsend (R-16) | |

## Commerce

| Majority Members | Minority Members |
|---|---|
| Warren H. Petersen (R-12) *Chair* | Diego Espinoza (D-19) |
| Jill Norgaard (R-18) *Vice Chair* | Stefanie Mach (D-10) |
| Jay Lawrence (R-23) | Celeste Plumlee (D-26) |
| Tony Rivero (R-21) | |
| Thomas "T.J." Shope (R-8) | |

## County and Municipal Affairs

| Majority Members | Minority Members |
|---|---|
| Doug Coleman (R-16) *Chair* | Lela Alston (D-24) |
| Tony Rivero (R-21) *Vice Chair* | Reginald Bolding, Jr. (D-27) |
| Paul Boyer (R-20) | Rosanna Gabaldón (D-2) |
| Karen Fann (R-1) | Celeste Plumlee (D-26) |
| Rick Gray (R-21) | |

## Education

| Majority Members | Minority Members |
|---|---|
| Paul Boyer (R-20) *Chair* | Reginald Bolding, Jr. (D-27) |
| Jay Lawrence (R-23) *Vice Chair* | Lisa Otondo (D-4) |
| Doug Coleman (R-16) | |
| Jill Norgaard (R-18) | |
| Bob Thorpe (R-6) | |

## Elections

| Majority Members | Minority Members |
|---|---|
| Michelle B. Ugenti-Rita (R-23) *Chair* | Ken Clark (D-24) |
| Javan D. "J. D." Mesnard (R-17) *Vice Chair* | Jonathan Larkin (D-30) |
| Dr. Heather Carter (R-15) | |
| Jeff Weninger (R-17) | |

**LEGISLATIVE BRANCH**

## Energy, Environment and Natural Resources

| Majority Members | Minority Members |
|---|---|
| Frank Pratt (R-8) *Chair* | Ken Clark (D-24) |
| Russell Wesley "Rusty" Bowers (R-25) *Vice Chair* | Matthew Kopec (D-9) |
| | Macario Saldate IV (D-3) |
| Brenda Barton (R-6) | |
| Dr. Heather Carter (R-15) | |
| Mark Finchem (R-11) | |
| Vince Leach (R-11) | |

## Federalism and States' Rights

| Majority Members | Minority Members |
|---|---|
| Kelly Townsend (R-16) *Chair* | Rebecca Rios (D-27) |
| Noel Campbell (R-1) *Vice Chair* | Ceci Velásquez (D-29) |
| Mark Finchem (R-11) | Bruce Wheeler (D-10) |
| Darin Mitchell (R-13) | |
| Bob Thorpe (R-6) | |

## Government and Higher Education

| Majority Members | Minority Members |
|---|---|
| Bob Thorpe (R-6) *Chair* | Randall Friese (D-9) |
| John Christopher Ackerley (R-2) *Vice Chair* | Jonathan Larkin (D-30) |
| | Macario Saldate IV (D-3) |
| Phil Lovas (R-22) | |
| Justin D. Olson (R-25) | |
| Warren H. Petersen (R-12) | |
| Kelly Townsend (R-16) | |

## Health

| Majority Members | Minority Members |
|---|---|
| Dr. Heather Carter (R-15) *Chair* | Randall Friese (D-9) |
| Regina Cobb (R-5) *Vice Chair* | Eric Meyer (D-28) |
| Paul Boyer (R-20) | |
| Jay Lawrence (R-23) | |

## Insurance

| Majority Members | Minority Members |
|---|---|
| Karen Fann (R-1) *Chair* | Jonathan Larkin (D-30) |
| David Livingston (R-22) *Vice Chair* | Debbie McCune-Davis (D-30) |
| Doug Coleman (R-16) | Lisa Otondo (D-4) |
| Phil Lovas (R-22) | |
| Bob Robson (R-18) | |

## Judiciary

| Majority Members | Minority Members |
|---|---|
| Edwin W. "Eddie" Farnsworth (R-12) *Chair* | Randall Friese (D-9) |
| | Albert Hale (D-7) |
| Sonny Borrelli (R-5) *Vice Chair* | |
| Anthony Kern (R-20) | |
| Javan D. "J. D." Mesnard (R-17) | |

## Military Affairs and Public Safety

| Majority Members | Minority Members |
|---|---|
| Sonny Borrelli (R-5) *Chair* | Richard C. Andrade (D-29) |
| Mark Finchem (R-11) *Vice Chair* | Mark A. Cardenas (D-19) |
| Noel Campbell (R-1) | Stefanie Mach (D-10) |
| Edwin W. "Eddie" Farnsworth (R-12) | |
| Anthony Kern (R-20) | |
| Frank Pratt (R-8) | |

## Rules

| Majority Members | Minority Members |
|---|---|
| David W. Stevens (R-14) *Chair* | Albert Hale (D-7) |
| Steve B. Montenegro (R-13) *Vice Chair* | Ceci Velásquez (D-29) |
| | Bruce Wheeler (D-10) |
| David M. Gowan, Sr. (R-14) | |
| Bob Robson (R-18) | |
| Bob Thorpe (R-6) | |

## Rural and Economic Development

| Majority Members | Minority Members |
|---|---|
| Thomas "T.J." Shope (R-8) *Chair* | Jennifer D. Benally (D-7) |
| Russell Wesley "Rusty" Bowers (R-25) *Vice Chair* | Sally Ann Gonzales (D-3) |
| | Juan Jose Mendez (D-26) |
| Brenda Barton (R-6) | |
| Vince Leach (R-11) | |
| Frank Pratt (R-8) | |

## Transportation and Infrastructure

| Majority Members | Minority Members |
|---|---|
| Rick Gray (R-21) *Chair* | Richard C. Andrade (D-29) |
| David W. Stevens (R-14) *Vice Chair* | Charlene R. Fernandez (D-4) |
| John Christopher Ackerley (R-2) | Matthew Kopec (D-9) |
| Sonny Borrelli (R-5) | |
| Noel Campbell (R-1) | |
| Karen Fann (R-1) | |

## Ways and Means

| Majority Members | Minority Members |
|---|---|
| Darin Mitchell (R-13) *Chair* | Bruce Wheeler (D-10) |
| Anthony Kern (R-20) *Vice Chair* | |
| Javan D. "J. D." Mesnard (R-17) | |
| Justin D. Olson (R-25) | |
| Michelle B. Ugenti-Rita (R-23) | |
| Jeff Weninger (R-17) | |

**LEGISLATIVE BRANCH**

# Arkansas General Assembly

Tel: (501) 682-6107  TTY: (501) 682-1952  Fax: (501) 682-2917
Internet: www.arkleg.state.ar.us

## Arkansas Senate

State Capitol Building, 500 Woodlane Street, Suite 320,
Little Rock, AR 72201
Tel: (501) 682-6107  TTY: (501) 682-1952  Fax: (501) 682-2917
Internet: www.arkleg.state.ar.us

President of the Senate
**LTC J. Timothy "Tim" Griffin, USAR** (R) . . . . . . . . . . .(501) 682-2144
  E-mail: tim.griffin@ark.org
  Education: Hendrix 1990 BA; Tulane 1994 JD
President Pro Tempore **Jonathan Dismang** (R) . . . . . . . . .(501) 776-8220
Assistant President Pro Tem - 1st District
  **Eddie Joe Williams** (R) . . . . . . . . . . . . . . . . . . . . . . . . . . (501) 286-9366
Assistant President Pro Tem - 2nd District
  **Jane English** (R) . . . . . . . . . . . . . . . . . . . . . . . . . . . . . . . (501) 257-7670
Assistant President Pro Tem - 3rd District
  **Cecile Bledsoe** (R) . . . . . . . . . . . . . . . . . . . . . . . . . . . . . (501) 682-5951
Majority Leader **Jim Hendren** (R) . . . . . . . . . . . . . . . . (479) 787-6222
  Education: Arkansas 1984 BSEE
Majority Whip **Jimmy Hickey, Jr.** (R) . . . . . . . . . . . . . . (870) 772-4444
Minority Leader **Keith M. Ingram** (D) . . . . . . . . . . . . . . (870) 735-9580
  Education: Mississippi BS
Minority Whip and Assistant President Pro Tem - 4th
  District **Bobby J. Pierce** (D) . . . . . . . . . . . . . . . . . . . . . .(870) 942-1031
Director, Arkansas Senate/Secretary of the Senate
  **Ann Cornwell** . . . . . . . . . . . . . . . . . . . . . . . . . . . . . . . . (501) 682-5951
  E-mail: ann.cornwell@senate.ar.gov
Constituency Services, Research and Special Projects
  Manager **Sabrina Lewellen** . . . . . . . . . . . . . . . . . . . . . . (501) 682-5608
  E-mail: lewellens@arkleg.state.ar.us
Public Information Officer **John Reed** . . . . . . . . . . . . . . . (501) 682-5954
  E-mail: john.reed@senate.ar.gov

## Senators

**Party Affiliation Statistics:** Republicans: 24, Democrats: 11

Senator **Cecile Bledsoe** (R-District 3) . . . . . . . . . . . . . . . .(501) 682-5951
  Counties Represented: Benton (part)
  Term Expires: 2019
  709 Sky Mountain Drive, Rogers, AR 72757
  E-mail: cecile.bledsoe@senate.ar.gov
  Committees: Joint Budget; Joint Energy; Joint Legislative Auditing;
  Joint Legislative Council; Public Health, Welfare and Labor; State
  Agencies and Governmental Affairs
Senator **David Burnett** (D-District 22) . . . . . . . . . . . . . . . (870) 563-5667
  Counties Represented: Craighead (part), Mississippi, Poinsett
  Term Expires: 2017
  P.O. Box 704, Osceola, AR 72730
  E-mail: david.burnett@senate.ar.gov
  Committees: Joint Budget; Joint Energy; Joint Legislative Auditing;
  Judiciary; State Agencies and Governmental Affairs
Senator **Ronald "Ron" Caldwell** (R-District 23) . . . . . . . .(501) 682-6107
  Counties Represented: Cross (part), Jackson, Lee (part), Monroe (part),
  St. Francis (part), White (part), Woodruff (part)
  Term Expires: 2017
  2490 Highway 284, Wynne, AR 72396
  E-mail: ronald.caldwell@senate.ar.gov
  Committees: Agriculture, Forestry and Economic Development; Joint
  Advanced Communications and Information Technology; Joint Budget;
  Joint Energy; Joint Legislative Council; Transportation, Technology and
  Legislative Affairs
  Education: Arkansas State BS
Senator **Eddie L. Cheatham** (D-District 26) . . . . . . . . . . . (870) 364-5659
  Counties Represented: Ashley, Bradley, Chicot, Cleveland (part), Desha
  (part), Drew, Lincoln (part)
  Term Expires: 2017
  2814 Ashley 239, Crossett, AR 71635
  E-mail: eddie.cheatham@senate.ar.gov
  Committees: Agriculture, Forestry and Economic Development;
  Education; Joint Legislative Auditing; Joint Public Retirement and
  Social Security Programs
  Education: Southern Arkansas U BS; Arkansas MEd

Senator **Linda Pondexter Chesterfield** (D-District 30) . . . .(501) 888-1859
  Counties Represented: Pulaski (part)
  Term Expires: 2019
  12 Keo Drive, Little Rock, AR 72206
  E-mail: linda.chesterfield@senate.ar.gov
  Committees: Children and Youth; Joint Budget; Joint Legislative
  Auditing; Judiciary; State Agencies and Governmental Affairs
Senator **Alan Clark** (R-District 13) . . . . . . . . . . . . . . . . . (501) 262-3360
  Counties Represented: Garland (part), Grant (part), Hot Spring, Saline
  (part)
  Term Expires: 2017
  P.O. Box 211, Lonsdale, AR 72087
  E-mail: alan.clark@senate.ar.gov
  Committees: Agriculture, Forestry and Economic Development;
  Children and Youth; Education; Joint Budget; Joint Legislative Council;
  Joint Performance Review
Senator **Linda Collins-Smith** (R-District 19) . . . . . . . . . . . (870) 378-1434
  Counties Represented: Fulton (part), Independence, Izard, Randolph
  (part), Sharp
  Term Expires: 2019
  P.O. Box 90, Pocahontas, AR 72455
  E-mail: linda.collins-smith@senate.ar.gov
  Committees: Children and Youth; City, County and Local Affairs; Joint
  Performance Review; Judiciary
Senator **John Cooper** (R-District 21) . . . . . . . . . . . . . . . . (501) 682-6107
  Counties Represented: Craighead (part)
  Term Expires: 2017
  P.O. Box 16801, Jonesboro, AR 72404
  E-mail: john.cooper@senate.ar.gov
  Committees: Agriculture, Forestry and Economic Development; Joint
  Budget; Joint Energy; Joint Legislative Council; Joint Performance
  Review; Public Health, Welfare and Labor
Senator **Jonathan Dismang** (R-District 28) . . . . . . . . . . . .(501) 776-8220
  Counties Represented: Arkansas (part), Lonoke (part), Monroe (part),
  Prairie, White (part), Woodruff (part)
  Term Expires: 2017
  P.O. Box 475, Beebe, AR 72012
  E-mail: jonathan.dismang@senate.ar.gov
  Committees: Children and Youth; Insurance and Commerce; Joint
  Budget; Joint Legislative Auditing; Joint Legislative Council; Revenue
  and Taxation
Senator **Joyce Elliott** (D-District 31) . . . . . . . . . . . . . . . . . (501) 603-9546
  Counties Represented: Pulaski (part)
  Term Expires: 2019
  P.O. Box 4248, Little Rock, AR 72214
  E-mail: joyce.elliott@senate.ar.gov
  Committees: Joint Budget; Joint Legislative Auditing; Joint Legislative
  Council; Joint Public Retirement and Social Security Programs;
  Judiciary; State Agencies and Governmental Affairs
Senator **Jane English** (R-District 34) . . . . . . . . . . . . . . . . . (501) 257-7670
  Counties Represented: Pulaski (part)
  Term Expires: 2017
  Three Great Oak Court, North Little Rock, AR 72116
  E-mail: jane.english@senate.ar.gov
  Committees: Children and Youth; Education; Insurance and Commerce;
  Joint Legislative Auditing; Joint Legislative Council; Joint Performance
  Review
Senator **Jake C. Files** (R-District 8) . . . . . . . . . . . . . . . . . . (479) 650-6899
  Counties Represented: Sebastian (part)
  Term Expires: 2019
  300 Free Ferry Landing, Fort Smith, AR 72903
  E-mail: jake.files@senate.ar.gov
  Committees: Joint Advanced Communications and Information
  Technology; Joint Budget; Joint Legislative Auditing; Revenue and
  Taxation; Transportation, Technology and Legislative Affairs
  Education: Arkansas State 1994 BS
Senator **Scott Flippo** (R-District 17) . . . . . . . . . . . . . . . . . .(870) 421-3420
  Counties Represented: Baxter (part), Boone (part), Marion (part)
  Term Expires: 2019
  E-mail: scott.flippo@senate.ar.gov
  Committees: City, County and Local Affairs; Joint Energy; Joint
  Legislative Council; Public Health, Welfare and Labor; Rules,
  Resolutions, and Memorials
Senator **Stephanie Flowers** (D-District 25) . . . . . . . . . . . . (501) 535-1032
  Counties Represented: Arkansas (part), Desha (part), Jefferson (part),
  Lincoln (part), Monroe (part), Phillips (part)
  Term Expires: 2017
  104 Maine Street, Pine Bluff, AR 71601
  E-mail: stephanie.flowers@senate.ar.gov
  Committees: Children and Youth; City, County and Local Affairs;
  Insurance and Commerce; Joint Budget; Joint Legislative Council;
  Public Health, Welfare and Labor

LEGISLATIVE BRANCH

Senator **Jim Hendren** (R-District 2) . . . . . . . . . . . . . . . . . (479) 787-6222
Counties Represented: Benton (part), Washington (part)
Term Expires: 2017
1607 Highway 72, SE, Gravette, AR 72736
E-mail: jim.hendren@senate.ar.gov
Committees: City, County and Local Affairs; Education; Joint
Advanced Communications and Information Technology; Joint Budget;
Joint Energy; Joint Legislative Council; Transportation, Technology and
Legislative Affairs

Senator **Bart Hester** (R-District 1) . . . . . . . . . . . . . . . . . . (479) 531-4176
Counties Represented: Benton (part), Washington (part)
Term Expires: 2017
2024 Shores Avenue, Cave Springs, AR 72718
E-mail: bart.hester@senate.ar.gov
Committees: Children and Youth; City, County and Local Affairs; Joint
Budget; Joint Legislative Auditing; Joint Legislative Council; Revenue
and Taxation
Education: Arkansas 2001

Senator **Jimmy Hickey, Jr.** (R-District 11) . . . . . . . . . . . . . (870) 772-4444
Counties Represented: Hempstead (part), Lafayette, Little River, Miller,
Sevier (part)
Term Expires: 2017
1600 Arkansas Boulevard, Texarkana, AR 71854
E-mail: jimmy.hickey@senate.ar.gov
Committees: Joint Advanced Communications and Information
Technology; Joint Energy; Joint Legislative Auditing; Revenue and
Taxation; Transportation, Technology and Legislative Affairs

Senator **Jeremy Hutchinson** (R-District 33) . . . . . . . . . . . (501) 773-3760
Counties Represented: Pulaski (part), Saline (part)
Term Expires: 2019
Three Chenal Wood Drive, Little Rock, AR 72223
E-mail: jeremy.hutchinson@senate.ar.gov
Committees: Insurance and Commerce; Joint Budget; Joint Legislative
Council; Joint Performance Review; Judiciary
Education: Harvard 1997 BBA; Arkansas (Little Rock) 2006 JD

Senator **Keith M. Ingram** (D-District 24) . . . . . . . . . . . . . . (870) 735-9580
Counties Represented: Crittenden, Cross (part), Lee (part), Phillips
(part), St. Francis (part)
Term Expires: 2019
P.O. 1028, West Memphis, AR 72303
E-mail: keith.ingram@senate.ar.gov
Committees: City, County and Local Affairs; Joint Budget; Joint
Legislative Auditing; Public Health, Welfare and Labor

Senator **Missy Thomas Irvin** (R-District 18) . . . . . . . . . . . (870) 269-2703
Counties Represented: Baxter (part), Cleburne, Faulkner (part), Fulton
(part), Marion (part), Searcy, Stone, Van Buren (part), White (part)
Term Expires: 2019
P.O. Box 106, Mountain View, AR 72560
E-mail: missy.irvin@senate.ar.gov
Committees: Children and Youth; City, County and Local Affairs; Joint
Budget; Joint Legislative Council; Joint Performance Review; Public
Health, Welfare and Labor

Senator **Blake Johnson** (R-District 20) . . . . . . . . . . . . . . . (870) 323-1766
Counties Represented: Clay, Craighead (part), Greene, Lawrence,
Randolph (part)
Term Expires: 2019
P.O. Box 8, Corning, AR 72422
E-mail: blake.johnson@senate.ar.gov
Committees: Agriculture, Forestry and Economic Development;
Education; Joint Legislative Auditing; Joint Public Retirement and
Social Security Programs
Education: Arkansas State 1993 BS

Senator **David Johnson** (D-District 32) . . . . . . . . . . . . . . . (501) 682-6107
Counties Represented: Pulaski (part)
Term Expires: 2017
State Capitol, Room 320, Little Rock, AR 72201
E-mail: david.johnson@senate.ar.gov
Committees: Joint Budget; Joint Public Retirement and Social Security
Programs; Judiciary; State Agencies and Governmental Affairs

Senator **Bryan B. King** (R-District 5) . . . . . . . . . . . . . . . . . (870) 438-4565
Counties Represented: Carroll (part), Crawford (part), Franklin (part),
Johnson (part), Madison, Sebastian (part), Washington (part)
Term Expires: 2019
874 County Road 814, Green Forest, AR 72638
E-mail: bryan.king@senate.ar.gov
Committees: Joint Advanced Communications and Information
Technology; Joint Energy; Joint Legislative Auditing; Joint Legislative
Council; Joint Performance Review; State Agencies and Governmental
Affairs; Transportation, Technology and Legislative Affairs

Senator **Uvalde Lindsey** (D-District 4) . . . . . . . . . . . . . . . . (479) 444-6752
Counties Represented: Washington (part)
Term Expires: 2019
2257 Gentle Oaks Lane, Fayetteville, AR 72703
E-mail: uvalde.lindsey@senate.ar.gov
Committees: Education; Insurance and Commerce; Joint Budget; Joint
Legislative Auditing; Joint Legislative Council; Joint Public Retirement
and Social Security Programs

Senator **Bruce Maloch** (D-District 12) . . . . . . . . . . . . . . . (870) 235-7040
Counties Represented: Clark (part), Columbia, Dallas, Grant (part),
Nevada (part), Ouachita (part)
Term Expires: 2017
650 Columbia Road 258, Magnolia, AR 71753
E-mail: bruce.maloch@senate.ar.gov
Committees: Agriculture, Forestry and Economic Development; Joint
Budget; Joint Public Retirement and Social Security Programs;
Revenue and Taxation
Education: Southern Arkansas U BBA; Arkansas JD

Senator **Bobby J. Pierce** (D-District 27) . . . . . . . . . . . . . . (870) 942-1031
Counties Represented: Calhoun, Cleveland (part), Grant (part),
Jefferson (part), Ouachita (part), Union
Term Expires: 2017
587 Grant 758, Sheridan, AR 72150
E-mail: bobby.pierce@senate.ar.gov
Committees: Children and Youth; Education; Joint Advanced
Communications and Information Technology; Joint Budget; Joint
Legislative Auditing; Joint Legislative Council; Transportation,
Technology and Legislative Affairs

Senator **Stanley Jason Rapert** (R-District 35) . . . . . . . . . (501) 336-0918
Counties Represented: Faulkner (part), Perry (part)
Term Expires: 2019
P.O. Box 10388, Conway, AR 72034
E-mail: jason.rapert@senate.ar.gov
Committees: Insurance and Commerce; Joint Budget; Joint Legislative
Council; Joint Public Retirement and Social Security Programs;
Revenue and Taxation

Senator **Terry Rice** (R-District 9) . . . . . . . . . . . . . . . . . . . . (479) 637-3100
Counties Represented: Crawford (part), Franklin (part), Scott, Sebastian
(part)
Term Expires: 2019
P.O. Box 2195, Waldron, AR 72958
E-mail: terry.rice@senate.ar.gov
Committees: Insurance and Commerce; Joint Legislative Auditing; Joint
Legislative Council; Judiciary

Senator **Bill Sample** (R-District 14) . . . . . . . . . . . . . . . . . . (501) 321-0040
Counties Represented: Garland (part), Saline (part)
Term Expires: 2019
2340 North Highway Seven, Hot Springs, AR 71909
E-mail: bill.sample@senate.ar.gov
Committees: Joint Advanced Communications and Information
Technology; Joint Legislative Auditing; Joint Legislative Council;
Joint Public Retirement and Social Security Programs; Revenue and
Taxation; Transportation, Technology and Legislative Affairs

Senator **David J. Sanders** (R-District 15) Room 320 . . . . . (501) 682-6107
Counties Represented: Conway, Faulkner (part), Perry (part), Pulaski
(part), Van Buren (part)
Term Expires: 2019
E-mail: davidjamessanders@gmail.com
Committees: Agriculture, Forestry and Economic Development; Joint
Legislative Auditing; Joint Legislative Council; Joint Performance
Review; Public Health, Welfare and Labor
Education: Ouachita Baptist 1997 BS

Senator **Greg Standridge** (R-District 16) . . . . . . . . . . . . . . (479) 968-1562
Counties Represented: Boone (part), Carroll (part), Newton, Pope, Van
Buren (part)
Term Expires: 2019
P.O. Box 1284, Russellville, AR 72811
E-mail: greg.standridge@senate.ar.gov
Committees: Children and Youth; City, County and Local Affairs;
Joint Advanced Communications and Information Technology;
Transportation, Technology and Legislative Affairs

Senator **Gary Stubblefield** (R-District 6) . . . . . . . . . . . . . . (479) 635-4314
Counties Represented: Franklin (part), Johnson (part), Logan, Yell
Term Expires: 2019
2542 Skeets Road, Branch, AR 72928
E-mail: gary.stubblefield@senate.ar.gov
Committees: Agriculture, Forestry and Economic Development; Joint
Budget; Joint Energy; Joint Legislative Council; Joint Performance
Review; Public Health, Welfare and Labor

*(continued on next page)*

**Senators** *continued*

Senator **Larry Teague** (D-District 10) . . . . . . . . . . . . . . . . . (870) 845-5303
  Counties Represented: Clark (part), Hempstead (part), Howard,
  Montgomery, Nevada (part), Pike, Polk, Sevier (part)
  Term Expires: 2019
  P.O. Box 903, Nashville, AR 71852
  E-mail: larry.teague@senate.ar.gov
  Committees: Insurance and Commerce; Joint Budget; Joint Legislative
  Auditing; Joint Public Retirement and Social Security Programs;
  Revenue and Taxation
Senator **Eddie Joe Williams** (R-District 29) . . . . . . . . . . . (501) 286-9366
  Counties Represented: Faulkner (part), Lonoke (part), Pulaski (part),
  White (part)
  Term Expires: 2017
  401 Cobblestone Drive, Cabot, AR 72023
  E-mail: eddiejoe.williams@senate.ar.gov
  Committees: Education; Joint Budget; Joint Energy; Joint Legislative
  Auditing; State Agencies and Governmental Affairs
Senator **Jon Woods** (R-District 7) . . . . . . . . . . . . . . . . . . (479) 200-3100
  Counties Represented: Washington (part)
  Term Expires: 2017
  P.O. Box 8082, Springdale, AR 72766
  E-mail: jon.woods@senate.ar.gov
  Committees: Joint Budget; Joint Legislative Council; Joint Public
  Retirement and Social Security Programs; Judiciary; State Agencies
  and Governmental Affairs

# Senate Standing Committees

## Agriculture, Forestry and Economic Development

| Majority Members | Minority Members |
|---|---|
| Ronald "Ron" Caldwell (R-23) *Chair* | Eddie L. Cheatham (D-26) |
| Alan Clark (R-13) *Vice Chair* | Bruce Maloch (D-12) |
| John Cooper (R-21) | |
| Blake Johnson (R-20) | |
| David J. Sanders (R-15) | |
| Gary Stubblefield (R-6) | |

## Children and Youth

| Majority Members | Minority Members |
|---|---|
| Bart Hester (R-1) *Vice Chair* | Stephanie Flowers (D-25) *Chair* |
| Alan Clark (R-13) | Linda Pondexter Chesterfield (D-30) |
| Linda Collins-Smith (R-19) | Bobby J. Pierce (D-27) |
| Jonathan Dismang (R-28) | |
| Jane English (R-34) | |
| Missy Thomas Irvin (R-18) | |
| Greg Standridge (R-16) | |

## City, County and Local Affairs

| Majority Members | Minority Members |
|---|---|
| Missy Thomas Irvin (R-18) *Chair* | Keith M. Ingram (D-24) *Vice Chair* |
| Linda Collins-Smith (R-19) | Stephanie Flowers (D-25) |
| Scott Flippo (R-17) | |
| Jim Hendren (R-2) | |
| Bart Hester (R-1) | |
| Greg Standridge (R-16) | |

## Education

| Majority Members | Minority Members |
|---|---|
| Jane English (R-34) *Chair* | Uvalde Lindsey (D-4) *Vice Chair* |
| Alan Clark (R-13) | Eddie L. Cheatham (D-26) |
| Jim Hendren (R-2) | Bobby J. Pierce (D-27) |
| Blake Johnson (R-20) | |
| Eddie Joe Williams (R-29) | |

## Insurance and Commerce

| Majority Members | Minority Members |
|---|---|
| Stanley Jason Rapert (R-35) *Chair* | Stephanie Flowers (D-25) |
| Terry Rice (R-9) *Vice Chair* | Uvalde Lindsey (D-4) |
| Jonathan Dismang (R-28) | Larry Teague (D-10) |
| Jane English (R-34) | |
| Jeremy Hutchinson (R-33) | |

## Judiciary

| Majority Members | Minority Members |
|---|---|
| Jeremy Hutchinson (R-33) *Chair* | David Burnett (D-22) |
| Linda Collins-Smith (R-19) | Linda Pondexter Chesterfield (D-30) |
| *Vice Chair* | Joyce Elliott (D-31) |
| Terry Rice (R-9) | David Johnson (D-32) |
| Jon Woods (R-7) | |

## Public Health, Welfare and Labor

| Majority Members | Minority Members |
|---|---|
| Cecile Bledsoe (R-3) *Chair* | Stephanie Flowers (D-25) |
| John Cooper (R-21) | *Vice Chair* |
| Scott Flippo (R-17) | Keith M. Ingram (D-24) |
| Missy Thomas Irvin (R-18) | |
| David J. Sanders (R-15) | |
| Gary Stubblefield (R-6) | |

## Revenue and Taxation

| Majority Members | Minority Members |
|---|---|
| Jake C. Files (R-8) *Chair* | Larry Teague (D-10) *Vice Chair* |
| Jonathan Dismang (R-28) | Bruce Maloch (D-12) |
| Bart Hester (R-1) | |
| Jimmy Hickey, Jr. (R-11) | |
| Stanley Jason Rapert (R-35) | |
| Bill Sample (R-14) | |

## State Agencies and Governmental Affairs

| Majority Members | Minority Members |
|---|---|
| Eddie Joe Williams (R-29) *Chair* | David Burnett (D-22) *Vice Chair* |
| Cecile Bledsoe (R-3) | Linda Pondexter Chesterfield (D-30) |
| Bryan B. King (R-5) | Joyce Elliott (D-31) |
| Jon Woods (R-7) | David Johnson (D-32) |

## Transportation, Technology and Legislative Affairs

| Majority Members | Minority Members |
|---|---|
| Bill Sample (R-14) *Chair* | Bobby J. Pierce (D-27) *Vice Chair* |
| Jake C. Files (R-8) | |
| Bryan B. King (R-5) | |
| Ronald "Ron" Caldwell (R-23) | |
| Jim Hendren (R-2) | |
| Jimmy Hickey, Jr. (R-11) | |
| Greg Standridge (R-16) | |

# Arkansas House of Representatives

State Capitol Building, Room 350, Little Rock, AR 72201-1089
Tel: (501) 682-6211 (In Session)  Tel: (501) 682-7771 (Out of Session)

Speaker of the House **Jeremy Gillam** (R) . . . . . . . . . . . . . (501) 729-0042
  Chief of Staff **Gabe Holstrom** . . . . . . . . . . . . . . . . . . . (501) 605-1346
Speaker Pro Tem **Jon Scott Eubanks** (R) . . . . . . . . . . . . . (479) 438-0533
  Assistant Speaker Pro Tem - 1st District
    **Monte Hodges** (D) . . . . . . . . . . . . . . . . . . . . . . . . . (870) 763-1322
    Education: Arkansas State BS
  Assistant Speaker Pro Tem - 2nd District
    **Warwick Sabin** (D) . . . . . . . . . . . . . . . . . . . . . . . . (501) 374-0000
    Education: Arkansas 1998; Oxford (UK) 2000 MA
  Assistant Speaker Pro Tem - 3rd District
    **Charlotte Vining Douglas** (R) . . . . . . . . . . . . . . . . . (479) 632-2187
    Education: Ouachita Baptist 1974 BSE
  Assistant Speaker Pro Tem - 4th District
    **Marcus E. Richmond, USMC (Ret)** (R) . . . . . . . . . . . (479) 299-4416
    Education: Arkansas Tech 1978 BS
Majority Leader **Ken Bragg** (R) . . . . . . . . . . . . . . . . . . . (870) 942-5269
  Education: Austin State BSF
Majority Whip **James "Jim" Dotson** (R) . . . . . . . . . . . . . (479) 644-0740
Minority Leader **Michael John Gray** (D) . . . . . . . . . . . . . (870) 347-6000
  Education: Arkansas State BS; Arkansas (Little Rock) JD
Minority Whip **David Jeffrey Whitaker** (D) . . . . . . . . . . . (501) 682-6107
  Education: U Mary Washington 1992 BA; Arkansas 1999 JD
Parliamentarian **Finos "Buddy" Johnson** . . . . . . . . . . . . . (501) 682-7771
  E-mail: buddy.johnson@arkansashouse.org
Chief Clerk of the House **Sherri Stacks** . . . . . . . . . . . . . . (501) 682-7771
  E-mail: sherri.stacks@arkansashouse.org

# Representatives

**Party Affiliation Statistics:** Republicans: 64, Democrats: 35, Independents: 1

Representative **Charles L. Armstrong** (D-District 30) . . . . . (501) 224-5071
Counties Represented: Pulaski (part)
Term Expires: 2017
9900 West 36th Street, Little Rock, AR 72204
E-mail: charles.armstrong@arkansashouse.org
Committees: Agriculture, Forestry and Economic Development;
Education; Joint Public Retirement and Social Security Programs

Representative **Eddie L. Armstrong III** (D-District 37) . . . . (501) 444-8468
Counties Represented: Pulaski (part)
Term Expires: 2017
P. O. Box 5323, North Little Rock, AR 72119
E-mail: eddie.armstrong@arkansashouse.org
Committees: Judiciary; State Agencies and Governmental Affairs
Education: Arkansas 2001

Representative **John Baine** (D-District 7) . . . . . . . . . . . . . . (870) 862-2002
Counties Represented: Calhoun (part), Ouachita (part), Union (part),
Washington (part)
Term Expires: 2017
P. O. Box 10056, El Dorado, AR 71730
E-mail: john.baine@arkansashouse.org
Committees: Insurance and Commerce; Joint Energy; Judiciary
Education: Mississippi BPA; Arkansas State MPA

Representative **Bob Ballinger** (R-District 97) . . . . . . . . . . . (501) 682-6107
Counties Represented: Carroll (part), Madison (part), Washington (part)
Term Expires: 2017
1757 Madison 7150, Hindsville, AR 72738
E-mail: bob.ballinger@arkansashouse.org
Committees: Joint Energy; Joint Legislative Council; Judiciary; State
Agencies and Governmental Affairs
Education: Northeastern State BA; Arkansas 2004 JD

Representative **Scott Baltz** (D-District 61) . . . . . . . . . . . . . (870) 378-1380
Counties Represented: Baxter (part), Fulton (part), Randolph (part),
Sharp (part)
Term Expires: 2017
4589 Highway 90 West, Pocahontas, AR 72455
E-mail: scott.baltz@arkansashouse.org
Committees: Education; Insurance and Commerce; Joint Legislative
Council; Joint Performance Review

Representative **Rick Beck** (R-District 65) . . . . . . . . . . . . . (501) 912-1441
Counties Represented: Conway (part), Perry (part)
Term Expires: 2017
E-mail: rick.beck@arkansashouse.org
Committees: Agriculture, Forestry and Economic Development; Joint
Energy; Joint Legislative Auditing; Judiciary

Representative **Nate Bell** (I-District 20) . . . . . . . . . . . . . . (479) 394-5665
Counties Represented: Clay (part), Craighead (part), Greene (part),
Lawrence (part), Montgomery (part), Polk (part), Randolph (part),
Sevier (part)
Term Expires: 2017
P.O. Box 2103, Mena, AR 71953
E-mail: nate.bell@arkansashouse.org
Committees: Education; Joint Legislative Council; State Agencies and
Governmental Affairs

Representative **Camille Bennett** (D-District 14) . . . . . . . . . (501) 257-7993
Counties Represented: Arkansas (part), Garland (part), Jefferson (part),
Lonoke (part), Prairie (part), Pulaski (part), Saline (part)
Term Expires: 2017
P.O. Box 414, Lonoke, AR 72068
E-mail: camille.bennett@arkansashouse.org
Committees: Judiciary; State Agencies and Governmental Affairs

Representative **Mary Bentley** (R-District 73) . . . . . . . . . . . (501) 333-2297
Counties Represented: Conway (part), Perry (part), Pope (part), Yell
(part)
Term Expires: 2017
142 Shady Lane, Perryville, AR 72126
E-mail: mary.bentley@arkansashouse.org
Committees: City, County and Local Affairs; Joint Legislative Auditing;
Public Health, Welfare and Labor
Education: Harding BSN

Representative **Charles Blake** (D-District 36) . . . . . . . . . . . (501) 425-9824
Counties Represented: Pulaski (part)
Term Expires: 2017
201 West Broadway Street, Suite G1, North Little Rock, AR 72114
E-mail: charles.blake@arkansashouse.org
Committees: City, County and Local Affairs; Joint Advanced
Communications and Information Technology; Public Transportation
Education: Grinnell

Representative
**Justin Boyd, PharmD, MBA** (R-District 77) . . . . . . . . . (479) 262-2156
Counties Represented: Sebastian (part)
Term Expires: 2017
1509 South 37th Street, Fort Smith, AR 72903
E-mail: justin.boyd.pharm.d@gmail.com
Committees: City, County and Local Affairs; Joint Legislative Auditing;
Public Health, Welfare and Labor
Education: Arkansas 2000 PharmD, 2007 MBA

Representative **Ken Bragg** (R-District 15) . . . . . . . . . . . . . . (870) 942-5269
Counties Represented: Conway (part), Faulkner (part), Grant (part), Hot
Spring (part), Jefferson (part), Perry (part), Pulaski (part), Van Buren
(part)
Term Expires: 2017
63 Pinecrest Circle, Sheridan, AR 72150
E-mail: ken.bragg@arkansashouse.org
Committees: Agriculture, Forestry and Economic Development; Public
Health, Welfare and Labor

Representative **David L. Branscum** (R-District 83) . . . . . . . (870) 448-2408
Counties Represented: Boone (part), Carroll (part),   Fax: (870) 448-5124
Newton (part), Pope (part), Searcy (part)
Term Expires: 2017
P.O. Box 370, Marshall, AR 72650
E-mail: davidlbranscum@hotmail.com
Committees: Agriculture, Forestry and Economic Development; Joint
Legislative Council; Public Health, Welfare and Labor

Representative **Mary Broadaway** (D-District 57) . . . . . . . . (870) 239-9800
Counties Represented: Greene (part)           Fax: (870) 236-4840
Term Expires: 2017
924 West Court Street, Paragould, AR 72450
E-mail: mary.broadaway@arkansashouse.org
Committees: Aging, Children and Youth, Legislative and Military
Affairs; Joint Legislative Auditing; Judiciary
Education: Trinity U; Arkansas JD

Representative **Karilyn Brown** (R-District 41) . . . . . . . . . . (501) 580-9000
Counties Represented: Pulaski (part)
Term Expires: 2017
P.O. Box 6677, Sherwood, AR 72124
E-mail: karilyn.brown@arkansashouse.org
Committees: Aging, Children and Youth, Legislative and Military
Affairs; Joint Public Retirement and Social Security Programs; Public
Transportation

Representative **Charlie Collins** (R-District 84) . . . . . . . . . . (479) 283-9303
Counties Represented: Washington (part)
Term Expires: 2017
3225 East Piper Glen, Fayetteville, AR 72703
E-mail: clcollins6@cox.net
Committees: Insurance and Commerce; Joint Budget; Revenue and
Taxation

Representative **Donnie Ray Copeland** (R-District 38) . . . . . (501) 297-4857
Counties Represented: Pulaski (part)
Term Expires: 2017
P.O. Box 15561, Little Rock, AR 72231
E-mail: donnie.copeland@arkansashouse.org
Committees: City, County and Local Affairs; Joint Public Retirement
and Social Security Programs; Judiciary

Representative **Bruce Cozart** (R-District 24) . . . . . . . . . . . (501) 627-3232
Counties Represented: Crittenden (part), Cross   Fax: (501) 760-2578
(part), Garland (part), Lee (part), Phillips (part), St. Francis (part)
Term Expires: 2017
420 Rock Creek Road, Hot Springs, AR 71913
E-mail: bruce.cozart@arkansashouse.org
Committees: Education; Insurance and Commerce; Joint Legislative
Auditing

Representative **Andy Davis** (R-District 31) . . . . . . . . . . . . . (501) 837-5109
Counties Represented: Pulaski (part), Saline (part)
Term Expires: 2017
P. O. Box 30248, Little Rock, AR 72260
E-mail: andy.davis@arkansashouse.org
Committees: Agriculture, Forestry and Economic Development; Joint
Legislative Auditing; Revenue and Taxation
Education: Arkansas BS, MS

Representative **Gary Deffenbaugh** (R-District 79) . . . . . . . . (479) 719-8197
Counties Represented: Crawford (part), Sebastian (part)
Term Expires: 2017
1424 North 9th Street, Van Buren, AR 72956
E-mail: gary.deffenbaugh@arkansashouse.org
Committees: City, County and Local Affairs; Education; Joint
Legislative Council; Joint Public Retirement and Social Security
Programs

*(continued on next page)*

**LEGISLATIVE BRANCH**

**Representatives** *continued*

Representative **Jana Della Rosa** (R-District 90) . . . . . . . . . (479) 236-3060
Counties Represented: Benton (part)
Term Expires: 2017
5409 South Pleasant Way, Rogers, AR 72758
E-mail: dellarosa4arkansas@gmail.com
Committees: City, County and Local Affairs; Joint Performance
Review; Public Transportation
Education: Arkansas 2000 BSIE

Representative **James "Jim" Dotson** (R-District 93) . . . . . (479) 644-0740
Counties Represented: Benton (part)
Term Expires: 2017
P. O. Box 651, Bentonville, AR 72712
E-mail: jim.dotson@arkansashouse.org
Committees: Joint Advanced Communications and Information
Technology; Joint Budget; Revenue and Taxation; State Agencies and
Governmental Affairs

Representative
**Charlotte Vining Douglas** (R-District 75) . . . . . . . . . . . (479) 632-2187
Counties Represented: Crawford (part), Sebastian (part)
Term Expires: 2017
5315 Ridge Road, Alma, AR 72921
E-mail: charlotte.douglas@arkansashouse.org
Committees: Education; Joint Budget; Joint Energy; State Agencies and
Governmental Affairs

Representative **Dan M. Douglas** (R-District 91) . . . . . . . . . (501) 682-6107
Counties Represented: Benton (part)
Term Expires: 2017
6251 Southwest Regional Airport Boulevard, Bentonville, AR 72712
E-mail: dan.douglas@arkansashouse.org
Committees: Agriculture, Forestry and Economic Development; Joint
Budget; Public Transportation

Representative **R. Trevor Drown** (R-District 68) . . . . . . . . (479) 857-2498
Counties Represented: Pope (part), Van Buren (part)
Term Expires: 2017
P.O. Box 1182, Dover, AR 72837
E-mail: trevor.drown@arkansashouse.org
Committees: Joint Energy; Joint Legislative Auditing; Judiciary; State
Agencies and Governmental Affairs

Representative **Lance Eads** (R-District 88) . . . . . . . . . . . . . (501) 682-7771
Counties Represented: Washington (part)
Term Expires: 2017
P.O. Box 8343, Springdale, AR 72766
E-mail: lance.eads@gmail.com
Committees: City, County and Local Affairs; Joint Performance
Review; Public Transportation

Representative **Les Eaves** (R-District 46) . . . . . . . . . . . . . . (501) 827-1344
Counties Represented: White (part)
Term Expires: 2017
102 Club Cove, Searcy, AR 72143
E-mail: les.eaves@arkansashouse.org
Committees: City, County and Local Affairs; Joint Legislative Auditing;
Revenue and Taxation

Representative **Jon Scott Eubanks** (R-District 74) . . . . . . . (479) 438-0533
Counties Represented: Franklin (part), Logan (part), Scott (part),
Sebastian (part)
Term Expires: 2017
2543 Greasy Valley Road, Paris, AR 72855
E-mail: jon.eubanks@arkansashouse.org
Committees: Agriculture, Forestry and Economic Development;
Education; Joint Budget

Representative **Joe Farrer** (R-District 44) . . . . . . . . . . . . . . (501) 743-6855
Counties Represented: Faulkner (part), Lonoke        Fax: (501) 605-8984
(part), White (part)
Term Expires: 2017
199 Lewisburg Road, Austin, AR 72007
E-mail: joe.farrer@arkansashouse.org
Committees: Insurance and Commerce; Joint Legislative Council;
Judiciary
Education: Central Arkansas 1988 BS

Representative **Dr. Deborah Ferguson** (D-District 51) . . . . (870) 735-7098
Counties Represented: Crittenden (part)
Term Expires: 2017
200 South Rhodes Street, Suite B, West Memphis, AR 72301
E-mail: deborah.ferguson@arkansashouse.org
Committees: Insurance and Commerce; Joint Budget; Public Health,
Welfare and Labor
Education: Mississippi 1976 BA; Tennessee Health Science 1979 DDS

Representative
**Kenneth B. "Ken" Ferguson** (D-District 16) . . . . . . . . . (870) 413-8942
Counties Represented: Boone (part), Carroll (part), Jefferson (part),
Lincoln (part), Newton (part), Pope (part), Van Buren (part)
Term Expires: 2017
E-mail: kenneth.ferguson@arkansashouse.org
Committees: City, County and Local Affairs; Joint Performance
Review; Revenue and Taxation

Representative **David Fielding** (D-District 5) . . . . . . . . . . . (870) 234-6143
Counties Represented: Carroll (part), Columbia (part), Crawford (part),
Franklin (part), Johnson (part), Lafayette (part), Madison (part), Nevada
(part), Ouachita (part), Sebastian (part), Washington (part)
Term Expires: 2017
909 South Vine, Magnolia, AR 71753
E-mail: david.fielding@arkansashouse.org
Committees: City, County and Local Affairs; Joint Energy; Joint
Legislative Council; Public Transportation

Representative **Charlene Fite** (R-District 80) . . . . . . . . . . . (479) 474-1818
Counties Represented: Crawford (part), Washington (part)
Term Expires: 2017
531 Pine Cliff Drive, Van Buren, AR 72956
E-mail: charlene.fite@arkansashouse.org
Committees: Aging, Children and Youth, Legislative and Military
Affairs; Joint Performance Review; Public Health, Welfare and Labor

Representative **Lanny Fite** (R-District 23) . . . . . . . . . . . . . . (501) 794-2228
Counties Represented: Cross (part), Jackson (part), Lee (part), Monroe
(part), Saline (part), St. Francis (part), White (part), Woodruff (part)
Term Expires: 2017
3324 Highway 5, Benton, AR 72019
E-mail: lanny.fite@att.net
Committees: Joint Legislative Council; Joint Public Retirement and
Social Security Programs; Revenue and Taxation; State Agencies and
Governmental Affairs

Representative **Vivian L. Flowers** (D-District 17) . . . . . . . . (870) 329-8356
Counties Represented: Baxter (part), Boone (part), Jefferson (part),
Marion (part)
Term Expires: 2017
E-mail: vivian.flowers@arkansashouse.org
Committees: Aging, Children and Youth, Legislative and Military
Affairs; Revenue and Taxation
Education: Arkansas (Little Rock)

Representative **Mickey Gates** (R-District 22) . . . . . . . . . . . (501) 623-1100
Counties Represented: Craighead (part), Garland (part), Mississippi
(part), Poinsett (part), Saline (part)
Term Expires: 2017
377 North Highway 7, Hot Springs, AR 71901
E-mail: mickey@mickeygates.com
Committees: Aging, Children and Youth, Legislative and Military
Affairs; Joint Performance Review; Public Transportation

Representative **Jeremy Gillam** (R-District 45) . . . . . . . . . . . (501) 729-0042
Counties Represented: White (part)                    Fax: (501) 729-3361
Term Expires: 2017
1825 Missle Base Road, Judsonia, AR 72081
E-mail: jeremy.gillam@arkansashouse.org
Committees: Education; Insurance and Commerce; Joint Budget

Representative **Justin Gonzales** (R-District 19) . . . . . . . . . . (870) 245-6365
Counties Represented: Clark (part), Fulton (part), Hempstead (part),
Howard (part), Independence (part), Izard (part), Nevada (part), Pike
(part), Randolph (part), Sharp (part)
Term Expires: 2017
E-mail: justinrroy@yahoo.com
Committees: City, County and Local Affairs; Joint Advanced
Communications and Information Technology; Joint Budget; Revenue
and Taxation

Representative **Bill Gossage** (R-District 82) . . . . . . . . . . . . (479) 667-2122
Counties Represented: Crawford (part), Franklin (part), Madison (part)
Term Expires: 2017
P.O. Box 221, Ozark, AR 72949
E-mail: bill.gossage@arkansashouse.org
Committees: Education; Insurance and Commerce
Education: Arkansas Tech 1979 BS; Arkansas 1992

Representative **Michael John Gray** (D-District 47) . . . . . . . (870) 347-6000
Counties Represented: Independence (part), Jackson (part), White
(part), Woodruff (part)
Term Expires: 2017
P.O. Box 360, Augusta, AR 72006
E-mail: michael.gray@arkansashouse.org
Committees: City, County and Local Affairs; Education; Joint
Advanced Communications and Information Technology

Representative **Michelle Gray** (R-District 62) . . . . . . . . . . (870) 368-4729
Counties Represented: Independence (part), Izard (part), Sharp (part), Stone (part)
Term Expires: 2017
58 Gray Manor Lane, Melbourne, AR 72556
E-mail: michelle.gray@arkansashouse.org
Committees: Joint Legislative Auditing; Joint Performance Review; Judiciary; State Agencies and Governmental Affairs

Representative **Kim Hammer** (R-District 28) . . . . . . . . . . . (501) 840-3841
Counties Represented: Arkansas (part), Lonoke (part), Monroe (part), Prairie (part), Saline (part), White (part), Woodruff (part)
Term Expires: 2017
1411 Edgehill, Benton, AR 72015
E-mail: kimdhammer@yahoo.com
Committees: City, County and Local Affairs; Joint Performance Review; Public Health, Welfare and Labor

Representative **Justin T. Harris** (R-District 81) . . . . . . . . . (479) 871-8542
Counties Represented: Crawford (part), Washington (part)
Term Expires: 2017
P.O. Box 880, West Fork, AR 72774
E-mail: justin.harris@arkansashouse.org
Committees: Aging, Children and Youth, Legislative and Military Affairs; Education; Joint Budget

Representative **Kenneth Henderson** (R-District 71) . . . . . . (479) 970-4850
Counties Represented: Pope (part)
Term Expires: 2017
311 Hickory Hills Drive, Russellville, AR 72802
E-mail: ken4arkansas@gmail.com
Committees: City, County and Local Affairs; Joint Energy; Public Health, Welfare and Labor

Representative **Kim Hendren** (R-District 92) . . . . . . . . . . . (479) 787-6500
Counties Represented: Benton (part)
Term Expires: 2017
E-mail: kim.hendren@arkansashouse.org
Committees: Agriculture, Forestry and Economic Development; Joint Energy; Joint Legislative Auditing; Revenue and Taxation
Education: Arkansas 1960 BS

Representative
**Mary P. "Prissy" Hickerson** (R-District 1) . . . . . . . . . . . (870) 773-1603
Counties Represented: Benton (part), Miller (part),    Fax: (870) 773-0439
Washington (part)
Term Expires: 2017
2805 Forest Avenue, Texarkana, AR 71854
E-mail: phickerson@valornet.com
Committees: Joint Legislative Auditing; Joint Performance Review; Public Transportation; State Agencies and Governmental Affairs

Representative **David Hillman** (D-District 13) . . . . . . . . . . (870) 830-3004
Counties Represented: Arkansas (part), Garland    Fax: (870) 992-3315
(part), Grant (part), Hot Spring (part), Lonoke (part), Prairie (part), Saline (part), White (part)
Term Expires: 2017
403 Essex Road, Almyra, AR 72003
E-mail: david.hillman@arkansashouse.org
Committees: Agriculture, Forestry and Economic Development; Joint Legislative Auditing; Public Transportation
Education: Ouachita Baptist

Representative **Grant Hodges** (R-District 96) . . . . . . . . . . (479) 381-9513
Counties Represented: Benton (part)
Term Expires: 2017
P.O. Box 2607, Rogers, AR 72757
E-mail: grant.hodges@arkansashouse.org
Committees: Education; Insurance and Commerce

Representative **Monte Hodges** (D-District 55) . . . . . . . . . . (870) 763-1322
Counties Represented: Crittenden (part), Mississippi (part)
Term Expires: 2017
P. O. Box 773, Blytheville, AR 72316
E-mail: monte.hodges@arkansashouse.org
Committees: City, County and Local Affairs; Joint Budget; Revenue and Taxation

Representative **Mike Holcomb** (R-District 10) . . . . . . . . . . (870) 879-6135
Counties Represented: Clark (part), Cleveland (part), Drew (part), Grant (part), Hempstead (part), Howard (part), Jefferson (part), Lincoln (part), Montgomery (part), Nevada (part), Pike (part), Polk (part), Sevier (part)
Term Expires: 2017
9108 Sulphur Springs Road, Pine Bluff, AR 71603
E-mail: mike.holcomb@arkansashouse.org
Committees: Public Transportation; State Agencies and Governmental Affairs

Representative **Douglas House** (R-District 40) . . . . . . . . . . (501) 590-1055
Counties Represented: Faulkner (part), Pulaski (part)
Term Expires: 2017
8923 Bridge Creek Road, North Little Rock, AR 72120
E-mail: douglas.house@arkansashouse.org
Committees: Agriculture, Forestry and Economic Development; Joint Budget; Joint Public Retirement and Social Security Programs; Judiciary
Education: Arkansas (Little Rock) 1976 BA, 1980 JD

Representative **Lane Jean** (R-District 2) . . . . . . . . . . . . . . . (870) 234-5433
Counties Represented: Benton (part), Columbia (part), Lafayette (part), Miller (part), Washington (part)
Term Expires: 2017
1105 Lawton Circle, Magnolia, AR 72753
E-mail: l_jean@sbcglobal.net
Committees: Agriculture, Forestry and Economic Development; Joint Budget; Revenue and Taxation

Representative **Joe Jett** (D-District 56) . . . . . . . . . . . . . . . . (870) 276-5319
Counties Represented: Clay (part), Greene (part), Lawrence (part), Randolph (part)
Term Expires: 2017
572 County Road 101, Success, AR 72470
E-mail: joe.jett@arkansashouse.org
Committees: Insurance and Commerce; Joint Budget; Revenue and Taxation

Representative **J.P. "Bob" Johnson** (D-District 42) . . . . . . (501) 982-1975
Counties Represented: Pulaski (part)
Term Expires: 2017
511 North First, Suite 8, Jacksonville, AR 72076
E-mail: bobjohnsoncpa@gmail.com
Committees: Aging, Children and Youth, Legislative and Military Affairs; Joint Public Retirement and Social Security Programs; Public Transportation

Representative **Jack Ladyman** (R-District 59) . . . . . . . . . . (870) 340-7280
Counties Represented: Craighead (part)
Term Expires: 2017
2204 Doral Drive, Jonesboro, AR 72404
E-mail: jackladyman@gmail.com
Committees: Joint Energy; Joint Legislative Auditing; Revenue and Taxation; State Agencies and Governmental Affairs

Representative **Sheilla E. Lampkin** (D-District 9) . . . . . . . . (870) 723-6449
Counties Represented: Ashley (part), Crawford (part), Drew (part), Franklin (part), Scott (part), Sebastian (part)
Term Expires: 2017
350 Rabb Road, Monticello, AR 71655
E-mail: sheilla.lampkin@arkansashouse.org
Committees: Agriculture, Forestry and Economic Development; Education; Joint Advanced Communications and Information Technology; Joint Legislative Council

Representative **Greg Leding** (D-District 86) . . . . . . . . . . . . (479) 966-9201
Counties Represented: Washington (part)
Term Expires: 2017
P.O. Box 1445, Fayetteville, AR 72702
E-mail: greg@gregleding.com
Committees: Education; Insurance and Commerce; Joint Legislative Council; Joint Public Retirement and Social Security Programs

Representative **Timothy "Tim" Lemons** (R-District 43) . . . (501) 605-7565
Counties Represented: Lonoke (part)
Term Expires: 2017
38 Brentwood Cove, Cabot, AR 72023
E-mail: arstrep43@gmail.com
Committees: City, County and Local Affairs; Joint Energy; Revenue and Taxation

Representative **Kelley Linck** (R-District 99) . . . . . . . . . . . . (870) 453-6149
Counties Represented: Baxter (part), Boone (part), Marion (part), Searcy (part)
Term Expires: 2017
13823 Highway 14 South, Yellville, AR 72687-7848
E-mail: kelley@kelleylinck.com
E-mail: kelley.linck@arkansashouse.org
Committees: Joint Legislative Council; Public Health, Welfare and Labor; State Agencies and Governmental Affairs

Representative **Fredrick J. "Fred" Love** (D-District 29) . . . (501) 612-3939
Counties Represented: Faulkner (part), Lonoke (part), Pulaski (part), White (part)
Term Expires: 2017
P.O. Box 4963, Little Rock, AR 72214
E-mail: fjlove@att.net
Committees: Insurance and Commerce; Joint Advanced Communications and Information Technology; Joint Budget; Public Health, Welfare and Labor

*(continued on next page)*

LEGISLATIVE BRANCH

**Representatives** *continued*

Representative **Mark Lowery** (R-District 39) . . . . . . . . . . . (501) 837-5221
Counties Represented: Pulaski (part)
Term Expires: 2017
229 Summit Valley Circle, Maumelle, AR 72113
E-mail: mark.lowery@arkansashouse.org
Committees: Education; Insurance and Commerce; Joint Legislative
Auditing; Joint Legislative Council
Education: Arkansas

Representative **Robin Lundstrum** (R-District 87) . . . . . . . . (479) 957-1959
Counties Represented: Benton (part), Washington (part)
Term Expires: 2017
1327 Elm Springs Road, Springdale, AR 72762
E-mail: robin.lundstrum@arkansashouse.org
Committees: Insurance and Commerce; Joint Energy; Public Health,
Welfare and Labor

Representative
**Dr. Stephen "Steve" Magie** (D-District 72) . . . . . . . . . (501) 327-4444
Counties Represented: Faulkner (part)          Fax: (501) 327-3962
Term Expires: 2017
P. O. Box 1506, Conway, AR 72033
E-mail: stephen.magie@arkansashouse.org
Committees: Joint Budget; Public Health, Welfare and Labor; State
Agencies and Governmental Affairs
Education: Central Arkansas BS; LSU Medical Center MD

Representative **Julie Mayberry** (R-District 27) . . . . . . . . . . (501) 888-8222
Counties Represented: Calhoun (part), Cleveland (part), Grant (part),
Jefferson (part), Ouachita (part), Pulaski (part), Saline (part), Union
(part)
Term Expires: 2017
3022 East Woodson Lateral Road, Hensley, AR 72065
E-mail: julie-mayberry@att.net
Committees: Aging, Children and Youth, Legislative and Military
Affairs; Joint Legislative Auditing; Public Transportation

Representative **Mark D. McElroy** (D-District 11) . . . . . . . . (870) 644-3822
Counties Represented: Ashley (part), Chicot (part), Desha (part),
Hempstead (part), Lafayette (part), Little River (part), Miller (part),
Sevier (part)
Term Expires: 2017
2645 Highway 138 East, Tillar, AR 71670
E-mail: mark.mcelroy@arkansashouse.org
Committees: Agriculture, Forestry and Economic Development;
Education; Joint Budget; Joint Energy

Representative **George B. McGill** (D-District 78) . . . . . . . .(479) 651-2107
Counties Represented: Sebastian (part)
Term Expires: 2017
P. O. Box 3858, Fort Smith, AR 72913
E-mail: george.mcgill@arkansashouse.org
Committees: Aging, Children and Youth, Legislative and Military
Affairs; Joint Legislative Council; Revenue and Taxation
Education: Arkansas MBA

Representative **Ron McNair** (R-District 98) . . . . . . . . . . . . (870) 754-7962
Counties Represented: Boone (part), Carroll (part)
Term Expires: 2017
E-mail: rmcnair1950@gmail.com
Committees: Agriculture, Forestry and Economic Development; Joint
Legislative Auditing; Joint Public Retirement and Social Security
Programs; Public Transportation

Representative **David Meeks** (R-District 70) . . . . . . . . . . . (501) 277-9340
Counties Represented: Faulkner (part), Perry (part)
Term Expires: 2017
2625 Donaghey Avenue, PMB 223, Conway, AR 72305
E-mail: david.meeks@arkansashouse.org
Committees: Aging, Children and Youth, Legislative and Military
Affairs; Joint Legislative Council; Joint Public Retirement and Social
Security Programs; Public Health, Welfare and Labor

Representative **Stephen Meeks** (R-District 67) . . . . . . . . . (501) 205-3272
Counties Represented: Faulkner (part)
Term Expires: 2017
522 Highway 225 East, Greenbrier, AR 72058
E-mail: stephen.meeks@arkansashouse.org
Committees: Agriculture, Forestry and Economic Development; Joint
Advanced Communications and Information Technology; Joint Budget;
Revenue and Taxation

Representative **Joshua "Josh" Miller** (R-District 66) . . . . . (501) 250-7039
Counties Represented: Cleburne (part), Faulkner (part), Van Buren
(part)
Term Expires: 2017
1008 Trailwood Drive, Heber Springs, AR 72543
E-mail: josh.miller@arkansashouse.org
Committees: Joint Legislative Council; Joint Performance Review;
Public Health, Welfare and Labor; State Agencies and Governmental
Affairs

Representative **Reginald K. Murdock** (D-District 48) . . . . . (870) 295-3208
Counties Represented: Lee (part), Monroe (part), St.     Fax: (870) 295-3162
Francis (part)
Term Expires: 2017
P.O. Box 1071, Marianna, AR 72360
E-mail: rkm_72360@yahoo.com
Committees: Education; Insurance and Commerce; Joint Budget

Representative **Micah S. Neal** (R-District 89) . . . . . . . . . . . (479) 935-5550
Counties Represented: Washington (part)
Term Expires: 2017
P. O. Box 1912, Springdale, AR 72765
E-mail: micah.neal@arkansashouse.org
Committees: Insurance and Commerce; Joint Budget; Joint Performance
Review; Revenue and Taxation

Representative **Milton Nicks, Jr.** (D-District 50) . . . . . . . . (870) 739-5360
Counties Represented: Crittenden (part), Cross (part)
Term Expires: 2017
247 Windover Lane, Marion, AR 72364
E-mail: milton.nicks@arkansashouse.org
Committees: City, County and Local Affairs; Joint Performance
Review; Public Transportation

Representative **Betty Overbey** (D-District 69) . . . . . . . . . . (479) 885-6479
Counties Represented: Johnson (part), Pope (part)
Term Expires: 2017
P.O. Box 177, Lamar, AR 72846
E-mail: betty.overbey@arkansashouse.org
Committees: City, County and Local Affairs; Joint Energy; Joint
Legislative Council; Public Health, Welfare and Labor

Representative **John Payton** (R-District 64) . . . . . . . . . . . . (501) 362-5815
Counties Represented: Baxter (part), Cleburne       Fax: (501) 362-3237
(part), Marion (part), Searcy (part), Stone (part)
Term Expires: 2017
P. O. Box 181, Wilburn, AR 72179
E-mail: john.payton@arkansashouse.org
Committees: Agriculture, Forestry and Economic Development; Joint
Budget; Public Health, Welfare and Labor

Representative **Rebecca Petty** (R-District 94) . . . . . . . . . . (479) 621-3464
Counties Represented: Benton (part)
Term Expires: 2017
1209 North Wren Drive, Rogers, AR 72756
E-mail: pettyforar@yahoo.com
Committees: Aging, Children and Youth, Legislative and Military
Affairs; Joint Advanced Communications and Information Technology;
Judiciary

Representative
**Mathew W. "Mat" Pitsch** (R-District 76) . . . . . . . . . . . (479) 883-2072
Counties Represented: Sebastian (part)
Term Expires: 2017
11215 Vista Ridge Court, Fort Smith, AR 72916
E-mail: mathew.pitsch@cox.net
Committees: Agriculture, Forestry and Economic Development; Joint
Advanced Communications and Information Technology; Public
Transportation

Representative **James Ratliff** (D-District 60) . . . . . . . . . . . (501) 454-5200
Counties Represented: Greene (part), Lawrence (part), Randolph (part),
Sharp (part)
Term Expires: 2017
P.O. Box 791, Imboden, AR 72434
E-mail: jamesratliff3468@yahoo.com
Committees: Agriculture, Forestry and Economic Development;
Education; Joint Legislative Council

Representative **Chris Richey** (D-District 12) . . . . . . . . . . . (870) 995-2499
Counties Represented: Arkansas (part), Clark (part), Columbia (part),
Dallas (part), Desha (part), Grant (part), Lincoln (part), Nevada (part),
Ouachita (part), Phillips (part)
Term Expires: 2017
P. O. Box 2356, West Helena, AR 72390
E-mail: chris.richey@arkansashouse.org
Committees: Joint Legislative Council; Public Health, Welfare and
Labor; State Agencies and Governmental Affairs
Education: Ouachita Baptist 1993 BA; Arkansas State 1996 MA

LEGISLATIVE BRANCH

Representative
**Marcus E. Richmond, USMC (Ret)** (R-District 21) . . . . . (479) 299-4416
Counties Represented: Craighead (part), Garland (part), Montgomery (part), Perry (part), Polk (part), Scott (part), Sebastian (part), Yell (part)
Term Expires: 2017
E-mail: marcus.richmond@arkansashouse.org
Committees: Aging, Children and Youth, Legislative and Military Affairs; Public Transportation

Representative **Laurie Rushing** (R-District 26) . . . . . . . . . . (501) 545-6066
Counties Represented: Ashley (part), Bradley (part), Chicot (part), Cleveland (part), Desha (part), Drew (part), Garland (part), Hot Spring (part), Lincoln (part)
Term Expires: 2017
134 Cannon Ridge Point, Hot Springs, AR 71913
E-mail: laurie.rushing@arkansashouse.org
Committees: Aging, Children and Youth, Legislative and Military Affairs; Joint Legislative Auditing; Judiciary

Representative **Warwick Sabin** (D-District 33) . . . . . . . . . (501) 374-0000
Counties Represented: Pulaski (part), Saline (part)
Term Expires: 2017
P. O. Box 250508, Little Rock, AR 72225
E-mail: warwick.sabin@arkansashouse.org
Committees: City, County and Local Affairs; Education; Joint Legislative Auditing

Representative **Sue Scott** (R-District 95) . . . . . . . . . . . . . . (479) 621-1265
Counties Represented: Benton (part)          Fax: (479) 636-8480
Term Expires: 2017
1412 Hilltop Farms Lane, Rogers, AR 72756
E-mail: sue.scott@arkansashouse.org
Committees: Aging, Children and Youth, Legislative and Military Affairs; Joint Legislative Auditing; Judiciary

Representative **Matthew J. Shepherd** (R-District 6) . . . . . (870) 862-2087
Counties Represented: Columbia (part), Franklin     Fax: (870) 862-2747
(part), Johnson (part), Logan (part), Ouachita (part), Union (part), Yell (part)
Term Expires: 2017
214 North Washington Avenue, Suite 302, El Dorado, AR 71730
E-mail: matthew.shepherd@arkansashouse.org
Committees: Agriculture, Forestry and Economic Development; Joint Budget; Judiciary

Representative **Brandt Smith** (R-District 58) . . . . . . . . . . . . (870) 351-7459
Counties Represented: Craighead (part)
Term Expires: 2017
3501 Ridgeway Circle, Jonesboro, AR 72404
E-mail: brandt.smith@arkansashouse.org
Committees: Aging, Children and Youth, Legislative and Military Affairs; Joint Advanced Communications and Information Technology; Public Transportation

Representative **James J. "Jim" Sorvillo** (R-District 32) . . (501) 682-7771
Counties Represented: Pulaski (part)
Term Expires: 2017
1925 Rainwood Cove Drive, Little Rock, AR 72212
E-mail: sorvillo4house@gmail.com
Committees: Insurance and Commerce; Joint Energy; Public Transportation

Representative **Nelda Speaks** (R-District 100) . . . . . . . . . . (870) 421-2552
Counties Represented: Baxter (part)
Term Expires: 2017
P.O. Box 1016, Mountain Home, AR 72654
E-mail: nelda@neldaspeaks.com
Committees: City, County and Local Affairs; Revenue and Taxation

Representative **James Sturch** (R-District 63) . . . . . . . . . . . . (870) 612-7589
Counties Represented: Independence (part)
Term Expires: 2017
Two Rick Road, Batesville, AR 72501
E-mail: jmsturch@yahoo.com
Committees: Aging, Children and Youth, Legislative and Military Affairs; Public Transportation
Education: Arkansas

Representative **Dan Sullivan** (R-District 53) . . . . . . . . . . . . (870) 275-2929
Counties Represented: Craighead (part)
Term Expires: 2017
P.O. Box 19406, Jonesboro, AR 72403
E-mail: dan.sullivan@arkansashouse.org
Committees: Aging, Children and Youth, Legislative and Military Affairs; Joint Performance Review; Public Health, Welfare and Labor

Representative **J. Brent Talley** (D-District 3) . . . . . . . . . . . . (870) 983-2717
Counties Represented: Benton (part), Hempstead (part), Nevada (part)
Term Expires: 2017
P.O. Box 256, Hope, AR 71802
E-mail: brent.talley@arkansashouse.org
Committees: Insurance and Commerce; Joint Energy; Judiciary
Education: Southern Arkansas U BS

Representative **Dwight Tosh** (R-District 52) . . . . . . . . . . . . . (870) 926-0423
Counties Represented: Craighead (part), Independence (part), Jackson (part), Poinsett (part)
Term Expires: 2017
4513 Butler Road, Jonesboro, AR 72404
E-mail: dwight.tosh@arkansashouse.org
Committees: Joint Legislative Auditing; Joint Performance Review; Judiciary; State Agencies and Governmental Affairs

Representative **Clarke Tucker** (D-District 35) . . . . . . . . . . . . (501) 379-1767
Counties Represented: Faulkner (part), Perry (part), Pulaski (part)
Term Expires: 2017
111 Center Street, Suite 1900, Little Rock, AR 72201
E-mail: clarke.tucker@arkansashouse.org
Committees: Aging, Children and Youth, Legislative and Military Affairs; Joint Performance Review; Revenue and Taxation

Representative **DeAnn Vaught** (R-District 4) . . . . . . . . . . . . (870) 832-2638
Counties Represented: Howard (part), Little River (part), Sevier (part), Washington (part)
Term Expires: 2017
E-mail: deann.vaught@arkansashouse.org
Committees: Aging, Children and Youth, Legislative and Military Affairs; Joint Legislative Auditing; Revenue and Taxation
Education: Southern Arkansas U

Representative **John T. Vines** (D-District 25) . . . . . . . . . . . . (501) 624-1252
Counties Represented: Arkansas (part), Desha (part), Garland (part), Jefferson (part), Lincoln (part), Monroe (part), Phillips (part)
Term Expires: 2017
123 Market Street, Hot Springs, AR 71901
E-mail: jtvines13@sbcglobal.net
Committees: Insurance and Commerce; Joint Budget; Judiciary

Representative **John W. Walker** (D-District 34) . . . . . . . . . (501) 614-9772
Counties Represented: Pulaski (part)          Fax: (501) 374-4787
Term Expires: 2017
1723 Broadway Street, Little Rock, AR 72206
E-mail: johnwalkeratty@aol.com
Committees: Education; Joint Budget; Joint Performance Review; State Agencies and Governmental Affairs

Representative **Dave Wallace** (R-District 54) . . . . . . . . . . . (870) 919-8046
Counties Represented: Mississippi (part), Poinsett (part)
Term Expires: 2017
E-mail: dave.wallace@arkansashouse.org
Committees: Aging, Children and Youth, Legislative and Military Affairs; Joint Performance Review; Public Transportation
Education: Arkansas State

Representative **Jeff R. Wardlaw** (D-District 8) . . . . . . . . . . (870) 226-9501
Counties Represented: Ashley (part), Bradley (part),      Fax: (870) 226-9500
Calhoun (part), Cleveland (part), Dallas (part), Drew (part), Sebastian (part)
Term Expires: 2017
801 East Church Street, Warren, AR 71671
E-mail: jeff.wardlaw@arkansashouse.org
E-mail: jeff@jeffwardlaw.com
Committees: Joint Legislative Council; Public Health, Welfare and Labor; State Agencies and Governmental Affairs

Representative **David Jeffrey Whitaker** (D-District 85) . . . (501) 682-6107
Counties Represented: Washington (part)
Term Expires: 2017
717 North Lewis Avenue, Fayetteville, AR 72701
E-mail: david.whitaker@arkansashouse.org
Committees: Agriculture, Forestry and Economic Development; Joint Performance Review; Judiciary

Representative **Richard Womack** (R-District 18) . . . . . . . . . (870) 403-6287
Counties Represented: Baxter (part), Clark (part), Cleburne (part), Dallas (part), Faulkner (part), Fulton (part), Garland (part), Hot Spring (part), Marion (part), Nevada (part), Searcy (part), Stone (part), Van Buren (part), White (part)
Term Expires: 2017
866 North 12th Street, Arkadelphia, AR 71923
E-mail: richard.womack@arkansashouse.org
Committees: Joint Budget; Joint Performance Review; Public Health, Welfare and Labor; State Agencies and Governmental Affairs
Education: Ouachita Baptist 1997

Representative **Marshall Wright** (D-District 49) . . . . . . . . . (870) 633-3141
Counties Represented: Cross (part), Monroe (part), St. Francis (part)
Term Expires: 2017
117 South Washington Street, Forrest City, AR 72335
E-mail: marshall.wright@arkansashouse.org
Committees: Insurance and Commerce; Joint Legislative Council; Judiciary

**LEGISLATIVE BRANCH**

# House Standing Committees

## Aging, Children and Youth, Legislative and Military Affairs

**Majority Members**
Justin T. Harris (R-81) *Vice Chair*
Karilyn Brown (R-41)
Charlene Fite (R-80)
Mickey Gates (R-22)
Julie Mayberry (R-27)
David Meeks (R-70)
Rebecca Petty (R-94)
Marcus E. Richmond (R-21)
Laurie Rushing (R-26)
Sue Scott (R-95)
Brandt Smith (R-58)
James Sturch (R-63)
Dan Sullivan (R-53)
DeAnn Vaught (R-4)
Dave Wallace (R-54)

**Minority Members**
George B. McGill (D-78) *Chair*
Mary Broadaway (D-57)
Vivian L. Flowers (D-17)
J.P. "Bob" Johnson (D-42)
Clarke Tucker (D-35)

## Agriculture, Forestry and Economic Development

**Majority Members**
Dan M. Douglas (R-91) *Chair*
Rick Beck (R-65)
Ken Bragg (R-15)
David L. Branscum (R-83)
Andy Davis (R-31)
Jon Scott Eubanks (R-74)
Kim Hendren (R-92)
Douglas House (R-40)
Lane Jean (R-2)
Ron McNair (R-98)
Stephen Meeks (R-67)
John Payton (R-64)
Mathew W. "Mat" Pitsch (R-76)
Matthew J. Shepherd (R-6)

**Minority Members**
David Hillman (D-13) *Vice Chair*
Charles L. Armstrong (D-30)
Sheilla E. Lampkin (D-9)
Mark D. McElroy (D-11)
James Ratliff (D-60)
David Jeffrey Whitaker (D-85)

## City, County and Local Affairs

**Majority Members**
Mary Bentley (R-73) *Vice Chair*
Justin Boyd (R-77)
Donnie Ray Copeland (R-38)
Gary Deffenbaugh (R-79)
Jana Della Rosa (R-90)
Lance Eads (R-88)
Les Eaves (R-46)
Justin Gonzales (R-19)
Kim Hammer (R-28)
Kenneth Henderson (R-71)
Timothy "Tim" Lemons (R-43)
Nelda Speaks (R-100)

**Minority Members**
Betty Overbey (D-69) *Chair*
Charles Blake (D-36)
Kenneth B. "Ken" Ferguson (D-16)
David Fielding (D-5)
Michael John Gray (D-47)
Monte Hodges (D-55)
Milton Nicks, Jr. (D-50)
Warwick Sabin (D-33)

## Education

**Majority Members**
Bruce Cozart (R-24) *Chair*
Gary Deffenbaugh (R-79)
Charlotte Vining Douglas (R-75)
Jon Scott Eubanks (R-74)
Jeremy Gillam (R-45)
Bill Gossage (R-82)
Justin T. Harris (R-81)
Grant Hodges (R-96)
Mark Lowery (R-39)

**Minority Members**
Sheilla E. Lampkin (D-9)
*Vice Chair*
Charles L. Armstrong (D-30)
Scott Baltz (D-61)
Michael John Gray (D-47)
Greg Leding (D-86)
Mark D. McElroy (D-11)
Reginald K. Murdock (D-48)
James Ratliff (D-60)
Warwick Sabin (D-33)
John W. Walker (D-34)

**Members**
Nate Bell (I-20)

## Insurance and Commerce

**Majority Members**
Charlie Collins (R-84) *Chair*
Bruce Cozart (R-24)
Joe Farrer (R-44)
Jeremy Gillam (R-45)
Bill Gossage (R-82)
Grant Hodges (R-96)
Mark Lowery (R-39)
Robin Lundstrum (R-87)
Micah S. Neal (R-89)
James J. "Jim" Sorvillo (R-32)

**Minority Members**
Reginald K. Murdock (D-48)
*Vice Chair*
John Baine (D-7)
Scott Baltz (D-61)
Dr. Deborah Ferguson (D-51)
Joe Jett (D-56)
Greg Leding (D-86)
Fredrick J. "Fred" Love (D-29)
J. Brent Talley (D-3)
John T. Vines (D-25)
Marshall Wright (D-49)

## Judiciary

**Majority Members**
Matthew J. Shepherd (R-6) *Chair*
Bob Ballinger (R-97)
Rick Beck (R-65)
Donnie Ray Copeland (R-38)
R. Trevor Drown (R-68)
Joe Farrer (R-44)
Michelle Gray (R-62)
Douglas House (R-40)
Rebecca Petty (R-94)
Laurie Rushing (R-26)
Sue Scott (R-95)
Dwight Tosh (R-52)

**Minority Members**
Marshall Wright (D-49) *Vice Chair*
Eddie L. Armstrong III (D-37)
John Baine (D-7)
Camille Bennett (D-14)
Mary Broadaway (D-57)
J. Brent Talley (D-3)
John T. Vines (D-25)
David Jeffrey Whitaker (D-85)

## Public Health, Welfare and Labor

**Majority Members**
Kelley Linck (R-99) *Chair*
Mary Bentley (R-73)
Justin Boyd (R-77)
Ken Bragg (R-15)
David L. Branscum (R-83)
Charlene Fite (R-80)
Kim Hammer (R-28)
Kenneth Henderson (R-71)
Robin Lundstrum (R-87)
David Meeks (R-70)
Joshua "Josh" Miller (R-66)
John Payton (R-64)
Dan Sullivan (R-53)
Richard Womack (R-18)

**Minority Members**
Dr. Deborah Ferguson (D-51)
*Vice Chair*
Fredrick J. "Fred" Love (D-29)
Dr. Stephen "Steve" Magie (D-72)
Betty Overbey (D-69)
Chris Richey (D-12)
Jeff R. Wardlaw (D-8)

## Public Transportation

**Majority Members**
Mary P. "Prissy" Hickerson (R-1)
*Chair*
Mike Holcomb (R-10) *Vice Chair*
Karilyn Brown (R-41)
Jana Della Rosa (R-90)
Dan M. Douglas (R-91)
Lance Eads (R-88)
Mickey Gates (R-22)
Julie Mayberry (R-27)
Ron McNair (R-98)
Mathew W. "Mat" Pitsch (R-76)
Marcus E. Richmond (R-21)
Brandt Smith (R-58)
James J. "Jim" Sorvillo (R-32)
James Sturch (R-63)
Dave Wallace (R-54)

**Minority Members**
Charles Blake (D-36)
David Fielding (D-5)
David Hillman (D-13)
J.P. "Bob" Johnson (D-42)
Milton Nicks, Jr. (D-50)

## Revenue and Taxation

**Majority Members**
Kim Hendren (R-92) *Vice Chair*
Charlie Collins (R-84)
Andy Davis (R-31)
James "Jim" Dotson (R-93)
Les Eaves (R-46)
Lanny Fite (R-23)
Justin Gonzales (R-19)
Lane Jean (R-2)
Jack Ladyman (R-59)
Timothy "Tim" Lemons (R-43)

**Minority Members**
Joe Jett (D-56) *Chair*
Kenneth B. "Ken" Ferguson (D-16)
Vivian L. Flowers (D-17)
Monte Hodges (D-55)
George B. McGill (D-78)
Clarke Tucker (D-35)

**Majority Members** *continued*
Stephen Meeks (R-67)
Micah S. Neal (R-89)
Nelda Speaks (R-100)
DeAnn Vaught (R-4)

## State Agencies and Governmental Affairs

**Majority Members**
Richard Womack (R-18) *Vice Chair*
Bob Ballinger (R-97)
James "Jim" Dotson (R-93)
Charlotte Vining Douglas (R-75)
R. Trevor Drown (R-68)
Lanny Fite (R-23)
Michelle Gray (R-62)
Mary P. "Prissy" Hickerson (R-1)
Mike Holcomb (R-10)
Jack Ladyman (R-59)
Kelley Linck (R-99)
Joshua "Josh" Miller (R-66)
Dwight Tosh (R-52)

**Minority Members**
Eddie L. Armstrong III (D-37)
Camille Bennett (D-14)
Dr. Stephen "Steve" Magie (D-72)
Chris Richey (D-12)
John W. Walker (D-34)
Jeff R. Wardlaw (D-8)

**Members**
Nate Bell (I-20) *Chair*

# California State Legislature

State Capitol, 1020 N Street, Sacramento, CA 95814-4900
Tel: (916) 651-4120   Internet: www.leginfo.ca.gov

## California State Senate

Tel: (916) 651-4120   Fax: (916) 445-1830   Internet: www.sen.ca.gov
President of the Senate
  **Gavin Christopher Newsom** (D) . . . . . . . . . . . . . . . . . . (916) 445-8994
    Education: Santa Clara U 1989 BA
President Pro Tem **Kevin de León** (D) . . . . . . . . . . . . . . . . (916) 651-4024
    Education: Pitzer BA
    Special Assistant to the President Pro Tempore
      **Nancy Lynott** . . . . . . . . . . . . . . . . . . . . . . . . . . . . . . . (916) 651-4006
Majority Leader **William W. "Bill" Monning** (D) . . . . . . . (916) 651-4017
    Education: UC Berkeley 1972 BA; U San Francisco 1976 JD
Majority Whip **Lois Wolk** (D) . . . . . . . . . . . . . . . . . . . . . . . (916) 651-4003
    Education: Antioch Col 1968 BA; Johns Hopkins 1971 MA
Majority Caucus Chair **Connie M. Leyva** (D) . . . . . . . . . . . (916) 651-4016
Minority Leader **Jean Fuller** (R) . . . . . . . . . . . . . . . . . . . . (916) 651-4029
    Education: Cal State (Fresno) BA; Cal State (Los Angeles) MPA
Minority Whip **Ted Gaines** (R) . . . . . . . . . . . . . . . . . . . . . . (916) 651-4001
    Education: Lewis & Clark BABA
Minority Caucus Chair **Tom Berryhill** (R) . . . . . . . . . . . . . (916) 651-4008
    Education: Cal Poly San Luis Obispo (Attended)
Secretary of the Senate **Daniel Alvarez** . . . . . . . . . . . . . . . (916) 651-4171
    E-mail: danny.alvarez@sen.ca.gov
Sergeant-at-Arms **Debbie Manning** . . . . . . . . . . . . . . . . . . (916) 651-4184
    E-mail: senate.sergeants@sen.ca.gov

## Senators

**Party Affiliation Statistics:** Republicans: 14, Democrats: 26
Senator **Benjamin "Ben" Allen** (D-District 26) . . . . . . . . . (916) 651-4026
    Counties Represented: Los Angeles (part)        Dist: (310) 318-6994
    Term Expires: 2018                              Fax: (916) 651-4926
    2512 Artesia Blvd, #320,                        Dist: (310) 318-6733
    Redondo Beach, CA 90278-3279
    E-mail: senator.allen@senate.ca.gov
    Committees: Budget and Fiscal Review; Elections and Constitutional
    Amendments; Natural Resources and Water; Transportation and
    Housing; Veterans Affairs
    Education: Harvard 2000 BA; Cambridge (UK) 2001 MPhil;
    Berkeley Law 2008 JD
Senator **Joel Anderson** (R-District 38) . . . . . . . . . . . . . . . . (916) 651-4038
    Counties Represented: San Diego (part)          Dist: (619) 596-3136
    Term Expires: 2018                                     (El Cajon)
    500 Fesler Street, Suite 201, El Cajon, CA 92020   Dist: (760) 510-2017
    One Civic Center Drive, Suite 320,                     (San Marcos)
    San Marcos, CA 92069                            Fax: (916) 447-9008
    E-mail: senator.anderson@senate.ca.gov          Dist: (619) 596-3140
    Committees: Budget and Fiscal Review; Elections and Constitutional
    Amendments; Judiciary; Public Safety
    Education: Cal Poly (Pomona) BS
Senator **Patricia C. "Pat" Bates** (R-District 38) . . . . . . . . (916) 651-4036
    Counties Represented: San Diego (part)          Dist: (949) 598-5850
    Term Expires: 2018                                    (Orange County)
    24031 El Toro Road, Suite 201A,                 Dist: (760) 931-2455
    Laguna Hills, CA 92653                                 (San Diego)
    169 Saxony Road, Suite 103, Encinitas, CA 92024  Fax: (916) 651-4936
    E-mail: senator.bates@senate.ca.gov             Dist: (949) 598-5855
    Committees: Appropriations; Business, Professions      (Orange County)
    and Economic Development; Environmental          Dist: (760) 931-2477
    Quality; Governmental Organization; Legislative       (San Diego County)
    Ethics; Transportation and Housing
    Education: Occidental 1961 BA
Senator **James T. "Jim" Beall, Jr.** (D-District 15) . . . . . . . (916) 651-4015
    Counties Represented: Santa Clara (part)        Dist: (408) 558-1295
    Term Expires: 2016                                     (Campbell)
    State Capitol, Room 2068, Sacramento, CA 95814  Dist: (408) 286-8318
    2105 South Bascom Avenue, Suite 154,                  (San Jose)
    Campbell, CA 95008                              Fax: (916) 651-4915
    100 Paseo De San Antonio, Suite 209,,           Dist: (408) 558-1296
    San Jose, CA 95113                              Dist: (408) 286-8318
    E-mail: senator.beall@senate.ca.gov
    Committees: Appropriations; Budget and Fiscal Review; Governance
    and Finance; Public Employment and Retirement; Transportation and
    Housing
    Education: San José State BA

*(continued on next page)*

LEGISLATIVE BRANCH

**LEGISLATIVE BRANCH**

**Senators** *continued*

**Senator Tom Berryhill** (R-District 8) . . . . . . . . . . . . . . . . . (916) 651-4008
Counties Represented: Amador, Calaveras, Fresno — Dist: (209) 848-8001
(part), Inyo, Madera (part), Mariposa, Mono, — (Oakdale)
Sacramento (part), Stanislaus (part), Tulare (part), — Dist: (559) 253-7122
Tuolumne — (Fresno)
Term Expires: 2018 — Dist: (209) 223-9140
4974 East Clinton Way, Fresno, CA 93727 — (Jackson)
4641 Spyres Road, Modesto, CA 95356 — Fax: (916) 651-4908
E-mail: senator.berryhill@senate.ca.gov — Dist: (209) 848-2013
Committees: Agriculture; Business, Professions — Dist: (559) 253-7127
and Economic Development; Governmental — Dist: (209) 762-8262
Organization; Human Services; Insurance

**Senator Martin "Marty" Block** (D-District 39)
Room 4072 . . . . . . . . . . . . . . . . . . . . . . . . . . . . (916) 651-4039
Counties Represented: San Diego (part) — Dist: (619) 645-3133
Term Expires: 2016 — Fax: (916) 651-4939
701 B Street, Suite 1840, San Diego, CA 92101 — Dist: (619) 645-3144
E-mail: senator.block@senate.ca.gov
Committees: Budget and Fiscal Review; Business, Professions and
Economic Development; Education; Governmental Organization
Education: Indiana BA; DePaul JD

**Senator Anthony Cannella** (R-District 12) . . . . . . . . . . . . . (916) 651-4012
Counties Represented: Fresno (part), Madera — Dist: (209) 577-6592
(part), Merced, Monterey (part), San Benito, — (Modesto)
Stanislaus (part) — Dist: (209) 726-5495
Term Expires: 2018 — (Merced)
918 15th Street, Modesto, CA 95354 — Dist: (831) 769-8040
1640 North Street, Suite 210, Merced, CA 95340 — (Salinas)
369 Main Street, Suite 208, Salinas, CA 93901 — Fax: (916) 445-0773
E-mail: senator.cannella@senate.ca.gov — Dist: (209) 577-4963
Committees: Agriculture; Energy, Utilities — (Modesto)
and Communications; Rules; Transportation and — Dist: (209) 726-5498
Housing — (Merced)
Education: UC Davis BSCE — Dist: (831) 769-8086
— (Salinas)

**Senator Kevin de León** (D-District 24) . . . . . . . . . . . . . . . (916) 651-4024
Counties Represented: Riverside (part) — Dist: (213) 483-9300
Term Expires: 2018 — Fax: (916) 327-8817
1808 W. Sunset Blvd, Los Angeles, CA 90026 — Dist: (213) 483-9305
E-mail: senator.deleon@senate.ca.gov
Committees: Rules

**Senator Jean Fuller** (R-District 16) . . . . . . . . . . . . . . . . . (916) 651-4016
Counties Represented: Kern (part), San Bernardino — Dist: (661) 323-0443
(part), Tulare (part) — Dist: (760) 228-3136
Term Expires: 2018 — Fax: (916) 651-4916
5701 Truxtun Avenue, Suite 150, — Dist: (661) 323-0446
Bakersfield, CA 93309
7248 Joshua Lane, Suite B, Yucca Valley, CA 92284
E-mail: senator.fuller@senate.ca.gov

**Senator Ted Gaines** (R-District 1) . . . . . . . . . . . . . . . . . (916) 651-4001
Counties Represented: Alpine, El Dorado, Lassen, — Dist: (916) 933-7213
Modoc, Nevada, Placer (part), Plumas, Sacramento — (El Dorado Hills)
(part), Shasta, Sierra, Siskiyou — Dist: (209) 224-7001
Term Expires: 2016 — (Jackson)
4359 Town Center Boulevard, Suite 112, — Fax: (916) 651-4901
El Dorado Hills, CA 95762 — Dist: (916) 933-7234
1900 Churn Creek, Suite 204, Redding, CA 96002 — (El Dorado Hills)
E-mail: senator.gaines@senate.ca.gov — Dist: (530) 225-3143
Committees: Energy, Utilities and Communications; — (Redding)
Environmental Quality; Governmental Organization; Insurance;
Legislative Ethics; Transportation and Housing

**Senator Cathleen Galgiani** (D-District 5) Room 2059 . . . . (916) 651-4005
Counties Represented: Sacramento (part), San — Dist: (209) 948-7930
Joaquin, Stanislaus (part) — (Stockton)
Term Expires: 2016 — Dist: (209) 576-6273
E-mail: senator.galgiani@senate.ca.gov — (Modesto)
Committees: Agriculture; Banking and Financial — Fax: (916) 651-4905
Institutions; Business, Professions and Economic — Dist: (209) 948-7993
Development; Governmental Organization; — (Stockton)
Transportation and Housing — Dist: (209) 576-6277
Education: Cal State (Sacramento) BA — (Modesto)

**Senator Steven M. "Steve" Glazer** (D-District 7) . . . . . . (916) 651-4007
Counties Represented: Alameda (part), Contra — Dist: (925) 942-6082
Costa (part) — Dist: (925) 754-1461
Term Expires: 2016 — Fax: (916) 651-4907
1350 Treat Boulevard, Suite 240, — Fax: (925) 942-6087
Walnut Creek, CA 94597
420 W. 3rd Street, Antioch, CA 94509
E-mail: senator.glazer@senate.ca.gov
Committees: Banking and Financial Institutions; Budget and Fiscal
Review; Governmental Organization; Insurance; Public Safety

**Senator Isadore Hall III** (D-District 35) . . . . . . . . . . . . . . (916) 651-4035
Counties Represented: Los Angeles (part) — Dist: (310) 514-8573
Term Expires: 2016 — Fax: (916) 651-4935
222 West 6th Street, Suite 320, — Dist: (310) 514-8578
San Pedro, CA 90731
E-mail: senator.hall@senate.ca.gov
Committees: Banking and Financial Institutions; Governmental
Organization; Health; Insurance; Public Employment and Retirement
Education: U Phoenix BBA; National U 2011 MPA; USC MA

**Senator Loni Hancock** (D-District 9) . . . . . . . . . . . . . . . . (916) 651-4009
Counties Represented: Alameda (part), Contra — Dist: (510) 286-1333
Costa (part) — Fax: (916) 651-4909
Term Expires: 2016 — Dist: (510) 286-3885
State Capitol, Room 3092, Sacramento, CA 95814
1515 Clay Street, Suite 2202, Oakland, CA 94612
E-mail: senator.hancock@senate.ca.gov
Committees: Budget and Fiscal Review; Education; Elections and
Constitutional Amendments; Human Services; Public Safety
Education: Ithaca 1963 BA; Wright Inst 1977 MA

**Senator Dr. Edward P. "Ed" Hernandez, O.D.** (D-District 22) . . . (916) 651-4022
Counties Represented: Los Angeles (part) — Dist: (626) 430-2499
Term Expires: 2018 — Fax: (916) 651-4922
100 South Vincent, West Covina, CA 91790 — Dist: (626) 430-2494
E-mail: senator.hernandez@senate.ca.gov
Committees: Business, Professions and Economic Development;
Governance and Finance; Governmental Organization; Health;
Insurance
Education: Cal State (Fullerton) BS; Indiana State OD

**Senator Robert M. "Bob" Hertzberg** (D-District 18) . . . . . (916) 651-4018
Counties Represented: Los Angeles (part) — Dist: (818) 901-5588
Term Expires: 2018 — Dist: (818) 901-5562
6150 Van Nuys Boulevard,, Suite 400, — Fax: (916) 651-4918
Van Nuys, CA 91401
E-mail: senator.hertzberg@senate.ca.gov
Committees: Elections and Constitutional Amendments; Energy,
Utilities and Communications; Governance and Finance; Judiciary;
Natural Resources and Water
Education: U Redlands 1976; Hastings 1979 JD

**Senator Jerry Hill** (D-District 13) Room 5064 . . . . . . . . . . (916) 651-4013
Counties Represented: San Mateo (part), Santa — Dist: (650) 212-3313
Clara (part) — Fax: (916) 651-4913
Term Expires: 2016 — Fax: (650) 212-3320
1528 South El Camino Real, Suite 303, San Mateo, CA 94402
E-mail: senator.hill@senate.ca.gov
Committees: Appropriations; Business, Professions and Economic
Development; Energy, Utilities and Communications; Environmental
Quality; Governmental Organization
Education: UC Berkeley BA

**Senator Ben Hueso** (D-District 40) Room 305 . . . . . . . . . . (916) 651-4040
Counties Represented: Imperial, San Diego (part) — Dist: (619) 409-7690
Term Expires: 2018 — (Chula Vista)
E-mail: senator.hueso@senate.ca.gov — Dist: (760) 335-3442
Committees: Banking and Financial Institutions; — (El Centro)
Energy, Utilities and Communications; — Fax: (916) 651-4940
Governmental Organization; Natural Resources — Dist: (619) 409-7688
and Water; Veterans Affairs — (Chula Vista)
Education: UCLA BA — Dist: (760) 335-3444
— (El Centro)

**Senator Robert "Bob" Huff** (R-District 29) . . . . . . . . . . . . (916) 651-4029
Counties Represented: Los Angeles (part), Orange — Dist: (714) 671-9474
(part), San Bernardino (part) — Fax: (916) 651-4929
Term Expires: 2016 — Dist: (714) 671-9750
State Capitol, Room 3048, Sacramento, CA 95814
20888 Amar Road, Suite 205, Walnut, CA 91789
E-mail: senator.huff@senate.ca.gov
Committees: Education
Education: Westmont BA

**Senator Hannah-Beth Jackson** (D-District 19)
Room 2032 . . . . . . . . . . . . . . . . . . . . . . . . . . . . (916) 651-4019
Counties Represented: Santa Barbara, Ventura (part) — Dist: (805) 965-0862
Term Expires: 2016 — Dist: (805) 988-1940
E-mail: senator.jackson@senate.ca.gov — Fax: (805) 965-0701
Committees: Business, Professions and Economic Development;
Environmental Quality; Judiciary; Labor and Industrial Relations;
Natural Resources and Water
Education: Scripps Col 1971 BS; Boston U 1975 JD

Senator **Ricardo Lara** (D-District 33) Room 5050 . . . . . . . (916) 651-4033
Counties Represented: Los Angeles (part)    Dist: (562) 256-7921
Term Expires: 2016    (Long Beach)
E-mail: senator.lara@senate.ca.gov    Dist: (323) 277-4560
Committees: Appropriations; Banking and Financial Institutions;
Energy, Utilities and Communications; Governance and Finance;
Governmental Organization
Education: San Diego State 1999 BAGS

Senator **Mark R. Leno** (D-District 11) . . . . . . . . . . . . . . . .(916) 651-4011
Counties Represented: San Francisco, San Mateo    Dist: (415) 479-6612
(part)    (San Rafael)
Term Expires: 2016    Dist: (415) 557-1300
Sacramento, CA 95814    (San Francisco)
3501 Civic Center Drive, San Rafael, CA 94903    Fax: (916) 445-4722
455 Golden Gate Avenue, San Francisco, CA 94102    Dist: (415) 479-1146
E-mail: senator.leno@sen.ca.gov    (San Rafael)
Committees: Budget and Fiscal Review;    Dist: (415) 557-1252
Environmental Quality; Judiciary; Labor and    (San Francisco)
Industrial Relations; Legislative Ethics; Public Safety
Education: American Col 1973 BA

Senator **Connie M. Leyva** (D-District 20) . . . . . . . . . . . . .(916) 651-4171
Counties Represented: Los Angeles (part), San Bernardino (part)
Term Expires: 2018
E-mail: senator.leyva@senate.ca.gov
Committees: Education; Energy, Utilities and Communications; Rules;
Transportation and Housing

Senator **Carol Liu** (D-District 25) . . . . . . . . . . . . . . . . . . . .(916) 651-4025
Counties Represented: Los Angeles (part), San    Dist: (818) 409-0400
Bernardino (part)    (Glendale)
Term Expires: 2016    Fax: (916) 324-7543
State Capitol, Room 5061, Sacramento, CA 95814    Dist: (818) 409-1256
710 South Central Avenue, Glendale, CA 91204    (Glendale)
E-mail: senator.liu@senate.ca.gov
Committees: Education; Elections and Constitutional Amendments;
Human Services; Insurance; Public Safety
Education: San José State Col 1963 BAE

Senator **Mike McGuire** (D-District 2) . . . . . . . . . . . . . . . . (916) 651-4171
Counties Represented: Del Norte, Humboldt, Lake, Marin, Mendocino,
Sonoma (part), Trinity
Term Expires: 2018
E-mail: senator.mcguire@senate.ca.gov
Committees: Appropriations; Energy, Utilities and Communications;
Governmental Organization; Human Services; Public Safety;
Transportation and Housing

Senator **Tony Mendoza** (D-District 32) . . . . . . . . . . . . . . .(916) 651-4171
Counties Represented: Los Angeles (part), Orange (part)
Term Expires: 2018
E-mail: senator.mendoza@senate.ca.gov
Committees: Appropriations; Business, Professions and Economic
Development; Education; Labor and Industrial Relations; Transportation
and Housing

Senator **Holly J. Mitchell** (D-District 30) . . . . . . . . . . . . . .(916) 651-4026
Counties Represented: Los Angeles (part)    Dist: (213) 745-6656
Term Expires: 2018
E-mail: senator.mitchell@senate.ca.gov
Committees: Budget and Fiscal Review; Health; Insurance; Labor and
Industrial Relations; Rules

Senator **William W. "Bill" Monning** (D-District 17)
Room 4066 . . . . . . . . . . . . . . . . . . . . . . . . . . . . . . . . . (916) 651-4017
Counties Represented: Monterey (part), San Luis Obispo, Santa Clara
(part), Santa Cruz
Term Expires: 2016
E-mail: senator.monning@senate.ca.gov
Committees: Budget and Fiscal Review; Education; Health; Judiciary;
Legislative Ethics; Natural Resources and Water; Public Safety

Senator **John M.W. Moorlach, CPA, CFP** (R-District 37) . .(916) 651-4037
Counties Represented: Orange (part)    Fax: (916) 651-4937
Term Expires: 2016
E-mail: senator.moorlach@senate.ca.gov
Committees: Budget and Fiscal Review; Governance and Finance;
Judiciary; Public Employment and Retirement
Education: Cal State (Long Beach) 1977

Senator **Mike Morrell** (R-District 23) Room 3056 . . . . . . . . (916) 651-4023
Counties Represented: Los Angeles (part), Riverside    Dist: (909) 919-7731
(part), San Bernardino (part)
Term Expires: 2016
Commerce Center Drive, Suite A-220, Rancho Cucamonga, CA 91730
E-mail: senator.morrell@senate.ca.gov
Committees: Banking and Financial Institutions; Energy, Utilities
and Communications; Legislative Ethics; Public Employment and
Retirement
Education: La Verne 1986 BABA

Senator **Janet Nguyen** (R-District 34) . . . . . . . . . . . . . . . . (916) 651-4034
Counties Represented: Los Angeles (part), Orange    Dist: (714) 741-1034
(part)    Fax: (916) 651-4934
Term Expires: 2018
10971 Garden Grove Boulevard, Suite D, Garden Grove, CA 92843
E-mail: senator.nguyen@senate.ca.gov
Committees: Budget and Fiscal Review; Governance and Finance;
Health; Human Services; Veterans Affairs

Senator **James Wiley "Jim" Nielsen** (R-District 4)
Room 4062 . . . . . . . . . . . . . . . . . . . . . . . . . . . . . . . . . .(916) 651-4171
Counties Represented: Butte, Colusa, Glenn, Placer (part), Sacramento
(part), Sutter, Tehama, Yuba
Term Expires: 2018
E-mail: senator.nielsen@senate.ca.gov
Committees: Appropriations; Budget and Fiscal Review; Health;
Veterans Affairs
Education: Cal State (Fresno) BA

Senator **Richard Pan** (D-District 6) . . . . . . . . . . . . . . . . . . .(916) 651-4171
Counties Represented: Sacramento (part), Yolo (part)
Term Expires: 2018
E-mail: senator.pan@senate.ca.gov
Committees: Agriculture; Budget and Fiscal Review; Education;
Health; Public Employment and Retirement
Education: Johns Hopkins BS; Harvard MA; Pittsburgh MD

Senator **Fran Pavley** (D-District 27) . . . . . . . . . . . . . . . . . .(916) 651-4027
Counties Represented: Los Angeles (part), Ventura    Dist: (310) 314-5214
(part)    (Santa Monica)
Term Expires: 2016    Fax: (916) 324-4823
State Capitol, Room 4035, Sacramento, CA 95814    Dist: (310) 314-5263
2716 Ocean Park Boulevard, Suite 3088,    (Santa Monica)
Santa Monica, CA 90405
E-mail: senator.pavley@senate.ca.gov
Committees: Budget and Fiscal Review; Energy, Utilities and
Communications; Environmental Quality; Governance and Finance;
Legislative Ethics; Natural Resources and Water
Education: Cal State (Fresno) 1970 BA;
Cal State (Northridge) 1985 MA

Senator **Richard D. Roth** (D-District 31) . . . . . . . . . . . . . . .(916) 651-4031
Counties Represented: Riverside (part)
Term Expires: 2016
3737 Main Street, Suite 104, Riverside, CA 92501
E-mail: senator.roth@senate.ca.gov
Committees: Budget and Fiscal Review; Health; Insurance;
Transportation and Housing; Veterans Affairs
Education: Miami U (OH) 1972; Emory 1974 JD

Senator **Sharon Runner** (R-District 21) . . . . . . . . . . . . . . .(916) 651-4021
Counties Represented: Los Angeles (part), San    Dist: (661) 729-6232
Bernardino (part)    Dist: (760) 843-8414
Term Expires: 2016    Dist: (661) 286-1471
848 W. Lancaster Boulevard, Suite 101,    Fax: (916) 651-4921
Lancaster, CA 93534
14343 Civic Drive, First Floor, Victorville, CA 92392
23920 Valencia Boulevard, Suite 250, Santa Clarita, CA 91355
E-mail: senator.runner@senate.ca.gov
Committees: Rules

Senator **Jeff Stone** (R-District 28) . . . . . . . . . . . . . . . . . . . . (916) 651-4171
Counties Represented: Riverside (part)
Term Expires: 2018
E-mail: senator.stone@senate.ca.gov
Committees: Budget and Fiscal Review; Labor and Industrial Relations;
Natural Resources and Water; Public Safety

Senator **Andrew James "Andy" Vidak** (R-District 14) . . . (916) 651-4016
Counties Represented: Fresno (part), Kern (part),    Dist: (661) 395-2620
Kings, Tulare (part)    Dist: (559) 585-7161
Term Expires: 2018
1122 Truxtun Avenue, Bakersfield, CA 93301
E-mail: senator.vidak@senate.ca.gov
Committees: Banking and Financial Institutions; Education;
Governmental Organization; Natural Resources and Water
Education: Texas Tech BS

Senator **Bob Wieckowski** (D-District 10) . . . . . . . . . . . . . .(916) 651-4010
Counties Represented: Alameda (part), Santa Clara    Dist: (510) 794-3900
(part)
Term Expires: 2018
39510 Paseo Padre Parkway, Suite 280, Fremont, CA 64538
E-mail: senator.wieckowski@senate.ca.gov
Committees: Business, Professions and Economic Development;
Environmental Quality; Insurance; Judiciary; Transportation and
Housing
Education: UC Berkeley BA; Santa Clara U JD

*(continued on next page)*

**Senators** *continued*

Senator **Lois Wolk** (D-District 3) . . . . . . . . . . . . . . . . . . . . . (916) 651-4003
  Counties Represented: Contra Costa (part), Napa,     Dist: (707) 454-3808
  Sacramento (part), Solano, Sonoma (part), Yolo                    (Vacaville)
  (part)                                               Dist: (209) 948-7930
  Term Expires: 2016                                                (Stockton)
  State Capitol, Room 4032, Sacramento, CA 95814       Fax: (916) 323-2304
  555 Mason Street, Suite 230, Vacaville, CA 95688     Dist: (707) 454-3811
  31 East Channel Street, Room 440,                                (Vacaville)
  Stockton, CA 95202                                   Dist: (209) 948-7993
  E-mail: senator.wolk@senate.ca.gov                               (Stockton)
  Committees: Agriculture; Budget and Fiscal Review; Energy, Utilities
  and Communications; Health; Natural Resources and Water

# Senate Standing Committees

## Agriculture

1020 N Street, Room 583, Sacramento, CA 95814

**Majority Members**
Cathleen Galgiani (D-5) *Chair*
Richard Pan (D-6)
Lois Wolk (D-3)

**Minority Members**
Anthony Cannella (R-12)
  *Vice Chair*
Tom Berryhill (R-8)

## Appropriations

State Capitol, Room 2206, Sacramento, CA 95814

**Majority Members**
Ricardo Lara (D-33) *Chair*
James T. "Jim" Beall, Jr. (D-15)
Jerry Hill (D-13)
Mike McGuire (D-2)
Tony Mendoza (D-32)

**Minority Members**
Patricia C. "Pat" Bates (R-38)
  *Vice Chair*
James Wiley "Jim" Nielsen (R-4)

## Banking and Financial Institutions

State Capitol, Room 112, Sacramento, CA 95814

**Majority Members**
Steven M. "Steve" Glazer (D-7)
  *Chair*
Cathleen Galgiani (D-5)
Ben Hueso (D-40)
Isadore Hall III (D-35)
Ricardo Lara (D-33)

**Minority Members**
Andrew James "Andy"
  Vidak (R-14)
  *Vice Chair*
Mike Morrell (R-23)

## Budget and Fiscal Review

State Capitol, Room 4203, Sacramento, CA 95814

**Majority Members**
Mark R. Leno (D-11) *Chair*
James T. "Jim" Beall, Jr. (D-15)
Martin "Marty" Block (D-39)
Steven M. "Steve" Glazer (D-7)
Loni Hancock (D-9)
Benjamin "Ben" Allen (D-26)
Holly J. Mitchell (D-30)
William W. "Bill" Monning (D-17)
Richard Pan (D-6)
Fran Pavley (D-27)
Richard D. Roth (D-31)
Lois Wolk (D-3)

**Minority Members**
James Wiley "Jim" Nielsen (R-4)
  *Vice Chair*
Joel Anderson (R-38)
John M.W. Moorlach (R-37)
Janet Nguyen (R-34)
Jeff Stone (R-28)

## Business, Professions and Economic Development

State Capitol, Room 3191, Sacramento, CA 95814

**Majority Members**
Jerry Hill (D-13) *Chair*
Martin "Marty" Block (D-39)
Cathleen Galgiani (D-5)
Dr. Edward P. "Ed" Hernandez
  (D-22)
Hannah-Beth Jackson (D-19)
Tony Mendoza (D-32)
Bob Wieckowski (D-10)

**Minority Members**
Patricia C. "Pat" Bates (R-38)
  *Vice Chair*
Tom Berryhill (R-8)

## Education

Room 2083, Sacramento, CA 95814

**Majority Members**
Carol Liu (D-25) *Chair*
Martin "Marty" Block (D-39)
Loni Hancock (D-9)
Connie M. Leyva (D-20)
Tony Mendoza (D-32)
William W. "Bill" Monning (D-17)
Richard Pan (D-6)

**Minority Members**
Robert "Bob" Huff (R-29)
Andrew James "Andy" Vidak
  (R-14)

## Elections and Constitutional Amendments

State Capitol, Room 3191, Sacramento, CA 95814

**Majority Members**
Benjamin "Ben" Allen (D-26)
  *Chair*
Loni Hancock (D-9)
Robert M. "Bob" Hertzberg (D-18)
Carol Liu (D-25)

**Minority Members**
Joel Anderson (R-38) *Vice Chair*

## Energy, Utilities and Communications

State Capitol, Room 4035, Sacramento, CA 95814

**Majority Members**
Ben Hueso (D-40) *Chair*
Jerry Hill (D-13)
Robert M. "Bob" Hertzberg (D-18)
Ricardo Lara (D-33)
Connie M. Leyva (D-20)
Mike McGuire (D-2)
Fran Pavley (D-27)
Lois Wolk (D-3)

**Minority Members**
Mike Morrell (R-23) *Vice Chair*
Anthony Cannella (R-12)
Ted Gaines (R-1)

## Environmental Quality

State Capitol, Room 2205, Sacramento, CA 95814

**Majority Members**
Bob Wieckowski (D-10) *Chair*
Jerry Hill (D-13)
Hannah-Beth Jackson (D-19)
Mark R. Leno (D-11)
Fran Pavley (D-27)

**Minority Members**
Ted Gaines (R-1) *Vice Chair*
Patricia C. "Pat" Bates (R-38)

## Governmental Organization

1020 N Street, Room 4203, Sacramento, CA 95814

**Majority Members**
Isadore Hall III (D-35) *Chair*
Martin "Marty" Block (D-39)
Cathleen Galgiani (D-5)
Steven M. "Steve" Glazer (D-7)
Dr. Edward P. "Ed" Hernandez
  (D-22)
Jerry Hill (D-13)
Ben Hueso (D-40)
Ricardo Lara (D-33)
Mike McGuire (D-2)

**Minority Members**
Tom Berryhill (R-8) *Vice Chair*
Patricia C. "Pat" Bates (R-38)
Ted Gaines (R-1)
Andrew James "Andy" Vidak
  (R-14)

## Governance and Finance

**Majority Members**
Robert M. "Bob" Hertzberg (D-18)
  *Chair*
James T. "Jim" Beall, Jr. (D-15)
Dr. Edward P. "Ed" Hernandez
  (D-22)
Ricardo Lara (D-33)
Fran Pavley (D-27)

**Minority Members**
Janet Nguyen (R-34) *Vice Chair*
John M.W. Moorlach (R-37)

# Health
State Capitol, Room 2191, Sacramento, CA 95814

| Majority Members | Minority Members |
|---|---|
| Dr. Edward P. "Ed" Hernandez (D-22) *Chair* | Janet Nguyen (R-34) *Vice Chair* |
| | James Wiley "Jim" Nielsen (R-4) |
| Isadore Hall III (D-35) | |
| Holly J. Mitchell (D-30) | |
| William W. "Bill" Monning (D-17) | |
| Richard Pan (D-6) | |
| Richard D. Roth (D-31) | |
| Lois Wolk (D-3) | |

# Human Services
State Capitol, Room 3191, Sacramento, CA 95814

| Majority Members | Minority Members |
|---|---|
| Mike McGuire (D-2) *Chair* | Tom Berryhill (R-8) *Vice Chair* |
| Loni Hancock (D-9) | Janet Nguyen (R-34) |
| Carol Liu (D-25) | |

# Insurance
State Capitol, 1020 N Street, Room 2195, Sacramento, CA 95814-4900

| Majority Members | Minority Members |
|---|---|
| Richard D. Roth (D-31) *Chair* | Ted Gaines (R-1) *Vice Chair* |
| Steven M. "Steve" Glazer (D-7) | Tom Berryhill (R-8) |
| Isadore Hall III (D-35) | |
| Dr. Edward P. "Ed" Hernandez (D-22) | |
| Carol Liu (D-25) | |
| Holly J. Mitchell (D-30) | |
| Bob Wieckowski (D-10) | |

# Judiciary
State Capitol, Room 112, Sacramento, CA 95814

| Majority Members | Minority Members |
|---|---|
| Hannah-Beth Jackson (D-19) *Chair* | John M.W. Moorlach (R-37) *Vice Chair* |
| Robert M. "Bob" Hertzberg (D-18) | Joel Anderson (R-38) |
| Mark R. Leno (D-11) | |
| William W. "Bill" Monning (D-17) | |
| Bob Wieckowski (D-10) | |

# Labor and Industrial Relations
State Capitol, Room 2040, Sacramento, CA 95814

| Majority Members | Minority Members |
|---|---|
| Tony Mendoza (D-32) *Chair* | Jeff Stone (R-28) *Vice Chair* |
| Hannah-Beth Jackson (D-19) | |
| Mark R. Leno (D-11) | |
| Holly J. Mitchell (D-30) | |

# Legislative Ethics
1020 N Street, Room 238, Sacramento, CA 95814-4900

| Majority Members | Minority Members |
|---|---|
| William W. "Bill" Monning (D-17) *Chair* | Mike Morrell (R-23) *Vice Chair* |
| Mark R. Leno (D-11) | Patricia C. "Pat" Bates (R-38) |
| Fran Pavley (D-27) | Ted Gaines (R-1) |

# Natural Resources and Water
State Capitol, Room 5046, Sacramento, CA 95814

| Majority Members | Minority Members |
|---|---|
| Fran Pavley (D-27) *Chair* | Jeff Stone (R-28) *Vice Chair* |
| Benjamin "Ben" Allen (D-26) | Andrew James "Andy" Vidak (R-14) |
| Robert M. "Bob" Hertzberg (D-18) | |
| Ben Hueso (D-40) | |
| Hannah-Beth Jackson (D-19) | |
| William W. "Bill" Monning (D-17) | |
| Lois Wolk (D-3) | |

# Public Employment and Retirement
State Capitol, Room 2040, Sacramento, CA 95814

| Majority Members | Minority Members |
|---|---|
| Richard Pan (D-6) *Chair* | Mike Morrell (R-23) *Vice Chair* |
| James T. "Jim" Beall, Jr. (D-15) | John M.W. Moorlach (R-37) |
| Isadore Hall III (D-35) | |

# Public Safety
State Capitol, Room 4203, Sacramento, CA 95814

| Majority Members | Minority Members |
|---|---|
| Loni Hancock (D-9) *Chair* | Joel Anderson (R-38) *Vice Chair* |
| Steven M. "Steve" Glazer (D-7) | Jeff Stone (R-28) |
| Mark R. Leno (D-11) | |
| Carol Liu (D-25) | |
| Mike McGuire (D-2) | |
| William W. "Bill" Monning (D-17) | |

# Rules
State Capitol, Room 113, Sacramento, CA 95814

| Majority Members | Minority Members |
|---|---|
| Kevin de León (D-24) *Chair* | Sharon Runner (R-21) *Vice Chair* |
| Holly J. Mitchell (D-30) | Anthony Cannella (R-12) |
| Connie M. Leyva (D-20) | |

# Transportation and Housing
State Capitol, Room 4203, Sacramento, CA 95814

| Majority Members | Minority Members |
|---|---|
| James T. "Jim" Beall, Jr. (D-15) *Chair* | Anthony Cannella (R-12) *Vice Chair* |
| Benjamin "Ben" Allen (D-26) | Patricia C. "Pat" Bates (R-38) |
| Cathleen Galgiani (D-5) | Ted Gaines (R-1) |
| Connie M. Leyva (D-20) | |
| Mike McGuire (D-2) | |
| Tony Mendoza (D-32) | |
| Richard D. Roth (D-31) | |
| Bob Wieckowski (D-10) | |

# Veterans Affairs
1020 N Street, Room 2040, Sacramento, CA 95814

| Majority Members | Minority Members |
|---|---|
| Ben Hueso (D-40) *Vice Chair* | James Wiley "Jim" Nielsen (R-4) *Chair* |
| Benjamin "Ben" Allen (D-26) | Janet Nguyen (R-34) |
| Richard D. Roth (D-31) | |

# California State Assembly
P.O. Box 942849, Sacramento, CA 94249
Internet: www.assembly.ca.gov

Speaker of the Assembly **Anthony Rendon** (D) . . . . . . . . (916) 319-2063
   Education: Cal State (Fullerton) BA, MA; UC Riverside PhD
   Chief of Staff **Carrie Cornwell** . . . . . . . . . . . . . . . . . . . . . (916) 319-3770
Speaker Pro Tempore **Kevin Mullin** (D) . . . . . . . . . . . . . . (916) 319-2022
   Education: U San Francisco BA; San Francisco State U MPA
Assistant Speaker Pro Tempore **Autumn R. Burke** (D) . . . . (916) 319-2062
Majority Floor Leader **Ian Charles Calderon** (D) . . . . . . . (916) 319-2057
   Education: Cal State (Long Beach) 2008 BA
Assistant Majority Floor Leader
   **James "Jim" Cooper** (D) . . . . . . . . . . . . . . . . . . . . . . (916) 319-2058
Majority Whip **Miguel Santiago** (D) . . . . . . . . . . . . . . . . . (916) 319-2053
   Education: UCLA BA
Assistant Majority Whip **Evan Low** (D) . . . . . . . . . . . . . . . (916) 319-2028
Majority Caucus Chair **Mike A. Gipson** (D) . . . . . . . . . . . (916) 319-2013
   Education: U Phoenix BS; Los Angeles Southwest AA
Minority Caucus Chair **Scott Wilk** (R) . . . . . . . . . . . . . . . . (916) 319-2038
   Education: Bakersfield BA
Minority Leader **Chad Mayes** (R) . . . . . . . . . . . . . . . . . . . . (916) 319-2012
Republican Floor Leader **Marie Waldron** (R) . . . . . . . . . . . (916) 319-2075
   Education: St John's U (NY) 1982 BS
Deputy Republican Floor Leader **James Gallagher** (R) . . . (916) 319-2003
Assistant Republican Leader **Travis Allen** (R) . . . . . . . . . . (916) 319-2072
   Education: Cal State (Long Beach) BA
Assistant Republican Leader **Franklin E. Bigelow** (R) . . . . (916) 319-2005
Assistant Republican Leader **Jay Obernolte** (R) . . . . . . . . (916) 319-2033
Chief Republican Whip **Chad Mayes** (R) . . . . . . . . . . . . . . (916) 319-2042
Republican Whip **Ling-Ling Chang** (R) . . . . . . . . . . . . . . . (916) 319-2055
Republican Whip **Beth B. Gaines** (R) . . . . . . . . . . . . . . . . . (916) 319-2006
Chief Clerk of the Assembly **E. Dotson Wilson** . . . . . . . . . (916) 319-2856
Chief Sergeant-at-Arms **Ronald E. Pane** . . . . . . . . . . . . . . (916) 319-2808

# Assembly Members
P.O. Box 942849, Sacramento, CA 94249-0072

**Party Affiliation Statistics:** Republicans: 28, Democrats: 52

Assembly Member
**K. H. "Katcho" Achadjian** (R-District 35) . . . . . . . . . . . (916) 319-2035
Counties Represented: San Luis Obispo (part),   Dist: (805) 549-3381
Santa Barbara (part)   Fax: (916) 319-2133
Term Expires: 2016   Dist: (805) 549-3400
1150 Osos Street, Suite 207, San Luis Obispo, CA 93401
E-mail: assemblymember.achadjian@assembly.ca.gov
Committees: Banking and Finance; Utilities and Commerce; Veterans
Affairs
Education: Cal Poly San Luis Obispo BBA

Assembly Member **Luis A. Alejo** (D-District 30) . . . . . . . . (916) 319-2030
Counties Represented: Monterey (part), San Benito,   Dist: (831) 759-8676
Santa Clara (part), Santa Cruz (part)   (Salinas)
Term Expires: 2016   Dist: (831) 638-3228
100 West Alisal Street, Suite 103,   (Hollister)
Salinas, CA 93901   Dist: (831) 761-7428
365 Fourth Street, Hollister, CA 95023   (Watsonville)
275 Main Street, Suite 104, Watsonville, CA 95076   Fax: (916) 319-2130
E-mail: assemblymember.alejo@assembly.ca.gov   Dist: (831) 759-2961
Committees: Environmental Safety and Toxic   (Salinas)
Materials; Governmental Organization; Judiciary;   Dist: (831) 638-3226
Local Government; Veterans Affairs   (Hollister)
Education: UC Berkeley BA; Harvard JD   Dist: (831) 761-7426

Assembly Member **Travis Allen** (R-District 72) . . . . . . . . (916) 319-2072
Counties Represented: Orange (part)   Fax: (916) 319-2172
Term Expires: 2016
17011 Beach Blvd, Suite 1120, Huntington Beach, CA 92647
E-mail: assemblymember.allen@assembly.ca.gov
Committees: Banking and Finance; Budget; Elections and Redistricting;
Insurance

Assembly Member
**Dr. Joaquin Arambula, MD** (D-District 31) . . . . . . . . . . (916) 319-2031
Counties Represented: Fresno (part)   Dist: (559) 445-5532
P.O. Box 942849, Sacramento, CA 94249-0031   Fax: (916) 319-2131
Hugh Burns State Building, 2550 Mariposa Mall,   Dist: (559) 445-6006
Fresno, CA 93721
E-mail: assemblymember.arambula@assembly.ca.gov
Committees: Environmental Safety and Toxic Materials; Human
Services; Rules; Veterans Affairs

Assembly Member **Toni G. Atkins** (D-District 78) . . . . . . . (916) 319-2078
Counties Represented: San Diego (part)   Dist: (619) 645-3090
Term Expires: 2016   (San Diego)
P.O. Box 942849, Sacramento, CA 94249-0078   Fax: (916) 319-2178
2455 Fifth Avenue, Suite 401,   Dist: (619) 645-3094
San Diego, CA 92101   (San Diego)
E-mail: assemblymember.atkins@assembly.ca.gov
Education: Emory & Henry BA

Assembly Member **Catharine B. Baker** (R-District 16) . . . . (916) 319-2016
Counties Represented: Alameda (part), Contra Costa   Dist: (925) 328-1515
(part)
Term Expires: 2016
P.O. Box 942849, Sacramento, CA 94249-0016
2694 Bishop Drive, Suite 275, San Ramon, CA 94583
E-mail: assemblymember.baker@assembly.ca.gov
Committees: Business and Professions; Higher Education;
Transportation

Assembly Member **Franklin E. Bigelow** (R-District 5) . . . . (916) 319-2005
Counties Represented: Alpine, Amador, Calaveras,   Dist: (530) 295-5505
El Dorado (part), Madera, Mariposa, Mono, Placer   Fax: (916) 319-2105
(part), Tuolumne
Term Expires: 2016
2441 Headington Road, Placerville, CA 95667
E-mail: assemblymember.bigelow@assembly.ca.gov
Committees: Appropriations; Budget; Governmental Organization;
Water, Parks and Wildlife

Assembly Member **Richard Bloom** (D-District 50) . . . . . . . (916) 319-2050
Counties Represented: Los Angeles (part)   Fax: (916) 319-2150
Term Expires: 2016
2800 28th Street, Suite 150, Santa Monica, CA 90405
E-mail: assemblymember.bloom@assembly.ca.gov
Committees: Appropriations; Budget; Business and Professions; Higher
Education; Transportation
Education: UC Berkeley 1975 BA; Loyola Law 1978 JD

Assembly Member **Susan Bonilla** (D-District 14) . . . . . . . . (916) 319-2014
Counties Represented: Contra Costa (part), Solano   Dist: (925) 521-1511
(part)   (Concord)
Term Expires: 2016   Fax: (916) 319-2114
P.O. Box 942849, Sacramento, CA 94249-0014   Dist: (925) 602-1536
2151 Salvio Street, Concord, CA 94520   (Concord)
E-mail: assemblymember.bonilla@assembly.ca.gov
Committees: Appropriations; Health; Human Services; Local
Government; Utilities and Commerce
Education: Azusa Pacific 1982 BA

Assembly Member **Rob Bonta** (D-District 18) . . . . . . . . . . (916) 319-2018
Counties Represented: Alameda (part)   Fax: (916) 319-2118
Term Expires: 2016
1515 Clay Street, Suite 2204, Oakland, CA 94612
E-mail: assemblymember.bonta@assembly.ca.gov
Committees: Appropriations; Budget; Governmental Organization;
Public Employees, Retirement and Social Security
Education: Yale, JD

Assembly Member
**William P. "Bill" Brough** (R-District 73) . . . . . . . . . . . . (916) 319-2073
Counties Represented: Orange (part)   Dist: (949) 347-7301
Term Expires: 2016
P.O. Box 942849, Sacramento, CA 94249-0073
29122 Rancho Viejo Road, Suite 111, San Juan Capistrano, CA 92675
E-mail: assemblymember.brough@assembly.ca.gov
Committees: Accountability and Administrative Review; Business and
Professions; Jobs, Economic Development and the Economy; Revenue
and Taxation; Veterans Affairs
Education: Connecticut 1995 BA

Assembly Member **Cheryl R. Brown** (D-District 47) . . . . . (916) 319-2047
Counties Represented: San Bernardino (part)   Dist: (909) 381-3238
Term Expires: 2016   (San Bernardino)
P.O. Box 942849, Sacramento, CA 94249-0047   Dist: (909) 350-7646
290 North D Street, Suite 903,   (Fontana)
San Bernardino, CA 92401   Fax: (916) 319-2147
Fontana City Hall, 8353 Sierra Avenue,   Dist: (909) 885-8589
Fontana, CA 92335   (San Bernardino)
E-mail: assemblymember.brown@assembly.ca.gov
Committees: Aging and Long-Term Care; Banking and Finance; Jobs,
Economic Development and the Economy; Transportation
Education: Cal State (San Bernardino) BA

Assembly Member **Autumn R. Burke** (D-District 62) . . . . . (916) 319-2062
Counties Represented: Los Angeles (part)   Dist: (310) 412-6400
Term Expires: 2016   Fax: (916) 319-2162
P.O. Box 942849, Sacramento, CA 94249-0062   Dist: (310) 412-6354
One Manchester Boulevard, Suite 601, Inglewood, CA 90301
E-mail: assemblymember.burke@assembly.ca.gov
Committees: Accountability and Administrative Review; Health;
Housing and Community Development

Assembly Member **Ian Charles Calderon** (D-District 57) . . (916) 319-2057
Counties Represented: Los Angeles (part)   Dist: (562) 692-5858
Term Expires: 2016   Fax: (916) 319-2157
P.O. Box 942849, Sacramento, CA 94249-0057   Dist: (562) 695-5852
13181 Crossroads Parkway, Suite 160,
City of Industry, CA 91746-3497
E-mail: assemblymember.calderon@assembly.ca.gov
Committees: Appropriations; Arts, Entertainment, Sports, Tourism and
Internet Media; Insurance

Assembly Member **Nora E. Campos** (D-District 27) . . . . . . (916) 319-2027
Counties Represented: Santa Clara (part)   Dist: (408) 277-1220
Term Expires: 2016   (San Jose)
P.O. Box 942849, Sacramento, CA 94249-0027   Fax: (916) 319-2127
100 Paseo De San Antonio, Suite 300,   Dist: (408) 277-1036
San Jose, CA 95113   (San Jose)
E-mail: assemblymember.campos@assembly.ca.gov
Committees: Budget; Business and Professions; Governmental
Organization; Health
Education: San Francisco State U BA

Assembly Member **Ling-Ling Chang** (R-District 55) . . . . . . (916) 319-2055
Counties Represented: Los Angeles (part), Orange   Dist: (909) 627-7021
(part), San Bernardino (part)   Fax: (916) 319-2155
Term Expires: 2016   Dist: (909) 627-1841
P.O. Box 942849, Sacramento, CA 94249-0055
13920 City Center Drive, Suite 260, Chino Hills, CA 91709
E-mail: assemblymember.chang@assembly.ca.gov
Committees: Appropriations; Business and Professions; Rules

LEGISLATIVE BRANCH

Assembly Member **Edwin "Ed" Chau** (D-District 49) .... (916) 319-2049
Counties Represented: Los Angeles (part)          Dist: (323) 264-4949
Term Expires: 2016                                Fax: (916) 319-2149
P.O. Box 942849, Sacramento, CA 94249-0049        Dist: (323) 264-4916
1255 Corporate Center Drive, Suite 306, Monterey Park, CA 91754
E-mail: assemblymember.chau@assembly.ca.gov
Committees: Banking and Finance; Housing and Community
Development; Jobs, Economic Development and the Economy;
Judiciary
Education: USC; Southwestern Law JD

Assembly Member **Rocky J. Chávez** (R-District 76) ...... (916) 319-2076
Counties Represented: San Diego (part)            Dist: (760) 929-7998
Term Expires: 2016                                Fax: (916) 319-2176
P.O. Box 942849, Sacramento, CA 94249-0078        Dist: (760) 929-7999
1910 Palomar Point Way, Suite 106, Carlsbad, CA 92008
E-mail: assemblymember.chavez@assembly.ca.gov
Committees: Budget; Health; Higher Education; Veterans Affairs
Education: Cal State (Chico) 1973 BA; Marine Corps Command U;
Air War Col

Assembly Member **David Chiu** (D-District 17) ........... (916) 319-2017
Counties Represented: San Francisco (part)        Dist: (415) 557-3013
Term Expires: 2016                                Fax: (916) 319-2117
P.O. Box 942849, Sacramento, CA 94249-0017        Dist: (415) 557-3015
455 Golden Gate Avenue, Suite 14300, San Francisco, CA 94102
E-mail: assemblymember.chiu@assembly.ca.gov
Committees: Budget; Health; Housing and Community Development;
Judiciary; Local Government

Assembly Member **Kansen Chu** (D-District 25) ......... (916) 319-2025
Counties Represented: Alameda (part), Santa        Dist: (408) 262-2501
Clara (part)                                       Fax: (916) 319-2125
Term Expires: 2016                                 Dist: (408) 262-2512
P.O. Box 942849, Sacramento, CA 94249-0025
1313 N. Milpitas Boulevard, Suite 255, Milpitas, CA 95035
E-mail: assemblymember.chu@assembly.ca.gov
Committees: Arts, Entertainment, Sports, Tourism and Internet Media;
Insurance; Labor and Employment; Transportation

Assembly Member **Ken Cooley** (D-District 8) ........... (916) 319-2008
Counties Represented: Sacramento (part)            Dist: (916) 464-1910
Term Expires: 2016                                 Fax: (916) 319-2108
P.O. Box 942849, Sacramento, CA 94249-0008         Dist: (916) 464-1915
2729 Prospect Park Drive, Suite 130, Rancho Cordova, CA 95670
E-mail: assemblymember.cooley@assembly.ca.gov
Committees: Governmental Organization; Insurance; Local
Government; Public Employees, Retirement and Social Security; Rules
Education: UC Berkeley 1977 BA; McGeorge 1984 JD

Assembly Member **James "Jim" Cooper** (D-District 9) .. (916) 319-2009
Counties Represented: Sacramento (part), San       Dist: (916) 262-0999
Joaquin (part)                                     Fax: (916) 319-2109
Term Expires: 2016
P.O. Box 942849, Sacramento, CA 94249-0009
2251 Florin Road, Suite 156, Sacramento, CA 95822
9250 Laguna Springs Drive, Elk Grove, CA 95758
E-mail: assemblymember.cooper@assembly.ca.gov
Committees: Agriculture; Budget; Governmental Organization;
Insurance; Public Employees, Retirement and Social Security

Assembly Member
**Matthew M. "Matt" Dababneh** (D-District 45) ....... (916) 319-2045
Counties Represented: Los Angeles (part), Ventura   Fax: (916) 319-2145
(part)
Term Expires: 2016
P.O. Box 942849, Sacramento, CA 94249-0045
6150 Van Nuys Boulevard, #400, Van Nuys, CA 91401
E-mail: assemblymember.dababneh@asm.ca.gov
Committees: Banking and Finance; Insurance; Revenue and Taxation;
Water, Parks and Wildlife
Education: UCLA

Assembly Member **Brian D. Dahle** (R-District 1) ........ (916) 319-2001
Counties Represented: Butte (part), Lassen, Modoc,  Dist: (530) 223-6300
Nevada, Placer (part), Plumas, Shasta, Sierra,      Fax: (530) 223-6737
Siskiyou                                            Dist: (916) 319-2101
Term Expires: 2016
P.O. Box 942849, Sacramento, CA 94249-0001
280 Hemsted Drive, Suite 110, Redding, CA 96002
E-mail: assemblymember.dahle@assembly.ca.gov
Committees: Aging and Long-Term Care; Environmental Safety and
Toxic Materials; Insurance; Utilities and Commerce; Water, Parks and
Wildlife

Assembly Member **Tom Daly** (D-District 69) ........... (916) 319-2069
Counties Represented: Orange (part)               Fax: (916) 319-2169
Term Expires: 2016
P.O. Box 942849, Sacramento, CA 94249-0069
2400 East Katella Avenue, Suite 640, Anaheim, CA 92806
E-mail: assemblymember.daly@assembly.ca.gov
Committees: Appropriations; Governmental Organization; Insurance;
Transportation; Veterans Affairs
Education: Harvard 1976 BA

Assembly Member **Bill Dodd** (D-District 4) ............. (916) 319-2004
Counties Represented: Colusa (part), Lake, Napa, Solano (part),
Sonoma (part), Yolo (part)
Term Expires: 2016
P.O. Box 942849, Sacramento, CA 94249-0004
4381 Broadway Street, Suite 108, American Canyon, CA 94503
725 Main Street, Suite 206, Woodland, CA 95695
E-mail: assemblymember.dodd@assembly.ca.gov
Committees: Agriculture; Business and Professions; Rules;
Transportation; Water, Parks and Wildlife

Assembly Member
**Susan Talamantes Eggman** (D-District 13) .......... (916) 319-2013
Counties Represented: San Joaquin (part)           Dist: (209) 948-7479
Term Expires: 2016                                 Fax: (916) 319-2113
P.O. Box 942849, Sacramento, CA 94249-0013         Dist: (209) 465-5058
31 East Channel Street, Suite 306, Stockton, CA 95202
E-mail: assemblymember.talamanteseggman@assembly.ca.gov
Committees: Agriculture; Appropriations; Business and Professions;
Local Government; Utilities and Commerce
Education: Cal State (Stanislaus) BA, MSW; Portland State PhD

Assembly Member **Jim Frazier** (D-District 11) .......... (916) 319-2011
Counties Represented: Contra Costa (part),          Dist: (707) 399-3011
Sacramento (part), Solano (part)                           (Fairfield)
Term Expires: 2016                                  Dist: (925) 513-0411
P.O. Box 942849, Sacramento, CA 94249-0014                 (Antioch)
1261 Travis Boulevard, Suite 110,                   Fax: (916) 319-2111
Fairfield, CA 94533                                 Dist: (707) 399-3030
150 City Park Way, Brentwood, CA 94513                     (Fairfield)
E-mail: assemblymember.frazier@assembly.ca.gov      Dist: (925) 513-3511
Committees: Accountability and Administrative Review; Insurance;
Transportation; Veterans Affairs

Assembly Member **Beth B. Gaines** (R-District 6) ....... (916) 319-2006
Counties Represented: El Dorado (part), Placer       Dist: (916) 774-4430
(part), Sacramento (part)                            Fax: (916) 319-2106
Term Expires: 2016                                   Dist: (916) 774-4433
P.O. Box 942849, Sacramento, CA 94249-0006
8799-A Auburn Folsom Road, Granite Bay, CA 95746
E-mail: assemblymember.gaines@assembly.ca.gov
Committees: Accountability and Administrative Review; Housing
and Community Development; Local Government; Water, Parks and
Wildlife

Assembly Member **James Gallagher** (R-District 3) ...... (916) 319-2003
Counties Represented: Butte (part), Colusa (part),   Dist: (530) 895-4217
Glenn, Sutter, Tehama, Yuba
Term Expires: 2016
P.O. Box 942849, Sacramento, CA 94249-0003
150 Amber Grove Drive, Suite 154, Chico, CA 95973
E-mail: assemblymember.gallagher@assembly.ca.gov
Committees: Agriculture; Appropriations; Environmental Safety and
Toxic Materials; Governmental Organization; Judiciary

Assembly Member **Cristina Garcia** (D-District 58) ....... (916) 319-2058
Counties Represented: Los Angeles (part)            Fax: (916) 319-2158
Term Expires: 2016
P.O. Box 942849, Sacramento, CA 94249-0058
8255 Firestone Boulevard, Suite 203, Downey, CA 90241
E-mail: assemblymember.garcia@assembly.ca.gov
Committees: Accountability and Administrative Review; Governmental
Organization; Judiciary; Natural Resources; Public Employees,
Retirement and Social Security; Utilities and Commerce; Water, Parks
and Wildlife
Education: Pomona 1999 BA; USC PhD; Claremont Graduate U MA;
UCLA MA

Assembly Member **Eduardo Garcia** (D-District 56) ...... (916) 319-2056
Counties Represented: Imperial, Riverside (part)    Fax: (916) 319-2156
Term Expires: 2016
P.O. Box 942849, Sacramento, CA 94249-0056
1625 West Main Street, Suite 220, El Centro, CA 92243
45-677 Oasis Street, Indio, CA 92201
E-mail: assemblymember.eduardo.garcia@assembly.ca.gov
Committees: Appropriations; Governmental Organization; Jobs,
Economic Development and the Economy; Transportation

*(continued on next page)*

**Assembly Members** *continued*

Assembly Member **Mike Gatto** (D-District 43) . . . . . . . . . (916) 319-2043
Counties Represented: Los Angeles (part)          Dist: (818) 558-3043
Term Expires: 2016                                Fax: (916) 319-2143
State Capitol, Room 2114, Sacramento, CA 95814    Dist: (818) 558-3042
300 East Magnolia Boulevard, Suite 504, Burbank, CA 91502
P.O. Box 942849, Sacramento, CA 94249-0043
E-mail: assemblymember.gatto@assembly.ca.gov
Committees: Banking and Finance; Business and Professions;
Insurance; Utilities and Commerce
Education: UCLA 1996 BA; Loyola Law 2004 JD

Assembly Member **Mike A. Gipson** (D-District 64) . . . . . . (916) 319-2064
Counties Represented: Los Angeles (part)
Term Expires: 2016
P.O. Box 942849, Sacramento, CA 94249-0064
2200 W. Artesia Boulevard, Suite 210, Sacramento, CA 90220
E-mail: assemblymember.gipson@assembly.ca.gov
Committees: Aging and Long-Term Care; Governmental Organization;
Jobs, Economic Development and the Economy; Revenue and Taxation

Assembly Member **Jimmy Gomez** (D-District 51) . . . . . . . (916) 319-2051
Counties Represented: Los Angeles (part)          Dist: (213) 483-5151
Term Expires: 2016                                Fax: (916) 319-2151
P.O. Box 942849, Sacramento, CA 94249-0051        Fax: (213) 483-5166
1910 West Sunset Boulevard, Suite 810, Los Angeles, CA 90026
E-mail: assemblymember.gomez@assembly.ca.gov
Committees: Health; Natural Resources; Rules; Transportation; Water,
Parks and Wildlife
Education: UCLA 1999 BA; JFK School Govt 2003 MPP

Assembly Member **Lorena S. Gonzalez** (D-District 80) . . . (916) 319-2080
Counties Represented: San Diego (part)            Dist: (619) 338-8090
Term Expires: 2016                                Fax: (916) 319-2180
P.O. Box 942849, Sacramento, CA 94249-0080        Dist: (619) 338-8099
1350 Front Street, Suite 6022, San Diego, CA 92101
E-mail: assemblymember.gonzalez@assembly.ca.gov
Committees: Appropriations; Environmental Safety and Toxic
Materials; Health; Insurance

Assembly Member **Richard S. Gordon** (D-District 24) . . . . (916) 319-2024
Counties Represented: San Mateo (part), Santa     Dist: (650) 691-2121
Clara (part)                                              (Los Altos)
Term Expires: 2016                                Fax: (916) 319-2124
P.O. Box 942849, Sacramento, CA 94249-0021        Dist: (650) 691-2120
5050 El Camino Real, Suite 117, Los Altos, CA 94022
E-mail: assemblymember.gordon@assembly.ca.gov
Committees: Budget; Elections and Redistricting; Local Government;
Rules
Education: USC 1970 BA; Garrett-Evangelical 1973 MDiv

Assembly Member **Adam C. Gray** (D-District 21) . . . . . . . . (916) 319-2021
Counties Represented: Merced, Stanislaus (part)   Dist: (209) 726-5465
Term Expires: 2016                                       (Merced)
P.O. Box 942849, Sacramento, CA 94249-0021        Dist: (209) 521-2111
690 West 16th Street, Merced, CA 95340                   (Modesto)
1010 Tenth Street, Modesto, CA 95354              Fax: (916) 319-2121
E-mail: assemblymember.gray@assembly.ca.gov       Dist: (209) 726-5469
Committees: Aging and Long-Term Care;                    (Merced)
Environmental Safety and Toxic Materials;         Dist: (209) 521-2102
Governmental Organization                                (Modesto)
Education: UC Santa Barbara 2000 (Attended)

Assembly Member **Shannon L. Grove** (R-District 34) . . . . (916) 319-2034
Counties Represented: Kern (part)                 Dist: (661) 395-2995
Term Expires: 2016                                       (Bakersfield)
State Capitol, Room 3098, Sacramento, CA 95814    Fax: (916) 319-2134
4900 California Avenue, Suite 100-B,              Dist: (661) 395-3883
Bakersfield, CA 93309                                    (Bakersfield)
P.O. Box 942849, Sacramento, CA 94249-0032
E-mail: assemblymember.grove@assembly.ca.gov
Committees: Agriculture; Budget; Elections and Redistricting; Human
Services

Assembly Member **David Hadley** (R-District 66) . . . . . . . . (916) 319-2066
Counties Represented: Los Angeles (part)          Dist: (310) 375-0691
Term Expires: 2016                                Fax: (916) 319-2166
23211 Hawthorne Boulevard, Suite 200A,            Dist: (310) 375-8245
Torrance, CA 90505
E-mail: assemblymember.hadley@assembly.ca.gov
Committees: Aging and Long-Term Care; Arts, Entertainment, Sports,
Tourism and Internet Media; Banking and Finance; Natural Resources;
Utilities and Commerce

Assembly Member **Matthew Harper** (R-District 74) . . . . . . (916) 319-2074
Counties Represented: Orange (part)               Dist: (714) 668-2100
Term Expires: 2016
P.O. Box 942849, Sacramento, CA 94249-0074
1503 South Coast Drive, Suite 205, Costa Mesa, CA 92626
E-mail: assemblymember.harper@assembly.ca.gov
Committees: Budget; Natural Resources; Water, Parks and Wildlife
Education: USC

Assembly Member **Roger Hernández** (D-District 48) . . . . . (916) 319-2048
Counties Represented: Los Angeles (part)          Dist: (626) 915-5801
Term Expires: 2016                                       (West Covina)
P.O. Box 942849, Sacramento, CA 94249-0057        Fax: (916) 319-2148
100 North Barranca Street, Suite 895,             Dist: (626) 915-6048
West Covina, CA 91791                                    (West Covina)
E-mail: assemblymember.hernandez@assembly.ca.gov
Committees: Appropriations; Governmental Organization; Health;
Labor and Employment; Utilities and Commerce
Education: UC Riverside BA; La Verne MPA

Assembly Member **Chris R. Holden** (D-District 41) . . . . . . (916) 319-2041
Counties Represented: Los Angeles (part), San     Dist: (626) 351-1917
Bernardino (part)                                        (Pasadena)
Term Expires: 2016                                Dist: (909) 624-7876
600 Rosemead Boulevard, Suite 117,                       (Claremont)
Pasadena, CA 91107                                Fax: (916) 319-2141
415 W. Foothill Boulevard, Suite 124,             Dist: (626) 351-6176
Claremont, CA 91711                                      (Pasadena)
P.O. Box 942849, Sacramento, CA 94249-0041        Dist: (909) 626-2548
E-mail: assemblymember.holden@assembly.ca.gov            (Claremont)
Committees: Appropriations; Budget; Business and Professions;
Judiciary; Rules
Education: San Diego State 1982 BB

Assembly Member **Jacqui V. Irwin** (D-District 44) . . . . . . . (916) 319-2044
Counties Represented: Los Angeles (part), Ventura Fax: (916) 319-2144
(part)
Term Expires: 2016
P.O. Box 942849, Sacramento, CA 94249-0044
2301 East Daily Drive, Suite 200, Camarillo, CA 93010
E-mail: assemblymember.irwin@assembly.ca.gov
Committees: Accountability and Administrative Review; Agriculture;
Budget; Higher Education; Jobs, Economic Development and the
Economy; Veterans Affairs

Assembly Member **Brian W. Jones** (R-District 71) . . . . . . . (916) 319-2071
Counties Represented: Riverside (part), San Diego Dist: (619) 258-7737
(part)                                                   (Santee)
Term Expires: 2016                                Fax: (916) 319-2171
P.O. Box 942849, Sacramento, CA 94249-0071        Dist: (619) 258-7739
10152 Mission Gorge Road, Santee, CA 92071               (Santee)
E-mail: assemblymember.jones@assembly.ca.gov
Committees: Appropriations; Natural Resources; Rules
Education: San Diego State BSBA

Assembly Member
**Reginald Byron Jones-Sawyer, Sr.** (D-District 59) . . . . (916) 319-2059
Counties Represented: Los Angeles (part)          Fax: (916) 319-2159
Term Expires: 2016
P.O. Box 942849, Sacramento, CA 94249-0059
700 Exposition Park Drive, Los Angeles, CA 90037
E-mail: assemblymember.jones.sawyer@assembly.ca.gov
Committees: Governmental Organization; Higher Education; Public
Safety
Education: USC BA

Assembly Member **Young O. Kim** (R-District 65) . . . . . . . . (916) 319-2065
Counties Represented: Orange (part)               Dist: (714) 521-6505
Term Expires: 2016                                Fax: (916) 319-2165
P.O. Box 942849, Sacramento, CA 94249-0065        Dist: (714) 521-6515
6281 Beach Boulevard, Suite 304, Buena Park, CA 90621
E-mail: assemblymember.kim@assembly.ca.gov
Committees: Banking and Finance; Budget; Education; Jobs, Economic
Development and the Economy; Transportation

Assembly Member **Tom Lackey** (R-District 36) . . . . . . . . . (916) 319-2036
Counties Represented: Kern (part), Los Angeles    Dist: (661) 267-7636
(part), San Bernardino (part)                     Fax: (916) 319-2136
Term Expires: 2016                                Dist: (661) 267-7636
P.O. Box 942849, Sacramento, CA 94249-0036
41319 12th Street West, Suite 105, Palmdale, CA 93551
E-mail: assemblymember.lackey@assembly.ca.gov
Committees: Accountability and Administrative Review; Budget;
Health; Public Safety

LEGISLATIVE BRANCH

Assembly Member **Marc Levine** (D-District 10) . . . . . . . . (916) 319-2010
Counties Represented: Marin, Sonoma (part)        Dist: (415) 479-4920
Term Expires: 2016                                          (San Rafael)
3501 Civic Center Drive, Suite 412,              Dist: (707) 773-0606
San Rafael, CA 94903                                        (Petaluma)
11 English Street, Petaluma, CA 94952            Dist: (707) 576-2631
50 D Street, Suite 301, Santa Rosa, CA 95404               (Santa Rosa)
E-mail: assemblymember.levine@assembly.ca.gov     Fax: (916) 319-2110
Committees: Aging and Long-Term Care; Arts,      Dist: (415) 479-2123
Entertainment, Sports, Tourism and Internet Media;         (San Rafael)
Governmental Organization; Higher Education;     Dist: (707) 773-1033
Water, Parks and Wildlife                                   (Petaluma)
Education: Cal State (Northridge) 1996;           Dist: (707) 576-2735
Naval Postgrad 1999                                         (Santa Rosa)

Assembly Member **Eric Linder** (R-District 60) . . . . . . . . . . (916) 319-2060
Counties Represented: Riverside (part)           Dist: (951) 371-6860
Term Expires: 2016                                Fax: (916) 319-2061
P.O. Box 942849, Sacramento, CA 94249-0060       Dist: (951) 734-4160
4740 Green River Road, Corona, CA 92880
E-mail: assemblymember.linder@assembly.ca.gov
Committees: Governmental Organization; Higher Education; Labor and
Employment; Local Government; Transportation

Assembly Member **Patty Lopez** (D-District 39) . . . . . . . . . . (916) 319-2039
Counties Represented: Los Angeles (part)         Dist: (818) 504-3911
Term Expires: 2016                                Fax: (916) 319-2139
9300 Laurel Canyon Boulevard, 1st Floor,         Dist: (818) 504-3912
Arleta, CA 91331
302 S. Brand Boulevard, Suite 212, San Fernando, CA 91340
E-mail: assemblymember.lopez@assembly.ca.gov
Committees: Aging and Long-Term Care; Housing and Community
Development; Human Services; Public Safety; Rules; Water, Parks and
Wildlife

Assembly Member **Evan Low** (D-District 28) . . . . . . . . . . . (916) 319-2028
Counties Represented: Santa Clara (part)         Dist: (408) 371-2802
Term Expires: 2016                                Fax: (916) 319-2128
P.O. Box 942849, Sacramento, CA 94249-0028       Dist: (408) 371-2809
2105 South Bascom Avenue, Suite 160, Campbell, CA 95008
E-mail: assemblymember.low@assembly.ca.gov
Committees: Banking and Finance; Elections and Redistricting; Higher
Education; Public Safety

Assembly Member **Brian Maienschein** (R-District 77) . . . . (916) 319-2077
Counties Represented: San Diego (part)           Dist: (858) 675-0077
Term Expires: 2016                                Fax: (916) 319-2177
P.O. Box 942849, Sacramento, CA 94249-0077       Dist: (858) 675-0688
12396 World Trade Drive, Suite 118, San Diego, CA 92128
E-mail: assemblymember.maienschein@assembly.ca.gov
Committees: Governmental Organization; Health; Human Services;
Judiciary
Education: UC Santa Barbara 1991 BA; Cal Western 1994 JD

Assembly Member **Devon J. Mathis** (R-District 26) . . . . . . (916) 319-2026
Counties Represented: Inyo, Kern (part), Tulare (part)
Term Expires: 2016
P.O. Box 942849, Sacramento, CA 94249-0026
113 North Church Street, Suite 505, Visalia, CA 93291
E-mail: assemblymember.mathis@assembly.ca.gov
Committees: Agriculture; Jobs, Economic Development and the
Economy; Transportation; Veterans Affairs; Water, Parks and Wildlife

Assembly Member **Chad Mayes** (R-District 42) . . . . . . . . . (916) 319-2042
Counties Represented: Riverside (part), San      Dist: (760) 346-6342
Bernardino (part)                                Fax: (916) 319-2142
Term Expires: 2016                               Fax: (760) 346-6506
P.O. Box 942849, Sacramento, CA 94249-0026
41608 Indian Trail Road, Suite D-1, Rancho Mirage, CA 92270
E-mail: assemblymember.mayes@assembly.ca.gov
Committees: Insurance; Rules

Assembly Member **Kevin McCarty** (D-District 7) . . . . . . . . (916) 319-2007
Counties Represented: Sacramento (part), Yolo    Dist: (916) 324-4676
(part)                                           Fax: (916) 319-2107
Term Expires: 2016                               Dist: (916) 327-3338
P.O. Box 942849, Sacramento, CA 94249-0007
915 L Street, Suite 110, Sacramento, CA 95814
E-mail: assemblymember.mccarty@assembly.ca.gov
Committees: Budget; Education; Environmental Safety and Toxic
Materials; Labor and Employment; Natural Resources

Assembly Member **Jose Medina** (D-District 61) . . . . . . . . . (916) 319-2061
Counties Represented: Riverside (part)           Dist: (951) 369-6644
Term Expires: 2016                               Fax: (916) 319-2161
P.O. Box 94249, Sacramento, CA 94249-0061        Dist: (951) 369-0366
1223 University Avenue, Suite 230, Riverside, CA 92507
E-mail: assemblymember.medina@assembly.ca.gov
Committees: Accountability and Administrative Review; Arts,
Entertainment, Sports, Tourism and Internet Media; Higher Education;
Transportation; Water, Parks and Wildlife
Education: UC Riverside 1974 BA, MA

Assembly Member **Melissa Melendez** (R-District 67) . . . . (916) 319-2067
Counties Represented: Riverside (part)           Dist: (951) 894-1232
Term Expires: 2016                               Fax: (916) 319-2167
P.O. Box 942849, Sacramento, CA 94249-0067       Dist: (951) 894-5053
41391 Kalmia Street, Suite 220, Murrieta, CA 92562
E-mail: assemblymember.melendez@assembly.ca.gov
Committees: Budget; Insurance; Public Safety; Transportation
Education: Chaminade BA; U Phoenix 2008 MBA

Assembly Member **Kevin Mullin** (D-District 22) . . . . . . . . (916) 319-2022
Counties Represented: San Mateo (part)           Dist: (650) 349-2200
Term Expires: 2016                               Fax: (916) 319-2122
P.O. Box 942849, Sacramento, CA 94249-2022       Dist: (650) 341-4676
1528 South El Camino Real, Suite 302, San Mateo, CA 94022
E-mail: assemblymember.mullin@assembly.ca.gov
Committees: Budget; Business and Professions; Elections and
Redistricting; Housing and Community Development; Revenue and
Taxation

Assembly Member **Adrin Nazarian** (D-District 46) . . . . . . (916) 319-2046
Counties Represented: Los Angeles (part)         Dist: (818) 376-4246
Term Expires: 2016                               Fax: (916) 319-2146
6150 Van Nuys Boulevard,, Suite 300,             Dist: (818) 376-4252
Van Nuys, CA 91401
P.O. Box 942849, Sacramento, CA 94249-0046
E-mail: assemblymember.nazarian@assembly.ca.gov
Committees: Arts, Entertainment, Sports, Tourism and Internet Media;
Budget; Health; Transportation
Education: UCLA 1986 BA

Assembly Member **Patrick O'Donnell** (D-District 70) . . . . . (916) 319-2070
Counties Represented: Los Angeles (part)         Dist: (562) 495-2915
Term Expires: 2016                                          (Long Beach)
P.O. Box 942849, Sacramento, CA 94249-0070       Dist: (310) 548-6420
110 Pine Avenue, Suite 804,                                 (San Pedro)
Long Beach, CA 90802
461 West 6th Street, Suite 209, San Pedro, CA 90731
E-mail: assemblymember.odonnell@assembly.ca.gov
Committees: Budget; Education; Labor and Employment; Public
Employees, Retirement and Social Security; Revenue and Taxation;
Transportation

Assembly Member **Jay Obernolte** (R-District 33) . . . . . . . . (916) 319-2033
Counties Represented: San Bernardino (part)      Dist: (760) 244-5277
Term Expires: 2016                               Fax: (916) 319-2133
P.O. Box 942849, Sacramento, CA 94249-0033       Dist: (760) 244-5447
15900 Smoketree Street, Suite 100, Hesperia, CA 92345
E-mail: assemblymember.obernolte@assembly.ca.gov
Committees: Appropriations; Arts, Entertainment, Sports, Tourism and
Internet Media; Budget; Rules; Utilities and Commerce

Assembly Member **Kristin Olsen** (R-District 12) . . . . . . . . (916) 319-2012
Counties Represented: San Joaquin (part),        Dist: (209) 576-6425
Stanislaus (part)                                           (Modesto)
Term Expires: 2016                               Fax: (916) 319-2112
P.O. Box 942849, Sacramento, CA 94249-0012       Dist: (209) 576-6426
3719 Tully Road, Modesto, CA 95356                          (Modesto)
E-mail: assemblymember.olsen@assembly.ca.gov
Committees: Education; Higher Education
Education: Westmont 1996 BA

Assembly Member **Jim Patterson** (R-District 23) . . . . . . . . (916) 319-2023
Counties Represented: Fresno (part), Tulare (part)  Dist: (559) 446-2029
Term Expires: 2016                               Fax: (916) 319-2123
P.O. Box 942849, Sacramento, CA 94249-0027       Dist: (559) 446-2028
6245 N. Fresno Street, Suite 106, Fresno, CA 93710
E-mail: assemblymember.patterson@assembly.ca.gov
Committees: Budget; Health; Labor and Employment; Revenue and
Taxation; Utilities and Commerce
Education: Cal State (Fresno) 1992 BS

Assembly Member **Bill Quirk** (D-District 20) . . . . . . . . . . . (916) 319-2020
Counties Represented: Alameda (part)             Dist: (510) 583-8818
Term Expires: 2016                               Fax: (916) 319-2120
P.O. Box 942849, Sacramento, CA 94249-0020       Dist: (510) 583-8800
22320 Foothill Boulevard, Suite 540, Hayward, CA 94541
E-mail: assemblymember.quirk@assembly.ca.gov
Committees: Agriculture; Appropriations; Public Safety; Revenue and
Taxation; Rules; Utilities and Commerce
Education: Columbia 1967 SB, 1970 ScD

*(continued on next page)*

**Assembly Members** *continued*

Assembly Member **Anthony Rendon** (D-District 63) . . . . . (916) 319-2063
Counties Represented: Los Angeles (part)  Dist: (562) 529-3250
Term Expires: 2016  Fax: (916) 319-2163
12132 South Garfield Avenue,  Dist: (562) 529-3255
South Gate, CA 90280
P.O. Box 942849, Sacramento, CA 94249-0063
E-mail: assemblymember.rendon@assembly.ca.gov

Assembly Member
**Sebastian Ridley-Thomas** (D-District 54) . . . . . . . . . . . (916) 319-2054
Counties Represented: Los Angeles (part)  Dist: (310) 342-1070
Term Expires: 2016  Fax: (916) 319-2154
300 Corporate Pointe, Suite 380,  Dist: (310) 342-1078
Culver City, CA 90230
P.O. Box 942849, Sacramento, CA 94249-0054
E-mail: assemblymember.ridley-thomas@assembly.ca.gov
Committees: Banking and Finance; Health; Revenue and Taxation
Education: Morehouse Col 2009 BA

Assembly Member **Freddie Rodriguez** (D-District 52) . . . . (916) 319-2052
Counties Represented: Los Angeles (part), San  Dist: (909) 902-9606
Bernardino (part)  Fax: (916) 319-2152
Term Expires: 2016  Dist: (909) 902-9761
P.O. Box 942849, Sacramento, CA 94249-0052
13160 7th Street, Chino, CA 91710
E-mail: assemblymember.rodriguez@assembly.ca.gov
Committees: Accountability and Administrative Review; Budget;
Health; Insurance; Rules

Assembly Member **Rudy Salas, Jr.** (D-District 32) . . . . . . . (916) 319-2032
Counties Represented: Kern (part), Kings  Dist: (661) 335-0302
Term Expires: 2016  (Bakersfield)
1430 Truxtun Avenue, Suite 803,  Dist: (559) 585-7170
Bakersfield, CA 93301  Fax: (916) 319-2132
E-mail: assemblymember.salas@assembly.ca.gov  Dist: (661) 335-0361
Committees: Agriculture; Business and Professions;  (Bakersfield)
Governmental Organization; Veterans Affairs;  Dist: (559) 585-7175
Water, Parks and Wildlife  (Hanford)
Education: UCLA 2000 BA

Assembly Member **Miguel Santiago** (D-District 53) . . . . . (916) 319-2053
Counties Represented: Los Angeles (part)  Dist: (213) 620-4646
Term Expires: 2016  Fax: (916) 319-2153
P.O. Box 942849, Sacramento, CA 94249-0053  Dist: (213) 620-6319
320 West 4th Street, Room 1050, Los Angeles, CA 90013
E-mail: assemblymember.santiago@assembly.ca.gov
Committees: Appropriations; Education; Health; Higher Education;
Public Safety; Utilities and Commerce

Assembly Member **Marc Steinorth** (R-District 40) . . . . . . (916) 319-2040
Counties Represented: San Bernardino (part)  Dist: (909) 466-9096
Term Expires: 2016
P.O. Box 942849, Sacramento, CA 94249-0040
10350 Commerce Center Drive, Suite A-200,
Rancho Cucamonga, CA 91730
E-mail: assemblymember.steinorth@assembly.ca.gov
Committees: Governmental Organization; Health; Housing and
Community Development

Assembly Member **Mark W. Stone** (D-District 29) . . . . . . . (916) 319-2029
Counties Represented: Monterey (part), Santa  Dist: (831) 425-1503
Clara (part), Santa Cruz (part)  (Santa Cruz)
Term Expires: 2016  Dist: (831) 649-2832
P.O. Box 942849, Sacramento, CA 94249-0029  (Monterey)
701 Ocean Street, Suite 318-B,  Fax: (916) 319-2129
Santa Cruz, CA 95060  Dist: (831) 425-2570
99 Pacific Street, Suite 555D, Monterey, CA 93940  (Santa Cruz)
E-mail: assemblymember.stone@assembly.ca.gov  Dist: (831) 649-2935
Committees: Banking and Finance; Human  (Monterey)
Services; Judiciary; Natural Resources
Education: UC Berkeley 1979 BA; Santa Clara U 1988 JD

Assembly Member **Tony Thurmond** (D-District 15) . . . . . . (916) 319-2015
Counties Represented: Alameda (part), Contra  Dist: (510) 286-1400
Costa (part)  Fax: (916) 319-2115
Term Expires: 2016  Dist: (510) 286-1406
P.O. Box 942849, Sacramento, CA 94249-0015
1515 Clay Street, Suite 2201, Oakland, CA 94612
E-mail: assemblymember.thurmond@assembly.ca.gov
Committees: Budget; Education; Health; Human Services; Labor and
Employment

Assembly Member **Philip Y. "Phil" Ting** (D-District 19) . . (916) 319-2019
Counties Represented: San Francisco (part), San  Dist: (415) 557-2312
Mateo (part)  Fax: (916) 319-2119
Term Expires: 2016  Dist: (415) 557-1178
P.O. Box 942849, Sacramento, CA 94249-0019
455 Golden Gate Avenue, San Francisco, CA 94102
E-mail: assemblymember.ting@assembly.ca.gov
Committees: Budget; Business and Professions; Judiciary; Utilities and
Commerce
Education: UC Berkeley 1991; JFK School Govt 1994 MA

Assembly Member
**Donald P. "Don" Wagner, JD** (R-District 68) . . . . . . . . (916) 319-2068
Counties Represented: Orange (part)  Dist: (949) 863-7070
Term Expires: 2016  (Irvine)
State Capitol, Room 4153, Sacramento, CA 95814  Fax: (916) 319-2168
3 Park Plaza, Suite 150, Irvine, CA 92614  Dist: (949) 863-9337
P.O. Box 942849, Sacramento, CA 94249-0068  (Irvine)
E-mail: assemblymember.wagner@assembly.ca.gov
Committees: Appropriations; Judiciary; Public Employees, Retirement
and Social Security; Revenue and Taxation
Affiliation: Of Counsel, Irvine, CA Office, Buchalter Nemer
18400 Von Karman Avenue, Suite 800, Irvine, CA 92612-0514
Education: UCLA 1983 BA, 1987 JD

Assembly Member **Marie Waldron** (R-District 75) . . . . . . . (916) 319-2075
Counties Represented: Riverside (part), San Diego  Dist: (760) 480-7570
(part)  Fax: (916) 319-2175
Term Expires: 2016  Dist: (760) 480-7516
P.O. Box 942849, Sacramento, CA 94249-0075
350 West 5th Avenue, Suite 110, Escondido, CA 92025
E-mail: assemblymember.waldron@assembly.ca.gov
Committees: Governmental Organization; Health; Local Government;
Public Employees, Retirement and Social Security; Rules

Assembly Member
**Dr. Shirley Weber, PhD** (D-District 79) . . . . . . . . . . . . . . (916) 319-2079
Counties Represented: San Diego (part)  Dist: (619) 531-7913
Term Expires: 2016  Fax: (916) 319-2179
P.O. Box 942849, Sacramento, CA 94249-0079  Dist: (619) 531-7924
1350 Front Street, Suite 6046, Sacramento, CA 92101
E-mail: assemblymember.weber@assembly.ca.gov
Committees: Appropriations; Education; Elections and Redistricting;
Higher Education
Education: UCLA 1970 BA, 1971 MA, 1975 PhD

Assembly Member **Scott Wilk** (R-District 38) . . . . . . . . . . (916) 319-2038
Counties Represented: Los Angeles (part), Ventura  Dist: (661) 286-1565
(part)  Fax: (916) 319-2138
Term Expires: 2016  Dist: (661) 286-1408
27441 Tourney Road, Suite 160, Valencia, CA 91355
P.O. Box 942849, Sacramento, CA 94249-0038
E-mail: assemblymember.wilk@assembly.ca.gov
Committees: Budget; Business and Professions; Governmental
Organization

Assembly Member **Das Williams** (D-District 37) . . . . . . . . (916) 319-2037
Counties Represented: San Luis Obispo (part),  Dist: (805) 564-1649
Santa Barbara (part), Ventura (part)  (Santa Barbara)
Term Expires: 2016  Dist: (805) 483-9808
101 West Anapamu Street, Suite A,  (Oxnard)
Santa Barbara, CA 93101  Fax: (916) 319-2137
P.O. Box 942849, Sacramento, CA 94249-0037  Dist: (805) 564-1651
E-mail: assemblymember.williams@assembly.ca.gov  (Santa Barbara)
Committees: Budget; Higher Education; Natural  Dist: (805) 483-8182
Resources; Utilities and Commerce; Water, Parks and Wildlife
Education: UC Santa Barbara MM, MS

Assembly Member **Jim Wood** (D-District 2) . . . . . . . . . . . . (916) 319-2002
Counties Represented: Del Norte, Humboldt,  Dist: (707) 576-2526
Mendocino, Sonoma (part), Trinity  (Santa Rosa)
Term Expires: 2016  Dist: (707) 445-7014
P.O. Box 942849, Sacramento, CA 94249-0002  (Eureka)
50 D Street, Suite 450, Santa Rosa, CA 95404  Dist: (707) 463-5770
710 E Street, Suite 150, Eureka, CA 95501  (Ukiah)
200 S School Street, Suite D, Ukiah, CA 95482  Fax: (916) 319-2102
E-mail: assemblymember.wood@assembly.ca.gov  Dist: (707) 576-2297
Committees: Appropriations; Business and  (Santa Rosa)
Professions; Health; Natural Resources  Dist: (707) 445-6607
Education: UC Riverside 1982; Loma Linda 1986  (Eureka)
Dist: (707) 463-5773

**LEGISLATIVE BRANCH**

# Assembly Standing Committees

## Accountability and Administrative Review
1020 North Street, Room 357, Sacramento, CA 95814

**Majority Members**
Cristina Garcia (D-58) *Chair*
Autumn R. Burke (D-62)
Jim Frazier (D-11)
Jacqui V. Irwin (D-44)
Jose Medina (D-61)
Freddie Rodriguez (D-52)

**Minority Members**
Tom Lackey (R-36) *Vice Chair*
William P. "Bill" Brough (R-73)
Beth B. Gaines (R-6)

## Aging and Long-Term Care
1020 N Street, Room 360 A, Sacramento, CA 95814

**Majority Members**
Cheryl R. Brown (D-47) *Chair*
Mike A. Gipson (D-64)
Adam C. Gray (D-21)
Marc Levine (D-10)
Patty Lopez (D-39)

**Minority Members**
David Hadley (R-66) *Vice Chair*
Brian D. Dahle (R-1)

## Agriculture
1020 N Street, Room 362, Sacramento, CA 95814

**Majority Members**
Bill Dodd (D-4) *Chair*
James "Jim" Cooper (D-9)
Susan Talamantes Eggman (D-13)
Jacqui V. Irwin (D-44)
Bill Quirk (D-20)
Rudy Salas, Jr. (D-32)

**Minority Members**
Devon J. Mathis (R-26) *Vice Chair*
James Gallagher (R-3)
Shannon L. Grove (R-34)

## Appropriations
State Capitol, Room 2114, Sacramento, CA 95814

**Majority Members**
Lorena S. Gonzalez (D-80) *Chair*
Richard Bloom (D-50)
Susan Bonilla (D-14)
Rob Bonta (D-18)
Ian Charles Calderon (D-57)
Tom Daly (D-69)
Susan Talamantes Eggman (D-13)
Eduardo Garcia (D-56)
Roger Hernández (D-48)
Chris R. Holden (D-41)
Bill Quirk (D-20)
Miguel Santiago (D-53)
Dr. Shirley Weber (D-79)
Jim Wood (D-2)

**Minority Members**
Franklin E. Bigelow (R-5)
*Vice Chair*
Ling-Ling Chang (R-55)
James Gallagher (R-3)
Brian W. Jones (R-71)
Jay Obernolte (R-33)
Donald P. "Don" Wagner (R-68)

## Arts, Entertainment, Sports, Tourism and Internet Media
1020 N Street, Room 152, Sacramento, CA 95814

**Majority Members**
Ian Charles Calderon (D-57) *Chair*
Kansen Chu (D-25)
Marc Levine (D-10)
Jose Medina (D-61)
Adrin Nazarian (D-46)

**Minority Members**
Jay Obernolte (R-33) *Vice Chair*
David Hadley (R-66)

## Banking and Finance
1020 N Street, Room 360B, Sacramento, CA 95814

**Majority Members**
Matthew M. "Matt" Dababneh (D-45)
*Chair*
Cheryl R. Brown (D-47)
Edwin "Ed" Chau (D-49)
Mike Gatto (D-43)
Evan Low (D-28)
Sebastian Ridley-Thomas (D-54)
Mark W. Stone (D-29)

**Minority Members**
Travis Allen (R-72) *Vice Chair*
K. H. "Katcho" Achadjian (R-35)
David Hadley (R-66)
Young O. Kim (R-65)

## Budget
State Capitol, Room 6026, Sacramento, CA 95814

**Majority Members**
Philip Y. "Phil" Ting (D-19) *Chair*
Richard Bloom (D-50)
Rob Bonta (D-18)
Nora E. Campos (D-27)
David Chiu (D-17)
James "Jim" Cooper (D-9)
Richard S. Gordon (D-24)
Chris R. Holden (D-41)
Jacqui V. Irwin (D-44)
Kevin McCarty (D-7)
Kevin Mullin (D-22)
Adrin Nazarian (D-46)
Patrick O'Donnell (D-70)
Freddie Rodriguez (D-52)
Tony Thurmond (D-15)
Das Williams (D-37)

**Minority Members**
Jay Obernolte (R-33) *Vice Chair*
Travis Allen (R-72)
Franklin E. Bigelow (R-5)
Rocky J. Chávez (R-76)
Shannon L. Grove (R-34)
Matthew Harper (R-74)
Young O. Kim (R-65)
Tom Lackey (R-36)
Melissa Melendez (R-67)
Jim Patterson (R-23)
Scott Wilk (R-38)

## Business and Professions
State Capitol, Room 3013, Sacramento, CA 95814

**Majority Members**
Rudy Salas, Jr. (D-32) *Chair*
Richard Bloom (D-50)
Nora E. Campos (D-27)
Susan Talamantes Eggman (D-13)
Mike Gatto (D-43)
Chris R. Holden (D-41)
Kevin Mullin (D-22)
Philip Y. "Phil" Ting (D-19)
Jim Wood (D-2)
Bill Dodd (D-4)

**Minority Members**
William P. "Bill" Brough (R-73)
*Vice Chair*
Catharine B. Baker (R-16)
Ling-Ling Chang (R-55)
Scott Wilk (R-38)

## Education
1020 N Street, Room 159, Sacramento, CA 95814

**Majority Members**
Patrick O'Donnell (D-70) *Chair*
Kevin McCarty (D-7)
Miguel Santiago (D-53)
Tony Thurmond (D-15)
Dr. Shirley Weber (D-79)

**Minority Members**
Kristin Olsen (R-12) *Vice Chair*
Young O. Kim (R-65)

## Elections and Redistricting
1020 N Street, Room 365, Sacramento, CA 95814

**Majority Members**
Dr. Shirley Weber (D-79) *Chair*
Evan Low (D-28)
Richard S. Gordon (D-24)
Kevin Mullin (D-22)

**Minority Members**
Shannon L. Grove (R-34)
*Vice Chair*
Travis Allen (R-72)

## Environmental Safety and Toxic Materials
1020 N Street, Room 171, Sacramento, CA 95814

**Majority Members**
Luis A. Alejo (D-30) *Chair*
Dr. Joaquin Arambula (D-31)
Lorena S. Gonzalez (D-80)
Adam C. Gray (D-21)
Kevin McCarty (D-7)

**Minority Members**
Brian D. Dahle (R-1) *Vice Chair*
James Gallagher (R-3)

## Governmental Organization
1020 N Street, Room 156, Sacramento, CA 95814

**Majority Members**
Adam C. Gray (D-21) *Chair*
Luis A. Alejo (D-30)
Rob Bonta (D-18)
Nora E. Campos (D-27)
Ken Cooley (D-8)
James "Jim" Cooper (D-9)
Tom Daly (D-69)
Cristina Garcia (D-58)
Eduardo Garcia (D-56)
Mike A. Gipson (D-64)
Roger Hernández (D-48)

**Minority Members**
Franklin E. Bigelow (R-5)
*Vice Chair*
James Gallagher (R-3)
Eric Linder (R-60)
Brian Maienschein (R-77)
Marc Steinorth (R-40)
Marie Waldron (R-75)
Scott Wilk (R-38)

*(continued on next page)*

**Governmental Organization** *continued*

**Majority Members** *continued*

Reginald Byron Jones-Sawyer, Sr.
  (D-59)
Marc Levine (D-10)
Rudy Salas, Jr. (D-32)

## Health

State Capitol, Room 6005, Sacramento, CA 95814

| **Majority Members** | **Minority Members** |
| --- | --- |
| Jim Wood (D-2) *Chair* | Brian Maienschein (R-77) |
| Susan Bonilla (D-14) | *Vice Chair* |
| Autumn R. Burke (D-62) | Rocky J. Chávez (R-76) |
| Nora E. Campos (D-27) | Tom Lackey (R-36) |
| David Chiu (D-17) | Jim Patterson (R-23) |
| Jimmy Gomez (D-51) | Marc Steinorth (R-40) |
| Lorena S. Gonzalez (D-80) | Marie Waldron (R-75) |
| Roger Hernández (D-48) | |
| Adrin Nazarian (D-46) | |
| Sebastian Ridley-Thomas (D-54) | |
| Freddie Rodriguez (D-52) | |
| Miguel Santiago (D-53) | |
| Tony Thurmond (D-15) | |

## Higher Education

1020 N Street, Room 173, Sacramento, CA 95814

| **Majority Members** | **Minority Members** |
| --- | --- |
| Jose Medina (D-61) *Chair* | Catharine B. Baker (R-16) |
| Richard Bloom (D-50) | *Vice Chair* |
| Jacqui V. Irwin (D-44) | Rocky J. Chávez (R-76) |
| Reginald Byron Jones-Sawyer, Sr. | Eric Linder (R-60) |
|   (D-59) | Kristin Olsen (R-12) |
| Marc Levine (D-10) | |
| Evan Low (D-28) | |
| Miguel Santiago (D-53) | |
| Dr. Shirley Weber (D-79) | |
| Das Williams (D-37) | |

## Housing and Community Development

1020 N Street, Room 162, Sacramento, CA 95814

| **Majority Members** | **Minority Members** |
| --- | --- |
| David Chiu (D-17) *Chair* | Marc Steinorth (R-40) *Vice Chair* |
| Autumn R. Burke (D-62) | Beth B. Gaines (R-6) |
| Edwin "Ed" Chau (D-49) | |
| Patty Lopez (D-39) | |
| Kevin Mullin (D-22) | |

## Human Services

1020 North Street, Room 124, Sacramento, CA 95814

| **Majority Members** | **Minority Members** |
| --- | --- |
| Susan Bonilla (D-14) *Chair* | Shannon L. Grove (R-34) |
| Dr. Joaquin Arambula (D-31) | *Vice Chair* |
| Patty Lopez (D-39) | Brian Maienschein (R-77) |
| Mark W. Stone (D-29) | |
| Tony Thurmond (D-15) | |

## Insurance

1020 N Street, Room 369, Sacramento, CA 95814

| **Majority Members** | **Minority Members** |
| --- | --- |
| Tom Daly (D-69) *Chair* | Melissa Melendez (R-67) |
| Ian Charles Calderon (D-57) | *Vice Chair* |
| Kansen Chu (D-25) | Travis Allen (R-72) |
| Ken Cooley (D-8) | Brian D. Dahle (R-1) |
| James "Jim" Cooper (D-9) | Chad Mayes (R-42) |
| Matthew M. "Matt" Dababneh | |
|   (D-45) | |
| Jim Frazier (D-11) | |
| Mike Gatto (D-43) | |
| Lorena S. Gonzalez (D-80) | |
| Freddie Rodriguez (D-52) | |

## Jobs, Economic Development and the Economy

1020 N Street, Room 359, Sacramento, CA 95814

| **Majority Members** | **Minority Members** |
| --- | --- |
| Eduardo Garcia (D-56) *Chair* | Young O. Kim (R-65) *Vice Chair* |
| Cheryl R. Brown (D-47) | William P. "Bill" Brough (R-73) |
| Edwin "Ed" Chau (D-49) | Devon J. Mathis (R-26) |
| Mike A. Gipson (D-64) | |
| Jacqui V. Irwin (D-44) | |

## Judiciary

1020 N Street, Room 104, Sacramento, CA 95814

| **Majority Members** | **Minority Members** |
| --- | --- |
| Mark W. Stone (D-29) *Chair* | Donald P. "Don" Wagner (R-68) |
| Luis A. Alejo (D-30) | *Vice Chair* |
| Edwin "Ed" Chau (D-49) | James Gallagher (R-3) |
| David Chiu (D-17) | Brian Maienschein (R-77) |
| Cristina Garcia (D-58) | |
| Chris R. Holden (D-41) | |
| Philip Y. "Phil" Ting (D-19) | |

## Labor and Employment

1020 N Street, Room 155, Sacramento, CA 95814

| **Majority Members** | **Minority Members** |
| --- | --- |
| Roger Hernández (D-48) *Chair* | Jim Patterson (R-23) *Vice Chair* |
| Kansen Chu (D-25) | Eric Linder (R-60) |
| Kevin McCarty (D-7) | |
| Patrick O'Donnell (D-70) | |
| Tony Thurmond (D-15) | |

## Local Government

1020 N Street, Room 157, Sacramento, CA 95814

| **Majority Members** | **Minority Members** |
| --- | --- |
| Susan Talamantes Eggman (D-13) | Marie Waldron (R-75) *Vice Chair* |
|   *Chair* | Beth B. Gaines (R-6) |
| Luis A. Alejo (D-30) | Eric Linder (R-60) |
| Susan Bonilla (D-14) | Marie Waldron (R-75) |
| David Chiu (D-17) | |
| Ken Cooley (D-8) | |
| Richard S. Gordon (D-24) | |

## Natural Resources

1020 N Street, Room 164, Sacramento, CA 95814

| **Majority Members** | **Minority Members** |
| --- | --- |
| Das Williams (D-37) *Chair* | Brian W. Jones (R-71) *Vice Chair* |
| Cristina Garcia (D-58) | David Hadley (R-66) |
| Jimmy Gomez (D-51) | Matthew Harper (R-74) |
| Kevin McCarty (D-7) | |
| Mark W. Stone (D-29) | |
| Jim Wood (D-2) | |

## Public Employees, Retirement and Social Security

1020 N Street, Room 153, Sacramento, CA 95814

| **Majority Members** | **Minority Members** |
| --- | --- |
| Rob Bonta (D-18) *Chair* | Marie Waldron (R-75) *Vice Chair* |
| James "Jim" Cooper (D-9) | Donald P. "Don" Wagner (R-68) |
| Ken Cooley (D-8) | |
| Cristina Garcia (D-58) | |
| Patrick O'Donnell (D-70) | |

## Public Safety

1020 N Street, Room 111, Sacramento, CA 95814

| **Majority Members** | **Minority Members** |
| --- | --- |
| Reginald Byron Jones-Sawyer, Sr. (D-59) | Melissa Melendez (R-67) |
|   *Chair* | *Vice Chair* |
| Bill Quirk (D-20) | Tom Lackey (R-36) |
| Evan Low (D-28) | |
| Patty Lopez (D-39) | |
| Miguel Santiago (D-53) | |

## Revenue and Taxation
1020 N Street, Room 167A, Sacramento, CA 95814

**Majority Members**
Sebastian Ridley-Thomas (D-54)
  *Chair*
Matthew M. "Matt" Dababneh
  (D-45)
Mike A. Gipson (D-64)
Kevin Mullin (D-22)
Patrick O'Donnell (D-70)
Bill Quirk (D-20)

**Minority Members**
William P. "Bill" Brough (R-73)
  *Vice Chair*
Jim Patterson (R-23)
Donald P. "Don" Wagner (R-68)

## Rules
State Capitol, Room 3016, Sacramento, CA 95814

**Majority Members**
Richard S. Gordon (D-24) *Chair*
Dr. Joaquin Arambula (D-31)
Ken Cooley (D-8)
Bill Dodd (D-4)
Jimmy Gomez (D-51)
Chris R. Holden (D-41)
Patty Lopez (D-39)
Bill Quirk (D-20)
Freddie Rodriguez (D-52)

**Minority Members**
Ling-Ling Chang (R-55) *Vice Chair*
Brian W. Jones (R-71)
Chad Mayes (R-42)
Jay Obernolte (R-33)
Marie Waldron (R-75)

## Transportation
1020 N Street, Room 112, Sacramento, CA 95814

**Majority Members**
Jim Frazier (D-11) *Chair*
Richard Bloom (D-50)
Cheryl R. Brown (D-47)
Kansen Chu (D-25)
Tom Daly (D-69)
Bill Dodd (D-4)
Eduardo Garcia (D-56)
Jimmy Gomez (D-51)
Jose Medina (D-61)
Adrin Nazarian (D-46)
Patrick O'Donnell (D-70)

**Minority Members**
Eric Linder (R-60) *Vice Chair*
Catharine B. Baker (R-16)
Young O. Kim (R-65)
Devon J. Mathis (R-26)
Melissa Melendez (R-67)

## Utilities and Commerce
State Capitol, Room 5136, Sacramento, CA 95814

**Majority Members**
Mike Gatto (D-43) *Chair*
Susan Bonilla (D-14)
Susan Talamantes Eggman (D-13)
Cristina Garcia (D-58)
Roger Hernández (D-48)
Bill Quirk (D-20)
Miguel Santiago (D-53)
Philip Y. "Phil" Ting (D-19)
Das Williams (D-37)

**Minority Members**
Jim Patterson (R-23) *Vice Chair*
K. H. "Katcho" Achadjian (R-35)
Brian D. Dahle (R-1)
David Hadley (R-66)
Jay Obernolte (R-33)

## Veterans Affairs
1020 N Street, Room 389, Sacramento, CA 95814

**Majority Members**
Jacqui V. Irwin (D-44) *Chair*
Luis A. Alejo (D-30)
Dr. Joaquin Arambula (D-31)
Tom Daly (D-69)
Jim Frazier (D-11)
Rudy Salas, Jr. (D-32)

**Minority Members**
Rocky J. Chávez (R-76) *Vice Chair*
K. H. "Katcho" Achadjian (R-35)
William P. "Bill" Brough (R-73)
Devon J. Mathis (R-26)

## Water, Parks and Wildlife
1020 N Street, Room 160, Sacramento, CA 95814

**Majority Members**
Marc Levine (D-10) *Chair*
Matthew M. "Matt" Dababneh
  (D-45)
Cristina Garcia (D-58)
Jimmy Gomez (D-51)
Patty Lopez (D-39)
Jose Medina (D-61)
Rudy Salas, Jr. (D-32)
Das Williams (D-37)
Bill Dodd (D-4)

**Minority Members**
Franklin E. Bigelow (R-5)
  *Vice Chair*
Brian D. Dahle (R-1)
Beth B. Gaines (R-6)
Matthew Harper (R-74)
Devon J. Mathis (R-26)

# Colorado General Assembly
State Capitol, 200 East Colfax Avenue, Denver, CO 80203
Tel: (888) 473-8136  Internet: www.leg.state.co.us

## Colorado Senate
State Capitol, 200 East Colfax Avenue, Denver, CO 80203
Tel: (303) 866-2316  Fax: (303) 866-4543 (Democrat)
Fax: (303) 866-2012 (Republican)

President of the Senate **Bill Cadman** (R) . . . . . . . . . . . . . (303) 866-4880
President Pro Tem **Ellen S. Roberts** (R) . . . . . . . . . . . . . (303) 866-4884
  Education: Cornell 1981 BS; Colorado 1986 JD
Majority Leader **Mark Scheffel** (R) . . . . . . . . . . . . . . . . (303) 866-4869
Assistant Majority Leader **Kevin Lundberg** (R) . . . . . . . . . (303) 866-4853
Majority Caucus Chair **Vicki Marble** (R) . . . . . . . . . . . . (303) 866-4876
Majority Whip **Randy L. Baumgardner** (R) . . . . . . . . . . (303) 866-5292
Minority Leader **Lucía Guzmán** (D) . . . . . . . . . . . . . . . . (303) 866-4862
  Education: Sam Houston State 1973 BS; Iliff Theol 1989 MDiv
Assistant Minority Leader **Rollie Heath** (D) . . . . . . . . . . (303) 866-4872
Minority Caucus Chair **Jessie Ulibarri** (D) . . . . . . . . . . . (303) 866-4857
  Education: Colorado 2006 BA
Minority Whip **Matt Jones** (D) . . . . . . . . . . . . . . . . . . . (303) 866-5291
  Education: Colorado State 1977 BA, 1983 MA
Secretary of the Senate **Effie Ameen** . . . . . . . . . . . . . . . (303) 866-4838
  E-mail: effie.ameen@state.co.us
Chief Sergeant-at-Arms **Philip "Phil" Brown** . . . . . . . . . . (303) 866-4837
  E-mail: senate.sergeants@state.co.us

## Senators
**Party Affiliation Statistics:** Republicans: 18, Democrats: 17

Senator **Irene Aguilar** (D-District 32) . . . . . . . . . . . . . . . (303) 866-4852
  Counties Represented: Denver (part)
  Term Expires: 2019
  E-mail: irene.aguilar.senate@state.co.us
  Committees: Business, Labor and Technology; Health and Human
  Services
  Education: Chicago 1985 MD
Senator **Randy L. Baumgardner** (R-District 8) . . . . . . . . . (303) 866-5292
  Counties Represented: Garfield, Grand, Jackson, Moffat, Rio Blanco,
  Routt, Summit
  Term Expires: 2017
  E-mail: randy.baumgardner.senate@state.co.us
  Committees: Agriculture, Natural Resources, and Energy; Business,
  Labor and Technology; Transportation
Senator **Bill Cadman** (R-District 12) . . . . . . . . . . . . . . . . (303) 866-4880
  Counties Represented: El Paso (part)
  Term Expires: 2017
  E-mail: bill.cadman.senate@state.co.us
  Committees: Joint Legislative Council
Senator **Morgan Carroll** (D-District 29) . . . . . . . . . . . . . (303) 866-4879
  Counties Represented: Arapahoe (part)
  Term Expires: 2017
  E-mail: morgan.carroll.senate@state.co.us
  Committees: Joint Legislative Audit
Senator **John B. Cooke** (R-District 13) . . . . . . . . . . . . . . (303) 866-4451
  Counties Represented: Weld (part)
  Term Expires: 2019
  E-mail: john.cooke.senate@state.co.us
  Committees: Agriculture, Natural Resources, and Energy; Judiciary;
  Transportation
Senator **Larry W. Crowder** (R-District 35) . . . . . . . . . . . (303) 866-4875
  Counties Represented: Alamosa, Baca, Bent, Conejos, Costilla,
  Crowley, Custer, Huerfano, Kiowa, Las Animas, Mineral, Otero,
  Prowers, Pueblo (part), Rio Grande, Saguache
  Term Expires: 2017
  E-mail: larry.crowder.senate@state.co.us
  Committees: Health and Human Services; Local Government
Senator **Kerry Donovan** (D-District 5) . . . . . . . . . . . . . . (303) 866-4871
  Counties Represented: Chaffee, Delta, Eagle, Gunnison, Hinsdale,
  Lake, Pitkin
  Term Expires: 2019
  E-mail: kerry.donovan.senate@state.co.us
  Committees: Agriculture, Natural Resources, and Energy; Local
  Government
  Education: Notre Dame BS

*(continued on next page)*

LEGISLATIVE BRANCH

**Senators** *continued*

Senator **Leroy M. Garcia, Jr.** (D-District 3) . . . . . . . . . . . (303) 866-4878
Counties Represented: Pueblo (part)
Term Expires: 2019
E-mail: leroy.garcia.senate@state.co.us
Committees: Agriculture, Natural Resources, and Energy;
Transportation
Education: U Phoenix

Senator **Kevin J. Grantham** (R-District 2) . . . . . . . . . . . (303) 866-4877
Counties Represented: Clear Creek, El Paso (part), Fremont, Park,
Teller
Term Expires: 2019
E-mail: kevin.grantham.senate@state.co.us
Committees: Appropriations; Joint Budget
Education: Liberty 1992 BA

Senator **Lucía Guzmán** (D-District 34) . . . . . . . . . . . . . . (303) 866-4862
Counties Represented: Denver (part)
Term Expires: 2019
E-mail: lucia.guzman.senate@state.co.us
Committees: Joint Legislative Council; Judiciary

Senator **Rollie Heath** (D-District 18) . . . . . . . . . . . . . . . (303) 866-4872
Counties Represented: Boulder (part)
Term Expires: 2017
E-mail: rollie.heath.senate@state.co.us
Committees: Appropriations; Business, Labor and Technology; Joint
Legislative Council

Senator **Owen Hill** (R-District 10) . . . . . . . . . . . . . . . . . (303) 866-2737
Counties Represented: El Paso (part)
Term Expires: 2017
E-mail: owen.hill.senate@state.co.us
Committees: Education; Finance; State, Veterans and Military Affairs
Education: Air Force Acad

Senator **Mary Hodge** (D-District 25) . . . . . . . . . . . . . . . (303) 866-4855
Counties Represented: Adams (part)
Term Expires: 2017
E-mail: mary.hodge.senate@state.co.us
Committees: Agriculture, Natural Resources, and Energy;
Appropriations

Senator **Chris Holbert** (R-District 30) . . . . . . . . . . . . . . . (303) 866-4881
Counties Represented: Douglas (part)
Term Expires: 2019
E-mail: chris.holbert.senate@state.co.us
Committees: Business, Labor and Technology; Education; Finance;
Joint Legislative Audit

Senator **Cheri E. Jahn** (D-District 20) . . . . . . . . . . . . . . . (303) 866-4856
Counties Represented: Jefferson (part)
Term Expires: 2019
E-mail: cheri.jahn.senate@state.co.us
Committees: Business, Labor and Technology; Joint Legislative Audit
Education: Comm Col Denver 2003

Senator **Michael "Mike" Johnston** (D-District 33) . . . . . . (303) 866-4864
Counties Represented: Denver (part)
Term Expires: 2017
E-mail: mike.johnston.senate@state.co.us
Committees: Education; Finance; Joint Legal Services
Education: Vail Mountain (Vail, CO); Yale 1997 BP; Harvard; Yale JD

Senator **Matt Jones** (D-District 17) . . . . . . . . . . . . . . . . (303) 866-5291
Counties Represented: Boulder (part), Broomfield (part)
Term Expires: 2017
E-mail: senatormattjones@gmail.com
Committees: Agriculture, Natural Resources, and Energy; Joint
Legislative Council; State, Veterans and Military Affairs

Senator **John Michael Kefalas** (D-District 14) . . . . . . . . . (303) 866-4841
Counties Represented: Larimer (part)
Term Expires: 2017
E-mail: john.kefalas.senate@state.co.us
Committees: Local Government
Education: Colorado State 1978

Senator **Andrew "Andy" Kerr** (D-District 22) . . . . . . . . . (303) 866-4859
Counties Represented: Jefferson (part)
Term Expires: 2019
E-mail: andy.kerr.senate@state.co.us
Committees: Education; Finance
Education: Colorado BA, MA

Senator **Kent D. Lambert** (R-District 9) . . . . . . . . . . . . . (303) 866-4835
Counties Represented: El Paso (part)
Term Expires: 2019
E-mail: senatorlambert@comcast.net
Committees: Appropriations; Joint Budget
Education: Air Force Acad 1974 BS; USC MA;
Air Force Inst Tech MS; Air War Col

Senator **Kevin Lundberg** (R-District 15) . . . . . . . . . . . . . (303) 866-4853
Counties Represented: Larimer (part)
Term Expires: 2019
E-mail: solidprinciples@gmail.com
Committees: Health and Human Services; Joint Legislative Council;
Judiciary

Senator **Vicki Marble** (R-District 23) . . . . . . . . . . . . . . . (303) 866-4876
Counties Represented: Broomfield (part), Larimer (part), Weld (part)
Term Expires: 2019
E-mail: vicki.marble.senate@state.co.us
Committees: Education; Joint Legislative Council; Local Government

Senator **Beth Martinez Humenik** (R-District 24) . . . . . . . (303) 866-4863
Counties Represented: Adams (part)
Term Expires: 2019
E-mail: beth.martinezhumenik.senate@state.co.us
Committees: Health and Human Services; Local Government
Education: Colorado State BS, MA

Senator **Michael Merrifield** (D-District 11) . . . . . . . . . . . (303) 866-6364
Counties Represented: El Paso (part)
Term Expires: 2019
E-mail: michael.merrifield.senate@state.co.us
Committees: Education; Judiciary

Senator **Tim Neville** (R-District 16) . . . . . . . . . . . . . . . . (303) 866-4873
Counties Represented: Boulder (part), Denver (part), Gilpin, Jefferson
(part)
Term Expires: 2019
E-mail: tim.neville.senate@state.co.us
Committees: Business, Labor and Technology; Education; Finance;
Joint Legislative Audit
Education: Regis U BBA

Senator **Linda M. Newell** (D-District 26) . . . . . . . . . . . . . (303) 866-4846
Counties Represented: Arapahoe (part)
Term Expires: 2017
E-mail: linda.newell.senate@gmail.com
Committees: Business, Labor and Technology; Health and Human
Services

Senator **Ellen S. Roberts** (R-District 6) . . . . . . . . . . . . . . (303) 866-4884
Counties Represented: Archuleta, Dolores, La Plata, Montezuma,
Montrose, Ouray, San Juan, San Miguel
Term Expires: 2019
E-mail: ellen.roberts.senate@state.co.us
Committees: Agriculture, Natural Resources, and Energy; Joint Legal
Services; Joint Legislative Council; Judiciary

Senator **Mark Scheffel** (R-District 4) . . . . . . . . . . . . . . . (303) 866-4869
Counties Represented: Douglas (part)
Term Expires: 2017
E-mail: mark.scheffel.senate@state.co.us
Committees: Joint Legal Services; Joint Legislative Council

Senator **Ray Scott** (R-District 7) . . . . . . . . . . . . . . . . . . (303) 866-3077
Counties Represented: Mesa
Term Expires: 2019
E-mail: ray.scott.senate@state.co.us
Committees: Agriculture, Natural Resources, and Energy; Joint Legal
Services; State, Veterans and Military Affairs; Transportation

Senator **Jerry Sonnenberg** (R-District 1) . . . . . . . . . . . . . (303) 866-6360
Counties Represented: Cheyenne, Elbert, Kit Carson, Lincoln, Logan,
Morgan, Phillips, Sedgwick, Washington, Weld (part), Yuma
Term Expires: 2019
E-mail: senatorsonnenberg@gmail.com
Committees: Agriculture, Natural Resources, and Energy;
Appropriations; State, Veterans and Military Affairs

Senator **M. Patrick "Pat" Steadman** (D-District 31) . . . . . (303) 866-4861
Counties Represented: Arapahoe (part), Denver (part)
Term Expires: 2017
E-mail: pat.steadman.senate@state.co.us
Committees: Appropriations; Joint Budget; Joint Legal Services
Education: Regis Col (MA); Colorado JD

Senator **Jack Tate** (R-District 27) . . . . . . . . . . . . . . . . . . (303) 866-4883
Counties Represented: Arapahoe (part)
Term Expires: 2017
E-mail: jack.tate.senate@state.co.us
Committees: Business, Labor and Technology; Local Government

Senator **Nancy J. Todd** (D-District 28) . . . . . . . . . . . . . . (303) 866-3432
Counties Represented: Arapahoe (part)
Term Expires: 2017
E-mail: nancy.todd.senate@state.co.us
Committees: Education; Transportation
Education: Kansas 1970; Northern Colorado 1990

LEGISLATIVE BRANCH

Senator **Jessie Ulibarri** (D-District 21) . . . . . . . . . . . . . . . (303) 866-4857
    Counties Represented: Adams (part)
    Term Expires: 2017
    E-mail: jessie.ulibarri.senate@state.co.us
    Committees: Joint Legislative Council; Local Government; State,
    Veterans and Military Affairs

Senator **Laura Woods** (R-District 19) . . . . . . . . . . . . . . . . (303) 866-4840
    Counties Represented: Jefferson (part)
    Term Expires: 2019
    E-mail: laura.woods.senate@state.co.us
    Committees: Appropriations; Business, Labor and Technology;
    Education

# Senate Standing Committees

## Agriculture, Natural Resources, and Energy

| Majority Members | Minority Members |
|---|---|
| Jerry Sonnenberg (R-1) *Chair* | Mary Hodge (D-25) |
| Ellen S. Roberts (R-6) *Vice Chair* | *Ranking Member* |
| Randy L. Baumgardner (R-8) | Kerry Donovan (D-5) |
| John B. Cooke (R-13) | Leroy M. Garcia, Jr. (D-3) |
| Ray Scott (R-7) | Matt Jones (D-17) |

## Appropriations

| Majority Members | Minority Members |
|---|---|
| Kevin J. Grantham (R-2) *Chair* | M. Patrick "Pat" Steadman (D-31) |
| Kent D. Lambert (R-9) *Vice Chair* | *Ranking Member* |
| Jerry Sonnenberg (R-1) | Rollie Heath (D-18) |
| Laura Woods (R-19) | Mary Hodge (D-25) |

## Business, Labor and Technology

| Majority Members | Minority Members |
|---|---|
| Chris Holbert (R-30) *Chair* | Rollie Heath (D-18) |
| Laura Woods (R-19) *Vice Chair* | *Ranking Member* |
| Randy L. Baumgardner (R-8) | Irene Aguilar (D-32) |
| Tim Neville (R-16) | Cheri E. Jahn (D-20) |
| Jack Tate (R-27) | Linda M. Newell (D-26) |

## Education

| Majority Members | Minority Members |
|---|---|
| Owen Hill (R-10) *Chair* | Andrew "Andy" Kerr (D-22) |
| Vicki Marble (R-23) *Vice Chair* | *Ranking Member* |
| Chris Holbert (R-30) | Michael "Mike" Johnston (D-33) |
| Tim Neville (R-16) | Michael Merrifield (D-11) |
| Laura Woods (R-19) | Nancy J. Todd (D-28) |

## Finance

| Majority Members | Minority Members |
|---|---|
| Tim Neville (R-16) *Chair* | Michael "Mike" Johnston (D-33) |
| Owen Hill (R-10) *Vice Chair* | *Ranking Member* |
| Chris Holbert (R-30) | Andrew "Andy" Kerr (D-22) |

## Health and Human Services

| Majority Members | Minority Members |
|---|---|
| Kevin Lundberg (R-15) *Chair* | Irene Aguilar (D-32) |
| Larry W. Crowder (R-35) | *Ranking Member* |
|   *Vice Chair* | Linda M. Newell (D-26) |
| Beth Martinez Humenik (R-24) | |

## Judiciary

| Majority Members | Minority Members |
|---|---|
| Ellen S. Roberts (R-6) *Chair* | Lucía Guzmán (D-34) |
| Kevin Lundberg (R-15) *Vice Chair* | *Ranking Member* |
| John B. Cooke (R-13) | Michael Merrifield (D-11) |

## Local Government

| Majority Members | Minority Members |
|---|---|
| Vicki Marble (R-23) *Chair* | John Michael Kefalas (D-14) |
| Larry W. Crowder (R-35) | *Ranking Member* |
|   *Vice Chair* | Kerry Donovan (D-5) |
| Beth Martinez Humenik (R-24) | Jessie Ulibarri (D-21) |
| Jack Tate (R-27) | |

## State, Veterans and Military Affairs

| Majority Members | Minority Members |
|---|---|
| Ray Scott (R-7) *Chair* | Jessie Ulibarri (D-21) |
| Jerry Sonnenberg (R-1) *Vice Chair* | *Ranking Member* |
| Owen Hill (R-10) | Matt Jones (D-17) |

## Transportation

| Majority Members | Minority Members |
|---|---|
| Randy L. Baumgardner (R-8) *Chair* | Nancy J. Todd (D-28) |
| Ray Scott (R-7) *Vice Chair* | *Ranking Member* |
| John B. Cooke (R-13) | Leroy M. Garcia, Jr. (D-3) |

# Colorado House of Representatives

200 East Colfax Avenue, Denver, CO 80203
Tel: (303) 866-2904  Tel: (800) 811-7647 (Outside Denver)
Fax: (303) 866-2218

Speaker of the House **Dickey Lee Hullinghorst** (D) . . . . . . (303) 866-2348
    Education: Wyoming 1965 BA
Speaker Pro Tem **Daniel R. "Dan" Pabon** (D) . . . . . . . . . (303) 866-2954
    Education: Colorado 2001 BSME, 2005 JD
Majority Leader **Crisanta Duran** (D) . . . . . . . . . . . . . . . . (303) 866-2925
    Education: Denver; Colorado 2005 JD
Assistant Majority Leader **Dominick Moreno** (D) . . . . . . . (303) 866-2964
    Education: Georgetown 2008 BA
Majority Whip **Su Ryden** (D) . . . . . . . . . . . . . . . . . . . . . (303) 866-2942
Deputy Majority Whip **Brittany Pettersen** (D) . . . . . . . . . (303) 866-2939
Majority Caucus Chairman **Angela Williams** (D) . . . . . . . . (303) 866-2909
    Education: Northeastern BA
Majority Caucus Assistant Chairman **Mike Foote** (D) . . . . . (303) 866-2920
    Education: Indiana BA; Denver MA; Colorado JD
Minority Leader **Brian DelGrosso** (R) . . . . . . . . . . . . . . . (303) 866-2947
Assistant Minority Leader **Polly Lawrence** (R) . . . . . . . . . (303) 866-2935
    Education: Colorado State
Minority Whip **Perry L. Buck** (R) . . . . . . . . . . . . . . . . . . (303) 866-2907
Minority Caucus Chairman **Lois Landgraf** (R) . . . . . . . . . . (303) 866-2946
    Education: Maryland; U Washington MBA
Chief Clerk of the House **Marilyn Eddins** . . . . . . . . . . . . . (303) 866-2345
    E-mail: marilyn.eddins@state.co.us
Chief Sergeant-at-Arms **John Wallin** . . . . . . . . . . . . . . . . (303) 866-2971
    E-mail: jmalecka@msn.com

## Representatives

**Party Affiliation Statistics:** Republicans: 31, Democrats: 34

Representative **Jeni Arndt** (D-District 53) . . . . . . . . . . . . . (303) 866-2917
    Counties Represented: Larimer (part)
    Term Expires: 2017
    E-mail: jeni.arndt.house@state.co.us
    Committees: Agriculture, Livestock and Natural Resources; Business
    Affairs and Labor; Local Government
Representative **Jon J. Becker** (R-District 65) . . . . . . . . . . . (303) 866-3706
    Counties Represented: Cheyenne, Kit Carson, Logan, Morgan, Phillips,
    Sedgwick, Yuma
    Term Expires: 2017
    E-mail: jon.becker.house@state.co.us
    Committees: Agriculture, Livestock and Natural Resources;
    Appropriations; Transportation and Energy
    Education: Morgan Comm Col AA; Colorado State BSBA;
    Colorado Christian MBA
Representative **KC Becker** (D-District 13) . . . . . . . . . . . . . (303) 866-2578
    Counties Represented: Boulder (part), Clear Creek, Gilpin, Grand,
    Jackson
    Term Expires: 2017
    E-mail: kcbecker.house@state.co.us
    Committees: Agriculture, Livestock and Natural Resources; Finance
    Education: William & Mary 1991 BA; Lewis & Clark 1996 JD;
    Denver 2005 MS
Representative **J. Paul Brown** (R-District 59) . . . . . . . . . . . (303) 866-2914
    Counties Represented: Archuleta, Gunnison (part), Hinsdale, La Plata,
    Ouray, San Juan
    Term Expires: 2017
    E-mail: jpaul.brown.house@state.co.us
    Committees: Agriculture, Livestock and Natural Resources; Health,
    Insurance and Environment
    Education: New Mexico State 1975 BS

*(continued on next page)*

LEGISLATIVE BRANCH

**Representatives** *continued*

Representative **Perry L. Buck** (R-District 49) . . . . . . . . . . . (303) 866-2907
Counties Represented: Larimer (part), Weld (part)
Term Expires: 2017
E-mail: perrybuck49@gmail.com
Committees: Agriculture, Livestock and Natural Resources; Joint
Legislative Council; Transportation and Energy

Representative **Janet P. Buckner** (D-District 40) . . . . . . . . (303) 866-2944
Counties Represented: Arapahoe (part)
Term Expires: 2017
E-mail: janet.buckner.house@state.co.us
Committees: Education; Health, Insurance and Environment

Representative **Terri Carver** (R-District 20) . . . . . . . . . . . . (303) 866-2191
Counties Represented: El Paso (part)
Term Expires: 2017
E-mail: terri.carver.house@state.co.us
Committees: Judiciary; Transportation and Energy

Representative **Kathleen Conti** (R-District 38) . . . . . . . . . (303) 866-2953
Counties Represented: Arapahoe (part)
Term Expires: 2017
E-mail: kathleen.conti.house@state.co.us
Committees: Finance; Public Health Care and Human Services

Representative **Don Coram** (R-District 58) . . . . . . . . . . . . (303) 866-2955
Counties Represented: Dolores, Montezuma, Montrose, San Miguel
Term Expires: 2017
E-mail: don.coram.house@state.co.us
Committees: Agriculture, Livestock and Natural Resources;
Transportation and Energy

Representative **Lois Court** (D-District 6) . . . . . . . . . . . . . . (303) 866-2967
Counties Represented: Denver (part)
Term Expires: 2017
E-mail: lois.court.house@state.co.us
Committees: Finance; Joint Legislative Council; Judiciary

Representative **Jessie Danielson** (D-District 24) . . . . . . . . (303) 866-5522
Counties Represented: Jefferson (part)
Term Expires: 2017
E-mail: jessie.danielson.house@state.co.us
Committees: Agriculture, Livestock and Natural Resources; Local
Government; Public Health Care and Human Services
Education: Colorado

Representative **Brian DelGrosso** (R-District 51) . . . . . . . . (303) 866-2947
Counties Represented: Larimer (part)
Term Expires: 2017
E-mail: brian.delgrosso.house@state.co.us
Committees: Joint Legislative Council

Representative **Tim Dore** (R-District 64) . . . . . . . . . . . . . . (303) 866-2398
Counties Represented: Baca, Bent, Crowley, Elbert, Kiowa, Las
Animas, Lincoln, Prowers, Washington
Term Expires: 2017
E-mail: tim.dore.house@state.co.us
Committees: Agriculture, Livestock and Natural Resources;
Appropriations; Joint Legal Services; Judiciary
Education: Denver 2000 JD

Representative **Crisanta Duran** (D-District 5) . . . . . . . . . . (303) 866-2925
Counties Represented: Denver (part)
Term Expires: 2017
E-mail: crisanta.duran.house@state.co.us
Committees: Joint Legislative Council

Representative **Daneya Esgar** (D-District 46) . . . . . . . . . . . (303) 866-2968
Counties Represented: Pueblo (part)
Term Expires: 2017
E-mail: daneya.esgar.house@state.co.us
Committees: Health, Insurance and Environment; Transportation and
Energy
Education: Colorado State Pueblo

Representative **Justin Everett** (R-District 22) . . . . . . . . . . (303) 866-2927
Counties Represented: Jefferson (part)
Term Expires: 2017
E-mail: justin.everett.house@state.co.us
Committees: Appropriations; Education; Public Health Care and Human
Services
Education: Chapman BA; Colorado (Denver) MBA

Representative **Rhonda C. Fields** (D-District 42) . . . . . . . . (303) 866-3911
Counties Represented: Arapahoe (part)
Term Expires: 2017
E-mail: rhonda.fields.house@state.co.us
Committees: Education; Local Government
Education: Northern Colorado BE, MA

Representative **Mike Foote** (D-District 12) . . . . . . . . . . . . (303) 866-2920
Counties Represented: Boulder (part)
Term Expires: 2017
E-mail: mike.foote.house@state.co.us
Committees: Finance; Joint Legal Services; Judiciary; State, Veterans
and Military Affairs

Representative **Alec Garnett** (D-District 2) . . . . . . . . . . . . (303) 866-2911
Counties Represented: Denver (part)
Term Expires: 2017
E-mail: alec.garnett.house@state.co.us
Committees: Business Affairs and Labor; Education; Finance
Education: Wooster 2005 AB; Colorado 2006 MPAff

Representative **Joann Ginal** (D-District 52) . . . . . . . . . . . . (303) 866-4569
Counties Represented: Larimer (part)
Term Expires: 2017
E-mail: joann.ginal.house@state.co.us
Committees: Agriculture, Livestock and Natural Resources; Health,
Insurance and Environment; Public Health Care and Human Services
Education: New Hampshire BS; Iowa State; Colorado State 1997 PhD

Representative **Millie Hamner** (D-District 61) . . . . . . . . . . (303) 866-2952
Counties Represented: Delta (part), Gunnison (part), Lake, Pitkin,
Summit
Term Expires: 2017
E-mail: millie.hamner.house@state.co.us
Committees: Appropriations; Joint Budget

Representative **Dickey Lee Hullinghorst** (D-District 10) . . . (303) 866-2348
Counties Represented: Boulder (part)
Term Expires: 2017
E-mail: dl.hullinghorst.house@state.co.us
Committees: Joint Legislative Council

Representative
**Stephen "Steve" Humphrey** (R-District 48) . . . . . . . . . (303) 866-2943
Counties Represented: Weld (part)
Term Expires: 2017
E-mail: rephumphrey48@yahoo.com
Committees: Health, Insurance and Environment; State, Veterans and
Military Affairs

Representative **Janak Joshi, MD** (R-District 16) . . . . . . . . (303) 866-2937
Counties Represented: El Paso (part)
Term Expires: 2017
E-mail: janak.joshi.house@state.co.us
Committees: Appropriations; Health, Insurance and Environment;
Public Health Care and Human Services
Education: Gujarat (India) MD; Northern Colorado MSHA

Representative **Daniel Kagan** (D-District 3) . . . . . . . . . . . . (303) 866-2921
Counties Represented: Arapahoe (part)
Term Expires: 2017
E-mail: repkagan@gmail.com
Committees: Finance; Joint Legal Services; Judiciary

Representative **Gordon Klingenschmitt** (R-District 15) . . . (303) 866-5525
Counties Represented: El Paso (part)
Term Expires: 2017
E-mail: klingenschmitt.house@state.co.us
Committees: Local Government

Representative **Tracy Kraft-Tharp** (D-District 29) . . . . . . . (303) 866-2950
Counties Represented: Jefferson (part)
Term Expires: 2017
E-mail: reptracy29@gmail.com
Committees: Business Affairs and Labor; Transportation and Energy

Representative **Lois Landgraf** (R-District 21) . . . . . . . . . . . (303) 866-2946
Counties Represented: El Paso (part)
Term Expires: 2017
E-mail: lois.landgraf.house@state.co.us
Committees: Health, Insurance and Environment; Joint Legislative
Council; Public Health Care and Human Services

Representative **Polly Lawrence** (R-District 39) . . . . . . . . . (303) 866-2935
Counties Represented: Douglas (part), Teller
Term Expires: 2017
E-mail: polly.lawrence.house@state.co.us
Committees: Joint Legislative Council; Judiciary

Representative **Steve Lebsock** (D-District 34) . . . . . . . . . . (303) 866-2931
Counties Represented: Adams (part)
Term Expires: 2017
E-mail: steve.lebsock.house@state.co.us
Committees: Agriculture, Livestock and Natural Resources; Local
Government
Education: Metropolitan State U 1998 BA

**LEGISLATIVE BRANCH**

Representative **Sanford E. "Pete" Lee** (D-District 18) .... (303) 866-2932
Counties Represented: El Paso (part)
Term Expires: 2017
E-mail: pete.lee.house@state.co.us
Committees: Education; Judiciary
Education: Ohio Wesleyan 1970 BA; Pennsylvania 1971 (Attended);
Akron 1975 JD

Representative **Timothy Leonard** (R-District 25) ........(303) 866-2582
Counties Represented: Jefferson (part)
Term Expires: 2017
E-mail: tim.leonard.house@state.co.us
Committees: Public Health Care and Human Services; State, Veterans
and Military Affairs

Representative **Susan Lontine** (D-District 1) ...........(303) 866-2966
Counties Represented: Denver (part), Jefferson (part)
Term Expires: 2017
E-mail: susan.lontine.house@state.co.us
Committees: Health, Insurance and Environment; State, Veterans and
Military Affairs

Representative **Paul Lundeen** (R-District 19) ...........(303) 866-2924
Counties Represented: El Paso (part)
Term Expires: 2017
E-mail: paul.lundeen.house@state.co.us
Committees: Education; Judiciary
Education: NYU

Representative **Elizabeth "Beth" McCann** (D-District 8) .. (303) 866-2959
Counties Represented: Denver (part)
Term Expires: 2017
E-mail: beth.mccann.house@state.co.us
Committees: Appropriations; Health, Insurance and Environment; Joint
Legal Services

Representative **Jovan Melton** (D-District 41) ...........(303) 866-2919
Counties Represented: Arapahoe (part)
Term Expires: 2017
E-mail: jovan.melton.house@state.co.us
Committees: Joint Legislative Council; Judiciary; Public Health Care
and Human Services; Transportation and Energy
Education: Colorado BA

Representative **Diane E. Mitsch Bush** (D-District 26) .....(303) 866-2923
Counties Represented: Eagle, Routt
Term Expires: 2017
E-mail: diane.mitschbush.house@state.co.us
Committees: Agriculture, Livestock and Natural Resources;
Transportation and Energy
Education: Minnesota 1975 BA, 1979 PhD

Representative **Dominick Moreno** (D-District 32) ........(303) 866-2964
Counties Represented: Adams (part)
Term Expires: 2017
E-mail: dominick.moreno.house@state.co.us
Committees: Education; Public Health Care and Human Services;
Transportation and Energy

Representative **Clarice Navarro-Ratzlaff** (R-District 47) ... (303) 866-2905
Counties Represented: Fremont (part), Otero, Pueblo (part)
Term Expires: 2017
E-mail: clarice.navarro.house@state.co.us
Committees: Business Affairs and Labor; Local Government

Representative **Patrick Neville** (R-District 45) ..........(303) 866-2948
Counties Represented: Douglas (part)
Term Expires: 2017
E-mail: patrick.neville.house@state.co.us
Committees: State, Veterans and Military Affairs; Transportation and
Energy

Representative
**Daniel P. "Dan" Nordberg** (R-District 14) ...........(303) 866-2965
Counties Represented: El Paso (part)
Term Expires: 2017
E-mail: dan.nordberg.house@state.co.us
Committees: Business Affairs and Labor; Joint Legislative Audit;
Transportation and Energy
Education: Colorado State

Representative **Daniel R. "Dan" Pabon** (D-District 4) .... (303) 866-2954
Counties Represented: Denver (part)
Term Expires: 2017
E-mail: dan.pabon.house@state.co.us
Committees: Appropriations; Business Affairs and Labor; Finance

Representative **Brittany Pettersen** (D-District 28) ........(303) 866-2939
Counties Represented: Jefferson (part)
Term Expires: 2017
E-mail: brittany.pettersen.house@state.co.us
Committees: Appropriations; Education

Representative **Dianne Primavera** (D-District 33) .......(303) 866-4667
Counties Represented: Boulder (part), Broomfield, Weld (part)
Term Expires: 2017
E-mail: dianne.primavera.house@state.co.us
Committees: Health, Insurance and Environment; Joint Legislative
Audit; Public Health Care and Human Services; State, Veterans and
Military Affairs
Education: Regis U 1972 BS; Northern Colorado 1975 MA

Representative **Kevin Priola** (R-District 56) .............(303) 866-2912
Counties Represented: Adams (part), Arapahoe (part)
Term Expires: 2017
E-mail: kpriola@gmail.com
Committees: Education

Representative **Bob Rankin** (R-District 57).............(303) 866-2949
Counties Represented: Garfield, Moffat, Rio Blanco
Term Expires: 2017
E-mail: bob.rankin.house@state.co.us
Committees: Appropriations; Joint Budget

Representative **Kim Ransom** (R-District 44) ...........(303) 866-2933
Counties Represented: Douglas (part)
Term Expires: 2017
E-mail: kim.ransom.house@state.co.us
Committees: Health, Insurance and Environment; Local Government

Representative **Paul Rosenthal** (D-District 9) ...........(303) 866-2910
Counties Represented: Arapahoe (part), Denver (part)
Term Expires: 2017
E-mail: paul.rosenthal.house@state.co.us
Committees: Business Affairs and Labor; Local Government
Education: U San Francisco 1990 BA; Denver 1997 MA

Representative **Kit Roupe** (R-District 17) .............(303) 866-3069
Counties Represented: El Paso (part)
Term Expires: 2017
E-mail: kit.roupe.house@state.co.us
Committees: Business Affairs and Labor; Finance

Representative **Su Ryden** (D-District 36) .............(303) 866-2942
Counties Represented: Arapahoe (part)
Term Expires: 2017
E-mail: su.ryden.house@state.co.us
Committees: Health, Insurance and Environment; Joint Legislative
Audit; State, Veterans and Military Affairs

Representative **Lori Saine** (R-District 63) ..............(303) 866-2906
Counties Represented: Weld (part)
Term Expires: 2017
E-mail: lori.saine.house@state.co.us
Committees: Agriculture, Livestock and Natural Resources; Joint
Legislative Audit; Local Government

Representative **Joseph A. "Joe" Salazar** (D-District 31) .. (303) 866-2918
Counties Represented: Adams (part)
Term Expires: 2017
E-mail: joseph.salazar.house@state.co.us
Committees: Judiciary
Education: Colorado; Denver JD

Representative
**Langhorne C. "Lang" Sias** (R-District 27) ..........(303) 866-2962
Counties Represented: Jefferson (part)
Term Expires: 2017
E-mail: lang.sias.house@state.co.us
Committees: Business Affairs and Labor; Finance; Health, Insurance
and Environment
Education: Vassar BA; London School Econ (UK) MSc; Michigan JD

Representative **Jonathan Singer** (D-District 11) ........(303) 866-2780
Counties Represented: Boulder (part)
Term Expires: 2017
E-mail: jonathan.singer.house@state.co.us
Committees: Appropriations; Local Government; Public Health Care
and Human Services

Representative **Dan Thurlow** (R-District 55) ...........(303) 866-3068
Counties Represented: Mesa (part)
Term Expires: 2017
E-mail: danthurlow55@gmail.com
Committees: Business Affairs and Labor; Local Government

Representative **Max Tyler** (D-District 23) ..............(303) 866-2951
Counties Represented: Jefferson (part)
Term Expires: 2017
E-mail: max@maxtyler.us
Committees: Public Health Care and Human Services; State, Veterans
and Military Affairs; Transportation and Energy

Representative **Kevin Van Winkle** (R-District 43) ........(303) 866-2936
Counties Represented: Douglas (part)
Term Expires: 2017
E-mail: kevin.vanwinkle.house@state.co.us
Committees: Finance

*(continued on next page)*

**Representatives** *continued*

Representative **Edward Vigil** (D-District 62) . . . . . . . . . . . . (303) 866-2916
   Counties Represented: Alamosa, Conejos, Costilla, Huerfano, Mineral,
   Pueblo (part), Rio Grande, Saguache
   Term Expires: 2017
   E-mail: edvigil1@gmail.com
   Committees: Agriculture, Livestock and Natural Resources

Representative **Yeulin Willett** (R-District 54) . . . . . . . . . . . (303) 866-2583
   Counties Represented: Delta (part), Mesa (part)
   Term Expires: 2017
   E-mail: yeulin.willett.house@state.co.us
   Committees: Joint Legal Services; Judiciary

Representative **Angela Williams** (D-District 7) . . . . . . . . . (303) 866-2909
   Counties Represented: Denver (part)
   Term Expires: 2017
   E-mail: angela.williams.house@state.co.us
   Committees: Business Affairs and Labor; Joint Legislative Council

Representative **James D. "Jim" Wilson** (R-District 60) . . . (303) 866-2747
   Counties Represented: Chaffee, Custer, Fremont (part), Park
   Term Expires: 2017
   E-mail: james.wilson.house@state.co.us
   Committees: Appropriations; Education; Finance

Representative **JoAnn Windholz** (R-District 30) . . . . . . . . (303) 866-2945
   Counties Represented: Adams (part)
   Term Expires: 2017
   E-mail: joann.windholz.house@state.co.us
   Committees: Education; Public Health Care and Human Services

Representative **Faith Winter** (D-District 35) . . . . . . . . . . . . (303) 866-2843
   Counties Represented: Adams (part)
   Term Expires: 2017
   E-mail: faith.winter.house@state.co.us
   Committees: Appropriations; Business Affairs and Labor;
   Transportation and Energy

Representative **Cole Wist** (R-District 37) . . . . . . . . . . . . . . (303) 866-5510
   Counties Represented: Arapahoe (part)
   Term Expires: 2017
   E-mail: cole.wist.house@state.co.us
   Committees: Business Affairs and Labor; State, Veterans and Military
   Affairs

Representative **Dave Young** (D-District 50) . . . . . . . . . . . . (303) 866-2929
   Counties Represented: Weld (part)
   Term Expires: 2017
   E-mail: dave.young.house@state.co.us
   Committees: Appropriations; Joint Budget
   Education: Colorado State 1975 BS; Colorado (Denver) 2000 MA

# House Standing Committees

## Agriculture, Livestock and Natural Resources

**Majority Members**
Edward Vigil (D-62) *Chair*
KC Becker (D-13) *Vice Chair*
Jeni Arndt (D-53)
Jessie Danielson (D-24)
Joann Ginal (D-52)
Steve Lebsock (D-34)
Diane E. Mitsch Bush (D-26)

**Minority Members**
Jon J. Becker (R-65)
J. Paul Brown (R-59)
Perry L. Buck (R-49)
Don Coram (R-58)
Tim Dore (R-64)
Lori Saine (R-63)

## Appropriations

**Majority Members**
Dave Young (D-50) *Chair*
Millie Hamner (D-61) *Vice Chair*
Elizabeth "Beth" McCann (D-8)
Daniel R. "Dan" Pabon (D-4)
Brittany Pettersen (D-28)
Jonathan Singer (D-11)
Faith Winter (D-35)

**Minority Members**
Jon J. Becker (R-65)
Tim Dore (R-64)
Justin Everett (R-22)
Janak Joshi (R-16)
Bob Rankin (R-57)
James D. "Jim" Wilson (R-60)

## Business Affairs and Labor

**Majority Members**
Angela Williams (D-7) *Chair*
Tracy Kraft-Tharp (D-29)
  *Vice Chair*
Jeni Arndt (D-53)
Alec Garnett (D-2)
Daniel R. "Dan" Pabon (D-4)
Paul Rosenthal (D-9)
Faith Winter (D-35)

**Minority Members**
Clarice Navarro-Ratzlaff (R-47)
Daniel P. "Dan" Nordberg (R-14)
Kit Roupe (R-17)
Langhorne C. "Lang" Sias (R-27)
Dan Thurlow (R-55)
Cole Wist (R-37)

# Education

**Majority Members**
Brittany Pettersen (D-28) *Chair*
Sanford E. "Pete" Lee (D-18)
  *Vice Chair*
Janet P. Buckner (D-40)
Rhonda C. Fields (D-42)
Alec Garnett (D-2)
Dominick Moreno (D-32)

**Minority Members**
Justin Everett (R-22)
Paul Lundeen (R-19)
Kevin Priola (R-56)
James D. "Jim" Wilson (R-60)
JoAnn Windholz (R-30)

# Finance

**Majority Members**
Lois Court (D-6) *Chair*
Mike Foote (D-12) *Vice Chair*
KC Becker (D-13)
Alec Garnett (D-2)
Daniel Kagan (D-3)
Daniel R. "Dan" Pabon (D-4)

**Minority Members**
Kathleen Conti (R-38)
Kit Roupe (R-17)
Langhorne C. "Lang" Sias (R-27)
James D. "Jim" Wilson (R-60)
Kevin Van Winkle (R-43)

# Health, Insurance and Environment

**Majority Members**
Elizabeth "Beth" McCann (D-8)
  *Chair*
Joann Ginal (D-52) *Vice Chair*
Janet P. Buckner (D-40)
Daneya Esgar (D-46)
Susan Lontine (D-1)
Dianne Primavera (D-33)
Su Ryden (D-36)

**Minority Members**
J. Paul Brown (R-59)
Stephen "Steve" Humphrey (R-48)
Janak Joshi (R-16)
Lois Landgraf (R-21)
Kim Ransom (R-44)
Langhorne C. "Lang" Sias (R-27)

# Judiciary

**Majority Members**
Daniel Kagan (D-3) *Chair*
Sanford E. "Pete" Lee (D-18)
  *Vice Chair*
Lois Court (D-6)
Mike Foote (D-12)
Jovan Melton (D-41)
Joseph A. "Joe" Salazar (D-31)

**Minority Members**
Terri Carver (R-20)
Tim Dore (R-64)
Polly Lawrence (R-39)
Paul Lundeen (R-19)
Yeulin Willett (R-54)

# Local Government

**Majority Members**
Rhonda C. Fields (D-42) *Chair*
Steve Lebsock (D-34) *Vice Chair*
Jeni Arndt (D-53)
Jessie Danielson (D-24)
Paul Rosenthal (D-9)
Jonathan Singer (D-11)

**Minority Members**
Gordon Klingenschmitt (R-15)
Clarice Navarro-Ratzlaff (R-47)
Kim Ransom (R-44)
Lori Saine (R-63)
Dan Thurlow (R-55)

# Public Health Care and Human Services

**Majority Members**
Dianne Primavera (D-33) *Chair*
Jonathan Singer (D-11) *Vice Chair*
Jessie Danielson (D-24)
Joann Ginal (D-52)
Jovan Melton (D-41)
Dominick Moreno (D-32)
Max Tyler (D-23)

**Minority Members**
Kathleen Conti (R-38)
Justin Everett (R-22)
Janak Joshi (R-16)
Lois Landgraf (R-21)
Timothy Leonard (R-25)
JoAnn Windholz (R-30)

# State, Veterans and Military Affairs

**Majority Members**
Su Ryden (D-36) *Chair*
Susan Lontine (D-1) *Vice Chair*
Mike Foote (D-12)
Dianne Primavera (D-33)
Max Tyler (D-23)

**Minority Members**
Stephen "Steve" Humphrey (R-48)
Timothy Leonard (R-25)
Patrick Neville (R-45)
Cole Wist (R-37)

# Transportation and Energy

**Majority Members**
Max Tyler (D-23) *Chair*
Diane E. Mitsch Bush (D-26)
  *Vice Chair*
Daneya Esgar (D-46)
Tracy Kraft-Tharp (D-29)
Jovan Melton (D-41)
Dominick Moreno (D-32)
Faith Winter (D-35)

**Minority Members**
Jon J. Becker (R-65)
Perry L. Buck (R-49)
Terri Carver (R-20)
Don Coram (R-58)
Patrick Neville (R-45)
Daniel P. "Dan" Nordberg (R-14)

**LEGISLATIVE BRANCH**

# Connecticut General Assembly

Legislative Office Building, Room 5100, Hartford, CT 06106
Tel: (860) 240-0100  Tel: (860) 240-8888 (Legislative Library)
Tel: (860) 240-8400 (Legislative Research Office)  Fax: (860) 240-0122
E-mail: jclm@cga.ct.gov  Internet: www.cga.ct.gov

## Connecticut State Senate

State Capitol, Room 305, Hartford, CT 06106-1591
Tel: (860) 240-0500  Tel: (860) 240-8600 (Senate Democrats)
Tel: (860) 240-8800 (Senate Republicans)

President of the Senate **Nancy Wyman** (D) . . . . . . . . . . . . . (860) 524-7384
President Pro Tem **Martin M. Looney** (D) . . . . . . . . . . . . . (860) 240-8629
  Education: Fairfield BA; Connecticut MA, 1985 JD
Chief Deputy President Pro Tem and Federal Relations
  Liaison **Joseph J. "Joe" Crisco, Jr.** (D) . . . . . . . . . . . .(860) 240-0189
  Education: Connecticut BS; Trinity Col (CT)
Deputy President Pro Tem **Eric D. Coleman** (D) . . . . . . . . (860) 240-5328
  Education: Pomfret (Pomfret, CT); Columbia BA; Connecticut 1977 JD
Deputy President Pro Tem **John W. Fonfara** (D) . . . . . . . . (860) 240-0043
  Education: Connecticut BS; Trinity Col (CT) MS
Deputy President Pro Tem **Joan V. Hartley** (D) . . . . . . . . (860) 240-0006
Deputy President Pro Tem **Carlo Leone** (D) . . . . . . . . . . . (203) 323-2138
  Education: Sacred Heart U BBA, MBA
Assistant President Pro Tem
  **Stephen T. "Steve" Cassano** (D) . . . . . . . . . . . . . . . . .(860) 478-5535
Assistant President Pro Tem
  **Catherine A. "Cathy" Osten** (D) . . . . . . . . . . . . . . . . .(860) 240-0579
Majority Leader **Robert "Bob" Duff** (D) . . . . . . . . . . . . . (860) 240-0414
  Education: Lynchburg BA
Deputy Majority Leader **Beth Bye** (D) . . . . . . . . . . . . . . . (860) 240-0428
  Education: New Hampshire BA, MA
Deputy Majority Leader **Paul R. Doyle** (D) . . . . . . . . . . . (860) 240-0475
  Education: Colby BA; Connecticut JD; U Col Galway
Deputy Majority Leader **Edwin A. "Ed" Gomes** (D) . . . . . (860) 240-0500
Deputy Majority Leader **Andrew M. Maynard** (D) . . . . . . . (860) 240-0591
  Education: Connecticut Col BA
Assistant Majority Leader **Dante Bartolomeo** (D) . . . . . . . (860) 240-0441
  Education: Colby 1991 BA
Assistant Majority Leader
  **Theresa Bielinski "Terry" Gerratana** (D) . . . . . . . . . . . (860) 240-0584
Assistant Majority Leader **Gayle S. Slossberg** (D) . . . . . . .(860) 240-0482
  Education: Cornell 1987 BS; NYU 1990 JD
Assistant Majority Leader **Gary A. Winfield** (D) . . . . . . . . (860) 240-0500
  Education: Navy Nuclear Power
Majority Whip **Mae Flexer** (D) . . . . . . . . . . . . . . . . . . . . . (860) 240-8634
Majority Whip **Edward M. "Ted" Kennedy, Jr.** (D) . . . . . (860) 240-0455
  Education: Wesleyan U 1983 BA; Yale 1991 MES; Connecticut 1997
Majority Whip **Timothy D. "Tim" Larson** (D) . . . . . . . . . (860) 240-0511
  Education: Eastern Connecticut State BA
Majority Whip **Marilyn Moore** (D) . . . . . . . . . . . . . . . . . . (860) 240-0584
Minority Leader **Leonard A. "Len" Fasano** (R) . . . . . . . . (860) 240-8800
  Education: Yale 1981 BS; Quinnipiac 1984 JD; Boston U 1985 LLM
Minority Leader Pro Tem **Kevin Witkos** (R) . . . . . . . . . . . (860) 240-0436
  Education: Connecticut 2007 BA
Deputy Minority Leader Pro Tem and Minority Caucus
  Chairman **Robert J. Kane** (R) . . . . . . . . . . . . . . . . . . . (860) 240-8875
  Education: Central Conn State U; New Haven 2009 MBA
Chief Deputy Minority Leader
  **Antonietta "Toni" Boucher** (R) . . . . . . . . . . . . . . . . . . (203) 762-3232
  Education: Connecticut MBA
Chief Deputy Minority Leader
  **Anthony "Tony" Guglielmo** (R) . . . . . . . . . . . . . . . . . . (860) 684-4164
  Education: Connecticut BA; Trinity Col (CT) MA
Chief Deputy Minority Leader **John A. Kissel** (R) . . . . . . . (860) 240-0531
  Education: Connecticut 1981 BS; Western New England 1984 JD
Deputy Minority Leader **Clark J. Chapin** (R) . . . . . . . . . . .(860) 240-8800
  Education: Rhode Island BS; Iowa State MS
Deputy Minority Leader **L. Scott Frantz** (R) . . . . . . . . . . .(860) 842-1421
Deputy Minority Leader **Michael A. McLachlan** (R) . . . . . .(860) 240-0068
Assistant Minority Leader **Tony Hwang** (R) . . . . . . . . . . . (860) 240-8800
  Education: Cornell BS
Assistant Minority Leader **Kevin C. Kelly** (R) . . . . . . . . . . (860) 240-8800

Assistant Minority Leader **Arthur "Art" Linares** (R) . . . . . .(860) 240-8800
  Education: Tampa 2011
Assistant Minority Leader and Screening Chairman
  **Joe Markley** (R) . . . . . . . . . . . . . . . . . . . . . . . . . . . . . (860) 240-0381
Minority Whip **Paul Formica** (R) . . . . . . . . . . . . . . . . . . . (860) 240-8800
Minority Whip **Henri Martin** (R) . . . . . . . . . . . . . . . . . . . (860) 240-8800
Clerk of the Senate **Garey E. Coleman** . . . . . . . . . . . . . . . (860) 240-0500
Assistant Clerk of the Senate **Cynthia J. Dunne** . . . . . . . . (860) 240-0500

## Senators

**Party Affiliation Statistics:** Republicans: 15, Democrats: 20,
Independents: 1

Senator **Dante Bartolomeo** (D-District 13)
  Legislative Office Building, Room 3200 . . . . . . . . . . . . . . (860) 240-0441
  Counties Represented: Middlesex (part), New Haven (part)
  Term Expires: 2017
  E-mail: dante.bartolomeo@cga.ct.gov
  Committees: Appropriations; Children; Education; Higher Education
  and Employment Advancement
Senator **Antonietta "Toni" Boucher** (R-District 26) . . . . . .(203) 762-3232
  Counties Represented: Fairfield (part)
  Term Expires: 2017
  5 Wicks End Lane, Wilton, CT 06897
  E-mail: toni.boucher@cga.ct.gov
  Committees: Education; Finance, Revenue and Bonding; Judiciary;
  Transportation
Senator **Beth Bye** (D-District 5) . . . . . . . . . . . . . . . . . . . . (860) 240-0428
  Counties Represented: Hartford (part)
  Term Expires: 2017
  99 Outlook Avenue, West Hartford, CT 06119
  E-mail: beth.bye@cga.ct.gov
  Committees: Appropriations; Children; Education; Judiciary; Legislative
  Management
Senator **Stephen T. "Steve" Cassano** (D-District 4) . . . . . (860) 478-5535
  Counties Represented: Hartford (part), Tolland   Res: (860) 646-6882
  (part)
  Term Expires: 2017
  1109 East Middle Turnpike, Manchester, CT 06040
  E-mail: steve.cassano@cga.ct.gov
  Committees: Finance, Revenue and Bonding; Government
  Administration and Elections; Planning and Development;
  Transportation
Senator **Clark J. Chapin** (R-District 30) . . . . . . . . . . . . . . (860) 240-8800
  Counties Represented: Fairfield (part), Litchfield (part)
  Term Expires: 2017
  300 Capitol Avenue, Hartford, CT 06106-1591
  E-mail: clark.chapin@cga.ct.gov
  Committees: Appropriations; Environment; Regulation Review
Senator **Eric D. Coleman** (D-District 2)
  Legislative Office Building, Room 2500 . . . . . . . . . . . . . . (860) 240-5328
  Counties Represented: Hartford (part)
  Term Expires: 2017
  E-mail: eric.coleman@cga.ct.gov
  Committees: Finance, Revenue and Bonding; Judiciary; Legislative
  Management; Program Review and Investigations; Public Safety and
  Security
Senator **Joseph J. "Joe" Crisco, Jr.** (D-District 17)
  Legislative Office Building, Room 2800 . . . . . . . . . . . . . . (860) 240-0189
  Counties Represented: New Haven (part)
  Term Expires: 2017
  E-mail: crisco@senatedems.ct.gov
  Committees: Banks; Commerce; Executive and Legislative
  Nominations; Insurance and Real Estate; Legislative Management;
  Public Health
Senator **Paul R. Doyle** (D-District 9)
  Legislative Office Building, Room 3500 . . . . . . . . . . . . . . (860) 240-0475
  Counties Represented: Hartford (part), Middlesex (part)
  Term Expires: 2017
  E-mail: doyle@senatedems.ct.gov
  Committees: Energy and Technology; Executive and Legislative
  Nominations; Judiciary; Regulation Review
Senator **Robert "Bob" Duff** (D-District 25) . . . . . . . . . . . (860) 240-0414
  Counties Represented: Fairfield (part)   Res: (203) 840-1333
  Term Expires: 2017
  300 Capitol Avenue, Hartford, CT 06106
  E-mail: duff@senatedems.ct.gov
  Committees: Executive and Legislative Nominations; Legislative
  Management; Regulation Review

*(continued on next page)*

**Senators** *continued*

Senator **Leonard A. "Len" Fasano** (R-District 34)
  Legislative Office Building, Room 3400 . . . . . . . . . . . . . . (860) 240-8800
  Counties Represented: Middlesex (part), New Haven (part)
  Term Expires: 2017
  E-mail: len.fasano@cga.ct.gov
  Committees: Executive and Legislative Nominations; Legislative
  Management

Senator **Mae Flexer** (D-District 29) . . . . . . . . . . . . . . . . . . . . (860) 240-8634
  Counties Represented: Tolland (part), Windham (part)
  Term Expires: 2017
  E-mail: mae.flexer@cga.ct.gov
  Committees: Aging; Appropriations; Higher Education and
  Employment Advancement; Judiciary; Veterans' Affairs

Senator **John W. Fonfara** (D-District 1)
  Legislative Office Building, Room 3900 . . . . . . . . . . . . . . (860) 240-0043
  Counties Represented: Hartford (part)
  Term Expires: 2017
  E-mail: fonfara@senatedems.ct.gov
  Committees: Finance, Revenue and Bonding; Legislative Management;
  Planning and Development; Program Review and Investigations

Senator **Paul Formica** (R-District 20) . . . . . . . . . . . . . . . . . (860) 240-8800
  Counties Represented: Middlesex (part), New London (part)
  Term Expires: 2017
  E-mail: paul.formica@cga.ct.gov
  Committees: Appropriations; Energy and Technology; Public Safety and
  Security

Senator **L. Scott Frantz** (R-District 36)
  Legislative Office Building, Room 3400 . . . . . . . . . . . . . . (860) 842-1421
  Counties Represented: Fairfield (part)
  Term Expires: 2017
  E-mail: scott.frantz@cga.ct.gov
  Committees: Commerce; Finance, Revenue and Bonding; Legislative
  Management; Transportation

Senator
  **Theresa Bielinski "Terry" Gerratana** (D-District 6) . . . . (860) 240-0584
  Counties Represented: Hartford (part)
  Term Expires: 2017
  674 Lincoln Street, New Britain, CT 06052
  E-mail: terry.gerratana@cga.ct.gov
  Committees: Appropriations; Government Administration and Elections;
  Judiciary; Public Health

Senator **Edwin A. "Ed" Gomes** (D-District 23) . . . . . . . . (860) 240-0500
  Counties Represented: Fairfield (part)
  Term Expires: 2017
  E-mail: ed.gomes@cga.ct.gov
  Committees: Labor and Public Employees; Public Safety and Security;
  Veterans' Affairs

Senator **Anthony "Tony" Guglielmo** (R-District 35) . . . . . (860) 684-4164
  Counties Represented: Tolland (part), Windham    Res: (860) 684-4878
  (part)
  Term Expires: 2017
  100 Stafford Street, Stafford Springs, CT 06076
  E-mail: anthony.guglielmo@cga.ct.gov
  Committees: Executive and Legislative Nominations; Program Review
  and Investigations; Public Safety and Security

Senator **Joan V. Hartley** (D-District 15)
  Legislative Office Building, Room 1800 . . . . . . . . . . . . . . (860) 240-0006
  Counties Represented: New Haven (part)
  Term Expires: 2017
  E-mail: hartley@senatedems.ct.gov
  Committees: Appropriations; Commerce; Executive and Legislative
  Nominations; Insurance and Real Estate; Legislative Management;
  Public Safety and Security

Senator **Tony Hwang** (R-District 28) . . . . . . . . . . . . . . . . . . (860) 240-8800
  Counties Represented: Fairfield (part)
  Term Expires: 2017
  E-mail: tony.hwang@cga.ct.gov
  Committees: Commerce; Housing; Labor and Public Employees;
  Veterans' Affairs

Senator **Robert J. Kane** (R-District 32) . . . . . . . . . . . . . . . (860) 240-8875
  Counties Represented: Litchfield (part), New Haven (part)
  Term Expires: 2017
  P.O. Box 232, Watertown, CT 06795
  E-mail: rob.kane@cga.ct.gov
  Committees: Appropriations; Executive and Legislative Nominations;
  Public Health

Senator **Kevin C. Kelly** (R-District 21)
  Legislative Office Building, Room 3400 . . . . . . . . . . . . . . (860) 240-8800
  Counties Represented: Fairfield (part), New Haven (part)
  Term Expires: 2017
  E-mail: kevin.kelly@cga.ct.gov
  Committees: Aging; Insurance and Real Estate; Legislative
  Management; Regulation Review

Senator **Edward M. "Ted" Kennedy, Jr.** (D-District 12) . . (860) 240-0455
  Counties Represented: Middlesex (part), New Haven (part)
  Term Expires: 2017
  E-mail: ted.kennedy@cga.ct.gov
  Committees: Environment; Public Health; Transportation

Senator **John A. Kissel** (R-District 7) . . . . . . . . . . . . . . . . . (860) 240-0531
  Counties Represented: Hartford (part), Tolland    Res: (860) 745-0668
  (part)
  Term Expires: 2017
  16 Frew Terrace, Enfield, CT 06082
  E-mail: john.a.kissel@cga.ct.gov
  Committees: Appropriations; General Law; Judiciary; Program Review
  and Investigations
  Affiliation: Attorney, Fallon, Barbieri & Gilcreast, P.C.

Senator **Timothy D. "Tim" Larson** (D-District 3) . . . . . . . . (860) 240-0511
  Counties Represented: Hartford (part), Tolland (part)
  Term Expires: 2017
  E-mail: timothy.larson@cga.ct.gov
  Committees: Commerce; Energy and Technology; General Law

Senator **Carlo Leone** (D-District 27) . . . . . . . . . . . . . . . . . . (203) 323-2138
  Counties Represented: Fairfield (part)
  Term Expires: 2017
  88 Houston Terrace, Stamford, CT 06902
  E-mail: carlo.leone@cga.ct.gov
  Committees: Banks; Finance, Revenue and Bonding; General Law;
  Regulation Review; Transportation

Senator **Arthur "Art" Linares** (R-District 33) . . . . . . . . . . . (860) 240-8800
  Counties Represented: Middlesex (part), New London (part)
  Term Expires: 2017
  300 Capitol Avenue, Hartford, CT 06106
  E-mail: art.linares@cga.ct.gov
  Committees: Education; Judiciary; Planning and Development
  Affiliation: Co-Founder, Business Development, Greenskies Renewable
  Energy LLC
  10 Main Street, Suite E, Middletown, CT 06457

Senator **Martin M. Looney** (D-District 11)
  Legislative Office Building, Room 3300 . . . . . . . . . . . . . . (860) 240-8629
  Counties Represented: New Haven (part)
  Term Expires: 2017
  E-mail: looney@senatedems.ct.gov
  Committees: Executive and Legislative Nominations; Legislative
  Management
  Affiliation: Attorney, Keyes & Looney

Senator **Joe Markley** (R-District 16) . . . . . . . . . . . . . . . . . . (860) 240-0381
  Counties Represented: Hartford (part), New Haven (part)
  Term Expires: 2017
  47 Elm Street, Plantsville, CT 06479
  E-mail: joe.markley@cga.ct.gov
  Committees: Appropriations; Human Services; Program Review and
  Investigations; Public Health

Senator **Henri Martin** (R-District 31) . . . . . . . . . . . . . . . . . . (860) 240-8800
  Counties Represented: Hartford (part), Litchfield (part)
  Term Expires: 2017
  E-mail: henri.martin@cga.ct.gov
  Committees: Banks; Children; Transportation; Veterans' Affairs

Senator **Andrew M. Maynard** (D-District 18)
  Legislative Office Building, Room 2300 . . . . . . . . . . . . . . (860) 240-0591
  Counties Represented: New London (part), Windham (part)
  Term Expires: 2017
  E-mail: maynard@senatedems.ct.gov
  Committees: Program Review and Investigations; Transportation

Senator **Michael A. McLachlan** (R-District 24)
  Legislative Office Building, Room 3400 . . . . . . . . . . . . . . (860) 240-0068
  Counties Represented: Fairfield (part)
  Term Expires: 2017
  E-mail: michael.mclachlan@cga.ct.gov
  Committees: Finance, Revenue and Bonding; Government
  Administration and Elections; Judiciary

Senator **Marilyn Moore** (D-District 22) . . . . . . . . . . . . . . . . (860) 240-0584
  Counties Represented: Fairfield (part)
  Term Expires: 2017
  E-mail: marilyn.moore@cga.ct.gov
  Committees: Environment; Finance, Revenue and Bonding; Human
  Services; Public Health

**LEGISLATIVE BRANCH**

Senator **Catherine A. "Cathy" Osten** (D-District 19)
Legislative Office Building, Room 3800 . . . . . . . . . . . . . (860) 240-0579
Counties Represented: Hartford (part), New London (part), Tolland (part)
Term Expires: 2017
E-mail: catherine.osten@cga.ct.gov
Committees: Aging; Housing; Labor and Public Employees; Planning and Development; Transportation

Senator **Gayle S. Slossberg** (D-District 14)
Legislative Office Building, Room 2200 . . . . . . . . . . . . . (860) 240-0482
Counties Represented: New Haven (part)          Res: (203) 878-6412
Term Expires: 2017
E-mail: slossberg@senatedems.ct.gov
Committees: Appropriations; Education; General Law; Human Services

Senator **Gary A. Winfield** (D-District 10)
Legislative Office Building, Room 3800 . . . . . . . . . . . . . (860) 240-0500
Counties Represented: New Haven (part)
Term Expires: 2017
E-mail: gary.holder-winfield@cga.ct.gov
Committees: Appropriations; Education; Finance, Revenue and Bonding; Housing; Judiciary; Public Safety and Security

Senator **Kevin Witkos** (R-District 8)
Legislative Office Building, Room 3400 . . . . . . . . . . . . . (860) 240-0436
Counties Represented: Hartford (part), Litchfield (part)
Term Expires: 2017
E-mail: kevin.witkos@cga.ct.gov
Committees: General Law; Higher Education and Employment Advancement; Legislative Management; Regulation Review

# Connecticut House of Representatives

Tel: (860) 240-0400  Tel: (860) 240-8500 (Democratic Leadership)
Tel: (860) 240-8585 (House Democrats)
Tel: (860) 240-8700 (Republican Leadership)
Tel: (860) 240-8787 (House Republicans)

Speaker of the House **J. Brendan Sharkey** (D) . . . . . . . . (203) 281-4647
Education: Georgetown 1984 BA; Connecticut 1989 JD

Deputy Speaker of the House **Linda M. Gentile** (D) . . . . . (203) 732-8386

Deputy Speaker of the House
**Robert D. "Bob" Godfrey** (D) . . . . . . . . . . . . . . . . . . . . (203) 778-5127
Education: Fordham 1970 AB; Connecticut 1985 JD

Deputy Speaker of the House **Patricia Billie Miller** (D) . . . (860) 240-8585
Education: Moravian BS

Deputy Speaker of the House **Linda A. Orange** (D) . . . . . . (860) 537-3936

Deputy Speaker of the House **Kevin Ryan** (D) . . . . . . . . . . (860) 848-0790
Education: Villanova 1974 BA, 1974 BS;
Penn Col Optometry 1976 BS, 1978 OD; New Haven 1989 AM

Deputy Speaker of the House **Peggy Sayers** (D) . . . . . . . . (860) 623-3868

Assistant Deputy Speaker of the House
**Emil "Buddy" Altobello, Jr.** (D) . . . . . . . . . . . . . . . . . . . (203) 634-1692

Assistant Deputy Speaker of the House
**Louis P. "Lou" Esposito, Jr.** (D) . . . . . . . . . . . . . . . . . . . (860) 240-8500

Assistant Deputy Speaker of the House
**Mary G. Fritz** (D) . . . . . . . . . . . . . . . . . . . . . . . . . . . . . (203) 269-1169
Education: Emmanuel (MA) 1959 BA; Boston Col; Trinity Col (CT); Fairfield

Majority Leader **Joe Aresimowicz** (D) . . . . . . . . . . . . . . . (860) 371-6887

Deputy Majority Leader **Juan R. Candelaria** (D) . . . . . . . . (860) 240-8585

Deputy Majority Leader **Michelle L. Cook** (D) . . . . . . . . . (860) 240-8585
Education: Central Conn State U BS

Deputy Majority Leader **Gregory "Gregg" Haddad** (D) . . (860) 429-8517

Deputy Majority Leader **Susan M. Johnson** (D) . . . . . . . . (860) 240-8585
Education: Eastern Connecticut State 1974; Western New England JD

Deputy Majority Leader **Douglas McCrory** (D) . . . . . . . . . (860) 560-0242
Education: Hartford BA, MBA; Sacred Heart U MEA

Deputy Majority Leader **Russell A. Morin** (D) . . . . . . . . . (860) 257-3876

Deputy Majority Leader **Jason Rojas** (D) . . . . . . . . . . . . . (860) 240-0549
Education: Connecticut BA; Trinity Col (CT) MPP

Assistant Majority Leader **Angel Arce** (D) . . . . . . . . . . . . (860) 240-8585

Assistant Majority Leader **David Arconti, Jr.** (D) . . . . . . . (860) 240-8466
Education: Southern Connecticut State U 2008 BS

Assistant Majority Leader
**Michael V. "Mike" Demicco** (D) . . . . . . . . . . . . . . . . . . . (860) 240-8585
Education: Wesleyan U 1980 BA

Assistant Majority Leader **John K. Hampton** (D) . . . . . . . . (860) 240-8585
Education: Hartford 1990 BA

Assistant Majority Leader **Ernest Hewett** (D) . . . . . . . . . . (860) 240-8585

Assistant Majority Leader **Rick Lopes** (D) . . . . . . . . . . . . (860) 229-7721

Assistant Majority Leader **Brandon McGee** (D) . . . . . . . . (860) 240-8585
Education: Alabama State 2006 BS; Albertus Magnus 2013 MS

Assistant Majority Leader **Frank N. Nicastro, Sr.** (D) . . . . . (860) 585-6070

Assistant Majority Leader **Emmett D. Riley** (D) . . . . . . . . (860) 240-8585
Education: Eastern Connecticut State BA

Assistant Majority Leader
**Daniel S. "Danny" Rovero** (D) . . . . . . . . . . . . . . . . . . . (860) 774-3792

Assistant Majority Leader
**Robert "Bobby" Sanchez** (D) . . . . . . . . . . . . . . . . . . . (860) 225-4807

Assistant Majority Leader **Hilda E. Santiago** (D) . . . . . . . (860) 240-8585
Education: Southern Connecticut State U BS

Majority Caucus Chair **Roland J. Lemar** (D) . . . . . . . . . . (203) 903-5003

Deputy Majority Caucus Chair
**Elizabeth A. "Betty" Boukus** (D) . . . . . . . . . . . . . . . . . (860) 240-8585
Education: Central Conn State U BS; Hartford MEd

Chief Majority Whip **Minnie Gonzalez** (D) . . . . . . . . . . . (860) 236-9654

Majority Whip at Large **Jonathan Steinberg** (D) . . . . . . . (203) 722-7477

Deputy Majority Whip at Large
**David William Kiner** (D) . . . . . . . . . . . . . . . . . . . . . . . . (860) 265-3366

Deputy Majority Whip at Large **Joe Verrengia** (D) . . . . . . (860) 240-8585

Deputy Majority Whip **Henry J. Genga** (D) . . . . . . . . . . . (860) 569-8008
Education: Hartford BA; New Haven MEd

Deputy Majority Whip **Ezequiel Santiago** (D) . . . . . . . . . (860) 240-8585

Assistant Majority Whip **Patricia A. Dillon** (D) . . . . . . . . (203) 387-6159
Education: Ohio State; Yale

Assistant Majority Whip **Daniel J. Fox** (D) . . . . . . . . . . . . (203) 324-6777
Education: Loyola Col (MD) BA; New England JD

Assistant Majority Whip **Mary M. Mushinsky** (D) . . . . . . . (203) 269-8378

Assistant Majority Whip **Kim Rose** (D) . . . . . . . . . . . . . . (203) 283-7885

Assistant Majority Whip
**Charles L. "Charlie" Stallworth** (D) . . . . . . . . . . . . . . . (860) 240-8585

Minority Leader **Themis Klarides** (R) . . . . . . . . . . . . . . . (860) 240-8700
Education: Trinity Col (CT) BA; Quinnipiac U 1992 JD

Deputy Minority Leader
**Vincent J. "Vinny" Candelora** (R) . . . . . . . . . . . . . . . . . (860) 240-8700
Education: Connecticut Col 1992; Dickinson Law 1995

Deputy Minority Leader **Laura Hoydick** (R) . . . . . . . . . . . (860) 240-8700
Education: Sacred Heart U BA

Deputy Minority Leader **Craig A. Miner** (R) . . . . . . . . . . . (860) 240-8700

Deputy Minority Leader At Large **Arthur J. O'Neill** (R) . . . (860) 240-8700
Education: Connecticut; Rutgers JD

Assistant Minority Leader **Mike Alberts** (R) . . . . . . . . . . . (860) 240-8700
Education: Connecticut 1980 BA, 1987 MBA

Assistant Minority Leader **William "Bill" Aman** (R) . . . . . (860) 240-8700
Education: Ithaca 1968 BS; Long Island 1972 MBA

Assistant Minority Leader **Livvy R. Floren** (R) . . . . . . . . . (860) 240-8700
Education: Vassar AB; Adelphi MBA; Manhattanville MAT

Assistant Minority Leader **Janice R. Giegler** (R) . . . . . . . . (860) 240-8700
Education: Ohio State BA; Green Mountain

Assistant Minority Leader **Craig A. Miner** (R) . . . . . . . . . . (860) 240-8700

Assistant Minority Leader **Jason D. Perillo, CPA** (R) . . . . . (860) 240-8700
Education: Georgetown BA; Boston Col 2005 MBA; Harvard MPA

Senior Minority Whip **John E. Piscopo** (R) . . . . . . . . . . . (860) 240-8700
Education: Eastern Connecticut State 1977 BA

Minority Whip **Anthony J. "Tony" D'Amelio** (R) . . . . . . . (860) 240-8700

Minority Whip **John H. Frey** (R) . . . . . . . . . . . . . . . . . . . (860) 240-8700
Education: Western Connecticut St

Minority Whip **David K. Labriola** (R) . . . . . . . . . . . . . . . . (860) 240-8700
Education: Yale 1982 BA; Connecticut 1985 JD

Minority Whip **Selim G. Noujaim** (R) . . . . . . . . . . . . . . . (860) 240-8700
Education: Central Conn State U BS; New Haven MBA

Clerk of the House **Martin J. Dunleavy** . . . . . . . . . . . . . . (860) 240-0401

# Representatives

**Party Affiliation Statistics:** Republicans: 64, Democrats: 87

Representative
**Catherine F. "Cathy" Abercrombie** (D-District 83) . . . . (203) 634-8770
Counties Represented: Hartford (part), New Haven (part)
Term Expires: 2017
64 Parker Avenue, Meriden, CT 06450
E-mail: catherine.abercrombie@cga.ct.gov
Committees: Appropriations; Human Services; Insurance and Real Estate

*(continued on next page)*

LEGISLATIVE BRANCH

**Representatives** *continued*

Representative **Timothy Ackert** (R-District 8) . . . . . . . . . . (860) 742-5287
  Counties Represented: Tolland (part)
  Term Expires: 2017
  67 Deer Lane, Coventry, CT 06238
  E-mail: tim.ackert@housegop.ct.gov
  Committees: Education; Energy and Technology; Higher Education and
  Employment Advancement

Representative **Terry B. Adams** (D-District 14) . . . . . . . . . (860) 240-8533
  Counties Represented: Hartford (part)
  Term Expires: 2017
  E-mail: terry.b.adams@cga.ct.gov
  Committees: Banks; Housing; Public Safety and Security

Representative **Alfred "Al" Adinolfi** (R-District 103) . . . . . .(860) 240-8700
  Counties Represented: Hartford (part), New Haven (part)
  Term Expires: 2017
  Legislative Office Building, Room 4200, Hartford, CT 06106-1591
  E-mail: al.adinolfi@housegop.ct.gov
  Committees: Aging; Judiciary; Public Health; Veterans' Affairs

Representative **Mike Alberts** (R-District 50) Room 4200 . . (860) 240-8700
  Counties Represented: Tolland (part), Windham (part)
  Term Expires: 2017
  E-mail: mike.alberts@housegop.ct.gov
  Committees: Banks; Commerce; Higher Education and Employment
  Advancement

Representative **James M. Albis** (D-District 99)
  Room 5005 . . . . . . . . . . . . . . . . . . . . . . . . . . . . . . . . . . . . (860) 240-8585
  Counties Represented: New Haven (part)
  Term Expires: 2017
  E-mail: james.albis@cga.ct.gov
  Committees: Environment; Executive and Legislative Nominations;
  Finance, Revenue and Bonding; Judiciary

Representative
**Capt David Alexander, USMCR** (D-District 58) . . . . . . . (860) 240-8585
  Counties Represented: Hartford (part)
  Term Expires: 2017
  27 Peral Street, Enfield, CT 06082
  E-mail: david.alexander@cga.ct.gov
  Committees: Finance, Revenue and Bonding; Government
  Administration and Elections; Public Health; Veterans' Affairs
  Education: Trinity Col (CT) 2003 BA; Connecticut 2006 JD

Representative
**Emil "Buddy" Altobello, Jr.** (D-District 82) . . . . . . . . . (203) 634-1692
  Counties Represented: Middlesex (part), New Haven (part)
  Term Expires: 2017
  Legislative Office Building, Room 4015, Hartford, CT 06106-1591
  E-mail: emil.altobello@cga.ct.gov
  Committees: Finance, Revenue and Bonding; General Law; Regulation
  Review

Representative **William "Bill" Aman** (R-District 14)
  Room 4200 . . . . . . . . . . . . . . . . . . . . . . . . . . . . . . . . . . . . (860) 240-8700
  Counties Represented: Hartford (part)
  Term Expires: 2017
  E-mail: bill.aman@cga.ct.gov
  Committees: Appropriations; General Law; Judiciary; Planning and
  Development

Representative **Angel Arce** (D-District 4) . . . . . . . . . . . . . (860) 240-8585
  Counties Represented: Hartford (part)
  Term Expires: 2017
  248 Franklin Avenue, Hartford, CT 06114
  E-mail: angel.arce@cga.ct.gov
  Committees: Finance, Revenue and Bonding; Housing; Transportation

Representative **David Arconti, Jr.** (D-District 109) . . . . . . . (860) 240-8466
  Counties Represented: Fairfield (part)
  Term Expires: 2017
  141 Great Plain Road, Danbury, CT 06811
  E-mail: david.arconti@cga.ct.gov
  Committees: Environment; General Law; Housing; Public Safety and
  Security

Representative **Joe Aresimowicz** (D-District 30)
  Room 4110 . . . . . . . . . . . . . . . . . . . . . . . . . . . . . . . . . . . . (860) 371-6887
  Counties Represented: Hartford (part)
  Term Expires: 2017
  248 Lower Lane, Berlin, CT 06037
  E-mail: joe.aresimowicz@cga.ct.gov
  Committees: Legislative Management

Representative **Andre F. Baker, Jr.** (D-District 124) . . . . . .(860) 240-8585
  Counties Represented: Fairfield (part)
  Term Expires: 2017
  E-mail: andre.baker@cga.ct.gov
  Committees: Appropriations; Education; Public Health

Representative **David A. Baram** (D-District 15) . . . . . . . . . (860) 240-8500
  Counties Represented: Hartford (part)
  Term Expires: 2017
  Legislative Office Building, Room 5006, Hartford, CT 06106-1591
  E-mail: david.baram@cga.ct.gov
  Committees: Banks; General Law; Judiciary
  Education: Connecticut 1975 BA

Representative **Brian Becker** (D-District 19) . . . . . . . . . . . .(860) 240-8585
  Counties Represented: Hartford (part)           Res: (860) 233-3615
  Term Expires: 2017
  14 Candlewood Drive, West Hartford, CT 06117
  E-mail: brian.becker@cga.ct.gov
  Committees: Commerce; Energy and Technology; Government
  Administration and Elections; Regulation Review

Representative **Sam Belsito** (R-District 53) Room 4200 . . .(860) 240-8700
  Counties Represented: Tolland (part), Windham     Dist: (860) 454-8002
  (part)
  Term Expires: 2017
  55 Lee Lane, Tolland, CT 06084
  E-mail: sam.belsito@housegop.ct.gov
  Committees: Appropriations; Planning and Development

Representative **Jeffrey J. Berger** (D-District 73) . . . . . . . . . (860) 240-8500
  Counties Represented: New Haven (part)
  Term Expires: 2017
  134 Gaylord Avenue, Waterbury, CT 06708
  E-mail: jeffrey.berger@cga.ct.gov
  Committees: Executive and Legislative Nominations; Finance, Revenue
  and Bonding; Judiciary

Representative **Eric C. Berthel** (R-District 68) . . . . . . . . . . (860) 240-8700
  Counties Represented: Litchfield (part)
  Term Expires: 2017
  E-mail: eric.berthel@housegop.ct.gov
  Committees: Education; Finance, Revenue and Bonding; Public Health

Representative **Whit Betts** (R-District 78) . . . . . . . . . . . . . (860) 240-8700
  Counties Represented: Hartford (part), Litchfield     Res: (860) 582-7105
  (part)
  Term Expires: 2017
  1924 Perkins Street, Bristol, CT 06010
  E-mail: whit.betts@housegop.ct.gov
  Committees: Appropriations; Higher Education and Employment
  Advancement; Program Review and Investigations; Public Health

Representative **Mike Bocchino** (R-District 15) . . . . . . . . . . (860) 240-8700
  Counties Represented: Hartford (part)
  Term Expires: 2017
  E-mail: mike.bocchino@housegop.ct.gov
  Committees: Children; Energy and Technology; Higher Education and
  Employment Advancement

Representative **Mitch Bolinsky** (R-District 106) . . . . . . . . . (800) 842-1423
  Counties Represented: Fairfield (part)
  Term Expires: 2017
  Legislative Office Building, Room 4200, Hartford, CT 06106-1591
  E-mail: mitch.bolinsky@housegop.ct.gov
  Committees: Aging; Appropriations; Education
  Education: SUNY (Buffalo) (Attended);
  Wisconsin (Whitewater) 1980 BBA

Representative
**Elizabeth A. "Betty" Boukus** (D-District 22) . . . . . . . . . (860) 240-8585
  Counties Represented: Hartford (part)
  Term Expires: 2017
  43 Hollyberry Lane, Plainville, CT 06062
  E-mail: betty.boukus@cga.ct.gov
  Committees: Finance, Revenue and Bonding; Public Safety and
  Security

Representative **Paul Brycki** (D-District 45) . . . . . . . . . . . . . (860) 240-8585
  Counties Represented: New London (part), Windham (part)
  Term Expires: 2017
  E-mail: paul.brycki@cga.ct.gov
  Committees: Commerce; Finance, Revenue and Bonding; Housing

Representative **Cecilia Buck-Taylor** (R-District 67) . . . . . . . (800) 842-1423
  Counties Represented: Litchfield (part)
  Term Expires: 2017
  Legislative Office Building, Room 4200, Hartford, CT 06106-1591
  E-mail: cecilia.buck-taylor@housegop.ct.gov
  Committees: Executive and Legislative Nominations; Human Services;
  Judiciary
  Education: SUNY (Albany) BA; Fordham 1991 JD

Representative **Aundré Bumgardner** (R-District 41) . . . . . . (860) 240-0401
  Counties Represented: New London (part)
  Term Expires: 2017
  E-mail: aundre.bumgardner@housegop.ct.gov
  Committees: Education; Finance, Revenue and Bonding; Transportation

Representative **Larry B. Butler** (D-District 72) . . . . . . . . . . (203) 754-4773
Counties Represented: New Haven (part)
Term Expires: 2017
70 Blackman Road, Waterbury, CT 06704
E-mail: larry.butler@cga.ct.gov
Committees: Finance, Revenue and Bonding; Housing; Human Services
Education: Central Conn State U

Representative **Gary Byron** (R-District 27) . . . . . . . . . . . . (860) 240-8700
Counties Represented: Hartford (part)
Term Expires: 2017
E-mail: gary.byron@housegop.ct.gov
Committees: Environment; Housing; Human Services

Representative **Fred Camillo** (R-District 151)
Room 4200 . . . . . . . . . . . . . . . . . . . . . . . . . . . . . . . . . . . . (860) 240-8700
Counties Represented: Fairfield (part)
Term Expires: 2017
E-mail: fred.camillo@housegop.ct.gov
Committees: Banks; Commerce; Executive and Legislative Nominations
Education: Manhattanville 1996 BA

Representative **Juan R. Candelaria** (D-District 95) . . . . . . . (860) 240-8585
Counties Represented: New Haven (part)
Term Expires: 2017
28 Arch Street, New Haven, CT 06519
E-mail: juan.candelaria@cga.ct.gov
Committees: Appropriations; Children; Education; Higher Education
and Employment Advancement; Legislative Management

Representative
**Vincent J. "Vinny" Candelora** (R-District 86)
Room 4200 . . . . . . . . . . . . . . . . . . . . . . . . . . . . . . . . . . . . (860) 240-8700
Counties Represented: Middlesex (part), New Haven (part)
Term Expires: 2017
E-mail: vincent.candelora@housegop.ct.gov
Committees: Finance, Revenue and Bonding; Judiciary; Legislative
Management; Public Health; Regulation Review

Representative **Devin R. Carney** (R-District 23) . . . . . . . . . (860) 240-0401
Counties Represented: Middlesex (part), New London (part)
Term Expires: 2017
E-mail: devin.carney@housegop.ct.gov
Committees: Environment; Higher Education and Employment
Advancement; Transportation

Representative **Christie Carpino** (R-District 32) . . . . . . . . . (860) 635-8725
Counties Represented: Middlesex (part)
Term Expires: 2017
29 Sovereign Ridge, Cromwell, CT 06416
E-mail: christie.carpino@housegop.ct.gov
Committees: Judiciary; Program Review and Investigations; Public
Health

Representative **Dan Carter** (R-District 2) . . . . . . . . . . . . . . (860) 240-8700
Counties Represented: Fairfield (part)                Res: (203) 917-5027
Term Expires: 2017
P.O. Box 907, Bethel, CT 06801
E-mail: dan.carter@housegop.ct.gov
Committees: Education; Finance, Revenue and Bonding; General Law

Representative **Jay M. Case** (R-District 63) . . . . . . . . . . . . (860) 842-1423
Counties Represented: Litchfield (part)
Term Expires: 2017
Legislative Office Building, Room 4200, Hartford, CT 06106-1591
E-mail: jay.case@housegop.ct.gov
Committees: Appropriations; Environment; Human Services

Representative **Theresa W. Conroy** (D-District 105)
Room 4000 . . . . . . . . . . . . . . . . . . . . . . . . . . . . . . . . . . . . (860) 240-8585
Counties Represented: New Haven (part)
Term Expires: 2017
177 Skokorat Street, Seymour, CT 06483
E-mail: theresa.conroy@cga.ct.gov
Committees: Planning and Development; Public Health; Veterans'
Affairs
Education: Quinnipiac AA; Southern Connecticut State U BA;
Fairfield MA

Representative **Michelle L. Cook** (D-District 65) . . . . . . . . (860) 240-8585
Counties Represented: Litchfield (part)
Term Expires: 2017
Legislative Office Building, Room 4044, Hartford, CT 06106-1591
499 Charles Street, Torrington, CT 06790
E-mail: michelle.cook@cga.ct.gov
Committees: Aging; Education; Human Services; Legislative
Management; Public Health

Representative **Jeffrey Currey** (D-District 11) . . . . . . . . . . (860) 240-8585
Counties Represented: Hartford (part)
Term Expires: 2017
E-mail: jeff.currey@cga.ct.gov
Committees: Education; Insurance and Real Estate; Judiciary

Representative **Michael C. D'Agostino** (D-District 91) . . . . (860) 240-8585
Counties Represented: New Haven (part)
Term Expires: 2017
575 Ridge Road, Hamden, CT 06517
E-mail: michael.dagostino@cga.ct.gov
Committees: Education; Finance, Revenue and Bonding; Planning and
Development
Education: Virginia 1993 BA, 1996 JD

Representative
**Anthony J. "Tony" D'Amelio** (R-District 71)
Room 4200 . . . . . . . . . . . . . . . . . . . . . . . . . . . . . . . . . . . . (860) 240-8700
Counties Represented: New Haven (part)
Term Expires: 2017
E-mail: anthony.damelio@housegop.ct.gov
Committees: Commerce; General Law; Public Safety and Security

Representative **Stephen D. Dargan** (D-District 115) . . . . . . (203) 937-1985
Counties Represented: New Haven (part)
Term Expires: 2017
215 Beach Street, West Haven, CT 06516
E-mail: stephen.dargan@cga.ct.gov
Committees: Executive and Legislative Nominations; Insurance and
Real Estate; Public Safety and Security
Education: Quinnipiac

Representative **Christopher Davis** (R-District 57)
Room 4200 . . . . . . . . . . . . . . . . . . . . . . . . . . . . . . . . . . . . (860) 240-8700
Counties Represented: Hartford (part), Tolland (part)
Term Expires: 2017
E-mail: christopher.davis@housegop.ct.gov
Committees: Finance, Revenue and Bonding; Housing; Insurance and
Real Estate

Representative
**Michael V. "Mike" Demicco** (D-District 21) . . . . . . . . . (860) 240-8585
Counties Represented: Hartford (part)
Term Expires: 2017
6 Deborah Lane, Farmington, CT 06032
E-mail: mike.demicco@cga.ct.gov
Committees: Energy and Technology; Environment; Public Health

Representative **Laura Devlin** (R-District 13) . . . . . . . . . . . . (860) 240-8700
Counties Represented: Hartford (part)
Term Expires: 2017
E-mail: laura.devlin@housegop.ct.gov
Committees: Finance, Revenue and Bonding; Government
Administration and Elections; Transportation

Representative **Patricia A. Dillon** (D-District 92) . . . . . . . . (203) 387-6159
Counties Represented: New Haven (part)
Term Expires: 2017
68 West Rock Avenue, New Haven, CT 06515
E-mail: patricia.dillon@cga.ct.gov
Committees: Appropriations; Environment; Higher Education and
Employment Advancement; Judiciary

Representative **Doug Dubitsky** (R-District 47) . . . . . . . . . . (860) 240-8700
Counties Represented: New London (part), Windham (part)
Term Expires: 2017
E-mail: doug.dubitsky@housegop.ct.gov
Committees: Environment; Judiciary; Planning and Development
Education: SUNY (Purchase) BFA; Utah 1999 JD

Representative
**Louis P. "Lou" Esposito, Jr.** (D-District 116) . . . . . . . . . (860) 240-8500
Counties Represented: New Haven (part)
Term Expires: 2017
56 Lakeview Avenue, West Haven, CT 06516
E-mail: lou.esposito@cga.ct.gov
Committees: General Law; Labor and Public Employees; Legislative
Management; Public Safety and Security

Representative **Charles J. Ferraro** (R-District 11) . . . . . . . . (860) 240-8700
Counties Represented: Hartford (part)
Term Expires: 2017
E-mail: charles.ferraro@housegop.ct.gov
Committees: Appropriations; Public Safety and Security

Representative **Andrew M. Fleischmann** (D-District 18) . . (860) 240-0420
Counties Represented: Hartford (part)            Fax: (860) 240-0206
Term Expires: 2017
Legislative Office Building, Room 3101, Hartford, CT 06106-1591
E-mail: andrew.fleischmann@cga.ct.gov
Committees: Appropriations; Education
Education: Princeton 1986 BS; Stanford MA

Representative **Livvy R. Floren** (R-District 149)
Room 4200 . . . . . . . . . . . . . . . . . . . . . . . . . . . . . . . . . . . . (860) 240-8700
Counties Represented: Fairfield (part)
Term Expires: 2017
E-mail: livvy.floren@housegop.ct.gov
Committees: Finance, Revenue and Bonding; Insurance and Real Estate

*(continued on next page)*

**Representatives** *continued*

Representative **Daniel J. Fox** (D-District 148) . . . . . . . . . . (203) 324-6777
Counties Represented: Fairfield (part)
Term Expires: 2017
14 Carter Drive, Apartment 2H, Stamford, CT 06902
E-mail: dan.fox@cga.ct.gov
Committees: Finance, Revenue and Bonding; Judiciary; Planning and
Development

Representative **Mike France** (R-District 42) . . . . . . . . . . . . (860) 240-8700
Counties Represented: New London (part)
Term Expires: 2017
E-mail: mike.france@housegop.ct.gov
Committees: Appropriations; Government Administration and Elections;
Planning and Development

Representative **John H. Frey** (R-District 111)
Room 4200 . . . . . . . . . . . . . . . . . . . . . . . . . . . . . . . (860) 240-8700
Counties Represented: Fairfield (part)
Term Expires: 2017
E-mail: john.frey@housegop.ct.gov
Committees: Banks; Finance, Revenue and Bonding; Housing

Representative **Mary G. Fritz** (D-District 90) . . . . . . . . . . . (203) 269-1169
Counties Represented: New Haven (part)
Term Expires: 2017
43 Grove Street, Yalesville, CT 06492
E-mail: mary.fritz@cga.ct.gov
Committees: Judiciary; Planning and Development

Representative **Henry J. Genga** (D-District 10) . . . . . . . . . . (860) 569-8008
Counties Represented: Hartford (part)
Term Expires: 2017
Five Elaine Drive, East Hartford, CT 06118-3515
E-mail: henry.genga@cga.ct.gov
E-mail: hgenga@sbcglobal.net
Committees: Appropriations; Education; Program Review and
Investigations; Public Health

Representative **Linda M. Gentile** (D-District 104) . . . . . . . . (203) 732-8386
Counties Represented: New Haven (part)
Term Expires: 2017
158 Hodge Avenue, Ansonia, CT 06401
E-mail: linda.gentile@cga.ct.gov
Committees: Commerce; Higher Education and Employment
Advancement; Legislative Management

Representative **Janice R. Giegler** (R-District 138)
Room 4200 . . . . . . . . . . . . . . . . . . . . . . . . . . . . . . . (860) 240-8700
Counties Represented: Fairfield (part)
Term Expires: 2017
E-mail: janice.giegler@housegop.ct.gov
Committees: Executive and Legislative Nominations; Public Safety and
Security; Transportation

Representative
**Robert D. "Bob" Godfrey** (D-District 110) . . . . . . . . . . (203) 778-5127
Counties Represented: Fairfield (part)
Term Expires: 2017
13 Stillman Avenue, Danbury, CT 06810-8007
E-mail: bob.godfrey@cga.ct.gov
E-mail: bobgodfrey110@hotmail.com
Committees: Executive and Legislative Nominations; Judiciary;
Legislative Management; Regulation Review

Representative **Minnie Gonzalez** (D-District 3) . . . . . . . . . (860) 236-9654
Counties Represented: Hartford (part)
Term Expires: 2017
97 Amity Street, Hartford, CT 06106
E-mail: minnie.gonzalez@cga.ct.gov
Committees: Appropriations; Judiciary; Public Safety and Security

Representative **Joe Gresko** (D-District 121) . . . . . . . . . . . . (860) 240-0400
Counties Represented: Fairfield (part)
Term Expires: 2017
E-mail: joseph.gresko@cga.ct.gov
Committees: Energy and Technology; Environment; Judiciary

Representative
**Antonio "Tony" Guerrera** (D-District 29) . . . . . . . . . . . (860) 513-1406
Counties Represented: Hartford (part)
Term Expires: 2017
194 Catherine Drive, Rocky Hill, CT 06067
E-mail: tony.guerrera@cga.ct.gov
Committees: Banks; Transportation; Veterans' Affairs
Education: Eastern Connecticut State BA

Representative
**Gregory "Gregg" Haddad** (D-District 54) . . . . . . . . . . . (860) 429-8517
Counties Represented: Tolland (part)
Term Expires: 2017
28 Storrs Heights Road, Storrs, CT 06268
E-mail: gregory.haddad@cga.ct.gov
Committees: Appropriations; Government Administration and Elections;
Higher Education and Employment Advancement

Representative **John K. Hampton** (D-District 16) . . . . . . . . (860) 240-8585
Counties Represented: Hartford (part)        Dist: (860) 240-8659
Term Expires: 2017
33 West Mountain, Simsbury, CT 06092
E-mail: john.hampton@cga.ct.gov
Committees: Aging; Banks; Children; Planning and Development

Representative **Stephen Harding** (R-District 107) . . . . . . . . (860) 240-0400
Counties Represented: Fairfield (part)
Term Expires: 2017
E-mail: stephen.harding@cga.ct.gov
Committees: Energy and Technology; Finance, Revenue and Bonding;
Judiciary

Representative
**John F. "Jack" Hennessy** (D-District 127) . . . . . . . . . . . (860) 240-8585
Counties Represented: Fairfield (part)
Term Expires: 2017
556 Savoy Street, Bridgeport, CT 06606
E-mail: jack.hennessy@cga.ct.gov
Committees: Environment; Finance, Revenue and Bonding; Veterans'
Affairs
Education: Boston Col 1974 BS

Representative **Ernest Hewett** (D-District 39) . . . . . . . . . . . (860) 240-8585
Counties Represented: New London (part)
Term Expires: 2017
Legislative Office Building, Room 4040, Hartford, CT 06106-1591
E-mail: ernest.hewett@cga.ct.gov
Committees: Appropriations; Banks; Judiciary; Regulation Review

Representative **Laura Hoydick** (R-District 120)
Room 4200 . . . . . . . . . . . . . . . . . . . . . . . . . . . . . . . (860) 240-8700
Counties Represented: Fairfield (part)
Term Expires: 2017
E-mail: laura.hoydick@cga.ct.gov
Committees: Banks; Energy and Technology; Finance, Revenue and
Bonding; Legislative Management

Representative **Claire L. Janowski** (D-District 56) . . . . . . . (860) 240-8585
Counties Represented: Tolland (part)
Term Expires: 2017
Legislative Office Building, Room 1003, Hartford, CT 06106-1591
E-mail: claire.janowski@cga.ct.gov
Committees: Executive and Legislative Nominations; Higher Education
and Employment Advancement; Transportation
Education: Trinity Col (CT) 1988 BA

Representative **Susan M. Johnson** (D-District 49) . . . . . . . (860) 240-8585
Counties Represented: Windham (part)
Term Expires: 2017
Legislative Office Building, Room 5007, Hartford, CT 06106-1591
120 Bolivia Street, Willimantic, CT 06226
E-mail: susan.johnson@cga.ct.gov
Committees: Appropriations; Education; Insurance and Real Estate

Representative **Ed Jutila** (D-District 37) . . . . . . . . . . . . . . . (860) 240-8585
Counties Represented: New London (part)
Term Expires: 2017
23 Brainard Road, Niantic, CT 06357
E-mail: ed.jutila@cga.ct.gov
Committees: Government Administration and Elections; Transportation
Education: Connecticut 1978 BA, 1985 JD

Representative **David William Kiner** (D-District 59) . . . . . . (860) 265-3366
Counties Represented: Hartford (part)
Term Expires: 2017
5 Cranberry Hollow, Enfield, CT 06082
E-mail: david.kiner@cga.ct.gov
Committees: General Law; Labor and Public Employees; Public Safety
and Security

Representative **Themis Klarides** (R-District 114)
Room 4200 . . . . . . . . . . . . . . . . . . . . . . . . . . . . . . . (860) 240-8700
Counties Represented: New Haven (part)
Term Expires: 2017
E-mail: themis.klarides@housegop.ct.gov
Committees: Legislative Management

Representative **Noreen S. Kokoruda** (R-District 101) . . . . . (203) 245-9054
Counties Represented: Middlesex (part), New Haven (part)
Term Expires: 2017
85 Liberty Street, Madison, CT 06443
E-mail: noreen.kokoruda@housegop.ct.gov
Committees: Aging; Appropriations; Children; Education

Representative **Brenda L. Kupchick** (R-District 132) . . . . . . (860) 240-8700
Counties Represented: Fairfield (part)     Res: (203) 336-1724
Term Expires: 2017
213 Farist Road, Fairfield, CT 06825
E-mail: brenda.kupchick@housegop.ct.gov
Committees: Energy and Technology; Housing; Insurance and Real Estate

Representative **David K. Labriola** (R-District 131)
Room 4200 . . . . . . . . . . . . . . . . . . . . . . . . . . . . . . . . (860) 240-8700
Counties Represented: New Haven (part)
Term Expires: 2017
E-mail: david.labriola@housegop.ct.gov
Committees: Government Administration and Elections; Judiciary; Transportation

Representative **Gail Lavielle** (R-District 143) . . . . . . . . . . (860) 240-8700
Counties Represented: Fairfield (part)     Res: (203) 726-7373
Term Expires: 2017
109 Hickory Hill, Wilton, CT 06897
E-mail: gail.lavielle@housegop.ct.gov
Committees: Appropriations; Education; Transportation

Representative
**Timothy B. "Tim" LeGeyt** (R-District 17) Room 4200 . . (860) 240-8700
Counties Represented: Hartford (part)
Term Expires: 2017
E-mail: tim.legeyt@housegop.ct.gov
Committees: Appropriations; Education; Higher Education and Employment Advancement
Education: Central Conn State U 1975; Western New England 1988 JD

Representative **Roland J. Lemar** (D-District 96) . . . . . . . . (203) 903-5003
Counties Represented: New Haven (part)
Term Expires: 2017
6 Eld Street, New Haven, CT 06511
E-mail: roland.lemar@cga.ct.gov
Committees: Education; Finance, Revenue and Bonding; Judiciary; Transportation

Representative **Matthew Lesser** (D-District 100) . . . . . . . . (860) 240-8585
Counties Represented: Middlesex (part)
Term Expires: 2017
Legislative Office Building, Room 4014, Hartford, CT 06106-1591
1160 South Main Street, Middletown, CT 06457
E-mail: matthew.lesser@cga.ct.gov
Committees: Appropriations; Banks; Government Administration and Elections

Representative **Rick Lopes** (D-District 24) . . . . . . . . . . . . . (860) 229-7721
Counties Represented: Hartford (part)
Term Expires: 2017
208 South Mountain Drive, New Britain, CT 06052
E-mail: rick.lopes@cga.ct.gov
Committees: Finance, Revenue and Bonding; Higher Education and Employment Advancement; Transportation

Representative **Kelly Luxenberg** (D-District 12) . . . . . . . . (860) 240-8585
Counties Represented: Hartford (part)
Term Expires: 2017
E-mail: kelly.luxenberg@cga.ct.gov
Committees: Aging; Labor and Public Employees

Representative **Jesse MacLachlan** (R-District 35) . . . . . . . . (860) 240-8700
Counties Represented: Middlesex (part)
Term Expires: 2017
E-mail: jesse.maclachlan@housegop.ct.gov
Committees: Energy and Technology; Higher Education and Employment Advancement

Representative **Cristin McCarthy Vahey** (D-District 13) . . . (860) 240-8585
Counties Represented: Hartford (part)
Term Expires: 2017
E-mail: cristin.mccarthyvahey@cga.ct.gov
Committees: Appropriations; Education; Transportation

Representative **Kathleen M. McCarty** (R-District 38) . . . . . (860) 240-8700
Counties Represented: New London (part)
Term Expires: 2017
E-mail: kathleen.mccarty@housegop.ct.gov
Committees: Appropriations; Education; Public Health

Representative **Douglas McCrory** (D-District 7) . . . . . . . . (860) 560-0242
Counties Represented: Hartford (part)
Term Expires: 2017
235 Blue Hills Avenue, Hartford, CT 06112
E-mail: douglas.mccrory@cga.ct.gov
Committees: Appropriations; Education; Higher Education and Employment Advancement; Legislative Management

Representative **Brandon McGee** (D-District 5) . . . . . . . . . (860) 240-8585
Counties Represented: Hartford (part)
Term Expires: 2017
43 Warren Street, Hartford, CT 06120
E-mail: brandon.mcgee@cga.ct.gov
Committees: Education; Human Services; Labor and Public Employees

Representative **Ben McGorty** (R-District 122) . . . . . . . . . . (860) 240-8700
Counties Represented: Fairfield (part)
Term Expires: 2017
E-mail: ben.mcgorty@housegop.ct.gov
Committees: Appropriations; Environment; Judiciary

Representative **Robert W. Megna** (D-District 97) . . . . . . . (860) 240-8585
Counties Represented: New Haven (part)
Term Expires: 2017
40 Foxon Hill Road, Number 54, New Haven, CT 06513
E-mail: robert.megna@cga.ct.gov
Committees: Energy and Technology; Environment; Insurance and Real Estate
Education: Oregon State 1982 BSBA

Representative **Patricia Billie Miller** (D-District 145) . . . . . (860) 240-8585
Counties Represented: Fairfield (part)
Term Expires: 2017
Legislative Office Building, Room 4016, Hartford, CT 06106-1591
95 Liberty Street, Room A4, Stamford, CT 06902
E-mail: patricia.miller@cga.ct.gov
Committees: Appropriations; Education; Government Administration and Elections

Representative **Philip J. Miller** (D-District 36) . . . . . . . . . . (860) 240-8585
Counties Represented: Middlesex (part)
Term Expires: 2017
24 Bushy Hill Road, Ivoryton, CT 06442
E-mail: philip.miller@cga.ct.gov
Committees: Environment; Planning and Development; Program Review and Investigations
Education: Assumption Col 1981 BA

Representative **Craig A. Miner** (R-District 66)
Room 4200 . . . . . . . . . . . . . . . . . . . . . . . . . . . . . . . . . (860) 240-8700
Counties Represented: Litchfield (part)
Term Expires: 2017
E-mail: craig.miner@housegop.ct.gov
Committees: Appropriations; Environment; Labor and Public Employees; Legislative Management; Public Safety and Security

Representative **Russell A. Morin** (D-District 28) . . . . . . . . (860) 257-3876
Counties Represented: Hartford (part)
Term Expires: 2017
495 Brimfield Road, Wethersfield, CT 06109-3209
E-mail: russell.morin@cga.ct.gov
Committees: Commerce; Finance, Revenue and Bonding; Legislative Management; Transportation

Representative **Bruce V. Morris** (D-District 140) . . . . . . . . (203) 979-9261
Counties Represented: Fairfield (part)
Term Expires: 2017
17 Sention Avenue, Norwalk, CT 06850-3207
E-mail: bruce.morris@cga.ct.gov
Committees: Energy and Technology; Human Services; Judiciary
Education: Connecticut

Representative **Gayle Mulligan** (R-District 55) . . . . . . . . . (860) 240-8700
Counties Represented: Hartford (part), Tolland (part)
Term Expires: 2017
E-mail: gayle.mulligan@housegop.ct.gov
Committees: Appropriations; Education

Representative **Mary M. Mushinsky** (D-District 85) . . . . . . (203) 269-8378
Counties Represented: New Haven (part)
Term Expires: 2017
188 South Cherry Street, Wallingford, CT 06492
E-mail: mary.mushinsky@cga.ct.gov
Committees: Environment; Finance, Revenue and Bonding; Program Review and Investigations

Representative **Frank N. Nicastro, Sr.** (D-District 79) . . . . . (860) 585-6070
Counties Represented: Hartford (part)
Term Expires: 2017
80 Beleden Gardens Drive, Bristol, CT 06708
E-mail: frank.nicastro@cga.ct.gov
Committees: Energy and Technology; General Law; Public Safety and Security; Veterans' Affairs

Representative **Selim G. Noujaim** (R-District 74)
Room 4200 . . . . . . . . . . . . . . . . . . . . . . . . . . . . . . . . . (860) 240-8700
Counties Represented: New Haven (part)
Term Expires: 2017
E-mail: selim.noujaim@housegop.ct.gov
Committees: Commerce; Insurance and Real Estate
Affiliation: Executive Vice President, Noujaim Tool Company, Inc.

*(continued on next page)*

**Representatives** *continued*

Representative **Tom O'Dea** (R-District 125) Room 4200 . . . (800) 842-1423
Counties Represented: Fairfield (part)
Term Expires: 2017
E-mail: tom.odea@housegop.ct.gov
Committees: Judiciary; Regulation Review; Transportation
Education: Providence 1988 BA; Columbus Law 1991 JD

Representative **Arthur J. O'Neill** (R-District 69)
Room 4200 . . . . . . . . . . . . . . . . . . . . . . . . . . . . . . . . . . . (860) 240-8700
Counties Represented: Litchfield (part), New Haven (part)
Term Expires: 2017
E-mail: arthur.oneill@housegop.ct.gov
Committees: Appropriations; Judiciary; Legislative Management;
Regulation Review

Representative **Linda A. Orange** (D-District 48) . . . . . . . . . (860) 537-3936
Counties Represented: New London (part), Tolland (part), Windham
(part)
Term Expires: 2017
52 Standish Road, Colchester, CT 06415
E-mail: linda.orange@cga.ct.gov
Committees: Appropriations; General Law; Legislative Management;
Public Safety and Security

Representative **Cara Christine Pavalock** (R-District 77) . . . (860) 240-8700
Counties Represented: Hartford (part)
Term Expires: 2017
E-mail: cara.pavalock@housegop.ct.gov
Committees: Aging; Commerce; Program Review and Investigations

Representative **Jason D. Perillo, CPA** (R-District 113)
Room 4200 . . . . . . . . . . . . . . . . . . . . . . . . . . . . . . . . . . . (860) 240-8700
Counties Represented: Fairfield (part)
Term Expires: 2017
E-mail: jason.perillo@housegop.ct.gov
Committees: Executive and Legislative Nominations; Finance, Revenue
and Bonding; Public Health

Representative **Christopher R. Perone** (D-District 137) . . . (203) 840-1643
Counties Represented: Fairfield (part)
Term Expires: 2017
Eight East Rocks Road, Norwalk, CT 06851
E-mail: chris.perone@cga.ct.gov
Committees: Commerce; Energy and Technology
Education: Syracuse BA

Representative **John E. Piscopo** (R-District 76)
Room 4200 . . . . . . . . . . . . . . . . . . . . . . . . . . . . . . . . . . . (860) 240-8700
Counties Represented: Hartford (part), Litchfield (part)
Term Expires: 2017
E-mail: john.piscopo@housegop.ct.gov
Committees: Energy and Technology; Environment; Finance, Revenue
and Bonding; Legislative Management

Representative **Robyn A. Porter** (D-District 94) . . . . . . . . . (860) 240-8585
Counties Represented: New Haven (part)
Term Expires: 2017
Legislative Office Building, 300 Capitol Avenue, Room 4006,
Hartford, CT 06106
E-mail: robyn.porter@cga.ct.gov
Committees: Appropriations; Human Services; Judiciary

Representative **Christine Randall** (D-District 44) . . . . . . . . (860) 240-8585
Counties Represented: Windham (part)
Term Expires: 2017
E-mail: christine.randall@cga.ct.gov
Committees: Energy and Technology; Insurance and Real Estate

Representative **Rosa C. Rebimbas** (R-District 70)
Room 4200 . . . . . . . . . . . . . . . . . . . . . . . . . . . . . . . . . . . (860) 240-8700
Counties Represented: New Haven (part)
Term Expires: 2017
E-mail: rosa.rebimbas@housegop.ct.gov
Committees: Finance, Revenue and Bonding; Government
Administration and Elections; Judiciary
Education: Fairfield BA; Utah JD

Representative **Lonnie Reed** (D-District 102) . . . . . . . . . . . (860) 240-8585
Counties Represented: New Haven (part)
Term Expires: 2017
Legislative Office Building, Room 4026, Hartford, CT 06106-1591
460 Maple Street, Apartment 44, Branford, CT 06405
E-mail: lonnie.reed@cga.ct.gov
Committees: Energy and Technology; Finance, Revenue and Bonding;
Planning and Development

Representative **Geraldo Reyes, Jr.** (D-District 75) . . . . . . . (800) 842-8267
Counties Represented: New Haven (part)
E-mail: geraldo.reyes@cga.ct.gov

Representative **Emmett D. Riley** (D-District 46) . . . . . . . . (860) 240-8585
Counties Represented: New London (part)
Term Expires: 2017
150 Yantic Street, Suite 160, Norwich, CT 06360
E-mail: emmett.riley@cga.ct.gov
Committees: Energy and Technology; Insurance and Real Estate;
Judiciary; Public Health

Representative **Matthew D. Ritter** (D-District 1) . . . . . . . . (860) 251-5000
Counties Represented: Hartford (part)      Res: (860) 519-5685
Term Expires: 2017
169 North Beacon Street, Hartford, CT 06105
E-mail: matthew.ritter@cga.ct.gov
Committees: Banks; Planning and Development; Public Health

Representative **Jason Rojas** (D-District 9) . . . . . . . . . . . . . (860) 240-0549
Counties Represented: Hartford (part)
Term Expires: 2017
Legislative Office Building, Room 4001, Hartford, CT 06106-1591
558 Oak Street, East Hartford, CT 06118
E-mail: jason.rojas@cga.ct.gov
Committees: Education; Finance, Revenue and Bonding; Planning and
Development

Representative **Christopher Rosario** (D-District 128) . . . . . (860) 240-8585
Counties Represented: Fairfield (part)
Term Expires: 2017
E-mail: christopher.rosario@cga.ct.gov
Committees: Appropriations; Energy and Technology; Transportation

Representative **Kim Rose** (D-District 118) . . . . . . . . . . . . . (203) 283-7885
Counties Represented: New Haven (part)
Term Expires: 2017
292 Naugatuck Avenue, Milford, CT 06460
E-mail: kim.rose@cga.ct.gov
Committees: Children; Housing; Veterans' Affairs

Representative
**Daniel S. "Danny" Rovero** (D-District 51) . . . . . . . . . . (860) 774-3792
Counties Represented: Windham (part)
Term Expires: 2017
181 Laurel Point Road, Dayville, CT 06241
E-mail: danny.rovero@cga.ct.gov
Committees: Aging; General Law; Public Safety and Security

Representative **David Rutigliano** (R-District 123) . . . . . . . . (800) 842-1423
Counties Represented: Fairfield (part)      Tel: (203) 247-3663
Term Expires: 2017
Legislative Office Building, Room 4200, Hartford, CT 06106-1591
E-mail: dave.rutigliano@housegop.ct.gov
Committees: Finance, Revenue and Bonding; General Law; Labor and
Public Employees

Representative **Kevin Ryan** (D-District 139) . . . . . . . . . . . . (860) 848-0790
Counties Represented: New London (part)
Term Expires: 2017
21 Terrace Drive, Oakdale, CT 06370
E-mail: kevin.ryan@cga.ct.gov
Committees: Appropriations; Environment; Legislative Management;
Public Health

Representative **Robert C. Sampson** (R-District 80)
Room 4200 . . . . . . . . . . . . . . . . . . . . . . . . . . . . . . . . . . . (203) 879-3202
Counties Represented: Hartford (part), New Haven (part)
Term Expires: 2017
E-mail: rob.sampson@housegop.ct.gov
Committees: Commerce; Insurance and Real Estate; Judiciary

Representative
**Robert "Bobby" Sanchez** (D-District 25) . . . . . . . . . . . (860) 225-4807
Counties Represented: Hartford (part)
Term Expires: 2017
269 Washington Street, New Britain, CT 06051
E-mail: bobby.sanchez@cga.ct.gov
Committees: Education; Finance, Revenue and Bonding; Higher
Education and Employment Advancement

Representative **Ezequiel Santiago** (D-District 130) . . . . . . . (860) 240-8585
Counties Represented: Fairfield (part)      Dist: (203) 345-5976
Term Expires: 2017
Legislative Office Building, Room 3802, Hartford, CT 06106-1591
991 State Street, Bridgeport, CT 06605
E-mail: ezequiel.santiago@cga.ct.gov
Committees: Appropriations; Commerce

Representative **Hilda E. Santiago** (D-District 84) . . . . . . . . (860) 240-8585
Counties Represented: New Haven (part)
Term Expires: 2017
Legislative Office Building, Room 4200, Hartford, CT 06106-1591
E-mail: hilda.santiago@cga.ct.gov
Committees: Banks; Finance, Revenue and Bonding; Human Services

LEGISLATIVE BRANCH

Representative **Peggy Sayers** (D-District 60) . . . . . . . . . . (860) 623-3868
Counties Represented: Hartford (part)
Term Expires: 2017
81 Spring Street, Windsor Locks, CT 06096
E-mail: peggy.sayers@cga.ct.gov
Committees: Commerce; Public Health; Transportation

Representative **Sean Scanlon** (D-District 98) . . . . . . . . . . (860) 240-8585
Counties Represented: New Haven (part)
Term Expires: 2017
E-mail: sean.scanlon@cga.ct.gov
Committees: Environment; Public Health; Transportation

Representative **John F. Scott** (R-District 40) . . . . . . . . . . (860) 240-8700
Counties Represented: New London (part)
Term Expires: 2017
E-mail: john.scott@housegop.ct.gov
Committees: Banks; Energy and Technology; Insurance and Real Estate

Representative **Joseph C. Serra** (D-District 33) . . . . . . . . . (860) 347-0119
Counties Represented: Middlesex (part)
Term Expires: 2017
P.O. Box 233, Middletown, CT 06457
E-mail: joseph.serra@cga.ct.gov
Committees: Aging; Judiciary; Transportation
Education: Hartford 1975 BS

Representative **John T. Shaban** (R-District 135) . . . . . . . . (860) 240-8700
Counties Represented: Fairfield (part)        Res: (203) 664-1015
Term Expires: 2017
29 Ledgewood Road, Redding, CT 06896
E-mail: john.shaban@housegop.ct.gov
Committees: Environment; Finance, Revenue and Bonding; Judiciary

Representative **J. Brendan Sharkey** (D-District 88) . . . . . . (203) 281-4647
Counties Represented: New Haven (part)
Term Expires: 2017
600 Mount Carmel Avenue, Hamden, CT 06518
E-mail: brendan.sharkey@cga.ct.gov
Committees: Legislative Management

Representative **Bill Simanski** (R-District 62) . . . . . . . . . . (860) 240-8700
Counties Represented: Hartford (part), Litchfield        Res: (860) 653-0686
(part)
Term Expires: 2017
12 Kilmer Lane, Granby, CT 06035
E-mail: bill.simanski@housegop.ct.gov
Committees: Banks; Planning and Development; Transportation

Representative **Caroline B. Simmons** (D-District 14) . . . . . (860) 240-8585
Counties Represented: Hartford (part)
Term Expires: 2017
E-mail: caroline.simmons@cga.ct.gov
Committees: Commerce; Judiciary; Public Safety and Security
Education: Harvard BA; George Washington MA

Representative **Richard A. Smith** (R-District 108) . . . . . . . (860) 240-8700
Counties Represented: Fairfield (part), Litchfield        Tel: (203) 746-6656
(part)                                                    Res: (203) 460-4871
Term Expires: 2017
25 Jeremy Drive, New Fairfield, CT 06812
E-mail: richard.smith@housegop.ct.gov
Committees: Government Administration and Elections; Judiciary;
Labor and Public Employees

Representative **J.P. Sredzinski** (R-District 11) . . . . . . . . . . (860) 240-8700
Counties Represented: Hartford (part)
Term Expires: 2017
E-mail: jp.sredzinski@housegop.ct.gov
Committees: Commerce; Public Safety and Security

Representative **Prasad Srinivasan, MD** (R-District 31) . . . . (860) 240-8700
Counties Represented: Hartford (part)
Term Expires: 2017
Legislative Office Building, Room 4200, Hartford, CT 06106-1591
E-mail: prasad.srinivasan@housegop.ct.gov
Committees: Finance, Revenue and Bonding; Planning and
Development; Public Health

Representative **Steven Stafstrom** (D-District 129) . . . . . . . (860) 240-8700
Counties Represented: Fairfield (part)
Term Expires: 2017
E-mail: steven.stafstrom@cga.ct.gov
Committees: Environment; Finance, Revenue and Bonding; Judiciary

Representative
**Charles L. "Charlie" Stallworth** (D-District 126) . . . . . . (860) 240-8585
Counties Represented: Fairfield (part)        Tel: (203) 345-7254
Term Expires: 2017
Legislative Office Building, Room 4050, Hartford, CT 06106-1591
35 Wickliffe Circle, Bridgeport, CT 06606
E-mail: charlie.stallworth@cga.ct.gov
Committees: Banks; Finance, Revenue and Bonding; Human Services

Representative **Pam Staneski** (R-District 11) . . . . . . . . . . (860) 240-8700
Counties Represented: Hartford (part)
Term Expires: 2017
E-mail: pam.staneski@housegop.ct.gov
Committees: Children; Education; Veterans' Affairs

Representative **Jonathan Steinberg** (D-District 136) . . . . . (203) 722-7477
Counties Represented: Fairfield (part)        Res: (203) 226-6749
Term Expires: 2017
1 Bushy Ridge Road, Westport, CT 06880
E-mail: jonathan.steinberg@cga.ct.gov
Committees: Energy and Technology; Finance, Revenue and Bonding;
Transportation

Representative **Peter A. Tercyak** (D-District 26) . . . . . . . . (860) 240-8585
Counties Represented: Hartford (part)
Term Expires: 2017
150 Belridge Road, New Britain, CT 06053
E-mail: peter.tercyak@cga.ct.gov
Committees: Appropriations; Labor and Public Employees; Public
Health
Education: Connecticut

Representative **William M. Tong** (D-District 147) . . . . . . . (860) 240-8585
Counties Represented: Fairfield (part)
Term Expires: 2017
99 Chestnut Hill Road, Stamford, CT 06903-4030
E-mail: william.tong@cga.ct.gov
Committees: Environment; Judiciary
Education: Phillips Acad (Andover, MA); Brown U 1995 AB;
Chicago 2000 JD

Representative **Mark Tweedie** (R-District 13) . . . . . . . . . . (860) 240-8700
Counties Represented: Hartford (part)
Term Expires: 2017
E-mail: mark.tweedie@housegop.ct.gov
Committees: Appropriations; Environment; Veterans' Affairs

Representative **Diana S. Urban** (D-District 43) . . . . . . . . . (860) 535-4868
Counties Represented: New London (part)
Term Expires: 2017
146 Babcock Road, North Stonington, CT 06359
E-mail: diana.urban@cga.ct.gov
Committees: Appropriations; Children; Environment
Education: Long Island BA; SUNY (Stony Brook) MA;
Chadwick MEM; Rhode Island

Representative **Kurt Vail** (R-District 52) . . . . . . . . . . . . . . (860) 240-8700
Counties Represented: Tolland (part)
Term Expires: 2017
E-mail: kurt.vail@housegop.ct.gov
Committees: Insurance and Real Estate; Labor and Public Employees;
Public Safety and Security

Representative **Edwin Vargas** (D-District 6) . . . . . . . . . . . (860) 240-8585
Counties Represented: Hartford (part)
Term Expires: 2017
141 Douglas Street, Hartford, CT 06114
E-mail: edwin.vargas@cga.ct.gov
Committees: Appropriations; Children; Commerce; Executive and
Legislative Nominations
Education: Hartford BS, MPA

Representative **Joe Verrengia** (D-District 20) . . . . . . . . . . (860) 240-8585
Counties Represented: Hartford (part)        Res: (860) 982-5282
Term Expires: 2017
143 Elmfield Street, West Hartford, CT 06117
Legislative Office Building, Room 4048, Hartford, CT 06106-1591
E-mail: joe.verrengia@cga.ct.gov
Committees: Finance, Revenue and Bonding; Judiciary; Public Safety
and Security; Transportation

Representative **Toni Edmonds Walker** (D-District 93) . . . . (860) 240-8585
Counties Represented: New Haven (part)
Term Expires: 2017
1643 Ella Grasso Boulevard, New Haven, CT 06511
E-mail: toni.walker@cga.ct.gov
Committees: Appropriations; Higher Education and Employment
Advancement; Judiciary
Education: Southern Connecticut State U BA; Fordham MA

Representative **Roberta B. Willis** (D-District 64) . . . . . . . . (860) 240-8585
Counties Represented: Litchfield (part)
Term Expires: 2017
P.O. Box 1733, Lakeville, CT 06039-1733
E-mail: roberta.willis@cga.ct.gov
Committees: Appropriations; Environment; Higher Education and
Employment Advancement

Representative **Frederick N. Wilms** (R-District 142) . . . . . (860) 240-8700
Counties Represented: Fairfield (part)
Term Expires: 2017
E-mail: fred.wilms@housegop.ct.gov
Committees: Appropriations; Public Health; Transportation

*(continued on next page)*

**LEGISLATIVE BRANCH**

**Representatives** *continued*

Representative **Terrie E. Wood** (R-District 141)
Room 4200 . . . . . . . . . . . . . . . . . . . . . . . . . . . . . . . . . . . . . (860) 240-8700
Counties Represented: Fairfield (part)
Term Expires: 2017
E-mail: terrie.wood@housegop.ct.gov
Committees: Finance, Revenue and Bonding; Human Services;
Regulation Review

Representative **Dave Yaccarino** (R-District 87) . . . . . . . . . . (860) 240-8700
Counties Represented: New Haven (part)     Tel: (203) 234-2989
Term Expires: 2017     Res: (203) 980-0030
Legislative Office Building, Room 4200, Hartford, CT 06106-1591
1 Lincoln Street, North Haven, CT 06473
E-mail: david.yaccarino@housegop.ct.gov
Committees: Energy and Technology; Finance, Revenue and Bonding;
Public Safety and Security; Veterans' Affairs

Representative **Tami Zawistowski** (R-District 61)
Room 4200 . . . . . . . . . . . . . . . . . . . . . . . . . . . . . . . . . . . . . (860) 240-8700
Counties Represented: Hartford (part)     Dist: (860) 658-1191
Term Expires: 2017
11 Seymour Road, Glastonbury, CT 06026
E-mail: tami.zawistowski@housegop.ct.gov
Committees: Appropriations; Planning and Development;
Transportation
Education: Connecticut 1978

Representative **Melissa H. Ziobron** (R-District 34) . . . . . . . (800) 842-1423
Counties Represented: Middlesex (part), New London (part)
Term Expires: 2017
Legislative Office Building, Room 4200, Hartford, CT 06106-1591
E-mail: melissa.ziobron@cga.ct.gov
Committees: Appropriations; Children; Environment
Education: Central Conn State U BA

Representative **David Zoni** (D-District 81) Room 4000 . . . . (860) 240-0401
Counties Represented: Hartford (part)
Term Expires: 2017
P.O. Box 834, Southington, CT 06489
E-mail: david.zoni@cga.ct.gov
Committees: Aging; Finance, Revenue and Bonding; Insurance and
Real Estate; Public Health
Education: Quinnipiac (Attended)

Representative **Lezlye Zupkus** (R-District 89)
Room 4200 . . . . . . . . . . . . . . . . . . . . . . . . . . . . . . . . . . . . . (203) 758-4219
Counties Represented: New Haven (part)
Term Expires: 2017
E-mail: lezlye.zupkus@housegop.ct.gov
Committees: General Law; Human Services; Public Safety and Security

# Standing Joint Committees

## Aging
Capitol Building, Room 011, Hartford, CT 06106

### Senate Members

| **Majority Members** | **Minority Members** |
|---|---|
| Mae Flexer (D-29) *Co-Chair* | Kevin C. Kelly (R-21) |
| Catherine A. "Cathy" Osten (D-19) *Vice Chair* | *Ranking Member* |

### House Members

| **Majority Members** | **Minority Members** |
|---|---|
| Joseph C. Serra (D-33) *Co-Chair* | Mitch Bolinsky (R-106) |
| Daniel S. "Danny" Rovero (D-51) *Vice Chair* | *Ranking Member* |
| Michelle L. Cook (D-65) | Alfred "Al" Adinolfi (R-103) |
| John K. Hampton (D-16) | Noreen S. Kokoruda (R-101) |
| Kelly Luxenberg (D-12) | Cara Christine Pavalock (R-77) |
| David Zoni (D-81) | |

## Appropriations
Legislative Office Building, Room 2700, Hartford, CT 06106-1591

### Senate Members

| **Majority Members** | **Minority Members** |
|---|---|
| Beth Bye (D-5) *Co-Chair* | Robert J. Kane (R-32) |
| Joan V. Hartley (D-15) *Vice Chair* | *Ranking Member* |
| Dante Bartolomeo (D-13) | Clark J. Chapin (R-30) |
| Mae Flexer (D-29) | Paul Formica (R-20) |
| Theresa Bielinski "Terry" Gerratana (D-6) | John A. Kissel (R-7) |
| Gayle S. Slossberg (D-14) | Joe Markley (R-16) |
| Gary A. Winfield (D-10) | |

### House Members

| **Majority Members** | **Minority Members** |
|---|---|
| Toni Edmonds Walker (D-93) *Co-Chair* | Melissa H. Ziobron (R-34) *Ranking Member* |
| Henry J. Genga (D-10) *Vice Chair* | William "Bill" Aman (R-14) |
| Robyn A. Porter (D-94) *Vice Chair* | Sam Belsito (R-53) |
| Catherine F. "Cathy" Abercrombie (D-83) | Whit Betts (R-78) |
| Andre F. Baker, Jr. (D-124) | Mitch Bolinsky (R-106) |
| Juan R. Candelaria (D-95) | Jay M. Case (R-63) |
| Patricia A. Dillon (D-92) | Charles J. Ferraro (R-11) |
| Andrew M. Fleischmann (D-18) | Mike France (R-42) |
| Minnie Gonzalez (D-3) | Noreen S. Kokoruda (R-101) |
| Gregory "Gregg" Haddad (D-54) | Gail Lavielle (R-143) |
| Ernest Hewett (D-39) | Timothy B. "Tim" LeGeyt (R-17) |
| Susan M. Johnson (D-49) | Kathleen M. McCarty (R-38) |
| Matthew Lesser (D-100) | Ben McGorty (R-122) |
| Cristin McCarthy Vahey (D-13) | Craig A. Miner (R-66) |
| Douglas McCrory (D-7) | Gayle Mulligan (R-55) |
| Patricia Billie Miller (D-145) | Arthur J. O'Neill (R-69) |
| Linda A. Orange (D-48) | Mark Tweedie (R-13) |
| Christopher Rosario (D-128) | Frederick N. Wilms (R-142) |
| Kevin Ryan (D-139) | Tami Zawistowski (R-61) |
| Ezequiel Santiago (D-130) | |
| Peter A. Tercyak (D-26) | |
| Diana S. Urban (D-43) | |
| Edwin Vargas (D-6) | |
| Roberta B. Willis (D-64) | |

## Banks
Legislative Office Building, Room 2400, Hartford, CT 06106-1591

### Senate Members

| **Majority Members** | **Minority Members** |
|---|---|
| Carlo Leone (D-27) *Co-Chair* | Henri Martin (R-31) |
| Joseph J. "Joe" Crisco, Jr. (D-17) *Vice Chair* | *Ranking Member* |

### House Members

| **Majority Members** | **Minority Members** |
|---|---|
| Matthew Lesser (D-100) *Co-Chair* | Bill Simanski (R-62) |
| Charles L. "Charlie" Stallworth (D-126) *Vice Chair* | *Ranking Member* |
| Terry B. Adams (D-14) | Mike Alberts (R-50) |
| David A. Baram (D-15) | Fred Camillo (R-151) |
| Antonio "Tony" Guerrera (D-29) | John H. Frey (R-111) |
| John K. Hampton (D-16) | Laura Hoydick (R-120) |
| Ernest Hewett (D-39) | John F. Scott (R-40) |
| Matthew D. Ritter (D-1) | |
| Hilda E. Santiago (D-84) | |

## Children
Capitol Building, Room 011, Hartford, CT 06106

### Senate Members

| **Majority Members** | **Minority Members** |
|---|---|
| Dante Bartolomeo (D-13) *Co-Chair* | Henri Martin (R-31) |
| Beth Bye (D-5) *Vice Chair* | *Ranking Member* |

### House Members

| **Majority Members** | **Minority Members** |
|---|---|
| Diana S. Urban (D-43) *Co-Chair* | Noreen S. Kokoruda (R-101) |
| John K. Hampton (D-16) *Vice Chair* | *Ranking Member* |
| Juan R. Candelaria (D-95) | Mike Bocchino (R-15) |
| Kim Rose (D-118) | Pam Staneski (R-11) |
| Edwin Vargas (D-6) | Melissa H. Ziobron (R-34) |

## Commerce
State Capitol, Room 110, Hartford, CT 06106

### Senate Members

| **Majority Members** | **Minority Members** |
|---|---|
| Joan V. Hartley (D-15) *Co-Chair* | L. Scott Frantz (R-36) |
| Joseph J. "Joe" Crisco, Jr. (D-17) *Vice Chair* | *Ranking Member* |
| Timothy D. "Tim" Larson (D-3) | Tony Hwang (R-28) |

**House Members**

**Majority Members**
Christopher R. Perone (D-137) *Co-Chair*
Edwin Vargas (D-6) *Vice Chair*
Brian Becker (D-19)
Paul Brycki (D-45)
Linda M. Gentile (D-104)
Russell A. Morin (D-28)
Ezequiel Santiago (D-130)
Peggy Sayers (D-60)
Caroline B. Simmons (D-14)

**Minority Members**
Fred Camillo (R-151) *Ranking Member*
Mike Alberts (R-50)
Anthony J. "Tony" D'Amelio (R-71)
Selim G. Noujaim (R-74)
Cara Christine Pavalock (R-77)
Robert C. Sampson (R-80)
J.P. Sredzinski (R-11)

## Education
Legislative Office Building, Room 3100, Hartford, CT 06106-1591

**Senate Members**

**Majority Members**
Gayle S. Slossberg (D-14) *Co-Chair*
Gary A. Winfield (D-10) *Vice Chair*
Dante Bartolomeo (D-13)
Beth Bye (D-5)

**Minority Members**
Antonietta Boucher (R-26) *Ranking Member*
Arthur Linares (R-33)

**House Members**

**Majority Members**
Andrew M. Fleischmann (D-18) *Co-Chair*
Robert "Bobby" Sanchez (D-25) *Vice Chair*
Andre F. Baker, Jr. (D-124)
Juan R. Candelaria (D-95)
Michelle L. Cook (D-65)
Jeffrey Currey (D-11)
Michael C. D'Agostino (D-91)
Henry J. Genga (D-10)
Susan M. Johnson (D-49)
Roland J. Lemar (D-96)
Cristin McCarthy Vahey (D-13)
Douglas McCrory (D-7)
Brandon McGee (D-5)
Patricia Billie Miller (D-145)
Jason Rojas (D-9)

**Minority Members**
Gail Lavielle (R-143) *Ranking Member*
Timothy Ackert (R-8)
Aundré Bumgardner (R-41)
Eric C. Berthel (R-68)
Mitch Bolinsky (R-106)
Dan Carter (R-2)
Noreen S. Kokoruda (R-101)
Timothy B. "Tim" LeGeyt (R-17)
Kathleen M. McCarty (R-38)
Gayle Mulligan (R-55)
Pam Staneski (R-11)

## Energy and Technology
Legislative Office Building, Room 3900, Hartford, CT 06106-1591

**Senate Members**

**Majority Members**
Paul R. Doyle (D-9) *Co-Chair*
Timothy D. "Tim" Larson (D-3) *Vice Chair*

**Minority Members**
Paul Formica (R-20) *Ranking Member*

**House Members**

**Majority Members**
Lonnie Reed (D-102) *Co-Chair*
Michael V. "Mike" Demicco (D-21) *Vice Chair*
Brian Becker (D-19)
Joe Gresko (D-121)
Robert W. Megna (D-97)
Bruce V. Morris (D-140)
Frank N. Nicastro, Sr. (D-79)
Christopher R. Perone (D-137)
Christine Randall (D-44)
Emmett D. Riley (D-46)
Christopher Rosario (D-128)
Jonathan Steinberg (D-136)

**Minority Members**
Timothy Ackert (R-8) *Ranking Member*
Mike Bocchino (R-15)
Stephen Harding (R-107)
Laura Hoydick (R-120)
Brenda L. Kupchick (R-132)
Jesse MacLachlan (R-35)
John E. Piscopo (R-76)
John F. Scott (R-40)
Dave Yaccarino (R-87)

## Environment
Legislative Office Building, Room 3200, Hartford, CT 06106-1591

**Senate Members**

**Majority Members**
Edward M. "Ted" Kennedy, Jr. (D-12) *Co-Chair*
Marilyn Moore (D-22) *Vice Chair*

**Minority Members**
Clark J. Chapin (R-30) *Ranking Member*

**House Members**

**Majority Members**
James M. Albis (D-99) *Co-Chair*
David Arconti, Jr. (D-109) *Vice Chair*
Michael V. "Mike" Demicco (D-21)
Patricia A. Dillon (D-92)
Joe Gresko (D-121)
John F. "Jack" Hennessy (D-127)
Robert W. Megna (D-97)
Philip J. Miller (D-36)
Mary M. Mushinsky (D-85)
Kevin Ryan (D-139)
Sean Scanlon (D-98)
Steven Stafstrom (D-129)
William M. Tong (D-147)
Diana S. Urban (D-43)
Roberta B. Willis (D-64)

**Minority Members**
John T. Shaban (R-135) *Ranking Member*
Gary Byron (R-27)
Devin R. Carney (R-23)
Jay M. Case (R-63)
Doug Dubitsky (R-47)
Ben McGorty (R-122)
Craig A. Miner (R-66)
John E. Piscopo (R-76)
Mark Tweedie (R-13)
Melissa H. Ziobron (R-34)

## Executive and Legislative Nominations
Legislative Office Building, Room 1000, Hartford, CT 06106-1591

**Senate Members**

**Majority Members**
Robert "Bob" Duff (D-25) *Co-Chair*
Martin M. Looney (D-11) *Vice Chair*
Joseph J. "Joe" Crisco, Jr. (D-17)
Paul R. Doyle (D-9)
Joan V. Hartley (D-15)

**Minority Members**
Robert J. Kane (R-32) *Ranking Member*
Leonard A. Fasano (R-34)
Anthony Guglielmo (R-35)

**House Members**

**Majority Members**
Claire L. Janowski (D-56) *Co-Chair*
Edwin Vargas (D-6) *Vice Chair*
James M. Albis (D-99)
Jeffrey J. Berger (D-73)
Stephen D. Dargan (D-115)
Robert D. "Bob" Godfrey (D-110)

**Minority Members**
Cecilia Buck-Taylor (R-67) *Ranking Member*
Fred Camillo (R-151)
Janice R. Giegler (R-138)
Jason D. Perillo (R-113)

## Finance, Revenue and Bonding
Legislative Office Building, Room 3700, Hartford, CT 06106-1591

**Senate Members**

**Majority Members**
John W. Fonfara (D-1) *Co-Chair*
Carlo Leone (D-27) *Vice Chair*
Stephen T. "Steve" Cassano (D-4)
Eric D. Coleman (D-2)
Marilyn Moore (D-22)
Gary A. Winfield (D-10)

**Minority Members**
L. Scott Frantz (R-36) *Ranking Member*
Antonietta Boucher (R-26)
Michael A. McLachlan (R-24)

**House Members**

**Majority Members**
Jeffrey J. Berger (D-73) *Co-Chair*
Roland J. Lemar (D-96) *Vice Chair*
Hilda E. Santiago (D-84) *Vice Chair*
James M. Albis (D-99)
Capt David Alexander (D-58)
Emil "Buddy" Altobello, Jr. (D-82)
Angel Arce (D-4)
Elizabeth A. "Betty" Boukus (D-22)
Paul Brycki (D-45)
Larry B. Butler (D-72)
Michael C. D'Agostino (D-91)
Daniel J. Fox (D-148)
John F. "Jack" Hennessy (D-127)
Rick Lopes (D-24)
Russell A. Morin (D-28)
Mary M. Mushinsky (D-85)
Lonnie Reed (D-102)
Jason Rojas (D-9)
Robert "Bobby" Sanchez (D-25)
Steven Stafstrom (D-129)
Charles L. "Charlie" Stallworth (D-126)
Jonathan Steinberg (D-136)
Joe Verrengia (D-20)
David Zoni (D-81)

**Minority Members**
Christopher Davis (R-57) *Ranking Member*
Eric C. Berthel (R-68)
Aundré Bumgardner (R-41)
Vincent J. "Vinny" Candelora (R-86)
Dan Carter (R-2)
Laura Devlin (R-13)
Livvy R. Floren (R-149)
John H. Frey (R-111)
Stephen Harding (R-107)
Laura Hoydick (R-120)
Jason D. Perillo (R-113)
John E. Piscopo (R-76)
Rosa C. Rebimbas (R-70)
David Rutigliano (R-123)
John T. Shaban (R-135)
Prasad Srinivasan (R-31)
Terrie E. Wood (R-141)
Dave Yaccarino (R-87)

## General Law

Legislative Office Building, Room 3500, Hartford, CT 06106-1591

### Senate Members

**Majority Members**
Carlo Leone (D-27) *Co-Chair*
Timothy D. "Tim" Larson (D-3)
  *Vice Chair*
Gayle S. Slossberg (D-14)

**Minority Members**
Kevin Witkos (R-8)
  *Ranking Member*
John A. Kissel (R-7)

### House Members

**Majority Members**
David A. Baram (D-15) *Co-Chair*
David William Kiner (D-59)
  *Vice Chair*
Emil "Buddy" Altobello, Jr. (D-82)
David Arconti, Jr. (D-109)
Louis P. "Lou" Esposito, Jr. (D-116)
Frank N. Nicastro, Sr. (D-79)
Linda A. Orange (D-48)
Daniel S. "Danny" Rovero (D-51)

**Minority Members**
Dan Carter (R-2) *Ranking Member*
William "Bill" Aman (R-14)
Anthony J. "Tony" D'Amelio
  (R-71)
David Rutigliano (R-123)
Lezlye Zupkus (R-89)

## Government Administration and Elections

Legislative Office Building, Room 2200, Hartford, CT 06106-1591

### Senate Members

**Majority Members**
Stephen T. "Steve" Cassano (D-4)
  *Co-Chair*
Theresa Bielinski
  "Terry" Gerratana (D-6)
  *Vice Chair*

**Minority Members**
Michael A. McLachlan (R-24)
  *Ranking Member*

### House Members

**Majority Members**
Ed Jutila (D-37) *Co-Chair*
Capt David Alexander (D-58)
  *Vice Chair*
Brian Becker (D-19)
Gregory "Gregg" Haddad (D-54)
Matthew Lesser (D-100)
Patricia Billie Miller (D-145)

**Minority Members**
Richard A. Smith (R-108)
  *Ranking Member*
Laura Devlin (R-13)
Mike France (R-42)
David K. Labriola (R-131)
Rosa C. Rebimbas (R-70)

## Higher Education and Employment Advancement

Legislative Office Building, Room 1800, Hartford, CT 06106

### Senate Members

**Majority Members**
Dante Bartolomeo (D-13) *Co-Chair*
Mae Flexer (D-29) *Vice Chair*

**Minority Members**
Kevin Witkos (R-8)
  *Ranking Member*

### House Members

**Majority Members**
Roberta B. Willis (D-64) *Co-Chair*
Rick Lopes (D-24) *Vice Chair*
Juan R. Candelaria (D-95)
Patricia A. Dillon (D-92)
Linda M. Gentile (D-104)
Gregory "Gregg" Haddad (D-54)
Claire L. Janowski (D-56)
Douglas McCrory (D-7)
Robert "Bobby" Sanchez (D-25)
Toni Edmonds Walker (D-93)

**Minority Members**
Whit Betts (R-78) *Ranking Member*
Timothy Ackert (R-8)
Mike Alberts (R-50)
Mike Bocchino (R-15)
Devin R. Carney (R-23)
Timothy B. "Tim" LeGeyt (R-17)
Jesse MacLachlan (R-35)

## Housing

Capitol Building, Room 2700, Hartford, CT 06106

### Senate Members

**Majority Members**
Gary A. Winfield (D-10) *Co-Chair*
Catherine A. "Cathy" Osten (D-19)
  *Vice Chair*

**Minority Members**
Tony Hwang (R-28)
  *Ranking Member*

### House Members

**Majority Members**
Larry B. Butler (D-72) *Co-Chair*
Kim Rose (D-118) *Vice Chair*
Terry B. Adams (D-14)
Angel Arce (D-4)
David Arconti, Jr. (D-109)
Paul Brycki (D-45)

**Minority Members**
Brenda L. Kupchick (R-132)
  *Ranking Member*
Gary Byron (R-27)
Christopher Davis (R-57)
John H. Frey (R-111)

## Human Services

Legislative Office Building, Room 2000, Hartford, CT 06106-1591

### Senate Members

**Majority Members**
Marilyn Moore (D-22) *Co-Chair*
Gayle S. Slossberg (D-14)
  *Vice Chair*

**Minority Members**
Joe Markley (R-16)
  *Ranking Member*

### House Members

**Majority Members**
Catherine F. "Cathy"
  Abercrombie (D-83)
  *Co-Chair*
Brandon McGee (D-5) *Vice Chair*
Larry B. Butler (D-72)
Michelle L. Cook (D-65)
Bruce V. Morris (D-140)
Robyn A. Porter (D-94)
Hilda E. Santiago (D-84)
Charles L. "Charlie" Stallworth
  (D-126)

**Minority Members**
Terrie E. Wood (R-141)
  *Ranking Member*
Cecilia Buck-Taylor (R-67)
Gary Byron (R-27)
Jay M. Case (R-63)
Lezlye Zupkus (R-89)

## Insurance and Real Estate

Legislative Office Building, Room 2800, Hartford, CT 06106-1591

### Senate Members

**Majority Members**
Joseph J. "Joe" Crisco, Jr. (D-17)
  *Co-Chair*
Joan V. Hartley (D-15) *Vice Chair*

**Minority Members**
Kevin C. Kelly (R-21)
  *Ranking Minority Member*

### House Members

**Majority Members**
Robert W. Megna (D-97) *Co-Chair*
David Zoni (D-81) *Vice Chair*
Catherine F. "Cathy" Abercrombie
  (D-83)
Jeffrey Currey (D-11)
Stephen D. Dargan (D-115)
Susan M. Johnson (D-49)
Emmett D. Riley (D-46)
Christine Randall (D-44)

**Minority Members**
Robert C. Sampson (R-80)
  *Ranking Minority Member*
Christopher Davis (R-57)
Livvy R. Floren (R-149)
Brenda L. Kupchick (R-132)
Selim G. Noujaim (R-74)
John F. Scott (R-40)
Kurt Vail (R-52)

## Judiciary

Legislative Office Building, Room 2500, Hartford, CT 06106-1591

### Senate Members

**Majority Members**
Eric D. Coleman (D-2) *Co-Chair*
Paul R. Doyle (D-9) *Vice Chair*
Beth Bye (D-5)
Mae Flexer (D-29)
Theresa Bielinski "Terry" Gerratana
  (D-6)
Gary A. Winfield (D-10)

**Minority Members**
John A. Kissel (R-7)
  *Ranking Member*
Antonietta Boucher (R-26)
Arthur Linares (R-33)
Michael A. McLachlan (R-24)

### House Members

**Majority Members**
William M. Tong (D-147) *Co-Chair*
Daniel J. Fox (D-148) *Vice Chair*
James M. Albis (D-99)
David A. Baram (D-15)
Jeffrey J. Berger (D-73)
Jeffrey Currey (D-11)
Patricia A. Dillon (D-92)
Mary G. Fritz (D-90)
Robert D. "Bob" Godfrey (D-110)
Minnie Gonzalez (D-3)
Joe Gresko (D-121)
Ernest Hewett (D-39)
Roland J. Lemar (D-96)
Bruce V. Morris (D-140)
Robyn A. Porter (D-94)
Emmett D. Riley (D-46)
Joseph C. Serra (D-33)
Caroline B. Simmons (D-144)
Steven Stafstrom (D-129)
Joe Verrengia (D-20)
Toni Edmonds Walker (D-93)

**Minority Members**
Rosa C. Rebimbas (R-70)
  *Ranking Member*
Alfred "Al" Adinolfi (R-103)
William "Bill" Aman (R-14)
Cecilia Buck-Taylor (R-67)
Vincent J. "Vinny" Candelora
  (R-86)
Christie Carpino (R-32)
Doug Dubitsky (R-47)
Stephen Harding (R-107)
David K. Labriola (R-131)
Ben McGorty (R-122)
Tom O'Dea (R-125)
Arthur J. O'Neill (R-69)
Robert C. Sampson (R-80)
John T. Shaban (R-135)
Richard A. Smith (R-108)

## Labor and Public Employees

Legislative Office Building, Room 3800, Hartford, CT 06106-1591

### Senate Members

**Majority Members**
Edwin A. "Ed" Gomes (D-23)
  *Co-Chair*
Catherine A. "Cathy" Osten (D-19)
  *Vice Chair*

**Minority Members**
Tony Hwang (R-28)
  *Ranking Member*

### House Members

**Majority Members**
Peter A. Tercyak (D-26) *Co-Chair*
Louis P. "Lou" Esposito, Jr. (D-116)
David William Kiner (D-59)
Kelly Luxenberg (D-12)
Brandon McGee (D-5)

**Minority Members**
David Rutigliano (R-123)
  *Ranking Member*
Craig A. Miner (R-66)
Richard A. Smith (R-108)
Kurt Vail (R-52)

## Legislative Management

Legislative Office Building, Room 5100, Hartford, CT 06106-1591

### Senate Members

**Majority Members**
Martin M. Looney (D-11) *Co-Chair*
Robert "Bob" Duff (D-25)
  *Vice Chair*
Beth Bye (D-5)
Eric D. Coleman (D-2)
Joseph J. "Joe" Crisco, Jr. (D-17)
John W. Fonfara (D-1)
Joan V. Hartley (D-15)

**Minority Members**
Leonard A. Fasano (R-34)
  *Ranking Member*
L. Scott Frantz (R-36)
Kevin C. Kelly (R-21)
Kevin Witkos (R-8)

### House Members

**Majority Members**
J. Brendan Sharkey (D-88)
  *Co-Chair*
Joe Aresimowicz (D-30) *Vice Chair*
Juan R. Candelaria (D-95)
Michelle L. Cook (D-65)
Louis P. "Lou" Esposito, Jr. (D-116)
Linda M. Gentile (D-104)
Robert D. "Bob" Godfrey (D-110)
Douglas McCrory (D-7)
Russell A. Morin (D-28)
Linda A. Orange (D-48)
Kevin Ryan (D-139)

**Minority Members**
Themis Klarides (R-114)
  *Ranking Member*
Vincent J. "Vinny" Candelora
  (R-86)
Laura Hoydick (R-120)
Craig A. Miner (R-66)
Arthur J. O'Neill (R-69)
John E. Piscopo (R-76)

## Planning and Development

Legislative Office Building, Room 2100, Hartford, CT 06106-1591

### Senate Members

**Majority Members**
Catherine A. "Cathy" Osten (D-19)
  *Co-Chair*
Stephen T. "Steve" Cassano (D-4)
  *Vice Chair*
John W. Fonfara (D-1)

**Minority Members**
Arthur Linares (R-33)
  *Ranking Member*

### House Members

**Majority Members**
Philip J. Miller (D-36) *Co-Chair*
Michael C. D'Agostino (D-91)
  *Vice Chair*
Theresa W. Conroy (D-105)
Daniel J. Fox (D-148)
Mary G. Fritz (D-90)
John K. Hampton (D-16)
Lonnie Reed (D-102)
Matthew D. Ritter (D-1)
Jason Rojas (D-9)

**Minority Members**
William "Bill" Aman (R-14)
  *Ranking Member*
Sam Belsito (R-53)
Doug Dubitsky (R-47)
Mike France (R-42)
Bill Simanski (R-62)
Prasad Srinivasan (R-31)
Tami Zawistowski (R-61)

## Program Review and Investigations

State Capitol, Room 506, Hartford, CT 06106

### Senate Members

**Majority Members**
John W. Fonfara (D-1) *Co-Chair*
Eric D. Coleman (D-2)
Andrew M. Maynard (D-18)

**Minority Members**
John A. Kissel (R-7)
  *Ranking Member*
Anthony Guglielmo (R-35)
Joe Markley (R-16)

### House Members

**Majority Members**
Mary M. Mushinsky (D-85)
  *Ranking Member*
Henry J. Genga (D-10)
Philip J. Miller (D-36)

**Minority Members**
Christie Carpino (R-32) *Co-Chair*
Whit Betts (R-78)
Cara Christine Pavalock (R-77)

## Public Health

Legislative Office Building, Room 3000, Hartford, CT 06106-1591

### Senate Members

**Majority Members**
Theresa Bielinski
  "Terry" Gerratana (D-6)
  *Co-Chair*
Joseph J. "Joe" Crisco, Jr. (D-17)
  *Vice Chair*
Edward M. "Ted" Kennedy, Jr.
  (D-12)
Marilyn Moore (D-22)

**Minority Members**
Joe Markley (R-16)
  *Ranking Member*
Robert J. Kane (R-32)

### House Members

**Majority Members**
Matthew D. Ritter (D-1) *Co-Chair*
Emmett D. Riley (D-46) *Vice Chair*
Capt David Alexander (D-58)
Andre F. Baker, Jr. (D-124)
Theresa W. Conroy (D-105)
Michelle L. Cook (D-65)
Michael V. "Mike" Demicco (D-21)
Henry J. Genga (D-10)
Kevin Ryan (D-139)
Peggy Sayers (D-60)
Sean Scanlon (D-98)
Peter A. Tercyak (D-26)
David Zoni (D-81)

**Minority Members**
Prasad Srinivasan (R-31)
  *Ranking Member*
Alfred "Al" Adinolfi (R-103)
Eric C. Berthel (R-68)
Whit Betts (R-78)
Vincent J. "Vinny" Candelora
  (R-86)
Christie Carpino (R-32)
Kathleen M. McCarty (R-38)
Jason D. Perillo (R-113)
Frederick N. Wilms (R-142)

## Public Safety and Security

Legislative Office Building, Room 3600, Hartford, CT 06106-1591

### Senate Members

**Majority Members**
Joan V. Hartley (D-15) *Co-Chair*
Eric D. Coleman (D-2) *Vice Chair*
Edwin A. "Ed" Gomes (D-23)
Gary A. Winfield (D-10)

**Minority Members**
Anthony Guglielmo (R-35)
  *Ranking Minority Member*
Paul Formica (R-20)

### House Members

**Majority Members**
Stephen D. Dargan (D-115)
  *Co-Chair*
Joe Verrengia (D-20) *Vice Chair*
Terry B. Adams (D-14)
David Arconti, Jr. (D-109)
Elizabeth A. "Betty" Boukus (D-22)
Louis P. "Lou" Esposito, Jr. (D-116)
Minnie Gonzalez (D-3)
David William Kiner (D-59)
Frank N. Nicastro, Sr. (D-79)
Linda A. Orange (D-48)
Daniel S. "Danny" Rovero (D-51)
Caroline B. Simmons (D-14)

**Minority Members**
Lezlye Zupkus (R-89)
  *Ranking Minority Member*
Anthony J. "Tony" D'Amelio
  (R-71)
Charles J. Ferraro (R-11)
Janice R. Giegler (R-138)
Craig A. Miner (R-66)
J.P. Sredzinski (R-11)
Kurt Vail (R-52)
Dave Yaccarino (R-87)

## Regulation Review

Capitol Building, Room 011, Hartford, CT 06106

### Senate Members

**Majority Members**
Paul R. Doyle (D-9)
  *Ranking Member*
Carlo Leone (D-27)
Robert "Bob" Duff (D-25)

**Minority Members**
Clark J. Chapin (R-30) *Co-Chair*
Kevin C. Kelly (R-21)
Kevin Witkos (R-8)

### House Members

**Majority Members**
Brian Becker (D-19) *Co-Chair*
Emil "Buddy" Altobello, Jr. (D-82)
Robert D. "Bob" Godfrey (D-110)
Ernest Hewett (D-39)

**Minority Members**
Arthur J. O'Neill (R-69)
  *Ranking Member*
Vincent J. "Vinny" Candelora
  (R-86)
Tom O'Dea (R-125)
Terrie E. Wood (R-141)

**LEGISLATIVE BRANCH**

# Transportation

Legislative Office Building, Room 2300, Hartford, CT 06106-1591

### Senate Members
#### Majority Members
Andrew M. Maynard (D-18)
  *Co-Chair*
Carlo Leone (D-27) *Vice Chair*
Stephen T. "Steve" Cassano (D-4)
Edward M. "Ted" Kennedy, Jr.
  (D-12)
Catherine A. "Cathy" Osten (D-19)

#### Minority Members
Antonietta Boucher (R-26)
  *Ranking Member*
L. Scott Frantz (R-36)
Henri Martin (R-31)

### House Members
#### Majority Members
Antonio "Tony" Guerrera (D-29)
  *Co-Chair*
Angel Arce (D-4) *Vice Chair*
Claire L. Janowski (D-56)
Ed Jutila (D-37)
Roland J. Lemar (D-96)
Rick Lopes (D-24)
Cristin McCarthy Vahey (D-13)
Russell A. Morin (D-28)
Christopher Rosario (D-128)
Peggy Sayers (D-60)
Sean Scanlon (D-98)
Joseph C. Serra (D-33)
Jonathan Steinberg (D-136)
Joe Verrengia (D-20)

#### Minority Members
Tom O'Dea (R-125)
  *Ranking Member*
Aundré Bumgardner (R-41)
Devin R. Carney (R-23)
Laura Devlin (R-13)
Janice R. Giegler (R-138)
David K. Labriola (R-131)
Gail Lavielle (R-143)
Bill Simanski (R-62)
Frederick N. Wilms (R-142)
Tami Zawistowski (R-61)

# Veterans' Affairs

Capitol, Room 509A, Hartford, CT 06106

### Senate Members
#### Majority Members
Mae Flexer (D-29) *Co-Chair*
Edwin A. "Ed" Gomes (D-23)
  *Vice Chair*

#### Minority Members
Henri Martin (R-31)
  *Ranking Member*
Tony Hwang (R-28)

### House Members
#### Majority Members
John F. "Jack" Hennessy (D-127)
  *Co-Chair*
Frank N. Nicastro, Sr. (D-79)
  *Vice Chair*
Capt David Alexander (D-58)
Theresa W. Conroy (D-105)
Antonio "Tony" Guerrera (D-29)
Kim Rose (D-118)

#### Minority Members
Dave Yaccarino (R-87)
  *Ranking Member*
Alfred "Al" Adinolfi (R-103)
Pam Staneski (R-11)
Mark Tweedie (R-13)

# Delaware General Assembly

411 Legislative Hall, Dover, DE 19901
P.O. Box 1401, Dover, DE 19903
Tel: (302) 744-4114  Fax: (302) 739-3895
Internet: http://legis.delaware.gov

# Delaware State Senate

411 Legislative Avenue, Dover, DE 19901
820 North French Street, Wilmington, DE 19801
Tel: (302) 744-4286  Fax: (302) 739-6890 (Democrats)
Fax: (302) 739-5049 (Republicans)

President of the Senate (**Vacant**) . . . . . . . . . . . . . . . . . . . . (302) 739-4151
President Pro Tempore **Patricia M. "Patti" Blevins** (D) . . . (302) 744-4133
  Education: Temple BA
  Special Assistant **Carling Ryan** . . . . . . . . . . . . . . . . . . . . (302) 744-4133
Majority Leader **David B. McBride** (D) . . . . . . . . . . . . . . (302) 744-4167
  Education: Delaware BS, MSCE
Majority Whip **Margaret Rose Henry** (D) . . . . . . . . . . . . . (302) 744-4191
  Education: Texas Southern BA; Springfield (IL) MA
Minority Leader **F. Gary Simpson** (R) . . . . . . . . . . . . . . . (302) 744-4134
  Education: Delaware 1969 BS, 1972 MS
Minority Whip **Gregory F. Lavelle** (R) . . . . . . . . . . . . . . . (302) 744-4048
  Education: Delaware BSBEd; Pennsylvania MS
Secretary of the Senate **Bernard J. Brady** . . . . . . . . . . . . . (302) 744-4129

## Senators

**Party Affiliation Statistics:** Republicans: 9, Democrats: 12

Senator **Patricia M. "Patti" Blevins** (D-District 7)
  Carvel State Office Building, Floor 11 . . . . . . . . . . . . . . . (302) 744-4133
  Counties Represented: New Castle (part)      Dist: (302) 577-8542
  Term Expires: 2017                              (Wilmington)
  E-mail: patricia.blevins@state.de.us          Fax: (302) 577-3269
  Committees: Administrative Services/Elections; Banking and Business;
  Ethics; Executive; Judiciary; Legislative Council; Permanent Rules
Senator **Colin R. J. Bonini** (R-District 16) . . . . . . . . . . . . . (302) 744-4169
  Counties Represented: Kent (part)             Dist: (302) 698-0960
  Term Expires: 2019                            Fax: (302) 739-5049
  E-mail: colin.bonini@state.de.us              Dist: (302) 698-3688
  Committees: Banking and Business; Bond; Highways and
  Transportation; Insurance and Telecommunications
  Education: Wesley Col (DE) BA
Senator **Brian J. Bushweller** (D-District 17) . . . . . . . . . . . (302) 744-4162
  Counties Represented: Kent (part)             Dist: (302) 674-5442
  Term Expires: 2019                            Fax: (302) 739-6890
  E-mail: brian.bushweller@state.de.us
  Committees: Adult and Juvenile Corrections; Bond; Community/County
  Affairs; Finance; Highways and Transportation; Insurance and
  Telecommunications; Joint Finance; Public Safety
  Education: Oklahoma City BA; Stanford MA
Senator **Catherine A. Cloutier** (R-District 5) Floor 11 . . . . (302) 744-4197
  Counties Represented: New Castle (part)       Dist: (302) 577-8517
  Term Expires: 2017                              (Wilmington)
  E-mail: catherine.cloutier@state.de.us        Fax: (302) 739-5049
  Committees: Children, Youth and Families; Energy and Transit;
  Finance; Insurance and Telecommunications; Joint Finance; Labor and
  Industrial Relations
Senator **Bruce C. Ennis** (D-District 14) . . . . . . . . . . . . . . . .(302) 744-4310
  Counties Represented: Kent (part), New Castle  Dist: (302) 653-7566
  (part)                                        Fax: (302) 739-6890
  Term Expires: 2017                            Dist: (302) 653-6541
  E-mail: bruce.ennis@state.de.us
  Committees: Adult and Juvenile Corrections; Agriculture; Finance;
  Joint Finance; Natural Resources and Environmental Control; Veterans
  Affairs
Senator **Bethany A. Hall-Long** (D-District 10) . . . . . . . . . (302) 744-4286
  Counties Represented: New Castle (part)
  Term Expires: 2019
  Carvel State Office Building, 820 N. French Street, 11th Floor,
  Wilmington, DE 19801
  E-mail: bethany.hall-long@state.de.us
  Committees: Agriculture; Banking and Business; Bond;
  Community/County Affairs; Education; Health and Social Services;
  Highways and Transportation; Insurance and Telecommunications;
  Veterans Affairs
  Education: Thomas Jefferson BSN; Medical U (SC) MSN;
  George Mason PhD

Senator **Margaret Rose Henry** (D-District 2) . . . . . . . . . . (302) 744-4191
Counties Represented: New Castle (part)  Dist: (302) 577-8719
Term Expires: 2019  (Wilmington)
Carvel State Office Building, 820 N. French Street, 11th Floor,
Wilmington, DE 19801
E-mail: margaretrose.henry@state.de.us
Committees: Administrative Services/Elections; Community/County
Affairs; Education; Ethics; Executive; Health and Social Services;
Judiciary; Legislative Council; Permanent Rules

Senator **Gerald W. Hocker** (R-District 20) . . . . . . . . . . . . . (302) 744-4144
Counties Represented: Sussex (part)  Dist: (302) 537-6016
Term Expires: 2017  Dist: (302) 539-4140
E-mail: gerald.hocker@state.de.us  Dist: (302) 539-9662
Committees: Administrative Services/Elections;  Fax: (302) 539-6206
Adult and Juvenile Corrections; Bond; Labor and  Dist: (302) 539-2507
Industrial Relations; Natural Resources and Environmental Control
Education: Delaware BSBA

Senator **Gregory F. Lavelle** (R-District 4)
Carvel State Office Building, 11th Floor . . . . . . . . . . . . . . (302) 744-4048
Counties Represented: New Castle (part)  Dist: (302) 577-8714
Term Expires: 2019  Dist: (302) 478-6128
E-mail: greg.lavelle@state.de.us  Fax: (302) 739-5049
Committees: Ethics; Executive; Health and Social Services; Judiciary;
Legislative Council; Permanent Rules

Senator **David G. Lawson** (R-District 15) . . . . . . . . . . . . . (302) 744-4237
Counties Represented: Kent (part)  Res: (302) 492-1511
Term Expires: 2017  Fax: (302) 492-1453
E-mail: dave.lawson@state.de.us
Committees: Adult and Juvenile Corrections; Community/County
Affairs; Finance; Joint Finance; Public Safety; Veterans Affairs

Senator **Ernesto B. Lopez** (R-District 6) . . . . . . . . . . . . . . (302) 744-4136
Counties Represented: New Castle (part), Sussex  Dist: (302) 598-7669
(part)  Fax: (302) 739-5049
Term Expires: 2019
E-mail: ernesto.lopez@state.de.us
Committees: Children, Youth and Families; Education; Health and
Social Services; Joint Sunset; Natural Resources and Environmental
Control; Sunset
Education: Gettysburg BA; Delaware MA, EdD

Senator **Robert I. Marshall** (D-District 3) . . . . . . . . . . . . (302) 744-4168
Counties Represented: New Castle (part)  Dist: (302) 577-8519
Term Expires: 2019
Carvel State Office Building, 820 N. French Street, 11th Floor,
Wilmington, DE 19801
E-mail: robert.marshall@state.de.us
Committees: Bond; Children, Youth and Families; Education; Health
and Social Services; Labor and Industrial Relations; Natural Resources
and Environmental Control; Public Safety
Education: Thomas Edison State BA

Senator **David B. McBride** (D-District 13)
Carvel State Office Building, 11th Floor . . . . . . . . . . . . . . (302) 744-4167
Counties Represented: New Castle (part)  Dist: (302) 577-8744
Term Expires: 2017  (Wilmington)
E-mail: david.mcbride@state.de.us
Committees: Adult and Juvenile Corrections; Agriculture; Ethics;
Executive; Highways and Transportation; Labor and Industrial
Relations; Legislative Council; Natural Resources and Environmental
Control; Permanent Rules; Public Safety; Veterans Affairs

Senator **Harris B. McDowell III** (D-District 1)
Carvel State Office Building, 11th Floor . . . . . . . . . . . . . . (302) 744-4147
Counties Represented: New Castle (part)  Dist: (302) 577-8744
Term Expires: 2017  (Wilmington)
E-mail: harris.mcdowell@state.de.us
Committees: Banking and Business; Children, Youth and Families;
Energy and Transit; Ethics; Executive; Finance; Health and Social
Services; Insurance and Telecommunications; Joint Finance; Judiciary;
Permanent Rules
Education: Delaware (Attended); Georgetown (Attended)

Senator **Karen E. Peterson** (D-District 9)
Carvel State Office Building, 11th Floor . . . . . . . . . . . . . . (302) 744-4163
Counties Represented: New Castle (part)  Dist: (302) 999-7522
Term Expires: 2017  (Wilmington)
E-mail: karen.peterson@state.de.us
Committees: Adult and Juvenile Corrections; Community/County
Affairs; Finance; Health and Social Services; Highways and
Transportation; Joint Finance; Labor and Industrial Relations; Natural
Resources and Environmental Control; Veterans Affairs
Education: Neumann BS

Senator **Brian G. Pettyjohn** (R-District 19) . . . . . . . . . . . (302) 744-4048
Counties Represented: Kent (part), Sussex (part)  Dist: (302) 858-0694
Term Expires: 2017
E-mail: brian.pettyjohn@state.de.us
Committees: Agriculture; Community/County Affairs; Education; Joint
Sunset; Public Safety; Sunset; Veterans Affairs
Education: Delaware (Attended)

Senator **Nicole Poore** (D-District 12) . . . . . . . . . . . . . . . . . (302) 744-4164
Counties Represented: New Castle (part)  Dist: (302) 577-8740
Term Expires: 2017  Fax: (302) 739-6890
Carvel State Office Building, 820 N. French Street,  Dist: (302) 577-7204
11th Floor, Wilmington, DE 19801
E-mail: nicole.poore@state.de.us
Committees: Administrative Services/Elections; Children, Youth and
Families; Education; Energy and Transit; Health and Social Services;
Joint Sunset; Labor and Industrial Relations; Sunset
Education: Wilmington Col (DE) 1994 BS

Senator **Bryant L. Richardson** (R-District 21) . . . . . . . . . . (302) 629-7513
Counties Represented: Sussex (part)  Tel: (302) 245-0109
Term Expires: 2019
E-mail: bryant.richardson@state.de.us
Committees: Administrative Services/Elections; Agriculture; Energy
and Transit; Highways and Transportation

Senator **F. Gary Simpson** (R-District 18) . . . . . . . . . . . . . . (302) 744-4134
Counties Represented: Kent (part), Sussex (part)  Fax: (302) 739-5049
Term Expires: 2019
E-mail: gsimpson@udel.edu
Committees: Ethics; Executive; Judiciary; Legislative Council;
Permanent Rules

Senator **David P. Sokola** (D-District 8) . . . . . . . . . . . . . . . . (302) 744-4139
Counties Represented: New Castle (part)  Dist: (302) 577-8744
Term Expires: 2017  (Wilmington)
Carvel State Office Building, 820 N. French Street,  Dist: (302) 695-7366
11th Floor, Wilmington, DE 19801  Dist: (302) 239-2193
E-mail: david.sokola@state.de.us
Committees: Administrative Services/Elections; Banking and
Business; Bond; Education; Energy and Transit; Insurance and
Telecommunications; Joint Sunset; Sunset
Education: Delaware 1977 BSPE

Senator **Bryan Townsend** (D-District 11) . . . . . . . . . . . . . . (302) 744-4165
Counties Represented: New Castle (part)  Dist: (302) 577-5316
Term Expires: 2019  Dist: (302) 709-1516
Carvel State Office Building, 820 N. French Street, 11th Floor,
Wilmington, DE 19801
E-mail: bryan.townsend@state.de.us
Committees: Adult and Juvenile Corrections; Banking and Business;
Education; Joint Sunset; Judiciary; Public Safety; Sunset; Veterans
Affairs
Education: Delaware 2003 BS, 2004 BA; Cambridge (UK) 2006 PhM;
Yale 2009 JD

# Senate Standing Committees
## Administrative Services/Elections

| Majority Members | Minority Members |
|---|---|
| Margaret Rose Henry (D-2) | Gerald W. Hocker (R-20) |
| *Chairman* | Bryant L. Richardson (R-21) |
| Patricia M. "Patti" Blevins (D-7) | |
| Nicole Poore (D-12) | |
| David P. Sokola (D-8) | |

## Adult and Juvenile Corrections

| Majority Members | Minority Members |
|---|---|
| Bruce C. Ennis (D-14) *Chairman* | Gerald W. Hocker (R-20) |
| Brian J. Bushweller (D-17) | David G. Lawson (R-15) |
| David B. McBride (D-13) | |
| Karen E. Peterson (D-9) | |
| Bryan Townsend (D-11) | |

## Agriculture

| Majority Members | Minority Members |
|---|---|
| Bruce C. Ennis (D-14) *Chairman* | Brian G. Pettyjohn (R-19) |
| Bethany A. Hall-Long (D-10) | Bryant L. Richardson (R-21) |
| David B. McBride (D-13) | |

## Banking and Business

**Majority Members**
Bryan Townsend (D-11) *Chairman*
Patricia M. "Patti" Blevins (D-7)
Bethany A. Hall-Long (D-10)
Harris B. McDowell III (D-1)
David P. Sokola (D-8)

**Minority Members**
Colin R. J. Bonini (R-16)

## Bond

**Majority Members**
David P. Sokola (D-8) *Chairman*
Brian J. Bushweller (D-17)
Bethany A. Hall-Long (D-10)
Robert I. Marshall (D-3)

**Minority Members**
Colin R. J. Bonini (R-16)
Gerald W. Hocker (R-20)

## Children, Youth and Families

**Majority Members**
Harris B. McDowell III (D-1)
 *Chairman*
Robert I. Marshall (D-3)
Nicole Poore (D-12)

**Minority Members**
Catherine A. Cloutier (R-5)
Ernesto B. Lopez (R-6)

## Community/County Affairs

**Majority Members**
Bethany A. Hall-Long (D-10)
 *Chairman*
Brian J. Bushweller (D-17)
Margaret Rose Henry (D-2)
Karen E. Peterson (D-9)

**Minority Members**
David G. Lawson (R-15)
Brian G. Pettyjohn (R-19)

## Education

**Majority Members**
David P. Sokola (D-8) *Chairman*
Bethany A. Hall-Long (D-10)
Margaret Rose Henry (D-2)
Robert I. Marshall (D-3)
Nicole Poore (D-12)
Bryan Townsend (D-11)

**Minority Members**
Ernesto B. Lopez (R-6)
Brian G. Pettyjohn (R-19)

## Energy and Transit

**Majority Members**
Harris B. McDowell III (D-1)
 *Chairman*
Nicole Poore (D-12)
David P. Sokola (D-8)

**Minority Members**
Catherine A. Cloutier (R-5)
Bryant L. Richardson (R-21)

## Ethics

**Majority Members**
Patricia M. "Patti" Blevins (D-7)
 *Chairman*
Margaret Rose Henry (D-2)
David B. McBride (D-13)
Harris B. McDowell III (D-1)

**Minority Members**
Gregory F. Lavelle (R-4)
F. Gary Simpson (R-18)

## Executive

**Majority Members**
Patricia M. "Patti" Blevins (D-7)
 *Chairman*
Margaret Rose Henry (D-2)
David B. McBride (D-13)
Harris B. McDowell III (D-1)

**Minority Members**
Gregory F. Lavelle (R-4)
F. Gary Simpson (R-18)

## Finance

**Majority Members**
Harris B. McDowell III (D-1)
 *Chairman*
Brian J. Bushweller (D-17)
Bruce C. Ennis (D-14)
Karen E. Peterson (D-9)

**Minority Members**
Catherine A. Cloutier (R-5)
David G. Lawson (R-15)

## Health and Social Services

**Majority Members**
Bethany A. Hall-Long (D-10)
 *Chairman*
Margaret Rose Henry (D-2)
Robert I. Marshall (D-3)
Harris B. McDowell III (D-1)
Karen E. Peterson (D-9)
Nicole Poore (D-12)

**Minority Members**
Gregory F. Lavelle (R-4)
Ernesto B. Lopez (R-6)

## Highways and Transportation

**Majority Members**
Karen E. Peterson (D-9) *Chairman*
Brian J. Bushweller (D-17)
Bethany A. Hall-Long (D-10)
David B. McBride (D-13)

**Minority Members**
Colin R. J. Bonini (R-16)
Bryant L. Richardson (R-21)

## Insurance and Telecommunications

**Majority Members**
Brian J. Bushweller (D-17)
 *Chairman*
Bethany A. Hall-Long (D-10)
Harris B. McDowell III (D-1)
David P. Sokola (D-8)

**Minority Members**
Colin R. J. Bonini (R-16)
Catherine A. Cloutier (R-5)

## Judiciary

**Majority Members**
Margaret Rose Henry (D-2)
 *Chairman*
Patricia M. "Patti" Blevins (D-7)
Harris B. McDowell III (D-1)
Bryan Townsend (D-11)

**Minority Members**
Gregory F. Lavelle (R-4)
F. Gary Simpson (R-18)

## Labor and Industrial Relations

**Majority Members**
Robert I. Marshall (D-3) *Chairman*
David B. McBride (D-13)
Karen E. Peterson (D-9)
Nicole Poore (D-12)

**Minority Members**
Catherine A. Cloutier (R-5)
Gerald W. Hocker (R-20)

## Legislative Council

**Majority Members**
Patricia M. "Patti" Blevins (D-7)
 *Chairman*
Margaret Rose Henry (D-2)
David B. McBride (D-13)

**Minority Members**
F. Gary Simpson (R-18)
Gregory F. Lavelle (R-4)

## Natural Resources and Environmental Control

**Majority Members**
David B. McBride (D-13) *Chairman*
Bruce C. Ennis (D-14)
Robert I. Marshall (D-3)
Karen E. Peterson (D-9)

**Minority Members**
Gerald W. Hocker (R-20)
Ernesto B. Lopez (R-6)

## Permanent Rules

**Majority Members**
Patricia M. "Patti" Blevins (D-7)
 *Chairman*
Margaret Rose Henry (D-2)
David B. McBride (D-13)
Harris B. McDowell III (D-1)

**Minority Members**
Gregory F. Lavelle (R-4)
F. Gary Simpson (R-18)

## Public Safety

**Majority Members**
Robert I. Marshall (D-3) *Chairman*
Brian J. Bushweller (D-17)
David B. McBride (D-13)
Bryan Townsend (D-11)

**Minority Members**
David G. Lawson (R-15)
Brian G. Pettyjohn (R-19)

## Sunset

**Majority Members**
Nicole Poore (D-12) *Chairman*
David P. Sokola (D-8)
Bryan Townsend (D-11)

**Minority Members**
Ernesto B. Lopez (R-6)
Brian G. Pettyjohn (R-19)

## Veterans Affairs

**Majority Members**
Bruce C. Ennis (D-14) *Chairman*
Bethany A. Hall-Long (D-10)
David B. McBride (D-13)
Karen E. Peterson (D-9)
Bryan Townsend (D-11)

**Minority Members**
David G. Lawson (R-15)
Brian G. Pettyjohn (R-19)

# Delaware House of Representatives

Tel: (302) 744-4087   Fax: (302) 739-2313
Fax: (302) 739-2773 (Republicans)   Fax: (302) 739-2313 (Democrats)

Speaker of the House
**Peter C. "Pete" Schwartzkopf** (D) . . . . . . . . . . . . . . . . . (302) 744-4351
   Education: Wilmington Col (DE) 1994 BA
Speaker Pro Tempore **Helene M. Keeley** (D) . . . . . . . . . . . (302) 744-4351
Majority Leader **Valerie J. Longhurst** (D) . . . . . . . . . . . . . (302) 744-4047
   Education: West Chester 1988 (Attended)
Majority Whip **John J. Viola** (D) . . . . . . . . . . . . . . . . . . . . (302) 744-4351
Minority Leader **Daniel B. Short** (R) . . . . . . . . . . . . . . . . (302) 744-4297
   Education: Delaware AA
Minority Whip **Deborah D. Hudson** (R) . . . . . . . . . . . . . (302) 744-4171
   Education: Delaware 1974 BS
Chief Clerk of the House **Richard L. Puffer** . . . . . . . . . . . . (302) 744-4087
   E-mail: richard.puffer@state.de.us

## Representatives

**Party Affiliation Statistics:** Republicans: 16, Democrats: 25

Representative
**Paul S. Baumbach, CFA, CFP, ChFC** (D-District 23) . . . . (302) 744-4351
   Counties Represented: New Castle (part)      Dist: (302) 577-8342
   Term Expires: 2017                            Fax: (302) 739-2313
   411 Legislative Avenue, Dover, DE 19901       Dist: (302) 577-6701
   E-mail: paul.baumbach@state.de.us
   Committees: Economic Development, Banking and Insurance; Housing
   and Community Affairs; Manufactured Housing; Revenue and Finance;
   Telecommunications, Internet and Technology
   Education: Delaware 1983 BS; Villanova 1988 MS

Representative **Andria L. Bennett** (D-District 32) . . . . . . . . (302) 744-4351
   Counties Represented: Kent (part)            Fax: (302) 739-2313
   Term Expires: 2017
   411 Legislative Avenue, Dover, DE 19901
   E-mail: andria.bennett@state.de.us
   Committees: Agriculture; Economic Development, Banking and
   Insurance; Housing and Community Affairs; Joint Sunset; Policy
   Analysis and Government Accountability; Revenue and Finance;
   Telecommunications, Internet and Technology; Veterans Affairs

Representative **David S. Bentz** (D-District 18) . . . . . . . . . . (302) 744-4351
   Counties Represented: New Castle (part)      Tel: (302) 577-8476
   Term Expires: 2017
   411 Legislative Avenue, Dover, DE 19901
   E-mail: david.bentz@state.de.us
   Committees: Education; Energy; Health and Human Development;
   Labor; Natural Resources

Representative **Stephanie T. Bolden** (D-District 2) . . . . . . . (302) 744-4351
   Counties Represented: New Castle (part)      Dist: (302) 577-8476
   Term Expires: 2017                            (Wilmington)
   411 Legislative Avenue, Dover, DE 19901       Res: (302) 428-1269
   E-mail: stephaniet.bolden@state.de.us        Fax: (302) 739-2313
   Committees: Education; Gaming and Parimutuels;   Dist: (302) 577-6701
   Health and Human Development; Housing and Community Affairs;
   Joint Sunset; Labor; Policy Analysis and Government Accountability;
   Revenue and Finance; Veterans Affairs
   Education: Delaware State 1969 BS; Boston Col 1974 MEd

Representative **Gerald L. Brady** (D-District 4) . . . . . . . . . . (302) 744-4351
   Counties Represented: New Castle (part)      Dist: (302) 577-8476
   Term Expires: 2017
   411 Legislative Avenue, Dover, DE 19901
   E-mail: gerald.brady@state.de.us
   Committees: Corrections; Joint Sunset; Judiciary; Labor; Natural
   Resources; Policy Analysis and Government Accountability; Public
   Safety and Homeland Security; Transportation, Land Use and
   Infrastructure; Veterans Affairs

Representative **Ruth Briggs-King** (R-District 37) . . . . . . . . (302) 744-4251
   Counties Represented: Sussex (part)          Dist: (302) 856-2772
   Term Expires: 2017                            Fax: (302) 739-2773
   411 Legislative Avenue, Dover, DE 19901
   E-mail: ruth.king@state.de.us
   Committees: Health and Human Development; Manufactured Housing;
   Public Safety and Homeland Security; Transportation, Land Use and
   Infrastructure; Veterans Affairs
   Education: Wilmington Col (DE) BA, MA

Representative **William J. Carson, Jr.** (D-District 28) . . . . . (302) 744-4113
   Counties Represented: Kent (part)            Fax: (302) 739-2313
   Term Expires: 2017
   411 Legislative Avenue, Dover, DE 19901
   E-mail: william.carson@state.de.us
   Committees: Agriculture; Appropriations; Corrections; Joint Finance;
   Manufactured Housing; Natural Resources; Public Safety and
   Homeland Security; Transportation, Land Use and Infrastructure;
   Veterans Affairs

Representative **Richard G. Collins** (R-District 41) . . . . . . . . (302) 744-4087
   Counties Represented: Sussex (part)
   Term Expires: 2017
   E-mail: richard.collins@state.de.us
   Committees: Agriculture; Energy; Telecommunications, Internet and
   Technology; Transportation, Land Use and Infrastructure

Representative **Timothy D. Dukes** (R-District 40) . . . . . . . . (302) 744-4171
   Counties Represented: Sussex (part)          Fax: (302) 875-7207
   Term Expires: 2017
   411 Legislative Avenue, Dover, DE 19901
   E-mail: timothy.dukes@state.de.us
   Committees: Education; Gaming and Parimutuels; Health and Human
   Development; Joint Sunset; Natural Resources; Policy Analysis and
   Government Accountability; Telecommunications, Internet and
   Technology; Veterans Affairs
   Education: Valley Forge Christian BSc

Representative **Ronald E. Gray** (R-District 38) . . . . . . . . . . (302) 744-4171
   Counties Represented: Sussex (part)
   Term Expires: 2017
   411 Legislative Avenue, Dover, DE 19901
   E-mail: ronald.gray@state.de.us
   Committees: Economic Development, Banking and Insurance; Housing
   and Community Affairs; Labor; Natural Resources; Revenue and
   Finance; Veterans Affairs
   Education: Delaware BCE

Representative **Debra J. Heffernan** (D-District 6) . . . . . . . . (302) 744-4351
   Counties Represented: New Castle (part)      Dist: (302) 577-8476
   Term Expires: 2017                            Res: (302) 762-3478
   411 Legislative Avenue, Dover, DE 19901
   E-mail: debra.heffernan@state.de.us
   Committees: Appropriations; Education; Energy; Health and Human
   Development; Joint Finance; Natural Resources; Veterans Affairs
   Education: Delaware BS; Duke MS

Representative **Kevin S. Hensley** (R-District 9) . . . . . . . . . . (302) 744-4087
   Counties Represented: New Castle (part)
   Term Expires: 2017
   E-mail: kevin.hensley@state.de.us
   Committees: Economic Development, Banking and Insurance;
   Education; Health and Human Development; Housing and Community
   Affairs; Veterans Affairs

Representative **Deborah D. Hudson** (R-District 12) . . . . . . (302) 744-4171
   Counties Represented: New Castle (part)      Dist: (302) 577-8723
   Term Expires: 2017                            (Wilmington)
   1022 Oriente Avenue, Wilmington, DE 19807-2261   Fax: (302) 577-6396
   E-mail: deborah.hudson@state.de.us
   Committees: Ethics; House Administration; House Rules;
   Telecommunications, Internet and Technology

Representative **Earl G. Jaques, Jr.** (D-District 27) . . . . . . . . (302) 744-4142
   Counties Represented: New Castle (part)      Dist: (302) 577-8476
   Term Expires: 2017                            Fax: (302) 739-2313
   411 Legislative Avenue, Dover, DE 19901
   E-mail: earl.jaques@state.de.us
   Committees: Education; Health and Human Development; Labor;
   Transportation, Land Use and Infrastructure; Veterans Affairs
   Education: Columbia Southern BS

Representative **James J. Johnson** (D-District 16) . . . . . . . . (302) 744-4351
   Counties Represented: New Castle (part)      Dist: (302) 577-8476
   Term Expires: 2017                            Fax: (302) 739-2313
   411 Legislative Avenue, Dover, DE 19901       Dist: (302) 577-6701
   E-mail: jj.johnson@state.de.us
   Committees: Appropriations; Corrections; Gaming and Parimutuels;
   Joint Finance; Judiciary; Labor; Public Safety and Homeland Security;
   Revenue and Finance; Veterans Affairs
   Education: Goldey-Beacom 1975 AS

*(continued on next page)*

**LEGISLATIVE BRANCH**

**Representatives** *continued*

Representative **S. Quinton Johnson** (D-District 8) . . . . . . . (302) 744-4351
Counties Represented: New Castle (part)          Dist: (302) 577-8476
Term Expires: 2017                                Dist: (302) 378-2681
411 Legislative Avenue, Dover, DE 19901           Fax: (302) 739-2313
E-mail: quinton.johnson@state.de.us
Committees: Agriculture; Capital Infrastructure; Economic
Development, Banking and Insurance; Gaming and Parimutuels; Health
and Human Development; Natural Resources; Revenue and Finance;
Veterans Affairs
Education: Salisbury State U BS

Representative **Helene M. Keeley** (D-District 3) . . . . . . . . (302) 744-4351
Counties Represented: New Castle (part)          Dist: (302) 577-8476
Term Expires: 2017                                      (Wilmington)
2119 Gilles Street, Wilmington, DE 19805          Fax: (302) 577-6701
E-mail: helene.keeley@state.de.us
Committees: Economic Development, Banking and Insurance; Gaming
and Parimutuels; Housing and Community Affairs; Labor; Revenue and
Finance

Representative **Harvey R. Kenton** (R-District 36) . . . . . . . (302) 744-4171
Counties Represented: Sussex (part)               Res: (302) 422-6155
Term Expires: 2017                                Fax: (302) 739-2773
411 Legislative Avenue, Dover, DE 19901
E-mail: harvey.kenton@state.de.us
Committees: Agriculture; Appropriations; Education; Joint Finance;
Natural Resources; Veterans Affairs

Representative **John A. Kowalko, Jr.** (D-District 25) . . . . . (302) 744-4351
Counties Represented: New Castle (part)          Dist: (302) 577-8342
Term Expires: 2017                                Fax: (302) 739-2313
411 Legislative Avenue, Dover, DE 19901           Dist: (302) 577-6701
E-mail: john.kowalko@state.de.us
Committees: Energy; Health and Human Development; Labor;
Manufactured Housing; Natural Resources

Representative **Valerie J. Longhurst** (D-District 15) . . . . . (302) 744-4047
Counties Represented: New Castle (part)          Dist: (302) 577-8475
Term Expires: 2017
411 Legislative Avenue, Dover, DE 19901
E-mail: valerie.longhurst@state.de.us
Committees: Ethics; House Administration; House Rules; Manufactured
Housing

Representative **Sean M. Lynn** (D-District 31) . . . . . . . . . . (302) 744-4351
Counties Represented: Kent (part)                Dist: (302) 744-4177
Term Expires: 2017
E-mail: sean.lynn@state.de.us
Committees: Agriculture; Education; Energy; Health and Human
Development; Judiciary; Telecommunications, Internet and Technology;
Veterans Affairs
Education: Marymount Manhattan

Representative **Sean Matthews** (D-District 10) . . . . . . . . . (302) 744-4351
Counties Represented: New Castle (part)          Dist: (302) 577-8476
Term Expires: 2017                                Dist: (302) 331-1020
E-mail: sean.matthews@state.de.us
Committees: Education; Health and Human Development; Housing and
Community Affairs; Labor; Revenue and Finance; Veterans Affairs

Representative **Joseph E. Miro** (R-District 22) . . . . . . . . . (302) 744-4171
Counties Represented: New Castle (part)          Tel: (302) 577-8723
Term Expires: 2017                                      (Wilmington)
5 Firechase Circle, Newark, DE 19711
E-mail: joseph.miro@state.de.us
Committees: Appropriations; Education; Health and Human
Development; Joint Finance
Education: Lincoln U (PA) 1970 BA; West Chester 1975 MA

Representative **John L. Mitchell, Jr.** (D-District 13) . . . . . . (302) 744-4351
Counties Represented: New Castle (part)          Dist: (302) 577-8342
Term Expires: 2017                                Fax: (302) 739-2313
411 Legislative Avenue, Dover, DE 19901           Dist: (302) 577-6701
E-mail: john.l.mitchell@state.de.us
Committees: Capital Infrastructure; Corrections; Gaming and
Parimutuels; Judiciary; Public Safety and Homeland Security

Representative **Michael P. Mulrooney** (D-District 17) . . . . . (302) 744-4351
Counties Represented: New Castle (part)          Tel: (302) 577-8476
Term Expires: 2017                                      (Wilmington)
32 Saratoga Drive, New Castle, DE 19720
E-mail: michael.mulrooney@state.de.us
Committees: Agriculture; Capital Infrastructure; Corrections; Energy;
Labor; Natural Resources; Public Safety and Homeland Security;
Veterans Affairs

Representative **Edward S. Osienski** (D-District 24) . . . . . . (302) 744-4351
Counties Represented: New Castle (part)          Dist: (302) 577-8476
Term Expires: 2017                                Res: (302) 292-8903
411 Legislative Avenue, Dover, DE 19901           Fax: (302) 739-2313
E-mail: edward.osienski@state.de.us               Dist: (302) 577-6701
Committees: Education; Health and Human Development; Labor;
Public Safety and Homeland Security; Transportation, Land Use and
Infrastructure; Veterans Affairs

Representative
**William R. "Bobby" Outten** (R-District 30) . . . . . . . . . (302) 744-4083
Counties Represented: Kent (part)                Dist: (302) 398-3816
Term Expires: 2017                                Fax: (302) 739-2773
411 Legislative Avenue, Dover, DE 19901
E-mail: bobby.outten@state.de.us
Committees: Agriculture; Corrections; Judiciary; Public Safety and
Homeland Security; Veterans Affairs

Representative
**W. Charles "Trey" Paradee** (D-District 29) . . . . . . . . . . (302) 744-4351
Counties Represented: Kent (part)                Fax: (302) 739-2313
Term Expires: 2017
411 Legislative Avenue, Dover, DE 19901
E-mail: trey.paradee@state.de.us
Committees: Agriculture; Economic Development, Banking and
Insurance; Energy; Judiciary; Natural Resources; Telecommunications,
Internet and Technology; Veterans Affairs
Education: Delaware 1991 BA, 1998 MBA

Representative **Harold J. Peterman** (R-District 33) . . . . . . (302) 744-4171
Counties Represented: Kent (part)                Res: (302) 335-4261
Term Expires: 2017                                Fax: (302) 739-2773
411 Legislative Avenue, Dover, DE 19901
E-mail: jack.peterman@state.de.us
Committees: Agriculture; Housing and Community Affairs; Natural
Resources; Veterans Affairs

Representative **Charles Potter, Jr.** (D-District 1) . . . . . . . . (302) 744-4351
Counties Represented: New Castle (part)          Dist: (302) 577-5312
Term Expires: 2017                                Dist: (302) 762-8322
411 Legislative Avenue, Dover, DE 19901           Fax: (302) 739-2313
E-mail: charles.potter@state.de.us                Dist: (302) 652-2411
Committees: Capital Infrastructure; Education;    Dist: (302) 577-6701
Gaming and Parimutuels; Judiciary; Revenue and Finance
Education: Wilmington Col (DE) 1982 BA

Representative
**Michael J. "Mike" Ramone** (R-District 21) . . . . . . . . . . (302) 744-4108
Counties Represented: New Castle (part)          Dist: (302) 577-8723
Term Expires: 2017                                Dist: (302) 584-8601
Carvel State Office Building, 820 North French    Fax: (302) 739-2773
Street, Wilmington, DE 19801                      Dist: (302) 577-6396
E-mail: michael.ramone@state.de.us
Committees: Capital Infrastructure; Economic Development, Banking
and Insurance; Education; Gaming and Parimutuels; Labor; Revenue
and Finance; Veterans Affairs
Education: Delaware 1982 (Attended)

Representative
**Peter C. "Pete" Schwartzkopf** (D-District 14) . . . . . . . . (302) 744-4351
Counties Represented: Sussex (part)
Term Expires: 2017
411 Legislative Avenue, Dover, DE 19901
E-mail: peter.schwartzkopf@state.de.us
Committees: Ethics; House Administration; House Rules

Representative **Bryon H. Short** (D-District 7) . . . . . . . . . . (302) 744-4297
Counties Represented: New Castle (part)          Dist: (302) 577-8480
Term Expires: 2017                                Dist: (302) 475-2552
411 Legislative Avenue, Dover, DE 19901
E-mail: bryon.short@state.de.us
Committees: Economic Development, Banking and Insurance; Housing
and Community Affairs; Revenue and Finance; Veterans Affairs
Education: Salisbury State U 1988 BA

Representative **Daniel B. Short** (R-District 39) . . . . . . . . . (302) 744-4172
Counties Represented: Sussex (part)              Dist: (302) 628-5222
Term Expires: 2017                                Fax: (302) 739-2773
133 N. Cannon St., Seaford, DE 19973
E-mail: daniel.short@state.de.us
Committees: Ethics; Gaming and Parimutuels; House Administration;
House Rules; Veterans Affairs

Representative
**Melanie George Smith, JD** (D-District 5) . . . . . . . . . . . (302) 744-4126
Counties Represented: New Castle (part)          Dist: (302) 577-8476
Term Expires: 2017                                      (Wilmington)
411 Legislative Avenue, Dover, DE 19901           Fax: (302) 739-2313
E-mail: melanie.g.smith@state.de.us               Dist: (302) 577-6701
Committees: Appropriations; Joint Finance; Judiciary; Public Safety
and Homeland Security; Veterans Affairs
Education: Pennsylvania BA; Georgetown JD

Representative **Stephen T. Smyk** (R-District 20) . . . . . . . . (302) 744-4321
  Counties Represented: Sussex (part)          Dist: (302) 577-8723
  Term Expires: 2017                            Fax: (302) 739-2773
  411 Legislative Avenue, Dover, DE 19901       Fax: (302) 257-7639
  E-mail: steve.smyk@state.de.us
  Committees: Corrections; Energy; Judiciary; Public Safety and
  Homeland Security
Representative **Jeffrey N. Spiegelman** (R-District 11) . . . . (302) 744-4171
  Counties Represented: Kent (part), New Castle   Dist: (302) 577-8723
  (part)
  Term Expires: 2017
  411 Legislative Avenue, Dover, DE 19901
  E-mail: jeff.spiegelman@state.de.us
  Committees: Economic Development, Banking and Insurance; Housing
  and Community Affairs; Joint Sunset; Judiciary; Policy Analysis and
  Government Accountability; Revenue and Finance; Veterans Affairs
Representative **John J. Viola** (D-District 26) . . . . . . . . . . . (302) 744-4351
  Counties Represented: New Castle (part)      Dist: (302) 577-8187
  Term Expires: 2017                            Fax: (302) 577-6701
  Carvel State Office Building, 820 North French Street,
  Wilmington, DE 19801
  E-mail: john.viola@state.de.us
  Committees: Ethics; House Administration; House Rules;
  Telecommunications, Internet and Technology
Representative **Kimberly Williams** (D-District 19) . . . . . . . (302) 744-4351
  Counties Represented: New Castle (part)      Dist: (302) 577-8476
  Term Expires: 2017
  411 Legislative Avenue, Dover, DE 19901
  E-mail: kimberly.williams@state.de.us
  Committees: Education; Housing and Community Affairs; Labor;
  Telecommunications, Internet and Technology; Veterans Affairs
Representative **David L. Wilson** (R-District 35) . . . . . . . . . (302) 744-4150
  Counties Represented: Sussex (part)          Dist: (302) 422-9270
  Term Expires: 2017                            Fax: (302) 739-2773
  411 Legislative Avenue, Dover, DE 19901       Dist: (302) 422-0462
  E-mail: david.l.wilson@state.de.us
  Committees: Agriculture; Capital Infrastructure; Corrections; Judiciary;
  Public Safety and Homeland Security; Veterans Affairs
Representative **Lyndon D. Yearick** (R-District 34) . . . . . . . (302) 744-4171
  Counties Represented: Kent (part)            Dist: (302) 387-2510
  Term Expires: 2017
  E-mail: lyndon.yearick@state.de.us
  Committees: Health and Human Development; Manufactured Housing;
  Revenue and Finance; Telecommunications, Internet and Technology;
  Veterans Affairs
  Education: Penn State MBA; Bloomsburg BS

## House Standing Committees

### Agriculture

**Majority Members**
William J. Carson, Jr. (D-28) *Chair*
S. Quinton Johnson (D-8)
  *Vice Chair*
Andria L. Bennett (D-32)
Sean M. Lynn (D-31)
Michael P. Mulrooney (D-17)
W. Charles "Trey" Paradee (D-29)

**Minority Members**
Richard G. Collins (R-41)
Harvey R. Kenton (R-36)
William R. "Bobby" Outten (R-30)
Harold J. Peterman (R-33)
David L. Wilson (R-35)

### Appropriations

**Majority Members**
Melanie George Smith (D-5) *Chair*
James J. Johnson (D-16) *Vice Chair*
William J. Carson, Jr. (D-28)
Debra J. Heffernan (D-6)

**Minority Members**
Harvey R. Kenton (R-36)
Joseph E. Miro (R-22)

### Capital Infrastructure

**Majority Members**
S. Quinton Johnson (D-8) *Chair*
Michael P. Mulrooney (D-17)
  *Vice Chair*
John L. Mitchell, Jr. (D-13)
Charles Potter, Jr. (D-1)

**Minority Members**
Michael J. "Mike" Ramone (R-21)
David L. Wilson (R-35)

### Corrections

**Majority Members**
James J. Johnson (D-16) *Chair*
John L. Mitchell, Jr. (D-13)
  *Vice Chair*
Gerald L. Brady (D-4)
William J. Carson, Jr. (D-28)
Michael P. Mulrooney (D-17)

**Minority Members**
William R. "Bobby" Outten (R-30)
Stephen T. Smyk (R-20)
David L. Wilson (R-35)

### Economic Development, Banking and Insurance

**Majority Members**
Bryon H. Short (D-7) *Chair*
Andria L. Bennett (D-32)
  *Vice Chair*
Paul S. Baumbach (D-23)
S. Quinton Johnson (D-8)
Helene M. Keeley (D-3)
W. Charles "Trey" Paradee (D-29)

**Minority Members**
Ronald E. Gray (R-38)
Kevin S. Hensley (R-9)
Michael J. "Mike" Ramone (R-21)
Jeffrey N. Spiegelman (R-11)

### Education

**Majority Members**
Earl G. Jaques, Jr. (D-27) *Chair*
Kimberly Williams (D-19)
  *Vice Chair*
David S. Bentz (D-18)
Stephanie T. Bolden (D-2)
Debra J. Heffernan (D-6)
Sean M. Lynn (D-31)
Sean Matthews (D-10)
Edward S. Osienski (D-24)
Charles Potter, Jr. (D-1)

**Minority Members**
Timothy D. Dukes (R-40)
Kevin S. Hensley (R-9)
Harvey R. Kenton (R-36)
Joseph E. Miro (R-22)
Michael J. "Mike" Ramone (R-21)

### Energy

**Majority Members**
W. Charles "Trey" Paradee (D-29)
  *Chair*
Sean M. Lynn (D-31) *Vice Chair*
David S. Bentz (D-18)
Debra J. Heffernan (D-6)
John A. Kowalko, Jr. (D-25)
Michael P. Mulrooney (D-17)

**Minority Members**
Richard G. Collins (R-41)
Stephen T. Smyk (R-20)

### Ethics

**Majority Members**
Valerie J. Longhurst (D-15)
  *Chairman*
Peter C. "Pete"
  Schwartzkopf (D-14)
  *Vice Chairman*
John J. Viola (D-26)

**Minority Members**
Deborah D. Hudson (R-12)
Daniel B. Short (R-39)

### Gaming and Parimutuels

**Majority Members**
Charles Potter, Jr. (D-1) *Chairman*
Helene M. Keeley (D-3)
  *Vice Chairman*
Stephanie T. Bolden (D-2)
James J. Johnson (D-16)
S. Quinton Johnson (D-8)
John L. Mitchell, Jr. (D-13)

**Minority Members**
Timothy D. Dukes (R-40)
Michael J. "Mike" Ramone (R-21)
Daniel B. Short (R-39)

### Health and Human Development

**Majority Members**
Debra J. Heffernan (D-6) *Chair*
David S. Bentz (D-18) *Vice Chair*
Stephanie T. Bolden (D-2)
Earl G. Jaques, Jr. (D-27)
S. Quinton Johnson (D-8)
John A. Kowalko, Jr. (D-25)
Sean M. Lynn (D-31)
Sean Matthews (D-10)
Edward S. Osienski (D-24)

**Minority Members**
Ruth Briggs-King (R-37)
Timothy D. Dukes (R-40)
Kevin S. Hensley (R-9)
Joseph E. Miro (R-22)
Lyndon D. Yearick (R-34)

**LEGISLATIVE BRANCH**

## House Administration

| Majority Members | Minority Members |
|---|---|
| Valerie J. Longhurst (D-15) *Chair* | Deborah D. Hudson (R-12) |
| John J. Viola (D-26) | Daniel B. Short (R-39) |
| Peter C. "Pete" Schwartzkopf (D-14) | |

## House Rules

| Majority Members | Minority Members |
|---|---|
| Valerie J. Longhurst (D-15) *Chairman* | Deborah D. Hudson (R-12) |
| Peter C. "Pete" Schwartzkopf (D-14) | Daniel B. Short (R-39) |
| John J. Viola (D-26) | |

## Housing and Community Affairs

| Majority Members | Minority Members |
|---|---|
| Stephanie T. Bolden (D-2) *Chair* | Ronald E. Gray (R-38) |
| Andria L. Bennett (D-32) *Vice Chair* | Kevin S. Hensley (R-9) |
| Paul S. Baumbach (D-23) | Harold J. Peterman (R-33) |
| Helene M. Keeley (D-3) | Jeffrey N. Spiegelman (R-11) |
| Sean Matthews (D-10) | |
| Bryon H. Short (D-7) | |
| Kimberly Williams (D-19) | |

## Judiciary

| Majority Members | Minority Members |
|---|---|
| John L. Mitchell, Jr. (D-13) *Chair* | William R. "Bobby" Outten (R-30) |
| Melanie George Smith (D-5) *Vice Chair* | Stephen T. Smyk (R-20) |
| Gerald L. Brady (D-4) | Jeffrey N. Spiegelman (R-11) |
| James J. Johnson (D-16) | David L. Wilson (R-35) |
| Sean M. Lynn (D-31) | |
| W. Charles "Trey" Paradee (D-29) | |
| Charles Potter, Jr. (D-1) | |

## Labor

| Majority Members | Minority Members |
|---|---|
| Michael P. Mulrooney (D-17) *Chair* | Ronald E. Gray (R-38) |
| Edward S. Osienski (D-24) *Vice Chair* | Michael J. "Mike" Ramone (R-21) |
| David S. Bentz (D-18) | |
| Stephanie T. Bolden (D-2) | |
| Gerald L. Brady (D-4) | |
| Earl G. Jaques, Jr. (D-27) | |
| James J. Johnson (D-16) | |
| Helene M. Keeley (D-3) | |
| John A. Kowalko, Jr. (D-25) | |
| Sean Matthews (D-10) | |
| Kimberly Williams (D-19) | |

## Manufactured Housing

| Majority Members | Minority Members |
|---|---|
| Paul S. Baumbach (D-23) *Chair* | Ruth Briggs-King (R-37) |
| William J. Carson, Jr. (D-28) *Vice Chair* | Lyndon D. Yearick (R-34) |
| John A. Kowalko, Jr. (D-25) | |
| Valerie J. Longhurst (D-15) | |

## Natural Resources

| Majority Members | Minority Members |
|---|---|
| Debra J. Heffernan (D-6) *Chair* | Timothy D. Dukes (R-40) |
| Michael P. Mulrooney (D-17) *Vice Chair* | Ronald E. Gray (R-38) |
| David S. Bentz (D-18) | Harvey R. Kenton (R-36) |
| Gerald L. Brady (D-4) | Harold J. Peterman (R-33) |
| William J. Carson, Jr. (D-28) | |
| S. Quinton Johnson (D-8) | |
| John A. Kowalko, Jr. (D-25) | |
| W. Charles "Trey" Paradee (D-29) | |

## Policy Analysis and Government Accountability

| Majority Members | Minority Members |
|---|---|
| Gerald L. Brady (D-4) *Chair* | Timothy D. Dukes (R-40) |
| Andria L. Bennett (D-32) | Jeffrey N. Spiegelman (R-11) |
| Stephanie T. Bolden (D-2) | |

## Public Safety and Homeland Security

| Majority Members | Minority Members |
|---|---|
| John L. Mitchell, Jr. (D-13) *Chair* | Ruth Briggs-King (R-37) |
| Michael P. Mulrooney (D-17) *Vice Chair* | William R. "Bobby" Outten (R-30) |
| Gerald L. Brady (D-4) | Stephen T. Smyk (R-20) |
| William J. Carson, Jr. (D-28) | David L. Wilson (R-35) |
| James J. Johnson (D-16) | |
| Edward S. Osienski (D-24) | |
| Melanie George Smith (D-5) | |

## Revenue and Finance

| Majority Members | Minority Members |
|---|---|
| Helene M. Keeley (D-3) *Chair* | Ronald E. Gray (R-38) |
| Bryon H. Short (D-7) *Vice Chair* | Michael J. "Mike" Ramone (R-21) |
| Paul S. Baumbach (D-23) | Jeffrey N. Spiegelman (R-11) |
| Andria L. Bennett (D-32) | Lyndon D. Yearick (R-34) |
| Stephanie T. Bolden (D-2) | |
| James J. Johnson (D-16) | |
| S. Quinton Johnson (D-8) | |
| Sean Matthews (D-10) | |
| Charles Potter, Jr. (D-1) | |

## Telecommunications, Internet and Technology

| Majority Members | Minority Members |
|---|---|
| Andria L. Bennett (D-32) *Chair* | Richard G. Collins (R-41) |
| W. Charles "Trey" Paradee (D-29) *Vice Chair* | Timothy D. Dukes (R-40) |
| Paul S. Baumbach (D-23) | Deborah D. Hudson (R-12) |
| Sean M. Lynn (D-31) | Lyndon D. Yearick (R-34) |
| John J. Viola (D-26) | |
| Kimberly Williams (D-19) | |

## Transportation, Land Use and Infrastructure

| Majority Members | Minority Members |
|---|---|
| Edward S. Osienski (D-24) *Chair* | Ruth Briggs-King (R-37) |
| William J. Carson, Jr. (D-28) *Vice Chair* | Richard G. Collins (R-41) |
| Gerald L. Brady (D-4) | |
| Earl G. Jaques, Jr. (D-27) | |

## Veterans Affairs

| Majority Members | Minority Members |
|---|---|
| Earl G. Jaques, Jr. (D-27) *Chair* | Ruth Briggs-King (R-37) |
| Gerald L. Brady (D-4) *Vice Chair* | Timothy D. Dukes (R-40) |
| Andria L. Bennett (D-32) | Ronald E. Gray (R-38) |
| Stephanie T. Bolden (D-2) | Kevin S. Hensley (R-9) |
| William J. Carson, Jr. (D-28) | Harvey R. Kenton (R-36) |
| Debra J. Heffernan (D-6) | William R. "Bobby" Outten (R-30) |
| James J. Johnson (D-16) | Harold J. Peterman (R-33) |
| S. Quinton Johnson (D-8) | Michael J. "Mike" Ramone (R-21) |
| Sean M. Lynn (D-31) | Daniel B. Short (R-39) |
| Sean Matthews (D-10) | Jeffrey N. Spiegelman (R-11) |
| Michael P. Mulrooney (D-17) | David L. Wilson (R-35) |
| Edward S. Osienski (D-24) | Lyndon D. Yearick (R-34) |
| W. Charles "Trey" Paradee (D-29) | |
| Bryon H. Short (D-7) | |
| Melanie George Smith (D-5) | |
| Kimberly Williams (D-19) | |

# Florida Legislature

Tel: (850) 488-1234  Internet: www.leg.state.fl.us

## Florida Senate

The Capitol, 404 South Monroe Street, Tallahassee, FL 32399-1100
Tel: (850) 487-5270  Fax: (850) 487-5174  Internet: www.flsenate.gov

President of the Senate **Andy Gardiner** (R) . . . . . . . . . . . . (850) 487-5013
  Education: Stetson 1992 BS
  Chief of Staff **Reynold David Meyer** . . . . . . . . . . . . . . . (850) 487-5013
President Pro Tempore **Garrett S. Richter** (R) . . . . . . . . . . (850) 487-5023
  Education: Pittsburgh 1981 BS
Majority Leader **Bill Galvano** (R) . . . . . . . . . . . . . . . . . . . (850) 487-5026
  Education: Florida 1989 BA; Miami 1992 JD
Deputy Majority Leader **Denise Grimsley** (R) . . . . . . . . . . (850) 487-5021
  Education: Warner Southern BA; Miami MBA
Minority Leader **Arthenia L. Joyner** (D) . . . . . . . . . . . . . . (850) 487-5019
  Education: Florida A&M 1964 BS, 1968 JD
Minority Leader Pro Tempore **Oscar Braynon II** (D) . . . . . . (850) 487-5036
  Education: Florida State BS
Minority Whip **Joseph Abruzzo** (D) . . . . . . . . . . . . . . . . . (850) 487-5025
  Education: Lynn 2003 BA
Minority Deputy Whip **Maria Lorts Sachs** (D) . . . . . . . . . . (850) 487-5833
  Education: Maryland BA; Boston U MA; Miami JD
Secretary of the Senate **Debbie Brown** . . . . . . . . . . . . . . . (850) 487-5270
Sergeant-at-Arms **Tim Hay** . . . . . . . . . . . . . . . . . . . . . . . (850) 487-5224

## Senators

**Party Affiliation Statistics: Republicans: 26, Democrats: 14**

Senator **Joseph Abruzzo** (D-District 25)
  222 Senate Office Building . . . . . . . . . . . . . . . . . . (850) 487-5025
  Counties Represented: Palm Beach (part)   Dist: (561) 791-4774
  Term Expires: 2016   Fax: (888) 284-6495
  12300 West Forest Hill Boulevard, Suite 200,
  Wellington, FL 33414-5785
  E-mail: abruzzo.joseph.web@flsenate.gov
  Committees: Communications, Energy and Public Utilities; Community
  Affairs; Finance and Tax; Fiscal Policy; Joint Legislative Auditing;
  Regulated Industries

Senator **Thad Altman** (R-District 16)
  314 Senate Office Building . . . . . . . . . . . . . . . . . . (850) 487-5016
  Counties Represented: Brevard (part), Indian   Dist: (321) 868-2132
  River (part)   Fax: (888) 263-3815
  Term Expires: 2018
  8910 Astronaut Boulevard, Suite 210, Cape Canaveral, FL 32920
  E-mail: altman.thad.web@flsenate.gov
  Committees: Appropriations; Children, Families and Elder Affairs;
  Environmental Preservation and Conservation; Finance and Tax;
  Military and Veterans Affairs, Space, and Domestic Security
  Education: Brevard Com Col 1975 AA; Rollins 1987 BS

Senator **Aaron P. Bean** (R-District 4) . . . . . . . . . . . . . . . (850) 487-5004
  Counties Represented: Duval (part), Nassau   Dist: (904) 346-5039
  Term Expires: 2018   Fax: (888) 263-1578
  1919 Atlantic Boulevard, Jacksonville, FL 32207
  302 Senate Office Building, 404 South Monroe,
  Tallahassee, FL 32399-1100
  E-mail: bean.aaron.web@flsenate.gov
  Committees: Commerce and Tourism; Fiscal Policy; Health Policy;
  Judiciary; Regulated Industries
  Education: Jacksonville U 1989 BS

Senator **Lizbeth Benacquisto** (R-District 30)
  326 Senate Office Building . . . . . . . . . . . . . . . . . . (850) 487-5030
  Counties Represented: Charlotte (part), Lee (part)   Dist: (239) 338-2570
  Term Expires: 2018
  2310 First Street, Unit 305, Fort Myers, FL 33901
  E-mail: benacquisto.lizbeth.web@flsenate.gov
  Committees: Appropriations; Banking and Insurance; Education Pre-K
  -12; Higher Education; Joint Legislative Auditing; Judiciary; Rules
  Education: Palm Beach Atlantic BA

Senator **Rob Bradley** (R-District 7)
  208 Senate Office Building . . . . . . . . . . . . . . . . . . (850) 487-5007
  Counties Represented: Alachua, Bradford, Clay   Dist: (904) 278-2085
  Term Expires: 2016   Fax: (888) 263-0641
  2233 Park Avenue, Suite 303, Orange Park, FL 32073
  E-mail: bradley.rob.web@flsenate.gov
  Committees: Communications, Energy and Public Utilities; Community
  Affairs; Criminal Justice; Fiscal Policy; Joint Legislative Auditing;
  Reapportionment; Regulated Industries
  Education: Florida 1992 BS, 1996 JD

Senator **Jeffrey P. "Jeff" Brandes** (R-District 22)
  318 Senate Office Building . . . . . . . . . . . . . . . . . . (850) 487-5022
  Counties Represented: Hillsborough (part), Pinellas   Dist: (727) 563-2100
  (part)   Fax: (305) 654-7152
  Term Expires: 2018
  9800 Fourth Street North, Suite 200, St. Petersburg, FL 33702
  E-mail: brandes.jeff.web@flsenate.gov
  Committees: Community Affairs; Criminal Justice; Education Pre-K
  -12; Judiciary; Transportation
  Education: Carson-Newman 1999 BS

Senator **Oscar Braynon II** (D-District 36) . . . . . . . . . . . . . (850) 487-5036
  Counties Represented: Broward (part), Miami-Dade   Dist: (305) 654-7150
  (part)   Fax: (305) 654-7152
  Term Expires: 2018
  606 Northwest 183rd Street, Miami Gardens, FL 33169
  213 Senate Office Building, 404 Monroe Street,
  Tallahassee, FL 32399-1100
  E-mail: braynon.oscar.web@flsenate.gov
  Committees: Ethics and Elections; Health Policy; Higher Education;
  Joint Legislative Budget Commission; Reapportionment; Regulated
  Industries; Transportation

Senator **Dwight M. Bullard** (D-District 39) . . . . . . . . . . . . (850) 487-5039
  Counties Represented: Collier (part), Hendry,   Dist: (305) 234-2208
  Miami-Dade (part), Monroe   Fax: (305) 234-2210
  Term Expires: 2016
  218 Senate Office Building, 404 Monroe Street,
  Tallahassee, FL 32399-1100
  10720 Caribbean Boulevard, Suite 435, Cutler Bay, FL 33189
  E-mail: bullard.dwight.web@flsenate.gov
  Committees: Agriculture; Education Pre-K -12; Governmental
  Oversight and Accountability; Transportation
  Education: Florida A&M 1999 BS

Senator **Jeff Clemens** (D-District 27)
  226 Senate Office Building . . . . . . . . . . . . . . . . . . (850) 487-5027
  Counties Represented: Palm Beach (part)   Dist: (561) 540-1140
  Term Expires: 2016   Fax: (561) 540-1143
  508 Lake Avenue, Unit C, Lake Worth, FL 33460
  E-mail: clemens.jeff.web@flsenate.gov
  Committees: Banking and Insurance; Criminal Justice; Education Pre-K
  -12; Ethics and Elections; Fiscal Policy
  Education: Michigan State 1992 BA

Senator **Charles S. "Charlie" Dean, Sr.** (R-District 5)
  311 Senate Office Building . . . . . . . . . . . . . . . . . . (850) 487-5005
  Counties Represented: Baker, Citrus, Columbia,   Dist: (352) 860-5175
  Dixie, Gilchrist, Lafayette, Levy, Marion (part), Suwannee, Union
  Term Expires: 2017
  405 Tompkins Street, Inverness, FL 34450
  E-mail: dean.charles.web@flsenate.gov
  Committees: Agriculture; Children, Families and Elder Affairs;
  Communications, Energy and Public Utilities; Community Affairs;
  Environmental Preservation and Conservation
  Education: Florida State 1963 BS; Rollins 1976 MS

Senator **Nancy C. Detert** (R-District 28)
  416 Senate Office Building . . . . . . . . . . . . . . . . . . (850) 487-5028
  Counties Represented: Charlotte (part), Sarasota   Dist: (941) 480-3547
  Term Expires: 2018   Fax: (941) 480-3549
  417 Commercial Court, Suite D, Venice, FL 34292
  E-mail: detert.nancy.web@flsenate.gov
  Committees: Banking and Insurance; Children, Families and Elder
  Affairs; Commerce and Tourism; Education Pre-K -12

Senator **Miguel Diaz de la Portilla** (R-District 40)
  406 Senate Office Building . . . . . . . . . . . . . . . . . . (850) 487-5040
  Counties Represented: Miami-Dade (part)   Dist: (305) 643-7200
  Term Expires: 2018
  2100 Coral Way, Suite 505, Miami, FL 33145-2657
  E-mail: portilla.miguel.web@flsenate.gov
  Committees: Community Affairs; Finance and Tax; Judiciary;
  Regulated Industries; Rules
  Education: Miami 1984 BA, 1987 JD

Senator **Greg Evers** (R-District 2)
  308 Senate Office Building . . . . . . . . . . . . . . . . . . (850) 487-5002
  Counties Represented: Escambia, Okaloosa (part),   Dist: (850) 595-0213
  Santa Rosa   (Crestview)
  Term Expires: 2018   Fax: (888) 263-0013
  5234 Willing Street Street, Milton, FL 32570
  E-mail: evers.greg.web@flsenate.gov
  Committees: Communications, Energy and Public Utilities; Criminal
  Justice; Environmental Preservation and Conservation; Military and
  Veterans Affairs, Space, and Domestic Security; Transportation

*(continued on next page)*

**Senators** *continued*

Senator **Anitere Flores** (R-District 37)
413 Senate Office Building . . . . . . . . . . . . . . . . . . . . . (850) 487-5037
Counties Represented: Miami-Dade (part)   Dist: (305) 270-6550
Term Expires: 2016
10691 North Kendall Drive, Suite 309, Miami, FL 33176
E-mail: flores.anitere.web@flsenate.gov
Committees: Appropriations; Ethics and Elections; Finance and Tax;
Fiscal Policy; Health Policy; Regulated Industries
Education: Florida International 1997 BA; Florida 2001 JD

Senator **Don Gaetz** (R-District 1)
420 Senate Office Building . . . . . . . . . . . . . . . . . . . . . (850) 487-5001
Counties Represented: Bay, Holmes, Jackson,   Dist: (850) 897-5747
Okaloosa (part), Walton, Washington   Fax: (888) 263-2259
Term Expires: 2016
4300 Legendary Drive, Suite 230, Destin, FL 32541
E-mail: gaetz.don.web@flsenate.gov
Committees: Appropriations; Education Pre-K -12; Ethics and
Elections; Health Policy; Higher Education; Rules

Senator **Bill Galvano** (R-District 26) . . . . . . . . . . . . . . . . . (850) 487-5026
Counties Represented: Charlotte (part), DeSoto,   Dist: (941) 741-3401
Glades, Hardee, Highlands (part), Hillsborough   Fax: (305) 364-3110
(part), Manatee (part)
Term Expires: 2018
1023 Manatee Avenue West, Suite 201, Bradenton, FL 34205
330 Senate Office Building, 404 Monroe Street,
Tallahassee, FL 32399-1100
E-mail: galvano.bill.web@flsenate.gov
Committees: Agriculture; Appropriations; Education Pre-K -12; Health
Policy; Joint Legislative Budget Commission; Reapportionment; Rules

Senator **Rene Garcia** (R-District 38) . . . . . . . . . . . . . . . . . (850) 487-5038
Counties Represented: Miami-Dade (part)   Dist: (305) 364-3100
Term Expires: 2018   Fax: (305) 364-3110
1490 West 68th Street, Suite 201, Hialeah, FL 33014
310 Senate Office Building, 404 Monroe Street,
Tallahassee, FL 32399-1100
E-mail: garcia.rene.web@flsenate.gov
Committees: Agriculture; Appropriations; Children, Families and Elder
Affairs; Communications, Energy and Public Utilities; Education Pre-K
-12; Health Policy; Joint Legislative Budget Commission
Education: Florida International 1999 BA; Miami 2004 MBA

Senator **Andy Gardiner** (R-District 13)
409 Senate Office Building . . . . . . . . . . . . . . . . . . . . . (850) 487-5013
Counties Represented: Brevard (part), Orange (part)   Dist: (407) 428-5800
Term Expires: 2016
1013 East Michigan Street, Orlando, FL 32806
E-mail: gardiner.andy.web@flsenate.gov

Senator **Audrey Gibson** (D-District 9)
205 Senate Office Building . . . . . . . . . . . . . . . . . . . . . (850) 487-5009
Counties Represented: Duval (part)   Dist: (904) 359-2553
Term Expires: 2016   Fax: (904) 359-2532
101 East Union Street, Suite 104, Jacksonville, FL 32202-3065
E-mail: gibson.audrey.web@flsenate.gov
Committees: Communications, Energy and Public Utilities; Criminal
Justice; Joint Legislative Auditing; Military and Veterans Affairs,
Space, and Domestic Security; Reapportionment; Rules
Education: Florida State 1978 BS

Senator **Denise Grimsley** (R-District 21)
306 Senate Office Building . . . . . . . . . . . . . . . . . . . . . (850) 487-5021
Counties Represented: Highlands (part), Martin   Dist: (863) 386-6016
(part), Okeechobee, Osceola (part), Polk (part), St. Lucie (part)
Term Expires: 2016
205 South Commerce Avenue, Suite A, Sebring, FL 33870
E-mail: grimsley.denise.web@flsenate.gov
Committees: Agriculture; Appropriations; Communications, Energy and
Public Utilities; Health Policy; Joint Legislative Budget Commission;
Transportation

Senator **Dixon Alan Hays** (R-District 11)
320 Senate Office Building . . . . . . . . . . . . . . . . . . . . . (850) 487-5011
Counties Represented: Lake (part), Marion (part),   Dist: (352) 742-6441
Orange (part), Sumter (part)   (Umatilla)
Term Expires: 2016   Dist: (352) 360-6739
871 South Central Avenue,   (The Villages)
Umatilla, FL 32784-9290   Fax: (352) 360-6748
1104 Main Street, The Villages, FL 32159   (The Villages)
E-mail: hays.alan.web@flsenate.gov
Committees: Appropriations; Environmental Preservation and
Conservation; Ethics and Elections; Fiscal Policy; Governmental
Oversight and Accountability
Education: Florida 1976 DMD

Senator **Dorothy L. Hukill** (R-District 8)
305 Senate Office Building . . . . . . . . . . . . . . . . . . . . . (850) 487-5008
Counties Represented: Lake (part), Marion (part),   Dist: (386) 304-7630
Volusia (part)   Fax: (888) 263-3818
Term Expires: 2018
209 Dunlawton Avenue, Unit 17, Port Orange, FL 32127
E-mail: hukill.dorothy.web@flsenate.gov
Committees: Appropriations; Banking and Insurance; Communications,
Energy and Public Utilities; Finance and Tax; Fiscal Policy
Education: Hunter 1967 BA; St John's U (NY) 1978 JD;
Columbia 1970 MA

Senator **Travis Hutson** (R-District 6) . . . . . . . . . . . . . . . . . (850) 487-5006
Counties Represented: Flagler, Putnam, St. Johns,   Dist: (850) 446-7610
Volusia (part)   Fax: (888) 263-3475
Term Expires: 2018
312 Senate Office Building, 404 Monroe Street,
Tallahassee, FL 32399-1100
4875 Palm Coast Parkway NW, Suite 5, Palm Coast, FL 32137
E-mail: hutson.travis.web@flsenate.gov
Committees: Children, Families and Elder Affairs; Commerce and
Tourism; Communications, Energy and Public Utilities; Community
Affairs; Environmental Preservation and Conservation
Education: Lafayette BSE

Senator **Arthenia L. Joyner** (D-District 19)
200 Senate Office Building . . . . . . . . . . . . . . . . . . . . . (850) 487-5019
Counties Represented: Hillsborough (part), Manatee   Dist: (813) 233-4277
(part), Pinellas (part)   Fax: (813) 233-4280
Term Expires: 2016
508 West Dr. Martin Luther King Jr. Boulevard, Suite C,
Tampa, FL 33603
E-mail: joyner.arthenia.web@flsenate.gov
Committees: Appropriations; Health Policy; Higher Education; Joint
Legislative Budget Commission; Judiciary; Rules

Senator **Jack Latvala** (R-District 20)
408 Senate Office Building . . . . . . . . . . . . . . . . . . . . . (850) 487-5020
Counties Represented: Pinellas (part)   Dist: (727) 793-2797
Term Expires: 2018   Fax: (727) 793-2799
26133 U.S. Highway 19 North, Suite 201, Clearwater, FL 33763
E-mail: latvala.jack.web@flsenate.gov
Committees: Appropriations; Commerce and Tourism; Governmental
Oversight and Accountability; Regulated Industries; Rules
Education: Stetson 1973 BA

Senator **Thomas A. "Tom" Lee** (R-District 24)
418 Senate Office Building . . . . . . . . . . . . . . . . . . . . . (850) 487-5024
Counties Represented: Hillsborough (part)   Tel: (813) 653-7061
Term Expires: 2018
915 Oakfield Drive, Suite D, Brandon, FL 33511
E-mail: lee.tom.web@flsenate.gov
Committees: Appropriations; Banking and Insurance; Joint Legislative
Budget Commission; Reapportionment; Rules
Education: Tampa 1984 BS

Senator **John Legg** (R-District 17)
316 Senate Office Building . . . . . . . . . . . . . . . . . . . . . (850) 487-5017
Counties Represented: Hillsborough (part), Pasco   Dist: (813) 909-9919
(part)   Fax: (888) 263-3681
Term Expires: 2016
262 Crystal Grove Boulevard, Lutz, FL 33548
E-mail: legg.john.web@flsenate.gov
Committees: Education Pre-K -12; Ethics and Elections; Fiscal Policy;
Governmental Oversight and Accountability; Higher Education
Education: South Florida 1996 BSW

Senator **Gwen Margolis** (D-District 35)
414 Senate Office Building . . . . . . . . . . . . . . . . . . . . . (850) 487-5035
Counties Represented: Miami-Dade (part)   Dist: (305) 571-5777
Term Expires: 2016
3050 Biscayne Boulevard, Suite 600, Miami, FL 33137
E-mail: margolis.gwen.web@flsenate.gov
Committees: Appropriations; Banking and Insurance; Finance and Tax;
Fiscal Policy; Regulated Industries
Education: Temple

Senator **Bill Montford** (D-District 3)
214 Senate Office Building . . . . . . . . . . . . . . . . . . . . . (850) 487-5003
Counties Represented: Calhoun, Franklin, Gadsden,   Dist: (850) 627-9100
Gulf, Hamilton, Jefferson, Leon, Liberty, Madison,   Fax: (850) 627-5086
Taylor, Wakulla
Term Expires: 2016
20 East Washington Street, Suite D, Quincy, FL 32351
E-mail: montford.bill.web@flsenate.gov
Committees: Agriculture; Appropriations; Banking and Insurance;
Education Pre-K -12; Reapportionment; Rules
Education: Florida State 1969 BS

LEGISLATIVE BRANCH

Senator **Joe Negron** (R-District 32)
412 Senate Office Building . . . . . . . . . . . . . . . . . . . . . (850) 487-5032
Counties Represented: Indian River (part), Martin    Dist: (772) 219-1665
(part), Palm Beach (part), St. Lucie (part)    Fax: (772) 219-1666
Term Expires: 2018
3500 SW Corporate Parkway, Suite 204, Palm City, FL 34990
E-mail: negron.joe.web@flsenate.gov
Committees: Appropriations; Banking and Insurance; Ethics and
Elections; Higher Education; Regulated Industries; Rules
Education: Stetson 1983 BA; Emory 1986 JD

Senator **Garrett S. Richter** (R-District 23)
404 Senate Office Building . . . . . . . . . . . . . . . . . . . . . (850) 487-5023
Counties Represented: Collier (part), Lee (part)    Dist: (239) 417-6205
Term Expires: 2016    (Naples)
3299 East Tamiami Trail, Suite 203,    Dist: (239) 338-2777
Naples, FL 34112-4961    (Cape Coral)
25 Homestead Road North, Suite 42B,    Fax: (888) 263-7893
Lehigh Acres, FL 33936
E-mail: richter.garrett.web@flsenate.gov
Committees: Appropriations; Banking and Insurance; Commerce and
Tourism; Ethics and Elections; Regulated Industries; Rules

Senator **Jeremy Ring** (D-District 29)
405 Senate Office Building . . . . . . . . . . . . . . . . . . . . . (850) 487-5029
Counties Represented: Broward (part)    Dist: (954) 917-1392
Term Expires: 2016    Fax: (954) 917-1394
5790 Margate Boulevard, Margate, FL 33063
E-mail: ring.jeremy.web@flsenate.gov
Committees: Appropriations; Children, Families and Elder Affairs;
Commerce and Tourism; Governmental Oversight and Accountability;
Judiciary

Senator **Maria Lorts Sachs** (D-District 34)
216 Senate Office Building . . . . . . . . . . . . . . . . . . . . . (850) 487-5034
Counties Represented: Broward (part), Palm Beach    Dist: (561) 279-1427
(part)    Fax: (561) 279-1429
Term Expires: 2018
Delray Beach City Hall, 100 NW 1st Avenue, Delray Beach, FL 33444
E-mail: sachs.maria.web@flsenate.gov
Committees: Communications, Energy and Public Utilities; Fiscal
Policy; Higher Education; Military and Veterans Affairs, Space, and
Domestic Security; Regulated Industries

Senator **David H. Simmons** (R-District 10)
400 Senate Office Building . . . . . . . . . . . . . . . . . . . . . (850) 487-5010
Counties Represented: Seminole, Volusia (part)    Dist: (407) 262-7578
Term Expires: 2018
251 Maitland Avenue, Suite 304, Altamonte Springs, FL 32701
E-mail: simmons.david.web@flsenate.gov
Committees: Appropriations; Banking and Insurance; Environmental
Preservation and Conservation; Higher Education; Joint Legislative
Budget Commission; Judiciary; Reapportionment; Rules
Education: Tennessee Tech 1974 BS; Vanderbilt 1977 JD

Senator **Wilton Simpson** (R-District 18)
322 Senate Office Building . . . . . . . . . . . . . . . . . . . . . (850) 487-5018
Counties Represented: Hernando, Pasco (part),    Dist: (727) 816-1120
Sumter (part)    Fax: (888) 263-4821
Term Expires: 2018
P.O. Box 787, New Port Richey, FL 34656-0787
E-mail: simpson.wilton.web@flsenate.gov
Committees: Community Affairs; Environmental Preservation and
Conservation; Finance and Tax; Joint Legislative Auditing; Judiciary;
Transportation

Senator **Christopher L. "Chris" Smith** (D-District 31)
202 Senate Office Building . . . . . . . . . . . . . . . . . . . . . (850) 487-5031
Counties Represented: Broward (part)    Dist: (954) 321-2705
Term Expires: 2016    Fax: (954) 321-2707
2151 NW 6th Street, Fort Lauderdale, FL 33311
E-mail: smith.chris.web@flsenate.gov
Committees: Appropriations; Banking and Insurance; Environmental
Preservation and Conservation; Ethics and Elections
Education: Johnson C Smith 1992 BS; Florida State 1995 JD

Senator **Eleanor Sobel** (D-District 33)
410 Senate Office Building . . . . . . . . . . . . . . . . . . . . . (850) 487-5033
Counties Represented: Broward (part)    Dist: (954) 924-3693
Term Expires: 2016    Fax: (954) 924-3695
The "Old" Library, 2600 Hollywood Boulevard, First Floor,
Hollywood, FL 33020
E-mail: sobel.eleanor.web@flsenate.gov
Committees: Agriculture; Children, Families and Elder Affairs;
Education Pre-K -12; Health Policy
Education: Brooklyn 1967 BA; CUNY 1968 MA; Columbia 1975 MA

Senator **Darren Soto** (D-District 14)
220 Senate Office Building . . . . . . . . . . . . . . . . . . . . . (850) 487-5014
Counties Represented: Orange (part), Osceola    Dist: (407) 846-5187
(part), Polk (part)    Fax: (407) 846-5188
Term Expires: 2018
Kissimmee City Halll, 101 North Church Street, Suite 305,
Kissimmee, FL 34741
E-mail: soto.darren.web@flsenate.gov
Committees: Environmental Preservation and Conservation; Finance
and Tax; Judiciary; Rules
Education: Rutgers 2000 BA; George Washington 2004 JD

Senator **Kelli Stargel** (R-District 15)
324 Senate Office Building . . . . . . . . . . . . . . . . . . . . . (850) 487-5015
Counties Represented: Orange (part), Osceola (part),    Dist: (863) 668-3028
Polk (part)
Term Expires: 2016
2033 East Edgewood Drive, Suite 1, Lakeland, FL 33803
E-mail: stargel.kelli.web@flsenate.gov
Committees: Fiscal Policy; Higher Education; Judiciary; Military and
Veterans Affairs, Space, and Domestic Security; Regulated Industries

Senator **Geraldine F. "Geri" Thompson** (D-District 12)
210 Senate Office Building . . . . . . . . . . . . . . . . . . . . . (850) 487-5012
Counties Represented: Orange (part)    Tel: (407) 245-1511
Term Expires: 2018    Fax: (407) 245-1513
511 West South Street, Suite 204, Orlando, FL 32805
E-mail: thompson.geraldine.web@flsenate.gov
Committees: Commerce and Tourism; Community Affairs; Ethics and
Elections; Transportation
Education: Miami 1970 BE; Florida State 1973 MS

## Senate Standing Committees

### Agriculture
335 Knott Building, 404 South Monroe Street,
Tallahassee, FL 32399-1100

| Majority Members | Minority Members |
|---|---|
| Charles S. "Charlie" Dean, Sr. (R-5) *Vice Chair* | Bill Montford (D-3) *Chair* |
| Bill Galvano (R-26) | Dwight M. Bullard (D-39) |
| Rene Garcia (R-38) | Eleanor Sobel (D-33) |
| Denise Grimsley (R-21) | |

### Appropriations
201 The Capitol, 404 South Monroe Street, Tallahassee, FL 32239-1100

| Majority Members | Minority Members |
|---|---|
| Thomas A. "Tom" Lee (R-24) *Chair* | Arthenia L. Joyner (D-19) |
| Lizbeth Benacquisto (R-30) *Vice Chair* | Gwen Margolis (D-35) |
| Thad Altman (R-16) | Bill Montford (D-3) |
| Anitere Flores (R-37) | Jeremy Ring (D-29) |
| Don Gaetz (R-1) | Christopher L. "Chris" Smith (D-31) |
| Bill Galvano (R-26) | |
| Rene Garcia (R-38) | |
| Denise Grimsley (R-21) | |
| Dixon Alan Hays (R-11) | |
| Dorothy L. Hukill (R-8) | |
| Jack Latvala (R-20) | |
| Joe Negron (R-32) | |
| Garrett S. Richter (R-23) | |
| David H. Simmons (R-10) | |

### Banking and Insurance
320 Knott Building, 404 South Monroe Street,
Tallahassee, FL 32399-1100

| Majority Members | Minority Members |
|---|---|
| Lizbeth Benacquisto (R-30) *Chair* | Jeff Clemens (D-27) |
| Garrett S. Richter (R-23) *Vice Chair* | Gwen Margolis (D-35) |
| Nancy C. Detert (R-28) | Bill Montford (D-3) |
| Dorothy L. Hukill (R-8) | Christopher L. "Chris" Smith (D-31) |
| Thomas A. "Tom" Lee (R-24) | |
| Joe Negron (R-32) | |
| David H. Simmons (R-10) | |

## Children, Families and Elder Affairs

520 Knott Building, 404 South Monroe Street,
Tallahassee, FL 32399-1100

| **Majority Members** | **Minority Members** |
| --- | --- |
| Thad Altman (R-16) *Vice Chair* | Eleanor Sobel (D-33) *Chair* |
| Charles S. "Charlie" Dean, Sr. | Jeremy Ring (D-29) |
| (R-5) | |
| Nancy C. Detert (R-28) | |
| Rene Garcia (R-38) | |
| Travis Hutson (R-6) | |

## Commerce and Tourism

310 Knott Building, 404 South Monroe Street,
Tallahassee, FL 32399-1100

| **Majority Members** | **Minority Members** |
| --- | --- |
| Nancy C. Detert (R-28) *Chair* | Geraldine F. "Geri" |
| Aaron P. Bean (R-4) | Thompson (D-12) |
| Travis Hutson (R-6) | *Vice Chair* |
| Jack Latvala (R-20) | Jeremy Ring (D-29) |
| Garrett S. Richter (R-23) | |

## Communications, Energy and Public Utilities

337 Knott Building, 404 South Monroe Street,
Tallahassee, FL 32399-1100

| **Majority Members** | **Minority Members** |
| --- | --- |
| Denise Grimsley (R-21) *Chair* | Joseph Abruzzo (D-25) |
| Dorothy L. Hukill (R-8) *Vice Chair* | Audrey Gibson (D-9) |
| Rob Bradley (R-7) | Maria Lorts Sachs (D-34) |
| Charles S. "Charlie" Dean, Sr. | |
| (R-5) | |
| Greg Evers (R-2) | |
| Rene Garcia (R-38) | |
| Travis Hutson (R-6) | |

## Community Affairs

315 Knott Building, 404 South Monroe Street,
Tallahassee, FL 32399-1100

| **Majority Members** | **Minority Members** |
| --- | --- |
| Wilton Simpson (R-18) *Chair* | Joseph Abruzzo (D-25) |
| Jeffrey P. "Jeff" Brandes (R-22) | Geraldine F. "Geri" Thompson |
| *Vice Chair* | (D-12) |
| Rob Bradley (R-7) | |
| Charles S. "Charlie" Dean, Sr. | |
| (R-5) | |
| Miguel Diaz de la Portilla (R-40) | |
| Travis Hutson (R-6) | |

## Criminal Justice

510 Knott Building, 404 South Monroe Street,
Tallahassee, FL 32399-1100

| **Majority Members** | **Minority Members** |
| --- | --- |
| Greg Evers (R-2) *Chair* | Audrey Gibson (D-9) *Vice Chair* |
| Rob Bradley (R-7) | Jeff Clemens (D-27) |
| Jeffrey P. "Jeff" Brandes (R-22) | |

## Education Pre-K -12

415 Knott Building, 404 South Monroe Street,
Tallahassee, FL 32399-1100

| **Majority Members** | **Minority Members** |
| --- | --- |
| John Legg (R-17) *Chair* | Dwight M. Bullard (D-39) |
| Nancy C. Detert (R-28) *Vice Chair* | Jeff Clemens (D-27) |
| Lizbeth Benacquisto (R-30) | Bill Montford (D-3) |
| Jeffrey P. "Jeff" Brandes (R-22) | Eleanor Sobel (D-33) |
| Don Gaetz (R-1) | |
| Bill Galvano (R-26) | |
| Rene Garcia (R-38) | |

## Environmental Preservation and Conservation

325 Knott Building, 404 South Monroe Street,
Tallahassee, FL 32399-1100

| **Majority Members** | **Minority Members** |
| --- | --- |
| Charles S. "Charlie" | Christopher L. "Chris" Smith |
| Dean, Sr. (R-5) | (D-31) |
| *Chair* | Darren Soto (D-14) |
| Wilton Simpson (R-18) *Vice Chair* | |
| Thad Altman (R-16) | |
| Greg Evers (R-2) | |
| Dixon Alan Hays (R-11) | |
| Travis Hutson (R-6) | |
| David H. Simmons (R-10) | |

## Ethics and Elections

420 Knott Building, 404 South Monroe Street,
Tallahassee, FL 32399-1100

| **Majority Members** | **Minority Members** |
| --- | --- |
| Garrett S. Richter (R-23) *Chair* | Oscar Braynon II (D-36) |
| John Legg (R-17) *Vice Chair* | Jeff Clemens (D-27) |
| Anitere Flores (R-37) | Christopher L. "Chris" Smith |
| Don Gaetz (R-1) | (D-31) |
| Dixon Alan Hays (R-11) | Geraldine F. "Geri" Thompson |
| Joe Negron (R-32) | (D-12) |

## Finance and Tax

207 The Capitol, 404 South Monroe Street, Tallahassee, FL 32399-1100

| **Majority Members** | **Minority Members** |
| --- | --- |
| Dorothy L. Hukill (R-8) *Chair* | Joseph Abruzzo (D-25) *Vice Chair* |
| Thad Altman (R-16) | Gwen Margolis (D-35) |
| Miguel Diaz de la Portilla (R-40) | Darren Soto (D-14) |
| Anitere Flores (R-37) | |
| Wilton Simpson (R-18) | |

## Fiscal Policy

225 Knott Building, 404 South Monroe Street,
Tallahassee, FL 32399-1100

| **Majority Members** | **Minority Members** |
| --- | --- |
| Anitere Flores (R-37) *Chair* | Joseph Abruzzo (D-25) |
| Rob Bradley (R-7) *Vice Chair* | Jeff Clemens (D-27) |
| Aaron P. Bean (R-4) | Gwen Margolis (D-35) |
| Dixon Alan Hays (R-11) | Maria Lorts Sachs (D-34) |
| Dorothy L. Hukill (R-8) | |
| John Legg (R-17) | |
| Kelli Stargel (R-15) | |

## Governmental Oversight and Accountability

525 Knott Building, 404 South Monroe Street,
Tallahassee, FL 32399-1100

| **Majority Members** | **Minority Members** |
| --- | --- |
| Dixon Alan Hays (R-11) *Vice Chair* | Jeremy Ring (D-29) *Chair* |
| Jack Latvala (R-20) | Dwight M. Bullard (D-39) |
| John Legg (R-17) | |

## Health Policy

530 Knott Building, 404 South Monroe Street,
Tallahassee, FL 32399-1100

| **Majority Members** | **Minority Members** |
| --- | --- |
| Aaron P. Bean (R-4) *Chair* | Eleanor Sobel (D-33) *Vice Chair* |
| Anitere Flores (R-37) | Oscar Braynon II (D-36) |
| Don Gaetz (R-1) | Arthenia L. Joyner (D-19) |
| Bill Galvano (R-26) | |
| Rene Garcia (R-38) | |
| Denise Grimsley (R-21) | |

## Higher Education
415 Knott Building, 404 South Monroe Street,
Tallahassee, FL 32399-1100

| **Majority Members** | **Minority Members** |
| --- | --- |
| Kelli Stargel (R-15) *Chair* | Maria Lorts Sachs (D-34) |
| Lizbeth Benacquisto (R-30) | *Vice Chair* |
| Don Gaetz (R-1) | Oscar Braynon II (D-36) |
| John Legg (R-17) | Arthenia L. Joyner (D-19) |
| Joe Negron (R-32) | |
| David H. Simmons (R-10) | |

## Judiciary
515 Knott Building, 404 South Monroe Street,
Tallahassee, FL 32399-1100

| **Majority Members** | **Minority Members** |
| --- | --- |
| Miguel Diaz de la Portilla (R-40) | Jeremy Ring (D-29) *Vice Chair* |
| *Chair* | Arthenia L. Joyner (D-19) |
| Aaron P. Bean (R-4) | Darren Soto (D-14) |
| Lizbeth Benacquisto (R-30) | |
| Jeffrey P. "Jeff" Brandes (R-22) | |
| David H. Simmons (R-10) | |
| Wilton Simpson (R-18) | |
| Kelli Stargel (R-15) | |

## Military and Veterans Affairs, Space, and Domestic Security
215 Knott Building, 404 South Monroe Street,
Tallahassee, FL 32399-1100

| **Majority Members** | **Minority Members** |
| --- | --- |
| Thad Altman (R-16) *Chair* | Audrey Gibson (D-9) *Vice Chair* |
| Greg Evers (R-2) | Maria Lorts Sachs (D-34) |
| Kelli Stargel (R-15) | |

## Reapportionment
2000 The Capitol, 404 South Monroe Street, Tallahassee, FL 32399-1100

| **Majority Members** | **Minority Members** |
| --- | --- |
| Bill Galvano (R-26) *Chair* | Oscar Braynon II (D-36) *Vice Chair* |
| Rob Bradley (R-7) | Audrey Gibson (D-9) |
| Thomas A. "Tom" Lee (R-24) | Bill Montford (D-3) |
| David H. Simmons (R-10) | |

## Regulated Industries
330 Knott Building, 404 South Monroe Street,
Tallahassee, FL 32399-1100

| **Majority Members** | **Minority Members** |
| --- | --- |
| Rob Bradley (R-7) *Chair* | Gwen Margolis (D-35) *Vice Chair* |
| Aaron P. Bean (R-4) | Joseph Abruzzo (D-25) |
| Miguel Diaz de la Portilla (R-40) | Oscar Braynon II (D-36) |
| Anitere Flores (R-37) | Maria Lorts Sachs (D-34) |
| Jack Latvala (R-20) | |
| Joe Negron (R-32) | |
| Garrett S. Richter (R-23) | |
| Kelli Stargel (R-15) | |

## Rules
402 Senate Office Building, 404 South Monroe Street,
Tallahassee, FL 32399-1100

| **Majority Members** | **Minority Members** |
| --- | --- |
| David H. Simmons (R-10) *Chair* | Darren Soto (D-14) *Vice Chair* |
| Lizbeth Benacquisto (R-30) | Audrey Gibson (D-9) |
| Miguel Diaz de la Portilla (R-40) | Arthenia L. Joyner (D-19) |
| Don Gaetz (R-1) | Bill Montford (D-3) |
| Bill Galvano (R-26) | |
| Jack Latvala (R-20) | |
| Thomas A. "Tom" Lee (R-24) | |
| Joe Negron (R-32) | |
| Garrett S. Richter (R-23) | |

## Transportation
410 Knott Building, 404 South Monroe Street,
Tallahassee, FL 32399-1100

| **Majority Members** | **Minority Members** |
| --- | --- |
| Jeffrey P. "Jeff" Brandes (R-22) | Dwight M. Bullard (D-39) |
| *Chair* | *Vice Chair* |
| Greg Evers (R-2) | Oscar Braynon II (D-36) |
| Denise Grimsley (R-21) | Geraldine F. "Geri" Thompson |
| Wilton Simpson (R-18) | (D-12) |

# Florida House of Representatives
The Capitol, 402 South Monroe Street, Tallahassee, FL 32399-1300
Tel: (850) 488-7475 (Documents Division)
Tel: (850) 488-5644 (House Bill Drafting)  Tel: (850) 488-2812 (Library)

Speaker of the House **Steve Crisafulli** (R) . . . . . . . . . . . . . (850) 717-5051
  Education: Central Florida BA
Speaker Pro Tempore **Matt Hudson** (R) . . . . . . . . . . . . . . . (850) 717-5080
  Education: Barry 2007
Majority Leader **Dana D. Young** (R) . . . . . . . . . . . . . . . . . . (850) 717-5060
  Education: Florida State 1985 BS; Virginia 1993 JD
Deputy Majority Leader **Jim Boyd** (R) . . . . . . . . . . . . . . . . (850) 717-5071
  Education: Florida State 1978 BS
Majority Whip **Jim Boyd** (R) . . . . . . . . . . . . . . . . . . . . . . . . (850) 717-5071
Deputy Majority Whip **David Santiago** (R) . . . . . . . . . . . . (850) 717-5027
Minority Leader **Mark S. Pafford** (D) . . . . . . . . . . . . . . . . . (850) 717-5086
  Education: Miami Dade Comm Col 1986 AA;
  Florida International 1988 BA
Minority Leader Pro Tempore **Mia L. Jones** (D) . . . . . . . . . (850) 717-5014
  Education: Florida A&M 1991 BS, 1992 MBA
Minority Whip **Alan B. Williams, MBA** (D) . . . . . . . . . . . (850) 717-5008
  Education: Florida A&M 1998 BS, 2003 MBA
Deputy Minority Whip **Hazelle P. "Hazel" Rogers** (D) . . . (850) 717-5095
  Education: U Phoenix 2003 BS
Clerk of the House **Robert L. "Bob" Ward** . . . . . . . . . . . . (850) 717-5400
Sergeant-at-Arms **Russell Hosford** . . . . . . . . . . . . . . . . . . (850) 488-8224

## Representatives
**Party Affiliation Statistics:** Republicans: 82, Democrats: 38

Representative **Janet H. Adkins** (R-District 11)
  Room 313 . . . . . . . . . . . . . . . . . . . . . . . . . . . . . . . . . . . . (850) 717-5011
  Counties Represented: Duval (part), Nassau    Dist: (904) 491-3664
  Term Expires: 2016    (Fernandina Beach)
  905 South Eighth Street,    Dist: (904) 246-0532
  Fernandina Beach, FL 32034-3706    (Starke)
  945 North Temple Avenue, Starke, FL 32091-2110
  E-mail: janet.adkins@myfloridahouse.gov
  Committees: Appropriations; Education; Rules and Calendar
  Education: North Florida 1987 BS, 1990 MBA
Representative
**Lawrence T. "Larry" Ahern** (R-District 66)
  Room 1102 . . . . . . . . . . . . . . . . . . . . . . . . . . . . . . . . . . . (850) 717-5066
  Counties Represented: Pinellas (part)    Dist: (727) 395-2512
  Term Expires: 2016
  8383 Seminole Boulevard, Suite B, Seminole, FL 33772-4392
  E-mail: larry.ahern@myfloridahouse.gov
  Committees: Local and Federal Affairs
Representative **Ben Albritton** (R-District 56) Room 222 . . . (850) 717-5056
  Counties Represented: DeSoto, Hardee, Polk (part)    Dist: (863) 534-0073
  Term Expires: 2016    (Bartow)
  150 Noth Central Avenue, Bartow, FL 33830-4742    Dist: (863) 993-4536
  E-mail: ben.albritton@myfloridahouse.gov    (DeSoto County)
  Committees: Appropriations; Rules and Calendar; State Affairs
  Education: Florida Southern 1990 BS
Representative **Bruce Antone** (D-District 46) . . . . . . . . . . . (850) 717-5046
  Counties Represented: Orange (part)    Dist: (407) 245-0303
  Term Expires: 2016
  Tampa Avenue Complex, 434 North Tampa Avenue,
  Orlando, FL 32805-1220
  E-mail: bruce.antone@myfloridahouse.gov
  Committees: Education
  Education: Tuskegee 1983 BSEE

*(continued on next page)*

**Representatives** *continued*

Representative **Frank Artiles** (R-District 118)
Room 1102 . . . . . . . . . . . . . . . . . . . . . . . . . . . . . (850) 717-5118
Counties Represented: Miami-Dade (part)          Dist: (305) 252-4300
Term Expires: 2016
13501 SW 128th Street, Suite 115A, Miami, FL 33186-5862
E-mail: frank.artiles@myfloridahouse.gov
Committees: Economic Affairs; Finance and Tax; Rules and Calendar
Education: Florida State 1995 BS; St Thomas (Cuba) 2000 JD;
Miami 2001 LLM

Representative **Bryan Avila** (R-District 111) Room 1301 . . . (850) 717-5111
Counties Represented: Miami-Dade (part)          Dist: (305) 953-2932
Term Expires: 2016
E-mail: bryan.avila@myfloridahouse.gov
Committees: Economic Affairs; Health and Human Services
Education: Miami 2006 BA; Florida International 2010 MPA

Representative **Dennis K. Baxley** (R-District 23)
Room 214 . . . . . . . . . . . . . . . . . . . . . . . . . . . . . (850) 717-5023
Counties Represented: Marion (part)          Dist: (352) 732-1313
Term Expires: 2016
315 SE 25th Avenue, Ocala, FL 34471-2689
E-mail: dennis.baxley@myfloridahouse.gov
Committees: Local and Federal Affairs; Rules and Calendar
Education: Florida State 1974 BA

Representative **Lori Berman** (D-District 90) Room 1401 . . . (850) 717-5090
Counties Represented: Palm Beach (part)          Dist: (561) 374-7850
Term Expires: 2016
2300 High Ridge Road, Suite 161, Boynton Beach, FL 33426
E-mail: lori.berman@myfloridahouse.gov
Committees: Energy and Utilities; Finance and Tax; Health and Human
Services; Rules and Calendar
Education: Tufts 1980 BA; George Washington 1983 JD;
Miami 2002 LLM

Representative **Halsey Beshears** (R-District 7) . . . . . . . . . (850) 717-5007
Counties Represented: Calhoun, Franklin, Gulf,          Dist: (850) 584-2828
Jefferson, Lafayette, Leon (part), Liberty, Madison,          Dist: (850) 342-0016
Taylor, Wakulla
Term Expires: 2016
2191 South Jefferson, Monticello, FL 32344-5132
115 west Green Street, Suite 228, Perry, FL 32347-3226
E-mail: halsey.beshears@myfloridahouse.gov
Committees: Agriculture and Natural Resources; Energy and Utilities;
Regulatory Affairs
Education: Florida State BS; Florida 2009 MS

Representative **Michael Bileca** (R-District 105)
Room 1003 . . . . . . . . . . . . . . . . . . . . . . . . . . . . . (850) 717-5115
Counties Represented: Broward (part), Collier          Dist: (305) 273-3235
(part), Miami-Dade (part)          Dist: (305) 273-3236
Term Expires: 2016
9955 North Kendall Drive, Suite 201, Miami, FL 33176-1700
E-mail: michael.bileca@myfloridahouse.gov
Committees: Education; State Affairs
Education: Tulane 1992 BS; Northwestern 2002 MBA

Representative **Jim Boyd** (R-District 71) Room 1102 . . . . . (850) 717-5071
Counties Represented: Manatee (part), Sarasota          Dist: (941) 708-4968
(part)
Term Expires: 2016
717 Manatee Avenue West, Suite 100, Bradenton, FL 34205-8654
E-mail: jim.boyd@myfloridahouse.gov
Committees: Agriculture and Natural Resources; Appropriations;
Regulatory Affairs; Rules and Calendar

Representative **Randolph Bracy III** (D-District 45) . . . . . . . (850) 717-5045
Counties Represented: Orange (part)          Dist: (407) 660-6670
Term Expires: 2016
1800 Pembrook Drive, Orlando, FL 32810-6378
E-mail: randolph.bracy@myfloridahouse.gov
Committees: Economic Affairs; Finance and Tax; Regulatory Affairs
Education: William & Mary 1999 BS; Central Florida 2006 MBA,
2006 MSA

Representative **Jason T. Brodeur** (R-District 28)
Room 1003 . . . . . . . . . . . . . . . . . . . . . . . . . . . . . (850) 717-5028
Counties Represented: Seminole (part)          Dist: (407) 302-4800
Term Expires: 2016
114 West First Street, Suite 208, Sanford, FL 32771-1273
E-mail: jason.brodeur@myfloridahouse.gov
Committees: Finance and Tax; Health and Human Services; Health
Care Appropriations
Education: Florida 1997 BS, 2003 MBA

Representative
**Douglas Vaughn "Doug" Broxson** (R-District 3)
Room 1003 . . . . . . . . . . . . . . . . . . . . . . . . . . . . . (850) 717-5003
Counties Represented: Okaloosa (part), Santa          Dist: (850) 626-3113
Rosa (part)          (Milton)
Term Expires: 2016          Dist: (850) 916-5436
Pensacola State College, Milton Campus, Building 4000,          (Gulf Breeze)
5988 Highway 90, Room 4013, Milton, FL 32583-1713
E-mail: doug.broxson@myfloridahouse.gov
Committees: Local and Federal Affairs
Education: Evangel U 1971 BS

Representative **Daniel "Danny" Burgess** (R-District 38)
1301 The Capitol . . . . . . . . . . . . . . . . . . . . . . . . . (850) 717-5038
Counties Represented: Pasco (part)          Dist: (813) 780-0667
Term Expires: 2016
E-mail: danny.burgess@myfloridahouse.gov
Committees: Local and Federal Affairs
Education: South Florida 2008 BA; Barry 2012 JD

Representative **Colleen Burton** (R-District 40)
Room 1301 . . . . . . . . . . . . . . . . . . . . . . . . . . . . . (850) 717-5040
Counties Represented: Polk (part)          Dist: (863) 413-2640
Term Expires: 2016
100 South Kentucky Avenue, Lakeland, FL 33801-5093
E-mail: colleen.burton@myfloridahouse.gov
Committees: Health and Human Services; Judiciary

Representative
**Matthew H. "Matt" Caldwell** (R-District 79)
Room 1102 . . . . . . . . . . . . . . . . . . . . . . . . . . . . . (850) 717-5079
Counties Represented: Lee (part)          Dist: (239) 694-0161
Term Expires: 2016
Building A, 15191 Homestead Road, Lehigh Acres, FL 33971-9749
E-mail: matt.caldwell@myfloridahouse.gov
Committees: Agriculture and Natural Resources; Rules and Calendar;
State Affairs
Education: Florida Gulf Coast 2004 BA

Representative
**Daphne D. Campbell, RN** (D-District 108)
Room 1401 . . . . . . . . . . . . . . . . . . . . . . . . . . . . . (850) 717-5108
Counties Represented: Miami-Dade (part)          Dist: (305) 795-1210
Term Expires: 2016
9999 North East Second Avenue, Suite 309,
Miami Shores, FL 33138-2346
E-mail: daphne.campbell@myfloridahouse.gov
Committees: Health and Human Services Quality; Local and Federal
Affairs

Representative
**Gwyndolen "Gwyn" Clarke-Reed** (D-District 92)
Room 1302 . . . . . . . . . . . . . . . . . . . . . . . . . . . . . (850) 717-5092
Counties Represented: Broward (part)          Dist: (954) 786-4848
Term Expires: 2016
Pompano Beach City Hall, 100 West Atlantic Boulevard,
Pompano Beach, FL 33060
E-mail: gwyn.clarke-reed@myfloridahouse.gov
Committees: Appropriations; Health and Human Services
Education: Brooklyn 1973 BS; Adelphi 1979 MEd

Representative **Neil Combee** (R-District 39)
319 The Capitol . . . . . . . . . . . . . . . . . . . . . . . . . . (850) 717-5039
Counties Represented: Osceola (part), Polk (part)          Dist: (863) 968-5666
Term Expires: 2016
E-mail: neil.combee@myfloridahouse.gov
Committees: Local and Federal Affairs; State Affairs
Education: Florida State (Attended)

Representative **Richard Corcoran** (R-District 37)
Room 1101 . . . . . . . . . . . . . . . . . . . . . . . . . . . . . (850) 717-5037
Counties Represented: Pasco (part)          Dist: (813) 792-5177
Term Expires: 2016
17953 Hunting Bow Circle, Suite 101, Lutz, FL 33558-5375
E-mail: richard.corcoran@myfloridahouse.gov
Committees: Appropriations; Joint Legislative Budget Commission
Education: St Leo Col 1989 BA; Regent U 1996 JD

Representative **John Cortes** (D-District 43) Room 1402 . . . (850) 717-5043
Counties Represented: Osceola (part)          Dist: (407) 846-5009
Term Expires: 2016          Dist: (407) 846-5010
231 Ruby Avenue, Suite A, Kissimmee, FL 34741-5640
E-mail: john.cortes@myfloridahouse.gov
Committees: State Affairs

Representative **Robert "Bob" Cortes** (R-District 30)
Room 1301 . . . . . . . . . . . . . . . . . . . . . . . . . . (850) 717-5030
Counties Represented: Orange (part), Seminole          Dist: (407) 659-4818
(part)
Term Expires: 2016
696 North Maitland Avenue, Maitland, FL 32751-4423
E-mail: bob.cortes@myfloridahouse.gov
Committees: Finance and Tax

Representative
**Fredrick W. "Fred" Costello** (R-District 25)
Room 1301 . . . . . . . . . . . . . . . . . . . . . . . . . . (850) 717-5025
Counties Represented: Volusia (part)          Dist: (386) 304-5511
Term Expires: 2016
209 Dunlawton Avenue, Unit 15, Port Orange, FL 32127
E-mail: fred.costello@myfloridahouse.gov
Committees: Health and Human Services; Rules and Calendar
Education: Graceland U 1970 BS; Iowa 1974 DDS

Representative **Steve Crisafulli** (R-District 51)
Room 303 . . . . . . . . . . . . . . . . . . . . . . . . . . . (850) 717-5051
Counties Represented: Brevard (part)          Dist: (321) 449-5111
Term Expires: 2016
2460 North Courtenay Parkway, Suite 108,
Merritt Island, FL 32953-4193
E-mail: steve.crisafulli@myfloridahouse.gov

Representative **Janet R. Cruz** (D-District 62) Room 1401 . . (850) 717-5062
Counties Represented: Hillsborough (part)          Dist: (813) 673-4673
Term Expires: 2016
2221 North Himes Avenue, Suite B, Tampa, FL 33607-3139
E-mail: janet.cruz@myfloridahouse.gov
Committees: Appropriations; Energy and Utilities; Health and Human
Services; Health Care Appropriations; Joint Legislative Budget
Commission

Representative
**Travis W. Cummings, CPA** (R-District 18) . . . . . . . . . . (850) 717-5018
Counties Represented: Clay (part)          Dist: (904) 278-5761
Term Expires: 2016
580 Wells Road, Suite 2, Orange Park, FL 32073-2979
E-mail: travis.cummings@myfloridahouse.gov
Committees: Health and Human Services; State Affairs
Education: Valdosta State U 1994 BAcc; North Florida 2002 MBA

Representative **Jose Felix Diaz, JD** (R-District 116)
Room 1101 . . . . . . . . . . . . . . . . . . . . . . . . . . (850) 717-5116
Counties Represented: Miami-Dade (part)          Dist: (305) 442-6800
Term Expires: 2016
7901 SW 24th Street, Miami, FL 33155-6524
E-mail: jose.diaz@myfloridahouse.gov
Committees: Energy and Utilities; Health Care Appropriations;
Regulatory Affairs
Education: Miami 2002 BA; Columbia 2005 JD

Representative
**Manuel "Manny" Diaz, Jr.** (R-District 103) . . . . . . . . . . (850) 717-5103
Counties Represented: Broward (part), Miami-Dade          Dist: (305) 364-3072
(part)
Term Expires: 2016
17680 Northwest 78th Avenue, Suite 104, Hialeah, FL 33015-3667
E-mail: manny.diaz@myfloridahouse.gov
Committees: Education; Health and Human Services Quality
Education: St Thomas U 1994 BA; Nova Southeastern 1998 MS

Representative **Brad Drake** (R-District 5)
1301 The Capitol . . . . . . . . . . . . . . . . . . . . . . . (850) 717-5005
Counties Represented: Bay (part), Holmes, Jackson,          Dist: (850) 718-0047
Walton, Washington
Term Expires: 2016
Chipola College Administration Building, 3094 Indian Circle,
Room 186, Marianna, FL 32446-1701
E-mail: brad.drake@myfloridahouse.gov
Committees: State Affairs
Education: Florida 2000 BS

Representative **Bobby B. DuBose** (D-District 94)
1402 The Capitol . . . . . . . . . . . . . . . . . . . . . . . (850) 717-5094
Counties Represented: Broward (part)          Dist: (954) 467-4206
Term Expires: 2016
E-mail: bobby.dubose@myfloridahouse.gov
Committees: Local and Federal Affairs
Education: Florida BA

Representative
**Dwight Richard Dudley, JD** (D-District 68) . . . . . . . . . . (850) 717-5068
Counties Represented: Pinellas (part)          Dist: (850) 552-2747
Term Expires: 2016          Dist: (727) 552-2748
3637 4th Street North, Suite 300, Saint Petersburg, FL 33704-1336
E-mail: dwight.dudley@myfloridahouse.gov
Committees: Judiciary
Education: Florida State 1980 BS, 1987 JD

Representative **Dane Eagle** (R-District 77) . . . . . . . . . . . . . (850) 717-5077
Counties Represented: Lee (part)          Dist: (239) 772-1291
Term Expires: 2016
1039 Southeast 9th Place, Cape Coral, FL 33990-3131
E-mail: dane.eagle@myfloridahouse.gov
Committees: Regulatory Affairs
Education: Florida 2005 BA

Representative **Katie A. Edwards** (D-District 98) . . . . . . . . (850) 717-5098
Counties Represented: Broward (part)          Dist: (954) 838-1371
Term Expires: 2016
777 Sawgrass Corporate Parkway, Sunrise, FL 33325-6256
E-mail: katie.edwards@myfloridahouse.gov
Committees: Agriculture and Natural Resources; Health and Human
Services; Judiciary
Education: Clemson 2002 BS; Florida International 2012 JD

Representative **Eric J. "E" Eisnaugle** (R-District 44)
1302 The Capitol . . . . . . . . . . . . . . . . . . . . . . . (850) 717-5044
Counties Represented: Orange (part)          Dist: (407) 355-5784
Term Expires: 2016
7009 Dr. Phillips Boulevard, Suite 270, Orlando, FL 32819-5124
E-mail: eric.eisnaugle@myfloridahouse.gov
Committees: Local and Federal Affairs; Rules and Calendar
Education: Florida Southern 2000 BS; Vanderbilt 2003 JD

Representative **Julian "Jay" Fant** (R-District 15)
Room 1301 . . . . . . . . . . . . . . . . . . . . . . . . . . (850) 717-5015
Counties Represented: Duval (part)          Dist: (904) 381-6011
Term Expires: 2016          Dist: (904) 381-6012
4114 Herschel Street, Jacksonville, FL 32210-2200
E-mail: jay.fant@myfloridahouse.gov
Committees: Finance and Tax; Judiciary
Education: Washington and Lee 1990 BSBA; Florida 1994 JD

Representative
**Heather Dawes Fitzenhagen, JD** (R-District 78)
1302 The Capitol . . . . . . . . . . . . . . . . . . . . . . . (850) 717-5078
Counties Represented: Lee (part)          Dist: (239) 533-2440
Term Expires: 2016
E-mail: heather.fitzenhagen@myfloridahouse.gov
Committees: Economic Affairs
Education: Hollins U 1982 BA; Nova Southeastern JD

Representative **Erik Fresen** (R-District 114) Room 313 . . . . (850) 717-5114
Counties Represented: Miami-Dade (part)          Dist: (305) 663-2011
Term Expires: 2016
6080 Bird Road, Suite 1, Miami, FL 33155-5249
P.O. Box 557622, Miami, FL 33255-7622
E-mail: erik.fresen@myfloridahouse.gov
Committees: Appropriations; Education; Joint Legislative Budget
Commission
Education: Florida State BS

Representative **Reggie Fullwood** (D-District 13)
Room 1003 . . . . . . . . . . . . . . . . . . . . . . . . . . (850) 717-5013
Counties Represented: Duval (part)
Term Expires: 2016
E-mail: reggie.fullwood@myfloridahouse.gov
Committees: Education; State Affairs

Representative **Matt Gaetz** (R-District 4) Room 1003 . . . . . (850) 717-5004
Counties Represented: Okaloosa (part)          Dist: (850) 833-9328
Term Expires: 2016
1188 Eglin Parkway, Shalimar, FL 32579
E-mail: matt.gaetz@myfloridahouse.gov
Committees: Finance and Tax; Health Care Appropriations; Regulatory
Affairs; State Affairs
Education: Florida State 2003 BS; William & Mary 2007 JD

Representative **Joseph S. "Joe" Geller** (D-District 100)
Room 1402 . . . . . . . . . . . . . . . . . . . . . . . . . . (850) 717-5100
Counties Represented: Broward (part), Miami-Dade          Dist: (954) 924-3708
(part)          Dist: (954) 924-3709
Term Expires: 2016
100 West Dania Beach Boulevard, Dania Beach, FL 33004-3643
E-mail: joseph.geller@myfloridahouse.gov
Committees: Economic Affairs; Education
Education: Florida State 1975 BA, 1979 JD

Representative **Julio Gonzalez** (R-District 74) . . . . . . . . . . (850) 717-5074
Counties Represented: Sarasota (part)          Dist: (941) 480-3560
Term Expires: 2016
333 Tamiami Trail Sout, Suite 284, Venice, FL 34285-2441
E-mail: julio.gonzalez@myfloridahouse.gov
Committees: Judiciary

*(continued on next page)*

**Representatives** *continued*

Representative **Tom Goodson** (R-District 50)
Room 1101 . . . . . . . . . . . . . . . . . . . . . . . . . . . . . . . . . (850) 717-5050
Counties Represented: Brevard (part), Orange (part)    Dist: (321) 383-5151
Term Expires: 2016
400 South Street, Titusville, FL 32780-7610
E-mail: tom.goodson@myfloridahouse.gov
Committees: Agriculture and Natural Resources
Education: Florida State 1975 BS

Representative
**James W. "J.W." Grant, JD** (R-District 64)
405 House Office Building . . . . . . . . . . . . . . . . . . . . . . (850) 717-5064
Counties Represented: Hillsborough (part), Pinellas (part)
Term Expires: 2016
E-mail: james.grant@myfloridahouse.gov
Committees: Rules and Calendar
Education: Auburn 2006 BS; Stetson 2009 JD

Representative **Bill Hager, JD** (R-District 89) Room 1101 . .(850) 717-5089
Counties Represented: Palm Beach (part)    Dist: (561) 470-6607
Term Expires: 2016
301 Yamato Road, Suite 1240, Boca Raton, FL 33431-4931
E-mail: bill.hager@myfloridahouse.gov
Committees: Education
Education: Northern Iowa 1969 BA; Hawaii 1972 MAED;
Illinois 1974 JD

Representative **Gayle B. Harrell** (R-District 83)
Room 417 . . . . . . . . . . . . . . . . . . . . . . . . . . . . . . . . . . (850) 717-5083
Counties Represented: Martin (part), St. Lucie    Dist: (772) 871-7660
(part)
Term Expires: 2016
751 SE Port St. Lucie Boulevard, Port St. Lucie, FL 34984-5211
E-mail: gayle.harrell@myfloridahouse.gov
Committees: Health and Human Services; Judiciary
Education: Florida 1964 BA, 1977 MA

Representative **Shawn Harrison** (R-District 63)
Suite 1102 . . . . . . . . . . . . . . . . . . . . . . . . . . . . . . . . . (850) 717-5063
Counties Represented: Hillsborough (part)    Dist: (813) 910-3277
Term Expires: 2016
15310 Amberly Drive, Suite 215, Tampa, FL 33647-2146
E-mail: shawn.harrison@myfloridahouse.gov
Committees: State Affairs
Education: South Florida 1987 BA; Florida 1990 JD

Representative **Walter Bryan "Mike" Hill** (R-District 2) . . . (850) 717-5002
Counties Represented: Escambia (part), Santa Rosa    Dist: (850) 595-0467
(part)
Term Expires: 2016
418 West Garden Street, Suite 403, Pensacola, FL 32502-4731
E-mail: mike.hill@myfloridahouse.gov
Committees: Health Care Appropriations; Local and Federal Affairs;
Rules and Calendar
Education: Air Force Acad 1980 BS; West Florida 1988 MBA

Representative **Matt Hudson** (R-District 80) Room 222 . . . (850) 717-5080
Counties Represented: Collier (part), Hendry    Dist: (239) 417-6270
Term Expires: 2016    Dist: (863) 675-5267
3299 East Tamiami Trail, Naples, FL 34112-4961
E-mail: matt.hudson@myfloridahouse.gov
Committees: Appropriations; Health Care Appropriations; Joint
Legislative Budget Commission; Judiciary

Representative **Blaise Ingoglia** (R-District 35)
Room 1101 . . . . . . . . . . . . . . . . . . . . . . . . . . . . . . . . . (850) 717-5035
Counties Represented: Hernando (part)    Dist: (352) 688-5004
Term Expires: 2016
2943 Landover Boulevard, Spring Hill, FL 34608-7258
E-mail: blaise.ingoglia@myfloridahouse.gov
Committees: Economic Affairs

Representative **Clay Ingram** (R-District 1) 222 . . . . . . . . . . (850) 717-5001
Counties Represented: Escambia (part)    Dist: (850) 494-7330
Term Expires: 2016
11000 University Parkway, Pensacola, FL 32514-5732
E-mail: clay.ingram@myfloridahouse.gov
Committees: Appropriations; Education; Energy and Utilities; Joint
Legislative Budget Commission
Education: Florida State 2000 BS

Representative **Kristin Diane Jacobs** (D-District 96)
Room 1402 . . . . . . . . . . . . . . . . . . . . . . . . . . . . . . . . . (850) 717-5096
Counties Represented: Broward (part)    Dist: (954) 956-5600
Term Expires: 2016
4800 West Copans Road, Coconut Creek, FL 33063-3879
E-mail: kristin.jacobs@myfloridahouse.gov
Committees: Local and Federal Affairs

Representative **Evan Jenne** (D-District 99) Room 316 . . . . (850) 717-5099
Counties Represented: Broward (part)    Dist: (954) 893-5000
Term Expires: 2016    Dist: (954) 893-5001
3107 Stirling Road, Suite 306, Hollywood, FL 33312-8502
E-mail: evan.jenne@myfloridahouse.gov
Committees: Economic Affairs; Regulatory Affairs; Rules and Calendar
Education: Florida State 1999 BS, 2002 MPA

Representative **Mia L. Jones** (D-District 14) Room 405 . . . (850) 717-5014
Counties Represented: Duval (part)    Dist: (904) 924-1615
Term Expires: 2016
3890 Dunn Avenue, Suite 901, Jacksonville, FL 32218-6431
E-mail: mia.jones@myfloridahouse.gov
Committees: Appropriations; Health and Human Services

Representative **Shevrin "Shev" Jones** (D-District 101)
1101 The Capitol . . . . . . . . . . . . . . . . . . . . . . . . . . . . . (850) 717-5101
Counties Represented: Broward (part)    Dist: (954) 893-5010
Term Expires: 2016
E-mail: shevrin.jones@myfloridahouse.gov
Committees: Health and Human Services
Education: Florida A&M 2006 BS; Florida Atlantic MS

Representative **Dave Kerner, JD** (D-District 87)
1101 The Capitol . . . . . . . . . . . . . . . . . . . . . . . . . . . . . (850) 717-5087
Counties Represented: Palm Beach (part)    Dist: (561) 641-3406
Term Expires: 2016
E-mail: dave.kerner@myfloridahouse.gov
Committees: Judiciary
Education: Florida 2006 BA, 2010 JD

Representative **Mike La Rosa** (R-District 42) . . . . . . . . . . . (850) 717-5042
Counties Represented: Osceola (part), Polk (part)    Dist: (407) 891-2555
Term Expires: 2016
201 West Central Avenue, Lake Wales, FL 33853-1013
E-mail: mike.larosa@myfloridahouse.gov
Committees: Energy and Utilities; Regulatory Affairs; State Affairs
Education: Central Florida 2004 BA

Representative
**Christopher "Chris" Latvala** (R-District 67)
Room 1101 . . . . . . . . . . . . . . . . . . . . . . . . . . . . . . . . . (850) 717-5067
Counties Represented: Pinellas (part)    Dist: (727) 724-3000
Term Expires: 2016
2963 Gulf to Bay Boulevard, Suite 206, Clearwater, FL 33759-4200
E-mail: chris.latvala@myfloridahouse.gov
Committees: Education
Education: Central Florida 2004 BA

Representative **Larry Lee, Jr.** (D-District 84)
1401 The Capitol . . . . . . . . . . . . . . . . . . . . . . . . . . . . . (850) 717-5084
Counties Represented: St. Lucie (part)    Dist: (772) 595-1391
Term Expires: 2016
E-mail: larry.lee@myfloridahouse.gov
Committees: Agriculture and Natural Resources
Education: Livingstone 1976 BS

Representative **MaryLynn "ML" Magar** (R-District 82) . . . (850) 717-5082
Counties Represented: Martin (part), Palm Beach    Dist: (772) 545-3481
(part)    Dist: (772) 545-3482
Term Expires: 2016
11704 Southeast Dixie Highway, Hobe Sound, FL 33475-5457
E-mail: marylynn.magar@myfloridahouse.gov
Committees: Economic Affairs; Health and Human Services; Health
Care Appropriations
Education: Radford 1985 BS

Representative **Debbie Mayfield** (R-District 54)
Room 317 . . . . . . . . . . . . . . . . . . . . . . . . . . . . . . . . . . (850) 717-5054
Counties Represented: Indian River, St. Lucie (part)    Dist: (772) 778-5077
Term Expires: 2016
1053 20th Place, Vero Beach, FL 32960-5359
E-mail: debbie.mayfield@myfloridahouse.gov
Committees: Economic Affairs; Energy and Utilities; Joint Legislative
Auditing; Local and Federal Affairs

Representative **Charles McBurney, JD** (R-District 16)
Room 412 . . . . . . . . . . . . . . . . . . . . . . . . . . . . . . . . . . (850) 717-5016
Counties Represented: Duval (part)    Dist: (904) 359-6090
Term Expires: 2016
76 South Laura Street, Suite 200, Jacksonville, FL 32202-3411
E-mail: charles.mcburney@myfloridahouse.gov
Committees: Appropriations; Judiciary; Rules and Calendar
Education: Florida 1979 BA, 1982 JD

LEGISLATIVE BRANCH

Representative
**Kionne Lamaine McGhee, JD, Esq.** (D-District 117) . . . (850) 717-5117
Counties Represented: Miami-Dade (part)       Dist: (305) 256-6300
Term Expires: 2016
South Dade Government Center, 10710 Southwest 211 Street,
Miami, FL 33189-2819
E-mail: kionne.mcghee@myfloridahouse.gov
Committees: Local and Federal Affairs
Education: Howard U 2000 BS; Texas Southern JD

Representative **Larry Metz, JD** (R-District 32)
Room 1101 . . . . . . . . . . . . . . . . . . . . . . . . . . . . . . (850) 717-5032
Counties Represented: Lake (part)       Dist: (352) 989-9134
Term Expires: 2016
301 West Ward Avenue, Eustis, FL 32726-4033
E-mail: larry.metz@myfloridahouse.gov
Committees: Appropriations; Joint Legislative Budget Commission;
Judiciary
Education: Florida 1976 BA; Florida State 1983 JD

Representative **Mike Miller** (R-District 47)
1101 The Capitol . . . . . . . . . . . . . . . . . . . . . . . . . (850) 717-5047
Counties Represented: Orange (part)       Dist: (407) 245-0588
Term Expires: 2016       Dist: (407) 245-0589
E-mail: mike.miller@myfloridahouse.gov
Committees: Regulatory Affairs
Education: Florida 1990; Rollins 2008 MBA

Representative
**George R. Moraitis, Jr., JD** (R-District 93)
Room 1101 . . . . . . . . . . . . . . . . . . . . . . . . . . . . . . (850) 717-5093
Counties Represented: Broward (part)       Dist: (954) 762-3757
Term Expires: 2016
2132 East Oakland Park Boulevard, Suite 2,
Fort Lauderdale, FL 33306-1109
E-mail: george.moraitis@myfloridahouse.gov
Committees: Appropriations
Education: Naval Acad 1988 BS; Florida 2002 JD

Representative **Jared Evan Moskowitz** (D-District 97) . . . . (850) 717-5097
Counties Represented: Broward (part)       Dist: (954) 346-2848
Term Expires: 2016
2850 University Drive, Coral Springs, FL 33065-1425
E-mail: jared.moskowitz@myfloridahouse.gov
Committees: Finance and Tax; Health Care Appropriations; Judiciary;
Regulatory Affairs

Representative **Amanda Murphy** (D-District 36)
Suite 1402 . . . . . . . . . . . . . . . . . . . . . . . . . . . . . . (850) 717-5036
Counties Represented: Pasco (part)       Dist: (727) 848-5885
Term Expires: 2016
5509 Grand Boulevard, Suite 300, New Port Richey, FL 34652-3836
E-mail: amanda.murphy@myfloridahouse.gov
Committees: Health Care Appropriations; Joint Legislative Auditing;
State Affairs
Education: Florida State 1992 BS

Representative **Edwin "Ed" Narain** (D-District 61)
Suite 1402 . . . . . . . . . . . . . . . . . . . . . . . . . . . . . . (850) 717-5061
Counties Represented: Hillsborough (part)       Dist: (813) 241-8024
Term Expires: 2016
2109 East Palm Avenue, Suite 201, Tampa, FL 33605-3909
E-mail: edwin.narain@myfloridahouse.gov
Committees: Economic Affairs
Education: St Leo U 2009 MBA; Stetson 2013 JD

Representative **Jeanette M. Nuñez** (R-District 119)
Room 308 . . . . . . . . . . . . . . . . . . . . . . . . . . . . . . (850) 717-5119
Counties Represented: Miami-Dade (part)       Dist: (305) 227-7630
Term Expires: 2016       (Miami)
2450 Southwest 137th Avenue, Suite 205, Miami, FL 33175-6312
E-mail: jeanette.nunez@myfloridahouse.gov
Committees: Appropriations
Education: Florida International 1994 BS, 1998 MS

Representative **H. Marlene O'Toole** (R-District 33)
Room 313 . . . . . . . . . . . . . . . . . . . . . . . . . . . . . . (850) 717-5033
Counties Represented: Lake (part), Marion (part),       Dist: (352) 315-4445
Sumter
Term Expires: 2016
916 Avenida Central, The Villages, FL 32159-5704
E-mail: marlene.otoole@myfloridahouse.gov
Committees: Appropriations; Education; Rules and Calendar

Representative **Jose R. Oliva** (R-District 110)
Room 1301 . . . . . . . . . . . . . . . . . . . . . . . . . . . . . . (850) 717-5110
Counties Represented: Miami-Dade (part)       Dist: (305) 361-3114
Term Expires: 2016
3798 West 12th Avenue, Hialeah, FL 32399-1300
E-mail: jose.oliva@myfloridahouse.gov
Committees: Appropriations; Economic Affairs; Rules and Calendar
Education: St Thomas U 1994 BA

Representative **Mark S. Pafford** (D-District 86)
Room 1402 . . . . . . . . . . . . . . . . . . . . . . . . . . . . . . (850) 717-5086
Counties Represented: Palm Beach (part)       Dist: (561) 682-0156
Term Expires: 2016
2240 Palm Beach Lakes Boulevard, Suite 102,
West Palm Beach, FL 33409-3403
E-mail: mark.pafford@myfloridahouse.gov
Committees: Appropriations; Rules and Calendar

Representative
**Kathleen C. Passidomo, JD** (R-District 106)
Room 324 . . . . . . . . . . . . . . . . . . . . . . . . . . . . . . (850) 717-5106
Counties Represented: Collier (part)       Dist: (239) 417-6200
Term Expires: 2016
3299 Tamiami Trail East, Suite 304, Naples, FL 34112-5746
E-mail: kathleen.passidomo@myfloridahouse.gov
Committees: Judiciary
Education: Trinity U 1975 BA; Stetson 1978 JD

Representative **Keith W. Perry** (R-District 21)
Room 1301 . . . . . . . . . . . . . . . . . . . . . . . . . . . . . . (850) 717-5021
Counties Represented: Alachua (part), Dixie,       Dist: (352) 873-6544
Gilchrist
Term Expires: 2016
2440 SW 76th Street, Suite 120, Gainesville, FL 32608-0345
City Hall-Cross City, 99 Northeast 210 Avenue, Cross City, FL 32628
E-mail: keith.perry@myfloridahouse.gov
Committees: Education

Representative **Kathleen Mick Peters** (R-District 69) . . . . . (850) 717-5069
Counties Represented: Pinellas (part)       Dist: (727) 341-7385
Term Expires: 2016
1700 66th Street North, Suite 203, St. Petersburg, FL 32710
E-mail: kathleen.peters@myfloridahouse.gov
Committees: Economic Affairs
Education: St Petersburg AA; Eckerd 1999 BA

Representative **Dr. Cary Pigman, MD** (R-District 55)
Room 400 . . . . . . . . . . . . . . . . . . . . . . . . . . . . . . (850) 717-5055
Counties Represented: Glades, Highlands,       Dist: (863) 386-6000
Okeechobee, St. Lucie (part)
Term Expires: 2016
205 South Commerce Avenue, Suite B, Sebring, FL 33870-3626
E-mail: cary.pigman@myfloridahouse.gov
Committees: Agriculture and Natural Resources; Health and Human
Services
Education: Edgecliff Col 1980 BSChem; Ohio State 1983 MD

Representative **Ray Pilon** (R-District 72) Room 1101 . . . . . (850) 717-5072
Counties Represented: Sarasota (part)       Dist: (941) 955-8077
Term Expires: 2016
1660 Ringling Boulevard, Suite 310-311, Sarasota, FL 34236-6808
E-mail: ray.pilon@myfloridahouse.gov
Committees: Agriculture and Natural Resources; State Affairs
Education: Northern Michigan 1968 BS

Representative **Scott Plakon** (R-District 29) Room 1101 . . (850) 717-5029
Counties Represented: Seminole (part)       Dist: (407) 262-7423
Term Expires: 2016
1855 West State Road 434, Suite 222, Longwood, FL 32750-5071
E-mail: scott.plakon@myfloridahouse.gov
Committees: Judiciary
Education: Stetson 1981 BS

Representative **Rene Plasencia** (R-District 49)
Room 1101 . . . . . . . . . . . . . . . . . . . . . . . . . . . . . . (850) 717-5049
Counties Represented: Orange (part)       Dist: (407) 207-7283
Term Expires: 2016
7217 East Colonial Drive, Suite 216, Orlando, FL 32807-6379
E-mail: rene.plasencia@myfloridahouse.gov
Committees: Economic Affairs
Education: Central Florida BA

Representative **Elizabeth W. Porter** (R-District 10)
Room 1301 . . . . . . . . . . . . . . . . . . . . . . . . . . . . . . (850) 717-5010
Counties Represented: Alachua (part), Baker,       Dist: (386) 719-4600
Columbia, Hamilton, Suwannee
Term Expires: 2016
678 SE Baya Drive, Lake City, FL 32025-6038
E-mail: elizabeth.porter@myfloridahouse.gov
Committees: Agriculture and Natural Resources; Appropriations;
Education
Education: Florida State BA

*(continued on next page)*

**Representatives** *continued*

Representative **Bobby Powell** (D-District 88)
Room 1401 . . . . . . . . . . . . . . . . . . . . . . . . . . . . . . . . . . . (850) 717-5088
Counties Represented: Palm Beach (part)          Dist: (561) 650-6880
Term Expires: 2016
2715 North Australian Avenue, Suite 105,
West Palm Beach, FL 33407-4500
E-mail: bobby.powell@myfloridahouse.gov
Committees: Economic Affairs
Education: Florida A&M BS; Florida State MUP

Representative **Sharon Pritchett** (D-District 102)
1402 The Capitol . . . . . . . . . . . . . . . . . . . . . . . . . . . . . . (850) 717-5102
Counties Represented: Broward (part), Miami-Dade      Dist: (954) 432-1557
(part)
Term Expires: 2016
8910 Miramar Parkway, Suite 309, Miramar, FL 33025-4188
E-mail: sharon.pritchett@myfloridahouse.gov
Committees: Local and Federal Affairs; Rules and Calendar
Education: St Thomas U 1978 BSCrimJ, 1980 MS

Representative
**Jacob William "Jake" Raburn** (R-District 57) . . . . . . . (850) 717-5057
Counties Represented: Hillsborough (part)         Dist: (813) 653-7097
Term Expires: 2016
3618 Erindale Drive, Valrico, FL 33596-6311
E-mail: jake.raburn@myfloridahouse.gov
Committees: Regulatory Affairs; State Affairs
Education: Florida 2007 BS

Representative **Kevin J.G. Rader** (D-District 81) . . . . . . . . (850) 717-5081
Counties Represented: Palm Beach (part)         Dist: (561) 279-1633
Term Expires: 2016                        (Boynton Beach)
9045 La Fontana Boulevard, Suite 117,            Dist: (772) 595-1391
Boca Raton, FL 33434-5641                     (Fort Pierce)
110 Dr. Martin Luther King Jr. Boulevard, Belle Glade, FL 33430-3900
E-mail: kevin.rader@myfloridahouse.gov
Committees: Agriculture and Natural Resources; Appropriations; Health
and Human Services Quality; Local and Federal Affairs
Education: Boston U 1990 BS, 1990 BA

Representative **Holly Merrill Raschein** (R-District 120) . . . (850) 717-5120
Counties Represented: Miami-Dade (part), Monroe      Dist: (305) 453-1202
Term Expires: 2016
99198 Overseas Highway, Suite 10, Key Largo, FL 33037-2437
43 North Krome Avenue, Suite 202, Homestead, FL 33030-6014
E-mail: holly.raschein@myfloridahouse.gov
Committees: Appropriations; Regulatory Affairs
Education: Florida State 2003 BS

Representative
**Daniel "Danny" Raulerson, CPA** (R-District 58)
1102 The Capitol . . . . . . . . . . . . . . . . . . . . . . . . . . . . . . (850) 717-5058
Counties Represented: Hillsborough (part)         Dist: (813) 757-9110
Term Expires: 2016
E-mail: dan.raulerson@myfloridahouse.gov
Committees: Education; Health and Human Services Quality; Joint
Legislative Auditing
Education: Florida State 1979 BSAcc

Representative **Lake Ray** (R-District 12) Room 317 . . . . . . (850) 717-5012
Counties Represented: Duval (part)            Dist: (850) 723-5300
Term Expires: 2016
1615 Huffingham Road, Jacksonville, FL 32216-2792
E-mail: lake.ray@myfloridahouse.gov
Committees: Local and Federal Affairs; Rules and Calendar
Education: Florida 1981 BSCE

Representative
**Michelle Rehwinkel Vasilinda** (D-District 9)
Room 1001 . . . . . . . . . . . . . . . . . . . . . . . . . . . . . . . . . . . (850) 717-5009
Counties Represented: Leon (part)
Term Expires: 2016
E-mail: michelle.rehwinkel@myfloridahouse.gov
Committees: Education; Energy and Utilities; Judiciary
Education: South Florida 1982 BA; Florida 1985 JD

Representative **Paul Renner** (R-District 24) Room 1102 . . . (850) 717-5024
Counties Represented: Flagler, St. Johns (part), Volusia (part)
Term Expires: 2016
E-mail: paul.renner@myfloridahouse.gov
Committees: Health and Human Services
Education: Davidson 1989 BA; Florida 1994 JD

Representative **David Richardson, CPA** (D-District 113)
Room 1301 . . . . . . . . . . . . . . . . . . . . . . . . . . . . . . . . . . . (850) 717-5113
Counties Represented: Miami-Dade (part)          Dist: (305) 535-5426
Term Expires: 2016                        Dist: (305) 624-2437
1701 Meridian Avenue, Miami Beach, FL 33139-1890
970 Southwest 1st Street, Miami, FL 33130-1169
E-mail: david.richardson@myfloridahouse.gov
Committees: Appropriations; Health Care Appropriations; Regulatory
Affairs; Rules and Calendar
Education: Central Florida 1979 BS, 1983 BSBA; Florida 1987 MBA

Representative
**Kenneth L. "Ken" Roberson** (R-District 75)
Room 214 . . . . . . . . . . . . . . . . . . . . . . . . . . . . . . . . . . . (850) 717-5075
Counties Represented: Charlotte             Dist: (941) 613-0914
Term Expires: 2016
17825 Murdock Circle, Suite B, Port Charlotte, FL 33948-4090
E-mail: ken.roberson@myfloridahouse.gov
Committees: Appropriations; Health and Human Services; Health and
Human Services Quality

Representative **Ray Wesley Rodrigues** (R-District 76) . . . . (850) 717-5076
Counties Represented: Lee (part)              Dist: (239) 433-6501
Term Expires: 2016
17595 South Tamiami Trail, Suite 216, 217, 218,
Fort Myers, FL 33908-4570
E-mail: ray.rodrigues@myfloridahouse.gov
Committees: Energy and Utilities; Finance and Tax; Joint Legislative
Auditing; Regulatory Affairs
Education: Berry 1992 BA

Representative
**José Javier Rodríguez, JD** (D-District 112) . . . . . . . . . . (850) 717-5112
Counties Represented: Miami-Dade (part)          Dist: (305) 854-0365
Term Expires: 2016
2100 Coral Way, Suite 601, Miami, FL 33145-2657
E-mail: jose.rodriguez@myfloridahouse.gov
Committees: Finance and Tax; Health and Human Services Quality;
Judiciary; Rules and Calendar
Education: Brown U 2000 BA; Harvard 2006 JD

Representative
**Hazelle P. "Hazel" Rogers** (D-District 95) Room 1101 . . (850) 717-5095
Counties Represented: Broward (part)           Dist: (954) 497-3367
Term Expires: 2016
3800 Inverrary Blvd, Suite 100-J, Lauderhill, FL 33319-4359
E-mail: hazelle.rogers@myfloridahouse.gov
Committees: Finance and Tax

Representative
**Patrick Joseph "Pat" Rooney, Jr.** (R-District 85)
Room 324 . . . . . . . . . . . . . . . . . . . . . . . . . . . . . . . . . . . (850) 717-5085
Counties Represented: Palm Beach (part)          Dist: (531) 625-5176
Term Expires: 2016
3970 RCA Boulevard, Suite 7001,
Palm Beach Gardens, FL 33410-4231
E-mail: pat.rooney@myfloridahouse.gov
Committees: Economic Affairs; Health and Human Services Quality
Education: Clemson 1986 BA; Villanova 1989 JD; Lehigh 1992 MBA

Representative **Darryl Ervin Rouson, JD** (D-District 70)
Room 405 . . . . . . . . . . . . . . . . . . . . . . . . . . . . . . . . . . . (850) 717-5070
Counties Represented: Hillsborough (part), Manatee    Dist: (727) 906-3200
(part), Pinellas (part), Sarasota (part)         Dist: (941) 708-8570
Term Expires: 2016
6501 25th Way South, Suite D, Saint Petersburg, FL 33712-5665
302 Manatee Avenue East, Suite 304, Bradenton, FL 34208-1901
E-mail: darryl.rouson@myfloridahouse.gov
Committees: Appropriations; Regulatory Affairs
Education: Florida 1981 JD

Representative **David Santiago** (R-District 27) . . . . . . . . . (850) 717-5027
Counties Represented: Volusia (part)           Dist: (386) 575-0387
Term Expires: 2016
777 Deltona Boulevard, Deltona, FL 32725-7175
E-mail: david.santiago@myfloridahouse.gov
Committees: Local and Federal Affairs

Representative **Irving L. "Irv" Slosberg** (D-District 91)
Room 1402 . . . . . . . . . . . . . . . . . . . . . . . . . . . . . . . . . . . (850) 717-5091
Counties Represented: Palm Beach (part)          Dist: (561) 496-5940
Term Expires: 2016
7499 West Atlantic Avenue, Suite 200, Delray Beach, FL 33446-1394
E-mail: irving.slosberg@myfloridahouse.gov
Committees: Regulatory Affairs; State Affairs
Education: Roosevelt 1970 BS

Representative **Jimmie Todd Smith** (R-District 34)
Room 1003 . . . . . . . . . . . . . . . . . . . . . . . . (850) 717-5034
Counties Represented: Citrus, Hernando (part)　　Dist: (352) 560-6020
Term Expires: 2016
591 East Gulf to Lake Highway, Lecanto, FL 34461-9392
E-mail: jimmie.smith@myfloridahouse.gov
Committees: Local and Federal Affairs

Representative **Ross Spano** (R-District 59) . . . . . . . . . . . . (850) 717-5059
Counties Represented: Hillsborough (part)　　Dist: (813) 655-3742
Term Expires: 2016
11256 Winthrop Main Street, Unit A, Riverview, FL 33578-4267
E-mail: ross.spano@myfloridahouse.gov
Committees: Education; Health and Human Services Quality
Education: South Florida 1994 BA; Florida State 1998 JD

Representative **Chris Sprowls** (R-District 65)
1101 The Capitol . . . . . . . . . . . . . . . . . . . . . . . . (850) 717-5065
Counties Represented: Pinellas (part)　　Dist: (727) 793-2810
Term Expires: 2016
E-mail: chris.sprowls@myfloridahouse.gov
Committees: Health and Human Services
Education: South Florida 2006 BA; Stetson 2009 JD

Representative **Cynthia A. Stafford, JD** (D-District 109)
Room 1401 . . . . . . . . . . . . . . . . . . . . . . . . (850) 717-5109
Counties Represented: Miami-Dade (part)　　Dist: (305) 953-3086
Term Expires: 2016
13300 Northwest 27th Avenue, Suite 5, Opa Locka, FL 33054-4827
E-mail: cynthia.stafford@myfloridahouse.gov
Committees: Appropriations; Joint Legislative Auditing
Education: St Thomas (Cuba) 1993 BA, 1999 JD

Representative **Richard N. "Rick" Stark** (D-District 104)
Room 1302 . . . . . . . . . . . . . . . . . . . . . . . . (850) 717-5104
Counties Represented: Broward (part)　　Dist: (954) 217-0287
Term Expires: 2016
1730 Main Street, Suite 202, Weston, FL 33326-3676
E-mail: richard.stark@myfloridahouse.gov
Committees: Finance and Tax
Education: Denver 1974 BA

Representative
**Gregory W. "Greg" Steube, JD** (R-District 73)
Room 1102 . . . . . . . . . . . . . . . . . . . . . . . . (850) 717-5073
Counties Represented: Manatee (part), Sarasota　　Dist: (941) 907-2810
(part)
Term Expires: 2016
722 Apex Road, Unit A, Sarasota, FL 34240-1713
E-mail: greg.steube@myfloridahouse.gov
Committees: Appropriations; Economic Affairs
Education: Florida 2000 BS, 2003 JD

Representative **Cyndi Stevenson, CPA** (R-District 17)
1102 The Capitol . . . . . . . . . . . . . . . . . . . . . . . . (850) 717-5017
Counties Represented: St. Johns (part)
Term Expires: 2016
E-mail: cyndi.stevenson@myfloridahouse.gov
Committees: Economic Affairs
Education: Stetson 1981 BBA

Representative **Charlie Stone** (R-District 22) . . . . . . . . . . . . (850) 717-5022
Counties Represented: Levy, Marion (part)　　Dist: (352) 291-4436
Term Expires: 2016
3001 Southwest College Road, Suite 104, Ocala, FL 34474-4415
E-mail: charlie.stone@myfloridahouse.gov
Committees: Judiciary

Representative **Jennifer Sullivan** (R-District 31)
Room 1101 . . . . . . . . . . . . . . . . . . . . . . . . (850) 717-5031
Counties Represented: Lake (part), Orange (part)　　Dist: (352) 742-6275
Term Expires: 2016
2755 South Bay Street, Unit D, Eustis, FL 32726-6587
E-mail: jennifer.sullivan@myfloridahouse.gov
Committees: Finance and Tax

Representative **Dwayne L. Taylor** (D-District 26)
Room 1302 . . . . . . . . . . . . . . . . . . . . . . . . (850) 717-5026
Counties Represented: Volusia (part)　　Dist: (386) 239-6202
Term Expires: 2016
1020 West International Speedway Boulevard, Suite 103,
Daytona Beach, FL 32114-4773
E-mail: dwayne.taylor@myfloridahouse.gov
Committees: State Affairs
Education: Central Florida BS

Representative **John Tobia** (R-District 53) Room 323 . . . . . (850) 717-5053
Counties Represented: Brevard (part)　　Dist: (321) 984-4848
Term Expires: 2016
8060 South Highway A1A, Melbourne, FL 32951-3948
E-mail: john.tobia@myfloridahouse.gov
Committees: Finance and Tax
Education: Florida 1999 BA, 1999 MA

Representative
**Victor Manuel "Vic" Torres, Jr.** (D-District 48) . . . . . . . (850) 717-5048
Counties Represented: Orange (part)　　Dist: (407) 730-3422
Term Expires: 2016
5425 South Semoran Boulevard, Suite 1-C, Orlando, FL 32822-1751
E-mail: victor.torres@myfloridahouse.gov
Committees: Education

Representative **Carlos Trujillo, JD** (R-District 105)
Room 204 . . . . . . . . . . . . . . . . . . . . . . . . (850) 717-5105
Counties Represented: Broward (part), Collier　　Dist: (305) 470-5070
(part), Miami-Dade (part)　　Dist: (239) 434-5094
Term Expires: 2016
2500 NW 107th Avenue, Suite 204, Doral, FL 33172-5923
Collier County Administration Building, Suite 305,
Naples, FL 34112-5746
E-mail: carlos.trujillo@myfloridahouse.gov
Committees: Judiciary
Education: Spring Hill 2004 BS; Florida State 2007 JD

Representative **Jay Trumbull, Jr.** (R-District 6)
Room 1101 . . . . . . . . . . . . . . . . . . . . . . . . (850) 717-5006
Counties Represented: Bay (part)　　Dist: (850) 914-6300
Term Expires: 2016
455 Harrison Avenue, Suite A, Panama City, FL 32401-2731
E-mail: jay.trumbull@myfloridahouse.gov
Committees: Finance and Tax; Health and Human Services
Education: Auburn BS

Representative **Charles E. Van Zant** (R-District 19)
Room 410 . . . . . . . . . . . . . . . . . . . . . . . . (850) 717-5019
Counties Represented: Bradford, Clay (part),　　Dist: (386) 312-2272
Putnam, Union
Term Expires: 2016
3841 Reid Street, Suite 5, Palatka, FL 32177-2509
E-mail: charles.vanzant@myfloridahouse.gov
Committees: Finance and Tax; Local and Federal Affairs
Education: Florida 1968 BARCH; Southern Baptist 1974 MDiv;
Midwestern Baptist 2001 ThD

Representative **Barbara Watson** (D-District 107)
Room 1401 . . . . . . . . . . . . . . . . . . . . . . . . (850) 717-5107
Counties Represented: Miami-Dade (part)　　Dist: (305) 654-7100
Term Expires: 2016
610 Northwest 183rd Street, Suite 204,
Miami Gardens, FL 33169-4472
E-mail: barbara.watson@myfloridahouse.gov
Committees: Rules and Calendar

Representative **Clovis Watson, Jr., MBA** (D-District 20) . . (850) 717-5020
Counties Represented: Alachua (part), Marion (part)　　Dist: (352) 264-4001
Term Expires: 2016
2815 Northwest 13th Street, Suite 202, Gainesville, FL 32609-2865
E-mail: clovis.watson@myfloridahouse.gov
Committees: State Affairs
Education: Alabama BA; Mountain State MA; North Central U MBA

Representative **Alan B. Williams, MBA** (D-District 8)
Room 1001 . . . . . . . . . . . . . . . . . . . . . . . . (850) 717-5008
Counties Represented: Gadsden, Leon (part)
Term Expires: 2016
E-mail: alan.williams@myfloridahouse.gov
Committees: Appropriations; Economic Affairs; Education; Energy and
Utilities; Joint Legislative Budget Commission

Representative **John Wood, JD** (R-District 41)
Room 214 . . . . . . . . . . . . . . . . . . . . . . . . (850) 717-5041
Counties Represented: Polk (part)　　Dist: (863) 298-5300
Term Expires: 2016
20 3rd Street Southwest, Suite 300, Winter Haven, FL 33880-2905
E-mail: john.wood@myfloridahouse.gov
Committees: Appropriations; Health Care Appropriations; Judiciary;
Regulatory Affairs
Education: Columbia 1974 BA; Florida State 1977 JD

Representative **Ritch Workman** (R-District 52)
Room 218 . . . . . . . . . . . . . . . . . . . . . . . . (850) 717-5052
Counties Represented: Brevard (part)　　Dist: (321) 757-7019
Term Expires: 2016
33 Suntree Place, Suite D, Melbourne, FL 32940-7602
E-mail: ritch.workman@myfloridahouse.gov
Committees: Finance and Tax; Regulatory Affairs; Rules and Calendar
Education: Appalachian State 1995 BS

Representative **Dana D. Young** (R-District 60)
Room 1101 . . . . . . . . . . . . . . . . . . . . . . . . (850) 717-5060
Counties Represented: Hillsborough (part)　　Dist: (813) 835-2270
Term Expires: 2016
2909 West Bay to Bay Boulevard, Suite 202, Tampa, FL 33629-8175
E-mail: dana.young@myfloridahouse.gov
Committees: Appropriations

**LEGISLATIVE BRANCH**

**LEGISLATIVE BRANCH**

# House Committees
## Appropriations
221 The Capitol, 402 South Monroe Street, Tallahassee, FL 32399-1300

**Majority Members**
Richard Corcoran (R-37) *Chair*
Jim Boyd (R-71) *Vice Chair*
Janet H. Adkins (R-11)
Ben Albritton (R-56)
Erik Fresen (R-114)
Matt Hudson (R-80)
Clay Ingram (R-1)
Charles McBurney (R-16)
Larry Metz (R-32)
George R. Moraitis, Jr. (R-93)
Jeanette M. Nuñez (R-119)
H. Marlene O'Toole (R-33)
Jose R. Oliva (R-110)
Elizabeth W. Porter (R-10)
Holly Merrill Raschein (R-120)
Kenneth L. "Ken" Roberson (R-75)
Gregory W. "Greg" Steube (R-73)
John Wood (R-41)
Dana D. Young (R-60)

**Minority Members**
Janet R. Cruz (D-62)
    *Democratic Ranking Member*
Gwyndolen "Gwyn" Clarke-Reed
    (D-92)
Mia L. Jones (D-14)
Mark S. Pafford (D-86)
Kevin J.G. Rader (D-81)
David Richardson (D-113)
Darryl Ervin Rouson (D-70)
Cynthia A. Stafford (D-109)
Alan B. Williams (D-8)

## Economic Affairs
203 House Office Building, 402 South Monroe Street, Tallahassee, FL 32399-1300

**Majority Members**
Jose R. Oliva (R-110) *Chair*
MaryLynn "ML" Magar (R-82)
    *Vice Chair*
Frank Artiles (R-118)
Bryan Avila (R-111)
Heather Dawes Fitzenhagen (R-78)
Blaise Ingoglia (R-35)
Debbie Mayfield (R-54)
Kathleen Mick Peters (R-69)
Rene Plasencia (R-49)
Patrick Joseph "Pat" Rooney, Jr.
    (R-85)
Gregory W. "Greg" Steube (R-73)
Cyndi Stevenson (R-17)

**Minority Members**
Alan B. Williams (D-8)
    *Democratic Ranking Member*
Randolph Bracy III (D-45)
Joseph S. "Joe" Geller (D-100)
Evan Jenne (D-99)
Edwin "Ed" Narain (D-61)
Bobby Powell (D-88)

## Education
313 House Office Building, 402 South Monroe Street, Tallahassee, FL 32399-1300

**Majority Members**
H. Marlene O'Toole (R-33) *Chair*
Keith W. Perry (R-21) *Vice Chair*
Janet H. Adkins (R-11)
Michael Bileca (R-105)
Manuel "Manny" Diaz, Jr. (R-103)
Erik Fresen (R-114)
Bill Hager (R-89)
Clay Ingram (R-1)
Christopher "Chris" Latvala (R-67)
Elizabeth W. Porter (R-10)
Daniel "Danny" Raulerson (R-58)
Ross Spano (R-59)

**Minority Members**
Reggie Fullwood (D-13)
    *Democratic Ranking Member*
Bruce Antone (D-46)
Joseph S. "Joe" Geller (D-100)
Michelle Rehwinkel Vasilinda (D-9)
Victor Manuel "Vic" Torres, Jr.
    (D-48)
Alan B. Williams (D-8)

## Finance and Tax
221 The Capitol, 402 South Monroe Street, Tallahassee, FL 32399-1300

**Majority Members**
Matt Gaetz (R-4) *Chair*
Ray Wesley Rodrigues (R-76)
    *Vice Chair*
Frank Artiles (R-118)
Jason T. Brodeur (R-28)
Robert "Bob" Cortes (R-30)
Julian "Jay" Fant (R-15)
Jennifer Sullivan (R-31)
John Tobia (R-53)
Jay Trumbull, Jr. (R-6)
Charles E. Van Zant (R-19)
Ritch Workman (R-52)

**Minority Members**
José Javier Rodríguez (D-112)
    *Democratic Ranking Member*
Lori Berman (D-90)
Randolph Bracy III (D-45)
Jared Evan Moskowitz (D-97)
Hazelle P. "Hazel" Rogers (D-95)
Richard N. "Rick" Stark (D-104)

## Health and Human Services
214 House Office Building, 402 South Monroe Street, Tallahassee, FL 32399-1300

**Majority Members**
Jason T. Brodeur (R-28) *Chair*
MaryLynn "ML" Magar (R-82)
    *Vice Chair*
Bryan Avila (R-111)
Colleen Burton (R-40)
Fredrick W. "Fred" Costello (R-25)
Travis W. Cummings (R-18)
Gayle B. Harrell (R-83)
Dr. Cary Pigman (R-55)
Paul Renner (R-24)
Kenneth L. "Ken" Roberson (R-75)
Chris Sprowls (R-65)
Jay Trumbull, Jr. (R-6)

**Minority Members**
Mia L. Jones (D-14)
    *Democratic Ranking Member*
Lori Berman (D-90)
Gwyndolen "Gwyn" Clarke-Reed
    (D-92)
Janet R. Cruz (D-62)
Katie A. Edwards (D-98)
Shevrin "Shev" Jones (D-101)

## Judiciary
412 House Office Building, 402 South Monroe Street, Tallahassee, FL 32399-1300

**Majority Members**
Charles McBurney (R-16) *Chair*
Kathleen C. Passidomo (R-106)
    *Vice Chair*
Colleen Burton (R-40)
Julian "Jay" Fant (R-15)
Julio Gonzalez (R-74)
Gayle B. Harrell (R-83)
Matt Hudson (R-80)
Larry Metz (R-32)
Scott Plakon (R-29)
Charlie Stone (R-22)
Carlos Trujillo (R-105)
John Wood (R-41)

**Minority Members**
Dave Kerner (D-87)
    *Democratic Ranking Member*
Dwight Richard Dudley (D-68)
Katie A. Edwards (D-98)
Jared Evan Moskowitz (D-97)
Michelle Rehwinkel Vasilinda (D-9)
José Javier Rodríguez (D-112)

## Local and Federal Affairs
317 House Office Building, 402 South Monroe Street, Tallahassee, FL 32399-1300

**Majority Members**
Dennis K. Baxley (R-23) *Chair*
Debbie Mayfield (R-54) *Vice Chair*
Lawrence T. "Larry" Ahern (R-66)
Douglas Vaughn "Doug" Broxson
    (R-3)
Daniel "Danny" Burgess (R-38)
Neil Combee (R-39)
Eric J. "E" Eisnaugle (R-44)
Walter Bryan "Mike" Hill (R-2)
Lake Ray (R-12)
David Santiago (R-27)
Jimmie Todd Smith (R-34)
Charles E. Van Zant (R-19)

**Minority Members**
Sharon Pritchett (D-102)
    *Democratic Ranking Member*
Daphne D. Campbell (D-108)
Bobby B. DuBose (D-94)
Kristin Diane Jacobs (D-96)
Kionne Lamaine McGhee (D-117)
Kevin J.G. Rader (D-81)

## Regulatory Affairs
303 House Office Building, 402 South Monroe Street, Tallahassee, FL 32399-1300

**Majority Members**
Jose Felix Diaz (R-116) *Chair*
Mike La Rosa (R-42) *Vice Chair*
Halsey Beshears (R-7)
Jim Boyd (R-71)
Dane Eagle (R-77)
Matt Gaetz (R-4)
Mike Miller (R-47)
Jacob William "Jake" Raburn
    (R-57)
Holly Merrill Raschein (R-120)
Ray Wesley Rodrigues (R-76)
John Wood (R-41)
Ritch Workman (R-52)

**Minority Members**
Jared Evan Moskowitz (D-97)
    *Democratic Ranking Member*
Randolph Bracy III (D-45)
Evan Jenne (D-99)
David Richardson (D-113)
Darryl Ervin Rouson (D-70)
Irving L. "Irv" Slosberg (D-91)

## Rules and Calendar
422 The Capitol, 402 South Monroe Street, Tallahassee, FL 32399-1300

**Majority Members**
Ritch Workman (R-52) *Chair*
Eric J. "E" Eisnaugle (R-44)
  *Vice Chair*
Janet H. Adkins (R-11)
Ben Albritton (R-56)
Frank Artiles (R-118)
Dennis K. Baxley (R-23)
Jim Boyd (R-71)
Matthew H. "Matt" Caldwell (R-79)
Fredrick W. "Fred" Costello (R-25)
James W. "J.W." Grant (R-64)
Walter Bryan "Mike" Hill (R-2)
Charles McBurney (R-16)
H. Marlene O'Toole (R-33)
Jose R. Oliva (R-110)
Lake Ray (R-12)

**Minority Members**
David Richardson (D-113)
  *Democratic Ranking Member*
Lori Berman (D-90)
Evan Jenne (D-99)
Mark S. Pafford (D-86)
Sharon Pritchett (D-102)
José Javier Rodríguez (D-112)
Barbara Watson (D-107)

## State Affairs
218 House Office Building, 402 South Monroe Street,
Tallahassee, FL 32399-1300

**Majority Members**
Matthew H. "Matt" Caldwell (R-79)
  *Chair*
Neil Combee (R-39) *Vice Chair*
Ben Albritton (R-56)
Michael Bileca (R-105)
Travis W. Cummings (R-18)
Brad Drake (R-5)
Matt Gaetz (R-4)
Shawn Harrison (R-63)
Mike La Rosa (R-42)
Ray Pilon (R-72)
Jacob William "Jake" Raburn
  (R-57)

**Minority Members**
Dwayne L. Taylor (D-26)
  *Democratic Ranking Member*
John Cortes (D-43)
Reggie Fullwood (D-13)
Amanda Murphy (D-36)
Irving L. "Irv" Slosberg (D-91)
Clovis Watson, Jr. (D-20)

# General Assembly of Georgia
State Capitol, Atlanta, GA 30334
Tel: (404) 656-5000  Internet: www.legis.state.ga.us

## Georgia Senate
Tel: (404) 656-5040  Fax: (404) 656-5043

President of the Senate **Casey Cagle** (R) . . . . . . . . . . . . . . (404) 656-5030
  Affiliation: Lieutenant Governor, Office of the Lieutenant Governor,
  State of Georgia
  240 State Capitol, Atlanta, GA 30334
  Education: Georgia Southern (Attended)
President Pro Tem **David J. Shafer** (R) . . . . . . . . . . . . . . . (404) 656-0048
  Education: Georgia
Majority Leader **William S. "Bill" Cowsert** (R) . . . . . . . . (404) 463-1383
  Education: Georgia JD
Majority Caucus Chair **William T. Ligon, Jr.** (R) . . . . . . . . (404) 656-0045
Majority Whip **Steve Gooch** (R) . . . . . . . . . . . . . . . . . . . (404) 656-9221
  Education: North Georgia MPA
Deputy Majority Whip **G.M. "Greg" Kirk** (R) . . . . . . . . . (404) 463-5258
Administration Floor Leader **Mike Dugan** (R) . . . . . . . . . (404) 656-0036
  Education: West Georgia 1986 BA, 1989 MA
Administration Floor Leader **William "Bill" Jackson** (R) . . (404) 651-7738
Administration Floor Leader
  **John Flanders Kennedy** (R) . . . . . . . . . . . . . . . . . . . . (404) 656-7454
Administration Floor Leader **Butch Miller** (R) . . . . . . . . . . (404) 651-7738
  Education: North Georgia BS
Minority Leader **Steve Henson** (D) . . . . . . . . . . . . . . . . . . (404) 656-0085
Minority Caucus Chairman **Horacena Tate** (D) . . . . . . . . . (404) 463-8053
  Education: Georgia 1977 BS; Atlanta 1987 MAED;
  Clark Atlanta 1992 EdD
Minority Caucus Secretary **Nan Grogan Orrock** (D) . . . . . . (404) 463-8054
  Education: Mary Washington Col BA
Minority Whip **Vincent D. Fort** (D) . . . . . . . . . . . . . . . . . (404) 656-5091
Secretary of the Senate **David A. Cook** . . . . . . . . . . . . . . . (404) 656-5040
  E-mail: david.cook@senate.ga.gov
  Education: Georgia Southern 1976; Georgia 1982 JD
Sergeant-at-Arms **John Long** . . . . . . . . . . . . . . . . . . . . . . (404) 656-5040

## Senators
**Party Affiliation Statistics:** Republicans: 39, Democrats: 17

Senator **John Albers** (R-District 56) . . . . . . . . . . . . . . . . (404) 463-8055
  Counties Represented: Cherokee (part), Fulton       Dist: (678) 667-3656
  (part)                                              Fax: (404) 656-6484
  Term Expires: 2017                                  Dist: (404) 806-4385
  885 Woodstock Road #215, Suite 430, Roswell, GA 30075
  E-mail: john.albers@senate.ga.gov
  Committees: Appropriations; Finance; Public Safety; State and Local
  Governmental Operations
  Education: Louisville; Georgia
Senator **Brandon L. Beach** (R-District 21)
  Coverdell Legislative Office Bldg., Room 303-B . . . . . . . . (404) 656-5040
  Counties Represented: Cherokee (part), Fulton (part)
  Term Expires: 2017
  E-mail: brandon.beach@senate.ga.gov
  Committees: Higher Education; Regulated Industries and Utilities;
  Science and Technology; Transportation
  Education: LSU (Alexandria) BA; Centenary (LA) MBA
Senator **Charles "Charlie" Bethel** (R-District 54) . . . . . . . (404) 656-6436
  Counties Represented: Gordon (part), Murray,        Dist: (706) 270-1685
  Pickens (part), Whitfield                           Fax: (404) 656-6484
  Term Expires: 2017
  1701 Briarcliff Circle, Dalton, GA 30720
  E-mail: charlie.bethel@senate.ga.gov
  Committees: Appropriations; Insurance and Labor; Judiciary; Judiciary
  Non-Civil; Reapportionment and Redistricting
  Education: Georgia 1998 BBA, 2001 JD
Senator **Ellis Black** (D-District 8) . . . . . . . . . . . . . . . . . . (404) 656-3932
  Counties Represented: Brooks, Clinch, Cook, Echols, Lanier, Lowndes,
  Thomas (part)
  Term Expires: 2017
  E-mail: ellis.black@senate.ga.gov
  Committees: Agriculture and Consumer Affairs; Education and Youth;
  Retirement; State Institutions and Property
  Education: Georgia BSA

*(continued on next page)*

**LEGISLATIVE BRANCH**

**Senators** *continued*

**Senator Dean Burke** (R-District 11)
Coverdell Legislative Office Bldg., 305-A . . . . . . . . . . . . (404) 656-0040
Counties Represented: Colquitt, Decatur, Early,    Dist: (229) 243-6267
Grady, Miller, Mitchell (part), Seminole, Thomas (part)
Term Expires: 2017
E-mail: dean.burke@senate.ga.gov
Committees: Agriculture and Consumer Affairs; Appropriations; Ethics;
Health and Human Services
Education: Georgia Southwestern 1977 BS;
Medical Col (GA) 1981 MD

**Senator Gloria S. Butler** (D-District 55) . . . . . . . . . . . . . (404) 656-0075
Counties Represented: DeKalb (part), Gwinnett    Fax: (404) 657-9728
(part)
Term Expires: 2017
6241 Southland Trace, Stone Mountain, GA 30087
E-mail: gloria.butler@senate.ga.gov
Committees: Ethics; Health and Human Services; Joint Metropolitan
Atlanta Rapid Transit Oversight; Rules; State and Local Governmental
Operations; Transportation; Urban Affairs
Education: Georgia Perimeter 1984 AA

**Senator William S. "Bill" Cowsert** (R-District 46) . . . . . . (404) 463-1383
Counties Represented: Clarke (part), Oconee,    Dist: (706) 543-7700
Walton (part)    Fax: (404) 651-6768
Term Expires: 2017    Dist: (706) 202-3211
P.O. Box 512, Athens, GA 30603
E-mail: bill.cowsert@senate.ga.gov
Committees: Administrative Affairs; Appropriations; Finance; Health
and Human Services; Judiciary; Reapportionment and Redistricting;
Regulated Industries and Utilities; Rules

**Senator Michael Robert "Mike" Crane** (R-District 28) . . . (404) 656-6446
Counties Represented: Carroll (part), Coweta,    Fax: (404) 463-1381
Fulton (part), Heard, Troup (part)
Term Expires: 2017
PO Box 700, Newnan, GA 30264
E-mail: michael.crane@senate.ga.gov
Committees: Appropriations; Judiciary Non-Civil; Reapportionment and
Redistricting; Retirement
Education: Georgia Tech 1987 BIM

**Senator Gail Davenport** (D-District 44) . . . . . . . . . . . . . . (404) 463-5260
Counties Represented: Clayton (part), DeKalb (part)    Dist: (678) 215-9974
Term Expires: 2017    Fax: (404) 656-6579
P. O. Box 1074, Jonesboro, GA 30236
E-mail: gail.davenport@senate.ga.gov
Committees: Appropriations; State Institutions and Property; Urban
Affairs; Veterans, Military and Homeland Security

**Senator Mike Dugan** (R-District 30) . . . . . . . . . . . . . . . . (404) 656-0036
Counties Represented: Carroll (part), Douglas (part), Paulding (part)
Term Expires: 2017
106 Champion Drive, Carrollton, GA 30116
E-mail: mike.dugan@senate.ga.gov
Committees: Economic Development and Tourism; Public Safety;
Transportation; Veterans, Military and Homeland Security

**Senator Vincent D. Fort** (D-District 39) 121-G . . . . . . . . . (404) 656-5091
Counties Represented: Fulton (part)    Fax: (404) 651-7078
Term Expires: 2017
E-mail: vincent.fort@senate.ga.gov
Committees: Appropriations; Education and Youth; Interstate
Cooperation; Judiciary; Judiciary Non-Civil; Reapportionment and
Redistricting; Urban Affairs

**Senator Frank Ginn** (R-District 47) . . . . . . . . . . . . . . . . . (404) 656-4700
Counties Represented: Barrow, Clarke (part),    Dist: (706) 680-4466
Jackson (part), Madison    Fax: (404) 657-3248
Term Expires: 2017
P. O. Box 1136, Danielsville, GA 30633
E-mail: frank.ginn@senate.ga.gov
Committees: Appropriations; Economic Development and Tourism;
Natural Resources and the Environment; Regulated Industries and
Utilities; Transportation
Education: Georgia 1985 BSAE

**Senator Steve Gooch** (R-District 51) . . . . . . . . . . . . . . . . (404) 656-9221
Counties Represented: Dawson, Fannin, Forsyth    Fax: (404) 657-3248
(part), Gilmer, Lumpkin, Pickens (part), Union, White
Term Expires: 2017
P. O. Box 600, Dahlonega, GA 30533
E-mail: steve.gooch@senate.ga.gov
Committees: Appropriations; Finance; Joint Metropolitan Atlanta
Rapid Transit Oversight; Regulated Industries and Utilities; Rules;
Transportation

**Senator M.H. "Marty" Harbin** (R-District 16) . . . . . . . . . . (404) 656-0078
Counties Represented: Fayette (part), Lamar, Pike,    Fax: (404) 656-6484
Spalding
Term Expires: 2017
E-mail: marty.harbin@senate.ga.gov
Committees: Banking and Financial Institutions; Government Oversight;
Insurance and Labor; State and Local Governmental Operations

**Senator Ed Harbison** (D-District 15) . . . . . . . . . . . . . . . . (404) 656-0074
Counties Represented: Chattahoochee, Macon,    Fax: (404) 463-5547
Marion, Muscogee (part), Schley, Talbot, Taylor
Term Expires: 2017
P.O. Box 1292, Columbus, GA 31902
E-mail: ed.harbison@senate.ga.gov
Committees: Banking and Financial Institutions; Ethics; Insurance and
Labor; Interstate Cooperation; Reapportionment and Redistricting;
Regulated Industries and Utilities; State Institutions and Property;
Veterans, Military and Homeland Security

**Senator Tyler Harper** (R-District 7) . . . . . . . . . . . . . . . . . (404) 656-5263
Counties Represented: Atkinson, Bacon, Ben Hill,    Dist: (229) 425-4840
Berrien, Charlton (part), Coffee, Irwin, Pierce, Tift    Fax: (404) 463-4161
(part), Ware
Term Expires: 2017
PO Box 798, Ocilla, GA 31774
E-mail: tyler.harper@senate.ga.gov
Committees: Agriculture and Consumer Affairs; Natural Resources and
the Environment; Public Safety; Retirement
Education: Georgia BSAE

**Senator Bill Heath** (R-District 31) . . . . . . . . . . . . . . . . . . (404) 656-3943
Counties Represented: Haralson, Paulding (part),    Dist: (770) 537-5234
Polk    Fax: (404) 463-4161
Term Expires: 2017    Dist: (770) 537-6383
2225 Cashtown Road, Bremen, GA 30110
E-mail: billheath@billheath.net
Committees: Agriculture and Consumer Affairs; Appropriations;
Finance; Government Oversight; Rules; Transportation

**Senator Steve Henson** (D-District 41) . . . . . . . . . . . . . . . (404) 656-0085
Counties Represented: DeKalb (part), Gwinnett    Dist: (404) 243-5107
(part)    Res: (770) 939-5969
Term Expires: 2017    Fax: (404) 463-2071
2643 Sterling Acres Drive, Tucker, GA 30084    Dist: (678) 937-1672
E-mail: steve.henson@senate.ga.gov
Committees: Administrative Affairs; Health and Human Services;
Natural Resources and the Environment; Reapportionment and
Redistricting; Regulated Industries and Utilities; Rules; Urban Affairs

**Senator Hunter Hill** (R-District 6) . . . . . . . . . . . . . . . . . . (404) 463-2518
Counties Represented: Cobb (part), Fulton (part)    Dist: (404) 414-1891
Term Expires: 2017
2451 Cumberland Parkway, Suite 3439, Atlanta, GA 30339
E-mail: hunter.hill@senate.ga.gov
Committees: Appropriations; Finance; Joint Metropolitan Atlanta
Rapid Transit Oversight; Judiciary Non-Civil; Reapportionment and
Redistricting; Retirement; Rules; Veterans, Military and Homeland
Security
Education: West Point BS

**Senator Jack Hill** (R-District 4) . . . . . . . . . . . . . . . . . . . . (404) 656-5038
Counties Represented: Bulloch, Candler, Effingham,    Dist: (912) 557-3811
Emanuel (part), Evans, Tattnall (part)    Fax: (404) 657-7094
Term Expires: 2017    Dist: (912) 557-3522
P.O. Box 486, Reidsville, GA 30453
E-mail: jack.hill@senate.ga.gov
Committees: Appropriations; Finance; Natural Resources and the
Environment; Regulated Industries and Utilities; Rules

**Senator Judson Hill** (R-District 32) . . . . . . . . . . . . . . . . . (404) 656-0150
Counties Represented: Cobb (part), Fulton (part)    Dist: (770) 565-0024
Term Expires: 2017    Fax: (404) 461-6768
3102 Raines Court, Marietta, GA 30062    Dist: (770) 234-5378
E-mail: judson.hill@senate.ga.gov
Committees: Appropriations; Finance; Health and Human Services;
Rules
Education: Emory 1982 BSE, 1982 BA

**Senator Chuck Hufstetler** (R-District 52) . . . . . . . . . . . . . (404) 656-0034
Counties Represented: Bartow (part), Chattooga    Dist: (706) 291-6191
(part), Floyd, Gordon (part)    Fax: (404) 463-1388
Term Expires: 2017
3 Orchard Spring Drive, Rome, GA 30165
E-mail: chuck.hufstetler@senate.ga.gov
Committees: Appropriations; Education and Youth; Health and Human
Services; Retirement

LEGISLATIVE BRANCH

Senator **Lester G. Jackson III** (D-District 2)
Coverdell Legislative Office Building, Room 110-D . . . . . (404) 463-5261
Counties Represented: Chatham (part)　　　　Dist: (912) 233-7970
Term Expires: 2017　　　　　　　　　　　　　Fax: (404) 463-1386
1501 Abercorn Street, Savannah, GA 31401　　Dist: (912) 201-0431
E-mail: lester.jackson@senate.ga.gov
Committees: Agriculture and Consumer Affairs; Economic
Development and Tourism; Finance; Health and Human Services;
Higher Education; Urban Affairs

Senator **William "Bill" Jackson** (R-District 24) . . . . . . . . (404) 651-7738
Counties Represented: Columbia (part), Elbert,　Dist: (706) 863-5818
Hart, Lincoln, Oglethorpe, Taliaferro, Wilkes　　Tel: (404) 651-5795
Term Expires: 2017　　　　　　　　　　　　　Fax: (706) 541-0197
P.O. Box 528, Appling, GA 30802
E-mail: bill.jackson@senate.ga.gov
Committees: Administrative Affairs; Appropriations; Ethics;
Reapportionment and Redistricting; Rules; Transportation

Senator **Donzella James** (D-District 35) . . . . . . . . . . . . . (404) 463-1379
Counties Represented: Douglas (part), Fulton (part)　Fax: (404) 656-6579
Term Expires: 2017
PO Box 311225, College Park, GA 30349
E-mail: donzella.james@senate.ga.gov
Committees: Economic Development and Tourism; Education and
Youth; Interstate Cooperation
Education: Morris Brown BA

Senator **Rick Jeffares** (R-District 17) . . . . . . . . . . . . . . . (404) 656-0503
Counties Represented: Henry (part), Newton　　Dist: (678) 432-7676
(part), Rockdale (part)　　　　　　　　　　　Fax: (404) 463-1388
Term Expires: 2017　　　　　　　　　　　　　Dist: (678) 432-5133
300 Lester Mill Road, Suite 200-E, Locust Grove, GA 30248
P. O. Box 270, Locust Grove, GA 30248
E-mail: rick.jeffares@senate.ga.gov
Committees: Economic Development and Tourism; Ethics; Natural
Resources and the Environment; Regulated Industries and Utilities;
State Institutions and Property
Education: Clayton State BA

Senator **Burt Jones** (R-District 25) . . . . . . . . . . . . . . . . . . (404) 656-0082
Counties Represented: Baldwin, Bibb (part), Butts,　Dist: (770) 775-4880
Greene, Jasper, Jones (part), Morgan, Putnam,　Fax: (770) 234-6752
Walton (part)
Term Expires: 2017
407 East Second Street, Jackson, GA 30233
E-mail: burt.jones@senate.ga.gov
Committees: Banking and Financial Institutions; Higher Education;
Insurance and Labor; Regulated Industries and Utilities; Transportation
Education: Georgia

Senator **Emanuel Jones** (D-District 10) . . . . . . . . . . . . . . (404) 656-0502
Counties Represented: DeKalb (part), Henry (part)　Dist: (770) 964-8888
Term Expires: 2017　　　　　　　　　　　　　Fax: (404) 657-9728
P.O. Box 370244, Decatur, GA 30037　　　　　Dist: (770) 964-7162
E-mail: emanuel.jones@senate.ga.gov
Committees: Banking and Financial Institutions; Economic
Development and Tourism; Interstate Cooperation; Retirement
Education: Pennsylvania 1981 BSEE; Columbia 1986 MBA

Senator **Harold V. Jones II** (D-District 22) . . . . . . . . . . . . (404) 463-3942
Counties Represented: Richmond (part)
Term Expires: 2017
E-mail: harold.jones@senate.ga.gov
Committees: Judiciary Non-Civil; Public Safety

Senator **John Flanders Kennedy** (R-District 18) . . . . . . . . (404) 656-7454
Counties Represented: Bibb (part), Crawford,　Fax: (404) 651-5795
Houston (part), Monroe, Peach, Upson
Term Expires: 2017
E-mail: john.kennedy@senate.ga.gov
Committees: Banking and Financial Institutions; Judiciary; Judiciary
Non-Civil; Science and Technology

Senator **G.M. "Greg" Kirk** (R-District 13) . . . . . . . . . . . . . (404) 463-5258
Counties Represented: Crisp, Dodge, Dooly, Lee, Sumter (part), Tift
(part), Turner, Wilcox, Worth
Term Expires: 2017
E-mail: greg.kirk@senate.ga.gov
Committees: Agriculture and Consumer Affairs; Government Oversight;
Health and Human Services; Natural Resources and the Environment;
State and Local Governmental Operations

Senator **William T. Ligon, Jr.** (R-District 3) . . . . . . . . . . . (404) 656-0045
Counties Represented: Brantley, Camden, Charlton　Dist: (912) 261-2263
(part), Glynn, McIntosh　　　　　　　　　　　Fax: (404) 463-2535
Term Expires: 2017　　　　　　　　　　　　　Dist: (912) 261-0463
158 Scranton Connector, Brunswick, GA 31521
P. O. Box 10450, Savannah, GA 31521
E-mail: william.ligon@senate.ga.gov
Committees: Appropriations; Ethics; Health and Human Services; Joint
Metropolitan Atlanta Rapid Transit Oversight; Judiciary; Judiciary
Non-Civil; Rules

Senator **David E. Lucas, Sr.** (D-District 26) . . . . . . . . . . . . (404) 656-5035
Counties Represented: Bibb (part), Hancock,　Dist: (478) 254-7600
Houston (part), Jones (part), Twiggs, Washington, Wilkinson
Term Expires: 2017
2594 Saratoga Drive, Macon, GA 31211
E-mail: david.lucas@senate.ga.gov
Committees: Economic Development and Tourism; Regulated Industries
and Utilities; Retirement; State Institutions and Property; Urban Affairs

Senator **P.K. Martin IV** (R-District 9) . . . . . . . . . . . . . . . . .(404) 656-3933
Counties Represented: Gwinnett (part)
Term Expires: 2017
E-mail: p.k.martin@senate.ga.gov
Committees: Economic Development and Tourism; Higher Education;
Insurance and Labor; State and Local Governmental Operations

Senator **Joshua McKoon** (R-District 29) . . . . . . . . . . . . . . (404) 463-3931
Counties Represented: Harris, Meriwether,　Dist: (706) 442-9130
Muscogee (part), Troup (part)　　　　　　　　Fax: (404) 657-3217
Term Expires: 2017
P. O. Box 2565, Columbus, GA 31902
E-mail: josh.mckoon@senate.ga.gov
Committees: Ethics; Higher Education; Insurance and Labor; Judiciary;
Judiciary Non-Civil; Regulated Industries and Utilities
Education: Furman 2001 BA; Alabama 2003 JD

Senator **Fran Millar** (R-District 40) . . . . . . . . . . . . . . . . . . (404) 463-2260
Counties Represented: DeKalb (part), Fulton　Dist: (404) 923-3607
(part), Gwinnett (part)　　　　　　　　　　　Fax: (404) 657-3217
Term Expires: 2017
P. O. Box 88096, Atlanta, GA 30356
E-mail: fran.millar@senate.ga.gov
Committees: Education and Youth; Health and Human Services; Higher
Education; Joint Metropolitan Atlanta Rapid Transit Oversight; Rules
Education: West Virginia Wesleyan BEc

Senator **Butch Miller** (R-District 49)
Coverdell Legislative Office Building, Room 325-B . . . . . (404) 651-7738
Counties Represented: Hall (part)　　　　　　Dist: (678) 989-5301
Term Expires: 2017　　　　　　　　　　　　　Fax: (404) 651-5795
2420 Browns Bridge Road, Gainesville, GA 30504
E-mail: butch.miller@senate.ga.gov
Committees: Appropriations; Banking and Financial Institutions;
Ethics; Joint Metropolitan Atlanta Rapid Transit Oversight; Regulated
Industries and Utilities; Rules

Senator **Jeff E. Mullis** (R-District 53) . . . . . . . . . . . . . . . . (404) 656-0057
Counties Represented: Catoosa, Chattooga (part),　Dist: (706) 375-1776
Dade, Walker　　　　　　　　　　　　　　　Fax: (404) 651-6767
Term Expires: 2017
212 English Avenue, Chickamauga, GA 30707
E-mail: jeff.mullis@senate.ga.gov
Committees: Appropriations; Economic Development and Tourism;
Regulated Industries and Utilities; Rules

Senator **Nan Grogan Orrock** (D-District 36) . . . . . . . . . . . (404) 463-8054
Counties Represented: Fulton (part)　　　　　Dist: (404) 524-5999
Term Expires: 2017　　　　　　　　　　　　　Res: (404) 622-6687
1070 Delaware Avenue SE, Atlanta, GA 30316　Fax: (404) 463-2279
E-mail: nan.orrock@senate.ga.gov　　　　　　Res: (404) 622-0486
Committees: Agriculture and Consumer Affairs; Health and Human
Services; Higher Education; Urban Affairs

Senator **Elena Parent** (D-District 42) . . . . . . . . . . . . . . . . (404) 656-5109
Counties Represented: DeKalb (part)
Term Expires: 2017
E-mail: elena.parent@senate.ga.gov
Committees: Government Oversight; Judiciary Non-Civil; Science and
Technology

Senator **Michael A. "Doc" Rhett** (D-District 33) . . . . . . . . (404) 656-0054
Counties Represented: Cobb (part)
Term Expires: 2017
E-mail: michael.rhett@senate.ga.gov
Committees: Banking and Financial Institutions; Economic
Development and Tourism; Retirement; Veterans, Military and
Homeland Security

*(continued on next page)*

**Senators** *continued*

**Senator Valencia Seay** (D-District 34) . . . . . . . . . . . . . . . . (404) 656-5095
Counties Represented: Clayton (part), Fayette (part)    Dist: (770) 909-9912
Term Expires: 2017                                        Fax: (404) 657-9728
P.O. Box 960008, Riverdale, GA 30274
E-mail: valencia.seay@senate.ga.gov
Committees: Appropriations; Government Oversight; Public Safety;
Science and Technology; Transportation
Education: DeKalb; Clayton State

**Senator David J. Shafer** (R-District 48) . . . . . . . . . . . . . . (404) 656-0048
Counties Represented: Fulton (part), Gwinnett (part)    Dist: (770) 497-0048
Term Expires: 2017                                        Fax: (404) 651-6768
P.O. Box 880, Duluth, GA 30096
E-mail: david.shafer@senate.ga.gov
Committees: Administrative Affairs; Appropriations; Banking and
Financial Institutions; Finance; Health and Human Services; Insurance
and Labor; Reapportionment and Redistricting; Regulated Industries
and Utilities; Rules

**Senator Freddie Powell Sims** (D-District 12)
Coverdell Legislative Office Building, Room 305-A . . . . . (404) 463-5259
Counties Represented: Baker, Calhoun, Clay,              Fax: (404) 657-7266
Dougherty, Mitchell (part), Quitman, Randolph, Stewart, Sumter (part),
Terrell, Webster
Term Expires: 2017
5377 Goose Hollow Road, Dawson, GA 31742
E-mail: freddie.sims@senate.ga.gov
Committees: Appropriations; Education and Youth; Finance; Interstate
Cooperation; Natural Resources and the Environment

**Senator Jesse C. Stone** (R-District 23) . . . . . . . . . . . . . . . (404) 463-1314
Counties Represented: Burke, Columbia (part),           Dist: (478) 237-7029
Emanuel (part), Glascock, Jefferson, Jenkins,           Fax: (478) 463-1388
Johnson, McDuffie, Richmond (part), Screven,            Dist: (478) 237-9211
Warren
Term Expires: 2017
642 Liberty Street, Waynesboro, GA 30830
E-mail: jesse.stone@senate.ga.gov
Committees: Appropriations; Banking and Financial Institutions;
Education and Youth; Ethics; Judiciary; Judiciary Non-Civil
Education: Georgia MBA, JD

**Senator Horacena Tate** (D-District 38) . . . . . . . . . . . . . . . (404) 463-8053
Counties Represented: Cobb (part), Fulton (part)        Dist: (404) 557-5609
Term Expires: 2017                                        Fax: (404) 463-7783
201 Joseph E. Lowery Boulevard NW, Atlanta, GA 30314
E-mail: horacena.tate@senate.ga.gov
Committees: Appropriations; Education and Youth; Reapportionment
and Redistricting; Rules; State and Local Governmental Operations;
Urban Affairs

**Senator Bruce Thompson** (R-District 14) . . . . . . . . . . . . . (404) 656-0065
Counties Represented: Bartow (part), Cherokee           Dist: (770) 546-7565
(part), Cobb (part)
Term Expires: 2017
25 Hawks Branch Lane, White, GA 30184-3244
E-mail: bruce.thompson@senate.ga.gov
Committees: Banking and Financial Institutions; Finance; Higher
Education; Science and Technology

**Senator Curt Thompson** (D-District 5) . . . . . . . . . . . . . . . (404) 463-1318
Counties Represented: Gwinnett (part)                   Res: (770) 696-4777
Term Expires: 2017                                        Fax: (404) 651-7078
6320 Glenbrook Drive, Tucker, GA 30084
E-mail: curt.thompson@senate.ga.gov
Committees: Appropriations; Ethics; Judiciary; Natural Resources and
the Environment
Education: American U 1990 BA; Georgia State 1992 JD

**Senator Lindsey Tippins** (R-District 37) . . . . . . . . . . . . . . (404) 657-0406
Counties Represented: Cobb (part)                       Dist: (770) 424-2700
Term Expires: 2017                                        Fax: (404) 657-0459
139 Midway Road, Marietta, GA 30064                     Dist: (770) 424-2777
E-mail: lindsey.tippins@senate.ga.gov
Committees: Administrative Affairs; Appropriations; Education and
Youth; Natural Resources and the Environment; Transportation
Education: Georgia State 1971 BBA; Woodrow Wilson Law 1978 JD

**Senator Renee S. Unterman** (R-District 45) . . . . . . . . . . . (404) 463-1368
Counties Represented: Gwinnett (part)                   Dist: (770) 945-1887
Term Expires: 2017                                        Fax: (404) 651-6767
P.O. Box 508, Buford, GA 30518
E-mail: renee.unterman@senate.ga.gov
Committees: Administrative Affairs; Appropriations; Finance; Health
and Human Services; Insurance and Labor; Regulated Industries and
Utilities; Rules
Education: Georgia State; Georgia

**Senator JaNice VanNess** (R-District 43) . . . . . . . . . . . . . (404) 463-2598
Counties Represented: DeKalb (part), Newton (part), Rockdale (part)
Term Expires: 2017
2731 Pitlochry Street, Conyers, GA 30094
E-mail: janice.vanness@senate.ga.gov
Committees: Economic Development and Tourism; Education and
Youth; Health and Human Services; State Institutions and Property

**Senator Larry Walker III** (R-District 20) . . . . . . . . . . . . . . (404) 656-0081
Counties Represented: Bleckley, Houston (part), Laurens, Pulaski
Term Expires: 2017
1110 Washington Street, Perry, GA 31069
E-mail: larry.walker@senate.ga.gov
Committees: Agriculture and Consumer Affairs; Insurance and Labor;
State Institutions and Property; Veterans, Military and Homeland
Security

**Senator Ben Watson** (R-District 1) . . . . . . . . . . . . . . . . . . (404) 656-7880
Counties Represented: Bryan, Chatham (part), Liberty (part)
Term Expires: 2017
E-mail: ben.watson@senate.ga.gov
Committees: Economic Development and Tourism; Ethics; Health
and Human Services; Public Safety; State Institutions and Property;
Transportation

**Senator John Wilkinson** (R-District 50) . . . . . . . . . . . . . . (706) 886-1898
Counties Represented: Banks, Franklin, Habersham,       Fax: (706) 886-1898
Hall (part), Jackson (part), Rabun, Stephens, Towns
Term Expires: 2017
PO Box 2227, Toccoa, GA 30577
E-mail: john.wilkinson@senate.ga.gov
Committees: Agriculture and Consumer Affairs; Appropriations;
Education and Youth; Natural Resources and the Environment; Rules
Education: Georgia BSA, MEd

**Senator Michael E. Williams** (R-District 27) . . . . . . . . . . . (404) 656-7127
Counties Represented: Forsyth (part)
Term Expires: 2017
E-mail: michael.williams@senate.ga.gov
Committees: Ethics; Finance; Higher Education; Public Safety; State
and Local Governmental Operations

**Senator Tommie Williams** (R-District 19) . . . . . . . . . . . . . (404) 656-0089
Counties Represented: Appling, Jeff Davis, Liberty      Dist: (912) 526-7444
(part), Long, Montgomery, Tattnall (part), Telfair,     Fax: (404) 463-5220
Toombs, Treutlen, Wayne, Wheeler                        Dist: (912) 526-8730
Term Expires: 2017
148 Williams Avenue, Lyons, GA 30436
E-mail: tommie.williams@senate.ga.gov
Committees: Appropriations; Judiciary; Natural Resources and the
Environment; Reapportionment and Redistricting; Transportation
Education: Georgia; Georgia Southern

# Senate Standing Committees

## Administrative Affairs
State Capitol, Room 321, Atlanta, GA 30334
Tel: (404) 656-0048  Fax: (404) 651-6768

| **Majority Members** | **Minority Members** |
|---|---|
| David J. Shafer (R-48) *Chair* | Steve Henson (D-41) |
| William S. "Bill" Cowsert (R-46) | |
| William "Bill" Jackson (R-24) | |
| Lindsey Tippins (R-37) | |
| Renee S. Unterman (R-45) | |

## Agriculture and Consumer Affairs
State Capitol, Room 110-B, Atlanta, GA 30334
Tel: (404) 656-0040  Fax: (404) 463-2279

| **Majority Members** | **Minority Members** |
|---|---|
| John Wilkinson (R-50) *Chair* | Ellis Black (D-8) *Secretary* |
| Tyler Harper (R-7) *Vice Chair* | Lester G. Jackson III (D-2) |
| Dean Burke (R-11) | Nan Grogan Orrock (D-36) |
| G.M. "Greg" Kirk (R-13) | |
| Larry Walker III (R-20) | |
| Bill Heath (R-31) | |
| *Ex-Officio Member* | |

LEGISLATIVE BRANCH

## Appropriations

State Capitol, Room 234, Atlanta, GA 30334
Tel: (404) 656-5038  Fax: (404) 657-7094

| **Majority Members** | **Minority Members** |
| --- | --- |
| Jack Hill (R-4) *Chairman* | Gail Davenport (D-44) |
| Renee S. Unterman (R-45) | Vincent D. Fort (D-39) |
|   *Vice Chair* | Valencia Seay (D-34) |
| Charles "Charlie" Bethel (R-54) | Freddie Powell Sims (D-12) |
|   *Secretary* | Horacena Tate (D-38) |
| John Albers (R-56) | Curt Thompson (D-5) |
| Dean Burke (R-11) | |
| William S. "Bill" Cowsert (R-46) | |
| Michael Robert "Mike" Crane | |
|   (R-28) | |
| Frank Ginn (R-47) | |
| Steve Gooch (R-51) | |
| Bill Heath (R-31) | |
| Hunter Hill (R-6) | |
| Judson Hill (R-32) | |
| Chuck Hufstetler (R-52) | |
| William "Bill" Jackson (R-24) | |
| William T. Ligon, Jr. (R-3) | |
| Butch Miller (R-49) | |
| Jeff E. Mullis (R-53) | |
| David J. Shafer (R-48) | |
| Jesse C. Stone (R-23) | |
| Lindsey Tippins (R-37) | |
| John Wilkinson (R-50) | |
| Tommie Williams (R-19) | |

## Banking and Financial Institutions

State Capitol, Room 121-H, Atlanta, GA 30334
Tel: (404) 656-0036  Fax: (404) 651-6767

| **Majority Members** | **Minority Members** |
| --- | --- |
| Burt Jones (R-25) *Chair* | Ed Harbison (D-15) |
| Jesse C. Stone (R-23) *Vice Chair* | Emanuel Jones (D-10) |
| Butch Miller (R-49) *Secretary* | Michael A. "Doc" Rhett (D-33) |
| M.H. "Marty" Harbin (R-16) | |
| John Flanders Kennedy (R-18) | |
| Bruce Thompson (R-14) | |
| David J. Shafer (R-48) | |
|   *Ex-Officio Member* | |

## Economic Development and Tourism

Coverdell Legislative Office Building, Room 321-B, Atlanta, GA 30334
Tel: (404) 656-9221  Fax: (404) 657-3248

| **Majority Members** | **Minority Members** |
| --- | --- |
| Frank Ginn (R-47) *Chairman* | Emanuel Jones (D-10) *Secretary* |
| Ben Watson (R-1) *Vice Chairman* | Lester G. Jackson III (D-2) |
| Mike Dugan (R-30) | Donzella James (D-35) |
| Rick Jeffares (R-17) | David E. Lucas, Sr. (D-26) |
| P.K. Martin IV (R-9) | Michael A. "Doc" Rhett (D-33) |
| Jeff E. Mullis (R-53) | |
| JaNice VanNess (R-43) | |

## Education and Youth

Coverdell Legislative Office Building, Room 301-B, Atlanta, GA 30334
Tel: (404) 463-2260  Fax: (404) 463-4161

| **Majority Members** | **Minority Members** |
| --- | --- |
| Lindsey Tippins (R-37) *Chairman* | Freddie Powell Sims (D-12) |
| John Wilkinson (R-50) |   *Secretary* |
|   *Vice Chairman* | Ellis Black (D-8) |
| Chuck Hufstetler (R-52) | Vincent D. Fort (D-39) |
| Fran Millar (R-40) | Donzella James (D-35) |
| Jesse C. Stone (R-23) | Horacena Tate (D-38) |
| JaNice VanNess (R-43) | |

## Ethics

State Capitol, Room 321, Atlanta, GA 30334
Tel: (404) 656-0089  Fax: (404) 463-5220

| **Majority Members** | **Minority Members** |
| --- | --- |
| Dean Burke (R-11) *Chairman* | Gloria S. Butler (D-55) *Secretary* |
| Michael E. Williams (R-27) | Ed Harbison (D-15) |
|   *Vice Chair* | Curt Thompson (D-5) |
| William "Bill" Jackson (R-24) | |
| Rick Jeffares (R-17) | |
| William T. Ligon, Jr. (R-3) | |
| Joshua McKoon (R-29) | |
| Butch Miller (R-49) | |
| Jesse C. Stone (R-23) | |
| Ben Watson (R-1) | |

## Finance

Coverdell Legislative Office Building, Room 319-B, Atlanta, GA 30334
Tel: (404) 463-1366  Fax: (404) 657-0797

| **Majority Members** | **Minority Members** |
| --- | --- |
| Judson Hill (R-32) *Chair* | Lester G. Jackson III (D-2) |
| Hunter Hill (R-6) *Vice Chair* | Freddie Powell Sims (D-12) |
| John Albers (R-56) *Secretary* | |
| Steve Gooch (R-51) | |
| Bill Heath (R-31) | |
| David J. Shafer (R-48) | |
| Bruce Thompson (R-14) | |
| Michael E. Williams (R-27) | |
| William S. "Bill" Cowsert (R-46) | |
|   *Ex-Officio Member* | |
| Jack Hill (R-4) *Ex-Officio Member* | |
| Renee S. Unterman (R-45) | |
|   *Ex-Officio Member* | |

## Government Oversight

State Capitol, Room 421-B, Atlanta, GA 30334
Tel: (404) 463-1368  Fax: (404) 651-6768

| **Majority Members** | **Minority Members** |
| --- | --- |
| Bill Heath (R-31) *Chair* | Elena Parent (D-42) |
| M.H. "Marty" Harbin (R-16) | Valencia Seay (D-34) |
|   *Vice Chair* | |
| G.M. "Greg" Kirk (R-13) *Secretary* | |

## Health and Human Services

State Capitol, Room 121-G, Atlanta, GA 30334
Tel: (404) 656-6436  Fax: (404) 651-6767

| **Majority Members** | **Minority Members** |
| --- | --- |
| Renee S. Unterman (R-45) | Gloria S. Butler (D-55) |
|   *Chairman* | Steve Henson (D-41) |
| Chuck Hufstetler (R-52) *Vice Chair* | Lester G. Jackson III (D-2) |
| Fran Millar (R-40) *Secretary* | Nan Grogan Orrock (D-36) |
| Dean Burke (R-11) | |
| William S. "Bill" Cowsert (R-46) | |
| Judson Hill (R-32) | |
| G.M. "Greg" Kirk (R-13) | |
| William T. Ligon, Jr. (R-3) | |
| David J. Shafer (R-48) | |
| JaNice VanNess (R-43) | |
| Ben Watson (R-1) | |

## Higher Education

State Capitol, Room 121-D, Atlanta, GA 30334
Tel: (404) 463-3931  Fax: (404) 651-6767

| **Majority Members** | **Minority Members** |
| --- | --- |
| Fran Millar (R-40) *Chair* | Lester G. Jackson III (D-2) |
| P.K. Martin IV (R-9) *Vice Chair* | Nan Grogan Orrock (D-36) |
| Burt Jones (R-25) *Secretary* | |
| Brandon L. Beach (R-21) | |
| Joshua McKoon (R-29) | |
| Bruce Thompson (R-14) | |
| Michael E. Williams (R-27) | |

**LEGISLATIVE BRANCH**

## Insurance and Labor

State Capitol, Room 110-A, Atlanta, GA 30334
Tel: (404) 656-4700  Fax: (404) 463-2279

| **Majority Members** | **Minority Members** |
|---|---|
| Charles "Charlie" Bethel (R-54) *Chair* | Ed Harbison (D-15) |
| David J. Shafer (R-48) *Vice Chair* | |
| P.K. Martin IV (R-9) *Secretary* | |
| M.H. "Marty" Harbin (R-16) | |
| Burt Jones (R-25) | |
| Joshua McKoon (R-29) | |
| Renee S. Unterman (R-45) | |
| Larry Walker III (R-20) | |

## Interstate Cooperation

State Capitol, Room 432, Atlanta, GA 30334
Tel: (404) 656-0074  Fax: (404) 463-5547

**Minority Members**
Donzella James (D-35) *Chair*
Freddie Powell Sims (D-12) *Vice Chair*
Emanuel Jones (D-10) *Secretary*
Vincent D. Fort (D-39)
Ed Harbison (D-15)

## Judiciary

Coverdell Legislative Office Building, Room 301-A, Atlanta, GA 30334
Tel: (404) 656-0034  Fax: (404) 463-4161

| **Majority Members** | **Minority Members** |
|---|---|
| Joshua McKoon (R-29) *Chair* | Vincent D. Fort (D-39) |
| William S. "Bill" Cowsert (R-46) *Vice Chair* | Curt Thompson (D-5) |
| Charles "Charlie" Bethel (R-54) *Secretary* | |
| John Flanders Kennedy (R-18) | |
| William T. Ligon, Jr. (R-3) | |
| Tommie Williams (R-19) | |
| Jesse C. Stone (R-23) *Ex-Officio* | |

## Judiciary Non-Civil

Coverdell Legislative Office Building, Room 320-B, Atlanta, GA 30334
Tel: (404) 463-1314  Fax: (404) 463-1388

| **Majority Members** | **Minority Members** |
|---|---|
| Jesse C. Stone (R-23) *Chair* | Vincent D. Fort (D-39) |
| William T. Ligon, Jr. (R-3) *Vice Chair* | Harold V. Jones II (D-22) |
| John Flanders Kennedy (R-18) *Secretary* | Elena Parent (D-42) |
| Charles "Charlie" Bethel (R-54) | |
| Michael Robert "Mike" Crane (R-28) | |
| Hunter Hill (R-6) | |
| Joshua McKoon (R-29) *Ex-Officio Member* | |

## Natural Resources and the Environment

State Capitol, Room 121-C, Atlanta, GA 30334
Tel: (404) 656-0081  Fax: (404) 651-6767

| **Majority Members** | **Minority Members** |
|---|---|
| Rick Jeffares (R-17) *Vice Chair* | Steve Henson (D-41) |
| Tyler Harper (R-7) *Secretary* | Freddie Powell Sims (D-12) |
| Frank Ginn (R-47) | Curt Thompson (D-5) |
| Jack Hill (R-4) | |
| G.M. "Greg" Kirk (R-13) | |
| Lindsey Tippins (R-37) | |
| John Wilkinson (R-50) | |
| Tommie Williams (R-19) | |

## Public Safety

Coverdell Legislative Office Building, Room 304-B, Atlanta, GA 30334
Tel: (404) 656-7127  Fax: (404) 463-1381

| **Majority Members** | **Minority Members** |
|---|---|
| Tyler Harper (R-7) *Chair* | Harold V. Jones II (D-22) |
| John Albers (R-56) *Vice Chair* | Valencia Seay (D-34) |
| Mike Dugan (R-30) *Secretary* | |
| Ben Watson (R-1) | |
| Michael E. Williams (R-27) | |

## Reapportionment and Redistricting

Coverdell Legislative Office Building, Room 325-A, Atlanta, GA 30334
Tel: (404) 656-0150  Fax: (404) 463-2535

| **Majority Members** | **Minority Members** |
|---|---|
| Michael Robert "Mike" Crane (R-28) *Chair* | Horacena Tate (D-38) *Secretary* |
| Charles "Charlie" Bethel (R-54) *Vice Chair* | Vincent D. Fort (D-39) |
| William S. "Bill" Cowsert (R-46) | Ed Harbison (D-15) |
| Hunter Hill (R-6) | Steve Henson (D-41) |
| William "Bill" Jackson (R-24) | |
| David J. Shafer (R-48) | |
| Tommie Williams (R-19) | |

## Regulated Industries and Utilities

State Capitol, Room 421-F, Atlanta, GA 30334
Tel: (404) 656-0048  Fax: (404) 651-6768

| **Majority Members** | **Minority Members** |
|---|---|
| Rick Jeffares (R-17) *Chair* | Steve Henson (D-41) |
| Frank Ginn (R-47) *Vice Chair* | David E. Lucas, Sr. (D-26) |
| Joshua McKoon (R-29) *Secretary* | Ed Harbison (D-15) *Ex Officio Member* |
| Brandon L. Beach (R-21) | |
| William S. "Bill" Cowsert (R-46) | |
| Steve Gooch (R-51) | |
| Jack Hill (R-4) | |
| Butch Miller (R-49) | |
| Jeff E. Mullis (R-53) | |
| Burt Jones (R-25) | |
| David J. Shafer (R-48) *Ex Officio Member* | |
| Renee S. Unterman (R-45) *Ex Officio Member* | |

## Retirement

State Capitol, Room 109, Atlanta, GA 30334
Tel: (404) 651-7738  Fax: (404) 651-5795

| **Majority Members** | **Minority Members** |
|---|---|
| Chuck Hufstetler (R-52) *Chair* | Ellis Black (D-8) *Vice Chair* |
| Michael Robert "Mike" Crane (R-28) | Emanuel Jones (D-10) *Secretary* |
| Tyler Harper (R-7) | David E. Lucas, Sr. (D-26) |
| Hunter Hill (R-6) *Ex-Officio Member* | Michael A. "Doc" Rhett (D-33) |

## Rules

State Capitol, Room 453, Atlanta, GA 30334
Tel: (404) 656-0095  Fax: (404) 656-6581

| **Majority Members** | **Minority Members** |
|---|---|
| Jeff E. Mullis (R-53) *Chairman* | Gloria S. Butler (D-55) |
| William "Bill" Jackson (R-24) *Secretary* | Steve Henson (D-41) |
| Bill Heath (R-31) | Horacena Tate (D-38) |
| Jack Hill (R-4) | |
| Judson Hill (R-32) | |
| Fran Millar (R-40) | |
| Butch Miller (R-49) | |
| Renee S. Unterman (R-45) | |
| William S. "Bill" Cowsert (R-46) *Ex-Officio Member* | |
| Steve Gooch (R-51) *Ex-Officio Member* | |
| Hunter Hill (R-6) *Ex-Officio Member* | |
| William T. Ligon, Jr. (R-3) *Ex-Officio Member* | |
| David J. Shafer (R-48) *Ex-Officio Member* | |
| John Wilkinson (R-50) *Ex-Officio Member* | |

## Science and Technology

Coverdell Legislative Office Building, Room 303-B, Atlanta, GA 30334
Tel: (404) 656-5039  Fax: (404) 656-6484

| **Majority Members** | **Minority Members** |
|---|---|
| Brandon L. Beach (R-21) *Chairman* | Elena Parent (D-42) |
| Bruce Thompson (R-14) | Valencia Seay (D-34) |
| *Vice Chairman* | |
| John Flanders Kennedy (R-18) | |
| *Secretary* | |

## State and Local Governmental Operations

Coverdell Legislative Office Building, Room 325-B, Atlanta, GA 30334
Tel: (404) 463-5257  Fax: (404) 463-2535

| **Majority Members** | **Minority Members** |
|---|---|
| John Albers (R-56) *Chair* | Gloria S. Butler (D-55) |
| G.M. "Greg" Kirk (R-13) | Horacena Tate (D-38) |
| *Vice Chair* | |
| Michael E. Williams (R-27) | |
| *Secretary* | |
| M.H. "Marty" Harbin (R-16) | |
| P.K. Martin IV (R-9) | |

## State Institutions and Property

Coverdell Legislative Office Building, Room 321-A, Atlanta, GA 30334
Tel: (404) 656-0082  Fax: (404) 657-3248

| **Majority Members** | **Minority Members** |
|---|---|
| Rick Jeffares (R-17) *Vice Chair* | Ed Harbison (D-15) *Chair* |
| Ben Watson (R-1) *Secretary* | Ellis Black (D-8) |
| JaNice VanNess (R-43) | Gail Davenport (D-44) |
| Larry Walker III (R-20) | David E. Lucas, Sr. (D-26) |

## Transportation

State Capitol, Room 110 - B, Atlanta, GA 30334
Tel: (404) 656-0057  Fax: (404) 651-6768

| **Majority Members** | **Minority Members** |
|---|---|
| Tommie Williams (R-19) *Chair* | Gloria S. Butler (D-55) |
| Steve Gooch (R-51) *Vice Chair* | Valencia Seay (D-34) |
| Brandon L. Beach (R-21) *Secretary* | *Ex-Officio Member* |
| Mike Dugan (R-30) | |
| William "Bill" Jackson (R-24) | |
| Burt Jones (R-25) | |
| Lindsey Tippins (R-37) | |
| Ben Watson (R-1) | |
| Frank Ginn (R-47) | |
| *Ex-Officio Member* | |
| Bill Heath (R-31) | |
| *Ex-Officio Member* | |

## Urban Affairs

State Capitol, Room 420-C, Atlanta, GA 30334
Tel: (404) 656-0075  Fax: (404) 657-9728

**Minority Members**
Lester G. Jackson III (D-2) *Chairman*
Steve Henson (D-41) *Vice Chairman*
Gloria S. Butler (D-55) *Secretary*
Gail Davenport (D-44)
Vincent D. Fort (D-39)
David E. Lucas, Sr. (D-26)
Nan Grogan Orrock (D-36)
Horacena Tate (D-38)

## Veterans, Military and Homeland Security

Coverdell Legislative Office Building, Room 302-A, Atlanta, GA 30334
Tel: (404) 656-0503  Fax: (404) 657-3217

| **Majority Members** | **Minority Members** |
|---|---|
| Hunter Hill (R-6) *Chair* | Ed Harbison (D-15) *Vice Chair* |
| Mike Dugan (R-30) *Secretary* | Gail Davenport (D-44) |
| Larry Walker III (R-20) | Michael A. "Doc" Rhett (D-33) |

# Georgia House of Representatives

Tel: (404) 656-0305  Fax: (404) 656-6412

Speaker of the House **David Ralston** (R) . . . . . . . . . . . . . . (404) 656-5020
Speaker Pro Tem **Jan Jones** (R) . . . . . . . . . . . . . . . . . . . (404) 656-5072
Majority Leader **Jon G. Burns** (R) . . . . . . . . . . . . . . . . . (404) 656-5099

Majority Whip **Matt Ramsey** (R) . . . . . . . . . . . . . . . . . . . (404) 656-7146
Education: Georgia Southern 1998 BA; Georgia State 2005 JD
Chief Deputy Majority Whip **Katie M. Dempsey** (R) . . . . . (404) 463-2247
Deputy Majority Whip **Stephen Allison** (R) . . . . . . . . . . . (404) 656-0188
Deputy Majority Whip **Paul R. Battles** (R) . . . . . . . . . . . . (404) 463-3793
Deputy Majority Whip **James "Bubber" Epps** (R) . . . . . . . (404) 656-0298
Deputy Majority Whip **Randy Nix** (R) . . . . . . . . . . . . . . . (404) 656-0177
Education: Troy State BA
Deputy Majority Whip **Barbara Sims** (R) . . . . . . . . . . . . . (404) 656-0213
Deputy Majority Whip **Tom Weldon, Jr.** (R) . . . . . . . . . . . (404) 656-0152
Majority Caucus Chairman **Matt Hatchett** (R) . . . . . . . . . (404) 651-7737
Education: Presbyterian Col BS
Majority Caucus Vice Chairman **Sam Teasley** (R) . . . . . . . (404) 656-0177
Majority Caucus Secretary and Treasurer
**Bruce Williamson** (R) . . . . . . . . . . . . . . . . . . . . . . . . . . . (404) 656-7859
Education: Furman 1976 BABA
Administration Floor Leader **Robert Dickey** (R) . . . . . . . . (404) 651-7737
Administration Floor Leader **Chad Nimmer** (R) . . . . . . . . (404) 656-0287
Administration Floor Leader **Terry Rogers** (R) . . . . . . . . . (404) 656-0178
Minority Leader **Stacey Y. Abrams** (D) . . . . . . . . . . . . . . (404) 656-5058
Education: Spelman 1995 BA; Texas 1998 MPAff; Yale 1999 JD
Minority Whip **Carolyn Fleming Hugley** (D) . . . . . . . . . . (404) 656-5058
Education: Arkansas BA; Mississippi State MPA
Chief Deputy Minority Whip **Scott Holcomb** (D) . . . . . . . . (404) 656-6372
Education: Connecticut BA; West Virginia JD
Minority Caucus Chairman **Virgil Fludd** (D) . . . . . . . . . . . (404) 656-0314
Education: Davidson 1980 BA
Minority Caucus Vice Chairman **Billy Mitchell** (D) . . . . . . (404) 656-0126
Minority Caucus Secretary **Debbie G. Buckner** (D) . . . . . . (404) 656-0116
Minority Caucus Treasurer **David Wilkerson** (D) . . . . . . . (404) 656-0116
Clerk of the House **Bill Reilly** . . . . . . . . . . . . . . . . . . . . . (404) 656-5015
Education: Western St Orange County 1983 JD
Assistant Clerk of the House **Christel Raasch** . . . . . . . . . . (404) 656-5015
E-mail: christel.raasch@house.ga.gov

# Representatives

**Party Affiliation Statistics:** Republicans: 119, Democrats: 60, Independents: 1

Representative **Stacey Y. Abrams** (D-District 89) . . . . . . . . (404) 656-5058
Counties Represented: DeKalb (part)       Dist: (404) 378-9434
Term Expires: 2017                        Fax: (404) 378-3328
1912 Hosea Williams Drive, Atlanta, GA 30317
E-mail: staceyabrams@gmail.com
Committees: Appropriations; Ethics; Judiciary Non-Civil; Rules; Ways and Means

Representative **Kimberly Alexander** (D-District 66) . . . . . . (404) 656-7859
Counties Represented: Douglas (part), Paulding (part)
Term Expires: 2017
PO Box 393, Hiram, GA 30141
E-mail: kimberly.alexander@house.ga.gov
Committees: Code Revision; Intragovernmental Coordination; Legislative and Congressional Reapportionment; Motor Vehicles
Education: Morris Brown BA; Central Michigan MS

Representative **Stephen Allison** (R-District 8)
Coverdell Legislative Office Building, Room 501 . . . . . . . (404) 656-0188
Counties Represented: Rabun, Towns, Union, White     Dist: (706) 781-3929
(part)
Term Expires: 2017
90 Blue Ridge Street, Blairsville, GA 30512
E-mail: stephen.allison@house.ga.gov
Committees: Appropriations; Energy, Utilities and Telecommunications; Judiciary; Juvenile Justice; Special Rules

Representative **Alex Atwood** (R-District 179) . . . . . . . . . . (404) 656-0152
Counties Represented: Glynn (part)       Dist: (912) 264-4211
Term Expires: 2017
300 Main Street, Suite 201, Saint Simons Island, GA 31522
E-mail: alex.atwood@house.ga.gov
Committees: Appropriations; Insurance; Judiciary Non-Civil; Juvenile Justice; Public Safety and Homeland Security
Education: Georgia State BS

Representative **Mandi Ballinger** (R-District 23) . . . . . . . . . (404) 656-0254
Counties Represented: Cherokee (part)
Term Expires: 2017
PO Box 5123, Canton, GA 30114
E-mail: mandi.ballinger@house.ga.gov
Committees: Appropriations; Budget and Fiscal Affairs Oversight; Information and Audits; Judiciary Non-Civil; Juvenile Justice; Rules; Transportation
Education: Kennesaw State U BA

*(continued on next page)*

**LEGISLATIVE BRANCH**

**Representatives** *continued*

Representative **Timothy Barr** (R-District 103)
  Coverdell Legislative Office Building, Room 612-E . . . . . (404) 656-0325
  Counties Represented: Gwinnett (part), Hall (part)
  Term Expires: 2017
  E-mail: timothy.barr@house.ga.gov
  Committees: Appropriations; Code Revision; Health and Human Services; Motor Vehicles; Natural Resources and Environment

Representative **Paul R. Battles** (R-District 15)
  Coverdell Legislative Office Building, Room 404 . . . . . . . (404) 463-3793
  Counties Represented: Bartow (part)          Res: (770) 382-9965
  Term Expires: 2017
  208 Road #2 Southwest, Cartersville, GA 30120
  E-mail: paul.battles@house.ga.gov
  E-mail: p.battles@yahoo.com
  Committees: Appropriations; Economic Development and Tourism; Motor Vehicles; Retirement; Ways and Means

Representative **Sharon Beasley-Teague** (D-District 65) . . . (404) 656-0220
  Counties Represented: Douglas (part), Fulton (part)
  Term Expires: 2017
  P.O. Box 488, Red Oak, GA 30272-0488
  E-mail: sharon.beasley-teague@house.ga.gov
  Committees: Game, Fish and Parks; Human Relations and Aging; Legislative and Congressional Reapportionment; Ways and Means

Representative **D.C. "Dave" Belton** (R-District 112) . . . . . . (404) 656-5015
  Counties Represented: Morgan, Newton (part)
  Term Expires: 2017
  E-mail: dave.belton@house.ga.gov
  Committees: Economic Development and Tourism; Education; Interstate Cooperation

Representative **Karen Bennett** (D-District 94) . . . . . . . . . . (404) 656-0202
  Counties Represented: DeKalb (part), Gwinnett (part)
  Term Expires: 2017
  6909 Springbank Way, Stone Mountain, GA 30087
  E-mail: karen.bennett@house.ga.gov
  Committees: Code Revision; Economic Development and Tourism; Health and Human Services; Regulated Industries
  Education: Howard U 1979 BS; Georgia State MS; Emory 2008 MDiv

Representative **Taylor J. Bennett** (D-District 80) . . . . . . . . (404) 656-0220
  Counties Represented: DeKalb (part), Fulton (part)
  Term Expires: 2017
  E-mail: taylor.bennett@house.ga.gov
  Committees: Budget and Fiscal Affairs Oversight; Judiciary; Small Business Development

Representative **Patty Bentley** (D-District 139) . . . . . . . . . . (404) 656-0287
  Counties Represented: Dooly, Macon, Peach (part), Taylor
  Term Expires: 2017
  PO Box 811, Reynolds, GA 31006
  E-mail: patty.bentley@house.ga.gov
  Committees: Agriculture and Consumer Affairs; Higher Education; Intragovernmental Coordination; Retirement
  Education: Georgia Tech 2008 (Attended)

Representative **Tommy Benton** (R-District 31) . . . . . . . . . (404) 656-0213
  Counties Represented: Jackson (part)          Res: (706) 367-5891
  Term Expires: 2017
  177 Martin Street, Jefferson, GA 30549
  E-mail: tommy.benton@house.ga.gov
  Committees: Appropriations; Education; Human Relations and Aging; Retirement; Rules; Transportation
  Education: West Georgia Col 1972 AB; Brenau Col 1983

Representative **Beth Beskin** (D-District 54) . . . . . . . . . . . . (404) 656-0254
  Counties Represented: Fulton (part)
  Term Expires: 2017
  809 Peachtree Battle Avenue, Atlanta, GA 30327
  E-mail: beth.beskin@house.ga.gov
  Committees: Education; Joint Metropolitan Atlanta Rapid Transit Oversight; Judiciary; State Planning and Community Affairs

Representative **James Beverly** (D-District 143) . . . . . . . . . (404) 656-0220
  Counties Represented: Bibb (part)          Fax: (478) 803-0001
  Term Expires: 2017
  PO Box 13451, Macon, GA 31208
  E-mail: james.beverly@house.ga.gov
  Committees: Health and Human Services; Retirement; Small Business Development; Special Rules

Representative **Z. Shaw Blackmon** (R-District 146) . . . . . . (404) 656-0177
  Counties Represented: Houston (part)
  Term Expires: 2017
  E-mail: shaw.blackmon@house.ga.gov
  Committees: Economic Development and Tourism; Insurance; Special Rules

Representative **Bruce Broadrick** (R-District 4) . . . . . . . . . . (404) 656-0202
  Counties Represented: Whitfield (part)
  Term Expires: 2017
  PO Box 947, Dalton, GA 30722-0947
  E-mail: bruce.broadrick@house.ga.gov
  Committees: Game, Fish and Parks; Health and Human Services; Industry and Labor; Intragovernmental Coordination
  Education: Middle Georgia; Georgia

Representative **Buzz Brockway** (R-District 102) . . . . . . . . . (404) 656-0188
  Counties Represented: Gwinnett (part)
  Term Expires: 2017
  P. O. Box 491355, Lawrenceville, GA 30049
  E-mail: buzz.brockway@house.ga.gov
  Committees: Appropriations; Economic Development and Tourism; Governmental Affairs; Insurance
  Education: Georgia Tech 1990 BSMS

Representative **Roger B. Bruce** (D-District 61) . . . . . . . . . . (404) 656-0314
  Counties Represented: Cobb (part), Douglas (part), Fulton (part)
  Term Expires: 2017
  410 Stone Arbor Court, Atlanta, GA 30331
  E-mail: rbruce5347@aol.com
  Committees: Game, Fish and Parks; Human Relations and Aging; Judiciary; Small Business Development

Representative **Debbie G. Buckner** (D-District 137) . . . . . . (404) 656-0116
  Counties Represented: Harris (part), Meriwether       Dist: (706) 269-3630
  (part), Muscogee (part), Talbot                        Fax: (706) 327-0131
  Term Expires: 2017
  780 Fielder's Mill Road, Junction City, GA 31812
  E-mail: debbie.buckner@house.ga.gov
  Committees: Natural Resources and Environment; Retirement; State Properties

Representative **Jon G. Burns** (R-District 159) . . . . . . . . . . (404) 656-5099
  Counties Represented: Bulloch (part), Effingham       Dist: (912) 754-3439
  (part), Screven
  Term Expires: 2017
  5829 Clyo Kildare Road, Newington, GA 30446
  E-mail: jon.burns@house.ga.gov
  Committees: Agriculture and Consumer Affairs; Appropriations; Economic Development and Tourism; Ethics; Game, Fish and Parks; Rules; State Properties; Transportation

Representative **Johnnie Caldwell, Jr.** (R-District 131) . . . . (404) 656-0325
  Counties Represented: Lamar (part), Pike, Upson
  Term Expires: 2017
  2430 Woodland Road, Thomaston, GA 30286
  E-mail: johnnie.caldwell@house.ga.gov
  Committees: Appropriations; Banks and Banking; Insurance; Judiciary; Motor Vehicles
  Education: Georgia; Mercer JD

Representative **Michael Caldwell** (R-District 20) . . . . . . . . (404) 656-7859
  Counties Represented: Cherokee (part)
  Term Expires: 2017
  3044 Lexington Avenue, Woodstock, GA 30189
  E-mail: michael.caldwell@house.ga.gov
  Committees: Budget and Fiscal Affairs Oversight; Code Revision; Economic Development and Tourism; State Planning and Community Affairs
  Education: Kennesaw State U 2010 BA

Representative **Park Cannon** (D-District 58) . . . . . . . . . . . (404) 656-7859
  Counties Represented: Fulton (part)
  Term Expires: 2017
  E-mail: park.cannon@house.ga.gov

Representative
**Wesley E. "Wes" Cantrell** (R-District 22) . . . . . . . . . . . (404) 656-0202
  Counties Represented: Cherokee (part), Forsyth (part), Fulton (part)
  Term Expires: 2017
  1044 Meadow Brook Drive, Woodstock, GA 30188
  E-mail: wesley.cantrell@house.ga.gov
  Committees: Education; Juvenile Justice; Small Business Development

Representative **John Carson, CPA** (R-District 46) . . . . . . . (404) 656-0287
  Counties Represented: Cherokee (part), Cobb (part)     Dist: (404) 575-2785
  Term Expires: 2017
  3605 Sandy Plains Road, Marietta, GA 30066
  E-mail: john.carson@house.ga.gov
  Committees: Energy, Utilities and Telecommunications; Insurance; Intragovernmental Coordination; Transportation; Ways and Means
  Education: Georgia State 1994 BAcc; Kennesaw State Col MBA

Representative **Amy Alexander Carter** (R-District 175) . . . (404) 651-7737
Counties Represented: Brooks, Lowndes (part),    Dist: (229) 245-2733
Thomas (part)    Fax: (229) 245-8890
Term Expires: 2017
P.O. Box 4930, Valdosta, GA 31604-4930
E-mail: amy.carter@house.ga.gov
Committees: Agriculture and Consumer Affairs; Appropriations;
Education; Governmental Affairs; Higher Education; Small Business
Development
Education: Valdosta State U 1993 BSEd

Representative **Doreen Carter, CIA** (D-District 92) . . . . . . (404) 656-0220
Counties Represented: DeKalb (part), Rockdale (part)
Term Expires: 2017
E-mail: doreen.carter@house.ga.gov
Committees: Code Revision; Small Business Development; Special
Rules
Education: Georgia State 1989 BBA; Kennesaw State U 2012 MBA

Representative **David S. Casas** (R-District 107) . . . . . . . . .(404) 656-0254
Counties Represented: Gwinnett (part)    Dist: (770) 931-8033
Term Expires: 2017    Fax: (770) 931-8839
P.O. Box 283, Lilburn, GA 30048-0283
E-mail: david.casas@house.ga.gov
Committees: Appropriations; Code Revision; Education; Higher
Education
Education: Georgia State 1996 BA

Representative **Joyce Chandler** (R-District 105) . . . . . . . . . (404) 656-0254
Counties Represented: Gwinnett (part)
Term Expires: 2017
PO Box 1371, Gray, GA 30017
E-mail: joyce.chandler@house.ga.gov
Committees: Education; Higher Education; Juvenile Justice; Regulated
Industries
Education: Georgia PhD

Representative **Mike Cheokas** (R-District 138) . . . . . . . . . (404) 656-0298
Counties Represented: Chattahoochee, Marion,    Dist: (229) 924-7823
Schley, Sumter (part)    Fax: (229) 924-7893
Term Expires: 2017
P.O. Box 824, Americus, GA 31709
E-mail: mike.cheokas@house.ga.gov
Committees: Appropriations; Budget and Fiscal Affairs Oversight;
Health and Human Services; Information and Audits; Insurance; State
Properties

Representative **David Clark** (R-District 98) . . . . . . . . . . . . .(404) 656-0325
Counties Represented: Gwinnett (part)
Term Expires: 2017
420 South Hill Street, Buford, GA 30518
E-mail: david.clark@house.ga.gov
Committees: Defense and Veterans Affairs; Small Business
Development; State Properties

Representative **Heath N. Clark** (R-District 147) . . . . . . . . .(404) 656-0109
Counties Represented: Houston (part)
Term Expires: 2017
113 Mary Jay Drive, Warner Robins, GA 30188
E-mail: heath.clark@house.ga.gov
Committees: Defense and Veterans Affairs; Public Safety and
Homeland Security; Science and Technology

Representative **Valerie Clark** (R-District 101) . . . . . . . . . . .(404) 656-0202
Counties Represented: Gwinnett (part)
Term Expires: 2017
252 Regal Drive, Lawrenceville, GA 30046
E-mail: valerie.clark@house.ga.gov
Committees: Appropriations; Education; Health and Human Services;
Human Relations and Aging; Transportation
Education: SUNY (Plattsburgh); North Carolina MEd; Georgia PhD

Representative **Brooks P. Coleman, Jr.** (R-District 97) . . . . (404) 656-9210
Counties Represented: Gwinnett (part)    Res: (770) 476-4471
Term Expires: 2017
3919 Hillside Drive, Duluth, GA 30096
E-mail: brooks.coleman@house.ga.gov
Committees: Appropriations; Education; Intragovernmental
Coordination; Natural Resources and Environment; Retirement
Education: Mercer BA; Georgia MEd; Georgia State EdS, PhD

Representative **Kevin Cooke** (R-District 18) . . . . . . . . . . . . .(404) 656-0188
Counties Represented: Carroll (part), Haralson (part)
Term Expires: 2017
342 Mill Pond Crossing, Carrollton, GA 30116
E-mail: kevin.cooke@house.ga.gov
Committees: Agriculture and Consumer Affairs; Appropriations;
Interstate Cooperation; Legislative and Congressional Reapportionment;
Public Safety and Homeland Security; Regulated Industries; State
Planning and Community Affairs
Education: Georgia

Representative **Christian Coomer** (R-District 14) . . . . . . . (404) 656-0109
Counties Represented: Bartow (part), Floyd (part)    Dist: (770) 383-9171
Term Expires: 2017    Fax: (770) 383-9170
14 Claire Cove, Cartersville, GA 30120
E-mail: christian.coomer@house.ga.gov
Committees: Appropriations; Banks and Banking; Judiciary Non-Civil;
Juvenile Justice; Retirement; Transportation

Representative **Sharon Cooper** (R-District 43) . . . . . . . . . (404) 656-5069
Counties Represented: Cobb (part)    Dist: (770) 956-8357
Term Expires: 2017    Res: (770) 951-2841
1234 Powers Ferry Commons, Marietta, GA 30067    Fax: (770) 956-9693
E-mail: sharon.cooper@house.ga.gov
Committees: Health and Human Services; Judiciary Non-Civil;
Regulated Industries; Rules

Representative **John L. Corbett** (R-District 174) . . . . . . . . . (404) 656-0287
Counties Represented: Camden (part), Charlton (part), Clinch, Echols,
Lowndes (part), Ware (part)
Term Expires: 2017
E-mail: john.corbett@house.ga.gov
Committees: Game, Fish and Parks; Intragovernmental Coordination;
Natural Resources and Environment

Representative
**Dorothy "Dee" Dawkins-Haigler** (D-District 91) . . . . . . (404) 656-0287
Counties Represented: DeKalb (part), Rockdale    Res: (770) 987-1491
(part)    Fax: (770) 676-0576
Term Expires: 2017
6050 Kingston Wood Way, Lithonia, GA 30038
E-mail: dee.dawkins-haigler@house.ga.gov
Committees: Banks and Banking; Human Relations and Aging;
Industry and Labor; Science and Technology
Education: Kentucky State; Interdenominational MDiv

Representative **John Deffenbaugh** (R-District 1) . . . . . . . . (404) 656-0202
Counties Represented: Dade, Walker (part)
Term Expires: 2017
97 Wayside Lane, Lookout Mountain, GA 30750
E-mail: john.deffenbaugh@house.ga.gov
Committees: Banks and Banking; Defense and Veterans Affairs;
Regulated Industries; Small Business Development; Transportation
Education: Covenant Col 1970 BA

Representative **Katie M. Dempsey** (R-District 13) . . . . . . . (404) 463-2247
Counties Represented: Floyd (part)
Term Expires: 2017
811 Highland Avenue, Rome, GA 30161
E-mail: katie.dempsey@house.ga.gov
Committees: Appropriations; Economic Development and Tourism;
Energy, Utilities and Telecommunications; Health and Human Services;
Higher Education; Rules; Transportation

Representative
**Pamela "Pam" Dickerson** (D-District 113) . . . . . . . . . . . (404) 656-0314
Counties Represented: Newton (part), Rockdale    Res: (770) 602-0085
(part)
Term Expires: 2017
P. O. Box 1016, Conyers, GA 30013
E-mail: pam.dickerson@house.ga.gov
Committees: Education; Game, Fish and Parks; Judiciary Non-Civil;
Juvenile Justice; Legislative and Congressional Reapportionment; State
Planning and Community Affairs
Education: Southern U (New Orleans) BS

Representative **Robert Dickey** (R-District 140) . . . . . . . . . . (404) 651-7737
Counties Represented: Bibb (part), Crawford,    Dist: (478) 836-3136
Houston (part), Monroe (part), Peach (part)
Term Expires: 2017
3440 Old Highway 341 North, Musella, GA 30710
E-mail: robert.dickey@house.ga.gov
Committees: Agriculture and Consumer Affairs; Appropriations; Banks
and Banking; Energy, Utilities and Telecommunications; Higher
Education; Natural Resources and Environment

Representative **Tom Dickson** (R-District 6) . . . . . . . . . . . . . (404) 463-2247
Counties Represented: Murray (part), Whitfield    Res: (706) 694-3908
(part)
Term Expires: 2017
5043 Village Drive, Cohutta, GA 30710
E-mail: tom.dickson@house.ga.gov
Committees: Appropriations; Economic Development and Tourism;
Education; Legislative and Congressional Reapportionment; Regulated
Industries; Rules

*(continued on next page)*

**LEGISLATIVE BRANCH**

**Representatives** *continued*

Representative **Matt Dollar** (R-District 45)
Coverdell Legislative Office Building, Room 601 . . . . . . (404) 656-0254
Counties Represented: Cobb (part), Fulton (part)
Term Expires: 2017
PO Box 681746, Marietta, GA 30068
E-mail: matt.dollar@house.ga.gov
Committees: Appropriations; Energy, Utilities and Telecommunications; Insurance; Interstate Cooperation; Legislative and Congressional Reapportionment

Representative **Demetrius Douglas** (D-District 78) . . . . . . (404) 656-7859
Counties Represented: Clayton (part), Henry (part)
Term Expires: 2017
PO Box 131, Stockbridge, GA 30281
E-mail: demetrius.douglas@house.ga.gov
Committees: Banks and Banking; Health and Human Services; Intragovernmental Coordination; Motor Vehicles
Education: Georgia BS

Representative **Karla Lea Drenner** (D-District 85) . . . . . . (404) 656-0202
Counties Represented: DeKalb (part)
Term Expires: 2017
P.O. Box 348, Avondale Estates, GA 30002
E-mail: dren16999@aol.com
Committees: Energy, Utilities and Telecommunications; Health and Human Services; Natural Resources and Environment; Rules; Small Business Development

Representative **Mike Dudgeon** (R-District 25) . . . . . . . . . (404) 656-0298
Counties Represented: Forsyth (part), Fulton (part)
Term Expires: 2017
608 Coverdell Legislative Office Building, Atlanta, GA 30334
10075 Normandy Lane, Suwanee, GA 30024
E-mail: mike.dudgeon@house.ga.gov
Committees: Appropriations; Education; Energy, Utilities and Telecommunications; Science and Technology; Small Business Development

Representative **Winfred J. Dukes** (D-District 154) . . . . . . .(404) 656-0126
Counties Represented: Baker, Dougherty (part),          Dist: (229) 432-9891
Miller, Seminole          Fax: (229) 883-2188
Term Expires: 2017
920 Highland Avenue, Albany, GA 31701
E-mail: winfred.dukes@house.ga.gov
Committees: Agriculture and Consumer Affairs; Economic Development and Tourism; Special Rules; State Planning and Community Affairs

Representative **Emory Dunahoo, Jr.** (R-District 30) . . . . . . (404) 656-0126
Counties Represented: Hall (part)
Term Expires: 2017
4720 Walnut Lane, Gainesville, GA 30507
E-mail: emory.dunahoo@house.ga.gov
Committees: Agriculture and Consumer Affairs; Banks and Banking; Game, Fish and Parks; Information and Audits; State Properties

Representative **Geoff L. Duncan** (R-District 26) . . . . . . . . (404) 656-7859
Counties Represented: Forsyth (part)
Term Expires: 2017
PO Box 3483, Cumming, GA 30028
E-mail: geoff.duncan@house.ga.gov
Committees: Banks and Banking; Information and Audits; Interstate Cooperation; Science and Technology; Ways and Means
Education: Georgia Tech

Representative **Darrel Bush Ealum** (D-District 153) . . . . . . (404) 656-0116
Counties Represented: Dougherty (part)
Term Expires: 2017
521 Honeysuckle Drive, Albany, GA 31705
E-mail: darrel.ealum@house.ga.gov
Committees: Defense and Veterans Affairs; Human Relations and Aging; State Properties

Representative **Chuck Efstration** (R-District 104) . . . . . . . (404) 656-0305
Counties Represented: Gwinnett (part)
Term Expires: 2017
P.O. Box 1615, Dacula, GA 30019
E-mail: chuck.eftration@house.ga.gov
Committees: Appropriations; Defense and Veterans Affairs; Insurance; Juvenile Justice; Legislative and Congressional Reapportionment

Representative **Earl Ehrhart** (R-District 36) . . . . . . . . . . . (404) 463-2247
Counties Represented: Cobb (part)          Res: (770) 437-7536
Term Expires: 2017
5500 Wright Road, Powder Springs, GA 30127
E-mail: earl.ehrhart@house.ga.gov
Committees: Appropriations; Banks and Banking; Game, Fish and Parks; Higher Education; Legislative and Congressional Reapportionment; Rules
Education: Georgia 1980 BA

Representative **Terry Lamar England** (R-District 116) . . . . (404) 463-2247
Counties Represented: Barrow (part)          Dist: (770) 867-1601
Term Expires: 2017          Res: (770) 867-8096
1060 Old Hog Mountain Road, Auburn, GA 30011          Fax: (770) 867-2160
E-mail: englandhomeport2@windstream.net
Committees: Agriculture and Consumer Affairs; Appropriations; Education; Industry and Labor; Natural Resources and Environment; Ways and Means

Representative **James "Bubber" Epps** (R-District 144) . . . (404) 656-0298
Counties Represented: Bibb (part), Bleckley,          Res: (478) 474-7932
Houston (part), Jones (part), Laurens (part), Twiggs, Wilkinson
Term Expires: 2017
P.O. Box 121, Macon, GA 31202-0121
E-mail: bubberepps@gmail.com
Committees: Agriculture and Consumer Affairs; Appropriations; Insurance; Motor Vehicles; Natural Resources and Environment; Small Business Development; Transportation

Representative **Stacey Evans** (D-District 42) . . . . . . . . . . . (404) 656-6372
Counties Represented: Cobb (part)          Dist: (770) 710-4087
Term Expires: 2017
P. O. Box 2523, Smyrna, GA 30081
E-mail: stacey.evans@house.ga.gov
Committees: Appropriations; Interstate Cooperation; Judiciary; Juvenile Justice; Rules

Representative **Barry A. Fleming** (R-District 121)
Coverdell Legislative Office Building, Room 401-H . . . . . (404) 656-0152
Counties Represented: Columbia (part), McDuffie (part)
Term Expires: 2017
E-mail: barry.fleming@house.ga.gov
Committees: Governmental Affairs; Industry and Labor; Judiciary; Rules
Education: Georgia 1988, 1994 JD

Representative **Hugh Floyd** (D-District 99) . . . . . . . . . . . . .(404) 656-0314
Counties Represented: Gwinnett (part)          Res: (770) 921-2735
Term Expires: 2017          Fax: (770) 921-2645
744 Omaha Drive, Norcross, GA 30093
E-mail: hughfloyd@mindspring.com
Committees: Economic Development and Tourism; Education; Governmental Affairs; Industry and Labor
Education: Davidson 1980 BA

Representative **Virgil Fludd** (D-District 64) . . . . . . . . . . . . (404) 656-0314
Counties Represented: Fayette (part), Fulton (part)          Dist: (770) 683-8711
Term Expires: 2017          Fax: (770) 651-8086
P.O. Box 670, Tyrone, GA 30290
E-mail: vfludd@mindspring.com
Committees: Banks and Banking; Ethics; Regulated Industries; Small Business Development; Ways and Means

Representative **Gloria Frazier** (D-District 126) . . . . . . . . . . (404) 656-0265
Counties Represented: Burke, Richmond (part)          Res: (706) 560-9709
Term Expires: 2017
2717 Willis Foreman Road, Hephzibah, GA 30815
E-mail: frazier26@comcast.net
Committees: Banks and Banking; Budget and Fiscal Affairs Oversight; Energy, Utilities and Telecommunications; Public Safety and Homeland Security

Representative **Spencer Frye** (D-District 118) . . . . . . . . . . . (404) 656-0265
Counties Represented: Clarke (part)
Term Expires: 2017
PO Box 8101, Athens, GA 30603
E-mail: spencer.frye@house.ga.gov
Committees: Budget and Fiscal Affairs Oversight; Health and Human Services; Human Relations and Aging; Science and Technology

Representative **Pat Gardner** (D-District 57) . . . . . . . . . . . . (404) 656-0265
Counties Represented: Fulton (part)
Term Expires: 2017
668 East Pelham Road, Atlanta, GA 30324
E-mail: pat@patgardner.org
Committees: Appropriations; Ethics; Higher Education; Natural Resources and Environment; Transportation

Representative **Dan Gasaway** (R-District 28) . . . . . . . . . . .(404) 656-0325
Counties Represented: Banks, Habersham (part), Stephens
Term Expires: 2017
PO Box 700, Homer, GA 30547
E-mail: dan.gasaway@house.ga.gov
Committees: Budget and Fiscal Affairs Oversight; Higher Education; Human Relations and Aging; Insurance; Natural Resources and Environment
Education: Georgia Tech 1988 BS

Representative **Carl Gillard** (D-District 162) . . . . . . . . . . . . (404) 656-0305
Counties Represented: Chatham (part)
Term Expires: 2017
E-mail: carl.gilliard@house.ga.gov

Representative **Sheri Gilligan** (R-District 24) . . . . . . . . . . . (404) 656-0305
Counties Represented: Forsyth (part)
Term Expires: 2017
E-mail: sheri.gilligan@house.ga.gov
Committees: Code Revision; Human Relations and Aging; Natural
Resources and Environment

Representative **Mike Glanton, Sr.** (D-District 75) . . . . . . . . (404) 656-0325
Counties Represented: Clayton (part)
Term Expires: 2017
PO Box 216, Jonesboro, GA 30236
E-mail: mike.glanton@house.ga.gov
Committees: Appropriations; Defense and Veterans Affairs; Education;
Public Safety and Homeland Security
Education: Liberty; Fayetteville State; Georgia Military

Representative **Rich Golick** (R-District 40) . . . . . . . . . . . . . (404) 656-5943
Counties Represented: Cobb (part), Fulton (part)      Res: (770) 319-7200
Term Expires: 2017                                    Fax: (770) 319-0970
2372 Simpson Farm Way, Smyrna, GA 30080
E-mail: rich.golick@house.ga.gov
Committees: Appropriations; Insurance; Judiciary; Judiciary Non-Civil;
Regulated Industries; Rules

Representative **J. Craig Gordon** (D-District 163) . . . . . . . . (404) 656-0287
Counties Represented: Chatham (part)             Dist: (912) 231-8958
Term Expires: 2017
102 Oglethorpe Professional Court, Savannah, GA 31406
E-mail: craig.gordon@house.ga.gov
Committees: Economic Development and Tourism; Health and Human
Services; Retirement; Special Rules

Representative **Micah Gravley** (R-District 67) . . . . . . . . . . (404) 656-0325
Counties Represented: Douglas (part), Paulding (part)
Term Expires: 2017
94 Bridge Place, Douglasville, GA 30134
E-mail: micah.gravley@house.ga.gov
Committees: Code Revision; Economic Development and Tourism;
Judiciary Non-Civil; Public Safety and Homeland Security
Education: Emmanuel (GA) 1997 BS

Representative **Gerald E. Greene** (R-District 151) . . . . . . . (404) 656-0202
Counties Represented: Calhoun, Clay, Dougherty    Res: (229) 732-2750
(part), Early, Quitman, Randolph, Stewart, Terrell,  Fax: (229) 732-2973
Webster
Term Expires: 2017
Route 3, Cuthbert, GA 39840
E-mail: gerald.greene@house.ga.gov
Committees: Appropriations; Code Revision; Economic Development
and Tourism; Public Safety and Homeland Security; Retirement; Rules;
State Properties
Education: Georgia Southern BA; Georgia Southwestern MEd

Representative
**Oren H. "Buddy" Harden** (R-District 148) . . . . . . . . . . (404) 656-0188
Counties Represented: Crisp, Houston (part),     Res: (229) 535-6050
Pulaski, Wilcox
Term Expires: 2017
458 Lakeshore Way, Cordele, GA 31015
E-mail: bharden@planttel.net
Committees: Agriculture and Consumer Affairs; Appropriations; Banks
and Banking; Health and Human Services; Natural Resources and
Environment; Small Business Development

Representative **Brett Harrell** (R-District 106) . . . . . . . . . . . (404) 656-7859
Counties Represented: Gwinnett (part)
Term Expires: 2017
P. O. Box 1135, Snellville, GA 30078
E-mail: brett.harrell@house.ga.gov
Committees: Budget and Fiscal Affairs Oversight; Regulated Industries;
Transportation; Ways and Means

Representative **Matt Hatchett** (R-District 150) . . . . . . . . . . (404) 651-7737
Counties Represented: Johnson (part), Laurens    Fax: (478) 275-3455
(part), Treutlen
Term Expires: 2017
100 Canterbury Road, Dublin, GA 31021
E-mail: matt.hatchett@house.ga.gov
Committees: Appropriations; Economic Development and Tourism;
Energy, Utilities and Telecommunications; Ethics; Health and Human
Services; Rules

Representative **Lee Hawkins** (R-District 27) . . . . . . . . . . . (404) 656-0213
Counties Represented: Hall (part), White (part)
Term Expires: 2017
4710 Jim Hood Road, Gainesville, GA 30506
E-mail: lee.hawkins@house.ga.gov
Committees: Appropriations; Health and Human Services; Insurance;
Regulated Industries
Education: Georgia; Emory DDS

Representative **Michele D. Henson** (D-District 86) . . . . . . (404) 656-7859
Counties Represented: DeKalb (part)             Res: (404) 296-1442
Term Expires: 2017                              Fax: (404) 651-8086
4140 Creek Stone Court, Stone Mountain, GA 30083
E-mail: michele.henson@house.ga.gov
Committees: Appropriations; Economic Development and Tourism;
Health and Human Services; Small Business Development
Education: Miami BA

Representative
**Dustin "Dusty" Hightower** (R-District 68) . . . . . . . . . . (404) 657-1803
Counties Represented: Carroll (part), Douglas (part)   Dist: (404) 285-1445
Term Expires: 2017
3443 Hog Liver Road, Carrollton, GA 30117
E-mail: dustin.hightower@house.ga.gov
Committees: Appropriations; Governmental Affairs; Judiciary
Non-Civil; Public Safety and Homeland Security; Special Rules
Education: State U West Georgia 2004; John Marshall 2008 JD

Representative
**Col. William "Bill" Hitchens** (R-District 161) . . . . . . . . (404) 656-0178
Counties Represented: Chatham (part), Effingham (part)
Term Expires: 2017
2440 Rincon-Stillwell Road, Rincon, GA 31326
E-mail: bill.hitchens@house.ga.gov
Committees: Appropriations; Defense and Veterans Affairs; Economic
Development and Tourism; Public Safety and Homeland Security
Education: Georgia Southern

Representative **Scott Holcomb** (D-District 81) . . . . . . . . . . (404) 656-6372
Counties Represented: DeKalb (part), Gwinnett (part)
Term Expires: 2017
2306 Briarcliff Commons, Atlanta, GA 31064
E-mail: scott.holcomb@house.ga.gov
Committees: Defense and Veterans Affairs; Higher Education; Juvenile
Justice; Public Safety and Homeland Security

Representative **Susan Dykes Holmes** (R-District 129) . . . . (404) 656-0178
Counties Represented: Butts (part), Jasper, Jones (part), Monroe (part)
Term Expires: 2017
PO Box 151, Monticello, GA 31064
E-mail: susan.holmes@house.ga.gov
Committees: Agriculture and Consumer Affairs; Economic
Development and Tourism; Energy, Utilities and Telecommunications;
Legislative and Congressional Reapportionment; Special Rules
Education: Georgia BS

Representative **Penny Houston** (R-District 170) . . . . . . . . (404) 463-2247
Counties Represented: Berrien, Cook, Tift (part)   Res: (229) 686-2467
Term Expires: 2017
8395 Highway 129, Nashville, GA 31639
E-mail: penny.houston@house.ga.gov
Committees: Appropriations; Banks and Banking; Budget and Fiscal
Affairs Oversight; Economic Development and Tourism; Ways and
Means

Representative
**Henry "Wayne" Howard** (D-District 124) . . . . . . . . . . . (404) 656-6372
Counties Represented: Richmond (part)           Dist: (706) 722-1123
Term Expires: 2017                              Res: (706) 724-7828
2047B Martin Luther King Jr. Boulevard, Augusta, GA 30901
E-mail: wayne.howard@house.ga.gov
Committees: Appropriations; Education; Health and Human Services;
Juvenile Justice; Motor Vehicles

Representative
**Carolyn Fleming Hugley** (D-District 136) . . . . . . . . . . . (404) 656-5058
Counties Represented: Muscogee (part)           Dist: (706) 687-4327
Term Expires: 2017                              Res: (706) 685-8065
P.O. Box 6342, Columbus, GA 31917-6342         Fax: (706) 687-5582
E-mail: carolyn.hugley@house.ga.gov
Committees: Appropriations; Ethics; Insurance; Rules

Representative **Mack Jackson** (D-District 128) . . . . . . . . . . (404) 656-0314
Counties Represented: Glascock, Hancock, Jefferson (part), Johnson
(part), McDuffie (part), Warren, Washington
Term Expires: 2017
733 Evelyn Street, Sandersville, GA 31082
E-mail: mack.jackson@house.ga.gov
Committees: Legislative and Congressional Reapportionment; Public
Safety and Homeland Security; Rules; Small Business Development;
State Planning and Community Affairs

Representative **Rick Jasperse** (R-District 11) . . . . . . . . . . . (404) 656-0188
Counties Represented: Gordon (part), Murray (part),  Res: (770) 893-2039
Pickens
Term Expires: 2017
89 Apple Valley Farm Lane, Jasper, GA 30143
E-mail: rick.jasperse@house.ga.gov
Committees: Agriculture and Consumer Affairs; Appropriations; Health
and Human Services; Human Relations and Aging; Public Safety and
Homeland Security; Special Rules

*(continued on next page)*

**Representatives** *continued*

Representative **J.B. "Jeff" Jones** (R-District 167) . . . . . . . (404) 656-0126
Counties Represented: Glynn (part), Long, McIntosh
Term Expires: 2017
139-358 Altama Connector, Brunswick, GA 31525
E-mail: jb.jones@house.ga.gov
Committees: Interstate Cooperation; Motor Vehicles; Natural Resources and Environment

Representative **Jan Jones** (R-District 47) . . . . . . . . . . . . . . (404) 656-5072
Counties Represented: Fulton (part)          Fax: (404) 657-0498
Term Expires: 2017
12850 Highway 9, Alpharetta, GA 30004
E-mail: jan.jones@house.ga.gov
Committees: Appropriations; Education; Ethics; Legislative and Congressional Reapportionment; Rules

Representative **LaDawn Jones** (D-District 62) . . . . . . . . . . (404) 656-7859
Counties Represented: Douglas (part), Fulton (part)
Term Expires: 2017
PO Box 44824, Atlanta, GA 30349
E-mail: ladawn.jones@house.ga.gov
Committees: Budget and Fiscal Affairs Oversight; Judiciary; Small Business Development; State Properties

Representative **Sheila Jones** (D-District 53) . . . . . . . . . . . (404) 656-0323
Counties Represented: Cobb (part), Fulton (part)
Term Expires: 2017
P.O. Box 784, Smyrna, GA 30081-0784
E-mail: sheila.jones@house.ga.gov
Committees: Appropriations; Health and Human Services; Juvenile Justice; Transportation

Representative **Darryl Jordan** (D-District 77) . . . . . . . . . . . (404) 656-0116
Counties Represented: Clayton (part)
Term Expires: 2017
316 Herring Way, Riverdale, GA 30274
E-mail: darryl.jordan@house.ga.gov
Committees: Banks and Banking; Budget and Fiscal Affairs Oversight; Motor Vehicles; Transportation

Representative **Margaret D. Kaiser** (D-District 59) . . . . . . (404) 656-0265
Counties Represented: Fulton (part)          Res: (404) 223-6269
Term Expires: 2017
504 Hill Street SE, Atlanta, GA 30312
E-mail: mkaiser2@comcast.net
Committees: Agriculture and Consumer Affairs; Appropriations; Education; Health and Human Services

Representative **Trey Kelley** (R-District 16) . . . . . . . . . . . . . (404) 656-0287
Counties Represented: Bartow (part), Haralson (part), Polk
Term Expires: 2017
836 North College Drive, Cedartown, GA 30125
E-mail: trey.kelley@house.ga.gov
Committees: Banks and Banking; Code Revision; Energy, Utilities and Telecommunications; Health and Human Services; Higher Education; Judiciary; Ways and Means
Education: Shorter Col (GA)

Representative **Dar'shun N. Kendrick** (D-District 93) . . . . . (404) 656-0109
Counties Represented: DeKalb (part), Gwinnett          Dist: (678) 739-8109
(part)
Term Expires: 2017
P. O. Box 630, Lithonia, GA 30058
E-mail: darshun.kendrick@house.ga.gov
Committees: Interstate Cooperation; Judiciary Non-Civil; Juvenile Justice; Small Business Development
Education: Oglethorpe 2004 BA

Representative **E. Culver "Rusty" Kidd** (I-District 145) . . . (404) 656-0202
Counties Represented: Baldwin, Putnam (part)          Dist: (478) 452-1354
Term Expires: 2017          Res: (478) 454-0151
102 South Wayne Street, Milledgeville, GA 31061          Fax: (478) 452-3493
E-mail: rusty.kidd@house.ga.gov
Committees: Governmental Affairs; Health and Human Services; Science and Technology; State Properties

Representative **Tom Kirby** (R-District 114) . . . . . . . . . . . . . (404) 656-0177
Counties Represented: Barrow (part), Gwinnett          Fax: (404) 651-8086
(part), Rockdale (part), Walton (part)
Term Expires: 2017
PO Box 1416, Loganville, GA 30052
E-mail: tom.kirby@house.ga.gov
Committees: Agriculture and Consumer Affairs; Human Relations and Aging; Industry and Labor; Retirement; Small Business Development; Special Rules
Education: Kentucky BS

Representative **David Knight** (R-District 130) . . . . . . . . . . (404) 656-7855
Counties Represented: Henry (part), Lamar (part),          Dist: (678) 464-4926
Spalding (part)
Term Expires: 2017
526 Brook Circle, Griffin, GA 30224
E-mail: david.knight@house.ga.gov
Committees: Banks and Banking; Game, Fish and Parks; Higher Education; Rules; Small Business Development; Ways and Means

Representative **Dominic F. LaRiccia** (R-District 169) . . . . . (404) 656-0287
Counties Represented: Bacon, Coffee (part), Jeff Davis (part)
Term Expires: 2017
P.O. Box 1156, Douglas, GA 31534
E-mail: dominic.lariccia@house.ga.gov
Committees: Agriculture and Consumer Affairs; Game, Fish and Parks; Special Rules

Representative **Jodi Lott** (R-District 122) . . . . . . . . . . . . . . (404) 656-0177
Counties Represented: Columbia (part)
Term Expires: 2017
P.O. Box 86, Evans, GA 30809
E-mail: jodi.lott@house.ga.gov
Committees: Health and Human Services; Intragovernmental Coordination; Juvenile Justice

Representative **Eddie Lumsden** (R-District 12)
Coverdell Legislative Office Building, Room 612-B . . . . . (404) 656-0325
Counties Represented: Chattooga, Floyd (part)
Term Expires: 2017
E-mail: eddie.lumsden@house.ga.gov
Committees: Appropriations; Budget and Fiscal Affairs Oversight; Governmental Affairs; Insurance; Public Safety and Homeland Security; State Properties
Education: Floyd 1974 AA; Berry 1985 BS

Representative **Ronnie Mabra** (D-District 63) . . . . . . . . . . . (404) 656-7859
Counties Represented: Clayton (part), Fayette (part), Fulton (part)
Term Expires: 2017
1415 Highway 85 North, Suite 310-304, Fayetteville, GA 30214
E-mail: ronnie.mabra@house.ga.gov
Committees: Code Revision; Governmental Affairs; Higher Education; Judiciary
Education: Georgia Tech BS; Georgia JD

Representative **Pedro "Pete" Marin** (D-District 96) . . . . . . (404) 656-0314
Counties Represented: Gwinnett (part)          Fax: (770) 422-0408
Term Expires: 2017
4370 Satellite Boulevard, Apt. 1101, Duluth, GA 30096
E-mail: marinstatehouse@aol.com
Committees: Banks and Banking; Economic Development and Tourism; Industry and Labor; Science and Technology

Representative
**Charles E. "Chuck" Martin, Jr.** (R-District 49) . . . . . . . . (404) 656-5064
Counties Represented: Fulton (part)
Term Expires: 2017
11770 Haynes Bridge Road, Suite 205-544, Alpharetta, GA 30009
E-mail: chuck@martinforgeorgia.com
Committees: Appropriations; Budget and Fiscal Affairs Oversight; Energy, Utilities and Telecommunications; Regulated Industries; Science and Technology; Ways and Means
Education: Georgia 1983 BBA

Representative **Howard R. Maxwell** (R-District 17) . . . . . . (404) 656-5143
Counties Represented: Paulding (part)          Dist: (770) 386-5420
Term Expires: 2017          Res: (770) 445-3318
716 Graham Road, Dallas, GA 30132
E-mail: howard.maxwell@house.ga.gov
Committees: Appropriations; Education; Insurance; Regulated Industries; Retirement

Representative **Rahn Mayo** (D-District 84)
Coverdell Legislative Office Building, Room 511 . . . . . . . (404) 656-6372
Counties Represented: DeKalb (part)          Fax: (404) 591-8693
Term Expires: 2017
P.O. Box 360549, Decatur, GA 30036
E-mail: rahnmayo@gmail.com
Committees: Appropriations; Education; Insurance; Legislative and Congressional Reapportionment

Representative **Tom McCall** (R-District 33) . . . . . . . . . . . . (404) 656-5099
Counties Represented: Columbia (part), Elbert,          Res: (706) 283-5436
Lincoln, Madison (part), Wilkes (part)          Fax: (706) 283-6656
Term Expires: 2017
2835 Washington Highway, Elberton, GA 30635
E-mail: tommccall@bellsouth.net
Committees: Agriculture and Consumer Affairs; Game, Fish and Parks; Natural Resources and Environment; Transportation

Representative **Dewey McClain** (D-District 100) . . . . . . . . (404) 656-0220
Counties Represented: Gwinnett (part)        Dist: (404) 525-3659
Term Expires: 2017
1032 Flagg Way, Lawrenceville, GA 30044
P.O. Box 1621, Lilburn, GA 30048
E-mail: dewey.mcclain@house.ga.gov
Committees: Industry and Labor; Interstate Cooperation; State Planning
and Community Affairs

Representative **John D. Meadows III** (R-District 5) . . . . . . (404) 656-5141
Counties Represented: Gordon (part), Murray (part)    Dist: (706) 629-4441
Term Expires: 2017        Fax: (706) 629-3631
110 Victory Court, Calhoun, GA 30701
E-mail: john.meadows@house.ga.gov
Committees: Game, Fish and Parks; Governmental Affairs; Industry
and Labor; Insurance; Retirement; Rules

Representative **Marie R. Metze** (D-District 55) . . . . . . . . . (404) 656-0305
Counties Represented: Fulton (part)
Term Expires: 2017
E-mail: marie.metze@house.ga.gov
Committees: Economic Development and Tourism; Interstate
Cooperation; Special Rules

Representative **Billy Mitchell** (D-District 88) . . . . . . . . . . . (404) 656-0126
Counties Represented: DeKalb (part)        Res: (770) 465-8800
Term Expires: 2017        Fax: (770) 465-8888
P.O. Box 88, Stone Mountain, GA 30086
E-mail: billy.mitchell@house.ga.gov
Committees: Health and Human Services; Joint Metropolitan Atlanta
Rapid Transit Oversight; Regulated Industries

Representative **Greg Morris** (R-District 156) . . . . . . . . . . . . (404) 656-5115
Counties Represented: Appling (part), Jeff Davis    Dist: (912) 538-1062
(part), Montgomery, Toombs
Term Expires: 2017
P.O. Box 1749, Vidalia, GA 30475
E-mail: greg.morris@house.ga.gov
Committees: Appropriations; Banks and Banking; Code Revision;
Natural Resources and Environment; Rules

Representative **Howard Mosby** (D-District 83) . . . . . . . . . . (404) 656-0287
Counties Represented: DeKalb (part)
Term Expires: 2017
2101 Sugar Creek Falls Drive, Atlanta, GA 30316
E-mail: howard.mosby@house.ga.gov
Committees: Governmental Affairs; Health and Human Services; Ways
and Means

Representative **Chad Nimmer** (R-District 178) . . . . . . . . . . (404) 656-0287
Counties Represented: Appling (part), Brantley,    Dist: (912) 449-6190
Pierce, Wayne (part)
Term Expires: 2017
PO Box 1174, Blackshear, GA 31516
E-mail: chad.nimmer@house.ga.gov
Committees: Appropriations; Game, Fish and Parks; Industry and
Labor; Natural Resources and Environment; Transportation

Representative **Randy Nix** (R-District 69) . . . . . . . . . . . . . . (404) 656-0177
Counties Represented: Carroll (part), Heard, Troup    Res: (706) 845-9853
(part)        Fax: (404) 463-2796
Term Expires: 2017
219 East Yorktown Drive, LaGrange, GA 30240
E-mail: randy.nix@house.ga.gov
Committees: Appropriations; Banks and Banking; Economic
Development and Tourism; Education; Legislative and Congressional
Reapportionment; Natural Resources and Environment

Representative **Mary Margaret Oliver** (D-District 82) . . . . . (404) 656-0265
Counties Represented: DeKalb (part)        Dist: (404) 377-0485
Term Expires: 2017        Fax: (404) 377-0486
150 East Ponce de Leon Avenue, Decatur, GA 30030
E-mail: mmo@mmolaw.com
Committees: Appropriations; Governmental Affairs; Judiciary; Juvenile
Justice; Science and Technology

Representative **Byung "B.J." Pak** (R-District 108) . . . . . . . . (404) 656-0254
Counties Represented: Gwinnett (part)
Term Expires: 2017
1034 Morgan Garner Drive Southwest, Lilburn, GA 30047
E-mail: bj.pak@house.ga.gov
Committees: Code Revision; Health and Human Services; Judiciary
Non-Civil; Ways and Means

Representative **Larry J. "Butch" Parrish** (R-District 158) . . (404) 463-2247
Counties Represented: Bulloch (part), Candler,    Dist: (478) 237-7032
Emanuel, Jenkins
Term Expires: 2017
224 West Main Street, Swainsboro, GA 30401
E-mail: butch.parrish@house.ga.gov
Committees: Appropriations; Banks and Banking; Economic
Development and Tourism; Rules
Education: Georgia 1964 BS

Representative **Don Parsons** (R-District 44) . . . . . . . . . . . . (404) 656-9198
Counties Represented: Cobb (part)        Dist: (770) 977-4426
Term Expires: 2017
3167 Sycamore Lane, Marietta, GA 30066
E-mail: don.parsons@house.ga.gov
Committees: Appropriations; Energy, Utilities and Telecommunications;
Health and Human Services; Ways and Means

Representative **Allen M. Peake** (R-District 141) . . . . . . . . . (404) 656-5025
Counties Represented: Bibb (part), Monroe (part)    Dist: (478) 474-5633
Term Expires: 2017        ext. 12
103 Colony Court, Macon, GA 31210        Res: (478) 474-9105
E-mail: allen.peake@house.ga.gov
Committees: Appropriations; Health and Human Services; Rules; Small
Business Development; Ways and Means
Education: Mercer BBA

Representative **Jesse L. Petrea** (R-District 166) . . . . . . . . . (404) 656-0109
Counties Represented: Bryan (part), Chatham (part)
Term Expires: 2017
108 Loyer Lane, Savannah, GA 31411
E-mail: jesse.petrea@house.ga.gov
Committees: Health and Human Services; Human Relations and Aging;
Public Safety and Homeland Security

Representative **John David Pezold** (R-District 133)
Coverdell Legislative Office Building, Room 509-D . . . . . (404) 656-0220
Counties Represented: Harris (part), Muscogee (part), Troup (part)
Term Expires: 2017
E-mail: john.pezold@house.ga.gov
Committees: Defense and Veterans Affairs; Health and Human
Services; Higher Education; Small Business Development
Education: Auburn 2001 BS; Columbus State 2005 MBA

Representative **Clay Pirkle** (R-District 155) . . . . . . . . . . . . . (404) 656-0188
Counties Represented: Ben Hill, Coffee (part), Irwin, Tift (part), Turner
Term Expires: 2017
E-mail: clay.pirkle@house.ga.gov
Committees: Agriculture and Consumer Affairs; Science and
Technology; State Properties

Representative **Alan Powell** (R-District 32) . . . . . . . . . . . . . (404) 656-0202
Counties Represented: Franklin, Hart, Madison    Dist: (706) 376-4422
(part)
Term Expires: 2017
P.O. Box 248, Hartwell, GA 30643-0248
E-mail: alanpowell23@hotmail.com
Committees: Appropriations; Governmental Affairs; Motor Vehicles;
Public Safety and Homeland Security; Regulated Industries; Rules;
Small Business Development
Education: Georgia Southwestern BS

Representative **Jay Powell** (R-District 171) . . . . . . . . . . . . . (404) 656-7146
Counties Represented: Colquitt (part), Decatur    Dist: (229) 336-3962
(part), Mitchell
Term Expires: 2017
P.O. Box 188, Camilla, GA 31730
E-mail: jay.powell@house.ga.gov
Committees: Appropriations; Governmental Affairs; Judiciary; Rules;
Ways and Means

Representative **Betty Price** (R-District 48) . . . . . . . . . . . . . (404) 656-0305
Counties Represented: Fulton (part)
Term Expires: 2017
E-mail: betty.price@house.ga.gov
Committees: Governmental Affairs; Health and Human Services

Representative **Brian Prince** (D-District 127)
Coverdell Legislative Office Bldg., Room 409-D . . . . . . . . (404) 656-0116
Counties Represented: Jefferson (part), Richmond    Dist: (706) 364-4230
(part)
Term Expires: 2017
P.O. Box 14264, Augusta, GA 30919
E-mail: brian.prince@house.ga.gov
Committees: Defense and Veterans Affairs; Motor Vehicles; Special
Rules; Transportation

Representative **Jimmy Pruett** (R-District 149) . . . . . . . . . . (404) 656-0202
Counties Represented: Dodge, Jeff Davis (part),    Dist: (478) 374-4316
Laurens (part), Telfair, Wheeler
Term Expires: 2017
PO Box 459, Eastman, GA 31023
E-mail: jimmy.pruett@house.ga.gov
Committees: Appropriations; Economic Development and Tourism;
Game, Fish and Parks; Health and Human Services; Industry and
Labor; Joint Metropolitan Atlanta Rapid Transit Oversight; State
Planning and Community Affairs

*(continued on next page)*

**LEGISLATIVE BRANCH**

**Representatives** *continued*

Representative **Regina Quick** (R-District 117) . . . . . . . . . . (404) 656-0220
Counties Represented: Barrow (part), Clarke (part), Jackson (part), Oconee (part)
Term Expires: 2017
150 East Washington Street, Athens, GA 30601
E-mail: regina.quick@house.ga.gov
Committees: Agriculture and Consumer Affairs; Appropriations; Juvenile Justice; State Planning and Community Affairs
Education: Georgia JD

Representative **Brad Raffensperger** (R-District 50) . . . . . . . (404) 656-0325
Counties Represented: Fulton (part)
Term Expires: 2017
10335 Balladrum, Johns Creek, GA 30022
E-mail: brad.raffensperger@house.ga.gov
Committees: Energy, Utilities and Telecommunications; Intragovernmental Coordination; Juvenile Justice

Representative **Paulette Rakestraw** (R-District 19) . . . . . . (404) 656-0177
Counties Represented: Paulding (part)          Res: (770) 439-9056
Term Expires: 2017
PO Box 580, Powder Springs, GA 30127
E-mail: paulette.braddock@house.ga.gov
Committees: Economic Development and Tourism; Juvenile Justice; Regulated Industries; Science and Technology; Small Business Development; Special Rules

Representative **David Ralston** (R-District 7) . . . . . . . . . . . . (404) 656-5020
Counties Represented: Dawson (part), Fannin,        Dist: (706) 632-2221
Gilmer                                              Fax: (706) 632-6193
Term Expires: 2017
P.O. Box 1196, Blue Ridge, GA 30513
E-mail: david.ralston@house.ga.gov

Representative **Matt Ramsey** (R-District 72) . . . . . . . . . . . (404) 656-7146
Counties Represented: Coweta (part), Fayette (part)     Res: (770) 487-0182
Term Expires: 2017
200 Terrane Ridge, Peachtree City, GA 30269
E-mail: matt.ramsey@house.ga.gov
Committees: Appropriations; Ethics; Higher Education; Judiciary Non-Civil; Regulated Industries; Rules; Ways and Means

Representative **Nikki T. Randall** (D-District 142) . . . . . . . . (404) 656-0109
Counties Represented: Bibb (part)              Res: (478) 474-7932
Term Expires: 2017
P.O. Box 121, Macon, GA 31202-0121
E-mail: nikki.randall@house.ga.gov
Committees: Health and Human Services; Information and Audits; Insurance; Judiciary Non-Civil

Representative **Albert T. "Bert" Reeves** (R-District 34) . . . (404) 656-0287
Counties Represented: Cobb (part)
Term Expires: 2017
890 Crossfire Ridge, Marietta, GA 30064
E-mail: bert.reeves@house.ga.gov
Committees: Insurance; Interstate Cooperation; Judiciary Non-Civil

Representative **Trey Rhodes** (R-District 120) . . . . . . . . . . . (404) 656-0325
Counties Represented: Greene, Oglethorpe, Putnam (part), Taliaferro, Wilkes (part)
Term Expires: 2017
103 West Second Street, Greensboro, GA 30642
E-mail: trey.rhodes@house.ga.gov
Committees: Banks and Banking; Economic Development and Tourism; Special Rules

Representative **Tom Rice** (R-District 95) . . . . . . . . . . . . . . . (404) 656-5912
Counties Represented: Fulton (part), Gwinnett (part)     Res: (770) 447-9646
Term Expires: 2017
4151 Blue Iris Hollow, Norcross, GA 30092
E-mail: tom.rice@house.ga.gov
Committees: Appropriations; Motor Vehicles; Rules; Ways and Means
Education: Temple BA

Representative **Carl W. Rogers** (R-District 29) . . . . . . . . . . (404) 656-5146
Counties Represented: Hall (part)              Res: (770) 535-0994
Term Expires: 2017                             Fax: (770) 535-0996
P.O. Box 639, Gainesville, GA 30503
E-mail: carl.rogers@house.ga.gov
Committees: Appropriations; Health and Human Services; Higher Education; Insurance; Rules

Representative **Terry Rogers** (R-District 10) . . . . . . . . . . . . (404) 656-0178
Counties Represented: Habersham (part), White      Dist: (706) 754-0706
(part)
Term Expires: 2017
2403 New Liberty Road, Clarkesville, GA 30523
E-mail: terry.rogers@house.ga.gov
Committees: Defense and Veterans Affairs; Economic Development and Tourism; Human Relations and Aging; Regulated Industries; Rules; State Planning and Community Affairs

Representative **Dale Rutledge** (R-District 109) . . . . . . . . . . (404) 656-0109
Counties Represented: Henry (part), Newton (part), Rockdale (part)
Term Expires: 2017
1320 Lakehaven Parkway, McDonough, GA 30253
E-mail: dale.rutledge@house.ga.gov
Committees: Agriculture and Consumer Affairs; Judiciary; Regulated Industries; Transportation; Ways and Means

Representative **Ed Rynders** (R-District 152) . . . . . . . . . . . . (404) 463-2247
Counties Represented: Lee, Sumter (part), Worth     Res: (229) 436-7455
Term Expires: 2017
423 Martindale Drive, Albany, GA 31721
E-mail: erynders@bellsouth.net
Committees: Appropriations; Governmental Affairs; Health and Human Services; Intragovernmental Coordination; Legislative and Congressional Reapportionment; Transportation; Ways and Means

Representative **Sandra G. Scott** (D-District 76)
611 Coverdell Legislative Office Building . . . . . . . . . . . . . (404) 656-0314
Counties Represented: Clayton (part), Henry (part)
Term Expires: 2017
E-mail: sandra.scott@house.ga.gov
Committees: Human Relations and Aging; Legislative and Congressional Reapportionment; Science and Technology; Special Rules

Representative **Ed Setzler** (R-District 35) . . . . . . . . . . . . . . (404) 656-0178
Counties Represented: Cobb (part)              Dist: (404) 630-8452
Term Expires: 2017
1555 Boxwood Trace, Acworth, GA 30102
E-mail: ed.setzler@house.ga.gov
Committees: Appropriations; Education; Judiciary Non-Civil; Legislative and Congressional Reapportionment; Rules; Science and Technology; Transportation

Representative **Dexter Sharper** (D-District 177) . . . . . . . . . (404) 656-0126
Counties Represented: Lowndes (part)
Term Expires: 2017
19 Sharper Circle, Valdosta, GA 31601
E-mail: dexter.sharper@house.ga.gov
Committees: Health and Human Services; Information and Audits; Juvenile Justice; Small Business Development

Representative **Jason "Jay" Shaw** (D-District 176) . . . . . . (404) 656-0213
Counties Represented: Atkinson, Lanier, Lowndes     Dist: (229) 482-3505
(part), Ware (part)                                 Fax: (229) 482-8043
Term Expires: 2017
39 Valdosta Road, Lakeland, GA 31635
E-mail: jay.shaw@house.ga.gov
Committees: Appropriations; Economic Development and Tourism; Game, Fish and Parks; Industry and Labor; Insurance; Small Business Development

Representative **Barbara Sims** (R-District 123) . . . . . . . . . . . (404) 656-0213
Counties Represented: Columbia (part), Richmond     Fax: (404) 657-7775
(part)
Term Expires: 2017
10 Retreat, Augusta, GA 30909
E-mail: barbara.sims@house.ga.gov
Committees: Appropriations; Economic Development and Tourism; Health and Human Services; Rules; Science and Technology; State Properties; Transportation

Representative **Earnest G. Smith** (D-District 125) . . . . . . . (404) 656-6372
Counties Represented: Richmond (part)
Term Expires: 2017
253 Greene Street, Augusta, GA 30901-1616
E-mail: ma1027@aol.com
Committees: Banks and Banking; Defense and Veterans Affairs; Energy, Utilities and Telecommunications; Game, Fish and Parks

Representative **Lynn Ratigan Smith** (R-District 70) . . . . . . (404) 656-7149
Counties Represented: Carroll (part), Coweta (part)
Term Expires: 2017
Eight Evergreen Drive, Newnan, GA 30263
E-mail: lynn.smith@house.ga.gov
Committees: Appropriations; Legislative and Congressional Reapportionment; Natural Resources and Environment; Rules
Affiliation: Co-Owner, Murray Printing Co.

Representative **Michael Smith** (D-District 41)
Coverdell Legislative Office Building, Room 604-F . . . . . . (404) 656-0265
Counties Represented: Cobb (part)              Dist: (404) 652-9227
Term Expires: 2017
E-mail: michael.smith@house.ga.gov
Committees: Code Revision; Science and Technology; Special Rules; State Properties
Education: Kennesaw State U

LEGISLATIVE BRANCH

Representative **Richard H. Smith** (R-District 134) . . . . . . . . (404) 656-6831
Counties Represented: Harris (part), Muscogee (part)
Term Expires: 2017
P.O. Box 2122, Columbus, GA 31902-2122
E-mail: richard@smithforgeorgia.com
Committees: Appropriations; Insurance; Legislative and Congressional
Reapportionment; Natural Resources and Environment; Rules
Education: LSU 1968 BS; Florida 1970 MS

Representative **Calvin Smyre** (D-District 135) . . . . . . . . . . (404) 656-0116
Counties Represented: Muscogee (part)                    Dist: (706) 649-2243
Term Expires: 2017                                       Res: (706) 563-1794
P.O. Box 181, Columbus, GA 31902                         Fax: (706) 649-2479
E-mail: calvinsmyre@synovus.com
Committees: Appropriations; Higher Education; Rules
Education: Fort Valley State 1970 BS

Representative **Jason Spencer** (R-District 180) . . . . . . . . . (404) 656-0126
Counties Represented: Camden (part), Charlton           Res: (912) 576-5810
(part), Ware (part)
Term Expires: 2017
28 Yachtsmen Court, Woodbine, GA 31569
E-mail: jason.spencer@house.ga.gov
Committees: Game, Fish and Parks; Human Relations and Aging;
Juvenile Justice; Science and Technology; Special Rules
Education: Georgia BS

Representative
**Edward "Mickey" Stephens** (D-District 165) . . . . . . . . (404) 656-0116
Counties Represented: Chatham (part)                     Dist: (912) 661-1733
Term Expires: 2017
P.O. Box 5485, Savannah, GA 31414
E-mail: mickey.stephens@house.ga.gov
Committees: Health and Human Services; Insurance; Legislative and
Congressional Reapportionment; Regulated Industries; Ways and Means

Representative **Ron Stephens** (R-District 164) . . . . . . . . . (404) 656-5115
Counties Represented: Bryan (part), Chatham             Dist: (912) 966-5665
(part), Liberty (part)                                   Res: (912) 964-0061
Term Expires: 2017                                       Fax: (912) 964-9699
45 Cove Drive, Savannah, GA 31419
E-mail: ron.stephens@house.ga.gov
Committees: Appropriations; Economic Development and Tourism;
Rules; Ways and Means

Representative **Pam S. Stephenson** (D-District 90) . . . . . . (404) 656-0126
Counties Represented: DeKalb (part), Henry              Dist: (404) 243-0200
(part), Rockdale (part)                                  Fax: (404) 243-0307
Term Expires: 2017
14153 C Flat Shoals Parkway, Decatur, GA 30034
E-mail: pamelann@bellsouth.net
Committees: Code Revision; Health and Human Services;
Intragovernmental Coordination; Judiciary

Representative **Valencia Stovall** (D-District 74) . . . . . . . . . (404) 656-0314
Counties Represented: Clayton (part)
Term Expires: 2017
PO Box 842, Ellenwood, GA 30294
E-mail: valencia.stovall@house.ga.gov
Committees: Code Revision; Education; Interstate Cooperation; Small
Business Development
Education: Fort Valley State; Georgia State

Representative **David J. Stover** (R-District 71) . . . . . . . . . . (404) 656-0126
Counties Represented: Coweta (part), Fayette (part)
Term Expires: 2017
3150 East Highway 34, Suite 209-155, Newnan, GA 30265
E-mail: david.stover@house.ga.gov
Committees: Energy, Utilities and Telecommunications; Motor Vehicles;
Science and Technology; Small Business Development

Representative **R. Brian Strickland** (R-District 111) . . . . . , (404) 656-0109
Counties Represented: Henry (part)
Term Expires: 2017
PO Box 1803, McDonough, GA 30253
E-mail: brian.strickland@house.ga.gov
Committees: Appropriations; Banks and Banking; Economic
Development and Tourism; Industry and Labor; Intragovernmental
Coordination; Judiciary Non-Civil
Education: Valdosta State U BBA; Florida Coastal JD

Representative **Jan Tankersley** (R-District 160) . . . . . . . . . (404) 656-0254
Counties Represented: Bryan (part), Bulloch (part)      Res: (912) 842-5512
Term Expires: 2017
P. O. Box 187, Brooklet, GA 30415
E-mail: jan.tankersley@house.ga.gov
Committees: Agriculture and Consumer Affairs; Appropriations;
Intragovernmental Coordination; Natural Resources and Environment

Representative **Kevin K. Tanner** (R-District 9) . . . . . . . . . . (404) 656-0152
Counties Represented: Dawson (part), Forsyth (part), Lumpkin
Term Expires: 2017
PO Box 1885, Dawsonville, GA 30534
E-mail: kevin.tanner@house.ga.gov
Committees: Appropriations; Education; Intragovernmental
Coordination; Motor Vehicles; Natural Resources and Environment;
Special Rules

Representative **Steve Tarvin** (R-District 2)
Coverdell Legislative Office Bldg., Room 404-F . . . . . . . (404) 656-0109
Counties Represented: Catoosa (part), Walker (part),     Dist: (423) 605-7328
Whitfield (part)
Term Expires: 2017
P.O. Box 750, Chickamauga, GA 30707
E-mail: steve.tarvin@house.ga.gov
Committees: Budget and Fiscal Affairs Oversight; Defense and
Veterans Affairs; Game, Fish and Parks; Insurance; Small Business
Development

Representative **Darlene K. Taylor** (R-District 173) . . . . . . . (404) 656-0178
Counties Represented: Decatur (part), Grady,             Dist: (229) 225-9943
Thomas (part)
Term Expires: 2017
100 Town Court, Thomasville, GA 31792
E-mail: darlene.taylor@house.ga.gov
Committees: Agriculture and Consumer Affairs; Appropriations;
Governmental Affairs; Insurance; Public Safety and Homeland Security

Representative **Tom Taylor** (R-District 79) . . . . . . . . . . . . . (404) 656-0152
Counties Represented: DeKalb (part)
Term Expires: 2017
4926 Four Oaks Court, Dunwoody, GA 30360
E-mail: tom.taylor@house.ga.gov
Committees: Appropriations; Economic Development and Tourism;
Governmental Affairs; Joint Metropolitan Atlanta Rapid Transit
Oversight; Regulated Industries
Education: Georgia State

Representative **Sam Teasley** (R-District 37) . . . . . . . . . . . . (404) 656-0177
Counties Represented: Cobb (part)
Term Expires: 2017
P. O. Box 670051, Marietta, GA 30066
E-mail: sam.teasley@house.ga.gov
Committees: Banks and Banking; Education; Energy, Utilities and
Telecommunications; Ethics; Insurance; Ways and Means

Representative **Erica R. Thomas** (D-District 39) . . . . . . . . . (404) 656-7859
Counties Represented: Cobb (part)
Term Expires: 2017
P.O. Box 564, Austell, GA 30168
E-mail: erica.thomas@house.ga.gov
Committees: Budget and Fiscal Affairs Oversight; Juvenile Justice;
Science and Technology

Representative **Mable "Able" Thomas** (D-District 56)
Coverdell Legislative Office Building, Room 511-B . . . . . (404) 656-6372
Counties Represented: Fulton (part)
Term Expires: 2017
E-mail: mable.thomas@house.ga.gov
Committees: Economic Development and Tourism; Legislative and
Congressional Reapportionment; Natural Resources and Environment;
Science and Technology

Representative
**Robert T. "Bob" Trammell, Jr.** (D-District 132) . . . . . . . (404) 656-0314
Counties Represented: Coweta (part), Meriwether (part), Troup (part)
Term Expires: 2017
E-mail: bob.trammell@house.ga.gov
Committees: Information and Audits; Judiciary Non-Civil; Motor
Vehicles

Representative **Scot Turner** (R-District 21)
Coverdell Legislative Office Bldg., Room 611-G . . . . . . . . (404) 656-5015
Counties Represented: Cherokee (part)
Term Expires: 2017
508 Blue Ridge Terrace, Canton, GA 30114
E-mail: scot.turner@house.ga.gov
Committees: Agriculture and Consumer Affairs; Science and
Technology; Special Rules; State Planning and Community Affairs

Representative **Keisha Waites** (D-District 60) . . . . . . . . . . . (404) 656-0220
Counties Represented: Clayton (part), Fulton (part)
Term Expires: 2017
509 Coverdell Legislative Office Building, Atlanta, GA 30334
PO Box 3249, Atlanta, GA 30302
E-mail: keisha.waites@house.ga.gov
Committees: Interstate Cooperation; Juvenile Justice; Public Safety and
Homeland Security; Special Rules; Transportation

*(continued on next page)*

**LEGISLATIVE BRANCH**

**Representatives** *continued*

Representative **Sam Watson** (R-District 172) . . . . . . . . . . (404) 656-0177
Counties Represented: Colquitt (part), Thomas (part), Tift (part)
Term Expires: 2017
PO Box 3914, Moultrie, GA 31776
E-mail: sam.watson@house.ga.gov
Committees: Agriculture and Consumer Affairs; Appropriations;
Juvenile Justice; Natural Resources and Environment; Retirement;
Special Rules; Transportation
Education: Abraham Baldwin AS; Georgia BS

Representative
**Andrew J. "Andy" Welch III** (R-District 110) . . . . . . . . (404) 656-0109
Counties Represented: Butts (part), Henry (part),    Tel: (770) 957-3937
Newton (part)                     Fax: (678) 593-4888
Term Expires: 2017
404 Coverdell Legislative Office Building, Atlanta, GA 30334
PO Box 2871, McDonough, GA 30253
E-mail: andy.welch@house.ga.gov
Committees: Appropriations; Code Revision; Judiciary; Juvenile
Justice; Regulated Industries

Representative **Tom Weldon, Jr.** (R-District 3) . . . . . . . . . (404) 656-0152
Counties Represented: Catoosa (part)
Term Expires: 2017
P.O. Box 1459, Ringgold, GA 30736
E-mail: tom.weldon@house.ga.gov
Committees: Appropriations; Banks and Banking; Code Revision;
Judiciary; Juvenile Justice; Retirement; Rules

Representative
**William A. "Bill" Werkheiser** (R-District 157) . . . . . . . . (404) 656-0126
Counties Represented: Evans, Tattnall, Wayne (part)
Term Expires: 2017
P.O. Box 27, Glennville, GA 30427
E-mail: bill.werkheiser@house.ga.gov
Committees: Industry and Labor; Information and Audits; State
Properties

Representative **David Wilkerson** (D-District 38) . . . . . . . . . (404) 656-0116
Counties Represented: Cobb (part)
Term Expires: 2017
909 Tranquil Drive, Austell, GA 30106
E-mail: david.wilkerson@house.ga.gov
Committees: Budget and Fiscal Affairs Oversight; Juvenile Justice;
Retirement; Science and Technology

Representative
**Joseph B. "Joe" Wilkinson, Jr.** (R-District 52)
Room 415 . . . . . . . . . . . . . . . . . . . . . . . . . . . . . . . . . (404) 463-8143
Counties Represented: Fulton (part)         Dist: (404) 398-7383
Term Expires: 2017
200 River Vista Drive, Unit 203, Atlanta, GA 30339
E-mail: joe.wilkinson@house.ga.gov
Committees: Economic Development and Tourism; Ethics; Health and
Human Services; Insurance; Judiciary

Representative **Wendell Willard** (R-District 51) . . . . . . . . . (404) 656-5125
Counties Represented: Fulton (part)       Dist: (770) 481-7100
Term Expires: 2017                     Res: (770) 392-0676
755 River Gate Drive, Sandy Springs, GA 30350    Fax: (770) 481-7111
E-mail: wendell.willard@house.ga.gov
Committees: Appropriations; Ethics; Judiciary; Judiciary Non-Civil;
Rules; Ways and Means

Representative **Al Williams** (D-District 168) . . . . . . . . . . . . (404) 656-6372
Counties Represented: Liberty (part)       Dist: (912) 977-5600
Term Expires: 2017                     Fax: (912) 368-4982
9041 East Oglethorpe Highway, Midway, GA 31320
E-mail: al.williams@house.ga.gov
Committees: Economic Development and Tourism; Game, Fish and
Parks; Rules; Transportation

Representative **Chuck Williams** (R-District 119) . . . . . . . . (404) 656-0254
Counties Represented: Clarke (part), Oconee (part)
Term Expires: 2017
P.O. Box 1365, Watkinsville, GA 30677
E-mail: chuck.williams@house.ga.gov
Committees: Agriculture and Consumer Affairs; Appropriations; Higher
Education; Information and Audits; Natural Resources and Environment

Representative
**Earnest "Coach" Williams** (D-District 87) . . . . . . . . . . . (404) 656-0202
Counties Represented: DeKalb (part)
Term Expires: 2017
P.O. Box 436, Avondale Estates, GA 30002
E-mail: earnest.williams@house.ga.gov
Committees: Budget and Fiscal Affairs Oversight; Energy, Utilities and
Telecommunications; Retirement; State Planning and Community
Affairs

Representative **Bruce Williamson** (R-District 115) . . . . . . . (404) 656-7859
Counties Represented: Walton (part)       Dist: (770) 267-2566
Term Expires: 2017
P. O. Box 430, Monroe, GA 30655
E-mail: bruce.williamson@house.ga.gov
Committees: Banks and Banking; Governmental Affairs; Insurance;
Ways and Means

Representative **John Phillip Yates** (R-District 73) . . . . . . . (404) 656-5126
Counties Represented: Fayette (part), Henry (part),   Dist: (770) 412-7166
Spalding (part)                    Res: (770) 227-1474
Term Expires: 2017
961 Birdie Road, Griffin, GA 30223
E-mail: john.yates@house.ga.gov
Committees: Appropriations; Defense and Veterans Affairs; Legislative
and Congressional Reapportionment; Motor Vehicles
Education: Georgia State 1959 BBA

# House Standing Committees

## Agriculture and Consumer Affairs

| **Majority Members** | **Minority Members** |
|---|---|
| Tom McCall (R-33) *Chair* | Patty Bentley (D-139) |
| Oren H. "Buddy" Harden (R-148) | Winfred J. Dukes (D-154) |
| *Vice Chair* | Margaret D. Kaiser (D-59) |
| Robert Dickey (R-140) *Secretary* | |
| Jon G. Burns (R-159) | |
| Amy Alexander Carter (R-175) | |
| Kevin Cooke (R-18) | |
| Emory Dunahoo, Jr. (R-30) | |
| Terry Lamar England (R-116) | |
| James "Bubber" Epps (R-144) | |
| Susan Dykes Holmes (R-129) | |
| Rick Jasperse (R-11) | |
| Tom Kirby (R-114) | |
| Dominic F. LaRiccia (R-169) | |
| Clay Pirkle (R-155) | |
| Regina Quick (R-117) | |
| Dale Rutledge (R-109) | |
| Jan Tankersley (R-160) | |
| Darlene K. Taylor (R-173) | |
| Scot Turner (R-21) | |
| Sam Watson (R-172) | |
| Chuck Williams (R-119) | |

## Appropriations

| **Majority Members** | **Minority Members** |
|---|---|
| Terry Lamar England (R-116) *Chair* | Stacey Y. Abrams (D-89) |
| Chad Nimmer (R-178) *Vice Chair* | Stacey Evans (D-42) |
| Ed Rynders (R-152) *Secretary* | Pat Gardner (D-57) |
| Stephen Allison (R-8) | Mike Glanton, Sr. (D-75) |
| Alex Atwood (R-179) | Michele D. Henson (D-86) |
| Mandi Ballinger (R-23) | Henry "Wayne" Howard (D-124) |
| Timothy Barr (R-103) | Carolyn Fleming Hugley (D-136) |
| Paul R. Battles (R-15) | Sheila Jones (D-53) |
| Tommy Benton (R-31) | Margaret D. Kaiser (D-59) |
| Buzz Brockway (R-102) | Rahn Mayo (D-84) |
| Jon G. Burns (R-159) | Mary Margaret Oliver (D-82) |
| Johnnie Caldwell, Jr. (R-131) | Jason "Jay" Shaw (D-176) |
| Amy Alexander Carter (R-175) | Calvin Smyre (D-135) |
| David S. Casas (R-107) | |
| Mike Cheokas (R-138) | |
| Valerie Clark (R-101) | |
| Brooks P. Coleman, Jr. (R-97) | |
| Kevin Cooke (R-18) | |
| Christian Coomer (R-14) | |
| Katie M. Dempsey (R-13) | |
| Robert Dickey (R-140) | |
| Tom Dickson (R-6) | |
| Matt Dollar (R-45) | |
| Mike Dudgeon (R-25) | |
| Chuck Efstration (R-104) | |
| Earl Ehrhart (R-36) | |
| James "Bubber" Epps (R-144) | |
| Rich Golick (R-40) | |
| Gerald E. Greene (R-151) | |
| Oren H. "Buddy" Harden (R-148) | |
| Matt Hatchett (R-150) | |
| Lee Hawkins (R-27) | |
| Dustin "Dusty" Hightower (R-68) | |

**Majority Members** *continued*

Col. William "Bill" Hitchens
  (R-161)
Penny Houston (R-170)
Rick Jasperse (R-11)
Jan Jones (R-47)
Eddie Lumsden (R-12)
Charles E. "Chuck" Martin, Jr.
  (R-49)
Howard R. Maxwell (R-17)
Greg Morris (R-156)
Randy Nix (R-69)
Larry J. "Butch" Parrish (R-158)
Don Parsons (R-44)
Alan Powell (R-32)
Jimmy Pruett (R-149)
Regina Quick (R-117)
Matt Ramsey (R-72)
Tom Rice (R-95)
Carl W. Rogers (R-29)
Ed Setzler (R-35)
Barbara Sims (R-123)
Lynn Ratigan Smith (R-70)
Richard H. Smith (R-134)
Ron Stephens (R-164)
R. Brian Strickland (R-111)
Jan Tankersley (R-160)
Kevin K. Tanner (R-9)
Darlene K. Taylor (R-173)
Tom Taylor (R-79)
Sam Watson (R-172)
Andrew J. "Andy" Welch III
  (R-110)
Tom Weldon, Jr. (R-3)
Wendell Willard (R-51)
Chuck Williams (R-119)
John Phillip Yates (R-73)
Allen M. Peake (R-141)
  *Ex-Officio Member*
Jay Powell (R-171)
  *Ex-Officio Member*

## Banks and Banking

**Majority Members**

Greg Morris (R-156) *Chair*
R. Brian Strickland (R-111)
  *Vice Chair*
Randy Nix (R-69) *Secretary*
Johnnie Caldwell, Jr. (R-131)
Christian Coomer (R-14)
John Deffenbaugh (R-1)
Robert Dickey (R-140)
Emory Dunahoo, Jr. (R-30)
Geoff L. Duncan (R-26)
Earl Ehrhart (R-36)
Oren H. "Buddy" Harden (R-148)
Penny Houston (R-170)
Trey Kelley (R-16)
David Knight (R-130)
Larry J. "Butch" Parrish (R-158)
Trey Rhodes (R-120)
Sam Teasley (R-37)
Tom Weldon, Jr. (R-3)
Bruce Williamson (R-115)

**Minority Members**

Dorothy "Dee" Dawkins-Haigler
  (D-91)
Demetrius Douglas (D-78)
Virgil Fludd (D-64)
Gloria Frazier (D-126)
Darryl Jordan (D-77)
Pedro "Pete" Marin (D-96)
Earnest G. Smith (D-125)

## Budget and Fiscal Affairs Oversight

**Majority Members**

Charles E. "Chuck"
  Martin, Jr. (R-49)
  *Chair*
Brett Harrell (R-106) *Vice Chair*
Mandi Ballinger (R-23) *Secretary*
Mike Cheokas (R-138)
Michael Caldwell (R-20)
Dan Gasaway (R-28)
Penny Houston (R-170)
Eddie Lumsden (R-12)
Steve Tarvin (R-2)

**Minority Members**

Taylor J. Bennett (D-80)
Gloria Frazier (D-126)
Spencer Frye (D-118)
LaDawn Jones (D-62)
Darryl Jordan (D-77)
Erica R. Thomas (D-39)
David Wilkerson (D-38)
Earnest "Coach" Williams (D-87)

## Code Revision

**Majority Members**

Gerald E. Greene (R-151) *Chair*
Micah Gravley (R-67) *Vice Chair*
Byung "B.J." Pak (R-108) *Secretary*
Timothy Barr (R-103)
Michael Caldwell (R-20)
David S. Casas (R-107)
Sheri Gilligan (R-24)
Trey Kelley (R-16)
Greg Morris (R-156)
Andrew J. "Andy" Welch III
  (R-110)
Tom Weldon, Jr. (R-3)

**Minority Members**

Kimberly Alexander (D-66)
Karen Bennett (D-94)
Doreen Carter (D-92)
Ronnie Mabra (D-63)
Michael Smith (D-41)
Pam S. Stephenson (D-90)
Valencia Stovall (D-74)

## Defense and Veterans Affairs

**Majority Members**

John Phillip Yates (R-73) *Chair*
Col. William "Bill"
  Hitchens (R-161)
  *Vice Chair*
John David Pezold (R-133)
  *Secretary*
David Clark (R-98)
Heath N. Clark (R-147)
John Deffenbaugh (R-1)
Chuck Efstration (R-104)
Terry Rogers (R-10)
Steve Tarvin (R-2)

**Minority Members**

Darrel Bush Ealum (D-153)
Mike Glanton, Sr. (D-75)
Scott Holcomb (D-81)
Brian Prince (D-127)
Earnest G. Smith (D-125)

## Economic Development and Tourism

**Majority Members**

Ron Stephens (R-164) *Chair*
Terry Rogers (R-10) *Vice Chair*
Barbara Sims (R-123) *Secretary*
Paul R. Battles (R-15)
D.C. "Dave" Belton (R-112)
Z. Shaw Blackmon (R-146)
Buzz Brockway (R-102)
Jon G. Burns (R-159)
Michael Caldwell (R-20)
Katie M. Dempsey (R-13)
Tom Dickson (R-6)
Micah Gravley (R-67)
Gerald E. Greene (R-151)
Matt Hatchett (R-150)
Col. William "Bill" Hitchens
  (R-161)
Susan Dykes Holmes (R-129)
Penny Houston (R-170)
Randy Nix (R-69)
Larry J. "Butch" Parrish (R-158)
Jimmy Pruett (R-149)
Paulette Rakestraw (R-19)
Trey Rhodes (R-120)
R. Brian Strickland (R-111)
Tom Taylor (R-79)
Joseph B. "Joe" Wilkinson, Jr.
  (R-52)

**Minority Members**

Karen Bennett (D-94)
Winfred J. Dukes (D-154)
Hugh Floyd (D-99)
J. Craig Gordon (D-163)
Michele D. Henson (D-86)
Pedro "Pete" Marin (D-96)
Marie R. Metze (D-55)
Jason "Jay" Shaw (D-176)
Mable "Able" Thomas (D-56)
Al Williams (D-168)

## Education

**Majority Members**

Brooks P. Coleman, Jr. (R-97)
  *Chair*
Mike Dudgeon (R-25) *Vice Chair*
Tommy Benton (R-31) *Secretary*
D.C. "Dave" Belton (R-112)
Wesley E. "Wes" Cantrell (R-22)
Amy Alexander Carter (R-175)
David S. Casas (R-107)
Joyce Chandler (R-105)
Valerie Clark (R-101)
Tom Dickson (R-6)
Terry Lamar England (R-116)
Jan Jones (R-47)
Howard R. Maxwell (R-17)
Randy Nix (R-69)

**Minority Members**

Beth Beskin (D-54)
Pamela "Pam" Dickerson (D-113)
Hugh Floyd (D-99)
Mike Glanton, Sr. (D-75)
Henry "Wayne" Howard (D-124)
Margaret D. Kaiser (D-59)
Rahn Mayo (D-84)
Valencia Stovall (D-74)

*(continued on next page)*

**Education** *continued*

**Majority Members** *continued*

Ed Setzler (R-35)
Kevin K. Tanner (R-9)
Sam Teasley (R-37)

## Energy, Utilities and Telecommunications

| **Majority Members** | **Minority Members** |
| --- | --- |
| Don Parsons (R-44) *Chair* | Karla Lea Drenner (D-85) |
| John Carson (R-46) *Vice Chair* | Gloria Frazier (D-126) |
| Mike Dudgeon (R-25) *Secretary* | Earnest G. Smith (D-125) |
| Stephen Allison (R-8) | Earnest "Coach" Williams (D-87) |
| Katie M. Dempsey (R-13) | |
| Robert Dickey (R-140) | |
| Matt Dollar (R-45) | |
| Matt Hatchett (R-150) | |
| Susan Dykes Holmes (R-129) | |
| Trey Kelley (R-16) | |
| Charles E. "Chuck" Martin, Jr. (R-49) | |
| Brad Raffensperger (R-50) | |
| David J. Stover (R-71) | |
| Sam Teasley (R-37) | |

## Ethics

| **Majority Members** | **Minority Members** |
| --- | --- |
| Joseph B. "Joe" Wilkinson, Jr. (R-52) *Chair* | Stacey Y. Abrams (D-89) *Vice Chair* |
| Jon G. Burns (R-159) | Virgil Fludd (D-64) |
| Matt Hatchett (R-150) | Pat Gardner (D-57) |
| Jan Jones (R-47) | Carolyn Fleming Hugley (D-136) |
| Matt Ramsey (R-72) | |
| Sam Teasley (R-37) | |
| Wendell Willard (R-51) | |

## Game, Fish and Parks

| **Majority Members** | **Minority Members** |
| --- | --- |
| David Knight (R-130) *Chair* | Sharon Beasley-Teague (D-65) |
| Bruce Broadrick (R-4) *Vice Chair* | Roger B. Bruce (D-61) |
| Jimmy Pruett (R-149) *Secretary* | Pamela "Pam" Dickerson (D-113) |
| Jon G. Burns (R-159) | Jason "Jay" Shaw (D-176) |
| John L. Corbett (R-174) | Earnest G. Smith (D-125) |
| Emory Dunahoo, Jr. (R-30) | Al Williams (D-168) |
| Earl Ehrhart (R-36) | |
| Dominic F. LaRiccia (R-169) | |
| Tom McCall (R-33) | |
| John D. Meadows III (R-5) | |
| Chad Nimmer (R-178) | |
| Jason Spencer (R-180) | |
| Steve Tarvin (R-2) | |

## Governmental Affairs

| **Majority Members** | **Minority Members** |
| --- | --- |
| Ed Rynders (R-152) *Chair* | Hugh Floyd (D-99) |
| Buzz Brockway (R-102) *Vice Chair* | Ronnie Mabra (D-63) |
| Darlene K. Taylor (R-173) *Secretary* | Howard Mosby (D-83) |
| Amy Alexander Carter (R-175) | Mary Margaret Oliver (D-82) |
| Barry A. Fleming (R-121) | |
| Dustin "Dusty" Hightower (R-68) | |
| Eddie Lumsden (R-12) | |
| John D. Meadows III (R-5) | |
| Alan Powell (R-32) | |
| Jay Powell (R-171) | |
| Betty Price (R-48) | |
| Tom Taylor (R-79) | |
| Bruce Williamson (R-115) | |

**Members**

E. Culver "Rusty" Kidd (I-145)

## Health and Human Services

| **Majority Members** | **Minority Members** |
| --- | --- |
| Sharon Cooper (R-43) *Chair* | Karen Bennett (D-94) |
| Lee Hawkins (R-27) *Vice Chair* | James Beverly (D-143) |
| Ed Rynders (R-152) *Secretary* | Demetrius Douglas (D-78) |
| Timothy Barr (R-103) | Karla Lea Drenner (D-85) |
| Bruce Broadrick (R-4) | Spencer Frye (D-118) |
| Mike Cheokas (R-138) | J. Craig Gordon (D-163) |
| Valerie Clark (R-101) | Michele D. Henson (D-86) |
| Katie M. Dempsey (R-13) | Henry "Wayne" Howard (D-124) |
| Oren H. "Buddy" Harden (R-148) | Sheila Jones (D-53) |
| Matt Hatchett (R-150) | Margaret D. Kaiser (D-59) |
| Rick Jasperse (R-11) | Billy Mitchell (D-88) |
| Trey Kelley (R-16) | Howard Mosby (D-83) |
| Jodi Lott (R-122) | Nikki T. Randall (D-142) |
| Byung "B.J." Pak (R-108) | Dexter Sharper (D-177) |
| Don Parsons (R-44) | Edward "Mickey" Stephens (D-165) |
| Allen M. Peake (R-141) | Pam S. Stephenson (D-90) |
| Jesse L. Petrea (R-166) | |
| John David Pezold (R-133) | |
| Betty Price (R-48) | |
| Jimmy Pruett (R-149) | |
| Carl W. Rogers (R-29) | |
| Barbara Sims (R-123) | |
| Joseph B. "Joe" Wilkinson, Jr. (R-52) | |

**Members**

E. Culver "Rusty" Kidd (I-145)

## Higher Education

| **Majority Members** | **Minority Members** |
| --- | --- |
| Carl W. Rogers (R-29) *Chair* | Patty Bentley (D-139) |
| Chuck Williams (R-119) *Vice Chair* | Pat Gardner (D-57) |
| Trey Kelley (R-16) *Secretary* | Scott Holcomb (D-81) |
| Amy Alexander Carter (R-175) | Ronnie Mabra (D-63) |
| David S. Casas (R-107) | Calvin Smyre (D-135) |
| Joyce Chandler (R-105) | |
| Katie M. Dempsey (R-13) | |
| Robert Dickey (R-140) | |
| Earl Ehrhart (R-36) | |
| Dan Gasaway (R-28) | |
| David Knight (R-130) | |
| John David Pezold (R-133) | |
| Matt Ramsey (R-72) | |

## Human Relations and Aging

| **Majority Members** | **Minority Members** |
| --- | --- |
| Tommy Benton (R-31) *Chair* | Darrel Bush Ealum (D-153) |
| Tom Kirby (R-114) *Vice Chair* | Sharon Beasley-Teague (D-65) |
| Dan Gasaway (R-28) *Secretary* | Roger B. Bruce (D-61) |
| Valerie Clark (R-101) | Dorothy "Dee" Dawkins-Haigler (D-91) |
| Sheri Gilligan (R-24) | Spencer Frye (D-118) |
| Rick Jasperse (R-11) | Sandra G. Scott (D-76) |
| Jesse L. Petrea (R-166) | |
| Terry Rogers (R-10) | |
| Jason Spencer (R-180) | |

## Industry and Labor

| **Majority Members** | **Minority Members** |
| --- | --- |
| Chad Nimmer (R-178) *Vice Chair* | Jason "Jay" Shaw (D-176) *Chair* |
| Tom Kirby (R-114) *Secretary* | Dorothy "Dee" Dawkins-Haigler (D-91) |
| Bruce Broadrick (R-4) | Hugh Floyd (D-99) |
| Terry Lamar England (R-116) | Pedro "Pete" Marin (D-96) |
| Barry A. Fleming (R-121) | Dewey McClain (D-100) |
| John D. Meadows III (R-5) | |
| Jimmy Pruett (R-149) | |
| R. Brian Strickland (R-111) | |
| William A. "Bill" Werkheiser (R-157) | |

## Information and Audits

| Majority Members | Minority Members |
| --- | --- |
| Mike Cheokas (R-138) *Chair* | Nikki T. Randall (D-142) |
| Geoff L. Duncan (R-26) *Vice Chair* | Dexter Sharper (D-177) |
| Emory Dunahoo, Jr. (R-30) *Secretary* | Robert T. "Bob" Trammell, Jr. (D-132) |
| Mandi Ballinger (R-23) | |
| William A. "Bill" Werkheiser (R-157) | |
| Chuck Williams (R-119) | |

## Insurance

| Majority Members | Minority Members |
| --- | --- |
| Richard H. Smith (R-134) *Chair* | Carolyn Fleming Hugley (D-136) |
| Johnnie Caldwell, Jr. (R-131) *Vice Chair* | Rahn Mayo (D-84) |
| John Carson (R-46) *Secretary* | Nikki T. Randall (D-142) |
| Alex Atwood (R-179) | Jason "Jay" Shaw (D-176) |
| Z. Shaw Blackmon (R-146) | Edward "Mickey" Stephens (D-165) |
| Buzz Brockway (R-102) | |
| Mike Cheokas (R-138) | |
| Matt Dollar (R-45) | |
| Chuck Efstration (R-104) | |
| James "Bubber" Epps (R-144) | |
| Dan Gasaway (R-28) | |
| Rich Golick (R-40) | |
| Lee Hawkins (R-27) | |
| Eddie Lumsden (R-12) | |
| Howard R. Maxwell (R-17) | |
| John D. Meadows III (R-5) | |
| Albert T. "Bert" Reeves (R-34) | |
| Carl W. Rogers (R-29) | |
| Steve Tarvin (R-2) | |
| Darlene K. Taylor (R-173) | |
| Sam Teasley (R-37) | |
| Joseph B. "Joe" Wilkinson, Jr. (R-52) | |
| Bruce Williamson (R-115) | |

## Interstate Cooperation

| Majority Members | Minority Members |
| --- | --- |
| Matt Dollar (R-45) *Chair* | Stacey Evans (D-42) |
| Kevin Cooke (R-18) *Vice Chair* | Dar'shun N. Kendrick (D-93) |
| Geoff L. Duncan (R-26) *Secretary* | Marie R. Metze (D-55) |
| D.C. "Dave" Belton (R-112) | Dewey McClain (D-100) |
| J.B. "Jeff" Jones (R-167) | Valencia Stovall (D-74) |
| Albert T. "Bert" Reeves (R-34) | Keisha Waites (D-60) |

## Intragovernmental Coordination

| Majority Members | Minority Members |
| --- | --- |
| Jan Tankersley (R-160) *Chair* | Kimberly Alexander (D-66) |
| John Carson (R-46) *Vice Chair* | Patty Bentley (D-139) |
| Kevin K. Tanner (R-9) *Secretary* | Demetrius Douglas (D-78) |
| Bruce Broadrick (R-4) | Pam S. Stephenson (D-90) |
| Brooks P. Coleman, Jr. (R-97) | |
| John L. Corbett (R-174) | |
| Jodi Lott (R-122) | |
| Brad Raffensperger (R-50) | |
| Ed Rynders (R-152) | |
| R. Brian Strickland (R-111) | |

## Judiciary

| Majority Members | Minority Members |
| --- | --- |
| Wendell Willard (R-51) *Chair* | Beth Beskin (D-54) |
| Barry A. Fleming (R-121) *Vice Chair* | Taylor J. Bennett (D-80) |
| Stephen Allison (R-8) *Secretary* | Roger B. Bruce (D-61) |
| Johnnie Caldwell, Jr. (R-131) | Stacey Evans (D-42) |
| Trey Kelley (R-16) | LaDawn Jones (D-62) |
| Jay Powell (R-171) | Ronnie Mabra (D-63) |
| Dale Rutledge (R-109) | Mary Margaret Oliver (D-82) |
| Andrew J. "Andy" Welch III (R-110) | Pam S. Stephenson (D-90) |
| Tom Weldon, Jr. (R-3) | |
| Rich Golick (R-40) *Ex-Officio Member* | |
| Joseph B. "Joe" Wilkinson, Jr. (R-52) *Ex-Officio Member* | |

## Judiciary Non-Civil

| Majority Members | Minority Members |
| --- | --- |
| Rich Golick (R-40) *Chair* | Stacey Y. Abrams (D-89) |
| Byung "B.J." Pak (R-108) *Vice Chair* | Pamela "Pam" Dickerson (D-113) |
| Dustin "Dusty" Hightower (R-68) *Secretary* | Dar'shun N. Kendrick (D-93) |
| Alex Atwood (R-179) | Nikki T. Randall (D-142) |
| Mandi Ballinger (R-23) | Robert T. "Bob" Trammell, Jr. (D-132) |
| Christian Coomer (R-14) | |
| Sharon Cooper (R-43) | |
| Micah Gravley (R-67) | |
| Matt Ramsey (R-72) | |
| Albert T. "Bert" Reeves (R-34) | |
| Ed Setzler (R-35) | |
| R. Brian Strickland (R-111) | |
| Wendell Willard (R-51) *Ex-Officio Member* | |

## Juvenile Justice

| Majority Members | Minority Members |
| --- | --- |
| Tom Weldon, Jr. (R-3) *Chair* | Pamela "Pam" Dickerson (D-113) |
| Mandi Ballinger (R-23) *Vice Chair* | Stacey Evans (D-42) |
| Paulette Rakestraw (R-19) *Secretary* | Scott Holcomb (D-81) |
| Stephen Allison (R-8) | Henry "Wayne" Howard (D-124) |
| Alex Atwood (R-179) | Sheila Jones (D-53) |
| Wesley E. "Wes" Cantrell (R-22) | Dar'shun N. Kendrick (D-93) |
| Joyce Chandler (R-105) | Mary Margaret Oliver (D-82) |
| Christian Coomer (R-14) | Dexter Sharper (D-177) |
| Chuck Efstration (R-104) | Erica R. Thomas (D-39) |
| Jodi Lott (R-122) | Keisha Waites (D-60) |
| Regina Quick (R-117) | David Wilkerson (D-38) |
| Brad Raffensperger (R-50) | |
| Jason Spencer (R-180) | |
| Sam Watson (R-172) | |
| Andrew J. "Andy" Welch III (R-110) | |

## Legislative and Congressional Reapportionment

| Majority Members | Minority Members |
| --- | --- |
| Randy Nix (R-69) *Chair* | Kimberly Alexander (D-66) |
| Susan Dykes Holmes (R-129) *Vice Chair* | Sharon Beasley-Teague (D-65) |
| Ed Rynders (R-152) *Secretary* | Pamela "Pam" Dickerson (D-113) |
| Kevin Cooke (R-18) | Mack Jackson (D-128) |
| Tom Dickson (R-6) | Rahn Mayo (D-84) |
| Matt Dollar (R-45) | Sandra G. Scott (D-76) |
| Earl Ehrhart (R-36) | Edward "Mickey" Stephens (D-165) |
| Jan Jones (R-47) | Mable "Able" Thomas (D-56) |
| Chuck Efstration (R-104) | |
| Ed Setzler (R-35) | |
| Lynn Ratigan Smith (R-70) | |
| Richard H. Smith (R-134) | |
| John Phillip Yates (R-73) | |

## Motor Vehicles

| Majority Members | Minority Members |
| --- | --- |
| Tom Rice (R-95) *Chair* | Kimberly Alexander (D-66) |
| Kevin K. Tanner (R-9) *Vice Chair* | Demetrius Douglas (D-78) |
| Paul R. Battles (R-15) *Secretary* | Henry "Wayne" Howard (D-124) |
| Timothy Barr (R-103) | Darryl Jordan (D-77) |
| Johnnie Caldwell, Jr. (R-131) | Brian Prince (D-127) |
| James "Bubber" Epps (R-144) | Robert T. "Bob" Trammell, Jr. (D-132) |
| J.B. "Jeff" Jones (R-167) | |
| Alan Powell (R-32) | |
| David J. Stover (R-71) | |
| John Phillip Yates (R-73) | |

LEGISLATIVE BRANCH

## Natural Resources and Environment

**Majority Members**
Lynn Ratigan Smith (R-70) *Chair*
Oren H. "Buddy" Harden (R-148)
   *Vice Chair*
Sam Watson (R-172) *Secretary*
Timothy Barr (R-103)
Brooks P. Coleman, Jr. (R-97)
John L. Corbett (R-174)
Robert Dickey (R-140)
Terry Lamar England (R-116)
James "Bubber" Epps (R-144)
Dan Gasaway (R-28)
Sheri Gilligan (R-24)
J.B. "Jeff" Jones (R-167)
Tom McCall (R-33)
Greg Morris (R-156)
Chad Nimmer (R-178)
Randy Nix (R-69)
Richard H. Smith (R-134)
Jan Tankersley (R-160)
Kevin K. Tanner (R-9)
Chuck Williams (R-119)

**Minority Members**
Debbie G. Buckner (D-137)
Karla Lea Drenner (D-85)
Pat Gardner (D-57)
Mable "Able" Thomas (D-56)

## Public Safety and Homeland Security

**Majority Members**
Alan Powell (R-32) *Chair*
Darlene K. Taylor (R-173)
   *Vice Chair*
Alex Atwood (R-179) *Secretary*
Heath N. Clark (R-147)
Kevin Cooke (R-18)
Micah Gravley (R-67)
Gerald E. Greene (R-151)
Dustin "Dusty" Hightower (R-68)
Col. William "Bill" Hitchens
   (R-161)
Rick Jasperse (R-11)
Eddie Lumsden (R-12)
Jesse L. Petrea (R-166)

**Minority Members**
Gloria Frazier (D-126)
Mike Glanton, Sr. (D-75)
Scott Holcomb (D-81)
Mack Jackson (D-128)
Keisha Waites (D-60)

## Regulated Industries

**Majority Members**
Howard R. Maxwell (R-17) *Chair*
Brett Harrell (R-106) *Vice Chair*
Tom Dickson (R-6) *Secretary*
Joyce Chandler (R-105)
Kevin Cooke (R-18)
Sharon Cooper (R-43)
John Deffenbaugh (R-1)
Rich Golick (R-40)
Lee Hawkins (R-27)
Charles E. "Chuck" Martin, Jr.
   (R-49)
Alan Powell (R-32)
Paulette Rakestraw (R-19)
Matt Ramsey (R-72)
Terry Rogers (R-10)
Dale Rutledge (R-109)
Tom Taylor (R-79)
Andrew J. "Andy" Welch III
   (R-110)

**Minority Members**
Karen Bennett (D-94)
Virgil Fludd (D-64)
Billy Mitchell (D-88)
Edward "Mickey" Stephens (D-165)

## Retirement

**Majority Members**
Paul R. Battles (R-15) *Chair*
Tom Kirby (R-114) *Vice Chair*
Sam Watson (R-172) *Secretary*
Tommy Benton (R-31)
Brooks P. Coleman, Jr. (R-97)
Christian Coomer (R-14)
Gerald E. Greene (R-151)
Howard R. Maxwell (R-17)
John D. Meadows III (R-5)
Tom Weldon, Jr. (R-3)

**Minority Members**
Patty Bentley (D-139)
James Beverly (D-143)
Debbie G. Buckner (D-137)
J. Craig Gordon (D-163)
David Wilkerson (D-38)
Earnest "Coach" Williams (D-87)

## Rules

**Majority Members**
John D. Meadows III (R-5) *Chair*
Allen M. Peake (R-141) *Vice Chair*
Richard H. Smith (R-134) *Secretary*
Mandi Ballinger (R-23)
Tommy Benton (R-31)
Jon G. Burns (R-159)
Sharon Cooper (R-43)
Katie M. Dempsey (R-13)
Tom Dickson (R-6)
Earl Ehrhart (R-36)
Barry A. Fleming (R-121)
Rich Golick (R-40)
Gerald E. Greene (R-151)
Matt Hatchett (R-150)
Jan Jones (R-47)
David Knight (R-130)
Greg Morris (R-156)
Larry J. "Butch" Parrish (R-158)
Alan Powell (R-32)
Jay Powell (R-171)
Matt Ramsey (R-72)
Tom Rice (R-95)
Carl W. Rogers (R-29)
Terry Rogers (R-10)
Ed Setzler (R-35)
Barbara Sims (R-123)
Lynn Ratigan Smith (R-70)
Ron Stephens (R-164)
Tom Weldon, Jr. (R-3)
Wendell Willard (R-51)

**Minority Members**
Stacey Y. Abrams (D-89)
Karla Lea Drenner (D-85)
Stacey Evans (D-42)
Carolyn Fleming Hugley (D-136)
Mack Jackson (D-128)
Calvin Smyre (D-135)
Al Williams (D-168)

## Science and Technology

**Majority Members**
Ed Setzler (R-35) *Chair*
Paulette Rakestraw (R-19)
   *Vice Chair*
David J. Stover (R-71) *Secretary*
Heath N. Clark (R-147)
Mike Dudgeon (R-25)
Geoff L. Duncan (R-26)
Charles E. "Chuck" Martin, Jr.
   (R-49)
Clay Pirkle (R-155)
Barbara Sims (R-123)
Jason Spencer (R-180)
Scot Turner (R-21)

**Members**
E. Culver "Rusty" Kidd (I-145)

**Minority Members**
Dorothy "Dee" Dawkins-Haigler
   (D-91)
Spencer Frye (D-118)
Pedro "Pete" Marin (D-96)
Mary Margaret Oliver (D-82)
Sandra G. Scott (D-76)
Michael Smith (D-41)
Erica R. Thomas (D-39)
Mable "Able" Thomas (D-56)
David Wilkerson (D-38)

## Small Business Development

**Majority Members**
James "Bubber" Epps (R-144)
   *Chair*
John Deffenbaugh (R-1) *Vice Chair*
Oren H. "Buddy" Harden (R-148)
   *Secretary*
Wesley E. "Wes" Cantrell (R-22)
Amy Alexander Carter (R-175)
David Clark (R-98)
Mike Dudgeon (R-25)
Tom Kirby (R-114)
David Knight (R-130)
Allen M. Peake (R-141)
John David Pezold (R-133)
Alan Powell (R-32)
Paulette Rakestraw (R-19)
David J. Stover (R-71)
Steve Tarvin (R-2)

**Minority Members**
Taylor J. Bennett (D-80)
James Beverly (D-143)
Roger B. Bruce (D-61)
Doreen Carter (D-92)
Karla Lea Drenner (D-85)
Virgil Fludd (D-64)
Michele D. Henson (D-86)
Mack Jackson (D-128)
LaDawn Jones (D-62)
Dar'shun N. Kendrick (D-93)
Dexter Sharper (D-177)
Jason "Jay" Shaw (D-176)
Valencia Stovall (D-74)

## Special Rules

**Majority Members**
Rick Jasperse (R-11) *Chair*
Sam Watson (R-172) *Vice Chair*
Jason Spencer (R-180) *Secretary*
Stephen Allison (R-8)
Z. Shaw Blackmon (R-146)
Susan Dykes Holmes (R-129)
Dustin "Dusty" Hightower (R-68)
Tom Kirby (R-114)
Dominic F. LaRiccia (R-169)
Paulette Rakestraw (R-19)
Trey Rhodes (R-120)
Kevin K. Tanner (R-9)
Scot Turner (R-21)

**Minority Members**
James Beverly (D-143)
Doreen Carter (D-92)
Winfred J. Dukes (D-154)
J. Craig Gordon (D-163)
Marie R. Metze (D-55)
Brian Prince (D-127)
Sandra G. Scott (D-76)
Michael Smith (D-41)
Keisha Waites (D-60)

## State Planning and Community Affairs

**Majority Members**
Jimmy Pruett (R-149) *Chair*
Terry Rogers (R-10) *Vice Chair*
Regina Quick (R-117) *Secretary*
Michael Caldwell (R-20)
Kevin Cooke (R-18)
Scot Turner (R-21)

**Minority Members**
Beth Beskin (D-54)
Pamela "Pam" Dickerson (D-113)
Winfred J. Dukes (D-154)
Mack Jackson (D-128)
Dewey McClain (D-100)
Earnest "Coach" Williams (D-87)

## State Properties

**Majority Members**
Barbara Sims (R-123) *Chair*
Emory Dunahoo, Jr. (R-30)
  *Vice Chair*
Gerald E. Greene (R-151) *Secretary*
Jon G. Burns (R-159)
Mike Cheokas (R-138)
David Clark (R-98)
Eddie Lumsden (R-12)
Clay Pirkle (R-155)
William A. "Bill" Werkheiser
  (R-157)

**Minority Members**
Debbie G. Buckner (D-137)
Darrel Bush Ealum (D-153)
LaDawn Jones (D-62)
Michael Smith (D-41)

**Members**
E. Culver "Rusty" Kidd (I-145)

## Transportation

**Majority Members**
Christian Coomer (R-14) *Chair*
Valerie Clark (R-101) *Vice Chair*
James "Bubber" Epps (R-144)
  *Secretary*
Mandi Ballinger (R-23)
Tommy Benton (R-31)
Jon G. Burns (R-159)
John Carson (R-46)
John Deffenbaugh (R-1)
Katie M. Dempsey (R-13)
Brett Harrell (R-106)
Tom McCall (R-33)
Chad Nimmer (R-178)
Dale Rutledge (R-109)
Ed Rynders (R-152)
Ed Setzler (R-35)
Barbara Sims (R-123)
Sam Watson (R-172)

**Minority Members**
Pat Gardner (D-57)
Sheila Jones (D-53)
Darryl Jordan (D-77)
Brian Prince (D-127)
Keisha Waites (D-60)
Al Williams (D-168)

## Ways and Means

**Majority Members**
Jay Powell (R-171) *Chair*
Allen M. Peake (R-141) *Vice Chair*
Brett Harrell (R-106) *Secretary*
Paul R. Battles (R-15)
John Carson (R-46)
Geoff L. Duncan (R-26)
Penny Houston (R-170)
Trey Kelley (R-16)
David Knight (R-130)
Charles E. "Chuck" Martin, Jr.
  (R-49)
Byung "B.J." Pak (R-108)

**Minority Members**
Stacey Y. Abrams (D-89)
Sharon Beasley-Teague (D-65)
Virgil Fludd (D-64)
Howard Mosby (D-83)
Edward "Mickey" Stephens (D-165)

**Majority Members** *continued*
Don Parsons (R-44)
Matt Ramsey (R-72)
Tom Rice (R-95)
Dale Rutledge (R-109)
Ed Rynders (R-152)
Ron Stephens (R-164)
Sam Teasley (R-37)
Wendell Willard (R-51)
Bruce Williamson (R-115)
Terry Lamar England (R-116)
  *Ex-Officio Member*

# Guam Legislature

155 Hessler Place, Hagatna, GU 96910
Tel: (671) 472-7679   Tel: (671) 472-3499 (Protocol Office)
Fax: (671) 472-3459   Internet: www.guamlegislature.com

Speaker of the Legislature **Judith T. Won Pat** (D) . . . . . . . (671) 472-3586
  155 Hesler Street, Hagatna, GU 96910
  Education: San Diego EdD
Vice Speaker of the Legislature **Benjamin J.F. Cruz** (D) . . . (671) 477-2520
  Education: Santa Clara U 1975 JD
Legislative Secretary **Tina Rose Muña-Barnes** (D) . . . . . . . (671) 472-3455
Majority Leader **Rory J. Respicio** (D) . . . . . . . . . . . . . . (671) 472-7679
  Education: Maryland University Col BS
Assistant Majority Leader **Thomas C. "Tom" Ada** (D) . . . (671) 473-3301
Majority Whip **Dennis G. Rodriguez, Jr.** (D) . . . . . . . . . . (671) 649-8638
Assistant Majority Whip **Michael F.Q. San Nicolas** (D) . . . (671) 472-6453
Minority Leader **V. Anthony "Tony" Ada** (R) . . . . . . . . . . (671) 472-9681
Assistant Minority Leader **Brant McCreadie** (R) . . . . . . . . (671) 472-3462
Minority Whip **Mary Camacho Torres** (R) . . . . . . . . . . . (671) 475-6279
Assistant Minority Whip
  **Thomas "Tommy" Morrison** (R) . . . . . . . . . . . . . . . . (671) 478-8669
Executive Director **Vince P. Arriola** . . . . . . . . . . . . . . . . . (671) 472-3545
  E-mail: vparriola1@gmail.com
Parliamentarian of the Legislature
  **Benjamin J.F. Cruz** (D) . . . . . . . . . . . . . . . . . . . . . . . (671) 477-2520
Clerk of the Legislature **Rennae V. Meno** . . . . . . . . . . . . . (671) 472-3541
  E-mail: rennae@guamlegislature.org    Fax: (671) 472-3524
Sergeant-at-Arms **Thomas Unsiog** . . . . . . . . . . . . . . . . . . (671) 472-3540
  E-mail: sgtarms@guamlegislature.org
Legislative Counsel **Therese Terlaje** . . . . . . . . . . . . . . . . (671) 477-8894
  Union Bank Building, 194 Hernan Cortes Avenue,    Fax: (671) 472-8896
  Suite 209, Hagatna, GU 96910
  E-mail: tterlaje@guam.net

## Senators

**Party Affiliation Statistics:** Republicans: 6, Democrats: 9

Senator **Thomas C. "Tom" Ada** (D-At-Large) . . . . . . . . . . (671) 473-3301
  Counties Represented: At Large    Fax: (671) 473-3303
  Term Expires: 2017
  Ada Plaza Center, 173 Aspinall Avenue, Suite 207, Hagatna, GU 96910
  E-mail: tom@senatorada.org
  Committees: Early Learning, Juvenile Justice, Public Education and
  First Generation Initiatives; Finance and Taxation, General Government
  Operations, and Youth Development; Guam U.S. Military Relocation,
  Public Safety, and Judiciary; Health, Economic Development,
  Homeland Security, and Senior Citizens; Rules, Federal, Foreign and
  Micronesian Affairs, Human and Natural Resources, Election Reform,
  and Capitol District; Transportation, Infrastructure, Lands, Border
  Protection, Veterans' Affairs and Procurement
Senator **V. Anthony "Tony" Ada** (R-At-Large) . . . . . . . . . (671) 472-9681
  Counties Represented: At Large    Tel: (671) 472-9682
  Term Expires: 2017    Fax: (671) 472-9683
  140 Aspinall Avenue, Suite 202, Hagatna, GU 96910
  E-mail: senatortonyada@guamlegislature.org
  Committees: Appropriations and Adjudication; Early Learning, Juvenile
  Justice, Public Education and First Generation Initiatives; Guam U.S.
  Military Relocation, Public Safety, and Judiciary; Health, Economic
  Development, Homeland Security, and Senior Citizens; Higher
  Education, Culture, Public Libraries, and Women's Affairs; Municipal
  Affairs, Tourism, Housing and Historic Preservation; Rules, Federal,
  Foreign and Micronesian Affairs, Human and Natural Resources,
  Election Reform, and Capitol District
Senator **Frank B. Aguon, Jr.** (D-At-Large) . . . . . . . . . . . . (671) 472-4861
  Counties Represented: At Large    Tel: (671) 472-4862
  Term Expires: 2017
  DNA Building, 238 Archbishop Flores Street, Suite 907,
  Hagatna, GU 96910
  E-mail: aguon4guam@gmail.com
  Committees: Appropriations and Adjudication; Early Learning, Juvenile
  Justice, Public Education and First Generation Initiatives; Finance and
  Taxation, General Government Operations, and Youth Development;
  Guam U.S. Military Relocation, Public Safety, and Judiciary; Health,
  Economic Development, Homeland Security, and Senior Citizens;
  Rules, Federal, Foreign and Micronesian Affairs, Human and Natural
  Resources, Election Reform, and Capitol District; Transportation,
  Infrastructure, Lands, Border Protection, Veterans' Affairs and
  Procurement

Senator **Frank F. Blas, Jr.** (R-At-Large) . . . . . . . . . . . . . . (671) 475-2527
  Counties Represented: At Large    Fax: (671) 475-2422
  Term Expires: 2017
  238 Archbishop Flores Street, Suite 801, Hagatna, GU 96910
  E-mail: frank.blasjr@gmail.com
  Committees: Guam U.S. Military Relocation, Public Safety, and
  Judiciary; Municipal Affairs, Tourism, Housing and Historic
  Preservation; Transportation, Infrastructure, Lands, Border Protection,
  Veterans' Affairs and Procurement
Senator **Benjamin J.F. Cruz** (D-At-Large) Suite 107 . . . . . (671) 477-2520
  Counties Represented: At Large    Tel: (671) 477-2521
  Term Expires: 2017    Fax: (671) 477-2522
  E-mail: senator@senatorbjcruz.com
  Committees: Appropriations and Adjudication; Early Learning, Juvenile
  Justice, Public Education and First Generation Initiatives; Finance and
  Taxation, General Government Operations, and Youth Development;
  Guam U.S. Military Relocation, Public Safety, and Judiciary; Health,
  Economic Development, Homeland Security, and Senior Citizens;
  Higher Education, Culture, Public Libraries, and Women's Affairs;
  Municipal Affairs, Tourism, Housing and Historic Preservation; Rules,
  Federal, Foreign and Micronesian Affairs, Human and Natural
  Resources, Election Reform, and Capitol District; Transportation,
  Infrastructure, Lands, Border Protection, Veterans' Affairs and
  Procurement
Senator **James V. "Jim" Espaldon** (R-At-Large) . . . . . . . . (671) 475-4546
  Counties Represented: At Large    Fax: (671) 475-2422
  Term Expires: 2017
  238 Archbishop Flores Street, Suite 801, Hagatna, GU 96910
  E-mail: jespaldonesq@gmail.com
  Committees: Finance and Taxation, General Government Operations,
  and Youth Development; Guam U.S. Military Relocation, Public Safety,
  and Judiciary; Municipal Affairs, Tourism, Housing and Historic
  Preservation; Transportation, Infrastructure, Lands, Border Protection,
  Veterans' Affairs and Procurement
Senator **Brant McCreadie** (R-At-Large) . . . . . . . . . . . . . . (671) 472-3462
  Counties Represented: At Large    Tel: (671) 472-3463
  Term Expires: 2017
  De La Corte Building, 167 East Marine Corp Drive, Suite 102,
  Hagatna, GU 96910
  E-mail: brantforguam@gmail.com
  Committees: Early Learning, Juvenile Justice, Public Education and
  First Generation Initiatives; Guam U.S. Military Relocation, Public
  Safety, and Judiciary; Health, Economic Development, Homeland
  Security, and Senior Citizens; Municipal Affairs, Tourism, Housing and
  Historic Preservation
Senator **Thomas "Tommy" Morrison** (R-At-Large) . . . . . . (671) 478-8669
  Counties Represented: At Large
  Term Expires: 2017
  Ada Plaza Center Building B, 173 Aspinall Avenue, Suite 202 & 203B,
  Hagatna, GU 96910
  E-mail: tommy@senatormorrison.com
  Committees: Appropriations and Adjudication; Early Learning, Juvenile
  Justice, Public Education and First Generation Initiatives; Health,
  Economic Development, Homeland Security, and Senior Citizens
Senator **Tina Rose Muña-Barnes** (D-At-Large)
  Suite 101 . . . . . . . . . . . . . . . . . . . . . . . . . . . . . . . . . . (671) 472-3455
  Counties Represented: At Large    Tel: (671) 472-3456
  Term Expires: 2017    Fax: (671) 472-3400
  E-mail: tinamunabarnes@gmail.com
  Committees: Appropriations and Adjudication; Early Learning, Juvenile
  Justice, Public Education and First Generation Initiatives; Finance and
  Taxation, General Government Operations, and Youth Development;
  Health, Economic Development, Homeland Security, and Senior
  Citizens; Higher Education, Culture, Public Libraries, and Women's
  Affairs; Municipal Affairs, Tourism, Housing and Historic Preservation;
  Rules, Federal, Foreign and Micronesian Affairs, Human and Natural
  Resources, Election Reform, and Capitol District
Senator **Rory J. Respicio** (D-At-Large) Suite 302 . . . . . . . . (671) 472-7679
  Counties Represented: At Large    Tel: (671) 472-3545
  Term Expires: 2017    Tel: (671) 472-3546
  E-mail: roryforguam@gmail.com    Fax: (671) 472-3547
  Committees: Early Learning, Juvenile Justice, Public Education and
  First Generation Initiatives; Finance and Taxation, General Government
  Operations, and Youth Development; Guam U.S. Military Relocation,
  Public Safety, and Judiciary; Health, Economic Development,
  Homeland Security, and Senior Citizens; Higher Education, Culture,
  Public Libraries, and Women's Affairs; Municipal Affairs, Tourism,
  Housing and Historic Preservation; Rules, Federal, Foreign and
  Micronesian Affairs, Human and Natural Resources, Election Reform,
  and Capitol District; Transportation, Infrastructure, Lands, Border
  Protection, Veterans' Affairs and Procurement

**LEGISLATIVE BRANCH**

Senator **Dennis G. Rodriguez, Jr.** (D-At-Large) . . . . . . . . (671) 649-8638
  Counties Represented: At Large
  Term Expires: 2017
  176 Serenu Avenue, Suite 107, Tamuning, GU 96931
  Tel: (671) 649-0511
  Fax: (671) 649-0520
  E-mail: senatordrodriguez@gmail.com
  Committees: Appropriations and Adjudication; Finance and Taxation,
  General Government Operations, and Youth Development; Guam U.S.
  Military Relocation, Public Safety, and Judiciary; Health, Economic
  Development, Homeland Security, and Senior Citizens; Municipal
  Affairs, Tourism, Housing and Historic Preservation; Rules, Federal,
  Foreign and Micronesian Affairs, Human and Natural Resources,
  Election Reform, and Capitol District; Transportation, Infrastructure,
  Lands, Border Protection, Veterans' Affairs and Procurement

Senator **Michael F.Q. San Nicolas** (D-At-Large) . . . . . . . . (671) 472-6453
  Counties Represented: At Large
  Term Expires: 2017
  E-mail: senatorsannicolas@gmail.com
  Committees: Appropriations and Adjudication; Early Learning, Juvenile
  Justice, Public Education and First Generation Initiatives; Finance and
  Taxation, General Government Operations, and Youth Development;
  Rules, Federal, Foreign and Micronesian Affairs, Human and Natural
  Resources, Election Reform, and Capitol District

Senator **Mary Camacho Torres** (R-At-Large) . . . . . . . . . . (671) 475-6279
  Counties Represented: At Large
  Term Expires: 2017
  238 Archbishop Flores Street, Suite 801, Hagatna, GU 96910
  Fax: (671) 475-2422
  E-mail: marycamachotorres@gmail.com
  Committees: Appropriations and Adjudication; Early Learning, Juvenile
  Justice, Public Education and First Generation Initiatives; Finance and
  Taxation, General Government Operations, and Youth Development;
  Higher Education, Culture, Public Libraries, and Women's Affairs;
  Municipal Affairs, Tourism, Housing and Historic Preservation; Rules,
  Federal, Foreign and Micronesian Affairs, Human and Natural
  Resources, Election Reform, and Capitol District; Transportation,
  Infrastructure, Lands, Border Protection, Veterans' Affairs and
  Procurement

Senator
**Nerissa Bretania Underwood, PhD** (D-At-Large)
  Suite 104 . . . . . . . . . . . . . . . . . . . . . . . . . . . . . . . . . . . (671) 969-0973
  Counties Represented: At Large
  Term Expires: 2017
  E-mail: senatorunderwood@guamlegislature.org
  Committees: Appropriations and Adjudication; Early Learning, Juvenile
  Justice, Public Education and First Generation Initiatives; Finance and
  Taxation, General Government Operations, and Youth Development;
  Guam U.S. Military Relocation, Public Safety, and Judiciary; Health,
  Economic Development, Homeland Security, and Senior Citizens;
  Higher Education, Culture, Public Libraries, and Women's Affairs;
  Municipal Affairs, Tourism, Housing and Historic Preservation; Rules,
  Federal, Foreign and Micronesian Affairs, Human and Natural
  Resources, Election Reform, and Capitol District; Transportation,
  Infrastructure, Lands, Border Protection, Veterans' Affairs and
  Procurement
  Education: U Guam 1981 BA; Oregon 1985 MS, 1989 PhD

Senator **Judith T. Won Pat** (D-At-Large) Suite 201 . . . . . (671) 472-3586
  Counties Represented: At Large
  Term Expires: 2017
  E-mail: speaker@judiwonpat.com
  Tel: (671) 472-3587
  Tel: (671) 472-3588
  Fax: (671) 472-3589
  Committees: Early Learning, Juvenile Justice, Public Education and
  First Generation Initiatives; Finance and Taxation, General Government
  Operations, and Youth Development; Higher Education, Culture, Public
  Libraries, and Women's Affairs; Municipal Affairs, Tourism, Housing
  and Historic Preservation; Rules, Federal, Foreign and Micronesian
  Affairs, Human and Natural Resources, Election Reform, and Capitol
  District

## Senate Standing Committees

Tel: (671) 472-3499  Fax: (671) 472-3403

## Appropriations and Adjudication

| Majority Members | Minority Members |
|---|---|
| Benjamin J.F. Cruz (D) *Chairperson* | V. Anthony "Tony" Ada (R) |
| Frank B. Aguon, Jr. (D) | Thomas "Tommy" Morrison (R) |
| *Vice Chairperson* | Mary Camacho Torres (R) |
| Tina Rose Muña-Barnes (D) | |
| Dennis G. Rodriguez, Jr. (D) | |
| Michael F.Q. San Nicolas (D) | |
| Nerissa Bretania Underwood (D) | |

## Early Learning, Juvenile Justice, Public Education and First Generation Initiatives

| Majority Members | Minority Members |
|---|---|
| Nerissa Bretania Underwood (D) | V. Anthony "Tony" Ada (R) |
| *Chairperson* | Brant McCreadie (R) |
| Judith T. Won Pat (D) | Thomas "Tommy" Morrison (R) |
| *Vice Chairperson* | Mary Camacho Torres (R) |
| Thomas C. "Tom" Ada (D) | |
| Frank B. Aguon, Jr. (D) | |
| Benjamin J.F. Cruz (D) | |
| Tina Rose Muña-Barnes (D) | |
| Rory J. Respicio (D) | |
| Michael F.Q. San Nicolas (D) | |

## Finance and Taxation, General Government Operations, and Youth Development

| Majority Members | Minority Members |
|---|---|
| Michael F.Q. San Nicolas (D) | Mary Camacho Torres (R) |
| *Chairperson* | *Vice Chairperson* |
| Thomas C. "Tom" Ada (D) | James V. "Jim" Espaldon (R) |
| Frank B. Aguon, Jr. (D) | |
| Benjamin J.F. Cruz (D) | |
| Tina Rose Muña-Barnes (D) | |
| Rory J. Respicio (D) | |
| Dennis G. Rodriguez, Jr. (D) | |
| Nerissa Bretania Underwood (D) | |
| Judith T. Won Pat (D) | |

## Health, Economic Development, Homeland Security, and Senior Citizens

| Majority Members | Minority Members |
|---|---|
| Dennis G. Rodriguez, Jr. (D) | V. Anthony "Tony" Ada (R) |
| *Chairperson* | *Vice Chairperson* |
| Thomas C. "Tom" Ada (D) | Brant McCreadie (R) |
| Frank B. Aguon, Jr. (D) | Thomas "Tommy" Morrison (R) |
| Benjamin J.F. Cruz (D) | |
| Tina Rose Muña-Barnes (D) | |
| Rory J. Respicio (D) | |
| Nerissa Bretania Underwood (D) | |

## Higher Education, Culture, Public Libraries, and Women's Affairs

| Majority Members | Minority Members |
|---|---|
| Judith T. Won Pat (D) *Chairperson* | V. Anthony "Tony" Ada (R) |
| Nerissa Bretania Underwood (D) | Mary Camacho Torres (R) |
| *Vice Chairperson* | |
| Benjamin J.F. Cruz (D) | |
| Tina Rose Muña-Barnes (D) | |
| Rory J. Respicio (D) | |

## Guam U.S. Military Relocation, Public Safety, and Judiciary

| Majority Members | Minority Members |
|---|---|
| Frank B. Aguon, Jr. (D) | V. Anthony "Tony" Ada (R) |
| *Chairperson* | Frank F. Blas (R) |
| Thomas C. "Tom" Ada (D) | James V. "Jim" Espaldon (R) |
| *Vice Chairperson* | Brant McCreadie (R) |
| Benjamin J.F. Cruz (D) | |
| Rory J. Respicio (D) | |
| Dennis G. Rodriguez, Jr. (D) | |
| Nerissa Bretania Underwood (D) | |

## Municipal Affairs, Tourism, Housing and Historic Preservation

| Majority Members | Minority Members |
|---|---|
| Tina Rose Muña-Barnes (D) | V. Anthony "Tony" Ada (R) |
| *Chairperson* | Frank F. Blas, Jr. (R) |
| Benjamin J.F. Cruz (D) | James V. "Jim" Espaldon (R) |
| *Vice Chairperson* | Brant McCreadie (R) |
| Rory J. Respicio (D) | Mary Camacho Torres (R) |
| Dennis G. Rodriguez, Jr. (D) | |
| Nerissa Bretania Underwood (D) | |
| Judith T. Won Pat (D) | |

## Rules, Federal, Foreign and Micronesian Affairs, Human and Natural Resources, Election Reform, and Capitol District

**Majority Members**
Rory J. Respicio (D) *Chairperson*
Thomas C. "Tom" Ada (D)
  *Vice Chairperson*
Frank B. Aguon, Jr. (D)
Benjamin J.F. Cruz (D)
Tina Rose Muña-Barnes (D)
Dennis G. Rodriguez, Jr. (D)
Michael F.Q. San Nicolas (D)
Nerissa Bretania Underwood (D)
Judith T. Won Pat (D)

**Minority Members**
V. Anthony "Tony" Ada (R)
Mary Camacho Torres (R)

## Transportation, Infrastructure, Lands, Border Protection, Veterans' Affairs and Procurement

**Majority Members**
Thomas C. "Tom" Ada (D)
  *Chairperson*
Rory J. Respicio (D)
  *Vice Chairperson*
Frank B. Aguon, Jr. (D)
Benjamin J.F. Cruz (D)
Dennis G. Rodriguez, Jr. (D)
Nerissa Bretania Underwood (D)

**Minority Members**
Frank F. Blas, Jr. (R)
James V. "Jim" Espaldon (R)
Mary Camacho Torres (R)

# Hawaii Legislature

State Capitol, 415 South Beretania Street, Honolulu, HI 96813
Tel: (808) 587-0666 (Legislative Reference Bureau)
Tel: (808) 587-0690 (Legislative Reference Bureau Library)
Internet: www.capitol.hawaii.gov

## Hawaii Senate

Tel: (808) 586-6720  Fax: (808) 586-6719
E-mail: sens@capitol.hawaii.gov

President of the Senate **Ronald D. "Ron" Kouchi** (D) .... (808) 586-6030
Vice President of the Senate **Will Espero** (D) ........... (808) 586-6360
  Education: Seattle 1982 BA
Majority Leader **J. Kalani English** (D) ................. (808) 587-7225
  Education: Hawaii 1989 BA, 1995 MA
Majority Floor Leader and Majority Whip
  **Josh Green** (D) .................................... (808) 586-9385
  Education: Penn State 1997 MD
Majority Caucus Leader **Brickwood Galuteria** (D) ....... (808) 586-6740
  Education: Pacific U 1974 BS
Majority Whip **Donovan M. Dela Cruz** (D) ............... (808) 586-6090
  Education: Oregon 1994 BA
Minority Leader **Sam Slom** (R) ........................ (808) 586-8420
  Education: Hawaii 1963 BA; La Salle U 1966 LLB
Minority Floor Leader **Sam Slom** (R) .................. (808) 586-8420
Chief Clerk of the Senate **Carol Taniguchi** ........... (808) 586-6720
  E-mail: sclerk@capitol.hawaii.gov
Sergeant-at-Arms **Bienvenido C. Villaflor** ............ (808) 586-6725
                                              Fax: (808) 586-6659

## Senators

**Party Affiliation Statistics:** Republicans: 1, Democrats: 24

Senator **Rosalyn H. Baker** (D-District 6)
  Hawaii State Capitol, Room 230 .................... (808) 586-6070
  Counties Represented: Maui (part)         Fax: (808) 586-6071
  Term Expires: 2018
  E-mail: senbaker@capitol.hawaii.gov
  Committees: Commerce, Consumer Protection and Health; Economic
  Development, Environment, and Technology; Public Safety,
  Intergovernmental, and Military Affairs
  Education: Southwest Texas State 1968 BA

Senator **Suzanne Chun Oakland** (D-District 13)
  Hawaii State Capitol, Room 226 ................... (808) 586-6130
  Counties Represented: Honolulu (part)     Fax: (808) 586-6131
  Term Expires: 2016
  E-mail: senchunoakland@capitol.hawaii.gov
  Committees: Education; Human Services; Transportation and Energy;
  Ways and Means
  Education: Hawaii 1983 BA

Senator **Donovan M. Dela Cruz** (D-District 22)
  Hawaii State Capitol, Room 202 ................... (808) 586-6090
  Counties Represented: Honolulu (part)     Fax: (808) 586-6091
  Term Expires: 2016
  E-mail: sendelacruz@capitol.hawaii.gov
  Committees: Education; Government Operations; Water, Land, and
  Agriculture; Ways and Means

Senator **J. Kalani English** (D-District 7)
  Hawaii State Capitol, Room 205 ................... (808) 587-7225
  Counties Represented: Maui (part)         Fax: (808) 587-7230
  Term Expires: 2018
  E-mail: senenglish@capitol.hawaii.gov
  Committees: Hawaiian Affairs; Tourism and International Affairs;
  Transportation and Energy; Ways and Means

Senator **Will Espero** (D-District 19)
  Hawaii State Capitol, Room 206 ................... (808) 586-6360
  Counties Represented: Honolulu (part)     Fax: (808) 586-6361
  Term Expires: 2016
  E-mail: senespero@capitol.hawaii.gov
  Committees: Commerce, Consumer Protection and Health; Economic
  Development, Environment, and Technology; Public Safety,
  Intergovernmental, and Military Affairs

Senator **Gerald M. "Mike" Gabbard** (D-District 20)
Hawaii State Capitol, Room 201 . . . . . . . . . . . . . . . . . . (808) 586-6830
Counties Represented: Honolulu (part)        Fax: (808) 586-6679
Term Expires: 2016
E-mail: sengabbard@capitol.hawaii.gov
Committees: Higher Education and the Arts; Judiciary and Labor;
Transportation and Energy; Water, Land, and Agriculture
Education: Sonoma State 1971 BA; Oregon State 1980 MEd

Senator **Brickwood Galuteria** (D-District 12)
Hawaii State Capitol, Room 223 . . . . . . . . . . . . . . . . . . (808) 586-6740
Counties Represented: Honolulu (part)        Fax: (808) 586-6829
Term Expires: 2018
E-mail: sengaluteria@capitol.hawaii.gov
Committees: Economic Development, Environment, and Technology;
Housing; Tourism and International Affairs; Ways and Means

Senator **Josh Green** (D-District 3)
Hawaii State Capitol, Room 407 . . . . . . . . . . . . . . . . . . (808) 586-9385
Counties Represented: Hawaii (part)        Fax: (808) 586-9391
Term Expires: 2018
E-mail: sengreen@capitol.hawaii.gov
Committees: Housing; Human Services; Tourism and International
Affairs

Senator **Breene Y. Harimoto** (D-District 16)
Hawaii State Capitol, Room 215 . . . . . . . . . . . . . . . . . . (808) 586-6230
Counties Represented: Honolulu (part)        Fax: (808) 586-6231
Term Expires: 2018
E-mail: senharimoto@capitol.hawaii.gov
Committees: Education; Housing; Human Services; Ways and Means

Senator **Les Ihara, Jr.** (D-District 10)
Hawaii State Capitol, Room 220 . . . . . . . . . . . . . . . . . . (808) 586-6250
Counties Represented: Honolulu (part)        Fax: (808) 586-6251
Term Expires: 2016
E-mail: senihara@capitol.hawaii.gov
Committees: Commerce, Consumer Protection and Health; Economic
Development, Environment, and Technology; Government Operations;
Housing
Education: Hawaii 1975 BA

Senator **Lorraine R. Inouye** (D-District 4)
Hawaii State Capitol, Room 210 . . . . . . . . . . . . . . . . . . (808) 586-7335
Counties Represented: Hawaii (part)        Fax: (808) 586-7339
Term Expires: 2018
E-mail: seninouye@capitol.hawaii.gov
Committees: Hawaiian Affairs; Public Safety, Intergovernmental, and
Military Affairs; Transportation and Energy; Ways and Means

Senator **Kaialii "Kai" Kahele** (D-District 1) . . . . . . . . . . . . (808) 586-6760
Counties Represented: Hawaii (part)        Fax: (808) 586-6689
Term Expires: 2018
E-mail: senkahele@capitol.hawaii.gov
Committees: Education; Higher Education and the Arts; Judiciary and
Labor; Tourism and International Affairs
Education: Hawaii BA

Senator **Gilbert S. C. Keith-Agaran** (D-District 5)
Hawaii State Capitol, Room 221 . . . . . . . . . . . . . . . . . . (808) 586-7344
Counties Represented: Maui (part)        Fax: (808) 586-7348
Term Expires: 2018
E-mail: senkeithagaran@capitol.hawaii.gov
Committees: Economic Development, Environment, and Technology;
Government Operations; Judiciary and Labor
Education: Yale 1984 BA; Boalt Hall 1987 JD

Senator **Michelle N. Kidani** (D-District 18)
Hawaii State Capitol, Room 228 . . . . . . . . . . . . . . . . . . (808) 586-7100
Counties Represented: Honolulu (part)        Fax: (808) 586-7109
Term Expires: 2018
E-mail: senkidani@capitol.hawaii.gov
Committees: Commerce, Consumer Protection and Health; Education;
Higher Education and the Arts; Transportation and Energy
Education: Kennedy-Western 1993 BS

Senator **Donna Mercado Kim** (D-District 14)
Hawaii State Capitol, Room 218 . . . . . . . . . . . . . . . . . . (808) 587-7200
Counties Represented: Honolulu (part)        Fax: (808) 587-7205
Term Expires: 2016
E-mail: senkim@capitol.hawaii.gov
Committees: Government Operations; Hawaiian Affairs; Judiciary and
Labor; Tourism and International Affairs
Education: Washington State 1974 BA

Senator **Ronald D. "Ron" Kouchi** (D-District 8)
Hawaii State Capitol, Room 409 . . . . . . . . . . . . . . . . . . (808) 586-6030
Counties Represented: Kauai        Fax: (808) 586-6031
Term Expires: 2016
E-mail: senkouchi@capitol.hawaii.gov

Senator **Clarence K. Nishihara** (D-District 17)
Hawaii State Capitol, Room 204 . . . . . . . . . . . . . . . . . . (808) 586-6970
Counties Represented: Honolulu (part)        Fax: (808) 586-6879
Term Expires: 2018
E-mail: sennishihara@capitol.hawaii.gov
Committees: Commerce, Consumer Protection and Health; Public
Safety, Intergovernmental, and Military Affairs; Transportation and
Energy; Water, Land, and Agriculture

Senator **Gil Riviere** (D-District 23)
Hawaii State Capitol, Room 217 . . . . . . . . . . . . . . . . . . (808) 586-7330
Counties Represented: Honolulu (part)        Fax: (808) 586-7334
Term Expires: 2018
E-mail: senriviere@capitol.hawaii.gov
Committees: Education; Human Services; Water, Land, and Agriculture;
Ways and Means

Senator **Russell E. Ruderman** (D-District 2)
Hawaii State Capitol, Room 203 . . . . . . . . . . . . . . . . . . (808) 586-6890
Counties Represented: Hawaii (part)        Fax: (808) 586-6899
Term Expires: 2016
E-mail: senruderman@capitol.hawaii.gov
Committees: Commerce, Consumer Protection and Health; Economic
Development, Environment, and Technology; Human Services; Water,
Land, and Agriculture
Education: Penn State 1975 BS

Senator **Maile S. L. Shimabukuro** (D-District 21)
Hawaii State Capitol, Room 222 . . . . . . . . . . . . . . . . . . (808) 586-7793
Counties Represented: Honolulu (part)        Fax: (808) 586-7797
Term Expires: 2018
E-mail: senshimabukuro@capitol.hawaii.gov
Committees: Government Operations; Hawaiian Affairs; Judiciary and
Labor; Water, Land, and Agriculture
Education: Colorado Col 1992 BA; Hawaii 2000 JD

Senator **Sam Slom** (R-District 9)
Hawaii State Capitol, Room 214 . . . . . . . . . . . . . . . . . . (808) 586-8420
Counties Represented: Honolulu (part)        Fax: (808) 586-8426
Term Expires: 2016
E-mail: senslom@capitol.hawaii.gov
Committees: Commerce, Consumer Protection and Health; Economic
Development, Environment, and Technology; Education; Government
Operations; Hawaiian Affairs; Higher Education and the Arts; Housing;
Human Services; Judiciary and Labor; Public Safety, Intergovernmental,
and Military Affairs; Tourism and International Affairs; Transportation
and Energy; Water, Land, and Agriculture; Ways and Means

Senator **Brian T. Taniguchi** (D-District 11)
Hawaii State Capitol, Room 219 . . . . . . . . . . . . . . . . . . (808) 586-6460
Counties Represented: Honolulu (part)        Fax: (808) 586-6461
Term Expires: 2016
E-mail: sentaniguchi@capitol.hawaii.gov
Committees: Higher Education and the Arts; Housing; Ways and Means
Education: Hawaii 1973 BA, 1978 JD

Senator **Laura H. Thielen** (D-District 25)
Hawaii State Capitol, Room 231 . . . . . . . . . . . . . . . . . . (808) 587-8388
Counties Represented: Honolulu (part)        Fax: (808) 587-7240
Term Expires: 2016
E-mail: senthielen@capitol.hawaii.gov
Committees: Economic Development, Environment, and Technology;
Human Services; Judiciary and Labor; Water, Land, and Agriculture
Education: Colorado 1984 BA; Case Western JD; Georgetown MPP

Senator **Jill N. Tokuda** (D-District 24)
Hawaii State Capitol, Room 207 . . . . . . . . . . . . . . . . . . (808) 587-7215
Counties Represented: Honolulu (part)        Fax: (808) 587-7220
Term Expires: 2018
E-mail: sentokuda@capitol.hawaii.gov
Committees: Government Operations; Tourism and International
Affairs; Ways and Means
Education: George Washington 1998 BA

Senator **Glenn Wakai** (D-District 15)
Hawaii State Capitol, Room 216 . . . . . . . . . . . . . . . . . . (808) 586-8585
Counties Represented: Honolulu (part)        Fax: (808) 586-8588
Term Expires: 2016
E-mail: senwakai@capitol.hawaii.gov
Committees: Economic Development, Environment, and Technology;
Housing; Water, Land, and Agriculture; Ways and Means
Education: USC 1990 BA

# Senate Standing Committees

## Commerce, Consumer Protection and Health

**Majority Members**
Rosalyn H. Baker (D-6) *Chair*
Michelle N. Kidani (D-18)
  *Vice Chair*
Will Espero (D-19)
Les Ihara, Jr. (D-10)
Clarence K. Nishihara (D-17)
Russell E. Ruderman (D-2)

**Minority Members**
Sam Slom (R-9)

## Economic Development, Environment, and Technology

**Majority Members**
Glenn Wakai (D-15) *Chair*
Rosalyn H. Baker (D-6)
Will Espero (D-19)
Brickwood Galuteria (D-12)
Les Ihara, Jr. (D-10)
Gilbert S. C. Keith-Agaran (D-5)
Russell E. Ruderman (D-2)
Laura H. Thielen (D-25)

**Minority Members**
Sam Slom (R-9) *Vice Chair*

## Education

**Majority Members**
Michelle N. Kidani (D-18) *Chair*
Breene Y. Harimoto (D-16)
  *Vice Chair*
Suzanne Chun Oakland (D-13)
Donovan M. Dela Cruz (D-22)
Kaialii "Kai" Kahele (D-1)
Gil Riviere (D-23)

**Minority Members**
Sam Slom (R-9)

## Government Operations

**Majority Members**
Donna Mercado Kim (D-14) *Chair*
Les Ihara, Jr. (D-10) *Vice Chair*
Donovan M. Dela Cruz (D-22)
Gilbert S. C. Keith-Agaran (D-5)
Maile S. L. Shimabukuro (D-21)
Jill N. Tokuda (D-24)

**Minority Members**
Sam Slom (R-9)

## Hawaiian Affairs

**Majority Members**
Maile S. L. Shimabukuro (D-21)
  *Chair*
J. Kalani English (D-7) *Vice Chair*
Lorraine R. Inouye (D-4)
Donna Mercado Kim (D-14)

**Minority Members**
Sam Slom (R-9)

## Housing

**Majority Members**
Breene Y. Harimoto (D-16) *Chair*
Brickwood Galuteria (D-12)
  *Vice Chair*
Josh Green (D-3)
Les Ihara, Jr. (D-10)
Brian T. Taniguchi (D-11)
Glenn Wakai (D-15)

**Minority Members**
Sam Slom (R-9)

## Higher Education and the Arts

**Majority Members**
Brian T. Taniguchi (D-11) *Chair*
Michelle N. Kidani (D-18)
  *Vice Chair*
Gerald M. "Mike" Gabbard (D-20)
Kaialii "Kai" Kahele (D-1)

**Minority Members**
Sam Slom (R-9)

## Human Services

**Majority Members**
Suzanne Chun Oakland (D-13)
  *Chair*
Gil Riviere (D-23) *Vice Chair*
Josh Green (D-3)
Breene Y. Harimoto (D-16)
Russell E. Ruderman (D-2)
Laura H. Thielen (D-25)

**Minority Members**
Sam Slom (R-9)

## Judiciary and Labor

**Majority Members**
Gilbert S. C. Keith-Agaran (D-5)
  *Chair*
Maile S. L. Shimabukuro (D-21)
  *Vice Chair*
Gerald M. "Mike" Gabbard (D-20)
Kaialii "Kai" Kahele (D-1)
Donna Mercado Kim (D-14)
Laura H. Thielen (D-25)

**Minority Members**
Sam Slom (R-9)

## Public Safety, Intergovernmental, and Military Affairs

**Majority Members**
Clarence K. Nishihara (D-17) *Chair*
Will Espero (D-19) *Vice Chair*
Rosalyn H. Baker (D-6)
Lorraine R. Inouye (D-4)

**Minority Members**
Sam Slom (R-9)

## Tourism and International Affairs

**Majority Members**
J. Kalani English (D-7) *Vice Chair*
Brickwood Galuteria (D-12)
Josh Green (D-3)
Kaialii "Kai" Kahele (D-1)
Donna Mercado Kim (D-14)
Jill N. Tokuda (D-24)

**Minority Members**
Sam Slom (R-9)

## Transportation and Energy

**Majority Members**
Lorraine R. Inouye (D-4) *Chair*
Gerald M. "Mike" Gabbard (D-20)
  *Vice Chair*
Suzanne Chun Oakland (D-13)
J. Kalani English (D-7)
Michelle N. Kidani (D-18)
Clarence K. Nishihara (D-17)

**Minority Members**
Sam Slom (R-9)

## Water, Land, and Agriculture

**Majority Members**
Gerald M. "Mike" Gabbard (D-20)
  *Chair*
Clarence K. Nishihara (D-17)
  *Vice Chair*
Donovan M. Dela Cruz (D-22)
Gil Riviere (D-23)
Russell E. Ruderman (D-2)
Maile S. L. Shimabukuro (D-21)
Laura H. Thielen (D-25)
Glenn Wakai (D-15)

**Minority Members**
Sam Slom (R-9)

## Ways and Means

**Majority Members**
Jill N. Tokuda (D-24) *Chair*
Donovan M. Dela Cruz (D-22)
  *Vice Chair*
Suzanne Chun Oakland (D-13)
J. Kalani English (D-7)
Brickwood Galuteria (D-12)
Breene Y. Harimoto (D-16)
Lorraine R. Inouye (D-4)
Gil Riviere (D-23)
Brian T. Taniguchi (D-11)
Glenn Wakai (D-15)

**Minority Members**
Sam Slom (R-9)

# Hawaii House of Representatives

Tel: (808) 586-6400  Fax: (808) 586-6401
Internet: www.capitol.hawaii.gov/house.aspx

Speaker of the House **Joseph M. Souki** (D) . . . . . . . . . . . (808) 586-6100
  Education: Woodbury 1954 BA
Vice Speaker of the House **John M. Mizuno** (D) . . . . . . . (808) 586-6050
Majority Leader **Scott K. Saiki** (D) . . . . . . . . . . . . . . . . . (808) 586-8485
  Education: Hawaii BA, 1991 JD
Assistant Majority Leader **Chris Lee** (D) . . . . . . . . . . . . . (808) 586-9450
Assistant Majority Leader **Roy M. Takumi** (D) . . . . . . . . (808) 586-6170
  Education: Long Island BA; Hawaii MPA
Majority Floor Leader **Cindy Evans** (D) . . . . . . . . . . . . . (808) 586-8510
  Education: Evergreen State BA
Majority Whip **Ken Ito** (D) . . . . . . . . . . . . . . . . . . . . . (808) 586-8470
  Education: Hawaii 1970 BEd
Minority Leader **Beth Fukumoto Chang** (R) . . . . . . . . . (808) 586-9460
  Education: Hawaii 2006 BA; Georgetown 2008 MA
Assistant Minority Leader **Bob McDermott** (R) . . . . . . . . (808) 586-9730
  Education: Chaminade MBA
Assistant Minority Floor Leader **Cynthia Thielen** (R) . . . . . (808) 586-6480
  Education: Hawaii 1975 BA, JD
Minority Floor Leader **Feki Pouha** (R) . . . . . . . . . . . . . (808) 586-6380
Minority Whip **Lauren Kealohilani Matsumoto** (R) . . . . . (808) 586-9490
  Education: Hawaii 2009 BA
Minority Policy Leader and Minority Leader Emeritus
  **Gene Ward** (R) . . . . . . . . . . . . . . . . . . . . . . . . . . (808) 586-6420
  Education: Hawaii BA, 1980 MA, 1983 PhD
Minority Policy Leader **Andria P.L. Tupola** (R) . . . . . . . . (808) 586-8465
Chief Clerk of the House **Brian L. Takeshita** . . . . . . . . . . (808) 586-6400
Sergeant-at-Arms **Kevin R. Kuroda** . . . . . . . . . . . . . . . . (808) 586-6500
  E-mail: kuroda@capitol.hawaii.gov          Fax: (808) 586-6501
  Education: U Washington BA

# Representatives

**Party Affiliation Statistics:** Republicans: 7, Democrats: 44
Representative **Henry J. C. Aquino** (D-District 38)
  Hawaii State Capitol, Room 419 . . . . . . . . . . . . . . . . . (808) 586-6520
  Counties Represented: Honolulu (part)          Fax: (808) 586-6521
  Term Expires: 2016
  E-mail: repaquino@capitol.hawaii.gov
  Committees: Education; Higher Education; Labor and Public
  Employment; Public Safety; Transportation
Representative **Della Au Belatti** (D-District 24)
  Hawaii State Capitol, Room 426 . . . . . . . . . . . . . . . . . (808) 586-9425
  Counties Represented: Honolulu (part)          Fax: (808) 586-9431
  Term Expires: 2016
  E-mail: repbelatti@capitol.hawaii.gov
  Committees: Consumer Protection and Commerce; Health; Housing;
  Human Services; Judiciary
  Education: Princeton 1996 AB; Hawaii (Hilo) 2003 JD
Representative **Tom Brower** (D-District 22)
  Hawaii State Capitol, Room 315 . . . . . . . . . . . . . . . . . (808) 586-8520
  Counties Represented: Honolulu (part)
  Term Expires: 2016
  E-mail: repbrower@capitol.hawaii.gov
  Committees: Agriculture; Consumer Protection and Commerce;
  Economic Development and Business; Judiciary; Tourism; Veterans,
  Military, and International Affairs
Representative **Romy M. Cachola** (D-District 30)
  Hawaii State Capitol, Room 435 . . . . . . . . . . . . . . . . . (808) 586-6010
  Counties Represented: Honolulu (part)          Fax: (808) 586-6011
  Term Expires: 2016
  E-mail: repcachola@capitol.hawaii.gov
  Committees: Agriculture; Economic Development and Business;
  Finance; Tourism; Veterans, Military, and International Affairs
Representative **Isaac W. Choy** (D-District 23)
  Hawaii State Capitol, Room 404 . . . . . . . . . . . . . . . . . (808) 586-8475
  Counties Represented: Honolulu (part)          Fax: (808) 586-8479
  Term Expires: 2016
  E-mail: repchoy@capitol.hawaii.gov
  Committees: Agriculture; Economic Development and Business;
  Education; Higher Education; Tourism; Veterans, Military, and
  International Affairs
  Education: San José State BS

Representative **Richard P. Creagan** (D-District 5)
  Hawaii State Capitol, Room 317 . . . . . . . . . . . . . . . . . (808) 586-9605
  Counties Represented: Hawaii (part)
  Term Expires: 2016
  E-mail: repcreagan@capitol.hawaii.gov
  Committees: Consumer Protection and Commerce; Health; Housing;
  Human Services; Judiciary
  Education: Yale 1969 BS; Connecticut 1978 MD
Representative **Ty Cullen** (D-District 39)
  Hawaii State Capitol, Room 316 . . . . . . . . . . . . . . . . . (808) 586-8490
  Counties Represented: Honolulu (part)          Fax: (808) 586-8494
  Term Expires: 2016
  E-mail: repcullen@capitol.hawaii.gov
  Committees: Energy and Environmental Protection; Finance; Ocean,
  Marine Resources and Hawaiian Affairs; Water and Land
Representative **Lynn DeCoite** (D-District 13)
  Hawaii State Capitol, Room 405 . . . . . . . . . . . . . . . . . (808) 586-6790
  Counties Represented: Maui (part)          Fax: (808) 586-6779
  Term Expires: 2016
  E-mail: repdecoite@capitol.hawaii.gov
  Committees: Agriculture; Economic Development and Business;
  Finance; Tourism; Veterans, Military, and International Affairs
Representative **Cindy Evans** (D-District 7)
  Hawaii State Capitol, Room 425 . . . . . . . . . . . . . . . . . (808) 586-8510
  Counties Represented: Hawaii (part)          Fax: (808) 586-8514
  Term Expires: 2016
  E-mail: repevans@capitol.hawaii.gov
  Committees: Energy and Environmental Protection; Legislative
  Management; Ocean, Marine Resources and Hawaiian Affairs; Water
  and Land
Representative **Beth Fukumoto Chang** (R-District 36)
  Hawaii State Capitol, Room 333 . . . . . . . . . . . . . . . . . (808) 586-9460
  Counties Represented: Honolulu (part)
  Term Expires: 2016
  E-mail: repfukumoto@capitol.hawaii.gov
  Committees: Consumer Protection and Commerce; Health; Housing;
  Human Services; Legislative Management
Representative **Sharon E. Har** (D-District 42)
  Hawaii State Capitol, Room 418 . . . . . . . . . . . . . . . . . (808) 586-8500
  Counties Represented: Honolulu (part)          Fax: (808) 586-8504
  Term Expires: 2016
  E-mail: rephar@capitol.hawaii.gov
  Committees: Consumer Protection and Commerce; Labor and Public
  Employment; Public Safety; Transportation
Representative **Mark J. Hashem** (D-District 18)
  Hawaii State Capitol, Room 424 . . . . . . . . . . . . . . . . . (808) 586-6510
  Counties Represented: Honolulu (part)          Fax: (808) 586-6511
  Term Expires: 2016
  E-mail: rephashem@capitol.hawaii.gov
  Committees: Consumer Protection and Commerce; Health; Housing;
  Human Services; Judiciary
Representative **Linda Ichiyama** (D-District 32)
  Hawaii State Capitol, Room 327 . . . . . . . . . . . . . . . . . (808) 586-6220
  Counties Represented: Honolulu (part)          Fax: (808) 586-6221
  Term Expires: 2016
  E-mail: repichiyama@capitol.hawaii.gov
  Committees: Education; Higher Education; Labor and Public
  Employment; Public Safety; Transportation
Representative **Kaniela Ing** (D-District 11)
  Hawaii State Capitol, Room 311 . . . . . . . . . . . . . . . . . (808) 586-8525
  Counties Represented: Maui (part)          Fax: (808) 586-8529
  Term Expires: 2016
  E-mail: reping@capitol.hawaii.gov
  Committees: Education; Energy and Environmental Protection; Higher
  Education; Ocean, Marine Resources and Hawaiian Affairs; Water and
  Land
  Education: Hawaii, MPA
Representative **Ken Ito** (D-District 49)
  Hawaii State Capitol, Room 432 . . . . . . . . . . . . . . . . . (808) 586-8470
  Counties Represented: Honolulu (part)          Fax: (808) 586-8474
  Term Expires: 2016
  E-mail: repito@capitol.hawaii.gov
  Committees: Agriculture; Economic Development and Business;
  Education; Higher Education; Tourism; Veterans, Military, and
  International Affairs
Representative **Aaron Ling Johanson** (D-District 31)
  Hawaii State Capitol, Room 427 . . . . . . . . . . . . . . . . . (808) 586-9470
  Counties Represented: Honolulu (part)          Fax: (808) 586-9476
  Term Expires: 2016
  E-mail: repjohanson@capitol.hawaii.gov
  Committees: Finance; Labor and Public Employment; Public Safety;
  Transportation

*(continued on next page)*

LEGISLATIVE BRANCH

**Representatives** *continued*

Representative **Jo Jordan** (D-District 44)
Hawaii State Capitol, Room 323 . . . . . . . . . . . . . . . . . . . . (808) 586-8460
Counties Represented: Honolulu (part)          Fax: (808) 586-8464
Term Expires: 2016
E-mail: repjordan@capitol.hawaii.gov
Committees: Finance; Health; Housing; Human Services

Representative **Derek S. K. Kawakami** (D-District 14)
Hawaii State Capitol, Room 314 . . . . . . . . . . . . . . . . . . . . (808) 586-8435
Counties Represented: Kauai (part)          Fax: (808) 586-8437
Term Expires: 2016
E-mail: repkawakami@capitol.hawaii.gov
Committees: Agriculture; Consumer Protection and Commerce;
Economic Development and Business; Judiciary; Tourism; Veterans,
Military, and International Affairs
Education: Chaminade 2001 BA

Representative **Jarrett K. Keohokalole** (D-District 48)
Hawaii State Capitol, Room 310 . . . . . . . . . . . . . . . . . . . . (808) 586-8540
Counties Represented: Honolulu (part)          Fax: (808) 586-8544
Term Expires: 2016
E-mail: repkeohokalole@capitol.hawaii.gov
Committees: Finance; Labor and Public Employment; Public Safety;
Transportation

Representative
**Bertrand A. Kobayashi, Jr.** (D-District 19)
Hawaii State Capitol, Room 304 . . . . . . . . . . . . . . . . . . . . (808) 586-6310
Counties Represented: Honolulu (part)          Fax: (808) 586-6311
Term Expires: 2016
E-mail: repkobayashi@capitol.hawaii.gov
Committees: Finance; Health; Housing; Human Services

Representative **Sam Satoru Kong** (D-District 33)
Room 313 . . . . . . . . . . . . . . . . . . . . . . . . . . . . . . . . . . (808) 586-8455
Counties Represented: Honolulu (part)          Fax: (808) 586-8459
Term Expires: 2016
E-mail: repkong@capitol.hawaii.gov
Committees: Agriculture; Economic Development and Business;
Education; Higher Education; Tourism; Veterans, Military, and
International Affairs

Representative **Chris Lee** (D-District 51)
Hawaii State Capitol, Room 313 . . . . . . . . . . . . . . . . . . . . (808) 586-9450
Counties Represented: Honolulu (part)          Fax: (808) 586-9456
Term Expires: 2016
E-mail: repclee@capitol.hawaii.gov
Committees: Consumer Protection and Commerce; Energy and
Environmental Protection; Judiciary; Ocean, Marine Resources and
Hawaiian Affairs; Water and Land

Representative **Matthew S. LoPresti** (D-District 41)
Room 328 . . . . . . . . . . . . . . . . . . . . . . . . . . . . . . . . . . (808) 586-6400
Counties Represented: Honolulu (part)          Fax: (808) 586-6081
Term Expires: 2016
E-mail: replopresti@capitol.hawaii.gov
Committees: Finance; Labor and Public Employment; Transportation

Representative **Nicole E. Lowen** (D-District 6)
Hawaii State Capitol, Room 425 . . . . . . . . . . . . . . . . . . . . (808) 586-8400
Counties Represented: Hawaii (part)
Term Expires: 2016
E-mail: replowen@capitol.hawaii.gov
Committees: Energy and Environmental Protection; Finance; Ocean,
Marine Resources and Hawaiian Affairs; Water and Land
Education: Pennsylvania BA

Representative **Sylvia Luke** (D-District 25) . . . . . . . . . . . . . (808) 586-6200
Counties Represented: Honolulu (part)
Term Expires: 2016
Hawaii State Capitol, 415 S. Beretania Street, Room 306,
Honolulu, HI 96813
E-mail: repluke@capitol.hawaii.gov
Committees: Finance
Education: Hawaii 1989 BA; U San Francisco 1995 JD

Representative
**Lauren Kealohilani Matsumoto** (R-District 45)
Hawaii State Capitol, Room 303 . . . . . . . . . . . . . . . . . . . . (808) 586-9490
Counties Represented: Honolulu (part)
Term Expires: 2016
E-mail: repmatsumoto@capitol.hawaii.gov
Committees: Agriculture; Economic Development and Business;
Education; Higher Education; Tourism; Veterans, Military, and
International Affairs

Representative **Bob McDermott** (R-District 40)
Hawaii State Capitol, Room 330 . . . . . . . . . . . . . . . . . . . . (808) 586-9730
Counties Represented: Honolulu (part)          Fax: (808) 586-9738
Term Expires: 2016
E-mail: repmcdermott@capitol.hawaii.gov
Committees: Consumer Protection and Commerce; Judiciary

Representative **Angus L.K. McKelvey** (D-District 10)
Hawaii State Capitol, Room 427 . . . . . . . . . . . . . . . . . . . . (808) 586-6160
Counties Represented: Maui (part)          Fax: (808) 586-6161
Term Expires: 2016
E-mail: repmckelvey@capitol.hawaii.gov
Committees: Consumer Protection and Commerce

Representative **John M. Mizuno** (D-District 28)
Hawaii State Capitol, Room 439 . . . . . . . . . . . . . . . . . . . . (808) 586-6050
Counties Represented: Honolulu (part)          Fax: (808) 586-6051
Term Expires: 2016
E-mail: repmizuno@capitol.hawaii.gov
Committees: Legislative Management

Representative **Dee Morikawa** (D-District 16)
Hawaii State Capitol, Room 310 . . . . . . . . . . . . . . . . . . . . (808) 586-6280
Counties Represented: Kauai (part)          Fax: (808) 586-6281
Term Expires: 2016
E-mail: repmorikawa@capitol.hawaii.gov
Committees: Health; Housing; Human Services; Judiciary

Representative **Mark M. Nakashima** (D-District 1)
Hawaii State Capitol, Room 406 . . . . . . . . . . . . . . . . . . . . (808) 586-6680
Counties Represented: Hawaii (part)          Fax: (808) 586-6684
Term Expires: 2016
E-mail: repnakashima@capitol.hawaii.gov
Committees: Consumer Protection and Commerce; Judiciary; Labor and
Public Employment; Public Safety; Transportation

Representative **Scott Y. Nishimoto** (D-District 21)
Hawaii State Capitol, Room 441 . . . . . . . . . . . . . . . . . . . . (808) 586-8515
Counties Represented: Honolulu (part)          Fax: (808) 586-8519
Term Expires: 2016
E-mail: repnishimoto@capitol.hawaii.gov
Committees: Energy and Environmental Protection; Finance; Legislative
Management; Ocean, Marine Resources and Hawaiian Affairs; Water
and Land
Education: Hawaii 1997 BA, 2002 JD

Representative **Takashi Ohno** (D-District 27)
Hawaii State Capitol, Room 332 . . . . . . . . . . . . . . . . . . . . (808) 586-9415
Counties Represented: Honolulu (part)          Fax: (808) 586-9421
Term Expires: 2016
E-mail: repohno@capitol.hawaii.gov
Committees: Agriculture; Economic Development and Business;
Education; Higher Education; Tourism; Veterans, Military, and
International Affairs
Education: Linfield BA; Chaminade MEd

Representative **Richard Onishi** (D-District 3)
Hawaii State Capitol, Room 441 . . . . . . . . . . . . . . . . . . . . (808) 586-6120
Counties Represented: Hawaii (part)          Fax: (808) 586-6121
Term Expires: 2016
E-mail: reponishi@capitol.hawaii.gov
Committees: Agriculture; Economic Development and Business;
Finance; Tourism; Veterans, Military, and International Affairs
Education: Hawaii (Hilo) 1986 BBA

Representative **Marcus R. Oshiro** (D-District 46)
Hawaii State Capitol, Room 441 . . . . . . . . . . . . . . . . . . . . (808) 586-6700
Counties Represented: Honolulu (part)          Fax: (808) 586-6702
Term Expires: 2016
E-mail: repmoshiro@capitol.hawaii.gov
Committees: Consumer Protection and Commerce; Health; Housing;
Human Services
Education: Hawaii BA; Willamette 1988 JD

Representative **Feki Pouha** (R-District 47)
Hawaii State Capitol, Room 319 . . . . . . . . . . . . . . . . . . . . (808) 586-6380
Counties Represented: Honolulu (part)          Fax: (808) 586-6381
Term Expires: 2016
E-mail: reppouha@capitol.hawaii.gov
Committees: Energy and Environmental Protection; Finance; Ocean,
Marine Resources and Hawaiian Affairs; Water and Land

Representative **Karl Rhoads** (D-District 29)
Hawaii State Capitol, Room 302 . . . . . . . . . . . . . . . . . . . . (808) 586-6180
Counties Represented: Honolulu (part)
Term Expires: 2016
E-mail: reprhoads@capitol.hawaii.gov
Committees: Judiciary

Representative **Scott K. Saiki** (D-District 26)
Hawaii State Capitol, Room 434 . . . . . . . . . . . . . . . . . . . (808) 586-8485
Counties Represented: Honolulu (part)        Fax: (808) 586-8489
Term Expires: 2016
E-mail: repsaiki@capitol.hawaii.gov
Committees: Legislative Management

Representative **Joy San Buenaventura** (D-District 4)
Hawaii State Capitol, Room 305 . . . . . . . . . . . . . . . . . . . (808) 586-6400
Counties Represented: Hawaii (part)
Term Expires: 2016
E-mail: repsanbuenaventura@capitol.hawaii.gov
Committees: Consumer Protection and Commerce; Judiciary; Labor and
Public Employment; Public Safety; Transportation

Representative **Calvin K. Y. Say** (D-District 20)
Hawaii State Capitol, Room 431 . . . . . . . . . . . . . . . . . . . (808) 586-6900
Counties Represented: Honolulu (part)        Fax: (808) 586-6910
Term Expires: 2016
E-mail: repsay@capitol.hawaii.gov
Committees: Education; Energy and Environmental Protection; Higher
Education; Ocean, Marine Resources and Hawaiian Affairs; Water and
Land
Education: Hawaii 1974 BEd

Representative **Joseph M. Souki** (D-District 8)
Hawaii State Capitol, Room 433 . . . . . . . . . . . . . . . . . . . (808) 586-6100
Counties Represented: Maui (part)        Fax: (808) 586-6101
Term Expires: 2016
E-mail: repsouki@capitol.hawaii.gov

Representative **Gregg Takayama** (D-District 34)
Hawaii State Capitol, Room 324 . . . . . . . . . . . . . . . . . . . (808) 586-6340
Counties Represented: Honolulu (part)        Fax: (808) 586-6341
Term Expires: 2016
E-mail: reptakayama@capitol.hawaii.gov
Committees: Consumer Protection and Commerce; Judiciary; Public
Safety; Transportation
Education: Hawaii BA

Representative **Roy M. Takumi** (D-District 35)
Hawaii State Capitol, Room 444 . . . . . . . . . . . . . . . . . . . (808) 586-6170
Counties Represented: Honolulu (part)        Fax: (808) 586-6171
Term Expires: 2016
E-mail: reptakumi@capitol.hawaii.gov
Committees: Education; Higher Education; Labor and Public
Employment; Public Safety; Transportation

Representative **Cynthia Thielen** (R-District 50)
Hawaii State Capitol, Room 443 . . . . . . . . . . . . . . . . . . . (808) 586-6480
Counties Represented: Honolulu (part)        Fax: (808) 586-6481
Term Expires: 2016
E-mail: repthielen@capitol.hawaii.gov
Committees: Energy and Environmental Protection; Judiciary; Ocean,
Marine Resources and Hawaiian Affairs; Water and Land

Representative **James Kunane Tokioka** (D-District 15)
Hawaii State Capitol, Room 322 . . . . . . . . . . . . . . . . . . . (808) 586-6270
Counties Represented: Kauai (part)        Fax: (808) 586-6271
Term Expires: 2016
E-mail: reptokioka@capitol.hawaii.gov
Committees: Agriculture; Economic Development and Business;
Finance; Tourism; Veterans, Military, and International Affairs

Representative **Clift Tsuji** (D-District 2)
Hawaii State Capitol, Room 402 . . . . . . . . . . . . . . . . . . . (808) 586-8480
Counties Represented: Hawaii (part)        Fax: (808) 586-8484
Term Expires: 2016
E-mail: reptsuji@capitol.hawaii.gov
Committees: Agriculture; Economic Development and Business;
Education; Higher Education; Tourism; Veterans, Military, and
International Affairs
Education: Hawaii 1966 BA

Representative **Andria P.L. Tupola** (R-District 43)
Room 317 . . . . . . . . . . . . . . . . . . . . . . . . . . . . . . . . . . . . (808) 586-8465
Counties Represented: Honolulu (part)        Fax: (808) 586-8469
Term Expires: 2016
E-mail: reptupola@capitol.hawaii.gov
Committees: Education; Health; Higher Education; Labor and Public
Employment; Public Safety; Transportation

Representative **Gene Ward** (R-District 17)
Hawaii State Capitol, Room 318 . . . . . . . . . . . . . . . . . . . (808) 586-6420
Counties Represented: Honolulu (part)        Fax: (808) 586-6421
Term Expires: 2016
E-mail: repward@capitol.hawaii.gov
Committees: Agriculture; Economic Development and Business;
Finance; Tourism; Veterans, Military, and International Affairs

Representative **Justin H. Woodson** (D-District 9)
Hawaii State Capitol, Room 305 . . . . . . . . . . . . . . . . . . . (808) 586-6210
Counties Represented: Maui (part)        Fax: (808) 586-6211
Term Expires: 2016
E-mail: repwoodson@capitol.hawaii.gov
Committees: Agriculture; Consumer Protection and Commerce;
Economic Development and Business; Judiciary; Tourism; Veterans,
Military, and International Affairs
Education: Cal State (Fullerton)

Representative **Ryan I. Yamane** (D-District 37)
Hawaii State Capitol, Room 420 . . . . . . . . . . . . . . . . . . . (808) 586-6150
Counties Represented: Honolulu (part)        Fax: (808) 586-6151
Term Expires: 2016
E-mail: repyamane@capitol.hawaii.gov
Committees: Consumer Protection and Commerce; Energy and
Environmental Protection; Ocean, Marine Resources and Hawaiian
Affairs; Water and Land
Education: Hawaii 1992 BA, 1996 MSW, 2002 MBA

Representative **Kyle T. Yamashita** (D-District 12)
Hawaii State Capitol, Room 422 . . . . . . . . . . . . . . . . . . . (808) 586-6330
Counties Represented: Maui (part)        Fax: (808) 586-6331
Term Expires: 2016
E-mail: repyamashita@capitol.hawaii.gov
Committees: Finance; Labor and Public Employment; Public Safety;
Transportation

# House Standing Committees

## Agriculture

| Majority Members | Minority Members |
|---|---|
| Clift Tsuji (D-2) *Chair* | Lauren Kealohilani Matsumoto |
| Richard Onishi (D-3) *Vice Chair* | (R-45) |
| Tom Brower (D-22) | Gene Ward (R-17) |
| Romy M. Cachola (D-30) | |
| Isaac W. Choy (D-23) | |
| Lynn DeCoite (D-13) | |
| Ken Ito (D-49) | |
| Derek S. K. Kawakami (D-14) | |
| Sam Satoru Kong (D-33) | |
| Takashi Ohno (D-27) | |
| James Kunane Tokioka (D-15) | |
| Justin H. Woodson (D-9) | |

## Consumer Protection and Commerce

| Majority Members | Minority Members |
|---|---|
| Angus L.K. McKelvey (D-10) *Chair* | Beth Fukumoto Chang (R-36) |
| Justin H. Woodson (D-9) *Vice Chair* | Bob McDermott (R-40) |
| Della Au Belatti (D-24) | |
| Tom Brower (D-22) | |
| Richard P. Creagan (D-5) | |
| Sharon E. Har (D-42) | |
| Mark J. Hashem (D-18) | |
| Derek S. K. Kawakami (D-14) | |
| Chris Lee (D-51) | |
| Mark M. Nakashima (D-1) | |
| Marcus R. Oshiro (D-46) | |
| Joy San Buenaventura (D-4) | |
| Gregg Takayama (D-34) | |
| Ryan I. Yamane (D-37) | |

## Economic Development and Business

| Majority Members | Minority Members |
|---|---|
| Derek S. K. Kawakami (D-14) *Chair* | Lauren Kealohilani Matsumoto (R-45) |
| Sam Satoru Kong (D-33) *Vice Chair* | Gene Ward (R-17) |
| Tom Brower (D-22) | |
| Romy M. Cachola (D-30) | |
| Isaac W. Choy (D-23) | |
| Lynn DeCoite (D-13) | |
| Ken Ito (D-49) | |
| Takashi Ohno (D-27) | |
| Richard Onishi (D-3) | |
| James Kunane Tokioka (D-15) | |
| Clift Tsuji (D-2) | |
| Justin H. Woodson (D-9) | |

LEGISLATIVE BRANCH

## Education

**Majority Members**
Roy M. Takumi (D-35) *Chair*
Takashi Ohno (D-27) *Vice Chair*
Henry J. C. Aquino (D-38)
Isaac W. Choy (D-23)
Linda Ichiyama (D-32)
Kaniela Ing (D-11)
Ken Ito (D-49)
Sam Satoru Kong (D-33)
Calvin K. Y. Say (D-20)
Clift Tsuji (D-2)

**Minority Members**
Lauren Kealohilani Matsumoto (R-45)
Andria P.L. Tupola (R-43)

## Energy and Environmental Protection

**Majority Members**
Chris Lee (D-51) *Chair*
Nicole E. Lowen (D-6) *Vice Chair*
Ty Cullen (D-39)
Cindy Evans (D-7)
Kaniela Ing (D-11)
Scott Y. Nishimoto (D-21)
Calvin K. Y. Say (D-20)
Ryan I. Yamane (D-37)

**Minority Members**
Feki Pouha (R-47)
Cynthia Thielen (R-50)

## Finance

**Majority Members**
Sylvia Luke (D-25) *Chair*
Scott Y. Nishimoto (D-21) *Vice Chair*
Romy M. Cachola (D-30)
Ty Cullen (D-39)
Lynn DeCoite (D-13)
Jo Jordan (D-44)
Jarrett K. Keohokalole (D-48)
Bertrand A. Kobayashi, Jr. (D-19)
Matthew S. LoPresti (D-41)
Nicole E. Lowen (D-6)
Richard Onishi (D-3)
James Kunane Tokioka (D-15)
Kyle T. Yamashita (D-12)

**Minority Members**
Aaron Ling Johanson (D-31)
Feki Pouha (R-47)
Gene Ward (R-17)

## Health

**Majority Members**
Della Au Belatti (D-24) *Chair*
Richard P. Creagan (D-5) *Vice Chair*
Mark J. Hashem (D-18)
Jo Jordan (D-44)
Bertrand A. Kobayashi, Jr. (D-19)
Dee Morikawa (D-16)
Marcus R. Oshiro (D-46)

**Minority Members**
Beth Fukumoto Chang (R-36)
Andria P.L. Tupola (R-43)

## Higher Education

**Majority Members**
Isaac W. Choy (D-23) *Chair*
Linda Ichiyama (D-32) *Vice Chair*
Henry J. C. Aquino (D-38)
Kaniela Ing (D-11)
Ken Ito (D-49)
Sam Satoru Kong (D-33)
Takashi Ohno (D-27)
Calvin K. Y. Say (D-20)
Roy M. Takumi (D-35)
Clift Tsuji (D-2)

**Minority Members**
Lauren Kealohilani Matsumoto (R-45)
Andria P.L. Tupola (R-43)

## Housing

**Majority Members**
Mark J. Hashem (D-18) *Chair*
Jo Jordan (D-44) *Vice Chair*
Della Au Belatti (D-24)
Richard P. Creagan (D-5)
Bertrand A. Kobayashi, Jr. (D-19)
Dee Morikawa (D-16)
Marcus R. Oshiro (D-46)

**Minority Members**
Beth Fukumoto Chang (R-36)

## Human Services

**Majority Members**
Dee Morikawa (D-16) *Chair*
Bertrand A. Kobayashi, Jr. (D-19) *Vice Chair*
Della Au Belatti (D-24)
Richard P. Creagan (D-5)
Mark J. Hashem (D-18)
Jo Jordan (D-44)
Marcus R. Oshiro (D-46)

**Minority Members**
Beth Fukumoto Chang (R-36)

## Judiciary

**Majority Members**
Karl Rhoads (D-29) *Chair*
Joy San Buenaventura (D-4) *Vice Chair*
Della Au Belatti (D-24)
Tom Brower (D-22)
Richard P. Creagan (D-5)
Mark J. Hashem (D-18)
Derek S. K. Kawakami (D-14)
Chris Lee (D-51)
Dee Morikawa (D-16)
Mark M. Nakashima (D-1)
Gregg Takayama (D-34)
Justin H. Woodson (D-9)

**Minority Members**
Bob McDermott (R-40)
Cynthia Thielen (R-50)

## Labor and Public Employment

**Majority Members**
Mark M. Nakashima (D-1) *Chair*
Jarrett K. Keohokalole (D-48) *Vice Chair*
Henry J. C. Aquino (D-38)
Sharon E. Har (D-42)
Linda Ichiyama (D-32)
Matthew S. LoPresti (D-41)
Joy San Buenaventura (D-4)
Roy M. Takumi (D-35)
Kyle T. Yamashita (D-12)

**Minority Members**
Aaron Ling Johanson (D-31)
Andria P.L. Tupola (R-43)

## Legislative Management

**Majority Members**
Scott Y. Nishimoto (D-21) *Chair*
John M. Mizuno (D-28) *Vice Chair*
Cindy Evans (D-7)
Scott K. Saiki (D-26)

**Minority Members**
Beth Fukumoto Chang (R-36)

## Ocean, Marine Resources and Hawaiian Affairs

**Majority Members**
Kaniela Ing (D-11) *Chair*
Nicole E. Lowen (D-6) *Vice Chair*
Ty Cullen (D-39)
Cindy Evans (D-7)
Chris Lee (D-51)
Scott Y. Nishimoto (D-21)
Calvin K. Y. Say (D-20)
Ryan I. Yamane (D-37)

**Minority Members**
Feki Pouha (R-47)
Cynthia Thielen (R-50)

## Public Safety

**Majority Members**
Gregg Takayama (D-34) *Chair*
Kyle T. Yamashita (D-12) *Vice Chair*
Henry J. C. Aquino (D-38)
Sharon E. Har (D-42)
Linda Ichiyama (D-32)
Jarrett K. Keohokalole (D-48)
Mark M. Nakashima (D-1)
Joy San Buenaventura (D-4)
Roy M. Takumi (D-35)

**Minority Members**
Aaron Ling Johanson (D-31)
Andria P.L. Tupola (R-43)

## Tourism

**Majority Members**
Tom Brower (D-22) *Chair*
Takashi Ohno (D-27) *Vice Chair*
Romy M. Cachola (D-30)
Isaac W. Choy (D-23)
Lynn DeCoite (D-13)
Ken Ito (D-49)
Derek S. K. Kawakami (D-14)
Sam Satoru Kong (D-33)
Richard Onishi (D-3)
James Kunane Tokioka (D-15)
Clift Tsuji (D-2)
Justin H. Woodson (D-9)

**Minority Members**
Lauren Kealohilani Matsumoto
(R-45)
Gene Ward (R-17)

## Transportation

**Majority Members**
Henry J. C. Aquino (D-38) *Chair*
Matthew S. LoPresti (D-41)
*Vice Chair*
Sharon E. Har (D-42)
Linda Ichiyama (D-32)
Jarrett K. Keohokalole (D-48)
Mark M. Nakashima (D-1)
Joy San Buenaventura (D-4)
Gregg Takayama (D-34)
Roy M. Takumi (D-35)
Kyle T. Yamashita (D-12)

**Minority Members**
Aaron Ling Johanson (D-31)
Andria P.L. Tupola (R-43)

## Veterans, Military, and International Affairs

**Majority Members**
Ken Ito (D-49) *Chair*
James Kunane Tokioka (D-15)
*Vice Chair*
Tom Brower (D-22)
Romy M. Cachola (D-30)
Isaac W. Choy (D-23)
Lynn DeCoite (D-13)
Derek S. K. Kawakami (D-14)
Sam Satoru Kong (D-33)
Takashi Ohno (D-27)
Richard Onishi (D-3)
Clift Tsuji (D-2)
Justin H. Woodson (D-9)

**Minority Members**
Lauren Kealohilani Matsumoto
(R-45)
Gene Ward (R-17)

## Water and Land

**Majority Members**
Ryan I. Yamane (D-37) *Chair*
Ty Cullen (D-39) *Vice Chair*
Cindy Evans (D-7)
Kaniela Ing (D-11)
Chris Lee (D-51)
Nicole E. Lowen (D-6)
Scott Y. Nishimoto (D-21)
Calvin K. Y. Say (D-20)

**Minority Members**
Feki Pouha (R-47)
Cynthia Thielen (R-50)

# Idaho Legislature

Tel: (208) 332-1000  TTY: (800) 626-0471  Fax: (208) 334-5397
E-mail: idleginfo@lso.idaho.gov  Internet: www.legislature.idaho.gov

## Idaho Senate

P.O. Box 83720 State Capitol Building, Boise, ID 83720-0081
Tel: (208) 332-1300 (In Session Phone)  Fax: (208) 332-1422 (Interim)
Fax: (208) 332-2320 (Session)

President of the Senate **Brad J. Little** (R) . . . . . . . . . . . . . . (208) 334-2200
 Education: Idaho 1977 BS
President Pro Tem **Brent Hill** (R) . . . . . . . . . . . . . . . . . . . . (208) 332-1315
 Education: Utah State 1973 BS
Majority Leader **Bart M. Davis** (R) . . . . . . . . . . . . . . . . . . (208) 332-1305
 Education: BYU 1977 BA; Idaho 1980 JD
Assistant Majority Leader **Chuck Winder** (R) . . . . . . . . . . (208) 332-1354
 Education: Col Idaho BA
Majority Caucus Chair **Todd M. Lakey** (R) . . . . . . . . . . . . (208) 332-1304
 Education: BYU 1990 BS; Lewis & Clark 1993 JD
Minority Leader **Michelle Stennett** (D) . . . . . . . . . . . . . . . (208) 726-8106
 Education: Oregon BA
Assistant Minority Leader **Cherie Buckner-Webb** (D) . . . . (208) 332-1309
 Education: George Fox U BS; Northwest Nazarene U MSW
Minority Caucus Chair **Grant Burgoyne** (D) . . . . . . . . . . . (208) 287-8787
 Education: Idaho BA; Kansas JD
Secretary of the Senate **Jennifer Novak** . . . . . . . . . . . . . . (208) 332-1309
 E-mail: jnovak@senate.idaho.gov
Assistant Secretary of the Senate **Rusti Horton** . . . . . . . . (208) 332-1311
Sergeant-at-Arms **Sarah Jane McDonald** . . . . . . . . . . . . . (208) 332-1400
 Education: Idaho State

## Senators

**Party Affiliation Statistics:** Republicans: 28, Democrats: 7

Senator **Kelly Arthur Anthon** (R-District 27) . . . . . . . . . . (208) 332-1300
 Counties Represented: Cassia, Minidoka       Dist: (208) 654-4099
 Term Expires: 2016
 725 East 300 South, Burley, ID 83318
 E-mail: kanthon@senate.idaho.gov
 Committees: Education; Judiciary and Rules
 Education: BYU (Idaho) 1998 BA; Idaho 2002 JD
Senator **R. Steven Bair** (R-District 31) . . . . . . . . . . . . . . . (208) 332-1346
 Counties Represented: Bingham       Res: (208) 684-5209
 Term Expires: 2016
 947 West 200 South, Blackfoot, ID 83221
 E-mail: sbair@senate.idaho.gov
 Committees: Finance; Resources and Environment
 Education: Ricks (Attended)
Senator **Clifford R. "Cliff" Bayer** (R-District 21) . . . . . . . . (208) 332-1309
 Counties Represented: Ada (part)       Res: (208) 362-5058
 Term Expires: 2016
 592 Saint Kitts Drive, Meridian, ID 83642
 E-mail: cbayer@senate.idaho.gov
 Committees: Agricultural Affairs; Local Government and Taxation;
 Resources and Environment
 Education: Boise State 1987 BS
Senator **Bert Brackett** (R-District 23) . . . . . . . . . . . . . . . . (208) 332-1336
 Counties Represented: Elmore, Owyhee, Twin Falls       Res: (208) 857-2217
 (part)
 Term Expires: 2016
 48331 Three Creek Highway, Rogerson, ID 83302
 E-mail: bbrackett@senate.idaho.gov
 Committees: Finance; Transportation
 Education: Idaho BSA
Senator **Cherie Buckner-Webb** (D-District 19) . . . . . . . . . (208) 332-1309
 Counties Represented: Ada (part)       Dist: (208) 861-5482
 Term Expires: 2016
 2304 West Bella Street, Boise, ID 83702
 E-mail: cbucknerwebb@senate.idaho.gov
 Committees: Education; Transportation
Senator **Grant Burgoyne** (D-District 16) . . . . . . . . . . . . . . (208) 287-8787
 Counties Represented: Ada (part)       Res: (208) 377-5729
 Term Expires: 2016
 E-mail: gburgoyne@senate.idaho.gov
 Committees: Agricultural Affairs; Judiciary and Rules; Local
 Government and Taxation

*(continued on next page)*

**LEGISLATIVE BRANCH**

**LEGISLATIVE BRANCH**

**Senators** *continued*

Senator **Bart M. Davis** (R-District 33) . . . . . . . . . . . . . . . . (208) 332-1305
  Counties Represented: Bonneville (part)       Tel: (208) 522-8100
  Term Expires: 2016                         Res: (208) 529-4993
  2638 Bellin Circle, Idaho Falls, ID 83402      Fax: (208) 522-1334
  E-mail: bmdavis@senate.idaho.gov
  Committees: Judiciary and Rules; State Affairs

Senator **Lori Den Hartog** (R-District 22) . . . . . . . . . . . . . . (208) 779-2022
  Counties Represented: Ada (part)
  Term Expires: 2016
  P.O. Box 267, Meridian, ID 83680
  E-mail: ldenhartog@senate.idaho.gov
  Committees: Agricultural Affairs; Education; Transportation

Senator **Jim Guthrie** (R-District 28) . . . . . . . . . . . . . . . . . (208) 332-1309
  Counties Represented: Bannock (part), Power   Res: (208) 254-3605
  Term Expires: 2016
  425 West Goodenough Road, McCammon, ID 83250
  E-mail: jguthrie@senate.idaho.gov
  Committees: Commerce and Human Resources; Finance; Local
  Government and Taxation

Senator **Marv Hagedorn** (R-District 14) . . . . . . . . . . . . . . (208) 332-1309
  Counties Represented: Ada (part)         Res: (208) 867-5643
  Term Expires: 2016
  5285 West Ridgeside Street, Meridian, ID 83646
  E-mail: mhagedorn@senate.idaho.gov
  Committees: Health and Welfare; Resources and Environment;
  Transportation
  Education: Maryland (Attended)

Senator **Mark Harris** (R-District 32) . . . . . . . . . . . . . . . . . (208) 332-1300
  Counties Represented: Bear Lake, Bonneville (part), Caribou, Franklin,
  Oneida, Teton
  Term Expires: 2016
  E-mail: mharris@senate.idaho.gov
  Committees: Agricultural Affairs; Health and Welfare
  Education: Utah State 1998 BA

Senator **Lee Heider** (R-District 24) . . . . . . . . . . . . . . . . . . (208) 332-1309
  Counties Represented: Twin Falls (part)    Res: (208) 734-8864
  Term Expires: 2016
  1631 Richmond Drive, Twin Falls, ID 83301
  E-mail: lheider@senate.idaho.gov
  Committees: Commerce and Human Resources; Health and Welfare;
  Resources and Environment
  Education: BYU BA; Ball State MPA

Senator **Brent Hill** (R-District 34) . . . . . . . . . . . . . . . . . . (208) 332-1315
  Counties Represented: Bonneville (part), Madison   Tel: (208) 356-3677
  Term Expires: 2016                      Res: (208) 356-7495
  1010 South 2nd East, Rexburg, ID 83440      Fax: (208) 356-3689
  E-mail: bhill@senate.idaho.gov
  Committees: State Affairs

Senator **Dan G. Johnson** (R-District 6) . . . . . . . . . . . . . . . (208) 332-1308
  Counties Represented: Lewis, Nez Perce    Dist: (208) 816-1164
  Term Expires: 2016
  PO Box 2117, Lewiston, ID 83501
  E-mail: djohnson@senate.idaho.gov
  Committees: Finance; Judiciary and Rules; Local Government and
  Taxation
  Education: Idaho 1989 BSF; Virginia Tech 1991 MA

Senator **Maryanne Jordan** (D-District 17) . . . . . . . . . . . . . (208) 332-1300
  Counties Represented: Ada (part)         Res: (208) 859-1931
  Term Expires: 2016
  312 N. Atlantic Street, Boise, ID 83706
  E-mail: mjordan@senate.idaho.gov
  Committees: Health and Welfare; Judiciary and Rules

Senator **Shawn Keough** (R-District 1) . . . . . . . . . . . . . . . . (208) 332-1349
  Counties Represented: Bonner (part), Boundary   Res: (208) 263-1839
  Term Expires: 2016
  P.O. Box 101, Sandpoint, ID 83864
  E-mail: skeough@senate.idaho.gov
  Committees: Finance; Transportation
  Education: North Idaho (Attended)

Senator **Roy Lacey** (D-District 29) . . . . . . . . . . . . . . . . . . (208) 332-1309
  Counties Represented: Bannock (part)    Res: (208) 232-7053
  Term Expires: 2016
  13774 West Trail Creek Road, Pocatello, ID 83204
  E-mail: rlacey@senate.idaho.gov
  Committees: Finance; Resources and Environment; Transportation
  Education: Idaho State (Attended)

Senator **Todd M. Lakey** (R-District 12) . . . . . . . . . . . . . . . (208) 332-1304
  Counties Represented: Canyon (part)
  Term Expires: 2016
  34 South Bingham Street, Nampa, ID 83651
  E-mail: tlakey@senate.idaho.gov
  Committees: Commerce and Human Resources; State Affairs

Senator **Abby Lee** (R-District 9) . . . . . . . . . . . . . . . . . . . . (208) 250-6744
  Counties Represented: Adams, Canyon (part), Payette, Valley (part),
  Washington
  Term Expires: 2016
  E-mail: alee@senate.idaho.gov
  Committees: Agricultural Affairs; Health and Welfare; Judiciary and
  Rules

Senator **Patti Anne Lodge** (R-District 11) . . . . . . . . . . . . . (208) 332-1319
  Counties Represented: Canyon (part)    Res: (208) 459-7158
  Term Expires: 2016
  P.O. Box 96, Huston, ID 83630
  E-mail: palodge@senate.idaho.gov
  Committees: Health and Welfare; Judiciary and Rules; State Affairs
  Education: Marylhurst 1964 BA

Senator **Fred S. Martin** (R-District 15) . . . . . . . . . . . . . . . (208) 332-1309
  Counties Represented: Ada (part)         Res: (208) 447-9000
  Term Expires: 2016
  3672 Tumbleweed Place, Boise, ID 83713
  E-mail: fmartin@senate.idaho.gov
  Committees: Commerce and Human Resources; Health and Welfare
  Education: Ricks (Attended); Idaho State (Attended)

Senator **Curt McKenzie** (R-District 13) . . . . . . . . . . . . . . . (208) 332-1326
  Counties Represented: Canyon (part)    Tel: (208) 334-4379
  Term Expires: 2016                     Fax: (208) 331-2150
  412 West Fort Street, Boise, ID 83702
  E-mail: cmckenzie@senate.idaho.gov
  Committees: Local Government and Taxation; State Affairs
  Education: Northwest Nazarene U 1992 BA; Georgetown 1995 JD

Senator **Dean M. Mortimer** (R-District 30) . . . . . . . . . . . . (208) 332-1358
  Counties Represented: Bonneville (part)   Tel: (208) 524-9000
  Term Expires: 2016                     Res: (208) 528-6377
  7403 South 1st East, Idaho Falls, ID 83404   Fax: (208) 524-9999
  E-mail: dmortimer@senate.idaho.gov
  Committees: Education; Finance
  Education: Ricks AA; Utah State BA, MA

Senator **Bob Nonini** (R-District 3) . . . . . . . . . . . . . . . . . . (208) 332-1309
  Counties Represented: Kootenai (part)    Res: (208) 765-1904
  Term Expires: 2016                     Fax: (208) 292-4310
  5875 West Harbor Drive, Coeur d'Alene, ID 83814
  E-mail: bnonini@senate.idaho.gov
  Committees: Education; Judiciary and Rules; Transportation
  Education: North Idaho (Attended)

Senator **Sheryl L. Nuxoll** (R-District 7) . . . . . . . . . . . . . . (208) 332-1309
  Counties Represented: Bonner (part), Clearwater,   Res: (208) 962-7718
  Idaho, Shoshone
  Term Expires: 2016
  P.O. Box 187, Cottonwood, ID 83522
  E-mail: snuxoll@senate.idaho.gov
  Committees: Finance; Health and Welfare; Resources and Environment
  Education: Gonzaga 1973 BS

Senator **Jim Patrick** (R-District 25) . . . . . . . . . . . . . . . . . . (208) 726-8106
  Counties Represented: Jerome, Twin Falls (part)   Fax: (208) 733-6897
  Term Expires: 2016
  2231 East 3200 North, Twin Falls, ID 83301
  E-mail: jpatrick@senate.idaho.gov
  Committees: Agricultural Affairs; Commerce and Human Resources;
  Education
  Education: Idaho 1968 BS

Senator **Jim Rice** (R-District 10) . . . . . . . . . . . . . . . . . . . . (208) 455-3950
  Counties Represented: Canyon (part)    Dist: (208) 891-4178
  Term Expires: 2016
  2319 Polk Street, Caldwell, ID 83605
  E-mail: jrice@senate.idaho.gov
  Committees: Agricultural Affairs; Commerce and Human Resources;
  Local Government and Taxation
  Education: BYU; William Howard Taft JD

Senator **Dan J. Schmidt** (D-District 5) . . . . . . . . . . . . . . . (208) 332-1309
  Counties Represented: Benewah, Latah    Res: (208) 882-6328
  Term Expires: 2016
  267 Circle Drive, Moscow, ID 83843
  E-mail: dschmidt@senate.idaho.gov
  Committees: Commerce and Human Resources; Finance; Health and
  Welfare
  Education: Stanford 1976 BS; U Washington 1986 MD

Senator **Jeffery C. "Jeff" Siddoway** (R-District 35)......(208) 332-1342
Counties Represented: Butte, Clark, Fremont,    Res: (208) 663-4585
Jefferson       Fax: (208) 663-4428
Term Expires: 2016
1764 East 1200 North, Terreton, ID 83450
E-mail: jsiddoway@senate.idaho.gov
Committees: Local Government and Taxation; Resources and
Environment; State Affairs

Senator **Mary Souza** (R-District 4).................(208) 661-4388
Counties Represented: Kootenai (part)
Term Expires: 2016
E-mail: msouza@senate.idaho.gov
Committees: Agricultural Affairs; Education; Judiciary and Rules

Senator **Michelle Stennett** (D-District 26).............(208) 726-8106
Counties Represented: Blaine, Camas, Gooding, Lincoln
Term Expires: 2016
P.O. Box 475, Ketchum, ID 83340
E-mail: mstennett@senate.idaho.gov
Committees: Local Government and Taxation; Resources and
Environment; State Affairs

Senator **Steven P. Thayn** (R-District 8) ...............(208) 332-1309
Counties Represented: Boise, Custer, Gem, Lemhi,    Res: (208) 365-6614
Valley (part)
Term Expires: 2016
5655 Hillview Road, Emmett, ID 83617
E-mail: sthayn@senate.idaho.gov
Committees: Commerce and Human Resources; Education; Finance
Education: Boise State BS

Senator **Steve Vick** (R-District 2)..................(208) 332-1309
Counties Represented: Kootenai (part)    Res: (208) 819-4189
Term Expires: 2016
2140 East Hanley Avenue, Dalton Gardens, ID 83815
E-mail: sjvick@senate.idaho.gov
Committees: Local Government and Taxation; Resources and
Environment; Transportation
Education: Montana State 1979 BS

Senator **Janie Ward-Engelking** (D-District 18).........(208) 332-1309
Counties Represented: Ada (part)    Res: (208) 385-9564
Term Expires: 2016
3578 South Crosspoint Ave, Boise, ID 83706
PO Box 170117, Boise, ID 83717
E-mail: jwardengelking@senate.idaho.gov
Committees: Agricultural Affairs; Commerce and Human Resources;
Education
Education: Idaho State BS; Boise State MS

Senator **Chuck Winder** (R-District 20)...............(208) 332-1354
Counties Represented: Ada (part)    Tel: (208) 866-0113
Term Expires: 2016      Res: (208) 853-9090
5528 North Ebbetts Avenue, Boise, ID 83713    Fax: (208) 389-2088
E-mail: cwinder@senate.idaho.gov
Committees: State Affairs; Transportation

# Senate Standing Committees

## Agricultural Affairs
State Capitol Building, Room WW53, Boise, ID 83720-0081
Tel: (208) 332-1330

**Majority Members** | **Minority Members**
Jim Rice (R-10) *Chair* | Grant Burgoyne (D-16)
Clifford R. "Cliff" Bayer (R-21) | Janie Ward-Engelking (D-18)
  *Vice Chair*
Lori Den Hartog (R-22)
Mark Harris (R-32)
Abby Lee (R-9)
Jim Patrick (R-25)
Mary Souza (R-4)

## Commerce and Human Resources
State Capitol Building, Room WW54, Boise, ID 83720-0081
Tel: (208) 332-1333

**Majority Members** | **Minority Members**
Jim Patrick (R-25) *Chair* | Dan J. Schmidt (D-5)
Fred S. Martin (R-15) *Vice Chair* | Janie Ward-Engelking (D-18)
Jim Guthrie (R-28)
Lee Heider (R-24)
Todd M. Lakey (R-12)
Jim Rice (R-10)
Steven P. Thayn (R-8)

## Education
State Capitol Building, Room WW55, Boise, ID 83720-0081
Tel: (208) 332-1321

**Majority Members** | **Minority Members**
Dean M. Mortimer (R-30) *Chair* | Cherie Buckner-Webb (D-19)
Steven P. Thayn (R-8) *Vice Chair* | Janie Ward-Engelking (D-18)
Kelly Arthur Anthon (R-27)
Lori Den Hartog (R-22)
Bob Nonini (R-3)
Jim Patrick (R-25)
Mary Souza (R-4)

## Finance
State Capitol Building, Room C310, Boise, ID 83720-0081
Tel: (208) 334-4735

**Majority Members** | **Minority Members**
Shawn Keough (R-1) *Chair* | Roy Lacey (D-29)
Dan G. Johnson (R-6) *Vice Chair* | Dan J. Schmidt (D-5)
R. Steven Bair (R-31)
Bert Brackett (R-23)
Jim Guthrie (R-28)
Dean M. Mortimer (R-30)
Sheryl L. Nuxoll (R-7)
Steven P. Thayn (R-8)

## Health and Welfare
State Capitol Building, Room WW54, Boise, ID 83720-0081
Tel: (208) 332-1319

**Majority Members** | **Minority Members**
Lee Heider (R-24) *Chair* | Maryanne Jordan (D-17)
Sheryl L. Nuxoll (R-7) *Vice Chair* | Dan J. Schmidt (D-5)
Marv Hagedorn (R-14)
Mark Harris (R-32)
Abby Lee (R-9)
Patti Anne Lodge (R-11)
Fred S. Martin (R-15)

## Judiciary and Rules
State Capitol Building, Room WW54, Boise, ID 83720-0081
Tel: (208) 332-1317

**Majority Members** | **Minority Members**
Patti Anne Lodge (R-11) *Chair* | Grant Burgoyne (D-16)
Bob Nonini (R-3) *Vice Chair* | Maryanne Jordan (D-17)
Kelly Arthur Anthon (R-27)
Bart M. Davis (R-33)
Dan G. Johnson (R-6)
Abby Lee (R-9)
Mary Souza (R-4)

## Local Government and Taxation
State Capitol Building, Room WW53, Boise, ID 83720-0081
Tel: (208) 332-1315

**Majority Members** | **Minority Members**
Jeffery C. "Jeff" Siddoway (R-35) | Grant Burgoyne (D-16)
  *Chair* | Michelle Stennett (D-26)
Jim Guthrie (R-28) *Vice Chair*
Clifford R. "Cliff" Bayer (R-21)
Dan G. Johnson (R-6)
Curt McKenzie (R-13)
Jim Rice (R-10)
Steve Vick (R-2)

## Resources and Environment
State Capitol Building, Room WW55, Boise, ID 83720-0081
Tel: (208) 332-1323

**Majority Members** | **Minority Members**
R. Steven Bair (R-31) *Chair* | Roy Lacey (D-29)
Steve Vick (R-2) *Vice Chair* | Michelle Stennett (D-26)
Clifford R. "Cliff" Bayer (R-21)
Marv Hagedorn (R-14)
Lee Heider (R-24)
Sheryl L. Nuxoll (R-7)
Jeffery C. "Jeff" Siddoway (R-35)

LEGISLATIVE BRANCH

## State Affairs

State Capitol Building, Room WW55, Boise, ID 83720-0081
Tel: (208) 332-1326

| **Majority Members** | **Minority Members** |
|---|---|
| Curt McKenzie (R-13) *Chair* | Michelle Stennett (D-26) |
| Patti Anne Lodge (R-11) *Vice Chair* | |
| Bart M. Davis (R-33) | |
| Brent Hill (R-34) | |
| Todd M. Lakey (R-12) | |
| Jeffery C. "Jeff" Siddoway (R-35) | |
| Chuck Winder (R-20) | |

## Transportation

State Capitol Building, Room WW53, Boise, ID 83720-0081
Tel: (208) 332-1332

| **Majority Members** | **Minority Members** |
|---|---|
| Bert Brackett (R-23) *Chair* | Cherie Buckner-Webb (D-19) |
| Marv Hagedorn (R-14) *Vice Chair* | Roy Lacey (D-29) |
| Lori Den Hartog (R-22) | |
| Shawn Keough (R-1) | |
| Bob Nonini (R-3) | |
| Steve Vick (R-2) | |
| Chuck Winder (R-20) | |

# Idaho House of Representatives

P.O. Box 83720 State Capitol Building, Boise, ID 83720-0038

Speaker of the House **Scott Bedke** (R)..................(208) 332-1120
   Education: BYU BA
   Administrative Assistant **Susan Frieders**..............(208) 332-1111
Majority Leader **Michael "Mike" Moyle** (R)............(208) 332-1120
   Education: BYU (Attended)
Assistant Majority Leader **Brent J. Crane** (R)...........(208) 332-1058
   Education: Boise State 2005 BA
Majority Caucus Chairman **John Vander Woude** (R).....(208) 332-1141
Minority Leader **John Rusche** (D)...................(208) 332-1130
   Education: Notre Dame 1973 BS; Washington U (MO) 1977 MD
   Chief of Staff **Morgan Hill**.........................(208) 332-1132
Assistant Minority Leader **Mathew Erpelding** (D).......(208) 332-1141
   Education: Idaho State BA; Idaho MA
Minority Caucus Chairman **Donna L. Pence** (D).........(208) 332-1032
   Education: Idaho 1964 BS; Idaho State 1966 MA
Chief Clerk of the House **Bonnie Alexander**............(208) 332-1141
Sergeant-at-Arms **Claudia Howell**....................(208) 332-1150
Chief Fiscal Officer **Terri Franks-Smith**................(208) 332-1112

## Representatives

**Party Affiliation Statistics:** Republicans: 56, Democrats: 14

Representative **Neil A. Anderson** (R-District 31A).......(208) 332-1141
   Counties Represented: Bingham (part)    Res: (208) 684-3723
   Term Expires: 2016
   71 South 700 West, Blackfoot, ID 83221
   E-mail: nanderson@house.idaho.gov
   Committees: Commerce and Human Resources; Revenue and Taxation
   Education: Idaho State BA
Representative **Robert Anderst** (R-District 12A).........(208) 332-1141
   Counties Represented: Canyon (part)    Res: (208) 442-1092
   Term Expires: 2016
   7401 East Grey Lag Drive, Nampa, ID 83687
   E-mail: randerst@house.idaho.gov
   Committees: Business; Environment, Energy and Technology; Revenue and Taxation
   Education: Idaho State 1992 AA
Representative **Ken Andrus** (R-District 28A)............(208) 332-1046
   Counties Represented: Bannock (part), Power (part)    Tel: (208) 244-2057
   Term Expires: 2016    Res: (208) 776-5380
   6948 East Old Oregon Trail Road, Lava Hot Springs, ID 83246
   E-mail: kandrus@house.idaho.gov
   Committees: Agricultural Affairs; Resources and Conservation; State Affairs
   Education: BYU 1960 BS
Representative **Vito Barbieri** (R-District 2A)............(208) 332-1141
   Counties Represented: Kootenai (part)    Res: (208) 762-3737
   Term Expires: 2016
   564 East Prairie Avenue, Dalton Gardens, ID 83815
   E-mail: vbar@house.idaho.gov
   Committees: Business; Local Government; State Affairs
   Education: Western St Orange County JD

Representative **Linden B. Bateman** (R-District 33B)......(208) 332-1141
   Counties Represented: Bonneville (part)    Res: (208) 524-0927
   Term Expires: 2016
   170 East 23rd Street, Idaho Falls, ID 83404
   E-mail: lbateman@house.idaho.gov
   Committees: Resources and Conservation; State Affairs; Transportation and Defense
   Education: BYU BA
Representative **Gayle Batt** (R-District 11A)............(208) 332-1047
   Counties Represented: Canyon (part)    Res: (208) 337-5600
   Term Expires: 2016
   25253 Graphic Lane, Wilder, ID 83676
   E-mail: gbatt@house.idaho.gov
   Committees: Agricultural Affairs; Business; State Affairs
   Education: Oregon State BA
Representative **Scott Bedke** (R-District 27A)...........(208) 332-1120
   Counties Represented: Cassia (part), Minidoka    Res: (208) 862-3619
   (part)    Fax: (208) 862-3688
   Term Expires: 2016
   P.O. Box 89, Oakley, ID 83346
   E-mail: sbedke@house.idaho.gov
Representative **Maxine T. Bell** (R-District 25A).........(208) 334-4734
   Counties Represented: Jerome (part), Twin Falls    Res: (208) 324-4296
   (part)
   Term Expires: 2016
   194 South 300 East, Jerome, ID 83338
   E-mail: mbell@house.idaho.gov
   Committees: Agricultural Affairs; Appropriations
Representative **Merrill Beyeler** (R-District 8B)...........(208) 768-2651
   Counties Represented: Boise (part), Custer (part), Gem (part), Lemhi (part), Valley (part)
   Term Expires: 2016
   E-mail: mbeyeler@house.idaho.gov
   Committees: Business; Environment, Energy and Technology; Health and Welfare
Representative **Judy Boyle** (R-District 9B)..............(208) 332-1064
   Counties Represented: Adams (part), Canyon (part),    Res: (208) 355-3225
   Payette (part), Washington (part)
   Term Expires: 2016
   2301 Valley Road, Midvale, ID 83645
   E-mail: jboyle@house.idaho.gov
   Committees: Agricultural Affairs; Education; Resources and Conservation
Representative **Van Burtenshaw** (R-District 35A)........(208) 663-4607
   Counties Represented: Butte (part), Clark (part),    Fax: (208) 663-4760
   Fremont (part), Jefferson (part)
   Term Expires: 2016
   E-mail: vburtenshaw@house.idaho.gov
   Committees: Agricultural Affairs; Appropriations; Resources and Conservation
Representative **Greg Chaney** (R-District 10B)...........(208) 585-8708
   Counties Represented: Canyon (part)
   Term Expires: 2016
   E-mail: gchaney@house.idaho.gov
   Committees: Commerce and Human Resources; Environment, Energy and Technology; Revenue and Taxation
Representative **Don Cheatham** (R-District 3B).........(208) 332-1000
   Counties Represented: Kootenai (part)
   Term Expires: 2016
   E-mail: dcheatham@house.idaho.gov
   Committees: Judiciary, Rules and Administration; Local Government; State Affairs
Representative **Susan B. "Sue" Chew** (D-District 17B)...(208) 332-1030
   Counties Represented: Ada (part)    Res: (208) 344-0098
   Term Expires: 2016
   1304 Lincoln Avenue, Boise, ID 83706
   E-mail: schew@house.idaho.gov
   Committees: Commerce and Human Resources; Health and Welfare
   Education: UC Berkeley BS; UC San Francisco PharmD
Representative **Lance W. Clow** (R-District 24A).........(208) 332-1141
   Counties Represented: Twin Falls (part)    Res: (208) 733-5767
   Term Expires: 2016
   2170 Bitterroot Drive, Twin Falls, ID 83301
   E-mail: lclow@house.idaho.gov
   Committees: Business; Education; Local Government
   Education: Cal Lutheran U 1969 BA
Representative **Gary E. Collins** (R-District 13B).........(208) 332-1063
   Counties Represented: Canyon (part)    Res: (208) 466-5460
   Term Expires: 2016
   2019 East Massachusetts, Nampa, ID 83686
   E-mail: gcollins@house.idaho.gov
   Committees: Business; Local Government; Revenue and Taxation

Representative **Brent J. Crane** (R-District 13A) . . . . . . . . .(208) 332-1058
Counties Represented: Canyon (part)                Tel: (208) 466-0613
Term Expires: 2016                                 Fax: (208) 461-4815
P.O. Box 86, Nampa, ID 83653
E-mail: bcrane@house.idaho.gov
Committees: Business; State Affairs; Ways and Means

Representative
**Thomas E. "Tom" Dayley** (R-District 21B) . . . . . . . . . .(208) 332-1141
Counties Represented: Ada (part)                   Res: (208) 562-0276
Term Expires: 2016
4892 South Willandra Way, Boise, ID 83709
E-mail: tdayley@house.idaho.gov
Committees: Agricultural Affairs; Judiciary, Rules and Administration;
Revenue and Taxation
Education: BYU BA; USC MA

Representative **Reed DeMordaunt** (R-District 14B) . . . . . . (208) 332-1141
Counties Represented: Ada (part)                   Dist: (888) 340-9866
Term Expires: 2016                                 Res: (208) 938-4845
1017 South Arbor Island Way, Eagle, ID 83616
E-mail: reedd@house.idaho.gov
Committees: Business; Education
Education: BYU BA; South Carolina MA; American U (Cairo) MA

Representative **Sage Dixon** (R-District 1B) . . . . . . . . . . . . (208) 265-2547
Counties Represented: Bonner (part), Boundary (part)
Term Expires: 2016
E-mail: sdixon@house.idaho.gov
Committees: Business; Education; Transportation and Defense

Representative **Mathew Erpelding** (D-District 19A) . . . . . . (208) 332-1141
Counties Represented: Ada (part)                   Res: (208) 856-0291
Term Expires: 2016
2519 West Idaho Street, Boise, ID 83702
E-mail: merpelding@house.idaho.gov
Committees: Agricultural Affairs; Resources and Conservation;
Revenue and Taxation; Ways and Means

Representative **John L. Gannon** (D-District 17A) . . . . . . . (208) 332-1141
Counties Represented: Ada (part)                   Res: (208) 343-1608
Term Expires: 2016
2104 South Pond Street, Boise, ID 83705
E-mail: jgannon@house.idaho.gov
Committees: Appropriations; Judiciary, Rules and Administration
Education: UC Davis BA; Hastings JD

Representative **Terry Gestrin** (R-District 8A) . . . . . . . . . . . (208) 332-1120
Counties Represented: Boise (part), Custer (part),   Res: (208) 325-8844
Gem (part), Lemhi (part), Valley (part)
Term Expires: 2016
P.O. Box 399, Donnelly, ID 83615
E-mail: tgestrin@house.idaho.gov
Committees: Education; Resources and Conservation; Transportation
and Defense
Education: Idaho State BABA

Representative **Marc Gibbs** (R-District 32A) . . . . . . . . . . . (208) 332-1042
Counties Represented: Bear Lake (part), Bonneville   Res: (208) 425-3385
(part), Caribou (part), Franklin (part), Oneida (part),   Fax: (208) 425-3329
Teton (part)
Term Expires: 2016
632 Highway 34, Grace, ID 83241
E-mail: mgibbs@house.idaho.gov
Committees: Appropriations; Resources and Conservation
Education: Utah State BA

Representative **Steven C. Harris** (R-District 21A) . . . . . . . (208) 332-1141
Counties Represented: Ada (part)                   Res: (208) 888-5838
Term Expires: 2016
851 East Martinique Drive, Meridian, ID 83642
E-mail: sharris@house.idaho.gov
Committees: Commerce and Human Resources; Education;
Transportation and Defense
Education: BYU MS

Representative **Stephen Hartgen** (R-District 24B) . . . . . . . (208) 332-1061
Counties Represented: Twin Falls (part)            Res: (208) 733-5790
Term Expires: 2016
1681 West Wildflower Lane, Twin Falls, ID 83301
E-mail: shartgen@house.idaho.gov
Committees: Commerce and Human Resources; Environment, Energy
and Technology; Revenue and Taxation
Education: Amherst BA; Minnesota PhD

Representative **Brandon A. Hixon** (R-District 10A) . . . . . . .(208) 332-1141
Counties Represented: Canyon (part)                Res: (208) 440-1074
Term Expires: 2016
910 North Plateau Avenue, Caldwell, ID 83605
E-mail: bhixon@house.idaho.gov
Committees: Business; Health and Welfare; Transportation and Defense

Representative **James Holtzclaw** (R-District 20B) . . . . . . . (208) 332-1141
Counties Represented: Ada (part)                   Res: (208) 284-9542
Term Expires: 2016
3720 North Heritage View Avenue, Meridian, ID 83646
E-mail: jholtzclaw@house.idaho.gov
Committees: Commerce and Human Resources; State Affairs;
Transportation and Defense
Education: George Fox U BA

Representative **Wendy Horman** (R-District 30B) . . . . . . . . (208) 332-1141
Counties Represented: Bonneville (part)            Res: (208) 522-4387
Term Expires: 2016
1860 Heather Circle, Idaho Falls, ID 83406
E-mail: wendyhorman@house.idaho.gov
Committees: Appropriations; Commerce and Human Resources; Local
Government

Representative **Paulette Emily Jordan** (D-District 5A) . . . . (208) 819-3773
Counties Represented: Benewah (part), Latah (part)
Term Expires: 2016
E-mail: pjordan@house.idaho.gov
Committees: Business; Environment, Energy and Technology; State
Affairs

Representative **Clark Kauffman** (R-District 25B) . . . . . . . . (208) 332-1141
Counties Represented: Jerome (part), Twin Falls   Res: (208) 326-4131
(part)
Term Expires: 2016
3791 North 2100 East, Filer, ID 83328
E-mail: ckauffman@house.idaho.gov
Committees: Business; Revenue and Taxation; Transportation and
Defense

Representative **Ryan Kerby** (R-District 9A) . . . . . . . . . . . . (208) 739-0190
Counties Represented: Adams (part), Canyon (part), Payette (part),
Washington (part)
Term Expires: 2016
E-mail: rkerby@house.idaho.gov
Committees: Agricultural Affairs; Education; Judiciary, Rules and
Administration

Representative **Phylis K. King** (D-District 18B) . . . . . . . . . (208) 332-1080
Counties Represented: Ada (part)                   Res: (208) 344-0202
Term Expires: 2016
2107 Palouse, Boise, ID 83705
E-mail: pking@house.idaho.gov
Committees: Appropriations; Commerce and Human Resources;
Transportation and Defense
Education: Colorado State 1968 BS

Representative **Hy Kloc** (D-District 16B) . . . . . . . . . . . . . . .(208) 332-1141
Counties Represented: Ada (part)                   Res: (208) 343-8465
Term Expires: 2016
3932 Oak Park Place, Boise, ID 83703
E-mail: hkloc@house.idaho.gov
Committees: Education; Local Government
Education: Western Michigan 1970 BA

Representative
**Thomas F. "Tom" Loertscher** (R-District 32B) . . . . . . . (208) 332-1183
Counties Represented: Bear Lake (part), Bonneville   Res: (208) 522-3072
(part), Caribou (part), Franklin (part), Oneida (part),   Fax: (208) 522-1141
Teton (part)
Term Expires: 2016
1357 Bone Road, Iona, ID 83427
E-mail: tloertscher@house.idaho.gov
Committees: Local Government; State Affairs
Education: Utah BS

Representative **Lynn M. Luker** (R-District 15A) . . . . . . . . . .(208) 332-1039
Counties Represented: Ada (part)                   Tel: (208) 343-0022
Term Expires: 2016                                 Res: (208) 375-8254
514 South El Blanco Drive, Boise, ID 83709        Fax: (208) 375-0501
E-mail: lluker@house.idaho.gov
Committees: Local Government; State Affairs
Education: UC Berkeley 1977 BA; Idaho 1980 JD

Representative **Luke Malek** (R-District 4A) . . . . . . . . . . . . (208) 332-1141
Counties Represented: Kootenai (part)              Res: (208) 661-3881
Term Expires: 2016
P.O. Box 363, Coeur d'Alene, ID 83816
E-mail: lmalek@house.idaho.gov
Committees: Appropriations; Judiciary, Rules and Administration;
Local Government
Education: Col Idaho 2004 BA; Idaho 2010 JD

Representative **John McCrostie** (D-District 16A) . . . . . . . . (208) 440-8317
Counties Represented: Ada (part)
Term Expires: 2016
E-mail: jmccrostie@house.idaho.gov
Committees: Judiciary, Rules and Administration; Local Government;
State Affairs

*(continued on next page)*

LEGISLATIVE BRANCH

**Representatives** *continued*

Representative **Patrick E. McDonald** (R-District 15B).....(208) 332-1000
Counties Represented: Ada (part)          Res: (208) 938-1329
Term Expires: 2016
13359 West Annabrook Drive, Boise, ID 83713
E-mail: pmcdonald@house.idaho.gov
Committees: Education; Judiciary, Rules and Administration;
Transportation and Defense
Education: Idaho State BS, MEd

Representative **Shannon McMillan** (R-District 7A).......(208) 332-1141
Counties Represented: Bonner (part), Clearwater    Dist: (208) 752-1800
(part), Idaho (part), Shoshone (part)             Fax: (208) 752-1900
Term Expires: 2016
P.O. Box 26, Silverton, ID 83867
E-mail: smcmillan@house.idaho.gov
Committees: Agricultural Affairs; Judiciary, Rules and Administration;
State Affairs

Representative **Ron Mendive** (R-District 3A)...........(208) 332-1141
Counties Represented: Kootenai (part)          Res: (208) 667-9330
Term Expires: 2016
3732 South Dusty Lane, Coeur d'Alene, ID 83814
E-mail: rmendive@house.idaho.gov
Committees: Education; Environment, Energy and Technology;
Resources and Conservation
Education: North Idaho

Representative **Steven Miller** (R-District 26A)..........(208) 332-1141
Counties Represented: Blaine (part), Camas (part),    Res: (208) 764-2560
Gooding (part), Lincoln (part)
Term Expires: 2016
1208 East 200 North, Fairfield, ID 83327
E-mail: smiller@house.idaho.gov
Committees: Agricultural Affairs; Appropriations; Resources and
Conservation
Education: Idaho BS

Representative **Jason Monks** (R-District 22B)...........(208) 332-1141
Counties Represented: Ada (part)
Term Expires: 2016
1002 West Washington Drive, Meridian, ID 83642
E-mail: jmonks@house.idaho.gov
Committees: Appropriations; Business; Transportation and Defense
Education: BYU BA

Representative **Michael "Mike" Moyle** (R-District 14A) .. (208) 332-1120
Counties Represented: Ada (part)          Res: (208) 286-7842
Term Expires: 2016                        Fax: (208) 286-9540
480 North Plummer Road, Star, ID 83669
E-mail: mmoyle@house.idaho.gov
Committees: Resources and Conservation; Revenue and Taxation; Ways
and Means

Representative **Ronald M. Nate** (R-District 34A) ........ (208) 403-3609
Counties Represented: Bonneville (part), Madison (part)
Term Expires: 2016
E-mail: nater@house.idaho.gov
Committees: Environment, Energy and Technology; Judiciary, Rules
and Administration; Revenue and Taxation

Representative **Peter "Pete" Nielsen** (R-District 23B) .... (208) 332-1054
Counties Represented: Elmore (part), Owyhee    Res: (208) 832-4382
(part), Twin Falls (part)
Term Expires: 2016
4303 Southwest Easy Street, Mountain Home, ID 83647
E-mail: pnielsen@house.idaho.gov
Committees: Commerce and Human Resources; Environment, Energy
and Technology; State Affairs

Representative **Mark Nye** (D-District 29A)..............(208) 221-6109
Counties Represented: Bannock (part)
Term Expires: 2016
E-mail: mnye@house.idaho.gov
Committees: Judiciary, Rules and Administration; Local Government;
Revenue and Taxation

Representative **Kelley Packer** (R-District 28B)...........(208) 332-1141
Counties Represented: Bannock (part), Power (part)    Res: (208) 254-3953
Term Expires: 2016
104 Mountain View Drive, McCammon, ID 83250
E-mail: kpacker@house.idaho.gov
Committees: Commerce and Human Resources; Health and Welfare;
Transportation and Defense
Education: American InterContinental AA

Representative **Joe A. Palmer** (R-District 20A) .........(208) 332-1062
Counties Represented: Ada (part)          Tel: (208) 887-9488
Term Expires: 2016                        Fax: (208) 884-0181
1524 North Meridian Road, Meridian, ID 83642
E-mail: jpalmer@house.idaho.gov
Committees: Business; State Affairs; Transportation and Defense
Education: Boise State (Attended)

Representative **Donna L. Pence** (D-District 26B).........(208) 332-1032
Counties Represented: Blaine (part), Camas (part),    Res: (208) 934-5302
Gooding (part), Lincoln (part)
Term Expires: 2016
1960 U.S. Highway 26, Gooding, ID 83330
E-mail: dpence@house.idaho.gov
Committees: Agricultural Affairs; Education; Resources and
Conservation; Ways and Means

Representative **Christy Perry** (R-District 11B) ..........(208) 332-1141
Counties Represented: Canyon (part)          Res: (208) 880-9720
Term Expires: 2016
8791 Elkhorn Lane, Nampa, ID 83686
E-mail: cperry@house.idaho.gov
Committees: Judiciary, Rules and Administration; Local Government;
Ways and Means
Education: Boise State BA, MA

Representative **Dell Raybould** (R-District 34B) ..........(208) 332-1173
Counties Represented: Bonneville (part), Madison    Res: (208) 356-6837
(part)
Term Expires: 2016
3215 North 2000 West, Rexburg, ID 83440
E-mail: draybould@house.idaho.gov
Committees: Resources and Conservation; Revenue and Taxation
Education: Ricks (Attended)

Representative **Eric Redman** (R-District 2B) ...........(208) 623-6383
Counties Represented: Kootenai (part)
Term Expires: 2016
E-mail: eredman@house.idaho.gov
Committees: Commerce and Human Resources; Health and Welfare;
Local Government

Representative **Paul Romrell** (R-District 35B) ..........(208) 332-1141
Counties Represented: Butte (part), Clark (part), Fremont (part),
Jefferson (part)
Term Expires: 2016
512 Park Street, St. Anthony, ID 83445
E-mail: promrell@house.idaho.gov
Committees: Agricultural Affairs; Commerce and Human Resources;
Health and Welfare

Representative **Ilana Rubel** (D-District 18A) ...........(208) 332-1141
Counties Represented: Ada (part)          Res: (208) 866-4776
Term Expires: 2016
2750 Migratory Drive, Boise, ID 83706
E-mail: irubel@house.idaho.gov
Committees: Education; Environment, Energy and Technology;
Resources and Conservation

Representative **Dan Rudolph** (D-District 6A)............(208) 413-6337
Counties Represented: Lewis (part), Nez Perce (part)
Term Expires: 2016
E-mail: drudolph@house.idaho.gov
Committees: Commerce and Human Resources; Revenue and Taxation;
Transportation and Defense

Representative **John Rusche** (D-District 6B) ...........(208) 332-1130
Counties Represented: Lewis (part), Nez Perce    Res: (208) 743-1339
(part)                                          Fax: (866) 821-0184
Term Expires: 2016
1405 27th Avenue, Lewiston, ID 83501
E-mail: jrusche@house.idaho.gov
Committees: Business; Environment, Energy and Technology; Health
and Welfare; Ways and Means

Representative **Heather Scott** (R-District 1A) ..........(208) 920-3120
Counties Represented: Bonner (part), Boundary (part)
Term Expires: 2016
E-mail: hscott@house.idaho.gov
Committees: Environment, Energy and Technology; Judiciary, Rules
and Administration; Revenue and Taxation

Representative **Paul E. Shepherd** (R-District 7B) ........(208) 332-1067
Counties Represented: Bonner (part), Clearwater    Res: (208) 628-3695
(part), Idaho (part), Shoshone (part)
Term Expires: 2016
P.O. Box 277, Riggins, ID 83549
E-mail: pshepherd@house.idaho.gov
Committees: Education; Resources and Conservation; Transportation
and Defense

Representative **Kathleen Sims** (R-District 4B) . . . . . . . . . (208) 332-1141
Counties Represented: Kootenai (part)          Dist: (208) 765-5005
Term Expires: 2016                              Res: (208) 540-1154
PO Box 399, Coeur d'Alene, ID 83816
E-mail: ksims@house.idaho.gov
Committees: Judiciary, Rules and Administration; Local Government;
State Affairs
Education: North Idaho AA

Representative **Elaine Smith** (D-District 29B) . . . . . . . . . . (208) 332-1031
Counties Represented: Bannock (part)           Tel: (208) 235-3231
Term Expires: 2016                             Res: (208) 237-1462
3759 Heron Avenue, Pocatello, ID 83201         Fax: (208) 235-3280
E-mail: esmith@house.idaho.gov
Committees: Business; Environment, Energy and Technology; State
Affairs
Education: Idaho State 1968 BA

Representative **Jeff Thompson** (R-District 30A) . . . . . . . . (208) 332-1081
Counties Represented: Bonneville (part)        Tel: (208) 681-4310
Term Expires: 2016                             Res: (208) 524-7367
1739 Peggy's Lane, Idaho Falls, ID 83402
E-mail: jthompson@house.idaho.gov
Committees: Business; Environment, Energy and Technology; Revenue
and Taxation
Education: Liberty 1986 BA; Idaho State 2006 MBA

Representative **Caroline Nilsson Troy** (R-District 5B) . . . . . (208) 285-0182
Counties Represented: Benewah (part), Latah (part)
Term Expires: 2016
E-mail: cntroy@house.idaho.gov
Committees: Agricultural Affairs; Business; Health and Welfare

Representative **Janet Trujillo** (R-District 33A) . . . . . . . . . . (208) 332-1141
Counties Represented: Bonneville (part)        Res: (208) 419-8266
Term Expires: 2016
3144 Disney Drive, Idaho Falls, ID 83404
E-mail: jtrujillo@house.idaho.gov
Committees: Environment, Energy and Technology; Judiciary, Rules
and Administration; Revenue and Taxation

Representative **Julie Van Orden** (R-District 31B) . . . . . . . . (208) 332-1141
Counties Represented: Bingham (part)           Res: (208) 684-4052
Term Expires: 2016
425 South 1100 West, Pingree, ID 83262
E-mail: jvanorden@house.idaho.gov
Committees: Agricultural Affairs; Education; Resources and
Conservation

Representative **John Vander Woude** (R-District 22A) . . . . (208) 332-1141
Counties Represented: Ada (part)               Tel: (208) 888-3003
Term Expires: 2016                             Res: (208) 888-4210
5311 Ridgewood Road, Nampa, ID 83687           Fax: (208) 888-9268
E-mail: jvanderwoude@house.idaho.gov
Committees: Environment, Energy and Technology; Health and
Welfare; Resources and Conservation; Ways and Means

Representative **Richard Wills** (R-District 23A) . . . . . . . . . . (208) 332-1181
Counties Represented: Elmore (part), Owyhee    Tel: (208) 484-0403
(part), Twin Falls (part)                      Res: (208) 366-7408
Term Expires: 2016                             Fax: (208) 366-2457
P.O. Box 602, Glenns Ferry, ID 83623
E-mail: rwills@house.idaho.gov
Committees: Education; Judiciary, Rules and Administration;
Transportation and Defense

Representative **Melissa Wintrow** (D-District 19B) . . . . . . . (208) 949-0279
Counties Represented: Ada (part)
Term Expires: 2016
E-mail: mwintrow@house.idaho.gov
Committees: Judiciary, Rules and Administration; State Affairs;
Transportation and Defense

Representative **Fred Wood** (R-District 27B) . . . . . . . . . . . . (208) 332-1074
Counties Represented: Cassia (part), Minidoka  Res: (208) 312-1056
(part)                                         Fax: (208) 677-3136
Term Expires: 2016
P.O. Box 1207, Burley, ID 83318-0828
E-mail: fwood@house.idaho.gov
Committees: Health and Welfare
Education: Tulane BS, MD

Representative **Rick D. Youngblood** (R-District 12B) . . . . . (208) 332-1141
Counties Represented: Canyon (part)            Res: (208) 412-5107
Term Expires: 2016
12612 Smith Avenue, Nampa, ID 83651
E-mail: ryoungblood@house.idaho.gov
Committees: Appropriations; Business; Resources and Conservation;
Transportation and Defense
Education: North Idaho (Attended); Col Idaho (Attended)

# House Standing Committees
## Agricultural Affairs
State Capitol Building, Room EW20, Boise, ID 83720-0038
Tel: (208) 332-1137

**Majority Members**
Ken Andrus (R-28A) *Chair*
Judy Boyle (R-9B) *Vice Chair*
Gayle Batt (R-11A)
Maxine T. Bell (R-25A)
Van Burtenshaw (R-35A)
Thomas E. "Tom" Dayley (R-21B)
Ryan Kerby (R-9A)
Shannon McMillan (R-7A)
Steven Miller (R-26A)
Paul Romrell (R-35B)
Caroline Nilsson Troy (R-5B)
Julie Van Orden (R-31B)

**Minority Members**
Mathew Erpelding (D-19A)
Donna L. Pence (D-26B)

## Appropriations
State Capitol Building, Room C310, Boise, ID 83720-0038
Tel: (208) 334-4736

**Majority Members**
Maxine T. Bell (R-25A) *Chair*
Marc Gibbs (R-32A)
Van Burtenshaw (R-35A)
Wendy Horman (R-30B)
Luke Malek (R-4A)
Steven Miller (R-26A)
Jason Monks (R-22B)
Rick D. Youngblood (R-12B)

**Minority Members**
John L. Gannon (D-17A)
Phylis K. King (D-18B)

## Business
State Capitol Building, Room EW41, Boise, ID 83720-0038
Tel: (208) 332-1139

**Majority Members**
Vito Barbieri (R-2A) *Chair*
Lance W. Clow (R-24A) *Vice Chair*
Robert Anderst (R-12A)
Gayle Batt (R-11A)
Merrill Beyeler (R-8B)
Gary E. Collins (R-13B)
Brent J. Crane (R-13A)
Reed DeMordaunt (R-14B)
Sage Dixon (R-1B)
Brandon A. Hixon (R-10A)
Clark Kauffman (R-25B)
Jason Monks (R-22B)
Joe A. Palmer (R-20A)
Jeff Thompson (R-30A)
Caroline Nilsson Troy (R-5B)
Rick D. Youngblood (R-12B)

**Minority Members**
Paulette Emily Jordan (D-5A)
John Rusche (D-6B)
Elaine Smith (D-29B)

## Commerce and Human Resources
State Capitol Building, Room EW05, Boise, ID 83720-0038
Tel: (208) 332-1147

**Majority Members**
Stephen Hartgen (R-24B) *Chair*
Neil A. Anderson (R-31A)
  *Vice Chair*
Greg Chaney (R-10B)
Steven C. Harris (R-21A)
James Holtzclaw (R-20B)
Wendy Horman (R-30B)
Peter "Pete" Nielsen (R-23B)
Kelley Packer (R-28B)
Eric Redman (R-2B)
Paul Romrell (R-35B)

**Minority Members**
Susan B. "Sue" Chew (D-17B)
Phylis K. King (D-18B)
Dan Rudolph (D-6A)

**LEGISLATIVE BRANCH**

**LEGISLATIVE BRANCH**

# Education

State Capitol Building, Room EW41, Boise, ID 83720-0038
Tel: (208) 332-1148

| **Majority Members** | **Minority Members** |
|---|---|
| Reed DeMordaunt (R-14B) *Chair* | Hy Kloc (D-16B) |
| Julie Van Orden (R-31B) *Vice Chair* | Donna L. Pence (D-26B) |
| Judy Boyle (R-9B) | Ilana Rubel (D-18A) |
| Lance W. Clow (R-24A) | |
| Sage Dixon (R-1B) | |
| Terry Gestrin (R-8A) | |
| Steven C. Harris (R-21A) | |
| Ryan Kerby (R-9A) | |
| Patrick E. McDonald (R-15B) | |
| Ron Mendive (R-3A) | |
| Paul E. Shepherd (R-7B) | |
| Richard Wills (R-23A) | |

# Environment, Energy and Technology

State Capitol Building, Room EW41, Boise, ID 83720-0038
Tel: (208) 332-1128

| **Majority Members** | **Minority Members** |
|---|---|
| Jeff Thompson (R-30A) *Chair* | Paulette Emily Jordan (D-5A) |
| Robert Anderst (R-12A) *Vice Chair* | Ilana Rubel (D-18A) |
| Merrill Beyeler (R-8B) | John Rusche (D-6B) |
| Greg Chaney (R-10B) | Elaine Smith (D-29B) |
| Stephen Hartgen (R-24B) | |
| Ron Mendive (R-3A) | |
| Ronald M. Nate (R-34A) | |
| Peter "Pete" Nielsen (R-23B) | |
| Heather Scott (R-1A) | |
| Janet Trujillo (R-33A) | |
| John Vander Woude (R-22A) | |

# Health and Welfare

State Capitol Building, Room EW42, Boise, ID 83720-0038
Tel: (208) 332-1138

| **Majority Members** | **Minority Members** |
|---|---|
| Fred Wood (R-27B) *Chair* | Susan B. "Sue" Chew (D-17B) |
| Kelley Packer (R-28B) *Vice Chair* | John Rusche (D-6B) |
| Merrill Beyeler (R-8B) | |
| Brandon A. Hixon (R-10A) | |
| Eric Redman (R-2B) | |
| Paul Romrell (R-35B) | |
| Caroline Nilsson Troy (R-5B) | |
| John Vander Woude (R-22A) | |

# Judiciary, Rules and Administration

State Capitol Building, Room EW42, Boise, ID 83720-0038
Tel: (208) 332-1127

| **Majority Members** | **Minority Members** |
|---|---|
| Richard Wills (R-23A) *Chair* | John L. Gannon (D-17A) |
| Thomas E. "Tom" Dayley (R-21B) *Vice Chair* | John McCrostie (D-16A) |
| Don Cheatham (R-3B) | Mark Nye (D-29A) |
| Ryan Kerby (R-9A) | Melissa Wintrow (D-19B) |
| Luke Malek (R-4A) | |
| Patrick E. McDonald (R-15B) | |
| Shannon McMillan (R-7A) | |
| Ronald M. Nate (R-34A) | |
| Christy Perry (R-11B) | |
| Heather Scott (R-1A) | |
| Kathleen Sims (R-4B) | |
| Janet Trujillo (R-33A) | |

# Local Government

State Capitol Building, Room EW05, Boise, ID 83720-0038
Tel: (208) 332-1147

| **Majority Members** | **Minority Members** |
|---|---|
| Lynn M. Luker (R-15A) *Chair* | Hy Kloc (D-16B) |
| Kathleen Sims (R-4B) *Vice Chair* | John McCrostie (D-16A) |
| Vito Barbieri (R-2A) | Mark Nye (D-29A) |
| Don Cheatham (R-3B) | |
| Lance W. Clow (R-24A) | |
| Gary E. Collins (R-13B) | |
| Wendy Horman (R-30B) | |
| Thomas F. "Tom" Loertscher (R-32B) | |
| Luke Malek (R-4A) | |
| Christy Perry (R-11B) | |
| Eric Redman (R-2B) | |

# Resources and Conservation

State Capitol Building, Room EW40, Boise, ID 83720-0038
Tel: (208) 332-1136

| **Majority Members** | **Minority Members** |
|---|---|
| Dell Raybould (R-34B) *Chair* | Mathew Erpelding (D-19A) |
| Terry Gestrin (R-8A) *Vice Chair* | Donna L. Pence (D-26B) |
| Ken Andrus (R-28A) | Ilana Rubel (D-18A) |
| Linden B. Bateman (R-33B) | |
| Judy Boyle (R-9B) | |
| Van Burtenshaw (R-35A) | |
| Marc Gibbs (R-32A) | |
| Ron Mendive (R-3A) | |
| Steven Miller (R-26A) | |
| Michael "Mike" Moyle (R-14A) | |
| Paul E. Shepherd (R-7B) | |
| John Vander Woude (R-22A) | |
| Julie Van Orden (R-31B) | |
| Rick D. Youngblood (R-12B) | |

# Revenue and Taxation

State Capitol, Room EW42, Boise, ID 83720-0038
Tel: (208) 332-1125

| **Majority Members** | **Minority Members** |
|---|---|
| Gary E. Collins (R-13B) *Chair* | Mathew Erpelding (D-19A) |
| Janet Trujillo (R-33A) *Vice Chair* | Mark Nye (D-29A) |
| Neil A. Anderson (R-31A) | Dan Rudolph (D-6A) |
| Robert Anderst (R-12A) | |
| Greg Chaney (R-10B) | |
| Thomas E. "Tom" Dayley (R-21B) | |
| Stephen Hartgen (R-24B) | |
| Clark Kauffman (R-25B) | |
| Michael "Mike" Moyle (R-14A) | |
| Ronald M. Nate (R-34A) | |
| Dell Raybould (R-34B) | |
| Heather Scott (R-1A) | |
| Jeff Thompson (R-30A) | |

# State Affairs

State Capitol Building, Room EW40, Boise, ID 83720-0038
Tel: (208) 332-1145

| **Majority Members** | **Minority Members** |
|---|---|
| Thomas F. "Tom" Loertscher (R-32B) *Chair* | Elaine Smith (D-29B) |
| Gayle Batt (R-11A) *Vice Chair* | Paulette Emily Jordan (D-5A) |
| Ken Andrus (R-28A) | John McCrostie (D-16A) |
| Vito Barbieri (R-2A) | Melissa Wintrow (D-19B) |
| Linden B. Bateman (R-33B) | |
| Don Cheatham (R-3B) | |
| Brent J. Crane (R-13A) | |
| James Holtzclaw (R-20B) | |
| Lynn M. Luker (R-15A) | |
| Shannon McMillan (R-7A) | |
| Peter "Pete" Nielsen (R-23B) | |
| Joe A. Palmer (R-20A) | |
| Kathleen Sims (R-4B) | |

## Transportation and Defense
State Capitol Building, Room EW40, Boise, ID 83720-0038
Tel: (208) 332-1146

**Majority Members**
Joe A. Palmer (R-20A) *Chair*
Paul E. Shepherd (R-7B) *Vice Chair*
Linden B. Bateman (R-33B)
Sage Dixon (R-1B)
Terry Gestrin (R-8A)
Steven C. Harris (R-21A)
Brandon A. Hixon (R-10A)
James Holtzclaw (R-20B)
Clark Kauffman (R-25B)
Patrick E. McDonald (R-15B)
Jason Monks (R-22B)
Kelley Packer (R-28B)
Richard Wills (R-23A)
Rick D. Youngblood (R-12B)

**Minority Members**
Phylis K. King (D-18B)
Dan Rudolph (D-6A)
Melissa Wintrow (D-19B)

## Ways and Means
State Capitol Building, Room E403, Boise, ID 83720-0038
Tel: (208) 332-1120

**Majority Members**
Christy Perry (R-11B) *Chair*
Brent J. Crane (R-13A)
Michael "Mike" Moyle (R-14A)
John Vander Woude (R-22A)

**Minority Members**
Mathew Erpelding (D-19A)
Donna L. Pence (D-26B)
John Rusche (D-6B)

# Illinois General Assembly
Tel: (217) 782-2000  Internet: www.ilga.gov

## Illinois Senate
State House, Springfield, IL 62706
Tel: (217) 782-5715

President of the Senate **John J. Cullerton** (D)...........(217) 782-2728
  Education: Loyola U (Chicago) 1970 BA, 1974 JD
President Pro Tem **Don Harmon** (D)....................(217) 782-8176
  Education: Knox (IL) 1988 BA; Chicago JD, MBA
Majority Leader **James F. Clayborne, Jr.** (D)..........(217) 782-5399
Assistant Majority Leader **Kimberly A. Lightford** (D)....(217) 782-8505
Assistant Majority Leader **Terry Link** (D).............(217) 782-8181
Assistant Majority Leader **Antonio "Tony" Muñoz** (D)...(217) 782-9415
Assistant Majority Leader **John M. Sullivan** (D)........(217) 782-2479
Assistant Majority Leader **Donne E. Trotter** (D).........(217) 782-3201
Majority Caucus Chair **Ira I. Silverstein** (D)...........(217) 782-5500
  Education: John Marshall 1985 JD
Majority Caucus Whip **William R. "Bill" Haine** (D)......(217) 782-5247
Majority Caucus Whip **Mattie Hunter** (D)..............(217) 782-5966
Majority Caucus Whip **Iris Y. Martinez** (D)............(217) 782-8191
Minority Leader **Christine Radogno** (R)...............(217) 782-9407
  Education: Loyola U (Chicago) BA, MSW
Deputy Minority Leader **Matt Murphy** (R).............(217) 782-4471
Assistant Minority Leader **William E. "Bill" Brady** (R)...(217) 782-6216
Assistant Minority Leader **David S. Luechtefeld** (R).....(217) 782-8137
Assistant Minority Leader **Sue Rezin** (R)..............(217) 782-3840
Assistant Minority Leader **Dave Syverson** (R)..........(217) 782-5413
Minority Caucus Chair **Pamela J. Althoff** (R)...........(217) 782-8000
Minority Caucus Whip **Chapin Rose** (R)...............(217) 558-1006
Sergeant-at-Arms **Claricel "Joe" Dominguez**...........(217) 782-5715
  Assistant Sergeant-at-Arms **Dirk R. Eilers**............(217) 782-5715
Secretary of the Senate **Tim Anderson**................(217) 782-5715
  Education: Illinois 1991 BA
  Assistant Secretary of Senate **Scott Kaiser**...........(217) 782-5715

## Senators
**Party Affiliation Statistics:** Republicans: 19, Democrats: 39,
Independents: 1

Senator **Pamela J. Althoff** (R-District 32)...........(217) 782-8000
  Counties Represented: Lake (part), McHenry (part)  Dist: (815) 455-6330
  Term Expires: 2017  Fax: (815) 679-6756
  5400 W. Elm street, Suite 103, McHenry, IL 60050
  E-mail: pamela@pamelaalthoff.net
  Committees: Appropriations II; Assignments; Committee of the Whole;
  Executive Appointments; Labor; Licensed Activities and Pensions;
  Revenue; Transportation
Senator **Neil Anderson** (R-District 36)...............(217) 782-5957
  Counties Represented: Carroll (part), Henry (part),  Dist: (309) 736-7084
  Rock Island, Whiteside (part)  Fax: (217) 782-0116
  Term Expires: 2019
  1825 Avenue of the Cities, Suite 1, Moline, IL 61265
  E-mail: neil@electneil.com
  Committees: Agriculture; Committee of the Whole; Energy and Public
  Utilities; Higher Education; Local Government; Transportation
Senator **Jason Barickman** (R-District 53)............(217) 782-6597
  Counties Represented: Ford, Iroquois, Livingston  Dist: (309) 661-2788
  (part), McLean (part), Vermilion (part), Woodford  Fax: (309) 210-5544
  (part)
  Term Expires: 2017
  2401 E Washington Street, Suite 201, Bloomington, IL 61704
  E-mail: jason@jasonbarickman.org
  Committees: Appropriations I; Commerce and Economic Development;
  Committee of the Whole; Education; Judiciary; Licensed Activities and
  Pensions
  Education: Illinois State 1998 BS; Illinois 2005 JD
Senator **Scott M. Bennett** (D-District 52)............(217) 782-5715
  Counties Represented: Champaign (part), Vermilion  Dist: (217) 355-5252
  (part)  Fax: (217) 355-5255
  Term Expires: 2019
  Committees: Agriculture; Appropriations II; Committee of the Whole;
  Criminal Law; Environment and Conservation; Higher Education;
  Labor
  Education: Illinois State BA

*(continued on next page)*

**Senators** *continued*

Senator **Jennifer Bertino-Tarrant** (D-District 49) . . . . . . . (217) 782-0052
Counties Represented: Kendall (part), Will (part)    Dist: (815) 254-4211
Term Expires: 2017    Fax: (815) 254-4213
15300 Route 59, Unit 202, Plainfield, IL 60544
E-mail: jbertino-tarrant@senatedem.ilga.gov
Committees: Appropriations II; Committee of the Whole; Education;
Labor; Licensed Activities and Pensions; Local Government;
Transportation
Education: Illinois State BS; U St Francis MS;
Loyola U (Chicago) 2006 EdD

Senator **Daniel Biss** (D-District 9) . . . . . . . . . . . . . . . . . . . . (217) 782-2119
Counties Represented: Cook (part)    Dist: (847) 568-1250
Term Expires: 2019    Fax: (847) 568-1256
3706 Dempster Street, Skokie, IL 60076
E-mail: dbiss@senatedem.ilga.gov
Committees: Appropriations I; Committee of the Whole; Education;
Financial Institutions; Human Services; Revenue
Education: Harvard 1998 BA; MIT 2002 PhD

Senator **Tim Bivins** (R-District 45) . . . . . . . . . . . . . . . . . . . (217) 782-0180
Counties Represented: Carroll (part), DeKalb    Dist: (815) 284-0045
(part), Jo Daviess, La Salle (part), Lee (part), Ogle,    Fax: (815) 284-0207
Stephenson, Whiteside (part), Winnebago (part)
Term Expires: 2019
629 North Galena, Dixon, IL 61021
E-mail: senatorbivins@grics.net
Committees: Appropriations I; Committee of the Whole; Environment
and Conservation; Human Services; Insurance; Local Government

Senator **William E. "Bill" Brady** (R-District 44) . . . . . . . . (217) 782-6216
Counties Represented: Logan, McLean (part),    Dist: (309) 664-4440
Menard, Sangamon (part), Tazewell (part)    Fax: (309) 664-8597
Term Expires: 2017
2203 Eastland Drive, Suite 3, Bloomington, IL 61704
E-mail: billbrady@senatorbillbrady.com
Committees: Commerce and Economic Development; Committee
of the Whole; Energy and Public Utilities; Executive; Insurance;
Transportation

Senator **Melinda Bush** (D-District 31) . . . . . . . . . . . . . . . . (217) 782-7353
Counties Represented: Lake (part)    Dist: (847) 548-5631
Term Expires: 2017    Fax: (217) 782-2115
10 North Lake Street, Suite 112, Grayslake, IL 60030
E-mail: mbush@senatedem.ilga.gov
Committees: Commerce and Economic Development; Committee of the
Whole; Education; Environment and Conservation; Human Services;
Revenue; State Government and Veterans Affairs

Senator **James F. Clayborne, Jr.** (D-District 57) . . . . . . . . (217) 782-5399
Counties Represented: Madison (part), St. Clair    Dist: (618) 875-1212
(part)    Fax: (618) 274-3010
Term Expires: 2019
10 Collinsville Avenue, Suite 210A, East St. Louis, IL 62201
E-mail: clayborne@senatedem.ilga.gov
Committees: Assignments; Committee of the Whole; Energy and Public
Utilities; Executive; Insurance

Senator **Jacqueline Y. "Jacqui" Collins** (D-District 16) . . . (217) 782-1607
Counties Represented: Cook (part)    Dist: (773) 224-2830
Term Expires: 2017    Fax: (773) 224-2855
1155 West 79th Street, Chicago, IL 60620
E-mail: jcollins@senatedem.ilga.gov
Committees: Commerce and Economic Development; Committee of the
Whole; Financial Institutions; Higher Education; Insurance; Public
Health; Transportation
Education: John F Kennedy MA; Spertus MA; Harvard MA

Senator **Michael G. Connelly** (R-District 21) . . . . . . . . . . . (217) 782-8192
Counties Represented: DuPage (part), Will (part)    Dist: (630) 682-8101
Term Expires: 2019    Fax: (630) 682-8108
1725 South Naperville Road, Suite 200, Wheaton, IL 60189
E-mail: senatorconnelly21@gmail.com
Committees: Commerce and Economic Development; Committee of the
Whole; Criminal Law; Judiciary; Labor; Licensed Activities and
Pensions

Senator **John J. Cullerton** (D-District 6) . . . . . . . . . . . . . . (217) 782-2728
Counties Represented: Cook (part)    Dist: (773) 883-0770
Term Expires: 2019    Fax: (773) 880-9083
1726 West Belmont, Chicago, IL 60657
E-mail: john@senatorcullerton.com
Committees: Committee of the Whole; Executive

Senator **Thomas E. "Tom" Cullerton** (D-District 23) . . . . . (217) 782-9463
Counties Represented: Cook (part), DuPage (part)    Dist: (630) 903-6662
Term Expires: 2017    Fax: (630) 903-6643
338 South Ardmore, Villa Park, IL 60181
E-mail: tcullerton@senatedem.ilga.gov
Committees: Appropriations II; Committee of the Whole; Energy and
Public Utilities; Labor; Local Government; State Government and
Veterans Affairs; Transportation

Senator **William "Bill" Cunningham** (D-District 18) . . . . . (217) 782-5745
Counties Represented: Cook (part)    Dist: (773) 445-8128
Term Expires: 2019    Fax: (773) 672-5143
10400 South Western Avenue, Chicago, IL 60643
E-mail: bcunningham@senatedem.ilga.gov
Committees: Agriculture; Appropriations II; Committee of the Whole;
Criminal Law; Higher Education; Labor; Transportation

Senator **William "Willie" Delgado** (D-District 2) . . . . . . . . (217) 782-5652
Counties Represented: Cook (part)    Dist: (773) 292-0202
Term Expires: 2017    Fax: (773) 292-1903
4150 West Armitage Street, Chicago, IL 60639
E-mail: wdelgado@senatedem.ilga.gov
Committees: Appropriations I; Committee of the Whole; Education;
Human Services
Education: Northeastern BA

Senator **Gary F. Forby** (D-District 59) . . . . . . . . . . . . . . . . (217) 782-5509
Counties Represented: Alexander, Franklin, Gallatin,    Dist: (618) 439-2504
Hamilton, Hardin, Jackson (part), Johnson, Massac,    Fax: (618) 438-3704
Pope, Pulaski, Saline, Union (part), Williamson
Term Expires: 2017
903 West Washington Street, Suite 5, Benton, IL 62812
E-mail: gforby@senatedem.ilga.gov
Committees: Committee of the Whole; Energy and Public Utilities;
Insurance; Labor; Licensed Activities and Pensions

Senator **William R. "Bill" Haine** (D-District 56) . . . . . . . . (217) 782-5247
Counties Represented: Jersey (part), Madison    Dist: (618) 465-4764
(part), St. Clair (part)    Fax: (618) 465-4816
Term Expires: 2017
307 Henry Street, Suite 210, Alton, IL 62002
E-mail: williamh@ilga.gov
Committees: Committee of the Whole; Criminal Law; Insurance;
Judiciary; Licensed Activities and Pensions

Senator **Don Harmon** (D-District 39) . . . . . . . . . . . . . . . . . (217) 782-8176
Counties Represented: Cook (part), DuPage (part)    Dist: (708) 848-2002
Term Expires: 2019    Fax: (708) 848-2022
6933 West North Avenue, Oak Park, IL 60302
E-mail: dharmon@senatedem.ilga.gov
Committees: Assignments; Committee of the Whole; Executive;
Judiciary

Senator **Napoleon B. Harris III** (D-District 15) . . . . . . . . . . (217) 782-8066
Counties Represented: Cook (part), Will (part)    Dist: (708) 893-0552
Term Expires: 2019    Fax: (708) 566-4108
369 East 147th Street, Unit H, Harvey, IL 60426
E-mail: nharris@senatedem.ilga.gov
Committees: Commerce and Economic Development; Committee of the
Whole; Insurance; Licensed Activities and Pensions; Public Health;
Transportation
Education: Northwestern BComm

Senator **Michael E. Hastings** (D-District 19) . . . . . . . . . . . (217) 782-9595
Counties Represented: Cook (part), Will (part)    Dist: (708) 283-4125
Term Expires: 2017    Fax: (708) 253-1313
813 School Road, Matteson, IL 60443
E-mail: mhastings@senatedem.ilga.gov
Committees: Appropriations I; Appropriations II; Committee of the
Whole; Financial Institutions; Insurance; Judiciary; State Government
and Veterans Affairs
Education: West Point BS; Illinois MS

Senator **Linda Holmes** (D-District 42) . . . . . . . . . . . . . . . . (217) 782-0422
Counties Represented: DuPage (part), Kane (part),    Dist: (630) 801-8985
Kendall (part), Will (part)    Fax: (630) 801-8987
Term Expires: 2019
765 LaSalle Street, Suite 202, Aurora, IL 60505
E-mail: lholmes@senatedem.ilga.gov
Committees: Agriculture; Commerce and Economic Development;
Committee of the Whole; Environment and Conservation; Insurance;
Labor; Local Government

Senator **Mattie Hunter** (D-District 3) . . . . . . . . . . . . . . . . . (217) 782-5966
Counties Represented: Cook (part)    Dist: (312) 949-1908
Term Expires: 2019    Fax: (312) 949-1958
2929 South Wabash Avenue, 102, Chicago, IL 60616
E-mail: mhunter@senatedem.ilga.gov
Committees: Appropriations I; Committee of the Whole; Energy and
Public Utilities; Executive; Human Services; Public Health

*LEGISLATIVE BRANCH*

Senator **Toi W. Hutchinson** (D-District 40) . . . . . . . . . . . . (217) 782-7419
Counties Represented: Cook (part), Grundy (part),    Dist: (708) 756-0882
Kankakee (part), Will (part)    Fax: (708) 756-0885
Term Expires: 2017
222 Vollmer Road, Suite 2C, Chicago Heights, IL 60411
E-mail: thutchinson@senatedem.ilga.gov
Committees: Appropriations II; Committee of the Whole; Judiciary;
Labor; Licensed Activities and Pensions; Revenue; Transportation

Senator **Emil Jones III** (D-District 14) . . . . . . . . . . . . . . (217) 782-9573
Counties Represented: Cook (part)    Dist: (773) 995-7748
Term Expires: 2017    Fax: (773) 995-9061
507 West 111th Street, Chicago, IL 60628
E-mail: ejones@senatedem.ilga.gov
Committees: Committee of the Whole; Financial Institutions; Licensed
Activities and Pensions; Local Government; Revenue; Transportation

Senator **David M. Koehler** (D-District 46) . . . . . . . . . . . . (217) 782-8250
Counties Represented: Fulton (part), Peoria (part),    Dist: (309) 677-0120
Tazewell (part)
Term Expires: 2017
400 NE Jefferson Avenue, Suite 200, Peoria, IL 61603
E-mail: 46illinois@gmail.com
Committees: Agriculture; Committee of the Whole; Environment and
Conservation; Labor; Local Government; Transportation
Education: Yankton 1971 BA; United Sem MDiv

Senator **Steven M. Landek** (D-District 12) . . . . . . . . . . . . (217) 782-0054
Counties Represented: Cook (part)    Dist: (708) 430-2510
Term Expires: 2019    Fax: (708) 430-2610
6215 W. 79th Steet, Suite 1A, Burbank, IL 60459
E-mail: slandek@senatedem.ilga.gov
Committees: Appropriations II; Committee of the Whole; Local
Government; Revenue; State Government and Veterans Affairs

Senator **Kimberly A. Lightford** (D-District 4) . . . . . . . . . . (217) 782-8505
Counties Represented: Cook (part)    Dist: (708) 343-7444
Term Expires: 2017    Fax: (708) 343-7400
10001 West Roosevelt Road, Suite 202, Westchester, IL 60154
E-mail: klightford@senatedem.ilga.gov
Committees: Assignments; Committee of the Whole; Education; Energy
and Public Utilities; Executive; Executive Appointments; Labor

Senator **Terry Link** (D-District 30) . . . . . . . . . . . . . . . . . . . (217) 782-8181
Counties Represented: Cook (part), Lake (part)    Dist: (847) 821-1811
Term Expires: 2019    Fax: (847) 821-1815
100 South Greenleaf Street, Gurnee, IL 60031
E-mail: senator@link30.org
Committees: Committee of the Whole; Energy and Public Utilities;
Executive; Financial Institutions; Insurance

Senator **David S. Luechtefeld** (R-District 58) . . . . . . . . . . (217) 782-8137
Counties Represented: Jackson (part), Jefferson,    Dist: (618) 243-9014
Monroe, Perry, Randolph, St. Clair (part), Union    Fax: (618) 243-5376
(part), Washington (part)
Term Expires: 2017
700 North Front Street, Okawville, IL 62271
E-mail: sendavel@midwest.net
Committees: Agriculture; Committee of the Whole; Education;
Executive; Financial Institutions; Higher Education

Senator **Andy Manar** (D-District 48) . . . . . . . . . . . . . . . . . (217) 782-0228
Counties Represented: Christian, Macon (part),    Dist: (217) 429-8110
Macoupin (part), Madison (part), Montgomery,    Fax: (217) 524-0374
Sangamon (part)    Dist: (217) 429-8018
Term Expires: 2019
Macon County Office Building, 141 S. Main St., Decatur, IL 62523
E-mail: amanar@senatedem.ilga.gov
Committees: Agriculture; Appropriations I; Appropriations II;
Committee of the Whole; Education; Executive Appointments; Higher
Education; Labor

Senator **Iris Y. Martinez** (D-District 20) . . . . . . . . . . . . . . (217) 782-8191
Counties Represented: Cook (part)    Dist: (773) 463-0720
Term Expires: 2017    Fax: (773) 463-0795
2845 North Kedzie Avenue, Chicago, IL 60618
E-mail: imartinez@senatedem.ilga.gov
Committees: Commerce and Economic Development; Committee of the
Whole; Education; Energy and Public Utilities; Labor; Licensed
Activities and Pensions; Transportation

Senator **William Sam McCann** (R-District 50) . . . . . . . . . (217) 782-8206
Counties Represented: Calhoun, Greene, Jersey    Dist: (217) 245-0050
(part), Macoupin (part), Madison (part), Morgan,    Fax: (217) 245-0021
Pike, Sangamon (part), Scott
Term Expires: 2017
221 Dunlap Court, Jacksonville, IL 62650
E-mail: senatorsam@frontier.com
Committees: Agriculture; Committee of the Whole; Environment and
Conservation; Higher Education; Local Government; Public Health

Senator **Kyle McCarter** (R-District 54) . . . . . . . . . . . . . . . (217) 782-5755
Counties Represented: Bond, Clinton, Effingham    Dist: (618) 283-3000
(part), Fayette, Madison (part), Marion, St. Clair    Fax: (618) 283-9750
(part), Washington (part)
Term Expires: 2019
310 W. Gallatin, Vandalia, IL 62471
E-mail: mccarter51@att.net
Committees: Agriculture; Committee of the Whole; Environment and
Conservation; Higher Education; Labor; State Government and Veterans
Affairs

Senator **Dan McConchie** (I-District 26) . . . . . . . . . . . . . . . (217) 782-8010
Counties Represented: Cook (part), Kane (part),    Dist: (224) 662-4544
Lake (part), McHenry (part)
Term Expires: 2017
105B Capitol Building, 401 S. Spring Street, Springfield, IL 62706
325 N. Rand Road, Suite B, Lake Zurich, IL 60047
Committees: Appropriations I; Commerce and Economic Development;
Labor; State Government and Veterans Affairs

Senator **Karen McConnaughay** (R-District 33) . . . . . . . . . (217) 782-1977
Counties Represented: Kane (part), McHenry (part)    Dist: (847) 214-8245
Term Expires: 2019
81 S McLean Boulevard, South Elgin, IL 60177
E-mail: karenmcconnaughay33@gmail.com
Committees: Commerce and Economic Development; Committee of the
Whole; Education; Energy and Public Utilities; Financial Institutions;
Revenue; Transportation

Senator **Patrick "Pat" McGuire** (D-District 43) . . . . . . . . . (217) 782-8800
Counties Represented: DuPage (part), Will (part)    Dist: (815) 207-4445
Term Expires: 2017    Fax: (815) 207-4446
2200 Weber Road, Crest Hill, IL 60403
E-mail: pmcguire@senatedem.ilga.gov
Committees: Appropriations II; Committee of the Whole; Environment
and Conservation; Higher Education; Revenue; State Government and
Veterans Affairs; Transportation

Senator **Julie A. Morrison** (D-District 29) . . . . . . . . . . . . . (217) 782-3650
Counties Represented: Cook (part), Lake (part)    Dist: (847) 945-5200
Term Expires: 2017    Fax: (847) 845-5214
700 Osterman Avenue, Deerfield, IL 60015
E-mail: jmorrison@senatedem.ilga.gov
Committees: Commerce and Economic Development; Committee of the
Whole; Education; Environment and Conservation; Human Services;
Transportation
Education: Knox (IL) 1978 BA

Senator **John G. Mulroe** (D-District 10) . . . . . . . . . . . . . . . (217) 782-1035
Counties Represented: Cook (part)    Dist: (773) 763-3810
Term Expires: 2017    Fax: (773) 763-3881
6107 B North Highway, Chicago, IL 60631
E-mail: jmulroe@senatedem.ilga.gov
Committees: Commerce and Economic Development; Committee of
the Whole; Criminal Law; Energy and Public Utilities; Insurance;
Judiciary; Public Health
Education: Loyola U (Chicago) BBA, JD

Senator **Antonio "Tony" Muñoz** (D-District 1) . . . . . . . . . (217) 782-9415
Counties Represented: Cook (part)    Dist: (773) 869-9050
Term Expires: 2017    Fax: (773) 869-9046
1836 West 35th Street, 1st Floor, Chicago, IL 60609
E-mail: amunoz@senatedem.ilga.gov
Committees: Committee of the Whole; Energy and Public Utilities;
Executive; Executive Appointments; Insurance

Senator **Laura M. Murphy** (D-District 28) . . . . . . . . . . . . . (217) 782-3875
Counties Represented: Cook (part), DuPage (part)    Dist: (847) 656-5414
Term Expires: 2017
350 S. Northwest Highway, Park Ridge, IL 60068
Committees: Appropriations I; Appropriations II; Criminal Law; Higher
Education; Revenue
Education: Illinois State BA

Senator **Matt Murphy** (R-District 27) . . . . . . . . . . . . . . . . . (217) 782-4471
Counties Represented: Cook (part)    Dist: (847) 776-1490
Term Expires: 2019    Fax: (847) 776-1494
1 East Northwest Highway, Suite 109, Palatine, IL 60067
E-mail: senatormattmurphy@sbcglobal.net
Committees: Appropriations I; Appropriations II; Committee of
the Whole; Energy and Public Utilities; Executive; Executive
Appointments; Insurance

Senator **Michael Noland, USN (Ret)** (D-District 22) . . . . . (217) 782-7746
Counties Represented: Cook (part), Kane (part)    Dist: (847) 214-8864
Term Expires: 2017    Fax: (847) 214-8867
The Professional Building, 164 Division Street, Suite 102,
Elgin, IL 60120
E-mail: mnoland@senatedem.ilga.gov
Committees: Committee of the Whole; Criminal Law; Education;
Energy and Public Utilities; Judiciary; Revenue
Education: Illinois (Chicago) BA, MBA; John Marshall JD

*(continued on next page)*

**LEGISLATIVE BRANCH**

**Senators** *continued*

**Senator Chris Nybo** (R-District 24) . . . . . . . . . . . . . . . . (217) 782-8148
Counties Represented: Cook (part), DuPage (part)    Dist: (630) 969-0990
Term Expires: 2019    Fax: (217) 782-4079
309J Capitol Building, Springfield, IL 62706    Dist: (630) 969-1007
One South Cass Avenue, Westmont, IL 60559
E-mail: chris@chrisnybo.org
Committees: Committee of the Whole; Criminal Law; Energy
and Public Utilities; Financial Institutions; Judiciary; Revenue;
Transportation
Education: Dartmouth 1999 BA; Chicago 2002 JD

**Senator James D. "Jim" Oberweis** (R-District 25) . . . . . . (217) 782-0471
Counties Represented: Cook (part), DuPage (part),    Dist: (630) 800-1992
Kane (part), Kendall (part)
Term Expires: 2017
959 Oak Street, North Aurora, IL 60542
E-mail: senatoroberweis@gmail.com
Committees: Appropriations II; Committee of the Whole; Labor; Local
Government; State Government and Veterans Affairs; Transportation
Education: Illinois BA; Chicago 1980 MBA

**Senator Christine Radogno** (R-District 41) . . . . . . . . . . . (217) 782-9407
Counties Represented: Cook (part), DuPage (part),    Dist: (630) 243-0800
Will (part)    Fax: (217) 782-7818
Term Expires: 2017    Dist: (630) 243-0808
1011 State Street, Suite 210, Lemont, IL 60439
E-mail: christine@senatorradogno.com
Committees: Committee of the Whole; Executive

**Senator Kwame Y. Raoul** (D-District 13) . . . . . . . . . . . . . (217) 782-5338
Counties Represented: Cook (part)    Dist: (773) 363-1996
Term Expires: 2017    Fax: (773) 681-7166
1509 East 53rd Street, 2nd Floor, Chicago, IL 60615
E-mail: kraoul@senatedem.ilga.gov
Committees: Committee of the Whole; Criminal Law; Energy and
Public Utilities; Executive; Judiciary; Public Health
Education: DePaul BA; Chicago-Kent 1993 JD

**Senator Sue Rezin** (R-District 38) . . . . . . . . . . . . . . . . . (217) 782-3840
Counties Represented: Bureau (part), Grundy (part),    Dist: (815) 220-8720
Kendall (part), La Salle (part), Livingston (part),    Fax: (815) 220-8721
Putnam, Will (part)
Term Expires: 2017
103 Fifth Street P.O. Box 260, Peru, IL 61354
E-mail: suerezin@gmail.com
Committees: Appropriations II; Committee of the Whole; Education;
Energy and Public Utilities; Executive; Financial Institutions;
Transportation

**Senator Dale A. Righter** (R-District 55) . . . . . . . . . . . . . (217) 782-6674
Counties Represented: Clark, Clay, Coles, Crawford,    Dist: (217) 235-6033
Cumberland, Edgar (part), Edwards, Effingham    Fax: (217) 235-6052
(part), Jasper, Lawrence, Richland, Wabash, Wayne, White
Term Expires: 2017
88 Broadway Avenue, Suite 1, Mattoon, IL 61938
E-mail: drighter@consolidated.net
Committees: Appropriations II; Assignments; Committee of the Whole;
Criminal Law; Environment and Conservation; Human Services;
Revenue
Education: Saint Louis U JD

**Senator Chapin Rose** (R-District 51) . . . . . . . . . . . . . . . (217) 558-1006
Counties Represented: Champaign (part), De Witt,    Dist: (217) 607-1853
Douglas, Edgar (part), Macon (part), McLean (part),    Fax: (217) 607-5471
Moultrie, Piatt, Shelby, Vermilion (part)
Term Expires: 2019
510 South Staley Road, Suite D, Champaign, IL 61822
E-mail: cr@chapinrose.org
Committees: Appropriations I; Appropriations II; Committee of the
Whole; Education; Insurance

**Senator Martin A. Sandoval** (D-District 11) . . . . . . . . . . (217) 782-5304
Counties Represented: Cook (part)    Dist: (708) 656-2002
Term Expires: 2017    Fax: (708) 656-7608
5807 West 35th Street, Cicero, IL 60804
E-mail: msandoval@senatedem.ilga.gov
Committees: Committee of the Whole; Energy and Public Utilities;
Licensed Activities and Pensions; Local Government; Transportation

**Senator Ira I. Silverstein** (D-District 8) . . . . . . . . . . . . . (217) 782-5500
Counties Represented: Cook (part)    Dist: (773) 743-5015
Term Expires: 2017    Fax: (773) 743-4750
2951 West Devon Avenue, Chicago, IL 60659
E-mail: isilverstein@senatedem.ilga.gov
Committees: Committee of the Whole; Executive; Executive
Appointments; Financial Institutions; Insurance; Judiciary

**Senator Steve Stadelman** (D-District 34) . . . . . . . . . . . . (217) 782-8022
Counties Represented: Winnebago (part)    Dist: (815) 987-7557
Term Expires: 2017    Fax: (815) 987-7529
200 South Wyman Street, Suite 301, Rockford, IL 61101
E-mail: sstadelman@senatedem.ilga.gov
Committees: Appropriations I; Commerce and Economic Development;
Committee of the Whole; Education; Higher Education; Transportation

**Senator Heather A. Steans** (D-District 7) . . . . . . . . . . . . (217) 782-8492
Counties Represented: Cook (part)    Dist: (773) 769-1717
Term Expires: 2017    Fax: (773) 769-6901
5533 North Broadway Street, Chicago, IL 60640
E-mail: hsteans@senatedem.ilga.gov
Committees: Appropriations I; Appropriations II; Committee of the
Whole; Environment and Conservation; Executive; Human Services
Education: Princeton BA; Harvard MA

**Senator John M. Sullivan** (D-District 47) . . . . . . . . . . . . (217) 782-2479
Counties Represented: Adams, Brown, Cass, Fulton    Dist: (217) 222-2295
(part), Hancock, Henderson, Knox (part), Mason,    Fax: (217) 222-2944
McDonough, Schuyler, Warren
Term Expires: 2017
926 Broadway, Suite 6, Quincy, IL 62301
E-mail: jsullivan@senatedem.ilga.gov
Committees: Agriculture; Committee of the Whole; Environment and
Conservation; Financial Institutions; Higher Education; Insurance; State
Government and Veterans Affairs; Transportation

**Senator Dave Syverson** (R-District 35) . . . . . . . . . . . . . (217) 782-5413
Counties Represented: Boone, DeKalb (part),    Dist: (815) 987-7555
Kane (part), Winnebago (part)    Fax: (815) 987-7563
Term Expires: 2017
200 S. Wyman St., Suite 302, Rockford, IL 61101
E-mail: info@senatordavesyverson.com
Committees: Committee of the Whole; Energy and Public Utilities;
Executive; Human Services; Insurance; Public Health

**Senator Donne E. Trotter** (D-District 17) . . . . . . . . . . . . (217) 782-3201
Counties Represented: Cook (part), Kankakee    Dist: (773) 933-7715
(part), Will (part)    Fax: (773) 933-5498
Term Expires: 2017
86585 Cottage Grove Avenue, Chicago, IL 60619
E-mail: dtrotter@senatedem.ilga.gov
Committees: Appropriations I; Appropriations II; Committee of the
Whole; Energy and Public Utilities; Executive

**Senator Patricia Van Pelt, CPA** (D-District 5) . . . . . . . . . (217) 782-6252
Counties Represented: Cook (part)    Dist: (312) 888-9191
Term Expires: 2017    Fax: (312) 277-3716
1016 W. Jackson Boulevard, Chicago, IL 60607
E-mail: pvanpelt@senatedem.ilga.gov
Committees: Appropriations I; Commerce and Economic Development;
Committee of the Whole; Criminal Law; Energy and Public Utilities;
Public Health
Education: Roosevelt 1996 BA; Spertus 1996 MA;
Capella U 2009 PhD

**Senator Chuck Weaver** (R-District 37) . . . . . . . . . . . . . . (217) 782-1942
Counties Represented: Bureau (part), Henry (part), Knox (part),
La Salle (part), Lee (part), Marshall, Mercer, Peoria (part), Stark,
Woodford (part)
Term Expires: 2017
Committees: Commerce and Economic Development; Criminal Law;
Insurance; Judiciary; Licensed Activities and Pensions; Public Health

# Senate Standing Committees

## Agriculture

**Majority Members**

William "Bill" Cunningham (D-18)
*Chairperson*
John M. Sullivan (D-47)
*Vice Chairperson*
Scott M. Bennett (D-52)
Linda Holmes (D-42)
David M. Koehler (D-46)
Andy Manar (D-48)

**Minority Members**

Neil Anderson (R-36)
*Minority Spokesperson*
David S. Luechtefeld (R-58)
William Sam McCann (R-50)
Kyle McCarter (R-54)

LEGISLATIVE BRANCH

## Appropriations I
**Majority Members**
Heather A. Steans (D-7)
  *Chairperson*
Donne E. Trotter (D-17)
  *Vice Chairperson*
Daniel Biss (D-9)
William "Willie" Delgado (D-2)
Michael E. Hastings (D-19)
Mattie Hunter (D-3)
Andy Manar (D-48)
Laura M. Murphy (D-28)
Steve Stadelman (D-34)
Patricia Van Pelt (D-5)

**Members**
Dan McConchie (I-26)

**Minority Members**
Matt Murphy (R-27)
  *Minority Spokesman*
Jason Barickman (R-53)
Tim Bivins (R-45)
Chapin Rose (R-51)

## Appropriations II
**Majority Members**
Donne E. Trotter (D-17)
  *Chairperson*
Heather A. Steans (D-7)
  *Vice Chairperson*
Scott M. Bennett (D-52)
Jennifer Bertino-Tarrant (D-49)
Thomas E. "Tom" Cullerton (D-23)
William "Bill" Cunningham (D-18)
Michael E. Hastings (D-19)
Toi W. Hutchinson (D-40)
Steven M. Landek (D-12)
Andy Manar (D-48)
Patrick "Pat" McGuire (D-43)
Laura M. Murphy (D-28)

**Minority Members**
Chapin Rose (R-51)
  *Minority Spokesperson*
Pamela J. Althoff (R-32)
Matt Murphy (R-27)
James D. "Jim" Oberweis (R-25)
Sue Rezin (R-38)
Dale A. Righter (R-55)

## Assignments
**Majority Members**
James F. Clayborne, Jr. (D-57)
  *Chairperson*
Don Harmon (D-39)
  *Vice Chairperson*
Kimberly A. Lightford (D-4)

**Minority Members**
Dale A. Righter (R-55)
  *Minority Spokesperson*
Pamela J. Althoff (R-32)

## Commerce and Economic Development
**Majority Members**
Linda Holmes (D-42) *Chairperson*
Melinda Bush (D-31)
  *Vice Chairperson*
Jacqueline Y. "Jacqui" Collins
  (D-16)
Napoleon B. Harris III (D-15)
Iris Y. Martinez (D-20)
Julie A. Morrison (D-29)
John G. Mulroe (D-10)
Steve Stadelman (D-34)
Patricia Van Pelt (D-5)

**Members**
Dan McConchie (I-26)

**Minority Members**
Chuck Weaver (R-37)
  *Minority Spokesperson*
Jason Barickman (R-53)
William E. "Bill" Brady (R-44)
Michael G. Connelly (R-21)
Karen McConnaughay (R-33)

## Committee of the Whole
**Majority Members**
Scott M. Bennett (D-52)
Jennifer Bertino-Tarrant (D-49)
Daniel Biss (D-9)
Melinda Bush (D-31)
James F. Clayborne, Jr. (D-57)
Jacqueline Y. "Jacqui" Collins
  (D-16)
John J. Cullerton (D-6)
Thomas E. "Tom" Cullerton (D-23)
William "Bill" Cunningham (D-18)
William "Willie" Delgado (D-2)
Gary F. Forby (D-59)
William R. "Bill" Haine (D-56)
Don Harmon (D-39)
Napoleon B. Harris III (D-15)
Michael E. Hastings (D-19)

**Minority Members**
Pamela J. Althoff (R-32)
Neil Anderson (R-36)
Jason Barickman (R-53)
Tim Bivins (R-45)
William E. "Bill" Brady (R-44)
Michael G. Connelly (R-21)
David S. Luechtefeld (R-58)
William Sam McCann (R-50)
Kyle McCarter (R-54)
Karen McConnaughay (R-33)
Matt Murphy (R-27)
Chris Nybo (R-24)
James D. "Jim" Oberweis (R-25)
Christine Radogno (R-41)
Sue Rezin (R-38)
Dale A. Righter (R-55)

**Majority Members** *continued*
Linda Holmes (D-42)
Mattie Hunter (D-3)
Toi W. Hutchinson (D-40)
Emil Jones III (D-14)
David M. Koehler (D-46)
Steven M. Landek (D-12)
Kimberly A. Lightford (D-4)
Terry Link (D-30)
Andy Manar (D-48)
Iris Y. Martinez (D-20)
Patrick "Pat" McGuire (D-43)
Julie A. Morrison (D-29)
John G. Mulroe (D-10)
Antonio "Tony" Muñoz (D-1)
Michael Noland (D-22)
Kwame Y. Raoul (D-13)
Martin A. Sandoval (D-11)
Ira I. Silverstein (D-8)
Steve Stadelman (D-34)
Heather A. Steans (D-7)
John M. Sullivan (D-47)
Donne E. Trotter (D-17)
Patricia Van Pelt (D-5)

**Minority Members** *continued*
Chapin Rose (R-51)
Dave Syverson (R-35)

## Criminal Law
**Majority Members**
Michael Noland (D-22)
  *Chairperson*
Kwame Y. Raoul (D-13)
  *Vice Chairperson*
Scott M. Bennett (D-52)
William "Bill" Cunningham (D-18)
William R. "Bill" Haine (D-56)
John G. Mulroe (D-10)
Laura M. Murphy (D-28)
Patricia Van Pelt (D-5)

**Minority Members**
Michael G. Connelly (R-21)
  *Minority Spokesperson*
Chris Nybo (R-24)
Dale A. Righter (R-55)
Chuck Weaver (R-37)

## Education
**Majority Members**
William "Willie" Delgado (D-2)
  *Chairperson*
Kimberly A. Lightford (D-4)
  *Vice Chairperson*
Jennifer Bertino-Tarrant (D-49)
Daniel Biss (D-9)
Melinda Bush (D-31)
Andy Manar (D-48)
Iris Y. Martinez (D-20)
Julie A. Morrison (D-29)
Michael Noland (D-22)
Steve Stadelman (D-34)

**Minority Members**
David S. Luechtefeld (R-58)
  *Minority Spokesperson*
Jason Barickman (R-53)
Karen McConnaughay (R-33)
Sue Rezin (R-38)
Chapin Rose (R-51)

## Energy and Public Utilities
**Majority Members**
Mattie Hunter (D-3) *Chairperson*
Iris Y. Martinez (D-20)
  *Vice Chairperson*
James F. Clayborne, Jr. (D-57)
Thomas E. "Tom" Cullerton (D-23)
Gary F. Forby (D-59)
Kimberly A. Lightford (D-4)
Terry Link (D-30)
John G. Mulroe (D-10)
Antonio "Tony" Muñoz (D-1)
Michael Noland (D-22)
Kwame Y. Raoul (D-13)
Martin A. Sandoval (D-11)
Donne E. Trotter (D-17)
Patricia Van Pelt (D-5)

**Minority Members**
Sue Rezin (R-38)
  *Minority Spokesperson*
Neil Anderson (R-36)
William E. "Bill" Brady (R-44)
Karen McConnaughay (R-33)
Matt Murphy (R-27)
Chris Nybo (R-24)
Dave Syverson (R-35)

**LEGISLATIVE BRANCH**

## Environment and Conservation

**Majority Members**
David M. Koehler (D-46)
*Chairperson*
Heather A. Steans (D-7)
*Vice Chairperson*
Scott M. Bennett (D-52)
Melinda Bush (D-31)
Linda Holmes (D-42)
Patrick "Pat" McGuire (D-43)
Julie A. Morrison (D-29)
John M. Sullivan (D-47)

**Minority Members**
Kyle McCarter (R-54)
*Minority Spokesperson*
Tim Bivins (R-45)
William Sam McCann (R-50)
Dale A. Righter (R-55)

## Executive

**Majority Members**
Don Harmon (D-39) *Chairperson*
Ira I. Silverstein (D-8)
*Vice Chairperson*
James F. Clayborne, Jr. (D-57)
John J. Cullerton (D-6)
Mattie Hunter (D-3)
Kimberly A. Lightford (D-4)
Terry Link (D-30)
Antonio "Tony" Muñoz (D-1)
Kwame Y. Raoul (D-13)
Heather A. Steans (D-7)
Donne E. Trotter (D-17)

**Minority Members**
Matt Murphy (R-27)
*Minority Spokesperson*
William E. "Bill" Brady (R-44)
David S. Luechtefeld (R-58)
Christine Radogno (R-41)
Sue Rezin (R-38)
Dave Syverson (R-35)

## Executive Appointments

**Majority Members**
Antonio "Tony" Muñoz (D-1)
*Chairperson*
Andy Manar (D-48)
*Vice Chairperson*
Kimberly A. Lightford (D-4)
Ira I. Silverstein (D-8)

**Minority Members**
Matt Murphy (R-27)
*Minority Spokesperson*
Pamela J. Althoff (R-32)

## Financial Institutions

**Majority Members**
Jacqueline Y. "Jacqui"
Collins (D-16)
*Chairperson*
Terry Link (D-30) *Vice Chairperson*
Daniel Biss (D-9)
Michael E. Hastings (D-19)
Emil Jones III (D-14)
Ira I. Silverstein (D-8)
John M. Sullivan (D-47)

**Minority Members**
Chris Nybo (R-24)
*Minority Spokesperson*
David S. Luechtefeld (R-58)
Karen McConnaughay (R-33)
Sue Rezin (R-38)

## Higher Education

**Majority Members**
Patrick "Pat" McGuire (D-43)
*Chairperson*
William "Bill" Cunningham (D-18)
*Vice Chairperson*
Scott M. Bennett (D-52)
Jacqueline Y. "Jacqui" Collins
(D-16)
Andy Manar (D-48)
Laura M. Murphy (D-28)
Steve Stadelman (D-34)
John M. Sullivan (D-47)

**Minority Members**
David S. Luechtefeld (R-58)
*Minority Spokesperson*
Neil Anderson (R-36)
William Sam McCann (R-50)
Kyle McCarter (R-54)

## Human Services

**Majority Members**
Daniel Biss (D-9) *Chairperson*
Julie A. Morrison (D-29)
*Vice Chairperson*
Melinda Bush (D-31)
William "Willie" Delgado (D-2)
Mattie Hunter (D-3)
Heather A. Steans (D-7)

**Minority Members**
Dave Syverson (R-35)
*Minority Spokesperson*
Tim Bivins (R-45)
Dale A. Righter (R-55)

## Insurance

**Majority Members**
William R. "Bill" Haine (D-56)
*Chairperson*
Napoleon B. Harris III (D-15)
*Vice Chairperson*
James F. Clayborne, Jr. (D-57)
Jacqueline Y. "Jacqui" Collins
(D-16)
Michael E. Hastings (D-19)
Linda Holmes (D-42)
Terry Link (D-30)
John G. Mulroe (D-10)
Antonio "Tony" Muñoz (D-1)
Ira I. Silverstein (D-8)
John M. Sullivan (D-47)

**Minority Members**
William E. "Bill" Brady (R-44)
*Minority Spokesman*
Tim Bivins (R-45)
Matt Murphy (R-27)
Chapin Rose (R-51)
Dave Syverson (R-35)
Chuck Weaver (R-37)

## Judiciary

**Majority Members**
Kwame Y. Raoul (D-13)
*Chairperson*
Michael E. Hastings (D-19)
*Vice Chairperson*
William R. "Bill" Haine (D-56)
Don Harmon (D-39)
Toi W. Hutchinson (D-40)
John G. Mulroe (D-10)
Michael Noland (D-22)
Ira I. Silverstein (D-8)

**Minority Members**
Jason Barickman (R-53)
*Minority Spokesperson*
Michael G. Connelly (R-21)
Chris Nybo (R-24)
Chuck Weaver (R-37)

## Labor

**Majority Members**
Gary F. Forby (D-59) *Chairperson*
Jennifer Bertino-Tarrant (D-49)
*Vice Chairperson*
Scott M. Bennett (D-52)
Thomas E. "Tom" Cullerton (D-23)
William "Bill" Cunningham (D-18)
Linda Holmes (D-42)
Toi W. Hutchinson (D-40)
David M. Koehler (D-46)
Kimberly A. Lightford (D-4)
Andy Manar (D-48)
Iris Y. Martinez (D-20)

**Members**
Dan McConchie (I-26)

**Minority Members**
James D. "Jim" Oberweis (R-25)
*Minority Spokesperson*
Pamela J. Althoff (R-32)
Michael G. Connelly (R-21)
Kyle McCarter (R-54)

## Licensed Activities and Pensions

**Majority Members**
Iris Y. Martinez (D-20) *Chairperson*
Emil Jones III (D-14)
*Vice Chairperson*
Jennifer Bertino-Tarrant (D-49)
Gary F. Forby (D-59)
William R. "Bill" Haine (D-56)
Napoleon B. Harris III (D-15)
Toi W. Hutchinson (D-40)
Martin A. Sandoval (D-11)

**Minority Members**
Pamela J. Althoff (R-32)
*Minority Spokesperson*
Jason Barickman (R-53)
Michael G. Connelly (R-21)
Chuck Weaver (R-37)

## Local Government

**Majority Members**
Emil Jones III (D-14) *Chairperson*
Thomas E. "Tom" Cullerton (D-23)
*Vice Chairperson*
Jennifer Bertino-Tarrant (D-49)
Linda Holmes (D-42)
David M. Koehler (D-46)
Steven M. Landek (D-12)
Martin A. Sandoval (D-11)

**Minority Members**
Tim Bivins (R-45)
*Minority Spokesperson*
Neil Anderson (R-36)
William Sam McCann (R-50)
James D. "Jim" Oberweis (R-25)

## Public Health

**Majority Members**
John G. Mulroe (D-10) *Chairperson*
Patricia Van Pelt (D-5)
  *Vice Chairperson*
Jacqueline Y. "Jacqui" Collins
  (D-16)
Napoleon B. Harris III (D-15)
Mattie Hunter (D-3)
Kwame Y. Raoul (D-13)

**Minority Members**
Dave Syverson (R-35)
  *Minority Spokesperson*
William Sam McCann (R-50)
Chuck Weaver (R-37)

## Revenue

**Majority Members**
Toi W. Hutchinson (D-40)
  *Chairperson*
Michael Noland (D-22)
  *Vice Chairperson*
Daniel Biss (D-9)
Melinda Bush (D-31)
Emil Jones III (D-14)
Steven M. Landek (D-12)
Patrick "Pat" McGuire (D-43)
Laura M. Murphy (D-28)

**Minority Members**
Pamela J. Althoff (R-32)
  *Minority Spokesperson*
Karen McConnaughay (R-33)
Chris Nybo (R-24)
Dale A. Righter (R-55)

## State Government and Veterans Affairs

**Majority Members**
Steven M. Landek (D-12)
  *Chairperson*
Patrick "Pat" McGuire (D-43)
  *Vice Chairperson*
Melinda Bush (D-31)
Thomas E. "Tom" Cullerton (D-23)
Michael E. Hastings (D-19)
John M. Sullivan (D-47)

**Minority Members**
Kyle McCarter (R-54)
James D. "Jim" Oberweis (R-25)

**Members**
Dan McConchie (I-26) *Minority Spokesperson*

## Transportation

**Majority Members**
Martin A. Sandoval (D-11)
  *Chairperson*
Steve Stadelman (D-34)
  *Vice Chairperson*
Jennifer Bertino-Tarrant (D-49)
Jacqueline Y. "Jacqui" Collins
  (D-16)
Thomas E. "Tom" Cullerton (D-23)
William "Bill" Cunningham (D-18)
Napoleon B. Harris III (D-15)
Toi W. Hutchinson (D-40)
Emil Jones III (D-14)
David M. Koehler (D-46)
Iris Y. Martinez (D-20)
Patrick "Pat" McGuire (D-43)
Julie A. Morrison (D-29)
John M. Sullivan (D-47)

**Minority Members**
Karen McConnaughay (R-33)
  *Minority Spokesperson*
Neil Anderson (R-36)
Pamela J. Althoff (R-32)
William E. "Bill" Brady (R-44)
Chris Nybo (R-24)
James D. "Jim" Oberweis (R-25)
Sue Rezin (R-38)

# Illinois House of Representatives

State Capitol, 401 S. Spring Street, Springfield, IL 62706
240-W Stratton Office Building, 401 S. Spring Street,
Springfield, IL 62706
Tel: (217) 782-8223  Fax: (217) 782-3885

**Michael J. Madigan**
Speaker of the House

Began Service: 1971
Date of Birth: April 19, 1942
Education: Notre Dame 1964 BS;
Loyola U (Chicago) 1967 JD

Speaker of the House **Michael J. Madigan** (D) . . . . . . . . . (217) 782-5350
  Chief of Staff **Timothy Mapes** . . . . . . . . . . . . . . . . . . . . . (217) 782-6360

Chief Legal Counsel to the Speaker
  **Heather Wier Vaught** . . . . . . . . . . . . . . . . . . . . . . . . . (217) 782-7600
Majority Leader **Barbara Flynn Currie** (D) . . . . . . . . . . . (217) 782-8121
  Education: Chicago 1968 BA, 1973 MA
Deputy Majority Leader **Louis I. "Lou" Lang** (D) . . . . . . . (217) 782-1252
  Education: Illinois 1971 BA; DePaul 1974 JD
Assistant Majority Leader **Edward J. Acevedo** (D) . . . . . . (217) 782-2855
Assistant Majority Leader **John E. Bradley** (D) . . . . . . . . . (217) 782-1051
  Education: Southeastern Illinois AA; Texas BA; Illinois 1996 JD
Assistant Majority Leader **Daniel J. Burke** (D) . . . . . . . . . (217) 782-1117
  Education: Loyola U (Chicago) (Attended); DePaul (Attended)
Assistant Majority Leader **Sara Feigenholtz** (D) . . . . . . . . (217) 782-8062
  Education: Northeastern 1979 BA
Assistant Majority Leader **Jehan A. Gordon-Booth** (D) . . (217) 782-3186
Assistant Majority Leader **Elaine Nekritz** (D) . . . . . . . . . . (217) 558-1004
  Education: Michigan JD
Assistant Majority Leader **Al Riley** (D) . . . . . . . . . . . . . . . (217) 558-1007
  Education: Chicago State 1974 BA; Illinois (Chicago) 1978 MUP
Assistant Majority Leader **Arthur L. Turner** (D) . . . . . . . . (217) 782-8116
Minority Leader **Jim Durkin** (R) . . . . . . . . . . . . . . . . . . . . (217) 782-0494
  Education: Illinois State 1984 BS; John Marshall 1989 JD
Deputy Minority Leader **Patricia R. "Patti" Bellock** (R) . . (217) 782-1448
  Education: St Norbert BA
Deputy Minority Leader **David R. Leitch** (R) . . . . . . . . . . . (217) 782-8108
  Education: Kalamazoo BA
Assistant Minority Leader **Dan Brady** (R) . . . . . . . . . . . . . (217) 782-1118
  Education: St Ambrose 1983 BA; Southern Illinois 1982 AA
Assistant Minority Leader **Norine Hammond** (R) . . . . . . . . (217) 782-0416
Assistant Minority Leader **Chad D. Hays** (R) . . . . . . . . . . . (217) 782-4811
  Education: Southern Illinois 1986 (Attended)
Assistant Minority Leader **Bill Mitchell** (R) . . . . . . . . . . . . (217) 782-8163
  Education: Eastern Illinois 1982 BA
Assistant Minority Leader **Ed Sullivan, Jr.** (R) . . . . . . . . . (217) 782-3696
Assistant Minority Leader **Michael W. Tryon** (R) . . . . . . . (217) 782-0432
Chief Doorkeeper **Lee A. Crawford** . . . . . . . . . . . . . . . . . (217) 782-8223
Parliamentarian **Heather Wier Vaught** . . . . . . . . . . . . . . . (217) 782-5350
Clerk of the House **Timothy Mapes** . . . . . . . . . . . . . . . . . . (217) 782-8223
  E-mail: tim.mapes@ilga.gov
  Assistant Clerk of the House **Bradley S. Bolin** . . . . . . . . (217) 782-8223

# Representatives

**Party Affiliation Statistics:** Republicans: 47, Democrats: 71

Representative **Edward J. Acevedo** (D-District 2) . . . . . . . (217) 782-2855
  Counties Represented: Cook (part)          Dist: (773) 843-1200
  Term Expires: 2017                         Fax: (217) 557-5148
  1836 West 35th Street, Chicago, IL 60609   Dist: (773) 843-9500
  E-mail: eacevedoed@ilga.gov
  Committees: Appropriations - Elementary and Secondary Education;
  Appropriations - Human Services; Executive; Health and Healthcare
  Disparities
Representative **Carol Ammons** (D-District 103) . . . . . . . . (217) 558-1009
  Counties Represented: Champaign (part)     Dist: (217) 531-1660
  Term Expires: 2017                         Fax: (217) 666-7521
  E-mail: csrepammons@gmail.com
  Committees: Appropriations - Elementary and Secondary Education;
  Community College Access and Affordability; Environment; Higher
  Education; Human Services; Personnel and Pensions; Small Business
  Empowerment and Workforce Development; Special Needs Services
Representative
  **Steven A. "Steve" Andersson** (R-District 65) . . . . . . . . (217) 782-5457
  Counties Represented: Kane (part), McHenry (part)   Dist: (630) 457-5460
  Term Expires: 2017
  127 S. 1st Street, Suite 204, Geneva, IL 60134
  E-mail: steven.andersson@hds.ilga.gov
  Committees: Appropriations - General Services; Cities and Villages;
  Judiciary - Civil; Museums, Arts, and Cultural Enhancement;
  Renewable Energy and Sustainability; Small Business Empowerment
  and Workforce Development; Transportation: Regulation, Roads &
  Bridges
Representative **Jaime M. Andrade, Jr.** (D-District 40)
  247-E William G. Stratton Building . . . . . . . . . . . . . . . . . . (217) 782-8117
  Counties Represented: Cook (part)          Dist: (773) 267-2880
  Term Expires: 2017                         Fax: (217) 558-4551
  E-mail: staterep40@gmail.com               Dist: (773) 267-2840
  Committees: Consumer Protection; Economic Development and
  Housing; Human Services; Intermodal Infrastructure; State Government
  Administration; Transportation: Regulation, Roads & Bridges
  Education: DePaul BSB

*(continued on next page)*

LEGISLATIVE BRANCH

**Representatives** *continued*

Representative **John D. Anthony** (R-District 75) . . . . . . . . (217) 782-5997
Counties Represented: Grundy (part), Kendall          Dist: (815) 416-1475
(part), La Salle (part), Will (part)                  Fax: (217) 782-3189
Term Expires: 2017
3605 North State Road 47, Morris, IL 60450
E-mail: johna@ilga.gov
Committees: Agriculture and Conservation; Appropriations - Public
Safety; Elementary and Secondary Education: Charter School Policy;
Energy; Judiciary - Criminal; Restorative Justice; Special Needs
Services

Representative **Luis Arroyo** (D-District 3) . . . . . . . . . . . . . (217) 782-0480
Counties Represented: Cook (part)                     Dist: (773) 627-2000
Term Expires: 2017                                    Fax: (217) 557-9609
4502 Fullerton Avenue, Chicago, IL 60639             Dist: (773) 637-2002
E-mail: RepDistrict3@gmail.com
Committees: Appropriations - Public Safety; Executive; Labor and
Commerce; Public Utilities; Tollway Oversight; Veterans' Affairs

Representative **Mark Batinick** (R-District 97) . . . . . . . . . . . (217) 782-1331
Counties Represented: Kendall (part), Will (part)     Dist: (815) 254-0000
Term Expires: 2017
E-mail: mark.batinick@hds.ilga.gov
Committees: Appropriations - Higher Education; Business and
Occupational Licenses; Elementary and Secondary Education: School
Curriculum & Policies; Environment; Insurance; Veterans' Affairs

Representative **Daniel V. Beiser** (D-District 111) . . . . . . . . (217) 782-5996
Counties Represented: Jersey (part), Madison (part)   Dist: (618) 465-5900
Term Expires: 2017                                    Fax: (217) 558-0493
528 Henry Street, Alton, IL 62022                     Dist: (618) 465-5150
E-mail: dvbeiser@sbcglobal.net
Committees: Appropriations - Public Safety; Environment; Intermodal
Infrastructure; Transportation: Regulation, Roads & Bridges;
Transportation: Vehicles and Safety
Education: Southern Illinois BS, MS

Representative
**Patricia R. "Patti" Bellock** (R-District 47) . . . . . . . . . . . (217) 782-1448
Counties Represented: Cook (part), DuPage (part)      Dist: (630) 852-8633
Term Expires: 2017                                    Fax: (217) 782-2289
1 South Cass Avenue, Suite 205,                       Dist: (630) 852-6530
Westmont, IL 60559
E-mail: rep@pbellock.com
Committees: Appropriations - Human Services; Financial Institutions;
Health and Healthcare Disparities; Human Services; Labor and
Commerce; Special Needs Services

Representative **Thomas M. Bennett** (R-District 106) . . . . . (217) 558-1039
Counties Represented: Ford, Iroquois, Livingston      Dist: (815) 432-0106
(part), Vermilion (part), Woodford (part)
Term Expires: 2017
E-mail: thomas.bennett@hds.ilga.gov
Committees: Appropriations - Elementary and Secondary Education;
Appropriations - Higher Education; Consumer Protection; Elementary
and Secondary Education: School Curriculum & Policies; Higher
Education; Renewable Energy and Sustainability; State Government
Administration

Representative **Avery Bourne** (R-District 95) . . . . . . . . . . . (217) 782-8071
Counties Represented: Christian (part), Macoupin      Dist: (217) 324-5200
(part), Madison (part), Montgomery                    Fax: (217) 324-5201
Term Expires: 2017
206-N Stratton Office Building, Springfield, IL 62706
E-mail: bourne@ilhousegop.org
Committees: Agriculture and Conservation; Consumer Protection;
Counties and Townships

Representative **John E. Bradley** (D-District 117) . . . . . . . . (217) 782-1051
Counties Represented: Franklin, Hamilton (part),      Dist: (618) 997-9697
Williamson                                            Fax: (217) 782-0882
Term Expires: 2017                                    Dist: (618) 997-9807
1301 Enterprise Way, Suite 40A, Marion, IL 62959
E-mail: repjohnbradley@mychoice.net
Committees: Agriculture and Conservation; Judiciary - Civil; Labor and
Commerce; Revenue and Finance

Representative **Dan Brady** (R-District 105) . . . . . . . . . . . . . (217) 782-1118
Counties Represented: Livingston (part), McLean       Dist: (309) 662-1100
(part)                                                Fax: (217) 558-6271
Term Expires: 2017                                    Dist: (309) 662-1150
104 W. North Street, Bloomingdale, IL 61761
E-mail: dan@rep-danbrady.com
Committees: Appropriations - Higher Education; Community College
Access and Affordability; Higher Education; Insurance; Labor and
Commerce; Special Needs Services; Transportation: Vehicles and
Safety

Representative **Peter Breen** (R-District 48) . . . . . . . . . . . . . (217) 782-8037
Counties Represented: DuPage (part)                   Dist: (630) 403-8135
Term Expires: 2017
E-mail: peter.breen@hds.ilga.gov
Committees: Consumer Protection; Economic Development and
Housing; Energy; Insurance; Judiciary - Civil; Labor and Commerce;
Restorative Justice

Representative **Adam Brown** (R-District 102) . . . . . . . . . . . (217) 782-8398
Counties Represented: Champaign (part), Douglas,      Dist: (217) 607-5104
Edgar (part), Macon (part), Moultrie, Shelby,         Fax: (217) 782-7012
Vermilion (part)                                      Fax: (217) 607-5471
Term Expires: 2017
101 South Main, Decatur, IL 62523
E-mail: staterepbrown@gmail.com
Committees: Appropriations - General Services; Economic
Development and Housing; Financial Institutions; Health Care
Licenses; Public Utilities; Youth and Young Adults
Education: Richland Col 2005 (Attended); Illinois 2007 BS

Representative **Terri Bryant** (R-District 115) . . . . . . . . . . . . (217) 782-0387
Counties Represented: Jackson (part), Jefferson,      Dist: (618) 242-8115
Perry (part), Union (part), Washington (part)         Fax: (618) 242-8118
Term Expires: 2017
E-mail: staterepterribryant@gmail.com
Committees: Appropriations - Public Safety; Intermodal Infrastructure;
Judiciary - Criminal; Juvenile Justice and System-Involved Youth;
Tourism and Conventions; Veterans' Affairs; Youth and Young Adults

Representative **Daniel J. Burke** (D-District 1) . . . . . . . . . . . (217) 782-1117
Counties Represented: Cook (part)                     Dist: (773) 471-2299
Term Expires: 2017                                    Fax: (217) 782-0927
2650 West 51st Street, Chicago, IL 60632             Dist: (773) 471-1648
E-mail: burkedj2@ilga.gov
Committees: Elementary and Secondary Education: Charter School
Policy; Executive; Financial Institutions

Representative **Kelly M. Burke** (D-District 36) . . . . . . . . . . . (217) 782-0515
Counties Represented: Cook (part)                     Dist: (708) 425-0571
Term Expires: 2017                                    Fax: (217) 558-4553
5144 West 95th Street, Oak Lawn, IL 60453            Dist: (708) 425-0642
E-mail: kellyb@ilga.gov
Committees: Agriculture and Conservation; Appropriations - Higher
Education; Health Care Licenses; Higher Education; Labor and
Commerce; Museums, Arts, and Cultural Enhancement; Tollway
Oversight
Education: Illinois BA; John Marshall JD

Representative **Timothy J. "Tim" Butler** (R-District 87) . . (217) 782-0053
Counties Represented: Logan, Menard, Sangamon         Fax: (217) 782-0897
(part), Tazewell (part)
Term Expires: 2017
Committees: Environment; Museums, Arts, and Cultural Enhancement;
Tourism and Conventions; Transportation: Vehicles and Safety
Education: Eastern Illinois 1990 BA

Representative **John M. Cabello** (R-District 68) . . . . . . . . . (217) 782-0455
Counties Represented: Winnebago (part)                Dist: (815) 282-0083
Term Expires: 2017                                    Fax: (217) 782-1141
1941 Harlem Road, Loves, Loves Park, IL 61111        Dist: (815) 282-0085
E-mail: johncabello@aol.com
Committees: Appropriations - Public Safety; Intermodal Infrastructure;
Judiciary - Criminal; Labor and Commerce; Public Utilities; Tollway
Oversight

Representative **Kelly Cassidy** (D-District 14) . . . . . . . . . . . (217) 782-8088
Counties Represented: Cook (part)                     Dist: (773) 784-2002
Term Expires: 2017                                    Dist: (773) 784-2060
5533 North Broadway Street, Chicago, IL 60640        Fax: (217) 782-6592
E-mail: repcassidy@gmail.com
Committees: Appropriations - Public Safety; Community College
Access and Affordability; Human Services; Judiciary - Criminal;
Juvenile Justice and System-Involved Youth; Labor and Commerce;
Renewable Energy and Sustainability; Restorative Justice

Representative **John D. Cavaletto** (R-District 107) . . . . . . . (217) 782-0066
Counties Represented: Bond, Clinton (part),           Dist: (618) 548-9080
Effingham (part), Fayette, Marion                     Fax: (217) 782-1336
Term Expires: 2017                                    Dist: (618) 548-9087
1370 West Main Street, Suite A, Salem, IL 62881
E-mail: john@johncavaletto.com
Committees: Appropriations - Public Safety; Counties and Townships;
Elementary and Secondary Education: School Curriculum & Policies;
Small Business Empowerment and Workforce Development; Special
Needs Services
Education: Southern Illinois BS, MS

Representative **Linda Chapa-LaVia** (D-District 83) . . . . . . . (217) 558-1002
Counties Represented: Kane (part)　　　　Dist: (630) 264-6855
Term Expires: 2017　　　　　　　　　　　Fax: (217) 782-0927
8 East Galena Boulevard, Suite 240,　　　Dist: (630) 264-6752
Aurora, IL 60506
E-mail: chapa-laviali@ilga.gov
Committees: Appropriations - Higher Education; Elementary and
Secondary Education: Charter School Policy; Elementary and
Secondary Education: School Curriculum & Policies; Energy; Financial
Institutions; Public Utilities; Small Business Empowerment and
Workforce Development; Veterans' Affairs
Education: Illinois (Chicago) 1991 BA

Representative
**Katherine "Kate" Cloonen** (D-District 79)
235-E Stratton Office Building . . . . . . . . . . . . . . . . . . . . (217) 782-5981
Counties Represented: Grundy (part), Kankakee　Dist: (815) 939-1983
(part), Will (part)　　　　　　　　　　　　　　Fax: (815) 939-0081
Term Expires: 2017
E-mail: staterepcloonen79@att.net
Committees: Agriculture and Conservation; Elementary and Secondary
Education: School Curriculum & Policies; Intermodal Infrastructure;
State Government Administration; Veterans' Affairs
Education: Ball State BA

Representative **Deborah O'Keefe Conroy** (D-District 46)
244-W Stratton Office Building. . . . . . . . . . . . . . . . . . . .(217) 782-8158
Counties Represented: DuPage (part)　　　Dist: (630) 415-3520
Term Expires: 2017　　　　　　　　　　　Fax: (630) 415-3522
E-mail: repdebconroy@gmail.com
Committees: Counties and Townships; Elementary and Secondary
Education: School Curriculum & Policies; Health Care Availability and
Access; Higher Education; Juvenile Justice and System-Involved Youth;
Youth and Young Adults

Representative **Jerry F. Costello II** (D-District 116)
200-5S Stratton Office Building. . . . . . . . . . . . . . . . . . . .(217) 782-1018
Counties Represented: Monroe, Perry (part),　Dist: (618) 282-7284
Randolph, St. Clair (part)　　　　　　　　　　Fax: (217) 558-4502
Term Expires: 2017　　　　　　　　　　　　　Fax: (618) 282-7286
E-mail: staterepcostello@gmail.com
Committees: Agriculture and Conservation; Consumer Protection;
International Trade and Commerce; Tourism and Conventions;
Veterans' Affairs

Representative **Fred Crespo** (D-District 44)　. . . . . . . . . . . . (217) 782-0347
Counties Represented: Cook (part)　　　　Dist: (630) 372-3340
Term Expires: 2017　　　　　　　　　　　Fax: (217) 557-4622
1014 East Schaumburg, Streator, IL 60107　Fax: (630) 372-3342
E-mail: fred@fredcrespo.com
Committees: Appropriations - General Services; Community College
Access and Affordability; Elementary and Secondary Education: School
Curriculum & Policies; Financial Institutions; Public Utilities; Special
Needs Services

Representative **Barbara Flynn Currie** (D-District 25) . . . . . (217) 782-8121
Counties Represented: Cook (part)　　　　Dist: (773) 667-0550
Term Expires: 2017　　　　　　　　　　　Fax: (217) 524-1794
1303 East 53rd Street, Chicago, IL 60615　Dist: (773) 667-3010
E-mail: repcurrie@sbcglobal.net
Committees: Elementary and Secondary Education: Licensing
Oversight; Revenue and Finance; Rules

Representative **John D'Amico** (D-District 15) . . . . . . . . . . . (217) 782-8198
Counties Represented: Cook (part)　　　　Dist: (773) 736-0218
Term Expires: 2017　　　　　　　　　　　Fax: (217) 782-2906
4404 West Lawrence Avenue, Chicago, IL 60630　Dist: (773) 736-2333
E-mail: johnd@ilga.gov
Committees: Consumer Protection; Labor and Commerce;
Transportation: Regulation, Roads & Bridges; Transportation: Vehicles
and Safety; Veterans' Affairs

Representative
**Christopher "C.D." Davidsmeyer** (R-District 100) . . . . . (217) 782-1840
Counties Represented: Calhoun, Greene, Jersey　Dist: (217) 243-6221
(part), Macoupin (part), Madison (part), Morgan,　Fax: (217) 558-3743
Pike, Sangamon (part), Scott　　　　　　　　　Dist: (217) 245-2071
Term Expires: 2017
22-N Stratton Office Building, Springfield, IL 62706
E-mail: repcddavidsmeyer@gmail.com
Committees: Appropriations - Human Services; Business and
Occupational Licenses; Energy; Financial Institutions; Health Care
Licenses; Insurance; Veterans' Affairs; Youth and Young Adults
Education: Miami 2002 BA

Representative **Monique D. Davis** (D-District 27) . . . . . . . (217) 782-0010
Counties Represented: Cook (part)　　　　Dist: (773) 445-9700
Term Expires: 2017　　　　　　　　　　　Fax: (217) 782-1795
1234 West 95th Street, Chicago, IL 60643　Dist: (773) 445-5755
E-mail: davismd@ilga.gov
Committees: Appropriations - Higher Education; Community College
Access and Affordability; Elementary and Secondary Education:
Charter School Policy; Insurance; Museums, Arts, and Cultural
Enhancement; Restorative Justice
Education: Roosevelt 1967 BS, 1974 MS

Representative **William "Will" Davis** (D-District 30) . . . . . (217) 782-8197
Counties Represented: Cook (part)　　　　Dist: (708) 799-7300
Term Expires: 2017　　　　　　　　　　　Fax: (217) 782-3220
1912 West 174th Street, Suite 200,　　　　Dist: (708) 799-7377
Hazelcrest, IL 60429
E-mail: williamd@ilga.gov
Committees: Appropriations - Elementary and Secondary Education;
Appropriations - Higher Education; Appropriations - Public Safety;
Health and Healthcare Disparities; International Trade and Commerce;
Labor and Commerce
Education: Southern Illinois 1989 BA

Representative **Anthony DeLuca** (D-District 80) . . . . . . . . . (217) 782-1719
Counties Represented: Cook (part), Will (part)　Dist: (708) 754-7999
Term Expires: 2017　　　　　　　　　　　　　Fax: (217) 558-4944
195 West Joe Orr Road, Suite 201,　　　　　　Dist: (708) 754-7904
Chicago, IL 60411
E-mail: repdeluca@sbcglobal.net
Committees: Appropriations - Public Safety; Business and Occupational
Licenses; Cities and Villages; Insurance; Tollway Oversight

Representative **Tom Demmer** (R-District 90)
222-N Stratton Office Building . . . . . . . . . . . . . . . . . . . . (217) 782-0535
Counties Represented: DeKalb (part), La Salle　Dist: (815) 561-3690
(part), Lee (part), Ogle (part), Winnebago (part)　Fax: (815) 561-3691
Term Expires: 2017
E-mail: rep@tomdemmer.com
Committees: Agriculture and Conservation; Appropriations -
Elementary and Secondary Education; Appropriations - Human
Services; Elementary and Secondary Education: Charter School Policy;
Health and Healthcare Disparities; Higher Education; Human Services;
Youth and Young Adults
Education: Dayton 2008 BA

Representative **Scott R. Drury** (D-District 58) . . . . . . . . . . . (217) 782-0902
Counties Represented: Cook (part), Lake (part)　Dist: (847) 681-8580
Term Expires: 2017
Stratton Office Building, 250-W, Springfield, IL 62706
425 Sheridan Road, Highwood, IL 60040
E-mail: repdrury@gmail.com
Committees: Elementary and Secondary Education: Charter School
Policy; Judiciary - Criminal; Personnel and Pensions

Representative **Kenneth "Ken" Dunkin** (D-District 5) . . . . (217) 782-4535
Counties Represented: Cook (part)　　　　Dist: (773) 363-1411
Term Expires: 2017　　　　　　　　　　　Fax: (773) 363-6003
2059 East 75th Street, Chicago, IL 60649　Dist: (312) 266-0699
E-mail: ken@repkendunkin.com
Committees: Appropriations - Higher Education; Appropriations -
Public Safety; Elementary and Secondary Education: School
Curriculum & Policies; Financial Institutions; Health and Healthcare
Disparities; Insurance; Tourism and Conventions
Education: Harold Washington AA; Morehouse Col BA; Chicago MA

Representative **Jim Durkin** (R-District 82) . . . . . . . . . . . . . (217) 782-0494
Counties Represented: Cook (part), DuPage (part),　Dist: (630) 325-2068
Will (part)　　　　　　　　　　　　　　　　　　Fax: (708) 246-1173
Term Expires: 2017　　　　　　　　　　　　　　Dist: (630) 325-2291
16W281 83rd Street, Suite C, Burr Ridge, IL 60527
E-mail: jimd@ilga.gov

Representative **Marcus C. Evans, Jr.** (D-District 33)
276-S Stratton Office Building. . . . . . . . . . . . . . . . . . . . .(217) 782-8272
Counties Represented: Cook (part)　　　　Dist: (773) 783-8492
Term Expires: 2017　　　　　　　　　　　Fax: (217) 782-2404
E-mail: repevans33@gmail.com　　　　　　Dist: (773) 783-8625
Committees: Agriculture and Conservation; Appropriations - General
Services; Business and Occupational Licenses; Economic Development
and Housing; Financial Institutions; Revenue and Finance

Representative **Sara Feigenholtz** (D-District 12) . . . . . . . . . (217) 782-8062
Counties Represented: Cook (part)　　　　Dist: (773) 296-4141
Term Expires: 2017　　　　　　　　　　　Fax: (773) 442-0200
3223 N. Sheffied, Chicago, IL 60657
E-mail: sara@staterepsara.com
Committees: Adoption Reform; Appropriations - Human Services;
Insurance; Special Needs Services; Tourism and Conventions

*(continued on next page)*

**Representatives** *continued*

Representative **Laura Fine** (D-District 17) . . . . . . . . . . . . (217) 782-4194
Counties Represented: Cook (part)  Dist: (847) 998-1717
Term Expires: 2017  Fax: (217) 524-0449
Stratton Office Building, 231-E,  Dist: (847) 998-1707
Springfield, IL 62706
E-mail: repfine@gmail.com
Committees: Appropriations - Higher Education; Environment; Higher
Education; Human Services; Insurance; Youth and Young Adults
Education: Northeastern Illinois 1999 MA

Representative **Mary E. Flowers** (D-District 31) . . . . . . . . (217) 782-4207
Counties Represented: Cook (part)  Dist: (773) 471-5200
Term Expires: 2017  Fax: (217) 782-1130
2525 West 79th Street, Chicago, IL 60652  Dist: (773) 471-1036
E-mail: flowersme@ilga.gov
Committees: Economic Development and Housing; Health and
Healthcare Disparities; Health Care Availability and Access; Higher
Education; Human Services; Juvenile Justice and System-Involved
Youth; Restorative Justice; Small Business Empowerment and
Workforce Development; Special Needs Services; Youth and Young
Adults
Education: Chicago (Attended); Kennedy-King (Attended)

Representative **LaShawn K. Ford** (D-District 8) . . . . . . . . (217) 782-5962
Counties Represented: Cook (part)  Dist: (773) 378-5902
Term Expires: 2017  Fax: (217) 557-4502
4800 West Chicago Avenue, 2nd Floor,  Dist: (773) 378-5903
Chicago, IL 60651
E-mail: repford@lashawnford.com
Committees: Appropriations - General Services; Appropriations -
Human Services; Economic Development and Housing; Health Care
Availability and Access; International Trade and Commerce; Restorative
Justice; Small Business Empowerment and Workforce Development;
Tourism and Conventions; Veterans' Affairs

Representative **Mike Fortner** (R-District 49) . . . . . . . . . . . (217) 782-1653
Counties Represented: Cook (part), DuPage (part),  Dist: (630) 293-9344
Kane (part)  Fax: (217) 782-1275
Term Expires: 2017  Dist: (630) 293-9785
135 Freemont Street, West Chicago, IL 60185
E-mail: mike.fortner@sbcglobal.net
Committees: Cities and Villages; Energy; Intermodal Infrastructure;
Renewable Energy and Sustainability; Tollway Oversight;
Transportation: Regulation, Roads & Bridges

Representative **Jack D. Franks** (D-District 63) . . . . . . . . . . (217) 782-1717
Counties Represented: McHenry (part)  Dist: (815) 334-0063
Term Expires: 2017  Fax: (217) 557-2118
180 South Eastwood Drive, Woodstock, IL 60098  Dist: (815) 334-9147
E-mail: jack@jackfranks.org
Committees: International Trade and Commerce; Public Utilities; State
Government Administration; Tollway Oversight; Veterans' Affairs
Education: Wisconsin BA; American U JD

Representative **Randy E. Frese** (R-District 94) . . . . . . . . . . (217) 782-8096
Counties Represented: Adams, Hancock, Henderson,  Dist: (217) 223-0833
Warren (part)
Term Expires: 2017
E-mail: randy.frese@hds.ilga.gov
Committees: Agriculture and Conservation; Appropriations - Human
Services; Consumer Protection; Elementary and Secondary Education:
School Curriculum & Policies; Small Business Empowerment and
Workforce Development; Veterans' Affairs

Representative **Robyn Gabel** (D-District 18)
248-W Stratton Office Building . . . . . . . . . . . . . . . . . . . . (217) 782-8052
Counties Represented: Cook (part)  Dist: (847) 424-9898
Term Expires: 2017  Fax: (217) 558-4553
E-mail: staterepgabel@robyngabel.com  Dist: (847) 424-9828
Committees: Appropriations - General Services; Human Services; Environment; Human
Services; Insurance; Juvenile Justice and System-Involved Youth;
Museums, Arts, and Cultural Enhancement; Renewable Energy and
Sustainability; Small Business Empowerment and Workforce
Development; Youth and Young Adults

Representative **Jehan A. Gordon-Booth** (D-District 92) . . (217) 782-3186
Counties Represented: Peoria (part)  Dist: (309) 681-1992
Term Expires: 2017  Fax: (217) 558-4552
300 East War Memorial Drive, Suite 303,  Dist: (309) 681-8572
Peoria, IL 61614
E-mail: repjgordon@gmail.com
Committees: Appropriations - Higher Education; Appropriations -
Public Safety; Financial Institutions; Public Utilities

Representative **Will Guzzardi** (D-District 39) . . . . . . . . . . (217) 558-1032
Counties Represented: Cook (part)  Dist: (773) 227-9720
Term Expires: 2017
E-mail: will@repguzzardi.com
Committees: Economic Development and Housing; Elementary and
Secondary Education: School Curriculum & Policies; Energy;
Environment; Juvenile Justice and System-Involved Youth; Renewable
Energy and Sustainability; Special Needs Services

Representative **Norine Hammond** (R-District 93) . . . . . . . (217) 782-0416
Counties Represented: Brown, Cass, Fulton (part),  Dist: (309) 836-2707
Knox (part), Mason, McDonough, Schuyler, Warren  Fax: (217) 557-4530
(part)  Dist: (309) 836-2231
Term Expires: 2017
311 Noth Lafayette Street, Macomb, IL 61455
E-mail: rephammond@macomb.com
Committees: Appropriations - Higher Education; Community College
Access and Affordability; Consumer Protection; Higher Education;
Human Services; Insurance; Transportation: Regulation, Roads &
Bridges

Representative **Sonya M. Harper** (D-District 6) . . . . . . . . . (217) 782-8223
Counties Represented: Cook (part)
Term Expires: 2017
E-mail: repsonyaharper@gmail.com
Committees: Economic Development and Housing; Elementary and
Secondary Education: School Curriculum & Policies; Environment;
Renewable Energy and Sustainability; Restorative Justice

Representative **MG David Harris, ARNG** (R-District 53) . . (217) 782-3739
Counties Represented: Cook (part)  Dist: (224) 635-2010
Term Expires: 2017
800 West Central Road, Mount Prospect, IL 60056
E-mail: repharris@yahoo.com
Committees: Appropriations - General Services; Financial Institutions;
Renewable Energy and Sustainability; Revenue and Finance; State
Government Administration; Tollway Oversight; Transportation:
Regulation, Roads & Bridges

Representative
**Gregory S. "Greg" Harris** (D-District 13) . . . . . . . . . . . (217) 782-3835
Counties Represented: Cook (part)  Dist: (773) 348-3434
Term Expires: 2017  Fax: (217) 557-6470
1967 West Montrose, Chicago, IL 60613  Dist: (773) 348-3475
E-mail: greg@gregharris.org
Committees: Appropriations - Human Services; Executive; Insurance;
Restorative Justice; Tourism and Conventions

Representative **Chad D. Hays** (R-District 104) . . . . . . . . . . (217) 782-4811
Counties Represented: Champaign (part), Vermilion  Dist: (217) 477-0104
(part)  Fax: (217) 477-0102
Term Expires: 2017
7 East Fairchild Street, Danville, IL 61832
E-mail: chad@rephays.com
Committees: Executive; Health Care Availability and Access; Health
Care Licenses; Higher Education; Juvenile Justice and System-Involved
Youth

Representative
**Elizabeth "Lisa" Hernandez** (D-District 24) . . . . . . . . . (217) 782-8173
Counties Represented: Cook (part)  Dist: (708) 222-5240
Term Expires: 2017  Fax: (217) 558-1844
2137 South Lombard Street, Suite 205,  Dist: (708) 222-5241
Cicero, IL 60804
E-mail: repehernandez@yahoo.com
Committees: Appropriations - Elementary and Secondary Education;
Appropriations - Human Services; Consumer Protection; Health and
Healthcare Disparities; Higher Education; Labor and Commerce; Small
Business Empowerment and Workforce Development

Representative **Jay C. Hoffman** (D-District 113) . . . . . . . . (217) 782-0104
Counties Represented: Madison (part), St. Clair  Dist: (618) 416-7407
(part)  Fax: (217) 782-1333
Term Expires: 2017  Dist: (618) 416-7409
312 South High Street, Belleville, IL 62220
E-mail: repjayhoffman@gmail.com
Committees: Appropriations - Public Safety; Judiciary - Civil; Labor
and Commerce; Public Utilities
Education: Illinois State BS; Saint Louis U JD

Representative **Frances Ann Hurley** (D-District 35)
252-W Stratton Office Building . . . . . . . . . . . . . . . . . . . . (217) 782-8200
Counties Represented: Cook (part)  Dist: (773) 445-8128
Term Expires: 2017  Fax: (773) 672-5144
E-mail: repfranhurley@gmail.com
Committees: Appropriations - General Services; Consumer Protection;
Health Care Licenses; Labor and Commerce; Special Needs Services;
Transportation: Regulation, Roads & Bridges; Youth and Young Adults

Representative **Jeanne M. Ives** (R-District 42)
230-N Stratton Office Building . . . . . . . . . . . . . . . . . . . . . . (217) 558-1037
Counties Represented: DuPage (part)     Dist: (630) 384-1108
Term Expires: 2017     Fax: (217) 782-1275
E-mail: repjeanneives@gmail.com
Committees: Appropriations - Elementary and Secondary Education;
Cities and Villages; Community College Access and Affordability;
Intermodal Infrastructure; Juvenile Justice and System-Involved Youth;
Labor and Commerce; Personnel and Pensions; Youth and Young
Adults

Representative **Eddie Lee Jackson, Sr.** (D-District 114) . . . (217) 782-5951
Counties Represented: St. Clair (part)
Term Expires: 2017     Fax: (217) 782-8794
4700 State Street, Suite 2, East St. Louis, IL 62205    Dist: (618) 875-9870
E-mail: bbsty2010@gmail.com
Committees: Appropriations - Elementary and Secondary Education;
Consumer Protection; Counties and Townships; Energy; Executive
Education: Southern IL Edwardsville BS, MCP

Representative **Sheri L. Jesiel** (R-District 61) . . . . . . . . . . (217) 782-8151
Counties Represented: Lake (part)     Dist: (847) 855-8600
Term Expires: 2017     Fax: (217) 557-7207
Warren Township Center, 17801 West Washington    Dist: (847) 855-6042
Street, Gurnee, IL 60031
E-mail: jesiel@ilhousegop.org
Committees: Appropriations - Human Services; Appropriations - Public
Safety; Elementary and Secondary Education: School Curriculum &
Policies; Human Services; Juvenile Justice and System-Involved Youth;
Personnel and Pensions; Small Business Empowerment and Workforce
Development; Special Needs Services
Education: Carthage BBA

Representative **Thaddeus Jones** (D-District 29) . . . . . . . . (217) 782-8087
Counties Represented: Cook (part), Will (part)    Dist: (708) 933-6018
Term Expires: 2017     Fax: (217) 558-6433
1910 Sibley Boulevard, Calumet City, IL 60409    Dist: (708) 933-6284
E-mail: repjones.jones@gmail.com
Committees: Appropriations - Higher Education; Appropriations -
Public Safety; Community College Access and Affordability; Labor and
Commerce

Representative **Dwight Kay** (R-District 112) . . . . . . . . . . . (217) 782-8018
Counties Represented: Madison (part), St. Clair    Dist: (618) 307-9200
(part)     Fax: (618) 307-9202
Term Expires: 2017
9 Junction Drive West, Suite 5, Glen Carbon, IL 62034
E-mail: dwightkay112@gmail.com
Committees: Appropriations - Human Services; Appropriations - Public
Safety; Economic Development and Housing; Insurance; International
Trade and Commerce; Judiciary - Civil; Labor and Commerce

Representative **Stephanie A. Kifowit** (D-District 84)
200-3S Stratton Office Building. . . . . . . . . . . . . . . . . . . . . (217) 782-8028
Counties Represented: DuPage (part), Kane (part),    Dist: (630) 585-1308
Kendall (part), Will (part)     Fax: (630) 585-1357
Term Expires: 2017
E-mail: stephanie.kifowit@att.net
Committees: Appropriations - General Services; Financial Institutions;
Health Care Licenses; Intermodal Infrastructure
Education: Northern Illinois BS, MPA

Representative **Louis I. "Lou" Lang** (D-District 16) . . . . . . (217) 782-1252
Counties Represented: Cook (part)     Dist: (847) 673-1131
Term Expires: 2017     Fax: (217) 782-9903
4528 West Oakton Street, Skokie, IL 60076    Dist: (847) 982-0393
E-mail: langli@ilga.gov
E-mail: reploulang@aol.com
Committees: Rules

Representative **David R. Leitch** (R-District 73) . . . . . . . . . (217) 782-8108
Counties Represented: Bureau (part), La Salle    Dist: (309) 690-7373
(part), Marshall, Peoria (part), Stark, Woodford    Fax: (217) 557-3047
(part)     Dist: (309) 690-7375
Term Expires: 2017
5407 North University, Suite B, Peoria, IL 61614
E-mail: repdavidleitch@gmail.com
Committees: Appropriations - Human Services; Community College
Access and Affordability; Financial Institutions; Health and Healthcare
Disparities; Public Utilities; Rules

Representative **Camille Lilly** (D-District 78) . . . . . . . . . . . . (217) 782-6400
Counties Represented: Cook (part)     Dist: (773) 473-7300
Term Expires: 2017     Fax: (217) 558-1054
5755 West Division, Chicago, IL 60651    Dist: (773) 473-7378
E-mail: statereplilly@yahoo.com
Committees: Appropriations - Human Services; Appropriations - Public
Safety; Elementary and Secondary Education: School Curriculum &
Policies; Health and Healthcare Disparities; Juvenile Justice and
System-Involved Youth; Museums, Arts, and Cultural Enhancement;
Transportation: Regulation, Roads & Bridges

Representative **Michael J. Madigan** (D-District 22) . . . . . . (217) 782-5350
Counties Represented: Cook (part)     Dist: (773) 581-8000
6500 South Pulaski Road, Chicago, IL 60629    Fax: (217) 524-1794
E-mail: mmadigan@hds.ilga.gov    Dist: (773) 581-9414

Representative **Natalie Manley** (D-District 98)
242A-W Stratton Office Building . . . . . . . . . . . . . . . . . . . (217) 782-3316
Counties Represented: Will (part)     Dist: (815) 725-2741
Term Expires: 2017     Fax: (815) 725-5269
E-mail: repmanley@gmail.com
Committees: Appropriations - General Services; Appropriations -
Human Services; Business and Occupational Licenses; Consumer
Protection; Small Business Empowerment and Workforce Development;
Transportation: Regulation, Roads & Bridges; Transportation: Vehicles
and Safety; Youth and Young Adults
Education: U St Francis BA

Representative **Robert F. Martwick, Jr.** (D-District 19)
282-S Stratton Office Building. . . . . . . . . . . . . . . . . . . . . (217) 782-8400
Counties Represented: Cook (part)     Dist: (773) 286-1115
Term Expires: 2017     Fax: (773) 545-7106
E-mail: repmartwick@gmail.com
Committees: Appropriations - General Services; Economic
Development and Housing; Elementary and Secondary Education:
Charter School Policy; Financial Institutions; Insurance; Judiciary -
Civil; Museums, Arts, and Cultural Enhancement; Renewable Energy
and Sustainability; Veterans' Affairs
Education: Boston Col BA; John Marshall JD

Representative **Rita Mayfield** (D-District 60) . . . . . . . . . . . (217) 558-1012
Counties Represented: Lake (part)     Dist: (847) 599-2800
Term Expires: 2017     Fax: (217) 558-1092
415 Washington Street, Suite 203,    Dist: (847) 599-2955
Waukegan, IL 60085
E-mail: 60thdistrict@gmail.com
Committees: Appropriations - Human Services; Appropriations - Public
Safety; Business and Occupational Licenses; Community College
Access and Affordability; Elementary and Secondary Education:
Licensing Oversight; Health and Healthcare Disparities; Judiciary -
Criminal; Public Utilities
Education: Columbia Col (IL) BS; Benedictine U MS

Representative **Emily McAsey** (D-District 85) . . . . . . . . . . (217) 782-4179
Counties Represented: DuPage (part), Will (part)    Dist: (815) 588-0085
Term Expires: 2017     Fax: (217) 557-7204
209 West Romero Road, Romeoville, IL 60446    Dist: (815) 372-0080
E-mail: repemily@gmail.com
Committees: Appropriations - Elementary and Secondary Education;
Elementary and Secondary Education: Charter School Policy;
Environment; Renewable Energy and Sustainability; Veterans' Affairs

Representative **Michael P. McAuliffe** (R-District 20) . . . . . . (217) 782-8182
Counties Represented: Cook (part)     Dist: (773) 444-0611
Term Expires: 2017     Fax: (217) 558-1073
6650 North Northwest Highway, First Floor,    Dist: (773) 444-0711
Chicago, IL 60631
E-mail: mmcauliffe20@yahoo.com
Committees: Appropriations - Public Safety; Health Care Availability
and Access; Health Care Licenses; Museums, Arts, and Cultural
Enhancement; Public Utilities; Tourism and Conventions; Veterans'
Affairs

Representative **Margo McDermed** (R-District 37) . . . . . . . (217) 782-0424
Counties Represented: Cook (part), Will (part)    Dist: (815) 277-2079
Term Expires: 2017     Fax: (815) 277-2079
E-mail: margo.mcdermed@hds.ilga.gov
Committees: Appropriations - General Services; Counties and
Townships; Environment; Health Care Licenses; Intermodal
Infrastructure; Juvenile Justice and System-Involved Youth; State
Government Administration

Representative **David McSweeney** (R-District 52)
226-N Stratton Office Building . . . . . . . . . . . . . . . . . . . . . (217) 782-1517
Counties Represented: Cook (part), Kane (part),    Dist: (847) 516-0052
Lake (part), McHenry (part)     Fax: (847) 516-8164
Term Expires: 2017
E-mail: ilhouse52@gmail.com
Committees: Appropriations - Elementary and Secondary Education;
Consumer Protection; Economic Development and Housing; State
Government Administration
Education: Duke 1987 BA; Fuqua 1988 MBA

*(continued on next page)*

**Representatives** *continued*

Representative
**Charles E. "Charlie" Meier** (R-District 108)
206-N Stratton Office Building . . . . . . . . . . . . . . . . . . . . . (217) 782-6401
Counties Represented: Clinton (part), Madison   Dist: (618) 651-0405
(part), St. Clair (part), Washington (part)   Fax: (618) 651-0413
Term Expires: 2017
E-mail: repcmeier@gmail.com
Committees: Agriculture and Conservation; Appropriations - Human
Services; Community College Access and Affordability; Elementary
and Secondary Education: School Curriculum & Policies; Environment;
Special Needs Services

Representative **Bill Mitchell** (R-District 101) . . . . . . . . . . . . (217) 782-8163
Counties Represented: Champaign (part), De   Dist: (217) 876-1968
Witt, Macon (part), McLean (part), Piatt   Fax: (217) 557-0571
Term Expires: 2017   Dist: (217) 876-1973
5130 Hickory Point Frontage Road, Decatur, IL 62526
E-mail: repmitchell@earthlink.net
Committees: Elementary and Secondary Education: Licensing
Oversight; Energy; Environment; Health and Healthcare Disparities;
Public Utilities

Representative **Christian L. Mitchell** (D-District 26) . . . . . . (217) 782-2023
Counties Represented: Cook (part)   Dist: (773) 924-1755
Term Expires: 2017   Fax: (217) 558-1092
449 E. 35th Street, Chicago, IL 60616   Dist: (773) 924-1775
E-mail: mitchelldistrict26@att.net
Committees: Elementary and Secondary Education: School Curriculum
& Policies; Judiciary - Criminal; Juvenile Justice and System-Involved
Youth; Renewable Energy and Sustainability; Revenue and Finance;
State Government Administration
Education: Chicago BA

Representative **Anna Moeller** (D-District 43) . . . . . . . . . . . .(217) 782-8020
Counties Represented: Cook (part), Kane (part)   Dist: (847) 841-7130
Term Expires: 2017   Fax: (217) 557-4459
249-E Stratton Office Building,   Dist: (847) 841-7140
Springfield, IL 62706
164 Division Street, Elgin, IL 60120
E-mail: staterepmoeller@gmail.com
Committees: Adoption Reform; Agriculture and Conservation;
Appropriations - General Services; Elementary and Secondary
Education: Charter School Policy; Environment; Health Care Licenses;
Renewable Energy and Sustainability

Representative **Donald L. Moffitt** (R-District 74) . . . . . . . .(217) 782-8032
Counties Represented: Bureau (part), Henry (part),   Dist: (309) 343-8000
Knox (part), Lee (part), Mercer   Fax: (217) 577-0179
Term Expires: 2017   Dist: (309) 343-2683
64 S. Prairie Street., Suite 5, Galesburg, IL 61401
E-mail: moffitt@grics.net
Committees: Agriculture and Conservation; Appropriations - Public
Safety; Counties and Townships; Elementary and Secondary Education:
School Curriculum & Policies; Financial Institutions; Intermodal
Infrastructure; Veterans' Affairs
Education: Illinois BS

Representative **Thomas "Tom" Morrison** (R-District 54) . .(217) 782-8026
Counties Represented: Cook (part)   Dist: (847) 202-6584
Term Expires: 2017   Fax: (217) 782-1275
11 East Palatine Road, Suite 106, Palatine, IL 60067
E-mail: repmorrison54@gmail.com
Committees: Appropriations - General Services; Environment;
Personnel and Pensions; Renewable Energy and Sustainability; State
Government Administration
Education: Hillsdale (Attended)

Representative
**Martin J. "Marty" Moylan** (D-District 55)
242-W Stratton Office Building . . . . . . . . . . . . . . . . . . . . . (217) 782-8007
Counties Represented: Cook (part)   Dist: (847) 635-6821
Term Expires: 2017   Fax: (847) 635-8565
E-mail: staterepmoylan@gmail.com
Committees: Cities and Villages; Intermodal Infrastructure;
Tollway Oversight; Transportation: Regulation, Roads & Bridges;
Transportation: Vehicles and Safety; Veterans' Affairs; Youth and
Young Adults

Representative **Michelle Mussman** (D-District 56) . . . . . . (217) 782-3725
Counties Represented: Cook (part), DuPage (part)   Dist: (847) 923-9104
Term Expires: 2017   Fax: (847) 923-9105
15 West Weathersfield Way, Schaumburg, IL 60193
E-mail: staterepmussman@gmail.com
Committees: Appropriations - Elementary and Secondary Education;
Appropriations - Human Services; Community College Access and
Affordability; Elementary and Secondary Education: School Curriculum
& Policies; Energy; Special Needs Services; State Government
Administration

Representative **Elaine Nekritz** (D-District 57) . . . . . . . . . . (217) 558-1004
Counties Represented: Cook (part), Lake (part)   Dist: (847) 229-5499
Term Expires: 2017   Fax: (217) 558-4554
24 South Des Plaines River Road, Suite 400,   Dist: (847) 229-5487
Des Plaines, IL 60016
E-mail: enekritz@repnekritz.org
Committees: Appropriations - Public Safety; Judiciary - Civil;
Personnel and Pensions; Public Utilities; Special Needs Services

Representative **Brandon W. Phelps** (D-District 118) . . . . . . (217) 782-5131
Counties Represented: Alexander, Gallatin,   Dist: (618) 253-4189
Hamilton (part), Hardin, Jackson (part), Johnson,   Fax: (847) 855-6042
Massac, Pope, Pulaski, Saline, Union (part)   Dist: (618) 253-3136
Term Expires: 2017
607 S. Commercial Street, Suite B, Harrisburg, IL 62946
E-mail: bphelps118@gmail.com
Committees: Appropriations - Higher Education; Appropriations -
Public Safety; Environment; Health Care Licenses; Labor and
Commerce; Public Utilities; Veterans' Affairs
Education: Eastern Illinois BA

Representative
**Reginald "Reggie" Phillips** (R-District 110) . . . . . . . . . (217) 558-1040
Counties Represented: Clark, Coles, Crawford,   Dist: (217) 348-1110
Cumberland, Edgar (part), Lawrence (part)
Term Expires: 2017
E-mail: reginald.phillips@hds.ilga.gov
Committees: Appropriations - Higher Education; Counties and
Townships; Environment; Health and Healthcare Disparities; Labor and
Commerce; Transportation: Regulation, Roads & Bridges

Representative **Robert W. Pritchard** (R-District 70) . . . . . . (217) 782-0425
Counties Represented: Boone (part), DeKalb   Dist: (815) 748-3494
(part), Kane (part)   Fax: (217) 782-1275
Term Expires: 2017   Dist: (815) 748-4630
2600 DeKalb Avenue, Suite C, Sycamore, IL 60178
E-mail: bob@pritchardstaterep.com
Committees: Appropriations - Elementary and Secondary Education;
Appropriations - Higher Education; Elementary and Secondary
Education: Licensing Oversight; Elementary and Secondary Education:
School Curriculum & Policies; Higher Education; State Government
Administration
Education: Illinois 1967 BS, 1968 MS

Representative **Pamela Reaves-Harris** (D-District 10) . . . . . (217) 782-8077
Counties Represented: Cook (part)   Dist: (312) 877-5074
Term Expires: 2017   Fax: (217) 524-0448
E-mail: repreavesharris@gmail.com   Dist: (312) 877-5165
Committees: Energy; Intermodal Infrastructure; Judiciary - Civil;
Tourism and Conventions
Education: Chicago-Kent JD

Representative **David Reis** (R-District 109) . . . . . . . . . . . . .(217) 782-2087
Counties Represented: Clay, Edwards, Effingham   Dist: (618) 392-0108
(part), Jasper, Lawrence (part), Richland, Wabash,   Fax: (217) 557-0571
Wayne, White   Dist: (618) 392-0107
Term Expires: 2017
219 East Main, Olney, IL 62450
P.O. Box 189, Olney, IL 62450
E-mail: david@davidreis.org
Committees: Appropriations - Public Safety; Economic Development
and Housing; Financial Institutions; Insurance
Education: Illinois BS

Representative **Al Riley** (D-District 38) . . . . . . . . . . . . . . . (217) 558-1007
Counties Represented: Cook (part), Will (part)   Dist: (708) 799-4364
Term Expires: 2017   (Matteson)
600 Holiday Plaza Drive, Suite 535,   Fax: (217) 558-1664
Matteson, IL 60443   Dist: (708) 799-4481
E-mail: rep.riley38@sbcglobal.net   (Matteson)
Committees: Appropriations - Elementary and Secondary Education;
Appropriations - Public Safety; Cities and Villages; Counties and
Townships; Transportation: Vehicles and Safety

Representative **Robert "Bob" Rita** (D-District 28)
281-S Stratton Office Building . . . . . . . . . . . . . . . . . . . . . .(217) 558-1000
Counties Represented: Cook (part)   Dist: (708) 396-2822
Term Expires: 2017   Fax: (217) 558-1091
E-mail: robertbobrita@aol.com   Dist: (708) 396-2898
Committees: Appropriations - Public Safety; Business and Occupational
Licenses; Consumer Protection; Executive; Insurance; Revenue and
Finance; Tollway Oversight

Representative **Ronald "Ron" Sandack** (R-District 81) ... (217) 782-6578
Counties Represented: DuPage (part), Will (part)   Dist: (630) 737-0504
Term Expires: 2017   Fax: (630) 737-0509
632 Capitol Building, 401 S 2nd Steet, Springfield, IL 62706
E-mail: repsandack@gmail.com
Committees: Community College Access and Affordability; Elementary
and Secondary Education: School Curriculum & Policies; Judiciary -
Civil; Judiciary - Criminal; Public Utilities; Renewable Energy and
Sustainability; Restorative Justice
Education: DePaul 1989 JD; Illinois 1986 BA

Representative **Sue Scherer** (D-District 96)
E-2 Stratton Office Building ........................ (217) 524-0353
Counties Represented: Christian (part), Macon   Dist: (217) 877-9636
(part), Sangamon (part)   Fax: (217) 524-0354
Term Expires: 2017   Dist: (217) 877-9659
E-mail: staterepsue@gmail.com
Committees: Agriculture and Conservation; Consumer Protection;
Elementary and Secondary Education: Licensing Oversight; Elementary
and Secondary Education: School Curriculum & Policies; Intermodal
Infrastructure; Small Business Empowerment and Workforce
Development

Representative **Carol A. Sente** (D-District 59) .......... (217) 782-0499
Counties Represented: Cook (part), Lake (part)   Dist: (847) 478-9909
Term Expires: 2017   Fax: (217) 524-0443
430 N. Milwaukee Ave., Suite 8,   Dist: (847) 478-9960
Lincolnshire, IL 60069
E-mail: repsente@gmail.com
Committees: Elementary and Secondary Education: School Curriculum
& Policies; Environment; Personnel and Pensions; State Government
Administration; Veterans' Affairs
Education: Indiana 1983 BS

Representative **Elgie R. Sims, Jr.** (D-District 34)
200-1S Stratton Office Building ....................(217) 782-6476
Counties Represented: Cook (part), Kankakee   Dist: (773) 783-8800
(part), Will (part)   Fax: (217) 782-0952
Term Expires: 2017   Dist: (773) 783-8773
E-mail: Repsims34@gmail.com
Committees: Business and Occupational Licenses; Elementary and
Secondary Education: School Curriculum & Policies; Higher
Education; Judiciary - Criminal; Revenue and Finance; Transportation:
Regulation, Roads & Bridges
Education: Illinois State 1993 BS; Illinois (Springfield) 1997 MPA;
Loyola U (Chicago) 2007 JD

Representative
**Andrew F. "Andy" Skoog** (D-District 76) ............ (217) 782-0140
Counties Represented: Bureau (part), La Salle   Dist: (815) 664-2717
(part), Livingston (part), Putnam   Fax: (815) 663-1629
Term Expires: 2017
Committees: Agriculture and Conservation; Elementary and Secondary
Education: School Curriculum & Policies; Higher Education; Small
Business Empowerment and Workforce Development; Veterans' Affairs

Representative **Mike Smiddy** (D-District 71)
284-S Stratton Office Building ....................(217) 782-3992
Counties Represented: Carroll (part), Henry (part),   Dist: (309) 848-9098
Rock Island (part), Whiteside (part)   Fax: (217) 524-0443
Term Expires: 2017   Dist: (309) 848-9101
E-mail: repsmiddy@gmail.com
Committees: Appropriations - Higher Education; Community College
Access and Affordability; Elementary and Secondary Education: School
Curriculum & Policies; Juvenile Justice and System-Involved Youth;
Labor and Commerce; Transportation: Regulation, Roads & Bridges

Representative **Keith P. Sommer** (R-District 88) ........ (217) 782-0221
Counties Represented: McLean (part), Tazewell   Dist: (309) 263-9242
(part)   Fax: (217) 557-1098
Term Expires: 2017   Dist: (309) 263-8187
121 West Jefferson Street, Morton, IL 61550
E-mail: sommer@mtco.com
Committees: Adoption Reform; Business and Occupational Licenses;
Insurance; International Trade and Commerce
Education: Virginia BA

Representative **Joe Sosnowski** (R-District 69) ......... (217) 782-0548
Counties Represented: Boone (part), Winnebago   Dist: (815) 547-3436
(part)   Fax: (217) 782-1141
Term Expires: 2017   Dist: (815) 516-8434
305 Amphiteater Drive, Rockford, IL 61107
E-mail: repsosnowski@gmail.com
Committees: Appropriations - Elementary and Secondary Education;
Appropriations - Higher Education; Elementary and Secondary
Education: Charter School Policy; Elementary and Secondary
Education: School Curriculum & Policies; Executive; Revenue and
Finance; Tollway Oversight
Education: Northern Illinois 1999 BA

Representative **Cynthia Soto** (D-District 4) ............. (217) 782-0150
Counties Represented: Cook (part)   Dist: (773) 252-0402
Term Expires: 2017   Fax: (217) 557-7210
2615 West Division Street, Chicago, IL 60622   Dist: (312) 829-3707
E-mail: 4repsoto@gmail.com
Committees: Appropriations - Elementary and Secondary Education;
Appropriations - Higher Education; Financial Institutions; Health and
Healthcare Disparities; Human Services

Representative **Brian W. Stewart** (R-District 89)..........(815) 232-0774
Counties Represented: Carroll (part), Jo Daviess,   Fax: (815) 232-0777
Ogle (part), Stephenson, Whiteside (part), Winnebago (part)
Term Expires: 2017
50 West Douglas Street, Suite 1001, Freeport, IL 61032
E-mail: repstewart@gmail.com
Committees: Agriculture and Conservation; Appropriations - Public
Safety; Human Services; Judiciary - Criminal; Labor and Commerce;
Revenue and Finance; Veterans' Affairs

Representative **Ed Sullivan, Jr.** (R-District 51)...........(217) 782-3696
Counties Represented: Cook (part), Lake (part)   Dist: (847) 566-5115
Term Expires: 2017   Fax: (217) 782-7012
700 North Lake Street, Suite 101,   Dist: (847) 566-5155
Mundelein, IL 60060
E-mail: ilhouse51@sbcglobal.net
Committees: Elementary and Secondary Education: Charter School
Policy; Executive; Financial Institutions; Public Utilities; Revenue and
Finance; Rules

Representative **Silvana Tabares** (D-District 21)
280-S Stratton Office Building......................(217) 782-7752
Counties Represented: Cook (part)   Dist: (773) 522-1315
Term Expires: 2017   Fax: (217) 524-0450
E-mail: rep.tabares@gmail.com   Dist: (773) 522-1317
Committees: Financial Institutions; Labor and Commerce;
Transportation: Regulation, Roads & Bridges

Representative **André M. Thapedi** (D-District 32)........(217) 782-1702
Counties Represented: Cook (part)   Dist: (773) 873-4444
Term Expires: 2017   Fax: (217) 557-0543
371 East 75th Street, Chicago, IL 60619   Dist: (773) 873-4445
E-mail: rep32district@gmail.com
Committees: Energy; Financial Institutions; International Trade and
Commerce; Judiciary - Civil; Public Utilities

Representative **Michael W. Tryon** (R-District 66) ........ (217) 782-0432
Counties Represented: Kane (part), McHenry (part)   Dist: (815) 459-6453
Term Expires: 2017   Fax: (217) 782-1141
One North Virginia, Crystal Lake, IL 60014   Dist: (815) 356-0643
E-mail: mike@miketryon.com
Committees: Environment; Executive; Juvenile Justice and
System-Involved Youth; Labor and Commerce; Renewable Energy and
Sustainability; Revenue and Finance

Representative **Arthur L. Turner** (D-District 9)...........(217) 782-8116
Counties Represented: Cook (part)   Dist: (773) 277-4700
Term Expires: 2017   Fax: (217) 782-0888
3849 West Ogden Avenue, Chicago, IL 60623   Dist: (773) 277-4703
E-mail: arthurt@ilga.gov
Committees: Economic Development and Housing; Executive;
Insurance; Judiciary - Criminal; Juvenile Justice and System-Involved
Youth; Revenue and Finance; Rules

Representative **Michael Unes** (R-District 91)
232-N Stratton Office Building ....................(217) 782-8152
Counties Represented: Fulton (part), Peoria (part),   Dist: (309) 620-8631
Tazewell (part)   Fax: (217) 782-1275
Term Expires: 2017   Dist: (309) 349-3046
E-mail: repunes@gmail.com
Committees: Appropriations - Human Services; Financial Institutions;
Human Services; Insurance; International Trade and Commerce;
Tourism and Conventions; Transportation: Vehicles and Safety;
Veterans' Affairs

Representative **Patrick J. Verschoore** (D-District 72) ..... (217) 782-5970
Counties Represented: Rock Island (part)   Dist: (309) 558-3612
Term Expires: 2017   Fax: (217) 558-1253
County Office Building, 1504 3rd Avenue,   Dist: (309) 793-4764
Rock Island, IL 61201
E-mail: repverschoore@72nddistrict.org
Committees: Appropriations - Public Safety; Counties and Townships;
Environment; Health Care Licenses; Public Utilities; Veterans' Affairs

Representative **Litesa E. Wallace** (D-District 67)........(217) 782-3167
Counties Represented: Winnebago (part)   Dist: (217) 782-8223
Term Expires: 2017   Fax: (217) 557-7654
200 S. Wyman, Suite 304, Rockford, IL 61101   Dist: (815) 987-7225
E-mail: litesa@staterepwallace.com
Committees: Agriculture and Conservation; Economic Development
and Housing; Financial Institutions; Human Services; Renewable
Energy and Sustainability

*(continued on next page)*

LEGISLATIVE BRANCH

**Representatives** *continued*

Representative
**Lawrence "Larry" Walsh, Jr.** (D-District 86) . . . . . . . . . (217) 782-8090
Counties Represented: Will (part)             Dist: (815) 730-8600
Term Expires: 2017                            Fax: (217) 782-0952
121 Springfield Avenue, Joliet, IL 60435      Dist: (815) 730-8121
E-mail: statereplarrywalshjr@gmail.com
Committees: Appropriations - General Services; Counties and
Townships; Intermodal Infrastructure; Labor and Commerce;
Transportation: Regulation, Roads & Bridges

Representative **Grant Wehrli** (R-District 41) . . . . . . . . . . . . (217) 782-6507
Counties Represented: DuPage (part), Will (part)   Dist: (630) 696-4160
Term Expires: 2017
E-mail: grant.wehrli@hds.ilga.gov
Committees: Appropriations - Higher Education; Consumer Protection;
Personnel and Pensions; Public Utilities; Small Business Empowerment
and Workforce Development; Special Needs Services

Representative **Emanuel Chris Welch** (D-District 7)
266-S Stratton Office Building . . . . . . . . . . . . . . . . . . . . . (217) 782-8120
Counties Represented: Cook (part)             Dist: (708) 450-1000
Term Expires: 2017                            Fax: (217) 524-0448
E-mail: repwelch@emanuelchriswelch.com        Fax: (708) 450-1104
Committees: Appropriations - Elementary and Secondary Education;
Appropriations - Higher Education; Elementary and Secondary
Education: School Curriculum & Policies; Higher Education; Judiciary
- Criminal; Labor and Commerce
Education: Northwestern 1993; John Marshall 1997 JD

Representative **Barbara M. Wheeler** (R-District 64) . . . . . . (217) 782-1664
Counties Represented: Lake (part), McHenry (part)   Dist: (847) 973-0064
Term Expires: 2017                            Fax: (217) 558-7016
550 West Woodstock, Crystal Lake, IL 60014
E-mail: repwheeler64@gmail.com
Committees: Adoption Reform; Appropriations - Elementary and
Secondary Education; Elementary and Secondary Education: Charter
School Policy; Elementary and Secondary Education: School
Curriculum & Policies; Health and Healthcare Disparities; Higher
Education; Judiciary - Criminal; Museums, Arts, and Cultural
Enhancement

Representative **Keith Wheeler** (R-District 50) . . . . . . . . . . (217) 782-1486
Counties Represented: Kane (part), Kendall (part)   Dist: (630) 345-3464
Term Expires: 2017
E-mail: office@repkeithwheeler.org
Committees: Appropriations - General Services; Economic
Development and Housing; Labor and Commerce; Public Utilities;
Restorative Justice; Small Business Empowerment and Workforce
Development; Transportation: Regulation, Roads & Bridges

Representative **Ann Williams** (D-District 11) . . . . . . . . . . . (217) 782-2458
Counties Represented: Cook (part)             Dist: (773) 880-9082
Term Expires: 2017                            Fax: (217) 557-7214
1726 West Belmont, Chicago, IL 60657          Dist: (773) 880-9083
E-mail: ann@repannwilliams.com
Committees: Adoption Reform; Insurance; Judiciary - Civil; Labor and
Commerce; Renewable Energy and Sustainability
Education: Iowa BA; Drake JD

Representative **Kathleen Willis** (D-District 77)
264-S Stratton Office Building . . . . . . . . . . . . . . . . . . . . . (217) 782-3374
Counties Represented: Cook (part), DuPage (part)   Dist: (708) 562-6970
Term Expires: 2017                            Fax: (217) 524-0448
E-mail: repwillis77@gmail.com                 Dist: (708) 562-6974
Committees: Appropriations - Human Services; Cities and Villages;
Elementary and Secondary Education: School Curriculum & Policies;
Higher Education; Special Needs Services; State Government
Administration

Representative
**Christine Jennifer Winger** (R-District 45) . . . . . . . . . . . (217) 782-4014
Counties Represented: Cook (part), DuPage (part)   Dist: (847) 252-9311
Term Expires: 2017                            Fax: (217) 782-1336
One Tiffany Pointe, Suite G3, Bloomingdale, IL 60108
E-mail: winger@ilhousegop.com
Committees: Appropriations - General Services; Financial Institutions;
Insurance; Renewable Energy and Sustainability; Small Business
Empowerment and Workforce Development; Veterans' Affairs

Representative **Sara Wojcicki Jimenez** (R-District 99) . . . . (217) 782-0044
Counties Represented: Sangamon (part)         Fax: (217) 782-0897
Term Expires: 2017
Committees: Agriculture and Conservation; Appropriations -
Higher Education; Business and Occupational Licenses; Economic
Development and Housing; International Trade and Commerce

Representative **Sam Yingling** (D-District 62)
258-W Stratton Office Building . . . . . . . . . . . . . . . . . . . . (217) 782-7320
Counties Represented: Lake (part)             Dist: (847) 231-6262
Term Expires: 2017                            Fax: (847) 231-6102
E-mail: repsamyingling@gmail.com
Committees: Appropriations - General Services; Counties and
Townships; Financial Institutions; Renewable Energy and Sustainability;
State Government Administration

Representative **Michael J. Zalewski** (D-District 23) . . . . . . (217) 782-5280
Counties Represented: Cook (part)             Dist: (708) 442-6500
Term Expires: 2017                            Fax: (217) 524-0449
3rd Floor South, 1 Riverside Road,           Dist: (708) 442-6501
Riverside, IL 60546
E-mail: repzalewski@gmail.com
Committees: Health Care Licenses; Insurance; Judiciary - Criminal;
Personnel and Pensions; Revenue and Finance
Education: Illinois BA; John Marshall JD

# House Standing Committees

## Adoption Reform

| Majority Members | Minority Members |
|---|---|
| Sara Feigenholtz (D-12) | Keith P. Sommer (R-88) |
| *Chairperson* | *Republican Spokesperson* |
| Anna Moeller (D-43) | Barbara M. Wheeler (R-64) |
| *Vice Chairperson* | |
| Ann Williams (D-11) | |

## Agriculture and Conservation

| Majority Members | Minority Members |
|---|---|
| Jerry F. Costello II (D-116) | Donald L. Moffitt (R-74) |
| *Chairperson* | *Republican Spokesperson* |
| Katherine "Kate" Cloonen (D-79) | John D. Anthony (R-75) |
| *Vice Chairperson* | Avery Bourne (R-95) |
| John E. Bradley (D-117) | Tom Demmer (R-90) |
| Kelly M. Burke (D-36) | Randy E. Frese (R-94) |
| Marcus C. Evans, Jr. (D-33) | Charles E. "Charlie" Meier (R-108) |
| Anna Moeller (D-43) | Brian W. Stewart (R-89) |
| Sue Scherer (D-96) | Sara Wojcicki Jimenez (R-99) |
| Andrew F. "Andy" Skoog (D-76) | |
| Litesa E. Wallace (D-67) | |

## Appropriations - Elementary and Secondary Education

| Majority Members | Minority Members |
|---|---|
| William "Will" Davis (D-30) | Robert W. Pritchard (R-70) |
| *Chairperson* | *Republican Spokesperson* |
| Elizabeth "Lisa" Hernandez (D-24) | Thomas M. Bennett (R-106) |
| *Vice Chairperson* | Tom Demmer (R-90) |
| Edward J. Acevedo (D-2) | Jeanne M. Ives (R-42) |
| Carol Ammons (D-103) | David McSweeney (R-52) |
| Eddie Lee Jackson, Sr. (D-114) | Joe Sosnowski (R-69) |
| Emily McAsey (D-85) | Barbara M. Wheeler (R-64) |
| Michelle Mussman (D-56) | |
| Al Riley (D-38) | |
| Cynthia Soto (D-4) | |
| Emanuel Chris Welch (D-7) | |

## Appropriations - General Services

| Majority Members | Minority Members |
|---|---|
| Fred Crespo (D-44) *Chairperson* | Thomas "Tom" Morrison (R-54) |
| Stephanie A. Kifowit (D-84) | *Republican Spokesperson* |
| *Vice Chairperson* | Steven A. "Steve" Andersson (R-65) |
| Marcus C. Evans, Jr. (D-33) | Adam Brown (R-102) |
| LaShawn K. Ford (D-8) | MG David Harris (R-53) |
| Frances Ann Hurley (D-35) | Margo McDermed (R-37) |
| Natalie Manley (D-98) | Keith Wheeler (R-50) |
| Robert F. Martwick, Jr. (D-19) | Christine Jennifer Winger (R-45) |
| Anna Moeller (D-43) | |
| Lawrence "Larry" Walsh, Jr. (D-86) | |
| Sam Yingling (D-62) | |

## Appropriations - Higher Education

**Majority Members**
Kenneth "Ken" Dunkin (D-5)
*Chairman*
Cynthia Soto (D-4)
*Vice Chairperson*
Kelly M. Burke (D-36)
Linda Chapa-LaVia (D-83)
Monique D. Davis (D-27)
William "Will" Davis (D-30)
Laura Fine (D-17)
Jehan A. Gordon-Booth (D-92)
Thaddeus Jones (D-29)
Brandon W. Phelps (D-118)
Mike Smiddy (D-71)
Emanuel Chris Welch (D-7)

**Minority Members**
Dan Brady (R-105)
*Republican Spokesperson*
Mark Batinick (R-97)
Thomas M. Bennett (R-106)
Norine Hammond (R-93)
Reginald "Reggie" Phillips (R-110)
Robert W. Pritchard (R-70)
Joe Sosnowski (R-69)
Grant Wehrli (R-41)
Sara Wojcicki Jimenez (R-99)

## Appropriations - Human Services

**Majority Members**
Gregory S. "Greg" Harris (D-13)
*Chairperson*
Robyn Gabel (D-18)
*Vice Chairperson*
Edward J. Acevedo (D-2)
Sara Feigenholtz (D-12)
LaShawn K. Ford (D-8)
Elizabeth "Lisa" Hernandez (D-24)
Camille Lilly (D-78)
Natalie Manley (D-98)
Rita Mayfield (D-60)
Michelle Mussman (D-56)
Kathleen Willis (D-77)

**Minority Members**
Patricia R. "Patti" Bellock (R-47)
*Republican Spokesperson*
Christopher "C.D." Davidsmeyer (R-100)
Tom Demmer (R-90)
Randy E. Frese (R-94)
Sheri L. Jesiel (R-61)
Dwight Kay (R-112)
David R. Leitch (R-73)
Charles E. "Charlie" Meier (R-108)
Michael Unes (R-91)

## Appropriations - Public Safety

**Majority Members**
Luis Arroyo (D-3) *Chairperson*
Jay C. Hoffman (D-113)
*Vice Chairperson*
Daniel V. Beiser (D-111)
Kelly Cassidy (D-14)
William "Will" Davis (D-30)
Anthony DeLuca (D-80)
Kenneth "Ken" Dunkin (D-5)
Jehan A. Gordon-Booth (D-92)
Thaddeus Jones (D-29)
Camille Lilly (D-78)
Rita Mayfield (D-60)
Elaine Nekritz (D-57)
Brandon W. Phelps (D-118)
Al Riley (D-38)
Robert "Bob" Rita (D-28)
Patrick J. Verschoore (D-72)

**Minority Members**
John M. Cabello (R-68)
*Republican Spokesperson*
John D. Anthony (R-75)
Terri Bryant (R-115)
John D. Cavaletto (R-107)
Sheri L. Jesiel (R-61)
Dwight Kay (R-112)
Michael P. McAuliffe (R-20)
Donald L. Moffitt (R-74)
David Reis (R-109)
Brian W. Stewart (R-89)

## Business and Occupational Licenses

**Majority Members**
Robert "Bob" Rita (D-28)
*Chairperson*
Marcus C. Evans, Jr. (D-33)
*Vice Chairperson*
Anthony DeLuca (D-80)
Natalie Manley (D-98)
Rita Mayfield (D-60)
Elgie R. Sims, Jr. (D-34)

**Minority Members**
Keith P. Sommer (R-88)
*Republican Spokesperson*
Mark Batinick (R-97)
Christopher "C.D." Davidsmeyer (R-100)
Sara Wojcicki Jimenez (R-99)

## Cities and Villages

**Majority Members**
Anthony DeLuca (D-80)
*Chairperson*
Kathleen Willis (D-77)
*Vice Chairperson*
Martin J. "Marty" Moylan (D-55)
Al Riley (D-38)

**Minority Members**
Mike Fortner (R-49)
*Republican Spokesperson*
Steven A. "Steve" Andersson (R-65)
Jeanne M. Ives (R-42)

## Community College Access and Affordability

**Majority Members**
Thaddeus Jones (D-29) *Chairperson*
Mike Smiddy (D-71)
*Vice Chairperson*
Carol Ammons (D-103)
Kelly Cassidy (D-14)
Fred Crespo (D-44)
Monique D. Davis (D-27)
Rita Mayfield (D-60)
Michelle Mussman (D-56)

**Minority Members**
Dan Brady (R-105)
*Republican Spokesperson*
Norine Hammond (R-93)
Jeanne M. Ives (R-42)
David R. Leitch (R-73)
Charles E. "Charlie" Meier (R-108)
Ronald "Ron" Sandack (R-81)

## Consumer Protection

**Majority Members**
Elizabeth "Lisa" Hernandez (D-24)
*Chairperson*
Eddie Lee Jackson, Sr. (D-114)
*Vice Chairperson*
Jaime M. Andrade, Jr. (D-40)
Jerry F. Costello II (D-116)
John D'Amico (D-15)
Frances Ann Hurley (D-35)
Natalie Manley (D-98)
Robert "Bob" Rita (D-28)
Sue Scherer (D-96)

**Minority Members**
Norine Hammond (R-93)
*Republican Spokesperson*
Thomas M. Bennett (R-106)
Peter Breen (R-48)
Avery Bourne (R-95)
Randy E. Frese (R-94)
David McSweeney (R-52)
Grant Wehrli (R-41)

## Counties and Townships

**Majority Members**
Eddie Lee Jackson, Sr. (D-114)
*Chairman*
Patrick J. Verschoore (D-72)
*Vice Chairperson*
Deborah O'Keefe Conroy (D-46)
Al Riley (D-38)
Lawrence "Larry" Walsh, Jr. (D-86)
Sam Yingling (D-62)

**Minority Members**
Donald L. Moffitt (R-74)
*Republican Spokesperson*
Avery Bourne (R-95)
John D. Cavaletto (R-107)
Margo McDermed (R-37)
Reginald "Reggie" Phillips (R-110)

## Economic Development and Housing

**Majority Members**
Marcus C. Evans, Jr. (D-33)
*Chairperson*
Jaime M. Andrade, Jr. (D-40)
*Vice Chairperson*
Mary E. Flowers (D-31)
LaShawn K. Ford (D-8)
Will Guzzardi (D-39)
Sonya M. Harper (D-6)
Robert F. Martwick, Jr. (D-19)
Arthur L. Turner (D-9)
Litesa E. Wallace (D-67)

**Minority Members**
David McSweeney (R-52)
*Republican Spokesperson*
Peter Breen (R-48)
Adam Brown (R-102)
Dwight Kay (R-112)
David Reis (R-109)
Keith Wheeler (R-50)
Sara Wojcicki Jimenez (R-99)

## Elementary and Secondary Education: Charter School Policy

**Majority Members**
Emily McAsey (D-85) *Chairperson*
Robert F. Martwick, Jr. (D-19)
*Vice Chairperson*
Daniel J. Burke (D-1)
Linda Chapa-LaVia (D-83)
Monique D. Davis (D-27)
Scott R. Drury (D-58)
Anna Moeller (D-43)

**Minority Members**
Joe Sosnowski (R-69)
*Republican Spokesperson*
John D. Anthony (R-75)
Tom Demmer (R-90)
Ed Sullivan, Jr. (R-51)
Barbara M. Wheeler (R-64)

## Elementary and Secondary Education: Licensing Oversight

**Majority Members**
Rita Mayfield (D-60) *Chairperson*
Sue Scherer (D-96)
*Vice Chairperson*
Barbara Flynn Currie (D-25)

**Minority Members**
Bill Mitchell (R-101)
*Republican Spokesperson*
Robert W. Pritchard (R-70)

**LEGISLATIVE BRANCH**

## Elementary and Secondary Education: School Curriculum & Policies

**Majority Members**
Fred Crespo (D-44) *Chairperson*
Linda Chapa-LaVia (D-83)
  *Vice Chairperson*
Katherine "Kate" Cloonen (D-79)
Deborah O'Keefe Conroy (D-46)
Kenneth "Ken" Dunkin (D-5)
Will Guzzardi (D-39)
Sonya M. Harper (D-6)
Camille Lilly (D-78)
Christian L. Mitchell (D-26)
Michelle Mussman (D-56)
Sue Scherer (D-96)
Carol A. Sente (D-59)
Elgie R. Sims, Jr. (D-34)
Andrew F. "Andy" Skoog (D-76)
Mike Smiddy (D-71)
Emanuel Chris Welch (D-7)
Kathleen Willis (D-77)

**Minority Members**
Robert W. Pritchard (R-70)
  *Republican Spokesperson*
Mark Batinick (R-97)
Thomas M. Bennett (R-106)
John D. Cavaletto (R-107)
Randy E. Frese (R-94)
Sheri L. Jesiel (R-61)
Charles E. "Charlie" Meier (R-108)
Donald L. Moffitt (R-74)
Ronald "Ron" Sandack (R-81)
Joe Sosnowski (R-69)
Barbara M. Wheeler (R-64)

## Energy

**Majority Members**
Linda Chapa-LaVia (D-83)
  *Chairperson*
Michelle Mussman (D-56)
  *Vice Chairperson*
Will Guzzardi (D-39)
Eddie Lee Jackson, Sr. (D-114)
Pamela Reaves-Harris (D-10)
André M. Thapedi (D-32)

**Minority Members**
Christopher "C.D."
  Davidsmeyer (R-100)
  *Republican Spokesperson*
John D. Anthony (R-75)
Peter Breen (R-48)
Mike Fortner (R-49)
Bill Mitchell (R-101)

## Environment

**Majority Members**
Patrick J. Verschoore (D-72)
  *Chairperson*
Carol A. Sente (D-59)
  *Vice Chairperson*
Carol Ammons (D-103)
Daniel V. Beiser (D-111)
Laura Fine (D-17)
Robyn Gabel (D-18)
Will Guzzardi (D-39)
Sonya M. Harper (D-6)
Emily McAsey (D-85)
Anna Moeller (D-43)
Brandon W. Phelps (D-118)

**Minority Members**
Michael W. Tryon (R-66)
  *Republican Spokesperson*
Mark Batinick (R-97)
Timothy J. "Tim" Butler (R-87)
Margo McDermed (R-37)
Charles E. "Charlie" Meier (R-108)
Bill Mitchell (R-101)
Thomas "Tom" Morrison (R-54)
Reginald "Reggie" Phillips (R-110)

## Executive

**Majority Members**
Daniel J. Burke (D-1) *Chairperson*
Robert "Bob" Rita (D-28)
  *Vice Chairperson*
Edward J. Acevedo (D-2)
Luis Arroyo (D-3)
Gregory S. "Greg" Harris (D-13)
Eddie Lee Jackson, Sr. (D-114)
Arthur L. Turner (D-9)

**Minority Members**
Chad D. Hays (R-104)
  *Republican Spokesperson*
Joe Sosnowski (R-69)
Ed Sullivan, Jr. (R-51)
Michael W. Tryon (R-66)

## Financial Institutions

**Majority Members**
Cynthia Soto (D-4) *Chairperson*
Silvana Tabares (D-21)
  *Vice Chairperson*
Daniel J. Burke (D-1)
Linda Chapa-LaVia (D-83)
Fred Crespo (D-44)
Kenneth "Ken" Dunkin (D-5)
Marcus C. Evans, Jr. (D-33)
Jehan A. Gordon-Booth (D-92)
Stephanie A. Kifowit (D-84)
Robert F. Martwick, Jr. (D-19)
André M. Thapedi (D-32)
Litesa E. Wallace (D-67)
Sam Yingling (D-62)

**Minority Members**
Adam Brown (R-102)
  *Republican Spokesperson*
Patricia R. "Patti" Bellock (R-47)
Christopher "C.D." Davidsmeyer
  (R-100)
MG David Harris (R-53)
David R. Leitch (R-73)
Donald L. Moffitt (R-74)
David Reis (R-109)
Ed Sullivan, Jr. (R-51)
Michael Unes (R-91)
Christine Jennifer Winger (R-45)

## Health and Healthcare Disparities

**Majority Members**
William "Will" Davis (D-30)
  *Chairperson*
Camille Lilly (D-78)
  *Vice Chairperson*
Edward J. Acevedo (D-2)
Kenneth "Ken" Dunkin (D-5)
Mary E. Flowers (D-31)
Elizabeth "Lisa" Hernandez (D-24)
Rita Mayfield (D-60)
Cynthia Soto (D-4)

**Minority Members**
David R. Leitch (R-73)
  *Republican Spokesperson*
Patricia R. "Patti" Bellock (R-47)
Tom Demmer (R-90)
Bill Mitchell (R-101)
Reginald "Reggie" Phillips (R-110)
Barbara M. Wheeler (R-64)

## Health Care Availability and Access

**Majority Members**
Mary E. Flowers (D-31)
  *Chairperson*
LaShawn K. Ford (D-8)
  *Vice Chairperson*
Deborah O'Keefe Conroy (D-46)

**Minority Members**
Chad D. Hays (R-104)
  *Republican Spokesperson*
Michael P. McAuliffe (R-20)

## Health Care Licenses

**Majority Members**
Michael J. Zalewski (D-23)
  *Chairperson*
Patrick J. Verschoore (D-72)
  *Vice Chairperson*
Kelly M. Burke (D-36)
Frances Ann Hurley (D-35)
Stephanie A. Kifowit (D-84)
Anna Moeller (D-43)
Brandon W. Phelps (D-118)

**Minority Members**
Michael P. McAuliffe (R-20)
  *Republican Spokesperson*
Adam Brown (R-102)
Christopher "C.D." Davidsmeyer
  (R-100)
Chad D. Hays (R-104)
Margo McDermed (R-37)

## Higher Education

**Majority Members**
Kelly M. Burke (D-36) *Chairperson*
Emanuel Chris Welch (D-7)
  *Vice Chairperson*
Carol Ammons (D-103)
Deborah O'Keefe Conroy (D-46)
Laura Fine (D-17)
Mary E. Flowers (D-31)
Elizabeth "Lisa" Hernandez (D-24)
Elgie R. Sims, Jr. (D-34)
Andrew F. "Andy" Skoog (D-76)
Kathleen Willis (D-77)

**Minority Members**
Norine Hammond (R-93)
  *Republican Spokesperson*
Thomas M. Bennett (R-106)
Dan Brady (R-105)
Tom Demmer (R-90)
Chad D. Hays (R-104)
Robert W. Pritchard (R-70)
Barbara M. Wheeler (R-64)

## Human Services

**Majority Members**
Robyn Gabel (D-18) *Chairperson*
Litesa E. Wallace (D-67)
  *Vice Chairperson*
Carol Ammons (D-103)
Jaime M. Andrade, Jr. (D-40)
Kelly Cassidy (D-14)
Laura Fine (D-17)
Mary E. Flowers (D-31)
Cynthia Soto (D-4)

**Minority Members**
Patricia R. "Patti" Bellock (R-47)
  *Republican Spokesperson*
Tom Demmer (R-90)
Norine Hammond (R-93)
Sheri L. Jesiel (R-61)
Brian W. Stewart (R-89)
Michael Unes (R-91)

## Insurance

**Majority Members**
Monique D. Davis (D-27)
  *Chairperson*
Gregory S. "Greg" Harris (D-13)
  *Vice Chairperson*
Anthony DeLuca (D-80)
Kenneth "Ken" Dunkin (D-5)
Sara Feigenholtz (D-12)
Laura Fine (D-17)
Gary F. Forby (D-59)
Robyn Gabel (D-18)
Robert F. Martwick, Jr. (D-19)
Robert "Bob" Rita (D-28)
Arthur L. Turner (D-9)
Ann Williams (D-11)
Michael J. Zalewski (D-23)

**Minority Members**
David Reis (R-109)
  *Republican Spokesperson*
Mark Batinick (R-97)
Dan Brady (R-105)
Peter Breen (R-48)
Christopher "C.D." Davidsmeyer
  (R-100)
Norine Hammond (R-93)
Dwight Kay (R-112)
Keith P. Sommer (R-88)
Michael Unes (R-91)
Christine Jennifer Winger (R-45)

LEGISLATIVE BRANCH

## Intermodal Infrastructure

**Majority Members**
Lawrence "Larry" Walsh, Jr. (D-86)
*Chairperson*
Martin J. "Marty" Moylan (D-55)
*Vice Chairperson*
Jaime M. Andrade, Jr. (D-40)
Daniel V. Beiser (D-111)
Katherine "Kate" Cloonen (D-79)
Stephanie A. Kifowit (D-84)
Pamela Reaves-Harris (D-10)
Sue Scherer (D-96)

**Minority Members**
Mike Fortner (R-49)
*Republican Spokesperson*
Terri Bryant (R-115)
John M. Cabello (R-68)
Jeanne M. Ives (R-42)
Margo McDermed (R-37)
Donald L. Moffitt (R-74)

## International Trade and Commerce

**Majority Members**
André M. Thapedi (D-32)
*Chairperson*
Jack D. Franks (D-63)
*Vice Chairperson*
Jerry F. Costello II (D-116)
William "Will" Davis (D-30)
LaShawn K. Ford (D-8)

**Minority Members**
Keith P. Sommer (R-88)
*Republican Spokesperson*
Dwight Kay (R-112)
Michael Unes (R-91)
Sara Wojcicki Jimenez (R-99)

## Judiciary - Civil

**Majority Members**
Elaine Nekritz (D-57) *Chairperson*
Ann Williams (D-11)
*Vice-Chairperson*
John E. Bradley (D-117)
Jay C. Hoffman (D-113)
Robert F. Martwick, Jr. (D-19)
Pamela Reaves-Harris (D-10)
André M. Thapedi (D-32)

**Minority Members**
Ronald "Ron" Sandack (R-81)
*Ranking Minority Member*
Steven A. "Steve" Andersson
(R-65)
Peter Breen (R-48)
Dwight Kay (R-112)

## Judiciary - Criminal

**Majority Members**
Elgie R. Sims, Jr. (D-34)
*Chairperson*
Scott R. Drury (D-58)
*Vice Chairperson*
Kelly Cassidy (D-14)
Rita Mayfield (D-60)
Christian L. Mitchell (D-26)
Arthur L. Turner (D-9)
Emanuel Chris Welch (D-7)
Michael J. Zalewski (D-23)

**Minority Members**
John M. Cabello (R-68)
*Republican Spokesperson*
John D. Anthony (R-75)
Terri Bryant (R-115)
Ronald "Ron" Sandack (R-81)
Brian W. Stewart (R-89)
Barbara M. Wheeler (R-64)

## Juvenile Justice and System-Involved Youth

**Majority Members**
Kelly Cassidy (D-14) *Chairperson*
Christian L. Mitchell (D-26)
*Vice Chairperson*
Deborah O'Keefe Conroy (D-46)
Mary E. Flowers (D-31)
Robyn Gabel (D-18)
Will Guzzardi (D-39)
Camille Lilly (D-78)
Mike Smiddy (D-71)
Arthur L. Turner (D-9)

**Minority Members**
Michael W. Tryon (R-66)
*Republican Spokesperson*
Terri Bryant (R-115)
Chad D. Hays (R-104)
Jeanne M. Ives (R-42)
Sheri L. Jesiel (R-61)
Margo McDermed (R-37)

## Labor and Commerce

**Majority Members**
Jay C. Hoffman (D-113)
*Chairperson*
Thaddeus Jones (D-29)
*Vice Chairperson*
Luis Arroyo (D-3)
John E. Bradley (D-117)
Kelly M. Burke (D-36)
Kelly Cassidy (D-14)
John D'Amico (D-15)
William "Will" Davis (D-30)
Elizabeth "Lisa" Hernandez (D-24)
Frances Ann Hurley (D-35)
Brandon W. Phelps (D-118)

**Minority Members**
Dwight Kay (R-112)
*Republican Spokesperson*
Patricia R. "Patti" Bellock (R-47)
Dan Brady (R-105)
Peter Breen (R-48)
John M. Cabello (R-68)
Jeanne M. Ives (R-42)
Reginald "Reggie" Phillips (R-110)
Brian W. Stewart (R-89)
Michael W. Tryon (R-66)
Keith Wheeler (R-50)

**Majority Members** *continued*
Mike Smiddy (D-71)
Silvana Tabares (D-21)
Lawrence "Larry" Walsh, Jr. (D-86)
Emanuel Chris Welch (D-7)
Ann Williams (D-11)

## Museums, Arts, and Cultural Enhancement

**Majority Members**
Camille Lilly (D-78) *Chairperson*
Robyn Gabel (D-18)
*Vice Chairperson*
Kelly M. Burke (D-36)
Monique D. Davis (D-27)
Robert F. Martwick, Jr. (D-19)

**Minority Members**
Michael P. McAuliffe (R-20)
*Republican Spokesperson*
Steven A. "Steve" Andersson
(R-65)
Timothy J. "Tim" Butler (R-87)
Barbara M. Wheeler (R-64)

## Personnel and Pensions

**Majority Members**
Elaine Nekritz (D-57) *Chairperson*
Michael J. Zalewski (D-23)
*Vice Chairperson*
Carol Ammons (D-103)
Scott R. Drury (D-58)
Carol A. Sente (D-59)

**Minority Members**
Thomas "Tom" Morrison (R-54)
*Republican Spokesperson*
Jeanne M. Ives (R-42)
Sheri L. Jesiel (R-61)
Grant Wehrli (R-41)

## Public Utilities

**Majority Members**
Brandon W. Phelps (D-118)
*Chairperson*
André M. Thapedi (D-32)
*Vice Chairperson*
Luis Arroyo (D-3)
Linda Chapa-LaVia (D-83)
Fred Crespo (D-44)
Jack D. Franks (D-63)
Jehan A. Gordon-Booth (D-92)
Jay C. Hoffman (D-113)
Rita Mayfield (D-60)
Elaine Nekritz (D-57)
Patrick J. Verschoore (D-72)

**Minority Members**
Ed Sullivan, Jr. (R-51)
*Republican Spokesperson*
Adam Brown (R-102)
John M. Cabello (R-68)
David R. Leitch (R-73)
Michael P. McAuliffe (R-20)
Bill Mitchell (R-101)
Ronald "Ron" Sandack (R-81)
Grant Wehrli (R-41)
Keith Wheeler (R-50)

## Renewable Energy and Sustainability

**Majority Members**
Ann Williams (D-11) *Chairperson*
Emily McAsey (D-85)
*Vice Chairperson*
Kelly Cassidy (D-14)
Robyn Gabel (D-18)
Will Guzzardi (D-39)
Sonya M. Harper (D-6)
Robert F. Martwick, Jr. (D-19)
Christian L. Mitchell (D-26)
Anna Moeller (D-43)
Litesa E. Wallace (D-67)
Sam Yingling (D-62)

**Minority Members**
Thomas "Tom" Morrison (R-54)
*Republican Spokesperson*
Steven A. "Steve" Andersson
(R-65)
Thomas M. Bennett (R-106)
Mike Fortner (R-49)
MG David Harris (R-53)
Ronald "Ron" Sandack (R-81)
Michael W. Tryon (R-66)
Christine Jennifer Winger (R-45)

## Restorative Justice

**Majority Members**
LaShawn K. Ford (D-8)
*Chairperson*
Kelly Cassidy (D-14)
*Vice Chairperson*
Monique D. Davis (D-27)
Mary E. Flowers (D-31)
Sonya M. Harper (D-6)
Gregory S. "Greg" Harris (D-13)

**Minority Members**
Ronald "Ron" Sandack (R-81)
*Republican Spokesperson*
John D. Anthony (R-75)
Peter Breen (R-48)
Keith Wheeler (R-50)

## Revenue and Finance

**Majority Members**
John E. Bradley (D-117)
  *Chairperson*
Michael J. Zalewski (D-23)
  *Vice Chairperson*
Barbara Flynn Currie (D-25)
Marcus C. Evans, Jr. (D-33)
Christian L. Mitchell (D-26)
Elgie R. Sims, Jr. (D-34)
Robert "Bob" Rita (D-28)
Arthur L. Turner (D-9)

**Minority Members**
MG David Harris (R-53)
  *Republican Spokesperson*
Joe Sosnowski (R-69)
Brian W. Stewart (R-89)
Ed Sullivan, Jr. (R-51)
Michael W. Tryon (R-66)

## Rules

**Majority Members**
Barbara Flynn Currie (D-25)
  *Chairperson*
Louis I. "Lou" Lang (D-16)
Arthur L. Turner (D-9)

**Minority Members**
Ed Sullivan, Jr. (R-51)
  *Republican Spokesperson*
David R. Leitch (R-73)

## Small Business Empowerment and Workforce Development

**Majority Members**
LaShawn K. Ford (D-8)
  *Chairperson*
Natalie Manley (D-98)
  *Vice Chairperson*
Carol Ammons (D-103)
Linda Chapa-LaVia (D-83)
Mary E. Flowers (D-31)
Robyn Gabel (D-18)
Elizabeth "Lisa" Hernandez (D-24)
Sue Scherer (D-96)
Andrew F. "Andy" Skoog (D-76)

**Minority Members**
John D. Cavaletto (R-107)
  *Republican Spokesperson*
Steven A. "Steve" Andersson
  (R-65)
Randy E. Frese (R-94)
Sheri L. Jesiel (R-61)
Grant Wehrli (R-41)
Keith Wheeler (R-50)
Christine Jennifer Winger (R-45)

## Special Needs Services

**Majority Members**
Michelle Mussman (D-56)
  *Chairperson*
Frances Ann Hurley (D-35)
  *Vice Chairperson*
Carol Ammons (D-103)
Fred Crespo (D-44)
Sara Feigenholtz (D-12)
Mary E. Flowers (D-31)
Will Guzzardi (D-39)
Elaine Nekritz (D-57)
Kathleen Willis (D-77)

**Minority Members**
John D. Cavaletto (R-107)
  *Republican Spokesperson*
John D. Anthony (R-75)
Patricia R. "Patti" Bellock (R-47)
Dan Brady (R-105)
Sheri L. Jesiel (R-61)
Charles E. "Charlie" Meier (R-108)
Grant Wehrli (R-41)

## State Government Administration

**Majority Members**
Jack D. Franks (D-63) *Chairperson*
Sam Yingling (D-62)
  *Vice Chairperson*
Jaime M. Andrade, Jr. (D-40)
Katherine "Kate" Cloonen (D-79)
Christian L. Mitchell (D-26)
Michelle Mussman (D-56)
Carol A. Sente (D-59)
Kathleen Willis (D-77)

**Minority Members**
Robert W. Pritchard (R-70)
  *Republican Spokesperson*
Thomas M. Bennett (R-106)
MG David Harris (R-53)
Margo McDermed (R-37)
David McSweeney (R-52)
Thomas "Tom" Morrison (R-54)

## Tollway Oversight

**Majority Members**
Robert "Bob" Rita (D-28)
  *Chairperson*
Kelly M. Burke (D-36)
  *Vice Chairperson*
Luis Arroyo (D-3)
Anthony DeLuca (D-80)
Jack D. Franks (D-63)
Martin J. "Marty" Moylan (D-55)

**Minority Members**
Mike Fortner (R-49)
  *Republican Spokesperson*
John M. Cabello (R-68)
MG David Harris (R-53)
Joe Sosnowski (R-69)

## Tourism and Conventions

**Majority Members**
Kenneth "Ken" Dunkin (D-5)
  *Chairperson*
Gregory S. "Greg" Harris (D-13)
  *Vice Chairperson*
Jerry F. Costello II (D-116)
Sara Feigenholtz (D-12)
LaShawn K. Ford (D-8)
Pamela Reaves-Harris (D-10)

**Minority Members**
Michael Unes (R-91)
  *Republican Spokesperson*
Terri Bryant (R-115)
Timothy J. "Tim" Butler (R-87)
Michael P. McAuliffe (R-20)

## Transportation: Regulation, Roads & Bridges

**Majority Members**
Daniel V. Beiser (D-111)
  *Chairperson*
John D'Amico (D-15)
  *Vice Chairperson*
Jaime M. Andrade, Jr. (D-40)
Frances Ann Hurley (D-35)
Camille Lilly (D-78)
Natalie Manley (D-98)
Martin J. "Marty" Moylan (D-55)
Mike Smiddy (D-71)
Elgie R. Sims, Jr. (D-34)
Silvana Tabares (D-21)
Lawrence "Larry" Walsh, Jr. (D-86)

**Minority Members**
Mike Fortner (R-49)
  *Republican Spokesperson*
Steven A. "Steve" Andersson
  (R-65)
Norine Hammond (R-93)
MG David Harris (R-53)
Reginald "Reggie" Phillips (R-110)
Keith Wheeler (R-50)

## Transportation: Vehicles and Safety

**Majority Members**
John D'Amico (D-15) *Chairperson*
Daniel V. Beiser (D-111)
  *Vice Chairperson*
Natalie Manley (D-98)
Martin J. "Marty" Moylan (D-55)
Al Riley (D-38)

**Minority Members**
Michael Unes (R-91)
  *Republican Spokesperson*
Dan Brady (R-105)
Timothy J. "Tim" Butler (R-87)

## Veterans' Affairs

**Majority Members**
Linda Chapa-LaVia (D-83)
  *Chairperson*
Jerry F. Costello II (D-116)
  *Vice Chairperson*
Luis Arroyo (D-3)
Katherine "Kate" Cloonen (D-79)
John D'Amico (D-15)
LaShawn K. Ford (D-8)
Jack D. Franks (D-63)
Robert F. Martwick, Jr. (D-19)
Emily McAsey (D-85)
Martin J. "Marty" Moylan (D-55)
Brandon W. Phelps (D-118)
Carol A. Sente (D-59)
Andrew F. "Andy" Skoog (D-76)
Patrick J. Verschoore (D-72)

**Minority Members**
Michael P. McAuliffe (R-20)
  *Republican Spokesperson*
Mark Batinick (R-97)
Terri Bryant (R-115)
Christopher "C.D." Davidsmeyer
  (R-100)
Randy E. Frese (R-94)
Donald L. Moffitt (R-74)
Brian W. Stewart (R-89)
Michael Unes (R-91)
Christine Jennifer Winger (R-45)

## Youth and Young Adults

**Majority Members**
Laura Fine (D-17) *Chairperson*
Deborah O'Keefe Conroy (D-46)
  *Vice Chairperson*
Mary E. Flowers (D-31)
Robyn Gabel (D-18)
Frances Ann Hurley (D-35)
Natalie Manley (D-98)
Martin J. "Marty" Moylan (D-55)

**Minority Members**
Christopher "C.D."
  Davidsmeyer (R-100)
  *Republican Spokesperson*
Adam Brown (R-102)
Terri Bryant (R-115)
Tom Demmer (R-90)
Jeanne M. Ives (R-42)

# Indiana General Assembly

State House, 200 West Washington Street, Indianapolis, IN 46204
Tel: (317) 232-9400  TTY: (317) 232-0404  Fax: (317) 232-2554
Internet: www.state.in.us/legislative

## Indiana Senate

200 West Washington Street, Indianapolis, IN 46204
Tel: (317) 232-9400  Fax: (317) 234-9240

President of the Senate **Eric Holcomb** (R) . . . . . . . . . . . . . (765) 643-9503
President Pro Tem **David C. Long** (R) . . . . . . . . . . . . . . . (317) 232-9416
  Education: UC Davis BA; Santa Clara U JD
Assistant President Pro Tem **Patricia L. "Pat" Miller** (R) . . (317) 232-9489
  Education: Indiana BS
Majority Floor Leader **Brandt Hershman** (R) . . . . . . . . . . (317) 232-9840
  Education: Purdue BA; Indiana 2013 JD
Majority Floor Leader Emeritus
  **Joseph C. "Joe" Zakas** (R) . . . . . . . . . . . . . . . . . . . . . (317) 232-9490
  Education: Illinois 1972 BA; Notre Dame 1980 MBA, 1980 JD
Assistant Majority Floor Leader, Communications
  **Randall "Randy" Head** (R) . . . . . . . . . . . . . . . . . . . (317) 232-9488
  Education: Wabash Col 1991 BA; Indiana 1994 JD
Assistant Majority Floor Leader, Parliamentarian
  **Brent E. Steele** (R) . . . . . . . . . . . . . . . . . . . . . . . . . . . . (317) 232-9814
  Education: Indiana 1969 BS, 1972 JD
Majority Caucus Chair **James W. "Jim" Merritt, Jr.** (R) . . (317) 232-9533
  Education: Indiana 1981 BA
Assistant Majority Caucus Chair **Rodric D. Bray** (R) . . . . . (317) 232-9426
  Education: Indiana 1991 BA; Valparaiso 1994 JD
Assistant Majority Caucus Chair **Jim Tomes** (R) . . . . . . . . (317) 232-9414
Majority Whip **Ryan D. Mishler** (R) . . . . . . . . . . . . . . . . . (317) 233-0930
  Education: USC BSBA
Assistant Majority Whip **Travis Holdman** (R) . . . . . . . . . . (317) 232-9807
  Education: Southeast Missouri State 1972 BA; St Francis U 1977 MS;
  Indiana 1990 JD
Minority Floor Leader **Timothy S. Lanane** (D) . . . . . . . . . . (317) 232-9534
  Education: Wabash Col 1974 BS; Indiana 1977 JD
Assistant Minority Floor Leader **Jean D. Breaux** (D) . . . . . (317) 232-9461
Minority Caucus Chair **James "Jim" Arnold** (D) . . . . . . . . (317) 232-9441
  Education: Valparaiso BA
Assistant Minority Caucus Chair **Frank Mrvan, Jr.** (D) . . . . (317) 232-9432
Minority Whip **Earline S. Rogers** (D) . . . . . . . . . . . . . . . . (317) 232-9491
  Education: Indiana BS, MS
Principal Secretary of the Senate **Jennifer L. Mertz** . . . . . . (317) 232-9421
  E-mail: jennifer.mertz@iga.in.gov

## Senators

**Party Affiliation Statistics: Republicans: 40, Democrats: 10**

Senator **Ronnie J. Alting** (R-District 22) . . . . . . . . . . . . . . (317) 232-9517
  Counties Represented: Tippecanoe (part)          Tel: (765) 449-5865
  Term Expires: 2018
  3600 Cedar Lane, Lafayette, IN 47905-3914
  E-mail: senator.alting@iga.in.gov
  Committees: Civil Law; Elections; Public Policy
  Education: Purdue 1996 BPE
Senator **James "Jim" Arnold** (D-District 8) . . . . . . . . . . . (317) 232-9441
  Counties Represented: LaPorte (part), St. Joseph    Res: (219) 326-5826
  (part), Starke (part)
  Term Expires: 2016
  5698 West Johnson Road, LaPorte, IN 46350-8185
  E-mail: s8@in.gov
  Committees: Agriculture; Ethics; Homeland Security and
  Transportation; Insurance and Financial Institutions; Pensions and
  Labor; Public Policy; Rules and Legislative Procedure; Veterans Affairs
  and the Military
Senator **James E. "Jim" Banks** (R-District 17) . . . . . . . . . (317) 232-9808
  Counties Represented: Grant (part), Huntington    Res: (260) 248-8406
  (part), Wabash, Whitley (part)
  Term Expires: 2018
  238 South Eagle Glen Trail, Columbia City, IN 46725-7532
  E-mail: senator.banks@iga.in.gov
  Committees: Education and Career Development; Homeland Security
  and Transportation; Pensions and Labor; Veterans Affairs and the
  Military

Senator **Eric Bassler** (R-District 39) . . . . . . . . . . . . . . . . . (317) 232-9400
  Counties Represented: Clay (part), Daviess, Greene, Knox (part),
  Martin, Owen (part), Sullivan
  Term Expires: 2018
  E-mail: senator.bassler@iga.in.gov
  Committees: Education and Career Development; Environmental
  Affairs; Pensions and Labor
Senator **Vaneta G. Becker** (R-District 50) . . . . . . . . . . . . . (317) 232-9494
  Counties Represented: Vanderburgh (part), Warrick    Tel: (812) 473-0123
  (part)                                              Res: (812) 479-3776
  Term Expires: 2016
  4017 Cobble Field Drive, Evansville, IN 47711-7703
  E-mail: s50@in.gov
  Committees: Family and Children Services; Health and Provider
  Services; Public Policy
  Education: Southern Indiana BS
Senator **Phil L. Boots** (R-District 23) . . . . . . . . . . . . . . . . (317) 234-9054
  Counties Represented: Boone (part), Fountain,       Tel: (765) 362-1504
  Montgomery, Parke, Vermillion, Warren               Res: (765) 866-7520
  Term Expires: 2018
  P.O. Box 793, Crawfordsville, IN 47933-0793
  E-mail: senator.boots@iga.in.gov
  Committees: Appropriations; Environmental Affairs; Pensions and
  Labor; Public Policy
Senator **Rodric D. Bray** (R-District 37) . . . . . . . . . . . . . . . (317) 234-9426
  Counties Represented: Johnson (part), Morgan, Owen (part), Putnam
  (part)
  Term Expires: 2016
  210 East Morgan Street, Martinsville, IN 46151
  E-mail: senator.bray@iga.in.gov
  Committees: Civil Law; Corrections and Criminal Law; Elections;
  Judiciary
Senator **Jean D. Breaux** (D-District 34) . . . . . . . . . . . . . . (317) 232-9461
  Counties Represented: Marion (part)                Res: (317) 543-2883
  Term Expires: 2016
  P.O. Box 26267, Indianapolis, IN 46226-0267
  E-mail: s34@in.gov
  Committees: Commerce and Technology; Ethics; Family and Children
  Services; Health and Provider Services; Joint Rules; Local Government;
  Rules and Legislative Procedure; Tax and Fiscal Policy; Utilities
Senator **John E. Broden** (D-District 10) . . . . . . . . . . . . . . (317) 232-9849
  Counties Represented: Elkhart (part), St. Joseph    Tel: (574) 234-8050
  (part)                                              Res: (574) 289-0401
  Term Expires: 2016
  1319 Ostego Street, South Bend, IN 46617-1121
  E-mail: s10@in.gov
  Committees: Commerce and Technology; Environmental Affairs;
  Judiciary; Local Government; Tax and Fiscal Policy; Utilities
  Education: Notre Dame BA; Indiana JD
Senator **Elizabeth "Liz" Brown** (R-District 15) . . . . . . . . (317) 232-9400
  Counties Represented: Allen (part)
  Term Expires: 2018
  E-mail: senator.brown@iga.in.gov
  Committees: Environmental Affairs; Health and Provider Services;
  Insurance and Financial Institutions
  Education: Notre Dame BS; Iowa 1983 JD
Senator **James R. "Jim" Buck** (R-District 21) . . . . . . . . . (317) 232-9466
  Counties Represented: Clinton (part), Grant (part),  Tel: (800) 382-9437
  Hamilton (part), Howard, Tipton                     Res: (765) 453-9216
  Term Expires: 2018
  4407 McKibben Drive, Kokomo, IN 46902-4719
  E-mail: senator.buck@iga.in.gov
  Committees: Civil Law; Commerce and Technology; Elections; Local
  Government; Tax and Fiscal Policy; Utilities
  Education: Indiana Wesleyan BS, BA, MBA
Senator **Edward "Ed" Charbonneau** (R-District 5) . . . . . . (317) 232-9494
  Counties Represented: Jasper (part), LaPorte        Tel: (219) 508-4356
  (part), Porter (part), Pulaski, Starke (part)       Res: (219) 462-0031
  Term Expires: 2016
  2503 Sherwood Drive, Valparaiso, IN 46385-2861
  E-mail: s5@iga.in.gov
  Committees: Appropriations; Environmental Affairs; Health and
  Provider Services; Rules and Legislative Procedure; Tax and Fiscal
  Policy
  Education: Wabash Col; Loyola U (Chicago) MBA; South Texas JD
Senator **Michael R. "Mike" Crider** (R-District 28)
  State House . . . . . . . . . . . . . . . . . . . . . . . . . . . . . . . . . . (317) 232-9493
  Counties Represented: Hancock, Marion (part), Shelby (part)
  Term Expires: 2016
  E-mail: senator.crider@iga.in.gov
  Committees: Agriculture; Health and Provider Services; Homeland
  Security and Transportation; Natural Resources; Veterans Affairs and
  the Military

*(continued on next page)*

LEGISLATIVE BRANCH

**Senators** continued

Senator **Michael A. "Mike" Delph** (R-District 29)
State House ........................................ (317) 232-9488
Counties Represented: Boone (part), Hamilton        Res: (317) 843-9808
(part), Marion (part)
Term Expires: 2018
E-mail: s29@in.gov
E-mail: senator.delph@iga.in.gov
Committees: Commerce and Technology; Judiciary; Utilities
Education: Indiana 1992 BA, 1996 MS, 1996 MPA, 2010 JD

Senator **Gene Douglas Eckerty** (R-District 26) ... ...... (317) 232-9466
Counties Represented: Delaware (part), Henry        Res: (765) 744-6364
(part), Madison (part)
Term Expires: 2018
P.O. Box 55, Yorktown, IN 47396-0055
E-mail: senator.eckerty@iga.in.gov
Committees: Appropriations; Environmental Affairs; Ethics; Homeland
Security and Transportation; Local Government; Rules and Legislative
Procedure; Veterans Affairs and the Military

Senator **Jon Ford** (R-District 38) ..................... (317) 232-9400
Counties Represented: Clay (part), Vigo
Term Expires: 2018
E-mail: senator.ford@iga.in.gov
Committees: Family and Children Services; Homeland Security and
Transportation; Public Policy; Veterans Affairs and the Military

Senator **C. Susan "Sue" Glick** (R-District 13) .......... (317) 232-9493
Counties Represented: DeKalb (part), Lagrange,      Tel: (800) 382-9467
Noble, Steuben                                      Res: (260) 463-7414
Term Expires: 2016
113 West Spring Street, LaGrange, IN 46761-1843
E-mail: senator.glick@iga.in.gov
Committees: Agriculture; Corrections and Criminal Law; Judiciary;
Natural Resources
Education: Indiana AB; Indiana (Indianapolis) JD

Senator **Ronald T. Grooms** (R-District 46) ............ (317) 234-9425
Counties Represented: Clark (part), Floyd          Tel: (800) 382-9467
Term Expires: 2018                                 Res: (812) 282-6108
3104 Autumn Green Way, Jeffersonville, IN 47310-7548
E-mail: senator.grooms@iga.in.gov
Committees: Family and Children Services; Health and Provider
Services; Homeland Security and Transportation; Veterans Affairs and
the Military
Education: Butler 1972 BS

Senator **Randall "Randy" Head** (R-District 18) ........ (317) 232-9488
Counties Represented: Carroll (part), Cass, Fulton,  Tel: (574) 737-8529
Kosciusko (part), Marshall (part), Miami
Term Expires: 2016
5003 Waterbury Court, Logansport, IN 46947-2449
E-mail: senator.head@iga.in.gov
Committees: Civil Law; Commerce and Technology; Elections;
Judiciary; Local Government; Utilities

Senator **Brandt Hershman** (R-District 7) .............. (317) 232-9840
Counties Represented: Boone (part), Carroll (part),  Dist: (574) 581-2000
Clinton (part), Jasper (part), Tippecanoe (part), White
Term Expires: 2016
P.O. Box 177, Buck Creek, IN 47924-0177
E-mail: senator.hershman@iga.in.gov
Committees: Appropriations; Joint Rules; Local Government; Rules and
Legislative Procedure; Tax and Fiscal Policy

Senator **Travis Holdman** (R-District 19) .............. (317) 232-9807
Counties Represented: Adams, Blackford, Grant        Dist: (260) 436-1333
(part), Huntington (part), Jay, Wells                Res: (260) 638-4420
Term Expires: 2018
2467 West 1000 North-90, Markle, IN 46770-9797
E-mail: senator.holdman@iga.in.gov
Committees: Family and Children Services; Insurance and Financial
Institutions; Rules and Legislative Procedure; Tax and Fiscal Policy

Senator **Erin Houchin** (R-District 47) ................. (317) 232-9400
Counties Represented: Crawford, Dubois (part), Harrison, Orange,
Perry, Washington
Term Expires: 2018
E-mail: senator.houchin@iga.in.gov
Committees: Commerce and Technology; Family and Children Services;
Local Government; Utilities

Senator **Luke Kenley** (R-District 20) .................. (317) 232-9453
Counties Represented: Hamilton (part)               Tel: (317) 773-2980
Term Expires: 2016                                  Res: (317) 877-1171
102 Harbour Trees Lane, Noblesville, IN 46062-9079
E-mail: senator.kenley@iga.in.gov
Committees: Appropriations; Tax and Fiscal Policy
Affiliation: President, Cambridge Investments Inc.
Education: Miami 1967 AB; Harvard 1972 JD

Senator **Dennis K. Kruse** (R-District 14) .............. (317) 233-0930
Counties Represented: Allen (part), DeKalb (part)   Tel: (260) 927-9999
Term Expires: 2018                                  Res: (260) 925-0000
6704 County Road 31, Auburn, IN 46706-9635
E-mail: senator.kruse@iga.in.gov
Committees: Education and Career Development; Family and Children
Services; Pensions and Labor; Rules and Legislative Procedure
Education: Indiana 1970 BS

Senator **Timothy S. Lanane** (D-District 25) ........... (317) 232-9534
Counties Represented: Delaware (part), Madison      Tel: (765) 644-4415
(part)                                              Res: (765) 649-0858
Term Expires: 2018
34 West 8th Street, Anderson, IN 46016-1406
E-mail: s25@in.gov
Committees: Civil Law; Corrections and Criminal Law; Elections;
Ethics; Insurance and Financial Institutions; Joint Rules; Public Policy;
Rules and Legislative Procedure

Senator **Jean Leising** (R-District 42) ................. (317) 234-9054
Counties Represented: Decatur (part), Fayette (part),  Tel: (317) 439-1835
Franklin (part), Henry (part), Ripley (part), Rush,   Res: (812) 934-4118
Shelby (part)
Term Expires: 2016
5268 Stockpile Road, Oldenburg, IN 47036-9713
E-mail: senator.leising@iga.in.gov
Committees: Agriculture; Commerce and Technology; Education and
Career Development; Natural Resources; Utilities

Senator **David C. Long** (R-District 16) ............... (317) 232-9416
Counties Represented: Allen (part), Whitley (part)   Dist: (260) 436-7100
Term Expires: 2016
7100 West Jefferson Boulevard, Fort Wayne, IN 46804-6236
E-mail: senator.long@iga.in.gov
Committees: Joint Rules; Rules and Legislative Procedure

Senator **James W. "Jim" Merritt, Jr.** (R-District 31) ..... (317) 232-9533
Counties Represented: Hamilton (part), Marion (part)
Term Expires: 2018
State House, 200 West Washington Street, Indianapolis, IN 46204-2785
E-mail: senator.merritt@iga.in.gov
Committees: Commerce and Technology; Homeland Security and
Transportation; Joint Rules; Public Policy; Rules and Legislative
Procedure; Utilities; Veterans Affairs and the Military

Senator **Mark Brian Messmer, PE** (R-District 48) ........ (317) 232-9400
Counties Represented: Dubois (part), Gibson (part), Knox (part), Pike,
Spencer, Warrick (part)
Term Expires: 2018
E-mail: senator.messmer@iga.in.gov
Committees: Agriculture; Insurance and Financial Institutions; Natural
Resources; Public Policy
Education: Purdue 1985 BSME

Senator **Patricia L. "Pat" Miller** (R-District 32) .......... (317) 232-9489
Counties Represented: Marion (part)                 Res: (317) 894-7023
Term Expires: 2016
1041 South Muesing Road, Indianapolis, IN 46239-9614
E-mail: senator.miller@iga.in.gov
Committees: Appropriations; Family and Children Services; Health and
Provider Services

Senator **Peter Miller** (R-District 24) ................. (317) 232-9414
Counties Represented: Hendricks (part), Putnam      Res: (317) 838-8697
(part)
Term Expires: 2016
6455 Valleywood Court, Avon, IN 46123-7397
E-mail: sen.petemiller@iga.in.gov
Committees: Civil Law; Education and Career Development; Elections;
Tax and Fiscal Policy
Education: Purdue BS

Senator **Ryan D. Mishler** (R-District 9) ............... (317) 233-0930
Counties Represented: Elkhart (part), Kosciusko     Tel: (574) 546-5265
(part), Marshall (part), St. Joseph (part)
Term Expires: 2016
P.O. Box 202, Bremen, IN 46506-0202
E-mail: senator.mishler@iga.in.gov
Committees: Appropriations; Health and Provider Services; Tax and
Fiscal Policy

Senator **Frank Mrvan, Jr.** (D-District 1) ............... (317) 232-9432
Counties Represented: Lake (part)                   Res: (219) 844-3375
Term Expires: 2018
6732 Maryland Avenue, Hammond, IN 46323-1825
E-mail: s1@in.gov
Committees: Agriculture; Education and Career Development; Health
and Provider Services; Insurance and Financial Institutions; Natural
Resources; Tax and Fiscal Policy

**LEGISLATIVE BRANCH**

Senator **Rick Niemeyer** (R-District 6) . . . . . . . . . . . . . . . . (317) 232-9490
  Counties Represented: Benton, Lake (part), Newton
  Term Expires: 2018
  E-mail: senator.niemeyer@iga.in.gov
  Committees: Environmental Affairs; Health and Provider Services;
  Public Policy

Senator **Clyde Allen "Chip" Perfect, Jr.** (R-District 43) . . . (317) 232-9541
  Counties Represented: Bartholomew (part), Dearborn (part), Decatur
  (part), Jackson (part), Jennings, Ohio, Ripley (part)
  Term Expires: 2018
  E-mail: senator.perfect@iga.in.gov
  Committees: Agriculture; Local Government; Natural Resources;
  Pensions and Labor

Senator **Jeffrey Raatz** (R-District 27) . . . . . . . . . . . . . . . . (317) 232-9400
  Counties Represented: Dearborn (part), Fayette (part), Franklin (part),
  Randolph, Union, Wayne
  Term Expires: 2018
  E-mail: senator.raatz@iga.in.gov
  Committees: Corrections and Criminal Law; Education and Career
  Development; Insurance and Financial Institutions

Senator **Lonnie Marcus Randolph** (D-District 2) . . . . . . . (317) 232-9847
  Counties Represented: Lake (part)        Tel: (219) 397-5531
  Term Expires: 2016                        Res: (219) 397-5540
  1919 East Columbus Drive, East Chicago, IN 46312-2827
  E-mail: s2@in.gov
  Committees: Civil Law; Commerce and Technology; Elections;
  Judiciary; Natural Resources; Public Policy; Tax and Fiscal Policy;
  Utilities

Senator **Earline S. Rogers** (D-District 3) . . . . . . . . . . . . . (317) 232-9491
  Counties Represented: Lake (part)        Res: (219) 949-7578
  Term Expires: 2016
  3636 West 15th Avenue, Gary, IN 46404-1828
  E-mail: s3@in.gov
  Committees: Appropriations; Education and Career Development;
  Family and Children Services; Homeland Security and Transportation;
  Pensions and Labor; Veterans Affairs and the Military

Senator **Scott M. Schneider** (R-District 30) . . . . . . . . . . . (317) 232-9808
  Counties Represented: Hamilton (part), Marion (part)
  Term Expires: 2016
  State House, 200 West Washington Street, Indianapolis, IN 46204-2785
  E-mail: senator.schneider@iga.in.gov
  Committees: Education and Career Development; Environmental
  Affairs
  Education: Indiana Wesleyan BS

Senator **James C. "Jim" Smith, Jr.** (R-District 45) . . . . . . (317) 234-9426
  Counties Represented: Clark (part), Jackson (part),    Tel: (800) 382-9467
  Jefferson, Scott, Switzerland                           Res: (812) 248-9008
  Term Expires: 2018
  6103 Welsh Landing, Charlestown, IN 47111-8759
  E-mail: senator.smith@iga.in.gov
  Committees: Local Government; Pensions and Labor; Tax and Fiscal
  Policy
  Education: Louisville, MBA

Senator **Brent E. Steele** (R-District 44) . . . . . . . . . . . . . . (317) 232-9814
  Counties Represented: Bartholomew (part), Brown,    Res: (812) 275-4220
  Jackson (part), Lawrence, Monroe (part)
  Term Expires: 2016
  714 Leatherwood Road, Bedford, IN 47421-8753
  E-mail: senator.steele@iga.in.gov
  Committees: Agriculture; Corrections and Criminal Law; Ethics;
  Insurance and Financial Institutions; Judiciary; Natural Resources;
  Rules and Legislative Procedure

Senator **Mark Stoops** (D-District 40) . . . . . . . . . . . . . . . . (317) 232-9847
  Counties Represented: Monroe (part)
  Term Expires: 2016
  E-mail: s40@iga.in.gov
  Committees: Appropriations; Education and Career Development;
  Environmental Affairs; Health and Provider Services; Homeland
  Security and Transportation; Veterans Affairs and the Military

Senator **Karen Tallian** (D-District 4) . . . . . . . . . . . . . . . . (317) 232-9532
  Counties Represented: LaPorte (part), Porter (part)    Tel: (219) 764-0434
  Term Expires: 2018                                      Res: (219) 762-3248
  6195 Central Avenue, Portage, IN 46368-3645
  E-mail: s4@in.gov
  Committees: Appropriations; Corrections and Criminal Law;
  Environmental Affairs; Pensions and Labor; Rules and Legislative
  Procedure
  Education: Chicago 1972 BA; Valparaiso 1990 JD

Senator **Gregory G. "Greg" Taylor** (D-District 33) . . . . . . (317) 232-9847
  Counties Represented: Marion (part)          Tel: (317) 955-1080
  Term Expires: 2016                            Res: (317) 925-1182
  3855 North Delaware Street, Indianapolis, IN 46205-2647
  E-mail: s33@in.gov
  Committees: Appropriations; Civil Law; Corrections and Criminal Law;
  Elections; Judiciary; Local Government
  Education: Indiana JD

Senator **Jim Tomes** (R-District 49) . . . . . . . . . . . . . . . . . . (317) 232-9414
  Counties Represented: Gibson (part), Posey,    Res: (812) 985-5473
  Vanderburgh (part)
  Term Expires: 2018
  9412 Highway 66, Wadesville, IN 47638-9010
  E-mail: senator.tomes@iga.in.gov
  Committees: Agriculture; Commerce and Technology; Corrections and
  Criminal Law; Natural Resources; Utilities

Senator **Greg Walker** (R-District 41) . . . . . . . . . . . . . . . . . (317) 232-9984
  Counties Represented: Bartholomew (part), Johnson    Tel: (812) 603-6952
  (part)
  Term Expires: 2018
  3129 25th Street, Unit 342, Columbus, IN 47203-2436
  E-mail: senator.walker@iga.in.gov
  Committees: Civil Law; Elections; Ethics; Insurance and Financial
  Institutions; Pensions and Labor; Tax and Fiscal Policy
  Education: Indiana BA

Senator **Brent Waltz** (R-District 36) . . . . . . . . . . . . . . . . . (317) 232-9246
  Counties Represented: Johnson (part), Marion (part)    Res: (317) 435-0195
  Term Expires: 2016
  P.O. Box 7274, Greenwood, IN 46142-6423
  E-mail: senator.waltz@iga.in.gov
  Committees: Corrections and Criminal Law; Insurance and Financial
  Institutions; Pensions and Labor
  Education: Wabash Col 1996 BA

Senator **Carlin J. Yoder** (R-District 12) . . . . . . . . . . . . . . . (317) 232-9984
  Counties Represented: Elkhart (part), Kosciusko    Dist: (574) 642-3940
  (part)                                              Res: (574) 370-9110
  Term Expires: 2016
  59246 State Road 13, Middlebury, IN 46540-9774
  E-mail: senator.yoder@iga.in.gov
  Committees: Appropriations; Education and Career Development;
  Homeland Security and Transportation; Veterans Affairs and the
  Military
  Education: Indiana (South Bend)

Senator **R. Michael "Mike" Young** (R-District 35) . . . . . . . (317) 232-9517
  Counties Represented: Hendricks (part), Marion    Res: (317) 297-2544
  (part)
  Term Expires: 2016
  3102 Columbine Circle, Indianapolis, IN 46224-2020
  E-mail: s35@in.gov
  Committees: Civil Law; Corrections and Criminal Law; Elections;
  Judiciary

Senator **Joseph C. "Joe" Zakas** (R-District 11) . . . . . . . . . (317) 232-9490
  Counties Represented: Elkhart (part), St. Joseph    Tel: (574) 294-7473
  (part)                                              Res: (574) 277-5155
  Term Expires: 2018
  16372 Wild Cherry Drive, Granger, IN 46530-8544
  E-mail: senator.zakas@iga.in.gov
  Committees: Appropriations; Judiciary

# Senate Standing Committees

## Agriculture

**Majority Members**                    **Minority Members**
Jean Leising (R-42) *Chair*             Frank Mrvan, Jr. (D-1)
C. Susan "Sue" Glick (R-13)               *Ranking Minority Member*
  *Ranking Member*                      James "Jim" Arnold (D-8)
Michael R. "Mike" Crider (R-28)
Mark Brian Messmer (R-48)
Clyde Allen "Chip" Perfect, Jr.
  (R-43)
Brent E. Steele (R-44)
Jim Tomes (R-49)

# Appropriations

**Majority Members**
Luke Kenley (R-20) *Chair*
Ryan D. Mishler (R-9)
  *Ranking Member*
Phil L. Boots (R-23)
Edward "Ed" Charbonneau (R-5)
Gene Douglas Eckerty (R-26)
Brandt Hershman (R-7)
Patricia L. "Pat" Miller (R-32)
Carlin J. Yoder (R-12)
Joseph C. "Joe" Zakas (R-11)

**Minority Members**
Karen Tallian (D-4)
  *Ranking Minority Member*
Earline S. Rogers (D-3)
Mark Stoops (D-40)
Gregory G. "Greg" Taylor (D-33)

# Civil Law

**Majority Members**
Rodric D. Bray (R-37) *Chair*
Greg Walker (R-41)
  *Ranking Member*
Ronnie J. Alting (R-22)
James R. "Jim" Buck (R-21)
Randall "Randy" Head (R-18)
Peter Miller (R-24)
R. Michael "Mike" Young (R-35)

**Minority Members**
Gregory G. "Greg" Taylor (D-33)
  *Ranking Minority Member*
Timothy S. Lanane (D-25)
Lonnie Marcus Randolph (D-2)

# Commerce and Technology

**Majority Members**
James R. "Jim" Buck (R-21) *Chair*
James W. "Jim" Merritt, Jr. (R-31)
  *Ranking Member*
Michael A. "Mike" Delph (R-29)
Randall "Randy" Head (R-18)
Erin Houchin (R-47)
Jean Leising (R-42)
Jim Tomes (R-49)

**Minority Members**
Jean D. Breaux (D-34)
  *Ranking Minority Member*
John E. Broden (D-10)
Lonnie Marcus Randolph (D-2)

# Corrections and Criminal Law

**Majority Members**
R. Michael "Mike" Young (R-35)
  *Chair*
Rodric D. Bray (R-37)
  *Ranking Member*
C. Susan "Sue" Glick (R-13)
Jeffrey Raatz (R-27)
Brent E. Steele (R-44)
Jim Tomes (R-49)
Brent Waltz (R-36)

**Minority Members**
Gregory G. "Greg" Taylor (D-33)
  *Ranking Minority Member*
Timothy S. Lanane (D-25)
Karen Tallian (D-4)

# Education and Career Development

**Majority Members**
Dennis K. Kruse (R-14) *Chair*
Carlin J. Yoder (R-12)
  *Ranking Member*
James E. "Jim" Banks (R-17)
Eric Bassler (R-39)
Jean Leising (R-42)
Peter Miller (R-24)
Jeffrey Raatz (R-27)
Scott M. Schneider (R-30)

**Minority Members**
Earline S. Rogers (D-3)
  *Ranking Minority Member*
Frank Mrvan, Jr. (D-1)
Mark Stoops (D-40)

# Elections

**Majority Members**
Greg Walker (R-41) *Chair*
Rodric D. Bray (R-37)
  *Ranking Member*
Ronnie J. Alting (R-22)
James R. "Jim" Buck (R-21)
Randall "Randy" Head (R-18)
Peter Miller (R-24)
R. Michael "Mike" Young (R-35)

**Minority Members**
Gregory G. "Greg" Taylor (D-33)
  *Ranking Minority Member*
Timothy S. Lanane (D-25)
Lonnie Marcus Randolph (D-2)

# Environmental Affairs

**Majority Members**
Edward "Ed" Charbonneau (R-5)
  *Chair*
Gene Douglas Eckerty (R-26)
  *Ranking Member*
Eric Bassler (R-39)
Phil L. Boots (R-23)
Elizabeth "Liz" Brown (R-15)
Rick Niemeyer (R-6)
Scott M. Schneider (R-30)

**Minority Members**
Mark Stoops (D-40)
  *Ranking Minority Member*
John E. Broden (D-10)
Karen Tallian (D-4)

# Ethics

**Majority Members**
Gene Douglas Eckerty (R-26) *Chair*
Greg Walker (R-41)
  *Ranking Member*
Brent E. Steele (R-44)

**Minority Members**
James "Jim" Arnold (D-8)
  *Ranking Minority Member*
Jean D. Breaux (D-34)
Timothy S. Lanane (D-25)

# Family and Children Services

**Majority Members**
Ronald T. Grooms (R-46) *Chair*
Vaneta G. Becker (R-50)
  *Ranking Member*
Jon Ford (R-38)
Travis Holdman (R-19)
Erin Houchin (R-47)
Dennis K. Kruse (R-14)
Patricia L. "Pat" Miller (R-32)

**Minority Members**
Earline S. Rogers (D-3)
  *Ranking Minority Member*
Jean D. Breaux (D-34)

# Health and Provider Services

**Majority Members**
Patricia L. "Pat" Miller (R-32)
  *Chair*
Ryan D. Mishler (R-9)
  *Ranking Member*
Vaneta G. Becker (R-50)
Elizabeth "Liz" Brown (R-15)
Edward "Ed" Charbonneau (R-5)
Michael R. "Mike" Crider (R-28)
Ronald T. Grooms (R-46)
Rick Niemeyer (R-6)

**Minority Members**
Jean D. Breaux (D-34)
  *Ranking Minority Member*
Frank Mrvan, Jr. (D-1)
Mark Stoops (D-40)

# Homeland Security and Transportation

**Majority Members**
Carlin J. Yoder (R-12) *Chair*
Michael R. "Mike" Crider (R-28)
  *Ranking Member*
James E. "Jim" Banks (R-17)
Gene Douglas Eckerty (R-26)
Jon Ford (R-38)
Ronald T. Grooms (R-46)
James W. "Jim" Merritt, Jr. (R-31)

**Minority Members**
James "Jim" Arnold (D-8)
  *Ranking Minority Member*
Earline S. Rogers (D-3)
Mark Stoops (D-40)

# Insurance and Financial Institutions

**Majority Members**
Travis Holdman (R-19) *Chair*
Greg Walker (R-41)
  *Ranking Member*
Elizabeth "Liz" Brown (R-15)
Mark Brian Messmer (R-48)
Jeffrey Raatz (R-27)
Brent E. Steele (R-44)
Brent Waltz (R-36)

**Minority Members**
Frank Mrvan, Jr. (D-1)
  *Ranking Minority Member*
James "Jim" Arnold (D-8)
Timothy S. Lanane (D-25)

# Judiciary

**Majority Members**
Brent E. Steele (R-44) *Chair*
R. Michael "Mike" Young (R-35)
  *Ranking Member*
Rodric D. Bray (R-37)
Michael A. "Mike" Delph (R-29)
C. Susan "Sue" Glick (R-13)
Randall "Randy" Head (R-18)
Joseph C. "Joe" Zakas (R-11)

**Minority Members**
Lonnie Marcus Randolph (D-2)
  *Ranking Minority Member*
John E. Broden (D-10)
Gregory G. "Greg" Taylor (D-33)

## Local Government

**Majority Members**
Randall "Randy" Head (R-18)
  *Chair*
James C. "Jim" Smith, Jr. (R-45)
  *Ranking Member*
James R. "Jim" Buck (R-21)
Gene Douglas Eckerty (R-26)
Brandt Hershman (R-7)
Erin Houchin (R-47)
Clyde Allen "Chip" Perfect, Jr.
  (R-43)

**Minority Members**
John E. Broden (D-10)
  *Ranking Minority Member*
Jean D. Breaux (D-34)
Gregory G. "Greg" Taylor (D-33)

## Natural Resources

**Majority Members**
C. Susan "Sue" Glick (R-13) *Chair*
Jean Leising (R-42)
  *Ranking Member*
Michael R. "Mike" Crider (R-28)
Mark Brian Messmer (R-48)
Clyde Allen "Chip" Perfect, Jr.
  (R-43)
Brent E. Steele (R-44)
Jim Tomes (R-49)

**Minority Members**
Frank Mrvan, Jr. (D-1)
  *Ranking Minority Member*
Lonnie Marcus Randolph (D-2)

## Pensions and Labor

**Majority Members**
Phil L. Boots (R-23) *Chair*
Brent Waltz (R-36)
  *Ranking Member*
James E. "Jim" Banks (R-17)
Eric Bassler (R-39)
Dennis K. Kruse (R-14)
Clyde Allen "Chip" Perfect, Jr.
  (R-43)
James C. "Jim" Smith, Jr. (R-45)
Greg Walker (R-41)

**Minority Members**
Karen Tallian (D-4)
  *Ranking Minority Member*
James "Jim" Arnold (D-8)
Earline S. Rogers (D-3)

## Public Policy

**Majority Members**
Ronnie J. Alting (R-22) *Chair*
Mark Brian Messmer (R-48)
  *Ranking Member*
Vaneta G. Becker (R-50)
Phil L. Boots (R-23)
Jon Ford (R-38)
James W. "Jim" Merritt, Jr. (R-31)
Rick Niemeyer (R-6)

**Minority Members**
James "Jim" Arnold (D-8)
  *Ranking Minority Member*
Timothy S. Lanane (D-25)
Lonnie Marcus Randolph (D-2)

## Rules and Legislative Procedure

**Majority Members**
David C. Long (R-16) *Chair*
Travis Holdman (R-19)
  *Ranking Member*
Edward "Ed" Charbonneau (R-5)
Gene Douglas Eckerty (R-26)
Brandt Hershman (R-7)
Dennis K. Kruse (R-14)
James W. "Jim" Merritt, Jr. (R-31)
Brent E. Steele (R-44)

**Minority Members**
Timothy S. Lanane (D-25)
  *Ranking Minority Member*
James "Jim" Arnold (D-8)
Jean D. Breaux (D-34)
Karen Tallian (D-4)

## Tax and Fiscal Policy

**Majority Members**
Brandt Hershman (R-7) *Chair*
Travis Holdman (R-19)
  *Ranking Member*
James R. "Jim" Buck (R-21)
Edward "Ed" Charbonneau (R-5)
Luke Kenley (R-20)
Peter Miller (R-24)
Ryan D. Mishler (R-9)
James C. "Jim" Smith, Jr. (R-45)
Greg Walker (R-41)

**Minority Members**
John E. Broden (D-10)
  *Ranking Minority Member*
Jean D. Breaux (D-34)
Frank Mrvan, Jr. (D-1)
Lonnie Marcus Randolph (D-2)

## Utilities

**Majority Members**
James W. "Jim" Merritt, Jr. (R-31)
  *Chair*
James R. "Jim" Buck (R-21)
  *Ranking Member*
Michael A. "Mike" Delph (R-29)
Randall "Randy" Head (R-18)
Erin Houchin (R-47)
Jean Leising (R-42)
Jim Tomes (R-49)

**Minority Members**
Jean D. Breaux (D-34)
  *Ranking Minority Member*
John E. Broden (D-10)
Lonnie Marcus Randolph (D-2)

## Veterans Affairs and the Military

**Majority Members**
James E. "Jim" Banks (R-17) *Chair*
Carlin J. Yoder (R-12)
  *Ranking Member*
Michael R. "Mike" Crider (R-28)
Gene Douglas Eckerty (R-26)
Jon Ford (R-38)
Ronald T. Grooms (R-46)
James W. "Jim" Merritt, Jr. (R-31)

**Minority Members**
James "Jim" Arnold (D-8)
  *Ranking Minority Member*
Earline S. Rogers (D-3)
Mark Stoops (D-40)

# Indiana House of Representatives

200 West Washington Street, Indianapolis, IN 46204
Tel: (317) 232-9600  TTY: (317) 233-5733  Fax: (317) 232-9679
Fax: (317) 232-7644 (Republican Leadership)
Fax: (317) 232-9792 (Democrat Leadership)

Speaker of the House **Brian C. Bosma** (R) . . . . . . . . . . . . .(317) 232-9657
  Education: Purdue 1981 BSE; Indiana 1984 JD
Speaker Pro Tem **William C. "Bill" Friend** (R) . . . . . . . . . (317) 232-9600
  Education: Indianapolis 1971 BA
Deputy Speaker Pro Tem
  **Michael "Mike" Karickhoff** (R) . . . . . . . . . . . . . . . . . . .(317) 234-9380
  Education: Missouri BS
Majority Floor Leader **Matthew S. Lehman** (R) . . . . . . . .(317) 234-9499
  Education: Vincennes 1984 AS
Assistant Majority Leader **David N. Frizzell** (R) . . . . . . . . (317) 232-9981
  Education: Loyola Col (MD) 1973 BA
Assistant Majority Leader **Peggy Mayfield** (R) . . . . . . . . . .(317) 232-9608
Assistant Majority Leader **Edmond L. "Ed" Soliday** (R) . . (317) 232-9850
Majority Caucus Chair **Kathy Kreag Richardson** (R) . . . . .(317) 232-9600
Assistant Majority Caucus Chair **Eric Allan Koch** (R) . . . . .(317) 232-9600
  Education: Georgetown 1987 BSBA; Indiana 1989 JD
Assistant Majority Caucus Chair
  **Gregory Earl "Greg" Steuerwald** (R) . . . . . . . . . . . . . . (317) 232-9600
  Education: Indiana State 1974 BS; Alabama 1977 MS;
  IU-Purdue U Indianapolis 1981 JD
Majority Whip **Bob Heaton** (R) . . . . . . . . . . . . . . . . . . . . (317) 232-9620
  Education: Indiana State 1980 BSBA
Assistant Majority Whip **Thomas "Tom" Dermody** (R) . . (317) 232-9619
Assistant Majority Whip **Sharon Negele** (R) . . . . . . . . . . .(317) 232-9816
  Education: Western Michigan 1982; Houston 1990 MBA
Assistant Majority Whip **David L. Ober** (R) . . . . . . . . . . . .(317) 232-9643
  Education: Purdue (Calumet) BS
Minority Leader **Scott D. Pelath** (D) . . . . . . . . . . . . . . . . (317) 232-9600
  Education: Indiana 1992 BS
Assistant Minority Leader
  **Phillip K. "Phil" GiaQuinta** (D) . . . . . . . . . . . . . . . . . . (317) 232-9600
  Education: Indiana
Minority Floor Leader **Linda C. Lawson** (D) . . . . . . . . . . .(317) 232-9600
Assistant Minority Floor Leader **Ryan M. Dvorak** (D) . . . . (317) 232-9600
  Education: Notre Dame 1996 BA
Minority Caucus Chair **John Bartlett** (D) . . . . . . . . . . . . . (317) 232-9600
Assistant Minority Caucus Chair **Robin Shackleford** (D) . . (317) 232-9608
  Education: Indiana 1993 BS; IU-Purdue U Indianapolis 1999 MPA
Minority Whip **Terri J. Austin** (D) . . . . . . . . . . . . . . . . . . (317) 234-9047
  Education: Ball State 1977 BA, 1981 MA
Assistant Minority Whip **David L. Niezgodski** (D) . . . . . . . (317) 232-9756
Principal Clerk of the House **M. Caroline Spotts** . . . . . . . .(317) 232-9608
  E-mail: caroline.spotts@iga.in.gov

LEGISLATIVE BRANCH

# Representatives

Tel: (800) 382-9841 (In-State)

**Party Affiliation Statistics:** Republicans: 71, Democrats: 29

Representative **Lloyd Arnold** (R-District 74) Suite 401-2 . . (317) 232-9815
Counties Represented: Crawford, Dubois (part), Orange (part), Perry, Spencer (part)
Term Expires: 2016
E-mail: h74@iga.in.gov
Committees: Agriculture and Rural Development; Elections and Apportionment; Natural Resources; Veterans Affairs and Public Safety

Representative **Terri J. Austin** (D-District 36)
Room 336-19 . . . . . . . . . . . . . . . . . . . . . . . . . . . . . . (317) 234-9047
Counties Represented: Madison (part)
Term Expires: 2016
E-mail: h36@iga.in.gov
E-mail: taustin@iga.state.in.us
Committees: Education; Insurance; Public Policy; Rules and Legislative Procedures

Representative **Michael J. Aylesworth** (R-District 11) . . . . (317) 234-9447
Counties Represented: Lake (part), Porter (part)
Term Expires: 2016
E-mail: h11@iga.in.gov
Committees: Environmental Affairs; Local Government; Natural Resources
Education: Indiana BS

Representative **Ronald "Ron" Bacon** (R-District 75)
Suite 401 . . . . . . . . . . . . . . . . . . . . . . . . . . . . . . . . . (317) 232-9674
Counties Represented: Pike (part), Spencer (part), Warrick (part)
Term Expires: 2016
E-mail: h75@iga.in.gov
Committees: Family, Children and Human Affairs; Public Health

Representative **James R. "Jim" Baird** (R-District 44) . . . . (317) 232-9671
Counties Represented: Clay (part), Morgan (part), Owen (part), Parke (part), Putnam
Term Expires: 2016
E-mail: h44@in.gov
Committees: Agriculture and Rural Development; Statutory Committee on Interstate and International Cooperation; Ways and Means
Education: Purdue BS, MS; Kentucky PhD

Representative **John Bartlett** (D-District 95)
Room 336-15 . . . . . . . . . . . . . . . . . . . . . . . . . . . . . . (317) 232-9600
Counties Represented: Marion (part)    Tel: (800) 382-9842
Term Expires: 2016
E-mail: h95@in.gov
Committees: Elections and Apportionment; Employment, Labor and Pensions; Government and Regulatory Reform

Representative **B. Patrick "Pat" Bauer** (D-District 6)
Room 3A-1 . . . . . . . . . . . . . . . . . . . . . . . . . . . . . . . . (317) 232-9600
Counties Represented: St. Joseph (part)    Tel: (800) 382-9842
Term Expires: 2016
E-mail: h6@in.gov
Committees: Environmental Affairs; Joint Rules; Judiciary; Public Health
Affiliation: Dean of External Affairs, Ivy Tech State College
Education: Notre Dame 1966 BA; Indiana 1968 MS

Representative
**Robert W. "Bob" Behning** (R-District 91)
Suite 401-3 . . . . . . . . . . . . . . . . . . . . . . . . . . . . . . . (317) 232-9981
Counties Represented: Hendricks (part), Marion    Tel: (800) 382-9841
(part)
Term Expires: 2016
E-mail: h91@in.gov
Committees: Education; Public Health; Utilities, Energy, and Telecommunications
Affiliation: Owner, Berkshire Florists
Education: Indiana 1976 BS

Representative **Greg Beumer** (R-District 33) Suite 401 . . . . (317) 234-3827
Counties Represented: Blackford (part), Delaware (part), Jay, Randolph
Term Expires: 2016
E-mail: h33@iga.in.gov
Committees: Agriculture and Rural Development; Environmental Affairs; Financial Institutions

Representative **Bruce A. Borders** (R-District 45) . . . . . . . . (317) 234-9499
Counties Represented: Daviess (part), Greene (part), Knox (part), Sullivan, Vigo (part)
Term Expires: 2016
E-mail: h45@iga.in.gov
Committees: Insurance; Local Government; Veterans Affairs and Public Safety
Education: Evangel Col BBA

Representative **Brian C. Bosma** (R-District 88) . . . . . . . . . (317) 232-9657
Counties Represented: Hamilton (part), Hancock (part), Marion (part)
Term Expires: 2016
111 Monument Circle, Suite 900, Indianapolis, IN 46204
E-mail: h88@in.gov
Committees: Joint Rules

Representative **Mike Braun** (R-District 63) . . . . . . . . . . . . . (317) 234-9447
Counties Represented: Daviess (part), Dubois (part), Martin (part), Pike (part)
Term Expires: 2016
E-mail: h63@iga.in.gov
Committees: Education; Roads and Transportation; Ways and Means
Education: Wabash Col

Representative **Charlie Brown** (D-District 3) Room 4A-3 . . (317) 232-9600
Counties Represented: Lake (part)    Tel: (800) 382-9842
Term Expires: 2016
E-mail: h3@in.gov
Committees: Public Health; Public Policy; Roads and Transportation; Statutory Committee on Interstate and International Cooperation
Education: Cheyney 1961 BS; Indiana 1982 MPA

Representative
**Timothy N. "Tim" Brown** (R-District 41) . . . . . . . . . . . (317) 232-9651
Counties Represented: Boone (part), Montgomery    Dist: (765) 362-7024
(part), Tippecanoe (part)
Term Expires: 2016
P.O. Box 861, Crawfordsville, IN 47933
E-mail: h41@in.gov
Committees: Ways and Means
Affiliation: Physician, Crawfordsville Family Care/American Health
Education: Illinois Wesleyan 1978 BA; Illinois 1982 MD

Representative
**Charles W. "Woody" Burton** (R-District 58) . . . . . . . . . (317) 232-9863
Counties Represented: Bartholomew (part), Hancock    Dist: (317) 881-0400
(part), Johnson (part)
Term Expires: 2016
69 Meadow Lane, Whiteland, IN 46184-9625
E-mail: h58@in.gov
Committees: Education; Elections and Apportionment; Financial Institutions; Insurance; Rules and Legislative Procedures

Representative **Martin Carbaugh** (R-District 81)
Room 150 . . . . . . . . . . . . . . . . . . . . . . . . . . . . . . . . . (317) 232-9643
Counties Represented: Allen (part)
Term Expires: 2016
E-mail: h81@in.gov
Committees: Employment, Labor and Pensions; Insurance; Veterans Affairs and Public Safety

Representative **Robert W. "Bob" Cherry** (R-District 53) . . (317) 232-9619
Counties Represented: Hancock (part), Madison (part)
Term Expires: 2016
3118 East 100 South, Greenfield, IN 46140
E-mail: h53@in.gov
Committees: Local Government; Rules and Legislative Procedures; Ways and Means
Education: Purdue 1969 BS

Representative **Edward D. "Ed" Clere** (R-District 72) . . . . (317) 232-9841
Counties Represented: Floyd (part)    Dist: (812) 987-4333
Term Expires: 2016
1701 DePauw Avenue, New Albany, IN 47150
E-mail: h72@in.gov
Committees: Public Health; Public Policy; Ways and Means
Education: Indiana Southeast BS

Representative **Anthony "Tony" Cook** (R-District 32) . . . . (317) 232-9600
Counties Represented: Delaware (part), Grant (part),    Tel: (800) 382-9841
Hamilton (part), Howard (part), Madison (part), Tipton
Term Expires: 2016
E-mail: h32@in.gov
Committees: Education; Elections and Apportionment; Statutory Committee on Interstate and International Cooperation

Representative **Casey B. Cox** (R-District 85)
Room 336-22 . . . . . . . . . . . . . . . . . . . . . . . . . . . . . . (317) 232-9600
Counties Represented: Allen (part)
Term Expires: 2016
E-mail: h85@in.gov
Committees: Courts and Criminal Code; Elections and Apportionment; Family, Children and Human Affairs; Judiciary
Education: Indiana 2004 BA, 2007 JD

Representative **Wesley H. "Wes" Culver** (R-District 49)
Room 4A-6 . . . . . . . . . . . . . . . . . . . . . . . . . . . . . (317) 232-9678
Counties Represented: Elkhart (part)          Tel: (800) 382-9841
Term Expires: 2016                                    (In-State)
E-mail: h49@in.gov
Committees: Commerce, Small Business and Economic Development;
Financial Institutions; Statutory Committee on Interstate and
International Cooperation
Representative
**Steven J. "Steve" Davisson** (R-District 73)
Room 4-2 . . . . . . . . . . . . . . . . . . . . . . . . . . . . . . (317) 232-9600
Counties Represented: Clark (part), Harrison (part), Jackson (part),
Lawrence (part), Orange (part), Washington
Term Expires: 2016
E-mail: h73@in.gov
Committees: Public Health; Ways and Means
Education: Purdue 1981 BS
Representative
**Edward O. "Ed" DeLaney** (D-District 86)
Room 336-14 . . . . . . . . . . . . . . . . . . . . . . . . . . . (317) 232-9600
Counties Represented: Marion (part)
Term Expires: 2016
E-mail: h86@in.gov
Committees: Courts and Criminal Code; Judiciary; Ways and Means
Education: SUNY (Binghamton) BA, MA; Harvard 1973 JD
Representative
**Thomas "Tom" Dermody** (R-District 20) Room 405 . . . (317) 232-9619
Counties Represented: LaPorte (part), Starke (part)     Tel: (800) 382-9841
Term Expires: 2016
E-mail: h20@in.gov
Committees: Commerce, Small Business and Economic Development;
Public Policy
Representative **Dale R. DeVon** (R-District 5) . . . . . . . . . . . (317) 232-9678
Counties Represented: St. Joseph (part)
Term Expires: 2016
200 West Washington Street, Indianapolis, IN 46204-2789
E-mail: h5@iga.in.gov
Committees: Education; Family, Children and Human Affairs; Utilities,
Energy, and Telecommunications
Representative **Ryan M. Dvorak** (D-District 8) Room 4-1 . . (317) 232-9600
Counties Represented: LaPorte (part), St. Joseph     Tel: (800) 382-9842
(part)
Term Expires: 2016
E-mail: h8@in.gov
Committees: Courts and Criminal Code; Environmental Affairs; Natural
Resources; Rules and Legislative Procedures
Representative **Sean R. Eberhart** (R-District 57)
Suite 401 . . . . . . . . . . . . . . . . . . . . . . . . . . . . . . (317) 232-9600
Counties Represented: Shelby          Tel: (800) 382-9841
Term Expires: 2016
E-mail: h57@in.gov
Committees: Environmental Affairs; Natural Resources; Public Policy
Education: Purdue 1988 BSIE; Indiana 1996 MBA
Representative **Jeff Ellington** (R-District 62) Room 149 . . . (317) 232-9600
Counties Represented: Daviess (part), Greene (part), Martin (part),
Monroe (part)
Term Expires: 2016
E-mail: h62@in.gov
Committees: Natural Resources; Public Policy; Statutory Committee on
Interstate and International Cooperation
Representative **Sue Errington** (D-District 34)
Room 336-7 . . . . . . . . . . . . . . . . . . . . . . . . . . . . (317) 232-9608
Counties Represented: Delaware (part)
Term Expires: 2016
E-mail: h34@in.gov
Committees: Education; Environmental Affairs; Government and
Regulatory Reform; Natural Resources
Education: Indiana 1964 AB; Michigan 1965 MA
Representative **William "Bill" Fine** (R-District 12) . . . . . . . (317) 234-9380
Counties Represented: Lake (part)
Term Expires: 2016
E-mail: h12@iga.in.gov
Committees: Commerce, Small Business and Economic Development;
Education; Judiciary
Representative **Daniel "Dan" Forestal** (D-District 100)
Room 336-10 . . . . . . . . . . . . . . . . . . . . . . . . . . . (317) 232-9608
Counties Represented: Marion (part)
Term Expires: 2016
E-mail: h100@iga.in.gov
Committees: Commerce, Small Business and Economic Development;
Roads and Transportation; Utilities, Energy, and Telecommunications

Representative **William C. "Bill" Friend** (R-District 23) . . . (317) 232-9600
Counties Represented: Cass (part), Fulton (part),     Tel: (765) 985-3885
Miami          Tel: (800) 382-9841
Term Expires: 2016
3340 West 900 North, Macy, IN 46951
E-mail: h23@in.gov
Committees: Agriculture and Rural Development; Environmental
Affairs
Representative **David N. Frizzell** (R-District 93) . . . . . . . . . (317) 232-9981
Counties Represented: Johnson (part), Marion (part)     Dist: (317) 882-2146
Term Expires: 2016          Tel: (800) 382-9841
8310 Hill Gail Drive, Indianapolis, IN 46217
E-mail: h93@in.gov
Committees: Family, Children and Human Affairs; Public Health;
Utilities, Energy, and Telecommunications
Representative **Randall L. "Randy" Frye** (R-District 67)
Room 336 . . . . . . . . . . . . . . . . . . . . . . . . . . . . . (317) 232-9600
Counties Represented: Dearborn (part), Decatur     Dist: (812) 663-7083
(part), Jefferson (part), Jennings (part), Ohio, Ripley (part), Switzerland
Term Expires: 2016
E-mail: h67@in.gov
Committees: Roads and Transportation; Utilities, Energy, and
Telecommunications; Veterans Affairs and Public Safety
Education: Cincinnati Christian 1995 AS
Representative
**Phillip K. "Phil" GiaQuinta** (D-District 80) Room 4-1 . . (317) 232-9600
Counties Represented: Allen (part)          Tel: (800) 382-9842
Term Expires: 2016
E-mail: h80@in.gov
Committees: Elections and Apportionment; Financial Institutions;
Public Policy
Representative **Terry A. Goodin** (D-District 66)
Room 4A-1 . . . . . . . . . . . . . . . . . . . . . . . . . . . . (317) 232-9600
Counties Represented: Clark (part), Jefferson (part),     Tel: (800) 382-9842
Scott
Term Expires: 2016
E-mail: h66@in.gov
Committees: Statutory Committee on Interstate and International
Cooperation; Ways and Means
Education: Eastern Kentucky 1989 BA, 1990 MA; Indiana 1995 DEd
Representative
**Douglas L. "Doug" Gutwein** (R-District 16)
Room 4A-7 . . . . . . . . . . . . . . . . . . . . . . . . . . . . (317) 232-9509
Counties Represented: Fulton (part), Jasper (part), Newton (part),
Pulaski, Starke (part)
Term Expires: 2016
E-mail: h16@in.gov
Committees: Agriculture and Rural Development; Employment, Labor
and Pensions; Veterans Affairs and Public Safety
Representative **Christina Hale** (D-District 87) Room 336 . . (317) 232-9608
Counties Represented: Marion (part)
Term Expires: 2016
E-mail: h87@in.gov
Committees: Commerce, Small Business and Economic Development;
Insurance; Utilities, Energy, and Telecommunications
Education: Purdue
Representative **Richard "Dick" Hamm** (R-District 56)
Room 336 . . . . . . . . . . . . . . . . . . . . . . . . . . . . . (317) 232-9850
Counties Represented: Wayne (part)
Term Expires: 2016
E-mail: h56@in.gov
Committees: Agriculture and Rural Development; Financial Institutions;
Insurance; Statutory Committee on Interstate and International
Cooperation
Representative **Timothy P. Harman** (R-District 17)
Room 336-41 . . . . . . . . . . . . . . . . . . . . . . . . . . . (317) 232-9608
Counties Represented: Fulton (part), Marshall
Term Expires: 2016
E-mail: h17@in.gov
Committees: Commerce, Small Business and Economic Development;
Employment, Labor and Pensions; Government and Regulatory Reform
Education: Florida Atlantic 1992; Florida State 1994 MEd
Representative **Donna J. Harris** (D-District 2)
Room 3A-1 . . . . . . . . . . . . . . . . . . . . . . . . . . . . (317) 232-9600
Counties Represented: Lake (part)          Tel: (800) 382-9842
Term Expires: 2016
E-mail: h2@in.gov
Committees: Government and Regulatory Reform; Judiciary; Natural
Resources; Statutory Committee on Interstate and International
Cooperation

*(continued on next page)*

**Representatives** *continued*

Representative **Bob Heaton** (R-District 46) Room 149 .... (317) 232-9620
Counties Represented: Clay (part), Monroe (part), Owen (part), Vigo (part)
Term Expires: 2016
E-mail: h46@in.gov
Committees: Financial Institutions; Insurance; Natural Resources

Representative **Todd Huston** (R-District 37)
Room 336-25 ..................................... (317) 232-9380
Counties Represented: Hamilton (part)
Term Expires: 2016
E-mail: h37@in.gov
Committees: Public Policy; Ways and Means
Education: Indiana

Representative **Christopher Judy** (R-District 83) ....... (317) 232-9600
Counties Represented: Allen (part), Whitley (part)
Term Expires: 2016
E-mail: h83@iga.in.gov
Committees: Agriculture and Rural Development; Natural Resources; Veterans Affairs and Public Safety

Representative
**Michael "Mike" Karickhoff** (R-District 30) .......... (317) 234-9380
Counties Represented: Grant (part), Howard (part)    Dist: (765) 860-7160
Term Expires: 2016
2504 Greenstree Lane, Kokomo, IN 46902
E-mail: h30@in.gov
Committees: Natural Resources; Ways and Means

Representative **Clyde Kersey** (D-District 43)
Room 336-21 ..................................... (317) 232-9600
Counties Represented: Vigo (part)
Term Expires: 2016
E-mail: h43@in.gov
Committees: Elections and Apportionment; Natural Resources; Statutory Committee on Ethics; Statutory Committee on Interstate and International Cooperation
Education: Indiana State 1971 BS, 1975 MS

Representative
**Cynthia L. "Cindy" Kirchhofer** (R-District 89)
Suite 401-2 ...................................... (317) 232-9600
Counties Represented: Marion (part)    Tel: (800) 382-9841
Term Expires: 2016
E-mail: h89@in.gov
Committees: Courts and Criminal Code; Government and Regulatory Reform; Public Health

Representative **Sheila Klinker** (D-District 27)
Room 4A-3 ....................................... (317) 232-9600
Counties Represented: Tippecanoe (part)    Tel: (800) 382-9842
Term Expires: 2016
E-mail: h27@in.gov
Committees: Agriculture and Rural Development; Family, Children and Human Affairs; Veterans Affairs and Public Safety; Ways and Means
Education: Purdue 1961 BA, 1976 MS, 1981 MS

Representative **Eric Allan Koch** (R-District 65) .. ✓ ...... (317) 232-9600
Counties Represented: Brown, Jackson (part),    Dist: (812) 279-6367
Johnson (part), Lawrence (part), Monroe (part)    Tel: (800) 382-9841
Term Expires: 2016
P.O. Box 372, Bedford, IN 47421
E-mail: h65@in.gov
Committees: Judiciary; Rules and Legislative Procedures; Statutory Committee on Ethics; Utilities, Energy, and Telecommunications
Affiliation: Attorney, Applegate McDonald & Koch, P.C.

Representative **Linda C. Lawson** (D-District 1)
Room 3-3 ........................................ (317) 232-9600
Counties Represented: Lake (part)    Tel: (800) 382-9842
Term Expires: 2016
E-mail: h1@in.gov
Committees: Courts and Criminal Code; Employment, Labor and Pensions; Veterans Affairs and Public Safety

Representative **Donald J. "Don" Lehe** (R-District 25) .... (317) 234-2993
Counties Represented: Carroll (part), Cass (part),    Dist: (765) 563-3620
Clinton (part), Tippecanoe (part), White (part)
Term Expires: 2016
10644 South 100 East, Brookston, IN 47923
E-mail: h25@in.gov
Committees: Agriculture and Rural Development; Environmental Affairs; Public Health
Education: Purdue 1970 BS

Representative **Matthew S. Lehman** (R-District 79).....(317) 234-9499
Counties Represented: Adams, Allen (part), Wells    Tel: (800) 382-9841
(part)
Term Expires: 2016
663 Lehman Street, Berne, IN 46711
E-mail: h79@in.gov
Committees: Courts and Criminal Code; Insurance; Public Policy

Representative
**Daniel Joseph "Dan" Leonard** (R-District 50) ........ (317) 232-9600
Counties Represented: Allen (part), Huntington,    Dist: (260) 356-5122
Wells (part)
Term Expires: 2016
6274 North Goshen Road, Huntington, IN 46750
E-mail: h50@in.gov
Committees: Judiciary; Ways and Means
Education: Purdue 1971 BS

Representative **Jim Lucas** (R-District 69) Room 336-36 ... (317) 232-9671
Counties Represented: Bartholomew (part), Jackson (part), Jefferson (part), Jennings (part)
Term Expires: 2016
E-mail: h69@in.gov
Committees: Education; Government and Regulatory Reform; Public Policy

Representative **Randall Lyness** (R-District 68)...........(317) 234-9380
Counties Represented: Dearborn (part), Franklin (part), Union
Term Expires: 2016
E-mail: h68@iga.in.gov
Committees: Courts and Criminal Code; Employment, Labor and Pensions; Statutory Committee on Interstate and International Cooperation
Education: Indiana State BS

Representative **Karlee D. Macer** (D-District 92)
Room 336-11 ..................................... (317) 232-9707
Counties Represented: Marion (part)
Term Expires: 2016
E-mail: h92@in.gov
Committees: Commerce, Small Business and Economic Development; Family, Children and Human Affairs; Veterans Affairs and Public Safety

Representative **Kevin A. Mahan** (R-District 31)
Room 149 ........................................ (317) 232-9509
Counties Represented: Blackford (part), Delaware (part), Grant (part), Wells (part)
Term Expires: 2016
E-mail: h31@in.gov
Committees: Family, Children and Human Affairs; Government and Regulatory Reform; Insurance

Representative **Peggy Mayfield** (R-District 60)
Room 336-32 ..................................... (317) 232-9608
Counties Represented: Monroe (part), Morgan (part)
Term Expires: 2016
E-mail: h60@in.gov
Committees: Insurance; Ways and Means

Representative **Wendy M. McNamara** (R-District 76) ✓
Room 336-34 ..................................... (317) 232-9671
Counties Represented: Posey (part), Vanderburgh (part)
Term Expires: 2016
E-mail: h76@in.gov
Committees: Courts and Criminal Code; Government and Regulatory Reform; Judiciary

Representative **Douglas Miller** (R-District 48) ........... (317) 232-9620
Counties Represented: Elkhart (part)
Term Expires: 2016
E-mail: h48@iga.in.gov
Committees: Commerce, Small Business and Economic Development; Environmental Affairs; Government and Regulatory Reform

Representative **Justin Moed** (D-District 97) Room 336-9 .. (317) 232-9608
Counties Represented: Marion (part)
Term Expires: 2016
E-mail: h97@in.gov
Committees: Agriculture and Rural Development; Education; Financial Institutions; Local Government
Education: Butler 2006

Representative **Robert "Bob" Morris** (R-District 84) ..... (317) 232-9600
Counties Represented: Allen (part)    Tel: (800) 382-9841
Term Expires: 2016    (In-State)
6344 East State Boulevard, Fort Wayne, IN 46815
E-mail: h84@in.gov
Committees: Commerce, Small Business and Economic Development; Employment, Labor and Pensions; Roads and Transportation
Education: Indiana BS

Representative **Alan P. Morrison** (R-District 42)
Room 336-23 . . . . . . . . . . . . . . . . . . . . . . . . . . . . . . . . . (317) 234-2993
Counties Represented: Clay (part), Fountain (part), Parke (part),
Vermillion, Vigo (part), Warren (part)
Term Expires: 2016
E-mail: h42@in.gov
Committees: Agriculture and Rural Development; Natural Resources;
Utilities, Energy, and Telecommunications
Education: Slippery Rock U BS; Indiana State MA

Representative **Charles Moseley** (D-District 10)
Room 336-12 . . . . . . . . . . . . . . . . . . . . . . . . . . . . . (317) 232-9600
Counties Represented: Porter (part)          Tel: (800) 382-9842
Term Expires: 2016
E-mail: h10@in.gov
Committees: Elections and Apportionment; Employment, Labor and
Pensions; Veterans Affairs and Public Safety

Representative **Sharon Negele** (R-District 13)
Room 150 . . . . . . . . . . . . . . . . . . . . . . . . . . . . . . . (317) 232-9816
Counties Represented: Benton, Fountain (part), Jasper (part),
Montgomery (part), Newton (part), Tippecanoe (part), Warren (part),
White (part)
Term Expires: 2016
401 East Pike Street, Attica, IN 47918
E-mail: h13@iga.in.gov
Committees: Financial Institutions; Ways and Means

Representative **David L. Niezgodski** (D-District 7)
Room 4-1 . . . . . . . . . . . . . . . . . . . . . . . . . . . . . . . (317) 232-9756
Counties Represented: St. Joseph (part)          Tel: (800) 382-9842
Term Expires: 2016
E-mail: h7@in.gov
Committees: Agriculture and Rural Development; Employment, Labor
and Pensions; Ways and Means

Representative **Curt L. Nisly** (R-District 22) . . . . . . . . . (317) 232-9678
Counties Represented: Elkhart (part), Kosciusko (part)
Term Expires: 2016
E-mail: h22@iga.in.gov
Committees: Roads and Transportation; Statutory Committee on
Interstate and International Cooperation

Representative **David L. Ober** (R-District 82)
Room 336-40 . . . . . . . . . . . . . . . . . . . . . . . . . . . . (317) 232-9643
Counties Represented: Allen (part), Elkhart (part), Lagrange (part),
Noble, Whitley (part)
Term Expires: 2016
E-mail: h82@iga.in.gov
Committees: Employment, Labor and Pensions; Rules and Legislative
Procedures; Ways and Means

Representative **Julie Olthoff** (R-District 19) . . . . . . . . . . . (317) 232-9850
Counties Represented: Lake (part), Porter (part)
Term Expires: 2016
E-mail: h19@iga.in.gov
Committees: Commerce, Small Business and Economic Development;
Family, Children and Human Affairs; Government and Regulatory
Reform

Representative **Scott D. Pelath** (D-District 9) Room 3-2 . . (317) 232-9600
Counties Represented: LaPorte (part), Porter (part)     Tel: (800) 382-9842
Term Expires: 2016
E-mail: h9@in.gov

Representative **Matt Pierce** (D-District 61) Room 336-20 . . (317) 232-9600
Counties Represented: Monroe (part)          Tel: (800) 382-9842
Term Expires: 2016
E-mail: h61@in.gov
Committees: Courts and Criminal Code; Environmental Affairs;
Joint Rules; Rules and Legislative Procedures; Utilities, Energy, and
Telecommunications
Education: Indiana 1984 BA, 1987 JD

Representative
**Gregory W. "Greg" Porter** (D-District 96)
Room 4A-2 . . . . . . . . . . . . . . . . . . . . . . . . . . . . . . (317) 232-9600
Counties Represented: Marion (part)          Tel: (800) 382-9842
Term Expires: 2016
E-mail: h96@in.gov
Committees: Insurance; Public Health; Ways and Means
Education: Earlham 1978 BA

Representative **John L. Price** (R-District 47)
Room 336-26 . . . . . . . . . . . . . . . . . . . . . . . . . . . . (317) 232-9608
Counties Represented: Johnson (part), Morgan (part)
Term Expires: 2016
E-mail: h47@iga.in.gov
Committees: Financial Institutions; Local Government; Veterans Affairs
and Public Safety

Representative **Cherrish Pryor** (D-District 94)
Room 4A-1 . . . . . . . . . . . . . . . . . . . . . . . . . . . . . . (317) 232-9600
Counties Represented: Marion (part)
Term Expires: 2016
E-mail: h94@in.gov
Committees: Local Government; Roads and Transportation; Utilities,
Energy, and Telecommunications; Ways and Means
Education: Indiana BS; IU-Purdue U Indianapolis MPA

Representative **Rhonda J. Rhoads** (R-District 70) . . . . . . . . (317) 234-3827
Counties Represented: Clark (part), Floyd (part), Harrison (part)
Term Expires: 2016
525 Capitol Avenue, Covington, IN 47112
E-mail: h70@in.gov
Committees: Courts and Criminal Code; Education; Family, Children
and Human Affairs
Education: Indiana State BS; Indiana MSE

Representative **Kathy Kreag Richardson** (R-District 29) . . (317) 232-9600
Counties Represented: Hamilton (part)          Dist: (317) 773-6123
Term Expires: 2016
1363 Grant Street, Noblesville, IN 46060
E-mail: h29@in.gov
Committees: Elections and Apportionment; Judiciary; Statutory
Committee on Ethics

Representative **Gail C. Riecken** (D-District 77)
Room 336-18 . . . . . . . . . . . . . . . . . . . . . . . . . . . . (317) 232-9600
Counties Represented: Vanderburgh (part)
Term Expires: 2016
E-mail: h77@in.gov
Committees: Financial Institutions; Government and Regulatory
Reform; Statutory Committee on Ethics; Ways and Means
Education: Indiana BS

Representative
**Thomas E. "Tom" Saunders** (R-District 54) . . . . . . . . . (317) 232-9600
Counties Represented: Henry, Rush (part), Wayne     Dist: (765) 987-7572
(part)
Term Expires: 2016
P.O. Box 218, Lewisville, IN 47352
E-mail: h54@in.gov
Committees: Local Government; Roads and Transportation; Statutory
Committee on Interstate and International Cooperation

Representative **Donna Schaibley** (R-District 24) . . . . . . . . (317) 232-9863
Counties Represented: Boone (part), Hamilton (part)
Term Expires: 2016
E-mail: h24@iga.in.gov
Committees: Environmental Affairs; Financial Institutions; Statutory
Committee on Interstate and International Cooperation

Representative **Robin Shackleford** (D-District 98)
Room 336-8 . . . . . . . . . . . . . . . . . . . . . . . . . . . . . . (317) 232-9608
Counties Represented: Marion (part)
Term Expires: 2016
E-mail: h98@in.gov
Committees: Commerce, Small Business and Economic Development;
Financial Institutions; Public Health

Representative **Harold "Hal" Slager** (R-District 15)
Room 401-4 . . . . . . . . . . . . . . . . . . . . . . . . . . . . . . (317) 232-9608
Counties Represented: Lake (part)
Term Expires: 2016
E-mail: h15@iga.in.gov
Committees: Public Health; Ways and Means
Education: Butler 1981

Representative **Ben Smaltz** (R-District 52) Room 336-42 . . (317) 232-9648
Counties Represented: Allen (part), DeKalb, Steuben (part)
Term Expires: 2016
E-mail: h52@iga.in.gov
Committees: Commerce, Small Business and Economic Development;
Joint Rules; Public Policy; Roads and Transportation
Education: Ball State

Representative **Milo Smith** (R-District 59) . . . . . . . . . . . . (317) 232-9600
Counties Represented: Bartholomew (part)          Dist: (812) 372-2121
Term Expires: 2016
632 3rd Street, Columbus, IN 47201
E-mail: h59@in.gov
Committees: Elections and Apportionment; Family, Children and
Human Affairs

Representative **Vernon G. Smith** (D-District 14)
Room 3A-1 . . . . . . . . . . . . . . . . . . . . . . . . . . . . . . (317) 232-9600
Counties Represented: Lake (part)          Tel: (800) 382-9842
Term Expires: 2016
E-mail: h14@in.gov
Committees: Education; Judiciary; Local Government
Education: Indiana 1966 BS, 1969 MS, 1978 EdD

*(continued on next page)*

**LEGISLATIVE BRANCH**

**Representatives** *continued*

Representative **Edmond L. "Ed" Soliday** (R-District 4)
Room 405 . . . . . . . . . . . . . . . . . . . . . . . . . . . . (317) 232-9850
Counties Represented: Porter (part)          Tel: (800) 382-9841
Term Expires: 2016
E-mail: h4@in.gov
Committees: Elections and Apportionment; Roads and Transportation;
Rules and Legislative Procedures; Utilities, Energy, and
Telecommunications; Veterans Affairs and Public Safety

Representative **Michael "Mike" Speedy** (R-District 90)
Room 336-24 . . . . . . . . . . . . . . . . . . . . . . . . . . (317) 232-9600
Counties Represented: Marion (part)
Term Expires: 2016
E-mail: h90@in.gov
Committees: Employment, Labor and Pensions; Roads and
Transportation; Utilities, Energy, and Telecommunications
Education: Indiana BS

Representative **Steven R. Stemler** (D-District 71)
Room 336-16 . . . . . . . . . . . . . . . . . . . . . . . . . . (317) 232-9600
Counties Represented: Clark (part)          Tel: (800) 382-9842
Term Expires: 2016
E-mail: h71@in.gov
Committees: Roads and Transportation; Statutory Committee on Ethics;
Ways and Means

Representative
**Gregory Earl "Greg" Steuerwald** (R-District 40) . . . . . . (317) 232-9600
Counties Represented: Hendricks (part)        Dist: (317) 745-4485
Term Expires: 2016
P.O. Box 503, Danville, IN 46122-0503
E-mail: h40@in.gov
Committees: Courts and Criminal Code; Judiciary; Rules and
Legislative Procedures; Statutory Committee on Ethics

Representative **Holli Sullivan** (R-District 78) . . . . . . . . . . . (800) 382-9841
Counties Represented: Vanderburgh (part), Warrick (part)
Term Expires: 2016
E-mail: h78@in.gov
Committees: Roads and Transportation; Ways and Means
Education: Missouri BS

Representative **Vanessa Summers** (D-District 99)
Room 3A-3 . . . . . . . . . . . . . . . . . . . . . . . . . . . (317) 232-9600
Counties Represented: Marion (part)          Tel: (800) 382-9842
Term Expires: 2016
E-mail: h99@in.gov
Committees: Family, Children and Human Affairs; Public Policy
Affiliation: Special Projects Coordinator, The Julian Center

Representative
**Jeffrey A. "Jeff" Thompson** (R-District 28) . . . . . . . . . (317) 232-9790
Counties Represented: Boone (part), Hendricks   Dist: (317) 994-6239
(part)
Term Expires: 2016
6001 North State Road 39, Lizton, IN 46149
E-mail: h28@in.gov
Committees: Education; Elections and Apportionment; Ways and
Means
Education: Purdue 1978 BS

Representative **Gerald R. "Jerry" Torr** (R-District 39)
Room 3A-4 . . . . . . . . . . . . . . . . . . . . . . . . . . . (317) 232-9677
Counties Represented: Hamilton (part)         Tel: (800) 682-9841
Term Expires: 2016
E-mail: h39@in.gov
Committees: Commerce, Small Business and Economic Development;
Employment, Labor and Pensions; Insurance; Joint Rules; Judiciary;
Rules and Legislative Procedures
Affiliation: Claims Adjuster, Monroe Guaranty Insurance

Representative
**Randolph P. "Randy" Truitt** (R-District 26)
Room 4A-8 . . . . . . . . . . . . . . . . . . . . . . . . . . . (317) 232-9600
Counties Represented: Tippecanoe (part)
Term Expires: 2016
E-mail: h26@in.gov
Committees: Government and Regulatory Reform; Local Government;
Ways and Means
Education: Purdue BS; Indiana Wesleyan 2002 MBA

Representative **Heath R. VanNatter** (R-District 38)
Room 149 . . . . . . . . . . . . . . . . . . . . . . . . . . . . (317) 232-9600
Counties Represented: Carroll (part), Cass (part), Clinton (part),
Howard (part)
Term Expires: 2016
E-mail: h38@in.gov
Committees: Environmental Affairs; Local Government; Utilities,
Energy, and Telecommunications

Representative
**Thomas "Tom" Washburne** (R-District 64)
Room 336-30 . . . . . . . . . . . . . . . . . . . . . . . . . . (317) 234-2993
Counties Represented: Gibson, Knox (part), Pike (part), Posey (part),
Vanderburgh (part)
Term Expires: 2016
E-mail: h64@iga.in.gov
Committees: Courts and Criminal Code; Financial Institutions;
Judiciary
Education: Purdue 1986 BSE; Indiana 1990 JD

Representative **Timothy "Tim" Wesco** (R-District 21)
Room 4-2 . . . . . . . . . . . . . . . . . . . . . . . . . . . . (317) 234-3827
Counties Represented: Elkhart (part), St. Joseph (part)
Term Expires: 2016
E-mail: h21@in.gov
Committees: Elections and Apportionment; Employment, Labor and
Pensions; Local Government; Public Policy

Representative **David A. Wolkins** (R-District 18) . . . . . . . . (317) 232-9815
Counties Represented: Grant (part), Kosciusko   Tel: (800) 382-9841
(part), Wabash                    Dist: (574) 269-2639
Term Expires: 2016
501 Pierceton Road, Winona Lake, IN 46590
E-mail: h18@in.gov
Committees: Environmental Affairs; Government and Regulatory
Reform; Natural Resources
Education: Greenville Col 1966 BS; St Francis Col (IN) 1972 MS

Representative **Melanie M. Wright** (D-District 35) . . . . . . . (800) 382-9842
Counties Represented: Delaware (part), Jackson (part), Madison (part)
Term Expires: 2016
E-mail: h35@iga.in.gov
Committees: Agriculture and Rural Development; Family, Children and
Human Affairs; Insurance; Local Government

Representative **Dennis J. Zent** (R-District 51)
Room 336-28 . . . . . . . . . . . . . . . . . . . . . . . . . . (317) 232-9833
Counties Represented: Lagrange (part), Steuben (part)
Term Expires: 2016
E-mail: h51@iga.in.gov
Committees: Local Government; Public Health; Veterans Affairs and
Public Safety

Representative **Cindy Meyer Ziemke** (R-District 55)
Room 150 . . . . . . . . . . . . . . . . . . . . . . . . . . . . (317) 232-9850
Counties Represented: Decatur (part), Fayette, Franklin (part), Ripley
(part), Rush (part)
Term Expires: 2016
E-mail: h55@iga.in.gov
Committees: Courts and Criminal Code; Family, Children and Human
Affairs

# House Standing Committees
## Agriculture and Rural Development

**Majority Members**
Donald J. "Don" Lehe (R-25) *Chair*
Alan P. Morrison (R-42) *Vice Chair*
Lloyd Arnold (R-74)
James R. "Jim" Baird (R-44)
Greg Beumer (R-33)
William C. "Bill" Friend (R-23)
Douglas L. "Doug" Gutwein (R-16)
Richard "Dick" Hamm (R-56)
Christopher Judy (R-83)

**Minority Members**
Melanie M. Wright (D-35)
 *Ranking Minority Member*
Sheila Klinker (D-27)
Justin Moed (D-97)
David L. Niezgodski (D-7)

## Commerce, Small Business and Economic Development

**Majority Members**
Ben Smaltz (R-52) *Chair*
Robert "Bob" Morris (R-84)
 *Vice Chair*
Wesley H. "Wes" Culver (R-49)
Thomas "Tom" Dermody (R-20)
William "Bill" Fine (R-12)
Timothy P. Harman (R-17)
Douglas Miller (R-48)
Julie Olthoff (R-19)
Gerald R. "Jerry" Torr (R-39)

**Minority Members**
Karlee D. Macer (D-92)
 *Ranking Minority Member*
Daniel "Dan" Forestal (D-100)
Christina Hale (D-87)
Robin Shackleford (D-98)

# Courts and Criminal Code

**Majority Members**
Thomas "Tom" Washburne (R-64)
*Chair*
Wendy M. McNamara (R-76)
*Vice Chair*
Casey B. Cox (R-85)
Cynthia L. "Cindy" Kirchhofer (R-89)
Matthew S. Lehman (R-79)
Randall Lyness (R-68)
Rhonda J. Rhoads (R-70)
Gregory Earl "Greg" Steuerwald (R-40)
Cindy Meyer Ziemke (R-55)

**Minority Members**
Matt Pierce (D-61)
*Ranking Minority Member*
Edward O. "Ed" DeLaney (D-86)
Ryan M. Dvorak (D-8)
Linda C. Lawson (D-1)

# Education

**Majority Members**
Robert W. "Bob" Behning (R-91)
*Chair*
Rhonda J. Rhoads (R-70)
*Vice Chair*
Mike Braun (R-63)
Charles W. "Woody" Burton (R-58)
Anthony "Tony" Cook (R-32)
Dale R. DeVon (R-5)
William "Bill" Fine (R-12)
Jim Lucas (R-69)
Jeffrey A. "Jeff" Thompson (R-28)

**Minority Members**
Vernon G. Smith (D-14)
*Ranking Minority Member*
Terri J. Austin (D-36)
Sue Errington (D-34)
Justin Moed (D-97)

# Elections and Apportionment

**Majority Members**
Milo Smith (R-59) *Chair*
Kathy Kreag Richardson (R-29)
*Vice Chair*
Lloyd Arnold (R-74)
Charles W. "Woody" Burton (R-58)
Anthony "Tony" Cook (R-32)
Casey B. Cox (R-85)
Edmond L. "Ed" Soliday (R-4)
Jeffrey A. "Jeff" Thompson (R-28)
Timothy "Tim" Wesco (R-21)

**Minority Members**
John Bartlett (D-95)
*Ranking Minority Member*
Phillip K. "Phil" GiaQuinta (D-80)
Clyde Kersey (D-43)
Charles Moseley (D-10)

# Employment, Labor and Pensions

**Majority Members**
Douglas L. "Doug" Gutwein (R-16)
*Chair*
Timothy P. Harman (R-17)
*Vice Chair*
Martin Carbaugh (R-81)
Randall Lyness (R-68)
Robert "Bob" Morris (R-84)
David L. Ober (R-82)
Michael "Mike" Speedy (R-90)
Gerald R. "Jerry" Torr (R-39)
Timothy "Tim" Wesco (R-21)

**Minority Members**
Charles Moseley (D-10)
*Ranking Minority Member*
John Bartlett (D-95)
Linda C. Lawson (D-1)
David L. Niezgodski (D-7)

# Environmental Affairs

**Majority Members**
David A. Wolkins (R-18) *Chair*
Greg Beumer (R-33) *Vice Chair*
Michael J. Aylesworth (R-11)
Sean R. Eberhart (R-57)
William C. "Bill" Friend (R-23)
Donald J. "Don" Lehe (R-25)
Douglas Miller (R-48)
Donna Schaibley (R-24)
Heath R. VanNatter (R-38)

**Minority Members**
Sue Errington (D-34)
*Ranking Minority Member*
B. Patrick "Pat" Bauer (D-6)
Ryan M. Dvorak (D-8)
Matt Pierce (D-61)

# Family, Children and Human Affairs

**Majority Members**
David N. Frizzell (R-93) *Chair*
Cindy Meyer Ziemke (R-55)
*Vice Chair*
Ronald "Ron" Bacon (R-75)
Casey B. Cox (R-85)
Dale R. DeVon (R-5)
Kevin A. Mahan (R-31)
Julie Olthoff (R-19)
Rhonda J. Rhoads (R-70)
Milo Smith (R-59)

**Minority Members**
Vanessa Summers (D-99)
*Ranking Minority Member*
Sheila Klinker (D-27)
Karlee D. Macer (D-92)
Melanie M. Wright (D-35)

# Financial Institutions

**Majority Members**
Charles W. "Woody" Burton (R-58)
*Chair*
Bob Heaton (R-46) *Vice Chair*
Greg Beumer (R-33)
Wesley H. "Wes" Culver (R-49)
Richard "Dick" Hamm (R-56)
Sharon Negele (R-13)
John L. Price (R-47)
Donna Schaibley (R-24)
Thomas "Tom" Washburne (R-64)

**Minority Members**
Justin Moed (D-97)
*Ranking Minority Member*
Phillip K. "Phil" GiaQuinta (D-80)
Gail C. Riecken (D-77)
Robin Shackleford (D-98)

# Government and Regulatory Reform

**Majority Members**
Kevin A. Mahan (R-31) *Chair*
Jim Lucas (R-69) *Vice Chair*
Timothy P. Harman (R-17)
Cynthia L. "Cindy" Kirchhofer (R-89)
Wendy M. McNamara (R-76)
Douglas Miller (R-48)
Julie Olthoff (R-19)
Randolph P. "Randy" Truitt (R-26)
David A. Wolkins (R-18)

**Minority Members**
Gail C. Riecken (D-77)
*Ranking Minority Member*
John Bartlett (D-95)
Sue Errington (D-34)
Donna J. Harris (D-2)

# Insurance

**Majority Members**
Martin Carbaugh (R-81) *Chair*
Richard "Dick" Hamm (R-56)
*Vice Chair*
Bruce A. Borders (R-45)
Charles W. "Woody" Burton (R-58)
Bob Heaton (R-46)
Matthew S. Lehman (R-79)
Kevin A. Mahan (R-31)
Peggy Mayfield (R-60)
Gerald R. "Jerry" Torr (R-39)

**Minority Members**
Christina Hale (D-87)
*Ranking Minority Member*
Terri J. Austin (D-36)
Gregory W. "Greg" Porter (D-96)
Melanie M. Wright (D-35)

# Judiciary

**Majority Members**
Gregory Earl "Greg" Steuerwald (R-40)
*Chair*
Casey B. Cox (R-85) *Vice Chair*
William "Bill" Fine (R-12)
Eric Allan Koch (R-65)
Daniel Joseph "Dan" Leonard (R-50)
Wendy M. McNamara (R-76)
Kathy Kreag Richardson (R-29)
Gerald R. "Jerry" Torr (R-39)
Thomas "Tom" Washburne (R-64)

**Minority Members**
B. Patrick "Pat" Bauer (D-6)
*Ranking Minority Member*
Edward O. "Ed" DeLaney (D-86)
Donna J. Harris (D-2)
Vernon G. Smith (D-14)

# Local Government

**Majority Members**
John L. Price (R-47) *Chair*
Michael J. Aylesworth (R-11)
*Vice Chair*
Bruce A. Borders (R-45)
Robert W. "Bob" Cherry (R-53)
Thomas E. "Tom" Saunders (R-54)
Randolph P. "Randy" Truitt (R-26)
Heath R. VanNatter (R-38)
Timothy "Tim" Wesco (R-21)
Dennis J. Zent (R-51)

**Minority Members**
Cherrish Pryor (D-94)
*Ranking Minority Member*
Justin Moed (D-97)
Vernon G. Smith (D-14)
Melanie M. Wright (D-35)

**LEGISLATIVE BRANCH**

## Natural Resources

**Majority Members**
Sean R. Eberhart (R-57) *Chair*
Lloyd Arnold (R-74) *Vice Chair*
Michael J. Aylesworth (R-11)
Jeff Ellington (R-62)
Bob Heaton (R-46)
Christopher Judy (R-83)
Michael "Mike" Karickhoff (R-30)
Alan P. Morrison (R-42)
David A. Wolkins (R-18)

**Minority Members**
Clyde Kersey (D-43)
 *Ranking Minority Member*
Ryan M. Dvorak (D-8)
Sue Errington (D-34)
Donna J. Harris (D-2)

## Public Health

**Majority Members**
Cynthia L. "Cindy"
 Kirchhofer (R-89)
 *Chair*
Dennis J. Zent (R-51) *Vice Chair*
Ronald "Ron" Bacon (R-75)
Robert W. "Bob" Behning (R-91)
Edward D. "Ed" Clere (R-72)
Steven J. "Steve" Davisson (R-73)
David N. Frizzell (R-93)
Donald J. "Don" Lehe (R-25)
Harold "Hal" Slager (R-15)

**Minority Members**
Charlie Brown (D-3)
 *Ranking Minority Member*
B. Patrick "Pat" Bauer (D-6)
Gregory W. "Greg" Porter (D-96)
Robin Shackleford (D-98)

## Public Policy

**Majority Members**
Thomas "Tom" Dermody (R-20)
 *Chair*
Timothy "Tim" Wesco (R-21)
 *Vice Chair*
Edward D. "Ed" Clere (R-72)
Sean R. Eberhart (R-57)
Jeff Ellington (R-62)
Todd Huston (R-37)
Matthew S. Lehman (R-79)
Jim Lucas (R-69)
Ben Smaltz (R-52)

**Minority Members**
Phillip K. "Phil" GiaQuinta (D-80)
 *Ranking Minority Member*
Terri J. Austin (D-36)
Charlie Brown (D-3)
Vanessa Summers (D-99)

## Roads and Transportation

**Majority Members**
Edmond L. "Ed" Soliday (R-4)
 *Chair*
Michael "Mike" Speedy (R-90)
 *Vice Chair*
Mike Braun (R-63)
Randall L. "Randy" Frye (R-67)
Robert "Bob" Morris (R-84)
Curt L. Nisly (R-22)
Thomas E. "Tom" Saunders (R-54)
Ben Smaltz (R-52)
Holli Sullivan (R-78)

**Minority Members**
Daniel "Dan" Forestal (D-100)
 *Ranking Minority Member*
Charlie Brown (D-3)
Cherrish Pryor (D-94)
Steven R. Stemler (D-71)

## Rules and Legislative Procedures

**Majority Members**
Gerald R. "Jerry" Torr (R-39) *Chair*
Gregory Earl "Greg"
 Steuerwald (R-40)
 *Vice Chair*
Charles W. "Woody" Burton (R-58)
Robert W. "Bob" Cherry (R-53)
Eric Allan Koch (R-65)
David L. Ober (R-82)
Edmond L. "Ed" Soliday (R-4)

**Minority Members**
Matt Pierce (D-61)
 *Ranking Minority Member*
Terri J. Austin (D-36)
Ryan M. Dvorak (D-8)

## Statutory Committee on Ethics

**Majority Members**
Gregory Earl "Greg"
 Steuerwald (R-40)
 *Chair*
Eric Allan Koch (R-65)
Kathy Kreag Richardson (R-29)

**Minority Members**
Clyde Kersey (D-43) *Vice Chair*
Gail C. Riecken (D-77)
Steven R. Stemler (D-71)

## Statutory Committee on Interstate and International Cooperation

**Majority Members**
Wesley H. "Wes" Culver (R-49)
 *Chair*
Thomas E. "Tom" Saunders (R-54)
 *Vice Chair*
James R. "Jim" Baird (R-44)
Anthony "Tony" Cook (R-32)
Jeff Ellington (R-62)
Richard "Dick" Hamm (R-56)
Randall Lyness (R-68)
Curt L. Nisly (R-22)
Donna Schaibley (R-24)

**Minority Members**
Donna J. Harris (D-2)
 *Ranking Minority Member*
Charlie Brown (D-3)
Terry A. Goodin (D-66)
Clyde Kersey (D-43)

## Utilities, Energy, and Telecommunications

**Majority Members**
Eric Allan Koch (R-65) *Chair*
Heath R. VanNatter (R-38)
 *Vice Chair*
Robert W. "Bob" Behning (R-91)
Dale R. DeVon (R-5)
David N. Frizzell (R-93)
Randall L. "Randy" Frye (R-67)
Alan P. Morrison (R-42)
Edmond L. "Ed" Soliday (R-4)
Michael "Mike" Speedy (R-90)

**Minority Members**
Christina Hale (D-87)
 *Ranking Minority Member*
Daniel "Dan" Forestal (D-100)
Matt Pierce (D-61)
Cherrish Pryor (D-94)

## Veterans Affairs and Public Safety

**Majority Members**
Randall L. "Randy" Frye (R-67)
 *Chair*
Bruce A. Borders (R-45) *Vice Chair*
Lloyd Arnold (R-74)
Martin Carbaugh (R-81)
Douglas L. "Doug" Gutwein (R-16)
Christopher Judy (R-83)
John L. Price (R-47)
Edmond L. "Ed" Soliday (R-4)
Dennis J. Zent (R-51)

**Minority Members**
Karlee D. Macer (D-92)
 *Ranking Minority Member*
Sheila Klinker (D-27)
Linda C. Lawson (D-1)
Charles Moseley (D-10)

## Ways and Means

**Majority Members**
Timothy N. "Tim" Brown (R-41)
 *Chair*
Robert W. "Bob" Cherry (R-53)
 *Vice Chair*
James R. "Jim" Baird (R-44)
Mike Braun (R-63)
Edward D. "Ed" Clere (R-72)
Steven J. "Steve" Davisson (R-73)
Todd Huston (R-37)
Michael "Mike" Karickhoff (R-30)
Daniel Joseph "Dan" Leonard
 (R-50)
Peggy Mayfield (R-60)
Sharon Negele (R-13)
David L. Ober (R-82)
Harold "Hal" Slager (R-15)
Holli Sullivan (R-78)
Jeffrey A. "Jeff" Thompson (R-28)
Randolph P. "Randy" Truitt (R-26)

**Minority Members**
Gregory W. "Greg" Porter (D-96)
 *Ranking Minority Member*
Edward O. "Ed" DeLaney (D-86)
Terry A. Goodin (D-66)
Sheila Klinker (D-27)
David L. Niezgodski (D-7)
Cherrish Pryor (D-94)
Gail C. Riecken (D-77)
Steven R. Stemler (D-71)

# Iowa General Assembly

State Capitol, Des Moines, IA 50319
Tel: (515) 281-5129

## Iowa Senate

Tel: (515) 281-3371  Fax: (515) 242-6108  TTY: (515) 281-3789
President of the Senate **Pam Jochum** (D) . . . . . . . . . . . . . (563) 556-6530
  Administrative Assistant **Steve Conway** . . . . . . . . . . . . . . (515) 281-3371
  Administrative Assistant **Kay Kibbie** . . . . . . . . . . . . . . . . (515) 281-3371
President Pro Tem **Steven J. "Steve" Sodders** (D) . . . . . . (641) 483-2383
Majority Leader **Michael E. "Mike" Gronstal** (D) . . . . . . . (515) 281-4610
  Education: Antioch U BA
Majority Whip **Joseph L. "Joe" Bolkcom** (D) . . . . . . . . . (319) 337-6280
  Education: St Ambrose 1983 BA; Iowa 1988 MPA
Assistant Majority Leader
  **William A. "Bill" Dotzler, Jr.** (D) . . . . . . . . . . . . . . . . . (319) 296-2947
  Education: Northern Iowa 1975 BA
Assistant Majority Leader
  **Matthew W. "Matt" McCoy** (D) . . . . . . . . . . . . . . . . . (515) 681-9327
  Education: Briar Cliff Col 1988 BA
Assistant Majority Leader **Amanda Ragan** (D) . . . . . . . . . (641) 424-2316
Assistant Majority Leader **Mary Jo Wilhelm** (D) . . . . . . . (319) 547-4156
Republican Floor Leader **Bill C. Dix** (R) . . . . . . . . . . . . . . (319) 885-6790
Republican Whip **Jack Whitver** (R) . . . . . . . . . . . . . . . . . (515) 865-6394
Republican Assistant Leader **Rick Bertrand** (R) . . . . . . . . . (712) 253-7069
  Education: Northern Iowa 1993 BA
Republican Assistant Leader **Randy Feenstra** (R) . . . . . . . (712) 439-1244
Republican Assistant Leader **Tim L. Kapucian** (R) . . . . . . . (319) 442-5337
Republican Assistant Leader **Dan Zumbach** (R) . . . . . . . . (563) 920-5094
Secretary of the Senate **Michael E. "Mike" Marshall** . . . . (515) 281-5307
  E-mail: mike.marshall@legis.iowa.gov
Sergeant-at-Arms **William L. "Bill" Krieg** . . . . . . . . . . . . (515) 281-3371

## Senators

**Party Affiliation Statistics:** Republicans: 24, Democrats: 26

Senator **Chaz Allen** (D-District 15) . . . . . . . . . . . . . . . . . (641) 521-6297
  Counties Represented: Jasper (part), Polk (part)
  Term Expires: 2019
  1438 North 7th Avenue E, Newton, IA 50208
  E-mail: chaz.allen@legis.iowa.gov
  Committees: Joint Administration and Regulation Appropriations; Local Government; Veterans Affairs; Ways and Means
Senator **Bill Anderson** (R-District 3) . . . . . . . . . . . . . . . . (712) 898-2505
  Counties Represented: Plymouth (part), Woodbury (part)
  Term Expires: 2019
  1138 Mason Avenue, Pierson, IA 51048
  E-mail: bill.anderson@legis.iowa.gov
  Committees: Agriculture; Commerce; Economic Growth/Rebuild Iowa; Joint Transportation, Infrastructure, and Capitals Appropriations; Ways and Means
Senator **Jerry Behn** (R-District 24) . . . . . . . . . . . . . . . . . (515) 281-5307
  Counties Represented: Boone, Greene, Hamilton,   Res: (515) 432-7327
  Story (part), Webster (part)
  Term Expires: 2017
  1313 Quill Avenue, Boone, IA 50036
  E-mail: jerry.behn@legis.iowa.gov
  Committees: Education; Ethics; Natural Resources and Environment; Ways and Means
Senator **Rick Bertrand** (R-District 7) . . . . . . . . . . . . . . . . (712) 253-7069
  Counties Represented: Woodbury (part)
  Term Expires: 2019
  1501 Peavey Street, Sioux City, IA 51105
  E-mail: rick.bertrand@legis.iowa.gov
  Committees: Commerce; Labor and Business Relations; State Government
Senator **Tony Bisignano** (D-District 17) . . . . . . . . . . . . . . (515) 244-9530
  Counties Represented: Polk (part)
  Term Expires: 2019
  E-mail: tony.bisignano@legis.iowa.gov
  Committees: Economic Growth/Rebuild Iowa; Joint Economic Development Appropriations; Judiciary; Labor and Business Relations; Local Government

Senator **Joseph L. "Joe" Bolkcom** (D-District 43) . . . . . . (319) 337-6280
  Counties Represented: Johnson (part)
  Term Expires: 2019
  728 Second Avenue, Iowa City, IA 52245
  E-mail: joe.bolkcom@legis.iowa.gov
  Committees: Appropriations; Commerce; Human Resources; Joint Health and Human Services Appropriations; Natural Resources and Environment; Ways and Means
Senator **Tod R. Bowman** (D-District 29) . . . . . . . . . . . . . (563) 652-5499
  Counties Represented: Dubuque (part), Jackson, Jones (part)
  Term Expires: 2019
  812 Grant Street, Maquoketa, IA 52060
  E-mail: tod.bowman@legis.iowa.gov
  Committees: Agriculture; Economic Growth/Rebuild Iowa; Education; Joint Transportation, Infrastructure, and Capitals Appropriations; State Government; Transportation
Senator **Chris Brase** (D-District 46) . . . . . . . . . . . . . . . . . (563) 260-5416
  Counties Represented: Muscatine (part), Scott (part)
  Term Expires: 2017
  972 Newell Ave, Muscatine, IA 52761
  E-mail: chris.brase@legis.iowa.gov
  Committees: Agriculture; Joint Administration and Regulation Appropriations; Labor and Business Relations; Natural Resources and Environment; Transportation
  Education: Iowa (Attended)
Senator **Michael Breitbach** (R-District 28) . . . . . . . . . . . . (563) 933-6486
  Counties Represented: Allamakee, Clayton, Fayette (part), Winneshiek (part)
  Term Expires: 2017
  301 W Mission Street, Strawberry Point, IA 52076
  E-mail: michael.breitbach@legis.iowa.gov
  Committees: Economic Growth/Rebuild Iowa; Local Government; Transportation; Ways and Means
  Education: Loras 1978 BAcc
Senator **Jacob "Jake" Chapman** (R-District 10) . . . . . . . (515) 650-3942
  Counties Represented: Adair, Cass (part), Dallas (part), Guthrie, Polk (part)
  Term Expires: 2017
  1206 Lynne Drive, Adel, IA 50003
  E-mail: jake.chapman@legis.iowa.gov
  Committees: Appropriations; Economic Growth/Rebuild Iowa; Rules and Administration; State Government
Senator **Mark Chelgren** (R-District 41) . . . . . . . . . . . . . . (641) 777-7047
  Counties Represented: Davis, Jefferson (part), Van Buren, Wapello (part)
  Term Expires: 2019
  819 Hutchinson, Ottumwa, IA 52501
  E-mail: mark.chelgren@legis.iowa.gov
  Committees: Economic Growth/Rebuild Iowa; Human Resources; Joint Justice System Appropriations; Veterans Affairs
Senator **Mark Costello** (R-District 12) . . . . . . . . . . . . . . . (515) 281-3371
  Counties Represented: Fremont, Mills, Montgomery, Page, Ringgold, Taylor
  Term Expires: 2017
  E-mail: mark.costello@legis.iowa.gov
  Committees: Human Resources; Labor and Business Relations; Veterans Affairs
  Education: Northern Iowa 1984 BA
Senator **Thomas G. "Tom" Courtney** (D-District 44) . . . . (319) 759-5334
  Counties Represented: Des Moines, Louisa, Muscatine (part)
  Term Expires: 2017
  2200 Summer Street, Burlington, IA 52601
  E-mail: thomas.courtney@legis.iowa.gov
  E-mail: senate44@msn.com
  Committees: Appropriations; Commerce; Joint Justice System Appropriations; Rules and Administration; State Government
Senator **Jeff Danielson** (D-District 30) . . . . . . . . . . . . . . . (319) 231-7192
  Counties Represented: Black Hawk (part)   Dist: (319) 236-0611
  Term Expires: 2017
  P.O. Box 1191, Cedar Falls, IA 50613-1191
  E-mail: jeff@jeffdanielson.org
  E-mail: jeff.danielson@legis.iowa.gov
  Committees: Appropriations; Economic Growth/Rebuild Iowa; Joint Administration and Regulation Appropriations; State Government; Transportation; Veterans Affairs
  Education: Northern Iowa BA

*(continued on next page)*

LEGISLATIVE BRANCH

**Senators** *continued*

**Senator Dick L. Dearden** (D-District 16) . . . . . . . . . . . . . (515) 262-1203
Counties Represented: Polk (part)
Term Expires: 2017
3113 Kinsey, Des Moines, IA 50317
E-mail: dick.dearden@legis.iowa.gov
Committees: Ethics; Joint Agriculture and Natural Resources
Appropriations; Natural Resources and Environment; Rules and
Administration; State Government; Transportation

**Senator Bill C. Dix** (R-District 25) . . . . . . . . . . . . . . . . . (319) 885-6790
Counties Represented: Butler (part), Grundy, Hardin, Story (part)
Term Expires: 2019
317 South Walnut Street, Shell Rock, IA 50670
E-mail: bill.dix@legis.iowa.gov
Committees: Rules and Administration

**Senator William A. "Bill" Dotzler, Jr.** (D-District 31) . . . . (319) 296-2947
Counties Represented: Black Hawk (part)
Term Expires: 2019
2837 Cedar Terrace Drive, Waterloo, IA 50702-4513
E-mail: bill.dotzler@legis.iowa.gov
Committees: Appropriations; Economic Growth/Rebuild Iowa; Human
Resources; Joint Economic Development Appropriations; Labor and
Business Relations; Ways and Means

**Senator Robert E. Dvorsky** (D-District 37) . . . . . . (319) 625-2650 ext. 125
Counties Represented: Cedar, Johnson (part),        Res: (319) 351-0988
Muscatine (part)
Term Expires: 2019
412 Sixth Street, Coralville, IA 52241
E-mail: robert.dvorsky@legis.iowa.gov
Committees: Appropriations; Education; Joint Health and Human
Services Appropriations; Rules and Administration; State Government;
Transportation
Education: Iowa 1972 BS, 1984 MPA

**Senator Randy Feenstra** (R-District 2) . . . . . . . . . . . . . . . (712) 439-1244
Counties Represented: Cherokee, Plymouth (part), Sioux
Term Expires: 2017
641 Second Street, Hull, IA 51239
E-mail: randy.feenstra@legis.iowa.gov
Committees: State Government; Transportation; Ways and Means

**Senator Julian B. Garrett** (R-District 13) . . . . . . . . . . . . . (515) 971-0883
Counties Represented: Madison, Warren (part)
Term Expires: 2019
19978 - 115 Avenue, Indianola, IA 50125
E-mail: julian.garrett@legis.iowa.gov
Committees: Appropriations; Government Oversight; Human
Resources; Joint Justice System Appropriations; Judiciary

**Senator Michael E. "Mike" Gronstal** (D-District 8) . . . . . . (515) 281-4610
Counties Represented: Pottawattamie (part)        Res: (712) 328-2808
Term Expires: 2017                                Fax: (515) 281-3361
220 Bennett Avenue, Council Bluffs, IA 51503
E-mail: mike.gronstal@legis.iowa.gov
Committees: Rules and Administration

**Senator Dennis Guth** (R-District 4) . . . . . . . . . . . . . . . . . (641) 430-0424
Counties Represented: Emmet, Hancock, Kossuth, Winnebago, Wright
Term Expires: 2017
1770 Taft Avenue, Klemme, IA 50449
E-mail: dennis.guth@legis.iowa.gov
Committees: Economic Growth/Rebuild Iowa; Joint Administration
and Regulation Appropriations; Local Government; Rules and
Administration
Education: Iowa State 1977 BA

**Senator Rita Hart** (D-District 49) . . . . . . . . . . . . . . . . . . . (563) 374-1368
Counties Represented: Clinton, Scott (part)
Term Expires: 2017
2764 - 130th Ave, Wheatland, IA 52777
E-mail: rita.hart@legis.iowa.gov
Committees: Agriculture; Economic Growth/Rebuild Iowa; Education;
Joint Economic Development Appropriations; Local Government;
Veterans Affairs
Education: Northern Iowa BA; Iowa 1988 MA

**Senator Robert M. Hogg** (D-District 33) . . . . . . . . . . . . . (319) 247-0223
Counties Represented: Linn (part)
Term Expires: 2019
2750 Otis Road SE, Cedar Rapids, IA 52403
E-mail: robert.hogg@legis.iowa.gov
Committees: Appropriations; Education; Government Oversight; Joint
Justice System Appropriations; Judiciary; Ways and Means

**Senator Wally E. Horn** (D-District 35) . . . . . . . . . . . . . . . (319) 396-3131
Counties Represented: Linn (part)                Fax: (319) 396-0691
Term Expires: 2019
101 Stoney Point Road, SW, Cedar Rapids, IA 52404
E-mail: wally.horn@legis.iowa.gov
Committees: Ethics; Joint Education Appropriations; Judiciary; State
Government; Transportation; Veterans Affairs
Education: Northeast Missouri State 1958 BS; Texas A&M 1962 MA

**Senator Pam Jochum** (D-District 50) . . . . . . . . . . . . . . . . (563) 556-6530
Counties Represented: Dubuque (part)
Term Expires: 2017
2368 Jackson St., Dubuque, IA 52001-3525
E-mail: pam.jochum@legis.iowa.gov
Committees: Human Resources; Rules and Administration; Ways and
Means

**Senator David J. "Dave" Johnson** (R-District 1) . . . . . . . . (712) 348-2953
Counties Represented: Clay, Dickinson, Lyon, Osceola, Palo Alto
Term Expires: 2019
P.O. Box 279, Ocheyedan, IA 51354-0279
E-mail: david.johnson@legis.iowa.gov
Committees: Education; Human Resources; Joint Health and Human
Services Appropriations; Natural Resources and Environment; State
Government
Education: Beloit 1973 BA

**Senator Tim L. Kapucian** (R-District 38) . . . . . . . . . . . . . (319) 442-5337
Counties Represented: Benton, Iowa, Poweshiek
Term Expires: 2017
1275 - 69th Street, Keystone, IA 52249
E-mail: tim.kapucian@legis.iowa.gov
E-mail: tkgrainandlvstk@hotmail.com
Committees: Agriculture; Appropriations; Joint Transportation,
Infrastructure, and Capitals Appropriations; Transportation

**Senator Kevin Kinney** (D-District 17) . . . . . . . . . . . . . . . . (319) 631-4667
Counties Represented: Polk (part)
Term Expires: 2019
4321 Calkins Ave SW, Oxford, IA 52322
E-mail: kevin.kinney@legis.iowa.gov
Committees: Agriculture; Education; Government Oversight; Joint
Agriculture and Natural Resources Appropriations; Judiciary; Natural
Resources and Environment

**Senator Tim Kraayenbrink** (R-District 5) . . . . . . . . . . . . . (515) 576-0444
Counties Represented: Calhoun, Humboldt,        Res: (515) 576-0417
Pocahontas, Webster (part)
Term Expires: 2019
1561 National Ave, Fort Dodge, IA 50501
E-mail: tim.kraayenbrink@legis.iowa.gov
Committees: Appropriations; Education; Joint Education
Appropriations; Transportation

**Senator Liz Mathis** (D-District 34) . . . . . . . . . . . . . . . . . . (319) 361-1725
Counties Represented: Linn (part)
Term Expires: 2017
1725 Mackenzie Drive Northeast, Cedar Rapids, IA 52411
E-mail: liz.mathis@legis.iowa.gov
Committees: Appropriations; Commerce; Economic Growth/Rebuild
Iowa; Education; Human Resources; Veterans Affairs

**Senator Matthew W. "Matt" McCoy** (D-District 21) . . . . . (515) 681-9327
Counties Represented: Polk (part), Warren (part)
Term Expires: 2019
110 - 35th Street, Des Moines, IA 50312
E-mail: matt.mccoy@legis.iowa.gov
Committees: Appropriations; Commerce; Joint Transportation,
Infrastructure, and Capitals Appropriations; State Government;
Transportation; Ways and Means

**Senator Janet A. Petersen** (D-District 18) . . . . . . . . . . . . . (515) 442-0120
Counties Represented: Polk (part)                Res: (515) 279-9063
Term Expires: 2017
4300 Beaver Hills Drive, Des Moines, IA 50310
E-mail: janet.petersen@legis.iowa.gov
Committees: Commerce; Joint Transportation, Infrastructure, and
Capitals Appropriations; Judiciary; State Government; Ways and Means
Education: Northern Iowa 1992 BA; Drake 1999 MA

**Senator Herman C. Quirmbach** (D-District 23) . . . . . . . . . (515) 292-8984
Counties Represented: Story (part)
Term Expires: 2019
1002 Jarrett Circle, Ames, IA 50014
E-mail: hcqbach@gmail.com
Committees: Education; Joint Education Appropriations; Judiciary;
Local Government; Transportation; Ways and Means
Education: Harvard 1972 BA; Princeton 1980 MEcon, 1983 PhD

LEGISLATIVE BRANCH

Senator **Amanda Ragan** (D-District 27) . . . . . . . . . . . . . (641) 424-2316
Counties Represented: Butler (part), Cerro Gordo     Res: (641) 424-0874
(part), Franklin
Term Expires: 2019
361 S Pennsylvania Ave 1-D, Mason City, IA 50401
E-mail: amanda.ragan@legis.iowa.gov
Committees: Agriculture; Appropriations; Human Resources; Joint
Health and Human Services Appropriations; Natural Resources and
Environment; Rules and Administration; Veterans Affairs
Affiliation: Director, Community Kitchen of North Iowa

Senator **Ken Rozenboom** (R-District 40) . . . . . . . . . . . . . . (641) 295-6551
Counties Represented: Appanoose, Mahaska, Marion (part), Monroe,
Wapello (part)
Term Expires: 2017
2200 Oxford Ave, Oskaloosa, IA 52577
E-mail: ken.rozenboom@legis.iowa.gov
Committees: Agriculture; Appropriations; Joint Agriculture and Natural
Resources Appropriations; Natural Resources and Environment;
Veterans Affairs
Education: Calvin Col (Attended)

Senator **Charles Schneider** (R-District 22) . . . . . . . . . (515) 281-5307
Counties Represented: Dallas (part), Polk (part)
Term Expires: 2017
7887 Cody Drive, West Des Moines, IA 50266
E-mail: charles.schneider@legis.iowa.gov
Committees: Commerce; Economic Growth/Rebuild Iowa; Joint
Economic Development Appropriations; Judiciary

Senator **Brian H. Schoenjahn** (D-District 32) . . . . . . . . . . (563) 933-2218
Counties Represented: Black Hawk (part), Bremer,     Res: (563) 633-4065
Buchanan (part), Fayette (part)
Term Expires: 2017
P.O. Box 132, Arlington, IA 50606
E-mail: brian.schoenjahn@legis.iowa.gov
Committees: Appropriations; Commerce; Education; Government
Oversight; Joint Education Appropriations; Natural Resources and
Environment; State Government

Senator **Jason Schultz** (R-District 9) . . . . . . . . . . . . . . . . (712) 269-2178
Counties Represented: Crawford (part), Harrison, Ida, Monona, Shelby,
Woodbury (part)
Term Expires: 2019
E-mail: jason.schultz@legis.iowa.gov
Committees: Education; Ethics; Joint Agriculture and Natural
Resources Appropriations; State Government; Ways and Means

Senator **Mark Segebart** (R-District 6) . . . . . . . . . . . . . . . (712) 269-4519
Counties Represented: Audubon, Buena Vista, Carroll, Crawford (part),
Sac
Term Expires: 2017
1820 - 350th Street, Vail, IA 51465
E-mail: mark.segebart@legis.iowa.gov
E-mail: mareseg@iowatelecom.net
Committees: Appropriations; Human Resources; Joint Health and
Human Services Appropriations; Veterans Affairs

Senator **Dr. Joseph M. "Joe" Seng** (D-District 45) . . . . . . (563) 322-5522
Counties Represented: Scott (part)     Res: (563) 391-1627
Term Expires: 2019     Fax: (563) 322-9534
4804 Northwest Boulevard, Davenport, IA 52806
E-mail: joe.seng@legis.iowa.gov
Committees: Agriculture; Commerce; Ethics; Labor and Business
Relations; Natural Resources and Environment; Ways and Means
Education: Iowa State BS

Senator **Tom Shipley** (R-District 11) . . . . . . . . . . . . . . . . . (712) 785-3583
Counties Represented: Adams, Cass (part), Pottawattamie (part), Union
Term Expires: 2019
E-mail: tom.shipley@legis.iowa.gov
Committees: Agriculture; Judiciary; Labor and Business Relations;
Natural Resources and Environment

Senator **Amy Sinclair** (R-District 14) . . . . . . . . . . . . . . . . (641) 870-0199
Counties Represented: Clarke, Decatur, Jasper (part), Lucas, Marion
(part), Wayne
Term Expires: 2017
1255 King Road, Allerton, IA 50008
E-mail: amy.sinclair@legis.iowa.gov
Committees: Commerce; Education; Joint Education Appropriations;
Local Government

Senator **Roby Smith** (R-District 47) . . . . . . . . . . . . . . . . . (563) 386-0179
Counties Represented: Scott (part)
Term Expires: 2019
2036 East 48th Street, Davenport, IA 52807
E-mail: roby.smith@legis.iowa.gov
Committees: Commerce; Joint Economic Development Appropriations;
Local Government; Transportation; Ways and Means

Senator **Steven J. "Steve" Sodders** (D-District 36) . . . . . (641) 483-2383
Counties Represented: Black Hawk (part), Marshall, Tama
Term Expires: 2017
2667 Iowa Avenue, Mount Pleasant, IA 52641
E-mail: steve.sodders@legis.iowa.gov
Committees: Agriculture; Commerce; Economic Growth/Rebuild Iowa;
Judiciary; Labor and Business Relations; Rules and Administration;
Veterans Affairs

Senator **Rich Taylor** (D-District 42) . . . . . . . . . . . . . . . . . . (319) 931-1568
Counties Represented: Henry, Jefferson (part), Lee, Washington (part)
Term Expires: 2017
2667 Iowa Avenue, Mount Pleasant, IA 52641
E-mail: rich.taylor@legis.iowa.gov
Committees: Agriculture; Economic Growth/Rebuild Iowa; Joint Justice
System Appropriations; Judiciary; Local Government

Senator **Jack Whitver** (R-District 19) . . . . . . . . . . . . . . . . (515) 865-6394
Counties Represented: Polk (part)
Term Expires: 2019
2819 Southwest Chestnut, Ankeny, IA 50023
E-mail: jack.whitver@legis.iowa.gov
Committees: Government Oversight; Judiciary; Labor and Business
Relations; Rules and Administration; State Government

Senator **Mary Jo Wilhelm** (D-District 26) . . . . . . . . . . . . . (563) 547-4156
Counties Represented: Cerro Gordo (part), Chickasaw, Floyd, Howard,
Mitchell, Winneshiek (part), Worth
Term Expires: 2017
414 North Elm, Cresco, IA 52136
E-mail: mary.jo.wilhelm@legis.iowa.gov
E-mail: mjwilhelm414@msn.com
Committees: Economic Growth/Rebuild Iowa; Education; Joint
Agriculture and Natural Resources Appropriations; Local Government

Senator **Brad Zaun** (R-District 20) . . . . . . . . . . . . . . . . . . (515) 223-4500
Counties Represented: Polk (part)     Res: (515) 276-2025
Term Expires: 2017
7032 Holcomb Avenue, Urbandale, IA 50322
E-mail: brad.zaun@legis.iowa.gov
Committees: Education; Ethics; Judiciary

Senator **Dan Zumbach** (R-District 48) . . . . . . . . . . . . . . . (563) 920-5094
Counties Represented: Buchanan (part), Delaware, Jones (part), Linn
(part)
Term Expires: 2017
2618 - 140th Ave, Ryan, IA 52330
E-mail: dan.zumbach@legis.iowa.gov
Committees: Agriculture; Appropriations; Commerce; Joint
Administration and Regulation Appropriations; Natural Resources and
Environment

# Senate Standing Committees

## Agriculture

| Majority Members | Minority Members |
|---|---|
| Dr. Joseph M. "Joe" Seng (D-45) *Chair* | Dan Zumbach (R-48) *Ranking Member* |
| Amanda Ragan (D-27) *Vice Chair* | Bill Anderson (R-3) |
| Tod R. Bowman (D-29) | Tim L. Kapucian (R-38) |
| Chris Brase (D-46) | Ken Rozenboom (R-40) |
| Rita Hart (D-49) | Tom Shipley (R-11) |
| Kevin Kinney (D-17) | |
| Steven J. "Steve" Sodders (D-36) | |
| Rich Taylor (D-42) | |

## Appropriations

| Majority Members | Minority Members |
|---|---|
| Robert E. Dvorsky (D-37) *Chair* | Jacob "Jake" Chapman (R-10) *Ranking Member* |
| Jeff Danielson (D-30) *Vice Chair* | Julian B. Garrett (R-13) |
| Joseph L. "Joe" Bolkcom (D-43) | Tim L. Kapucian (R-38) |
| Thomas G. "Tom" Courtney (D-44) | Tim Kraayenbrink (R-5) |
| William A. "Bill" Dotzler, Jr. (D-31) | Ken Rozenboom (R-40) |
| Robert M. Hogg (D-33) | Mark Segebart (R-6) |
| Liz Mathis (D-34) | Dan Zumbach (R-48) |
| Matthew W. "Matt" McCoy (D-21) | |
| Amanda Ragan (D-27) | |
| Brian H. Schoenjahn (D-32) | |

## Commerce

**Majority Members**
Janet A. Petersen (D-18) *Chair*
Matthew W. "Matt" McCoy (D-21) *Vice Chair*
Joseph L. "Joe" Bolkcom (D-43)
Thomas G. "Tom" Courtney (D-44)
Liz Mathis (D-34)
Brian H. Schoenjahn (D-32)
Dr. Joseph M. "Joe" Seng (D-45)
Steven J. "Steve" Sodders (D-36)

**Minority Members**
Bill Anderson (R-3) *Ranking Member*
Rick Bertrand (R-7)
Charles Schneider (R-22)
Amy Sinclair (R-14)
Roby Smith (R-47)
Dan Zumbach (R-48)

## Economic Growth/Rebuild Iowa

**Majority Members**
Rita Hart (D-49) *Chair*
Steven J. "Steve" Sodders (D-36) *Vice Chair*
Tony Bisignano (D-17)
Tod R. Bowman (D-29)
Jeff Danielson (D-30)
William A. "Bill" Dotzler, Jr. (D-31)
Liz Mathis (D-34)
Rich Taylor (D-42)
Mary Jo Wilhelm (D-26)

**Minority Members**
Mark Chelgren (R-41) *Ranking Member*
Jacob "Jake" Chapman (R-10)
Bill Anderson (R-3)
Michael Breitbach (R-28)
Dennis Guth (R-4)
Charles Schneider (R-22)

## Education

**Majority Members**
Herman C. Quirmbach (D-23) *Chair*
Brian H. Schoenjahn (D-32) *Vice Chair*
Tod R. Bowman (D-29)
Robert E. Dvorsky (D-37)
Rita Hart (D-49)
Robert M. Hogg (D-33)
Kevin Kinney (D-17)
Liz Mathis (D-34)
Mary Jo Wilhelm (D-26)

**Minority Members**
Amy Sinclair (R-14) *Ranking Member*
Jerry Behn (R-24)
David J. "Dave" Johnson (R-1)
Tim Kraayenbrink (R-5)
Jason Schultz (R-9)
Brad Zaun (R-20)

## Ethics

**Majority Members**
Wally E. Horn (D-35) *Chair*
Dick L. Dearden (D-16) *Vice Chair*
Dr. Joseph M. "Joe" Seng (D-45)

**Minority Members**
Jason Schultz (R-9) *Ranking Member*
Jerry Behn (R-24)
Brad Zaun (R-20)

## Government Oversight

**Majority Members**
Robert M. Hogg (D-33) *Chair*
Brian H. Schoenjahn (D-32) *Vice Chair*
Kevin Kinney (D-17)

**Minority Members**
Julian B. Garrett (R-13) *Ranking Member*
Jack Whitver (R-19)

## Human Resources

**Majority Members**
Liz Mathis (D-34) *Chair*
Amanda Ragan (D-27) *Vice Chair*
Joseph L. "Joe" Bolkcom (D-43)
William A. "Bill" Dotzler, Jr. (D-31)
Pam Jochum (D-50)

**Minority Members**
David J. "Dave" Johnson (R-1) *Ranking Member*
Mark Chelgren (R-41)
Mark Costello (R-12)
Julian B. Garrett (R-13)
Mark Segebart (R-6)

## Judiciary

**Majority Members**
Steven J. "Steve" Sodders (D-36) *Chair*
Robert M. Hogg (D-33) *Vice Chair*
Tony Bisignano (D-17)
Wally E. Horn (D-35)
Kevin Kinney (D-17)
Janet A. Petersen (D-18)
Herman C. Quirmbach (D-23)
Rich Taylor (D-42)

**Minority Members**
Charles Schneider (R-22) *Ranking Member*
Julian B. Garrett (R-13)
Tom Shipley (R-11)
Jack Whitver (R-19)
Brad Zaun (R-20)

## Labor and Business Relations

**Majority Members**
Tony Bisignano (D-17) *Chair*
Dr. Joseph M. "Joe" Seng (D-45) *Vice Chair*
Chris Brase (D-46)
William A. "Bill" Dotzler, Jr. (D-31)
Steven J. "Steve" Sodders (D-36)

**Minority Members**
Tom Shipley (R-11) *Ranking Member*
Rick Bertrand (R-7)
Mark Costello (R-12)
Jack Whitver (R-19)

## Local Government

**Majority Members**
Rich Taylor (D-42) *Chair*
Mary Jo Wilhelm (D-26) *Vice Chair*
Chaz Allen (D-15)
Tony Bisignano (D-17)
Rita Hart (D-49)
Herman C. Quirmbach (D-23)

**Minority Members**
Roby Smith (R-47) *Ranking Member*
Michael Breitbach (R-28)
Dennis Guth (R-4)
Amy Sinclair (R-14)

## Natural Resources and Environment

**Majority Members**
Dick L. Dearden (D-16) *Chair*
Chris Brase (D-46) *Vice Chair*
Joseph L. "Joe" Bolkcom (D-43)
Kevin Kinney (D-17)
Amanda Ragan (D-27)
Brian H. Schoenjahn (D-32)
Dr. Joseph M. "Joe" Seng (D-45)

**Minority Members**
Ken Rozenboom (R-40) *Ranking Member*
Jerry Behn (R-24)
David J. "Dave" Johnson (R-1)
Tom Shipley (R-11)
Dan Zumbach (R-48)

## Rules and Administration

**Majority Members**
Michael E. "Mike" Gronstal (D-8) *Chair*
Pam Jochum (D-50) *Vice Chair*
Thomas G. "Tom" Courtney (D-44)
Dick L. Dearden (D-16)
Robert E. Dvorsky (D-37)
Amanda Ragan (D-27)
Steven J. "Steve" Sodders (D-36)

**Minority Members**
Bill C. Dix (R-25) *Ranking Member*
Jacob "Jake" Chapman (R-10)
Dennis Guth (R-4)
Jack Whitver (R-19)

## State Government

**Majority Members**
Jeff Danielson (D-30) *Chair*
Thomas G. "Tom" Courtney (D-44) *Vice Chair*
Tod R. Bowman (D-29)
Dick L. Dearden (D-16)
Robert E. Dvorsky (D-37)
Wally E. Horn (D-35)
Matthew W. "Matt" McCoy (D-21)
Janet A. Petersen (D-18)
Brian H. Schoenjahn (D-32)

**Minority Members**
Rick Bertrand (R-7) *Ranking Member*
Jacob "Jake" Chapman (R-10)
Randy Feenstra (R-2)
David J. "Dave" Johnson (R-1)
Jason Schultz (R-9)
Jack Whitver (R-19)

## Transportation

**Majority Members**
Tod R. Bowman (D-29) *Chair*
Robert E. Dvorsky (D-37) *Vice Chair*
Chris Brase (D-46)
Jeff Danielson (D-30)
Dick L. Dearden (D-16)
Wally E. Horn (D-35)
Matthew W. "Matt" McCoy (D-21)
Herman C. Quirmbach (D-23)

**Minority Members**
Tim L. Kapucian (R-38) *Ranking Member*
Michael Breitbach (R-28)
Randy Feenstra (R-2)
Tim Kraayenbrink (R-5)
Roby Smith (R-47)

## Veterans Affairs

**Majority Members**
Wally E. Horn (D-35) *Chair*
Jeff Danielson (D-30) *Vice Chair*
Chaz Allen (D-15)
Rita Hart (D-49)
Liz Mathis (D-34)
Steven J. "Steve" Sodders (D-36)
Amanda Ragan (D-27)

**Minority Members**
Mark Segebart (R-6) *Ranking Member*
Mark Chelgren (R-41)
Mark Costello (R-12)
Ken Rozenboom (R-40)

## Ways and Means

| Majority Members | Minority Members |
|---|---|
| Joseph L. "Joe" Bolkcom (D-43) *Chair* | Randy Feenstra (R-2) *Ranking Member* |
| Chaz Allen (D-15) *Vice Chair* | Bill Anderson (R-3) |
| William A. "Bill" Dotzler, Jr. (D-31) | Jerry Behn (R-24) |
| Robert M. Hogg (D-33) | Michael Breitbach (R-28) |
| Pam Jochum (D-50) | Jason Schultz (R-9) |
| Matthew W. "Matt" McCoy (D-21) | Roby Smith (R-47) |
| Janet A. Petersen (D-18) | |
| Herman C. Quirmbach (D-23) | |
| Dr. Joseph M. "Joe" Seng (D-45) | |

# Iowa House of Representatives

Tel: (515) 281-3221

Speaker of the House **Linda L. Upmeyer** (R) . . . . . . . . . . (641) 923-3398
Speaker Pro Tem **Matt W. Windschitl** (R) . . . . . . . . . . . . (712) 642-4334
Majority Leader **Chris Hagenow** (R) . . . . . . . . . . . . . . . . (641) 923-3398
Majority Whip **Joel Fry** (R) . . . . . . . . . . . . . . . . . . . . . . . (515) 274-1652
Assistant Majority Leader **Lee Hein** (R) . . . . . . . . . . . . . . (515) 281-3221
Assistant Majority Leader **Jarad Klein** (R) . . . . . . . . . . . . (515) 281-3221
Assistant Majority Leader **Zach Nunn** (R) . . . . . . . . . . . . (515) 281-3221
Assistant Majority Leader **Walt Rogers** (R) . . . . . . . . . . . (515) 281-3221
  Education: Northern Iowa 1984 BTech
Minority Leader **Mark D. Smith, ACSW, LISW** (D) . . . . . . (515) 281-3221
  Education: Graceland Col BA; Iowa MSW
Assistant Minority Leader **Ako Abdul-Samad** (D) . . . . . . . (515) 281-4280
Assistant Minority Leader **Mary Gaskill** (D) . . . . . . . . . . . (641) 682-6417
Assistant Minority Leader **Todd Prichard** (D) . . . . . . . . . . (515) 281-3221
  Education: Iowa 1998 BA, 2004 JD
Assistant Minority Leader **Sharon S. Steckman** (D) . . . . . (641) 424-9362
Chief Clerk of the House **Carmine R. Boal** (R) . . . . . . . . . (515) 281-5381
Sergeant-at-Arms **Donald L. "Don" Wederquist** . . . . . . . . (515) 281-5381

## Representatives

**Party Affiliation Statistics:** Republicans: 57, Democrats: 43

Representative **Ako Abdul-Samad** (D-District 35) . . . . . . . (515) 281-4280
  Counties Represented: Polk (part)        Res: (515) 288-3066
  Term Expires: 2017
  E-mail: ako.abdul-samad@legis.iowa.gov
  Committees: Administration and Rules; Education; Human Resources;
  Public Safety

Representative **Marti Anderson** (D-District 36) . . . . . . . . . (515) 281-3221
  Counties Represented: Polk (part)
  Term Expires: 2017
  E-mail: marti.anderson@legis.iowa.gov
  Committees: Administration and Rules; Environmental Protection;
  Human Resources; Joint Justice System Appropriations; Judiciary;
  Public Safety
  Education: Northern Iowa BSocW; Iowa MSSW

Representative **Robert Bacon** (R-District 48) . . . . . . . . . . . (515) 387-8969
  Counties Represented: Boone (part), Hamilton, Story (part), Webster
  (part)
  Term Expires: 2017
  302 3rd Avenue,, #1, Slater, IA 50244
  E-mail: rob.bacon@legis.iowa.gov
  Committees: Appropriations; Human Resources; Joint Health and
  Human Services Appropriations; Natural Resources; State Government

Representative **Chip Baltimore** (R-District 47) . . . . . . . . . . (515) 281-3221
  Counties Represented: Boone (part), Greene
  Term Expires: 2017
  521 South Delaware Street, Boone, IA 50036
  E-mail: chip.baltimore@legis.iowa.gov
  Committees: Commerce; Joint Justice System Appropriations;
  Judiciary; Ways and Means

Representative **Clel E. Baudler** (R-District 20) . . . . . . . . . . (515) 281-3221
  Counties Represented: Adair, Cass (part), Dallas    Res: (641) 743-6327
  (part), Guthrie
  Term Expires: 2017
  2260 Highway 25, Greenfield, IA 50849
  E-mail: clel.baudler@legis.iowa.gov
  Committees: Environmental Protection; Government Oversight; Natural
  Resources; Public Safety

Representative **Terry C. Baxter** (R-District 8) . . . . . . . . . . . (515) 281-3221
  Counties Represented: Hancock, Kossuth (part), Wright
  Term Expires: 2017
  E-mail: terry.baxter@legis.iowa.gov
  Committees: Environmental Protection; Joint Economic Development
  Appropriations; Judiciary; Local Government; Public Safety

Representative **Bruce Bearinger** (D-District 64) . . . . . . . . . (515) 281-4280
  Counties Represented: Buchanan (part), Fayette (part)
  Term Expires: 2017
  E-mail: bruce.bearinger@legis.iowa.gov
  Committees: Agriculture; Appropriations; Economic Growth/Rebuild
  Iowa; Veterans Affairs
  Education: Iowa State MS

Representative **Liz Bennett** (D-District 65) . . . . . . . . . . . . . (515) 281-3221
  Counties Represented: Linn (part)
  Term Expires: 2017
  E-mail: liz.bennett@legis.iowa.gov
  Committees: Economic Growth/Rebuild Iowa; Environmental Protection

Representative **Deborah L. Berry** (D-District 62) . . . . . . . . . (319) 233-9934
  Counties Represented: Black Hawk (part)
  Term Expires: 2017
  208 Greenbrier Road, Waterloo, IA 50703
  E-mail: deborah.berry@legis.iowa.gov
  Committees: Administration and Rules; Ethics; Joint Administration
  and Regulation Appropriations; Judiciary; State Government

Representative **Brian Best** (R-District 12) . . . . . . . . . . . . . . (515) 281-3221
  Counties Represented: Audubon, Carroll, Crawford (part)
  Term Expires: 2017
  E-mail: brian.best@legis.iowa.gov
  Committees: Economic Growth/Rebuild Iowa; Human Resources; Joint
  Health and Human Services Appropriations; Natural Resources;
  Transportation

Representative **Darrel Branhagen** (R-District 55) . . . . . . . . (515) 281-3221
  Counties Represented: Clayton (part), Fayette (part), Winneshiek (part)
  Term Expires: 2017
  E-mail: darrel.branhagen@legis.iowa.gov
  Committees: Joint Justice System Appropriations; Judiciary; Local
  Government; State Government; Veterans Affairs

Representative **Timi Brown-Powers** (D-District 61) . . . . . . (515) 281-3221
  Counties Represented: Black Hawk (part)
  Term Expires: 2017
  E-mail: timi.brown-powers@legis.iowa.gov
  Committees: Education; Human Resources; Joint Administration and
  Regulation Appropriations; Public Safety; Ways and Means

Representative **Joshua Byrnes** (R-District 51) . . . . . . . . . . . (515) 281-3221
  Counties Represented: Howard, Mitchell, Winneshiek (part), Worth
  Term Expires: 2017
  1479 - 308th Street, Osage, IA 50461
  E-mail: josh.byrnes@legis.iowa.gov
  Committees: Agriculture; Education; Transportation; Ways and Means

Representative **Gary Carlson** (R-District 91) . . . . . . . . . . . . (515) 281-3221
  Counties Represented: Muscatine (part)
  Term Expires: 2017
  E-mail: gary.carlson@legis.iowa.gov
  Committees: Commerce; Economic Growth/Rebuild Iowa;
  Joint Economic Development Appropriations; Local Government;
  Transportation

Representative **Dennis M. Cohoon** (D-District 87) . . . . . . . (319) 753-2211
  Counties Represented: Des Moines (part)     Res: (319) 752-5057
  Term Expires: 2017
  816 Randall Lane, Burlington, IA 52601
  E-mail: dennis.cohoon@legis.iowa.gov
  Committees: Education; Joint Transportation, Infrastructure, and
  Capitals Appropriations; State Government; Transportation
  Education: Iowa Wesleyan 1977 BA

Representative **Peter Cownie** (R-District 42) . . . . . . . . . . . . (515) 281-3221
  Counties Represented: Polk (part), Warren (part)    Res: (515) 664-8341
  Term Expires: 2017
  686 58th Place, Des Moines, IA 50266
  E-mail: peter.cownie@legis.iowa.gov
  Committees: Agriculture; Commerce; Ways and Means

Representative
**David Alan "Dave" Dawson** (D-District 14) . . . . . . . . . . (515) 281-4280
  Counties Represented: Woodbury (part)
  Term Expires: 2017
  400 Essex Street, Sioux City, IA 51103
  E-mail: dave.dawson@legis.iowa.gov
  Committees: Commerce; Ethics; Human Resources; Joint
  Transportation, Infrastructure, and Capitals Appropriations; Judiciary;
  Transportation
  Education: Iowa State 1996 BS; UCLA 1999 JD

*(continued on next page)*

**Representatives** *continued*

Representative **Dave Deyoe** (R-District 49) . . . . . . . . . . . (515) 382-2382
Counties Represented: Hardin (part), Story (part)   Dist: (515) 291-3289
Term Expires: 2017   Res: (515) 382-2352
911 Shagbark Drive, Nevada, IA 50201
E-mail: dave.deyoe@legis.iowa.gov
Committees: Agriculture; Appropriations; Economic Growth/Rebuild
Iowa; Environmental Protection; Joint Economic Development
Appropriations

Representative **Cecil Dolecheck** (R-District 24) . . . . . . . . . (515) 281-3221
Counties Represented: Montgomery (part), Page,   Tel: (641) 464-2913
Ringgold, Taylor
Term Expires: 2017
703 North Fillmore, Mount Ayr, IA 50854
E-mail: cecil.dolecheck@legis.iowa.gov
Committees: Agriculture; Appropriations; Education; Joint Education
Appropriations

Representative **Nancy A. Dunkel** (D-District 57) . . . . . . . . (515) 281-4280
Counties Represented: Dubuque (part)
Term Expires: 2017
E-mail: nancy.dunkel@legis.iowa.gov
Committees: Agriculture; Appropriations; Economic Growth/Rebuild
Iowa; Joint Transportation, Infrastructure, and Capitals Appropriations;
Veterans Affairs
Education: Loras (Attended)

Representative **Abby Finkenauer** (R-District 99) . . . . . . . . (515) 281-3221
Counties Represented: Dubuque (part)
Term Expires: 2017
E-mail: abby.finkenauer@legis.iowa.gov
Committees: Economic Growth/Rebuild Iowa; Joint Economic
Development Appropriations; Labor; Transportation; Ways and Means

Representative **Dean C. Fisher** (R-District 72) . . . . . . . . . . (515) 281-4280
Counties Represented: Black Hawk (part), Marshall (part), Tama
Term Expires: 2017
E-mail: dean.fisher@legis.iowa.gov
Committees: Appropriations; Joint Education Appropriations; Natural
Resources; Public Safety
Education: DeVry Inst 1978 BEE

Representative **John Forbes** (D-District 40) . . . . . . . . . . . . (515) 281-4280
Counties Represented: Polk (part)
Term Expires: 2017
E-mail: john.forbes@legis.iowa.gov
Committees: Appropriations; Commerce; Joint Health and Human
Services Appropriations; Local Government
Education: Drake 1980 BSPh

Representative **Greg Forristall** (R-District 22) . . . . . . . . . . (515) 281-3221
Counties Represented: Pottawattamie (part)   Res: (712) 486-2271
Term Expires: 2017
11917 370th Street, Macedonia, IA 51549
E-mail: greg.forristall@legis.iowa.gov
Committees: Education; Human Resources; Labor; Ways and Means

Representative **Joel Fry** (R-District 27) . . . . . . . . . . . . . . . (515) 281-3221
Counties Represented: Clarke, Decatur, Lucas   Res: (641) 342-1017
(part), Wayne
Term Expires: 2017
1473 195th Avenue, Osceola, IA 50213
E-mail: joel.fry@legis.iowa.gov
Committees: Administration and Rules; Education; Human Resources;
Labor; Public Safety

Representative **Ruth Ann Gaines** (D-District 32) . . . . . . . . (515) 281-3221
Counties Represented: Polk (part)
Term Expires: 2017
3501 Oxford, Des Moines, IA 50313
E-mail: ruthann.gaines@legis.iowa.gov
Committees: Education; Government Oversight; Human Resources;
Public Safety; Veterans Affairs

Representative **Mary Gaskill** (D-District 81) . . . . . . . . . . . . (641) 682-6417
Counties Represented: Wapello (part)
Term Expires: 2017
509 East 4th Street, Ottumwa, IA 52501
E-mail: mary.gaskill@legis.iowa.gov
Committees: Administration and Rules; Economic Growth/Rebuild
Iowa; Local Government; Ways and Means

Representative **Tedd Gassman** (R-District 7) . . . . . . . . . . . (515) 281-4280
Counties Represented: Emmet, Kossuth (part), Winnebago
Term Expires: 2017
E-mail: tedd.gassman@legis.iowa.gov
Committees: Education; Environmental Protection; Joint Administration
and Regulation Appropriations; Labor; Local Government

Representative **Patrick "Pat" Grassley** (R-District 50) . . . . (515) 281-3221
Counties Represented: Butler (part), Grundy, Hardin   Res: (319) 983-9019
(part)
Term Expires: 2017
30601 Deer Trail Drive, New Hartford, IA 50660
E-mail: pat.grassley@legis.iowa.gov
Committees: Appropriations; Commerce

Representative **Stan Gustafson** (R-District 25) . . . . . . . . . (515) 281-3221
Counties Represented: Madison, Warren (part)
Term Expires: 2017
19978 - 115 Avenue, Indianola, IA 50125
E-mail: stan.gustafson@legis.iowa.gov
Committees: Economic Growth/Rebuild Iowa; Human Resources; Joint
Justice System Appropriations; Judiciary; Veterans Affairs

Representative **Chris Hagenow** (R-District 43) . . . . . . . . . (515) 281-3221
Counties Represented: Polk (part)   Res: (515) 274-1652
Term Expires: 2017
1915 69th Street, Des Moines, IA 50322
E-mail: chris.hagenow@legis.iowa.gov
Committees: Administration and Rules

Representative **Christopher "Chris" Hall** (D-District 13) . . (515) 281-3221
Counties Represented: Woodbury (part)
Term Expires: 2017
3800 Glen Oaks Boulevard, Sioux City, IA 51104
E-mail: chris.hall@legis.iowa.gov
Committees: Appropriations; Commerce; Natural Resources

Representative **Curtis "Curt" Hanson** (D-District 82) . . . . (515) 281-3221
Counties Represented: Davis, Jefferson (part), Van Buren
Term Expires: 2017
801 North Court Street, Fairfield, IA 52556
E-mail: curt.hanson@legis.iowa.gov
Committees: Agriculture; Education; Environmental Protection; Joint
Education Appropriations; Natural Resources

Representative **Mary Ann Hanusa** (R-District 16) . . . . . . . (515) 281-3221
Counties Represented: Pottawattamie (part)
Term Expires: 2017
121 Fox Haven Drive, Council Bluffs, IA 51503
E-mail: maryann.hanusa@legis.iowa.gov
Committees: Economic Growth/Rebuild Iowa; Education; Joint
Economic Development Appropriations; Labor; Transportation

Representative **Greg T. Heartsill** (R-District 28) . . . . . . . . . (515) 281-4280
Counties Represented: Jasper (part), Lucas (part), Marion (part)
Term Expires: 2017
E-mail: greg.heartsill@legis.iowa.gov
Committees: Environmental Protection; Government Oversight;
Judiciary; Local Government; Public Safety
Education: Buena Vista Col 1993 BBA

Representative **David E. Heaton** (R-District 84) . . . . . . . . . (319) 385-2241
Counties Represented: Henry, Jefferson (part), Lee   Res: (319) 385-9342
(part), Washington (part)
Term Expires: 2017
510 East Washington Street, Mount Pleasant, IA 52641
E-mail: dave.heaton@legis.iowa.gov
Committees: Appropriations; Human Resources; Joint Health and
Human Services Appropriations; Judiciary
Education: Iowa Wesleyan 1964 BA

Representative **Lisa Heddens** (D-District 46) . . . . . . . . . . . (515) 281-3221
Counties Represented: Story (part)   Tel: (515) 243-1713
Term Expires: 2017   Res: (515) 292-1748
4541 513th Avenue, Ames, IA 50010
E-mail: lisa.heddens@legis.iowa.gov
Committees: Appropriations; Human Resources; Joint Health and
Human Services Appropriations; Natural Resources

Representative **Lee Hein** (R-District 96) . . . . . . . . . . . . . . . (515) 281-3221
Counties Represented: Delaware, Jones (part)
Term Expires: 2017
11989 Richland Road, Monticello, IA 52310
E-mail: lee.hein@legis.iowa.gov
Committees: Agriculture; State Government; Transportation; Ways and
Means

Representative **Jake Highfill** (R-District 39) . . . . . . . . . . . . (515) 281-4280
Counties Represented: Polk (part)
Term Expires: 2017
9805 Skyline Circle, Johnston, IA 50131
E-mail: jake.highfill@legis.iowa.gov
Committees: Education; Government Oversight; Joint Transportation,
Infrastructure, and Capitals Appropriations; Local Government; State
Government
Education: Iowa BB

Representative **Steven Holt** (R-District 18) . . . . . . . . . . . . (515) 281-3221
Counties Represented: Crawford (part), Harrison (part), Shelby
Term Expires: 2017
E-mail: steven.holt@legis.iowa.gov
Committees: Commerce; Joint Justice System Appropriations; Labor;
Public Safety; Veterans Affairs

Representative **Charles "Chuck" Holz** (R-District 5) . . . . . (515) 281-4280
Counties Represented: Plymouth (part), Woodbury (part)
Term Expires: 2017
17585 Lake Avenue, Le Mars, IA 51031
E-mail: chuck.holz@legis.iowa.gov
Committees: Agriculture; Commerce; Economic Growth/Rebuild Iowa;
Transportation

Representative **Bruce L. Hunter** (D-District 34) . . . . . . . . . (515) 256-8010
Counties Represented: Polk (part)
Term Expires: 2017
452 Wilmers Avenue, Des Moines, IA 50315
E-mail: bruce.hunter@legis.iowa.gov
Committees: Joint Administration and Regulation Appropriations;
Labor; Local Government; State Government

Representative **Daniel A. Huseman** (R-District 3) . . . . . . . (515) 281-4280
Counties Represented: Cherokee, Plymouth (part),　　Res: (712) 434-5880
Sioux (part)
Term Expires: 2017
6144 Y Avenue, Aurelia, IA 51005
E-mail: dan.huseman@legis.iowa.gov
Committees: Appropriations; Joint Transportation, Infrastructure, and
Capitals Appropriations; Natural Resources; Transportation

Representative
**Charles "Chuck" Isenhart** (D-District 100) . . . . . . . . . . (515) 281-3221
Counties Represented: Dubuque (part)　　Res: (563) 557-1261
Term Expires: 2017
P.O. Box 3353, Dubuque, IA 52004
E-mail: charles.isenhart@legis.iowa.gov
Committees: Economic Growth/Rebuild Iowa; Environmental
Protection; Joint Agriculture and Natural Resources Appropriations;
Ways and Means

Representative **David "Dave" Jacoby** (D-District 74) . . . . . (319) 354-2272
Counties Represented: Johnson (part)　　Res: (319) 358-8538
Term Expires: 2017
2308 Northridge Drive, Coralville, IA 52241
E-mail: david.jacoby@legis.iowa.gov
Committees: Commerce; Transportation; Ways and Means
Education: Northern Iowa BA

Representative **Megan Jones** (R-District 2) . . . . . . . . . . . . (515) 281-4280
Counties Represented: Clay, Dickinson (part), Palo Alto
Term Expires: 2017
606 11th Ave SW, Spencer, IA 51301
E-mail: megan.hess@legis.iowa.gov
Committees: Environmental Protection; Joint Agriculture and Natural
Resources Appropriations; Judiciary; Local Government
Education: William Mitchell 2011 (Attended); Drake BA

Representative **Ron Jorgensen** (R-District 6) . . . . . . . . . . (515) 281-3221
Counties Represented: Woodbury (part)
Term Expires: 2017
5921 Pine View Drive, Sioux City, IA 51106
E-mail: ron.jorgensen@legis.iowa.gov
Committees: Economic Growth/Rebuild Iowa; Education; Ethics; Labor

Representative **Bobby Kaufmann** (R-District 73) . . . . . . . (515) 281-4280
Counties Represented: Cedar, Johnson (part), Muscatine (part)
Term Expires: 2017
1527 330th Street, Wilton, IA 52778
E-mail: bobby.kaufmann@legis.iowa.gov
Committees: Commerce; Government Oversight; Judiciary; Local
Government; Veterans Affairs

Representative **Jerry A. Kearns** (D-District 83) . . . . . . . . . (515) 281-3221
Counties Represented: Lee (part)　　Res: (319) 524-1570
Term Expires: 2017
402 Hickory Terrace, Keokuk, IA 52632
E-mail: jerry.kearns@legis.iowa.gov
Committees: Agriculture; Joint Justice System Appropriations; Labor;
Veterans Affairs; Ways and Means

Representative **Daniel Kelley** (D-District 29) . . . . . . . . . . . (515) 281-3221
Counties Represented: Jasper (part)
Term Expires: 2017
P.O. Box 333, Newton, IA 50208
E-mail: dan.kelley@legis.iowa.gov
Committees: Agriculture; Environmental Protection; Joint
Administration and Regulation Appropriations; State Government;
Ways and Means

Representative **Jarad Klein** (R-District 78) . . . . . . . . . . . . . (515) 281-3221
Counties Represented: Keokuk, Washington (part)
Term Expires: 2017
1744 Keokuk Washington Road, Keota, IA 52248
E-mail: jarad.klein@legis.iowa.gov
Committees: Administration and Rules; Agriculture; Environmental
Protection; Natural Resources; Public Safety

Representative **Kevin Koester** (R-District 38) . . . . . . . . . . (515) 281-3221
Counties Represented: Polk (part)　　Res: (515) 963-9996
Term Expires: 2017
E-mail: kevin.koester@legis.iowa.gov
Committees: Education; Local Government; Natural Resources; State
Government

Representative **John Kooiker** (R-District 4) . . . . . . . . . . . . (515) 281-3221
Counties Represented: Sioux (part)
Term Expires: 2017
E-mail: john.kooiker@legis.iowa.gov
Committees: Joint Transportation, Infrastructure, and Capitals
Appropriations; Labor; Local Government; Public Safety; Veterans
Affairs

Representative **Bob M. Kressig** (D-District 59) . . . . . . . . . (515) 281-3221
Counties Represented: Black Hawk (part)　　Res: (319) 266-9021
Term Expires: 2017
3523 Veralta Drive, Cedar Falls, IA 50613
E-mail: bob.kressig@legis.iowa.gov
Committees: Commerce; Environmental Protection; Joint Economic
Development Appropriations; Local Government; Public Safety

Representative **John Landon** (R-District 37) . . . . . . . . . . . (515) 281-4280
Counties Represented: Polk (part)
Term Expires: 2017
525 NE Stone Valley Drive, Ankeny, IA 50021
E-mail: john.landon@legis.iowa.gov
Committees: Appropriations; Commerce; Joint Administration and
Regulation Appropriations; Transportation
Education: Iowa State BSA

Representative **Vicki S. Lensing** (D-District 85) . . . . . . . . (319) 338-8171
Counties Represented: Johnson (part)　　Res: (319) 338-6148
Term Expires: 2017
2408 Mayfield Road, Iowa City, IA 52245
E-mail: vicki.lensing@legis.iowa.gov
Committees: Environmental Protection; Government Oversight; Local
Government; State Government

Representative **Jim Lykam** (D-District 89) . . . . . . . . . . . . . (563) 391-1919
Counties Represented: Scott (part)
Term Expires: 2017
2906 West 35th Street, Davenport, IA 52806
E-mail: jim.lykam@legis.iowa.gov
Committees: Commerce; Joint Transportation, Infrastructure, and
Capitals Appropriations; Natural Resources; Transportation

Representative **Mary S. Mascher** (D-District 86) . . . . . . . . (319) 351-2826
Counties Represented: Johnson (part)
Term Expires: 2017
40 Gryn Court, Iowa City, IA 52246
E-mail: mary.mascher@legis.iowa.gov
Committees: Appropriations; Education; Local Government; State
Government

Representative
**David E. "Dave" Maxwell** (R-District 76) . . . . . . . . . . . (515) 281-4280
Counties Represented: Iowa (part), Poweshiek
Term Expires: 2017
E-mail: dave.maxwell@legis.iowa.gov
Committees: Agriculture; Joint Transportation, Infrastructure, and
Capitals Appropriations; Natural Resources; Transportation; Ways and
Means

Representative **Charlie McConkey** (D-District 15) . . . . . . . . (515) 281-3221
Counties Represented: Pottawattamie (part)
Term Expires: 2017
E-mail: charlie.mcconkey@legis.iowa.gov
Committees: Economic Growth/Rebuild Iowa; Human Resources;
Labor; Ways and Means

Representative **Brian Meyer** (D-District 33) . . . . . . . . . . . . (515) 281-3054
Counties Represented: Polk (part)　　Res: (515) 953-5221
Term Expires: 2017
E-mail: brian.meyer@legis.iowa.gov
Committees: Commerce; Joint Justice System Appropriations;
Judiciary; Local Government; Veterans Affairs

Representative **Helen Miller** (D-District 9) . . . . . . . . . . . . . (515) 281-3221
Counties Represented: Webster (part)　　Tel: (515) 570-3535
Term Expires: 2017
P.O. Box 675, Fort Dodge, IA 50501
E-mail: helen.miller@legis.iowa.gov
Committees: Agriculture; Economic Growth/Rebuild Iowa; Joint
Agriculture and Natural Resources Appropriations; Natural Resources

*LEGISLATIVE BRANCH*

*(continued on next page)*

**Representatives** *continued*

Representative **Linda J. Miller** (R-District 94) . . . . . . . . . . (515) 281-3221
Counties Represented: Scott (part)          Res: (563) 449-9956
Term Expires: 2017
6766 Ridges Court, Bettendorf, IA 52722
E-mail: linda.miller@legis.iowa.gov
Committees: Human Resources; Joint Health and Human Services
Appropriations; State Government; Ways and Means
Education: Drake; Iowa 1968

Representative **Norlin Mommsen** (R-District 97) . . . . . . . . (515) 281-3221
Counties Represented: Clinton (part), Scott (part)
Term Expires: 2017
E-mail: norlin.mommsen@legis.iowa.gov
Committees: Agriculture; Appropriations; Joint Agriculture and Natural
Resources Appropriations; Natural Resources

Representative **Brian Moore** (R-District 58) . . . . . . . . . . . (515) 281-3221
Counties Represented: Dubuque (part), Jackson, Jones (part)
Term Expires: 2017
8054 Warren Drive, Des Moines, IA 50320
E-mail: brian.moore@legis.iowa.gov
Committees: Agriculture; Natural Resources; Public Safety;
Transportation; Ways and Means

Representative **Tom Moore** (R-District 21) . . . . . . . . . . . . . (515) 281-5381
Counties Represented: Adams, Cass (part), Pottawattamie (part), Union
Term Expires: 2017
E-mail: tom.moore@legis.iowa.gov
Committees: Education; Environmental Protection; Human Resources;
State Government

Representative **Zach Nunn** (R-District 30) . . . . . . . . . . . . . (515) 281-3221
Counties Represented: Polk (part)
Term Expires: 2017
E-mail: zach.nunn@legis.iowa.gov
Committees: Administration and Rules; Commerce; Economic
Growth/Rebuild Iowa; Joint Education Appropriations; Judiciary;
Veterans Affairs; Ways and Means

Representative **Jo Oldson** (D-District 42) . . . . . . . . . . . . . . (515) 255-2805
Counties Represented: Polk (part), Warren (part)
Term Expires: 2017
4004 Grand Avenue, Des Moines, IA 50312
E-mail: jo.oldson@legis.iowa.gov
Committees: Appropriations; Commerce; Judiciary; Transportation

Representative **Rick Olson** (D-District 31) . . . . . . . . . . . . . (515) 281-3221
Counties Represented: Polk (part)          Tel: (515) 265-7658
Term Expires: 2017
E-mail: rick.olson@legis.iowa.gov
Committees: Judiciary; Public Safety; Transportation

Representative **Scott Ourth** (D-District 26) . . . . . . . . . . . . (515) 281-4280
Counties Represented: Warren (part)
Term Expires: 2017
E-mail: scott.ourth@legis.iowa.gov
Committees: Agriculture; Commerce; Joint Agriculture and Natural
Resources Appropriations; Natural Resources
Education: Graceland U 1981 BA; Central Michigan 1985 (Attended)

Representative **Kraig Paulsen** (R-District 67) . . . . . . . . . . . (515) 281-3521
Counties Represented: Linn (part)          Res: (319) 294-2062
Term Expires: 2017
1305 Cress Parkway, Hiawatha, IA 52233
E-mail: kraig.paulsen@legis.iowa.gov
Committees: Judiciary; Transportation

Representative **Ross C. Paustian** (R-District 92) . . . . . . . . (515) 281-3221
Counties Represented: Scott (part)
Term Expires: 2017
E-mail: ross.paustian@legis.iowa.gov
Committees: Agriculture; Environmental Protection; Joint Agriculture
and Natural Resources Appropriations; Natural Resources

Representative **Dawn E. Pettengill** (R-District 75) . . . . . . . (319) 475-2276
Counties Represented: Benton, Iowa (part)
Term Expires: 2017
905 D Avenue, Mount Auburn, IA 52349
P.O. Box 76, Mount Auburn, IA 52313
E-mail: dawn.pettengill@legis.iowa.gov
Committees: Commerce; Government Oversight; State Government;
Ways and Means

Representative **Todd Prichard** (D-District 52) . . . . . . . . . . . (515) 281-3221
Counties Represented: Cerro Gordo (part), Chickasaw, Floyd
Term Expires: 2017
1011 Sunset Street, New Hampton, IA 50659
E-mail: todd.prichard@legis.iowa.gov
Committees: Administration and Rules; Agriculture; Judiciary; State
Government; Veterans Affairs; Ways and Means

Representative
**Col Kenneth R. "Ken" Rizer, USAF** (R-District 68) . . . . (515) 281-3221
Counties Represented: Linn (part)
Term Expires: 2017
E-mail: ken.rizer@legis.iowa.gov
Committees: Appropriations; Commerce; Human Resources; Joint
Health and Human Services Appropriations; Judiciary
Education: Air Force Acad 1987 BS; JFK School Govt 2001 MPA

Representative **Walt Rogers** (R-District 60) . . . . . . . . . . . . (515) 281-3221
Counties Represented: Black Hawk (part)
Term Expires: 2017
4202 Briarwood Drive, Cedar Falls, IA 50613
E-mail: walt.rogers@legis.iowa.gov
Committees: Administration and Rules; Appropriations; Economic
Growth/Rebuild Iowa; Judiciary; Local Government

Representative **Patti Ruff** (D-District 56) . . . . . . . . . . . . . . (515) 281-4280
Counties Represented: Allamakee, Clayton (part)
Term Expires: 2017
E-mail: patti.ruff@legis.iowa.gov
Committees: Agriculture; Education; Joint Agriculture and Natural
Resources Appropriations; Natural Resources; Ways and Means
Education: Loras 1995 BA

Representative
**Kirsten A. Running-Marquardt** (D-District 69) . . . . . . . (319) 393-7337
Counties Represented: Linn (part)
Term Expires: 2017
3515 Fieldstone Place SW, Cedar Rapids, IA 52404
E-mail: kirsten.running-marquardt@legis.iowa.gov
Committees: Appropriations; Economic Growth/Rebuild Iowa; Joint
Economic Development Appropriations; Labor

Representative **Sandy Salmon** (R-District 63) . . . . . . . . . . . (515) 281-4280
Counties Represented: Black Hawk (part), Bremer
Term Expires: 2017
E-mail: sandy.salmon@legis.iowa.gov
Committees: Education; Human Resources; Joint Administration and
Regulation Appropriations; Public Safety; Veterans Affairs
Education: Northern Iowa 1977 BA

Representative **Thomas R. "Tom" Sands** (R-District 88) . . (319) 728-2436
Counties Represented: Des Moines (part), Louisa,     Res: (319) 729-2280
Muscatine (part)
Term Expires: 2017
13247 - 130th Street, Wapello, IA 52653
E-mail: tom.sands@legis.iowa.gov
Committees: Commerce; Ethics; Ways and Means

Representative **Mike Sexton** (R-District 10) . . . . . . . . . . . . (515) 281-3221
Counties Represented: Calhoun, Humboldt, Pocahontas, Webster (part)
Term Expires: 2017
E-mail: mike.sexton@legis.iowa.gov
Committees: Agriculture; Appropriations; Joint Education
Appropriations; Labor; State Government

Representative **Larry Sheets** (R-District 80) . . . . . . . . . . . . (515) 281-3221
Counties Represented: Appanoose, Mahaska (part), Monroe, Wapello
(part)
Term Expires: 2017
E-mail: larry.sheets@legis.iowa.gov
Committees: Economic Growth/Rebuild Iowa; Environmental
Protection; Joint Economic Development Appropriations; Labor; Local
Government
Education: Purdue 1966 BS; Michigan 1968 MS;
Illinois Tech 1987 MBA

Representative **David Sieck** (R-District 23) . . . . . . . . . . . . . (515) 281-3221
Counties Represented: Fremont, Mills, Montgomery (part)
Term Expires: 2017
E-mail: david.sieck@legis.iowa.gov
Committees: Education; Environmental Protection; Human Resources;
Joint Administration and Regulation Appropriations; Public Safety

Representative
**Mark D. Smith, ACSW, LISW** (D-District 71) . . . . . . . . (641) 750-9278
Counties Represented: Marshall (part)
Term Expires: 2017
816 Roberts Terrace, Marshalltown, IA 50158
E-mail: mark.smith@legis.iowa.gov
E-mail: representativemarksmith@gmail.com
Committees: Administration and Rules

Representative **Art Staed** (D-District 66) . . . . . . . . . . . . . . (515) 281-4280
Counties Represented: Linn (part)
Term Expires: 2017
2905 Alleghany Dr NE, Cedar Falls, IA 52402
E-mail: art.staed@legis.iowa.gov
Committees: Education; Joint Education Appropriations; Local
Government; Public Safety; Veterans Affairs
Education: Rockhurst U BA; Missouri (Kansas City) MEd;
East Central U MA

Representative **Quentin Stanerson** (R-District 95) . . . . . . (515) 281-4280
Counties Represented: Buchanan (part), Linn (part)
Term Expires: 2017
E-mail: quentin.stanerson@legis.iowa.gov
Committees: Education; Joint Transportation, Infrastructure, and Capitals Appropriations; State Government; Veterans Affairs; Ways and Means
Education: Coe BA; Grand Canyon MA

Representative **Sharon S. Steckman** (D-District 53) . . . . . (641) 424-9362
Counties Represented: Cerro Gordo (part)
Term Expires: 2017
1038 15th St. NE, Mason City, IA 50401
E-mail: sharon.steckman@legis.iowa.gov
Committees: Administration and Rules; Education; Environmental Protection; Labor; Ways and Means

Representative **Sally Stutsman** (D-District 77) . . . . . . . . . (515) 281-4280
Counties Represented: Johnson (part)
Term Expires: 2017
E-mail: sally.stutsman@legis.iowa.gov
Committees: Agriculture; Appropriations; Joint Health and Human Services Appropriations; State Government; Transportation
Education: Iowa State BA

Representative **Rob Taylor** (R-District 44) . . . . . . . . . . . . . (515) 281-4280
Counties Represented: Dallas (part)
Term Expires: 2017
495 77th Place, West Des Moines, IA 50266
E-mail: rob.taylor@legis.iowa.gov
Committees: Appropriations; Economic Growth/Rebuild Iowa; Ethics; Human Resources; Joint Education Appropriations
Education: Upper Iowa BS; William Penn MA

Representative **Todd E. Taylor** (D-District 70) . . . . . . . . . . (319) 396-8587
Counties Represented: Linn (part)
Term Expires: 2017
1416 - A Avenue, Cedar Rapids, IA 52405
E-mail: todd.taylor@legis.iowa.gov
Committees: Appropriations; Joint Justice System Appropriations; Labor; State Government

Representative **Phyllis Thede** (D-District 93) . . . . . . . . . . . (515) 281-3221
Counties Represented: Scott (part)                    Res: (563) 441-0630
Term Expires: 2017
2343 Hawthorne Court, Bettendorf, IA 52722
E-mail: phyllis.thede@legis.iowa.gov
Committees: Appropriations; Ethics; Government Oversight; Local Government; Natural Resources

Representative **Linda L. Upmeyer** (R-District 54) . . . . . . . (641) 923-3398
Counties Represented: Butler (part), Cerro Gordo (part), Franklin
Term Expires: 2017
2175 Pine Avenue, Garner, IA 50438
E-mail: linda.upmeyer@legis.iowa.gov
Committees: Administration and Rules

Representative **Guy Vander Linden** (R-District 79) . . . . . . (515) 281-3221
Counties Represented: Mahaska (part), Marion (part)
Term Expires: 2017
1610 Carbonado Road, Oskaloosa, IA 52577
E-mail: guy.vanderlinden@legis.iowa.gov
Committees: Commerce; Joint Administration and Regulation Appropriations; State Government; Ways and Means

Representative **Ralph C. Watts** (R-District 19) . . . . . . . . . . (515) 281-4280
Counties Represented: Dallas (part), Polk (part)       Tel: (515) 993-4850
Term Expires: 2017
28232 Prospect Avenue, Adel, IA 50003
E-mail: ralph.watts@legis.iowa.gov
Committees: Commerce; Labor; State Government; Veterans Affairs

Representative **Beth Wessel-Kroeschell** (D-District 45) . . . (515) 292-2904
Counties Represented: Story (part)
Term Expires: 2017
518 Ash Avenue, Ames, IA 50014
E-mail: beth.wessel-kroeschell@legis.iowa.gov
Committees: Environmental Protection; Human Resources; Joint Health and Human Services Appropriations; Public Safety

Representative **John H. Wills** (R-District 1) . . . . . . . . . . . . . (515) 281-3221
Counties Represented: Dickinson (part), Lyon, Osceola
Term Expires: 2017
E-mail: john.wills@legis.iowa.gov
Committees: Administration and Rules; Agriculture; Environmental Protection; Joint Agriculture and Natural Resources Appropriations; Natural Resources; State Government

Representative
**Cindy L. Winckler** (D-District 90) . . . . . . . . . . . (563) 391-9161 ext. 103
Counties Represented: Scott (part)                    Res: (563) 324-7927
Term Expires: 2017                                     Fax: (563) 323-1020
Six Thode Court, Davenport, IA 52802
E-mail: cindy.winckler@legis.iowa.gov
Committees: Education; Human Resources; Joint Education Appropriations; State Government
Education: Northeast Missouri State BSE; Northern Iowa MS

Representative **Matt W. Windschitl** (R-District 17) . . . . . . (712) 642-4334
Counties Represented: Harrison (part), Ida, Monona, Woodbury (part)
Term Expires: 2017
222 West Huron, Missouri Valley, IA 51555
E-mail: matt.windschitl@legis.iowa.gov
Committees: Administration and Rules; Judiciary; Veterans Affairs; Ways and Means

Representative **Mary Lynn Wolfe** (D-District 98) . . . . . . . . (515) 281-3221
Counties Represented: Clinton (part)
Term Expires: 2017
337 Fourth Avenue South, Clinton, IA 52732
E-mail: mary.wolfe@legis.iowa.gov
Committees: Government Oversight; Judiciary; Public Safety; Transportation

Representative **Gary Worthan** (R-District 11) . . . . . . . . . . (515) 281-4280
Counties Represented: Buena Vista, Sac              Tel: (712) 732-6340
Term Expires: 2017
5647 105th Avenue, Storm Lake, IA 50588
E-mail: gary.worthan@legis.iowa.gov
Committees: Appropriations; Joint Justice System Appropriations; Public Safety; Transportation

# House Standing Committees
## Administration and Rules

| Majority Members | Minority Members |
|---|---|
| Walt Rogers (R-60) *Chair* | Marti Anderson (D-36) |
| Jarad Klein (R-78) *Vice Chair* | *Ranking Member* |
| Joel Fry (R-27) | Ako Abdul-Samad (D-35) |
| Chris Hagenow (R-43) | Deborah L. Berry (D-62) |
| Zach Nunn (R-30) | Mary Gaskill (D-81) |
| Linda L. Upmeyer (R-54) | Todd Prichard (D-52) |
| John H. Wills (R-1) | Mark D. Smith (D-71) |
| Matt W. Windschitl (R-17) | Sharon S. Steckman (D-53) |

## Agriculture

| Majority Members | Minority Members |
|---|---|
| Lee Hein (R-96) *Chair* | Helen Miller (D-9) |
| Ross C. Paustian (R-92) *Vice Chair* | *Ranking Member* |
| Joshua Byrnes (R-51) | Bruce Bearinger (D-64) |
| Peter Cownie (R-42) | Nancy A. Dunkel (D-57) |
| Dave Deyoe (R-49) | Curtis "Curt" Hanson (D-82) |
| Cecil Dolecheck (R-24) | Jerry A. Kearns (D-83) |
| Charles "Chuck" Holz (R-5) | Daniel Kelley (D-29) |
| Jarad Klein (R-78) | Scott Ourth (D-26) |
| David E. "Dave" Maxwell (R-76) | Todd Prichard (D-52) |
| Norlin Mommsen (R-97) | Patti Ruff (D-56) |
| Brian Moore (R-58) | Sally Stutsman (D-77) |
| Mike Sexton (R-10) | |
| John H. Wills (R-1) | |

## Appropriations

| Majority Members | Minority Members |
|---|---|
| Patrick "Pat" Grassley (R-50) *Chair* | Christopher "Chris" Hall (D-13) |
| Col Kenneth R. "Ken" Rizer (R-68) *Vice Chair* | *Ranking Member* |
| Robert Bacon (R-48) | Bruce Bearinger (D-64) |
| Dave Deyoe (R-49) | Nancy A. Dunkel (D-57) |
| Cecil Dolecheck (R-24) | John Forbes (D-40) |
| Dean C. Fisher (R-72) | Lisa Heddens (D-46) |
| David E. Heaton (R-84) | Mary S. Mascher (D-86) |
| Daniel A. Huseman (R-3) | Jo Oldson (D-42) |
| John Landon (R-37) | Kirsten A. Running-Marquardt (D-69) |
| Norlin Mommsen (R-97) | Sally Stutsman (D-77) |
| Walt Rogers (R-60) | Todd E. Taylor (D-70) |
| Mike Sexton (R-10) | Phyllis Thede (D-93) |
| Rob Taylor (R-44) | |
| Gary Worthan (R-11) | |

**LEGISLATIVE BRANCH**

## Commerce

**Majority Members**
Peter Cownie (R-42) *Chair*
Gary Carlson (R-91) *Vice Chair*
Chip Baltimore (R-47)
Patrick "Pat" Grassley (R-50)
Steven Holt (R-18)
Charles "Chuck" Holz (R-5)
Bobby Kaufmann (R-73)
John Landon (R-37)
Zach Nunn (R-30)
Dawn E. Pettengill (R-75)
Col Kenneth R. "Ken" Rizer (R-68)
Thomas R. "Tom" Sands (R-88)
Guy Vander Linden (R-79)
Ralph C. Watts (R-19)

**Minority Members**
Jo Oldson (D-42) *Ranking Member*
David Alan "Dave" Dawson (D-14)
John Forbes (D-40)
Christopher "Chris" Hall (D-13)
David "Dave" Jacoby (D-74)
Bob M. Kressig (D-59)
Jim Lykam (D-89)
Brian Meyer (D-33)
Scott Ourth (D-26)

## Economic Growth/Rebuild Iowa

**Majority Members**
Mary Ann Hanusa (R-16) *Chair*
Rob Taylor (R-44) *Vice Chair*
Brian Best (R-12)
Gary Carlson (R-91)
Dave Deyoe (R-49)
Abby Finkenauer (R-99)
Stan Gustafson (R-25)
Charles "Chuck" Holz (R-5)
Ron Jorgensen (R-6)
Zach Nunn (R-30)
Walt Rogers (R-60)
Larry Sheets (R-80)

**Minority Members**
Nancy A. Dunkel (D-57)
 *Ranking Member*
Bruce Bearinger (D-64)
Liz Bennett (D-65)
Mary Gaskill (D-81)
Charles "Chuck" Isenhart (D-100)
Charlie McConkey (D-15)
Helen Miller (D-9)
Kirsten A. Running-Marquardt
 (D-69)

## Education

**Majority Members**
Ron Jorgensen (R-6) *Chair*
Tedd Gassman (R-7) *Vice Chair*
Joshua Byrnes (R-51)
Cecil Dolecheck (R-24)
Greg Forristall (R-22)
Joel Fry (R-27)
Mary Ann Hanusa (R-16)
Jake Highfill (R-39)
Kevin Koester (R-38)
Tom Moore (R-21)
Sandy Salmon (R-63)
David Sieck (R-23)
Quentin Stanerson (R-95)

**Minority Members**
Patti Ruff (D-56) *Ranking Member*
Ako Abdul-Samad (D-35)
Timi Brown-Powers (D-61)
Dennis M. Cohoon (D-87)
Ruth Ann Gaines (D-32)
Curtis "Curt" Hanson (D-82)
Mary S. Mascher (D-86)
Art Staed (D-66)
Sharon S. Steckman (D-53)
Cindy L. Winckler (D-90)

## Environmental Protection

**Majority Members**
Megan Jones (R-2) *Chair*
Ross C. Paustian (R-92) *Vice Chair*
Clel E. Baudler (R-20)
Terry C. Baxter (R-8)
Dave Deyoe (R-49)
Tedd Gassman (R-7)
Greg T. Heartsill (R-28)
Jarad Klein (R-78)
Tom Moore (R-21)
Larry Sheets (R-80)
David Sieck (R-23)
John H. Wills (R-1)

**Minority Members**
Charles "Chuck" Isenhart (D-100)
 *Ranking Member*
Marti Anderson (D-36)
Liz Bennett (D-65)
Curtis "Curt" Hanson (D-82)
Daniel Kelley (D-29)
Bob M. Kressig (D-59)
Vicki S. Lensing (D-85)
Sharon S. Steckman (D-53)
Beth Wessel-Kroeschell (D-45)

## Ethics

**Majority Members**
Rob Taylor (R-44) *Chair*
Ron Jorgensen (R-6) *Vice Chair*
Thomas R. "Tom" Sands (R-88)

**Minority Members**
Phyllis Thede (D-93)
 *Ranking Member*
Deborah L. Berry (D-62)
David Alan "Dave" Dawson (D-14)

## Government Oversight

**Majority Members**
Bobby Kaufmann (R-73) *Chair*
Greg T. Heartsill (R-28) *Vice Chair*
Clel E. Baudler (R-20)
Jake Highfill (R-39)
Dawn E. Pettengill (R-75)

**Minority Members**
Ruth Ann Gaines (D-32)
 *Ranking Member*
Vicki S. Lensing (D-85)
Mary Lynn Wolfe (D-98)
Phyllis Thede (D-93)

## Human Resources

**Majority Members**
Linda J. Miller (R-94) *Chair*
Robert Bacon (R-48) *Vice Chair*
Brian Best (R-12)
Greg Forristall (R-22)
Joel Fry (R-27)
Stan Gustafson (R-25)
David E. Heaton (R-84)
Tom Moore (R-21)
Col Kenneth R. "Ken" Rizer (R-68)
Sandy Salmon (R-63)
David Sieck (R-23)
Rob Taylor (R-44)

**Minority Members**
Beth Wessel-Kroeschell (D-45)
 *Ranking Member*
Ako Abdul-Samad (D-35)
Marti Anderson (D-36)
Timi Brown-Powers (D-61)
David Alan "Dave" Dawson (D-14)
Ruth Ann Gaines (D-32)
Lisa Heddens (D-46)
Charlie McConkey (D-15)
Cindy L. Winckler (D-90)

## Judiciary

**Majority Members**
Chip Baltimore (R-47) *Chair*
Stan Gustafson (R-25) *Vice Chair*
Terry C. Baxter (R-8)
Darrel Branhagen (R-55)
Greg T. Heartsill (R-28)
David E. Heaton (R-84)
Megan Jones (R-2)
Bobby Kaufmann (R-73)
Zach Nunn (R-30)
Kraig Paulsen (R-67)
Col Kenneth R. "Ken" Rizer (R-68)
Walt Rogers (R-60)
Matt W. Windschitl (R-17)

**Minority Members**
Mary Lynn Wolfe (D-98)
 *Ranking Member*
Marti Anderson (D-36)
Deborah L. Berry (D-62)
David Alan "Dave" Dawson (D-14)
Brian Meyer (D-33)
Jo Oldson (D-42)
Rick Olson (D-31)
Todd Prichard (D-52)

## Labor

**Majority Members**
Greg Forristall (R-22) *Chair*
Larry Sheets (R-80) *Vice Chair*
Abby Finkenauer (R-99)
Joel Fry (R-27)
Tedd Gassman (R-7)
Mary Ann Hanusa (R-16)
Steven Holt (R-18)
Ron Jorgensen (R-6)
John Kooiker (R-4)
Mike Sexton (R-10)
Ralph C. Watts (R-19)

**Minority Members**
Bruce L. Hunter (D-34)
 *Ranking Member*
Jerry A. Kearns (D-83)
Charlie McConkey (D-15)
Kirsten A. Running-Marquardt
 (D-69)
Sharon S. Steckman (D-53)
Todd E. Taylor (D-70)

## Local Government

**Majority Members**
Kevin Koester (R-38) *Chair*
Greg T. Heartsill (R-28) *Vice Chair*
Terry C. Baxter (R-8)
Darrel Branhagen (R-55)
Gary Carlson (R-91)
Tedd Gassman (R-7)
Jake Highfill (R-39)
Megan Jones (R-2)
Bobby Kaufmann (R-73)
John Kooiker (R-4)
Walt Rogers (R-60)
Larry Sheets (R-80)

**Minority Members**
Art Staed (D-66) *Ranking Member*
John Forbes (D-40)
Mary Gaskill (D-81)
Bruce L. Hunter (D-34)
Bob M. Kressig (D-59)
Vicki S. Lensing (D-85)
Mary S. Mascher (D-86)
Brian Meyer (D-33)
Phyllis Thede (D-93)

## Natural Resources

**Majority Members**
Brian Moore (R-58) *Chair*
Dean C. Fisher (R-72) *Vice Chair*
Robert Bacon (R-48)
Clel E. Baudler (R-20)
Brian Best (R-12)
Daniel A. Huseman (R-3)
Jarad Klein (R-78)
Kevin Koester (R-38)
David E. "Dave" Maxwell (R-76)
Norlin Mommsen (R-97)
Ross C. Paustian (R-92)
John H. Wills (R-1)

**Minority Members**
Curtis "Curt" Hanson (D-82)
 *Ranking Member*
Christopher "Chris" Hall (D-13)
Lisa Heddens (D-46)
Jim Lykam (D-89)
Helen Miller (D-9)
Scott Ourth (D-26)
Patti Ruff (D-56)
Phyllis Thede (D-93)

## Public Safety

**Majority Members**
Clel E. Baudler (R-20) *Chair*
Steven Holt (R-18) *Vice Chair*
Terry C. Baxter (R-8)
Dean C. Fisher (R-72)
Joel Fry (R-27)
Greg T. Heartsill (R-28)
Jarad Klein (R-78)
John Kooiker (R-4)
Brian Moore (R-58)
Sandy Salmon (R-63)
David Sieck (R-23)
Gary Worthan (R-11)

**Minority Members**
Bob M. Kressig (D-59)
  *Ranking Member*
Ako Abdul-Samad (D-35)
Marti Anderson (D-36)
Timi Brown-Powers (D-61)
Ruth Ann Gaines (D-32)
Rick Olson (D-31)
Art Staed (D-66)
Beth Wessel-Kroeschell (D-45)
Mary Lynn Wolfe (D-98)

## State Government

**Majority Members**
Guy Vander Linden (R-79) *Chair*
Mike Sexton (R-10) *Vice Chair*
Robert Bacon (R-48)
Darrel Branhagen (R-55)
Lee Hein (R-96)
Jake Highfill (R-39)
Kevin Koester (R-38)
Linda J. Miller (R-94)
Tom Moore (R-21)
Dawn E. Pettengill (R-75)
Quentin Stanerson (R-95)
Ralph C. Watts (R-19)
John H. Wills (R-1)

**Minority Members**
Vicki S. Lensing (D-85)
  *Ranking Member*
Deborah L. Berry (D-62)
Dennis M. Cohoon (D-87)
Bruce L. Hunter (D-34)
Daniel Kelley (D-29)
Mary S. Mascher (D-86)
Todd Prichard (D-52)
Sally Stutsman (D-77)
Todd E. Taylor (D-70)
Cindy L. Winckler (D-90)

## Transportation

**Majority Members**
Joshua Byrnes (R-51) *Chair*
Brian Best (R-12) *Vice Chair*
Gary Carlson (R-91)
Abby Finkenauer (R-99)
Mary Ann Hanusa (R-16)
Lee Hein (R-96)
Charles "Chuck" Holz (R-5)
Daniel A. Huseman (R-3)
John Landon (R-37)
David E. "Dave" Maxwell (R-76)
Brian Moore (R-58)
Kraig Paulsen (R-67)
Gary Worthan (R-11)

**Minority Members**
Jim Lykam (D-89) *Ranking Member*
Dennis M. Cohoon (D-87)
David Alan "Dave" Dawson (D-14)
David "Dave" Jacoby (D-74)
Jo Oldson (D-42)
Rick Olson (D-31)
Sally Stutsman (D-77)
Mary Lynn Wolfe (D-98)

## Veterans Affairs

**Majority Members**
Quentin Stanerson (R-95) *Chair*
Sandy Salmon (R-63) *Vice Chair*
Darrel Branhagen (R-55)
Stan Gustafson (R-25)
Steven Holt (R-18)
Bobby Kaufmann (R-73)
John Kooiker (R-4)
Zach Nunn (R-30)
Ralph C. Watts (R-19)
Matt W. Windschitl (R-17)

**Minority Members**
Jerry A. Kearns (D-83)
  *Ranking Member*
Bruce Bearinger (D-64)
Nancy A. Dunkel (D-57)
Ruth Ann Gaines (D-32)
Brian Meyer (D-33)
Todd Prichard (D-52)
Art Staed (D-66)

## Ways and Means

**Majority Members**
Thomas R. "Tom" Sands (R-88)
  *Chair*
David E. "Dave" Maxwell (R-76)
  *Vice Chair*
Chip Baltimore (R-47)
Joshua Byrnes (R-51)
Peter Cownie (R-42)
Abby Finkenauer (R-99)
Greg Forristall (R-22)
Lee Hein (R-96)
Linda J. Miller (R-94)
Brian Moore (R-58)
Zach Nunn (R-30)
Dawn E. Pettengill (R-75)
Quentin Stanerson (R-95)
Guy Vander Linden (R-79)
Matt W. Windschitl (R-17)

**Minority Members**
David "Dave" Jacoby (D-74)
  *Ranking Member*
Timi Brown-Powers (D-61)
Mary Gaskill (D-81)
Charles "Chuck" Isenhart (D-100)
Jerry A. Kearns (D-83)
Daniel Kelley (D-29)
Charlie McConkey (D-15)
Todd Prichard (D-52)
Patti Ruff (D-56)
Sharon S. Steckman (D-53)

# Kansas Legislature

Statehouse, 300 Southwest 10th Avenue, Topeka, KS 66612-1504
Tel: (785) 296-2391  Fax: (785) 296-1153  TTY: (785) 296-8430
Internet: www.kslegislature.org

# Kansas Senate

300 Southwest 10th Avenue, Topeka, KS 66612-1504
Tel: (785) 296-2456  Fax: (785) 296-6718

President of the Senate **Susan Wagle** (R) . . . . . . . . . . . . . (785) 296-2419
  Education: Wichita State 1979 BA
  Chief of Staff **Harrison Hems** . . . . . . . . . . . . . . . . . . . . (785) 296-2419
Vice President of the Senate **Jeff King** (R) . . . . . . . . . . . . . (785) 296-7361
Majority Leader **Terry Bruce** (R) . . . . . . . . . . . . . . . . . . . . (785) 296-2497
Assistant Majority Leader **Julia Lynn** (R) . . . . . . . . . . . . . (785) 296-7382
  Education: Kansas 1980 BA
Majority Whip **Garrett Love** (R) . . . . . . . . . . . . . . . . . . . . (785) 296-7359
Minority Leader **Anthony Hensley** (D) . . . . . . . . . . . . . (785) 296-3245
  Education: Washburn 1975 BA; Kansas State 1988 MS
Assistant Minority Leader **Marci Francisco** (D) . . . . . . . . (785) 296-7364
  Education: Kansas AB
Minority Agenda Chair **Tom Holland** (D) . . . . . . . . . . . . (785) 296-7372
  Education: Indiana 1982 BS; Minnesota 1987 MBA
Minority Caucus Chairman **Tom Hawk** (D) . . . . . . . . . . . (785) 296-7360
  Education: Kansas State 1968 BS, 1970 MS, 1983 PhD
Minority Whip **Laura Jeanne Kelly** (D) . . . . . . . . . . . . . . (785) 296-7365
  Education: Bradley 1971 BS; Indiana 1976 MS
Secretary of the Senate **Corey Carnahan** . . . . . . . . . . . . . (785) 296-2456
  E-mail: corey.carnahan@senate.ks.gov
Sergeant-at-Arms **Charles Nicolay** . . . . . . . . . . . . . . . . . (785) 296-7344

# Senators

**Party Affiliation Statistics:** Republicans: 32, Democrats: 8

Senator **Steve E. Abrams** (R-District 32) Room 224-E . . . . (785) 296-7381
  Counties Represented: Barber, Comanche, Cowley (part), Harper,
  Kingman (part), Sedgwick (part), Sumner
  Term Expires: 2017
  6964 252nd Road, Arkansas City, KS 67005
  E-mail: steve.abrams@senate.ks.gov
  E-mail: sabrams@hit.net
  Committees: Agriculture; Assessment and Taxation; Education
  Education: Kansas State 1971 BS, 1977 DVM
Senator **Tom Arpke** (R-District 24) Room 135-E . . . . . . . . (785) 296-7369
  Counties Represented: Dickinson (part), Saline      Res: (785) 827-8940
  Term Expires: 2017
  512 West Iron Avenue, Salina, KS 67402-3003
  E-mail: tom.arpke@senate.ks.gov
  Committees: Education; Ethics and Elections; Local Government;
  Natural Resources; Ways and Means
  Education: Florida State 1974 BS
Senator **Molly Baumgardner** (R-District 37)
  Room 224-E . . . . . . . . . . . . . . . . . . . . . . . . . . . . . . . . . . (785) 296-7368
  Counties Represented: Johnson (part), Miami (part)
  Term Expires: 2017
  E-mail: molly.baumgardner@senate.ks.gov
  Committees: Commerce; Corrections and Juvenile Oversight;
  Education; Joint Corrections and Juvenile Justice Oversight
  Education: Missouri (Kansas City)
Senator **Elaine S. Bowers** (R-District 36) Room 223-E . . . (785) 296-7389
  Counties Represented: Cloud, Jewell, Lincoln,      Res: (785) 243-4256
  Marshall (part), Mitchell, Osborne, Ottawa, Phillips (part), Republic,
  Rooks, Russell, Smith, Washington
  Term Expires: 2017
  1326 North 150th Road, Concordia, KS 66901
  E-mail: elaine.bowers@senate.ks.gov
  E-mail: elaine@concordiaautomart.com
  Committees: Agriculture; Financial Institutions and Insurance; Joint
  State-Tribal Relations; Public Health and Welfare
Senator **Terry Bruce** (R-District 34) Room 330-E . . . . . . . . (785) 296-2497
  Counties Represented: Kingman (part), Reno      Res: (888) 224-0291
  Term Expires: 2017
  P.O. Box 726, Hutchinson, KS 67501
  E-mail: terry.bruce@senate.ks.gov
  Committees: Assessment and Taxation; Confirmation Oversight;
  Interstate Cooperation; Joint Legislative Coordinating Council; Joint
  Special Claims Against the State; Judiciary; Organization, Calendar and
  Rules

*(continued on next page)*

LEGISLATIVE BRANCH

**Senators** *continued*

Senator **Jim Denning** (R-District 8) Room 541-E . . . . . . . (785) 296-7394
Counties Represented: Johnson (part)     Res: (913) 345-9416
Term Expires: 2017
8416 West 115th Street, Overland Park, KS 66210
E-mail: jim.denning@senate.ks.gov
E-mail: jdenning@discovervision.com
Committees: Commerce; Financial Institutions and Insurance; Public
Health and Welfare; Ways and Means
Education: Fort Hays State 1980 BS

Senator **Leslie D. "Les" Donovan, Sr.** (R-District 27)
Room 123-E . . . . . . . . . . . . . . . . . . . . . . . . . . . . . . . . (785) 296-7385
Counties Represented: Sedgwick (part)     Tel: (316) 942-1271
Term Expires: 2017     Fax: (316) 942-1278
314 North Rainbow Lake Road, Wichita, KS 67235-8502
E-mail: les.donovan@senate.ks.gov
Committees: Assessment and Taxation; Transportation

Senator **Oletha Faust-Goudeau** (D-District 29)
Room 124-E . . . . . . . . . . . . . . . . . . . . . . . . . . . . . . . (785) 296-7387
Counties Represented: Sedgwick (part)     Res: (316) 652-9067
Term Expires: 2017
4158 Regents Lane, Wichita, KS 67208-2141
E-mail: oletha.faust-goudeau@senate.ks.gov
E-mail: oletha29th@aol.com
Committees: Commerce; Ethics and Elections; Federal and State
Affairs; Joint Administrative Rules and Regulations; Local Government

Senator **Steve Fitzgerald** (R-District 5) Room 135-E . . . . . (785) 296-7357
Counties Represented: Leavenworth (part),     Res: (913) 306-1838
Wyandotte (part)
Term Expires: 2017
3100 Tonganoxie Road, Leavenworth, KS 66048
E-mail: steve.fitzgerald@senate.ks.gov
E-mail: fitz_steve@hotmail.com
Committees: Education; Ethics and Elections; Joint Corrections and
Juvenile Justice Oversight; Local Government; Transportation; Ways
and Means
Education: US Army Command; Central Michigan MA

Senator **Marci Francisco** (D-District 2) Room 134-E . . . . . (785) 296-7364
Counties Represented: Douglas (part), Jefferson     Res: (785) 842-6402
(part)
Term Expires: 2017
1101 Ohio, Lawrence, KS 66044
E-mail: marci.francisco@senate.ks.gov
Committees: Agriculture; Joint Information Technology; Joint State
Building Construction; Natural Resources; Utilities; Ways and Means

Senator **David Barton Haley** (D-District 4) Room 134-E . . (785) 296-7376
Counties Represented: Wyandotte (part)     Res: (913) 321-3210
Term Expires: 2017     Fax: (913) 321-3110
936 Cleveland Avenue, Kansas City, KS 66101
E-mail: david.haley@senate.ks.gov
Committees: Ethics and Elections; Joint Special Claims Against the
State; Joint State-Tribal Relations; Judiciary; Local Government; Public
Health and Welfare
Education: Howard U 1984 JD; Morehouse Col 1980

Senator **Tom Hawk** (D-District 22) Room 124-E . . . . . . . . (785) 296-7360
Counties Represented: Clay, Geary (part), Riley     Res: (785) 537-8000
Term Expires: 2017
2600 Woodhaven Court, Manhattan, KS 66502
E-mail: tom.hawk@senate.ks.gov
E-mail: tom@tomhawk.com
Committees: Agriculture; Financial Institutions and Insurance; Joint
Administrative Rules and Regulations; Natural Resources; Utilities

Senator **Anthony Hensley** (D-District 19) Room 318-E . . . (785) 296-3245
Counties Represented: Douglas (part), Jefferson     Res: (785) 232-1944
(part), Osage, Shawnee (part)     Fax: (785) 296-0103
Term Expires: 2017
2226 Southeast Virginia Avenue, Topeka, KS 66605-1357
E-mail: anthony.hensley@senate.ks.gov
E-mail: anthony.hensley@hotmail.com
Committees: Assessment and Taxation; Confirmation Oversight;
Education; Interstate Cooperation; Joint Kansas Security; Joint
Legislative Coordinating Council; Joint Legislative Post Audit;
Transportation

Senator **Tom Holland** (D-District 3) Room 134-E . . . . . . . . (785) 296-7372
Counties Represented: Douglas (part), Leavenworth     Dist: (785) 865-0660
(part)     Res: (785) 865-2786
Term Expires: 2017     Fax: (785) 865-0989
961 East 1600 Road, Baldwin City, KS 66006
E-mail: tom.holland@senate.ks.gov
Committees: Assessment and Taxation; Commerce; Federal and State
Affairs; Interstate Cooperation; Joint Information Technology

Senator **Mitch Holmes** (R-District 33) Room 237-E . . . . . . (785) 296-7667
Counties Represented: Barton, Edwards, Hodgeman     Res: (620) 234-5834
(part), Kiowa, Lane, Ness, Pawnee, Pratt, Rice (part), Rush, Scott,
Stafford
Term Expires: 2017
211 Southeast 20th Avenue, Saint John, KS 67576
E-mail: mitch.holmes@senate.ks.gov
E-mail: mitch@mitchholmes.com
Committees: Agriculture; Ethics and Elections; Federal and State
Affairs; Joint Kansas Security; Local Government; Public Health and
Welfare
Education: Friends 1989 BS

Senator **Laura Jeanne Kelly** (D-District 18)
Room 125-E . . . . . . . . . . . . . . . . . . . . . . . . . . . . . . . (785) 296-7365
Counties Represented: Pottawatomie (part), Shawnee     Res: (785) 357-5304
(part), Wabaunsee (part)
Term Expires: 2017
234 Southwest Greenwood, Topeka, KS 66606
E-mail: laura.kelly@senate.ks.gov
E-mail: laura@laurakelly.org
Committees: Financial Institutions and Insurance; Joint Legislative Post
Audit; Joint State Building Construction; Public Health and Welfare;
Ways and Means

Senator **Dan N. Kerschen** (R-District 26) Suite 225-E . . . . (785) 296-7353
Counties Represented: Sedgwick (part)     Res: (316) 535-2310
Term Expires: 2017
645 South 236 West, Garden City, KS 67050
E-mail: dan.kerschen@senate.ks.gov
E-mail: dnk7@pixius.net
Committees: Agriculture; Education; Joint Special Claims Against the
State; Natural Resources; Ways and Means
Education: Kansas State 1974 BS

Senator **Jeff King** (R-District 15) Room 341-E . . . . . . . . . . (785) 296-7361
Counties Represented: Allen (part), Labette (part),     Res: (620) 331-9888
Montgomery (part), Neosho
Term Expires: 2017
1212 North Second Street, Independence, KS 67301
E-mail: jeff.king@senate.ks.gov
Committees: Confirmation Oversight; Corrections and Juvenile
Oversight; Interstate Cooperation; Judiciary; Organization, Calendar
and Rules; Transportation

Senator **Forrest J. Knox** (R-District 14) Room 234-E . . . . . (785) 296-7678
Counties Represented: Butler (part), Chautauqua, Coffey, Cowley (part),
Elk, Greenwood, Labette (part), Montgomery (part), Wilson, Woodson
Term Expires: 2017
17120 Udall Road, Altoona, KS 66710
E-mail: forrest.knox@senate.ks.gov
E-mail: senatorforrestknox@gmail.com
Committees: Agriculture; Corrections and Juvenile Oversight; Joint
Corrections and Juvenile Justice Oversight; Joint State Building
Construction; Joint State-Tribal Relations; Judiciary
Education: Kansas State 1978 BS; Technion-Israel Tech 1989 MS

Senator **Jacob LaTurner** (R-District 13) Room 135-E . . . . . (785) 296-7370
Counties Represented: Bourbon (part), Cherokee,     Res: (620) 249-1929
Crawford, Labette (part)
Term Expires: 2017
204 East Euclid, Pittsburg, KS 66762
E-mail: Jacob.laturner@senate.ks.gov
E-mail: jacoblaturner@yahoo.com
Committees: Federal and State Affairs; Financial Institutions and
Insurance; Joint Corrections and Juvenile Justice Oversight; Public
Health and Welfare; Transportation
Education: Pittsburg State 2011 BA

Senator **Jeff Longbine** (R-District 17) Room 235-E . . . . . . (785) 296-7384
Counties Represented: Geary (part), Lyon,     Fax: (620) 342-3073
Pottawatomie (part), Wabaunsee (part)
Term Expires: 2017
2801 Lakeridge Road, Emporia, KS 66801
E-mail: jeff.longbine@senate.ks.gov
E-mail: jlongbine@longbineauto.com
Committees: Commerce; Federal and State Affairs; Financial
Institutions and Insurance; Joint Legislative Post Audit; Utilities
Education: Emporia State (Attended)

Senator **Garrett Love** (R-District 38) Room 237-E . . . . . . . (785) 296-7359
Counties Represented: Clark, Ford, Gray, Hodgeman     Res: (620) 846-0223
(part), Meade, Seward
Term Expires: 2017
P.O. Box 1, Montezuma, KS 67867-0001
E-mail: garrett.love@senate.ks.gov
Committees: Agriculture; Ethics and Elections; Interstate Cooperation;
Joint Administrative Rules and Regulations; Joint Information
Technology; Judiciary; Local Government; Public Health and Welfare

Senator **Julia Lynn** (R-District 9) Room 445-E . . . . . . . . . (785) 296-7382
 Counties Represented: Johnson (part)   Res: (913) 832-5311
 Term Expires: 2017
 18837 W 115th Terrace, Olathe, KS 66061
 E-mail: julia.lynn@senate.ks.gov
 Committees: Assessment and Taxation; Commerce; Interstate
 Cooperation; Joint Legislative Post Audit; Judiciary; Utilities

Senator **Ty Masterson** (R-District 16) Room 545-E . . . . . . (785) 296-7388
 Counties Represented: Butler (part), Sedgwick   Res: (316) 573-9987
 (part)                                         Fax: (316) 462-0712
 Term Expires: 2017
 P.O. Box 424, Andover, KS 67002
 E-mail: ty.masterson@senate.ks.gov
 Committees: Confirmation Oversight; Utilities; Ways and Means
 Education: Kansas State (Attended)

Senator **Carolyn McGinn** (R-District 31) Room 223-E . . . . (785) 296-7377
 Counties Represented: Harvey, Sedgwick (part)   Res: (316) 772-0147
 Term Expires: 2017
 P.O. Box A, Sedgwick, KS 67135
 E-mail: carolyn.mcginn@senate.ks.gov
 Committees: Agriculture; Corrections and Juvenile Oversight; Joint
 Corrections and Juvenile Justice Oversight; Judiciary; Natural
 Resources
 Education: Wichita State 1983 BBA

Senator **Jeff Melcher** (R-District 11) Room 541-E . . . . . . (785) 296-7301
 Counties Represented: Johnson (part)   Res: (913) 390-3931
 Term Expires: 2017
 11424 Canterbury Circle, Leawood, KS 66211
 E-mail: jeff.melcher@senate.ks.gov
 E-mail: jeff@melcherforsenate.com
 Committees: Assessment and Taxation; Commerce; Education; Joint
 Information Technology; Ways and Means
 Education: Missouri Science and Tech BME

Senator **Michael O'Donnell II** (R-District 25)
 Room 225-E . . . . . . . . . . . . . . . . . . . . . . . . . . (785) 296-7391
 Counties Represented: Sedgwick (part)
 Term Expires: 2017
 E-mail: michael.odonnell@senate.ks.gov
 E-mail: michael@michaelforkansas.com
 Committees: Ethics and Elections; Joint Legislative Post Audit; Local
 Government; Natural Resources; Public Health and Welfare; Ways and
 Means
 Education: Friends

Senator **Robert S. "Rob" Olson** (R-District 23)
 Room 236-E . . . . . . . . . . . . . . . . . . . . . . . . . . (785) 296-7358
 Counties Represented: Johnson (part)   Res: (913) 302-3135
 Term Expires: 2017
 19050 West 161st Street, Olathe, KS 66062
 E-mail: rob.olson@senate.ks.gov
 Committees: Commerce; Confirmation Oversight; Federal and State
 Affairs; Financial Institutions and Insurance; Utilities

Senator **Ralph Ostmeyer** (R-District 40) Room 136-E . . . . (785) 296-7399
 Counties Represented: Cheyenne, Decatur, Ellis,   Res: (785) 824-3773
 Gove, Graham, Logan, Norton, Phillips (part), Rawlins, Sheridan,
 Sherman, Thomas, Trego, Wallace
 Term Expires: 2017
 P.O. Box 97, Grinnell, KS 67738
 E-mail: ralph.ostmeyer@senate.ks.gov
 Committees: Agriculture; Corrections and Juvenile Oversight; Federal
 and State Affairs; Joint Administrative Rules and Regulations; Joint
 State-Tribal Relations; Natural Resources

Senator **Mike Petersen** (R-District 28) Room 345-S . . . . . (785) 296-7355
 Counties Represented: Sedgwick (part)   Res: (316) 264-1817
 Term Expires: 2017
 2608 Southeast Drive, Wichita, KS 67216-2140
 E-mail: mike.petersen@senate.ks.gov
 Committees: Assessment and Taxation; Joint Information Technology;
 Joint Kansas Security; Judiciary; Transportation; Utilities

Senator **Pat Huggins Pettey** (D-District 6) Room 125-E . . (785) 296-7375
 Counties Represented: Johnson (part), Wyandotte   Res: (913) 579-3741
 (part)
 Term Expires: 2017
 5316 Lakewood Street, Kansas City, KS 66106
 E-mail: pat.pettey@senate.ks.gov
 E-mail: jmphp42@yahoo.com
 Committees: Corrections and Juvenile Oversight; Education; Joint
 Corrections and Juvenile Justice Oversight; Joint Kansas Security; Joint
 State-Tribal Relations; Judiciary; Transportation
 Education: Kansas 1968 BS, MS

Senator **Mary Pilcher-Cook** (R-District 10) Room 441-E . . (785) 296-7362
 Counties Represented: Johnson (part), Wyandotte   Res: (913) 268-9306
 (part)
 Term Expires: 2017
 13910 West 58th Place, Shawnee, KS 66216
 E-mail: mary.pilchercook@senate.ks.gov
 Committees: Assessment and Taxation; Commerce; Judiciary

Senator **Larry R. Powell** (R-District 39) Room 237-E . . . . . (785) 296-7694
 Counties Represented: Finney, Grant, Greeley,   Tel: (620) 275-6789
 Hamilton, Haskell, Kearny, Morton, Stanton, Stevens, Wichita
 Term Expires: 2017
 2209 Grandview Drive, East, Garden City, KS 67846
 E-mail: larry.powell@senate.ks.gov
 E-mail: lpowell18@cox.net
 Committees: Agriculture; Assessment and Taxation; Joint State
 Building Construction; Natural Resources; Utilities; Ways and Means
 Education: Kansas State

Senator **Dennis D. Pyle** (R-District 1) Room 234-E . . . . . . (785) 296-7379
 Counties Represented: Atchison, Brown, Doniphan,   Res: (785) 742-3780
 Jackson, Marshall (part), Nemaha, Pottawatomie (part)
 Term Expires: 2017
 2979 Kingfisher Road, Hiawatha, KS 66434
 E-mail: dennis.pyle@senate.ks.gov
 Committees: Education; Local Government; Natural Resources

Senator **Vicki Schmidt** (R-District 20) Room 445-S . . . . . . (785) 296-7374
 Counties Represented: Shawnee (part), Wabaunsee   Res: (785) 267-4686
 (part)                                          Fax: (785) 266-6760
 Term Expires: 2017
 5906 Southwest 43rd Court, Topeka, KS 66610-1632
 E-mail: vicki.schmidt@senate.ks.gov
 Committees: Education; Financial Institutions and Insurance; Joint
 Administrative Rules and Regulations; Transportation
 Education: Kansas 1978 BPharm

Senator **Greg Smith** (R-District 21) Room 441-E . . . . . . . . (785) 296-7367
 Counties Represented: Johnson (part)   Res: (913) 383-1574
 Term Expires: 2017
 8605 Robinson, Overland Park, KS 66212
 E-mail: greg.smith@senate.ks.gov
 E-mail: greg4ks@gmail.com
 Committees: Corrections and Juvenile Oversight; Joint Corrections and
 Juvenile Justice Oversight; Joint Kansas Security; Judiciary; Natural
 Resources; Utilities
 Education: Avila U 2006 BA, 2010 MA

Senator **Caryn Tyson** (R-District 12) Room 236-E . . . . . . . (785) 296-6838
 Counties Represented: Allen (part), Anderson, Bourbon (part), Franklin,
 Linn, Miami (part)
 Term Expires: 2017
 E-mail: caryn.tyson@senate.ks.gov
 Committees: Assessment and Taxation; Education; Natural Resources;
 Ways and Means
 Education: Kansas State 1987 BS

Senator **Susan Wagle** (R-District 30) Room 333-E . . . . . . . (785) 296-2419
 Counties Represented: Sedgwick (part)   Res: (316) 733-5698
 Term Expires: 2017
 Four North Sagebrush, Wichita, KS 67230
 E-mail: susan.wagle@senate.ks.gov
 Committees: Commerce; Confirmation Oversight; Ethics and Elections;
 Interstate Cooperation; Joint Legislative Coordinating Council;
 Organization, Calendar and Rules; Public Health and Welfare

Senator **Richard "Rick" Wilborn** (R-District 35)
 Room 541-E . . . . . . . . . . . . . . . . . . . . . . . . . . (785) 296-2456
 Counties Represented: Wyandotte (part)
 Term Expires: 2017
 E-mail: richard.wilborn@senate.ks.gov
 Committees: Commerce; Federal and State Affairs; Financial
 Institutions and Insurance; Utilities
 Education: Kansas State

Senator **Kay Wolf** (R-District 7) Room 235-E . . . . . . . . . . . (785) 296-2456
 Counties Represented: Johnson (part)
 Term Expires: 2017
 8339 Roe Avenue, Prairie Village, KS 66207
 E-mail: kay.wolf@senate.ks.gov
 Committees: Ethics and Elections; Federal and State Affairs; Joint State
 Building Construction; Local Government; Transportation
 Education: Oklahoma BA

**LEGISLATIVE BRANCH**

**LEGISLATIVE BRANCH**

# Senate Standing Committees
## Agriculture
**Majority Members**
Garrett Love (R-38) *Chair*
Dan N. Kerschen (R-26) *Vice Chair*
Steve E. Abrams (R-32)
Elaine S. Bowers (R-36)
Mitch Holmes (R-33)
Forrest J. Knox (R-14)
Carolyn McGinn (R-31)
Ralph Ostmeyer (R-40)
Larry R. Powell (R-39)

**Minority Members**
Marci Francisco (D-2)
   *Ranking Minority Member*
Tom Hawk (D-22)

## Assessment and Taxation
**Majority Members**
Leslie D. "Les" Donovan, Sr. (R-27)
   *Chair*
Caryn Tyson (R-12) *Vice Chair*
Steve E. Abrams (R-32)
Terry Bruce (R-34)
Julia Lynn (R-9)
Jeff Melcher (R-11)
Mike Petersen (R-28)
Mary Pilcher-Cook (R-10)
Larry R. Powell (R-39)

**Minority Members**
Tom Holland (D-3)
   *Ranking Minority Member*
Anthony Hensley (D-19)

## Commerce
**Majority Members**
Julia Lynn (R-9) *Chair*
Susan Wagle (R-30) *Vice Chair*
Molly Baumgardner (R-37)
Jim Denning (R-8)
Jeff Longbine (R-17)
Jeff Melcher (R-11)
Robert S. "Rob" Olson (R-23)
Mary Pilcher-Cook (R-10)
Richard "Rick" Wilborn (R-35)

**Minority Members**
Tom Holland (D-3)
   *Ranking Minority Member*
Oletha Faust-Goudeau (D-29)

## Confirmation Oversight
**Majority Members**
Terry Bruce (R-34) *Chair*
Jeff King (R-15)
Ty Masterson (R-16)
Robert S. "Rob" Olson (R-23)
Susan Wagle (R-30)

**Minority Members**
Anthony Hensley (D-19) *Vice Chair*

## Corrections and Juvenile Oversight
**Majority Members**
Greg Smith (R-21) *Chair*
Forrest J. Knox (R-14) *Vice Chair*
Molly Baumgardner (R-37)
Jeff King (R-15)
Carolyn McGinn (R-31)
Ralph Ostmeyer (R-40)

**Minority Members**
Pat Huggins Pettey (D-6)
   *Ranking Minority Member*

## Education
**Majority Members**
Steve E. Abrams (R-32) *Chair*
Tom Arpke (R-24) *Vice Chair*
Molly Baumgardner (R-37)
Steve Fitzgerald (R-5)
Dan N. Kerschen (R-26)
Jeff Melcher (R-11)
Dennis D. Pyle (R-1)
Vicki Schmidt (R-20)
Caryn Tyson (R-12)

**Minority Members**
Anthony Hensley (D-19)
   *Ranking Minority Member*
Pat Huggins Pettey (D-6)

## Ethics and Elections
**Majority Members**
Mitch Holmes (R-33) *Chair*
Steve Fitzgerald (R-5) *Vice Chair*
Tom Arpke (R-24)
Garrett Love (R-38)
Michael O'Donnell II (R-25)
Susan Wagle (R-30)
Kay Wolf (R-7)

**Minority Members**
Oletha Faust-Goudeau (D-29)
   *Ranking Minority Member*
David Barton Haley (D-4)

## Federal and State Affairs
**Majority Members**
Ralph Ostmeyer (R-40) *Chair*
Jacob LaTurner (R-13) *Vice Chair*
Mitch Holmes (R-33)
Jeff Longbine (R-17)
Robert S. "Rob" Olson (R-23)
Richard "Rick" Wilborn (R-35)
Kay Wolf (R-7)

**Minority Members**
Oletha Faust-Goudeau (D-29)
   *Ranking Minority Member*
Tom Holland (D-3)

## Financial Institutions and Insurance
**Majority Members**
Jeff Longbine (R-17) *Chair*
Elaine S. Bowers (R-36) *Vice Chair*
Jim Denning (R-8)
Jacob LaTurner (R-13)
Robert S. "Rob" Olson (R-23)
Vicki Schmidt (R-20)
Richard "Rick" Wilborn (R-35)

**Minority Members**
Tom Hawk (D-22)
   *Ranking Minority Member*
Laura Jeanne Kelly (D-18)

## Interstate Cooperation
**Majority Members**
Susan Wagle (R-30) *Chair*
Terry Bruce (R-34) *Vice Chair*
Jeff King (R-15)
Garrett Love (R-38)
Julia Lynn (R-9)

**Minority Members**
Anthony Hensley (D-19)
   *Ranking Minority Member*
Tom Holland (D-3)

## Judiciary
**Majority Members**
Jeff King (R-15) *Chair*
Greg Smith (R-21) *Vice Chair*
Terry Bruce (R-34)
Forrest J. Knox (R-14)
Garrett Love (R-38)
Julia Lynn (R-9)
Carolyn McGinn (R-31)
Mike Petersen (R-28)
Mary Pilcher-Cook (R-10)

**Minority Members**
David Barton Haley (D-4)
   *Ranking Minority Member*
Pat Huggins Pettey (D-6)

## Local Government
**Majority Members**
Dennis D. Pyle (R-1) *Chair*
Steve Fitzgerald (R-5) *Vice Chair*
Tom Arpke (R-24)
Mitch Holmes (R-33)
Garrett Love (R-38)
Michael O'Donnell II (R-25)
Kay Wolf (R-7)

**Minority Members**
Oletha Faust-Goudeau (D-29)
   *Ranking Minority Member*
David Barton Haley (D-4)

## Natural Resources
**Majority Members**
Larry R. Powell (R-39) *Chair*
Dan N. Kerschen (R-26) *Vice Chair*
Tom Arpke (R-24)
Carolyn McGinn (R-31)
Michael O'Donnell II (R-25)
Ralph Ostmeyer (R-40)
Dennis D. Pyle (R-1)
Greg Smith (R-21)
Caryn Tyson (R-12)

**Minority Members**
Marci Francisco (D-2)
   *Ranking Minority Member*
Tom Hawk (D-22)

## Organization, Calendar and Rules
**Majority Members**
Susan Wagle (R-30) *Chair*
Terry Bruce (R-34) *Vice Chair*
Jeff King (R-15)

## Public Health and Welfare
**Majority Members**
Michael O'Donnell II (R-25) *Chair*
Elaine S. Bowers (R-36) *Vice Chair*
Jim Denning (R-8)
Mitch Holmes (R-33)
Jacob LaTurner (R-13)
Garrett Love (R-38)
Susan Wagle (R-30)

**Minority Members**
Laura Jeanne Kelly (D-18)
   *Ranking Minority Member*
David Barton Haley (D-4)

## Transportation

**Majority Members**
Mike Petersen (R-28) *Chair*
Kay Wolf (R-7) *Vice Chair*
Leslie D. "Les" Donovan, Sr. (R-27)
Steve Fitzgerald (R-5)
Jeff King (R-15)
Jacob LaTurner (R-13)
Vicki Schmidt (R-20)

**Minority Members**
Pat Huggins Pettey (D-6)
    *Ranking Minority Member*
Anthony Hensley (D-19)

## Utilities

**Majority Members**
Robert S. "Rob" Olson (R-23)
    *Chair*
Mike Petersen (R-28) *Vice Chair*
Forrest J. Knox (R-14)
Jeff Longbine (R-17)
Julia Lynn (R-9)
Ty Masterson (R-16)
Larry R. Powell (R-39)
Greg Smith (R-21)
Richard "Rick" Wilborn (R-35)

**Minority Members**
Marci Francisco (D-2)
    *Ranking Minority Member*
Tom Hawk (D-22)

## Ways and Means

**Majority Members**
Ty Masterson (R-16) *Chair*
Jim Denning (R-8) *Vice Chair*
Tom Arpke (R-24)
Steve Fitzgerald (R-5)
Dan N. Kerschen (R-26)
Jeff Melcher (R-11)
Michael O'Donnell II (R-25)
Larry R. Powell (R-39)
Caryn Tyson (R-12)

**Minority Members**
Laura Jeanne Kelly (D-18)
    *Ranking Minority Member*
Marci Francisco (D-2)

# Kansas House of Representatives

Tel: (785) 296-7633  Fax: (785) 296-1153

Speaker of the House **Ray Merrick** (R) . . . . . . . . . . . . . . (785) 296-2302
    Education: Washburn 1965 BBA
Speaker Pro Tem **Peggy Mast** (R) . . . . . . . . . . . . . . . . . . (785) 296-7685
Majority Leader **Jene Vickrey** (R) . . . . . . . . . . . . . . . . . (785) 291-3500
Assistant Majority Leader **Mario Goico** (R) . . . . . . . . . . . . (785) 296-7663
    Education: Wichita State 1973 BAE, 1985 MBA
Majority Whip **Willie Dove** (R) . . . . . . . . . . . . . . . . . . (785) 296-7677
Majority Caucus Chair **Daniel "Dan" Hawkins** (R) . . . . . . (785) 296-7631
    Education: Emporia State 1983 BSB; American Col
Minority Leader **Tom Burroughs** (D) . . . . . . . . . . . . . . . (785) 296-7885
Assistant Minority Leader **Louis E. Ruiz** (D) . . . . . . . . . . . (785) 296-7122
Minority Caucus Chair **Barbara W. Ballard** (D) . . . . . . . . (785) 296-7697
    Education: Webster 1967; Kansas State 1976 MS, 1980 PhD
Minority Agenda Chair **Brandon Whipple** (D) . . . . . . . . . (785) 296-7366
    Education: Wichita State 2005 BGS, 2007 MA
Minority Policy Chair **John Wilson** (D) . . . . . . . . . . . . . (785) 296-7652
    Education: Kansas 2006 BFA
Minority Whip **Ed Trimmer** (D) . . . . . . . . . . . . . . . . . . (785) 296-7122
    Education: Emporia State 1974 BS
Chief Clerk of the House **Susan Kannarr** . . . . . . . . . . . . . (785) 296-7633
    E-mail: susan.kannarr@house.ks.gov        Fax: (785) 291-3531
    Education: Kansas BA, JD
Sergeant-at-Arms (Interim) **Mike Lietz** . . . . . . . . . . . . . . (785) 296-7629

## Representatives

**Party Affiliation Statistics:** Republicans: 98, Democrats: 27

Representative **John Alcala** (D-District 57) . . . . . . . . . . . (785) 296-7371
    Counties Represented: Shawnee (part)        Res: (785) 640-7396
    Term Expires: 2017
    520 Northeast Lake, Topeka, KS 66616
    E-mail: john.alcala@house.ks.gov
    E-mail: jalcala3@cox.net
    Committees: Elections; Joint State Building Construction; Local
    Government; Pensions and Benefits; Taxation

Representative **Steve Alford** (R-District 124) . . . . . . . . . . . (785) 296-7696
    Counties Represented: Grant (part), Haskell (part),        Res: (620) 356-1361
    Morton, Seward (part), Stanton, Stevens
    Term Expires: 2017
    4179 East Road 19, Ulysses, KS 67880
    E-mail: j.stephen.alford@house.ks.gov
    Committees: Corrections and Juvenile Justice; Joint State Building
    Construction; Judiciary; Utilities and Telecommunications

Representative **Steven Anthimides** (R-District 98) . . . . . . . (785) 296-3971
    Counties Represented: Sedgwick (part)
    Term Expires: 2017
    1052 Southwest Christine, Wichita, KS 67218
    E-mail: steven.anthimides@house.ks.gov
    Committees: Corrections and Juvenile Justice; Insurance and Financial
    Institutions; Utilities and Telecommunications

Representative **Barbara W. Ballard** (D-District 44) . . . . . . . (785) 296-7697
    Counties Represented: Douglas (part)        Res: (785) 841-0063
    Term Expires: 2017        Fax: (785) 864-1414
    1532 Alvamar Drive, Lawrence, KS 66047-1605
    E-mail: barbara.ballard@house.ks.gov
    Committees: Appropriations; Social Services Budget; Transportation

Representative **John E. Barker** (R-District 70) . . . . . . . . . . (785) 296-7674
    Counties Represented: Clay (part), Dickinson (part),        Res: (785) 479-7519
    Marion (part)
    Term Expires: 2017
    103 Wassinger Avenue, Abilene, KS 67410
    E-mail: john.barker@house.ks.gov
    Committees: Appropriations; Education; Joint Legislative Post Audit;
    Judiciary

Representative **Tony Barton** (R-District 41)
    Room 559-W . . . . . . . . . . . . . . . . . . . . . . . . . . . . . . . . (785) 296-7522
    Counties Represented: Leavenworth (part)
    Term Expires: 2017
    1402 Franklin Street, Leavenworth, KS 66048
    E-mail: tony.barton@house.ks.gov
    Committees: Education; Energy and Environment; Insurance and
    Financial Institutions; Veterans, Military and Homeland Security

Representative **Steven R. Becker** (R-District 104) . . . . . . . . (785) 296-7196
    Counties Represented: Reno (part)        Res: (620) 543-2297
    Term Expires: 2017
    P.O. Box 384, Buhler, KS 67522-0384
    E-mail: steven.becker@house.ks.gov
    E-mail: steveb@embarqmail.com
    Committees: Corrections and Juvenile Justice; Federal and State
    Affairs; Judiciary

Representative **Rick Billinger** (R-District 120)
    Room 168-W . . . . . . . . . . . . . . . . . . . . . . . . . . . . . . . . (785) 296-4683
    Counties Represented: Cheyenne, Decatur, Rawlins,        Res: (785) 899-4700
    Sherman, Thomas (part), Wallace
    Term Expires: 2017
    310 Acacia Drive, Goodland, KS 67735
    E-mail: rick.billinger@house.ks.gov
    Committees: Commerce, Labor and Economic Development; Insurance
    and Financial Institutions; Pensions and Benefits

Representative **Sue Ellen Boldra** (R-District 111) . . . . . . . . (785) 296-4683
    Counties Represented: Ellis (part)        Res: (785) 625-2250
    Term Expires: 2017
    2406 General Custer Road, Hays, KS 67601
    E-mail: sue.boldra@house.ks.gov
    E-mail: sueboldra@gmail.com
    Committees: Agriculture and Natural Resources; Education; Utilities
    and Telecommunications
    Education: McPherson 1971 BAEd; Fort Hays State MA

Representative **Barbara Bollier** (R-District 21) . . . . . . . . . . (785) 296-7686
    Counties Represented: Johnson (part)        Res: (913) 485-2121
    Term Expires: 2017
    6910 Overhill Road, Mission Hills, KS 66208
    E-mail: barbara.bollier@house.ks.gov
    Committees: Education Budget; Elections; Vision 2020
    Education: Kansas 1980 BS, MD

Representative **John Bradford** (R-District 40) . . . . . . . . . . (785) 296-7653
    Counties Represented: Leavenworth (part)        Res: (913) 683-0871
    Term Expires: 2017        Fax: (913) 351-3688
    125 Rock Creek Loop, Lansing, KS 66043
    E-mail: john.bradford@house.ks.gov
    E-mail: jbrad125@gmail.com
    Committees: Education; Federal and State Affairs; Insurance and
    Financial Institutions
    Education: Chaminade 1977 BS; Florida Tech 1987 MS

*(continued on next page)*

**Representatives** *continued*

Representative **Rob Bruchman** (R-District 20)..........(785) 296-7653
Counties Represented: Johnson (part)         Res: (913) 709-0766
Term Expires: 2017
5016 West 108th Terrace, Suite 522, Overland Park, KS 66211
E-mail: rob.bruchman@house.ks.gov
Committees: Education; Energy and Environment; Social Services
Budget; Utilities and Telecommunications
Education: Kansas 2001 BA, 2004 JD

Representative **Tom Burroughs** (D-District 33) ..........(785) 296-7885
Counties Represented: Wyandotte (part)      Dist: (913) 963-7415
Term Expires: 2017                          Res: (913) 375-1956
3131 South 73rd Terrace, Kansas City, KS 66106
E-mail: tom.burroughs@house.ks.gov
Committees: Calendar and Printing; Interstate Cooperation; Joint
Legislative Coordinating Council; Joint Legislative Post Audit; Joint
State-Tribal Relations; Legislative Budget

Representative **Larry L. Campbell** (R-District 26) ........(785) 296-7654
Counties Represented: Johnson (part), Miami (part)
Term Expires: 2017
15803 South Avalon, Olathe, KS 66062
E-mail: larry.campbell@house.ks.gov
Committees: Elections; Insurance and Financial Institutions; Local
Government; Vision 2020
Education: Southern Nazarene BA; MidAmerica Nazarene MA

Representative **Sydney Carlin** (D-District 66) ..........(785) 296-7657
Counties Represented: Pottawatomie (part), Riley   Res: (785) 539-1702
(part)
Term Expires: 2017
1650 Sunny Slope Lane, Manhattan, KS 66502
E-mail: sydney.carlin@house.ks.gov
Committees: Agriculture and Natural Resources; Agriculture and
Natural Resources Budget; Appropriations; Joint Corrections and
Juvenile Justice Oversight
Education: Kansas State 2000 BS

Representative **John L. Carmichael** (D-District 92).......(785) 296-7650
Counties Represented: Sedgwick (part)
Term Expires: 2017
1475 North Lieunett Street, Wichita, KS 67203
E-mail: john.carmichael@house.ks.gov
Committees: Elections; Energy and Environment; Judiciary; Local
Government
Education: Wichita State 1980 BS; Kansas 1982 JD

Representative **Blake Carpenter** (R-District 81)
Room 167-W ....................................(785) 296-7567
Counties Represented: Sedgwick (part)
Term Expires: 2017
E-mail: blake.carpenter@house.ks.gov
Committees: Health and Human Services; Judiciary; Veterans, Military
and Homeland Security

Representative **Will Carpenter** (R-District 75) ..........(785) 296-7673
Counties Represented: Butler (part)         Tel: (316) 541-2932
Term Expires: 2017
6965 SW 18th Street, El Dorado, KS 67042
E-mail: will.carpenter@house.ks.gov
E-mail: carpfam6965@sbcglobal.net
Committees: Appropriations; Commerce, Labor and Economic
Development; Joint State Building Construction; Social Services
Budget

Representative **Jeremy "J.R." Claeys** (R-District 69) .....(785) 296-7670
Counties Represented: Saline (part)         Res: (785) 250-5758
Term Expires: 2017
2356 Montclair Drive, Salina, KS 67401
E-mail: jrclaeys@house.ks.gov
E-mail: jr@claeys.com
Committees: Appropriations; Commerce, Labor and Economic
Development; Joint Information Technology; Transportation and Public
Safety Budget
Education: Kansas State 2001 BA; George Washington 2004 MPA

Representative **Lonnie G. Clark** (R-District 65)
Room 352-S ....................................(785) 296-7483
Counties Represented: Geary (part)
Term Expires: 2017
E-mail: lonnie.clark@house.ks.gov
Committees: Agriculture and Natural Resources; Agriculture and
Natural Resources Budget; Veterans, Military and Homeland Security

Representative **Stephanie Clayton** (R-District 19) .......(785) 296-7655
Counties Represented: Johnson (part)        Res: (913) 205-4970
Term Expires: 2017
9825 Woodson Drive, Overland Park, KS 66207
E-mail: stephanie.clayton@house.ks.gov
E-mail: stephaniesawyerclayton@gmail.com
Committees: Agriculture and Natural Resources Budget; Federal and
State Affairs; Social Services Budget
Education: Emporia State 2000 BA

Representative **Susan Concannon** (R-District 107).......(785) 296-7644
Counties Represented: Cloud, Lincoln (part),   Res: (785) 738-8087
Mitchell, Ottawa
Term Expires: 2017
P.O. Box 65, Beloit, KS 67420
E-mail: susan.concannon@house.ks.gov
E-mail: sconcannon@nckcn.com
Committees: Agriculture and Natural Resources; Federal and State
Affairs; General Government Budget
Education: Bethany (KS) 1980 BA

Representative **Ken Corbet** (R-District 54) .............(785) 296-7633
Counties Represented: Douglas (part), Osage (part), Shawnee (part)
Term Expires: 2017
10351 Southwest 61st Street, Topeka, KS 66610
E-mail: ken.corbet@house.ks.gov
Committees: Commerce, Labor and Economic Development; Energy
and Environment; Taxation; Utilities and Telecommunications

Representative **Pam Curtis** (D-District 32) .............(785) 296-7371
Counties Represented: Wyandotte (part)
Term Expires: 2017
22 North 16th Street, Kansas City, KS 66102
E-mail: pam.curtis@house.ks.gov
Committees: General Government Budget; Judiciary; Local
Government; Vision 2020

Representative **Erin Davis** (R-District 15) ..............(785) 296-7658
Counties Represented: Johnson (part)        Res: (913) 768-6408
Term Expires: 2017
12018 South Clinton Street, Olathe, KS 66061
E-mail: erin.davis@house.ks.gov
Committees: Children and Seniors; Commerce, Labor and Economic
Development; Judiciary; Pensions and Benefits

Representative **Peter DeGraaf** (R-District 82) ...........(785) 296-7693
Counties Represented: Sedgwick (part), Sumner   Tel: (316) 777-1414
(part)                                      Res: (316) 777-0715
Term Expires: 2017
1545 East 119th, Mulvane, KS 67110
E-mail: peter.degraaf@house.ks.gov
E-mail: petedegraaf@att.net
Committees: Federal and State Affairs; Joint Corrections and Juvenile
Justice Oversight
Education: Air Force Acad 1979 BS

Representative **Diana K. Dierks** (R-District 71) ..........(785) 296-7642
Counties Represented: Saline (part)         Res: (785) 820-7504
Term Expires: 2017                          Fax: (785) 820-8066
1221 Sunset Drive, Salina, KS 67401
E-mail: diana.dierks@house.ks.gov
E-mail: dierks@salinahomes.com
Committees: Agriculture and Natural Resources; Elections; Veterans,
Military and Homeland Security
Education: Butler County Com Col (KS) 1984 AA

Representative **John Doll** (R-District 123) ..............(785) 296-7380
Counties Represented: Finney (part)         Res: (620) 275-9304
Term Expires: 2017
2927 Cliff Place, Garden City, KS 67846
E-mail: john.doll@house.ks.gov
Committees: Insurance and Financial Institutions; Transportation;
Utilities and Telecommunications
Education: St Mary Plains 1979 BA

Representative **Willie Dove** (R-District 38) .............(785) 296-7677
Counties Represented: Johnson (part), Leavenworth   Tel: (913) 422-8317
(part)                                      Res: (913) 909-5866
Term Expires: 2017
14715 Timber Lanek, Bonner Springs, KS 66012
E-mail: willie.dove@house.ks.gov
E-mail: williedove@sunflower.net
Committees: Children and Seniors; Health and Human Services;
Insurance and Financial Institutions

Representative **John T. Edmonds** (R-District 112) . . . . . . (785) 296-5593
Counties Represented: Barton (part) Tel: (620) 792-6552
Term Expires: 2017 Res: (620) 792-4121
209 Northeast Ten Road, Great Bend, KS 67530 Fax: (620) 792-2999
E-mail: john.edmonds@house.ks.gov
E-mail: jtedmonds@aol.com
Committees: Health and Human Services; Pensions and Benefits; Taxation
Education: Missouri (Kansas City) MAcc

Representative **Keith Esau** (R-District 14) . . . . . . . . . . . . . (785) 296-7631
Counties Represented: Johnson (part) Res: (913) 515-2135
Term Expires: 2017
11702 South Winchester Street, Olathe, KS 66061
E-mail: keith.esau@house.ks.gov
Committees: Elections; Energy and Environment; Insurance and Financial Institutions; Joint Information Technology; Local Government
Education: Tabor 1982 BA

Representative **Bud Estes** (R-District 119) . . . . . . . . . . . (785) 296-6287
Counties Represented: Ford (part) Res: (620) 371-6262
Term Expires: 2017
1405 Elbow Bend, Dodge City, KS 67801
E-mail: bud.estes@house.ks.gov
Committees: Federal and State Affairs; Health and Human Services; Insurance and Financial Institutions

Representative **John L. Ewy** (R-District 117) . . . . . . . . . . . (785) 296-7105
Counties Represented: Edwards, Finney (part), Ford Res: (620) 357-6417
(part), Hodgeman, Kiowa, Ness, Pawnee (part), Rush (part)
Term Expires: 2017
801 Roughton Street, Jetmore, KS 67854
E-mail: john.ewy@house.ks.gov
Committees: Agriculture and Natural Resources; Federal and State Affairs; Joint State-Tribal Relations; Transportation
Education: Fort Hays State BA; Kansas State 1980 MEd

Representative **Shannon Francis** (R-District 125)
Room 167-W . . . . . . . . . . . . . . . . . . . . . . . . . . . . . . . (785) 296-7655
Counties Represented: Seward (part)
Term Expires: 2017
E-mail: shannon.francis@house.ks.gov
Committees: Agriculture and Natural Resources; Local Government; Vision 2020

Representative **Blaine Finch** (R-District 59) . . . . . . . . . . . . (785) 296-7655
Counties Represented: Franklin (part), Osage (part) Res: (785) 242-3343
Term Expires: 2017 Fax: (785) 242-3058
Five Southwest Fairview Drive, Ottawa, KS 66067
E-mail: blaine.finch@house.ks.gov
E-mail: blainefinch@gmail.com
Committees: Corrections and Juvenile Justice; Judiciary; Utilities and Telecommunications
Education: Ottawa U 2000 BA; Washburn 2002 JD

Representative **Gail Finney** (D-District 84) . . . . . . . . . . . . (785) 296-7649
Counties Represented: Sedgwick (part) Res: (316) 768-0615
Term Expires: 2017
1745 North Madison Street, Wichita, KS 67214
E-mail: gail.finney@house.ks.gov
E-mail: gafinney5@yahoo.com
Committees: Appropriations; Corrections and Juvenile Justice; Transportation and Public Safety Budget
Education: Wichita State 1984 BBA; Friends MBA

Representative **Stan Frownfelter** (D-District 37) . . . . . . . . (785) 296-7648
Counties Represented: Wyandotte (part) Res: (913) 262-9659
Term Expires: 2017
5225 Crest Drive, Kansas City, KS 66106
E-mail: stan.frownfelter@house.ks.gov
Committees: Commerce, Labor and Economic Development; Insurance and Financial Institutions; Utilities and Telecommunications
Education: Emporia State 1976 BSB

Representative **Linda J. Gallagher** (R-District 23)
Room 167-W . . . . . . . . . . . . . . . . . . . . . . . . . . . . . (785) 296-7548
Counties Represented: Johnson (part)
Term Expires: 2017
E-mail: linda.gallagher@house.ks.gov
Committees: Agriculture and Natural Resources Budget; Children and Seniors; Social Services Budget
Education: Kansas 1979 BS

Representative **Randy Garber** (R-District 62) . . . . . . . . . . . (785) 296-6014
Counties Represented: Atchison (part), Brown, Res: (785) 284-2472
Jackson (part), Nemaha
Term Expires: 2017
2424 Timberlane Terr, Sabetha, KS 66534
E-mail: randy.garber@house.ks.gov
Committees: Children and Seniors; General Government Budget; Social Services Budget; Vision 2020

Representative **Mario Goico** (R-District 94) . . . . . . . . . . . . (785) 296-7663
Counties Represented: Sedgwick (part) Res: (316) 721-3682
Term Expires: 2017
1254 North Pine Grove Court, Wichita, KS 67212
E-mail: mario.goico@house.ks.gov
Committees: Calendar and Printing; Insurance and Financial Institutions; Interstate Cooperation; Joint Kansas Security; Legislative Budget; Transportation; Veterans, Military and Homeland Security

Representative **Ramon Gonzalez, Jr.** (R-District 47) . . . . . (785) 296-7677
Counties Represented: Jefferson, Shawnee (part) Res: (785) 597-5917
Term Expires: 2017
P.O. Box 12, Perry, KS 66073
E-mail: ramon.gonzalezjr@house.ks.gov
Committees: Corrections and Juvenile Justice; Joint Corrections and Juvenile Justice Oversight; Transportation and Public Safety Budget; Utilities and Telecommunications

Representative **Amanda Grosserode** (R-District 16) . . . . . . (785) 296-7659
Counties Represented: Johnson (part) Res: (913) 438-2870
Term Expires: 2017
12601 West 99th Street, Lenexa, KS 66215
E-mail: amanda.grosserode@house.ks.gov
Committees: Appropriations; Education; Education Budget; Joint Corrections and Juvenile Justice Oversight
Education: Nebraska Christian AS; Wayne State U 2000 BS

Representative **Daniel "Dan" Hawkins** (R-District 100) . . . (785) 296-7631
Counties Represented: Sedgwick (part) Res: (316) 371-1667
Term Expires: 2017 Fax: (877) 722-7073
9406 Harvest Lane, Wichita, KS 67212
E-mail: dan.hawkins@house.ks.gov
E-mail: danhawkinskansas@gmail.com
Committees: Appropriations; Health and Human Services; Insurance and Financial Institutions

Representative **Dennis Hedke** (R-District 99) . . . . . . . . . . . (785) 296-7699
Counties Represented: Butler (part), Sedgwick Res: (316) 634-6970
(part)
Term Expires: 2017
1669 North Sagebrush, Wichita, KS 67230
E-mail: dennis.hedke@house.ks.gov
Committees: Education; Energy and Environment; Taxation
Education: Kansas State 1976 BS

Representative **Henry Helgerson** (D-District 83) . . . . . . . . (785) 296-7668
Counties Represented: Sedgwick (part)
Term Expires: 2017
12 East Peach Tree Lane, Eastborough, KS 67207
E-mail: henry.helgerson@house.ks.gov
Committees: Taxation; Transportation; Veterans, Military and Homeland Security

Representative **Lane Hemsley** (R-District 56)
Room 165-W . . . . . . . . . . . . . . . . . . . . . . . . . . . . . . (785) 296-7460
Counties Represented: Shawnee (part)
Term Expires: 2017
E-mail: lane.hemsley@house.ks.gov
Committees: Commerce, Labor and Economic Development; Federal and State Affairs; Taxation

Representative **Broderick T. Henderson** (D-District 35) . . . (785) 296-7697
Counties Represented: Wyandotte (part) Res: (913) 342-2614
Term Expires: 2017
2710 North Eighth Street, Kansas City, KS 66101-1110
E-mail: broderick.henderson@house.ks.gov
Committees: Federal and State Affairs; Health and Human Services; Insurance and Financial Institutions

Representative **Gerald T. "Jerry" Henry** (D-District 63) . . . (785) 296-7688
Counties Represented: Atchison (part), Doniphan Res: (913) 367-2050
Term Expires: 2017
3515 Neosho Road, Cummings, KS 66016-9173
E-mail: jerry.henry@house.ks.gov
Committees: Agriculture and Natural Resources Budget; Appropriations; Education Budget; Joint Corrections and Juvenile Justice Oversight

Representative **Larry Paul Hibbard** (R-District 13) . . . . . . . (785) 296-7380
Counties Represented: Elk (part), Greenwood, Res: (620) 637-2454
Neosho (part), Wilson, Woodson
Term Expires: 2017
858 EE 75 Road, Toronto, KS 66777
E-mail: larry.hibbard@house.ks.gov
E-mail: lphibbard@yahoo.com
Committees: Agriculture and Natural Resources; Agriculture and Natural Resources Budget; Utilities and Telecommunications

*(continued on next page)*

**LEGISLATIVE BRANCH**

**Representatives** continued

Representative
**Dennis "Boog" Highberger** (D-District 46)
Room 174-W . . . . . . . . . . . . . . . . . . . . . . . . . . . . . . . . . (785) 296-7122
Counties Represented: Douglas (part)
Term Expires: 2017
E-mail: dennis.boog.highberger@house.ks.gov
Committees: Corrections and Juvenile Justice; Energy and Environment; Judiciary

Representative **Ron Highland** (R-District 51) . . . . . . . . . . . (785) 296-7310
Counties Represented: Lyon (part), Pottawatomie      Res: (785) 456-9799
(part), Riley (part), Shawnee (part), Wabaunsee
Term Expires: 2017
27487 Wells Creek Road, Wamego, KS 66547
E-mail: ron.highland@house.ks.gov
E-mail: rlhighland@wamego.net
Committees: Appropriations; Education; Taxation
Education: Kansas State 1973 BS, 1975 DVM, 1985 PhD

Representative **Brett Hildabrand** (R-District 17) . . . . . . . . (785) 296-7659
Counties Represented: Johnson (part)      Res: (913) 449-6697
Term Expires: 2017
16820 West 67th Street, Shawnee, KS 66217
E-mail: brett.hildabrand@house.ks.gov
E-mail: hildabrand2010@gmail.com
Committees: Education Budget; Federal and State Affairs; Health and Human Services; Joint Information Technology
Education: Kansas State 2004 BS

Representative **Don Hill** (R-District 60) . . . . . . . . . . . . . . . (785) 296-7636
Counties Represented: Lyon (part)      Res: (620) 342-3046
Term Expires: 2017
1720 Luther Street, Emporia, KS 66801
E-mail: don.hill@house.ks.gov
Committees: Elections; Insurance and Financial Institutions; Pensions and Benefits
Education: Kansas 1971 BPharm

Representative **Don Hineman** (R-District 118) . . . . . . . . . . (785) 296-7636
Counties Represented: Gove, Graham (part), Lane,      Res: (620) 397-2504
Logan, Rooks (part), Scott, Sheridan, Thomas (part), Trego, Wichita
Term Expires: 2017
116 South Longhorn Road, Dighton, KS 67839
E-mail: don.hineman@house.ks.gov
E-mail: dhineman@st-tel.net
Committees: Federal and State Affairs; General Government Budget; Taxation
Education: Kansas 1969 BS; Michigan 1970 MBA, 1973 MS

Representative **Kyle Hoffman** (R-District 116) . . . . . . . . . . (785) 296-7643
Counties Represented: Barber, Comanche (part),      Res: (620) 582-2217
Harper, Sumner (part)
Term Expires: 2017
1318 Avenue T, Coldwater, KS 67029
E-mail: kyle.hoffman@house.ks.gov
Committees: Agriculture and Natural Resources Budget; Appropriations; Judiciary
Education: Kansas State 1994 BA

Representative **Michael Houser** (R-District 1) . . . . . . . . . . (785) 296-7679
Counties Represented: Cherokee, Labette (part)      Res: (620) 704-3817
Term Expires: 2017
6891 Southwest 10th Street, Columbus, KS 66725
E-mail: michael.houser@house.ks.gov
E-mail: mhouser_2010@yahoo.com
Committees: Federal and State Affairs; Joint Special Claims Against the State; Transportation; Transportation and Public Safety Budget

Representative **Roderick A. Houston** (D-District 89) . . . . . (785) 296-7652
Counties Represented: Sedgwick (part)      Res: (316) 691-8450
Term Expires: 2017      Fax: (316) 267-1870
4902 East Looman Street, Wichita, KS 67220
E-mail: roderick.houston@house.ks.gov
E-mail: rep.houston@gmail.com
Committees: Health and Human Services; Insurance and Financial Institutions; Veterans, Military and Homeland Security; Vision 2020
Education: Wichita State

Representative **Steve Huebert** (R-District 90) . . . . . . . . . . (785) 296-1754
Counties Represented: Sedgwick (part)      Res: (316) 755-1943
Term Expires: 2017
619 North Birch Street, Valley Center, KS 67147
E-mail: steve.huebert@house.ks.gov
Committees: Education Budget; Elections; Joint Administrative Rules and Regulations; Local Government
Education: Wichita State 1982 BS

Representative **Becky J. Hutchins** (R-District 61)
Room 176-W . . . . . . . . . . . . . . . . . . . . . . . . . . . . . . . . . (785) 296-3971
Counties Represented: Jackson (part), Pottawatomie (part)
Term Expires: 2017
E-mail: becky.hutchins@house.ks.gov
Committees: Education; Judiciary; Pensions and Benefits; Veterans, Military and Homeland Security

Representative **Mark E. Hutton** (R-District 105) . . . . . . . . . (785) 296-7658
Counties Represented: Sedgwick (part)      Res: (316) 721-1571
Term Expires: 2017
7118 Clearmeadow Circle, Wichita, KS 67205
E-mail: mark.hutton@house.ks.gov
E-mail: mhutton881@cox.net
Committees: Appropriations; Commerce, Labor and Economic Development; Joint State Building Construction; Taxation
Education: Kansas State 1977 BS

Representative **J. Russell Jennings** (R-District 122) . . . . . . (785) 296-7196
Counties Represented: Finney (part), Grant (part),      Res: (620) 290-1545
Greeley, Hamilton, Haskell (part), Kearny
Term Expires: 2017
P.O. Box 295, Lakin, KS 67860
E-mail: russ.jennings@house.ks.gov
E-mail: jrussj@gmail.com
Committees: Corrections and Juvenile Justice; Energy and Environment; Transportation and Public Safety Budget
Education: Friends BS

Representative **Steven C. Johnson** (R-District 108) . . . . . . (785) 296-7696
Counties Represented: Ellsworth, McPherson (part),      Res: (785) 667-6601
Rice (part), Saline (part)
Term Expires: 2017
10197 South Hopkins Road, Assaria, KS 67416
E-mail: steven.johnson@house.ks.gov
Committees: Agriculture and Natural Resources Budget; Pensions and Benefits; Taxation
Education: Kansas State 1988; Chicago 1993 MBA

Representative **Dick Jones** (R-District 52) Room 352-S . . . (785) 296-7483
Counties Represented: Shawnee (part)
Term Expires: 2017
E-mail: dick.jones@house.ks.gov
Committees: Federal and State Affairs; Health and Human Services; Insurance and Financial Institutions

Representative **Kevin Jones** (R-District 5) . . . . . . . . . . . . . (785) 296-6287
Counties Represented: Anderson (part), Franklin      Res: (316) 259-9505
(part), Linn (part), Miami (part)
Term Expires: 2017
416 East 7th Street, Wellsville, KS 66092
E-mail: kevin.jones@house.ks.gov
E-mail: kevinjonesforkansas@gmail.com
Committees: Education; Insurance and Financial Institutions; Joint Kansas Security; Pensions and Benefits; Veterans, Military and Homeland Security
Education: Johnson County Comm Col 1995 AA; Kansas 1998 BS; Southwestern Christian MA

Representative **Mark A. Kahrs** (R-District 87) . . . . . . . . . . (785) 296-5593
Counties Represented: Sedgwick (part)      Res: (316) 684-0104
Term Expires: 2017
P.O. Box, Wichita, KS 67278
E-mail: mark.kahrs@house.ks.gov
E-mail: mark@kahrsforkansas.com
Committees: Appropriations; Elections; Judiciary; Local Government; Rules and Journal
Education: Wichita State 1986 BBA; Washburn 1991 JD

Representative **Kasha Kelley** (R-District 80) . . . . . . . . . . . . (785) 296-7671
Counties Represented: Cowley (part), Sumner (part)      Res: (316) 772-0513
Term Expires: 2017
P.O. Box 1111, Arkansas City, KS 67005
E-mail: kasha.kelley@house.ks.gov
Committees: Education; Energy and Environment; Taxation
Education: Kansas BS

Representative **Jim Kelly** (R-District 11) . . . . . . . . . . . . . . . (785) 296-6014
Counties Represented: Montgomery (part)      Res: (620) 331-7874
Term Expires: 2017
309 South 5th Street, Independence, KS 67301
E-mail: jim.kelly@house.ks.gov
Committees: Health and Human Services; Insurance and Financial Institutions; Pensions and Benefits

LEGISLATIVE BRANCH

Representative **Mike Kiegerl** (R-District 121) . . . . . . . . . . . . (785) 296-7636
Counties Represented: Johnson (part)          Res: (913) 764-3291
Term Expires: 2017
2350 Golf Course Road, Olathe, KS 66061
E-mail: mike.kiegerl@house.ks.gov
Committees: Children and Seniors; Energy and Environment; Local
Government; Transportation and Public Safety Budget
Education: Illinois 1975 BA;
American Grad International Mgmt 1977 MBA

Representative **Marvin G. Kleeb** (R-District 48) . . . . . . . . (785) 296-7680
Counties Represented: Johnson (part)          Tel: (913) 707-4535
Term Expires: 2017                            Res: (913) 681-9135
14206 Eby, Overland Park, KS 66221
E-mail: marvin.kleeb@house.ks.gov
E-mail: marvin@marvinkleeb.com
Committees: Appropriations; Commerce, Labor and Economic
Development; Taxation

Representative **Annie Kuether** (D-District 55) . . . . . . . . . . (785) 296-7669
Counties Represented: Shawnee (part)          Res: (785) 232-0717
Term Expires: 2017
1346 Southwest Wayne, Topeka, KS 66604-2606
E-mail: annie.kuether@house.ks.gov
Committees: Corrections and Juvenile Justice; Energy and
Environment; Judiciary; Utilities and Telecommunications

Representative **Greg Lewis** (R-District 113) . . . . . . . . . . . . (785) 296-7682
Counties Represented: Barton (part), Pawnee (part), Pratt, Rice (part),
Stafford
Term Expires: 2017
910 Northeast 30th Avenue, Saint John, KS 67576
E-mail: greg.lewis@house.ks.gov
Committees: Agriculture and Natural Resources; Local Government;
Vision 2020

Representative **Jerry Lunn** (R-District 28) . . . . . . . . . . . . . (785) 296-7675
Counties Represented: Johnson (part)          Res: (816) 582-5268
Term Expires: 2017
14512 Horton, Overland Park, KS 66223
E-mail: jerry.lunn@house.ks.gov
E-mail: jlunn@brushcreekpartners.com
Committees: Appropriations; Education; Joint Administrative Rules and
Regulations; Taxation

Representative **Nancy Lusk** (D-District 22) . . . . . . . . . . . . . (785) 296-7651
Counties Represented: Johnson (part)          Tel: (913) 648-2616
Term Expires: 2017
7700 West 83rd Street, Overland Park, KS 66204
E-mail: nancy.lusk@house.ks.gov
E-mail: nnlusk@kc.rr.com
Committees: Education; Federal and State Affairs; Social Services
Budget
Education: Wichita State 1975 BFA

Representative **Adam Lusker** (D-District 2) . . . . . . . . . . . . (785) 296-7698
Counties Represented: Allen (part), Bourbon (part), Crawford (part),
Neosho (part)
Term Expires: 2017
452 South 210th Street, Frontenac, KS 66763
E-mail: adam.lusker@house.ks.gov
Committees: Agriculture and Natural Resources; Joint Kansas Security;
Joint State Building Construction; Transportation; Veterans, Military
and Homeland Security

Representative **Charles W. Macheers** (R-District 39) . . . . . (785) 296-7675
Counties Represented: Johnson (part)          Tel: (913) 396-9662
Term Expires: 2017                            Fax: (913) 432-9933
21704 West 57th Terrance, Shawnee, KS 66218
E-mail: charles.macheers@house.ks.gov
E-mail: charles@macheers.com
Committees: Appropriations; Education; Joint State-Tribal Relations;
Judiciary; Rules and Journal
Education: Kansas 1991 BS; Thomas M Cooley 1996 JD

Representative **Les Mason** (R-District 73) . . . . . . . . . . . . . (785) 296-7684
Counties Represented: McPherson (part)
Term Expires: 2017
108 Arcadian Court, McPherson, KS 67460
E-mail: les.mason@house.ks.gov
Committees: Commerce, Labor and Economic Development; Energy
and Environment; Taxation

Representative **Peggy Mast** (R-District 76) . . . . . . . . . . . . . (785) 296-7685
Counties Represented: Coffey, Lyon (part), Osage    Res: (620) 343-2465
(part)                                              Fax: (620) 343-1559
Term Expires: 2017
765 Road 110, Emporia, KS 66801
E-mail: peggy.mast@house.ks.gov
E-mail: pmast@ink.org
Committees: Calendar and Printing; Interstate Cooperation; Joint
Kansas Security; Joint Legislative Coordinating Council; Joint
Legislative Post Audit; Legislative Budget; Social Services Budget

Representative **Craig McPherson** (R-District 8) . . . . . . . . . .(785) 296-7695
Counties Represented: Johnson (part)          Res: (913) 735-6804
Term Expires: 2017
P.O. Box 23442, Overland Park, KS 66283
E-mail: craig.mcpherson@house.ks.gov
E-mail: craig@craigmcpherson.com
Committees: Energy and Environment; General Government Budget;
Joint Special Claims Against the State; Judiciary
Education: Claremont McKenna 2006 BA; George Mason JD

Representative **Ray Merrick** (R-District 27) . . . . . . . . . . . . (785) 296-2302
Counties Represented: Johnson (part)          Res: (913) 897-4014
Term Expires: 2017
6874 West 164th Terrace, Stilwell, KS 66085
E-mail: ray.merrick@house.ks.gov
E-mail: merrickrf@sbcglobal.net
Committees: Calendar and Printing; Interstate Cooperation; Joint
Legislative Coordinating Council; Legislative Budget

Representative **Tom Moxley** (R-District 68) . . . . . . . . . . . . (785) 296-7689
Counties Represented: Chase, Dickinson (part),    Res: (620) 787-2277
Geary (part), Morris
Term Expires: 2017
1852 South 200 Road, Council Grove, KS 66846
E-mail: tom.moxley@house.ks.gov
Committees: Agriculture and Natural Resources; Corrections and
Juvenile Justice; Energy and Environment
Education: Kansas State 1969 BA

Representative **Connie O'Brien** (R-District 42) . . . . . . . . . (785) 296-7671
Counties Represented: Douglas (part), Leavenworth    Res: (913) 702-2396
(part)
Term Expires: 2017
22123 211th Street, Tonganoxie, KS 66089
E-mail: connie.obrien@house.ks.gov
E-mail: connie@connieobrien.net
Committees: Children and Seniors; Education Budget; Elections; Vision
2020
Education: St Mary Col 1996 BA

Representative **Leslie Osterman** (R-District 97) . . . . . . . . . (785) 296-7659
Counties Represented: Sedgwick (part)          Res: (316) 269-2640
Term Expires: 2017
1401 West Dallas, Wichita, KS 67217
E-mail: leslie.osterman@house.ks.gov
Committees: Health and Human Services; Joint State-Tribal Relations;
Judiciary; Veterans, Military and Homeland Security
Education: George Washington 1991 BS

Representative **Jarrod Ousley** (D-District 24)
Room 173-W . . . . . . . . . . . . . . . . . . . . . . . . . . . . . . . (785) 296-7366
Counties Represented: Johnson (part)
Term Expires: 2017
E-mail: jarrod.ousley@house.ks.gov
Committees: Children and Seniors; Education; Insurance and Financial
Institutions; Vision 2020

Representative **Fred Patton** (R-District 50) . . . . . . . . . . . . .(785) 296-7460
Counties Represented: Shawnee (part)
Term Expires: 2017
E-mail: fred.patton@house.ks.gov
Committees: Commerce, Labor and Economic Development; Judiciary;
Veterans, Military and Homeland Security; Vision 2020
Education: Washburn BBA; Kansas JD

Representative **Janice L. Pauls** (R-District 102) . . . . . . . . .(785) 296-7645
Counties Represented: Reno (part)          Res: (620) 663-8961
Term Expires: 2017
1634 North Baker Street, Hutchinson, KS 67501-5621
E-mail: jan.pauls@house.ks.gov
Committees: Corrections and Juvenile Justice; Federal and State
Affairs; Joint Administrative Rules and Regulations; Judiciary; Rules
and Journal

*(continued on next page)*

**LEGISLATIVE BRANCH**

**Representatives** *continued*

Representative **Virgil Peck, Jr.** (R-District 12) . . . . . . . . . . (785) 296-7641
Counties Represented: Butler (part), Chautauqua,          Res: (620) 289-2334
Cowley (part), Elk (part), Montgomery (part)
Term Expires: 2017
P.O. Box 277, Tyro, KS 67364
E-mail: virgil.peck@house.ks.gov
Committees: Education Budget; Elections; Joint Legislative Post Audit;
Local Government; Pensions and Benefits

Representative **Tom Phillips** (R-District 67) . . . . . . . . . . . . (785) 296-7690
Counties Represented: Riley (part)          Res: (785) 537-2194
Term Expires: 2017
1530 Barrington Drive, Manhattan, KS 66503
E-mail: tom.phillips@house.ks.gov
Committees: Children and Seniors; Energy and Environment; Local
Government; Taxation
Education: Kansas State 1980 BS, 1983 MS

Representative **Randy Powell** (R-District 30)
Room 165-W . . . . . . . . . . . . . . . . . . . . . . . . . . . . . (785) 296-5593
Counties Represented: Johnson (part)
Term Expires: 2017
E-mail: randy.powell@house.ks.gov
Committees: Energy and Environment; Health and Human Services;
Judiciary

Representative **Richard Proehl** (R-District 7) . . . . . . . . . . (785) 296-7639
Counties Represented: Labette (part), Montgomery          Res: (620) 421-1804
(part)          Fax: (620) 421-2042
Term Expires: 2017
510 Pine Ridge Road, Parsons, KS 67357
E-mail: richard.proehl@house.ks.gov
Committees: Appropriations; Transportation; Transportation and Public
Safety Budget
Education: Kansas State 1967 BS, 1972 MS

Representative **Ken Rahjes** (R-District 110) . . . . . . . . . . . . (785) 296-7676
Counties Represented: Ellis (part), Graham (part), Norton, Phillips,
Rooks (part)
Term Expires: 2017
1798 East 900 Road, Agra, KS 67621
E-mail: ken.rahjes@house.ks.gov
Committees: Agriculture and Natural Resources; Children and Seniors;
General Government Budget

Representative **Marty Read** (R-District 4) . . . . . . . . . . . . . . (785) 296-7310
Counties Represented: Anderson (part), Bourbon          Res: (620) 224-6495
(part), Linn (part)          Fax: (913) 795-2508
Term Expires: 2017
18244 Kansas Highway 52, Mound City, KS 66056
E-mail: marty.read@house.ks.gov
E-mail: bjread2@embarqmail.com
Committees: Agriculture and Natural Resources; Federal and State
Affairs; Transportation
Education: Kansas State 1971 BS

Representative **Marc Rhoades** (R-District 72) . . . . . . . . . . (785) 296-7682
Counties Represented: Butler (part), Harvey (part)          Res: (316) 284-9725
Term Expires: 2017
1006 Lazy Creek Drive, Newton, KS 67114
E-mail: marc.rhoades@house.ks.gov
Committees: Appropriations; Education; Taxation
Education: Kansas State 1983 ScB; Liberty 1992 MRE;
Friends 2000 MABA

Representative **Melissa Rooker** (R-District 25) . . . . . . . . . . (785) 296-7686
Counties Represented: Johnson (part)          Res: (913) 384-7371
Term Expires: 2017
4124 Brookridge Drive, Fairway, KS 66205
E-mail: melissa.rooker@house.ks.gov
E-mail: melissa@melissarooker.com
Committees: Transportation; Transportation and Public Safety Budget;
Vision 2020
Education: Kansas 1986 BFA

Representative **John J. Rubin** (R-District 18) . . . . . . . . . . (785) 296-7690
Counties Represented: Johnson (part)          Res: (913) 962-4295
Term Expires: 2017
13803 West 53rd Street, Shawnee, KS 66216
E-mail: john.rubin@house.ks.gov
Committees: Joint Corrections and Juvenile Justice Oversight;
Judiciary; Veterans, Military and Homeland Security
Education: Boston Col 1970 BA; Washington U (MO) 1973 JD

Representative **Louis E. Ruiz** (D-District 31) . . . . . . . . . . . (785) 296-7122
Counties Represented: Wyandotte (part)          Res: (913) 262-1634
Term Expires: 2017
2914 West 46th Avenue, Kansas City, KS 66103
E-mail: louis.ruiz@house.ks.gov
Committees: Calendar and Printing; Commerce, Labor and Economic
Development; Legislative Budget

Representative
**Ronald W. "Ron" Ryckman, Jr.** (R-District 78) . . . . . . . (785) 296-5481
Counties Represented: Johnson (part)          Res: (913) 768-7760
Term Expires: 2017
14234 West 158th Street, Olathe, KS 66062
E-mail: ron.ryckman@house.ks.gov
E-mail: ron@ronryckman.com
Committees: Appropriations; Legislative Budget
Education: MidAmerica Nazarene 1994 BBA

Representative **Ronald Ryckman, Sr.** (R-District 115) . . . . (785) 296-7658
Counties Represented: Clark, Comanche (part), Ford          Res: (620) 873-5273
(part), Gray, Haskell (part), Meade
Term Expires: 2017
P.O. Box 192, Meade, KS 67864
E-mail: ronald.ryckman@house.ks.gov
Committees: Taxation; Transportation; Utilities and
Telecommunications
Education: Central Michigan 1970 BSEd; Bob Jones U 1979 MSEd

Representative **Michael "Tom" Sawyer** (D-District 95) . . . (785) 296-7691
Counties Represented: Sedgwick (part)          Res: (316) 265-7096
Term Expires: 2017
1041 South Elizabeth, Wichita, KS 67213
E-mail: tom.sawyer@house.ks.gov
E-mail: shocker3@cox.net
Committees: Elections; Rules and Journal; Taxation
Education: Wichita State 1984 BBA

Representative **Joseph Scapa** (R-District 88)
Room 166-W . . . . . . . . . . . . . . . . . . . . . . . . . . . . . (785) 296-7682
Counties Represented: Sedgwick (part)
Term Expires: 2017
E-mail: joseph.scapa@house.ks.gov
Committees: Elections; Federal and State Affairs; Insurance and
Financial Institutions; Local Government
Education: Wichita State (Attended); Tabor (Attended)

Representative **Don Schroeder** (R-District 74) . . . . . . . . . . (785) 296-7500
Counties Represented: Harvey (part), Marion (part),          Res: (620) 327-4427
McPherson (part)
Term Expires: 2017
708 Charles Street, Hesston, KS 67062
E-mail: don.schroeder@house.ks.gov
Committees: Agriculture and Natural Resources; Agriculture and
Natural Resources Budget; Utilities and Telecommunications
Education: Wichita State 2005 MPA

Representative **Scott Schwab** (R-District 49) . . . . . . . . . . (785) 296-7632
Counties Represented: Johnson (part)          Res: (913) 302-7916
Term Expires: 2017
14953 West 140th Terrace, Olathe, KS 66062
E-mail: scott.schwab@house.ks.gov
E-mail: scott@scottschwab.com
Committees: Health and Human Services; Insurance and Financial
Institutions; Rules and Journal; Utilities and Telecommunications
Education: Fort Hays State 1994 BA

Representative **Sharon Schwartz** (R-District 106) . . . . . . . (785) 296-7637
Counties Represented: Jewell (part), Marshall,          Res: (785) 325-2568
Republic, Washington
Term Expires: 2017
2051 20th Road, Washington, KS 66968-8648
E-mail: sharon.schwartz@house.ks.gov
Committees: Agriculture and Natural Resources; Appropriations;
Joint Administrative Rules and Regulations; Legislative Budget;
Transportation
Affiliation: Business Manager, Divers Farm

Representative **Ben Scott** (D-District 58) . . . . . . . . . . . . . . (785) 296-7649
Counties Represented: Shawnee (part)
Term Expires: 2017
3024 Southeast Minnesota Avenue, Topeka, KS 66605
E-mail: ben.scott@house.ks.gov
Committees: Federal and State Affairs; Insurance and Financial
Institutions

Representative **Joe Seiwert** (R-District 101) . . . . . . . . . . . (785) 296-7647
Counties Represented: Reno (part), Sedgwick (part)          Res: (620) 459-6927
Term Expires: 2017
1111 East Boundary Road, Pretty Prairie, KS 67570
E-mail: joe.seiwert@house.ks.gov
Committees: Agriculture and Natural Resources; Transportation;
Utilities and Telecommunications

LEGISLATIVE BRANCH

Representative **Thomas "Tom" Sloan** (R-District 45) .... (785) 296-7632
Counties Represented: Douglas (part)       Res: (785) 841-1526
Term Expires: 2017                          Fax: (785) 841-3105
772 Highway 40, Lawrence, KS 66049
E-mail: tom.sloan@house.ks.gov
Committees: Agriculture and Natural Resources; Transportation; Vision
2020
Education: Syracuse 1968 BA; Central Michigan MA;
North Carolina PhD

Representative **Charles "Chuck" Smith** (R-District 3)
Room 559-W ...................................... (785) 296-7522
Counties Represented: Crawford (part)
Term Expires: 2017
E-mail: chuck.smith@house.ks.gov
Committees: Children and Seniors; Education; Insurance and Financial
Institutions

Representative **Gene Suellentrop** (R-District 91) ....... (785) 296-7680
Counties Represented: Sedgwick (part)       Res: (316) 260-3663
Term Expires: 2017
6813 West Northwind Circle, Wichita, KS 67205
E-mail: gene.suellentrop@house.ks.gov
Committees: Appropriations; Commerce, Labor and Economic
Development; Taxation

Representative **William M. Sutton** (R-District 43) ....... (913) 856-4421
Counties Represented: Johnson (part)
Term Expires: 2017
301 West Westhoff Place, Gardner, KS 66030
E-mail: william.m.sutton@gmail.com
Committees: Education Budget; Energy and Environment; General
Government Budget

Representative **Susie Swanson** (R-District 64)
Room 519-N ...................................... (785) 296-7642
Counties Represented: Clay (part), Riley (part)
Term Expires: 2017
E-mail: susie.swanson@house.ks.gov
Committees: Agriculture and Natural Resources; Children and Seniors;
Corrections and Juvenile Justice; Vision 2020

Representative **Jack Thimesch** (R-District 114) ......... (785) 296-7105
Counties Represented: Kingman, Reno (part), Rice     Res: (620) 318-6020
(part)
Term Expires: 2017
P.O. Box 177, Cunningham, KS 67035
E-mail: jack.thimesch@house.ks.gov
E-mail: jackthimesch@live.com
Committees: Agriculture and Natural Resources; Transportation;
Utilities and Telecommunications

Representative **Kent Thompson** (R-District 9) ........... (785) 296-7673
Counties Represented: Allen (part), Neosho (part)
Term Expires: 2017
P.O. Box, Iola, KS 66749
E-mail: kent.thompson@house.ks.gov
Committees: Health and Human Services; Pensions and Benefits;
Taxation; Utilities and Telecommunications

Representative **Annie Tietze** (D-District 53) ............. (785) 296-7648
Counties Represented: Shawnee (part)       Res: (785) 273-5296
Term Expires: 2017
329 South West Yorkshire Road, Topeka, KS 66606
E-mail: annie.tietze@house.ks.gov
E-mail: atietze@cox.net
Committees: Commerce, Labor and Economic Development; Federal
and State Affairs; Interstate Cooperation; Transportation and Public
Safety Budget
Education: Emporia State 1972 BSEd; Kansas MA

Representative **James Todd** (R-District 29) ............. (785) 296-7695
Counties Represented: Johnson (part)       Res: (913) 568-8738
Term Expires: 2017
9812 West 118th Street, Overland Park, KS 66210
E-mail: james.todd@house.ks.gov
E-mail: jameserictodd@gmail.com
Committees: Federal and State Affairs; Joint Special Claims Against
the State; Judiciary; Rules and Journal; Transportation
Education: Kansas 2004 BA, 2009 JD

Representative **Ed Trimmer** (D-District 79) ............. (785) 296-7122
Counties Represented: Cowley (part), Sumner (part)   Res: (620) 221-7146
Term Expires: 2017                          Fax: (620) 221-2777
1402 East 9th, Winfield, KS 67156
E-mail: ed.trimmer@house.ks.gov
Committees: Agriculture and Natural Resources; Education; Joint
Administrative Rules and Regulations; Joint Legislative Post
Audit; Pensions and Benefits; Rules and Journal; Utilities and
Telecommunications

Representative **Jene Vickrey** (R-District 6) ............. (785) 291-3500
Counties Represented: Miami (part)         Res: (913) 837-2585
Term Expires: 2017
502 South Countryside, Louisburg, KS 66053-9805
E-mail: jene.vickrey@house.ks.gov
E-mail: vickrey@jenevickrey.org
Committees: Calendar and Printing; Interstate Cooperation; Joint
Legislative Coordinating Council; Legislative Budget

Representative **Ponka-We Victors** (D-District 103) ...... (785) 296-7651
Counties Represented: Sedgwick (part)      Res: (316) 831-9483
Term Expires: 2017
P.O. Box 48081, Wichita, KS 67201
E-mail: ponka-we.victors@house.ks.gov
Committees: Agriculture and Natural Resources; Children and Seniors;
Joint State-Tribal Relations; Transportation
Education: Wichita State 2008 MPA

Representative **Jim Ward** (D-District 86) ............... (785) 296-7697
Counties Represented: Sedgwick (part)      Res: (316) 683-3609
Term Expires: 2017
3100 East Clark, Wichita, KS 67211
E-mail: jim.ward@house.ks.gov
Committees: Health and Human Services; Joint Administrative Rules
and Regulations; Joint Corrections and Juvenile Justice Oversight;
Judiciary; Pensions and Benefits
Education: Creighton 1981 BA; Washburn 1985 JD

Representative **Troy L. Waymaster** (R-District 109) ...... (785) 296-7672
Counties Represented: Barton (part), Jewell (part),   Res: (785) 698-2545
Lincoln (part), Osborne, Rush (part), Russell, Smith  Fax: (785) 483-3801
Term Expires: 2017
P.O. Box 283, Luray, KS 67649
E-mail: troy.waymaster@house.ks.gov
E-mail: twaymaster@aol.com
Committees: Agriculture and Natural Resources; Appropriations;
General Government Budget
Education: Kansas 2000 BA

Representative **Chuck Weber** (R-District 85) ............ (785) 296-7688
Counties Represented: Butler (part), Sedgwick (part)
Term Expires: 2017
2331 North Winstead Circle, Wichita, KS 67226
E-mail: chuck.weber@house.ks.gov
Committees: Commerce, Labor and Economic Development; Federal
and State Affairs; Taxation

Representative **Brandon Whipple** (D-District 96) ........ (785) 296-7366
Counties Represented: Sedgwick (part)      Res: (316) 290-9447
Term Expires: 2017
2925 South Walnut, Wichita, KS 67217
E-mail: brandon.whipple@house.ks.gov
E-mail: brandon@whippleforkansas.com
Committees: Commerce, Labor and Economic Development; Joint
Information Technology; Taxation; Utilities and Telecommunications

Representative **John Whitmer** (R-District 93) ........... (785) 296-7633
Counties Represented: Sedgwick (part)
Term Expires: 2017
P.O. Box 2862, Wichita, KS 67201
E-mail: john.whitmer@house.ks.gov
Committees: Energy and Environment; Health and Human Services;
Judiciary

Representative **Kristey Williams** (R-District 77)
Room 519-N ...................................... (785) 296-3971
Counties Represented: Butler (part)
Term Expires: 2017
E-mail: kristey.williams@house.ks.gov
Committees: Commerce, Labor and Economic Development; Federal
and State Affairs; Social Services Budget

Representative **John Wilson** (D-District 10) ............. (785) 296-7652
Counties Represented: Douglas (part)
Term Expires: 2017
1923 Ohio Street, Lawrence, KS 66046
E-mail: john.wilson@house.ks.gov
Committees: Agriculture and Natural Resources; Children and Seniors;
Health and Human Services; Joint Information Technology

Representative **Dr. Valdenia Winn** (D-District 34) ........ (785) 296-7657
Counties Represented: Wyandotte (part)     Res: (913) 321-2620
Term Expires: 2017
1044 Washington Boulevard, Kansas City, KS 66102
E-mail: valdenia.winn@house.ks.gov
Committees: Education; Education Budget; Federal and State Affairs;
Joint Administrative Rules and Regulations
Education: Kansas 1972 BSEd, 1975 MA, 1993 PhD

*(continued on next page)*

**LEGISLATIVE BRANCH**

Representatives *continued*

Representative **Kathy Wolfe Moore** (D-District 36).......(785) 296-7687
  Counties Represented: Wyandotte (part)   Res: (913) 721-3655
  Term Expires: 2017
  3209 North 131st Street, Kansas City, KS 66109
  E-mail: kathy.wolfemoore@house.ks.gov
  Committees: Appropriations; General Government Budget; Joint
  Special Claims Against the State; Taxation

# House Standing Committees
## Agriculture and Natural Resources

**Majority Members**
Sharon Schwartz (R-106) *Chair*
Sue Ellen Boldra (R-111)
  *Vice Chair*
Lonnie G. Clark (R-65)
Susan Concannon (R-107)
Diana K. Dierks (R-71)
John L. Ewy (R-117)
Shannon Francis (R-125)
Larry Paul Hibbard (R-13)
Greg Lewis (R-113)
Tom Moxley (R-68)
Ken Rahjes (R-110)
Marty Read (R-4)
Don Schroeder (R-74)
Joe Seiwert (R-101)
Thomas "Tom" Sloan (R-45)
Susie Swanson (R-64)
Jack Thimesch (R-114)
Troy L. Waymaster (R-109)

**Minority Members**
Ponka-We Victors (D-103)
  *Ranking Minority Member*
Sydney Carlin (D-66)
Adam Lusker (D-2)
Ed Trimmer (D-79)
John Wilson (D-10)

## Agriculture and Natural Resources Budget

**Majority Members**
Kyle Hoffman (R-116) *Chair*
Don Schroeder (R-74) *Vice Chair*
Lonnie G. Clark (R-65)
Stephanie Clayton (R-19)
Linda J. Gallagher (R-23)
Larry Paul Hibbard (R-13)
Steven C. Johnson (R-108)

**Minority Members**
Sydney Carlin (D-66)
  *Ranking Minority Member*
Gerald T. "Jerry" Henry (D-63)

## Appropriations

**Majority Members**
Ronald W. "Ron"
  Ryckman, Jr. (R-78)
  *Chair*
Sharon Schwartz (R-106)
  *Vice Chair*
John E. Barker (R-70)
Will Carpenter (R-75)
Jeremy "J.R." Claeys (R-69)
Amanda Grosserode (R-16)
Daniel "Dan" Hawkins (R-100)
Ron Highland (R-51)
Kyle Hoffman (R-116)
Mark E. Hutton (R-105)
Mark A. Kahrs (R-87)
Marvin G. Kleeb (R-48)
Jerry Lunn (R-28)
Charles W. Macheers (R-39)
Richard Proehl (R-7)
Marc Rhoades (R-72)
Gene Suellentrop (R-91)
Troy L. Waymaster (R-109)

**Minority Members**
Gerald T. "Jerry" Henry (D-63)
  *Ranking Minority Member*
Barbara W. Ballard (D-44)
Sydney Carlin (D-66)
Gail Finney (D-84)
Kathy Wolfe Moore (D-36)

## Calendar and Printing

**Majority Members**
Jene Vickrey (R-6) *Chair*
Ray Merrick (R-27) *Vice Chair*
Mario Goico (R-94)
Peggy Mast (R-76)

**Minority Members**
Tom Burroughs (D-33)
  *Ranking Minority Member*
Louis E. Ruiz (D-31)

## Children and Seniors

**Majority Members**
Connie O'Brien (R-42) *Chair*
Erin Davis (R-15) *Vice Chair*
Willie Dove (R-38)
Linda J. Gallagher (R-23)
Randy Garber (R-62)
Mike Kiegerl (R-121)
Tom Phillips (R-67)
Ken Rahjes (R-110)
Charles "Chuck" Smith (R-3)
Susie Swanson (R-64)

**Minority Members**
Ponka-We Victors (D-103)
  *Ranking Minority Member*
Jarrod Ousley (D-24)
John Wilson (D-10)

## Commerce, Labor and Economic Development

**Majority Members**
Mark E. Hutton (R-105) *Chair*
Les Mason (R-73) *Vice Chair*
Rick Billinger (R-120)
Will Carpenter (R-75)
Jeremy "J.R." Claeys (R-69)
Ken Corbet (R-54)
Erin Davis (R-15)
Lane Hemsley (R-56)
Marvin G. Kleeb (R-48)
Fred Patton (R-50)
Gene Suellentrop (R-91)
Chuck Weber (R-85)
Kristey Williams (R-77)

**Minority Members**
Stan Frownfelter (D-37)
  *Ranking Minority Member*
Louis E. Ruiz (D-31)
Annie Tietze (D-53)
Brandon Whipple (D-96)

## Corrections and Juvenile Justice

**Majority Members**
Ramon Gonzalez, Jr. (R-47) *Chair*
Janice L. Pauls (R-102) *Vice Chair*
Steve Alford (R-124)
Steven Anthimides (R-98)
Steven R. Becker (R-104)
Blaine Finch (R-59)
J. Russell Jennings (R-122)
Tom Moxley (R-68)
Susie Swanson (R-64)

**Minority Members**
Dennis "Boog" Highberger (D-46)
  *Ranking Minority Member*
Gail Finney (D-84)
Annie Kuether (D-55)

## Education

**Majority Members**
Ron Highland (R-51) *Chair*
Jerry Lunn (R-28) *Vice Chair*
John E. Barker (R-70)
Tony Barton (R-41)
Sue Ellen Boldra (R-111)
John Bradford (R-40)
Rob Bruchman (R-20)
Amanda Grosserode (R-16)
Dennis Hedke (R-99)
Becky J. Hutchins (R-61)
Kevin Jones (R-5)
Kasha Kelley (R-80)
Charles W. Macheers (R-39)
Marc Rhoades (R-72)
Charles "Chuck" Smith (R-3)

**Minority Members**
Dr. Valdenia Winn (D-34)
  *Ranking Minority Member*
Nancy Lusk (D-22)
Jarrod Ousley (D-24)
Ed Trimmer (D-79)

## Education Budget

**Majority Members**
Amanda Grosserode (R-16) *Chair*
William M. Sutton (R-43)
  *Vice Chair*
Barbara Bollier (R-21)
Brett Hildabrand (R-17)
Steve Huebert (R-90)
Connie O'Brien (R-42)
Virgil Peck, Jr. (R-12)

**Minority Members**
Dr. Valdenia Winn (D-34)
  *Ranking Minority Member*
Gerald T. "Jerry" Henry (D-63)

# Elections

**Majority Members**
Mark A. Kahrs (R-87) *Chair*
Keith Esau (R-14) *Vice Chair*
Barbara Bollier (R-21)
Larry L. Campbell (R-26)
Diana K. Dierks (R-71)
Don Hill (R-60)
Steve Huebert (R-90)
Connie O'Brien (R-42)
Virgil Peck, Jr. (R-12)
Joseph Scapa (R-88)

**Minority Members**
Michael "Tom" Sawyer (D-95)
 *Ranking Minority Member*
John Alcala (D-57)
John L. Carmichael (D-92)

# Energy and Environment

**Majority Members**
Dennis Hedke (R-99) *Chair*
Ken Corbet (R-54) *Vice Chair*
Tony Barton (R-41)
Rob Bruchman (R-20)
Keith Esau (R-14)
J. Russell Jennings (R-122)
Kasha Kelley (R-80)
Mike Kiegerl (R-121)
Les Mason (R-73)
Craig McPherson (R-8)
Tom Moxley (R-68)
Tom Phillips (R-67)
Randy Powell (R-30)
William M. Sutton (R-43)
John Whitmer (R-93)

**Minority Members**
Annie Kuether (D-55)
 *Ranking Minority Member*
John L. Carmichael (D-92)
Dennis "Boog" Highberger (D-46)

# Federal and State Affairs

**Majority Members**
Janice L. Pauls (R-102) *Chair*
James Todd (R-29) *Vice Chair*
Steven R. Becker (R-104)
John Bradford (R-40)
Stephanie Clayton (R-19)
Susan Concannon (R-107)
Peter DeGraaf (R-82)
Bud Estes (R-119)
John L. Ewy (R-117)
Lane Hemsley (R-56)
Brett Hildabrand (R-17)
Don Hineman (R-118)
Michael Houser (R-1)
Dick Jones (R-52)
Marty Read (R-4)
Joseph Scapa (R-88)
Chuck Weber (R-85)
Kristey Williams (R-77)

**Minority Members**
Annie Tietze (D-53)
 *Ranking Minority Member*
Broderick T. Henderson (D-35)
Nancy Lusk (D-22)
Ben Scott (D-58)
Dr. Valdenia Winn (D-34)

# Insurance and Financial Institutions

**Majority Members**
Scott Schwab (R-49) *Chair*
Jim Kelly (R-11) *Vice Chair*
Steven Anthimides (R-98)
Tony Barton (R-41)
Rick Billinger (R-120)
John Bradford (R-40)
Larry L. Campbell (R-26)
John Doll (R-123)
Willie Dove (R-38)
Keith Esau (R-14)
Bud Estes (R-119)
Mario Goico (R-94)
Daniel "Dan" Hawkins (R-100)
Don Hill (R-60)
Dick Jones (R-52)
Kevin Jones (R-5)
Joseph Scapa (R-88)
Charles "Chuck" Smith (R-3)

**Minority Members**
Roderick A. Houston (D-89)
 *Ranking Minority Member*
Stan Frownfelter (D-37)
Broderick T. Henderson (D-35)
Jarrod Ousley (D-24)
Ben Scott (D-58)

# General Government Budget

**Majority Members**
Troy L. Waymaster (R-109) *Chair*
Craig McPherson (R-8) *Vice Chair*
Susan Concannon (R-107)
Randy Garber (R-62)
Don Hineman (R-118)
Ken Rahjes (R-110)
William M. Sutton (R-43)

**Minority Members**
Kathy Wolfe Moore (D-36)
 *Ranking Minority Member*
Pam Curtis (D-32)

# Health and Human Services

**Majority Members**
Daniel "Dan" Hawkins (R-100)
 *Chair*
Willie Dove (R-38) *Vice Chair*
Blake Carpenter (R-81)
John T. Edmonds (R-112)
Bud Estes (R-119)
Brett Hildabrand (R-17)
Dick Jones (R-52)
Jim Kelly (R-11)
Leslie Osterman (R-97)
Randy Powell (R-30)
Scott Schwab (R-49)
Kent Thompson (R-9)
John Whitmer (R-93)

**Minority Members**
Jim Ward (D-86)
 *Ranking Minority Member*
Broderick T. Henderson (D-35)
Roderick A. Houston (D-89)
John Wilson (D-10)

# Interstate Cooperation

**Majority Members**
Ray Merrick (R-27) *Chair*
Peggy Mast (R-76) *Vice Chair*
Mario Goico (R-94)
Jene Vickrey (R-6)

**Minority Members**
Tom Burroughs (D-33)
 *Ranking Minority Member*
Annie Tietze (D-53)

# Judiciary

**Majority Members**
John E. Barker (R-70) *Chair*
Charles W. Macheers (R-39)
 *Vice Chair*
Steve Alford (R-124)
Steven R. Becker (R-104)
Blake Carpenter (R-81)
Erin Davis (R-15)
Blaine Finch (R-59)
Kyle Hoffman (R-116)
Becky J. Hutchins (R-61)
Mark A. Kahrs (R-87)
Craig McPherson (R-8)
Leslie Osterman (R-97)
Fred Patton (R-50)
Janice L. Pauls (R-102)
Randy Powell (R-30)
John J. Rubin (R-18)
James Todd (R-29)
John Whitmer (R-93)

**Minority Members**
John L. Carmichael (D-92)
 *Ranking Minority Member*
Pam Curtis (D-32)
Dennis "Boog" Highberger (D-46)
Annie Kuether (D-55)
Jim Ward (D-86)

# Legislative Budget

**Majority Members**
Ronald W. "Ron"
 Ryckman, Jr. (R-78)
 *Chair*
Sharon Schwartz (R-106)
 *Vice Chair*
Mario Goico (R-94)
Peggy Mast (R-76)
Ray Merrick (R-27)
Jene Vickrey (R-6)

**Minority Members**
Tom Burroughs (D-33)
 *Ranking Minority Member*
Louis E. Ruiz (D-31)

LEGISLATIVE BRANCH

## Local Government

**Majority Members**
Steve Huebert (R-90) *Chair*
Tom Phillips (R-67) *Vice Chair*
Larry L. Campbell (R-26)
Keith Esau (R-14)
Shannon Francis (R-125)
Mark A. Kahrs (R-87)
Mike Kiegerl (R-121)
Greg Lewis (R-113)
Virgil Peck, Jr. (R-12)
Joseph Scapa (R-88)

**Minority Members**
John Alcala (D-57)
 *Ranking Minority Member*
John L. Carmichael (D-92)
Pam Curtis (D-32)

## Pensions and Benefits

**Majority Members**
Steven C. Johnson (R-108) *Chair*
Kent Thompson (R-9) *Vice Chair*
Rick Billinger (R-120)
Erin Davis (R-15)
John T. Edmonds (R-112)
Don Hill (R-60)
Becky J. Hutchins (R-61)
Kevin Jones (R-5)
Jim Kelly (R-11)
Virgil Peck, Jr. (R-12)

**Minority Members**
Ed Trimmer (D-79)
 *Ranking Minority Member*
John Alcala (D-57)
Jim Ward (D-86)

## Rules and Journal

**Majority Members**
Janice L. Pauls (R-102) *Chair*
Mark A. Kahrs (R-87)
Charles W. Macheers (R-39)
Scott Schwab (R-49)
James Todd (R-29)

**Minority Members**
Michael "Tom" Sawyer (D-95)
 *Vice Chair*
Ed Trimmer (D-79)

## Social Services Budget

**Majority Members**
Will Carpenter (R-75) *Chair*
Peggy Mast (R-76) *Vice Chair*
Rob Bruchman (R-20)
Stephanie Clayton (R-19)
Linda J. Gallagher (R-23)
Randy Garber (R-62)
Kristey Williams (R-77)

**Minority Members**
Barbara W. Ballard (D-44)
 *Ranking Minority Member*
Nancy Lusk (D-22)

## Taxation

**Majority Members**
Marvin G. Kleeb (R-48) *Chair*
Gene Suellentrop (R-91) *Vice Chair*
Ken Corbet (R-54)
John T. Edmonds (R-112)
Dennis Hedke (R-99)
Lane Hemsley (R-56)
Ron Highland (R-51)
Don Hineman (R-118)
Mark E. Hutton (R-105)
Steven C. Johnson (R-108)
Kasha Kelley (R-80)
Jerry Lunn (R-28)
Les Mason (R-73)
Tom Phillips (R-67)
Marc Rhoades (R-72)
Ronald Ryckman, Sr. (R-115)
Kent Thompson (R-9)
Chuck Weber (R-85)

**Minority Members**
Henry Helgerson (D-83)
Michael "Tom" Sawyer (D-95)
 *Ranking Minority Member*
John Alcala (D-57)
Brandon Whipple (D-96)
Kathy Wolfe Moore (D-36)

## Transportation

**Majority Members**
Richard Proehl (R-7) *Chair*
Ronald Ryckman, Sr. (R-115)
 *Vice Chair*
John Doll (R-123)
John L. Ewy (R-117)
Mario Goico (R-94)
Michael Houser (R-1)
Marty Read (R-4)
Melissa Rooker (R-25)

**Minority Members**
Adam Lusker (D-2)
 *Ranking Minority Member*
Barbara W. Ballard (D-44)
Henry Helgerson (D-83)
Ponka-We Victors (D-103)

**Majority Members** *continued*
Sharon Schwartz (R-106)
Joe Seiwert (R-101)
Thomas "Tom" Sloan (R-45)
Jack Thimesch (R-114)
James Todd (R-29)

## Transportation and Public Safety Budget

**Majority Members**
Jeremy "J.R." Claeys (R-69) *Chair*
J. Russell Jennings (R-122)
 *Vice Chair*
Ramon Gonzalez, Jr. (R-47)
Michael Houser (R-1)
Mike Kiegerl (R-121)
Richard Proehl (R-7)
Melissa Rooker (R-25)

**Minority Members**
Gail Finney (D-84)
 *Ranking Minority Member*
Annie Tietze (D-53)

## Utilities and Telecommunications

**Majority Members**
Joe Seiwert (R-101) *Chair*
Steve Alford (R-124) *Vice Chair*
Steven Anthimides (R-98)
Sue Ellen Boldra (R-111)
Rob Bruchman (R-20)
Ken Corbet (R-54)
John Doll (R-123)
Blaine Finch (R-59)
Ramon Gonzalez, Jr. (R-47)
Larry Paul Hibbard (R-13)
Ronald Ryckman, Sr. (R-115)
Don Schroeder (R-74)
Scott Schwab (R-49)
Jack Thimesch (R-114)
Kent Thompson (R-9)

**Minority Members**
Annie Kuether (D-55)
 *Ranking Minority Member*
Stan Frownfelter (D-37)
Ed Trimmer (D-79)
Brandon Whipple (D-96)

## Veterans, Military and Homeland Security

**Majority Members**
Mario Goico (R-94) *Chair*
Leslie Osterman (R-97) *Vice Chair*
Tony Barton (R-41)
Blake Carpenter (R-81)
Lonnie G. Clark (R-65)
Diana K. Dierks (R-71)
Becky J. Hutchins (R-61)
Kevin Jones (R-5)
Fred Patton (R-50)
John J. Rubin (R-18)

**Minority Members**
Adam Lusker (D-2)
 *Ranking Minority Member*
Henry Helgerson (D-83)
Roderick A. Houston (D-89)

## Vision 2020

**Majority Members**
Larry L. Campbell (R-26) *Chair*
Thomas "Tom" Sloan (R-45)
 *Vice Chair*
Barbara Bollier (R-21)
Shannon Francis (R-125)
Randy Garber (R-62)
Greg Lewis (R-113)
Connie O'Brien (R-42)
Fred Patton (R-50)
Melissa Rooker (R-25)
Susie Swanson (R-64)

**Minority Members**
Pam Curtis (D-32)
 *Ranking Minority Member*
Roderick A. Houston (D-89)
Jarrod Ousley (D-24)

# Kentucky General Assembly

State Capitol, Room 300, Frankfort, KY 40601
Tel: (502) 564-8100  Fax: (502) 223-5094  Internet: www.lrc.ky.gov

## Kentucky Senate

Tel: (502) 564-5320  Fax: (502) 563-8317

President of the Senate **Robert Stivers** (R) . . . . . . . . . . . . . (606) 598-2322
  Education: Sue Bennett BS; Kentucky JD
President Pro Tem **David P. Givens** (R) . . . . . . . . . . . . . . . (502) 564-3120
Majority Floor Leader **Damon Thayer** (R) . . . . . . . . . . . . . (502) 564-2450
Majority Caucus Chairman **Dan "Malano" Seum** (R) . . . . (502) 564-2450
Majority Whip **Jimmy Higdon** (R) . . . . . . . . . . . . (502) 564-8100 ext. 623
  Education: Morehead State BS
Minority Floor Leader **Ray S. Jones II** (D) . . . . . . (502) 564-8100 ext. 681
  Education: Eastern Kentucky BA; Louisville JD
Minority Caucus Chairman **Gerald A. Neal** (D) . . . (502) 564-8100 ext. 718
  Education: Kentucky State BA; Louisville JD
Minority Whip **Julian M. Carroll** (D) . . . . . . . . . . (502) 564-8100 ext. 651
  Education: Kentucky BA, LLD
Chief Clerk of the Senate **Donna Holiday** . . . . . . . . . . . . . (502) 564-2450
  E-mail: donna.holiday@lrc.ky.gov

## Senators

**Party Affiliation Statistics:** Republicans: 27, Democrats: 11

Senator **Julie Raque Adams** (R-District 36) . . . . . (502) 564-8100 ext. 682
  Counties Represented: Jefferson (part)
  Term Expires: 2019
  E-mail: julie.adams@lrc.ky.gov
  Committees: Banking and Insurance; Education; Health and Welfare;
  State and Local Government
Senator **Ralph Alvarado** (R-District 28) . . . . . . . . (502) 564-8100 ext. 681
  Counties Represented: Clark, Fayette (part), Montgomery
  Term Expires: 2019
  E-mail: ralph.alvarado@lrc.ky.gov
  Committees: Appropriations and Revenue; Health and Welfare; State
  and Local Government
Senator **Joe Bowen** (R-District 8) . . . . . . . . . . . . . . (502) 564-8100 ext. 662
  Counties Represented: Daviess, Hancock, McLean    Res: (270) 685-1859
  Term Expires: 2019
  2031 Fieldcrest Drive, Owensboro, KY 42301
  E-mail: joe.bowen@lrc.ky.gov
  Committees: Licensing, Occupations and Administrative Regulations;
  State and Local Government; Transportation
  Education: Kentucky BS
Senator **Tom Buford** (R-District 22) . . . . . . . . . . . (502) 564-8100 ext. 610
  Counties Represented: Fayette (part), Garrard,    Res: (859) 885-0606
  Jessamine, Mercer, Washington    Fax: (502) 564-2466
  Term Expires: 2019
  409 West Maple Street, Nicholasville, KY 40356
  E-mail: tom.buford@lrc.ky.gov
  Committees: Banking and Insurance; Health and Welfare; Licensing,
  Occupations and Administrative Regulations
  Education: Kentucky BS
Senator **Jared K. Carpenter** (R-District 34) . . . . . . (502) 564-8100 ext. 730
  Counties Represented: Fayette (part), Madison,    Res: (859) 623-7199
  Rockcastle
  Term Expires: 2019
  138 Legacy Drive, Berea, KY 40403
  E-mail: jared.carpenter@lrc.ky.gov
  Committees: Banking and Insurance; Education; Natural Resources and
  Energy; Transportation
Senator **Danny Carroll** (R-District 2) . . . . . . . . . . . (502) 564-8100 ext. 712
  Counties Represented: Ballard, Carlisle, Marshall, McCracken
  Term Expires: 2019
  E-mail: danny.carroll@lrc.ky.gov
  Committees: Appropriations and Revenue; Education; Health and
  Welfare; Judiciary
Senator **Julian M. Carroll** (D-District 7) . . . . . . . . (502) 564-8100 ext. 651
  Counties Represented: Anderson, Franklin, Gallatin, Owen, Woodford
  Term Expires: 2017
  702 Capitol Avenue, Annex Room 229, Frankfort, KY 40601
  E-mail: julian.carroll@lrc.ky.gov
  Committees: Committee on Committees; Health and Welfare;
  Licensing, Occupations and Administrative Regulations; Rules;
  Veterans, Military Affairs and Public Protection

Senator **Perry B. Clark** (D-District 37) . . . . . . . . . . (502) 564-8100 ext. 715
  Counties Represented: Jefferson (part)    Res: (502) 366-1247
  Term Expires: 2017
  5716 New Cut Road, Louisville, KY 40214
  E-mail: perry.clark@lrc.ky.gov
  Committees: Economic Development, Tourism and Labor; Judiciary;
  Veterans, Military Affairs and Public Protection
Senator **C. B. Embry, Jr.** (R-District 6) . . . . . . . . . (502) 564-8100 ext. 710
  Counties Represented: Butler, Hopkins, Muhlenberg, Ohio
  Term Expires: 2017
  Committees: Agriculture; Natural Resources and Energy;
  Transportation; Veterans, Military Affairs and Public Protection
  Education: Western Kentucky BS
Senator **Carroll Gibson** (R-District 5) . . . . . . . . . . . . . . . . (502) 564-2450
  Counties Represented: Breckinridge, Edmonson,    Res: (270) 230-5866
  Grayson, Hart, Larue, Meade
  Term Expires: 2017
  P.O. Box 506, Leitchfield, KY 42755
  E-mail: carroll.gibson@lrc.ky.gov
  Committees: Economic Development, Tourism and Labor; Judiciary;
  Veterans, Military Affairs and Public Protection
  Education: Western Kentucky BS
Senator
  **Christopher "Chris" Girdler** (R-District 15) . . . . (502) 564-8100 ext. 656
  Counties Represented: Boyle, Lincoln, Pulaski
  Term Expires: 2017
  PO Box 395, Somerset, KY 42502
  E-mail: christopher.girdler@lrc.ky.gov
  Committees: Agriculture; Appropriations and Revenue; Banking and
  Insurance; Economic Development, Tourism and Labor; Natural
  Resources and Energy
  Education: Eastern Kentucky BA
Senator **David P. Givens** (R-District 9) . . . . . . . . . . . . . . . (502) 564-3120
  Counties Represented: Allen, Barren, Green, Metcalfe, Monroe,
  Simpson
  Term Expires: 2017
  P.O. Box 12, Greensburg, KY 42743
  E-mail: david.givens@lrc.ky.gov
  Committees: Agriculture; Appropriations and Revenue; Committee on
  Committees; Education; Enrollment; Health and Welfare; Rules
Senator **Denise Harper Angel** (D-District 35) . . . . (502) 564-8100 ext. 633
  Counties Represented: Jefferson (part)    Res: (502) 452-9130
  Term Expires: 2017
  2521 Ransdell Avenue, Louisville, KY 40204
  E-mail: denise.harperangel@lrc.ky.gov
  Committees: Economic Development, Tourism and Labor; Health and
  Welfare; Licensing, Occupations and Administrative Regulations; State
  and Local Government
Senator **Ernie Harris** (R-District 26) . . . . . . . . . . . (502) 564-8100 ext. 605
  Counties Represented: Jefferson (part), Oldham    Res: (502) 241-8307
  Term Expires: 2019
  P.O. Box 1073, Crestwood, KY 40014
  E-mail: ernie.harris@lrc.ky.gov
  Committees: Economic Development, Tourism and Labor; Natural
  Resources and Energy; Transportation; Veterans, Military Affairs and
  Public Protection
  Education: Kentucky BA; Webster MA
Senator **Jimmy Higdon** (R-District 14) . . . . . . . . . (502) 564-8100 ext. 623
  Counties Represented: Casey, Jefferson (part),    Tel: (270) 692-6945
  Marion, Nelson, Spencer    Fax: (270) 692-1111
  Term Expires: 2019
  344 North Spalding Street, Lebanon, KY 40033
  E-mail: jimmy.higdon@lrc.ky.gov
  Committees: Committee on Committees; Economic Development,
  Tourism and Labor; Education; Health and Welfare; Licensing,
  Occupations and Administrative Regulations; Rules; Transportation
Senator **Paul Hornback** (R-District 20) . . . . . . . . . (502) 564-8100 ext. 648
  Counties Represented: Carroll, Henry, Jefferson    Res: (502) 461-9005
  (part), Shelby, Trimble    Fax: (502) 461-7799
  Term Expires: 2019
  6102 Cropper Road, Shelbyville, KY 40065
  E-mail: paul.hornback@lrc.ky.gov
  Committees: Agriculture; Licensing, Occupations and Administrative
  Regulations; Natural Resources and Energy
Senator **Stan Humphries** (R-District 1) . . . . . . . . . (502) 564-8100 ext. 870
  Counties Represented: Calloway, Fulton, Graves,    Res: (270) 522-0195
  Hickman, Lyon, Trigg
  Term Expires: 2019
  702 Capitol Avenue, Annex Room 209, Frankfort, KY 40601
  E-mail: stan.humphries@lrc.ky.gov
  Committees: Agriculture; Appropriations and Revenue; State and Local
  Government; Veterans, Military Affairs and Public Protection
  Education: Murray State U BS

*(continued on next page)*

**LEGISLATIVE BRANCH**

**Senators** *continued*

Senator **Ray S. Jones II** (D-District 31) ........ (502) 564-8100 ext. 681
Counties Represented: Elliott, Lawrence, Martin,   Tel: (606) 432-5777
Morgan, Pike   Fax: (606) 432-5154
Term Expires: 2017
P.O. Drawer 3850, Pikeville, KY 41502
E-mail: ray.jones@lrc.ky.gov
Committees: Committee on Committees; Judiciary; Licensing, Occupations and Administrative Regulations; Natural Resources and Energy; Transportation

Senator **Alice Forgy Kerr** (R-District 12) ........ (502) 564-8100 ext. 625
Counties Represented: Fayette (part)   Res: (859) 223-3274
Term Expires: 2019
3274 Gondola Drive, Lexington, KY 40513
E-mail: alice.kerr@lrc.ky.gov
Committees: Economic Development, Tourism and Labor; Education; Health and Welfare; Judiciary
Education: Western Kentucky BSEd, MA

Senator
**Christian "Chris" McDaniel** (R-District 23) .... (502) 564-8100 ext. 615
Counties Represented: Kenton (part)
Term Expires: 2017
PO Box, Latonia, KY 41015
E-mail: christian.mcdaniel@lrc.ky.gov
Committees: Appropriations and Revenue; Banking and Insurance; Licensing, Occupations and Administrative Regulations; State and Local Government; Veterans, Military Affairs and Public Protection
Education: Citadel 1997 BS; Northern Kentucky MBA

Senator **Morgan McGarvey** (D-District 19) ...... (502) 564-8100 ext. 621
Counties Represented: Jefferson (part)   Res: (502) 589-2780
Term Expires: 2017
2250 Winston Avenue, Louisville, KY 40205
E-mail: morgan.mcgarvey@lrc.ky.gov
Committees: Appropriations and Revenue; Banking and Insurance; State and Local Government
Education: Missouri BA; Kentucky JD

Senator **Gerald A. Neal** (D-District 33) ........ (502) 564-8100 ext. 718
Counties Represented: Jefferson (part)   Tel: (502) 584-8500
Term Expires: 2017   Res: (502) 776-1222
Meidinger Tower, 462 South Fourth Street,   Fax: (502) 584-1119
Suite 2150, Louisville, KY 40202
E-mail: gerald.neal@lrc.ky.gov
Committees: Education; Rules; Transportation; Veterans, Military Affairs and Public Protection

Senator **Dennis Parrett** (D-District 10) ......... (502) 564-8100 ext. 645
Counties Represented: Hardin, Jefferson (part)   Res: (270) 765-4565
Term Expires: 2019
731 Thomas Road, Elizabethtown, KY 42701
E-mail: dennis.parrett@lrc.ky.gov
Committees: Agriculture; Appropriations and Revenue; Banking and Insurance; Enrollment; Veterans, Military Affairs and Public Protection

Senator **J. Dorsey Ridley** (D-District 4) ........ (502) 564-8100 ext. 655
Counties Represented: Caldwell, Crittenden,   Tel: (270) 869-0505
Henderson, Livingston, Union, Webster   Res: (270) 826-5402
Term Expires: 2019   Fax: (270) 869-0340
4030 Hidden Creek Drive, Henderson, KY 42420
Committees: Agriculture; Banking and Insurance; State and Local Government; Transportation
Education: Western Kentucky BSBA

Senator **Albert L. Robinson** (R-District 21) ...... (502) 564-8100 ext. 604
Counties Represented: Bath, Estill, Jackson, Laurel,   Res: (606) 878-6877
Menifee, Powell
Term Expires: 2017
1249 South Main Street, London, KY 40741
E-mail: albert.robinson@lrc.ky.gov
Committees: Banking and Insurance; State and Local Government; Transportation; Veterans, Military Affairs and Public Protection
Education: Cumberland Col BS

Senator **John Schickel** (R-District 11) ......... (502) 564-8100 ext. 617
Counties Represented: Boone   Res: (859) 384-7506
Term Expires: 2017
702 Capitol Avenue, Annex Room 209, Frankfort, KY 40601
P.O. Box 991, Union, KY 41091
E-mail: john.schickel@lrc.ky.gov
Committees: Banking and Insurance; Judiciary; Licensing, Occupations and Administrative Regulations; Natural Resources and Energy
Education: Northern Kentucky BA, MPA

Senator **Wil Schroder** (R-District 24) .......... (502) 564-8100 ext. 624
Counties Represented: Bracken, Campbell, Pendleton
Term Expires: 2019
E-mail: wil.schroder@lrc.ky.gov
Committees: Appropriations and Revenue; Economic Development, Tourism and Labor; Judiciary
Education: Kentucky 1968, 1970 JD; Missouri (Kansas City) 1971 LLM

Senator **Dan "Malano" Seum** (R-District 38) .......... (502) 564-2450
Counties Represented: Bullitt, Jefferson (part)   Res: (502) 749-2859
Term Expires: 2019
1107 Holly Avenue, Fairdale, KY 40118
E-mail: dan.seum@lrc.ky.gov
Committees: Banking and Insurance; Committee on Committees; Judiciary; Licensing, Occupations and Administrative Regulations; Rules; State and Local Government; Veterans, Military Affairs and Public Protection

Senator **Brandon Smith** (R-District 30) ........ (502) 564-8100 ext. 661
Counties Represented: Bell, Breathitt, Johnson,   Res: (606) 436-4526
Leslie, Magoffin, Perry   Fax: (606) 436-4526
Term Expires: 2019
PO Box 846, Hazard, KY 41701
E-mail: brandon.smith@lrc.ky.gov
Committees: Appropriations and Revenue; Natural Resources and Energy; Transportation

Senator **Robert Stivers** (R-District 25) ................ (606) 598-2322
Counties Represented: Clay, Knox, Lee, Owsley,   Res: (606) 598-8575
Whitley, Wolfe   Fax: (606) 598-2357
Term Expires: 2017
207 Main Street, Manchester, KY 40962
E-mail: robert.stivers@lrc.ky.gov
Committees: Committee on Committees; Judiciary; Rules

Senator **Damon Thayer** (R-District 17) ................ (502) 564-2450
Counties Represented: Grant, Kenton (part), Scott   Res: (859) 621-6956
Term Expires: 2017   Fax: (502) 868-6086
102 Grayson Way, Georgetown, KY 40324
E-mail: damon.thayer@lrc.ky.gov
Committees: Agriculture; Committee on Committees; Licensing, Occupations and Administrative Regulations; Rules; State and Local Government

Senator **Reginald Thomas** (D-District 13) ....... (502) 564-8100 ext. 608
Counties Represented: Fayette (part)
Term Expires: 2017
702 Capitol Avenue, Annex Room 229, Frankfort, KY 40601
E-mail: reginald.thomas@lrc.ky.gov
Committees: Economic Development, Tourism and Labor; Education; Health and Welfare

Senator **Johnny Ray Turner** (D-District 29) ..... (502) 564-8100 ext. 2470
Counties Represented: Floyd, Harlan, Knott, Letcher   Res: (606) 889-6568
Term Expires: 2017
849 Crestwood Drive, Prestonsburg, KY 41653
Committees: Appropriations and Revenue; Education; Natural Resources and Energy; Transportation
Education: Morehead State BA, MA

Senator **Robin L. Webb** (D-District 18) ......... (502) 564-8100 ext. 676
Counties Represented: Boyd, Carter, Greenup   Res: (606) 474-5380
Term Expires: 2019
404 West Main Street, Grayson, KY 41143
E-mail: robin.webb@lrc.ky.gov
Committees: Agriculture; Appropriations and Revenue; Judiciary; Natural Resources and Energy
Education: Morehead State BS; Northern Kentucky JD

Senator **Stephen "Steve" West** (R-District 27) .. (502) 564-8100 ext. 806
Counties Represented: Bourbon, Fleming, Harrison, Lewis, Mason, Nicholas, Robertson, Rowan
Term Expires: 2017
702 Capitol Avenue, Annex Room 229, Frankfort, KY 40601
202 Vimont Lane, Paris, KY 40361
E-mail: steve.west@lrc.ky.gov
Committees: Agriculture; Appropriations and Revenue; Education
Education: Eastern Kentucky 1993 BA; Salmon P Chase 1996 JD

Senator **Whitney H. Westerfield** (R-District 3) ... (502) 564-8100 ext. 622
Counties Represented: Christian, Logan, Todd
Term Expires: 2017
PO Box 340, Hopkinsville, KY 42241
E-mail: whitney.westerfield@lrc.ky.gov
Committees: Agriculture; Judiciary; Natural Resources and Energy; Transportation; Veterans, Military Affairs and Public Protection
Education: Kentucky 2003 BS; Southern Illinois 2006 JD

Senator **Mike Wilson** (R-District 32)............(502) 564-8100 ext. 717
Counties Represented: Warren
Term Expires: 2019
635 Crossings Court, Bowling Green, KY 42104
E-mail: mike.wilson@lrc.ky.gov
Committees: Economic Development, Tourism and Labor; Education; Transportation; Veterans, Military Affairs and Public Protection

Res: (270) 781-7326
Fax: (270) 781-8005

Senator
**George Maxwell "Max" Wise** (R-District 16)..(502) 564-8100 ext. 673
Counties Represented: Adair, Clinton, Cumberland, McCreary, Russell, Taylor, Wayne
Term Expires: 2019
Committees: Appropriations and Revenue; Economic Development, Tourism and Labor; Education; Enrollment; Health and Welfare; Veterans, Military Affairs and Public Protection

# Senate Standing Committees

## Agriculture

**Majority Members**
Paul Hornback (R-20) *Chair*
Stephen "Steve" West (R-27)
  *Vice Chair*
C. B. Embry, Jr. (R-6)
Christopher "Chris" Girdler (R-15)
David P. Givens (R-9)
Stan Humphries (R-1)
Damon Thayer (R-17)
Whitney H. Westerfield (R-3)

**Minority Members**
Dennis Parrett (D-10)
J. Dorsey Ridley (D-4)
Robin L. Webb (D-18)

## Appropriations and Revenue

**Majority Members**
Christian "Chris" McDaniel (R-23)
  *Chair*
Stan Humphries (R-1) *Vice Chair*
Ralph Alvarado (R-28)
Danny Carroll (R-2)
Christopher "Chris" Girdler (R-15)
David P. Givens (R-9)
Wil Schroder (R-24)
Brandon Smith (R-30)
Stephen "Steve" West (R-27)
George Maxwell "Max" Wise
  (R-16)

**Minority Members**
Morgan McGarvey (D-19)
Dennis Parrett (D-10)
Johnny Ray Turner (D-29)
Robin L. Webb (D-18)

## Banking and Insurance

**Majority Members**
Tom Buford (R-22) *Chair*
Jared K. Carpenter (R-34)
  *Vice Chair*
Julie Raque Adams (R-36)
Christopher "Chris" Girdler (R-15)
Christian "Chris" McDaniel (R-23)
Albert L. Robinson (R-21)
John Schickel (R-11)
Dan "Malano" Seum (R-38)

**Minority Members**
Morgan McGarvey (D-19)
Dennis Parrett (D-10)
J. Dorsey Ridley (D-4)

## Committee on Committees

**Majority Members**
Robert Stivers (R-25) *Chair*
David P. Givens (R-9) *Vice Chair*
Jimmy Higdon (R-14)
Dan "Malano" Seum (R-38)
Damon Thayer (R-17)

**Minority Members**
Julian M. Carroll (D-7)
Ray S. Jones II (D-31)

## Economic Development, Tourism and Labor

**Majority Members**
Alice Forgy Kerr (R-12) *Chair*
Christopher "Chris" Girdler (R-15)
  *Vice Chair*
Carroll Gibson (R-5)
Ernie Harris (R-26)
Jimmy Higdon (R-14)
Wil Schroder (R-24)
Mike Wilson (R-32)
George Maxwell "Max" Wise
  (R-16)

**Minority Members**
Perry B. Clark (D-37)
Denise Harper Angel (D-35)
Reginald Thomas (D-13)

## Education

**Majority Members**
Mike Wilson (R-32) *Chair*
George Maxwell
  "Max" Wise (R-16)
  *Vice Chair*
Julie Raque Adams (R-36)
Jared K. Carpenter (R-34)
Danny Carroll (R-2)
David P. Givens (R-9)
Jimmy Higdon (R-14)
Alice Forgy Kerr (R-12)
Stephen "Steve" West (R-27)

**Minority Members**
Gerald A. Neal (D-33)
Reginald Thomas (D-13)
Johnny Ray Turner (D-29)

## Enrollment

**Majority Members**
George Maxwell
  "Max" Wise (R-16)
  *Chair*
David P. Givens (R-9)

**Minority Members**
Dennis Parrett (D-10)

## Health and Welfare

**Majority Members**
Julie Raque Adams (R-36) *Chair*
Ralph Alvarado (R-28) *Vice Chair*
Tom Buford (R-22)
Danny Carroll (R-2)
David P. Givens (R-9)
Jimmy Higdon (R-14)
Alice Forgy Kerr (R-12)
George Maxwell "Max" Wise
  (R-16)

**Minority Members**
Julian M. Carroll (D-7)
Denise Harper Angel (D-35)
Reginald Thomas (D-13)

## Judiciary

**Majority Members**
Whitney H. Westerfield (R-3) *Chair*
Wil Schroder (R-24) *Vice Chair*
Danny Carroll (R-2)
Carroll Gibson (R-5)
Alice Forgy Kerr (R-12)
John Schickel (R-11)
Dan "Malano" Seum (R-38)
Robert Stivers (R-25)

**Minority Members**
Perry B. Clark (D-37)
Ray S. Jones II (D-31)
Robin L. Webb (D-18)

## Licensing, Occupations and Administrative Regulations

**Majority Members**
John Schickel (R-11) *Chair*
Paul Hornback (R-20) *Vice Chair*
Joe Bowen (R-8)
Tom Buford (R-22)
Jimmy Higdon (R-14)
Christian "Chris" McDaniel (R-23)
Dan "Malano" Seum (R-38)
Damon Thayer (R-17)

**Minority Members**
Julian M. Carroll (D-7)
Denise Harper Angel (D-35)
Ray S. Jones II (D-31)

## Natural Resources and Energy

**Majority Members**
Jared K. Carpenter (R-34) *Chair*
Brandon Smith (R-30) *Vice Chair*
C. B. Embry, Jr. (R-6)
Christopher "Chris" Girdler (R-15)
Ernie Harris (R-26)
Paul Hornback (R-20)
John Schickel (R-11)
Whitney H. Westerfield (R-3)

**Minority Members**
Ray S. Jones II (D-31)
Johnny Ray Turner (D-29)
Robin L. Webb (D-18)

## Rules

**Majority Members**
Robert Stivers (R-25) *Chair*
David P. Givens (R-9) *Vice Chair*
Jimmy Higdon (R-14)
Dan "Malano" Seum (R-38)
Damon Thayer (R-17)

**Minority Members**
Julian M. Carroll (D-7)
Gerald A. Neal (D-33)

**LEGISLATIVE BRANCH**

## State and Local Government

| Majority Members | Minority Members |
|---|---|
| Joe Bowen (R-8) *Chair* | Denise Harper Angel (D-35) |
| Stan Humphries (R-1) *Vice Chair* | Morgan McGarvey (D-19) |
| Julie Raque Adams (R-36) | J. Dorsey Ridley (D-4) |
| Ralph Alvarado (R-28) | |
| Christian "Chris" McDaniel (R-23) | |
| Albert L. Robinson (R-21) | |
| Dan "Malano" Seum (R-38) | |
| Damon Thayer (R-17) | |

## Transportation

| Majority Members | Minority Members |
|---|---|
| Ernie Harris (R-26) *Chair* | Ray S. Jones II (D-31) |
| Brandon Smith (R-30) *Vice Chair* | Gerald A. Neal (D-33) |
| Joe Bowen (R-8) | J. Dorsey Ridley (D-4) |
| Jared K. Carpenter (R-34) | Johnny Ray Turner (D-29) |
| C. B. Embry, Jr. (R-6) | |
| Jimmy Higdon (R-14) | |
| Albert L. Robinson (R-21) | |
| Whitney H. Westerfield (R-3) | |
| Mike Wilson (R-32) | |

## Veterans, Military Affairs and Public Protection

| Majority Members | Minority Members |
|---|---|
| Albert L. Robinson (R-21) *Chair* | Julian M. Carroll (D-7) |
| C. B. Embry, Jr. (R-6) *Vice Chair* | Perry B. Clark (D-37) |
| Carroll Gibson (R-5) | Gerald A. Neal (D-33) |
| Ernie Harris (R-26) | Dennis Parrett (D-10) |
| Stan Humphries (R-1) | |
| Christian "Chris" McDaniel (R-23) | |
| Dan "Malano" Seum (R-38) | |
| Whitney H. Westerfield (R-3) | |
| Mike Wilson (R-32) | |
| George Maxwell "Max" Wise (R-16) | |

# Kentucky House of Representatives

Tel: (502) 564-8100 Fax: (502) 564-6543

Speaker of the House **Gregory D. "Greg" Stumbo** (D) . . . (502) 564-2363
  Education: Kentucky BA; Louisville JD
  Chief of Staff **Steve Collins** . . . . . . . . . . . . . . . . (502) 564-8100 ext. 699
    E-mail: steve.collins@lrc.ky.gov
Speaker Pro Tem **Jody Richards** (D) . . . . . . . . . . . . . . . (502) 564-2363
  Education: Kentucky Wesleyan AB; Missouri 1962 MA
Majority Floor Leader **Rocky Adkins** (D) . . . . . . . . . . . . . .(502) 564-5565
  Education: Morehead State BA, MA
Majority Caucus Chairman **Sannie Overly** (D) . . . (502) 564-8100 ext. 752
Majority Whip **Johnny W. Bell** (D) . . . . . . . . . . . (502) 564-8100 ext. 688
  Education: Western Kentucky BS; Salmon P Chase JD
Minority Floor Leader **Jeffrey H. Hoover** (R) . . . . . . . . . . . (502) 564-0521
  Education: Centre; Cumberland JD
Minority Caucus Chairman **J. Stan Lee** (R) . . . . . . . . . . . . .(502) 564-5391
  Education: Kentucky 1983 BS, 1988 JD
Minority Whip **James "Jim" DeCesare** (R) . . . . . (502) 564-8100 ext. 660
Chief Clerk of the House **Jean Burgin** . . . . . . . . . . . . . . . .(502) 564-3900
  E-mail: jean.burgin@lrc.ky.gov
Sergeant-at-Arms **Dale Rogers** . . . . . . . . . . . . . . . . . . . . (502) 564-8100

# Representatives

**Party Affiliation Statistics:** Republicans: 47, Democrats: 53

Representative **Rocky Adkins** (D-District 99) . . . . . . . . . . .(502) 564-5565
  Counties Represented: Elliott, Lewis, Rowan          Tel: (606) 928-3433
  Term Expires: 2017                                    Res: (606) 738-4242
  P.O. Box 688, Sandy Hook, KY 41171                   Fax: (606) 929-5913
  E-mail: rocky.adkins@lrc.ky.gov
  Committees: Committees; Enrollment; Rules
Representative **Lynn Bechler** (R-District 4) . . . . . . (502) 564-8100 ext. 665
  Counties Represented: Caldwell, Christian (part),     Res: (270) 988-4171
  Crittenden, Livingston
  Term Expires: 2017
  2359 Brown Mines Road, Marion, KY 42064
  E-mail: lynn.bechler@lrc.ky.gov
  Committees: Agriculture and Small Business; Economic Development;
  Labor and Industry

Representative
  **Linda Howlett Belcher** (D-District 49) . . . . . . . . (502) 564-8100 ext. 651
  Counties Represented: Bullitt (part)
  Term Expires: 2017
  E-mail: linda.belcher@lrc.ky.gov
  Committees: Appropriations and Revenue; Education; Labor and
  Industry; Local Government
Representative **Johnny W. Bell** (D-District 23) . . . (502) 564-8100 ext. 688
  Counties Represented: Barren, Warren (part)          Tel: (270) 651-7005
  Term Expires: 2017                                    Res: (270) 590-0110
  108 North Green Street, Glasgow, KY 42141
  E-mail: johnny.bell@lrc.ky.gov
  Committees: Agriculture and Small Business; Banking and
  Insurance; Committees; Elections, Constitutional Amendments and
  Intergovernmental Affairs; Judiciary; Rules; State Government;
  Veterans, Military Affairs and Public Safety
Representative
  **Robert J. Benvenuti III** (R-District 88) . . . . . . . . (502) 564-8100 ext. 628
  Counties Represented: Fayette (part)
  Term Expires: 2017
  702 Capitol Avenue, Annex Room 429J, Frankfort, KY 40601
  2384 Abbeywood Road, Lexington, KY 40515
  E-mail: robert.benvenuti@lrc.ky.gov
  Committees: Health and Welfare; Judiciary; Veterans, Military Affairs
  and Public Safety
  Education: Kentucky 1988 BS, 1991 MPA, 1998 JD
Representative **Kevin D. Bratcher** (R-District 29) . . . . . (502) 564-8100 ext.
680
  Counties Represented: Jefferson (part)               Res: (502) 231-3311
  Term Expires: 2017
  10215 Landwood Drive, Louisville, KY 40291
  E-mail: kevin.bratcher@lrc.ky.gov
  Committees: Elections, Constitutional Amendments and
  Intergovernmental Affairs; State Government; Tourism Development
  and Energy
  Education: Embry-Riddle BS
Representative
  **George A. Brown, Jr.** (D-District 77) . . . . . . . . . (502) 564-8100 ext. 620
  Counties Represented: Fayette (part)
  Term Expires: 2017
  E-mail: george.brown@lrc.ky.gov
  Committees: Economic Development; Education; Health and Welfare
  Education: Tennessee State BBA
Representative **Regina Bunch** (R-District 82) . . . . . (502) 564-8100 ext. 683
  Counties Represented: Laurel (part), Whitley
  Term Expires: 2017
  1051 Old Corbin Pike Road, Williamsburg, KY 40769
  E-mail: regina.bunch@lrc.ky.gov
  Committees: Education; Labor and Industry; Veterans, Military Affairs
  and Public Safety
Representative
  **Thomas J. "Tom" Burch** (D-District 30) . . . . . . (502) 564-8100 ext. 601
  Counties Represented: Jefferson (part)               Res: (502) 454-4002
  Term Expires: 2017
  4012 Lambert Avenue, Louisville, KY 40218
  E-mail: tom.burch@lrc.ky.gov
  Committees: Health and Welfare; Licensing and Occupations; Veterans,
  Military Affairs and Public Safety
  Education: Bellarmine BA
Representative
  **Denver "Denny" Butler** (R-District 38) . . . . . . . (502) 564-8100 ext. 670
  Counties Represented: Jefferson (part)
  Term Expires: 2017
  PO Box 9041, Louisville, KY 40209
  E-mail: denny.butler@lrc.ky.gov
  Committees: Appropriations and Revenue; Labor and Industry;
  Licensing and Occupations; Transportation; Veterans, Military Affairs
  and Public Safety
  Education: Louisville 2005 BS
Representative
  **John "Bam" Carney** (R-District 51) . . . . . . . . . (502) 564-8100 ext. 708
  Counties Represented: Adair, Taylor                  Res: (270) 465-5400
  Term Expires: 2017
  702 Capitol Avenue, Annex Room 413A, Frankfort, KY 40601
  341 Pembroke Way, Campbellsville, KY 42718
  E-mail: john.carney@lrc.ky.gov
  Committees: Appropriations and Revenue; Education; State
  Government

LEGISLATIVE BRANCH

Representative **Lawrence "Larry" Clark** (D-District 46) . . . (502) 564-7520
Counties Represented: Jefferson (part)　　Res: (502) 968-3546
Term Expires: 2017
5913 Whispering Hills Boulevard, Louisville, KY 40219
E-mail: larry.clark@lrc.ky.gov
Committees: Appropriations and Revenue; Licensing and Occupations;
Rules; Tourism Development and Energy; Veterans, Military Affairs
and Public Safety

Representative **Hubert Collins** (D-District 97) . . . . (502) 564-8100 ext. 654
Counties Represented: Johnson, Morgan, Wolfe　　Res: (606) 297-3152
Term Expires: 2017
72 Collins Drive, Wittensville, KY 41274
E-mail: hubert.collins@lrc.ky.gov
Committees: Education; Natural Resources and Environment; Tourism
Development and Energy; Transportation
Education: Morehead State BA, MA

Representative **Leslie A. Combs** (D-District 94) . . (502) 564-8100 ext. 669
Counties Represented: Letcher, Pike (part)　　Tel: (606) 433-4317
Term Expires: 2017　　Res: (606) 477-6672
245 East Cedar Drive, Pikeville, KY 41501
E-mail: leslie.combs@lrc.ky.gov
Committees: Appropriations and Revenue; Education; State
Government; Tourism Development and Energy; Transportation;
Veterans, Military Affairs and Public Safety
Education: Transylvania BBA

Representative **Tim Couch** (R-District 90) . . . . . . . (502) 564-8100 ext. 632
Counties Represented: Clay, Laurel (part), Leslie　　Res: (606) 672-8998
Term Expires: 2017　　Fax: (606) 672-8998
P.O. Box 710, Hyden, KY 41749
E-mail: tim.couch@lrc.ky.gov
Committees: Natural Resources and Environment; State Government;
Transportation; Veterans, Military Affairs and Public Safety
Education: Cumberland Col

Representative
**William R. Coursey** (D-District 6) . . . . . . . . . . . (502) 564-8100 ext. 659
Counties Represented: Lyon, Marshall, McCracken　　Tel: (270) 527-4610
(part)
Term Expires: 2017
285 Oak-Level Elva Road, Symsonia, KY 42082
Committees: Agriculture and Small Business; Banking and Insurance;
Labor and Industry; State Government; Transportation; Veterans,
Military Affairs and Public Safety

Representative
**Ronald "Ron" Crimm** (R-District 33) . . . . . . . . (502) 564-8100 ext. 706
Counties Represented: Jefferson (part), Oldham　　Tel: (502) 245-2118
(part)　　Res: (502) 245-8905
Term Expires: 2017
P.O. Box 43244, Louisville, KY 40253
E-mail: ron.crimm@lrc.ky.gov
Committees: Appropriations and Revenue; Banking and Insurance;
Local Government; Veterans, Military Affairs and Public Safety
Education: Shippensburg BS

Representative
**James "Jim" DeCesare** (R-District 17) . . . . . . . (502) 564-8100 ext. 660
Counties Represented: Butler, Warren (part)　　Tel: (270) 792-5779
Term Expires: 2017　　Fax: (888) 275-1182
136 Cedar Trail Avenue, Bowling Green, KY 42101
P.O. Box 122, Rockfield, KY 42274
E-mail: jim.decesare@lrc.ky.gov
Committees: Economic Development; Education; Rules

Representative
**Mitchel B. "Mike" Denham** (D-District 70) . . . . (502) 564-8100 ext. 696
Counties Represented: Bracken, Fleming, Mason,　　Tel: (606) 759-5167
Robertson
Term Expires: 2017
306 Old Hill City Road, Maysville, KY 41056
E-mail: mitchel.denham@lrc.ky.gov
Committees: Agriculture and Small Business; Appropriations and
Revenue; Banking and Insurance; Economic Development; Local
Government

Representative **Bob M. DeWeese** (R-District 48) . . . . . . . . (502) 564-5391
Counties Represented: Jefferson (part), Oldham　　Tel: (502) 564-4334
(part)　　Res: (502) 426-5565
Term Expires: 2017
6206 Glen Hill Road, Louisville, KY 40222
E-mail: bob.deweese@lrc.ky.gov
Committees: Appropriations and Revenue; Economic Development;
Health and Welfare; Rules
Education: Kentucky BS; Louisville MD

Representative
**Jeffery M. Donohue** (D-District 37) . . . . . . . . . (502) 564-8100 ext. 629
Counties Represented: Jefferson (part)　　Tel: (502) 439-6175
Term Expires: 2017
702 Capitol Avenue, Annex Room 324C, Frankfort, KY 40601
P.O. Box 509, Fairdale, KY 40118
E-mail: jeffery.donohue@lrc.ky.gov
Committees: Appropriations and Revenue; Economic Development;
Education; Labor and Industry; Licensing and Occupations

Representative **Myron B. Dossett** (R-District 9) . . (502) 564-8100 ext. 657
Counties Represented: Christian (part), Hopkins　　Res: (270) 475-9503
(part)
Term Expires: 2017
491 East Nashville Street, Pembroke, KY 42266
E-mail: myron.dossett@lrc.ky.gov
Committees: Agriculture and Small Business; Appropriations and
Revenue; Tourism Development and Energy; Veterans, Military Affairs
and Public Safety

Representative **Jim DuPlessis** (R-District 25) . . . . . (502) 564-8100 ext. 650
Counties Represented: Hardin (part)
Term Expires: 2017
E-mail: jim.duplessis@lrc.ky.gov
Committees: Natural Resources and Environment

Representative **Daniel B. Elliott** (R-District 54) . . . . . . . . . (502) 564-8100
Counties Represented: Boyle, Casey
Term Expires: 2017

Representative
**Joseph M. Fischer** (R-District 68) . . . . . . . . . . . (502) 564-8100 ext. 742
Counties Represented: Campbell (part)　　Tel: (513) 794-6442
Term Expires: 2017　　Res: (859) 781-6965
126 Dixie Place, Fort Thomas, KY 41075
E-mail: joe.fischer@lrc.ky.gov
Committees: Banking and Insurance; Elections, Constitutional
Amendments and Intergovernmental Affairs; Judiciary
Education: Holy Cross Col BA; Cincinnati JD

Representative **Kelly Flood** (D-District 75) . . . . . . . (502) 564-8100 ext. 675
Counties Represented: Fayette (part)　　Res: (859) 221-3107
Term Expires: 2017
702 Capitol Avenue, Annex Room 357A, Frankfort, KY 40601
121 Arcadia Park, Lexington, KY 40503
E-mail: kelly.flood@lrc.ky.gov
Committees: Appropriations and Revenue; Education; Judiciary

Representative
**David W. Floyd, USAF (Ret)** (R-District 50) . . . (502) 564-8100 ext. 698
Counties Represented: Nelson　　Res: (502) 350-0986
Term Expires: 2017
102 Maywood Avenue, Bardstown, KY 40004
E-mail: david.floyd@lrc.ky.gov
Committees: Licensing and Occupations; Transportation; Veterans,
Military Affairs and Public Safety
Education: Air Force Acad BS; Embry-Riddle MAS

Representative **Jim Glenn** (D-District 13) . . . . . . . . (502) 564-8100 ext. 705
Counties Represented: Daviess (part)　　Res: (270) 686-8760
Term Expires: 2017
P.O. Box 21562, Owensboro, KY 42304
E-mail: jim.glenn@lrc.ky.gov
Committees: Agriculture and Small Business; Appropriations and
Revenue; Education; State Government; Veterans, Military Affairs and
Public Safety
Education: Wisconsin (Oshkosh) MBA

Representative **James Gooch, Jr.** (R-District 12) . . (502) 564-8100 ext. 687
Counties Represented: Daviess (part), Hopkins　　Tel: (270) 635-1139
(part), McLean, Webster　　Res: (270) 667-7327
Term Expires: 2017　　Fax: (270) 667-5111
17 North Broadway B2, Providence, KY 42450
E-mail: jim.gooch@lrc.ky.gov
Committees: Banking and Insurance; Natural Resources and
Environment; State Government; Tourism Development and Energy
Affiliation: Vice President, West Kentucky Steel Construction Company,
Inc.

Representative
**Derrick W. Graham** (D-District 57)
702 Capitol Annex, Room 329J . . . . . . . . . . . . . . (502) 564-8100 ext. 639
Counties Represented: Franklin (part)　　Res: (502) 223-1769
Term Expires: 2017
E-mail: derrick.graham@lrc.ky.gov
Committees: Agriculture and Small Business; Education; Elections,
Constitutional Amendments and Intergovernmental Affairs; State
Government
Education: Kentucky State BA; Ohio State MA

*(continued on next page)*

LEGISLATIVE BRANCH

**Representatives** *continued*

Representative **Jeff Greer** (D-District 27) . . . . . . . (502) 564-8100 ext. 603
Counties Represented: Hardin (part), Meade     Res: (270) 422-3764
Term Expires: 2017     Fax: (270) 422-5010
2125 Highway 79, Brandenburg, KY 40108
E-mail: jeff.greer@lrc.ky.gov
Committees: Banking and Insurance; Labor and Industry; Veterans,
Military Affairs and Public Safety
Education: Eastern Kentucky BBA

Representative **David Hale** (R-District 74) . . . . . . . (502) 564-8100 ext. 642
Counties Represented: Menifee, Montgomery, Powell
Term Expires: 2017
E-mail: david.hale@lrc.ky.gov
Committees: Agriculture and Small Business

Representative **Chris Harris** (D-District 93) . . . . . . (502) 564-8100 ext. 635
Counties Represented: Martin, Pike (part)
Term Expires: 2017
E-mail: chris.harris@lrc.ky.gov
Committees: Banking and Insurance; Judiciary; Natural Resources and
Environment; Tourism Development and Energy

Representative **Richard Heath** (R-District 2) . . . . . (502) 564-9100 ext. 638
Counties Represented: Graves, McCracken (part)
Term Expires: 2017
438 Millers Chapel Road, Mayfield, KY 42066
E-mail: richard.heath@lrc.ky.gov
Committees: Agriculture and Small Business; Economic Development
Education: Murray State U 1984 BS, 1989 MA

Representative **Jeffrey H. Hoover** (R-District 83) . . . . . . . (502) 564-0521
Counties Represented: Clinton, Cumberland,     Tel: (270) 343-5588
Pulaski (part), Russell     Res: (270) 343-2264
Term Expires: 2017
P.O. Box 985, Jamestown, KY 42629
E-mail: jeff.hoover@lrc.ky.gov
Committees: Committees; Enrollment; Judiciary; Rules

Representative
**Dennis Horlander** (D-District 40) . . . . . . . . . . . (502) 564-8100 ext. 636
Counties Represented: Jefferson (part)     Tel: (502) 447-2498
Term Expires: 2017     Res: (502) 447-6122
1806 Farnsley Road, Suite 6, Shively, KY 40216     Fax: (502) 447-4715
E-mail: dennis.horlander@lrc.ky.gov
Committees: Banking and Insurance; Economic Development; Labor
and Industry; Licensing and Occupations
Affiliation: President, Horlander & Associates
Education: Louisville

Representative **Cluster Howard** (D-District 91) . . . (502) 564-8100 ext. 641
Counties Represented: Breathitt, Estill, Lee, Madison (part), Owsley
Term Expires: 2017
E-mail: cluster.howard@lrc.ky.gov
Committees: Economic Development; Education; Local Government;
Natural Resources and Environment

Representative **Kenny Imes** (D-District 5) . . . . . . . (502) 564-8100 ext. 611
Counties Represented: Calloway, Trigg (part)
Term Expires: 2017
4064 US 641 North, Murray, KY 42071
E-mail: kenny.imes@lrc.ky.gov
Committees: State Government; Veterans, Military Affairs and Public
Safety
Education: Murray State U 1969 (Attended)

Representative **Joni L. Jenkins** (D-District 44) . . . (502) 564-8100 ext. 692
Counties Represented: Jefferson (part)     Res: (502) 447-4324
Term Expires: 2017
2010 O'Brien Court, Shively, KY 40216
E-mail: joni.jenkins@lrc.ky.gov
Committees: Appropriations and Revenue; Health and Welfare;
Judiciary; Labor and Industry; Licensing and Occupations; Rules
Education: Kentucky BA

Representative **James Kay** (D-District 56) . . . . . . . . . . . . . (859) 846-4407
Counties Represented: Fayette (part), Franklin (part), Woodford
Term Expires: 2017
702 Capitol Avenue, Annex Room 451A, Frankfort, KY 40601
P.O. Box 1536, Versailles, KY 40383
E-mail: james.kay@lrc.ky.gov
Committees: Agriculture and Small Business; Education; Tourism
Development and Energy

Representative **Dennis Keene** (D-District 67) . . . . . (502) 564-8100 ext. 626
Counties Represented: Campbell (part)     Res: (859) 411-5894
Term Expires: 2017
1040 John Hill Road, Wilder, KY 41076
E-mail: dennis.keene@lrc.ky.gov
Committees: Banking and Insurance; Economic Development;
Licensing and Occupations

Representative
**Thomas Robert "Tom" Kerr** (R-District 64) . . . (502) 564-8100 ext. 694
Counties Represented: Campbell (part), Kenton     Tel: (859) 431-2222
(part)     Res: (859) 356-1344
Term Expires: 2017     Fax: (859) 431-3463
5415 Old Taylor Mill Road, Taylor Mill, KY 41015
E-mail: thomas.kerr@lrc.ky.gov
Committees: Banking and Insurance; Economic Development;
Judiciary; Labor and Industry; Tourism Development and Energy
Education: Kentucky BBA; Salmon P Chase JD

Representative **Kim King** (R-District 55) . . . . . . . . (502) 564-8100 ext. 763
Counties Represented: Jessamine (part), Mercer,     Res: (859) 734-2173
Washington
Term Expires: 2017
250 Bright Leaf Drive, Harrodsburg, KY 40330
E-mail: kim.king@lrc.ky.gov
Committees: Agriculture and Small Business; Economic Development;
Tourism Development and Energy

Representative
**Martha Jane King** (D-District 16) . . . . . . . . . . . (502) 564-8100 ext. 618
Counties Represented: Logan, Todd, Warren (part)     Res: (270) 657-2707
Term Expires: 2017     Fax: (270) 657-2755
702 Capitol Avenue, Annex Room 329J, Frankfort, KY 40601
Lake Malone, 633 Little Cliff Estates, Lewisburg, KY 42256
E-mail: marthajane.king@lrc.ky.gov
Committees: Agriculture and Small Business; Appropriations and
Revenue; State Government; Tourism Development and Energy;
Veterans, Military Affairs and Public Safety

Representative **Adam Koenig** (R-District 69) . . . . . (502) 564-8100 ext. 689
Counties Represented: Boone (part), Kenton (part)     Res: (859) 578-9258
Term Expires: 2017
3346 Canterbury Court, Erlanger, KY 41018
E-mail: adam.koenig@lrc.ky.gov
Committees: Banking and Insurance; Labor and Industry; Licensing
and Occupations; Local Government
Education: Miami U (OH) 1993 BA

Representative **J. Stan Lee** (R-District 45) . . . . . . . . . . . . . (502) 564-5391
Counties Represented: Fayette (part)     Tel: (502) 564-4334
Term Expires: 2017     Res: (859) 252-2202
P.O. Box 2090, Lexington, KY 40588     Fax: (859) 259-2927
E-mail: stan.lee@lrc.ky.gov
Committees: Judiciary; Local Government; Rules

Representative **Brian E. Linder** (R-District 61) . . . . (502) 564-8100 ext. 627
Counties Represented: Boone (part), Grant, Kenton (part), Scott (part)
Term Expires: 2017
16 Ridgeview Circle, Dry Ridge, KY 41035
E-mail: brian.linder@lrc.ky.gov
Committees: Education; Local Government; Tourism Development and
Energy
Education: Kentucky 1996 BA; Thomas More Col 2000 MBA

Representative
**Mary Lou Marzian** (D-District 34) . . . . . . . . . . (502) 564-8100 ext. 643
Counties Represented: Jefferson (part)     Res: (502) 451-5032
Term Expires: 2017
2007 Tyler Lane, Louisville, KY 40205
E-mail: marylou.marzian@lrc.ky.gov
Committees: Education; Elections, Constitutional Amendments and
Intergovernmental Affairs; Health and Welfare; Judiciary; Labor and
Industry
Education: Louisville BS

Representative **Donna Mayfield** (R-District 73) . . . (502) 564-8100 ext. 630
Counties Represented: Clark, Madison (part)     Res: (859) 745-5941
Term Expires: 2017
2059 Elkin Station Road, Winchester, KY 40391
E-mail: donna.mayfield@lrc.ky.gov
Committees: Education; Transportation; Veterans, Military Affairs and
Public Safety

Representative
**Thomas M. McKee** (D-District 78) . . . . . . . . . . (502) 564-8100 ext. 667
Counties Represented: Harrison, Pendleton, Scott     Res: (859) 234-5879
(part)     Fax: (859) 234-3332
Term Expires: 2017
1053 Cook Road, Cynthiana, KY 41031
E-mail: tom.mckee@lrc.ky.gov
Committees: Agriculture and Small Business; Local Government;
Tourism Development and Energy; Transportation
Education: Centre BA

LEGISLATIVE BRANCH

Representative **David Meade** (R-District 80) . . . . . (502) 564-8100 ext. 661
Counties Represented: Lincoln, Pulaski (part)
Term Expires: 2017
702 Capitol Ave, Room 405A, Frankfort, KY 40601
E-mail: david.meade@lrc.ky.gov
Committees: Banking and Insurance; Licensing and Occupations; State Government

Representative
**Reginald K. Meeks** (D-District 42) . . . . . . . . . . (502) 564-8100 ext. 653
Counties Represented: Jefferson (part)          Res: (502) 772-1095
Term Expires: 2017
P.O. Box 757, Louisville, KY 40210
E-mail: reginald.meeks@lrc.ky.gov
E-mail: srmeeks42@aol.com
Committees: Appropriations and Revenue; Education; Health and Welfare; Judiciary; Licensing and Occupations; Natural Resources and Environment
Education: Wabash Col BA; Iowa JD

Representative
**Michael Lee Meredith** (R-District 19) . . . . . . . . (502) 564-8100 ext. 719
Counties Represented: Edmonson, Warren (part)    Dist: (270) 597-6049
Term Expires: 2017
P.O. Box 292, Brownsville, KY 42210
E-mail: michael.meredith@lrc.ky.gov
Committees: Agriculture and Small Business; Banking and Insurance; Local Government

Representative **Russ A. Meyer** (D-District 39) . . . . (502) 564-8100 ext. 623
Counties Represented: Fayette (part), Jessamine (part)
Term Expires: 2017
E-mail: russ.meyer@lrc.ky.gov
Committees: Banking and Insurance; Local Government; Transportation

Representative **Suzanne Miles** (R-District 7) . . . . . (502) 564-8100 ext. 709
Counties Represented: Daviess (part), Henderson (part), Union
Term Expires: 2017
702 Capitol Avenue, Annex Room 451E, Frankfort, KY 40601
E-mail: suzanne.miles@lrc.ky.gov
Committees: Agriculture and Small Business; Judiciary; State Government

Representative **Charles W. Miller** (D-District 28) . . (502) 564-8100 ext. 631
Counties Represented: Jefferson (part)          Res: (502) 937-7788
Term Expires: 2017
3608 Gateview Circle, Louisville, KY 40272
E-mail: charlie.miller@lrc.ky.gov
Committees: Education; Labor and Industry; Licensing and Occupations; Transportation
Education: Western Kentucky BA, MA

Representative **Jerry T. Miller** (R-District 36) . . . . . (502) 564-8100 ext. 718
Counties Represented: Jefferson (part), Oldham (part)
Term Expires: 2017
E-mail: jerry.miller@lrc.ky.gov
Committees: Labor and Industry; Transportation

Representative **Terry Mills** (D-District 24) . . . . . . . (502) 564-8100 ext. 684
Counties Represented: Green, Larue, Marion      Res: (270) 692-2757
Term Expires: 2017
695 McElroy Pike, Lebanon, KY 40033
E-mail: terry.mills@lrc.ky.gov
Committees: Agriculture and Small Business; Appropriations and Revenue; Economic Development; Labor and Industry; Transportation; Veterans, Military Affairs and Public Safety

Representative **Phil Moffett** (R-District 32) . . . . . . (502) 564-8100 ext. 708
Counties Represented: Jefferson (part)
Term Expires: 2017
E-mail: phil.moffett@lrc.ky.gov
Committees: Health and Welfare

Representative **Brad Montell** (R-District 58) . . . . . (502) 564-8100 ext. 609
Counties Represented: Shelby              Tel: (502) 633-7017
Term Expires: 2017                        Res: (502) 633-7533
543 Main Street, Shelbyville, KY 40065
P.O. 1016, Shelbyville, KY 40066
E-mail: brad.montell@lrc.ky.gov
Committees: Banking and Insurance; State Government
Education: Western Kentucky BA, MA

Representative **Tim Moore** (R-District 18) . . . . . . . (502) 564-8100 ext. 702
Counties Represented: Grayson, Hardin (part)    Res: (502) 769-5878
Term Expires: 2017
417 Bates Road, Elizabethtown, KY 42701
E-mail: tim.moore@lrc.ky.gov
Committees: Health and Welfare; Natural Resources and Environment; Veterans, Military Affairs and Public Safety
Education: Air Force Acad 1988 BS; Arkansas MS

Representative **Rick G. Nelson** (D-District 87) . . . . (502) 564-8100 ext. 612
Counties Represented: Bell, Harlan (part)       Res: (606) 248-8828
Term Expires: 2017                              Fax: (606) 248-8828
Route 3, Box 686, Middlesboro, KY 40965
E-mail: rick.nelson@lrc.ky.gov
Committees: Education; Labor and Industry; Transportation; Veterans, Military Affairs and Public Safety
Education: Cumberland Col BS; Eastern Kentucky MA

Representative **Lew Nicholls** (D-District 98) . . . . . . . . . . . (502) 564-8100
Counties Represented: Boyd (part), Greenup
Term Expires: 2017

Representative **David Osborne** (R-District 59) . . . . (502) 564-8100 ext. 679
Counties Represented: Oldham (part)             Tel: (502) 645-2186
Term Expires: 2017                              Res: (502) 228-3201
P.O. Box 8, Prospect, KY 40059
E-mail: david.osborne@lrc.ky.gov
Committees: Agriculture and Small Business; Banking and Insurance; Licensing and Occupations; Rules; Tourism Development and Energy
Education: Kentucky BS

Representative **Sannie Overly** (D-District 72) . . . . (502) 564-8100 ext. 752
Counties Represented: Bath, Bourbon, Fayette    Res: (859) 987-9879
(part), Nicholas
Term Expires: 2017
340 Main Street, Paris, KY 40361
E-mail: sannie.overly@lrc.ky.gov
Committees: Agriculture and Small Business; Banking and Insurance; Committees; Elections, Constitutional Amendments and Intergovernmental Affairs; Enrollment; Rules

Representative **Darryl T. Owens** (D-District 43) . . . (502) 564-8100 ext. 685
Counties Represented: Jefferson (part)          Tel: (502) 584-6341
Term Expires: 2017                              Fax: (502) 584-6342
1300 West Broadway, Louisville, KY 40203
E-mail: darryl.owens@lrc.ky.gov
Committees: Elections, Constitutional Amendments and Intergovernmental Affairs; Health and Welfare; Judiciary; Licensing and Occupations
Education: Central State BA; Howard U JD

Representative
**Ruth Ann Palumbo** (D-District 76) . . . . . . . . . . (502) 564-8100 ext. 600
Counties Represented: Fayette (part)            Tel: (606) 299-2598
Term Expires: 2017                              Res: (606) 299-2597
10 Deepwood Drive, Lexington, KY 40505
E-mail: ruthann.palumbo@lrc.ky.gov
Committees: Banking and Insurance; Economic Development; Education; Health and Welfare; Licensing and Occupations; Rules
Education: Kentucky BA

Representative **Marie L. Rader** (R-District 89) . . . . (502) 564-8100 ext. 720
Counties Represented: Jackson, Laurel (part),   Res: (606) 287-7303
Madison (part)                                  Fax: (606) 287-3300
Term Expires: 2017
P.O. Box 323, McKee, KY 40447
E-mail: marie.rader@lrc.ky.gov
Committees: Appropriations and Revenue; Education; Natural Resources and Environment; Transportation
Education: Berea

Representative **Rick W. Rand** (D-District 47) . . . . . (502) 564-8100 ext. 619
Counties Represented: Carroll, Gallatin, Henry,  Tel: (502) 255-3286
Trimble                                          Res: (502) 255-3392
Term Expires: 2017                               Fax: (502) 255-9911
P.O. Box 273, Bedford, KY 40006
E-mail: rick.rand@lrc.ky.gov
Committees: Appropriations and Revenue
Education: Hanover BA

Representative **Jody Richards** (D-District 20) . . . . . . . . . . . (502) 564-2363
Counties Represented: Warren (part)             Tel: (270) 781-9946
Term Expires: 2017                              Res: (270) 842-6731
817 Culpeper Street, Bowling Green, KY 42103   Fax: (270) 781-9963
E-mail: jody.richards@lrc.ky.gov
Committees: Banking and Insurance; Committees; Education; Local Government; Rules; State Government
Affiliation: Owner, Superior Books

Representative **Steven Riggs** (D-District 31) . . . . . (502) 564-8100 ext. 674
Counties Represented: Jefferson (part)          Fax: (502) 564-6543
Term Expires: 2017
8108 Thornwood Road, Louisville, KY 40220
Committees: Banking and Insurance; Local Government; Rules; Transportation
Education: Kentucky BBA

*(continued on next page)*

**LEGISLATIVE BRANCH**

**Representatives** *continued*

Representative **Tom Riner** (D-District 41) . . . . . . . . (502) 564-8100 ext. 606
Counties Represented: Jefferson (part)         Res: (502) 584-3639
Term Expires: 2017
1143 East Broadway, Louisville, KY 40204
E-mail: tom.riner@lrc.ky.gov
Committees: Agriculture and Small Business; Education; Judiciary;
Labor and Industry; State Government; Veterans, Military Affairs and
Public Safety

Representative **Bart T. Rowland** (R-District 21) . . . (502) 564-8100 ext. 613
Counties Represented: Hardin (part), Hart, Metcalfe,    Res: (270) 407-3233
Monroe
Term Expires: 2017
3823 Poplar Log Church Road, Tompkinsville, KY 42167
E-mail: bart.rowland@lrc.ky.gov
Committees: Agriculture and Small Business; Banking and Insurance;
Education

Representative **Steven Jack Rudy** (R-District 1) . . (502) 564-8100 ext. 637
Counties Represented: Ballard, Carlisle, Fulton,    Res: (270) 744-8137
Hickman, McCracken (part)
Term Expires: 2017
3430 Blue Ridge, West Paducah, KY 42086
E-mail: steven.rudy@lrc.ky.gov
Committees: Agriculture and Small Business; Appropriations and
Revenue; Rules; State Government
Education: Murray State U

Representative **Sal Santoro** (R-District 60) . . . . . . (502) 564-8100 ext. 691
Counties Represented: Boone (part)         Res: (859) 371-8840
Term Expires: 2017              Fax: (859) 371-4060
596 Walterlot Court, Florence, KY 41042
E-mail: sal.santoro@lrc.ky.gov
Committees: Appropriations and Revenue; Education; Licensing and
Occupations; State Government; Transportation
Education: Cincinnati BA; Xavier (OH) MA

Representative **Dean Schamore** (D-District 10) . . . (502) 564-8100 ext. 704
Counties Represented: Breckinridge, Hancock, Hardin (part)
Term Expires: 2017
E-mail: dean.schamore@lrc.ky.gov
Committees: Agriculture and Small Business; Economic Development;
Tourism Development and Energy

Representative **Jonathan Shell** (R-District 71) . . . . (502) 564-8100 ext. 649
Counties Represented: Garrard, Madison (part), Rockcastle
Term Expires: 2017
702 Capitol Avenue, Annex Room 432B, Frankfort, KY 40601
P.O. Box 138, Lancaster, KY 40444
E-mail: jonathan.shell@lrc.ky.gov
Committees: Banking and Insurance; Local Government
Education: Eastern Kentucky BS

Representative **John W. Short** (D-District 92) . . . . (502) 564-8100 ext. 668
Counties Represented: Knott, Magoffin, Pike (part)    Dist: (606) 785-9018
Term Expires: 2017
240 Briarwood Lane, Mallie, KY 41836
E-mail: john.short@lrc.ky.gov
Committees: Agriculture and Small Business; Economic Development;
Natural Resources and Environment; Tourism Development and Energy;
Transportation

Representative
**Arnold R. Simpson** (D-District 65) . . . . . . . . . . (502) 564-8100 ext. 695
Counties Represented: Kenton (part)         Tel: (859) 261-6577
Term Expires: 2017              Res: (859) 581-6521
702 Capitol Avenue, Annex Room 357B, Frankfort, KY 40601
E-mail: arnold.simpson@lrc.ky.gov
Committees: Appropriations and Revenue; Economic Development;
Licensing and Occupations; Local Government; Rules; Transportation
Education: Kentucky State BA; Kentucky JD

Representative
**Kevin P. Sinnette** (D-District 100) . . . . . . . . . . . (502) 564-8100 ext. 703
Counties Represented: Boyd (part)         Res: (606) 324-5711
Term Expires: 2017              Fax: (606) 329-1430
702 Capitol Avenue, Annex Room 316E, Frankfort, KY 40601
P.O. Box 1358, Ashland, KY 41105
E-mail: kevin.sinnette@lrc.ky.gov
Committees: Banking and Insurance; Local Government; Natural
Resources and Environment; Rules

Representative **Rita H. Smart** (D-District 81) . . . . . (502) 564-8100 ext. 607
Counties Represented: Madison (part)         Res: (859) 623-7876
Term Expires: 2017
419 West Main Street, Richmond, KY 40475
E-mail: rita.smart@lrc.ky.gov
Committees: Agriculture and Small Business; Appropriations and
Revenue; Education; Local Government; Veterans, Military Affairs and
Public Safety

Representative **Diane St. Onge** (R-District 63) . . . (502) 564-8100 ext. 701
Counties Represented: Boone (part), Kenton (part)
Term Expires: 2017
PO Box 17351, Lakeside Park, KY 41017
E-mail: diane.st.onge@lrc.ky.gov
Committees: Licensing and Occupations; State Government;
Transportation
Education: Northern Kentucky BA; Salmon P Chase JD

Representative **Fitz Steele** (D-District 84) . . . . . . . (502) 564-8100 ext. 697
Counties Represented: Harlan (part), Perry    Res: (606) 439-0556
Term Expires: 2017              Fax: (606) 439-0556
702 Capitol Avenue, Annex Room 316B, Frankfort, KY 40601
176 Woodland Avenue, Hazard, KY 41701
E-mail: fitz.steele@lrc.ky.gov
Committees: Appropriations and Revenue; Banking and Insurance;
Natural Resources and Environment; Tourism Development and Energy;
Transportation

Representative **Jim Stewart III** (R-District 86) . . . . (502) 564-8100 ext. 690
Counties Represented: Knox, Laurel (part)    Res: (606) 542-5210
Term Expires: 2017
141 KY 223, Flat Lick, KY 40935
E-mail: jim.stewart@lrc.ky.gov
Committees: Appropriations and Revenue; Education; Labor and
Industry; Natural Resources and Environment; Transportation

Representative **Wilson Stone** (D-District 22) . . . . . (502) 564-8100 ext. 672
Counties Represented: Allen, Simpson, Warren    Res: (270) 622-5054
(part)
Term Expires: 2017
702 Capitol Avenue, Annex Room 329A, Frankfort, KY 40601
1481 Jefferson School Road, Scottsville, KY 42164
E-mail: wilson.stone@lrc.ky.gov
Committees: Agriculture and Small Business; Appropriations and
Revenue; Banking and Insurance; Economic Development; Education

Representative
**Gregory D. "Greg" Stumbo** (D-District 95) . . . . . . . . . . (502) 564-2363
Counties Represented: Floyd, Pike (part)    Res: (606) 886-9953
Term Expires: 2017
108 Kassidy Drive, P.O. Box 1473, Prestonsburg, KY 41653
Committees: Committees; Rules

Representative **Chuck Tackett** (D-District 62) . . . . . . . . . . (502) 564-8100
Counties Represented: Fayette (part), Owen, Scott (part)
Term Expires: 2017
E-mail: chuck.tackett@lrc.ky.gov

Representative **Jeffery R. Taylor** (D-District 8) . . . . . . . . . (502) 564-8100
Counties Represented: Christian (part), Trigg (part)
Term Expires: 2017

Representative **Thomas N. "Tommy"
Thompson** (D-District 14) . . . . . . . . . . . . . . . . (502) 564-8100 ext. 664
Counties Represented: Daviess (part), Ohio    Res: (270) 926-1740
Term Expires: 2017              Fax: (270) 685-3242
P.O. Box 458, Owensboro, KY 42303
E-mail: tommy.thompson@lrc.ky.gov
Committees: Banking and Insurance; Economic Development; Rules;
State Government
Education: Florida 1970 BSBA; Indiana 1972 MBA

Representative **James A. Tipton** (R-District 53) . . (502) 564-8100 ext. 793
Counties Represented: Anderson, Bullitt (part), Spencer
Term Expires: 2017
E-mail: james.tipton@lrc.ky.gov
Committees: Agriculture and Small Business

Representative **Tommy Turner** (R-District 85) . . . . (502) 564-8100 ext. 716
Counties Represented: Laurel (part), Pulaski (part)    Res: (606) 274-5175
Term Expires: 2017
175 Clifty Grove Church Road, Somerset, KY 42501
E-mail: tommy.turner@lrc.ky.gov
Committees: Agriculture and Small Business; Appropriations and
Revenue; Rules; State Government; Transportation

Representative **Ken Upchurch** (R-District 52) . . . . . . . . . . (502) 564-3900
Counties Represented: McCreary, Pulaski (part), Wayne
Term Expires: 2017
702 Capitol Avenue, Annex Room 451C, Frankfort, KY 40601
P.O. Box 969, Monticello, KY 42633
E-mail: ken.upchurch@lrc.ky.gov
Committees: Banking and Insurance; Judiciary; State Government
Education: Eastern Kentucky BA

Representative

**Dr. David Allen Watkins** (D-District 11)....... (502) 564-8100 ext. 700
Counties Represented: Daviess (part), Henderson (part)   Res: (270) 826-0952
Fax: (270) 826-3338
Term Expires: 2017
5600 Timberlane Drive, Henderson, KY 42420
E-mail: david.watkins@lrc.ky.gov
Committees: Appropriations and Revenue; Education; Health and
Welfare; Tourism Development and Energy; Transportation
Education: Western Kentucky BS, MA; Louisville MD

Representative **Gerald Watkins** (D-District 3) ........... (502) 564-3900
Counties Represented: McCracken (part)
Term Expires: 2017
702 Capitol Avenue, Annex Room 332A, Frankfort, KY 40601
E-mail: gerald.watkins@lrc.ky.gov
Committees: Education; Judiciary; Tourism Development and Energy
Education: Murray State U 1981 BS, 1984 MBA

Representative **Jim Wayne** (D-District 35)....... (502) 564-8100 ext. 616
Counties Represented: Jefferson (part)   Res: (502) 451-8262
Term Expires: 2017
1280 Royal Avenue, Louisville, KY 40204
E-mail: jim.wayne@lrc.ky.gov
Committees: Appropriations and Revenue; Local Government; State
Government
Affiliation: President, Wayne & Associates, Inc.
Education: Maryknoll BA, MA; Smith MSW

Representative **Russell Webber** (R-District 26) ... (502) 564-8100 ext. 663
Counties Represented: Bullitt (part), Hardin (part)
Term Expires: 2017
PO Box 6605, Shepherdsville, KY 40165
E-mail: russell.webber@lrc.ky.gov
Committees: Economic Development; Health and Welfare; Veterans,
Military Affairs and Public Safety
Education: Kentucky 1989 BA

Representative **Susan Westrom** (D-District 79)... (502) 564-8100 ext. 740
Counties Represented: Fayette (part)   Res: (859) 266-7581
Term Expires: 2017
P.O. Box 22778, Lexington, KY 40522-2778
E-mail: susan.westrom@lrc.ky.gov
Committees: Appropriations and Revenue; Enrollment; Health and
Welfare; Licensing and Occupations; Local Government
Education: Kentucky BA, MA

Representative

**Addia Kathryn Wuchner** (R-District 66)...... (502) 564-8100 ext. 707
Counties Represented: Boone (part)   Res: (859) 525-6698
Term Expires: 2017
P.O. Box 911, Burlington, KY 41005
E-mail: addia.wuchner@lrc.ky.gov
Committees: Appropriations and Revenue; Education; Health and
Welfare; Transportation

Representative **Brent Yonts** (D-District 15)...... (502) 564-8100 ext. 686
Counties Represented: Hopkins (part), Muhlenberg   Tel: (270) 338-0816
Term Expires: 2017   Res: (270) 338-6790
232 Norman Circle, Greenville, KY 42345   Fax: (270) 338-1639
E-mail: brent.yonts@lrc.ky.gov
Committees: Judiciary; Labor and Industry; State Government
Education: Murray State U BS; Kentucky JD

Representative **Jill York** (R-District 96)................ (606) 474-7263
Counties Represented: Carter, Lawrence   Tel: (502) 564-8100
Term Expires: 2017   ext. 602
P.O. Box 591, Grayson, KY 41143   Fax: (606) 474-7638
E-mail: jill.york@lrc.ky.gov
Committees: Appropriations and Revenue; Education; Natural
Resources and Environment; Tourism Development and Energy

# House Standing Committees

## Agriculture and Small Business

**Majority Members**
Thomas M. McKee (D-78) *Chair*
Mitchel B. "Mike" Denham (D-70)
  *Vice Chair*
James Kay (D-56) *Vice Chair*
Terry Mills (D-24) *Vice Chair*
Wilson Stone (D-22) *Vice Chair*
Johnny W. Bell (D-23)
William R. Coursey (D-6)
Jim Glenn (D-13)
Derrick W. Graham (D-57)

**Minority Members**
Lynn Bechler (R-4) *Vice Chair*
Richard Heath (R-2) *Vice Chair*
Myron B. Dossett (R-9)
David Hale (R-74)
Kim King (R-55)
Michael Lee Meredith (R-19)
Suzanne Miles (R-7)
David Osborne (R-59)
Bart T. Rowland (R-21)
Steven Jack Rudy (R-1)

**Majority Members** *continued*
Martha Jane King (D-16)
Sannie Overly (D-72)
Tom Riner (D-41)
Dean Schamore (D-10)
John W. Short (D-92)
Rita H. Smart (D-81)

**Minority Members** *continued*
James A. Tipton (R-53)
Tommy Turner (R-85)

## Appropriations and Revenue

**Majority Members**
Rick W. Rand (D-47) *Chair*
Arnold R. Simpson (D-65)
  *Vice Chair*
Linda Howlett Belcher (D-49)
Lawrence "Larry" Clark (D-46)
Leslie A. Combs (D-94)
Mitchel B. "Mike" Denham (D-70)
Jeffery M. Donohue (D-37)
Kelly Flood (D-75)
Jim Glenn (D-13)
Joni L. Jenkins (D-44)
Martha Jane King (D-16)
Reginald K. Meeks (D-42)
Terry Mills (D-24)
Rita H. Smart (D-81)
Fitz Steele (D-84)
Wilson Stone (D-22)
Dr. David Allen Watkins (D-11)
Jim Wayne (D-35)
Susan Westrom (D-79)

**Minority Members**
Denver "Denny" Butler (R-38)
Bob M. DeWeese (R-48) *Vice Chair*
John "Bam" Carney (R-51)
Ronald "Ron" Crimm (R-33)
Myron B. Dossett (R-9)
Marie L. Rader (R-89)
Steven Jack Rudy (R-1)
Sal Santoro (R-60)
Jim Stewart III (R-86)
Tommy Turner (R-85)
Addia Kathryn Wuchner (R-66)
Jill York (R-96)

## Banking and Insurance

**Majority Members**
Jeff Greer (D-27) *Chair*
William R. Coursey (D-6)
  *Vice Chair*
Mitchel B. "Mike" Denham (D-70)
  *Vice Chair*
Steven Riggs (D-31) *Vice Chair*
Kevin P. Sinnette (D-100)
  *Vice Chair*
Johnny W. Bell (D-23)
Chris Harris (D-93)
Dennis Horlander (D-40)
Dennis Keene (D-67)
Russ A. Meyer (D-39)
Sannie Overly (D-72)
Ruth Ann Palumbo (D-76)
Jody Richards (D-20)
Fitz Steele (D-84)
Wilson Stone (D-22)
Thomas N. "Tommy" Thompson
  (D-14)

**Minority Members**
James Gooch, Jr. (R-12)
Ronald "Ron" Crimm (R-33)
  *Vice Chair*
David Osborne (R-59) *Vice Chair*
Bart T. Rowland (R-21) *Vice Chair*
Joseph M. Fischer (R-68)
Thomas Robert "Tom" Kerr (R-64)
Adam Koenig (R-69)
David Meade (R-80)
Michael Lee Meredith (R-19)
Brad Montell (R-58)
Jonathan Shell (R-71)
Ken Upchurch (R-52)

## Committees

**Majority Members**
Gregory D. "Greg" Stumbo (D-95)
  *Chair*
Rocky Adkins (D-99)
Johnny W. Bell (D-23)
Sannie Overly (D-72)
Jody Richards (D-20)

**Minority Members**
Jeffrey H. Hoover (R-83)

## Economic Development

**Majority Members**
Ruth Ann Palumbo (D-76) *Chair*
Dennis Keene (D-67) *Vice Chair*
George A. Brown, Jr. (D-77)
Mitchel B. "Mike" Denham (D-70)
Jeffery M. Donohue (D-37)
Dennis Horlander (D-40)
Cluster Howard (D-91)
Terry Mills (D-24)
Dean Schamore (D-10)
John W. Short (D-92)
Arnold R. Simpson (D-65)
Wilson Stone (D-22)
Thomas N. "Tommy" Thompson
  (D-14)

**Minority Members**
Russell Webber (R-26) *Vice Chair*
Lynn Bechler (R-4)
James "Jim" DeCesare (R-17)
Bob M. DeWeese (R-48)
Richard Heath (R-2)
Thomas Robert "Tom" Kerr (R-64)
Kim King (R-55)

**LEGISLATIVE BRANCH**

## Education

**Majority Members**
Derrick W. Graham (D-57) *Chair*
Charles W. Miller (D-28)
  *Vice Chair*
Rick G. Nelson (D-87) *Vice Chair*
Tom Riner (D-41) *Vice Chair*
Wilson Stone (D-22) *Vice Chair*
Gerald Watkins (D-3) *Vice Chair*
Linda Howlett Belcher (D-49)
George A. Brown, Jr. (D-77)
Hubert Collins (D-97)
Leslie A. Combs (D-94)
Jeffery M. Donohue (D-37)
Kelly Flood (D-75)
Jim Glenn (D-13)
Cluster Howard (D-91)
James Kay (D-56)
Mary Lou Marzian (D-34)
Reginald K. Meeks (D-42)
Ruth Ann Palumbo (D-76)
Jody Richards (D-20)
Rita H. Smart (D-81)
Dr. David Allen Watkins (D-11)

**Minority Members**
John "Bam" Carney (R-51)
  *Vice Chair*
Jill York (R-96) *Vice Chair*
Regina Bunch (R-82)
James "Jim" DeCesare (R-17)
Brian E. Linder (R-61)
Donna Mayfield (R-73)
Marie L. Rader (R-89)
Bart T. Rowland (R-21)
Sal Santoro (R-60)
Jim Stewart III (R-86)
Addia Kathryn Wuchner (R-66)

## Elections, Constitutional Amendments and Intergovernmental Affairs

**Majority Members**
Darryl T. Owens (D-43) *Chair*
Mary Lou Marzian (D-34)
  *Vice Chair*
Johnny W. Bell (D-23)
Derrick W. Graham (D-57)
Sannie Overly (D-72)

**Minority Members**
Kevin D. Bratcher (R-29)
  *Vice Chair*
Joseph M. Fischer (R-68)
  *Vice Chair*

## Enrollment

**Majority Members**
Susan Westrom (D-79) *Chair*
Rocky Adkins (D-99)
Sannie Overly (D-72)

**Minority Members**
Jeffrey H. Hoover (R-83)

## Health and Welfare

**Majority Members**
Thomas J. "Tom" Burch (D-30)
  *Chair*
Dr. David Allen Watkins (D-11)
  *Vice Chair*
George A. Brown, Jr. (D-77)
Joni L. Jenkins (D-44)
Mary Lou Marzian (D-34)
Reginald K. Meeks (D-42)
Darryl T. Owens (D-43)
Ruth Ann Palumbo (D-76)
Susan Westrom (D-79)

**Minority Members**
Robert J. Benvenuti III (R-88)
  *Vice Chair*
Addia Kathryn Wuchner (R-66)
  *Vice Chair*
Bob M. DeWeese (R-48)
Phil Moffett (R-32)
Tim Moore (R-18)
Russell Webber (R-26)

## Judiciary

**Majority Members**
Darryl T. Owens (D-43) *Chair*
Brent Yonts (D-15) *Vice Chair*
Johnny W. Bell (D-23)
Kelly Flood (D-75)
Chris Harris (D-93)
Joni L. Jenkins (D-44)
Mary Lou Marzian (D-34)
Reginald K. Meeks (D-42)
Tom Riner (D-41)
Gerald Watkins (D-3)

**Minority Members**
Joseph M. Fischer (R-68)
  *Vice Chair*
Robert J. Benvenuti III (R-88)
Jeffrey H. Hoover (R-83)
Thomas Robert "Tom" Kerr (R-64)
J. Stan Lee (R-45)
Suzanne Miles (R-7)
Ken Upchurch (R-52)

## Labor and Industry

**Majority Members**
Rick G. Nelson (D-87) *Chair*
Jeffery M. Donohue (D-37)
  *Vice Chair*
Joni L. Jenkins (D-44) *Vice Chair*
Charles W. Miller (D-28)
  *Vice Chair*
William R. Coursey (D-6)
Jeff Greer (D-27)
Dennis Horlander (D-40)
Mary Lou Marzian (D-34)
Terry Mills (D-24)
Tom Riner (D-41)
Brent Yonts (D-15)
Linda Howlett Belcher (D-49)

**Minority Members**
Adam Koenig (R-69) *Vice Chair*
Lynn Bechler (R-4)
Regina Bunch (R-82)
Denver "Denny" Butler (R-38)
Thomas Robert "Tom" Kerr (R-64)
Jerry T. Miller (R-36)
Jim Stewart III (R-86)

## Licensing and Occupations

**Majority Members**
Dennis Keene (D-67) *Chair*
Reginald K. Meeks (D-42)
  *Vice Chair*
Charles W. Miller (D-28)
  *Vice Chair*
Susan Westrom (D-79) *Vice Chair*
Thomas J. "Tom" Burch (D-30)
Lawrence "Larry" Clark (D-46)
Jeffery M. Donohue (D-37)
Dennis Horlander (D-40)
Joni L. Jenkins (D-44)
Darryl T. Owens (D-43)
Ruth Ann Palumbo (D-76)
Arnold R. Simpson (D-65)

**Minority Members**
Denver "Denny" Butler (R-38)
  *Vice Chair*
David Meade (R-80) *Vice Chair*
David Osborne (R-59) *Vice Chair*
David W. Floyd (R-50)
Adam Koenig (R-69)
Sal Santoro (R-60)
Diane St. Onge (R-63)

## Local Government

**Majority Members**
Steven Riggs (D-31) *Chair*
Mitchel B. "Mike" Denham (D-70)
  *Vice Chair*
Jim Wayne (D-35) *Vice Chair*
Linda Howlett Belcher (D-49)
Cluster Howard (D-91)
Thomas M. McKee (D-78)
Russ A. Meyer (D-39)
Jody Richards (D-20)
Arnold R. Simpson (D-65)
Kevin P. Sinnette (D-100)
Rita H. Smart (D-81)
Susan Westrom (D-79)

**Minority Members**
Michael Lee Meredith (R-19)
  *Vice Chair*
Jonathan Shell (R-71) *Vice Chair*
Ronald "Ron" Crimm (R-33)
Adam Koenig (R-69)
J. Stan Lee (R-45)
Brian E. Linder (R-61)

## Natural Resources and Environment

**Majority Members**
Fitz Steele (D-84) *Vice Chair*
Hubert Collins (D-97)
Chris Harris (D-93)
Cluster Howard (D-91)
Reginald K. Meeks (D-42)
Kevin P. Sinnette (D-100)
John W. Short (D-92)

**Minority Members**
James Gooch, Jr. (R-12) *Chair*
Tim Couch (R-90) *Vice Chair*
Jim Stewart III (R-86) *Vice Chair*
Jim DuPlessis (R-25)
Tim Moore (R-18)
Marie L. Rader (R-89)
Jill York (R-96)

## Rules

**Majority Members**
Gregory D. "Greg" Stumbo (D-95)
  *Chair*
Rocky Adkins (D-99)
Johnny W. Bell (D-23)
Lawrence "Larry" Clark (D-46)
Joni L. Jenkins (D-44)
Sannie Overly (D-72)
Ruth Ann Palumbo (D-76)
Jody Richards (D-20)
Steven Riggs (D-31)
Arnold R. Simpson (D-65)
Kevin P. Sinnette (D-100)
Thomas N. "Tommy" Thompson
  (D-14)

**Minority Members**
James "Jim" DeCesare (R-17)
Bob M. DeWeese (R-48)
Jeffrey H. Hoover (R-83)
J. Stan Lee (R-45)
David Osborne (R-59)
Steven Jack Rudy (R-1)
Tommy Turner (R-85)

## State Government

**Majority Members**

Brent Yonts (D-15) *Chair*
Jim Glenn (D-13) *Vice Chair*
Derrick W. Graham (D-57)
  *Vice Chair*
Kenny Imes (D-5) *Vice Chair*
Johnny W. Bell (D-23)
Leslie A. Combs (D-94)
William R. Coursey (D-6)
Martha Jane King (D-16)
Jody Richards (D-20)
Tom Riner (D-41)
Thomas N. "Tommy" Thompson
  (D-14)
Jim Wayne (D-35)

**Minority Members**

James Gooch, Jr. (R-12)
Steven Jack Rudy (R-1) *Vice Chair*
Kevin D. Bratcher (R-29)
John "Bam" Carney (R-51)
Tim Couch (R-90)
David Meade (R-80)
Suzanne Miles (R-7)
Brad Montell (R-58)
Sal Santoro (R-60)
Diane St. Onge (R-63)
Tommy Turner (R-85)
Ken Upchurch (R-52)

## Tourism Development and Energy

**Majority Members**

John W. Short (D-92) *Chair*
Fitz Steele (D-84) *Vice Chair*
Dr. David Allen Watkins (D-11)
  *Vice Chair*
Gerald Watkins (D-3) *Vice Chair*
Lawrence "Larry" Clark (D-46)
Hubert Collins (D-97)
Leslie A. Combs (D-94)
Chris Harris (D-93)
James Kay (D-56)
Martha Jane King (D-16)
Thomas M. McKee (D-78)
Dean Schamore (D-10)

**Minority Members**

James Gooch, Jr. (R-12)
Brian E. Linder (R-61) *Vice Chair*
Kevin D. Bratcher (R-29)
Myron B. Dossett (R-9)
Thomas Robert "Tom" Kerr (R-64)
Kim King (R-55)
David Osborne (R-59)
Jill York (R-96)

## Transportation

**Majority Members**

Hubert Collins (D-97) *Chair*
Leslie A. Combs (D-94) *Vice Chair*
Charles W. Miller (D-28)
  *Vice Chair*
William R. Coursey (D-6)
Thomas M. McKee (D-78)
Russ A. Meyer (D-39)
Terry Mills (D-24)
Rick G. Nelson (D-87)
Steven Riggs (D-31)
John W. Short (D-92)
Arnold R. Simpson (D-65)
Fitz Steele (D-84)
Dr. David Allen Watkins (D-11)

**Minority Members**

Marie L. Rader (R-89) *Vice Chair*
Diane St. Onge (R-63) *Vice Chair*
Denver "Denny" Butler (R-38)
Tim Couch (R-90)
David W. Floyd (R-50)
Donna Mayfield (R-73)
Jerry T. Miller (R-36)
Sal Santoro (R-60)
Jim Stewart III (R-86)
Tommy Turner (R-85)
Addia Kathryn Wuchner (R-66)

## Veterans, Military Affairs and Public Safety

**Majority Members**

Jeff Greer (D-27) *Vice Chair*
Johnny W. Bell (D-23)
Thomas J. "Tom" Burch (D-30)
Lawrence "Larry" Clark (D-46)
Leslie A. Combs (D-94)
William R. Coursey (D-6)
Jim Glenn (D-13)
Kenny Imes (D-5)
Martha Jane King (D-16)
Terry Mills (D-24)
Rick G. Nelson (D-87)
Tom Riner (D-41)
Rita H. Smart (D-81)

**Minority Members**

Myron B. Dossett (R-9) *Vice Chair*
David W. Floyd (R-50) *Vice Chair*
Robert J. Benvenuti III (R-88)
Regina Bunch (R-82)
Denver "Denny" Butler (R-38)
Tim Couch (R-90)
Ronald "Ron" Crimm (R-33)
Donna Mayfield (R-73)
Tim Moore (R-18)
Russell Webber (R-26)

# Louisiana Legislature

State Capitol, 900 North Third Street, Baton Rouge, LA 70804
Fax: (225) 342-9784  Internet: www.legis.la.gov

## Louisiana State Senate

P.O. Box 94183, Baton Rouge, LA 70804
Tel: (225) 342-2040  Fax: (225) 342-9784
E-mail: websen@legis.state.la.us  Internet: www.senate.legis.state.la.us

President of the Senate **John A. Alario, Jr.** (R) . . . . . . . . . (504) 340-2221
  Education: Southeastern Louisiana 1965 BA
President Pro Tem **Gerald Long** (R) . . . . . . . . . . . . . . . . . . (318) 628-5799
  Education: Northwestern State 1966 BEd
Secretary of the Senate **Glenn Koepp** . . . . . . . . . . . . . . . (225) 342-5997
  E-mail: koeppg@legis.state.la.us
  Education: LSU BA, JD
Sergeant-at-Arms **John Keller** . . . . . . . . . . . . . . . . . . . . . (225) 342-6198
  E-mail: kellerj@legis.state.la.us
Parliamentarian **Daniel R. "Danny" Martiny** (R) . . . . . . . . (225) 342-2366
  Education: LSU 1973 BA; Loyola U (New Orleans) 1976 JD

## Senators

**Party Affiliation Statistics:** Republicans: 25, Democrats: 14

Senator **John A. Alario, Jr.** (R-District 8) . . . . . . . . . . . . . (225) 342-2040
  Parishes Represented: Jefferson Parish (part),        Dist: (504) 340-2221
  Plaquemines Parish (part)                             Fax: (504) 341-0794
  Term Expires: 2020
  1063 Muller Parkway, Westwego, LA 70094
  E-mail: alarioj@legis.la.gov
  Committees: Joint Legislative Capital Outlay

Senator **Robert L. "Bret" Allain** (R-District 21) . . . . . . . . (225) 342-2040
  Parishes Represented: Iberia Parish (part),           Dist: (337) 828-9107
  Lafourche Parish (part), St. Mary Parish,             Fax: (337) 828-9108
  Terrebonne Parish (part)
  Term Expires: 2020
  600 Main Street, Suite One, Franklin, LA 70804
  E-mail: allainb@legis.la.gov
  Committees: Agriculture, Forestry, Aquaculture, and Rural
  Development; Commerce, Consumer Protection, and International
  Affairs; Finance; Natural Resources
  Education: LSU 1981 BS

Senator **Conrad H. Appel III** (R-District 9) . . . . . . . . . . . . (225) 342-2040
  Parishes Represented: Jefferson Parish (part),        Dist: (504) 838-5550
  Orleans Parish (part)
  Term Expires: 2020
  721 Papworth Avenue, Suite 102A, Metairie, LA 70005
  E-mail: appelc@legis.la.gov
  Committees: Commerce, Consumer Protection, and International
  Affairs; Education; Environmental Quality; Finance
  Education: LSU 1973 BSEE

Senator **Regina Ashford Barrow** (D-District 15) . . . . . . . . (225) 359-9400
  Parishes Represented: East Baton Rouge Parish         Fax: (225) 359-9402
  (part)
  Term Expires: 2020
  4811 Harding Boulevard, Baton Rouge, LA 70811
  E-mail: barrowr@legis.la.gov
  Committees: Finance; Health and Welfare; Judiciary C; Labor and
  Industrial Relations

Senator **Wesley T. Bishop** (D-District 4) . . . . . . . . . . . . . (504) 242-4198
  Parishes Represented: Orleans Parish (part)           Fax: (504) 242-6116
  Term Expires: 2020
  7240 Crowder Boulevard, Suite 402, New Orleans, LA 70127
  E-mail: bishopw@legis.la.gov
  Committees: Finance; Judiciary A; Labor and Industrial Relations;
  Senate and Governmental Affairs
  Education: Southern U (New Orleans) 1990 BS;
  Mississippi 1991 MPA; Ohio State 1995 JD

Senator **Gerald Boudreaux** (D-District 24) . . . . . . . . . . . . (337) 267-7520
  Parishes Represented: Lafayette Parish (part), St.    Fax: (337) 267-7522
  Landry Parish (part), St. Martin Parish (part)
  Term Expires: 2020
  2900 Moss Street, Suite B, Lafayette, LA 70501
  E-mail: boudreauxg@legis.la.gov
  Committees: Education; Health and Welfare; Retirement

*(continued on next page)*

LEGISLATIVE BRANCH

**Senators** *continued*

Senator **Troy E. Brown** (D-District 2) . . . . . . . . . . . . . . . (225) 342-2040
  Parishes Represented: Ascension Parish (part),      Dist: (985) 369-3333
  Assumption Parish (part), Iberville Parish (part),      Fax: (985) 369-3334
  Lafourche Parish (part), St. Charles Parish (part), St. James Parish
  (part), St. John the Baptist Parish (part), West Baton Rouge Parish
  (part)
  Term Expires: 2020
  P.O. Box 974, Napoleonville, LA 70390
  E-mail: brownte@legis.la.gov
  Committees: Environmental Quality; Health and Welfare; Joint
  Legislative Capital Outlay; Revenue and Fiscal Affairs; Transportation,
  Highways and Public Works
  Education: Southern U (New Orleans) BS

Senator **Troy A. Carter** (D-District 7) . . . . . . . . . . . . . . . (225) 342-2040
  Parishes Represented: Jefferson Parish (part),      Dist: (504) 302-3682
  Orleans Parish (part), Plaquemines Parish (part)      Fax: (504) 324-0708
  Term Expires: 2020
  P.O. Box 50730, New Orleans, LA 70150
  E-mail: cartert@legis.la.gov
  Committees: Joint Legislative Capital Outlay; Judiciary C; Labor
  and Industrial Relations; Revenue and Fiscal Affairs; Senate and
  Governmental Affairs

Senator **Norby Chabert** (R-District 20) . . . . . . . . . . . . . . (225) 342-2040
  Parishes Represented: Lafourche Parish (part),      Dist: (985) 858-2927
  Terrebonne Parish (part)      Fax: (985) 858-2930
  Term Expires: 2020
  P.O. Box 2417, Houma, LA 70361
  E-mail: chabertn@legis.la.gov
  Committees: Health and Welfare; Judiciary B; Natural Resources;
  Retirement
  Education: Nicholls State 2001 BA

Senator **Dan Claitor** (R-District 16) . . . . . . . . . . . . . . . . . (225) 342-2040
  Parishes Represented: East Baton Rouge Parish      Dist: (225) 342-7602
  (part)      Fax: (225) 342-7603
  Term Expires: 2020
  320 Somerulos Street, Baton Rouge, LA 70802
  E-mail: claitord@legis.la.gov
  Committees: Health and Welfare; Judiciary C
  Education: LSU 1983 BS; Loyola U (New Orleans) 1987 JD

Senator **Patrick "Page" Cortez** (R-District 23) . . . . . . . . . (225) 342-2040
  Parishes Represented: Lafayette Parish (part)      Dist: (337) 993-7430
  Term Expires: 2020
  Building Five, 101 West Farrell Road, Suite 100, Lafayette, LA 70508
  E-mail: cortezp@legis.la.gov
  Committees: Commerce, Consumer Protection, and International
  Affairs; Retirement; Transportation, Highways and Public Works
  Education: Louisiana (Lafayette) 1986 BBS, 1988 BAE

Senator **John Leo "Jack" Donahue** (R-District 11) . . . . . . (225) 342-2040
  Parishes Represented: St. Tammany Parish (part),      Dist: (985) 727-7949
  Tangipahoa Parish (part)      Fax: (985) 727-9904
  Term Expires: 2020
  P.O. Box 896, Mandeville, LA 70470
  3030 East Causeway Approach, Mandeville, LA 70448
  E-mail: donahuej@legis.la.gov
  Committees: Finance; Judiciary A; Local and Municipal Affairs; Senate
  and Governmental Affairs
  Education: LSU 1967 BSCE

Senator **Yvonne Colomb** (D-District 14) . . . . . . . . . . . . . . (225) 342-2040
  Parishes Represented: East Baton Rouge Parish      Dist: (225) 342-9700
  (part)
  Term Expires: 2020
  1520 Thomas H. Delpit Drive, Suite 226, Baton Rouge, LA 70802
  E-mail: colomby@legis.la.gov
  Committees: Health and Welfare; Joint Legislative Capital Outlay;
  Judiciary C; Local and Municipal Affairs; Revenue and Fiscal Affairs
  Education: LSU 2008 BS

Senator **Dale M. Erdey** (R-District 13) . . . . . . . . . . . . . . . (225) 342-2040
  Parishes Represented: East Baton Rouge Parish      Dist: (225) 686-2881
  (part), Livingston Parish (part), Tangipahoa Parish      Fax: (225) 686-7353
  (part)
  Term Expires: 2020
  P.O. Box 908, Livingston, LA 70754
  E-mail: erdeyd@legis.la.gov
  Committees: Environmental Quality; Health and Welfare; Joint
  Legislative Capital Outlay; Revenue and Fiscal Affairs; Transportation,
  Highways and Public Works
  Education: LSU 1976 BS

Senator **James R. "Jim" Fannin** (R-District 35) . . . . . . . . . (318) 259-6620
  Parishes Represented: Grant Parish (part), Jackson      Fax: (318) 259-6645
  Parish (part), Lincoln Parish (part), Ouachita Parish (part), Rapides
  Parish (part), Winn Parish (part)
  Term Expires: 2020
  320 Sixth Street, Jonesboro, LA 71251
  E-mail: fanninj@legis.la.gov
  Committees: Agriculture, Forestry, Aquaculture, and Rural
  Development; Finance; Joint Legislative Capital Outlay; Senate and
  Governmental Affairs; Transportation, Highways and Public Works

Senator **Ryan Gatti** (R-District 36) . . . . . . . . . . . . . . . . . . (225) 342-2040
  Parishes Represented: Bienville Parish (part),      Dist: (318) 746-0861
  Bossier Parish (part), Claiborne Parish (part),      Fax: (318) 746-3955
  Webster Parish
  Term Expires: 2020
  2123 Shed Road, Bossier City, LA 71111
  E-mail: gattir@legis.la.gov
  Committees: Insurance; Judiciary A; Natural Resources

Senator **Sharon Hewitt** (R-District 1) . . . . . . . . . . . . . . . . (225) 342-2040
  Parishes Represented: Orleans Parish (part),      Dist: (985) 646-6490
  Plaquemines Parish (part), St. Bernard Parish (part),      Fax: (985) 646-6497
  St. Tammany Parish (part)
  Term Expires: 2020
  2055 Second Street, Suite A, Slidell, LA 70458
  E-mail: hewitts@legis.la.gov
  Committees: Environmental Quality; Finance; Transportation, Highways
  and Public Works

Senator **Ronnie S. Johns** (R-District 27) . . . . . . . . . . . . . . (225) 342-2040
  Parishes Represented: Calcasieu Parish (part)      Dist: (337) 491-2016
  Term Expires: 2020
  1011 Lakeshore Drive, Suite 515, Lake Charles, LA 70601
  E-mail: johnsr@legis.la.gov
  Committees: Finance; Insurance; Joint Legislative Capital Outlay;
  Judiciary B; Labor and Industrial Relations
  Education: Northeast Louisiana 1972 BS

Senator **Eric LaFleur** (D-District 28) . . . . . . . . . . . . . . . . . (225) 342-2040
  Parishes Represented: Acadia Parish (part), Allen      Dist: (337) 363-5019
  Parish, Avoyelles Parish (part), Evangeline Parish,      Fax: (337) 363-6812
  St. Landry Parish (part)
  Term Expires: 2020
  P.O. Box 617, Ville Platte, LA 70586
  E-mail: lafleure@legis.la.gov
  Committees: Finance; Insurance; Joint Legislative Capital Outlay;
  Judiciary B
  Education: Tulane BA, 1991 JD

Senator **Eddie J. Lambert** (R-District 18) . . . . . . . . . . . . . (225) 673-5048
  Parishes Represented: Ascension Parish (part),      Fax: (225) 673-6980
  Livingston Parish (part), St. James Parish (part)
  Term Expires: 2020
  P.O. Box 241, Gonzales, LA 70707
  E-mail: lamberte@legis.la.gov
  Committees: Environmental Quality; Insurance; Joint Legislative
  Capital Outlay; Natural Resources; Revenue and Fiscal Affairs
  Education: LSU 1978 BA, 1982 JD

Senator **Gerald Long** (R-District 31) . . . . . . . . . . . . . . . . . (225) 342-2040
  Parishes Represented: Grant Parish (part),      Dist: (318) 628-5799
  Natchitoches Parish (part), Rapides Parish (part),      Fax: (318) 628-6120
  Red River Parish, Sabine Parish, Winn Parish (part)
  Term Expires: 2020
  P.O. Box 151, Winnfield, LA 71483
  E-mail: longg@legis.la.gov
  Committees: Agriculture, Forestry, Aquaculture, and Rural
  Development; Insurance; Retirement; Transportation, Highways and
  Public Works

Senator **Jay Luneau** (D-District 29) . . . . . . . . . . . . . . . . . . (318) 484-2288
  Parishes Represented: Bienville Parish (part), Grant      Fax: (318) 484-2287
  Parish (part), Jackson Parish (part), Lincoln Parish (part), Natchitoches
  Parish (part), Rapides Parish (part), Winn Parish (part)
  Term Expires: 2020
  711 Washington Street, Alexandria, LA 71301
  E-mail: luneauj@legis.la.gov
  Committees: Health and Welfare; Joint Legislative Capital Outlay;
  Judiciary A; Natural Resources; Revenue and Fiscal Affairs

Senator **Daniel R. "Danny" Martiny** (R-District 10) . . . . . . (225) 342-2366
  Parishes Represented: Jefferson Parish (part)      Dist: (504) 834-7676
  Term Expires: 2020      Fax: (504) 834-5409
  131 Airline Highway, Suite 201, Metairie, LA 70001
  E-mail: martinyd@legis.la.gov
  Committees: Commerce, Consumer Protection, and International
  Affairs; Judiciary A; Local and Municipal Affairs

Senator **John Milkovich** (D-District 38) . . . . . . . . . . . . . . (225) 342-2040
  Parishes Represented: Caddo Parish (part), De     Dist: (318) 676-7877
  Soto Parish        Fax: (318) 676-7879
  Term Expires: 2020
  656 Jordan Street, Shreveport, LA 71101
  E-mail: milkovichj@legis.la.gov
  Committees: Education; Judiciary A; Retirement

Senator **Fred H. Mills, Jr.** (R-District 22) . . . . . . . . . . . . . (225) 342-2040
  Parishes Represented: Iberia Parish (part), Lafayette    Dist: (337) 365-8484
  Parish (part), St. Landry Parish (part), St. Martin    Dist: (337) 845-4240
  Parish (part)        Fax: (337) 365-2730
  Term Expires: 2020        Dist: (337) 845-4095
  800 South Lewis Street, New Iberia, LA 70560
  1010 Martin Street, Parks, LA 70582
  E-mail: millsf@legis.la.gov
  Committees: Health and Welfare; Judiciary C; Local and Municipal
  Affairs
  Education: Louisiana (Monroe) 1976 BPharm

Senator **Beth Mizell** (R-District 12) . . . . . . . . . . . . . . . . . . (985) 839-3936
  Parishes Represented: St. Tammany Parish (part),     Fax: (985) 839-7714
  Tangipahoa Parish (part), Washington Parish
  Term Expires: 2020
  1051 Main Street, Franklinton, LA 70438
  E-mail: mizellb@legis.la.gov
  Committees: Commerce, Consumer Protection, and International
  Affairs; Education; Retirement

Senator **Jean-Paul J. "JP" Morrell** (D-District 3) . . . . . . . (225) 342-2040
  Parishes Represented: Jefferson Parish (part),     Dist: (504) 284-4794
  Orleans Parish (part), St. Bernard Parish (part)     Fax: (504) 284-4796
  Term Expires: 2020
  New Orleans Lakefront Terminal Building, 6001 Stars and Stripes
  Boulevard, Suite 221, New Orleans, LA 70126
  E-mail: morrelljp@legis.la.gov
  Committees: Joint Legislative Capital Outlay; Judiciary B; Labor
  and Industrial Relations; Revenue and Fiscal Affairs; Senate and
  Governmental Affairs
  Education: Spring Hill 2004 BS; Tulane 2004 JD

Senator **Dan W. "Blade" Morrish** (R-District 25) . . . . . . . (225) 342-2040
  Parishes Represented: Acadia Parish (part),     Dist: (337) 824-3979
  Calcasieu Parish (part), Cameron Parish, Jefferson    Fax: (337) 824-5898
  Davis Parish
  Term Expires: 2020
  119 West Nezpique Street, Jennings, LA 70546
  E-mail: morrishd@legis.la.gov
  Committees: Education; Environmental Quality; Insurance
  Education: McNeese State BS

Senator **Barrow Peacock** (R-District 37) . . . . . . . . . . . . . . (225) 342-2040
  Parishes Represented: Bossier Parish (part), Caddo    Dist: (318) 741-7180
  Parish (part)
  Term Expires: 2020
  1619 Jimmie Davis Highway, Bossier City, LA 71112
  E-mail: peacockb@legis.la.gov
  Committees: Agriculture, Forestry, Aquaculture, and Rural
  Development; Commerce, Consumer Protection, and International
  Affairs; Joint Legislative Capital Outlay; Labor and Industrial
  Relations; Retirement
  Education: Southern Methodist 1992 BABA; LSU 1996 MBA

Senator **Jonathan W. "JP" Perry** (R-District 26) . . . . . . . . (225) 342-2040
  Parishes Represented: Acadia Parish (part),     Dist: (337) 643-6425
  Lafayette Parish (part), St. Landry Parish (part),    Fax: (337) 740-6400
  Vermilion Parish
  Term Expires: 2020
  P.O. Box 100, Kaplan, LA 70548
  E-mail: perryj@legis.la.gov
  Committees: Commerce, Consumer Protection, and International
  Affairs; Judiciary C; Local and Municipal Affairs
  Education: Louisiana (Monroe) 1995 BA;
  Southern U (New Orleans) JD

Senator **Karen Carter Peterson** (D-District 5) . . . . . . . . . . (504) 342-2040
  Parishes Represented: Jefferson Parish (part),     Dist: (504) 568-8346
  Orleans Parish (part)        Fax: (504) 568-8405
  Term Expires: 2020
  1010 Common Street, Suite 2510, New Orleans, LA 70112
  E-mail: petersonk@legis.la.gov
  Committees: Joint Legislative Capital Outlay; Judiciary B; Local
  and Municipal Affairs; Revenue and Fiscal Affairs; Senate and
  Governmental Affairs
  Education: Howard U 1991 BBA; Tulane 1995 JD

Senator **Hartwell Neil Riser, Jr.** (R-District 32) . . . . . . . . . (225) 342-2040
  Parishes Represented: Avoyelles Parish (part),     Dist: (318) 649-0977
  Caldwell Parish, Catahoula Parish, Concordia Parish    Fax: (318) 649-0979
  (part), Franklin Parish, La Salle Parish, Ouachita Parish (part), Rapides
  Parish (part), Richland Parish (part), West Feliciana Parish (part)
  Term Expires: 2020
  P.O. Box 117, Columbia, LA 71418
  E-mail: risern@legis.la.gov
  Committees: Agriculture, Forestry, Aquaculture, and Rural
  Development; Joint Legislative Capital Outlay; Labor and Industrial
  Relations; Revenue and Fiscal Affairs; Senate and Governmental
  Affairs
  Education: Northeast Louisiana 1984 BSBusMgt

Senator **Gary L. Smith, Jr.** (D-District 19) . . . . . . . . . . . . . (225) 342-2040
  Parishes Represented: Jefferson Parish (part),     Dist: (985) 764-9122
  Lafourche Parish (part), St. Charles Parish (part), St. John the Baptist
  Parish (part)
  Term Expires: 2020
  P.O. Box 189, Norco, LA 70079
  E-mail: smithgl@legis.la.gov
  Committees: Insurance; Joint Legislative Capital Outlay; Judiciary B;
  Revenue and Fiscal Affairs
  Education: LSU 1994 BS; Loyola U (New Orleans) 1998 JD;
  Tulane 1999 LLM

Senator **John R. Smith** (R-District 30) . . . . . . . . . . . . . . . . (225) 342-2040
  Parishes Represented: Beauregard Parish, Calcasieu    Dist: (337) 238-2709
  Parish (part), Vernon Parish     Fax: (337) 238-6444
  Term Expires: 2020
  611-B South Fifth Street, Leesville, LA 71446
  E-mail: smithj@legis.la.gov
  Committees: Agriculture, Forestry, Aquaculture, and Rural
  Development; Insurance; Joint Legislative Capital Outlay; Local and
  Municipal Affairs; Revenue and Fiscal Affairs
  Education: Loyola U (New Orleans) BS, MBA

Senator **Greg Tarver** (D-District 39) . . . . . . . . . . . . . . . . . . (225) 342-2040
  Parishes Represented: Caddo Parish (part)     Dist: (318) 227-1499
  Term Expires: 2020
  1024 Pierre Avenue, Shreveport, LA 71103
  E-mail: tarverg@legis.la.gov
  Committees: Finance; Judiciary B; Natural Resources; Senate and
  Governmental Affairs
  Education: Grambling State

Senator **Francis C. Thompson** (D-District 34) . . . . . . . . . . . (225) 342-2040
  Parishes Represented: Concordia Parish (part), East    Dist: (318) 878-9408
  Carroll Parish, Madison Parish, Morehouse Parish    Fax: (318) 878-5650
  (part), Ouachita Parish (part), Richland Parish (part), Tensas Parish
  Term Expires: 2020
  P.O. Box 68, Delhi, LA 71232
  E-mail: thompsof@legis.la.gov
  Committees: Agriculture, Forestry, Aquaculture, and Rural
  Development; Commerce, Consumer Protection, and International
  Affairs
  Education: Louisiana Tech U 1963 BS, 1971 MS;
  Northeast Louisiana 1977 EdD

Senator **Mike A. Walsworth** (R-District 33) . . . . . . . . . . . . (225) 342-2040
  Parishes Represented: Claiborne Parish (part),     Dist: (318) 340-6453
  Lincoln Parish (part), Morehouse Parish (part),    Fax: (318) 396-0192
  Ouachita Parish (part), Union Parish, West Carroll Parish
  Term Expires: 2020
  4007 White's Ferry Road, Suite A, West Monroe, LA 71291
  E-mail: walsworthm@legis.la.gov
  Committees: Education; Environmental Quality; Senate and
  Governmental Affairs
  Education: Northeast Louisiana 1978 BA

Senator **Richard "Rick" Ward III** (R-District 17) . . . . . . . . (225) 342-2040
  Parishes Represented: Assumption Parish (part),    Dist: (225) 246-8838
  East Baton Rouge Parish (part), East Feliciana Parish, Iberville Parish
  (part), Pointe Coupee Parish, St. Helena Parish (part), St. Martin Parish
  (part), West Baton Rouge Parish (part), West Feliciana Parish (part)
  Term Expires: 2020
  3741 Highway One, Port Allen, LA 70767
  E-mail: wardr@legis.la.gov
  Committees: Insurance; Judiciary A; Natural Resources
  Education: LSU; LSU Hebert Law 2008 JD

*(continued on next page)*

**LEGISLATIVE BRANCH**

**Senators** *continued*

Senator **Mack A. "Bodi" White, Jr.** (R-District 6) . . . . . . . (225) 342-2040
Parishes Represented: East Baton Rouge Parish          Dist: (225) 272-1324
(part), Livingston Parish (part), St. Helena Parish (part), Tangipahoa
Parish (part)
Term Expires: 2020
808 O'Neal Lane, Baton Rouge, LA 70816
E-mail: whitem@legis.la.gov
Committees: Commerce, Consumer Protection, and International
Affairs; Education; Finance; Joint Legislative Capital Outlay; Judiciary
C
Education: Southeastern Louisiana 1978 BA

# Senate Standing Committees
## Agriculture, Forestry, Aquaculture, and Rural Development

| Majority Members | Minority Members |
|---|---|
| James R. "Jim" Fannin (R-35) *Vice Chair* | Francis C. Thompson (D-34) *Chair* |
| Robert L. "Bret" Allain (R-21) | |
| Gerald Long (R-31) | |
| Barrow Peacock (R-37) | |
| Hartwell Neil Riser, Jr. (R-32) | |
| John R. Smith (R-30) | |

## Commerce, Consumer Protection, and International Affairs

| Majority Members | Minority Members |
|---|---|
| Daniel R. "Danny" Martiny (R-10) *Chair* | Francis C. Thompson (D-34) |
| Mack A. "Bodi" White, Jr. (R-6) *Vice Chair* | |
| Robert L. "Bret" Allain (R-21) | |
| Conrad H. Appel III (R-9) | |
| Patrick "Page" Cortez (R-23) | |
| Beth Mizell (R-12) | |
| Barrow Peacock (R-37) | |
| Jonathan W. "JP" Perry (R-26) | |

## Education

| Majority Members | Minority Members |
|---|---|
| Dan W. "Blade" Morrish (R-25) *Chair* | John Milkovich (D-38) *Vice Chair* |
| Conrad H. Appel III (R-9) | Gerald Boudreaux (D-24) |
| Beth Mizell (R-12) | |
| Mike A. Walsworth (R-33) | |
| Mack A. "Bodi" White, Jr. (R-6) | |

## Environmental Quality

| Majority Members | Minority Members |
|---|---|
| Mike A. Walsworth (R-33) *Chair* | Troy E. Brown (D-2) |
| Conrad H. Appel III (R-9) *Vice Chair* | |
| Dale M. Erdey (R-13) | |
| Sharon Hewitt (R-1) | |
| Eddie J. Lambert (R-18) | |
| Dan W. "Blade" Morrish (R-25) | |

## Finance

| Majority Members | Minority Members |
|---|---|
| Robert L. "Bret" Allain (R-21) *Vice Chair* | Eric LaFleur (D-28) *Chair* |
| Conrad H. Appel III (R-9) | Regina Ashford Barrow (D-15) |
| John Leo "Jack" Donahue (R-11) | Wesley T. Bishop (D-4) |
| James R. "Jim" Fannin (R-35) | Greg Tarver (D-39) |
| Sharon Hewitt (R-1) | |
| Ronnie S. Johns (R-27) | |
| Mack A. "Bodi" White, Jr. (R-6) | |

## Health and Welfare

| Majority Members | Minority Members |
|---|---|
| Fred H. Mills, Jr. (R-22) *Chair* | Regina Ashford Barrow (D-15) *Vice Chair* |
| Norby Chabert (R-20) | Gerald Boudreaux (D-24) |
| Dan Claitor (R-16) | Troy E. Brown (D-2) |
| Dale M. Erdey (R-13) | Yvonne Colomb (D-14) |
| | Jay Luneau (D-29) |

# Insurance

| Majority Members | Minority Members |
|---|---|
| John R. Smith (R-30) *Chair* | Eric LaFleur (D-28) |
| Ryan Gatti (R-36) *Vice Chair* | Gary L. Smith, Jr. (D-19) |
| Ronnie S. Johns (R-27) | |
| Eddie J. Lambert (R-18) | |
| Gerald Long (R-31) | |
| Dan W. "Blade" Morrish (R-25) | |
| Richard "Rick" Ward III (R-17) | |

## Judiciary A

| Majority Members | Minority Members |
|---|---|
| Richard "Rick" Ward III (R-17) *Chair* | Jay Luneau (D-29) *Vice Chair* |
| John Leo "Jack" Donahue (R-11) | Wesley T. Bishop (D-4) |
| Ryan Gatti (R-36) | John Milkovich (D-38) |
| Daniel R. "Danny" Martiny (R-10) | |

## Judiciary B

| Majority Members | Minority Members |
|---|---|
| Ronnie S. Johns (R-27) *Vice Chair* | Gary L. Smith, Jr. (D-19) *Chair* |
| Norby Chabert (R-20) | Eric LaFleur (D-28) |
| | Jean-Paul J. "JP" Morrell (D-3) |
| | Karen Carter Peterson (D-5) |
| | Greg Tarver (D-39) |

## Judiciary C

| Majority Members | Minority Members |
|---|---|
| Dan Claitor (R-16) *Chair* | Regina Ashford Barrow (D-15) |
| Jonathan W. "JP" Perry (R-26) *Vice Chair* | Troy A. Carter (D-7) |
| Fred H. Mills, Jr. (R-22) | Yvonne Colomb (D-14) |
| Mack A. "Bodi" White, Jr. (R-6) | |

## Labor and Industrial Relations

| Majority Members | Minority Members |
|---|---|
| Hartwell Neil Riser, Jr. (R-32) *Chair* | Troy A. Carter (D-7) *Vice Chair* |
| Ronnie S. Johns (R-27) | Regina Ashford Barrow (D-15) |
| Barrow Peacock (R-37) | Wesley T. Bishop (D-4) |
| | Jean-Paul J. "JP" Morrell (D-3) |

## Local and Municipal Affairs

| Majority Members | Minority Members |
|---|---|
| John Leo "Jack" Donahue (R-11) *Vice Chair* | Yvonne Colomb (D-14) *Chair* |
| Daniel R. "Danny" Martiny (R-10) | Karen Carter Peterson (D-5) |
| Fred H. Mills, Jr. (R-22) | |
| Jonathan W. "JP" Perry (R-26) | |
| John R. Smith (R-30) | |

## Natural Resources

| Majority Members | Minority Members |
|---|---|
| Norby Chabert (R-20) *Chair* | Jay Luneau (D-29) |
| Eddie J. Lambert (R-18) *Vice Chair* | Greg Tarver (D-39) |
| Robert L. "Bret" Allain (R-21) | |
| Ryan Gatti (R-36) | |
| Richard "Rick" Ward III (R-17) | |

## Retirement

| Majority Members | Minority Members |
|---|---|
| Barrow Peacock (R-37) *Chair* | Gerald Boudreaux (D-24) *Vice Chair* |
| Norby Chabert (R-20) | John Milkovich (D-38) |
| Patrick "Page" Cortez (R-23) | |
| Gerald Long (R-31) | |
| Beth Mizell (R-12) | |

## Revenue and Fiscal Affairs

| Majority Members | Minority Members |
|---|---|
| Dale M. Erdey (R-13) *Vice Chair* | Jean-Paul J. "JP" Morrell (D-3) *Chair* |
| Eddie J. Lambert (R-18) | Troy E. Brown (D-2) |
| Hartwell Neil Riser, Jr. (R-32) | Troy A. Carter (D-7) |
| John R. Smith (R-30) | Yvonne Colomb (D-14) |
| | Jay Luneau (D-29) |
| | Karen Carter Peterson (D-5) |
| | Gary L. Smith, Jr. (D-19) |

## Senate and Governmental Affairs

**Majority Members**
John Leo "Jack" Donahue (R-11)
James R. "Jim" Fannin (R-35)
Hartwell Neil Riser, Jr. (R-32)
Mike A. Walsworth (R-33)

**Minority Members**
Karen Carter Peterson (D-5) *Chair*
Wesley T. Bishop (D-4) *Vice Chair*
Troy A. Carter (D-7)
Jean-Paul J. "JP" Morrell (D-3)
Greg Tarver (D-39)

## Transportation, Highways and Public Works

**Majority Members**
Patrick "Page" Cortez (R-23) *Chair*
Sharon Hewitt (R-1) *Vice Chair*
Dale M. Erdey (R-13)
James R. "Jim" Fannin (R-35)
Gerald Long (R-31)

**Minority Members**
Troy E. Brown (D-2)

# Louisiana House of Representatives

P.O. Box 94062, Baton Rouge, LA 70804
Tel: (225) 342-6945  Fax: (225) 342-5045
Internet: www.house.louisiana.gov

Speaker of the House **Taylor F. Barras** (R) . . . . . . . . . . . . . . (225) 342-7263
    Education: LSU 1979 BS
Speaker Pro Tem **Walter "Walt" Leger III** (D) . . . . . . . . . (225) 342-8385
    Education: LSU 2000 BA; Tulane 2003 JD
Majority Leader **Lance Harris** (R) . . . . . . . . . . . . . . . . . . . . (318) 767-6095
Clerk of the House **Alfred W. Speer** . . . . . . . . . . . . . . . . . (225) 342-7259
    P.O. Box 44281, Baton Rouge, LA 70804
    E-mail: speera@legis.la.gov
Chief Sergeant at Arms **Clarence Russ** . . . . . . . . . . . . . . . (225) 342-1228
    E-mail: russc@legis.la.gov
Library Director **Frances Thomas** . . . . . . . . . . . . . . . . . . . (225) 342-2430
    E-mail: thomasf@legis.la.gov                          Fax: (225) 342-2431

## Representatives

**Party Affiliation Statistics:** Republicans: 61, Democrats: 42,
Independents: 2

Representative **Mark T. Abraham** (R-District 36) . . . . . . . . (337) 475-3016
    Parishes Represented: Calcasieu Parish (part)
    Term Expires: 2020
    130 Jamestown Road, Lake Charles, LA 70605
    E-mail: abrahamm@legis.la.gov
    Committees: Appropriations; Insurance; Retirement
    Education: LSU BS
Representative **Neil C. Abramson** (D-District 98) . . . . . . . . (504) 275-8051
    Parishes Represented: Orleans Parish (part)      Fax: (504) 568-3342
    Term Expires: 2020
    601 Poydras Street, Suite 1635, New Orleans, LA 70130
    E-mail: abramson@legis.la.gov
    Committees: Joint Legislative Capital Outlay; Ways and Means
    Education: Dartmouth 1989 BA; LSU 1992 JD
Representative **Bryan Adams** (R-District 85) . . . . . . . . . . . (504) 361-6013
    Parishes Represented: Jefferson Parish (part)    Fax: (504) 361-6687
    Note: On May 17, 2016, State Representative Bryan Adams announced
    his resignation from the Louisiana House of Representatives, effective
    at the end of the special legislative session.
    Term Expires: 2020
    P.O. Box 1387, Gretna, LA 70054
    E-mail: adamsb@legis.la.gov
    Committees: Administration of Criminal Justice; Judiciary;
    Transportation, Highways, and Public Works
    Education: LSU 1984 (Attended)
Representative **Beryl Adams Amedée** (R-District 51) . . . . (985) 858-2967
    Parishes Represented: Assumption Parish (part), Lafourche Parish
    (part), St. Mary Parish (part), Terrebonne Parish (part)
    Term Expires: 2020
    302 School Street, Houma, LA 70360
    E-mail: amedeeb@legis.la.gov
    Committees: Agriculture, Forestry, Aquaculture, and Rural
    Development; Appropriations; Education

Representative **John F. "Andy" Anders** (D-District 21) . . . (318) 336-5865
    Parishes Represented: Catahoula Parish (part),    Fax: (318) 336-9268
    Concordia Parish, East Carroll Parish (part), Madison Parish (part),
    Tensas Parish (part)
    Term Expires: 2020
    200 Advocate Row, Suite D, Vidalia, LA 71373
    E-mail: larep021@legis.la.gov
    Committees: Agriculture, Forestry, Aquaculture, and Rural
    Development; Commerce; Insurance
    Education: Louisiana Tech U 1979 BS
Representative **James K. Armes III** (D-District 30) . . . . . . . (337) 238-7004
    Parishes Represented: Beauregard Parish (part),  Fax: (337) 238-7007
    Vernon Parish (part)
    Term Expires: 2020
    2255 University Parkway, Leesville, LA 71446
    E-mail: armesj@legis.la.gov
    Committees: Appropriations; Natural Resources and Environment
    Education: McNeese State 1974 BS
Representative **Tony Bacala** (R-District 59) . . . . . . . . . . . . . (225) 677-8020
    Parishes Represented: Ascension Parish (part)
    Term Expires: 2020
    15482 Airline Highway, Suite A, Prairieville, LA 70769
    E-mail: bacalat@legis.la.gov
    Committees: Administration of Criminal Justice; Appropriations;
    Retirement
Representative
**Lawrence A. "Larry" Bagley** (R-District 7) . . . . . . . . . . (318) 925-9588
    Parishes Represented: Caddo Parish (part), De Soto Parish (part),
    Sabine Parish (part)
    Term Expires: 2020
    671 Highway 171, Suite E, Stonewall, LA 71078
    E-mail: bagleyl@legis.la.gov
    Committees: Appropriations; Health and Welfare; Labor and Industrial
    Relations
Representative **John Bagneris** (D-District 100) . . . . . . . . . (504) 243-7783
    Parishes Represented: Orleans Parish (part)
    Term Expires: 2020
    5555 Bullard Avenue, Suite 101, New Orleans, LA 70128
    E-mail: bagnerisj@legis.la.gov
    Committees: Administration of Criminal Justice; Judiciary
    Education: Southern U (New Orleans)
Representative **Taylor F. Barras** (R-District 48) . . . . . . . . . (225) 342-7263
    Parishes Represented: Iberia Parish (part), Lafayette    Dist: (337) 373-4051
    Parish (part), St. Martin Parish (part)         Fax: (225) 342-8336
    Term Expires: 2020                              Dist: (337) 373-4053
    800 South Lewis Street, Second Floor, Suite 206,
    New Iberia, LA 70560
    E-mail: barrast@legis.la.gov
    Committees: Joint Legislative Capital Outlay
Representative
**John A. "Johnny" Berthelot** (R-District 88) . . . . . . . . . (225) 647-5646
    Parishes Represented: Ascension Parish (part)   Fax: (225) 644-7207
    Term Expires: 2020
    1024 S. Purpera, Gonzalez, LA 70737
    E-mail: berthelotj@legis.la.gov
    Committees: Appropriations; Municipal, Parochial and Cultural Affairs
    Education: LSU (Attended)
Representative **Robert E. Billiot** (D-District 83) . . . . . . . . . (504) 436-8929
    Parishes Represented: Jefferson Parish (part)   Fax: (504) 436-8994
    Term Expires: 2020
    10 Westbank Expressway, Westwego, LA 70094
    E-mail: billiotr@legis.la.gov
    Committees: Appropriations; Municipal, Parochial and Cultural Affairs;
    Natural Resources and Environment
    Education: Nicholls State 1976 BA
Representative **Stuart J. Bishop** (R-District 43) . . . . . . . . . (337) 981-7409
    Parishes Represented: Lafayette Parish (part)   Fax: (337) 981-7411
    Term Expires: 2020
    P.O. Box 80993, Lafayette, LA 70508
    E-mail: bishops@legis.la.gov
    Committees: Natural Resources and Environment
    Education: LSU 1997 BA
Representative **Joseph Bouie, Jr.** (D-District 97) . . . . . . . . (504) 286-1033
    Parishes Represented: Orleans Parish (part)     Fax: (504) 286-1035
    Term Expires: 2020
    6305 Elysian Field Avenue, Suite 404, New Orleans, LA 70122
    E-mail: bouiej@legis.la.gov
    Committees: Education; Joint Legislative Capital Outlay; Municipal,
    Parochial and Cultural Affairs; Ways and Means
    Education: Southern U (New Orleans) BA; Tulane MSW;
    Clark Atlanta PhD

*(continued on next page)*

**Representatives** *continued*

Representative **Chris Broadwater** (R-District 86) ........ (985) 543-4900
Parishes Represented: Tangipahoa Parish (part)     Fax: (985) 543-4902
Term Expires: 2020
P.O. Box 157, Hahnville, LA 70404
E-mail: broadwaterc@legis.la.gov
Committees: Education; Joint Legislative Capital Outlay; Labor and
Industrial Relations; Ways and Means
Education: Louisiana Col 1995 BA; New Orleans Baptist 1998 MDiv;
LSU Hebert Law 2002 JD

Representative **Chad M. Brown** (D-District 60) ......... (225) 687-2410
Parishes Represented: Assumption Parish (part), Iberville Parish (part)
Term Expires: 2020
57835 Plaquemine Street, Plaquemine, LA 70764
E-mail: brownc@legis.la.gov
Committees: Commerce; Insurance; Judiciary
Education: LSU 1992 BS; Southern U Law 1996 JD

Representative **Terry R. Brown** (I-District 22) ........... (855) 261-6566
Parishes Represented: Grant Parish, LaSalle Parish     Fax: (318) 627-5155
(part), Natchitoches Parish (part), Red River Parish (part), Winn Parish
(part)
Term Expires: 2020
510 Main Street, Colfax, LA 71417
E-mail: browntr@legis.la.gov
Committees: Administration of Criminal Justice; Agriculture, Forestry,
Aquaculture, and Rural Development; Natural Resources and
Environment; Transportation, Highways, and Public Works
Education: Northwestern State 1969 BA

Representative **Thomas G. Carmody, Jr.** (R-District 6) ... (318) 862-9956
Parishes Represented: Bossier Parish (part), Caddo     Fax: (318) 862-9958
Parish (part)
Term Expires: 2020
5918 Fairfield Avenue, Shreveport, LA 71106
E-mail: carmodyt@legis.la.gov
Committees: Commerce
Education: LSU (Shreveport) 1983 BFA

Representative **Barbara Carpenter** (D-District 63) ....... (225) 771-5674
Parishes Represented: East Baton Rouge Parish (part)
Term Expires: 2020
1975 Harding Boulevard, Baton Rouge, LA 70807
E-mail: carpenterb@legis.la.gov
Committees: Administration of Criminal Justice; Retirement;
Transportation, Highways, and Public Works
Education: Southern U A&M MEd; Kansas State PhD

Representative **Gary M. Carter, Jr.** (D-District 102) ...... (504) 361-6600
Parishes Represented: Orleans Parish (part)
Term Expires: 2020
3520 General DeGaulle, Suite 3071, New Orleans, LA 70114
E-mail: carterg@legis.la.gov
Committees: Appropriations; House and Governmental Affairs;
Judiciary
Education: Xavier (LA) 1996 BA; Tulane 2002 JD

Representative
**Robert J. "Robby" Carter** (D-District 72) ............ (985) 748-2245
Parishes Represented: East Feliciana Parish (part), St. Helena Parish,
Tangipahoa Parish (part)
Term Expires: 2020
225 Northwest Central Avenue, Amite, LA 70422
E-mail: carterr@legis.la.gov
Committees: Civil Law and Procedure; Insurance; Judiciary
Education: Southeastern Louisiana BA; LSU JD

Representative
**Stephen F. "Steve" Carter** (R-District 68) ............ (225) 362-5305
Parishes Represented: East Baton Rouge Parish     Fax: (225) 362-5306
(part)
Term Expires: 2020
3115 Old Forge, Baton Rouge, LA 70808
E-mail: carters@legis.la.gov
Committees: Education; Transportation, Highways, and Public Works

Representative
**Charles R. "Bubba" Chaney** (R-District 19) ......... (318) 728-5875
Parishes Represented: East Carroll Parish (part),     Fax: (318) 728-5876
Madison Parish (part), Morehouse Parish (part), Ouachita Parish (part),
Richland Parish, West Carroll Parish
Term Expires: 2020
P.O. Box 8, Rayville, LA 71269
E-mail: chaneyb@legis.la.gov
Committees: Agriculture, Forestry, Aquaculture, and Rural
Development; Appropriations; Natural Resources and Environment

Representative **Patrick Connick** (R-District 84) .......... (504) 371-0240
Parishes Represented: Jefferson Parish (part)     Fax: (504) 371-0242
Term Expires: 2020
5201 Westbank Expressway, Suite 100, Marrero, LA 70072
E-mail: connickp@legis.la.gov
Committees: Commerce; Natural Resources and Environment

Representative **Jean-Paul Coussan** (R-District 45) ....... (337) 262-2400
Parishes Represented: Lafayette Parish (part)
Term Expires: 2020
P.O. Box 52001, Lafayette, LA 70505
E-mail: coussanjp@legis.la.gov
Committees: Commerce; Judiciary; Natural Resources and Environment

Representative **Lt. Col. Kenny R. Cox** (D-District 23) ..... (855) 844-8583
Parishes Represented: De Soto Parish (part),     Fax: (318) 357-3208
Natchitoches Parish (part), Red River Parish (part)
Term Expires: 2020
781 Highway 494, Natchitoches, LA 71457
E-mail: coxk@legis.la.gov
Committees: Commerce; Health and Welfare; Labor and Industrial
Relations

Representative **Gregory Cromer** (R-District 90) ......... (985) 645-3592
Parishes Represented: St. Tammany Parish (part)     Fax: (985) 645-3594
Term Expires: 2020
P.O. Box 2088, Slidell, LA 70459
E-mail: cromerg@legis.la.gov
Committees: Civil Law and Procedure; Insurance; Labor and Industrial
Relations

Representative **Michael E. Danahay** (D-District 33) ...... (337) 527-5581
Parishes Represented: Calcasieu Parish (part)     Fax: (337) 527-5803
Term Expires: 2020
1625 Beglis Parkway, Sulphur, LA 70663
E-mail: danahaym@legis.la.gov
Committees: House and Governmental Affairs

Representative **Paula Davis** (R-District 69) ............. (225) 362-5301
Parishes Represented: East Baton Rouge Parish (part)
Term Expires: 2020
7902 Wrenwood Boulevard, Suite D, Baton Rouge, LA 70809
E-mail: davisp@legis.la.gov
Committees: Insurance; Joint Legislative Capital Outlay; Municipal,
Parochial and Cultural Affairs; Ways and Means
Education: LSU BA

Representative **Phillip DeVillier** (R-District 41) .......... (337) 457-0194
Parishes Represented: Acadia Parish (part), Evangeline Parish (part), St.
Landry Parish (part)
Term Expires: 2020
P.O. Box 986, Eunice, LA 70535
E-mail: devillierp@legis.la.gov
Committees: Agriculture, Forestry, Aquaculture, and Rural
Development; Joint Legislative Capital Outlay; Natural Resources and
Environment; Ways and Means
Education: LSU

Representative **Stephen Dwight** (R-District 35) ......... (337) 491-2315
Parishes Represented: Beauregard Parish (part), Calcasieu Parish (part)
Term Expires: 2020
P.O. Box 12703, Lake Charles, LA 70612
E-mail: dwights@legis.la.gov
Committees: Administration of Criminal Justice; Joint Legislative
Capital Outlay; Municipal, Parochial and Cultural Affairs; Ways and
Means
Education: LSU; Southern U Law JD

Representative **Rick Edmonds** (R-District 66) ........... (225) 295-9240
Parishes Represented: East Baton Rouge Parish (part)
Term Expires: 2020
3931 South Sherwood Forest Boulevard, Baton Rouge, LA 70816
E-mail: edmondsr@legis.la.gov
Committees: Appropriations; Education; Municipal, Parochial and
Cultural Affairs
Education: East Texas Baptist BA; New Orleans Baptist MDiv

Representative **Julie Emerson** (R-District 39) ........... (337) 886-4687
Parishes Represented: Lafayette Parish (part), St. Landry Parish (part)
Term Expires: 2020
306 North Church Street, Carencro, LA 70520
E-mail: emersonj@legis.la.gov
Committees: Agriculture, Forestry, Aquaculture, and Rural
Development; Civil Law and Procedure; Education
Education: Louisiana (Lafayette) BS; South Carolina MBA

Representative **R. Reid Falconer** (R-District 89) ........ (985) 792-5185
Parishes Represented: St. Tammany Parish (part)
Term Expires: 2020
4990 Highway 22, Suite E, Mandeville, LA 70471
E-mail: falconerr@legis.la.gov
Committees: Commerce; Education; Labor and Industrial Relations
Education: LSU 1979 BArch, 1984 MS, 1984 MBA

Representative **Franklin J. Foil** (R-District 70) . . . . . . . . . . (225) 342-6777
Parishes Represented: East Baton Rouge Parish    Fax: (225) 342-6785
(part)
Term Expires: 2020
412 North Fourth Street, Suite 220, Baton Rouge, LA 70802
E-mail: foilf@legis.la.gov
Committees: Appropriations; Natural Resources and Environment
Education: LSU 1987 BA; Loyola U (New Orleans) 1991 JD

Representative **A. B. Franklin** (D-District 34) . . . . . . . . . . . (337) 491-2320
Parishes Represented: Calcasieu Parish (part)    Fax: (337) 491-2020
Term Expires: 2020
2808 East Broad Street, Lake Charles, LA 70615
E-mail: franklina@legis.la.gov
Committees: Transportation, Highways, and Public Works

Representative **Randal L. Gaines** (D-District 57) . . . . . . . . (985) 652-1228
Parishes Represented: St. Charles Parish (part), St.    Fax: (985) 652-1229
John the Baptist Parish (part)
Term Expires: 2020
301 West Airline Highway, Suite 210, La Place, LA 70068
E-mail: gainesr@legis.la.gov
Committees: Administration of Criminal Justice; Civil Law and
Procedure; Judiciary
Education: Southern U Law 1984 JD

Representative
**Raymond "Ray" Garofalo** (R-District 103) . . . . . . . . . . (504) 277-4729
Parishes Represented: Orleans Parish (part),    Fax: (504) 278-6597
Plaquemines Parish (part), St. Bernard Parish
Term Expires: 2020
9000 West Saint Bernard Highway, Suite 40, Chalmette, LA 70043
E-mail: garofalor@legis.la.gov
Committees: Civil Law and Procedure
Education: Loyola U (New Orleans) 1980 BA, 1992 JD

Representative **Jerry "Truck" Gisclair** (D-District 54) . . . . . (985) 798-7707
Parishes Represented: Jefferson Parish (part),    Fax: (985) 798-7757
Lafourche Parish (part)
Term Expires: 2020
P.O. Drawer 1448, Larose, LA 70373-1448
E-mail: gisclairj@legis.la.gov
Committees: Agriculture, Forestry, Aquaculture, and Rural
Development; Natural Resources and Environment; Transportation,
Highways, and Public Works

Representative **Cedric B. Glover** (D-District 4) . . . . . . . . . (318) 221-7775
Parishes Represented: Caddo Parish (part)
Term Expires: 2020
1341 Russell Road, Shreveport, LA 71107
E-mail: gloverc@legis.la.gov
Committees: Commerce; Insurance; Municipal, Parochial and Cultural
Affairs

Representative **John E. "Johnny" Guinn** (R-District 37) . . (337) 824-0376
Parishes Represented: Calcasieu Parish (part),    Fax: (337) 824-4780
Jefferson Davis Parish
Term Expires: 2020
P.O. Box 287, Jennings, LA 70546
E-mail: guinnj@legis.la.gov
Committees: Agriculture, Forestry, Aquaculture, and Rural
Development; Natural Resources and Environment; Transportation,
Highways, and Public Works

Representative **Jeffrey "Jeff" Hall** (D-District 26) . . . . . . . (318) 487-5661
Parishes Represented: Rapides Parish (part)
Term Expires: 2020
1811 MacArthur Drive, Alexandria, LA 71301
E-mail: hallj@legis.la.gov
Committees: Agriculture, Forestry, Aquaculture, and Rural
Development; Education; Transportation, Highways, and Public Works

Representative **James "Jimmy" Harris** (D-District 99) . . . (504) 243-1960
Parishes Represented: Orleans Parish (part)
Term Expires: 2020
7240 Crowder Boulevard, Suite 406, New Orleans, LA 70127
E-mail: harrisj@legis.la.gov
Committees: House and Governmental Affairs; Joint Legislative Capital
Outlay; Judiciary; Ways and Means
Education: Morehouse Col BA; Southern U Law JD

Representative **Lance Harris** (R-District 25) . . . . . . . . . . . . (318) 767-6095
Parishes Represented: Rapides Parish (part)    Fax: (318) 767-6097
Term Expires: 2020
P.O. Box 13555, Alexandria, LA 71315
E-mail: harrisl@legis.la.gov
Committees: Appropriations; House and Governmental Affairs

Representative
**Kenneth E. "Kenny" Havard** (R-District 62) . . . . . . . . . (225) 634-7470
Parishes Represented: East Baton Rouge Parish    Fax: (225) 634-7477
(part), East Feliciana Parish (part), West Feliciana Parish (part)
Term Expires: 2020
P.O. Box 217, Jackson, LA 70748
E-mail: havardk@legis.la.gov
Committees: Joint Legislative Capital Outlay; Transportation,
Highways, and Public Works

Representative
**Lowell Christopher "Chris" Hazel** (R-District 27) . . . . . (318) 767-6082
Parishes Represented: Rapides Parish (part)    Fax: (318) 767-6084
Term Expires: 2020
1013 Main Street, Pineville, LA 71360
E-mail: hazelc@legis.la.gov
Committees: Administration of Criminal Justice; Judiciary
Education: Thomas M Cooley 2000 JD; New Orleans 1990 AB

Representative **Cameron Henry** (R-District 82) . . . . . . . . . (504) 838-5433
Parishes Represented: Jefferson Parish (part)    Fax: (504) 838-5435
Term Expires: 2020
1539 Metairie Road, Suite A, Metairie, LA 70005
E-mail: henryc@legis.la.gov
Committees: Appropriations; Joint Legislative Capital Outlay

Representative **Bob Hensgens** (R-District 47) . . . . . . . . . . (337) 893-5035
Parishes Represented: Calcasieu Parish (part),    Fax: (337) 898-1160
Cameron Parish, Vermilion Parish (part)
Term Expires: 2020
407 Charity Street, Abbeville, LA 70510
E-mail: hensgensb@legis.la.gov
Committees: Agriculture, Forestry, Aquaculture, and Rural
Development; Appropriations; Health and Welfare

Representative **Stephanie Hilferty** (R-District 94) . . . . . . . (504) 885-4154
Parishes Represented: Jefferson Parish (part), Orleans Parish (part)
Term Expires: 2020
3331 Severn Avenue, Suite 206, Metairie, LA 70002
E-mail: hilfertys@legis.la.gov
Committees: Education; Joint Legislative Capital Outlay; Municipal,
Parochial and Cultural Affairs; Ways and Means
Education: Loyola U (New Orleans) BA

Representative **Dorothy Sue Hill** (D-District 32) . . . . . . . . (800) 259-2118
Parishes Represented: Allen Parish, Beauregard    Fax: (337) 639-4045
Parish (part), Calcasieu Parish (part)
Term Expires: 2020
529 Tramel Road, Dry Creek, LA 70637
E-mail: hilld@legis.la.gov
Committees: Agriculture, Forestry, Aquaculture, and Rural
Development; House and Governmental Affairs; Transportation,
Highways, and Public Works

Representative **Valarie Hodges** (R-District 64) . . . . . . . . . . (225) 791-2199
Parishes Represented: East Baton Rouge Parish    Fax: (225) 791-9203
(part), Livingston Parish (part)
Term Expires: 2020
35055 LA Highway 16, Suite 2A, Denham Springs, LA 70706
E-mail: hodgesv@legis.la.gov
Committees: Administration of Criminal Justice; Appropriations;
Judiciary

Representative **Frank A. Hoffmann** (R-District 15) . . . . . . . (318) 362-4130
Parishes Represented: Ouachita Parish (part)    Fax: (318) 362-4131
Term Expires: 2020
204 North Third Street, Suite A, West Monroe, LA 71291
E-mail: hoffmanf@legis.la.gov
Committees: Health and Welfare
Education: Louisiana (Monroe) 1966 BA, MEd, EdD

Representative **Paul Hollis** (R-District 104) . . . . . . . . . . . . . (985) 871-4680
Parishes Represented: St. Tammany Parish (part)    Fax: (985) 871-4682
Term Expires: 2020
2000 Preserve Lake Drive, Suite B, Covington, LA 70433
E-mail: hollisp@legis.la.gov
Committees: Commerce; Insurance; Retirement
Education: LSU 1994 BA

Representative **Dodie Horton** (R-District 9) . . . . . . . . . . . . (318) 949-2463
Parishes Represented: Bossier Parish (part)
Term Expires: 2020
954 Highway 80, Suite 400, Haughton, LA 71037
E-mail: hortond@legis.la.gov
Committees: Health and Welfare; Joint Legislative Capital Outlay;
Labor and Industrial Relations; Ways and Means

*(continued on next page)*

**LEGISLATIVE BRANCH**

**Representatives** *continued*

Representative **Frank A. Howard** (R-District 24) . . . . . . . . (318) 256-4135
Parishes Represented: Natchitoches Parish (part),     Fax: (318) 256-4137
Sabine Parish (part), Vernon Parish (part)
Term Expires: 2020
1601 Texas Highway, Many, LA 71449
E-mail: howardf@legis.la.gov
Committees: Administration of Criminal Justice; Agriculture, Forestry,
Aquaculture, and Rural Development; Transportation, Highways, and
Public Works

Representative **Marcus Hunter** (D-District 17) . . . . . . . . . . (318) 362-3440
Parishes Represented: Ouachita Parish (part)     Fax: (318) 362-3450
Term Expires: 2020
900 Saint John Street, Monroe, LA 71201
E-mail: hunterm@legis.la.gov
Committees: Health and Welfare; Joint Legislative Capital Outlay;
Labor and Industrial Relations; Ways and Means
Education: Southern U Law 2005 JD

Representative **Mike Pete Huval** (R-District 46) . . . . . . . . (337) 332-3331
Parishes Represented: Iberia Parish (part), St.     Fax: (337) 332-3341
Landry Parish (part), St. Martin Parish (part)
Term Expires: 2020
391 Cannery Road, Breaux Bridge, LA 70517
E-mail: huvalm@legis.la.gov
Committees: Insurance; Joint Legislative Capital Outlay; Municipal,
Parochial and Cultural Affairs; Ways and Means
Education: Louisiana (Lafayette) (Attended)

Representative **Barry Ivey** (R-District 65) . . . . . . . . . . . . . . (225) 261-5739
Parishes Represented: East Baton Rouge Parish     Fax: (225) 261-5741
(part)
Term Expires: 2020
P.O. Box 78286, Baton Rouge, LA 70837
E-mail: iveyb@legis.la.gov
Committees: House and Governmental Affairs; Joint Legislative Capital
Outlay; Retirement; Ways and Means
Education: LSU 2003 BS

Representative **Katrina R. Jackson** (D-District 16) . . . . . . . (318) 362-5123
Parishes Represented: Morehouse Parish (part),     Fax: (318) 362-5125
Ouachita Parish (part)
Term Expires: 2020
1051 Kansas Lane, Monroe, LA 71203
E-mail: jacksonk@legis.la.gov
Committees: Health and Welfare; Judiciary
Education: Louisiana (Monroe); Southern U Law 2004 JD

Representative **Edward "Ted" James** (D-District 101) . . . . (225) 343-3633
Parishes Represented: East Baton Rouge Parish     Fax: (225) 336-4667
(part)
Term Expires: 2020
830 Main Street, Baton Rouge, LA 70802
E-mail: james.ted@legis.la.gov
Committees: Joint Legislative Capital Outlay; Labor and Industrial
Relations; Ways and Means
Education: Cal Southern BSAcc; Southern U Law 2006 JD

Representative **Patrick O. Jefferson** (D-District 11) . . . . . . (318) 927-2519
Parishes Represented: Bienville Parish (part),     Fax: (318) 927-6564
Claiborne Parish, Lincoln Parish (part)
Term Expires: 2020
700 Main Street, Homer, LA 71040
E-mail: jeffersonpo@legis.la.gov
Committees: Commerce; Labor and Industrial Relations
Education: Dillard 1990 BA; Ohio State 1994 JD

Representative **Sam L. Jenkins, Jr.** (D-District 2) . . . . . . . . (318) 632-5970
Parishes Represented: Bossier Parish (part), Caddo Parish (part)
Term Expires: 2020
2419 Kings Highway, Shreveport, LA 71103
E-mail: jenkinss@legis.la.gov
Committees: Civil Law and Procedure; House and Governmental
Affairs; Municipal, Parochial and Cultural Affairs
Education: Southern U Law JD

Representative **Michael "Mike" Johnson** (R-District 8) . . . (318) 741-2790
Parishes Represented: Bossier Parish (part)
Term Expires: 2020
2250 Hospital Drive, Suite 248, Bossier City, LA 71111
E-mail: johnsonmi@legis.la.gov
Committees: Civil Law and Procedure; Health and Welfare; Judiciary
Education: LSU 1995 BS; LSU Hebert Law 1998 JD

Representative **Robert A. Johnson** (D-District 28) . . . . . . (318) 253-8891
Parishes Represented: Avoyelles Parish     Fax: (318) 253-6377
Term Expires: 2020
P.O. Box 467, Marksville, LA 71351
E-mail: johnsoro@legis.la.gov
Committees: Health and Welfare; Joint Legislative Capital Outlay;
Judiciary; Ways and Means
Education: Loyola U (New Orleans) 1997 BA, 2000 JD

Representative **Sam Jones** (D-District 50) . . . . . . . . . . . . . (337) 828-7778
Parishes Represented: St. Martin Parish (part), St.     Fax: (337) 828-4511
Mary Parish (part)
Term Expires: 2020
733 Main Street, Franklin, LA 70538
E-mail: joness@legis.la.gov
Committees: Retirement
Education: Nicholls State 1975 BA

Representative **Edmond Jordan** (D-District 29) . . . . . . . . (225) 356-6200
Parishes Represented: East Baton Rouge Parish     Fax: (225) 356-6202
(part), West Baton Rouge Parish (part)
Term Expires: 2020
5905 Hooper Road, Baton Rouge, LA 70811
E-mail: jordane@legis.la.gov
Education: Southern U Law JD

Representative **Nancy Landry** (R-District 31) . . . . . . . . . . . (337) 262-2252
Parishes Represented: Lafayette Parish (part),     Fax: (337) 262-2254
Vermilion Parish (part)
Term Expires: 2020
109 South College Road, Lafayette, LA 70503
E-mail: landryn@legis.la.gov
Committees: Education
Education: LSU 1985 BA, 1990 JD

Representative **Col. Terry Landry** (D-District 96) . . . . . . . . (337) 373-9380
Parishes Represented: Iberia Parish (part), Lafayette     Fax: (337) 373-9382
Parish (part), St. Martin Parish (part)
Term Expires: 2020
800 South Lewis Street, Suite 201-B, New Iberia, LA 70560
E-mail: landryt@legis.la.gov
Committees: Administration of Criminal Justice; Joint Legislative
Capital Outlay; Transportation, Highways, and Public Works

Representative **H. Bernard LeBas** (D-District 38) . . . . . . . . (337) 363-0152
Parishes Represented: Evangeline Parish (part), St.     Fax: (337) 363-0179
Landry Parish (part)
Term Expires: 2020
115 Southwest Railroad Avenue, Ville Platte, LA 70586
E-mail: lebasb@legis.la.gov
Committees: Agriculture, Forestry, Aquaculture, and Rural
Development; Health and Welfare; Transportation, Highways, and
Public Works
Education: Louisiana (Monroe) 1968 BS

Representative **Walter "Walt" Leger III** (D-District 91) . . . (225) 342-8385
Parishes Represented: Orleans Parish (part)     Dist: (504) 556-9970
Term Expires: 2020     Fax: (225) 342-7043
600 Carondelet Street, Ninth Floor,     Dist: (504) 556-9972
New Orleans, LA 70130
E-mail: legerw@legis.la.gov
Committees: Appropriations; Education

Representative **Chris Leopold** (R-District 105) . . . . . . . . . . (504) 393-5649
Parishes Represented: Jefferson Parish (part),     Fax: (504) 393-5603
Orleans Parish (part), Plaquemines Parish (part)
Term Expires: 2020
1500 Woodland Highway, Suite A, Belle Chasse, LA 70037
E-mail: leopoldc@legis.la.gov
Committees: Commerce; Joint Legislative Capital Outlay; Judiciary;
Natural Resources and Environment
Education: Southeastern Louisiana 1990 BA

Representative **Joseph P. Lopinto III** (R-District 80) . . . . . . (504) 838-5430
Parishes Represented: Jefferson Parish (part)     Fax: (504) 834-5409
Note: On May 17, 2016, Joseph Lopinto announced his resignation
from the Louisiana House of Representatives, effective at the end of the
special legislative session.
Term Expires: 2020
131 Airline Highway, Suite 201, Metairie, LA 70001
E-mail: lopintoj@legis.la.gov
Committees: Administration of Criminal Justice; Commerce; Judiciary
Education: Loyola U (New Orleans) 2005 JD

Representative **Rodney Lyons, Sr.** (D-District 87) . . . . . . . . (504) 510-5417
Parishes Represented: Jefferson Parish (part)
Term Expires: 2020
2100 Woodmere Boulevard, Suite 160, Harvey, LA 70058
E-mail: lyonsr@legis.la.gov
Committees: Commerce; Municipal, Parochial and Cultural Affairs;
Natural Resources and Environment

Representative **Sherman Q. Mack** (R-District 95) . . . . . . . (225) 567-3677
Parishes Represented: Livingston Parish (part)    Fax: (225) 567-3679
Term Expires: 2020
P.O. Box 115, Albany, LA 70711
E-mail: macks@legis.la.gov
Committees: Administration of Criminal Justice
Education: Southeastern Louisiana 1995; Southern U Law 1999 JD

Representative **Tanner Magee** (R-District 53) . . . . . . . . . . (985) 858-2970
Parishes Represented: Lafourche Parish (part), Terrebonne Parish (part)
Term Expires: 2020
7833 West Main Street, Houma, LA 70360
E-mail: mageet@legis.la.gov
Committees: Civil Law and Procedure; Health and Welfare; Judiciary
Education: LSU BS, MPA, JD

Representative **C. Denise Marcelle** (D-District 61) . . . . . . (225) 342-8003
Parishes Represented: East Baton Rouge Parish (part)
Term Expires: 2020
1824 North Acadian Thruway, Baton Rouge, LA 70802
E-mail: marcelled@legis.la.gov
Committees: Administration of Criminal Justice; Municipal, Parochial
and Cultural Affairs; Transportation, Highways, and Public Works

Representative **Jack G. McFarland** (R-District 13) . . . . . . . (318) 259-4275
Parishes Represented: Bienville Parish (part), Jackson Parish, Ouachita
Parish (part), Winn Parish (part)
Term Expires: 2020
P.O. Box 143, Jonesboro, LA 71251
E-mail: mcfarlandj@legis.la.gov
Committees: Appropriations; Labor and Industrial Relations; Natural
Resources and Environment
Education: Arkansas (Monticello) BS

Representative **Blake Miguez** (R-District 49) . . . . . . . . . . . (337) 937-8827
Parishes Represented: Iberia Parish (part), Vermilion Parish (part)
Term Expires: 2020
401 North Broadway Street, Erath, LA 70533
E-mail: miguezb@legis.la.gov
Committees: Appropriations; Labor and Industrial Relations; Natural
Resources and Environment

Representative **Dustin Miller** (D-District 4) . . . . . . . . . . . . (337) 943-2900
Parishes Represented: Orleans Parish (part)
Term Expires: 2020
1115 South Union Street, Opelousas, LA 70570
E-mail: millerd@legis.la.gov
Committees: Agriculture, Forestry, Aquaculture, and Rural
Development; Appropriations; Health and Welfare
Education: Louisiana (Lafayette) BSN

Representative
**Gregory A. "Greg" Miller** (R-District 56) . . . . . . . . . . . (985) 764-9991
Parishes Represented: St. Charles Parish (part), St.    Fax: (985) 764-9993
John the Baptist Parish (part)
Term Expires: 2020
P.O. Box 190, Norco, LA 70079
E-mail: millerg@legis.la.gov
Committees: Civil Law and Procedure; House and Governmental
Affairs; Retirement
Education: LSU; LSU Hebert Law 1988 JD

Representative **Jack Montoucet** (D-District 42) . . . . . . . . (337) 783-2999
Parishes Represented: Acadia Parish (part),    Fax: (337) 788-4957
Lafayette Parish (part)
Term Expires: 2020
112 East Hutchinson Avenue, Crowley, LA 70526
E-mail: montoucj@legis.la.gov
Committees: Natural Resources and Environment; Retirement;
Transportation, Highways, and Public Works

Representative **Helena Moreno** (D-District 93) . . . . . . . . . (504) 568-2740
Parishes Represented: Orleans Parish (part)    Fax: (504) 568-2744
Term Expires: 2020
643 Magazine Street, Suite 302, New Orleans, LA 70130
E-mail: morenoh@legis.la.gov
Committees: Commerce; Health and Welfare
Education: Southern Methodist 1999 BA

Representative **James H. "Jim" Morris** (R-District 1) . . . . (318) 995-6852
Parishes Represented: Bossier Parish (part), Caddo    Fax: (318) 995-6890
Parish (part)
Term Expires: 2020
P.O. Box 217, Oil City, LA 71061
E-mail: larep001@legis.la.gov
Committees: Joint Legislative Capital Outlay; Natural Resources and
Environment; Ways and Means
Education: Henderson State 1976 BSEd

Representative **John C. "Jay" Morris III** (R-District 14) . . . (318) 362-4270
Parishes Represented: Morehouse Parish (part),    Fax: (318) 362-4277
Ouachita Parish (part)
Term Expires: 2020
2309 Oliver Road, Room One, Monroe, LA 71201
E-mail: morrisjc@legis.la.gov
Committees: House and Governmental Affairs; Joint Legislative Capital
Outlay; Judiciary; Ways and Means
Education: LSU 1980 BA, 1983 JD

Representative **Barbara Norton** (D-District 3) . . . . . . . . . . . (318) 632-5887
Parishes Represented: Caddo Parish (part)    Fax: (318) 632-5889
Term Expires: 2020
3245 Hollywood Avenue, Shreveport, LA 71108
E-mail: nortonb@legis.la.gov
Committees: Administration of Criminal Justice; Municipal, Parochial
and Cultural Affairs; Transportation, Highways, and Public Works

Representative **J. Kevin Pearson** (R-District 76) . . . . . . . . . (985) 646-6487
Parishes Represented: St. Tammany Parish (part)    Fax: (985) 646-6489
Term Expires: 2020
1349 Corporate Square, Suite 6, Slidell, LA 70458
E-mail: pearsonk@legis.la.gov
Committees: Commerce; Retirement

Representative **Vincent J. Pierre** (D-District 44) . . . . . . . . . (337) 262-2330
Parishes Represented: Lafayette Parish (part)    Fax: (337) 262-2332
Term Expires: 2020
800 West Congress Street, Suite A, Lafayette, LA 70501
E-mail: pierrev@legis.la.gov
Committees: Insurance; Labor and Industrial Relations; Transportation,
Highways, and Public Works

Representative **J. Rogers Pope** (R-District 71) . . . . . . . . . . (225) 667-3588
Parishes Represented: Livingston Parish (part)    Fax: (225) 667-3590
Term Expires: 2020
P.O. Box 555, Denham Springs, LA 70727
E-mail: poper@legis.la.gov
Committees: Health and Welfare; Transportation, Highways, and Public
Works
Education: Southeastern Louisiana BEd, MEd

Representative **Edward J. Price** (D-District 58) . . . . . . . . . . (225) 644-6738
Parishes Represented: Ascension Parish (part),    Fax: (225) 644-6750
Iberville Parish (part), St. James Parish (part)
Term Expires: 2020
2109 South Burnside Avenue, Suite C, Gonzales, LA 70737
E-mail: pricee@legis.la.gov
Committees: Commerce; Education; Labor and Industrial Relations

Representative **Stephen E. Pugh** (R-District 73) . . . . . . . . . (985) 386-7844
Parishes Represented: Tangipahoa Parish (part)    Fax: (985) 386-5669
Term Expires: 2020
114 Northeast Railroad Avenue, Ponchatoula, LA 70454
E-mail: pughs@legis.la.gov
Committees: Commerce; House and Governmental Affairs; Municipal,
Parochial and Cultural Affairs
Education: Col Financial Planning 2001 PMD

Representative **Steve E. Pylant** (R-District 20) . . . . . . . . . . (318) 435-7313
Parishes Represented: Caldwell Parish, Catahoula    Fax: (318) 435-2994
Parish (part), Franklin Parish, LaSalle Parish (part), Tensas Parish (part)
Term Expires: 2020
805 Jackson Street, Suite A, Winnsboro, LA 71295
E-mail: plyants@legis.la.gov
Committees: Administration of Criminal Justice; Agriculture, Forestry,
Aquaculture, and Rural Development; Appropriations

Representative
**H. Eugene "Gene" Reynolds** (D-District 10) . . . . . . . . . (318) 371-3092
Parishes Represented: Bossier Parish (part), Webster    Fax: (318) 371-3093
Parish
Term Expires: 2020
736 Main Street, Minden, LA 71055
E-mail: reynoldsg@legis.la.gov
Committees: Agriculture, Forestry, Aquaculture, and Rural
Development; Commerce; Education

Representative **Jerome "Dee" Richard** (I-District 55) . . . . (985) 447-0999
Parishes Represented: Lafourche Parish (part)    Fax: (985) 447-0998
Term Expires: 2020
907 Jackson Street, Thibodaux, LA 70301
E-mail: richardj@legis.la.gov
Committees: Appropriations; Insurance; Municipal, Parochial and
Cultural Affairs
Education: LSU 1978 BS

*(continued on next page)*

**LEGISLATIVE BRANCH**

**Representatives** *continued*

Representative **Clay Schexnayder** (R-District 81) . . . . . . . (225) 473-6016
Parishes Represented: Ascension Parish (part),       Fax: (225) 473-6018
Livingston Parish (part), St. James Parish (part), St. John the Baptist
Parish (part)
Term Expires: 2020
6473 Highway 44, Suite 205, Gonzales, LA 70737
E-mail: schexnayderc@legis.la.gov
Committees: Agriculture, Forestry, Aquaculture, and Rural
Development; Civil Law and Procedure

Representative **John M. Schroder, Sr.** (R-District 77) . . . . . (985) 893-6262
Parishes Represented: St. Tammany Parish (part)       Fax: (985) 893-6261
Term Expires: 2020
522 North New Hampshire Street, Covington, LA 70433
E-mail: schrodoj@legis.la.gov
Committees: Appropriations; House and Governmental Affairs
Education: Southeastern Louisiana BS

Representative **Alan T. Seabaugh** (R-District 5) . . . . . . . . (318) 676-7990
Parishes Represented: Caddo Parish (part)       Fax: (318) 676-7992
Term Expires: 2020
601 Marshall Street, Suite 701, Shreveport, LA 71101
E-mail: seabaugha@legis.la.gov
Committees: Civil Law and Procedure; Insurance; Labor and Industrial
Relations
Education: LSU 1990 BA, 1993 JD

Representative **Rob Shadoin** (R-District 12) . . . . . . . . . . . (318) 251-5039
Parishes Represented: Lincoln Parish (part), Union       Fax: (318) 251-5091
Parish
Term Expires: 2020
207 West Mississippi, Suite 300, Ruston, LA 71270
E-mail: shadoinr@legis.la.gov
Committees: Commerce; House and Governmental Affairs; Judiciary

Representative **Scott M. Simon** (R-District 74) . . . . . . . . . (985) 893-6246
Parishes Represented: St. Tammany Parish (part),       Fax: (985) 893-6247
Tangipahoa Parish (part), Washington Parish (part)
Term Expires: 2020
P.O. Box 1297, Abita Springs, LA 70420
E-mail: simons@legis.la.gov
Committees: Appropriations; Education; Labor and Industrial Relations

Representative **Patricia Haynes Smith** (D-District 67) . . . . (225) 342-7106
Parishes Represented: East Baton Rouge Parish       Fax: (225) 342-7117
(part)
Term Expires: 2020
251 Florida Street, Suite 300, Baton Rouge, LA 70801
E-mail: smithp@legis.la.gov
Committees: Appropriations; Education; Municipal, Parochial and
Cultural Affairs

Representative **Julie Stokes, CPA** (R-District 79) . . . . . . . . (504) 456-3173
Parishes Represented: Jefferson Parish (part)       Fax: (504) 456-3175
Term Expires: 2020
4425 Clearview Parkway, Suite D, Metairie, LA 70006
E-mail: stokesj@legis.la.gov
Committees: Health and Welfare; Joint Legislative Capital Outlay;
Ways and Means
Education: New Orleans 1992 BS

Representative **Kirk Talbot** (R-District 78) . . . . . . . . . . . . . (504) 736-7299
Parishes Represented: Jefferson Parish (part)       Fax: (504) 736-7113
Term Expires: 2020
9523 Jefferson Highway, Suite B, River Ridge, LA 70123
E-mail: talbotk@legis.la.gov
Committees: Insurance

Representative **Major Thibaut** (D-District 18) . . . . . . . . . . . (225) 638-3811
Parishes Represented: Iberville Parish (part), Pointe       Fax: (225) 638-2952
Coupee Parish, West Baton Rouge Parish (part), West Feliciana Parish
(part)
Term Expires: 2020
2004 False River Drive, New Roads, LA 70760
E-mail: thibautm@legis.la.gov
Committees: Insurance; Joint Legislative Capital Outlay; Ways and
Means
Education: LSU 1999 BS

Representative
**Malinda Brumfield White** (D-District 75) . . . . . . . . . . . (985) 730-2147
Parishes Represented: St. Tammany Parish (part), Washington Parish
(part)
Term Expires: 2020
116 Georgia Avenue, Suite 40, Bogalusa, LA 70427
E-mail: whitema@legis.la.gov
Committees: Municipal, Parochial and Cultural Affairs; Natural
Resources and Environment; Transportation, Highways, and Public
Works

Representative **Thomas P. Willmott** (R-District 92) . . . . . . (504) 465-3479
Parishes Represented: Jefferson Parish (part), St.       Fax: (504) 465-3481
Charles Parish (part)
Term Expires: 2020
2002 20th Street, Suite 204-A, Kenner, LA 70062
E-mail: willmott@legis.la.gov
Committees: Health and Welfare; Joint Legislative Capital Outlay;
Municipal, Parochial and Cultural Affairs; Ways and Means

Representative **Jerome "Zee" Zeringue** (R-District 52) . . . (985) 876-8823
Parishes Represented: Lafourche Parish (part), Terrebonne Parish (part)
Term Expires: 2020
E-mail: zeringuej@legis.la.gov
Committees: Appropriations; Judiciary; Natural Resources and
Environment
Education: LSU BS, MS

# House Standing Committees
## Administration of Criminal Justice

| Majority Members | Minority Members |
|---|---|
| Sherman Q. Mack (R-95) *Chair* | John Bagneris (D-100) |
| Steve E. Pylant (R-20) *Vice Chair* | Barbara Carpenter (D-63) |
| Bryan Adams (R-85) | Randal L. Gaines (D-57) |
| Tony Bacala (R-59) | Col. Terry Landry (D-96) |
| Stephen Dwight (R-35) | C. Denise Marcelle (D-61) |
| Lowell Christopher "Chris" Hazel (R-27) | Barbara Norton (D-3) |
| Valarie Hodges (R-64) | |
| Frank A. Howard (R-24) | |
| Joseph P. Lopinto III (R-80) | |

**Members**
Terry R. Brown (I-22)

## Agriculture, Forestry, Aquaculture, and Rural Development

| Majority Members | Minority Members |
|---|---|
| Clay Schexnayder (R-81) *Chair* | John F. "Andy" Anders (D-21) *Vice Chair* |
| Beryl Adams Amedée (R-51) | |
| Charles R. "Bubba" Chaney (R-19) | Jerry "Truck" Gisclair (D-54) |
| Phillip DeVillier (R-41) | Jeffrey "Jeff" Hall (D-26) |
| Julie Emerson (R-39) | Dorothy Sue Hill (D-32) |
| John E. "Johnny" Guinn (R-37) | H. Bernard LeBas (D-38) |
| Bob Hensgens (R-47) | Dustin Miller (D-4) |
| Frank A. Howard (R-24) | H. Eugene "Gene" Reynolds (D-10) |
| Steve E. Pylant (R-20) | |

**Members**
Terry R. Brown (I-22)

## Appropriations

| Majority Members | Minority Members |
|---|---|
| Cameron Henry (R-82) *Chair* | James K. Armes III (D-30) |
| Franklin J. Foil (R-70) *Vice Chair* | Robert E. Billiot (D-83) |
| Mark T. Abraham (R-36) | Gary M. Carter, Jr. (D-102) |
| Beryl Adams Amedée (R-51) | Walter "Walt" Leger III (D-91) |
| Tony Bacala (R-59) | Dustin Miller (D-4) |
| Lawrence A. "Larry" Bagley (R-7) | Patricia Haynes Smith (D-67) |
| John A. "Johnny" Berthelot (R-88) | |
| Charles R. "Bubba" Chaney (R-19) | |
| Rick Edmonds (R-66) | |
| Lance Harris (R-25) | |
| Bob Hensgens (R-47) | |
| Valarie Hodges (R-64) | |
| Jack G. McFarland (R-13) | |
| Blake Miguez (R-49) | |
| Steve E. Pylant (R-20) | |
| Scott M. Simon (R-74) | |
| John M. Schroder, Sr. (R-77) | |
| Jerome "Zee" Zeringue (R-52) | |

**Members**
Jerome "Dee" Richard (I-55)

## Civil Law and Procedure

**Majority Members**
Raymond "Ray" Garofalo (R-103) *Chair*
Gregory Cromer (R-90)
Julie Emerson (R-39)
Michael "Mike" Johnson (R-8)
Tanner Magee (R-53)
Gregory A. "Greg" Miller (R-56)
Clay Schexnayder (R-81)
Alan T. Seabaugh (R-5)

**Minority Members**
Randal L. Gaines (D-57) *Vice Chair*
Robert J. "Robby" Carter (D-72)
Sam L. Jenkins, Jr. (D-2)

## Commerce

**Majority Members**
Thomas G. Carmody, Jr. (R-6) *Chair*
Paul Hollis (R-104) *Vice Chair*
Patrick Connick (R-84)
Jean-Paul Coussan (R-45)
R. Reid Falconer (R-89)
Chris Leopold (R-105)
Joseph P. Lopinto III (R-80)
J. Kevin Pearson (R-76)
Stephen E. Pugh (R-73)
Rob Shadoin (R-12)

**Minority Members**
John F. "Andy" Anders (D-21)
Chad M. Brown (D-60)
Lt. Col. Kenny R. Cox (D-23)
Cedric B. Glover (D-4)
Patrick O. Jefferson (D-11)
Rodney Lyons, Sr. (D-87)
Helena Moreno (D-93)
Edward J. Price (D-58)
H. Eugene "Gene" Reynolds (D-10)

## Education

**Majority Members**
Nancy Landry (R-31) *Chair*
Beryl Adams Amedée (R-51)
Chris Broadwater (R-86)
Stephen F. "Steve" Carter (R-68)
Rick Edmonds (R-66)
Julie Emerson (R-39)
R. Reid Falconer (R-89)
Stephanie Hilferty (R-94)
Scott M. Simon (R-74)

**Minority Members**
Edward J. Price (D-58) *Vice Chair*
Joseph Bouie, Jr. (D-97)
Jeffrey "Jeff" Hall (D-26)
Walter "Walt" Leger III (D-91)
H. Eugene "Gene" Reynolds (D-10)
Patricia Haynes Smith (D-67)

## Health and Welfare

**Majority Members**
Frank A. Hoffmann (R-15) *Chair*
Thomas P. Willmott (R-92) *Vice Chair*
Lawrence A. "Larry" Bagley (R-7)
Dodie Horton (R-9)
Bob Hensgens (R-47)
Michael "Mike" Johnson (R-8)
Tanner Magee (R-53)
J. Rogers Pope (R-71)
Julie Stokes (R-79)

**Minority Members**
Lt. Col. Kenny R. Cox (D-23)
Marcus Hunter (D-17)
Katrina R. Jackson (D-16)
Robert A. Johnson (D-28)
H. Bernard LeBas (D-38)
Dustin Miller (D-4)
Helena Moreno (D-93)

## House and Governmental Affairs

**Majority Members**
Stephen E. Pugh (R-73) *Vice Chair*
Lance Harris (R-25)
Barry Ivey (R-65)
Gregory A. "Greg" Miller (R-56)
John C. "Jay" Morris III (R-14)
John M. Schroder, Sr. (R-77)
Rob Shadoin (R-12)

**Minority Members**
Michael E. Danahay (D-33) *Chair*
Gary M. Carter, Jr. (D-102)
James "Jimmy" Harris (D-99)
Dorothy Sue Hill (D-32)
Sam L. Jenkins, Jr. (D-2)

## Insurance

**Majority Members**
Kirk Talbot (R-78) *Chair*
Mark T. Abraham (R-36)
Gregory Cromer (R-90)
Paula Davis (R-69)
Paul Hollis (R-104)
Mike Pete Huval (R-46)
Alan T. Seabaugh (R-5)

**Members**
Jerome "Dee" Richard (I-55)

**Minority Members**
Major Thibaut (D-18) *Vice Chair*
John F. "Andy" Anders (D-21)
Chad M. Brown (D-60)
Robert J. "Robby" Carter (D-72)
Cedric B. Glover (D-4)
Vincent J. Pierre (D-44)

## Judiciary

**Majority Members**
Michael "Mike" Johnson (R-8) *Vice Chair*
Bryan Adams (R-85)
Jean-Paul Coussan (R-45)
Lowell Christopher "Chris" Hazel (R-27)
Valarie Hodges (R-64)
Chris Leopold (R-105)
Joseph P. Lopinto III (R-80)
Tanner Magee (R-53)
John C. "Jay" Morris III (R-14)
Rob Shadoin (R-12)
Jerome "Zee" Zeringue (R-52)

**Minority Members**
Katrina R. Jackson (D-16) *Chair*
John Bagneris (D-100)
Chad M. Brown (D-60)
Gary M. Carter, Jr. (D-102)
Robert J. "Robby" Carter (D-72)
Randal L. Gaines (D-57)
James "Jimmy" Harris (D-99)
Robert A. Johnson (D-28)

## Labor and Industrial Relations

**Majority Members**
Chris Broadwater (R-86) *Vice Chair*
Lawrence A. "Larry" Bagley (R-7)
Gregory Cromer (R-90)
R. Reid Falconer (R-89)
Dodie Horton (R-9)
Jack G. McFarland (R-13)
Blake Miguez (R-49)
Alan T. Seabaugh (R-5)
Scott M. Simon (R-74)

**Minority Members**
Patrick O. Jefferson (D-11) *Chair*
Lt. Col. Kenny R. Cox (D-23)
Marcus Hunter (D-17)
Edward "Ted" James (D-101)
Vincent J. Pierre (D-44)
Edward J. Price (D-58)

## Municipal, Parochial and Cultural Affairs

**Majority Members**
John A. "Johnny" Berthelot (R-88) *Chair*
Mike Pete Huval (R-46) *Vice Chair*
Paula Davis (R-69)
Stephen Dwight (R-35)
Rick Edmonds (R-66)
Stephanie Hilferty (R-94)
Stephen E. Pugh (R-73)
Thomas P. Willmott (R-92)

**Members**
Jerome "Dee" Richard (I-55)

**Minority Members**
Robert E. Billiot (D-83)
Joseph Bouie, Jr. (D-97)
Cedric B. Glover (D-4)
Sam L. Jenkins, Jr. (D-2)
Rodney Lyons, Sr. (D-87)
C. Denise Marcelle (D-61)
Barbara Norton (D-3)
Patricia Haynes Smith (D-67)
Malinda Brumfield White (D-75)

## Natural Resources and Environment

**Majority Members**
Stuart J. Bishop (R-43) *Chair*
Chris Leopold (R-105) *Vice Chair*
Charles R. "Bubba" Chaney (R-19)
Patrick Connick (R-84)
Jean-Paul Coussan (R-45)
Phillip DeVillier (R-41)
Franklin J. Foil (R-70)
John E. "Johnny" Guinn (R-37)
Jack G. McFarland (R-13)
Blake Miguez (R-49)
James H. "Jim" Morris (R-1)
Jerome "Zee" Zeringue (R-52)

**Members**
Terry R. Brown (I-22)

**Minority Members**
James K. Armes III (D-30)
Robert E. Billiot (D-83)
Jerry "Truck" Gisclair (D-54)
Rodney Lyons, Sr. (D-87)
Jack Montoucet (D-42)
Malinda Brumfield White (D-75)

## Retirement

**Majority Members**
J. Kevin Pearson (R-76) *Chair*
Mark T. Abraham (R-36)
Tony Bacala (R-59)
Paul Hollis (R-104)
Barry Ivey (R-65)
Gregory A. "Greg" Miller (R-56)

**Minority Members**
Jack Montoucet (D-42) *Vice Chair*
Barbara Carpenter (D-63)
Sam Jones (D-50)

## Transportation, Highways, and Public Works

**Majority Members**

Kenneth E. "Kenny" Havard (R-62)
  *Chair*
Bryan Adams (R-85)
Stephen F. "Steve" Carter (R-68)
John E. "Johnny" Guinn (R-37)
Frank A. Howard (R-24)
J. Rogers Pope (R-71)

**Members**

Terry R. Brown (I-22)

**Minority Members**

Col. Terry Landry (D-96)
  *Vice Chair*
Barbara Carpenter (D-63)
A. B. Franklin (D-34)
Jerry "Truck" Gisclair (D-54)
Jeffrey "Jeff" Hall (D-26)
Dorothy Sue Hill (D-32)
H. Bernard LeBas (D-38)
C. Denise Marcelle (D-61)
Jack Montoucet (D-42)
Barbara Norton (D-3)
Vincent J. Pierre (D-44)
Malinda Brumfield White (D-75)

## Ways and Means

**Majority Members**

James H. "Jim" Morris (R-1)
  *Vice Chair*
Chris Broadwater (R-86)
Paula Davis (R-69)
Phillip DeVillier (R-41)
Stephen Dwight (R-35)
Stephanie Hilferty (R-94)
Dodie Horton (R-9)
Mike Pete Huval (R-46)
Barry Ivey (R-65)
John C. "Jay" Morris III (R-14)
Julie Stokes (R-79)
Thomas P. Willmott (R-92)

**Minority Members**

Neil C. Abramson (D-98) *Chair*
Joseph Bouie, Jr. (D-97)
James "Jimmy" Harris (D-99)
Marcus Hunter (D-17)
Edward "Ted" James (D-101)
Robert A. Johnson (D-28)
Major Thibaut (D-18)

# Maine Legislature

TTY: (207) 287-4469  Fax: (207) 287-1456
E-mail: webmaster_legis@legislature.maine.gov
Internet: www.maine.gov/legis

## Maine Senate

3 State House Station, Augusta, ME 04333-0003
Tel: (207) 287-1540  TTY: (207) 287-1583  Fax: (207) 287-1900
E-mail: webmaster_senate@legislature.maine.gov
E-mail: webmaster_sendems@legislature.maine.gov (Democrat Office)
E-mail: webmaster_senreps@legislature.maine.gov (Republican Office)

President of the Senate **Michael D. Thibodeau** (R) . . . . . . . (207) 223-5177
Majority Leader **Garrett Paul Mason** (R) . . . . . . . . . . . . . (207) 287-1505
  Education: Pensacola Christian 2006 BS
Assistant Majority Leader **Andre E. Cushing III** (R) . . . . . . (207) 287-1540
  Education: Maine
Minority Leader **Justin L. Alfond** (D) . . . . . . . . . . . . . . . (207) 828-0277
  Education: Tulane 1998 BABA
Assistant Minority Leader **Dawn Hill** (D) . . . . . . . . . . . . . (207) 337-0368
  Education: West Virginia 1979 JD
Secretary of the Senate **Joseph G. Carleton** . . . . . . . . . . . (207) 287-1540
Assistant Secretary of the Senate **David R. Madore** . . . . . . (207) 287-1540

## Senators

**Party Affiliation Statistics:** Republicans: 20, Democrats: 15

Senator **Justin L. Alfond** (D-District 27) . . . . . . . . . . . . . . (207) 828-0277
  Counties Represented: Cumberland (part)
  Term Expires: 2016
  134 Sheridan Street, Portland, ME 04101
  E-mail: justin@justinalfond.com
  Committees: Joint Regulatory Fairness and Reform
Senator **Linda Baker** (R-District 23) . . . . . . . . . . . . . . . . . (207) 287-1505
  Counties Represented: Lincoln (part), Sagadahoc
  Term Expires: 2016
  E-mail: linda.baker@legislature.maine.gov
  Committees: Bills in Second Reading; Joint Insurance and Financial
  Services; Joint Marine Resources
Senator **Eric Brakey** (R-District 20) . . . . . . . . . . . . . . . . . (207) 287-1505
  Counties Represented: Androscoggin (part), Cumberland (part)
  Term Expires: 2016
  E-mail: sen.eric.brakey@gmail.com
  Committees: Joint Environment and Natural Resources; Joint Health
  and Human Services
Senator **Catherine Breen** (D-District 25) . . . . . . . . . . . . . . (207) 287-1515
  Counties Represented: Cumberland (part)
  Term Expires: 2016
  E-mail: cathy.breen@legislature.maine.gov
  Committees: Joint Environment and Natural Resources
Senator **David C. Burns** (R-District 6) . . . . . . . . . . . . . . . (207) 287-1540
  Counties Represented: Hancock (part), Washington
  Term Expires: 2016
  159 Dodge Road, Whiting, ME 04691
  E-mail: sendavid.burns@legislature.maine.gov
  Committees: Conduct and Ethics; Joint Criminal Justice and Public
  Safety; Joint Government Oversight Committee; Joint Judiciary
Senator **Ronald F. Collins** (R-District 34) . . . . . . . . . . . . . (207) 985-2485
  Counties Represented: York (part)
  Term Expires: 2016
  401 Harriseckett Road, Wells, ME 04090
  E-mail: rcollins7@maine.rr.com
  Committees: Conduct and Ethics; Joint Transportation; Joint Veterans
  and Legal Affairs
Senator **Andre E. Cushing III** (R-District 10) . . . . . . . . . . . (207) 287-1540
  Counties Represented: Penobscot (part)
  Term Expires: 2016
  PO Box 211, Hampden, ME 04444
  E-mail: andre@andrecushing.com
  Committees: Joint Labor, Commerce, Research and Economic
  Development; Senate Rules; Senatorial Vote
Senator **Scott Cyrway** (R-District 16) . . . . . . . . . . . . . . . . (207) 287-1505
  Counties Represented: Kennebec (part), Somerset (part)
  Term Expires: 2016
  E-mail: scyrway@roadrunner.com
  Committees: Joint Inland Fisheries and Wildlife; Joint Veterans and
  Legal Affairs

Senator **Paul T. Davis, Sr.** (R-District 4) . . . . . . . . . . . . . .(207) 287-1505
Counties Represented: Penobscot (part), Piscataquis, Somerset (part)
Term Expires: 2016
E-mail: sendavis@myottmail.com
Committees: Joint Inland Fisheries and Wildlife; Joint Taxation

Senator **Susan Deschambault** (D-District 32) . . . . . . . . . .(207) 287-1515
Counties Represented: York (part)
Term Expires: 2016
9 Porter Street, Biddeford, ME 04005
E-mail: susan.deschambault@legislature.maine.gov
Committees: Joint Inland Fisheries and Wildlife

Senator **G. William "Bill" Diamond** (D-District 26) . . . . . .(207) 287-1515
Counties Represented: Cumberland (part)
Term Expires: 2016
E-mail: diamondhollyd@aol.com
Committees: Joint Transportation; Senatorial Vote

Senator **James F. Dill** (D-District 5) . . . . . . . . . . . . . . . . .(207) 287-1515
Counties Represented: Penobscot (part)
Term Expires: 2016
E-mail: jdill@umext.maine.edu
Committees: Joint Agriculture, Conservation and Forestry
Education: Maine BS, MS; Purdue 1979 PhD

Senator **Peter E. Edgecomb** (R-District 1) . . . . . . . . . . . . .(207) 287-1505
Counties Represented: Aroostook (part)
Term Expires: 2016
E-mail: peter.edgecomb@legislature.maine.gov
Committees: Joint Agriculture, Conservation and Forestry; Joint
Education and Cultural Affairs
Education: Maine 1988 CAS; New Hampshire MA

Senator **Stan J. Gerzofsky** (D-District 24) . . . . . . . . . . . . .(207) 373-1328
Counties Represented: Cumberland (part)
Term Expires: 2016
Three Federal Street, Brunswick, ME 04011
E-mail: stan1340@aol.com
Committees: Joint Criminal Justice and Public Safety; Joint Rules;
Senate Rules; Senatorial Vote
Education: Pasadena City 1965 (Attended)

Senator **Geoffrey Gratwick** (D-District 9) . . . . . . . . . . . . .(207) 287-1540
Counties Represented: Penobscot (part)
Term Expires: 2016
1230 Kenduskeag Avenue, Bangor, ME 04401
E-mail: sengeoff.gratwick@legislature.maine.gov
Committees: Engrossed Bills; Joint Insurance and Financial Services

Senator **James Michael Hamper** (R-District 19) . . . . . . . .(207) 287-1540
Counties Represented: Cumberland (part), Oxford (part)
Term Expires: 2016
1023 King Street, Oxford, ME 04270
E-mail: senatorhamp@gmail.com
Committees: Joint Appropriations and Financial Affairs
Education: Maine 2001 AA

Senator **Anne M. Haskell** (D-District 28) . . . . . . . . . . . . . .(207) 287-1540
Counties Represented: Cumberland (part)
Term Expires: 2016
31 Higgins Street, Portland, ME 04101
E-mail: annehask@maine.rr.com
Committees: Conduct and Ethics; Joint Health and Human Services

Senator **Dawn Hill** (D-District 35) . . . . . . . . . . . . . . . . . . .(207) 337-0368
Counties Represented: York (part)
Term Expires: 2016
P.O. Box 701, Cape Neddick, ME 03902
E-mail: sendawn.hill@legislature.maine.gov
Committees: Joint Energy, Utilities and Technology; Senate Rules;
Senatorial Vote

Senator **Christopher K. Johnson** (D-District 13) . . . . . . . .(207) 832-4135
Counties Represented: Kennebec (part), Knox (part), Lincoln (part)
Term Expires: 2016
3 State House Station, Augusta, ME 04333
E-mail: chris@dirigo.net
Committees: Joint Government Oversight Committee; Joint Judiciary
Education: Maine BA

Senator **Roger J. Katz** (R-District 15) . . . . . . . . . . . . . . . .(207) 485-2394
Counties Represented: Kennebec (part)
Term Expires: 2016
Three Westview Street, Augusta, ME 04330
E-mail: rkatz@lipmankatzmckee.com
Committees: Joint Appropriations and Financial Affairs; Joint
Government Oversight Committee; Senate Rules; Senatorial Vote
Education: Harvard 1971 BA; Boston U 1975 JD

Senator **Brian D. Langley** (R-District 7) . . . . . . . . . . . . . . .(207) 667-0625
Counties Represented: Hancock (part)
Term Expires: 2016
11 South Street, Ellsworth, ME 04605
E-mail: langley4legislature@myfairpoint.net
Committees: Conduct and Ethics; Joint Education and Cultural Affairs;
Joint Marine Resources
Education: Southern Maine; Syracuse BS

Senator **Nathan L. Libby** (D-District 21) . . . . . . . . . . . . . .(207) 287-1515
Counties Represented: Androscoggin (part)
Term Expires: 2016
E-mail: nathan.libby@gmail.com
Committees: Joint State and Local Government; Joint Taxation
Education: Bates 2007 BA

Senator **Garrett Paul Mason** (R-District 22) . . . . . . . . . . .(207) 287-1505
Counties Represented: Androscoggin (part),   Tel: (207) 577-1251
Kennebec (part)
Term Expires: 2016
312 Ridge Road, Lisbon Falls, ME 04252
E-mail: garrettpaulmason@gmail.com
Committees: Joint Energy, Utilities and Technology; Senate Rules;
Senatorial Vote

Senator **Earle L. McCormick** (R-District 14) . . . . . . . . . . .(207) 287-1505
Counties Represented: Kennebec (part)
Term Expires: 2016
E-mail: demccormick@tds.net
Committees: Joint Health and Human Services; Joint Taxation

Senator **Rebecca Millett** (D-District 29) . . . . . . . . . . . . . . .(207) 287-1540
Counties Represented: Cumberland (part)
Term Expires: 2016
12 Waumbek Road, Cape Elizabeth, ME 04107
E-mail: senrebeccamillett@gmail.com
Committees: Bills in Second Reading; Joint Education and Cultural
Affairs
Education: American U BA, BS; Chicago MBA

Senator **David Miramant** (D-District 12) . . . . . . . . . . . . . .(207) 287-1515
Counties Represented: Knox (part)
Term Expires: 2016
E-mail: davemiramant@gmail.com
Committees: Bills in Second Reading; Joint Marine Resources

Senator **John L. Patrick** (D-District 18) . . . . . . . . . . . . . . .(207) 364-7666
Counties Represented: Androscoggin (part), Oxford (part)
Term Expires: 2016
Three State House Station, Augusta, ME 04333
E-mail: senjohn.patrick@legislature.maine.gov
Committees: Joint Labor, Commerce, Research and Economic
Development; Joint Veterans and Legal Affairs

Senator **Kimberley C. Rosen** (R-District 8) . . . . . . . . . . . .(207) 287-1505
Counties Represented: Hancock (part), Hancock (part)
Term Expires: 2016
E-mail: kimberley.rosen@legislature.maine.gov
Committees: Engrossed Bills; Joint Criminal Justice and Public Safety;
Joint Transportation

Senator **Thomas B. Saviello** (R-District 17) . . . . . . . . . . . .(207) 645-3420
Counties Represented: Franklin, Kennebec (part)
Term Expires: 2016
60 Applegate Lane, Wilton, ME 04294
E-mail: drtom16@hotmail.com
Committees: Bills in Second Reading; Joint Agriculture, Conservation
and Forestry; Joint Environment and Natural Resources; Joint
Regulatory Fairness and Reform; Senatorial Vote
Education: Maine 1974 MS, 1978 PhD

Senator **Michael D. Thibodeau** (R-District 11) . . . . . . . . . .(207) 223-5177
Counties Represented: Waldo
Term Expires: 2016
169 Coles Corner Road, Winterport, ME 04496
E-mail: senatorthibodeau@aol.com

Senator **Linda M. Valentino** (D-District 31) . . . . . . . . . . . .(207) 287-1540
Counties Represented: York (part)
Term Expires: 2016
PO Box 1049, Saco, ME 04072
E-mail: senatorvalentino@gmail.com
Committees: Conduct and Ethics; Joint Appropriations and Financial
Affairs

Senator **Amy Fern Volk** (R-District 30) . . . . . . . . . . . . . . . .(207) 287-1505
Counties Represented: Cumberland (part), York (part)
Term Expires: 2016
E-mail: amy.volk@legislature.maine.gov
Committees: Joint Judiciary; Joint Labor, Commerce, Research and
Economic Development

*(continued on next page)*

**LEGISLATIVE BRANCH**

**Senators** *continued*

Senator **Rodney L. Whittemore** (R-District 3) . . . . . . . . . (207) 474-6703
Counties Represented: Kennebec (part), Somerset (part)
Term Expires: 2016
P.O. Box 96, Skowhegan, ME 04976
E-mail: rodwhittemore@gmail.com
Committees: Joint Insurance and Financial Services; Joint State and
Local Government

Senator **Michael J. Willette** (R-District 2) . . . . . . . . . . . . . (207) 287-1505
Counties Represented: Aroostook (part), Penobscot (part)
Term Expires: 2016
E-mail: mikeblackbear@gmail.com
Committees: Joint State and Local Government

Senator **David Woodsome** (R-District 33) . . . . . . . . . . . . (207) 287-1505
Counties Represented: York (part)
Term Expires: 2016
E-mail: david.woodsome@legislature.maine.gov
Committees: Engrossed Bills; Joint Energy, Utilities and Technology

# Senate Standing Committees

## Bills in Second Reading

| Majority Members | Minority Members |
| --- | --- |
| Thomas B. Saviello (R-17) *Chair* | Rebecca Millett (D-29) |
| Linda Baker (R-23) | David Miramant (D-12) |

## Conduct and Ethics

| Majority Members | Minority Members |
| --- | --- |
| David C. Burns (R-6) *Chair* | Anne M. Haskell (D-28) |
| Ronald F. Collins (R-34) | Linda M. Valentino (D-31) |
| Brian D. Langley (R-7) | |

## Engrossed Bills

| Majority Members | Minority Members |
| --- | --- |
| Kimberley C. Rosen (R-8) *Chair* | Geoffrey Gratwick (D-9) |
| David Woodsome (R-33) | |

## Senate Rules

| Majority Members | Minority Members |
| --- | --- |
| Garrett Paul Mason (R-22) *Chair* | Stan J. Gerzofsky (D-24) |
| Andre E. Cushing III (R-10) | Dawn Hill (D-35) |
| Roger J. Katz (R-15) | |

## Senatorial Vote

| Majority Members | Minority Members |
| --- | --- |
| Roger J. Katz (R-15) *Chair* | G. William "Bill" Diamond (D-26) |
| Andre E. Cushing III (R-10) | Stan J. Gerzofsky (D-24) |
| Garrett Paul Mason (R-22) | Dawn Hill (D-35) |
| Thomas B. Saviello (R-17) | |

# Maine House of Representatives

2 State House Station, Augusta, ME 04333-0002
Tel: (207) 287-1400   TTY: (207) 287-4469   Fax: (207) 287-1456
E-mail: webmaster_house@legislature.maine.gov

Speaker of the House **Mark W. Eves** (D) . . . . . . . . . . . . . (207) 287-1300
Education: Louisville BA; Louisville Sem MA
Chief of Staff to the Speaker **Ana Hicks** . . . . . . . . . . . . (207) 287-1300
E-mail: ana.hicks@legislature.maine.gov       Fax: (207) 287-1308
Majority Leader **Jeff M. McCabe** (D) . . . . . . . . . . . . . . . . (207) 474-5402
Assistant Majority Leader **Sara Gideon** (D) . . . . . . . . . . . (207) 865-9593
Education: George Washington 2004 BA
Minority Leader
**LtCol Kenneth Wade Fredette, ANG** (R) . . . . . . . . . . . (207) 287-1440
Education: Maine (Machias) BS; Southern Maine; Maine JD
Assistant Minority Leader
**Eleanor M. "Ellie" Espling** (R) . . . . . . . . . . . . . . . . . . . . (207) 926-6082
Education: Southern Maine ABA
Clerk of the House **Robert B. Hunt** (D) . . . . . . . . . . . . . . . (207) 287-1400
E-mail: rob.hunt@legislature.maine.gov
Assistant Clerk of the House **Jennifer McGowan** . . . . . . . (207) 287-1400
E-mail: jennifer.mcgowan@legislature.maine.gov

# Representatives

**Party Affiliation Statistics:** Republicans: 69, Democrats: 78,
Independents: 4

Representative **Robert Alley** (D-District 138) . . . . . . . . . . . (207) 287-1400
Counties Represented: Washington (part)
Term Expires: 2016
E-mail: robert.alley@legislature.maine.gov
Committees: Joint Inland Fisheries and Wildlife; Joint Marine
Resources

Representative **Susan M. W. Austin** (R-District 67) . . . . . (207) 287-1400
Counties Represented: Cumberland (part)
Term Expires: 2016
E-mail: susan.austin@legislature.maine.gov
Committees: Joint Labor, Commerce, Research and Economic
Development

Representative **Christopher W. Babbidge** (D-District 8) . . (207) 287-1400
Counties Represented: York (part)
Term Expires: 2016
E-mail: christopher.babbidge@legislature.maine.gov
Committees: Joint Energy, Utilities and Technology; Joint State and
Local Government

Representative **Dillon Bates** (D-District 118) . . . . . . . . . . . (207) 287-1400
Counties Represented: Franklin (part), Piscataquis (part), Somerset
(part)
Term Expires: 2016
E-mail: dillon.bates@legislature.maine.gov
Committees: Engrossed Bills; Joint Labor, Commerce, Research and
Economic Development

Representative **Kevin Battle** (R-District 33) . . . . . . . . . . . . (207) 287-1400
Counties Represented: Cumberland (part)
Term Expires: 2016
E-mail: kevin.battle@legislature.maine.gov
Committees: Joint Marine Resources

Representative **Roberta B. Beavers** (D-District 2) . . . . . . . . (207) 748-3432
Counties Represented: York (part)
Term Expires: 2016
72 Woodland Hills, South Berwick, ME 03908
E-mail: repbobbi.beavers@legislature.maine.gov
Committees: Bills in Second Reading; Joint Energy, Utilities and
Technology
Education: Rutgers BA; Lehigh 1979 MBA;
Montclair State U 1996 MA

Representative **Henry E. M. Beck** (D-District 110) . . . . . . . (207) 837-4343
Counties Represented: Kennebec (part)
Term Expires: 2016
P.O. Box 1723, Waterville, ME 04903
E-mail: rephenry.beck@legislature.maine.gov
Committees: Elections; Joint Insurance and Financial Services

Representative
**Anne H. "Pinny" Beebe-Center** (D-District 93) . . . . . . . (207) 287-1400
Counties Represented: Knox (part)                    Res: (207) 596-3937
Term Expires: 2016
E-mail: anne.beebe-center@legislature.maine.gov
Committees: Joint State and Local Government

Representative **Bruce A. Bickford** (R-District 63) . . . . . . . . (207) 287-1400
Counties Represented: Androscoggin (part)
Term Expires: 2016
E-mail: bruce.bickford@legislature.maine.gov
Committees: Joint Taxation

Representative **Russell J. Black** (R-District 114) . . . . . . . . . (207) 645-2990
Counties Represented: Franklin (part)
Term Expires: 2016
123 Black Road, Wilton, ME 04294
E-mail: russell.black@legislature.maine.gov
Committees: Joint Agriculture, Conservation and Forestry
Education: Wentworth Inst (Attended)

Representative **Lydia Blume** (D-District 3) . . . . . . . . . . . . . (207) 287-1400
Counties Represented: York (part)
Term Expires: 2016
E-mail: lydia.blume@legislature.maine.gov
Committees: Bills in Second Reading; Joint Marine Resources

Representative **Heidi Brooks** (D-District 61) . . . . . . . . . . . (207) 287-1400
Counties Represented: Androscoggin (part)
Term Expires: 2016
E-mail: heidi.brooks@legislature.maine.gov
Committees: Joint Insurance and Financial Services

Representative **Mark E. Bryant** (D-District 24) . . . . . . . . . (207) 287-1400
  Counties Represented: Cumberland (part)
  Term Expires: 2016
  E-mail: mark.bryant@legislature.maine.gov
  Committees: Ethics; Joint State and Local Government; Joint Transportation

Representative
  **Andrew Russell Buckland** (R-District 113) . . . . . . . . . . (207) 287-1400
  Counties Represented: Franklin (part)
  Term Expires: 2016
  E-mail: andrew.buckland@legislature.maine.gov
  Committees: Joint Environment and Natural Resources

Representative **Christine Burstein** (D-District 96) . . . . . . . . (207) 287-1400
  Counties Represented: Waldo (part)
  Term Expires: 2016
  E-mail: christine.burstein@legislature.maine.gov
  Committees: Joint Health and Human Services; Leaves of Absence

Representative **James J. Campbell, Sr.** (I-District 21) . . . . (207) 793-2396
  Counties Represented: York (part)
  Term Expires: 2016
  PO Box 29, West Newfield, ME 04095
  Committees: Joint Labor, Commerce, Research and Economic Development

Representative
  **Richard H. "Dick" Campbell** (R-District 130) . . . . . . . . (207) 745-7748
  Counties Represented: Hancock (part), Penobscot      Tel: (207) 287-1440
  (part)                                                    ((In-Session))
  Term Expires: 2016                                    Fax: (207) 825-4861
  321 River Road, Orrington, ME 04474
  E-mail: richard.campbell@legislature.maine.gov
  Committees: Joint Environment and Natural Resources
  Education: Maine

Representative **Paul Chace, RPh** (R-District 46) . . . . . . . . (207) 287-1400
  Counties Represented: Androscoggin (part), Cumberland (part)
  Term Expires: 2016
  E-mail: paul.chace@legislature.maine.gov
  Committees: Elections; Joint Taxation

Representative **Ralph Chapman** (D-District 133) . . . . . . . . (207) 326-0899
  Counties Represented: Hancock (part)
  Term Expires: 2016
  455 Varnumville Road, Brooksville, ME 04617
  E-mail: repralph.chapman@legislature.maine.gov
  Committees: Joint Agriculture, Conservation and Forestry
  Education: Tufts BS

Representative **Justin Mark Chenette** (D-District 15) . . . . (207) 590-3266
  Counties Represented: York (part)
  Term Expires: 2016
  19 Buckthorn Circle, Saco, ME 04072
  E-mail: repjustin.chenette@legislature.maine.gov
  Committees: Joint Criminal Justice and Public Safety
  Education: Lyndon State 2011 BA

Representative **Benjamin M. Chipman** (D-District 119) . . . (207) 318-4961
  Counties Represented: Piscataquis (part)
  Term Expires: 2016
  5 Mayo Street, Portland, ME 04101
  E-mail: repben.chipman@legislature.maine.gov
  Committees: Joint Environment and Natural Resources

Representative **Janice E. Cooper** (D-District 47) . . . . . . . . (207) 847-3193
  Counties Represented: Cumberland (part)
  Term Expires: 2016
  53 West Elm Street, Yarmouth, ME 04096
  E-mail: repjanice.cooper@legislature.maine.gov
  Committees: Joint Insurance and Financial Services
  Education: Yale 1971 JD

Representative **Patrick Corey** (R-District 25) . . . . . . . . . . . (207) 287-1400
  Counties Represented: Cumberland (part)
  Term Expires: 2016
  E-mail: patrick.corey@legislature.maine.gov
  Committees: Joint Inland Fisheries and Wildlife

Representative **Dale J. Crafts** (R-District 57) . . . . . . . . . . . (207) 729-6565
  Counties Represented: Androscoggin (part)       Res: (207) 353-5469
  Term Expires: 2016                              Fax: (207) 729-0118
  2 Passing Lane, Lisbon Falls, ME 04252
  E-mail: repdale.crafts@legislature.maine.gov
  Committees: Joint Inland Fisheries and Wildlife

Representative **Matthea Elisabeth "Mattie" Daughtry**
  (D-District 49) . . . . . . . . . . . . . . . . . . . . . . . . . . . . . . . (207) 522-0913
  Counties Represented: Cumberland (part)
  Term Expires: 2016
  11B Everett Street, Brunswick, ME 04011
  E-mail: repmattie.daughtry@legislature.maine.gov
  Committees: Joint Education and Cultural Affairs

Representative **James E. Davitt** (D-District 101) . . . . . . . . (207) 287-1400
  Counties Represented: Penobscot (part)
  Term Expires: 2016
  E-mail: james.davitt@legislature.maine.gov
  Committees: Joint Criminal Justice and Public Safety

Representative **Jennifer DeChant** (D-District 52) . . . . . . . . (207) 442-8486
  Counties Represented: Sagadahoc (part)
  Term Expires: 2016
  1008 Middle Street, Bath, ME 04530
  E-mail: repjennifer.dechant@legislature.maine.gov
  Committees: Joint Energy, Utilities and Technology
  Education: Heidelberg BA; Franklin U MBA

Representative
  **Michael Gilbert "Mick" Devin** (D-District 90) . . . . . . . . (207) 563-3132
  Counties Represented: Lincoln (part)
  Term Expires: 2016
  1 Hillcrest Road, Newcastle, ME 04553
  E-mail: michael.devin@legislature.maine.gov
  Committees: Joint Marine Resources
  Education: Naval Acad; Florida Tech MS

Representative
  **Kathleen Jackson Dillingham** (R-District 72) . . . . . . . . . (207) 287-1400
  Counties Represented: Androscoggin (part), Oxford (part)
  Term Expires: 2016
  E-mail: kathleen.dillingham@legislature.maine.gov
  Committees: Joint Veterans and Legal Affairs

Representative **Mark N. Dion** (D-District 43) . . . . . . . . . . . (207) 797-6341
  Counties Represented: Cumberland (part)
  Term Expires: 2016
  45 Allison Avenue, Portland, ME 04103
  E-mail: repmark.dion@legislature.maine.gov
  Committees: Joint Energy, Utilities and Technology
  Education: Maine 2005 JD

Representative **Donna R. Doore** (D-District 85) . . . . . . . . . (207) 287-1400
  Counties Represented: Kennebec (part)
  Term Expires: 2016
  E-mail: donna.doore@legislature.maine.gov
  Committees: Joint State and Local Government

Representative **Robert S. Duchesne** (D-District 121) . . . . . (207) 287-1400
  Counties Represented: Penobscot (part)
  Term Expires: 2016
  E-mail: robert.duchesne@legislature.maine.gov
  Committees: Joint Environment and Natural Resources

Representative **Larry C. Dunphy** (I-District 118) . . . . . . . . (207) 635-2831
  Counties Represented: Franklin (part), Piscataquis (part), Somerset (part)
  Term Expires: 2016
  P.O. Box 331, North Anson, ME 04958
  E-mail: larry.dunphy@legislature.maine.gov
  Committees: Joint Energy, Utilities and Technology

Representative **Michelle Ann Dunphy** (D-District 122) . . . (207) 287-1400
  Counties Represented: Penobscot (part)
  Term Expires: 2016
  E-mail: michelle.dunphy@legislature.maine.gov
  Committees: Joint Agriculture, Conservation and Forestry

Representative **Anthony Edgecomb** (R-District 148) . . . . . (207) 287-1400
  Counties Represented: Aroostook (part)
  Term Expires: 2016
  E-mail: anthony.edgecomb@legislature.maine.gov
  Committees: Engrossed Bills; Joint Agriculture, Conservation and Forestry

Representative
  **Eleanor M. "Ellie" Espling** (R-District 65) . . . . . . . . . . . (207) 926-6082
  Counties Represented: Androscoggin (part), Cumberland (part)
  Term Expires: 2016
  12 Lewiston Road, New Gloucester, ME 04260
  E-mail: ellie.espling@legislature.maine.gov
  Committees: Elections; Rules and Business of the House

Representative **Jeffrey Evangelos** (I-District 91) . . . . . . . . (207) 287-1400
  Counties Represented: Knox (part), Lincoln (part)
  Term Expires: 2016
  E-mail: jeffrey.evangelos@legislature.maine.gov
  Committees: Ethics; Joint Judiciary; Joint State and Local Government
  Education: Maine 1974 MA

Representative **Mark W. Eves** (D-District 6) . . . . . . . . . . . . (207) 287-1300
  Counties Represented: York (part)
  Term Expires: 2016
  29 Acorn Lane, North Berwick, ME 03906
  E-mail: repmark.eves@legislature.maine.gov
  Committees: Rules and Business of the House

*(continued on next page)*

**LEGISLATIVE BRANCH**

**LEGISLATIVE BRANCH**

**Representatives** *continued*

Representative **Richard R. Farnsworth** (D-District 37) .... (207) 874-6399
Counties Represented: Cumberland (part)
Term Expires: 2016
55 Old Mast Road, Portland, ME 04102
E-mail: richard.farnsworth@legislature.maine.gov
Committees: Joint Education and Cultural Affairs

Representative **Bradlee Thomas Farrin** (R-District 111) ... (207) 287-1400
Counties Represented: Somerset (part)
Term Expires: 2016
E-mail: bradlee.farrin@legislature.maine.gov
Committees: Joint Transportation

Representative **Ryan Fecteau** (D-District 11) ........... (207) 287-1400
Counties Represented: York (part)
Term Expires: 2016
E-mail: ryan.fecteau@legislature.maine.gov
Committees: Joint Labor, Commerce, Research and Economic
Development; Leaves of Absence

Representative **Robert Foley** (R-District 7) ............. (207) 287-1400
Counties Represented: York (part)
Term Expires: 2016
E-mail: robert.foley@legislature.maine.gov
Committees: Ethics; Joint Insurance and Financial Services

Representative **Lori Fowle** (D-District 80) ............. (207) 872-7268
Counties Represented: Kennebec (part), Lincoln (part)
Term Expires: 2016
305 Taber Hill Road, Vassalboro, ME 04989
E-mail: replori.fowle@legislature.maine.gov
Committees: Joint Criminal Justice and Public Safety

Representative
**LtCol Kenneth Wade Fredette, ANG** (R-District 100) .. (207) 287-1440
Counties Represented: Penobscot (part)
Term Expires: 2016
P.O. Box 70, Newport, ME 04953
E-mail: repkenneth.fredette@legislature.maine.gov
Committees: Ethics; Rules and Business of the House

Representative **Aaron M. Frey** (D-District 124) ......... (207) 249-9969
Counties Represented: Penobscot (part)
Term Expires: 2016
PO Box 74, Bangor, ME 04402
E-mail: repaaron.frey@legislature.maine.gov
Committees: Joint Appropriations and Financial Affairs
Education: St Anselm 2001 BA; Roger Williams 2008 JD

Representative **Drew Gattine** (D-District 34) ........... (207) 409-3477
Counties Represented: Cumberland (part)
Term Expires: 2016
529 Stroudwater Street, Westbrook, ME 04092
E-mail: repdrew.gattine@legislature.maine.gov
Committees: Joint Health and Human Services
Education: Colgate 1983 BA; Columbia 1987 JD

Representative **Karen Gerrish** (R-District 20) ........... (207) 287-1400
Counties Represented: York (part)
Term Expires: 2016
E-mail: karen.gerrish@legislature.maine.gov
Committees: Joint Criminal Justice and Public Safety

Representative **Sara Gideon** (D-District 48) ............. (207) 865-9593
Counties Represented: Cumberland (part)
Term Expires: 2016
37 South Freeport Road, Freeport, ME 04032
E-mail: repsara.gideon@legislature.maine.gov
Committees: Elections

Representative **Paul E. Gilbert** (D-District 74) ........... (207) 897-5143
Counties Represented: Androscoggin (part), Franklin (part)
Term Expires: 2016
P.O. Box 186, Jay, ME 04239
E-mail: reppaul.gilbert@legislature.maine.gov
Committees: Joint Labor, Commerce, Research and Economic
Development

Representative **James S. Gillway** (R-District 98) ........ (207) 548-6372
Counties Represented: Waldo (part)                Res: (207) 548-6429
Term Expires: 2016                                Fax: (207) 548-2305
79 Bowen Road, Searsport, ME 04974
E-mail: repjames.gillway@legislature.maine.gov
Committees: Ethics; Joint Transportation

Representative **Phyllis Ginzler** (R-District 69) ........... (207) 287-1400
Counties Represented: Cumberland (part), Oxford (part)
Term Expires: 2016
E-mail: phyllis.ginzler@legislature.maine.gov
Committees: Joint Judiciary; Leaves of Absence

Representative
**Jared Golden, USMC (Ret)** (D-District 60) .......... (207) 287-1400
Counties Represented: Androscoggin (part)
Term Expires: 2016
E-mail: jared.golden@legislature.maine.gov
Committees: Joint Transportation; Joint Veterans and Legal Affairs
Education: Bates 2011

Representative **Adam A. Goode** (D-District 127) ........ (207) 991-7000
Counties Represented: Penobscot (part)
Term Expires: 2016
P.O. Box 2681, Bangor, ME 04402
E-mail: repadam.goode@legislature.maine.gov
Committees: Joint Taxation

Representative **Gay M. Grant** (D-District 83) ........... (207) 582-5882
Counties Represented: Kennebec (part)           Fax: (207) 582-5882
Term Expires: 2016
PO Box 4, South Gardiner, ME 04359
E-mail: repgay.grant@legislature.maine.gov
Committees: Joint Appropriations and Financial Affairs
Education: Southern Maine BA

Representative
**Randall Adam Greenwood** (R-District 82) .......... (207) 287-1400
Counties Represented: Androscoggin (part), Kennebec (part)
Term Expires: 2016
E-mail: randall.greenwood@legislature.maine.gov
Committees: Joint State and Local Government

Representative **Martin Grohman** (D-District 12) ........ (207) 287-1400
Counties Represented: York (part)
Term Expires: 2016
E-mail: martin.grohman@legislature.maine.gov
Committees: Joint Energy, Utilities and Technology

Representative **Stacey K. Guerin** (R-District 102) ........ (207) 884-7118
Counties Represented: Penobscot (part)
Term Expires: 2016
79 Phillips Road, Glenburn, ME 04401
E-mail: repstacey.guerin@legislature.maine.gov
Committees: Joint Judiciary

Representative **Scott M. Hamann** (D-District 32) ........ (207) 233-2951
Counties Represented: Cumberland (part)
Term Expires: 2016
60 Thornton Avenue, South Portland, ME 04106
E-mail: repscott.hamann@legislature.maine.gov
Committees: Bills in Second Reading; Joint Health and Human
Services
Education: Montana State BA

Representative **Sheldon Hanington** (R-District 142) ...... (207) 287-1400
Counties Represented: Penobscot (part)
Term Expires: 2016
E-mail: sheldon.hanington@legislature.maine.gov
Committees: Joint Veterans and Legal Affairs; Leaves of Absence

Representative **Jeff Hanley** (R-District 87) ............. (207) 287-1400
Counties Represented: Kennebec (part), Lincoln (part)
Term Expires: 2016
E-mail: jeffery.hanley@legislature.maine.gov
Committees: Joint Environment and Natural Resources

Representative **Denise Patricia Harlow** (D-District 36) .... (207) 409-0870
Counties Represented: Cumberland (part)
Term Expires: 2016
36 Broadway, Portland, ME 04103
E-mail: repdenise.harlow@legislature.maine.gov
Committees: Joint Environment and Natural Resources

Representative **Matthew A. Harrington** (R-District 19) ... (800) 423-2900
Counties Represented: York (part)
Term Expires: 2016
E-mail: matthew.harrington@legislature.maine.gov
Committees: Joint State and Local Government

Representative **Stephanie Hawke** (R-District 89) ........ (207) 633-4600
Counties Represented: Lincoln (part)
Term Expires: 2016
E-mail: stephanie.hawke@legislature.maine.gov
Committees: Joint Marine Resources

Representative **Frances Head** (R-District 117) ........... (207) 287-4469
Counties Represented: Franklin (part), Oxford (part)
Term Expires: 2016
E-mail: frances.head@legislature.maine.gov
Committees: Ethics; Joint Health and Human Services

Representative **Erin D. Herbig** (D-District 97) . . . . . . . . . . (207) 542-7654
Counties Represented: Waldo (part)
Term Expires: 2016
PO Box 1015, Belfast, ME 04915
E-mail: reperin.herbig@legislature.maine.gov
Committees: Joint Labor, Commerce, Research and Economic
Development

Representative **Lloyd Herrick** (R-District 73) . . . . . . . . . . . (207) 287-1400
Counties Represented: Oxford (part)
Term Expires: 2016
E-mail: lloyd.herrick@legislature.maine.gov
Committees: Joint Judiciary

Representative **Craig V. Hickman** (D-District 81) . . . . . . . . (207) 377-3276
Counties Represented: Kennebec (part)　　　Fax: (207) 377-3226
Term Expires: 2016
192 Annabessacook Road, Winthrop, ME 04364
E-mail: repcraig.hickman@legislature.maine.gov
Committees: Joint Agriculture, Conservation and Forestry
Education: Harvard 1990 BA

Representative **Norman E. Higgins** (R-District 120) . . . . . . (207) 287-1400
Counties Represented: Piscataquis (part)
Term Expires: 2016
E-mail: norman.higgins@legislature.maine.gov
Committees: Joint Energy, Utilities and Technology

Representative **Gary Hilliard** (R-District 76) . . . . . . . . . . . . (207) 287-1400
Counties Represented: Kennebec (part)
Term Expires: 2016
E-mail: gary.hilliard@legislature.maine.gov
Committees: Joint Inland Fisheries and Wildlife

Representative **Brian Hobart** (R-District 55) . . . . . . . . . . . . (207) 287-1400
Counties Represented: Sagadahoc (part)
Term Expires: 2016
E-mail: brian.hobart@legislature.maine.gov
Committees: Joint Transportation

Representative **Barry J. Hobbins** (D-District 14) . . . . . . . . (207) 282-5985
Counties Represented: York (part)
Term Expires: 2016
22 Glenhaven Circle, Saco, ME 04072
E-mail: barry.hobbins@legislature.maine.gov
Committees: Joint Judiciary
Education: Maine 1973 BA; Pierce Law 1977 JD

Representative **George Hogan** (D-District 13) . . . . . . . . . . . (207) 287-1400
Counties Represented: York (part)
Term Expires: 2016
E-mail: george.hogan@legislature.maine.gov
Committees: Joint Transportation

Representative **Brian L. Hubbell** (D-District 135) . . . . . . . (207) 409-3477
Counties Represented: Hancock (part)
Term Expires: 2016
529 Stroudwater Street, Westbrook, ME 04092
E-mail: repbrian.hubbell@legislature.maine.gov
Committees: Joint Education and Cultural Affairs
Education: MIT 1980 BS

Representative **Patricia Hymanson** (D-District 4) . . . . . . . . (207) 287-1400
Counties Represented: York (part)
Term Expires: 2016
E-mail: patricia.hymanson@legislature.maine.gov
Committees: Engrossed Bills; Joint Health and Human Services

Representative **Erik C. Jorgensen** (D-District 41) . . . . . . . . (207) 939-7120
Counties Represented: Cumberland (part)
Term Expires: 2016
83 Highland Street, Portland, ME 04103
E-mail: reperik.jorgensen@legislature.maine.gov
Committees: Joint Appropriations and Financial Affairs
Education: Bowdoin 1987 AB; Harvard 1999 MPA

Representative **Jonathan L. Kinney** (R-District 22) . . . . . . . (207) 637-2366
Counties Represented: Cumberland (part), York (part)
Term Expires: 2016
179 Beaver Berry Road, Limington, ME 04049
E-mail: repjonathan.kinney@legislature.maine.gov
Committees: Joint Veterans and Legal Affairs

Representative **MaryAnne Kinney** (R-District 99) . . . . . . . . (207) 287-1400
Counties Represented: Waldo (part)
Term Expires: 2016
E-mail: maryanne.kinney@legislature.maine.gov
Committees: Joint Agriculture, Conservation and Forestry

Representative
**Victoria P. "Tori" Kornfield** (D-District 125) . . . . . . . . . . (207) 947-7224
Counties Represented: Penobscot (part)
Term Expires: 2016
48 Madison Street, Bangor, ME 04401
E-mail: reptori.kornfield@legislature.maine.gov
Committees: Joint Education and Cultural Affairs

Representative
**Charles B. "Chuck" Kruger** (D-District 92) . . . . . . . . . . (207) 354-8928
Counties Represented: Knox (part)　　　Res: (207) 354-8239
Term Expires: 2016
37 Green Street, Thomaston, ME 04861
E-mail: repchuck.kruger@legislature.maine.gov
Committees: Joint Government Oversight Committee

Representative **Walter A. Kumiega III** (D-District 134) . . . . (207) 348-2548
Counties Represented: Hancock (part), Knox (part)
Term Expires: 2016
36 Cedar Lane, Little Deer Isle, ME 04650
E-mail: repwalter.kumiega@legislature.maine.gov
Committees: Engrossed Bills; Joint Marine Resources

Representative **Michel A. Lajoie** (D-District 58) . . . . . . . . . (207) 783-1927
Counties Represented: Androscoggin (part)
Term Expires: 2016
279 Old Greene Road, Lewiston, ME 04240
E-mail: repmichel.lajoie@legislature.maine.gov
Committees: Joint Criminal Justice and Public Safety

Representative **Lawrence E. Lockman** (R-District 137) . . . (207) 584-5900
Counties Represented: Hancock (part), Penobscot (part), Washington
(part)
Term Expires: 2016
10 Perry Lane, Amherst, ME 05605
E-mail: replawrence.lockman@legislature.maine.gov
Committees: Joint Labor, Commerce, Research and Economic
Development
Education: Covenant Col (Attended); Pasadena City (Attended)

Representative **Ricky D. Long** (R-District 145) . . . . . . . . . . (207) 365-4704
Counties Represented: Aroostook (part), Penobscot (part)
Term Expires: 2016
756 Island Falls Road, Sherman, ME 04776
E-mail: reprick.long@legislature.maine.gov
Committees: Joint Criminal Justice and Public Safety

Representative
**Thomas R. W. Longstaff** (D-District 109) . . . . . . . . . . . . (207) 872-6617
Counties Represented: Kennebec (part)
Term Expires: 2016
39 Pleasant Street, Waterville, ME 04901
E-mail: thomas.longstaff@legislature.maine.gov
Committees: Engrossed Bills; Joint Veterans and Legal Affairs; Leaves
of Absence

Representative **Louis J. Luchini** (D-District 132) . . . . . . . . (207) 664-4699
Counties Represented: Hancock (part)
Term Expires: 2016
P.O. Box 1311, Ellsworth, ME 04605
E-mail: replouis.luchini@legislature.maine.gov
Committees: Ethics; Joint Veterans and Legal Affairs

Representative **Peter Lyford** (R-District 129) . . . . . . . . . . . (207) 848-3335
Counties Represented: Penobscot (part)
Term Expires: 2016
E-mail: peter.lyford@legislature.maine.gov
Committees: Joint Inland Fisheries and Wildlife

Representative **Joyce A. Maker** (R-District 140) . . . . . . . . . (207) 454-2327
Counties Represented: Washington (part)
Term Expires: 2016
89 Lafayette Street, Calais, ME 04619
E-mail: repjoyce.maker@legislature.maine.gov
Committees: Joint Education and Cultural Affairs

Representative **Richard S. Malaby** (R-District 136) . . . . . . . (207) 422-6806
Counties Represented: Hancock (part), Washington　　Res: (207) 422-3146
(part)　　　　　　　　　　　　　　　　　　　　　　Fax: (207) 422-3105
Term Expires: 2016
52 Cross Road, Hancock, ME 04640
E-mail: reprichard.malaby@legislature.maine.gov
Committees: Engrossed Bills; Joint Health and Human Services

Representative **Donald G. Marean** (R-District 16) . . . . . . . . (207) 727-5527
Counties Represented: York (part)
Term Expires: 2016
233 Bonny Eagle Road, Hollis Center, ME 04042
E-mail: repdon.marean@legislature.maine.gov
Committees: Joint Agriculture, Conservation and Forestry; Joint
Taxation

*(continued on next page)*

**Representatives** *continued*

Representative **John L. Martin** (D-District 151) . . . . . . . . . (207) 834-7568
  Counties Represented: Aroostook (part)          Res: (207) 444-5556
  Term Expires: 2016
  E-mail: john.martin@legislature.maine.gov
  Committees: Elections; Joint Appropriations and Financial Affairs;
  Joint Environment and Natural Resources

Representative
  **Roland D. "Danny" Martin** (D-District 150) . . . . . . . . . (207) 543-6165
  Counties Represented: Aroostook (part)
  Term Expires: 2016
  E-mail: roland.martin@legislature.maine.gov
  Committees: Joint Inland Fisheries and Wildlife; Joint State and Local
  Government

Representative **Anne-Marie Mastraccio** (D-District 18) . . . (207) 249-9969
  Counties Represented: York (part)
  Term Expires: 2016
  PO Box 74, Bangor, ME 04402
  E-mail: repannemarie.mastraccio@legislature.maine.gov
  Committees: Joint Labor, Commerce, Research and Economic
  Development

Representative **Jeff M. McCabe** (D-District 107) . . . . . . . . (207) 474-5402
  Counties Represented: Somerset (part)
  Term Expires: 2016
  13 Olive Street, Skowhegan, ME 04976
  E-mail: repjeff.mccabe@legislature.maine.gov
  Committees: Rules and Business of the House

Representative **Michael D. McClellan** (R-District 66) . . . . . (207) 329-6148
  Counties Represented: Androscoggin (part),       Res: (207) 655-4438
  Cumberland (part)
  Term Expires: 2016
  27 Pismire Mountain Road, Raymond, ME 04071
  E-mail: repmichael.mcclellan@legislature.maine.gov
  Committees: Joint Education and Cultural Affairs; Joint Regulatory
  Fairness and Reform

Representative **Joyce "Jay" McCreight** (D-District 51) . . . (207) 449-3293
  Counties Represented: Cumberland (part), Sagadahoc (part)
  Term Expires: 2016
  E-mail: joyce.mccreight@legislature.maine.gov
  Committees: Joint Judiciary; Joint Marine Resources

Representative **Carol A. McElwee** (R-District 149) . . . . . . (207) 498-8605
  Counties Represented: Aroostook (part)
  Term Expires: 2016
  54 Pioneer Avenue, Caribou, ME 04736
  E-mail: carol.mcelwee@legislature.maine.gov
  Committees: Bills in Second Reading; Joint Agriculture, Conservation
  and Forestry

Representative **Andrew J. McLean** (D-District 27) . . . . . . (207) 939-8482
  Counties Represented: Cumberland (part)
  Term Expires: 2016
  114 Johnson Road, Gorham, ME 04038
  E-mail: repandrew.mclean@legislature.maine.gov
  Committees: Bills in Second Reading; Joint Transportation
  Education: Plymouth State U; Southern Maine MPP

Representative **Gina Melaragno** (D-District 62) . . . . . . . . (207) 740-8860
  Counties Represented: Androscoggin (part)
  Term Expires: 2016
  E-mail: gina.melaragno@legislature.maine.gov
  Committees: Joint Insurance and Financial Services

Representative **Kimberly Monaghan** (D-District 30) . . . . . . (207) 584-5900
  Counties Represented: Cumberland (part)
  Term Expires: 2016
  10 Perry Lane, Amherst, ME 05605
  E-mail: repkim.monaghan-derrig@legislature.maine.gov
  Committees: Ethics; Joint Judiciary; Joint Veterans and Legal Affairs

Representative **Matthew W. Moonen** (D-District 38) . . . . . (207) 332-7823
  Counties Represented: Cumberland (part)
  Term Expires: 2016
  17 Pine Street, Portland, ME 04102
  E-mail: repmatt.moonen@legislature.maine.gov
  Committees: Elections; Joint Judiciary; Joint Taxation
  Education: Northwestern BA

Representative **Terry K. Morrison** (D-District 31) . . . . . . . (207) 831-0828
  Counties Represented: Cumberland (part)
  Term Expires: 2016
  13 Ocean Street, South Portland, ME 04106
  E-mail: repterry.morrison@legislature.maine.gov
  Committees: Joint Insurance and Financial Services

Representative **Catherine M. Nadeau** (D-District 78) . . . . . (207) 873-2025
  Counties Represented: Kennebec (part)
  Term Expires: 2016
  23 Patterson Avenue, Winslow, ME 04901
  E-mail: repcatherine.nadeau@legislature.maine.gov
  Committees: Joint Criminal Justice and Public Safety

Representative **Robert W. Nutting** (R-District 77) . . . . . . . (207) 465-7139
  Counties Represented: Kennebec (part)
  Term Expires: 2016
  P.O. Box 100, Oakland, ME 04963
  E-mail: robert.nutting@legislature.maine.gov
  Committees: Joint Appropriations and Financial Affairs

Representative **Beth A. O'Connor** (R-District 5) . . . . . . . . (207) 698-7899
  Counties Represented: York (part)
  Term Expires: 2016
  E-mail: beth.o'connor@legislature.maine.gov
  Committees: Joint Energy, Utilities and Technology

Representative **Lester Ordway** (R-District 23) . . . . . . . . . (800) 423-2900
  Counties Represented: Cumberland (part)         Res: (207) 642-3491
  Term Expires: 2016
  E-mail: lester.ordway@legislature.maine.gov
  Committees: Joint State and Local Government

Representative **Wayne R. Parry** (R-District 10) . . . . . . . . . (207) 286-9145
  Counties Represented: York (part)
  Term Expires: 2016
  851 Alfred Road, Arundel, ME 04046
  E-mail: repwayne.parry@legislature.maine.gov
  Committees: Joint Transportation

Representative
  **Matthew J. Peterson** (D-District 115) . . . . . . . . . (207) 776-8051 (Cell)
  Counties Represented: Oxford (part)
  Term Expires: 2016
  1106 Route 2, Rumford, ME 04276
  E-mail: matthew.peterson@legislature.maine.gov
  Committees: Joint Government Oversight Committee; Joint Health and
  Human Services

Representative **John J. Picchiotti** (R-District 108) . . . . . . . (207) 453-2137
  Counties Represented: Somerset (part)
  Term Expires: 2016
  E-mail: john.picchiotti@legislature.maine.gov
  Committees: Joint Insurance and Financial Services

Representative **Richard A. Pickett** (R-District 116) . . . . . . (207) 562-4517
  Counties Represented: Oxford (part)             Res: (207) 645-4893
  Term Expires: 2016
  E-mail: richard.pickett@legislature.maine.gov
  Committees: Joint State and Local Government

Representative **Jeffrey Pierce** (R-District 53) . . . . . . . . . . . (207) 737-9051
  Counties Represented: Lincoln (part), Sagadahoc (part)
  Term Expires: 2016
  E-mail: jeffrey.pierce@legislature.maine.gov
  Committees: Joint Marine Resources

Representative **Teresa Pierce** (D-District 44) . . . . . . . . . . . (207) 781-7144
  Counties Represented: Cumberland (part)
  Term Expires: 2016
  E-mail: teresa.pierce@legislature.maine.gov
  Committees: Leaves of Absence

Representative
  **Matthew G. "Matt" Pouliot** (R-District 86) . . . . . . . . . (207) 287-1440
  Counties Represented: Kennebec (part)          Res: (207) 441-9418
  Term Expires: 2016                             Fax: (207) 623-8520
  14 Winthrop Court, Augusta, ME 04330
  E-mail: matthew.pouliot@legislature.maine.gov
  Committees: Joint Education and Cultural Affairs
  Education: Maine (Augusta) 2009 BSBA

Representative **Christine B. Powers** (D-District 68) . . . . . . (207) 318-2511
  Counties Represented: Cumberland (part), York (part)
  Term Expires: 2016
  E-mail: christine.powers@legislature.maine.gov
  Committees: Joint Transportation

Representative **Dwayne Prescott** (R-District 17) . . . . . . . . (800) 423-2900
  Counties Represented: York (part)
  Term Expires: 2016
  E-mail: dwayne.prescott@legislature.maine.gov
  Committees: Joint Insurance and Financial Services

Representative **Roger E. Reed** (R-District 103) . . . . . . . . . (207) 848-5136
  Counties Represented: Penobscot (part)
  Term Expires: 2016
  278 Murray Road, Carmel, ME 04419
  E-mail: reproger.reed@legislature.maine.gov
  Committees: Elections; Joint Inland Fisheries and Wildlife
  Education: Maine (Farmington) 1965 BS; Southern Maine 1975 MEd

Representative **Margaret R. Rotundo** (D-District 59) . . . . . (207) 784-3259
Counties Represented: Androscoggin (part)
Term Expires: 2016
446 College Street, Lewiston, ME 04240
E-mail: margaret.rotundo@legislature.maine.gov
Committees: Joint Appropriations and Financial Affairs

Representative **Diane Russell** (D-District 39) . . . . . . . . . . . (207) 272-9182
Counties Represented: Cumberland (part)
Term Expires: 2016
28 Vesper Street, Portland, ME 04101
E-mail: repdiane.russell@legislature.maine.gov
Committees: Joint Taxation

Representative **Deane Rykerson** (D-District 1) . . . . . . . . . (207) 439-8755
Counties Represented: York (part)          Fax: (888) 620-8146
Term Expires: 2016
One Salt Marsh Lane, Kittery Point, ME 03905
E-mail: repdeane.rykerson@legislature.maine.gov
Committees: Joint Energy, Utilities and Technology
Education: SUNY (Stony Brook) 1972 BA; Boston Arch Ctr 1989 BA;
Harvard 1996 MA

Representative **Linda F. Sanborn** (D-District 26) . . . . . . . . (207) 939-2879
Counties Represented: Cumberland (part)
Term Expires: 2016
170 Spiller Road, Gorham, ME 04038
E-mail: replinda.sanborn@legislature.maine.gov
Committees: Joint Appropriations and Financial Affairs

Representative **Deborah J. Sanderson** (R-District 88) . . . . (207) 623-2168
Counties Represented: Kennebec (part), Lincoln (part)
Term Expires: 2016
64 Whittier Drive, Chelsea, ME 04330
E-mail: deborah.sanderson@legislature.maine.gov
Committees: Joint Health and Human Services

Representative **Robert J. Saucier** (D-District 147) . . . . . . . (207) 227-1160
Counties Represented: Aroostook (part)
Term Expires: 2016
117 Lombard Street, Presque Isle, ME 04769
E-mail: saucierforpi@gmail.com
Committees: Joint Agriculture, Conservation and Forestry; Joint
Veterans and Legal Affairs
Education: Southern Maine BS

Representative **David Sawicki** (R-District 64) . . . . . . . . . . (207) 753-6312
Counties Represented: Androscoggin (part)
Term Expires: 2016
E-mail: david.sawicki@legislature.maine.gov
Committees: Joint Marine Resources

Representative **John C. Schneck** (D-District 126) . . . . . . . . (207) 942-7886
Counties Represented: Penobscot (part)
Term Expires: 2016
2078 Ohio Street, Bangor, ME 04401
E-mail: repjohn.schneck@legislature.maine.gov
Committees: Joint Veterans and Legal Affairs
Education: Insurance 1983 BBA

Representative **H. Stedman Seavey, Jr.** (R-District 9) . . . . (207) 967-5991
Counties Represented: York (part)
Term Expires: 2016
E-mail: stedman.seavey@legislature.maine.gov
Committees: Joint Taxation

Representative **Roger L. Sherman** (R-District 144) . . . . . . . (207) 532-7073
Counties Represented: Aroostook (part)
Term Expires: 2016
E-mail: roger.sherman@legislature.maine.gov
Committees: Joint Judiciary
Education: Ricker 1962; Maine 1967 JD; New Hampshire 1972 MS

Representative
**Stanley Byron Short, Jr.** (D-District 106) . . . . . . . . . . . (207) 487-4944
Counties Represented: Kennebec (part), Somerset (part)
Term Expires: 2016
PO Box 103, Pittsfield, ME 04967
E-mail: repstanley.short@legislature.maine.gov
Committees: Joint Inland Fisheries and Wildlife

Representative **Heather W. Sirocki** (R-District 28) . . . . . . . (207) 883-5609
Counties Represented: Cumberland (part)
Term Expires: 2016
32 Glendale Circle, Scarborough, ME 04074
E-mail: heather.sirocki@legislature.maine.gov
Committees: Joint Appropriations and Financial Affairs; Leaves of
Absence

Representative **Thomas Skolfield** (R-District 112) . . . . . . . (207) 585-2638
Counties Represented: Franklin (part), Somerset (part)
Term Expires: 2016
E-mail: thomas.skolfield@legislature.maine.gov
Committees: Bills in Second Reading; Joint Taxation

Representative **Stephen S. Stanley** (D-District 143) . . . . . . (207) 723-2712
Counties Represented: Penobscot (part)          Res: (207) 746-5371
Term Expires: 2016
614 Pattagumpus Road, Medway, ME 04460
E-mail: stephen.stanley@legislature.maine.gov
Committees: Joint Taxation

Representative **Paul Stearns** (R-District 119) . . . . . . . . . . . (207) 876-3242
Counties Represented: Piscataquis (part)
Term Expires: 2016
E-mail: paul.stearns@legislature.maine.gov
Committees: Joint Education and Cultural Affairs

Representative **Joel Stetkis** (R-District 105) . . . . . . . . . . . (800) 423-2900
Counties Represented: Somerset (part)
Term Expires: 2016
E-mail: joel.stetkis@legislature.maine.gov
Committees: Engrossed Bills; Joint Labor, Commerce, Research and
Economic Development

Representative **Peter C. Stuckey** (D-District 42) . . . . . . . . (207) 773-3345
Counties Represented: Cumberland (part)
Term Expires: 2016
20 Vaill Street, Portland, ME 04103
E-mail: reppeter.stuckey@legislature.maine.gov
Committees: Joint Health and Human Services

Representative **Gary E. Sukeforth** (I-District 95) . . . . . . . . (800) 423-2900
Counties Represented: Knox (part)          Fax: (207) 785-6801
Term Expires: 2016
E-mail: gary.sukeforth@legislature.maine.gov
Committees: Joint Taxation

Representative **Denise Tepler** (D-District 54) . . . . . . . . . . . (207) 729-4018
Counties Represented: Sagadahoc (part)
Term Expires: 2016
E-mail: denise.tepler@legislature.maine.gov
Committees: Joint Taxation

Representative **Timothy Theriault** (R-District 79) . . . . . . . (207) 437-2073
Counties Represented: Kennebec (part)          Res: (207) 968-2641
Term Expires: 2016
E-mail: timothy.theriault@legislature.maine.gov
Committees: Joint Criminal Justice and Public Safety

Representative **Jeffrey L. Timberlake** (R-District 75) . . . . . (207) 225-6000
Counties Represented: Androscoggin (part)          Res: (207) 225-6016
Term Expires: 2016          Fax: (207) 255-2166
284 Ricker Hill Road, Turner, ME 04282
E-mail: jeffrey.timberlake@legislature.maine.gov
Committees: Joint Appropriations and Financial Affairs; Leaves of
Absence

Representative **Michael Timmons** (R-District 45) . . . . . . . . (207) 829-4856
Counties Represented: Cumberland (part)          Fax: (207) 829-3205
Term Expires: 2016
E-mail: michael.timmons@legislature.maine.gov
Committees: Elections; Joint Criminal Justice and Public Safety

Representative **Ryan D. Tipping-Spitz** (D-District 123) . . . (207) 866-4333
Counties Represented: Penobscot (part)
Term Expires: 2016
279 Main Street, Orono, ME 04473
E-mail: ryan.tipping-spitz@legislature.maine.gov
Committees: Joint Taxation
Education: Acadia U (Canada)

Representative **Ralph Tucker** (D-District 50) . . . . . . . . . . . (207) 725-7639
Counties Represented: Cumberland (part)
Term Expires: 2016
E-mail: ralph.tucker@legislature.maine.gov
Committees: Joint Environment and Natural Resources; Joint Insurance
and Financial Services

Representative **William Tuell** (R-District 139) . . . . . . . . . . (800) 423-2900
Counties Represented: Washington (part)
Term Expires: 2016
E-mail: william.tuell@legislature.maine.gov
Committees: Joint Marine Resources; Joint State and Local
Government

Representative **Beth P. Turner** (R-District 141) . . . . . . . . . . (207) 732-4625
Counties Represented: Penobscot (part), Washington (part)
Term Expires: 2016
P. O. Box 65, Burlington, ME 04417
E-mail: repbeth.turner@legislature.maine.gov
Committees: Bills in Second Reading; Joint State and Local
Government; Joint Veterans and Legal Affairs

Representative **Karen Vachon** (R-District 29) . . . . . . . . . . . (207) 883-4715
Counties Represented: Cumberland (part)
Term Expires: 2016
E-mail: karen.vachon@legislature.maine.gov
Committees: Joint Health and Human Services

*(continued on next page)*

**LEGISLATIVE BRANCH**

**Representatives** *continued*

Representative **Arthur C. Verow** (D-District 128) . . . . . . . . (207) 989-7032
  Counties Represented: Penobscot (part)
  Term Expires: 2016
  E-mail: arthur.verow@legislature.maine.gov
  Committees: Joint Transportation

Representative **Nathan Wadsworth** (R-District 70) . . . . . . (207) 838-7451
  Counties Represented: Oxford (part)
  Term Expires: 2016
  E-mail: nathan.wadsworth@legislature.maine.gov
  Committees: Bills in Second Reading; Joint Energy, Utilities and
  Technology

Representative
  **Raymond A. "Ray" Wallace** (R-District 104) . . . . . . . . (207) 270-8041
  Counties Represented: Penobscot (part)
  Term Expires: 2016
  83 Pine Street, Dexter, ME 04930
  E-mail: repray.wallace@legislature.maine.gov
  Committees: Joint Insurance and Financial Services

Representative **Karleton Ward** (R-District 131) . . . . . . . . . (207) 989-7400
  Counties Represented: Hancock (part), Waldo (part)   Res: (207) 843-7546
  Term Expires: 2016                                    Fax: (207) 989-7548
  E-mail: karleton.ward@legislature.maine.gov
  Committees: Joint Labor, Commerce, Research and Economic
  Development

Representative **Charlotte Warren** (D-District 84) . . . . . . . . (207) 441-9116
  Counties Represented: Kennebec (part)
  Term Expires: 2016
  E-mail: charlotte.warren@legislature.maine.gov
  Committees: Joint Criminal Justice and Public Safety; Joint Judiciary

Representative **Joan W. Welsh** (D-District 94) . . . . . . . . . . (207) 236-6554
  Counties Represented: Knox (part), Waldo (part)   Fax: (207) 236-6554
  Term Expires: 2016
  54 Sea Street, Rockport, ME 04856
  E-mail: repjoan.welsh@legislature.maine.gov
  Committees: Joint Environment and Natural Resources

Representative **Dustin Michael White** (R-District 146) . . . . (800) 423-2900
  Counties Represented: Aroostook (part)
  Term Expires: 2016
  E-mail: dustin.white@legislature.maine.gov
  Committees: Engrossed Bills; Joint Environment and Natural Resources

Representative **Tom J. Winsor** (R-District 71) . . . . . . . . . . (207) 527-2233
  Counties Represented: Oxford (part)              Fax: (207) 527-2233
  Term Expires: 2016
  107 Thurston Road, Norway, ME 04268
  E-mail: tom.winsor@legislature.maine.gov
  Committees: Joint Appropriations and Financial Affairs

Representative **Stephen J. Wood** (R-District 57) . . . . . . . . (207) 740-3723
  Counties Represented: Androscoggin (part)
  Term Expires: 2016
  P.O. Box 927, Sabattus, ME 04280
  E-mail: repsteve.wood@legislature.maine.gov
  Committees: Joint Inland Fisheries and Wildlife

# Tribal Representatives

Houlton Band of Maliseet Indians Representative
  **Henry John Bear** (I) . . . . . . . . . . . . . . . . . . . . . . . . . . . . . (207) 532-8368
  Term Expires: 2016
  41 Elm Street, Houlton, ME 04730
  E-mail: bearlaw2@yahoo.com
  Committees: Joint Veterans and Legal Affairs

Penobscot Nation Representative
  **Theodore Bear Mitchell, I** (I) . . . . . . . . . . . . . . . . . . . . . (207) 817-0392
  Term Expires: 2016
  14 Oak Hill Street, Penobscot Nation, Indian Island, ME 04468
  E-mail: theodore.mitchell@legislature.maine.gov
  Committees: Joint Judiciary

Passamaquoddy Tribe Representative
  **Matthew Dana II** (I) . . . . . . . . . . . . . . . . . . . . . . . . . . . . (800) 423-2900
  Term Expires: 2016                               Dist: (207) 796-2301
  Pleasant Point, PO Box 341, Perry, ME 04667
  E-mail: matthew.dana@legislature.maine.gov
  Committees: Joint Inland Fisheries and Wildlife

# House Standing Committees

## Bills in Second Reading

**Majority Members**
Andrew J. McLean (D-27) *Chair*
Roberta B. Beavers (D-2)
Lydia Blume (D-3)
Scott M. Hamann (D-32)

**Minority Members**
Carol A. McElwee (R-149)
Thomas Skolfield (R-112)
Beth P. Turner (R-141)
Nathan Wadsworth (R-70)

## Elections

**Majority Members**
Sara Gideon (D-48) *Chair*
Henry E. M. Beck (D-110)
John L. Martin (D-151)
Matthew W. Moonen (D-38)

**Minority Members**
Paul Chace (R-46)
Eleanor M. "Ellie" Espling (R-65)
Roger E. Reed (R-103)
Michael Timmons (R-45)

## Engrossed Bills

**Majority Members**
Walter A. Kumiega III (D-134)
  *Chair*
Dillon Bates (D-118)
Patricia Hymanson (D-4)
Thomas R. W. Longstaff (D-109)

**Minority Members**
Anthony Edgecomb (R-148)
Richard S. Malaby (R-136)
Joel Stetkis (R-105)
Dustin Michael White (R-146)

## Ethics

**Majority Members**
Louis J. Luchini (D-132) *Chair*
Mark E. Bryant (D-24)
Kimberly Monaghan (D-30)

**Minority Members**
Robert Foley (R-7)
LtCol Kenneth Wade Fredette
  (R-100)
James S. Gillway (R-98)
Frances Head (R-117)

**Members**
Jeffrey Evangelos (I-91)

## Leaves of Absence

**Majority Members**
Thomas R. W. Longstaff (D-109)
  *Chair*
Christine Burstein (D-96)
Ryan Fecteau (D-11)
Teresa Pierce (D-44)

**Minority Members**
Phyllis Ginzler (R-69)
Sheldon Hanington (R-142)
Heather W. Sirocki (R-28)
Jeffrey L. Timberlake (R-75)

## Rules and Business of the House

**Majority Members**
Mark W. Eves (D-6)
  *Ex Officio Member*
Jeff M. McCabe (D-107)

**Minority Members**
Eleanor M. "Ellie" Espling (R-65)
LtCol Kenneth Wade Fredette
  (R-100)

# Maryland General Assembly

Tel: (410) 841-3000  Tel: (410) 946-5401 (TTY)  Tel: (800) 492-7122
Fax: (410) 841-3850

## Maryland Senate

James Senate Office Building, 11 Bladen Street, Annapolis, MD 21401

**Thomas V. "Mike" Miller, Jr.**
President of the Senate

Began Service: 1975
Date of Birth: December 3, 1942
Education: Maryland 1964 BS, 1967 LLB, 1967 JD
Religion: Catholic

President of the Senate
  **Thomas V. "Mike" Miller, Jr.** (D) . . . . . . . . . . . . . . . . . (410) 841-3700
  Chief of Staff **Victoria L. Gruber** . . . . . . . . . . . . . . . . . (410) 841-3700
  Office Manager **Joy R. Walker** . . . . . . . . . . . . . . . . . (410) 841-3700
President Pro Tem **Nathaniel J. McFadden** (D) . . . . . . . . (410) 841-3165
  Education: Morgan State 1968 BA, 1972 MS
Majority Leader **Catherine E. Pugh** (D) . . . . . . . . . . . . . . (410) 841-3656
  Education: Morgan State BA
Deputy Majority Leader **Katherine A. Klausmeier** (D) . . . (410) 841-3620
Assistant Deputy Majority Leader **Nancy J. King** (D) . . . . . (410) 841-3686
Majority Whip **Lisa A. Gladden** (D) . . . . . . . . . . . . . . . . . (410) 841-3697
  Education: Duke 1986 AB; Maryland 1991 JD
Majority Whip **Jamin B. "Jamie" Raskin** (D) . . . . . . . . . (410) 841-3634
  Education: Harvard 1983 BA, 1987 JD
Deputy Majority Whip
  **James Carew "Jim" Rosapepe** (D) . . . . . . . . . . . . . . (410) 858-3141
Minority Leader **J. B. Jennings** (R) . . . . . . . . . . . . . . . . . (410) 841-3706
  Education: Baltimore 1997 BS
Minority Whip **Stephen S. "Steve" Hershey, Jr.** (R) . . . . (410) 841-3639
Secretary of the Senate **William B. C. Addison, Jr.** . . . . . . (410) 841-3908
Sergeant-at-Arms **Sgt George M. White** . . . . . . . . . . . . . (410) 841-3844

## Senators

**Party Affiliation Statistics:** Republicans: 14, Democrats: 33

Senator **John C. Astle** (D-District 30) Room 123 . . . . . . . . (410) 841-3578
  Counties Represented: Anne Arundel (part)    Fax: (410) 841-3156
  Term Expires: 2019
  E-mail: john.astle@senate.state.md.us
  Committees: Finance; Joint Administrative, Executive and Legislative
  Review; Joint Information Technology and Biotechnology Committee;
  Rules
  Education: Marshall 1966 BA
Senator **Gail H. Bates** (R-District 9) Room 401 . . . . . . . . . (410) 841-3671
  Counties Represented: Carroll (part), Howard (part)    Fax: (410) 841-3395
  Term Expires: 2019
  E-mail: gail.bates@senate.state.md.us
  Committees: Education, Health and Environmental Affairs; Joint
  Children, Youth and Families; Joint Protocol
  Education: Maryland 1968 BS
Senator **Joanne C. Benson** (D-District 24)
  James Senate Building, Room 214 . . . . . . . . . . . . . . . . . (410) 841-3148
  Counties Represented: Prince George's (part)    Tel: (301) 858-3148
  Term Expires: 2019                                 Fax: (410) 841-3149
  E-mail: joanne.benson@senate.state.md.us    Fax: (301) 858-3149
  Committees: Finance; Joint Children, Youth and Families; Joint Fair
  Practices and State Personnel Oversight; Joint Management of Public
  Funds; Joint Protocol
  Education: Bowie State 1961 BS; Catholic U 1972 MA
Senator **James "Jim" Brochin** (D-District 42)
  Room 221 . . . . . . . . . . . . . . . . . . . . . . . . . . . . . . . . (410) 841-3648
  Counties Represented: Baltimore (part)    Fax: (410) 841-3643
  Term Expires: 2019
  E-mail: jim.brochin@senate.state.md.us
  Committees: Executive Nominations; Joint Legislative Ethics; Judicial
  Proceedings
  Education: North Carolina Greensboro 1986 BA; Maryland 1990 MA

Senator **Joan Carter-Conway** (D-District 43) . . . . . . . . . . (410) 841-3145
  Counties Represented: Baltimore City (part)    Fax: (410) 841-3135
  Term Expires: 2019
  Miller Senate Office Building, 11 Bladen Street, Two West,
  Annapolis, MD 21401-1991
  E-mail: joan.carter.conway@senate.state.md.us
  Committees: Education, Health and Environmental Affairs; Executive
  Nominations; Joint Children, Youth and Families; Rules
  Education: Baltimore 1988 BA
Senator **Robert G. Cassilly** (R-District 34) . . . . . . . . . . . (410) 841-3158
  Counties Represented: Cecil (part), Harford (part)    Fax: (410) 841-3400
  Term Expires: 2019
  E-mail: bob.cassilly@senate.state.md.us
  Committees: Joint Administrative, Executive and Legislative Review;
  Judicial Proceedings
Senator **Ulysses Currie** (D-District 25) . . . . . . . . . . . . . . (410) 841-3127
  Counties Represented: Prince George's (part)    Fax: (410) 841-3733
  Term Expires: 2019
  Miller Senate Office Building, 11 Bladen Street, Room 201,
  Annapolis, MD 21401-1991
  E-mail: ulysses.currie@senate.state.md.us
  Committees: Budget and Taxation; Executive Nominations
  Education: North Carolina A&T 1959 BS; American U 1968 MA
Senator **James E. DeGrange, Sr.** (D-District 32)
  Room 101 . . . . . . . . . . . . . . . . . . . . . . . . . . . . . . . . (410) 841-3593
  Counties Represented: Anne Arundel (part)    Fax: (410) 841-3589
  Term Expires: 2019
  E-mail: james.degrange@senate.state.md.us
  Committees: Budget and Taxation; Executive Nominations; Joint
  Protocol; Joint Spending Affordability; Rules
Senator **Adelaide C. "Addie" Eckardt** (R-District 37) . . . . (410) 841-3590
  Counties Represented: Caroline (part), Dorchester,    Fax: (410) 841-3087
  Talbot, Wicomico (part)
  Term Expires: 2019
  E-mail: adelaide.eckardt@senate.state.md.us
  Committees: Budget and Taxation; Joint Administrative, Executive and
  Legislative Review; Joint Children, Youth and Families; Joint Fair
  Practices and State Personnel Oversight; Special Joint Pensions
  Education: Maryland 1978 BS, 1981 MS
Senator **George C. Edwards** (R-District 1) Room 322 . . . . (410) 841-3565
  Counties Represented: Allegany, Garrett,    Fax: (410) 841-3552
  Washington (part)
  Term Expires: 2019
  E-mail: george.edwards@senate.state.md.us
  Committees: Budget and Taxation; Executive Nominations; Joint Audit;
  Joint Protocol; Joint Spending Affordability; Rules
  Education: Fairmont State Col 1970 BS
Senator **Brian J. Feldman** (D-District 15) . . . . . . . . . . . . (410) 841-3169
  Counties Represented: Montgomery (part)    Tel: (301) 858-3169
  Term Expires: 2019                             Fax: (410) 841-3607
  James Senate Building, 11 Bladen Street,    Fax: (301) 858-3607
  Room 104, Annapolis, MD 21401-1991
  E-mail: brian.feldman@senate.state.md.us
  Committees: Finance; Joint Federal Relations; Joint Information
  Technology and Biotechnology Committee
  Education: Penn State 1983 BS; Pittsburgh 1986 JD;
  Johns Hopkins 2000 MA
Senator **William C. "Bill" Ferguson** (D-District 46)
  Miller Senate Building, Two West . . . . . . . . . . . . . . . . . (410) 841-3600
  Counties Represented: Baltimore City (part)    Tel: (301) 858-3600
  Term Expires: 2019                                 Fax: (410) 841-3161
  E-mail: bill.ferguson@senate.state.md.us    Fax: (301) 858-3161
  Committees: Budget and Taxation; Joint Children, Youth and Families;
  Special Joint Pensions
  Education: Davidson 2005 BA; Johns Hopkins 2007 MAT;
  Maryland 2010 JD
Senator **Lisa A. Gladden** (D-District 41) . . . . . . . . . . . . (410) 841-3697
  Counties Represented: Baltimore City (part)    Fax: (410) 841-3142
  Term Expires: 2019
  Miller Senate Building, 11 Bladen Street, Two East,
  Annapolis, MD 21401-1991
  E-mail: lisa.gladden@senate.state.md.us
  Committees: Budget and Taxation; Joint Administrative, Executive and
  Legislative Review
Senator **Guy J. Guzzone** (D-District 13) . . . . . . . . . . . . . (410) 841-3572
  Counties Represented: Howard (part)
  Term Expires: 2019
  E-mail: guy.guzzone@senate.state.md.us
  Committees: Budget and Taxation; Joint Administrative, Executive and
  Legislative Review; Joint Audit; Special Joint Pensions
  Education: Maryland BA, BA, MPM

*(continued on next page)*

**LEGISLATIVE BRANCH**

**Senators** *continued*

Senator
**Stephen S. "Steve" Hershey, Jr.** (R-District 36)
James Senate Office, Room 416 . . . . . . . . . . . . . . . . . . (410) 841-3639
Counties Represented: Caroline (part), Cecil          Tel: (301) 858-3639
(part), Kent, Queen Anne's                            Fax: (410) 841-3762
Term Expires: 2019                                    Fax: (301) 858-3762
E-mail: steve.hershey@senate.state.md.us
Committees: Executive Nominations; Finance; Joint Information
Technology and Biotechnology Committee; Joint Legislative Ethics;
Rules

Senator **Michael J. Hough** (R-District 4) . . . . . . . . . . . . . (410) 841-3704
Counties Represented: Carroll (part), Frederick       Fax: (410) 841-3713
(part)
Term Expires: 2019
E-mail: michael.hough@senate.state.md.us
Committees: Joint Children, Youth and Families; Judicial Proceedings
Education: Towson U 2007

Senator **J. B. Jennings** (R-District 7)
James Senate Office, Room 403 . . . . . . . . . . . . . . . . . . (410) 841-3706
Counties Represented: Baltimore (part), Harford       Tel: (301) 858-3706
(part)                                                Fax: (410) 841-3750
Term Expires: 2019                                    Fax: (301) 858-3750
E-mail: jb.jennings@senate.state.md.us
Committees: Executive Nominations; Finance; Rules

Senator **Cheryl Kagan** (D-District 17) . . . . . . . . . . . . . . . . (410) 841-3134
Counties Represented: Montgomery (part)               Fax: (410) 841-3665
Term Expires: 2019
E-mail: cheryl.kagan@senate.state.md.us
Committees: Education, Health and Environmental Affairs

Senator **Edward J. Kasemeyer** (D-District 12)
Miller Senate Office Building, Room 3 West . . . . . . . . . . (410) 841-3653
Counties Represented: Baltimore (part), Howard        Fax: (410) 841-3850
(part)
Term Expires: 2019
E-mail: edward.kasemeyer@senate.state.md.us
Committees: Budget and Taxation; Executive Nominations; Rules;
Special Joint Pensions
Education: Western Maryland 1967 BA

Senator **Delores G. Kelley** (D-District 10) Room 302 . . . . . (410) 841-3606
Counties Represented: Baltimore (part)                Fax: (410) 841-3399
Term Expires: 2019
E-mail: delores.kelley@senate.state.md.us
Committees: Executive Nominations; Finance
Education: Virginia State 1956 BA; NYU 1958 MA; Purdue 1972 MA;
Maryland 1977 PhD

Senator **Nancy J. King** (D-District 39) Room 222 . . . . . . . . (410) 841-3686
Counties Represented: Montgomery (part)               Fax: (410) 841-3670
Term Expires: 2019
E-mail: nancy.king@senate.state.md.us
Committees: Budget and Taxation; Joint Children, Youth and Families

Senator **Katherine A. Klausmeier** (D-District 8)
Room 103 . . . . . . . . . . . . . . . . . . . . . . . . . . . . . . . . . . (410) 841-3620
Counties Represented: Baltimore (part)                Fax: (410) 841-3085
Term Expires: 2019
E-mail: katherine.klausmeier@senate.state.md.us
Committees: Executive Nominations; Finance; Rules

Senator **Susan C. Lee** (D-District 16) . . . . . . . . . . . . . . . . . (410) 841-3124
Counties Represented: Montgomery (part)               Fax: (410) 841-3102
Term Expires: 2019
E-mail: susan.lee@senate.state.md.us
Committees: Judicial Proceedings
Education: Maryland 1976 BA; U San Francisco 1982 JD

Senator **Richard S. Madaleno, Jr.** (D-District 18)
Room 203 . . . . . . . . . . . . . . . . . . . . . . . . . . . . . . . . . . (410) 858-3137
Counties Represented: Montgomery (part)               Fax: (410) 841-3676
Term Expires: 2019
E-mail: richard.madaleno@senate.state.md.us
Committees: Budget and Taxation; Executive Nominations; Joint
Management of Public Funds; Joint Spending Affordability
Education: Syracuse 1987 BA, 1989 MA

Senator **Roger P. Manno** (D-District 19)
Miller Senate Building, Three West . . . . . . . . . . . . . . . . . (410) 841-3151
Counties Represented: Montgomery (part)               Tel: (301) 858-3151
Term Expires: 2019                                    Fax: (410) 841-3740
E-mail: roger.manno@senate.state.md.us               Fax: (301) 858-3740
Committees: Budget and Taxation; Joint Administrative, Executive
and Legislative Review; Joint Federal Relations; Joint Spending
Affordability; Special Joint Pensions
Education: Hunter BA; Franklin Pierce Col MIP, JD

Senator **James N. "Jim" Mathias, Jr.** (D-District 38) . . . . (410) 841-3645
Counties Represented: Somerset, Wicomico (part),     Dist: (410) 352-3096
Worcester                                             Fax: (410) 841-3006
Term Expires: 2019                                    Dist: (410) 352-3087
11941 Industrial Park Road, Unit 8, Bishopville, MD 21813
E-mail: james.mathias@senate.state.md.us
Committees: Executive Nominations; Finance; Joint Administrative,
Executive and Legislative Review; Joint Chesapeake and Atlantic
Coastal Bays Critical Area

Senator **Nathaniel J. McFadden** (D-District 45)
Miller Senate Building, Room 422 . . . . . . . . . . . . . . . . . . (410) 841-3165
Counties Represented: Baltimore City (part)           Fax: (410) 841-3138
Term Expires: 2019
E-mail: nathaniel.mcfadden@senate.state.md.us
Committees: Executive Nominations; Joint Audit; Joint Legislative
Ethics; Joint Spending Affordability; Judicial Proceedings; Rules;
Special Joint Pensions

Senator
**Thomas McLain "Mac" Middleton** (D-District 28) . . . . (410) 841-3616
Counties Represented: Charles (part)                  Fax: (410) 841-3682
Term Expires: 2019
Miller Senate Office Building, 11 Bladen Street, Three East,
Annapolis, MD 21401-1991
E-mail: thomas.mcclain.middleton@senate.state.md.us
Committees: Executive Nominations; Finance; Joint Spending
Affordability; Rules
Education: Mount St Mary's 1968 BS

Senator **Thomas V. "Mike" Miller, Jr.** (D-District 27) . . . . (410) 841-3700
Counties Represented: Calvert (part), Prince          Fax: (410) 841-3910
George's (part)
H-107 State House, State Circle, Annapolis, MD 21401-1991
E-mail: thomas.v.mike.miller@senate.state.md.us
Committees: Executive Nominations; Rules

Senator **C. Anthony Muse** (D-District 26) Room 304 . . . . . (410) 841-3092
Counties Represented: Prince George's (part)          Fax: (410) 841-3410
Term Expires: 2019
E-mail: anthony.muse@senate.state.md.us
Committees: Joint Fair Practices and State Personnel Oversight; Judicial
Proceedings
Education: Morgan State BA; Wesley Sem MDiv; Howard U DMin

Senator **Shirley Nathan-Pulliam** (D-District 44) . . . . . . . . (410) 841-3612
Counties Represented: Baltimore City (part)           Fax: (410) 841-3613
Term Expires: 2019
E-mail: shirley.nathan.pulliam@senate.state.md.us
Committees: Education, Health and Environmental Affairs; Joint
Chesapeake and Atlantic Coastal Bays Critical Area; Joint Children,
Youth and Families
Education: Maryland 1980 BSN; Johns Hopkins 1987 MAS

Senator **H. Wayne Norman, Jr.** (R-District 35) . . . . . . . . . . (410) 841-3603
Counties Represented: Harford (part)                  Fax: (410) 841-3190
Term Expires: 2019
E-mail: wayne.norman@senate.state.md.us
Committees: Joint Legislative Ethics; Judicial Proceedings

Senator **Douglas J. J. Peters** (D-District 23) Room 121 . . (410) 841-3631
Counties Represented: Prince George's (part)          Fax: (410) 841-3174
Term Expires: 2019
E-mail: douglas.peters@senate.state.md.us
Committees: Budget and Taxation; Joint Audit; Joint Federal Relations;
Joint Spending Affordability; Special Joint Pensions
Education: Maryland BS; Baltimore MBA

Senator **Paul G. Pinsky** (D-District 22) Room 220 . . . . . . . (410) 841-3155
Counties Represented: Prince George's (part)          Fax: (410) 841-3144
Term Expires: 2019
E-mail: paul.pinsky@senate.state.md.us
Committees: Education, Health and Environmental Affairs
Education: George Washington 1972 BA, 1978 MA

Senator **Catherine E. Pugh** (D-District 40)
Miller Senate Office Building, Room 3 East . . . . . . . . . . . (410) 841-3656
Counties Represented: Baltimore City (part)           Fax: (410) 841-3738
Term Expires: 2019
E-mail: catherine.pugh@senate.state.md.us
Committees: Executive Nominations; Finance; Joint Administrative,
Executive and Legislative Review; Joint Audit

Senator **Victor R. Ramirez** (D-District 47) Room 303 . . . . . (410) 841-3745
Counties Represented: Prince George's (part)          Tel: (301) 858-3745
Term Expires: 2019                                    Fax: (410) 841-3387
E-mail: victor.ramirez@senate.state.md.us            Fax: (301) 858-3387
Committees: Joint Administrative, Executive and Legislative Review;
Joint Federal Relations; Joint Legislative Ethics; Judicial Proceedings
Education: Frostburg State U 1996 BA; St Thomas U 2001 JD

**LEGISLATIVE BRANCH**

Senator **Jamin B. "Jamie" Raskin** (D-District 20)
  Room 122 . . . . . . . . . . . . . . . . . . . . . . . . . . . . . . . . . . . . (410) 841-3634
  Counties Represented: Montgomery (part)          Fax: (410) 841-3166
  Term Expires: 2019
  E-mail: jamie.raskin@senate.state.md.us
  Committees: Executive Nominations; Joint Chesapeake and Atlantic
  Coastal Bays Critical Area; Joint Federal Relations; Joint Legislative
  Ethics; Judicial Proceedings
Senator **Justin D. Ready** (R-District 5) Room 414 . . . . . . (410) 841-3683
  Counties Represented: Baltimore (part), Carroll (part)
  Term Expires: 2019
  E-mail: justin.ready@senate.state.md.us
  Committees: Judicial Proceedings
  Education: Salisbury U 2004 BA
Senator **Edward R. Reilly** (R-District 33) Room 321 . . . . . (410) 841-3568
  Counties Represented: Anne Arundel (part)          Fax: (410) 841-3067
  Term Expires: 2019
  E-mail: edward.reilly@senate.state.md.us
  Committees: Executive Nominations; Finance; Joint Management of
  Public Funds
Senator **James Carew "Jim" Rosapepe** (D-District 21)
  Room 314 . . . . . . . . . . . . . . . . . . . . . . . . . . . . . . . . . . . . (301) 858-3141
  Counties Represented: Anne Arundel (part), Prince     Fax: (410) 841-3195
  George's (part)
  Term Expires: 2019
  E-mail: jim.rosapepe@senate.state.md.us
  Committees: Education, Health and Environmental Affairs; Joint
  Information Technology and Biotechnology Committee; Joint
  Management of Public Funds
Senator **Johnny Ray Salling** (R-District 6) . . . . . . . . . . . . (410) 841-3587
  Counties Represented: Baltimore (part)          Fax: (410) 841-3218
  Term Expires: 2019
  E-mail: johnnyray.salling@senate.state.md.us
  Committees: Education, Health and Environmental Affairs; Joint
  Chesapeake and Atlantic Coastal Bays Critical Area; Joint Fair
  Practices and State Personnel Oversight
Senator **Andrew A. Serafini** (R-District 2) . . . . . . . . . . . . . (410) 841-3903
  Counties Represented: Washington (part)
  Term Expires: 2019
  E-mail: andrew.serafini@senate.state.md.us
  Committees: Budget and Taxation
Senator **Bryan W. Simonaire** (R-District 31) Room 414 . . (410) 841-3658
  Counties Represented: Anne Arundel (part)          Fax: (410) 841-3586
  Term Expires: 2019
  E-mail: bryan.simonaire@senate.state.md.us
  Committees: Education, Health and Environmental Affairs; Joint
  Chesapeake and Atlantic Coastal Bays Critical Area
  Education: Loyola Col (MD) MS
Senator **Steve Waugh** (R-District 29) . . . . . . . . . . . . . . . . (410) 841-3673
  Counties Represented: Calvert (part), Charles (part), St. Mary's
  Term Expires: 2019
  E-mail: steve.waugh@senate.state.md.us
  Committees: Education, Health and Environmental Affairs; Joint
  Administrative, Executive and Legislative Review
Senator **Ronald N. Young** (D-District 3) Room 316 . . . . . . (410) 841-3575
  Counties Represented: Frederick (part), Washington (part)
  Term Expires: 2019
  E-mail: ronald.young@senate.state.md.us
  Committees: Education, Health and Environmental Affairs; Joint
  Federal Relations
Senator **Robert A. "Bobby" Zirkin** (D-District 11)
  Room 301 . . . . . . . . . . . . . . . . . . . . . . . . . . . . . . . . . . . . (410) 841-3131
  Counties Represented: Baltimore (part)          Fax: (410) 841-3737
  Term Expires: 2019
  E-mail: bobby.zirkin@senate.state.md.us
  Committees: Executive Nominations; Judicial Proceedings
  Education: Johns Hopkins 1993 BA; Georgetown 1998 JD
Senator **Craig J. Zucker** (D-District 14) . . . . . . . . . . . . . . . (410) 841-3625
  Counties Represented: Montgomery (part)          Fax: (410) 841-3618
  Term Expires: 2019
  E-mail: craig.zucker@senate.state.md.us
  Committees: Education, Health and Environmental Affairs

# Senate Standing Committees

## Budget and Taxation
Miller Senate Office Building, 11 Bladen Street, Three West,
Annapolis, MD 21401-1991
Fax: (410) 841-3091

| **Majority Members** | **Minority Members** |
|---|---|
| Edward J. Kasemeyer (D-12) *Chair* | Adelaide C. "Addie" Eckardt (R-37) |
| Richard S. Madaleno, Jr. (D-18) | George C. Edwards (R-1) |
|   *Vice Chair* | Andrew A. Serafini (R-2) |
| Ulysses Currie (D-25) | |
| James E. DeGrange, Sr. (D-32) | |
| William C. "Bill" Ferguson (D-46) | |
| Lisa A. Gladden (D-41) | |
| Guy J. Guzzone (D-13) | |
| Nancy J. King (D-39) | |
| Roger P. Manno (D-19) | |
| Douglas J. J. Peters (D-23) | |

## Education, Health and Environmental Affairs
Miller Senate Office Building, 11 Bladen Street, Two West,
Annapolis, MD 21401-1991
Fax: (410) 841-3957   E-mail: ehe@mlis.state.md.us

| **Majority Members** | **Minority Members** |
|---|---|
| Joan Carter-Conway (D-43) *Chair* | Gail H. Bates (R-9) |
| Paul G. Pinsky (D-22) *Vice Chair* | Johnny Ray Salling (R-6) |
| Cheryl Kagan (D-17) | Bryan W. Simonaire (R-31) |
| Shirley Nathan-Pulliam (D-44) | Steve Waugh (R-29) |
| James Carew "Jim" Rosapepe (D-21) | |
| Ronald N. Young (D-3) | |
| Craig J. Zucker (D-14) | |

## Executive Nominations
James Senate Office Building, 11 Bladen Street, Annapolis, MD 21401

| **Majority Members** | **Minority Members** |
|---|---|
| Jamin B. "Jamie" Raskin (D-20) *Chair* | George C. Edwards (R-1) |
| Delores G. Kelley (D-10) *Vice Chair* | Stephen S. "Steve" Hershey, Jr. (R-36) |
| James "Jim" Brochin (D-42) | J. B. Jennings (R-7) |
| Joan Carter-Conway (D-43) | Edward R. Reilly (R-33) |
| Ulysses Currie (D-25) | |
| James E. DeGrange, Sr. (D-32) | |
| Edward J. Kasemeyer (D-12) | |
| Katherine A. Klausmeier (D-8) | |
| Richard S. Madaleno, Jr. (D-18) | |
| James N. "Jim" Mathias, Jr. (D-38) | |
| Nathaniel J. McFadden (D-45) | |
| Thomas McLain "Mac" Middleton (D-28) | |
| Thomas V. "Mike" Miller, Jr. (D-27) | |
| Catherine E. Pugh (D-40) | |
| Robert A. "Bobby" Zirkin (D-11) | |

## Finance
Miller Senate Office Building, 11 Bladen Street, Annapolis, MD 21401

| **Majority Members** | **Minority Members** |
|---|---|
| Thomas McLain "Mac" Middleton (D-28) *Chair* | Stephen S. "Steve" Hershey, Jr. (R-36) |
| John C. Astle (D-30) *Vice Chair* | J. B. Jennings (R-7) |
| Joanne C. Benson (D-24) | Edward R. Reilly (R-33) |
| Brian J. Feldman (D-15) | |
| Delores G. Kelley (D-10) | |
| Katherine A. Klausmeier (D-8) | |
| James N. "Jim" Mathias, Jr. (D-38) | |
| Catherine E. Pugh (D-40) | |

**LEGISLATIVE BRANCH**

**LEGISLATIVE BRANCH**

## Judicial Proceedings

Miller Senate Office Building, 11 Bladen Street, Annapolis, MD 21401

**Majority Members**
Robert A. "Bobby" Zirkin (D-11)
  *Chair*
James "Jim" Brochin (D-42)
Susan C. Lee (D-16)
Nathaniel J. McFadden (D-45)
C. Anthony Muse (D-26)
Victor R. Ramirez (D-47)
Jamin B. "Jamie" Raskin (D-20)

**Minority Members**
Robert G. Cassilly (R-34)
Michael J. Hough (R-4)
H. Wayne Norman, Jr. (R-35)
Justin D. Ready (R-5)

## Rules

State House, Annapolis, MD 21401
Fax: (410) 841-3910

**Majority Members**
Katherine A. Klausmeier (D-8)
  *Chair*
James E. DeGrange, Sr. (D-32)
  *Vice Chair*
John C. Astle (D-30)
Joan Carter-Conway (D-43)
Edward J. Kasemeyer (D-12)
Nathaniel J. McFadden (D-45)
Thomas McLain "Mac" Middleton
  (D-28)
Thomas V. "Mike" Miller, Jr.
  (D-27)

**Minority Members**
George C. Edwards (R-1)
Stephen S. "Steve" Hershey, Jr.
  (R-36)
J. B. Jennings (R-7)

## Maryland House of Delegates

House Office Building, 6 Bladen Street, Annapolis, MD 21401-1991

**Michael Erin Busch**
Speaker of the House

Education: Temple 1970 BS

Speaker of the House **Michael Erin Busch** (D) . . . . . . . . . (410) 841-3800
Chief of Staff **Alexandra M. Hughes** . . . . . . . . . . . . . . (410) 841-3916
Speaker Pro Tem **Adrienne A. Jones** (D) . . . . . . . . . . . . . (410) 841-3391
  Education: Maryland Baltimore County 1976 BA
Deputy Speaker Pro Tem **Carolyn J. B. Howard** (D) . . . . . (410) 841-3074
  Education: Florida A&M BS; Bowie State MEd
Majority Leader **Anne R. Kaiser** (D) . . . . . . . . . . . . . . (410) 841-3036
  Education: Chicago 1990 BA; Michigan 1995 MPP, 1995 MA
Deputy Majority Leader **Dan K. Morhaim** (D) . . . . . . . . . .(410) 841-3054
  Education: UCLA 1970 AB; New York Medical 1975 MD
Assistant Majority Floor Leader **Keith E. Haynes** (D) . . . . .(410) 841-3801
  Education: North Carolina State 1985 BA;
  North Carolina Central 1988 MPA; Baltimore 1991 JD
Majority Whip **Talmadge Branch** (D) . . . . . . . . . . . . . . (410) 841-3398
  Education: Salisbury State U 1981 BA
Chief Deputy Majority Whip
  **Benjamin S. "Ben" Barnes** (D) . . . . . . . . . . . . . . . (410) 841-3046
  Education: North Carolina Greensboro 1998 BA; Baltimore 2003 JD
Majority Parliamentarian **C. William "Bill" Frick** (D) . . . . (410) 841-3454
  Education: Northwestern 1997 AB; Harvard 2000 JD
Minority Leader **Nicholaus R. Kipke** (R) . . . . . . . . . . . . .(410) 841-3421
Assistant Minority Leader **Susan L. M. Aumann** (R) . . . . .(410) 841-3258
  Education: Col Notre Dame (MD) 1983 BA
Minority Whip **Kathryn "Kathy" Szeliga** (R) . . . . . . . . . . (410) 841-3698
  Education: Towson State U 1994 BA
Assistant Minority Whip **Neil C. Parrott** (R) . . . . . . . . . . . (410) 841-3636
  Education: Maryland 1994 BS; Mount St Mary's U 2006 MBA
Chief Deputy Minority Whip **Herbert H. McMillan** (R) . . . (410) 841-3211
  Education: Naval Acad 1980 BS
Minority Parliamentarian
  **Robert L. "Bob" Flanagan** (R) . . . . . . . . . . . . . . . . . (410) 841-3077
  Education: Harvard 1967 BA; Cornell 1974 JD

Chief Clerk of the House **Sylvia Siegert** . . . . . . . . . . . . . . (410) 841-3999
  E-mail: hseclerk@mlis.state.md.us
Sergeant-at-Arms **Robert Parham** . . . . . . . . . . . . . . . . . . . . (410) 841-3844

## Delegates

**Party Affiliation Statistics:** Republicans: 51, Democrats: 90

Delegate **Christopher T. Adams** (R-District 37B) . . . . . . . (410) 841-3343
  Counties Represented: Caroline (part), Dorchester   Fax: (410) 841-3299
  (part), Talbot, Wicomico (part)
  Term Expires: 2019
  E-mail: christopher.adams@house.state.md.us
  Committees: Economic Matters
Delegate **Kathryn L. "Kathy" Afzali** (R-District 4) . . . . . . (410) 841-3288
  Counties Represented: Carroll (part), Frederick   Fax: (410) 841-3184
  (part)
  Term Expires: 2019
  House Office Building, 6 Bladen Street, Room 319,
  Annapolis, MD 21401
  E-mail: kathy.afzali@house.state.md.us
  Committees: Joint Children, Youth and Families; Ways and Means
  Education: Mount St Mary BS
Delegate
  **Curtis Stovall "Curt" Anderson** (D-District 43) . . . . . . (410) 841-3291
  Counties Represented: Baltimore City (part)   Fax: (410) 841-3024
  Term Expires: 2019
  314 House Office Building, 6 Bladen Street, Annapolis, MD 21401
  3200 Barclay Street, Baltimore, MD 21218
  E-mail: curt.anderson@house.state.md.us
  Committees: Drug and Alcohol Abuse; Judiciary
  Education: Morgan State 1974 BA; Baltimore 1987 JD
Delegate **Carl Anderton, Jr.** (R-District 38B) . . . . . . . . . . .(410) 841-3431
  Counties Represented: Wicomico (part)   Fax: (410) 841-3434
  Term Expires: 2019
  E-mail: carl.anderton@house.state.md.us
  Committees: Environment and Transportation
Delegate **Angela Angel** (D-District 25) . . . . . . . . . . . . . . . (410) 841-3707
  Counties Represented: Prince George's (part)   Fax: (410) 841-3498
  Term Expires: 2019
  E-mail: angela.angel@house.state.md.us
  Committees: Health and Government Operations
  Education: Hampton BA
Delegate **Steven J. Arentz** (R-District 36) Room 308 . . . . .(410) 841-3543
  Counties Represented: Caroline (part), Cecil (part),   Tel: (301) 858-3543
  Kent, Queen Anne's
  Term Expires: 2019
  E-mail: steven.arentz@house.state.md.us
  Committees: Economic Matters
Delegate **Vanessa Atterbeary** (D-District 13) . . . . . . . . . . .(410) 841-3471
  Counties Represented: Howard (part)   Fax: (410) 841-3986
  Term Expires: 2019
  E-mail: vanessa.atterbeary@house.state.md.us
  Committees: Judiciary
Delegate **Susan L. M. Aumann** (R-District 42B) . . . . . . . . (410) 841-3258
  Counties Represented: Baltimore (part)   Tel: (301) 858-3258
  Term Expires: 2019   Fax: (301) 858-3163
  19222 Golden Meadow Drive,   Fax: (410) 841-3163
  Germantown, MD 20878
  E-mail: susan.aumann@house.state.md.us
  Committees: Economic Matters; Joint Legislative Ethics
Delegate **Charles E. Barkley** (D-District 39) . . . . . . . . . . . (301) 858-3001
  Counties Represented: Montgomery (part)   Dist: (301) 540-7071
  Term Expires: 2019   Fax: (410) 841-3009
  19222 Golden Meadow Drive, Germantown, MD 20878
  E-mail: charles.barkley@house.state.md.us
  Committees: Economic Matters
  Education: Towson State U 1972 BS; Western Maryland 1982 MEd
Delegate **Benjamin S. "Ben" Barnes** (D-District 21)
  151 House Office Building . . . . . . . . . . . . . . . . . . . . . . . .(301) 858-3046
  Counties Represented: Anne Arundel (part), Prince   Fax: (301) 858-3346
  George's (part)
  Term Expires: 2019
  E-mail: ben.barnes@house.state.md.us
  Committees: Appropriations; Drug and Alcohol Abuse; Joint Spending
  Affordability; Special Joint Pensions
Delegate **Darryl Barnes** (D-District 25) . . . . . . . . . . . . . . .(410) 841-3557
  Counties Represented: Prince George's (part)   Fax: (410) 841-3850
  Term Expires: 2019
  E-mail: darryl.barnes@house.state.md.us
  Committees: Ways and Means

Delegate **Erek Barron** (D-District 24) . . . . . . . . . . . . . . . . (410) 841-3692
  Counties Represented: Prince George's (part)
  Term Expires: 2019
  E-mail: erek.barron@house.state.md.us
  Committees: Health and Government Operations

Delegate **Kumar P. Barve** (D-District 17) . . . . . . . . . . . . . (410) 841-3464
  Counties Represented: Montgomery (part)      Dist: (301) 417-0158
  Term Expires: 2019                           Fax: (410) 841-3020
  426 Palmspring Drive, Gaithersburg, MD 20878
  E-mail: kumar.barve@house.state.md.us
  E-mail: kumarbarve@gmail.com
  Committees: Environment and Transportation; Rules and Executive
  Nominations
  Education: Georgetown 1980 BS

Delegate **Pamela G. Beidle** (D-District 32) Room 161 . . . . (410) 841-3370
  Counties Represented: Anne Arundel (part)    Fax: (410) 841-3347
  Term Expires: 2019
  E-mail: pamela.beidle@house.state.md.us
  Committees: Environment and Transportation
  Education: Towson U 1994 BS

Delegate **Wendell R. Beitzel** (R-District 1A)
  Room 410B . . . . . . . . . . . . . . . . . . . . . . . . . . . . . . . . . . (410) 841-3435
  Counties Represented: Allegany (part), Garrett    Fax: (410) 841-3040
  Term Expires: 2019
  E-mail: wendell.beitzel@house.state.md.us
  Committees: Appropriations; Joint Spending Affordability; Special Joint
  Pensions
  Education: Fairmont State Col 1964 BS; Frostburg State U 1988 MBA

Delegate **Talmadge Branch** (D-District 45) . . . . . . . . . . . . (410) 841-3398
  Counties Represented: Baltimore City (part)    Dist: (410) 563-4709
  Term Expires: 2019                             Fax: (410) 841-3550
  3224 Belair Road, Baltimore, MD 21213-1228     Dist: (410) 563-4708
  E-mail: talmadge.branch@house.state.md.us
  Committees: Economic Matters; Rules and Executive Nominations

Delegate **Eric M. Bromwell** (D-District 8) Room 415 . . . . . (410) 841-3766
  Counties Represented: Baltimore (part)    Fax: (410) 841-3850
  Term Expires: 2019
  E-mail: eric.bromwell@house.state.md.us
  Committees: Health and Government Operations; Joint Administrative,
  Executive and Legislative Review
  Education: Salisbury U 1998 BA

Delegate **Benjamin T. Brooks, Sr.** (D-District 10) . . . . . . . (410) 841-3352
  Counties Represented: Baltimore (part)    Fax: (410) 841-3132
  Term Expires: 2019
  E-mail: benjamin.brooks@house.state.md.us
  Committees: Economic Matters

Delegate **Jason C. Buckel** (R-District 1B) . . . . . . . . . . . . . (410) 841-3404
  Counties Represented: Allegany (part)    Fax: (410) 841-3484
  Term Expires: 2019
  E-mail: jason.buckel@house.state.md.us
  Committees: Ways and Means

Delegate **Michael Erin Busch** (D-District 30A) . . . . . . . . . (410) 841-3800
  Counties Represented: Anne Arundel (part)    Fax: (410) 841-3880
  State House, Room H-101, Annapolis, MD 21401-1991
  E-mail: michael.busch@house.state.md.us

Delegate **Edward P. "Ned" Carey** (D-District 31A) . . . . . . (410) 841-3047
  Counties Represented: Anne Arundel (part)    Fax: (410) 841-3386
  Term Expires: 2019
  E-mail: ned.carey@house.state.md.us
  Committees: Economic Matters

Delegate **Mary Beth Carozza** (R-District 38C) . . . . . . . . . (410) 841-3356
  Counties Represented: Wicomico (part), Worcester    Fax: (410) 841-3356
  (part)
  Term Expires: 2019
  E-mail: marybeth.carozza@house.state.md.us
  Committees: Appropriations
  Education: Catholic U 1983 BA, 1983 MA

Delegate **Alfred C. "Al" Carr, Jr.** (D-District 18)
  Room 222 . . . . . . . . . . . . . . . . . . . . . . . . . . . . . . . . . . . (410) 841-3638
  Counties Represented: Montgomery (part)    Fax: (410) 841-3053
  Term Expires: 2019
  E-mail: alfred.carr@house.state.md.us
  Committees: Environment and Transportation; Joint Chesapeake and
  Atlantic Coastal Bays Critical Area; Joint Federal Relations
  Education: Rochester 1988 BS

Delegate **Jill P. Carter** (D-District 41) . . . . . . . . . . . . . . . . (410) 841-3283
  Counties Represented: Baltimore City (part)    Fax: (410) 841-3251
  Term Expires: 2019
  3301 Liberty Heights Avenue, Baltimore, MD 21215
  E-mail: jill.carter@house.state.md.us
  Committees: Judiciary
  Education: Loyola Col (MD) 1988 BA; Baltimore 1992 JD

Delegate **Andrew P. Cassilly** (R-District 35B) . . . . . . . . . . (410) 841-3444
  Counties Represented: Cecil (part), Harford (part)    Fax: (410) 841-3244
  Term Expires: 2019
  E-mail: andrew.cassilly@house.state.md.us
  Committees: Environment and Transportation

Delegate **Mark S. Chang** (D-District 32) . . . . . . . . . . . . . . (410) 841-3511
  Counties Represented: Anne Arundel (part)    Fax: (410) 841-3235
  Term Expires: 2019
  E-mail: mark.chang@house.state.md.us
  Committees: Appropriations

Delegate **Barrie S. Ciliberti** (R-District 4) Room 324 . . . . . (301) 858-3080
  Counties Represented: Carroll (part), Frederick    Fax: (410) 841-3028
  (part)
  Term Expires: 2019
  E-mail: barrie.ciliberti@house.state.md.us
  Committees: Appropriations

Delegate **Luke Clippinger** (D-District 46) Room 316 . . . . . (410) 841-3303
  Counties Represented: Baltimore City (part)    Fax: (410) 841-3537
  Term Expires: 2019
  E-mail: luke.clippinger@house.state.md.us
  Committees: Economic Matters; Joint Administrative, Executive and
  Legislative Review
  Education: Earlham 1994 BA; Louisville 2005 JD

Delegate **John W. E. Cluster, Jr.** (R-District 8)
  Room 308 . . . . . . . . . . . . . . . . . . . . . . . . . . . . . . . . . . . (410) 841-3526
  Counties Represented: Baltimore (part)    Fax: (410) 841-3098
  Term Expires: 2019
  E-mail: john.cluster@house.state.md.us
  Committees: Judiciary

Delegate **Frank M. Conaway, Jr.** (D-District 40)
  Room 314 . . . . . . . . . . . . . . . . . . . . . . . . . . . . . . . . . . . (410) 841-3189
  Counties Represented: Baltimore City (part)    Fax: (410) 841-3213
  Term Expires: 2019
  E-mail: frank.conaway@house.state.md.us
  Committees: Judiciary
  Education: Sojourner-Douglass 1999 BA

Delegate **Bonnie L. Cullison** (D-District 19) Room 220 . . . (410) 841-3883
  Counties Represented: Montgomery (part)    Fax: (410) 841-3882
  Term Expires: 2019
  E-mail: bonnie.cullison@house.state.md.us
  Committees: Health and Government Operations; Joint Legislative
  Ethics

Delegate **Dereck E. Davis** (D-District 25) Room 231 . . . . . (410) 841-3519
  Counties Represented: Prince George's (part)    Fax: (410) 841-3558
  Term Expires: 2019
  E-mail: dereck.davis@house.state.md.us
  Committees: Economic Matters; Rules and Executive Nominations
  Education: Maryland 1989 BA, 1999 MPP

Delegate **Kathleen M. Dumais** (D-District 15)
  Room 101 . . . . . . . . . . . . . . . . . . . . . . . . . . . . . . . . . . . (410) 841-3052
  Counties Represented: Montgomery (part)    Fax: (410) 841-3219
  Term Expires: 2019
  E-mail: kathleen.dumais@house.state.md.us
  Committees: Drug and Alcohol Abuse; Joint Children, Youth and
  Families; Judiciary; Rules and Executive Nominations
  Education: Mount Vernon 1980 BA; Maryland 1983 JD

Delegate **Eric Ebersole** (D-District 12) . . . . . . . . . . . . . . . (410) 841-3328
  Counties Represented: Baltimore (part), Howard    Fax: (410) 841-3176
  (part)
  Term Expires: 2019
  E-mail: eric.ebersole@house.state.md.us
  Committees: Joint Children, Youth and Families; Ways and Means

Delegate **Diana M. Fennell** (D-District 47A) . . . . . . . . . . . (410) 841-3478
  Counties Represented: Prince George's (part)    Fax: (410) 841-3727
  Term Expires: 2019
  E-mail: diana.fennell@house.state.md.us
  Committees: Ways and Means

Delegate **Mark N. Fisher** (R-District 27C) Room 217 . . . . . (410) 841-3231
  Counties Represented: Calvert (part)    Fax: (410) 841-3335
  Term Expires: 2019
  E-mail: mark.fisher@house.state.md.us
  Committees: Economic Matters

Delegate **Robert L. "Bob" Flanagan** (R-District 9B) . . . . . (410) 841-3077
  Counties Represented: Howard (part)    Fax: (410) 841-3349
  Term Expires: 2019
  E-mail: bob.flanagan@house.state.md.us
  Committees: Environment and Transportation; Joint Administrative,
  Executive and Legislative Review

*(continued on next page)*

Delegates *continued*

Delegate **William "Bill" Folden** (R-District 3B) . . . . . . . . (410) 841-3240
Counties Represented: Frederick (part), Washington    Fax: (410) 841-3308
(part)
Term Expires: 2019
E-mail: william.folden@house.state.md.us
Committees: Judiciary

Delegate **David V. Fraser-Hidalgo** (D-District 15)
Room 350 . . . . . . . . . . . . . . . . . . . . . . . . . . . . . (410) 841-3186
Counties Represented: Montgomery (part)    Tel: (301) 858-3186
Term Expires: 2019    Fax: (410) 841-3112
E-mail: david.fraser.hidalgo@house.state.md.us    Fax: (301) 858-3112
Committees: Environment and Transportation

Delegate **C. William "Bill" Frick** (D-District 16)
Room 219 . . . . . . . . . . . . . . . . . . . . . . . . . . . . . (410) 841-3454
Counties Represented: Montgomery (part)    Fax: (410) 841-3457
Term Expires: 2019
E-mail: bill.frick@house.state.md.us
Committees: Economic Matters; Joint Legislative Ethics; Rules and
Executive Nominations

Delegate **Barbara A. Frush** (D-District 21) . . . . . . . . . . . . . (410) 841-3114
Counties Represented: Anne Arundel (part), Prince    Dist: (301) 572-4042
George's (part)    Fax: (410) 841-3850
Term Expires: 2019    Dist: (301) 572-7305
3019 Chapel View Drive, Beltsville, MD 20705-3429
E-mail: barbara.frush@house.state.md.us
Committees: Environment and Transportation; Joint Protocol

Delegate **Tawanna P. Gaines** (D-District 22) Room 416 . . . (410) 841-3058
Counties Represented: Prince George's (part)    Fax: (410) 841-3119
Term Expires: 2019
E-mail: tawanna.gaines@house.state.md.us
Committees: Appropriations; Joint Children, Youth and Families; Joint
Spending Affordability; Rules and Executive Nominations
Education: DC Teachers Col 1972 BA

Delegate **Jefferson L. Ghrist** (R-District 36) . . . . . . . . . . . (410) 841-3555
Counties Represented: Caroline (part), Cecil (part),    Fax: (410) 841-3434
Kent, Queen Anne's
Term Expires: 2019
E-mail: jeff.ghrist@house.state.md.us
Committees: Appropriations; Joint Fair Practices and State Personnel
Oversight

Delegate **James W. "Jim" Gilchrist** (D-District 17)
Room 221 . . . . . . . . . . . . . . . . . . . . . . . . . . . . . (410) 841-3744
Counties Represented: Montgomery (part)    Fax: (410) 841-3850
Term Expires: 2019
E-mail: jim.gilchrist@house.state.md.us
Committees: Environment and Transportation; Joint Federal Relations
Education: Grinnell 1987 BA; George Washington 1993 MBA

Delegate **Glen Glass** (R-District 34A) Room 325 . . . . . . . . (410) 841-3280
Counties Represented: Harford (part)    Fax: (410) 841-3190
Term Expires: 2019
E-mail: glen.glass@house.state.md.us
Committees: Joint Federal Relations; Judiciary

Delegate **Cheryl D. Glenn** (D-District 45) . . . . . . . . . . . . . (410) 841-3257
Counties Represented: Baltimore City (part)    Tel: (410) 563-0228
Term Expires: 2019
3301 Bel Air Road, Suite 2B, Baltimore, MD 21213
E-mail: cheryl.glenn@house.state.md.us
Committees: Economic Matters; Joint Protocol

Delegate **Robin L. Grammer, Jr.** (R-District 6) . . . . . . . . . (410) 841-3298
Counties Represented: Baltimore (part)    Fax: (410) 841-3007
Term Expires: 2019
E-mail: robin.grammer@house.state.md.us
Committees: Appropriations

Delegate **Ana Sol Gutierrez** (D-District 18) . . . . . . . . . . . . (410) 841-3181
Counties Represented: Montgomery (part)    Dist: (301) 718-0707
Term Expires: 2019    Fax: (410) 841-3232
3317 Turner Lane, Chevy Chase, MD 20815-3217
E-mail: ana.gutierrez@house.state.md.us
Committees: Appropriations; Joint Children, Youth and Families; Joint
Management of Public Funds
Education: Penn State BS; American U MS

Delegate **Peter A. Hammen** (D-District 46) . . . . . . . . . . . . (410) 841-3772
Counties Represented: Baltimore City (part)    Dist: (410) 631-7900
Term Expires: 2019    Fax: (410) 841-3409
6228 Eastern Avenue, Baltimore, MD 21224    Dist: (410) 631-7906
E-mail: peter.hammen@house.state.md.us
Committees: Health and Government Operations; Rules and Executive
Nominations
Education: Baltimore 1989 BS, 1993 MPA

Delegate **Antonio Hayes** (D-District 40) . . . . . . . . . . . . . (410) 841-3545
Counties Represented: Baltimore City (part)    Fax: (410) 841-3279
Term Expires: 2019
E-mail: antonio.hayes@house.state.md.us
Committees: Health and Government Operations; Joint Children, Youth
and Families

Delegate **Keith E. Haynes** (D-District 44A) . . . . . . . . . . . . (410) 841-3801
Independent Cities Represented: Baltimore    Dist: (410) 837-6189
Term Expires: 2019    Fax: (410) 841-3530
300 West Pratt Street, Baltimore, MD 21201-4310    Dist: (410) 837-8079
E-mail: keith.haynes@house.state.md.us
Committees: Appropriations; Special Joint Pensions

Delegate **Anne Healey** (D-District 22) Room 350 . . . . . . . . (410) 841-3961
Counties Represented: Prince George's (part)    Dist: (301) 779-4515
Term Expires: 2019    Fax: (410) 841-3223
E-mail: anne.healey@house.state.md.us    Dist: (301) 779-4515
Committees: Environment and Transportation; Rules and Executive
Nominations
Education: Marywood Col 1972 BA; Catholic U 1974 MA

Delegate **Shelly Hettleman** (D-District 11) . . . . . . . . . . . . (410) 841-3833
Counties Represented: Baltimore (part)    Fax: (410) 841-3373
Term Expires: 2019
E-mail: shelly.hettleman@house.state.md.us
Committees: Appropriations
Education: Northwestern BA

Delegate **Terri L. Hill** (D-District 12) . . . . . . . . . . . . . . . (410) 841-3378
Counties Represented: Baltimore (part), Howard    Fax: (410) 841-3007
(part)
Term Expires: 2019
E-mail: terri.hill@house.state.md.us
Committees: Health and Government Operations
Education: Harvard 1981 AB; Columbia 1985 MD

Delegate **Sheila Ellis Hixson** (D-District 20) Room 131 . . . (410) 841-3469
Counties Represented: Montgomery (part)    Fax: (410) 841-3777
Term Expires: 2019
E-mail: sheila.hixson@house.state.md.us
Committees: Joint Spending Affordability; Rules and Executive
Nominations; Ways and Means
Education: Northern State BA

Delegate **Marvin E. Holmes, Jr.** (D-District 23B)
Room 313 . . . . . . . . . . . . . . . . . . . . . . . . . . . . . (410) 841-3310
Counties Represented: Prince George's (part)    Tel: (301) 858-3310
Term Expires: 2019    Fax: (410) 841-3017
E-mail: marvin.holmes@house.state.md.us    Fax: (301) 858-3017
Committees: Environment and Transportation; Joint Administrative,
Executive and Legislative Review

Delegate **Kevin Bailey Hornberger** (R-District 35A) . . . . . . (410) 841-3284
Counties Represented: Cecil (part)    Fax: (410) 841-3190
Term Expires: 2019
E-mail: kevin.hornberger@house.state.md.us
Committees: Ways and Means

Delegate **Carolyn J. B. Howard** (D-District 24) . . . . . . . . . (410) 841-3919
Counties Represented: Prince George's (part)    Fax: (410) 841-3925
Term Expires: 2019
1891 Brightseat Road, Landover, MD 20785-4256
E-mail: carolyn.howard@house.state.md.us
Committees: Joint Management of Public Funds; Rules and Executive
Nominations; Ways and Means

Delegate **Seth Howard** (R-District 30B) . . . . . . . . . . . . . . (410) 841-3439
Counties Represented: Anne Arundel (part)    Fax: (410) 841-3256
Term Expires: 2019
E-mail: seth.howard@house.state.md.us
Committees: Economic Matters

Delegate **Richard K. "Rick" Impallaria** (R-District 7) . . . . . (410) 841-3289
Counties Represented: Baltimore (part), Harford    Fax: (410) 841-3598
(part)
Term Expires: 2019
5 Punte Lane, Baltimore, MD 21221
E-mail: rick.impallaria@house.state.md.us
Committees: Economic Matters

Delegate **Michael A. Jackson** (D-District 27B) . . . . . . . . . . (410) 841-3103
Counties Represented: Calvert (part), Prince    Fax: (410) 841-3105
George's (part)
Term Expires: 2019
E-mail: michael.jackson@house.state.md.us
Committees: Appropriations

Delegate **Jay A. Jacobs** (R-District 36) Room 321 . . . . . . . (410) 841-3449
Counties Represented: Caroline (part), Cecil (part),    Fax: (410) 841-3093
Kent, Queen Anne's
Term Expires: 2019
E-mail: jay.jacobs@house.state.md.us
Committees: Environment and Transportation; Joint Administrative,
Executive and Legislative Review

Delegate **Jay Jalisi** (D-District 10) . . . . . . . . . . . . . . . . . (410) 841-3358
 Counties Represented: Baltimore (part)    Fax: (410) 841-3850
 Term Expires: 2019
 E-mail: jay.jalisi@house.state.md.us
 Committees: Environment and Transportation

Delegate **Sally Y. Jameson** (D-District 28) Room 427 . . . . (410) 841-3337
 Counties Represented: Charles (part)    Fax: (410) 841-3277
 Term Expires: 2019
 E-mail: sally.jameson@house.state.md.us
 Committees: Economic Matters; Rules and Executive Nominations

Delegate **Adrienne A. Jones** (D-District 10) Room 312 . . . (410) 841-3391
 Counties Represented: Baltimore (part)    Fax: (410) 841-3157
 Term Expires: 2019
 E-mail: adrienne.jones@house.state.md.us
 Committees: Appropriations; Joint Fair Practices and State Personnel
 Oversight; Joint Legislative Ethics; Joint Spending Affordability; Rules
 and Executive Nominations

Delegate **Anne R. Kaiser** (D-District 14) Room 151 . . . . . (410) 841-3036
 Counties Represented: Montgomery (part)    Fax: (410) 841-3060
 Term Expires: 2019
 E-mail: anne.kaiser@house.state.md.us
 Committees: Ways and Means

Delegate **Ariana B. Kelly** (D-District 16) Room 210 . . . . . . (410) 841-3642
 Counties Represented: Montgomery (part)    Fax: (410) 841-3026
 Term Expires: 2019
 E-mail: ariana.kelly@house.state.md.us
 Committees: Health and Government Operations; Joint Children, Youth
 and Families; Joint Federal Relations
 Education: Wisconsin 2002 BA

Delegate **Nicholaus R. Kipke** (R-District 31B)
 Room 212 . . . . . . . . . . . . . . . . . . . . . . . . . . . . (410) 841-3421
 Counties Represented: Anne Arundel (part)    Tel: (301) 858-3421
 Term Expires: 2019    Fax: (410) 841-3553
 E-mail: nicholaus.kipke@house.state.md.us    Fax: (301) 858-3553
 Committees: Health and Government Operations; Rules and Executive
 Nominations

Delegate **Trent M. Kittleman** (R-District 9A) . . . . . . . . . . . (410) 841-3556
 Counties Represented: Carroll (part), Howard (part)    Fax: (410) 841-3571
 Term Expires: 2019
 E-mail: trent.kittleman@house.state.md.us
 Committees: Judiciary

Delegate **Tony Knotts** (D-District 26) . . . . . . . . . . . . . . . . (410) 841-3212
 Counties Represented: Prince George's (part)    Fax: (410) 841-3105
 Term Expires: 2019
 E-mail: tony.knotts@house.state.md.us
 Committees: Environment and Transportation
 Education: Bowie State

Delegate **Marc A. Korman** (D-District 16) . . . . . . . . . . . . (410) 841-3649
 Counties Represented: Montgomery (part)    Fax: (410) 841-3424
 Term Expires: 2019
 E-mail: marc.korman@house.state.md.us
 Committees: Appropriations; Joint Federal Relations
 Education: USC 2002 BA

Delegate **Benjamin F. Kramer** (D-District 19) Room 226 . . (410) 841-3485
 Counties Represented: Montgomery (part)    Fax: (410) 841-3875
 Term Expires: 2019
 E-mail: benjamin.kramer@house.state.md.us
 Committees: Economic Matters
 Education: Maryland BA

Delegate **Susan W. Krebs** (R-District 5) . . . . . . . . . . . . . . (410) 841-3200
 Counties Represented: Carroll (part)    Fax: (410) 841-3349
 Term Expires: 2019
 E-mail: susan.krebs@house.state.md.us
 Committees: Health and Government Operations
 Education: Towson State U 1981 BS

Delegate **Carol L. Krimm** (D-District 3A) . . . . . . . . . . . . . (410) 841-3472
 Counties Represented: Frederick (part)    Fax: (410) 841-3412
 Term Expires: 2019
 E-mail: carol.krimm@house.state.md.us
 Committees: Appropriations; Special Joint Pensions

Delegate **Stephen W. "Steve" Lafferty** (D-District 42A)
 Room 306 . . . . . . . . . . . . . . . . . . . . . . . . . . . . (410) 841-3487
 Counties Represented: Baltimore (part)    Fax: (410) 841-3501
 Term Expires: 2019
 E-mail: stephen.lafferty@house.state.md.us
 Committees: Environment and Transportation; Joint Chesapeake and
 Atlantic Coastal Bays Critical Area
 Education: Maryland 1971 BA; Bowling Green State MA;
 Baltimore JD

Delegate **Clarence Lam** (D-District 12) . . . . . . . . . . . . . . (410) 841-3205
 Counties Represented: Baltimore (part), Howard    Fax: (410) 841-3007
 (part)
 Term Expires: 2019
 E-mail: clarence.lam@house.state.md.us
 Committees: Environment and Transportation

Delegate **Brooke Elizabeth Lierman** (D-District 46) . . . . . (410) 841-3319
 Counties Represented: Baltimore City (part)
 Term Expires: 2019
 E-mail: brooke.lierman@house.state.md.us
 Committees: Appropriations; Joint Chesapeake and Atlantic Coastal
 Bays Critical Area; Special Joint Pensions

Delegate **Mary Ann Lisanti** (D-District 34A) . . . . . . . . . . . (410) 841-3331
 Counties Represented: Harford (part)    Fax: (410) 841-3002
 Term Expires: 2019
 E-mail: maryann.lisanti@house.state.md.us
 Committees: Economic Matters
 Education: Col Notre Dame (MD) 1989 BA;
 Central Michigan 1996 MS

Delegate **Robert B. "Bob" Long** (R-District 6) . . . . . . . . . (410) 841-3458
 Counties Represented: Baltimore (part)    Fax: (410) 841-3177
 Term Expires: 2019
 E-mail: bob.long@house.state.md.us
 Committees: Ways and Means

Delegate **Eric Luedtke** (D-District 14) Room 222 . . . . . . . . (410) 841-3110
 Counties Represented: Montgomery (part)    Fax: (410) 941-3053
 Term Expires: 2019
 E-mail: eric.luedtke@house.state.md.us
 Committees: Ways and Means
 Education: Maryland 2002 BA

Delegate **Michael Malone** (R-District 33) . . . . . . . . . . . . . (410) 841-3510
 Counties Represented: Anne Arundel (part)    Fax: (410) 841-3235
 Term Expires: 2019
 E-mail: michael.malone@house.state.md.us
 Committees: Judiciary

Delegate **John F. "Johnny" Mautz** (R-District 37B) . . . . (410) 841-3429
 Counties Represented: Caroline (part), Dorchester    Fax: (410) 841-3523
 (part), Talbot, Wicomico (part)
 Term Expires: 2019
 E-mail: johnny.mautz@house.state.md.us
 Committees: Economic Matters
 Education: Dayton 1994 BA; Ohio Northern 1997 JD

Delegate **Susan K. McComas** (R-District 34B) . . . . . . . . . (410) 841-3272
 Counties Represented: Harford (part)    Fax: (410) 841-3244
 Term Expires: 2019
 E-mail: susan.mccomas@house.state.md.us
 Committees: Joint Administrative, Executive and Legislative Review;
 Joint Legislative Ethics; Judiciary; Rules and Executive Nominations
 Education: Johns Hopkins 1974 BA; Wyoming 1980 JD

Delegate **Tony McConkey** (R-District 33) Room 216 . . . . . (410) 841-3406
 Counties Represented: Anne Arundel (part)    Fax: (410) 841-3209
 Term Expires: 2019
 E-mail: tony.mcconkey@house.state.md.us
 Committees: Appropriations; Special Joint Pensions
 Education: Maryland 1986 BA, 1986 BS, 1990 JD

Delegate **Cory V. McCray** (D-District 45) . . . . . . . . . . . . . (410) 841-3486
 Counties Represented: Baltimore City (part)    Fax: (410) 841-3467
 Term Expires: 2019
 E-mail: cory.mccray@house.state.md.us
 Committees: Environment and Transportation

Delegate **Patrick L. "Pat" McDonough** (R-District 7) . . . . (410) 841-3334
 Counties Represented: Baltimore (part), Harford    Dist: (410) 238-0025
 (part)    Fax: (410) 841-3598
 Term Expires: 2019    Dist: (410) 238-0035
 P.O. Box 15470, Baltimore, MD 21220
 E-mail: pat.mcdonough@house.state.md.us
 E-mail: patmcdee@comcast.net
 Committees: Health and Government Operations

Delegate **Maggie L. McIntosh** (D-District 43) Room 251 . . . . . . . . . (410)
 841-3407
 Counties Represented: Baltimore City (part)    Fax: (410) 841-3509
 Term Expires: 2019
 E-mail: maggie.mcintosh@house.state.md.us
 Committees: Appropriations; Rules and Executive Nominations
 Education: Wichita State 1970 BAE; Johns Hopkins 1987 MS,
 1987 ABS

Delegate **Michael W. McKay** (R-District 1C) . . . . . . . . . . . (410) 841-3321
 Counties Represented: Allegany (part), Washington (part)
 Term Expires: 2019
 E-mail: mike.mckay@house.state.md.us
 Committees: Appropriations

*(continued on next page)*

**Delegates** *continued*

Delegate **Herbert H. McMillan** (R-District 30A)
Room 164 . . . . . . . . . . . . . . . . . . . . . . . . (410) 841-3211
Counties Represented: Anne Arundel (part)    Fax: (410) 841-3386
Term Expires: 2019
E-mail: herb.mcmillan@house.state.md.us
Committees: Health and Government Operations

Delegate **Richard W. "Ric" Metzgar** (R-District 6) . . . . . . .(410) 841-3332
Counties Represented: Baltimore (part)
Term Expires: 2019
E-mail: ric.metzgar@house.state.md.us
Committees: Ways and Means

Delegate **Christian Miele** (R-District 8) . . . . . . . . . . . . . . (410) 841-3365
Counties Represented: Baltimore (part)    Fax: (410) 841-3034
Term Expires: 2019
E-mail: christian.miele@house.state.md.us
Committees: Health and Government Operations

Delegate **Aruna Miller** (D-District 15) Room 225 . . . . . . . . (410) 841-3090
Counties Represented: Montgomery (part)    Fax: (410) 841-3126
Term Expires: 2019
E-mail: aruna.miller@house.state.md.us
Committees: Appropriations; Joint Fair Practices and State Personnel Oversight
Education: Missouri (Rolla) 1989 BS

Delegate **Warren E. Miller** (R-District 9A) Room 202 . . . . .(410) 841-3582
Counties Represented: Carroll (part), Howard (part)    Fax: (410) 841-3571
Term Expires: 2019
E-mail: warren.miller@house.state.md.us
Committees: Economic Matters; Rules and Executive Nominations
Education: Towson State U 1987 BS

Delegate **David Moon** (D-District 20) . . . . . . . . . . . . . . . . .(410) 841-3474
Counties Represented: Montgomery (part)    Fax: (410) 841-3445
Term Expires: 2019
E-mail: david.moon@house.state.md.us
Committees: Judiciary

Delegate **Marice I. Morales** (D-District 19) . . . . . . . . . . . . (410) 841-3528
Counties Represented: Montgomery (part)    Fax: (410) 841-3011
Term Expires: 2019
E-mail: marice.morales@house.state.md.us
Committees: Judiciary

Delegate **Matt Morgan** (R-District 29A) . . . . . . . . . . . . . . (410) 841-3170
Counties Represented: St. Mary's (part)    Fax: (410) 841-3252
Term Expires: 2019
E-mail: matt.morgan@house.state.md.us
Committees: Health and Government Operations

Delegate **Dan K. Morhaim** (D-District 11) . . . . . . . . . . . . . (410) 841-3054
Counties Represented: Baltimore (part)    Fax: (410) 841-3385
Term Expires: 2019
8 Park Center Court, Room 100, Owings Mills, MD 21117-5609
E-mail: dan.morhaim@house.state.md.us
Committees: Health and Government Operations; Joint Administrative, Executive and Legislative Review; Joint Information Technology and Biotechnology Committee

Delegate
**Anthony J. "Tony" O'Donnell** (R-District 29C) . . . . . . . (301) 858-3314
Counties Represented: Calvert (part), St. Mary's    Dist: (410) 326-0081
(part)    Fax: (410) 841-3451
Term Expires: 2019    Dist: (410) 326-9169
P.O. Box 865, Solomons, MD 20688-0865
E-mail: anthony.odonnell@house.state.md.us
Committees: Environment and Transportation; Rules and Executive Nominations
Education: SUNY (Albany) 1985 BS

Delegate **Nathaniel T. Oaks** (D-District 41) . . . . . . . . . . . .(410) 841-3283
Counties Represented: Baltimore City (part)    Dist: (410) 494-2192
Term Expires: 2019    Fax: (410) 841-3267
411 House Office Building, 6 Bladen Street, Annapolis, MD 21401
E-mail: nathaniel.oaks@house.state.md.us
Committees: Health and Government Operations; Joint Administrative, Executive and Legislative Review
Education: Morgan State 1974 BS

Delegate **Charles James Otto** (R-District 38A) . . . . . . . . . (410) 841-3433
Counties Represented: Somerset (part), Worcester    Dist: (410) 621-0200
(part)    Fax: (410) 841-3463
Term Expires: 2019
E-mail: charles.otto@house.state.md.us
Committees: Environment and Transportation; Joint Protocol
Education: Virginia Tech 1986 BS

Delegate **Neil C. Parrott** (R-District 2A) Room 213 . . . . . . (410) 841-3636
Counties Represented: Washington (part)    Fax: (410) 841-3273
Term Expires: 2019
E-mail: neil.parrott@house.state.md.us
Committees: Judiciary

Delegate **Edith Jerry Patterson** (D-District 28) . . . . . . . . .(410) 841-3247
Counties Represented: Charles (part)    Fax: (410) 841-3367
Term Expires: 2019
E-mail: edith.patterson@house.state.md.us
Committees: Ways and Means
Education: George Washington EdD

Delegate **Joseline Peña-Melnyk** (D-District 21)
Room 157 . . . . . . . . . . . . . . . . . . . . . . . . . . . . (410) 841-3502
Counties Represented: Anne Arundel (part), Prince    Fax: (410) 841-3342
George's (part)
Term Expires: 2019
E-mail: joseline.pena.melnyk@house.state.md.us
Committees: Health and Government Operations
Education: SUNY (Buffalo State Col) BA; SUNY (Buffalo) JD

Delegate **Shane E. Pendergrass** (D-District 13)
Room 241 . . . . . . . . . . . . . . . . . . . . . . . . . . . . (410) 841-3139
Counties Represented: Howard (part)    Fax: (410) 841-3409
Term Expires: 2019
E-mail: shane.pendergrass@house.state.md.us
Committees: Health and Government Operations; Rules and Executive Nominations
Education: Illinois 1973 BFA, 1974 MA

Delegate **Andrew Joseph Platt** (D-District 17) . . . . . . . . . .(410) 841-3037
Counties Represented: Montgomery (part)    Fax: (410) 841-3003
Term Expires: 2019
E-mail: andrew.platt@house.state.md.us
Committees: Ways and Means

Delegate **Elizabeth G. "Susie" Proctor** (D-District 27A) . .(410) 841-3083
Counties Represented: Charles (part), Prince    Fax: (410) 841-3459
George's (part)
Term Expires: 2019
E-mail: susie.proctor@house.state.md.us
Committees: Judiciary

Delegate **Pamela E. "Pam" Queen** (D-District 14) . . . . . . .(410) 841-3380
Counties Represented: Montgomery (part)    Fax: (410) 841-3266
Term Expires: 2019
E-mail: pam.queen@house.state.md.us
Committees: Judiciary
Education: Tuskegee BS; Johns Hopkins MS; George Washington PhD

Delegate **Teresa Reilly** (R-District 35B) . . . . . . . . . . . . . . (410) 841-3278
Counties Represented: Cecil (part), Harford (part)    Fax: (410) 841-3190
Term Expires: 2019
E-mail: teresa.reilly@house.state.md.us
Committees: Ways and Means

Delegate **Deborah C. "Deb" Rey** (R-District 29B) . . . . . . . (410) 841-3227
Counties Represented: St. Mary's (part)    Fax: (410) 841-3051
Term Expires: 2019
E-mail: deborah.rey@house.state.md.us
Committees: Judiciary

Delegate **Kirill Reznik** (D-District 39) Room 225 . . . . . . . . (410) 841-3039
Counties Represented: Montgomery (part)    Dist: (301) 540-0054
Term Expires: 2019    Fax: (410) 841-3126
E-mail: kirill.reznik@house.state.md.us    Dist: (301) 540-0911
Committees: Appropriations; Joint Administrative, Executive and Legislative Review; Joint Federal Relations

Delegate **A. Shane Robinson** (D-District 39) Room 223 . . (410) 841-3021
Counties Represented: Montgomery (part)    Fax: (410) 841-3375
Term Expires: 2019
E-mail: shane.robinson@house.state.md.us
Committees: Environment and Transportation
Education: Nevada (Reno) 2000 BS

Delegate **Barbara A. Robinson** (D-District 40)
Room 315 . . . . . . . . . . . . . . . . . . . . . . . . . . . . (410) 841-3520
Counties Represented: Baltimore City (part)    Fax: (410) 841-3199
Term Expires: 2019
E-mail: barbara.robinson@house.state.md.us
Committees: Appropriations; Joint Fair Practices and State Personnel Oversight; Special Joint Pensions

Delegate **April Rose** (R-District 5) . . . . . . . . . . . . . . . . . . (410) 841-3070
Counties Represented: Carroll (part)    Fax: (410) 841-3349
Term Expires: 2019
E-mail: april.rose@house.state.md.us
Committees: Health and Government Operations

LEGISLATIVE BRANCH

Delegate
**Samuel I. "Sandy" Rosenberg** (D-District 41) . . . . . . . (410) 841-3297
Counties Represented: Baltimore City (part)          Dist: (410) 664-2646
Term Expires: 2019                                    Fax: (410) 841-3179
4811 Liberty Heights Avenue,                          Dist: (410) 467-4968
Baltimore, MD 21207
E-mail: samuel.rosenberg@house.state.md.us
Committees: Joint Administrative, Executive and Legislative Review;
Joint Spending Affordability; Judiciary; Rules and Executive
Nominations
Education: Amherst 1972 BA; Columbia 1975 JD

Delegate **Sid Saab** (R-District 33) . . . . . . . . . . . . . . . . . . . (410) 841-3551
Counties Represented: Anne Arundel (part)          Fax: (410) 841-3235
Term Expires: 2019
E-mail: sid.saab@house.state.md.us
Committees: Health and Government Operations

Delegate **Sheree Sample-Hughes** (D-District 37A) . . . . . . (410) 841-3427
Counties Represented: Dorchester (part), Wicomico     Fax: (410) 841-3780
(part)
Term Expires: 2019
E-mail: sheree.sample.hughes@house.state.md.us
Committees: Health and Government Operations

Delegate **Carlo Sanchez** (D-District 47B) Room 206 . . . . . (410) 841-3340
Counties Represented: Prince George's (part)
Term Expires: 2019
E-mail: carlo.sanchez@house.state.md.us
Committees: Judiciary

Delegate **Haven N. Shoemaker, Jr.** (R-District 5) . . . . . . . . (410) 841-3359
Counties Represented: Carroll (part)          Fax: (410) 841-3349
Term Expires: 2019
E-mail: haven.shoemaker@house.state.md.us
Committees: Ways and Means
Education: Maryland Baltimore County 1987 BA; Widener 1992 JD

Delegate **Meagan "Meg" Simonaire** (R-District 31B) . . . . (410) 841-3206
Counties Represented: Anne Arundel (part)          Fax: (410) 841-3764
Term Expires: 2019
E-mail: meagan.simonaire@house.state.md.us
Committees: Joint Children, Youth and Families; Ways and Means

Delegate **William C. "Will" Smith, Jr.** (D-District 20) . . . . (410) 841-3493
Counties Represented: Montgomery (part)          Fax: (410) 841-3445
Term Expires: 2019
E-mail: will.smith@house.state.md.us
Committees: Judiciary

Delegate **Theodore J. Sophocleus** (D-District 32)
Room 162 . . . . . . . . . . . . . . . . . . . . . . . . . . . . . . . . . (410) 841-3372
Counties Represented: Anne Arundel (part)          Fax: (410) 841-3437
Term Expires: 2019
E-mail: ted.sophocleus@house.state.md.us
Committees: Appropriations
Education: Maryland 1962 BSPh

Delegate **Dana M. Stein** (D-District 11) Room 304 . . . . . . (410) 841-3527
Counties Represented: Baltimore (part)          Fax: (410) 841-3373
Term Expires: 2019
E-mail: dana.stein@house.state.md.us
Committees: Environment and Transportation; Joint Chesapeake and
Atlantic Coastal Bays Critical Area; Rules and Executive Nominations
Education: Harvard 1981 BA; Princeton 1985 MPA; Columbia 1985 JD

Delegate **Charles E. Sydnor III** (D-District 44B) . . . . . . . . (410) 841-3802
Counties Represented: Baltimore (part)          Fax: (410) 841-3537
Term Expires: 2019
E-mail: charles.sydnor@house.state.md.us
Committees: Judiciary

Delegate **Kathryn "Kathy" Szeliga** (R-District 7)
House Office Building,, Room 212 . . . . . . . . . . . . . . . . (410) 841-3698
Counties Represented: Baltimore (part), Harford     Fax: (410) 841-3023
(part)
Term Expires: 2019
E-mail: kathy.szeliga@house.state.md.us
Committees: Environment and Transportation; Rules and Executive
Nominations

Delegate **Jimmy Tarlau** (D-District 47A) . . . . . . . . . . . . . . (410) 841-3326
Counties Represented: Prince George's (part)          Fax: (410) 841-3727
Term Expires: 2019
E-mail: jimmy.tarlau@house.state.md.us
Committees: Ways and Means

Delegate **Frank S. Turner** (D-District 13) Room 131 . . . . . . (410) 841-3246
Counties Represented: Howard (part)          Fax: (410) 841-3986
Term Expires: 2019
E-mail: frank.turner@house.state.md.us
Committees: Rules and Executive Nominations; Ways and Means
Education: North Carolina Central 1968 BA, 1973 JD

Delegate **Kriselda Valderrama** (D-District 26)
House Office Building,, Room 205 . . . . . . . . . . . . . . . . . . (410) 841-3210
Counties Represented: Prince George's (part)          Fax: (410) 841-3525
Term Expires: 2019
E-mail: kris.valderrama@house.state.md.us
Committees: Economic Matters
Education: Salisbury State U BS

Delegate **Geraldine Valentino-Smith** (D-District 23A)
Room 209 . . . . . . . . . . . . . . . . . . . . . . . . . . . . . . . . . (410) 841-3101
Counties Represented: Prince George's (part)          Fax: (410) 841-3850
Term Expires: 2019
E-mail: geraldine.valentino.smith@house.state.md.us
Committees: Appropriations
Education: Catholic U 1987 BS; Columbia 1992 JD

Delegate **Joseph F. Vallario, Jr.** (D-District 23B)
Room 325 . . . . . . . . . . . . . . . . . . . . . . . . . . . . . . . . . (410) 841-3488
Counties Represented: Prince George's (part)          Dist: (301) 423-8100
Term Expires: 2019                                    Fax: (410) 841-3495
E-mail: joseph.vallario@house.state.md.us
Committees: Judiciary; Rules and Executive Nominations
Education: Franklin U 1959 BCS, 1959 MCS; Eastern Col 1963 LLB,
1963 JD

Delegate **Michael L. Vaughn** (D-District 24) . . . . . . . . . . . (410) 841-3691
Counties Represented: Prince George's (part)          Fax: (410) 841-3055
Term Expires: 2019
1891 Brightseat Road, Landover, MD 20785
E-mail: michael.vaughn@house.state.md.us
Committees: Economic Matters

Delegate **David Edward Vogt III** (R-District 4) . . . . . . . . . (410) 841-3118
Counties Represented: Carroll (part), Frederick     Fax: (410) 841-3349
(part)
Term Expires: 2019
E-mail: david.vogt@house.state.md.us
Committees: Appropriations; Joint Management of Public Funds

Delegate
**Jeffrey D. "Jeff" Waldstreicher** (D-District 18)
Room 221 . . . . . . . . . . . . . . . . . . . . . . . . . . . . . . . . . (410) 841-3130
Counties Represented: Montgomery (part)          Fax: (410) 841-3233
Term Expires: 2019
E-mail: jeff.waldstreicher@house.state.md.us
Committees: Economic Matters
Education: Emory BA; Boalt Hall JD

Delegate **Jay Walker** (D-District 26) Room 430 . . . . . . . . . (410) 841-3581
Counties Represented: Prince George's (part)          Fax: (410) 841-3078
Term Expires: 2019
E-mail: jay.walker@house.state.md.us
Committees: Rules and Executive Nominations; Ways and Means
Education: Howard U BA

Delegate **Alonzo T. Washington** (D-District 22)
Room 204B . . . . . . . . . . . . . . . . . . . . . . . . . . . . . . . . (410) 841-3652
Counties Represented: Prince George's (part)          Fax: (410) 841-3699
Term Expires: 2019
E-mail: alonzo.washington@house.state.md.us
Committees: Joint Children, Youth and Families; Joint Federal
Relations; Joint Management of Public Funds; Ways and Means
Education: Maryland 2007 BA

Delegate **Mary L. Washington** (D-District 43)
Room 315 . . . . . . . . . . . . . . . . . . . . . . . . . . . . . . . . . (410) 841-3476
Counties Represented: Baltimore City (part)          Fax: (410) 841-3295
Term Expires: 2019
E-mail: mary.washington@house.state.md.us
Committees: Joint Children, Youth and Families; Ways and Means
Education: Antioch Col 1989 BA; Johns Hopkins 1992 MA, 1997 PhD

Delegate **Christopher R. West** (R-District 42B) . . . . . . . . . (410) 841-3793
Counties Represented: Baltimore (part)
Term Expires: 2019
E-mail: chris.west@house.state.md.us
Committees: Health and Government Operations; Joint Federal
Relations
Education: Williams 1972 BA; Pennsylvania 1975 JD

Delegate **Brett Wilson** (R-District 2B) . . . . . . . . . . . . . . . . (410) 841-3125
Counties Represented: Washington (part)          Fax: (410) 841-3414
Term Expires: 2019
E-mail: brett.wilson@house.state.md.us
Committees: Judiciary

Delegate **C. T. Wilson** (D-District 28) Room 152 . . . . . . . . (410) 841-3325
Counties Represented: Charles (part)          Fax: (410) 841-3367
Term Expires: 2019
E-mail: ct.wilson@house.state.md.us
Committees: Economic Matters

*(continued on next page)*

**LEGISLATIVE BRANCH**

**Delegates** *continued*

Delegate **William J. "Bill" Wivell** (R-District 2A) . . . . . . . (410) 841-3447
  Counties Represented: Washington (part)      Fax: (410) 841-3273
  Term Expires: 2019
  E-mail: william.wivell@house.state.md.us
  Committees: Environment and Transportation

Delegate **Karen Lewis Young** (D-District 3A) . . . . . . . . . . (410) 841-3436
  Counties Represented: Frederick (part)      Fax: (410) 841-3028
  Term Expires: 2019
  E-mail: karen.young@house.state.md.us
  Committees: Health and Government Operations
  Education: Franklin & Marshall 1973 BA; Columbia 1974 MA,
  1977 MBA

Delegate **Patrick G. Young** (D-District 44B) . . . . . . . . . . . (410) 841-3544
  Counties Represented: Baltimore (part)
  Term Expires: 2019
  E-mail: pat.young@house.state.md.us
  Committees: Appropriations

## House Standing Committees

### Appropriations
121 House Office Building, Annapolis, MD 21401
Fax: (410) 841-3416

| Majority Members | Minority Members |
| --- | --- |
| Maggie L. McIntosh (D-43) *Chair* | Wendell R. Beitzel (R-1A) |
| Tawanna P. Gaines (D-22) *Vice Chair* | Mary Beth Carozza (R-38C) |
| | Barrie S. Ciliberti (R-4) |
| Benjamin S. "Ben" Barnes (D-21) | Jefferson L. Ghrist (R-36) |
| Mark S. Chang (D-32) | Robin L. Grammer, Jr. (R-6) |
| Ana Sol Gutierrez (D-18) | Tony McConkey (R-33) |
| Keith E. Haynes (D-44A) | Michael W. McKay (R-1C) |
| Shelly Hettleman (D-11) | David Edward Vogt III (R-4) |
| Michael A. Jackson (D-27B) | |
| Adrienne A. Jones (D-10) | |
| Marc A. Korman (D-16) | |
| Carol L. Krimm (D-3A) | |
| Brooke Elizabeth Lierman (D-46) | |
| Aruna Miller (D-15) | |
| Kirill Reznik (D-39) | |
| Barbara A. Robinson (D-40) | |
| Theodore J. Sophocleus (D-32) | |
| Geraldine Valentino-Smith (D-23A) | |
| Patrick G. Young (D-44B) | |

### Economic Matters
231 House Office Building, Annapolis, MD 21401
Fax: (410) 841-3558

| Majority Members | Minority Members |
| --- | --- |
| Dereck E. Davis (D-25) *Chair* | Christopher T. Adams (R-37B) |
| Sally Y. Jameson (D-28) *Vice Chair* | Steven J. Arentz (R-36) |
| Charles E. Barkley (D-39) | Susan L. M. Aumann (R-42B) |
| Talmadge Branch (D-45) | Mark N. Fisher (R-27C) |
| Benjamin T. Brooks, Sr. (D-10) | Seth Howard (R-30B) |
| Edward P. "Ned" Carey (D-31A) | Richard K. "Rick" Impallaria (R-7) |
| Luke Clippinger (D-46) | John F. "Johnny" Mautz (R-37B) |
| C. William "Bill" Frick (D-16) | Warren E. Miller (R-9A) |
| Cheryl D. Glenn (D-45) | |
| Mary Ann Lisanti (D-34A) | |
| Kriselda Valderrama (D-26) | |
| Michael L. Vaughn (D-24) | |
| Jeffrey D. "Jeff" Waldstreicher (D-18) | |
| C. T. Wilson (D-28) | |
| Benjamin F. Kramer (D-19) | |

### Environment and Transportation
251 House Office Building, Annapolis, MD 21401
Fax: (410) 841-3509

| Majority Members | Minority Members |
| --- | --- |
| Kumar P. Barve (D-17) *Chair* | Carl Anderton, Jr. (R-38B) |
| Dana M. Stein (D-11) *Vice Chair* | Andrew P. Cassilly (R-35B) |
| Pamela G. Beidle (D-32) | Robert L. "Bob" Flanagan (R-9B) |
| Alfred C. "Al" Carr, Jr. (D-18) | Jay A. Jacobs (R-36) |
| David V. Fraser-Hidalgo (D-15) | Anthony J. "Tony" O'Donnell (R-29C) |
| Barbara A. Frush (D-21) | Charles James Otto (R-38A) |
| James W. "Jim" Gilchrist (D-17) | Kathryn "Kathy" Szeliga (R-7) |
| Anne Healey (D-22) | William J. "Bill" Wivell (R-2A) |
| Marvin E. Holmes, Jr. (D-23B) | |
| Jay Jalisi (D-10) | |
| Tony Knotts (D-26) | |
| Stephen W. "Steve" Lafferty (D-42A) | |
| Clarence Lam (D-12) | |
| Cory V. McCray (D-45) | |
| A. Shane Robinson (D-39) | |

### Health and Government Operations
241 House Office Building, Annapolis, MD 21401
Fax: (410) 841-3409

| Majority Members | Minority Members |
| --- | --- |
| Peter A. Hammen (D-46) *Chair* | Nicholaus R. Kipke (R-31B) |
| Shane E. Pendergrass (D-13) *Vice Chair* | Susan W. Krebs (R-5) |
| | Patrick L. "Pat" McDonough (R-7) |
| Angela Angel (D-25) | Herbert H. McMillan (R-30A) |
| Erek Barron (D-24) | Christian Miele (R-8) |
| Eric M. Bromwell (D-8) | Matt Morgan (R-29A) |
| Bonnie L. Cullison (D-19) | April Rose (R-5) |
| Antonio Hayes (D-40) | Sid Saab (R-33) |
| Terri L. Hill (D-12) | Christopher R. West (R-42B) |
| Ariana B. Kelly (D-16) | |
| Dan K. Morhaim (D-11) | |
| Nathaniel T. Oaks (D-41) | |
| Joseline Peña-Melnyk (D-21) | |
| Sheree Sample-Hughes (D-37A) | |
| Karen Lewis Young (D-3A) | |

### Judiciary
101 House Office Building, Annapolis, MD 21401
Fax: (410) 841-3850

| Majority Members | Minority Members |
| --- | --- |
| Joseph F. Vallario, Jr. (D-23B) *Chair* | John W. E. Cluster, Jr. (R-8) |
| Kathleen M. Dumais (D-15) *Vice Chair* | William "Bill" Folden (R-3B) |
| | Glen Glass (R-34A) |
| Curtis Stovall "Curt" Anderson (D-43) | Trent M. Kittleman (R-9A) |
| Vanessa Atterbeary (D-13) | Michael Malone (R-33) |
| Jill P. Carter (D-41) | Susan K. McComas (R-34B) |
| Frank M. Conaway, Jr. (D-40) | Neil C. Parrott (R-2A) |
| David Moon (D-20) | Deborah C. "Deb" Rey (R-29B) |
| Marice I. Morales (D-19) | Brett Wilson (R-2B) |
| Elizabeth G. "Susie" Proctor (D-27A) | |
| Pamela E. "Pam" Queen (D-14) | |
| Samuel I. "Sandy" Rosenberg (D-41) | |
| Carlo Sanchez (D-47B) | |
| William C. "Will" Smith, Jr. (D-20) | |
| Charles E. Sydnor III (D-44B) | |

## Rules and Executive Nominations

145 House Office Building, Annapolis, MD 21401

**Majority Members**
Anne Healey (D-22) *Chair*
Jay Walker (D-26) *Vice Chairman*
Kumar P. Barve (D-17)
Talmadge Branch (D-45)
Dereck E. Davis (D-25)
Kathleen M. Dumais (D-15)
C. William "Bill" Frick (D-16)
Tawanna P. Gaines (D-22)
Peter A. Hammen (D-46)
Sheila Ellis Hixson (D-20)
Carolyn J. B. Howard (D-24)
Sally Y. Jameson (D-28)
Adrienne A. Jones (D-10)
Maggie L. McIntosh (D-43)
Shane E. Pendergrass (D-13)
Samuel I. "Sandy" Rosenberg (D-41)
Dana M. Stein (D-11)
Frank S. Turner (D-13)
Joseph F. Vallario, Jr. (D-23B)

**Minority Members**
Nicholaus R. Kipke (R-31B)
Susan K. McComas (R-34B)
Warren E. Miller (R-9A)
Anthony J. "Tony" O'Donnell (R-29C)
Kathryn "Kathy" Szeliga (R-7)

## Ways and Means

131 House Office Building, Annapolis, MD 21401
Fax: (410) 841-3777

**Majority Members**
Sheila Ellis Hixson (D-20) *Chair*
Frank S. Turner (D-13) *Vice Chair*
Darryl Barnes (D-25)
Eric Ebersole (D-12)
Diana M. Fennell (D-47A)
Carolyn J. B. Howard (D-24)
Anne R. Kaiser (D-14)
Eric Luedtke (D-14)
Edith Jerry Patterson (D-28)
Andrew Joseph Platt (D-17)
Jimmy Tarlau (D-47A)
Jay Walker (D-26)
Alonzo T. Washington (D-22)
Mary L. Washington (D-43)

**Minority Members**
Kathryn L. "Kathy" Afzali (R-4)
Jason C. Buckel (R-1B)
Kevin Bailey Hornberger (R-35A)
Robert B. "Bob" Long (R-6)
Richard W. "Ric" Metzgar (R-6)
Teresa Reilly (R-35B)
Haven N. Shoemaker, Jr. (R-5)
Meagan "Meg" Simonaire (R-31B)

# Massachusetts General Court

State House, Boston, MA 02133
Tel: (617) 722-2000  TTY: (617) 722-2539  Fax: (617) 367-8658

## Massachusetts Senate

State House, Boston, MA 02133
Tel: (617) 722-1455  Fax: (617) 722-2845

President of the Senate **Stanley C. Rosenberg** (D) . . . . . . (617) 722-1500
Education: UMass (Amherst) 1977 BA
President Pro Tempore **Marc R. Pacheco** (D). . . . . . . . . . .(617) 722-1551
Education: UMass (Amherst) 1973 AS; New Hampshire Col 1986 BS; Suffolk 1989 MPA
Majority Leader **Harriette L. Chandler** (D) . . . . . . . . . . . . (617) 722-1544
Education: Wellesley 1959 BAA; Clark U 1973 PhD; Simmons 1983 MBA
Assistant Majority Leader **Cynthia Stone Creem** (D) . . . . (617) 722-1639
Education: Boston U 1964 BS, 1966 JD
Assistant Majority Leader **Mark C. Montigny** (D). . . . . . .(617) 722-1440
Majority Whip **Kenneth J. Donnelly** (D). . . . . . . . . . . . . .(617) 722-1432
Education: UMass (Amherst) BA
Assistant Majority Whip **Michael J. Rodrigues** (D) . . . . . (617) 722-1114
Education: SE Massachusetts BS
Minority Leader **Bruce E. Tarr** (R) . . . . . . . . . . . . . . . . . . (617) 722-1600
Education: Suffolk 1987 BA, 1990 JD
Assistant Minority Leader **Richard J. Ross** (R) . . . . . . . . . (617) 722-1555
Minority Whip **Donald F. Humason, Jr.** (R) . . . . . . . . . . . (617) 722-1415
Education: Westfield State Col 1989 BS
Assistant Minority Whip **Ryan C. Fattman** (R) . . . . . . . . . (617) 722-1420
Clerk of the Senate **William F. Welch** . . . . . . . . . . . . . . . .(617) 722-1276
E-mail: william.welch@masenate.gov

## Senators

**Party Affiliation Statistics:** Republicans: 6, Democrats: 34

Senator **Michael J. "Mike" Barrett** (D-Third Middlesex)
Room 416 . . . . . . . . . . . . . . . . . . . . . . . . . . . . . . . . . . . . .(617) 722-1572
Counties Represented: Middlesex (part)       Fax: (617) 626-0898
Term Expires: 2017
E-mail: mike.barrett@masenate.gov
Committees: Global Warming and Climate Change; Joint Economic Development and Emerging Technologies; Joint Elder Affairs; Joint Health Care Financing; Joint Labor and Workforce Development; Joint Public Service; Joint State Administration and Regulatory Oversight; Joint Veterans and Federal Affairs; Post Audit and Oversight
Education: Harvard 1970 AB; Northeastern 1977 JD
Senator
**Joseph A. Boncore** (D-First Suffolk, Middlesex)
Room 109D. . . . . . . . . . . . . . . . . . . . . . . . . . . . . . . . . . .(617) 722-1634
Counties Represented: Middlesex (part), Suffolk (part)
Term Expires: 2017
E-mail: joseph.boncore@masenate.gov
Education: Massachusetts Law JD
Senator **Michael D. Brady** (D-Second Plymouth, Bristol)
Room 109-E . . . . . . . . . . . . . . . . . . . . . . . . . . . . . . . . . .(617) 722-1200
Counties Represented: Bristol (part), Plymouth (part)
Term Expires: 2017
E-mail: michael.brady@masenate.gov
Committees: Joint Election Laws; Joint Public Service; Joint Veterans and Federal Affairs
Senator **William N. Brownsberger**
(D-Second Suffolk, Middlesex) Room 504 . . . . . . . . . . . .(617) 722-1280
Counties Represented: Middlesex (part), Suffolk (part)
Term Expires: 2017
E-mail: william.brownsberger@masenate.gov
Committees: Ethics; Joint Election Laws; Joint Judiciary; Joint Municipalities and Regional Government; Joint Ways and Means; Ways and Means
Education: Harvard 1978 BA, 1983 JD
Senator **Harriette L. Chandler** (D-First Worcester)
Room 333 . . . . . . . . . . . . . . . . . . . . . . . . . . . . . . . . . . . .(617) 722-1544
Counties Represented: Worcester (part)       Fax: (617) 722-1357
Term Expires: 2017
E-mail: harriette.chandler@masenate.gov
Committees: Ethics; Joint Housing; Joint Rules; Rules

LEGISLATIVE BRANCH

*(continued on next page)*

**Senators** *continued*

Senator **Sonia Rosa Chang-Diaz** (D-Second Suffolk)
Room 111 . . . . . . . . . . . . . . . . . . . . . . . . . . . . . . . . . (617) 722-1673
Counties Represented: Suffolk (part)
Term Expires: 2017
E-mail: sonia.chang-diaz@masenate.gov
Committees: Bonding, Capital Expenditures and State Assets; Joint
Children, Families and Persons With Disabilities; Joint Education; Joint
Judiciary; Joint Public Safety and Homeland Security; Joint Ways and
Means; Redistricting; Steering and Policy; Ways and Means
Education: Virginia 2000 BA

Senator
**Cynthia Stone Creem** (D-First Middlesex, Norfolk)
Room 312A . . . . . . . . . . . . . . . . . . . . . . . . . . . . . . . (617) 722-1639
Counties Represented: Middlesex (part), Norfolk (part)
Term Expires: 2017
E-mail: cynthia.creem@masenate.gov
Committees: Bills in the Third Reading; Ethics; Joint Judiciary; Joint
Rules

Senator **Viriato Manuel "Vinny" deMacedo**
(R-Plymouth, Barnstable) Room 313C . . . . . . . . . . . . . . (617) 722-1330
Counties Represented: Barnstable (part), Plymouth (part)
Term Expires: 2017
E-mail: vinny.demacedo@masenate.gov
Committees: Bonding, Capital Expenditures and State Assets; Joint
Community Development and Small Businesses; Joint Economic
Development and Emerging Technologies; Joint Financial Services;
Joint Municipalities and Regional Government; Joint Rules; Joint
Tourism, Arts and Cultural Development; Joint Ways and Means;
Personnel and Administration; Rules; Ways and Means
Education: King's Col (NY) 1987 BS

Senator **Sal DiDomenico** (D-Middlesex, Suffolk)
Room 208 . . . . . . . . . . . . . . . . . . . . . . . . . . . . . . . . . (617) 722-1650
Counties Represented: Middlesex (part), Suffolk (part)
Term Expires: 2017
E-mail: sal.didomenico@masenate.gov
Committees: Ethics; Joint Election Laws; Joint Ways and Means; Ways
and Means

Senator **Kenneth J. Donnelly** (D-Fourth Middlesex)
Room 413-D . . . . . . . . . . . . . . . . . . . . . . . . . . . . . . . (617) 722-1432
Counties Represented: Middlesex (part)          Fax: (617) 722-1004
Term Expires: 2017
E-mail: kenneth.donnelly@masenate.gov
Committees: Bonding, Capital Expenditures and State Assets; Joint
Election Laws; Joint Mental Health and Substance Abuse; Joint Public
Service; Joint Ways and Means; Personnel and Administration; Ways
and Means

Senator **Eileen M. Donoghue** (D-First Middlesex)
Room 112 . . . . . . . . . . . . . . . . . . . . . . . . . . . . . . . . . (617) 722-1630
Counties Represented: Middlesex (part)          Fax: (617) 722-1001
Term Expires: 2017
E-mail: eileen.donoghue@masenate.gov
Committees: Bonding, Capital Expenditures and State Assets;
Joint Economic Development and Emerging Technologies; Joint
Higher Education; Joint Labor and Workforce Development; Joint
Municipalities and Regional Government; Joint Transportation; Joint
Ways and Means; Personnel and Administration; Rules; Ways and
Means
Education: UMass (Amherst) 1976 BA; Suffolk 1979 JD

Senator **Benjamin Brackett Downing**
(D-Berkshire, Hampshire, Franklin, Hampden)
Room 413F . . . . . . . . . . . . . . . . . . . . . . . . . . . . . . . . (617) 722-1625
Counties Represented: Berkshire, Franklin (part),     Dist: (413) 442-4008
Hampden (part), Hampshire (part)                Fax: (617) 722-1523
Term Expires: 2017                              Dist: (413) 422-4077
E-mail: benjamin.downing@masenate.gov
Committees: Bills in the Third Reading; Global Warming and
Climate Change; Joint Higher Education; Joint Revenue; Joint
Telecommunications, Utilities and Energy; Joint Tourism, Arts and
Cultural Development; Joint Ways and Means; Post Audit and
Oversight; Redistricting; Ways and Means
Education: Providence 2003 BA; Tufts 2008 MA

Senator **James B. Eldridge** (D-Middlesex, Worcester)
Room 218 . . . . . . . . . . . . . . . . . . . . . . . . . . . . . . . . . (617) 722-1120
Counties Represented: Middlesex (part), Worcester     Fax: (617) 722-1089
(part)
Term Expires: 2017
E-mail: james.eldridge@masenate.gov
Committees: Global Warming and Climate Change; Joint Environment,
Natural Resources and Agriculture; Joint Financial Services; Joint
Mental Health and Substance Abuse; Joint State Administration and
Regulatory Oversight; Joint Tourism, Arts and Cultural Development
Education: Johns Hopkins 1995 BA; Boston Col 2000 JD

Senator **Ryan C. Fattman** (R-Worcester, Norfolk)
Room 213A . . . . . . . . . . . . . . . . . . . . . . . . . . . . . . . (617) 722-1420
Counties Represented: Norfolk (part), Worcester (part)
Term Expires: 2017
E-mail: ryan.fattman@masenate.gov
Committees: Global Warming and Climate Change; Joint Consumer
Protection and Professional Licensure; Joint Elder Affairs; Joint
Election Laws; Joint Environment, Natural Resources and Agriculture;
Joint Revenue; Joint Telecommunications, Utilities and Energy;
Personnel and Administration; Post Audit and Oversight

Senator **Jennifer L. Flanagan** (D-Worcester, Middlesex)
Room 312D . . . . . . . . . . . . . . . . . . . . . . . . . . . . . . . (617) 722-1230
Counties Represented: Middlesex (part), Worcester     Fax: (617) 722-1130
(part)
Term Expires: 2017
E-mail: jennifer.flanagan@masenate.gov
Committees: Joint Children, Families and Persons With Disabilities;
Joint Mental Health and Substance Abuse; Joint Public Health; Joint
Public Safety and Homeland Security
Education: UMass (Boston) BA; Fitchburg State MS

Senator **Linda Dorcena Forry** (D-First Suffolk)
Room 410 . . . . . . . . . . . . . . . . . . . . . . . . . . . . . . . . . (617) 722-1150
Counties Represented: Suffolk (part)
Term Expires: 2017
E-mail: linda.dorcenaforry@masenate.gov
Committees: Intergovernmental Affairs; Joint Education; Joint Health
Care Financing; Joint Housing; Joint Mental Health and Substance
Abuse; Joint Transportation

Senator **Anne M. Gobi**
(D-Worcester, Hampden, Hampshire, Middlesex)
Room 513 . . . . . . . . . . . . . . . . . . . . . . . . . . . . . . . . . (617) 722-1540
Counties Represented: Hampden (part), Hampshire (part), Middlesex
(part), Worcester (part)
Term Expires: 2017
E-mail: anne.gobi@masenate.gov
Committees: Intergovernmental Affairs; Joint Economic Development
and Emerging Technologies; Joint Elder Affairs; Joint Environment,
Natural Resources and Agriculture; Joint Housing; Joint
Telecommunications, Utilities and Energy; Joint Veterans and Federal
Affairs
Education: Worcester State Col BS; UMass (Amherst) JD

Senator **Donald F. Humason, Jr.**
(R-Second Hampden, Hampshire) Room 313-A . . . . . . . . (617) 722-1415
Counties Represented: Hampden (part), Hampshire     Fax: (617) 722-1506
(part)
Term Expires: 2017
E-mail: donald.humason@masenate.gov
Committees: Bonding, Capital Expenditures and State Assets;
Intergovernmental Affairs; Joint Children, Families and Persons With
Disabilities; Joint Education; Joint Public Service; Joint Transportation;
Joint Veterans and Federal Affairs; Joint Ways and Means; Ways and
Means

Senator **Patricia D. "Pat" Jehlen** (D-Second Middlesex)
Room 424 . . . . . . . . . . . . . . . . . . . . . . . . . . . . . . . . . (617) 722-1578
Counties Represented: Middlesex (part)          Fax: (617) 722-1117
Term Expires: 2017
E-mail: patricia.jehlen@masenate.gov
Committees: Joint Education; Joint Elder Affairs; Joint Housing; Joint
Judiciary; Joint Ways and Means; Ways and Means
Education: Swarthmore BA; Harvard 1969 MAT

Senator **Brian A. Joyce** (D-Norfolk, Bristol, Plymouth)
Room 320 . . . . . . . . . . . . . . . . . . . . . . . . . . . . . . . . . (617) 722-1643
Counties Represented: Bristol (part), Norfolk (part), Plymouth (part)
Term Expires: 2017
E-mail: brian.a.joyce@masenate.gov
Committees: Joint Health Care Financing; Redistricting
Education: Boston Col 1984 BS; Suffolk 1990 JD

Senator **John F. Keenan** (D-Norfolk, Plymouth)
Room 413-B . . . . . . . . . . . . . . . . . . . . . . . . . . . . . . . (617) 722-1494
Counties Represented: Norfolk (part), Plymouth     Fax: (617) 722-1055
(part)
Term Expires: 2017
E-mail: john.keenan@masenate.gov
Committees: Bills in the Third Reading; Bonding, Capital Expenditures
and State Assets; Joint Children, Families and Persons With
Disabilities; Joint Economic Development and Emerging Technologies;
Joint Financial Services; Joint Housing; Joint Judiciary; Joint State
Administration and Regulatory Oversight; Joint Transportation; Joint
Ways and Means; Ways and Means

Senator
**Barbara A. L'Italien** (D-Second Essex, Middlesex)
Room 413C . . . . . . . . . . . . . . . . . . . . . . . . . . . . . . . . . . (617) 722-1612
Counties Represented: Essex (part), Middlesex (part)
Term Expires: 2017
E-mail: barbara.l'italien@masenate.gov
Committees: Intergovernmental Affairs; Joint Community Development
and Small Businesses; Joint Consumer Protection and Professional
Licensure; Joint Education; Joint Elder Affairs; Joint Health Care
Financing; Joint Higher Education; Joint Municipalities and Regional
Government; Redistricting

Senator **Eric P. Lesser** (D-First Hampden, Hampshire)
Room 519 . . . . . . . . . . . . . . . . . . . . . . . . . . . . . . . . . . (617) 722-1291
Counties Represented: Hampden (part), Hampshire (part)
Term Expires: 2017
E-mail: eric.lesser@masenate.gov
Committees: Joint Economic Development and Emerging Technologies;
Joint Elder Affairs; Joint Financial Services; Joint Public Health;
Joint Revenue; Joint Tourism, Arts and Cultural Development; Joint
Transportation; Joint Veterans and Federal Affairs
Education: Harvard 2007 BA

Senator **Jason M. Lewis** (D-Fifth Middlesex)
Room 511-B . . . . . . . . . . . . . . . . . . . . . . . . . . . . . . . . (617) 722-1206
Counties Represented: Middlesex (part)
Term Expires: 2017
E-mail: jason.lewis@masenate.gov
Committees: Joint Children, Families and Persons With Disabilities;
Joint Education; Joint Labor and Workforce Development; Joint Public
Health; Post Audit and Oversight; Steering and Policy
Education: Harvard 1990, 1995 MBA

Senator **Joan B. Lovely** (D-Second Essex) . . . . . . . . . . . . (617) 722-1410
Counties Represented: Essex (part)          Fax: (617) 722-1347
Term Expires: 2017
State House, Room 413A, Boston, MA 02133
E-mail: joan.lovely@masenate.gov
Committees: Joint Children, Families and Persons With Disabilities;
Joint Mental Health and Substance Abuse; Joint Municipalities and
Regional Government; Joint Public Health; Joint State Administration
and Regulatory Oversight; Joint Tourism, Arts and Cultural
Development; Joint Ways and Means; Ways and Means
Education: Salem State U 2006 BS; Massachusetts Law 2009 JD

Senator **Thomas M. McGee** (D-Third Essex) . . . . . . . . . . (617) 722-1350
Counties Represented: Essex (part)
Term Expires: 2017
State House, Room 109-C, Boston, MA 02133
E-mail: thomas.mcgee@masenate.gov
Committees: Global Warming and Climate Change; Joint Economic
Development and Emerging Technologies; Joint Environment, Natural
Resources and Agriculture; Joint Transportation; Joint Ways and
Means; Ways and Means
Education: Lowell BA; New England 1987 JD

Senator
**Mark C. Montigny** (D-Second Bristol, Plymouth)
Room 312C . . . . . . . . . . . . . . . . . . . . . . . . . . . . . . . . . . (617) 722-1440
Counties Represented: Bristol (part), Plymouth     Fax: (617) 722-1068
(part)
Term Expires: 2017
E-mail: mark.montigny@masenate.gov
Committees: Joint Health Care Financing; Joint Rules; Rules

Senator **Michael O. Moore** (D-Second Worcester)
Room 109-B . . . . . . . . . . . . . . . . . . . . . . . . . . . . . . . . . (617) 722-1485
Counties Represented: Worcester (part)     Fax: (617) 722-1066
Term Expires: 2017
E-mail: michael.moore@masenate.gov
Committees: Bonding, Capital Expenditures and State Assets;
Intergovernmental Affairs; Joint Higher Education; Joint Labor and
Workforce Development; Joint Public Safety and Homeland Security;
Joint Ways and Means; Post Audit and Oversight; Ways and Means
Education: Western New England, MA

Senator **Patrick O'Connor** (R-Plymouth, Norfolk)
Room 520 . . . . . . . . . . . . . . . . . . . . . . . . . . . . . . . . . . . (617) 722-1646
Counties Represented: Norfolk (part), Plymouth (part)
Term Expires: 2017
E-mail: patrick.o'connor@masenate.gov

Senator **Kathleen O'Connor Ives** (D-First Essex)
Room 215 . . . . . . . . . . . . . . . . . . . . . . . . . . . . . . . . . . (617) 722-1604
Counties Represented: Essex (part)          Fax: (617) 722-1999
Term Expires: 2017
E-mail: kathleen.oconnorives@masenate.gov
Committees: Joint Community Development and Small Businesses;
Joint Consumer Protection and Professional Licensure; Joint Financial
Services; Joint Higher Education; Joint Ways and Means; Personnel and
Administration; Steering and Policy; Ways and Means; Ways and
Means
Education: Mount Holyoke 1999 BA; Pace 2007 JD

Senator **Marc R. Pacheco** (D-First Plymouth, Bristol) . . . . . (617) 722-1551
Counties Represented: Bristol (part), Plymouth (part)
Term Expires: 2017
State House, Room 312-B, Boston, MA 02133
E-mail: marc.pacheco@masenate.gov
Committees: Global Warming and Climate Change; Joint
Telecommunications, Utilities and Energy; Personnel and
Administration

Senator
**Michael J. Rodrigues** (D-First Bristol, Plymouth)
Room 213-B . . . . . . . . . . . . . . . . . . . . . . . . . . . . . . . . (617) 722-1114
Counties Represented: Bristol (part), Plymouth     Dist: (508) 646-0650
(part)                                        Fax: (617) 722-1498
Term Expires: 2017
E-mail: michael.rodrigues@masenate.gov
Committees: Intergovernmental Affairs; Joint Community Development
and Small Businesses; Joint Consumer Protection and Professional
Licensure; Joint Financial Services; Joint Public Service; Joint
Revenue; Joint State Administration and Regulatory Oversight; Joint
Telecommunications, Utilities and Energy

Senator **Stanley C. Rosenberg**
(D-Hampshire, Franklin, Worcester) Room 332 . . . . . . . . (617) 722-1500
Counties Represented: Franklin (part), Hampshire     Fax: (617) 722-1062
(part), Worcester (part)
Term Expires: 2017
E-mail: stan.rosenberg@masenate.gov

Senator **Richard J. Ross** (R-Norfolk, Bristol, Middlesex)
Room 419 . . . . . . . . . . . . . . . . . . . . . . . . . . . . . . . . . . (617) 722-1555
Counties Represented: Bristol (part), Middlesex (part), Norfolk (part)
Term Expires: 2017
E-mail: richard.ross@masenate.gov
Committees: Ethics; Joint Higher Education; Joint Housing; Joint
Judiciary; Joint Mental Health and Substance Abuse; Joint Public
Health; Joint Public Safety and Homeland Security; Joint Ways and
Means; Ways and Means

Senator **Michael F. Rush** (D-Norfolk, Suffolk)
Room 511C . . . . . . . . . . . . . . . . . . . . . . . . . . . . . . . . . (617) 722-1348
Counties Represented: Norfolk (part), Suffolk (part)     Fax: (617) 722-1071
Term Expires: 2017
E-mail: mike.rush@masenate.gov
Committees: Joint Community Development and Small Businesses;
Joint Environment, Natural Resources and Agriculture; Joint
Transportation; Joint Veterans and Federal Affairs; Joint Ways and
Means; Personnel and Administration; Ways and Means
Education: Providence BA, MA; S New England Law JD

Senator **Karen E. Spilka** (D-Second Middlesex, Norfolk)
Room 212 . . . . . . . . . . . . . . . . . . . . . . . . . . . . . . . . . . (617) 722-1640
Counties Represented: Middlesex (part), Norfolk     Dist: (508) 872-6677
(part)                                        Fax: (617) 722-1077
Term Expires: 2017
E-mail: karen.spilka@masenate.gov
Committees: Joint Rules; Joint Ways and Means; Rules; Ways and
Means
Education: Cornell 1975 BA; Northeastern 1980 JD

Senator **Bruce E. Tarr** (R-First Essex, Middlesex)
Room 308 . . . . . . . . . . . . . . . . . . . . . . . . . . . . . . . . . . (617) 722-1600
Counties Represented: Essex (part), Middlesex     Fax: (617) 722-2845
(part)
Term Expires: 2017
E-mail: bruce.tarr@masenate.gov
Committees: Bills in the Third Reading; Ethics; Joint Health Care
Financing; Joint Labor and Workforce Development; Joint State
Administration and Regulatory Oversight; Post Audit and Oversight;
Redistricting; Steering and Policy

*(continued on next page)*

**Senators** *continued*

**Senator James E. Timilty** (D-Bristol, Norfolk)
Room 507 . . . . . . . . . . . . . . . . . . . . . . . . . . . . . . . . (617) 722-1222
Counties Represented: Bristol (part), Norfolk (part)     Fax: (617) 722-1056
Term Expires: 2017
E-mail: james.timilty@masenate.gov
Committees: Joint Consumer Protection and Professional Licensure;
Joint Environment, Natural Resources and Agriculture; Joint
Municipalities and Regional Government; Joint Public Health; Joint
Public Safety and Homeland Security; Joint Public Service; Joint
Revenue; Joint Ways and Means; Redistricting; Ways and Means

**Senator James T. Welch** (D-Hampden) Room 309 . . . . . . (617) 722-1660
Counties Represented: Hampden (part)     Dist: (413) 737-7756
Term Expires: 2017     Fax: (413) 737-7747
722 Union Street, West Springfield, MA 01089
E-mail: james.welch@masenate.gov
Committees: Joint Election Laws; Joint Health Care Financing; Joint
Public Safety and Homeland Security; Post Audit and Oversight
Education: Westfield State Col BS

**Senator Daniel A. "Dan" Wolf** (D-Cape and Islands)
Room 405 . . . . . . . . . . . . . . . . . . . . . . . . . . . . . . . . (617) 722-1570
Counties Represented: Barnstable (part), Dukes,     Dist: (508) 775-0162
Nantucket     Fax: (617) 722-1271
Term Expires: 2017
E-mail: daniel.wolf@masenate.gov
Committees: Joint Community Development and Small Businesses;
Joint Labor and Workforce Development; Joint Revenue; Joint
Telecommunications, Utilities and Energy; Joint Tourism, Arts and
Cultural Development; Steering and Policy
Education: Germantown (Philadelphia, PA); Wesleyan U

# Senate Standing Committees

## Bills in the Third Reading
State House, Room 109-D, Boston, MA 02133
Tel: (617) 722-1634

| **Majority Members** | **Minority Members** |
| --- | --- |
| Cynthia Stone Creem (D) *Vice Chair* | Bruce E. Tarr (R) |
| Benjamin Brackett Downing (D) | |
| John F. Keenan (D) | |

## Bonding, Capital Expenditures and State Assets
State House, Room 413B, Boston, MA 02133
Tel: (617) 722-1494

| **Majority Members** | **Minority Members** |
| --- | --- |
| John F. Keenan (D) *Chair* | Viriato Manuel "Vinny" deMacedo (R) |
| Sonia Rosa Chang-Diaz (D) *Vice Chair* | Donald F. Humason, Jr. (R) |
| Kenneth J. Donnelly (D) | |
| Eileen M. Donoghue (D) | |
| Michael O. Moore (D) | |

## Ethics
State House, Room 333, Boston, MA 02133
Tel: (617) 722-1639

| **Majority Members** | **Minority Members** |
| --- | --- |
| Cynthia Stone Creem (D) *Chair* | Richard J. Ross (R) |
| William N. Brownsberger (D) *Vice Chair* | Bruce E. Tarr (R) |
| Harriette L. Chandler (D) | |
| Sal DiDomenico (D) | |

## Global Warming and Climate Change
State House, Room 312-B, Boston, MA 02133
Tel: (617) 722-1551

| **Majority Members** | **Minority Members** |
| --- | --- |
| Marc R. Pacheco (D) *Chair* | Ryan C. Fattman (R) |
| James B. Eldridge (D) *Vice Chair* | |
| Michael J. "Mike" Barrett (D) | |
| Benjamin Brackett Downing (D) | |
| Thomas M. McGee (D) | |

## Intergovernmental Affairs
State House, Room 419, Boston, MA 02133
Tel: (617) 722-1150

| **Majority Members** | **Minority Members** |
| --- | --- |
| Linda Dorcena Forry (D) *Chair* | Donald F. Humason, Jr. (R) |
| Barbara A. L'Italien (D) *Vice Chair* | |
| Anne M. Gobi (D) | |
| Michael O. Moore (D) | |
| Michael J. Rodrigues (D) | |

## Personnel and Administration
State House, Room 504, Boston, MA 02133
Tel: (617) 722-1348

| **Majority Members** | **Minority Members** |
| --- | --- |
| Michael F. Rush (D) *Chair* | Viriato Manuel "Vinny" deMacedo (R) |
| Kathleen O'Connor Ives (D) *Vice Chair* | Ryan C. Fattman (R) |
| Kenneth J. Donnelly (D) | |
| Eileen M. Donoghue (D) | |
| Marc R. Pacheco (D) | |

## Post Audit and Oversight
State House, Room 313A, Boston, MA 02133
Tel: (617) 722-1572

| **Majority Members** | **Minority Members** |
| --- | --- |
| Michael J. "Mike" Barrett (D) *Chair* | Bruce E. Tarr (R) *Ranking Minority Member* |
| Benjamin Brackett Downing (D) *Vice Chair* | Ryan C. Fattman (R) |
| Jason M. Lewis (D) | |
| Michael O. Moore (D) | |
| James T. Welch (D) | |

## Redistricting
State House, Room 413F, Boston, MA 02133
Tel: (617) 722-1625

| **Majority Members** | **Minority Members** |
| --- | --- |
| Benjamin Brackett Downing (D) *Chair* | Bruce E. Tarr (R) |
| Brian A. Joyce (D) *Vice Chair* | |
| Sonia Rosa Chang-Diaz (D) | |
| Barbara A. L'Italien (D) | |
| James E. Timilty (D) | |

## Rules
State House, Room 312-C, Boston, MA 02133
Tel: (617) 722-1440

| **Majority Members** | **Minority Members** |
| --- | --- |
| Mark C. Montigny (D) *Chair* | Viriato Manuel "Vinny" deMacedo (R) |
| Eileen M. Donoghue (D) *Vice Chair* | |
| Harriette L. Chandler (D) | |
| Karen E. Spilka (D) | |

## Steering and Policy
State House, Room 405, Boston, MA 02133
Tel: (617) 722-1570

| **Majority Members** | **Minority Members** |
| --- | --- |
| Daniel A. "Dan" Wolf (D) *Chair* | Bruce E. Tarr (R) |
| Jason M. Lewis (D) *Vice Chair* | |
| Sonia Rosa Chang-Diaz (D) | |
| Kathleen O'Connor Ives (D) | |

## Ways and Means

State House, Room 212, Boston, MA 02133
Tel: (617) 722-1481

| Majority Members | Minority Members |
|---|---|
| Karen E. Spilka (D) *Chair* | Viriato Manuel "Vinny" deMacedo |
| Sal DiDomenico (D) *Vice Chair* | (R) |
| Patricia D. "Pat" Jehlen (D) | Donald F. Humason, Jr. (R) |
| *Assistant Vice Chair* | Richard J. Ross (R) |
| William N. Brownsberger (D) | |
| Sonia Rosa Chang-Diaz (D) | |
| Kenneth J. Donnelly (D) | |
| Eileen M. Donoghue (D) | |
| Benjamin Brackett Downing (D) | |
| John F. Keenan (D) | |
| Joan B. Lovely (D) | |
| Thomas M. McGee (D) | |
| Michael O. Moore (D) | |
| Kathleen O'Connor Ives (D) | |
| Michael F. Rush (D) | |
| James E. Timilty (D) | |

# Massachusetts House of Representatives

State House, Boston, MA 02133
Tel: (617) 722-2000  Fax: (617) 722-2798

Speaker of the House **Robert A. DeLeo** (D) . . . . . . . . . . . (617) 722-2500
  Education: Northeastern BA; Suffolk JD
Speaker Pro Tem **Patricia A. Haddad** (D) . . . . . . . . . . . . (617) 722-2600
  Education: Bridgewater State Col 1972 BS
Majority Leader **Ronald Mariano** (D) . . . . . . . . . . . . . . . .(617) 722-2300
  Education: Northeastern BS; UMass (Boston) 1972 MEd
Assistant Majority Leader **Byron Rushing** (D) . . . . . . . . . .(617) 722-2783
Second Assistant Majority Leader
  **Garrett J. Bradley** (D) . . . . . . . . . . . . . . . . . . . . (617) 722-2520
  Education: Boston Col 1992 BA, 1995 JD
Second Assistant Majority Leader **Paul J. Donato** (D) . . . . (617) 722-2180
Minority Leader **Bradley H. Jones, Jr.** (R) . . . . . . . . . . . . (617) 722-2100
  Education: Harvard 1988 ALB
Assistant Minority Leader **Bradford R. Hill** (R) . . . . . . . . . (617) 722-2100
Second Assistant Minority Leader
  **Elizabeth A. Poirier** (R) . . . . . . . . . . . . . . . . . . . . . (617) 722-2100
Third Assistant Minority Leader **Paul K. Frost** (R) . . . . . . . (617) 722-2489
  Education: UMass (Amherst) 1993 BA
Third Assistant Minority Leader
  **Susan Williams Gifford** (R) . . . . . . . . . . . . . . . . . . . . . (617) 722-2976
  Education: Western Michigan BA
Clerk of the House **Steven T. James** . . . . . . . . . . . . . . . . . (617) 722-2356

## Representatives

**Party Affiliation Statistics:** Republicans: 34, Democrats: 126

Representative **James Arciero** (D-Middlesex-2)
  Room 172 . . . . . . . . . . . . . . . . . . . . . . . . . . . . . . . . . . . (617) 722-2019
  Counties Represented: Middlesex (part)
  Term Expires: 2017
  E-mail: james.arciero@mahouse.gov
  Committees: Joint Consumer Protection and Professional Licensure;
  Joint Higher Education; Joint Revenue; Joint Veterans and Federal
  Affairs
Representative **Brian M. Ashe** (D-Hampden-2)
  Room 466 . . . . . . . . . . . . . . . . . . . . . . . . . . . . . . . . . . (617) 722-2017
  Counties Represented: Hampden (part)          Dist: (413) 754-4184
  Term Expires: 2017                            Fax: (617) 722-2848
  E-mail: brian.ashe@mahouse.gov
  Committees: Joint Election Laws; Personnel and Administration;
  Redistricting; Steering, Policy and Scheduling
Representative **Cory Atkins** (D-Middlesex-14) Room 195 . .(617) 722-2692
  Counties Represented: Middlesex (part)        Dist: (978) 369-5299
  Term Expires: 2017                            Fax: (617) 722-2822
  1540 Monument Street, Concord, MA 01742
  E-mail: cory.atkins@mahouse.gov
  Committees: Joint Tourism, Arts and Cultural Development
  Education: UMass (Boston) BS

Representative **Bruce J. Ayers** (D-Norfolk-1) . . . . . . . . . . .(617) 722-2230
  Counties Represented: Norfolk (part)
  Term Expires: 2017
  State House, Room 167, Boston, MA 02133
  E-mail: bruce.ayers@mahouse.gov
  Committees: Joint Elder Affairs; Joint Public Safety and Homeland
  Security; Joint Tourism, Arts and Cultural Development; Steering,
  Policy and Scheduling
Representative **Ruth Brim Balser** (D-Middlesex-12) . . . . . . (617) 722-2396
  Counties Represented: Middlesex (part)        Fax: (617) 626-0119
  Term Expires: 2017
  State House, Room 136, Boston, MA 02133
  E-mail: ruth.balser@mahouse.gov
  Committees: Joint Mental Health and Substance Abuse; Joint Public
  Health; Joint Ways and Means; Technology and Intergovernmental
  Affairs; Ways and Means
  Education: Rochester AB; NYU 1978 PhD
Representative **Christine P. Barber** (D-Middlesex-34)
  Room 236 . . . . . . . . . . . . . . . . . . . . . . . . . . . . . . . . (617) 722-2430
  Counties Represented: Middlesex (part)
  Term Expires: 2017
  E-mail: christine.barber@mahouse.gov
  Committees: Joint Environment, Natural Resources and Agriculture;
  Joint Health Care Financing; Joint Public Health; Personnel and
  Administration
  Education: Holy Cross Col BA; UMass (Amherst) MPA
Representative **Fred Jay Barrows** (R-Bristol-1)
  Room 542 . . . . . . . . . . . . . . . . . . . . . . . . . . . . . . . . . . (617) 722-2488
  Counties Represented: Bristol (part), Norfolk (part)   Fax: (617) 722-2390
  Term Expires: 2017
  E-mail: f.jay.barrows@mahouse.gov
  Committees: Ethics; Joint Health Care Financing
Representative **Jennifer E. Benson** (D-Middlesex-37)
  Room 42 . . . . . . . . . . . . . . . . . . . . . . . . . . . . . . . . . . (617) 722-2014
  Counties Represented: Middlesex (part), Worcester   Dist: (978) 582-4146
  (part)                                                ext. 450
  Term Expires: 2017                            Fax: (617) 722-2813
  960 Massachusetts Avenue, Lunenburg, MA 01462-1300
  E-mail: jennifer.benson@mahouse.gov
  Committees: Joint Consumer Protection and Professional Licensure
  Education: Florida Atlantic 1995 BA
Representative
  **Donald R. Berthiaume, Jr.** (R-Worcester-5) Room 540 . .(617) 722-2090
  Counties Represented: Hampshire (part), Worcester (part)
  Term Expires: 2017
  E-mail: donald.berthiaume@mahouse.gov
  Committees: Joint Environment, Natural Resources and Agriculture;
  Joint Veterans and Federal Affairs; Personnel and Administration
Representative **Nicholas A. Boldyga** (R-Hampden-3)
  Room 167 . . . . . . . . . . . . . . . . . . . . . . . . . . . . . . . . . (617) 722-2810
  Counties Represented: Hampden (part)          Fax: (617) 626-0137
  Term Expires: 2017
  E-mail: nicholas.boldyga@mahouse.gov
  Committees: Bonding, Capital Expenditures and State Assets; Joint
  Ways and Means; Ways and Means
Representative **Garrett J. Bradley** (D-Plymouth-3)
  Room 479 . . . . . . . . . . . . . . . . . . . . . . . . . . . . . . . . . (617) 722-2520
  Counties Represented: Norfolk (part), Plymouth   Dist: (781) 749-3331
  (part)
  Term Expires: 2017
  88 Chief Justice Cushing Highway, Hingham, MA 08043
  E-mail: garrett.bradley@mahouse.gov
  Committees: Ethics; Joint Rules; Rules
Representative **Paul Brodeur** (D-Middlesex-32)
  Room 160 . . . . . . . . . . . . . . . . . . . . . . . . . . . . . . . . . (617) 722-2304
  Counties Represented: Middlesex (part)        Fax: (617) 626-0142
  Term Expires: 2017
  E-mail: paul.brodeur@mahouse.gov
  Committees: Joint Health Care Financing; Joint Public Service; Joint
  Telecommunications, Utilities and Energy; Joint Ways and Means;
  Ways and Means
Representative **Antonio F. D. Cabral** (D-Bristol-13)
  Room 466 . . . . . . . . . . . . . . . . . . . . . . . . . . . . . . . . . (617) 722-2017
  Counties Represented: Bristol (part)          Fax: (617) 722-2813
  Term Expires: 2017
  E-mail: antonio.cabral@mahouse.gov
  Committees: Bonding, Capital Expenditures and State Assets
  Education: UMass (Dartmouth) 1978 BA

*(continued on next page)*

**LEGISLATIVE BRANCH**

**Representatives** continued

Representative **Daniel F. "Dan" Cahill** (D-Essex-10) . . . . . (617) 722-2020
Counties Represented: Essex (part)
Term Expires: 2017
E-mail: daniel.cahill@mahouse.gov
Committees: Joint Labor and Workforce Development; Joint Public Service; Personnel and Administration
Education: Northeastern BS; Suffolk MS, JD

Representative **Thomas J. Calter III** (D-Plymouth-12)
Room 446 . . . . . . . . . . . . . . . . . . . . . . . . . . . . . . . . . . (617) 722-2460
Counties Represented: Plymouth (part)          Dist: (508) 732-0034
Term Expires: 2017                             Fax: (617) 722-2598
E-mail: thomas.calter@mahouse.gov             Dist: (508) 732-0035
Committees: Global Warming and Climate Change; Joint Community Development and Small Businesses; Joint Economic Development and Emerging Technologies; Joint Higher Education

Representative **Kate Campanale** (R-Worcester-17)
Room 542 . . . . . . . . . . . . . . . . . . . . . . . . . . . . . . . . . . (617) 722-2488
Counties Represented: Worcester (part)
Term Expires: 2017
E-mail: kate.campanale@mahouse.gov
Committees: Joint Health Care Financing; Joint Ways and Means; Ways and Means

Representative **Linda Dean Campbell** (D-Essex-15)
Room 236 . . . . . . . . . . . . . . . . . . . . . . . . . . . . . . . . . . (617) 722-2430
Counties Represented: Essex (part)            Fax: (617) 722-9278
Term Expires: 2017
42 Sugar Pine Lane, Methuen, MA 01844
E-mail: linda.dean.campbell@mahouse.gov
Committees: Joint Economic Development and Emerging Technologies; Joint Public Safety and Homeland Security; Joint State Administration and Regulatory Oversight; Joint Ways and Means; Ways and Means

Representative **James M. Cantwell** (D-Plymouth-4)
Room 22 . . . . . . . . . . . . . . . . . . . . . . . . . . . . . . . . . . . (617) 722-2140
Counties Represented: Plymouth (part)         Fax: (617) 626-0835
Term Expires: 2017
988 Plain Street, Marshfield, MA 02050
E-mail: james.cantwell@mahouse.gov
Committees: Joint Environment, Natural Resources and Agriculture; Joint Financial Services; Joint Public Safety and Homeland Security; Joint Ways and Means; Ways and Means

Representative **Gailanne M. Cariddi** (D-Berkshire-1)
Room 36 . . . . . . . . . . . . . . . . . . . . . . . . . . . . . . . . . . . (617) 722-2370
Counties Represented: Berkshire (part)        Fax: (617) 626-0143
Term Expires: 2017
E-mail: gailanne.cariddi@mahouse.gov
Committees: Joint Economic Development and Emerging Technologies

Representative **Evandro C. Carvalho** (D-Suffolk-5)
Room 446 . . . . . . . . . . . . . . . . . . . . . . . . . . . . . . . . . . (617) 722-2460
Counties Represented: Suffolk (part)
Term Expires: 2017
E-mail: evandro.carvalho@mahouse.gov
Committees: Joint Consumer Protection and Professional Licensure; Joint Economic Development and Emerging Technologies; Joint Judiciary; Joint Transportation
Education: UMass (Amherst); Howard U JD

Representative
**Gerard J. "Gerry" Cassidy** (D-Plymouth-9)
Room 134 . . . . . . . . . . . . . . . . . . . . . . . . . . . . . . . . . . (617) 722-2400
Counties Represented: Plymouth (part)
Term Expires: 2017
E-mail: gerard.cassidy@mahouse.gov
Committees: Joint Higher Education; Post Audit and Oversight

Representative **Tackey Chan** (D-Norfolk-2) . . . . . . . . . . . (617) 722-2430
Counties Represented: Norfolk (part)          Fax: (617) 626-0146
Term Expires: 2017
State House, Room 236, Boston, MA 02133
E-mail: tackey.chan@mahouse.gov
Committees: Joint Community Development and Small Businesses; Joint Consumer Protection and Professional Licensure; Joint Telecommunications, Utilities and Energy; Joint Ways and Means; Ways and Means

Representative **Nick Collins** (D-Suffolk-4) Room 39 . . . . . . (617) 722-2014
Counties Represented: Suffolk (part)          Fax: (617) 626-0154
Term Expires: 2017
E-mail: nick.collins@mahouse.gov
Committees: Joint Ways and Means; Personnel and Administration; Redistricting; Technology and Intergovernmental Affairs; Ways and Means

Representative **Edward Coppinger** (D-Suffolk-10) . . . . . . (617) 722-2080
Counties Represented: Norfolk (part), Suffolk (part)   Fax: (617) 626-0158
Term Expires: 2017
State House, Room 26, Boston, MA 02133
E-mail: edward.coppinger@mahouse.gov
Committees: Redistricting

Representative **Brendan P. Crighton** (D-Essex-11)
Room 130 . . . . . . . . . . . . . . . . . . . . . . . . . . . . . . . . . . (617) 722-2130
Counties Represented: Essex (part)
Term Expires: 2017
E-mail: brendan.crighton@mahouse.gov
Committees: Joint Community Development and Small Businesses; Joint Economic Development and Emerging Technologies; Joint Public Health; Post Audit and Oversight

Representative **Claire D. Cronin** (D-Plymouth-11)
Room 136 . . . . . . . . . . . . . . . . . . . . . . . . . . . . . . . . . . (617) 722-2396
Counties Represented: Bristol (part), Plymouth (part)
Term Expires: 2017
E-mail: claire.cronin@mahouse.gov
Committees: Joint Judiciary; Joint Telecommunications, Utilities and Energy; Joint Ways and Means; Post Audit and Oversight; Ways and Means
Education: Stonehill 1982 BA; Suffolk 1985 JD

Representative **Daniel R. Cullinane** (D-Suffolk-12)
Room 121 . . . . . . . . . . . . . . . . . . . . . . . . . . . . . . . . . . (617) 722-2006
Counties Represented: Norfolk (part), Suffolk (part)   Fax: (617) 626-0456
Term Expires: 2017
E-mail: daniel.cullinane@mahouse.gov
Committees: Joint Elder Affairs; Joint Financial Services; Joint Health Care Financing; Post Audit and Oversight
Education: Providence 2007

Representative **Mark J. Cusack** (D-Norfolk-5) . . . . . . . . . . (617) 722-2400
Counties Represented: Norfolk (part)          Fax: (617) 626-0159
Term Expires: 2017
State House, Room 134, Boston, MA 02133
E-mail: mark.cusack@mahouse.gov
Committees: Technology and Intergovernmental Affairs

Representative **Josh S. Cutler** (D-Plymouth-6)
Suite 473F . . . . . . . . . . . . . . . . . . . . . . . . . . . . . . . . . (617) 722-2210
Counties Represented: Plymouth (part)         Fax: (617) 626-0325
Term Expires: 2017
235 Washington Street, Pembroke, MA 02359
E-mail: josh.cutler@mahouse.gov
Committees: Bonding, Capital Expenditures and State Assets; Joint Environment, Natural Resources and Agriculture; Joint Telecommunications, Utilities and Energy; Post Audit and Oversight
Education: Skidmore 1994 BA; Suffolk 2001 JD

Representative **Angelo D'Emilia** (R-Plymouth-8) . . . . . . . . (617) 722-2488
Counties Represented: Bristol (part), Plymouth   Dist: (508) 697-2700
(part)                                          Fax: (617) 626-0170
Term Expires: 2017
State House, Room 548, Boston, MA 02133
31 Perkins Street, Bridgewater, MA 02324
E-mail: angelo.d'emilia@mahouse.gov
Committees: Bills in the Third Reading; Joint Community Development and Small Businesses; Joint Ways and Means; Ways and Means

Representative **Michael Day** (D-Middlesex-31)
Room 448 . . . . . . . . . . . . . . . . . . . . . . . . . . . . . . . . . . (617) 722-2582
Counties Represented: Middlesex (part)
Term Expires: 2017
E-mail: michael.day@mahouse.gov
Committees: Joint Education; Joint Judiciary; Joint Mental Health and Substance Abuse; Post Audit and Oversight

Representative **Marjorie C. Decker** (D-Middlesex-25)
Room 155 . . . . . . . . . . . . . . . . . . . . . . . . . . . . . . . . . . (617) 722-2450
Counties Represented: Middlesex (part)        Fax: (617) 626-0337
Term Expires: 2017
E-mail: marjorie.decker@mahouse.gov
Committees: Global Warming and Climate Change; Joint Health Care Financing; Joint Housing; Joint Ways and Means; Ways and Means
Education: UMass (Amherst) BA; Harvard 2007 MA

Representative **David F. DeCoste** (R-Plymouth-5)
Room 236 . . . . . . . . . . . . . . . . . . . . . . . . . . . . . . . . . . (617) 722-2430
Counties Represented: Plymouth (part)
Term Expires: 2017
E-mail: david.decoste@mahouse.gov
Committees: Joint Housing; Joint Public Service; Joint Veterans and Federal Affairs

LEGISLATIVE BRANCH

Representative **Robert A. DeLeo** (D-Suffolk-19)
Room 356 . . . . . . . . . . . . . . . . . . . . . . . . . . . . . (617) 722-2500
Counties Represented: Suffolk (part)     Dist: (781) 289-8965
Term Expires: 2017                        Fax: (617) 722-2008
220 Beach Street, Revere, MA 02151        Dist: (781) 289-0582
E-mail: robert.deleo@mahouse.gov

Representative **Brian S. Dempsey** (D-Essex-3)
Room 243 . . . . . . . . . . . . . . . . . . . . . . . . . . . . . (617) 722-2990
Counties Represented: Essex (part)        Fax: (617) 722-2215
Term Expires: 2017
E-mail: brian.dempsey@mahouse.gov
Committees: Joint Ways and Means; Ways and Means
Education: UMass (Lowell) BA

Representative **Marcos A. Devers** (D-Essex-16)
Room 43 . . . . . . . . . . . . . . . . . . . . . . . . . . . . . . (617) 722-2030
Counties Represented: Essex (part)        Fax: (617) 722-2238
Term Expires: 2017
E-mail: marcos.devers@mahouse.gov
Committees: Joint Education; Joint Housing; Joint Labor and
Workforce Development; Joint Ways and Means; Ways and Means
Education: U A Santo Domingo 1978 BCE

Representative **Geoffrey "Geoff" Diehl** (R-Plymouth-7) . . . (617) 722-2810
Counties Represented: Plymouth (part)     Dist: (781) 261-3103
Term Expires: 2017
529 Washington Street, Whitman, MA 02382
State House, Room 167, Boston, MA 02133
E-mail: geoff.diehl@mahouse.gov
Committees: Global Warming and Climate Change; Joint Housing;
Personnel and Administration

Representative **Diana DiZoglio** (D-Essex-14) Room 33 . . . . (617) 722-2060
Counties Represented: Essex (part)
Term Expires: 2017
E-mail: diana.dizoglio@mahouse.gov
Committees: Joint Education; Joint Election Laws; Joint Mental Health
and Substance Abuse; Steering, Policy and Scheduling
Education: Wellesley BA

Representative **Daniel M. Donahue** (D-Worcester-16)
Room 122 . . . . . . . . . . . . . . . . . . . . . . . . . . . . . (617) 722-2006
Counties Represented: Worcester (part)    Fax: (617) 626-0457
Term Expires: 2017
E-mail: daniel.donahue@mahouse.gov
Committees: Bonding, Capital Expenditures and State Assets; Joint
Labor and Workforce Development; Joint Telecommunications, Utilities
and Energy; Joint Transportation
Education: Col Holy Cross 2009

Representative **Paul J. Donato** (D-Middlesex-35)
Room 481 . . . . . . . . . . . . . . . . . . . . . . . . . . . . . (617) 722-2180
Counties Represented: Middlesex (part)    Dist: (781) 395-1683
Term Expires: 2017                        Fax: (617) 722-2347
271 Spring Street, Medford, MA 02155      Dist: (781) 395-2871
E-mail: paul.donato@mahouse.gov
Committees: Ethics; Joint Rules; Rules

Representative **Shawn Dooley** (R-Norfolk-9) Room 167 . . (617) 722-2810
Counties Represented: Norfolk (part)
Term Expires: 2017
E-mail: shawn.dooley@mahouse.gov
Committees: Joint Financial Services; Joint Revenue; Joint Ways and
Means; Ways and Means
Education: Auburn BA

Representative **Michelle M. DuBois** (D-Plymouth-10)
Room 146 . . . . . . . . . . . . . . . . . . . . . . . . . . . . . (617) 722-2011
Counties Represented: Plymouth (part)
Term Expires: 2017
E-mail: michelle.dubois@mahouse.gov
Committees: Bonding, Capital Expenditures and State Assets; Joint
Children, Families and Persons With Disabilities; Joint Public Service;
Joint State Administration and Regulatory Oversight

Representative **Peter J. Durant** (R-Worcester-6)
Room 33 . . . . . . . . . . . . . . . . . . . . . . . . . . . . . . (617) 722-2060
Counties Represented: Worcester (part)
Term Expires: 2017
E-mail: peter.durant@mahouse.gov
Committees: Joint Ways and Means; Post Audit and Oversight; Ways
and Means

Representative **James J. Dwyer** (D-Middlesex-30)
Room 254 . . . . . . . . . . . . . . . . . . . . . . . . . . . . . (617) 722-2220
Counties Represented: Middlesex (part)    Fax: (617) 626-0831
Term Expires: 2017
E-mail: james.dwyer@mahouse.gov
Committees: Bonding, Capital Expenditures and State Assets; Joint
Public Safety and Homeland Security; Joint Revenue; Steering, Policy
and Scheduling

Representative **Carolyn C. Dykema** (D-Middlesex-8)
Room 127 . . . . . . . . . . . . . . . . . . . . . . . . . . . . . (617) 722-2680
Counties Represented: Middlesex (part), Worcester    Fax: (617) 722-2239
(part)
Term Expires: 2017
E-mail: carolyn.dykema@mahouse.gov
Committees: Joint Children, Families and Persons With Disabilities;
Joint Environment, Natural Resources and Agriculture; Joint Housing;
Joint Ways and Means; Ways and Means

Representative **Lori A. Ehrlich** (D-Essex-8) Room 236 . . . . (617) 722-2430
Counties Represented: Essex (part)
Term Expires: 2017
E-mail: lori.ehrlich@mahouse.gov
Committees: Joint Health Care Financing

Representative **Tricia Farley-Bouvier** (D-Berkshire-3)
Room 156 . . . . . . . . . . . . . . . . . . . . . . . . . . . . . (617) 722-2240
Counties Represented: Berkshire (part)
Term Expires: 2017
113 Oliver Avenue, Pittsfield, MA 01201
E-mail: tricia.farley-bouvier@mahouse.gov
Committees: Global Warming and Climate Change; Joint Children,
Families and Persons With Disabilities; Joint Mental Health and
Substance Abuse; Steering, Policy and Scheduling

Representative **Kimberly Ferguson** (R-Worcester-1) . . . . . . (617) 722-2236
Counties Represented: Worcester (part)    Fax: (617) 626-0182
Term Expires: 2017
State House, Room 473B, Boston, MA 02133
E-mail: kimberly.ferguson@mahouse.gov
Committees: Joint Children, Families and Persons With Disabilities;
Joint Education; Ways and Means

Representative **John V. Fernandes** (D-Worcester-10)
Room 136 . . . . . . . . . . . . . . . . . . . . . . . . . . . . . (617) 722-2396
Counties Represented: Norfolk (part), Worcester    Dist: (508) 473-3063
(part)                                    Fax: (617) 626-0706
Term Expires: 2017                        Dist: (508) 478-4420
12 Main Street, Milford, MA 01757
E-mail: john.fernandes@mahouse.gov
Committees: Joint Judiciary

Representative **Ann-Margaret Ferrante** (D-Essex-5)
Room 26 . . . . . . . . . . . . . . . . . . . . . . . . . . . . . . (617) 722-2080
Counties Represented: Essex (part)        Fax: (617) 722-2339
Term Expires: 2017
E-mail: ann-margaret.ferrante@mahouse.gov
Committees: Joint Community Development and Small Businesses

Representative **Michael J. Finn** (D-Hampden-6) . . . . . . . . . (617) 722-2400
Counties Represented: Hampden (part)      Fax: (617) 626-0189
Term Expires: 2017
State House, Room 134, Boston, MA 02133
E-mail: michael.finn@mahouse.gov
Committees: Joint Health Care Financing; Joint Tourism, Arts and
Cultural Development; Joint Transportation; Joint Ways and Means;
Ways and Means

Representative **Carole A. Fiola** (D-Bristol-6) Room 443 . . . (617) 722-2460
Counties Represented: Bristol (part)      Fax: (617) 626-0460
Term Expires: 2017
E-mail: carole.fiola@mahouse.gov
Committees: Joint Economic Development and Emerging Technologies;
Joint Mental Health and Substance Abuse; Joint Municipalities and
Regional Government; Joint Public Service
Education: UMass (Amherst) 1982 BA

Representative **Gloria L. Fox** (D-Suffolk-7) Room 167 . . . . (617) 722-2810
Counties Represented: Suffolk (part)      Fax: (617) 722-2846
Term Expires: 2017
Seven Harold Park, Boston, MA 02119
E-mail: gloria.fox@mahouse.gov
Committees: Joint Elder Affairs; Joint Veterans and Federal Affairs;
Joint Ways and Means; Redistricting; Ways and Means

Representative **Paul K. Frost** (R-Worcester-7) Room 542 . . (617) 722-2489
Counties Represented: Worcester (part)
Term Expires: 2017
E-mail: paul.frost@mahouse.gov
Committees: Joint Election Laws; Joint Rules; Redistricting

Representative **William C. Galvin** (D-Norfolk-6)
Room 166 . . . . . . . . . . . . . . . . . . . . . . . . . . . . . (617) 722-2692
Counties Represented: Norfolk (part)
Term Expires: 2017
E-mail: william.galvin@mahouse.gov
Committees: Joint Rules; Rules

*(continued on next page)*

**LEGISLATIVE BRANCH**

**Representatives** *continued*

Representative **Sean Garballey** (D-Middlesex-23)
Room 540 . . . . . . . . . . . . . . . . . . . . . . . . . . . . . . . (617) 722-2090
Counties Represented: Middlesex (part)     Fax: (617) 722-2850
Term Expires: 2017
E-mail: sean.garballey@mahouse.gov
Committees: Joint Higher Education; Joint Municipalities and Regional Government; Joint Ways and Means; Technology and Intergovernmental Affairs; Ways and Means

Representative **Denise C. Garlick** (D-Norfolk-13)
Room 167 . . . . . . . . . . . . . . . . . . . . . . . . . . . . . . . (617) 722-2810
Counties Represented: Norfolk (part)     Fax: (617) 626-0197
Term Expires: 2017
E-mail: denise.garlick@mahouse.gov
Committees: Joint Elder Affairs

Representative **Colleen M. Garry** (D-Middlesex-36)
Room 238 . . . . . . . . . . . . . . . . . . . . . . . . . . . . . . . (617) 722-2380
Counties Represented: Middlesex (part)     Fax: (617) 722-2847
Term Expires: 2017
E-mail: colleen.garry@mahouse.gov
Committees: Joint Judiciary; Joint Ways and Means; Personnel and Administration; Redistricting; Ways and Means
Education: Lowell BS; Suffolk JD

Representative **Carmine Gentile** (D-Middlesex-13)
Room 39 . . . . . . . . . . . . . . . . . . . . . . . . . . . . . . . (617) 722-2014
Counties Represented: Middlesex (part)
Term Expires: 2017
E-mail: carmine.gentile@mahouse.gov
Committees: Global Warming and Climate Change; Joint Elder Affairs; Joint Higher Education; Technology and Intergovernmental Affairs

Representative **Susan Williams Gifford** (R-Plymouth-2)
Room 124 . . . . . . . . . . . . . . . . . . . . . . . . . . . . . . . (617) 722-2976
Counties Represented: Plymouth (part)     Dist: (508) 295-5999
Term Expires: 2017     Fax: (617) 722-2848
191 Main Street, Suite 213F, Wareham, MA 02571     Dist: (508) 295-5993
E-mail: susan.gifford@mahouse.gov
Committees: Steering, Policy and Scheduling

Representative
**Thomas A. Golden, Jr.** (D-Middlesex-16) Room 473B . . (617) 722-2263
Counties Represented: Middlesex (part)     Fax: (617) 570-6578
Term Expires: 2017
E-mail: thomas.golden@mahouse.gov
Committees: Joint Telecommunications, Utilities and Energy

Representative **Carlos Gonzalez** (D-Hampden-10)
Room 26 . . . . . . . . . . . . . . . . . . . . . . . . . . . . . . . (617) 722-2080
Counties Represented: Hampden (part)
Term Expires: 2017
E-mail: carlos.gonzalez@mahouse.gov
Committees: Joint Community Development and Small Businesses; Joint Economic Development and Emerging Technologies; Joint Housing; Joint Judiciary

Representative **Kenneth I. Gordon** (D-Middlesex-21)
Room 472 . . . . . . . . . . . . . . . . . . . . . . . . . . . . . . . (617) 722-2013
Counties Represented: Middlesex (part)
Term Expires: 2017
E-mail: ken.gordon@mahouse.gov
Committees: Global Warming and Climate Change; Joint Election Laws; Joint State Administration and Regulatory Oversight; Joint Transportation

Representative **Danielle W. Gregoire** (D-Middlesex-4)
Room 473G . . . . . . . . . . . . . . . . . . . . . . . . . . . . . . . (617) 722-2070
Counties Represented: Middlesex (part), Worcester     Fax: (617) 626-0323
(part)
Term Expires: 2017
E-mail: danielle.gregoire@mahouse.gov
Committees: Joint Children, Families and Persons With Disabilities; Joint Education; Joint Financial Services; Joint Labor and Workforce Development
Education: St Anselm 2001 BA; Suffolk 2006 JD

Representative **Patricia A. Haddad** (D-Bristol-5)
Room 370 . . . . . . . . . . . . . . . . . . . . . . . . . . . . . . . (617) 722-2600
Counties Represented: Bristol (part)     Dist: (508) 646-2821
Term Expires: 2017     Fax: (617) 722-2313
Town Office Building, 140 Wood Street, Room 11,     Dist: (508) 324-0993
Somerset, MA 02726
E-mail: patricia.haddad@mahouse.gov
Committees: Ethics; Joint Rules; Rules

Representative **Sheila C. Harrington** (R-Middlesex-1)
Room 237 . . . . . . . . . . . . . . . . . . . . . . . . . . . . . . . (617) 722-2305
Counties Represented: Middlesex (part)     Fax: (617) 626-0199
Term Expires: 2017
E-mail: sheila.harrington@mahouse.gov
Committees: Joint Judiciary; Joint Rules; Joint Ways and Means; Rules

Representative **Stephan Hay** (D-Worcester-3) Room 33 . . . (617) 722-2060
Counties Represented: Worcester (part)
Term Expires: 2017
E-mail: stephan.hay@mahouse.gov
Committees: Joint Election Laws; Joint Municipalities and Regional Government

Representative **Jonathan Hecht** (D-Middlesex-29)
Room 22 . . . . . . . . . . . . . . . . . . . . . . . . . . . . . . . (617) 722-2140
Counties Represented: Middlesex (part)     Dist: (617) 926-5171
Term Expires: 2017     Fax: (617) 626-0199
E-mail: johnathan.hecht@mahouse.gov
Committees: Global Warming and Climate Change; Joint Children, Families and Persons With Disabilities; Joint Elder Affairs; Joint Public Health

Representative **Paul Heroux** (D-Bristol-2) Room 540 . . . . . (617) 722-2090
Counties Represented: Bristol (part)     Fax: (617) 626-0335
Term Expires: 2017
E-mail: paul.heroux@mahouse.gov
Committees: Bonding, Capital Expenditures and State Assets; Joint Municipalities and Regional Government; Joint Public Safety and Homeland Security; Steering, Policy and Scheduling
Education: USC 2001 BA; Pennsylvania MA; London School Econ (UK); Harvard MPA

Representative **Bradford R. Hill** (R-Essex-4) Room 128 . . . (617) 722-2100
Counties Represented: Essex (part)     Dist: (978) 356-9008
Term Expires: 2017
P.O. Box 556, Ipswich, MA 01938
E-mail: brad.hill@mahouse.gov
Committees: Steering, Policy and Scheduling

Representative **Kate Hogan** (D-Middlesex-3) Room 130 . . . (617) 722-2130
Counties Represented: Middlesex (part), Worcester (part)
Term Expires: 2017
E-mail: kate.hogan@mahouse.gov
Committees: Joint Public Health
Education: UMass (Amherst) BA

Representative **Russell E. Holmes** (D-Suffolk-6)
Room 254 . . . . . . . . . . . . . . . . . . . . . . . . . . . . . . . (617) 722-2220
Counties Represented: Suffolk (part)     Fax: (617) 626-0205
Term Expires: 2017
E-mail: russell.holmes@mahouse.gov
Committees: Joint Financial Services; Joint Housing; Joint Public Service; Joint Ways and Means; Ways and Means

Representative **Kevin G. Honan** (D-Suffolk-17) Room 38 . . (617) 722-2470
Counties Represented: Suffolk (part)     Dist: (617) 254-6457
Term Expires: 2017     Fax: (617) 722-2162
192 Faneuil Street, Brighton, MA 02135
E-mail: kevin.honan@mahouse.gov
Committees: Joint Housing
Education: Boston Col 1981 BA; Lesley Col 1991 MMgmtS; John F Kennedy 1999 MPA

Representative **Steven S. Howitt** (R-Bristol-4) . . . . . . . . . . (617) 722-2305
Counties Represented: Bristol (part)     Fax: (617) 626-0211
Term Expires: 2017
State House, Room 237, Boston, MA 02133
E-mail: steven.howitt@mahouse.gov
Committees: Joint Consumer Protection and Professional Licensure; Joint Tourism, Arts and Cultural Development; Joint Transportation

Representative **Daniel J. Hunt** (D-Suffolk-13)
Room 473B . . . . . . . . . . . . . . . . . . . . . . . . . . . . . . . (617) 722-2263
Counties Represented: Norfolk (part), Suffolk (part)
Term Expires: 2017
E-mail: dan.hunt@mahouse.gov
Committees: Joint Consumer Protection and Professional Licensure; Joint Election Laws; Joint Health Care Financing; Joint State Administration and Regulatory Oversight
Education: Suffolk JD

Representative
**Frank Randal "Randy" Hunt** (R-Barnstable-5) . . . . . . . . (617) 722-2396
Counties Represented: Barnstable (part), Plymouth     Dist: (508) 888-2158
(part)     Fax: (617) 626-0218
Term Expires: 2017
93 Route 6A, Sandwich, MA 02563
State House, Room 136, Boston, MA 02133
E-mail: randy.hunt@mahouse.gov
Committees: Joint Mental Health and Substance Abuse; Joint Revenue; Joint Telecommunications, Utilities and Energy

LEGISLATIVE BRANCH

Representative **Bradley H. Jones, Jr.** (R-Middlesex-20)
Room 124 . . . . . . . . . . . . . . . . . . . . . . . . . . . . . . . . (617) 722-2100
Counties Represented: Essex (part)          Dist: (978) 664-5936
Term Expires: 2017                          Fax: (617) 722-2390
249 Park Street, North Reading, MA 01864
E-mail: bradley.jones@mahouse.gov

Representative **Louis L. Kafka** (D-Norfolk-8) Room 185 . . . (617) 722-2960
Counties Represented: Bristol (part), Norfolk (part)     Fax: (617) 722-2713
Term Expires: 2017
E-mail: louis.kafka@mahouse.gov
Committees: Joint Rules; Rules

Representative **Hannah Kane** (R-Worcester-11)
Room 238 . . . . . . . . . . . . . . . . . . . . . . . . . . . . . . . . (617) 722-2430
Counties Represented: Worcester (part)
Term Expires: 2017
E-mail: hannah.kane@mahouse.gov
Committees: Joint Public Health; Joint Transportation; Personnel and
Administration; Redistricting

Representative **Jay R. Kaufman** (D-Middlesex-15)
Room 34 . . . . . . . . . . . . . . . . . . . . . . . . . . . . . . . . . (617) 722-2320
Counties Represented: Middlesex (part)       Dist: (781) 862-6181
Term Expires: 2017                           Fax: (617) 722-2415
E-mail: jay.kaufman@mahouse.gov
Committees: Joint Revenue
Education: Brandeis BA, MA; NYU MA

Representative **Mary S. Keefe** (D-Worcester-15)
Room 473F . . . . . . . . . . . . . . . . . . . . . . . . . . . . . . . (617) 722-2210
Counties Represented: Worcester (part)
Term Expires: 2017
E-mail: mary.keefe@mahouse.gov
Committees: Joint Environment, Natural Resources and Agriculture;
Joint Labor and Workforce Development; Joint Public Health; Joint
Tourism, Arts and Cultural Development

Representative **James M. Kelcourse** (R-Essex-1)
Room 130 . . . . . . . . . . . . . . . . . . . . . . . . . . . . . . . . (617) 722-2130
Counties Represented: Essex (part)
Term Expires: 2017
E-mail: james.kelcourse@mahouse.gov
Committees: Joint Economic Development and Emerging Technologies;
Joint Education; Joint Environment, Natural Resources and Agriculture

Representative **Kay S. Khan** (D-Middlesex-11)
Room 146 . . . . . . . . . . . . . . . . . . . . . . . . . . . . . . . . (617) 722-2011
Counties Represented: Middlesex (part)       Dist: (617) 527-1451
Term Expires: 2017                           Fax: (617) 722-2338
18 Saint Mary's Street, Newton, MA 02462     Dist: (617) 965-4162
E-mail: kay.khan@mahouse.gov
Committees: Joint Children, Families and Persons With Disabilities
Education: Boston U BS, MS

Representative **Peter V. Kocot** (D-Hampshire-1)
Room 22 . . . . . . . . . . . . . . . . . . . . . . . . . . . . . . . . . (617) 722-2140
Counties Represented: Hampden (part), Hampshire     Fax: (617) 722-2347
(part)
Term Expires: 2017
E-mail: peter.kocot@mahouse.gov
Committees: Ethics; Joint State Administration and Regulatory
Oversight

Representative **Robert M. Koczera** (D-Bristol-11)
Room 448 . . . . . . . . . . . . . . . . . . . . . . . . . . . . . . . . (617) 722-2582
Counties Represented: Bristol (part)
Term Expires: 2017
119 Jarry Street, New Bedford, MA 02745
E-mail: robert.koczera@mahouse.gov
Committees: Joint Education; Joint Environment, Natural Resources
and Agriculture; Joint Ways and Means; Steering, Policy and
Scheduling; Ways and Means
Education: UMass (Dartmouth) 1975 BA; Suffolk MPA

Representative **Stephen Kulik** (D-Franklin-1) Room 238 . . (617) 722-2380
Counties Represented: Franklin (part), Hampden     Dist: (413) 665-7200
(part), Hampshire (part)                           Fax: (617) 722-2847
Term Expires: 2017                                 Dist: (413) 665-7101
One Sugarloaf Street, South Deerfield, MA 01373
E-mail: stephen.kulik@mahouse.gov
Committees: Joint Ways and Means; Ways and Means
Education: Northeastern 1972 (Attended); UMass (Amherst) (Attended)

Representative **Kevin J. Kuros** (R-Worcester-8) . . . . . . . . . (617) 722-2460
Counties Represented: Norfolk (part), Worcester     Fax: (617) 722-2353
(part)
Term Expires: 2017
State House, Room 443, Boston, MA 02133
E-mail: kevin.kuros@mahouse.gov
Committees: Joint Economic Development and Emerging Technologies;
Joint Municipalities and Regional Government; Technology and
Intergovernmental Affairs

Representative **John J. Lawn** (D-Middlesex-10)
Room 254 . . . . . . . . . . . . . . . . . . . . . . . . . . . . . . . . (617) 722-2220
Counties Represented: Middlesex (part)       Fax: (617) 626-0150
Term Expires: 2017
E-mail: john.lawn@mahouse.gov
Committees: Joint Financial Services

Representative **David Paul Linsky** (D-Middlesex-5)
Room 146 . . . . . . . . . . . . . . . . . . . . . . . . . . . . . . . . (617) 722-2575
Counties Represented: Middlesex (part), Norfolk     Fax: (617) 722-2238
(part)
Term Expires: 2017
E-mail: david.linsky@mahouse.gov
Committees: Post Audit and Oversight
Education: Colby 1979 BA; Boston Col 1982 JD

Representative
**James D. "Jay" Livingstone** (D-Suffolk-8)
Room 136 . . . . . . . . . . . . . . . . . . . . . . . . . . . . . . . . (617) 722-2396
Counties Represented: Middlesex (part), Suffolk (part)
Term Expires: 2017
E-mail: jay.livingstone@mahouse.gov
Committees: Joint Community Development and Small Businesses;
Joint Environment, Natural Resources and Agriculture; Joint Housing;
Joint State Administration and Regulatory Oversight
Education: Connecticut 1995 BA; George Washington 1998 JD

Representative **Marc T. Lombardo** (R-Middlesex-22)
Room 443 . . . . . . . . . . . . . . . . . . . . . . . . . . . . . . . . (617) 722-2460
Counties Represented: Middlesex (part)       Fax: (617) 626-0240
Term Expires: 2017
E-mail: marc.lombardo@mahouse.gov
Committees: Ethics; Joint Election Laws; Technology and
Intergovernmental Affairs

Representative **James J. Lyons** (R-Essex-18) Room 443 . . (617) 722-2460
Counties Represented: Essex (part), Middlesex     Fax: (617) 626-0246
(part)
Term Expires: 2017
12 High Vale Lane, Andover, MA 01810
E-mail: james.lyons@mahouse.gov
Committees: Joint Judiciary; Joint Public Health; Personnel and
Administration
Education: Brandeis 1975 BA

Representative **Adrian Madaro** (D-Suffolk-1) Room 544 . . (617) 722-2637
Counties Represented: Suffolk (part)
Term Expires: 2017
E-mail: adrian.madaro@mahouse.gov
Committees: Joint Health Care Financing; Joint Municipalities and
Regional Government; Joint State Administration and Regulatory
Oversight; Technology and Intergovernmental Affairs
Education: Tufts BA

Representative
**Timothy R. Madden** (D-Barnstable, Dukes, Nantucket)
Room 167 . . . . . . . . . . . . . . . . . . . . . . . . . . . . . . . . (617) 722-2810
Counties Represented: Barnstable (part), Dukes,     Fax: (617) 722-2846
Nantucket
Term Expires: 2017
E-mail: timothy.madden@mahouse.gov
Committees: Bills in the Third Reading; Joint Financial Services; Joint
Transportation; Joint Ways and Means; Ways and Means

Representative **John J. Mahoney** (D-Worcester-13)
Room 443 . . . . . . . . . . . . . . . . . . . . . . . . . . . . . . . . (617) 722-2460
Counties Represented: Worcester (part)       Fax: (617) 626-0247
Term Expires: 2017
E-mail: john.mahoney@mahouse.gov
Committees: Joint Election Laws

Representative **Elizabeth A. Malia** (D-Suffolk-11)
Room 33 . . . . . . . . . . . . . . . . . . . . . . . . . . . . . . . . . (617) 722-2060
Counties Represented: Suffolk (part)
Term Expires: 2017
E-mail: liz.malia@mahouse.gov
Committees: Joint Mental Health and Substance Abuse
Education: Boston Col

Representative **Brian R. Mannal** (D-Barnstable-2)
Room 473F . . . . . . . . . . . . . . . . . . . . . . . . . . . . . . . (617) 722-2210
Counties Represented: Barnstable (part)       Fax: (617) 626-0166
Term Expires: 2017
E-mail: brian.mannal@mahouse.gov
Committees: Joint Environment, Natural Resources and Agriculture;
Joint Tourism, Arts and Cultural Development; Personnel and
Administration; Redistricting
Education: Wooster 1999 BA; Capital U 2008 JD

*(continued on next page)*

*LEGISLATIVE BRANCH*

**Representatives** *continued*

### Representative **Ronald Mariano** (D-Norfolk-3)
Room 343 . . . . . . . . . . . . . . . . . . . . . . . . . . . . . (617) 722-2300
Counties Represented: Norfolk (part)    Fax: (617) 722-2750
Term Expires: 2017
E-mail: ronald.mariano@mahouse.gov
Committees: Joint Rules; Rules

### Representative **Paul W. Mark** (D-Berkshire-2) Room 166 . . (617) 722-2692
Counties Represented: Berkshire (part), Franklin    Dist: (413) 496-9666
(part)    Fax: (617) 626-0249
Term Expires: 2017
P.O. Box 114, Dalton, MA 01227
E-mail: paul.mark@mahouse.gov
Committees: Joint Rules; Rules

### Representative **Christopher M. Markey** (D-Bristol-9)
Room 527A . . . . . . . . . . . . . . . . . . . . . . . . . . . . (617) 722-2020
Counties Represented: Bristol (part)    Fax: (617) 626-0250
Term Expires: 2017
E-mail: christopher.markey@mahouse.gov
Committees: Ethics

### Representative **Joseph "Joe" McGonagle** (D-Middlesex-28)
Room 134 . . . . . . . . . . . . . . . . . . . . . . . . . . . . (617) 722-2400
Counties Represented: Middlesex (part)
Term Expires: 2017
E-mail: joseph.mcgonagle@mahouse.gov
Committees: Joint Elder Affairs; Joint Housing; Joint Transportation;
Steering, Policy and Scheduling

### Representative **Joseph "Joe" McKenna** (R-Worcester-18) Room 33 . . . (617) 722-2060
Counties Represented: Worcester (part)
Term Expires: 2017
E-mail: joseph.mckenna@mahouse.gov
Committees: Joint Consumer Protection and Professional Licensure;
Joint Labor and Workforce Development

### Representative **Paul McMurtry** (D-Norfolk-11)
Room 448 . . . . . . . . . . . . . . . . . . . . . . . . . . . . (617) 722-2582
Counties Represented: Norfolk (part)    Dist: (781) 320-8683
Term Expires: 2017    Fax: (617) 722-2353
580 High Street, Dedham, MA 02026
E-mail: paul.mcmurtry@mahouse.gov
Committees: Personnel and Administration

### Representative **James R. Miceli** (D-Middlesex-19)
Room 237 . . . . . . . . . . . . . . . . . . . . . . . . . . . . (617) 722-2305
Counties Represented: Middlesex (part)    Dist: (978) 658-9797
Term Expires: 2017
11 Webber Street, Wilmington, MA 01887
E-mail: james.miceli@mahouse.gov
Committees: Joint Elder Affairs; Joint Election Laws; Joint Public
Service; Joint Ways and Means; Ways and Means
Education: Northeastern 1958 BS, 1958 BA

### Representative **Aaron M. Michlewitz** (D-Suffolk-3)
Room 254 . . . . . . . . . . . . . . . . . . . . . . . . . . . . (617) 722-2220
Counties Represented: Suffolk (part)    Fax: (617) 570-6575
Term Expires: 2017
E-mail: aaron.m.michlewitz@mahouse.gov
Committees: Joint Financial Services
Education: Northeastern BA

### Representative **Leonard Mirra** (R-Essex-2) Room 548 . . . . (617) 722-2488
Counties Represented: Essex (part)    Fax: (617) 626-0339
Term Expires: 2017
E-mail: leonard.mirra@mahouse.gov
Committees: Ethics; Joint Community Development and Small
Businesses; Joint Telecommunications, Utilities and Energy
Education: Boston Col 1986 BA

### Representative **Rady Mom** (D-Middlesex-18) Room 443 . . (617) 722-2460
Counties Represented: Middlesex (part)
Term Expires: 2017
E-mail: rady.mom@mahouse.gov
Committees: Joint Education; Joint Election Laws; Joint Public Safety
and Homeland Security; Joint Telecommunications, Utilities and Energy

### Representative **Frank A. Moran** (D-Essex-17)
State House 443, Room 279 . . . . . . . . . . . . . . . (617) 722-2017
Counties Represented: Essex (part)    Fax: (617) 626-0288
Term Expires: 2017
E-mail: frank.moran@mahouse.gov
Committees: Bonding, Capital Expenditures and State Assets;
Joint Community Development and Small Businesses; Joint
Consumer Protection and Professional Licensure; Technology and
Intergovernmental Affairs

### Representative **Michael J. Moran** (D-Suffolk-18)
Room 42 . . . . . . . . . . . . . . . . . . . . . . . . . . . . . (617) 722-2014
Counties Represented: Norfolk (part), Suffolk (part)
Term Expires: 2017
E-mail: michael.moran@mahouse.gov
Committees: Joint Rules; Rules

### Representative **David K. "Dave" Muradian, Jr.** (R-Worcester-9)
Room 156 . . . . . . . . . . . . . . . . . . . . . . . . . . . . (617) 722-2240
Counties Represented: Worcester (part)
Term Expires: 2017
E-mail: david.muradian@mahouse.gov
Committees: Joint Higher Education; Joint Transportation

### Representative **Mathew "Matt" Muratore** (R-Plymouth-1) Room 39 . . . (617) 722-2014
Counties Represented: Plymouth (part)
Term Expires: 2017
E-mail: mathew.muratore@mahouse.gov
Committees: Joint Health Care Financing; Joint State Administration
and Regulatory Oversight; Joint Tourism, Arts and Cultural
Development

### Representative **James Michael Murphy** (D-Norfolk-4)
Room 156 . . . . . . . . . . . . . . . . . . . . . . . . . . . . (617) 722-2240
Counties Represented: Norfolk (part), Plymouth (part)
Term Expires: 2017
E-mail: james.murphy@mahouse.gov
Committees: Joint Public Service
Education: Merrimack BA; Suffolk JD

### Representative **David M. Nangle** (D-Middlesex-17)
Room 146 . . . . . . . . . . . . . . . . . . . . . . . . . . . . (617) 722-2575
Counties Represented: Middlesex (part)    Fax: (617) 722-2215
Term Expires: 2017
E-mail: david.nangle@mahouse.gov
Committees: Steering, Policy and Scheduling

### Representative **Harold P. Naughton, Jr.** (D-Worcester-12) Room 167 . . . (617) 722-2230
Counties Represented: Worcester (part)    Dist: (978) 365-1955
Term Expires: 2017    Fax: (617) 722-9278
200 High Street, 1st Floor, Clinton, MA 01510    Dist: (978) 368-8458
E-mail: harold.naughton@mahouse.gov
Committees: Joint Public Safety and Homeland Security
Education: Assumption Col 1982 BA; Suffolk 1991 JD

### Representative **Shaunna O'Connell** (R-Bristol-3)
Room 237 . . . . . . . . . . . . . . . . . . . . . . . . . . . . (617) 722-2305
Counties Represented: Bristol (part)
Term Expires: 2017
141 Oak Street, Taunton, MA 02780
E-mail: shaunna.o'connell@mahouse.gov
Committees: Global Warming and Climate Change; Joint Children,
Families and Persons With Disabilities; Post Audit and Oversight

### Representative **James J. O'Day** (D-Worcester-14)
Room 540 . . . . . . . . . . . . . . . . . . . . . . . . . . . . (617) 722-2090
Counties Represented: Worcester (part)    Fax: (617) 626-0884
Term Expires: 2017
E-mail: james.o'day@mahouse.gov
Committees: Joint Municipalities and Regional Government

### Representative **Keiko M. Orrall** (R-Bristol-12) Room 540 . . (617) 722-2090
Counties Represented: Bristol (part)    Fax: (617) 626-0477
Term Expires: 2017
E-mail: keiko.orrall@mahouse.gov
Committees: Joint Economic Development and Emerging Technologies;
Joint Labor and Workforce Development
Education: Smith

### Representative **Jerald A. Parisella** (D-Essex-6)
Room 174 . . . . . . . . . . . . . . . . . . . . . . . . . . . . (617) 722-2460
Counties Represented: Essex (part)    Fax: (617) 626-0261
Term Expires: 2017
E-mail: jerald.parisella@mahouse.gov
Committees: Joint Veterans and Federal Affairs

### Representative **Sarah K. Peake** (D-Barnstable-4)
Room 163 . . . . . . . . . . . . . . . . . . . . . . . . . . . . (617) 722-2040
Counties Represented: Barnstable (part)    Dist: (508) 487-5694
Term Expires: 2017    Fax: (617) 722-2239
E-mail: sarah.peake@mahouse.gov
Education: Colgate AB; Pace JD

### Representative **Alice Hanlon Peisch** (D-Norfolk-14)
Room 473-G . . . . . . . . . . . . . . . . . . . . . . . . . . (617) 722-2070
Counties Represented: Middlesex (part), Norfolk (part)
Term Expires: 2017
E-mail: alice.peisch@mahouse.gov
Committees: Joint Education
Education: Smith BA; Suffolk JD

Representative **Thomas M. Petrolati** (D-Hampden-7)
Room 171 . . . . . . . . . . . . . . . . . . . . . . . . . . . . . . . . (617) 722-2255
Counties Represented: Hampden (part), Hampshire    Dist: (413) 589-7303
(part)    Fax: (617) 722-2846
Term Expires: 2017    Dist: (413) 547-0435
116 Sewall Street, Ludlow, MA 01056
E-mail: thomas.petrolati@mahouse.gov
Committees: Joint Rules; Joint Telecommunications, Utilities and
Energy; Rules; Ways and Means
Education: Western New England BA

Representative
**William Smitty Pignatelli** (D-Berkshire-4) Room 466 . . (617) 722-2582
Counties Represented: Berkshire (part), Hampden    Dist: (413) 637-0631
(part)    Fax: (617) 722-2879
Term Expires: 2017
P.O. Box 2228, Lenox, MA 01240
E-mail: rep.pignatelli@mahouse.gov
Committees: Joint Higher Education; Joint Tourism, Arts and Cultural
Development; Joint Ways and Means; Redistricting; Ways and Means

Representative **Elizabeth A. Poirier** (R-Bristol-14)
Room 124 . . . . . . . . . . . . . . . . . . . . . . . . . . . . . . . . (617) 722-2100
Counties Represented: Bristol (part)    Dist: (508) 695-3296
Term Expires: 2017    Fax: (617) 626-0108
53 Ledgebrook Drive, North Attleborough, MA 02760
E-mail: elizabeth.poirier@mahouse.gov
Committees: Ethics

Representative **Denise Provost** (D-Middlesex-27)
Room 473-B . . . . . . . . . . . . . . . . . . . . . . . . . . . . . . (617) 722-2263
Counties Represented: Middlesex (part)    Fax: (617) 626-0548
Term Expires: 2017
E-mail: denise.provost@mahouse.gov
Committees: Global Warming and Climate Change; Joint Higher
Education; Joint Revenue; Joint State Administration and Regulatory
Oversight

Representative **Angelo J. Puppolo, Jr.** (D-Hampden-12)
Room 540 . . . . . . . . . . . . . . . . . . . . . . . . . . . . . . . . (617) 722-2430
Counties Represented: Hampden (part)    Dist: (413) 596-4333
Term Expires: 2017    Fax: (617) 722-2848
2341 Boston Road, Suite 236, Wilbraham, MA 01095
E-mail: angelo.puppolo@mahouse.gov
Committees: Joint State Administration and Regulatory Oversight

Representative **David M. Rogers** (D-Middlesex-24)
Room 472 . . . . . . . . . . . . . . . . . . . . . . . . . . . . . . . . (617) 722-2013
Counties Represented: Middlesex (part)
Term Expires: 2017
E-mail: dave.rogers@mahouse.gov
Committees: Joint Children, Families and Persons With Disabilities;
Joint Housing; Joint Municipalities and Regional Government;
Technology and Intergovernmental Affairs

Representative **John H. Rogers** (D-Norfolk-12)
Room 162 . . . . . . . . . . . . . . . . . . . . . . . . . . . . . . . . (617) 722-2092
Counties Represented: Norfolk (part)    Fax: (617) 722-2347
Term Expires: 2017
E-mail: john.rogers@mahouse.gov
Committees: Joint Children, Families and Persons With Disabilities;
Joint Education; Joint Labor and Workforce Development; Personnel
and Administration
Education: Brandeis 1987 BA; Suffolk 1992 JD

Representative **Dennis A. Rosa** (D-Worcester-4)
Room 136 . . . . . . . . . . . . . . . . . . . . . . . . . . . . . . . . (617) 722-2396
Counties Represented: Worcester (part)    Dist: (978) 534-6946
Term Expires: 2017
24 House Street, Room 27, Leominster, MA 01453
E-mail: dennis.rosa@mahouse.gov
Committees: Joint Community Development and Small Businesses;
Joint Election Laws; Joint Mental Health and Substance Abuse; Joint
Veterans and Federal Affairs

Representative **Jeffrey N. Roy** (D-Norfolk-10)
Room 527A . . . . . . . . . . . . . . . . . . . . . . . . . . . . . . . (617) 722-2020
Counties Represented: Norfolk (part)
Term Expires: 2017
E-mail: jeffrey.roy@mahouse.gov
Committees: Ethics; Joint Judiciary; Joint Labor and Workforce
Development; Joint Ways and Means; Ways and Means
Education: Bates 1983; Boston Col 1986 JD

Representative **Byron Rushing** (D-Suffolk-9) Room 234 . . (617) 722-2783
Counties Represented: Suffolk (part)    Fax: (617) 722-2238
Term Expires: 2017
E-mail: byron.rushing@mahouse.gov
Committees: Ethics; Joint Rules; Rules

Representative **Daniel "Danny" Ryan** (D-Suffolk-2)
Room 146 . . . . . . . . . . . . . . . . . . . . . . . . . . . . . . . . (617) 722-2575
Counties Represented: Suffolk (part)
Term Expires: 2017
E-mail: dan.ryan@mahouse.gov
Committees: Joint Labor and Workforce Development; Joint
Transportation; Joint Veterans and Federal Affairs; Technology and
Intergovernmental Affairs

Representative **Jeffrey Sánchez** (D-Suffolk-15)
Room 236 . . . . . . . . . . . . . . . . . . . . . . . . . . . . . . . . (617) 722-2430
Counties Represented: Norfolk (part), Suffolk (part)
Term Expires: 2017
E-mail: jeffrey.sanchez@mahouse.gov
Committees: Joint Health Care Financing

Representative
**Thomas "Tom" Sannicandro** (D-Middlesex-7)
Room 472 . . . . . . . . . . . . . . . . . . . . . . . . . . . . . . . . (617) 722-2013
Counties Represented: Middlesex (part)    Fax: (617) 722-2239
Term Expires: 2017
E-mail: tom.sannicandro@mahouse.gov
Committees: Joint Higher Education

Representative **Angelo M. Scaccia** (D-Suffolk-14)
Room 33 . . . . . . . . . . . . . . . . . . . . . . . . . . . . . . . . . (617) 722-2060
Counties Represented: Suffolk (part)    Dist: (617) 361-4331
Term Expires: 2017    Fax: (617) 722-2849
59 Readville Street, Readville, MA 02136
E-mail: angelo.scaccia@mahouse.gov
Committees: Bonding, Capital Expenditures and State Assets; Joint
Mental Health and Substance Abuse; Joint Veterans and Federal
Affairs; Joint Ways and Means; Ways and Means
Education: Boston Col BS; Suffolk JD

Representative **Paul A. Schmid III** (D-Bristol-8)
Room 39 . . . . . . . . . . . . . . . . . . . . . . . . . . . . . . . . . (617) 722-2014
Counties Represented: Bristol (part)    Fax: (617) 626-0267
Term Expires: 2017
E-mail: paul.schmid@mahouse.gov
Committees: Joint Environment, Natural Resources and Agriculture

Representative **John W. Scibak** (D-Hampshire-2)
Room 43 . . . . . . . . . . . . . . . . . . . . . . . . . . . . . . . . . (617) 722-2240
Counties Represented: Hampshire (part)    Dist: (413) 539-6566
Term Expires: 2017    Fax: (617) 722-2215
P.O. Box 136, South Hadley, MA 01075    Dist: (413) 539-5855
E-mail: john.scibak@mahouse.gov
Committees: Joint Labor and Workforce Development
Education: Notre Dame BA, MA, PhD

Representative **Alan Silvia** (D-Bristol-7) Room 174 . . . . . . (617) 722-2877
Counties Represented: Bristol (part)    Dist: (774) 526-1122
Term Expires: 2017    Fax: (617) 626-0168
1664 South Main Street, Fall River, MA 02724
E-mail: alan.silvia@mahouse.gov
Committees: Joint Public Safety and Homeland Security; Joint
Revenue; Joint Veterans and Federal Affairs; Joint Ways and Means;
Ways and Means
Education: Northeastern 1975 BS; Salve Regina U 1982 MS

Representative **Frank Israel Smizik** (D-Norfolk-15)
Room 274 . . . . . . . . . . . . . . . . . . . . . . . . . . . . . . . . (617) 722-2676
Counties Represented: Norfolk (part)    Fax: (617) 722-2239
Term Expires: 2017
42 Russell Street, Brookline, MA 02446
E-mail: frank.smizik@mahouse.gov
Committees: Global Warming and Climate Change
Education: Pittsburgh BA; Duquesne JD

Representative **Todd M. Smola** (R-Hampden-1)
Room 124 . . . . . . . . . . . . . . . . . . . . . . . . . . . . . . . . (617) 722-2240
Counties Represented: Hampden (part), Hampshire (part), Worcester
(part)
Term Expires: 2017
E-mail: todd.smola@mahouse.gov
Committees: Joint Ways and Means; Ways and Means

Representative **Theodore C. Speliotis** (D-Essex-13)
Room 43 . . . . . . . . . . . . . . . . . . . . . . . . . . . . . . . . . (617) 722-2030
Counties Represented: Essex (part)
Term Expires: 2017
E-mail: theodore.speliotis@mahouse.gov
Committees: Bills in the Third Reading

*(continued on next page)*

**LEGISLATIVE BRANCH**

**Representatives** *continued*

Representative **Thomas M. Stanley** (D-Middlesex-9)
Room 167 . . . . . . . . . . . . . . . . . . . . . . . . . . . (617) 722-2810
Counties Represented: Middlesex (part)
Term Expires: 2017
E-mail: thomas.stanley@mahouse.gov
Committees: Joint Municipalities and Regional Government; Joint
Revenue; Joint Ways and Means; Post Audit and Oversight; Ways and
Means
Education: Bentley Col BS; Suffolk MPA

Representative **Ellen Story** (D-Hampshire-3) Room 277 . . . (617) 722-2012
Counties Represented: Hampshire (part)            Fax: (617) 576-6577
Term Expires: 2017
E-mail: ellen.story@mahouse.gov
Committees: Joint Rules; Rules
Education: Texas BA; Cambridge MEd

Representative **William M. Straus** (D-Bristol-10)
Room 134 . . . . . . . . . . . . . . . . . . . . . . . . . . . (617) 722-2400
Counties Represented: Bristol (part), Plymouth      Tel: (617) 722-2387
(part)
Term Expires: 2017
E-mail: william.straus@mahouse.gov
Committees: Joint Transportation
Education: Middlebury BA; Georgetown 1982 JD

Representative **Benjamin Swan** (D-Hampden-11)
Room 238 . . . . . . . . . . . . . . . . . . . . . . . . . . . (617) 722-2380
Counties Represented: Hampden (part)         Dist: (413) 739-8547
Term Expires: 2017                           Fax: (617) 722-2846
815 State Street, Springfield, MA 01109      Dist: (413) 739-8572
E-mail: benjamin.swan@mahouse.gov
Committees: Joint Ways and Means; Ways and Means
Education: UMass (Amherst) MEd

Representative **Walter F. Timilty, Jr.** (D-Norfolk-7)
Room 167 . . . . . . . . . . . . . . . . . . . . . . . . . . . (617) 722-2230
Counties Represented: Norfolk (part)
Term Expires: 2017
E-mail: walter.timilty@mahouse.gov
Committees: Joint Municipalities and Regional Government; Joint
Revenue; Joint Veterans and Federal Affairs; Redistricting

Representative
**Timothy J. Toomey, Jr.** (D-Middlesex-26) Room 238 . . . (617) 722-2380
Counties Represented: Middlesex (part)       Dist: (617) 491-1846
Term Expires: 2017                           Fax: (617) 626-0668
500 Cambridge Street, Cambridge, MA 02141
E-mail: timothy.toomey@mahouse.gov
Committees: Joint Revenue
Education: Suffolk BS

Representative **Jose F. Tosado** (D-Hampden-9) Room 34 . . (617) 722-2320
Counties Represented: Hampden (part)
Term Expires: 2017
E-mail: jose.tosado@mahouse.gov
Committees: Joint Consumer Protection and Professional Licensure;
Joint Financial Services; Joint Mental Health and Substance Abuse;
Redistricting

Representative **Paul Tucker** (D-Essex-7) Room 134 . . . . . . . (617) 722-2400
Counties Represented: Essex (part)
Term Expires: 2017
E-mail: paul.tucker@mahouse.gov
Committees: Joint Education; Joint Judiciary; Joint Public Health; Joint
Public Safety and Homeland Security

Representative **Steven Ultrino, EdD** (D-Middlesex-33)
Room 443 . . . . . . . . . . . . . . . . . . . . . . . . . . . (617) 722-2460
Counties Represented: Middlesex (part)
Term Expires: 2017
E-mail: steven.ultrino@mahouse.gov
Committees: Joint Elder Affairs; Joint Health Care Financing; Joint
Public Health; Joint Tourism, Arts and Cultural Development

Representative **Aaron Vega** (D-Hampden-5) Room 146 . . . (617) 722-2011
Counties Represented: Hampden (part)         Fax: (617) 626-2224
Term Expires: 2017
E-mail: aaron.vega@mahouse.gov
Committees: Joint Children, Families and Persons With Disabilities;
Joint Economic Development and Emerging Technologies; Joint Public
Service; Personnel and Administration

Representative **John C. Velis** (D-Hampden-4) Room 448 . . (617) 722-2582
Counties Represented: Hampden (part)
Term Expires: 2017
E-mail: john.velis@mahouse.gov
Committees: Joint Judiciary; Joint Public Health; Joint
Telecommunications, Utilities and Energy; Joint Veterans and Federal
Affairs
Education: South Florida BS; Suffolk JD

Representative **David T. Vieira** (R-Barnstable-3)
Room 167 . . . . . . . . . . . . . . . . . . . . . . . . . . . (617) 722-2810
Counties Represented: Barnstable (part)
Term Expires: 2017
E-mail: david.vieira@mahouse.gov
Committees: Bonding, Capital Expenditures and State Assets; Joint
Public Safety and Homeland Security; Joint Rules; Rules

Representative **RoseLee Vincent** (D-Suffolk-16)
Room 473F . . . . . . . . . . . . . . . . . . . . . . . . . . . (617) 722-2210
Counties Represented: Essex (part), Suffolk (part)
Term Expires: 2017
E-mail: roselee.vincent@mahouse.gov
Committees: Joint Consumer Protection and Professional Licensure;
Joint Economic Development and Emerging Technologies; Joint
Tourism, Arts and Cultural Development; Joint Transportation

Representative **Joseph F. Wagner** (D-Hampden-8)
Room 42 . . . . . . . . . . . . . . . . . . . . . . . . . . . (617) 722-2370
Counties Represented: Hampden (part)         Dist: (413) 592-7857
Term Expires: 2017                           Fax: (413) 592-1354
333 Front Street, Suite 3, Chicopee, MA 01013
E-mail: joseph.wagner@mahouse.gov
Committees: Joint Economic Development and Emerging Technologies;
Joint Rules; Rules

Representative **Chris Walsh** (D-Middlesex-6) Room 472 . . . (617) 722-2013
Counties Represented: Middlesex (part)        Fax: (617) 626-0291
Term Expires: 2017
Nine Vernon Street, Framingham, MA 01701
E-mail: chris.walsh@mahouse.gov
Committees: Joint Financial Services; Joint Public Service; Joint
Transportation; Joint Ways and Means; Ways and Means

Representative **Thomas Walsh** (D-Essex-12) Room 276 . . . (617) 722-2676
Counties Represented: Essex (part)
Term Expires: 2017
E-mail: thomas.walsh@mahouse.gov
Committees: Joint Revenue; Joint Tourism, Arts and Cultural
Development

Representative
**Timothy R. "Tim" Whelan** (R-Barnstable-1) Room 39 . . (617) 722-2014
Counties Represented: Barnstable (part)
Term Expires: 2017
E-mail: timothy.whelan@mahouse.gov
Committees: Joint Higher Education; Joint Public Safety and Homeland
Security; Joint Public Service

Representative **Susannah Whipps Lee** (R-Franklin-2)
Room 540 . . . . . . . . . . . . . . . . . . . . . . . . . . . (617) 722-2090
Counties Represented: Franklin (part), Hampshire (part), Worcester
(part)
Term Expires: 2017
E-mail: susannah.whippslee@mahouse.gov
Committees: Joint Elder Affairs; Joint Mental Health and Substance
Abuse; Joint Municipalities and Regional Government; Joint State
Administration and Regulatory Oversight

Representative **Donald H. Wong** (R-Essex-9) Room 541 . . (617) 722-2488
Counties Represented: Essex (part), Middlesex      Fax: (617) 626-0299
(part)
Term Expires: 2017
E-mail: donald.wong@mahouse.gov
Committees: Joint Financial Services; Joint Ways and Means; Ways and
Means

Representative **Jonathan "Jon" Zlotnik** (D-Worcester-2)
Room 26 . . . . . . . . . . . . . . . . . . . . . . . . . . . (617) 722-2080
Counties Represented: Worcester (part)        Fax: (617) 626-0333
Term Expires: 2017
95 Pleasant Street, Room 212, Gardner, MA 01440
E-mail: jon.zlotnik@mahouse.gov
Committees: Global Warming and Climate Change; Joint Community
Development and Small Businesses; Joint Consumer Protection and
Professional Licensure; Joint Higher Education
Education: UMass (Lowell) 2012 BA

# House Standing Committees
## Bills in the Third Reading
State House, Room 312B, Boston, MA 02133

| **Majority Members** | **Minority Members** |
| --- | --- |
| Theodore C. Speliotis (D) *Chair* | Angelo D'Emilia (R) |
| Timothy R. Madden (D) *Vice Chair* | |

LEGISLATIVE BRANCH

## Bonding, Capital Expenditures and State Assets

State House, Room 446, Boston, MA 02133

| **Majority Members** | **Minority Members** |
| --- | --- |
| Antonio F. D. Cabral (D) *Chair* | Nicholas A. Boldyga (R) |
| Josh S. Cutler (D) | David T. Vieira (R) |
| Daniel M. Donahue (D) | |
| Michelle M. DuBois (D) | |
| James J. Dwyer (D) | |
| Paul Heroux (D) | |
| Frank A. Moran (D) | |
| Angelo M. Scaccia (D) | |

## Ethics

State House, Room 504, Boston, MA 02133

| **Majority Members** | **Minority Members** |
| --- | --- |
| Christopher M. Markey (D) *Chair* | Fred Jay Barrows (R) |
| Jeffrey N. Roy (D) *Vice Chair* | Marc T. Lombardo (R) |
| Garrett J. Bradley (D) | Leonard Mirra (R) |
| Paul J. Donato (D) | Elizabeth A. Poirier (R) |
| Patricia A. Haddad (D) | |
| Peter V. Kocot (D) | |
| Byron Rushing (D) | |

## Global Warming and Climate Change

State House, Room 234, Boston, MA 02133

| **Majority Members** | **Minority Members** |
| --- | --- |
| Frank Israel Smizik (D) *Chair* | Geoffrey "Geoff" Diehl (R) |
| Marjorie C. Decker (D) *Vice Chair* | Shaunna O'Connell (R) |
| Thomas J. Calter III (D) | |
| Tricia Farley-Bouvier (D) | |
| Carmine Gentile (D) | |
| Kenneth I. Gordon (D) | |
| Jonathan Hecht (D) | |
| Denise Provost (D) | |
| Jonathan "Jon" Zlotnik (D) | |

## Personnel and Administration

State House, Room 448, Boston, MA 02133

| **Majority Members** | **Minority Members** |
| --- | --- |
| Paul McMurtry (D) *Chair* | Donald R. Berthiaume, Jr. (R) |
| Nick Collins (D) *Vice Chair* | Geoffrey "Geoff" Diehl (R) |
| Brian M. Ashe (D) | Hannah Kane (R) |
| Christine P. Barber (D) | James J. Lyons (R) |
| Daniel F. "Dan" Cahill (D) | |
| Colleen M. Garry (D) | |
| Brian R. Mannal (D) | |
| John H. Rogers (D) | |
| Aaron Vega (D) | |

## Post Audit and Oversight

State House, Room 146, Boston, MA 02133

| **Majority Members** | **Minority Members** |
| --- | --- |
| David Paul Linsky (D) *Chair* | Peter J. Durant (R) |
| Gerard J. "Gerry" Cassidy (D) | Shaunna O'Connell (R) |
| Brendan P. Crighton (D) | |
| Claire D. Cronin (D) | |
| Daniel R. Cullinane (D) | |
| Josh S. Cutler (D) | |
| Michael Day (D) | |
| Thomas M. Stanley (D) | |

## Redistricting

State House, Room 160, Boston, MA 02133

| **Majority Members** | **Minority Members** |
| --- | --- |
| Edward Coppinger (D) *Chair* | Paul K. Frost (R) |
| Brian M. Ashe (D) *Vice Chair* | Hannah Kane (R) |
| Nick Collins (D) | |
| Gloria L. Fox (D) | |
| Colleen M. Garry (D) | |
| Brian R. Mannal (D) | |
| William Smitty Pignatelli (D) | |
| Walter F. Timilty, Jr. (D) | |
| Jose F. Tosado (D) | |

## Rules

State House, Room 166, Boston, MA 02133

| **Majority Members** | **Minority Members** |
| --- | --- |
| William C. Galvin (D) *Chair* | Sheila C. Harrington (R) |
| Paul W. Mark (D) *Vice Chair* | David T. Vieira (R) |
| Garrett J. Bradley (D) | |
| Paul J. Donato (D) | |
| Patricia A. Haddad (D) | |
| Louis L. Kafka (D) | |
| Ronald Mariano (D) | |
| Michael J. Moran (D) | |
| Thomas M. Petrolati (D) | |
| Byron Rushing (D) | |
| Ellen Story (D) | |
| Joseph F. Wagner (D) | |

## Steering, Policy and Scheduling

State House, Room 146, Boston, MA 02133

| **Majority Members** | **Minority Members** |
| --- | --- |
| David M. Nangle (D) *Chair* | Susan Williams Gifford (R) |
| Robert M. Koczera (D) *Vice Chair* | Bradford R. Hill (R) |
| Brian M. Ashe (D) | |
| Bruce J. Ayers (D) | |
| Diana DiZoglio (D) | |
| James J. Dwyer (D) | |
| Tricia Farley-Bouvier (D) | |
| Paul Heroux (D) | |
| Joseph "Joe" McGonagle (D) | |

## Technology and Intergovernmental Affairs

State House, Room 544, Boston, MA 02133

| **Majority Members** | **Minority Members** |
| --- | --- |
| Mark J. Cusack (D) *Chair* | Kevin J. Kuros (R) |
| David M. Rogers (D) *Vice Chair* | Marc T. Lombardo (R) |
| Ruth Brim Balser (D) | |
| Nick Collins (D) | |
| Sean Garballey (D) | |
| Carmine Gentile (D) | |
| Adrian Madaro (D) | |
| Frank A. Moran (D) | |
| Daniel "Danny" Ryan (D) | |

## Ways and Means

State House, Room 237, Boston, MA 02133

| **Majority Members** | **Minority Members** |
| --- | --- |
| Brian S. Dempsey (D) *Chair* | Nicholas A. Boldyga (R) |
| Stephen Kulik (D) *Vice Chair* | Kate Campanale (R) |
| Benjamin Swan (D) | Angelo D'Emilia (R) |
|   *Assistant Vice Chair* | Shawn Dooley (R) |
| Ruth Brim Balser (D) | Peter J. Durant (R) |
| Paul Brodeur (D) | Kimberly Ferguson (R) |
| Linda Dean Campbell (D) | Todd M. Smola (R) |
| James M. Cantwell (D) | Donald H. Wong (R) |
| Tackey Chan (D) | |
| Nick Collins (D) | |
| Claire D. Cronin (D) | |
| Marjorie C. Decker (D) | |
| Marcos A. Devers (D) | |
| Carolyn C. Dykema (D) | |
| Michael J. Finn (D) | |
| Gloria L. Fox (D) | |
| Sean Garballey (D) | |
| Colleen M. Garry (D) | |
| Russell E. Holmes (D) | |
| Robert M. Koczera (D) | |
| Timothy R. Madden (D) | |
| James R. Miceli (D) | |
| Kathleen O'Connor Ives (D) | |
| Thomas M. Petrolati (D) | |
| William Smitty Pignatelli (D) | |
| Jeffrey N. Roy (D) | |
| Angelo M. Scaccia (D) | |
| Alan Silvia (D) | |
| Thomas M. Stanley (D) | |
| Chris Walsh (D) | |

# Michigan Legislature

Tel: (517) 373-0170  TTY: (517) 373-0543  Fax: (517) 373-0171
Internet: www.legislature.mi.gov

## Michigan Senate

123 West Allegan Street, Lansing, MI 48933
Tel: (517) 373-2400  Fax: (517) 373-9635
E-mail: sensecretary@senate.michigan.gov
Internet: www.senate.michigan.gov

President of the Senate **Brian Calley** (R) . . . . . . . . . . . . . . (517) 373-3400
  Education: Michigan State BS, MBA
President Pro Tem **Tonya Schuitmaker** (R) . . . . . . . . . . . . (517) 373-0793
Assistant President Pro Tem **Margaret O'Brien** (R) . . . . . . (517) 373-5100
Associate President Pro Tem **Hoon-Yung Hopgood** (D) . . . (517) 373-7800
  Education: Michigan 1996 BA
Majority Leader **Arlan B. Meekhof** (R) . . . . . . . . . . . . . . (517) 373-6920
  Education: Davenport 1994 (Attended)
Assistant Majority Leader **Goeff Hansen** (R) . . . . . . . . . . . (517) 373-1635
Majority Floor Leader **Michael W. "Mike" Kowall** (R) . . . (517) 373-1758
Assistant Majority Floor Leader **Jim Stamas** (R) . . . . . . . . (517) 373-7946
Majority Caucus Chairperson **David B. Robertson** (R) . . . . (517) 373-1636
Assistant Majority Caucus Chairman **Rick Jones** (R) . . . . . (517) 373-3447
  Education: Michigan State 1980 AB
Majority Whip **Jack Brandenburg** (R) . . . . . . . . . . . . . . . (517) 373-7670
  Education: Ashland 1974 BS
Assistant Majority Whip **Darwin L. Booher** (R) . . . . . . . . (517) 373-1725
  Education: Graceland U; Michigan State MA; Grand Valley State MA
Minority Leader **Jim Ananich** (D) . . . . . . . . . . . . . . . . . . (517) 373-0142
  Education: Michigan State 1998 BA; Michigan (Flint) 2005 MPA
Assistant Minority Leader **Steven M. Bieda** (D) . . . . . . . . (517) 373-8360
  Education: Wayne State U BA; Detroit Mercy JD
Minority Floor Leader **Morris W. Hood III** (D) . . . . . . . . . (517) 373-0990
Assistant Minority Floor Leader
  **Coleman A. Young II** (D) . . . . . . . . . . . . . . . . . . . . . (517) 373-7346
Minority Caucus Chair **David M. Knezek, Jr.** (D) . . . . . . . (517) 373-0994
  Education: Michigan (Dearborn) 2012 BA
Assistant Minority Caucus Chairman
  **Vincent Gregory** (D) . . . . . . . . . . . . . . . . . . . . . . . . (517) 373-7888
  Education: Madonna 2007 BS
Minority Whip **Curtis Hertel, Jr.** (D) . . . . . . . . . . . . . . . . (517) 373-1734
  Education: Michigan State 2000 BA
Secretary of the Senate **Jeff Cobb** . . . . . . . . . . . . . . . . . . (517) 373-2400
  E-mail: sensecretary@senate.michigan.gov
  E-mail: jcobb@senate.michigan.gov
Assistant Secretary of the Senate **Adam W. Reames** . . . . . (517) 373-2400
  E-mail: sensecretary@senate.michigan.gov
  Education: Michigan BA; Claremont Graduate U MPP;
  Wayne State U JD

## Senators

**Party Affiliation Statistics:** Republicans: 27, Democrats: 10,
Vacancies: 1

Senator **Jim Ananich** (D-District 27)
  Farnum Building, Room 315 . . . . . . . . . . . . . . . . . . . . . (517) 373-0142
  Counties Represented: Genesee (part)    Fax: (517) 373-3938
  Term Expires: 2019
  E-mail: senjananich@senate.michigan.gov
  Committees: Government Operations

Senator **Steven M. Bieda** (D-District 9)
  Farnum Building, Room 310 . . . . . . . . . . . . . . . . . . . . . (517) 373-8360
  Counties Represented: Macomb (part)    Fax: (517) 373-9230
  Term Expires: 2019
  E-mail: sensbieda@senate.michigan.gov
  Committees: Economic Development; Energy and Technology; Finance;
  Insurance; Judiciary

Senator **Darwin L. Booher** (R-District 35)
  Farnum Building, Room 520 . . . . . . . . . . . . . . . . . . . . . (517) 373-1725
  Counties Represented: Benzie, Crawford, Kalkaska,    Fax: (517) 373-0741
  Lake, Leelanau, Manistee, Mason, Missaukee, Ogemaw, Osceola,
  Roscommon, Wexford
  Term Expires: 2019
  E-mail: sendbooher@senate.michigan.gov
  Committees: Agriculture; Appropriations; Banking and Financial
  Institutions; Education

Senator **Jack Brandenburg** (R-District 8) . . . . . . . . . . . . . (517) 373-7670
  Counties Represented: Macomb (part)    Fax: (517) 373-5958
  Term Expires: 2019
  P.O. Box 30036, Lansing, MI 48909-7536
  E-mail: senjbrandenburg@senate.michigan.gov
  Committees: Economic Development; Finance; Insurance; Local
  Government and Elections

Senator **Thomas A. "Tom" Casperson** (R-District 38)
  Farnum Building, Room 705 . . . . . . . . . . . . . . . . . . . . . (517) 373-7840
  Counties Represented: Alger, Baraga, Delta,    Fax: (517) 373-3932
  Dickinson, Gogebic, Houghton, Iron, Keweenaw, Marquette,
  Menominee, Ontonagon, Schoolcraft
  Term Expires: 2019
  Farnum Building, 705, Lansing, MI 48909
  E-mail: sentcasperson@senate.michigan.gov
  Committees: Families, Seniors and Human Services; Finance; Natural
  Resources; Transportation

Senator **Patrick Colbeck** (R-District 7)
  Farnum Building, Room 1020 . . . . . . . . . . . . . . . . . . . . (517) 373-7350
  Counties Represented: Wayne (part)    Fax: (517) 373-9228
  Term Expires: 2019
  E-mail: senpcolbeck@senate.michigan.gov
  Committees: Education; Elections and Government Reform; Judiciary;
  Veterans, Military Affairs and Homeland Security
  Education: Michigan 1987 BSE, 1988 MSE

Senator **Judy K. Emmons** (R-District 33)
  Farnum Building, Room 1005 . . . . . . . . . . . . . . . . . . . . (517) 373-3760
  Counties Represented: Clare, Gratiot, Isabella,    Fax: (517) 373-8661
  Mecosta, Montcalm
  Term Expires: 2019
  E-mail: senjemmons@senate.michigan.gov
  Committees: Economic Development; Elections and Government
  Reform; Families, Seniors and Human Services; Veterans, Military
  Affairs and Homeland Security

Senator **Mike Green** (R-District 31)
  Farnum Building, Room 805 . . . . . . . . . . . . . . . . . . . . . (517) 373-1777
  Counties Represented: Bay, Lapeer, Tuscola    Fax: (517) 373-5871
  Term Expires: 2019
  E-mail: senmgreen@senate.michigan.gov
  Committees: Agriculture; Appropriations; Outdoor Recreation and
  Tourism

Senator **Vincent Gregory** (D-District 11)
  Farnum Building, Room 1015 . . . . . . . . . . . . . . . . . . . . (517) 373-7888
  Counties Represented: Oakland (part)    Fax: (517) 373-2983
  Term Expires: 2019
  E-mail: senvgregory@senate.michigan.gov
  Committees: Appropriations; Oversight

Senator **Goeff Hansen** (R-District 34)
  Farnum Building, Room 420 . . . . . . . . . . . . . . . . . . . . . (517) 373-1635
  Counties Represented: Muskegon, Newaygo, Oceana    Fax: (517) 373-3300
  Term Expires: 2019
  E-mail: senghansen@senate.michigan.gov
  Committees: Appropriations; Government Operations; Outdoor
  Recreation and Tourism

Senator **Curtis Hertel, Jr.** (D-District 23)
  Farnum Building, Room 315 . . . . . . . . . . . . . . . . . . . . . (517) 373-1734
  Counties Represented: Ingham (part)    Fax: (517) 373-5397
  Term Expires: 2019
  E-mail: senchertel@senate.michigan.gov
  Committees: Appropriations; Banking and Financial Institutions;
  Commerce; Health Policy; Joint Administrative Rules; Regulatory
  Reform

Senator **Dave Hildenbrand** (R-District 29)
  Farnum Building, Room 920 . . . . . . . . . . . . . . . . . . . . . (517) 373-1801
  Counties Represented: Kent (part)    Fax: (517) 373-5801
  Term Expires: 2019
  E-mail: sendhildenbrand@senate.michigan.gov
  Committees: Appropriations
  Education: Michigan State 1996 BS

Senator **Morris W. Hood III** (D-District 3)
  Farnum Building, Room 710 . . . . . . . . . . . . . . . . . . . . . (517) 373-0990
  Counties Represented: Wayne (part)    Fax: (517) 373-5338
  Term Expires: 2019
  E-mail: senmhood@senate.michigan.gov
  Committees: Elections and Government Reform; Government
  Operations; Joint Administrative Rules; Joint Legislative Council

Senator **Hoon-Yung Hopgood** (D-District 6)
  Farnum Building, Room 515 . . . . . . . . . . . . . . . . . . . . . (517) 373-7800
  Counties Represented: Wayne (part)    Fax: (517) 373-9310
  Term Expires: 2019
  E-mail: senhhopgood@senate.michigan.gov
  Committees: Appropriations; Energy and Technology; Health Policy;
  Transportation

LEGISLATIVE BRANCH

Senator **Kenneth Horn** (R-District 32)
Farnum Building, Room 1010 . . . . . . . . . . . . . . . . . . . . . . (517) 373-1760
Counties Represented: Genesee (part), Saginaw    Fax: (517) 373-3487
Term Expires: 2019
E-mail: senkhorn@senate.michigan.gov
Committees: Economic Development; Energy and Technology;
Insurance; Transportation

Senator **Joe Hune** (R-District 22)
Farnum Building, Room 505 . . . . . . . . . . . . . . . . . . . . . . . (517) 373-2420
Counties Represented: Livingston, Washtenaw (part)    Fax: (517) 373-2764
Term Expires: 2019
E-mail: senjhune@senate.michigan.gov
Committees: Agriculture; Energy and Technology; Health Policy;
Insurance; Regulatory Reform
Education: Cleary U BS

Senator
**Bertram Courtney "Bert" Johnson** (D-District 2)
Farnum Building, Room 220 . . . . . . . . . . . . . . . . . . . . . . . (517) 373-7748
Counties Represented: Wayne (part)    Fax: (517) 373-1387
Term Expires: 2019
E-mail: senbjohnson@senate.michigan.gov
Committees: Agriculture; Families, Seniors and Human Services;
Insurance; Outdoor Recreation and Tourism; Regulatory Reform
Education: Detroit Mercy

Senator **Rick Jones** (R-District 24)
Farnum Building, Room 915 . . . . . . . . . . . . . . . . . . . . . . . (517) 373-3447
Counties Represented: Clinton, Eaton, Ingham    Fax: (517) 373-5849
(part), Shiawassee
Term Expires: 2019
E-mail: senrjones@senate.michigan.gov
Committees: Families, Seniors and Human Services; Health Policy;
Insurance; Judiciary; Regulatory Reform

Senator **David M. Knezek, Jr.** (D-District 5)
Farnum Building, Room 610 . . . . . . . . . . . . . . . . . . . . . . . (517) 373-0994
Counties Represented: Wayne (part)    Fax: (517) 373-5981
Term Expires: 2019
E-mail: sendknezek@senate.michigan.gov
Committees: Appropriations; Education; Energy and Technology;
Health Policy; Veterans, Military Affairs and Homeland Security

Senator **Martin J. "Marty" Knollenberg** (R-District 13)
Farnum Building, Room 520 . . . . . . . . . . . . . . . . . . . . . . . (517) 373-2523
Counties Represented: Oakland (part)    Fax: (517) 373-5669
Term Expires: 2019
E-mail: senmknollenberg@senate.michigan.gov
Committees: Appropriations; Education; Finance; Regulatory Reform
Education: Albion 2006 BA

Senator **Michael W. "Mike" Kowall** (R-District 15)
Farnum Building, Room 305 . . . . . . . . . . . . . . . . . . . . . . . (517) 373-1758
Counties Represented: Oakland (part)    Fax: (517) 373-0938
Term Expires: 2019
E-mail: senmkowall@senate.michigan.gov
Committees: Commerce; Government Operations; Joint Administrative
Rules; Oversight; Regulatory Reform

Senator **Peter MacGregor** (R-District 28)
Farnum Building, Room 715 . . . . . . . . . . . . . . . . . . . . . . . (517) 373-0797
Counties Represented: Kent (part)    Fax: (517) 373-5236
Term Expires: 2019
E-mail: senpmacgregor@senate.michigan.gov
Committees: Appropriations; Banking and Financial Institutions;
Commerce; Oversight; Regulatory Reform
Education: Michigan State 1988

Senator **James Jim Marleau** (R-District 12)
Farnum Building, Room 1010 . . . . . . . . . . . . . . . . . . . . . . (517) 373-2417
Counties Represented: Oakland (part)    Fax: (517) 373-2694
Term Expires: 2019
E-mail: senjmarleau@senate.michigan.gov
Committees: Appropriations; Health Policy; Insurance; Transportation
Education: Toledo AAS

Senator **Arlan B. Meekhof** (R-District 30) . . . . . . . . . . . . . (517) 373-6920
Counties Represented: Ottawa    Fax: (517) 373-2751
Term Expires: 2019
Capitol Building, 100 N Capitol Ave, Room S-8, Lansing, MI 48909
E-mail: senameekhof@senate.michigan.gov
Committees: Government Operations; Joint Legislative Council

Senator **Mike Nofs** (R-District 19) . . . . . . . . . . . . . . . . . . (517) 373-2426
Counties Represented: Barry, Calhoun, Ionia    Fax: (517) 373-2964
Term Expires: 2019
Capital Building, 100 N Capitol Ave, Room S-132, Lansing, MI 48909
E-mail: senmnofs@senate.michigan.gov
Committees: Appropriations; Banking and Financial Institutions;
Energy and Technology
Education: Spring Arbor U 1991 BA

Senator **Margaret O'Brien** (R-District 20)
Farnum Building, Room 910 . . . . . . . . . . . . . . . . . . . . . . . (517) 373-5100
Counties Represented: Kalamazoo    Fax: (517) 373-5115
Term Expires: 2019
E-mail: senmobrien@senate.michigan.gov
Committees: Banking and Financial Institutions; Commerce; Health
Policy; Insurance; Veterans, Military Affairs and Homeland Security

Senator **Phillip "Phil" Pavlov** (R-District 25)
Farnum Building, Room 505 . . . . . . . . . . . . . . . . . . . . . . . (517) 373-7708
Counties Represented: Huron, Macomb (part),    Fax: (517) 373-1450
Sanilac, St. Clair
Term Expires: 2019
E-mail: senppavlov@senate.michigan.gov
Committees: Education; Families, Seniors and Human Services; Natural
Resources; Transportation

Senator **John Proos IV** (R-District 21)
Farnum Building, Room 820 . . . . . . . . . . . . . . . . . . . . . . . (517) 373-6960
Counties Represented: Berrien, Cass, St. Joseph    Fax: (517) 373-0897
Term Expires: 2019
E-mail: senjproos@senate.michigan.gov
Committees: Appropriations; Energy and Technology; Finance; Local
Government and Elections; Michigan Competitiveness

Senator **David B. Robertson** (R-District 14)
Farnum Building, Room 305 . . . . . . . . . . . . . . . . . . . . . . . (517) 373-1636
Counties Represented: Genesee (part), Oakland    Fax: (517) 373-1453
(part)
Term Expires: 2019
E-mail: sendrobertson@senate.michigan.gov
Committees: Elections and Government Reform; Finance; Health
Policy; Michigan Competitiveness; Natural Resources

Senator **Tory Rocca** (R-District 10)
Farnum Building, Room 205 . . . . . . . . . . . . . . . . . . . . . . . (517) 373-7315
Counties Represented: Macomb (part)    Fax: (517) 373-3126
Term Expires: 2019
E-mail: sentrocca@senate.michigan.gov
Committees: Banking and Financial Institutions; Joint Administrative
Rules; Joint Legislative Council; Judiciary; Local Government and
Elections; Regulatory Reform

Senator **Wayne A. Schmidt** (R-District 37)
Farnum Building, Room 820 . . . . . . . . . . . . . . . . . . . . . . . (517) 373-2413
Counties Represented: Antrim, Charlevoix,    Fax: (517) 373-5144
Cheboygan, Chippewa, Emmet, Grand Traverse, Luce, Mackinac
Term Expires: 2019
E-mail: senwschmidt@senate.michigan.gov
Committees: Agriculture; Commerce; Economic Development;
Insurance; Joint Legislative Council; Outdoor Recreation and Tourism

Senator **Tonya Schuitmaker** (R-District 26)
Farnum Building, Room 405 . . . . . . . . . . . . . . . . . . . . . . . (517) 373-0793
Counties Represented: Allegan, Kent (part), Van    Fax: (517) 373-5607
Buren
Term Expires: 2019
E-mail: sentschuitmaker@senate.michigan.gov
Committees: Appropriations; Energy and Technology; Judiciary;
Oversight

Senator **Michael "Mike" Shirkey** (R-District 16)
Farnum Building, Room 320 . . . . . . . . . . . . . . . . . . . . . . . (517) 373-5932
Counties Represented: Branch, Hillsdale, Jackson    Fax: (517) 373-5944
Term Expires: 2019
E-mail: senmshirkey@senate.michigan.gov
Committees: Appropriations; Elections and Government Reform;
Energy and Technology; Health Policy; Michigan Competitiveness

Senator **Jim Stamas** (R-District 36)
Farnum Building, Room 920 . . . . . . . . . . . . . . . . . . . . . . . (517) 373-7946
Counties Represented: Alcona, Alpena, Arenac,    Fax: (517) 373-2678
Gladwin, Iosco, Midland, Montmorency, Oscoda, Otsego, Presque Isle
Term Expires: 2019
E-mail: senjstamas@senate.michigan.gov
Committees: Appropriations; Economic Development; Health Policy;
Joint Administrative Rules; Joint Legislative Council; Michigan
Competitiveness; Natural Resources; Oversight

Senator **Rebekah Warren** (D-District 18)
Farnum Building, Room 415 . . . . . . . . . . . . . . . . . . . . . . . (517) 373-2406
Counties Represented: Washtenaw (part)    Fax: (517) 373-5679
Term Expires: 2019
E-mail: senrwarren@senate.michigan.gov
Committees: Economic Development; Finance; Michigan
Competitiveness; Natural Resources; Regulatory Reform

*(continued on next page)*

**LEGISLATIVE BRANCH**

**Senators** *continued*

Senator **Coleman A. Young II** (D-District 1)
Farnum Building, Room 410 . . . . . . . . . . . . . . . . . . . . . . . (517) 373-7346
Counties Represented: Wayne (part)          Fax: (517) 373-9320
Term Expires: 2019
E-mail: sencyoung@senate.michigan.gov
Committees: Appropriations; Banking and Financial Institutions;
Insurance; Local Government and Elections

Senator **Dale Zorn** (R-District 17)
Farnum Building, Room 710 . . . . . . . . . . . . . . . . . . . . . . . (517) 373-3543
Counties Represented: Lenawee, Monroe          Fax: (517) 373-0927
Term Expires: 2019
E-mail: sendzorn@senate.michigan.gov
Committees: Banking and Financial Institutions; Energy and
Technology; Local Government and Elections; Outdoor Recreation and
Tourism; Veterans, Military Affairs and Homeland Security

District 4 **(Vacant)** . . . . . . . . . . . . . . . . . . . . . . . . . . . . . (517) 373-7918
Note: A special election to fill this legislative vacancy will be held on
November 8, 2016.

# Senate Standing Committees

## Agriculture

**Majority Members**
Joe Hune (R-22) *Chair*
Mike Green (R-31)
  *Majority Vice Chair*
Darwin L. Booher (R-35)
Wayne A. Schmidt (R-37)

**Minority Members**
Bertram Courtney
  "Bert" Johnson (D-2)
  *Minority Vice Chair*

## Appropriations

**Majority Members**
Dave Hildenbrand (R-29) *Chair*
Peter MacGregor (R-28)
  *Majority Vice Chair*
Darwin L. Booher (R-35)
Mike Green (R-31)
Goeff Hansen (R-34)
Martin J. "Marty" Knollenberg
  (R-13)
James Jim Marleau (R-12)
Mike Nofs (R-19)
John Proos IV (R-21)
Tonya Schuitmaker (R-26)
Michael "Mike" Shirkey (R-16)
Jim Stamas (R-36)

**Minority Members**
Vincent Gregory (D-11)
  *Minority Vice Chair*
Curtis Hertel, Jr. (D-23)
Hoon-Yung Hopgood (D-6)
David M. Knezek, Jr. (D-5)
Coleman A. Young II (D-1)

## Banking and Financial Institutions

**Majority Members**
Darwin L. Booher (R-35) *Chair*
Margaret O'Brien (R-20)
  *Majority Vice Chair*
Peter MacGregor (R-28)
Mike Nofs (R-19)
Tory Rocca (R-10)
Dale Zorn (R-17)

**Minority Members**
Curtis Hertel, Jr. (D-23)
  *Minority Vice Chair*
Coleman A. Young II (D-1)

## Commerce

**Majority Members**
Wayne A. Schmidt (R-37) *Chair*
Michael W. "Mike" Kowall (R-15)
  *Majority Vice Chair*
Peter MacGregor (R-28)
Margaret O'Brien (R-20)

**Minority Members**
Curtis Hertel, Jr. (D-23)
  *Minority Vice Chair*

## Economic Development

**Majority Members**
Kenneth Horn (R-32) *Chair*
Wayne A. Schmidt (R-37)
  *Majority Vice Chair*
Jack Brandenburg (R-8)
Judy K. Emmons (R-33)
Jim Stamas (R-36)

**Minority Members**
Rebekah Warren (D-18)
  *Minority Vice Chair*
Steven M. Bieda (D-9)

## Education

**Majority Members**
Phillip "Phil" Pavlov (R-25) *Chair*
Martin J. "Marty"
  Knollenberg (R-13)
  *Majority Vice Chair*
Darwin L. Booher (R-35)
Patrick Colbeck (R-7)

**Minority Members**
David M. Knezek, Jr. (D-5)
  *Minority Vice Chair*

## Elections and Government Reform

**Majority Members**
David B. Robertson (R-14) *Chair*
Patrick Colbeck (R-7)
  *Majority Vice Chair*
Judy K. Emmons (R-33)
Michael "Mike" Shirkey (R-16)

**Minority Members**
Morris W. Hood III (D-3)
  *Minority Vice Chair*

## Energy and Technology

**Majority Members**
Mike Nofs (R-19) *Chair*
John Proos IV (R-21)
  *Majority Vice Chair*
Kenneth Horn (R-32)
Joe Hune (R-22)
Tonya Schuitmaker (R-26)
Michael "Mike" Shirkey (R-16)
Dale Zorn (R-17)

**Minority Members**
Hoon-Yung Hopgood (D-6)
  *Minority Vice Chair*
Steven M. Bieda (D-9)
David M. Knezek, Jr. (D-5)

## Families, Seniors and Human Services

**Majority Members**
Judy K. Emmons (R-33) *Chair*
Phillip "Phil" Pavlov (R-25)
  *Majority Vice Chair*
Thomas A. "Tom" Casperson
  (R-38)
Rick Jones (R-24)

**Minority Members**
Bertram Courtney
  "Bert" Johnson (D-2)
  *Minority Vice Chair*

## Finance

**Majority Members**
Jack Brandenburg (R-8) *Chair*
David B. Robertson (R-14)
  *Majority Vice Chair*
Thomas A. "Tom" Casperson
  (R-38)
Martin J. "Marty" Knollenberg
  (R-13)
John Proos IV (R-21)

**Minority Members**
Steven M. Bieda (D-9)
  *Minority Vice Chair*
Rebekah Warren (D-18)

## Government Operations

**Majority Members**
Arlan B. Meekhof (R-30) *Chair*
Goeff Hansen (R-34)
  *Majority Vice Chair*
Michael W. "Mike" Kowall (R-15)

**Minority Members**
Jim Ananich (D-27)
  *Minority Vice Chair*
Morris W. Hood III (D-3)

## Health Policy

**Majority Members**
Michael "Mike" Shirkey (R-16)
  *Chair*
Joe Hune (R-22)
  *Majority Vice Chair*
Rick Jones (R-24)
James Jim Marleau (R-12)
Margaret O'Brien (R-20)
David B. Robertson (R-14)
Jim Stamas (R-36)

**Minority Members**
Curtis Hertel, Jr. (D-23)
  *Minority Vice Chair*
Hoon-Yung Hopgood (D-6)
David M. Knezek, Jr. (D-5)

## Insurance

**Majority Members**
Joe Hune (R-22) *Chair*
Jack Brandenburg (R-8)
  *Majority Vice Chair*
Kenneth Horn (R-32)
Rick Jones (R-24)
James Jim Marleau (R-12)
Margaret O'Brien (R-20)
Wayne A. Schmidt (R-37)

**Minority Members**
Steven M. Bieda (D-9)
  *Minority Vice Chair*
Bertram Courtney "Bert" Johnson
  (D-2)
Coleman A. Young II (D-1)

## Judiciary

| Majority Members | Minority Members |
|---|---|
| Rick Jones (R-24) *Chair* | Steven M. Bieda (D-9) |
| Tonya Schuitmaker (R-26) | *Minority Vice Chair* |
| *Majority Vice Chair* | |
| Patrick Colbeck (R-7) | |
| Tory Rocca (R-10) | |

## Local Government and Elections

| Majority Members | Minority Members |
|---|---|
| Dale Zorn (R-17) *Chair* | Coleman A. Young II (D-1) |
| John Proos IV (R-21) | *Minority Vice Chair* |
| *Majority Vice Chair* | |
| Jack Brandenburg (R-8) | |
| Tory Rocca (R-10) | |

## Michigan Competitiveness

| Majority Members | Minority Members |
|---|---|
| Michael "Mike" Shirkey (R-16) | Rebekah Warren (D-18) |
| *Chair* | *Minority Vice Chair* |
| Jim Stamas (R-36) | |
| *Majority Vice Chair* | |
| John Proos IV (R-21) | |
| David B. Robertson (R-14) | |

## Natural Resources

| Majority Members | Minority Members |
|---|---|
| Thomas A. "Tom" | Rebekah Warren (D-18) |
| Casperson (R-38) | *Minority Vice Chair* |
| *Chair* | |
| Phillip "Phil" Pavlov (R-25) | |
| *Majority Vice Chair* | |
| David B. Robertson (R-14) | |
| Jim Stamas (R-36) | |

## Outdoor Recreation and Tourism

| Majority Members | Minority Members |
|---|---|
| Goeff Hansen (R-34) *Chair* | Bertram Courtney |
| Dale Zorn (R-17) | "Bert" Johnson (D-2) |
| *Majority Vice Chair* | *Minority Vice Chair* |
| Mike Green (R-31) | |
| Wayne A. Schmidt (R-37) | |

## Oversight

| Majority Members | Minority Members |
|---|---|
| Peter MacGregor (R-28) *Chair* | Vincent Gregory (D-11) |
| Michael W. "Mike" Kowall (R-15) | *Minority Vice Chair* |
| *Majority Vice Chair* | |
| Jim Stamas (R-36) | |
| Tonya Schuitmaker (R-26) | |

## Regulatory Reform

| Majority Members | Minority Members |
|---|---|
| Tory Rocca (R-10) *Chair* | Rebekah Warren (D-18) |
| Rick Jones (R-24) | *Minority Vice Chair* |
| *Majority Vice Chair* | Curtis Hertel, Jr. (D-23) |
| Joe Hune (R-22) | Bertram Courtney "Bert" Johnson |
| Martin J. "Marty" Knollenberg | (D-2) |
| (R-13) | |
| Michael W. "Mike" Kowall (R-15) | |
| Peter MacGregor (R-28) | |

## Transportation

| Majority Members | Minority Members |
|---|---|
| Thomas A. "Tom" | Hoon-Yung Hopgood (D-6) |
| Casperson (R-38) | *Minority Vice Chair* |
| *Chair* | |
| Kenneth Horn (R-32) | |
| *Majority Vice Chair* | |
| James Jim Marleau (R-12) | |
| Phillip "Phil" Pavlov (R-25) | |

## Veterans, Military Affairs and Homeland Security

| Majority Members | Minority Members |
|---|---|
| Margaret O'Brien (R-20) *Chair* | David M. Knezek, Jr. (D-5) |
| Judy K. Emmons (R-33) | *Minority Vice Chair* |
| *Majority Vice Chair* | |
| Patrick Colbeck (R-7) | |
| Dale Zorn (R-17) | |

# Michigan House of Representatives

Anderson House Office Building, 124 North Capitol Avenue,
Lansing, MI 48909-7514
P.O. Box 30014, Lansing, MI 48909-7514
Tel: (517) 373-0135  Fax: (517) 373-5930
Internet: www.house.michigan.gov

Speaker of the House **Kevin Cotter** (R) . . . . . . . . . . . . . . (517) 373-1789
Speaker Pro Tem **Tom Leonard, JD** (R) . . . . . . . . . . . . . . (517) 373-1778
  Education: Michigan BA; Michigan State JD
Majority Floor Leader **Aric Nesbitt** (R) . . . . . . . . . . . . . . (517) 373-0839
  Education: Hillsdale BA
Assistant Majority Floor Leader **Ken Yonker** (R) . . . . . . . . . (517) 373-0840
Majority Whip **Rob VerHeulen, JD** (R) . . . . . . . . . . . . . . (517) 373-8900
  Education: Grand Rapids Comm Col (Attended); Michigan (Attended);
  Wayne State U JD
Assistant Majority Whip **Jon Bumstead** (R) . . . . . . . . . . . (517) 373-7317
Minority Leader **Tim Greimel** (D) . . . . . . . . . . . . . . . . . . (517) 373-0475
Minority Floor Leader **Sam Singh** (D) . . . . . . . . . . . . . . . (517) 373-1786
  Education: Michigan State 1994 BA
Clerk of the House **Gary L. Randall** . . . . . . . . . . . . . . . . . (517) 373-0135
  E-mail: clerk@house.mi.gov
Assistant Clerk of the House **Rich Brown** . . . . . . . . . . . . . (517) 373-0135
  E-mail: clerk@house.mi.gov

## Representatives

**Party Affiliation Statistics:** Republicans: 63, Democrats: 46,
Vacancies: 1

Representative **Chris Afendoulis** (R-District 73) . . . . . . . . (517) 373-0218
  Counties Represented: Kent (part)
  Term Expires: 2017
  E-mail: chrisafendoulis@house.mi.gov
  Committees: Appropriations
  Education: Michigan 1984 BBA
Representative **Brian Banks** (D-District 1)
  S585 House Office Building . . . . . . . . . . . . . . . . . . . . . (517) 373-0154
  Counties Represented: Wayne (part)
  Term Expires: 2017
  E-mail: brianbanks@house.mi.gov
  Committees: Appropriations; Insurance
  Education: Wayne State U BS, MAED; Michigan State JD
Representative **Tom Barrett** (R-District 71) . . . . . . . . . . . . (517) 373-0853
  Counties Represented: Eaton (part)
  Term Expires: 2017
  E-mail: tombarrett@house.mi.gov
  Committees: Commerce and Trade; Energy Policy; Insurance
Representative **Dr. John Bizon** (R-District 62) . . . . . . . . . . (517) 373-0555
  Counties Represented: Calhoun (part)
  Term Expires: 2017
  E-mail: drjohnbizon@house.mi.gov
  Committees: Appropriations; Health Policy
Representative **Winnie Brinks** (D-District 76)
  N1095 House Office Building . . . . . . . . . . . . . . . . . . . . (517) 373-0822
  Counties Represented: Kent (part)
  Term Expires: 2017
  E-mail: winniebrinks@house.mi.gov
  Committees: Education; Health Policy; Workforce and Talent
  Development
  Education: Calvin Col 1990 BA
Representative **Charles Brunner** (D-District 96)
  S1285 House Office Building . . . . . . . . . . . . . . . . . . . . (517) 373-0158
  Counties Represented: Bay (part)    Fax: (517) 373-8881
  Term Expires: 2017
  E-mail: charlesbrunner@house.mi.gov
  Committees: Agriculture; Energy Policy; Local Government; Tourism

*(continued on next page)*

**LEGISLATIVE BRANCH**

**Representatives** *continued*

Representative **Jon Bumstead** (R-District 100)
S1289 House Office Building . . . . . . . . . . . . . . . . . . . . . (517) 373-7317
Counties Represented: Lake, Newaygo, Oceana
Term Expires: 2017
E-mail: jonbumstead@house.mi.gov
Committees: Appropriations

Representative **Wendell Byrd** (D-District 3) . . . . . . . . . . . . (517) 373-0144
Counties Represented: Wayne (part)
Term Expires: 2017
E-mail: wendellbyrd@house.mi.gov
Committees: Commerce and Trade; Energy Policy; Financial Liability
Reform; Tax Policy

Representative **Mike Callton** (R-District 87)
N1191 House Office Building . . . . . . . . . . . . . . . . . . . . . (517) 373-0842
Counties Represented: Barry, Ionia (part)          Fax: (517) 373-6979
Term Expires: 2017
E-mail: mikecallton@house.mi.gov
Committees: Commerce and Trade; Education; Financial Services;
Health Policy

Representative **Edward J. Canfield, DO** (R-District 84) . . . (517) 373-0476
Counties Represented: Huron, Tuscola
Term Expires: 2017
E-mail: edwardcanfield@house.mi.gov
Committees: Appropriations
Education: Lake Superior State 1983 BS; Michigan State 1988 DO

Representative **Stephanie Chang** (D-District 6) . . . . . . . . (517) 373-0823
Counties Represented: Wayne (part)
Term Expires: 2017
E-mail: stephaniechang@house.mi.gov
Committees: Criminal Justice; Education; Judiciary
Education: Michigan 2005 BA, 2014 MPP, 2014 MSW

Representative **Lee Chatfield** (R-District 107) . . . . . . . . . . (517) 373-2629
Counties Represented: Cheboygan (part), Chippewa, Emmet, Mackinac
Term Expires: 2017
E-mail: leechatfield@house.mi.gov
Committees: Education; Health Policy; Local Government; Tax Policy
Education: Liberty MA

Representative **John Chirkun** (D-District 22) . . . . . . . . . . . (517) 373-0854
Counties Represented: Macomb (part)
Term Expires: 2017
E-mail: johnchirkun@house.mi.gov
Committees: Financial Liability Reform; Regulatory Reform

Representative **Paul Clemente** (D-District 14)
N693 House Office Building . . . . . . . . . . . . . . . . . . . . . . (517) 373-0140
Counties Represented: Wayne (part)          Fax: (517) 373-5924
Term Expires: 2017
E-mail: paulclemente@house.mi.gov
Committees: Financial Services; Insurance; Tax Policy

Representative **Tom Cochran** (D-District 67)
S1086 House Office Building . . . . . . . . . . . . . . . . . . . . . (517) 373-0587
Counties Represented: Ingham (part)
Term Expires: 2017
E-mail: tomcochran@house.mi.gov
Committees: Energy Policy; Health Policy; Insurance
Education: Siena Heights BA

Representative **Triston Cole** (R-District 105) . . . . . . . . . . . (517) 373-0829
Counties Represented: Antrim, Charlevoix, Montmorency, Oscoda,
Otsego
Term Expires: 2017
E-mail: tristoncole@house.mi.gov
Committees: Agriculture; Energy Policy; Judiciary; Transportation and
Infrastructure

Representative **Kevin Cotter** (R-District 99)
S1288 House Office Building . . . . . . . . . . . . . . . . . . . . . (517) 373-1789
Counties Represented: Isabella, Midland (part)          Fax: (517) 373-5924
Term Expires: 2017
E-mail: kevincotter@house.mi.gov
Committees: Joint Legislative Council

Representative **Laura Cox** (R-District 19) . . . . . . . . . . . . . (517) 373-3920
Counties Represented: Wayne (part)
Term Expires: 2017
E-mail: lauracox@house.mi.gov
Committees: Appropriations
Education: Michigan State

Representative **Kathy S. Crawford** (R-District 38) . . . . . . . . (517) 373-0827
Counties Represented: Oakland (part)
Term Expires: 2017
E-mail: kathycrawford@house.mi.gov
Committees: Families, Children, and Seniors; Health Policy; Regulatory
Reform; Workforce and Talent Development

Representative **George Darany** (D-District 15)
N694 House Office Building . . . . . . . . . . . . . . . . . . . . . . (517) 373-0847
Counties Represented: Wayne (part)          Fax: (517) 373-7538
Term Expires: 2017
E-mail: georgetdarany@house.mi.gov
Committees: Agriculture; Health Policy; Regulatory Reform

Representative **Scott Dianda** (D-District 110)
S1489 House Office Building . . . . . . . . . . . . . . . . . . . . . (517) 373-0850
Counties Represented: Baraga, Gogebic, Houghton, Iron, Keweenaw,
Marquette (part), Ontonagon
Term Expires: 2017
E-mail: scottdianda@house.mi.gov
Committees: Energy Policy; Regulatory Reform; Transportation and
Infrastructure
Education: Lake Superior State BA; Harvard (Attended)

Representative **Gretchen Driskell** (D-District 52)
S986 House Office Building . . . . . . . . . . . . . . . . . . . . . . (517) 373-0828
Counties Represented: Washtenaw (part)
Term Expires: 2017
E-mail: gretchendriskell@house.mi.gov
Committees: Agriculture
Education: Lynchburg 1980 BA; George Washington MBA

Representative **Fred Durhal III** (D-District 5) . . . . . . . . . . . (517) 373-0844
Counties Represented: Wayne (part)
Term Expires: 2017
E-mail: freddurhal@house.mi.gov
Committees: Appropriations

Representative **Pam Faris** (D-District 48)
N897 House Office Building . . . . . . . . . . . . . . . . . . . . . . (517) 373-7557
Counties Represented: Genesee (part)
Term Expires: 2017
E-mail: pamfaris@house.mi.gov
Committees: Appropriations
Education: Baker Col BA

Representative **Jeff Farrington** (R-District 30)
N0794 House Office Building . . . . . . . . . . . . . . . . . . . . . (517) 373-7768
Counties Represented: Macomb (part)
Term Expires: 2017
E-mail: jefffarrington@house.mi.gov
Committees: Financial Liability Reform; Tax Policy; Transportation and
Infrastructure; Workforce and Talent Development

Representative **Anthony Forlini** (R-District 24)
S0788 House Office Building . . . . . . . . . . . . . . . . . . . . . (517) 373-0113
Counties Represented: Macomb (part)
Term Expires: 2017
E-mail: anthonyforlini@house.mi.gov
Committees: Families, Children, and Seniors; Financial Services;
Natural Resources

Representative **Ray Franz** (R-District 101)
S1385 House Office Building . . . . . . . . . . . . . . . . . . . . . (517) 373-0825
Counties Represented: Benzie, Leelanau, Manistee, Mason
Term Expires: 2017
E-mail: rayfranz@house.mi.gov
Committees: Agriculture; Insurance; Regulatory Reform

Representative **Daniela García** (R-District 90) . . . . . . . . . . (517) 373-0830
Counties Represented: Ottawa (part)
Term Expires: 2017
E-mail: danielagarcia@house.mi.gov
Committees: Appropriations; Commerce and Trade; Education; Health
Policy; Regulatory Reform
Education: Michigan 2001 BA

Representative **LaTanya Garrett** (D-District 7) . . . . . . . . . . (517) 373-2276
Counties Represented: Wayne (part)
Term Expires: 2017
E-mail: latanyagarrett@house.mi.gov
Committees: Agriculture; Commerce and Trade; Energy Policy

Representative **Sherry Gay-Dagnogo** (D-District 8) . . . . . . (517) 373-3815
Counties Represented: Wayne (part)
Term Expires: 2017
E-mail: sherrygay-dagnogo@house.mi.gov
Committees: Financial Services

Representative **Erika Geiss** (D-District 12) . . . . . . . . . . . . . (517) 373-0852
Counties Represented: Wayne (part)
Term Expires: 2017
E-mail: erikageiss@house.mi.gov
Committees: Commerce and Trade; Health Policy; Joint Administrative
Rules; Workforce and Talent Development
Education: Brandeis 1992 BA; Tufts 1998 MA

Representative **Ben Glardon** (R-District 85)
S1189 House Office Building . . . . . . . . . . . . . . . . . . . . . . (517) 373-0841
Counties Represented: Saginaw (part), Shiawassee
Term Expires: 2017
E-mail: benglardon@house.mi.gov
Committees: Agriculture; Insurance; Transportation and Infrastructure

Representative **Gary Glenn** (R-District 98) . . . . . . . . . . . . (517) 373-1791
Counties Represented: Bay (part), Midland (part)
Term Expires: 2017
E-mail: garyglenn@house.mi.gov
Committees: Commerce and Trade; Energy Policy; Tax Policy

Representative **Ken Goike** (R-District 33)
N0797 House Office Building . . . . . . . . . . . . . . . . . . . . . . (517) 373-0820
Counties Represented: Macomb (part)
Term Expires: 2017
E-mail: kengoike@house.mi.gov
Committees: Insurance; Joint Administrative Rules; Natural Resources;
Tourism; Transportation and Infrastructure

Representative **Joseph Graves** (R-District 51) Suite 985 . . (517) 373-1780
Counties Represented: Genesee (part), Oakland (part)
Term Expires: 2017
E-mail: josephgraves@house.mi.gov
Committees: Commerce and Trade; Financial Services; Health Policy;
Oversight and Ethics

Representative **Christine Greig** (D-District 37) . . . . . . . . . (517) 373-1793
Counties Represented: Oakland (part)
Term Expires: 2017
E-mail: christinegreig@house.mi.gov
Committees: Education; Joint Legislative Council; Workforce and
Talent Development

Representative **Tim Greimel** (D-District 29) . . . . . . . . . . . . (517) 373-0475
Counties Represented: Oakland (part)          Fax: (517) 373-5061
Term Expires: 2017
E-mail: timgreimel@house.mi.gov
Committees: Government Operations

Representative **Vanessa Guerra** (D-District 95) . . . . . . . . . (517) 373-0152
Counties Represented: Saginaw (part)
Term Expires: 2017
E-mail: vanessaguerra@house.mi.gov
Committees: Criminal Justice; Judiciary
Education: Michigan BA

Representative **Kurt Heise** (R-District 20) . . . . . . . . . . . . . (517) 373-3816
Counties Represented: Wayne (part)
Term Expires: 2017
E-mail: kurtheise@house.mi.gov
Committees: Criminal Justice; Judiciary; Local Government

Representative **Jon Hoadley** (D-District 60) . . . . . . . . . . . . (517) 373-1785
Counties Represented: Kalamazoo (part)
Term Expires: 2017
E-mail: jonhoadley@house.mi.gov
Committees: Appropriations

Representative **Thomas "Tom" Hooker** (R-District 77)
N1096 House Office Building . . . . . . . . . . . . . . . . . . . . . . (517) 373-2277
Counties Represented: Kent (part)
Term Expires: 2017
E-mail: thomashooker@house.mi.gov
Committees: Education; Families, Children, and Seniors; Health Policy

Representative **Marcia Hovey-Wright** (D-District 92)
N1196 House Office Building . . . . . . . . . . . . . . . . . . . . . . (517) 373-2646
Counties Represented: Muskegon (part)          Fax: (517) 373-9646
Term Expires: 2017
E-mail: marciahoveywright@house.mi.gov
Committees: Criminal Justice; Families, Children, and Seniors; Joint
Administrative Rules

Representative **Gary Howell** (R-District 82) . . . . . . . . . . . . (517) 373-0135
Counties Represented: Lapeer
Term Expires: 2017
E-mail: garyhowell@house.mi.gov
Committees: Criminal Justice

Representative **Martin Howrylak, CPA** (R-District 41)
N0890 House Office Building . . . . . . . . . . . . . . . . . . . . . . (517) 373-1783
Counties Represented: Oakland (part)
Term Expires: 2017
E-mail: martinhowrylak@house.mi.gov
Committees: Criminal Justice; Joint Administrative Rules; Judiciary;
Oversight and Ethics; Tax Policy
Education: Michigan 1998 BS, 2003 MAcc

Representative **Holly Hughes** (R-District 91) . . . . . . . . . . . (517) 373-3436
Counties Represented: Muskegon (part)
Term Expires: 2017
E-mail: hollyhughes@house.mi.gov
Committees: Agriculture; Commerce and Trade; Energy Policy; Health
Policy

Representative **Brandt Iden** (R-District 61) . . . . . . . . . . . . (517) 373-1774
Counties Represented: Kalamazoo (part)
Term Expires: 2017
E-mail: brandtiden@house.mi.gov
Committees: Regulatory Reform; Tax Policy; Workforce and Talent
Development

Representative **Larry Inman** (R-District 104) . . . . . . . . . . . (517) 373-1766
Counties Represented: Grand Traverse
Term Expires: 2017
E-mail: larryinman@house.mi.gov
Committees: Appropriations

Representative **Jeff Irwin** (D-District 53)
S0987 House Office Building . . . . . . . . . . . . . . . . . . . . . . (517) 373-2577
Counties Represented: Washtenaw (part)          Fax: (517) 373-5808
Term Expires: 2017
E-mail: jeffirwin@house.mi.gov
Committees: Appropriations; Judiciary

Representative **Bradford C. Jacobsen** (R-District 46)
N0895 House Office Building . . . . . . . . . . . . . . . . . . . . . . (517) 373-1798
Counties Represented: Oakland (part)
Term Expires: 2017
E-mail: bradjacobsen@house.mi.gov
Committees: Energy Policy; Government Operations; Joint Legislative
Council; Transportation and Infrastructure

Representative **Nancy Jenkins** (R-District 57)
N0991 House Office Building . . . . . . . . . . . . . . . . . . . . . . (517) 373-1706
Counties Represented: Lenawee (part)
Term Expires: 2017
E-mail: nancyjenkins@house.mi.gov
Committees: Appropriations; Commerce and Trade

Representative **Joel Johnson** (R-District 97)
S1286 House Office Building . . . . . . . . . . . . . . . . . . . . . . (517) 373-8962
Counties Represented: Arenac, Clare, Gladwin, Osceola (part)
Term Expires: 2017
E-mail: joeljohnson@house.mi.gov
Committees: Agriculture; Commerce and Trade; Judiciary; Workforce
and Talent Development

Representative **Tim Kelly** (R-District 94)
N1198 House Office Building . . . . . . . . . . . . . . . . . . . . . . (517) 373-0837
Counties Represented: Saginaw (part)
Term Expires: 2017
E-mail: timkelly@house.mi.gov
Committees: Appropriations; Education
Education: Denver 1984 BA

Representative **Klint Kesto** (R-District 39)
S0888 House Office Building . . . . . . . . . . . . . . . . . . . . . . (517) 373-1799
Counties Represented: Oakland (part)
Term Expires: 2017
E-mail: klintkesto@house.mi.gov
Committees: Health Policy; Judiciary; Regulatory Reform
Education: Michigan 2002 BA; Wayne State U 2006 JD

Representative **John Kivela** (D-District 109)
S1488 House Office Building . . . . . . . . . . . . . . . . . . . . . . (517) 373-0498
Counties Represented: Alger, Luce, Marquette (part), Schoolcraft
Term Expires: 2017
E-mail: johnkivela@house.mi.gov
Committees: Energy Policy; Natural Resources; Tourism

Representative **Robert L. Kosowski** (D-District 16)
N0695 House Office Building . . . . . . . . . . . . . . . . . . . . . . (517) 373-2576
Counties Represented: Wayne (part)
Term Expires: 2017
E-mail: robertkosowski@house.mi.gov
Committees: Energy Policy; Insurance; Tourism

Representative **Andrea LaFontaine** (R-District 32)
N0796 House Office Building . . . . . . . . . . . . . . . . . . . . . . (517) 373-8931
Counties Represented: Macomb (part), St. Clair (part)
Term Expires: 2017
E-mail: andrealafontaine@house.mi.gov
Committees: Energy Policy; Financial Liability Reform; Government
Operations; Insurance; Joint Legislative Council; Natural Resources

Representative **David LaGrand** (D-District 75) . . . . . . . . . . (517) 373-0135
Counties Represented: Kent (part)
Term Expires: 2017
E-mail: davidlagrand@house.mi.gov
Committees: Transportation and Infrastructure
Education: Calvin Col 1988 BA; Chicago 1992 JD

*(continued on next page)*

**Representatives** *continued*

Representative **Marilyn Lane** (D-District 31)
N0795 House Office Building . . . . . . . . . . . . . . . . . . . . . (517) 373-0159
Counties Represented: Macomb (part)          Fax: (517) 373-5893
Term Expires: 2017
E-mail: marilynlane@house.mi.gov
Committees: Energy Policy; Regulatory Reform; Transportation and Infrastructure

Representative **Dan V. Lauwers** (R-District 81)
S1185 House Office Building . . . . . . . . . . . . . . . . . . . . . (517) 373-1790
Counties Represented: St. Clair (part)
Term Expires: 2017
E-mail: danlauwers@house.mi.gov
Committees: Agriculture; Regulatory Reform; Transportation and Infrastructure; Workforce and Talent Development
Education: Michigan State 1985 BS, 1985 BS

Representative **Bill Lavoy** (D-District 17)
N0696 House Office Building . . . . . . . . . . . . . . . . . . . . . (517) 373-1530
Counties Represented: Monroe (part), Wayne (part)
Term Expires: 2017
E-mail: billlavoy@house.mi.gov
Committees: Agriculture; Energy Policy; Tax Policy
Education: Michigan BA

Representative **Tom Leonard, JD** (R-District 93)
N1197 House Office Building . . . . . . . . . . . . . . . . . . . . . (517) 373-1778
Counties Represented: Clinton, Gratiot (part)
Term Expires: 2017
E-mail: tomleonard@house.mi.gov
Committees: Insurance

Representative **Eric Leutheuser** (R-District 58) . . . . . . . . . (517) 373-1794
Counties Represented: Branch, Hillsdale
Term Expires: 2017
E-mail: ericleutheuser@house.mi.gov
Committees: Commerce and Trade; Financial Liability Reform

Representative **Frank Liberati** (D-District 13) . . . . . . . . . . . (517) 373-0845
Counties Represented: Wayne (part)
Term Expires: 2017
E-mail: frankliberati@house.mi.gov
Committees: Families, Children, and Seniors; Health Policy; Workforce and Talent Development

Representative **Leslie Love** (D-District 10) . . . . . . . . . . . . . (517) 373-0857
Counties Represented: Wayne (part)
Term Expires: 2017
E-mail: leslielove@house.mi.gov
Committees: Commerce and Trade; Financial Services; Workforce and Talent Development

Representative **Peter J. Lucido** (R-District 36) . . . . . . . . . . (517) 373-0843
Counties Represented: Macomb (part)
Term Expires: 2017
E-mail: peterlucido@house.mi.gov
Committees: Criminal Justice; Energy Policy; Financial Services; Judiciary
Education: Central Michigan 1984 MB; Detroit Law 1988 JD

Representative **David C. Maturen** (R-District 63) . . . . . . . (517) 373-1787
Counties Represented: Calhoun (part), Kalamazoo (part)
Term Expires: 2017
E-mail: davidmaturen@house.mi.gov
Committees: Energy Policy; Local Government; Tax Policy; Transportation and Infrastructure

Representative **Ed McBroom** (R-District 108)
S1487 House Office Building . . . . . . . . . . . . . . . . . . . . . (517) 373-0156
Counties Represented: Delta, Dickinson, Menominee
Term Expires: 2017
E-mail: edmcbroom@house.mi.gov
Committees: Education; Energy Policy; Natural Resources; Oversight and Ethics

Representative
**Michael D. "Mike" McCready** (R-District 40)
S0889 House Office Building . . . . . . . . . . . . . . . . . . . . . (517) 373-8670
Counties Represented: Oakland (part)
Term Expires: 2017
E-mail: mikemccready@house.mi.gov
Committees: Appropriations; Transportation and Infrastructure
Education: Michigan 1983 BS

Representative **Aaron Miller** (R-District 59) . . . . . . . . . . . . (517) 373-0832
Counties Represented: Cass (part), St. Joseph
Term Expires: 2017
E-mail: aaronmiller@house.mi.gov
Committees: Appropriations
Education: Western Michigan 2010 BA; Bethel Col (IN) 2014 MEd

Representative **Jeremy Moss** (D-District 35) . . . . . . . . . . . (517) 373-1788
Counties Represented: Oakland (part)
Term Expires: 2017
E-mail: jeremymoss@house.mi.gov
Committees: Commerce and Trade; Local Government; Regulatory Reform

Representative **Paul Muxlow** (R-District 83)
S1187 House Office Building . . . . . . . . . . . . . . . . . . . . . (517) 373-0835
Counties Represented: Sanilac, St. Clair (part)
Term Expires: 2017
E-mail: paulmuxlow@house.mi.gov
Committees: Appropriations
Education: Eastern Michigan BA; Michigan MA

Representative **Sheldon Neeley** (D-District 34) . . . . . . . . . (517) 373-8808
Counties Represented: Genesee (part)
Term Expires: 2017
E-mail: sheldonneeley@house.mi.gov
Committees: Health Policy; Local Government; Transportation and Infrastructure

Representative **Aric Nesbitt** (R-District 66)
S1085 House Office Building . . . . . . . . . . . . . . . . . . . . . (517) 373-0839
Counties Represented: Kalamazoo (part), Van Buren
Term Expires: 2017
E-mail: aricnesbitt@house.mi.gov
Committees: Energy Policy

Representative **Rick Outman** (R-District 70)
S1089 House Office Building . . . . . . . . . . . . . . . . . . . . . (517) 373-0834
Counties Represented: Gratiot (part), Montcalm
Term Expires: 2017
E-mail: rickoutman@house.mi.gov
Committees: Agriculture; Energy Policy

Representative **Kristy Pagan** (D-District 21) . . . . . . . . . . . . (517) 373-2575
Counties Represented: Wayne (part)
Term Expires: 2017
E-mail: kristypagan@house.mi.gov
Committees: Appropriations; Oversight and Ethics

Representative **Dave Pagel** (R-District 78)
N1097 House Office Building . . . . . . . . . . . . . . . . . . . . . (517) 373-1796
Counties Represented: Berrien (part), Cass (part)
Term Expires: 2017
E-mail: davepagel@house.mi.gov
Committees: Appropriations; Tourism
Education: Michigan State 1976 BS

Representative **Peter Pettalia** (R-District 106)
S1485 House Office Building . . . . . . . . . . . . . . . . . . . . . (517) 373-0833
Counties Represented: Alcona, Alpena, Cheboygan (part), Iosco, Presque Isle
Term Expires: 2017
E-mail: peterpettalia@house.mi.gov
Committees: Energy Policy; Financial Services; Tourism; Transportation and Infrastructure

Representative **Phil Phelps** (D-District 49)
N0898 House Office Building . . . . . . . . . . . . . . . . . . . . . (517) 373-7515
Counties Represented: Genesee (part)
Term Expires: 2017
E-mail: repphelps@house.mi.gov
Committees: Health Policy
Education: Michigan (Flint)

Representative **Julie Plawecki** (D-District 11) . . . . . . . . . . . (517) 373-0849
Counties Represented: Wayne (part)
Term Expires: 2017
E-mail: julieplawecki@house.mi.gov
Committees: Energy Policy; Natural Resources
Education: Oakland U BS

Representative **Earl Poleski** (R-District 64)
N0998 House Office Building . . . . . . . . . . . . . . . . . . . . . (517) 373-1795
Counties Represented: Jackson (part)
Term Expires: 2017
E-mail: earlpoleski@house.mi.gov
Committees: Appropriations; Financial Liability Reform

Representative **Lisa Posthumus Lyons** (R-District 86)
N1190 House Office Building . . . . . . . . . . . . . . . . . . . . . (517) 373-0846
Counties Represented: Ionia (part), Kent (part)
Term Expires: 2017
E-mail: lisalyons@house.mi.gov
Committees: Financial Liability Reform; Insurance

Representative **Phil Potvin** (R-District 102)
S1386 House Office Building . . . . . . . . . . . . . . . . . . . . . (517) 373-1747
Counties Represented: Mecosta, Osceola (part), Wexford
Term Expires: 2017
E-mail: philpotvin@house.mi.gov
Committees: Appropriations

Representative **Amanda Price** (R-District 89)
N1193 House Office Building . . . . . . . . . . . . . . . . . . . . . . (517) 373-0838
Counties Represented: Ottawa (part)
Term Expires: 2017
E-mail: amandaprice@house.mi.gov
Committees: Education; Joint Administrative Rules; Local Government;
Workforce and Talent Development

Representative **Al Pscholka** (R-District 79)
N1098 House Office Building . . . . . . . . . . . . . . . . . . . . . . (517) 373-1403
Counties Represented: Berrien (part)
Term Expires: 2017
E-mail: alpscholka@house.mi.gov
Committees: Appropriations

Representative **Bruce Rendon** (R-District 103)
S1387 House Office Building . . . . . . . . . . . . . . . . . . . . . . (517) 373-3817
Counties Represented: Crawford, Kalkaska, Missaukee, Ogemaw,
Roscommon
Term Expires: 2017
E-mail: brucerendon@house.mi.gov
Committees: Agriculture; Commerce and Trade; Natural Resources;
Tourism

Representative **Brett Roberts** (R-District 65) . . . . . . . . . . . (517) 373-1775
Counties Represented: Eaton (part), Jackson (part), Lenawee (part)
Term Expires: 2017
E-mail: bettroberts@house.mi.gov
Committees: Agriculture; Energy Policy; Regulatory Reform;
Workforce and Talent Development

Representative **Sarah Roberts** (D-District 18)
N0697 House Office Building . . . . . . . . . . . . . . . . . . . . . . (517) 373-1180
Counties Represented: Macomb (part)
Term Expires: 2017
E-mail: sarahroberts@house.mi.gov
Committees: Appropriations
Education: Iowa 2000 BA

Representative **Rose Mary Robinson** (D-District 4)
S0588 House Office Building . . . . . . . . . . . . . . . . . . . . . . (517) 373-1008
Counties Represented: Wayne (part)
Term Expires: 2017
E-mail: rosemaryrobinson@house.mi.gov
Committees: Judiciary; Oversight and Ethics
Education: Wayne State U 1972 JD

Representative **Jim Runestad** (R-District 44) . . . . . . . . . . . (517) 373-2616
Counties Represented: Oakland (part)
Term Expires: 2017
E-mail: jimrunestad@house.mi.gov
Committees: Families, Children, and Seniors; Insurance; Judiciary;
Local Government
Education: Central Michigan BS

Representative **David Rutledge** (D-District 54)
S0988 House Office Building . . . . . . . . . . . . . . . . . . . . . . (517) 373-1771
Counties Represented: Washtenaw (part)
Term Expires: 2017
E-mail: davidrutledge@house.mi.gov
Committees: Joint Legislative Council; Local Government;
Transportation and Infrastructure

Representative **Harvey Santana** (D-District 9)
S0688 House Office Building . . . . . . . . . . . . . . . . . . . . . . (517) 373-6990
Counties Represented: Wayne (part)
Term Expires: 2017
E-mail: harveysantana@house.mi.gov
Committees: Appropriations; Education

Representative **Andy Schor** (D-District 68)
S1087 House Office Building . . . . . . . . . . . . . . . . . . . . . . (517) 373-0826
Counties Represented: Ingham (part)
Term Expires: 2017
E-mail: andyschor@house.mi.gov
Committees: Commerce and Trade; Education; Regulatory Reform
Education: Michigan 1997 BA

Representative **Jason Sheppard** (R-District 56) . . . . . . . . (517) 373-2617
Counties Represented: Monroe (part)
Term Expires: 2017
E-mail: jasonsheppard@house.mi.gov
Committees: Agriculture; Commerce and Trade; Energy Policy; Local
Government

Representative **Sam Singh** (D-District 69)
S1088 House Office Building . . . . . . . . . . . . . . . . . . . . . . (517) 373-1786
Counties Represented: Ingham (part)
Term Expires: 2017
E-mail: samsingh@house.mi.gov
Committees: Appropriations; Government Operations

Representative **Charles Smiley** (D-District 50)
N0899 House Office Building . . . . . . . . . . . . . . . . . . . . . . (517) 373-3906
Counties Represented: Genesee (part)
Term Expires: 2017
E-mail: charlessmiley@house.mi.gov
Committees: Natural Resources; Transportation and Infrastructure

Representative **Pat Somerville** (R-District 23)
S0787 House Office Building . . . . . . . . . . . . . . . . . . . . . . (517) 373-0855
Counties Represented: Wayne (part)
Term Expires: 2017
E-mail: patsomerville@house.mi.gov
Committees: Commerce and Trade; Education; Financial Liability
Reform; Tax Policy

Representative **Jim Tedder** (R-District 43) . . . . . . . . . . . . . (517) 373-0615
Counties Represented: Oakland (part)
Term Expires: 2017
E-mail: jimtedder@house.mi.gov
Committees: Education; Health Policy; Workforce and Talent
Development

Representative **Lana Theis** (R-District 42) . . . . . . . . . . . . . (517) 373-1784
Counties Represented: Livingston (part)
Term Expires: 2017
E-mail: lanatheis@house.mi.gov
Committees: Financial Services; Insurance; Local Government;
Oversight and Ethics

Representative **Alberta Tinsley-Talabi** (D-District 2)
S0586 House Office Building . . . . . . . . . . . . . . . . . . . . . . (517) 373-1776
Counties Represented: Wayne (part)
Term Expires: 2017
E-mail: albertatalabi@house.mi.gov
Committees: Agriculture; Families, Children, and Seniors
Education: Eastern Michigan BA

Representative **Jim Townsend** (D-District 26)
N790 House Office Building . . . . . . . . . . . . . . . . . . . . . . (517) 373-3818
Counties Represented: Oakland (part)
Term Expires: 2017
E-mail: jimtownsend@house.mi.gov
Committees: Commerce and Trade; Tax Policy; Workforce and Talent
Development

Representative **Dr. Henry "Hank" Vaupel** (R-District 47) . . . . . . . . (517)
373-8835
Counties Represented: Livingston (part)
Term Expires: 2017
E-mail: hankvaupel@house.mi.gov
Committees: Agriculture; Families, Children, and Seniors; Health
Policy; Insurance
Education: Michigan State DVM

Representative **Rob VerHeulen, JD** (R-District 74)
N1093 House Office Building . . . . . . . . . . . . . . . . . . . . . . (517) 373-8900
Counties Represented: Kent (part)
Term Expires: 2017
E-mail: robverheulen@house.mi.gov
Committees: Appropriations; Health Policy; Joint Legislative Council

Representative **Roger Victory** (R-District 88)
N1192 House Office Building . . . . . . . . . . . . . . . . . . . . . . (517) 373-1830
Counties Represented: Ottawa (part)
Term Expires: 2017
E-mail: rogervictory@house.mi.gov
Committees: Appropriations
Education: Davenport 1989 BA

Representative **Michael Webber** (R-District 45) . . . . . . . . (517) 373-1773
Counties Represented: Oakland (part)
Term Expires: 2017
E-mail: michaelwebber@house.mi.gov
Committees: Criminal Justice; Energy Policy; Government Operations;
Insurance; Tax Policy

Representative **Mary Whiteford** (R-District 80) . . . . . . . . . (517) 373-0135
Counties Represented: Allegan (part)
Term Expires: 2017
E-mail: marywhiteford@house.mi.gov
Committees: Natural Resources

Representative **Robert Wittenberg** (D-District 27) . . . . . . . (517) 373-0478
Counties Represented: Oakland (part)
Term Expires: 2017
E-mail: robertwittenberg@house.mi.gov
Committees: Financial Liability Reform; Health Policy; Insurance

Representative **Henry Yanez** (D-District 25)
S789 House Office Building . . . . . . . . . . . . . . . . . . . . . . (517) 373-2275
Counties Represented: Macomb (part)
Term Expires: 2017
E-mail: henryyanez@house.mi.gov
Committees: Appropriations; Financial Services

*(continued on next page)*

**LEGISLATIVE BRANCH**

**Representatives** *continued*

Representative **Ken Yonker** (R-District 72)
N-1091 House Office Building . . . . . . . . . . . . . . . . . . . . . . (517) 373-0840
Counties Represented: Allegan (part), Kent (part)
Term Expires: 2017
E-mail: kenyonker@house.mi.gov
Committees: Education; Health Policy; Regulatory Reform; Tax Policy;
Transportation and Infrastructure

Representative **Adam Zemke** (D-District 55)
S989 House Office Building . . . . . . . . . . . . . . . . . . . . . . . (517) 373-1792
Counties Represented: Washtenaw (part)
Term Expires: 2017
E-mail: adamzemke@house.mi.gov
Committees: Appropriations; Education
Education: Michigan State 2008 MME, 2005 BSME

District 28 **(Vacant)** . . . . . . . . . . . . . . . . . . . . . . . . . . . . . (517) 373-0135
Note: A general election to fill this legislative vacancy will be held on
November 8, 2016.

# House Standing Committees

## Agriculture

**Majority Members**
Dan V. Lauwers (R-81) *Chair*
Triston Cole (R-105)
 *Majority Vice Chair*
Ray Franz (R-101)
Ben Glardon (R-85)
Joel Johnson (R-97)
Holly Hughes (R-91)
Rick Outman (R-70)
Bruce Rendon (R-103)
Brett Roberts (R-65)
Jason Sheppard (R-56)
Dr. Henry "Hank" Vaupel (R-47)

**Minority Members**
Charles Brunner (D-96)
 *Minority Vice Chair*
George Darany (D-15)
Gretchen Driskell (D-52)
LaTanya Garrett (D-7)
Bill Lavoy (D-17)
Alberta Tinsley-Talabi (D-2)

## Appropriations

**Majority Members**
Al Pscholka (R-79) *Chair*
Jon Bumstead (R-100)
 *Majority Vice Chair*
Chris Afendoulis (R-73)
Dr. John Bizon (R-62)
Edward J. Canfield (R-84)
Laura Cox (R-19)
Daniela García (R-90)
Larry Inman (R-104)
Nancy Jenkins (R-57)
Tim Kelly (R-94)
Michael D. "Mike" McCready
 (R-40)
Aaron Miller (R-59)
Paul Muxlow (R-83)
Dave Pagel (R-78)
Earl Poleski (R-64)
Phil Potvin (R-102)
Rob VerHeulen (R-74)
Roger Victory (R-88)

**Minority Members**
Harvey Santana (D-9)
 *Minority Vice Chair*
Brian Banks (D-1)
Fred Durhal III (D-5)
Pam Faris (D-48)
Jon Hoadley (D-60)
Jeff Irwin (D-53)
Kristy Pagan (D-21)
Sarah Roberts (D-18)
Sam Singh (D-69)
Henry Yanez (D-25)
Adam Zemke (D-55)

## Commerce and Trade

**Majority Members**
Joseph Graves (R-51) *Chair*
Jason Sheppard (R-56)
 *Majority Vice Chair*
Tom Barrett (R-71)
Mike Callton (R-87)
Daniela García (R-90)
Gary Glenn (R-98)
Holly Hughes (R-91)
Nancy Jenkins (R-57)
Joel Johnson (R-97)
Eric Leutheuser (R-58)
Bruce Rendon (R-103)
Pat Somerville (R-23)

**Minority Members**
Andy Schor (D-68)
 *Minority Vice Chair*
Wendell Byrd (D-3)
LaTanya Garrett (D-7)
Erika Geiss (D-12)
Leslie Love (D-10)
Jeremy Moss (D-35)
Jim Townsend (D-26)

## Criminal Justice

**Majority Members**
Kurt Heise (R-20) *Chair*
Michael Webber (R-45)
 *Majority Vice Chair*
Gary Howell (R-82)
Martin Howrylak (R-41)
Peter J. Lucido (R-36)

**Minority Members**
Vanessa Guerra (D-95)
 *Minority Vice Chair*
Stephanie Chang (D-6)
Marcia Hovey-Wright (D-92)

## Education

**Majority Members**
Amanda Price (R-89) *Chair*
Daniela García (R-90)
 *Majority Vice-Chair*
Mike Callton (R-87)
Lee Chatfield (R-107)
Thomas "Tom" Hooker (R-77)
Tim Kelly (R-94)
Ed McBroom (R-108)
Pat Somerville (R-23)
Jim Tedder (R-43)
Ken Yonker (R-72)

**Minority Members**
Adam Zemke (D-55)
 *Minority Vice Chair*
Winnie Brinks (D-76)
Stephanie Chang (D-6)
Christine Greig (D-37)
Harvey Santana (D-9)
Andy Schor (D-68)

## Energy Policy

**Majority Members**
Aric Nesbitt (R-66) *Chair*
Gary Glenn (R-98)
 *Majority Vice Chair*
Tom Barrett (R-71)
Triston Cole (R-105)
Holly Hughes (R-91)
Bradford C. Jacobsen (R-46)
Andrea LaFontaine (R-32)
Peter J. Lucido (R-36)
David C. Maturen (R-63)
Ed McBroom (R-108)
Rick Outman (R-70)
Peter Pettalia (R-106)
Brett Roberts (R-65)
Jason Sheppard (R-56)
Michael Webber (R-45)

**Minority Members**
Tom Cochran (D-67)
Bill Lavoy (D-17)
 *Minority Vice Chair*
Charles Brunner (D-96)
Wendell Byrd (D-3)
Scott Dianda (D-110)
LaTanya Garrett (D-7)
John Kivela (D-109)
Robert L. Kosowski (D-16)
Marilyn Lane (D-31)
Julie Plawecki (D-11)

## Families, Children, and Seniors

**Majority Members**
Thomas "Tom" Hooker (R-77)
 *Chair*
Jim Runestad (R-44)
 *Majority Vice Chair*
Kathy S. Crawford (R-38)
Anthony Forlini (R-24)
Dr. Henry "Hank" Vaupel (R-47)

**Minority Members**
Marcia Hovey-Wright (D-92)
 *Minority Vice Chair*
Frank Liberati (D-13)
Alberta Tinsley-Talabi (D-2)

## Financial Liability Reform

**Majority Members**
Pat Somerville (R-23) *Chair*
Eric Leutheuser (R-58)
 *Majority Vice Chair*
Jeff Farrington (R-30)
Andrea LaFontaine (R-32)
Lisa Posthumus Lyons (R-86)
Earl Poleski (R-64)

**Minority Members**
Robert Wittenberg (D-27)
 *Minority Vice Chair*
Wendell Byrd (D-3)
John Chirkun (D-22)

## Financial Services

**Majority Members**
Anthony Forlini (R-24) *Chair*
Peter Pettalia (R-106)
 *Majority Vice Chair*
Mike Callton (R-87)
Joseph Graves (R-51)
Peter J. Lucido (R-36)
Lana Theis (R-42)

**Minority Members**
Henry Yanez (D-25)
 *Minority Vice Chair*
Paul Clemente (D-14)
Sherry Gay-Dagnogo (D-8)
Leslie Love (D-10)

## Government Operations

**Majority Members**
Bradford C. Jacobsen (R-46) *Chair*
Michael Webber (R-45)
 *Majority Vice Chair*
Andrea LaFontaine (R-32)

**Minority Members**
Tim Greimel (D-29)
 *Minority Vice Chair*
Sam Singh (D-69)

## Health Policy

**Majority Members**
Mike Callton (R-87) *Chair*
Dr. Henry "Hank" Vaupel (R-47)
  *Majority Vice Chair*
Dr. John Bizon (R-62)
Lee Chatfield (R-107)
Kathy S. Crawford (R-38)
Daniela García (R-90)
Joseph Graves (R-51)
Thomas "Tom" Hooker (R-77)
Holly Hughes (R-91)
Klint Kesto (R-39)
Jim Tedder (R-43)
Rob VerHeulen (R-74)
Ken Yonker (R-72)

**Minority Members**
George Darany (D-15)
  *Minority Vice Chair*
Winnie Brinks (D-76)
Tom Cochran (D-67)
Erika Geiss (D-12)
Frank Liberati (D-13)
Sheldon Neeley (D-34)
Phil Phelps (D-49)
Robert Wittenberg (D-27)

## Insurance

**Majority Members**
Tom Leonard (R-93) *Chair*
Lana Theis (R-42)
  *Majority Vice Chair*
Tom Barrett (R-71)
Ray Franz (R-101)
Ben Glardon (R-85)
Ken Goike (R-33)
Andrea LaFontaine (R-32)
Lisa Posthumus Lyons (R-86)
Jim Runestad (R-44)
Dr. Henry "Hank" Vaupel (R-47)
Michael Webber (R-45)

**Minority Members**
Tom Cochran (D-67)
  *Minority Vice Chair*
Brian Banks (D-1)
Paul Clemente (D-14)
Robert L. Kosowski (D-16)
Robert Wittenberg (D-27)

## Judiciary

**Majority Members**
Klint Kesto (R-39) *Chair*
Peter J. Lucido (R-36)
  *Majority Vice Chair*
Triston Cole (R-105)
Kurt Heise (R-20)
Martin Howrylak (R-41)
Joel Johnson (R-97)
Jim Runestad (R-44)

**Minority Members**
Jeff Irwin (D-53)
  *Minority Vice Chair*
Stephanie Chang (D-6)
Vanessa Guerra (D-95)
Rose Mary Robinson (D-4)

## Local Government

**Majority Members**
Lee Chatfield (R-107) *Chair*
Amanda Price (R-89)
  *Majority Vice Chair*
Kurt Heise (R-20)
David C. Maturen (R-63)
Jim Runestad (R-44)
Jason Sheppard (R-56)
Lana Theis (R-42)

**Minority Members**
Jeremy Moss (D-35)
  *Minority Vice Chair*
Charles Brunner (D-96)
Sheldon Neeley (D-34)
David Rutledge (D-54)

## Natural Resources

**Majority Members**
Andrea LaFontaine (R-32) *Chair*
Bruce Rendon (R-103)
  *Majority Vice Chair*
Anthony Forlini (R-24)
Ken Goike (R-33)
Ed McBroom (R-108)
Mary Whiteford (R-80)

**Minority Members**
John Kivela (D-109)
  *Minority Vice Chair*
Julie Plawecki (D-11)
Charles Smiley (D-50)

## Oversight and Ethics

**Majority Members**
Ed McBroom (R-108) *Chair*
Martin Howrylak (R-41)
  *Majority Vice Chair*
Joseph Graves (R-51)
Lana Theis (R-42)

**Minority Members**
Rose Mary Robinson (D-4)
  *Minority Vice Chair*
Kristy Pagan (D-21)

## Regulatory Reform

**Majority Members**
Ray Franz (R-101) *Chair*
Brett Roberts (R-65)
  *Majority Vice Chair*
Kathy S. Crawford (R-38)
Daniela García (R-90)
Brandt Iden (R-61)
Klint Kesto (R-39)
Dan V. Lauwers (R-81)
Ken Yonker (R-72)

**Minority Members**
Scott Dianda (D-110)
  *Minority Vice Chair*
John Chirkun (D-22)
George Darany (D-15)
Marilyn Lane (D-31)
Jeremy Moss (D-35)
Andy Schor (D-68)

## Tax Policy

**Majority Members**
Jeff Farrington (R-30) *Chair*
David C. Maturen (R-63)
  *Majority Vice Chair*
Lee Chatfield (R-107)
Gary Glenn (R-98)
Martin Howrylak (R-41)
Brandt Iden (R-61)
Pat Somerville (R-23)
Michael Webber (R-45)
Ken Yonker (R-72)

**Minority Members**
Jim Townsend (D-26)
  *Minority Vice Chair*
Wendell Byrd (D-3)
Paul Clemente (D-14)
Bill Lavoy (D-17)

## Transportation and Infrastructure

**Majority Members**
Peter Pettalia (R-106) *Chair*
Ben Glardon (R-85)
  *Majority Vice Chair*
Triston Cole (R-105)
Jeff Farrington (R-30)
Ken Goike (R-33)
Bradford C. Jacobsen (R-46)
Dan V. Lauwers (R-81)
David C. Maturen (R-63)
Michael D. "Mike" McCready
  (R-40)
Ken Yonker (R-72)

**Minority Members**
Marilyn Lane (D-31)
  *Minority Vice Chair*
David LaGrand (D-75)
Scott Dianda (D-110)
Sheldon Neeley (D-34)
David Rutledge (D-54)
Charles Smiley (D-50)

## Tourism

**Majority Members**
Peter Pettalia (R-106) *Chair*
Ken Goike (R-33)
  *Majority Vice Chair*
Dave Pagel (R-78)
Bruce Rendon (R-103)

**Minority Members**
Robert L. Kosowski (D-16)
  *Minority Vice Chair*
Charles Brunner (D-96)
John Kivela (D-109)

## Workforce and Talent Development

**Majority Members**
Joel Johnson (R-97) *Chair*
Jim Tedder (R-43)
  *Majority Vice Chair*
Kathy S. Crawford (R-38)
Jeff Farrington (R-30)
Brandt Iden (R-61)
Dan V. Lauwers (R-81)
Amanda Price (R-89)
Brett Roberts (R-65)

**Minority Members**
Winnie Brinks (D-76)
  *Minority Vice Chair*
Erika Geiss (D-12)
Christine Greig (D-37)
Frank Liberati (D-13)
Leslie Love (D-10)
Jim Townsend (D-26)

# Minnesota Legislature

Tel: (651) 296-8338 (Legislative Reference Desk)
Internet: www.leg.state.mn.us

## Minnesota Senate

Minnesota Senate Building, 95 University Avenue West,
Saint Paul, MN 55155
State Office Building, 100 Rev. Dr. Martin Luther King Jr. Boulevard,
St. Paul, MN 55155-1206
Tel: (651) 296-0504  Tel: (651) 296-8088 (Committee Hotline)
TTY: (651) 296-0250  Fax: (651) 296-6511  Internet: www.senate.mn

President of the Senate **Sandra L. Pappas** (DFL) . . . . . . . (651) 296-1802
  Education: Metropolitan State U 1986 BA;
  JFK School Govt 1994 MPA
President Pro Tem **Ann H. Rest** (DFL) . . . . . . . . . . . . . . . . (651) 296-2889
  Education: Northwestern BA; Chicago MA; Minnesota MBT;
  Harvard 1970 MAT; JFK School Govt MPA
Majority Leader **Thomas M. "Tom" Bakk** (DFL) . . . . . . . (651) 296-8881
  Education: Minnesota (Duluth) BA
Deputy Majority Leader **Jeff Hayden** (DFL) . . . . . . . . . . . (651) 296-4261
  Education: Bethel U BA
Assistant Majority Leader **Katie Sieben** (DFL) . . . . . . . . . (651) 296-8060
  Education: Colorado Col BA; JFK School Govt 2008 MPA
Majority Whip **Chris A. Eaton** (DFL) . . . . . . . . . . . . . . . . (651) 296-8869
Majority Whip **Lyle J. Koenen** (DFL) . . . . . . . . . . . . . . . . (651) 296-5094
Minority Leader **David W. Hann** (R) . . . . . . . . . . . . . . . . (651) 296-1749
  Education: Gustavus Adolphus 1973 BA
Assistant Minority Leader **Michelle R. Benson** (R) . . . . . . (651) 296-3219
Assistant Minority Leader **Gary H. Dahms** (R) . . . . . . . . . (651) 296-8138
Assistant Minority Leader **Paul E. Gazelka** (R) . . . . . . . . . (651) 296-4875
  Education: Oral Roberts BS
Assistant Minority Leader **Bill G. Ingebrigtsen** (R) . . . . . . (651) 297-8063
  Education: Alexandria Tech AA
Assistant Minority Leader **Warren Limmer** (R) . . . . . . . . . (651) 296-2159
  Education: St Cloud State BA
Assistant Minority Leader **Carrie Ruud** (R) . . . . . . . . . . . . (651) 296-4913
Minority Whip **David J. Osmek** (R) . . . . . . . . . . . . . . . . . . (651) 296-1282
  Education: St Cloud State BES
Secretary of the Senate **JoAnne Zoff** . . . . . . . . . . . . . . . . (651) 296-2344
  E-mail: joanne.zoff@senate.mn

## Senators

**Party Affiliation Statistics: Republicans: 28, Democrats: 39**

Senator **Jim Abeler** (R-District 35) Room 127 . . . . . . . . . . (651) 296-3733
  Counties Represented: Anoka (part)
  Term Expires: 2017
  E-mail: sen.jim.abeler@senate.mn
  Committees: Higher Education and Workforce Development; State and
  Local Government
  Education: Northwestern Col (MN) 1979 DC
Senator **Bruce D. Anderson** (R-District 29) Room 133 . . . . (651) 296-5981
  Counties Represented: Hennepin (part), Wright    Res: (763) 682-1480
  (part)
  Term Expires: 2017
  E-mail: sen.bruce.anderson@senate.mn
  Committees: Finance; State and Local Government
  Education: Northwestern Col (MN) 1999 BSBA
Senator **Thomas M. "Tom" Bakk** (DFL-District 3)
  Room 3113 . . . . . . . . . . . . . . . . . . . . . . . . . . . . . . . . . . . . . . (651) 296-8881
  Counties Represented: Cook, Koochiching, Lake,  Dist: (218) 741-6010
  St. Louis (part)    Res: (218) 666-5041
  Term Expires: 2017
  E-mail: sen.tom.bakk@senate.mn
  Committees: Rules and Administration; Taxes
Senator **Michelle R. Benson** (R-District 31) Room 115 . . . (651) 296-3219
  Counties Represented: Anoka (part), Isanti (part), Sherburne (part)
  Term Expires: 2017
  E-mail: sen.michelle.benson@senate.mn
  Committees: Environment and Energy; Health, Human Services and
  Housing

Senator **Terri E. Bonoff** (DFL-District 44) Room 3105 . . . . (651) 296-4314
  Counties Represented: Hennepin (part)    Res: (952) 935-5168
  Term Expires: 2017
  E-mail: sen.terri.bonoff@senate.mn
  Committees: Finance; Higher Education and Workforce Development;
  Jobs, Agriculture and Rural Development
  Education: Clark U BA
Senator **David M. "Dave" Brown** (R-District 15)
  Room 109 . . . . . . . . . . . . . . . . . . . . . . . . . . . . . . . . . . . . . . (651) 296-8075
  Counties Represented: Benton (part), Kanabec (part), Mille Lacs,
  Morrison (part), Sherburne (part), Wright (part)
  Term Expires: 2017
  E-mail: sen.david.brown@senate.mn
  Committees: Commerce; Environment and Energy
Senator **Jim Carlson** (DFL-District 51) Room 3215 . . . . . . (651) 279-8073
  Counties Represented: Dakota (part)
  Term Expires: 2017
  E-mail: sen.jim.carlson@senate.mn
  Committees: Commerce; Education; Transportation
  Education: Minnesota BME
Senator **Roger C. Chamberlain** (R-District 38)
  Room 129 . . . . . . . . . . . . . . . . . . . . . . . . . . . . . . . . . . . . . . (651) 296-1253
  Counties Represented: Anoka (part), Ramsey (part), Washington (part)
  Term Expires: 2017
  E-mail: sen.roger.chamberlain@senate.mn
  Committees: Education
Senator **Bobby Joe Champion** (DFL-District 59)
  Room 3207 . . . . . . . . . . . . . . . . . . . . . . . . . . . . . . . . . . . . . (651) 296-9246
  Counties Represented: Hennepin (part)
  Term Expires: 2017
  1501 Hall Curve North, Minneapolis, MN 55411
  E-mail: sen.bobby.champion@senate.mn
  Committees: Capital Investment; Finance; Judiciary; Transportation
  Education: Macalester 1979 BA; William Mitchell 1995 JD
Senator **Greg D. Clausen** (DFL-District 57) Room 3103 . . (651) 296-4210
  Counties Represented: Dakota (part)    Dist: (651) 423-7719
  Term Expires: 2017
  E-mail: sen.greg.clausen@senate.mn
  Committees: Education; Higher Education and Workforce Development
  Education: Augsburg 1969 BA; U St Thomas (MN) 1973 MA,
  1983 EdD
Senator **Richard J. "Dick" Cohen** (DFL-District 64)
  Room 3235 . . . . . . . . . . . . . . . . . . . . . . . . . . . . . . . . . . . . . (651) 296-5931
  Counties Represented: Ramsey (part)    Dist: (651) 645-0511
  Term Expires: 2017    Res: (651) 699-4476
  E-mail: sen.richard.cohen@senate.mn
  Committees: Capital Investment; Finance; Rules and Administration
  Education: Northwestern BA; William Mitchell JD
Senator **Kevin L. Dahle** (DFL-District 20) Room 3217 . . . . (651) 296-1279
  Counties Represented: Le Sueur (part), Rice  Dist: (507) 663-0630
  (part), Scott (part)    Res: (507) 645-0910
  Term Expires: 2017
  E-mail: sen.kevin.dahle@senate.mn
  Committees: Commerce; Education; State and Local Government
  Education: Northern Iowa 1982 BS; St Mary's U (MN) 2004 MA
Senator **Gary H. Dahms** (R-District 16) Room 121 . . . . . . (651) 296-8138
  Counties Represented: Brown, Lac qui Parle, Lyon  Res: (507) 641-5269
  (part), Redwood (part), Renville (part), Yellow Medicine
  Term Expires: 2017
  E-mail: sen.gary.dahms@senate.mn
  Committees: Commerce; Jobs, Agriculture and Rural Development
Senator **D. Scott Dibble** (DFL-District 61) . . . . . . . . . . . . . (651) 296-4191
  Counties Represented: Hennepin (part)
  Term Expires: 2017
  E-mail: sen.scott.dibble@senate.mn
  Committees: Environment and Energy; Finance; Transportation
Senator **Kari Dziedzic** (DFL-District 60) Room 3213 . . . . . (651) 296-7809
  Counties Represented: Hennepin (part)
  Term Expires: 2017
  E-mail: sen.kari.dziedzic@senate.mn
  Committees: Judiciary; Taxes
  Education: Minnesota
Senator **Chris A. Eaton** (DFL-District 40) Room 3413 . . . . (651) 296-8869
  Counties Represented: Hennepin (part)
  Term Expires: 2017
  E-mail: sen.chris.eaton@senate.mn
  Committees: Environment and Energy; Health, Human Services and
  Housing; State and Local Government; Taxes

LEGISLATIVE BRANCH

Senator **Kent Eken** (DFL-District 4) Room 3107 . . . . . . . . (651) 296-3205
  Counties Represented: Becker (part), Clay, Norman
  Term Expires: 2017
  E-mail: sen.kent.eken@senate.mn
  Committees: Capital Investment; Higher Education and Workforce
  Development; Jobs, Agriculture and Rural Development
  Education: Concordia Col St Paul MN BA; St Cloud State MA

Senator **Michelle L. Fischbach** (R-District 13) Room 15 . . (651) 296-2084
  Counties Represented: Benton (part), Stearns (part)    Res: (320) 243-7052
  Term Expires: 2017
  E-mail: sen.michelle.fischbach@senate.mn
  Committees: Finance; Rules and Administration
  Education: St Cloud State 1989 BA; William Mitchell 2010 JD

Senator **Melisa Franzen** (DFL-District 49) Room 3403 . . . . (651) 296-6238
  Counties Represented: Hennepin (part)
  Term Expires: 2017
  E-mail: sen.melisa.franzen@senate.mn
  Committees: Education; Higher Education and Workforce Development;
  Transportation
  Education: Minnesota MPP; Hamline 2006 JD

Senator **Paul E. Gazelka** (R-District 9) Room 145 . . . . . . . (651) 296-4875
  Counties Represented: Cass (part), Morrison (part),    Dist: (218) 829-9694
  Todd, Wadena (part)
  Term Expires: 2017
  E-mail: sen.paul.gazelka@senate.mn
  Committees: Commerce; Rules and Administration; Taxes

Senator **Barbara J. "Barb" Goodwin** (DFL-District 41)
  Room 2101 . . . . . . . . . . . . . . . . . . . . . . . . . . . . . (651) 296-4334
  Counties Represented: Anoka (part), Hennepin    Res: (763) 571-1716
  (part), Ramsey (part)
  Term Expires: 2017
  E-mail: sen.barb.goodwin@senate.mn
  Committees: Commerce; Judiciary
  Education: Hamline 1985 BA

Senator **Dan D. Hall** (R-District 56) Room 103 . . . . . . . . . (651) 296-5975
  Counties Represented: Dakota (part), Scott (part)
  Term Expires: 2017
  E-mail: sen.dan.hall@senate.mn
  Committees: Judiciary; State and Local Government

Senator **David W. Hann** (R-District 48) Room 147 . . . . . . . (651) 296-1749
  Counties Represented: Hennepin (part)    Dist: (612) 554-9579
  Term Expires: 2017    Res: (952) 934-0361
  E-mail: sen.david.hann@senate.mn
  Committees: Rules and Administration

Senator **Foung Hawj** (DFL-District 67) Room 2403 . . . . . . (651) 296-5285
  Counties Represented: Ramsey (part)
  Term Expires: 2017
  E-mail: sen.foung.hawj@senate.mn
  Committees: Environment and Energy; Jobs, Agriculture and Rural
  Development
  Education: Kansas 1990 BA; RIT 2001 MS

Senator **Jeff Hayden** (DFL-District 62) Room 3109 . . . . . . (651) 296-4261
  Counties Represented: Hennepin (part)
  Term Expires: 2017
  E-mail: sen.jeff.hayden@senate.mn
  Committees: Capital Investment; Health, Human Services and Housing;
  State and Local Government

Senator **John A. Hoffman** (DFL-District 36) Room 3227 . . (651) 296-4154
  Counties Represented: Anoka (part), Hennepin (part)
  Term Expires: 2017
  E-mail: sen.john.hoffman@senate.mn
  Committees: Environment and Energy; Health, Human Services and
  Housing
  Education: St Mary's U (MN) 1988 BA

Senator **Karin Housley** (R-District 39) Room 21 . . . . . . . . (651) 296-4351
  Counties Represented: Chisago (part), Washington (part)
  Term Expires: 2017
  E-mail: sen.karin.housley@senate.mn
  Committees: Commerce; State and Local Government
  Education: SUNY Col (Buffalo) 1988 BA

Senator **Bill G. Ingebrigtsen** (R-District 8) Room 143 . . . . (651) 297-8063
  Counties Represented: Douglas (part), Otter Tail    Res: (320) 846-1893
  (part)
  Term Expires: 2017
  E-mail: sen.bill.ingebrigtsen@senate.mn
  Committees: Capital Investment; Finance

Senator **Vicki Jensen** (DFL-District 24) Room 3229 . . . . . . (651) 296-9457
  Counties Represented: Dodge (part), Rice (part), Steele (part), Waseca
  (part)
  Term Expires: 2017
  E-mail: sen.vicki.jensen@senate.mn
  Committees: Commerce; Transportation

Senator **Alice M. Johnson** (DFL-District 37)
  Room 3111 . . . . . . . . . . . . . . . . . . . . . . . . . . . . . (651) 296-2556
  Counties Represented: Anoka (part)    Res: (763) 786-2025
  Term Expires: 2017
  E-mail: sen.alice.johnson@senate.mn
  Committees: Education; State and Local Government
  Education: Metropolitan State U (Attended);
  Concordia Col Moorhead MN BA; Harvard 1996 MA

Senator **Susan Kent** (DFL-District 53) Room 3409 . . . . . . . (651) 296-4166
  Counties Represented: Ramsey (part), Washington (part)
  Term Expires: 2017
  E-mail: sen.susan.kent@senate.mn
  Committees: Education; Higher Education and Workforce Development;
  Transportation
  Education: Texas 1985 BS

Senator **Mary Kiffmeyer** (R-District 30) Room 123 . . . . . . (651) 296-5655
  Counties Represented: Hennepin (part), Sherburne    Res: (763) 263-3876
  (part), Wright (part)
  Term Expires: 2017
  E-mail: sen.mary.kiffmeyer@senate.mn
  Committees: Capital Investment; Transportation

Senator **Lyle J. Koenen** (DFL-District 17) Room 3201 . . . . (651) 296-5094
  Counties Represented: Chippewa, Kandiyohi,    Res: (320) 847-4305
  Renville (part), Swift
  Term Expires: 2017
  E-mail: sen.lyle.koenen@senate.mn
  Committees: Environment and Energy; Jobs, Agriculture and Rural
  Development; Taxes

Senator **Ronald "Ron" Latz** (DFL-District 46)
  Room 2109 . . . . . . . . . . . . . . . . . . . . . . . . . . . . . (651) 297-8065
  Counties Represented: Hennepin (part)    Dist: (952) 224-9052
  Term Expires: 2017    Res: (952) 545-9065
  E-mail: sen.ron.latz@senate.mn
  Committees: Commerce; Finance; Judiciary
  Education: Wisconsin 1985 BA; Harvard 1988 JD

Senator **Warren Limmer** (R-District 34) Room 153 . . . . . . (651) 296-2159
  Counties Represented: Hennepin (part)    Res: (763) 493-9646
  Term Expires: 2017
  E-mail: sen.warren.limmer@senate.mn
  Committees: Finance; Judiciary; Rules and Administration

Senator **Tony Lourey** (DFL-District 11) Room 2105 . . . . . . (651) 296-0293
  Counties Represented: Carlton, Kanabec (part),    Res: (218) 496-5893
  Pine, St. Louis (part)
  Term Expires: 2017
  E-mail: sen.tony.lourey@senate.mn
  Committees: Finance; Health, Human Services and Housing
  Education: Minnesota BA

Senator **John Marty** (DFL-District 66) Room 3233 . . . . . . . (651) 296-5645
  Counties Represented: Ramsey (part)    Res: (651) 633-8934
  Term Expires: 2017
  E-mail: sen.john.marty@senate.mn
  Committees: Environment and Energy; Finance; Health, Human
  Services and Housing; Rules and Administration

Senator **James P. "Jim" Metzen** (DFL-District 52)
  Room 2113 . . . . . . . . . . . . . . . . . . . . . . . . . . . . . (651) 296-4370
  Counties Represented: Dakota (part)    Res: (651) 451-0174
  Term Expires: 2017
  312 Deerwood Court, South St. Paul, MN 55075
  E-mail: sen.jim.metzen@senate.mn
  Committees: Capital Investment; Commerce; Rules and Administration
  Education: Minnesota BA

Senator **Jeremy R. Miller** (R-District 28) Room 135 . . . . . . (651) 296-5649
  Counties Represented: Fillmore, Houston, Winona    Dist: (507) 452-2067
  (part)    Res: (507) 474-2562
  Term Expires: 2017
  E-mail: sen.jeremy.miller@senate.mn
  Committees: Capital Investment; Finance; Higher Education and
  Workforce Development

Senator **Carla J. Nelson** (R-District 26) Room 117 . . . . . . . (651) 296-4848
  Counties Represented: Olmsted (part)    Dist: (507) 281-1262
  Term Expires: 2017    Res: (507) 288-2159
  E-mail: sen.carla.nelson@senate.mn
  Committees: Capital Investment; Education; Health, Human Services
  and Housing; Higher Education and Workforce Development; Jobs,
  Agriculture and Rural Development; Taxes
  Education: Drake 1979 BSEd; Minnesota 1997 MEd

*(continued on next page)*

**Senators** *continued*

Senator **Scott J. Newman** (R-District 18) Room 141 . . . . . (651) 296-4131
  Counties Represented: McLeod, Meeker, Sibley,    Res: (320) 587-5965
  Wright (part)
  Term Expires: 2017
  E-mail: sen.scott.newman@senate.mn
  Committees: Capital Investment; Finance; Judiciary; Rules and
  Administration; Transportation
  Education: Minnesota St (Mankato) BA; William Mitchell JD

Senator **Sean R. Nienow** (R-District 32) Room 105 . . . . . . (651) 296-5419
  Counties Represented: Chisago (part), Isanti (part)    Res: (763) 689-1623
  Term Expires: 2017
  E-mail: sen.sean.nienow@senate.mn
  Committees: Education; Finance; Health, Human Services and Housing

Senator **Julianne E. Ortman** (R-District 47) Room 119 . . . (651) 296-4837
  Counties Represented: Carver (part)    Res: (952) 906-9891
  Term Expires: 2017
  E-mail: sen.julianne.ortman@senate.mn
  Committees: Higher Education and Workforce Development; Taxes
  Education: Macalester BA; Pennsylvania 1989 JD

Senator **David J. Osmek** (R-District 33) Room 19 . . . . . . (651) 296-1282
  Counties Represented: Carver (part), Hennepin    Res: (952) 472-1238
  (part)
  Term Expires: 2017
  4933 Crestview Road, Mound, MN 55364
  E-mail: sen.david.osmek@senate.mn
  Committees: Environment and Energy; Transportation

Senator **Sandra L. Pappas** (DFL-District 65)
  Room 3205 . . . . . . . . . . . . . . . . . . . . . . . . . . . (651) 296-1802
  Counties Represented: Ramsey (part)    Res: (651) 227-6032
  Term Expires: 2017
  E-mail: sen.sandra.pappas@senate.mn
  Committees: Capital Investment; Commerce; Finance; Rules and
  Administration; State and Local Government

Senator **John C. Pederson** (R-District 14) Room 27 . . . . . . (651) 296-6455
  Counties Represented: Benton (part), Sherburne    Dist: (320) 529-6932
  (part), Stearns (part)    Res: (320) 654-8558
  Term Expires: 2017
  E-mail: sen.john.pederson@senate.mn
  Committees: Capital Investment; Finance; Transportation
  Education: Northwestern Col (MN) BSBA; Cardinal Stritch U MBA

Senator **Eric R. Pratt** (R-District 55) Room 23 . . . . . . . . . . (651) 296-4123
  Counties Represented: Scott (part)    Res: (651) 849-2918
  Term Expires: 2017
  E-mail: sen.eric.pratt@senate.mn
  Committees: Commerce; Higher Education and Workforce
  Development; Transportation
  Education: Colorado 1987 BA; U St Thomas (MN) 1993 MBA

Senator **Roger J. Reinert** (DFL-District 7) Room 3101 . . . (651) 296-4188
  Counties Represented: St. Louis (part)    Dist: (218) 733-2037
  Term Expires: 2017
  E-mail: sen.roger.reinert@senate.mn
  Committees: Commerce; Taxes; Transportation
  Education: Minnesota 1992 BS; Mankato State 1994 MS

Senator **Ann H. Rest** (DFL-District 45) Room 3209 . . . . . . (651) 296-2889
  Counties Represented: Hennepin (part)    Res: (763) 545-8057
  Term Expires: 2017
  E-mail: sen.ann.rest@senate.mn
  Committees: Taxes; Transportation

Senator **Julie A. Rosen** (R-District 23) Room 139 . . . . . . . (651) 296-5713
  Counties Represented: Blue Earth (part), Faribault    Res: (507) 238-2304
  (part), Jackson (part), Le Sueur (part), Martin, Waseca (part),
  Watonwan
  Term Expires: 2017
  E-mail: sen.julie.rosen@senate.mn
  Committees: Capital Investment; Environment and Energy; Health,
  Human Services and Housing
  Education: Colorado State BS

Senator **Carrie Ruud** (R-District 10) Room 25 . . . . . . . . . . (651) 296-4913
  Counties Represented: Aitkin, Crow Wing
  Term Expires: 2017
  E-mail: sen.carrie.ruud@senate.mn
  Committees: Education; Jobs, Agriculture and Rural Development

Senator **Tom Saxhaug** (DFL-District 5) Room 2111 . . . . . . (651) 296-4136
  Counties Represented: Beltrami (part), Cass (part),    Res: (218) 326-8163
  Hubbard (part), Itasca (part)
  Term Expires: 2017
  E-mail: sen.tom.saxhaug@senate.mn
  Committees: Finance
  Education: St Olaf 1970 BA

Senator **Bev Scalze** (DFL-District 42) Room 3231 . . . . . . . (651) 296-5537
  Counties Represented: Ramsey (part)
  Term Expires: 2017
  969 Bean Avenue, Little Canada, MN 55109
  E-mail: sen.bev.scalze@senate.mn
  Committees: Capital Investment; Environment and Energy; State and
  Local Government

Senator **Matt Schmit** (DFL-District 21) Room 3441 . . . . . . (651) 296-4264
  Counties Represented: Dodge (part), Goodhue (part), Wabasha, Winona
  (part)
  Term Expires: 2017
  E-mail: sen.matt.schmit@senate.mn
  Committees: Capital Investment; Environment and Energy; Jobs,
  Agriculture and Rural Development
  Education: St John's U (MN) 2002 BA; Minnesota 2003 MPP

Senator **David H. Senjem** (R-District 25) Room 113 . . . . . (651) 296-3903
  Counties Represented: Dodge (part), Olmsted (part)
  Term Expires: 2017
  2423 - 12th Avenue, Northwest, Rochester, MN 55901
  E-mail: sen.david.senjem@senate.mn
  Committees: Capital Investment; Taxes; Transportation
  Education: Luther Col BA

Senator **Kathy Sheran** (DFL-District 19) Room 2103 . . . . . (651) 296-6153
  Counties Represented: Blue Earth (part), Le Sueur    Res: (507) 344-2155
  (part), Nicollet
  Term Expires: 2017
  E-mail: sen.kathy.sheran@senate.mn
  Committees: Health, Human Services and Housing; Higher Education
  and Workforce Development; Judiciary
  Education: St Teresa BSN; Minnesota St (Mankato) MS

Senator **Katie Sieben** (DFL-District 54) Room 3203 . . . . . . (651) 297-8060
  Counties Represented: Dakota (part), Washington    Res: (651) 458-3194
  (part)
  Term Expires: 2017
  P.O. Box 227, Newport, MN 55055
  E-mail: sen.katie.sieben@senate.mn
  Committees: Capital Investment; Environment and Energy; Finance;
  Rules and Administration

Senator **Rod Skoe** (DFL-District 2) Room 3211 . . . . . . . . (651) 296-4196
  Counties Represented: Becker (part), Beltrami    Res: (218) 776-3420
  (part), Clearwater, Hubbard (part), Lake of the Woods, Mahnomen,
  Otter Tail (part), Wadena (part)
  Term Expires: 2017
  E-mail: sen.rod.skoe@senate.mn
  Committees: Rules and Administration; Taxes
  Education: Augsburg BA

Senator **Dan Sparks** (DFL-District 27) Room 2401 . . . . . . (651) 296-9248
  Counties Represented: Dodge (part), Faribault    Res: (507) 438-2898
  (part), Freeborn, Mower, Steele (part)
  Term Expires: 2017
  E-mail: sen.dan.sparks@senate.mn
  Committees: Capital Investment; Higher Education and Workforce
  Development; Jobs, Agriculture and Rural Development; Taxes

Senator **LeRoy A. Stumpf** (DFL-District 1) Room 3221 . . . (651) 296-8660
  Counties Represented: Kittson, Marshall,    Res: (218) 465-4655
  Pennington, Polk, Red Lake, Roseau
  Term Expires: 2017
  E-mail: sen.leroy.stumpf@senate.mn
  Committees: Capital Investment; Finance; Rules and Administration
  Education: St Paul Theol BA; Syracuse 1991 MPA

Senator **David "Dave" Thompson** (R-District 58)
  Room 131 . . . . . . . . . . . . . . . . . . . . . . . . . . . (651) 296-5252
  Counties Represented: Dakota (part), Goodhue    Dist: (612) 385-5950
  (part)
  Term Expires: 2017
  E-mail: sen.dave.thompson@senate.mn
  Committees: Education; State and Local Government; Taxes
  Education: North Dakota 1984 BA; Minnesota 1987 JD

Senator **David J. Tomassoni** (DFL-District 6)
  Room 3401 . . . . . . . . . . . . . . . . . . . . . . . . . . . (651) 296-8017
  Counties Represented: Itasca (part), St. Louis (part)    Res: (218) 254-3430
  Term Expires: 2017
  E-mail: sen.david.tomassoni@senate.mn
  Committees: Capital Investment; Finance; Transportation
  Education: Denver BA, BS

Senator **Patricia Torres Ray** (DFL-District 63)
  Room 3225 . . . . . . . . . . . . . . . . . . . . . . . . . . . (651) 296-4274
  Counties Represented: Hennepin (part)    Res: (612) 722-1068
  Term Expires: 2017
  E-mail: sen.patricia.torres.ray@senate.mn
  Committees: Education; Higher Education and Workforce Development;
  State and Local Government
  Education: Minnesota BA, 2004 MPA

Senator **William V. "Bill" Weber** (R-District 22)
Room 125 . . . . . . . . . . . . . . . . . . . . . . . . . . . . . . . . . . (651) 296-5650
Counties Represented: Cottonwood, Jackson (part),       Dist: (507) 283-2391
Lincoln, Lyon (part), Murray, Nobles, Pipestone, Redwood (part), Rock
Term Expires: 2017
E-mail: sen.bill.weber@senate.mn
Committees: Environment and Energy; Jobs, Agriculture and Rural
Development

Senator **Torrey Westrom** (R-District 12) Room 107 . . . . . . (651) 296-3826
Counties Represented: Big Stone, Douglas (part),       Res: (218) 685-6299
Grant, Pope, Stearns (part), Stevens, Traverse, Wilkin
Term Expires: 2017
E-mail: sen.torrey.westrom@senate.mn
Committees: Finance; Transportation
Education: Bemidji State 1994 BA; William Mitchell 2003 JD

Senator **Charles W. "Chuck" Wiger** (DFL-District 43)
Room 3219 . . . . . . . . . . . . . . . . . . . . . . . . . . . . . . . . . (651) 296-6820
Counties Represented: Ramsey (part), Washington    Dist: (651) 665-4851
(part)                                             Res: (651) 770-0283
Term Expires: 2017
E-mail: sen.chuck.wiger@senate.mn
Committees: Education; Finance; Transportation
Education: Hamline 1974 BA, 1977 JD

Senator **Melissa H. Wiklund** (DFL-District 50)
Room 2409 . . . . . . . . . . . . . . . . . . . . . . . . . . . . . . . . . (651) 296-8061
Counties Represented: Hennepin (part)          Res: (952) 884-0767
Term Expires: 2017
9943 Wentworth Avenue, South, Bloomington, MN 55420
E-mail: sen.melissa.wiklund@senate.mn
Committees: Education; Health, Human Services and Housing; State
and Local Government
Education: Minnesota 1991 BEE

# Senate Standing Committees

## Capital Investment
State Capitol, 75 Rev. Dr. MLK Jr., Blvd., Room 121,
St. Paul, MN 55155-1606
Tel: (651) 296-5440

**Majority Members**
LeRoy A. Stumpf (DFL-1) *Chair*
Bev Scalze (DFL-42) *Vice Chair*
Bobby Joe Champion (DFL-59)
Richard J. "Dick" Cohen (DFL-64)
Kent Eken (DFL-4)
Jeff Hayden (DFL-62)
James P. "Jim" Metzen (DFL-52)
Sandra L. Pappas (DFL-65)
Matt Schmit (DFL-21)
Katie Sieben (DFL-54)
Dan Sparks (DFL-27)
David J. Tomassoni (DFL-6)

**Minority Members**
David H. Senjem (R-25)
   *Ranking Minority Member*
Bill G. Ingebrigtsen (R-8)
Mary Kiffmeyer (R-30)
Jeremy R. Miller (R-28)
Carla J. Nelson (R-26)
Scott J. Newman (R-18)
John C. Pederson (R-14)
Julie A. Rosen (R-23)

## Commerce
State Capitol, 75 Rev. Dr. MLK Jr., Blvd., Room 120,
St. Paul, MN 55155-1606
Tel: (651) 296-4175

**Majority Members**
James P. "Jim" Metzen (DFL-52)
   *Chair*
Vicki Jensen (DFL-24) *Vice Chair*
Jim Carlson (DFL-51)
Kevin L. Dahle (DFL-20)
Barbara J. "Barb" Goodwin
   (DFL-41)
Ronald "Ron" Latz (DFL-46)
Sandra L. Pappas (DFL-65)
Roger J. Reinert (DFL-7)

**Minority Members**
Paul E. Gazelka (R-9)
   *Ranking Minority Member*
David M. "Dave" Brown (R-15)
Gary H. Dahms (R-16)
Karin Housley (R-39)
Eric R. Pratt (R-55)

## Education
State Capitol, 75 Rev. Dr. MLK Jr., Blvd., Room 235,
St. Paul, MN 55155-1606
Tel: (651) 296-5312

**Majority Members**
Patricia Torres Ray (DFL-63) *Chair*
Kevin L. Dahle (DFL-20)
   *Vice Chair*
Jim Carlson (DFL-51)
Greg D. Clausen (DFL-57)
Melisa Franzen (DFL-49)
Alice M. Johnson (DFL-37)
Susan Kent (DFL-53)
Charles W. "Chuck" Wiger
   (DFL-43)
Melissa H. Wiklund (DFL-50)

**Minority Members**
Carla J. Nelson (R-26)
   *Ranking Minority Member*
Roger C. Chamberlain (R-38)
Sean R. Nienow (R-32)
Carrie Ruud (R-10)
David "Dave" Thompson (R-58)

## Environment and Energy
75 Rev. Dr. Martin Luther King Jr. Boulevard, Room 322,
St. Paul, MN 55155
Tel: (651) 296-7593

**Majority Members**
John Marty (DFL-66) *Chair*
John A. Hoffman (DFL-36)
   *Vice Chair*
D. Scott Dibble (DFL-61)
Chris A. Eaton (DFL-40)
Foung Hawj (DFL-67)
Lyle J. Koenen (DFL-17)
Bev Scalze (DFL-42)
Matt Schmit (DFL-21)
Katie Sieben (DFL-54)

**Minority Members**
David M. "Dave" Brown (R-15)
   *Ranking Minority Member*
Michelle R. Benson (R-31)
David J. Osmek (R-33)
Julie A. Rosen (R-23)
William V. "Bill" Weber (R-22)

## Finance
75 Rev. Dr. Martin Luther King Jr. Boulevard, Room 226,
St. Paul, MN 55155
Tel: (651) 296-5308

**Majority Members**
Richard J. "Dick" Cohen (DFL-64)
   *Chair*
Bobby Joe Champion (DFL-59)
   *Vice Chair*
Terri E. Bonoff (DFL-44)
D. Scott Dibble (DFL-61)
Ronald "Ron" Latz (DFL-46)
Tony Lourey (DFL-11)
John Marty (DFL-66)
Sandra L. Pappas (DFL-65)
Tom Saxhaug (DFL-5)
Katie Sieben (DFL-54)
LeRoy A. Stumpf (DFL-1)
David J. Tomassoni (DFL-6)
Charles W. "Chuck" Wiger
   (DFL-43)

**Minority Members**
Michelle L. Fischbach (R-13)
   *Ranking Minority Member*
Bruce D. Anderson (R-29)
Bill G. Ingebrigtsen (R-8)
Warren Limmer (R-34)
Jeremy R. Miller (R-28)
Scott J. Newman (R-18)
Sean R. Nienow (R-32)
John C. Pederson (R-14)
Torrey Westrom (R-12)

## Health, Human Services and Housing
75 Rev. Dr. Martin Luther King Jr. Boulevard, Room 328,
St. Paul, MN 55155
Tel: (651) 296-4151

**Majority Members**
Kathy Sheran (DFL-19) *Chair*
Melissa H. Wiklund (DFL-50)
   *Vice Chair*
Chris A. Eaton (DFL-40)
Jeff Hayden (DFL-62)
John A. Hoffman (DFL-36)
Tony Lourey (DFL-11)
John Marty (DFL-66)

**Minority Members**
Michelle R. Benson (R-31)
   *Ranking Minority Member*
Carla J. Nelson (R-26)
Sean R. Nienow (R-32)
Julie A. Rosen (R-23)

**LEGISLATIVE BRANCH**

## Higher Education and Workforce Development
75 Rev. Dr. Martin Luther King Jr. Boulevard, Room 226,
St. Paul, MN 55155
Tel: (651) 296-5538

**Majority Members**
Terri E. Bonoff (DFL-44) *Chair*
Greg D. Clausen (DFL-57)
  *Vice Chair*
Kent Eken (DFL-4)
Melisa Franzen (DFL-49)
Susan Kent (DFL-53)
Kathy Sheran (DFL-19)
Dan Sparks (DFL-27)
Patricia Torres Ray (DFL-63)

**Minority Members**
Jeremy R. Miller (R-28)
  *Ranking Minority Member*
Jim Abeler (R-35)
Carla J. Nelson (R-26)
Julianne E. Ortman (R-47)
Eric R. Pratt (R-55)

## Jobs, Agriculture and Rural Development
75 Rev. Dr. Martin Luther King Jr. Boulevard, Room 205,
St. Paul, MN 55155
Tel: (651) 296-5968

**Majority Members**
Dan Sparks (DFL-27) *Chair*
Matt Schmit (DFL-21) *Vice Chair*
Terri E. Bonoff (DFL-44)
Kent Eken (DFL-4)
Foung Hawj (DFL-67)
Lyle J. Koenen (DFL-17)

**Minority Members**
Gary H. Dahms (R-16)
  *Ranking Minority Member*
Carla J. Nelson (R-26)
Carrie Ruud (R-10)
William V. "Bill" Weber (R-22)

## Judiciary
State Capitol, 75 Rev. Dr. MLK Jr., Blvd., Room 122,
St. Paul, MN 55155-1606
Tel: (651) 296-4842

**Majority Members**
Ronald "Ron" Latz (DFL-46) *Chair*
Barbara J. "Barb"
  Goodwin (DFL-41)
  *Vice Chair*
Bobby Joe Champion (DFL-59)
Kari Dziedzic (DFL-60)
Kathy Sheran (DFL-19)

**Minority Members**
Warren Limmer (R-34)
  *Ranking Minority Member*
Dan D. Hall (R-56)
Scott J. Newman (R-18)

## Rules and Administration
State Capitol, 75 Rev. Dr. MLK Jr., Blvd., Room 208,
St. Paul, MN 55155-1606
Tel: (651) 296-2577

**Majority Members**
Thomas M. "Tom" Bakk (DFL-3)
  *Chair*
Katie Sieben (DFL-54) *Vice Chair*
Richard J. "Dick" Cohen (DFL-64)
John Marty (DFL-66)
James P. "Jim" Metzen (DFL-52)
Sandra L. Pappas (DFL-65)
Rod Skoe (DFL-2)
LeRoy A. Stumpf (DFL-1)

**Minority Members**
David W. Hann (R-48)
  *Ranking Minority Member*
Michelle L. Fischbach (R-13)
Paul E. Gazelka (R-9)
Warren Limmer (R-34)
Scott J. Newman (R-18)

## State and Local Government
75 Rev. Dr. Martin Luther King Jr. Boulevard, Room 328,
St. Paul, MN 55155
Tel: (651) 296-1113

**Majority Members**
Patricia Torres Ray (DFL-63) *Chair*
Chris A. Eaton (DFL-40)
  *Vice Chair*
Kevin L. Dahle (DFL-20)
Jeff Hayden (DFL-62)
Alice M. Johnson (DFL-37)
Sandra L. Pappas (DFL-65)
Bev Scalze (DFL-42)
Melissa H. Wiklund (DFL-50)

**Minority Members**
Dan D. Hall (R-56)
  *Ranking Minority Member*
Jim Abeler (R-35)
Bruce D. Anderson (R-29)
Karin Housley (R-39)
David "Dave" Thompson (R-58)

## Taxes
State Capitol, 75 Rev. Dr. MLK Jr., Blvd., Room 120,
St. Paul, MN 55155-1606
Tel: (651) 296-5640

**Majority Members**
Rod Skoe (DFL-2) *Chair*
Ann H. Rest (DFL-45) *Vice Chair*
Thomas M. "Tom" Bakk (DFL-3)
Kari Dziedzic (DFL-60)
Chris A. Eaton (DFL-40)
Lyle J. Koenen (DFL-17)
Roger J. Reinert (DFL-7)
Dan Sparks (DFL-27)

**Minority Members**
Julianne E. Ortman (R-47)
  *Ranking Minority Member*
Paul E. Gazelka (R-9)
Carla J. Nelson (R-26)
David H. Senjem (R-25)
David "Dave" Thompson (R-58)

## Transportation
75 Rev. Dr. Martin Luther King Jr. Boulevard, Room 303,
St. Paul, MN 55155
Tel: (651) 296-1738

**Majority Members**
D. Scott Dibble (DFL-61) *Chair*
Susan Kent (DFL-53) *Vice Chair*
Jim Carlson (DFL-51)
Bobby Joe Champion (DFL-59)
Melisa Franzen (DFL-49)
Vicki Jensen (DFL-24)
Roger J. Reinert (DFL-7)
Ann H. Rest (DFL-45)
David J. Tomassoni (DFL-6)
Charles W. "Chuck" Wiger
  (DFL-43)

**Minority Members**
Scott J. Newman (R-18)
  *Ranking Minority Member*
Mary Kiffmeyer (R-30)
David J. Osmek (R-33)
John C. Pederson (R-14)
Eric R. Pratt (R-55)
David H. Senjem (R-25)
Torrey Westrom (R-12)

# Minnesota House of Representatives
State Office Building, 100 Rev. Dr. Martin Luther King Jr. Boulevard,
St. Paul, MN 55155-1206
Tel: (651) 296-2146  TTY: (651) 296-9896
Internet: www.house.leg.state.mn.us

Speaker of the House **Kurt Daudt** (R) . . . . . . . . . . . . . . . . . (651) 296-5364
  Education: North Dakota
Majority Leader **Joyce Peppin** (R) . . . . . . . . . . . . . . . . . . . (651) 296-7806
  Education: Minnesota (Duluth) 1992 BA;
  U St Thomas (MN) 2007 MBA
Majority Whip **Dan Fabian** (R) . . . . . . . . . . . . . . . . . . . . . (651) 296-9635
  Education: North Dakota State MA
Assistant Majority Leader **Dave Baker** (R) . . . . . . . . . . . . . (651) 296-6206
Assistant Majority Leader **Debra "Deb" Kiel** (R) . . . . . . . . . (651) 296-5091
Assistant Majority Leader **Ron Kresha** (R). . . . . . . . . . . . . (651) 296-4247
  Education: St Cloud State 1994 BA; Bellevue U 2010 MBA
Assistant Majority Leader **Kathy Lohmer** (R) . . . . . . . . . . . (651) 296-4244
Assistant Majority Leader **Tim Sanders** (R) . . . . . . . . . . . . (651) 296-4226
Assistant Majority Leader **Chris Swedzinski** (R). . . . . . . . . (651) 296-5374
Minority Leader **Paul C. Thissen** (DFL). . . . . . . . . . . . . . . (651) 296-5375
  Education: Harvard 1989 AB; Chicago 1992 JD
Deputy Minority Leader **Melissa Hortman** (DFL) . . . . . . . (651) 296-4280
  Education: Boston U 1991 BA; Minnesota 1995 JD
Deputy Minority Leader **Paul Marquart** (DFL) . . . . . . . . . . (651) 296-6829
  Education: North Dakota BS; Tri-College MS
Deputy Minority Leader **Erin Murphy** (DFL) . . . . . . . . . . . (651) 296-8799
Chief Clerk of the House **Patrick D. Murphy** . . . . . . . . . . . (651) 296-2314
  E-mail: pat.murphy@house.mn

## Representatives
**Party Affiliation Statistics:** Republicans: 73, Democrats: 61

Representative **Tony Albright** (R-District 55B) . . . . . . . . . . (651) 296-5185
  Counties Represented: Scott (part)      Res: (612) 801-9401
  Term Expires: 2017
  E-mail: rep.tony.albright@house.mn
  Committees: Capital Investment; Government Operations and Elections
  Policy; Health and Human Services Reform; Rules and Legislative
  Administration; State Government Finance; Ways and Means
  Education: Minnesota St (Moorhead) 1984 BS

*LEGISLATIVE BRANCH*

Representative **Susan Allen** (DFL-District 62B) . . . . . . . . (651) 296-7152
Counties Represented: Hennepin (part)          Res: (612) 559-3172
Term Expires: 2017
E-mail: rep.susan.allen@house.mn
Committees: Agriculture Policy; Health and Human Services Finance;
Health and Human Services Reform
Education: Augsburg 1992 BA; New Mexico 1995 JD;
William Mitchell 2000 LLM

Representative **Chad Anderson** (R-District 50B) . . . . . . . . (651) 296-4218
Counties Represented: Hennepin (part)
Term Expires: 2017
10437 Fifth Avenue Circle, Bloomington, MN 55420
E-mail: rep.chad.anderson@house.mn
Committees: Aging and Long-Term Care Policy; Government
Operations and Elections Policy; Transportation Policy and Finance
Education: Bethel U BA

Representative **Mark Anderson** (R-District 9A) . . . . . . . . . (651) 296-4293
Counties Represented: Cass (part), Todd (part), Wadena (part)
Term Expires: 2017
8182 County Road, Room 401, Lake Lillian, MN 56468
E-mail: rep.mark.anderson@house.mn
Committees: Agriculture Finance; Agriculture Policy; Mining and
Outdoor Recreation Policy; State Government Finance; Transportation
Policy and Finance
Education: North Dakota BS

Representative **Paul H. Anderson** (R-District 12B) . . . . . . . (651) 296-4317
Counties Represented: Douglas (part), Pope (part),          Res: (320) 239-2726
Stearns (part)
Term Expires: 2017
E-mail: rep.paul.anderson@house.mn
Committees: Agriculture Finance; Agriculture Policy; Education
Finance
Education: Minnesota (Morris) BA

Representative **Sarah Anderson** (R-District 44A) . . . . . . . (651) 296-5511
Counties Represented: Hennepin (part)          Res: (763) 383-9504
Term Expires: 2017
5050 Holly Lane North, Plymouth, MN 55446
E-mail: rep.sarah.anderson@house.mn
Committees: Commerce and Regulatory Reform; State Government
Finance; Taxes; Ways and Means
Education: Minnesota (Duluth) BA

Representative **Tom Anzelc** (DFL-District 5B) . . . . . . . . . . (651) 296-4936
Counties Represented: Cass (part), Itasca (part)          Res: (218) 327-7924
Term Expires: 2017
44205 Burrows Lake Lane, Bovey, MN 55709
E-mail: rep.tom.anzelc@house.mn
Committees: Education Finance; Mining and Outdoor Recreation
Policy; Taxes
Education: St Cloud State 1968 BS

Representative **Jon Applebaum** (DFL-District 44B) . . . . . . (651) 296-9934
Counties Represented: Hennepin (part)
Term Expires: 2017
E-mail: rep.jon.applebaum@house.mn
Committees: Agriculture Finance; Civil Law and Data Practices;
Commerce and Regulatory Reform
Education: Vanderbilt BA; Minnesota JD

Representative **Joe Atkins** (DFL-District 52B) . . . . . . . . . . (651) 296-4192
Counties Represented: Dakota (part)          Dist: (651) 451-6411
Term Expires: 2017          Res: (651) 451-3837
2463 - 78th Street East, Inver Grove Heights, MN 55076
E-mail: rep.joe.atkins@house.mn
Committees: Capital Investment; Commerce and Regulatory Reform;
Transportation Policy and Finance
Education: Minnesota 1988 BA; William Mitchell 1991 JD

Representative **Jeff Backer** (R-District 12A) . . . . . . . . . . . (651) 296-4929
Counties Represented: Big Stone, Douglas (part), Grant, Pope (part),
Stevens, Traverse, Wilkin
Term Expires: 2017
E-mail: rep.jeff.backer@house.mn
Committees: Agriculture Policy; Health and Human Services Finance;
Health and Human Services Reform
Education: St Cloud State 1991 BS

Representative **Dave Baker** (R-District 17B) . . . . . . . . . . . . (651) 296-6206
Counties Represented: Kandiyohi (part)
Term Expires: 2017
E-mail: rep.dave.baker@house.mn
Committees: Aging and Long-Term Care Policy; Health and Human
Services Reform; Job Growth and Energy Affordability Policy and
Finance

Representative **Bob Barrett** (R-District 32B) . . . . . . . . . . . (651) 296-5377
Counties Represented: Chisago (part)
Term Expires: 2017
E-mail: rep.bob.barrett@house.mn
Committees: Greater Minnesota Economic and Workforce Development
Policy; Higher Education Policy and Finance; Taxes
Education: Minnesota St (Moorhead) 1989 BA

Representative **Peggy Bennett** (R-District 27A) . . . . . . . . . (651) 296-8216
Counties Represented: Dodge (part), Freeborn (part), Mower (part),
Steele (part)
Term Expires: 2017
E-mail: rep.peggy.bennett@house.mn
Committees: Agriculture Finance; Education Finance; Education
Innovation Policy

Representative **Connie Bernardy** (DFL-District 41A) . . . . . (651) 296-5510
Counties Represented: Anoka (part), Ramsey (part)          Res: (763) 571-0015
Term Expires: 2017
6840 Siverts Lane, NE, Fridley, MN 55432
E-mail: rep.connie.bernardy@house.mn
Committees: Higher Education Policy and Finance; Rules and
Legislative Administration; Transportation Policy and Finance
Education: Minnesota BA; U St Thomas (MN) 1988 MBA

Representative **David Bly** (DFL-District 20B) . . . . . . . . . . . (651) 296-0171
Counties Represented: Le Sueur (part), Rice (part)          Res: (612) 327-0119
Term Expires: 2017
211 North Lincoln Street, Northfield, MN 55057
E-mail: rep.david.bly@house.mn
Committees: Agriculture Finance; Agriculture Policy; Education
Innovation Policy
Education: St Olaf 1974 BA; St Mary's U (MN) 2004 MA

Representative
**Lyndon R. Carlson, Sr.** (DFL-District 45A) . . . . . . . . . . (651) 296-4255
Counties Represented: Hennepin (part)          Res: (763) 533-9779
Term Expires: 2017
8216 - 35th Avenue North, Crystal, MN 55427
E-mail: rep.lyndon.carlson@house.mn
Committees: State Government Finance; Taxes; Ways and Means
Education: Minnesota St (Mankato) 1964 BS

Representative **Drew Christensen** (R-District 56A) . . . . . . . (651) 296-4212
Counties Represented: Dakota (part), Scott (part)
Term Expires: 2017
E-mail: rep.drew.christensen@house.mn
Committees: Aging and Long-Term Care Policy; Education Finance;
Education Innovation Policy; Higher Education Policy and Finance

Representative **Karen Clark** (DFL-District 62A) . . . . . . . . . (651) 296-0294
Counties Represented: Hennepin (part)          Res: (612) 722-7728
Term Expires: 2017
E-mail: rep.karen.clark@house.mn
Committees: Agriculture Finance; Environment and Natural Resources
Policy and Finance; Job Growth and Energy Affordability Policy and
Finance
Education: St Teresa 1967 BS; JFK School Govt 1996 MPA

Representative
**John "Jack" Considine** (DFL-District 19B) . . . . . . . . . (651) 296-3248
Counties Represented: Blue Earth (part)
Term Expires: 2017
E-mail: rep.jack.considine@house.mn
Committees: Aging and Long-Term Care Policy; Mining and Outdoor
Recreation Policy; Public Safety and Crime Prevention Policy and
Finance
Education: Georgia BA

Representative **Tony Cornish** (R-District 23B) . . . . . . . . . . (651) 296-4240
Counties Represented: Blue Earth (part), Le Sueur          Res: (507) 549-3349
(part), Waseca (part), Watonwan (part)
Term Expires: 2017
E-mail: rep.tony.cornish@house.mn
Committees: Environment and Natural Resources Policy and Finance;
Mining and Outdoor Recreation Policy; Public Safety and Crime
Prevention Policy and Finance; Ways and Means

Representative **Brian Daniels** (R-District 24B) . . . . . . . . . . (651) 296-8237
Counties Represented: Dodge (part), Rice (part), Steele (part)
Term Expires: 2017
E-mail: rep.brian.daniels@house.mn
Committees: Aging and Long-Term Care Policy; Agriculture Finance;
Higher Education Policy and Finance; Legacy Funding Finance

Representative **Kurt Daudt** (R-District 31A) . . . . . . . . . . . . (651) 296-5364
Counties Represented: Anoka (part), Isanti (part),          Res: (763) 634-2616
Sherburne (part)
Term Expires: 2017
E-mail: rep.kurt.daudt@house.mn

*(continued on next page)*

*LEGISLATIVE BRANCH*

**Representatives** *continued*

Representative
**Gregory M. "Greg" Davids** (R-District 28B) . . . . . . . . . (651) 296-9278
Counties Represented: Fillmore, Houston          Res: (507) 951-3893
Term Expires: 2017
P.O. Box 32, Preston, MN 55965
E-mail: rep.greg.davids@house.mn
Committees: Commerce and Regulatory Reform; Taxes; Veterans
Affairs Division; Ways and Means
Education: Winona State 1979 BS

Representative **Jim Davnie** (DFL-District 63A) . . . . . . . . . (651) 296-0173
Counties Represented: Hennepin (part)
Term Expires: 2017
2741 - 39th Avenue South, Minneapolis, MN 55406
E-mail: rep.jim.davnie@house.mn
Committees: Education Finance; Education Innovation Policy; Taxes
Education: Minnesota 1988 BS, 1995 BA

Representative **Matt Dean** (R-District 38B) . . . . . . . . . . . . (651) 296-3018
Counties Represented: Ramsey (part), Washington (part)
Term Expires: 2017
P.O. Box 669, Willernie, MN 55090
E-mail: rep.matt.dean@house.mn
Committees: Health and Human Services Finance; Health and Human
Services Reform; Ways and Means
Education: Minnesota BARCH

Representative **Raymond Dehn** (DFL-District 59B) . . . . . . (651) 296-8659
Counties Represented: Hennepin (part)          Dist: (612) 310-3346
Term Expires: 2017          Res: (612) 588-7741
1211 Upton Avenue, North, Minneapolis, MN 55411
E-mail: rep.raymond.dehn@house.mn
Committees: Capital Investment; Commerce and Regulatory Reform;
Ethics; Public Safety and Crime Prevention Policy and Finance
Education: Minnesota 1996 BA

Representative **Bob Dettmer** (R-District 39A) . . . . . . . . . . (651) 296-4124
Counties Represented: Chisago (part), Washington          Res: (651) 464-4475
(part)
Term Expires: 2017
20617 Everton Court North, Forest Lake, MN 55025
E-mail: rep.bob.dettmer@house.mn
Committees: Education Finance; State Government Finance; Veterans
Affairs Division; Ways and Means
Education: Bemidji State 1973 BS; U St Thomas (MN) MA

Representative **Steve Drazkowski** (R-District 21B) . . . . . . . (651) 296-2273
Counties Represented: Dodge (part), Goodhue          Res: (651) 564-0638
(part), Lyon (part), Murray, Wabasha (part), Winona (part)
Term Expires: 2017
1646 Cherry Street, East, Mazeppa, MN 55956-3032
E-mail: rep.steve.drazkowski@house.mn
Committees: Taxes; Transportation Policy and Finance; Ways and
Means
Education: Wisconsin (River Falls) 1989 BS; Minnesota MEd

Representative **Rob Ecklund** (DFL-District 3A) . . . . . . . . . (651) 296-2190
Counties Represented: Cook, Koochiching, Lake (part), St. Louis (part)
Term Expires: 2017
4647 Highway 11, International Falls, MN 56649
E-mail: rep.rob.ecklund@house.mn
Committees: Agriculture Finance; Environment and Natural Resources
Policy and Finance; Greater Minnesota Economic and Workforce
Development Policy; Mining and Outdoor Recreation Policy

Representative **Ron Erhardt** (DFL-District 49A) . . . . . . . . (651) 296-4363
Counties Represented: Hennepin (part)          Res: (952) 927-9437
Term Expires: 2017
4214 Sunnyside Road, Edina, MN 55424
E-mail: rep.ron.erhardt@house.mn
Committees: State Government Finance; Taxes; Transportation Policy
and Finance
Education: Minnesota BA, 1958 BBA

Representative **Sondra Erickson** (R-District 15A) . . . . . . . . (651) 296-6746
Counties Represented: Kanabec (part), Mille Lacs,          Res: (763) 389-4498
Sherburne (part)
Term Expires: 2017
1947 Ridge Road, Princeton, MN 55371
E-mail: rep.sondra.erickson@house.mn
Committees: Education Finance; Education Innovation Policy; Ethics;
Taxes
Education: Concordia Col Moorhead MN BA

Representative **Dan Fabian** (R-District 1A) . . . . . . . . . . . . (651) 296-9635
Counties Represented: Kittson, Marshall,          Res: (218) 463-1208
Pennington (part), Roseau          Fax: (651) 297-5378
Term Expires: 2017
705 Maine Avenue, South, Roseau, MN 56751
E-mail: rep.dan.fabian@house.mn
Committees: Agriculture Finance; Environment and Natural Resources
Policy and Finance; Job Growth and Energy Affordability Policy and
Finance

Representative **Kelly Fenton** (R-District 53B) . . . . . . . . . . . (651) 296-1147
Counties Represented: Washington (part)
Term Expires: 2017
E-mail: rep.kelly.fenton@house.mn
Committees: Education Finance; Environment and Natural Resources
Policy and Finance; Government Operations and Elections Policy;
Rules and Legislative Administration

Representative **Peter M. Fischer** (DFL-District 43A) . . . . . (651) 296-5363
Counties Represented: Ramsey (part), Washington          Dist: (612) 522-1690
(part)          Res: (651) 770-4984
Term Expires: 2017
2443 Standridge Avenue, Maplewood, MN 55109
E-mail: rep.peter.fischer@house.mn
Committees: Environment and Natural Resources Policy and Finance;
Health and Human Services Reform; Veterans Affairs Division
Education: U St Thomas (MN) 1981 BA

Representative **Peggy Flanagan** (DFL-District 46A) . . . . . . (651) 296-7026
Counties Represented: Hennepin (part)
Term Expires: 2017
E-mail: rep.peggy.flanagan@house.mn
Committees: Education Innovation Policy; Public Safety and Crime
Prevention Policy and Finance; Rules and Legislative Administration
Education: Minnesota 2002 BA

Representative **Mary Franson** (R-District 8B) . . . . . . . . . . . (651) 296-3201
Counties Represented: Douglas (part), Otter Tail          Res: (320) 304-4001
(part)
Term Expires: 2017
2470 Le Homme Dieu Hights, Northeast, Alexandria, MN 56308
E-mail: rep.mary.franson@house.mn
Committees: Aging and Long-Term Care Policy; Agriculture Policy;
Health and Human Services Finance; Health and Human Services
Reform
Education: Minnesota (Duluth) BA

Representative **Mike Freiberg** (DFL-District 45B) . . . . . . . . (651) 296-4176
Counties Represented: Hennepin (part)          Res: (763) 234-8749
Term Expires: 2017
6601 Olympia Street, Golden Valley, MN 55427
E-mail: rep.mike.freiberg@house.mn
Committees: Health and Human Services Reform; Legacy Funding
Finance; Rules and Legislative Administration
Education: Georgetown BA; William Mitchell 2005 JD

Representative **Pat Garofalo** (R-District 58B) . . . . . . . . . . . (651) 296-1069
Counties Represented: Dakota (part), Goodhue          Res: (651) 463-2112
(part)
Term Expires: 2017
5997 - 193rd Street West, Farmington, MN 55024
E-mail: rep.pat.garofalo@house.mn
Committees: Greater Minnesota Economic and Workforce Development
Policy; Job Growth and Energy Affordability Policy and Finance; Rules
and Legislative Administration; Taxes; Ways and Means
Education: Minnesota St (Mankato) 1994 BS

Representative **Steve Green** (R-District 2B) . . . . . . . . . . . . (651) 296-9918
Counties Represented: Becker (part), Clearwater          Res: (218) 435-6401
(part), Hubbard (part), Mahnomen, Otter Tail (part), Wadena (part)
Term Expires: 2017
2465 102nd Street, Fosston, MN 56542
E-mail: rep.steve.green@house.mn
Committees: Environment and Natural Resources Policy and Finance;
Greater Minnesota Economic and Workforce Development Policy;
Legacy Funding Finance

Representative **Glenn Gruenhagen** (R-District 18B) . . . . . . (651) 296-4229
Counties Represented: McLeod (part), Sibley          Res: (320) 864-3911
Term Expires: 2017
16367 441st Avenue, Glencoe, MN 55336-5124
E-mail: rep.glenn.gruenhagen@house.mn
Committees: Agriculture Finance; Civil Law and Data Practices; Health
and Human Services Finance; Higher Education Policy and Finance

LEGISLATIVE BRANCH

Representative **Bob Gunther** (R-District 23A) . . . . . . . . . . . (651) 296-3240
Counties Represented: Blue Earth (part), Jackson    Res: (507) 235-6154
(part), Martin, Watonwan (part)
Term Expires: 2017
530 Kings Road, Fairmont, MN 56031
E-mail: rep.bob.gunther@house.mn
Committees: Aging and Long-Term Care Policy; Greater Minnesota
Economic and Workforce Development Policy; Job Growth and Energy
Affordability Policy and Finance; Rules and Legislative Administration;
Ways and Means
Education: St Cloud State BS

Representative **Tom Hackbarth** (R-District 31B) . . . . . . . . (651) 296-2439
Counties Represented: Anoka (part)    Res: (763) 753-3215
Term Expires: 2017
19255 Eidelweiss Street, NW, Cedar, MN 55011
E-mail: rep.tom.hackbarth@house.mn
Committees: Environment and Natural Resources Policy and Finance;
Mining and Outdoor Recreation Policy; Taxes; Ways and Means

Representative **Laurie Halverson** (DFL-District 51B) . . . . . (651) 296-4128
Counties Represented: Dakota (part)    Res: (651) 249-9245
Term Expires: 2017
680 Brockton Curve, Eagan, MN 55123
E-mail: rep.laurie.halverson@house.mn
Committees: Commerce and Regulatory Reform; Government
Operations and Elections Policy; Health and Human Services Finance
Education: Col St Catherine 2001 BS; Minnesota 2007 MPA

Representative **Rod Hamilton** (R-District 22B) . . . . . . . . . . (651) 296-5373
Counties Represented: Cottonwood, Faribault (part),    Res: (507) 427-3916
Jackson (part), Nobles (part), Redwood (part)
Term Expires: 2017
1717 Second Avenue, Mountain Lake, MN 56159
E-mail: rep.rod.hamilton@house.mn
Committees: Agriculture Finance; Agriculture Policy; Health and
Human Services Finance; Ways and Means

Representative **David Hancock** (R-District 2A) . . . . . . . . . (651) 296-4265
Counties Represented: Beltrami (part), Clearwater (part), Hubbard
(part), Lake of the Woods
Term Expires: 2017
E-mail: rep.dave.hancock@house.mn
Committees: Environment and Natural Resources Policy and Finance;
Greater Minnesota Economic and Workforce Development Policy;
Veterans Affairs Division
Education: Anderson U 1968 BA

Representative **Rick Hansen** (DFL-District 52A) . . . . . . . . (651) 296-6828
Counties Represented: Dakota (part)    Res: (651) 451-1189
Term Expires: 2017
1007 - 15th Avenue North, South St. Paul, MN 55075
E-mail: rep.rick.hansen@house.mn
Committees: Agriculture Finance; Capital Investment; Environment and
Natural Resources Policy and Finance
Education: Upper Iowa BS; Iowa State MS

Representative **Alice Hausman** (DFL-District 66A) . . . . . . (651) 296-3824
Counties Represented: Ramsey (part)    Res: (651) 646-6220
Term Expires: 2017
1447 Chelmsford Street, St. Paul, MN 55108
E-mail: rep.alice.hausman@house.mn
Committees: Capital Investment; Environment and Natural Resources
Policy and Finance; Transportation Policy and Finance
Education: Concordia Col (NE) BS; Concordia U (IL) MA

Representative **Josh Heintzeman** (R-District 10A) . . . . . . (651) 296-4333
Counties Represented: Crow Wing (part)
Term Expires: 2017
E-mail: rep.josh.heintzeman@house.mn
Committees: Environment and Natural Resources Policy and Finance;
Higher Education Policy and Finance; Legacy Funding Finance

Representative **Jerry Hertaus** (R-District 33A) . . . . . . . . . (651) 296-9188
Counties Represented: Hennepin (part)    Res: (763) 477-6950
Term Expires: 2017
8055 Davis Street, Greenfield, MN 55357
E-mail: rep.jerry.hertaus@house.mn
Committees: Education Finance; Mining and Outdoor Recreation
Policy; Public Safety and Crime Prevention Policy and Finance
Education: St Mary's Col (MN) BN

Representative **Debra Hilstrom** (DFL-District 40B) . . . . . . (651) 296-3709
Counties Represented: Hennepin (part)    Res: (763) 561-6487
Term Expires: 2017
E-mail: rep.debra.hilstrom@house.mn
Committees: Civil Law and Data Practices; Public Safety and Crime
Prevention Policy and Finance; Ways and Means
Education: Minnesota BA; William Mitchell 2010 JD

Representative **Joe Hoppe** (R-District 47B) . . . . . . . . . . . . (651) 296-5066
Counties Represented: Carver (part)    Res: (952) 368-9617
Term Expires: 2017
935 Weston Ridge Parkway, Chaska, MN 55318
E-mail: rep.joe.hoppe@house.mn
Committees: Civil Law and Data Practices; Commerce and Regulatory
Reform; Rules and Legislative Administration
Education: St John's U (MN) 1987 BA

Representative **Frank Hornstein** (DFL-District 61A) . . . . . . (651) 296-9281
Counties Represented: Hennepin (part)    Res: (612) 926-3406
Term Expires: 2017
4344 Drew Avenue South, Minneapolis, MN 55410
E-mail: rep.frank.hornstein@house.mn
Committees: Environment and Natural Resources Policy and Finance;
Transportation Policy and Finance; Ways and Means
Education: Macalester 1981 BA; Tufts 1985 MA

Representative **Melissa Hortman** (DFL-District 36B) . . . . . (651) 296-4280
Counties Represented: Anoka (part), Hennepin    Res: (763) 425-5279
(part)
Term Expires: 2017
8710 Windsor Terrace, Brooklyn Park, MN 55443
E-mail: rep.melissa.hortman@house.mn
Committees: Job Growth and Energy Affordability Policy and Finance;
Rules and Legislative Administration

Representative **Jeff Howe** (R-District 13A) . . . . . . . . . . . . (651) 296-4373
Counties Represented: Stearns (part)
Term Expires: 2017
P.O. Box 84, Rockford, MN 56369
E-mail: rep.jeff.howe@house.mn
Committees: Capital Investment; Public Safety and Crime Prevention
Policy and Finance; State Government Finance; Transportation Policy
and Finance
Education: St Cloud State BA

Representative **Jason Isaacson** (DFL-District 42B) . . . . . . (651) 296-7153
Counties Represented: Ramsey (part)    Res: (612) 600-5778
Term Expires: 2017
E-mail: rep.jason.isaacson@house.mn
Committees: Higher Education Policy and Finance; Job Growth and
Energy Affordability Policy and Finance; Rules and Legislative
Administration
Education: North Dakota State 1998 BS, 2005 MS;
Minnesota 2012 (ABD)

Representative **Brian Johnson** (R-District 32A) . . . . . . . . . (651) 296-4346
Counties Represented: Chisago (part), Isanti (part)    Res: (763) 202-4731
Term Expires: 2017
31840 Lakeway Drive, NE, Cambridge, MN 55008
E-mail: rep.brian.johnson@house.mn
Committees: Civil Law and Data Practices; Greater Minnesota
Economic and Workforce Development Policy; Mining and Outdoor
Recreation Policy; Public Safety and Crime Prevention Policy and
Finance

Representative **Clark Johnson** (DFL-District 19A) . . . . . . . (651) 296-8634
Counties Represented: Blue Earth (part), Le Sueur (part), Nicollet
Term Expires: 2017
E-mail: rep.clark.johnson@house.mn
Committees: Agriculture Finance; Agriculture Policy; Environment and
Natural Resources Policy and Finance; Transportation Policy and
Finance
Education: Michigan State 1974 BA

Representative **Sheldon Johnson** (DFL-District 67B) . . . . (651) 296-4201
Counties Represented: Ramsey (part)    Res: (651) 738-3143
Term Expires: 2017
2031 Howard Street South, St. Paul, MN 55119
E-mail: rep.sheldon.johnson@house.mn
Committees: Commerce and Regulatory Reform; Job Growth and
Energy Affordability Policy and Finance; State Government Finance
Education: Bethel Col (MN) BA; St Thomas U MA

Representative **Phyllis Kahn** (DFL-District 60B) . . . . . . . . (651) 296-4257
Counties Represented: Hennepin (part)    Res: (612) 378-2591
Term Expires: 2017
115 West Island Avenue, Minneapolis, MN 55401
E-mail: rep.phyllis.kahn@house.mn
Committees: Legacy Funding Finance; State Government Finance;
Ways and Means
Education: Cornell BA; Yale 1962 PhD; Harvard 1986 MPA

Representative **Tim Kelly** (R-District 21A) . . . . . . . . . . . . . (651) 296-8635
Counties Represented: Goodhue (part), Wabasha    Res: (651) 380-4345
(part)
Term Expires: 2017
P.O. Box 412, Red Wing, MN 55066
E-mail: rep.tim.kelly@house.mn
Committees: Health and Human Services Reform; Rules and
Legislative Administration; Transportation Policy and Finance

*(continued on next page)*

**Representatives** *continued*

Representative **Debra "Deb" Kiel** (R-District 1B) . . . . . . . (651) 296-5091
Counties Represented: Pennington (part), Polk, Red Lake
Term Expires: 2017
36044 275th Avenue, Southwest, Crookston, MN 56716
E-mail: rep.deb.kiel@house.mn
Committees: Aging and Long-Term Care Policy; Agriculture Finance;
Greater Minnesota Economic and Workforce Development Policy;
Mining and Outdoor Recreation Policy

Representative **Jim Knoblach** (R-District 14B) . . . . . . . . . (651) 296-6612
Counties Represented: Benton (part), Sherburne        Res: (320) 252-8084
(part), Stearns (part)
Term Expires: 2017
6179 45th Avenue Southeast, St. Cloud, MN 56304
E-mail: rep.jim.knoblach@house.mn
Committees: Taxes; Ways and Means
Education: St John's U (MN) BS; Harvard 1981 MBA;
Georgetown 1987 MA

Representative **Jon Koznick** (R-District 58A) . . . . . . . . . . . (651) 296-6926
Counties Represented: Dakota (part)
Term Expires: 2017
E-mail: rep.jon.koznick@house.mn
Committees: Taxes; Transportation Policy and Finance
Education: St Cloud State BS

Representative **Ron Kresha** (R-District 9B) . . . . . . . . . . . . (651) 296-4247
Counties Represented: Morrison (part), Todd (part)     Res: (320) 761-6133
Term Expires: 2017
214 Lindbergh Drive, NW, Little Falls, MN 56345
E-mail: rep.ron.kresha@house.mn
Committees: Commerce and Regulatory Reform; Education Finance;
Education Innovation Policy; Rules and Legislative Administration

Representative **Carolyn Laine** (DFL-District 41B) . . . . . . . (651) 296-4331
Counties Represented: Anoka (part), Hennepin     Res: (763) 788-1864
(part), Ramsey (part)
Term Expires: 2017
1908 - 41st Avenue, N.E., Columbia Heights, MN 55421
E-mail: rep.carolyn.laine@house.mn
Committees: Government Operations and Elections Policy; Health and
Human Services Finance; State Government Finance
Education: Minnesota BS; St Mary's Col (MN) 2003 MA

Representative **John Lesch** (DFL-District 66B) . . . . . . . . . (651) 296-4224
Counties Represented: Ramsey (part)               Dist: (651) 266-8740
Term Expires: 2017                                 Res: (651) 489-7238
1254 Dale Street North, St. Paul, MN 55117
E-mail: rep.john.lesch@house.mn
Committees: Civil Law and Data Practices; Taxes; Veterans Affairs
Division
Education: Saint Louis U 1995 BA; Hamline 1998 JD

Representative **Tina Liebling** (DFL-District 26A) . . . . . . . (651) 296-0573
Counties Represented: Olmsted (part)               Tel: (507) 289-4664
Term Expires: 2017
P.O. Box 6332, Rochester, MN 55903
E-mail: rep.tina.liebling@house.mn
Committees: Aging and Long-Term Care Policy; Health and Human
Services Finance; Health and Human Services Reform; Ways and
Means
Education: Minnesota BA; Boston U JD

Representative **Ben Lien** (DFL-District 4A) . . . . . . . . . . . . (651) 296-5515
Counties Represented: Clay (part)                 Res: (218) 443-4813
Term Expires: 2017
424 11th Street, North, Apartment #7, Moorhead, MN 56560
E-mail: rep.ben.lien@house.mn
Committees: Greater Minnesota Economic and Workforce Development
Policy; Higher Education Policy and Finance
Education: Minnesota St (Moorhead) 2008 BA

Representative **Leon M. Lillie** (DFL-District 43B) . . . . . . . (651) 296-1188
Counties Represented: Ramsey (part), Washington    Res: (651) 770-9260
(part)
Term Expires: 2017
2667 East First Avenue, St. Paul, MN 55109
E-mail: rep.leon.lillie@house.mn
Committees: Aging and Long-Term Care Policy; Capital Investment;
Commerce and Regulatory Reform; Legacy Funding Finance
Education: Luther Col BS

Representative **Diane Loeffler** (DFL-District 60A) . . . . . . . (651) 296-4219
Counties Represented: Hennepin (part)             Res: (612) 781-1307
Term Expires: 2017
2245 Ulysses Street NE, Apartment 2, Minneapolis, MN 55418
E-mail: rep.diane.loeffler@house.mn
Committees: Health and Human Services Finance; Health and Human
Services Reform; Taxes
Education: Augsburg 1975 BA

Representative **Kathy Lohmer** (R-District 39B) . . . . . . . . . (651) 296-4244
Counties Represented: Washington (part)            Res: (651) 342-0924
Term Expires: 2017
8199 Hill Train, North, Lake Elmo, MN 55042
E-mail: rep.kathy.lohmer@house.mn
Committees: Civil Law and Data Practices; Health and Human Services
Finance; Health and Human Services Reform; Public Safety and Crime
Prevention Policy and Finance

Representative **Jenifer W. Loon** (R-District 48B) . . . . . . . . (651) 296-7449
Counties Represented: Hennepin (part)
Term Expires: 2017
E-mail: rep.jenifer.loon@house.mn
Committees: Commerce and Regulatory Reform; Education Finance;
Taxes; Ways and Means
Education: Augustana (SD) 1985 BA

Representative **Bob Loonan** (R-District 55A) . . . . . . . . . . . (651) 296-8872
Counties Represented: Scott (part)
Term Expires: 2017
E-mail: rep.bob.loonan@house.mn
Committees: Commerce and Regulatory Reform; Job Growth and
Energy Affordability Policy and Finance; State Government Finance

Representative **Eric Lucero** (R-District 30B) . . . . . . . . . . . (651) 296-1534
Counties Represented: Hennepin (part), Wright (part)
Term Expires: 2017
E-mail: rep.eric.lucero@house.mn
Committees: Education Innovation Policy; Mining and Outdoor
Recreation Policy; Public Safety and Crime Prevention Policy and
Finance; Transportation Policy and Finance

Representative **Dale Lueck** (R-District 10B) . . . . . . . . . . . (651) 296-2365
Counties Represented: Aitkin, Crow Wing (part)
Term Expires: 2017
E-mail: rep.dale.lueck@house.mn
Committees: Agriculture Finance; Agriculture Policy; Mining and
Outdoor Recreation Policy; Veterans Affairs Division

Representative **Tara Mack** (R-District 57A) . . . . . . . . . . . (651) 296-5506
Counties Represented: Dakota (part)
Term Expires: 2017
E-mail: rep.tara.mack@house.mn
Committees: Health and Human Services Finance; Health and Human
Services Reform; Rules and Legislative Administration

Representative **Tim Mahoney** (DFL-District 67A) . . . . . . . (651) 296-4277
Counties Represented: Ramsey (part)               Res: (651) 776-3200
Term Expires: 2017
1091 Hyacinth, St. Paul, MN 55106
E-mail: rep.tim.mahoney@house.mn
Committees: Greater Minnesota Economic and Workforce Development
Policy; Job Growth and Energy Affordability Policy and Finance; Ways
and Means

Representative **Carlos Mariani** (DFL-District 65B) . . . . . . . (651) 296-9714
Counties Represented: Ramsey (part)               Res: (651) 224-6647
Term Expires: 2017
187 West Congress, St. Paul, MN 55107
E-mail: rep.carlos.mariani@house.mn
Committees: Agriculture Policy; Education Finance; Education
Innovation Policy
Education: Macalester 1979 BA; Minnesota JD

Representative **Paul Marquart** (DFL-District 4B) . . . . . . . . (651) 296-6829
Counties Represented: Becker (part), Clay (part),    Res: (218) 233-9200
Norman
Term Expires: 2017
605 First Street, N.E., Dilworth, MN 56529
E-mail: rep.paul.marquart@house.mn
Committees: Agriculture Policy; Education Finance

Representative **Sandra A. Masin** (DFL-District 51A) . . . . . (651) 296-3533
Counties Represented: Dakota (part)               Res: (651) 452-3411
Term Expires: 2017
E-mail: rep.sandra.masin@house.mn
Committees: Aging and Long-Term Care Policy; Health and Human
Services Reform; Transportation Policy and Finance
Education: Valparaiso 1964 BA

Representative **Joe McDonald** (R-District 29A) . . . . . . . . . (651) 296-4336
Counties Represented: Hennepin (part), Wright      Res: (612) 910-0310
(part)
Term Expires: 2017
E-mail: rep.joe.mcdonald@house.mn
Committees: Health and Human Services Finance; Higher Education
Policy and Finance; Taxes

Representative **Denny McNamara** (R-District 54B) . . . . . . (651) 296-3135
Counties Represented: Dakota (part), Washington   Res: (651) 437-2597
(part)
Term Expires: 2017
1368 Featherstone Court, Hastings, MN 55033
E-mail: rep.denny.mcnamara@house.mn
Committees: Environment and Natural Resources Policy and Finance;
Mining and Outdoor Recreation Policy; Transportation Policy and
Finance; Ways and Means
Education: Minnesota 1976 BSBA

Representative **Carly Melin** (DFL-District 6A) . . . . . . . . . . (651) 296-0172
Counties Represented: Itasca (part), St. Louis (part)   Res: (218) 263-1502
Term Expires: 2017
E-mail: rep.carly.melin@house.mn
Committees: Capital Investment; Mining and Outdoor Recreation
Policy; Taxes
Education: Bemidji State BA; Hamline JD

Representative **Jason Metsa** (DFL-District 6B) . . . . . . . . . (651) 296-0170
Counties Represented: St. Louis (part)   Res: (218) 741-5692
Term Expires: 2017
810 Fifth Street, South, Virginia, MN 55792
E-mail: rep.jason.metsa@house.mn
Committees: Agriculture Finance; Job Growth and Energy Affordability
Policy and Finance; Mining and Outdoor Recreation Policy

Representative **Tim Miller** (R-District 17A) . . . . . . . . . . . . (651) 296-4228
Counties Represented: Chippewa, Kandiyohi (part), Renville (part),
Swift
Term Expires: 2017
E-mail: rep.tim.miller@house.mn
Committees: Aging and Long-Term Care Policy; Agriculture Finance;
Greater Minnesota Economic and Workforce Development Policy;
Legacy Funding Finance

Representative **Rena Moran** (DFL-District 65A) . . . . . . . . . (651) 296-5158
Counties Represented: Ramsey (part)
Term Expires: 2017
671 Aurora Avenue, West, St. Paul, MN 55104
E-mail: rep.rena.moran@house.mn
Committees: Education Innovation Policy; Greater Minnesota Economic
and Workforce Development Policy; Health and Human Services
Reform

Representative **Joe Mullery** (DFL-District 59A) . . . . . . . . (651) 296-4262
Counties Represented: Hennepin (part)   Res: (612) 521-4921
Term Expires: 2017
4101 Vincent Avenue North, Minneapolis, MN 55412
E-mail: rep.joe.mullery@house.mn
Committees: Education Finance; Government Operations and Elections
Policy; Health and Human Services Reform
Education: Minnesota BA, 1971 JD

Representative **Erin Murphy** (DFL-District 64A) . . . . . . . . (651) 296-8799
Counties Represented: Ramsey (part)   Res: (651) 235-7104
Term Expires: 2017
898 Osceola Avenue, Saint Paul, MN 55105
E-mail: rep.erin.murphy@house.mn
Committees: Health and Human Services Finance; Legacy Funding
Finance

Representative **Mary Murphy** (DFL-District 3B) . . . . . . . . (651) 296-2676
Counties Represented: Lake (part), St. Louis (part)   Res: (218) 729-6399
Term Expires: 2017
5180 West Arrowhead Road, Hermantown, MN 55811
E-mail: rep.mary.murphy@house.mn
Committees: Education Finance; Ethics; Legacy Funding Finance; Ways
and Means
Education: Col St Scholastica BA

Representative **Jim Nash** (R-District 47A) . . . . . . . . . . . . . (651) 296-4282
Counties Represented: Carver (part)
Term Expires: 2017
E-mail: rep.jim.nash@house.mn
Committees: Government Operations and Elections Policy; State
Government Finance; Transportation Policy and Finance

Representative
**Michael V. "Mike" Nelson** (DFL-District 40A) . . . . . . . (651) 296-3751
Counties Represented: Hennepin (part)   Res: (763) 561-2795
Term Expires: 2017
7441 Hampshire Avenue North, Brooklyn Park, MN 55428
E-mail: rep.michael.nelson@house.mn
Committees: Government Operations and Elections Policy; Rules and
Legislative Administration; State Government Finance

Representative
**James "Jim" Newberger** (R-District 15B) . . . . . . . . . . (651) 296-2451
Counties Represented: Benton (part), Morrison   Res: (763) 482-9486
(part), Sherburne (part), Wright (part)
Term Expires: 2017
14225 Balsam Boulevard, Becker, MN 55308
E-mail: rep.jim.newberger@house.mn
Committees: Environment and Natural Resources Policy and Finance;
Job Growth and Energy Affordability Policy and Finance; Public Safety
and Crime Prevention Policy and Finance
Education: St Cloud State BA

Representative **Jerry Newton** (DFL-District 37A) . . . . . . . . (651) 296-5369
Counties Represented: Anoka (part)   Res: (763) 755-2161
Term Expires: 2017
12095 Dogwood Street, NW, Coon Rapids, MN 55448
E-mail: rep.jerry.newton@house.mn
Committees: Aging and Long-Term Care Policy; Education Finance;
Veterans Affairs Division
Education: Maryland 1973 BA; Boston U 1975 MA

Representative **Bud Nornes** (R-District 8A) . . . . . . . . . . . . (651) 296-4946
Counties Represented: Otter Tail (part)   Res: (218) 736-7777
Term Expires: 2017
22195 River Oaks Drive, Fergus Falls, MN 56537
E-mail: rep.bud.nornes@house.mn
Committees: Agriculture Policy; Education Finance; Education
Innovation Policy; Higher Education Policy and Finance; Ways and
Means

Representative **Kim Norton** (DFL-District 25B) . . . . . . . . . (651) 296-9249
Counties Represented: Olmsted (part)   Res: (507) 990-0276
Term Expires: 2017
1721 Wilshire Drive, Northeast, Rochester, MN 55906
E-mail: rep.kim.norton@house.mn
Committees: Greater Minnesota Economic and Workforce Development
Policy; Higher Education Policy and Finance; Transportation Policy and
Finance
Education: Nebraska 1981 BS

Representative **Tim O'Driscoll** (R-District 13B) . . . . . . . . . (651) 296-7808
Counties Represented: Benton (part), Stearns (part)
Term Expires: 2017
P.O. Box 225, Sartell, MN 53677
E-mail: rep.tim.odriscoll@house.mn
Committees: Capital Investment; Commerce and Regulatory Reform;
Government Operations and Elections Policy; Rules and Legislative
Administration; Veterans Affairs Division

Representative **Marion O'Neill** (R-District 29B) . . . . . . . . . (651) 296-5063
Counties Represented: Wright (part)
Term Expires: 2017
E-mail: rep.marion.oneill@house.mn
Committees: Greater Minnesota Economic and Workforce Development
Policy; Higher Education Policy and Finance; Job Growth and Energy
Affordability Policy and Finance; Public Safety and Crime Prevention
Policy and Finance; Rules and Legislative Administration
Education: Bemidji State 1992 BA; Regent U 1995 MA

Representative **Gene Pelowski, Jr.** (DFL-District 28A) . . . (651) 296-8637
Counties Represented: Winona (part)   Res: (507) 454-3282
Term Expires: 2017
257 Wilson Street, Winona, MN 55987
E-mail: rep.gene.pelowski@house.mn
Committees: Capital Investment; Higher Education Policy and Finance;
Rules and Legislative Administration; Ways and Means
Education: Winona State 1975 BS, 1998 MS

Representative **Joyce Peppin** (R-District 34A) . . . . . . . . . . (651) 296-7806
Counties Represented: Hennepin (part)   Res: (763) 428-4626
Term Expires: 2017
14535 Edgewood Road, Rogers, MN 55374
E-mail: rep.joyce.peppin@house.mn
Committees: Rules and Legislative Administration

Representative **John Persell** (DFL-District 5A) . . . . . . . . . . (651) 296-5516
Counties Represented: Beltrami (part), Cass (part),   Res: (218) 751-2770
Hubbard (part), Itasca (part)
Term Expires: 2017
2435 Steghorn Lane, Bemidji, MN 56601
E-mail: rep.john.persell@house.mn
Committees: Environment and Natural Resources Policy and Finance;
Health and Human Services Finance; Veterans Affairs Division
Education: Bemidji State 1978 BS

*(continued on next page)*

**Representatives** *continued*

Representative **John Petersburg** (R-District 24A) . . . . . . . (651) 296-5368
Counties Represented: Steele (part), Waseca (part)    Res: (507) 835-5082
Term Expires: 2017
700 19th Avenue, NE, Waseca, MN 56093
E-mail: rep.john.petersburg@house.mn
Committees: State Government Finance; Taxes; Transportation Policy
and Finance
Education: Minnesota St (Mankato) BS

Representative **Roz Peterson** (R-District 56B) . . . . . . . . . . (651) 296-5387
Counties Represented: Dakota (part)
Term Expires: 2017
E-mail: rep.roz.peterson@house.mn
Committees: Education Finance; Education Innovation Policy; Health
and Human Services Reform
Education: Gustavus Adolphus BA

Representative **Nels Pierson** (R-District 26B) . . . . . . . . . . (651) 296-4378
Counties Represented: Faribault (part), Olmsted (part)
Term Expires: 2017
E-mail: rep.nels.pierson@house.mn
Committees: Agriculture Finance; Education Innovation Policy; Health
and Human Services Finance; Health and Human Services Reform

Representative **David Pinto** (DFL-District 64B) . . . . . . . . . . (651) 296-4199
Counties Represented: Ramsey (part)
Term Expires: 2017
E-mail: rep.dave.pinto@house.mn
Committees: Civil Law and Data Practices; Rules and Legislative
Administration
Education: Harvard BA; Virginia 2001 JD, 2001 MBA

Representative **Jeanne Poppe** (DFL-District 27B) . . . . . . . . (651) 296-4193
Counties Represented: Dodge (part), Freeborn    Res: (507) 438-7857
(part), Mower (part)
Term Expires: 2017
900 Fourth Street NW, Austin, MN 55912
E-mail: rep.jeanne.poppe@house.mn
Committees: Agriculture Finance; Agriculture Policy; Capital
Investment; Environment and Natural Resources Policy and Finance;
Ways and Means
Education: Wisconsin (River Falls) 1980 BA; Winona State 1984 MS

Representative **Cindy Pugh** (R-District 33B) . . . . . . . . . . . (651) 296-4315
Counties Represented: Carver (part), Hennepin (part)
Term Expires: 2017
E-mail: rep.cindy.pugh@house.mn
Committees: Government Operations and Elections Policy; Higher
Education Policy and Finance; State Government Finance; Veterans
Affairs Division
Education: Wisconsin 1979 BS

Representative **Duane Quam** (R-District 25A) . . . . . . . . . . (651) 296-9236
Counties Represented: Dodge (part), Olmsted (part)    Res: (507) 775-6043
Term Expires: 2017
415 4th Avenue, Northeast, Byron, MN 55920-1453
E-mail: rep.duane.quam@house.mn
Committees: Education Finance; Health and Human Services Reform;
Public Safety and Crime Prevention Policy and Finance

Representative **Jason Rarick** (R-District 11B) . . . . . . . . . . (651) 296-0518
Counties Represented: Kanabec (part), Pine (part)
Term Expires: 2017
E-mail: rep.jason.rarick@house.mn
Committees: Agriculture Policy; Capital Investment; Environment and
Natural Resources Policy and Finance

Representative **Paul Rosenthal** (DFL-District 49B) . . . . . . . (651) 296-7803
Counties Represented: Hennepin (part)    Res: (651) 271-8131
Term Expires: 2017
4721 Hibiscus Avenue, Edina, MN 55435
E-mail: rep.paul.rosenthal@house.mn
Committees: Aging and Long-Term Care Policy; Higher Education
Policy and Finance; Public Safety and Crime Prevention Policy and
Finance
Education: NYU BA

Representative **Linda Runbeck** (R-District 38A) . . . . . . . . (651) 296-2907
Counties Represented: Anoka (part), Washington    Res: (763) 784-8822
(part)
Term Expires: 2017
48 East Golden Lake Road, Circle Pines, MN 55014
E-mail: rep.linda.runbeck@house.mn
Committees: Capital Investment; Government Operations and Elections
Policy; State Government Finance; Transportation Policy and Finance

Representative **Tim Sanders** (R-District 37B) . . . . . . . . . . (651) 296-4226
Counties Represented: Anoka (part)    Res: (612) 877-1283
Term Expires: 2017
2064 - 119th Avenue, Northeast, Blaine, MN 55449
E-mail: rep.tim.sanders@house.mn
Committees: Commerce and Regulatory Reform; Government
Operations and Elections Policy; Rules and Legislative Administration;
Transportation Policy and Finance

Representative **Dan Schoen** (DFL-District 54A) . . . . . . . . (651) 296-4342
Counties Represented: Dakota (part), Washington    Res: (651) 459-3753
(part)
Term Expires: 2017
938 Selby Avenue, Saint Paul Park, MN 55071
E-mail: rep.dan.schoen@house.mn
Committees: Civil Law and Data Practices; Health and Human Services
Finance; Public Safety and Crime Prevention Policy and Finance

Representative **Joe Schomacker** (R-District 22A) . . . . . . . . (651) 296-5505
Counties Represented: Lincoln, Nobles (part),    Res: (507) 935-0308
Pipestone, Rock
Term Expires: 2017
518 North Freeman Avenue, Luverne, MN 56156
E-mail: rep.joe.schomacker@house.mn
Committees: Aging and Long-Term Care Policy; Agriculture Policy;
Health and Human Services Finance; Health and Human Services
Reform

Representative **Jennifer Schultz** (DFL-District 7A) . . . . . . . (651) 296-2228
Counties Represented: St. Louis (part)
Term Expires: 2017
E-mail: rep.jennifer.schultz@house.mn
Committees: Agriculture Policy; Health and Human Services Reform;
State Government Finance
Education: Minnesota PhD

Representative **Peggy Scott** (R-District 35B) . . . . . . . . . . (651) 296-4231
Counties Represented: Anoka (part)    Res: (763) 238-7322
Term Expires: 2017
1363 146th Avenue, Andover, MN 55304
E-mail: rep.peggy.scott@house.mn
Committees: Civil Law and Data Practices; Commerce and Regulatory
Reform; Government Operations and Elections Policy; Job Growth
and Energy Affordability Policy and Finance; Rules and Legislative
Administration

Representative **Yvonne Selcer** (DFL-District 48A) . . . . . . . (651) 296-3964
Counties Represented: Hennepin (part)    Res: (952) 912-0473
Term Expires: 2017
14518 Rocksborough Road, Minnetonka, MN 55345
E-mail: rep.yvonne.selcer@house.mn
Committees: Education Finance; Education Innovation Policy;
Government Operations and Elections Policy
Education: St Teresa 1975 BSEd

Representative **Erik Simonson** (DFL-District 7B) . . . . . . . . (651) 296-4246
Counties Represented: St. Louis (part)
Term Expires: 2017
E-mail: rep.erik.simonson@house.mn
Committees: Job Growth and Energy Affordability Policy and Finance;
Taxes

Representative **Linda Slocum** (DFL-District 50A) . . . . . . . . (651) 296-7158
Counties Represented: Hennepin (part)    Res: (612) 718-1950
Term Expires: 2017
6421 12th Avenue, South, Richfield, MN 55423
E-mail: rep.linda.slocum@house.mn
Committees: Commerce and Regulatory Reform; Education Finance;
Taxes

Representative **Dennis Smith** (R-District 34B) . . . . . . . . . (651) 296-5502
Counties Represented: Hennepin (part)
Term Expires: 2017
E-mail: rep.dennis.smith@house.mn
Committees: Capital Investment; Civil Law and Data Practices;
Commerce and Regulatory Reform; Job Growth and Energy
Affordability Policy and Finance
Education: North Dakota BS; William Mitchell JD

Representative **Mike Sundin** (DFL-District 11A) . . . . . . . . (651) 296-4308
Counties Represented: Carlton, Pine (part), St.    Res: (218) 391-5911
Louis (part)
Term Expires: 2017
33 Thomson Road, Esko, MN 55733
E-mail: rep.mike.sundin@house.mn
Committees: Agriculture Finance; Commerce and Regulatory Reform;
Greater Minnesota Economic and Workforce Development Policy;
Transportation Policy and Finance

Representative **Chris Swedzinski** (R-District 16A) . . . . . . (651) 296-5374
  Counties Represented: Lac qui Parle, Lyon (part),    Res: (507) 829-7754
  Redwood (part), Yellow Medicine
  Term Expires: 2017
  1673 County Road Eight, Ghent, MN 56239-1130
  E-mail: rep.chris.swedzinski@house.mn
  Committees: Capital Investment; Commerce and Regulatory Reform;
  Job Growth and Energy Affordability Policy and Finance; Rules and
  Legislative Administration; Taxes

Representative **Tama Theis** (R-District 14A) . . . . . . . . . . (651) 296-6316
  Counties Represented: Stearns (part)
  Term Expires: 2017
  E-mail: rep.tama.theis@house.mn
  Committees: Aging and Long-Term Care Policy; Capital Investment;
  Commerce and Regulatory Reform; Government Operations and
  Elections Policy

Representative **Paul C. Thissen** (DFL-District 61B) . . . . . . (651) 296-5375
  Counties Represented: Hennepin (part)    Res: (612) 824-6697
  Term Expires: 2017
  1219 West 51st Street, Minneapolis, MN 55419
  E-mail: rep.paul.thissen@house.mn
  Committees: Rules and Legislative Administration

Representative **Paul Torkelson** (R-District 16B) . . . . . . . . . (651) 296-9303
  Counties Represented: Brown, Redwood (part),    Res: (507) 375-7315
  Renville (part)
  Term Expires: 2017
  71664 320th Street, Saint James, MN 56081
  E-mail: rep.paul.torkelson@house.mn
  Committees: Capital Investment; Environment and Natural Resources
  Policy and Finance; Ethics; Legacy Funding Finance; Taxes; Ways and
  Means
  Education: Gustavus Adolphus BA

Representative **Mark Uglem** (R-District 36A) . . . . . . . . . . (651) 296-5513
  Counties Represented: Anoka (part), Hennepin (part)
  Term Expires: 2017
  11623 Oakview Court, Champlin, MN 55316
  E-mail: rep.mark.uglem@house.mn
  Committees: Capital Investment; Environment and Natural Resources
  Policy and Finance; Transportation Policy and Finance
  Education: Minnesota (Duluth) BA

Representative **Dean Urdahl** (R-District 18A) . . . . . . . . . . (651) 296-4344
  Counties Represented: McLeod (part), Meeker,    Res: (320) 857-2600
  Wright (part)
  Term Expires: 2017
  54880 253rd Street, Grove City, MN 56243
  E-mail: rep.dean.urdahl@house.mn
  Committees: Capital Investment; Education Innovation Policy; Legacy
  Funding Finance; Ways and Means
  Education: St Cloud State BS

Representative **Bob Vogel** (R-District 20A) . . . . . . . . . . . . (651) 296-7065
  Counties Represented: Le Sueur (part), Scott (part)
  Term Expires: 2017
  E-mail: rep.bob.vogel@house.mn
  Committees: Capital Investment; Civil Law and Data Practices; Job
  Growth and Energy Affordability Policy and Finance

Representative **Jean Wagenius** (DFL-District 63B) . . . . . . . (651) 296-4200
  Counties Represented: Hennepin (part)    Res: (612) 822-3347
  Term Expires: 2017
  4804 - 11th Avenue South, Minneapolis, MN 55417
  E-mail: rep.jean.wagenius@house.mn
  Committees: Capital Investment; Job Growth and Energy Affordability
  Policy and Finance; Ways and Means
  Education: George Washington 1963 BA; William Mitchell 1983 JD

Representative **JoAnn Ward** (DFL-District 53A) . . . . . . . . . (651) 296-7807
  Counties Represented: Ramsey (part), Washington (part)
  Term Expires: 2017
  7817 Somerset Circle, Woodbury, MN 55125
  E-mail: rep.joann.ward@house.mn
  Committees: Education Innovation Policy; Public Safety and Crime
  Prevention Policy and Finance; Veterans Affairs Division
  Education: Kansas State BS; U St Thomas (MN) 1994 MAEd

Representative **Abigail Whelan** (R-District 35A) . . . . . . . . . (651) 296-1729
  Counties Represented: Anoka (part)
  Term Expires: 2017
  E-mail: rep.abigail.whelan@house.mn
  Committees: Education Innovation Policy; Higher Education Policy and
  Finance; Transportation Policy and Finance

Representative **Anna Wills** (R-District 57B) . . . . . . . . . . . . (651) 296-4306
  Counties Represented: Dakota (part)    Res: (612) 564-9447
  Term Expires: 2017
  E-mail: rep.anna.wills@house.mn
  Committees: Education Finance; Education Innovation Policy; Legacy
  Funding Finance; Taxes
  Education: Northwestern Col (MN) 2002 (Attended)

Representative **Barb Yarusso** (DFL-District 42A) . . . . . . . . (651) 296-0141
  Counties Represented: Ramsey (part)    Res: (651) 486-8328
  Term Expires: 2017
  E-mail: rep.barb.yarusso@house.mn
  Committees: Aging and Long-Term Care Policy; Education Innovation
  Policy; Mining and Outdoor Recreation Policy
  Education: Minnesota 1978 BChE; Wisconsin 1985 PhD

Representative **Cheryl Youakim** (DFL-District 46B) . . . . . . (651) 296-9889
  Counties Represented: Hennepin (part)
  Term Expires: 2017
  E-mail: rep.cheryl.youakim@house.mn
  Committees: Government Operations and Elections Policy; Higher
  Education Policy and Finance
  Education: Minnesota BA

Representative **Nick Zerwas** (R-District 30A) . . . . . . . . . . (651) 296-4237
  Counties Represented: Sherburne (part), Wright    Res: (763) 441-3935
  (part)
  Term Expires: 2017
  12778 183rd Court, NW, Elk River, MN 55330
  E-mail: rep.nick.zerwas@house.mn
  Committees: Civil Law and Data Practices; Health and Human Services
  Finance; Health and Human Services Reform; Public Safety and Crime
  Prevention Policy and Finance
  Education: Hamline 2003 BS; U Phoenix MBA

# House Standing Committees

## Aging and Long-Term Care Policy

| Majority Members | Minority Members |
|---|---|
| Joe Schomacker (R-22A) *Chair* | Leon M. Lillie (DFL-43B) |
| Tama Theis (R-14A) *Vice Chair* | *DFL Lead* |
| Chad Anderson (R-50B) | John "Jack" Considine (DFL-19B) |
| Dave Baker (R-17B) | Tina Liebling (DFL-26A) |
| Drew Christensen (R-56A) | Sandra A. Masin (DFL-51A) |
| Brian Daniels (R-24B) | Jerry Newton (DFL-37A) |
| Mary Franson (R-8B) | Paul Rosenthal (DFL-49B) |
| Bob Gunther (R-23A) | Barb Yarusso (DFL-42A) |
| Debra "Deb" Kiel (R-1B) | |
| Tim Miller (R-17A) | |

## Agriculture Finance

| Majority Members | Minority Members |
|---|---|
| Rod Hamilton (R-22B) *Chair* | Jeanne Poppe (DFL-27B) *DFL Lead* |
| Debra "Deb" Kiel (R-1B) | Jon Applebaum (DFL-44B) |
|  *Vice Chair* | David Bly (DFL-20B) |
| Mark Anderson (R-9A) | Karen Clark (DFL-62A) |
| Paul H. Anderson (R-12B) | Rob Ecklund (DFL-3A) |
| Peggy Bennett (R-27A) | Rick Hansen (DFL-52A) |
| Brian Daniels (R-24B) | Clark Johnson (DFL-19A) |
| Dan Fabian (R-1A) | Jason Metsa (DFL-6B) |
| Glenn Gruenhagen (R-18B) | Mike Sundin (DFL-11A) |
| Dale Lueck (R-10B) | |
| Tim Miller (R-17A) | |
| Nels Pierson (R-26B) | |

## Agriculture Policy

| Majority Members | Minority Members |
|---|---|
| Paul H. Anderson (R-12B) *Chair* | David Bly (DFL-20B) *DFL Lead* |
| Mary Franson (R-8B) *Vice Chair* | Susan Allen (DFL-62B) |
| Mark Anderson (R-9A) | Clark Johnson (DFL-19A) |
| Jeff Backer (R-12A) | Carlos Mariani (DFL-65B) |
| Rod Hamilton (R-22B) | Paul Marquart (DFL-4B) |
| Dale Lueck (R-10B) | Jeanne Poppe (DFL-27B) |
| Bud Nornes (R-8A) | Jennifer Schultz (DFL-7A) |
| Jason Rarick (R-11B) | |
| Joe Schomacker (R-22A) | |

## Capital Investment

**Majority Members**
Paul Torkelson (R-16B) *Chair*
Chris Swedzinski (R-16A)
  *Vice Chair*
Tony Albright (R-55B)
Jeff Howe (R-13A)
Tim O'Driscoll (R-13B)
Jason Rarick (R-11B)
Linda Runbeck (R-38A)
Dennis Smith (R-34B)
Tama Theis (R-14A)
Mark Uglem (R-36A)
Dean Urdahl (R-18A)
Bob Vogel (R-20A)

**Minority Members**
Alice Hausman (DFL-66A)
  *DFL Lead*
Joe Atkins (DFL-52B)
Raymond Dehn (DFL-59B)
Rick Hansen (DFL-52A)
Leon M. Lillie (DFL-43B)
Carly Melin (DFL-6A)
Gene Pelowski, Jr. (DFL-28A)
Jeanne Poppe (DFL-27B)
Jean Wagenius (DFL-63B)

## Civil Law and Data Practices

**Majority Members**
Peggy Scott (R-35B) *Chair*
Dennis Smith (R-34B) *Vice Chair*
Glenn Gruenhagen (R-18B)
Joe Hoppe (R-47B)
Brian Johnson (R-32A)
Kathy Lohmer (R-39B)
Bob Vogel (R-20A)
Nick Zerwas (R-30A)

**Minority Members**
John Lesch (DFL-66B) *DFL Lead*
Jon Applebaum (DFL-44B)
Debra Hilstrom (DFL-40B)
David Pinto (DFL-64B)
Dan Schoen (DFL-54A)

## Commerce and Regulatory Reform

**Majority Members**
Joe Hoppe (R-47B) *Chair*
Tim O'Driscoll (R-13B) *Vice Chair*
Sarah Anderson (R-44A)
Gregory M. "Greg" Davids (R-28B)
Ron Kresha (R-9B)
Jenifer W. Loon (R-48B)
Bob Loonan (R-55A)
Tim Sanders (R-37B)
Peggy Scott (R-35B)
Dennis Smith (R-34B)
Chris Swedzinski (R-16A)
Tama Theis (R-14A)

**Minority Members**
Joe Atkins (DFL-52B) *DFL Lead*
Jon Applebaum (DFL-44B)
Raymond Dehn (DFL-59B)
Laurie Halverson (DFL-51B)
Sheldon Johnson (DFL-67B)
Leon M. Lillie (DFL-43B)
Linda Slocum (DFL-50A)
Mike Sundin (DFL-11A)

## Education Finance

**Majority Members**
Jenifer W. Loon (R-48B) *Chair*
Ron Kresha (R-9B) *Vice Chair*
Paul H. Anderson (R-12B)
Peggy Bennett (R-27A)
Drew Christensen (R-56A)
Bob Dettmer (R-39A)
Sondra Erickson (R-15A)
Kelly Fenton (R-53B)
Jerry Hertaus (R-33A)
Bud Nornes (R-8A)
Roz Peterson (R-56B)
Duane Quam (R-25A)
Anna Wills (R-57B)

**Minority Members**
Mary Murphy (DFL-3B) *DFL Lead*
Tom Anzelc (DFL-5B)
Jim Davnie (DFL-63A)
Carlos Mariani (DFL-65B)
Paul Marquart (DFL-4B)
Joe Mullery (DFL-59A)
Jerry Newton (DFL-37A)
Yvonne Selcer (DFL-48A)
Linda Slocum (DFL-50A)

## Education Innovation Policy

**Majority Members**
Sondra Erickson (R-15A) *Chair*
Peggy Bennett (R-27A) *Vice Chair*
Drew Christensen (R-56A)
Ron Kresha (R-9B)
Eric Lucero (R-30B)
Bud Nornes (R-8A)
Roz Peterson (R-56B)
Nels Pierson (R-26B)
Dean Urdahl (R-18A)
Abigail Whelan (R-35A)
Anna Wills (R-57B)

**Minority Members**
Carlos Mariani (DFL-65B)
  *DFL Lead*
David Bly (DFL-20B)
Jim Davnie (DFL-63A)
Peggy Flanagan (DFL-46A)
Rena Moran (DFL-65A)
Yvonne Selcer (DFL-48A)
JoAnn Ward (DFL-53A)
Barb Yarusso (DFL-42A)

## Environment and Natural Resources Policy and Finance

**Majority Members**
Denny McNamara (R-54B) *Chair*
Dan Fabian (R-1A) *Vice Chair*
Tony Cornish (R-23B)
Kelly Fenton (R-53B)
Steve Green (R-2B)
Tom Hackbarth (R-31B)
David Hancock (R-2A)
Josh Heintzeman (R-10A)
James "Jim" Newberger (R-15B)
Jason Rarick (R-11B)
Paul Torkelson (R-16B)
Mark Uglem (R-36A)

**Minority Members**
Rick Hansen (DFL-52A) *DFL Lead*
Karen Clark (DFL-62A)
Rob Ecklund (DFL-3A)
Peter M. Fischer (DFL-43A)
Alice Hausman (DFL-66A)
Frank Hornstein (DFL-61A)
Clark Johnson (DFL-19A)
John Persell (DFL-5A)
Jeanne Poppe (DFL-27B)

## Ethics

**Majority Members**
Sondra Erickson (R-15A) *Chair*
Paul Torkelson (R-16B)

**Minority Members**
Mary Murphy (DFL-3B) *DFL Lead*
Raymond Dehn (DFL-59B)

## Government Operations and Elections Policy

**Majority Members**
Tim Sanders (R-37B) *Chair*
Cindy Pugh (R-33B) *Vice Chair*
Tony Albright (R-55B)
Chad Anderson (R-50B)
Kelly Fenton (R-53B)
Jim Nash (R-47A)
Tim O'Driscoll (R-13B)
Linda Runbeck (R-38A)
Peggy Scott (R-35B)
Tama Theis (R-14A)

**Minority Members**
Michael V. "Mike"
  Nelson (DFL-40A)
  *DFL Lead*
Laurie Halverson (DFL-51B)
Carolyn Laine (DFL-41B)
Joe Mullery (DFL-59A)
Yvonne Selcer (DFL-48A)
Cheryl Youakim (DFL-46B)

## Greater Minnesota Economic and Workforce Development Policy

**Majority Members**
Bob Gunther (R-23A) *Chair*
Steve Green (R-2B) *Vice Chair*
Bob Barrett (R-32B)
Pat Garofalo (R-58B)
David Hancock (R-2A)
Brian Johnson (R-32A)
Debra "Deb" Kiel (R-1B)
Tim Miller (R-17A)
Marion O'Neill (R-29B)

**Minority Members**
Kim Norton (DFL-25B) *DFL Lead*
Rob Ecklund (DFL-3A)
Ben Lien (DFL-4A)
Tim Mahoney (DFL-67A)
Rena Moran (DFL-65A)
Mike Sundin (DFL-11A)

## Health and Human Services Finance

**Majority Members**
Matt Dean (R-38B) *Chair*
Joe McDonald (R-29A) *Vice Chair*
Jeff Backer (R-12A)
Mary Franson (R-8B)
Glenn Gruenhagen (R-18B)
Rod Hamilton (R-22B)
Kathy Lohmer (R-39B)
Tara Mack (R-57A)
Nels Pierson (R-26B)
Joe Schomacker (R-22A)
Nick Zerwas (R-30A)

**Minority Members**
Tina Liebling (DFL-26A) *DFL Lead*
Diane Loeffler (DFL-60A)
  *DFL Lead*
Susan Allen (DFL-62B)
Laurie Halverson (DFL-51B)
Carolyn Laine (DFL-41B)
Erin Murphy (DFL-64A)
John Persell (DFL-5A)
Dan Schoen (DFL-54A)

## Health and Human Services Reform

**Majority Members**
Tara Mack (R-57A) *Chair*
Roz Peterson (R-56B) *Vice Chair*
Tony Albright (R-55B)
Jeff Backer (R-12A)
Dave Baker (R-17B)
Matt Dean (R-38B)
Mary Franson (R-8B)
Tim Kelly (R-21A)
Kathy Lohmer (R-39B)
Nels Pierson (R-26B)
Duane Quam (R-25A)
Joe Schomacker (R-22A)
Nick Zerwas (R-30A)

**Minority Members**
Joe Mullery (DFL-59A) *DFL Lead*
Susan Allen (DFL-62B)
Peter M. Fischer (DFL-43A)
Mike Freiberg (DFL-45B)
Tina Liebling (DFL-26A)
Diane Loeffler (DFL-60A)
Sandra A. Masin (DFL-51A)
Rena Moran (DFL-65A)
Jennifer Schultz (DFL-7A)

## Higher Education Policy and Finance

| Majority Members | Minority Members |
|---|---|
| Bud Nornes (R-8A) *Chair* | Gene Pelowski, Jr. (DFL-28A) |
| Marion O'Neill (R-29B) *Vice Chair* | *DFL Lead* |
| Bob Barrett (R-32B) | Connie Bernardy (DFL-41A) |
| Drew Christensen (R-56A) | Jason Isaacson (DFL-42B) |
| Brian Daniels (R-24B) | Ben Lien (DFL-4A) |
| Glenn Gruenhagen (R-18B) | Kim Norton (DFL-25B) |
| Josh Heintzeman (R-10A) | Paul Rosenthal (DFL-49B) |
| Joe McDonald (R-29A) | Cheryl Youakim (DFL-46B) |
| Cindy Pugh (R-33B) | |
| Abigail Whelan (R-35A) | |

## Job Growth and Energy Affordability Policy and Finance

| Majority Members | Minority Members |
|---|---|
| Pat Garofalo (R-58B) *Chair* | Tim Mahoney (DFL-67A) |
| Dave Baker (R-17B) *Vice Chair* | *DFL Lead* |
| Dan Fabian (R-1A) | Karen Clark (DFL-62A) *DFL Lead* |
| Bob Gunther (R-23A) | Melissa Hortman (DFL-36B) |
| Bob Loonan (R-55A) | Jason Isaacson (DFL-42B) |
| James "Jim" Newberger (R-15B) | Sheldon Johnson (DFL-67B) |
| Marion O'Neill (R-29B) | Jason Metsa (DFL-6B) |
| Peggy Scott (R-35B) | Erik Simonson (DFL-7B) |
| Dennis Smith (R-34B) | Jean Wagenius (DFL-63B) |
| Chris Swedzinski (R-16A) | |
| Bob Vogel (R-20A) | |

## Legacy Funding Finance

| Majority Members | Minority Members |
|---|---|
| Dean Urdahl (R-18A) *Chair* | Phyllis Kahn (DFL-60B) *DFL Lead* |
| Josh Heintzeman (R-10A) | Mike Freiberg (DFL-45B) |
| *Vice Chair* | Leon M. Lillie (DFL-43B) |
| Brian Daniels (R-24B) | Erin Murphy (DFL-64A) |
| Steve Green (R-2B) | Mary Murphy (DFL-3B) |
| Tim Miller (R-17A) | |
| Paul Torkelson (R-16B) | |
| Anna Wills (R-57B) | |

## Mining and Outdoor Recreation Policy

| Majority Members | Minority Members |
|---|---|
| Tom Hackbarth (R-31B) *Chair* | Tom Anzelc (DFL-5B) *DFL Lead* |
| Dale Lueck (R-10B) *Vice Chair* | John "Jack" Considine (DFL-19B) |
| Mark Anderson (R-9A) | Rob Ecklund (DFL-3A) |
| Tony Cornish (R-23B) | Carly Melin (DFL-6A) |
| Jerry Hertaus (R-33A) | Jason Metsa (DFL-6B) |
| Brian Johnson (R-32A) | Barb Yarusso (DFL-42A) |
| Debra "Deb" Kiel (R-1B) | |
| Eric Lucero (R-30B) | |
| Denny McNamara (R-54B) | |

## Public Safety and Crime Prevention Policy and Finance

| Majority Members | Minority Members |
|---|---|
| Tony Cornish (R-23B) *Chair* | Debra Hilstrom (DFL-40B) |
| Brian Johnson (R-32A) *Vice Chair* | *DFL Lead* |
| Jerry Hertaus (R-33A) | John "Jack" Considine (DFL-19B) |
| Jeff Howe (R-13A) | Raymond Dehn (DFL-59B) |
| Kathy Lohmer (R-39B) | Peggy Flanagan (DFL-46A) |
| Eric Lucero (R-30B) | Paul Rosenthal (DFL-49B) |
| James "Jim" Newberger (R-15B) | Dan Schoen (DFL-54A) |
| Marion O'Neill (R-29B) | JoAnn Ward (DFL-53A) |
| Duane Quam (R-25A) | |
| Nick Zerwas (R-30A) | |

## Rules and Legislative Administration

| Majority Members | Minority Members |
|---|---|
| Joyce Peppin (R-34A) *Chair* | Paul C. Thissen (DFL-61B) |
| Kelly Fenton (R-53B) *Vice Chair* | *DFL Lead* |
| Tony Albright (R-55B) | Connie Bernardy (DFL-41A) |
| Pat Garofalo (R-58B) | Peggy Flanagan (DFL-46A) |
| Bob Gunther (R-23A) | Mike Freiberg (DFL-45B) |
| Joe Hoppe (R-47B) | Melissa Hortman (DFL-36B) |
| Tim Kelly (R-21A) | Jason Isaacson (DFL-42B) |
| Ron Kresha (R-9B) | |

| Majority Members *continued* | Minority Members *continued* |
|---|---|
| Tara Mack (R-57A) | Michael V. "Mike" Nelson |
| Tim O'Driscoll (R-13B) | (DFL-40A) |
| Marion O'Neill (R-29B) | Gene Pelowski, Jr. (DFL-28A) |
| Tim Sanders (R-37B) | David Pinto (DFL-64B) |
| Peggy Scott (R-35B) | |
| Chris Swedzinski (R-16A) | |

## State Government Finance

| Majority Members | Minority Members |
|---|---|
| Sarah Anderson (R-44A) *Chair* | Sheldon Johnson (DFL-67B) |
| Jeff Howe (R-13A) *Vice Chair* | *DFL Lead* |
| Tony Albright (R-55B) | Lyndon R. Carlson, Sr. (DFL-45A) |
| Mark Anderson (R-9A) | Ron Erhardt (DFL-49A) |
| Bob Dettmer (R-39A) | Phyllis Kahn (DFL-60B) |
| Bob Loonan (R-55A) | Carolyn Laine (DFL-41B) |
| Jim Nash (R-47A) | Michael V. "Mike" Nelson |
| John Petersburg (R-24A) | (DFL-40A) |
| Cindy Pugh (R-33B) | Jennifer Schultz (DFL-7A) |
| Linda Runbeck (R-38A) | |

## Taxes

| Majority Members | Minority Members |
|---|---|
| Gregory M. "Greg" Davids (R-28B) | Tom Anzelc (DFL-5B) |
| *Chair* | Lyndon R. Carlson, Sr. (DFL-45A) |
| Bob Barrett (R-32B) *Vice Chair* | Jim Davnie (DFL-63A) |
| Sarah Anderson (R-44A) | Ron Erhardt (DFL-49A) |
| Steve Drazkowski (R-21B) | John Lesch (DFL-66B) |
| Sondra Erickson (R-15A) | Diane Loeffler (DFL-60A) |
| Pat Garofalo (R-58B) | Carly Melin (DFL-6A) |
| Tom Hackbarth (R-31B) | Erik Simonson (DFL-7B) |
| Jim Knoblach (R-14B) | Linda Slocum (DFL-50A) |
| Jon Koznick (R-58A) | |
| Jenifer W. Loon (R-48B) | |
| Joe McDonald (R-29A) | |
| John Petersburg (R-24A) | |
| Chris Swedzinski (R-16A) | |
| Paul Torkelson (R-16B) | |
| Anna Wills (R-57B) | |

## Transportation Policy and Finance

| Majority Members | Minority Members |
|---|---|
| Tim Kelly (R-21A) *Chair* | Ron Erhardt (DFL-49A) |
| John Petersburg (R-24A) *Vice Chair* | *Co-DFL Lead* |
| Chad Anderson (R-50B) | Frank Hornstein (DFL-61A) |
| Mark Anderson (R-9A) | *Co-DFL Lead* |
| Steve Drazkowski (R-21B) | Joe Atkins (DFL-52B) |
| Jeff Howe (R-13A) | Connie Bernardy (DFL-41A) |
| Jon Koznick (R-58A) | Alice Hausman (DFL-66A) |
| Eric Lucero (R-30B) | Clark Johnson (DFL-19A) |
| Denny McNamara (R-54B) | Sandra A. Masin (DFL-51A) |
| Jim Nash (R-47A) | Kim Norton (DFL-25B) |
| Linda Runbeck (R-38A) | Mike Sundin (DFL-11A) |
| Tim Sanders (R-37B) | |
| Mark Uglem (R-36A) | |
| Abigail Whelan (R-35A) | |

## Veterans Affairs Division

| Majority Members | Minority Members |
|---|---|
| Bob Dettmer (R-39A) *Chair* | John Persell (DFL-5A) *DFL Lead* |
| David Hancock (R-2A) *Vice Chair* | Peter M. Fischer (DFL-43A) |
| Gregory M. "Greg" Davids (R-28B) | John Lesch (DFL-66B) |
| Dale Lueck (R-10B) | Jerry Newton (DFL-37A) |
| Tim O'Driscoll (R-13B) | JoAnn Ward (DFL-53A) |
| Cindy Pugh (R-33B) | |

## Ways and Means

| Majority Members | Minority Members |
|---|---|
| Jim Knoblach (R-14B) *Chair* | Lyndon R. Carlson, Sr. (DFL-45A) |
| Tony Albright (R-55B) *Vice Chair* | *DFL Lead* |
| Sarah Anderson (R-44A) | Debra Hilstrom (DFL-40B) |
| Tony Cornish (R-23B) | Frank Hornstein (DFL-61A) |
| Gregory M. "Greg" Davids (R-28B) | Phyllis Kahn (DFL-60B) |
| Matt Dean (R-38B) | Tina Liebling (DFL-26A) |
| Bob Dettmer (R-39A) | Tim Mahoney (DFL-67A) |
| Steve Drazkowski (R-21B) | Mary Murphy (DFL-3B) |

*(continued on next page)*

**LEGISLATIVE BRANCH**

**Ways and Means** *continued*

**Majority Members** *continued*

Pat Garofalo (R-58B)
Bob Gunther (R-23A)
Tom Hackbarth (R-31B)
Rod Hamilton (R-22B)
Jenifer W. Loon (R-48B)
Denny McNamara (R-54B)
Bud Nornes (R-8A)
Paul Torkelson (R-16B)
Dean Urdahl (R-18A)

**Minority Members** *continued*

Gene Pelowski, Jr. (DFL-28A)
Jeanne Poppe (DFL-27B)
Jean Wagenius (DFL-63B)

# Mississippi Legislature

New Capitol, Jackson, MS 39215-1018
P.O. Box 1018, Jackson, MS 39215-1018
Internet: www.legislature.ms.gov

## Mississippi State Senate

New Capitol, Jackson, MS 39215-1018
Tel: (601) 359-3770  Fax: (601) 359-3935

President of the Senate **Tate Reeves, CFA** (R) . . . . . . . . . . . (601) 359-3200
  Education: Millsaps 1996 BA
President Pro Tem **Terry Clark Burton** (R) . . . . . . . . . . . . . (601) 359-3234
Secretary of the Senate **Liz Welch** . . . . . . . . . . . . . . . . . . . (601) 359-3229
  E-mail: lwelch@senate.ms.gov

## Senators

**Party Affiliation Statistics:** Republicans: 32, Democrats: 20

Senator **Juan Barnett** (D-District 34) . . . . . . . . . . . . . . . . . (601) 359-3221
  Counties Represented: Jasper, Jones (part), Scott (part), Smith
  Term Expires: 2020
  E-mail: jbarnett@senate.ms.gov
  Committees: Agriculture; Constitution; Economic Development;
  Environment Protection, Conservation and Water Resources; Finance;
  Judiciary A; Municipalities; Veterans and Military Affairs

Senator **Barbara Blackmon** (R-District 21) . . . . . . . . . . . . . (601) 359-3237
  Counties Represented: Attala (part), Holmes (part), Madison (part),
  Yazoo (part)
  Term Expires: 2020
  E-mail: bblackmon@senate.ms.gov
  Committees: County Affairs; Enrolled Bills; Executive Contingent
  Fund; Finance; Highways and Transportation; Insurance; Judiciary A;
  Medicaid

Senator **Kevin Blackwell** (R-District 19) . . . . . . . . . . . . . . . (601) 359-3234
  Counties Represented: DeSoto (part)
  Term Expires: 2020
  E-mail: kblackwell@senate.ms.gov
  Committees: Business and Financial Institutions; Drug Policy;
  Economic Development; Education; Finance; Insurance; Judiciary B;
  Medicaid

Senator **David Blount** (D-District 29) . . . . . . . . . . . . . . . . . (601) 359-3232
  Counties Represented: Hinds (part)          Fax: (601) 359-5957
  Term Expires: 2020
  1305 Saint Mary Street, Jackson, MS 39202
  E-mail: dblount@senate.ms.gov
  Committees: Accountability, Efficiency, Transparency; Education;
  Elections; Ethics; Finance; Judiciary B; Public Health and Welfare;
  Public Property
  Education: Davidson BA; Virginia MA

Senator **Jenifer B. Branning** (R-District 18) . . . . . . . . . . . (601) 359-3246
  Counties Represented: Leake, Neshoba, Winston (part)
  Term Expires: 2020
  E-mail: jbranning@senate.ms.gov
  Committees: Agriculture; Appropriations; Business and Financial
  Institutions; Ethics; Forestry; Judiciary A; Municipalities; Wildlife,
  Fisheries, and Parks

Senator **Nickey Reed Browning** (R-District 3) . . . . . . . . . (601) 359-3246
  Counties Represented: Calhoun (part), Pontotoc     Res: (662) 489-5979
  (part), Union                                       Fax: (601) 359-3063
  Term Expires: 2020
  P. O. Box 1051, Pontotoc, MS 38863
  E-mail: nbrowning@senate.ms.gov
  Committees: Business and Financial Institutions; County Affairs; Drug
  Policy; Energy; Finance; Forestry; Highways and Transportation;
  Insurance

Senator **Hob Bryan** (D-District 7) . . . . . . . . . . . . . . . . . . . (601) 359-3237
  Counties Represented: Itawamba (part), Lee (part),   Tel: (662) 256-9601
  Monroe                                               Res: (662) 256-9989
  Term Expires: 2020                                   Fax: (601) 359-2879
  P.O. Box 75, Amory, MS 38821
  E-mail: hbryan@senate.ms.gov
  Committees: Constitution; Elections; Finance; Highways and
  Transportation; Judiciary B; Local and Private; Medicaid; Public Health
  and Welfare
  Education: Mississippi State BA; Virginia 1977 JD

Senator **Terry Clark Burton** (R-District 31) . . . . . . . . . . . . (601) 359-3234
Counties Represented: Lauderdale (part), Newton,     Tel: (601) 683-6695
Scott (part)     Res: (601) 683-7050
Term Expires: 2020     Fax: (601) 359-5345
101 Rew St., Newton, MS 39345
E-mail: tburton@senate.ms.gov
Committees: Accountability, Efficiency, Transparency; Appropriations;
Education; Energy; Medicaid; Municipalities; Public Health and
Welfare; Rules; Universities and Colleges

Senator **Albert Butler** (D-District 36) . . . . . . . . . . . . . . . (601) 359-3232
Counties Represented: Claiborne, Copiah (part),     Res: (601) 437-4089
Hinds (part), Jefferson     Fax: (601) 359-5957
Term Expires: 2020
P.O. Box 614, Port Gibson, MS 39150
E-mail: abutler@senate.ms.gov
Committees: Appropriations; Drug Policy; Environment Protection,
Conservation and Water Resources; Ethics; Forestry; Labor; Public
Property; State Library; Tourism

Senator **Fredie Videt Carmichael** (R-District 33) . . . . . . . (601) 359-3244
Counties Represented: Clarke, Lauderdale (part)     Res: (601) 693-2750
Term Expires: 2020     Fax: (601) 359-9210
5396 Springhill Loop, Meridian, MS 39301
E-mail: vcarmichael@senate.ms.gov
Committees: Appropriations; Business and Financial Institutions;
Corrections; Energy; Insurance; Investigative State Offices; Ports and
Marine Resources
Education: Mississippi State BS, MEd

Senator **Chris Caughman** (R-District 35) . . . . . . . . . . . . . . (601) 359-3244
Counties Represented: Copiah (part), Covington (part), Rankin (part),
Simpson (part)
Term Expires: 2020
E-mail: ccaughman@senate.ms.gov
Committees: Agriculture; Business and Financial Institutions;
Education; Finance; Investigative State Offices; Medicaid; Public Health
and Welfare; Universities and Colleges; Wildlife, Fisheries, and Parks

Senator **Lydia Graves Chassaniol** (R-District 14) . . . . . . . (601) 359-3246
Counties Represented: Attala (part), Carroll,     Res: (662) 453-3172
Grenada (part), Leflore (part), Montgomery (part),     Fax: (601) 359-3063
Tallahatchie (part)
Term Expires: 2020
PO BOX 211, Winona, MS 38967
E-mail: lchassaniol@senate.ms.gov
Committees: Agriculture; Corrections; Drug Policy; Elections; Ethics;
Finance; Investigative State Offices; Municipalities; Tourism

Senator **Eugene S. "Buck" Clarke** (R-District 22) . . . . . . . (601) 359-3250
Counties Represented: Bolivar (part), Humphreys     Tel: (662) 827-7261
(part), Sharkey, Washington (part), Yazoo (part)     Res: (662) 827-5685
Term Expires: 2020     Fax: (601) 827-7264
P. O. Box 668, Hollandale, MS 38748     Fax: (601) 359-5110
E-mail: bclarke@senate.ms.gov
Committees: Accountability, Efficiency, Transparency; Agriculture;
Appropriations; Education; Insurance; Judiciary A; Medicaid

Senator **Deborah Jeanne Dawkins** (D-District 48) . . . . . . . (601) 359-3237
Counties Represented: Harrison (part)     Res: (228) 452-5182
Term Expires: 2020     Fax: (601) 359-2879
111 Lang Avenue, Number 3, Pass Christian, MS 39571
E-mail: ddawkins@senate.ms.gov
Committees: Drug Policy; Environment Protection, Conservation
and Water Resources; Finance; Forestry; Investigative State Offices;
Medicaid; Ports and Marine Resources; State Library
Education: Southern Mississippi BS

Senator **Bob M. Dearing** (D-District 37) . . . . . . . . . . . . . . (601) 369-3244
Counties Represented: Adams (part), Amite (part), Pike (part)
Term Expires: 2020
E-mail: bdearing@senate.ms.gov
Committees: Appropriations; Constitution; Energy; Highways and
Transportation; Insurance; Ports and Marine Resources; Public Health
and Welfare; Public Property
Education: Delta State BSE; Southern Mississippi ME

Senator **Dennis DeBar** (R-District 43) . . . . . . . . . . . . . . . (601) 359-3221
Counties Represented: George, Greene, Stone (part), Wayne
Term Expires: 2020
E-mail: ddebar@senate.ms.gov
Committees: Appropriations; Corrections; Drug Policy; Energy;
Enrolled Bills; Highways and Transportation; Judiciary A; Judiciary B

Senator **Sally Doty** (R-District 39) . . . . . . . . . . . . . . . . . . (601) 359-3237
Counties Represented: Lawrence, Lincoln, Simpson     Res: (601) 835-4175
(part)     Dist: (601) 757-7446
Term Expires: 2020     Fax: (601) 359-2879
PO Box 4662, Brookhaven, MS 39603
E-mail: sdoty@senate.ms.gov
Committees: Business and Financial Institutions; Drug Policy;
Economic Development; Elections; Energy; Finance; Highways and
Transportation; Judiciary A; Public Health and Welfare; Public Property

Senator **Joey Fillingane** (R-District 41) . . . . . . . . . . . . . . . (601) 359-3246
Counties Represented: Covington (part), Forrest     Tel: (601) 271-2070
(part), Lamar (part), Marion (part)     Fax: (601) 359-3063
Term Expires: 2020     Fax: (601) 264-3323
8 Westbrook Drive, Sumrall, MS 39482
E-mail: jfillingane@senate.ms.gov
Committees: Constitution; Economic Development; Elections; Finance;
Judiciary A; Judiciary B; Public Health and Welfare; Universities and
Colleges

Senator **Hillman Terome Frazier** (D-District 27) . . . . . . . . (601) 359-3246
Counties Represented: Hinds (part)     Res: (601) 982-1871
Term Expires: 2020     Fax: (601) 359-3063
2066 Queensroad Avenue, Jackson, MS 39213
E-mail: hfrazier@senate.ms.gov
Committees: Appropriations; Elections; Housing; Interstate and Federal
Cooperation; Investigative State Offices; Judiciary A; Public Health and
Welfare; Universities and Colleges
Education: Jackson State U BA; George Washington 1974 JD

Senator **Tommy Arlin Gollott** (R-District 50) . . . . . . . . . . (601) 359-2886
Counties Represented: Harrison (part)     Res: (228) 374-1431
Term Expires: 2020     Fax: (601) 359-2889
235 Bayview Avenue, Biloxi, MS 39530     Fax: (601) 432-0083
E-mail: tgollott@senate.ms.gov
Committees: Appropriations; Economic Development; Elections;
Highways and Transportation; Local and Private; Ports and Marine
Resources; Rules; Tourism

Senator **Josh Harkins** (R-District 20) . . . . . . . . . . . . . . . . (601) 359-2886
Counties Represented: Madison (part), Rankin (part)     Fax: (601) 359-2889
Term Expires: 2020
PO Box 320374, Flowood, MS 39232
E-mail: jharkins@senate.ms.gov
Committees: Business and Financial Institutions; Energy; Finance;
Highways and Transportation; Public Health and Welfare; Public
Property; Rules; Tourism; Universities and Colleges

Senator **Angela Burks Hill** (R-District 40) . . . . . . . . . . . . . (601) 798-3195
Counties Represented: Marion (part), Pearl River     Tel: (601) 359-2886
(part), Walthall (part)     Fax: (601) 359-2889
Term Expires: 2020
54 Watts Road, Picayune, MS 39466
E-mail: ahill@senate.ms.gov
Committees: Agriculture; Appropriations; Education; Environment
Protection, Conservation and Water Resources; Insurance; Investigative
State Offices; Judiciary B; Wildlife, Fisheries, and Parks

Senator **W. Briggs Hopson III** (R-District 23) . . . . . . . . . . (601) 359-3237
Counties Represented: Issaquena, Warren, Yazoo     Fax: (601) 359-2879
(part)
Term Expires: 2020
1202 Cherry Street, Vicksburg, MS 39183
E-mail: bhopson@senate.ms.gov
Committees: Accountability, Efficiency, Transparency; Appropriations;
Education; Energy; Environment Protection, Conservation and Water
Resources; Judiciary A; Judiciary B; Public Health and Welfare;
Tourism; Universities and Colleges

Senator **John Horhn** (D-District 26) . . . . . . . . . . . . . . . . . (601) 359-3237
Counties Represented: Hinds (part), Madison (part)     Tel: (601) 366-4285
Term Expires: 2020     Res: (601) 362-1045
P.O. Box 2030, Jackson, MS 39225     Fax: (601) 359-2879
E-mail: jhorhn@senate.ms.gov
Committees: Appropriations; Economic Development; Environment
Protection, Conservation and Water Resources; Highways and
Transportation; Insurance; Public Health and Welfare; Rules; State
Library; Tourism
Education: Centre BA

Senator **Billy Hudson** (R-District 45) . . . . . . . . . . . . . . . . (601) 359-2395
Counties Represented: Forrest (part), Lamar (part),     Res: (601) 794-0606
Pearl River (part), Perry (part), Stone (part)     Fax: (601) 359-3938
Term Expires: 2020
27 Troon Circle, Hattiesburg, MS 39401
E-mail: bhudson@senate.ms.gov
Committees: Agriculture; County Affairs; Education; Environment
Protection, Conservation and Water Resources; Finance; Highways and
Transportation; Labor; Veterans and Military Affairs

*(continued on next page)*

LEGISLATIVE BRANCH

**Senators** *continued*

Senator **Gary Jackson** (R-District 15) . . . . . . . . . . . . . . (601) 359-3234
Counties Represented: Attala (part), Choctaw,          Res: (662) 547-6684
Montgomery (part), Oktibbeha (part), Webster,          Fax: (601) 359-5345
Winston (part)
Term Expires: 2020
P.O. Box 40, French Camp, MS 39745
E-mail: gjackson@senate.ms.gov
Committees: Appropriations; Business and Financial Institutions;
Energy; Ethics; Local and Private; Public Health and Welfare;
Universities and Colleges; Wildlife, Fisheries, and Parks

Senator **Robert L. Jackson** (D-District 11) . . . . . . . . . . . (601) 359-3221
Counties Represented: Coahoma, Quitman, Tate          Tel: (662) 326-4000
(part), Tunica                                        Res: (662) 326-4611
Term Expires: 2020                                    Fax: (601) 359-2611
P.O. Box 383, Marks, MS 38646
E-mail: rjackson@senate.ms.gov
Committees: Agriculture; Appropriations; Business and Financial
Institutions; Energy; Interstate and Federal Cooperation; Labor; Ports
and Marine Resources; Public Property

Senator **Sampson Jackson II** (D-District 32) . . . . . . . . . . .(601) 359-2886
Counties Represented: Kemper, Lauderdale (part),       Tel: (601) 743-5900
Noxubee (part), Winston (part)                         Res: (601) 677-2305
Term Expires: 2020                                     Fax: (601) 359-2889
749 Matthew Jackson Road, Preston, MS 39354
E-mail: sjackson@senate.ms.gov
Committees: Appropriations; Business and Financial Institutions;
Corrections; Energy; Interstate and Federal Cooperation; Judiciary B;
Veterans and Military Affairs; Wildlife, Fisheries, and Parks

Senator **Russell Jolly** (D-District 8) . . . . . . . . . . . . . . . . (662) 542-6701
Counties Represented: Calhoun (part), Chickasaw,       Res: (662) 456-3118
Grenada (part), Lee (part)                             Tel: (601) 359-2886
Term Expires: 2020                                     Fax: (601) 359-2889
369 Highway 47, Houston, MS 38851
E-mail: rjolly@senate.ms.gov
Committees: Agriculture; County Affairs; Energy; Environment
Protection, Conservation and Water Resources; Ethics; Finance;
Highways and Transportation

Senator **David Lee Jordan** (D-District 24) . . . . . . . . . . . . (601) 359-3244
Counties Represented: Holmes (part), Leflore           Tel: (662) 453-2246
(part), Tallahatchie (part)                            Res: (662) 453-5361
Term Expires: 2020                                     Fax: (601) 359-9210
P.O. Box 8173, Greenwood, MS 38930
E-mail: djordan@senate.ms.gov
Committees: Agriculture; Drug Policy; Education; Environment
Protection, Conservation and Water Resources; Finance; Forestry;
Housing; Municipalities; Tourism
Education: Wyoming BS

Senator **Dean Kirby** (R-District 30) . . . . . . . . . . . . . . . . . (601) 359-3234
Counties Represented: Rankin (part)                    Tel: (601) 939-5968
Term Expires: 2020                                     Res: (601) 932-1966
P.O. Box 54099, Pearl, MS 39288                        Fax: (601) 359-5345
E-mail: dkirby@senate.ms.gov
Committees: Corrections; Finance; Highways and Transportation;
Housing; Insurance; Interstate and Federal Cooperation; Judiciary A;
Public Health and Welfare

Senator **Chris Massey** (R-District 1) . . . . . . . . . . . . . . . . . (601) 550-0334
Counties Represented: DeSoto (part)                    Tel: (601) 359-2886
Term Expires: 2020                                     Fax: (601) 359-2889
PO Box 208, Nesbit, MS 38651
E-mail: cmassey@senate.ms.gov
Committees: Education; Ethics; Finance; Highways and Transportation;
Housing; Labor; Municipalities; Tourism; Wildlife, Fisheries, and Parks

Senator **Chris McDaniel** (R-District 42) . . . . . . . . . . . . . . (601) 359-2395
Counties Represented: Jones (part)                     Tel: (601) 477-2291
Term Expires: 2020                                     Tel: (601) 580-5833
506 South Court Street, Ellisville, MS 39437           Fax: (601) 359-3938
E-mail: cmcdaniel@senate.ms.gov
Committees: Appropriations; Constitution; Drug Policy; Judiciary B;
Labor; Municipalities
Education: William Carey; Mississippi JD

Senator **Chad McMahan** (R-District 6) . . . . . . . . . . . . . . .(601) 359-3244
Counties Represented: Lee (part), Pontotoc (part)
Term Expires: 2020
E-mail: cmcmahan@senate.ms.gov
Committees: Economic Development; Ethics; Finance; Housing;
Judiciary A; Labor; Municipalities; Tourism

Senator **J. Walter Michel** (R-District 25) . . . . . . . . . . . . . (601) 359-3770
Counties Represented: Hinds (part), Madison (part)
Term Expires: 2020

Senator **Philip Moran** (R-District 46) . . . . . . . . . . . . . . . . (228) 255-3700
Counties Represented: Hancock, Harrison (part)         Tel: (601) 359-3221
Term Expires: 2020                                     Fax: (601) 359-2166
18403 Old Joe Moran Road, Kiln, MS 39556
E-mail: pmoran@senate.ms.gov
Committees: County Affairs; Economic Development; Enrolled Bills;
Finance; Highways and Transportation; Investigative State Offices;
Labor; Veterans and Military Affairs; Wildlife, Fisheries, and Parks

Senator **Sollie B. Norwood** (D-District 28) . . . . . . . . . . . . (601) 969-9088
Counties Represented: Hinds (part)                     Tel: (601) 359-3221
Term Expires: 2020                                     Fax: (601) 359-2166
PO Box 20192, Jackson, MS 39289
E-mail: snorwood@senate.ms.gov
Committees: Appropriations; Corrections; Education; Housing;
Interstate and Federal Cooperation; Labor; Medicaid

Senator **Dr. David L. Parker, DO** (R-District 2) . . . . . . . . . (601) 359-2886
Counties Represented: Benton, Marshall, Tippah        Dist: (662) 893-3300
(part)                                                 Fax: (601) 359-2889
Term Expires: 2020
E-mail: dparker@senate.ms.gov
Committees: Economic Development; Elections; Finance; Housing;
Judiciary A; Local and Private; Public Health and Welfare; Universities
and Colleges; Veterans and Military Affairs
Education: Christian Brothers U 1991 BS;
Southern Col Optometry 1995 DO

Senator **Rita P. Parks** (R-District 4) . . . . . . . . . . . . . . . . . (662) 287-6323
Counties Represented: Alcorn, Tippah (part),           Tel: (601) 359-3232
Tishomingo (part)                                      Fax: (601) 359-5957
Term Expires: 2020
150 CR 632, Corinth, MS 38834
E-mail: rparks@senate.ms.gov
Committees: Accountability, Efficiency, Transparency; Business and
Financial Institutions; Economic Development; Finance; Highways and
Transportation; Insurance; Medicaid; Public Health and Welfare;
Veterans and Military Affairs

Senator **John A. Polk** (R-District 44) . . . . . . . . . . . . . . . . (601) 261-5613
Counties Represented: Forrest (part), Lamar (part),    Tel: (601) 359-3246
Perry (part)                                           Fax: (601) 359-3063
Term Expires: 2020
53 Tidewater Road, Hattiesburg, MS 39402
E-mail: jpolk@senate.ms.gov
Committees: Accountability, Efficiency, Transparency; County Affairs;
Education; Elections; Energy; Finance; Housing; Insurance; Universities
and Colleges

Senator **Joseph Seymour** (R-District 47) . . . . . . . . . . . . . (601) 359-2886
Counties Represented: Harrison (part), Jackson (part), Pearl River
(part), Stone (part)
Term Expires: 2020
E-mail: mseymour@senate.ms.gov
Committees: Agriculture; Appropriations; County Affairs; Environment
Protection, Conservation and Water Resources; Executive Contingent
Fund; Forestry; Ports and Marine Resources; Public Property

Senator **Derrick T. Simmons** (D-District 12) . . . . . . . . . . . (601) 359-3221
Counties Represented: Bolivar (part), Washington       Tel: (662) 334-1666
(part)                                                 Tel: (662) 378-8764
Term Expires: 2020                                     Fax: (601) 359-2166
P.O. Box 1854, Greenville, MS 38702
E-mail: dsimmons@senate.ms.gov
Committees: Corrections; Enrolled Bills; Finance; Insurance; Judiciary
A; Judiciary B; Labor; Wildlife, Fisheries, and Parks

Senator **Willie Lee Simmons** (D-District 13) . . . . . . . . . . .(601) 359-3237
Counties Represented: Bolivar (part), Humphreys        Tel: (662) 846-7434
(part), Sunflower                                      Fax: (601) 359-2879
Term Expires: 2020                                     Fax: (601) 846-7011
P.O. Box 297, Cleveland, MS 38732-0297
E-mail: wsimmons@senate.ms.gov
Committees: Agriculture; Appropriations; Corrections; Highways
and Transportation; Ports and Marine Resources; Public Health and
Welfare; State Library; Tourism
Education: Alcorn State BS; Delta State MS

Senator **Bill Stone** (D-District 10) . . . . . . . . . . . . . . . . . . . (601) 562-5948
Counties Represented: Panola, Tate (part)              Tel: (601) 359-3221
Term Expires: 2020                                     Res: (662) 224-3949
E-mail: bstone@senate.ms.gov                           Fax: (601) 359-2166
Committees: Constitution; County Affairs; Executive Contingent Fund;
Finance; Forestry; Highways and Transportation; Municipalities;
Universities and Colleges; Wildlife, Fisheries, and Parks

Senator **Sean J. Tindell** (R-District 49) . . . . . . . . . . . . . . . (228) 342-5963
Counties Represented: Harrison (part)     Tel: (601) 359-2395
Term Expires: 2020     Fax: (601) 359-3938
PO Box 784, Gulfport, MS 39507
E-mail: stindell@senate.ms.gov
Committees: Accountability, Efficiency, Transparency; Appropriations;
Corrections; Energy; Environment Protection, Conservation and Water
Resources; Judiciary A; Judiciary B; Ports and Marine Resources;
Tourism

Senator **Gray Tollison** (R-District 9) . . . . . . . . . . . . . . . . (601) 359-3244
Counties Represented: Lafayette, Tallahatchie     Tel: (662) 234-7070
(part), Yalobusha     Res: (662) 234-8395
Term Expires: 2020     Fax: (601) 359-9210
P.O. Box 1216, Oxford, MS 38655
E-mail: gtollison@senate.ms.gov
Committees: Appropriations; Constitution; Education; Executive
Contingent Fund; Judiciary B; Public Health and Welfare; Rules;
Universities and Colleges; Wildlife, Fisheries, and Parks
Education: Rhodes BA; Mississippi JD

Senator **Angela Turner** (D-District 16) . . . . . . . . . . . . . . . (601) 359-3237
Counties Represented: Clay, Lowndes (part),     Dist: (662) 494-6611
Noxubee (part), Oktibbeha (part)     Fax: (601) 359-2879
Term Expires: 2020
PO Drawer 1500, West Point, MS 39773
E-mail: aturner@senate.ms.gov
Committees: Accountability, Efficiency, Transparency; Appropriations;
Constitution; Ethics; Judiciary A; Judiciary B; Veterans and Military
Affairs

Senator **Michael Watson** (R-District 51) . . . . . . . . . . . . . . (601) 359-2395
Counties Represented: Jackson (part)     Tel: (228) 762-2272
Term Expires: 2020     Fax: (601) 359-3938
PO Box 964, Pascagoula, MS 39568
E-mail: mwatson@senate.ms.gov
Committees: Drug Policy; Environment Protection, Conservation
and Water Resources; Finance; Forestry; Investigative State Offices;
Judiciary B; Ports and Marine Resources; Wildlife, Fisheries, and Parks

Senator **Brice Wiggins** (R-District 52) . . . . . . . . . . . . . . . . (228) 696-9545
Counties Represented: Jackson (part)     Tel: (601) 359-3232
Term Expires: 2020     Fax: (601) 510-9378
1501 Roswell Street, Pascagoula, MS 39581     Fax: (601) 359-5957
E-mail: bwiggins@senate.ms.gov
Committees: Appropriations; Corrections; Education; Environment
Protection, Conservation and Water Resources; Judiciary B; Medicaid;
Ports and Marine Resources; Public Health and Welfare

Senator **J. P. Wilemon, Jr.** (D-District 5) . . . . . . . . . . . . . . (601) 359-3232
Counties Represented: Itawamba (part), Prentiss,     Res: (662) 454-7585
Tishomingo (part)     Fax: (601) 359-5957
Term Expires: 2020
P.O. Box 82, Belmont, MS 38827
E-mail: jwilemon@senate.ms.gov
Committees: Accountability, Efficiency, Transparency; Appropriations;
Business and Financial Institutions; Drug Policy; Education; Enrolled
Bills; Investigative State Offices; Municipalities; Universities and
Colleges

Senator **Tammy Witherspoon** (D-District 38) . . . . . . . . . . (601) 359-3221
Counties Represented: Adams (part), Amite (part), Pike (part), Walthall
(part)
Term Expires: 2020
E-mail: twitherspoon@senate.ms.gov
Committees: Corrections; Environment Protection, Conservation and
Water Resources; Finance; Municipalities; Ports and Marine Resources;
State Library; Universities and Colleges

Senator **Charles "Chuck" Younger** (R-District 17) . . . . . . . (601) 359-2395
Counties Represented: Lowndes (part)     Res: (662) 329-3430
Term Expires: 2020     Fax: (601) 359-3938
E-mail: cyounger@senate.ms.gov
Committees: Agriculture; Appropriations; County Affairs; Economic
Development; Environment Protection, Conservation and Water
Resources; Forestry; Highways and Transportation; Housing; Medicaid;
Public Health and Welfare

## Senate Standing Committees

## Accountability, Efficiency, Transparency

**Majority Members**
John A. Polk (R-44) *Chair*
Terry Clark Burton (R-31)
Eugene S. "Buck" Clarke (R-22)
W. Briggs Hopson III (R-23)
Rita P. Parks (R-4)
Sean J. Tindell (R-49)

**Minority Members**
J. P. Wilemon, Jr. (D-5) *Vice Chair*
David Blount (D-29)
Angela Turner (D-16)

## Agriculture

**Majority Members**
Billy Hudson (R-45) *Chair*
Jenifer B. Branning (R-18)
Chris Caughman (R-35)
Lydia Graves Chassaniol (R-14)
Eugene S. "Buck" Clarke (R-22)
Angela Burks Hill (R-40)
Joseph Seymour (R-47)
Charles "Chuck" Younger (R-17)

**Minority Members**
Russell Jolly (D-8) *Vice Chair*
Juan Barnett (D-34)
Robert L. Jackson (D-11)
David Lee Jordan (D-24)
Willie Lee Simmons (D-13)

## Appropriations

**Majority Members**
Eugene S. "Buck" Clarke (R-22)
  *Chair*
W. Briggs Hopson III (R-23)
  *Vice Chair*
Jenifer B. Branning (R-18)
Terry Clark Burton (R-31)
Fredie Videt Carmichael (R-33)
Dennis DeBar (R-43)
Tommy Arlin Gollott (R-50)
Angela Burks Hill (R-40)
Gary Jackson (R-15)
Chris McDaniel (R-42)
Joseph Seymour (R-47)
Sean J. Tindell (R-49)
Gray Tollison (R-9)
Brice Wiggins (R-52)
Charles "Chuck" Younger (R-17)

**Minority Members**
Albert Butler (D-36)
Bob M. Dearing (D-37)
Hillman Terome Frazier (D-27)
John Horhn (D-26)
Robert L. Jackson (D-11)
Sampson Jackson II (D-32)
Sollie B. Norwood (D-28)
Willie Lee Simmons (D-13)
Angela Turner (D-16)
J. P. Wilemon, Jr. (D-5)

## Business and Financial Institutions

**Majority Members**
Rita P. Parks (R-4) *Chair*
Kevin Blackwell (R-19)
Jenifer B. Branning (R-18)
Nickey Reed Browning (R-3)
Fredie Videt Carmichael (R-33)
Chris Caughman (R-35)
Sally Doty (R-39)
Josh Harkins (R-20)
Gary Jackson (R-15)

**Minority Members**
Robert L. Jackson (D-11)
Sampson Jackson II (D-32)
J. P. Wilemon, Jr. (D-5)

## Constitution

**Majority Members**
Chris McDaniel (R-42) *Chair*
Joey Fillingane (R-41)
Gray Tollison (R-9)

**Minority Members**
Angela Turner (D-16) *Vice Chair*
Juan Barnett (D-34)
Hob Bryan (D-7)
Bob M. Dearing (D-37)
Bill Stone (D-10)

## Corrections

**Majority Members**
Lydia Graves Chassaniol (R-14)
  *Vice Chair*
Fredie Videt Carmichael (R-33)
Dennis DeBar (R-43)
Dean Kirby (R-30)
Sean J. Tindell (R-49)
Brice Wiggins (R-52)

**Minority Members**
Sampson Jackson II (D-32) *Chair*
Sollie B. Norwood (D-28)
Derrick T. Simmons (D-12)
Willie Lee Simmons (D-13)
Tammy Witherspoon (D-38)

## County Affairs

**Majority Members**
Charles "Chuck" Younger (R-17)
  *Chair*
Billy Hudson (R-45) *Vice Chair*
Barbara Blackmon (R-21)
Nickey Reed Browning (R-3)
Philip Moran (R-46)
John A. Polk (R-44)
Joseph Seymour (R-47)

**Minority Members**
Russell Jolly (D-8)
Bill Stone (D-10)

**LEGISLATIVE BRANCH**

## Drug Policy

| Majority Members | Minority Members |
|---|---|
| Michael Watson (R-51) *Vice Chairman* | David Lee Jordan (D-24) *Chairman* |
| Kevin Blackwell (R-19) | Albert Butler (D-36) |
| Nickey Reed Browning (R-3) | Deborah Jeanne Dawkins (D-48) |
| Lydia Graves Chassaniol (R-14) | J. P. Wilemon, Jr. (D-5) |
| Dennis DeBar (R-43) | |
| Sally Doty (R-39) | |
| Chris McDaniel (R-42) | |

## Economic Development

| Majority Members | Minority Members |
|---|---|
| Kevin Blackwell (R-19) | John Horhn (D-26) *Chairman* |
| Sally Doty (R-39) | Juan Barnett (D-34) *Vice Chair* |
| Joey Fillingane (R-41) | |
| Tommy Arlin Gollott (R-50) | |
| Chad McMahan (R-6) | |
| Philip Moran (R-46) | |
| Dr. David L. Parker (R-2) | |
| Rita P. Parks (R-4) | |
| Charles "Chuck" Younger (R-17) | |

## Education

| Majority Members | Minority Members |
|---|---|
| Gray Tollison (R-9) *Chair* | David Blount (D-29) |
| Chris Caughman (R-35) *Vice Chair* | David Lee Jordan (D-24) |
| Kevin Blackwell (R-19) | Sollie B. Norwood (D-28) |
| Terry Clark Burton (R-31) | J. P. Wilemon, Jr. (D-5) |
| Eugene S. "Buck" Clarke (R-22) | |
| Angela Burks Hill (R-40) | |
| W. Briggs Hopson III (R-23) | |
| Billy Hudson (R-45) | |
| Chris Massey (R-1) | |
| John A. Polk (R-44) | |
| Brice Wiggins (R-52) | |

## Elections

| Majority Members | Minority Members |
|---|---|
| Sally Doty (R-39) *Chair* | David Blount (D-29) *Vice Chair* |
| Lydia Graves Chassaniol (R-14) | Hob Bryan (D-7) |
| Joey Fillingane (R-41) | Hillman Terome Frazier (D-27) |
| Tommy Arlin Gollott (R-50) | |
| Dr. David L. Parker (R-2) | |
| John A. Polk (R-44) | |

## Energy

| Majority Members | Minority Members |
|---|---|
| W. Briggs Hopson III (R-23) *Chair* | Bob M. Dearing (D-37) |
| Josh Harkins (R-20) *Vice Chair* | Robert L. Jackson (D-11) |
| Nickey Reed Browning (R-3) | Sampson Jackson II (D-32) |
| Terry Clark Burton (R-31) | Russell Jolly (D-8) |
| Fredie Videt Carmichael (R-33) | |
| Dennis DeBar (R-43) | |
| Sally Doty (R-39) | |
| Gary Jackson (R-15) | |
| John A. Polk (R-44) | |
| Sean J. Tindell (R-49) | |

## Enrolled Bills

| Majority Members | Minority Members |
|---|---|
| Barbara Blackmon (R-21) *Vice Chair* | Derrick T. Simmons (D-12) *Chair* |
| Dennis DeBar (R-43) | J. P. Wilemon, Jr. (D-5) |
| Philip Moran (R-46) | |

## Environment Protection, Conservation and Water Resources

| Majority Members | Minority Members |
|---|---|
| Michael Watson (R-51) *Chair* | Tammy Witherspoon (D-38) *Vice Chair* |
| Angela Burks Hill (R-40) | Juan Barnett (D-34) |
| W. Briggs Hopson III (R-23) | Albert Butler (D-36) |
| Billy Hudson (R-45) | Deborah Jeanne Dawkins (D-48) |
| Joseph Seymour (R-47) | John Horhn (D-26) |
| Sean J. Tindell (R-49) | Russell Jolly (D-8) |
| Brice Wiggins (R-52) | David Lee Jordan (D-24) |
| Charles "Chuck" Younger (R-17) | |

## Ethics

| Majority Members | Minority Members |
|---|---|
| Chris Massey (R-1) *Chair* | David Blount (D-29) |
| Gary Jackson (R-15) *Vice Chair* | Albert Butler (D-36) |
| Jenifer B. Branning (R-18) | Russell Jolly (D-8) |
| Lydia Graves Chassaniol (R-14) | Angela Turner (D-16) |
| Chad McMahan (R-6) | |

## Executive Contingent Fund

| Majority Members | Minority Members |
|---|---|
| Gray Tollison (R-9) *Vice Chair* | Bill Stone (D-10) *Chair* |
| Barbara Blackmon (R-21) | |
| Joseph Seymour (R-47) | |

## Finance

| Majority Members | Minority Members |
|---|---|
| Joey Fillingane (R-41) *Chair* | Juan Barnett (D-34) |
| Dean Kirby (R-30) *Vice Chair* | David Blount (D-29) |
| Barbara Blackmon (R-21) | Hob Bryan (D-7) |
| Kevin Blackwell (R-19) | Deborah Jeanne Dawkins (D-48) |
| Nickey Reed Browning (R-3) | Russell Jolly (D-8) |
| Chris Caughman (R-35) | David Lee Jordan (D-24) |
| Lydia Graves Chassaniol (R-14) | Derrick T. Simmons (D-12) |
| Sally Doty (R-39) | Bill Stone (D-10) |
| Josh Harkins (R-20) | Tammy Witherspoon (D-38) |
| Billy Hudson (R-45) | |
| Chris Massey (R-1) | |
| Chad McMahan (R-6) | |
| Philip Moran (R-46) | |
| Dr. David L. Parker (R-2) | |
| Rita P. Parks (R-4) | |
| John A. Polk (R-44) | |
| Michael Watson (R-51) | |

## Forestry

| Majority Members | Minority Members |
|---|---|
| Nickey Reed Browning (R-3) *Chair* | Albert Butler (D-36) |
| Jenifer B. Branning (R-18) *Vice Chair* | Deborah Jeanne Dawkins (D-48) |
| Joseph Seymour (R-47) | David Lee Jordan (D-24) |
| Michael Watson (R-51) | Bill Stone (D-10) |
| Charles "Chuck" Younger (R-17) | |

## Highways and Transportation

| Majority Members | Minority Members |
|---|---|
| Dennis DeBar (R-43) *Vice Chair* | Willie Lee Simmons (D-13) *Chair* |
| Nickey Reed Browning (R-3) | Hob Bryan (D-7) |
| Barbara Blackmon (R-21) | Bob M. Dearing (D-37) |
| Sally Doty (R-39) | John Horhn (D-26) |
| Tommy Arlin Gollott (R-50) | Russell Jolly (D-8) |
| Josh Harkins (R-20) | Bill Stone (D-10) |
| Billy Hudson (R-45) | |
| Dean Kirby (R-30) | |
| Chris Massey (R-1) | |
| Philip Moran (R-46) | |
| Rita P. Parks (R-4) | |
| Charles "Chuck" Younger (R-17) | |

## Housing

| Majority Members | Minority Members |
|---|---|
| Chris Massey (R-1) *Vice Chair* | Hillman Terome Frazier (D-27) *Chair* |
| Dean Kirby (R-30) | David Lee Jordan (D-24) |
| Chad McMahan (R-6) | Sollie B. Norwood (D-28) |
| Dr. David L. Parker (R-2) | |
| John A. Polk (R-44) | |
| Charles "Chuck" Younger (R-17) | |

## Insurance

| Majority Members | Minority Members |
|---|---|
| Fredie Videt Carmichael (R-33) *Chair* | Bob M. Dearing (D-37) |
| Kevin Blackwell (R-19) *Vice Chair* | John Horhn (D-26) |
| Barbara Blackmon (R-21) | Derrick T. Simmons (D-12) |
| Nickey Reed Browning (R-3) | |
| Eugene S. "Buck" Clarke (R-22) | |
| Angela Burks Hill (R-40) | |
| Dean Kirby (R-30) | |
| Rita P. Parks (R-4) | |
| John A. Polk (R-44) | |

## Interstate and Federal Cooperation

**Majority Members**
Dean Kirby (R-30)

**Minority Members**
Robert L. Jackson (D-11) *Chair*
Sampson Jackson II (D-32)
   *Vice Chair*
Hillman Terome Frazier (D-27)
Sollie B. Norwood (D-28)

## Investigative State Offices

**Majority Members**
Angela Burks Hill (R-40) *Chair*
Fredie Videt Carmichael (R-33)
   *Vice Chair*
Chris Caughman (R-35)
Lydia Graves Chassaniol (R-14)
Philip Moran (R-46)
Michael Watson (R-51)

**Minority Members**
Deborah Jeanne Dawkins (D-48)
Hillman Terome Frazier (D-27)
J. P. Wilemon, Jr. (D-5)

## Judiciary A

**Majority Members**
Sean J. Tindell (R-49) *Chair*
Sally Doty (R-39) *Vice Chair*
Barbara Blackmon (R-21)
Jenifer B. Branning (R-18)
Eugene S. "Buck" Clarke (R-22)
Dennis DeBar (R-43)
Joey Fillingane (R-41)
W. Briggs Hopson III (R-23)
Dean Kirby (R-30)
Chad McMahan (R-6)
Dr. David L. Parker (R-2)

**Minority Members**
Juan Barnett (D-34)
Hillman Terome Frazier (D-27)
Derrick T. Simmons (D-12)
Angela Turner (D-16)

## Judiciary B

**Majority Members**
Chris McDaniel (R-42) *Vice Chair*
Kevin Blackwell (R-19)
Dennis DeBar (R-43)
Angela Burks Hill (R-40)
Joey Fillingane (R-41)
W. Briggs Hopson III (R-23)
Sean J. Tindell (R-49)
Gray Tollison (R-9)
Michael Watson (R-51)
Brice Wiggins (R-52)

**Minority Members**
Hob Bryan (D-7) *Chair*
David Blount (D-29)
Sampson Jackson II (D-32)
Derrick T. Simmons (D-12)
Angela Turner (D-16)

## Labor

**Majority Members**
Billy Hudson (R-45)
Chris Massey (R-1)
Chad McMahan (R-6)
Philip Moran (R-46)
Chris McDaniel (R-42)

**Minority Members**
Albert Butler (D-36) *Chair*
Sollie B. Norwood (D-28)
   *Vice Chair*
Robert L. Jackson (D-11)
Derrick T. Simmons (D-12)

## Local and Private

**Majority Members**
Gary Jackson (R-15) *Chair*
Dr. David L. Parker (R-2)
   *Vice Chair*
Tommy Arlin Gollott (R-50)

**Minority Members**
Hob Bryan (D-7)

## Medicaid

**Majority Members**
Brice Wiggins (R-52) *Chair*
Barbara Blackmon (R-21)
Kevin Blackwell (R-19)
Terry Clark Burton (R-31)
Chris Caughman (R-35)
Eugene S. "Buck" Clarke (R-22)
Rita P. Parks (R-4)
Charles "Chuck" Younger (R-17)

**Minority Members**
Hob Bryan (D-7) *Vice Chair*
Deborah Jeanne Dawkins (D-48)
Sollie B. Norwood (D-28)

## Municipalities

**Majority Members**
Chad McMahan (R-6) *Vice Chair*
Jenifer B. Branning (R-18)
Terry Clark Burton (R-31)
Lydia Graves Chassaniol (R-14)
Chris Massey (R-1)
Chris McDaniel (R-42)

**Minority Members**
J. P. Wilemon, Jr. (D-5) *Chair*
Juan Barnett (D-34)
David Lee Jordan (D-24)
Bill Stone (D-10)
Tammy Witherspoon (D-38)

## Ports and Marine Resources

**Majority Members**
Tommy Arlin Gollott (R-50) *Chair*
Joseph Seymour (R-47) *Vice Chair*
Fredie Videt Carmichael (R-33)
Sean J. Tindell (R-49)
Michael Watson (R-51)
Brice Wiggins (R-52)

**Minority Members**
Deborah Jeanne Dawkins (D-48)
Bob M. Dearing (D-37)
Robert L. Jackson (D-11)
Willie Lee Simmons (D-13)
Tammy Witherspoon (D-38)

## Public Health and Welfare

**Majority Members**
Dean Kirby (R-30) *Chair*
Brice Wiggins (R-52) *Vice Chair*
Terry Clark Burton (R-31)
Chris Caughman (R-35)
Sally Doty (R-39)
Joey Fillingane (R-41)
Josh Harkins (R-20)
W. Briggs Hopson III (R-23)
Gary Jackson (R-15)
Dr. David L. Parker (R-2)
Rita P. Parks (R-4)
Gray Tollison (R-9)
Charles "Chuck" Younger (R-17)

**Minority Members**
Hob Bryan (D-7)
David Blount (D-29)
Bob M. Dearing (D-37)
Hillman Terome Frazier (D-27)
John Horhn (D-26)
Willie Lee Simmons (D-13)

## Public Property

**Majority Members**
Sally Doty (R-39)
Josh Harkins (R-20)
Joseph Seymour (R-47)

**Minority Members**
David Blount (D-29) *Chair*
Bob M. Dearing (D-37) *Vice Chair*
Albert Butler (D-36)
Robert L. Jackson (D-11)

## Rules

**Majority Members**
Terry Clark Burton (R-31) *Chair*
Gray Tollison (R-9) *Vice Chair*
Tommy Arlin Gollott (R-50)
Josh Harkins (R-20)

**Minority Members**
John Horhn (D-26)

## State Library

**Minority Members**
Deborah Jeanne Dawkins (D-48) *Chair*
Albert Butler (D-36) *Vice Chair*
John Horhn (D-26)
Willie Lee Simmons (D-13)
Tammy Witherspoon (D-38)

## Tourism

**Majority Members**
Lydia Graves Chassaniol (R-14)
   *Chair*
Sean J. Tindell (R-49) *Vice Chair*
Tommy Arlin Gollott (R-50)
Josh Harkins (R-20)
W. Briggs Hopson III (R-23)
Chris Massey (R-1)
Chad McMahan (R-6)

**Minority Members**
Albert Butler (D-36)
John Horhn (D-26)
David Lee Jordan (D-24)
Willie Lee Simmons (D-13)

## Universities and Colleges

**Majority Members**
Josh Harkins (R-20) *Chair*
Terry Clark Burton (R-31)
Chris Caughman (R-35)
Joey Fillingane (R-41)
W. Briggs Hopson III (R-23)
Gary Jackson (R-15)
Dr. David L. Parker (R-2)
John A. Polk (R-44)
Gray Tollison (R-9)

**Minority Members**
Hillman Terome Frazier (D-27)
   *Vice Chair*
Bill Stone (D-10)
J. P. Wilemon, Jr. (D-5)
Tammy Witherspoon (D-38)

## Veterans and Military Affairs

| Majority Members | Minority Members |
|---|---|
| Dr. David L. Parker (R-2) *Chair* | Juan Barnett (D-34) |
| Philip Moran (R-46) *Vice Chair* | Sampson Jackson II (D-32) |
| Billy Hudson (R-45) | Angela Turner (D-16) |
| Rita P. Parks (R-4) | |

## Wildlife, Fisheries, and Parks

| Majority Members | Minority Members |
|---|---|
| Philip Moran (R-46) *Chair* | Sampson Jackson II (D-32) |
| Angela Burks Hill (R-40) *Vice Chair* | Derrick T. Simmons (D-12) |
| | Bill Stone (D-10) |
| Jenifer B. Branning (R-18) | |
| Chris Caughman (R-35) | |
| Gary Jackson (R-15) | |
| Chris Massey (R-1) | |
| Gray Tollison (R-9) | |
| Michael Watson (R-51) | |

# Mississippi House of Representatives

Tel: (601) 359-3360  Fax: (601) 359-3728

Speaker of the House **Philip Gunn** (R) . . . . . . . . . . . . . . . . (601) 355-8321
Speaker Pro Tem **Greg Snowden** (R) . . . . . . . . . . . . . . . (601) 693-5700
Majority Leader **Tyrone Ellis** (D) . . . . . . . . . . . . . . . . . . . . (662) 359-4084
Clerk of the House **Don Richardson** . . . . . . . . . . . . . . . . . (601) 359-3360
   Education: Mississippi State BS, MBA, MS

## Representatives

**Party Affiliation Statistics:** Republicans: 74, Democrats: 47, Vacancies: 1

Representative **Shane Aguirre** (R-District 17) . . . . . . . . . . (601) 359-3360
   Counties Represented: Lee (part)
   Term Expires: 2020
   E-mail: saguirre@house.ms.gov
   Committees: Banking and Financial Services; Gaming; Judiciary A; Judiciary En Banc; Public Health and Human Services; Universities and Colleges

Representative **Jeramey Anderson** (D-District 110) . . . . . . (855) 537-2639
   Counties Represented: Jackson (part)
   Term Expires: 2020
   4219 Joseph Street, Moss Point, MS 39562
   E-mail: janderson@house.ms.gov
   Committees: Investigative State Offices; Judiciary B; Judiciary En Banc; Marine Resources; Universities and Colleges

Representative **William Tracy Arnold** (R-District 3) . . . . . . (662) 728-9951
   Counties Represented: Alcorn (part), Prentiss (part)
   Term Expires: 2020
   301 Wyninegar Road, Booneville, MS 38829
   E-mail: warnold@house.ms.gov
   Committees: Appropriations; Banking and Financial Services; Judiciary B; Judiciary En Banc; Transportation; Universities and Colleges

Representative **Willie L. Bailey** (D-District 49) . . . . . . . . . . (662) 335-5310
   Counties Represented: Washington (part)
   Term Expires: 2020
   P.O. Box 189, Greenville, MS 38702-0189
   E-mail: wbailey@house.ms.gov
   Committees: Apportionment and Elections; County Affairs; Gaming; Interstate Cooperation; Judiciary B; Judiciary En Banc; Ports, Harbors and Airports; Tourism; Ways and Means
   Education: George Washington 1972 JD; Tougaloo 1969 BA

Representative **Nick Bain** (D-District 2) . . . . . . . . . . . . . . . (662) 287-1620
   Counties Represented: Alcorn (part)
   Term Expires: 2020
   516 North Fillmore Street, Corinth, MS 38839
   E-mail: nbain@house.ms.gov
   Committees: Agriculture; Judiciary B; Judiciary En Banc; Public Health and Human Services

Representative **Mark Baker** (R-District 74) . . . . . . . . . . . . . (601) 824-7455
   Counties Represented: Madison (part), Rankin (part)   Res: (601) 824-3297
   Term Expires: 2020
   P.O. Box 947, Brandon, MS 39043-0947
   E-mail: mbaker@house.ms.gov
   Committees: Banking and Financial Services; Investigative State Offices; Judiciary A; Judiciary En Banc; Transportation; Ways and Means
   Education: U Memphis BA; Mississippi Col JD

Representative **Earle S. Banks** (D-District 67) . . . . . . . . . . (601) 359-9392
   Counties Represented: Hinds (part)      Tel: (601) 713-2223
   Term Expires: 2020        Res: (601) 355-5574
   P.O. Box 2539, Jackson, MS 39207
   E-mail: ebanksjax@aol.com
   Committees: Appropriations; Insurance; Judiciary A; Judiciary En Banc; Public Property; Public Utilities
   Education: Jackson State U BS; Mississippi Col JD

Representative **David Baria** (D-District 122) . . . . . . . . . . . . (228) 466-0815
   Counties Represented: Hancock (part)
   Term Expires: 2020
   544 Main Street, Bay Saint Louis, MS 39520
   E-mail: dbaria@house.ms.gov
   Committees: Judiciary B; Judiciary En Banc; Public Utilities; Universities and Colleges; Youth and Family Affairs

Representative **Toby Barker** (R-District 102) . . . . . . . . . . . (601) 307-3802
   Counties Represented: Forrest (part), Lamar (part)
   Term Expires: 2020
   409 South 21st Avenue, Hattiesburg, MS 39401
   E-mail: tbarker@house.ms.gov
   Committees: Apportionment and Elections; Appropriations; Education; Medicaid; Public Health and Human Services

Representative **Shane Barnett** (R-District 86) . . . . . . . . . . (601) 735-4047
   Counties Represented: Clarke (part), Perry (part), Wayne (part)
   Term Expires: 2020
   P.O. Box 621, Waynesboro, MS 39367
   E-mail: sbarnett@house.ms.gov
   Committees: Conservation and Water Resources; Forestry; Judiciary B; Judiciary En Banc; Marine Resources; Wildlife, Fisheries and Parks

Representative **Manly Barton** (R-District 109) . . . . . . . . . . (228) 588-2763
   Counties Represented: George (part), Jackson (part)
   Term Expires: 2020
   7905 Pecan Ridge, Moss Point, MS 39562
   E-mail: mbarton@house.ms.gov
   Committees: Agriculture; Conservation and Water Resources; County Affairs; Local and Private Legislation; Military Affairs; Ports, Harbors and Airports; Rules; Transportation

Representative **Charles Jim Beckett** (R-District 23) . . . . . (662) 983-7358
   Counties Represented: Calhoun (part), Clay (part),   Res: (662) 983-2451
   Oktibbeha (part), Webster (part)
   Term Expires: 2020
   P.O. Box 722, Bruce, MS 38915
   E-mail: jbeckett@house.ms.gov
   Committees: Apportionment and Elections; Appropriations; Banking and Financial Services; Insurance; Judiciary A; Judiciary En Banc; Public Utilities; Rules; Universities and Colleges
   Education: Mississippi BA, JD

Representative **Christopher M. Bell** (D-District 65) . . . . . . (601) 359-3360
   Counties Represented: Hinds (part), Madison (part)
   Term Expires: 2020
   E-mail: cbell@house.ms.gov
   Committees: Constitution; Executive Contingent Fund; Gaming; Insurance; Public Health and Human Services

Representative **Donnie Bell** (R-District 21) . . . . . . . . . . . . . (601) 862-3385
   Counties Represented: Itawamba (part), Monroe (part)
   Term Expires: 2020
   836 Tucker Road, Fulton, MS 38843
   E-mail: dbell@house.ms.gov
   Committees: Agriculture; Banking and Financial Services; Universities and Colleges; Ways and Means; Workforce Development

Representative **Richard Bennett** (R-District 120) . . . . . . . . (228) 863-6483
   Counties Represented: Harrison (part)
   Term Expires: 2020
   20108 Daugherty Road, Long Beach, MS 39560
   E-mail: rbennett@house.ms.gov
   Committees: Appropriations; Education; Gaming; Local and Private Legislation; Management; Medicaid; Public Utilities; Tourism

Representative **Edward Blackmon, Jr.** (D-District 57) . . . . (601) 859-1567
   Counties Represented: Madison (part)      Res: (601) 859-4202
   Term Expires: 2020
   P.O. Drawer 105, Canton, MS 39046
   E-mail: eblackmon@house.ms.gov
   Committees: Apportionment and Elections; Judiciary A; Judiciary En Banc; Municipalities; Rules; Ways and Means
   Education: Tougaloo 1970 BA; George Washington 1973 JD

Representative **Joel Bomgar** (R-District 58) . . . . . . . . . . . . (601) 359-3360
   Counties Represented: Madison (part)
   Term Expires: 2020
   E-mail: jbomgar@house.ms.gov
   Committees: Corrections; Education; Judiciary B; Judiciary En Banc; Medicaid; Municipalities; Public Property; Youth and Family Affairs

Representative **C. Scott Bounds** (R-District 44) . . . . . . . . (601) 656-1765
Counties Represented: Neshoba (part)
Term Expires: 2020
45 Carla Drive, Philadelphia, MS 39350
E-mail: sbounds@house.ms.gov
Committees: Appropriations; Banking and Financial Services; Judiciary
A; Management; Public Health and Human Services; Wildlife, Fisheries
and Parks

Representative **Randy P. Boyd** (R-District 19) . . . . . . . . . . (662) 231-0133
Counties Represented: Itawamba (part), Lee (part), Tishomingo (part)
Term Expires: 2020
PO Box 157, Mantachie, MS 38855
E-mail: rboyd@house.ms.gov
Committees: Education; Forestry; Investigative State Offices; Public
Property

Representative **Chris Brown** (R-District 20) . . . . . . . . . . . (662) 369-8745
Counties Represented: Lowndes (part), Monroe (part)
Term Expires: 2020
52160 Highway Eight, Aberdeen, MS 39730
E-mail: crbrown@house.ms.gov
Committees: Appropriations; Banking and Financial Services;
Conservation and Water Resources; Constitution; Management;
Medicaid; Public Health and Human Services

Representative **Cedric Burnett** (D-District 9) . . . . . . . . . . (601) 359-3360
Counties Represented: Coahoma (part), Panola (part), Quitman (part),
Tate (part), Tunica (part)
Term Expires: 2020
E-mail: cburnett@house.ms.gov
Committees: Banking and Financial Services; Executive Contingent
Fund; Judiciary B; Judiciary En Banc; Public Health and Human
Services; Transportation

Representative **Charles Busby** (R-District 111) . . . . . . . . . (228) 769-0501
Counties Represented: Jackson (part)
Term Expires: 2020
907 Grant Avenue, Pascagoula, MS 39567
E-mail: cbusby@house.ms.gov
Committees: Appropriations; Conservation and Water Resources;
Education; Insurance; Ports, Harbors and Airports; Transportation

Representative **Larry Byrd** (R-District 104) . . . . . . . . . . . . (601) 544-1877
Counties Represented: Forrest (part), Lamar (part)
Term Expires: 2020
17 Byrd Road, Petal, MS 39465
E-mail: lbyrd@house.ms.gov
Committees: Banking and Financial Services; Conservation and Water
Resources; County Affairs; Management; Public Health and Human
Services; Transportation

Representative **Credell Calhoun** (D-District 68) . . . . . . . . . (601) 948-1217
Counties Represented: Hinds (part)          Res: (601) 949-7561
Term Expires: 2020
P.O. Box 3406, Jackson, MS 39207
E-mail: ccalhoun@house.ms.gov
Committees: Education; Insurance; Military Affairs; Universities and
Colleges; Ways and Means
Education: Prairie View A&M BA, MA

Representative **Kimberly L. Campbell** (D-District 72) . . . . . (601) 956-5771
Counties Represented: Hinds (part), Madison (part)     Res: (601) 982-4277
Term Expires: 2020
1062 Devonshire Drive, Jackson, MS 39206
E-mail: kcampbell@house.ms.gov
Committees: Banking and Financial Services; Compilation, Revision
and Publication; Judiciary B; Judiciary En Banc; Public Utilities
Education: Mississippi State 1994 BA; Auburn 1998 MA;
Mississippi 2001 JD

Representative **Lester Carpenter** (R-District 1) . . . . . . . . . (662) 427-8281
Counties Represented: Alcorn (part), Tishomingo (part)
Term Expires: 2020
8 Carpenter Drive, Burnsville, MS 38833
E-mail: lcarpenter@house.ms.gov
Committees: Agriculture; Banking and Financial Services; County
Affairs; Judiciary A; Municipalities; Tourism; Ways and Means;
Wildlife, Fisheries and Parks

Representative **Gary Alan Chism** (R-District 37) . . . . . . . . (662) 327-0777
Counties Represented: Clay (part), Lowndes (part),       Res: (662) 328-7769
Oktibbeha (part)
Term Expires: 2020
P.O. Box 2343, Columbus, MS 39704-2343
E-mail: gchism@house.ms.gov
Committees: Conservation and Water Resources; Education; Insurance;
Judiciary A; Judiciary En Banc; Local and Private Legislation; Public
Utilities; Ways and Means

Representative **Bryant W. Clark** (D-District 47) . . . . . . . . . (662) 834-6133
Counties Represented: Attala (part), Holmes (part),      Res: (662) 834-4074
Yazoo (part)
Term Expires: 2020
271 Clark Road, Pickens, MS 39146
E-mail: bclark@house.ms.gov
Committees: Apportionment and Elections; Conservation and Water
Resources; Judiciary A; Judiciary En Banc; Public Health and Human
Services; Transportation; Wildlife, Fisheries and Parks
Education: Mississippi State BS; Mississippi Col JD

Representative **Alyce Griffin Clarke** (D-District 69) . . . . . . (601) 359-3096
Counties Represented: Hinds (part)            Res: (601) 354-5453
Term Expires: 2020
1053 Arbor Vista Boulevard, Jackson, MS 39209
E-mail: aclarke@house.ms.gov
Committees: Appropriations; Banking and Financial Services;
Education; Universities and Colleges; Youth and Family Affairs
Education: Alcorn State BS

Representative **Angela Cockerham** (D-District 96) . . . . . . . (601) 783-6600
Counties Represented: Adams (part), Amite (part),       Res: (601) 783-4979
Pike (part), Wilkinson
Term Expires: 2020
P.O. Box 613, Magnolia, MS 39652
E-mail: acockerham@house.ms.gov
Committees: Apportionment and Elections; Appropriations;
Compilation, Revision and Publication; Ethics; Judiciary A; Judiciary
En Banc; Management; Wildlife, Fisheries and Parks

Representative **Carolyn Crawford** (R-District 121) . . . . . . . (228) 452-5029
Counties Represented: Harrison (part)
Term Expires: 2020
23155 Stablewood Circle, Pass Christian, MS 39571
E-mail: ccrawford@house.ms.gov
Committees: Education; Gaming; Judiciary A; Marine Resources;
Universities and Colleges; Ways and Means

Representative **Dana Criswell** (R-District 6) . . . . . . . . . . . . (601) 359-3360
Counties Represented: DeSoto (part)
Term Expires: 2020
E-mail: dcriswell@house.ms.gov
Committees: Constitution; Education; Judiciary A; Judiciary En Banc;
Tourism; Transportation; Universities and Colleges

Representative **Becky Currie** (R-District 92) . . . . . . . . . . . . (601) 833-5953
Counties Represented: Copiah (part), Franklin (part), Lincoln (part)
Term Expires: 2020
407 Oliver Drive, Brookhaven, MS 39601
E-mail: bcurrie@house.ms.gov
Committees: Apportionment and Elections; Appropriations; Education;
Medicaid; Rules; Tourism

Representative **Scott DeLano** (R-District 117) . . . . . . . . . . (228) 806-7418
Counties Represented: Harrison (part)         Res: (228) 806-8087
Term Expires: 2020
P.O. Box 4524, Biloxi, MS 39535
E-mail: sdelano@house.ms.gov
Committees: Appropriations; Education; Gaming; Insurance
Education: Southern Mississippi BA

Representative
**William C. "Bill" Denny, Jr.** (R-District 64) . . . . . . . . . . (601) 359-3369
Counties Represented: Hinds (part), Madison (part)     Res: (601) 956-6807
Term Expires: 2020
P.O. Box 12185, Jackson, MS 39236-2185
E-mail: bdenny@house.ms.gov
Committees: Apportionment and Elections; Appropriations;
Constitution; Judiciary A; Judiciary En Banc; Municipalities
Education: Maryland BS

Representative **Oscar Denton** (D-District 55) . . . . . . . . . . . (601) 630-8004
Counties Represented: Warren (part)
Term Expires: 2020
5024 Rollingwood E. Drive, Vicksburg, MS 39180
P.O. Box 1018, Jackson, MS 39180
E-mail: odenton@house.ms.gov
Committees: Gaming; Insurance; Tourism; Transportation; Workforce
Development

Representative **Deborah Butler Dixon** (D-District 63) . . . . (601) 371-9119
Counties Represented: Hinds (part)
Term Expires: 2020
PO Box 106, Raymond, MS 39204
E-mail: ddixon@house.ms.gov
Committees: Agriculture; Corrections; Gaming; Judiciary B; Judiciary
En Banc; Public Health and Human Services; Youth and Family Affairs

*(continued on next page)*

LEGISLATIVE BRANCH

**Representatives** *continued*

Representative **Jarvis Dortch** (D-District 66) . . . . . . . . . . . (601) 359-3360
Counties Represented: Hinds (part)
Term Expires: 2020
E-mail: jdortch@house.ms.gov
Committees: Agriculture; Education; Insurance; Medicaid; Public
Health and Human Services

Representative **Tyrone Ellis** (D-District 38) . . . . . . . . . . . (662) 359-4084
Counties Represented: Clay (part), Lowndes (part),    Res: (662) 323-6564
Noxubee (part), Oktibbeha (part)
Term Expires: 2020
P.O. Box 892, Starkville, MS 39760
E-mail: tellis@house.ms.gov
Committees: Apportionment and Elections; Corrections; Judiciary B;
Judiciary En Banc; Ways and Means

Representative **Dan Eubanks** (R-District 25) . . . . . . . . . . . (601) 359-3360
Counties Represented: Coahoma (part), DeSoto (part), Tunica (part)
Term Expires: 2020
E-mail: deubanks@house.ms.gov
Committees: Agriculture; Banking and Financial Services; Constitution;
Insurance; Public Health and Human Services; Youth and Family
Affairs

Representative **Casey Eure** (R-District 116) . . . . . . . . . . . . (228) 297-2849
Counties Represented: Harrison (part)
Term Expires: 2020
13372 Damon Court, Biloxi, MS 39532
E-mail: ceure@house.ms.gov
Committees: Appropriations; Banking and Financial Services;
Conservation and Water Resources; Gaming; Marine Resources; Public
Utilities; Tourism

Representative **Michael T. Evans** (D-District 45) . . . . . . . . (662) 773-3543
Counties Represented: Leake (part), Neshoba (part), Rankin (part),
Scott (part)
Term Expires: 2020
1147 Mount Harmony Road, Preston, MS 39354
E-mail: mevans@house.ms.gov
Committees: Agriculture; Conservation and Water Resources; Public
Utilities; Wildlife, Fisheries and Parks

Representative
**Robert Emil "Bob" Evans** (D-District 91) . . . . . . . . . . . (601) 587-0615
Counties Represented: Copiah (part), Covington    Res: (601) 587-9313
(part), Jefferson Davis (part), Lawrence (part), Simpson (part)
Term Expires: 2020
P.O. Box 636, Monticello, MS 39654
E-mail: bevans@house.ms.gov
Committees: Banking and Financial Services; Education; Judiciary A;
Judiciary En Banc; Universities and Colleges

Representative **John Gary Faulkner** (D-District 5) . . . . . . . (601) 359-4085
Counties Represented: Benton (part), Marshall (part)
Term Expires: 2020
P. O. Box 1018, Jackson, MS 39215
P.O. Box 942, Holly Springs, MS 38635
E-mail: jfaulkner@house.ms.gov
Committees: Military Affairs; Transportation; Universities and
Colleges; Youth and Family Affairs

Representative **Mark S. Formby** (R-District 108) . . . . . . . . (601) 798-3800
Counties Represented: Pearl River (part)    Res: (601) 798-8917
Term Expires: 2020
911 Highway 43 North, Picayune, MS 39466
E-mail: mformby@house.ms.gov
Committees: Education; Insurance; Marine Resources; Public Utilities;
Ways and Means
Affiliation: Real Estate Agent, Formby & Associates
Education: Mississippi State BA

Representative **Robert Foster** (R-District 28) . . . . . . . . . . . (601) 359-3360
Counties Represented: Bolivar (part), Sunflower (part), Washington
(part)
Term Expires: 2020
E-mail: rfoster@house.ms.gov
Committees: Agriculture; Constitution; Local and Private Legislation;
Municipalities; Transportation; Workforce Development

Representative **Herb Frierson** (R-District 106) . . . . . . . . . . (601) 795-6285
Counties Represented: Lamar (part), Pearl River    Res: (601) 795-1675
(part)
Note: On March 24, 2016, Governor Phil Bryant appointed Herb
Frierson to serve as Commissioner of the Department of Revenue.
Representative Frierson will depart from the Mississippi House of
Representatives effective June 30, 2016.
Term Expires: 2020
12 Trailwood Lane, Poplarville, MS 39470
E-mail: hfrierson@house.ms.gov
Committees: Appropriations; Education; Wildlife, Fisheries and Parks;
Workforce Development
Education: Mississippi State BS

Representative **Karl Gibbs** (D-District 36) . . . . . . . . . . . . . (662) 494-6559
Counties Represented: Clay (part), Lowndes (part), Monroe (part)
Term Expires: 2020
5543 George Walker Road, West Point, MS 39773
P. O. Box 1018, Jackson, MS 39215
E-mail: kgibbs@house.ms.gov
Committees: Agriculture; Military Affairs; Wildlife, Fisheries and
Parks; Youth and Family Affairs

Representative **Andrew "Andy" Gipson** (R-District 77) . . . (601) 949-4789
Counties Represented: Rankin (part), Simpson    Res: (601) 847-0417
(part), Smith (part)
Term Expires: 2020
414 Holly Grove Circle, Braxton, MS 39044
E-mail: agipson@house.ms.gov
Committees: Agriculture; Appropriations; Compilation, Revision and
Publication; County Affairs; Ethics; Insurance; Judiciary B; Judiciary
En Banc; Municipalities; Transportation

Representative **Jeffrey S. "Jeff" Guice** (R-District 114) . . . (228) 875-1131
Counties Represented: Harrison (part), Jackson    Res: (228) 872-2994
(part)
Term Expires: 2020
2016 Bienville Boulevard, Ocean Springs, MS 39564
E-mail: jguice@house.ms.gov
Committees: Education; Insurance; Interstate Cooperation; Ports,
Harbors and Airports; Public Health and Human Services; Tourism;
Ways and Means

Representative **Philip Gunn** (R-District 56) . . . . . . . . . . . . (601) 355-8321
Counties Represented: Hinds (part), Madison (part),    Res: (601) 924-8438
Yazoo (part)
Term Expires: 2020
101 Pinehaven Cove, Clinton, MS 39056
E-mail: pgunn@house.ms.gov
Committees: Compilation, Revision and Publication; Rules

Representative **Jeff Hale** (R-District 24) . . . . . . . . . . . . . . . (601) 359-3360
Counties Represented: Calhoun (part), Grenada (part), Yalobusha (part)
Term Expires: 2020
E-mail: jhale@house.ms.gov
Committees: Apportionment and Elections; Banking and Financial
Services; Insurance; Public Property; Workforce Development

Representative **Greg Haney** (R-District 118) . . . . . . . . . . . (228) 864-9095
Counties Represented: Harrison (part)
Term Expires: 2020
106 45th Street, Gulfport, MS 39507
E-mail: ghaney@house.ms.gov
Committees: Judiciary A; Marine Resources; Ports, Harbors and
Airports; Tourism; Workforce Development

Representative **Ashley Henley** (R-District 40) . . . . . . . . . . (601) 359-3360
Counties Represented: DeSoto (part)
Term Expires: 2020
E-mail: ahenley@house.ms.gov
Committees: Apportionment and Elections; Constitution; Corrections;
Education; Military Affairs; Tourism; Workforce Development; Youth
and Family Affairs

Representative **John Wesley Hines, Sr.** (D-District 50) . . . (662) 334-9444
Counties Represented: Washington (part)    Res: (662) 335-9704
Term Expires: 2020
P.O. Box 114, Greenville, MS 38701
E-mail: jhines@house.ms.gov
Committees: Banking and Financial Services; Gaming; Insurance;
Management; Public Utilities
Affiliation: Investigator, McTeer Associates

Representative
**Daniel Stephen "Steve" Holland** (D-District 16) . . . . . . (662) 840-5000
Counties Represented: Lee (part)    Res: (662) 844-2004
Term Expires: 2020
P.O. Box 2, Plantersville, MS 38862
E-mail: sholland@house.ms.gov
Committees: Appropriations; Banking and Financial Services;
Conservation and Water Resources; Medicaid; Transportation
Affiliation: Co-Owner, Lee Memorial Funeral Home

LEGISLATIVE BRANCH

Representative **Gregory Holloway, Sr.** (D-District 76) . . . . (601) 359-2435
Counties Represented: Claiborne (part), Copiah  Res: (601) 894-4228
(part), Hinds (part)
Term Expires: 2020
115 Edgewood Drive, Hazlehurst, MS 39083
E-mail: gholloway@house.ms.gov
Committees: Agriculture; Education; Municipalities; Public Property;
Rules; Universities and Colleges

Representative **Joey Hood** (R-District 35) . . . . . . . . . . . . . (662) 285-4663
Counties Represented: Choctaw (part), Grenada (part), Oktibbeha
(part), Webster (part)
Term Expires: 2020
PO Box 759, Ackerman, MS 39735
E-mail: jhood@house.ms.gov
Committees: Banking and Financial Services; Judiciary B; Judiciary En
Banc; Medicaid; Public Health and Human Services; Public Utilities;
Ways and Means
Education: Mississippi State 1999 BA; Mississippi Col 2003 JD

Representative **Steve Hopkins** (R-District 7) . . . . . . . . . . . (601) 359-3360
Counties Represented: DeSoto (part)
Term Expires: 2020
E-mail: shopkins@house.ms.gov
Committees: County Affairs; Education; Interstate Cooperation;
Military Affairs; Municipalities; Universities and Colleges; Wildlife,
Fisheries and Parks

Representative **Kevin Horan** (D-District 34) . . . . . . . . . . . . (662) 226-1817
Counties Represented: Carroll (part), Holmes (part), Humphreys (part),
Leflore (part), Montgomery (part), Washington (part)
Term Expires: 2020
PO Box 2166, Grenada, MS 38901
E-mail: khoran@house.ms.gov
Committees: Banking and Financial Services; Corrections; Judiciary B;
Judiciary En Banc

Representative **Stephen A. Horne** (R-District 81) . . . . . . . (601) 482-1456
Counties Represented: Clarke (part), Lauderdale  Res: (601) 644-9974
(part)
Term Expires: 2020
5904 Causeyville Road, Meridian, MS 39301
E-mail: shorne@house.ms.gov
Committees: Enrolled Bills; Executive Contingent Fund; Interstate
Cooperation; Investigative State Offices; Ways and Means

Representative **Mac Huddleston** (R-District 15) . . . . . . . . (662) 489-5157
Counties Represented: Pontotoc (part)
Term Expires: 2020
P.O. Box 300, Pontotoc, MS 38863
E-mail: mhuddleston@house.ms.gov
Committees: Agriculture; Apportionment and Elections; Appropriations;
Ethics; Military Affairs; Public Health and Human Services; Rules;
Universities and Colleges

Representative **Robert E. Huddleston** (D-District 30) . . . . . (662) 375-8692
Counties Represented: Bolivar (part), Leflore (part), Quitman (part),
Sunflower (part), Tallahatchie (part)
Term Expires: 2020
P.O. Box 426, Sumner, MS 38957
E-mail: rhuddleston@house.ms.gov
Committees: Agriculture; Apportionment and Elections; Appropriations;
Corrections; County Affairs; Workforce Development
Affiliation: Construction Supervisor, Talla Housing

Representative **Jay P. Hughes, Jr.** (D-District 12) . . . . . . . . (601) 359-3360
Counties Represented: Lafayette (part)
Term Expires: 2020
E-mail: jhughes@house.ms.gov
Committees: Constitution; Judiciary A; Judiciary En Banc; Medicaid

Representative **Lataisha Jackson** (D-District 11) . . . . . . . (662) 578-4300
Counties Represented: Panola (part), Tate (part)
Term Expires: 2020
P. O. Box 1018, Jackson, MS 39215
E-mail: ljackson@house.ms.gov
Committees: Agriculture; Local and Private Legislation; Public
Property; Universities and Colleges

Representative **Chris Johnson** (R-District 87) . . . . . . . . . . (601) 359-3360
Counties Represented: Jasper (part), Jones (part), Newton (part)
Term Expires: 2020
E-mail: cjohnson@house.ms.gov
Committees: Agriculture; Banking and Financial Services; Corrections;
Education; Public Health and Human Services; Transportation

Representative **Robert L. Johnson III** (D-District 94) . . . . . (601) 442-9371
Counties Represented: Adams (part), Claiborne  Res: (601) 445-5690
(part), Jefferson (part)
Term Expires: 2020
P.O. Box 1678, Natchez, MS 39121
E-mail: rjohnson@house.ms.gov
Committees: Gaming; Judiciary A; Judiciary En Banc; Medicaid;
Transportation; Ways and Means; Wildlife, Fisheries and Parks

Representative **Kabir Karriem** (D-District 41) . . . . . . . . . . . (601) 359-3360
Counties Represented: Lowndes (part)
Term Expires: 2020
E-mail: kkarriem@house.ms.gov
Committees: Military Affairs; Municipalities; Ports, Harbors and
Airports; Tourism

Representative **Bill Kinkade** (R-District 52) . . . . . . . . . . . . (901) 365-4830
Counties Represented: DeSoto (part), Marshall (part)
Term Expires: 2020
PO Box 1018, Jackson, MS 39215
E-mail: bkinkade@house.ms.gov
Committees: Agriculture; Corrections; Forestry; Ways and Means;
Wildlife, Fisheries and Parks
Education: New Mexico (Attended)

Representative **John "Timmy" Ladner** (R-District 93) . . . . (228) 518-0878
Counties Represented: Forrest (part), Hancock (part), Harrison (part),
Lamar (part), Pearl River (part), Stone (part)
Term Expires: 2020
6 Michael D. Smith Road, Poplarville, MS 39470
E-mail: tladner@house.ms.gov
Committees: Agriculture; Appropriations; Gaming; Investigative State
Offices; Judiciary B; Judiciary En Banc; Marine Resources; Workforce
Development

Representative
**John Thomas "Trey" Lamar III** (R-District 8) . . . . . . . . . (662) 562-6537
Counties Represented: DeSoto (part), Tate (part)
Term Expires: 2020
213 South Ward Street, Senatobia, MS 38668
E-mail: jlamar@house.ms.gov
Committees: Agriculture; County Affairs; Judiciary A; Judiciary En
Banc; Universities and Colleges; Ways and Means; Wildlife, Fisheries
and Parks
Education: Mississippi BBA; Mississippi Col JD;
Washington U (MO) MLaw

Representative **Vince Mangold** (R-District 53) . . . . . . . . . (601) 359-3360
Counties Represented: Amite (part), Franklin (part), Lawrence (part),
Lincoln (part), Pike (part)
Term Expires: 2020
E-mail: vmangold@house.ms.gov
Committees: Agriculture; Conservation and Water Resources;
Education; Forestry; Marine Resources; Military Affairs;
Transportation; Wildlife, Fisheries and Parks

Representative **Steve Massengill** (R-District 13) . . . . . . . . (662) 815-5000
Counties Represented: Benton (part), Lafayette (part), Marshall (part),
Union (part)
Term Expires: 2020
424 Massengill Road, Hickory Flat, MS 38633
E-mail: smassengill@house.ms.gov
Committees: Agriculture; Public Utilities; Tourism; Transportation;
Workforce Development

Representative **Doug McLeod** (R-District 107) . . . . . . . . . (601) 947-3125
Counties Represented: Forrest (part), George (part), Jackson (part),
Stone (part)
Term Expires: 2020
1211 Bexley Church Road, Lucedale, MS 39452
E-mail: dmcleod@house.ms.gov
Committees: Agriculture; Corrections; Medicaid; Public Health and
Human Services; Transportation; Ways and Means; Workforce
Development

Representative **Roun McNeal** (R-District 105) . . . . . . . . . . (601) 359-3360
Counties Represented: Forrest (part), George (part), Greene, Perry
(part), Wayne (part)
Term Expires: 2020
E-mail: rmcneal@house.ms.gov
Committees: Corrections; County Affairs; Forestry; Judiciary B;
Judiciary En Banc; Municipalities; Universities and Colleges;
Workforce Development

*(continued on next page)*

LEGISLATIVE BRANCH

**Representatives** *continued*

Representative **H. Nolan Mettetal** (R-District 10) . . . . . . . (662) 487-1512
Counties Represented: Lafayette (part), Panola (part), Tallahatchie (part)
Term Expires: 2020
PO Box 414, Sardis, MS 38666
E-mail: nmettetal@house.ms.gov
Committees: Appropriations; Banking and Financial Services; Medicaid; Public Health and Human Services; Public Property; Universities and Colleges

Representative **Carl L. Mickens** (D-District 42) . . . . . . . . . (601) 359-3360
Counties Represented: Kemper (part), Lauderdale (part), Noxubee (part)
Term Expires: 2020
E-mail: cmickens@house.ms.gov
Committees: Conservation and Water Resources; Constitution; Corrections; Education; Public Utilities; Workforce Development

Representative
**America "Chuck" Middleton** (D-District 85) . . . . . . . . (601) 529-9928
Counties Represented: Adams (part), Claiborne    Res: (601) 437-8502
(part), Hinds (part), Jefferson (part), Warren (part)
Term Expires: 2020
P.O. Box 685, Port Gibson, MS 39150
E-mail: amiddleton@house.ms.gov
Committees: Constitution; Enrolled Bills; Forestry; Gaming; Interstate Cooperation; Investigative State Offices; State Library; Tourism; Ways and Means

Representative **Tom Miles** (D-District 75) . . . . . . . . . . . . . . (601) 732-9511
Counties Represented: Scott (part)
Term Expires: 2020
807 Highway 35 South, Forest, MS 39074
E-mail: tmiles@house.ms.gov
Committees: Public Utilities

Representative **Sam C. Mims V** (R-District 97) . . . . . . . . . (601) 684-0281
Counties Represented: Adams (part), Amite (part), Franklin (part), Lawrence (part), Pike (part), Walthall (part)
Term Expires: 2020
605 Lakeshore Drive, McComb, MS 39648
E-mail: smims@house.ms.gov
Committees: Appropriations; Judiciary B; Judiciary En Banc; Medicaid; Public Health and Human Services

Representative **Alex Monsour** (R-District 54) . . . . . . . . . . (601) 415-7274
Counties Represented: Issaquena (part), Sharkey (part), Warren (part)
Term Expires: 2020
112 Villanova Drive, Vicksburg, MS 39183
E-mail: amonsour@house.ms.gov
Committees: Appropriations; Constitution; Gaming; Insurance; Judiciary B; Judiciary En Banc; Ports, Harbors and Airports; Tourism; Transportation

Representative **John L. Moore** (R-District 60) . . . . . . . . . . (601) 359-3311
Counties Represented: Rankin (part), Simpson (part)    Tel: (601) 591-4100
Term Expires: 2020
P.O. Box 20, Brandon, MS 39043
E-mail: jmoore@house.ms.gov
Committees: Appropriations; Education; Insurance; Judiciary B; Judiciary En Banc; Rules; Transportation

Representative **Ken Morgan** (R-District 100) . . . . . . . . . . . (601) 736-9688
Counties Represented: Jefferson Davis (part), Lamar (part), Marion (part)
Term Expires: 2020
1640 Highway 587, Morgantown, MS 39483
E-mail: kmorgan@house.ms.gov
Committees: Agriculture; Conservation and Water Resources; Forestry; Public Property; State Library; Ways and Means; Wildlife, Fisheries and Parks

Representative **David W. Myers** (D-District 98) . . . . . . . . . (601) 684-4000
Counties Represented: Pike (part), Walthall (part)    Res: (601) 684-1709
Term Expires: 2020
808 North Cherry Street, McComb, MS 39648
E-mail: dmyers@house.ms.gov
Committees: Appropriations; Medicaid; Military Affairs; Municipalities; Public Utilities

Representative **Karl Oliver** (R-District 46) . . . . . . . . . . . . . (601) 359-3360
Counties Represented: Attala (part), Carroll (part), Grenada (part), Leflore (part), Montgomery (part)
Term Expires: 2020
E-mail: koliver@house.ms.gov
Committees: Agriculture; Corrections; Forestry; Military Affairs; Public Property; Wildlife, Fisheries and Parks

Representative **Orlando Paden** (D-District 26) . . . . . . . . . . (601) 359-3360
Counties Represented: Coahoma (part), Quitman (part)
Term Expires: 2020
E-mail: opaden@house.ms.gov
Committees: Agriculture; Education; Enrolled Bills; Public Health and Human Services; Tourism; Universities and Colleges

Representative **Randall H. Patterson** (R-District 115) . . . . . (228) 432-8480
Counties Represented: Harrison (part)    Res: (228) 273-2017
Term Expires: 2020
1352 Kensington Drive, Biloxi, MS 39530
E-mail: rhpatterson@house.ms.gov
Committees: Enrolled Bills; Executive Contingent Fund; Investigative State Offices; Marine Resources; Tourism; Ways and Means

Representative **Willie J. Perkins, Sr.** (D-District 32) . . . . . (662) 455-1211
Counties Represented: Leflore (part)    Res: (662) 453-4108
Term Expires: 2020    Fax: (662) 453-9159
P.O. Box 8404, Greenwood, MS 38935-8404
E-mail: wperkins@house.ms.gov
Committees: Appropriations; County Affairs; Gaming; Insurance; Judiciary A; Judiciary En Banc; Management; Municipalities; Ways and Means
Education: Tougaloo BA, BS; Mississippi JD

Representative **Bill Pigott** (R-District 99) . . . . . . . . . (601) 303-0988 (Cell)
Counties Represented: Lamar (part), Marion (part), Pike (part), Walthall (part)
Term Expires: 2020
92 Pigott-Easterling Road, Tylertown, MS 39667
E-mail: bpigott@house.ms.gov
Committees: Agriculture; Conservation and Water Resources; Forestry; Interstate Cooperation

Representative **Brent L. Powell** (R-District 59) . . . . . . . . . (601) 359-3360
Counties Represented: Rankin (part)
Term Expires: 2020
PO Box 5454, Brandon, MS 39047
E-mail: bpowell@house.ms.gov
Committees: Constitution; Judiciary A; Judiciary En Banc; Public Health and Human Services; Transportation; Ways and Means
Education: Mississippi State BS

Representative **John O. Read** (R-District 112) . . . . . . . . . . (228) 497-4090
Counties Represented: Jackson (part)    Res: (228) 497-9852
Term Expires: 2020
2396 Robert Hiram Drive, Gautier, MS 39552
E-mail: jread@house.ms.gov
Committees: Appropriations; Conservation and Water Resources; Gaming; Ports, Harbors and Airports; Public Property; Rules
Education: Northeast Louisiana BS

Representative
**Thomas Upton "Tom" Reynolds** (D-District 33) . . . . . (662) 647-3203
Counties Represented: Lafayette (part), Tallahatchie    Res: (662) 473-2571
(part), Yalobusha (part)
Term Expires: 2020
P.O. Drawer 220, Charleston, MS 38921
E-mail: treynolds@house.ms.gov
Committees: Apportionment and Elections; Compilation, Revision and Publication; Constitution; County Affairs; Judiciary A; Judiciary En Banc; Transportation; Ways and Means
Education: Mississippi BA, JD

Representative **Lyod B. "Rob" Roberson** (R-District 43) . . (601) 359-3360
Counties Represented: Kemper (part), Noxubee (part), Winston
Term Expires: 2020
E-mail: rroberson@house.ms.gov
Committees: County Affairs; Education; Judiciary A; Judiciary En Banc; Local and Private Legislation; Municipalities; Transportation

Representative **Margaret Ellis Rogers** (R-District 14) . . . . . (662) 534-8886
Counties Represented: Pontotoc (part), Union (part)
Term Expires: 2020
619 Owen Road, New Albany, MS 38652
E-mail: mrogers@house.ms.gov
Committees: Banking and Financial Services; Public Utilities; State Library; Ways and Means

Representative **Ray Rogers** (R-District 61) . . . . . . . . . . . . . (601) 939-9633
Counties Represented: Rankin (part)    Fax: (601) 932-1060
Term Expires: 2020
3403 Lanell Lane, Pearl, MS 39208
E-mail: rrogers@house.ms.gov
Committees: Banking and Financial Services; County Affairs; Ethics; Investigative State Offices; Management; Military Affairs; Public Property; Ways and Means

Representative **Randy Rushing** (R-District 78) . . . . . . . . . (601) 635-2044
Counties Represented: Neshoba (part), Newton (part), Scott (part)
Term Expires: 2020
672 North 8th Avenue, Decatur, MS 39327
PO Box 424, Decatur, MS 39327
E-mail: rrushing@house.ms.gov
Committees: Corrections; County Affairs; Military Affairs;
Municipalities; Ways and Means

Representative **Noah L. Sanford** (R-District 90) . . . . . . . . . (601) 359-3360
Counties Represented: Covington (part), Forrest (part), Jefferson Davis
(part), Marion (part), Simpson (part)
Term Expires: 2020
E-mail: nsanford@house.ms.gov
Committees: Agriculture; Apportionment and Elections; County
Affairs; Judiciary B; Judiciary En Banc; Public Health and Human
Services; Public Utilities

Representative **Omeria McDonald Scott** (D-District 80) . . (601) 649-7677
Counties Represented: Clarke (part), Jasper (part), Jones (part)
Term Expires: 2020
615 East 19th Street, Laurel, MS 39440
E-mail: oscott@house.ms.gov
Committees: Insurance; Medicaid; Public Health and Human Services;
Tourism; Ways and Means

Representative **William Shirley** (R-District 84) . . . . . . . . . (601) 776-3428
Counties Represented: Clarke (part), Jasper (part), Lauderdale (part),
Newton (part)
Term Expires: 2020
911 CR 140, Quitman, MS 39355
E-mail: wshirley@house.ms.gov
Committees: Enrolled Bills; Insurance; Judiciary B; Judiciary En Banc;
Medicaid

Representative **Bobby Shows** (R-District 89) . . . . . . . . . . (601) 477-9225
Counties Represented: Jones (part)
Term Expires: 2020
P.O. Box 373, Ellisville, MS 39437
E-mail: bshows@house.ms.gov
Committees: Agriculture; Appropriations; County Affairs; Executive
Contingent Fund; Public Health and Human Services; Public Utilities;
Universities and Colleges

Representative **Jeffrey C. "Jeff" Smith** (R-District 39) . . . (662) 328-2711
Counties Represented: Lowndes (part)                 Res: (662) 327-0407
Term Expires: 2020                                   Fax: (662) 328-0745
P.O. Box 681, Columbus, MS 39703
E-mail: jsmith@house.ms.gov
Committees: Constitution; Judiciary A; Judiciary En Banc; Ways and
Means
Education: Mississippi State BS; Mississippi JD

Representative **Greg Snowden** (R-District 83) . . . . . . . . . (601) 693-5700
Counties Represented: Clarke (part), Lauderdale (part)
Term Expires: 2020
P.O. Box 3807, Meridian, MS 39303-3857
E-mail: gsnowden@house.ms.gov
E-mail: greg@gregsnowden.com
Committees: Appropriations; Compilation, Revision and Publication;
Judiciary A; Judiciary En Banc; Management; Rules

Representative **Gary V. Staples** (R-District 88) . . . . . . . . . (601) 649-4972
Counties Represented: Jones (part), Perry (part)
Term Expires: 2020
366 Forest Road, Laurel, MS 39443
E-mail: gstaples@house.ms.gov
Committees: Agriculture; Appropriations; Banking and Financial
Services; Public Utilities

Representative **Jody Steverson** (R-District 4) . . . . . . . . . . (662) 837-0194
Counties Represented: Benton (part), Tippah, Union (part)
Term Expires: 2020
125 Woodridge, Ripley, MS 38663
E-mail: jsteverson@house.ms.gov
Committees: Constitution; Insurance; Public Utilities; Transportation;
Universities and Colleges; Ways and Means

Representative **Rufus "Pete" Straughter** (D-District 51) . . (662) 247-2728
Counties Represented: Humphreys (part), Issaquena (part), Sharkey
(part), Washington (part), Yazoo (part)
Term Expires: 2020
107 Van Buren Street, Belzoni, MS 39038
E-mail: rstraughter@house.ms.gov
Committees: Education; Local and Private Legislation; Universities and
Colleges; Ways and Means
Education: Delta State BA; Jackson State U MBA, MS

Representative **Preston E. Sullivan** (D-District 22) . . . . . . (662) 447-5719
Counties Represented: Calhoun (part), Chickasaw, Pontotoc (part)
Term Expires: 2020
1601 Country Road 410, Okolona, MS 38860
E-mail: psullivan@house.ms.gov
Committees: Agriculture; Appropriations; Conservation and Water
Resources; County Affairs; Forestry; Public Property; Transportation

Representative **Kathy Sykes** (D-District 70) . . . . . . . . . . . (601) 359-3360
Counties Represented: Hinds (part)
Term Expires: 2020
E-mail: ksykes@house.ms.gov
Committees: Banking and Financial Services; Interstate Cooperation;
Public Health and Human Services; Public Utilities; Workforce
Development

Representative
**Sara Richardson Thomas** (D-District 31) . . . . . . . . . . (662) 887-2628
Counties Represented: Sunflower (part)
Term Expires: 2020
512 B. B. King Road, Indianola, MS 38751
E-mail: sthomas@house.ms.gov
Committees: Agriculture; Education; Ethics; Investigative State Offices;
Public Property; Tourism; Youth and Family Affairs

Representative **Brad A. Touchstone** (R-District 101) . . . . . (601) 359-3360
Counties Represented: Forrest (part), Lamar (part)
Term Expires: 2020
E-mail: btouchstone@house.ms.gov
Committees: Education; Insurance; Judiciary A; Judiciary En Banc;
Public Health and Human Services; Public Utilities; Transportation;
Youth and Family Affairs
Education: Mississippi Col JD; Millsaps BA

Representative **Mark K Tullos** (R-District 79) . . . . . . . . . . . (601) 359-3360
Counties Represented: Covington (part), Jones (part), Smith (part)
Term Expires: 2020
P.O. Box 1018, Jackson, MS 39180
E-mail: mtullos@house.ms.gov
Committees: Corrections; County Affairs; Judiciary A; Judiciary En
Banc; Military Affairs; Municipalities; Youth and Family Affairs

Representative **Jerry R. Turner** (R-District 18) . . . . . . . . . . (662) 365-8484
Counties Represented: Lee (part), Prentiss (part)     Res: (662) 365-5135
Term Expires: 2020
1290 Carrollville Avenue, Baldwyn, MS 38824
E-mail: jturner@house.ms.gov
Committees: Agriculture; Appropriations; Banking and Financial
Services; Conservation and Water Resources; Insurance; Management;
Transportation

Representative **Kenneth Walker** (D-District 27) . . . . . . . . . (601) 359-3360
Counties Represented: Attala (part), Leake (part), Madison (part),
Yazoo (part)
Term Expires: 2020
E-mail: kwalker@house.ms.gov
Committees: Agriculture; Conservation and Water Resources;
Education; Forestry; Workforce Development
Education: Jackson State U 1978

Representative **Percy W. Watson** (D-District 103) . . . . . . . . (601) 545-1051
Counties Represented: Forrest (part)                  Res: (601) 544-6490
Term Expires: 2020
P.O. Box 1767, Hattiesburg, MS 39403-1767
E-mail: pwatson@house.ms.gov
Committees: Appropriations; Ethics; Insurance; Judiciary A; Judiciary
En Banc; Public Health and Human Services; Public Utilities
Education: Iowa BA, JD

Representative **Tom Weathersby** (R-District 62) . . . . . . . . . (601) 845-2017
Counties Represented: Copiah (part), Rankin (part), Simpson (part)
Term Expires: 2020
3806 Highway 49 South, Florence, MS 39073
E-mail: tweathersby@house.ms.gov
Committees: Banking and Financial Services; Insurance; Public
Property; Ways and Means
Education: Southern Mississippi BS; Mississippi Col MEd

Representative **Jason White** (R-District 48) . . . . . . . . . . . . (662) 967-2015
Counties Represented: Attala (part), Carroll (part), Choctaw (part),
Holmes (part), Humphreys (part), Leake (part)
Term Expires: 2020
PO Box 246, West, MS 39192
E-mail: jwhite@house.ms.gov
Committees: Apportionment and Elections; Ethics; Judiciary B;
Judiciary En Banc; Medicaid; Public Health and Human Services;
Rules; Universities and Colleges; Ways and Means

*(continued on next page)*

**LEGISLATIVE BRANCH**

**Representatives** *continued*

Representative **Sonya Williams-Barnes** (D-District 119) . . (228) 863-7712
Counties Represented: Harrison (part)
Term Expires: 2020
2317 Searle Avenue, Gulfport, MS 39507
E-mail: swilliamsbarnes@house.ms.gov
Committees: Education; Gaming; Marine Resources; Ports, Harbors and Airports; Tourism

Representative **Patricia H. Willis** (R-District 95) . . . . . . . . (228) 867-6005
Counties Represented: Hancock (part), Harrison (part)
Term Expires: 2020
5565 Diamondhead Drive East, Diamondhead, MS 39525
P. O. Box 1018, Jackson, MS 39215
E-mail: pwillis@house.ms.gov
Committees: Corrections; Gaming; Judiciary B; Judiciary En Banc; Marine Resources; Military Affairs; Ports, Harbors and Airports; Tourism

Representative **Cory Wilson** (R-District 73) . . . . . . . . . . . . (601) 359-3360
Counties Represented: Hinds (part)
Term Expires: 2020
E-mail: cwilson@house.ms.gov
Committees: Apportionment and Elections; Compilation, Revision and Publication; Conservation and Water Resources; Ethics; Judiciary A; Judiciary En Banc; Transportation; Universities and Colleges

Representative **Adrienne Wooten** (D-District 71) . . . . . . . (601) 707-5705
Counties Represented: Hinds (part), Rankin (part)     Res: (601) 502-2444
Term Expires: 2020
P.O. Box 1617, Canton, MS 39046
E-mail: awooten@house.ms.gov
Committees: Insurance; Judiciary B; Judiciary En Banc; Municipalities; Public Health and Human Services; Universities and Colleges

Representative **Charles Young, Jr.** (D-District 82) . . . . . . . (601) 693-1961
Counties Represented: Lauderdale (part)
Term Expires: 2020
PO Box 5393, Meridian, MS 39301
E-mail: cyoung@house.ms.gov
Committees: Corrections; Medicaid; Public Property; Universities and Colleges

Representative
**Henry B. "Hank" Zuber III** (R-District 113) . . . . . . . . . . (228) 875-1097
Counties Represented: Jackson (part)     Res: (228) 875-4866
Term Expires: 2020
429 Hanley Road, Ocean Springs, MS 39564
E-mail: hzuber@house.ms.gov
Committees: Banking and Financial Services; Gaming; Insurance; Judiciary B; Judiciary En Banc; Medicaid; Ways and Means

District 29 **(Vacant)** . . . . . . . . . . . . . . . . . . . . . . . . . . . . . . (601) 359-3360
Note: A special election to fill this legislative vacancy will be held June 7, 2016.

# House Standing Committees

## Agriculture

**Majority Members**
Bill Pigott (R-99) *Chairman*
Vince Mangold (R-53)
  *Vice Chairman*
Manly Barton (R-109)
Donnie Bell (R-21)
Lester Carpenter (R-1)
Dan Eubanks (R-25)
Robert Foster (R-28)
Andrew "Andy" Gipson (R-77)
Mac Huddleston (R-15)
Chris Johnson (R-87)
Bill Kinkade (R-52)
John "Timmy" Ladner (R-93)
John Thomas "Trey" Lamar III
  (R-8)
Steve Massengill (R-13)
Doug McLeod (R-107)
Ken Morgan (R-100)
Karl Oliver (R-46)
Noah L. Sanford (R-90)
Bobby Shows (R-89)
Gary V. Staples (R-88)
Jerry R. Turner (R-18)

**Minority Members**
Nick Bain (D-2)
Deborah Butler Dixon (D-63)
Jarvis Dortch (D-66)
Michael T. Evans (D-45)
Karl Gibbs (D-36)
Gregory Holloway, Sr. (D-76)
Robert E. Huddleston (D-30)
Lataisha Jackson (D-11)
Orlando Paden (D-26)
Preston E. Sullivan (D-22)
Kenneth Walker (D-27)
Sara Richardson Thomas (D-31)

## Apportionment and Elections

**Majority Members**
William C. "Bill" Denny, Jr. (R-64)
  *Chairman*
Toby Barker (R-102)
Charles Jim Beckett (R-23)
Becky Currie (R-92)
Jeff Hale (R-24)
Ashley Henley (R-40)
Mac Huddleston (R-15)
Noah L. Sanford (R-90)
Jason White (R-48)
Cory Wilson (R-73)

**Minority Members**
Thomas Upton "Tom"
  Reynolds (D-33)
  *Vice Chairman*
Willie L. Bailey (D-49)
Edward Blackmon, Jr. (D-57)
Bryant W. Clark (D-47)
Angela Cockerham (D-96)
Tyrone Ellis (D-38)
Robert E. Huddleston (D-30)

## Appropriations

**Majority Members**
Herb Frierson (R-106) *Chairman*
Mac Huddleston (R-15)
  *Vice Chairman*
William Tracy Arnold (R-3)
Toby Barker (R-102)
Charles Jim Beckett (R-23)
Richard Bennett (R-120)
C. Scott Bounds (R-44)
Chris Brown (R-20)
Charles Busby (R-111)
Becky Currie (R-92)
Scott DeLano (R-117)
William C. "Bill" Denny, Jr. (R-64)
Casey Eure (R-116)
Andrew "Andy" Gipson (R-77)
John "Timmy" Ladner (R-93)
H. Nolan Mettetal (R-10)
Sam C. Mims V (R-97)
Alex Monsour (R-54)
John L. Moore (R-60)
John O. Read (R-112)
Bobby Shows (R-89)
Greg Snowden (R-83)
Gary V. Staples (R-88)
Jerry R. Turner (R-18)

**Minority Members**
Earle S. Banks (D-67)
Alyce Griffin Clarke (D-69)
Angela Cockerham (D-96)
Daniel Stephen "Steve" Holland
  (D-16)
Robert E. Huddleston (D-30)
David W. Myers (D-98)
Willie J. Perkins, Sr. (D-32)
Preston E. Sullivan (D-22)
Percy W. Watson (D-103)

## Banking and Financial Services

**Majority Members**
Henry B. "Hank" Zuber III (R-113)
  *Chairman*
Shane Aguirre (R-17)
William Tracy Arnold (R-3)
Mark Baker (R-74)
Charles Jim Beckett (R-23)
Donnie Bell (R-21)
C. Scott Bounds (R-44)
Chris Brown (R-20)
Larry Byrd (R-104)
Lester Carpenter (R-1)
Dan Eubanks (R-25)
Casey Eure (R-116)
Jeff Hale (R-24)
Joey Hood (R-35)
Chris Johnson (R-87)
H. Nolan Mettetal (R-10)
Margaret Ellis Rogers (R-14)
Ray Rogers (R-61)
Gary V. Staples (R-88)
Jerry R. Turner (R-18)
Tom Weathersby (R-62)

**Minority Members**
Kimberly L. Campbell (D-72)
  *Vice Chairman*
Cedric Burnett (D-9)
Alyce Griffin Clarke (D-69)
Robert Emil "Bob" Evans (D-91)
John Wesley Hines, Sr. (D-50)
Daniel Stephen "Steve" Holland
  (D-16)
Kevin Horan (D-34)
Kathy Sykes (D-70)

## Compilation, Revision and Publication

**Majority Members**
Philip Gunn (R-56) *Chairman*
Andrew "Andy" Gipson (R-77)
Greg Snowden (R-83)
Cory Wilson (R-73)

**Minority Members**
Kimberly L. Campbell (D-72)
Angela Cockerham (D-96)
Thomas Upton "Tom" Reynolds
  (D-33)

## Conservation and Water Resources

**Majority Members**
John O. Read (R-112) *Chairman*
Shane Barnett (R-86)
Manly Barton (R-109)
Chris Brown (R-20)
Charles Busby (R-111)
Larry Byrd (R-104)
Gary Alan Chism (R-37)
Casey Eure (R-116)
Vince Mangold (R-53)
Ken Morgan (R-100)
Bill Pigott (R-99)
Jerry R. Turner (R-18)
Cory Wilson (R-73)

**Minority Members**
Bryant W. Clark (D-47)
 *Vice Chairman*
Michael T. Evans (D-45)
Daniel Stephen "Steve" Holland
 (D-16)
Carl L. Mickens (D-42)
Preston E. Sullivan (D-22)
Kenneth Walker (D-27)

## Constitution

**Majority Members**
Brent L. Powell (R-59) *Chairman*
Dana Criswell (R-6) *Vice Chairman*
Chris Brown (R-20)
William C. "Bill" Denny, Jr. (R-64)
Dan Eubanks (R-25)
Robert Foster (R-28)
Ashley Henley (R-40)
Alex Monsour (R-54)
Jeffrey C. "Jeff" Smith (R-39)
Jody Steverson (R-4)

**Minority Members**
Christopher M. Bell (D-65)
Jay P. Hughes, Jr. (D-12)
Carl L. Mickens (D-42)
America "Chuck" Middleton (D-85)
Thomas Upton "Tom" Reynolds
 (D-33)

## Corrections

**Majority Members**
Bill Kinkade (R-52) *Chairman*
Joel Bomgar (R-58)
Ashley Henley (R-40)
Chris Johnson (R-87)
Doug McLeod (R-107)
Roun McNeal (R-105)
Karl Oliver (R-46)
Randy Rushing (R-78)
Mark K Tullos (R-79)
Patricia H. Willis (R-95)

**Minority Members**
Deborah Butler Dixon (D-63)
Tyrone Ellis (D-38)
Kevin Horan (D-34)
Robert E. Huddleston (D-30)
Carl L. Mickens (D-42)
Charles Young, Jr. (D-82)

## County Affairs

**Majority Members**
Larry Byrd (R-104) *Chairman*
Roun McNeal (R-105)
 *Vice Chairman*
Manly Barton (R-109)
Lester Carpenter (R-1)
Andrew "Andy" Gipson (R-77)
Steve Hopkins (R-7)
John Thomas "Trey" Lamar III
 (R-8)
Lyod B. "Rob" Roberson (R-43)
Ray Rogers (R-61)
Randy Rushing (R-78)
Noah L. Sanford (R-90)
Bobby Shows (R-89)
Mark K Tullos (R-79)

**Minority Members**
Willie L. Bailey (D-49)
Robert E. Huddleston (D-30)
Willie J. Perkins, Sr. (D-32)
Thomas Upton "Tom" Reynolds
 (D-33)
Preston E. Sullivan (D-22)

## Education

**Majority Members**
John L. Moore (R-60) *Chairman*
Lyod B. "Rob" Roberson (R-43)
 *Vice Chairman*
Toby Barker (R-102)
Richard Bennett (R-120)
Joel Bomgar (R-58)
Randy P. Boyd (R-19)
Charles Busby (R-111)
Gary Alan Chism (R-37)
Carolyn Crawford (R-121)
Dana Criswell (R-6)
Becky Currie (R-92)
Scott DeLano (R-117)
Mark S. Formby (R-108)
Herb Frierson (R-106)

**Minority Members**
Credell Calhoun (D-68)
Alyce Griffin Clarke (D-69)
Jarvis Dortch (D-66)
Robert Emil "Bob" Evans (D-91)
Gregory Holloway, Sr. (D-76)
Carl L. Mickens (D-42)
Orlando Paden (D-26)
Rufus "Pete" Straughter (D-51)
Sara Richardson Thomas (D-31)
Kenneth Walker (D-27)
Sonya Williams-Barnes (D-119)

**Majority Members** *continued*
Jeffrey S. "Jeff" Guice (R-114)
Ashley Henley (R-40)
Steve Hopkins (R-7)
Chris Johnson (R-87)
Vince Mangold (R-53)
Brad A. Touchstone (R-101)

## Enrolled Bills

**Majority Members**
Stephen A. Horne (R-81) *Chairman*
William Shirley (R-84)
 *Vice Chairman*
Randall H. Patterson (R-115)

**Minority Members**
America "Chuck" Middleton (D-85)
Orlando Paden (D-26)

## Ethics

**Majority Members**
Andrew "Andy" Gipson (R-77)
 *Chairman*
Mac Huddleston (R-15)
Ray Rogers (R-61)
Jason White (R-48)
Cory Wilson (R-73)

**Minority Members**
Percy W. Watson (D-103)
 *Vice Chairman*
Angela Cockerham (D-96)
Sara Richardson Thomas (D-31)

## Executive Contingent Fund

**Majority Members**
Bobby Shows (R-89) *Chairman*
Stephen A. Horne (R-81)
Randall H. Patterson (R-115)

**Minority Members**
Christopher M. Bell (D-65)
 *Vice Chairman*
Cedric Burnett (D-9)

## Forestry

**Majority Members**
Ken Morgan (R-100) *Chairman*
Karl Oliver (R-46) *Vice Chairman*
Shane Barnett (R-86)
Randy P. Boyd (R-19)
Bill Kinkade (R-52)
Vince Mangold (R-53)
Roun McNeal (R-105)
Bill Pigott (R-99)

**Minority Members**
America "Chuck" Middleton (D-85)
Preston E. Sullivan (D-22)
Kenneth Walker (D-27)

## Gaming

**Majority Members**
Richard Bennett (R-120) *Chairman*
John "Timmy" Ladner (R-93)
 *Vice Chairman*
Shane Aguirre (R-17)
Carolyn Crawford (R-121)
Scott DeLano (R-117)
Casey Eure (R-116)
Alex Monsour (R-54)
John O. Read (R-112)
Patricia H. Willis (R-95)
Henry B. "Hank" Zuber III (R-113)

**Minority Members**
Willie L. Bailey (D-49)
Christopher M. Bell (D-65)
Oscar Denton (D-55)
Deborah Butler Dixon (D-63)
John Wesley Hines, Sr. (D-50)
Robert L. Johnson III (D-94)
America "Chuck" Middleton (D-85)
Willie J. Perkins, Sr. (D-32)
Sonya Williams-Barnes (D-119)

## Insurance

**Majority Members**
Gary Alan Chism (R-37) *Chairman*
Brad A. Touchstone (R-101)
 *Vice Chairman*
Charles Jim Beckett (R-23)
Charles Busby (R-111)
Scott DeLano (R-117)
Dan Eubanks (R-25)
Mark S. Formby (R-108)
Andrew "Andy" Gipson (R-77)
Jeffrey S. "Jeff" Guice (R-114)
Jeff Hale (R-24)
Alex Monsour (R-54)
John L. Moore (R-60)
William Shirley (R-84)
Jody Steverson (R-4)
Jerry R. Turner (R-18)
Tom Weathersby (R-62)
Henry B. "Hank" Zuber III (R-113)

**Minority Members**
Earle S. Banks (D-67)
Christopher M. Bell (D-65)
Credell Calhoun (D-68)
Oscar Denton (D-55)
Jarvis Dortch (D-66)
John Wesley Hines, Sr. (D-50)
Willie J. Perkins, Sr. (D-32)
Omeria McDonald Scott (D-80)
Percy W. Watson (D-103)
Adrienne Wooten (D-71)

## Interstate Cooperation

**Majority Members**
Jeffrey S. "Jeff" Guice (R-114)
  *Chairman*
Steve Hopkins (R-7)
Stephen A. Horne (R-81)
Bill Pigott (R-99)

**Minority Members**
Kathy Sykes (D-70) *Vice Chairman*
Willie L. Bailey (D-49)
America "Chuck" Middleton (D-85)

## Investigative State Offices

**Majority Members**
Randall H. Patterson (R-115)
  *Chairman*
Mark Baker (R-74)
Randy P. Boyd (R-19)
Stephen A. Horne (R-81)
John "Timmy" Ladner (R-93)
Ray Rogers (R-61)

**Minority Members**
America "Chuck" Middleton (D-85)
  *Vice Chairman*
Jeramey Anderson (D-110)
Sara Richardson Thomas (D-31)

## Judiciary A

**Majority Members**
Mark Baker (R-74) *Chairman*
Cory Wilson (R-73) *Vice Chairman*
Shane Aguirre (R-17)
Charles Jim Beckett (R-23)
C. Scott Bounds (R-44)
Lester Carpenter (R-1)
Gary Alan Chism (R-37)
Carolyn Crawford (R-121)
Dana Criswell (R-6)
William C. "Bill" Denny, Jr. (R-64)
Greg Haney (R-118)
John Thomas "Trey" Lamar III
  (R-8)
Brent L. Powell (R-59)
Lyod B. "Rob" Roberson (R-43)
Jeffrey C. "Jeff" Smith (R-39)
Greg Snowden (R-83)
Brad A. Touchstone (R-101)
Mark K Tullos (R-79)

**Minority Members**
Earle S. Banks (D-67)
Edward Blackmon, Jr. (D-57)
Bryant W. Clark (D-47)
Angela Cockerham (D-96)
Robert Emil "Bob" Evans (D-91)
Jay P. Hughes, Jr. (D-12)
Robert L. Johnson III (D-94)
Willie J. Perkins, Sr. (D-32)
Thomas Upton "Tom" Reynolds
  (D-33)
Percy W. Watson (D-103)

## Judiciary B

**Majority Members**
Andrew "Andy" Gipson (R-77)
  *Chairman*
Joey Hood (R-35) *Vice Chairman*
William Tracy Arnold (R-3)
Shane Barnett (R-86)
Joel Bomgar (R-58)
John "Timmy" Ladner (R-93)
Roun McNeal (R-105)
Sam C. Mims V (R-97)
Alex Monsour (R-54)
John L. Moore (R-60)
Noah L. Sanford (R-90)
William Shirley (R-84)
Jason White (R-48)
Patricia H. Willis (R-95)
Henry B. "Hank" Zuber III (R-113)

**Minority Members**
Jeramey Anderson (D-110)
Willie L. Bailey (D-49)
Nick Bain (D-2)
David Baria (D-122)
Cedric Burnett (D-9)
Kimberly L. Campbell (D-72)
Deborah Butler Dixon (D-63)
Tyrone Ellis (D-38)
Kevin Horan (D-34)
Adrienne Wooten (D-71)

## Judiciary En Banc

**Majority Members**
Mark Baker (R-74) *Chairman*
Andrew "Andy" Gipson (R-77)
  *Vice Chairman*
Shane Aguirre (R-17)
William Tracy Arnold (R-3)
Shane Barnett (R-86)
Charles Jim Beckett (R-23)
Joel Bomgar (R-58)
Gary Alan Chism (R-37)
William C. "Bill" Denny, Jr. (R-64)
Dana Criswell (R-6)
Joey Hood (R-35)
John "Timmy" Ladner (R-93)
John Thomas "Trey" Lamar III
  (R-8)
Roun McNeal (R-105)

**Minority Members**
Jeramey Anderson (D-110)
Willie L. Bailey (D-49)
Nick Bain (D-2)
Earle S. Banks (D-67)
David Baria (D-122)
Edward Blackmon, Jr. (D-57)
Cedric Burnett (D-9)
Kimberly L. Campbell (D-72)
Bryant W. Clark (D-47)
Angela Cockerham (D-96)
Deborah Butler Dixon (D-63)
Tyrone Ellis (D-38)
Robert Emil "Bob" Evans (D-91)
Kevin Horan (D-34)
Jay P. Hughes, Jr. (D-12)
Robert L. Johnson III (D-94)

**Majority Members** *continued*
Sam C. Mims V (R-97)
Alex Monsour (R-54)
John L. Moore (R-60)
Brent L. Powell (R-59)
Lyod B. "Rob" Roberson (R-43)
Noah L. Sanford (R-90)
William Shirley (R-84)
Jeffrey C. "Jeff" Smith (R-39)
Greg Snowden (R-83)
Brad A. Touchstone (R-101)
Mark K Tullos (R-79)
Jason White (R-48)
Patricia H. Willis (R-95)
Cory Wilson (R-73)
Henry B. "Hank" Zuber III (R-113)

**Minority Members** *continued*
Willie J. Perkins, Sr. (D-32)
Thomas Upton "Tom" Reynolds
  (D-33)
Percy W. Watson (D-103)
Adrienne Wooten (D-71)

## Local and Private Legislation

**Majority Members**
Manly Barton (R-109) *Chairman*
Richard Bennett (R-120)
Gary Alan Chism (R-37)
Robert Foster (R-28)
Lyod B. "Rob" Roberson (R-43)

**Minority Members**
Lataisha Jackson (D-11)
  *Vice Chairman*
Rufus "Pete" Straughter (D-51)

## Management

**Majority Members**
Greg Snowden (R-83) *Chairman*
Richard Bennett (R-120)
C. Scott Bounds (R-44)
Chris Brown (R-20)
Larry Byrd (R-104)
Ray Rogers (R-61)
Jerry R. Turner (R-18)

**Minority Members**
Angela Cockerham (D-96)
  *Vice Chairman*
John Wesley Hines, Sr. (D-50)
Willie J. Perkins, Sr. (D-32)

## Marine Resources

**Majority Members**
Casey Eure (R-116) *Chairman*
Carolyn Crawford (R-121)
  *Vice Chairman*
Shane Barnett (R-86)
Mark S. Formby (R-108)
Greg Haney (R-118)
John "Timmy" Ladner (R-93)
Vince Mangold (R-53)
Randall H. Patterson (R-115)
Patricia H. Willis (R-95)

**Minority Members**
Jeramey Anderson (D-110)
Sonya Williams-Barnes (D-119)

## Medicaid

**Majority Members**
Chris Brown (R-20) *Chairman*
Joel Bomgar (R-58) *Vice Chairman*
Toby Barker (R-102)
Richard Bennett (R-120)
Becky Currie (R-92)
Joey Hood (R-35)
Doug McLeod (R-107)
H. Nolan Mettetal (R-10)
Sam C. Mims V (R-97)
William Shirley (R-84)
Jason White (R-48)
Henry B. "Hank" Zuber III (R-113)

**Minority Members**
Jarvis Dortch (D-66)
Daniel Stephen "Steve" Holland
  (D-16)
Jay P. Hughes, Jr. (D-12)
Robert L. Johnson III (D-94)
David W. Myers (D-98)
Omeria McDonald Scott (D-80)
Charles Young, Jr. (D-82)

## Military Affairs

**Majority Members**
Ray Rogers (R-61) *Chair*
Ashley Henley (R-40) *Vice Chair*
Manly Barton (R-109)
Steve Hopkins (R-7)
Mac Huddleston (R-15)
Vince Mangold (R-53)
Karl Oliver (R-46)
Randy Rushing (R-78)
Mark K Tullos (R-79)
Patricia H. Willis (R-95)

**Minority Members**
Credell Calhoun (D-68)
John Gary Faulkner (D-5)
Karl Gibbs (D-36)
Kabir Karriem (D-41)
David W. Myers (D-98)

## Municipalities

**Majority Members**
Randy Rushing (R-78) *Chairman*
Steve Hopkins (R-7) *Vice Chairman*
Joel Bomgar (R-58)
Lester Carpenter (R-1)
William C. "Bill" Denny, Jr. (R-64)
Robert Foster (R-28)
Andrew "Andy" Gipson (R-77)
Roun McNeal (R-105)
Lyod B. "Rob" Roberson (R-43)
Mark K Tullos (R-79)

**Minority Members**
Gregory Holloway, Sr. (D-76)
Edward Blackmon, Jr. (D-57)
Kabir Karriem (D-41)
David W. Myers (D-98)
Willie J. Perkins, Sr. (D-32)
Adrienne Wooten (D-71)

## Ports, Harbors and Airports

**Majority Members**
Alex Monsour (R-54) *Chairman*
Manly Barton (R-109)
Charles Busby (R-111)
Jeffrey S. "Jeff" Guice (R-114)
Greg Haney (R-118)
John O. Read (R-112)
Patricia H. Willis (R-95)

**Minority Members**
Sonya Williams-Barnes (D-119)
   *Vice Chair*
Willie L. Bailey (D-49)
Kabir Karriem (D-41)

## Public Health and Human Services

**Majority Members**
Sam C. Mims V (R-97) *Chairman*
Chris Johnson (R-87)
   *Vice Chairman*
Shane Aguirre (R-17)
Toby Barker (R-102)
C. Scott Bounds (R-44)
Chris Brown (R-20)
Larry Byrd (R-104)
Dan Eubanks (R-25)
Jeffrey S. "Jeff" Guice (R-114)
Joey Hood (R-35)
Mac Huddleston (R-15)
Doug McLeod (R-107)
H. Nolan Mettetal (R-10)
Brent L. Powell (R-59)
Noah L. Sanford (R-90)
Bobby Shows (R-89)
Brad A. Touchstone (R-101)
Jason White (R-48)

**Minority Members**
Bryant W. Clark (D-47)
Nick Bain (D-2)
Christopher M. Bell (D-65)
Cedric Burnett (D-9)
Deborah Butler Dixon (D-63)
Jarvis Dortch (D-66)
Orlando Paden (D-26)
Omeria McDonald Scott (D-80)
Kathy Sykes (D-70)
Percy W. Watson (D-103)
Adrienne Wooten (D-71)

## Public Property

**Majority Members**
Tom Weathersby (R-62) *Chairman*
Jeff Hale (R-24) *Vice Chairman*
Joel Bomgar (R-58)
Randy P. Boyd (R-19)
H. Nolan Mettetal (R-10)
Ken Morgan (R-100)
Karl Oliver (R-46)
John O. Read (R-112)
Ray Rogers (R-61)

**Minority Members**
Earle S. Banks (D-67)
Gregory Holloway, Sr. (D-76)
Lataisha Jackson (D-11)
Preston E. Sullivan (D-22)
Sara Richardson Thomas (D-31)
Charles Young, Jr. (D-82)

## Public Utilities

**Majority Members**
Charles Jim Beckett (R-23)
   *Chairman*
Jody Steverson (R-4)
   *Vice Chairman*
Richard Bennett (R-120)
Gary Alan Chism (R-37)
Casey Eure (R-116)
Mark S. Formby (R-108)
Joey Hood (R-35)
Steve Massengill (R-13)
Margaret Ellis Rogers (R-14)
Noah L. Sanford (R-90)
Bobby Shows (R-89)
Gary V. Staples (R-88)
Brad A. Touchstone (R-101)

**Minority Members**
Earle S. Banks (D-67)
David Baria (D-122)
Kimberly L. Campbell (D-72)
Michael T. Evans (D-45)
John Wesley Hines, Sr. (D-50)
Carl L. Mickens (D-42)
Tom Miles (D-75)
David W. Myers (D-98)
Kathy Sykes (D-70)
Percy W. Watson (D-103)

## Rules

**Majority Members**
Jason White (R-48) *Chairman*
John O. Read (R-112)
   *Vice Chairman*
Manly Barton (R-109)
Charles Jim Beckett (R-23)
Becky Currie (R-92)
Philip Gunn (R-56)
Mac Huddleston (R-15)
John L. Moore (R-60)
Greg Snowden (R-83)

**Minority Members**
Edward Blackmon, Jr. (D-57)
Gregory Holloway, Sr. (D-76)

## State Library

**Majority Members**
Margaret Ellis Rogers (R-14)
   *Chairman*
Ken Morgan (R-100)

**Minority Members**
America "Chuck" Middleton (D-85)

## Tourism

**Majority Members**
Becky Currie (R-92) *Chairman*
Richard Bennett (R-120)
Lester Carpenter (R-1)
Dana Criswell (R-6)
Casey Eure (R-116)
Jeffrey S. "Jeff" Guice (R-114)
Greg Haney (R-118)
Ashley Henley (R-40)
Steve Massengill (R-13)
Alex Monsour (R-54)
Randall H. Patterson (R-115)
Patricia H. Willis (R-95)

**Minority Members**
Sara Richardson Thomas (D-31)
   *Vice Chairman*
Willie L. Bailey (D-49)
Oscar Denton (D-55)
Kabir Karriem (D-41)
America "Chuck" Middleton (D-85)
Orlando Paden (D-26)
Omeria McDonald Scott (D-80)
Sonya Williams-Barnes (D-119)

## Transportation

**Majority Members**
Charles Busby (R-111) *Chairman*
Steve Massengill (R-13)
   *Vice Chairman*
William Tracy Arnold (R-3)
Mark Baker (R-74)
Manly Barton (R-109)
Larry Byrd (R-104)
Dana Criswell (R-6)
Robert Foster (R-28)
Andrew "Andy" Gipson (R-77)
Chris Johnson (R-87)
Vince Mangold (R-53)
Doug McLeod (R-107)
Alex Monsour (R-54)
John L. Moore (R-60)
Brent L. Powell (R-59)
Lyod B. "Rob" Roberson (R-43)
Jody Steverson (R-4)
Brad A. Touchstone (R-101)
Jerry R. Turner (R-18)
Cory Wilson (R-73)

**Minority Members**
Cedric Burnett (D-9)
Bryant W. Clark (D-47)
Oscar Denton (D-55)
John Gary Faulkner (D-5)
Daniel Stephen "Steve" Holland
   (D-16)
Robert L. Johnson III (D-94)
Thomas Upton "Tom" Reynolds
   (D-33)
Preston E. Sullivan (D-22)

## Universities and Colleges

**Majority Members**
H. Nolan Mettetal (R-10) *Chairman*
Shane Aguirre (R-17)
William Tracy Arnold (R-3)
Charles Jim Beckett (R-23)
Donnie Bell (R-21)
Carolyn Crawford (R-121)
Dana Criswell (R-6)
Steve Hopkins (R-7)
Mac Huddleston (R-15)
John Thomas "Trey" Lamar III
   (R-8)
Roun McNeal (R-105)
Bobby Shows (R-89)
Jody Steverson (R-4)
Jason White (R-48)
Cory Wilson (R-73)

**Minority Members**
Gregory Holloway, Sr. (D-76)
   *Vice Chair*
Jeramey Anderson (D-110)
David Baria (D-122)
Credell Calhoun (D-68)
Alyce Griffin Clarke (D-69)
Robert Emil "Bob" Evans (D-91)
John Gary Faulkner (D-5)
Lataisha Jackson (D-11)
Orlando Paden (D-26)
Rufus "Pete" Straughter (D-51)
Adrienne Wooten (D-71)
Charles Young, Jr. (D-82)

**LEGISLATIVE BRANCH**

# Ways and Means

**Majority Members**
Jeffrey C. "Jeff" Smith (R-39)
  *Chairman*
John Thomas "Trey"
  Lamar III (R-8)
  *Vice Chairman*
Mark Baker (R-74)
Donnie Bell (R-21)
Lester Carpenter (R-1)
Gary Alan Chism (R-37)
Carolyn Crawford (R-121)
Mark S. Formby (R-108)
Jeffrey S. "Jeff" Guice (R-114)
Joey Hood (R-35)
Stephen A. Horne (R-81)
Bill Kinkade (R-52)
Doug McLeod (R-107)
Ken Morgan (R-100)
Randall H. Patterson (R-115)
Brent L. Powell (R-59)
Margaret Ellis Rogers (R-14)
Ray Rogers (R-61)
Randy Rushing (R-78)
Jody Steverson (R-4)
Tom Weathersby (R-62)
Jason White (R-48)
Henry B. "Hank" Zuber III (R-113)

**Minority Members**
Willie L. Bailey (D-49)
Edward Blackmon, Jr. (D-57)
Credell Calhoun (D-68)
Tyrone Ellis (D-38)
Robert L. Johnson III (D-94)
America "Chuck" Middleton (D-85)
Willie J. Perkins, Sr. (D-32)
Thomas Upton "Tom" Reynolds
  (D-33)
Omeria McDonald Scott (D-80)
Rufus "Pete" Straughter (D-51)

# Wildlife, Fisheries and Parks

**Majority Members**
C. Scott Bounds (R-44) *Chairman*
Shane Barnett (R-86)
  *Vice Chairman*
Lester Carpenter (R-1)
Herb Frierson (R-106)
Steve Hopkins (R-7)
Bill Kinkade (R-52)
John Thomas "Trey" Lamar III
  (R-8)
Vince Mangold (R-53)
Ken Morgan (R-100)
Karl Oliver (R-46)

**Minority Members**
Bryant W. Clark (D-47)
Angela Cockerham (D-96)
Michael T. Evans (D-45)
Karl Gibbs (D-36)
Robert L. Johnson III (D-94)

# Workforce Development

**Majority Members**
Donnie Bell (R-21) *Chair*
Doug McLeod (R-107) *Vice Chair*
Robert Foster (R-28)
Herb Frierson (R-106)
Jeff Hale (R-24)
Greg Haney (R-118)
Ashley Henley (R-40)
John "Timmy" Ladner (R-93)
Steve Massengill (R-13)
Roun McNeal (R-105)

**Minority Members**
Oscar Denton (D-55)
Robert E. Huddleston (D-30)
Carl L. Mickens (D-42)
Kathy Sykes (D-70)
Kenneth Walker (D-27)

# Youth and Family Affairs

**Majority Members**
Joel Bomgar (R-58)
Dan Eubanks (R-25)
Ashley Henley (R-40)
Brad A. Touchstone (R-101)
Mark K Tullos (R-79)

**Minority Members**
Deborah Butler Dixon (D-63) *Chair*
Karl Gibbs (D-36) *Vice Chair*
David Baria (D-122)
Alyce Griffin Clarke (D-69)
John Gary Faulkner (D-5)
Sara Richardson Thomas (D-31)

# Missouri General Assembly

State Capitol Building, Jefferson City, MO 65101
Tel: (573) 751-3824  Internet: www.moga.mo.gov

# Missouri Senate

State Capitol Building, 201 West Capitol Avenue,
Jefferson City, MO 65101
Tel: (573) 751-3824  Fax: (573) 751-2230  Internet: www.senate.mo.gov

President of the Senate **Peter D. Kinder** (R) . . . . . . . . . . . . (573) 751-4727
  Affiliation: Lieutenant Governor, Office of the Lieutenant Governor,
  State of Missouri
  State Capitol, Room 224, Jefferson City, MO 65101
  Education: St Mary's U (TX) 1979 JD
President Pro Tem **Ronald "Ron" Richard** (R) . . . . . . . . . (573) 751-2173
  Education: Missouri Southern State Col 1969 BA;
  Southwest Missouri State 1971 MA
Majority Floor Leader **Mike Kehoe** (R) . . . . . . . . . . . . . . . (573) 751-2076
Assistant Majority Floor Leader
  **Robert F. "Bob" Onder** (R) . . . . . . . . . . . . . . . . . . . . . (573) 751-3824
Majority Caucus Chairman **Eric Schmitt** (R) . . . . . . . . . . . (573) 751-2853
Majority Caucus Secretary **Jay Wasson** (R) . . . . . . . . . . . . (573) 751-1503
Majority Caucus Whip **Brian Munzlinger** (R) . . . . . . . . . . (573) 751-7985
  Education: Missouri 1978 BSAg
Minority Floor Leader **Joseph "Joe" Keaveny** (D) . . . . . . (573) 751-3599
Assistant Minority Floor Leader
  **Regina "Gina" Walsh** (D) . . . . . . . . . . . . . . . . . . . . . . (573) 751-2420
Minority Caucus Chair **Shalonn "Kiki" Curls** (D) . . . . . . . (573) 751-3158
Minority Caucus Secretary **Jason R. Holsman** (D) . . . . . . . (573) 751-6607
  Education: Kansas BA; Norwich 2003 MA
Minority Caucus Whip **Maria N. Chappelle-Nadal** (D) . . . (573) 751-4106
Secretary of the Senate **Nancy Sell** . . . . . . . . . . . . . . . . . . (573) 751-3766
  E-mail: nancy.sell@senate.mo.gov

# Senators

**Party Affiliation Statistics:** Republicans: 24, Democrats: 8, Vacancies: 2

Senator **Dan W. Brown** (R-District 16) Room 419 . . . . . . . (573) 751-5713
  Counties Represented: Camden, Crawford, Dent, Phelps, Pulaski
  Term Expires: 2019
  E-mail: dan.brown@senate.mo.gov
  Committees: Agriculture, Food Production and Outdoor Resources;
  Appropriations; Education; Joint MO Health Net; Veterans' Affairs and
  Health
Senator **Maria N. Chappelle-Nadal** (D-District 14)
  Room 330 . . . . . . . . . . . . . . . . . . . . . . . . . . . . . . . . . (573) 751-4106
  Counties Represented: St. Louis (part)        Fax: (573) 751-0467
  Term Expires: 2019
  E-mail: maria.chappellenadal@senate.mo.gov
  Committees: Education; Joint Public Employee Retirement;
  Joint Transportation Oversight; Seniors, Families and Children;
  Transportation, Infrastructure, and Public Safety; Veterans' Affairs and
  Health
Senator **Mike Cunningham** (R-District 33) Room 331 . . . . (573) 751-1882
  Counties Represented: Douglas, Howell, Ozark, Ripley, Texas, Webster,
  Wright
  Term Expires: 2017
  E-mail: mike.cunningham@senate.mo.gov
  Committees: Commerce, Consumer Protection, Energy and the
  Environment; Financial and Governmental Organizations and Elections;
  Governmental Accountability and Fiscal Oversight; Veterans' Affairs
  and Health
  Education: Truman State 1972 BSBA
Senator **Shalonn "Kiki" Curls** (D-District 9) Room 434 . . . (573) 751-3158
  Counties Represented: Jackson (part)
  Term Expires: 2017
  E-mail: shalonn.curls@senate.mo.gov
  Committees: Agriculture, Food Production and Outdoor Resources;
  Appropriations; Gubernatorial Appointments; Jobs, Economic
  Development and Local Government; Joint Capital Improvements and
  Leases Oversight; Joint Corrections; Joint MO Health Net; Small
  Business, Insurance and Industry; Transportation, Infrastructure, and
  Public Safety

Senator **Bob Dixon** (R-District 30) Room 332 . . . . . . . . . . . (573) 751-2583
Counties Represented: Greene (part)  Fax: (573) 526-1305
Term Expires: 2019
E-mail: bob.dixon@senate.mo.gov
Committees: Jobs, Economic Development and Local Government;
Joint Transportation Oversight; Judiciary and Civil and Criminal
Jurisprudence; Rules, Joint Rules, Resolutions and Ethics;
Transportation, Infrastructure, and Public Safety; Ways and Means
Education: Drury Col 1997 BSBA; Drury U 2009 MEd

Senator **Edgar G. H. "Ed" Emery** (R-District 31)
Room 431 . . . . . . . . . . . . . . . . . . . . . . . . . . . . . . . . . . (573) 751-2108
Counties Represented: Barton, Bates, Cass, Henry, Vernon
Term Expires: 2017
E-mail: ed.emery@senate.mo.gov
Committees: Commerce, Consumer Protection, Energy and the
Environment; Education; Gubernatorial Appointments; Judiciary and
Civil and Criminal Jurisprudence; Ways and Means
Education: Missouri (Rolla) 1972 BS

Senator **Dan Hegeman** (R-District 12) . . . . . . . . . . . . . . . (573) 751-3824
Counties Represented: Andrew, Atchison, Clay (part), Clinton, Daviess,
DeKalb, Gentry, Grundy, Harrison, Holt, Mercer, Nodaway, Putnam,
Sullivan, Worth
Term Expires: 2019
E-mail: dan.hegeman@senate.mo.gov
Committees: Agriculture, Food Production and Outdoor Resources;
Financial and Governmental Organizations and Elections; General Laws
and Pensions; Jobs, Economic Development and Local Government

Senator **Jason R. Holsman** (D-District 7) Room 329 . . . . . (573) 751-6607
Counties Represented: Jackson (part)
Term Expires: 2017
E-mail: jason.holsman@senate.mo.gov
Committees: Agriculture, Food Production and Outdoor Resources;
Commerce, Consumer Protection, Energy and the Environment;
Education; Jobs, Economic Development and Local Government; Joint
Education

Senator **Joseph "Joe" Keaveny** (D-District 4)
Room 428 . . . . . . . . . . . . . . . . . . . . . . . . . . . . . . . . . . (573) 751-3599
Counties Represented: St. Louis (part), St. Louis  Fax: (573) 751-0266
City (part)
Term Expires: 2019
E-mail: joseph.keaveny@senate.mo.gov
Committees: Administration; Commerce, Consumer Protection, Energy
and the Environment; Financial and Governmental Organizations
and Elections; General Laws and Pensions; Joint Public Employee
Retirement; Judiciary and Civil and Criminal Jurisprudence; Progress
and Development; Rules, Joint Rules, Resolutions and Ethics

Senator **Mike Kehoe** (R-District 6) Room 220 . . . . . . . . . . (573) 751-2076
Counties Represented: Cole, Gasconade, Maries,  Fax: (573) 751-2582
Miller, Moniteau, Morgan, Osage
Term Expires: 2019
E-mail: mike.kehoe@senate.mo.gov
Committees: Administration; Appropriations; Commerce, Consumer
Protection, Energy and the Environment; Governmental Accountability
and Fiscal Oversight; Joint Corrections; Joint Public Employee
Retirement; Joint Transportation Oversight

Senator **Will Kraus** (R-District 8) Room 418 . . . . . . . . . . . (573) 751-1464
Counties Represented: Jackson (part)
Term Expires: 2019
E-mail: will.kraus@senate.mo.gov
Committees: Commerce, Consumer Protection, Energy and the
Environment; Financial and Governmental Organizations and Elections;
Jobs, Economic Development and Local Government; Seniors, Families
and Children; Ways and Means

Senator **Doug Libla** (R-District 25) Room 226 . . . . . . . . . . (573) 751-4843
Counties Represented: Butler, Carter, Dunklin, Mississippi, New
Madrid, Pemiscot, Shannon, Stoddard
Term Expires: 2017
E-mail: doug.libla@senate.mo.gov
Committees: Agriculture, Food Production and Outdoor Resources;
Education; Joint Transportation Oversight; Rules, Joint Rules,
Resolutions and Ethics; Seniors, Families and Children; Small
Business, Insurance and Industry; Transportation, Infrastructure, and
Public Safety

Senator **Brian Munzlinger** (R-District 18) Room 331A . . . . (573) 751-7985
Counties Represented: Adair, Chariton, Clark,  Fax: (573) 522-3722
Knox, Lewis, Linn, Macon, Marion, Pike, Ralls, Randolph, Schuyler,
Scotland, Shelby
Term Expires: 2019
E-mail: brian.munzlinger@senate.mo.gov
Committees: Agriculture, Food Production and Outdoor Resources;
Gubernatorial Appointments; Joint Transportation Oversight; Small
Business, Insurance and Industry; Transportation, Infrastructure, and
Public Safety

Senator **Jamilah Nasheed** (D-District 5) Room 328 . . . . . . (573) 751-4415
Counties Represented: St. Louis City (part)
Term Expires: 2017
E-mail: jamilah.nasheed@senate.mo.gov
Committees: Appropriations; Governmental Accountability and Fiscal
Oversight; Gubernatorial Appointments; Jobs, Economic Development
and Local Government; Joint Corrections; Joint Education

Senator **Robert F. "Bob" Onder** (R-District 2) . . . . . . . . . . (573) 751-3824
Counties Represented: St. Charles (part)
Term Expires: 2019
E-mail: bob.onder@senate.mo.gov
Committees: Education; General Laws and Pensions; Judiciary and
Civil and Criminal Jurisprudence; Veterans' Affairs and Health; Ways
and Means

Senator **Michael "Mike" Parson** (R-District 28)
Room 420 . . . . . . . . . . . . . . . . . . . . . . . . . . . . . . . . . . (573) 751-8793
Counties Represented: Benton, Cedar, Dallas, Hickory, Laclede, Pettis,
Polk, St. Clair
Term Expires: 2019
E-mail: mparson@senate.mo.gov
Committees: Agriculture, Food Production and Outdoor Resources;
Appropriations; Small Business, Insurance and Industry

Senator **David Pearce** (R-District 21) Room 227 . . . . . . . . (573) 751-2272
Counties Represented: Caldwell, Carroll, Howard,  Fax: (573) 526-7381
Johnson, Lafayette, Livingston, Ray, Saline
Term Expires: 2017
E-mail: david.pearce@senate.mo.gov
Committees: Agriculture, Food Production and Outdoor Resources;
Appropriations; Education; Joint Capital Improvements and Leases
Oversight; Joint Education
Education: Missouri 1984 BS

Senator **Ronald "Ron" Richard** (R-District 32)
Room 321 . . . . . . . . . . . . . . . . . . . . . . . . . . . . . . . . . . (573) 751-2173
Counties Represented: Dade, Jasper, Newton
Term Expires: 2019
E-mail: ronald.richard@senate.mo.gov
Committees: Administration; Gubernatorial Appointments; Rules, Joint
Rules, Resolutions and Ethics

Senator **Jeanie Riddle** (R-District 10) . . . . . . . . . . . . . . . . (573) 751-3824
Counties Represented: Audrain, Callaway, Lincoln, Monroe,
Montgomery, Warren
Term Expires: 2019
E-mail: jeanie.riddle@senate.mo.gov
Committees: Commerce, Consumer Protection, Energy and the
Environment; Financial and Governmental Organizations and Elections;
Governmental Accountability and Fiscal Oversight; Joint Child Abuse
and Neglect; Joint Education; Seniors, Families and Children

Senator **Gary Romine** (R-District 3) Room 334 . . . . . . . . . (573) 751-4008
Counties Represented: Iron, Jefferson (part), Reynolds, St. Francois,
Ste. Genevieve, Washington
Term Expires: 2017
E-mail: gary.romine@senate.mo.gov
Committees: Commerce, Consumer Protection, Energy and the
Environment; Education; Jobs, Economic Development and Local
Government; Joint Education; Seniors, Families and Children;
Transportation, Infrastructure, and Public Safety
Education: Central Missouri State 1978 BS

Senator **David Sater** (R-District 29) Room 433 . . . . . . . . . (573) 751-1480
Counties Represented: Barry, Lawrence, McDonald, Stone, Taney
Term Expires: 2017
E-mail: davidds@centurytel.net
E-mail: david.sater@senate.mo.gov
Committees: Appropriations; Financial and Governmental Organizations
and Elections; Joint Gaming and Wagering; Seniors, Families and
Children; Veterans' Affairs and Health
Education: Southwest Missouri State 1969 BS;
Missouri (Kansas City) 1972

Senator **Robert "Rob" Schaaf** (R-District 34)
Room 319 . . . . . . . . . . . . . . . . . . . . . . . . . . . . . . . . . . (573) 751-2183
Counties Represented: Buchanan, Platte
Term Expires: 2019
Committees: Appropriations; General Laws and Pensions; Gubernatorial
Appointments; Joint Public Employee Retirement; Veterans' Affairs and
Health
Education: Missouri Western State Col 1979 BS;
Saint Louis U 1983 MD

*(continued on next page)*

LEGISLATIVE BRANCH

**Senators** *continued*

Senator **Kurt Schaefer** (R-District 19) Room 221 . . . . . . . (573) 751-3931
Counties Represented: Boone, Cooper     Fax: (573) 751-4320
Term Expires: 2017
E-mail: kurt.schaefer@senate.mo.gov
Committees: Appropriations; Gubernatorial Appointments; Joint Capital
Improvements and Leases Oversight; Joint Education; Joint MO Health
Net; Judiciary and Civil and Criminal Jurisprudence
Education: Missouri 1990 BA; Vermont Law 1995 JD, 1996 MSL

Senator **Dave Schatz** (R-District 26) . . . . . . . . . . . . . . . . . (573) 751-3824
Counties Represented: Franklin, St. Louis (part)
Term Expires: 2019
E-mail: dave.schatz@senate.mo.gov
Committees: Commerce, Consumer Protection, Energy and the
Environment; General Laws and Pensions; Gubernatorial Appointments;
Jobs, Economic Development and Local Government; Joint
Transportation Oversight; Transportation, Infrastructure, and Public
Safety

Senator **Eric Schmitt** (R-District 15) Room 320 . . . . . . . . (573) 751-2853
Counties Represented: St. Louis (part)
Term Expires: 2017
E-mail: eschmitt@senate.mo.gov
Committees: Gubernatorial Appointments; Jobs, Economic
Development and Local Government; Joint MO Health Net; Judiciary
and Civil and Criminal Jurisprudence; Veterans' Affairs and Health

Senator **Jill Schupp** (D-District 24) . . . . . . . . . . . . . . . . . . (573) 751-3824
Counties Represented: St. Louis (part)
Term Expires: 2019
E-mail: jill.schupp@senate.mo.gov
Committees: General Laws and Pensions; Progress and Development;
Seniors, Families and Children; Veterans' Affairs and Health

Senator **Scott Sifton** (D-District 1) Room 425 . . . . . . . . . . (573) 751-0220
Counties Represented: St. Louis (part)
Term Expires: 2017
E-mail: scott.sifton@senate.mo.gov
Committees: Commerce, Consumer Protection, Energy and the
Environment; Financial and Governmental Organizations and Elections;
Judiciary and Civil and Criminal Jurisprudence; Veterans' Affairs and
Health; Ways and Means
Education: Truman State 1996 BS; Michigan 1999 JD

Senator **Ryan Silvey** (R-District 17) Room 429 . . . . . . . . . (573) 751-5282
Counties Represented: Clay (part)
Term Expires: 2017
E-mail: ryan.silvey@senate.mo.gov
Committees: Appropriations; Governmental Accountability and Fiscal
Oversight; Joint Capital Improvements and Leases Oversight; Joint
Gaming and Wagering; Progress and Development; Veterans' Affairs
and Health
Education: Bob Jones U

Senator **Wayne Wallingford** (R-District 27) Room 225 . . . . (573) 751-2459
Counties Represented: Bollinger, Cape Girardeau, Madison, Perry,
Scott, Wayne
Term Expires: 2017
E-mail: wayne.wallingford@senate.mo.gov
Committees: Commerce, Consumer Protection, Energy and the
Environment; Financial and Governmental Organizations and Elections;
Joint Public Employee Retirement; Progress and Development; Rules,
Joint Rules, Resolutions and Ethics; Small Business, Insurance and
Industry; Ways and Means
Education: Nebraska (Omaha) 1968 BS; Central Michigan 1983 MA

Senator **Regina "Gina" Walsh** (D-District 13)
Room 427 . . . . . . . . . . . . . . . . . . . . . . . . . . . . . . . . . . . . . (573) 751-2420
Counties Represented: St. Louis (part)    Fax: (573) 751-1598
Term Expires: 2017
E-mail: gina.walsh@senate.mo.gov
Committees: Administration; Appropriations; Joint Capital
Improvements and Leases Oversight; Joint Public Employee
Retirement; Progress and Development; Rules, Joint Rules, Resolutions
and Ethics; Small Business, Insurance and Industry

Senator **Jay Wasson** (R-District 20) Room 323 . . . . . . . . . (573) 751-1503
Counties Represented: Christian, Greene (part)
Term Expires: 2019
E-mail: jay.wasson@senate.mo.gov
Committees: Financial and Governmental Organizations and Elections;
Governmental Accountability and Fiscal Oversight; Jobs, Economic
Development and Local Government; Joint Corrections; Small
Business, Insurance and Industry

Senator **Paul Wieland** (R-District 22) . . . . . . . . . . . . . . . . . (573) 751-3824
Counties Represented: Jefferson (part)
Term Expires: 2019
E-mail: paul.wieland@senate.mo.gov
Committees: Financial and Governmental Organizations and Elections;
General Laws and Pensions; Jobs, Economic Development and Local
Government; Joint Education; Small Business, Insurance and Industry

District 11 **(Vacant)** . . . . . . . . . . . . . . . . . . . . . . . . . . . . . . (573) 751-3824
Note: A general election to fill this legislative vacancy will be held on
November 8, 2016.

District 23 **(Vacant)** . . . . . . . . . . . . . . . . . . . . . . . . . . . . . . (573) 751-3824
Note: A general election to fill this legislative vacancy will be held on
November 8, 2016.

# Senate Standing Committees

## Administration

| Majority Members | Minority Members |
|---|---|
| Ronald "Ron" Richard (R-32) *Vice Chair* | Joseph "Joe" Keaveny (D-4) |
| Mike Kehoe (R-6) | Regina "Gina" Walsh (D-13) |

## Agriculture, Food Production and Outdoor Resources

| Majority Members | Minority Members |
|---|---|
| Brian Munzlinger (R-18) *Chair* | Shalonn "Kiki" Curls (D-9) |
| Doug Libla (R-25) *Vice Chair* | Jason R. Holsman (D-7) |
| Dan W. Brown (R-16) | |
| Dan Hegeman (R-12) | |
| Michael "Mike" Parson (R-28) | |
| David Pearce (R-21) | |

## Appropriations

| Majority Members | Minority Members |
|---|---|
| Kurt Schaefer (R-19) *Chair* | Shalonn "Kiki" Curls (D-9) |
| Ryan Silvey (R-17) *Vice Chair* | Jamilah Nasheed (D-5) |
| Dan W. Brown (R-16) | Regina "Gina" Walsh (D-13) |
| Mike Kehoe (R-6) | |
| Michael "Mike" Parson (R-28) | |
| David Pearce (R-21) | |
| David Sater (R-29) | |
| Robert "Rob" Schaaf (R-34) | |

## Commerce, Consumer Protection, Energy and the Environment

| Majority Members | Minority Members |
|---|---|
| Mike Kehoe (R-6) *Chair* | Jason R. Holsman (D-7) |
| Edgar G. H. "Ed" Emery (R-31) *Vice Chair* | Joseph "Joe" Keaveny (D-4) |
| Mike Cunningham (R-33) | Scott Sifton (D-1) |
| Will Kraus (R-8) | |
| Jeanie Riddle (R-10) | |
| Gary Romine (R-3) | |
| Dave Schatz (R-26) | |
| Wayne Wallingford (R-27) | |

## Education

| Majority Members | Minority Members |
|---|---|
| David Pearce (R-21) *Chair* | Maria N. Chappelle-Nadal (D-14) |
| Gary Romine (R-3) *Vice Chair* | Jason R. Holsman (D-7) |
| Dan W. Brown (R-16) | |
| Edgar G. H. "Ed" Emery (R-31) | |
| Doug Libla (R-25) | |
| Robert F. "Bob" Onder (R-2) | |

## Financial and Governmental Organizations and Elections

| Majority Members | Minority Members |
|---|---|
| Jay Wasson (R-20) *Chair* | Joseph "Joe" Keaveny (D-4) |
| Mike Cunningham (R-33) *Vice Chair* | Scott Sifton (D-1) |
| Dan Hegeman (R-12) | |
| Will Kraus (R-8) | |
| Jeanie Riddle (R-10) | |
| David Sater (R-29) | |
| Wayne Wallingford (R-27) | |
| Paul Wieland (R-22) | |

## General Laws and Pensions

| Majority Members | Minority Members |
|---|---|
| Robert "Rob" Schaaf (R-34) *Chair* | Joseph "Joe" Keaveny (D-4) |
| Paul Wieland (R-22) *Vice Chair* | Jill Schupp (D-24) |
| Dan Hegeman (R-12) | |
| Robert F. "Bob" Onder (R-2) | |
| Dave Schatz (R-26) | |

## Governmental Accountability and Fiscal Oversight

| Majority Members | Minority Members |
|---|---|
| Mike Cunningham (R-33) *Chair* | Jamilah Nasheed (D-5) |
| Ryan Silvey (R-17) *Vice Chair* | |
| Mike Kehoe (R-6) | |
| Jeanie Riddle (R-10) | |
| Jay Wasson (R-20) | |

## Gubernatorial Appointments

| Majority Members | Minority Members |
|---|---|
| Ronald "Ron" Richard (R-32) *Vice Chair* | Shalonn "Kiki" Curls (D-9) |
| | Jamilah Nasheed (D-5) |
| Edgar G. H. "Ed" Emery (R-31) | |
| Brian Munzlinger (R-18) | |
| Robert "Rob" Schaaf (R-34) | |
| Kurt Schaefer (R-19) | |
| Dave Schatz (R-26) | |
| Eric Schmitt (R-15) | |

## Jobs, Economic Development and Local Government

| Majority Members | Minority Members |
|---|---|
| Eric Schmitt (R-15) *Chair* | Shalonn "Kiki" Curls (D-9) |
| Dan Hegeman (R-12) *Vice Chair* | Jason R. Holsman (D-7) |
| Bob Dixon (R-30) | Jamilah Nasheed (D-5) |
| Will Kraus (R-8) | |
| Gary Romine (R-3) | |
| Dave Schatz (R-26) | |
| Jay Wasson (R-20) | |
| Paul Wieland (R-22) | |

## Judiciary and Civil and Criminal Jurisprudence

| Majority Members | Minority Members |
|---|---|
| Bob Dixon (R-30) *Chair* | Joseph "Joe" Keaveny (D-4) |
| Robert F. "Bob" Onder (R-2) *Vice Chair* | Scott Sifton (D-1) |
| Edgar G. H. "Ed" Emery (R-31) | |
| Kurt Schaefer (R-19) | |
| Eric Schmitt (R-15) | |

## Progress and Development

| Majority Members | Minority Members |
|---|---|
| Ryan Silvey (R-17) | Joseph "Joe" Keaveny (D-4) *Chair* |
| Wayne Wallingford (R-27) | Regina "Gina" Walsh (D-13) *Vice Chair* |
| | Jill Schupp (D-24) |

## Rules, Joint Rules, Resolutions and Ethics

| Majority Members | Minority Members |
|---|---|
| Ronald "Ron" Richard (R-32) *Chair* | Joseph "Joe" Keaveny (D-4) |
| Bob Dixon (R-30) | Regina "Gina" Walsh (D-13) |
| Doug Libla (R-25) | |
| Wayne Wallingford (R-27) | |

## Seniors, Families and Children

| Majority Members | Minority Members |
|---|---|
| David Sater (R-29) *Chair* | Maria N. Chappelle-Nadal (D-14) |
| Jeanie Riddle (R-10) *Vice Chair* | Jill Schupp (D-24) |
| Will Kraus (R-8) | |
| Doug Libla (R-25) | |
| Gary Romine (R-3) | |

## Small Business, Insurance and Industry

| Majority Members | Minority Members |
|---|---|
| Michael "Mike" Parson (R-28) *Chair* | Shalonn "Kiki" Curls (D-9) |
| | Regina "Gina" Walsh (D-13) |
| Brian Munzlinger (R-18) | |
| Doug Libla (R-25) | |
| Wayne Wallingford (R-27) | |
| Jay Wasson (R-20) | |
| Paul Wieland (R-22) | |

## Transportation, Infrastructure, and Public Safety

| Majority Members | Minority Members |
|---|---|
| Doug Libla (R-25) *Chair* | Maria N. Chappelle-Nadal (D-14) |
| Dave Schatz (R-26) *Vice Chair* | Shalonn "Kiki" Curls (D-9) |
| Bob Dixon (R-30) | |
| Brian Munzlinger (R-18) | |
| Gary Romine (R-3) | |

## Veterans' Affairs and Health

| Majority Members | Minority Members |
|---|---|
| Dan W. Brown (R-16) *Chair* | Maria N. Chappelle-Nadal (D-14) |
| Robert "Rob" Schaaf (R-34) *Vice Chair* | Jill Schupp (D-24) |
| | Scott Sifton (D-1) |
| Mike Cunningham (R-33) | |
| Robert F. "Bob" Onder (R-2) | |
| David Sater (R-29) | |
| Eric Schmitt (R-15) | |
| Ryan Silvey (R-17) | |

## Ways and Means

| Majority Members | Minority Members |
|---|---|
| Will Kraus (R-8) *Chair* | Scott Sifton (D-1) |
| Wayne Wallingford (R-27) *Vice Chair* | |
| Bob Dixon (R-30) | |
| Edgar G. H. "Ed" Emery (R-31) | |
| Robert F. "Bob" Onder (R-2) | |

# Missouri House of Representatives

201 West Capitol Avenue, Room 306C, Jefferson City, MO 65101
Tel: (573) 751-3829  Internet: www.house.mo.gov

Speaker of the House **Todd Richardson** (R) . . . . . . . . . . . .(573) 751-4039
Speaker Pro Tem **Denny L. Hoskins** (R) . . . . . . . . . . . . . (573) 751-4302
Majority Floor Leader **Mike Cierpiot** (R) . . . . . . . . . . . . . .(573) 751-0907
Majority Whip **Delus Johnson** (R) . . . . . . . . . . . . . . . . . .(573) 751-3666
Majority Caucus Chair **Shelley "White" Keeney** (R) . . . . .(573) 751-5912
Majority Caucus Secretary **Mike Bernskoetter** (R) . . . . . . .(573) 751-0665
Minority Leader **Jacob Hummel** (D) . . . . . . . . . . . . . . . . .(573) 751-0438
Assistant Minority Floor Leader
  **Gail McCann Beatty** (D) . . . . . . . . . . . . . . . . . . . . . . . (573) 751-2124
Minority Whip **John Joseph Rizzo** (D) . . . . . . . . . . . . . . .(573) 751-3310
Minority Caucus Chair **Gina Mitten** (D) . . . . . . . . . . . . . .(573) 751-2883
  Education: Missouri (St Louis) 2001 BGS;
  Washington U (MO) 2005 JD
Minority Caucus Vice Chair **Jon Carpenter** (D) . . . . . . . . (573) 751-4787
  Education: USC 2010 BA
Minority Caucus Secretary **Karla May** (D) . . . . . . . . . . . . .(573) 751-2198
Chief Clerk of the House **D. Adam Crumbliss** . . . . . . . . . .(573) 751-3829

# Representatives

**Party Affiliation Statistics:** Republicans: 116, Democrats: 45, Independents: 1, Vacancies: 1

Representative **Joe Adams** (D-District 86) Room 105-H . . (573) 751-4265
  Counties Represented: St. Louis County (part)
  Term Expires: 2017
  E-mail: joe.adams@house.mo.gov
  Committees: Appropriations - Higher Education; Local Government; Telecommunications

Representative **Justin Alferman** (R-District 61)
  Room 116-2 . . . . . . . . . . . . . . . . . . . . . . . . . . . . . . . . . .(573) 751-6668
  Counties Represented: Franklin (part), Gasconade (part), Osage (part)
  Term Expires: 2017
  E-mail: justin.alferman@house.mo.gov
  Committees: Budget; Employment Security; Fiscal Review; Property, Casualty, and Life Insurance; State and Local Governments

*(continued on next page)*

LEGISLATIVE BRANCH

**Representatives** *continued*

Representative **Susan "Sue" Allen** (R-District 100)
Room 303A . . . . . . . . . . . . . . . . . . . . . . . . . . . . . . . . . . .(573) 751-9765
Counties Represented: St. Louis County (part)
Term Expires: 2017
E-mail: sue.allen@house.mo.gov
Committees: Budget; Employment Security; Fiscal Review; Joint
Legislative Research; Social Services

Representative **Ira Anders** (D-District 21) . . . . . . . . . . . . . .(573) 751-5701
Counties Represented: Jackson (part)                    Res: (816) 254-5865
Term Expires: 2017
731 North Spring Street, Independence, MO 64050
E-mail: ira.anders@house.mo.gov
Committees: Elementary and Secondary Education; Financial
Institutions and Taxation; Joint Public Employee Retirement; Pensions;
Utility Infrastructure

Representative **Sonya Anderson** (R-District 131)
Room 135AA . . . . . . . . . . . . . . . . . . . . . . . . . . . . . . . . . .(573) 751-2948
Counties Represented: Greene (part)
Term Expires: 2017
E-mail: sonya.anderson@house.mo.gov
Committees: Agriculture; Appropriations - Agriculture, Conservation
and Natural Resources; Conservation and Natural Resources; Fiscal
Review
Education: Southwest Missouri State (Attended)

Representative **Allen Andrews** (R-District 1)
Room 135-AB . . . . . . . . . . . . . . . . . . . . . . . . . . . . . . . . . .(573) 751-9465
Counties Represented: Atchison, Holt, Nodaway, Worth
Term Expires: 2017
E-mail: allen.andrews@house.mo.gov
Committees: Civil and Criminal Proceedings; Conservation and Natural
Resources; Consumer Affairs; Corrections

Representative **Lauren Arthur** (D-District 18)
Room 109-H . . . . . . . . . . . . . . . . . . . . . . . . . . . . . . . . . .(573) 751-2199
Counties Represented: Clay (part)
Term Expires: 2017
E-mail: lauren.arthur@house.mo.gov
Committees: Elementary and Secondary Education; Ethics; Health and
Mental Health Policy; Higher Education

Representative **Kevin Austin** (R-District 136)
Room 135AC . . . . . . . . . . . . . . . . . . . . . . . . . . . . . . . . . . (573) 751-0232
Counties Represented: Greene (part)
Term Expires: 2017
E-mail: kevin.austin@house.mo.gov
Committees: Economic Development and Business Attraction and
Retention; Judiciary; Local Government; Professional Registration and
Licensing
Education: Missouri State U 1998 BS; Missouri 1996 JD

Representative **Kurt Bahr** (R-District 102) . . . . . . . . . . . . . (573) 751-9768
Counties Represented: St. Charles (part)               Dist: (636) 695-4188
Term Expires: 2017
1001 Boardwalk Springs Place, O'Fallon, MO 63368
E-mail: kurt.bahr@house.mo.gov
Committees: Appropriations - Elementary and Secondary Education;
Budget; Emerging Issues in Education; Social Services

Representative **Jay Barnes** (R-District 60) Room 415B . . . .(573) 751-2412
Counties Represented: Cole (part)
Term Expires: 2017
E-mail: jay.barnes@house.mo.gov
Committees: Appropriations - General Administration; Consumer
Affairs; Ethics; Government Oversight and Accountability

Representative **Charles "Chuck" Basye** (R-District 47)
Room 201-G . . . . . . . . . . . . . . . . . . . . . . . . . . . . . . . . . . .(573) 751-1501
Counties Represented: Boone (part), Cooper (part), Howard (part),
Randolph (part)
Term Expires: 2017
E-mail: chuck.basye@house.mo.gov
Committees: Appropriations - Agriculture, Conservation and Natural
Resources; Appropriations - Revenue, Transportation and Economic
Development; Energy and the Environment; Veterans

Representative **Nathan Beard** (R-District 52)
Room 409-A . . . . . . . . . . . . . . . . . . . . . . . . . . . . . . . . . . .(573) 751-9774
Counties Represented: Johnson (part), Pettis (part)
Term Expires: 2017
E-mail: nathan.beard@house.mo.gov
Committees: Children and Families; Economic Development and
Business Attraction and Retention; Ethics; Professional Registration and
Licensing; Veterans

Representative **Mike Bernskoetter** (R-District 59)
Room 414 . . . . . . . . . . . . . . . . . . . . . . . . . . . . . . . . . .(573) 751-0665
Counties Represented: Cole (part), Miller (part)
Term Expires: 2017
E-mail: mike.bernskoetter@house.mo.gov
Committees: Agriculture; Ethics; Joint Public Employee Retirement;
Small Business; Utility Infrastructure

Representative **T.J. Berry** (R-District 38) . . . . . . . . . . . . . .(573) 751-2238
Counties Represented: Clay (part)                   Dist: (816) 665-6323
Term Expires: 2017                                   Fax: (816) 628-6268
P.O. Box 512, Kearney, MO 64060
E-mail: tj.berry@house.mo.gov
Committees: Consumer Affairs; Financial Institutions and Taxation;
Trade and Tourism; Utilities

Representative **Linda R. Black** (D-District 117)
Room 105F . . . . . . . . . . . . . . . . . . . . . . . . . . . . . . . . . . .(573) 751-2317
Counties Represented: St. Francois (part)
Term Expires: 2017
E-mail: linda.black@house.mo.gov
Committees: Agriculture; Agriculture Policy; Corrections; Joint
Corrections; Public Safety and Emergency Preparedness

Representative **Jack Bondon** (R-District 56)
Room 201-F . . . . . . . . . . . . . . . . . . . . . . . . . . . . . . . . . . .(573) 751-2175
Counties Represented: Bates (part), Cass (part), Jackson (part)
Term Expires: 2017
E-mail: jack.bondon@house.mo.gov
Committees: Emerging Issues; Emerging Issues in Education; Energy
and the Environment

Representative **Rick Brattin** (R-District 55) . . . . . . . . . . . . .(573) 751-3783
Counties Represented: Cass (part)
Term Expires: 2017
P. O. Box 766, Harrisonville, MO 64701
E-mail: rick.brattin@house.mo.gov
Committees: Children and Families; Consumer Affairs; Corrections;
Workforce Standards and Development

Representative **Cloria Brown** (R-District 94)
Room 406-A . . . . . . . . . . . . . . . . . . . . . . . . . . . . . . . . . . .(573) 751-3719
Counties Represented: St. Louis County (part)
Term Expires: 2017
E-mail: cloria.brown@house.mo.gov
Committees: Budget; Children and Families; Financial Institutions and
Taxation; Higher Education

Representative **Wanda Brown** (R-District 57)
Room 412B . . . . . . . . . . . . . . . . . . . . . . . . . . . . . . . . . . .(573) 751-3971
Counties Represented: Bates (part), Benton (part), Cass (part), Henry
Term Expires: 2017
E-mail: wanda.brown@house.mo.gov
Committees: Consumer Affairs; Employment Security; Labor and
Industrial Relations

Representative **Eric Burlison** (R-District 133)
Room 313-3 . . . . . . . . . . . . . . . . . . . . . . . . . . . . . . . . . . .(573) 751-0136
Counties Represented: Greene (part)
Term Expires: 2017
E-mail: eric.burlison@house.mo.gov
Committees: Budget; Elementary and Secondary Education; General
Laws; Labor and Industrial Relations; Professional Registration and
Licensing

Representative **Bob Burns** (D-District 93) Room 109E . . . . (573) 751-0211
Counties Represented: St. Louis City (part), St. Louis County (part)
Term Expires: 2017
E-mail: bob.burns@house.mo.gov
Committees: Insurance; Property, Casualty, and Life Insurance;
Transportation; Veterans; Workforce Standards and Development

Representative **Michael Butler** (D-District 79)
Room 109D . . . . . . . . . . . . . . . . . . . . . . . . . . . . . . . . . .(573) 751-6800
Counties Represented: St. Louis City (part)
Term Expires: 2017
E-mail: michael.butler@house.mo.gov
Committees: Commerce; Economic Development and Business
Attraction and Retention; Emerging Issues in Education; Small
Business
Education: Alabama A&M BA

Representative **Jon Carpenter** (D-District 15)
Room 105J . . . . . . . . . . . . . . . . . . . . . . . . . . . . . . . . . . .(573) 751-4787
Counties Represented: Clay (part)
Term Expires: 2017
E-mail: jon.carpenter@house.mo.gov
Committees: Financial Institutions and Taxation; General Laws;
Professional Registration and Licensing; Ways and Means

LEGISLATIVE BRANCH

Representative **Jason Chipman** (R-District 120)
Room 115-H . . . . . . . . . . . . . . . . . . . . . . . . . . . . . . . . (573) 751-1688
Counties Represented: Crawford (part), Phelps (part)
Term Expires: 2017
E-mail: jason.chipman@house.mo.gov
Committees: Appropriations - Revenue, Transportation and Economic
Development; Conservation and Natural Resources; Corrections;
Elections

Representative **Mike Cierpiot** (R-District 30)
Room 302B . . . . . . . . . . . . . . . . . . . . . . . . . . . . . . . . . . (573) 751-0907
Counties Represented: Jackson (part)
Term Expires: 2017
E-mail: mike.cierpiot@house.mo.gov
Committees: Administration and Accounts; Ethics; Utility Infrastructure

Representative **Mike Colona** (D-District 80) Room 107 . . . (573) 751-6736
Counties Represented: St. Louis City (part)          Fax: (573) 526-9844
Term Expires: 2017
E-mail: mike.colona@house.mo.gov
Committees: Civil and Criminal Proceedings; Energy and the
Environment; Judiciary; Property, Casualty, and Life Insurance; Utilities

Representative **Kathie Conway** (R-District 104) . . . . . . . . . (573) 751-2250
Counties Represented: St. Charles (part)
Term Expires: 2017
3904 Cambridge Crossing Drive, Saint Charles, MO 63304
E-mail: kathie.conway@house.mo.gov
Committees: Appropriations - Public Safety and Corrections; Budget;
Fiscal Review; Public Safety and Emergency Preparedness

Representative **Pat Conway** (D-District 10) . . . . . . . . . . . . (573) 751-9755
Counties Represented: Buchanan (part)
Term Expires: 2017
712B Francis Street, St. Joseph, MO 64501
E-mail: pat.conway@house.mo.gov
Committees: Administration and Accounts; Appropriations - General
Administration; Elections; Ethics; Joint Legislative Oversight; Social
Services; Veterans

Representative **Steve Cookson** (R-District 153)
Room 201CA . . . . . . . . . . . . . . . . . . . . . . . . . . . . . . . . . (573) 751-1066
Counties Represented: Butler (part), Carter, Ripley, Wayne (part)
Term Expires: 2017
E-mail: steve.cookson@house.mo.gov
Committees: Conservation and Natural Resources; Education; Higher
Education; Joint Education

Representative **Kevin Corlew** (R-District 14)
Room 201-A . . . . . . . . . . . . . . . . . . . . . . . . . . . . . . . . . . (573) 751-3618
Counties Represented: Clay (part), Platte (part)
Term Expires: 2017
E-mail: kevin.corlew@house.mo.gov
Committees: Civil and Criminal Proceedings; Economic Development
and Business Attraction and Retention; Energy and the Environment;
Judiciary

Representative **Robert Cornejo** (R-District 64)
Room 115J . . . . . . . . . . . . . . . . . . . . . . . . . . . . . . . . . . . (573) 751-1484
Counties Represented: Lincoln (part), St. Charles (part)
Term Expires: 2017
E-mail: robert.cornejo@house.mo.gov
Committees: Civil and Criminal Proceedings; Government Oversight
and Accountability; Health Insurance; Judiciary; Professional
Registration and Licensing
Education: Washington U (MO) BA; Missouri 2008 JD

Representative **Sandy Crawford** (R-District 129)
Room 302-1 . . . . . . . . . . . . . . . . . . . . . . . . . . . . . . . . . . (573) 751-1167
Counties Represented: Dallas, Laclede (part)
Term Expires: 2017
E-mail: sandy.crawford@house.mo.gov
Committees: Ethics; Financial Institutions and Taxation;
Telecommunications; Utilities

Representative **Gary Cross** (R-District 35) . . . . . . . . . . . . . (573) 751-1459
Counties Represented: Jackson (part)          Dist: (816) 525-3186
Term Expires: 2017
P.O. Box 1737, Lees Summit, MO 64063
E-mail: gary.cross@house.mo.gov
Committees: Emerging Issues; Local Government; Small Business;
Ways and Means

Representative **Courtney Allen Curtis** (D-District 73)
Room 116-5 . . . . . . . . . . . . . . . . . . . . . . . . . . . . . . . . . . (573) 751-0855
Counties Represented: St. Louis County (part)
Term Expires: 2017
E-mail: courtney.curtis@house.mo.gov
Committees: Appropriations - Health, Mental Health and Social
Services; Government Oversight and Accountability; Joint Education;
Ways and Means
Education: Columbia Col (MO); Missouri

Representative **Paul Curtman** (R-District 109)
Room 403A . . . . . . . . . . . . . . . . . . . . . . . . . . . . . . . . . . (573) 751-3776
Counties Represented: Franklin (part)
Term Expires: 2017
E-mail: paul.curtman@house.mo.gov
Committees: Appropriations - Public Safety and Corrections; General
Laws; Government Efficiency; Ways and Means

Representative **Charlie Davis** (R-District 162) . . . . . . . . . . (573) 751-7082
Counties Represented: Jasper (part), Newton (part)     Res: (417) 825-1193
Term Expires: 2017
1624 Lakeview Drive, Webb City, MO 64870
E-mail: charlie.davis@house.mo.gov
Committees: Employment Security; Social Services; Utility
Infrastructure; Veterans

Representative **Shamed Dogan** (R-District 98)
Room 201-C . . . . . . . . . . . . . . . . . . . . . . . . . . . . . . . . . (573) 751-4392
Counties Represented: St. Louis County (part)
Term Expires: 2017
E-mail: shamed.dogan@house.mo.gov
Committees: Economic Development and Business Attraction and
Retention; Elections; Elementary and Secondary Education; Utility
Infrastructure

Representative **Dean A. Dohrman** (R-District 51)
Room 115G . . . . . . . . . . . . . . . . . . . . . . . . . . . . . . . . . . (573) 751-2204
Counties Represented: Johnson (part), Pettis (part), Saline (part)
Term Expires: 2017
E-mail: dean.dohrman@house.mo.gov
Committees: Appropriations - Elementary and Secondary Education;
Elementary and Secondary Education; Higher Education; Veterans;
Workforce Standards and Development
Education: Missouri (Kansas City) 2004 PhD

Representative **Tony Dugger** (R-District 141) Room 300 . . (573) 751-2205
Counties Represented: Webster, Wright
Term Expires: 2017
E-mail: tony.dugger@house.mo.gov
Committees: Elections; Financial Institutions and Taxation;
Telecommunications; Utility Infrastructure

Representative **Randy D. Dunn** (D-District 23)
Room 116-1 . . . . . . . . . . . . . . . . . . . . . . . . . . . . . . . . . . (573) 751-0538
Counties Represented: Jackson (part)
Term Expires: 2017
E-mail: randy.dunn@house.mo.gov
Committees: Appropriations - Revenue, Transportation and Economic
Development; Economic Development and Business Attraction and
Retention
Education: Missouri (Kansas City) BA, MPA

Representative **J. Eggleston** (R-District 2) Room 406-B . . . (573) 751-4285
Counties Represented: Daviess, DeKalb, Gentry, Harrison
Term Expires: 2017
E-mail: j.eggleston@house.mo.gov
Committees: Agriculture; Agriculture Policy; Health Insurance;
Insurance

Representative **Brandon Ellington** (D-District 22)
Room 116-4 . . . . . . . . . . . . . . . . . . . . . . . . . . . . . . . . . . (573) 751-3129
Counties Represented: Jackson (part)
Term Expires: 2017
E-mail: brandon.ellington@house.mo.gov
Committees: Appropriations - Public Safety and Corrections; Energy
and the Environment; Joint Corrections; Small Business; Ways and
Means

Representative **Kevin Engler** (R-District 116)
Room 411-2 . . . . . . . . . . . . . . . . . . . . . . . . . . . . . . . . . . (573) 751-3455
Counties Represented: Perry (part), St. Francois (part), Ste. Genevieve
(part)
Term Expires: 2017
E-mail: kevin.engler@house.mo.gov
Committees: General Laws; Health Insurance; Local Government;
Rules
Education: Southwest Missouri State 1981 BS

Representative **Keith English** (I-District 68)
Room 116A-2 . . . . . . . . . . . . . . . . . . . . . . . . . . . . . . . . . (573) 751-9628
Counties Represented: St. Louis County (part)
Term Expires: 2017
E-mail: keith.english@house.mo.gov
Committees: Insurance; Joint Gaming and Wagering; Small Business;
Utilities
Education: Saint Louis U (Attended)

*(continued on next page)*

**Representatives** *continued*

Representative **Sue Entlicher** (R-District 128) . . . . . . . . . (573) 751-1347
Counties Represented: Cedar (part), Polk (part)    Res: (417) 326-4791
Term Expires: 2017
4853 South 127 Road, Bolivar, MO 65613
E-mail: sue.entlicher@house.mo.gov
Committees: Agriculture Policy; Elections; Health and Mental Health
Policy; State and Local Governments; Transportation

Representative **Scott Fitzpatrick** (R-District 158) . . . . . . . (573) 751-1488
Counties Represented: Barry, Lawrence (part),    Dist: (417) 858-8814
Stone (part)    Fax: (417) 858-6885
Term Expires: 2017
27882 Highway 39 South, Shell Knob, MO 65747
E-mail: scott.fitzpatrick@house.mo.gov
Committees: Budget; Employment Security; Fiscal Review;
Government Oversight and Accountability; Joint Legislative Research
Education: Missouri 2010 BA

Representative **Paul Fitzwater** (R-District 144)
Room 415B . . . . . . . . . . . . . . . . . . . . . . . . . . . . . . . . . (573) 751-2112
Counties Represented: Iron, Reynolds (part), Washington (part), Wayne
(part)
Term Expires: 2017
E-mail: paul.fitzwater@house.mo.gov
Committees: Appropriations - Public Safety and Corrections;
Corrections; Higher Education; Joint Corrections; Judiciary

Representative **Travis Fitzwater** (R-District 49)
Room 116-A2 . . . . . . . . . . . . . . . . . . . . . . . . . . . . . . . (573) 751-5226
Counties Represented: Callaway (part), Cole (part)
Term Expires: 2017
E-mail: travis.fitzwater@house.mo.gov
Committees: Property, Casualty, and Life Insurance; Social Services;
Trade and Tourism; Utility Infrastructure

Representative **Tom Flanigan** (R-District 163)
Room 110B . . . . . . . . . . . . . . . . . . . . . . . . . . . . . . . . . (573) 751-5458
Counties Represented: Jasper (part)
Term Expires: 2017
E-mail: thomas.flanigan@house.mo.gov
Committees: Budget; Employment Security; Joint Legislative Research;
Telecommunications

Representative **Lyndall Fraker** (R-District 137) . . . . . . . . . (573) 751-3819
Counties Represented: Greene (part)    Dist: (417) 838-2756
Term Expires: 2017    Fax: (417) 859-0460
P.O. Box 130, Marshfield, MO 65706
E-mail: lyndall.fraker@house.mo.gov
Committees: Professional Registration and Licensing; Small Business;
Utilities; Utility Infrastructure; Workforce Standards and Development

Representative **Diane Franklin** (R-District 123)
Room 206B . . . . . . . . . . . . . . . . . . . . . . . . . . . . . . . . . (573) 751-1119
Counties Represented: Camden (part), Laclede (part)
Term Expires: 2017
E-mail: diane.franklin@house.mo.gov
Committees: Appropriations - Elementary and Secondary Education;
Children and Families; Professional Registration and Licensing; Social
Services

Representative **Keith Frederick** (R-District 121)
Room 403B . . . . . . . . . . . . . . . . . . . . . . . . . . . . . . . . . (573) 751-3834
Counties Represented: Phelps (part), Pulaski (part)
Term Expires: 2017
E-mail: keith.frederick@house.mo.gov
Committees: Appropriations - Health, Mental Health and Social
Services; Health and Mental Health Policy; Professional Registration
and Licensing; Social Services

Representative
**Elaine Freeman Gannon** (R-District 115) Room 203C . . (573) 751-7735
Counties Represented: Jefferson (part), St. Francois (part), Ste.
Genevieve (part)
Term Expires: 2017
E-mail: elaine.gannon@house.mo.gov
Committees: Appropriations - Elementary and Secondary Education;
Children and Families; Emerging Issues in Education; Trade and
Tourism
Education: Southwest Missouri State 1975 BS;
Missouri Baptist 1994 MS

Representative **Kimberly M. Gardner** (D-District 77)
Room 109I . . . . . . . . . . . . . . . . . . . . . . . . . . . . . . . . . (573) 751-1400
Counties Represented: St. Louis City (part)
Term Expires: 2017
E-mail: kimberly.gardner@house.mo.gov
Committees: Appropriations - Agriculture, Conservation and Natural
Resources; Civil and Criminal Proceedings; Corrections; Judiciary;
Rules
Education: Harris-Stowe State 1999 BS; Saint Louis U 2003 JD,
2012 MS

Representative **Alan K. Green** (D-District 67)
Room 102BA . . . . . . . . . . . . . . . . . . . . . . . . . . . . . . . (573) 751-3829
Counties Represented: St. Louis County (part)
Term Expires: 2017
E-mail: alan.green@house.mo.gov
Committees: Appropriations - General Administration; Government
Efficiency; Small Business
Education: National-Louis; Lindenwood U; United Sem PhD

Representative **Elijah Haahr** (R-District 134) Room 409B . . (573) 751-2210
Counties Represented: Greene (part)
Term Expires: 2017
E-mail: elijah.haahr@house.mo.gov
Committees: Emerging Issues; General Laws; Government Oversight
and Accountability; Utility Infrastructure
Education: Missouri Western State Col 2005 BA;
Missouri State U 2008 JD

Representative **Marsha Haefner** (R-District 95)
Room 305A . . . . . . . . . . . . . . . . . . . . . . . . . . . . . . . . . (573) 751-3762
Counties Represented: St. Louis County (part)
Term Expires: 2017
E-mail: marsha.haefner@house.mo.gov
Committees: Appropriations - Health, Mental Health and Social
Services; Budget; Children and Families; Health and Mental Health
Policy; Social Services

Representative **Jim Hansen** (R-District 40) Room 405A . . . (573) 751-4028
Counties Represented: Lincoln (part), Monroe (part), Pike, Ralls
Term Expires: 2017
E-mail: jim.hansen@house.mo.gov
Committees: Economic Development and Business Attraction and
Retention; Emerging Issues; Health Insurance; Insurance; Small
Business
Education: Arizona 1969 BS, MS

Representative **Ben Harris** (D-District 118) . . . . . . . . . . . . (573) 751-2398
Counties Represented: Jefferson (part), Washington    Dist: (636) 221-1798
(part)    Fax: (636) 944-3522
Term Expires: 2017
7158 White Road, Hillsboro, MO 63050
E-mail: ben.harris@house.mo.gov
Committees: Agriculture; Agriculture Policy; Appropriations -
Agriculture, Conservation and Natural Resources; Conservation and
Natural Resources; Small Business

Representative **Ron Hicks** (R-District 107) Room 115F . . . . (573) 751-1470
Counties Represented: St. Charles (part)
Term Expires: 2017
E-mail: ron.hicks@house.mo.gov
Committees: Appropriations - Revenue, Transportation and Economic
Development; Emerging Issues; Telecommunications; Utility
Infrastructure

Representative **Galen Wayne Higdon, Jr.** (R-District 11)
Room 412A . . . . . . . . . . . . . . . . . . . . . . . . . . . . . . . . . (573) 751-3643
Counties Represented: Buchanan (part), Platte (part)    Res: (816) 676-8817
Term Expires: 2017
E-mail: galen.higdon@house.mo.gov
Committees: Appropriations - Public Safety and Corrections; Civil and
Criminal Proceedings; Public Safety and Emergency Preparedness;
Ways and Means

Representative **Justin S. Hill** (R-District 108)
Room 116-A1 . . . . . . . . . . . . . . . . . . . . . . . . . . . . . . . (573) 751-3572
Counties Represented: St. Charles (part)
Term Expires: 2017
E-mail: justin.hill@house.mo.gov
Committees: Appropriations - Public Safety and Corrections;
Corrections; Health Insurance; Public Safety and Emergency
Preparedness

Representative **Dave Hinson** (R-District 119)
Room 411A . . . . . . . . . . . . . . . . . . . . . . . . . . . . . . . . . (573) 751-0549
Counties Represented: Franklin (part), Washington (part)
Term Expires: 2017
E-mail: dave.hinson@house.mo.gov
Committees: Emerging Issues in Education; Local Government; State
and Local Governments

Representative **Denny L. Hoskins** (R-District 54)
Room 301 . . . . . . . . . . . . . . . . . . . . . . . . . . . . . . . . . . (573) 751-4302
Counties Represented: Johnson (part), Pettis (part)
Term Expires: 2017
E-mail: denny.hoskins@house.mo.gov
Committees: Higher Education

Representative **Lincoln Hough** (R-District 135)
Room 411B . . . . . . . . . . . . . . . . . . . . . . . . . . . . . . . . . (573) 751-9809
Counties Represented: Greene (part)
Term Expires: 2017
E-mail: lincoln.hough@house.mo.gov
Committees: Appropriations - Revenue, Transportation and Economic
Development; Budget; Pensions; Transportation

Representative **Jay D. Houghton** (R-District 43)
Room 236A . . . . . . . . . . . . . . . . . . . . . . . . . . . . . . . . (573) 751-3649
Counties Represented: Audrain, Callaway (part)
Term Expires: 2017
E-mail: jay.houghton@house.mo.gov
Committees: Agriculture; Agriculture Policy; Appropriations -
Agriculture, Conservation and Natural Resources; Appropriations -
General Administration

Representative **Penny V. Hubbard** (D-District 78)
Room 317B . . . . . . . . . . . . . . . . . . . . . . . . . . . . . . . . (573) 751-2383
Counties Represented: St. Louis City (part)
Term Expires: 2017
E-mail: penny.hubbard@house.mo.gov
Committees: Corrections; Government Oversight and Accountability;
Joint Corrections; Public Safety and Emergency Preparedness

Representative **Tila Hubrecht** (R-District 151)
Room 407-C . . . . . . . . . . . . . . . . . . . . . . . . . . . . . . . . (573) 751-1494
Counties Represented: Scott (part), Stoddard
Term Expires: 2017
E-mail: tila.hubrecht@house.mo.gov
Committees: Elementary and Secondary Education; Energy and the
Environment; Health and Mental Health Policy; Ways and Means
Education: Southeast Missouri State BE

Representative **Jacob Hummel** (D-District 81)
Room 204 . . . . . . . . . . . . . . . . . . . . . . . . . . . . . . . . . . (573) 751-0438
Counties Represented: St. Louis City (part)        Fax: (573) 526-2038
Term Expires: 2017
E-mail: jacob.hummel@house.mo.gov
Committees: Appropriations - General Administration; Local
Government; Rules; Utilities

Representative **Tom Hurst** (R-District 62) Room 115E . . . . (573) 751-1344
Counties Represented: Cole (part), Crawford (part), Gasconade (part),
Maries, Miller (part), Osage (part), Phelps (part)
Term Expires: 2017
E-mail: tom.hurst@house.mo.gov
Committees: Agriculture Policy; Government Oversight and
Accountability; Trade and Tourism; Workforce Standards and
Development
Education: Missouri 1988 BS

Representative **Delus Johnson** (R-District 9)
Room 233B . . . . . . . . . . . . . . . . . . . . . . . . . . . . . . . . (573) 751-3666
Counties Represented: Andrew, Buchanan (part)
Term Expires: 2017
E-mail: delus.johnson@house.mo.gov
Committees: Administration and Accounts; Economic Development and
Business Attraction and Retention; Government Efficiency

Representative **Caleb Jones** (R-District 50) Room 233A . . (573) 751-2134
Counties Represented: Boone (part), Cole (part), Cooper (part),
Moniteau (part)
Term Expires: 2017
E-mail: caleb.jones@house.mo.gov
Committees: Budget; General Laws; Joint Gaming and Wagering;
Pensions; Transportation

Representative **Jeffery "Jeff" Justus** (R-District 156)
Room 115H . . . . . . . . . . . . . . . . . . . . . . . . . . . . . . . . (573) 751-1309
Counties Represented: Taney (part)
Term Expires: 2017
E-mail: jeffery.justus@house.mo.gov
Committees: Appropriations - General Administration; Commerce;
Pensions; Trade and Tourism

Representative
**Shelley "White" Keeney** (R-District 145) . . . . . . . . . . (573) 751-5912
Counties Represented: Bollinger, Madison, Perry    Res: (573) 275-8202
(part)                                              Fax: (573) 526-9804
Term Expires: 2017
P.O. Box 3140, Marble Hill, MO 63764
E-mail: shelley.keeney@house.mo.gov
Committees: Administration and Accounts; Budget; Judiciary;
Professional Registration and Licensing

Representative **Mike Kelley** (R-District 127) Room 201F . . (573) 751-2165
Counties Represented: Barton, Cedar (part), Dade, Jasper (part), Polk
(part)
Term Expires: 2017
E-mail: mike.kelley@house.mo.gov
Committees: Education; Government Efficiency; Labor and Industrial
Relations; Ways and Means; Workforce Standards and Development

Representative **Kip Kendrick** (D-District 45)
Room 106-B . . . . . . . . . . . . . . . . . . . . . . . . . . . . . . . (573) 751-4189
Counties Represented: Boone (part)
Term Expires: 2017
E-mail: kip.kendrick@house.mo.gov
Committees: Appropriations - Elementary and Secondary Education;
Conservation and Natural Resources; Health Insurance; Pensions

Representative **Bill E. Kidd** (R-District 20) . . . . . . . . . . . . (573) 751-3674
Counties Represented: Jackson (part)
Term Expires: 2017
E-mail: bill.kidd@house.mo.gov
Committees: Appropriations - Revenue, Transportation and Economic
Development; Elections; Telecommunications

Representative **S. Nick King** (R-District 17)
Room 201-CA . . . . . . . . . . . . . . . . . . . . . . . . . . . . . . . (573) 751-1218
Counties Represented: Clay (part)
Term Expires: 2017
E-mail: nick.king@house.mo.gov
Committees: Budget; Commerce; Local Government; Small Business

Representative **Jeanne Kirkton** (D-District 91)
Room 135BC . . . . . . . . . . . . . . . . . . . . . . . . . . . . . . . (573) 751-1285
Counties Represented: St. Louis City (part), St.    Res: (314) 968-0124
Louis County (part)                                 Fax: (573) 522-9394
Term Expires: 2017
E-mail: jeanne.kirkton@house.mo.gov
Committees: Appropriations - Health, Mental Health and Social
Services; Budget; Health and Mental Health Policy; Social Services

Representative **Andrew Koenig** (R-District 99)
Room 312 . . . . . . . . . . . . . . . . . . . . . . . . . . . . . . . . . . (573) 751-5568
Counties Represented: St. Louis County (part)
Term Expires: 2017
E-mail: andrew.koenig@house.mo.gov
Committees: Emerging Issues in Education; Financial Institutions and
Taxation; Government Efficiency; Ways and Means

Representative **Glenn Kolkmeyer** (R-District 53)
Room 400CA . . . . . . . . . . . . . . . . . . . . . . . . . . . . . . . (573) 751-1462
Counties Represented: Jackson (part), Johnson (part), Lafayette (part)
Term Expires: 2017
E-mail: glen.kolkmeyer@house.mo.gov
Committees: Elections; Energy and the Environment; Joint
Transportation Oversight; State and Local Governments; Transportation

Representative **Bart Korman** (R-District 42) Room 113 . . . (573) 751-2689
Counties Represented: Montgomery, St. Charles    Res: (636) 585-2700
(part), Warren (part)
Term Expires: 2017
E-mail: bart.korman@house.mo.gov
Committees: Agriculture Policy; Joint Transportation Oversight;
Telecommunications; Transportation; Utilities; Utility Infrastructure

Representative **Michele Kratky** (D-District 82) . . . . . . . . . (573) 751-4220
Counties Represented: St. Louis City (part)      Res: (314) 481-0444
Term Expires: 2017                               Fax: (573) 522-6170
6001 Bishops Place, St. Louis, MO 63109
E-mail: michele.kratky@house.mo.gov
Committees: Administration and Accounts; Commerce; Economic
Development and Business Attraction and Retention; Joint Gaming and
Wagering; Professional Registration and Licensing; Trade and Tourism

Representative **Jeremy LaFaver** (D-District 25)
Room 116A-1 . . . . . . . . . . . . . . . . . . . . . . . . . . . . . . . (573) 751-2437
Counties Represented: Jackson (part)
Term Expires: 2017
E-mail: jeremy.lafaver@house.mo.gov
Committees: Appropriations - Higher Education; Budget; Emerging
Issues; General Laws; Joint Capital Improvements and Leases
Oversight

Representative **Mike Lair** (R-District 7) Room 400 . . . . . . . (573) 751-2917
Counties Represented: Grundy, Linn (part), Livingston
Term Expires: 2017
E-mail: mike.lair@house.mo.gov
Committees: Consumer Affairs; Education; Joint Education; Pensions;
Rules

*(continued on next page)*

**Representatives** *continued*

Representative **Bill Lant** (R-District 159) . . . . . . . . . . . . . . (573) 751-9801
Counties Represented: McDonald, Newton (part)     Dist: (417) 776-8088
Term Expires: 2017     Res: (417) 623-5286
5528 Gum Road, Joplin, MO 64865
E-mail: bill.lant@house.mo.gov
Committees: Emerging Issues; Joint Transportation Oversight; Labor and Industrial Relations; Property, Casualty, and Life Insurance; Transportation; Workforce Standards and Development

Representative **Jeanie Lauer** (R-District 32) . . . . . . . . . . . (573) 751-1487
Counties Represented: Jackson (part)     Res: (816) 228-9152
Term Expires: 2017
1413 NW Wildwood Drive, Blue Springs, MO 64015
E-mail: jeanie.lauer@house.mo.gov
Committees: Appropriations - Higher Education; Children and Families; Commerce; Public Safety and Emergency Preparedness; Rules

Representative **Deb Lavender** (D-District 90)
Room 109-F . . . . . . . . . . . . . . . . . . . . . . . . . . . . . . . . . . (573) 751-4069
Counties Represented: St. Louis County (part)
Term Expires: 2017
E-mail: deb.lavender@house.mo.gov
Committees: Agriculture Policy; Fiscal Review; Rules; Small Business

Representative **Mike Leara** (R-District 96) Room 313-2 . . . (573) 751-2150
Counties Represented: St. Louis County (part)
Term Expires: 2017
E-mail: mike.leara@house.mo.gov
Committees: Administration and Accounts; Joint Public Employee Retirement; Pensions; Rules; Utilities

Representative **Donna Lichtenegger** (R-District 146)
Room 314 . . . . . . . . . . . . . . . . . . . . . . . . . . . . . . . . . . . (573) 751-6662
Counties Represented: Cape Girardeau (part)
Term Expires: 2017
E-mail: donna.lichtenegger@house.mo.gov
Committees: Appropriations - Higher Education; Budget; Economic Development and Business Attraction and Retention; Education; Higher Education

Representative **Warren D. Love** (R-District 125)
Room 201A . . . . . . . . . . . . . . . . . . . . . . . . . . . . . . . . . . (573) 751-4065
Counties Represented: Benton (part), Cedar (part), Hickory, St. Clair
Term Expires: 2017
E-mail: warren.love@house.mo.gov
Committees: Agriculture Policy; Appropriations - General Administration; Emerging Issues in Education; Telecommunications
Education: Central Missouri (Attended)

Representative **Steve Lynch** (R-District 122)
Room 203A . . . . . . . . . . . . . . . . . . . . . . . . . . . . . . . . . . (573) 751-1446
Counties Represented: Laclede (part), Pulaski (part)
Term Expires: 2017
E-mail: steve.lynch@house.mo.gov
Committees: Appropriations - Elementary and Secondary Education; Insurance; Small Business; Veterans; Workforce Standards and Development

Representative **Nick Marshall** (R-District 13) . . . . . . . . . . . (573) 751-6593
Counties Represented: Platte (part)     Dist: (816) 243-5603
Term Expires: 2017     Res: (816) 729-2022
11724 Northwest Plaze Circle, Kansas City, MO 64153
E-mail: nick.marshall@house.mo.gov
Committees: Civil and Criminal Proceedings; Energy and the Environment; Local Government; Property, Casualty, and Life Insurance

Representative **Kirk Mathews** (R-District 110)
Room 203-A . . . . . . . . . . . . . . . . . . . . . . . . . . . . . . . . . (573) 751-0562
Counties Represented: Franklin (part), St. Louis County (part)
Term Expires: 2017
E-mail: kirk.mathews@house.mo.gov
Committees: Appropriations - General Administration; Budget; General Laws; Transportation

Representative **Karla May** (D-District 84) Room 101J . . . . . (573) 751-2198
Counties Represented: St. Louis City (part)
Term Expires: 2017
E-mail: karla.may@house.mo.gov
Committees: Appropriations - Revenue, Transportation and Economic Development; Budget; Employment Security; Joint Transportation Oversight; Transportation

Representative **John C. McCaherty** (R-District 97) . . . . . . . (573) 751-3751
Counties Represented: Jefferson (part), St. Louis     Tel: (636) 671-7448
County (part)
Term Expires: 2017
4202 Wilderness Lane, High Ridge, MO 63049
E-mail: john.mccaherty@house.mo.gov
Committees: Commerce; Small Business; Trade and Tourism; Veterans

Representative **Gail McCann Beatty** (D-District 26) . . . . . . (573) 751-2124
Counties Represented: Jackson (part)
Term Expires: 2017
P.O. Box 22333, Kansas City, MO 64113
E-mail: gail.beatty@house.mo.gov
Committees: Budget; Professional Registration and Licensing

Representative **Tracy McCreery** (D-District 88)
Room 105-E . . . . . . . . . . . . . . . . . . . . . . . . . . . . . . . . . . (573) 751-7535
Counties Represented: St. Louis County (part)
Term Expires: 2017
E-mail: tracy.mccreery@house.mo.gov
Committees: Agriculture; Agriculture Policy; Appropriations - Agriculture, Conservation and Natural Resources; General Laws; Government Efficiency; Utility Infrastructure

Representative **Andrew McDaniel** (R-District 150)
Room 115-I . . . . . . . . . . . . . . . . . . . . . . . . . . . . . . . . . . (573) 751-3629
Counties Represented: Dunklin (part), Pemiscot (part)
Term Expires: 2017
E-mail: andrew.mcdaniel@house.mo.gov
Committees: Civil and Criminal Proceedings; Higher Education; Public Safety and Emergency Preparedness; Utilities

Representative **Tom McDonald** (D-District 29)
Room 135BA . . . . . . . . . . . . . . . . . . . . . . . . . . . . . . . . . (573) 751-9851
Counties Represented: Jackson (part)
Term Expires: 2017
E-mail: tom.mcdonald@house.mo.gov
Committees: Emerging Issues; Fiscal Review; Joint Transportation Oversight; State and Local Governments; Trade and Tourism; Transportation; Utility Infrastructure

Representative **Joe Don McGaugh** (R-District 39)
Room 115D . . . . . . . . . . . . . . . . . . . . . . . . . . . . . . . . . . (573) 751-1468
Counties Represented: Carroll (part), Chariton (part), Ray (part)
Term Expires: 2017
E-mail: joedon.mcgaugh@house.mo.gov
Committees: Agriculture Policy; Civil and Criminal Proceedings; Elections; Judiciary
Education: Missouri 2006 BA; Missouri (Kansas City) 2010 JD

Representative **DaRon McGee** (D-District 36) . . . . . . . . . . (573) 751-3829
Counties Represented: Jackson (part)
Term Expires: 2017
E-mail: daron.mcgee@house.mo.gov
Committees: Consumer Affairs; Local Government; Professional Registration and Licensing

Representative **Margo McNeil** (D-District 69)
Room 103BC . . . . . . . . . . . . . . . . . . . . . . . . . . . . . . . . . (573) 751-5365
Counties Represented: St. Louis County (part)
Term Expires: 2017
E-mail: margo.mcneil@house.mo.gov
Committees: Appropriations - Elementary and Secondary Education; Emerging Issues in Education; Energy and the Environment; Health Insurance; Insurance

Representative **Susan "Sue" Meredith** (D-District 71)
Room 103BB . . . . . . . . . . . . . . . . . . . . . . . . . . . . . . . . . (573) 751-4183
Counties Represented: St. Louis County (part)
Term Expires: 2017
E-mail: susan.meredith@house.mo.gov
Committees: Agriculture; Children and Families; Conservation and Natural Resources; Social Services
Education: Webster 1983 BA, 1998 MA

Representative
**Jeffrey "Jeff" Messenger** (R-District 130)
Room 410B . . . . . . . . . . . . . . . . . . . . . . . . . . . . . . . . . . (573) 751-2381
Counties Represented: Greene (part)
Term Expires: 2017
E-mail: jeff.messenger@house.mo.gov
Committees: Appropriations - Public Safety and Corrections; Budget; Government Oversight and Accountability; Labor and Industrial Relations; Small Business

Representative **Rocky Miller** (R-District 124)
Room 115B . . . . . . . . . . . . . . . . . . . . . . . . . . . . . . . . . . (573) 751-3604
Counties Represented: Camden (part), Miller (part)
Term Expires: 2017
E-mail: rocky.miller@house.mo.gov
Committees: Energy and the Environment; Trade and Tourism; Utilities; Utility Infrastructure
Education: Missouri Science and Tech 1988 BS; St Ambrose (Attended)

LEGISLATIVE BRANCH

Representative **Bonnaye V. Mims** (D-District 27)
Room 116-3 . . . . . . . . . . . . . . . . . . . . . . . . . . . . . (573) 751-7639
Counties Represented: Jackson (part)
Term Expires: 2017
E-mail: bonnaye.mims@house.mo.gov
Committees: Appropriations - Health, Mental Health and Social
Services; Corrections; Ethics; Higher Education; Joint Education
Education: Park U BA, MPA

Representative **Gina Mitten** (D-District 83) Room 109H . . (573) 751-2883
Counties Represented: St. Louis City (part), St.          Tel: (314) 644-0919
Louis County (part)
Term Expires: 2017
E-mail: gina.mitten@house.mo.gov
Committees: Civil and Criminal Proceedings; Consumer Affairs; Ethics;
Government Oversight and Accountability; Health Insurance; Judiciary

Representative **Genise Montecillo** (D-District 92)
Room 130D-B . . . . . . . . . . . . . . . . . . . . . . . . . . . . . (573) 751-9472
Counties Represented: St. Louis County (part)
Term Expires: 2017
E-mail: genise.montecillo@house.mo.gov
Committees: Appropriations - Elementary and Secondary Education;
Budget; Education; Elementary and Secondary Education

Representative **Mike Moon** (R-District 157) . . . . . . . . . . . . (573) 751-4077
Counties Represented: Lawrence (part)
Term Expires: 2017
6935 Lawrence 1222, Ash Grove, MO 65604
E-mail: mike.moon@house.mo.gov
Committees: Appropriations - Agriculture, Conservation and Natural
Resources; Professional Registration and Licensing; Property, Casualty,
and Life Insurance; Ways and Means
Education: Southwest Missouri State BS

Representative **Judy Morgan** (D-District 24)
Room 101G . . . . . . . . . . . . . . . . . . . . . . . . . . . . . . . . (573) 751-4485
Counties Represented: Jackson (part)
Term Expires: 2017
E-mail: judy.morgan@house.mo.gov
Committees: Education; Emerging Issues in Education; Fiscal Review;
Pensions

Representative **Lynn Morris** (R-District 140)
Room 200BC . . . . . . . . . . . . . . . . . . . . . . . . . . . . . . . (573) 751-2565
Counties Represented: Christian (part)
Term Expires: 2017
E-mail: lynn.morris@house.mo.gov
Committees: Appropriations - Elementary and Secondary Education;
Appropriations - Health, Mental Health and Social Services; Health and
Mental Health Policy; Health Insurance; Rules
Education: Missouri (Kansas City) BS; Southwest Baptist 2000 MHA

Representative **Dave Muntzel** (R-District 48)
Room 201E . . . . . . . . . . . . . . . . . . . . . . . . . . . . . . . . (573) 751-0169
Counties Represented: Carroll (part), Chariton (part), Cooper (part),
Howard (part), Pettis (part), Randolph (part), Saline (part)
Term Expires: 2017
E-mail: dave.muntzel@house.mo.gov
Committees: Agriculture Policy; Appropriations - Higher Education;
Emerging Issues; Property, Casualty, and Life Insurance
Education: Central Missouri State 1973 BAA

Representative **James W. "Jim" Neely** (R-District 8)
Room 115C . . . . . . . . . . . . . . . . . . . . . . . . . . . . . . . . (573) 751-0246
Counties Represented: Caldwell, Clay (part), Clinton, Ray (part)
Term Expires: 2017
E-mail: jim.neely@house.mo.gov
Committees: Appropriations - Health, Mental Health and Social
Services; Appropriations - Higher Education; Children and Families;
Small Business
Education: Missouri; Kansas City Med DO

Representative **Stacey Newman** (D-District 87)
Room 101K . . . . . . . . . . . . . . . . . . . . . . . . . . . . . . . . (573) 751-0100
Counties Represented: St. Louis County (part)          Fax: (573) 526-9866
Term Expires: 2017
E-mail: stacey.newman@house.mo.gov
Committees: Appropriations - General Administration; Children and
Families; Elections; Ethics; State and Local Governments

Representative **Mary Nichols** (D-District 72) . . . . . . . . . . . . (573) 751-1832
Counties Represented: St. Louis County (part)          Res: (314) 770-9992
Term Expires: 2017
11610 Mack Avenue, Maryland Heights, MO 63043
E-mail: mary.nichols@house.mo.gov
Committees: Appropriations - Public Safety and Corrections; Financial
Institutions and Taxation; Telecommunications

Representative **Charlie Norr** (D-District 132)
Room 105D . . . . . . . . . . . . . . . . . . . . . . . . . . . . . . . . (573) 751-3795
Counties Represented: Greene (part)
Term Expires: 2017
E-mail: charlie.norr@house.mo.gov
Committees: Children and Families; Commerce; Public Safety and
Emergency Preparedness; Trade and Tourism
Education: Maryland (Attended); Baltimore Poly (Attended)

Representative **Bill Otto** (D-District 70) Room 116-2 . . . . . (573) 751-4163
Counties Represented: St. Charles (part), St. Louis County (part)
Term Expires: 2017
E-mail: bill.otto@house.mo.gov
Committees: Consumer Affairs; Insurance; Property, Casualty, and Life
Insurance; Veterans
Education: Embry-Riddle (Attended)

Representative **Sharon L. Pace** (D-District 74)
Room 105G . . . . . . . . . . . . . . . . . . . . . . . . . . . . . . . . (573) 751-4726
Counties Represented: St. Louis County (part)
Term Expires: 2017
E-mail: sharon.pace@house.mo.gov
Committees: Appropriations - Revenue, Transportation and Economic
Development; Emerging Issues; Health and Mental Health Policy;
Telecommunications; Utilities

Representative **Mark A. Parkinson** (R-District 105) . . . . . . . (573) 751-2949
Counties Represented: St. Charles (part)
Term Expires: 2017
3429 Indiana Avenue, Saint Charles, MO 63303
E-mail: mark.parkinson@house.mo.gov
Committees: Appropriations - Higher Education; Consumer Affairs;
Employment Security; Joint Capital Improvements and Leases
Oversight; Judiciary

Representative **Joshua "Josh" Peters** (D-District 76)
Room 109F . . . . . . . . . . . . . . . . . . . . . . . . . . . . . . . . (573) 751-3829
Counties Represented: St. Louis City (part)
Term Expires: 2017
E-mail: joshua.peters@house.mo.gov
Committees: Agriculture Policy; Appropriations - Public Safety and
Corrections; Professional Registration and Licensing; Utility
Infrastructure

Representative **Donna Pfautsch** (R-District 33)
Room 236B . . . . . . . . . . . . . . . . . . . . . . . . . . . . . . . . (573) 751-9766
Counties Represented: Cass (part), Jackson (part), Lafayette (part)
Term Expires: 2017
E-mail: donna.pfautsch@house.mo.gov
Committees: Appropriations - Elementary and Secondary Education;
Economic Development and Business Attraction and Retention; Rules;
State and Local Governments
Education: Central Missouri BA, MA

Representative
**Donald E. "Don" Phillips** (R-District 138) . . . . . . . . . . . (573) 751-3851
Counties Represented: Christian (part), Stone (part),     Res: (417) 739-4771
Taney (part)
Term Expires: 2017
18 Midview Drive, Kimberling City, MO 65686
E-mail: donald.phillips@house.mo.gov
Committees: Commerce; Conservation and Natural Resources; Rules;
Trade and Tourism

Representative **Tommie Pierson** (D-District 66)
Room 101H . . . . . . . . . . . . . . . . . . . . . . . . . . . . . . . . (573) 751-6845
Counties Represented: St. Louis City (part), St. Louis County (part)
Term Expires: 2017
E-mail: tommie.pierson@house.mo.gov
Committees: Agriculture Policy; Education; Elementary and Secondary
Education; Higher Education; Joint Education; Joint Public Employee
Retirement

Representative **Randy Pietzman** (R-District 41)
Room 201-D . . . . . . . . . . . . . . . . . . . . . . . . . . . . . . . (573) 751-9459
Counties Represented: Lincoln (part)
Term Expires: 2017
E-mail: randy.pietzman@house.mo.gov
Committees: Conservation and Natural Resources; Financial Institutions
and Taxation; Property, Casualty, and Life Insurance; Small Business

Representative **Patricia Pike** (R-District 126) . . . . . . . . . . . (573) 751-5388
Counties Represented: Bates (part), Vernon
Term Expires: 2017
E-mail: patricia.pike@house.mo.gov
Committees: Agriculture Policy; Appropriations - General
Administration; Government Efficiency; Veterans

*(continued on next page)*

**Representatives** *continued*

Representative **Dean Plocher** (R-District 89) . . . . . . . . . . . (573) 751-1544
  Counties Represented: St. Louis County (part)
  Term Expires: 2017
  E-mail: dean.plocher@house.mo.gov
  Committees: Appropriations - Revenue, Transportation and Economic
  Development; Consumer Affairs; Professional Registration and
  Licensing

Representative **Jeffrey "Jeff" Pogue** (R-District 143)
  Room 400CC . . . . . . . . . . . . . . . . . . . . . . . . . . . . . . . . . (573) 751-2264
  Counties Represented: Dent, Oregon, Reynolds (part), Shannon
  Term Expires: 2017
  E-mail: jeff.pogue@house.mo.gov
  Committees: Appropriations - Higher Education; Government
  Efficiency; Ways and Means
  Education: Southwest Baptist 2012 AA

Representative **Craig Redmon** (R-District 4) . . . . . . . . . . . (573) 751-3644
  Counties Represented: Adair (part), Clark, Knox,     Dist: (573) 288-5983
  Lewis, Schuyler, Scotland
  Term Expires: 2017
  30391 Pear Street, Canton, MO 63435
  E-mail: craig.redmon@house.mo.gov
  Committees: Agriculture Policy; Appropriations - Agriculture,
  Conservation and Natural Resources; Budget; Energy and the
  Environment

Representative **Holly Rehder** (R-District 148)
  Room 406A . . . . . . . . . . . . . . . . . . . . . . . . . . . . . . . . . . (573) 751-5471
  Counties Represented: Mississippi (part), Scott (part)
  Term Expires: 2017
  E-mail: holly.rehder@house.mo.gov
  Committees: Appropriations - Health, Mental Health and Social
  Services; Appropriations - Revenue, Transportation and Economic
  Development; Health and Mental Health Policy; Labor and Industrial
  Relations; Utility Infrastructure
  Education: Southwest Missouri State BS

Representative **Bill Reiboldt** (R-District 160)
  Room 235BB . . . . . . . . . . . . . . . . . . . . . . . . . . . . . . . (573) 751-9781
  Counties Represented: Newton (part)
  Term Expires: 2017
  E-mail: bill.reiboldt@house.mo.gov
  Committees: Agriculture; Appropriations - Agriculture, Conservation
  and Natural Resources; Consumer Affairs; Corrections

Representative **Tim Remole** (R-District 6) Room 201G . . . (573) 751-6566
  Counties Represented: Linn (part), Macon, Randolph (part)
  Term Expires: 2017
  E-mail: tim.remole@house.mo.gov
  Committees: Children and Families; Conservation and Natural
  Resources; Energy and the Environment; Utility Infrastructure

Representative **Shawn Rhoads** (R-District 154)
  Room 406B . . . . . . . . . . . . . . . . . . . . . . . . . . . . . . . . . (573) 751-1455
  Counties Represented: Howell (part)
  Term Expires: 2017
  E-mail: shawn.rhoads@house.mo.gov
  Committees: Fiscal Review; Joint Corrections; Pensions; Public Safety
  and Emergency Preparedness; State and Local Governments

Representative **Todd Richardson** (R-District 152)
  Room 404A . . . . . . . . . . . . . . . . . . . . . . . . . . . . . . . . . (573) 751-4039
  Counties Represented: Butler (part), Dunklin (part)
  Term Expires: 2017
  E-mail: todd.richardson@house.mo.gov
  Committees: Joint Government Accountability

Representative **John Joseph Rizzo** (D-District 19)
  Room 102BB . . . . . . . . . . . . . . . . . . . . . . . . . . . . . . . . (573) 751-3310
  Counties Represented: Jackson (part)
  Term Expires: 2017
  E-mail: john.rizzo@house.mo.gov
  Committees: Budget; Economic Development and Business Attraction
  and Retention; Local Government; Rules

Representative **Shane Roden** (R-District 111)
  Room 115-J . . . . . . . . . . . . . . . . . . . . . . . . . . . . . . . . . (573) 751-4567
  Counties Represented: Jefferson (part)
  Term Expires: 2017
  E-mail: shane.roden@house.mo.gov
  Committees: Appropriations - Public Safety and Corrections;
  Corrections; Public Safety and Emergency Preparedness; Veterans

Representative **Rebecca Roeber** (R-District 34)
  Room 116-3 . . . . . . . . . . . . . . . . . . . . . . . . . . . . . . . . (573) 751-1456
  Counties Represented: Jackson (part)
  Term Expires: 2017
  E-mail: rebecca.roeber@house.mo.gov
  Committees: Elementary and Secondary Education; Health Insurance;
  Insurance; Transportation

Representative **Don Rone** (R-District 149) Room 116-1 . . . (573) 751-4085
  Counties Represented: Mississippi (part), New Madrid, Pemiscot (part),
  Scott (part)
  Term Expires: 2017
  E-mail: don.rone@house.mo.gov
  Committees: Agriculture Policy; Appropriations - Agriculture,
  Conservation and Natural Resources; Joint Transportation Oversight;
  Telecommunications; Transportation

Representative **Robert Ross** (R-District 142)
  Room 114A . . . . . . . . . . . . . . . . . . . . . . . . . . . . . . . . . (573) 751-1490
  Counties Represented: Howell (part), Laclede (part), Phelps (part),
  Pulaski (part), Texas
  Term Expires: 2017
  E-mail: robert.ross@house.mo.gov
  Committees: Appropriations - General Administration; Budget;
  Conservation and Natural Resources; Joint Capital Improvements and
  Leases Oversight; Professional Registration and Licensing
  Education: Missouri State U 2003 BS

Representative **Caleb Rowden** (R-District 44)
  Room 201C . . . . . . . . . . . . . . . . . . . . . . . . . . . . . . . . . (573) 751-1169
  Counties Represented: Boone (part), Randolph (part)
  Term Expires: 2017
  E-mail: caleb.rowden@house.mo.gov
  Committees: Budget; Commerce; Economic Development and Business
  Attraction and Retention; Emerging Issues
  Education: Missouri (Attended)

Representative **Lyle Rowland** (R-District 155)
  Room 413A . . . . . . . . . . . . . . . . . . . . . . . . . . . . . . . . . (573) 751-2042
  Counties Represented: Douglas, Ozark, Taney (part)    Res: (417) 794-3493
  Term Expires: 2017
  E-mail: lyle.rowland@house.mo.gov
  Committees: Conservation and Natural Resources; Education; Emerging
  Issues in Education; Pensions

Representative **Rory Rowland** (D-District 29) . . . . . . . . . . . (573) 751-3623
  Counties Represented: Jackson (part)
  Term Expires: 2017
  E-mail: rory.rowland@house.mo.gov
  Committees: Government Efficiency

Representative **Joe Runions** (D-District 37) Room 101F . . (573) 751-0238
  Counties Represented: Cass (part), Jackson (part)
  Term Expires: 2017
  E-mail: joe.runions@house.mo.gov
  Committees: Employment Security; Energy and the Environment;
  Government Efficiency; Joint Public Employee Retirement

Representative **Becky Ruth** (R-District 114) Room 115-F . . (573) 751-4451
  Counties Represented: Jefferson (part)
  Term Expires: 2017
  E-mail: becky.ruth@house.mo.gov
  Committees: Appropriations - Health, Mental Health and Social
  Services; Elementary and Secondary Education; Health and Mental
  Health Policy; Insurance; Local Government

Representative **Dan Shaul** (R-District 113) Room 116-5 . . . (573) 751-2504
  Counties Represented: Jefferson (part)
  Term Expires: 2017
  E-mail: dan.shaul@house.mo.gov
  Committees: Elections; Emerging Issues in Education; Small Business;
  Ways and Means

Representative **Noel J. Shull** (R-District 16) Room 201B . . (573) 751-9458
  Counties Represented: Clay (part)
  Term Expires: 2017
  E-mail: noel.shull@house.mo.gov
  Committees: Appropriations - Revenue, Transportation and Economic
  Development; Insurance; Property, Casualty, and Life Insurance

Representative **Lindell F. Shumake** (R-District 5)
  Room 407B . . . . . . . . . . . . . . . . . . . . . . . . . . . . . . . . . (573) 751-3613
  Counties Represented: Marion, Monroe (part), Shelby
  Term Expires: 2017
  E-mail: lindell.shumake@house.mo.gov
  Committees: Administration and Accounts; Agriculture; Corrections;
  Small Business; Veterans

Representative **Clem Smith** (D-District 85) . . . . . . . . . . . . (573) 751-4468
  Counties Represented: St. Louis County (part)
  Term Expires: 2017
  P.O. Box 210851, St. Louis, MO 63121
  E-mail: clem.smith@house.mo.gov
  Committees: Elections; Labor and Industrial Relations; Utilities; Utility
  Infrastructure; Workforce Standards and Development

Representative **Sheila Solon** (R-District 31) Room 305B . . (573) 751-8636
  Counties Represented: Jackson (part)
  Term Expires: 2017
  E-mail: sheila.solon@house.mo.gov
  Committees: Government Efficiency; State and Local Governments;
  Veterans

Representative **Chrissy Sommer** (R-District 106)
Room 304B . . . . . . . . . . . . . . . . . . . . . . . . . . . . . . (573) 751-1452
Counties Represented: St. Charles (part)
Term Expires: 2017
E-mail: chrissy.sommer@house.mo.gov
Committees: General Laws; Higher Education; Professional
Registration and Licensing; Property, Casualty, and Life Insurance

Representative **Bryan Spencer** (R-District 63)
Room 201D . . . . . . . . . . . . . . . . . . . . . . . . . . . . . . (573) 751-1460
Counties Represented: St. Charles (part), Warren (part)
Term Expires: 2017
E-mail: bryan.spencer@house.mo.gov
Committees: Agriculture Policy; Elementary and Secondary Education;
Employment Security; Utility Infrastructure
Education: Culver-Stockton 1989 BS; Missouri (St Louis) 2001 MA

Representative **Kathryn "Kathy" Swan** (R-District 147)
Room 115I . . . . . . . . . . . . . . . . . . . . . . . . . . . . . . (573) 751-1443
Counties Represented: Cape Girardeau (part)
Term Expires: 2017
E-mail: kathryn.swan@house.mo.gov
Committees: Budget; Education; Elementary and Secondary Education;
Joint Education; Professional Registration and Licensing
Education: Southeast Missouri State BS

Representative **Jered Taylor** (R-District 139)
Room 116-4 . . . . . . . . . . . . . . . . . . . . . . . . . . . . . . (573) 751-3833
Counties Represented: Christian (part)
Term Expires: 2017
E-mail: jered.taylor@house.mo.gov
Committees: Appropriations - Higher Education; Consumer Affairs;
Elections; Telecommunications

Representative **Rob Vescovo** (R-District 112)
Room 409-B . . . . . . . . . . . . . . . . . . . . . . . . . . . . . . (573) 751-3607
Counties Represented: Jefferson (part)
Term Expires: 2017
E-mail: rob.vescovo@house.mo.gov
Committees: Civil and Criminal Proceedings; Government Efficiency;
Government Oversight and Accountability; Labor and Industrial
Relations

Representative **Nate Walker** (R-District 3) Room 405B . . . (573) 751-3647
Counties Represented: Adair (part), Mercer, Putnam, Sullivan
Term Expires: 2017
E-mail: nate.walker@house.mo.gov
Committees: Financial Institutions and Taxation; Higher Education;
Joint Public Employee Retirement; Pensions; Workforce Standards and
Development
Education: Missouri BS, MS; Duke (Attended)

Representative **Rochelle Walton Gray** (D-District 75)
Room 105E . . . . . . . . . . . . . . . . . . . . . . . . . . . . . . (573) 751-5538
Counties Represented: St. Louis County (part)
Term Expires: 2017
E-mail: rochelle.gray@house.mo.gov
Committees: Professional Registration and Licensing; Public Safety and
Emergency Preparedness

Representative **Stephen Webber** (D-District 46)
Room 106A . . . . . . . . . . . . . . . . . . . . . . . . . . . . . . (573) 751-9753
Counties Represented: Boone (part)
Term Expires: 2017
E-mail: stephen.webber@house.mo.gov
Committees: Appropriations - Higher Education; Budget; Consumer
Affairs; Labor and Industrial Relations; Workforce Standards and
Development

Representative **William "Bill" White** (R-District 161)
Room 407A . . . . . . . . . . . . . . . . . . . . . . . . . . . . . . (573) 751-3791
Counties Represented: Jasper (part), Newton (part)    Res: (417) 623-0038
Term Expires: 2017                                    Fax: (417) 623-0008
E-mail: bill.white@house.mo.gov
Committees: Civil and Criminal Proceedings; Health and Mental Health
Policy; Health Insurance; Pensions

Representative **John D. Wiemann** (R-District 103)
Room 135-AC . . . . . . . . . . . . . . . . . . . . . . . . . . . . . (573) 751-2176
Counties Represented: St. Charles (part)
Term Expires: 2017
E-mail: john.wiemann@house.mo.gov
Committees: Appropriations - Health, Mental Health and Social
Services; Employment Security; Health Insurance; Professional
Registration and Licensing

Representative **Kenneth "Ken" Wilson** (R-District 12)
Room 410A . . . . . . . . . . . . . . . . . . . . . . . . . . . . . . (573) 751-9760
Counties Represented: Clay (part), Platte (part)
Term Expires: 2017
E-mail: ken.wilson@house.mo.gov
Committees: Appropriations - Public Safety and Corrections;
Government Efficiency; Local Government; Public Safety and
Emergency Preparedness
Education: Missouri Western State Col BA

Representative **David Wood** (R-District 58) Room 115A . . (573) 751-2077
Counties Represented: Miller (part), Moniteau (part), Morgan
Term Expires: 2017
E-mail: david.wood@house.mo.gov
Committees: Appropriations - Health, Mental Health and Social
Services; Education; Emerging Issues in Education; Joint Education;
Trade and Tourism
Education: Central Missouri BA

Representative **Anne Zerr** (R-District 65) Room 315 . . . . . . (573) 751-3717
Counties Represented: St. Charles (part)
Term Expires: 2017
E-mail: anne.zerr@house.mo.gov
Committees: Commerce; Emerging Issues; Fiscal Review; Health and
Mental Health Policy; Joint Gaming and Wagering

District 101 **(Vacant)** . . . . . . . . . . . . . . . . . . . . . . . . . . (573) 751-3829
Note: A general election to fill this legislative vacancy will be held on
November 8, 2016.

# House Standing Committees

## Administration and Accounts

| Majority Members | Minority Members |
| --- | --- |
| Mike Leara (R-96) *Chair* | Pat Conway (D-10) |
| Lindell F. Shumake (R-5) *Vice Chair* | Michele Kratky (D-82) |
| Mike Cierpiot (R-30) | |
| Delus Johnson (R-9) | |
| Shelley "White" Keeney (R-145) | |

## Agriculture

| Majority Members | Minority Members |
| --- | --- |
| Bill Reiboldt (R-160) *Chair* | Linda R. Black (D-117) *Vice Chair* |
| Sonya Anderson (R-131) | Ben Harris (D-118) |
| Mike Bernskoetter (R-59) | Tracy McCreery (D-88) |
| J. Eggleston (R-2) | Susan "Sue" Meredith (D-71) |
| Jay D. Houghton (R-43) | |
| Lindell F. Shumake (R-5) | |

## Agriculture Policy

| Majority Members | Minority Members |
| --- | --- |
| Jay D. Houghton (R-43) *Chair* | Linda R. Black (D-117) |
| Tom Hurst (R-62) *Vice-Chair* | Ben Harris (D-118) |
| J. Eggleston (R-2) | Deb Lavender (D-90) |
| Sue Entlicher (R-128) | Tracy McCreery (D-88) |
| Bart Korman (R-42) | Joshua "Josh" Peters (D-76) |
| Warren D. Love (R-125) | Tommie Pierson (D-66) |
| Joe Don McGaugh (R-39) | |
| Dave Muntzel (R-48) | |
| Patricia Pike (R-126) | |
| Craig Redmon (R-4) | |
| Don Rone (R-149) | |
| Bryan Spencer (R-63) | |

## Appropriations - Agriculture, Conservation and Natural Resources

| Majority Members | Minority Members |
| --- | --- |
| Craig Redmon (R-4) *Chair* | Kimberly M. Gardner (D-77) |
| Don Rone (R-149) *Vice-Chair* | Ben Harris (D-118) |
| Sonya Anderson (R-131) | Tracy McCreery (D-88) |
| Charles "Chuck" Basye (R-47) | |
| Jay D. Houghton (R-43) | |
| Mike Moon (R-157) | |
| Bill Reiboldt (R-160) | |

## Appropriations - Elementary and Secondary Education

**Majority Members**
Kurt Bahr (R-102) *Chair*
Elaine Freeman Gannon (R-115)
  *Vice Chair*
Dean A. Dohrman (R-51)
Diane Franklin (R-123)
Steve Lynch (R-122)
Lynn Morris (R-140)
Donna Pfautsch (R-33)

**Minority Members**
Kip Kendrick (D-45)
Margo McNeil (D-69)
Genise Montecillo (D-92)

## Appropriations - General Administration

**Majority Members**
Robert Ross (R-142) *Chair*
Jeffery "Jeff" Justus (R-156)
  *Vice-Chair*
Jay Barnes (R-60)
Jay D. Houghton (R-43)
Warren D. Love (R-125)
Kirk Mathews (R-110)
Patricia Pike (R-126)

**Minority Members**
Pat Conway (D-10)
Alan K. Green (D-67)
Jacob Hummel (D-81)
Stacey Newman (D-87)

## Appropriations - Health, Mental Health and Social Services

**Majority Members**
Marsha Haefner (R-95) *Chair*
David Wood (R-58) *Vice Chair*
Keith Frederick (R-121)
Lynn Morris (R-140)
James W. "Jim" Neely (R-8)
Holly Rehder (R-148)
Becky Ruth (R-114)
John D. Wiemann (R-103)

**Minority Members**
Courtney Allen Curtis (D-73)
Jeanne Kirkton (D-91)
Bonnaye V. Mims (D-27)

## Appropriations - Higher Education

**Majority Members**
Donna Lichtenegger (R-146) *Chair*
Jeanie Lauer (R-32) *Vice Chair*
Dave Muntzel (R-48)
James W. "Jim" Neely (R-8)
Mark A. Parkinson (R-105)
Jeffrey "Jeff" Pogue (R-143)
Jered Taylor (R-139)

**Minority Members**
Joe Adams (D-86)
Jeremy LaFaver (D-25)
Stephen Webber (D-46)

## Appropriations - Public Safety and Corrections

**Majority Members**
Kathie Conway (R-104) *Chair*
Kenneth "Ken" Wilson (R-12)
  *Vice Chair*
Paul Curtman (R-109)
Paul Fitzwater (R-144)
Galen Wayne Higdon, Jr. (R-11)
Justin S. Hill (R-108)
Jeffrey "Jeff" Messenger (R-130)
Shane Roden (R-111)

**Minority Members**
Brandon Ellington (D-22)
Mary Nichols (D-72)
Joshua "Josh" Peters (D-76)

## Appropriations - Revenue, Transportation and Economic Development

**Majority Members**
Lincoln Hough (R-135) *Chair*
Charles "Chuck" Basye (R-47)
  *Vice Chair*
Jason Chipman (R-120)
Ron Hicks (R-107)
Bill E. Kidd (R-20)
Dean Plocher (R-89)
Holly Rehder (R-148)
Noel J. Shull (R-16)

**Minority Members**
Randy D. Dunn (D-23)
Karla May (D-84)
Sharon L. Pace (D-74)

## Budget

**Majority Members**
Tom Flanigan (R-163) *Chair*
Scott Fitzpatrick (R-158) *Vice-Chair*
Justin Alferman (R-61)
Susan "Sue" Allen (R-100)
Kurt Bahr (R-102)
Cloria Brown (R-94)
Eric Burlison (R-133)
Kathie Conway (R-104)
Marsha Haefner (R-95)
Lincoln Hough (R-135)
Caleb Jones (R-50)
Shelley "White" Keeney (R-145)
S. Nick King (R-17)
Donna Lichtenegger (R-146)
Kirk Mathews (R-110)
Jeffrey "Jeff" Messenger (R-130)
Craig Redmon (R-4)
Robert Ross (R-142)
Caleb Rowden (R-44)
Kathryn "Kathy" Swan (R-147)

**Minority Members**
Jeanne Kirkton (D-91)
Jeremy LaFaver (D-25)
Karla May (D-84)
Gail McCann Beatty (D-26)
Genise Montecillo (D-92)
John Joseph Rizzo (D-19)
Stephen Webber (D-46)

## Children and Families

**Majority Members**
Diane Franklin (R-123) *Chair*
James W. "Jim" Neely (R-8)
  *Vice-Chair*
Nathan Beard (R-52)
Rick Brattin (R-55)
Cloria Brown (R-94)
Elaine Freeman Gannon (R-115)
Marsha Haefner (R-95)
Jeanie Lauer (R-32)
Tim Remole (R-6)

**Minority Members**
Susan "Sue" Meredith (D-71)
Stacey Newman (D-87)
Charlie Norr (D-132)

## Civil and Criminal Proceedings

**Majority Members**
Joe Don McGaugh (R-39) *Chair*
Rob Vescovo (R-112) *Vice Chair*
Allen Andrews (R-1)
Kevin Corlew (R-14)
Robert Cornejo (R-64)
Galen Wayne Higdon, Jr. (R-11)
Nick Marshall (R-13)
Andrew McDaniel (R-150)
William "Bill" White (R-161)

**Minority Members**
Mike Colona (D-80)
Kimberly M. Gardner (D-77)
Gina Mitten (D-83)

## Commerce

**Majority Members**
Anne Zerr (R-65) *Chair*
Jeanie Lauer (R-32) *Vice Chair*
Jeffery "Jeff" Justus (R-156)
S. Nick King (R-17)
John C. McCaherty (R-97)
Donald E. "Don" Phillips (R-138)
Caleb Rowden (R-44)

**Minority Members**
Michael Butler (D-79)
Michele Kratky (D-82)
Charlie Norr (D-132)

## Conservation and Natural Resources

**Majority Members**
Sonya Anderson (R-131) *Chair*
Tim Remole (R-6) *Vice Chair*
Allen Andrews (R-1)
Jason Chipman (R-120)
Steve Cookson (R-153)
Donald E. "Don" Phillips (R-138)
Randy Pietzman (R-41)
Robert Ross (R-142)
Lyle Rowland (R-155)

**Minority Members**
Ben Harris (D-118)
Kip Kendrick (D-45)
Susan "Sue" Meredith (D-71)

## Consumer Affairs

**Majority Members**
Mark A. Parkinson (R-105) *Chair*
Rick Brattin (R-55) *Vice Chair*
Allen Andrews (R-1)
Jay Barnes (R-60)
T.J. Berry (R-38)
Wanda Brown (R-57)
Mike Lair (R-7)
Dean Plocher (R-89)
Bill Reiboldt (R-160)
Jered Taylor (R-139)

**Minority Members**
DaRon McGee (D-36)
Gina Mitten (D-83)
Bill Otto (D-70)
Stephen Webber (D-46)

## Corrections

**Majority Members**
Paul Fitzwater (R-144) *Chair*
Rick Brattin (R-55) *Vice-Chair*
Allen Andrews (R-1)
Jason Chipman (R-120)
Justin S. Hill (R-108)
Bill Reiboldt (R-160)
Shane Roden (R-111)
Lindell F. Shumake (R-5)

**Minority Members**
Linda R. Black (D-117)
Kimberly M. Gardner (D-77)
Penny V. Hubbard (D-78)
Bonnaye V. Mims (D-27)

## Economic Development and Business Attraction and Retention

**Majority Members**
Caleb Rowden (R-44) *Chair*
Kevin Corlew (R-14) *Vice-Chair*
Kevin Austin (R-136)
Nathan Beard (R-52)
Shamed Dogan (R-98)
Jim Hansen (R-40)
Delus Johnson (R-9)
Donna Lichtenegger (R-146)
Donna Pfautsch (R-33)

**Minority Members**
Michael Butler (D-79)
Randy D. Dunn (D-23)
Michele Kratky (D-82)
John Joseph Rizzo (D-19)

## Education

**Majority Members**
Mike Lair (R-7) *Chair*
David Wood (R-58) *Vice Chair*
Steve Cookson (R-153)
Mike Kelley (R-127)
Donna Lichtenegger (R-146)
Lyle Rowland (R-155)
Kathryn "Kathy" Swan (R-147)

**Minority Members**
Genise Montecillo (D-92)
Judy Morgan (D-24)
Tommie Pierson (D-66)

## Elections

**Majority Members**
Sue Entlicher (R-128) *Chair*
Shamed Dogan (R-98) *Vice Chair*
Jason Chipman (R-120)
Tony Dugger (R-141)
Bill E. Kidd (R-20)
Glenn Kolkmeyer (R-53)
Joe Don McGaugh (R-39)
Dan Shaul (R-113)
Jered Taylor (R-139)

**Minority Members**
Pat Conway (D-10)
Stacey Newman (D-87)
Clem Smith (D-85)

## Elementary and Secondary Education

**Majority Members**
Kathryn "Kathy" Swan (R-147)
    *Chair*
Bryan Spencer (R-63) *Vice-Chair*
Eric Burlison (R-133)
Shamed Dogan (R-98)
Dean A. Dohrman (R-51)
Tila Hubrecht (R-151)
Rebecca Roeber (R-34)
Becky Ruth (R-114)

**Minority Members**
Ira Anders (D-21)
Lauren Arthur (D-18)
Genise Montecillo (D-92)
Tommie Pierson (D-66)

## Emerging Issues

**Majority Members**
Elijah Haahr (R-134) *Chair*
Gary Cross (R-35) *Vice Chair*
Jack Bondon (R-56)
Jim Hansen (R-40)
Ron Hicks (R-107)
Bill Lant (R-159)
Dave Muntzel (R-48)
Caleb Rowden (R-44)
Anne Zerr (R-65)

**Minority Members**
Jeremy LaFaver (D-25)
Tom McDonald (D-29)
Sharon L. Pace (D-74)

## Emerging Issues in Education

**Majority Members**
Lyle Rowland (R-155) *Chair*
Elaine Freeman Gannon (R-115)
    *Vice Chair*
Kurt Bahr (R-102)
Jack Bondon (R-56)
Dave Hinson (R-119)
Andrew Koenig (R-99)
Warren D. Love (R-125)
Dan Shaul (R-113)
David Wood (R-58)

**Minority Members**
Michael Butler (D-79)
Margo McNeil (D-69)
Judy Morgan (D-24)

## Employment Security

**Majority Members**
Wanda Brown (R-57) *Chair*
Bryan Spencer (R-63) *Vice Chair*
Justin Alferman (R-61)
Susan "Sue" Allen (R-100)
Charlie Davis (R-162)
Scott Fitzpatrick (R-158)
Tom Flanigan (R-163)
Mark A. Parkinson (R-105)
John D. Wiemann (R-103)

**Minority Members**
Karla May (D-84)
Joe Runions (D-37)

## Energy and the Environment

**Majority Members**
Rocky Miller (R-124) *Chair*
Nick Marshall (R-13) *Vice Chair*
Charles "Chuck" Basye (R-47)
Jack Bondon (R-56)
Kevin Corlew (R-14)
Tila Hubrecht (R-151)
Glenn Kolkmeyer (R-53)
Craig Redmon (R-4)
Tim Remole (R-6)

**Minority Members**
Mike Colona (D-80)
Brandon Ellington (D-22)
Margo McNeil (D-69)
Joe Runions (D-37)

## Ethics

**Majority Members**
Mike Cierpiot (R-30) *Chair*
Jay Barnes (R-60)
Nathan Beard (R-52)
Mike Bernskoetter (R-59)
Sandy Crawford (R-129)

**Minority Members**
Gina Mitten (D-83) *Vice Chair*
Lauren Arthur (D-18)
Pat Conway (D-10)
Bonnaye V. Mims (D-27)
Stacey Newman (D-87)

## Financial Institutions and Taxation

**Majority Members**
Tony Dugger (R-141) *Chair*
Cloria Brown (R-94) *Vice Chair*
T.J. Berry (R-38)
Sandy Crawford (R-129)
Andrew Koenig (R-99)
Randy Pietzman (R-41)
Nate Walker (R-3)

**Minority Members**
Ira Anders (D-21)
Jon Carpenter (D-15)
Mary Nichols (D-72)

## Fiscal Review

**Majority Members**
Susan "Sue" Allen (R-100) *Chair*
Scott Fitzpatrick (R-158) *Vice-Chair*
Justin Alferman (R-61)
Sonya Anderson (R-131)
Kathie Conway (R-104)
Shawn Rhoads (R-154)
Anne Zerr (R-65)

**Minority Members**
Deb Lavender (D-90)
Tom McDonald (D-29)
Judy Morgan (D-24)

LEGISLATIVE BRANCH

## General Laws

**Majority Members**
Caleb Jones (R-50) *Chair*
Kirk Mathews (R-110) *Vice Chair*
Eric Burlison (R-133)
Paul Curtman (R-109)
Kevin Engler (R-116)
Elijah Haahr (R-134)
Chrissy Sommer (R-106)

**Minority Members**
Jon Carpenter (D-15)
Jeremy LaFaver (D-25)
Tracy McCreery (D-88)

## Government Efficiency

**Majority Members**
Paul Curtman (R-109) *Chair*
Mike Kelley (R-127) *Vice Chair*
Delus Johnson (R-9)
Andrew Koenig (R-99)
Patricia Pike (R-126)
Jeffrey "Jeff" Pogue (R-143)
Sheila Solon (R-31)
Rob Vescovo (R-112)
Kenneth "Ken" Wilson (R-12)

**Minority Members**
Alan K. Green (D-67)
Tracy McCreery (D-88)
Rory Rowland (D-29)
Joe Runions (D-37)

## Government Oversight and Accountability

**Majority Members**
Jay Barnes (R-60) *Chair*
Tom Hurst (R-62) *Vice Chair*
Robert Cornejo (R-64)
Scott Fitzpatrick (R-158)
Elijah Haahr (R-134)
Jeffrey "Jeff" Messenger (R-130)
Rob Vescovo (R-112)

**Minority Members**
Courtney Allen Curtis (D-73)
Penny V. Hubbard (D-78)
Gina Mitten (D-83)

## Health and Mental Health Policy

**Majority Members**
Keith Frederick (R-121) *Chair*
Sue Entlicher (R-128)
Marsha Haefner (R-95)
Tila Hubrecht (R-151)
Lynn Morris (R-140)
Holly Rehder (R-148)
Becky Ruth (R-114)
William "Bill" White (R-161)
Anne Zerr (R-65)

**Minority Members**
Lauren Arthur (D-18) *Vice-Chair*
Jeanne Kirkton (D-91)
Sharon L. Pace (D-74)

## Health Insurance

**Majority Members**
Jim Hansen (R-40) *Chair*
Lynn Morris (R-140) *Vice Chair*
Robert Cornejo (R-64)
J. Eggleston (R-2)
Kevin Engler (R-116)
Justin S. Hill (R-108)
Rebecca Roeber (R-34)
William "Bill" White (R-161)
John D. Wiemann (R-103)

**Minority Members**
Kip Kendrick (D-45)
Margo McNeil (D-69)
Gina Mitten (D-83)

## Higher Education

**Majority Members**
Steve Cookson (R-153) *Chair*
Cloria Brown (R-94)
Dean A. Dohrman (R-51)
Paul Fitzwater (R-144)
Denny L. Hoskins (R-54)
Donna Lichtenegger (R-146)
Andrew McDaniel (R-150)
Chrissy Sommer (R-106)
Nate Walker (R-3)

**Minority Members**
Lauren Arthur (D-18) *Vice Chair*
Bonnaye V. Mims (D-27)
Tommie Pierson (D-66)

## Insurance

**Majority Members**
Rebecca Roeber (R-34) *Vice Chair*
J. Eggleston (R-2)
Jim Hansen (R-40)
Steve Lynch (R-122)
Becky Ruth (R-114)
Noel J. Shull (R-16)

**Minority Members**
Bob Burns (D-93)
Margo McNeil (D-69)
Bill Otto (D-70)

**Members**
Keith English (I-68)

## Judiciary

**Majority Members**
Kevin Austin (R-136) *Chair*
Joe Don McGaugh (R-39)
   *Vice Chair*
Kevin Corlew (R-14)
Robert Cornejo (R-64)
Paul Fitzwater (R-144)
Shelley "White" Keeney (R-145)
Mark A. Parkinson (R-105)

**Minority Members**
Mike Colona (D-80)
Kimberly M. Gardner (D-77)
Gina Mitten (D-83)

## Labor and Industrial Relations

**Majority Members**
Holly Rehder (R-148) *Chair*
Mike Kelley (R-127) *Vice Chair*
Wanda Brown (R-57)
Eric Burlison (R-133)
Bill Lant (R-159)
Jeffrey "Jeff" Messenger (R-130)
Rob Vescovo (R-112)

**Minority Members**
Stephen Webber (D-46)
Clem Smith (D-85)

## Local Government

**Majority Members**
Dave Hinson (R-119) *Chair*
Kenneth "Ken" Wilson (R-12)
   *Vice Chair*
Kevin Austin (R-136)
Gary Cross (R-35)
Kevin Engler (R-116)
S. Nick King (R-17)
Nick Marshall (R-13)
Becky Ruth (R-114)

**Minority Members**
Joe Adams (D-86)
Jacob Hummel (D-81)
DaRon McGee (D-36)
John Joseph Rizzo (D-19)

## Pensions

**Majority Members**
Nate Walker (R-3) *Chair*
William "Bill" White (R-161)
   *Vice Chair*
Lincoln Hough (R-135)
Caleb Jones (R-50)
Jeffery "Jeff" Justus (R-156)
Mike Lair (R-7)
Mike Leara (R-96)
Shawn Rhoads (R-154)
Lyle Rowland (R-155)

**Minority Members**
Ira Anders (D-21)
Kip Kendrick (D-45)
Judy Morgan (D-24)

## Professional Registration and Licensing

**Majority Members**
Eric Burlison (R-133) *Chair*
Chrissy Sommer (R-106)
   *Vice Chair*
Kevin Austin (R-136)
Nathan Beard (R-52)
Robert Cornejo (R-64)
Lyndall Fraker (R-137)
Diane Franklin (R-123)
Keith Frederick (R-121)
Shelley "White" Keeney (R-145)
Mike Moon (R-157)
Dean Plocher (R-89)
Robert Ross (R-142)
Kathryn "Kathy" Swan (R-147)
John D. Wiemann (R-103)

**Minority Members**
Jon Carpenter (D-15)
Michele Kratky (D-82)
Gail McCann Beatty (D-26)
DaRon McGee (D-36)
Joshua "Josh" Peters (D-76)
Rochelle Walton Gray (D-75)

## Property, Casualty, and Life Insurance

**Majority Members**
Noel J. Shull (R-16) *Chair*
Dave Muntzel (R-48) *Vice Chair*
Justin Alferman (R-61)
Travis Fitzwater (R-49)
Bill Lant (R-159)
Nick Marshall (R-13)
Mike Moon (R-157)
Randy Pietzman (R-41)
Chrissy Sommer (R-106)

**Minority Members**
Bob Burns (D-93)
Mike Colona (D-80)
Bill Otto (D-70)

## Public Safety and Emergency Preparedness

**Majority Members**
Shawn Rhoads (R-154) *Chair*
Galen Wayne Higdon, Jr. (R-11) *Vice Chair*
Kathie Conway (R-104)
Justin S. Hill (R-108)
Jeanie Lauer (R-32)
Andrew McDaniel (R-150)
Shane Roden (R-111)
Kenneth "Ken" Wilson (R-12)

**Minority Members**
Linda R. Black (D-117)
Penny V. Hubbard (D-78)
Charlie Norr (D-132)
Rochelle Walton Gray (D-75)

## Rules

**Majority Members**
Kevin Engler (R-116) *Chair*
Donna Pfautsch (R-33) *Vice-Chair*
Mike Lair (R-7)
Jeanie Lauer (R-32)
Mike Leara (R-96)
Lynn Morris (R-140)
Donald E. "Don" Phillips (R-138)

**Minority Members**
Kimberly M. Gardner (D-77)
Jacob Hummel (D-81)
Deb Lavender (D-90)
John Joseph Rizzo (D-19)

## Small Business

**Majority Members**
John C. McCaherty (R-97) *Chair*
Gary Cross (R-35) *Vice Chair*
Mike Bernskoetter (R-59)
Lyndall Fraker (R-137)
Jim Hansen (R-40)
S. Nick King (R-17)
Steve Lynch (R-122)
Jeffrey "Jeff" Messenger (R-130)
James W. "Jim" Neely (R-8)
Randy Pietzman (R-41)
Dan Shaul (R-113)
Lindell F. Shumake (R-5)

**Members**
Keith English (I-68)

**Minority Members**
Michael Butler (D-79)
Brandon Ellington (D-22)
Alan K. Green (D-67)
Ben Harris (D-118)
Deb Lavender (D-90)

## Social Services

**Majority Members**
Susan "Sue" Allen (R-100) *Chair*
Marsha Haefner (R-95) *Vice Chair*
Kurt Bahr (R-102)
Charlie Davis (R-162)
Travis Fitzwater (R-49)
Diane Franklin (R-123)
Keith Frederick (R-121)

**Minority Members**
Pat Conway (D-10)
Jeanne Kirkton (D-91)
Susan "Sue" Meredith (D-71)

## State and Local Governments

**Majority Members**
Sheila Solon (R-31) *Chair*
Glenn Kolkmeyer (R-53) *Vice Chair*
Justin Alferman (R-61)
Sue Entlicher (R-128)
Dave Hinson (R-119)
Donna Pfautsch (R-33)
Shawn Rhoads (R-154)

**Minority Members**
Tom McDonald (D-29)
Stacey Newman (D-87)

## Telecommunications

**Majority Members**
Bart Korman (R-42) *Chair*
Ron Hicks (R-107) *Vice Chair*
Sandy Crawford (R-129)
Tony Dugger (R-141)
Tom Flanigan (R-163)
Bill E. Kidd (R-20)
Warren D. Love (R-125)
Don Rone (R-149)
Jered Taylor (R-139)

**Minority Members**
Joe Adams (D-86)
Mary Nichols (D-72)
Sharon L. Pace (D-74)

## Trade and Tourism

**Majority Members**
Donald E. "Don" Phillips (R-138) *Chair*
Jeffery "Jeff" Justus (R-156) *Vice Chair*
T.J. Berry (R-38)
Travis Fitzwater (R-49)
Elaine Freeman Gannon (R-115)
Tom Hurst (R-62)
John C. McCaherty (R-97)
Rocky Miller (R-124)
David Wood (R-58)

**Minority Members**
Michele Kratky (D-82)
Tom McDonald (D-29)
Charlie Norr (D-132)

## Transportation

**Majority Members**
Glenn Kolkmeyer (R-53) *Chair*
Bart Korman (R-42) *Vice Chair*
Sue Entlicher (R-128)
Lincoln Hough (R-135)
Caleb Jones (R-50)
Bill Lant (R-159)
Kirk Mathews (R-110)
Rebecca Roeber (R-34)
Don Rone (R-149)

**Minority Members**
Bob Burns (D-93)
Karla May (D-84)
Tom McDonald (D-29)

## Utilities

**Majority Members**
T.J. Berry (R-38) *Chair*
Sandy Crawford (R-129) *Vice Chair*
Lyndall Fraker (R-137)
Bart Korman (R-42)
Mike Leara (R-96)
Andrew McDaniel (R-150)
Rocky Miller (R-124)

**Members**
Keith English (I-68)

**Minority Members**
Mike Colona (D-80)
Jacob Hummel (D-81)
Sharon L. Pace (D-74)
Clem Smith (D-85)

## Utility Infrastructure

**Majority Members**
Lyndall Fraker (R-137) *Chair*
Tim Remole (R-6) *Vice Chair*
Mike Bernskoetter (R-59)
Mike Cierpiot (R-30)
Charlie Davis (R-162)
Shamed Dogan (R-98)
Tony Dugger (R-141)
Travis Fitzwater (R-49)
Elijah Haahr (R-134)
Ron Hicks (R-107)
Bart Korman (R-42)
Rocky Miller (R-124)
Holly Rehder (R-148)
Bryan Spencer (R-63)

**Minority Members**
Ira Anders (D-21)
Tracy McCreery (D-88)
Tom McDonald (D-29)
Joshua "Josh" Peters (D-76)
Clem Smith (D-85)

## Veterans

**Majority Members**
Charlie Davis (R-162) *Chair*
Steve Lynch (R-122) *Vice Chair*
Charles "Chuck" Basye (R-47)
Nathan Beard (R-52)
Dean A. Dohrman (R-51)
John C. McCaherty (R-97)
Patricia Pike (R-126)
Shane Roden (R-111)
Lindell F. Shumake (R-5)
Sheila Solon (R-31)

**Minority Members**
Bob Burns (D-93)
Pat Conway (D-10)
Bill Otto (D-70)

## Ways and Means

**Majority Members**
Andrew Koenig (R-99) *Chair*
Mike Moon (R-157) *Vice Chair*
Gary Cross (R-35)
Paul Curtman (R-109)
Galen Wayne Higdon, Jr. (R-11)
Tila Hubrecht (R-151)
Mike Kelley (R-127)
Jeffrey "Jeff" Pogue (R-143)
Dan Shaul (R-113)

**Minority Members**
Jon Carpenter (D-15)
Courtney Allen Curtis (D-73)
Brandon Ellington (D-22)

**LEGISLATIVE BRANCH**

## Workforce Standards and Development

**Majority Members**
Bill Lant (R-159) *Chair*
Dean A. Dohrman (R-51)
*Vice Chair*
Rick Brattin (R-55)
Lyndall Fraker (R-137)
Tom Hurst (R-62)
Mike Kelley (R-127)
Steve Lynch (R-122)
Nate Walker (R-3)

**Minority Members**
Bob Burns (D-93)
Clem Smith (D-85)
Stephen Webber (D-46)

# State Legislature of Montana

Capitol Station, Helena, MT 59620
Tel: (406) 444-4800 (In Session only)
Tel: (406) 444-3064 (Legislative Services)  Fax: (406) 444-3036

## Montana Senate

Fax: (406) 444-4875 (In Session Only)
President of the Senate **Debby Barrett** (R) . . . . . . . . . . . . . (406) 681-3177
President Pro Tem **Frederick "Eric" Moore** (R) . . . . . . . . . (406) 234-3562
Majority Leader **Matthew M. Rosendale, Sr.** (R) . . . . . . . (406) 687-3549
Majority Whip **Edward Buttrey** (R) . . . . . . . . . . . . . . . . . (406) 750-6798
Majority Whip **Cary L. Smith** (R) . . . . . . . . . . . . . . . . . . (406) 698-9307
Minority Leader **Jon C. Sesso** (D) . . . . . . . . . . . . . . . . . (406) 490-7405
  Education: Wisconsin 1975 BA, 1978 MA
Minority Whip **Robyn Driscoll** (D) . . . . . . . . . . . . . . . . . (406) 272-2403
  Education: Rocky Mt Col (MT) 1992 BA
Minority Whip **Tom Facey** (D) . . . . . . . . . . . . . . . . . . . . (406) 240-4242
Secretary of the Senate **Marilyn Miller** . . . . . . . . . . . . . . (406) 444-4801
Sergeant-at-Arms **Carl Spencer** . . . . . . . . . . . . . . . . . . . (406) 444-4878
  E-mail: carlspencer@mt.gov

## Senators

**Party Affiliation Statistics:** Republicans: 29, Democrats: 21

Senator **Duane Ankney** (R-District 20) . . . . . . . . . . . . . . (406) 740-0629
  Counties Represented: Custer (part), Musselshell,    Tel: (406) 748-4328
  Rosebud (part), Treasure, Yellowstone (part)
  Term Expires: 2019
  P.O. Box 2138, Colstrip, MT 59323-2138
  E-mail: goodwind1.duane@gmail.com
  Committees: Energy and Telecommunications; Natural Resources; Taxation

Senator **Elsie Arntzen** (R-District 26) . . . . . . . . . . . . . . . (406) 534-2780
  Counties Represented: Yellowstone (part)    Tel: (406) 698-7845
  Term Expires: 2017
  2323 Azalea Lane, Billings, MT 59102-2516
  E-mail: emarntzen@gmail.com
  Committees: Business, Labor and Economic Affairs; Ethics; Highways and Transportation
  Education: Montana State 1992 BSEd; Montana 1978 BA

Senator **Debby Barrett** (R-District 36) . . . . . . . . . . . . . . (406) 681-3177
  Counties Represented: Beaverhead, Jefferson (part), Madison, Silver Bow (part)
  Term Expires: 2017
  18580 Mt. Highway 324, Dillon, MT 59725-8031
  E-mail: sen.debby.barrett@mt.gov
  Committees: Rules

Senator **Dick Barrett** (D-District 47) . . . . . . . . . . . . . . . . (406) 396-3256
  Counties Represented: Lake (part), Missoula (part)
  Term Expires: 2017
  219 Agnes Avenue, Missoula, MT 59801-8730
  E-mail: rnewbar@gmail.com
  Committees: Highways and Transportation; Local Government; Rules; Taxation
  Education: Swarthmore 1964 BA; Wisconsin 1970 PhD

Senator **Mark Blasdel** (R-District 4) . . . . . . . . . . . . . . . . (406) 261-3269
  Counties Represented: Flathead (part)
  Term Expires: 2019
  P.O. Box 1493, Kalispell, MT 59903-1493
  E-mail: sen.mark.blasdel@mt.gov
  Committees: Education and Cultural Resources; Energy and Telecommunications; Finance and Claims; Rules; Taxation
  Education: UNLV 1997 BS

Senator **John C. Brenden** (R-District 18) . . . . . . . . . . . . (406) 783-8394
  Counties Represented: Dawson, Richland, Wibaux
  Term Expires: 2017
  P.O. Box 970, Scobey, MT 59263-0970
  E-mail: senatorbrenden@gmail.com
  Committees: Committee on Committees; Finance and Claims; Fish and Game; Judiciary

Senator **Dee L. Brown** (R-District 2) . . . . . . . . . . . . . . . . (406) 387-9494
  Counties Represented: Flathead (part)
  Term Expires: 2017
  P.O. Box 444, Hungry Horse, MT 59919-0444
  Committees: Business, Labor and Economic Affairs; Committee on Committees; Ethics; Highways and Transportation; State Administration
  Education: Montana 1971 BA; Northern Montana 1986 MA

Senator **Taylor Brown** (R-District 28) . . . . . . . . . . . . . . . .(406) 348-2070
Counties Represented: Yellowstone (part)
Term Expires: 2017
775 Squaw Creek Road, Huntley, MT 59037-9219
E-mail: taylor@northernbroadcasting.com
Committees: Agriculture, Livestock, and Irrigation; Education and
Cultural Resources; Legislative Administration; Taxation

Senator **Edward Buttrey** (R-District 11) . . . . . . . . . . . . . . .(406) 750-6798
Counties Represented: Cascade (part)
Term Expires: 2019
27 Granite Hill Lane, Great Falls, MT 59405-8041
E-mail: ebuttrey@cteq.com
Committees: Business, Labor and Economic Affairs; Local
Government; Rules

Senator **Mary M. Caferro** (D-District 41) . . . . . . . . . . . . .(406) 461-2384
Counties Represented: Lewis and Clark (part)
Term Expires: 2019
607 North Davis Street, Helena, MT 59601-3737
E-mail: marycaferro@gmail.com
Committees: Agriculture, Livestock, and Irrigation; Finance and
Claims; Public Health, Welfare and Safety

Senator **Jill Cohenour** (D-District 42) . . . . . . . . . . . . . . .(406) 227-1144
Counties Represented: Lewis and Clark (part)
Term Expires: 2019
2610 Colt Drive, East Helena, MT 59635
E-mail: sen.jill.cohenour@mt.gov
Committees: Agriculture, Livestock, and Irrigation; Education and
Cultural Resources; Taxation

Senator **Patrick "Pat" Connell** (R-District 43) . . . . . . . . . .(406) 370-8682
Counties Represented: Ravalli (part)
Term Expires: 2019
567 Tiffany Lane, Hamilton, MT 59840
E-mail: connell4sd43@yahoo.com
Committees: Business, Labor and Economic Affairs; Energy and
Telecommunications; Natural Resources

Senator **Robyn Driscoll** (D-District 26) . . . . . . . . . . . . . . .(406) 272-2403
Counties Represented: Yellowstone (part)
Term Expires: 2017
404 Moule Drive, Billings, MT 59102-4861
E-mail: robyn@robyndriscoll.com
Committees: Energy and Telecommunications; Judiciary

Senator **Tom Facey** (D-District 50) . . . . . . . . . . . . . . . . . .(406) 728-6814
Counties Represented: Missoula (part)          Tel: (406) 240-4242
Term Expires: 2019
418 Plymouth Street, Missoula, MT 59801-4133
E-mail: facey_tom@hotmail.com
Committees: Business, Labor and Economic Affairs; Education and
Cultural Resources; Ethics; Fish and Game

Senator **Jennifer Fielder** (R-District 7) . . . . . . . . . . . . . . .(406) 444-4801
Counties Represented: Flathead (part), Mineral, Missoula (part),
Sanders
Term Expires: 2017
P.O. Box 2558, Thompson Falls, MT 59873-2558
E-mail: sen.jennifer.fielder@mt.gov
Committees: Fish and Game; Judiciary; Legislative Administration;
Natural Resources
Education: Wenatchee Valley 1987 AAS, 1988 AA;
Western State Col 1990 BS

Senator **Bradley Maxon Hamlett** (D-District 10) . . . . . . . .(406) 799-5885
Counties Represented: Cascade (part)
Term Expires: 2017
P.O. Box 49, Cascade, MT 59421-0049
E-mail: senatorhamlett@gmail.com
Committees: Finance and Claims; Fish and Game; Natural Resources

Senator **Kristin "Kris" Hansen** (R-District 14) . . . . . . . . . .(406) 262-7514
Counties Represented: Cascade (part), Chouteau (part), Hill (part),
Liberty
Term Expires: 2019
P.O. Box 1957, Havre, MT 59501
Committees: Agriculture, Livestock, and Irrigation; Committee on
Committees; Education and Cultural Resources; Finance and Claims;
Judiciary; Rules

Senator **Jedediah Hinkle** (R-District 32) . . . . . . . . . . . . . .(406) 585-0722
Counties Represented: Gallatin (part)
Term Expires: 2019
2451 Daws Drive, Apt B, Bozeman, MT 59718-6982
E-mail: sen.jedediah.hinkle@mt.gov
Committees: Fish and Game; Judiciary; State Administration

Senator **Brian E. Hoven** (R-District 13) . . . . . . . . . . . . . . .(406) 761-8533
Counties Represented: Cascade (part)          Tel: (406) 899-5000
Term Expires: 2019
1501 Meadowlark Drive, Great Falls, MT 59404
E-mail: brian@hovenequipment.com
Committees: Agriculture, Livestock, and Irrigation; Natural Resources;
Taxation

Senator **David Howard** (R-District 29) . . . . . . . . . . . . . . . .(406) 444-4800
Counties Represented: Carbon, Stillwater, Sweet Grass (part)
Term Expires: 2019
P.O. Box 10, Park City, MT 59063
E-mail: sendavidhoward@gmail.com
Committees: Agriculture, Livestock, and Irrigation; Finance and
Claims; Public Health, Welfare and Safety

Senator **Llew Jones** (R-District 9) . . . . . . . . . . . . . . . . . . .(406) 289-0345
Counties Represented: Glacier (part), Lewis and Clark (part), Pondera
(part), Teton, Toole
Term Expires: 2019
1102 Fourth Avenue SW, Conrad, MT 59425-1919
E-mail: sen.llew.jones@mt.gov
Committees: Education and Cultural Resources; Energy and
Telecommunications; Finance and Claims

Senator **Douglas "Doug" Kary** (R-District 22) . . . . . . . . .(406) 698-1478
Counties Represented: Yellowstone (part)
Term Expires: 2019
415 West Wicks Lane, Billings, MT 59105
E-mail: sen.doug.kary@mt.gov
Committees: Energy and Telecommunications; Judiciary; State
Administration

Senator **Christine Kaufmann** (D-District 40) . . . . . . . . . . .(406) 439-0256
Counties Represented: Lewis and Clark (part), Powell (part)
Term Expires: 2017
825 Breckenridge Street, Helena, MT 59601-4433
E-mail: kaufmann@mt.net
Committees: Highways and Transportation; Natural Resources; Taxation

Senator **Jim Keane** (D-District 38) . . . . . . . . . . . . . . . . . . .(406) 723-8378
Counties Represented: Jefferson (part), Silver Bow (part)
Term Expires: 2019
2131 Wall Street, Butte, MT 59701-5527
Committees: Energy and Telecommunications; Finance and Claims;
Natural Resources

Senator **Bob Keenan** (R-District 5) . . . . . . . . . . . . . . . . . .(406) 250-4111
Counties Represented: Flathead (part), Lake (part)   Tel: (406) 837-4989
Term Expires: 2019
P.O. Box 697, Bigfork, MT 59911
E-mail: bob@bobkeenan.us
Committees: Education and Cultural Resources; Energy and
Telecommunications; Finance and Claims; Rules

Senator **Cliff Larsen** (D-District 47) . . . . . . . . . . . . . . . . . .(406) 544-6263
Counties Represented: Lake (part), Missoula (part)
Term Expires: 2017
8925 LaValle Creek Road, Missoula, MT 59808-9324
E-mail: cliff@larsenusa.com
Committees: Energy and Telecommunications; Judiciary; Natural
Resources

Senator **Sue Malek** (D-District 46) . . . . . . . . . . . . . . . . . . .(406) 370-2424
Counties Represented: Missoula (part)
Term Expires: 2017
1400 Prairie Way, Missoula, MT 59802-3420
E-mail: suemalek@gmail.com
Committees: Ethics; Highways and Transportation; Local Government;
State Administration; Taxation

Senator **Mary McNally** (D-District 24) . . . . . . . . . . . . . . . .(406) 671-1376
Counties Represented: Yellowstone (part)
Term Expires: 2019
P.O. Box 20584, Billings, MT 59104
E-mail: sen.mary.mcnally@mt.gov
Committees: Energy and Telecommunications; Judiciary; Local
Government

Senator **Mary Sheehy Moe** (D-District 12) . . . . . . . . . . . .(406) 444-4800
Counties Represented: Cascade (part)
Term Expires: 2019
8 Prospect Drive, Great Falls, MT 59405-4120
E-mail: moe.mt.senate@gmail.com
Committees: Education and Cultural Resources; Judiciary; Rules

Senator **Frederick "Eric" Moore** (R-District 19) . . . . . . . .(406) 234-3562
Counties Represented: Carter, Custer (part), Fallon, Garfield, McCone,
Powder River (part), Prairie
Term Expires: 2019
487 Signal Butte Road, Miles City, MT 59301-9205
E-mail: mail@senatorericmoore.com
Committees: Agriculture, Livestock, and Irrigation; Finance and
Claims; Rules

*(continued on next page)*

**Senators** *continued*

Senator **Mike Phillips** (D-District 31) . . . . . . . . . . . . . . . . (406) 599-5857
Counties Represented: Gallatin (part)
Term Expires: 2017
9 West Arnold Street, Bozeman, MT 59715-6127
Committees: Finance and Claims; Fish and Game; Rules

Senator **Jennifer "JP" Pomnichowski** (D-District 33) . . . . (406) 444-4800
Counties Represented: Gallatin (part)
Term Expires: 2019
222 Westridge Drive, Bozeman, MT 59715-6025
E-mail: sen.jp@mt.gov
Committees: Agriculture, Livestock, and Irrigation; Legislative
Administration; Local Government; Taxation
Education: Montana State 1991 BS

Senator **Rick Ripley** (R-District 10) . . . . . . . . . . . . . . . . . . (406) 562-3502
Counties Represented: Cascade (part)
Term Expires: 2017
8920 MT Highway 200, Wolf Creek, MT 59648-8639
E-mail: ripley@3rivers.net
Committees: Committee on Committees; Finance and Claims; Fish and
Game; Natural Resources; Rules

Senator **Matthew M. Rosendale, Sr.** (R-District 17) . . . . . (406) 687-3549
Counties Represented: Blaine (part), Daniels, Hill (part), Phillips (part),
Roosevelt (part), Sheridan, Valley (part)
Term Expires: 2017
1954 Highway 16, Glendive, MT 59330-9218
E-mail: mattrosendale@midrivers.com
Committees: Finance and Claims; Rules

Senator **Scott Sales** (R-District 35) . . . . . . . . . . . . . . . . . . (406) 579-7994
Counties Represented: Broadwater, Gallatin (part), Lewis and Clark
(part)
Term Expires: 2017
P.O. Box 11163, Bozeman, MT 59719-1163
E-mail: sales4mtsenate@hotmail.com
Committees: Highways and Transportation; Judiciary; Local
Government
Education: Boise State 1982 BBA

Senator **Diane Sands** (D-District 49) . . . . . . . . . . . . . . . . . (406) 444-4800
Counties Represented: Missoula (part)
Term Expires: 2019
4487 Nicole Court, Missoula, MT 59803-2791
E-mail: senatorsands@gmail.com
Committees: Highways and Transportation; Judiciary; Public Health,
Welfare and Safety
Education: Montana 1974 AB

Senator **Jon C. Sesso** (D-District 37) . . . . . . . . . . . . . . . . . (406) 490-7405
Counties Represented: Silver Bow (part)
Term Expires: 2017
811 W Galena Street, Butte, MT 59701-1540
E-mail: jonsesso@yahoo.com
Committees: Finance and Claims; Rules

Senator **Cary L. Smith** (R-District 27) . . . . . . . . . . . . . . . . (406) 698-9307
Counties Represented: Yellowstone (part)
Term Expires: 2019
3650 Decathlon Parkway, Apt 9, Billings, MT 59102-7215
E-mail: sen.cary.smith@mt.gov
Committees: Business, Labor and Economic Affairs; Finance and
Claims; Fish and Game; Public Health, Welfare and Safety; Rules

Senator **Sharon Stewart-Peregoy** (D-District 21) . . . . . . . . (406) 639-2198
Counties Represented: Big Horn, Powder River (part), Rosebud (part),
Yellowstone (part)
Term Expires: 2017
P.O. Box 211, Crow Agency, MT 29022-0211
Committees: Agriculture, Livestock, and Irrigation; Business, Labor
and Economic Affairs; Education and Cultural Resources

Senator **Nels Swandal** (R-District 30) . . . . . . . . . . . . . . . . (406) 444-4800
Counties Represented: Gallatin (part), Park, Sweet Grass (part)
Term Expires: 2019
P.O. Box 147, Wilsall, MT 59086
E-mail: sen.nels.swandal@mt.gov
Committees: Agriculture, Livestock, and Irrigation; Judiciary; Public
Health, Welfare and Safety

Senator **Janna Taylor** (R-District 6) . . . . . . . . . . . . . . . . . . (406) 253-8766
Counties Represented: Flathead (part), Lake (part)
Term Expires: 2017
P.O. Box 233, Dayton, MT 59914-0233
E-mail: sen.janna.taylor@mt.gov
Committees: Committee on Committees; Finance and Claims;
Highways and Transportation; Local Government; Taxation

Senator **Fred A. Thomas** (R-District 45) . . . . . . . . . . . . . . (406) 370-4001
Counties Represented: Missoula (part)         Tel: (406) 777-4000
Term Expires: 2017
1004 South Burnt Fork Road, Stevensville, MT 59870-6658
E-mail: sfredthomas@yahoo.com
Committees: Highways and Transportation; Public Health, Welfare and
Safety; Rules; Taxation
Education: Montana State 1981

Senator **Bruce Tutvedt** (R-District 3) . . . . . . . . . . . . . . . . (406) 257-9732
Counties Represented: Flathead (part)
Term Expires: 2017
2335 West Valley Drive, Kalispell, MT 59901
E-mail: tutvedt@montanasky.us
Committees: Energy and Telecommunications; Legislative
Administration; Local Government; Taxation

Senator **Gordon Vance** (R-District 34) . . . . . . . . . . . . . . . . (406) 587-8608
Counties Represented: Gallatin (part)
Term Expires: 2019
305 Stillwater Avenue, Bozeman, MT 59718-1917
E-mail: vancesd34@gmail.com
Committees: Business, Labor and Economic Affairs; Highways and
Transportation; Local Government

Senator **Chas V. Vincent** (R-District 1) . . . . . . . . . . . . . . . (406) 293-1575
Counties Represented: Lincoln
Term Expires: 2017
34 Paul Bunyan Lane, Libby, MT 59923-7990
E-mail: cvvincent@hotmail.com
Committees: Committee on Committees; Fish and Game; Judiciary;
Natural Resources

Senator **Gene Vuckovich** (D-District 39) . . . . . . . . . . . . . . (406) 563-2313
Counties Represented: Deer Lodge, Granite, Powell (part), Silver Bow
(part)
Term Expires: 2017
1205 West Third Street, Anaconda, MT 59711-1801
E-mail: sen.gene.vuckovich@mt.gov
Committees: Business, Labor and Economic Affairs; Fish and Game;
Legislative Administration; Local Government

Senator **Roger Webb** (R-District 23) . . . . . . . . . . . . . . . . . (406) 861-9322
Counties Represented: Yellowstone (part)         Fax: (406) 248-1953
Term Expires: 2017
1132 Ginger Avenue, Billings, MT 59105-2062
E-mail: webb4mt@hotmail.com
Committees: Energy and Telecommunications; Finance and Claims;
State Administration

Senator **Lea Whitford** (D-District 8) . . . . . . . . . . . . . . . . . (406) 450-4057
Counties Represented: Flathead (part), Glacier (part), Lake (part),
Pondera (part)
Term Expires: 2019
221 Ed Williams Road, Cut Bank, MT 59427
Committees: Business, Labor and Economic Affairs; Highways and
Transportation; State Administration

Senator **Jonathan Windy Boy** (D-District 16) . . . . . . . . . . (406) 444-3064
Counties Represented: Blaine (part), Chouteau (part), Hill (part),
Phillips (part), Roosevelt (part), Valley (part)
Term Expires: 2017
P.O. Box 269, Box Elder, MT 59521-0195
E-mail: senatorjwb@gmail.com
Committees: Energy and Telecommunications; Finance and Claims;
Public Health, Welfare and Safety

Senator **Cynthia Wolken** (D-District 48) . . . . . . . . . . . . . . (406) 444-4800
Counties Represented: Missoula (part)
Term Expires: 2019
P.O. Box 16503, Missoula, MT 59808
E-mail: sen.cynthia.wolken@mt.gov
Committees: Agriculture, Livestock, and Irrigation; Finance and
Claims; Rules

# Senate Standing Committees

## Agriculture, Livestock, and Irrigation

| **Majority Members** | **Minority Members** |
| --- | --- |
| Taylor Brown (R-28) *Chair* | Mary M. Caferro (D-41) |
| Brian E. Hoven (R-13) *Vice Chair* | Jill Cohenour (D-42) |
| Kristin "Kris" Hansen (R-14) | Jennifer "JP" Pomnichowski (D-33) |
| David Howard (R-29) | Sharon Stewart-Peregoy (D-21) |
| Frederick "Eric" Moore (R-19) | Cynthia Wolken (D-48) |
| Nels Swandal (R-30) | |

## Business, Labor and Economic Affairs

**Majority Members**
Edward Buttrey (R-11) *Chair*
Elsie Arntzen (R-26) *Vice Chair*
Dee L. Brown (R-2)
Patrick "Pat" Connell (R-43)
Cary L. Smith (R-27)
Gordon Vance (R-34)

**Minority Members**
Tom Facey (D-50)
Sharon Stewart-Peregoy (D-21)
Gene Vuckovich (D-39)
Lea Whitford (D-8)

## Committee on Committees

**Majority Members**
John C. Brenden (R-18) *Chair*
Dee L. Brown (R-2)
Kristin "Kris" Hansen (R-14)
Rick Ripley (R-10)
Janna Taylor (R-6)
Chas V. Vincent (R-1)

## Education and Cultural Resources

**Majority Members**
Taylor Brown (R-28) *Chair*
Mark Blasdel (R-4) *Vice Chair*
Kristin "Kris" Hansen (R-14)
Llew Jones (R-9)
Bob Keenan (R-5)

**Minority Members**
Jill Cohenour (D-42)
Tom Facey (D-50)
Mary Sheehy Moe (D-12)
Sharon Stewart-Peregoy (D-21)

## Energy and Telecommunications

**Majority Members**
Roger Webb (R-23) *Chair*
Duane Ankney (R-20) *Vice Chair*
Mark Blasdel (R-4)
Patrick "Pat" Connell (R-43)
Llew Jones (R-9)
Douglas "Doug" Kary (R-22)
Bob Keenan (R-5)
Bruce Tutvedt (R-3)

**Minority Members**
Robyn Driscoll (D-26)
Jim Keane (D-38)
Cliff Larsen (D-47)
Mary McNally (D-24)
Jonathan Windy Boy (D-16)

## Ethics

**Majority Members**
Elsie Arntzen (R-26) *Chair*
Dee L. Brown (R-2) *Vice Chair*

**Minority Members**
Tom Facey (D-50)
Sue Malek (D-46)

## Finance and Claims

**Majority Members**
Llew Jones (R-9) *Chair*
Bob Keenan (R-5) *Vice Chair*
Mark Blasdel (R-4)
John C. Brenden (R-18)
Kristin "Kris" Hansen (R-14)
David Howard (R-29)
Frederick "Eric" Moore (R-19)
Rick Ripley (R-10)
Matthew M. Rosendale, Sr. (R-17)
Cary L. Smith (R-27)
Janna Taylor (R-6)
Roger Webb (R-23)

**Minority Members**
Jonathan Windy Boy (D-16)
Mary M. Caferro (D-41)
Bradley Maxon Hamlett (D-10)
Jim Keane (D-38)
Mike Phillips (D-31)
Jon C. Sesso (D-37)
Cynthia Wolken (D-48)

## Fish and Game

**Majority Members**
John C. Brenden (R-18) *Chair*
Rick Ripley (R-10) *Vice Chair*
Jennifer Fielder (R-7)
Jedediah Hinkle (R-32)
Cary L. Smith (R-27)
Chas V. Vincent (R-1)

**Minority Members**
Tom Facey (D-50)
Bradley Maxon Hamlett (D-10)
Mike Phillips (D-31)
Gene Vuckovich (D-39)

## Highways and Transportation

**Majority Members**
Elsie Arntzen (R-26) *Chair*
Gordon Vance (R-34) *Vice Chair*
Dee L. Brown (R-2)
Scott Sales (R-35)
Janna Taylor (R-6)
Fred A. Thomas (R-45)

**Minority Members**
Diane Sands (D-49)
Dick Barrett (D-47)
Christine Kaufmann (D-40)
Sue Malek (D-46)
Lea Whitford (D-8)

## Judiciary

**Majority Members**
Scott Sales (R-35) *Chair*
Jennifer Fielder (R-7) *Vice Chair*
John C. Brenden (R-18)
Kristin "Kris" Hansen (R-14)
Jedediah Hinkle (R-32)
Douglas "Doug" Kary (R-22)
Nels Swandal (R-30)
Chas V. Vincent (R-1)

**Minority Members**
Robyn Driscoll (D-26)
Cliff Larsen (D-47)
Mary McNally (D-24)
Mary Sheehy Moe (D-12)
Diane Sands (D-49)

## Legislative Administration

**Majority Members**
Jennifer Fielder (R-7) *Chair*
Taylor Brown (R-28) *Vice Chair*
Bruce Tutvedt (R-3)

**Minority Members**
Jennifer "JP" Pomnichowski (D-33)
Gene Vuckovich (D-39)

## Local Government

**Majority Members**
Janna Taylor (R-6) *Chair*
Edward Buttrey (R-11) *Vice Chair*
Scott Sales (R-35)
Bruce Tutvedt (R-3)
Gordon Vance (R-34)

**Minority Members**
Dick Barrett (D-47)
Sue Malek (D-46)
Mary McNally (D-24)
Jennifer "JP" Pomnichowski (D-33)
Gene Vuckovich (D-39)

## Natural Resources

**Majority Members**
Chas V. Vincent (R-1) *Chair*
Rick Ripley (R-10) *Vice Chair*
Duane Ankney (R-20)
Patrick "Pat" Connell (R-43)
Jennifer Fielder (R-7)
Brian E. Hoven (R-13)

**Minority Members**
Bradley Maxon Hamlett (D-10)
Christine Kaufmann (D-40)
Jim Keane (D-38)
Cliff Larsen (D-47)

## Public Health, Welfare and Safety

**Majority Members**
Fred A. Thomas (R-45) *Chair*
David Howard (R-29) *Vice Chair*
Cary L. Smith (R-27)
Nels Swandal (R-30)

**Minority Members**
Mary M. Caferro (D-41)
Diane Sands (D-49)
Jonathan Windy Boy (D-16)

## Rules

**Majority Members**
Matthew M. Rosendale, Sr. (R-17) *Chair*
Frederick "Eric" Moore (R-19) *Vice Chair*
Debby Barrett (R-36)
Mark Blasdel (R-4)
Edward Buttrey (R-11)
Kristin "Kris" Hansen (R-14)
Bob Keenan (R-5)
Rick Ripley (R-10)
Cary L. Smith (R-27)
Fred A. Thomas (R-45)

**Minority Members**
Dick Barrett (D-47)
Mary Sheehy Moe (D-12)
Mike Phillips (D-31)
Jon C. Sesso (D-37)
Cynthia Wolken (D-48)

## State Administration

**Majority Members**
Dee L. Brown (R-2) *Chair*
Roger Webb (R-23) *Vice Chair*
Jedediah Hinkle (R-32)
Douglas "Doug" Kary (R-22)

**Minority Members**
Sue Malek (D-46)
Lea Whitford (D-8)

## Taxation

**Majority Members**
Bruce Tutvedt (R-3) *Chair*
Fred A. Thomas (R-45) *Vice Chair*
Duane Ankney (R-20)
Mark Blasdel (R-4)
Taylor Brown (R-28)
Brian E. Hoven (R-13)
Janna Taylor (R-6)

**Minority Members**
Dick Barrett (D-47)
Jill Cohenour (D-42)
Christine Kaufmann (D-40)
Sue Malek (D-46)
Jennifer "JP" Pomnichowski (D-33)

**LEGISLATIVE BRANCH**

# Montana House of Representatives

1301 East 6th Avenue, Helena, MT 59601

Tel: (406) 444-4800 (In Session) Fax: (406) 444-1865 (In Session)

Speaker of the House **Austin Knudsen** (R) . . . . . . . . . . . . (406) 539-4268
Speaker Pro Tem **Lee Randall** (R) . . . . . . . . . . . . . . . . . . . . (406) 436-2807
Majority Leader **Keith Regier** (R) . . . . . . . . . . . . . . . . . . . (406) 756-6141
Majority Whip **Gerald A. "Jerry" Bennett** (R) . . . . . . . . (406) 293-7012
Majority Whip **Alan Doane** (R) . . . . . . . . . . . . . . . . . . . . . (406) 583-7546
   Education: Dawson Comm Col 2006
Majority Whip **Greg Hertz** (R) . . . . . . . . . . . . . . . . . . . . . . (406) 253-9505
   Education: Montana 1980 BA
Majority Whip **Sarah Laszloffy** (R) . . . . . . . . . . . . . . . . . . (406) 530-7013
Minority Leader **Chuck Hunter** (D) . . . . . . . . . . . . . . . . . (406) 202-2030
   Education: Elmira BA; Colorado 1982 MA
Minority Caucus Chair **Carolyn Pease-Lopez** (D) . . . . . . . (406) 245-2265
Minority Whip **Bryce Bennett** (D) . . . . . . . . . . . . . . . . . . . (406) 546-3629
Minority Whip **Jenny Eck** (D) . . . . . . . . . . . . . . . . . . . . . . (406) 459-1082
   Education: Smith BA
Minority Whip **Margaret "Margie" MacDonald** (D) . . . . . (406) 698-4917
Sergeant-at-Arms **Dennis Robert Lenz** (R) . . . . . . . . . . . . (406) 444-4200
   E-mail: dlenz@mt.gov
   Education: Texas Christian (Attended)
Chief Clerk of the House **Lindsey Grovom** . . . . . . . . . . . . (406) 444-4819
   E-mail: lgrovom@mt.gov

# Representatives

**Party Affiliation Statistics:** Republicans: 59, Democrats: 41

Representative **Nancy Ballance** (R-District 87) . . . . . . . . . (406) 444-4800
   Counties Represented: Ravalli (part)    Tel: (406) 444-4819
   Term Expires: 2017
   388 Hawk Point Lane, Hamilton, MT 59840-9269
   E-mail: nancyballance@aol.com
   Committees: Appropriations

Representative **Bryce Bennett** (D-District 91) . . . . . . . . . . (406) 546-3629
   Counties Represented: Missoula (part)
   Term Expires: 2017
   P.O. Box 9062, Missoula, MT 59807-9062
   P.O. Box 200400, Helena, MT 59620-0400
   E-mail: bennettforhouse@gmail.com
   Committees: Education; Ethics

Representative **Gerald A. "Jerry" Bennett** (R-District 1) . . . . . . . . . (406) 293-7012
   Counties Represented: Lincoln (part)
   Term Expires: 2017
   784 Taylor Road, Libby, MT 59923-8458
   E-mail: jbenhd1@hotmail.com
   Committees: Judiciary; Legislative Administration; Rules

Representative **Seth Berglee** (R-District 58) . . . . . . . . . . . (406) 690-9329
   Counties Represented: Carbon
   Term Expires: 2017
   P.O. Box 340, Joliet, MT 59041
   E-mail: rep.seth.berglee@mt.gov
   Committees: Agriculture; Human Services; Judiciary

Representative **Tom Berry** (R-District 40) . . . . . . . . . . . . . (406) 698-3940
   Counties Represented: Musselshell, Yellowstone   Res: (406) 323-3151
   (part)
   Term Expires: 2017
   P.O. Box 157, Roundup, MT 59072-0157
   E-mail: tom@tomberrymt.com
   Committees: Business and Labor; Federal Relations, Energy and Telecommunications; Local Government

Representative **Randy Brodehl** (R-District 9) . . . . . . . . . . . (406) 751-1612
   Counties Represented: Flathead (part)
   Term Expires: 2017
   16 White Bark, Kalispell, MT 59901-2122
   E-mail: randybrodehl57@gmail.com
   Committees: Appropriations

Representative **Bob Brown** (R-District 13) . . . . . . . . . . . . . (406) 827-9894
   Counties Represented: Flathead (part), Sanders   Tel: (406) 242-0141
   (part)
   Term Expires: 2017
   P.O. Box 1907, Thompson Falls, MT 59873-1907
   E-mail: rep.bob.brown@mt.gov
   Committees: Fish, Wildlife and Parks; Natural Resources; State Administration
   Education: Montana State 1970 BA, 1974 BA; Montana 1988 MEd

Representative **Zach Brown** (D-District 63) . . . . . . . . . . . . (406) 579-5697
   Counties Represented: Gallatin (part)
   Term Expires: 2017
   503 S Willson Avenue, Bozeman, MT 59715-5236
   E-mail: brownformontana@gmail.com
   Committees: Fish, Wildlife and Parks; Natural Resources; Taxation
   Education: Montana

Representative **Tom Burnett** (R-District 67) . . . . . . . . . . . (406) 459-6148
   Counties Represented: Gallatin (part)    Tel: (406) 539-7075
   Term Expires: 2017
   4143 Rain Roper Drive, Bozeman, MT 59715-0634
   E-mail: burnetthd67@gmail.com
   Committees: Appropriations

Representative **Christy Clark** (R-District 17) . . . . . . . . . . . (406) 466-2483
   Counties Represented: Lewis and Clark (part), Pondera (part), Teton
   Term Expires: 2017
   P.O. Box 423, Choteau, MT 59422-0423
   E-mail: christy_clark@ymail.com
   Committees: Agriculture; Business and Labor; Legislative Administration; Transportation
   Education: Cal State (Sacramento) BA

Representative **Rob Cook** (R-District 18) . . . . . . . . . . . . . (406) 868-3426
   Counties Represented: Glacier (part), Pondera   Tel: (406) 278-7535
   (part), Toole
   Term Expires: 2017
   223 First Avenue SW, Conrad, MT 59425-3426
   E-mail: robc_hd27@itbusa.com
   Committees: Fish, Wildlife and Parks; Taxation; Transportation

Representative **Virginia Court** (D-District 50) . . . . . . . . . . (406) 259-5099
   Counties Represented: Yellowstone (part)
   Term Expires: 2017
   18 Heatherwood Lane, Billings, MT 59102-2449
   E-mail: vjchd52@yahoo.com
   Committees: Fish, Wildlife and Parks; Judiciary; Natural Resources

Representative **Mike Cuffe** (R-District 2) . . . . . . . . . . . . . (406) 293-1247
   Counties Represented: Lincoln (part)    Tel: (406) 889-5777
   Term Expires: 2017
   P.O. Box 1685, Eureka, MT 59917-1685
   E-mail: rep.mike.cuffe@mt.gov
   Committees: Appropriations; Legislative Administration

Representative **Willis Curdy** (D-District 98) . . . . . . . . . . . (406) 546-0523
   Counties Represented: Missoula (part)   Tel: (406) 728-0981
   Term Expires: 2017
   11280 Kona Ranch Road, Missoula, MT 59804
   E-mail: rep.willis.curdy@mt.gov
   Committees: Agriculture; Business and Labor; Transportation

Representative **Geraldine Custer** (R-District 39) . . . . . . . . (406) 351-1235
   Counties Represented: Custer (part), Rosebud (part), Treasure, Yellowstone (part)
   Term Expires: 2017
   P.O. Box 1075, Forsyth, MT 59327
   E-mail: rep.geraldine.custer@mt.gov
   Committees: Federal Relations, Energy and Telecommunications; Local Government; Taxation

Representative **Alan Doane** (R-District 36) . . . . . . . . . . . . (406) 583-7546
   Counties Represented: Dawson, Wibaux
   Term Expires: 2017
   268 Country Road 521, Bloomfield, MT 59315-9500
   E-mail: alandoane@midrivers.com
   Committees: Human Services; Judiciary; Legislative Administration; Rules

Representative **Kimberly Dudik** (D-District 94) . . . . . . . . . (406) 459-6148
   Counties Represented: Missoula (part)
   Term Expires: 2017
   P.O. Box 16712, Missoula, MT 59808-6712
   E-mail: kimberly.dudik@gmail.com
   Committees: Appropriations; Rules
   Education: Montana 2003 JD; Montana State BSN

Representative **Mary Ann Dunwell** (D-District 84) . . . . . . . (406) 459-6148
   Counties Represented: Lewis and Clark (part)
   Term Expires: 2017
   2520 Lookout Circle, Helena, MT 59601
   E-mail: rep.maryann.dunwell@mt.gov
   Committees: Legislative Administration; Natural Resources; Taxation

Representative **Jenny Eck** (D-District 79) . . . . . . . . . . . . . (406) 459-1082
   Counties Represented: Lewis and Clark (part)
   Term Expires: 2017
   P.O. 1206, Helena, MT 59624-1206
   E-mail: jennyleeeck@hotmail.com
   Committees: Human Services; Judiciary; Rules

Representative **Ron Ehli** (R-District 86) . . . . . . . . . . . . . . (406) 363-3130
Counties Represented: Ravalli (part)     Tel: (406) 360-5789
Term Expires: 2017
P.O. Box 765, Hamilton, MT 59840-0765
E-mail: rep.ron.ehli@mt.gov
Committees: Appropriations

Representative **Janet Ellis** (D-District 81) . . . . . . . . . . . . . . (406) 459-6148
Counties Represented: Lewis and Clark (part)
Term Expires: 2017
P.O. Box 385, Helena, MT 59624
E-mail: rep.janet.ellis@mt.gov
Committees: Appropriations

Representative **Jeff Essmann** (R-District 54) . . . . . . . . . . . (406) 534-3345
Counties Represented: Yellowstone (part)
Term Expires: 2017
P.O. Box 80945, Billings, MT 59108
E-mail: jessmann@mt.gov
Committees: Education; Rules; State Administration

Representative **Clayton Fiscus** (R-District 43) . . . . . . . . . . (406) 860-6400
Counties Represented: Yellowstone (part)     Tel: (406) 252-6400
Term Expires: 2017
1800 Mary Street, Billings, MT 59105-4804
E-mail: fiscusrlty@aol.com
Committees: Fish, Wildlife and Parks; Judiciary; Transportation

Representative **Steve Fitzpatrick** (R-District 20) . . . . . . . . (406) 727-0826
Counties Represented: Cascade (part)
Term Expires: 2017
3203 15th Avenue South, Great Falls, MT 59405-5416
E-mail: fitzpatricks@bresnan.net
Committees: Business and Labor; Local Government; Natural
Resources

Representative **Kelly Flynn** (R-District 70) . . . . . . . . . . . . . (406) 266-3322
Counties Represented: Broadwater, Lewis and Clark (part)
Term Expires: 2017
P.O. Box 233, Townsend, MT 59644-0233
E-mail: hideaway1987@centurylink.net
Committees: Fish, Wildlife and Parks; Natural Resources

Representative **Moffie Funk** (D-District 82) . . . . . . . . . . . . . (406) 461-6788
Counties Represented: Lewis and Clark (part)
Term Expires: 2017
P.O. Box 925, Helena, MT 59624
E-mail: rep.moffie.funk@mt.gov
Committees: Education; Local Government; State Administration

Representative **Frank Garner** (R-District 7) . . . . . . . . . . . . (406) 471-7197
Counties Represented: Flathead (part)
Term Expires: 2017
P.O. Box 10176, Kalispell, MT 59904-0176
E-mail: rep.frank.garner@mt.gov
Committees: Local Government; State Administration; Transportation

Representative **Carl Glimm** (R-District 6) . . . . . . . . . . . . . . (406) 751-7334
Counties Represented: Flathead (part)
Term Expires: 2017
5107 Ashley Road, Kila, MT 59920
E-mail: rep.carl.glimm@mt.gov
Committees: Appropriations
Education: Montana State 1997 BS

Representative **Edward Greef** (R-District 88) . . . . . . . . . . . (406) 370-0581
Counties Represented: Ravalli (part)     Tel: (406) 273-7733
Term Expires: 2017
P.O. Box 1327, Florence, MT 29833-1327
E-mail: edgreef@hotmail.com
Committees: Education; Local Government; State Administration

Representative **Dave Hagstrom** (R-District 52) . . . . . . . . . (406) 698-7380
Counties Represented: Yellowstone (part)     Tel: (406) 248-7380
Term Expires: 2017
324 South 31st Street, Billings, MT 59101-3942
E-mail: drhagstrom@gmail.com
Committees: Appropriations
Education: Eastern Montana 1979 BA

Representative **Bill Harris** (R-District 29) . . . . . . . . . . . . . . (406) 429-2091
Counties Represented: Fergus (part), Petroleum     Tel: (406) 366-6775
Term Expires: 2017
P.O. Box 205, Winnett, MT 59087-0205
E-mail: rep.bill.harris@mt.gov
Committees: Agriculture; Ethics; Human Services; State Administration

Representative **Denise Hayman** (D-District 66) . . . . . . . . . (406) 579-1986
Counties Represented: Gallatin (part)     Tel: (406) 587-7229
Term Expires: 2017
120 Sourdough Ridge, Bozeman, MT 59715
E-mail: rep.denise.hayman@mt.gov
Committees: Human Services; Local Government; State Administration

Representative **Greg Hertz** (R-District 12) . . . . . . . . . . . . . (406) 253-9505
Counties Represented: Lake (part)     Tel: (406) 883-6296
Term Expires: 2017
38258 Pinewood Drive, Polson, MT 59860-8789
E-mail: greghertz11@gmail.com
Committees: Agriculture; Education; Rules; Taxation

Representative **Stephanie Hess** (R-District 28) . . . . . . . . . (406) 459-6148
Counties Represented: Hill (part)
Term Expires: 2017
P.O. Box 28, Havre, MT 59501
E-mail: rep.stephanie.hess@mt.gov
Committees: Fish, Wildlife and Parks; Human Services; Judiciary

Representative **Ellie Boldman Hill** (D-District 90) . . . . . . . (406) 218-9608
Counties Represented: Missoula (part)
Term Expires: 2017
501 Daly Avenue, Missoula, MT 59801-4412
E-mail: elliehillhd94@gmail.com
Committees: Human Services; Judiciary

Representative **Roy Hollandsworth** (R-District 27) . . . . . . (406) 627-2446
Counties Represented: Cascade (part), Chouteau     Tel: (406) 788-5027
(part), Liberty
Term Expires: 2017
1463 Prairie Dr., Brady, MT 59416-8928
E-mail: hgrain@3rivers.net
Committees: Appropriations

Representative **Kenneth Holmlund** (R-District 38) . . . . . . (406) 234-2956
Counties Represented: Custer (part)     Tel: (406) 951-6764
Term Expires: 2017
1612 Tompy Street, Miles City, MT 59301
E-mail: rep.kenneth.holmlund@mt.gov
Committees: Appropriations

Representative **Chuck Hunter** (D-District 83) . . . . . . . . . . . (406) 202-2030
Counties Represented: Lewis and Clark (part)     Tel: (406) 449-2327
Term Expires: 2017
717 Dearborn Ave., Helena, MT 59601-2712
E-mail: chunter717@bresnan.net
Committees: Business and Labor; Rules

Representative **Tom Jacobson** (D-District 21) . . . . . . . . . . . (406) 868-9814
Counties Represented: Cascade (part)
Term Expires: 2017
521 Riverview Drive E, Great Falls, MT 59404-1634
E-mail: tomjacobsonmt@gmail.com
Committees: Fish, Wildlife and Parks; Human Services; Taxation
Education: U Great Falls 2001 BBA; Wyoming 2003 MPA

Representative **Donald "Don" Jones** (R-District 46) . . . . . (406) 690-1434
Counties Represented: Yellowstone (part)
Term Expires: 2017
1945 Clarke Avenue, Billings, MT 59102-4019
E-mail: djjones@syntiros.com
Committees: Appropriations

Representative **Jessica Karjala** (D-District 48) . . . . . . . . . . (406) 459-6148
Counties Represented: Yellowstone (part)
Term Expires: 2017
6125 Masters Boulevard, Billings, MT 59106
E-mail: rep.jessica.karjala@mt.gov
Committees: Agriculture; Human Services; State Administration

Representative **Katharin Kelker, EdD** (D-District 47) . . . . . (406) 652-6716
Counties Represented: Yellowstone (part)     Tel: (406) 698-5610
Term Expires: 2017
2438 Rimrock Road, Billings, MT 59102
E-mail: rep.katharin.kelker@mt.gov
Committees: Education; Judiciary; Local Government

Representative **George G. Kipp III** (D-District 15) . . . . . . . (406) 229-1045
Counties Represented: Flathead (part), Glacier     Tel: (406) 338-2298
(part), Lake (part), Pondera (part)
Term Expires: 2017
P.O. Box 191, Heart Butte, MT 59448
E-mail: rep.george.kipp@mt.gov
Committees: Business and Labor; Transportation

Representative **Austin Knudsen** (R-District 34) . . . . . . . . . (406) 539-4268
Counties Represented: Daniels, Roosevelt (part), Sheridan, Valley (part)
Term Expires: 2017
P.O. Box 624, Culbertson, MT 59218-0624
E-mail: austinforhouse@yahoo.com
Committees: Business and Labor; Federal Relations, Energy and
Telecommunications; Rules

Representative **Debra Lamm** (R-District 60) . . . . . . . . . . . . (406) 223-9368
Counties Represented: Park (part)
Term Expires: 2017
P.O. Box 1390, Livingston, MT 59047-1390
E-mail: rep.debra.lamm@mt.gov
Committees: Education; Local Government; State Administration

*(continued on next page)*

**LEGISLATIVE BRANCH**

**Representatives** *continued*

Representative **Mike L. Lang** (R-District 33) . . . . . . . . . . (406) 654-7357
Counties Represented: Blaine (part), Hill (part), Phillips (part), Valley (part)
Term Expires: 2017
P.O. Box 109, Malta, MT 59538-7357
E-mail: rep.mike.lang@mt.gov
Committees: Agriculture; Business and Labor; Federal Relations, Energy and Telecommunications; Legislative Administration

Representative **Sarah Laszloffy** (R-District 53) . . . . . . . . . (406) 530-7013
Counties Represented: Yellowstone (part)
Term Expires: 2017
3165 US Highway 212 S, Laurel, MT 59044-8911
E-mail: sarah.laszloffy@gmail.com
Committees: Education; Judiciary; Rules

Representative **Steve Lavin** (R-District 8) . . . . . . . . . . . . . (406) 212-0699
Counties Represented: Flathead (part)
Term Expires: 2017
P.O. Box 11241, Kalispell, MT 59904-4241
E-mail: stevelavin4hd8@gmail.com
Committees: Local Government; Taxation; Transportation

Representative **Ed Lieser** (D-District 5) . . . . . . . . . . . . . . .(406) 471-2082
Counties Represented: Flathead (part)
Term Expires: 2017
1355 Lion Mountain Drive, Whitefish, MT 59937-8072
E-mail: liesered@yahoo.com
Committees: Fish, Wildlife and Parks; Natural Resources; Taxation
Education: Minnesota (Duluth) BS

Representative **Ryan Lynch** (D-District 76) . . . . . . . . . . . . .(406) 498-6625
Counties Represented: Silver Bow (part)
Term Expires: 2017
P.O. Box 934, Butte, MT 59703-0934
E-mail: lynchryan@gmail.com
Committees: Business and Labor; Federal Relations, Energy and Telecommunications
Education: Gonzaga 2004 BBA

Representative
**Margaret "Margie" MacDonald** (D-District 51) . . . . . . . (406) 698-4917
Counties Represented: Yellowstone (part)          Res: (406) 652-6625
Term Expires: 2017
P.O. Box 245, Billings, MT 59103-0245
E-mail: macmargaret@gmail.com
Committees: Agriculture; Judiciary; Rules; Transportation

Representative **Forrest Mandeville** (R-District 57) . . . . . . . (406) 690-1933
Counties Represented: Stillwater, Sweet Grass (part)
Term Expires: 2017
P.O. Box 337, Columbus, MT 59019-0337
E-mail: rep.forrest.mandeville@mt.gov
Committees: Human Services; Local Government; State Administration

Representative **Theresa Manzella** (R-District 85) . . . . . . . . (406) 546-9462
Counties Represented: Ravalli (part)          Tel: (406) 363-2898
Term Expires: 2017
640 Gold Creek Loop, Hamilton, MT 59840
E-mail: rep.theresa.manzella@mt.gov
Committees: Agriculture; Judiciary; Natural Resources

Representative **Kelly McCarthy** (D-District 49) . . . . . . . . . (406) 839-0071
Counties Represented: Yellowstone (part)
Term Expires: 2017
625 Yellowstone Avenue, Billings, MT 59101-1624
E-mail: kelly@kellyformontana.org
Committees: Appropriations
Education: Embry-Riddle 1999 BS; Texas (Dallas) 2006 MBA

Representative **Edith "Edie" McClafferty** (D-District 73) . . (406) 490-5873
Counties Represented: Silver Bow (part)          Tel: (406) 782-2700
Term Expires: 2017
1311 Stuart Avenue, Butte, MT 59701-5014
E-mail: edie.mcclafferty@gmail.com
Committees: Education; Legislative Administration; Taxation

Representative **Nate McConnell** (D-District 89) . . . . . . . . (406) 214-2445
Counties Represented: Missoula (part)
Term Expires: 2017
P.O. Box 8511, Missoula, MT 59807
E-mail: rep.nate.mcconnell@mt.gov
Committees: Judiciary; Local Government; Natural Resources

Representative **Wendy McKamey** (R-District 23) . . . . . . . . (406) 868-5006
Counties Represented: Cascade (part)          Tel: (406) 866-3300
Term Expires: 2017
33 Upper Millegan Road, Great Falls, MT 59405
E-mail: rep.wendy.mckamey@mt.gov
Committees: Agriculture; State Administration; Transportation

Representative **Robert "Bob" Mehlhoff** (D-District 22) . . . (406) 453-3526
Counties Represented: Cascade (part)
Term Expires: 2017
407 9th Street NW, Great Falls, MT 59404-2333
E-mail: rmehlhoff@yahoo.com
Committees: Appropriations

Representative **Gilbert Bruce Meyers** (R-District 32) . . . . . (406) 399-7776
Counties Represented: Blaine (part), Chouteau          Tel: (406) 395-4922
(part), Hill (part), Phillips (part)
Term Expires: 2017
P.O. Box 3016, Box Elder, MT 59521
E-mail: rep.gbruce.meyers@mt.gov
Committees: Education; Fish, Wildlife and Parks; Judiciary

Representative **Mike Miller** (R-District 80) . . . . . . . . . . . . (406) 793-5860
Counties Represented: Lewis and Clark (part), Powell (part)
Term Expires: 2017
20906 MT Highway 141, Helmville, MT 59843-9025
E-mail: mike4hd84@blackfoot.net
Committees: Rules; Taxation; Transportation

Representative **Matthew Monforton** (R-District 69) . . . . . .(406) 570-2949
Counties Represented: Gallatin (part)
Term Expires: 2017
32 Kelly Court, Bozeman, MT 59719-7630
E-mail: rep.matthew.monforton@mt.gov
Committees: Agriculture; Education; Judiciary

Representative **David "Doc" Moore** (R-District 92) . . . . . . (406) 239-3499
Counties Represented: Missoula (part)
Term Expires: 2017
3919 Paxson Street, Missoula, MT 59801-8941
E-mail: mooreformontana@gmail.com
Committees: Business and Labor; Federal Relations, Energy and Telecommunications
Education: Montana 1987 BA, 1991 BS, 2012 MPA

Representative **Dale Mortensen** (R-District 44) . . . . . . . . . (406) 855-1424
Counties Represented: Yellowstone (part)          Tel: (406) 256-0640
Term Expires: 2017
446 Caravan Avenue, Billings, MT 59105
E-mail: rep.dale.mortensen@mt.gov
Committees: Agriculture; Natural Resources; State Administration

Representative **Mark Noland** (R-District 10) . . . . . . . . . . . (406) 837-4810
Counties Represented: Flathead (part), Lake (part)          Tel: (406) 253-8982
Term Expires: 2017
PO Box 1852, Bigfork, MT 59911-1852
E-mail: marknolandhd10@gmail.com
Committees: Business and Labor; Fish, Wildlife and Parks; Natural Resources

Representative **Pat Noonan** (D-District 74) . . . . . . . . . . . . (406) 565-0518
Counties Represented: Silver Bow (part)
Term Expires: 2017
PO Box 90, Ramsay, MT 59748-0090
E-mail: pnoonan73@yahoo.com
Committees: Appropriations

Representative **Andrea Olsen** (D-District 100) . . . . . . . . . .(406) 459-6148
Counties Represented: Missoula (part)
Term Expires: 2017
622 Rollins Street, Missoula, MT 59801
E-mail: rep.andrea.olsen@mt.gov
Committees: Agriculture; Business and Labor; Natural Resources

Representative **Albert Olszewski** (R-District 11) . . . . . . . . . (406) 253-8248
Counties Represented: Flathead (part)
Term Expires: 2017
P.O. Box 11243, Kalispell, MT 59904
E-mail: rep.albert.olszewski@mt.gov
Committees: Agriculture; Human Services; Taxation

Representative **Ryan Osmundson** (R-District 30) . . . . . . . . (406) 374-2449
Counties Represented: Cascade (part), Fergus (part)          Tel: (406) 949-3715
Golden Valley, Judith Basin, Meagher, Wheatland
Term Expires: 2017
1394 S Buffalo Canyon Road, Buffalo, MT 59418-8005
E-mail: ryanosmundson@gmail.com
Committees: Appropriations

Representative **Carolyn Pease-Lopez** (D-District 42) . . . . . (406) 245-2265
Counties Represented: Big Horn (part), Yellowstone (part)
Term Expires: 2017
5723 US Highway 87 E, Billings, MT 59101-9074
E-mail: rep.carolyn.pease-lopez@mt.gov
Committees: Agriculture; Ethics; Human Services; Judiciary

Representative **Patricia Rae Peppers** (D-District 41)......(406) 697-0565
Counties Represented: Big Horn (part), Powder        Tel: (406) 477-8226
River (part), Rosebud (part)
Term Expires: 2017
P.O. Box 497, Lame Deer, MT 59043-0497
E-mail: peppers@rangeweb.net
Committees: Appropriations

Representative **Zac Perry** (D-District 3)................(406) 459-6148
Counties Represented: Flathead (part)
Term Expires: 2017
P.O. Box 268, Hungry Horse, MT 59919
E-mail: rep.zac.perry@mt.gov
Committees: Agriculture; Federal Relations, Energy and
Telecommunications; Judiciary; Legislative Administration

Representative **Andrew Person** (D-District 96) ......... (406) 210-0161
Counties Represented: Missoula (part)
Term Expires: 2017
P.O. Box 8452, Missoula, MT 59807-8452
E-mail: james.a.person@gmail.com
Committees: Federal Relations, Energy and Telecommunications; Fish,
Wildlife and Parks; Judiciary

Representative **Gordon Pierson, Jr.** (D-District 78) ...... (406) 846-3335
Counties Represented: Deer Lodge (part), Powell (part), Silver Bow
(part)
Term Expires: 2017
603 Washinton Street, Deer Lodge, MT 59722-1347
E-mail: rep.gordon.pierson@mt.gov
Committees: Agriculture; Business and Labor; Human Services;
Legislative Administration

Representative **Randy Pinocci** (R-District 19) ........... (406) 264-5391
Counties Represented: Cascade (part)        Tel: (406) 899-1947
Term Expires: 2017
E-mail: rep.randy.pinocci@mt.gov
Committees: Federal Relations, Energy and Telecommunications; Fish,
Wildlife and Parks; Judiciary

Representative **Christopher S. Pope** (D-District 65) ...... (406) 581-8739
Counties Represented: Gallatin (part)
Term Expires: 2017
1508 South Willson Avenue, Bozeman, MT 59715-5563
E-mail: rep.christopher.pope@mt.gov
Committees: Business and Labor; Federal Relations, Energy and
Telecommunications; Local Government

Representative **Jean Price** (D-District 24)...............(406) 452-9315
Counties Represented: Cascade (part)
Term Expires: 2017
422 15th Street South, Great Falls, MT 59405-2424
E-mail: jeanbigskybigwin@gmail.com
Committees: Education; Fish, Wildlife and Parks; State Administration

Representative **Lee Randall** (R-District 37) ............. (406) 436-2807
Counties Represented: Carter, Custer (part), Fallon, Garfield, McCone,
Powder River (part), Prairie
Term Expires: 2017
101 Randall Lane, Broadus, MT 59317-9519
E-mail: leerandall_2003@hotmail.com
Committees: Rules; Taxation

Representative **Alan Redfield** (R-District 59) ............(406) 333-4353
Counties Represented: Gallatin (part), Park (part),        Tel: (406) 444-4819
Sweet Grass (part)
Term Expires: 2017
538 Mill Creek Road, Livingston, MT 59047
E-mail: redfieldhd61@gmail.com
Committees: Agriculture; Human Services; Taxation
Education: Montana State 1975 BS

Representative **Keith Regier** (R-District 4) ..............(406) 756-6141
Counties Represented: Flathead (part)
Term Expires: 2017
1078 Stillwater Road, Kalispell, MT 59901-6902
E-mail: rep.keith.regier@mt.gov
Committees: Judiciary; Natural Resources; Rules

Representative **Vince Ricci** (R-District 55) .............(406) 855-9153
Counties Represented: Yellowstone (part)        Tel: (406) 628-7028
Term Expires: 2017
1231 Fifth Avenue, Laurel, MT 59044
E-mail: rep.vince.ricci@mt.gov
Committees: Business and Labor; Human Services; Local Government

Representative **Tom Richmond** (R-District 56) ......... (406) 208-5588
Counties Represented: Yellowstone (part)        Tel: (406) 656-1309
Term Expires: 2017
3103 Westfield Drive, Billings, MT 59106-1402
E-mail: tomrichmondmt@gmail.com
Committees: Federal Relations, Energy and Telecommunications; Local
Government

Representative **Daniel Salomon** (R-District 93) ......... (406) 675-0150
Counties Represented: Lake (part)        Tel: (406) 253-9724
Term Expires: 2017
42470 Salomon Road, Ronan, MT 59864-9272
E-mail: dansalomon12@gmail.com
Committees: Agriculture; Business and Labor; Education

Representative **Casey Schreiner** (D-District 25) ......... (406) 565-0372
Counties Represented: Cascade (part)
Term Expires: 2017
2223 6th Avenue N, Great Falls, MT 59401-1819
E-mail: rep.casey.schreiner@mt.gov
Committees: Federal Relations, Energy and Telecommunications; State
Administration

Representative **Nicholas Schwaderer** (R-District 14) ..... (406) 493-7835
Counties Represented: Mineral, Missoula (part), Sanders (part)
Term Expires: 2017
P.O. Box 370, Superior, MT 59872-0370
E-mail: nick.schwadererhd14@gmail.com
Committees: Education; Ethics; Local Government; Taxation

Representative **Ray L. Shaw** (R-District 72).............(406) 842-5039
Counties Represented: Beaverhead, Silver Bow (part)
Term Expires: 2017
251 Bivens Creek Road, Sheridan, MT 59749-9639
E-mail: shaw@3rivers.net
Committees: Fish, Wildlife and Parks; Natural Resources; State
Administration

Representative **Bridget Smith** (D-District 31) .......... (406) 230-2268
Counties Represented: Roosevelt (part), Valley        Tel: (406) 653-1234
(part)
Term Expires: 2017
516 Hill Street, Wolf Point, MT 59201-1245
E-mail: repbsmith@gmail.com
Committees: Fish, Wildlife and Parks; Taxation; Transportation

Representative **Scott Staffanson** (R-District 35) ......... (406) 798-3354
Counties Represented: Richland        Tel: (406) 480-0467
Term Expires: 2017
34704 County Road 122, Sidney, MT 59270-6353
E-mail: scottstaffanson@gmail.com
Committees: Agriculture; Business and Labor; Natural Resources

Representative **Tom Steenberg** (D-District 99) ......... (406) 721-5869
Counties Represented: Missoula (part)
Term Expires: 2017
4802 Aspen Drive, Missoula, MT 59802-5218
E-mail: mtsteenberg@bresnan.net
Committees: Business and Labor; Federal Relations, Energy and
Telecommunications; Local Government

Representative **Kathy Swanson** (D-District 77).......... (406) 563-5312
Counties Represented: Deer Lodge (part), Granite
Term Expires: 2017
308 E 6th Street, Anaconda, MT 59711-3016
E-mail: rep.kathy.swanson@mt.gov
Committees: Local Government; State Administration; Transportation

Representative **Mitch Tropila** (D-District 26) ............ (406) 899-3474
Counties Represented: Cascade (part)
Term Expires: 2017
P.O. Box 929, Great Falls, MT 59403-0929
E-mail: tropila@mt.net
Committees: Appropriations; Legislative Administration

Representative **Brad Tschida** (R-District 97) ........... (406) 546-4349
Counties Represented: Missoula (part)
Term Expires: 2017
10825 Mullan Road, Missoula, MT 59808
E-mail: rep.brad.tschida@mt.gov
Committees: Appropriations

Representative **Kirk B. Wagoner** (R-District 75) ......... (406) 465-8291
Counties Represented: Jefferson (part)
Term Expires: 2017
One Jackson Creek Road, #2347, Montana City, MT 59634-9714
E-mail: kirk@kirkbwagoner.org
Committees: Fish, Wildlife and Parks; Human Services; Judiciary

Representative **Susan Webber** (D-District 16)...........(406) 338-2159
Counties Represented: Glacier (part)        Tel: (406) 450-1894
Term Expires: 2017
P.O. Box 1011, Browning, MT 59417-1011
E-mail: rep.susan.webber@mt.gov
Committees: Agriculture; Education; Legislative Administration; State
Administration
Education: Montana BA; Montana State MPA

*(continued on next page)*

LEGISLATIVE BRANCH

**Representatives** *continued*

Representative **Jeffrey W. Welborn** (R-District 72) . . . . . . . (406) 949-6070
  Counties Represented: Beaverhead, Silver Bow (part)
  Term Expires: 2017
  P.O. Box 790, Dillon, MT 59725-0790
  E-mail: jeffwelborn@hotmail.com
  Committees: Business and Labor; Federal Relations, Energy
  and Telecommunications; Fish, Wildlife and Parks; Legislative
  Administration

Representative **Kerry E. White** (R-District 64) . . . . . . . . . . (406) 587-3653
  Counties Represented: Gallatin (part)
  Term Expires: 2017
  4000 Blackwood Road, Bozeman, MT 59718-7621
  E-mail: winwithwhite@gmail.com
  Committees: Fish, Wildlife and Parks; Natural Resources; Taxation

Representative **Kathleen Williams** (D-District 61) . . . . . . . (406) 570-1917
  Counties Represented: Gallatin (part)
  Term Expires: 2017
  P.O. Box 548, Bozeman, MT 59771-0548
  E-mail: kathleenhd65@bresnan.net
  Committees: Agriculture; Natural Resources; Rules; Taxation

Representative **Nancy Wilson** (D-District 95) . . . . . . . . . . (406) 531-6994
  Counties Represented: Missoula (part)
  Term Expires: 2017
  332 S First Street W, Apt A, Missoula, MT 59801-1802
  E-mail: nwilsonhd95@gmail.com
  Committees: Local Government; Taxation; Transportation

Representative **Art Wittich** (R-District 68) . . . . . . . . . . . . (406) 599-9836
  Counties Represented: Gallatin (part)
  Term Expires: 2017
  3116 Sourdough Road, Bozeman, MT 59715
  E-mail: rep.art.wittich@mt.gov
  Committees: Human Services; Rules; State Administration

Representative **Tom Woods** (D-District 62) . . . . . . . . . . . . (406) 850-4461
  Counties Represented: Gallatin (part)
  Term Expires: 2017
  1122 N Spruce Drive, Bozeman, MT 59715-5949
  E-mail: tomwoods4mt@gmail.com
  Committees: Appropriations; Rules

Representative **Daniel Zolnikov** (R-District 45) . . . . . . . . . (406) 861-5210
  Counties Represented: Yellowstone (part)
  Term Expires: 2017
  P.O. Box 50403, Billings, MT 59105-0403
  E-mail: rep.daniel.zolnikov@mt.gov
  Committees: Federal Relations, Energy and Telecommunications;
  Legislative Administration; Local Government

# House Standing Committees

## Agriculture

| Majority Members | Minority Members |
|---|---|
| Alan Redfield (R-59) *Chair* | Margaret "Margie" |
| Christy Clark (R-17) *Vice Chair* | MacDonald (D-51) |
| Seth Berglee (R-58) | *Vice Chair* |
| Greg Hertz (R-12) | Willis Curdy (D-98) |
| Bill Harris (R-29) | Jessica Karjala (D-48) |
| Mike L. Lang (R-33) | Andrea Olsen (D-100) |
| Theresa Manzella (R-85) | Carolyn Pease-Lopez (D-42) |
| Matthew Monforton (R-69) | Zac Perry (D-3) |
| Dale Mortensen (R-44) | Gordon Pierson, Jr. (D-78) |
| Wendy McKamey (R-23) | Susan Webber (D-16) |
| Daniel Salomon (R-93) | Kathleen Williams (D-61) |
| Scott Staffanson (R-35) | |
| Albert Olszewski (R-11) | |

## Appropriations

| Majority Members | Minority Members |
|---|---|
| Nancy Ballance (R-87) *Chair* | Pat Noonan (D-74) *Vice Chair* |
| Ryan Osmundson (R-30) *Vice Chair* | Kimberly Dudik (D-94) |
| Randy Brodehl (R-9) | Janet Ellis (D-81) |
| Tom Burnett (R-67) | Kelly McCarthy (D-49) |
| Mike Cuffe (R-2) | Robert "Bob" Mehlhoff (D-22) |
| Ron Ehli (R-86) | Patricia Rae Peppers (D-41) |
| Carl Glimm (R-6) | Mitch Tropila (D-26) |
| Dave Hagstrom (R-52) | Tom Woods (D-62) |
| Kenneth Holmlund (R-38) | |
| Roy Hollandsworth (R-27) | |
| Donald "Don" Jones (R-46) | |
| Brad Tschida (R-97) | |

## Business and Labor

| Majority Members | Minority Members |
|---|---|
| Tom Berry (R-40) *Chair* | Ryan Lynch (D-76) *Vice Chair* |
| Jeffrey W. Welborn (R-72) | Willis Curdy (D-98) |
| *Vice Chair* | Chuck Hunter (D-83) |
| Christy Clark (R-17) | George G. Kipp III (D-15) |
| Steve Fitzpatrick (R-20) | Andrea Olsen (D-100) |
| Austin Knudsen (R-34) | Gordon Pierson, Jr. (D-78) |
| Mike L. Lang (R-33) | Christopher S. Pope (D-65) |
| David "Doc" Moore (R-92) | Tom Steenberg (D-99) |
| Mark Noland (R-10) | |
| Vince Ricci (R-55) | |
| Daniel Salomon (R-93) | |
| Scott Staffanson (R-35) | |

## Education

| Majority Members | Minority Members |
|---|---|
| Sarah Laszloffy (R-53) *Chair* | Edith "Edie" McClafferty (D-73) |
| Debra Lamm (R-60) *Vice Chair* | *Vice Chair* |
| Jeff Essmann (R-54) | Bryce Bennett (D-91) |
| Edward Greef (R-88) | Moffie Funk (D-82) |
| Greg Hertz (R-12) | Katharin Kelker (D-47) |
| Gilbert Bruce Meyers (R-32) | Jean Price (D-24) |
| Matthew Monforton (R-69) | Susan Webber (D-16) |
| Daniel Salomon (R-93) | |
| Nicholas Schwaderer (R-14) | |

## Ethics

| Majority Members | Minority Members |
|---|---|
| Bill Harris (R-29) *Chair* | Bryce Bennett (D-91) *Vice Chair* |
| Nicholas Schwaderer (R-14) | Carolyn Pease-Lopez (D-42) |
| *Vice Chair* | |

## Federal Relations, Energy and Telecommunications

| Majority Members | Minority Members |
|---|---|
| Mike L. Lang (R-33) *Chair* | Tom Steenberg (D-99) *Vice Chair* |
| Daniel Zolnikov (R-45) *Vice Chair* | Ryan Lynch (D-76) |
| Tom Berry (R-40) | Zac Perry (D-3) |
| Geraldine Custer (R-39) | Andrew Person (D-96) |
| Austin Knudsen (R-34) | Christopher S. Pope (D-65) |
| David "Doc" Moore (R-92) | Casey Schreiner (D-25) |
| Randy Pinocci (R-19) | |
| Tom Richmond (R-56) | |
| Jeffrey W. Welborn (R-72) | |

## Fish, Wildlife and Parks

| Majority Members | Minority Members |
|---|---|
| Kelly Flynn (R-70) *Chair* | Jean Price (D-24) *Vice Chair* |
| Jeffrey W. Welborn (R-72) | Zach Brown (D-63) |
| *Vice Chair* | Virginia Court (D-50) |
| Bob Brown (R-13) | Tom Jacobson (D-21) |
| Rob Cook (R-18) | Ed Lieser (D-5) |
| Clayton Fiscus (R-43) | Andrew Person (D-96) |
| Stephanie Hess (R-28) | Bridget Smith (D-31) |
| Gilbert Bruce Meyers (R-32) | |
| Mark Noland (R-10) | |
| Randy Pinocci (R-19) | |
| Ray L. Shaw (R-72) | |
| Kirk B. Wagoner (R-75) | |
| Kerry E. White (R-64) | |

## Human Services

| Majority Members | Minority Members |
|---|---|
| Art Wittich (R-68) *Chair* | Ellie Boldman Hill (D-90) |
| Kirk B. Wagoner (R-75) *Vice Chair* | *Vice Chair* |
| Seth Berglee (R-58) | Denise Hayman (D-66) |
| Alan Doane (R-36) | Jenny Eck (D-79) |
| Bill Harris (R-29) | Jessica Karjala (D-48) |
| Stephanie Hess (R-28) | Tom Jacobson (D-21) |
| Forrest Mandeville (R-57) | Carolyn Pease-Lopez (D-42) |
| Albert Olszewski (R-11) | Gordon Pierson, Jr. (D-78) |
| Alan Redfield (R-59) | |
| Vince Ricci (R-55) | |

## Judiciary

**Majority Members**
Gerald A. "Jerry" Bennett (R-1) *Chair*
Alan Doane (R-36) *Vice Chair*
Seth Berglee (R-58)
Clayton Fiscus (R-43)
Stephanie Hess (R-28)
Sarah Laszloffy (R-53)
Theresa Manzella (R-85)
Gilbert Bruce Meyers (R-32)
Matthew Monforton (R-69)
Randy Pinocci (R-19)
Keith Regier (R-4)
Kirk B. Wagoner (R-75)

**Minority Members**
Virginia Court (D-50) *Vice Chair*
Jenny Eck (D-79)
Ellie Boldman Hill (D-90)
Katharin Kelker (D-47)
Margaret "Margie" MacDonald (D-51)
Nate McConnell (D-89)
Carolyn Pease-Lopez (D-42)
Zac Perry (D-3)
Andrew Person (D-96)

## Legislative Administration

**Majority Members**
Jeffrey W. Welborn (R-72) *Chair*
Christy Clark (R-17) *Vice Chair*
Gerald A. "Jerry" Bennett (R-1)
Mike Cuffe (R-2)
Alan Doane (R-36)
Mike L. Lang (R-33)
Daniel Zolnikov (R-45)

**Minority Members**
Edith "Edie" McClafferty (D-73) *Vice Chair*
Mary Ann Dunwell (D-84)
Zac Perry (D-3)
Gordon Pierson, Jr. (D-78)
Mitch Tropila (D-26)
Susan Webber (D-16)

## Local Government

**Majority Members**
Edward Greef (R-88) *Chair*
Steve Fitzpatrick (R-20) *Vice Chair*
Tom Berry (R-40)
Geraldine Custer (R-39)
Frank Garner (R-7)
Steve Lavin (R-8)
Debra Lamm (R-60)
Forrest Mandeville (R-57)
Vince Ricci (R-55)
Tom Richmond (R-56)
Nicholas Schwaderer (R-14)
Daniel Zolnikov (R-45)

**Minority Members**
Kathy Swanson (D-77) *Vice Chair*
Moffie Funk (D-82)
Denise Hayman (D-66)
Katharin Kelker (D-47)
Nate McConnell (D-89)
Christopher S. Pope (D-65)
Tom Steenberg (D-99)
Nancy Wilson (D-95)

## Natural Resources

**Majority Members**
Kerry E. White (R-64) *Chair*
Steve Fitzpatrick (R-20) *Vice Chair*
Bob Brown (R-13)
Kelly Flynn (R-70)
Theresa Manzella (R-85)
Dale Mortensen (R-44)
Mark Noland (R-10)
Keith Regier (R-4)
Ray L. Shaw (R-72)
Scott Staffanson (R-35)

**Minority Members**
Virginia Court (D-50) *Vice Chair*
Zach Brown (D-63)
Mary Ann Dunwell (D-84)
Ed Lieser (D-5)
Nate McConnell (D-89)
Andrea Olsen (D-100)
Kathleen Williams (D-61)

## Rules

**Majority Members**
Jeff Essmann (R-54) *Chair*
Gerald A. "Jerry" Bennett (R-1) *Vice Chair*
Alan Doane (R-36)
Greg Hertz (R-12)
Austin Knudsen (R-34)
Sarah Laszloffy (R-53)
Mike Miller (R-80)
Lee Randall (R-37)
Keith Regier (R-4)
Art Wittich (R-68)

**Minority Members**
Chuck Hunter (D-83) *Vice Chair*
Kimberly Dudik (D-94)
Jenny Eck (D-79)
Margaret "Margie" MacDonald (D-51)
Kathleen Williams (D-61)
Tom Woods (D-62)

## State Administration

**Majority Members**
Jeff Essmann (R-54) *Chair*
Bill Harris (R-29) *Vice Chair*
Bob Brown (R-13)
Frank Garner (R-7)
Edward Greef (R-88)
Debra Lamm (R-60)
Forrest Mandeville (R-57)
Wendy McKamey (R-23)
Dale Mortensen (R-44)
Ray L. Shaw (R-72)
Art Wittich (R-68)

**Minority Members**
Casey Schreiner (D-25) *Vice Chair*
Moffie Funk (D-82)
Denise Hayman (D-66)
Jessica Karjala (D-48)
Jean Price (D-24)
Kathy Swanson (D-77)
Susan Webber (D-16)

## Taxation

**Majority Members**
Mike Miller (R-80) *Chair*
Greg Hertz (R-12) *Vice Chair*
Rob Cook (R-18)
Geraldine Custer (R-39)
Steve Lavin (R-8)
Albert Olszewski (R-11)
Lee Randall (R-37)
Alan Redfield (R-59)
Nicholas Schwaderer (R-14)
Kerry E. White (R-64)

**Minority Members**
Kathleen Williams (D-61) *Vice Chair*
Zach Brown (D-63)
Mary Ann Dunwell (D-84)
Tom Jacobson (D-21)
Ed Lieser (D-5)
Edith "Edie" McClafferty (D-73)
Bridget Smith (D-31)
Nancy Wilson (D-95)

## Transportation

**Majority Members**
Steve Lavin (R-8) *Chair*
Christy Clark (R-17) *Vice Chair*
Rob Cook (R-18)
Clayton Fiscus (R-43)
Frank Garner (R-7)
Wendy McKamey (R-23)
Mike Miller (R-80)

**Minority Members**
Nancy Wilson (D-95) *Vice Chair*
Willis Curdy (D-98)
George G. Kipp III (D-15)
Margaret "Margie" MacDonald (D-51)
Bridget Smith (D-31)
Kathy Swanson (D-77)

**LEGISLATIVE BRANCH**

# Nebraska Unicameral Legislature

State Capitol, Room 2018, Lincoln, NE 68509
P.O. Box 94604, Lincoln, NE 68509-4604
Tel: (402) 471-2271 Fax: (402) 471-2126
Internet: www.nebraskalegislature.gov

**Note:** The Nebraska Unicameral Legislature is a nonpartisan legislative body.

## Nebraska Legislature

President of the Legislature **Mike Foley** (R) . . . . . . . . . . . . (402) 471-2256
  E-mail: mike.foley@nebraska.gov
  Education: SUNY (Brockport) 1976 BS; Michigan State 1978 MBA
Speaker of the Legislature **Galen Hadley** (I) . . . . . . . . . . (402) 471-2726
  Education: Nebraska 1964 BS; Colorado 1969 MBA;
  Nebraska 1975 PhD
  Assistant to the Speaker **Jeannette Thiem** . . . . . . . . . . . (402) 471-2756
Clerk of the Legislature **Patrick J. O'Donnell** . . . . . . . . . . (402) 471-2271
Sergeant-at-Arms **Ron Witkowski** . . . . . . . . . . . . . . . . . . . (402) 471-2271

## Senators

Senator **Roy Baker** (I-District 30) Room 1522 . . . . . . . . . . . (402) 471-2620
  Counties Represented: Gage, Lancaster (part)
  Term Expires: 2019
  E-mail: rbaker@leg.ne.gov
  Committees: Education; Health and Human Services
Senator **Dave Bloomfield** (I-District 17) Room 1206 . . . . . (402) 471-2716
  Counties Represented: Dakota, Thurston, Wayne
  Term Expires: 2017
  E-mail: dbloomfield@leg.ne.gov
  Committees: Agriculture; Business and Labor; Government, Military and Veterans Affairs
Senator **Kate Bolz** (I-District 29) Room 1120 . . . . . . . . . . . . (402) 471-2734
  Counties Represented: Lancaster (part)
  Term Expires: 2017
  E-mail: kbolz@leg.ne.gov
  Committees: Appropriations
  Education: Nebraska Wesleyan 2001 BA; Michigan 2005 MSW
Senator **Lydia N. Brasch** (I-District 16) Room 1016 . . . . . . (402) 471-2728
  Counties Represented: Burt, Cuming, Washington
  Term Expires: 2019
  E-mail: lbrasch@leg.ne.gov
  Committees: Revenue; Transportation and Telecommunications
  Education: Nebraska 1989 BA
Senator **Patty Pansing Brooks** (I-District 28)
  Room 1523 . . . . . . . . . . . . . . . . . . . . . . . . . . . . . . . . . (402) 471-2633
  Counties Represented: Lancaster (part)
  Term Expires: 2019
  E-mail: ppansingbrooks@leg.ne.gov
  Committees: Education; Judiciary
Senator **Kathy Campbell** (I-District 25) Room 1402 . . . . . (402) 471-2731
  Counties Represented: Lancaster (part)   Res: (402) 423-3311
  Term Expires: 2017
  6111 Chartwell Lane, Lincoln, NE 68516
  E-mail: kcampbell@leg.ne.gov
  Committees: Banking, Commerce and Insurance; Executive Board of the Legislative Council; Health and Human Services
  Education: Nebraska 1969 BS, 1970 MEd
Senator **Ernie Chambers** (I-District 11) Room 1114 . . . . . . (402) 471-2612
  Counties Represented: Douglas (part)
  Term Expires: 2017
  Committees: Agriculture; Business and Labor; Executive Board of the Legislative Council; Judiciary
Senator **Colby Coash** (I-District 27) Room 2028 . . . . . . . . (402) 471-2632
  Counties Represented: Lancaster (part)
  Term Expires: 2017
  829 Mary Court, Lincoln, NE 68522
  E-mail: ccoash@leg.ne.gov
  Committees: Executive Board of the Legislative Council; General Affairs; Judiciary; Urban Affairs
  Education: Nebraska 1998 BA
Senator **Tanya Cook** (I-District 13) Room 2011 . . . . . . . . . . (402) 471-2727
  Counties Represented: Douglas (part)
  Term Expires: 2017
  E-mail: tcook@leg.ne.gov
  Committees: Education; Health and Human Services
  Education: Georgetown 1986 BA; Nebraska 1994 MA

Senator **Joni Craighead** (I-District 6) Room 1529 . . . . . . . . (402) 471-2714
  Counties Represented: Douglas (part)
  Term Expires: 2019
  E-mail: jcraighead@leg.ne.gov
  Committees: Banking, Commerce and Insurance; Government, Military and Veterans Affairs
Senator **Sue Crawford** (I-District 45) Room 1212 . . . . . . . . (402) 471-2615
  Counties Represented: Sarpy (part)
  Term Expires: 2017
  E-mail: scrawford@leg.ne.gov
  Committees: Business and Labor; Health and Human Services; Urban Affairs
  Education: Northeast Missouri State 1989 BS; Indiana 1995 PhD
Senator **Al Davis** (I-District 43) Room 1021 . . . . . . . . . . . . . (402) 471-2628
  Counties Represented: Blaine, Box Butte (part), Brown, Cherry, Dawes, Grant, Hooker, Keya Paha, Logan, Loup, McPherson, Sheridan, Thomas
  Term Expires: 2017
  E-mail: adavis@leg.ne.gov
  Committees: Nebraska Retirement Systems; Revenue; Transportation and Telecommunications
  Education: Denver 1978 BA; Creighton (Attended)
Senator **Laura Ebke** (I-District 32) Room 1101 . . . . . . . . . (402) 471-2711
  Counties Represented: Fillmore, Jefferson, Lancaster (part), Saline, Thayer
  Term Expires: 2019
  E-mail: lebke@leg.ne.gov
  Committees: Business and Labor; Judiciary; Urban Affairs
Senator **Nicole B. Fox** (I-District 7) Room 2004 . . . . . . . . . (402) 471-2721
  Counties Represented: Douglas (part)
  Term Expires: 2017
  P.O. Box 94604, Lincoln, NE 68509
  E-mail: nfox@leg.ne.gov
  Committees: Banking, Commerce and Insurance; Health and Human Services
  Education: Iowa State BS
Senator **Curtis Friesen** (I-District 34) Room 1403 . . . . . . . . (402) 471-2630
  Counties Represented: Hall (part), Hamilton, Merrick, Nance
  Term Expires: 2019
  E-mail: cfriesen@leg.ne.gov
  Committees: Natural Resources; Transportation and Telecommunications
Senator
**Col Tommy L. Garrett, USAF (Ret)** (I-District 3)
  Room 1208 . . . . . . . . . . . . . . . . . . . . . . . . . . . . . . . . . . (402) 471-2627
  Counties Represented: Sarpy (part)
  Term Expires: 2019
  E-mail: tgarrett@leg.ne.gov
  Committees: Government, Military and Veterans Affairs; Transportation and Telecommunications
  Education: Colorado State 1976 BS; Troy State 1986 MS; National War Col 2000 MS
Senator **Mike Gloor** (I-District 35) Room 1116 . . . . . . . . . (402) 471-2617
  Counties Represented: Hall (part)   Res: (308) 382-8572
  Term Expires: 2017
  3115 Brentwood Circle, Grand Island, NE 68801
  E-mail: mgloor@leg.ne.gov
  Committees: Banking, Commerce and Insurance; Revenue
  Education: Hastings Col 1972 BA; Utah 1976 MS; Minnesota 1987 MHA
Senator **Michael Groene** (I-District 42) Room 1101 . . . . . . (402) 471-2729
  Counties Represented: Lincoln (part)
  Term Expires: 2019
  E-mail: mgroene@leg.ne.gov
  Committees: Education; Government, Military and Veterans Affairs; Nebraska Retirement Systems
Senator **Ken Haar** (I-District 21) Room 1015 . . . . . . . . . . . . (402) 471-2673
  Counties Represented: Lancaster (part)   Res: (402) 796-2047
  Term Expires: 2017
  13901 NW 126th Street, Malcolm, NE 68402
  E-mail: khaar@leg.ne.gov
  Committees: Appropriations
  Education: Nebraska 1965 BS, 1973 MS
Senator **Galen Hadley** (I-District 37) Room 2103 . . . . . . . . (402) 471-2726
  Counties Represented: Buffalo (part)   Res: (308) 237-3794
  Term Expires: 2017
  3112 Country Club Lane, Kearney, NE 68845
  E-mail: ghadley@leg.ne.gov
  Committees: Executive Board of the Legislative Council; Legislative Performance Audit

Senator **Matt Hansen** (I-District 26) Room 1404 . . . . . . . . (402) 471-2610
Counties Represented: Lancaster (part)
Term Expires: 2019
E-mail: mhansen@leg.ne.gov
Committees: General Affairs; Government, Military and Veterans
Affairs; Urban Affairs
Education: Nebraska

Senator **Burke J. Harr** (I-District 8) Room 2010 . . . . . . . . (402) 471-2722
Counties Represented: Douglas (part)
Term Expires: 2019
E-mail: bharr@leg.ne.gov
Committees: Agriculture; Business and Labor; Revenue
Education: U St Thomas (MN) 1994 BA; Notre Dame 1998 JD

Senator **Robert "Bob" Hilkemann** (I-District 4)
Room 1115 . . . . . . . . . . . . . . . . . . . . . . . . . . . (402) 471-2621
Counties Represented: Douglas (part)
Term Expires: 2019
E-mail: rhilkemann@leg.ne.gov
Committees: Appropriations

Senator **Sara Howard** (I-District 9) Room 1012 . . . . . . . . (402) 471-2723
Counties Represented: Douglas (part)
Term Expires: 2017
E-mail: showard@leg.ne.gov
Committees: Banking, Commerce and Insurance; Health and Human
Services
Education: Smith 2003 BA; Loyola U (Chicago) 2008 JD

Senator **Dan Hughes** (I-District 44) Room 1117 . . . . . . . . (402) 471-2805
Counties Represented: Chase, Dundy, Frontier, Furnas, Gosper, Harlan,
Hayes, Hitchcock, Perkins, Red Willow
Term Expires: 2019
E-mail: dhughes@leg.ne.gov
Committees: General Affairs; Natural Resources; Urban Affairs

Senator **Jerry Johnson** (I-District 23) Room 1022 . . . . . . . (402) 471-2719
Counties Represented: Butler, Colfax (part), Saunders
Term Expires: 2017
E-mail: jjohnson@leg.ne.gov
Committees: Agriculture; Business and Labor; Natural Resources

Senator **Bill Kintner** (I-District 2) Room 1000 . . . . . . . . . . (402) 471-2613
Counties Represented: Cass, Sarpy (part)
Term Expires: 2019
E-mail: bkintner@leg.ne.gov
Committees: Appropriations
Education: Wright State 1983 BSB

Senator **Rick Kolowski** (I-District 31) Room 1018 . . . . . . . (402) 471-2327
Counties Represented: Douglas (part)
Term Expires: 2017
E-mail: rkolowski@leg.ne.gov
Committees: Education; Natural Resources; Nebraska Retirement
Systems
Education: Lake Forest Col 1966 BA; Nebraska (Omaha) 1970 MS;
Nebraska 1978 PhD

Senator **Mark Kolterman** (I-District 24) Room 1115 . . . . . . (402) 471-2756
Counties Represented: Polk, Seward, York
Term Expires: 2019
E-mail: mkolterman@leg.ne.gov
Committees: Agriculture; General Affairs; Health and Human Services;
Nebraska Retirement Systems

Senator **Robert "Bob" Krist** (I-District 10) Room 2108 . . . (402) 471-2718
Counties Represented: Douglas (part)
Term Expires: 2019
E-mail: bkrist@leg.ne.gov
Committees: Executive Board of the Legislative Council; General
Affairs; Judiciary; Legislative Performance Audit; Urban Affairs
Education: U St Thomas (TX) 1979 BA; Webster 1982 MA

Senator **John L. Kuehn** (I-District 38) Room 1117 . . . . . . . (402) 471-2732
Counties Represented: Buffalo (part), Clay, Franklin, Kearney,
Nuckolls, Phelps, Webster
Term Expires: 2019
E-mail: jkuehn@leg.ne.gov
Committees: Appropriations; Legislative Performance Audit

Senator **Tyson Larson** (I-District 40) Room 1019 . . . . . . . . (402) 471-2801
Counties Represented: Boyd, Cedar, Dixon, Holt, Knox, Rock
Term Expires: 2019
E-mail: tlarson@leg.ne.gov
Committees: Agriculture; Executive Board of the Legislative Council;
General Affairs; Government, Military and Veterans Affairs; Legislative
Performance Audit
Education: Georgetown 2008 BA

Senator **Brett Lindstrom** (I-District 18) Room 1202 . . . . . . (402) 471-2618
Counties Represented: Douglas (part)
Term Expires: 2019
E-mail: blindstrom@leg.ne.gov
Committees: Banking, Commerce and Insurance; Natural Resources
Education: Nebraska

Senator **John S. McCollister** (I-District 20) Room 1017 . . . (402) 471-2622
Counties Represented: Douglas (part)
Term Expires: 2019
E-mail: jmccollister@leg.ne.gov
Committees: Business and Labor; Natural Resources; Urban Affairs

Senator **Beau McCoy** (I-District 39) Room 2017 . . . . . . . . (402) 471-2885
Counties Represented: Douglas (part)
Term Expires: 2017
3922 South 190th Street, Omaha, NE 68130
E-mail: bmccoy@leg.ne.gov
Committees: Government, Military and Veterans Affairs; Transportation
and Telecommunications
Education: Bellevue U 2007 BA

Senator **Heath Mello** (I-District 5) Room 1004 . . . . . . . . . (402) 471-2710
Counties Represented: Douglas (part)
Term Expires: 2017
3084 South 40th Street, Number 11, Omaha, NE 68105
E-mail: hmello@leg.ne.gov
Committees: Appropriations; Executive Board of the Legislative
Council; Legislative Performance Audit; Nebraska Retirement Systems
Education: Nebraska 2002 BA

Senator **Adam Morfeld** (I-District 46) Room 1008 . . . . . . . (402) 471-2720
Counties Represented: Lincoln (part)
Term Expires: 2019
E-mail: amorfeld@leg.ne.gov
Committees: Education; Judiciary

Senator **John Murante** (I-District 49) Room 1423 . . . . . . . (402) 471-2725
Counties Represented: Sarpy (part)
Term Expires: 2017
E-mail: jmurante@leg.ne.gov
Committees: Executive Board of the Legislative Council; Government,
Military and Veterans Affairs; Transportation and Telecommunications
Education: Nebraska 2004 BA

Senator **Merv Riepe** (I-District 12) Room 1528 . . . . . . . . . (402) 471-2623
Counties Represented: Douglas (part)
Term Expires: 2019
E-mail: mriepe@leg.ne.gov
Committees: Agriculture; General Affairs; Health and Human Services

Senator **Jim Scheer** (I-District 19) Room 1401 . . . . . . . . . (402) 471-2929
Counties Represented: Madison, Stanton (part)
Term Expires: 2017
E-mail: jscheer@leg.ne.gov
Committees: Banking, Commerce and Insurance; Legislative
Performance Audit; Revenue
Education: Nebraska 1976 BS

Senator **Ken Schilz** (I-District 47) Room 1210 . . . . . . . . . . (402) 471-2616
Counties Represented: Arthur, Banner, Box Butte (part), Cheyenne,
Deuel, Garden, Keith, Kimball, Morrill, Sioux
Term Expires: 2017
E-mail: kschilz@leg.ne.gov
Committees: Agriculture; General Affairs; Natural Resources
Education: Nebraska 1992 BS

Senator **David A. Schnoor** (I-District 15) Room 1118 . . . . (402) 471-2625
Counties Represented: Dodge
Term Expires: 2017
E-mail: dschnoor@leg.ne.gov
Committees: Education; Natural Resources

Senator **Paul Schumacher** (I-District 22) Room 1124 . . . . . (402) 471-2715
Counties Represented: Colfax (part), Platte, Stanton (part)
Term Expires: 2019
E-mail: pschumacher@leg.ne.gov
Committees: Banking, Commerce and Insurance; Revenue
Education: Fort Hays State 1973 BS; Georgetown 1976 JD

Senator **Lester Seiler** (I-District 33) Room 1103 . . . . . . . . (402) 471-2712
Counties Represented: Adams, Hall (part)
Term Expires: 2017
E-mail: lseiler@leg.ne.gov
Committees: Judiciary; Transportation and Telecommunications
Education: Hastings Col; Wayne State Col 1960 BEc;
Nebraska 1966 JD

Senator **Jim Smith** (I-District 14) Room 1110 . . . . . . . . . . (402) 471-2730
Counties Represented: Sarpy (part)
Term Expires: 2019
E-mail: jsmith@leg.ne.gov
Committees: Revenue; Transportation and Telecommunications
Education: West Florida 1984 BAcc; Creighton 1996 MBA

*(continued on next page)*

**Senators** *continued*

Senator **John P. Stinner, Sr.** (I-District 48) Room 1406 . . . (402) 471-2802
  Counties Represented: Scotts Bluff
  Term Expires: 2019
  E-mail: jstinner@leg.ne.gov
  Committees: Appropriations

Senator **Kate Sullivan** (I-District 41) Room 1107 . . . . . . . . (402) 471-2631
  Counties Represented: Antelope, Boone, Garfield, Greeley, Howard,
  Pierce, Sherman, Valley, Wheeler
  Term Expires: 2017
  E-mail: ksullivan@leg.ne.gov
  Committees: Education; Revenue
  Education: Nebraska 1971 BS, 1975 MS

Senator **Dan Watermeier** (I-District 1) Room 2000 . . . . . . .(402) 471-2733
  Counties Represented: Johnson, Nemaha, Otoe, Pawnee, Richardson
  Term Expires: 2017
  E-mail: dwatermeier@leg.ne.gov
  Committees: Appropriations; Executive Board of the Legislative
  Council; Legislative Performance Audit
  Education: Nebraska 1983 BSA

Senator **Matthew H. "Matt" Williams** (I-District 36)
  Room 2015 . . . . . . . . . . . . . . . . . . . . . . . . . . . . . . . (402) 471-2642
  Counties Represented: Buffalo (part), Custer, Dawson
  Term Expires: 2019
  E-mail: mwilliams@leg.ne.gov
  Committees: Banking, Commerce and Insurance; Judiciary
  Education: Nebraska JD

## Standing Committees

### Agriculture
**Members**
Jerry Johnson (I-23) *Chair*
Dave Bloomfield (I-17)
Ernie Chambers (I-11)
Burke J. Harr (I-8)
Mark Kolterman (I-24)
Tyson Larson (I-40)
Merv Riepe (I-12)
Ken Schilz (I-47)

### Appropriations
**Members**
Heath Mello (I-5) *Chair*
Kate Bolz (I-29)
Ken Haar (I-21)
Robert "Bob" Hilkemann (I-4)
Bill Kintner (I-2)
John L. Kuehn (I-38)
John P. Stinner, Sr. (I-48)
Dan Watermeier (I-1)

### Banking, Commerce and Insurance
**Members**
Jim Scheer (I-19) *Chair*
Kathy Campbell (I-25)
Joni Craighead (I-6)
Nicole B. Fox (I-7)
Mike Gloor (I-35)
Sara Howard (I-9)
Brett Lindstrom (I-18)
Paul Schumacher (I-22)
Matthew H. "Matt" Williams (I-36)

### Business and Labor
**Members**
Burke J. Harr (I-8) *Chair*
Dave Bloomfield (I-17)
Ernie Chambers (I-11)
Sue Crawford (I-45)
Laura Ebke (I-32)
Jerry Johnson (I-23)
John S. McCollister (I-20)

### Education
**Members**
Kate Sullivan (I-41) *Chair*
Roy Baker (I-30)
Patty Pansing Brooks (I-28)
Tanya Cook (I-13)
Michael Groene (I-42)
Rick Kolowski (I-31)
Adam Morfeld (I-46)
David A. Schnoor (I-15)

### General Affairs
**Members**
Tyson Larson (I-40) *Chair*
Colby Coash (I-27)
Matt Hansen (I-26)
Dan Hughes (I-44)
Mark Kolterman (I-24)
Robert "Bob" Krist (I-10)
Merv Riepe (I-12)
Ken Schilz (I-47)

### Government, Military and Veterans Affairs
**Members**
John Murante (I-49) *Chair*
Dave Bloomfield (I-17)
Joni Craighead (I-6)
Col Tommy L. Garrett (I-3)
Michael Groene (I-42)
Matt Hansen (I-26)
Tyson Larson (I-40)
Beau McCoy (I-39)

### Health and Human Services
**Members**
Kathy Campbell (I-25) *Chair*
Roy Baker (I-30)
Tanya Cook (I-13)
Sue Crawford (I-45)
Nicole B. Fox (I-7)
Sara Howard (I-9)
Mark Kolterman (I-24)
Merv Riepe (I-12)

### Judiciary
**Members**
Lester Seiler (I-33) *Chair*
Patty Pansing Brooks (I-28)
Ernie Chambers (I-11)
Colby Coash (I-27)
Laura Ebke (I-32)
Robert "Bob" Krist (I-10)
Adam Morfeld (I-46)
Matthew H. "Matt" Williams (I-36)

### Natural Resources
**Members**
Ken Schilz (I-47) *Chair*
Curtis Friesen (I-34)
Dan Hughes (I-44)
Jerry Johnson (I-23)
Rick Kolowski (I-31)
Brett Lindstrom (I-18)
John S. McCollister (I-20)
David A. Schnoor (I-15)

### Nebraska Retirement Systems
**Members**
Al Davis (I-43)
Michael Groene (I-42)
Rick Kolowski (I-31)
Mark Kolterman (I-24)
Heath Mello (I-5)

LEGISLATIVE BRANCH

## Revenue

**Members**

Mike Gloor (I-35) *Chair*
Lydia N. Brasch (I-16)
Al Davis (I-43)
Burke J. Harr (I-8)
Jim Scheer (I-19)
Paul Schumacher (I-22)
Jim Smith (I-14)
Kate Sullivan (I-41)

## Transportation and Telecommunications

**Members**

Jim Smith (I-14) *Chair*
Lydia N. Brasch (I-16)
Al Davis (I-43)
Curtis Friesen (I-34)
Col Tommy L. Garrett (I-3)
Beau McCoy (I-39)
John Murante (I-49)
Lester Seiler (I-33)

## Urban Affairs

**Members**

Sue Crawford (I-45) *Chair*
Colby Coash (I-27)
Laura Ebke (I-32)
Matt Hansen (I-26)
Dan Hughes (I-44)
Robert "Bob" Krist (I-10)
John S. McCollister (I-20)

# Nevada Legislature

401 South Carson Street, Carson City, NV 89701-4747
Tel: (775) 684-6800  Internet: www.leg.state.nv.us

## Nevada Senate

401 South Carson Street, Carson City, NV 89701-4747
Tel: (775) 684-1400  Fax: (775) 684-6522  E-mail: senate@lcb.state.nv.us

President of the Senate **Mark Hutchison** (R) . . . . . . . . . . . . (775) 684-7111
  Affiliation: Lieutenant Governor, Office of the Lieutenant Governor,
  State of Nevada
  State Capitol Building, 101 North Carson Street, Suite 2,
  Carson City, NV 89701
  Education: UNLV BA; J Reuben Clark Law JD
President Pro Tem **Joseph P. "Joe" Hardy, MD** (R) . . . . . . (775) 684-1462
  Education: Nevada (Reno) BS; Washington U (MO) MD
Majority Floor Leader **Michael Roberson** (R) . . . . . . . . . . (775) 684-1481
Assistant Majority Floor Leader
  **Benjamin "Ben" Kieckhefer** (R) . . . . . . . . . . . . . . . . . . (775) 223-9618
  Education: DePaul BA; Illinois (Springfield) MPA
Majority Co-Whip **Scott Hammond** (R) . . . . . . . . . . . . . . (775) 684-1442
  Education: UNLV 1995 BA, 1997 MA
Majority Co-Whip **James Arnold Settelmeyer** (R) . . . . . . (775) 684-1470
Minority Floor Leader **Aaron D. Ford, JD** (D) . . . . . . . . . . (775) 684-6502
  Education: Texas A&M 1995 BS; George Washington 1997 MA;
  Ohio State 1998 MA, 2001 PhD, 2001 JD
Assistant Minority Floor Leader **Kelvin Atkinson** (D) . . . . (775) 684-1429
  Education: Howard U BA
Minority Co-Whip **Joyce Woodhouse** (D) . . . . . . . . . . . . (702) 896-1453
  Education: Carroll Col (MT) 1966 BA; UNLV 1983 MA
Minority Co-Whip **Ruben J. Kihuen** (D) . . . . . . . . . . . . . . (775) 684-1427
Secretary of the Senate **Claire J. Clift** . . . . . . . . . . . . . . . . . (775) 684-1401
  E-mail: claire.clift@sen.state.nv.us

## Senators

**Party Affiliation Statistics:** Republicans: 10, Democrats: 9, Vacancies: 2

Senator **Kelvin Atkinson** (D-District 4) . . . . . . . . . . . . . . . (775) 684-1429
  Counties Represented: Clark (part)          Fax: (702) 457-9995
  Term Expires: 2016
  4165 Fuselier Drive, North Las Vegas, NV 89032-3112
  E-mail: kelvin.atkinson@asm.state.nv.us
  Committees: Commerce, Labor and Energy; Government Affairs;
  Legislative Operations and Elections
Senator **Moises "Mo" Denis** (D-District 2) . . . . . . . . . . . . (775) 684-1431
  Counties Represented: Clark (part)          Res: (702) 657-6857
  Term Expires: 2018
  3204 Osage Avenue, Las Vegas, NV 89101-1838
  E-mail: moises.denis@sen.state.nv.us
  Committees: Education; Transportation
  Education: BYU BA
Senator **Patricia Farley** (R-District 8) . . . . . . . . . . . . . . . . . (775) 684-1445
  Counties Represented: Clark (part)          Tel: (702) 335-4794
  Term Expires: 2018
  1930 Village Center Circle, #3-619, Las Vegas, NV 89134
  E-mail: patricia.farley@sen.state.nv.us
  Committees: Commerce, Labor and Energy; Legislative Operations and
  Elections; Transportation
Senator **Aaron D. Ford, JD** (D-District 11) . . . . . . . . . . . . (775) 684-6502
  Counties Represented: Clark (part)
  Term Expires: 2016
  96003, Las Vegas, NV 89193-6003
  E-mail: aaron.ford@sen.state.nv.us
  Committees: Judiciary; Revenue and Economic Development
Senator **Peter J. "Pete" Goicoechea** (R-District 19) . . . . . (775) 684-1447
  Counties Represented: Clark (part), Elko, Eureka,     Tel: (775) 237-7383
  Lincoln, Nye (part), White Pine              Res: (775) 237-5300
  Term Expires: 2016                           Fax: (775) 237-5102
  P.O. Box 97, Eureka, NV 89316-0097
  E-mail: pete.goicoechea@sen.state.nv.us
  Committees: Finance; Government Affairs; Natural Resources
  Education: Utah State 1967 (Attended)
Senator **Donald G. "Don" Gustavson** (R-District 14) . . . . (775) 684-1480
  Counties Represented: Esmeralda, Humboldt, Lander, Mineral, Nye
  (part), Pershing, Washoe (part)
  Term Expires: 2018
  P.O. Box 51601, Sparks, NV 89435-1601
  E-mail: don.gustavson@sen.state.nv.us
  Committees: Education; Natural Resources; Transportation

*(continued on next page)*

**Senators** *continued*

Senator **Scott Hammond** (R-District 18) . . . . . . . . . . . . . . . (775) 684-1442
  Counties Represented: Clark (part)       Res: (702) 523-9055
  Term Expires: 2016
  8408 Gracious Pine Avenue, Las Vegas, NV 89143-4608
  E-mail: scott.hammond@sen.state.nv.us
  Committees: Education; Judiciary; Transportation

Senator **Joseph P. "Joe" Hardy, MD** (R-District 12) . . . . . (775) 684-1462
  Counties Represented: Clark (part)       Res: (702) 293-7506
  Term Expires: 2018               Fax: (702) 581-3066
  P.O. Box 60306, Boulder City, NV 89006-3606
  E-mail: joe.hardy@sen.state.nv.us
  Committees: Commerce, Labor and Energy; Government Affairs;
  Health and Human Services; Revenue and Economic Development

Senator **Becky Harris** (R-District 9) . . . . . . . . . . . . . . . . . . . (775) 684-1421
  Counties Represented: Clark (part)       Tel: (702) 324-0404
  Term Expires: 2018
  P.O. Box 401146, Las Vegas, NV 89140
  E-mail: becky.harris@sen.state.nv.us
  Committees: Commerce, Labor and Energy; Education; Judiciary

Senator **Benjamin "Ben" Kieckhefer** (R-District 16) . . . . . (775) 223-9618
  Counties Represented: Carson City, Washoe (part)
  Term Expires: 2018
  10045, Goler Wash Court, Reno, NV 89521-3029
  E-mail: ben.kieckhefer@sen.state.nv.us
  Committees: Finance; Health and Human Services; Revenue and
  Economic Development

Senator **Ruben J. Kihuen** (D-District 10) . . . . . . . . . . . . . . . (775) 684-1427
  Counties Represented: Clark (part)
  Term Expires: 2018
  P.O. Box 427, Las Vegas, NV 89125-0427
  E-mail: ruben.kihuen@sen.state.nv.us
  Committees: Judiciary; Revenue and Economic Development

Senator **Mark A. Lipparelli** (R-District 6) . . . . . . . . . . . . . . (775) 684-1475
  Counties Represented: Clark (part)       Fax: (775) 684-6522
  Term Expires: 2016
  E-mail: mark.lipparelli@sen.state.nv.us
  Committees: Education; Finance; Government Affairs; Health and
  Human Services

Senator **Mark A. Manendo** (D-District 21) . . . . . . . . . . . . . (775) 684-6503
  Counties Represented: Clark (part)       Res: (702) 451-8654
  Term Expires: 2018               Fax: (702) 451-9060
  4030 Beisner Street, Las Vegas, NV 89122-4634
  E-mail: mark.manendo@sen.state.nv.us
  Committees: Commerce, Labor and Energy; Natural Resources;
  Transportation

Senator **David R. Parks** (D-District 7) . . . . . . . . . . . . . . . . . (775) 684-6504
  Counties Represented: Clark (part)       Res: (702) 736-6929
  Term Expires: 2016
  P.O. Box 71887, Las Vegas, NV 89170-1887
  E-mail: david.parks@sen.state.nv.us
  Committees: Finance; Government Affairs
  Education: New Hampshire BS; UNLV MBA

Senator **Michael Roberson** (R-District 20) . . . . . . . . . . . . . (775) 684-1481
  Counties Represented: Clark (part)       Res: (702) 612-6929
  Term Expires: 2018
  P.O. Box 530940, Henderson, NV 89053-0940
  E-mail: michael.roberson@sen.state.nv.us
  Committees: Finance; Judiciary; Revenue and Economic Development

Senator **Richard S. "Tick" Segerblom** (D-District 3) . . . . . (775) 684-1422
  Counties Represented: Clark (part)       Tel: (702) 388-9600
  Term Expires: 2016               Fax: (702) 385-2909
  700 South Third Street, Las Vegas, NV 89101-6703
  E-mail: tsegerblom@asm.state.nv.us
  Committees: Education; Judiciary; Legislative Operations and Elections
  Education: Pomona BA; Denver JD

Senator **James Arnold Settelmeyer** (R-District 17) . . . . . . (775) 684-1470
  Counties Represented: Churchill, Douglas, Lyon,   Res: (775) 265-7739
  Storey
  Term Expires: 2018
  2388 Highway 395, Minden, NV 89423-8923
  E-mail: james.settelmeyer@sen.state.nv.us
  Committees: Commerce, Labor and Energy; Legislative Operations and
  Elections; Natural Resources

Senator **Pastor Patricia "Pat" Spearman** (D-District 1) . . (775) 684-1424
  Counties Represented: Clark (part)       Tel: (702) 701-0612
  Term Expires: 2016
  5575 Simmons Street, Suite 1-174, North Las Vegas, NV 89031-9009
  E-mail: pat.spearman@sen.state.nv.us
  Committees: Commerce, Labor and Energy; Revenue and Economic
  Development
  Education: Norfolk State BS; Episcopal Sem MDiv

Senator **Joyce Woodhouse** (D-District 5) . . . . . . . . . . . . . (702) 896-1453
  Counties Represented: Clark (part)
  Term Expires: 2016
  246 Garfield Drive, Henderson, NV 89074-1027
  E-mail: joyce.woodhouse@sen.state.nv.us
  Committees: Education; Finance; Health and Human Services

District 13 **(Vacant)** . . . . . . . . . . . . . . . . . . . . . . . . . . . . . . (775) 684-1401
  Note: A general election to fill this legislative vacancy will be held on
  November 8, 2016.

District 15 **(Vacant)**
  Note: A general election to fill this legislative vacancy will be held on
  November 8, 2016.

# Senate Standing Committees
## Commerce, Labor and Energy
401 South Carson Street, Room 2135, Carson City, NV 89701-4747
Tel: (775) 684-1461  E-mail: sencl@sen.state.nv.us

| **Majority Members** | **Minority Members** |
| --- | --- |
| James Arnold Settelmeyer (R-17) | Kelvin Atkinson (D-4) |
| *Chair* | Mark A. Manendo (D-21) |
| Patricia Farley (R-8) *Vice Chair* | Pastor Patricia "Pat" Spearman |
| Joseph P. "Joe" Hardy (R-12) | (D-1) |
| Becky Harris (R-9) | |

## Education
401 S. Carson St., Room 2149, Carson City, NV 89701-4747
Tel: (775) 684-1466  E-mail: sened@sen.state.nv.us

| **Majority Members** | **Minority Members** |
| --- | --- |
| Becky Harris (R-9) *Chair* | Moises "Mo" Denis (D-2) |
| Scott Hammond (R-18) *Vice Chair* | Richard S. "Tick" Segerblom (D-3) |
| Donald G. "Don" Gustavson (R-14) | Joyce Woodhouse (D-5) |
| Mark A. Lipparelli (R-6) | |

## Finance
401 S. Carson St., Room 2134, Carson City, NV 89701-4747
Tel: (775) 684-1423  E-mail: senfin@sen.state.nv.us

| **Majority Members** | **Minority Members** |
| --- | --- |
| Benjamin "Ben" Kieckhefer (R-16) | David R. Parks (D-7) |
| *Chair* | Joyce Woodhouse (D-5) |
| Michael Roberson (R-20) | |
| *Vice Chair* | |
| Peter J. "Pete" Goicoechea (R-19) | |
| Mark A. Lipparelli (R-6) | |

## Government Affairs
401 S. Carson St., Room 2144, Carson City, NV 89701-4747
Tel: (775) 684-1474  E-mail: senga@sen.state.nv.us

| **Majority Members** | **Minority Members** |
| --- | --- |
| Peter J. "Pete" Goicoechea (R-19) | Kelvin Atkinson (D-4) |
| *Chair* | David R. Parks (D-7) |
| Joseph P. "Joe" Hardy (R-12) | |
| *Vice Chair* | |
| Mark A. Lipparelli (R-6) | |

## Health and Human Services
401 South Carson Street, Room 2149, Carson City, NV 89701-4747
Tel: (775) 684-1441  E-mail: senhhs@sen.state.nv.us

| **Majority Members** | **Minority Members** |
| --- | --- |
| Joseph P. "Joe" Hardy (R-12) *Chair* | Joyce Woodhouse (D-5) |
| Benjamin "Ben" Kieckhefer (R-16) | |
| *Vice Chair* | |
| Mark A. Lipparelli (R-6) | |

## Judiciary
401 S. Carson St., Room 2149, Carson City, NV 89701-4747
Tel: (775) 684-1438  E-mail: senjud@sen.state.nv.us

| **Majority Members** | **Minority Members** |
| --- | --- |
| Becky Harris (R-9) *Vice Chair* | Aaron D. Ford (D-11) |
| Scott Hammond (R-18) | Ruben J. Kihuen (D-10) |
| Michael Roberson (R-20) | Richard S. "Tick" Segerblom (D-3) |

## Legislative Operations and Elections

401 S. Carson St., Room 2144, Carson City, NV 89701-4747
Tel: (775) 684-1465  E-mail: senloe@sen.state.nv.us

| Majority Members | Minority Members |
|---|---|
| Patricia Farley (R-8) *Chair* | Kelvin Atkinson (D-4) |
| James Arnold Settelmeyer (R-17) *Vice Chair* | Richard S. "Tick" Segerblom (D-3) |

## Natural Resources

401 S. Carson St., Room 2144, Carson City, NV 89701-4747
Tel: (775) 684-1453  E-mail: sennr@sen.state.nv.us

| Majority Members | Minority Members |
|---|---|
| Donald G. "Don" Gustavson (R-14) *Chair* | Mark A. Manendo (D-21) |
| Peter J. "Pete" Goicoechea (R-19) *Vice Chair* | |
| James Arnold Settelmeyer (R-17) | |

## Revenue and Economic Development

401 South Carson Street, Room 2134, Carson City, NV 89701-4747
Tel: (775) 684-1456  E-mail: senrev@sen.state.nv.us

| Majority Members | Minority Members |
|---|---|
| Michael Roberson (R-20) *Chair* | Aaron D. Ford (D-11) |
| Joseph P. "Joe" Hardy (R-12) | Ruben J. Kihuen (D-10) |
| Benjamin "Ben" Kieckhefer (R-16) | Pastor Patricia "Pat" Spearman (D-1) |

## Transportation

401 S. Carson St., Room 2135, Carson City, NV 89701-4747
Tel: (775) 684-1468  E-mail: sentrn@sen.state.nv.us

| Majority Members | Minority Members |
|---|---|
| Scott Hammond (R-18) *Chair* | Moises "Mo" Denis (D-2) |
| Donald G. "Don" Gustavson (R-14) *Vice Chair* | Mark A. Manendo (D-21) |
| Patricia Farley (R-8) | |

# Nevada Assembly

401 South Carson Street, Carson City, NV 89701-4747
Tel: (775) 684-8555  Fax: (775) 684-8533
Speaker of the Assembly **John Hambrick** (R) . . . . . . . . . . (775) 242-8580
Speaker Pro Tem **John Ellison** (R) . . . . . . . . . . . . . . . . . . (775) 738-6284
Majority Floor Leader **Dennis Paul Anderson** (R) . . . . . . . (702) 410-6645
  Education: Chapman 1996 BS
Assistant Majority Floor Leader **Ira Hansen** (R) . . . . . . . . (775) 221-2502
Majority Whip **Jim Wheeler** (R) . . . . . . . . . . . . . . . . . .(775) 546-3471
  Education: Pierce Col (Attended); USC (Attended)
Assistant Majority Whip **Jill Dickman** (R) . . . . . . . . . . . . . (775) 771-9579
Assistant Majority Whip **Victoria Seaman** (R) . . . . . . . . . (775) 466-0407
Minority Floor Leader **(Vacant)** . . . . . . . . . . . . . . . . . . . . (775) 684-8555
Assistant Minority Floor Leader
  **Teresa Benitez-Thompson** (D) . . . . . . . . . . . . . . . . . . . (775) 247-7665
Assistant Minority Floor Leader **Maggie Carlton** (D) . . . . . (702) 236-5401
Chief Clerk of the Assembly **Susan Furlong** . . . . . . . . . . . (775) 684-8555
  E-mail: susan.furlong@asm.state.nv.us

## Assembly Members

**Party Affiliation Statistics:** Republicans: 22, Democrats: 16,
Independents: 1, Vacancies: 3

Assembly Member
  **Dennis Paul Anderson** (R-District 13) . . . . . . . . . . . . . . (702) 410-6645
  Counties Represented: Clark (part)
  Term Expires: 2016
  10000 West Charleston Boulevard, Suite 100,
  Las Vegas, NV 89135-1006
  E-mail: paul.anderson@asm.state.nv.us
  Committees: Commerce and Labor; Ways and Means
Assembly Member **Elliot T. Anderson** (D-District 15) . . . . (775) 684-8835
  Counties Represented: Clark (part)          Res: (702) 733-4073
  Term Expires: 2016
  3135 South Mojave, Unit 227, Las Vegas, NV 89121-8315
  E-mail: elliot.anderson@asm.state.nv.us
  Committees: Education; Judiciary; Legislative Operations and Elections
  Education: UNLV BA

Assembly Member **Nelson Araujo** (D-District 3) . . . . . . . . (702) 900-2189
  Counties Represented: Clark (part)
  Term Expires: 2016
  P.O. Box 295, Las Vegas, NV 89125-0295
  E-mail: nelson.araujo@asm.state.nv.us
  Committees: Health and Human Services; Judiciary; Natural Resources,
  Agriculture and Mining; Transportation
  Education: UNLV BA, MPA
Assembly Member **Derek W. Armstrong** (R-District 21) . . (702) 216-1010
  Counties Represented: Clark (part)
  Term Expires: 2016
  2675 Windmill Parkway, Apt 2823, Henderson, NV 89074-1944
  E-mail: derek.armstrong@asm.state.nv.us
  Committees: Education; Taxation; Ways and Means
  Education: UNLV BA, JD
Assembly Member
  **Teresa Benitez-Thompson** (D-District 27) . . . . . . . . . . .(775) 684-8845
  Counties Represented: Washoe (part)          Res: (775) 247-7665
  Term Expires: 2016
  P.O. Box 5730, Reno, NV 89513-5730
  E-mail: teresa.benitezthompson@asm.state.nv.us
  Committees: Health and Human Services; Taxation; Ways and Means
Assembly Member
  **Irene Bustamante Adams** (D-District 42) . . . . . . . . . . . (775) 684-8803
  Counties Represented: Clark (part)          Res: (702) 542-3900
  Term Expires: 2016
  3800 Reflection Way, Las Vegas, NV 89147-4442
  E-mail: irene.bustamanteadams@asm.state.nv.us
  Committees: Commerce and Labor; Taxation; Ways and Means
  Education: Cal State (Fresno) BS; UNLV EMBA
Assembly Member **Maggie Carlton** (D-District 14) . . . . . . .(775) 684-8597
  Counties Represented: Clark (part)          Tel: (702) 236-5401
  Term Expires: 2016
  5540 East Cartwright Avenue, Las Vegas, NV 89110-3802
  E-mail: maggie.carlton@asm.state.nv.us
  Committees: Commerce and Labor; Natural Resources, Agriculture and
  Mining; Ways and Means
Assembly Member **Richard Carrillo** (D-District 18) . . . . . . .(775) 684-8801
  Counties Represented: Clark (part)          Res: (702) 273-8786
  Term Expires: 2016
  4819 Diza Court, Las Vegas, NV 89122-7574
  E-mail: richard.carrillo@asm.state.nv.us
  Committees: Government Affairs; Natural Resources, Agriculture and
  Mining; Transportation
Assembly Member **Olivia Diaz** (D-District 11) . . . . . . . . . .(775) 684-8553
  Counties Represented: Clark (part)          Res: (702) 501-8994
  Term Expires: 2016
  P.O. Box 365072, North Las Vegas, NV 89036-9072
  E-mail: olivia.diaz@asm.state.nv.us
  Committees: Commerce and Labor; Education; Judiciary; Taxation
  Education: UNLV BA; Nova Southeastern MS
Assembly Member **Jill Dickman** (R-District 31) . . . . . . . . . (775) 771-9579
  Counties Represented: Washoe (part)
  Term Expires: 2016
  1344 Disc Drive, Suite 201, Sparks, NV 89436-0684
  E-mail: jill.dickman@asm.state.nv.us
  Committees: Health and Human Services; Taxation; Transportation;
  Ways and Means
Assembly Member **Vicki Dooling** (R-District 41) . . . . . . . . (702) 808-2017
  Counties Represented: Clark (part)
  Term Expires: 2016
  2505 Anthem Village Drive, Suite 492, Henderson, NV 89052-5505
  E-mail: vicki.dooling@asm.state.nv.us
  Committees: Education; Government Affairs; Natural Resources,
  Agriculture and Mining; Transportation
Assembly Member **Chris Edwards** (R-District 19) . . . . . . . (702) 715-4308
  Counties Represented: Clark (part)
  Term Expires: 2016
  6088 Riflecrest Avenue, Las Vegas, NV 89156-4778
  E-mail: chris.edwards@asm.state.nv.us
  Committees: Education; Natural Resources, Agriculture and Mining;
  Ways and Means
  Education: Notre Dame BA; George Washington MPA
Assembly Member **John Ellison** (R-District 33) . . . . . . . . (775) 684-8831
  Counties Represented: Elko, Eureka, Lincoln (part),          Res: (775) 738-6284
  White Pine
  Term Expires: 2016
  P.O. Box 683, Elko, NV 89803-0683
  E-mail: john.ellison@asm.state.nv.us
  Committees: Commerce and Labor; Government Affairs; Natural
  Resources, Agriculture and Mining

*(continued on next page)*

LEGISLATIVE BRANCH

**Assembly Members** *continued*

Assembly Member **Michele Ann Fiore** (R-District 4) . . . . . (702) 210-8460
Counties Represented: Clark (part)
Term Expires: 2016
9085 West Rosada Way, Las Vegas, NV 89149-3556
E-mail: michele.fiore@asm.state.nv.us
Committees: Commerce and Labor; Judiciary; Legislative Operations
and Elections; Transportation

Assembly Member **Edgar R. Flores** (D-District 28) . . . . . . .(775) 684-8583
Counties Represented: Clark (part)                  Tel: (702) 308-0483
Term Expires: 2016
P.O. Box 42302, Las Vegas, NV 89116-0302
E-mail: edgar.flores@asm.state.nv.us
Committees: Education; Government Affairs; Transportation
Education: UNLV BA

Assembly Member **David M. Gardner** (R-District 9) . . . . . (702) 813-0271
Counties Represented: Clark (part)
Term Expires: 2016
9661 Waukegan Avenue, Las Vegas, NV 89148-5744
E-mail: david.gardner@asm.state.nv.us
Committees: Education; Health and Human Services; Judiciary; Natural
Resources, Agriculture and Mining

Assembly Member **John Hambrick** (R-District 2) . . . . . . . .(775) 684-8827
Counties Represented: Clark (part)                  Res: (702) 242-8580
Term Expires: 2016                                   Fax: (702) 242-3406
1930 Village Center Circle, Suite 3-419, Las Vegas, NV 89134-6245
E-mail: john.hambrick@asm.state.nv.us
Committees: Health and Human Services; Taxation; Ways and Means

Assembly Member **Ira Hansen** (R-District 32) . . . . . . . . . .(775) 684-8851
Counties Represented: Esmeralda, Humboldt,          Fax: (775) 322-8889
Lander, Mineral, Nye (part), Pershing, Washoe (part)
Term Expires: 2016
68 Amigo Court, Sparks, NV 89441-6213
E-mail: ira.hansen@asm.state.nv.us
Committees: Commerce and Labor; Judiciary; Natural Resources,
Agriculture and Mining

Assembly Member **Amber Joiner** (D-District 24) . . . . . . . . (775) 338-6733
Counties Represented: Washoe (part)
Term Expires: 2016
P.O. Box 9810, Reno, NV 89507-0810
E-mail: amber.joiner@asm.state.nv.us
Committees: Education; Government Affairs; Health and Human
Services

Assembly Member **Brent A. Jones** (R-District 35) . . . . . . . (702) 521-0632
Counties Represented: Clark (part)
Term Expires: 2016
4497 Via Bianca Avenue, Las Vegas, NV 89141-4256
E-mail: brent.jones@asm.state.nv.us
Committees: Health and Human Services; Judiciary; Transportation

Assembly Member
**Randall "Randy" Kirner** (R-District 26) . . . . . . . . . . . . .(775) 852-3857
Counties Represented: Washoe (part)                 Tel: (775) 684-8848
Term Expires: 2016
18124 Wedge Parkway, Suite 519, Reno, NV 89511-8134
E-mail: randy.kirner@asm.state.nv.us
Committees: Commerce and Labor; Taxation; Ways and Means
Education: North Georgia 1967; Georgia State 1968 MBA;
West Coast 1975 MS

Assembly Member **John Moore** (LIB-District 8) . . . . . . . . .(702) 482-7676
Counties Represented: Clark (part)
Term Expires: 2016
5155 W. Tropicana Avenue, Suite 2020, Las Vegas, NV 89103-7006
E-mail: john.moore@asm.state.nv.us
Committees: Government Affairs; Health and Human Services;
Legislative Operations and Elections

Assembly Member **Harvey Munford** (D-District 6) . . . . . . .(775) 684-8545
Counties Represented: Clark (part)                  Res: (702) 646-4265
Term Expires: 2016
809 Sunny Place, Las Vegas, NV 89106-3637
E-mail: harvey.munford@asm.state.nv.us
Committees: Education; Government Affairs; Legislative Operations
and Elections
Education: Montana State BA, MA

Assembly Member **Dina Neal** (D-District 7) . . . . . . . . . . . (775) 684-8587
Counties Represented: Clark (part)                  Res: (702) 738-5870
Term Expires: 2016                                   Fax: (702) 399-2114
3217 Brautigan Court, North Las Vegas, NV 89032-6030
E-mail: dina.neal@asm.state.nv.us
Committees: Commerce and Labor; Government Affairs; Taxation

Assembly Member **Philip "P.K." O'Neill** (R-District 40) . . . (775) 741-8309
Counties Represented: Carson City, Washoe (part)
Term Expires: 2016
1216 Sonoma Street, Carson City, NV 89701-6175
E-mail: pk.oneill@asm.state.nv.us
Committees: Commerce and Labor; Judiciary; Transportation
Education: Sierra Nevada BS

Assembly Member **James Ohrenschall** (D-District 12) . . . (775) 684-8819
Counties Represented: Clark (part)                  Res: (702) 432-6999
Term Expires: 2016
P.O. Box 97741, Las Vegas, NV 89193-7741
E-mail: james.ohrenschall@asm.state.nv.us
Committees: Commerce and Labor; Judiciary; Legislative Operations
and Elections
Education: UNLV BA, JD

Assembly Member **James Oscarson** (R-District 36) . . . . .(775) 513-7468
Counties Represented: Clark (part), Lincoln (part), Nye (part)
Term Expires: 2016
P.O. Box 1600, Pahrump, NV 89048-1600
E-mail: james.oscarson@asm.state.nv.us
Committees: Health and Human Services; Natural Resources,
Agriculture and Mining; Ways and Means
Education: Comm Col Southern Nevada (Attended)

Assembly Member **Victoria Seaman** (R-District 34) . . . . . .(702) 466-0407
Counties Represented: Clark (part)
Term Expires: 2016
8808 Rozetta Court, Las Vegas, NV 89134-6179
E-mail: victoria.seaman@asm.state.nv.us
Committees: Commerce and Labor; Judiciary; Legislative Operations
and Elections

Assembly Member **Shelly M. Shelton** (R-District 10) . . . . (702) 343-4546
Counties Represented: Clark (part)
Term Expires: 2016
845 S. Kenny Way, Las Vegas, NV 89107-4437
E-mail: shelly.shelton@asm.state.nv.us
Committees: Education; Government Affairs; Legislative Operations
and Elections

Assembly Member **Stephen Silberkraus** (R-District 29) . . (702) 900-0998
Counties Represented: Clark (part)
Term Expires: 2016
P.O. Box 530364, Henderson, NV 89053-0364
E-mail: stephen.silberkraus@asm.state.nv.us
Committees: Commerce and Labor; Government Affairs; Transportation

Assembly Member **Ellen Barre Spiegel** (D-District 20) . . . (775) 684-8577
Counties Represented: Clark (part)                  Tel: (702) 577-2167
Term Expires: 2016
2764 North Green Valley Parkway, #327, Henderson, NV 89014-2120
E-mail: ellen.spiegel@asm.state.nv.us
Committees: Government Affairs; Health and Human Services;
Transportation
Education: Cornell BS

Assembly Member
**Michael "Mike" Sprinkle** (D-District 30) . . . . . . . . . . . .(775) 742-5935
Counties Represented: Washoe (part)
Term Expires: 2016
P.O. Box 51202, Sparks, NV 89435-1202
E-mail: mike.sprinkle@asm.state.nv.us
Committees: Health and Human Services; Transportation; Ways and
Means
Education: Loyola Marymount 1991 BLA

Assembly Member **Lynn D. Stewart** (R-District 22) . . . . . .(775) 684-8823
Counties Represented: Clark (part)
Term Expires: 2016
2720 Cool Lilac Avenue, Henderson, NV 89052-3836
E-mail: lynn.stewart@asm.state.nv.us
Committees: Education; Government Affairs; Legislative Operations
and Elections
Education: BYU BS, MA

Assembly Member **Heidi Swank** (D-District 16) . . . . . . . . (775) 684-8595
Counties Represented: Clark (part)                  Tel: (702) 371-6217
Term Expires: 2016
546 Barbara Way, Las Vegas, NV 89104-2858
E-mail: heidi.swank@asm.state.nv.us
Committees: Education; Natural Resources, Agriculture and Mining;
Ways and Means
Education: Hamline BA; Northwestern 2000 MA, 2006 PhD

Assembly Member **Tyrone Thompson** (D-District 17) . . . . (775) 561-7976
Counties Represented: Clark (part)
Term Expires: 2016
117 Fox Crossing Avenue, North Las Vegas, NV 89084-5207
E-mail: tyrone.thompson@asm.state.nv.us
Committees: Health and Human Services; Judiciary; Legislative
Operations and Elections

Assembly Member **Robin L. Titus** (R-District 38) . . . . . . . (775) 465-2587
Counties Represented: Churchill, Lyon (part)
Term Expires: 2016
P.O. Box 377, Wellington, NV 89444-0377
E-mail: robin.titus@asm.state.nv.us
Committees: Health and Human Services; Natural Resources,
Agriculture and Mining; Ways and Means

Assembly Member **Glenn E. Trowbridge** (R-District 37) . . (702) 363-2183
Counties Represented: Clark (part)
Term Expires: 2016
1965 Verbania Drive, Las Vegas, NV 89134-2579
E-mail: glenn.trowbridge@asm.state.nv.us
Committees: Health and Human Services; Judiciary; Legislative
Operations and Elections; Taxation

Assembly Member **Jim Wheeler** (R-District 39) . . . . . . . . (775) 684-8843
Counties Represented: Douglas, Lyon (part), Storey     Tel: (775) 546-3471
Term Expires: 2016
P.O. Box 2135, Minden, NV 89423-2135
E-mail: jim.wheeler@asm.state.nv.us
Committees: Government Affairs; Natural Resources, Agriculture and
Mining; Transportation

Assembly Member **Melissa Woodbury** (R-District 23) . . . . (775) 684-8503
Counties Represented: Clark (part)                 Tel: (702) 580-6119
Term Expires: 2016                                 Fax: (702) 240-2332
10000 West Charleston Boulevard, Suite 100,
Las Vegas, NV 89135-1006
E-mail: melissa.woodbury@asm.state.nv.us
Committees: Education; Government Affairs; Transportation

District 1 **(Vacant)** . . . . . . . . . . . . . . . . . . . . . . . . . . . . . . (775) 684-8555
Note: A general election to fill this legislative vacancy will be held on
November 8, 2016.

District 5 **(Vacant)** . . . . . . . . . . . . . . . . . . . . . . . . . . . . . . (775) 684-8555
Note: A general election to fill this legislative vacancy will be held on
November 8, 2016.

District 25 **(Vacant)** . . . . . . . . . . . . . . . . . . . . . . . . . . . . . (775) 684-8555
Note: A general election to fill this legislative vacancy will be held on
November 8, 2016.

# Assembly Standing Committees
## Commerce and Labor
401 S. Carson St., Room 4100, Carson City, NV 89701-4747

**Majority Members**
Randall "Randy" Kirner (R-26)
  *Chair*
Victoria Seaman (R-34) *Vice Chair*
Dennis Paul Anderson (R-13)
John Ellison (R-33)
Michele Ann Fiore (R-4)
Ira Hansen (R-32)
Philip "P.K." O'Neill (R-40)
Stephen Silberkraus (R-29)

**Minority Members**
Irene Bustamante Adams (D-42)
Maggie Carlton (D-14)
Olivia Diaz (D-11)
Dina Neal (D-7)
James Ohrenschall (D-12)

## Education
401 S. Carson St., Room 3142, Carson City, NV 89701-4747

**Majority Members**
Melissa Woodbury (R-23) *Chair*
Lynn D. Stewart (R-22) *Vice Chair*
Derek W. Armstrong (R-21)
Vicki Dooling (R-41)
Chris Edwards (R-19)
David M. Gardner (R-9)
Shelly M. Shelton (R-10)

**Minority Members**
Elliot T. Anderson (D-15)
Olivia Diaz (D-11)
Edgar R. Flores (D-28)
Amber Joiner (D-24)
Harvey Munford (D-6)
Heidi Swank (D-16)

## Government Affairs
401 S. Carson St., Room 3143, Carson City, NV 89701-4747

**Majority Members**
John Ellison (R-33) *Chair*
Vicki Dooling (R-41)
Shelly M. Shelton (R-10)
Stephen Silberkraus (R-29)
Lynn D. Stewart (R-22)
Jim Wheeler (R-39)
Melissa Woodbury (R-23)

**Members**
John Moore (LIB-8) *Vice Chair*

**Minority Members**
Richard Carrillo (D-18)
Edgar R. Flores (D-28)
Amber Joiner (D-24)
Harvey Munford (D-6)
Dina Neal (D-7)
Ellen Barre Spiegel (D-20)

## Health and Human Services
401 S. Carson St., Room 3138, Carson City, NV 89701-4747

**Majority Members**
James Oscarson (R-36) *Chair*
Robin L. Titus (R-38) *Vice Chair*
Jill Dickman (R-31)
David M. Gardner (R-9)
John Hambrick (R-2)
Brent A. Jones (R-35)
Glenn E. Trowbridge (R-37)

**Members**
John Moore (LIB-8)

**Minority Members**
Nelson Araujo (D-3)
Teresa Benitez-Thompson (D-27)
Amber Joiner (D-24)
Ellen Barre Spiegel (D-20)
Michael "Mike" Sprinkle (D-30)
Tyrone Thompson (D-17)

## Judiciary
401 S. Carson St., Room 3138, Carson City, NV 89701-4747

**Majority Members**
Ira Hansen (R-32) *Chair*
Michele Ann Fiore (R-4)
David M. Gardner (R-9)
Brent A. Jones (R-35)
Philip "P.K." O'Neill (R-40)
Victoria Seaman (R-34)
Glenn E. Trowbridge (R-37)

**Minority Members**
Elliot T. Anderson (D-15)
Nelson Araujo (D-3)
Olivia Diaz (D-11)
James Ohrenschall (D-12)
Tyrone Thompson (D-17)

## Legislative Operations and Elections
401 S. Carson St., Room 3142, Carson City, NV 89701-4747

**Majority Members**
Lynn D. Stewart (R-22) *Chair*
Shelly M. Shelton (R-10)
  *Vice Chair*
Michele Ann Fiore (R-4)
Victoria Seaman (R-34)
Glenn E. Trowbridge (R-37)

**Members**
John Moore (LIB-8)

**Minority Members**
Elliot T. Anderson (D-15)
Harvey Munford (D-6)
James Ohrenschall (D-12)
Tyrone Thompson (D-17)

## Natural Resources, Agriculture and Mining
401 S. Carson St., Room 3138, Carson City, NV 89701-4747

**Majority Members**
Robin L. Titus (R-38) *Chair*
Jim Wheeler (R-39) *Vice Chair*
Vicki Dooling (R-41)
Chris Edwards (R-19)
John Ellison (R-33)
David M. Gardner (R-9)
Ira Hansen (R-32)
James Oscarson (R-36)

**Minority Members**
Nelson Araujo (D-3)
Maggie Carlton (D-14)
Richard Carrillo (D-18)
Heidi Swank (D-16)

## Taxation
401 S. Carson St., Suite 4109, Carson City, NV 89701-4747

**Majority Members**
Derek W. Armstrong (R-21) *Chair*
Randall "Randy" Kirner (R-26)
  *Vice Chair*
Jill Dickman (R-31)
John Hambrick (R-2)
Glenn E. Trowbridge (R-37)

**Minority Members**
Teresa Benitez-Thompson (D-27)
Irene Bustamante Adams (D-42)
Olivia Diaz (D-11)
Dina Neal (D-7)

## Transportation
401 S. Carson St., Room 3143, Carson City, NV 89701-4747

**Majority Members**
Jim Wheeler (R-39) *Chair*
Jill Dickman (R-31) *Vice Chair*
Vicki Dooling (R-41)
Michele Ann Fiore (R-4)
Brent A. Jones (R-35)
Philip "P.K." O'Neill (R-40)
Stephen Silberkraus (R-29)
Melissa Woodbury (R-23)

**Minority Members**
Nelson Araujo (D-3)
Richard Carrillo (D-18)
Edgar R. Flores (D-28)
Ellen Barre Spiegel (D-20)
Michael "Mike" Sprinkle (D-30)

## Ways and Means

401 S. Carson St., Room 3137, Carson City, NV 89701-4747

**Majority Members**
Dennis Paul Anderson (R-13) *Chair*
John Hambrick (R-2) *Vice Chair*
Derek W. Armstrong (R-21)
Jill Dickman (R-31)
Chris Edwards (R-19)
Randall "Randy" Kirner (R-26)
James Oscarson (R-36)
Robin L. Titus (R-38)

**Minority Members**
Teresa Benitez-Thompson (D-27)
Irene Bustamante Adams (D-42)
Maggie Carlton (D-14)
Michael "Mike" Sprinkle (D-30)
Heidi Swank (D-16)

# New Hampshire General Court

State House, 107 North Main Street, Concord, NH 03301
Tel: (603) 271-1110  Tel: (603) 271-2548 (House)
Tel: (603) 271-2111 (Senate)  Fax: (603) 271-3309 (House)
Internet: www.gencourt.state.nh.us

## New Hampshire Senate

Tel: (603) 271-2111  TTY: (800) 735-2964
Fax: (603) 271-2103 (Democrats)  Fax: (603) 271-2105 (Republicans)

President of the Senate **Charles W. "Chuck" Morse** (R) . . (603) 271-8472
  Education: Plymouth State Col 1984 BA
President Pro Tem **Sharon M. Carson** (R). . . . . . . . . . . . . (603) 271-1403
Deputy President Pro Tem **Russell Edward Prescott** (R). . (603) 271-3074
Majority Leader **Joseph E. "Jeb" Bradley** (R). . . . . . . . . (603) 271-2106
  Education: Tufts 1974 BA
Minority Leader **Jeff Woodburn** (D) . . . . . . . . . . . . . . . . . (603) 271-3207
Deputy Minority Leader
  **Louis C. "Lou" D'Allesandro** (D). . . . . . . . . . . . . . . . (603) 271-2117
  Education: New Hampshire
Assistant Minority Leader **Molly M. Kelly** (D). . . . . . . . . . (603) 271-3207
  Education: Keene State BA
Clerk of the Senate **Tammy L. Wright** . . . . . . . . . . . . . . . (603) 271-3050
  E-mail: tammy.wright@leg.state.nh.us        Fax: (603) 271-3545
Sergeant-at-Arms **Roger Amadon** . . . . . . . . . . . . . . . . . . (603) 271-3420

## Senators

**Party Affiliation Statistics:** Republicans: 14, Democrats: 10

Senator **Kevin Avard** (R-District 12) Room 105-A . . . . . . . . (603) 271-4151
  Counties Represented: Hillsborough (part)
  Term Expires: 2016
  E-mail: kevin.avard@leg.state.nh.us
  Committees: Education; Health and Human Services; Rules, Enrolled
  Bills and Internal Affairs
Senator **Regina Birdsell** (R-District 19) Room 105-A . . . . . (603) 271-4151
  Counties Represented: Rockingham (part)        Res: (603) 548-7118
  Term Expires: 2016
  24 Larson Drive, Hampstead, NH 03841-2263
  E-mail: regina.birdsell@leg.state.nh.us
  Committees: Public and Municipal Affairs; Transportation
Senator **David Richard Boutin** (R-District 16). . . . . . . . . . (603) 271-3092
  Counties Represented: Merrimack (part),        Res: (603) 203-5391
  Rockingham (part)
  Term Expires: 2016
  1465 Hookett Road, Suite 80, Hooksett, NH 03106
  E-mail: david.boutin@leg.state.nh.us
  Committees: Capital Budget; Public and Municipal Affairs; Ways and
  Means
  Education: Northeastern 1975 BSE; Rhode Island 1980 MCP
Senator **Joseph E. "Jeb" Bradley** (R-District 3). . . . . . . . (603) 271-2106
  Counties Represented: Carroll, Grafton (part),        Res: (603) 387-2365
  Strafford (part)
  Term Expires: 2016
  630 South Main, Wolfeboro, NH 03894
  E-mail: jeb.bradley@leg.state.nh.us
  Committees: Commerce; Energy and Natural Resources; Rules,
  Enrolled Bills and Internal Affairs
Senator **Sharon M. Carson** (R-District 14) Room 106 . . . . (603) 271-1403
  Counties Represented: Hillsborough (part), Rockingham (part)
  Term Expires: 2016
  19 Tokanel Road, Londonderry, NH 05053
  E-mail: sharon.carson@leg.state.nh.us
  Committees: Executive Departments and Administration; Health and
  Human Services; Judiciary
Senator **Sam A. Cataldo** (R-District 6) Room 107 . . . . . . . (603) 271-4063
  Counties Represented: Belknap (part), Strafford (part)
  Term Expires: 2016
  120 Hornetown Road, Farmington, NH 03835
  E-mail: sam.cataldo@leg.state.nh.us
  Committees: Commerce; Executive Departments and Administration;
  Judiciary
  Education: Lowell Tech; Northeastern; La Salle U

Senator **Martha Fuller Clark** (D-District 21) Room 115 . . . (603) 271-3076
Counties Represented: Rockingham (part), Strafford (part)
Term Expires: 2016
152 Middle Street, Portsmouth, NH 03801
E-mail: martha.fullerclark@leg.state.nh.us
Committees: Energy and Natural Resources; Health and Human
Services; Rules, Enrolled Bills and Internal Affairs
Education: Mills 1964 BA; Boston U 1977 BA

Senator **Louis C. "Lou" D'Allesandro** (D-District 20) . . . . (603) 271-2117
Counties Represented: Hillsborough (part)          Res: (603) 669-3494
Term Expires: 2016
332 Saint James Avenue, Manchester, NH 03102-4950
E-mail: dalas@leg.state.nh.us
Committees: Capital Budget; Finance; Ways and Means

Senator **Gary L. Daniels** (R-District 11) Room 302 . . . . . . (603) 271-3042
Counties Represented: Hillsborough (part)          Res: (603) 860-4482
Term Expires: 2016
127 Whitten Road, Milford, NH 03055
E-mail: gary.daniels@leg.state.nh.us
Committees: Capital Budget; Judiciary; Transportation

Senator **Dan Feltes** (D-District 11) . . . . . . . . . . . . . . . . . . . (603) 271-3067
Counties Represented: Hillsborough (part)
Term Expires: 2016
33 North State Street, Room 5, Concord, NH 03301
E-mail: dan.feltes@leg.state.nh.us
Committees: Energy and Natural Resources; Transportation; Ways and
Means

Senator **Jeanie Forrester** (R-District 2) Room 105 . . . . . . (603) 271-4980
Counties Represented: Belknap (part), Grafton (part), Merrimack (part)
Term Expires: 2016
E-mail: jeanie.forrester@leg.state.nh.us
Committees: Capital Budget; Finance
Education: New Hampshire BA, MBA

Senator **Andrew Hosmer** (D-District 7) . . . . . . . . . . . . . . . (603) 271-8631
Counties Represented: Belknap (part), Merrimack (part)
Term Expires: 2016
Legislative Office Building, 33 North State Street, Room 101-A,
Concord, NH 03301
E-mail: andrew.hosmer@leg.state.nh.us
Committees: Finance

Senator **Molly M. Kelly** (D-District 10) Room 120 . . . . . . . (603) 271-3207
Counties Represented: Cheshire (part)
Term Expires: 2016
E-mail: molly.kelly@leg.state.nh.us
Committees: Capital Budget; Education; Health and Human Services;
Public and Municipal Affairs

Senator **Bette R. Lasky** (D-District 13) Room 124 . . . . . . . (603) 271-3091
Counties Represented: Hillsborough (part)
Term Expires: 2016
E-mail: bette.lasky@leg.state.nh.us
Committees: Judiciary; Public and Municipal Affairs
Education: UMass (Amherst) 1968 BA

Senator **Gerald H. "Jerry" Little** (R-District 8)
Room 105-A . . . . . . . . . . . . . . . . . . . . . . . . . . . . . . . . . (603) 271-4151
Counties Represented: Cheshire (part), Hillsborough (part), Merrimack
(part), Sullivan (part)
Note: On April 6, 2016, the New Hampshire Executive Council
confirmed Gerald Little's nomination as Commissioner of the New
Hampshire Banking Department. Little will begin working at the
Banking Department on June 2, 2016. He will depart the New
Hampshire Senate at the end of May 2016.
Term Expires: 2016
E-mail: jerry.little@leg.state.nh.us
Committees: Energy and Natural Resources; Finance
Education: New Hampshire 1977 BA

Senator **Charles W. "Chuck" Morse** (R-District 22)
Room 302 . . . . . . . . . . . . . . . . . . . . . . . . . . . . . . . . . . . (603) 271-8472
Counties Represented: Hillsborough (part), Rockingham (part)
Term Expires: 2016
E-mail: chuck.morse@leg.state.nh.us
Committees: Finance; Ways and Means

Senator **David M. Pierce** (D-District 5) . . . . . . . . . . . . . . . . (603) 271-3067
Counties Represented: Grafton (part), Sullivan (part)
Term Expires: 2016
Legislative Office Building, 33 North State Street, Room 5,
Concord, NH 03301
E-mail: david.pierce@leg.state.nh.us
Committees: Commerce; Judiciary
Education: Baylor; George Washington JD, MBA

Senator **Russell Edward Prescott** (R-District 23)
Room 302 . . . . . . . . . . . . . . . . . . . . . . . . . . . . . . (603) 271-3074
Counties Represented: Rockingham (part)          Res: (603) 642-4243
Term Expires: 2016
Eight Farm Road, Kingston, NH 03848
E-mail: represcott@represcott.com
Committees: Commerce; Rules, Enrolled Bills and Internal Affairs

Senator **John Reagan** (R-District 17) Room 107 . . . . . . . . (603) 271-4063
Counties Represented: Merrimack (part), Rockingham (part), Strafford
(part)
Term Expires: 2016
E-mail: john.reagan111@gmail.com
Committees: Education; Executive Departments and Administration;
Finance

Senator **Andy Sanborn** (R-District 9) Room 302 . . . . . . . . (603) 271-2609
Counties Represented: Cheshire (part), Hillsborough (part)
Term Expires: 2016
E-mail: andy.sanborn@leg.state.nh.us
Committees: Energy and Natural Resources; Health and Human
Services; Ways and Means
Education: New England Col BA

Senator **Donna M. Soucy** (D-District 18) Room 120 . . . . . (603) 271-3207
Counties Represented: Hillsborough (part)
Term Expires: 2016
E-mail: donna.soucy@leg.state.nh.us
Committees: Commerce; Executive Departments and Administration;
Rules, Enrolled Bills and Internal Affairs
Education: St Anselm BA; New Hampshire 1999 JD

Senator **Nancy F. Stiles** (R-District 24) . . . . . . . . . . . . . . . (603) 271-3093
Counties Represented: Rockingham (part)
Term Expires: 2016
Legislative Office Building, 33 North State Street, Room 103-A,
Concord, NH 03301
E-mail: nancy.stiles@leg.state.nh.us
Committees: Education; Public and Municipal Affairs; Transportation

Senator **David H. Watters** (D-District 4) . . . . . . . . . . . . . . . (603) 271-8631
Counties Represented: Strafford (part)
Term Expires: 2016
Legislative Office Building, 33 North State Street, Room 101-A,
Concord, NH 03301
E-mail: david.watters@leg.state.nh.us
Committees: Education; Transportation
Education: Dartmouth 1972 BA; Brown U 1979 PhD

Senator **Jeff Woodburn** (D-District 1) Room 120 . . . . . . . . (603) 271-3207
Counties Represented: Coos, Grafton (part)
Term Expires: 2016
E-mail: jeff.woodburn@leg.state.nh.us
Committees: Executive Departments and Administration

# Senate Standing Committees
## Capital Budget
State House, 107 North Main Street, Room 103, Concord, NH 03301

| **Majority Members** | **Minority Members** |
| --- | --- |
| Gary L. Daniels (R-11) *Chair* | Louis C. "Lou" D'Allesandro |
| David Richard Boutin (R-16) | (D-20) |
| *Vice Chair* | Molly M. Kelly (D-10) |
| Jeanie Forrester (R-2) | |

## Commerce
State House, 107 North Main Street, Room 100, Concord, NH 03301

| **Majority Members** | **Minority Members** |
| --- | --- |
| Russell Edward Prescott (R-23) | David M. Pierce (D-5) |
| *Chair* | Donna M. Soucy (D-18) |
| Joseph E. "Jeb" Bradley (R-3) | |
| *Vice Chair* | |
| Sam A. Cataldo (R-6) | |

## Education
Legislative Office Building, 33 North State Street, Room 103,
Concord, NH 03301

| **Majority Members** | **Minority Members** |
| --- | --- |
| John Reagan (R-17) *Chair* | Molly M. Kelly (D-10) |
| Nancy F. Stiles (R-24) *Vice Chair* | David H. Watters (D-4) |
| Kevin Avard (R-12) | |

## Energy and Natural Resources

State House, 107 North Main Street, Room 100, Concord, NH 03301

**Majority Members**
Joseph E. "Jeb" Bradley (R-3)
  *Chair*
Gerald H. "Jerry" Little (R-8)
  *Vice Chair*
Andy Sanborn (R-9)

**Minority Members**
Martha Fuller Clark (D-21)
Dan Feltes (D-11)

## Executive Departments and Administration

Legislative Office Building, 33 North State Street, Room 101, Concord, NH 03301

**Majority Members**
Sharon M. Carson (R-14) *Chair*
John Reagan (R-17) *Vice Chair*
Sam A. Cataldo (R-6)

**Minority Members**
Donna M. Soucy (D-18)
Jeff Woodburn (D-1)

## Finance

State House, 107 North Main Street, Room 103, Concord, NH 03301

**Majority Members**
Jeanie Forrester (R-2) *Chair*
Gerald H. "Jerry" Little (R-8)
  *Vice Chair*
Charles W. "Chuck" Morse (R-22)
John Reagan (R-17)

**Minority Members**
Louis C. "Lou" D'Allesandro
  (D-20)
Andrew Hosmer (D-7)

## Health and Human Services

Legislative Office Building, 33 North State Street, Room 101, Concord, NH 03301

**Majority Members**
Andy Sanborn (R-9) *Chair*
Kevin Avard (R-12)
Sharon M. Carson (R-14)

**Minority Members**
Molly M. Kelly (D-10) *Vice Chair*
Martha Fuller Clark (D-21)

## Judiciary

State House, 107 North Main Street, Room 100, Concord, NH 03301

**Majority Members**
Sharon M. Carson (R-14) *Chair*
Sam A. Cataldo (R-6) *Vice Chair*
Gary L. Daniels (R-11)

**Minority Members**
Bette R. Lasky (D-13)
David M. Pierce (D-5)

## Public and Municipal Affairs

Legislative Office Building, 33 North State Street, Room 102, Concord, NH 03301

**Majority Members**
Regina Birdsell (R-19) *Chair*
David Richard Boutin (R-16)
  *Vice Chair*
Nancy F. Stiles (R-24)

**Minority Members**
Molly M. Kelly (D-10)
Bette R. Lasky (D-13)

## Rules, Enrolled Bills and Internal Affairs

State House, 107 North Main Street, Room 100, Concord, NH 03301

**Majority Members**
Russell Edward Prescott (R-23)
  *Chair*
Kevin Avard (R-12) *Vice Chair*
Joseph E. "Jeb" Bradley (R-3)

**Minority Members**
Martha Fuller Clark (D-21)
Donna M. Soucy (D-18)

## Transportation

Legislative Office Building, 33 North State Street, Room 103, Concord, NH 03301

**Majority Members**
Nancy F. Stiles (R-24) *Chair*
Regina Birdsell (R-19) *Vice Chair*
Gary L. Daniels (R-11)

**Minority Members**
David H. Watters (D-4)
Dan Feltes (D-11)

## Ways and Means

State House, 107 North Main Street, Room 103, Concord, NH 03301

**Majority Members**
David Richard Boutin (R-16) *Chair*
Charles W. "Chuck" Morse (R-22)
Andy Sanborn (R-9)

**Minority Members**
Louis C. "Lou"
  D'Allesandro (D-20)
  *Vice Chair*
Dan Feltes (D-11)

# New Hampshire House of Representatives

Tel: (603) 271-2548  Fax: (603) 271-3309

Speaker of the House **Shawn N. Jasper** (R) . . . . . . . . . . . . (603) 566-4348
Deputy Speaker of the House **Gene G. Chandler** (R) . . . . . (603) 374-6603
Speaker Pro Tempore **Sherman A. Packard** (R) . . . . . . . . (603) 432-3391
Majority Leader **Richard "Dick" Hinch** (R) . . . . . . . . . . . . (603) 261-6317
Deputy Majority Leader
  **Stephen J. "Steve" Schmidt** (R) . . . . . . . . . . . . . . . . . (603) 569-0848
Majority Whip **Kathleen Hoelzel** (R) . . . . . . . . . . . . . . . . . (603) 895-4172
Deputy Majority Whip **Claire Rouillard** (R) . . . . . . . . . . . . (603) 494-6144
Assistant Majority Whip **Peggy McCarthy** (R) . . . . . . . . . (603) 598-4966
Assistant Majority Whip **Terry Wolf** (R) . . . . . . . . . . . . . . . (603) 471-0240
Minority Leader **Stephen J. "Steve" Shurtleff** (D) . . . . . . (603) 753-4563
Deputy Minority Leader
  **Lucinda "Cindy" Rosenwald** (D) . . . . . . . . . . . . . . . . . (603) 595-9896
Senior Assistant Minority Leader **Jeffrey Goley** (D) . . . . . . (603) 669-2256
Minority Floor Leader **Susan Ford** (D) . . . . . . . . . . . . . . . (603) 823-5609
Deputy Minority Floor Leader
  **Andrew A. "Andy" White** (D) . . . . . . . . . . . . . . . . . . . (603) 252-0846
Clerk of the House **Paul C. Smith** . . . . . . . . . . . . . . . . . . (603) 271-2548
  E-mail: paul.smith@leg.state.nh.us
Assistant Clerk of the House **Michael Coe** . . . . . . . . . . . . (603) 271-2548
  E-mail: michael.coe@leg.state.nh.us
Sergeant-at-Arms **Walter Sword** . . . . . . . . . . . . . . . . . . . (603) 271-3315
  E-mail: walter.sword@leg.state.nh.us

## Representatives

**Party Affiliation Statistics:** Republicans: 236, Democrats: 160, Independents: 1, Vacancies: 3

Representative **Michael D. Abbott** (D-Cheshire-1) . . . . . . . (603) 336-7090
  Counties Represented: Cheshire (part)
  Term Expires: 2016
  P.O. Box 174, Hinsdale, NH 03451
  E-mail: michael.abbott@leg.state.nh.us
  Committees: Transportation
Representative **Richard Abel** (D-Grafton-13) . . . . . . . . . . . (603) 448-5831
  Counties Represented: Grafton (part)
  Term Expires: 2016
  112 Bank Street, Lebanon, NH 03766
  E-mail: richard.abel@leg.state.nh.us
  Committees: Commerce and Consumer Affairs
Representative **Patrick Abrami** (R-Rockingham-19) . . . . . . . (603) 772-3489
  Counties Represented: Rockingham (part)
  Term Expires: 2016
  Nine Tall Pines Drive, Stratham, NH 03885-2564
  E-mail: patrick.abrami@leg.state.nh.us
  Committees: Ways and Means
Representative **Max Abramson** (R-Rockingham-20) . . . . . . (603) 760-7090
  Counties Represented: Rockingham (part)
  Term Expires: 2016
  14 Charles Henry Way, Seabrook, NH 03874
  E-mail: maxabramson@gmx.com
Representative
  **Christopher R. Adams** (R-Hillsborough-26) . . . . . . . . . . (603) 673-3212
  Counties Represented: Hillsborough (part)
  Term Expires: 2016
  10 Sargent Road, Brookline, NH 03033
  E-mail: cradams13@charter.net
  Committees: Education
Representative **Glen Aldrich** (R-Belknap-2) . . . . . . . . . . . . (603) 527-8726
  Counties Represented: Belknap (part)
  Term Expires: 2016
  343 Old Lakeshore Road, Gilford, NH 03249
  E-mail: glenaldrich@gmail.com
  Committees: Science, Technology and Energy

Representative **Caroletta C. Alicea** (D-Merrimack-8) . . . . . (603) 271-2548
Counties Represented: Merrimack (part)
Term Expires: 2016
Four Stirrup Iron Road, Boscawen, NH 03303
E-mail: caroletta.alicea@leg.state.nh.us
Committees: Children and Family Law

Representative **Mary M. Allen** (R-Rockingham-5) . . . . . . . (603) 382-5665
Counties Represented: Rockingham (part)
Term Expires: 2016
39 Pond Street, Newton, NH 03858-3415
Committees: Finance

Representative **Susan W. Almy** (D-Grafton-13) . . . . . . . . . (603) 448-4769
Counties Represented: Grafton (part)
Term Expires: 2016
266 Poverty Lane, Lebanon, NH 03766-2730
E-mail: susan.almy@comcast.net
Committees: Ways and Means
Education: Stanford 1974 DPhil; Swarthmore 1968 AB

Representative **Richard Ames** (D-Cheshire-9) . . . . . . . . . . (603) 271-2548
Counties Represented: Cheshire (part)
Term Expires: 2016
12 Blackberry Lane, Jaffrey, NH 03452
E-mail: richard.ames@leg.state.nh.us
Committees: Ways and Means
Education: Harvard 1965 BS, 1968 JD

Representative **Keith Ammon** (R-Hillsborough-40) . . . . . . . (603) 296-9879
Counties Represented: Hillsborough (part)
Term Expires: 2016
P.O. Box, New Boston, NH 03070
E-mail: keith.ammon@leg.state.nh.us
Committees: Municipal and County Government

Representative **Lino Avellani** (R-Carroll-5) . . . . . . . . . . . . . (603) 858-5196
Counties Represented: Carroll (part)
Term Expires: 2016
P.O. Box 516, Sanbornville, NH 03872
E-mail: lino.avellani@leg.state.nh.us
Committees: Labor, Industrial and Rehabilitative Services

Representative **Gary Azarian** (R-Rockingham-8) . . . . . . . . (603) 890-8669
Counties Represented: Rockingham (part)
Term Expires: 2016
34 Ticklefancy Lane, Salem, NH 03079
E-mail: gazarian@comcast.net
Committees: Ways and Means

Representative **William "Bill" Baber** (D-Stafford-14) . . . . . (603) 271-2548
Counties Represented: Stafford (part)
Term Expires: 2016
Five Gerry's Lane, Dover, NH 03820
E-mail: bill.baber@leg.state.nh.us
Committees: Science, Technology and Energy
Education: Southern Illinois; Boston U

Representative
**Robert A. "Bob" Backus** (D-Hillsborough-19) . . . . . . . (603) 271-2548
Counties Represented: Hillsborough (part)
Term Expires: 2016
1318 Goffstown Drive, Manchester, NH 03102
E-mail: robert.backus@leg.state.nh.us
Committees: Science, Technology and Energy
Education: Harvard JD

Representative **Brad Bailey** (R-Grafton-14) . . . . . . . . . . . . . (603) 271-2548
Counties Represented: Grafton (part)          Res: (603) 638-2118
Term Expires: 2016
101 Smutty Hollow Road, Monroe, NH 03771
E-mail: brad.bailey@leg.state.nh.us
Committees: Legislative Administration

Representative **John L. Balcom** (R-Hillsborough-21) . . . . . (603) 424-8422
Counties Represented: Hillsborough (part)
Term Expires: 2016
85 Pond View Drive, Merrimack, NH 03054
E-mail: john.balcom@leg.state.nh.us
Committees: Education

Representative **Alfred P. Baldasaro** (R-Rockingham-5) . . . . (603) 425-6997
Counties Represented: Rockingham (part)
Term Expires: 2016
41 Hall Road, Londonderry, NH 03053
E-mail: al.baldasaro@leg.state.nh.us
Committees: State-Federal Relations and Veterans Affairs

Representative **Arthur E. Barnes III** (R-Rockingham-8) . . . . (603) 893-4754
Counties Represented: Rockingham (part)
Term Expires: 2016
174 Pelham Road, Salem, NH 03079
E-mail: arthur.barnes@leg.state.nh.us
Committees: Criminal Justice and Public Safety

Representative
**Benjamin C. Baroody** (D-Hillsborough-43) . . . . . . . . . . (603) 271-2548
Counties Represented: Hillsborough (part)
Term Expires: 2016
E-mail: ben.baroody@leg.state.nh.us
Committees: Fish, Game and Marine Resources

Representative
**Richard W. "Dick" Barry** (R-Hillsborough-21) . . . . . . . . (603) 320-1531
Counties Represented: Hillsborough (part)      Res: (603) 880-3731
Term Expires: 2016
12 Kyle Road, Merrimack, NH 03054-4528
E-mail: richardbarry@leg.state.nh.us
Committees: Finance; Rules

Representative **Christy D. Bartlett** (D-Merrimack-19) . . . . . (603) 271-2548
Counties Represented: Merrimack (part)      Res: (603) 224-3172
Term Expires: 2016
77 Sanborn Road, Concord, NH 03301
E-mail: christydbartlett@gmail.com
Committees: Environment and Agriculture

Representative **David Bates** (R-Rockingham-7) . . . . . . . . . . (603) 894-6987
Counties Represented: Rockingham (part)
Term Expires: 2016
12 Range Road, Windham, NH 03087
E-mail: rep.bates@live.com
Committees: Commerce and Consumer Affairs

Representative **Steven Beaudoin** (R-Stafford-9) . . . . . . . . (603) 271-2548
Counties Represented: Stafford (part)
Term Expires: 2016
24 Hemlock Street, Rochester, NH 03867
E-mail: steven.beaudoin@leg.state.nh.us
Committees: Executive Departments and Administration

Representative **Jane Beaulieu** (D-Hillsborough-45) . . . . . . . (603) 271-2548
Counties Represented: Hillsborough (part)      Res: (603) 203-8440
Term Expires: 2016
609 South Main Street, Manchester, NH 03102
E-mail: jane.beaulieu@leg.state.nh.us
Committees: Municipal and County Government

Representative
**James "Jim" Belanger** (R-Hillsborough-27) . . . . . . . . . . (603) 893-0659
Counties Represented: Hillsborough (part)
Term Expires: 2016
220 North Main Street, Salem, NH 03079-1719
E-mail: jim.belanger@leg.state.nh.us
Committees: Municipal and County Government

Representative **Ronald J. Belanger** (R-Rockingham-8) . . . . (603) 893-0659
Counties Represented: Rockingham (part)
Term Expires: 2016
220 North Main Street, Salem, NH 03079-1719
E-mail: ron.belanger@leg.state.nh.us
Committees: Commerce and Consumer Affairs

Representative **Travis Bennett** (D-Grafton-8) . . . . . . . . . . . (603) 686-0625
Counties Represented: Grafton (part)
Term Expires: 2016
4C Pleasant Street, Plymouth, NH 03264
E-mail: travisrbennett1@gmail.com
Committees: Election Law

Representative **Paul Berch** (D-Cheshire-1) . . . . . . . . . . . . . (603) 271-2548
Counties Represented: Cheshire (part)      Res: (603) 399-4960
Term Expires: 2016
956 River Road, Westmoreland, NH 03467
E-mail: pberch@myfairpoint.net
Committees: Judiciary
Education: George Washington 1967; Chicago 1970 JD

Representative **Skip Berrien** (D-Rockingham-18) . . . . . . . . (603) 580-1240
Counties Represented: Rockingham (part)
Term Expires: 2016
Seven Coach Road, Exeter, NH 03833
E-mail: skip.berrien@leg.state.nh.us
Committees: Children and Family Law

Representative **Roger R. Berube** (D-Stafford-18) . . . . . . . . (603) 692-5653
Counties Represented: Stafford (part)
Term Expires: 2016
15 Stackpole Road, Somersworth, NH 03878-1627
E-mail: rogerrberube@hotmail.com
Committees: Criminal Justice and Public Safety

Representative **David A. Bickford** (R-Strafford-3) . . . . . . . . (603) 271-2548
Counties Represented: Strafford (part)      Res: (603) 859-7899
Term Expires: 2016
183 Brackett Road, New Durham, NH 03855
E-mail: davidabickford51@yahoo.com
Committees: Municipal and County Government

*(continued on next page)*

## Representatives *continued*

Representative **Barbara Biggie** (R-Hillsborough-23) . . . . . . (603) 271-2548
Counties Represented: Hillsborough (part)
Term Expires: 2016
E-mail: barbara.biggie@leg.state.nh.us
Committees: Commerce and Consumer Affairs

Representative **Peter W. Bixby** (D-Stafford-17) . . . . . . . . . . (603) 271-2548
Counties Represented: Stafford (part)     Res: (603) 749-5659
Term Expires: 2016
69 Glenwood Avenue, Dover, NH 03820
E-mail: peter.bixby@leg.state.nh.us
Committees: Environment and Agriculture
Education: Yale BA; Indiana MA, PhD

Representative **Ralph G. Boehm** (R-Hillsborough-20) . . . . .(603) 860-6309
Counties Represented: Hillsborough (part)
Term Expires: 2016
Six Gibson Drive, Litchfield, NH 03052-2301
E-mail: ralph.boehm@leg.state.nh.us
Committees: Education

Representative **Efstathia Booras** (D-Hillsborough-33) . . . . (603) 271-2548
Counties Represented: Hillsborough (part)     Res: (603) 886-5886
Term Expires: 2016
44 Balcom Street, Nashua, NH 03060
E-mail: efstathia.booras@leg.state.nh.us
Committees: State-Federal Relations and Veterans Affairs

Representative **David A. Borden** (D-Rockingham-24) . . . . .(603) 271-2548
Counties Represented: Rockingham (part)     Res: (603) 436-4132
Term Expires: 2016
P.O. Box 167, New Castle, NH 03854
E-mail: david@davidbordennh.com
Committees: Science, Technology and Energy

Representative **John Bordenet** (D-Cheshire-5) . . . . . . . . . . (603) 271-2548
Counties Represented: Cheshire (part)
Term Expires: 2016
E-mail: john.bordenet@leg.state.nh.us
Committees: Commerce and Consumer Affairs

Representative **Amanda Bouldin** (D-Merrimack-12) . . . . . . (603) 271-2548
Counties Represented: Merrimack (part)
Term Expires: 2016
E-mail: amanda.bouldin@leg.state.nh.us
Committees: State-Federal Relations and Veterans Affairs

Representative **Paula Bradley** (D-Merrimack-18) . . . . . . . . (603) 271-2548
Counties Represented: Merrimack (part)
Term Expires: 2016
E-mail: paula.bradley@leg.state.nh.us
Committees: Resources, Recreation and Development

Representative **Michael Brewster** (R-Merrimack-21) . . . . . (603) 491-5927
Counties Represented: Merrimack (part)
Term Expires: 2016
Committees: Environment and Agriculture

Representative **Ernest H. "Ernie" Bridge** (R-Sullivan-6) . . .(603) 863-7203
Counties Represented: Sullivan (part)
Term Expires: 2016
E-mail: yankeeernie@gmail.com
Committees: Environment and Agriculture

Representative **Chris Brown** (D-Grafton-12) . . . . . . . . . . . . .(603) 271-2548
Counties Represented: Grafton (part)
Term Expires: 2016
E-mail: chris.brown@leg.state.nh.us
Committees: Municipal and County Government

Representative **Duane Brown** (R-Grafton-16) . . . . . . . . . . . (603) 271-2548
Counties Represented: Grafton (part)
Term Expires: 2016
E-mail: duane.brown@leg.state.nh.us
Committees: Election Law

Representative
**Pamela "Pam" Brown** (D-Hillsborough-31) . . . . . . . . . . .(603) 930-6999
Counties Represented: Hillsborough (part)
Term Expires: 2016
Two Clocktower Place, Apartment 209, Nashua, NH 03060-3351
E-mail: pam.brown@leg.state.nh.us
Committees: Transportation

Representative **Rebecca A. Brown** (D-Grafton-2) . . . . . . . (603) 271-2548
Counties Represented: Grafton (part)     Res: (603) 823-8119
Term Expires: 2016
80 Post Road, Sugar Hill, NH 03586
E-mail: rebecca.brown@leg.state.nh.us
Committees: Environment and Agriculture

Representative **Thomas "Tom" Buco** (D-Carroll-2) . . . . . . (603) 271-2548
Counties Represented: Carroll (part)     Res: (603) 986-5629
Term Expires: 2016
P.O. Box 3149, Conway, NH 03818
E-mail: tom.buco@leg.state.nh.us
Committees: Finance

Representative **John A. Burt** (R-Hillsborough-39) . . . . . . . . (603) 624-5084
Counties Represented: Hillsborough (part)
Term Expires: 2016
Seven Bay Street, Goffstown, NH 03045
E-mail: john.burt@leg.state.nh.us
Committees: Criminal Justice and Public Safety

Representative **Wayne M. Burton** (D-Strafford-6) . . . . . . . . (603) 271-2548
Counties Represented: Strafford (part)
Term Expires: 2016
E-mail: wayne.burton@leg.state.nh.us
Committees: Election Law

Representative **Carol Bush** (R-Rockingham-31) . . . . . . . . . (603) 271-2548
Counties Represented: Rockingham (part)
Term Expires: 2016
E-mail: carol.bush@leg.state.nh.us
Committees: Environment and Agriculture

Representative **Edward A. Butler** (D-Carrol-7) . . . . . . . . . (603) 271-6131
Counties Represented: Carroll (part)     Res: (603) 374-6131
Term Expires: 2016
Two Morey Road, Harts Location, NH 03812
E-mail: edward.butler@leg.state.nh.us
Committees: Commerce and Consumer Affairs
Education: Boston U 1978 BSN; NYU 1984 MN

Representative **Frank A. Byron** (R-Hillsborough-20) . . . . . . (603) 271-2548
Counties Represented: Hillsborough (part)     Res: (603) 889-7424
Term Expires: 2016
Eight Mallard Court, Litchfield, NH 03052
E-mail: frank.byron@leg.state.nh.us
Committees: Finance

Representative **Michael Cahill** (D-Rockingham-17) . . . . . . . (603) 659-2355
Counties Represented: Rockingham (part)
Term Expires: 2016
328 Ash Swamp Road, Newmarket, NH 03857
E-mail: michael.cahill@leg.state.nh.us
Committees: Labor, Industrial and Rehabilitative Services

Representative
**Jacqueline A. Cali-Pitts** (D-Rockingham-30) . . . . . . . . . (603) 431-7657
Counties Represented: Rockingham (part)
Term Expires: 2016
40 Bedford Way, Apartment 112, Portsmouth, NH 03801-3484
E-mail: jackie.cali-pitts@leg.state.nh.us
Committees: Science, Technology and Energy

Representative **G. Thomas Cardon** (R-Rockingham-6) . . . . (603) 271-2548
Counties Represented: Rockingham (part)
Term Expires: 2016
E-mail: thomas.cardon@leg.state.nh.us
Committees: Transportation

Representative **Clyde Carson** (D-Merrimack-7) . . . . . . . . . . (603) 271-2548
Counties Represented: Merrimack (part)     Tel: (603) 456-2562
Term Expires: 2016
33 Kearsage Mountain Road, Warner, NH 03278
E-mail: clyde.carson@leg.state.nh.us
Committees: Municipal and County Government

Representative **Gene G. Chandler** (R-Carroll-1) . . . . . . . . . (603) 374-6603
Counties Represented: Carroll (part)
Term Expires: 2016
General Delivery, Bartlett, NH 03812-9999
P.O. Box 296, Bartlett, NH 03812-0296
E-mail: gene.chandler@leg.state.nh.us
Committees: Public Works and Highways; Rules

Representative **Cynthia Chase** (D-Cheshire-8) . . . . . . . . . . .(603) 357-2381
Counties Represented: Cheshire (part)
Term Expires: 2016
110 Arch Street, Keene, NH 03431-2168
E-mail: cyndychase25@gmail.com
Committees: Children and Family Law

Representative **Francis Chase** (R-Rockingham-20) . . . . . . . (603) 944-0830
Counties Represented: Rockingham (part)
Term Expires: 2016
14 Lighthouse Way, Seabrook, NH 03874
E-mail: chd1500@outlook.com
Committees: Municipal and County Government

Representative **Catherine Cheney** (R-Stafford-17)........(603) 271-2548
Counties Represented: Stafford (part)
Term Expires: 2016
E-mail: catherine.cheney@leg.state.nh.us
Committees: Municipal and County Government

Representative **Brian Chirichiello** (R-Rockingham-6)......(603) 661-4835
Counties Represented: Rockingham (part)        Res: (603) 432-0799
Term Expires: 2016
Six Rollins Street, Derry, NH 03038-2318
E-mail: brian.chirichiello@verani.com
Committees: Transportation

Representative
**D. L. "Chris" Christensen** (R-Hillsborough-21)........(603) 271-2548
Counties Represented: Hillsborough (part)
Term Expires: 2016
E-mail: c.christensen@leg.state.nh.us
Committees: Resources, Recreation and Development

Representative **Lars T. Christiansen** (R-Hillsborough-37)..(603) 889-0481
Counties Represented: Hillsborough (part)
Term Expires: 2016
One Stone Wood Lane, Hudson, NH 03051
E-mail: lars@taybre.net
Committees: State-Federal Relations and Veterans Affairs

Representative **Andrew Christie, Jr.** (R-Rockingham-37)..(603) 271-2548
Counties Represented: Rockingham (part)
Term Expires: 2016
E-mail: andrew.christie@leg.state.nh.us
Committees: Executive Departments and Administration

Representative **Rick Christie** (R-Hillsborough-6).........(603) 626-5743
Counties Represented: Hillsborough (part)
Term Expires: 2016
149 Moose Club Park Road, Goffstown, NH 03045
E-mail: rick.christie@leg.state.nh.us
Committees: Election Law

Representative
**Jacalyn L. "Jackie" Cilley** (D-Strafford-4)...........(603) 664-5597
Counties Represented: Strafford (part)
Term Expires: 2016
Eight Oak Hill Road, Barrington, NH 03825
E-mail: jcilley@aol.com
Committees: Executive Departments and Administration

Representative **John R. Cloutier** (D-Sullivan-10)........(603) 477-3690
Counties Represented: Sullivan (part)        Res: (603) 542-6190
Term Expires: 2016
10 Spruce Avenue, Claremont, NH 03743-5306
E-mail: jocloutier@comcast.net
Committees: Public Works and Highways

Representative **James Coffey** (R-Hillsborough-25) ......(603) 785-5700
Counties Represented: Hillsborough (part)        Res: (603) 787-3173
Term Expires: 2016
P.O. Box 343, New Ipswich, NH 03071
E-mail: james.coffey@leg.state.nh.us
Committees: Municipal and County Government

Representative **Alan Cohen** (D-Hillsborough-30).........(603) 889-0965
Counties Represented: Hillsborough (part)
Term Expires: 2016
Four Monterey Avenue, Nashua, NH 03064
E-mail: alan.cohen@leg.state.nh.us
Committees: Transportation

Representative **Ed Comeau** (R-Carroll-5)..............(603) 522-2275
Counties Represented: Carroll (part)
Term Expires: 2016
212 Stoneham Road, Brookfield, NH 03872
E-mail: ed@edcomeau.org
Committees: Criminal Justice and Public Safety

Representative **Guy Comtois** (R-Belknap-7)............(603) 776-8989
Counties Represented: Belknap (part)
Term Expires: 2016
P.O. Box 186, Center Barnstead, NH 03225-0186
E-mail: gcomtois2010@gmail.com
Committees: Fish, Game and Marine Resources

Representative **Larry Converse** (D-Sullivan-4)..........(603) 542-2180
Counties Represented: Sullivan (part)
Term Expires: 2016
Seven Clover Street, Claremont, NH 03743
E-mail: lcallcone@aol.com
Committees: Labor, Industrial and Rehabilitative Services

Representative **Allen W. Cook** (R-Rockingham-11).......(603) 271-2548
Counties Represented: Rockingham (part)
Term Expires: 2016
E-mail: allen.cook@leg.state.nh.us
Committees: Education

Representative **Mary R. Cooney** (D-Grafton-8).........(603) 798-3700
Counties Represented: Grafton (part)        Res: (603) 536-1141
Term Expires: 2016
169 Dover Road, Chichester, NH 03258
78 Highland Street, Plymouth, NH 03264-1237
E-mail: mary.cooney@leg.state.nh.us
Committees: Ways and Means

Representative **Glenn Cordelli** (R-Carroll-4)...........(603) 271-2548
Counties Represented: Carroll (part)        Res: (603) 515-0008
Term Expires: 2016
P.O. Box 209, Center Tuftonboro, NH 03186
E-mail: glenn.cordelli@leg.state.nh.us
Committees: Education

Representative **Patricia Cornell** (D-Hillsborough-18)......(603) 271-2548
Counties Represented: Hillsborough (part)
Term Expires: 2016
E-mail: patricia.cornell@leg.state.nh.us
Committees: Municipal and County Government

Representative **David E. Cote** (D-Hillsborough-31) .......(603) 882-2244
Counties Represented: Hillsborough (part)
Term Expires: 2016
96 West Hollis Street, Nashua, NH 03060-3146
E-mail: david.cote@leg.state.nh.us
Committees: Election Law

Representative **Karel A. Crawford** (R-Carroll-4) ........(603) 271-2548
Counties Represented: Carroll (part)        Res: (603) 253-7857
Term Expires: 2016
P.O. Box 825, Center Harbor, NH 03226
E-mail: karel.crawford@leg.state.nh.us
Committees: Transportation

Representative **Robert Cushing** (D-Rockingham-21)......(603) 271-2548
Counties Represented: Rockingham (part)        Res: (603) 926-2737
Term Expires: 2016
395 Winnacunnet Road, Hampton, NH 03842
E-mail: renny.cushing@leg.state.nh.us
Committees: Criminal Justice and Public Safety

Representative **David J. Danielson** (R-Hillsborough-7)....(603) 271-2548
Counties Represented: Hillsborough (part)        Res: (603) 472-3833
Term Expires: 2016
Nine Darby Lane, Bedford, NH 03310
E-mail: david.danielson@leg.state.nh.us
Committees: Finance
Education: St Anselm 1969 BA; Rivier 1980 MBA

Representative **Stephen Darrow** (R-Grafton-17) ........(603) 271-2548
Counties Represented: Grafton (part)
Term Expires: 2016
E-mail: stephen.darrow@leg.state.nh.us
Committees: Environment and Agriculture

Representative **Yvonne Dean-Bailey** (R-Rockingham-32)..(603) 340-4073
Counties Represented: Rockingham (part)
363 First New Hampshire Turnpike, Northwood, NH 03261
E-mail: ydb@leg.state.nh.us
Committees: Election Law

Representative **Susan DeLemus** (R-Stafford-11).........(603) 335-5119
Counties Represented: Stafford (part)
Term Expires: 2016
14 Dustin Homestead, Rochester, NH 03867
E-mail: susan.delemus@leg.state.nh.us

Representative **Helen Deloge** (D-Merrimack-16).........(603) 271-2548
Counties Represented: Merrimack (part)
Term Expires: 2016
E-mail: helen.deloge@leg.state.nh.us
Committees: Health, Human Services and Elderly Affairs

Representative **Debra L. DeSimone** (R-Rockingham-14) ..(603) 362-4314
Counties Represented: Rockingham (part)
Term Expires: 2016
11 Providence Hill Road, Atkinson, NH 03811-2338
E-mail: debra.desimone@leg.state.nh.us
Committees: Children and Family Law

Representative
**James E. "Jim" Devine** (R-Rockingham-4)..........(603) 887-3569
Counties Represented: Rockingham (part)        Fax: (603) 887-4923
Term Expires: 2016
54 Hampstead, Sandown, NH 03873
E-mail: jim.devine@leg.state.nh.us
Committees: Science, Technology and Energy

Representative **Debbie DiFranco** (D-Rockingham-27).....(603) 271-2548
Counties Represented: Rockingham (part)
Term Expires: 2016
E-mail: debbie.difranco@leg.state.nh.us
Committees: Election Law

*(continued on next page)*

LEGISLATIVE BRANCH

**Representatives** *continued*

Representative **Len DiSesa** (D-Stafford-16) . . . . . . . . . . . . (603) 343-4344
Counties Represented: Stafford (part)
Term Expires: 2016
29 Pleasant Valley Road, Dover, NH 03820
E-mail: len.disesa@leg.state.nh.us
Committees: Criminal Justice and Public Safety

Representative **Linda A. DiSilvestro** (D-Hillsborough-9) . . (603) 271-2548
Counties Represented: Hillsborough (part)        Res: (603) 645-6729
Term Expires: 2016
145 Fox Hollow Way, Manchester, NH 03014
E-mail: linda.disilvestro@leg.state.nh.us
Committees: Labor, Industrial and Rehabilitative Services

Representative **David Doherty** (D-Merrimack-20) . . . . . . . . (603) 485-2788
Counties Represented: Merrimack (part)
Term Expires: 2016
242 Fourth Range Road, Pembroke, NH 03275
E-mail: david.doherty@leg.state.nh.us
Committees: Environment and Agriculture

Representative **Daniel Donovan** (R-Hillsborough-2) . . . . . . (603) 271-2548
Counties Represented: Hillsborough (part)
Term Expires: 2016
E-mail: daniel.donovan@leg.state.nh.us
Committees: Health, Human Services and Elderly Affairs

Representative **Fred Doucette** (R-Rockingham-8) . . . . . . . . (603) 271-2548
Counties Represented: Rockingham (part)
Term Expires: 2016
E-mail: fred.doucette@leg.state.nh.us
Committees: Labor, Industrial and Rehabilitative Services

Representative **Joseph "Joe" Duarte** (R-Rockingham-2) . . (603) 271-2548
Counties Represented: Rockingham (part)        Res: (603) 483-8454
Term Expires: 2016
Ten Critchett Road, Candia, NH 03034
E-mail: joe.duarte@leg.state.nh.us
Committees: Fish, Game and Marine Resources

Representative **Russell Dumais** (R-Belknap-2) . . . . . . . . . . (603) 293-2014
Counties Represented: Belknap (part)
Term Expires: 2016
Six Glidden Road, Gilford, NH 03249
E-mail: sundeedumais@metrocast.net
Committees: Transportation

Representative **Eric Eastman** (R-Hillsborough-28) . . . . . . . . (603) 271-2548
Counties Represented: Hillsborough (part)
Term Expires: 2016
E-mail: eric.eastman@leg.state.nh.us
Committees: State-Federal Relations and Veterans Affairs

Representative **Daniel Adams Eaton** (D-Cheshire-3) . . . . . (603) 271-2548
Counties Represented: Cheshire (part)        Res: (603) 446-3535
Term Expires: 2016
One Shedd Hill Road, Stoddard, NH 03464
E-mail: daniel.eaton@leg.state.nh.us
Committees: Finance

Representative **Karen Ebel** (D-Merrimack-5) . . . . . . . . . . . . (603) 271-2548
Counties Represented: Merrimack (part)        Res: (603) 748-3876
Term Expires: 2016
P.O. Box 714, New London, NH 03257
E-mail: karen.ebel@leg.state.nh.us
Committees: Public Works and Highways
Education: Trinity Col (VT) BS; Georgetown 1981 JD

Representative **Frank Edelblut** (R-Hillsborough-38) . . . . . . (603) 271-2548
Counties Represented: Hillsborough (part)
Term Expires: 2016
E-mail: frank.edelblut@leg.state.nh.us
Committees: Children and Family Law

Representative **Michael Edgar** (D-Rockingham-21) . . . . . . . (603) 395-3635
Counties Represented: Rockingham (part)
Term Expires: 2016
Seven Ann's Terrace, Hampton, NH 03842-1231
E-mail: michael.edgar@leg.state.nh.us
Committees: Labor, Industrial and Rehabilitative Services
Education: Connecticut 1970 BS

Representative **Elizabeth Edwards** (D-Hillsborough-11) . . . (603) 271-2548
Counties Represented: Hillsborough (part)
Term Expires: 2016
524 Wilson Street, #5, Manchester, NH 03103
E-mail: ecomstockedwards@gmail.com
Committees: State-Federal Relations and Veterans Affairs

Representative **Robert J. Elliott** (R-Rockingham-8) . . . . . . . (603) 893-0402
Counties Represented: Rockingham (part)
Term Expires: 2016
44 Centerville Drive, Salem, NH 03079
E-mail: bob.elliott@leg.state.nh.us
E-mail: thegfr@aol.com
Committees: Education
Education: Boston U 1958 BDiv

Representative **J. Tracy Emerick** (D-Rockingham-21) . . . . . (603) 271-2548
Counties Represented: Rockingham (part)        Res: (603) 926-8316
Term Expires: 2016
207 North Shore Road, Hampton, NH 03842
E-mail: tracy.emerick@leg.state.nh.us
Committees: Finance

Representative **Susan Emerson** (R-Cheshire-11) . . . . . . . . . (603) 899-6529
Counties Represented: Cheshire (part)
Term Expires: 2016
P.O. Box 646, Rindge, NH 03461-0646
E-mail: semerson435@aol.com
Committees: Health, Human Services and Elderly Affairs

Representative **Eric P. Estevez** (R-Hillsborough-37) . . . . . . (603) 402-0920
Counties Represented: Hillsborough (part)
Term Expires: 2016
P.O. Box 22, Pelham, NH 03076
E-mail: eric.estevez@leg.state.nh.us
Committees: Judiciary

Representative **Beverly Ann Ferrante** (R-Rockingham-6) . . (603) 434-8974
Counties Represented: Rockingham (part)
Term Expires: 2016
68 Chester Road, Derry, NH 03038-3901
E-mail: bevferrante@msn.com
Committees: Resources, Recreation and Development

Representative **Elizabeth Ferreira** (R-Hillsborough-28) . . . . (603) 320-8971
Counties Represented: Hillsborough (part)
Term Expires: 2016
325 Broad Stret, Nashua, NH 03063
E-mail: elizabeth.ferreira.nh@gmail.com
Committees: Children and Family Law

Representative **Robert M. "Bob" Fesh** (R-Merrimack-6) . . (603) 434-1550
Counties Represented: Merrimack (part)
Term Expires: 2016
27 Claire Avenue, Derry, NH 03038-4220
E-mail: rmfesh@comcast.net
Committees: Criminal Justice and Public Safety

Representative **Dennis H. Fields** (R-Belknap-4) . . . . . . . . . . (603) 528-6224
Counties Represented: Belknap (part)
Term Expires: 2016
429 Lower Bay Road, Sanbornton, NH 03269-2712
E-mail: dennis.fields@leg.state.nh.us
Committees: Criminal Justice and Public Safety

Representative **Jack Flanagan** (R-Hillsborough-26) . . . . . . . (603) 672-7175
Counties Represented: Hillsborough (part)
Term Expires: 2016
Four Sawtelle Road, Brookline, NH 03033-2511
E-mail: jack.flanagan@leg.state.nh.us
Committees: Labor, Industrial and Rehabilitative Services; Rules

Representative **Robert Z. Fisher** (R-Belknap-9) . . . . . . . . . (603) 271-2548
Counties Represented: Belknap (part)
Term Expires: 2016
E-mail: robert.fisher@leg.state.nh.us
Committees: Criminal Justice and Public Safety

Representative
**Donald H. "Don" Flanders** (R-Belknap-3) . . . . . . . . . . . . (603) 524-4242
Counties Represented: Belknap (part)        Res: (603) 524-5369
Term Expires: 2016        Fax: (603) 524-0748
19 Kensington Drive, Laconia, NH 03246-2910
208 Union Avenue, Laconia, NH 03246-3103
E-mail: dflanders@comcast.net
Committees: Commerce and Consumer Affairs

Representative **Susan Ford** (D-Grafton-3) . . . . . . . . . . . . . . (603) 823-5609
Counties Represented: Grafton (part)
Term Expires: 2016
557 Sugar Hill Road, Franconia, NH 03580
E-mail: susan.ford@leg.state.nh.us
Committees: Finance

Representative **Armand D. Forest** (D-Hillsborough-18) . . . (603) 271-2548
Counties Represented: Hillsborough (part)
Term Expires: 2016
E-mail: armand.forest@leg.state.nh.us
Committees: Fish, Game and Marine Resources

Representative **John J. Fothergill** (R-Coos-1) . . . . . . . . . (603) 271-2548
Counties Represented: Coos (part)
Term Expires: 2016
E-mail: john.fothergill@leg.state.nh.us
Committees: Health, Human Services and Elderly Affairs

Representative **Paula Francese** (D-Rockingham-18) . . . . . (603) 271-2548
Counties Represented: Rockingham (part)
Term Expires: 2016
E-mail: paula.francese@leg.state.nh.us
Committees: Resources, Recreation and Development

Representative **Valerie Fraser** (R-Belknap-1) . . . . . . . . . . (603) 271-2548
Counties Represented: Belknap (part)
Term Expires: 2016
E-mail: valerie.fraser@leg.state.nh.us
Committees: Commerce and Consumer Affairs

Representative **June M. Frazer** (D-Merrimack-13) . . . . . . . (603) 228-0048
Counties Represented: Merrimack (part)
Term Expires: 2016
27 Piscataqua Road, Concord, NH 03301-4632
E-mail: june.frazer@leg.state.nh.us
Committees: Education

Representative **Mary C. Freitas** (D-Hillsborough-14) . . . . . (603) 622-9056
Counties Represented: Hillsborough (part)
Term Expires: 2016
279 Candia Road, Manchester, NH 03109
E-mail: mary.freitas@leg.state.nh.us
Committees: Health, Human Services and Elderly Affairs

Representative
**Barbara Conner French** (D-Merrimack-6) . . . . . . . . . . (603) 428-3366
Counties Represented: Merrimack (part)
Term Expires: 2016
81 Fairview Avenue, Henniker, NH 03242
Committees: Health, Human Services and Elderly Affairs

Representative **Harold F. French** (R-Merrimack-2) . . . . . . . (603) 271-2548
Counties Represented: Merrimack (part)
Term Expires: 2016
E-mail: harold.french@leg.state.nh.us
Committees: Commerce and Consumer Affairs

Representative **William G. Friel** (R-Rockingham-14) . . . . . (603) 271-2548
Counties Represented: Rockingham (part)          Res: (603) 362-5423
Term Expires: 2016
Five Kelly Lane, Atkinson, NH 03811
E-mail: william.friel@leg.state.nh.us
Committees: Public Works and Highways

Representative **Alethea Lincoln Froburg** (D-Coos-3) . . . . . (603) 271-2548
Counties Represented: Coos (part)
Term Expires: 2016
E-mail: alethea.froburg@leg.state.nh.us
Committees: Children and Family Law

Representative **Bart Fromuth** (R-Hillsborough-7) . . . . . . . . (603) 203-1379
Counties Represented: Hillsborough (part)
Term Expires: 2016
38 Hawthorne Drive, Unit G, Bedford, NH 03110
E-mail: bart@voteforbart.com
Committees: Commerce and Consumer Affairs

Representative **Larry Gagne** (R-Hillsborough-13) . . . . . . . . (603) 625-9692
Counties Represented: Hillsborough (part)
Term Expires: 2016
126 Lakeside Drive, Manchester, NH 03104-5801
E-mail: lgagne25@comcast.net
Committees: Transportation

Representative **Raymond "Ray" Gagnon** (D-Sullivan-5) . . (603) 477-7135
Counties Represented: Sullivan (part)          Res: (603) 542-7286
Term Expires: 2016
Four Warren Street, Claremont, NH 03743
E-mail: raymond.gagnon@leg.state.nh.us
E-mail: gagnon1@adelphia.net
Committees: Executive Departments and Administration

Representative **Brian S. Gallagher** (R-Belknap-4) . . . . . . . (603) 271-2548
Counties Represented: Belknap (part)
Term Expires: 2016
E-mail: brian.gallagher@leg.state.nh.us
Committees: Ways and Means

Representative **William M. Gannon** (R-Rockingham-4) . . . (978) 384-0816
Counties Represented: Rockingham (part)
Term Expires: 2016
P.O. Box 71, Sandown, NH 03873
E-mail: contact@williamgannon.net
Committees: Election Law

Representative **Janice S. Gardner** (D-Stafford-15) . . . . . . (603) 271-2548
Counties Represented: Stafford (part)          Res: (603) 742-0205
Term Expires: 2016
165 Dover Point Road, Dover, NH 03820
E-mail: sparhwk@comcast.net
Committees: Environment and Agriculture

Representative **Carolyn M. Gargasz** (R-Hillsborough-27) . . (603) 465-7463
Counties Represented: Hillsborough (part)          Fax: (603) 465-7463
Term Expires: 2016
P.O. Box 1223, Hollis, NH 03049-1223
E-mail: cgargasz@cs.com
Committees: Children and Family Law

Representative **Kenneth N. Gidge** (D-Hillsborough-33) . . . (603) 271-2548
Counties Represented: Hillsborough (part)          Res: (603) 888-2355
Term Expires: 2016
22 Hayden Street, Nashua, NH 03060
E-mail: kenneth.gidge@leg.state.nh.us
Committees: Commerce and Consumer Affairs

Representative **Mary Stuart Gile** (D-Merrimack-27) . . . . . . (603) 224-2278
Counties Represented: Merrimack (part)
Term Expires: 2016
35 Penacook Street, Concord, NH 03301-4518
E-mail: mary.gile@leg.state.nh.us
Committees: Education

Representative **Edmond D. Gionet** (R-Grafton-5) . . . . . . . . (603) 745-2240
Counties Represented: Grafton (part)
Term Expires: 2016
P.O. Box 414, Lincoln, NH 03251-0414
E-mail: edmond.gionet@leg.state.nh.us
Committees: Public Works and Highways

Representative **Jeffrey Goley** (D-Hillsborough-8) . . . . . . . . (603) 669-2256
Counties Represented: Hillsborough (part)          Res: (603) 626-6659
Term Expires: 2016
100 Merrimack Street, Manchester, NH 03103
1683 North River Road, Manchester, NH 03104-1645
E-mail: jgoley03104@yahoo.com
Committees: Executive Departments and Administration

Representative **Carlos E. Gonzalez** (R-Hillsborough-45) . . . (603) 674-9696
Counties Represented: Hillsborough (part)
Term Expires: 2016
P.O. Box 154, Manchester, NH 03105
E-mail: cegonzalezj@comcast.net
Committees: Fish, Game and Marine Resources

Representative **Pamela S. Gordon** (D-Rockingham-29) . . . (603) 271-2548
Counties Represented: Rockingham (part)
Term Expires: 2016
E-mail: pamela.gordon@leg.state.nh.us
Committees: Health, Human Services and Elderly Affairs

Representative
**Richard E. "Dick" Gordon** (R-Rockingham-35) . . . . . . . . (603) 642-7252
Counties Represented: Rockingham (part)
Term Expires: 2016
Four Burnt Swamp Road, East Kingston, NH 03827
E-mail: dick.gordon@leg.state.nh.us
Committees: Environment and Agriculture

Representative **Mary J. Gorman** (D-Hillsborough-31) . . . . . (603) 886-1652
Counties Represented: Hillsborough (part)
Term Expires: 2016
44 1/2 Amherst Street, Nashua, NH 03064-2560
Committees: Education

Representative
**Suzanne H. "Sue" Gottling** (D-Sullivan-2) . . . . . . . . . . . (603) 271-2548
Counties Represented: Sullivan (part)          Res: (603) 763-5904
Term Expires: 2016
173 Lake Avenue, Sunapee, NH 03782
E-mail: sgottling@comcast.net
Committees: Resources, Recreation and Development

Representative **Linda Gould** (R-Hillsborough-7) . . . . . . . . . (603) 271-2548
Counties Represented: Hillsborough (part)
Term Expires: 2016
E-mail: linda.gould@leg.state.nh.us
Committees: Resources, Recreation and Development

Representative **Bill Goulette** (R-Hillsborough-23) . . . . . . . . (603) 271-2548
Counties Represented: Hillsborough (part)
Term Expires: 2016
E-mail: bill.goulette@leg.state.nh.us
Committees: Executive Departments and Administration

Representative **Robert Graham** (R-Strafford-1) . . . . . . . . . (603) 652-6520
Counties Represented: Strafford (part)
Term Expires: 2016
58 Bolan Road, Milton, NH 03851
E-mail: robert.graham@leg.state.nh.us

*(continued on next page)*

**Representatives** *continued*

Representative **James P. Gray** (R-Stafford-8) . . . . . . . . . . . (603) 332-7144
Counties Represented: Stafford (part)
Term Expires: 2016
21 Roulx Drive, Rochester, NH 03867
E-mail: james.gray@leg.state.nh.us
Committees: Children and Family Law; Election Law

Representative **Dennis Green** (R-Rockingham-13) . . . . . . . . (603) 340-4073
Counties Represented: Rockingham (part)
Term Expires: 2016
22 Corliss Way, Hampstead, NH 03841
E-mail: dennis.green@leg.state.nh.us
Committees: Criminal Justice and Public Safety

Representative **James "Jim" Grenier** (R-Sullivan-7) . . . . . (603) 863-5681
Counties Represented: Sullivan (part)
Term Expires: 2016
P.O. Box 29, Lempster, NH 03605
E-mail: jimgreniersullivan7@gmail.com
Committees: Education

Representative **Barbara Griffin** (R-Hillsborough-6) . . . . . . . (603) 271-2548
Counties Represented: Hillsborough (part)
Term Expires: 2016
E-mail: barbara.griffin@leg.state.nh.us
Committees: Election Law

Representative **Mary E. Griffin** (R-Rockingham-7) . . . . . . . .(603) 432-0959
Counties Represented: Rockingham (part)
Term Expires: 2016
Four Wynridge Road, Windham, NH 03087-1628
Committees: Ways and Means

Representative **Warren Groen** (R-Stafford-10) . . . . . . . . . . (603) 817-9353
Counties Represented: Stafford (part)          Res: (603) 332-8988
Term Expires: 2016
17 Alice Lane, Rochester, NH 03867-8502
E-mail: warrengroen@gmail.com
Committees: Environment and Agriculture

Representative **C. Lee Guerette** (D-Hillsborough-33) . . . . . (603) 271-2548
Counties Represented: Hillsborough (part)
Term Expires: 2016
E-mail: lee.guerette@leg.state.nh.us
Committees: Fish, Game and Marine Resources

Representative
**Joseph "Joe" Guthrie** (R-Rockingham-13) . . . . . . . . . . (603) 271-2548
Counties Represented: Rockingham (part)
Term Expires: 2016
E-mail: joseph.guthrie@leg.state.nh.us
Committees: Health, Human Services and Elderly Affairs

Representative
**Robert "Bob" Haefner** (R-Hillsborough-37) . . . . . . . . . (603) 930-8459
Counties Represented: Hillsborough (part)     Res: (603) 889-1553
Term Expires: 2016
One Saint John Street, Hudson, NH 03051
E-mail: bob.haefner@leg.state.nh.us
E-mail: bobhaefnerip@comcast.net
Committees: Environment and Agriculture

Representative **Joseph M. Hagan** (R-Rockingham-4) . . . . . (603) 542-1822
Counties Represented: Rockingham (part)      Res: (603) 887-4280
Term Expires: 2016
30 Chester Street, Chester, NH 03036-4305
E-mail: usrnnurse@msn.com
Committees: Judiciary

Representative **Carolyn Halstead** (R-Hillsborough-23) . . . . (603) 271-2548
Counties Represented: Hillsborough (part)
Term Expires: 2016
E-mail: carolyn.halstead@leg.state.nh.us
Committees: Science, Technology and Energy

Representative **Joe Hannon** (R-Stafford-25) . . . . . . . . . . . .(603) 292-5852
Counties Represented: Stafford (part)
Term Expires: 2016
One Thornton Lane, Lee, NH 03861
E-mail: joehannon4nh@gmail.com
Committees: Commerce and Consumer Affairs

Representative **Daniel C. Hansberry** (D-Hillsborough-35) . .(603) 888-5634
Counties Represented: Hillsborough (part)
Term Expires: 2016
20 Shelley Drive, Nashua, NH 03062
E-mail: daniel.hansberry@leg.state.nh.us
Committees: Executive Departments and Administration
Education: Keene State 1974 BSEd; Rivier 1979 MEd

Representative **Peter T. Hansen** (R-Hillsborough-22) . . . . . (603) 860-1106
Counties Represented: Hillsborough (part)      Res: (603) 673-5987
Term Expires: 2016
82 Amherst Street, Amherst, NH 03031-3032
E-mail: peter.hansen@leg.state.nh.us
Committees: Executive Departments and Administration

Representative **Jeffrey F. Harris** (R-Rockingham-9) . . . . . . . (603) 679-2331
Counties Represented: Rockingham (part)
Term Expires: 2016
146 Exeter Road, Epping, NH 03042
E-mail: jeffrey.harris@leg.state.nh.us
Committees: Municipal and County Government

Representative **Suzanne Harvey** (D-Hillsborough-29) . . . . . (603) 271-2548
Counties Represented: Hillsborough (part)
Term Expires: 2016
E-mail: suzanne.harvey@leg.state.nh.us
Committees: Science, Technology and Energy

Representative **William A. "Bill" Hatch** (D-Coos-6) . . . . . . (603) 306-6199
Counties Represented: Coos (part)          Res: (603) 466-9491
Term Expires: 2016
79 Promenade Street, Gorham, NH 03581
E-mail: william.hatch@leg.state.nh.us
E-mail: hatchbill@hotmail.com
Committees: Finance

Representative **Mary S. Heath** (D-Hillsborough-14) . . . . . . (603) 622-0895
Counties Represented: Hillsborough (part)
Term Expires: 2016
76 Island Pond Road, Manchester, NH 03109
E-mail: mary.heath@leg.state.nh.us
Committees: Education

Representative **Frank H. Heffron** (D-Rockingham-18) . . . . . (603) 772-4659
Counties Represented: Rockingham (part)
Term Expires: 2016
Four Minuteman Lane, Exeter, NH 03833
E-mail: frank.heffron@leg.state.nh.us
Committees: Judiciary
Education: Middlebury 1959 BA; Columbia 1962 LLB

Representative **Paul Henle** (D-Merrimack-12) . . . . . . . . . . . (603) 224-7756
Counties Represented: Merrimack (part)
Term Expires: 2016
11-2 Cabernet Drive, Concord, NH 03033
E-mail: paul.henle@leg.state.nh.us
Committees: Ways and Means

Representative **Erin Tapper Hennessey** (R-Grafton-1) . . . . (603) 271-2548
Counties Represented: Grafton (part)
Term Expires: 2016
E-mail: erin.hennessey@leg.state.nh.us
Committees: Public Works and Highways

Representative **Martha Hennessey** (D-Grafton-12) . . . . . . . (603) 271-2548
Counties Represented: Grafton (part)
Term Expires: 2016
E-mail: martha.hennessey@leg.state.nh.us
Committees: Children and Family Law
Education: Dartmouth 1976

Representative
**Christopher J. Herbert** (D-Hillsborough-43) . . . . . . . . . . (603) 271-2548
Counties Represented: Hillsborough (part)
Term Expires: 2016
E-mail: chris.herbert@leg.state.nh.us
Committees: Commerce and Consumer Affairs

Representative **David W. Hess** (R-Merrimack-24) . . . . . . . . (603) 485-9027
Counties Represented: Merrimack (part)       Fax: (603) 647-0900
Term Expires: 2016
68 Pine Street, Hooksett, NH 03106-1323
E-mail: dave.hess@leg.state.nh.us
Committees: Finance; Ways and Means

Representative **Patricia C. Higgins** (D-Grafton-12) . . . . . . . (603) 643-3989
Counties Represented: Grafton (part)
Term Expires: 2016
Eight Mink Drive, Hanover, NH 03755
E-mail: patricia.higgins@leg.state.nh.us
Committees: Public Works and Highways

Representative **Gregory Hill** (R-Merrimack-3) . . . . . . . . . . . (603) 271-2548
Counties Represented: Merrimack (part)
Term Expires: 2016
E-mail: greg.hill@leg.state.nh.us
Committees: Labor, Industrial and Rehabilitative Services

Representative
**Richard "Dick" Hinch** (R-Rockingham-21) . . . . . . . . . . . (603) 261-6317
Counties Represented: Rockingham (part)  Res: (603) 424-9690
Term Expires: 2016
14 Ichabod Drive, Merrimack, NH 03054-6226
E-mail: dick.hinch@leg.state.nh.us
Committees: Legislative Administration; Rules

Representative **Geoffrey Hirsch** (D-Merrimack-6) . . . . . . . . (603) 938-2833
Counties Represented: Merrimack (part)
Term Expires: 2016
P.O. Box 385, Bradford, NH 03221
E-mail: geoffrey.hirsch@leg.state.nh.us
Committees: Criminal Justice and Public Safety

Representative **Bruce Hodgdon** (R-Rockingham-1) . . . . . . . (603) 942-5264
Counties Represented: Rockingham (part)
Term Expires: 2016
P.O. Box 323, Northwood, NH 03261
E-mail: bruce.hodgdon@leg.state.nh.us
Committees: Transportation

Representative **J.R. Hoell** (R-Merrimack-23) . . . . . . . . . . . (603) 315-9002
Counties Represented: Merrimack (part)
Term Expires: 2016
32 Ordway Road, Dunbarton, NH 03046-4320
E-mail: jr.hoell@leg.state.nh.us
Committees: Executive Departments and Administration

Representative **Kathleen Hoelzel** (R-Rockingham-3) . . . . . . (603) 895-4172
Counties Represented: Rockingham (part)
Term Expires: 2016
15 Dudley Road, Raymond, NH 03077-1414
E-mail: kathleen.hoelzel@leg.state.nh.us
Committees: Election Law; Rules

Representative **Edith Hogan** (R-Hillsborough-34) . . . . . . . . (603) 271-2548
Counties Represented: Hillsborough (part)
Term Expires: 2016
E-mail: edith.hogan@leg.state.nh.us
Committees: Election Law

Representative **Gary S. Hopper** (R-Hillsborough-2) . . . . . . (603) 529-7728
Counties Represented: Hillsborough (part)
Term Expires: 2016
107 Buxton School Road, Weare, NH 03281-5806
E-mail: gary.hopper@leg.state.nh.us
Committees: Judiciary

Representative **Werner D. Horn** (R-Merrimack-2) . . . . . . . . (603) 271-2548
Counties Represented: Merrimack (part)
Term Expires: 2016
E-mail: werner.horn@leg.state.nh.us
Committees: Transportation

Representative **Timothy "Tim" Horrigan** (D-Strafford-6) . . (603) 868-3342
Counties Represented: Strafford (part)  Fax: (866) 542-0665
Term Expires: 2016
7-A Faculty Road, Durham, NH 03824-2706
E-mail: timothy.horrigan@alumni.usc.edu
Committees: Judiciary
Education: Columbia Col (CA) 1979 BA; Columbia 1982 MA;
USC 1984 MBA

Representative **Raymond Howard** (R-Belknap-8) . . . . . . . . (603) 875-4115
Counties Represented: Belknap (part)
Term Expires: 2016
311 Stockbridge Corner Road, Alton, NH 03809
E-mail: brhowardjr@yahoo.com
Committees: Environment and Agriculture

Representative **Robert Hull** (R-Grafton-9) . . . . . . . . . . . . . . (603) 271-2548
Counties Represented: Grafton (part)
Term Expires: 2016
E-mail: robert.hull@leg.state.nh.us
Committees: Judiciary

Representative **John B. Hunt** (R-Cheshire-11) . . . . . . . . . . . (603) 345-1129
Counties Represented: Cheshire (part)  Res: (603) 899-6000
Term Expires: 2016  Fax: (603) 899-6160
165 Sunridge Road, Rindge, NH 03461-3433
E-mail: jbhunt@prodigy.net
Committees: Commerce and Consumer Affairs

Representative **George Hurt** (R-Belknap-2) . . . . . . . . . . . . . (603) 271-2548
Counties Represented: Belknap (part)
Term Expires: 2016
P.O. Box 7481, Gilford, NH 03247
E-mail: ghurtstateleg@gmail.com
Committees: Commerce and Consumer Affairs

Representative **William J. Infantine** (R-Hillsborough-13) . . (603) 647-0800
Counties Represented: Hillsborough (part)  Res: (603) 622-3325
Term Expires: 2016
40 Stark Street, Manchester, NH 03101
89 Windward Lane, Manchester, NH 03104-4743
E-mail: winfantine@aspen-ins.com
Committees: Labor, Industrial and Rehabilitative Services

Representative **Paul C. Ingbretson** (R-Grafton-15) . . . . . . . (603) 989-3092
Counties Represented: Grafton (part)
Term Expires: 2016
P.O. Box 296, Pike, NH 03780
E-mail: ingbretson_studio@yahoo.com
Committees: Children and Family Law

Representative **Robert E. Introne** (R-Rockingham-5) . . . . . (603) 432-0345
Counties Represented: Rockingham (part)  Fax: (603) 434-6266
Term Expires: 2016
Eight Everts Street, Londonderry, NH 03053-3039
E-mail: reintrone@aol.com
Committees: Science, Technology and Energy

Representative **Virginia O'Brien Irwin** (D-Sullivan-9) . . . . . (603) 271-2548
Counties Represented: Sullivan (part)
Term Expires: 2016
E-mail: virginia.irwin@leg.state.nh.us
Committees: Public Works and Highways

Representative **Daniel C. Itse** (R-Rockingham-10) . . . . . . . . (603) 642-9403
Counties Represented: Rockingham (part)
Term Expires: 2016
P.O. Box 70, Fremont, NH 03044-0070
E-mail: itsenh@comcast.net
Committees: Children and Family Law

Representative **Martin I. Jack** (D-Hillsborough-36) . . . . . . . (603) 318-0457
Counties Represented: Hillsborough (part)
Term Expires: 2016
83 Cadogan Way, Nashua, NH 03062
E-mail: martin.jack@leg.state.nh.us
Committees: Public Works and Highways

Representative **Shawn N. Jasper** (R-Hillsborough-37) . . . . (603) 566-4348
Counties Represented: Hillsborough (part)  Res: (603) 595-9621
Term Expires: 2016  Fax: (603) 882-2056
83 Old Derry Road, Hudson, NH 03051-3017
E-mail: shawn.jasper@leg.state.nh.us
Committees: Rules

Representative **Jean L. Jeudy** (D-Hillsborough-10) . . . . . . . (603) 716-6369
Counties Represented: Hillsborough (part)  Res: (603) 645-5290
Term Expires: 2016
134 Calef Road, Manchester, NH 03103-6324
E-mail: jean.jeudy@gmail.com
Committees: Executive Departments and Administration

Representative **Gladys Johnsen** (D-Cheshire-7) . . . . . . . . . (603) 313-9290
Counties Represented: Cheshire (part)  Res: (603) 358-5164
Term Expires: 2016
417 Pako Avenue, Keene, NH 03431-5030
E-mail: johnsengladys@gmail.com
Committees: Transportation

Representative **Eric Johnson** (R-Grafton-7) . . . . . . . . . . . . . (603) 271-2548
Counties Represented: Grafton (part)
Term Expires: 2016
E-mail: eric.johnson@leg.state.nh.us
Committees: Resources, Recreation and Development

Representative **Laura Jones** (R-Stafford-24) . . . . . . . . . . . . . (603) 948-2264
Counties Represented: Stafford (part)
Term Expires: 2016
Nine Jackson Street, Rochester, NH 03867
E-mail: laurajonesnh@gmail.com
Committees: Commerce and Consumer Affairs
Education: Cal State (Fullerton) BA

Representative
**Thomas L. Kaczynski, Jr.** (R-Stafford-22) . . . . . . . . . . . (603) 332-7310
Counties Represented: Stafford (part)
Term Expires: 2016
112 Whitehall Road, Rochester, NH 03868
E-mail: hampoul@metrocast.net
Committees: Executive Departments and Administration

Representative **Naida L. Kaen** (D-Strafford-5) . . . . . . . . . . . (603) 868-5600
Counties Represented: Strafford (part)  Res: (603) 659-2205
Term Expires: 2016
22 Toon Lake, Lee, NH 03861
E-mail: naidakaen@hotmail.com
Committees: Children and Family Law
Education: Michigan BA; New Hampshire MBA

*(continued on next page)*

LEGISLATIVE BRANCH

**Representatives** *continued*

Representative
**Lawrence "Mike" Kappler** (R-Rockingham-3) . . . . . . . . (603) 303-8959
Counties Represented: Rockingham (part)        Res: (603) 895-4408
Term Expires: 2016
18 Agent Road, Raymond, NH 03077
E-mail: l.mikekappler@comcast.net
Committees: Municipal and County Government

Representative **David B. Karrick, Jr.** (D-Merrimack-25) . . . (603) 456-2772
Counties Represented: Merrimack (part)
Term Expires: 2016
P.O. Box 328, Warner, NH 03278
E-mail: david.karrick@leg.state.nh.us
Committees: Ways and Means
Education: Yale 1965 BA

Representative
**Phyllis M. Katsakiores** (R-Rockingham-6) . . . . . . . . . . . (603) 434-9587
Counties Represented: Rockingham (part)
Term Expires: 2016
One Bradford Street, Derry, NH 03038
E-mail: pkatsakiores@comcast.net
Committees: State-Federal Relations and Veterans Affairs

Representative
**Thomas Katsiantonis** (D-Hillsborough-15) . . . . . . . . . . (603) 606-4244
Counties Represented: Hillsborough (part)        Res: (603) 627-9652
Term Expires: 2016
45 Glen Bloom Drive, Manchester, NH 03109-5062
E-mail: thomaskatsiantonis@gmail.com
Committees: State-Federal Relations and Veterans Affairs

Representative **Shem Kellogg** (R-Rockingham-14) . . . . . . . (603) 560-8621
Counties Represented: Rockingham (part)
Term Expires: 2016
48 Westville Road, Plaistow, NH 03865
E-mail: shem.kellogg@leg.state.nh.us
Committees: Fish, Game and Marine Resources

Representative **Linda B. Kenison** (D-Merrimack-15) . . . . . . (603) 228-8348
Counties Represented: Merrimack (part)
Term Expires: 2016
Ten Marshall Street, Concord, NH 03301
E-mail: linda.kenison@leg.state.nh.us
Committees: Judiciary

Representative **David H. Kidder** (R-Merrimack-5) . . . . . . . . (603) 526-4680
Counties Represented: Merrimack (part)        Fax: (603) 526-2070
Term Expires: 2016
370 Main Street, New London, NH 03257
34 Blueberry Lane, New London, NH 03257-5511
E-mail: david.kidder@leg.state.nh.us
Committees: Fish, Game and Marine Resources

Representative **Robert Knowles** (R-Stafford-12) . . . . . . . . . (603) 335-0373
Counties Represented: Stafford (part)
Term Expires: 2016
22 Meadowbrook Village, Rochester, NH 03867
E-mail: rknowles@metrocast.net
Committees: Fish, Game and Marine Resources

Representative **Walter Kolodziej** (R-Rockingham-7) . . . . . . (603) 437-7936
Counties Represented: Rockingham (part)
Term Expires: 2016
Eight Kent Street, Windham, NH 03087-1645
Committees: Public Works and Highways

Representative **Frank R. Kotowski** (R-Merrimack-24) . . . . . (603) 485-9579
Counties Represented: Merrimack (part)
Term Expires: 2016
21 Pleasant Street, Hooksett, NH 03106-1453
E-mail: frank.kotowski@leg.state.nh.us
Committees: Health, Human Services and Elderly Affairs

Representative **Bill Kuch** (R-Merrimack-23) . . . . . . . . . . . . (603) 856-0957
Counties Represented: Merrimack (part)
Term Expires: 2016
82 Page Road, Bow, NH 03304
E-mail: bill.kuch@leg.state.nh.us
Committees: Public Works and Highways

Representative **Neal M. Kurk** (R-Hillsborough-2) . . . . . . . . (603) 529-7253
Counties Represented: Hillsborough (part)
Term Expires: 2016
Rural Route 1, Weare, NH 03281-5412
E-mail: rep03281@aol.com
Committees: Finance

Representative
**Roderick M. "Rick" Ladd, Jr.** (R-Grafton-4) . . . . . . . . . (603) 989-3268
Counties Represented: Grafton (part)
Term Expires: 2016
P.O. Box 67, Haverhill, NH 03765-0067
E-mail: ladd.nhhouse@charter.net
Committees: Education

Representative **Joseph LaChance** (R-Hillsborough-8) . . . . . (603) 271-2548
Counties Represented: Hillsborough (part)
Term Expires: 2016
E-mail: joseph.lachance@leg.state.nh.us
Committees: Ways and Means

Representative
**Thomas W. "Tom" Laware** (R-Sullivan-8) . . . . . . . . . . . (603) 826-3137
Counties Represented: Sullivan (part)
Term Expires: 2016
398 River Road, Charlestown, NH 03603
E-mail: thomas.laware@leg.state.nh.us
Committees: Transportation

Representative **Shari LeBreche** (R-Belknap-6) . . . . . . . . . . (603) 455-6186
Counties Represented: Belknap (part)
Term Expires: 2016
64 Tioga Drive, Belmont, NH 03220
E-mail: shari.lebreche@leg.state.nh.us
Committees: Fish, Game and Marine Resources

Representative
**Donald "Don" LeBrun** (R-Hillsborough-32) . . . . . . . . . . (603) 886-1725
Counties Represented: Hillsborough (part)
Term Expires: 2016
333 Candlewood Park, Nashua, NH 03062-4454
E-mail: donald.lebrun@leg.state.nh.us
Committees: Health, Human Services and Elderly Affairs

Representative **Don E. Leeman** (R-Stafford-23) . . . . . . . . . (603) 973-6009
Counties Represented: Stafford (part)
Term Expires: 2016
14 Partridge Green Way, Rochester, NH 03867
E-mail: don.leeman@leg.state.nh.us
Committees: Ways and Means

Representative **Peter R. Leishman** (D-Hillsborough-24) . . . (603) 365-0621
Counties Represented: Hillsborough (part)        Res: (603) 924-0004
Term Expires: 2016
39 Birch Road, Peterborough, NH 03458
E-mail: prleishman@aol.com
Committees: Finance
Education: Unity AA

Representative **Douglas A. Ley** (D-Cheshire-9) . . . . . . . . . (603) 532-8556
Counties Represented: Cheshire (part)
Term Expires: 2016
28 School Street, Jaffrey, NH 03452
E-mail: douglas.ley@leg.state.nh.us
Committees: Labor, Industrial and Rehabilitative Services

Representative **Douglas B. Long** (R-Merrimack-4) . . . . . . . (603) 927-4137
Counties Represented: Merrimack (part)
Term Expires: 2016
12 French Road, Wilmot, NH 03287
E-mail: longbroscon@mcttelecom.com
Committees: Fish, Game and Marine Resources

Representative **Patrick T. Long** (D-Hillsborough-10) . . . . . . (603) 668-1037
Counties Represented: Hillsborough (part)
Term Expires: 2016
112 Hollis Street, Manchester, NH 03101
E-mail: long55@comcast.net
Committees: Children and Family Law

Representative **Patricia Lovejoy** (D-Rockingham-36) . . . . . (603) 778-9662
Counties Represented: Rockingham (part)
Term Expires: 2016
21 Coach Road, Stratham, NH 03885-2258
E-mail: patty.lovejoy@leg.state.nh.us
Committees: Ways and Means

Representative **David Lundgren** (R-Rockingham-5) . . . . . . . (603) 432-1800
Counties Represented: Rockingham (part)        Res: (603) 432-3499
Term Expires: 2016                              Fax: (603) 432-4142
21 King John Drive, Londonderry, NH 03053
E-mail: qtipnh@aol.com
Committees: State-Federal Relations and Veterans Affairs

Representative **David Luneau** (I-Merrimack-10) . . . . . . . . . (603) 746-6484
Counties Represented: Merrimack (part)
Term Expires: 2016
211 Putney Hill Road, Hopkinton, NH 03229
E-mail: dluneaunh@gmail.com
Committees: Commerce and Consumer Affairs

Representative
**James R. "Jim" MacKay** (D-Merrimack-14) . . . . . . . . (603) 224-0623
Counties Represented: Merrimack (part)
Term Expires: 2016
139 North State Street, Concord, NH 03301-6431
E-mail: james.mackay@mygait.com
Committees: Health, Human Services and Elderly Affairs; Legislative
Administration

Representative **Kevin G. Maes** (D-Grafton-6) . . . . . . . . . . . (603) 786-9705
Counties Represented: Grafton (part)
Term Expires: 2016
P.O. Box 205, Rumney, NH 03266
E-mail: kevin.maes@leg.state.nh.us
Committees: Resources, Recreation and Development

Representative **Norman L. Major** (R-Rockingham-14) . . . . (603) 382-5429
Counties Represented: Rockingham (part)          Fax: (603) 382-8117
Term Expires: 2016
12 Kingston Road, Plaistow, NH 03865-2211
E-mail: norman.major@leg.state.nh.us
Committees: Ways and Means

Representative **Latha Mangipudi** (D-Hillsborough-35) . . . . (603) 891-1239
Counties Represented: Hillsborough (part)
Term Expires: 2016
20 Salmon Brook Drive, Nashua, NH 03062
E-mail: latha.mangipudi@leg.state.nh.us
Committees: Criminal Justice and Public Safety

Representative **Jonathan F. Manley** (D-Hillsborough-3) . . . (603) 588-2427
Counties Represented: Hillsborough (part)
Term Expires: 2016
227 Bible Hill Road, Bennington, NH 03442
E-mail: jonathan.manley@leg.state.nh.us
Committees: Fish, Game and Marine Resources
Education: Keene State

Representative **John E. Mann** (D-Cheshire-2) . . . . . . . . . . (603) 835-9095
Counties Represented: Cheshire (part)
Term Expires: 2016
35 Prentice Hill Road, Alstead, NH 03602
E-mail: john.mann@leg.state.nh.us
Committees: Science, Technology and Energy

Representative **John J. Manning, Jr.** (R-Rockingham-8) . . (603) 818-3188
Counties Represented: Rockingham (part)
Term Expires: 2016
30 Maclarnon Road, Salem, NH 03079
E-mail: john.manning@leg.state.nh.us
Committees: Ways and Means

Representative **Richard Marple** (R-Merrimack-24) . . . . . . . (603) 627-1837
Counties Represented: Merrimack (part)
Term Expires: 2016
11 Dartmouth Street, Hooksett, NH 03106
E-mail: dick.marple@leg.state.nh.us
Committees: State-Federal Relations and Veterans Affairs

Representative **Dick Marston** (R-Hillsborough-19) . . . . . . . (603) 666-7334
Counties Represented: Hillsborough (part)
Term Expires: 2016
25 English Village Road, #304, Manchester, NH 03102
E-mail: dick.marston.nhstaterep@gmail.com
Committees: Criminal Justice and Public Safety
Education: New Hampshire Col

Representative **André A. Martel** (R-Hillsborough-44) . . . . . (603) 218-3370
Counties Represented: Hillsborough (part)
Term Expires: 2016
81 Maurice Street, Manchester, NH 03103
E-mail: martel.andy@yahoo.com
Committees: Health, Human Services and Elderly Affairs
Education: Southern New Hampshire BS

Representative **John F. Martin** (R-Merrimack-24) . . . . . . . . (603) 271-2548
Counties Represented: Merrimack (part)
Term Expires: 2016
E-mail: john.martin@leg.state.nh.us
Committees: Criminal Justice and Public Safety

Representative **Linda Massimilla** (D-Grafton-1) . . . . . . . . (603) 444-5270
Counties Represented: Grafton (part)
Term Expires: 2016
197 Orchard Hill Road, Littleton, NH 03561
E-mail: linda.massimilla@leg.state.nh.us
Committees: State-Federal Relations and Veterans Affairs

Representative **Carolyn L. Matthews** (R-Rockingham-3) . . (603) 271-2548
Counties Represented: Rockingham (part)
Term Expires: 2016
E-mail: carolyn.matthews@leg.state.nh.us
Committees: Resources, Recreation and Development

Representative **Rebecca McBeath** (D-Rockingham-26) . . . . (603) 271-2548
Counties Represented: Rockingham (part)
Term Expires: 2016
E-mail: rebecca.mcbeath@leg.state.nh.us
Committees: Commerce and Consumer Affairs

Representative **Frank McCarthy** (R-Carroll-2) . . . . . . . . . . (603) 356-9160
Counties Represented: Carroll (part)
Term Expires: 2016
P.O. Box 876, Conway, NH 03818
E-mail: serendipity922@gmail.com
Committees: State-Federal Relations and Veterans Affairs

Representative **Peggy McCarthy** (R-Hillsborough-29) . . . . . (603) 598-4966
Counties Represented: Hillsborough (part)
Term Expires: 2016
34 Terry Street, Nashua, NH 03064
E-mail: mccarthy.peggy@gmail.com
Committees: State-Federal Relations and Veterans Affairs

Representative
**Donald B. McClarren** (R-Hillsborough-29) . . . . . . . . . . . (603) 883-9245
Counties Represented: Hillsborough (part)
Term Expires: 2016
39 Monza Road, Nashua, NH 03064
E-mail: dmcclarren@hotmail.com
Committees: Ways and Means

Representative **Mark E. McConkey** (R-Carroll-3) . . . . . . . . (603) 520-8275
Counties Represented: Carroll (part)
Term Expires: 2016
Ten Clover Lane, Freedom, NH 03836-4205
E-mail: mcconkey2@hotmail.com
Committees: Public Works and Highways

Representative
**James W. "Jim" McConnell** (R-Cheshire-12) . . . . . . . . . (603) 357-7150
Counties Represented: Cheshire (part)
Term Expires: 2016
P.O. Box G, Keene, NH 03431
E-mail: jim.mcconnell@leg.state.nh.us
Committees: Resources, Recreation and Development

Representative **Carol McGuire** (R-Merrimack-29) . . . . . . . . (603) 782-4918
Counties Represented: Merrimack (part)
Term Expires: 2016
700 Suncook Valley Highway, Epsom, NH 03234
E-mail: carol@mcguire4house.com
Committees: Resources, Recreation and Development

Representative **Dan McGuire** (R-Merrimack-21) . . . . . . . . . (603) 782-4918
Counties Represented: Merrimack (part)
Term Expires: 2016
700 Suncook Valley Highway, Epsom, NH 03234
E-mail: dan.mcguire@leg.state.nh.us
Committees: Finance

Representative **Betsy McKinney** (R-Rockingham-5) . . . . . . (603) 432-5232
Counties Represented: Rockingham (part)
Term Expires: 2016
Three Leelynn Circle, Londonderry, NH 03053-2326
E-mail: betsy.mckinney@leg.state.nh.us
Committees: Finance

Representative **Mark McLean** (R-Hillsborough-15) . . . . . . . (603) 668-0076
Counties Represented: Hillsborough (part)
Term Expires: 2016
43 Forest Hill Way, Manchester, NH 03109
E-mail: mark.mclean@leg.state.nh.us
Committees: Judiciary

Representative **Charles E. McMahon** (R-Rockingham-7) . . (603) 401-4646
Counties Represented: Rockingham (part)          Res: (603) 432-8877
Term Expires: 2016                                Fax: (603) 432-6854
P.O. Box 1024, Windham, NH 03087-1024
E-mail: cmcmahon55@gmail.com
Committees: Health, Human Services and Elderly Affairs

Representative **Richard McNamara** (D-Hillsborough-38) . . (603) 271-2548
Counties Represented: Hillsborough (part)
Term Expires: 2016
P.O. Box 1891, Hillsborough, NH 03244
E-mail: richard.mcnamara@leg.state.nh.us
Committees: Fish, Game and Marine Resources
Education: Worcester State Col BS; SUNY (Potsdam) MS

Representative **David Milz** (R-Rockingham-6) . . . . . . . . . . (603) 437-0030
Counties Represented: Rockingham (part)
Term Expires: 2016
12R Bonnie Lane, Derry, NH 03038
E-mail: david.milz@leg.state.nh.us
Committees: Public Works and Highways

*(continued on next page)*

LEGISLATIVE BRANCH

**Representatives** *continued*

**Representative Howard M. Moffett** (D-Merrimack-9) . . . . . (603) 783-4993
Counties Represented: Merrimack (part)
Term Expires: 2016
66 Cogswell Hill Road, Canterbury, NH 03224
E-mail: howard.moffett@leg.state.nh.us
Committees: Science, Technology and Energy
Education: Yale 1966 BA; Cambridge (UK) 1969 MA;
Boalt Hall 1975 JD

**Representative Josh Moore** (R-Hillsborough-21) . . . . . . . . (603) 361-0955
Counties Represented: Hillsborough (part)
Term Expires: 2016
14 Buttonwood Lane, Merrimack, NH 03054
E-mail: josh.moore@leg.state.nh.us
Committees: Education

**Representative Wayne Moynihan** (D-Coos-2) . . . . . . . . . . (603) 449-2058
Counties Represented: Coos (part)
Term Expires: 2016
138 Plain Road, Milan, NH 03588
E-mail: wayne.moynihan@leg.state.nh.us
Committees: Election Law

**Representative John Mullen, Jr.** (R-Strafford-1) . . . . . . . . (603) 755-9062
Counties Represented: Strafford (part)
Term Expires: 2016
34 Shore Drive, Middleton, NH 03887
E-mail: john.mullen@leg.state.nh.us
Committees: Resources, Recreation and Development

**Representative David Murotake** (R-Hillsborough-32) . . . . . (603) 889-4568
Counties Represented: Hillsborough (part)
Term Expires: 2016
17 Port Chester Drive, Nashua, NH 03062
E-mail: david.murotake@leg.state.nh.us
Committees: Science, Technology and Energy
Education: MIT 1977 SB, 1977 SM; Sloan 1990 PhD

**Representative Keith Murphy** (R-Hillsborough-7) . . . . . . . . (603) 644-3535
Counties Represented: Hillsborough (part)        Res: (603) 471-3043
Term Expires: 2016                              Fax: (603) 644-3537
13 Woburn Abbey Drive, Bedford, NH 03110-6234
E-mail: rep.keithmurphy@gmail.com
Committees: Labor, Industrial and Rehabilitative Services
Education: Baltimore 2002 BA; Maryland 2004 MCP

**Representative Mel Myler** (D-Merrimack-10) . . . . . . . . . . . (603) 746-5294
Counties Represented: Merrimack (part)
Term Expires: 2016
P.O. Box 82, Contoocook, NH 03229
E-mail: mel.myler@leg.state.nh.us
Committees: Education

**Representative Bill Nelson** (R-Carroll-5) . . . . . . . . . . . . . . (603) 522-5279
Counties Represented: Carroll (part)
Term Expires: 2016
98 Lyford Road, Brookfield, NH 03872
E-mail: bill.nelson@leg.state.nh.us
Committees: Health, Human Services and Elderly Affairs

**Representative**
**Robert "Bob" Nigrello** (R-Rockingham-16) . . . . . . . . . . (603) 394-7591
Counties Represented: Rockingham (part)
Term Expires: 2016
Two Pine Woods, East Kingston, NH 03827
E-mail: bob.nigrello@leg.state.nh.us
Committees: Ways and Means

**Representative Sharon L. Nordgren** (D-Grafton-12) . . . . . . (603) 381-2286
Counties Represented: Grafton (part)             Res: (603) 643-5068
Term Expires: 2016                              Fax: (603) 643-8567
23 Rope Ferry Road, Hanover, NH 03755-1404
E-mail: sharon.nordgren@leg.state.nh.us
Committees: Finance

**Representative Jeanine Notter** (R-Hillsborough-21) . . . . . . (603) 423-0408
Counties Represented: Hillsborough (part)
Term Expires: 2016
19 Whittier Road, Merrimack, NH 03054-4755
E-mail: jeanine.notter@leg.state.nh.us
Committees: Science, Technology and Energy

**Representative**
**Michael B. O'Brien, Sr.** (D-Hillsborough-37) . . . . . . . . . (603) 888-8051
Counties Represented: Hillsborough (part)
Term Expires: 2016
Four Woodfield Street, Nashua, NH 03062
E-mail: michael.o'brien@leg.state.nh.us
Committees: Transportation

**Representative**
**William L. "Bill" O'Brien** (R-Hillsborough-5) . . . . . . . . . (603) 271-3661
Counties Represented: Hillsborough (part)
Term Expires: 2016
P.O. Box 154, Mont Vernon, NH 03057-0154
E-mail: william.obrien@leg.state.nh.us

**Representative John O'Connor** (R-Rockingham-6) . . . . . . . (603) 459-3906
Counties Represented: Rockingham (part)         Res: (603) 434-8393
Term Expires: 2016
13 Arrowhead Road, Derry, NH 03038-3715
E-mail: john.oconnor@leg.state.nh.us
Committees: Environment and Agriculture

**Representative Andrew S. O'Hearne** (D-Sullivan-3) . . . . . . (603) 558-1038
Counties Represented: Sullivan (part)
Term Expires: 2016
120 Main Street, Claremont, NH 03743
E-mail: andrew.ohearne@leg.state.nh.us
Committees: Criminal Justice and Public Safety

**Representative William "Bill" O'Neil** (D-Hillsborough-9) . . (603) 644-5277
Counties Represented: Hillsborough (part)
Term Expires: 2016
309 Ash Street, Manchester, NH 03104-3203
E-mail: william.oneil@leg.state.nh.us
Committees: Labor, Industrial and Rehabilitative Services

**Representative Lynne M. Ober** (R-Hillsborough-37) . . . . . . (603) 883-9654
Counties Represented: Hillsborough (part)
Term Expires: 2016
Three Heritage Circle, Hudson, NH 03051-3410
E-mail: lynne.ober@leg.state.nh.us
E-mail: lynne.ober@comcast.net
Committees: Finance

**Representative Russell T. Ober III** (R-Hillsborough-37) . . . . (603) 883-9654
Counties Represented: Hillsborough (part)
Term Expires: 2016
3 Heritage Circle, Hudson, NH 03051
E-mail: thud007@hotmail.com
Committees: Legislative Administration; State-Federal Relations and
Veterans Affairs

**Representative Bill Ohm** (R-Hillsborough-36) . . . . . . . . . . . (603) 891-2306
Counties Represented: Hillsborough (part)
Term Expires: 2016
18 Mountain Laurels Drive, Unit 403, Nashua, NH 03062
E-mail: billohm2010@aol.com
Committees: Ways and Means

**Representative Jeffrey Oligny** (R-Rockingham-34) . . . . . . . (603) 339-2626
Counties Represented: Rockingham (part)
Term Expires: 2016
35 Forrest Street, East Hampstead, NH 03826-5418
E-mail: jeffrey.oligny@leg.state.nh.us
Committees: Children and Family Law

**Representative Jason Osborne** (R-Rockingham-4) . . . . . . . (603) 391-2138
Counties Represented: Rockingham (part)
Term Expires: 2016
65 Miner Road, Auburn, NH 03032
E-mail: jason@osborne4nh.com
Committees: Education

**Representative Lee Walker Oxenham** (D-Sullivan-1) . . . . . (603) 271-2548
Counties Represented: Sullivan (part)
Term Expires: 2016
E-mail: lee.oxenham@leg.state.nh.us
Committees: Resources, Recreation and Development

**Representative Sherman A. Packard** (R-Rockingham-5) . . . (603) 432-3391
Counties Represented: Rockingham (part)         Fax: (603) 421-0902
Term Expires: 2016
70 Old Derry Road, Londonderry, NH 03053-2218
E-mail: sherm_packard@juno.com
Committees: Legislative Administration; Transportation

**Representative Barry Palmer** (R-Hillsborough-32) . . . . . . . . (603) 889-0288
Counties Represented: Hillsborough (part)
Term Expires: 2016
123 Shore Drive, Nashua, NH 03062
Committees: Judiciary

**Representative Laura C. Pantelakos** (D-Rockingham-25) . . (603) 502-3184
Counties Represented: Rockingham (part)         Res: (603) 436-2148
Term Expires: 2016
528 Dennett Street, Portsmouth, NH 03801-3621
E-mail: lcpantelakos@comcast.net
Committees: Criminal Justice and Public Safety

LEGISLATIVE BRANCH

Representative **Jason R. Parent** (R-Merrimack-26) . . . . . . (603) 271-2548
Counties Represented: Merrimack (part)
Term Expires: 2016
E-mail: jason.parent@leg.state.nh.us
Committees: Children and Family Law

Representative
**James "Jim" Parison** (R-Hillsborough-25) . . . . . . . . . . (603) 468-8431
Counties Represented: Hillsborough (part)        Res: (603) 878-5001
Term Expires: 2016
40 Old Rindge Road, New Ipswich, NH 03071-3225
E-mail: james.parison@leg.state.nh.us
Committees: Science, Technology and Energy

Representative **Harold B. Parker** (R-Carrol-6) . . . . . . . . . . (603) 491-6807
Counties Represented: Carroll (part)
Term Expires: 2016
E-mail: hbpcd6@gmail.com
Committees: Criminal Justice and Public Safety; Executive Departments
and Administration

Representative **Henry A. L. Parkhurst** (D-Cheshire-13) . . . (603) 239-8945
Counties Represented: Cheshire (part)
Term Expires: 2016
One Parkhurst Place, Winchester, NH 03470-2460
E-mail: hank.parkhurst@leg.state.nh.us
Committees: Resources, Recreation and Development

Representative **Dick Patten** (D-Merrimack-17) . . . . . . . . . . (603) 496-2917
Counties Represented: Merrimack (part)        Res: (603) 228-1803
Term Expires: 2016                            Fax: (603) 715-1648
30 Pinewood Trail, Concord, NH 03301-5247
E-mail: dickpatten7@gmail.com
Committees: Transportation

Representative **Michele Peckham** (R-Rockingham-22) . . . . (603) 964-3736
Counties Represented: Rockingham (part)        Res: (603) 964-6422
Term Expires: 2016                            Fax: (603) 964-3744
82 Atlantic Avenue, North Hampton, NH 03862-2306
E-mail: michele.peckham@leg.state.nh.us
Committees: Environment and Agriculture

Representative **William Pearson** (D-Cheshire-4) . . . . . . . . (603) 714-9075
Counties Represented: Cheshire (part)
Term Expires: 2016
31 Elliot Street, Keene, NH 03431
E-mail: william.pearson@leg.state.nh.us
Committees: Election Law

Representative **Tony Pellegrino** (R-Hillsborough-21) . . . . . . (603) 424-7095
Counties Represented: Hillsborough (part)
Term Expires: 2016
35 Amherst Road, Merrimack, NH 03054-3927
E-mail: tony.pellegrino@leg.state.nh.us
Committees: Labor, Industrial and Rehabilitative Services; Legislative
Administration

Representative **Ken Peterson** (R-Merrimack-7) . . . . . . . . . . (603) 472-2913
Counties Represented: Merrimack (part)
Term Expires: 2016
43 Brick Mill Road, Bedford, NH 03110
E-mail: ken.peterson@leg.state.nh.us
Committees: Municipal and County Government

Representative **Larry Robert Phillips** (D-Cheshire-16) . . . . (603) 357-4315
Counties Represented: Cheshire (part)
Term Expires: 2016
171 Roxbury Street, Keene, NH 03431
E-mail: larry.phillips@leg.state.nh.us
Committees: Judiciary

Representative **David W. Pierce** (R-Hillsborough-6) . . . . . (603) 497-8278
Counties Represented: Hillsborough (part)
Term Expires: 2016
21 Mill Street, Goffstown, NH 03045
E-mail: david.w.pierce@leg.state.nh.us
Committees: Public Works and Highways

Representative **Wendy Piper** (D-Grafton-10) . . . . . . . . . . . (603) 632-7179
Counties Represented: Grafton (part)
Term Expires: 2016
P.O. Box 311, Enfield, NH 03748
E-mail: wendy.piper@leg.state.nh.us
Committees: Public Works and Highways

Representative **Joseph A. Pitre** (R-Strafford-2) . . . . . . . . . (603) 755-2447
Counties Represented: Strafford (part)
Term Expires: 2016
76 Cocheco Road, Farmington, NH 03835-3803
E-mail: joseph.pitre@leg.state.nh.us
Committees: Finance

Representative **Marjorie Porter** (D-Hillsborough-1) . . . . . . (603) 464-0225
Counties Represented: Hillsborough (part)
Term Expires: 2016
64 School Street, Hillsborough, NH 03244-4878
E-mail: marjorie.porter@leg.state.nh.us
Committees: Municipal and County Government

Representative **John Potucek** (R-Rockingham-6) . . . . . . . . (603) 432-9049
Counties Represented: Rockingham (part)
Term Expires: 2016
18 Sunset Avenue, Derry, NH 03038
E-mail: john.potucek@leg.state.nh.us
Committees: Resources, Recreation and Development

Representative **Anne K. Priestley** (R-Rockingham-8) . . . . . (603) 893-1214
Counties Represented: Rockingham (part)
Term Expires: 2016
Four Bluff Street, Salem, NH 03079
E-mail: kpanne@gmail.com
Committees: State-Federal Relations and Veterans Affairs

Representative **Mark Proulx** (R-Hillsborough-44) . . . . . . . . (603) 669-7179
Counties Represented: Hillsborough (part)
Term Expires: 2016
76 Janet Court, Manchester, NH 03103
Committees: Executive Departments and Administration

Representative
**Katherine Prudhomme-O'Brien** (R-Rockingham-6) . . . . (603) 425-6605
Counties Represented: Rockingham (part)
Term Expires: 2016
19 Beacon Hill Road, Derry, NH 03038
E-mail: kpo@leg.state.nh.us
Committees: Labor, Industrial and Rehabilitative Services

Representative **Laurence Rappaport** (R-Coos-1) . . . . . . . . (603) 237-4150
Counties Represented: Coos (part)        Res: (603) 237-4429
Term Expires: 2016
P.O. Box 158, Colebrook, NH 03576-0158
E-mail: rapp@lmr.com
Committees: Science, Technology and Energy

Representative **Mario Ratzki** (D-Merrimack-1) . . . . . . . . . . (603) 735-5440
Counties Represented: Merrimack (part)
Term Expires: 2016
P.O. Box 213, East Andover, NH 03231
E-mail: mario.ratzki@leg.state.nh.us
Committees: Public Works and Highways

Representative **Frederick Rice** (R-Rockingham-21) . . . . . . . (603) 929-9510
Counties Represented: Rockingham (part)        Res: (603) 929-1517
Term Expires: 2016                            Fax: (603) 929-9511
15 Heather Lane, Hampton, NH 03842-1118
E-mail: fred.rice@leg.state.nh.us
Committees: Resources, Recreation and Development

Representative **Harold L. "Chip" Rice** (D-Merrimack-27) . . (603) 224-2886
Counties Represented: Merrimack (part)
Term Expires: 2016
23 Wilson Avenue, Concord, NH 03301-2226
E-mail: chip.rice@leg.state.nh.us
Committees: Labor, Industrial and Rehabilitative Services

Representative **Kimberly Rice** (R-Hillsborough-37) . . . . . . . (603) 943-3369
Counties Represented: Hillsborough (part)
Term Expires: 2016
51 Belknap Road, Hudson, NH 03051
E-mail: kimberly.rice@leg.state.nh.us
Committees: Children and Family Law

Representative **Herbert D. Richardson** (R-Coos-4) . . . . . . . (603) 788-4065
Counties Represented: Coos (part)        Res: (603) 788-2442
Term Expires: 2016
34 William Street, Lancaster, NH 03584-3256
E-mail: honhdr@yahoo.com
Committees: Science, Technology and Energy

Representative **Leon H. Rideout** (R-Coos-7) . . . . . . . . . . . (603) 684-1102
Counties Represented: Coos (part)
Term Expires: 2016
28 Causeway Street, Lancaster, NH 03584
E-mail: leon.rideout@leg.state.nh.us
Committees: Labor, Industrial and Rehabilitative Services

Representative **Carol R. Roberts** (D-Hillsborough-4) . . . . . . (603) 271-2548
Counties Represented: Hillsborough (part)
Term Expires: 2016
E-mail: carol.roberts@leg.state.nh.us
Committees: Executive Departments and Administration

*(continued on next page)*

**Representatives** *continued*

Representative
**Lt. Col. Kris Edward Roberts** (D-Cheshire-16) . . . . . . . . (603) 352-1105
Counties Represented: Cheshire (part)
Term Expires: 2016
58 Grove Street, Keene, NH 03431
E-mail: kriseroberts@live.com
Committees: State-Federal Relations and Veterans Affairs

Representative
**Timothy N. "Tim" Robertson** (D-Cheshire-6) . . . . . . . .(603) 352-7006
Counties Represented: Cheshire (part)
Term Expires: 2016
Three James Hill Road, Keene, NH 03431
E-mail: timothyrbrtsn2@gmail.com
Committees: Criminal Justice and Public Safety

Representative **Katherine D. Rogers** (D-Merrimack-28) . . . (603) 496-8521
Counties Represented: Merrimack (part)
Term Expires: 2016
Four Jay Drive, Concord, NH 03301
E-mail: katherine.rogers@leg.state.nh.us
Committees: Finance
Education: Clark U 1977 BA; Suffolk 2002 JD

Representative
**Theodore "Ted" Rokas** (D-Hillsborough-12) . . . . . . . . . (603) 620-2228
Counties Represented: Hillsborough (part)
Term Expires: 2016
393 Wilson Street, Manchester, NH 03103-4913
E-mail: ted.rokas@leg.state.nh.us
Committees: Fish, Game and Marine Resources

Representative **Skip Rollins** (R-Sullivan-9) . . . . . . . . . . . . .(603) 863-6340
Counties Represented: Sullivan (part)
Term Expires: 2016
Five Willow Street, Newport, NH 03773
E-mail: skip@lavalleys.com
Committees: State-Federal Relations and Veterans Affairs

Representative **Deanna S. Rollo** (D-Stafford-18) . . . . . . . . . (603) 742-7511
Counties Represented: Stafford (part)
Term Expires: 2016
23 Heritage Drive, Rollinsford, NH 03869
E-mail: deanna1214@aol.com
Committees: Education

Representative
**Lucinda "Cindy" Rosenwald** (D-Hillsborough-30) . . . . . (603) 595-9896
Counties Represented: Hillsborough (part)
Term Expires: 2016
101 Wellington Street, Nashua, NH 03064-1616
E-mail: cindy.rosenwald@leg.state.nh.us
Committees: Finance; Rules

Representative **Claire Rouillard** (R-Hillsborough-6) . . . . . . .(603) 494-6144
Counties Represented: Hillsborough (part)
Term Expires: 2016
14 Jasmine Lane, Goffstown, NH 03045
E-mail: claire.rouillard@leg.state.nh.us
Committees: Judiciary

Representative **Robert H. Rowe** (R-Hillsborough-22) . . . . . (603) 673-2693
Counties Represented: Hillsborough (part)
Term Expires: 2016
18 Jones Road, Amherst, NH 03031-3213
P.O. Box 1117, Amherst, NH 03031-1117
E-mail: rhrowe@comcast.net
Committees: Judiciary

Representative **David H. Russell** (R-Belknap-5) . . . . . . . . . .(603) 364-7449
Counties Represented: Belknap (part)
Term Expires: 2016
P.O. Box 60, Gilmanton Iron Works, NH 03837
E-mail: russells@metrocast.net
Committees: Resources, Recreation and Development

Representative **Tara A. Sad** (D-Cheshire-1) . . . . . . . . . . . . (603) 321-1990
Counties Represented: Cheshire (part)              Res: (603) 756-4861
Term Expires: 2016
82 North Road, Walpole, NH 03608
P.O. Box 909, Walpole, NH 03608
E-mail: tara.eric@gmail.com
Committees: Environment and Agriculture

Representative **Laurie Sanborn** (R-Hillsborough-42) . . . . . .(603) 682-1557
Counties Represented: Hillsborough (part)
Term Expires: 2016
50 Campbell Road, Bedford, NH 03110
E-mail: laurie.sanborn@leg.state.nh.us
Committees: Commerce and Consumer Affairs
Education: Simmons

Representative
**Elisabeth N. "Betsy" Sanders** (R-Rockingham-12) . . . . (603) 642-5070
Counties Represented: Rockingham (part)
Term Expires: 2016
61 Beach Plain Road, Danville, NH 03819-5070
E-mail: elisabeth.sanders@leg.state.nh.us
Committees: Fish, Game and Marine Resources

Representative **George Saunderson** (D-Merrimack-9) . . . . (603) 783-4750
Counties Represented: Merrimack (part)
Term Expires: 2016
615 Lovejoy Road, Loudon, NH 03307
E-mail: george.saunderson@leg.state.nh.us
Committees: Environment and Agriculture

Representative **Eric Schleien** (R-Hillsborough-37) . . . . . . . .(914) 275-5696
Counties Represented: Hillsborough (part)
Term Expires: 2016
825 Fox Hollow Drive, Hudson, NH 03051
E-mail: eric.schleien@leg.state.nh.us
Committees: Children and Family Law

Representative **Andrew "Andy" Schmidt** (D-Sullivan-1) . . (603) 863-1247
Counties Represented: Sullivan (part)
Term Expires: 2016
P.O. Box 1747, Grantham, NH 03753-1747
E-mail: andrew.schmidt@leg.state.nh.us
Committees: Education

Representative **Peter B. Schmidt** (D-Stafford-19) . . . . . . . . (603) 743-3751
Counties Represented: Stafford (part)
Term Expires: 2016
P.O. Box 1468, Dover, NH 03821-1468
E-mail: reppbs@ttlc.net
E-mail: p.schmidt@ci.dover.nh.us
Committees: Executive Departments and Administration

Representative
**Stephen J. "Steve" Schmidt** (R-Carrol-6) . . . . . . . . . . (603) 569-0848
Counties Represented: Carroll (part)
Term Expires: 2016
59 Spruce Road, Wolfeboro, NH 03894-4113
E-mail: stephen.schmidt@leg.state.nh.us
Committees: Health, Human Services and Elderly Affairs

Representative **Adam Schroadter** (R-Rockingham-17) . . . . (603) 292-6058
Counties Represented: Rockingham (part)
Term Expires: 2016
P.O. Box 564, Newmarket, NH 03857
E-mail: repschroadter@gmail.com
Committees: Election Law

Representative **Dianne E. Schuett** (D-Merrimack-20) . . . . . (603) 224-0314
Counties Represented: Merrimack (part)
Term Expires: 2016
533 Pembroke Street, Pembroke, NH 03275
E-mail: dianne.schuett@leg.state.nh.us
Committees: Labor, Industrial and Rehabilitative Services; Legislative
Administration

Representative **Lisa Scontsas** (R-Hillsborough-30) . . . . . . .(603) 883-6869
Counties Represented: Hillsborough (part)
Term Expires: 2016
24 Courtland Street, Nashua, NH 03064
E-mail: lscontsas@gmail.com
Committees: Environment and Agriculture

Representative **G. Brian Seaworth** (R-Merrimack-20) . . . . (603) 485-8030
Counties Represented: Merrimack (part)
Term Expires: 2016
161 Buck Street, Pembroke, NH 03275
E-mail: brian.seaworth@leg.state.nh.us
Committees: Labor, Industrial and Rehabilitative Services

Representative **Carl W. Seidel** (R-Hillsborough-28) . . . . . . .(603) 598-2795
Counties Represented: Hillsborough (part)
Term Expires: 2016
39 Pilgrim Circle, Nashua, NH 03063
E-mail: seidel4staterep@mindspring.com
Committees: Public Works and Highways

Representative **Jeffrey Shackett** (R-Grafton-9) . . . . . . . . . (603) 744-2650
Counties Represented: Grafton (part)              Res: (603) 744-5895
Term Expires: 2016
E-mail: jeffrey.shackett@leg.state.nh.us
Committees: Executive Departments and Administration; Public Works
and Highways
Education: Plymouth State U 1987 BS

Representative
**Gilman C. "Gil" Shattuck** (D-Hillsborough-1)........(603) 464-3850
Counties Represented: Hillsborough (part)
Term Expires: 2016
571 Center Road, Hillsborough, NH 03244
E-mail: gilman.shattuck@leg.state.nh.us
Committees: Ways and Means
Education: Dartmouth 1949 AB; Tuck School 1950 MBA

Representative **Barbara E. Shaw** (D-Hillsborough-16) .... (603) 626-4681
Counties Represented: Hillsborough (part)
Term Expires: 2016
45 Randall Street, Manchester, NH 03103-6434
E-mail: beshaw3@aol.com
Committees: Education

Representative
**Marjorie "Marge" Shepardson** (D-Cheshire-10).......(603) 876-4027
Counties Represented: Cheshire (part)
Term Expires: 2016
94 Pleasant Street, Marlborough, NH 03455
E-mail: marge.shepardson@gmail.com
Committees: Science, Technology and Energy

Representative
**Thomas "Tom" Sherman** (D-Rockingham-24) ....... (603) 379-2248
Counties Represented: Rockingham (part)
Term Expires: 2016
296 Harbor Road, Rye, NH 03870
E-mail: thomas.sherman@leg.state.nh.us
Committees: Health, Human Services and Elderly Affairs

Representative
**Stephen J. "Steve" Shurtleff** (D-Merrimack-11) ...... (603) 753-4563
Counties Represented: Merrimack (part)
Term Expires: 2016
11 Vinton Drive, Penacook, NH 03303-1583
E-mail: steve.shurtleff@leg.state.nh.us
Committees: Legislative Administration; Rules

Representative **Tammy Simmons** (R-Hillsborough-17) .... (603) 235-9998
Counties Represented: Hillsborough (part)
Term Expires: 2016
142 Parker Street, Manchester, NH 03102
E-mail: tammy.simmons@leg.state.nh.us
Committees: Labor, Industrial and Rehabilitative Services

Representative **Alexis Simpson** (D-Rockingham-18)...... (603) 271-2548
Counties Represented: Rockingham (part)
Term Expires: 2016
E-mail: alexis.simpson@leg.state.nh.us
Committees: Environment and Agriculture

Representative **Peter Silva** (R-Hillsborough-35) ......... (603) 888-0558
Counties Represented: Hillsborough (part)
Term Expires: 2016
18 Masefield Road, Nashua, NH 03062
E-mail: psilva.nhstaterep@gmail.com
Committees: Fish, Game and Marine Resources

Representative **Gregory Smith** (R-Hillsborough-37) ...... (603) 635-3835
Counties Represented: Hillsborough (part)
Term Expires: 2016
Three Mountain View Road, Pelham, NH 03076
E-mail: gregory.smith@leg.state.nh.us
Committees: Executive Departments and Administration

Representative **Marjorie K. Smith** (D-Strafford-6) ........(603) 868-7500
Counties Represented: Strafford (part)
Term Expires: 2016
P.O. Box 136, Durham, NH 03824
E-mail: msmithpen@aol.com
Committees: Finance

Representative **Steven "Steve" Smith** (R-Sullivan-11) ... (603) 826-5996
Counties Represented: Sullivan (part)
Term Expires: 2016
P.O. Box 624, Charlestown, NH 03603-0624
E-mail: nhfirst@gmail.com
Committees: Transportation

Representative **Suzanne Smith** (D-Grafton-8) .......... (603) 744-9064
Counties Represented: Grafton (part)
Term Expires: 2016
20 Brookside Lane, Hebron, NH 03241-7200
E-mail: zanne1@metrocast.net
E-mail: suzanne.smith@leg.state.nh.us
Committees: Resources, Recreation and Development

Representative **Timothy J. Smith** (D-Hillsborough-17) .... (603) 657-0324
Counties Represented: Hillsborough (part)
Term Expires: 2016
494 South Main Street, Apt. 1, Manchester, NH 03102
E-mail: tim.smith@leg.state.nh.us
Committees: State-Federal Relations and Veterans Affairs

Representative **Kendall A. Snow** (D-Hillsborough-42) .... (603) 669-1075
Counties Represented: Hillsborough (part)
Term Expires: 2016
150 Birchwood Road, Manchester, NH 03104
E-mail: ken.snow@leg.state.nh.us
Committees: Health, Human Services and Elderly Affairs

Representative **Timothy M. Soucy** (D-Hillsborough-34) ... (603) 305-5012
Counties Represented: Hillsborough (part)
Term Expires: 2016
33 Gillis Street, Nashua, NH 03060
E-mail: timothy.soucy@leg.state.nh.us
Committees: Transportation
Education: Vermont BS; Boston U MPH

Representative **Tom Southworth** (D-Stafford-20) ........ (603) 742-0556
Counties Represented: Stafford (part)
Term Expires: 2016
56 Durham Road, Dover, NH 03820
E-mail: thomas.southworth@leg.state.nh.us
Committees: Ways and Means

Representative **Kathleen F. Souza** (R-Hillsborough-43) ... (603) 645-6131
Counties Represented: Hillsborough (part)
Term Expires: 2016
628 Belmont Street, Manchester, NH 03104-5167
Committees: Election Law

Representative **Judith T. Spang** (D-Strafford-6) ......... (603) 828-6419
Counties Represented: Strafford (part)          Res: (603) 659-5936
Term Expires: 2016
55 Wiswall Road, Durham, NH 03824-4420
E-mail: judith@kestrelnet.net
Committees: Resources, Recreation and Development

Representative **Peter Spanos** (R-Belknap-3) ............ (603) 524-2960
Counties Represented: Belknap (part)
Term Expires: 2016
E-mail: peterjspanos@gmail.com
Committees: Finance

Representative **James Spillane** (R-Rockingham-2) ....... (603) 463-5623
Counties Represented: Rockingham (part)
Term Expires: 2016
16 Swamp Road, Deerfield, NH 03037
E-mail: james@jamesspillane.org
Committees: Fish, Game and Marine Resources

Representative **Dale R. Sprague** (D-Stafford-18) ......... (603) 271-2548
Counties Represented: Stafford (part)
Term Expires: 2016
E-mail: dale.sprague@leg.state.nh.us
Committees: Public Works and Highways

Representative
**Stephen B. Stepanek** (R-Hillsborough-22) ........... (603) 673-7658
Counties Represented: Hillsborough (part)
Term Expires: 2016
P.O. Box 1015, Milford, NH 03055
E-mail: stephen.stepanek@leg.state.nh.us
Committees: Health, Human Services and Elderly Affairs

Representative **Franklin Sterling, Jr.** (R-Cheshire-14) ..... (603) 532-8284
Counties Represented: Cheshire (part)
Term Expires: 2016
63 Monadnock View Drive, Jaffrey, NH 03452
E-mail: fwsterling@comcast.net
Committees: Municipal and County Government

Representative **Audrey M. Stevens** (D-Strafford-7) ....... (603) 332-3863
Counties Represented: Strafford (part)
Term Expires: 2016
Eight Lisa Lane, Rochester, NH 03868
E-mail: audrey.stevens@leg.state.nh.us
Committees: Children and Family Law

Representative **Phillip Straight** (R-Hillsborough-21) ...... (603) 424-2043
Counties Represented: Hillsborough (part)
Term Expires: 2016
11 Spruce Street, Merrimack, NH 03054
E-mail: phil.straight@leg.state.nh.us
Committees: State-Federal Relations and Veterans Affairs

*(continued on next page)*

LEGISLATIVE BRANCH

**Representatives** *continued*

Representative
**Daniel J. "Dan" Sullivan** (D-Hillsborough-42) . . . . . . . (603) 627-5044
Counties Represented: Hillsborough (part)
Term Expires: 2016
172 Arah Street, Manchester, NH 03104-2119
E-mail: dan.sullivan@leg.state.nh.us
Committees: Executive Departments and Administration

Representative **Victoria L. Sullivan** (R-Hillsborough-16) . . . (603) 232-4382
Counties Represented: Hillsborough (part)
Term Expires: 2016
1056 South Beech Street, Manchester, NH 03103
E-mail: patchessul@comcast.net
Committees: Education

Representative **Joe Sweeney** (R-Rockingham-8) . . . . . . . . (603) 327-7184
Counties Represented: Rockingham (part)
Term Expires: 2016
29 Hunters Run, Salem, NH 03079
E-mail: josephfsweeney@gmail.com
Committees: Election Law

Representative **Shawn Sweeney** (R-Hillsborough-23) . . . . (603) 589-8015
Counties Represented: Hillsborough (part)
Term Expires: 2016
33 Orchard Street, Milford, NH 03055
E-mail: shawn.sweeney@leg.state.nh.us
Committees: Criminal Justice and Public Safety
Education: Daniel Webster 1998 BS; New Hampshire 2001 JD

Representative **George Sykes** (D-Grafton-13) . . . . . . . . . (603) 667-1834
Counties Represented: Grafton (part)
Term Expires: 2016
Three Avon Avenue, Lebanon, NH 03766
E-mail: george.sykes@leg.state.nh.us
Committees: Transportation

Representative **Michael Sylvia** (R-Belknap-6) . . . . . . . . . (603) 707-8594
Counties Represented: Belknap (part)
Term Expires: 2016
216 Farrarville Road, Belmont, NH 03220
E-mail: mike.sylvia@leg.state.nh.us
Committees: Judiciary

Representative **John Sytek** (R-Rockingham-8) . . . . . . . . . . (603) 505-0909
Counties Represented: Rockingham (part)                    Res: (603) 893-8889
Term Expires: 2016                                         Fax: (603) 893-0000
34 Town Village Drive, Salem, NH 03079
E-mail: john.sytek@leg.state.nh.us
Committees: Executive Departments and Administration

Representative **Charlene Takesian** (R-Hillsborough-37) . . . (603) 635-7215
Counties Represented: Hillsborough (part)
Term Expires: 2016
114 Jeremy Hill Road, Pelham, NH 03076
E-mail: charlene.takesian@leg.state.nh.us
Committees: Judiciary

Representative
**Daniel "Dan" Tamburello** (R-Rockingham-5) . . . . . . . . (603) 434-2940
Counties Represented: Rockingham (part)
Term Expires: 2016
Three Royal Lane, Londonderry, NH 03053-2507
E-mail: daniel.tamburello@leg.state.nh.us
Committees: Executive Departments and Administration

Representative **Bruce L. Tatro** (D-Cheshire-15) . . . . . . . . (603) 852-2624
Counties Represented: Cheshire (part)                      Res: (603) 352-3904
Term Expires: 2016
208 Old Richmond Road, Swanzey, NH 03446-5522
E-mail: bruce.tatro@leg.state.nh.us
Committees: Municipal and County Government

Representative **Robert L. Theberge** (D-Coos-3) . . . . . . . . (603) 723-8996
Counties Represented: Coos (part)                          Res: (603) 752-5672
Term Expires: 2016
P.O. Box 271, Berlin, NH 03570-0271
E-mail: robert.theberge@leg.state.nh.us
Committees: State-Federal Relations and Veterans Affairs

Representative **John E. Tholl, Jr.** (R-Coos-5) . . . . . . . . . . . (603) 837-2278
Counties Represented: Coos (part)
Term Expires: 2016
41 Kimball Hill Road, Whitefield, NH 03598
E-mail: jetjr2@msn.com
Committees: Criminal Justice and Public Safety

Representative **Doug Thomas** (R-Rockingham-5) . . . . . . . . (603) 490-3226
Counties Represented: Rockingham (part)
Term Expires: 2016
143 Mammoth Road, Londonderry, NH 03053
E-mail: doug.thomasnh@gmail.com
Committees: Science, Technology and Energy

Representative **Yvonne D. Thomas** (D-Coos-3) . . . . . . . . . (603) 496-3608
Counties Represented: Coos (part)                          Res: (603) 752-1816
Term Expires: 2016
557 Norway Street, Berlin, NH 03570
E-mail: yvonne.thomas@leg.state.nh.us
Committees: Resources, Recreation and Development

Representative **Susan Ticehurst** (D-Carroll-3) . . . . . . . . . (603) 323-8040
Counties Represented: Carroll (part)
Term Expires: 2016
334 Pease Hill Road, Tamworth, NH 03886
E-mail: ticehurstnhhouse@gmail.com
Committees: Health, Human Services and Elderly Affairs

Representative **Ben Tilton** (D-Cheshire-12) . . . . . . . . . . . . (603) 271-2548
Counties Represented: Cheshire (part)
Term Expires: 2016
E-mail: benjamin.tilton@leg.state.nh.us
Committees: Municipal and County Government

Representative **Franklin T. Tilton** (R-Belknap-3) . . . . . . . . (603) 528-8466
Counties Represented: Belknap (part)
Term Expires: 2016
56 Orchard Street, Laconia, NH 03246-3027
E-mail: frank.tilton@leg.state.nh.us
Committees: Public Works and Highways

Representative **Rio Tilton** (R-Rockingham-20) . . . . . . . . . . (603) 271-2548
Counties Represented: Rockingham (part)
Term Expires: 2016
Committees: Environment and Agriculture

Representative
**Charles "Chuck" Townsend** (D-Grafton-11) . . . . . . . . . (603) 381-0316
Counties Represented: Grafton (part)                       Res: (603) 632-7493
Term Expires: 2016                                         Fax: (603) 632-4471
49 Hall Road, Canaan, NH 03741-7408
E-mail: chuck.townsend@leg.state.nh.us
Committees: Science, Technology and Energy

Representative **Susan Treleaven** (D-Stafford-17) . . . . . . . . (603) 749-2347
Counties Represented: Stafford (part)
Term Expires: 2016
454 Sixth Street, Dover, NH 03820
E-mail: streleaven@comcast.net
Committees: Municipal and County Government

Representative **Chris True** (R-Rockingham-4) . . . . . . . . . . . (603) 271-2548
Counties Represented: Rockingham (part)
Term Expires: 2016
E-mail: chris.true@leg.state.nh.us
Committees: Transportation

Representative **Pamela J. Tucker** (R-Rockingham-23) . . . . . (603) 431-8982
Counties Represented: Rockingham (part)
Term Expires: 2016
15 Eagle Court, Greenland, NH 03840-2336
E-mail: pam.tucker@leg.state.nh.us
Committees: Commerce and Consumer Affairs; Legislative
Administration

Representative **Alan J. Turcotte** (D-Merrimack-22) . . . . . . . (603) 485-2349
Counties Represented: Merrimack (part)
Term Expires: 2016
Three High Ridge Trail, Allenstown, NH 03275
E-mail: alanturcotte4rep@gmail.com
Committees: Environment and Agriculture

Representative **Leonard "Len" Turcotte** (R-Strafford-4) . . . (603) 664-7715
Counties Represented: Strafford (part)
Term Expires: 2016
143 Beauty Hill Road, Barrington, NH 03825
E-mail: len.turcotte@leg.state.nh.us
Committees: Labor, Industrial and Rehabilitative Services

Representative
**Timothy "Tim" Twombly** (R-Hillsborough-34) . . . . . . . . (603) 888-4466
Counties Represented: Hillsborough (part)
Term Expires: 2016
120 East Hobart Street, Nashua, NH 03060
E-mail: timothy.twombly@leg.state.nh.us
Committees: Finance

Representative **Jordan G. Ulery** (R-Hillsborough-37) . . . . . (603) 231-7867
Counties Represented: Hillsborough (part)                  Res: (603) 882-8979
Term Expires: 2016                                         Fax: (603) 882-6863
P.O. Box 15, Hudson, NH 03051-0015
E-mail: jordanulery@myfairpoint.net
Committees: Ways and Means

Representative **Karen Umberger** (R-Carroll-2) . . . . . . . . . (603) 356-6881
Counties Represented: Carroll (part)
Term Expires: 2016
P.O. Box 186, Kearsarge, NH 03847-0186
E-mail: karenu@ncia.net
Committees: Finance

Representative **Herb Vadney** (R-Belknap-2) . . . . . . . . . . . . (603) 271-2548
Counties Represented: Belknap (part)
Term Expires: 2016
Ten Sleepy Hollow Road, Meredith, NH 03253
E-mail: herb.vadney@leg.state.nh.us
Committees: Science, Technology and Energy

Representative **Ivy Vann** (D-Hillsborough-24) . . . . . . . . . . . (603) 533-0357
Counties Represented: Hillsborough (part)
Term Expires: 2016
50 Summer Street, Peterborough, NH 03458
E-mail: ivy.vann@leg.state.nh.us
Committees: Fish, Game and Marine Resources

Representative **Peter Varney** (R-Belknap-5) . . . . . . . . . . . . (603) 765-6380
Counties Represented: Belknap (part)
Term Expires: 2016
P.O. Box 1059, Alton, NH 03809
E-mail: pvarney@atsnh.com
Committees: Municipal and County Government

Representative **James Verschueren** (D-Stafford-13) . . . . . . (603) 343-4652
Counties Represented: Stafford (part)
Term Expires: 2016
102-B Sixth Street, Dover, NH 03820
E-mail: james.verschueren@leg.state.nh.us
Committees: Education
Education: Oakland U BA; Fletcher Law & Diplomacy MS

Representative **Michael Vose** (R-Rockingham-9) . . . . . . . . . (603) 734-4084
Counties Represented: Rockingham (part)
Term Expires: 2016
75 Olde Bridge Lane, Epping, NH 03042
E-mail: michael.vose@leg.state.nh.us
Committees: Science, Technology and Energy

Representative **Janet G. Wall** (D-Strafford-6) . . . . . . . . . . . (603) 749-3051
Counties Represented: Strafford (part)
Term Expires: 2016
Nine Kelley Road, Madbury, NH 03823
E-mail: janet.wall@leg.state.nh.us
Committees: Judiciary
Education: New Hampshire

Representative **Mary Jane Wallner** (D-Merrimack-10) . . . . (603) 224-1632
Counties Represented: Merrimack (part)        Res: (603) 225-5249
Term Expires: 2016
19 North Fruit Street, Concord, NH 03301
Four Chestnut Pasture Road, Concord, NH 03301-7900
E-mail: maryjane.wallner@leg.state.nh.us
Committees: Finance; Rules

Representative
**Robert M. Walsh, Jr.** (D-Hillsborough-11) . . . . . . . . . . . (603) 759-9668
Counties Represented: Hillsborough (part)
Term Expires: 2016
114 Weston Street, Manchester, NH 03104
E-mail: bob.walsh@leg.state.nh.us
Committees: Finance
Education: Boston U 1955

Representative **Thomas C. Walsh** (R-Merrimack-24) . . . . . (603) 623-4104
Counties Represented: Merrimack (part)
Term Expires: 2016
15 Berry Hill Road, Hooksett, NH 03106
E-mail: tcwiv1966@aol.com
Committees: Transportation

Representative
**Gerald "Gerry" Ward** (D-Rockingham-28) . . . . . . . . . . . (603) 436-6142
Counties Represented: Rockingham (part)
Term Expires: 2016
16 Nixon Peak, Portsmouth, NH 03801
E-mail: ward4staterep@gmail.com
Committees: Election Law
Education: Harvard 1971 BA; Boston U 1984 PhD

Representative **Joanne Ward** (R-Rockingham-19) . . . . . . . . (603) 772-5145
Counties Represented: Rockingham (part)
Term Expires: 2016
Six Wedgewood Drive, Stratham, NH 03885
E-mail: joanne.ward@leg.state.nh.us
Committees: Health, Human Services and Elderly Affairs

Representative **Kenneth J. Ward** (D-Stafford-21) . . . . . . . (603) 988-7580
Counties Represented: Stafford (part)
Term Expires: 2016
P.O. Box 602, Rollinsford, NH 03869
E-mail: ken.ward@leg.state.nh.us
Committees: Fish, Game and Marine Resources

Representative **James Webb** (R-Rockingham-6) . . . . . . . . . (603) 595-1260
Counties Represented: Rockingham (part)        Res: (603) 845-3454
Term Expires: 2016
Six Independence Avenue, Derry, NH 03038-4364
E-mail: james.webb@leg.state.nh.us
Committees: Fish, Game and Marine Resources

Representative **Lucy McVitty Weber** (D-Cheshire-1) . . . . . (603) 756-4338
Counties Represented: Cheshire (part)
Term Expires: 2016
217 Old Keene Road, Walpole, NH 03608-4845
E-mail: lwmcv@comcast.net
Committees: Health, Human Services and Elderly Affairs; Legislative
Administration; Rules

Representative **David A. Welch** (R-Rockingham-13) . . . . . (603) 642-4402
Counties Represented: Rockingham (part)
Term Expires: 2016
P.O. Box 570, Kingston, NH 03848
E-mail: v-chcj@outlook.com
Committees: Criminal Justice and Public Safety

Representative **Kenneth L. Weyler** (R-Rockingham-13) . . . (603) 642-3518
Counties Represented: Rockingham (part)
Term Expires: 2016
23 Scotland Road, Kingston, NH 03848-3232
E-mail: kweyler@aol.com
Committees: Finance

Representative **Deborah H. Wheeler** (D-Merrimack-3) . . . . (603) 271-2548
Counties Represented: Merrimack (part)
Term Expires: 2016
E-mail: deborah.wheeler@leg.state.nh.us
Committees: Judiciary

Representative
**Andrew A. "Andy" White** (D-Grafton-13) . . . . . . . . . . . (603) 252-0846
Counties Represented: Grafton (part)        Res: (603) 727-9392
Term Expires: 2016
16 Young Street, Lebanon, NH 03766-1234
E-mail: awhite348@gmail.com
Committees: Labor, Industrial and Rehabilitative Services

Representative **Joshua Whitehouse** (R-Strafford-2) . . . . . . (603) 497-7091
Counties Represented: Strafford (part)
Term Expires: 2016
45 Foxtrot Drive, Farmington, NH 03835-3006
E-mail: joshua.whitehouse@leg.state.nh.us

Representative **Kermit R. Williams** (D-Hillsborough-4) . . . . (603) 654-7684
Counties Represented: Hillsborough (part)
Term Expires: 2016
55 Burns Hill Road, Wilton, NH 03086
E-mail: kermit.williams@leg.state.nh.us
Committees: Commerce and Consumer Affairs

Representative **Steven J. Woitkun** (R-Rockingham-33) . . . (603) 642-5154
Counties Represented: Rockingham (part)
Term Expires: 2016
85 Fairview Drive, Danville, NH 03819
E-mail: steven.woitkun@leg.state.nh.us
Committees: Executive Departments and Administration

Representative **Terry Wolf** (R-Hillsborough-7) . . . . . . . . . . (603) 471-0240
Counties Represented: Hillsborough (part)
Term Expires: 2016
61 Bracken Circle, Bedford, NH 03110
E-mail: terry.wolf@leg.state.nh.us
Committees: Education

Representative **David Woodbury** (D-Hillsborough-5) . . . . . (603) 487-2634
Counties Represented: Hillsborough (part)
Term Expires: 2016
37 McCurdy Road, New Boston, NH 03070
E-mail: david.woodbury@leg.state.nh.us
Committees: Judiciary
Education: Pennsylvania 1966

Representative **Donald S. "Ted." Wright** (R-Carroll-8) . . . . (603) 707-7869
Counties Represented: Carroll (part)
Term Expires: 2016
160 Sodom Road, Moultonboro, NH 03254
E-mail: donald.wright@leg.state.nh.us
Committees: Resources, Recreation and Development

*(continued on next page)*

**LEGISLATIVE BRANCH**

**Representatives** *continued*

Representative **Kurt Wuelper** (R-Strafford-3) . . . . . . . . . . . (603) 644-2927
  Counties Represented: Strafford (part)
  Term Expires: 2016
  1336 Parker Mountain Road, Strafford, NH 03884
  E-mail: kurt.wuelper@leg.state.nh.us
  Committees: Judiciary
Representative **Nick Zaricki** (R-Hillsborough-6) . . . . . . . . . (603) 660-3872
  Counties Represented: Hillsborough (part)
  Term Expires: 2016
  11 Hoyt Road, Goffstown, NH 03045
  E-mail: nick.zaricki@leg.state.nh.us
  Committees: Labor, Industrial and Rehabilitative Services
Belknap-3 **(Vacant)** . . . . . . . . . . . . . . . . . . . . . . . . . . . . . . . (603) 271-2548
  Note: A general election to fill this legislative vacancy will be held on
  November 8, 2016.
Rockingham-2 **(Vacant)** . . . . . . . . . . . . . . . . . . . . . . . . . . . (603) 271-2548
  Note: A general election to fill this legislative vacancy will be held on
  November 8, 2016.
Rockingham-17 **(Vacant)** . . . . . . . . . . . . . . . . . . . . . . . . . . (603) 271-2548
  Note: A general election to fill this legislative vacancy will be held on
  November 8, 2016.

# House Standing Committees
Legislative Office Bldg., 107 North Main Street, Concord, NH 03301

## Children and Family Law
Legislative Office Building, Room 206, Concord, NH 03301
Tel: (603) 271-3458

| **Majority Members** | **Minority Members** |
| --- | --- |
| Carolyn M. Gargasz (R) *Chair* | Patrick T. Long (D) *Clerk* |
| Debra L. DeSimone (R) *Vice Chair* | Caroletta C. Alicea (D) |
| Frank Edelblut (R) | Skip Berrien (D) |
| Elizabeth Ferreira (R) | Cynthia Chase (D) |
| James P. Gray (R) | Alethea Lincoln Froburg (D) |
| Paul C. Ingbretson (R) | Martha Hennessey (D) |
| Daniel C. Itse (R) | Naida L. Kaen (D) |
| Jeffrey Oligny (R) | Audrey M. Stevens (D) |
| Jason R. Parent (R) | |
| Eric Schleien (R) | |
| Kimberly Rice (R) | |

## Commerce and Consumer Affairs
Legislative Office Building, Room 302, Concord, NH 03301
Tel: (603) 271-3369

| **Majority Members** | **Minority Members** |
| --- | --- |
| John B. Hunt (R) *Chair* | Richard Abel (D) |
| Barbara Biggie (R) *Vice Chair* | John Bordenet (D) |
| Valerie Fraser (R) *Clerk* | Edward A. Butler (D) |
| David Bates (R) | Kenneth N. Gidge (D) |
| Ronald J. Belanger (R) | Christopher J. Herbert (D) |
| Donald H. "Don" Flanders (R) | David Luneau (I) |
| Harold F. French (R) | Rebecca McBeath (D) |
| Bart Fromuth (R) | Kermit R. Williams (D) |
| Joe Hannon (R) | |
| George Hurt (R) | |
| Laura Jones (R) | |
| Laurie Sanborn (R) | |
| Pamela J. Tucker (R) | |

## Criminal Justice and Public Safety
Legislative Office Building, Room 204, Concord, NH 03301
Tel: (603) 271-3419

| **Majority Members** | **Minority Members** |
| --- | --- |
| John E. Tholl, Jr. (R) *Chair* | Roger R. Berube (D) |
| David A. Welch (R) *Vice Chair* | Robert Cushing (D) |
| Dennis H. Fields (R) *Clerk* | Len DiSesa (D) |
| Arthur E. Barnes III (R) | Geoffrey Hirsch (D) |
| John A. Burt (R) | Latha Mangipudi (D) |
| Ed Comeau (R) | Andrew S. O'Hearne (D) |
| Robert M. "Bob" Fesh (R) | Laura C. Pantelakos (D) |
| Robert Z. Fisher (R) | Timothy N. "Tim" Robertson (D) |
| Dennis Green (R) | |
| Dick Marston (R) | |
| John F. Martin (R) | |
| Harold B. Parker (R) | |
| Shawn Sweeney (R) | |

## Education
Legislative Office Building, Room 207, Concord, NH 03301
Tel: (603) 271-3334

| **Majority Members** | **Minority Members** |
| --- | --- |
| Roderick M. "Rick" Ladd, Jr. (R) *Chair* | Barbara E. Shaw (D) *Clerk* |
| John L. Balcom (R) *Vice Chair* | June M. Frazer (D) |
| Christopher R. Adams (R) | Mary Stuart Gile (D) |
| Ralph G. Boehm (R) | Mary J. Gorman (D) |
| Allen W. Cook (R) | Mary S. Heath (D) |
| Glenn Cordelli (R) | Mel Myler (D) |
| Robert J. Elliott (R) | Deanna S. Rollo (D) |
| James "Jim" Grenier (R) | Andrew "Andy" Schmidt (D) |
| Josh Moore (R) | James Verschueren (D) |
| Jason Osborne (R) | |
| Victoria L. Sullivan (R) | |
| Terry Wolf (R) | |

## Election Law
Legislative Office Building, Room 308, Concord, NH 03301
Tel: (603) 271-3319

| **Majority Members** | **Minority Members** |
| --- | --- |
| Kathleen Hoelzel (R) *Chair* | Travis Bennett (D) |
| James P. Gray (R) *Vice Chair* | Wayne M. Burton (D) |
| Barbara Griffin (R) *Clerk* | David E. Cote (D) |
| Duane Brown (R) | Debbie DiFranco (D) |
| Rick Christie (R) | Wayne Moynihan (D) |
| Yvonne Dean-Bailey (R) | William Pearson (D) |
| William M. Gannon (R) | Gerald "Gerry" Ward (D) |
| Edith Hogan (R) | |
| Adam Schroadter (R) | |
| Kathleen F. Souza (R) | |
| Joe Sweeney (R) | |

## Environment and Agriculture
Legislative Office Building, Room 303, Concord, NH 03301
Tel: (603) 271-3125

| **Majority Members** | **Minority Members** |
| --- | --- |
| Robert "Bob" Haefner (R) *Chair* | Christy D. Bartlett (D) |
| John O'Connor (R) *Vice Chair* | Peter W. Bixby (D) |
| Michele Peckham (R) *Clerk* | Rebecca A. Brown (D) |
| Michael Brewster (R) | David Doherty (D) |
| Ernest H. "Ernie" Bridge (R) | Janice S. Gardner (D) |
| Carol Bush (R) | Tara A. Sad (D) |
| Stephen Darrow (R) | George Saunderson (D) |
| Richard E. "Dick" Gordon (R) | Alexis Simpson (D) |
| Warren Groen (R) | Alan J. Turcotte (D) |
| Raymond Howard (R) | |
| Lisa Scontsas (R) | |
| Rio Tilton (R) | |

## Executive Departments and Administration
Legislative Office Building, Room 306, Concord, NH 03301
Tel: (603) 271-3319

| **Majority Members** | **Minority Members** |
| --- | --- |
| Andrew Christie, Jr. (R) *Chair* | Jacalyn L. "Jackie" Cilley (D) |
| John Sytek (R) *Vice Chairman* | Raymond "Ray" Gagnon (D) |
| Steven Beaudoin (R) | Jeffrey Goley (D) |
| Bill Goulette (R) | Daniel C. Hansberry (D) |
| Peter T. Hansen (R) | Jean L. Jeudy (D) |
| J.R. Hoell (R) | Carol R. Roberts (D) |
| Thomas L. Kaczynski, Jr. (R) | Peter B. Schmidt (D) |
| Harold B. Parker (R) | Daniel J. "Dan" Sullivan (D) |
| Mark Proulx (R) | |
| Jeffrey Shackett (R) | |
| Gregory Smith (R) | |
| Daniel "Dan" Tamburello (R) | |
| Steven J. Woitkun (R) | |

## Finance

Legislative Office Building, Room 210-211, Concord, NH 03301
Tel: (603) 271-3165

| **Majority Members** | **Minority Members** |
|---|---|
| Neal M. Kurk (R) *Chair* | J. Tracy Emerick (D) |
| Lynne M. Ober (R) *Vice Chair* | Thomas "Tom" Buco (D) |
| Kenneth L. Weyler (R) *Clerk* | Daniel Adams Eaton (D) |
| Mary M. Allen (R) | Susan Ford (D) |
| Richard W. "Dick" Barry (R) | William A. "Bill" Hatch (D) |
| Frank A. Byron (R) | Peter R. Leishman (D) |
| David J. Danielson (R) | Sharon L. Nordgren (D) |
| David W. Hess (R) | Katherine D. Rogers (D) |
| Dan McGuire (R) | Lucinda "Cindy" Rosenwald (D) |
| Betsy McKinney (R) | Marjorie K. Smith (D) |
| Joseph A. Pitre (R) | Mary Jane Wallner (D) |
| Peter Spanos (R) | Robert M. Walsh, Jr. (D) |
| Timothy "Tim" Twombly (R) | |
| Karen Umberger (R) | |

## Fish, Game and Marine Resources

Legislative Office Building, Room 307, Concord, NH 03301
Tel: (603) 271-3125

| **Majority Members** | **Minority Members** |
|---|---|
| David H. Kidder (R) *Chair* | Jonathan F. Manley (D) *Clerk* |
| James Webb (R) *Vice Chair* | Benjamin C. Baroody (D) |
| Guy Comtois (R) | Armand D. Forest (D) |
| Joseph "Joe" Duarte (R) | C. Lee Guerette (D) |
| Carlos E. Gonzalez (R) | Richard McNamara (D) |
| Shem Kellogg (R) | Theodore "Ted" Rokas (D) |
| Robert Knowles (R) | Ivy Vann (D) |
| Shari LeBreche (R) | Kenneth J. Ward (D) |
| Douglas B. Long (R) | |
| Elisabeth N. "Betsy" Sanders (R) | |
| Peter Silva (R) | |
| James Spillane (R) | |

## Health, Human Services and Elderly Affairs

Legislative Office Building, Room 205, Concord, NH 03301
Tel: (603) 271-3334

| **Majority Members** | **Minority Members** |
|---|---|
| Frank R. Kotowski (R) *Chair* | Helen Deloge (D) |
| Donald "Don" LeBrun (R) *Vice Chair* | Barbara Conner French (D) |
| Bill Nelson (R) *Clerk* | Mary C. Freitas (D) |
| Daniel Donovan (R) | Pamela S. Gordon (D) |
| Susan Emerson (R) | James R. "Jim" MacKay (D) |
| John J. Fothergill (R) | Thomas "Tom" Sherman (D) |
| Joseph "Joe" Guthrie (R) | Kendall A. Snow (D) |
| André A. Martel (R) | Susan Ticehurst (D) |
| Charles E. McMahon (R) | Lucy McVitty Weber (D) |
| Stephen J. "Steve" Schmidt (R) | |
| Stephen B. Stepanek (R) | |
| Joanne Ward (R) | |

## Judiciary

Legislative Office Building, Room 208, Concord, NH 03301
Tel: (603) 271-3184

| **Majority Members** | **Minority Members** |
|---|---|
| Robert H. Rowe (R) *Chair* | Janet G. Wall (D) *Clerk* |
| Joseph M. Hagan (R) *Vice Chair* | Paul Berch (D) |
| Eric P. Estevez (R) | Frank H. Heffron (D) |
| Gary S. Hopper (R) | Timothy "Tim" Horrigan (D) |
| Robert Hull (R) | Linda B. Kenison (D) |
| Mark McLean (R) | Larry Robert Phillips (D) |
| Barry Palmer (R) | Deborah H. Wheeler (D) |
| Claire Rouillard (R) | David Woodbury (D) |
| Michael Sylvia (R) | |
| Charlene Takesian (R) | |
| Kurt Wuelper (R) | |

## Labor, Industrial and Rehabilitative Services

Legislative Office Building, Room 307, Concord, NH 03301
Tel: (603) 271-3125

| **Majority Members** | **Minority Members** |
|---|---|
| William J. Infantine (R) *Chair* | Michael Cahill (D) |
| Jack Flanagan (R) *Vice Chair* | Larry Converse (D) |
| G. Brian Seaworth (R) *Clerk* | Linda A. DiSilvestro (D) |
| Lino Avellani (R) | Michael Edgar (D) |
| Fred Doucette (R) | Douglas A. Ley (D) |
| Gregory Hill (R) | William "Bill" O'Neil (D) |
| Keith Murphy (R) | Dianne E. Schuett (D) |
| Tony Pellegrino (R) | Harold L. "Chip" Rice (D) |
| Katherine Prudhomme-O'Brien (R) | Andrew A. "Andy" White (D) |
| Leon H. Rideout (R) | |
| Tammy Simmons (R) | |
| Leonard "Len" Turcotte (R) | |
| Nick Zaricki (R) | |

## Legislative Administration

Legislative Office Building, Room 104, Concord, NH 03301
Tel: (603) 271-3125

| **Majority Members** | **Minority Members** |
|---|---|
| Richard "Dick" Hinch (R) *Chair* | Dianne E. Schuett (D) *Clerk* |
| Sherman A. Packard (R) *Vice Chair* | James R. MacKay (D) |
| Brad Bailey (R) | Stephen J. "Steve" Shurtleff (D) |
| Russell T. Ober III (R) | Lucy McVitty Weber (D) |
| Tony Pellegrino (R) | |
| Pamela J. Tucker (R) | |

## Municipal and County Government

Legislative Office Building, Room 301, Concord, NH 03301
Tel: (603) 271-3317

| **Majority Members** | **Minority Members** |
|---|---|
| James "Jim" Belanger (R) *Chair* | Marjorie Porter (D) *Clerk* |
| Franklin Sterling, Jr. (R) *Vice Chair* | Jane Beaulieu (D) |
| Keith Ammon (R) | Chris Brown (D) |
| David A. Bickford (R) | Clyde Carson (D) |
| Francis Chase (R) | Patricia Cornell (D) |
| Catherine Cheney (R) | Bruce L. Tatro (D) |
| James Coffey (R) | Ben Tilton (D) |
| Jeffrey F. Harris (R) | Susan Treleaven (D) |
| Lawrence "Mike" Kappler (R) | |
| Ken Peterson (R) | |
| Peter Varney (R) | |

## Public Works and Highways

Legislative Office Building, Room 201, Concord, NH 03301
Tel: (603) 271-3565

| **Majority Members** | **Minority Members** |
|---|---|
| Gene G. Chandler (R) *Chair* | Dale R. Sprague (D) |
| Mark E. McConkey (R) *Vice Chairman* | John R. Cloutier (D) |
| David Milz (R) *Clerk* | Karen Ebel (D) |
| William G. Friel (R) | Patricia C. Higgins (D) |
| Edmond D. Gionet (R) | Virginia O'Brien Irwin (D) |
| Erin Tapper Hennessey (R) | Martin l. Jack (D) |
| Walter Kolodziej (R) | Wendy Piper (D) |
| Bill Kuch (R) | Mario Ratzki (D) |
| David W. Pierce (R) | |
| Carl W. Seidel (R) | |
| Jeffrey Shackett (R) | |
| Franklin T. Tilton (R) | |

## Resources, Recreation and Development

Legislative Office Building, Room 305, Concord, NH 03301
Tel: (603) 271-3125

| **Majority Members** | **Minority Members** |
|---|---|
| D. L. "Chris" Christensen (R) *Chair* | Paula Bradley (D) |
| John Mullen, Jr. (R) *Vice Chair* | Paula Francese (D) |
| Carolyn L. Matthews (R) *Clerk* | Suzanne H. "Sue" Gottling (D) |
| Beverly Ann Ferrante (R) | Kevin G. Maes (D) |
| Linda Gould (R) | Lee Walker Oxenham (D) |
| Eric Johnson (R) | Henry A. L. Parkhurst (D) |
| James W. "Jim" McConnell (R) | Judith T. Spang (D) |
| Carol McGuire (R) | Suzanne Smith (D) |
| John Potucek (R) | Yvonne D. Thomas (D) |
| Frederick Rice (R) | |
| David H. Russell (R) | |
| Donald S. "Ted." Wright (R) | |

## Rules

Legislative Office Building, Room 104, Concord, NH 03301
Tel: (603) 271-3661

| **Majority Members** | **Minority Members** |
|---|---|
| Shawn N. Jasper (R) *Chair* | Lucinda "Cindy" Rosenwald (D) |
| Gene G. Chandler (R) *Vice Chair* | Stephen J. "Steve" Shurtleff (D) |
| Richard W. "Dick" Barry (R) | Mary Jane Wallner (D) |
| Jack Flanagan (R) | Lucy McVitty Weber (D) |
| Richard "Dick" Hinch (R) | |
| Kathleen Hoelzel (R) | |

## Science, Technology and Energy

Legislative Office Building, Room 304, Concord, NH 03301
Tel: (603) 271-3369

| **Majority Members** | **Minority Members** |
|---|---|
| Robert E. Introne (R) *Chairman* | William "Bill" Baber (D) |
| Herbert D. Richardson (R) *Vice Chairman* | Robert A. "Bob" Backus (D) |
| | David A. Borden (D) |
| James E. "Jim" Devine (R) *Clerk* | Jacqueline A. Cali-Pitts (D) |
| Glen Aldrich (R) | Suzanne Harvey (D) |
| Carolyn Halstead (R) | John E. Mann (D) |
| David Murotake (R) | Howard M. Moffett (D) |
| Jeanine Notter (R) | Marjorie "Marge" Shepardson (D) |
| James "Jim" Parison (R) | Charles "Chuck" Townsend (D) |
| Laurence Rappaport (R) | |
| Doug Thomas (R) | |
| Herb Vadney (R) | |
| Michael Vose (R) | |

## State-Federal Relations and Veterans Affairs

Legislative Office Building, Room 303, Concord, NH 03301
Tel: (603) 271-3317

| **Majority Members** | **Minority Members** |
|---|---|
| Russell T. Ober III (R) *Chair* | Robert L. Theberge (D) *Clerk* |
| Phillip Straight (R) *Vice Chair* | Efstathia Booras (D) |
| Alfred P. Baldasaro (R) | Amanda Bouldin (D) |
| Lars T. Christiansen (R) | Elizabeth Edwards (D) |
| Eric Eastman (R) | Thomas Katsiantonis (D) |
| Phyllis M. Katsakiores (R) | Linda Massimilla (D) |
| David Lundgren (R) | Lt. Col. Kris Edward Roberts (D) |
| Richard Marple (R) | Timothy J. Smith (D) |
| Frank McCarthy (R) | |
| Peggy McCarthy (R) | |
| Anne K. Priestley (R) | |
| Skip Rollins (R) | |

## Transportation

Legislative Office Building, Room 203, Concord, NH 03301
Tel: (603) 271-3565

| **Majority Members** | **Minority Members** |
|---|---|
| Steven "Steve" Smith (R) *Chair* | Michael D. Abbott (D) |
| Thomas C. Walsh (R) *Vice Chair* | Pamela "Pam" Brown (D) |
| Thomas W. "Tom" Laware (R) *Clerk* | Alan Cohen (D) |
| G. Thomas Cardon (R) | Gladys Johnsen (D) |
| Brian Chirichiello (R) | Michael B. O'Brien, Sr. (D) |
| Karel A. Crawford (R) | Dick Patten (D) |
| Russell Dumais (R) | Timothy M. Soucy (D) |
| Larry Gagne (R) | George Sykes (D) |
| Bruce Hodgdon (R) | |
| Werner D. Horn (R) | |
| Sherman A. Packard (R) | |
| Chris True (R) | |

## Ways and Means

Legislative Office Building, Room 202, Concord, NH 03301
Tel: (603) 271-3529

| **Majority Members** | **Minority Members** |
|---|---|
| Norman L. Major (R) *Chair* | Susan W. Almy (D) |
| Patrick Abrami (R) *Vice Chair* | Richard Ames (D) |
| Gary Azarian (R) *Clerk* | Mary R. Cooney (D) |
| Brian S. Gallagher (R) | Paul Henle (D) |
| Mary E. Griffin (R) | David B. Karrick, Jr. (D) |
| David W. Hess (R) | Patricia Lovejoy (D) |
| Joseph LaChance (R) | Gilman C. "Gil" Shattuck (D) |
| Don E. Leeman (R) | Tom Southworth (D) |
| John J. Manning, Jr. (R) | |
| Donald B. McClarren (R) | |
| Robert "Bob" Nigrello (R) | |
| Bill Ohm (R) | |
| Jordan G. Ulery (R) | |

# New Jersey State Legislature

125 West State Street, P.O. Box 099, Trenton, NJ 08625
Tel: (609) 292-4840  TTY: (609) 777-2744  Fax: (609) 777-2440
Internet: www.njleg.state.nj.us

## New Jersey Senate

President of the Senate
**Stephen M. "Steve" Sweeney** (D) . . . . . . . . . . . . . . . . (609) 292-5215
President Pro Tem **Nia H. Gill, Esq.** (D) . . . . . . . . . . . . . . (609) 292-5215
  Education: Upsala BA; Rutgers 1975 JD
Majority Leader **Loretta Weinberg** (D) . . . . . . . . . . . . . . (201) 928-0100
  Education: UCLA BA
Deputy Majority Leader **Paul A. Sarlo** (D) . . . . . . . . . . . . (201) 804-8118
  Education: NJIT BSCE, MSEE
Assistant Majority Leader **James Beach** (D) . . . . . . . . . . (856) 429-1572
  Education: Rowan U MA
Assistant Majority Leader **Linda R. Greenstein** (D) . . . . . . (609) 631-9988
  Education: Vassar AB; Johns Hopkins MA; Georgetown 1984 JD
Assistant Majority Leader **M. Teresa Ruiz** (D) . . . . . . . . . . (973) 484-1000
Majority Conference Leader **Robert M. Gordon** (D) . . . . . . (201) 703-9779
  Education: Williams BA; UC Berkeley MPP; Wharton 1978 MBA
Majority Whip **Sandra Bolden Cunningham** (D) . . . . . . . . (201) 451-5100
Minority Leader **Thomas H. Kean, Jr.** (R) . . . . . . . . . . . . . (609) 292-5199
  Education: Dartmouth 1990 AB; Tufts 1997 MALD, PhD
Deputy Minority Leader **Diane B. Allen** (R) . . . . . . . . . . . (609) 292-5199
  Education: Bucknell 1970 BA
Minority Conference Leader **Robert W. Singer** (R) . . . . . . (609) 292-5199
Deputy Minority Conference Leader **Jennifer Beck** (R) . . . (732) 933-1591
  Education: Boston Col 1989 BA, 1989 BS; Pennsylvania 1992 MGA
Minority Whip **Kevin O'Toole** (R) . . . . . . . . . . . . . . . . . . . (973) 237-1360
  Education: Seton Hall BA, JD
Republican Budget Officer **Anthony R. Bucco** (R) . . . . . . . (609) 292-5199
Secretary of the Senate **Jennifer A. McQuaid** . . . . . . . . . . (609) 847-3915
  Education: New Hampshire MA

## Senators

**Party Affiliation Statistics:** Republicans: 16, Democrats: 24

Senator **Dawn Marie Addiego** (R-District 8) . . . . . . . . . . . (609) 654-1498
  Counties Represented: Atlantic (part), Burlington (part), Camden (part)
  Term Expires: January 2018
  176 Route 70, Suite 13, Medford, NJ 08055
  E-mail: senaddiego@njleg.org
  Committees: Health, Human Services and Senior Citizens; Labor
  Education: Villanova BSAcc; Widener 1987 JD

Senator **Diane B. Allen** (R-District 7) . . . . . . . . . . . . . . . . (609) 292-5199
  Counties Represented: Burlington (part)   Dist: (856) 314-8835
  Term Expires: January 2018
  504 Route 130 North, Suite 100, Cinnaminson, NJ 08077
  E-mail: senallen@njleg.org
  Committees: Education; Health, Human Services and Senior Citizens;
  Joint Public Schools; Military and Veterans' Affairs
  Affiliation: President, VidComm, Inc.

Senator **Christopher "Kip" Bateman** (R-District 16) . . . . . (908) 526-3600
  Counties Represented: Hunterdon (part), Mercer (part), Middlesex
  (part), Somerset (part)
  Term Expires: January 2018
  36 East Main Street, Somerville, NJ 08876
  E-mail: senbateman@njleg.org
  Committees: Environment and Energy; Joint Public Schools; Judiciary;
  Law and Public Safety
  Education: Ithaca 1980 BA; Seton Hall 1984 JD

Senator **James Beach** (D-District 6) . . . . . . . . . . . . . . . . . (856) 429-1572
  Counties Represented: Burlington (part), Camden (part)
  Term Expires: January 2018
  1309 Route 70 East, Cherry Hill, NJ 08003
  E-mail: senbeach@njleg.org
  Committees: Commerce; Education; Joint Public Schools; Military and
  Veterans' Affairs

Senator **Jennifer Beck** (R-District 11) . . . . . . . . . . . . . . . . (732) 933-1591
  Counties Represented: Monmouth (part)
  Term Expires: January 2018
  32 Monmouth Street, Red Bank, NJ 07701
  E-mail: senbeck@njleg.org
  Committees: Budget and Appropriations; Community and Urban
  Affairs

Senator **Anthony R. Bucco** (R-District 25) . . . . . . . . . . . . (609) 292-5199
  Counties Represented: Morris (part), Somerset   Dist: (973) 627-9700
  (part)
  Term Expires: January 2018
  75 Bloomfield Avenue, Suite 302, 3rd Floor, Denville, NJ 07834
  E-mail: senbucco@njleg.org
  Committees: Budget and Appropriations; Joint Budget Oversight; Labor
  Affiliation: Executive Vice President, Thomas W. Dunn Corp.

Senator **Gerald Cardinale** (R-District 39) . . . . . . . . . . . . . (862) 248-0491
  Counties Represented: Bergen (part), Passaic (part)   Dist: (201) 567-2324
  Term Expires: January 2018
  350 Madison Avenue, Cresskill, NJ 07626
  E-mail: sencardinale@njleg.org
  Committees: Commerce; Judiciary
  Education: St John's U (NY) 1955 BS; NYU 1959 DDS

Senator **Richard J. Codey** (D-District 27) . . . . . . . . . . . . . (609) 292-5215
  Counties Represented: Essex (part), Morris (part)   Dist: (973) 535-5017
  Term Expires: January 2018
  66 West Mount Pleasant Avenue, Livingston, NJ 07039
  E-mail: sencodey@njleg.org
  Committees: Environment and Energy
  Education: Fairleigh Dickinson 1981 BA

Senator **Christopher J. Connors** (R-District 9) . . . . . . . . . (609) 693-6700
  Counties Represented: Atlantic (part), Burlington (part), Ocean (part)
  Term Expires: January 2018
  620 West Lacey Road, Forked River, NJ 08731
  E-mail: senconnors@njleg.org
  Committees: Community and Urban Affairs; Military and Veterans'
  Affairs
  Education: Stockton State 1978 BS; Rutgers 1987 MPA, 1995 JD

Senator **Nilsa J. Cruz-Perez** (D-District 5) . . . . . (856) 547-4800 (Audubon)
  Counties Represented: Camden (part), Gloucester   Tel: (856) 541-1251
  (part)                                                (Camden)
  Term Expires: January 2018                         Tel: (856) 853-2960
  Camden City Hall, 520 Market Street, Suite 104,    (Woodbury)
  Camden, NJ 08102
  Gloucester County Justice Complex Annex, 114 North Broad Street,
  Woodbury, NJ 08096
  515 White Horse Pike, Suite D-3, Audubon, NJ 08106
  E-mail: sencruzperez@njleg.org
  Committees: Economic Growth; Joint Housing Affordability; Joint
  Public Schools; Military and Veterans' Affairs; Transportation
  Education: Puerto Rico BA

Senator **Sandra Bolden Cunningham** (D-District 31) . . . . (201) 451-5100
  Counties Represented: Hudson (part)
  Term Expires: January 2018
  1738 Kennedy Boulevard, Jersey City, NJ 07305
  E-mail: sencunningham@njleg.org
  Committees: Budget and Appropriations; Higher Education; Labor

Senator **Patrick J. Diegnan, Jr.** (D-District 18) . . . . . . . . . (908) 757-1677
  Counties Represented: Middlesex (part)
  Term Expires: January 2018
  908 Oak Tree Avenue, South Plainfield, NJ 07080
  E-mail: sendiegnan@njleg.org
  Committees: Budget and Appropriations; Joint Public Schools; Law and
  Public Safety; State Government, Wagering, Tourism and Historic
  Preservation
  Education: Seton Hall BA, JD

Senator **Michael J. Doherty** (R-District 23) . . . . . . . . . . . . (908) 722-1365
  Counties Represented: Hunterdon (part), Somerset   Dist: (908) 835-0552
  (part), Warren (part)
  Term Expires: January 2018
  245 Route 22, Suite 208, Bridgewater, NJ 08807
  127 Belvidere Avenue, Second Floor, Washington, NJ 07882
  E-mail: sendoherty@njleg.org
  Committees: Education; Judiciary
  Education: West Point 1985 BS; Seton Hall 1993 JD

Senator **Nia H. Gill, Esq.** (D-District 34) . . . . . . . . . . . . . . (609) 292-5215
  Counties Represented: Essex (part), Passaic (part)   Dist: (973) 509-0388
  Term Expires: January 2018
  39 South Fullerton Avenue, Suite 7, Montclair, NJ 07042
  E-mail: sengill@njleg.org
  Committees: Commerce; Judiciary

Senator **Robert M. Gordon** (D-District 38) . . . (201) 703-9779 (Fair Lawn)
  Counties Represented: Bergen (part), Passaic (part)   Dist: (201) 374-2205
  Term Expires: January 2018                                     (Bergenfield)
  14-25 Plaza Road, Fair Lawn, NJ 07410
  P.O. Box 398, Fair Lawn, NJ 07410
  35 South Washington Street, Bergenfield, NJ 07671
  E-mail: sengordon@njleg.org
  Committees: Health, Human Services and Senior Citizens; Legislative
  Oversight; Transportation

*(continued on next page)*

**LEGISLATIVE BRANCH**

**Senators** *continued*

Senator **Linda R. Greenstein** (D-District 14) . . . . . . . . . . . . (609) 631-9988
Counties Represented: Mercer (part), Middlesex    Dist: (609) 395-9911
(part)
Term Expires: January 2018
7 Centre Drive, Suite 2, Monroe, NJ 08831
E-mail: sengreenstein@njleg.org
Committees: Budget and Appropriations; Environment and Energy;
Law and Public Safety

Senator **James W. Holzapfel** (R-District 10) . . . . . . . . . . . . (732) 840-9028
Counties Represented: Ocean (part)
Term Expires: January 2018
852 Highway 70, Brick, NJ 08724
E-mail: senholzapfel@njleg.org
Committees: Law and Public Safety; Transportation
Education: Monmouth Col (NJ) BA; Seton Hall JD

Senator **Thomas H. Kean, Jr.** (R-District 21) . . . . . . . . . . . (609) 292-5199
Counties Represented: Morris (part), Somerset    Dist: (908) 918-0414
(part), Union (part)                        (Summit)
Term Expires: January 2018        Dist: (908) 232-3673
425 North Avenue East, Suite C,       (Westfield)
Westfield, NJ 07090
E-mail: senkean@njleg.org
Committees: Commerce; Higher Education; Legislative Oversight

Senator **Joseph M. "Joe" Kyrillos, Jr.** (R-District 13) . . . . (609) 292-5199
Counties Represented: Monmouth (part)    Dist: (732) 671-3206
Term Expires: January 2018
10 Highway, 2nd Floor, Middletown, NJ 07701
E-mail: senkyrillos@njleg.org
Committees: Economic Growth; Judiciary; Legislative Oversight
Affiliation: Business Standards and Ethics Director, Mid-Atlantic
Health Group
Education: Hobart BA; Boston U MS

Senator **Raymond J. Lesniak** (D-District 20) . . . . . . . . . . (609) 292-5215
Counties Represented: Union (part)    Dist: (908) 624-0880
Term Expires: January 2018
985 Stuyesent Avenue, Union, NJ 07083
E-mail: senlesniak@njleg.org
Committees: Commerce; Economic Growth; Judiciary
Education: Rutgers 1971 AB; St John's U (NY) 1974 JD

Senator
**Fred H. Madden, Jr.** (D-District 4) . . (856) 232-6700 (Turnersville Office)
Counties Represented: Camden (part), Gloucester    Dist: (856) 401-3073
(part)                        (Laurel Springs
Term Expires: January 2018          Office)
129 Johnson Road, Suite 1, Turnersville, NJ 08012
1379 Chews Landing, Laurel Springs, NJ 08021
E-mail: senmadden@njleg.org
Committees: Health, Human Services and Senior Citizens; Labor

Senator **Kevin O'Toole** (R-District 40) . . . . . . . . . . . . . . . (973) 237-1360
Counties Represented: Bergen (part), Essex (part), Morris (part),
Passaic (part)
Term Expires: January 2018
Wayne Plaza II, 155 Route 46 West, Suite 108, Wayne, NJ 07470
E-mail: senotoole@njleg.org
Committees: Budget and Appropriations; Judiciary

Senator **Steven V. Oroho** (R-District 24) . . . . . . . . . . . . . (973) 300-0200
Counties Represented: Morris (part), Sussex,    Dist: (908) 441-6343
Warren (part)
Term Expires: January 2018
One Wilson Drive, Sparta, NJ 07871
E-mail: senoroho@njleg.org
Committees: Budget and Appropriations; Economic Growth; State
Government, Wagering, Tourism and Historic Preservation
Education: St Francis Col (PA) BSAcc

Senator **Joseph Pennacchio** (R-District 26) . . . . . . . . . . . (973) 227-4012
Counties Represented: Essex (part), Morris (part), Passaic (part)
Term Expires: January 2018
330 Changebridge Road, Suite 102, Pine Brook, NJ 07058
E-mail: senpennacchio@njleg.org
Committees: Transportation
Education: Brooklyn BS; NYU DDS

Senator **Nellie Pou** (D-District 35) . . . . . . . . . . . . . . . . . . (973) 247-1555
Counties Represented: Bergen (part), Passaic (part)
Term Expires: January 2018
100 Hamilton Plaza, Suite 1405, Paterson, NJ 07505
E-mail: senpou@njleg.org
Committees: Budget and Appropriations; Higher Education; Judiciary
Education: Kean Col; Rutgers; Virginia

Senator **Ronald L. Rice, Jr.** (D-District 28) . . . . . . . . . . . (609) 292-5215
Counties Represented: Essex (part)    Dist: (973) 371-5665
Term Expires: January 2018
1044 South Orange Avenue, Newark, NJ 07106
E-mail: senrice@njleg.org
Committees: Community and Urban Affairs; Health, Human Services
and Senior Citizens; Joint Public Schools
Education: John Jay Col BS; Rutgers MA

Senator **M. Teresa Ruiz** (D-District 29) . . . . . . . . . . . . . . . (973) 484-1000
Counties Represented: Essex (part)
Term Expires: January 2018
166 Bloomfield Avenue, Newark, NJ 07104
E-mail: senruiz@njleg.org
Committees: Budget and Appropriations; Education; Legislative
Oversight

Senator **Nicholas J. Sacco** (D-District 32) . . . . . . . . . . . . (609) 292-5215
Counties Represented: Bergen (part), Hudson (part)    Dist: (201) 295-0200
Term Expires: January 2018
9060 Palisade Avenue, North Bergen, NJ 07047
E-mail: sensacco@njleg.org
Committees: Law and Public Safety; Transportation
Education: Rutgers BA; Seton Hall MA

Senator **Paul A. Sarlo** (D-District 36) . . . . . . . . . . . . . . . . (201) 804-8118
Counties Represented: Bergen (part), Passaic (part)
Term Expires: January 2018
496 Columbia Boulevard, Floor 1, Wood Ridge, NJ 07075
E-mail: sensarlo@njleg.org
Committees: Budget and Appropriations; Higher Education; Joint
Budget Oversight; Judiciary; Legislative Oversight

Senator **Nicholas P. Scutari** (D-District 22) . . . . . . . . . . . (609) 292-5215
Counties Represented: Middlesex (part), Somerset    Dist: (908) 587-0404
(part), Union (part)
Term Expires: January 2018
1514 East St. Georges Avenue, 2nd Floor, Linden, NJ 07036
E-mail: senscutari@njleg.org
Committees: Commerce; Joint State Leasing and Space Utilization;
Judiciary
Education: Kean Col BA; Rutgers MEd; Thomas M Cooley JD

Senator **Robert W. Singer** (R-District 30) . . . . . . . . . . . . . (609) 292-5199
Counties Represented: Monmouth (part), Ocean    Dist: (732) 987-5669
(part)
Term Expires: January 2018
1771 Madison Avenue, Suite 202, Lakewood, NJ 08701
E-mail: sensinger@njleg.org
Committees: Health, Human Services and Senior Citizens; Higher
Education

Senator **Bob Smith** (D-District 17) . . . . . . . . . . . . . . . . . . . (732) 752-0770
Counties Represented: Middlesex (part), Somerset    Tel: (609) 292-5215
(part)
Term Expires: January 2018
216 Stelton Road, Suite E-5, Piscataway, NJ 08854
E-mail: senbsmith@njleg.org
Committees: Environment and Energy; Judiciary
Education: Scranton BA, MS; Rutgers MS; Seton Hall JD

Senator **Brian P. Stack** (D-District 33) . . . . . . . . . . . . . . . (201) 721-5263
Counties Represented: Hudson (part)
Term Expires: January 2018
411 Palisades Avenue, Jersey City, NJ 07307
E-mail: senstack@njleg.org
Committees: Budget and Appropriations; Community and Urban
Affairs; Judiciary

Senator **Stephen M. "Steve" Sweeney** (D-District 3) . . . . (609) 292-5215
Counties Represented: Cumberland (part),    Dist: (856) 339-0808
Gloucester (part), Salem                 (Salem)
Term Expires: January 2018       Dist: (856) 251-9801
199 East Broadway, Floor 1, Suite G,    (West Deptford)
Salem, NJ 08079
E-mail: sensweeney@njleg.org

Senator **Samuel D. Thompson** (R-District 12) . . . . . . . . . (732) 607-7580
Counties Represented: Burlington (part), Middlesex (part), Monmouth
(part), Ocean (part)
Term Expires: January 2018
2501 Highway 516, Suite 101, Old Bridge, NJ 08857
E-mail: senthompson@njleg.org
Committees: Budget and Appropriations; Environment and Energy;
Joint Housing Affordability; Joint Public Schools; State Government,
Wagering, Tourism and Historic Preservation
Education: Arkansas BS; LSU PhD

Senator **Shirley K. Turner** (D-District 15) . . . . . . . . . . . . . .(609) 323-7239
  Counties Represented: Hunterdon (part), Mercer (part)
  Term Expires: January 2018
  1440 Pennington Road, Ewing, NJ 08618
  E-mail: senturner@njleg.org
  Committees: Education; State Government, Wagering, Tourism and
  Historic Preservation
  Education: Trenton State BS; Rider MA
Senator
  **Jeff Van Drew** (D-District 1) . . . (609) 465-0700 (Cape May Court House)
  Counties Represented: Atlantic (part), Cape May,      Dist: (856) 765-0891
  Cumberland (part)                                          (Millville)
  Term Expires: January 2018                             Dist: (856) 696-7109
  School House Office Park, 211 S. Main St,                  (Vineland)
  Suite 104, Cape May Court House, NJ 08210
  219 High Street, Suite B, Millville, NJ 08332
  1117 E. Landis Avenue, Vineland, NJ 08360
  E-mail: senvandrew@njleg.org
  Committees: Budget and Appropriations; Community and Urban
  Affairs; Military and Veterans' Affairs
  Education: Rutgers BS; Fairleigh Dickinson DDS
Senator **Joseph F. Vitale** (D-District 19) . . . . . . . . . . . . . . (609) 292-5215
  Counties Represented: Middlesex (part)        Dist: (732) 855-7441
  Term Expires: January 2018
  569 Rahway Avenue, Woodbridge, NJ 07095
  E-mail: senvitale@njleg.org
  Committees: Health, Human Services and Senior Citizens; Labor
  Affiliation: President, Vitale Sign Corporation
Senator **Loretta Weinberg** (D-District 37) . . . . . . . . . . . . . (201) 928-0100
  Counties Represented: Bergen (part)
  Term Expires: January 2018
  545 Cedar Lane, Teaneck, NJ 07666
  E-mail: senweinberg@njleg.org
  Committees: Joint Budget Oversight; Judiciary; Legislative Oversight
Senator **James "Jim" Whelan** (D-District 2) . . . . . . . . . . . (609) 383-1388
  Counties Represented: Atlantic (part)
  Term Expires: January 2018
  511 Tilton Road, Northfield, NJ 08225
  E-mail: senwhelan@njleg.org
  Committees: Economic Growth; Health, Human Services and Senior
  Citizens; State Government, Wagering, Tourism and Historic
  Preservation
  Education: Temple

## Senate Standing Committees
### Budget and Appropriations

| Majority Members | Minority Members |
| --- | --- |
| Paul A. Sarlo (D-36) *Chair* | Jennifer Beck (R-11) |
| Brian P. Stack (D-33) *Vice Chair* | Anthony R. Bucco (R-25) |
| Sandra Bolden Cunningham (D-31) | Kevin O'Toole (R-40) |
| Patrick J. Diegnan, Jr. (D-18) | Steven V. Oroho (R-24) |
| Linda R. Greenstein (D-14) | Samuel D. Thompson (R-12) |
| Nellie Pou (D-35) | |
| M. Teresa Ruiz (D-29) | |
| Jeff Van Drew (D-1) | |

### Commerce

| Majority Members | Minority Members |
| --- | --- |
| Nia H. Gill (D-34) *Chair* | Gerald Cardinale (R-39) |
| Raymond J. Lesniak (D-20) *Vice Chair* | Thomas H. Kean, Jr. (R-21) |
| James Beach (D-6) | |
| Nicholas P. Scutari (D-22) | |

### Community and Urban Affairs

| Majority Members | Minority Members |
| --- | --- |
| Jeff Van Drew (D-1) *Chair* | Jennifer Beck (R-11) |
| Ronald L. Rice, Jr. (D-28) *Vice Chair* | Christopher J. Connors (R-9) |
| Brian P. Stack (D-33) | |

### Economic Growth

| Majority Members | Minority Members |
| --- | --- |
| Raymond J. Lesniak (D-20) *Chair* | Joseph M. "Joe" Kyrillos, Jr. (R-13) |
| Nilsa J. Cruz-Perez (D-5) *Vice Chair* | Steven V. Oroho (R-24) |
| James "Jim" Whelan (D-2) | |

### Education

| Majority Members | Minority Members |
| --- | --- |
| M. Teresa Ruiz (D-29) *Chair* | Diane B. Allen (R-7) |
| Shirley K. Turner (D-15) *Vice Chair* | Michael J. Doherty (R-23) |
| James Beach (D-6) | |

### Environment and Energy

| Majority Members | Minority Members |
| --- | --- |
| Bob Smith (D-17) *Chair* | Christopher "Kip" Bateman (R-16) |
| Linda R. Greenstein (D-14) *Vice Chair* | Samuel D. Thompson (R-12) |
| Richard J. Codey (D-27) | |

### Health, Human Services and Senior Citizens

| Majority Members | Minority Members |
| --- | --- |
| Joseph F. Vitale (D-19) *Chair* | Dawn Marie Addiego (R-8) |
| Fred H. Madden, Jr. (D-4) *Vice Chair* | Diane B. Allen (R-7) |
| Robert M. Gordon (D-38) | Robert W. Singer (R-30) |
| Ronald L. Rice, Jr. (D-28) | |
| James "Jim" Whelan (D-2) | |

### Higher Education

| Majority Members | Minority Members |
| --- | --- |
| Sandra Bolden Cunningham (D-31) *Chair* | Thomas H. Kean, Jr. (R-21) |
| Nellie Pou (D-35) *Vice Chair* | Robert W. Singer (R-30) |
| Paul A. Sarlo (D-36) | |

### Judiciary

| Majority Members | Minority Members |
| --- | --- |
| Nicholas P. Scutari (D-22) *Chair* | Christopher "Kip" Bateman (R-16) |
| Nia H. Gill (D-34) *Vice Chair* | Gerald Cardinale (R-39) |
| Raymond J. Lesniak (D-20) | Michael J. Doherty (R-23) |
| Nellie Pou (D-35) | Joseph M. "Joe" Kyrillos, Jr. (R-13) |
| Paul A. Sarlo (D-36) | Kevin O'Toole (R-40) |
| Bob Smith (D-17) | |
| Brian P. Stack (D-33) | |
| Loretta Weinberg (D-37) | |

### Labor

| Majority Members | Minority Members |
| --- | --- |
| Fred H. Madden, Jr. (D-4) *Chair* | Dawn Marie Addiego (R-8) |
| Joseph F. Vitale (D-19) *Vice Chair* | Anthony R. Bucco (R-25) |
| Sandra Bolden Cunningham (D-31) | |

### Law and Public Safety

| Majority Members | Minority Members |
| --- | --- |
| Linda R. Greenstein (D-14) *Chair* | Christopher "Kip" Bateman (R-16) |
| Patrick J. Diegnan, Jr. (D-18) *Vice Chair* | James W. Holzapfel (R-10) |
| Nicholas J. Sacco (D-32) | |

### Legislative Oversight

| Majority Members | Minority Members |
| --- | --- |
| Robert M. Gordon (D-38) *Chair* | Thomas H. Kean, Jr. (R-21) |
| Loretta Weinberg (D-37) *Vice Chair* | Joseph M. "Joe" Kyrillos, Jr. (R-13) |
| M. Teresa Ruiz (D-29) | |
| Paul A. Sarlo (D-36) | |

### Military and Veterans' Affairs

| Majority Members | Minority Members |
| --- | --- |
| James Beach (D-6) *Chair* | Diane B. Allen (R-7) |
| Jeff Van Drew (D-1) *Vice Chair* | Christopher J. Connors (R-9) |
| Nilsa J. Cruz-Perez (D-5) | |

### State Government, Wagering, Tourism and Historic Preservation

| Majority Members | Minority Members |
| --- | --- |
| James "Jim" Whelan (D-2) *Chair* | Steven V. Oroho (R-24) |
| Shirley K. Turner (D-15) *Vice Chair* | Samuel D. Thompson (R-12) |
| Patrick J. Diegnan, Jr. (D-18) | |

**LEGISLATIVE BRANCH**

## Transportation

**Majority Members**
Nicholas J. Sacco (D-32) *Chair*
Robert M. Gordon (D-38)
*Vice Chair*
Nilsa J. Cruz-Perez (D-5)

**Minority Members**
James W. Holzapfel (R-10)
Joseph Pennacchio (R-26)

# New Jersey General Assembly

Tel: (609) 847-3905  TTY: (800) 257-7490  Fax: (609) 777-2440

Speaker of the General Assembly **Vincent Prieto** (D) . . . . . (201) 770-1303
  Education: Middlesex County
Speaker Pro Tem **Gerald "Jerry" Green** (D) . . . . . . . . . . .(908) 561-5757
Deputy Speaker Pro Tempore **Daniel R. Benson** (D). . . . . .(609) 631-0198
  Education: Georgetown BS; Rutgers MPP
Speaker Emeritus **Sheila Y. Oliver** (D) . . . . . . . . . . . . . . (973) 395-1166
  Education: Lincoln U (PA) BA; Columbia 1976 MS
Deputy Speaker **John J. Burzichelli** (D) . . . . . . . . . . . . . . (856) 251-9801
Deputy Speaker **Wayne P. DeAngelo** (D). . . . . . . . . . . . .(609) 631-7501
Deputy Speaker **Gordon M. Johnson** (D) . . . . . . . . . . . . . (201) 530-0469
  Education: Aquinas Col BS; Seton Hall MA
Deputy Speaker **Pamela Rosen Lampitt** (D) . . . . . . . . . . (856) 435-1247
Deputy Speaker **Gary S. Schaer** (D). . . . . . . . . . . . . . . . .(973) 249-3665
  Education: American U
Deputy Speaker **L. Grace Spencer** (D). . . . . . . . . . . . . . .(973) 624-1730
Deputy Speaker **Valerie Vainieri Huttle** (D) . . . . . . . . . .(201) 541-1118
  Education: Fairleigh Dickinson BA
Deputy Speaker **Benjie E. Wimberly** (D) . . . . . . . . . . . . .(973) 925-7061
Deputy Speaker **John S. Wisniewski** (D) . . . . . . . . . . . . . (732) 432-8460
  Education: Rutgers BA; Seton Hall JD
Majority Leader **Louis D. Greenwald** (D) . . . . . . . . . . . . (856) 435-1247
  Education: Moravian BA; Seton Hall JD
Deputy Majority Leader **Joseph V. Egan** (D) . . . . . . . . . . (732) 249-4550
Deputy Majority Leader **Thomas P. Giblin** (D) . . . . . . . . .(973) 779-3125
  Education: Seton Hall BA
Deputy Majority Leader **Reed Gusciora** (D) . . . . . . . . . . . (609) 571-9638
  Education: Catholic U BA; Seton Hall JD
Deputy Majority Leader **Angelica M. Jimenez** (D) . . . . . . (201) 223-4247
Deputy Majority Leader **Annette Quijano** (D) . . . . . . . . . (908) 327-9119
Majority Conference Leader **Shavonda E. Sumter** (D) . . . (973) 925-7061
  Education: Kean U BA; Fairleigh Dickinson MBA
Deputy Conference Leader **Timothy J. Eustace** (D) . . . . . . (201) 576-9199
  Education: Ramapo 1978 BS
Deputy Parliamentarian **Craig J. Coughlin** (D) . . . . . . . . (732) 855-7441
Majority Whip **Herbert C. "Herb" Conaway, Jr.** (D) . . . . .(856) 461-3997
  Education: Princeton BA; Jefferson Col MD; Rutgers JD
Deputy Majority Whip **Ralph R. Caputo** (D). . . . . . . . . . .(973) 450-0484
  Education: Bloomfield 1963 BA; Seton Hall MS
Minority Leader **Jon M. Bramnick** (R) . . . . . . . . . . . . . .(908) 232-2073
  Education: Syracuse 1975 BA; Hofstra 1978 JD
Minority Conference Leader **David P. Rible** (R) . . . . . . . . (732) 974-0400
Deputy Minority Leader
  **Anthony M. "Tony" Bucco, Jr.** (R) . . . . . . . . . . . . (973) 927-2526
Deputy Minority Leader **Amy H. Handlin** (R) . . . . . . . . . (732) 383-7820
  Education: Harvard BA; Columbia MBA; NYU PhD
Deputy Minority Leader **David W. Wolfe** (R) . . . . . . . . . . (732) 840-9028
  Education: Westminster (PA) BA; Delaware MEd
Assistant Minority Leader **Chris A. Brown** (R) . . . . . . . . . (609) 677-8266
Parliamentarian **Michael Patrick Carroll** (R) . . . . . . . . . (973) 539-8113
  Education: Johns Hopkins BA; Rutgers JD
Minority Policy Co-Chair **DiAnne C. Gove** (R) . . . . . . . . .(609) 693-6700
Minority Policy Co-Chair **Brian E. Rumpf** (R). . . . . . . . . (609) 693-6700
  Education: Catholic U BA; Washington and Lee JD
Assistant Minority Whip **Jack M. Ciattarelli** (R). . . . . . . . (908) 450-7064
  Education: Seton Hall BS, MBA
Assistant Minority Whip **Erik C. Peterson** (R). . . . . . . . . .(908) 238-0251
Minority Whip **Scott T. Rumana** (R) . . . . . . . . . . . . . . . .(973) 237-1362
  Education: Hartwick 1987 BA; New York Law 1991 JD
Budget Officer **Declan J. O'Scanlon, Jr.** (R). . . . . . . . . . .(732) 933-1591
Appropriations Officer **John DiMaio** (R) . . . . . . . . . . . . .(908) 722-1365
Clerk of the General Assembly **Dana M. Burley** (D). . . . . .(609) 847-3115
  E-mail: dburley@njleg.org
  Education: Spelman BS

# Assembly Members

**Party Affiliation Statistics:** Republicans: 28, Democrats: 52

Assembly Member
  **Robert "Bob" Andrzejczak** (D-District 1) . . (609) 465-0700 (Cape May)
  Counties Represented: Atlantic (part), Cape May,    Dist: (856) 765-0891
  Cumberland (part)                                  (Millville)
  Term Expires: 2018
  211 S. Main St, Suite 104, Cape May Court House, NJ 08210
  219 High Street, Suite B, Millville, NJ 08332
  1117 E. Landis Avenue, Vineland, NJ 08360
  E-mail: asmandrzejczak@njleg.org
  Committees: Agriculture and Natural Resources; Military and Veterans'
  Affairs
Assembly Member **Robert "Bob" Auth** (R-District 39) . . . (862) 248-0491
  Counties Represented: Bergen (part), Passaic (part)
  Term Expires: 2018
  1069 Ringwood Avenue, Suite 312, Haskell, NJ 07420
  E-mail: asmauth@njleg.org
  Committees: Commerce and Economic Development; Education;
  Financial Institutions and Insurance
Assembly Member **Arthur Barclay** (D-District 5) . . . . . . . (856) 541-1251
  Counties Represented: Camden (part), Gloucester (part)
  Term Expires: 2018
  515 White Horse Pike, Audubon, NJ 08106
  231 Market Street, Camden, NJ 08102
  E-mail: asmbarclay@njleg.org
  Committees: Higher Education; Law and Public Safety
Assembly Member **Daniel R. Benson** (D-District 14) . . . . . (609) 631-0198
  Counties Represented: Mercer (part), Middlesex (part)
  Term Expires: 2018
  3691A Nottingham Way, Hamilton Square, NJ 08690
  E-mail: asmbenson@njleg.org
  Committees: Health and Senior Services; Law and Public Safety;
  Transportation and Independent Authorities
Assembly Member
  **Jon M. Bramnick** (R-District 21) . . . . . . . . . . .(908) 232-2073 (Westfield)
  Counties Represented: Morris (part), Somerset (part), Union (part)
  Term Expires: 2018
  251 North Avenue West, 2nd Floor, Westfield, NJ 07090
  E-mail: asmbramnick@njleg.org
Assembly Member **Chris A. Brown** (R-District 2) . . . . . . . (609) 677-8266
  Counties Represented: Atlantic (part)
  Term Expires: 2018
  2021 New Road, Suite 24, Linwood, NJ 08221
  E-mail: asmchrisabrown@njleg.org
  Committees: Regulatory Oversight and Reform and Federal Relations;
  Tourism and Gaming and the Arts
Assembly Member
  **Anthony M. "Tony" Bucco, Jr.** (R-District 25) . . . . . . . (973) 927-2526
  Counties Represented: Morris (part), Somerset (part)
  Term Expires: 2018
  1040 Route 10 West, Randolph, NJ 07869
  E-mail: asmbucco@njleg.org
  Committees: Budget; Commerce and Economic Development
Assembly Member
  **John J. Burzichelli** (D-District 3) . . . . . . . . . . . . .(856) 339-0808 (Salem)
  Counties Represented: Cumberland (part),    Dist: (856) 251-9801
  Gloucester (part), Salem                  (West Depford)
  Term Expires: 2018
  199 East Broadway, Suite G, Salem, NJ 08079
  935 Kings Highway, Suite 400, West Depford, NJ 08086
  E-mail: asmburzichelli@njleg.org
  Committees: Appropriations; Budget; Joint Budget Oversight; Tourism
  and Gaming and the Arts
Assembly Member **Ralph R. Caputo** (D-District 28) . . . . . .(973) 450-0484
  Counties Represented: Essex (part)
  Term Expires: 2018
  148-152 Franklin Street, Belleville, NJ 07109
  E-mail: asmcaputo@njleg.org
  Committees: Education; Joint Public Schools; Tourism and Gaming and
  the Arts
Assembly Member **Marlene Caride** (D-District 36) . . . . . . . (201) 943-0615
  Counties Represented: Bergen (part), Passaic (part)
  Term Expires: 2018
  613 Bergen Boulevard, Ridgefield, NJ 07657
  E-mail: aswcaride@njleg.org
  Committees: Financial Institutions and Insurance; Transportation and
  Independent Authorities

Assembly Member
**Michael Patrick Carroll** (R-District 25) . . . . . . . . . . . . . . (973) 539-8113
Counties Represented: Morris (part), Somerset (part)
Term Expires: 2018
146 Speedwell Avenue, Morris Plains, NJ 07950
E-mail: AsmCarroll@njleg.org
Committees: Judiciary; Law and Public Safety; State and Local
Government

Assembly Member **Annette Chaparro** (D-District 33) . . . . (201) 683-7917
Counties Represented: Hudson (part)
Term Expires: 2018
80 River Street, 2nd Floor, Hoboken, NJ 07030
E-mail: asmchaparro@njleg.org
Committees: Homeland Security and State Preparedness; Law and
Public Safety

Assembly Member
**Nicholas A. Chiaravalloti** (D-District 31) . . . . . . . . . . . . . (201) 471-2347
Counties Represented: Hudson (part)
Term Expires: 2018
836 Broadway, Bayonne, NJ 07002
E-mail: asmchiaravalloti@njleg.org
Committees: Commerce and Economic Development; Transportation
and Independent Authorities
Education: Catholic U 1994 BA; Rutgers (Newark) 1997 JD

Assembly Member **Jack M. Ciattarelli** (R-District 16) . . . . (908) 450-7064
Counties Represented: Hunterdon (part), Mercer (part), Middlesex
(part), Somerset (part)
Term Expires: 2018
50 Division Street, Suite 200, Somerville, NJ 08876
E-mail: asmciattarelli@njleg.org
Committees: Financial Institutions and Insurance; Regulated Professions

Assembly Member **Robert D. Clifton** (R-District 12) . . . . . (732) 970-6386
Counties Represented: Burlington (part), Middlesex (part), Monmouth
(part), Ocean (part)
Term Expires: 2018
935 Highway 34, Suite 3B, Matawan, NJ 07747
E-mail: asmclifton@njleg.org
Committees: Higher Education; Housing and Community Development;
Transportation and Independent Authorities

Assembly Member
**Herbert C. "Herb" Conaway, Jr.** (D-District 7) . . . . . . . . (856) 461-3997
Counties Represented: Burlington (part)
Term Expires: 2018
Delran Professional Center, Building C, 8008 Route 130 North,
Suite 450, Delran, NJ 08075
E-mail: asmconaway@njleg.org
Committees: Appropriations; Health and Senior Services; State and
Local Government

Assembly Member **Craig J. Coughlin** (D-District 19) . . . . . (732) 855-7441
Counties Represented: Middlesex (part)
Term Expires: 2018
569 Rahway Avenue, Woodbridge, NJ 07095
E-mail: asmcoughlin@njleg.org
Committees: Commerce and Economic Development; Financial
Institutions and Insurance; Labor

Assembly Member **Ronald S. Dancer** (R-District 12) . . . . . (609) 758-0205
Counties Represented: Burlington (part), Middlesex (part), Monmouth
(part), Ocean (part)
Term Expires: 2018
2110 West County Line Road, Jackson, NJ 08527
E-mail: asmdancer@njleg.org
Committees: Agriculture and Natural Resources; Labor; Tourism and
Gaming and the Arts
Education: Wesley Col (DE); Rutgers

Assembly Member
**Joseph "Joe" Danielsen** (D-District 17) . . . . . . . . . . . . . (732) 247-3999
Counties Represented: Middlesex (part), Somerset     Fax: (732) 247-4383
(part)
Term Expires: 2018
334 Elizabeth Avenue, Somerset, NJ 08873
E-mail: asmdanielsen@njleg.org
Committees: Financial Institutions and Insurance; Law and Public
Safety

Assembly Member **Wayne P. DeAngelo** (D-District 14) . . . (609) 631-7501
Counties Represented: Mercer (part), Middlesex (part)
Term Expires: 2018
4621A Nottingham Way, Hamilton Square, NJ 08690
E-mail: asmdeangelo@njleg.org
Committees: Military and Veterans' Affairs; Telecommunications and
Utilities

Assembly Member **BettyLou DeCroce** (R-District 26) . . . . (973) 265-0057
Counties Represented: Essex (part), Morris (part), Passaic (part)
Term Expires: 2018
1055 Parsippany Boulevard, Suite104, Parsippany, NJ 07054
E-mail: aswdecroce@njleg.org
Committees: Commerce and Economic Development; Health and
Senior Services; Joint Public Schools; Transportation and Independent
Authorities

Assembly Member **John DiMaio** (R-District 23) . . . . . . . . (908) 722-1365
Counties Represented: Hunterdon (part), Somerset (part), Warren (part)
Term Expires: 2018
245 Route 22, Suite 208, Bridgewater, NJ 08807
E-mail: asmdimaio@njleg.org
Committees: Appropriations; Budget

Assembly Member **Joann Downey** (D-District 11) . . . . . . . (732) 695-3371
Counties Represented: Monmouth (part)          Dist: (732) 333-0166
Term Expires: 2018
802 West Park Avenue, Suite 221, Ocean, NJ 07712
35 West Main Street, 1st Floor, Freehold, NJ 07728
E-mail: asmdowney@njleg.org
Committees: Financial Institutions and Insurance; Regulated
Professions; Women and Children

Assembly Member **Joseph V. Egan** (D-District 17) . . . . . . (732) 249-4550
Counties Represented: Middlesex (part), Somerset (part)
Term Expires: 2018
100 Bayard Street, New Brunswick, NJ 08901
E-mail: AsmEgan@njleg.org
Committees: Labor; Telecommunications and Utilities

Assembly Member **Timothy J. Eustace** (D-District 38) . . . (201) 576-9199
Counties Represented: Bergen (part), Passaic (part)     Fax: (201) 576-9432
Term Expires: 2018
205 Robin Road, Suite 222, Paramus, NJ 07652
E-mail: asmeustace@njleg.org
Committees: Commerce and Economic Development; Health and
Senior Services; State and Local Government

Assembly Member **Thomas P. Giblin** (D-District 34) . . . . . (973) 779-3125
Counties Represented: Essex (part), Passaic (part)
Term Expires: 2018
1333 Broad Street, Clifton, NJ 07013
E-mail: asmgiblin@njleg.org
Committees: Higher Education; Joint State Leasing and Space
Utilization; Regulated Professions; Transportation and Independent
Authorities

Assembly Member **DiAnne C. Gove** (R-District 9) . . . . . . . (609) 693-6700
Counties Represented: Atlantic (part), Burlington (part), Ocean (part)
Term Expires: 2018
620 West Lacey Road, Forked River, NJ 08731
E-mail: aswgove@njleg.org
Committees: Higher Education; Military and Veterans' Affairs

Assembly Member
**Gerald "Jerry" Green** (D-District 22) . . . . . . . . . . . . . . . (908) 561-5757
Counties Represented: Middlesex (part), Somerset (part), Union (part)
Term Expires: 2018
200 West Second Avenue, Suite 102, Plainfield, NJ 07060
E-mail: asmgreen@njleg.org
Committees: Health and Senior Services; Housing and Community
Development; Joint Housing Affordability

Assembly Member **Louis D. Greenwald** (D-District 6) . . . . (856) 435-1247
Counties Represented: Burlington (part), Camden (part)
Term Expires: 2018
1101 Laurel Oak Road, Suite 150, Voorhees, NJ 08043
E-mail: asmgreenwald@njleg.org

Assembly Member **Reed Gusciora** (D-District 15) . . . . . . . (609) 571-9638
Counties Represented: Hunterdon (part), Mercer (part)
Term Expires: 2018
144 W. State Street, Trenton, NJ 08608
E-mail: asmgusciora@njleg.org
E-mail: reednj15@aol.com
Committees: Financial Institutions and Insurance; Labor; Regulatory
Oversight and Reform and Federal Relations

Assembly Member **Amy H. Handlin** (R-District 13) . . . . . . (732) 383-7820
Counties Represented: Monmouth (part)
Term Expires: 2018
225 Route 35, Suite 202, Red Bank, NJ 07701
E-mail: aswhandlin@njleg.org
Committees: Financial Institutions and Insurance; Regulated Professions

*(continued on next page)*

LEGISLATIVE BRANCH

**Assembly Members** *continued*

Assembly Member

**Jamel C. Holley** (D-District 20) . . . . . . . . . . . . (908) 624-0880 (Union)
Counties Represented: Union (part)                     Dist: (908) 327-9119
Term Expires: 2018                                                    (Elizabeth)
985 Stuyesent Avenue, Union, NJ 07083            Fax: (908) 624-0587
E-mail: asmholley@njleg.org                                          (Union)
Committees: Higher Education; Housing and Community Development;
Women and Children
Education: New Jersey City U BA; Kean U MPA

Assembly Member **Eric Houghtaling** (D-District 11) . . . . . (732) 695-3371
Counties Represented: Monmouth (part)
Term Expires: 2018
802 West Park Avenue, Suite 221, Ocean, NJ 07712
35 West Main Street, 1st Floor, Freehold, NJ 07728
E-mail: asmhoughtaling@njleg.org
Committees: Agriculture and Natural Resources; Labor;
Telecommunications and Utilities

Assembly Member **Joe Howarth** (R-District 8) . . . . . . . . . (609) 654-1498
Counties Represented: Atlantic (part), Burlington (part), Camden (part)
Term Expires: 2018
176 Route 70, Suite 13, Medford, NJ 08055
E-mail: asmhowarth@njleg.org
Committees: Financial Institutions and Insurance; Human Services;
Military and Veterans' Affairs

Assembly Member **Mila M. Jasey** (D-District 27) . . . . . . . . (973) 762-1886
Counties Represented: Essex (part), Morris (part)
Term Expires: 2018
511 Valley Street, Maplewood, NJ 07040
E-mail: aswjasey@njleg.org
Committees: Education; Higher Education; Housing and Community
Development; Joint Public Schools

Assembly Member **Angelica M. Jimenez** (D-District 32) . . . . . . . . (201)
223-4247
Counties Represented: Bergen (part), Hudson (part)
Term Expires: 2018
5600 Kennedy Boulevard, Suite 104, West New York, NJ 07093
E-mail: aswjimenez@njleg.org
Committees: Education; Health and Senior Services; Regulated
Professions

Assembly Member

**Gordon M. Johnson** (D-District 37) . . . . . . . . (201) 530-0469 (Teaneck)
Counties Represented: Bergen (part)
Term Expires: 2018
545 Cedar Lane, Teaneck, NJ 07666
E-mail: asmjohnson@njleg.org
Committees: Budget; Commerce and Economic Development; Judiciary

Assembly Member

**Patricia Egan Jones** (D-District 5) . . . . . . . . (856) 547-4800 (Audubon)
Counties Represented: Camden (part), Gloucester      Dist: (856) 541-1251
(part)                                                               (Camden)
Term Expires: 2018                                     Dist: (856) 853-2960
Gloucester County Justice Complex Annex,                    (Woodbury)
114 North Broad Street, Woodbury, NJ 08096
231 Market Street, Camden, NJ 08102
515 White Horse Pike, Audubon, NJ 08106
E-mail: asmjones@njleg.org
Committees: Education; Housing and Community Development;
Human Services

Assembly Member **Robert J. Karabinchak** (D) . . . . . . . . . (732) 548-1406
Term Expires: 2018
3 Stephenville Parkway, Suite 2D, Edison, NJ 08820

Assembly Member **Sean T. Kean** (R-District 30) . . . . . . . . (732) 974-0400
Counties Represented: Monmouth (part), Ocean (part)
Term Expires: 2018
Building 2A, 1955 Highway 34, Wall, NJ 07719
E-mail: asmskean@njleg.org
Committees: Consumer Affairs; Regulated Professions
Education: Seton Hall BA; Columbia MALS; Seton Hall JD

Assembly Member **James J. Kennedy** (D-District 22) . . . . (732) 943-2660
Counties Represented: Middlesex (part), Somerset (part), Union (part)
Term Expires: 2018
E-mail: asmkennedy@njleg.org
Committees: Health and Senior Services; Transportation and
Independent Authorities

Assembly Member

**Joseph Lagana** (D-District 38) . . . . . . . . . . . . (201) 576-9199 (Paramus)
Counties Represented: Bergen (part), Passaic (part)    Tel: (201) 374-2205
Term Expires: 2018                                               (Bergenfield)
205 Robin Road, Suite 222, Paramus, NJ 07652
35 South Washington Street, Bergenfield, NJ 07671
E-mail: asmlagana@njleg.org
Committees: Appropriations; Financial Institutions and Insurance;
Judiciary
Education: Fordham BA; Thomas M Cooley JD

Assembly Member

**Pamela Rosen Lampitt** (D-District 6) . . . . . . . . . . . . . . . (856) 435-1247
Counties Represented: Burlington (part), Camden (part)
Term Expires: 2018
1101 Laurel Oak Road, Suite 150, Voorhees, NJ 08043
E-mail: aswlampitt@njleg.org
Committees: Appropriations; Financial Institutions and Insurance; Joint
Housing Affordability; Women and Children

Assembly Member **R. Bruce Land** (D-District 1) . . . . . . . . (856) 839-0305
Counties Represented: Atlantic (part), Cape May, Cumberland (part)
Term Expires: 2018
E-mail: asmland@njleg.org
Committees: Homeland Security and State Preparedness; Military and
Veterans' Affairs; Tourism and Gaming and the Arts

Assembly Member

**Vincent "Vince" Mazzeo** (D-District 2) . . . . . . . . . . . . . (609) 383-1388
Counties Represented: Atlantic (part)
Term Expires: 2018
507 Tilton Road, Northfield, NJ 08225
E-mail: asmmazzeo@njleg.org
Committees: Regulated Professions; Tourism and Gaming and the Arts
Education: Glassboro State BS

Assembly Member **Gregory P. McGuckin** (R-District 10) . . (732) 840-9028
Counties Represented: Ocean (part)
Term Expires: 2018
852 Highway 70, Brick, NJ 08724
E-mail: asmmcguckin@njleg.org
Committees: Homeland Security and State Preparedness; Transportation
and Independent Authorities

Assembly Member **John F. McKeon** (D-District 27) . . . . . . (973) 377-1606
Counties Represented: Essex (part), Morris (part)
Term Expires: 2018
221 Main Street, Madison, NJ 07940
E-mail: asmmckeon@njleg.org
Committees: Budget; Environment and Solid Waste; Financial
Institutions and Insurance; Judiciary
Education: Muhlenberg 1980 BA; Seton Hall 1983 JD

Assembly Member **Angela V. McKnight** (D-District 31) . . (201) 360-2502
Counties Represented: Hudson (part)
Term Expires: 2018
2324 John F. Kennedy Boulevard, Jersey City, NJ 07304
E-mail: asmmcknight@njleg.org
Committees: Education; Health and Senior Services; Human Services
Education: U Phoenix 2007 BS

Assembly Member **Paul D. Moriarty** (D-District 4) . . . . . . (856) 232-6700
Counties Represented: Camden (part), Gloucester (part)
Term Expires: 2018
129 Johnson Road, Suite 1, Turnersville, NJ 08012
E-mail: asmmoriarty@njleg.org
Committees: Consumer Affairs; Regulated Professions; Transportation
and Independent Authorities

Assembly Member **Gabriela Mosquera** (D-District 4) . . . . (856) 232-6700
Counties Represented: Camden (part), Gloucester      Dist: (856) 401-3073
(part)
Term Expires: 2018
129 Johnson Road, Suite 1, Turnersville, NJ 08012
1379 Chews Landing, Laurel Springs, NJ 08021
E-mail: aswmosquera@njleg.org
Committees: Appropriations; Higher Education; Women and Children

Assembly Member **Raj Mukherji** (D-District 33) . . . . . . . . (201) 626-4000
Counties Represented: Hudson (part)
Term Expires: 2018
433 Palisade Avenue, Jersey City, NJ 07307
E-mail: asmmukherji@njleg.org
Committees: Budget; Commerce and Economic Development; Labor

Assembly Member
**Nancy F. Munoz** (R-District 21) . . . . . . . . . . . (908) 918-0414 (Summitt)
Counties Represented: Morris (part), Somerset    Tel: (908) 232-3673
(part), Union (part)    (Westfield)
Term Expires: 2018    Tel: (908) 232-2073
57 Union Place, Suite 310, Summit, NJ 07901    (Westfield)
E-mail: aswmunoz@njleg.org
Committees: Commerce and Economic Development; Health and
Senior Services; Women and Children

Assembly Member
**Elizabeth Maher "Liz" Muoio** (D-District 15) . . . . . . . . (609) 571-9638
Counties Represented: Hunterdon (part), Mercer (part)
Term Expires: 2018
144 W. State Street, Trenton, NJ 08608
E-mail: aswmuoio@njleg.org
Committees: Budget; Commerce and Economic Development; Judiciary
Education: Wesleyan U BA; Georgetown JD

Assembly Member
**Declan J. O'Scanlon, Jr.** (R-District 13) . . . . (732) 933-1591 (Red Bank)
Counties Represented: Monmouth (part)
Term Expires: 2018
32 Monmouth Street, 3rd Floor, Red Bank, NJ 07701
E-mail: asmoscanlon@njleg.org
Committees: Budget; Joint Budget Oversight

Assembly Member **Sheila Y. Oliver** (D-District 34) . . . . . . . (973) 395-1166
Counties Represented: Essex (part), Passaic (part)
Term Expires: 2018
15-33 Halsted Street, Suite 202, East Orange, NJ 07018
E-mail: aswoliver@njleg.org
Committees: Commerce and Economic Development; Joint Public
Schools; Transportation and Independent Authorities
Affiliation: Assistant County Administrator, Office of the County
Administrator, County of Essex, New Jersey
Hall of Records, 465 Dr. Martin Luther King, Jr. Boulevard,
Room 510, Newark, NJ 07102

Assembly Member **Erik C. Peterson** (R-District 23) . . . . . . (908) 238-0251
Counties Represented: Hunterdon (part), Somerset (part), Warren (part)
Term Expires: 2018
178 Center Street, Suite 2B, Clinton, NJ 08809
E-mail: asmpeterson@njleg.org
Committees: Health and Senior Services; Judiciary; Law and Public
Safety

Assembly Member **Gail Phoebus** (R-District 24) . . . . . . . . (973) 300-0200
Counties Represented: Morris (part), Sussex,    Dist: (908) 441-6343
Warren (part)
Term Expires: 2018
One Wilson Drive, Suite 2B, Sparta, NJ 07871
1001 Route 517, Allamuchy, NJ 07820
P.O. Box 184, Allamuchy, NJ 07820
E-mail: asmphoebus@njleg.org
Committees: Appropriations; Human Services; Regulatory Oversight
and Reform and Federal Relations; Telecommunications and Utilities

Assembly Member **Nancy J. Pinkin** (D-District 18) . . . . . . (732) 548-1406
Counties Represented: Middlesex (part)
Term Expires: 2018
3 Stephenville Parkway, Suite 2D, Edison, NJ 08820
E-mail: aswpinkin@njleg.org
Committees: Health and Senior Services; Homeland Security and State
Preparedness; Law and Public Safety
Education: NYU MPA

Assembly Member **Eliana Pintor-Marin** (D-District 29) . . . (973) 589-0713
Counties Represented: Essex (part)
Term Expires: 2018
263 Lafayette Street, 1st Floor, Newark, NJ 07105
E-mail: aswpintormarin@njleg.org
Committees: Budget; Commerce and Economic Development;
Telecommunications and Utilities

Assembly Member **Vincent Prieto** (D-District 32) . . . . . . . . (201) 770-1303
Counties Represented: Bergen (part), Hudson (part)
Term Expires: 2018
1 Harmon Plaza, Suite 205, Secaucus, NJ 07094
E-mail: asmprieto@njleg.org

Assembly Member **Annette Quijano** (D-District 20) . . . . . . (908) 327-9119
Counties Represented: Union (part)
Term Expires: 2018
65 Jefferson Avenue, Suite B, Elizabeth, NJ 07201
985 Stuyesent Avenue, Union, NJ 07083
E-mail: aswquijano@njleg.org
Committees: Appropriations; Consumer Affairs; Homeland Security and
State Preparedness

Assembly Member **David P. Rible** (R-District 30) . . . . . . . (732) 974-0400
Counties Represented: Monmouth (part), Ocean (part)
Term Expires: 2018
1967 Highway 34 Building C, Suite 202, Wall, NJ 07719
E-mail: asmrible@njleg.org
Committees: Education; Higher Education; Joint Public Schools; Law
and Public Safety

Assembly Member
**Maria Rodriguez-Gregg** (R-District 8) . . . . . . . . . . . . . (609) 654-1498
Counties Represented: Atlantic (part), Burlington (part), Camden (part)
Term Expires: 2018
176 Route 70, Suite 13, Medford, NJ 08055
E-mail: aswrodriguezgregg@njleg.org
Committees: Budget; Housing and Community Development

Assembly Member **Scott T. Rumana** (R-District 40) . . . . . (973) 237-1362
Counties Represented: Bergen (part), Essex (part), Morris (part),
Passaic (part)
Term Expires: 2018
Wayne Plaza II, 155 Route 46 West, Suite 108, Wayne, NJ 07470
E-mail: asmrumana@njleg.org
Committees: Environment and Solid Waste; Transportation and
Independent Authorities

Assembly Member **Brian E. Rumpf** (R-District 9) . . . . . . . . (609) 693-6700
Counties Represented: Atlantic (part), Burlington (part), Ocean (part)
Term Expires: 2018
620 West Lacey Road, Forked River, NJ 08731
E-mail: asmrumpf@njleg.org
Committees: Regulatory Oversight and Reform and Federal Relations;
Telecommunications and Utilities

Assembly Member **David C. Russo** (R-District 40) . . . . . . (201) 444-9719
Counties Represented: Bergen (part), Essex (part), Morris (part),
Passaic (part)
Term Expires: 2018
201C Franklin Avenue, Midland Park, NJ 07432
E-mail: asmrusso@njleg.org
Committees: Homeland Security and State Preparedness
Affiliation: Attorney, Russo & Russo
Education: William & Mary BA; Seton Hall JD

Assembly Member **Gary S. Schaer** (D-District 36) . . . . . . (973) 249-3665
Counties Represented: Bergen (part), Passaic (part)
Term Expires: 2018
1 Howe Avenue, Suite 401, Passaic, NJ 07055
E-mail: asmschaer@njleg.org
Committees: Appropriations; Budget; Higher Education; Joint Budget
Oversight

Assembly Member **Holly Schepisi** (R-District 39) . . . . . . . . (201) 666-0881
Counties Represented: Bergen (part), Passaic (part)    Fax: (201) 666-5255
Term Expires: 2018
287 Kinderkamack Road, Westwood, NJ 07675
E-mail: aswschepisi@njleg.org
Committees: Appropriations; Health and Senior Services

Assembly Member **Troy E. Singleton** (D-District 7) . . . . . . (856) 234-2790
Counties Represented: Burlington (part)
Term Expires: 2018
400 N. Church Stree, Suite 260, Moorestown, NJ 08057
E-mail: asmsingleton@njleg.org
Committees: Budget; Education; State and Local Government
Education: Rowan

Assembly Member **F. Parker Space** (R-District 24) . . . . . . . (973) 300-0200
Counties Represented: Morris (part), Sussex,    Dist: (908) 441-6343
Warren (part)
Term Expires: 2018
One Wilson Drive, 2B, Sparta, NJ 07871
E-mail: asmspace@njleg.org
Committees: Agriculture and Natural Resources; Labor

Assembly Member **L. Grace Spencer** (D-District 29) . . . . . (973) 624-1730
Counties Represented: Essex (part)
Term Expires: 2018
223 Hawthorne Avenue, Newark, NJ 07112
E-mail: aswspencer@njleg.org
Committees: Appropriations; Environment and Solid Waste; Financial
Institutions and Insurance

Assembly Member **Shavonda E. Sumter** (D-District 35) . . (973) 925-7061
Counties Represented: Bergen (part), Passaic (part)
Term Expires: 2018
191 Market Street, Paterson, NJ 07505
E-mail: aswsumter@njleg.org
Committees: Health and Senior Services; Labor; Law and Public Safety

*(continued on next page)*

LEGISLATIVE BRANCH

**LEGISLATIVE BRANCH**

**Assembly Members** *continued*

Assembly Member
**Adam Joseph Taliaferro** (D-District 3) . . . . . . . (856) 339-0808 (Salem)
Counties Represented: Cumberland (part),            Tel: (856) 251-9801
Gloucester (part), Salem                                   (West Deptford)
Term Expires: 2018
935 Kings Highway, Suite 400, West Depford, NJ 08086
199 East Broadway, First floor, Suite G, Salem, NJ 08079
E-mail: asmtaliaferro@njleg.org
Committees: Agriculture and Natural Resources; Education
Education: Penn State 2005 BS; Rutgers JD

Assembly Member **Cleopatra G. Tucker** (D-District 28) . . . (973) 926-4320
Counties Represented: Essex (part)
Term Expires: 2018
400 Lyons Avenue, Newark, NJ 07112
E-mail: aswtucker@njleg.org
Committees: Human Services; Military and Veterans' Affairs;
Regulatory Oversight and Reform and Federal Relations

Assembly Member
**Valerie Vainieri Huttle** (D-District 37) . . . . . . . . . . . . . (201) 541-1118
Counties Represented: Bergen (part)             Dist: (201) 928-0100
Term Expires: 2018
One Engle Street, Suite 108, Englewood, NJ 07631
E-mail: aswvainierihuttle@njleg.org
Committees: Human Services; Tourism and Gaming and the Arts;
Transportation and Independent Authorities

Assembly Member **Jay Webber** (R-District 26) . . . . . . . . . . (973) 265-0057
Counties Represented: Essex (part), Morris (part), Passaic (part)
Term Expires: 2018
1055 Parsippany Boulevard, Suite 104, Parsippany, NJ 07054
E-mail: asmwebber@njleg.org
Committees: Labor; State and Local Government

Assembly Member **Benjie E. Wimberly** (D-District 35) . . . (973) 925-7061
Counties Represented: Bergen (part), Passaic (part)
Term Expires: 2018
191 Market Street, Paterson, NJ 07505
E-mail: asmwimberly@njleg.org
Committees: Budget; Joint Public Schools; Regulatory Oversight and
Reform and Federal Relations; Telecommunications and Utilities

Assembly Member **John S. Wisniewski** (D-District 19) . . . (732) 432-8460
Counties Represented: Middlesex (part)
Term Expires: 2018
132 Main Street, Suite A, Sayreville, NJ 08872
E-mail: asmwisniewski@njleg.org
Committees: Environment and Solid Waste; Transportation and
Independent Authorities

Assembly Member **David W. Wolfe** (R-District 10) . . . . . . . (732) 840-9028
Counties Represented: Ocean (part)
Term Expires: 2018
852 Highway 70, Brick, NJ 08724
E-mail: asmwolfe@njleg.org
Committees: Education; Environment and Solid Waste; Joint Public
Schools
Affiliation: Professor, Ocean County College, County of Ocean, New
Jersey
P.O. Box 2001, Toms River, NJ 08754-2001

Assembly Member **Andrew Zwicker** (D-District 16) . . . . . . (609) 454-3147
Counties Represented: Hunterdon (part), Mercer        Fax: (609) 580-1679
(part), Middlesex (part), Somerset (part)
Term Expires: 2018
23 Orchard Road, Suite 170, Skillman, NJ 08558
E-mail: asmzwicker@njleg.org
Committees: Environment and Solid Waste; Judiciary;
Telecommunications and Utilities
Education: Bard BS; Johns Hopkins PhD

# General Assembly Standing Committees

## Agriculture and Natural Resources

| Majority Members | Minority Members |
|---|---|
| Robert "Bob" Andrzejczak (D-1) *Chair* | Ronald S. Dancer (R-12) |
| Adam Joseph Taliaferro (D-3) *Vice Chair* | F. Parker Space (R-24) |
| Eric Houghtaling (D-11) | |

## Appropriations

| Majority Members | Minority Members |
|---|---|
| John J. Burzichelli (D-3) *Chair* | John DiMaio (R-23) |
| L. Grace Spencer (D-29) *Vice Chair* | Gail Phoebus (R-24) |
| Herbert C. "Herb" Conaway, Jr. (D-7) | Holly Schepisi (R-39) |
| Joseph Lagana (D-38) | |
| Pamela Rosen Lampitt (D-6) | |
| Gabriela Mosquera (D-4) | |
| Annette Quijano (D-20) | |
| Gary S. Schaer (D-36) | |

## Budget

| Majority Members | Minority Members |
|---|---|
| Gary S. Schaer (D-36) *Chair* | Anthony M. "Tony" Bucco, Jr. (R-25) |
| John J. Burzichelli (D-3) *Vice Chair* | John DiMaio (R-23) |
| Gordon M. Johnson (D-37) | Declan J. O'Scanlon, Jr. (R-13) |
| John F. McKeon (D-27) | Maria Rodriguez-Gregg (R-8) |
| Raj Mukherji (D-33) | |
| Elizabeth Maher "Liz" Muoio (D-15) | |
| Eliana Pintor-Marin (D-29) | |
| Troy E. Singleton (D-7) | |
| Benjie E. Wimberly (D-35) | |

## Commerce and Economic Development

| Majority Members | Minority Members |
|---|---|
| Gordon M. Johnson (D-37) *Chair* | Robert "Bob" Auth (R-39) |
| Eliana Pintor-Marin (D-29) *Vice Chair* | Anthony M. "Tony" Bucco, Jr. (R-25) |
| Nicholas A. Chiaravalloti (D-31) | BettyLou DeCroce (R-26) |
| Craig J. Coughlin (D-19) | Nancy F. Munoz (R-21) |
| Timothy J. Eustace (D-38) | |
| Raj Mukherji (D-33) | |
| Elizabeth Maher "Liz" Muoio (D-15) | |
| Sheila Y. Oliver (D-34) | |

## Consumer Affairs

| Majority Members | Minority Members |
|---|---|
| Paul D. Moriarty (D-4) *Chair* | Sean T. Kean (R-30) |
| Annette Quijano (D-20) | |

## Education

| Majority Members | Minority Members |
|---|---|
| Troy E. Singleton (D-7) *Vice Chair* | Robert "Bob" Auth (R-39) |
| Ralph R. Caputo (D-28) | David P. Rible (R-30) |
| Mila M. Jasey (D-27) | David W. Wolfe (R-10) |
| Angelica M. Jimenez (D-32) | |
| Patricia Egan Jones (D-5) | |
| Angela V. McKnight (D-31) | |
| Adam Joseph Taliaferro (D-3) | |

## Environment and Solid Waste

| Majority Members | Minority Members |
|---|---|
| L. Grace Spencer (D-29) *Chair* | Scott T. Rumana (R-40) |
| John F. McKeon (D-27) *Vice Chair* | David W. Wolfe (R-10) |
| John S. Wisniewski (D-19) | |
| Andrew Zwicker (D-16) | |

## Financial Institutions and Insurance

| Majority Members | Minority Members |
|---|---|
| Craig J. Coughlin (D-19) *Chair* | Robert "Bob" Auth (R-39) |
| Pamela Rosen Lampitt (D-6) *Vice Chair* | Jack M. Ciattarelli (R-16) |
| Marlene Caride (D-36) | Amy H. Handlin (R-13) |
| Joseph "Joe" Danielsen (D-17) | Joe Howarth (R-8) |
| Joann Downey (D-11) | |
| Reed Gusciora (D-15) | |
| Joseph Lagana (D-38) | |
| John F. McKeon (D-27) | |
| L. Grace Spencer (D-29) | |

## Health and Senior Services

| Majority Members | Minority Members |
|---|---|
| Herbert C. "Herb" Conaway, Jr. (D-7) *Chair* | BettyLou DeCroce (R-26) |
| Timothy J. Eustace (D-38) *Vice Chair* | Nancy F. Munoz (R-21) |
| Daniel R. Benson (D-14) | Erik C. Peterson (R-23) |
| Gerald "Jerry" Green (D-22) | Holly Schepisi (R-39) |
| Angelica M. Jimenez (D-32) | |
| Angela V. McKnight (D-31) | |
| James J. Kennedy (D-22) | |
| Nancy J. Pinkin (D-18) | |
| Shavonda E. Sumter (D-35) | |

## Higher Education

| Majority Members | Minority Members |
|---|---|
| Mila M. Jasey (D-27) *Chair* | Robert D. Clifton (R-12) |
| Thomas P. Giblin (D-34) *Vice Chair* | DiAnne C. Gove (R-9) |
| Arthur Barclay (D-5) | David P. Rible (R-30) |
| Jamel C. Holley (D-20) | |
| Gabriela Mosquera (D-4) | |
| Gary S. Schaer (D-36) | |

## Homeland Security and State Preparedness

| Majority Members | Minority Members |
|---|---|
| Annette Quijano (D-20) *Chair* | Gregory P. McGuckin (R-10) |
| Nancy J. Pinkin (D-18) *Vice Chair* | David C. Russo (R-40) |
| Annette Chaparro (D-33) | |
| R. Bruce Land (D-1) | |

## Housing and Community Development

| Majority Members | Minority Members |
|---|---|
| Gerald "Jerry" Green (D-22) *Chair* | Robert D. Clifton (R-12) |
| Mila M. Jasey (D-27) *Vice Chair* | Maria Rodriguez-Gregg (R-8) |
| Jamel C. Holley (D-20) | |
| Patricia Egan Jones (D-5) | |

## Human Services

| Majority Members | Minority Members |
|---|---|
| Valerie Vainieri Huttle (D-37) *Chair* | Joe Howarth (R-8) |
| Cleopatra G. Tucker (D-28) *Vice Chair* | Gail Phoebus (R-24) |
| Patricia Egan Jones (D-5) | |
| Angela V. McKnight (D-31) | |

## Judiciary

| Majority Members | Minority Members |
|---|---|
| John F. McKeon (D-27) *Chair* | Michael Patrick Carroll (R-25) |
| Gordon M. Johnson (D-37) *Vice Chair* | Erik C. Peterson (R-23) |
| Joseph Lagana (D-38) | |
| Elizabeth Maher "Liz" Muoio (D-15) | |
| Andrew Zwicker (D-16) | |

## Labor

| Majority Members | Minority Members |
|---|---|
| Joseph V. Egan (D-17) *Chair* | Ronald S. Dancer (R-12) |
| Shavonda E. Sumter (D-35) *Vice Chair* | F. Parker Space (R-24) |
| Craig J. Coughlin (D-19) | Jay Webber (R-26) |
| Reed Gusciora (D-15) | |
| Eric Houghtaling (D-11) | |
| Raj Mukherji (D-33) | |

## Law and Public Safety

| Majority Members | Minority Members |
|---|---|
| Daniel R. Benson (D-14) *Chair* | Michael Patrick Carroll (R-25) |
| Joseph "Joe" Danielsen (D-17) *Vice Chair* | Erik C. Peterson (R-23) |
| Arthur Barclay (D-5) | David P. Rible (R-30) |
| Annette Chaparro (D-33) | |
| Nancy J. Pinkin (D-18) | |
| Shavonda E. Sumter (D-35) | |

## Military and Veterans' Affairs

| Majority Members | Minority Members |
|---|---|
| Cleopatra G. Tucker (D-28) *Chair* | DiAnne C. Gove (R-9) |
| Wayne P. DeAngelo (D-14) *Vice Chairman* | Joe Howarth (R-8) |
| Robert "Bob" Andrzejczak (D-1) | |
| R. Bruce Land (D-1) | |

## Regulated Professions

| Majority Members | Minority Members |
|---|---|
| Thomas P. Giblin (D-34) *Chair* | Jack M. Ciattarelli (R-16) |
| Angelica M. Jimenez (D-32) *Vice Chair* | Amy H. Handlin (R-13) |
| Joann Downey (D-11) | Sean T. Kean (R-30) |
| Vincent "Vince" Mazzeo (D-2) | |
| Paul D. Moriarty (D-4) | |

## Regulatory Oversight and Reform and Federal Relations

| Majority Members | Minority Members |
|---|---|
| Reed Gusciora (D-15) *Chair* | Chris A. Brown (R-2) |
| Benjie E. Wimberly (D-35) *Vice Chair* | Gail Phoebus (R-24) |
| Cleopatra G. Tucker (D-28) | Brian E. Rumpf (R-9) |

## State and Local Government

| Majority Members | Minority Members |
|---|---|
| Troy E. Singleton (D-7) *Chair* | Michael Patrick Carroll (R-25) |
| Herbert C. "Herb" Conaway, Jr. (D-7) *Vice Chair* | Jay Webber (R-26) |
| Timothy J. Eustace (D-38) | |

## Telecommunications and Utilities

| Majority Members | Minority Members |
|---|---|
| Wayne P. DeAngelo (D-14) *Chair* | Gail Phoebus (R-24) |
| Benjie E. Wimberly (D-35) *Vice Chair* | Brian E. Rumpf (R-9) |
| Joseph V. Egan (D-17) | |
| Eric Houghtaling (D-11) | |
| Eliana Pintor-Marin (D-29) | |
| Andrew Zwicker (D-16) | |

## Tourism and Gaming and the Arts

| Majority Members | Minority Members |
|---|---|
| Ralph R. Caputo (D-28) *Chair* | Chris A. Brown (R-2) |
| Vincent "Vince" Mazzeo (D-2) *Vice Chair* | Ronald S. Dancer (R-12) |
| John J. Burzichelli (D-3) | |
| R. Bruce Land (D-1) | |
| Valerie Vainieri Huttle (D-37) | |

## Transportation and Independent Authorities

| Majority Members | Minority Members |
|---|---|
| John S. Wisniewski (D-19) *Chair* | Robert D. Clifton (R-12) |
| Marlene Caride (D-36) *Vice Chair* | BettyLou DeCroce (R-26) |
| Daniel R. Benson (D-14) | Gregory P. McGuckin (R-10) |
| Nicholas A. Chiaravalloti (D-31) | Scott T. Rumana (R-40) |
| Thomas P. Giblin (D-34) | |
| James J. Kennedy (D-22) | |
| Paul D. Moriarty (D-4) | |
| Sheila Y. Oliver (D-34) | |
| Valerie Vainieri Huttle (D-37) | |

## Women and Children

| Majority Members | Minority Members |
|---|---|
| Pamela Rosen Lampitt (D-6) *Chair* | Nancy F. Munoz (R-21) |
| Gabriela Mosquera (D-4) *Vice Chair* | |
| Joann Downey (D-11) | |
| Jamel C. Holley (D-20) | |

# New Mexico State Legislature

State Capitol, Room 411, Santa Fe, NM 87501
Tel: (505) 986-4300 Fax: (505) 986-4680
E-mail: lcs@nmlegis.gov (Legislative Council Service)
Internet: www.nmlegis.gov

## New Mexico Senate

State Capitol, Room 115, Santa Fe, NM 87501
Tel: (505) 986-4714 Fax: (505) 986-4280 E-mail: senate@nmlegis.gov

President of the Senate **John A. Sanchez** (R) . . . . . . . . . . (505) 476-2250
President Pro Tem **Mary Kay Papen** (D) . . . . . . . . . . . . . (505) 986-4270
Majority Floor Leader **Michael S. Sanchez** (D) . . . . . . . . (505) 986-4727
    Education: New Mexico BS, JD
Majority Whip **Michael Padilla** (D) . . . . . . . . . . . . . . . . . (505) 986-4726
    Education: New Mexico (Attended); U Phoenix (Attended)
Majority Caucus Chairman **Jacob R. Candelaria** (D) . . . . . (505) 986-4391
    Education: Princeton 2005 BA
Minority Floor Leader **Stuart Ingle** (R) . . . . . . . . . . . . . . (505) 986-4702
    Education: Oklahoma State 1970 BS
Minority Whip **William H. "Bill" Payne** (R) . . . . . . . . . . . (505) 986-4703
    Education: New Mexico BA, MA; Georgetown 1985 MA;
    New Mexico JD
Minority Caucus Chairman **Steven P. Neville** (R) . . . . . . . . (505) 986-4701
Chief Clerk of the Senate **Lenore M. Naranjo** . . . . . . . . . . (505) 986-4714
    E-mail: lenore.naranjo@nmlegis.gov
Sergeant-at-Arms **David G. Pacheco** . . . . . . . . . . . . . . . . (505) 986-4700

## Senators

**Party Affiliation Statistics: Republicans: 18, Democrats: 24**

Senator **Ted Barela** (R-District 39) . . . . . . . . . . . . . . . . . (505) 384-4307
    Counties Represented: Bernalillo (part), Lincoln (part), San Miguel
    (part), Santa Fe (part), Torrance (part), Valencia (part)
    Term Expires: 2017
    P.O. Box 225, Estancia, NM 87016
    E-mail: ted.barela@nmlegis.gov
    Committees: Public Affairs; Rules

Senator **Sue Wilson Beffort** (R-District 19) . . . . . . . . . . . (505) 986-4395
    Counties Represented: Bernalillo (part), Sandoval      Res: (505) 292-7116
    (part), Santa Fe (part), Torrance (part)
    Term Expires: 2017
    67 Raindance Road, Sandia Park, NM 87047
    E-mail: sue.beffort@nmlegis.gov
    Committees: Finance
    Education: Southern Methodist BA

Senator **Craig W. Brandt** (R-District 40) . . . . . . . . . . . . . (505) 986-4714
    Counties Represented: Sandoval (part)
    Term Expires: 2017
    7247 Milan Hills Road Northeast, Rio Rancho, NM 87144
    E-mail: craig.brandt@nmlegis.gov
    Committees: Education; Public Affairs
    Education: Oklahoma Baptist 2000 BA

Senator **William F. "Bill" Burt** (R-District 33) . . . . . . . . . (575) 434-6140
    Counties Represented: Chaves (part), Lincoln (part),   Dist: (575) 434-1414
    Otero (part)
    Term Expires: 2017
    P. O. Box 1848, Alamogordo, NM 88311
    E-mail: bill.burt@nmlegis.gov
    Committees: Finance
    Education: New Mexico State BA

Senator **Pete Campos** (D-District 8) . . . . . . . . . . . . . . . . (505) 986-4311
    Counties Represented: Colfax, Guadalupe, Harding,     Tel: (505) 454-2501
    Mora, Quay (part), San Miguel (part), Taos (part)      Res: (505) 425-0508
    Term Expires: 2017
    418 Raynolds Avenue, Las Vegas, NM 87701
    E-mail: petecampos@newmexico.com
    Committees: Committees' Committee; Finance
    Education: New Mexico BA, MA

Senator **Jacob R. Candelaria** (D-District 26) . . . . . . . . . . . (505) 986-4391
    Counties Represented: Bernalillo (part)
    Term Expires: 2017
    3501 Atrisco Drive Northwest, Number 423, Albuquerque, NM 87120
    E-mail: jacob.candelaria@nmlegis.gov
    Committees: Public Affairs; Rules

Senator **Joseph Cervantes** (D-District 31) . . . . . . . . . . . . (505) 986-4385
    Counties Represented: Dona Ana (part)
    Term Expires: 2017
    2610 South Espina, Las Cruces, NM 88001
    E-mail: joseph@cervanteslawnm.com
    Committees: Conservation; Judiciary
    Education: New Mexico 1983 BA;
    Cal Poly San Luis Obispo 1985 MA; New Mexico 1991 JD

Senator **Carlos R. Cisneros** (D-District 6) . . . . . . . . . . . . (505) 986-4362
    Counties Represented: Los Alamos (part), Rio      Res: (505) 670-5610
    Arriba (part), Santa Fe (part), Taos (part)
    Term Expires: 2017
    P.O. Box 1129, Questa, NM 87556
    E-mail: carlos.cisneros@nmlegis.gov
    Committees: Committees' Committee; Finance

Senator **Lee S. Cotter** (R-District 36) . . . . . . . . . . . . . . . (505) 986-4377
    Counties Represented: Dona Ana (part)
    Term Expires: 2017
    6670 Butterfield Ridge, Las Cruces, NM 88007
    E-mail: lee.cotter@nmlegis.gov
    Committees: Corporations and Transportation; Education
    Education: New Mexico State 1977 BS; Arizona 1991 MBA

Senator **Ron Griggs** (R-District 34) . . . . . . . . . . . . . . . . . (505) 986-4276
    Counties Represented: Dona Ana (part), Eddy (part), Otero (part)
    Term Expires: 2017
    2704 Birdie Loop, Alamogordo, NM 88310
    E-mail: ron.griggs@nmlegis.gov
    Committees: Judiciary; Public Affairs
    Education: New Mexico State 1974 BBA

Senator **Stuart Ingle** (R-District 27) . . . . . . . . . . . . . . . . (505) 986-4702
    Counties Represented: Chaves (part), Curry (part),     Tel: (575) 356-3088
    De Baca, Lea (part), Roosevelt                         (Res)
    Term Expires: 2017
    2106 West University Drive, Portales, NM 88130
    E-mail: stuart.ingle@nmlegis.gov
    Committees: Committees' Committee; Indian and Cultural Affairs;
    Rules

Senator **Daniel Ivey-Soto** (D-District 15) . . . . . . . . . . . . . (505) 986-4270
    Counties Represented: Bernalillo (part)
    Term Expires: 2017
    1420 Carlisle Boulevard Northeast, Suite 208,
    Albuquerque, NM 87110-5662
    E-mail: daniel.ivey-soto@nmlegis.gov
    Committees: Public Affairs; Rules

Senator **Gay G. Kernan** (R-District 42) . . . . . . . . . . . . . . (505) 986-4274
    Counties Represented: Chaves (part), Eddy (part),     Res: (575) 397-2536
    Lea (part)
    Term Expires: 2017
    928 West Mesa Verde, Hobbs, NM 88240
    E-mail: ggkern@valornet.com
    Committees: Education; Public Affairs

Senator **Carroll H. Leavell** (R-District 41) . . . . . . . . . . . . (505) 986-4278
    Counties Represented: Eddy (part), Lea (part)          Tel: (575) 393-2550
    Term Expires: 2017                                     Res: (575) 395-3154
    P.O. Drawer D, Jal, NM 88252
    E-mail: leavell4@leaco.net
    Committees: Finance
    Education: Eastern New Mexico BA

Senator **Linda M. Lopez** (D-District 11) . . . . . . . . . . . . . . (505) 986-4737
    Counties Represented: Bernalillo (part)               Res: (505) 831-4148
    Term Expires: 2017
    9132 Suncrest SW, Albuquerque, NM 87121
    E-mail: linda.lopez@nmlegis.gov
    Committees: Judiciary; Rules
    Education: Col Santa Fe BA, MBA

Senator **Richard C. Martinez** (D-District 5) . . . . . . . . . . . (505) 986-4487
    Counties Represented: Los Alamos (part), Rio          Tel: (575) 929-0125
    Arriba (part), Sandoval (part), Santa Fe (part)
    Term Expires: 2017
    P.O. Box 762, Espanola, NM 87532
    E-mail: richard.martinez@nmlegis.gov
    Committees: Conservation; Judiciary

Senator **Cisco McSorley** (D-District 16) . . . . . . . . . . . . . . (505) 986-4389
    Counties Represented: Bernalillo (part)               Res: (505) 266-0588
    Term Expires: 2017
    415 Wellesley Place NE, Albuquerque, NM 87106
    E-mail: cisco.mcsorley@nmlegis.gov
    Committees: Indian and Cultural Affairs; Judiciary
    Education: New Mexico 1974 BA, 1979 JD

LEGISLATIVE BRANCH

Senator **Mark Moores** (R-District 21) . . . . . . . . . . . . . . . . (505) 986-4859
    Counties Represented: Bernalillo (part)
    Term Expires: 2017
    9641 Seligman Avenue Northeast, Albuquerque, NM 87109
    E-mail: mark.moores@nmlegis.gov
    Committees: Corporations and Transportation; Rules
    Education: New Mexico BA, MBA

Senator **Howie C. Morales** (D-District 28) . . . . . . . . . . . . (505) 986-4863
    Counties Represented: Catron, Grant, Socorro (part)    Tel: (575) 574-0043
    Term Expires: 2017
    4285 North Swan, Silver City, NM 88061
    E-mail: howiemorales@yahoo.com
    Committees: Finance
    Education: Western New Mexico BS; New Mexico State PhD

Senator **George K. Munoz** (D-District 4) . . . . . . . . . . . . . . (505) 986-4387
    Counties Represented: Cibola (part), McKinley    Tel: (505) 722-6570
    (part), San Juan (part)    Res: (505) 722-0191
    Term Expires: 2017
    P.O. Box 2679, Gallup, NM 87305
    E-mail: munozgeo@gmail.com
    Committees: Committees' Committee; Finance

Senator **Steven P. Neville** (R-District 2) . . . . . . . . . . . . . . (505) 986-4701
    Counties Represented: San Juan (part)    Tel: (505) 327-5460
    Term Expires: 2017
    P.O. Box 1570, Aztec, NM 87410
    E-mail: nmsenate@msn.com
    Committees: Finance

Senator **Bill B. O'Neill** (D-District 13) . . . . . . . . . . . . . . . . (505) 986-4260
    Counties Represented: Bernalillo (part)
    Term Expires: 2017
    343 Sarah Lane Northwest, Albuquerque, NM 87114
    E-mail: oneillsd13@billoneillfornm.com
    Committees: Education; Public Affairs
    Education: Cornell (Attended)

Senator **Gerald Ortiz y Pino** (D-District 12) . . . . . . . . . . . (505) 986-4380
    Counties Represented: Bernalillo (part)    Res: (505) 243-1509
    Term Expires: 2017
    400 12th Street NW, Albuquerque, NM 87102
    E-mail: jortizyp@msn.com
    Committees: Public Affairs; Rules

Senator **Michael Padilla** (D-District 14) . . . . . . . . . . . . . . (505) 986-4726
    Counties Represented: Bernalillo (part)
    Term Expires: 2017
    PO Box 67545, Albuquerque, NM 87193
    E-mail: michael.padilla@nmlegis.gov
    Committees: Committees' Committee; Corporations and Transportation;
    Education

Senator **Mary Kay Papen** (D-District 38) . . . . . . . . . . . . . . (505) 986-4270
    Counties Represented: Dona Ana (part)    Res: (575) 524-4462
    Term Expires: 2017
    904 Conway Avenue, Las Cruces, NM 88005
    E-mail: marykay.papen@nmlegis.gov
    Committees: Committees' Committee; Corporations and Transportation;
    Indian and Cultural Affairs

Senator **William H. "Bill" Payne** (R-District 20) . . . . . . . . (505) 986-4703
    Counties Represented: Bernalillo (part)    Tel: (505) 884-6872
    Term Expires: 2017    Res: (505) 293-5703
    P.O. Box 14823, Albuquerque, NM 87191
    E-mail: william.payne@nmlegis.gov
    Committees: Committees' Committee; Conservation; Judiciary

Senator **John Pinto** (D-District 3) . . . . . . . . . . . . . . . . . . . . (505) 986-4835
    Counties Represented: McKinley (part), San Juan    Tel: (505) 371-8342
    (part)    Res: (505) 870-0823
    Term Expires: 2017
    509 West Morgan Avenue, Gallup, NM 87301
    E-mail: john.pinto@nmlegis.gov
    Committees: Education; Indian and Cultural Affairs
    Education: New Mexico BS, MA

Senator **Cliff R. Pirtle** (R-District 32) . . . . . . . . . . . . . . . . (505) 986-4862
    Counties Represented: Chaves (part), Eddy (part), Otero (part)
    Term Expires: 2017
    5507 Y.O. Road, Roswell, NM 88203
    E-mail: cliff.pirtle@nmlegis.gov
    Committees: Indian and Cultural Affairs; Rules

Senator **Nancy Rodriguez** (D-District 24) . . . . . . . . . . . . . (505) 986-4264
    Counties Represented: Santa Fe (part)    Res: (505) 983-8913
    Term Expires: 2017
    1838 Camino La Canada, Santa Fe, NM 87501
    E-mail: nancy.rodriguez@nmlegis.gov
    Committees: Finance

Senator **Sander Rue** (R-District 23) . . . . . . . . . . . . . . . . . . (505) 986-4375
    Counties Represented: Bernalillo (part)    Res: (505) 899-0288
    Term Expires: 2017
    7500 Rancho Solano Court NW, Albuquerque, NM 87120
    E-mail: sanderrue@comcast.net
    Committees: Corporations and Transportation; Rules

Senator **John C. Ryan** (R-District 10) . . . . . . . . . . . . . . . . (505) 986-4373
    Counties Represented: Bernalillo (part), Sandoval    Res: (505) 238-3733
    (part)
    Term Expires: 2017
    1020 Salamanca NW, Albuquerque, NM 87107
    E-mail: johnchrisryan@yahoo.com
    Committees: Conservation; Judiciary

Senator **Clemente Sanchez** (D-District 30) . . . . . . . . . . . . (505) 986-4369
    Counties Represented: Cibola (part), McKinley (part), Socorro (part),
    Valencia (part)
    Term Expires: 2017
    612 Inwood Avenue, Grants, NM 87020
    E-mail: clemente.sanchez@nmlegis.gov
    Committees: Committees' Committee; Corporations and Transportation;
    Rules
    Education: Eastern New Mexico 1981 BBA;
    New Mexico Highlands 1982 MBA

Senator **Michael S. Sanchez** (D-District 29) . . . . . . . . . . . (505) 986-4727
    Counties Represented: Bernalillo (part), Valencia    Tel: (505) 865-0688
    (part)    Res: (505) 865-5583
    Term Expires: 2017
    03 Bunton Road, Belen, NM 87002
    E-mail: senatormssanchez@aol.com
    Committees: Committees' Committee; Judiciary; Rules

Senator **John M. Sapien** (D-District 9) . . . . . . . . . . . . . . . (505) 986-4371
    Counties Represented: Bernalillo (part), Sandoval    Res: (505) 765-5662
    (part)
    Term Expires: 2017
    1600 West Ella, Corrales, NM 87048
    E-mail: john.sapien@nmlegis.gov
    Committees: Corporations and Transportation; Education

Senator **William E. Sharer** (R-District 1) . . . . . . . . . . . . . . (505) 986-4381
    Counties Represented: San Juan (part)    Tel: (505) 325-5055
    Term Expires: 2017    Res: (505) 564-8640
    P.O. Box 203, Farmington, NM 87499
    E-mail: bill@williamsharer.com
    Committees: Committees' Committee; Conservation; Corporations and
    Transportation
    Education: New Mexico State BA

Senator **Benny Shendo, Jr.** (D-District 22) . . . . . . . . . . . . (505) 986-4310
    Counties Represented: Bernalillo (part), McKinley (part), Rio Arriba
    (part), San Juan (part), Sandoval (part)
    Term Expires: 2017
    PO Box 634, Jemez Pueblo, NM 87024
    E-mail: benny.shendo@nmlegis.gov
    Committees: Conservation; Indian and Cultural Affairs

Senator **John Arthur Smith** (D-District 35) . . . . . . . . . . . . (505) 986-4365
    Counties Represented: Dona Ana (part), Hidalgo,    Tel: (575) 546-4979
    Luna, Sierra    Res: (575) 546-8546
    Term Expires: 2017
    P.O. Box 998, Deming, NM 88031
    E-mail: john.smith@nmlegis.gov
    Committees: Committees' Committee; Finance
    Education: New Mexico 1966 BS

Senator **William P. Soules** (D-District 37) . . . . . . . . . . . . . (505) 986-4856
    Counties Represented: Dona Ana (part)
    Term Expires: 2017
    5054 Silver King, Las Cruces, NM 88011
    E-mail: bill.soules@nmlegis.gov
    Committees: Conservation; Education
    Education: New Mexico State 1976 BA, 1980 MA, 1988 PhD

Senator **Mimi Stewart** (D-District 17) . . . . . . . . . . . . . . . . (505) 986-4714
    Counties Represented: Bernalillo (part)
    Term Expires: 2017
    E-mail: mimi.stewart@nmlegis.gov
    Committees: Corporations and Transportation; Public Affairs
    Education: Boston U 1971 BS; Wheelock 1977 MS

Senator **Lisa A. Torraco** (R-District 18) . . . . . . . . . . . . . . (505) 986-4266
    Counties Represented: Bernalillo (part)
    Term Expires: 2017
    1019 Second Street Northwest, Albuquerque, NM 87102
    E-mail: lisa.torraco@nmlegis.gov
    Committees: Indian and Cultural Affairs; Judiciary
    Education: New Mexico 1988 BA; San Diego 1991 JD

*(continued on next page)*

**Senators** *continued*

Senator **Peter Wirth** (D-District 25) . . . . . . . . . . . . . . . . . (505) 986-4276
  Counties Represented: Santa Fe (part)                Tel: (505) 988-1668
  Term Expires: 2017                                   Res: (505) 989-8667
  708 Paseo de Peralta, Santa Fe, NM 87501
  E-mail: peter.wirth@nmlegis.gov
  Committees: Conservation; Judiciary

Senator **Pat Woods** (R-District 7) Room 415D . . . . . . . . . (505) 986-4369
  Counties Represented: Curry (part), Quay (part), Union
  Term Expires: 2017
  E-mail: pat.woods@nmlegis.gov
  Committees: Conservation; Education

## Senate Standing Committees
### Committees' Committee
State Capitol, Room 311, Santa Fe, NM 87501

**Majority Members**
Mary Kay Papen (D-38) *Chair*
Michael S. Sanchez (D-29)
  *Vice Chair*
Pete Campos (D-8)
Carlos R. Cisneros (D-6)
George K. Munoz (D-4)
Michael Padilla (D-14)
Clemente Sanchez (D-30)
John Arthur Smith (D-35)

**Minority Members**
Stuart Ingle (R-27)
William H. "Bill" Payne (R-20)
William E. Sharer (R-1)

### Conservation
State Capitol, Room 311, Santa Fe, NM 87501

**Majority Members**
Peter Wirth (D-25) *Chair*
Benny Shendo, Jr. (D-22)
  *Vice Chair*
Joseph Cervantes (D-31)
Richard C. Martinez (D-5)
William P. Soules (D-37)

**Minority Members**
John C. Ryan (R-10)
  *Ranking Minority Member*
William H. "Bill" Payne (R-20)
William E. Sharer (R-1)
Pat Woods (R-7)

### Corporations and Transportation
State Capitol, Room 311, Santa Fe, NM 87501

**Majority Members**
Clemente Sanchez (D-30)
  *Vice Chair*
Michael Padilla (D-14)
Mary Kay Papen (D-38)
John M. Sapien (D-9)
Mimi Stewart (D-17)

**Minority Members**
William E. Sharer (R-1)
  *Ranking Minority Member*
Lee S. Cotter (R-36)
Mark Moores (R-21)
Sander Rue (R-23)

### Education
State Capitol, Room 311, Santa Fe, NM 87501

**Majority Members**
John M. Sapien (D-9) *Chair*
William P. Soules (D-37)
  *Vice Chair*
Bill B. O'Neill (D-13)
Michael Padilla (D-14)
John Pinto (D-3)

**Minority Members**
Gay G. Kernan (R-42)
  *Ranking Minority Member*
Craig W. Brandt (R-40)
Lee S. Cotter (R-36)
Pat Woods (R-7)

### Finance
State Capitol, Room 322, Santa Fe, NM 87501

**Majority Members**
John Arthur Smith (D-35) *Chair*
Carlos R. Cisneros (D-6)
  *Vice Chair*
Pete Campos (D-8)
Howie C. Morales (D-28)
George K. Munoz (D-4)
Nancy Rodriguez (D-24)

**Minority Members**
Sue Wilson Beffort (R-19)
  *Ranking Minority Member*
William F. "Bill" Burt (R-33)
Carroll H. Leavell (R-41)
Steven P. Neville (R-2)

### Indian and Cultural Affairs
State Capitol, Room 303, Santa Fe, NM 87501

**Majority Members**
John Pinto (D-3) *Chair*
Cisco McSorley (D-16) *Vice Chair*
Mary Kay Papen (D-38)
Benny Shendo, Jr. (D-22)

**Minority Members**
Cliff R. Pirtle (R-32)
  *Ranking Minority Member*
Stuart Ingle (R-27)
Lisa A. Torraco (R-18)

## Judiciary
State Capitol, Room 321, Santa Fe, NM 87501

**Majority Members**
Richard C. Martinez (D-5) *Chair*
Joseph Cervantes (D-31) *Vice Chair*
Linda M. Lopez (D-11)
Cisco McSorley (D-16)
Michael S. Sanchez (D-29)
Peter Wirth (D-25)

**Minority Members**
William H. "Bill" Payne (R-20)
  *Ranking Minority Member*
Ron Griggs (R-34)
John C. Ryan (R-10)
Lisa A. Torraco (R-18)

## Public Affairs
State Capitol, Room 321, Santa Fe, NM 87501

**Majority Members**
Gerald Ortiz y Pino (D-12) *Chair*
Bill B. O'Neill (D-13) *Vice Chair*
Jacob R. Candelaria (D-26)
Daniel Ivey-Soto (D-15)
Mimi Stewart (D-17)

**Minority Members**
Craig W. Brandt (R-40)
  *Ranking Minority Member*
Ted Barela (R-39)
Ron Griggs (R-34)
Gay G. Kernan (R-42)

## Rules
State Capitol, Room 321, Santa Fe, NM 87501

**Majority Members**
Linda M. Lopez (D-11) *Chair*
Daniel Ivey-Soto (D-15) *Vice Chair*
Jacob R. Candelaria (D-26)
Gerald Ortiz y Pino (D-12)
Clemente Sanchez (D-30)
Michael S. Sanchez (D-29)

**Minority Members**
Sander Rue (R-23)
  *Ranking Minority Member*
Ted Barela (R-39)
Stuart Ingle (R-27)
Mark Moores (R-21)
Cliff R. Pirtle (R-32)

# New Mexico House of Representatives
State Capitol, Santa Fe, NM 87501
Tel: (505) 986-4751  Fax: (505) 986-4755  E-mail: house@nmlegis.gov
Internet: www.nmlegis.gov

Speaker of the House **Don L. Tripp** (R) . . . . . . . . . . . . . . . .(505) 986-4220
  Chief of Staff **Regis Pecos** . . . . . . . . . . . . . . . . . . . . . . . (505) 986-4790
Majority Floor Leader **Nate Gentry** (R) . . . . . . . . . . . . . . .(505) 986-0782
Majority Whip **Alonzo Baldonado** (R). . . . . . . . . . . . . . . . (505) 986-4227
Minority Floor Leader **Brian F. Egolf, Jr.** (D) . . . . . . . . . . (505) 986-9641
Minority Whip **Sheryl Williams Stapleton** (D) . . . . . . . . (505) 986-4774
Chief Clerk of the House **Denise Ramonas** . . . . . . . . . . . .(505) 986-4751
  E-mail: denise.ramonas@nmlegis.gov
Sergeant-at-Arms **Gilbert J. Lopez** . . . . . . . . . . . . . . . . . . . (505) 986-4770
  E-mail: gilbert.lopez@nmlegis.gov

## Representatives
**Party Affiliation Statistics:** Republicans: 37, Democrats: 33

Representative **David Edward Adkins** (R-District 29) . . . . . (505) 239-3987
  Counties Represented: Bernalillo (part)
  Term Expires: 2017
  E-mail: david.adkins@nmlegis.gov
  Committees: Business and Employment; Judiciary

Representative **Eliseo Lee Alcon** (D-District 6) . . . . . . . . . (505) 285-6387
  Counties Represented: Cibola (part), McKinley (part)
  Term Expires: 2017
  P.O. Box 2134, Milan, NM 87021
  E-mail: eliseoalcon@msn.com
  Committees: Consumer and Public Affairs; Government, Elections, and
  Indian Affairs; Judiciary

Representative **Deborah A. Armstrong** (D-District 17) . . . (505) 795-5164
  Counties Represented: Bernalillo (part)
  Term Expires: 2017
  E-mail: deborah.armstrong@nmlegis.gov
  Committees: Health; Regulatory and Public Affairs
  Education: Michigan 1975 BS; New Mexico 2001 JD

Representative **Alonzo Baldonado** (R-District 8) . . . . . . . . (505) 986-4227
  Counties Represented: Valencia (part)          Dist: (505) 363-6214
  Term Expires: 2017
  P. O. Box 370, Los Lunas, NM 87031
  E-mail: zobaldonado@gmail.com
  Committees: Education; Safety and Civil Affairs

LEGISLATIVE BRANCH

Representative **Paul C. Bandy** (R-District 3) . . . . . . . . . . . (505) 986-4248
Counties Represented: San Juan (part)     Tel: (505) 334-0865
Term Expires: 2017
388 County Road 2900, Aztec, NM 87410
E-mail: paul@paulbandy.org
Committees: Agriculture and Water Resources; Appropriations and
Finance

Representative **Cathrynn N. Brown** (R-District 55) . . . . . . .(505) 986-4211
Counties Represented: Eddy (part)     Dist: (575) 302-2746
Term Expires: 2017
1814 North Guadalupe Street, Carlsbad, NM 88220
E-mail: c.brown.nm55@gmail.com
Committees: Judiciary; Transportation and Public Works

Representative **Gail Chasey** (D-District 18) . . . . . . . . . . (505) 986-4844
Counties Represented: Bernalillo (part)     Tel: (505) 266-5191
Term Expires: 2017
1206 Las Lomas Road NE, Albuquerque, NM 87106
E-mail: gailchasey@msn.com
Committees: Consumer and Public Affairs; Health; Judiciary

Representative
**Sharon E. Clahchischilliage** (R-District 4) . . . . . . . . . . . (505) 258-4342
Counties Represented: San Juan (part)     Tel: (505) 686-0836
Term Expires: 2017
PO Box 585, Kirtland AFB, NM 87417
E-mail: sharon.clahchischill@nmlegis.gov
Committees: Appropriations and Finance; Government, Elections, and
Indian Affairs
Education: Eastern New Mexico 1976 BS; Pennsylvania 1991 MA

Representative **Zachary J. Cook** (R-District 56) . . . . . . . . (505) 986-4454
Counties Represented: Lincoln (part), Otero (part)     Tel: (575) 258-9090
Term Expires: 2017
100 Sarah Lane, Ruidoso, NM 88435
E-mail: zachjcook@gmail.com
Committees: Government, Elections, and Indian Affairs; Judiciary
Education: New Mexico JD

Representative **Randal S. Crowder** (R-District 64) . . . . . . (575) 763-3901
Counties Represented: Curry (part)
Term Expires: 2017
E-mail: randal.crowder@nmlegis.gov
Committees: Agriculture and Water Resources; Ways and Means

Representative
**James Mitchell "Jim" Dines** (R-District 20) . . . . . . . . .(505) 400-8316
Counties Represented: Bernalillo (part)
Term Expires: 2017
E-mail: jim.dines@nmlegis.gov
Committees: Education; Judiciary

Representative **George Dodge, Jr.** (R-District 63) . . . . . . . (505) 986-4255
Counties Represented: Curry (part), De Baca,     Dist: (575) 472-5576
Guadalupe, Roosevelt (part), San Miguel (part)     Res: (575) 472-3798
Term Expires: 2017
P. O. Box 316, Santa Rosa, NM 88435
E-mail: georgedodge63@yahoo.com
Committees: Agriculture and Water Resources; Business and
Employment

Representative **Brian F. Egolf, Jr.** (D-District 47) . . . . . . . .(505) 986-9641
Counties Represented: Santa Fe (part)     Tel: (505) 986-4423
Term Expires: 2017
128 Grant Avenue, Suite 301, Santa Fe, NM 87501
E-mail: brian@brianegolf.com
Committees: Energy, Environment, and Natural Resources; Judiciary

Representative **Nora Espinoza** (R-District 59) . . . . . . . . . .(505) 986-4221
Counties Represented: Chaves (part), Lincoln (part)     Tel: (575) 623-5324
Term Expires: 2017
608 Golondrina, Roswell, NM 88201
E-mail: nora.espinoza@nmlegis.gov
Committees: Education; Regulatory and Public Affairs

Representative **Candy Spence Ezzell** (R-District 58) . . . . . (505) 986-4450
Counties Represented: Chaves (part)     Res: (575) 625-0550
Term Expires: 2017
P.O. Box 2125, Roswell, NM 88202
E-mail: csecows@aol.com
Committees: Agriculture and Water Resources; Business and
Employment

Representative **Kelly K. Fajardo** (R-District 7) . . . . . . . . . .(505) 573-0471
Counties Represented: Valencia (part)
Term Expires: 2017
1125 North Molina, Belen, NM 87002
E-mail: kelly.fajardo@nmlegis.gov
Committees: Government, Elections, and Indian Affairs; Health

Representative **David M. Gallegos** (R-District 61) . . . . . . .(575) 394-0099
Counties Represented: Lea (part)
Term Expires: 2017
PO Box 998, Eunice, NM 88231
E-mail: david.rsi@hotmail.com
Committees: Energy, Environment, and Natural Resources; Ways and
Means

Representative **Doreen Y. Gallegos** (D-District 52) . . . . . . .(575) 527-8511
Counties Represented: Dona Ana (part)     Tel: (575) 649-6325
Term Expires: 2017
3011 Broadmoor, Las Cruces, NM 88001
E-mail: doreen.gallegos@nmlegis.gov
Committees: Appropriations and Finance; Government, Elections, and
Indian Affairs
Education: New Mexico State BA, MA

Representative **Miguel P. Garcia** (D-District 14) . . . . . . . . (505) 986-4327
Counties Represented: Bernalillo (part)     Res: (505) 877-8131
Term Expires: 2017
1118 La Font Road SW, Albuquerque, NM 87105
E-mail: miguel.garcia@nmlegis.gov
Committees: Business and Employment; Ways and Means
Education: Eastern New Mexico 1973 BA; New Mexico 1993 MA

Representative
**Stephanie Garcia Richard** (D-District 43) . . . . . . . . . . . (505) 500-4343
Counties Represented: Los Alamos, Rio Arriba     Tel: (505) 672-4196
(part), Sandoval (part), Santa Fe (part)
Term Expires: 2017
PO Box 4657, Los Alamos, NM 87544
E-mail: stephanie.garciarichard@nmlegis.gov
Committees: Appropriations and Finance; Education
Education: Columbia 1996 BA

Representative **Nate Gentry** (R-District 30) . . . . . . . . . . . (505) 986-0782
Counties Represented: Bernalillo (part)     Res: (505) 508-0482
Term Expires: 2017
3716 Andrew Drive, NE, Albuquerque, NM 87110
E-mail: natefornm@gmail.com
Committees: Energy, Environment, and Natural Resources; Judiciary

Representative **Bealquin "Bill" Gomez** (D-District 34) . . . (575) 233-3040
Counties Represented: Dona Ana (part)
Term Expires: 2017
E-mail: bealquin.gomez@nmlegis.gov
Committees: Agriculture and Water Resources; Transportation and
Public Works

Representative
**Roberto J. "Bobby" Gonzales** (D-District 42) . . . . . . . . (505) 986-4425
Counties Represented: Taos (part)     Res: (575) 758-2674
Term Expires: 2017
Box 6193/NDCBU, Taos, NM 87571
E-mail: roberto.gonzales@nmlegis.gov
Committees: Agriculture and Water Resources; Transportation and
Public Works
Education: New Mexico BS; New Mexico Highlands MA

Representative **Jimmie C. Hall** (R-District 28) . . . . . . . . . . .(505) 986-4215
Counties Represented: Bernalillo (part)     Res: (505) 294-6178
Term Expires: 2017
13008 Gray Hills Road NE, Albuquerque, NM 87111
E-mail: jimmie.hall@nmlegis.gov
Committees: Appropriations and Finance; Education

Representative **Dianne Miller Hamilton** (R-District 38) . . . (505) 986-4221
Counties Represented: Grant (part), Hidalgo (part),     Res: (575) 538-9336
Sierra (part)
Term Expires: 2017
4132 North Gold Street, Silver City, NM 88061
E-mail: tavish38@gmail.com
Committees: Government, Elections, and Indian Affairs; Transportation
and Public Works

Representative **Jason Carl Harper** (R-District 57) . . . . . . . .(575) 554-7970
Counties Represented: Sandoval (part)
Term Expires: 2017
4917 Foxmoore Court Northeast, Rio Rancho, NM 87144
E-mail: jasonharpernm@gmail.com
Committees: Consumer and Public Affairs; Transportation and Public
Works; Ways and Means
Education: New Mexico Tech 2002 BS; Purdue 2004 MS;
New Mexico 2011 PhD

Representative **Yvette Herrell** (R-District 51) . . . . . . . . . . . (505) 986-4214
Counties Represented: Otero (part)
Term Expires: 2017
P. O. Box 4338, Alamogordo, NM 88311
E-mail: yherrell@yahoo.com
Committees: Business and Employment; Regulatory and Public Affairs

*(continued on next page)*

**Representatives** *continued*

Representative **Dona G. Irwin** (D-District 32) . . . . . . . . . . (505) 986-4234
Counties Represented: Grant (part), Hidalgo (part),      Tel: (575) 546-6016
Luna      Res: (575) 546-9376
Term Expires: 2017
420 South Slate Street, Deming, NM 88030
E-mail: donagale@zianet.com
Committees: Agriculture and Water Resources; Business and
Employment

Representative **Dr. Conrad D. James** (R-District 24) . . . . . (505) 750-7225
Counties Represented: Bernalillo (part)
Term Expires: 2017
E-mail: conradjamesforhd24@gmail.com
Committees: Appropriations and Finance; Business and Employment
Education: Cornell PhD

Representative **Doreen Wonda Johnson** (D-District 5) . . . (505) 986-4435
Counties Represented: McKinley (part), San Juan (part)
Term Expires: 2017
E-mail: dwonda.johnson@nmlegis.gov
Committees: Education; Regulatory and Public Affairs

Representative **Larry A. Larrañaga** (R-District 27) . . . . . . . (505) 986-4215
Counties Represented: Bernalillo (part)      Res: (505) 821-4948
Term Expires: 2017
7716 Lamplighter NE, Albuquerque, NM 87109
E-mail: larry@larranaga.com
Committees: Appropriations and Finance; Transportation and Public
Works
Education: New Mexico 1970 BS, 1978 MS

Representative **Idalia Lechuga-Tena** (D-District 21) . . . . . . (505) 986-4751
Counties Represented: Bernalillo (part)
Term Expires: 2017
E-mail: idalia.lechuga-tena@nmlegis.gov
Committees: Energy, Environment, and Natural Resources; Ways and
Means

Representative **Tim D. Lewis** (R-District 60) . . . . . . . . . . . (505) 986-4254
Counties Represented: Sandoval (part)
Term Expires: 2017
P. O. Box 45793, Rio Rancho, NM 87174
E-mail: lewisfornm@gmail.com
Committees: Business and Employment; Ways and Means

Representative **Rick L. Little** (R-District 53) . . . . . . . . . . . (575) 824-4063
Counties Represented: Dona Ana (part), Otero (part)
Term Expires: 2017
E-mail: rick.little@nmlegis.gov
Committees: Business and Employment; Safety and Civil Affairs

Representative **Georgene Louis** (D-District 26) . . . . . . . . . (505) 938-9144
Counties Represented: Bernalillo (part)      Tel: (505) 250-7932
Term Expires: 2017
PO Box 72123, Albuquerque, NM 87195
E-mail: georgene.louis@nmlegis.gov
Committees: Health; Judiciary
Education: New Mexico 2001 BA, 2004 JD

Representative **Patricia A. Lundstrom** (D-District 9) . . . . . (505) 986-4432
Counties Represented: McKinley (part), San Juan      Res: (505) 870-5915
(part)
Term Expires: 2017
3406 Bluehill Avenue, Gallup, NM 87301
E-mail: patricia.lundstrom@nmlegis.gov
Committees: Appropriations and Finance; Transportation and Public
Works

Representative **James Roger Madalena** (D-District 65) . . . (505) 986-4417
Counties Represented: Rio Arriba (part), San      Tel: (575) 867-3351
Juan (part), Sandoval (part)      Res: (575) 834-7005
Term Expires: 2017
373 Buffalo Hill Road, Jemez Pueblo, NM 87024
E-mail: james.madalena@nmlegis.gov
Committees: Government, Elections, and Indian Affairs; Health
Education: Eastern New Mexico 1973 BA

Representative **Antonio "Moe" Maestas** (D-District 16) . . (505) 986-4233
Counties Represented: Bernalillo (part)      Res: (505) 242-2279
Term Expires: 2017
544 61st Street NW, Albuquerque, NM 87105
E-mail: rep16@moejustice.com
Committees: Government, Elections, and Indian Affairs; Judiciary
Education: U Washington 1995 AB; New Mexico 1998 JD

Representative **Sarah Maestas Barnes** (R-District 15) . . . . (505) 847-6391
Counties Represented: Bernalillo (part)
Term Expires: 2017
E-mail: sarah.maestasbarnes@nmlegis.gov
Committees: Appropriations and Finance; Energy, Environment, and
Natural Resources
Education: New Mexico BA, JD

Representative **W. Ken Martinez** (D-District 69) . . . . . . . . (505) 986-4776
Counties Represented: Bernalillo (part), Cibola      Dist: (505) 287-8801
(part), McKinley (part), San Juan (part), Socorro      Res: (505) 287-0716
(part), Valencia (part)
Term Expires: 2017
P.O. Box 730, Grants, NM 87020
E-mail: kenmartmlo@gmail.com
Committees: Government, Elections, and Indian Affairs; Judiciary
Education: New Mexico BA; Notre Dame JD

Representative **Javier I. Martínez** (D-District 11) . . . . . . . (505) 289-3939
Counties Represented: Bernalillo (part)
Term Expires: 2017
E-mail: javier.martinez@nmlegis.gov
Committees: Energy, Environment, and Natural Resources; Ways and
Means

Representative **Bill McCamley** (D-District 33) . . . . . . . . . . . (575) 496-5731
Counties Represented: Dona Ana (part)
Term Expires: 2017
PO Box 458, Mesilla Park, NM 88048
E-mail: bill.mccamley@nmlegis.gov
Committees: Agriculture and Water Resources; Ways and Means
Education: New Mexico State 2001 BA; Harvard 2003

Representative **Terry H. McMillan** (R-District 37) . . . . . . . . (505) 986-4220
Counties Represented: Dona Ana (part)      Dist: (575) 635-0534
Term Expires: 2017
2001 East Lohman Avenue, #282, Las Cruces, NM 88001
E-mail: docmcmillan@msn.com
Committees: Health; Judiciary

Representative **Matthew McQueen** (D-District 50) . . . . . . (505) 986-4214
Counties Represented: Bernalillo (part), Santa Fe (part), Torrance
(part), Valencia (part)
Term Expires: 2017
E-mail: matthew.mcqueen@nmlegis.gov
Committees: Energy, Environment, and Natural Resources;
Transportation and Public Works

Representative **Rodney D. Montoya** (R-District 1) . . . . . . . (505) 360-1510
Counties Represented: San Juan (part)
Term Expires: 2017
E-mail: roddmontoya@gmail.com
Committees: Transportation and Public Works; Ways and Means

Representative **Andy Nuñez** (R-District 36) . . . . . . . . . . . . (575) 520-1654
Counties Represented: Dona Ana (part)
Term Expires: 2017
E-mail: annunez@zianet.com
Committees: Agriculture and Water Resources; Health
Education: New Mexico State 1962 BS, 1974 MS

Representative **Paul A. Pacheco** (R-District 23) . . . . . . . . . (505) 263-9235
Counties Represented: Bernalillo (part), Sandoval      Tel: (505) 922-0850
(part)
Term Expires: 2017
4216 Rancho grande Place Northwest, Albuquerque, NM 87120
E-mail: paul.pacheco@nmlegis.gov
Committees: Judiciary; Transportation and Public Works

Representative **Jane E. Powdrell-Culbert** (R-District 44) . . (505) 986-4467
Counties Represented: Sandoval (part)      Tel: (505) 890-5254
Term Expires: 2017
P.O. Box 2819, Corrales, NM 87048
E-mail: jpandp@comcast.net
Committees: Business and Employment; Government, Elections, and
Indian Affairs

Representative **William R. "Bill" Rehm** (R-District 31) . . . (505) 986-4248
Counties Represented: Bernalillo (part)      Tel: (505) 259-3398
Term Expires: 2017
P.O. Box 14768, Albuquerque, NM 87122
E-mail: bill.rehm@nmlegis.gov
Committees: Education; Safety and Civil Affairs

Representative **Dennis J. Roch** (R-District 67) . . . . . . . . . . (505) 986-4254
Counties Represented: Colfax (part), Curry (part),      Tel: (575) 799-7796
Harding, Quay, Roosevelt (part), San Miguel (part), Union
Term Expires: 2017
PO Box 355, Texico, NM 88135
E-mail: denroch@hotmail.com
Committees: Appropriations and Finance; Education

Representative **Debbie A. Rodella** (D-District 41) . . . . . . . . (505) 986-4329
Counties Represented: Rio Arriba (part), Santa Fe      Res: (505) 753-8247
(part), Taos (part)
Term Expires: 2017
16 Private Drive 1156, Espanola, NM 87532
E-mail: debbie.rodella@yahoo.com
Committees: Business and Employment; Government, Elections, and
Indian Affairs

LEGISLATIVE BRANCH

Representative **G. Andrés Romero** (D-District 10) . . . . . . (505) 514-9574
Counties Represented: Bernalillo (part)
Term Expires: 2017
E-mail: andres.romero@nmlegis.gov
Committees: Safety and Civil Affairs
Education: New Mexico 2010 BA

Representative
**Patricia A. Roybal Caballero** (D-District 13) . . . . . . . . . (505) 710-5996
Counties Represented: Bernalillo (part)
Term Expires: 2017
PO Box 72574, Albuquerque, NM 87195
E-mail: pat.roybalcaballero@nmlegis.gov
Committees: Consumer and Public Affairs; Regulatory and Public
Affairs; Safety and Civil Affairs
Education: New Mexico 2012 MPA

Representative **Patricio R. Ruiloba** (D-District 12) . . . . . . (505) 417-1749
Counties Represented: Bernalillo (part)
Term Expires: 2017
E-mail: patricio.ruiloba@nmlegis.gov
Committees: Safety and Civil Affairs; Transportation and Public Works

Representative **Nick L. Salazar** (D-District 40) . . . . . . . . . (505) 986-4433
Counties Represented: Colfax (part), Mora, Rio          Tel: (505) 663-5849
Arriba (part), San Miguel (part)                       Res: (505) 852-4178
Term Expires: 2017
P.O. Box 1076, Ohkay Owingeh, NM 87566
Committees: Appropriations and Finance; Health

Representative **Tomas E. Salazar** (D-District 70) . . . . . . . . (575) 421-2455
Counties Represented: San Miguel (part), Santa Fe (part), Torrance
(part)
Term Expires: 2017
PO Box 66, Las Vegas, NM 87701
E-mail: tomas.salazar@nmlegis.gov
Committees: Appropriations and Finance; Education
Education: New Mexico Highlands 1965 BS; Montana 1969 MA;
New Mexico 1976 PhD

Representative **Larry R. Scott** (R-District 62) . . . . . . . . . . . (575) 392-5960
Counties Represented: Lea (part)
Term Expires: 2017
E-mail: larry.scott@nmlegis.gov
Committees: Energy, Environment, and Natural Resources; Ways and
Means

Representative **James E. "Jim" Smith** (R-District 22) . . . . (505) 986-4467
Counties Represented: Bernalillo (part), Sandoval     Dist: (505) 934-1075
(part), Santa Fe (part)
Term Expires: 2017
P. O. Box 1783, Sandia Park, NM 87047
E-mail: jim@jimsmithnm.com
Committees: Government, Elections, and Indian Affairs; Regulatory
and Public Affairs

Representative
**Sheryl Williams Stapleton** (D-District 19) . . . . . . . . . (505) 986-4774
Counties Represented: Bernalillo (part)               Res: (505) 265-6089
Term Expires: 2017
P.O. Box 25385, Albuquerque, NM 87108
E-mail: sheryl.stapleton@nmlegis.gov
Committees: Education; Safety and Civil Affairs

Representative **Jeff Steinborn** (D-District 35) . . . . . . . . . . (575) 635-5615
Counties Represented: Dona Ana (part)
Term Expires: 2017
PO Box 562, Las Cruces, NM 88004
E-mail: jeff.steinborn@nmlegis.gov
Committees: Appropriations and Finance; Energy, Environment, and
Natural Resources
Education: Texas 1995 BA

Representative **James R.J. Strickler** (R-District 2) . . . . . . (505) 986-4227
Counties Represented: San Juan (part)                Res: (505) 327-4190
Term Expires: 2017
2204 North Santiago Avenue, Farmington, NM 87401
E-mail: jamesstrickler@msn.com
Committees: Energy, Environment, and Natural Resources; Ways and
Means

Representative **James G. Townsend** (R-District 54) . . . . . . (575) 703-0153
Counties Represented: Chaves (part), Eddy (part), Otero (part)
Term Expires: 2017
E-mail: james.townsend@nmlegis.gov
Committees: Energy, Environment, and Natural Resources; Safety and
Civil Affairs

Representative **Don L. Tripp** (R-District 49) . . . . . . . . . . . . (505) 986-4220
Counties Represented: Catron, Socorro (part),        Tel: (575) 835-2465
Valencia (part)                                      Res: (575) 835-0766
Term Expires: 2017
Box 1369, Socorro, NM 87801
E-mail: trippsdon@netscape.net
Committees: Health; Safety and Civil Affairs

Representative **Carl P. Trujillo** (D-District 46) . . . . . . . . . . (505) 699-6690
Counties Represented: Santa Fe (part)
Term Expires: 2017
11 West Gutierrez Street, Suite 3212, Santa Fe, NM 87506
E-mail: carl.trujillo@nmlegis.gov
Committees: Business and Employment; Ways and Means
Education: New Mexico BS

Representative **Christine V. Trujillo** (D-District 25) . . . . . . (505) 503-8600
Counties Represented: Bernalillo (part)
Term Expires: 2017
1923 Madeira Drive Northeast, Albuquerque, NM 87110
E-mail: christine.trujillo@nmlegis.gov
Committees: Appropriations and Finance; Education
Education: New Mexico Highlands BA; New Mexico MA

Representative **Jim R. Trujillo** (D-District 45) . . . . . . . . . . . (505) 986-4255
Counties Represented: Santa Fe (part)                Res: (505) 438-8890
Term Expires: 2017
1901 Morris Place, Santa Fe, NM 87505
E-mail: jimtrujillo@msn.com
Committees: Business and Employment; Ways and Means

Representative **Luciano "Lucky" Varela** (D-District 48) . . . (505) 986-4320
Counties Represented: Santa Fe (part)                Res: (505) 982-1292
Term Expires: 2017
1709 Callejon Zenaida, Santa Fe, NM 87501
E-mail: lucky4st@msn.com
Committees: Appropriations and Finance; Transportation and Public
Works
Education: Col Santa Fe 1968 BBA; La Salle U 1974 JD

Representative **Bob Wooley** (R-District 66) . . . . . . . . . . . . (505) 986-4453
Counties Represented: Chaves (part), Lea (part),     Res: (575) 627-6277
Roosevelt (part)
Term Expires: 2017
4504 Verdre Drive, Roswell, NM 88201
E-mail: bobwooley66@gmail.com
Committees: Agriculture and Water Resources; Regulatory and Public
Affairs
Education: New Mexico State BS

Representative **Monica Youngblood** (R-District 68) . . . . . . (505) 342-6250
Counties Represented: Bernalillo (part)
Term Expires: 2017
9832 Stone Street Northwest, Albuquerque, NM 87114
E-mail: monica@mynmstaterep.com
Committees: Appropriations and Finance; Education

Representative **John L. Zimmerman** (R-District 39) . . . . . . (575) 649-1217
Counties Represented: Dona Ana (part), Grant (part), Sierra (part)
Term Expires: 2017
E-mail: jzimmer_43@msn.com
Committees: Appropriations and Finance; Health

# House Standing Committees
## Agriculture and Water Resources
State Capitol, Room 318, Santa Fe, NM 87503

**Majority Members**
Candy Spence Ezzell (R-58) *Chair*
Andy Nuñez (R-36) *Vice Chair*
Paul C. Bandy (R-3)
Randal S. Crowder (R-64)
George Dodge, Jr. (R-63)
Bob Wooley (R-66)

**Minority Members**
Bealquin "Bill" Gomez (D-34)
Roberto J. "Bobby" Gonzales
(D-42)
Dona G. Irwin (D-32)
Bill McCamley (D-33)

## Appropriations and Finance
State Capitol, Room 307, Santa Fe, NM 87503

**Majority Members**
Larry A. Larrañaga (R-27) *Chair*
Paul C. Bandy (R-3) *Vice Chair*
Jimmie C. Hall (R-28)
*Deputy Chair*
Sharon E. Clahchischilliage (R-4)
Dr. Conrad D. James (R-24)
Sarah Maestas Barnes (R-15)
Dennis J. Roch (R-67)
Monica Youngblood (R-68)
John L. Zimmerman (R-39)

**Minority Members**
Doreen Y. Gallegos (D-52)
Stephanie Garcia Richard (D-43)
Patricia A. Lundstrom (D-9)
Nick L. Salazar (D-40)
Tomas E. Salazar (D-70)
Jeff Steinborn (D-35)
Christine V. Trujillo (D-25)
Luciano "Lucky" Varela (D-48)

LEGISLATIVE BRANCH

# Business and Employment
State Capitol, Room 309, Santa Fe, NM 87503

| Majority Members | Minority Members |
| --- | --- |
| Jane E. Powdrell-Culbert (R-44) *Chair* | Miguel P. García (D-14) |
| Dr. Conrad D. James (R-24) *Vice Chair* | Dona G. Irwin (D-32) |
| David Edward Adkins (R-29) | Debbie A. Rodella (D-41) |
| George Dodge, Jr. (R-63) | Carl P. Trujillo (D-46) |
| Candy Spence Ezzell (R-58) | Jim R. Trujillo (D-45) |
| Yvette Herrell (R-51) | |
| Rick L. Little (R-53) | |
| Tim D. Lewis (R-60) | |

# Consumer and Public Affairs
State Capitol, Room 315, Santa Fe, NM 87503

| Majority Members | Minority Members |
| --- | --- |
| Jason Carl Harper (R-57) | Eliseo Lee Alcon (D-6) *Chair* |
| | Patricia A. Roybal Caballero (D-13) *Vice Chair* |
| | Gail Chasey (D-18) |

# Education
State Capitol, Room 317, Santa Fe, NM 87503

| Majority Members | Minority Members |
| --- | --- |
| Nora Espinoza (R-59) *Chair* | Stephanie Garcia Richard (D-43) |
| Monica Youngblood (R-68) *Vice Chair* | Doreen Wonda Johnson (D-5) |
| Dennis J. Roch (R-67) *Deputy Chair* | Tomas E. Salazar (D-70) |
| Alonzo Baldonado (R-8) | Sheryl Williams Stapleton (D-19) |
| James Mitchell "Jim" Dines (R-20) | Christine V. Trujillo (D-25) |
| Jimmie C. Hall (R-28) | |
| William R. "Bill" Rehm (R-31) | |

# Energy, Environment, and Natural Resources
State Capitol, Room 315, Santa Fe, NM 87503

| Majority Members | Minority Members |
| --- | --- |
| James R.J. Strickler (R-2) *Chair* | Brian F. Egolf, Jr. (D-47) |
| David M. Gallegos (R-61) *Vice Chair* | Idalia Lechuga-Tena (D-21) |
| Nate Gentry (R-30) | Javier I. Martínez (D-11) |
| Sarah Maestas Barnes (R-15) | Matthew McQueen (D-50) |
| Larry R. Scott (R-62) | Jeff Steinborn (D-35) |
| James G. Townsend (R-54) | |

# Government, Elections, and Indian Affairs

| Majority Members | Minority Members |
| --- | --- |
| James E. "Jim" Smith (R-22) *Chair* | Eliseo Lee Alcon (D-6) |
| Sharon E. Clahchischilliage (R-4) *Vice Chair* | Doreen Y. Gallegos (D-52) |
| Zachary J. Cook (R-56) | James Roger Madalena (D-65) |
| Kelly K. Fajardo (R-7) | Antonio "Moe" Maestas (D-16) |
| Dianne Miller Hamilton (R-38) | W. Ken Martinez (D-69) |
| Jane E. Powdrell-Culbert (R-44) | Debbie A. Rodella (D-41) |

# Health
State Capitol, Room 309, Santa Fe, NM 87503

| Majority Members | Minority Members |
| --- | --- |
| Terry H. McMillan (R-37) *Chair* | Deborah A. Armstrong (D-17) |
| Kelly K. Fajardo (R-7) *Vice Chair* | Gail Chasey (D-18) |
| Andy Nuñez (R-36) | Georgene Louis (D-26) |
| Don L. Tripp (R-49) | James Roger Madalena (D-65) |
| John L. Zimmerman (R-39) | Nick L. Salazar (D-40) |

# Judiciary
State Capitol, Room 309, Santa Fe, NM 87503

| Majority Members | Minority Members |
| --- | --- |
| Zachary J. Cook (R-56) *Chair* | Eliseo Lee Alcon (D-6) |
| Paul A. Pacheco (R-23) *Vice Chair* | Gail Chasey (D-18) |
| David Edward Adkins (R-29) | Brian F. Egolf, Jr. (D-47) |
| Cathrynn N. Brown (R-55) | Georgene Louis (D-26) |
| James Mitchell "Jim" Dines (R-20) | Antonio "Moe" Maestas (D-16) |
| Nate Gentry (R-30) | W. Ken Martinez (D-69) |
| Terry H. McMillan (R-37) | |

# Regulatory and Public Affairs
State Capitol, Room 317, Santa Fe, NM 87503

| Majority Members | Minority Members |
| --- | --- |
| Yvette Herrell (R-51) *Chair* | Deborah A. Armstrong (D-17) |
| Bob Wooley (R-66) *Vice Chair* | Doreen Wonda Johnson (D-5) |
| Nora Espinoza (R-59) | Patricia A. Roybal Caballero (D-13) |
| James E. "Jim" Smith (R-22) | |

# Safety and Civil Affairs
State Capitol, Room 305, Santa Fe, NM 87503

| Majority Members | Minority Members |
| --- | --- |
| William R. "Bill" Rehm (R-31) *Chair* | G. Andrés Romero (D-10) |
| Rick L. Little (R-53) *Vice Chair* | Patricia A. Roybal Caballero (D-13) |
| Alonzo Baldonado (R-8) | Patricio R. Ruiloba (D-12) |
| James G. Townsend (R-54) | Sheryl Williams Stapleton (D-19) |
| Don L. Tripp (R-49) | |

# Transportation and Public Works
State Capitol, Room 315, Santa Fe, NM 87503

| Majority Members | Minority Members |
| --- | --- |
| Cathrynn N. Brown (R-55) *Chair* | Bealquin "Bill" Gomez (D-34) |
| Dianne Miller Hamilton (R-38) *Vice Chair* | Roberto J. "Bobby" Gonzales (D-42) |
| Jason Carl Harper (R-57) | Patricia A. Lundstrom (D-9) |
| Larry A. Larrañaga (R-27) | Matthew McQueen (D-50) |
| Rodney D. Montoya (R-1) | Patricio R. Ruiloba (D-12) |
| Paul A. Pacheco (R-23) | Luciano "Lucky" Varela (D-48) |

# Ways and Means
State Capitol, Room 305, Santa Fe, NM 87503

| Majority Members | Minority Members |
| --- | --- |
| Jason Carl Harper (R-57) *Chair* | Miguel P. García (D-14) |
| Tim D. Lewis (R-60) *Vice Chair* | Idalia Lechuga-Tena (D-21) |
| Randal S. Crowder (R-64) | Javier I. Martínez (D-11) |
| David M. Gallegos (R-61) | Bill McCamley (D-33) |
| Rodney D. Montoya (R-1) | Carl P. Trujillo (D-46) |
| Larry R. Scott (R-62) | Jim R. Trujillo (D-45) |
| James R.J. Strickler (R-2) | |

# New York State Legislature

Tel: (518) 455-2468 (Legislative Library)

## New York State Senate

Legislative Office Building, Albany, NY 12248
Tel: (518) 455-2800  Internet: www.senate.state.ny.us

Temporary President and Majority Leader
**John J. Flanagan** (R) . . . . . . . . . . . . . . . . . . . . . . . . . . . . .(518) 455-2071
Education: William & Mary 1990 BA; Touro 1990 JD

Vice President Pro Tempore **Hugh T. Farley** (R) . . . . . . . . (518) 455-2181
Education: SUNY (Albany) BA; American U JD

Majority Program Development Committee Chairman
**James L. Seward** (R) . . . . . . . . . . . . . . . . . . . . . . . . . . . . .(518) 455-3131
Education: Hartwick BA

Assistant Majority Leader on Conference Operations
**Kemp Hannon** (R) . . . . . . . . . . . . . . . . . . . . . . . . . . . . . . . (518) 455-2200
Education: Boston Col 1967 BA; Fordham 1970 JD

Deputy Majority Leader for Government Oversight and
Accountability **Andrew J. Lanza** (R) . . . . . . . . . . . . . . . . .(518) 455-3215
Education: St John's U (NY) BS; Fordham JD

Deputy Majority Leader for Legislative Operations
**John A. DeFrancisco** (R) . . . . . . . . . . . . . . . . . . . . . . . . . (518) 455-3511
Education: Syracuse 1968 BS; Duke 1971 JD

Deputy Majority Leader for State/Federal Relations
**John J. Bonacic** (R) . . . . . . . . . . . . . . . . . . . . . . . . . . . . . (518) 455-3181
Education: Iona 1964 BA; Fordham 1964 JD

Majority Conference Chair **Kenneth P. LaValle** (R) . . . . . . .(518) 455-3121
Education: Adelphi BA; SUNY (New Paltz) MS; Touro JD

Majority Conference Vice Chair **Carl L. Marcellino** (R) . . . (518) 455-2390
Education: NYU BA, MS

Majority Conference Secretary **Martin J. Golden** (R) . . . . .(518) 455-2730

Majority Whip **Michael F. Nozzolio** (R) . . . . . . . . . . . . . . .(518) 455-2366
Education: Cornell 1973 BS, 1977 MS; Syracuse JD

Deputy Majority Whip
**Elizabeth O'Connor "Betty" Little** (R) . . . . . . . . . . . . .(518) 455-2811

Assistant Majority Whip **Joseph A. Griffo** (R) . . . . . . . . . (518) 455-3334

Independent Democratic Conference Leader
**Jeffrey D. "Jeff" Klein** (D) . . . . . . . . . . . . . . . . . . . . . . .(518) 455-3595

Independent Democratic Conference Whip
**David Carlucci** (D) . . . . . . . . . . . . . . . . . . . . . . . . . . . . . .(518) 455-2991
Education: Cornell 2002 BS

Democratic Conference Leader
**Andrea Stewart-Cousins** (D) . . . . . . . . . . . . . . . . . . . . .(518) 455-2585
Education: Pace BS

Deputy Democratic Conference Leader
**Michael N. Gianaris** (D) . . . . . . . . . . . . . . . . . . . . . . . . . .(518) 455-3486
Education: Fordham 1990 BA; Harvard 1993 JD

Assistant Democratic Conference Leader for Conference
Operations **Toby Ann Stavisky** (D) . . . . . . . . . . . . . . . . .(518) 455-3461
Education: Syracuse BA

Assistant Democratic Conference Leader for Floor
Operations **Neil D. Breslin** (D) . . . . . . . . . . . . . . . . . . . .(518) 455-2225
Education: Fordham 1964 BS

Assistant Democratic Conference Leader for
Intergovernmental Affairs **Kevin S. Parker** (D) . . . . . . . . .(518) 455-2580
Education: Penn State BS; New School MS

Assistant Democratic Conference Leader for Policy and
Administration **Martin Malave Dilan** (D) . . . . . . . . . . . . .(518) 455-2177

Deputy Democratic Conference Floor Leader
**Daniel Squadron** (D) . . . . . . . . . . . . . . . . . . . . . . . . . . . .(518) 455-2625

Democratic Conference Chair **José M. Serrano** (D) . . . . . .(518) 455-2795
Education: Manhattan Col 1995 BA

Democratic Conference Vice Chair
**Ruth Hassell-Thompson** (D) . . . . . . . . . . . . . . . . . . . . . .(518) 455-2061

Democratic Conference Whip **Jose R. Peralta** (D) . . . . . . .(518) 455-2529
Education: Queens Col (NY) BA

Deputy Democratic Conference Whip **Bill Perkins** (D) . . . .(518) 455-2441
Education: Brown U BA

Assistant Democratic Conference Whip
**Timothy M. Kennedy** (D) . . . . . . . . . . . . . . . . . . . . . . . .(518) 455-2426

Democratic Conference Program Development Chair
**Gustavo Rivera** (D) . . . . . . . . . . . . . . . . . . . . . . . . . . . . .(518) 455-3395
Education: Puerto Rico

Secretary of the Senate **Francis W. Patience** . . . . . . . . . . .(518) 455-2051

Sergeant-at-Arms **Stephen F. Slagen** . . . . . . . . . . . . . . . . .(518) 455-2338

## Senators

**Party Affiliation Statistics:** Republicans: 31, Democrats: 27,
Independents: 5

Senator **Joseph P. Addabbo, Jr.** (D-District 15) . . . . . . . . . (518) 455-2322
Counties Represented: Queens (part)          Dist: (718) 738-1111
Term Expires: 2017                            Fax: (518) 426-6875
159-53 102nd Street, Howard Beach, NY 11414  Dist: (718) 322-5760
E-mail: addabbo@nysenate.gov
Committees: Aging; Civil Service and Pensions; Education;
Environmental Conservation; Labor; Racing, Gaming and Wagering;
Veterans, Homeland Security and Military Affairs
Education: St John's U (NY) BA; Touro JD

Senator **Frederick J. Akshar II** (R-District 52) . . . . . . . . . .(518) 455-2677
Counties Represented: Broome, Chenango (part),    Dist: (607) 773-8771
Delaware (part), Tioga                             Fax: (518) 426-6720
Term Expires: 2017                                 Dist: (607) 773-3688
44 Hawley Street, Binghamton, NY 13901
E-mail: akshar@nysenate.gov
Committees: Banks; Cities; Codes; Consumer Protection; Crime
Victims, Crime and Correction; Elections; Labor

Senator **George A. Amedore, Jr.** (R-District 46)
Room 802 . . . . . . . . . . . . . . . . . . . . . . . . . . . . . . . . . . . . . .(518) 455-2350
Counties Represented: Albany (part), Greene,      Fax: (518) 426-6751
Montgomery, Schenectady (part), Ulster (part)
Term Expires: 2017
E-mail: amedore@nysenate.gov
Committees: Alcoholism and Drug Abuse; Banks; Consumer
Protection; Corporations, Authorities and Commissions; Elections;
Judiciary; Social Services; Veterans, Homeland Security and Military
Affairs

Senator **Tony Avella** (D-District 11) . . . . . . . . . . . . . . . . . .(518) 455-2210
Counties Represented: Queens (part)               Dist: (718) 357-3094
Note: Democrat Tony Avella is part of the         Fax: (518) 426-6736
Independent Democratic Conference and will        Dist: (718) 357-3491
caucus with the Republican majority during the 2016 legislative
session.
Term Expires: 2017
38-50 Bell Boulevard, Suite C, Bayside, NY 11361
E-mail: avella@nysenate.gov
Committees: Banks; Children and Families; Cultural Affairs,
Tourism, Parks and Recreation; Education; Elections; Environmental
Conservation; Housing, Construction and Community Development;
Insurance; Judiciary; Transportation
Education: Hunter BA

Senator **John J. Bonacic** (R-District 42) . . . . . . . . . . . . . . . (518) 455-3181
Counties Represented: Delaware (part), Orange     Dist: (845) 344-3311
(part), Sullivan, Ulster (part)                   (Middletown Office)
Term Expires: 2017                                Dist: (607) 746-6675
201 Dolson Avenue, Suite F,                       (Delhi Office)
Middletown, NY 10940
111 Main Street, Delhi, NY 13753
E-mail: bonacic@nysenate.gov
Committees: Alcoholism and Drug Abuse; Banks; Children and
Families; Finance; Housing, Construction and Community
Development; Judiciary; Racing, Gaming and Wagering; Rules
Affiliation: Of Counsel, Bonacic, Lobiondo, Krahulik, LLP
90 Crystal Run Road, Suite 106, Middletown, NY 10941

Senator **Philip M. "Phil" Boyle** (R-District 4) . . . . . . . . . .(518) 455-3411
Counties Represented: Suffolk (part)              Dist: (631) 665-2311
Term Expires: 2017
69 West Main Street, Suite B, Bay Shore, NY 11706
E-mail: pboyle@nysenate.gov
Committees: Codes; Commerce, Economic Development and Small
Business; Consumer Protection; Finance; Housing, Construction and
Community Development; Judiciary; Local Government; Racing,
Gaming and Wagering
Education: North Carolina 1983 AB; SUNY (Albany) 1987 MPA;
Albany Law 1987 JD

Senator **Neil D. Breslin** (D-District 44) . . . . . . . . . . . . . . . (518) 455-2225
Counties Represented: Albany (part), Rensselaer   Fax: (518) 426-6807
(part)
Term Expires: 2017
State Capitol Building, Room 414, Albany, NY 12247
E-mail: breslin@nysenate.gov
Committees: Banks; Education; Finance; Higher Education; Insurance;
Judiciary; Rules

*(continued on next page)*

**LEGISLATIVE BRANCH**

**Senators** *continued*

Senator **David Carlucci** (D-District 38) . . . . . . . . . . . . . . . (518) 455-2991
Counties Represented: Rockland (part), Westchester    Dist: (845) 623-3627
(part)    Fax: (518) 426-6737
Note: Democrat David Carlucci is part of the    Dist: (845) 624-0424
Independent Democratic Conference and will caucus with the
Republican majority during the 2016 legislative session.
Term Expires: 2017
20 South Main Street, New City, NY 10956
E-mail: carlucci@nysenate.gov
Committees: Alcoholism and Drug Abuse; Energy and
Telecommunications; Infrastructure and Capital Investment; Insurance;
Investigations and Government Operations; Mental Health and
Developmental Disabilities; Racing, Gaming and Wagering; Rules;
Social Services; Veterans, Homeland Security and Military Affairs

Senator **Leroy G. Comrie, Jr.** (D-District 14) . . . . . . . . . . . (518) 455-2701
Counties Represented: Queens (part)    Dist: (718) 454-0162
Term Expires: 2017
Legislative Office Building, Room 617, Albany, NY 12247
E-mail: comrie@nysenate.gov
Committees: Agriculture; Civil Service and Pensions; Consumer
Protection; Elections; Infrastructure and Capital Investment; Judiciary;
Racing, Gaming and Wagering; Veterans, Homeland Security and
Military Affairs

Senator **Thomas D. Croci** (R-District 3) . . . . . . . . . . . . . . (518) 455-3570
Counties Represented: Suffolk (part)    Dist: (631) 360-3356
Term Expires: 2017
Legislative Office Building, Room 306, Albany, NY 12247
E-mail: croci@nysenate.gov
Committees: Alcoholism and Drug Abuse; Civil Service and Pensions;
Education; Energy and Telecommunications; Ethics; Higher Education;
Infrastructure and Capital Investment; Judiciary; Veterans, Homeland
Security and Military Affairs
Education: James Madison BS; New York Law JD

Senator **John A. DeFrancisco** (R-District 50) . . . . . . . . . . (518) 455-3511
Counties Represented: Cayuga (part), Onondaga    Dist: (315) 428-7632
(part)
Term Expires: 2017
800 State Office Building, 333 East Washington Street,
Syracuse, NY 13202
E-mail: jdefranc@nysenate.gov
Committees: Rules

Senator **Ruben Diaz, Sr.** (D-District 32) . . . . . . . . . . . . . . (518) 455-2511
Counties Represented: Bronx (part)    Dist: (718) 991-3161
Term Expires: 2017    Fax: (518) 426-6945
900 Rogers Place, Bronx, NY 10459    Dist: (718) 991-0309
E-mail: diaz@nysenate.gov
Committees: Aging; Banks; Finance; Investigations and Government
Operations; Judiciary; Transportation
Education: Lehman Col 1976 BD

Senator **Martin Malave Dilan** (D-District 18) . . . . . . . . . . (518) 455-2177
Counties Represented: Kings (part)    Dist: (718) 573-1726
Term Expires: 2017    Fax: (518) 426-6947
573 Metropolitan Avenue, Brooklyn, NY 11211    Dist: (718) 573-2407
E-mail: dilan@nysenate.gov
Committees: Elections; Energy and Telecommunications; Finance;
Infrastructure and Capital Investment; Judiciary; Labor; Rules;
Transportation

Senator **Adriano Espaillat** (D-District 31) . . . . . . . . . . . . . (518) 455-2041
Counties Represented: New York (part)    Dist: (212) 544-0173
Term Expires: 2017    Fax: (518) 426-6847
5030 Broadway, New York, NY 10034    Dist: (212) 544-0256
E-mail: espailla@nysenate.gov
Committees: Codes; Environmental Conservation; Finance; Higher
Education; Housing, Construction and Community Development;
Judiciary; Rules
Education: Queens Col (NY) 1978 BS

Senator **Hugh T. Farley** (R-District 49) . . . . . . . . . . . . . . (518) 455-2181
Counties Represented: Fulton, Hamilton, Herkimer    Dist: (518) 885-1829
(part), Saratoga (part), Schenectady (part)    (Ballston Spa Office)
Term Expires: 2017    Dist: (518) 762-3733
33 - 41 East Main Street City Hall,    (Johnstown Office)
Johnstown, NY 12095    Fax: (518) 455-2271
199 Milton Avenue, Suite 4,    Dist: (518) 885-1920
Ballston Spa, NY 12020    (Ballston Spa Office)
E-mail: farley@nysenate.gov    Dist: (518) 762-3721
Committees: Banks; Education; Ethics; Rules;    (Johnstown Office)
Social Services

Senator **Simcha Felder** (D-District 17) . . . . . . . . . . . . . . . (518) 455-2754
Counties Represented: Kings (part)    Dist: (718) 253-2015
Term Expires: 2017    Fax: (518) 426-6931
1412 Avenue, J Suite 2E, Brooklyn, NY 11230    Dist: (718) 253-2030
E-mail: felder@nysenate.gov
Committees: Aging; Cities; Commerce, Economic Development and
Small Business; Health; Infrastructure and Capital Investment; Mental
Health and Developmental Disabilities; Veterans, Homeland Security
and Military Affairs
Education: Touro BS; Baruch Col MBA

Senator **John J. Flanagan** (R-District 2) . . . . . . . . . . . . . . (518) 455-2071
Counties Represented: Suffolk (part)    Dist: (631) 361-2154
Term Expires: 2017    Fax: (518) 426-6904
260 Middle Country Road, Suite 102,    Dist: (631) 361-5367
Smithtown, NY 11787
E-mail: flanagan@nysenate.gov
Committees: Rules

Senator **Rich Funke** (R-District 55) . . . . . . . . . . . . . . . . . (518) 455-2215
Counties Represented: Monroe (part), Ontario (part)    Dist: (585) 223-1800
Term Expires: 2017    Fax: (518) 426-6745
230 Packett's Landing, Fairport, NY 14450    Dist: (585) 223-3157
E-mail: funke@nysenate.gov
Committees: Aging; Agriculture; Cities; Commerce, Economic
Development and Small Business; Consumer Protection; Cultural
Affairs, Tourism, Parks and Recreation; Environmental Conservation;
Higher Education

Senator **Patrick M. Gallivan** (R-District 59) . . . . . . . . . . . (518) 455-3471
Counties Represented: Erie (part), Livingston    Dist: (716) 656-8544
(part), Monroe (part), Wyoming    Fax: (518) 426-6949
Term Expires: 2017    Dist: (716) 656-8961
2721 Transit Road, Suite 116, Elma, NY 14059
E-mail: gallivan@nysenate.gov
Committees: Agriculture; Codes; Commerce, Economic Development
and Small Business; Crime Victims, Crime and Correction; Elections;
Finance; Higher Education; Housing, Construction and Community
Development; Infrastructure and Capital Investment; Labor;
Transportation
Education: SUNY (Albany) 1992 MA

Senator **Michael N. Gianaris** (D-District 12) . . . . . . . . . . . (518) 455-3486
Counties Represented: Queens (part)    Dist: (718) 728-0960
Term Expires: 2017    Fax: (518) 426-6929
31-19 Newtown Avenue, Suite 402,    Dist: (718) 728-0963
Astoria, NY 11102
E-mail: gianaris@nysenate.gov
Committees: Ethics; Rules

Senator **Martin J. Golden** (R-District 22) . . . . . . . . . . . . . (518) 455-2730
Counties Represented: Kings (part)    Dist: (718) 238-6044
Term Expires: 2017    Fax: (718) 238-6170
7408 Fifth Avenue, 1st Floor, Brooklyn, NY 11209
E-mail: golden@nysenate.gov
Committees: Aging; Banks; Civil Service and Pensions; Codes;
Finance; Health; Insurance; Investigations and Government Operations;
Veterans, Homeland Security and Military Affairs

Senator **Joseph A. Griffo** (R-District 47) . . . . . . . . . . . . . . (518) 455-3334
Counties Represented: Lewis, Oneida (part),    Dist: (315) 793-9072
St. Lawrence (part)    Fax: (518) 426-6921
Term Expires: 2017    Dist: (315) 793-0298
207 Genesee Street, Room 408, Utica, NY 13501
E-mail: griffo@nysenate.gov
Committees: Codes; Commerce, Economic Development and Small
Business; Crime Victims, Crime and Correction; Cultural Affairs,
Tourism, Parks and Recreation; Energy and Telecommunications;
Finance; Higher Education; Racing, Gaming and Wagering

Senator **Jesse E. Hamilton** (D-District 20) . . . . . . . . . . . . (518) 455-2431
Counties Represented: Kings (part)    Dist: (718) 284-4700
Term Expires: 2017
Legislative Office Building, Room 608, Albany, NY 12247
1669 Bedford Avenue, Second Floor, Brooklyn, NY 11225
E-mail: hamilton@nysenate.gov
Committees: Agriculture; Banks; Codes; Education; Energy and
Telecommunications; Insurance; Mental Health and Developmental
Disabilities

Senator **Kemp Hannon** (R-District 6) . . . . . . . . . . . . . . . . (518) 455-2200
Counties Represented: Nassau (part)    Dist: (516) 739-1700
Term Expires: 2017
595 Stewart Avenue, Suite 540, Garden City, NY 11530
E-mail: hannon@nysenate.gov
Committees: Finance; Health; Judiciary; Labor; Mental Health and
Developmental Disabilities; Rules

Senator **Ruth Hassell-Thompson** (D-District 36) ......... (518) 455-2061
Counties Represented: Bronx (part), Westchester   Dist: (718) 547-8854
(part)   (Bronx Office)
Note: On April 22, 2016, Ruth Hassell-Thompson   Dist: (914) 665-2400
was appointed Special Advisor for Policy and   (Mount Vernon
Community Affairs for New York State Homes   Office)
and Community Renewal. Hassell-Thompson's   Fax: (518) 426-6998
departure date from the New York State Senate   Dist: (718) 515-2718
has not yet been determined.   (Bronx Office)
Term Expires: 2017
959 East 233rd Street, Bronx, NY 10466
Doles Center, 250 South 6th Avenue, Mount Vernon, NY 10550
E-mail: hassellt@nysenate.gov
Committees: Commerce, Economic Development and Small Business;
Crime Victims, Crime and Correction; Finance; Health; Judiciary;
Rules

Senator **Brad Hoylman** (D-District 27) ................ (518) 455-2451
Counties Represented: New York (part)   Dist: (212) 633-8052
Term Expires: 2017   Fax: (518) 426-6846
322 Eighth Avenue, Suite 1700,   Dist: (212) 633-8096
New York, NY 10001
E-mail: hoylman@nysenate.gov
Committees: Aging; Cultural Affairs, Tourism, Parks and Recreation;
Environmental Conservation; Health; Investigations and Government
Operations; Judiciary
Education: West Virginia 1989 BA; Oxford (UK) 1992 MPhil;
Harvard JD

Senator **Todd Kaminsky** (D-District 9) ................ (518) 455-3401
Counties Represented: Nassau (part)   Fax: (518) 426-6914
Term Expires: 2017
55 Front Street, Rockville Centre, NY 11570-4040
E-mail: kaminsky@nysenate.gov
Committees: Alcoholism and Drug Abuse; Codes; Environmental
Conservation; Finance; Health; Local Government; Transportation;
Veterans, Homeland Security and Military Affairs
Education: Michigan; NYU JD

Senator **Timothy M. Kennedy** (D-District 63) .......... (518) 455-2426
Counties Represented: Erie (part)   Dist: (716) 826-2683
Term Expires: 2017   Fax: (518) 426-6851
2239 South Park Avenue, Buffalo, NY 14220   Dist: (716) 826-2793
E-mail: kennedy@nysenate.gov
Committees: Banks; Commerce, Economic Development and Small
Business; Cultural Affairs, Tourism, Parks and Recreation; Energy and
Telecommunications; Finance; Infrastructure and Capital Investment;
Insurance; Transportation

Senator **Jeffrey D. "Jeff" Klein** (D-District 34) ......... (518) 455-3595
Counties Represented: Bronx (part), Westchester   Dist: (718) 822-2049
(part)   Fax: (718) 822-2321
Note: Democrat Jeffrey Klein is part of the Independent Democratic
Conference and will caucus with the Republican majority during the
2016 legislative session.
Term Expires: 2017
1250 Waters Place, Suite 1202, Bronx, NY 10461
E-mail: jdklein@nysenate.gov

Senator **Liz Krueger** (D-District 28) ................... (518) 455-2297
Counties Represented: New York (part)   Dist: (212) 490-9535
Term Expires: 2017   Fax: (518) 426-6874
1850 Second Avenue, New York, NY 10128   Dist: (212) 490-2151
E-mail: lkrueger@nysenate.gov
Committees: Codes; Elections; Finance; Higher Education; Housing,
Construction and Community Development; Mental Health and
Developmental Disabilities; Rules
Education: Northwestern 1979 BS; Chicago 1981 MA

Senator **Andrew J. Lanza** (R-District 24) ............... (518) 455-3215
Counties Represented: Richmond (part)   Dist: (718) 984-4073
Term Expires: 2017   Fax: (518) 426-6852
3845 Richmond Avenue, Second Floor, Suite 2A,   Dist: (718) 984-4455
Staten Island, NY 10312
E-mail: lanza@nysenate.gov
Committees: Civil Service and Pensions; Codes; Education;
Ethics; Finance; Infrastructure and Capital Investment; Insurance;
Investigations and Government Operations; Judiciary; Rules

Senator **William J. Larkin, Jr.** (R-District 39) .......... (518) 455-2770
Counties Represented: Orange (part), Rockland   Dist: (845) 567-1270
(part), Ulster (part)
Term Expires: 2017
1093 Little Britain Road, New Windsor, NY 12553
E-mail: larkin@nysenate.gov
Committees: Corporations, Authorities and Commissions; Finance;
Health; Insurance; Rules; Transportation; Veterans, Homeland Security
and Military Affairs

Senator **George S. Latimer** (D-District 37) ............. (518) 455-2031
Counties Represented: Westchester (part)   Dist: (914) 934-5250
Term Expires: 2017   Fax: (914) 934-5256
222 Grace Church Street, Port Chester, NY 10573
E-mail: latimer@nysenate.gov
Committees: Banks; Consumer Protection; Education; Environmental
Conservation; Insurance; Local Government; Racing, Gaming and
Wagering
Education: Fordham 1974 BA; NYU 1976 MPA

Senator **Kenneth P. LaValle** (R-District 1) ............. (518) 455-3121
Counties Represented: Suffolk (part)   Dist: (631) 473-1461
Term Expires: 2017   Fax: (631) 473-1513
28 North Country Road, Suite 203, Mount Sinai, NY 11766
E-mail: lavalle@nysenate.gov
Committees: Aging; Education; Environmental Conservation; Finance;
Higher Education; Insurance; Judiciary; Rules; Social Services

Senator
**Elizabeth O'Connor "Betty" Little** (R-District 45) ..... (518) 455-2811
Counties Represented: Clinton, Essex, Franklin,   Dist: (518) 743-0968
St. Lawrence (part), Warren, Washington (part)   (Glens Falls Office)
Term Expires: 2017   Dist: (518) 561-2430
Five Warren Street, Glens Falls, NY 12801   (Plattsburgh Office)
137 Margaret Street, Plattsburgh, NY 12901
E-mail: little@nysenate.gov
Committees: Crime Victims, Crime and Correction; Cultural
Affairs, Tourism, Parks and Recreation; Education; Energy and
Telecommunications; Environmental Conservation; Finance; Health;
Housing, Construction and Community Development; Rules

Senator **Carl L. Marcellino** (R-District 5) ............. (518) 455-2390
Counties Represented: Nassau (part), Suffolk (part)   Dist: (516) 922-1811
Term Expires: 2017
250 Townsend Square, Oyster Bay, NY 11771
E-mail: marcelli@nysenate.gov
Committees: Banks; Cultural Affairs, Tourism, Parks and Recreation;
Education; Environmental Conservation; Finance; Labor; Rules;
Transportation

Senator
**Kathleen A. "Kathy" Marchione** (R-District 43) ...... (518) 455-2381
Counties Represented: Columbia, Rensselaer   Dist: (518) 371-2751
(part), Saratoga (part), Washington (part)   Fax: (518) 426-6985
Term Expires: 2017   Fax: (518) 371-2753
One Halfmoon Town Plaza, Halfmoon, NY 12065
E-mail: marchione@nysenate.gov
Committees: Aging; Banks; Cultural Affairs, Tourism, Parks and
Recreation; Elections; Finance; Local Government; Racing, Gaming
and Wagering; Veterans, Homeland Security and Military Affairs

Senator **Jack M. Martins** (R-District 7) ............... (518) 455-3265
Counties Represented: Nassau (part)   Dist: (516) 746-5924
Term Expires: 2017   Fax: (518) 426-6739
252 Mineola Boulevard, Mineola, NY 11501   Dist: (516) 740-0439
E-mail: martins@nysenate.gov
Committees: Banks; Civil Service and Pensions; Corporations,
Authorities and Commissions; Energy and Telecommunications;
Finance; Health; Insurance; Labor; Social Services; Transportation

Senator **Velmanette Montgomery** (D-District 25) ....... (518) 455-3451
Counties Represented: Kings (part)   Dist: (718) 643-6140
Term Expires: 2017   Fax: (518) 426-6845
30 Third Avenue, Brooklyn, NY 11217   Dist: (718) 237-4137
E-mail: montgome@nysenate.gov
Committees: Agriculture; Children and Families; Crime Victims, Crime
and Correction; Education; Finance; Health; Rules
Education: NYU MEd

Senator **Terrence P. Murphy** (R-District 40) ............ (518) 455-3111
Counties Represented: Dutchess (part), Putnam   Dist: (914) 962-2624
(part), Westchester (part)   Fax: (518) 426-6977
Term Expires: 2017   Fax: (914) 962-3505
691 East Main Street, Shrub Oak, NY 10588
E-mail: murphy@nysenate.gov
Committees: Banks; Ethics; Health; Insurance; Investigations and
Government Operations; Labor; Local Government; Mental Health and
Developmental Disabilities

Senator **Michael F. Nozzolio** (R-District 54) ........... (518) 455-2366
Counties Represented: Cayuga (part), Monroe   Dist: (315) 568-9816
(part), Ontario (part), Seneca, Tompkins (part),   Fax: (518) 426-6953
Wayne   Dist: (315) 568-2090
Term Expires: 2017
119 Fall Street, Seneca Falls, NY 13148
E-mail: nozzolio@nysenate.gov
Committees: Codes; Crime Victims, Crime and Correction; Elections;
Finance; Investigations and Government Operations; Judiciary; Racing,
Gaming and Wagering; Rules; Transportation

*(continued on next page)*

**Senators** *continued*

**Senator Thomas F. "Tom" O'Mara** (R-District 58) . . . . . . . (518) 455-2091
Counties Represented: Chemung, Schuyler, Steuben,    Dist: (607) 735-9671
Tompkins (part), Yates    Fax: (518) 426-6976
Term Expires: 2017    Dist: (607) 735-9675
333 East Water Street, Third Floor, Suite 301, Elma, NY 14901
E-mail: omara@nysenate.gov
Committees: Agriculture; Banks; Codes; Energy and
Telecommunications; Environmental Conservation; Finance; Insurance;
Investigations and Government Operations; Judiciary; Transportation
Education: Catholic U 1987 BA; Syracuse 1991 JD

**Senator Robert G. Ortt** (R-District 62) . . . . . . . . . . . . . . . (518) 455-2024
Counties Represented: Monroe (part), Niagara,    Dist: (716) 434-0680
Orleans    Fax: (716) 426-6987
Term Expires: 2017    Dist: (716) 434-3297
175 Walnut Street, Suite 6, Lockport, NY 14094
E-mail: ortt@nysenate.gov
Committees: Cities; Civil Service and Pensions; Corporations,
Authorities and Commissions; Environmental Conservation;
Higher Education; Labor; Local Government; Mental Health and
Developmental Disabilities; Veterans, Homeland Security and Military
Affairs

**Senator Marc C. Panepinto** (D-District 60) . . . . . . . . . . . . (518) 455-2760
Counties Represented: Erie (part)    Dist: (716) 854-8705
Term Expires: 2017    Fax: (518) 426-6760
65 Court Street, Room 213, Buffalo, NY 14202    Dist: (716) 854-3051
E-mail: panepinto@nysenate.gov
Committees: Agriculture; Housing, Construction and Community
Development; Insurance; Local Government

**Senator Kevin S. Parker** (D-District 21) . . . . . . . . . . . . . . (518) 455-2580
Counties Represented: Kings (part)    Dist: (718) 629-6401
Term Expires: 2017    Fax: (518) 426-6843
Shirley A. Chisholm SOB, 55 Hanson Place,    Dist: (718) 629-6420
Suite 650, Brooklyn, NY 11217
E-mail: parker@nysenate.gov
Committees: Alcoholism and Drug Abuse; Banks; Energy and
Telecommunications; Finance; Higher Education; Insurance; Rules

**Senator Jose R. Peralta** (D-District 13) . . . . . . . . . . . . . . . (518) 455-2529
Counties Represented: Queens (part)    Dist: (718) 205-3881
Term Expires: 2017    Fax: (518) 455-6909
32-37 Junction Boulevard,    Dist: (718) 205-4145
East Elmhurst, NY 11369
E-mail: jperalta@nysenate.gov
Committees: Cities; Consumer Protection; Crime Victims, Crime and
Correction; Education; Finance; Higher Education; Labor

**Senator Bill Perkins** (D-District 30) . . . . . . . . . . . . . . . . . (518) 455-2441
Counties Represented: New York (part)    Dist: (212) 222-7315
Term Expires: 2017    Fax: (518) 426-6809
163 West 125th Street, Harlem State Office    Dist: (212) 678-0001
Building, Suite 912, New York, NY 10027
E-mail: perkins@nysenate.gov
Committees: Codes; Corporations, Authorities and Commissions; Crime
Victims, Crime and Correction; Finance; Judiciary; Labor; Rules;
Transportation

**Senator Roxanne J. Persaud** (D-District 19) . . . . . . . . . . (518) 455-2788
Counties Represented: Kings (part)    Dist: (718) 649-7653
1222 East 96th Street, Brooklyn, NY 11236
E-mail: persaud@nysenate.gov
Committees: Children and Families; Cities; Civil Service and Pensions;
Commerce, Economic Development and Small Business; Cultural
Affairs, Tourism, Parks and Recreation; Health; Social Services
Education: Pace BS, MS

**Senator Michael H. Ranzenhofer** (R-District 61) . . . . . . . . (518) 455-3161
Counties Represented: Erie (part), Genesee, Monroe    Dist: (716) 631-8695
(part)    Fax: (518) 426-6963
Term Expires: 2017    Dist: (716) 634-4321
8203 Main Street, Suite 4, Williamsville, NY 14221
Legislative Office Building, Suite 609, Albany, NY 12247
E-mail: ranz@nysenate.gov
Committees: Agriculture; Corporations, Authorities and Commissions;
Education; Finance; Judiciary; Racing, Gaming and Wagering;
Transportation

**Senator Patricia Ritchie** (R-District 48) . . . . . . . . . . . . . . (518) 455-3438
Counties Represented: Jefferson, Oswego, St.    Dist: (315) 782-3418
Lawrence (part)    (Watertown Office)
Term Expires: 2017    Dist: (315) 342-2057
Dulles State Office Building, Room 418,    (Oswego Office)
Watertown, NY 13601    Dist: (315) 393-3024
46 East Bridge Street, 1st Floor,    (Ogdensburg Office)
Oswego, NY 13126    Fax: (518) 426-6740
330 Ford Street, Ogdensburg, NY 13669    Dist: (315) 782-6357
E-mail: ritchie@nysenate.gov    (Watertown Office)
Committees: Agriculture; Alcoholism and Drug Abuse; Civil Service
and Pensions; Crime Victims, Crime and Correction; Cultural Affairs,
Tourism, Parks and Recreation; Energy and Telecommunications;
Finance; Higher Education; Local Government; Transportation

**Senator Gustavo Rivera** (D-District 33) . . . . . . . . . . . . . . (518) 455-3395
Counties Represented: Bronx (part)    Dist: (718) 933-2034
Term Expires: 2017    Fax: (518) 426-6858
2432 Grand Concourse, Suite 506,    Dist: (718) 933-2825
Bronx, NY 10458
E-mail: grivera@nysenate.gov
Committees: Crime Victims, Crime and Correction; Ethics; Finance;
Health; Higher Education; Labor; Mental Health and Developmental
Disabilities

**Senator Joseph E. Robach** (R-District 56) . . . . . . . . . . . . (518) 455-2909
Counties Represented: Monroe (part)    Dist: (585) 225-3650
Term Expires: 2017
2300 West Ridge Road, Rochester, NY 14626
E-mail: robach@nysenate.gov
Committees: Commerce, Economic Development and Small Business;
Consumer Protection; Education; Finance; Higher Education;
Infrastructure and Capital Investment; Labor; Rules; Transportation
Education: Aquinas Inst Theol BS; SUNY (Brockport) MPA

**Senator James Sanders, Jr.** (D-District 10) . . . . . . . . . . . (518) 455-3531
Counties Represented: Queens (part)    Dist: (718) 523-3069
Term Expires: 2017    Fax: (518) 426-0529
142-01 Rockaway Boulevard, Jamaica, NY 11436    Fax: (718) 523-3670
E-mail: sanders@nysenate.gov
Committees: Banks; Civil Service and Pensions; Commerce, Economic
Development and Small Business; Cultural Affairs, Tourism, Parks and
Recreation; Insurance; Labor; Racing, Gaming and Wagering; Veterans,
Homeland Security and Military Affairs
Education: Brooklyn 1984 BA

**Senator Diane J. Savino** (D-District 23) . . . . . . . . . . . . . . (518) 455-2437
Counties Represented: Kings (part), Richmond    Dist: (718) 333-0311
(part)    (Brooklyn Office)
Note: Democrat Diane Savino is part of the    Dist: (718) 727-9406
Independent Democratic Conference and will    (Staten Island Office)
caucus with the Republican majority during the    Fax: (518) 426-6943
2016 legislative session.    Dist: (347) 492-3263
Term Expires: 2017    (Brooklyn Office)
2872 West 15th Street, Brooklyn, NY 11224-2602    Dist: (718) 727-9426
36 Richmond Terrace, Suite 112,    (Staten Island Office)
Staten Island, NY 10301
E-mail: savino@nysenate.gov
Committees: Banks; Children and Families; Cities; Civil Service and
Pensions; Codes; Consumer Protection; Crime Victims, Crime and
Correction; Finance; Judiciary; Labor

**Senator Susan Serino** (R-District 41) . . . . . . . . . . . . . . . . (518) 455-2945
Counties Represented: Dutchess (part), Putnam    Dist: (845) 229-0106
(part)    Fax: (845) 229-2586
Term Expires: 2017    Fax: (518) 426-6770
4254 Albany Post Road, Hyde Park, NY 12538
E-mail: serino@nysenate.gov
Committees: Aging; Children and Families; Cultural Affairs, Tourism,
Parks and Recreation; Education; Higher Education; Insurance;
Judiciary; Mental Health and Developmental Disabilities

**Senator José M. Serrano** (D-District 29) . . . . . . . . . . . . . . (518) 455-2795
Counties Represented: Bronx (part), New York    Dist: (212) 828-5829
(part)    Fax: (518) 426-6886
Term Expires: 2017    Dist: (212) 828-2420
1916 Park Avenue, Suite 202, New York, NY 10037
E-mail: serrano@nysenate.gov
Committees: Aging; Agriculture; Consumer Protection; Cultural
Affairs, Tourism, Parks and Recreation; Mental Health and
Developmental Disabilities; Veterans, Homeland Security and Military
Affairs

Senator **James L. Seward** (R-District 51) . . . . . . . . . . . . . (518) 455-3131
  Counties Represented: Cayuga (part), Chenango     Dist: (607) 432-5524
  (part), Cortland, Delaware (part), Herkimer (part),     (Oneonta Office)
  Otsego, Schoharie, Tompkins (part), Ulster (part)     Dist: (315) 866-1632
  Term Expires: 2017     (Herkimer Office)
  41 South Main Street, Oneonta, NY 13820     Dist: (607) 758-9005
  235 North Prospect Street, Herkimer, NY 13350     (Cortlandville Office)
  4030 West Road, Cortland, NY 13045
  E-mail: seward@nysenate.gov
  Committees: Agriculture; Education; Finance; Health; Higher
  Education; Insurance; Mental Health and Developmental Disabilities;
  Rules

Senator **Daniel Squadron** (D-District 26) . . . . . . . . . . . . . (518) 455-2625
  Counties Represented: Kings (part), New York     Dist: (718) 875-1517
  (part)     (Brooklyn Office)
  Term Expires: 2017     Dist: (212) 298-5565
  209 Joralemon Street, Brooklyn, NY 11201     (New York Office)
  250 Broadway, New York, NY 10007     Fax: (518) 426-6956
  E-mail: squadron@nysenate.gov     Dist: (212) 431-7836
  Committees: Codes; Corporations, Authorities and     (New York Office)
  Commissions; Finance; Investigations and Government Operations;
  Social Services; Transportation

Senator **Toby Ann Stavisky** (D-District 16) . . . . . . . . . . . (518) 455-3461
  Counties Represented: Queens (part)     Dist: (718) 445-0004
  Term Expires: 2017     Fax: (518) 426-6857
  142-29 37th Avenue, Suite One,     Dist: (718) 445-8398
  Flushing, NY 11354
  E-mail: stavisky@nysenate.gov
  Committees: Education; Finance; Health; Higher Education; Judiciary;
  Transportation

Senator **Andrea Stewart-Cousins** (D-District 35) . . . . . . . (518) 455-2585
  Counties Represented: Westchester (part)     Dist: (914) 423-4031
  Term Expires: 2017     Fax: (518) 426-6811
  28 Wells Avenue, Yonkers, NY 10701     Dist: (914) 423-0979
  E-mail: scousins@nysenate.gov
  Committees: Rules

Senator **David J. Valesky** (D-District 53) . . . . . . . . . . . . . (518) 455-2838
  Counties Represented: Madison, Oneida (part),     Dist: (315) 478-8745
  Onondaga (part)     Fax: (518) 426-6885
  Note: Democrat David Valesky is part of the     Dist: (315) 474-3804
  Independent Democratic Conference and will caucus with the
  Republican majority during the 2016 legislative session.
  Term Expires: 2017
  333 East Washington Street, Syracuse, NY 13202
  E-mail: valesky@nysenate.gov
  Committees: Aging; Agriculture; Commerce, Economic Development
  and Small Business; Education; Finance; Health; Higher Education;
  Local Government; Rules; Transportation

Senator **Michael Venditto** (R-District 8) . . . . . . . . . . . . . (518) 455-3341
  Counties Represented: Nassau (part), Suffolk (part)     Dist: (516) 882-0630
  Term Expires: 2017     Fax: (518) 426-6823
  5550 Merrick Road, Suite 205,     Dist: (516) 882-0636
  Massapequa, NY 11758
  E-mail: venditto@nysenate.gov
  Committees: Codes; Consumer Protection; Crime Victims, Crime and
  Correction; Higher Education; Insurance; Judiciary; Labor

Senator **Catharine M. Young** (R-District 57) . . . . . . . . . . . (518) 455-3563
  Counties Represented: Allegany, Cattaraugus,     Dist: (716) 372-4901
  Chautauqua, Livingston (part)     Fax: (518) 426-6905
  Term Expires: 2017     Dist: (716) 372-5740
  700 West State Street, Olean, NY 14760
  E-mail: cyoung@nysenate.gov
  Committees: Agriculture; Children and Families; Environmental
  Conservation; Finance; Health; Housing, Construction and Community
  Development; Transportation

# Senate Standing Committees

Legislative Office Building, Albany, NY 12247

## Aging

**Majority Members**
Susan Serino (R-41) *Chair*
Simcha Felder (D-17)
Rich Funke (R-55)
Martin J. Golden (R-22)
Kenneth P. LaValle (R-1)
Kathleen A. "Kathy" Marchione (R-43)
David J. Valesky (D-53)

**Minority Members**
Ruben Diaz, Sr. (D-32)
  *Ranking Member*
Joseph P. Addabbo, Jr. (D-15)
Brad Hoylman (D-27)
José M. Serrano (D-29)

## Agriculture

**Majority Members**
Patricia Ritchie (R-48) *Chair*
Rich Funke (R-55)
Patrick M. Gallivan (R-59)
Thomas F. "Tom" O'Mara (R-58)
Michael H. Ranzenhofer (R-61)
James L. Seward (R-51)
David J. Valesky (D-53)
Catharine M. Young (R-57)

**Minority Members**
Marc C. Panepinto (D-60)
  *Ranking Member*
Leroy G. Comrie, Jr. (D-14)
Jesse E. Hamilton (D-20)
Velmanette Montgomery (D-25)
José M. Serrano (D-29)

## Alcoholism and Drug Abuse

**Majority Members**
George A. Amedore, Jr. (R-46)
  *Chair*
John J. Bonacic (R-42)
David Carlucci (D-38)
Thomas D. Croci (R-3)
Patricia Ritchie (R-48)

**Minority Members**
Kevin S. Parker (D-21)
  *Ranking Member*
Todd Kaminsky (D-9)

## Banks

**Majority Members**
Diane J. Savino (D-23) *Chair*
Hugh T. Farley (R-49) *Vice Chair*
Frederick J. Akshar II (R-52)
George A. Amedore, Jr. (R-46)
Tony Avella (D-11)
John J. Bonacic (R-42)
Martin J. Golden (R-22)
Carl L. Marcellino (R-5)
Kathleen A. "Kathy" Marchione (R-43)
Jack M. Martins (R-7)
Terrence P. Murphy (R-40)
Thomas F. "Tom" O'Mara (R-58)

**Minority Members**
Jesse E. Hamilton (D-20)
  *Ranking Member*
Neil D. Breslin (D-44)
Ruben Diaz, Sr. (D-32)
Timothy M. Kennedy (D-63)
George S. Latimer (D-37)
Kevin S. Parker (D-21)
James Sanders, Jr. (D-10)

## Children and Families

**Majority Members**
Tony Avella (D-11) *Chair*
John J. Bonacic (R-42)
Diane J. Savino (D-23)
Susan Serino (R-41)
Catharine M. Young (R-57)

**Minority Members**
Velmanette Montgomery (D-25)
  *Ranking Member*
Roxanne J. Persaud (D-19)

## Cities

**Majority Members**
Simcha Felder (D-17) *Chair*
Frederick J. Akshar II (R-52)
Rich Funke (R-55)
Robert G. Ortt (R-62)
Diane J. Savino (D-23)

**Minority Members**
Roxanne J. Persaud (D-19)
  *Ranking Member*
Jose R. Peralta (D-13)

## Civil Service and Pensions

**Majority Members**
Martin J. Golden (R-22) *Chair*
Thomas D. Croci (R-3)
Andrew J. Lanza (R-24)
Jack M. Martins (R-7)
Robert G. Ortt (R-62)
Patricia Ritchie (R-48)
Diane J. Savino (D-23)

**Minority Members**
James Sanders, Jr. (D-10)
  *Ranking Member*
Joseph P. Addabbo, Jr. (D-15)
Leroy G. Comrie, Jr. (D-14)
Roxanne J. Persaud (D-19)

## Codes

**Majority Members**
Michael F. Nozzolio (R-54) *Chair*
Andrew J. Lanza (R-24) *Vice Chair*
Frederick J. Akshar II (R-52)
Philip M. "Phil" Boyle (R-4)
Patrick M. Gallivan (R-59)
Martin J. Golden (R-22)
Joseph A. Griffo (R-47)
Thomas F. "Tom" O'Mara (R-58)
Diane J. Savino (D-23)
Michael Venditto (R-8)

**Minority Members**
Daniel Squadron (D-26)
  *Ranking Member*
Adriano Espaillat (D-31)
Jesse E. Hamilton (D-20)
Todd Kaminsky (D-9)
Liz Krueger (D-28)
Bill Perkins (D-30)

## Commerce, Economic Development and Small Business

**Majority Members**
Philip M. "Phil" Boyle (R-4) *Chair*
Simcha Felder (D-17)
Rich Funke (R-55)
Patrick M. Gallivan (R-59)
Joseph A. Griffo (R-47)
Joseph E. Robach (R-56)
David J. Valesky (D-53)

**Minority Members**
Timothy M. Kennedy (D-63)
  *Ranking Member*
Ruth Hassell-Thompson (D-36)
Roxanne J. Persaud (D-19)
James Sanders, Jr. (D-10)

## Consumer Protection

**Majority Members**
Michael Venditto (R-8) *Chair*
Frederick J. Akshar II (R-52)
George A. Amedore, Jr. (R-46)
Philip M. "Phil" Boyle (R-4)
Rich Funke (R-55)
Joseph E. Robach (R-56)
Diane J. Savino (D-23)

**Minority Members**
Leroy G. Comrie, Jr. (D-14)
  *Ranking Member*
George S. Latimer (D-37)
Jose R. Peralta (D-13)
José M. Serrano (D-29)

## Corporations, Authorities and Commissions

**Majority Members**
Michael H. Ranzenhofer (R-61)
  *Chair*
George A. Amedore, Jr. (R-46)
William J. Larkin, Jr. (R-39)
Jack M. Martins (R-7)
Robert G. Ortt (R-62)

**Minority Members**
Bill Perkins (D-30)
  *Ranking Member*
Daniel Squadron (D-26)

## Crime Victims, Crime and Correction

**Majority Members**
Patrick M. Gallivan (R-59) *Chair*
Frederick J. Akshar II (R-52)
Joseph A. Griffo (R-47)
Elizabeth O'Connor "Betty" Little
  (R-45)
Michael F. Nozzolio (R-54)
Patricia Ritchie (R-48)
Diane J. Savino (D-23)
Michael Venditto (R-8)

**Minority Members**
Ruth Hassell-Thompson (D-36)
  *Ranking Member*
Velmanette Montgomery (D-25)
Jose R. Peralta (D-13)
Bill Perkins (D-30)
Gustavo Rivera (D-33)

## Cultural Affairs, Tourism, Parks and Recreation

**Majority Members**
Rich Funke (R-55) *Chair*
Tony Avella (D-11)
Joseph A. Griffo (R-47)
Elizabeth O'Connor "Betty" Little
  (R-45)
Carl L. Marcellino (R-5)
Kathleen A. "Kathy" Marchione
  (R-43)
Patricia Ritchie (R-48)
Susan Serino (R-41)

**Minority Members**
José M. Serrano (D-29)
  *Ranking Member*
Brad Hoylman (D-27)
Timothy M. Kennedy (D-63)
Roxanne J. Persaud (D-19)
James Sanders, Jr. (D-10)

## Education

**Majority Members**
Carl L. Marcellino (R-5) *Chair*
Tony Avella (D-11)
Thomas D. Croci (R-3)
Hugh T. Farley (R-49)
Andrew J. Lanza (R-24)
Kenneth P. LaValle (R-1)
Elizabeth O'Connor "Betty" Little
  (R-45)
Michael H. Ranzenhofer (R-61)
Joseph E. Robach (R-56)
Susan Serino (R-41)
James L. Seward (R-51)
David J. Valesky (D-53)

**Minority Members**
George S. Latimer (D-37)
  *Ranking Member*
Joseph P. Addabbo, Jr. (D-15)
Neil D. Breslin (D-44)
Jesse E. Hamilton (D-20)
Velmanette Montgomery (D-25)
Jose R. Peralta (D-13)
Toby Ann Stavisky (D-16)

## Elections

**Majority Members**
Frederick J. Akshar II (R-52) *Chair*
George A. Amedore, Jr. (R-46)
Tony Avella (D-11)
Patrick M. Gallivan (R-59)
Kathleen A. "Kathy" Marchione
  (R-43)
Michael F. Nozzolio (R-54)

**Minority Members**
Leroy G. Comrie, Jr. (D-14)
  *Ranking Member*
Martin Malave Dilan (D-18)
Liz Krueger (D-28)

## Energy and Telecommunications

**Majority Members**
Joseph A. Griffo (R-47) *Chair*
David Carlucci (D-38)
Thomas D. Croci (R-3)
Elizabeth O'Connor "Betty" Little
  (R-45)
Jack M. Martins (R-7)
Thomas F. "Tom" O'Mara (R-58)
Patricia Ritchie (R-48)

**Minority Members**
Kevin S. Parker (D-21)
  *Ranking Member*
Martin Malave Dilan (D-18)
Jesse E. Hamilton (D-20)
Timothy M. Kennedy (D-63)

## Environmental Conservation

**Majority Members**
Thomas F. "Tom" O'Mara (R-58)
  *Chair*
Tony Avella (D-11) *Vice Chair*
Rich Funke (R-55)
Kenneth P. LaValle (R-1)
Elizabeth O'Connor "Betty" Little
  (R-45)
Carl L. Marcellino (R-5)
Robert G. Ortt (R-62)
Catharine M. Young (R-57)

**Minority Members**
Brad Hoylman (D-27)
  *Ranking Member*
Joseph P. Addabbo, Jr. (D-15)
Adriano Espaillat (D-31)
Todd Kaminsky (D-9)
George S. Latimer (D-37)

## Ethics

**Majority Members**
Thomas D. Croci (R-3) *Chair*
Hugh T. Farley (R-49)
Andrew J. Lanza (R-24)
Terrence P. Murphy (R-40)

**Minority Members**
Michael N. Gianaris (D-12)
  *Ranking Member*
Gustavo Rivera (D-33)

## Finance

**Majority Members**
Catharine M. Young (R-57) *Chair*
John J. Bonacic (R-42)
Philip M. "Phil" Boyle (R-4)
Patrick M. Gallivan (R-59)
Martin J. Golden (R-22)
Joseph A. Griffo (R-47)
Kemp Hannon (R-6)
Andrew J. Lanza (R-24)
William J. Larkin, Jr. (R-39)
Kenneth P. LaValle (R-1)
Elizabeth O'Connor "Betty" Little
  (R-45)
Carl L. Marcellino (R-5)
Kathleen A. "Kathy" Marchione
  (R-43)
Jack M. Martins (R-7)
Michael F. Nozzolio (R-54)
Thomas F. "Tom" O'Mara (R-58)
Michael H. Ranzenhofer (R-61)
Patricia Ritchie (R-48)
Joseph E. Robach (R-56)
Diane J. Savino (D-23)
James L. Seward (R-51)
David J. Valesky (D-53)

**Minority Members**
Liz Krueger (D-28)
  *Ranking Member*
Neil D. Breslin (D-44)
Ruben Diaz, Sr. (D-32)
Martin Malave Dilan (D-18)
Adriano Espaillat (D-31)
Ruth Hassell-Thompson (D-36)
Todd Kaminsky (D-9)
Timothy M. Kennedy (D-63)
Velmanette Montgomery (D-25)
Kevin S. Parker (D-21)
Jose R. Peralta (D-13)
Bill Perkins (D-30)
Gustavo Rivera (D-33)
Daniel Squadron (D-26)
Toby Ann Stavisky (D-16)

## Health

**Majority Members**
Kemp Hannon (R-6) *Chair*
David J. Valesky (D-53) *Vice Chair*
Simcha Felder (D-17)
Martin J. Golden (R-22)
William J. Larkin, Jr. (R-39)
Elizabeth O'Connor "Betty" Little
  (R-45)
Jack M. Martins (R-7)
Terrence P. Murphy (R-40)
James L. Seward (R-51)
Catharine M. Young (R-57)

**Minority Members**
Gustavo Rivera (D-33)
  *Ranking Member*
Ruth Hassell-Thompson (D-36)
Brad Hoylman (D-27)
Todd Kaminsky (D-9)
Velmanette Montgomery (D-25)
Roxanne J. Persaud (D-19)
Toby Ann Stavisky (D-16)

## Higher Education

**Majority Members**
Kenneth P. LaValle (R-1) *Chair*
Thomas D. Croci (R-3)
Patrick M. Gallivan (R-59)
Joseph A. Griffo (R-47)
Rich Funke (R-55)
Robert G. Ortt (R-62)
Patricia Ritchie (R-48)
Joseph E. Robach (R-56)
Susan Serino (R-41)
James L. Seward (R-51)
David J. Valesky (D-53)
Michael Venditto (R-8)

**Minority Members**
Toby Ann Stavisky (D-16)
  *Ranking Member*
Neil D. Breslin (D-44)
Adriano Espaillat (D-31)
Liz Krueger (D-28)
Kevin S. Parker (D-21)
Jose R. Peralta (D-13)
Gustavo Rivera (D-33)

## Housing, Construction and Community Development

**Majority Members**
Elizabeth O'Connor
  "Betty" Little (R-45)
  *Chair*
Tony Avella (D-11)
John J. Bonacic (R-42)
Philip M. "Phil" Boyle (R-4)
Patrick M. Gallivan (R-59)
Catharine M. Young (R-57)

**Minority Members**
Adriano Espaillat (D-31)
  *Ranking Member*
Liz Krueger (D-28)
Marc C. Panepinto (D-60)

## Infrastructure and Capital Investment

**Majority Members**
Andrew J. Lanza (R-24) *Chair*
David Carlucci (D-38)
Thomas D. Croci (R-3)
Simcha Felder (D-17)
Patrick M. Gallivan (R-59)
Joseph E. Robach (R-56)

**Minority Members**
Timothy M. Kennedy (D-63)
  *Ranking Member*
Leroy G. Comrie, Jr. (D-14)
Martin Malave Dilan (D-18)

## Insurance

**Majority Members**
James L. Seward (R-51) *Chair*
Tony Avella (D-11)
David Carlucci (D-38)
Martin J. Golden (R-22)
Andrew J. Lanza (R-24)
William J. Larkin, Jr. (R-39)
Kenneth P. LaValle (R-1)
Jack M. Martins (R-7)
Terrence P. Murphy (R-40)
Thomas F. "Tom" O'Mara (R-58)
Susan Serino (R-41)
Michael Venditto (R-8)

**Minority Members**
Neil D. Breslin (D-44)
  *Ranking Member*
Jesse E. Hamilton (D-20)
Timothy M. Kennedy (D-63)
George S. Latimer (D-37)
Marc C. Panepinto (D-60)
Kevin S. Parker (D-21)
James Sanders, Jr. (D-10)

## Investigations and Government Operations

**Majority Members**
Andrew J. Lanza (R-24) *Chair*
David Carlucci (D-38)
Martin J. Golden (R-22)
Terrence P. Murphy (R-40)
Michael F. Nozzolio (R-54)
Thomas F. "Tom" O'Mara (R-58)

**Minority Members**
Brad Hoylman (D-27)
  *Ranking Member*
Ruben Diaz, Sr. (D-32)
Daniel Squadron (D-26)

## Judiciary

**Majority Members**
John J. Bonacic (R-42) *Chair*
George A. Amedore, Jr. (R-46)
Tony Avella (D-11)
Philip M. "Phil" Boyle (R-4)
Thomas D. Croci (R-3)
Kemp Hannon (R-6)
Andrew J. Lanza (R-24)
Kenneth P. LaValle (R-1)
Michael F. Nozzolio (R-54)
Thomas F. "Tom" O'Mara (R-58)
Michael H. Ranzenhofer (R-61)
Diane J. Savino (D-23)
Susan Serino (R-41)
Michael Venditto (R-8)

**Minority Members**
Ruth Hassell-Thompson (D-36)
  *Ranking Member*
Neil D. Breslin (D-44)
Leroy G. Comrie, Jr. (D-14)
Ruben Diaz, Sr. (D-32)
Martin Malave Dilan (D-18)
Adriano Espaillat (D-31)
Brad Hoylman (D-27)
Bill Perkins (D-30)
Toby Ann Stavisky (D-16)

## Labor

**Majority Members**
Jack M. Martins (R-7) *Chair*
Frederick J. Akshar II (R-52)
Patrick M. Gallivan (R-59)
Kemp Hannon (R-6)
Carl L. Marcellino (R-5)
Terrence P. Murphy (R-40)
Robert G. Ortt (R-62)
Joseph E. Robach (R-56)
Diane J. Savino (D-23)
Michael Venditto (R-8)

**Minority Members**
Jose R. Peralta (D-13)
  *Ranking Member*
Joseph P. Addabbo, Jr. (D-15)
Martin Malave Dilan (D-18)
Bill Perkins (D-30)
Gustavo Rivera (D-33)
James Sanders, Jr. (D-10)

## Local Government

**Majority Members**
Kathleen A. "Kathy"
  Marchione (R-43)
  *Chair*
Philip M. "Phil" Boyle (R-4)
Terrence P. Murphy (R-40)
Robert G. Ortt (R-62)
Patricia Ritchie (R-48)
David J. Valesky (D-53)

**Minority Members**
Todd Kaminsky (D-9)
  *Ranking Member*
George S. Latimer (D-37)
Marc C. Panepinto (D-60)

## Mental Health and Developmental Disabilities

**Majority Members**
Robert G. Ortt (R-62) *Chair*
David Carlucci (D-38)
Simcha Felder (D-17)
Kemp Hannon (R-6)
Terrence P. Murphy (R-40)
Susan Serino (R-41)
James L. Seward (R-51)

**Minority Members**
Jesse E. Hamilton (D-20)
  *Ranking Member*
Liz Krueger (D-28)
Gustavo Rivera (D-33)
José M. Serrano (D-29)

## Racing, Gaming and Wagering

**Majority Members**
John J. Bonacic (R-42) *Chair*
Philip M. "Phil" Boyle (R-4)
David Carlucci (D-38)
Joseph A. Griffo (R-47)
Kathleen A. "Kathy" Marchione
  (R-43)
Michael F. Nozzolio (R-54)
Michael H. Ranzenhofer (R-61)

**Minority Members**
Joseph P. Addabbo, Jr. (D-15)
  *Ranking Member*
Leroy G. Comrie, Jr. (D-14)
George S. Latimer (D-37)
James Sanders, Jr. (D-10)

## Rules

**Majority Members**
John J. Flanagan (R-2) *Chair*
John A. DeFrancisco (R-50)
  *Vice Chair*
John J. Bonacic (R-42)
David Carlucci (D-38)
Hugh T. Farley (R-49)
Kemp Hannon (R-6)
Andrew J. Lanza (R-24)
William J. Larkin, Jr. (R-39)
Kenneth P. LaValle (R-1)

**Minority Members**
Andrea Stewart-Cousins (D-35)
  *Ranking Member*
Neil D. Breslin (D-44)
Martin Malave Dilan (D-18)
Adriano Espaillat (D-31)
Michael N. Gianaris (D-12)
Ruth Hassell-Thompson (D-36)
Liz Krueger (D-28)
Velmanette Montgomery (D-25)
Kevin S. Parker (D-21)
Bill Perkins (D-30)

*(continued on next page)*

*LEGISLATIVE BRANCH*

**Rules** *continued*

**Majority Members** *continued*

Elizabeth O'Connor "Betty" Little
  (R-45)
Carl L. Marcellino (R-5)
Michael F. Nozzolio (R-54)
Joseph E. Robach (R-56)
James L. Seward (R-51)
David J. Valesky (D-53)

## Social Services

| **Majority Members** | **Minority Members** |
| --- | --- |
| David Carlucci (D-38) *Chair* | Roxanne J. Persaud (D-19) |
| George A. Amedore, Jr. (R-46) | *Ranking Member* |
| Hugh T. Farley (R-49) | Daniel Squadron (D-26) |
| Kenneth P. LaValle (R-1) | |
| Jack M. Martins (R-7) | |

## Transportation

| **Majority Members** | **Minority Members** |
| --- | --- |
| Joseph E. Robach (R-56) *Chair* | Martin Malave Dilan (D-18) |
| Carl L. Marcellino (R-5) *Vice Chair* | *Ranking Member* |
| Tony Avella (D-11) | Ruben Diaz, Sr. (D-32) |
| Patrick M. Gallivan (R-59) | Todd Kaminsky (D-9) |
| William J. Larkin, Jr. (R-39) | Timothy M. Kennedy (D-63) |
| Jack M. Martins (R-7) | Bill Perkins (D-30) |
| Michael F. Nozzolio (R-54) | Daniel Squadron (D-26) |
| Thomas F. "Tom" O'Mara (R-58) | Toby Ann Stavisky (D-16) |
| Michael H. Ranzenhofer (R-61) | |
| Patricia Ritchie (R-48) | |
| David J. Valesky (D-53) | |
| Catharine M. Young (R-57) | |

## Veterans, Homeland Security and Military Affairs

| **Majority Members** | **Minority Members** |
| --- | --- |
| Thomas D. Croci (R-3) *Chair* | Joseph P. Addabbo, Jr. (D-15) |
| George A. Amedore, Jr. (R-46) | *Ranking Member* |
| David Carlucci (D-38) | Leroy G. Comrie, Jr. (D-14) |
| Simcha Felder (D-17) | Todd Kaminsky (D-9) |
| Martin J. Golden (R-22) | James Sanders, Jr. (D-10) |
| William J. Larkin, Jr. (R-39) | José M. Serrano (D-29) |
| Kathleen A. "Kathy" Marchione | |
|   (R-43) | |
| Robert G. Ortt (R-62) | |

# New York State Assembly

Legislative Office Building, Albany, NY 12247
Tel: (518) 455-4100  Tel: (518) 455-4218 (Public Information)
Internet: www.assembly.state.ny.us

Speaker of the Assembly **Carl E. Heastie** (D) . . . . . . . . . . (518) 455-3791
  Education: SUNY (Stony Brook) BS; Baruch Col 2007 MBA
Deputy Speaker **Earlene Hooper** (D) . . . . . . . . . . . . . . . . (518) 455-5861
  Education: Norfolk State BA; Adelphi MSW; Five Towns PhD
Assistant Speaker **Felix W. Ortiz** (D) . . . . . . . . . . . . . . (518) 455-3821
  Education: Boricua 1983 BSBA; NYU 1986 MPA
Speaker Pro Tem **Jeffrion L. Aubry** (D) . . . . . . . . . . . (518) 455-4561
  Education: Col Santa Fe 1969 BA
Assistant Speaker Pro Tempore **N. Nick Perry** (D) . . . . . . . (518) 455-4166
  Education: Brooklyn 1978 BA, MPA
Majority Leader **Joseph D. Morelle** (D) . . . . . . . . . . . . . (518) 455-5373
  Education: SUNY (Geneseo) 1986 BA
Deputy Majority Leader **Philip R. Ramos** (D) . . . . . . . . . . (518) 455-5185
Assistant Majority Leader **Dov Hikind** (D) . . . . . . . . . . . . (518) 455-5721
  Education: CUNY; Queens Col (NY) BA; Brooklyn MURS
Majority Conference Chair **Michelle Schimel** (D) . . . . . . . . (518) 455-5192
  Education: Pennsylvania
Majority Conference Vice Chair **Aravella Simotas** (D) . . . (518) 455-5014
  Education: Fordham 1999 BA, 2002 JD
Majority Conference Secretary **David I. Weprin** (D) . . . . . . (518) 455-5806
  Education: SUNY (Albany) BA; Hofstra JD
Majority Whip **William Colton** (D) . . . . . . . . . . . . . . . . .(518) 455-5828
  Education: St John's U (NY) 1968 BA; Brooklyn MS;
  St John's U (NY) 1978 JD
Deputy Majority Whip **José Rivera** (D) . . . . . . . . . . . . . . (518) 455-5414

Assistant Majority Whip **Albert A. Stirpe, Jr.** (D) . . . . . . . .(518) 455-4505
  Education: Notre Dame 1975 BA
Majority Program Chair **Carmen E. Arroyo** (D) . . . . . . . . (518) 455-5402
  Education: New Rochelle 1980 BA
Majority Steering Chair **Barbara S. Lifton** (D) . . . . . . . . . (518) 455-5444
  Education: SUNY (Geneseo) 1973 BA, 1985 MA
Minority Leader **Brian M. Kolb** (R) . . . . . . . . . . . . . . . . (518) 455-3751
  Education: Roberts Wesleyan 1996 BS, 1998 MS
Minority Leader Pro Tempore **Jane L. Corwin** (R) . . . . . . . (518) 455-4601
  Education: SUNY (Albany) 1985 BA; Pace 1990 MBA
Assistant Minority Leader Pro Tempore
  **Thomas "Tom" McKevitt** (R) . . . . . . . . . . . . . . . . . . . . (518) 455-5341
  Education: Hofstra 1993 BA, 1996 JD
Deputy Minority Leader **William A. "Will" Barclay** (R) . . . (518) 455-5841
  Education: St Lawrence BA; Syracuse JD
Assistant Minority Leader **Gary D. Finch** (R) . . . . . . . . . . (518) 455-5878
  Education: SUNY (Empire State) 1989 BS
Assistant Minority Leader
  **Stephen "Steve" Hawley** (R) . . . . . . . . . . . . . . . . . . . (518) 455-5811
  Education: Toledo BSEd
Minority Conference Chair
  **Clifford W. "Cliff" Crouch** (R) . . . . . . . . . . . . . . . . . (518) 455-5741
  Education: Cornell 1965 AAS
Minority Conference Vice Chair
  **Peter D. "Pete" Lopez** (R) . . . . . . . . . . . . . . . . . . . . .(518) 455-5363
  Education: SUNY (Cobleskill) BA; SUNY (Albany) MPA
Minority Conference Secretary
  **Philip "Phil" Palmesano** (R) . . . . . . . . . . . . . . . . . . . (518) 455-5791
Minority Whip **James N. "Jim" Tedisco** (R) . . . . . . . . . . (518) 455-5772
  Education: Union Col (NY) 1972 BA
Deputy Minority Whip **Andrew P. Raia** (R) . . . . . . . . . . . (518) 455-5952
  Education: SUNY (New Paltz) 1991 BA
Assistant Minority Whip **Michael A. Montesano** (R) . . . . . (518) 455-4684
Minority Program Committee Chair
  **Joseph Saladino** (R) . . . . . . . . . . . . . . . . . . . . . . . . . (518) 455-5305
  Education: New York Inst Tech BS, MS
Minority Steering Chair **Joseph M. "Joe" Giglio** (R) . . . . (518) 455-5241
  Education: SUNY (Buffalo) BA
Clerk of the Assembly **Laurene R. Kretzler** . . . . . . . . . . . (518) 455-4242
  E-mail: kretzlerl@assembly.state.ny.us

## Assembly Members

**Party Affiliation Statistics:** Republicans: 43, Democrats: 105,
Vacancies: 2

Assembly Member **Peter J. Abbate, Jr.** (D-District 49) . . . (518) 455-3053
  Counties Represented: Kings (part)                Dist: (718) 236-1764
  Term Expires: 2017                                       (Brooklyn I)
  6605 Fort Hamilton Parkway, Brooklyn, NY 11219  Fax: (718) 234-0986
  E-mail: abbatep@assembly.state.ny.us
  Committees: Aging; Banks; Consumer Affairs and Protection;
  Governmental Employees; Labor
  Education: St John's U (NY) 1971 BA
Assembly Member **Thomas J. Abinanti** (D-District 92) . . . (518) 455-5753
  Counties Represented: Westchester (part)          Dist: (914) 631-1605
  Term Expires: 2017                                Fax: (914) 631-1609
  303 South Broadway, Suite 229, Tarrytown, NY 10591
  E-mail: abinantit@assembly.state.ny.us
  Committees: Codes; Corporations, Authorities and Commissions;
  Election Law; Environmental Conservation; Health; Libraries and
  Education Technology
  Education: Fordham BA; NYU 1972 JD
Assembly Member **Carmen E. Arroyo** (D-District 84) . . . . (518) 455-5402
  Counties Represented: Bronx (part)                Dist: (718) 292-2901
  Term Expires: 2017                                Fax: (518) 455-4681
  384 East 149th Street, Suite 301, Bronx, NY 10455
  E-mail: arroyoc@assembly.state.ny.us
  Committees: Aging; Alcoholism and Drug Abuse; Children and
  Families; Education
Assembly Member **Jeffrion L. Aubry** (D-District 35) . . . . (518) 455-4561
  Counties Represented: Queens (part)               Dist: (718) 457-3615
  Term Expires: 2017                                Fax: (518) 455-4565
  98-09 Northern Boulevard, Corona, NY 11368        Dist: (718) 457-3640
  E-mail: aubryj@assembly.state.ny.us
  Committees: Governmental Employees; Rules; Social Services; Ways
  and Means

Assembly Member
**William A. "Will" Barclay** (R-District 120) . . . . . . . . . . (518) 455-5841
Counties Represented: Jefferson (part), Onondaga      Dist: (315) 598-5185
(part), Oswego (part)
Term Expires: 2017
200 North Second Street, Fulton, NY 13069
E-mail: barclayw@assembly.state.ny.us
Committees: Energy; Insurance; Judiciary; Rules; Ways and Means

Assembly Member **Didi Barrett** (D-District 106) . . . . . . . . (518) 455-5177
Counties Represented: Columbia (part), Dutchess      Dist: (845) 454-1703
(part)                                                Fax: (518) 455-5418
Term Expires: 2017
12 Raymond Avenue, Suite 105, Poughkeepsie, NY 12603
E-mail: barrettd@assembly.state.ny.us
Committees: Aging; Agriculture; Economic Development, Job Creation,
Commerce and Industry; Mental Health; Tourism, Parks, Arts and
Sports Development; Veterans' Affairs

Assembly Member **Charles Barron** (D-District 60) . . . . . . . (518) 455-5912
Counties Represented: Kings (part)                   Dist: (718) 257-5824
Term Expires: 2017                                   Fax: (718) 257-2590
669 Vermont Street, Brooklyn, NY 11207
E-mail: barronc@assembly.state.ny.us
Committees: Aging; Alcoholism and Drug Abuse; Economic
Development, Job Creation, Commerce and Industry; Energy; Small
Business; Social Services
Education: Hunter BA

Assembly Member **Michael Benedetto** (D-District 82) . . . (518) 455-5296
Counties Represented: Bronx (part)                   Dist: (718) 320-2220
Term Expires: 2017                                   (Bronx Office I)
Bronx I: 177 Dreiser Loop, Room 12,                 Dist: (718) 892-2235
Bronx, NY 10475                                      (Bronx Office II)
Bronx II: 3602 East Tremont Avenue, Suite 201, Bronx, NY 10465
E-mail: benedettom@assembly.state.ny.us
Committees: Agriculture; Cities; Education; Governmental Operations;
Labor; Ways and Means

Assembly Member **Rodneyse Bichotte** (D-District 42) . . . . (518) 455-5385
Counties Represented: Kings (part)                   Dist: (718) 940-0428
Term Expires: 2017
1414 Cortelyou Road, Brooklyn, NY 11226
E-mail: bichotter@assembly.state.ny.us
Committees: Banks; Economic Development, Job Creation, Commerce
and Industry; Governmental Operations; Housing; Small Business;
Social Services
Education: SUNY (Buffalo) BSEE; Illinois Tech MSEE; Kellogg MBA

Assembly Member **Michael A. Blake** (D-District 79) . . . . . (518) 455-5272
Counties Represented: Bronx (part)                   Dist: (718) 538-3829
Term Expires: 2017                                   Fax: (718) 588-0159
780 Concourse Village West, Bronx, NY 10451
E-mail: blakem@assembly.state.ny.us
Committees: Banks; Correction; Election Law; Housing; Veterans'
Affairs
Education: Northwestern 2004 BJ

Assembly Member
**Kenneth Blankenbush** (R-District 117) . . . . . . . . . . . . . (518) 455-5797
Counties Represented: Jefferson (part), Lewis,       Dist: (315) 493-3909
Oneida (part), St. Lawrence (part)                   Fax: (315) 493-4045
Term Expires: 2017
40 Franklin Street, Suite Two, Carthage, NY 13619
E-mail: blankenbushk@assembly.state.ny.us
Committees: Agriculture; Corporations, Authorities and Commissions;
Insurance; Tourism, Parks, Arts and Sports Development

Assembly Member **Karl Brabenec** (R-District 98) . . . . . . . (518) 455-5991
Counties Represented: Orange (part), Rockland        Dist: (845) 544-7551
(part)                                               Fax: (845) 455-5929
Term Expires: 2017                                   Dist: (845) 544-7553
123 Route 94 South, Suite 2, Warwick, NY 10990
E-mail: brabeneck@assembly.state.ny.us
Committees: Aging; Cities; Election Law; Labor; Local Governments

Assembly Member **Edward Braunstein** (D-District 26) . . . (518) 455-5425
Counties Represented: Queens (part)                  Dist: (718) 357-3588
Term Expires: 2017
213-33 39th Avenue, Suite 238, Bayside, NY 11361
E-mail: braunsteine@assembly.state.ny.us
Committees: Aging; Cities; Health; Judiciary; Ways and Means
Education: SUNY (Albany) 2003 BS; New York Law 2008 JD

Assembly Member **James F. Brennan** (D-District 44) . . . . (518) 455-5377
Counties Represented: Kings (part)                   Dist: (718) 788-7221
Term Expires: 2017                                   (Brooklyn Office I)
Brooklyn I: 416 Seventh Avenue,                      Dist: (718) 940-0641
Brooklyn, NY 11215                                   (Brooklyn Office II)
1414 Cortelyou Road, Brooklyn, NY 11226             Fax: (518) 455-5592
E-mail: brennanj@assembly.state.ny.us
Committees: Codes; Corporations, Authorities and Commissions;
Education; Real Property Taxation
Education: Yale 1975 BA; Brooklyn Law 1982 JD

Assembly Member **Anthony J. Brindisi** (D-District 119) . . (518) 455-5454
Counties Represented: Herkimer (part), Oneida        Dist: (315) 732-1055
(part)                                               Fax: (518) 455-5928
Term Expires: 2017                                   Dist: (315) 732-1413
207 Genesee Street, Room 401, Utica, NY 13501
E-mail: brindisia@assembly.state.ny.us
Committees: Aging; Economic Development, Job Creation, Commerce
and Industry; Education; Higher Education; Transportation; Veterans'
Affairs
Education: Siena Col 2000 BA; Albany Law 2004 JD

Assembly Member **Harry B. Bronson** (D-District 138) . . . . (518) 455-4527
Counties Represented: Monroe (part)                  Dist: (585) 244-5255
Term Expires: 2017
840 University Avenue, Rochester, NY 14607
E-mail: bronsonh@assembly.state.ny.us
Committees: Agriculture; Economic Development, Job Creation,
Commerce and Industry; Labor; Local Governments; Transportation

Assembly Member **David Buchwald** (D-District 93) . . . . . . (518) 455-5397
Counties Represented: Westchester (part)             Dist: (914) 244-4450
Term Expires: 2017
125-131 East Main Street, Suite 204, Mount Kisco, NY 10549
E-mail: buchwaldd@assembly.state.ny.us
Committees: Consumer Affairs and Protection; Corporations,
Authorities and Commissions; Election Law; Governmental Operations;
Judiciary; Local Governments
Education: Yale 2000 BS; Harvard 2005 MPP, 2007 JD

Assembly Member **Marc W. Butler** (R-District 118) . . . . . . (518) 455-5393
Counties Represented: Fulton, Hamilton, Herkimer     Dist: (315) 866-1632
(part), Oneida (part), St. Lawrence (part)           (Herkimer Office)
Term Expires: 2017                                   Dist: (518) 762-6486
235 North Prospect Street, Herkimer, NY 13350       (Johnstown Office)
33-41 East Main Street, Johnstown, NY 12095         Fax: (518) 455-5889
E-mail: butlerm@assembly.state.ny.us                 Dist: (315) 866-5058
Committees: Agriculture; Economic Development,       (Herkimer Office)
Job Creation, Commerce and Industry; Environmental Conservation;
Higher Education; Insurance; Rules
Education: SUNY (Potsdam) BA

Assembly Member **Kevin A. Cahill** (D-District 103) . . . . . . (518) 455-4436
Counties Represented: Dutchess (part), Ulster (part)  Dist: (845) 338-9610
Term Expires: 2017                                   Fax: (518) 455-5576
Governor Clinton Building, One Albany Avenue,        Dist: (845) 338-9590
Suite G-4, Kingston, NY 12401
E-mail: cahillk@assembly.state.ny.us
Committees: Economic Development, Job Creation, Commerce and
Industry; Health; Higher Education; Insurance; Ways and Means
Education: SUNY (New Paltz) 1977 BA; Albany Law 1980 JD

Assembly Member **Alice Cancel** (D-District 65) . . . . . . . . (518) 455-3640
Counties Represented: New York (part)                Dist: (212) 312-1420
Term Expires: 2017
250 Broadway, Room 2212, New York, NY 10007
E-mail: cancela@assembly.state.ny.us
Committees: Banks; Cities; Housing; Social Services

Assembly Member **Ronald Castorina, Jr.** (R-District 63) . . (518) 455-4495
Counties Represented: Richmond (part)                Dist: (718) 967-5194
Term Expires: 2017                                   Fax: (518) 455-4501
101 Tyrellan Avenue, Suite 200,                      Dist: (718) 967-5282
Staten Island, NY 10309
E-mail: castorinar@nyassembly.gov

Assembly Member **John D. Ceretto** (D-District 145) . . . . . (518) 455-5284
Counties Represented: Erie (part), Niagara (part)    Dist: (716) 282-6062
Term Expires: 2017                                   Fax: (518) 455-5419
800 Main Street, Suite 2C, Niagara Falls, NY 14301
E-mail: cerettoj@assembly.state.ny.us
Committees: Energy; Libraries and Education Technology; Tourism,
Parks, Arts and Sports Development

Assembly Member **William Colton** (D-District 47) . . . . . . . (518) 455-5828
Counties Represented: Kings (part)                   Dist: (718) 236-1598
Term Expires: 2017                                   Fax: (518) 455-5706
155 Kings Highway, Brooklyn, NY 11223               Dist: (718) 236-6507
E-mail: coltonw@assembly.state.ny.us
Committees: Correction; Environmental Conservation; Governmental
Employees; Labor; Rules; Ways and Means

*(continued on next page)*

**Assembly Members** *continued*

Assembly Member **Vivian E. Cook** (D-District 32) . . . . . . (518) 455-4203
Counties Represented: Queens (part)  Dist: (718) 322-3975
Term Expires: 2017  Fax: (518) 455-3606
142-15 Rockaway Boulevard, Jamaica, NY 11436  Dist: (718) 322-4085
E-mail: cookv@assembly.state.ny.us
Committees: Codes; Corporations, Authorities and Commissions;
Housing; Insurance; Rules; Ways and Means

Assembly Member **Jane L. Corwin** (R-District 144) . . . . . (518) 455-4601
Counties Represented: Erie (part), Niagara (part),  Dist: (716) 839-4691
Orleans (part)
Term Expires: 2017
8180 Main Street, Clarence, NY 14221
E-mail: corwinj@assembly.state.ny.us
Committees: Corporations, Authorities and Commissions; Education;
Environmental Conservation; Mental Health; Ways and Means

Assembly Member **Marcos Crespo** (D-District 85) . . . . . . (518) 455-5514
Counties Represented: Bronx (part)  Dist: (718) 893-0202
Term Expires: 2017
1163 Manor Avenue, Bronx, NY 10472
E-mail: crespom@assembly.state.ny.us
Committees: Cities; Energy; Environmental Conservation; Insurance;
Transportation
Education: John Jay Col 2004 BA

Assembly Member
**Clifford W. "Cliff" Crouch** (R-District 122) . . . . . . . . . . (518) 455-5741
Counties Represented: Broome (part), Chenango  Dist: (607) 648-6080
(part), Delaware (part), Otsego (part)  Fax: (518) 455-5864
Term Expires: 2017  Dist: (607) 648-6089
One Kattelville Road, Binghamton, NY 13901
E-mail: crouchc@assembly.state.ny.us
Committees: Agriculture; Economic Development, Job Creation,
Commerce and Industry; Labor; Rules; Ways and Means

Assembly Member **Brian Curran** (R-District 21) . . . . . . . . (518) 455-4656
Counties Represented: Nassau (part)  Dist: (516) 561-8216
Term Expires: 2017
100 Merrick Road, Lynbrook, NY 11563
E-mail: curranb@assembly.state.ny.us
Committees: Banks; Ethics and Guidance; Insurance; Labor; Veterans'
Affairs
Education: Wilkes U 1990; CUNY 1994 JD

Assembly Member **Michael J. Cusick** (D-District 63) . . . . . (518) 455-5526
Counties Represented: Richmond (part)  Dist: (718) 370-1384
Term Expires: 2017
1911 Richmond Avenue, Staten Island, NY 10314
E-mail: cusickm@assembly.state.ny.us
Committees: Election Law; Governmental Employees; Higher
Education; Mental Health; Transportation; Veterans' Affairs; Ways and
Means
Education: Villanova 1991 BA

Assembly Member **Steven Cymbrowitz** (D-District 45) . . . (518) 455-5214
Counties Represented: Kings (part)  Dist: (718) 743-4078
Term Expires: 2017  Fax: (518) 455-5738
1800 Sheepshead Bay Road, Brooklyn, NY 11235  Dist: (718) 368-4391
E-mail: cymbrowitzs@assembly.state.ny.us
Committees: Aging; Codes; Environmental Conservation; Health;
Insurance
Education: Long Island BA; Adelphi MA; Brooklyn Law JD

Assembly Member **Maritza Davila** (D-District 53) . . . . . . . (518) 455-5537
Counties Represented: Kings (part)  Dist: (718) 443-1205
Term Expires: 2017  Fax: (518) 455-5789
249 Wilson Avenue, Brooklyn, NY 11237  Dist: (718) 443-1424
E-mail: davilam@assembly.state.ny.us
Committees: Alcoholism and Drug Abuse; Children and Families;
Correction; Economic Development, Job Creation, Commerce and
Industry; Housing; Social Services

Assembly Member **Michael DenDekker** (D-District 34) . . . (518) 455-4545
Counties Represented: Queens (part)  Dist: (718) 457-0384
Term Expires: 2017
75-35 31st Avenue, Suite 206B, East Elmhurst, NY 11370
E-mail: dendekkerm@assembly.state.ny.us
Committees: Aging; Alcoholism and Drug Abuse; Governmental
Employees; Labor; Transportation; Veterans' Affairs

Assembly Member **Erik Martin Dilan** (D-District 54) . . . . . (518) 455-5821
Counties Represented: Kings (part)  Dist: (718) 386-4576
Term Expires: 2017  Fax: (718) 386-4575
Legislative Office Building, Room 921, Albany, NY 12248
366 Cornelia Street, Brooklyn, NY 11237
E-mail: dilane@assembly.state.ny.us
Committees: Cities; Consumer Affairs and Protection; Corporations,
Authorities and Commissions; Governmental Operations; Housing;
Insurance

Assembly Member **Jeffrey Dinowitz** (D-District 81) . . . . . (518) 455-5965
Counties Represented: Bronx (part)  Dist: (718) 796-5345
Term Expires: 2017  Fax: (518) 455-4437
3107 Kingsbridge Avenue, Bronx, NY 10463  Dist: (718) 796-0694
E-mail: dinowitzj@assembly.state.ny.us
Committees: Consumer Affairs and Protection; Election Law; Health;
Judiciary; Rules
Education: CUNY 1975 BA; Brooklyn Law 1979 JD

Assembly Member **David J. DiPietro** (R-District 147) . . . . (518) 455-5314
Counties Represented: Erie (part), Wyoming  Dist: (585) 655-0951
Term Expires: 2017
411 Main Street, East Aurora, NY 14052
E-mail: dipietrod@assembly.state.ny.us
Committees: Alcoholism and Drug Abuse; Economic Development,
Job Creation, Commerce and Industry; Labor; Small Business;
Transportation
Education: Wittenberg BSBA

Assembly Member **Janet L. Duprey** (R-District 115) . . . . . (518) 455-5943
Counties Represented: Clinton, Franklin, St.  Dist: (518) 562-1986
Lawrence (part)
Term Expires: 2017
202 U.S. Oval, Plattsburgh, NY 12903
E-mail: dupreyj@assembly.state.ny.us
Committees: Correction; Governmental Operations; Health; Higher
Education; Labor; Rules; Ways and Means

Assembly Member
**Steven C. "Steve" Englebright** (D-District 4) . . . . . . . . (518) 455-4804
Counties Represented: Suffolk (part)  Dist: (631) 751-3094
Term Expires: 2017  Fax: (518) 455-5795
149 Main Street, East Setauket, NY 11733  Dist: (631) 751-3082
E-mail: englebrights@assembly.state.ny.us
Committees: Education; Energy; Environmental Conservation; Higher
Education; Rules
Education: Tennessee 1969 BS; SUNY (Stony Brook) 1974 MS

Assembly Member **Patricia Fahy** (D-District 109) . . . . . . . (518) 455-4178
Counties Represented: Albany (part)
Term Expires: 2017
Legislative Office Building, Room 452, Albany, NY 12248
E-mail: fahyp@assembly.state.ny.us
Committees: Banks; Children and Families; Environmental
Conservation; Higher Education; Tourism, Parks, Arts and Sports
Development
Education: Northern Illinois 1980 BS; Illinois (Chicago) 1985 MPA

Assembly Member
**Herman D. Farrell, Jr.** (D-District 71) . . . . . . . . . . . . . . (518) 455-5491
Counties Represented: New York (part)  Dist: (212) 234-1430
Term Expires: 2017  (New York Office I)
New York Office I: 2541-55 Adam Clayton Powell  Dist: (212) 568-2828
Jr. Boulevard, New York, NY 10039  (New York Office II)
E-mail: farrellhd@assembly.state.ny.us  Fax: (518) 455-5776
Committees: Rules; Ways and Means  Dist: (212) 234-1868
  (New York Office I)

Assembly Member **Gary D. Finch** (R-District 126) . . . . . . . (518) 455-5878
Counties Represented: Cayuga (part), Chenango  Dist: (315) 255-3045
(part), Cortland (part), Onondaga (part)  Fax: (518) 455-3895
Term Expires: 2017  Dist: (315) 255-3048
69 South Street, Auburn, NY 13021
E-mail: finchg@assembly.state.ny.us
Committees: Agriculture; Banks; Correction; Insurance; Rules

Assembly Member **Michael J. Fitzpatrick** (R-District 8) . . (518) 455-5021
Counties Represented: Suffolk (part)  Dist: (631) 724-2929
Term Expires: 2017
50 Route 111, Smithtown, NY 11787
E-mail: fitzpatrickm@assembly.state.ny.us
Committees: Higher Education; Housing; Labor; Ways and Means
Education: St Michael's BA

Assembly Member **Christopher Friend** (R-District 124) . . . (518) 455-4538
Counties Represented: Broome (part), Chemung  Dist: (607) 562-3602
(part), Tioga
Term Expires: 2017
476 Maple Street, Big Flats, NY 14814-9701
E-mail: friendc@assembly.state.ny.us
Committees: Aging; Children and Families; Corporations, Authorities
and Commissions; Housing; Local Governments
Education: New Hampshire BSChem; SUNY (Buffalo) MA, PhD

Assembly Member
**Sandra R. "Sandy" Galef** (D-District 95) . . . . . . . . . . . (518) 455-5348
Counties Represented: Putnam (part), Westchester    Dist: (914) 941-1111
(part)    Fax: (518) 455-5728
Term Expires: 2017    Dist: (914) 941-9132
Two Church Street, Ossining, NY 10562
E-mail: galefs@assembly.state.ny.us
Committees: Corporations, Authorities and Commissions; Election
Law; Governmental Operations; Health; Real Property Taxation
Education: Purdue 1962 BS; Virginia 1965 MEd

Assembly Member **David F. Gantt** (D-District 137) . . . . . . (518) 455-5606
Counties Represented: Monroe (part)    Dist: (585) 454-3670
Term Expires: 2017    Fax: (585) 454-5419
107 Liberty Pole Way, Rochester, NY 14604    Dist: (585) 454-3788
E-mail: ganttd@assembly.state.ny.us
Committees: Economic Development, Job Creation, Commerce and
Industry; Local Governments; Rules; Transportation; Ways and Means

Assembly Member **Andrew R. Garbarino** (R-District 7) . . (518) 455-4611
Counties Represented: Suffolk (part)    Dist: (631) 589-0348
Term Expires: 2017    Fax: (631) 589-0487
859 Montauk Highway, Suite One, Bayport, NY 11705
E-mail: garbarinoa@assembly.state.ny.us
Committees: Energy; Environmental Conservation; Health; Higher
Education; Racing and Wagering
Education: George Washington BA; Hofstra 2010 JD

Assembly Member
**Joseph M. "Joe" Giglio** (R-District 148) . . . . . . . . . . . . . (518) 455-5241
Counties Represented: Allegany, Cattaraugus,    Dist: (716) 373-7103
Steuben (part)
Term Expires: 2017
700 West State Street, Olean, NY 14760
E-mail: giglioj@assembly.state.ny.us
Committees: Aging; Children and Families; Codes; Correction; Ethics
and Guidance

Assembly Member **Mark Gjonaj** (D-District 80) . . . . . . . . . (518) 455-5844
Counties Represented: Bronx (part)    Dist: (718) 409-0109
Term Expires: 2017
1126 Pelham Parkway South, Bronx, NY 10461
E-mail: gjonajm@assembly.state.ny.us
Committees: Banks; Local Governments; Real Property Taxation; Small
Business; Tourism, Parks, Arts and Sports Development
Education: St John's U (NY) BS

Assembly Member **Deborah J. Glick** (D-District 66) . . . . . (518) 455-4841
Counties Represented: New York (part)    Dist: (212) 674-5153
Term Expires: 2017    Fax: (518) 455-4649
853 Broadway, Suite 2007, New York, NY 10003    Dist: (212) 674-5530
E-mail: glickd@assembly.state.ny.us
Committees: Environmental Conservation; Governmental Operations;
Higher Education; Rules; Ways and Means
Education: Queens Col (NY) 1978 BA; Fordham 1981 MBA

Assembly Member **Phillip Goldfeder** (D-District 23) . . . . . (518) 455-4292
Counties Represented: Queens (part)    Dist: (718) 641-8755
Term Expires: 2017    (Howard Beach)
162-38 Crossway Boulevard,    Dist: (718) 945-9550
Howard Beach, NY 11414    (Rockaway Beach)
95-16 Rockaway Beach Boulevard,    Fax: (718) 835-3190
Rockaway Beach, NY 11693    (Howard Beach)
E-mail: goldfederp@assembly.state.ny.us    Dist: (718) 945-9549
Committees: Aging; Corporations, Authorities and    (Rockaway Beach)
Commissions; Governmental Employees; Insurance; Racing and
Wagering
Education: Brooklyn 2004 BA

Assembly Member **Andrew Goodell** (R-District 150) . . . . . (518) 455-4511
Counties Represented: Chautauqua    Dist: (716) 664-7773
Term Expires: 2017
Fenton Building, Two East 2nd Street, Sutie 320,
Jamestown, NY 14701
E-mail: goodella@assembly.state.ny.us
Committees: Cities; Governmental Operations; Health; Judiciary; Social
Services

Assembly Member **Richard N. Gottfried** (D-District 75) . . (518) 455-4941
Counties Represented: New York (part)    Dist: (212) 807-7900
Term Expires: 2017    Fax: (518) 455-5939
242 West 27th Street, New York, NY 10001    Dist: (212) 243-2035
E-mail: gottfriedr@assembly.state.ny.us
Committees: Health; Higher Education; Rules
Education: Cornell 1968 BA; Columbia 1973 JD

Assembly Member **Alfred "Al" Graf** (R-District 5) . . . . . . . (518) 455-5937
Counties Represented: Suffolk (part)    Dist: (631) 585-0230
Term Expires: 2017
991 Main Street, Suite 202, Holbrook, NY 11741
E-mail: grafa@assembly.state.ny.us
Committees: Codes; Education; Housing; Judiciary

Assembly Member **Aileen M. Gunther** (D-District 100) . . . (518) 455-5355
Counties Represented: Orange (part), Sullivan (part)    Dist: (845) 342-9304
Term Expires: 2017    (Middletown Office)
19 South Street, Middletown, NY 10940    Dist: (845) 794-5807
18 Anawana Lake Road, Monticello, NY 12701    (Monticello Office)
E-mail: gunthera@assembly.state.ny.us
Committees: Agriculture; Environmental Conservation; Health; Mental
Health; Racing and Wagering; Real Property Taxation

Assembly Member **Pamela Harris** (D-District 46) . . . . . . . . (518) 455-4811
Counties Represented: Kings (part)    Dist: (718) 266-0267
Term Expires: 2017
2823 West 12th Street, Suite 1F, Brooklyn, NY 11224
E-mail: harrisp@nyassembly.gov
Committees: Alcoholism and Drug Abuse; Children and Families;
Higher Education

Assembly Member
**Stephen "Steve" Hawley** (R-District 139) . . . . . . . . . . (518) 455-5811
Counties Represented: Genesee, Monroe (part),    Dist: (585) 589-5780
Orleans (part)
Term Expires: 2017
121 North Main Street, Suite 100, Albion, NY 14411
E-mail: hawleys@assembly.state.ny.us
Committees: Agriculture; Insurance; Veterans' Affairs; Ways and
Means

Assembly Member **Carl E. Heastie** (D-District 83) . . . . . . . (518) 455-3791
Counties Represented: Bronx (part)    Dist: (718) 654-6539
Term Expires: 2017    Fax: (518) 455-4812
1446 East Gun Hill Road, Bronx, NY 10469    Dist: (718) 654-5836
E-mail: heastiec@assembly.state.ny.us
E-mail: speaker@assembly.state.ny.us
Committees: Rules

Assembly Member **Andrew Hevesi** (D-District 28) . . . . . . . (518) 455-4926
Counties Represented: Queens (part)    Dist: (718) 263-5595
Term Expires: 2017
70-50 Austin Street, Suite 118, Forest Hills, NY 11375
E-mail: hevesia@assembly.state.ny.us
Committees: Energy; Health; Insurance; Labor; Social Services
Education: Queens Col (NY) BA

Assembly Member **Dov Hikind** (D-District 48) . . . . . . . . . . (518) 455-5721
Counties Represented: Kings (part)    Dist: (718) 853-9616
Term Expires: 2017    Fax: (518) 455-5948
1310 48th Street, Brooklyn, NY 11219    Dist: (718) 436-5734
E-mail: hikindd@assembly.state.ny.us

Assembly Member **Earlene Hooper** (D-District 18) . . . . . . (518) 455-5861
Counties Represented: Nassau (part)    Dist: (516) 489-6610
Term Expires: 2017    Fax: (518) 455-4329
33 Front Street, Suite 104, Hempstead, NY 11550    Dist: (516) 538-3155
E-mail: hoopere@assembly.state.ny.us
Committees: Education; Rules; Ways and Means

Assembly Member **Pamela J. Hunter** (D-District 128) . . . . (518) 455-5383
Counties Represented: Onondaga (part)    Dist: (315) 449-9536
Term Expires: 2017
711 East Genesee Street, Suite 2, Syracuse, NY 13210
E-mail: hunterp@assembly.state.ny.us
Committees: Insurance; Social Services; Transportation; Veterans'
Affairs

Assembly Member **Alicia L. Hyndman** (D-District 29) . . . . (518) 455-4451
Counties Represented: Queens (part)    Dist: (718) 723-5412
Term Expires: 2017
232-06A Merrick Boulevard, Springfield Gardens, NY 11413
Committees: Economic Development, Job Creation, Commerce and
Industry; Small Business; Transportation
Education: SUNY (New Paltz) BA; Framingham State MPA

Assembly Member **Ellen C. Jaffee** (D-District 97) . . . . . . . . (518) 455-5118
Counties Represented: Rockland (part)    Dist: (845) 624-4601
Term Expires: 2017    Fax: (518) 455-5119
One Blue Hill Plaza, Suite 1116,    Dist: (845) 624-2911
Pearl River, NY 10965
P.O. Box 1549, Pearl River, NY 10965
E-mail: jaffeee@assembly.state.ny.us
Committees: Children and Families; Economic Development, Job
Creation, Commerce and Industry; Environmental Conservation;
Health; Higher Education; Mental Health; Oversight, Analysis and
Investigation
Education: Brooklyn 1965 BA; Fordham 1980 MS

*(continued on next page)*

**LEGISLATIVE BRANCH**

**Assembly Members** *continued*

Assembly Member **Kimberly Jean-Pierre** (D-District 11)
Room 530 . . . . . . . . . . . . . . . . . . . . . . . . . . . . . . . . . . (518) 455-5787
Counties Represented: Suffolk (part)          Dist: (631) 957-2087
Term Expires: 2017
640 West Montauk Highway, Lindenhurst, NY 11757
E-mail: jeanpierrek@assembly.state.ny.us
Committees: Banks; Economic Development, Job Creation, Commerce
and Industry; Local Governments; Mental Health; Transportation
Education: Brooklyn 2005 BFA; SUNY (Stony Brook) 2007 MS

Assembly Member **Mark Johns** (R-District 135) . . . . . . . . (518) 455-5784
Counties Represented: Monroe (part)          Dist: (585) 223-9130
Term Expires: 2017
268 Fairport Village Landing, Fairport, NY 14450
E-mail: johnsm@assembly.state.ny.us
Committees: Aging; Alcoholism and Drug Abuse; Governmental
Employees; Governmental Operations; Housing

Assembly Member **Latoya Joyner** (D-District 77) . . . . . . . . (518) 455-5671
Counties Represented: Bronx (part)          Dist: (718) 538-2000
Term Expires: 2017                           Fax: (518) 455-5461
910 Grand Concourse, Suite 1JK, Bronx, NY 10451    Dist: (718) 538-3128
E-mail: joynerl@assembly.state.ny.us
Committees: Aging; Consumer Affairs and Protection; Housing;
Insurance; Judiciary; Social Services

Assembly Member **Steven "Steve" Katz** (R-District 94) . . (518) 455-5783
Counties Represented: Putnam (part), Westchester    Dist: (845) 628-3781
(part)
Term Expires: 2017
947 South Lake Boulevard, Suite 1C, Mahopac, NY 10541
E-mail: katzs@assembly.state.ny.us
Committees: Aging; Alcoholism and Drug Abuse; Economic
Development, Job Creation, Commerce and Industry; Housing; Mental
Health

Assembly Member **Brian P. Kavanagh** (D-District 74) . . . . (518) 455-5506
Counties Represented: New York (part)          Dist: (212) 979-9696
Term Expires: 2017                           Fax: (518) 455-4801
237 1st Avenue (14th Street), Room 407,       Dist: (212) 979-0594
New York, NY 10003
E-mail: kavanaghb@assembly.state.ny.us
Committees: Cities; Corporations, Authorities and Commissions;
Election Law; Environmental Conservation; Housing; Labor
Education: Princeton BA; NYU 1998 JD

Assembly Member
**Michael P. "Mickey" Kearns** (D-District 142) . . . . . . . . (518) 455-4691
Counties Represented: Erie (part)          Dist: (716) 608-6099
Term Expires: 2017
1074 Union Road, West Seneca, NY 14224
E-mail: kearnsm@assembly.state.ny.us
Committees: Banks; Cities; Housing; Oversight, Analysis and
Investigation
Education: Canisius 1991 BA

Assembly Member **Ronald T. Kim** (D-District 40) . . . . . . . . (518) 455-5411
Counties Represented: Queens (part)          Dist: (718) 939-0195
Term Expires: 2017
136-20 38th Avenue, Suite 10A, Flushing, NY 11354
E-mail: kimr@assembly.state.ny.us
Committees: Corporations, Authorities and Commissions; Education;
Governmental Operations; Health; Housing; Social Services
Education: Hamilton 2002 BA; Baruch Col 2005 MPA

Assembly Member **Brian M. Kolb** (R-District 131) . . . . . . (518) 455-3751
Counties Represented: Ontario, Seneca (part)    Dist: (315) 781-2030
Term Expires: 2017                           Fax: (518) 455-3750
607 West Washington Street, Suite Two,        Dist: (315) 781-1746
Geneva, NY 14456
E-mail: kolbb@assembly.state.ny.us
Committees: Rules

Assembly Member
**Kieran Michael Lalor** (R-District 105) . . . . . . . . . . . . . . (518) 455-5725
Counties Represented: Dutchess (part)
Term Expires: 2017
Legislative Office Building, Room 531, Albany, NY 12248
North Hopewell Plaza, 1075 Route 82, Suite One,
Hopewell Junction, NY 12533
E-mail: lalork@assembly.state.ny.us
Committees: Banks; Governmental Operations; Real Property Taxation;
Small Business; Veterans' Affairs
Education: Pace JD

Assembly Member **Charles D. Lavine** (D-District 13) . . . . . (518) 455-5456
Counties Represented: Nassau (part)          Dist: (516) 676-0050
Term Expires: 2017                           Fax: (518) 455-5467
One School Street, Suite 303-B,              Dist: (516) 676-0071
Glen Cove, NY 11542
E-mail: lavinec@assembly.state.ny.us
Committees: Codes; Ethics and Guidance; Health; Higher Education;
Insurance; Judiciary
Education: Wisconsin 1969 BA; NYU 1972 JD

Assembly Member **Peter A. Lawrence** (R-District 134) . . . (518) 455-4664
Counties Represented: Monroe (part)          Dist: (585) 225-4190
Term Expires: 2017                           Fax: (518) 455-3093
2496 West Ridge Road, Rochester, NY 14626     Dist: (585) 225-6502
E-mail: lawrencep@assembly.state.ny.us
Committees: Ethics and Guidance; Higher Education; Oversight,
Analysis and Investigation; Racing and Wagering; Small Business

Assembly Member **Joseph R. Lentol** (D-District 50) . . . . . (518) 455-4477
Counties Represented: Kings (part)          Dist: (718) 383-7474
Term Expires: 2017                           Fax: (518) 455-4599
619 Lorimer Street, Brooklyn, NY 11211        Dist: (718) 383-1576
E-mail: lentolj@assembly.state.ny.us
Committees: Codes; Election Law; Rules; Ways and Means
Education: Dayton 1964 BA; Baltimore 1968 JD

Assembly Member **Barbara S. Lifton** (D-District 125) . . . . (518) 455-5444
Counties Represented: Cortland (part), Tompkins    Dist: (607) 277-8030
Term Expires: 2017                           Fax: (518) 455-4640
106 East Court Street, Ithaca, NY 14850
E-mail: liftonb@assembly.state.ny.us
Committees: Agriculture; Education; Election Law; Environmental
Conservation; Higher Education

Assembly Member **Guillermo Linares** (D-District 72) . . . . (518) 455-5807
Counties Represented: New York (part)          Dist: (212) 544-2278
Term Expires: 2017
210 Sherman Avenue, Suite A & C, New York, NY 10034
E-mail: linaresg@assembly.state.ny.us
Committees: Aging; Banks; Cities; Housing; Labor
Education: CCNY BA, MS; Teachers Col Columbia U EdD

Assembly Member
**Peter D. "Pete" Lopez** (R-District 102) . . . . . . . . . . . . . . (518) 455-5363
Counties Represented: Albany (part), Columbia    Dist: (518) 943-1371
(part), Delaware (part), Greene, Otsego (part),    (Catskill Office)
Schoharie, Ulster (part)                     Dist: (518) 295-7250
Term Expires: 2017                           (Schoharie Office)
45 Five Mile Woods Road, Suite Three, Catskill, NY 12414
113 Park Place, Schoharie, NY 12157
E-mail: lopezp@assembly.state.ny.us
Committees: Agriculture; Alcoholism and Drug Abuse; Corporations,
Authorities and Commissions; Education; Environmental Conservation

Assembly Member **Donna A. Lupardo** (D-District 123) . . . (518) 455-5431
Counties Represented: Broome (part)          Dist: (607) 723-9047
Term Expires: 2017
Binghamton, NY 13901
E-mail: lupardod@assembly.state.ny.us
Committees: Children and Families; Economic Development, Job
Creation, Commerce and Industry; Environmental Conservation; Higher
Education; Transportation
Education: Wagner 1976 BA; SUNY (Binghamton) 1984 MA

Assembly Member **Chad A. Lupinacci** (R-District 10) . . . . (518) 455-5732
Counties Represented: Suffolk (part)          Dist: (631) 271-8025
Term Expires: 2017
630 New York Avenue, Suite D, Huntington, NY 11743
E-mail: lupinaccic@assembly.state.ny.us
Committees: Election Law; Higher Education; Judiciary; Tourism,
Parks, Arts and Sports Development; Transportation
Education: Hofstra 2001 BA, JD, 2004 MPA

Assembly Member
**William "Bill" Magee** (D-District 121) . . . . . . . . . . . . . . (518) 455-4807
Counties Represented: Madison, Oneida (part),    Dist: (315) 361-4125
Otsego (part)                                Dist: (607) 432-1484
Term Expires: 2017                           (Oneonta)
214 Farrier Avenue, Oneida, NY 13421         Fax: (518) 455-5237
E-mail: mageew@assembly.state.ny.us          Dist: (315) 361-4222
Committees: Aging; Agriculture; Banks; Higher Education; Local
Governments
Education: Cornell 1961 BA

Assembly Member
**William B. Magnarelli** (D-District 129) . . . . . . . . . . . . . .(518) 455-4826
Counties Represented: Onondaga (part)　　　　　Dist: (315) 428-9651
Term Expires: 2017　　　　　　　　　　　　　　　Fax: (518) 455-5498
333 East Washington Street, Room 840,　　　　　Dist: (315) 428-1279
Syracuse, NY 13202
E-mail: magnarelliw@assembly.state.ny.us
Committees: Economic Development, Job Creation, Commerce and
Industry; Education; Local Governments; Oversight, Analysis and
Investigation; Rules
Education: Syracuse 1970 BA, 1973 JD

Assembly Member **Nicole Malliotakis** (R-District 64) . . . . (518) 455-5716
Counties Represented: Kings (part), Richmond　　Dist: (718) 987-0197
(part)　　　　　　　　　　　　　　　　　　　　Fax: (718) 987-0863
Term Expires: 2017
7408 Fifth Avenue, Brooklyn, NY 11209
11 Maplewood Place, Staten Island, NY 10306
E-mail: malliotakisn@assembly.state.ny.us
Committees: Banks; Corporations, Authorities and Commissions;
Governmental Employees; Transportation; Ways and Means
Education: Seton Hall BA; Wagner MBA

Assembly Member
**Margaret M. "Marge" Markey** (D-District 30) . . . . . . . . (518) 455-4755
Counties Represented: Queens (part)　　　　　　Dist: (718) 651-3185
Term Expires: 2017　　　　　　　　　　　　　　　Fax: (518) 455-5032
55-19 69th Street, Maspeth, NY 11378　　　　　　Dist: (718) 651-3027
E-mail: markeym@assembly.state.ny.us
Committees: Labor; Racing and Wagering; Rules; Tourism, Parks, Arts
and Sports Development; Ways and Means

Assembly Member **Shelley B. Mayer** (D-District 90) . . . . . (518) 455-3662
Counties Represented: Westchester (part)　　　　Dist: (914) 779-8805
Term Expires: 2017　　　　　　　　　　　　　　　Fax: (518) 455-5499
33 East Grassy Sprain Road, Room 406B,　　　　Dist: (914) 779-8859
Yonkers, NY 10710
E-mail: mayers@assembly.state.ny.us
Committees: Children and Families; Cities; Education; Health; Labor;
Social Services
Education: UCLA 1975 BA; SUNY (Buffalo) 1979 JD

Assembly Member
**John T. McDonald III** (D-District 108) . . . . . . . . . . . . . . (518) 455-4474
Counties Represented: Albany (part), Rensselaer (part), Saratoga (part)
Term Expires: 2017
Legislative Office Building, Room 417, Albany, NY 12248
E-mail: mcdonaldj@assembly.state.ny.us
Committees: Aging; Alcoholism and Drug Abuse; Cities; Insurance;
Mental Health; Real Property Taxation
Education: Albany Pharmacy 1985 BS

Assembly Member
**David G. McDonough** (R-District 14) . . . . . . . . . . . . . . .(518) 455-4633
Counties Represented: Nassau (part)　　　　　　Dist: (516) 409-2070
Term Expires: 2017
404 Bedford Avenue, Bellmore, NY 11710-3514
E-mail: mcdonoughd@assembly.state.ny.us
Committees: Consumer Affairs and Protection; Education; Health;
Transportation; Veterans' Affairs
Education: Columbia BA

Assembly Member
**Thomas "Tom" McKevitt** (R-District 17) . . . . . . . . . . . .(518) 455-5341
Counties Represented: Nassau (part)　　　　　　Dist: (516) 228-4960
Term Expires: 2017
1975 Hempstead Turnpike, Suite 202, East Meadow, NY 11554
E-mail: mckevitt@assembly.state.ny.us
Committees: Codes; Consumer Affairs and Protection; Election Law;
Local Governments

Assembly Member **Steven McLaughlin** (R-District 107) . . (518) 455-5777
Counties Represented: Columbia (part), Rensselaer　Dist: (518) 272-6149
(part), Washington (part)　　　　　　　　　　　Fax: (518) 272-6313
Term Expires: 2017
258 Hoosick Street, Suite 109, Troy, NY 12180
E-mail: mclaughlins@assembly.state.ny.us
Committees: Children and Families; Economic Development, Job
Creation, Commerce and Industry; Education; Energy; Social Services

Assembly Member
**Michael "Mike" Miller** (D-District 38) . . . . . . . . . . . . . . (518) 455-4621
Counties Represented: Queens (part)　　　　　　Dist: (718) 805-0950
Term Expires: 2017　　　　　　　　　　　　　　　Fax: (518) 455-5361
83-91 Woodhaven Boulevard,　　　　　　　　　　Dist: (718) 805-0953
Woodhaven, NY 11421
E-mail: millermg@assembly.state.ny.us
Committees: Aging; Banks; Education; Labor; Racing and Wagering;
Veterans' Affairs

Assembly Member
**Michael A. Montesano** (R-District 15) . . . . . . . . . . . . . .(518) 455-4684
Counties Represented: Nassau (part)　　　　　　Dist: (516) 937-3571
Term Expires: 2017
111 Levittown Parkway, Hicksville, NY 11801
E-mail: montesanom@assembly.state.ny.us
Committees: Codes; Corporations, Authorities and Commissions; Ethics
and Guidance; Judiciary; Oversight, Analysis and Investigation

Assembly Member **Joseph D. Morelle** (D-District 136) . . . (518) 455-5373
Counties Represented: Monroe (part)　　　　　　Dist: (585) 467-0410
Term Expires: 2017　　　　　　　　　　　　　　　Fax: (518) 455-5647
564 East Ridge Road, Suite 103,　　　　　　　　Dist: (585) 467-5342
Rochester, NY 14621
E-mail: morellej@assembly.state.ny.us
Committees: Rules

Assembly Member **Walter T. Mosley III** (D-District 57) . . . (518) 455-5325
Counties Represented: Kings (part)　　　　　　　Tel: (718) 596-0100
Term Expires: 2017
55 Hanson Place, Brooklyn, NY 11217
E-mail: mosleyw@assembly.state.ny.us
Committees: Banks; Codes; Correction; Education; Housing
Education: Penn State 1998; Howard U 1998 JD

Assembly Member **Francisco Moya** (D-District 39) . . . . . . (518) 455-4567
Counties Represented: Queens (part)　　　　　　Dist: (718) 458-5367
Term Expires: 2017　　　　　　　　　　　　　　　Fax: (718) 478-2371
82-11 37th Avenue, Suite 607, Jackson Heights, NY 11372
E-mail: moyaf@assembly.state.ny.us
Committees: Corporations, Authorities and Commissions; Energy;
Housing; Insurance; Labor; Ways and Means
Education: St John's U (NY)

Assembly Member **Dean Murray** (R-District 3) . . . . . . . . . (518) 455-4901
Counties Represented: Suffolk (part)　　　　　　Dist: (631) 207-0073
Term Expires: 2017　　　　　　　　　　　　　　　Fax: (518) 455-5908
1735 North Ocean Avenue, Suite A,　　　　　　　Dist: (631) 207-2006
Medford, NY 11763
E-mail: murrayd@assembly.state.ny.us
Committees: Aging; Education; Small Business; Tourism, Parks, Arts
and Sports Development; Transportation

Assembly Member
**William "Bill" Nojay** (R-District 133) . . . . . . . . . . . . . . .(518) 455-5662
Counties Represented: Livingston, Monroe (part),　Dist: (585) 218-0038
Steuben (part)　　　　　　　　　　　　　　　　　Fax: (585) 218-0063
Term Expires: 2017
30 Office Park Way, Pittsford, NY 14534
E-mail: nojayw@assembly.state.ny.us
Committees: Consumer Affairs and Protection; Election Law; Mental
Health; Transportation
Education: Colgate 1978 BA; Columbia 1982 MBA, 1982 JD

Assembly Member **Catherine T. Nolan** (D-District 37) . . . .(518) 455-4851
Counties Represented: Queens (part)　　　　　　Dist: (718) 784-3194
Term Expires: 2017　　　　　　　　　　　　　　(Long Island City
47-40 21 Street, Room 810,　　　　　　　　　　　　　　　　Office)
Long Island City, NY 11101
E-mail: nolanc@assembly.state.ny.us
Committees: Corporations, Authorities and Commissions; Education;
Rules; Veterans' Affairs; Ways and Means
Education: NYU 1979 BA

Assembly Member **Daniel J. O'Donnell** (D-District 69) . . . (518) 455-5603
Counties Represented: New York (part)　　　　　Dist: (212) 866-3970
Term Expires: 2017　　　　　　　　　　　　　　　Fax: (212) 864-1095
245 West 104th Street, New York, NY 10025
E-mail: odonnelld@assembly.state.ny.us
Committees: Codes; Correction; Education; Environmental
Conservation; Tourism, Parks, Arts and Sports Development
Education: George Washington 1982 BA; CUNY 1987 JD

Assembly Member
**Robert C. "Bob" Oaks** (R-District 130) . . . . . . . . . . . . . (518) 455-5655
Counties Represented: Cayuga (part), Oswego　　Dist: (315) 946-5166
(part), Wayne　　　　　　　　　　　　　　　　　Fax: (518) 455-5407
Term Expires: 2017　　　　　　　　　　　　　　　Dist: (315) 946-5229
10 Leach Road, Lyons, NY 14489
E-mail: oaksr@assembly.state.ny.us
Committees: Rules; Ways and Means
Education: Colgate 1974 BA; Montana 1976 MS

Assembly Member **Felix W. Ortiz** (D-District 51) . . . . . . . . (518) 455-3821
Counties Represented: Kings (part)　　　　　　　Dist: (718) 492-6334
Term Expires: 2017　　　　　　　　　　　　　　　Fax: (518) 455-3828
5004 4th Avenue, Brooklyn, NY 11220　　　　　　Dist: (718) 492-6435
E-mail: ortizf@assembly.state.ny.us
Committees: Correction; Labor; Rules; Ways and Means

*(continued on next page)*

**LEGISLATIVE BRANCH**

LEGISLATIVE BRANCH

**Assembly Members** continued

Assembly Member **Steven Otis** (D-District 91) . . . . . . . . . (518) 455-4897
Counties Represented: Westchester (part)          Dist: (914) 939-7028
Term Expires: 2017
222 Grace Church Street, Suite 305, Port Chester, NY 10573
E-mail: otiss@assembly.state.ny.us
Committees: Corporations, Authorities and Commissions; Education;
Environmental Conservation; Libraries and Education Technology;
Local Governments; Tourism, Parks, Arts and Sports Development
Education: Hobart & William Smith 1979 BA; NYU 1982 MPA;
Hofstra 1984 JD

Assembly Member
**Philip "Phil" Palmesano** (R-District 132) . . . . . . . . . . . (518) 455-5791
Counties Represented: Chemung (part), Schuyler,     Dist: (607) 776-9691
Seneca (part), Steuben (part), Yates                Fax: (518) 455-4644
Term Expires: 2017                                  Dist: (607) 776-5185
105 East Steuben Street, Bath, NY 14810
E-mail: palmesanop@assembly.state.ny.us
Committees: Corporations, Authorities and Commissions; Energy;
Libraries and Education Technology; Real Property Taxation; Tourism,
Parks, Arts and Sports Development

Assembly Member **Anthony H. Palumbo** (R-District 2) . . . (518) 455-5294
Counties Represented: Suffolk (part)               Dist: (631) 727-0204
Term Expires: 2017                                 Fax: (631) 727-0426
30 West Main Street, Suite 103, Riverhead, NY 11901
E-mail: palumboa@assembly.state.ny.us
Committees: Consumer Affairs and Protection; Environmental
Conservation; Governmental Employees; Judiciary; Social Services
Education: Lafayette; St John's U (NY) JD

Assembly Member **Amy R. Paulin** (D-District 88) . . . . . . . (518) 455-5585
Counties Represented: Westchester (part)           Dist: (914) 723-1115
Term Expires: 2017                                  Fax: (518) 455-5409
700 White Plains Road, Room 252,                    Dist: (914) 723-2665
Scarsdale, NY 10583
E-mail: paulina@assembly.state.ny.us
Committees: Education; Energy; Health; Higher Education
Education: SUNY (Albany) 1977 BA, MA

Assembly Member
**Crystal D. Peoples-Stokes** (D-District 141) . . . . . . . . . . (518) 455-5005
Counties Represented: Erie (part)                  Dist: (716) 897-9714
Term Expires: 2017
425 Michigan Avenue, Buffalo, NY 14203
E-mail: peoplec@assembly.state.ny.us
Committees: Alcoholism and Drug Abuse; Environmental
Conservation; Governmental Operations; Health; Higher Education;
Insurance
Education: SUNY (Buffalo) MSE, BE

Assembly Member **N. Nick Perry** (D-District 58) . . . . . . . . (518) 455-4166
Counties Represented: Kings (part)                 Dist: (718) 385-3336
Term Expires: 2017                                  Fax: (518) 455-5478
903 Utica Avenue, Brooklyn, NY 11203               Dist: (718) 385-3339
E-mail: perryn@assembly.state.ny.us
Committees: Banks; Codes; Labor; Rules; Transportation; Ways and
Means

Assembly Member **Victor M. Pichardo** (D-District 86) . . . . (518) 455-5511
Counties Represented: Bronx (part)                 Dist: (718) 933-6909
Term Expires: 2017
2175C Jerome Avenue, Bronx, NY 10453
E-mail: pichardov@assembly.state.ny.us
Committees: Cities; Higher Education; Housing; Real Property
Taxation; Small Business; Social Services
Education: Buffalo 2007

Assembly Member **J. Gary Pretlow, Sr.** (D-District 89) . . . (518) 455-5291
Counties Represented: Westchester (part)           Dist: (914) 667-0127
Term Expires: 2017                                  Fax: (518) 455-5447
Six Gramatan Avenue, Mount Vernon, NY 10550        Dist: (914) 667-0209
E-mail: pretlowj@assembly.state.ny.us
Committees: Codes; Insurance; Racing and Wagering; Rules; Ways and
Means
Education: Baruch Col 1974 BBA

Assembly Member **Dan Quart** (D-District 73) . . . . . . . . . . . (518) 455-4794
Counties Represented: New York (part)              Tel: (212) 605-0937
Term Expires: 2017                                  Fax: (212) 605-9948
353 Lexington Avenue, Suite 704, New York, NY 10016
E-mail: quartd@assembly.state.ny.us
Committees: Alcoholism and Drug Abuse; Consumer Affairs and
Protection; Corporations, Authorities and Commissions; Judiciary;
Tourism, Parks, Arts and Sports Development
Education: SUNY (Binghamton) 1994 BA; St John's U (NY) 1997 JD

Assembly Member **Edward Ra** (R-District 19) . . . . . . . . . . . (518) 455-4627
Counties Represented: Nassau (part)                Dist: (516) 535-4095
Term Expires: 2017
825 East Gate Boulevard, Suite 207, Garden City, NY 11530
E-mail: rae@assembly.state.ny.us
Committees: Codes; Education; Health; Higher Education;
Transportation
Education: St John's U (NY) 2007 JD; Cardozo 2008 LLM

Assembly Member **Andrew P. Raia** (R-District 12) . . . . . . . (518) 455-5952
Counties Represented: Suffolk (part)               Dist: (631) 261-4151
Term Expires: 2017
75 Woodbine Avenue, Northport, NY 11768
E-mail: raiaa@assembly.state.ny.us
Committees: Banks; Environmental Conservation; Health; Housing;
Rules

Assembly Member **Philip R. Ramos** (D-District 6) . . . . . . . (518) 455-5185
Counties Represented: Suffolk (part)               Dist: (631) 435-3214
Term Expires: 2017
1010 Suffolk Avenue, Brentwood, NY 11717
E-mail: ramosp@assembly.state.ny.us
Committees: Aging; Education; Local Governments; Ways and Means

Assembly Member **Diana C. Richardson** (D-District 43) . . (518) 455-5262
Counties Represented: Kings (part)                 Dist: (718) 771-3105
Term Expires: 2017                                  Fax: (718) 771-3276
1216 Union Street, Brooklyn, NY 11225
E-mail: district43@assembly.state.ny.us
Committees: Banks; Children and Families; Corporations, Authorities
and Commissions; Mental Health; Small Business
Education: Medgar Evers BPA; Baruch Col MPA

Assembly Member **José Rivera** (D-District 78) . . . . . . . . . (518) 455-5414
Counties Represented: Bronx (part)                 Dist: (718) 933-2204
Term Expires: 2017                                  Fax: (518) 455-5322
One Fordham Plaza, 10th Floor, Suite 1008,         Dist: (718) 933-2535
Bronx, NY 10458
E-mail: riveraj@assembly.state.ny.us
Committees: Aging; Agriculture; Insurance; Small Business

Assembly Member
**Annette M. Robinson** (D-District 56) . . . . . . . . . . . . . . . (518) 455-5474
Counties Represented: Kings (part)                 Dist: (718) 399-7630
Term Expires: 2017
1360 Fulton Street, Room 417, Brooklyn, NY 11216
E-mail: robinsona@assembly.state.ny.us
Committees: Aging; Banks; Children and Families; Housing; Real
Property Taxation; Small Business
Education: New Hampshire Col BS, MA

Assembly Member **Robert J. Rodriguez** (D-District 68) . . (518) 455-4781
Counties Represented: New York (part)              Dist: (212) 828-3953
Term Expires: 2017
55 East 115th Street, New York, NY 10029
E-mail: rrodriguez@assembly.state.ny.us
Committees: Banks; Corporations, Authorities and Commissions;
Housing; Labor; Mental Health; Ways and Means

Assembly Member **Linda B. Rosenthal** (D-District 67) . . . (518) 455-5802
Counties Represented: New York (part)              Dist: (212) 873-6368
Term Expires: 2017
230 West 72nd Street, Suite 2F, New York, NY 10023
E-mail: rosenthall@assembly.state.ny.us
Committees: Agriculture; Alcoholism and Drug Abuse; Education;
Energy; Health; Housing; Tourism, Parks, Arts and Sports Development
Education: Rochester 1980 BA

Assembly Member **Nily D. Rozic** (D-District 25) . . . . . . . . . (518) 455-5172
Counties Represented: Queens (part)                Dist: (718) 820-0241
Term Expires: 2017                                  Fax: (518) 455-5479
159-16 Union Turnpike, Suite 210,                  Dist: (718) 820-0414
Flushing, NY 11366
E-mail: rozicn@assembly.state.ny.us
Committees: Children and Families; Corporations, Authorities and
Commissions; Correction; Environmental Conservation; Labor
Education: NYU BA

Assembly Member
**Addie Jenne Russell** (D-District 116) . . . . . . . . . . . . . . . (518) 455-5545
Counties Represented: Jefferson (part), St. Lawrence   Dist: (315) 386-2037
(part)                                              (Canton Office)
Term Expires: 2017                                  Dist: (315) 786-0284
Three Remington Avenue, Suite One,                  (Watertown Office)
Canton, NY 13617                                    Fax: (315) 386-2041
Dulles State Office Building, 317 Washington        (Canton Office)
Street, Suite 210, Watertown, NY 13601             Fax: (315) 786-0287
E-mail: russella@assembly.state.ny.us              (Watertown Office)
Committees: Agriculture; Corporations, Authorities and Commissions;
Economic Development, Job Creation, Commerce and Industry;
Energy; Local Governments; Veterans' Affairs
Education: SUNY (Albany) 2000 BA; Syracuse 2003 JD

Assembly Member **Sean M. Ryan** (D-District 149) . . . . . . (518) 455-4886
Counties Represented: Erie (part)    Dist: (716) 885-9630
Term Expires: 2017    Fax: (518) 455-4890
936 Delaware Avenue, Buffalo, NY 14209    Dist: (716) 885-9636
E-mail: ryans@assembly.state.ny.us
Committees: Banks; Education; Energy; Environmental Conservation;
Local Governments; Veterans' Affairs
Education: SUNY (Fredonia); Brooklyn Law 1992 JD

Assembly Member **Joseph Saladino** (R-District 9) . . . . . (518) 455-5305
Counties Represented: Nassau (part), Suffolk (part)    Dist: (516) 541-4598
Term Expires: 2017
512 Park Boulevard, Massapequa Park, NY 11762
E-mail: saladinoj@assembly.state.ny.us
Committees: Environmental Conservation; Governmental Employees;
Labor; Libraries and Education Technology; Ways and Means

Assembly Member
**Angelo L. Santabarbara** (D-District 111) . . . . . . . . . . . .(518) 455-5197
Counties Represented: Albany (part), Montgomery,    Dist: (518) 843-0227
Schenectady (part)
Term Expires: 2017
2550 Riverfront Center, Amsterdam, NY 12010
E-mail: santabarbaraa@assembly.state.ny.us
Committees: Agriculture; Energy; Governmental Employees; Mental
Health; Racing and Wagering; Small Business; Veterans' Affairs
Education: SUNY (Albany) 2001 BS

Assembly Member **Michelle Schimel** (D-District 16) . . . . . (518) 455-5192
Counties Represented: Nassau (part)    Dist: (516) 482-6966
Term Expires: 2017
45 North Station Plaza, Suite 203, Great Neck, NY 11021
E-mail: schimelm@assembly.state.ny.us
Committees: Environmental Conservation; Governmental Operations;
Local Governments; Transportation; Veterans' Affairs

Assembly Member
**Robin L. Schimminger** (D-District 140) . . . . . . . . . . . . .(518) 455-4767
Counties Represented: Erie (part), Niagara (part)    Dist: (716) 873-2540
Term Expires: 2017    Fax: (518) 455-4724
3514 Delaware Avenue, Kenmore, NY 14217    Dist: (716) 873-5675
E-mail: schimmingerr@assembly.state.ny.us
Committees: Codes; Economic Development, Job Creation, Commerce
and Industry; Health; Ways and Means
Education: Canisius 1969 BA; NYU 1972 JD

Assembly Member **Rebecca Seawright** (D-District 76) . . . (518) 455-5676
Counties Represented: New York (part)    Dist: (212) 288-4607
Term Expires: 2017    Fax: (212) 288-4369
1365 First Avenue, New York, NY 10021
E-mail: seawrightr@assembly.state.ny.us
Committees: Banks; Consumer Affairs and Protection; Corporations,
Authorities and Commissions; Judiciary; Tourism, Parks, Arts and
Sports Development

Assembly Member **Luis Sepulveda** (D-District 87) . . . . . . (518) 455-5102
Counties Represented: Bronx (part)    Dist: (718) 931-2620
Term Expires: 2017    Fax: (518) 455-3693
1973 Westchester Avenue, Bronx, NY 10462    Dist: (718) 931-2915
E-mail: sepulvedal@assembly.state.ny.us
Committees: Aging; Agriculture; Banks; Correction; Housing; Mental
Health
Education: Hofstra 1988 BA, 1991 JD

Assembly Member
**Michael A. Simanowitz** (D-District 27) . . . . . . . . . . . . . (518) 455-4404
Counties Represented: Queens (part)    Dist: (718) 969-1508
Term Expires: 2017    Fax: (718) 969-8326
159-06 71st Avenue, Flushing, NY 11365
E-mail: simanowitzm@assembly.state.ny.us
Committees: Aging; Agriculture; Consumer Affairs and Protection;
Economic Development, Job Creation, Commerce and Industry; Higher
Education; Small Business
Education: Queens Col (NY) 1994 BA

Assembly Member **Jo Anne Simon** (D-District 52) . . . . . . (518) 455-5426
Counties Represented: Kings (part)    Dist: (718) 246-4889
Term Expires: 2017
341 Smith Street, Brooklyn, NY 11231
E-mail: simonj@assembly.state.ny.us
Committees: Consumer Affairs and Protection; Higher Education;
Judiciary; Labor; Transportation

Assembly Member **Aravella Simotas** (D-District 36) . . . . . (518) 455-5014
Counties Represented: Queens (part)    Dist: (718) 545-3889
Term Expires: 2017
31-19 Newtown Avenue, Suite 401, Astoria, NY 11102
E-mail: simotasa@assembly.state.ny.us
Committees: Banks; Consumer Affairs and Protection; Corporations,
Authorities and Commissions; Energy; Ethics and Guidance

Assembly Member **Frank Skartados** (D-District 104) . . . . . (518) 455-5762
Counties Represented: Dutchess (part), Orange    Fax: (518) 455-5593
(part), Ulster (part)
Term Expires: 2017
154 North Plank Road, Suite Two, Newburgh, NY 12550
E-mail: skartadosf@assembly.state.ny.us
Committees: Agriculture; Economic Development, Job Creation,
Commerce and Industry; Local Governments; Small Business; Tourism,
Parks, Arts and Sports Development; Transportation
Education: SUNY (New Paltz) 1985 BA;
Cal State (Sacramento) 1987 MA

Assembly Member **James G. Skoufis** (D-District 99) . . . . . (518) 455-5441
Counties Represented: Orange (part), Rockland    Dist: (845) 469-0914
(part)
Term Expires: 2017
11 Main Street, Chester, NY 10918
E-mail: skoufisj@assembly.state.ny.us
Committees: Agriculture; Insurance; Labor; Local Governments;
Transportation; Veterans' Affairs
Education: George Washington 2007 BA; Columbia MA

Assembly Member **Michaëlle C. Solages** (D-District 22) . . (518) 455-4465
Counties Represented: Nassau (part)    Fax: (518) 455-5560
Term Expires: 2017
1690 Central Court, Valley Stream, NY 11580
E-mail: solagesm@assembly.state.ny.us
Committees: Consumer Affairs and Protection; Governmental
Employees; Libraries and Education Technology; Racing and Wagering;
Social Services
Education: Hofstra 2007 BS

Assembly Member **Daniel G. Stec** (R-District 114) . . . . . . (518) 455-5565
Counties Represented: Essex, Saratoga (part),    Dist: (518) 792-4546
Warren, Washington (part)    (Glens Falls Office)
Term Expires: 2017    Dist: (518) 873-3803
140 Glen Street, Glens Falls, NY 12801    (Elizabethtown
7559 Court Street, Room 203,    Office)
Elizabethtown, NY 12921
E-mail: stecd@assembly.state.ny.us
Committees: Banks; Environmental Conservation; Local Governments;
Social Services; Tourism, Parks, Arts and Sports Development
Education: Clarkson U 1990 BS; Rhode Island 1997 MBA

Assembly Member
**Phillip G. "Phil" Steck** (D-District 110) . . . . . . . . . . . . . (518) 455-5931
Counties Represented: Albany (part), Schenectady    Dist: (518) 377-0902
(part)    Fax: (518) 455-5840
Term Expires: 2017    Dist: (518) 377-0458
1609 Union Street, Schenectady, NY 12309
E-mail: steckp@assembly.state.ny.us
Committees: Children and Families; Health; Insurance; Judiciary;
Transportation
Education: Harvard 1981 BA; Pennsylvania 1984 JD

Assembly Member **Albert A. Stirpe, Jr.** (D-District 130) . . (518) 455-4505
Counties Represented: Cayuga (part), Oswego    Dist: (315) 452-1115
(part), Wayne
Term Expires: 2017
7293 Buckley Road, Suite 201, North Syracuse, NY 13212
E-mail: stirpea@assembly.state.ny.us
Committees: Agriculture; Alcoholism and Drug Abuse; Economic
Development, Job Creation, Commerce and Industry; Higher Education;
Tourism, Parks, Arts and Sports Development

Assembly Member
**James N. "Jim" Tedisco** (R-District 112) . . . . . . . . . . . (518) 455-5772
Counties Represented: Saratoga (part), Schenectady    Dist: (518) 370-2812
(part)    Fax: (518) 455-4650
Term Expires: 2017    Dist: (518) 370-2862
636 Plank Road, Suite 101, Clifton Park, NY 12065
E-mail: tediscoj@assembly.state.ny.us
Committees: Banks; Economic Development, Job Creation, Commerce
and Industry; Racing and Wagering; Rules

Assembly Member **Claudia Tenney** (R-District 101) . . . . . . (518) 455-5334
Counties Represented: Delaware (part), Herkimer    Dist: (315) 736-3879
(part), Oneida (part), Orange (part), Otsego (part), Sullivan (part),
Ulster (part)
Term Expires: 2017
4747 Middle Settlement Road, New Hartford, NY 13413
E-mail: tenneyc@assembly.state.ny.us
Committees: Banks; Codes; Education; Social Services; Veterans'
Affairs

*(continued on next page)*

**LEGISLATIVE BRANCH**

**Assembly Members** *continued*

Assembly Member **Fred W. Thiele, Jr.** (I-District 1)......(518) 455-5997
Counties Represented: Suffolk (part)    Dist: (631) 537-2583
Term Expires: 2017    Fax: (518) 455-5963
2302 Main Street, Box 3062,    Dist: (631) 537-2836
Bridgehampton, NY 11932
E-mail: thielef@assembly.state.ny.us
Committees: Education; Environmental Conservation; Oversight,
Analysis and Investigation; Small Business; Transportation; Ways and
Means
Education: Long Island 1976 BA; Albany Law 1979 JD

Assembly Member **Matthew Titone** (D-District 61)......(518) 455-4677
Counties Represented: Richmond (part)    Dist: (718) 442-9932
Term Expires: 2017
853 Forest Avenue, Staten Island, NY 10310
E-mail: titonem@assembly.state.ny.us
Committees: Education; Environmental Conservation; Health; Judiciary;
Social Services; Tourism, Parks, Arts and Sports Development
Education: St John's U (NY) 1992 JD

Assembly Member **Michele R. Titus** (D-District 31)......(518) 455-5668
Counties Represented: Queens (part)    Dist: (718) 327-1845
Term Expires: 2017    (Far Rockaway
19-31 Mott Avenue, Room 301,    Office)
Far Rockaway, NY 11691    Dist: (718) 322-4958
131-17 Rockaway Boulevard,    (South Ozone Park
South Ozone Park, NY 11420    Office)
E-mail: titusm@assembly.state.ny.us
Committees: Children and Families; Codes; Education; Ethics and
Guidance; Judiciary; Labor
Education: SUNY (Binghamton) BA; Albany Law JD

Assembly Member **Latrice Walker** (D-District 55)........(518) 455-4466
Counties Represented: Kings (part)    Dist: (718) 498-8681
Term Expires: 2017    Fax: (718) 342-1258
400 Rockaway Avenue, Brooklyn, NY 11212
E-mail: walkerl@assembly.state.ny.us
Committees: Correction; Economic Development, Job Creation,
Commerce and Industry; Election Law; Energy; Housing
Education: Pace JD

Assembly Member
**Raymond W. "Ray" Walter** (R-District 146)..........(518) 455-4618
Counties Represented: Erie (part), Niagara (part)    Dist: (716) 634-1895
Term Expires: 2017    Fax: (518) 455-5023
5555 Main Street, Amherst, NY 14221
E-mail: walterr@assembly.state.ny.us
Committees: Economic Development, Job Creation, Commerce and
Industry; Health; Housing; Insurance; Ways and Means
Education: SUNY (Geneseo); Buffalo 2007 JD

Assembly Member **Helene E. Weinstein** (D-District 41) .. (518) 455-5462
Counties Represented: Kings (part)    Dist: (718) 648-4700
Term Expires: 2017    Fax: (518) 455-5752
3520 Nostrand Avenue, Brooklyn, NY 11229    Dist: (718) 769-4846
E-mail: weinsteinh@assembly.state.ny.us
Committees: Aging; Codes; Judiciary; Rules; Ways and Means
Education: American U 1973 BA; New England 1976 JD

Assembly Member **David I. Weprin** (D-District 24).......(518) 455-5806
Counties Represented: Queens (part)    Dist: (718) 454-3027
Term Expires: 2017
185-06 Union Turnpike, Fresh Meadows, NY 11366
E-mail: weprind@assembly.state.ny.us
Committees: Banks; Cities; Codes; Election Law; Judiciary; Ways and
Means

Assembly Member **Jaime R. Williams** (D-District 59) .... (518) 455-5211
Counties Represented: Kings (part)    Dist: (718) 252-2124
Term Expires: 2017    Fax: (718) 252-2417
5318 Avenue N, First Floor Store, Brooklyn, NY 11234
Committees: Children and Families; Environmental Conservation;
Tourism, Parks, Arts and Sports Development; Transportation

Assembly Member **Carrie Woerner** (D-District 113)......(518) 455-5404
Counties Represented: Saratoga (part), Washington    Dist: (518) 584-5493
(part)    Fax: (518) 455-3727
Term Expires: 2017    Dist: (518) 584-5496
112 Spring Street, Suite 109, Saratoga Springs, NY 12866
E-mail: woernerc@assembly.state.ny.us
Committees: Agriculture; Local Governments; Racing and Wagering;
Small Business; Tourism, Parks, Arts and Sports Development

Assembly Member **Angela Wozniak** (R-District 143).....(518) 455-5921
Counties Represented: Erie (part)    Dist: (716) 686-0080
Term Expires: 2017    Fax: (518) 455-3962
2562 Walden Avenue, Suite 102,    Dist: (716) 686-3752
Cheektowaga, NY 14225
E-mail: wozniaka@assembly.state.ny.us
Committees: Aging; Children and Families; Cities; Labor; Local
Governments

Assembly Member **Keith L. T. Wright** (D-District 70).....(518) 455-4793
Counties Represented: New York (part)    Dist: (212) 866-5809
Term Expires: 2017    Fax: (518) 455-3890
Adam Clayton Powell, Jr. Building,    Dist: (212) 864-1368
163 West 125th Street, Suite 911, New York, NY 10027
E-mail: wrightk@assembly.state.ny.us
Committees: Codes; Correction; Housing; Rules; Ways and Means
Education: Tufts 1977 MA; Rutgers 1982 JD

Assembly Member
**Kenneth P. Zebrowski** (D-District 96) ..............(518) 455-5735
Counties Represented: Rockland (part)    Dist: (845) 634-9791
Term Expires: 2017
67 North Main Street, New City, NY 10956
E-mail: zebrowskik@assembly.state.ny.us
Committees: Codes; Environmental Conservation; Ethics and Guidance;
Governmental Employees; Judiciary; Labor
Education: SUNY (Albany) BA; Seton Hall JD

District 20 **(Vacant)** ...................................(518) 455-4100
Note: A special election date has not yet been determined to fill this
legislative vacancy.

District 33 **(Vacant)** ...................................(518) 455-4100
Note: A special election date has not yet been determined to fill this
legislative vacancy.

# Assembly Standing Committees
Legislative Office Building, Albany, NY 12248

## Aging
State Capitol, Room 104A, Albany, NY 12248

**Majority Members**
Steven Cymbrowitz (D-45) *Chair*
Peter J. Abbate, Jr. (D-49)
Carmen E. Arroyo (D-84)
Didi Barrett (D-106)
Charles Barron (D-60)
Edward Braunstein (D-26)
Anthony J. Brindisi (D-119)
Michael DenDekker (D-34)
Phillip Goldfeder (D-23)
Latoya Joyner (D-77)
William "Bill" Magee (D-121)
John T. McDonald III (D-108)
Michael "Mike" Miller (D-38)
Philip R. Ramos (D-6)
José Rivera (D-78)
Annette M. Robinson (D-56)
Luis Sepulveda (D-87)
Michael A. Simanowitz (D-27)
Helene E. Weinstein (D-41)
Guillermo Linares (D-72)

**Minority Members**
Joseph M. "Joe" Giglio (R-148)
Karl Brabenec (R-98)
Christopher Friend (R-124)
Mark Johns (R-135)
Steven "Steve" Katz (R-94)
Dean Murray (R-3)
Angela Wozniak (R-143)

## Agriculture
Legislative Office Building, Room 829, Albany, NY 12248

**Majority Members**
William "Bill" Magee (D-121) *Chair*
Didi Barrett (D-106)
Michael Benedetto (D-82)
Harry B. Bronson (D-138)
Aileen M. Gunther (D-100)
Barbara S. Lifton (D-125)
José Rivera (D-78)
Linda B. Rosenthal (D-67)
Addie Jenne Russell (D-116)
Angelo L. Santabarbara (D-111)
Luis Sepulveda (D-87)
Michael A. Simanowitz (D-27)
Frank Skartados (D-104)
James G. Skoufis (D-99)
Albert A. Stirpe, Jr. (D-130)
Carrie Woerner (D-113)

**Minority Members**
Kenneth Blankenbush (R-117)
Marc W. Butler (R-118)
Clifford W. "Cliff" Crouch (R-122)
Gary D. Finch (R-126)
Stephen "Steve" Hawley (R-139)
Peter D. "Pete" Lopez (R-102)

## Alcoholism and Drug Abuse
Legislative Office Building, Room 630, Albany, NY 12248

**Majority Members**
Linda B. Rosenthal (D-67) *Chair*
Carmen E. Arroyo (D-84)
Charles Barron (D-60)
Maritza Davila (D-53)
Michael DenDekker (D-34)
Pamela Harris (D-46)
John T. McDonald III (D-108)
Crystal D. Peoples-Stokes (D-141)
Dan Quart (D-73)
Albert A. Stirpe, Jr. (D-130)

**Minority Members**
David J. DiPietro (R-147)
Mark Johns (R-135)
Steven "Steve" Katz (R-94)
Peter D. "Pete" Lopez (R-102)

## Banks
Legislative Office Building, Room 423, Albany, NY 12248

**Majority Members**
Annette M. Robinson (D-56) *Chair*
Peter J. Abbate, Jr. (D-49)
Rodneyse Bichotte (D-42)
Michael A. Blake (D-79)
Alice Cancel (D-65)
Patricia Fahy (D-109)
Mark Gjonaj (D-80)
Kimberly Jean-Pierre (D-11)
Michael P. "Mickey" Kearns (D-142)
Guillermo Linares (D-72)
William "Bill" Magee (D-121)
Michael "Mike" Miller (D-38)
Walter T. Mosley III (D-57)
N. Nick Perry (D-58)
Diana C. Richardson (D-43)
Robert J. Rodriguez (D-68)
Sean M. Ryan (D-149)
Rebecca Seawright (D-76)
Luis Sepulveda (D-87)
Aravella Simotas (D-36)
David I. Weprin (D-24)

**Minority Members**
Brian Curran (R-21)
Gary D. Finch (R-126)
Kieran Michael Lalor (R-105)
Nicole Malliotakis (R-64)
Andrew P. Raia (R-12)
Daniel G. Stec (R-114)
James N. "Jim" Tedisco (R-112)
Claudia Tenney (R-101)

## Children and Families
Legislative Office Building, Room 624, Albany, NY 12248

**Majority Members**
Donna A. Lupardo (D-123) *Chair*
Carmen E. Arroyo (D-84)
Maritza Davila (D-53)
Patricia Fahy (D-109)
Pamela Harris (D-46)
Ellen C. Jaffee (D-97)
Shelley B. Mayer (D-90)
Diana C. Richardson (D-43)
Annette M. Robinson (D-56)
Nily D. Rozic (D-25)
Phillip G. "Phil" Steck (D-110)
Michele R. Titus (D-31)
Jaime R. Williams (D-59)

**Minority Members**
Christopher Friend (R-124)
Joseph M. "Joe" Giglio (R-148)
Steven McLaughlin (R-107)
Angela Wozniak (R-143)

## Cities
Legislative Office Building, Room 843, Albany, NY 12248

**Majority Members**
Michael Benedetto (D-82) *Chair*
Edward Braunstein (D-26)
Alice Cancel (D-65)
Marcos Crespo (D-85)
Erik Martin Dilan (D-54)
Brian P. Kavanagh (D-74)
Michael P. "Mickey" Kearns (D-142)
Guillermo Linares (D-72)
Shelley B. Mayer (D-90)
John T. McDonald III (D-108)
Victor M. Pichardo (D-86)
David I. Weprin (D-24)

**Minority Members**
Karl Brabenec (R-98)
Andrew Goodell (R-150)
Angela Wozniak (R-143)

## Codes
Legislative Office Building, Room 630, Albany, NY 12248

**Majority Members**
Joseph R. Lentol (D-50) *Chair*
Thomas J. Abinanti (D-92)
James F. Brennan (D-44)
Vivian E. Cook (D-32)
Steven Cymbrowitz (D-45)
Charles D. Lavine (D-13)
Walter T. Mosley III (D-57)
Daniel J. O'Donnell (D-69)
N. Nick Perry (D-58)
J. Gary Pretlow, Sr. (D-89)
Robin L. Schimminger (D-140)
Michele R. Titus (D-31)
Helene E. Weinstein (D-41)
David I. Weprin (D-24)
Keith L. T. Wright (D-70)
Kenneth P. Zebrowski (D-96)

**Minority Members**
Joseph M. "Joe" Giglio (R-148)
Alfred "Al" Graf (R-5)
Thomas "Tom" McKevitt (R-17)
Michael A. Montesano (R-15)
Edward Ra (R-19)
Claudia Tenney (R-101)

## Consumer Affairs and Protection
Legislative Office Building, Room 942, Albany, NY 12248

**Majority Members**
Jeffrey Dinowitz (D-81) *Chair*
Peter J. Abbate, Jr. (D-49)
David Buchwald (D-93)
Erik Martin Dilan (D-54)
Latoya Joyner (D-77)
Dan Quart (D-73)
Rebecca Seawright (D-76)
Michael A. Simanowitz (D-27)
Jo Anne Simon (D-52)
Aravella Simotas (D-36)
Michaëlle C. Solages (D-22)

**Minority Members**
David G. McDonough (R-14)
Thomas "Tom" McKevitt (R-17)
William "Bill" Nojay (R-133)
Anthony H. Palumbo (R-2)

## Corporations, Authorities and Commissions
Legislative Office Building, Room 423, Albany, NY 12248

**Majority Members**
James F. Brennan (D-44) *Chair*
Thomas J. Abinanti (D-92)
David Buchwald (D-93)
Vivian E. Cook (D-32)
Brian P. Kavanagh (D-74)
Sandra R. "Sandy" Galef (D-95)
Phillip Goldfeder (D-23)
Erik Martin Dilan (D-54)
Ronald T. Kim (D-40)
Francisco Moya (D-39)
Catherine T. Nolan (D-37)
Steven Otis (D-91)
Dan Quart (D-73)
Diana C. Richardson (D-43)
Robert J. Rodriguez (D-68)
Nily D. Rozic (D-25)
Addie Jenne Russell (D-116)
Rebecca Seawright (D-76)
Aravella Simotas (D-36)

**Minority Members**
Kenneth Blankenbush (R-117)
Jane L. Corwin (R-144)
Christopher Friend (R-124)
Peter D. "Pete" Lopez (R-102)
Nicole Malliotakis (R-64)
Michael A. Montesano (R-15)
Philip "Phil" Palmesano (R-132)

## Correction
Legislative Office Building, Room 524, Albany, NY 12248

**Majority Members**
Daniel J. O'Donnell (D-69) *Chair*
Michael A. Blake (D-79)
William Colton (D-47)
Maritza Davila (D-53)
Walter T. Mosley III (D-57)
Felix W. Ortiz (D-51)
Nily D. Rozic (D-25)
Luis Sepulveda (D-87)
Latrice Walker (D-55)
Keith L. T. Wright (D-70)

**Minority Members**
Janet L. Duprey (R-115)
Gary D. Finch (R-126)
Joseph M. "Joe" Giglio (R-148)

## Economic Development, Job Creation, Commerce and Industry
Legislative Office Building, Room 846, Albany, NY 12248

**Majority Members**
Robin L. Schimminger (D-140)
  *Chair*
Didi Barrett (D-106)
Charles Barron (D-60)
Rodneyse Bichotte (D-42)
Anthony J. Brindisi (D-119)
Harry B. Bronson (D-138)
Kevin A. Cahill (D-103)
Maritza Davila (D-53)
David F. Gantt (D-137)
Alicia L. Hyndman (D-29)
Ellen C. Jaffee (D-97)
Kimberly Jean-Pierre (D-11)
Donna A. Lupardo (D-123)
William B. Magnarelli (D-129)
Addie Jenne Russell (D-116)
Michael A. Simanowitz (D-27)
Frank Skartados (D-104)
Albert A. Stirpe, Jr. (D-130)
Latrice Walker (D-55)

**Minority Members**
Marc W. Butler (R-118)
Clifford W. "Cliff" Crouch (R-122)
David J. DiPietro (R-147)
Steven "Steve" Katz (R-94)
Steven McLaughlin (R-107)
James N. "Jim" Tedisco (R-112)
Raymond W. "Ray" Walter (R-146)

## Education
Legislative Office Building, Room 835, Albany, NY 12248

**Majority Members**
Catherine T. Nolan (D-37) *Chair*
Carmen E. Arroyo (D-84)
Michael Benedetto (D-82)
James F. Brennan (D-44)
Anthony J. Brindisi (D-119)
Steven C. "Steve" Englebright (D-4)
Earlene Hooper (D-18)
Ronald T. Kim (D-40)
Barbara S. Lifton (D-125)
William B. Magnarelli (D-129)
Shelley B. Mayer (D-90)
Michael "Mike" Miller (D-38)
Walter T. Mosley III (D-57)
Daniel J. O'Donnell (D-69)
Steven Otis (D-91)
Amy R. Paulin (D-88)
Philip R. Ramos (D-6)
Linda B. Rosenthal (D-67)
Sean M. Ryan (D-149)
Matthew Titone (D-61)
Michele R. Titus (D-31)
Fred W. Thiele, Jr. (I-1)

**Minority Members**
Jane L. Corwin (R-144)
Alfred "Al" Graf (R-5)
Peter D. "Pete" Lopez (R-102)
David G. McDonough (R-14)
Steven McLaughlin (R-107)
Dean Murray (R-3)
Edward Ra (R-19)
Claudia Tenney (R-101)

## Election Law
Legislative Office Building, Room 715, Albany, NY 12248

**Majority Members**
Michael J. Cusick (D-63) *Chair*
Thomas J. Abinanti (D-92)
Michael A. Blake (D-79)
David Buchwald (D-93)
Jeffrey Dinowitz (D-81)
Sandra R. "Sandy" Galef (D-95)
Brian P. Kavanagh (D-74)
Joseph R. Lentol (D-50)
Barbara S. Lifton (D-125)
Latrice Walker (D-55)
David I. Weprin (D-24)

**Minority Members**
Karl Brabenec (R-98)
Chad A. Lupinacci (R-10)
Thomas "Tom" McKevitt (R-17)
William "Bill" Nojay (R-133)

## Energy
Legislative Office Building, Room 715, Albany, NY 12248

**Majority Members**
Amy R. Paulin (D-88) *Chair*
Charles Barron (D-60)
John D. Ceretto (D-145)
Marcos Crespo (D-85)
Steven C. "Steve" Englebright (D-4)
Andrew Hevesi (D-28)
Francisco Moya (D-39)
Linda B. Rosenthal (D-67)
Addie Jenne Russell (D-116)
Sean M. Ryan (D-149)
Angelo L. Santabarbara (D-111)
Aravella Simotas (D-36)
Latrice Walker (D-55)

**Minority Members**
Andrew R. Garbarino (R-7)
William A. "Will" Barclay (R-120)
Steven McLaughlin (R-107)
Philip "Phil" Palmesano (R-132)

## Environmental Conservation
Legislative Office Building, Room 623, Albany, NY 12248

**Majority Members**
Steven C. "Steve" Englebright (D-4)
  *Chair*
Thomas J. Abinanti (D-92)
William Colton (D-47)
Marcos Crespo (D-85)
Steven Cymbrowitz (D-45)
Patricia Fahy (D-109)
Deborah J. Glick (D-66)
Aileen M. Gunther (D-100)
Ellen C. Jaffee (D-97)
Brian P. Kavanagh (D-74)
Barbara S. Lifton (D-125)
Donna A. Lupardo (D-123)
Daniel J. O'Donnell (D-69)
Steven Otis (D-91)
Crystal D. Peoples-Stokes (D-141)
Nily D. Rozic (D-25)
Sean M. Ryan (D-149)
Michelle Schimel (D-16)
Matthew Titone (D-61)
Jaime R. Williams (D-59)
Kenneth P. Zebrowski (D-96)
Fred W. Thiele, Jr. (I-1)

**Minority Members**
Marc W. Butler (R-118)
Jane L. Corwin (R-144)
Andrew R. Garbarino (R-7)
Peter D. "Pete" Lopez (R-102)
Anthony H. Palumbo (R-2)
Andrew P. Raia (R-12)
Joseph Saladino (R-9)
Daniel G. Stec (R-114)

## Ethics and Guidance
Legislative Office Building, Room 557, Albany, NY 12248

**Majority Members**
Charles D. Lavine (D-13) *Chair*
Aravella Simotas (D-36)
Michele R. Titus (D-31)
Kenneth P. Zebrowski (D-96)

**Minority Members**
Brian Curran (R-21)
Joseph M. "Joe" Giglio (R-148)
Peter A. Lawrence (R-134)
Michael A. Montesano (R-15)

## Governmental Employees
Legislative Office Building, Room 840, Albany, NY 12248

**Majority Members**
Peter J. Abbate, Jr. (D-49) *Chair*
Jeffrion L. Aubry (D-35)
William Colton (D-47)
Michael J. Cusick (D-63)
Michael DenDekker (D-34)
Phillip Goldfeder (D-23)
Angelo L. Santabarbara (D-111)
Michaëlle C. Solages (D-22)
Kenneth P. Zebrowski (D-96)

**Minority Members**
Mark Johns (R-135)
Nicole Malliotakis (R-64)
Anthony H. Palumbo (R-2)
Joseph Saladino (R-9)

## Governmental Operations
Legislative Office Building, Room 623, Albany, NY 12248

**Majority Members**
Crystal D. Peoples-Stokes (D-141)
  *Chair*
Michael Benedetto (D-82)
Rodneyse Bichotte (D-42)
David Buchwald (D-93)
Erik Martin Dilan (D-54)
Sandra R. "Sandy" Galef (D-95)
Deborah J. Glick (D-66)
Ronald T. Kim (D-40)
Michelle Schimel (D-16)

**Minority Members**
Janet L. Duprey (R-115)
Andrew Goodell (R-150)
Mark Johns (R-135)
Kieran Michael Lalor (R-105)

# Health

Legislative Office Building, Room 823, Albany, NY 12248

| Majority Members | Minority Members |
|---|---|
| Richard N. Gottfried (D-75) *Chair* | Janet L. Duprey (R-115) |
| Thomas J. Abinanti (D-92) | Andrew R. Garbarino (R-7) |
| Edward Braunstein (D-26) | Andrew Goodell (R-150) |
| Kevin A. Cahill (D-103) | David G. McDonough (R-14) |
| Steven Cymbrowitz (D-45) | Edward Ra (R-19) |
| Jeffrey Dinowitz (D-81) | Andrew P. Raia (R-12) |
| Sandra R. "Sandy" Galef (D-95) | Raymond W. "Ray" Walter (R-146) |
| Aileen M. Gunther (D-100) | |
| Andrew Hevesi (D-28) | |
| Ellen C. Jaffee (D-97) | |
| Ronald T. Kim (D-40) | |
| Charles D. Lavine (D-13) | |
| Shelley B. Mayer (D-90) | |
| Amy R. Paulin (D-88) | |
| Crystal D. Peoples-Stokes (D-141) | |
| Linda B. Rosenthal (D-67) | |
| Robin L. Schimminger (D-140) | |
| Phillip G. "Phil" Steck (D-110) | |
| Matthew Titone (D-61) | |

# Higher Education

Legislative Office Building, Room 715, Albany, NY 12248

| Majority Members | Minority Members |
|---|---|
| Deborah J. Glick (D-66) *Chair* | Marc W. Butler (R-118) |
| Anthony J. Brindisi (D-119) | Janet L. Duprey (R-115) |
| Kevin A. Cahill (D-103) | Michael J. Fitzpatrick (R-8) |
| Michael J. Cusick (D-63) | Andrew R. Garbarino (R-7) |
| Steven C. "Steve" Englebright (D-4) | Peter A. Lawrence (R-134) |
| Patricia Fahy (D-109) | Chad A. Lupinacci (R-10) |
| Richard N. Gottfried (D-75) | Edward Ra (R-19) |
| Pamela Harris (D-46) | |
| Ellen C. Jaffee (D-97) | |
| Charles D. Lavine (D-13) | |
| Barbara S. Lifton (D-125) | |
| Donna A. Lupardo (D-123) | |
| William "Bill" Magee (D-121) | |
| Amy R. Paulin (D-88) | |
| Crystal D. Peoples-Stokes (D-141) | |
| Victor M. Pichardo (D-86) | |
| Michael A. Simanowitz (D-27) | |
| Jo Anne Simon (D-52) | |
| Albert A. Stirpe, Jr. (D-130) | |

# Housing

Legislative Office Building, Room 942, Albany, NY 12248

| Majority Members | Minority Members |
|---|---|
| Keith L. T. Wright (D-70) *Chair* | Michael J. Fitzpatrick (R-8) |
| Rodneyse Bichotte (D-42) | Christopher Friend (R-124) |
| Michael A. Blake (D-79) | Alfred "Al" Graf (R-5) |
| Alice Cancel (D-65) | Mark Johns (R-135) |
| Vivian E. Cook (D-32) | Steven "Steve" Katz (R-94) |
| Maritza Davila (D-53) | Andrew P. Raia (R-12) |
| Erik Martin Dilan (D-54) | Raymond W. "Ray" Walter (R-146) |
| Latoya Joyner (D-77) | |
| Brian P. Kavanagh (D-74) | |
| Michael P. "Mickey" Kearns (D-142) | |
| Ronald T. Kim (D-40) | |
| Guillermo Linares (D-72) | |
| Walter T. Mosley III (D-57) | |
| Francisco Moya (D-39) | |
| Victor M. Pichardo (D-86) | |
| Annette M. Robinson (D-56) | |
| Robert J. Rodriguez (D-68) | |
| Linda B. Rosenthal (D-67) | |
| Luis Sepulveda (D-87) | |
| Latrice Walker (D-55) | |

# Insurance

Legislative Office Building, Room 714, Albany, NY 12248

| Majority Members | Minority Members |
|---|---|
| Kevin A. Cahill (D-103) *Chair* | William A. "Will" Barclay (R-120) |
| Vivian E. Cook (D-32) | Kenneth Blankenbush (R-117) |
| Marcos Crespo (D-85) | Marc W. Butler (R-118) |
| Steven Cymbrowitz (D-45) | Brian Curran (R-21) |
| Erik Martin Dilan (D-54) | Gary D. Finch (R-126) |
| Phillip Goldfeder (D-23) | Stephen "Steve" Hawley (R-139) |
| Andrew Hevesi (D-28) | Raymond W. "Ray" Walter (R-146) |
| Pamela J. Hunter (D-128) | |
| Latoya Joyner (D-77) | |
| Charles D. Lavine (D-13) | |
| John T. McDonald III (D-108) | |
| Francisco Moya (D-39) | |
| Crystal D. Peoples-Stokes (D-141) | |
| J. Gary Pretlow, Sr. (D-89) | |
| José Rivera (D-78) | |
| James G. Skoufis (D-99) | |
| Phillip G. "Phil" Steck (D-110) | |

# Judiciary

Legislative Office Building, Room 832, Albany, NY 12248

| Majority Members | Minority Members |
|---|---|
| Helene E. Weinstein (D-41) *Chair* | William A. "Will" Barclay (R-120) |
| Edward Braunstein (D-26) | Andrew Goodell (R-150) |
| David Buchwald (D-93) | Alfred "Al" Graf (R-5) |
| Jeffrey Dinowitz (D-81) | Chad A. Lupinacci (R-10) |
| Latoya Joyner (D-77) | Michael A. Montesano (R-15) |
| Charles D. Lavine (D-13) | Anthony H. Palumbo (R-2) |
| Dan Quart (D-73) | |
| Rebecca Seawright (D-76) | |
| Jo Anne Simon (D-52) | |
| Phillip G. "Phil" Steck (D-110) | |
| Matthew Titone (D-61) | |
| Michele R. Titus (D-31) | |
| David I. Weprin (D-24) | |
| Kenneth P. Zebrowski (D-96) | |

# Labor

Legislative Office Building, Room 524, Albany, NY 12248

| Majority Members | Minority Members |
|---|---|
| Michele R. Titus (D-31) *Chair* | Karl Brabenec (R-98) |
| Peter J. Abbate, Jr. (D-49) | Clifford W. "Cliff" Crouch (R-122) |
| Michael Benedetto (D-82) | Brian Curran (R-21) |
| Harry B. Bronson (D-138) | David J. DiPietro (R-147) |
| William Colton (D-47) | Janet L. Duprey (R-115) |
| Michael DenDekker (D-34) | Michael J. Fitzpatrick (R-8) |
| Andrew Hevesi (D-28) | Joseph Saladino (R-9) |
| Brian P. Kavanagh (D-74) | Angela Wozniak (R-143) |
| Guillermo Linares (D-72) | |
| Margaret M. "Marge" Markey (D-30) | |
| Shelley B. Mayer (D-90) | |
| Michael "Mike" Miller (D-38) | |
| Francisco Moya (D-39) | |
| Felix W. Ortiz (D-51) | |
| N. Nick Perry (D-58) | |
| Robert J. Rodriguez (D-68) | |
| Nily D. Rozic (D-25) | |
| Jo Anne Simon (D-52) | |
| James G. Skoufis (D-99) | |
| Kenneth P. Zebrowski (D-96) | |

# Libraries and Education Technology

Legislative Office Building, Room 715, Albany, NY 12248

| Majority Members | Minority Members |
|---|---|
| Thomas J. Abinanti (D-92) *Chair* | Philip "Phil" Palmesano (R-132) |
| John D. Ceretto (D-145) | Joseph Saladino (R-9) |
| Steven Otis (D-91) | |
| Michaëlle C. Solages (D-22) | |

**LEGISLATIVE BRANCH**

## Local Governments

Legislative Office Building, Room 838, Albany, NY 12248

| Majority Members | Minority Members |
|---|---|
| William B. Magnarelli (D-129) *Chair* | Karl Brabenec (R-98) |
| Harry B. Bronson (D-138) | Christopher Friend (R-124) |
| David Buchwald (D-93) | Thomas "Tom" McKevitt (R-17) |
| David F. Gantt (D-137) | Daniel G. Stec (R-114) |
| Mark Gjonaj (D-80) | Angela Wozniak (R-143) |
| Kimberly Jean-Pierre (D-11) | |
| William "Bill" Magee (D-121) | |
| Steven Otis (D-91) | |
| Philip R. Ramos (D-6) | |
| Addie Jenne Russell (D-116) | |
| Sean M. Ryan (D-149) | |
| Michelle Schimel (D-16) | |
| Frank Skartados (D-104) | |
| James G. Skoufis (D-99) | |
| Carrie Woerner (D-113) | |

## Mental Health

Legislative Office Building, Room 825, Albany, NY 12248

| Majority Members | Minority Members |
|---|---|
| Aileen M. Gunther (D-100) *Chair* | Jane L. Corwin (R-144) |
| Didi Barrett (D-106) | Steven "Steve" Katz (R-94) |
| Michael J. Cusick (D-63) | William "Bill" Nojay (R-133) |
| Ellen C. Jaffee (D-97) | |
| Kimberly Jean-Pierre (D-11) | |
| John T. McDonald III (D-108) | |
| Diana C. Richardson (D-43) | |
| Robert J. Rodriguez (D-68) | |
| Angelo L. Santabarbara (D-111) | |
| Luis Sepulveda (D-87) | |

## Oversight, Analysis and Investigation

Legislative Office Building, Room 104, Albany, NY 12248

| Majority Members | Minority Members |
|---|---|
| Ellen C. Jaffee (D-97) *Chair* | Michael A. Montesano (R-15) |
| Michael P. "Mickey" Kearns (D-142) | Peter A. Lawrence (R-134) |
| William B. Magnarelli (D-129) | |
| Fred W. Thiele, Jr. (I-1) | |

## Racing and Wagering

Legislative Office Building, Room 846, Albany, NY 12248

| Majority Members | Minority Members |
|---|---|
| J. Gary Pretlow, Sr. (D-89) *Chair* | Andrew R. Garbarino (R-7) |
| Phillip Goldfeder (D-23) | Peter A. Lawrence (R-134) |
| Aileen M. Gunther (D-100) | James N. "Jim" Tedisco (R-112) |
| Margaret M. "Marge" Markey (D-30) | |
| Michael "Mike" Miller (D-38) | |
| Angelo L. Santabarbara (D-111) | |
| Michaëlle C. Solages (D-22) | |
| Carrie Woerner (D-113) | |

## Real Property Taxation

Legislative Office Building, Room 641-A, Albany, NY 12248

| Majority Members | Minority Members |
|---|---|
| Sandra R. "Sandy" Galef (D-95) *Chair* | Kieran Michael Lalor (R-105) |
| James F. Brennan (D-44) | Philip "Phil" Palmesano (R-132) |
| Mark Gjonaj (D-80) | |
| Aileen M. Gunther (D-100) | |
| John T. McDonald III (D-108) | |
| Victor M. Pichardo (D-86) | |
| Annette M. Robinson (D-56) | |

## Rules

| Majority Members | Minority Members |
|---|---|
| Carl E. Heastie (D-83) *Chair* | William A. "Will" Barclay (R-120) |
| Jeffrion L. Aubry (D-35) | Marc W. Butler (R-118) |
| William Colton (D-47) | Clifford W. "Cliff" Crouch (R-122) |
| Vivian E. Cook (D-32) | Janet L. Duprey (R-115) |
| Jeffrey Dinowitz (D-81) | Gary D. Finch (R-126) |
| Steven C. "Steve" Englebright (D-4) | Brian M. Kolb (R-131) |
| Herman D. Farrell, Jr. (D-71) | Robert C. "Bob" Oaks (R-130) |
| David F. Gantt (D-137) | Andrew P. Raia (R-12) |
| Deborah J. Glick (D-66) | James N. "Jim" Tedisco (R-112) |
| Richard N. Gottfried (D-75) | |
| Earlene Hooper (D-18) | |
| Joseph R. Lentol (D-50) | |
| William B. Magnarelli (D-129) | |
| Margaret M. "Marge" Markey (D-30) | |
| Joseph D. Morelle (D-136) | |
| Catherine T. Nolan (D-37) | |
| Felix W. Ortiz (D-51) | |
| N. Nick Perry (D-58) | |
| J. Gary Pretlow, Sr. (D-89) | |
| Helene E. Weinstein (D-41) | |
| Keith L. T. Wright (D-70) | |

## Small Business

Legislative Office Bldg., Room 624, Albany, NY 12248

| Majority Members | Minority Members |
|---|---|
| Fred W. Thiele, Jr. (I-1) *Chair* | David J. DiPietro (R-147) |
| Charles Barron (D-60) | Kieran Michael Lalor (R-105) |
| Rodneyse Bichotte (D-42) | Peter A. Lawrence (R-134) |
| Mark Gjonaj (D-80) | Dean Murray (R-3) |
| Alicia L. Hyndman (D-29) | |
| Victor M. Pichardo (D-86) | |
| Diana C. Richardson (D-43) | |
| José Rivera (D-78) | |
| Annette M. Robinson (D-56) | |
| Angelo L. Santabarbara (D-111) | |
| Michael A. Simanowitz (D-27) | |
| Frank Skartados (D-104) | |
| Carrie Woerner (D-113) | |

## Social Services

Legislative Office Building, Room 843, Albany, NY 12248

| Majority Members | Minority Members |
|---|---|
| Andrew Hevesi (D-28) *Chair* | Andrew Goodell (R-150) |
| Jeffrion L. Aubry (D-35) | Steven McLaughlin (R-107) |
| Charles Barron (D-60) | Anthony H. Palumbo (R-2) |
| Rodneyse Bichotte (D-42) | Daniel G. Stec (R-114) |
| Alice Cancel (D-65) | Claudia Tenney (R-101) |
| Maritza Davila (D-53) | |
| Pamela J. Hunter (D-128) | |
| Latoya Joyner (D-77) | |
| Ronald T. Kim (D-40) | |
| Shelley B. Mayer (D-90) | |
| Victor M. Pichardo (D-86) | |
| Michaëlle C. Solages (D-22) | |
| Matthew Titone (D-61) | |

## Tourism, Parks, Arts and Sports Development

Legislative Office Building, Room 714, Albany, NY 12248

| Majority Members | Minority Members |
|---|---|
| Margaret M. "Marge" Markey (D-30) *Chair* | Kenneth Blankenbush (R-117) |
| Didi Barrett (D-106) | Chad A. Lupinacci (R-10) |
| John D. Ceretto (D-145) | Dean Murray (R-3) |
| Patricia Fahy (D-109) | Philip "Phil" Palmesano (R-132) |
| Mark Gjonaj (D-80) | Daniel G. Stec (R-114) |
| Daniel J. O'Donnell (D-69) | |
| Steven Otis (D-91) | |
| Dan Quart (D-73) | |
| Linda B. Rosenthal (D-67) | |
| Rebecca Seawright (D-76) | |
| Frank Skartados (D-104) | |

**Majority Members** *continued*
Albert A. Stirpe, Jr. (D-130)
Matthew Titone (D-61)
Jaime R. Williams (D-59)
Carrie Woerner (D-113)

## Transportation
Legislative Office Building, Room 829, Albany, NY 12248

**Majority Members**
David F. Gantt (D-137) *Chair*
Anthony J. Brindisi (D-119)
Harry B. Bronson (D-138)
Marcos Crespo (D-85)
Michael J. Cusick (D-63)
Michael DenDekker (D-34)
Pamela J. Hunter (D-128)
Alicia L. Hyndman (D-29)
Kimberly Jean-Pierre (D-11)
Donna A. Lupardo (D-123)
N. Nick Perry (D-58)
Michelle Schimel (D-16)
Jo Anne Simon (D-52)
Frank Skartados (D-104)
James G. Skoufis (D-99)
Phillip G. "Phil" Steck (D-110)
Jaime R. Williams (D-59)
Fred W. Thiele, Jr. (I-1)

**Minority Members**
David J. DiPietro (R-147)
Chad A. Lupinacci (R-10)
Nicole Malliotakis (R-64)
David G. McDonough (R-14)
Dean Murray (R-3)
William "Bill" Nojay (R-133)
Edward Ra (R-19)

## Veterans' Affairs
Legislative Office Building, Room 840, Albany, NY 12248

**Majority Members**
Michael DenDekker (D-34) *Chair*
Didi Barrett (D-106)
Michael A. Blake (D-79)
Anthony J. Brindisi (D-119)
Michael J. Cusick (D-63)
Pamela J. Hunter (D-128)
Michael "Mike" Miller (D-38)
Catherine T. Nolan (D-37)
Addie Jenne Russell (D-116)
Sean M. Ryan (D-149)
Angelo L. Santabarbara (D-111)
Michelle Schimel (D-16)
James G. Skoufis (D-99)

**Minority Members**
Brian Curran (R-21)
Stephen "Steve" Hawley (R-139)
Kieran Michael Lalor (R-105)
David G. McDonough (R-14)
Claudia Tenney (R-101)

## Ways and Means
Legislative Office Building, Room 711-A, Albany, NY 12248

**Majority Members**
Herman D. Farrell, Jr. (D-71) *Chair*
Jeffrion L. Aubry (D-35)
Michael Benedetto (D-82)
Edward Braunstein (D-26)
Kevin A. Cahill (D-103)
William Colton (D-47)
Vivian E. Cook (D-32)
Michael J. Cusick (D-63)
David F. Gantt (D-137)
Deborah J. Glick (D-66)
Earlene Hooper (D-18)
Joseph R. Lentol (D-50)
Margaret M. "Marge" Markey (D-30)
Francisco Moya (D-39)
Catherine T. Nolan (D-37)
Felix W. Ortiz (D-51)
N. Nick Perry (D-58)
J. Gary Pretlow, Sr. (D-89)
Philip R. Ramos (D-6)
Robert J. Rodriguez (D-68)
Robin L. Schimminger (D-140)
Helene E. Weinstein (D-41)
David I. Weprin (D-24)
Keith L. T. Wright (D-70)
Fred W. Thiele, Jr. (I-1)

**Minority Members**
Robert C. "Bob" Oaks (R-130)
*Ranking Minority Member*
William A. "Will" Barclay (R-120)
Jane L. Corwin (R-144)
Clifford W. "Cliff" Crouch (R-122)
Janet L. Duprey (R-115)
Michael J. Fitzpatrick (R-8)
Stephen "Steve" Hawley (R-139)
Nicole Malliotakis (R-64)
Joseph Saladino (R-9)
Raymond W. "Ray" Walter (R-146)

# North Carolina General Assembly

Tel: (919) 733-4111   Fax: (919) 733-2599   Internet: www.ncleg.net

## North Carolina Senate
300 North Salisbury Street, Raleigh, NC 27603-5925
16 West Jones Street, Raleigh, NC 27601
Tel: (919) 733-7928   Fax: (919) 715-2880

President of the Senate **Dan Forest** (R)................(919) 733-7350
  Education: North Carolina Charlotte 1993 BA, MAArch
President Pro Tem **Philip E. "Phil" Berger** (R)..........(919) 733-5708
  Education: Averett Col 1980 BS; Wake Forest 1983 JD
Deputy President Pro Tem **Louis M. Pate, Jr.** (R).......(919) 733-5621
  Education: Golden Gate 1978 BS, 1980 MBA
Majority Leader **Harry Brown** (R)...................(919) 715-3034
  Education: Campbell 1992 BA, 1996 MBA
Majority Caucus Secretary
  **Fletcher L. "Fletch" Hartsell, Jr.** (R)..............(919) 733-7223
  Education: Davidson 1969 AB; North Carolina 1972 JD
Joint Majority Caucus Leader **Andrew C. Brock** (R).....(919) 715-0690
  Education: Western Carolina 1998 BS
Majority Whip **Jerry W. Tillman** (R).................(919) 733-5870
  Education: Elon Col 1965 BS; North Carolina Greensboro 1969 MSA
Minority Leader **Daniel Terry "Dan" Blue, Jr.** (D).....(919) 733-5752
  Education: North Carolina Central 1970; Duke 1973 JD
Deputy Minority Leader **Floyd B. McKissick, Jr.** (D).....(919) 733-4599
  Education: Clark U 1974 AB; North Carolina 1975 MRP;
  Harvard 1979 MPA; Duke 1983 JD
Deputy Minority Leader **Gladys Ashe Robinson** (D).....(919) 715-3042
  Education: Bennett 1971 BA; North Carolina A&T MEd, PhD
Minority Whip **Terry Van Duyn** (D)...................(919) 733-3001
Principal Clerk of the Senate **Sarah Lang**.............(919) 733-7761
Reading Clerk **Lee Settle**.........................(919) 733-7761
Sergeant-at-Arms **Philip King**.....................(919) 733-5946
Chaplain **Mike Morris**............................(919) 733-7761

## Senators
**Party Affiliation Statistics:** Republicans: 34, Democrats: 16
Senator **John M. Alexander, Jr.** (R-District 15).........(919) 733-5850
  Counties Represented: Wake (part)
  Term Expires: 2017
  E-mail: john.alexander@ncleg.net
  Committees: Agriculture/Environment/Natural Resources;
  Appropriations - Natural and Economic Resources; Commerce;
  Finance; Judiciary II; State and Local Government
Senator **Tom Apodaca** (R-District 48) Room 2010.......(919) 733-5745
  Counties Represented: Buncombe (part), Henderson,    Tel: (828) 696-0574
  Transylvania                                         Fax: (919) 755-2270
  Term Expires: 2017                                   Fax: (828) 696-7882
  1504 Fifth Avenue West, Hendersonville, NC 28792
  E-mail: tom.apodaca@ncleg.net
  Committees: Appropriations - Base Budget; Appropriations -
  Education/Higher Education; Appropriations - Justice and Public
  Safety; Commerce; Education/Higher Education; Finance; Insurance;
  Judiciary I; Pensions, Retirement and Aging; Redistricting; Rules and
  Operations of the Senate; Ways and Means
  Education: Western Carolina 1980 BS
Senator **Chad Barefoot** (R-District 18) Room 623........(919) 715-3036
  Counties Represented: Franklin, Wake (part)
  Term Expires: 2017
  E-mail: chad.barefoot@ncleg.net
  Committees: Agriculture/Environment/Natural Resources;
  Appropriations - Education/Higher Education; Education/Higher
  Education; Finance; Health Care; Judiciary II; Program Evaluation;
  Rules and Operations of the Senate
  Education: Appalachian State 2005 BA;
  Southeastern Baptist Sem 2009 MA
Senator **Tamara Patterson Barringer** (R-District 17).....(919) 733-5653
  Counties Represented: Wake (part)
  Term Expires: 2017
  300 North Salisbury Street, Room 309, Raleigh, NC 27603
  E-mail: tamara.barringer@ncleg.net
  Committees: Appropriations - Health and Human Services; Commerce;
  Education/Higher Education; Finance; Judiciary I; Judiciary II; State
  and Local Government
  Education: North Carolina 1981 BS, 1985 JD

*(continued on next page)*

**Senators** *continued*

Senator **Philip E. "Phil" Berger** (R-District 26)
Room 2008 . . . . . . . . . . . . . . . . . . . . . . . . . . . (919) 733-5708
Counties Represented: Guilford (part), Rockingham    Dist: (336) 623-5210
Term Expires: 2017                                   Fax: (336) 623-6313
P.O. Box 1309, Eden, NC 27289-1309
E-mail: phil.berger@ncleg.net

Senator **Stan Bingham** (R-District 33) Room 2117 . . . . . . (919) 733-5665
Counties Represented: Davidson, Montgomery          Tel: (336) 859-0999
Term Expires: 2017                                  Fax: (336) 857-3939
292 North Main Street, Denton, NC 27239
E-mail: stan.bingham@ncleg.net
Committees: Agriculture/Environment/Natural Resources;
Appropriations - Justice and Public Safety; Appropriations -
Transportation Department; Education/Higher Education; Health Care;
Judiciary II; Program Evaluation
Education: North Carolina 1968 BS

Senator **Daniel Terry "Dan" Blue, Jr.** (D-District 14)
Room 1117 . . . . . . . . . . . . . . . . . . . . . . . . . . (919) 733-5752
Counties Represented: Wake (part)                   Tel: (919) 833-1931
Term Expires: 2017
P.O. Box 1730, Raleigh, NC 27602
E-mail: dan.blue@ncleg.net
Committees: Appropriations - Base Budget; Appropriations -
Transportation Department; Commerce; Finance; Insurance; Judiciary I;
Rules and Operations of the Senate

Senator **Andrew C. Brock** (R-District 34) Room 521 . . . . . (919) 715-0690
Counties Represented: Davie, Iredell (part), Rowan   Tel: (336) 936-0180
(part)                                               Res: (336) 998-0298
Term Expires: 2017
160 New Hampshire Court, Mocksville, NC 27028
E-mail: andrew.brock@ncleg.net
Committees: Agriculture/Environment/Natural Resources;
Appropriations - Base Budget; Appropriations - General Government
and Information Technology; Appropriations - Natural and Economic
Resources; Commerce; Finance; Program Evaluation; Redistricting;
Rules and Operations of the Senate; Ways and Means

Senator **Harry Brown** (R-District 6) Room 300-B . . . . . . . (919) 715-3034
Counties Represented: Jones, Onslow                 Tel: (910) 347-3777
Term Expires: 2017                                  Fax: (910) 347-1060
2223 North Marine Boulevard, Jacksonville, NC 28546
E-mail: harry.brown@ncleg.net
Committees: Appropriations - Base Budget; Commerce;
Education/Higher Education; Finance; Judiciary I; Redistricting; Rules
and Operations of the Senate

Senator **Angela R. Bryant** (D-District 4) Room 520 . . . . . . (919) 715-3032
Counties Represented: Halifax, Nash (part), Vance,   Tel: (252) 442-4022
Warren, Wilson (part)
Term Expires: 2017
717 W. End Street, Rocky Mount, NC 27803
E-mail: angela.bryant@ncleg.net
Committees: Agriculture/Environment/Natural Resources;
Appropriations - Base Budget; Appropriations - Natural and Economic
Resources; Commerce; Education/Higher Education; Finance; Judiciary
II; Pensions, Retirement and Aging
Education: North Carolina 1976 BS, 1976 JD

Senator **Jay Chaudhuri** (D-District 16) . . . . . . . . . . . . . . (919) 715-6400
Counties Represented: Wake (part)
Term Expires: 2017
E-mail: jay.chaudhuri@ncleg.net

Senator **Robert B. "Ben" Clark III** (D-District 21)
Room 1121 . . . . . . . . . . . . . . . . . . . . . . . . . . (919) 733-9349
Counties Represented: Cumberland (part), Hoke
Term Expires: 2017
300 W. Hargett Street, #618, Raleigh, NC 27601
E-mail: ben.clark@ncleg.net
Committees: Appropriations - Natural and Economic Resources;
Commerce; Education/Higher Education; Finance; Judiciary I; Program
Evaluation; Redistricting; Rules and Operations of the Senate
Education: North Carolina A&T 1981 BS;
Southern IL Edwardsville MBA; George Washington (Attended)

Senator **Bill Cook** (R-District 1) Room 525 . . . . . . . . . . . . (919) 715-8293
Counties Represented: Beaufort, Camden, Currituck, Dare, Gates,
Hyde, Pasquotank, Perquimans
Term Expires: 2017
P.O. Box 267, Chocowinity, NC 27817
E-mail: bill.cook@ncleg.net
Committees: Agriculture/Environment/Natural Resources;
Appropriations - Natural and Economic Resources; Commerce;
Education/Higher Education; Finance; Judiciary II; Program Evaluation
Education: Maryland 1970 BS

Senator **Dr. David L. Curtis, DO** (R-District 44)
Room 410 . . . . . . . . . . . . . . . . . . . . . . . . . . . (919) 715-3038
Counties Represented: Gaston (part), Iredell (part),   Dist: (704) 483-2263
Lincoln
Term Expires: 2017
PO Box 278, Denver, NC 28037
E-mail: david.curtis@ncleg.net
Committees: Appropriations - Education/Higher Education;
Education/Higher Education; Finance; Health Care; Judiciary II;
Pensions, Retirement and Aging; State and Local Government
Education: North Carolina BEc; Southern Col Optometry 1978 DO

Senator **Warren "T." Daniel** (R-District 46) Room 1127 . . . (919) 715-7823
Counties Represented: Burke, Cleveland              Dist: (828) 433-0700
Term Expires: 2017                                  Fax: (919) 733-3113
309 West Union Street, Morganton, NC 28655         Dist: (828) 433-0703
E-mail: warren.daniel@ncleg.net
Committees: Appropriations - Transportation Department; Commerce;
Education/Higher Education; Finance; Judiciary II; Pensions,
Retirement and Aging; Transportation
Education: West Point 1991 BS; North Carolina 2000 JD

Senator **Donald G. "Don" Davis** (D-District 5) . . . . . . . . . (919) 715-8363
Counties Represented: Greene, Lenoir (part),        Dist: (252) 341-5548
Pitt (part), Wayne (part)                           Tel: (252) 747-2385
Term Expires: 2017
300 North Salisbury Street, Room 518, Raleigh, NC 27603
413 West Greene Street, Snow Hill, NC 28580
E-mail: don.davis@ncleg.net
Committees: Appropriations - Base Budget; Appropriations -
Education/Higher Education; Appropriations - Transportation
Department; Education/Higher Education; Health Care; State and Local
Government
Education: Air Force Acad 1994 BS; Central Michigan MS;
East Carolina MA, DEd

Senator **Jim Davis** (R-District 50) Room 2111 . . . . . . . . . . (919) 733-5875
Counties Represented: Cherokee, Clay, Graham,       Dist: (828) 342-4483
Haywood, Jackson, Macon, Swain                      Fax: (919) 733-5875
Term Expires: 2017
37 Georgia Road, Franklin, NC 28734
E-mail: jim.davis@ncleg.net
Committees: Appropriations - Base Budget; Appropriations - General
Government and Information Technology; Finance; Health Care;
Insurance; Judiciary II; State and Local Government; Transportation
Education: Southern Adventist U 1969 BA; Loma Linda 1974 DDS

Senator **Joel D. M. Ford** (D-District 38) Room 1119 . . . . . (919) 733-5955
Counties Represented: Mecklenburg (part)
Term Expires: 2017
PO Box 36391, Charlotte, NC 28236-6391
E-mail: joel.ford@ncleg.net
Committees: Agriculture/Environment/Natural Resources;
Appropriations - Base Budget; Appropriations - Transportation
Department; Commerce; Finance; Insurance; Rules and Operations of
the Senate; Transportation
Education: North Carolina A&T 1992 BABA

Senator **Valerie P. Foushee** (D-District 23) . . . . . . . . . . . . (919) 733-7928
Counties Represented: Chatham, Orange              Dist: (919) 942-2661
Term Expires: 2017
106 Claris Court, Chapel Hill, NC 27514
E-mail: valerie.foushee@ncleg.net
Committees: Agriculture/Environment/Natural Resources;
Appropriations - Base Budget; Appropriations - Justice and Public
Safety; Commerce; Education/Higher Education; Judiciary I; State and
Local Government
Education: North Carolina BA

Senator **Rick Gunn** (R-District 24) . . . . . . . . . . . . . . . . . . (919) 301-1446
Counties Represented: Alamance, Randolph (part)    Dist: (336) 229-6981
Term Expires: 2017
300 North Salisbury Street, Room 312, Raleigh, NC 27603
P. O. Box 308, Burlington, NC 27216
E-mail: rick.gunn@ncleg.net
Committees: Appropriations - Transportation Department; Commerce;
Insurance; Pensions, Retirement and Aging; Program Evaluation;
Transportation
Education: North Carolina 1990 BBA

Senator **Kathy Harrington** (R-District 43) Room 2113 . . . . (704) 460-2998
Counties Represented: Gaston (part)                 Dist: (919) 733-5734
Term Expires: 2017                                  Fax: (919) 733-2599
3324 Lincoln Lane, Gastonia, NC 28056
E-mail: kathy.harrington@ncleg.net
Committees: Appropriations - Base Budget; Commerce; Finance;
Judiciary I; Redistricting; Rules and Operations of the Senate;
Transportation
Education: Gaston 1979 (Attended)

LEGISLATIVE BRANCH

Senator **Fletcher L. "Fletch" Hartsell, Jr.** (R-District 36)
Room 300-C . . . . . . . . . . . . . . . . . . . . . . . . . . . . . . . . . . . . . . (919) 733-7223
Counties Represented: Cabarrus, Union (part)          Tel: (704) 786-5161
Term Expires: 2017                                    Fax: (704) 788-8058
P.O. Box 368, Concord, NC 28026-0368
E-mail: fletcher.hartsell@ncleg.net
Committees: Agriculture/Environment/Natural Resources;
Appropriations - Education/Higher Education; Appropriations - Justice
and Public Safety; Education/Higher Education; Finance; Health Care;
Judiciary I; Program Evaluation; State and Local Government

Senator **Ralph E. Hise, Jr.** (R-District 47) Room 1026 . . . . (919) 733-3460
Counties Represented: Madison, McDowell,             Tel: (828) 766-8329
Mitchell, Polk, Rutherford, Yancey                   Fax: (919) 733-2599
Term Expires: 2017
44 Hemlock Avenue, Spruce Pine, NC 28777
E-mail: ralph.hise@ncleg.net
Committees: Appropriations - Base Budget; Appropriations - Health
and Human Services; Finance; Health Care; Insurance; Redistricting;
Rules and Operations of the Senate; Transportation
Education: Appalachian State 2000 BS;
North Carolina State 2003 MEd

Senator **Brent Jackson** (R-District 10) Room 525 . . . . . . . . (919) 733-5705
Counties Represented: Duplin, Johnston (part),       Dist: (910) 567-2202
Sampson                                              Fax: (919) 715-5815
Term Expires: 2017
E-mail: brent.jackson@ncleg.net
Committees: Agriculture/Environment/Natural Resources;
Appropriations - Base Budget; Commerce; Finance; Judiciary I; Rules
and Operations of the Senate; State and Local Government
Education: North Carolina State (Attended)

Senator **Jeff Jackson** (D-District 37) Room 1102 . . . . . . . . (919) 715-8331
Counties Represented: Mecklenburg (part)             Dist: (704) 942-0118
Term Expires: 2017
2519 Cranbrook Lane, Charlotte, NC 28207
E-mail: jeff.jackson@ncleg.net
Committees: Agriculture/Environment/Natural Resources;
Appropriations - Justice and Public Safety; Finance; Judiciary II;
Pensions, Retirement and Aging; Program Evaluation

Senator **Joyce R. Krawiec** (R-District 31) Room 2022 . . . . (919) 733-7850
Counties Represented: Forsyth (part), Yadkin         Dist: (336) 996-3924
Term Expires: 2017
7030 Interlaken Drive, Kernersville, NC 27284
E-mail: joyce.krawiec@ncleg.net
Committees: Appropriations - Transportation Department; Commerce;
Education/Higher Education; Judiciary II; Program Evaluation;
Transportation

Senator **Michael V. Lee** (R-District 9)
Legislative Office Building, Room 406 . . . . . . . . . . . . . . . (919) 715-2525
Counties Represented: New Hanover (part)
Term Expires: 2017
E-mail: michael.lee@ncleg.net
Committees: Appropriations - Justice and Public Safety; Commerce;
Insurance; Program Evaluation; Redistricting
Education: North Carolina 1991 BA; Wake Forest 1997 JD

Senator **Paul A. Lowe** (D-District 32) . . . . . . . . . . . . . . . . (919) 733-5620
Counties Represented: Forsyth (part)
Term Expires: 2017
E-mail: paul.lowe@ncleg.net
Committees: Appropriations - Natural and Economic Resources;
Health Care; Judiciary II; Pensions, Retirement and Aging; Program
Evaluation; Transportation

Senator **Tom McInnis** (R-District 25) . . . . . . . . . . . . . . . . (919) 733-5953
Counties Represented: Anson, Richmond, Rowan (part), Scotland,
Stanly
Term Expires: 2017
E-mail: tom.mcinnis@ncleg.net
Committees: Agriculture/Environment/Natural Resources;
Appropriations - Natural and Economic Resources; Commerce;
Finance; Judiciary II; Program Evaluation

Senator **Floyd B. McKissick, Jr.** (D-District 20) . . . . . . . . . (919) 733-4599
Counties Represented: Durham (part), Granville       Dist: (919) 490-5373
Term Expires: 2017
300 North Salisbury Street, Room 520, Raleigh, NC 27603
4011 University Drive, Durham, NC 27707
E-mail: floyd.mckissick@ncleg.net
Committees: Appropriations - Health and Human Services; Commerce;
Finance; Health Care; Insurance; Redistricting; Rules and Operations of
the Senate

Senator **Wesley Meredith** (R-District 19) Room 2106 . . . . (919) 733-5776
Counties Represented: Cumberland (part)              Dist: (910) 867-9595
Term Expires: 2017                                   Tel: (919) 733-2599
P. O. Box 26210, Fayetteville, NC 28314
E-mail: wesley.meredith@ncleg.net
Committees: Appropriations - Transportation Department; Commerce;
Insurance; Rules and Operations of the Senate; Transportation
Education: Fayetteville Tech Comm Col 2004 AAS

Senator **E. S. "Buck" Newton** (R-District 11)
Room 408 . . . . . . . . . . . . . . . . . . . . . . . . . . . . . . . . . . . . . (919) 715-3030
Counties Represented: Johnston (part), Nash          Dist: (252) 291-3443
(part), Wilson (part)                                Fax: (919) 733-3113
Term Expires: 2017
E-mail: buck.newton@ncleg.net
Committees: Appropriations - Justice and Public Safety; Commerce;
Education/Higher Education; Finance; Judiciary I; Rules and
Operations of the Senate
Education: Appalachian State 1991 BS; Campbell 1999 JD

Senator **Louis M. Pate, Jr.** (R-District 7) Room 1028 . . . . . (919) 733-5621
Counties Represented: Lenoir (part), Pitt (part),    Dist: (919) 658-3637
Wayne (part)                                         Fax: (919) 733-3113
Term Expires: 2017
P.O. Box 945, Mount Olive, NC 28365
E-mail: louis.pate@ncleg.net
Committees: Appropriations - Base Budget; Appropriations - Health
and Human Services; Education/Higher Education; Health Care;
Pensions, Retirement and Aging; State and Local Government

Senator
**COL Ronald J. Rabin, USA (Ret)** (R-District 12)
Room 526 . . . . . . . . . . . . . . . . . . . . . . . . . . . . . . . . . . . . . (919) 733-5748
Counties Represented: Harnett, Johnston (part), Lee   Tel: (910) 489-4699
Term Expires: 2017
E-mail: ron.rabin@ncleg.net
Committees: Agriculture/Environment/Natural Resources;
Appropriations - Natural and Economic Resources; Education/Higher
Education; Finance; Health Care; Pensions, Retirement and Aging;
State and Local Government
Education: Southern Mississippi 1964 BA;
George Washington 1974 MS; National War Col (Attended)

Senator **Bill Rabon** (R-District 8) Room 2108 . . . . . . . . . . . (919) 733-5963
Counties Represented: Bladen, Brunswick, New         Fax: (919) 733-6595
Hanover (part), Pender
Term Expires: 2017
404 W Brunswick St., Southport, NC 28461
E-mail: bill.rabon@ncleg.net
Committees: Agriculture/Environment/Natural Resources;
Appropriations - Base Budget; Appropriations - Transportation
Department; Commerce; Finance; Rules and Operations of the Senate;
Transportation
Education: North Carolina State; Georgia 1976 DVM

Senator **Shirley Blackburn Randleman** (R-District 50) . . . (919) 733-5743
Counties Represented: Cherokee, Clay, Graham,        Tel: (336) 921-2043
Haywood, Jackson, Macon, Swain
Term Expires: 2017
300 North Salisbury Street, Room 308, Raleigh, NC 27603
487 Triple Cove Drive, Wilkesboro, NC 28697-7493
E-mail: shirley.randleman@ncleg.net
Committees: Agriculture/Environment/Natural Resources;
Appropriations - Base Budget; Appropriations - Justice and Public
Safety; Health Care; Judiciary II; Pensions, Retirement and Aging;
Program Evaluation

Senator **Gladys Ashe Robinson** (D-District 28)
Room 1120 . . . . . . . . . . . . . . . . . . . . . . . . . . . . . . . . . . . (919) 715-3042
Counties Represented: Guilford (part)                Fax: (919) 733-2599
Term Expires: 2017
E-mail: gladys.robinson@ncleg.net
Committees: Appropriations - Base Budget; Appropriations - Health
and Human Services; Education/Higher Education; Health Care;
Judiciary I; Program Evaluation

Senator **Robert A. "Bob" Rucho** (R-District 39)
Room 629 . . . . . . . . . . . . . . . . . . . . . . . . . . . . . . . . . . . . (919) 733-5655
Counties Represented: Mecklenburg (part)             Fax: (919) 733-2599
Term Expires: 2017
E-mail: bob.rucho@ncleg.net
Committees: Appropriations - Base Budget; Appropriations -
Education/Higher Education; Appropriations - Health and Human
Services; Commerce; Education/Higher Education; Finance; Health
Care; Insurance; Judiciary I; Redistricting
Education: Northeastern 1970 BS; Medical Col (VA) 1974 DDS;
North Carolina Charlotte 1994 MBA

*(continued on next page)*

*Legislative Branch* (side text)

**Senators** *continued*

Senator **Norman W. Sanderson** (R-District 2)
Room 629 . . . . . . . . . . . . . . . . . . . . . . (919) 733-5706
Counties Represented: Carteret, Craven, Pamlico      Dist: (252) 249-3749
Term Expires: 2017
269 Bennett Road, Arapahoe, NC 28510
E-mail: Norman.Sanderson@ncleg.net
Committees: Appropriations - General Government and Information Technology; Commerce; Finance; Insurance; Judiciary I; State and Local Government
Education: North Carolina State 1972 (Attended)

Senator **Jane W. Smith** (D-District 13) . . . . . . . . . . . . . (919) 733-5651
Counties Represented: Columbus, Robeson
Term Expires: 2017
E-mail: jane.smith@ncleg.net
Committees: Appropriations - Natural and Economic Resources; Commerce; Education/Higher Education; Pensions, Retirement and Aging; Redistricting; State and Local Government

Senator **Erica Smith-Ingram** (D-District 3) . . . . . . . . . . . (919) 715-3040
Counties Represented: Bertie, Chowan, Edgecombe, Hertford, Martin, Northampton, Tyrrell, Washington
Term Expires: 2017
E-mail: erica.smith-ingram@ncleg.net
Committees: Agriculture/Environment/Natural Resources; Appropriations - Education/Higher Education; Judiciary II; Redistricting; Transportation

Senator **Dan Soucek** (R-District 45) Room 310 . . . . . . . . . . (919) 733-5742
Counties Represented: Alleghany, Ashe, Avery,      Dist: (828) 773-6197
Caldwell, Watauga      Fax: (919) 733-2599
Term Expires: 2017
E-mail: dan.soucek@ncleg.net
Committees: Appropriations - Base Budget; Appropriations - Education/Higher Education; Commerce; Education/Higher Education; Finance; Judiciary I; Redistricting
Education: West Point 1991 BS

Senator **Jeff Tarte** (R-District 41) Room 2115 . . . . . . . . . . . (919) 715-3050
Counties Represented: Mecklenburg (part)      Dist: (704) 765-6167
Term Expires: 2017
19825 B North Cove Road, Cornelius, NC 28031
E-mail: jeff.tarte@ncleg.net
Committees: Appropriations - General Government and Information Technology; Education/Higher Education; Finance; Health Care; Pensions, Retirement and Aging; Program Evaluation; State and Local Government
Education: Illinois 1978 BEc

Senator **Jerry W. Tillman** (R-District 29) Room 627 . . . . . . (919) 733-5870
Counties Represented: Moore, Randolph (part)      Dist: (336) 431-5325
Term Expires: 2017      Fax: (919) 754-3339
1207 Dogwood Lane, Archdale, NC 27263
E-mail: jerry.tillman@ncleg.net
Committees: Appropriations - Base Budget; Appropriations - Education/Higher Education; Commerce; Education/Higher Education; Finance; Judiciary I; Program Evaluation

Senator **Tommy Tucker** (R-District 35) . . . . . . . . . . . . . (919) 733-7659
Counties Represented: Union (part)      Dist: (704) 243-6695
Term Expires: 2017      Fax: (919) 733-2599
300 North Salisbury Street, Room 311, Raleigh, NC 27603
1206 Rosehill Dr, Waxhaw, NC 28173
E-mail: tommy.tucker@ncleg.net
Committees: Agriculture/Environment/Natural Resources; Appropriations - Base Budget; Appropriations - Health and Human Services; Health Care; Rules and Operations of the Senate; Transportation
Education: North Carolina State (Attended)

Senator **Terry Van Duyn** (D-District 49) Room 515 . . . . . . . (919) 715-3001
Counties Represented: Buncombe (part)
Term Expires: 2017
E-mail: terry.vanduyn@ncleg.net
Committees: Appropriations - Health and Human Services; Finance; Health Care; Judiciary II; State and Local Government; Ways and Means

Senator **Joyce Waddell** (D-District 40) . . . . . . . . . . . . . . (919) 733-5650
Counties Represented: Mecklenburg (part)
Term Expires: 2017
E-mail: joyce.waddell@ncleg.net
Committees: Appropriations - Education/Higher Education; Commerce; Finance; Insurance; Pensions, Retirement and Aging; State and Local Government

Senator **Dr. Trudy Wade** (R-District 27) Room 2106 . . . . . . (919) 733-5856
Counties Represented: Guilford (part)      Dist: (336) 323-6480
Term Expires: 2017
1 Creswell Court, Greensboro, NC 27407
E-mail: trudy.wade@ncleg.net
Committees: Agriculture/Environment/Natural Resources; Appropriations - Base Budget; Appropriations - Natural and Economic Resources; Education/Higher Education; Finance; Health Care; Judiciary I; Rules and Operations of the Senate; State and Local Government
Education: Greensboro 1975 BS; Tuskegee 1980 DVM

Senator **W. Andrew "Andy" Wells, Jr.** (R-District 42) . . . . (919) 733-5876
Counties Represented: Alexander, Catawba
Term Expires: 2017
E-mail: andy.wells@ncleg.net
Committees: Appropriations - Health and Human Services; Education/Higher Education; Finance; Health Care; Judiciary II; Pensions, Retirement and Aging; Program Evaluation
Education: North Carolina State BS

Senator **Michael "Mike" Woodard** (D-District 22)
Room 575 . . . . . . . . . . . . . . . . . . . . . . . . . . (919) 733-4809
Counties Represented: Caswell, Durham (part),      Tel: (919) 599-5143
Person
Term Expires: 2017
762 Ninth Street, Durham, NC 27705
E-mail: mike.woodard@ncleg.net
Committees: Appropriations - General Government and Information Technology; Education/Higher Education; Finance; Health Care; Judiciary II; Program Evaluation
Education: Duke 1981 AB

# Senate Standing Committees
## Agriculture/Environment/Natural Resources
State Legislative Office Building, Room 544 LOB, Raleigh, NC 27603-5925

| **Majority Members** | **Minority Members** |
|---|---|
| Andrew C. Brock (R-34) *Co-Chair* | Angela R. Bryant (D-4) |
| Bill Cook (R-1) *Co-Chair* | Joel D. M. Ford (D-38) |
| Dr. Trudy Wade (R-27) *Co-Chair* | Valerie P. Foushee (D-23) |
| Fletcher L. "Fletch" Hartsell, Jr. (R-36) *Vice Chair* | Jeff Jackson (D-37) |
| | Erica Smith-Ingram (D-3) |
| Brent Jackson (R-10) *Vice Chair* | |
| John M. Alexander, Jr. (R-15) | |
| Chad Barefoot (R-18) | |
| Stan Bingham (R-33) | |
| Tom McInnis (R-25) | |
| COL Ronald J. Rabin (R-12) | |
| Bill Rabon (R-8) | |
| Shirley Blackburn Randleman (R-50) | |
| Tommy Tucker (R-35) | |

## Appropriations - Base Budget
State Legislative Office Building, Room 643 LOB, Raleigh, NC 27603-5925

| **Majority Members** | **Minority Members** |
|---|---|
| Harry Brown (R-6) *Co-Chair* | Daniel Terry "Dan" Blue, Jr. (D-14) |
| Kathy Harrington (R-43) *Co-Chair* | Angela R. Bryant (D-4) |
| Brent Jackson (R-10) *Co-Chair* | Donald G. "Don" Davis (D-5) |
| Tom Apodaca (R-48) | Joel D. M. Ford (D-38) |
| Andrew C. Brock (R-34) | Valerie P. Foushee (D-23) |
| Jim Davis (R-50) | Gladys Ashe Robinson (D-28) |
| Ralph E. Hise, Jr. (R-47) | |
| Louis M. Pate, Jr. (R-7) | |
| Bill Rabon (R-8) | |
| Shirley Blackburn Randleman (R-50) | |
| Robert A. "Bob" Rucho (R-39) | |
| Dan Soucek (R-45) | |
| Jerry W. Tillman (R-29) | |
| Tommy Tucker (R-35) | |
| Dr. Trudy Wade (R-27) | |

LEGISLATIVE BRANCH

## Appropriations - Education/Higher Education
State Legislative Office Building, Room 414 LOB, Raleigh, NC 27603-5925

| Majority Members | Minority Members |
|---|---|
| Tom Apodaca (R-48) *Co-Chair* | Donald G. "Don" Davis (D-5) |
| Dan Soucek (R-45) *Co-Chair* | Erica Smith-Ingram (D-3) |
| Chad Barefoot (R-18) *Co-Chair* | Joyce Waddell (D-40) |
| Dr. David L. Curtis (R-44) | |
| Fletcher L. "Fletch" Hartsell, Jr. (R-36) | |
| Robert A. "Bob" Rucho (R-39) | |
| Jerry W. Tillman (R-29) | |

## Appropriations - General Government and Information Technology
State Legislative Office Building, Room 1124 LB, Raleigh, NC 27603-5925

| Majority Members | Minority Members |
|---|---|
| Jim Davis (R-50) *Co-Chair* | Michael "Mike" Woodard (D-22) |
| Norman W. Sanderson (R-2) *Co-Chair* | |
| Andrew C. Brock (R-34) | |
| Jeff Tarte (R-41) | |

## Appropriations - Health and Human Services
State Legislative Office Building, Room 422 LOB, Raleigh, NC 27603-5925

| Majority Members | Minority Members |
|---|---|
| Ralph E. Hise, Jr. (R-47) *Co-Chair* | Floyd B. McKissick, Jr. (D-20) |
| Louis M. Pate, Jr. (R-7) *Co-Chair* | Gladys Ashe Robinson (D-28) |
| Tommy Tucker (R-35) *Co-Chair* | Terry Van Duyn (D-49) |
| Tamara Patterson Barringer (R-17) | |
| Robert A. "Bob" Rucho (R-39) | |
| W. Andrew "Andy" Wells, Jr. (R-42) | |

## Appropriations - Justice and Public Safety
State Legislative Office Building, Room 415 LOB, Raleigh, NC 27603-5925

| Majority Members | Minority Members |
|---|---|
| Stan Bingham (R-33) *Co-Chair* | Valerie P. Foushee (D-23) |
| E. S. "Buck" Newton (R-11) *Co-Chair* | Jeff Jackson (D-37) |
| Shirley Blackburn Randleman (R-50) *Co-Chair* | |
| Tom Apodaca (R-48) *Vice Chair* | |
| Fletcher L. "Fletch" Hartsell, Jr. (R-36) | |
| Michael V. Lee (R-9) | |

## Appropriations - Natural and Economic Resources
State Legislative Office Building, Room 423 LOB, Raleigh, NC 27603-5925

| Majority Members | Minority Members |
|---|---|
| Andrew C. Brock (R-34) *Co-Chair* | Angela R. Bryant (D-4) |
| Bill Cook (R-1) *Co-Chair* | Robert B. "Ben" Clark III (D-21) |
| Dr. Trudy Wade (R-27) *Co-Chair* | Paul A. Lowe (D-32) |
| John M. Alexander, Jr. (R-15) | Jane W. Smith (D-13) |
| Tom McInnis (R-25) | |
| COL Ronald J. Rabin (R-12) | |

## Appropriations - Transportation Department
State Legislative Office Building, Room 1027, Raleigh, NC 27601-2808

| Majority Members | Minority Members |
|---|---|
| Wesley Meredith (R-19) *Co-Chair* | Daniel Terry "Dan" Blue, Jr. (D-14) |
| Bill Rabon (R-8) *Co-Chair* | Donald G. "Don" Davis (D-5) |
| Warren "T." Daniel (R-46) *Vice Chair* | Joel D. M. Ford (D-38) |
| Stan Bingham (R-33) | |
| Rick Gunn (R-24) | |
| Joyce R. Krawiec (R-31) | |

## Commerce
State Legislative Office Building, Room 1027, Raleigh, NC 27601-2808

| Majority Members | Minority Members |
|---|---|
| Rick Gunn (R-24) *Co-Chair* | Daniel Terry "Dan" Blue, Jr. (D-14) |
| Wesley Meredith (R-19) *Co-Chair* | Angela R. Bryant (D-4) |
| Tamara Patterson Barringer (R-17) *Vice Chair* | Robert B. "Ben" Clark III (D-21) |
| Harry Brown (R-6) *Vice Chair* | Joel D. M. Ford (D-38) |
| John M. Alexander, Jr. (R-15) | Valerie P. Foushee (D-23) |
| Tom Apodaca (R-48) | Floyd B. McKissick, Jr. (D-20) |
| Andrew C. Brock (R-34) | Jane W. Smith (D-13) |
| Bill Cook (R-1) | Joyce Waddell (D-40) |
| Warren "T." Daniel (R-46) | |
| Kathy Harrington (R-43) | |
| Brent Jackson (R-10) | |
| Joyce R. Krawiec (R-31) | |
| Michael V. Lee (R-9) | |
| Tom McInnis (R-25) | |
| E. S. "Buck" Newton (R-11) | |
| Bill Rabon (R-8) | |
| Robert A. "Bob" Rucho (R-39) | |
| Norman W. Sanderson (R-2) | |
| Dan Soucek (R-45) | |
| Jerry W. Tillman (R-29) | |

## Education/Higher Education
State Legislative Office Building, Room 643, Raleigh, NC 27603-5925

| Majority Members | Minority Members |
|---|---|
| Dan Soucek (R-45) *Co-Chair* | Angela R. Bryant (D-4) |
| Jerry W. Tillman (R-29) *Co-Chair* | Robert B. "Ben" Clark III (D-21) |
| Dr. David L. Curtis (R-44) *Vice Chair* | Donald G. "Don" Davis (D-5) |
| Tom Apodaca (R-48) | Valerie P. Foushee (D-23) |
| Chad Barefoot (R-18) | Gladys Ashe Robinson (D-28) |
| Tamara Patterson Barringer (R-17) | Jane W. Smith (D-13) |
| Stan Bingham (R-33) | Michael "Mike" Woodard (D-22) |
| Harry Brown (R-6) | |
| Bill Cook (R-1) | |
| Warren "T." Daniel (R-46) | |
| Fletcher L. "Fletch" Hartsell, Jr. (R-36) | |
| Joyce R. Krawiec (R-31) | |
| E. S. "Buck" Newton (R-11) | |
| Louis M. Pate, Jr. (R-7) | |
| COL Ronald J. Rabin (R-12) | |
| Robert A. "Bob" Rucho (R-39) | |
| Jeff Tarte (R-41) | |
| Dr. Trudy Wade (R-27) | |
| W. Andrew "Andy" Wells, Jr. (R-42) | |

## Finance
State Legislative Office Building, Room 544 LOB, Raleigh, NC 27603-5925

| Majority Members | Minority Members |
|---|---|
| Bill Rabon (R-8) *Co-Chair* | Daniel Terry "Dan" Blue, Jr. (D-14) |
| Robert A. "Bob" Rucho (R-39) *Co-Chair* | Angela R. Bryant (D-4) |
| Jerry W. Tillman (R-29) *Co-Chair* | Robert B. "Ben" Clark III (D-21) |
| Dr. David L. Curtis (R-44) *Vice Chair* | Joel D. M. Ford (D-38) |
| | Jeff Jackson (D-37) |
| | Floyd B. McKissick, Jr. (D-20) |
| | Terry Van Duyn (D-49) |
| | Joyce Waddell (D-40) |

*(continued on next page)*

LEGISLATIVE BRANCH

## Finance *continued*

**Majority Members** *continued*

Fletcher L. "Fletch"
  Hartsell, Jr. (R-36)
  *Vice Chair*
COL Ronald J. Rabin (R-12)
  *Vice Chair*
John M. Alexander, Jr. (R-15)
Tom Apodaca (R-48)
Chad Barefoot (R-18)
Tamara Patterson Barringer (R-17)
Andrew C. Brock (R-34)
Harry Brown (R-6)
Bill Cook (R-1)
Warren "T." Daniel (R-46)
Jim Davis (R-50)
Kathy Harrington (R-43)
Ralph E. Hise, Jr. (R-47)
Brent Jackson (R-10)
Tom McInnis (R-25)
E. S. "Buck" Newton (R-11)
Norman W. Sanderson (R-2)
Dan Soucek (R-45)
Jeff Tarte (R-41)
Dr. Trudy Wade (R-27)
W. Andrew "Andy" Wells, Jr.
  (R-42)

**Minority Members** *continued*

Michael "Mike" Woodard (D-22)

## Health Care

State Legislative Office Building, Room 544 LOB,
Raleigh, NC 27603-5925

**Majority Members**

Ralph E. Hise, Jr. (R-47) *Co-Chair*
Louis M. Pate, Jr. (R-7) *Co-Chair*
Tommy Tucker (R-35) *Co-Chair*
Jeff Tarte (R-41) *Vice Chair*
Chad Barefoot (R-18)
Stan Bingham (R-33)
Dr. David L. Curtis (R-44)
Jim Davis (R-50)
Fletcher L. "Fletch" Hartsell, Jr.
  (R-36)
COL Ronald J. Rabin (R-12)
Shirley Blackburn Randleman
  (R-50)
Robert A. "Bob" Rucho (R-39)
Dr. Trudy Wade (R-27)
W. Andrew "Andy" Wells, Jr.
  (R-42)

**Minority Members**

Donald G. "Don" Davis (D-5)
Paul A. Lowe (D-32)
Floyd B. McKissick, Jr. (D-20)
Gladys Ashe Robinson (D-28)
Terry Van Duyn (D-49)
Michael "Mike" Woodard (D-22)

## Insurance

State Legislative Office Building, Room 1125, Raleigh, NC 27601-2808

**Majority Members**

Tom Apodaca (R-48) *Co-Chair*
Wesley Meredith (R-19) *Co-Chair*
Norman W. Sanderson (R-2)
  *Vice Chair*
Jim Davis (R-50)
Rick Gunn (R-24)
Ralph E. Hise, Jr. (R-47)
Michael V. Lee (R-9)
Robert A. "Bob" Rucho (R-39)

**Minority Members**

Daniel Terry "Dan" Blue, Jr. (D-14)
Joel D. M. Ford (D-38)
Floyd B. McKissick, Jr. (D-20)
Joyce Waddell (D-40)

## Judiciary I

State Legislative Office Building, Room 1027, Raleigh, NC 27601-2808

**Majority Members**

Fletcher L. "Fletch"
  Hartsell, Jr. (R-36)
  *Co-Chair*
E. S. "Buck" Newton (R-11)
  *Co-Chair*
Tom Apodaca (R-48)
Tamara Patterson Barringer (R-17)
Harry Brown (R-6)
Kathy Harrington (R-43)

**Minority Members**

Daniel Terry "Dan" Blue, Jr. (D-14)
Robert B. "Ben" Clark III (D-21)
Valerie P. Foushee (D-23)
Gladys Ashe Robinson (D-28)

## Majority Members *continued*

Brent Jackson (R-10)
Robert A. "Bob" Rucho (R-39)
Norman W. Sanderson (R-2)
Dan Soucek (R-45)
Jerry W. Tillman (R-29)
Dr. Trudy Wade (R-27)

## Judiciary II

State Legislative Office Building, Room 1124, Raleigh, NC 27601-2808

**Majority Members**

Tamara Patterson Barringer (R-17)
  *Co-Chair*
Warren "T." Daniel (R-46)
  *Co-Chair*
Shirley Blackburn
  Randleman (R-50)
  *Co-Chair*
John M. Alexander, Jr. (R-15)
Chad Barefoot (R-18)
Stan Bingham (R-33)
Bill Cook (R-1)
Dr. David L. Curtis (R-44)
Jim Davis (R-50)
Joyce R. Krawiec (R-31)
Tom McInnis (R-25)
W. Andrew "Andy" Wells, Jr.
  (R-42)

**Minority Members**

Angela R. Bryant (D-4)
Jeff Jackson (D-37)
Paul A. Lowe (D-32)
Erica Smith-Ingram (D-3)
Terry Van Duyn (D-49)
Michael "Mike" Woodard (D-22)

## Pensions, Retirement and Aging

State Legislative Office Building, Room 423, Raleigh, NC 27603-5925

**Majority Members**

Tom Apodaca (R-48) *Co-Chair*
Rick Gunn (R-24) *Co-Chair*
Dr. David L. Curtis (R-44)
Warren "T." Daniel (R-46)
Louis M. Pate, Jr. (R-7)
COL Ronald J. Rabin (R-12)
Shirley Blackburn Randleman
  (R-50)
Jeff Tarte (R-41)
W. Andrew "Andy" Wells, Jr.
  (R-42)

**Minority Members**

Angela R. Bryant (D-4)
Jeff Jackson (D-37)
Paul A. Lowe (D-32)
Jane W. Smith (D-13)
Joyce Waddell (D-40)

## Program Evaluation

**Majority Members**

Stan Bingham (R-33) *Co-Chair*
Fletcher L. "Fletch"
  Hartsell, Jr. (R-36)
  *Co-Chair*
Chad Barefoot (R-18)
Andrew C. Brock (R-34)
Bill Cook (R-1)
Rick Gunn (R-24)
Joyce R. Krawiec (R-31)
Michael V. Lee (R-9)
Tom McInnis (R-25)
Shirley Blackburn Randleman
  (R-50)
Jeff Tarte (R-41)
Jerry W. Tillman (R-29)
W. Andrew "Andy" Wells, Jr.
  (R-42)

**Minority Members**

Robert B. "Ben" Clark III (D-21)
Jeff Jackson (D-37)
Paul A. Lowe (D-32)
Gladys Ashe Robinson (D-28)
Michael "Mike" Woodard (D-22)

## Redistricting

**Majority Members**

Robert A. "Bob" Rucho (R-39)
  *Chair*
Andrew C. Brock (R-34) *Vice Chair*
Harry Brown (R-6) *Vice Chair*
Tom Apodaca (R-48)
Kathy Harrington (R-43)
Ralph E. Hise, Jr. (R-47)
Michael V. Lee (R-9)
Dan Soucek (R-45)

**Minority Members**

Robert B. "Ben" Clark III (D-21)
Floyd B. McKissick, Jr. (D-20)
Jane W. Smith (D-13)
Erica Smith-Ingram (D-3)

## Rules and Operations of the Senate

| Majority Members | Minority Members |
|---|---|
| Tom Apodaca (R-48) *Chair* | Daniel Terry "Dan" Blue, Jr. (D-14) |
| Tommy Tucker (R-35) *Vice Chair* | Robert B. "Ben" Clark III (D-21) |
| Chad Barefoot (R-18) | Joel D. M. Ford (D-38) |
| Andrew C. Brock (R-34) | Floyd B. McKissick, Jr. (D-20) |
| Harry Brown (R-6) | |
| Kathy Harrington (R-43) | |
| Ralph E. Hise, Jr. (R-47) | |
| Brent Jackson (R-10) | |
| Wesley Meredith (R-19) | |
| E. S. "Buck" Newton (R-11) | |
| Bill Rabon (R-8) | |
| Dr. Trudy Wade (R-27) | |

## State and Local Government

State Legislative Office Building, Room 1124, Raleigh, NC 27601-2808

| Majority Members | Minority Members |
|---|---|
| Jim Davis (R-50) *Co-Chair* | Donald G. "Don" Davis (D-5) |
| Norman W. Sanderson (R-2) *Co-Chair* | Valerie P. Foushee (D-23) |
| Dr. Trudy Wade (R-27) *Vice Chair* | Jane W. Smith (D-13) |
| John M. Alexander, Jr. (R-15) | Terry Van Duyn (D-49) |
| Tamara Patterson Barringer (R-17) | Joyce Waddell (D-40) |
| Dr. David L. Curtis (R-44) | |
| Fletcher L. "Fletch" Hartsell, Jr. (R-36) | |
| Brent Jackson (R-10) | |
| Louis M. Pate, Jr. (R-7) | |
| COL Ronald J. Rabin (R-12) | |
| Jeff Tarte (R-41) | |

## Transportation

State Legislative Office Building, Room 1027, Raleigh, NC 27601-2808

| Majority Members | Minority Members |
|---|---|
| Warren "T." Daniel (R-46) *Co-Chair* | Joel D. M. Ford (D-38) |
| Bill Rabon (R-8) *Co-Chair* | Paul A. Lowe (D-32) |
| Kathy Harrington (R-43) *Vice Chair* | Erica Smith-Ingram (D-3) |
| Wesley Meredith (R-19) *Vice Chair* | |
| Jim Davis (R-50) | |
| Rick Gunn (R-24) | |
| Ralph E. Hise, Jr. (R-47) | |
| Joyce R. Krawiec (R-31) | |
| Tommy Tucker (R-35) | |

## Ways and Means

| Majority Members | Minority Members |
|---|---|
| Tom Apodaca (R-48) *Chair* | Terry Van Duyn (D-49) |
| Andrew C. Brock (R-34) *Vice Chair* | |

# North Carolina House of Representatives

State Legislative Building, 16 West Jones Street, Raleigh, NC 27601
Tel: (919) 733-7928 Fax: (919) 733-2599

Speaker of the House **Tim K. Moore** (R) . . . . . . . . . . . . . . (919) 733-4838
Speaker Pro Tem **Paul Stam** (R) . . . . . . . . . . . . . . . . . . . . (919) 733-2962
  Education: Michigan State 1972 BS; North Carolina 1975 JD
Majority Leader **Mike Hager** (R) . . . . . . . . . . . . . . . . . . . . . (919) 733-5749
Deputy Majority Leader **Marilyn Avila** (R) . . . . . . . . . . . . . (919) 733-5530
Majority Whip **John R. Bell IV** (R) . . . . . . . . . . . . . . . . . . . (919) 715-3017
  Education: North Carolina Wilmington 2001 BA
Deputy Majority Whip
  **James L. "Jamie" Boles, Jr.** (R) . . . . . . . . . . . . . . . . . . (919) 733-5903
Deputy Majority Whip **Patricia "Pat" McElraft** (R) . . . . . . (919) 733-6275
Republican Conference Leader **Charles Jeter** (R) . . . . . . . . (919) 733-5654
  Education: Wofford 1995 BA
Joint Caucus Leader **Pat B. Hurley** (R) . . . . . . . . . . . . . . . (919) 733-5865
Republican Freshman Leader **John Fraley** (R) . . . . . . . . . . (919) 733-5741
Republican Freshman Whip **John R. Bradford III** (R) . . . . . (919) 733-5828
Minority Leader **Larry Dwight Hall** (D) . . . . . . . . . . . . . . . . (919) 733-5872
  Education: Johnson C Smith BS; North Carolina JD
Deputy Minority Leader **Susan C. Fisher** (D) . . . . . . . . . . . (919) 715-2013
Minority Whip **Rosa U. Gill** (D) . . . . . . . . . . . . . . . . . . . . . (919) 733-5880
Democratic Conference Co-Chair **Grier Martin** (D) . . . . . . . (919) 733-5773

Democratic Conference Co-Chair **Garland E. Pierce** (D) . . (919) 733-5803
Democratic Freshman Caucus Co-Chair
  **Graig R. Meyer** (D) . . . . . . . . . . . . . . . . . . . . . . . . . . . (919) 715-3019
Democratic Freshman Caucus Co-Chair
  **Robert T. Reives II** (D) . . . . . . . . . . . . . . . . . . . . . . . . (919) 733-7928
Principal Clerk of the House **Denise G. Weeks** . . . . . . . . . (919) 733-7760
Sergeant-at-Arms **Garland Shepheard** . . . . . . . . . . . . . . . (919) 733-5627

## Representatives

**Party Affiliation Statistics:** Republicans: 74, Democrats: 45,
Independents: 1

Representative **Jay Adams** (R-District 96) . . . . . . . . . . . . . (919) 733-5988
  Counties Represented: Catawba (part)
  Term Expires: 2017
  E-mail: jay.adams@ncleg.net
  Committees: Children, Youth and Families; Commerce and Job
  Development; Environment; Finance; Judiciary IV; Transportation;
  Wildlife Resources
Representative **Gale Adcock** (D-District 41) . . . . . . . . . . . . (919) 733-5602
  Counties Represented: Wake (part)
  Term Expires: 2017
  E-mail: gale.adcock@ncleg.net
  Committees: Appropriations; Health; Homeland Security, Military, and
  Veterans Affairs; Wildlife Resources
  Education: East Carolina BS; North Carolina MSN
Representative **John Ager** (D-District 115) . . . . . . . . . . . . . (919) 733-5746
  Counties Represented: Buncombe (part)
  Term Expires: 2017
  E-mail: john.ager@ncleg.net
  Committees: Agriculture; Appropriations; Children, Youth and Families;
  Education - K-12; Judiciary IV; Local Government; Wildlife Resources
Representative **Kelly M. Alexander, Jr.** (D-District 107) . . . (919) 733-5778
  Counties Represented: Mecklenburg (part)    Tel: (704) 333-1167
  Term Expires: 2017                          Fax: (704) 333-1173
  Legislative Office Building, 300 North Salisbury Street, Room 632,
  Raleigh, NC 27603-5925
  1424 Statesville Avenue, Charlotte, NC 28206
  E-mail: kelly.alexander@ncleg.net
  Committees: Alcoholic Beverage Control; Education - Community
  Colleges; Finance; Public Utilities; Transportation
  Education: North Carolina 1970 AB, 1973 MPA
Representative **Dean Arp** (R-District 69) . . . . . . . . . . . . . . (919) 715-3007
  Counties Represented: Union (part)          Tel: (704) 282-0418
  Term Expires: 2017
  PO Box 1511, Monroe, NC 28111-1511
  E-mail: dean.arp@ncleg.net
  Committees: Appropriations; Education - Community Colleges;
  Homeland Security, Military, and Veterans Affairs; Insurance; Judiciary
  I; Public Utilities; Transportation
  Education: Citadel 1988 BS; North Carolina Charlotte 1999 MS
Representative **Marilyn Avila** (R-District 40) Room 1017 . . (919) 733-5530
  Counties Represented: Wake (part)           Res: (919) 280-6084
  Term Expires: 2017
  E-mail: marilyn.avila@ncleg.net
  Committees: Appropriations; Children, Youth and Families; Commerce
  and Job Development; Health; Homeland Security, Military, and
  Veterans Affairs
Representative **Nathan A. Baskerville** (D-District 32) . . . . (919) 733-5824
  Counties Represented: Granville (part), Vance,  Dist: (252) 572-4495
  Warren
  Term Expires: 2017
  119 West Waycliff Road, Henderson, NC 27537
  E-mail: nathan.baskerville@ncleg.net
  Committees: Appropriations; Environment; Insurance; Judiciary III
  Education: Morehouse Col 2003 BA; North Carolina Central 2006 JD
Representative **John R. Bell IV** (R-District 10) . . . . . . . . . . (919) 715-3017
  Counties Represented: Craven (part), Greene (part),  Tel: (919) 344-6324
  Lenoir (part), Wayne (part)
  Term Expires: 2017
  501 Holland Hill Drive, Goldsboro, NC 27530
  E-mail: john.bell@ncleg.net
  Committees: Agriculture; Banking; Commerce and Job Development;
  Finance; Homeland Security, Military, and Veterans Affairs; Judiciary
  III; Public Utilities; Regulatory Reform; Rules, Calendar and
  Operations of the House

*(continued on next page)*

**LEGISLATIVE BRANCH**

**Representatives** *continued*

Representative **Larry M. Bell** (D-District 21) . . . . . . . . . . . (919) 733-5863
Counties Represented: Duplin (part), Sampson          Res: (910) 592-1177
(part), Wayne (part)                                  Fax: (910) 592-4637
Term Expires: 2017
Legislative Office Building, 300 North Salisbury Street, Room 538,
Raleigh, NC 27603-5925
908 Southwest Boulevard, Clinton, NC 28328
E-mail: larry.bell@ncleg.net
Committees: Agriculture; Appropriations; Commerce and Job
Development; Pensions and Retirement; State Personnel
Education: North Carolina A&T 1961 BS, 1976 MA;
East Carolina 1983 EdS

Representative **J. Daniel "Dan" Bishop** (R-District 104) . . (919) 715-3009
Counties Represented: Mecklenburg (part)
Term Expires: 2017
E-mail: dan.bishop@ncleg.net
Committees: Banking; Finance; Health; Judiciary IV; Pensions and
Retirement; Public Utilities; Regulatory Reform
Education: North Carolina 1986 BS, 1990 JD

Representative **Hugh Blackwell** (R-District 86) . . . . . . . . . (919) 733-5805
Counties Represented: Burke (part)                    Res: (828) 879-8454
Term Expires: 2017
Legislative Office Building, 300 North Salisbury Street, Room 606,
Raleigh, NC 27603-5925
321 Mountain View Avenue SE, Valdese, NC 28690
E-mail: hugh.blackwell@ncleg.net
Committees: Appropriations; Commerce and Job Development; Health;
Judiciary IV; Public Utilities; Regulatory Reform; Transportation

Representative **John M. Blust** (R-District 62)
Room 1109 . . . . . . . . . . . . . . . . . . . . . . . . . . . . . . . (919) 733-5781
Counties Represented: Guilford (part)                 Res: (336) 274-4658
Term Expires: 2017                                    Fax: (336) 274-4540
P.O. Box 8146, Greensboro, NC 27419
E-mail: john.blust@ncleg.net
Committees: Banking; Elections; Finance; Homeland Security, Military,
and Veterans Affairs; Judiciary II; Pensions and Retirement; Rules,
Calendar and Operations of the House
Education: North Carolina 1979 BA, 1982 JD

Representative
**James L. "Jamie" Boles, Jr.** (R-District 52) . . . . . . . . . (919) 733-5903
Counties Represented: Moore (part)                    Tel: (910) 692-6262
Term Expires: 2017
Legislative Office Building, 300 North Salisbury Street, Room 501,
Raleigh, NC 27603-5925
425 West Pennsylvania Avenue, Southern Pines, NC 28387
E-mail: jamie.boles@ncleg.net
Committees: Alcoholic Beverage Control; Appropriations; Commerce
and Job Development; Ethics; Insurance; Local Government; Rules,
Calendar and Operations of the House; Transportation

Representative **John R. Bradford III** (R-District 98) . . . . . . (919) 733-5828
Counties Represented: Mecklenburg (part)
Term Expires: 2017
E-mail: john.bradford@ncleg.net
Committees: Agriculture; Banking; Commerce and Job Development;
Environment; Finance; Public Utilities; Regulatory Reform

Representative **William "Bill" Brawley** (R-District 103)
Room 1313 . . . . . . . . . . . . . . . . . . . . . . . . . . . . . . . (919) 733-5800
Counties Represented: Mecklenburg (part)
Term Expires: 2017
E-mail: bill.brawley@ncleg.net
Committees: Appropriations; Commerce and Job Development;
Environment; Finance; Health; Insurance; Local Government;
Transportation

Representative **William D. Brisson** (D-District 22)
Room 1325 . . . . . . . . . . . . . . . . . . . . . . . . . . . . . . . (919) 733-5772
Counties Represented: Bladen (part), Johnston         Res: (910) 862-7007
(part), Sampson (part)                                Fax: (910) 862-3310
Term Expires: 2017
P.O. Box 531, Dublin, NC 28332
E-mail: william.brisson@ncleg.net
Committees: Agriculture; Appropriations; Environment; Ethics; Health;
Insurance; Regulatory Reform; Wildlife Resources

Representative **Cecil Antonio Brockman** (D-District 60) . . (919) 733-5825
Counties Represented: Guilford (part)
Term Expires: 2017
E-mail: cecil.brockman@ncleg.net
Committees: Agriculture; Appropriations; Commerce and Job
Development; Environment; Transportation

Representative **Mark Brody** (R-District 55) . . . . . . . . . . . . . (919) 715-3029
Counties Represented: Anson, Union (part)             Dist: (704) 965-6585
Term Expires: 2017
5315 Rocky River Road, Monroe, NC 28112
E-mail: mark.brody@ncleg.net
Committees: Agriculture; Appropriations; Commerce and Job
Development; Education - Community Colleges; Education -
Universities; Elections; Regulatory Reform
Education: Concordia U (WI) 1996 BA

Representative **Rayne Brown** (R-District 81) . . . . . . . . . . . (919) 715-0873
Counties Represented: Davidson (part)
Term Expires: 2017
300 North Salisbury Street, Room 638, Raleigh, NC 27603
E-mail: rayne.brown@ncleg.net
Committees: Appropriations; Education - Universities; Elections;
Ethics; Health; Judiciary III; Local Government; Transportation

Representative **Robert P. "Rob" Bryan III** (R-District 88) . . (919) 733-5607
Counties Represented: Mecklenburg (part)              Dist: (704) 331-4995
Term Expires: 2017
301 South College Street, Suite 3500, Charlotte, NC 28202
E-mail: rob.bryan@ncleg.net
Committees: Appropriations; Banking; Commerce and Job
Development; Education - K-12; Elections; Judiciary IV; Regulatory
Reform; University Board of Governors Nominating
Education: North Carolina 1993 BA; Duke 1998 JD

Representative **Dana Bumgardner** (R-District 109) . . . . . . (919) 733-5809
Counties Represented: Gaston (part)                   Tel: (704) 861-1648
Term Expires: 2017
3517 Lincoln Lane, Gastonia, NC 28056
E-mail: dana.bumgardner@ncleg.net
Committees: Appropriations; Banking; Insurance; Judiciary II; Public
Utilities; Rules, Calendar and Operations of the House; Transportation

Representative **Justin P. Burr** (R-District 67) . . . . . . . . . . . (919) 733-5908
Counties Represented: Montgomery (part), Stanly       Tel: (704) 983-4663
Term Expires: 2017
State Legislative Building, 16 West Jones Street, Room 1315,
Raleigh, NC 27601-1096
125 South Third Street, Albemarle, NC 28001
E-mail: justin.burr@ncleg.net
Committees: Appropriations; Elections; Health; Insurance; Judiciary I;
Local Government; Rules, Calendar and Operations of the House

Representative **Becky Carney** (D-District 102)
Room 1221 . . . . . . . . . . . . . . . . . . . . . . . . . . . . . . . (919) 733-5827
Counties Represented: Mecklenburg (part)              Fax: (704) 332-8339
Term Expires: 2017
P.O. Box 32873, Charlotte, NC 28232
E-mail: becky.carney@ncleg.net
Committees: Banking; Education - Universities; Environment; Ethics;
Finance; Health; Rules, Calendar and Operations of the House;
Transportation

Representative **Rick Catlin** (R-District 20) . . . . . . . . . . . . . (919) 733-5830
Counties Represented: New Hanover (part)              Dist: (910) 452-5861
Term Expires: 2017
220 Old Dairy Road, Wilmington, NC 28405
E-mail: rick.catlin@ncleg.net
Committees: Appropriations; Commerce and Job Development;
Environment; Public Utilities; Regulatory Reform; Transportation
Education: South Florida 1978 BS

Representative **George G. Cleveland** (R-District 14) . . . . . (919) 715-6707
Counties Represented: Onslow (part)                   Res: (910) 346-3866
Term Expires: 2017                                    Fax: (910) 346-3866
Legislative Office Building, 300 North Salisbury Street, Room 504,
Raleigh, NC 27603-5925
224 Campbell Place, Jacksonville, NC 28546
E-mail: george.cleveland@ncleg.net
Committees: Agriculture; Appropriations; Education - K-12;
Homeland Security, Military, and Veterans Affairs; Judiciary III; Local
Government; Transportation; Wildlife Resources

Representative **Jeffrey L. "Jeff" Collins** (R-District 25)
Room 1006 . . . . . . . . . . . . . . . . . . . . . . . . . . . . . . . (919) 733-5802
Counties Represented: Franklin (part), Nash (part)
Term Expires: 2017
E-mail: jeff.collins@ncleg.net
Committees: Agriculture; Alcoholic Beverage Control; Environment;
Finance; Insurance; Public Utilities; State Personnel

Representative **Debra Conrad** (R-District 74) . . . . . . . . . . . (919) 733-5787
Counties Represented: Forsyth (part)                  Dist: (336) 760-9653
Term Expires: 2017
4004 Pemberton Court, Winston-Salem, NC 27106
E-mail: debra.conrad@ncleg.net
Committees: Aging; Appropriations; Commerce and Job Development;
Elections; Insurance; Judiciary II; Public Utilities
Education: Wake Forest 1974 BS

Representative **Tricia Ann Cotham** (D-District 100) . . . . . . (919) 715-0706
Counties Represented: Mecklenburg (part)　　　Res: (704) 634-9400
Term Expires: 2017
Legislative Office Building, 300 North Salisbury Street, Room 418C,
Raleigh, NC 27603-5925
107 Sardis Grove Lane, Matthews, NC 28105
E-mail: tricia.cotham@ncleg.net
Committees: Children, Youth and Families; Education - K-12;
Elections; Ethics; Finance; Health; Regulatory Reform; Rules, Calendar
and Operations of the House; University Board of Governors
Nominating

Representative **Carla D. Cunningham** (D-District 106) . . . . (919) 733-5807
Counties Represented: Mecklenburg (part)　　　Dist: (704) 509-2939
Term Expires: 2017
6129 Sunbridge Court, Charlotte, NC 28269
E-mail: carla.cunningham@ncleg.net
Committees: Aging; Banking; Children, Youth and Families; Education
- Community Colleges; Finance; Public Utilities; Regulatory Reform
Education: Gaston 1996 AS; Winston-Salem State 2009 BSN

Representative **Namon Leo Daughtry** (R-District 26)
Room 1013 . . . . . . . . . . . . . . . . . . . . . . . . . . . . . . . . . (919) 733-5605
Counties Represented: Johnston (part)　　　Res: (919) 934-7265
Term Expires: 2017　　　Fax: (919) 934-9536
5 Lakeview Place, Smithfield, NC 27577
E-mail: leo.daughtry@ncleg.net
Committees: Agriculture; Alcoholic Beverage Control; Appropriations;
Education - Community Colleges; Ethics; Judiciary I; Rules, Calendar
and Operations of the House
Education: Wake Forest 1962 BA, 1965 LLB

Representative **Ted Davis, Jr.** (R-District 19) . . . . . . . . . . . (919) 733-5786
Counties Represented: New Hanover (part)　　　Dist: (910) 763-6249
Term Expires: 2017
PO Box 2535, Wilmington, NC 28402
E-mail: ted.davis@ncleg.net
Committees: Commerce and Job Development; Education -
Universities; Elections; Finance; Judiciary III; Local Government;
Rules, Calendar and Operations of the House; Wildlife Resources

Representative **Jimmy Dixon** (R-District 4) Room 1002 . . . (919) 715-3021
Counties Represented: Duplin (part), Wayne (part)
Term Expires: 2017
E-mail: jimmy.dixon@ncleg.net
Committees: Agriculture; Appropriations; Education - K-12; Elections;
Environment; Insurance; Regulatory Reform

Representative **Josh Dobson** (R-District 85) Room 1006 . . (919) 733-5862
Counties Represented: Avery, McDowell, Mitchell　　　Dist: (828) 442-4370
Term Expires: 2017
E-mail: josh.dobson@ncleg.net
Committees: Alcoholic Beverage Control; Appropriations; Banking;
Education - Community Colleges; Health; Insurance; State Personnel
Education: Gardner-Webb 2005 BA; Appalachian State 2008 MPA

Representative **Nelson Dollar** (R-District 36) . . . . . . . . . . . (919) 715-0795
Counties Represented: Wake (part)　　　Res: (919) 233-8399
Term Expires: 2017
P.O. Box 1369, Cary, NC 27512
E-mail: nelson.dollar@ncleg.net
Committees: Appropriations; Commerce and Job Development;
Finance; Health; Insurance; Judiciary IV; Public Utilities; Regulatory
Reform; Transportation; University Board of Governors Nominating

Representative **Beverly Miller Earle** (D-District 101) . . . . . (919) 715-2530
Counties Represented: Mecklenburg (part)　　　Res: (704) 333-7180
Term Expires: 2017　　　Fax: (704) 372-1994
Legislative Office Building, 300 North Salisbury Street, Room 634,
Raleigh, NC 27603-5925
312 South Clarkson Street, Charlotte, NC 28202
E-mail: beverly.earle@ncleg.net
Committees: Aging; Agriculture; Alcoholic Beverage Control;
Appropriations; Banking; Health; Insurance; Public Utilities

Representative **Jeffrey Elmore** (R-District 94) . . . . . . . . . . (919) 733-5935
Counties Represented: Alleghany, Wilkes (part)
Term Expires: 2017
PO Box 522, North Wilkesboro, NC 28659
E-mail: jeffrey.elmore@ncleg.net
Committees: Appropriations; Education - K-12; Education -
Universities; Pensions and Retirement; Public Utilities; State Personnel

Representative **John Faircloth** (R-District 61) . . . . . . . . . . (919) 733-5877
Counties Represented: Guilford (part)
Term Expires: 2017
300 North Salisbury Street, Room 306A3, Raleigh, NC 27603
E-mail: john.faircloth@ncleg.net
Committees: Appropriations; Elections; Ethics; Judiciary II; Local
Government; Transportation

Representative **Jean Farmer-Butterfield** (D-District 24) . . . (919) 733-5898
Counties Represented: Pitt (part), Wilson (part)　　　Res: (252) 291-0828
Term Expires: 2017　　　Fax: (919) 782-4634
Legislative Office Building, 300 North Salisbury Street, Room 528,
Raleigh, NC 27603-5925
E-mail: jean.farmer-butterfield@ncleg.net
Committees: Appropriations; Education - K-12; Health; Judiciary III;
Local Government

Representative **Susan C. Fisher** (D-District 114) . . . . . . . . (919) 715-2013
Counties Represented: Buncombe (part)　　　Res: (828) 258-5355
Term Expires: 2017
Legislative Office Building, 300 North Salisbury Street, Room 420,
Raleigh, NC 27603-5925
7 Maple Ridge Lane, Asheville, NC 28806
E-mail: susan.fisher@ncleg.net
Committees: Aging; Alcoholic Beverage Control; Appropriations;
Education - K-12; Elections; Local Government

Representative **Elmer Floyd** (D-District 43) . . . . . . . . . . . (919) 733-5959
Counties Represented: Cumberland (part)　　　Tel: (910) 488-6903
Term Expires: 2017
State Legislative Building, 17 West Jones Street, Room 1311,
Raleigh, NC 27601-1096
207 Courtney Street, Fayetteville, NC 28301
E-mail: elmer.floyd@ncleg.net
Committees: Appropriations; Commerce and Job Development;
Elections; Homeland Security, Military, and Veterans Affairs; Local
Government; Rules, Calendar and Operations of the House; State
Personnel

Representative **Carl Ford** (R-District 76) . . . . . . . . . . . . . . (919) 733-5881
Counties Represented: Cabarrus (part), Rowan　　　Dist: (704) 305-3541
(part)
Term Expires: 2017
320 Ketchie Estate Road, China Grove, NC 28023
E-mail: carl.ford@ncleg.net
Committees: Appropriations; Education - Community Colleges;
Elections; Health; Local Government; State Personnel; Transportation

Representative **John Fraley** (R-District 95) . . . . . . . . . . . . . (919) 733-5741
Counties Represented: Iredell (part)
Term Expires: 2017
E-mail: john.fraley@ncleg.net
Committees: Appropriations; Banking; Commerce and Job
Development; Education - Universities; Rules, Calendar and Operations
of the House; Transportation

Representative **Rosa U. Gill** (D-District 33) Room 1305 . . . (919) 733-5880
Counties Represented: Wake (part)　　　Tel: (919) 821-0425
Term Expires: 2017
2408 Foxtrot Road, Raleigh, NC 27610
E-mail: rosa.gill@ncleg.net
Committees: Alcoholic Beverage Control; Appropriations; Children,
Youth and Families; Elections; Insurance; Pensions and Retirement

Representative **Ken Goodman** (D-District 66)
Room 1111 . . . . . . . . . . . . . . . . . . . . . . . . . . . . . . . . . (919) 733-5823
Counties Represented: Hoke (part), Montgomery (part), Richmond
(part), Robeson (part), Scotland (part)
Term Expires: 2017
E-mail: ken.goodman@ncleg.net
Committees: Commerce and Job Development; Education - Community
Colleges; Finance; Health; Regulatory Reform; Rules, Calendar and
Operations of the House; Transportation

Representative **Charles Graham** (D-District 47)
Room 1315 . . . . . . . . . . . . . . . . . . . . . . . . . . . . . . . . . (919) 715-0875
Counties Represented: Robeson (part)
Term Expires: 2017
E-mail: charles.graham@ncleg.net
Committees: Agriculture; Appropriations; Commerce and Job
Development; Education - K-12; Insurance; Local Government;
Transportation

Representative **George W. Graham, Jr.** (D-District 12) . . . (919) 733-5995
Counties Represented: Craven (part), Greene (part),　　　Dist: (252) 527-6865
Lenoir (part)
Term Expires: 2017
PO Box 1082, Kinston, NC 28503
E-mail: george.graham@ncleg.net
Committees: Agriculture; Appropriations; Commerce and Job
Development; Elections; State Personnel
Education: Fayetteville State 1971 BS; North Carolina State 1975 MEd

Representative **Mike Hager** (R-District 112) . . . . . . . . . . . . (919) 733-5749
Counties Represented: Burke (part), Rutherford
Term Expires: 2017
300 North Salisbury Street, Room 306C, Raleigh, NC 27603
E-mail: mike.hager@ncleg.net
Committees: Commerce and Job Development; Environment; Finance;
Health; Judiciary IV; Public Utilities; Regulatory Reform

*(continued on next page)*

LEGISLATIVE BRANCH

**Representatives** *continued*

Representative **Duane R. Hall II** (D-District 11) . . . . . . . . . (919) 733-5755
    Counties Represented: Wake (part)       Dist: (919) 758-2111
    Term Expires: 2017
    4132 Brewster Drive, Raleigh, NC 27606
    E-mail: duane.hall@ncleg.net
    Committees: Appropriations; Education - Community Colleges;
    Judiciary III; Public Utilities; Transportation
    Education: North Carolina State BA; Florida State JD

Representative **Kyle Hall** (R-District 91) . . . . . . . . . . . . . . (919) 733-7928
    Counties Represented: Rockingham (part), Stokes
    Term Expires: 2017
    E-mail: kyle.hall@ncleg.net
    Committees: Appropriations; Commerce and Job Development;
    Insurance; Public Utilities
    Education: North Carolina BA

Representative **Larry Dwight Hall** (D-District 29) . . . . . . . (919) 733-5872
    Counties Represented: Durham (part)       Tel: (919) 682-8823
    Term Expires: 2017                         Fax: (919) 682-3821
    Legislative Office Building, 300 North Salisbury Street, Room 417B,
    Raleigh, NC 27603-5925
    P.O. Box 25308, Durham, NC 27702
    E-mail: larry.hall@ncleg.net
    Committees: Appropriations; Banking; Commerce and Job
    Development; Finance; Health; Homeland Security, Military, and
    Veterans Affairs; Insurance; Judiciary I; Regulatory Reform; Rules,
    Calendar and Operations of the House; University Board of Governors
    Nominating

Representative **Susi Hamilton** (D-District 18)
    Room 1319 . . . . . . . . . . . . . . . . . . . . . . . . . . . . . . . . . (919) 733-5754
    Counties Represented: Brunswick (part), New Hanover (part)
    Term Expires: 2017
    E-mail: susi.hamilton@ncleg.net
    Committees: Commerce and Job Development; Finance; Insurance;
    Judiciary IV; University Board of Governors Nominating

Representative **Edward F. Hanes, Jr.** (D-District 72) . . . . . (919) 733-5829
    Counties Represented: Forsyth (part)       Dist: (919) 632-4084
    Term Expires: 2017
    380-H Knollwood Street, Suite 191, Winston-Salem, NC 27103
    E-mail: edward.hanes@ncleg.net
    Committees: Alcoholic Beverage Control; Banking; Education - K-12;
    Ethics; Finance; Insurance; Public Utilities; Rules, Calendar and
    Operations of the House; University Board of Governors Nominating
    Education: North Carolina, JD; Harvard 1996 EdM

Representative **Jon Hardister** (R-District 59) . . . . . . . . . . . (919) 733-5191
    Counties Represented: Guilford (part)       Dist: (336) 404-8791
    Term Expires: 2017
    1709 Forest Valley Rd, Greensboro, NC 27410
    E-mail: jon.hardister@ncleg.net
    Committees: Alcoholic Beverage Control; Appropriations; Banking;
    Education - K-12; Elections; Judiciary I; Transportation
    Education: Greensboro BA

Representative
**Mary Price "Pricey" Harrison** (D-District 57)
    Room 2119 . . . . . . . . . . . . . . . . . . . . . . . . . . . . . . . . . (919) 733-5771
    Counties Represented: Guilford (part)       Res: (336) 274-5574
    Term Expires: 2017
    P.O. Box 9339, Greensboro, NC 27429-9339
    E-mail: pricey.harrison@ncleg.net
    Committees: Appropriations; Elections; Environment; Judiciary III;
    Public Utilities; Regulatory Reform

Representative **Kelly E. Hastings** (R-District 110)
    Room 2123 . . . . . . . . . . . . . . . . . . . . . . . . . . . . . . . . . (919) 715-2002
    Counties Represented: Cleveland (part), Gaston (part)
    Term Expires: 2017
    E-mail: kelly.hastings@ncleg.net
    Committees: Alcoholic Beverage Control; Education - Universities;
    Finance; Health; Insurance; Judiciary III; Public Utilities; Rules,
    Calendar and Operations of the House; University Board of Governors
    Nominating

Representative **Yvonne Lewis Holley** (D-District 38) . . . . . (919) 733-5758
    Counties Represented: Wake (part)       Dist: (919) 828-3873
    Term Expires: 2017
    1505 Tierney Circle, Raleigh, NC 27610
    E-mail: yvonne.holley@ncleg.net
    Committees: Aging; Agriculture; Alcoholic Beverage Control;
    Commerce and Job Development; Education - Community Colleges;
    Finance; Local Government; Pensions and Retirement; Transportation
    Education: Howard U

Representative **Craig Horn** (R-District 68) Room 1010 . . . . (919) 733-2406
    Counties Represented: Union (part)
    Term Expires: 2017
    E-mail: craig.horn@ncleg.net
    Committees: Appropriations; Children, Youth and Families; Commerce
    and Job Development; Education - K-12; Homeland Security, Military,
    and Veterans Affairs; Insurance; Judiciary III

Representative **Julia Craven Howard** (R-District 79)
    Room 1106 . . . . . . . . . . . . . . . . . . . . . . . . . . . . . . . . . (919) 733-5904
    Counties Represented: Davie, Forsyth (part)       Tel: (336) 751-3538
    Term Expires: 2017                          Fax: (336) 751-7632
    330 South Salisbury Street, Mocksville, NC 27028
    E-mail: julia.howard@ncleg.net
    Committees: Aging; Banking; Commerce and Job Development;
    Finance; Homeland Security, Military, and Veterans Affairs; Insurance;
    Judiciary I

Representative **Howard J. Hunter III** (D-District 5) . . . . . . (919) 733-5780
    Counties Represented: Bertie, Gates, Hertford, Pasquotank (part)
    Term Expires: 2017
    E-mail: howard.hunter@ncleg.net
    Committees: Agriculture; Appropriations; Commerce and Job
    Development; Elections; Judiciary IV; Transportation

Representative **Pat B. Hurley** (R-District 70) . . . . . . . . . . . (919) 733-5865
    Counties Represented: Randolph (part)       Res: (336) 625-9210
    Term Expires: 2017
    300 North Salisbury Street, Room 607, Raleigh, NC 27603-5925
    141 Ridgecrest Road, Asheboro, NC 27203
    E-mail: pat.hurley@ncleg.net
    Committees: Aging; Appropriations; Education - K-12; Judiciary II;
    Pensions and Retirement; State Personnel

Representative **Frank Iler** (R-District 17) . . . . . . . . . . . . . . (919) 301-1450
    Counties Represented: Brunswick (part)       Res: (910) 201-1007
    Term Expires: 2017
    Legislative Office Building, 300 North Salisbury Street, Room 306A2,
    Raleigh, NC 27603-5925
    2515 Marsh Hen Drive, Oak Island, NC 28465
    E-mail: frank.iler@ncleg.net
    Committees: Appropriations; Education - K-12; Elections;
    Environment; Insurance; Transportation

Representative **Verla C. Insko** (D-District 56) . . . . . . . . . . . (919) 733-7208
    Counties Represented: Orange (part)       Res: (919) 929-6115
    Term Expires: 2017
    Legislative Office Building, 300 North Salisbury Street, Room 307B1,
    Raleigh, NC 27603-5925
    610 Surry Road, Chapel Hill, NC 27514
    E-mail: verla.insko@ncleg.net
    Committees: Appropriations; Education - Universities; Environment;
    Health; Insurance; Judiciary III; State Personnel
    Education: Cal State (Fresno) 1959 AB; North Carolina 1993 MPA

Representative **Darren G. Jackson** (D-District 39) . . . . . . . (919) 733-5974
    Counties Represented: Wake (part)
    Term Expires: 2017
    Legislative Office Building, 300 North Salisbury Street, Room 301N,
    Raleigh, NC 27603-5925
    E-mail: darren.jackson@ncleg.net
    Committees: Appropriations; Commerce and Job Development;
    Education - Universities; Elections; Ethics; Insurance; Judiciary I;
    Rules, Calendar and Operations of the House
    Education: North Carolina; Duke JD

Representative **Charles Jeter** (R-District 92) . . . . . . . . . . . (919) 733-5654
    Counties Represented: Mecklenburg (part)       Dist: (704) 895-4884
    Term Expires: 2017
    15806 Brookway Drive, Suite 600, Huntersville, NC 28078
    E-mail: charles.jeter@ncleg.net
    Committees: Alcoholic Beverage Control; Banking; Children, Youth
    and Families; Finance; Local Government; Transportation; Wildlife
    Resources

Representative **Linda P. Johnson** (R-District 83)
    Room 1006 . . . . . . . . . . . . . . . . . . . . . . . . . . . . . . . . . (919) 733-5861
    Counties Represented: Cabarrus (part)       Res: (704) 932-1376
    Term Expires: 2017
    1205 Berkshire Drive, Kannapolis, NC 28081
    E-mail: linda.johnson2@ncleg.net
    Committees: Appropriations; Children, Youth and Families; Education -
    Community Colleges; Education - K-12; Education - Universities;
    Finance; Insurance; Judiciary I; Public Utilities; Rules, Calendar and
    Operations of the House

Representative **Bert Jones** (R-District 65) . . . . . . . . . . . . . (919) 733-5779
Counties Represented: Caswell, Rockingham (part)
Term Expires: 2017
300 North Salisbury Street, Room 306A1, Raleigh, NC 27603
E-mail: bert.jones@ncleg.net
Committees: Agriculture; Education - K-12; Elections; Finance; Health;
Judiciary IV; Regulatory Reform

Representative **Jonathan C. Jordan** (R-District 93) . . . . . . (919) 733-7727
Counties Represented: Ashe, Watauga
Term Expires: 2017
300 North Salisbury Street, Room 418C, Raleigh, NC 27603
P. O. Box 744, Jefferson, NC 28640
E-mail: jonathan.jordan@ncleg.net
Committees: Aging; Banking; Children, Youth and Families; Education
- Universities; Finance; Judiciary II; Regulatory Reform; University
Board of Governors Nominating

Representative **Donny C. Lambeth** (R-District 75) . . . . . . . (919) 733-5747
Counties Represented: Forsyth (part)          Dist: (336) 788-1041
Term Expires: 2017
4627 South Main Street, Winston-Salem, NC 27127
E-mail: donny.lambeth@ncleg.net
Committees: Aging; Appropriations; Education - K-12; Health;
Insurance; State Personnel
Education: High Point; Wake Forest MBA

Representative **James H. Langdon, Jr.** (R-District 28) . . . . (919) 733-5849
Counties Represented: Johnston (part)         Res: (919) 894-5797
Term Expires: 2017                            Fax: (919) 894-1464
Legislative Office Building, 300 North Salisbury Street, Room 610,
Raleigh, NC 27603-5925
10176 NC 50 Highway North, Angier, NC 27501
E-mail: james.langdon@ncleg.net
Committees: Agriculture; Appropriations; Education - K-12; Insurance;
Local Government; Pensions and Retirement; State Personnel; Wildlife
Resources
Education: North Carolina State 1960 BS, 1968 MEd

Representative **David R. Lewis** (R-District 53) . . . . . . . . . . (919) 715-3015
Counties Represented: Harnett (part)          Tel: (910) 892-6171
Term Expires: 2017                            Fax: (910) 892-4689
Legislative Office Building, 300 North Salisbury Street, Room 533,
Raleigh, NC 27603-5925
E-mail: david.lewis@ncleg.net
Committees: Agriculture; Alcoholic Beverage Control; Appropriations;
Commerce and Job Development; Education - Universities; Elections;
Finance; Health; Rules, Calendar and Operations of the House;
University Board of Governors Nominating

Representative **Marvin W. Lucas** (D-District 42) . . . . . . . . (919) 733-5775
Counties Represented: Cumberland (part)       Res: (910) 497-2733
Term Expires: 2017
Legislative Office Building, 300 North Salisbury Street, Room 417A,
Raleigh, NC 27603-5925
3318 Hedgemoor Circle, Spring Lake, NC 28390
E-mail: marvin.lucas@ncleg.net
Committees: Agriculture; Alcoholic Beverage Control; Appropriations;
Health; Homeland Security, Military, and Veterans Affairs; Insurance;
Wildlife Resources
Education: Fayetteville State 1964 BS;
North Carolina Central 1975 MA; East Carolina 1977 EdS

Representative **Paul Luebke** (D-District 30) . . . . . . . . . . . . (919) 733-7663
Counties Represented: Durham (part)           Res: (919) 286-0269
Term Expires: 2017
Legislative Office Building, 300 North Salisbury Street, Room 529,
Raleigh, NC 27603-5925
E-mail: paul.luebke@ncleg.net
Committees: Education - K-12; Environment; Finance; Local
Government; Public Utilities
Education: Valparaiso 1966 BA; Columbia 1975 PhD

Representative **Chris Malone** (R-District 35) . . . . . . . . . . . (919) 715-3010
Counties Represented: Wake (part)             Dist: (919) 395-4903
Term Expires: 2017
PO Box 967, Wake Forest, NC 27588
E-mail: chris.malone@ncleg.net
Committees: Alcoholic Beverage Control; Appropriations; Banking;
Commerce and Job Development; Education - K-12; Public Utilities;
Wildlife Resources
Education: St Mary Plains 1982 BA

Representative **Grier Martin** (D-District 34) Room 1023 . . . (919) 733-5773
Counties Represented: Wake (part)
Term Expires: 2017
E-mail: grier.martin@ncleg.net
Committees: Banking; Education - Community Colleges; Environment;
Homeland Security, Military, and Veterans Affairs; Judiciary I

Representative **Susan Martin** (R-District 8) . . . . . . . . . . . . (919) 715-3023
Counties Represented: Pitt (part), Wilson (part)    Dist: (252) 285-2060
Term Expires: 2017
1407 Kenan Street Northwest, Wilson, NC 27893
E-mail: susan.martin@ncleg.net
Committees: Agriculture; Appropriations; Commerce and Job
Development; Education - Universities; Elections; Finance; Health;
Homeland Security, Military, and Veterans Affairs; Public Utilities
Education: Richmond MBA

Representative **Patricia "Pat" McElraft** (R-District 13) . . . . (919) 733-6275
Counties Represented: Carteret, Jones         Tel: (252) 342-0693
Term Expires: 2017
Legislative Office Building, 300 North Salisbury Street, Room 603,
Raleigh, NC 27603-5925
P.O. Box 4477, Emerald Isle, NC 28594
E-mail: pat.mcelraft@ncleg.net
Committees: Appropriations; Commerce and Job Development;
Environment; Ethics; Insurance; Regulatory Reform; State Personnel

Representative **Chuck McGrady** (R-District 117) . . . . . . . . (919) 733-5956
Counties Represented: Henderson (part)
Term Expires: 2017
300 North Salisbury Street, Room 418A, Raleigh, NC 27603
E-mail: chuck.mcgrady@ncleg.net
Committees: Agriculture; Alcoholic Beverage Control; Appropriations;
Commerce and Job Development; Education - Universities;
Environment; Ethics; Judiciary II; Transportation; Wildlife Resources

Representative **Allen McNeill** (R-District 78) . . . . . . . . . . . (919) 715-4946
Counties Represented: Moore (part), Randolph      Dist: (336) 302-0263
(part)                                            Fax: (336) 629-2603
Term Expires: 2017
4172 NC Highway 49 South, Asheboro, NC 27205
E-mail: allen.mcneill@ncleg.net
Committees: Appropriations; Commerce and Job Development;
Education - Community Colleges; Judiciary I; Pensions and Retirement;
State Personnel; Transportation

Representative **Graig R. Meyer** (D-District 50) . . . . . . . . . . (919) 715-3019
Counties Represented: Durham (part), Orange (part)    Dist: (919) 967-6253
Term Expires: 2017
9603 Leslie Drive, Chapel Hill, NC 27516
E-mail: graig.meyer@ncleg.net
Committees: Aging; Education - K-12; Finance; Homeland Security,
Military, and Veterans Affairs; Public Utilities; Regulatory Reform

Representative
**Henry M. "Mickey" Michaux, Jr.** (D-District 31)
State Legislative Office Building, Room 1227 . . . . . . . . . (919) 715-2528
Counties Represented: Durham (part)           Tel: (919) 596-8181
Term Expires: 2017                            Fax: (919) 596-8183
P.O. Box 2152, Durham, NC 27702-2152
E-mail: mickey.michaux@ncleg.net
Committees: Appropriations; Education - Universities; Elections;
Judiciary II; Pensions and Retirement; State Personnel
Education: North Carolina Central 1952 BS, 1964 JD

Representative **Christopher W. Millis, PE** (R-District 16) . . (919) 715-9664
Counties Represented: Onslow (part), Pender       Dist: (910) 352-1740
Term Expires: 2017
PO Box 878, Hampstead, NC 28443
E-mail: chris.millis@ncleg.net
Committees: Appropriations; Commerce and Job Development;
Environment; Homeland Security, Military, and Veterans Affairs; Public
Utilities; Regulatory Reform
Education: North Carolina State 2005 BS

Representative **Rodney W. Moore** (D-District 99)
Room 1211 . . . . . . . . . . . . . . . . . . . . . . . . . . . . . . . . . (919) 733-5606
Counties Represented: Mecklenburg (part)
Term Expires: 2017
E-mail: rodney.moore@ncleg.net
Committees: Banking; Commerce and Job Development; Education
- Universities; Finance; Public Utilities; Regulatory Reform;
Transportation

Representative **Tim K. Moore** (R-District 111) . . . . . . . . . . (919) 733-4838
Counties Represented: Cleveland (part)        Tel: (704) 739-1221
Term Expires: 2017                            Fax: (704) 739-5051
Legislative Office Building, 300 North Salisbury Street, Room 604,
Raleigh, NC 27603-5925
E-mail: tim.moore@ncleg.net

Representative **Gregory F. Murphy** (R-District 9) . . . . . . . . (919) 733-5757
Counties Represented: Pitt (part)
E-mail: gregory.murphy@ncleg.net
Committees: Appropriations; Education - Universities; Health;
Transportation; University Board of Governors Nominating
Education: Davidson 1985

*(continued on next page)*

**LEGISLATIVE BRANCH**

**LEGISLATIVE BRANCH**

**Representatives** *continued*

Representative
**BG Gary H. Pendleton, USAR (Ret)** (R-District 49) .... (919) 733-5860
Counties Represented: Wake (part)              Dist: (919) 781-0995
Term Expires: 2017
300 North Salisbury Street, Room 602, Raleigh, NC 27603-5925
2908 Lake Boone Place, Raleigh, NC 27608
E-mail: gary.pendleton@ncleg.net
Committees: Appropriations; Banking; Health; Homeland Security,
Military, and Veterans Affairs; Insurance; Local Government; State
Personnel

Representative **Garland E. Pierce** (D-District 48) ....... (919) 733-5803
Counties Represented: Hoke (part), Richmond       Res: (910) 369-2844
(part), Robeson (part), Scotland (part)           Fax: (910) 369-2074
Term Expires: 2017
Legislative Office Building, 300 North Salisbury Street, Room 301 C,
Raleigh, NC 27603-5925
21981 Buie Street, Wagram, NC 28396
E-mail: garland.pierce@ncleg.net
Committees: Appropriations; Banking; Children, Youth and Families;
Commerce and Job Development; Homeland Security, Military, and
Veterans Affairs; Insurance

Representative **Larry Pittman, CCS** (R-District 82)
Room 1321 ............................................ (919) 715-2009
Counties Represented: Cabarrus (part)         Dist: (919) 782-3528
Term Expires: 2017
P.O. Box 5959, Concord, NC 28027
E-mail: larry.pittman@ncleg.net
Committees: Aging; Agriculture; Appropriations; Education - K-12;
Homeland Security, Military, and Veterans Affairs; Wildlife Resources

Representative **Michele D. Presnell** (R-District 118) ...... (919) 733-5732
Counties Represented: Haywood (part), Madison,    Dist: (828) 682-6342
Yancey
Term Expires: 2017
316 Woodstock Drive, Burnville, NC 28714
E-mail: michele.presnell@ncleg.net
Committees: Agriculture; Appropriations; Commerce and Job
Development; Transportation; Wildlife Resources

Representative **Joe Sam Queen** (D-District 119) ........ (919) 715-3005
Counties Represented: Haywood (part), Jackson,    Dist: (828) 452-4286
Swain
Term Expires: 2017
209 Hillview Circle, Waynesville, NC 28786
E-mail: joe.queen@ncleg.net
Committees: Aging; Agriculture; Appropriations; Judiciary II;
Regulatory Reform; Transportation
Education: North Carolina State 1972 BS, 1974 MS

Representative **Robert T. Reives II** (D-District 54)
Room 1319 ............................................ (919) 733-7928
Counties Represented: Chatham, Lee (part)
Term Expires: 2017
1502 Woodland Avenue, Sanford, NC 27330
E-mail: robert.reives@ncleg.net
Committees: Agriculture; Education - Community Colleges; Finance;
Homeland Security, Military, and Veterans Affairs; Judiciary II; Rules,
Calendar and Operations of the House

Representative **Bobbie Richardson** (D-District 7) ........ (919) 715-3032
Counties Represented: Franklin (part), Nash (part)   Dist: (919) 853-3617
Term Expires: 2017
7309 North Carolina Highway 561, Louisburg, NC 27549
E-mail: bobbie.richardson@ncleg.net
Committees: Appropriations; Commerce and Job Development;
Education - K-12; Elections; Judiciary IV

Representative
**William O. "Billy" Richardson** (D-District 44)
Room 1021 ............................................ (919) 733-5601
Counties Represented: Cumberland (part)        Dist: (910) 867-0371
3694 Glenbarry Place, Fayetteville, NC 28314
E-mail: william.richardson@ncleg.net
Committees: Education - K-12; Insurance; Judiciary II
Education: North Carolina 1977 BA; Campbell 1980 JD

Representative **Dennis Patrick Riddell** (R-District 64) .... (919) 733-5905
Counties Represented: Alamance (part)         Dist: (336) 222-1303
Term Expires: 2017
6343 Beale Road, Snow Hill, NC 27349
E-mail: dennis.riddell@ncleg.net
Committees: Agriculture; Appropriations; Children, Youth and Families;
Education - K-12; Elections; Judiciary IV; Public Utilities; Regulatory
Reform
Education: Cal Maritime Acad 1978 BS; Bob Jones U 1983 MA

Representative **George S. Robinson** (R-District 87) ...... (919) 733-5931
Counties Represented: Caldwell
Term Expires: 2017
E-mail: george.robinson@ncleg.net
Committees: Commerce and Job Development; Education - Community
Colleges; Finance; Judiciary I; Rules, Calendar and Operations of the
House; Transportation

Representative **Stephen M. Ross** (R-District 63) ......... (919) 733-5820
Counties Represented: Alamance (part)         Dist: (336) 269-3704
Term Expires: 2017
1314 McCuiston Drive, Burlington, NC 27215
E-mail: stephen.ross@ncleg.net
Committees: Banking; Commerce and Job Development; Finance;
Judiciary II; Local Government; Pensions and Retirement;
Transportation
Education: Elon U 1973 BA; North Carolina State

Representative **Jason Saine** (R-District 97) ............. (919) 733-5782
Counties Represented: Lincoln                  Dist: (704) 479-1803
Term Expires: 2017
7465 Bluff Point Lane, Denver, NC 28037
E-mail: jason.saine@ncleg.net
Committees: Alcoholic Beverage Control; Appropriations; Commerce
and Job Development; Elections; Finance; Health; Judiciary II; Rules,
Calendar and Operations of the House

Representative **Brad Salmon** (D-District 51) ............. (919) 715-3026
Counties Represented: Harnett (part), Lee (part)
Term Expires: 2017
E-mail: brad.salmon@ncleg.net
Committees: Agriculture; Appropriations; Children, Youth and Families;
Judiciary II

Representative
**Jacqueline Michelle Schaffer** (R-District 105) ........ (919) 733-5886
Counties Represented: Mecklenburg (part)
Term Expires: 2017
12113 Shoal Creek Court, Charlotte, NC 28277
E-mail: jacqueline.schaffer@ncleg.net
Committees: Commerce and Job Development; Elections; Ethics;
Finance; Homeland Security, Military, and Veterans Affairs; Judiciary
IV; Regulatory Reform; Rules, Calendar and Operations of the House;
Transportation
Education: Meredith BA; Regent U JD

Representative **Mitchell S. Setzer** (R-District 89)
State Legislative Office Building, Room 1023 .......... (919) 733-5773
Counties Represented: Catawba (part)          Res: (828) 241-3570
Term Expires: 2017                            Fax: (828) 241-2382
P.O. Box 416, Catawba, NC 28609
E-mail: mitchell.setzer@ncleg.net
Committees: Aging; Ethics; Finance; Health; Insurance; Judiciary IV;
Local Government

Representative
**Christopher "Chris" Sgro** (D-District 58) Room 1317 .. (919) 733-5902
Counties Represented: Guilford (part)
Term Expires: 2017
E-mail: chris.sgro@ncleg.net
Committees: Appropriations; Children, Youth and Families; Commerce
and Job Development; Education - K-12; Homeland Security, Military,
and Veterans Affairs
Education: American U

Representative **Phillip R. "Phil" Shepard** (R-District 15) .. (919) 715-9644
Counties Represented: Onslow (part)
Term Expires: 2017
300 North Salisbury Street, Room 301H, Raleigh, NC 27603
E-mail: phil.shepard@ncleg.net
Committees: Commerce and Job Development;
Education - Community Colleges; Homeland Security, Military, and
Veterans Affairs; Insurance; Transportation

Representative **Michael Speciale** (R-District 3) .......... (919) 733-5853
Counties Represented: Beaufort (part), Craven     Dist: (252) 635-5326
(part), Pamlico
Term Expires: 2017
803 Stately Pines Road, New Bern, NC 28560
E-mail: michael.speciale@ncleg.net
Committees: Appropriations; Elections; Homeland Security, Military,
and Veterans Affairs; Judiciary III; Regulatory Reform; Transportation

Representative **Paul Stam** (R-District 37) . . . . . . . . . . . . . . (919) 733-2962
  Counties Represented: Wake (part)                Tel: (919) 362-8873
  Term Expires: 2017                               Fax: (919) 387-1171
  Legislative Office Building, 300 North Salisbury Street, Room 613,
  Raleigh, NC 27603-5925
  P.O. Box 1600, Apex, NC 27502
  E-mail: paul.stam@ncleg.net
  Committees: Appropriations; Children, Youth and Families; Education -
  K-12; Elections; Finance; Judiciary II; Regulatory Reform; Rules,
  Calendar and Operations of the House

Representative **Bob Steinburg** (R-District 1) . . . . . . . . . . . (919) 733-0010
  Counties Represented: Camden, Chowan, Currituck,    Dist: (252) 482-2404
  Pasquotank (part), Perquimans, Tyrrell
  Term Expires: 2017
  103 South Granville Street, Edenton, NC 37932
  E-mail: bob.steinburg@ncleg.net
  Committees: Agriculture; Commerce and Job Development;
  Environment; Finance; Judiciary I; Transportation; Wildlife Resources
  Education: Upper Iowa 1990 BA

Representative **Sarah Stevens** (R-District 90) . . . . . . . . . . (919) 715-1883
  Counties Represented: Surry, Wilkes (part)        Tel: (336) 789-0639
  Term Expires: 2017
  Legislative Office Building, 300 North Salisbury Street, Room 509,
  Raleigh, NC 27603-5925
  2161 Margaret Drive, Mount Airy, NC 27030
  E-mail: sarah.stevens@ncleg.net
  Committees: Appropriations; Children, Youth and Families; Education -
  Community Colleges; Environment; Judiciary III; Regulatory Reform;
  State Personnel

Representative **John Szoka** (R-District 45) . . . . . . . . . . . . . (919) 733-9892
  Counties Represented: Cumberland (part)           Dist: (910) 583-2960
  Term Expires: 2017
  6922 Surrey Road, Fayetteville, NC 28306
  E-mail: john.szoka@ncleg.net
  Committees: Banking; Commerce and Job Development; Education -
  Community Colleges; Elections; Finance; Health; Homeland Security,
  Military, and Veterans Affairs; Judiciary I; Local Government; Rules,
  Calendar and Operations of the House

Representative **Evelyn A. Terry** (D-District 71) . . . . . . . . . (919) 733-5777
  Counties Represented: Forsyth (part)              Dist: (336) 788-5008
  Term Expires: 2017
  1224 Reynolds Forest Drive, Winston-Salem, NC 27107
  E-mail: evelyn.terry@ncleg.net
  Committees: Appropriations; Banking; Children, Youth and Families;
  Commerce and Job Development; Ethics; Judiciary IV; Transportation
  Education: Johnson C Smith BA; Appalachian State MA

Representative **Paul Tine** (I-District 6) . . . . . . . . . . . . . . . . (919) 733-5906
  Counties Represented: Beaufort (part), Dare, Hyde,    Dist: (252) 305-5133
  Washington
  Term Expires: 2017
  3040 Creek Road, Kitty Hawk, NC 27949
  E-mail: paul.tine@ncleg.net
  Committees: Alcoholic Beverage Control; Appropriations; Commerce
  and Job Development; Education - Community Colleges; Insurance;
  Judiciary IV; Rules, Calendar and Operations of the House;
  Transportation; Wildlife Resources
  Education: James Madison

Representative **John A. Torbett** (R-District 108) . . . . . . . . (919) 733-5868
  Counties Represented: Gaston (part)
  Term Expires: 2017
  300 North Salisbury Street, Room 537, Raleigh, NC 27603
  E-mail: john.torbett@ncleg.net
  Committees: Appropriations; Commerce and Job Development;
  Elections; Judiciary IV; Rules, Calendar and Operations of the House;
  Transportation

Representative **Brian Turner** (D-District 116) . . . . . . . . . . . (919) 715-3012
  Counties Represented: Buncombe (part)
  Term Expires: 2017
  E-mail: brian.turner@ncleg.net
  Committees: Appropriations; Homeland Security, Military, and Veterans
  Affairs

Representative **Rena W. Turner** (R-District 84) . . . . . . . . . (919) 733-5661
  Counties Represented: Iredell (part)              Dist: (704) 876-4948
  Term Expires: 2017
  247 Gethsemane Road, Olin, NC 28660
  E-mail: rena.turner@ncleg.net
  Committees: Aging; Agriculture; Appropriations; Education - K-12;
  Judiciary III; State Personnel; Transportation
  Education: Lenoir-Rhyne BA, MA

Representative **Ken Waddell** (D-District 46) Room 1311 . . (919) 733-5821
  Counties Represented: Bladen (part), Columbus,    Dist: (910) 654-3734
  Robeson (part)
  Term Expires: 2017
  E-mail: ken.waddell@ncleg.net
  Committees: Agriculture; Education - Community Colleges; Finance;
  Health; Pensions and Retirement; State Personnel; Transportation;
  Wildlife Resources
  Education: North Carolina State 1975 BS, 1985 MAgr

Representative **Harry Warren** (R-District 77) . . . . . . . . . . . (919) 733-5784
  Counties Represented: Rowan (part)
  Term Expires: 2017
  300 North Salisbury Street, Room 533, Raleigh, NC 27603
  E-mail: harry.warren@ncleg.net
  Committees: Aging; Elections; Finance; Insurance; Judiciary IV; Local
  Government; Public Utilities

Representative **Sam Watford** (R-District 80) . . . . . . . . . . . (919) 715-2526
  Counties Represented: Davidson (part)
  Term Expires: 2017
  E-mail: sam.watford@ncleg.net
  Committees: Agriculture; Appropriations; Children, Youth and Families;
  Education - Community Colleges; Local Government; Public Utilities

Representative **Roger West** (R-District 120)
  State Legislative Office Building, Room 1004 . . . . . . . . . (919) 733-5859
  Counties Represented: Cherokee, Clay, Graham,     Res: (828) 837-5246
  Macon                                             Fax: (828) 837-3776
  Term Expires: 2017
  P.O. Box 160, Marble, NC 28905
  E-mail: roger.west@ncleg.net
  Committees: Agriculture; Alcoholic Beverage Control; Appropriations;
  Environment; Homeland Security, Military, and Veterans Affairs;
  Wildlife Resources

Representative **Chris Whitmire** (R-District 113)
  Room 537 . . . . . . . . . . . . . . . . . . . . . . . . . . . . (919) 715-4466
  Counties Represented: Henderson (part), Polk,     Dist: (828) 862-4273
  Transylvania
  Term Expires: 2017
  E-mail: chris.whitmire@ncleg.net
  Committees: Agriculture; Appropriations; Education - K-12; Homeland
  Security, Military, and Veterans Affairs; Regulatory Reform; State
  Personnel
  Education: Air Force Acad 1990 BS; Columbia 1991 MS

Representative **Shelly Willingham** (D-District 23) . . . . . . . (919) 715-3024
  Counties Represented: Edgecombe, Martin
  Term Expires: 2017
  E-mail: shelly.willingham@ncleg.net
  Committees: Agriculture; Alcoholic Beverage Control; Banking;
  Education - Universities; Elections; Judiciary IV

Representative **Michael H. Wray** (D-District 27) . . . . . . . . (919) 733-5662
  Counties Represented: Halifax, Northampton        Res: (252) 535-3297
  Term Expires: 2017                                Fax: (252) 537-9456
  Legislative Office Building, 300 North Salisbury Street, Room 405,
  Raleigh, NC 27603-5925
  P.O. Box 904, Gaston, NC 27832
  E-mail: michael.wray@ncleg.net
  Committees: Appropriations; Commerce and Job Development;
  Education - Universities; Ethics; Health; Insurance; Public Utilities;
  Rules, Calendar and Operations of the House; Wildlife Resources

Representative **Larry Yarborough** (R-District 2) . . . . . . . . . (919) 715-0850
  Counties Represented: Granville (part), Person
  Term Expires: 2017
  E-mail: larry.yarborough@ncleg.net
  Committees: Agriculture; Alcoholic Beverage Control; Appropriations;
  Commerce and Job Development; Environment; Health; Transportation

Representative **Lee Zachary** (R-District 73) . . . . . . . . . . . . . (919) 715-8361
  Counties Represented: Alexander, Wilkes (part), Yadkin
  Term Expires: 2017
  E-mail: lee.zachary@ncleg.net
  Committees: Agriculture; Alcoholic Beverage Control; Banking;
  Finance; Judiciary III; Transportation; Wildlife Resources

**LEGISLATIVE BRANCH**

# House Standing Committees

## Aging

Legislative Office Building, Room 423, Raleigh, NC 27601-1096

**Majority Members**
Pat B. Hurley (R-70) *Chair*
Rena W. Turner (R-84) *Chair*
Debra Conrad (R-74)
Julia Craven Howard (R-79)
Jonathan C. Jordan (R-93)
Donny C. Lambeth (R-75)
Larry Pittman (R-82)
Mitchell S. Setzer (R-89)
Harry Warren (R-77)

**Minority Members**
Susan C. Fisher (D-114) *Vice Chair*
Yvonne Lewis Holley (D-38)
   *Vice Chair*
Joe Sam Queen (D-119) *Vice Chair*
Carla D. Cunningham (D-106)
Beverly Miller Earle (D-101)
Graig R. Meyer (D-50)

## Agriculture

Legislative Office Building, Room 1228, Raleigh, NC 27601-1096

**Majority Members**
Mark Brody (R-55) *Chair*
Jimmy Dixon (R-4) *Chair*
James H. Langdon, Jr. (R-28) *Chair*
Bob Steinburg (R-1) *Chair*
Larry Yarborough (R-2) *Vice Chair*
Lee Zachary (R-73) *Vice Chair*
John R. Bell IV (R-10)
John R. Bradford III (R-98)
George G. Cleveland (R-14)
Jeffrey L. "Jeff" Collins (R-25)
Namon Leo Daughtry (R-26)
Bert Jones (R-65)
David R. Lewis (R-53)
Susan Martin (R-8)
Chuck McGrady (R-117)
Larry Pittman (R-82)
Michele D. Presnell (R-118)
Dennis Patrick Riddell (R-64)
Rena W. Turner (R-84)
Sam Watford (R-80)
Roger West (R-120)
Chris Whitmire (R-113)

**Minority Members**
William D. Brisson (D-22)
   *Vice Chair*
Charles Graham (D-47) *Vice Chair*
George W. Graham, Jr. (D-12)
   *Vice Chair*
Marvin W. Lucas (D-42) *Vice Chair*
John Ager (D-115)
Larry M. Bell (D-21)
Cecil Antonio Brockman (D-60)
Beverly Miller Earle (D-101)
Yvonne Lewis Holley (D-38)
Howard J. Hunter III (D-5)
Joe Sam Queen (D-119)
Robert T. Reives II (D-54)
Brad Salmon (D-51)
Ken Waddell (D-46)
Shelly Willingham (D-23)

## Alcoholic Beverage Control

Legislative Office Building, Room 423, Raleigh, NC 27601-1096

**Majority Members**
James L. "Jamie" Boles, Jr. (R-52)
   *Chair*
Jon Hardister (R-59) *Chair*
Kelly E. Hastings (R-110)
   *Vice Chair*
Charles Jeter (R-92) *Vice Chair*
Jeffrey L. "Jeff" Collins (R-25)
Namon Leo Daughtry (R-26)
Josh Dobson (R-85)
David R. Lewis (R-53)
Chris Malone (R-35)
Chuck McGrady (R-117)
Jason Saine (R-97)
Roger West (R-120)
Larry Yarborough (R-2)
Lee Zachary (R-73)
Paul Tine (I-6)

**Minority Members**
Kelly M. Alexander, Jr. (D-107)
   *Vice Chair*
Marvin W. Lucas (D-42) *Vice Chair*
Beverly Miller Earle (D-101)
Susan C. Fisher (D-114)
Rosa U. Gill (D-33)
Edward F. Hanes, Jr. (D-72)
Yvonne Lewis Holley (D-38)
Shelly Willingham (D-23)

## Appropriations

Legislative Office Building, Room 643, Raleigh, NC 27601-1096

**Majority Members**
Nelson Dollar (R-36) *Senior Chair*
Linda P. Johnson (R-83) *Chair*
Donny C. Lambeth (R-75) *Chair*
Chuck McGrady (R-117) *Chair*
Dean Arp (R-69) *Vice Chair*
Marilyn Avila (R-40) *Vice Chair*
Hugh Blackwell (R-86) *Vice Chair*
James L. "Jamie" Boles, Jr. (R-52)
   *Vice Chair*
William "Bill" Brawley (R-103)
   *Vice Chair*

**Minority Members**
William D. Brisson (D-22)
   *Vice Chair*
Gale Adcock (D-41)
John Ager (D-115)
Nathan A. Baskerville (D-32)
Larry M. Bell (D-21)
Cecil Antonio Brockman (D-60)
Beverly Miller Earle (D-101)
Jean Farmer-Butterfield (D-24)
Susan C. Fisher (D-114)
Elmer Floyd (D-43)

**Majority Members** *continued*
Rayne Brown (R-81) *Vice Chair*
Robert P. "Rob" Bryan III (R-88)
   *Vice Chair*
Justin P. Burr (R-67) *Vice Chair*
George G. Cleveland (R-14)
   *Vice Chair*
Namon Leo Daughtry (R-26)
   *Vice Chair*
Jimmy Dixon (R-4) *Vice Chair*
John Faircloth (R-61) *Vice Chair*
Craig Horn (R-68) *Vice Chair*
Pat B. Hurley (R-70) *Vice Chair*
Frank Iler (R-17) *Vice Chair*
Chris Malone (R-35) *Vice Chair*
Patricia "Pat" McElraft (R-13)
   *Vice Chair*
Michele D. Presnell (R-118)
   *Vice Chair*
Dennis Patrick Riddell (R-64)
   *Vice Chair*
Jason Saine (R-97) *Vice Chair*
Phillip R. "Phil" Shepard (R-15)
   *Vice Chair*
Paul Tine (I-6) *Vice Chair*
John A. Torbett (R-108) *Vice Chair*
Roger West (R-120) *Vice Chair*
Mark Brody (R-55)
Dana Bumgardner (R-109)
Rick Catlin (R-20)
Debra Conrad (R-74)
Josh Dobson (R-85)
Jeffrey Elmore (R-94)
Carl Ford (R-76)
John Fraley (R-95)
Kyle Hall (R-91)
Jon Hardister (R-59)
James H. Langdon, Jr. (R-28)
David R. Lewis (R-53)
Susan Martin (R-8)
Allen McNeill (R-78)
Christopher W. Millis (R-16)
Gregory F. Murphy (R-9)
BG Gary H. Pendleton (R-49)
Larry Pittman (R-82)
Michael Speciale (R-3)
Paul Stam (R-37)
Sarah Stevens (R-90)
Rena W. Turner (R-84)
Sam Watford (R-80)
Chris Whitmire (R-113)
Larry Yarborough (R-2)

**Minority Members** *continued*
Rosa U. Gill (D-33)
Charles Graham (D-47)
George W. Graham, Jr. (D-12)
Duane R. Hall II (D-11)
Larry Dwight Hall (D-29)
Mary Price "Pricey" Harrison
   (D-57)
Howard J. Hunter III (D-5)
Verla C. Insko (D-56)
Darren G. Jackson (D-39)
Marvin W. Lucas (D-42)
Henry M. "Mickey" Michaux, Jr.
   (D-31)
Garland E. Pierce (D-48)
Joe Sam Queen (D-119)
Bobbie Richardson (D-7)
Brad Salmon (D-51)
Christopher "Chris" Sgro (D-58)
Evelyn A. Terry (D-71)
Brian Turner (D-116)
Michael H. Wray (D-27)

## Banking

Legislative Office Building, Room 1327, Raleigh, NC 27601-1096

**Majority Members**
Julia Craven Howard (R-79) *Chair*
Charles Jeter (R-92) *Chair*
J. Daniel "Dan" Bishop (R-104)
   *Vice Chair*
John Fraley (R-95) *Vice Chair*
John R. Bell IV (R-10)
John M. Blust (R-62)
John R. Bradford III (R-98)
Robert P. "Rob" Bryan III (R-88)
Dana Bumgardner (R-109)
Josh Dobson (R-85)
Jon Hardister (R-59)
Jonathan C. Jordan (R-93)
Chris Malone (R-35)
BG Gary H. Pendleton (R-49)
Stephen M. Ross (R-63)
John Szoka (R-45)
Lee Zachary (R-73)

**Minority Members**
Larry Dwight Hall (D-29)
   *Vice Chair*
Becky Carney (D-102)
Carla D. Cunningham (D-106)
Beverly Miller Earle (D-101)
Edward F. Hanes, Jr. (D-72)
Grier Martin (D-34)
Rodney W. Moore (D-99)
Garland E. Pierce (D-48)
Evelyn A. Terry (D-71)
Shelly Willingham (D-23)

## Children, Youth and Families
Legislative Office Building, Room 421, Raleigh, NC 27601-1096

**Majority Members**
Jonathan C. Jordan (R-93) *Chair*
Sarah Stevens (R-90) *Chair*
Jay Adams (R-96)
Marilyn Avila (R-40)
Craig Horn (R-68)
Charles Jeter (R-92)
Linda P. Johnson (R-83)
Dennis Patrick Riddell (R-64)
Paul Stam (R-37)
Sam Watford (R-80)

**Minority Members**
Tricia Ann Cotham (D-100)
 *Vice Chair*
John Ager (D-115)
Carla D. Cunningham (D-106)
Rosa U. Gill (D-33)
Garland E. Pierce (D-48)
Brad Salmon (D-51)
Christopher "Chris" Sgro (D-58)
Evelyn A. Terry (D-71)

## Commerce and Job Development
Legislative Office Building, Room 1228, Raleigh, NC 27601-1096

**Majority Members**
Debra Conrad (R-74) *Chair*
Michele D. Presnell (R-118) *Chair*
George S. Robinson (R-87) *Chair*
Stephen M. Ross (R-63) *Chair*
John R. Bradford III (R-98)
 *Vice Chair*
John Fraley (R-95) *Vice Chair*
Kyle Hall (R-91) *Vice Chair*
Susan Martin (R-8) *Vice Chair*
John Szoka (R-45) *Vice Chair*
Jay Adams (R-96)
Marilyn Avila (R-40)
John R. Bell IV (R-10)
Hugh Blackwell (R-86)
James L. "Jamie" Boles, Jr. (R-52)
William "Bill" Brawley (R-103)
Mark Brody (R-55)
Robert P. "Rob" Bryan III (R-88)
Rick Catlin (R-20)
Ted Davis, Jr. (R-19)
Nelson Dollar (R-36)
Mike Hager (R-112)
Craig Horn (R-68)
Julia Craven Howard (R-79)
David R. Lewis (R-53)
Chris Malone (R-35)
Patricia "Pat" McElraft (R-13)
Chuck McGrady (R-117)
Allen McNeill (R-78)
Christopher W. Millis (R-16)
Jason Saine (R-97)
Jacqueline Michelle Schaffer
 (R-105)
Phillip R. "Phil" Shepard (R-15)
Bob Steinburg (R-1)
Paul Tine (I-6)
John A. Torbett (R-108)
Larry Yarborough (R-2)

**Minority Members**
Ken Goodman (D-66) *Vice Chair*
Charles Graham (D-47) *Vice Chair*
Larry Dwight Hall (D-29)
 *Vice Chair*
Rodney W. Moore (D-99)
 *Vice Chair*
Bobbie Richardson (D-7)
 *Vice Chair*
Michael H. Wray (D-27) *Vice Chair*
Larry M. Bell (D-21)
Cecil Antonio Brockman (D-60)
Elmer Floyd (D-43)
George W. Graham, Jr. (D-12)
Susi Hamilton (D-18)
Yvonne Lewis Holley (D-38)
Howard J. Hunter III (D-5)
Darren G. Jackson (D-39)
Garland E. Pierce (D-48)
Christopher "Chris" Sgro (D-58)
Evelyn A. Terry (D-71)

## Education - Community Colleges
Legislative Office Building, Room 643, Raleigh, NC 27601-1096

**Majority Members**
Mark Brody (R-55) *Chair*
Allen McNeill (R-78) *Chair*
Josh Dobson (R-85) *Vice Chair*
Dean Arp (R-69)
Namon Leo Daughtry (R-26)
Carl Ford (R-76)
Linda P. Johnson (R-83)
George S. Robinson (R-87)
Phillip R. "Phil" Shepard (R-15)
Sarah Stevens (R-90)
John Szoka (R-45)
Paul Tine (I-6)
Sam Watford (R-80)

**Minority Members**
Yvonne Lewis Holley (D-38)
 *Vice Chair*
Robert T. Reives II (D-54)
 *Vice Chair*
Kelly M. Alexander, Jr. (D-107)
Carla D. Cunningham (D-106)
Ken Goodman (D-66)
Duane R. Hall II (D-11)
Grier Martin (D-34)
Ken Waddell (D-46)

## Education - K-12
Legislative Office Building, Room 643, Raleigh, NC 27601-1096

**Majority Members**
Jeffrey Elmore (R-94) *Chair*
Craig Horn (R-68) *Chair*
Linda P. Johnson (R-83) *Chair*
Robert P. "Rob" Bryan III (R-88)
George G. Cleveland (R-14)
Jimmy Dixon (R-4)
Jon Hardister (R-59)
Pat B. Hurley (R-70)
Frank Iler (R-17)
Bert Jones (R-65)
Donny C. Lambeth (R-75)
James H. Langdon, Jr. (R-28)
Chris Malone (R-35)
Larry Pittman (R-82)
Dennis Patrick Riddell (R-64)
Paul Stam (R-37)
Rena W. Turner (R-84)
Chris Whitmire (R-113)

**Minority Members**
Graig R. Meyer (D-50)
Tricia Ann Cotham (D-100)
 *Vice Chair*
Edward F. Hanes, Jr. (D-72)
 *Vice Chair*
John Ager (D-115)
Jean Farmer-Butterfield (D-24)
Susan C. Fisher (D-114)
Charles Graham (D-47)
Paul Luebke (D-30)
Bobbie Richardson (D-7)
William O. "Billy" Richardson
 (D-44)
Christopher "Chris" Sgro (D-58)

## Education - Universities
Legislative Office Building, Room 643, Raleigh, NC 27601-1096

**Majority Members**
John Fraley (R-95) *Chair*
Jonathan C. Jordan (R-93) *Chair*
Mark Brody (R-55)
Rayne Brown (R-81)
Ted Davis, Jr. (R-19)
Jeffrey Elmore (R-94)
Kelly E. Hastings (R-110)
Linda P. Johnson (R-83)
David R. Lewis (R-53)
Susan Martin (R-8)
Chuck McGrady (R-117)
Gregory F. Murphy (R-9)

**Minority Members**
Becky Carney (D-102)
Verla C. Insko (D-56)
Darren G. Jackson (D-39)
Henry M. "Mickey" Michaux, Jr.
 (D-31)
Rodney W. Moore (D-99)
Shelly Willingham (D-23)
Michael H. Wray (D-27)

## Elections
Legislative Office Building, Room 1425, Raleigh, NC 27601-1096

**Majority Members**
David R. Lewis (R-53) *Chair*
Bert Jones (R-65) *Chair*
John Szoka (R-45) *Vice Chair*
Harry Warren (R-77) *Vice Chair*
John M. Blust (R-62)
Mark Brody (R-55)
Rayne Brown (R-81)
Robert P. "Rob" Bryan III (R-88)
Justin P. Burr (R-67)
Debra Conrad (R-74)
Ted Davis, Jr. (R-19)
Jimmy Dixon (R-4)
John Faircloth (R-61)
Carl Ford (R-76)
Jon Hardister (R-59)
Frank Iler (R-17)
Susan Martin (R-8)
Dennis Patrick Riddell (R-64)
Jason Saine (R-97)
Jacqueline Michelle Schaffer
 (R-105)
Michael Speciale (R-3)
Paul Stam (R-37)
John A. Torbett (R-108)

**Minority Members**
Henry M. "Mickey"
 Michaux, Jr. (D-31)
 *Vice Chair*
Tricia Ann Cotham (D-100)
Susan C. Fisher (D-114)
Elmer Floyd (D-43)
Rosa U. Gill (D-33)
George W. Graham, Jr. (D-12)
Mary Price "Pricey" Harrison
 (D-57)
Howard J. Hunter III (D-5)
Darren G. Jackson (D-39)
Bobbie Richardson (D-7)
Shelly Willingham (D-23)

**LEGISLATIVE BRANCH**

# Environment
Legislative Office Building, Room 643, Raleigh, NC 27601-1096

**Majority Members**
Rick Catlin (R-20) *Chair*
Patricia "Pat" McElraft (R-13)
  *Chair*
Jay Adams (R-96) *Vice Chair*
Chuck McGrady (R-117)
  *Vice Chair*
John R. Bradford III (R-98)
William "Bill" Brawley (R-103)
Jeffrey L. "Jeff" Collins (R-25)
Jimmy Dixon (R-4)
Mike Hager (R-112)
Frank Iler (R-17)
Christopher W. Millis (R-16)
Bob Steinburg (R-1)
Sarah Stevens (R-90)
Roger West (R-120)
Larry Yarborough (R-2)

**Minority Members**
Mary Price "Pricey"
  Harrison (D-57)
  *Vice Chair*
Nathan A. Baskerville (D-32)
William D. Brisson (D-22)
Cecil Antonio Brockman (D-60)
Becky Carney (D-102)
Verla C. Insko (D-56)
Paul Luebke (D-30)
Grier Martin (D-34)

# Ethics
Legislative Office Building, Raleigh, NC 27601

**Majority Members**
John Faircloth (R-61) *Chair*
Namon Leo Daughtry (R-26)
  *Vice Chair*
James L. "Jamie" Boles, Jr. (R-52)
Rayne Brown (R-81)
Patricia "Pat" McElraft (R-13)
Chuck McGrady (R-117)
Jacqueline Michelle Schaffer
  (R-105)
Mitchell S. Setzer (R-89)

**Minority Members**
Becky Carney (D-102) *Vice Chair*
William D. Brisson (D-22)
Tricia Ann Cotham (D-100)
Edward F. Hanes, Jr. (D-72)
Darren G. Jackson (D-39)
Evelyn A. Terry (D-71)
Michael H. Wray (D-27)

# Finance
Legislative Office Building, Room 544, Raleigh, NC 27601-1096

**Majority Members**
William "Bill" Brawley (R-103)
  *Senior Chairman*
Jason Saine (R-97)
  *Senior Chairman*
Kelly E. Hastings (R-110) *Chair*
Susan Martin (R-8) *Chair*
Mitchell S. Setzer (R-89) *Chair*
John Szoka (R-45) *Chair*
John M. Blust (R-62) *Vice Chair*
Jeffrey L. "Jeff" Collins (R-25)
  *Vice Chair*
Nelson Dollar (R-36) *Vice Chair*
Mike Hager (R-112) *Vice Chair*
Linda P. Johnson (R-83) *Vice Chair*
Stephen M. Ross (R-63) *Vice Chair*
Harry Warren (R-77) *Vice Chair*
Jay Adams (R-96)
John R. Bell IV (R-10)
J. Daniel "Dan" Bishop (R-104)
John R. Bradford III (R-98)
Ted Davis, Jr. (R-19)
Julia Craven Howard (R-79)
Charles Jeter (R-92)
Bert Jones (R-65)
Jonathan C. Jordan (R-93)
David R. Lewis (R-53)
George S. Robinson (R-87)
Jacqueline Michelle Schaffer
  (R-105)
Paul Stam (R-37)
Bob Steinburg (R-1)
Lee Zachary (R-73)

**Minority Members**
Kelly M. Alexander, Jr. (D-107)
  *Vice Chair*
Paul Luebke (D-30) *Vice Chair*
Rodney W. Moore (D-99)
  *Vice Chair*
Becky Carney (D-102)
Tricia Ann Cotham (D-100)
Carla D. Cunningham (D-106)
Ken Goodman (D-66)
Larry Dwight Hall (D-29)
Susi Hamilton (D-18)
Edward F. Hanes, Jr. (D-72)
Yvonne Lewis Holley (D-38)
Graig R. Meyer (D-50)
Robert T. Reives II (D-54)
Ken Waddell (D-46)

# Health
Legislative Office Building, Room 544, Raleigh, NC 27601-1096

**Majority Members**
Justin P. Burr (R-67) *Chair*
Bert Jones (R-65) *Chair*
Donny C. Lambeth (R-75) *Chair*
Marilyn Avila (R-40) *Vice Chair*
Nelson Dollar (R-36) *Vice Chair*
J. Daniel "Dan" Bishop (R-104)
Hugh Blackwell (R-86)
William "Bill" Brawley (R-103)
Rayne Brown (R-81)
Josh Dobson (R-85)
Carl Ford (R-76)
Mike Hager (R-112)
Kelly E. Hastings (R-110)
David R. Lewis (R-53)
Susan Martin (R-8)
Gregory F. Murphy (R-9)
BG Gary H. Pendleton (R-49)
Jason Saine (R-97)
Mitchell S. Setzer (R-89)
John Szoka (R-45)
Larry Yarborough (R-2)

**Minority Members**
William D. Brisson (D-22)
  *Vice Chair*
Beverly Miller Earle (D-101)
  *Vice Chair*
Jean Farmer-Butterfield (D-24)
  *Vice Chair*
Gale Adcock (D-41)
Becky Carney (D-102)
Tricia Ann Cotham (D-100)
Ken Goodman (D-66)
Larry Dwight Hall (D-29)
Verla C. Insko (D-56)
Marvin W. Lucas (D-42)
Ken Waddell (D-46)
Michael H. Wray (D-27)

# Homeland Security, Military, and Veterans Affairs
Legislative Office Building, Room 1425, Raleigh, NC 27601-1096

**Majority Members**
George G. Cleveland (R-14) *Chair*
Michael Speciale (R-3) *Chair*
Chris Whitmire (R-113) *Chair*
Larry Pittman (R-82) *Chair*
Dean Arp (R-69)
Marilyn Avila (R-40)
John R. Bell IV (R-10)
John M. Blust (R-62)
Craig Horn (R-68)
Julia Craven Howard (R-79)
Susan Martin (R-8)
Christopher W. Millis (R-16)
BG Gary H. Pendleton (R-49)
Jacqueline Michelle Schaffer
  (R-105)
Phillip R. "Phil" Shepard (R-15)
John Szoka (R-45)
Roger West (R-120)

**Minority Members**
Larry Dwight Hall (D-29)
  *Vice Chair*
Grier Martin (D-34) *Vice Chair*
Garland E. Pierce (D-48)
  *Vice Chair*
Gale Adcock (D-41)
Elmer Floyd (D-43)
Marvin W. Lucas (D-42)
Graig R. Meyer (D-50)
Robert T. Reives II (D-54)
Christopher "Chris" Sgro (D-58)
Brian Turner (D-116)

# Insurance
Legislative Office Building, Room 1228, Raleigh, NC 27601-1096

**Majority Members**
Dana Bumgardner (R-109) *Chair*
Mitchell S. Setzer (R-89) *Chair*
BG Gary H. Pendleton (R-49)
  *Vice Chair*
Paul Tine (I-6) *Vice Chair*
Dean Arp (R-69)
James L. "Jamie" Boles, Jr. (R-52)
William "Bill" Brawley (R-103)
Justin P. Burr (R-67)
Jeffrey L. "Jeff" Collins (R-25)
Debra Conrad (R-74)
Jimmy Dixon (R-4)
Josh Dobson (R-85)
Nelson Dollar (R-36)
Kyle Hall (R-91)
Kelly E. Hastings (R-110)
Craig Horn (R-68)
Julia Craven Howard (R-79)
Frank Iler (R-17)
Linda P. Johnson (R-83)
Donny C. Lambeth (R-75)
James H. Langdon, Jr. (R-28)
Patricia "Pat" McElraft (R-13)
Phillip R. "Phil" Shepard (R-15)
Harry Warren (R-77)

**Minority Members**
Rosa U. Gill (D-33) *Vice Chair*
Nathan A. Baskerville (D-32)
William D. Brisson (D-22)
Beverly Miller Earle (D-101)
Charles Graham (D-47)
Larry Dwight Hall (D-29)
Susi Hamilton (D-18)
Edward F. Hanes, Jr. (D-72)
Verla C. Insko (D-56)
Darren G. Jackson (D-39)
Marvin W. Lucas (D-42)
Garland E. Pierce (D-48)
William O. "Billy" Richardson
  (D-44)
Michael H. Wray (D-27)

## Judiciary I
Legislative Office Building, Room 1228, Raleigh, NC 27601-1096

**Majority Members**
Namon Leo Daughtry (R-26) *Chair*
Justin P. Burr (R-67) *Vice Chair*
Dean Arp (R-69)
Jon Hardister (R-59)
Julia Craven Howard (R-79)
Linda P. Johnson (R-83)
Allen McNeill (R-78)
George S. Robinson (R-87)
Bob Steinburg (R-1)
John Szoka (R-45)

**Minority Members**
Darren G. Jackson (D-39)
*Vice Chair*
Larry Dwight Hall (D-29)
Grier Martin (D-34)

## Judiciary II
Legislative Office Building, Room 421, Raleigh, NC 27601-1096

**Majority Members**
John M. Blust (R-62) *Chair*
Jonathan C. Jordan (R-93) *Chair*
John Faircloth (R-61) *Vice Chair*
Pat B. Hurley (R-70) *Vice Chair*
Chuck McGrady (R-117)
*Vice Chair*
Paul Stam (R-37) *Vice Chair*
Dana Bumgardner (R-109)
Debra Conrad (R-74)
Stephen M. Ross (R-63)
Jason Saine (R-97)

**Minority Members**
Henry M. "Mickey"
Michaux, Jr. (D-31)
*Vice Chair*
Joe Sam Queen (D-119)
Robert T. Reives II (D-54)
William O. "Billy" Richardson
(D-44)
Brad Salmon (D-51)

## Judiciary III
Legislative Office Building, Room 421, Raleigh, NC 27601-1096

**Majority Members**
Ted Davis, Jr. (R-19) *Chair*
Sarah Stevens (R-90) *Chair*
Rena W. Turner (R-84) *Vice Chair*
John R. Bell IV (R-10)
Rayne Brown (R-81)
George G. Cleveland (R-14)
Kelly E. Hastings (R-110)
Craig Horn (R-68)
Michael Speciale (R-3)
Lee Zachary (R-73)

**Minority Members**
Nathan A. Baskerville (D-32)
*Vice Chair*
Duane R. Hall II (D-11) *Vice Chair*
Mary Price "Pricey"
Harrison (D-57)
*Vice Chair*
Jean Farmer-Butterfield (D-24)
Verla C. Insko (D-56)

## Judiciary IV
Legislative Building, 16 West Jones Street, Room 1327,
Raleigh, NC 27601

**Majority Members**
Hugh Blackwell (R-86) *Chair*
Robert P. "Rob" Bryan III (R-88)
*Chair*
Jacqueline Michelle
Schaffer (R-105)
*Chair*
Jay Adams (R-96)
J. Daniel "Dan" Bishop (R-104)
Nelson Dollar (R-36)
Mike Hager (R-112)
Bert Jones (R-65)
Dennis Patrick Riddell (R-64)
Mitchell S. Setzer (R-89)
Paul Tine (I-6)
John A. Torbett (R-108)
Harry Warren (R-77)

**Minority Members**
Susi Hamilton (D-18) *Vice Chair*
John Ager (D-115)
Howard J. Hunter III (D-5)
Bobbie Richardson (D-7)
Evelyn A. Terry (D-71)
Shelly Willingham (D-23)

## Local Government
Legislative Office Building, Room 425, Raleigh, NC 27601-1096

**Majority Members**
Ted Davis, Jr. (R-19) *Chair*
Carl Ford (R-76) *Chair*
James H. Langdon, Jr. (R-28)
*Vice Chair*
James L. "Jamie" Boles, Jr. (R-52)
William "Bill" Brawley (R-103)
Rayne Brown (R-81)
Justin P. Burr (R-67)

**Minority Members**
John Ager (D-115)
Jean Farmer-Butterfield (D-24)
Susan C. Fisher (D-114)
Elmer Floyd (D-43)
Charles Graham (D-47)
Yvonne Lewis Holley (D-38)
Paul Luebke (D-30)

**Majority Members** *continued*
George G. Cleveland (R-14)
John Faircloth (R-61)
Charles Jeter (R-92)
BG Gary H. Pendleton (R-49)
Stephen M. Ross (R-63)
Mitchell S. Setzer (R-89)
John Szoka (R-45)
Harry Warren (R-77)
Sam Watford (R-80)

## Pensions and Retirement
Legislative Office Building, Room 415, Raleigh, NC 27601-1096

**Majority Members**
Allen McNeill (R-78) *Chair*
Stephen M. Ross (R-63) *Chair*
J. Daniel "Dan" Bishop (R-104)
John M. Blust (R-62)
Jeffrey Elmore (R-94)
Pat B. Hurley (R-70)
James H. Langdon, Jr. (R-28)

**Minority Members**
Henry M. "Mickey"
Michaux, Jr. (D-31)
*Vice Chair*
Larry M. Bell (D-21)
Rosa U. Gill (D-33)
Yvonne Lewis Holley (D-38)
Ken Waddell (D-46)

## Public Utilities
Legislative Office Building, Room 643, Raleigh, NC 27601-1096

**Majority Members**
Dean Arp (R-69) *Chair*
Jeffrey L. "Jeff" Collins (R-25)
*Chair*
Harry Warren (R-77) *Chair*
Mike Hager (R-112) *Vice Chair*
Sam Watford (R-80) *Vice Chair*
John R. Bell IV (R-10)
J. Daniel "Dan" Bishop (R-104)
Hugh Blackwell (R-86)
John R. Bradford III (R-98)
Dana Bumgardner (R-109)
Rick Catlin (R-20)
Debra Conrad (R-74)
Nelson Dollar (R-36)
Jeffrey Elmore (R-94)
Kyle Hall (R-91)
Kelly E. Hastings (R-110)
Linda P. Johnson (R-83)
Chris Malone (R-35)
Susan Martin (R-8)
Christopher W. Millis (R-16)
Dennis Patrick Riddell (R-64)

**Minority Members**
Carla D. Cunningham (D-106)
*Vice Chair*
Edward F. Hanes, Jr. (D-72)
*Vice Chair*
Kelly M. Alexander, Jr. (D-107)
Beverly Miller Earle (D-101)
Duane R. Hall II (D-11)
Mary Price "Pricey" Harrison
(D-57)
Paul Luebke (D-30)
Graig R. Meyer (D-50)
Rodney W. Moore (D-99)
Michael H. Wray (D-27)

## Regulatory Reform
Legislative Office Building, Room 643, Raleigh, NC 27601-2808

**Majority Members**
John R. Bell IV (R-10) *Chair*
Christopher W. Millis (R-16) *Chair*
Dennis Patrick Riddell (R-64) *Chair*
Jonathan C. Jordan (R-93)
*Vice Chair*
Michael Speciale (R-3) *Vice Chair*
J. Daniel "Dan" Bishop (R-104)
Hugh Blackwell (R-86)
John R. Bradford III (R-98)
Mark Brody (R-55)
Robert P. "Rob" Bryan III (R-88)
Rick Catlin (R-20)
Jimmy Dixon (R-4)
Nelson Dollar (R-36)
Mike Hager (R-112)
Bert Jones (R-65)
Patricia "Pat" McElraft (R-13)
Jacqueline Michelle Schaffer
(R-105)
Paul Stam (R-37)
Sarah Stevens (R-90)
Chris Whitmire (R-113)

**Minority Members**
Ken Goodman (D-66) *Vice Chair*
William D. Brisson (D-22)
Tricia Ann Cotham (D-100)
Carla D. Cunningham (D-106)
Larry Dwight Hall (D-29)
Mary Price "Pricey" Harrison
(D-57)
Graig R. Meyer (D-50)
Rodney W. Moore (D-99)
Joe Sam Queen (D-119)

**LEGISLATIVE BRANCH**

# Rules, Calendar and Operations of the House

Legislative Office Building, Room 1327, Raleigh, NC 27601-2808

**Majority Members**
David R. Lewis (R-53) *Chair*
Namon Leo Daughtry (R-26)
  *Vice Chair*
Ted Davis, Jr. (R-19) *Vice Chair*
Paul Stam (R-37) *Vice Chair*
John A. Torbett (R-108) *Vice Chair*
John R. Bell IV (R-10)
John M. Blust (R-62)
James L. "Jamie" Boles, Jr. (R-52)
Dana Bumgardner (R-109)
Justin P. Burr (R-67)
John Fraley (R-95)
Kelly E. Hastings (R-110)
Linda P. Johnson (R-83)
George S. Robinson (R-87)
Jason Saine (R-97)
Jacqueline Michelle Schaffer
  (R-105)
John Szoka (R-45)
Paul Tine (I-6)

**Minority Members**
Becky Carney (D-102)
Tricia Ann Cotham (D-100)
Elmer Floyd (D-43)
Ken Goodman (D-66)
Larry Dwight Hall (D-29)
Edward F. Hanes, Jr. (D-72)
Darren G. Jackson (D-39)
Robert T. Reives II (D-54)
Michael H. Wray (D-27)

# State Personnel

Legislative Office Building, Room 424, Raleigh, NC 27601

**Majority Members**
Jeffrey L. "Jeff" Collins (R-25)
  *Chair*
James H. Langdon, Jr. (R-28) *Chair*
Josh Dobson (R-85)
Jeffrey Elmore (R-94)
Carl Ford (R-76)
Pat B. Hurley (R-70)
Donny C. Lambeth (R-75)
Patricia "Pat" McElraft (R-13)
Allen McNeill (R-78)
BG Gary H. Pendleton (R-49)
Sarah Stevens (R-90)
Rena W. Turner (R-84)
Chris Whitmire (R-113)

**Minority Members**
Larry M. Bell (D-21) *Vice Chair*
Elmer Floyd (D-43)
George W. Graham, Jr. (D-12)
Verla C. Insko (D-56)
Henry M. "Mickey" Michaux, Jr.
  (D-31)
Ken Waddell (D-46)

# Transportation

Legislative Office Building, Room 1228, Raleigh, NC 27601-1096

**Majority Members**
Frank Iler (R-17) *Chair*
Phillip R. "Phil" Shepard (R-15)
  *Chair*
John A. Torbett (R-108) *Chair*
George G. Cleveland (R-14)
  *Vice Chair*
Michael Speciale (R-3) *Vice Chair*
Jay Adams (R-96)
Dean Arp (R-69)
Hugh Blackwell (R-86)
James L. "Jamie" Boles, Jr. (R-52)
William "Bill" Brawley (R-103)
Rayne Brown (R-81)
Dana Bumgardner (R-109)
Rick Catlin (R-20)
Nelson Dollar (R-36)
John Faircloth (R-61)
Carl Ford (R-76)
John Fraley (R-95)
Jon Hardister (R-59)
Charles Jeter (R-92)
Chuck McGrady (R-117)
Allen McNeill (R-78)
Gregory F. Murphy (R-9)
Michele D. Presnell (R-118)
George S. Robinson (R-87)
Stephen M. Ross (R-63)
Jacqueline Michelle Schaffer
  (R-105)
Bob Steinburg (R-1)

**Minority Members**
Becky Carney (D-102) *Vice Chair*
Ken Waddell (D-46) *Vice Chair*
Kelly M. Alexander, Jr. (D-107)
Cecil Antonio Brockman (D-60)
Ken Goodman (D-66)
Charles Graham (D-47)
Duane R. Hall II (D-11)
Yvonne Lewis Holley (D-38)
Howard J. Hunter III (D-5)
Rodney W. Moore (D-99)
Joe Sam Queen (D-119)
Evelyn A. Terry (D-71)

**Majority Members** *continued*
Rena W. Turner (R-84)
Larry Yarborough (R-2)
Lee Zachary (R-73)
Paul Tine (I-6)

# University Board of Governors Nominating

**Majority Members**
Nelson Dollar (R-36) *Chair*
Kelly E. Hastings (R-110)
  *Vice Chair*
Robert P. "Rob" Bryan III (R-88)
Jonathan C. Jordan (R-93)
David R. Lewis (R-53)
Gregory F. Murphy (R-9)

**Minority Members**
Edward F. Hanes, Jr. (D-72)
  *Vice Chair*
Tricia Ann Cotham (D-100)
Larry Dwight Hall (D-29)
Susi Hamilton (D-18)

# Wildlife Resources

Legislative Office Building, Room 423, Raleigh, NC 27601-1096

**Majority Members**
Chris Malone (R-35) *Chair*
Roger West (R-120) *Chair*
Jay Adams (R-96)
George G. Cleveland (R-14)
Ted Davis, Jr. (R-19)
Charles Jeter (R-92)
James H. Langdon, Jr. (R-28)
Chuck McGrady (R-117)
Larry Pittman (R-82)
Michele D. Presnell (R-118)
Bob Steinburg (R-1)
Paul Tine (I-6)
Lee Zachary (R-73)

**Minority Members**
Michael H. Wray (D-27)
Ken Waddell (D-46) *Vice Chair*
Gale Adcock (D-41)
John Ager (D-115)
William D. Brisson (D-22)
Marvin W. Lucas (D-42)

# North Dakota Legislative Assembly

State Capitol, 600 East Boulevard Avenue, Bismarck, ND 58505-0360
Tel: (701) 328-2916  Fax: (701) 328-3615  Internet: www.legis.nd.gov

## North Dakota Senate

President of the Senate **Drew Howard Wrigley** (R) . . . . . . (701) 328-2200
  Education: North Dakota BA; Washington College of Law 1991 JD
President Pro Tem **Dick Dever** (R) . . . . . . . . . . . . . . . . . . (701) 222-2604
Interim President Pro Tem **Robert S. Erbele** (R) . . . . . . . . (701) 378-2272
Majority Leader **Rich Wardner** (R) . . . . . . . . . . . . . . . . . . (701) 483-6918
  Education: Dickinson State U BS; Northern State MS
Assistant Majority Leader **Jerry Klein** (R) . . . . . . . . . . . . (701) 547-3517
Minority Leader **Mac Schneider** (D) . . . . . . . . . . . . . . . . (701) 610-6092
Assistant Minority Leader **Joan Heckaman** (D) . . . . . . . . (701) 947-2106
Minority Caucus Leader **Philip M. Murphy** (D) . . . . . . . . . (701) 786-9043
Secretary of the Senate **William R. Horton** . . . . . . . . . . . . (701) 328-2916

## Senators

**Party Affiliation Statistics:** Republicans: 32, Democrats: 15

Senator **Howard C. Anderson, Jr., RPh** (R-District 8) . . . . (701) 861-9749
  Counties Represented: Burleigh (part), McLean (part)
  Term Expires: 2016
  2107 Seventh Street Northwest, Turtle Lake, ND 58575
  E-mail: hcanderson@nd.gov
  Committees: Correction and Revision of the Journal; Human Services;
  Political Subdivisions
  Education: North Dakota State

Senator **Kelly M. Armstrong** (R-District 36) . . . . . . . . . . . (701) 290-0447
  Counties Represented: Dunn (part), Hettinger (part),     Fax: (701) 483-8714
  Morton (part), Stark (part)
  Term Expires: 2016
  513 Elks Drive, Dickinson, ND 58601
  E-mail: karmstrong@nd.gov
  Committees: Energy and Natural Resources; Judiciary; Rules
  Education: North Dakota, 2003 JD

Senator **Tyler Axness** (D-District 16) . . . . . . . . . . . . . . . . (701) 388-1184
  Counties Represented: Cass (part)
  Term Expires: 2016
  752 51st Street South, Fargo, ND 58103
  E-mail: taxness@nd.gov
  Committees: Employment; Human Services; Transportation
  Education: North Dakota State BAA

Senator **Brad Bekkedahl** (R-District 1) . . . . . . . . . . . . . . (701) 774-3333
  Counties Represented: Williams (part)                    Res: (701) 572-6269
  Term Expires: 2018                                       Fax: (701) 572-1039
  E-mail: bbekkedahl@nd.gov
  Committees: Finance and Taxation; Political Subdivisions

Senator **Bill Bowman** (R-District 39) . . . . . . . . . . . . . . . . (701) 523-3188
  Counties Represented: Adams, Billings, Bowman, Dunn (part), Golden
  Valley, McKenzie (part), Slope
  Term Expires: 2018
  408 First Street SW, Bowman, ND 58623-9753
  E-mail: bbowman@nd.gov
  Committees: Appropriations
  Education: Dickinson State U BS

Senator **Randy Burckhard** (R-District 5) . . . . . . . . . . . . . (701) 838-1509
  Counties Represented: Ward (part)
  Term Expires: 2018
  1837 15th Street SW, Minot, ND 58701
  E-mail: raburckhard@nd.gov
  Committees: Industry, Business and Labor; Political Subdivisions

Senator **Tom Campbell** (R-District 19) . . . . . . . . . . . . . . . (701) 520-2727
  Counties Represented: Grand Forks (part), Walsh (part)
  Term Expires: 2018
  15135 County Road 11, Grafton, ND 58237
  E-mail: tomcampbell@nd.gov
  Committees: Industry, Business and Labor; Transportation
  Education: North Dakota State BS

Senator **Ron Carlisle** (R-District 30) . . . . . . . . . . . . . . . . (701) 202-7100
  Counties Represented: Burleigh (part)
  Term Expires: 2016
  P.O. Box 222, Bismarck, ND 58502
  E-mail: rcarlisle@nd.gov
  Committees: Appropriations

Senator **Jonathan Casper** (R-District 27) . . . . . . . . . . . . . (701) 893-8005
  Counties Represented: Cass (part)
  Term Expires: 2018
  E-mail: jcasper@nd.gov
  Committees: Judiciary; Transportation

Senator **Dwight Cook** (R-District 34) . . . . . . . . . . . . . . . . (701) 663-7421
  Counties Represented: Morton (part)
  Term Expires: 2016
  1408 - 17th Street SE, Mandan, ND 58554-4895
  E-mail: dcook@nd.gov
  Committees: Committees; Finance and Taxation; Government and
  Veterans Affairs
  Affiliation: Owner, Cook Industrial Sales

Senator **Kyle Davison** (R-District 41) . . . . . . . . . . . . . . . . (701) 261-8703
  Counties Represented: Cass (part)
  Term Expires: 2018
  E-mail: kdavison@nd.gov
  Committees: Education; Government and Veterans Affairs

Senator **Dick Dever** (R-District 32) . . . . . . . . . . . . . . . . . (701) 222-2604
  Counties Represented: Burleigh (part)
  Term Expires: 2016
  1416 Eastwood Street, Bismarck, ND 58504-6224
  E-mail: ddever@nd.gov
  Committees: Employment; Government and Veterans Affairs; Human
  Services

Senator **Jim Dotzenrod** (D-District 26) . . . . . . . . . . . . . . . (701) 439-2427
  Counties Represented: Dickey (part), Ransom (part), Richland (part),
  Sargent
  Term Expires: 2016
  P.O. Box 69, Wyndmere, ND 58081-0069
  E-mail: jdotzenrod@nd.gov
  Committees: Finance and Taxation; Political Subdivisions; Rules

Senator **Robert S. Erbele** (R-District 28) . . . . . . . . . . . . . (701) 378-2272
  Counties Represented: Burleigh (part), Dickey (part), Emmons,
  LaMoure (part), Logan, McIntosh
  Term Expires: 2016
  6512 - 51st Avenue SE, Lehr, ND 58460-9149
  E-mail: rerbele@nd.gov
  Committees: Appropriations; Rules

Senator **Tim Flakoll** (R-District 44) . . . . . . . . . . . . . . . . . (701) 367-5954
  Counties Represented: Cass (part)
  Term Expires: 2016
  1350 Second Street North, Fargo, ND 58102-2725
  E-mail: tflakoll@nd.gov
  Committees: Committees; Education; Employment; Government and
  Veterans Affairs
  Affiliation: Vice President and General Manager, FM RedHawks
  Professional Baseball
  Education: North Dakota State BS, MS; Somerset (UK) PhD

Senator **John Grabinger** (D-District 12) . . . . . . . . . . . . . . (701) 252-4824
  Counties Represented: Stutsman (part)               Fax: (701) 252-3708
  Term Expires: 2016
  1008 Eighth Avenue Northeast, Jamestown, ND 58401
  E-mail: jgrabinger@nd.gov
  Committees: Judiciary; Political Subdivisions

Senator **Joan Heckaman** (D-District 23) . . . . . . . . . . . . . . (701) 947-2106
  Counties Represented: Benson (part), Eddy, Griggs, Nelson, Steele
  Term Expires: 2016
  322 Second Avenue North, New Rockford, ND 58356-1712
  E-mail: jheckaman@nd.gov
  Committees: Appropriations; Committees

Senator **David Hogue** (R-District 38) . . . . . . . . . . . . . . . . (701) 852-0381
  Counties Represented: Ward (part)
  Term Expires: 2016
  P.O. Box 1000, Minot, ND 58703-1000
  E-mail: dhogue@nd.gov
  Committees: Arrangements for Senate Committee Rooms; Committees;
  Energy and Natural Resources; Judiciary; Rules

Senator **Ray Holmberg** (R-District 17) . . . . . . . . . . . . . . . (701) 775-9656
  Counties Represented: Grand Forks (part)
  Term Expires: 2018
  621 High Plains Court, Grand Forks, ND 58201-7717
  E-mail: rholmberg@nd.gov
  Committees: Appropriations; Rules
  Affiliation: Counselor, Grand Forks Public Schools
  2400 47th Avenue South, Grand Forks, ND 58201

Senator **Ralph L. Kilzer** (R-District 47) . . . . . . . . . . . . . . (701) 223-1572
  Counties Represented: Burleigh (part)
  Term Expires: 2018
  1982 Mesquite Loop, Bismarck, ND 58503-0198
  E-mail: rkilzer@nd.gov
  Committees: Appropriations; Employment
  Education: St John's U (MN) 1957 BA; Marquette 1966 MD

*(continued on next page)*

**Senators** *continued*

Senator **Jerry Klein** (R-District 14) . . . . . . . . . . . . . . . . . . . . (701) 547-3517
  Counties Represented: Benson (part), Kidder, Pierce, Sheridan, Wells
  Term Expires: 2016
  P.O. Box 265, Fessenden, ND 58438-0265
  E-mail: jklein@nd.gov
  Committees: Agriculture; Committees; Delayed Bills; Industry,
  Business and Labor; Rules

Senator **Karen K. Krebsbach** (R-District 40) . . . . . . . . . . . . (701) 838-0211
  Counties Represented: Ward (part)
  Term Expires: 2016
  P.O. Box 1767, Minot, ND 58702-1767
  E-mail: kkrebsbach@nd.gov
  Committees: Appropriations
  Affiliation: Vice President, Krebsbach Realty Company, Inc.
  Education: Minot State BS

Senator **Lonnie J. Laffen** (R-District 43) . . . . . . . . . . . . . . (701) 746-1727
  Counties Represented: Grand Forks (part)
  Term Expires: 2018
  3549 15th Avenue South, Grand Forks, ND 58201
  E-mail: llaffen@nd.gov
  Committees: Energy and Natural Resources; Finance and Taxation

Senator **Oley Larsen** (R-District 3) . . . . . . . . . . . . . . . . . . . . (701) 852-9006
  Counties Represented: Ward (part)
  Term Expires: 2018
  11051 20th Avenue SE, Minot, ND 58701
  E-mail: olarsen@nd.gov
  Committees: Agriculture; Human Services

Senator **Gary A. Lee** (R-District 22) . . . . . . . . . . . . . . . . . . (701) 347-4809
  Counties Represented: Cass (part)
  Term Expires: 2016
  P.O. Box 3, Casselton, ND 58012-0003
  E-mail: galee@nd.gov
  Committees: Appropriations; Delayed Bills

Senator **Judy Lee** (R-District 13) . . . . . . . . . . . . . . . . . . . . (701) 282-6512
  Counties Represented: Cass (part)
  Term Expires: 2018
  1822 Brentwood Court, West Fargo, ND 58078-4204
  E-mail: jlee@nd.gov
  Committees: Human Services; Political Subdivisions
  Education: North Dakota BS

Senator **Larry Luick** (R-District 25) . . . . . . . . . . . . . . . . . . (701) 474-5959
  Counties Represented: Cass (part), Richland (part)
  Term Expires: 2018
  17945 101st Street SE, Fairmount, ND 58030-9522
  E-mail: lluick@nd.gov
  Committees: Agriculture; Judiciary

Senator **Richard Marcellais** (D-District 9) . . . . . . . (701) 244-2400 ext. 104
  Counties Represented: Rolette                    Res: (701) 477-8985
  Term Expires: 2018
  Rural Route 1, Box 267A, Belcourt, ND 58316-9787
  E-mail: rmarcellais@nd.gov
  Committees: Education; Government and Veterans Affairs

Senator **Tim Mathern** (D-District 11) . . . . . . . . . . . . . . . . (701) 235-9817
  Counties Represented: Cass (part)
  Term Expires: 2018
  429 16th Avenue South, Fargo, ND 58103-4329
  E-mail: tmathern@nd.gov
  Committees: Appropriations; Delayed Bills
  Education: North Dakota State BA; Nebraska MSW;
  Harvard 2000 MPA

Senator **Joe Miller** (R-District 10) . . . . . . . . . . . . . . . . . . . . (701) 331-1491
  Counties Represented: Cavalier, Pembina, Walsh (part)
  Term Expires: 2016
  214 Harris Avenue North, Park River, ND 58270
  P.O. Box 151, Park River, ND 58270-0151
  E-mail: joetmiller@nd.gov
  Committees: Agriculture; Industry, Business and Labor
  Education: Valley City State BA

Senator **Philip M. Murphy** (D-District 20) . . . . . . . . . . . . (701) 786-9043
  Counties Represented: Cass (part), Grand Forks (part), Traill
  Term Expires: 2016
  1212 Parke Avenue, Portland, ND 58274
  E-mail: pmmurphy@nd.gov
  Committees: Committees; Energy and Natural Resources; Industry,
  Business and Labor

Senator **Carolyn C. Nelson** (D-District 21) . . . . . . . . . . . . (701) 235-5161
  Counties Represented: Cass (part)
  Term Expires: 2018
  One Second Street South, Room 5-402, Fargo, ND 58103-1959
  E-mail: cnelson@nd.gov
  Committees: Government and Veterans Affairs; Judiciary
  Education: North Dakota State BS, MS

Senator **David O'Connell** (D-District 6) . . . . . . . . . . . . . . . (701) 784-5441
  Counties Represented: Bottineau, McHenry, Renville
  Term Expires: 2016
  2624 County Road 30, Lansford, ND 58750-9737
  E-mail: doconnell@nd.gov
  Committees: Appropriations; Arrangements for Senate Committee
  Rooms

Senator **Erin Oban** (D-District 35) . . . . . . . . . . . . . . . . . . . . (701) 223-5613
  Counties Represented: Burleigh (part)            Res: (701) 955-3188
  Term Expires: 2018
  E-mail: eoban@nd.gov
  Committees: Agriculture; Education

Senator **Dave Oehlke** (R-District 15) . . . . . . . . . . . . . . . . (701) 662-8587
  Counties Represented: Ramsey, Towner
  Term Expires: 2018
  125 Woodlea Drive, Devils Lake, ND 58301-8545
  E-mail: doehlke@nd.gov
  Committees: Arrangements for Senate Committee Rooms; Finance and
  Taxation; Transportation

Senator **Nicole Poolman** (R-District 7) . . . . . . . . . . . . . . . (701) 250-6730
  Counties Represented: Burleigh (part)
  Term Expires: 2018
  6517 Misty Waters Drive, Bismarck, ND 58503
  E-mail: npoolman@nd.gov
  Committees: Correction and Revision of the Journal; Government and
  Veterans Affairs; Industry, Business and Labor
  Education: North Dakota BEd

Senator **Larry J. Robinson** (D-District 24) . . . . . . . . . . . . (701) 845-1428
  Counties Represented: Abbeville, Barnes, Cass (part), Ransom (part)
  Term Expires: 2016
  3584 Sheyenne Circle, Valley City, ND 58072-9545
  E-mail: lrobinson@nd.gov
  Committees: Appropriations; Rules
  Affiliation: Executive Director, Valley City State University Foundation
  101 College Street, SW, Valley City, ND 58072-4098
  Education: Valley City State BS; North Dakota State MS

Senator **David S. Rust** (R-District 2) . . . . . . . . . . . . . . . . . (701) 664-3508
  Counties Represented: Burke, Divide, Mountrail (part), Williams (part)
  Term Expires: 2016
  E-mail: drust@nd.gov
  Committees: Education; Transportation

Senator **Donald Schaible** (R-District 31) . . . . . . . . . . . . . . (701) 824-3168
  Counties Represented: Grant, Hettinger (part), Morton (part), Sioux
  Term Expires: 2018
  9115 Highway 21, Mott, ND 58646
  E-mail: dgschaible@nd.gov
  Committees: Education; Energy and Natural Resources

Senator **Mac Schneider** (D-District 42) . . . . . . . . . . . . . . (701) 610-6092
  Counties Represented: Grand Forks (part)
  Term Expires: 2016
  1806 University Drive, Grand Forks, ND 58203-3342
  E-mail: macschneider@nd.gov
  Committees: Committees; Employment

Senator **George B. Sinner** (D-District 46) . . . . . . . . . . . . . (701) 371-6236
  Counties Represented: Cass (part)
  Term Expires: 2016
  1806 Rose Creek Drive South, Fargo, ND 58104
  E-mail: georgesinner@nd.gov
  Committees: Correction and Revision of the Journal; Industry, Business
  and Labor; Transportation
  Education: North Dakota

Senator **Ronald Sorvaag** (R-District 45) . . . . . . . . . . . . . . (701) 235-9756
  Counties Represented: Cass (part)
  Term Expires: 2018
  3402 Birdie Street North, Fargo, ND 58102
  E-mail: rsorvaag@nd.gov
  Committees: Appropriations

Senator **Constance "Connie" Triplett** (D-District 18) . . . . (701) 772-8009
  Counties Represented: Grand Forks (part)
  Term Expires: 2016
  P.O. Box 5178, Grand Forks, ND 58206-5178
  E-mail: ctriplett@nd.gov
  Committees: Energy and Natural Resources; Finance and Taxation;
  Rules

LEGISLATIVE BRANCH

Senator **Jessica K. Unruh** (R-District 33) . . . . . . . . . . . . . .(701) 891-9708
  Counties Represented: Mercer (part), Morton (part), Oliver
  Term Expires: 2018
  213 10th Street Northeast, Beulah, ND 58523
  E-mail: jkunruh@nd.gov
  Committees: Energy and Natural Resources; Finance and Taxation
  Education: North Dakota State BS
Senator **Terry M. Wanzek** (R-District 29) . . . . . . . . . . . . .(701) 251-6113
  Counties Represented: Foster, LaMoure (part), Stutsman (part)
  Term Expires: 2018
  900 Seventh Avenue SW, Jamestown, ND 58401-4542
  E-mail: tmwanzek@nd.gov
  Committees: Appropriations; Delayed Bills
Senator **Rich Wardner** (R-District 37) . . . . . . . . . . . . . . .(701) 483-6918
  Counties Represented: Stark (part)
  Term Expires: 2018
  1042 - 12th Avenue West, Dickinson, ND 58601-3654
  E-mail: rwardner@nd.gov
  Committees: Committees
  Affiliation: Executive Director, Dickinson Area Chamber of Commerce
Senator **John M. Warner** (D-District 4) . . . . . . . . . . . . . . (701) 726-5663
  Counties Represented: Dunn (part), McKenzie (part), McLean (part),
  Mercer (part), Mountrail (part), Ward (part)
  Term Expires: 2016
  33200 331st Avenue SW, Ryder, ND 58779-9515
  E-mail: jwarner@nd.gov
  Committees: Agriculture; Delayed Bills; Human Services
  Education: Minot State; North Dakota State

# Senate Standing Committees

## Agriculture

**Majority Members**
Joe Miller (R-10) *Chairman*
Larry Luick (R-25) *Vice Chairman*
Jerry Klein (R-14)
Oley Larsen (R-3)

**Minority Members**
Erin Oban (D-35)
John M. Warner (D-4)

## Appropriations

**Majority Members**
Ray Holmberg (R-17) *Chairman*
Bill Bowman (R-39) *Vice Chairman*
Karen K. Krebsbach (R-40)
  *Vice Chairman*
Ron Carlisle (R-30)
Robert S. Erbele (R-28)
Ralph L. Kilzer (R-47)
Gary A. Lee (R-22)
Ronald Sorvaag (R-45)
Terry M. Wanzek (R-29)

**Minority Members**
Joan Heckaman (D-23)
Tim Mathern (D-11)
David O'Connell (D-6)
Larry J. Robinson (D-24)

## Education

**Majority Members**
Tim Flakoll (R-44) *Chairman*
David S. Rust (R-2) *Vice Chairman*
Kyle Davison (R-41)
Donald Schaible (R-31)

**Minority Members**
Richard Marcellais (D-9)
Erin Oban (D-35)

## Energy and Natural Resources

**Majority Members**
Donald Schaible (R-31) *Chairman*
Jessica K. Unruh (R-33)
  *Vice Chairman*
Kelly M. Armstrong (R-36)
David Hogue (R-38)
Lonnie J. Laffen (R-43)

**Minority Members**
Philip M. Murphy (D-20)
Constance "Connie" Triplett (D-18)

## Finance and Taxation

**Majority Members**
Dwight Cook (R-34) *Chairman*
Lonnie J. Laffen (R-43)
  *Vice Chairman*
Brad Bekkedahl (R-1)
Dave Oehlke (R-15)
Jessica K. Unruh (R-33)

**Minority Members**
Jim Dotzenrod (D-26)
Constance "Connie" Triplett (D-18)

## Government and Veterans Affairs

**Majority Members**
Dick Dever (R-32) *Chairman*
Nicole Poolman (R-7)
  *Vice Chairman*
Dwight Cook (R-34)
Kyle Davison (R-41)
Tim Flakoll (R-44)

**Minority Members**
Richard Marcellais (D-9)
Carolyn C. Nelson (D-21)

## Human Services

**Majority Members**
Judy Lee (R-13) *Chairman*
Oley Larsen (R-3) *Vice Chairman*
Howard C. Anderson, Jr. (R-8)
Dick Dever (R-32)

**Minority Members**
Tyler Axness (D-16)
John M. Warner (D-4)

## Industry, Business and Labor

**Majority Members**
Jerry Klein (R-14) *Chairman*
Tom Campbell (R-19)
  *Vice Chairman*
Randy Burckhard (R-5)
Joe Miller (R-10)
Nicole Poolman (R-7)

**Minority Members**
Philip M. Murphy (D-20)
George B. Sinner (D-46)

## Judiciary

**Majority Members**
David Hogue (R-38) *Chairman*
Kelly M. Armstrong (R-36)
  *Vice Chairman*
Jonathan Casper (R-27)
Larry Luick (R-25)

**Minority Members**
John Grabinger (D-12)
Carolyn C. Nelson (D-21)

## Political Subdivisions

**Majority Members**
Randy Burckhard (R-5) *Chairman*
Howard C. Anderson, Jr. (R-8)
  *Vice Chairman*
Brad Bekkedahl (R-1)
Judy Lee (R-13)

**Minority Members**
Jim Dotzenrod (D-26)
John Grabinger (D-12)

## Transportation

**Majority Members**
Dave Oehlke (R-15) *Chairman*
Jonathan Casper (R-27)
  *Vice Chairman*
Tom Campbell (R-19)
David S. Rust (R-2)

**Minority Members**
Tyler Axness (D-16)
George B. Sinner (D-46)

# Senate Procedural Committees

## Arrangements for Senate Committee Rooms

**Majority Members**
David Hogue (R-38) *Chairman*
Dave Oehlke (R-15)

**Minority Members**
David O'Connell (D-6)

## Committees

**Majority Members**
Rich Wardner (R-37) *Chairman*
Dwight Cook (R-34)
Tim Flakoll (R-44)
David Hogue (R-38)
Jerry Klein (R-14)

**Minority Members**
Philip M. Murphy (D-20)
Joan Heckaman (D-23)
Mac Schneider (D-42)

## Correction and Revision of the Journal

**Majority Members**
Nicole Poolman (R-7) *Chairman*
Howard C. Anderson, Jr. (R-8)

**Minority Members**
George B. Sinner (D-46)

## Delayed Bills

**Majority Members**
Jerry Klein (R-14) *Chairman*
Gary A. Lee (R-22)
Terry M. Wanzek (R-29)

**Minority Members**
Tim Mathern (D-11)
John M. Warner (D-4)

**LEGISLATIVE BRANCH**

## Employment

**Majority Members**
Dick Dever (R-32) *Chairman*
Tim Flakoll (R-44)
Ralph L. Kilzer (R-47)

**Minority Members**
Tyler Axness (D-16)
Mac Schneider (D-42)

## Rules

**Majority Members**
Ray Holmberg (R-17) *Chairman*
Kelly M. Armstrong (R-36)
Robert S. Erbele (R-28)
David Hogue (R-38)
Jerry Klein (R-14)

**Minority Members**
Jim Dotzenrod (D-26)
Larry J. Robinson (D-24)
Constance "Connie" Triplett (D-18)

# North Dakota House of Representatives

Speaker of the House **Wesley R. Belter** (R) . . . . . . . . . . . . (701) 532-0311
Majority Leader **Al Carlson** (R) . . . . . . . . . . . . . . . . . . . . . . (701) 232-5832
Assistant Majority Leader **Don Vigesaa** (R) . . . . . . . . . . . . (701) 797-2448
  Education: North Dakota State 1975 BSB
Majority Caucus Leader **Scott Louser** (R) . . . . . . . . . . . . . (701) 328-9587
  Education: Minot State 2001 MS
Minority Leader **Kenton Onstad** (D) . . . . . . . . . . . . . . . . . (701) 862-3445
Assistant Minority Leader **Corey Mock** (D) . . . . . . . . . . . . (701) 732-0085
Minority Caucus Co-Leader **Joshua A. Boschee** (D) . . . . . (701) 367-3513
  Education: North Dakota State BA, MEd
Minority Caucus Co-Leader **Ben Hanson** (D) . . . . . . . . . . (701) 446-8634
  Education: Minnesota St (Moorhead) BA
Chief Clerk of the House **Buell J. Reich** . . . . . . . . . . . . . . (701) 328-2916

## Representatives

**Party Affiliation Statistics:** Republicans: 71, Democrats: 23

Representative **Bill Amerman** (D-District 26) . . . . . . . . . . . (701) 724-3833
  Counties Represented: Dickey (part), Ransom (part), Richland (part), Sargent
  Term Expires: 2016
  P.O. Box 43, Forman, ND 58032-0043
  E-mail: bamerman@nd.gov
  Committees: Government and Veterans Affairs; Industry, Business and Labor

Representative **Bert Anderson** (R-District 2) . . . . . . . . . . . . (701) 965-6194
  Counties Represented: Burke, Divide, Mountrail (part), Williams (part)
  Term Expires: 2016
  P.O. Box 604, Crosby, ND 58730
  E-mail: bertanderson@nd.gov
  Committees: Agriculture; Human Services

Representative **Dick Anderson** (R-District 6) . . . . . . . . . . . (701) 366-4625
  Counties Represented: Bottineau, McHenry, Renville
  Term Expires: 2016
  1187 77th Street NE, Willow City, ND 58384
  E-mail: danderson@nd.gov
  Committees: Energy and Natural Resources; Human Services

Representative **Pamela Anderson** (D-District 41) . . . . . . . . (701) 306-3362
  Counties Represented: Cass (part)
  Term Expires: 2018
  3001 40th Avenue South, Fargo, ND 58104
  E-mail: pkanderson@nd.gov
  Committees: Judiciary; Political Subdivisions

Representative **Thomas Beadle** (R-District 27) . . . . . . . . . . (701) 235-2348
  Counties Represented: Cass (part)
  Term Expires: 2018
  4722 Townsite Place South, Fargo, ND 58104
  E-mail: tbeadle@nd.gov
  Committees: Industry, Business and Labor; Political Subdivisions

Representative **Richard S. Becker** (R-District 43) . . . . . . . . (701) 530-3333
  Counties Represented: Grand Forks (part)      Fax: (701) 530-3009
  Term Expires: 2018
  E-mail: rsbecker@nd.gov
  Committees: Human Services; Political Subdivisions

Representative **Rick C. Becker** (R-District 7) . . . . . . . . . . . (701) 527-6902
  Counties Represented: Burleigh (part)      Fax: (701) 530-3009
  Term Expires: 2018
  6140 Ponderosa Avenue, Bismarck, ND 58503
  E-mail: rcbecker@nd.gov
  Committees: Industry, Business and Labor; Transportation
  Education: North Dakota BS, MD

Representative **Larry Bellew** (R-District 38) . . . . . . . . . . . (701) 852-5786
  Counties Represented: Ward (part)
  Term Expires: 2016
  812 Bel Air Place, Minot, ND 58703-1751
  E-mail: lbellew@nd.gov
  Committees: Appropriations; Appropriations - Human Resources Division

Representative **Wesley R. Belter** (R-District 22) . . . . . . . . . (701) 532-0311
  Counties Represented: Cass (part)
  Term Expires: 2016
  4426 58th Street South, Fargo, ND 58104-6091
  E-mail: wbelter@nd.gov
  Committees: Committees; Delayed Bills; Rules

Representative **Tracy Boe** (D-District 9) . . . . . . . . . . . . . . . (701) 656-3427
  Counties Represented: Rolette
  Term Expires: 2018
  5125 89th Street, Mylo, ND 58353-9438
  E-mail: tboe@nd.gov
  Committees: Appropriations; Appropriations - Education and Environment Division; Employment

Representative **Randy Boehning** (R-District 27) . . . . . . . . . (701) 799-0108
  Counties Represented: Cass (part)
  Term Expires: 2018
  1781 39th Street Southwest, Room 201, Fargo, ND 58103-7178
  E-mail: rboehning@nd.gov
  Committees: Appropriations; Appropriations - Government Operations Division

Representative **Joshua A. Boschee** (D-District 44) . . . . . . . (701) 367-3513
  Counties Represented: Cass (part)
  Term Expires: 2016
  824 11th Street North, Fargo, ND 58102
  E-mail: jboschee@nd.gov
  Committees: Agriculture; Arrangements for House Committee Rooms; Committees; Industry, Business and Labor

Representative **Roger Brabandt** (R-District 5) . . . . . . . . . . (701) 839-6577
  Counties Represented: Ward (part)
  Term Expires: 2018
  1317 Third Street, SW, Minot, ND 58701
  E-mail: rbrabandt@nd.gov
  Committees: Energy and Natural Resources; Judiciary

Representative
**Michael Don "Mike" Brandenburg** (R-District 28) . . . . (701) 493-2915
  Counties Represented: Burleigh (part), Dickey (part), Emmons, LaMoure (part), Logan, McIntosh
  Term Expires: 2016
  8044 County Road 34, Edgeley, ND 58433-9761
  E-mail: mbrandenburg@nd.gov
  Committees: Appropriations; Appropriations - Government Operations Division

Representative **Al Carlson** (R-District 41) . . . . . . . . . . . . . . (701) 232-5832
  Counties Represented: Cass (part)
  Term Expires: 2018
  2548 Rose Creek Parkway South, Fargo, ND 58104-6699
  E-mail: acarlson@nd.gov
  Committees: Committees; Delayed Bills; Rules

Representative **Chuck Damschen** (R-District 10) . . . . . . . . (701) 868-3281
  Counties Represented: Cavalier, Pembina, Walsh (part)
  Term Expires: 2016
  9461 80th Street NE, Hampden, ND 58338-9351
  E-mail: cdamschen@nd.gov
  Committees: Energy and Natural Resources; Human Services

Representative **Lois Delmore** (D-District 43) . . . . . (701) 746-2407 ext. 321
  Counties Represented: Grand Forks (part)      Res: (701) 772-8428
  Term Expires: 2016
  714 South 22nd Street, Grand Forks, ND 58201-4138
  E-mail: ldelmore@nd.gov
  Committees: Employment; Judiciary; Transportation

Representative **Jeff Delzer** (R-District 8) . . . . . . . . . . . . . . (701) 442-5435
  Counties Represented: Burleigh (part), McLean (part)
  Term Expires: 2016
  2919 Fifth Street NW, Underwood, ND 58576-9603
  E-mail: jdelzer@nd.gov
  Committees: Appropriations

Representative **William R. "Bill" Devlin** (R-District 23) . . . (701) 524-2303
  Counties Represented: Benson (part), Eddy, Griggs, Nelson, Steele
  Term Expires: 2018
  P.O. Box 505, Finley, ND 58230
  E-mail: bdevlin@nd.gov
  Committees: Correction and Revision of the Journal; Energy and Natural Resources; Industry, Business and Labor

Representative **Jason Dockter** (R-District 6) . . . . . . . . . . . (701) 214-0486
  Counties Represented: Bottineau, McHenry, Renville
  Term Expires: 2016
  4443 Turnbow Lane, Bismarck, ND 58503
  E-mail: jddockter@nd.gov
  Committees: Finance and Taxation; Government and Veterans Affairs
  Education: North Dakota BSc

Representative **Mark A. Dosch** (R-District 32) . . . . . . . . . (701) 223-0569
  Counties Represented: Burleigh (part)
  Term Expires: 2016
  509 Cottonwood Loop, Bismarck, ND 58504-7411
  E-mail: mdosch@nd.gov
  Committees: Appropriations; Appropriations - Education and
  Environment Division; Arrangements for House Committee Rooms
  Education: North Dakota 1982 BSBA

Representative **Alan Fehr** (R-District 36) . . . . . . . . . . . . . (701) 590-0136
  Counties Represented: Dunn (part), Hettinger (part), Morton (part),
  Stark (part)
  Term Expires: 2016
  10641 Highway 10, Dickinson, ND 58601
  E-mail: afehr@nd.gov
  Committees: Agriculture; Human Services
  Education: North Dakota PhD

Representative **Robert "Bob" Frantsvog** (R-District 40) . . (701) 839-5307
  Counties Represented: Ward (part)
  Term Expires: 2016
  14 Ruyak Point, Minot, ND 58703-1232
  E-mail: rfrantsvog@nd.gov
  Committees: Industry, Business and Labor; Transportation

Representative **Glen Froseth** (R-District 4) . . . . . . . . . . . . (701) 385-4811
  Counties Represented: Dunn (part), McKenzie (part), McLean (part),
  Mercer (part), Mountrail (part), Ward (part)
  Term Expires: 2016
  P.O. Box 894, Kenmare, ND 58746-0894
  E-mail: gfroseth@nd.gov
  Committees: Energy and Natural Resources; Finance and Taxation

Representative **Eliot Glassheim** (D-District 18) . . . . . . . . . (701) 772-8840
  Counties Represented: Grand Forks (part)
  Term Expires: 2016
  619 North Third Street, Grand Forks, ND 58203-3203
  E-mail: eglassheim@nd.gov
  Committees: Appropriations; Appropriations - Government Operations
  Division

Representative **Ron Guggisberg** (D-District 11) . . . . . . . . . (701) 367-2478
  Counties Represented: Cass (part)
  Term Expires: 2018
  1621 17th Street South, Fargo, ND 58103
  E-mail: rguggisberg@nd.gov
  Committees: Appropriations; Appropriations - Education and
  Environment Division; Committees

Representative **Jessica Haak** (D-District 12) . . . . . . . . . . . (701) 320-5044
  Counties Represented: Stutsman (part)
  Term Expires: 2016
  PO Box 322, Jamestown, ND 58402
  E-mail: jehaak@nd.gov
  Committees: Agriculture; Finance and Taxation
  Education: Jamestown Col BA

Representative **Ben Hanson** (D-District 16) . . . . . . . . . . . . (701) 446-8634
  Counties Represented: Cass (part)
  Term Expires: 2016
  921 31st Avenue West, Fargo, ND 58078
  E-mail: bwhanson@nd.gov
  Committees: Industry, Business and Labor; Transportation

Representative **Patrick R. Hatlestad** (R-District 1) . . . . . . . (701) 577-6656
  Counties Represented: Williams (part)
  Term Expires: 2018
  P.O. Box 1342, Williston, ND 58802-1342
  E-mail: phatlestad@nd.gov
  Committees: Finance and Taxation; Political Subdivisions
  Education: North Dakota 1989 EdM

Representative **Kathy Hawken** (R-District 46) . . . . . . . . . . (701) 293-5483
  Counties Represented: Cass (part)
  Term Expires: 2016
  4442 Carrie Rose Lane South, Fargo, ND 58104-6818
  E-mail: khawken@nd.gov
  Committees: Employment; Judiciary; Transportation

Representative **Craig Headland** (R-District 29) . . . . . . . . . (701) 489-3184
  Counties Represented: Foster, LaMoure (part), Stutsman (part)
  Term Expires: 2018
  4950 - 92nd Avenue SE, Montpelier, ND 58472-9630
  E-mail: cheadland@nd.gov
  Committees: Agriculture; Committees; Finance and Taxation

Representative **Curt Hofstad** (R-District 15) . . . . . . . . . . . (701) 662-1151
  Counties Represented: Ramsey, Towner
  Term Expires: 2018
  1614 Third Street SE, Devils Lake, ND 58301-3450
  E-mail: chofstad@nd.gov
  Committees: Energy and Natural Resources; Human Services

Representative **Kathy Hogan** (D-District 21) . . . . . . . . . . . (701) 235-1916
  Counties Represented: Cass (part)
  Term Expires: 2018
  710 South University Drive, Fargo, ND 58103-2632
  E-mail: khogan@nd.gov
  Committees: Appropriations; Appropriations - Government Operations
  Division; Correction and Revision of the Journal

Representative
  **Richard G. "Rick" Holman** (D-District 20) . . . . . . . . . . (701) 788-2081
  Counties Represented: Cass (part), Grand Forks (part), Traill
  Term Expires: 2016
  622 153rd Avenue NE, Mayville, ND 58257-9000
  E-mail: rholman@nd.gov
  Committees: Appropriations; Appropriations - Human Resources
  Division; Committees

Representative **Bob Hunskor** (D-District 6) . . . . . . . . . . . . (701) 272-6283
  Counties Represented: Bottineau, McHenry, Renville
  Term Expires: 2016
  P.O. Box 1, Newburg, ND 58762-0001
  E-mail: bhunskor@nd.gov
  Committees: Education; Energy and Natural Resources

Representative **Dennis Johnson** (R-District 15) . . . . . . . . . (701) 662-4998
  Counties Represented: Ramsey, Towner
  Term Expires: 2018
  7871 - 45th Street NE, Devils Lake, ND 58301-9089
  E-mail: djohnson@nd.gov
  Committees: Agriculture; Education

Representative **Mary C. Johnson** (R-District 45) . . . . . . . . (701) 235-5912
  Counties Represented: Cass (part)                    Res: (701) 232-3080
  Term Expires: 2016
  E-mail: marycjohnson@nd.gov
  Committees: Government and Veterans Affairs; Judiciary

Representative **Tom Kading** (R-District 45) . . . . . . . . . . . . (701) 639-4849
  Counties Represented: Cass (part)
  Term Expires: 2018
  E-mail: tkading@nd.gov
  Committees: Agriculture; Finance and Taxation

Representative **Karen Karls** (R-District 35) . . . . . . . . . . . . (701) 258-6836
  Counties Represented: Burleigh (part)
  Term Expires: 2018
  2112 Senate Drive, Bismarck, ND 58501-1978
  E-mail: kkarls@nd.gov
  Committees: Government and Veterans Affairs; Judiciary

Representative **Jim Kasper** (R-District 46) . . . . . . . . . . . . (701) 799-9000
  Counties Represented: Cass (part)
  Term Expires: 2016
  1128 Westrac Drive, Fargo, ND 58103-2342
  E-mail: jkasper@nd.gov
  Committees: Committees; Government and Veterans Affairs; Industry,
  Business and Labor

Representative **George J. Keiser** (R-District 47) . . . . . . . . . (701) 258-0333
  Counties Represented: Burleigh (part)
  Term Expires: 2018
  422 Toronto Drive, Bismarck, ND 58503-0276
  E-mail: gkeiser@nd.gov
  Committees: Energy and Natural Resources; Industry, Business and
  Labor

Representative **Jerome "Jerry" Kelsh** (D-District 26) . . . . (701) 375-7521
  Counties Represented: Dickey (part), Ransom (part), Richland (part),
  Sargent
  Term Expires: 2016
  P.O. Box 27, Fullerton, ND 58441-0027
  E-mail: jkelsh@nd.gov
  Committees: Education; Political Subdivisions; Rules

Representative **Keith Kempenich** (R-District 39) . . . . . . . . (701) 523-3858
  Counties Represented: Adams, Billings, Bowman, Dunn (part), Golden
  Valley, McKenzie (part), Slope
  Term Expires: 2018
  9005 - 151st Avenue SW, Bowman, ND 58623-8857
  E-mail: kkempenich@nd.gov
  Committees: Appropriations; Appropriations - Government Operations
  Division

*(continued on next page)*

**LEGISLATIVE BRANCH**

**Representatives** *continued*

Representative **Dwight Kiefert** (R-District 24) . . . . . . . . . . (701) 845-0760
Counties Represented: Abbeville, Barnes, Cass     Fax: (701) 845-0760
(part), Ransom (part)
Term Expires: 2016
3721 115th Avenue Southeast, Valley City, ND 58072
E-mail: dhkiefert@nd.gov
Committees: Agriculture; Human Services

Representative
**Matthew M. "Matt" Klein** (R-District 40) . . . . . . . . . . . (701) 838-6309
Counties Represented: Ward (part)
Term Expires: 2016
1815 Seventh Street NW, Minot, ND 58703-1314
E-mail: mklein@nd.gov
Committees: Arrangements for House Committee Rooms; Finance and
Taxation; Political Subdivisions
Education: North Dakota State BSEE

Representative **Lawrence R. Klemin** (R-District 47) . . . . . . (701) 222-2577
Counties Represented: Burleigh (part)
Term Expires: 2018
1709 Montego Drive, Bismarck, ND 58503-0856
E-mail: lklemin@nd.gov
Committees: Correction and Revision of the Journal; Judiciary;
Political Subdivisions
Education: North Dakota 1967 BA, 1978 JD

Representative **Ben Koppelman** (R-District 16) . . . . . . . . . (701) 491-0665
Counties Represented: Cass (part)
Term Expires: 2016
205 36 1/2 Avenue Place East, West Fargo, ND 58078
E-mail: bkoppelman@nd.gov
Committees: Education; Government and Veterans Affairs
Education: North Dakota State (Attended)

Representative **Kim Koppelman** (R-District 13) . . . . . . . . . (701) 282-9267
Counties Represented: Cass (part)
Term Expires: 2018
513 First Avenue NW, West Fargo, ND 58078-1101
E-mail: kkoppelman@nd.gov
Committees: Judiciary; Political Subdivisions

Representative **Gary Kreidt** (R-District 33) . . . . . . . . . . . . (701) 843-7074
Counties Represented: Mercer (part), Morton (part), Oliver
Term Expires: 2016
3892 County Road 86, New Salem, ND 58563-9406
E-mail: gkreidt@nd.gov
Committees: Appropriations; Appropriations - Human Resources
Division

Representative **William E. Kretschmar** (R-District 28) . . . . (701) 684-7321
Counties Represented: Burleigh (part), Dickey (part), Emmons,
LaMoure (part), Logan, McIntosh
Term Expires: 2016
201 East Third Street, Venturia, ND 58413-4015
E-mail: wkretschmar@nd.gov
Committees: Correction and Revision of the Journal; Judiciary;
Political Subdivisions; Rules

Representative **Vernon R. Laning** (R-District 8) . . . . . . . . . (701) 226-2113
Counties Represented: Burleigh (part), McLean (part)
Term Expires: 2016
4121 78th Avenue Northeast, Bismarck, ND 58503
E-mail: vrlaning@nd.gov
Committees: Government and Veterans Affairs; Industry, Business and
Labor
Education: North Dakota State BS

Representative **Diane Larson** (R-District 30) . . . . . . . . . . . (701) 328-2916
Counties Represented: Burleigh (part)
Term Expires: 2016
2525 Larson Road, Bismarck, ND 58504
E-mail: dklarson@nd.gov
Committees: Agriculture; Judiciary
Education: Bismarck State AA; North Dakota BS

Representative **Mike Lefor** (R-District 37) . . . . . . . . . . . . . (701) 456-3069
Counties Represented: Stark (part)
Term Expires: 2018
E-mail: mlefor@nd.gov
Committees: Energy and Natural Resources; Industry, Business and
Labor

Representative **Alex Looysen** (R-District 12) . . . . . . . . . . . (701) 269-9482
Counties Represented: Stutsman (part)
Term Expires: 2016
PO Box 1035, Jamestown, ND 58401
E-mail: alooysen@nd.gov
Committees: Agriculture; Education

Representative **Scott Louser** (R-District 5) . . . . . . . . . . . . (701) 328-9587
Counties Represented: Ward (part)
Term Expires: 2018
1718 Birch Place SW, Minot, ND 58701
E-mail: sclouser@nd.gov
Committees: Committees; Government and Veterans Affairs; Industry,
Business and Labor

Representative **Andrew G. Maragos** (R-District 3) . . . . . . . (701) 825-3862
Counties Represented: Ward (part)
Term Expires: 2018
125 Sixth Avenue NE, Minot, ND 58703
E-mail: agmaragos@nd.gov
Committees: Employment; Judiciary; Political Subdivisions

Representative **Bob Martinson** (R-District 35) . . . . . . . . . . (701) 223-0835
Counties Represented: Burleigh (part)
Term Expires: 2018
2749 Pacific Avenue, Bismarck, ND 58501-2513
E-mail: bmartinson@nd.gov
Committees: Appropriations; Appropriations - Education and
Environment Division; Employment

Representative **Lisa M. Meier** (R-District 32) . . . . . . . . . . . (701) 202-7126
Counties Represented: Burleigh (part)
Term Expires: 2016
1713 South Third Street, Bismarck, ND 58504-7114
E-mail: lmeier@nd.gov
Committees: Education; Transportation

Representative **Alisa Mitskog** (D-District 25) . . . . . . . . . . . (701) 642-6480
Counties Represented: Cass (part), Richland (part)     Res: (701) 642-9023
Term Expires: 2018                                       Fax: (701) 642-6011
E-mail: amitskog@nd.gov
Committees: Agriculture; Finance and Taxation

Representative **Corey Mock** (D-District 42) . . . . . . . . . . . . (701) 732-0085
Counties Represented: Grand Forks (part)
Term Expires: 2016
P.O. Box 12542, Grand Forks, ND 58208-2542
E-mail: crmock@nd.gov
Committees: Delayed Bills; Education; Energy and Natural Resources

Representative **David Monson** (R-District 10) . . . . . . . . . . (701) 496-3394
Counties Represented: Cavalier, Pembina, Walsh (part)
Term Expires: 2016
P.O. Box 8, Osnabrock, ND 58269-0008
E-mail: dmonson@nd.gov
Committees: Appropriations; Appropriations - Education and
Environment Division

Representative **Gail Mooney** (D-District 20) . . . . . . . . . . . (701) 436-5010
Counties Represented: Cass (part), Grand Forks (part), Traill
Term Expires: 2016
680 166th Avenue Northeast, Cummings, ND 58223
E-mail: gmooney@nd.gov
Committees: Government and Veterans Affairs; Human Services

Representative **Naomi T. Muscha** (D-District 24) . . . . . . . . (701) 793-0326
Counties Represented: Abbeville, Barnes, Cass (part), Ransom (part)
Term Expires: 2016
221 Oehlke Avenue, Enderlin, ND 58027
E-mail: nmuscha@nd.gov
Committees: Energy and Natural Resources; Human Services
Education: Valley City State BS

Representative **Michael R. "Mike" Nathe** (R-District 30) . . . . . . . . . (701)
250-0645
Counties Represented: Burleigh (part)
Term Expires: 2016
1899 Bonn Boulevard, Bismarck, ND 58504-7019
E-mail: mrnathe@nd.gov
Committees: Committees; Education; Energy and Natural Resources

Representative **Jon Nelson** (R-District 14) . . . . . . . . . . . . . (701) 776-6738
Counties Represented: Benson (part), Kidder, Pierce, Sheridan, Wells
Term Expires: 2016
420 Sixth Avenue SE, Rugby, ND 58368-2320
E-mail: jonelson@nd.gov
Committees: Appropriations; Appropriations - Human Resources
Division

Representative **Marvin E. Nelson** (D-District 9) . . . . . . . . (701) 477-3422
Counties Represented: Rolette
Term Expires: 2018
P.O. Box 577, Rolla, ND 58367
E-mail: menelson@nd.gov
Committees: Industry, Business and Labor; Rules; Transportation

Representative **Christopher D. Olson** (R-District 13) . . . . . (701) 204-0424
Counties Represented: Cass (part)               Fax: (701) 204-0424
Term Expires: 2018
E-mail: cdolson@nd.gov
Committees: Education; Transportation

Representative **Kenton Onstad** (D-District 4) . . . . . . . . . . (701) 862-3445
Counties Represented: Dunn (part), McKenzie (part), McLean (part), Mercer (part), Mountrail (part), Ward (part)
Term Expires: 2016
3515 66th Avenue, NW, Parshall, ND 58770-9468
E-mail: konstad@nd.gov
Committees: Delayed Bills

Representative **Kylie Oversen** (D-District 42). . . . . . . . . . .(701) 328-2916
Counties Represented: Grand Forks (part)
Term Expires: 2016
PO Box 14382, Grand Forks, ND 58208
E-mail: koversen@nd.gov
Committees: Human Services; Political Subdivisions; Rules
Education: North Dakota BA, BS

Representative **Mark S. Owens** (R-District 17) . . . . . . . . . (701) 792-1819
Counties Represented: Grand Forks (part)
Term Expires: 2018
5865 Fountain Vista Drive, Grand Forks, ND 58201
E-mail: mowens@nd.gov
Committees: Finance and Taxation; Transportation

Representative **Gary Paur** (R-District 19) . . . . . . . . . . . . . (701) 869-2892
Counties Represented: Grand Forks (part), Walsh (part)
Term Expires: 2018
2710 28th Street NE, Gilby, ND 58235
E-mail: gpaur@nd.gov
Committees: Judiciary; Transportation

Representative **Chet Pollert** (R-District 29) . . . . . . . . . . . . (701) 652-2494
Counties Represented: Foster, LaMoure (part), Stutsman (part)
Term Expires: 2018
560 South Sixth Street, Carrington, ND 58421-2317
E-mail: cpollert@nd.gov
Committees: Appropriations; Appropriations - Human Resources Division

Representative **Todd Porter** (R-District 34). . . . . . . . . . . . .(701) 667-2922
Counties Represented: Morton (part)
Term Expires: 2016
4604 Borden Harbor Drive SE, Mandan, ND 58554-7961
E-mail: tkporter@nd.gov
Committees: Energy and Natural Resources; Human Services

Representative **Karen Rohr** (R-District 31) . . . . . . . . . . . . .(701) 202-1956
Counties Represented: Grant, Hettinger (part), Morton (part), Sioux
Term Expires: 2018
1704 Fourth Street NE, Mandan, ND 58554
E-mail: kmrohr@nd.gov
Committees: Education; Government and Veterans Affairs

Representative **Dan J. Ruby** (R-District 38) . . . . . . . . . . . . (701) 852-6132
Counties Represented: Ward (part)
Term Expires: 2016
4620 - 46th Avenue NW, Minot, ND 58703-8711
E-mail: druby@nd.gov
Committees: Committees; Industry, Business and Labor; Transportation

Representative **Mark Sanford** (R-District 17) . . . . . . . . . . . (701) 772-4236
Counties Represented: Grand Forks (part)
Term Expires: 2018
675 Vineyard Drive, Grand Forks, ND 58201
E-mail: masanford@nd.gov
Committees: Appropriations; Appropriations - Education and Environment Division

Representative **Mike Schatz** (R-District 36) . . . . . . . . . . . . (701) 579-4823
Counties Represented: Dunn (part), Hettinger (part), Morton (part), Stark (part)
Term Expires: 2016
400 Ninth Street East, New England, ND 58647-7528
E-mail: mischatz@nd.gov
Committees: Education; Transportation

Representative **James E. "Jim" Schmidt** (R-District 31) . .(701) 663-0009
Counties Represented: Grant, Hettinger (part), Morton (part), Sioux
Term Expires: 2018
5165 Highway 1806, Huff, ND 58554
E-mail: jeschmidt@nd.gov
Committees: Appropriations; Appropriations - Education and Environment Division

Representative **Mary Schneider** (D-District 21) . . . . . . . . .(701) 235-0316
Counties Represented: Cass (part)
Term Expires: 2018
E-mail: mschneider@nd.gov
Committees: Correction and Revision of the Journal; Finance and Taxation; Government and Veterans Affairs

Representative **Cynthia Schreiber Beck** (R-District 25) . . . (701) 642-5777
Counties Represented: Cass (part), Richland (part)
Term Expires: 2018
E-mail: cschreiberbeck@nd.gov
Committees: Agriculture; Education

Representative **Jay R. Seibel** (R-District 33) . . . . . . . . . . . (701) 873-2795
Counties Represented: Mercer (part), Morton (part), Oliver
Term Expires: 2018
E-mail: jayseibel@nd.gov
Committees: Government and Veterans Affairs; Human Services

Representative **Peter Silbernagel** (R-District 22) . . . . . . . . (701) 799-0689
Counties Represented: Cass (part)
Term Expires: 2016
PO Box 537, Casselton, ND 58012
E-mail: psilbernagel@nd.gov
Committees: Appropriations; Appropriations - Human Resources Division
Education: U Mary BA

Representative **Robert J. Skarphol** (R-District 2) . . . . . . . . (701) 664-3510
Counties Represented: Burke, Divide, Mountrail (part), Williams (part)
Term Expires: 2016
P.O. Box 725, Tioga, ND 58852-0725
E-mail: bskarphol@nd.gov
Committees: Appropriations; Appropriations - Government Operations Division

Representative **Vicky Steiner** (R-District 37) . . . . . . . . . . . (701) 225-4227
Counties Represented: Stark (part)
Term Expires: 2018
859 Senior Avenue, Dickinson, ND 58601
E-mail: vsteiner@nd.gov
Committees: Finance and Taxation; Government and Veterans Affairs; Judiciary

Representative **Roscoe Streyle** (R-District 3). . . . . . . . . . .(701) 351-0064
Counties Represented: Ward (part)
Term Expires: 2018
3108 15th Street SE, Minot, ND 58701
E-mail: rstreyle@nd.gov
Committees: Appropriations; Appropriations - Education and Environment Division

Representative **Marie Strinden** (D-District 18). . . . . . . . . .(917) 687-9245
Counties Represented: Grand Forks (part)
Term Expires: 2016
315 Kittson Avenue, Grand Forks, ND 58201
E-mail: mjstrinden@nd.gov
Committees: Finance and Taxation; Political Subdivisions
Education: NYU BFA

Representative **Gary R. Sukut** (R-District 1) . . . . . . . . . . . (701) 572-9607
Counties Represented: Williams (part)
Term Expires: 2018
1603 Fourth Avenue East, Williston, ND 58801-4324
E-mail: gsukut@nd.gov
Committees: Industry, Business and Labor; Transportation

Representative **Blair Thoreson** (R-District 44) . . . . . . . . . . (701) 234-0862
Counties Represented: Cass (part)
Term Expires: 2016
1246 Second Street North, Fargo, ND 58102-2723
E-mail: bthoreson@nd.gov
Committees: Appropriations; Appropriations - Government Operations Division

Representative **Nathan P. Toman** (R-District 34) . . . . . . . . (701) 516-4964
Counties Represented: Morton (part)
Term Expires: 2016
203 Fourth Avenue Northwest, Mandan, ND 58554
E-mail: nptoman@nd.gov
Committees: Finance and Taxation; Political Subdivisions
Education: Bismarck State AA

Representative **Wayne Trottier** (R-District 19) . . . . . . . . . . (701) 587-5040
Counties Represented: Grand Forks (part), Walsh (part)
Term Expires: 2018
115 North Lincoln Street, Northwood, ND 58267
E-mail: wtrottier@nd.gov
Committees: Agriculture; Finance and Taxation

Representative **Don Vigesaa** (R-District 23) . . . . . . . . . . . .(701) 797-2448
Counties Represented: Benson (part), Eddy, Griggs, Nelson, Steele
Term Expires: 2018
P.O. Box 763, Cooperstown, ND 58425-0763
E-mail: dwvigesaa@nd.gov
Committees: Appropriations; Appropriations - Government Operations Division; Committees; Delayed Bills; Rules

Representative **Kris Wallman** (D-District 11) . . . . . . . . . . . (701) 297-3549
Counties Represented: Cass (part)
Term Expires: 2018
E-mail: kwallman@nd.gov
Committees: Government and Veterans Affairs; Judiciary

*(continued on next page)*

**Representatives** *continued*

Representative **Robin Weisz** (R-District 14) . . . . . . . . . . . . . (701) 962-3799
  Counties Represented: Benson (part), Kidder, Pierce, Sheridan, Wells
  Term Expires: 2016
  50 Highway 3 South, Hurdsfield, ND 58451-9009
  E-mail: rweisz@nd.gov
  Committees: Human Services; Transportation

Representative **Denton B. Zubke** (R-District 39) . . . . . . . . (701) 444-6484
  Counties Represented: Adams, Billings, Bowman,    Res: (701) 842-3081
  Dunn (part), Golden Valley, McKenzie (part), Slope    Fax: (701) 444-3829
  Term Expires: 2018
  E-mail: dzubke@nd.gov
  Committees: Education; Political Subdivisions

# House Standing Committees

## Agriculture

| Majority Members | Minority Members |
| --- | --- |
| Dennis Johnson (R-15) *Chairman* | Joshua A. Boschee (D-44) |
| Wayne Trottier (R-19) | Jessica Haak (D-12) |
|   *Vice Chairman* | Alisa Mitskog (D-25) |
| Bert Anderson (R-2) | |
| Alan Fehr (R-36) | |
| Craig Headland (R-29) | |
| Tom Kading (R-45) | |
| Dwight Kiefert (R-24) | |
| Diane Larson (R-30) | |
| Alex Looysen (R-12) | |
| Cynthia Schreiber Beck (R-25) | |

## Appropriations

| Majority Members | Minority Members |
| --- | --- |
| Jeff Delzer (R-8) *Chairman* | Tracy Boe (D-9) |
| Keith Kempenich (R-39) | Eliot Glassheim (D-18) |
|   *Vice Chairman* | Ron Guggisberg (D-11) |
| Larry Bellew (R-38) | Kathy Hogan (D-21) |
| Randy Boehning (R-27) | Richard G. "Rick" Holman (D-20) |
| Michael Don "Mike" Brandenburg | |
|   (R-28) | |
| Mark A. Dosch (R-32) | |
| Gary Kreidt (R-33) | |
| Bob Martinson (R-35) | |
| David Monson (R-10) | |
| Jon Nelson (R-14) | |
| Chet Pollert (R-29) | |
| Mark Sanford (R-17) | |
| James E. "Jim" Schmidt (R-31) | |
| Peter Silbernagel (R-22) | |
| Robert J. Skarphol (R-2) | |
| Roscoe Streyle (R-3) | |
| Blair Thoreson (R-44) | |
| Don Vigesaa (R-23) | |

## Appropriations - Education and Environment Division

| Majority Members | Minority Members |
| --- | --- |
| David Monson (R-10) *Chairman* | Tracy Boe (D-9) |
| Roscoe Streyle (R-3) | Ron Guggisberg (D-11) |
|   *Vice Chairman* | |
| Mark A. Dosch (R-32) | |
| Bob Martinson (R-35) | |
| Mark Sanford (R-17) | |
| James E. "Jim" Schmidt (R-31) | |

## Appropriations - Government Operations Division

| Majority Members | Minority Members |
| --- | --- |
| Blair Thoreson (R-44) *Chairman* | Eliot Glassheim (D-18) |
| Michael Don "Mike" | Kathy Hogan (D-21) |
|   Brandenburg (R-28) | |
|   *Vice Chairman* | |
| Randy Boehning (R-27) | |
| Keith Kempenich (R-39) | |
| Robert J. Skarphol (R-2) | |
| Don Vigesaa (R-23) | |

## Appropriations - Human Resources Division

| Majority Members | Minority Members |
| --- | --- |
| Chet Pollert (R-29) *Chairman* | Richard G. "Rick" Holman (D-20) |
| Larry Bellew (R-38) *Vice Chairman* | |
| Gary Kreidt (R-33) | |
| Jon Nelson (R-14) | |
| Peter Silbernagel (R-22) | |

## Education

| Majority Members | Minority Members |
| --- | --- |
| Michael R. "Mike" Nathe (R-30) | Bob Hunskor (D-6) |
|   *Chairman* | Jerome "Jerry" Kelsh (D-26) |
| Mike Schatz (R-36) *Vice Chairman* | Corey Mock (D-42) |
| Dennis Johnson (R-15) | |
| Ben Koppelman (R-16) | |
| Alex Looysen (R-12) | |
| Lisa M. Meier (R-32) | |
| Christopher D. Olson (R-13) | |
| Karen Rohr (R-31) | |
| Cynthia Schreiber Beck (R-25) | |
| Denton B. Zubke (R-39) | |

## Energy and Natural Resources

| Majority Members | Minority Members |
| --- | --- |
| Todd Porter (R-34) *Chairman* | Bob Hunskor (D-6) |
| Chuck Damschen (R-10) | Corey Mock (D-42) |
|   *Vice Chairman* | Naomi T. Muscha (D-24) |
| Dick Anderson (R-6) | |
| Roger Brabandt (R-5) | |
| William R. "Bill" Devlin (R-23) | |
| Glen Froseth (R-4) | |
| Curt Hofstad (R-15) | |
| George J. Keiser (R-47) | |
| Mike Lefor (R-37) | |
| Michael R. "Mike" Nathe (R-30) | |

## Finance and Taxation

| Majority Members | Minority Members |
| --- | --- |
| Craig Headland (R-29) *Chairman* | Jessica Haak (D-12) |
| Mark S. Owens (R-17) | Alisa Mitskog (D-25) |
|   *Vice Chairman* | Mary Schneider (D-21) |
| Jason Dockter (R-6) | Marie Strinden (D-18) |
| Glen Froseth (R-4) | |
| Patrick R. Hatlestad (R-1) | |
| Tom Kading (R-45) | |
| Matthew M. "Matt" Klein (R-40) | |
| Vicky Steiner (R-37) | |
| Nathan P. Toman (R-34) | |
| Wayne Trottier (R-19) | |

## Government and Veterans Affairs

| Majority Members | Minority Members |
| --- | --- |
| Jim Kasper (R-46) *Chairman* | Bill Amerman (D-26) |
| Karen Rohr (R-31) *Vice Chairman* | Gail Mooney (D-20) |
| Jason Dockter (R-6) | Mary Schneider (D-21) |
| Mary C. Johnson (R-45) | Kris Wallman (D-11) |
| Karen Karls (R-35) | |
| Ben Koppelman (R-16) | |
| Vernon R. Laning (R-8) | |
| Scott Louser (R-5) | |
| Jay R. Seibel (R-33) | |
| Vicky Steiner (R-37) | |

## Human Services

| Majority Members | Minority Members |
| --- | --- |
| Robin Weisz (R-14) *Chairman* | Gail Mooney (D-20) |
| Curt Hofstad (R-15) *Vice Chairman* | Naomi T. Muscha (D-24) |
| Bert Anderson (R-2) | Kylie Oversen (D-42) |
| Dick Anderson (R-6) | |
| Richard S. Becker (R-43) | |
| Chuck Damschen (R-10) | |
| Alan Fehr (R-36) | |
| Dwight Kiefert (R-24) | |
| Todd Porter (R-34) | |
| Jay R. Seibel (R-33) | |

## Industry, Business and Labor

**Majority Members**
George J. Keiser (R-47) *Chairman*
Gary R. Sukut (R-1) *Vice Chairman*
Thomas Beadle (R-27)
Rick C. Becker (R-7)
William R. "Bill" Devlin (R-23)
Robert "Bob" Frantsvog (R-40)
Jim Kasper (R-46)
Vernon R. Laning (R-8)
Mike Lefor (R-37)
Scott Louser (R-5)
Dan J. Ruby (R-38)

**Minority Members**
Bill Amerman (D-26)
Joshua A. Boschee (D-44)
Ben Hanson (D-16)
Marvin E. Nelson (D-9)

## Judiciary

**Majority Members**
Kim Koppelman (R-13) *Chairman*
Karen Karls (R-35) *Vice Chairman*
Roger Brabandt (R-5)
Kathy Hawken (R-46)
Mary C. Johnson (R-45)
Lawrence R. Klemin (R-47)
William E. Kretschmar (R-28)
Diane Larson (R-30)
Andrew G. Maragos (R-3)
Gary Paur (R-19)
Vicky Steiner (R-37)

**Minority Members**
Pamela Anderson (D-41)
Lois Delmore (D-43)
Kris Wallman (D-11)

## Political Subdivisions

**Majority Members**
Lawrence R. Klemin (R-47)
  *Chairman*
Patrick R. Hatlestad (R-1)
  *Vice Chairman*
Thomas Beadle (R-27)
Richard S. Becker (R-43)
Matthew M. "Matt" Klein (R-40)
Kim Koppelman (R-13)
William E. Kretschmar (R-28)
Andrew G. Maragos (R-3)
Nathan P. Toman (R-34)
Denton B. Zubke (R-39)

**Minority Members**
Pamela Anderson (D-41)
Jerome "Jerry" Kelsh (D-26)
Kylie Oversen (D-42)
Marie Strinden (D-18)

## Transportation

**Majority Members**
Dan J. Ruby (R-38) *Chairman*
Lisa M. Meier (R-32)
  *Vice Chairman*
Rick C. Becker (R-7)
Robert "Bob" Frantsvog (R-40)
Kathy Hawken (R-46)
Christopher D. Olson (R-13)
Mark S. Owens (R-17)
Gary Paur (R-19)
Mike Schatz (R-36)
Gary R. Sukut (R-1)
Robin Weisz (R-14)

**Minority Members**
Lois Delmore (D-43)
Ben Hanson (D-16)
Marvin E. Nelson (D-9)

# House Procedural Committees

## Arrangements for House Committee Rooms

**Majority Members**
Matthew M. "Matt" Klein (R-40)
  *Chairman*
Mark A. Dosch (R-32)

**Minority Members**
Joshua A. Boschee (D-44)

## Committees

**Majority Members**
Al Carlson (R-41) *Chairman*
Wesley R. Belter (R-22)
Craig Headland (R-29)
Jim Kasper (R-46)
Scott Louser (R-5)
Michael R. "Mike" Nathe (R-30)
Dan J. Ruby (R-38)
Don Vigesaa (R-23)

**Minority Members**
Joshua A. Boschee (D-44)
Ron Guggisberg (D-11)
Richard G. "Rick" Holman (D-20)

## Correction and Revision of the Journal

**Majority Members**
William E. Kretschmar (R-28)
  *Chairman*
William R. "Bill" Devlin (R-23)
Lawrence R. Klemin (R-47)

**Minority Members**
Kathy Hogan (D-21)
Mary Schneider (D-21)

## Delayed Bills

**Majority Members**
Al Carlson (R-41) *Chairman*
Wesley R. Belter (R-22)
Don Vigesaa (R-23)

**Minority Members**
Corey Mock (D-42)
Kenton Onstad (D-4)

## Employment

**Majority Members**
Bob Martinson (R-35) *Chairman*
Kathy Hawken (R-46)
Andrew G. Maragos (R-3)

**Minority Members**
Tracy Boe (D-9)
Lois Delmore (D-43)

## Rules

**Majority Members**
Al Carlson (R-41) *Chairman*
Wesley R. Belter (R-22)
William E. Kretschmar (R-28)
Don Vigesaa (R-23)

**Minority Members**
Jerome "Jerry" Kelsh (D-26)
Marvin E. Nelson (D-9)
Kylie Oversen (D-42)

**LEGISLATIVE BRANCH**

# Ohio General Assembly

Tel: (614) 466-8842 (Legislative Information)
Tel: (614) 466-5312 (Legislative Service Library)  Tel: (614) 728-5100
(Lobbyist JLEC Registration/Legislative Inspector General)
Internet: www.legislature.state.oh.us

## Ohio Senate

State House, Columbus, OH 43215
Senate Building, 1 Capitol Square, Columbus, OH 43215
Tel: (614) 466-4900  Fax: (614) 466-8261

**Employees:** 125

President of the Senate **Keith L. Faber** (R) . . . . . . . . . . . . .(614) 466-7584
  Education: Oakland U BS; Ohio State JD
President Pro Tem **Larry J. Obhof, Jr.** (R) . . . . . . . . . . . . .(614) 466-7505
  Education: Ohio State BA; Yale 2003 JD
Majority Floor Leader **Thomas F. "Tom" Patton** (R) . . . . .(614) 466-8056
Majority Whip **Larry J. Obhof, Jr.** (R) . . . . . . . . . . . . . .(614) 466-7505
Minority Leader **Joseph "Joe" Schiavoni** (D) . . . . . . . . . .(614) 466-8285
  Education: Ohio 2001 BS; Capital U 2004 JD
Assistant Minority Leader **Charleta B. Tavares** (D) . . . . . .(614) 466-5131
Minority Whip **Edna R. Brown** (D) . . . . . . . . . . . . . . . . .(614) 466-5204
Assistant Minority Whip **Lou Gentile** (D) . . . . . . . . . . . . .(614) 466-6508
Clerk of the Senate **Vincent L. Keeran** . . . . . . . . . . . . . . .(614) 466-4900
  E-mail: keeran@ohiosenate.gov
Sergeant-at-Arms **Ken Mumper** . . . . . . . . . . . . . . . . . . . .(614) 466-4884
  E-mail: kmumper@mailr.sen.state.oh.us

## Senators

**Party Affiliation Statistics:** Republicans: 23, Democrats: 10

Senator **Kevin Bacon, JD** (R-District 3) Ground Floor . . . . (614) 466-8064
  Counties Represented: Franklin (part)
  Term Expires: 2019
  E-mail: bacon@ohiosenate.gov
  Committees: Civil Justice; Criminal Justice; Financial Institutions;
  Insurance; Public Utilities; Transportation, Commerce and Labor
  Education: Miami U (OH) 1994 BA; Capital U 1998 JD
Senator **Troy Balderson** (R-District 20) Ground Floor . . . . .(614) 466-8076
  Counties Represented: Athens (part), Fairfield, Guernsey, Hocking,
  Morgan, Muskingum, Pickaway (part)
  Term Expires: 2017
  E-mail: balderson@ohiosenate.gov
  Committees: Education; Energy and Natural Resources; Government
  Oversight and Reform; Insurance; Public Utilities; Ways and Means
  Education: Muskingum Col 1982 (Attended);
  Ohio State 1983 (Attended)
Senator **Bill Beagle** (R-District 5) 1st Floor . . . . . . . . . . . .(614) 466-6247
  Counties Represented: Darke (part), Miami, Montgomery (part), Preble
  Term Expires: 2019
  E-mail: beagle@ohiosenate.gov
  Committees: Agriculture; Finance; Financial Institutions; Health and
  Human Services; Insurance; Ways and Means
  Education: Miami Christian BS; Cleveland State MBA
Senator **Edna R. Brown** (D-District 11) 2nd Floor . . . . . . .(614) 466-5204
  Counties Represented: Lucas (part)
  Term Expires: 2019
  E-mail: brown@ohiosenate.gov
  Committees: Civil Justice; Government Oversight and Reform;
  Insurance; Rules and Reference; State and Local Government;
  Transportation, Commerce and Labor
Senator **David E. "Dave" Burke** (R-District 26)
  Ground Floor . . . . . . . . . . . . . . . . . . . . . . . . . . . . . . (614) 466-8049
  Counties Represented: Crawford, Marion, Morrow, Sandusky, Seneca,
  Union, Wyandot
  Term Expires: 2017
  E-mail: burke@ohiosenate.gov
  Committees: Agriculture; Finance; Financial Institutions; Government
  Oversight and Reform; Medicaid; Rules and Reference
  Education: Ohio Northern 1990 BSPh; Capital U 1994 MBA
Senator **Capri S. Cafaro** (D-District 32) Ground Floor . . . . (614) 466-7182
  Counties Represented: Ashtabula, Geauga (part), Trumbull
  Term Expires: 2017
  E-mail: cafaro@ohiosenate.gov
  Committees: Agriculture; Energy and Natural Resources; Health and
  Human Services; Medicaid; Transportation, Commerce and Labor;
  Ways and Means
  Education: Stanford 1997 BA; Georgetown 2001 MALS

Senator **William P. "Bill" Coley II** (R-District 4)
  1st Floor . . . . . . . . . . . . . . . . . . . . . . . . . . . . . . . . . (614) 466-8072
  Counties Represented: Butler (part)
  Term Expires: 2017
  E-mail: coley@ohiosenate.gov
  Committees: Civil Justice; Education; Finance; Government Oversight
  and Reform; Medicaid; Rules and Reference
  Education: Dayton BS; Cleveland-Marshall JD
Senator **John Eklund** (R-District 18) 1st Floor . . . . . . . . . (614) 644-7718
  Counties Represented: Geauga (part), Lake (part), Portage
  Term Expires: 2017
  E-mail: eklund@ohiosenate.gov
  Committees: Civil Justice; Criminal Justice; Financial Institutions;
  Public Utilities; Transportation, Commerce and Labor; Ways and Means
  Education: Washington and Lee JD
Senator **Keith L. Faber** (R-District 12)
  Statehouse, 2nd Floor . . . . . . . . . . . . . . . . . . . . . . . . . (614) 466-7584
  Counties Represented: Allen, Auglaize (part),          Fax: (614) 466-7339
  Champaign, Darke (part), Logan (part), Mercer, Shelby
  Term Expires: 2017
  E-mail: faber@ohiosenate.gov
  Committees: Rules and Reference
Senator **Randy L. Gardner** (R-District 2) 2nd Floor . . . . . . (614) 752-9777
  Counties Represented: Erie, Fulton (part), Lucas (part), Ottawa, Wood
  Term Expires: 2017
  E-mail: gardner@ohiosenate.gov
  Committees: Agriculture; Education; Energy and Natural Resources;
  Finance; Health and Human Services
  Education: Bowling Green State BS, MA
Senator **Lou Gentile** (D-District 30) Ground Floor . . . . . . . (614) 466-6508
  Counties Represented: Athens (part), Belmont, Carroll (part), Harrison,
  Jefferson, Meigs, Monroe, Noble, Vinton (part), Washington
  Term Expires: 2017
  E-mail: gentile@ohiosenate.gov
  Committees: Agriculture; Energy and Natural Resources; Finance;
  Financial Institutions; Rules and Reference; Transportation, Commerce
  and Labor
Senator **Robert D. "Bob" Hackett** (R-District 10) . . . . . . . (614) 466-3780
  Counties Represented: Clark, Greene, Madison
  Term Expires: 2017
  E-mail: hackett@ohiosenate.gov
  Committees: Agriculture; Civil Justice; Criminal Justice; Insurance;
  State and Local Government; Ways and Means
  Education: Columbia BA
Senator **Cliff Hite** (R-District 1) 1st Floor . . . . . . . . . . . . . (614) 466-8150
  Counties Represented: Auglaize (part), Defiance, Fulton (part),
  Hancock, Hardin, Henry, Logan (part), Paulding, Putnam, Van Wert,
  Williams
  Term Expires: 2017
  E-mail: hite@ohiosenate.gov
  Committees: Agriculture; Education; Energy and Natural Resources;
  Finance; Health and Human Services; Public Utilities; Rules and
  Reference
  Education: Kentucky 1977 BS
Senator **Jay Hottinger** (R-District 31) Ground Floor . . . . . .(614) 466-5838
  Counties Represented: Coshocton, Holmes (part), Licking, Perry,
  Tuscarawas
  Term Expires: 2019
  E-mail: hottinger@ohiosenate.gov
  Committees: Energy and Natural Resources; Financial Institutions;
  Health and Human Services; Insurance; State and Local Government;
  Transportation, Commerce and Labor
  Education: Capital U 1992 BA
Senator **James Michael "Jim" Hughes** (R-District 16)
  1st Floor . . . . . . . . . . . . . . . . . . . . . . . . . . . . . . . . . (614) 466-5981
  Counties Represented: Franklin (part)
  Term Expires: 2017
  E-mail: hughes@ohiosenate.gov
  Committees: Civil Justice; Criminal Justice; Finance; Financial
  Institutions; Insurance; Rules and Reference; State and Local
  Government
  Education: Ohio State BS, BSBA; Capital U 1994 JD
Senator **Shannon Jones** (R-District 7) 2nd Floor . . . . . . . . (614) 466-9737
  Counties Represented: Butler (part), Hamilton (part), Warren
  Term Expires: 2019
  E-mail: jones@ohiosenate.gov
  Committees: Energy and Natural Resources; Health and Human
  Services; Insurance; Medicaid; State and Local Government
  Education: Cincinnati BA

LEGISLATIVE BRANCH

Senator **Kris Jordan** (R-District 19) Ground Floor . . . . . . . (614) 466-8086
Counties Represented: Delaware, Franklin (part), Knox
Term Expires: 2019
E-mail: jordan@ohiosenate.gov
Committees: Education; Government Oversight and Reform; Medicaid;
State and Local Government; Ways and Means
Education: Ohio State BA

Senator **Frank LaRose** (R-District 27) 2nd Floor . . . . . . . . (614) 466-4823
Counties Represented: Stark (part), Wayne
Term Expires: 2019
E-mail: larose@ohiosenate.gov
Committees: Education; Financial Institutions; Government Oversight
and Reform; Insurance; State and Local Government; Transportation,
Commerce and Labor; Ways and Means
Education: Ohio State 2007 BS

Senator **Peggy Lehner** (R-District 6) Ground Floor . . . . . . (614) 466-4538
Counties Represented: Montgomery (part)
Term Expires: 2017
E-mail: lehner@ohiosenate.gov
Committees: Criminal Justice; Education; Health and Human Services;
Medicaid

Senator **Gayle L. Manning** (R-District 13) 1st Floor . . . . . . (614) 644-7613
Counties Represented: Huron, Lorain
Term Expires: 2019
E-mail: manning@ohiosenate.gov
Committees: Education; Health and Human Services; Medicaid; Rules
and Reference; Transportation, Commerce and Labor
Education: Kent State BA; Akron MA

Senator **Larry J. Obhof, Jr.** (R-District 22) 2nd Floor . . . . (614) 466-7505
Counties Represented: Ashland, Holmes (part), Medina, Richland
Term Expires: 2017
E-mail: obhof@ohiosenate.gov
Committees: Civil Justice; Financial Institutions; Government Oversight
and Reform; Rules and Reference

Senator **W. Scott Oelslager** (R-District 29) 1st Floor . . . . . (614) 466-0626
Counties Represented: Stark (part)
Term Expires: 2019
E-mail: oelslager@ohiosenate.gov
Committees: Civil Justice; Finance; Health and Human Services; Rules
and Reference
Education: Mount Union 1975 BA; Capital U JD

Senator **Thomas F. "Tom" Patton** (R-District 24)
1st Floor . . . . . . . . . . . . . . . . . . . . . . . . . . . . . . . (614) 466-8056
Counties Represented: Cuyahoga (part)
Term Expires: 2017
E-mail: patton@ohiosenate.gov
Committees: Energy and Natural Resources; Finance; Government
Oversight and Reform; Public Utilities; Rules and Reference;
Transportation, Commerce and Labor

Senator **Bob Peterson** (R-District 17) Ground Floor . . . . . (614) 466-8156
Counties Represented: Carroll (part), Clinton, Gallia, Highland,
Jackson, Lawrence (part), Pickaway (part), Pike, Ross, Vinton (part)
Term Expires: 2017
E-mail: peterson@ohiosenate.gov
Committees: Agriculture; Education; Finance; Government Oversight
and Reform; Insurance; Public Utilities; Rules and Reference; Ways
and Means
Education: Ohio State 1983 BS

Senator **Thomas "Tom" Sawyer** (D-District 28)
Ground Floor . . . . . . . . . . . . . . . . . . . . . . . . . . . (614) 466-7041
Counties Represented: Summit
Term Expires: 2017
E-mail: sawyer@ohiosenate.gov
Committees: Education; Finance; Public Utilities
Education: Akron 1968 BA, 1970 MA

Senator **Joseph "Joe" Schiavoni** (D-District 33)
Statehouse, 3rd Floor . . . . . . . . . . . . . . . . . . . . . . (614) 466-8285
Counties Represented: Columbiana, Mahoning
Term Expires: 2019
E-mail: schiavonni@ohiosenate.gov
Committees: Rules and Reference

Senator **William J. "Bill" Seitz III** (R-District 8)
1st Floor . . . . . . . . . . . . . . . . . . . . . . . . . . . . . . . (614) 466-8068
Counties Represented: Hamilton (part)
Term Expires: 2017
E-mail: seitz@ohiosenate.gov
Committees: Civil Justice; Criminal Justice; Energy and Natural
Resources; Government Oversight and Reform; Public Utilities; State
and Local Government
Education: Cincinnati 1975 BA, 1978 JD

Senator **Michael J. Skindell, JD** (D-District 23)
Ground Floor . . . . . . . . . . . . . . . . . . . . . . . . . . . . (614) 466-5123
Counties Represented: Cuyahoga (part)
Term Expires: 2019
E-mail: skindell@ohiosenate.gov
Committees: Agriculture; Civil Justice; Criminal Justice; Finance;
Government Oversight and Reform
Education: Walsh Col BA; Cleveland-Marshall JD

Senator **Charleta B. Tavares** (D-District 15) 2nd Floor . . . . (614) 466-5131
Counties Represented: Franklin (part)
Term Expires: 2019
E-mail: tavares@ohiosenate.gov
Committees: Finance; Health and Human Services; Medicaid; Rules
and Reference; Ways and Means

Senator **Cecil Thomas** (D-District 9) . . . . . . . . . . . . . . . . (614) 466-5980
Counties Represented: Hamilton (part)
Term Expires: 2019
E-mail: thomas@ohiosenate.gov
Committees: Civil Justice; Criminal Justice; Education; Financial
Institutions; Insurance; State and Local Government

Senator **Joseph W. "Joe" Uecker** (R-District 14)
1st Floor . . . . . . . . . . . . . . . . . . . . . . . . . . . . . . . (614) 466-4900
Counties Represented: Adams, Brown, Clermont, Lawrence (part),
Scioto
Term Expires: 2017
E-mail: uecker@ohiosenate.gov
Committees: Agriculture; Criminal Justice; Energy and Natural
Resources; Public Utilities; State and Local Government;
Transportation, Commerce and Labor
Education: Cincinnati 1977 AS; Northern Kentucky 1985 BS

Senator **Sandra R. Williams** (D-District 21) . . . . . . . . . . . (614) 466-4857
Counties Represented: Cuyahoga (part)
Term Expires: 2019
E-mail: williams@ohiosenate.gov
Committees: Criminal Justice; Education; Energy and Natural
Resources; Insurance; Public Utilities; Ways and Means
Education: Cleveland State BA; Tiffin MS

Senator **Kenny Yuko** (D-District 21) Ground Floor . . . . . . . (614) 466-4583
Counties Represented: Cuyahoga (part)
Term Expires: 2019
E-mail: yuko@ohiosenate.gov
Committees: Education; Financial Institutions; Government Oversight
and Reform; State and Local Government; Transportation, Commerce
and Labor

## Senate Standing Committees

### Agriculture

| **Majority Members** | **Minority Members** |
|---|---|
| Cliff Hite (R-1) *Chair* | Lou Gentile (D-30) |
| Robert D. "Bob" Hackett (R-10) | *Ranking Minority Member* |
| *Vice Chair* | Capri S. Cafaro (D-32) |
| Bill Beagle (R-5) | Michael J. Skindell (D-23) |
| David E. "Dave" Burke (R-26) | |
| Randy L. Gardner (R-2) | |
| Bob Peterson (R-17) | |
| Joseph W. "Joe" Uecker (R-14) | |

### Civil Justice

| **Majority Members** | **Minority Members** |
|---|---|
| Kevin Bacon (R-3) *Chair* | Michael J. Skindell (D-23) |
| W. Scott Oelslager (R-29) | *Ranking Minority Member* |
| *Vice Chair* | Edna R. Brown (D-11) |
| William P. "Bill" Coley II (R-4) | Cecil Thomas (D-9) |
| John Eklund (R-18) | |
| Robert D. "Bob" Hackett (R-10) | |
| James Michael "Jim" Hughes | |
| (R-16) | |
| Larry J. Obhof, Jr. (R-22) | |
| William J. "Bill" Seitz III (R-8) | |

## Criminal Justice

**Majority Members**
John Eklund (R-18) *Chair*
James Michael "Jim" Hughes (R-16) *Vice Chair*
Kevin Bacon (R-3)
Robert D. "Bob" Hackett (R-10)
Peggy Lehner (R-6)
William J. "Bill" Seitz III (R-8)
Joseph W. "Joe" Uecker (R-14)

**Minority Members**
Cecil Thomas (D-9) *Ranking Minority Member*
Michael J. Skindell (D-23)
Sandra R. Williams (D-21)

## Education

**Majority Members**
Peggy Lehner (R-6) *Chair*
Cliff Hite (R-1) *Vice Chair*
Troy Balderson (R-20)
William P. "Bill" Coley II (R-4)
Randy L. Gardner (R-2)
Kris Jordan (R-19)
Frank LaRose (R-27)
Gayle L. Manning (R-13)
Bob Peterson (R-17)

**Minority Members**
Thomas "Tom" Sawyer (D-28) *Ranking Minority Member*
Cecil Thomas (D-9)
Sandra R. Williams (D-21)
Kenny Yuko (D-21)

## Energy and Natural Resources

**Majority Members**
Troy Balderson (R-20) *Chair*
Shannon Jones (R-7) *Vice Chair*
Randy L. Gardner (R-2)
Cliff Hite (R-1)
Jay Hottinger (R-31)
Thomas F. "Tom" Patton (R-24)
William J. "Bill" Seitz III (R-8)
Joseph W. "Joe" Uecker (R-14)

**Minority Members**
Lou Gentile (D-30) *Ranking Minority Member*
Capri S. Cafaro (D-32)
Sandra R. Williams (D-21)

## Finance

**Majority Members**
W. Scott Oelslager (R-29) *Chair*
William P. "Bill" Coley II (R-4) *Vice Chair*
Bill Beagle (R-5)
David E. "Dave" Burke (R-26)
Randy L. Gardner (R-2)
Cliff Hite (R-1)
James Michael "Jim" Hughes (R-16)
Thomas F. "Tom" Patton (R-24)
Bob Peterson (R-17)

**Minority Members**
Michael J. Skindell (D-23) *Ranking Minority Member*
Lou Gentile (D-30)
Thomas "Tom" Sawyer (D-28)
Charleta B. Tavares (D-15)

## Financial Institutions

**Majority Members**
James Michael "Jim" Hughes (R-16) *Chair*
John Eklund (R-18) *Vice Chair*
Kevin Bacon (R-3)
Bill Beagle (R-5)
David E. "Dave" Burke (R-26)
Jay Hottinger (R-31)
Frank LaRose (R-27)
Larry J. Obhof, Jr. (R-22)

**Minority Members**
Kenny Yuko (D-21) *Ranking Minority Member*
Lou Gentile (D-30)
Cecil Thomas (D-9)

## Government Oversight and Reform

**Majority Members**
William P. "Bill" Coley II (R-4) *Chair*
William J. "Bill" Seitz III (R-8) *Vice Chair*
Troy Balderson (R-20)
David E. "Dave" Burke (R-26)
Kris Jordan (R-19)
Frank LaRose (R-27)
Larry J. Obhof, Jr. (R-22)
Bob Peterson (R-17)
Thomas F. "Tom" Patton (R-24)

**Minority Members**
Kenny Yuko (D-21) *Ranking Minority Member*
Edna R. Brown (D-11)
Michael J. Skindell (D-23)

## Health and Human Services

**Majority Members**
Shannon Jones (R-7) *Chair*
Peggy Lehner (R-6) *Vice Chair*
Bill Beagle (R-5)
Randy L. Gardner (R-2)
Cliff Hite (R-1)
Jay Hottinger (R-31)
Gayle L. Manning (R-13)
W. Scott Oelslager (R-29)

**Minority Members**
Charleta B. Tavares (D-15) *Ranking Minority Member*
Capri S. Cafaro (D-32)

## Insurance

**Majority Members**
Jay Hottinger (R-31) *Chair*
Kevin Bacon (R-3) *Vice Chair*
Troy Balderson (R-20)
Bill Beagle (R-5)
Robert D. "Bob" Hackett (R-10)
James Michael "Jim" Hughes (R-16)
Shannon Jones (R-7)
Frank LaRose (R-27)
Bob Peterson (R-17)

**Minority Members**
Edna R. Brown (D-11) *Ranking Minority Member*
Cecil Thomas (D-9)
Sandra R. Williams (D-21)

## Medicaid

**Majority Members**
David E. "Dave" Burke (R-26) *Chair*
Gayle L. Manning (R-13) *Vice Chair*
William P. "Bill" Coley II (R-4)
Shannon Jones (R-7)
Kris Jordan (R-19)
Peggy Lehner (R-6)

**Minority Members**
Capri S. Cafaro (D-32) *Ranking Minority Member*
Charleta B. Tavares (D-15)

## Public Utilities

**Majority Members**
William J. "Bill" Seitz III (R-8) *Chair*
Troy Balderson (R-20) *Vice Chair*
Kevin Bacon (R-3)
John Eklund (R-18)
Cliff Hite (R-1)
Thomas F. "Tom" Patton (R-24)
Bob Peterson (R-17)
Joseph W. "Joe" Uecker (R-14)

**Minority Members**
Sandra R. Williams (D-21) *Ranking Minority Member*
Thomas "Tom" Sawyer (D-28)

## Rules and Reference

**Majority Members**
Keith L. Faber (R-12) *Chair*
Larry J. Obhof, Jr. (R-22) *Vice Chair*
David E. "Dave" Burke (R-26)
William P. "Bill" Coley II (R-4)
Cliff Hite (R-1)
James Michael "Jim" Hughes (R-16)
Gayle L. Manning (R-13)
W. Scott Oelslager (R-29)
Bob Peterson (R-17)
Thomas F. "Tom" Patton (R-24)

**Minority Members**
Joseph "Joe" Schiavoni (D-33) *Ranking Minority Member*
Edna R. Brown (D-11)
Lou Gentile (D-30)
Charleta B. Tavares (D-15)

## State and Local Government

**Majority Members**
Joseph W. "Joe" Uecker (R-14) *Chair*
Jay Hottinger (R-31) *Vice Chair*
Robert D. "Bob" Hackett (R-10)
James Michael "Jim" Hughes (R-16)
Shannon Jones (R-7)
Kris Jordan (R-19)
Frank LaRose (R-27)
William J. "Bill" Seitz III (R-8)

**Minority Members**
Cecil Thomas (D-9) *Ranking Minority Member*
Edna R. Brown (D-11)
Kenny Yuko (D-21)

## Transportation, Commerce and Labor

**Majority Members**
Frank LaRose (R-27) *Chair*
Gayle L. Manning (R-13)
   *Vice Chair*
Kevin Bacon (R-3)
John Eklund (R-18)
Jay Hottinger (R-31)
Thomas F. "Tom" Patton (R-24)
Joseph W. "Joe" Uecker (R-14)

**Minority Members**
Capri S. Cafaro (D-32)
   *Ranking Minority Member*
Edna R. Brown (D-11)
Lou Gentile (D-30)
Kenny Yuko (D-21)

## Ways and Means

**Majority Members**
Bob Peterson (R-17) *Chair*
Bill Beagle (R-5) *Vice Chair*
Troy Balderson (R-20)
John Eklund (R-18)
Robert D. "Bob" Hackett (R-10)
Kris Jordan (R-19)
Frank LaRose (R-27)

**Minority Members**
Charleta B. Tavares (D-15)
   *Ranking Minority Member*
Capri S. Cafaro (D-32)
Sandra R. Williams (D-21)

# Ohio House of Representatives

77 South High Street, Columbus, OH 43215-6111
Tel: (614) 466-3357  Fax: (614) 644-9494

**Employees: 190**

Speaker of the House **Clifford A. Rosenberger** (R) . . . . . . .(614) 466-3506
   Majority Chief of Staff **Mike Dittoe** . . . . . . . . . . . . . . . .(614) 466-0980
Speaker Pro Tem **Ron Amstutz** (R) . . . . . . . . . . . . . . . . . .(614) 466-1474
   Education: Capital U 1986 BA
Majority Floor Leader **Barbara R. Sears** (R) . . . . . . . . . . .(614) 466-1731
   Education: Toledo 1983 AA
Assistant Majority Floor Leader **Jim "Jim" Buchy** (R) . . . (614) 466-6344
   Education: Wittenberg 1962 BS
Majority Whip **Michael D. "Mike" Dovilla** (R) . . . . . . . . .(614) 466-4895
   Education: Baldwin-Wallace 1997 BA; American U 1999 MPA
Assistant Majority Whip **Dorothy Liggett Pelanda** (R) . . . (614) 466-8147
Minority Leader **Frederick W. "Fred" Strahorn** (D) . . . . . .(614) 466-3357
   Education: Ohio State 1989 BA
Assistant Minority Leader
   **Nicholas J. Celebrezze, JD** (D) . . . . . . . . . . . . . . . . . . . (614) 466-3485
   Education: Akron BA; Cleveland-Marshall JD
Minority Whip **Nickie J. Antonio, MPA** (D) . . . . . . . . . . . (614) 466-5921
   Education: Cleveland State BSEd, 1991 MPA
Assistant Minority Whip **Jack R. Cera** (D) . . . . . . . . . . . . .(614) 466-3735
   Education: Brown U 1978 BA
Sergeant at Arms **Dan Lay** . . . . . . . . . . . . . . . . . . . . . . . .(614) 466-1500
Legislative Clerk **Brad Young** . . . . . . . . . . . . . . . . . . . . . .(614) 466-3357
Assistant to the Clerk **Ali Sagraves** . . . . . . . . . . . . . . . . . (614) 466-3357

# Representatives

**Party Affiliation Statistics: Republicans: 65, Democrats: 34**

Representative **Ron Amstutz** (R-District 1) . . . . . . . . . . . . (614) 466-1474
   Counties Represented: Wayne          Fax: (614) 719-0003
   Term Expires: 2017
   E-mail: rep01@ohiohouse.gov
   Committees: Public Utilities; Rules and Reference; Ways and Means

Representative **Marlene Anielski, CPM** (R-District 6) . . . . .(614) 466-6041
   Counties Represented: Cuyahoga (part)     Fax: (614) 719-6956
   Term Expires: 2017
   E-mail: rep06@ohiohouse.gov
   Committees: Armed Services, Veterans Affairs and Public Safety;
   Finance; Local Government
   Education: Akron BA; Cleveland State MBA

Representative **Niraj J. Antani** (R-District 42) . . . . . . . . . .(614) 466-6504
   Counties Represented: Montgomery (part)     Fax: (614) 719-6942
   Term Expires: 2017
   E-mail: rep42@ohiohouse.gov
   Committees: Community and Family Advancement; Economic and
   Workforce Development; Judiciary; Transportation and Infrastructure
   Education: Ohio State 2013 BA

Representative **Nickie J. Antonio, MPA** (D-District 13) . . . (614) 466-5921
   Counties Represented: Cuyahoga (part)     Fax: (614) 719-3913
   Term Expires: 2017
   E-mail: rep13@ohiohouse.gov
   Committees: Finance; Health and Aging; Rules and Reference

Representative **Steven Arndt** (R-District 89) . . . . . . . . . . . (614) 644-6011
   Counties Represented: Erie, Ottawa
   Term Expires: 2017
   E-mail: rep89@ohiohouse.gov
   Committees: Armed Services, Veterans Affairs and Public Safety;
   Commerce and Labor; Economic and Workforce Development; Local
   Government; Transportation and Infrastructure

Representative **Michael "Mike" Ashford** (D-District 44) . . (614) 466-1401
   Counties Represented: Lucas (part)     Fax: (614) 719-6948
   Term Expires: 2017
   E-mail: rep44@ohiohouse.gov
   Committees: Insurance; Local Government; Public Utilities
   Education: Nebraska (Omaha) BA

Representative **Nan A. Baker** (R-District 16) . . . . . . . . . . . (614) 466-0961
   Counties Represented: Cuyahoga (part)     Fax: (614) 719-3998
   Term Expires: 2017
   E-mail: rep16@ohiohouse.gov
   Committees: Economic and Workforce Development; Local
   Government; Ways and Means
   Education: Baldwin-Wallace 2008 BA

Representative **John E. Barnes, Jr.** (D-District 12) . . . . . . (614) 466-1408
   Counties Represented: Cuyahoga (part)     Fax: (614) 719-3912
   Term Expires: 2017
   E-mail: rep12@ohiohouse.gov
   Committees: Economic and Workforce Development; Health and
   Aging; Ways and Means
   Education: Case Western MS

Representative **John Becker** (R-District 65) . . . . . . . . . . . . (614) 466-8134
   Counties Represented: Clermont (part)     Fax: (614) 719-3966
   Term Expires: 2017
   E-mail: rep65@ohiohouse.gov
   Committees: Local Government; State Government; Transportation and
   Infrastructure
   Education: Xavier (OH) 1994 MBA; Northern Kentucky 1988 BA

Representative **Heather Bishoff** (D-District 20) . . . . . . . . . .(614) 644-6002
   Counties Represented: Franklin (part)     Fax: (614) 719-6959
   Term Expires: 2017
   E-mail: rep20@ohiohouse.gov
   Committees: Armed Services, Veterans Affairs and Public Safety;
   Health and Aging; Insurance
   Education: Baldwin-Wallace 1994 (Attended); Franklin U 1999 BS

Representative
   **Louis W. Blessing III, BCEE** (R-District 29) . . . . . . . . . .(614) 466-9091
   Counties Represented: Hamilton (part)     Fax: (614) 719-3583
   Term Expires: 2017
   3153 McGill Lane, Cincinnati, OH 45251
   E-mail: rep29@ohiohouse.gov
   Committees: Commerce and Labor; Education; Government
   Accountability and Oversight
   Education: Cincinnati BA, BSEE

Representative **John A. Boccieri, USAFR** (D-District 59) . . (614) 466-6107
   Counties Represented: Mahoning (part)
   Term Expires: 2017
   E-mail: rep59@ohiohouse.gov
   Committees: Public Utilities
   Education: St Bonaventure 1992 BS; Webster 1996 MA, 1996 MPA

Representative **Kristin Boggs** (D-District 18) . . . . . . . . . . .(614) 466-1896
   Counties Represented: Franklin (part)
   Term Expires: 2017
   E-mail: rep18@ohiohouse.gov
   Committees: State Government
   Education: Kent State (Attended); Cleveland-Marshall JD

Representative **Terry Boose, MBA** (R-District 57) . . . . . . . (614) 466-9628
   Counties Represented: Huron, Lorain (part)     Fax: (614) 719-3958
   Term Expires: 2017
   E-mail: rep57@ohiohouse.gov
   Committees: Agriculture and Rural Development; Local Government;
   Transportation and Infrastructure; Ways and Means
   Education: Bowling Green State 1978 BA; Texas Tech 1980 MBA

Representative **Kevin L. Boyce** (D-District 25) . . . . . . . . . .(614) 466-5343
   Counties Represented: Franklin (part)     Fax: (614) 719-3581
   Term Expires: 2017
   E-mail: rep25@ohiohouse.gov
   Committees: Community and Family Advancement; Finance; Rules and
   Reference
   Education: Toledo 1995 BA; Central Michigan 2004 MA

Representative **Janine R. Boyd** (D-District 9) . . . . . . . . . . .(614) 644-5079
   Counties Represented: Cuyahoga (part)
   Term Expires: 2017
   77 South High Street, 10th Floor, Columbus, OH 43215
   E-mail: rep09@ohiohouse.gov
   Committees: Community and Family Advancement; Education; Local
   Government

*(continued on next page)*

**LEGISLATIVE BRANCH**

**Representatives** *continued*

Representative **Andrew O. Brenner** (R-District 67) . . . . . . (614) 644-6711
Counties Represented: Delaware (part)          Fax: (614) 719-0002
Term Expires: 2017
77 South High Street, 13th Floor, Columbus, OH 43215
E-mail: rep67@ohiohouse.gov
Committees: Education; Rules and Reference
Education: Ohio State 1993 BS

Representative
**Thomas E. "Tom" Brinkman, Jr.** (R-District 27) . . . . . (614) 644-6886
Counties Represented: Hamilton (part)          Fax: (614) 719-3588
Term Expires: 2017
77 South High Street, 11th Floor, Columbus, OH 43215
E-mail: rep27@ohiohouse.gov
Committees: Commerce and Labor; Insurance; Public Utilities

Representative **Tim W. Brown** (R-District 3) . . . . . . . . . . (614) 466-8104
Counties Represented: Wood          Fax: (614) 719-0006
Term Expires: 2017
E-mail: rep03@ohiohouse.gov
Committees: Financial Institutions, Housing, and Urban Development;
Government Accountability and Oversight; Health and Aging
Education: Bowling Green State 1986 BB

Representative **Christie Bryant Kuhns** (D-District 32) . . . . (614) 466-1645
Counties Represented: Hamilton (part)          Fax: (614) 719-3586
Term Expires: 2017
E-mail: rep32@ohiohouse.gov
Committees: Financial Institutions, Housing, and Urban Development;
Health and Aging; Insurance
Education: Cincinnati 2001 BS, 2006 JD

Representative **Jim "Jim" Buchy** (R-District 84) . . . . . . . (614) 466-6344
Counties Represented: Auglaize (part), Darke (part),          Fax: (614) 719-3977
Mercer, Shelby (part)
Term Expires: 2017
E-mail: rep84@ohiohouse.gov
Committees: Agriculture and Rural Development; Government
Accountability and Oversight; Public Utilities

Representative **Tony Burkley** (R-District 82) . . . . . . . . . . . (614) 644-5091
Counties Represented: Auglaize (part), Defiance,          Fax: (614) 719-3974
Paulding, Van Wert
Term Expires: 2017
E-mail: rep82@ohiohouse.gov
Committees: Agriculture and Rural Development; Finance; Ways and
Means

Representative **James "Jim" Butler, JD** (R-District 41) . . . (614) 644-6008
Counties Represented: Montgomery (part)          Fax: (614) 719-3591
Term Expires: 2017
E-mail: rep41@ohiohouse.gov
Committees: Government Accountability and Oversight; Health and
Aging; Judiciary
Education: Naval Acad 1995 BA; Maryland 1996 MA;
Cincinnati 2005 JD

Representative
**Nicholas J. Celebrezze, JD** (D-District 15) . . . . . . . . . . (614) 466-3485
Counties Represented: Cuyahoga (part)          Fax: (614) 719-3911
Term Expires: 2017
E-mail: rep15@ohiohouse.gov
Committees: Judiciary; Rules and Reference

Representative **Jack R. Cera** (D-District 96) . . . . . . . . . . . . (614) 466-3735
Counties Represented: Belmont (part), Jefferson,          Fax: (614) 719-6995
Monroe
Term Expires: 2017
E-mail: rep96@ohiohouse.gov
Committees: Agriculture and Rural Development; Energy and Natural
Resources; Finance; Insurance; Ways and Means

Representative **Kathleen Clyde** (D-District 75) . . . . . . . . . . (614) 466-2004
Counties Represented: Portage (part)          Fax: (614) 719-3968
Term Expires: 2017
E-mail: rep75@ohiohouse.gov
Committees: Finance; Government Accountability and Oversight;
Public Utilities
Education: Wesleyan U 2001 BA; Ohio State 2008 JD

Representative **Margaret Conditt, PhD** (R-District 52) . . . . (614) 466-8550
Counties Represented: Butler (part)          Fax: (614) 719-6955
Term Expires: 2017
E-mail: rep52@ohiohouse.gov
Committees: Community and Family Advancement; Public Utilities
Education: Alabama BSChem; Colorado PhD

Representative **Hearcel F. Craig** (D-District 26) . . . . . . . . . . (614) 466-8010
Counties Represented: Franklin (part)
Term Expires: 2017
77 South High Street, 10th Floor, Columbus, OH 43215
E-mail: rep26@ohiohouse.gov
Committees: Armed Services, Veterans Affairs and Public Safety;
Economic and Workforce Development; Financial Institutions, Housing,
and Urban Development

Representative **Robert E. "Bob" Cupp** (R-District 4) . . . . . (614) 466-9624
Counties Represented: Allen          Fax: (614) 719-0004
Term Expires: 2017
77 South High Street, 13th Floor, Columbus, OH 43215
E-mail: rep04@ohiohouse.gov
Committees: Education; Finance; Judiciary; Public Utilities

Representative **Michael F. "Mike" Curtin** (D-District 17) . . (614) 644-6005
Counties Represented: Franklin (part)          Fax: (614) 719-6963
Term Expires: 2017
E-mail: rep17@ohiohouse.gov
Committees: Government Accountability and Oversight; State
Government; Ways and Means
Education: Ohio State 1973 BAJ

Representative **Bill Dean** (R-District 74) . . . . . . . . . . . . . . (614) 719-6984
Counties Represented: Clark (part), Greene (part),          Fax: (614) 719-0010
Madison
Term Expires: 2017
77 South High Street, 11th Floor, Columbus, OH 43215
E-mail: rep74@ohiohouse.gov
Committees: Insurance; State Government

Representative **Timothy Derickson** (R-District 53) . . . . . . . (614) 644-5094
Counties Represented: Butler (part)          Fax: (614) 719-6953
Term Expires: 2017
E-mail: rep53@ohiohouse.gov
Committees: Community and Family Advancement; Education;
Finance; Government Accountability and Oversight
Education: Clark State Com Col 1980 AS; Miami U (OH) 1984 BS

Representative **Jonathan Dever** (R-District 28) . . . . . . . . . . (614) 466-8120
Counties Represented: Hamilton (part)          Fax: (614) 719-3582
Term Expires: 2017
E-mail: rep28@ohiohouse.gov
Committees: Community and Family Advancement; Financial
Institutions, Housing, and Urban Development; Judiciary;
Transportation and Infrastructure; Ways and Means

Representative **Anthony "Tony" DeVitis** (R-District 36) . . (614) 466-1790
Counties Represented: Summit (part)          Fax: (614) 719-6943
Term Expires: 2017
E-mail: rep36@ohiohouse.gov
Committees: Commerce and Labor; Insurance; Transportation and
Infrastructure
Education: Akron

Representative **Michael D. "Mike" Dovilla** (R-District 7) . . (614) 466-4895
Counties Represented: Cuyahoga (part)          Fax: (614) 719-6957
Term Expires: 2017
E-mail: rep07@ohiohouse.gov
Committees: Finance; Financial Institutions, Housing, and Urban
Development; Public Utilities; Transportation and Infrastructure

Representative **Denise Driehaus** (D-District 31) . . . . . . . . . (614) 466-5786
Counties Represented: Hamilton (part)          Fax: (614) 719-3585
Term Expires: 2017
E-mail: rep31@ohiohouse.gov
Committees: Economic and Workforce Development; Finance; Ways
and Means
Education: Miami U (OH) 1985 BA

Representative **Mike Duffey** (R-District 21) . . . . . . . . . . . . (614) 644-6030
Counties Represented: Franklin (part)          Fax: (614) 719-6960
Term Expires: 2017
E-mail: rep21@ohiohouse.gov
Committees: Commerce and Labor; Finance; Health and Aging
Education: Michigan 2000 BS

Representative **Teresa Fedor** (D-District 45) . . . . . . . . . . . . (614) 644-6017
Counties Represented: Lucas (part)          Fax: (614) 719-6947
Term Expires: 2017
E-mail: rep45@ohiohouse.gov
Committees: Armed Services, Veterans Affairs and Public Safety;
Commerce and Labor; Education
Education: Toledo 1983 BS

Representative **Timothy E. "Tim" Ginter** (R-District 5) . . . (614) 466-8022
Counties Represented: Columbiana          Fax: (614) 719-6971
Term Expires: 2017
77 South High Street, 13th Floor, Columbus, OH 43215
E-mail: rep05@ohiohouse.gov
Committees: Community and Family Advancement; Health and Aging;
Public Utilities

Representative **Anne Gonzales** (R-District 19) . . . . . . . . . (614) 466-4847
Counties Represented: Franklin (part)          Fax: (614) 719-6958
Term Expires: 2017
E-mail: rep19@ohiohouse.gov
Committees: Health and Aging
Education: Otterbein BS

Representative **Doug Green** (R-District 66) . . . . . . . . . . . . (614) 644-6034
Counties Represented: Brown, Clermont (part)    Fax: (614) 719-6988
Term Expires: 2017
E-mail: rep66@ohiohouse.gov
Committees: Finance; Government Accountability and Oversight;
Transportation and Infrastructure

Representative **Cheryl L. Grossman** (R-District 23) . . . . . . (614) 466-9690
Counties Represented: Franklin (part)          Fax: (614) 719-6962
Term Expires: 2017
E-mail: rep23@ohiohouse.gov
Committees: Energy and Natural Resources; Finance; State Government

Representative **Christina M. Hagan** (R-District 50) . . . . . . (614) 466-9078
Counties Represented: Stark (part)             Fax: (614) 719-6950
Term Expires: 2017
E-mail: rep50@ohiohouse.gov
Committees: Agriculture and Rural Development; Community and
Family Advancement; Energy and Natural Resources; Public Utilities

Representative **David "Dave" Hall** (R-District 70) . . . . . . . (614) 466-2994
Counties Represented: Ashland, Holmes (part),   Fax: (614) 719-6997
Medina (part)
Term Expires: 2017
E-mail: rep70@ohiohouse.gov
Committees: Energy and Natural Resources; Finance; Public Utilities

Representative
**Stephen D. "Steve" Hambley** (R-District 69) . . . . . . . .(614) 466-8140
Counties Represented: Medina (part)            Fax: (614) 719-3969
Term Expires: 2017
E-mail: rep69@ohiohouse.gov
Committees: Financial Institutions, Housing, and Urban Development;
Judiciary; Local Government; State Government; Ways and Means
Education: Akron MA, PhD

Representative **Bill Hayes, JD** (R-District 72) . . . . . . . . . . .(614) 466-2500
Counties Represented: Coshocton, Licking (part),  Tel: (614) 719-6991
Perry
Term Expires: 2017
E-mail: rep72@ohiohouse.gov
Committees: Community and Family Advancement; Education; Rules
and Reference
Education: Capital U BS; Ohio State MA; Capital U JD

Representative **Michael Henne** (R-District 40) . . . . . . . . . . .(614) 644-8051
Counties Represented: Montgomery (part)         Fax: (614) 719-3590
Term Expires: 2017
E-mail: rep40@ohiohouse.gov
Committees: Education; Ways and Means
Education: Miami U (OH) 1985 BA

Representative **Brian D. Hill** (R-District 97) . . . . . . . . . . . . (614) 644-6014
Counties Represented: Guernsey, Muskingum (part)  Fax: (614) 719-6994
Term Expires: 2017
E-mail: rep97@ohiohouse.gov
Committees: Agriculture and Rural Development; Energy and Natural
Resources; Public Utilities

Representative **Ronald E. "Ron" Hood** (R-District 78) . . . .(614) 466-1464
Counties Represented: Athens (part), Fairfield (part),  Fax: (614) 719-3961
Hocking, Morgan, Muskingum (part), Pickaway (part)
Term Expires: 2017
E-mail: rep78@ohiohouse.gov
Committees: Commerce and Labor; Community and Family
Advancement; Rules and Reference; State Government
Education: Ohio State 1991 BSBA

Representative **Stephanie Howse** (D-District 11) . . . . . . . . (614) 466-1414
Counties Represented: Cuyahoga (part)          Fax: (614) 719-0011
Term Expires: 2017
E-mail: rep11@ohiohouse.gov
Committees: Community and Family Advancement; Energy and Natural
Resources; Transportation and Infrastructure

Representative **Stephen A. Huffman** (R-District 80) . . . . . .(614) 466-8114
Counties Represented: Darke (part), Miami       Fax: (614) 719-3979
Term Expires: 2017
77 South High Street, 11th Floor, Columbus, OH 43215
E-mail: rep80@ohiohouse.gov
Committees: Education; Health and Aging; State Government

Representative **Greta Johnson** (D-District 35) . . . . . . . . . .(614) 644-6037
Counties Represented: Summit (part)            Fax: (614) 719-6945
Term Expires: 2017
77 South High Street, 10th Floor, Columbus, OH 43215
E-mail: rep35@ohiohouse.gov
Committees: Armed Services, Veterans Affairs and Public Safety;
Judiciary; Transportation and Infrastructure

Representative **Terry Johnson, DO** (R-District 90) . . . . . . (614) 466-2124
Counties Represented: Adams, Lawrence (part),   Fax: (614) 719-6989
Scioto
Term Expires: 2017
E-mail: rep90@ohiohouse.gov
Committees: Armed Services, Veterans Affairs and Public Safety;
Health and Aging; Transportation and Infrastructure
Education: Ohio BA, 1991 DO

Representative **Kyle Koehler** (R-District 79) . . . . . . . . . . . .(614) 466-2038
Counties Represented: Clark (part)             Fax: (614) 719-3972
Term Expires: 2017
77 South High Street, 11th Floor, Columbus, OH 43215
E-mail: rep79@ohiohouse.gov
Committees: Agriculture and Rural Development; Commerce and
Labor; Economic and Workforce Development; Education

Representative **Stephanie Kunze** (R-District 24) . . . . . . . .(614) 466-8012
Counties Represented: Franklin (part)          Fax: (614) 719-0007
Term Expires: 2017
E-mail: rep24@ohiohouse.gov
Committees: Finance; Insurance
Education: Indiana BA

Representative **Al Landis** (R-District 98) . . . . . . . . . . . . . . .(614) 466-8035
Counties Represented: Holmes (part), Tuscarawas  Fax: (614) 719-6996
Term Expires: 2017
E-mail: rep98@ohiohouse.gov
Committees: Armed Services, Veterans Affairs and Public Safety;
Commerce and Labor; Energy and Natural Resources

Representative **Sarah LaTourette** (R-District 76) . . . . . . . .(614) 644-5088
Counties Represented: Geauga (part), Portage (part)  Fax: (614) 719-6998
Term Expires: 2017
77 South High Street, 11th Floor, Columbus, OH 43215
E-mail: rep76@ohiohouse.gov
Committees: Agriculture and Rural Development; Health and Aging;
Insurance; State Government

Representative **David Leland** (D-District 22) . . . . . . . . . . . (614) 466-2473
Counties Represented: Franklin (part)          Fax: (614) 719-6961
Term Expires: 2017
77 South High Street, 10th Floor, Columbus, OH 43215
E-mail: rep22@ohiohouse.gov
Committees: Energy and Natural Resources; Financial Institutions,
Housing, and Urban Development; Government Accountability and
Oversight

Representative **Michele Lepore-Hagan** (D-District 58) . . . . (614) 466-9435
Counties Represented: Mahoning (part)          Fax: (614) 719-3960
Term Expires: 2017
77 South High Street, 10th Floor, Columbus, OH 43215
E-mail: rep58@ohiohouse.gov
Committees: Commerce and Labor; Community and Family
Advancement; Health and Aging; Transportation and Infrastructure

Representative **Ron Maag** (R-District 62) . . . . . . . . . . . . . . .(614) 644-6023
Counties Represented: Warren (part)            Fax: (614) 719-3589
Term Expires: 2017
E-mail: rep62@ohiohouse.gov
Committees: Energy and Natural Resources; Finance; Health and
Aging; State Government
Education: Cincinnati BS

Representative **Nathan H. Manning** (R-District 55) . . . . . . (614) 644-5076
Counties Represented: Lorain (part)            Fax: (614) 719-3957
Term Expires: 2017
77 South High Street, 11th Floor, Columbus, OH 43215
E-mail: rep55@ohiohouse.gov
Committees: Education; Financial Institutions, Housing, and Urban
Development; Judiciary; Public Utilities

Representative **Jeffrey McClain** (R-District 87) . . . . . . . . . (614) 644-6265
Counties Represented: Crawford, Marion (part),   Fax: (614) 719-6982
Morrow, Seneca (part), Wyandot
Term Expires: 2017
E-mail: rep87@ohiohouse.gov
Committees: Community and Family Advancement; Finance; Ways and
Means

*(continued on next page)*

LEGISLATIVE BRANCH

**Representatives** *continued*

Representative **Robert McColley** (R-District 81) . . . . . . . . (614) 466-3760
Counties Represented: Fulton (part), Henry, Putnam,   Fax: (614) 719-3975
Williams
Term Expires: 2017
77 South High Street, 11th Floor, Columbus, OH 43215
E-mail: rep81@ohiohouse.gov
Committees: Government Accountability and Oversight; Judiciary;
Ways and Means

Representative **Michael J. O'Brien** (D-District 64) . . . . . . (614) 466-5358
Counties Represented: Ashtabula (part), Trumbull   Fax: (614) 719-3964
(part)
Term Expires: 2017
77 South High Street, 10th Floor, Columbus, OH 43215
E-mail: rep64@ohiohouse.gov
Committees: Armed Services, Veterans Affairs and Public Safety;
Finance

Representative **Sean O'Brien** (D-District 63) . . . . . . . . . . . (614) 466-3488
Counties Represented: Trumbull (part)   Fax: (614) 719-3965
Term Expires: 2017
E-mail: rep63@ohiohouse.gov
Committees: Agriculture and Rural Development; Energy and Natural
Resources; Public Utilities

Representative **Bill Patmon** (D-District 10) . . . . . . . . . . . . (614) 466-7954
Counties Represented: Cuyahoga (part)   Fax: (614) 719-0010
Term Expires: 2017
E-mail: rep10@ohiohouse.gov
Committees: Agriculture and Rural Development; Community and
Family Advancement; Education

Representative **John Patterson** (D-District 99) . . . . . . . . . (614) 466-1405
Counties Represented: Ashtabula (part), Geauga   Fax: (614) 719-6999
(part)
Term Expires: 2017
E-mail: rep99@ohiohouse.gov
Committees: Agriculture and Rural Development; Education; Finance
Education: Marietta; Kent State PhD

Representative **Dorothy Liggett Pelanda** (R-District 86) . . (614) 466-8147
Counties Represented: Marion (part), Union   Fax: (614) 719-6983
Term Expires: 2017
E-mail: rep86@ohiohouse.gov
Committees: Commerce and Labor; Government Accountability and
Oversight; Judiciary; Rules and Reference

Representative **Rick Perales** (R-District 73) . . . . . . . . . . . . (614) 466-6020
Counties Represented: Greene (part)   Fax: (614) 719-3970
Term Expires: 2017
E-mail: rep73@ohiohouse.gov
Committees: Armed Services, Veterans Affairs and Public Safety;
Economic and Workforce Development; Finance; State Government
Education: Auburn 1982 BS; Troy State 1992 MS

Representative **Debbie Phillips** (D-District 94) . . . . . . . . . (614) 466-2158
Counties Represented: Athens (part), Meigs, Vinton   Fax: (614) 719-6992
(part), Washington (part)
Term Expires: 2017
E-mail: rep94@ohiohouse.gov
Committees: Agriculture and Rural Development; Education; Finance
Education: Ohio BA

Representative **Dan Ramos** (D-District 56) . . . . . . . . . . . . . (614) 466-5141
Counties Represented: Lorain (part)   Fax: (614) 719-3956
Term Expires: 2017
E-mail: rep56@ohiohouse.gov
Committees: Education; Finance; Health and Aging; Rules and
Reference
Education: Ohio State 2003 BS

Representative **Alicia Reece** (D-District 33) 13th Floor . . . . (614) 466-1308
Counties Represented: Hamilton (part)   Fax: (614) 719-3587
Term Expires: 2017
E-mail: rep33@ohiohouse.gov
Committees: Commerce and Labor; Finance; Local Government
Education: Grambling State BA

Representative **William "Bill" Reineke** (R-District 88) . . . . (614) 466-1374
Counties Represented: Sandusky, Seneca (part)   Fax: (614) 719-6981
Term Expires: 2017
77 South High Street, 13th Floor, Columbus, OH 43215
E-mail: rep88@ohiohouse.gov
Committees: Finance; Financial Institutions, Housing, and Urban
Development; Ways and Means

Representative
**Richard Weston "Wes" Retherford** (R-District 51) . . . . (614) 466-6721
Counties Represented: Butler (part)   Fax: (614) 719-6954
Term Expires: 2017
E-mail: rep51@ohiohouse.gov
Committees: Agriculture and Rural Development; Armed Services,
Veterans Affairs and Public Safety; Insurance

Representative **Jeffery S. Rezabek** (R-District 43) . . . . . . . (614) 466-2960
Counties Represented: Montgomery (part), Preble   Fax: (614) 719-6940
Term Expires: 2017
E-mail: rep43@ohiohouse.gov
Committees: Agriculture and Rural Development; Judiciary; Local
Government

Representative **Kristina Roegner** (R-District 37) . . . . . . . . (614) 466-1177
Counties Represented: Summit (part)   Fax: (614) 719-6942
Term Expires: 2017
E-mail: rep37@ohiohouse.gov
Committees: Commerce and Labor; Public Utilities
Education: Tufts 1990 BSME; Pennsylvania 1995 MBA

Representative **John M. Rogers** (D-District 60) . . . . . . . . . (614) 466-7251
Counties Represented: Lake (part)   Fax: (614) 719-3962
Term Expires: 2017
E-mail: rep60@ohiohouse.gov
Committees: Local Government; Public Utilities; Ways and Means
Education: Cuyahoga Comm Col 1978 AS; Hiram 1982 BA;
John Carroll 1993 MBA; Cleveland-Marshall 2002 JD;
Alabama 2013 JD

Representative **Mark J. Romanchuk** (R-District 2) . . . . . . . (614) 466-5802
Counties Represented: Richland   Fax: (614) 719-3973
Term Expires: 2017
E-mail: rep02@ohiohouse.gov
Committees: Economic and Workforce Development; Finance; Public
Utilities
Education: DeVry U BSEE; Vanderbilt MBA

Representative **Clifford A. Rosenberger** (R-District 91) . . . (614) 466-3506
Counties Represented: Clinton, Highland, Pike, Ross   Fax: (614) 719-6986
(part)
Term Expires: 2017
E-mail: rep91@ohiohouse.gov
Committees: Rules and Reference

Representative **Margaret Ann Ruhl** (R-District 68) . . . . . . . (614) 466-1431
Counties Represented: Delaware (part), Knox   Fax: (614) 719-6990
Term Expires: 2017
E-mail: rep68@ohiohouse.gov
Committees: Agriculture and Rural Development; Local Government;
Transportation and Infrastructure

Representative **Scott K. Ryan** (R-District 71) . . . . . . . . . . . (614) 466-1482
Counties Represented: Licking (part)   Fax: (614) 719-3971
Term Expires: 2017
E-mail: rep71@ohiohouse.gov
Committees: Economic and Workforce Development; Finance; Public
Utilities; Ways and Means

Representative **Tim Schaffer** (R-District 77) . . . . . . . . . . . . (614) 466-8100
Counties Represented: Fairfield (part)   Fax: (614) 719-0005
Term Expires: 2017
E-mail: rep77@ohiohouse.gov
Committees: Agriculture and Rural Development; Public Utilities; Ways
and Means
Education: Mount Union 1985 BA

Representative **Gary Scherer, CPA** (R-District 92) . . . . . . . (614) 644-7928
Counties Represented: Carroll (part), Pickaway   Fax: (614) 719-6985
(part), Ross (part)
Term Expires: 2017
E-mail: rep92@ohiohouse.gov
Committees: Finance; Financial Institutions, Housing, and Urban
Development; Ways and Means
Education: Ohio State 1976 BAcc

Representative **J. Kirk Schuring** (R-District 48) . . . . . . . . . (614) 752-2438
Counties Represented: Stark (part)   Fax: (614) 719-6951
Term Expires: 2017
E-mail: rep48@ohiohouse.gov
Committees: Health and Aging

Representative **Barbara R. Sears** (R-District 47) . . . . . . . . (614) 466-1731
Counties Represented: Fulton (part), Lucas (part)   Fax: (614) 719-6946
Term Expires: 2017
E-mail: rep47@ohiohouse.gov
Committees: Finance; Health and Aging; Insurance

**LEGISLATIVE BRANCH**

Representative **Michael "Mike" Sheehy** (D-District 46)...(614) 466-1418
Counties Represented: Lucas (part)        Fax: (614) 719-6949
Term Expires: 2017
E-mail: rep46@ohiohouse.gov
Committees: Agriculture and Rural Development; Public Utilities;
Transportation and Infrastructure; Ways and Means
Education: Ohio State 1967 (Attended); Toledo 1971 BA

Representative **Marilyn Slaby** (R-District 38)...........(614) 644-5085
Counties Represented: Stark (part), Summit (part)   Fax: (614) 719-6941
Term Expires: 2017
E-mail: rep38@ohiohouse.gov
Committees: Education; Energy and Natural Resources; Ways and
Means

Representative **Stephen Slesnick** (D-District 49)........(614) 466-8030
Counties Represented: Stark (part)        Fax: (614) 719-6952
Term Expires: 2017
E-mail: rep49@ohiohouse.gov
Committees: Commerce and Labor; Public Utilities; State Government
Education: Ohio State BS

Representative **Kent Smith** (D-District 8)..............(614) 466-5441
Counties Represented: Cuyahoga (part)     Fax: (614) 719-0008
Term Expires: 2017
E-mail: rep08@ohiohouse.gov
Committees: Economic and Workforce Development; Education;
Financial Institutions, Housing, and Urban Development; Public
Utilities

Representative **Ryan Smith** (R-District 93) ............(614) 466-1366
Counties Represented: Gallia, Jackson, Lawrence   Fax: (614) 719-6987
(part), Vinton (part)
Term Expires: 2017
E-mail: rep93@ohiohouse.gov
Committees: Education; Finance; Government Accountability and
Oversight
Education: Ohio State 1995 BS

Representative **Robert Sprague** (R-District 83).........(614) 466-3819
Counties Represented: Hancock, Hardin, Logan   Fax: (614) 719-3976
(part)
Term Expires: 2017
E-mail: rep83@ohiohouse.gov
Committees: Finance; Financial Institutions, Housing, and Urban
Development; Health and Aging
Education: Duke BSME; North Carolina MBA

Representative
**Frederick W. "Fred" Strahorn** (D-District 39).........(614) 466-3357
Counties Represented: Montgomery (part)
Term Expires: 2017
E-mail: rep39@ohiohouse.gov
Committees: Rules and Reference

Representative **Martin J. Sweeney** (D-District 14).......(614) 466-3350
Counties Represented: Cuyahoga (part)     Fax: (614) 719-3910
Term Expires: 2017
77 South High Street, 11th Floor, Columbus, OH 43215
E-mail: rep14@ohiohouse.gov
Committees: Commerce and Labor; State Government; Transportation
and Infrastructure

Representative **Emilia Strong Sykes** (D-District 34)......(614) 466-3100
Counties Represented: Summit (part)       Fax: (614) 719-6944
Term Expires: 2017
77 South High Street, 10th Floor, Columbus, OH 43215
E-mail: rep34@ohiohouse.gov
Committees: Finance; Health and Aging; Judiciary; Ways and Means

Representative **Louis F. Terhar** (R-District 30) ...........(614) 466-8258
Counties Represented: Hamilton (part)     Fax: (614) 719-3584
Term Expires: 2017
E-mail: rep30@ohiohouse.gov
Committees: Armed Services, Veterans Affairs and Public Safety;
Energy and Natural Resources; Financial Institutions, Housing, and
Urban Development
Education: Naval Acad 1972 BS; Syracuse MBA; Harvard MA

Representative
**Andrew "Andy" Thompson** (R-District 95) .........(614) 644-8728
Counties Represented: Belmont (part), Carroll   Fax: (614) 719-6993
(part), Harrison, Noble, Washington (part)
Term Expires: 2017
E-mail: rep95@ohiohouse.gov
Committees: Agriculture and Rural Development; Energy and Natural
Resources; Finance
Education: Central Col (IA) 1985 BA

Representative **A. Nino Vitale** (R-District 85) ..........(614) 466-1507
Counties Represented: Champaign, Logan (part),   Fax: (614) 719-3978
Shelby (part)
Term Expires: 2017
77 South High Street, 11th Floor, Columbus, OH 43215
E-mail: rep85@ohiohouse.gov
Committees: Agriculture and Rural Development; Armed Services,
Veterans Affairs and Public Safety; Transportation and Infrastructure

Representative **Ron Young** (R-District 61) .............(614) 644-6074
Counties Represented: Lake (part)         Fax: (614) 719-3963
Term Expires: 2017
E-mail: rep61@ohiohouse.gov
Committees: Armed Services, Veterans Affairs and Public Safety;
Commerce and Labor; Community and Family Advancement;
Economic and Workforce Development
Education: Kent State 1973 BA

Representative **Paul Zeltwanger** (R-District 54) ........(614) 644-6027
Counties Represented: Butler (part), Warren (part)   Fax: (614) 719-3967
Term Expires: 2017
E-mail: rep54@ohiohouse.gov
Committees: Agriculture and Rural Development; Armed Services,
Veterans Affairs and Public Safety; Economic and Workforce
Development

# House Standing Committees

## Agriculture and Rural Development

| Majority Members | Minority Members |
|---|---|
| Brian D. Hill (R-97) *Chair* | John Patterson (D-99) |
| Tony Burkley (R-82) *Vice Chair* | *Ranking Minority Member* |
| Terry Boose (R-57) | Jack R. Cera (D-96) |
| Jim "Jim" Buchy (R-84) | Michael H. O'Brien (D-175) |
| Christina M. Hagan (R-50) | Sean O'Brien (D-63) |
| Kyle Koehler (R-79) | Bill Patmon (D-10) |
| Sarah LaTourette (R-76) | Debbie Phillips (D-94) |
| Richard Weston "Wes" Retherford (R-51) | Michael "Mike" Sheehy (D-46) |
| Jeffery S. Rezabek (R-43) | |
| Margaret Ann Ruhl (R-68) | |
| Tim Schaffer (R-77) | |
| Andrew "Andy" Thompson (R-95) | |
| A. Nino Vitale (R-85) | |
| Paul Zeltwanger (R-54) | |

## Armed Services, Veterans Affairs and Public Safety

| Majority Members | Minority Members |
|---|---|
| Terry Johnson (R-90) *Chair* | Hearcel F. Craig (D-26) |
| Louis F. Terhar (R-30) *Vice Chair* | *Ranking Minority Member* |
| Marlene Anielski (R-6) | Heather Bishoff (D-20) |
| Steven Arndt (R-89) | Teresa Fedor (D-45) |
| Al Landis (R-98) | Greta Johnson (D-35) |
| Rick Perales (R-73) | Michael J. O'Brien (D-64) |
| Richard Weston "Wes" Retherford (R-51) | |
| A. Nino Vitale (R-85) | |
| Ron Young (R-61) | |
| Paul Zeltwanger (R-54) | |

## Commerce and Labor

| Majority Members | Minority Members |
|---|---|
| Ron Young (R-61) *Chair* | Michele Lepore-Hagan (D-58) |
| Anthony "Tony" DeVitis (R-36) *Vice Chair* | *Ranking Minority Member* |
| Steven Arndt (R-89) | Teresa Fedor (D-45) |
| Louis W. Blessing III (R-29) | Alicia Reece (D-33) |
| Thomas E. "Tom" Brinkman, Jr. (R-27) | Stephen Slesnick (D-49) |
| Mike Duffey (R-21) | Martin J. Sweeney (D-14) |
| Ronald E. "Ron" Hood (R-78) | |
| Kyle Koehler (R-79) | |
| Al Landis (R-98) | |
| Dorothy Liggett Pelanda (R-86) | |
| Kristina Roegner (R-37) | |

## Community and Family Advancement

**Majority Members**
Timothy E. "Tim" Ginter (R-5)
  *Chair*
Margaret Conditt (R-52) *Vice Chair*
Niraj J. Antani (R-42)
Timothy Derickson (R-53)
Jonathan Dever (R-28)
Christina M. Hagan (R-50)
Bill Hayes (R-72)
Ronald E. "Ron" Hood (R-78)
Jeffrey McClain (R-87)
Ron Young (R-61)

**Minority Members**
Stephanie Howse (D-11)
  *Ranking Minority Member*
Kevin L. Boyce (D-25)
Janine R. Boyd (D-9)
Michele Lepore-Hagan (D-58)
Bill Patmon (D-10)

## Economic and Workforce Development

**Majority Members**
Mark J. Romanchuk (R-2) *Chair*
Rick Perales (R-73) *Vice Chair*
Niraj J. Antani (R-42)
Steven Arndt (R-89)
Nan A. Baker (R-16)
Kyle Koehler (R-79)
Scott K. Ryan (R-71)
Ron Young (R-61)
Paul Zeltwanger (R-54)

**Minority Members**
Kent Smith (D-8)
  *Ranking Minority Member*
John E. Barnes, Jr. (D-12)
Hearcel F. Craig (D-26)
Denise Driehaus (D-31)

## Education

**Majority Members**
Andrew O. Brenner (R-67) *Chair*
Timothy Derickson (R-53)
  *Vice Chair*
Louis W. Blessing III (R-29)
Robert E. "Bob" Cupp (R-4)
Bill Hayes (R-72)
Michael Henne (R-40)
Stephen A. Huffman (R-80)
Kyle Koehler (R-79)
Nathan H. Manning (R-55)
Marilyn Slaby (R-38)
Ryan Smith (R-93)

**Minority Members**
Teresa Fedor (D-45)
  *Ranking Minority Member*
Janine R. Boyd (D-9)
Bill Patmon (D-10)
John Patterson (D-99)
Debbie Phillips (D-94)
Dan Ramos (D-56)
Kent Smith (D-8)

## Energy and Natural Resources

**Majority Members**
Al Landis (R-98) *Chair*
Christina M. Hagan (R-50)
  *Vice Chair*
Cheryl L. Grossman (R-23)
David "Dave" Hall (R-70)
Brian D. Hill (R-97)
Ron Maag (R-62)
Marilyn Slaby (R-38)
Louis F. Terhar (R-30)
Andrew "Andy" Thompson (R-95)

**Minority Members**
Sean O'Brien (D-63)
  *Ranking Minority Member*
Jack R. Cera (D-96)
Stephanie Howse (D-11)
David Leland (D-22)

## Finance

**Majority Members**
Ryan Smith (R-93) *Chair*
Scott K. Ryan (R-71) *Vice Chair*
Marlene Anielski (R-6)
Tony Burkley (R-82)
Robert E. "Bob" Cupp (R-4)
Timothy Derickson (R-53)
Michael D. "Mike" Dovilla (R-7)
Mike Duffey (R-21)
Doug Green (R-66)
Cheryl L. Grossman (R-23)
David "Dave" Hall (R-70)
Stephanie Kunze (R-24)
Ron Maag (R-62)
Jeffrey McClain (R-87)
Rick Perales (R-73)
William "Bill" Reineke (R-88)
Mark J. Romanchuk (R-2)
Gary Scherer (R-92)
Barbara R. Sears (R-47)
Robert Sprague (R-83)
Andrew "Andy" Thompson (R-95)

**Minority Members**
Denise Driehaus (D-31)
  *Ranking Minority Member*
Nickie J. Antonio (D-13)
Kevin L. Boyce (D-25)
Jack R. Cera (D-96)
Kathleen Clyde (D-75)
Michael J. O'Brien (D-64)
John Patterson (D-99)
Debbie Phillips (D-94)
Dan Ramos (D-56)
Alicia Reece (D-33)
Emilia Strong Sykes (D-34)

## Financial Institutions, Housing, and Urban Development

**Majority Members**
Jonathan Dever (R-28) *Chair*
William "Bill" Reineke (R-88)
  *Vice Chair*
Tim W. Brown (R-3)
Michael D. "Mike" Dovilla (R-7)
Stephen D. "Steve" Hambley (R-69)
Nathan H. Manning (R-55)
Gary Scherer (R-92)
Robert Sprague (R-83)
Louis F. Terhar (R-30)

**Minority Members**
Christie Bryant Kuhns (D-32)
  *Ranking Minority Member*
Hearcel F. Craig (D-26)
David Leland (D-22)
Kent Smith (D-8)

## Government Accountability and Oversight

**Majority Members**
Tim W. Brown (R-3) *Chair*
Louis W. Blessing III (R-29)
  *Vice Chair*
Jim "Jim" Buchy (R-84)
James "Jim" Butler (R-41)
Timothy Derickson (R-53)
Doug Green (R-66)
Robert McColley (R-81)
Dorothy Liggett Pelanda (R-86)
Ryan Smith (R-93)

**Minority Members**
Kathleen Clyde (D-75)
  *Ranking Minority Member*
Michael F. "Mike" Curtin (D-17)
David Leland (D-22)

## Health and Aging

**Majority Members**
Anne Gonzales (R-19) *Chair*
Stephen A. Huffman (R-80)
  *Vice Chair*
Tim W. Brown (R-3)
James "Jim" Butler (R-41)
Mike Duffey (R-21)
Timothy E. "Tim" Ginter (R-5)
Terry Johnson (R-90)
Sarah LaTourette (R-76)
Ron Maag (R-62)
J. Kirk Schuring (R-48)
Barbara R. Sears (R-47)
Robert Sprague (R-83)

**Minority Members**
Nickie J. Antonio (D-13)
  *Ranking Minority Member*
John E. Barnes, Jr. (D-12)
Heather Bishoff (D-20)
Christie Bryant Kuhns (D-32)
Michele Lepore-Hagan (D-58)
Dan Ramos (D-56)
Emilia Strong Sykes (D-34)

## Insurance

**Majority Members**
Barbara R. Sears (R-47) *Chair*
Thomas E. "Tom"
  Brinkman, Jr. (R-27)
  *Vice Chair*
Bill Dean (R-74)
Anthony "Tony" DeVitis (R-36)
Stephanie Kunze (R-24)
Sarah LaTourette (R-76)
Richard Weston "Wes" Retherford
  (R-51)

**Minority Members**
Heather Bishoff (D-20)
  *Ranking Minority Member*
Michael "Mike" Ashford (D-44)
Christie Bryant Kuhns (D-32)
Jack R. Cera (D-96)

## Judiciary

**Majority Members**
James "Jim" Butler (R-41) *Chair*
Nathan H. Manning (R-55)
  *Vice Chair*
Niraj J. Antani (R-42)
Robert E. "Bob" Cupp (R-4)
Jonathan Dever (R-28)
Stephen D. "Steve" Hambley (R-69)
Robert McColley (R-81)
Dorothy Liggett Pelanda (R-86)
Jeffery S. Rezabek (R-43)

**Minority Members**
Greta Johnson (D-35)
  *Ranking Minority Member*
Nicholas J. Celebrezze (D-15)
Emilia Strong Sykes (D-34)

## Local Government

**Majority Members**
Marlene Anielski (R-6) *Chair*
Steven Arndt (R-89) *Vice Chair*
Nan A. Baker (R-16)
John Becker (R-65)
Terry Boose (R-57)
Stephen D. "Steve" Hambley (R-69)
Jeffery S. Rezabek (R-43)
Margaret Ann Ruhl (R-68)

**Minority Members**
John M. Rogers (D-60)
  *Ranking Minority Member*
Michael "Mike" Ashford (D-44)
Janine R. Boyd (D-9)
Alicia Reece (D-33)

## Medical Marijuana

Chair **J. Kirk Schuring** (R-District 48)
Vice Chair **Stephen A. Huffman** (R-District 80)
Member **Marlene Anielski, CPM** (R-District 6)
Member **Tim W. Brown** (R-District 3)
Member **Ryan Smith** (R-District 93)
Member **Louis F. Terhar** (R-District 30)
Ranking Minority Member
  **Dan Ramos** (D-District 56)
Member **Christie Bryant Kuhns** (D-District 32)
Member
  **Nicholas J. Celebrezze, JD** (D-District 15)

## Public Utilities

**Majority Members**
Michael D. "Mike" Dovilla (R-7)
  *Chair*
Kristina Roegner (R-37) *Vice Chair*
Ron Amstutz (R-1)
Thomas E. "Tom" Brinkman, Jr.
  (R-27)
Jim "Jim" Buchy (R-84)
Margaret Conditt (R-52)
Robert E. "Bob" Cupp (R-4)
Timothy E. "Tim" Ginter (R-5)
Christina M. Hagan (R-50)
David "Dave" Hall (R-70)
Brian D. Hill (R-97)
Nathan H. Manning (R-55)
Mark J. Romanchuk (R-2)
Scott K. Ryan (R-71)
Tim Schaffer (R-77)

**Minority Members**
John A. Boccieri (D-59)
Michael "Mike" Ashford (D-44)
  *Ranking Minority Member*
Kathleen Clyde (D-75)
Sean O'Brien (D-63)
John M. Rogers (D-60)
Michael "Mike" Sheehy (D-46)
Stephen Slesnick (D-49)
Kent Smith (D-8)

## Rules and Reference

**Majority Members**
Ron Amstutz (R-1) *Chair*
Clifford A. Rosenberger (R-91)
  *Vice Chair*
Andrew O. Brenner (R-67)
Bill Hayes (R-72)
Ronald E. "Ron" Hood (R-78)
Dorothy Liggett Pelanda (R-86)

**Minority Members**
Frederick W. "Fred"
  Strahorn (D-39)
  *Ranking Minority Member*
Nickie J. Antonio (D-13)
Kevin L. Boyce (D-25)
Nicholas J. Celebrezze (D-15)
Dan Ramos (D-56)

## State Government

**Majority Members**
Ron Maag (R-62) *Chair*
Stephen D. "Steve" Hambley (R-69)
  *Vice Chair*
John Becker (R-65)
Bill Dean (R-74)
Cheryl L. Grossman (R-23)
Ronald E. "Ron" Hood (R-78)
Stephen A. Huffman (R-80)
Sarah LaTourette (R-76)
Rick Perales (R-73)

**Minority Members**
Stephen Slesnick (D-49)
  *Ranking Minority Member*
Kristin Boggs (D-18)
Michael F. "Mike" Curtin (D-17)
Martin J. Sweeney (D-14)

## Transportation and Infrastructure

**Majority Members**
Terry Boose (R-57) *Chair*
Doug Green (R-66) *Vice Chair*
Niraj J. Antani (R-42)
Steven Arndt (R-89)
John Becker (R-65)
Jonathan Dever (R-28)
Anthony "Tony" DeVitis (R-36)
Michael D. "Mike" Dovilla (R-7)
Terry Johnson (R-90)
Margaret Ann Ruhl (R-68)
A. Nino Vitale (R-85)

**Minority Members**
Michael "Mike" Sheehy (D-46)
  *Ranking Minority Member*
Stephanie Howse (D-11)
Greta Johnson (D-35)
Michele Lepore-Hagan (D-58)
Martin J. Sweeney (D-14)

## Ways and Means

**Majority Members**
Tim Schaffer (R-77) *Chair*
Gary Scherer (R-92) *Vice Chair*
Ron Amstutz (R-1)
Nan A. Baker (R-16)
Terry Boose (R-57)
Tony Burkley (R-82)
Jonathan Dever (R-28)
Stephen D. "Steve" Hambley (R-69)
Michael Henne (R-40)
Jeffrey McClain (R-87)
Robert McColley (R-81)
William "Bill" Reineke (R-88)
Scott K. Ryan (R-71)
Marilyn Slaby (R-38)

**Minority Members**
Jack R. Cera (D-96)
  *Ranking Minority Member*
John E. Barnes, Jr. (D-12)
Michael F. "Mike" Curtin (D-17)
Denise Driehaus (D-31)
John M. Rogers (D-60)
Michael "Mike" Sheehy (D-46)
Emilia Strong Sykes (D-34)

LEGISLATIVE BRANCH

# Oklahoma Legislature

State Capitol Building, 2300 North Lincoln Boulevard,
Oklahoma City, OK 73105
Internet: www.lsb.state.ok.us

## Oklahoma State Senate

State Capitol Building, 2300 North Lincoln Boulevard,
Oklahoma City, OK 73105
Tel: (405) 524-0126  TTY: (405) 524-0126  Fax: (405) 521-5507
Internet: www.oksenate.gov

President Pro Tem **Brian Bingman** (R) . . . . . . . . . . . . . . . . . (405) 521-5528
  Education: Oklahoma 1976 BBA
Majority Floor Leader **Mike Schulz** (R) . . . . . . . . . . . . . . . (405) 521-5612
  Education: Oklahoma BS
Assistant Majority Floor Leader **Eddie Fields** (R) . . . . . . . (405) 521-5581
  Education: Oklahoma State 1990 BA
Assistant Majority Floor Leader **Anthony Sykes** (R) . . . . . (405) 521-5569
  Education: Oklahoma BPA, JD
Assistant Majority Floor Leader **Greg Treat** (R) . . . . . . . . . (405) 521-5632
  Education: Oklahoma 2000 BA
Majority Whip **Nathan Dahm** (R) . . . . . . . . . . . . . . . . . . . (405) 521-5551
Majority Whip **Kim David** (R) . . . . . . . . . . . . . . . . . . . . . . (405) 521-5590
Majority Whip **Frank Simpson** (R) . . . . . . . . . . . . . . . . . . (405) 521-5607
Majority Whip **Rob Standridge** (R) . . . . . . . . . . . . . . . . . . (405) 521-5535
  Education: Oklahoma 1993 BSPh
Majority Caucus Chairman **Bryce Marlatt** (R) . . . . . . . . . . (405) 521-5626
Majority Caucus Vice Chairman **Ann "AJ" Griffin** (R) . . . . (405) 521-5628
  Education: Oklahoma State BS; Central Oklahoma MS
Minority Floor Leader **John Sparks** (D) . . . . . . . . . . . . . . . (405) 521-5553
  Education: Harvard 1991 AB; Oklahoma 1994 JD
Assistant Minority Floor Leader **Kay Floyd** (D) . . . . . . . . . (405) 521-5610
  Education: Oklahoma State 1980 BS; Oklahoma 1983 JD
Assistant Minority Floor Leader **Earl Garrison** (D) . . . . . . . (405) 521-5533
  Education: Tulsa 1972 BFA; Oklahoma 1976 DEd
Assistant Minority Floor Leader **Susan Paddack** (D) . . . . . (405) 521-5541
  Education: Colorado BSEd; East Central U MEd
Assistant Minority Floor Leader
  **Charles "Charlie" Wyrick** (D) . . . . . . . . . . . . . . . . . . . (405) 524-5561
Minority Whip **Anastasia A. Pittman** (D) . . . . . . . . . . . . . (405) 521-5531
  Education: Oklahoma 1999 BA; Langston 2002 MA
Minority Caucus Chairman **Kay Floyd** (D) . . . . . . . . . . . . . (405) 521-5610
Minority Caucus Vice Chairman **Susan Paddack** (D) . . . . . (405) 521-5541
Secretary of the Senate **Paul Ziriax** . . . . . . . . . . . . . . . . . (405) 521-2391
  E-mail: ziriax@oksenate.gov

## Senators

**Party Affiliation Statistics:** Republicans: 39, Democrats: 9

Senator **Mark Allen** (R-District 4) Room 412 . . . . . . . . . . . (405) 521-5576
  Counties Represented: Leflore, Sequoyah
  Term Expires: 2018
  E-mail: allen@oksenate.gov
  Committees: Agriculture and Rural Development; Appropriations;
  Energy; Transportation
Senator **Patrick Anderson** (R-District 19) . . . . . . . . . . . . . . (405) 521-5630
  Counties Represented: Alfalfa, Garfield, Grant, Kay (part)
  Term Expires: 2016
  P.O. Box 5589, Enid, OK 73702
  E-mail: anderson@oksenate.gov
  Committees: Appropriations; Pensions; Tourism and Wildlife; Veterans
  and Military Affairs
  Education: Oklahoma State BS; Oklahoma JD
Senator **Don Barrington** (R-District 31) . . . . . . . . . . . . . . . (405) 521-5563
  Counties Represented: Comanche (part), Cotton, Jefferson, Stephens
  (part), Tillman
  Term Expires: 2016
  4506 Northeast Highlander Circle, Lawton, OK 73507
  E-mail: barrington@oksenate.gov
  Committees: Agriculture and Rural Development; Appropriations;
  Public Safety; Transportation
Senator **Randy Bass** (D-District 32) . . . . . . . . . . . . . . . . . . (405) 521-5567
  Counties Represented: Comanche (part)
  Term Expires: 2018
  2606 Northwest Lake Front Drive, Lawton, OK 73505
  E-mail: bass@oksenate.gov
  Committees: Appropriations; Energy; Insurance; Rules; Tourism and
  Wildlife; Veterans and Military Affairs

Senator **Stephanie Bice** (R-District 22) Room 531 . . . . . . . (405) 521-5592
  Counties Represented: Canadian (part), Oklahoma (part)
  Term Expires: 2018
  E-mail: bice@oksenate.gov
  Committees: Appropriations; Business and Commerce; General
  Government; Transportation
Senator **Brian Bingman** (R-District 12) . . . . . . . . . . . . . . . (405) 521-5528
  Counties Represented: Creek, Tulsa (part)    Dist: (918) 227-1856
  Term Expires: 2018
  1502 East McKinley, Sapulpa, OK 74066
  E-mail: bingman@oksenate.gov
Senator **Larry Boggs** (R-District 7) Room 513B . . . . . . . . . (405) 521-5604
  Counties Represented: Haskell, Hughes (part), Latimer, Okfuskee
  (part), Pittsburg
  Term Expires: 2016
  E-mail: boggs@oksenate.gov
  Committees: Agriculture and Rural Development; Appropriations;
  Tourism and Wildlife; Veterans and Military Affairs
  Education: Eastern Oklahoma State (Attended)
Senator **Joshua "Josh" Brecheen** (R-District 6)
  Room 513A . . . . . . . . . . . . . . . . . . . . . . . . . . . . . . . . . . (405) 521-5586
  Counties Represented: Atoka (part), Bryan, Coal, Johnston (part),
  Marshall
  Term Expires: 2018
  E-mail: brecheen@oksenate.gov
  Committees: Appropriations; Education; Public Safety; Tourism and
  Wildlife
  Education: Oklahoma State 2002 BS
Senator **Corey Brooks** (R-District 43) Room 520 . . . . . . . . (405) 521-5522
  Counties Represented: Garvin (part), McClain, Stephens (part)
  Term Expires: 2016
  E-mail: brooks@oksenate.gov
  Committees: Appropriations; General Government; Judiciary; Public
  Safety
  Education: Oklahoma Baptist 2001 BA; Naval War 2010 MA
Senator **Bill Brown** (R-District 36) Room 513A . . . . . . . . . . (405) 521-5602
  Counties Represented: Tulsa (part), Wagoner (part)    Dist: (918) 258-5526
  Term Expires: 2018
  E-mail: brownb@oksenate.gov
  Committees: Appropriations; Insurance; Pensions; Tourism and Wildlife
  Education: Northeastern BAEd
Senator **Brian A. Crain** (R-District 39) . . . . . . . . . . . . . . . . (405) 521-5620
  Counties Represented: Tulsa (part)
  Term Expires: 2016
  5305 East 37th Street, Tulsa, OK 74135
  E-mail: crain@oksenate.gov
  Committees: Appropriations; Energy; Health and Human Services;
  Judiciary
  Education: Oklahoma 1983 BBA; Tulsa 1991 JD
Senator **Nathan Dahm** (R-District 33) Room 533A . . . . . . (405) 521-5551
  Counties Represented: Tulsa (part)
  Term Expires: 2016
  E-mail: dahm@oksenate.gov
  Committees: Appropriations; Business and Commerce; Finance;
  General Government; Rules
Senator **Kim David** (R-District 18) Room 520 . . . . . . . . . . (405) 521-5590
  Counties Represented: Cherokee (part), Mayes (part), Muskogee (part),
  Tulsa (part), Wagoner (part)
  Term Expires: 2018
  E-mail: david@oksenate.gov
  Committees: Appropriations; Finance; Health and Human Services;
  Public Safety; Rules
Senator **J.J. Dossett** (D-District 34) Room 521A . . . . . . . . (405) 524-0126
  Counties Represented: Rogers (part), Tulsa (part)
  Term Expires: 2016
  E-mail: dossett@oksenate.gov
  Committees: Education; Pensions; Veterans and Military Affairs
  Education: Oklahoma State 2006 BA
Senator **Eddie Fields** (R-District 10) Room 514B . . . . . . . . (405) 521-5581
  Counties Represented: Kay (part), Osage (part)
  Term Expires: 2018
  E-mail: efields@oksenate.gov
  Committees: Agriculture and Rural Development; Appropriations;
  Energy; Rules; Tourism and Wildlife
Senator **Kay Floyd** (D-District 46) Room 522A . . . . . . . . . . (405) 521-5610
  Counties Represented: Oklahoma (part)
  Term Expires: 2018
  E-mail: floyd@oksenate.gov
  Committees: Appropriations; General Government; Health and Human
  Services; Judiciary; Rules

LEGISLATIVE BRANCH

Senator **John Ford** (R-District 29)....................(405) 521-5634
Counties Represented: Nowata, Rogers (part), Washington
Term Expires: 2016
748 Brookhollow Lane, Bartlesville, OK 74006
E-mail: fordj@oksenate.gov
Committees: Appropriations; Education; Finance; Public Safety
Education: Tulsa 1968 BS

Senator **Jack Fry** (R-District 42) Room 413A............(405) 521-5584
Counties Represented: Oklahoma (part)
Term Expires: 2018
E-mail: fry@oksenate.gov
Committees: Appropriations; General Government; Transportation;
Veterans and Military Affairs

Senator **Earl Garrison** (D-District 9)...................(405) 521-5533
Counties Represented: Cherokee (part), Muskogee (part)
Term Expires: 2016
3806 Club View Drive, Muskogee, OK 74403
E-mail: garrisone@oksenate.gov
Committees: Agriculture and Rural Development; Appropriations;
Education; Rules; Tourism and Wildlife

Senator **Ann "AJ" Griffin** (R-District 20)..............(405) 521-5628
Counties Represented: Kingfisher (part), Logan, Noble, Pawnee
Term Expires: 2018
P.O. Box 1233, Guthrie, OK 73044
E-mail: griffin@oksenate.gov
Committees: Appropriations; Energy; Health and Human Services;
Judiciary; Rules

Senator **James "Jim" Halligan** (R-District 21).........(405) 521-5572
Counties Represented: Payne
Term Expires: 2016
6321 West Coventry, Stillwater, OK 74074
E-mail: halligan@oksenate.gov
Committees: Appropriations; Business and Commerce; Education;
Finance
Education: Iowa 1962 BSChE, 1965 MSChE, 1967 PhD

Senator **David Holt** (R-District 30) Room 411A.........(405) 521-5636
Counties Represented: Oklahoma (part)
Term Expires: 2018
E-mail: holt@oksenate.gov
Committees: Appropriations; General Government; Judiciary; Public
Safety

Senator **Darcy A. Jech** (R-District 26) Room 528A......(405) 521-5545
Counties Represented: Beckham, Blaine, Caddo, Custer (part),
Kingfisher (part), Roger Mills
Term Expires: 2018
E-mail: jech@oksenate.gov
Committees: Appropriations; Finance; Insurance; Pensions

Senator **Clark Jolley** (R-District 41) ...................(405) 521-5622
Counties Represented: Oklahoma (part)
Term Expires: 2016
3016 Thornbrooke Boulevard, Edmond, OK 73013
E-mail: jolley@oksenate.gov
Committees: Appropriations; Education; Energy; Finance; Rules
Education: Oklahoma Baptist 1992 BA, 1992 BME;
Oklahoma 1995 JD

Senator **Ron Justice** (R-District 23) ...................(405) 521-5537
Counties Represented: Canadian (part), Grady, Kingfisher (part)
Term Expires: 2016
2209 County Street 2880, Chickasha, OK 73018
E-mail: justice@oksenate.gov
Committees: Agriculture and Rural Development; Appropriations;
Energy; Rules; Tourism and Wildlife
Education: Oklahoma State BS; Oklahoma MS

Senator **Kyle Loveless** (R-District 45) Room 531 ........ (405) 521-5618
Counties Represented: Canadian (part), Cleveland (part), Oklahoma
(part)
Term Expires: 2016
E-mail: loveless@oksenate.gov
Committees: Appropriations; Energy; Health and Human Services;
Transportation
Education: Georgetown 2000 BA

Senator **Kevin Matthews** (D-District 11) Room 518......(405) 521-5598
Counties Represented: Osage (part), Tulsa (part)
Term Expires: 2016
E-mail: matthews@oksenate.gov
Committees: General Government; Pensions; Public Safety;
Transportation
Education: Central State BS

Senator **Bryce Marlatt** (R-District 27) Room 427 ........ (405) 521-5626
Counties Represented: Beaver, Cimarron, Dewey, Ellis, Harper, Major,
Texas, Woods, Woodward
Term Expires: 2016
E-mail: marlatt@oksenate.gov
Committees: Appropriations; Energy; General Government; Rules;
Transportation

Senator **Mike Mazzei** (R-District 25) ................. (405) 521-5675
Counties Represented: Tulsa (part)
Term Expires: 2016
6528 East 101st Street, Suite D-1, PMB 220, Tulsa, OK 74133
1375 East 71st Street, Tulsa, OK 74136
E-mail: mazzei@oksenate.gov
Committees: Appropriations; Finance; Insurance; Pensions
Education: George Mason BA

Senator **Dan Newberry** (R-District 37) Room 414 ...... (405) 521-5600
Counties Represented: Tulsa (part)
Term Expires: 2016
E-mail: newberry@oksenate.gov
Committees: Appropriations; Business and Commerce; Pensions;
Transportation

Senator **Susan Paddack** (D-District 13)...............(405) 521-5541
Counties Represented: Garvin (part), Hughes (part),     Dist: (580) 332-7607
Pontotoc, Pottawatomie (part), Seminole (part)
Term Expires: 2016
500 Southeast County Road, Ada, OK 74820
E-mail: paddack@oksenate.gov
Committees: Appropriations; Education; Finance; Public Safety;
Transportation

Senator **Anastasia A. Pittman** (D-District 48)
Room 518 .................................................(405) 521-5531
Counties Represented: Oklahoma (part)
Term Expires: 2018
E-mail: pittman@oksenate.gov
Committees: Appropriations; Business and Commerce; Health and
Human Services; Transportation

Senator **Marty Quinn** (R-District 2) ...................(405) 521-5555
Counties Represented: Mayes (part), Rogers (part)
Term Expires: 2018
E-mail: quinn@oksenate.gov
Committees: Appropriations; Education; Finance; Insurance

Senator **Mike Schulz** (R-District 38) ...................(405) 521-5612
Counties Represented: Custer (part), Greer, Harmon, Jackson, Kiowa,
Washita
Term Expires: 2018
16830 SCR 209, Altus, OK 73521
E-mail: schulz@oksenate.gov

Senator **Ron Sharp** (R-District 17) Room 533 ...........(405) 521-5539
Counties Represented: Oklahoma (part), Pottawatomie (part)
Term Expires: 2016
E-mail: sharp@oksenate.gov
Committees: Appropriations; Business and Commerce; Education;
Tourism and Wildlife
Education: Southeastern Oklahoma St; Central State

Senator **Wayne Shaw** (R-District 3) Room 513A ........ (405) 521-5574
Counties Represented: Adair, Cherokee (part), Delaware (part), Mayes
(part), Rogers (part)
Term Expires: 2016
E-mail: shaw@oksenate.gov
Committees: Appropriations; Education; Public Safety; Tourism and
Wildlife
Education: Lamar; Lincoln Christian; Fuller Sem PhD

Senator **Ralph Shortey** (R-District 44) Room 514A ...... (405) 521-5557
Counties Represented: Canadian (part), Oklahoma (part)
Term Expires: 2018
E-mail: shortey@oksenate.gov
Committees: Appropriations; Energy; General Government;
Transportation

Senator **Joseph W. Silk** (R-District 5) Room 536 ........ (405) 521-5614
Counties Represented: Atoka (part), Choctaw, Le Flore (part),
McCurtain, Pushmataha
Term Expires: 2016
E-mail: silk@oksenate.gov
Committees: Agriculture and Rural Development; Appropriations;
Business and Commerce; Transportation

Senator **Frank Simpson** (R-District 14) Room 513B ......(405) 521-5607
Counties Represented: Carter, Johnston (part), Love, Murray
Term Expires: 2018
E-mail: simpson@oksenate.gov
Committees: Agriculture and Rural Development; Appropriations;
Finance; Rules; Veterans and Military Affairs

*(continued on next page)*

**LEGISLATIVE BRANCH**

**Senators** continued

Senator **Jason Smalley** (R-District 28) Room 416 . . . . . . . (405) 521-5547
  Counties Represented: Lincoln, Pottawatomie (part), Seminole (part)
  Term Expires: 2018
  E-mail: smalley@oksenate.gov
  Committees: Appropriations; Education; Pensions; Transportation;
  Veterans and Military Affairs
  Education: Oklahoma 2010 BA

Senator **John Sparks** (D-District 16) Room 533 . . . . . . . . (405) 521-5553
  Counties Represented: Cleveland (part)
  Term Expires: 2018
  E-mail: sparks@oksenate.gov
  Committees: Appropriations; Energy; Finance; Insurance; Judiciary

Senator **Rob Standridge** (R-District 15) Room 429 . . . . . . (405) 521-5535
  Counties Represented: Cleveland (part), Oklahoma (part)
  Term Expires: 2016
  E-mail: standridge@oksenate.gov
  Committees: Appropriations; Energy; Health and Human Services;
  Judiciary; Rules

Senator **Gary Stanislawski** (R-District 35) . . . . . . . . . . . . (405) 521-5624
  Counties Represented: Tulsa (part)      Dist: (918) 493-4190
  Term Expires: 2016
  6119 East 91st Street, Suite 300, Tulsa, OK 74137
  E-mail: stanislawski@oksenate.gov
  Committees: Appropriations; Education; Insurance; Transportation
  Education: Oregon State BSBA; Oral Roberts 1996 MA

Senator **Anthony Sykes** (R-District 24) . . . . . . . . . . . . . . (405) 521-5569
  Counties Represented: Cleveland (part)
  Term Expires: 2018
  1807 Southwest 24th Street, Moore, OK 73170
  E-mail: lewis@oksenate.gov
  Committees: Agriculture and Rural Development; Appropriations;
  Judiciary; Rules; Veterans and Military Affairs

Senator **Roger Thompson** (R-District 8) Room 527B . . . . . (405) 521-5588
  Counties Represented: McIntosh, Muskogee (part), Okfuskee (part),
  Okmulgee
  Term Expires: 2018
  E-mail: thompson@oksenate.gov
  Committees: Appropriations; Business and Commerce; Education;
  Judiciary

Senator **Greg Treat** (R-District 47) Room 530 . . . . . . . . . . (405) 521-5632
  Counties Represented: Oklahoma (part)
  Term Expires: 2016
  E-mail: treat@oksenate.gov
  Committees: Appropriations; Energy; Health and Human Services;
  Judiciary; Rules

Senator **Charles "Charlie" Wyrick** (D-District 1) . . . . . . . (405) 521-5561
  Counties Represented: Craig, Delaware (part), Mayes (part), Ottawa
  Term Expires: 2016
  58500 East 155 Road, Fairland, OK 74343-2702
  E-mail: wyrick@oksenate.gov
  Committees: Agriculture and Rural Development; Appropriations;
  Business and Commerce; Energy; Finance; Tourism and Wildlife

Senator **Ervin Yen** (R-District 40) Room 411A . . . . . . . . . . (405) 521-5543
  Counties Represented: Oklahoma (part)
  Term Expires: 2018
  E-mail: yen@oksenate.gov
  Committees: Appropriations; Business and Commerce; Finance; Health
  and Human Services

# Senate Standing Committees

## Agriculture and Rural Development

| Majority Members | Minority Members |
|---|---|
| Eddie Fields (R-10) *Chair* | Earl Garrison (D-9) |
| Mark Allen (R-4) *Vice Chair* | Charles "Charlie" Wyrick (D-1) |
| Don Barrington (R-31) | |
| Larry Boggs (R-7) | |
| Ron Justice (R-23) | |
| Joseph W. Silk (R-5) | |
| Frank Simpson (R-14) | |
| Anthony Sykes (R-24) | |

# Appropriations

| Majority Members | Minority Members |
|---|---|
| Clark Jolley (R-41) *Chair* | Randy Bass (D-32) |
| Greg Treat (R-47) *Vice Chair* | Kay Floyd (D-46) |
| Mark Allen (R-4) | Earl Garrison (D-9) |
| Patrick Anderson (R-19) | Susan Paddack (D-13) |
| Don Barrington (R-31) | Anastasia A. Pittman (D-48) |
| Stephanie Bice (R-22) | John Sparks (D-16) |
| Larry Boggs (R-7) | Charles "Charlie" Wyrick (D-1) |
| Joshua "Josh" Brecheen (R-6) | |
| Corey Brooks (R-43) | |
| Bill Brown (R-36) | |
| Brian A. Crain (R-39) | |
| Nathan Dahm (R-33) | |
| Kim David (R-18) | |
| Eddie Fields (R-10) | |
| John Ford (R-29) | |
| Jack Fry (R-42) | |
| Ann "AJ" Griffin (R-20) | |
| James "Jim" Halligan (R-21) | |
| David Holt (R-30) | |
| Darcy A. Jech (R-26) | |
| Ron Justice (R-23) | |
| Kyle Loveless (R-45) | |
| Bryce Marlatt (R-27) | |
| Mike Mazzei (R-25) | |
| Dan Newberry (R-37) | |
| Marty Quinn (R-2) | |
| Ron Sharp (R-17) | |
| Wayne Shaw (R-3) | |
| Ralph Shortey (R-44) | |
| Joseph W. Silk (R-5) | |
| Frank Simpson (R-14) | |
| Jason Smalley (R-28) | |
| Rob Standridge (R-15) | |
| Gary Stanislawski (R-35) | |
| Anthony Sykes (R-24) | |
| Roger Thompson (R-8) | |
| Ervin Yen (R-40) | |

# Business and Commerce

| Majority Members | Minority Members |
|---|---|
| Dan Newberry (R-37) *Chair* | Anastasia A. Pittman (D-48) |
| Stephanie Bice (R-22) *Vice Chair* | Charles "Charlie" Wyrick (D-1) |
| Nathan Dahm (R-33) | |
| James "Jim" Halligan (R-21) | |
| Ron Sharp (R-17) | |
| Joseph W. Silk (R-5) | |
| Roger Thompson (R-8) | |
| Ervin Yen (R-40) | |

# Education

| Majority Members | Minority Members |
|---|---|
| John Ford (R-29) *Chair* | J.J. Dossett (D-34) |
| Ron Sharp (R-17) *Vice Chair* | Earl Garrison (D-9) |
| Joshua "Josh" Brecheen (R-6) | Susan Paddack (D-13) |
| James "Jim" Halligan (R-21) | |
| Clark Jolley (R-41) | |
| Marty Quinn (R-2) | |
| Gary Stanislawski (R-35) | |
| Wayne Shaw (R-3) | |
| Jason Smalley (R-28) | |
| Roger Thompson (R-8) | |

# Energy

| Majority Members | Minority Members |
|---|---|
| Bryce Marlatt (R-27) *Chair* | Randy Bass (D-32) |
| Ann "AJ" Griffin (R-20) *Vice Chair* | John Sparks (D-16) |
| Mark Allen (R-4) | Charles "Charlie" Wyrick (D-1) |
| Brian A. Crain (R-39) | |
| Eddie Fields (R-10) | |
| Clark Jolley (R-41) | |
| Ron Justice (R-23) | |
| Kyle Loveless (R-45) | |
| Ralph Shortey (R-44) | |
| Rob Standridge (R-15) | |
| Greg Treat (R-47) | |

## Finance

**Majority Members**
Mike Mazzei (R-25) *Chair*
Marty Quinn (R-2) *Vice Chair*
Nathan Dahm (R-33)
Kim David (R-18)
John Ford (R-29)
James "Jim" Halligan (R-21)
Darcy A. Jech (R-26)
Clark Jolley (R-41)
Frank Simpson (R-14)
Ervin Yen (R-40)

**Minority Members**
Susan Paddack (D-13)
John Sparks (D-16)
Charles "Charlie" Wyrick (D-1)

## General Government

**Majority Members**
Nathan Dahm (R-33) *Chair*
Jack Fry (R-42) *Vice Chair*
Stephanie Bice (R-22)
Corey Brooks (R-43)
David Holt (R-30)
Bryce Marlatt (R-27)
Ralph Shortey (R-44)

**Minority Members**
Kay Floyd (D-46)
Kevin Matthews (D-11)

## Health and Human Services

**Majority Members**
Rob Standridge (R-15) *Chair*
Ervin Yen (R-40) *Vice Chair*
Brian A. Crain (R-39)
Kim David (R-18)
Ann "AJ" Griffin (R-20)
Kyle Loveless (R-45)
Greg Treat (R-47)

**Minority Members**
Kay Floyd (D-46)
Anastasia A. Pittman (D-48)

## Insurance

**Majority Members**
Bill Brown (R-36) *Chair*
Darcy A. Jech (R-26)
Mike Mazzei (R-25)
Marty Quinn (R-2)
Gary Stanislawski (R-35)

**Minority Members**
John Sparks (D-16) *Vice Chair*
Randy Bass (D-32)

## Judiciary

**Majority Members**
Anthony Sykes (R-24) *Chair*
Brian A. Crain (R-39) *Vice Chair*
Corey Brooks (R-43)
Ann "AJ" Griffin (R-20)
David Holt (R-30)
Rob Standridge (R-15)
Roger Thompson (R-8)
Greg Treat (R-47)

**Minority Members**
Kay Floyd (D-46)
John Sparks (D-16)

## Pensions

**Majority Members**
Jason Smalley (R-28) *Chair*
Darcy A. Jech (R-26) *Vice Chair*
Patrick Anderson (R-19)
Bill Brown (R-36)
Mike Mazzei (R-25)
Dan Newberry (R-37)

**Minority Members**
J.J. Dossett (D-34)
Kevin Matthews (D-11)

## Public Safety

**Majority Members**
Don Barrington (R-31) *Chair*
Corey Brooks (R-43) *Vice Chair*
Joshua "Josh" Brecheen (R-6)
Kim David (R-18)
John Ford (R-29)
David Holt (R-30)
Wayne Shaw (R-3)

**Minority Members**
Kevin Matthews (D-11)
Susan Paddack (D-13)

## Rules

**Majority Members**
Ron Justice (R-23) *Chair*
Eddie Fields (R-10) *Vice Chair*
Nathan Dahm (R-33)
Kim David (R-18)
Ann "AJ" Griffin (R-20)
Clark Jolley (R-41)
Bryce Marlatt (R-27)
Frank Simpson (R-14)
Rob Standridge (R-15)
Anthony Sykes (R-24)
Greg Treat (R-47)

**Minority Members**
Randy Bass (D-32)
Kay Floyd (D-46)
Earl Garrison (D-9)

## Tourism and Wildlife

**Majority Members**
Joshua "Josh" Brecheen (R-6)
   *Chair*
Larry Boggs (R-7) *Vice Chair*
Patrick Anderson (R-19)
Bill Brown (R-36)
Eddie Fields (R-10)
Ron Justice (R-23)
Ron Sharp (R-17)
Wayne Shaw (R-3)

**Minority Members**
Randy Bass (D-32)
Earl Garrison (D-9)
Charles "Charlie" Wyrick (D-1)

## Transportation

**Majority Members**
Gary Stanislawski (R-35) *Chair*
Joseph W. Silk (R-5) *Vice Chair*
Mark Allen (R-4)
Don Barrington (R-31)
Stephanie Bice (R-22)
Jack Fry (R-42)
Kyle Loveless (R-45)
Bryce Marlatt (R-27)
Dan Newberry (R-37)
Ralph Shortey (R-44)
Jason Smalley (R-28)

**Minority Members**
Kevin Matthews (D-11)
Susan Paddack (D-13)
Anastasia A. Pittman (D-48)

## Veterans and Military Affairs

**Majority Members**
Frank Simpson (R-14) *Chair*
Patrick Anderson (R-19) *Vice Chair*
Larry Boggs (R-7)
Jack Fry (R-42)
Jason Smalley (R-28)
Anthony Sykes (R-24)

**Minority Members**
Randy Bass (D-32)
J.J. Dossett (D-34)

# Oklahoma House of Representatives

State Capitol Building, 2300 North Lincoln Boulevard,
Oklahoma City, OK 73105
Tel: (405) 521-2711  Fax: (405) 557-7351  Internet: www.okhouse.gov

Speaker of the House **Jeffrey W. Hickman** (R) . . . . . . . . . . (405) 557-7339
   Education: Oklahoma 1996 BA
Speaker Pro Tempore **Lee R. Denney** (R) . . . . . . . . . . . . . . (405) 557-7304
   Education: Oklahoma State 1976 BS, 1978 DVM
Majority Floor Leader **Charles L. Ortega** (R) . . . . . . . . . . (405) 557-7369
Floor Leader **Lisa J. Billy** (R) . . . . . . . . . . . . . . . . . . . . . (405) 557-7365
   Education: Northeastern State BA; Oklahoma MEd
Floor Leader **Jason Nelson** (R) . . . . . . . . . . . . . . . . . . . . (405) 557-7335
Majority Whip **Gary W. Banz** (R) . . . . . . . . . . . . . . . . . . . .(405) 557-7395
   Education: Southern Nazarene 1968 BS; Central Oklahoma 1973 MEd
Assistant Majority Whip **Jadine Nollan** (R) . . . . . . . . . . . .(405) 557-7390
Majority Caucus Chairman **David Brumbaugh** (R) . . . . . . .(405) 557-7347
Majority Caucus Vice Chairman **Elise Hall** (R) . . . . . . . . . .(405) 557-7403
Majority Caucus Secretary **Katie Henke** (R) . . . . . . . . . . .(405) 557-7361
   Education: Cascia Hall Prep (Tulsa, OK) 1999 Dipl; Alabama 2003 BS
Minority Leader **Scott Inman** (D) . . . . . . . . . . . . . . . . . . . .(405) 557-7370
   Education: Oklahoma 2001 BA, 2004 JD
Assistant Minority Leader **Eric Proctor** (D) . . . . . . . . . . . .(405) 557-7410
   Education: Northeastern State BA
Minority Floor Leader **Ben Sherrer** (D) . . . . . . . . . . . . . . .(405) 557-7364
   Education: Oklahoma State 1991 BS; Oklahoma City 1997 JD

*(continued on next page)*

**LEGISLATIVE BRANCH**

**Oklahoma House of Representatives** *continued*

Minority Whip **Chuck Hoskin, USN** (D) . . . . . . . . . . . . . . (405) 557-7319
  Education: Northeastern Oklahoma A&M AA; Northeastern State BA, MEd

Minority Caucus Chairman **Jerry McPeak** (D) . . . . . . . . . . .(405) 557-7302
  Education: Oklahoma State 1969 BS; Northeastern State MS

Minority Caucus Vice Chairman **Steve Kouplen** (D) . . . . . (405) 557-7306
  Education: Oklahoma State 1973 BA, 1986 MA

Minority Caucus Secretary **David L. Perryman** (D) . . . . . . .(405) 557-7401
  Education: Eastern Oklahoma State 1977 AA;
  Oklahoma State 1980 BS; Oklahoma 1983 JD

Chief Clerk of the House **Jan Harrison** . . . . . . . . . . . . . . . (405) 557-7303
  E-mail: harrisonja@okhouse.gov

Sergeant-at-Arms **Dennis Baker** . . . . . . . . . . . . . . . . . . . . . (405) 557-7313
  E-mail: sgtdesk@okhouse.gov

# Representatives

**Party Affiliation Statistics:** Republicans: 71, Democrats: 30

Representative **Gary W. Banz** (R-District 101)
  Room 433 . . . . . . . . . . . . . . . . . . . . . . . . . . . . . . . . . . . . . . . . (405) 557-7395
  Counties Represented: Oklahoma (part)    Dist: (405) 769-5722
  Term Expires: 2016
  11061 Canterbury Lane, Midwest City, OK 73130
  E-mail: garybanz@okhouse.gov
  Committees: Elections and Ethics; Rules; Tourism and International Relations

Representative **John R. Bennett** (R-District 2)
  Room 300A . . . . . . . . . . . . . . . . . . . . . . . . . . . . . . . . . . . . . . .(405) 557-7315
  Counties Represented: Sequoyah (part)
  Term Expires: 2016
  E-mail: john.bennett@okhouse.gov
  Committees: Appropriations and Budget; Government Oversight and Accountability; Transportation

Representative **Scott R. Biggs** (R-District 51) Room 242 . . (405) 557-7405
  Counties Represented: Grady (part), McClain (part), Stephens (part)
  Term Expires: 2016
  E-mail: scott.biggs@okhouse.gov
  Committees: Agriculture and Rural Development; Criminal Justice and Corrections; Public Safety
  Education: Oklahoma State 2001 BA; Oklahoma 2006 JD

Representative **Lisa J. Billy** (R-District 42) Room 440 . . . . (405) 557-7365
  Counties Represented: Garvin (part), McClain (part)
  Term Expires: 2016
  P.O. Box 1412, Purcell, OK 73080
  E-mail: lisajbilly@okhouse.gov
  Committees: Appropriations and Budget; Criminal Justice and Corrections

Representative **Mike Brown** (D-District 4) Room 545 . . . . . (405) 557-7408
  Counties Represented: Cherokee (part)
  Term Expires: 2016
  E-mail: mikebrown@okhouse.gov
  Committees: Appropriations and Budget; Energy and Natural Resources; Wildlife

Representative **David Brumbaugh** (R-District 76)
  Room 400B . . . . . . . . . . . . . . . . . . . . . . . . . . . . . . . . . . . . . . .(405) 557-7347
  Counties Represented: Tulsa (part)
  Term Expires: 2016
  E-mail: david.brumbaugh@okhouse.gov
  Committees: Energy and Natural Resources; Transportation; Utilities

Representative **Chad Caldwell** (R-District 40)
  Room 329A . . . . . . . . . . . . . . . . . . . . . . . . . . . . . . . . . . . . . . .(405) 557-7317
  Counties Represented: Garfield (part)
  Term Expires: 2016
  E-mail: chad.caldwell@okhouse.gov
  Committees: Common Education; Rules; Utilities

Representative **Kevin J. Calvey** (R-District 82)
  Room 301A . . . . . . . . . . . . . . . . . . . . . . . . . . . . . . . . . . . . . . .(405) 557-7357
  Counties Represented: Oklahoma (part)
  Term Expires: 2016
  E-mail: kevin.calvey@okhouse.gov
  Committees: Energy and Natural Resources; Environmental Law; Judiciary and Civil Procedure
  Education: Dallas 1988 BA; Georgetown 1993 JD

Representative **Ed Cannaday, USA** (D-District 15)
  Room 546 . . . . . . . . . . . . . . . . . . . . . . . . . . . . . . . . . . . . (405) 557-7375
  Counties Represented: Haskell, Leflore (part), McIntosh (part), Muskogee (part), Pittsburg (part), Sequoyah (part)
  Term Expires: 2016
  E-mail: ed.cannaday@okhouse.gov
  Committees: Administrative Rules; Common Education; Utilities
  Education: Cameron 1964 AA; Tulsa 1968 BSEd, 1969 MA

Representative **Dennis Casey** (R-District 35) Room 337 . . .(405) 557-7344
  Counties Represented: Creek (part), Noble (part),    Dist: (405) 880-4708
  Osage (part), Pawnee, Payne (part)
  Term Expires: 2016
  43801 South 338 Road, Morrison, OK 73061
  E-mail: dennis.casey@okhouse.gov
  Committees: Agriculture and Rural Development; Appropriations and Budget; Common Education; Higher Education and Career Technology

Representative **Mike Christian** (R-District 93) Room 303 . . (405) 557-7371
  Counties Represented: Oklahoma (part)
  Term Expires: 2016
  648 Southwest 41st Street, Oklahoma City, OK 73109
  E-mail: mike.christian@okhouse.gov
  Committees: County and Municipal Government; Public Safety; Utilities

Representative **Bobby Cleveland** (R-District 20)
  Room 240 . . . . . . . . . . . . . . . . . . . . . . . . . . . . . . . . . . . . . . . (405) 557-7308
  Counties Represented: Cleveland (part), Garvin (part), McClain (part), Pottawatomie (part)
  Term Expires: 2016
  E-mail: bob.cleveland@okhouse.gov
  Committees: Criminal Justice and Corrections; Long-Term Care and Senior Services; Public Safety

Representative **Josh Cockroft** (R-District 27)
  Room 303A . . . . . . . . . . . . . . . . . . . . . . . . . . . . . . . . . . . . . . .(405) 557-7349
  Counties Represented: Cleveland (part), Pottawatomie (part)
  Term Expires: 2016
  E-mail: josh.cockroft@okhouse.gov
  Committees: County and Municipal Government; State Government Operations; Tourism and International Relations

Representative **Donnie Condit** (D-District 18) Room 502 . .(405) 557-7376
  Counties Represented: Coal, Hughes (part), McIntosh (part), Pittsburg (part)
  Term Expires: 2016
  E-mail: donnie.condit@okhouse.gov
  Committees: Common Education; Elections and Ethics; Rules

Representative **Ann Coody** (R-District 64) Room 439 . . . . .(405) 557-7398
  Counties Represented: Comanche (part)
  Term Expires: 2016
  104 South State Highway 65, Lawton, OK 73501
  E-mail: anncoody@okhouse.gov
  Committees: Appropriations and Budget; Common Education; Veterans and Military Affairs
  Education: Hardin-Simmons 1959 BA; Oklahoma MEd

Representative **Jeff Coody** (R-District 63) Room 338 . . . . . (405) 557-7307
  Counties Represented: Comanche (part), Tillman
  Term Expires: 2016
  E-mail: jeff.coody@okhouse.gov
  Committees: Agriculture and Rural Development; Environmental Law; Insurance

Representative **Marian Cooksey** (R-District 39)
  Room 409 . . . . . . . . . . . . . . . . . . . . . . . . . . . . . . . . . . . . . . . (405) 557-7342
  Counties Represented: Oklahoma (part)
  Term Expires: 2016
  1105 Columbia Court, Edmond, OK 73003
  E-mail: mariancooksey@okhouse.gov
  Committees: Criminal Justice and Corrections; Economic Development, Commerce and Real Estate; Energy and Natural Resources

Representative **Doug Cox** (R-District 5) Room 331 . . . . . . . (405) 557-7415
  Counties Represented: Delaware (part), Mayes (part)
  Term Expires: 2016
  33471 South 595 Road, Grove, OK 74344
  E-mail: dougcox@okhouse.gov
  Committees: Alcohol, Tobacco, and Controlled Substances; Appropriations and Budget; Public Health
  Education: Oklahoma State 1974 BS; Oklahoma 1978 MD

Representative **Lee R. Denney** (R-District 33) Room 411 . . (405) 557-7304
  Counties Represented: Logan (part), Payne (part)
  Term Expires: 2016
  834 East Sixth Street, Cushing, OK 74023
  E-mail: leedenney@okhouse.gov

Representative **David Derby** (R-District 74) Room 408 . . . . (405) 557-7377
Counties Represented: Rogers (part), Tulsa (part)
Term Expires: 2016
P.O. Box 2150, Owasso, OK 74055
E-mail: david.derby@okhouse.gov
Committees: Alcohol, Tobacco, and Controlled Substances; Public
Health; Public Safety
Education: Central Oklahoma 2000 BS

Representative **Travis Dunlap** (R-District 10)
Room 250A . . . . . . . . . . . . . . . . . . . . . . . . . . . . . . . . . . . . (405) 557-7402
Counties Represented: Nowata, Osage (part), Washington (part)
Term Expires: 2016
E-mail: travis.dunlap@okhouse.gov
Committees: Economic Development, Commerce and Real Estate;
Environmental Law; Tourism and International Relations

Representative **Jason Dunnington** (D-District 88)
Room 500A . . . . . . . . . . . . . . . . . . . . . . . . . . . . . . . . . . . (405) 557-7396
Counties Represented: Oklahoma (part)
Term Expires: 2016
E-mail: jason.dunnington@okhouse.gov
Committees: Environmental Law; State Government Operations

Representative
**Jonathan David "Jon" Echols** (R-District 91)
Room 248 . . . . . . . . . . . . . . . . . . . . . . . . . . . . . . . . . . . . (405) 557-7354
Counties Represented: Cleveland (part)
Term Expires: 2016
E-mail: jon.echols@okhouse.gov
Committees: Energy and Natural Resources; Judiciary and Civil
Procedure; Public Health
Education: Oklahoma 2002 BA; Oklahoma City 2005 JD

Representative **John T. Enns** (R-District 41) Room 434 . . . (405) 557-7321
Counties Represented: Canadian (part), Garfield (part), Kingfisher
(part), Oklahoma (part)
Term Expires: 2016
E-mail: john.enns@okhouse.gov
Committees: Agriculture and Rural Development; Alcohol, Tobacco,
and Controlled Substances; Veterans and Military Affairs
Education: Tabor BA

Representative **George E. Faught** (R-District 14)
Room 301B . . . . . . . . . . . . . . . . . . . . . . . . . . . . . . . . . . . (405) 557-7310
Counties Represented: Cherokee (part), Muskogee (part)
Term Expires: 2016
E-mail: george.faught@okhouse.gov
Committees: Administrative Rules; Transportation; Veterans and
Military Affairs

Representative **Dan Fisher** (R-District 60) Room 202 . . . . . (405) 557-7311
Counties Represented: Caddo (part), Canadian (part)
Term Expires: 2016
E-mail: dan.fisher@okhouse.gov
Committees: Administrative Rules; Common Education; State and
Federal Relations
Education: Arkansas Tech BS

Representative **William Fourkiller** (D-District 86)
Room 542 . . . . . . . . . . . . . . . . . . . . . . . . . . . . . . . . . . . . (405) 557-7394
Counties Represented: Adair, Cherokee (part), Delaware (part)
Term Expires: 2016
E-mail: will.fourkiller@okhouse.gov
Committees: Alcohol, Tobacco, and Controlled Substances; Business,
Labor, and Retirement Laws; Public Health

Representative **Regina Goodwin** (D-District 73)
Room 510 . . . . . . . . . . . . . . . . . . . . . . . . . . . . . . . . . . . . (405) 557-7406
Counties Represented: Osage (part), Tulsa (part)
Term Expires: 2016
E-mail: regina.goodwin@okhouse.gov
Committees: County and Municipal Government; Economic
Development, Commerce and Real Estate; Tourism and International
Relations
Education: Kansas BFA

Representative **Randy Grau** (R-District 81) Room 330 . . . . (405) 557-7360
Counties Represented: Oklahoma (part)
Term Expires: 2016
E-mail: randy.grau@okhouse.gov
Committees: Alcohol, Tobacco, and Controlled Substances; Criminal
Justice and Corrections; Judiciary and Civil Procedure

Representative **Claudia Griffith** (D-District 45)
Room 539 . . . . . . . . . . . . . . . . . . . . . . . . . . . . . . . . . . . . (405) 557-7386
Counties Represented: Cleveland (part)
Term Expires: 2016
E-mail: claudia.griffith@okhouse.gov
Committees: Alcohol, Tobacco, and Controlled Substances; Public
Health

Representative **Elise Hall** (R-District 100) Room 200A . . . . (405) 557-7403
Counties Represented: Oklahoma (part)
Term Expires: 2016
E-mail: elise.hall@okhouse.gov
Committees: Economic Development, Commerce and Real Estate;
Government Oversight and Accountability; Public Health

Representative **Tommy C. Hardin** (R-District 49)
Room 336 . . . . . . . . . . . . . . . . . . . . . . . . . . . . . . . . . . . . (405) 557-7383
Counties Represented: Carter (part), Love, Marshall
Term Expires: 2016
E-mail: tommy.hardin@okhouse.gov
Committees: Energy and Natural Resources; Rules; Wildlife

Representative **Katie Henke** (R-District 71) Room 244B . . . (405) 557-7361
Counties Represented: Tulsa (part)
Term Expires: 2016
E-mail: katie.henke@okhouse.gov
Committees: Common Education; Higher Education and Career
Technology; Transportation

Representative **Jeffrey W. Hickman** (R-District 58)
Room 401 . . . . . . . . . . . . . . . . . . . . . . . . . . . . . . . . . . . . (405) 557-7339
Counties Represented: Alfalfa, Major, Woods, Woodward (part)
Term Expires: 2016
E-mail: jwhickman@okhouse.gov

Representative **Chuck Hoskin, USN** (D-District 6)
Room 509 . . . . . . . . . . . . . . . . . . . . . . . . . . . . . . . . . . . . (405) 557-7319
Counties Represented: Craig, Mayes (part), Rogers (part)
Term Expires: 2016
E-mail: chuck.hoskin@okhouse.gov
Committees: Appropriations and Budget; Veterans and Military Affairs

Representative **Scott Inman** (D-District 94) Room 548 . . . . (405) 557-7370
Counties Represented: Oklahoma (part)
Term Expires: 2016
E-mail: scott.inman@okhouse.gov
Committees: Appropriations and Budget; Energy and Natural Resources

Representative **Dennis Johnson** (R-District 50)
Suite 407 . . . . . . . . . . . . . . . . . . . . . . . . . . . . . . . . . . . . (405) 557-7327
Counties Represented: Jefferson, Stephens (part)
Term Expires: 2016
E-mail: dennis.johnson@okhouse.gov
Committees: Appropriations and Budget; Energy and Natural
Resources; Public Safety
Education: Weber State 1975 BS

Representative **John Paul Jordan** (R-District 43)
Room 328B . . . . . . . . . . . . . . . . . . . . . . . . . . . . . . . . . . . (405) 557-7352
Counties Represented: Canadian (part), Oklahoma (part)
Term Expires: 2016
E-mail: jp.jordan@okhouse.gov
Committees: Children, Youth, and Family Services; Common
Education; Government Oversight and Accountability

Representative **Charles "Charlie" Joyner** (R-District 95)
Room 436 . . . . . . . . . . . . . . . . . . . . . . . . . . . . . . . . . . . . (405) 557-7314
Counties Represented: Oklahoma (part)
Term Expires: 2016
3500 Bella Vista Drive, Midwest City, OK 73110
E-mail: charlie.joyner@okhouse.gov
Committees: Business, Labor, and Retirement Laws; Elections and
Ethics; Transportation

Representative **Chris Kannady** (R-District 91)
Room 246A . . . . . . . . . . . . . . . . . . . . . . . . . . . . . . . . . . . (405) 557-7337
Counties Represented: Cleveland (part)
Term Expires: 2016
E-mail: chris.kannady@okhouse.gov
Committees: Higher Education and Career Technology; Judiciary and
Civil Procedure; Rules

Representative **Sally Kern** (R-District 84) Room 304 . . . . . . (405) 557-7348
Counties Represented: Oklahoma (part)
Term Expires: 2016
2713 Sterling Avenue, Oklahoma City, OK 73127
E-mail: sallykern@okhouse.gov
Committees: Children, Youth, and Family Services; Common
Education; State and Federal Relations
Education: Texas 1971 BA

Representative **Dan Kirby** (R-District 75) Room 302A . . . . (405) 557-7356
Counties Represented: Tulsa (part)
Term Expires: 2016
12208 East 38th Place, Tulsa, OK 74146
E-mail: dan.kirby@okhouse.gov
Committees: County and Municipal Government; Economic
Development, Commerce and Real Estate; Insurance

*(continued on next page)*

LEGISLATIVE BRANCH

**Representatives** *continued*

Representative **Steve Kouplen** (D-District 24) Room 541 . . (405) 557-7306
Counties Represented: Hughes (part), Okfuskee, Okmulgee (part)
Term Expires: 2016
5910 Garfied Road, Beggs, OK 74421
E-mail: steve.kouplen@okhouse.gov
Committees: Agriculture and Rural Development; Energy and Natural Resources; Insurance

Representative **James Leewright** (R-District 29)
Room 204B . . . . . . . . . . . . . . . . . . . . . . . . . . . . . . . . . . . (405) 557-7353
Counties Represented: Creek (part), Tulsa (part)
Term Expires: 2016
E-mail: james.leewright@okhouse.gov
Committees: Banking and Financial Services; Government Oversight and Accountability; Higher Education and Career Technology

Representative **Mark Lepak** (R-District 9) Room 328A . . . . (405) 557-7380
Counties Represented: Rogers (part)
Term Expires: 2016
E-mail: mark.lepak@okhouse.gov
Committees: State and Federal Relations; State Government Operations; Tourism and International Relations

Representative **James Lockhart** (D-District 3)
Room 505 . . . . . . . . . . . . . . . . . . . . . . . . . . . . . . . . . . . (405) 557-7413
Counties Represented: Leflore (part)
Term Expires: 2016
E-mail: james.lockhart@okhouse.gov
Committees: Transportation; Utilities; Wildlife

Representative **Ben Loring** (D-District 7) Room 539B . . . . . (405) 557-7399
Counties Represented: Delaware (part), Ottawa
Term Expires: 2016
E-mail: ben.loring@okhouse.gov
Committees: Public Safety; Tourism and International Relations

Representative **Scott Martin** (R-District 46) Room 441 . . . (405) 557-7329
Counties Represented: Cleveland (part)
Term Expires: 2016
E-mail: scott.martin@okhouse.gov
Committees: Appropriations and Budget; Banking and Financial Services; State Government Operations
Education: Oklahoma 1995 BS

Representative **Mark McBride** (R-District 53) Room 248 . . (405) 557-7346
Counties Represented: Cleveland (part)
Term Expires: 2016
E-mail: mark.mcbride@okhouse.gov
Committees: Business, Labor, and Retirement Laws; Energy and Natural Resources; Utilities
Education: Northwestern Oklahoma St (Attended)

Representative **Charles A. McCall III** (R-District 22)
Room 244 . . . . . . . . . . . . . . . . . . . . . . . . . . . . . . . . . . . (405) 557-7412
Counties Represented: Atoka (part), Garvin (part), Johnston, Murray (part)
Term Expires: 2016
E-mail: charles.mccall@okhouse.gov
Committees: Appropriations and Budget; Banking and Financial Services; Economic Development, Commerce and Real Estate
Education: Oklahoma 1992 BBA; Colorado 2000

Representative **Mark E. McCullough** (R-District 30)
Room 435A . . . . . . . . . . . . . . . . . . . . . . . . . . . . . . . . . . (405) 557-7414
Counties Represented: Creek (part), Tulsa (part)
Term Expires: 2016
E-mail: mark.mccullough@okhouse.gov
Committees: Appropriations and Budget; Criminal Justice and Corrections; Judiciary and Civil Procedure
Education: Oklahoma 1989 BS, 1992 MS; Tulsa 1998 JD

Representative **Jeannie McDaniel** (D-District 78)
Room 508 . . . . . . . . . . . . . . . . . . . . . . . . . . . . . . . . . . . (405) 557-7334
Counties Represented: Tulsa (part)
Term Expires: 2016
1416 South Marion Avenue, Tulsa, OK 74112
E-mail: jeanniemcdaniel@okhouse.gov
Committees: Appropriations and Budget; Common Education; Long-Term Care and Senior Services; Public Health
Education: Oklahoma 2004 BLS

Representative **Randy McDaniel** (R-District 83)
Room 438 . . . . . . . . . . . . . . . . . . . . . . . . . . . . . . . . . . . (405) 557-7409
Counties Represented: Oklahoma (part)
Term Expires: 2016
E-mail: randy.mcdaniel@okhouse.gov
Committees: Appropriations and Budget; Business, Labor, and Retirement Laws; Economic Development, Commerce and Real Estate; Insurance
Affiliation: First Vice President of Investments, Wachovia Securities Financial Holdings, LLC
Education: Oklahoma 1990 BA; Cambridge (UK) MPhil

Representative **Jerry McPeak** (D-District 13) Room 503 . . . (405) 557-7302
Counties Represented: McIntosh (part), Muskogee (part)
Term Expires: 2016
P.O. Box 63, Warner, OK 74469
E-mail: jerrymcpeak@okhouse.gov
Committees: Appropriations and Budget; Energy and Natural Resources; Transportation

Representative **John Michael Montgomery** (R-District 62)
Room 329B . . . . . . . . . . . . . . . . . . . . . . . . . . . . . . . . . . (405) 557-7374
Counties Represented: Comanche (part)
Term Expires: 2016
E-mail: john.montgomery@okhouse.gov
Committees: Administrative Rules; Environmental Law; Tourism and International Relations

Representative **Lewis H. Moore** (R-District 96)
Room 329 . . . . . . . . . . . . . . . . . . . . . . . . . . . . . . . . . . . (405) 557-7400
Counties Represented: Oklahoma (part)
Term Expires: 2016
10100 Sunday Drive, Arcadia, OK 73007
E-mail: lewis.moore@okhouse.gov
Committees: Environmental Law; Insurance; State and Federal Relations
Education: Arkansas BA

Representative **Richard Daniel Morrissette** (D-District 92) Room 543 . . (405) 557-7404
Counties Represented: Oklahoma (part)                    Dist: (405) 634-7166
Term Expires: 2016
6609 South Harvey Avenue, Oklahoma City, OK 73139
E-mail: richardmorrissette@okhouse.gov
Committees: Appropriations and Budget; Economic Development, Commerce and Real Estate; Judiciary and Civil Procedure; State Government Operations
Education: New Hampshire 1979 BA; Tulsa 1984 JD

Representative **Glen Mulready** (R-District 68) Room 200 . . (405) 557-7340
Counties Represented: Creek (part), Tulsa (part)
Term Expires: 2016
E-mail: glen.mulready@okhouse.gov
Committees: Administrative Rules; Insurance; Public Health

Representative **Cyndi Munson** (D-District 85) . . . . . . . . . . (405) 557-7392
Counties Represented: Oklahoma (part)
Term Expires: 2016
E-mail: cyndi.munson@okhouse.gov
Committees: Criminal Justice and Corrections; Higher Education and Career Technology; Veterans and Military Affairs

Representative **William Casey Murdock** (R-District 61)
Room 301 . . . . . . . . . . . . . . . . . . . . . . . . . . . . . . . . . . . (405) 557-7384
Counties Represented: Beaver, Cimarron, Ellis, Harper, Texas, Woodward (part)
Term Expires: 2016
E-mail: casey.murdock@okhouse.gov
Committees: Transportation; Utilities; Wildlife

Representative **Jason W. Murphey** (R-District 31)
Room 437 . . . . . . . . . . . . . . . . . . . . . . . . . . . . . . . . . . . (405) 557-7350
Counties Represented: Logan (part), Oklahoma (part)
Term Expires: 2016
E-mail: jason.murphey@okhouse.gov
Committees: County and Municipal Government; State and Federal Relations; State Government Operations
Education: Charter Oak State 2006 BA

Representative **Jason Nelson** (R-District 87)
Room 305A . . . . . . . . . . . . . . . . . . . . . . . . . . . . . . . . . . (405) 557-7335
Counties Represented: Oklahoma (part)
Term Expires: 2016
4117 Northwest 58th Street, Oklahoma City, OK 73112-1513
E-mail: jason.nelson@okhouse.gov
Committees: Appropriations and Budget; Children, Youth, and Family Services; Common Education; Rules

LEGISLATIVE BRANCH

Representative **Tom Newell** (R-District 28) Room 302 . . . . (405) 557-7372
Counties Represented: Pottawatomie (part), Seminole
Term Expires: 2016
E-mail: tom.newell@okhouse.gov
Committees: Business, Labor, and Retirement Laws; Children, Youth, and Family Services; Government Oversight and Accountability

Representative **Jadine Nollan** (R-District 66) Room 333 . . (405) 557-7390
Counties Represented: Osage (part), Tulsa (part)
Term Expires: 2016
E-mail: jadine.nollan@okhouse.gov
Committees: Alcohol, Tobacco, and Controlled Substances; Common Education; Long-Term Care and Senior Services

Representative **Terry S. O'Donnell** (R-District 23)
Room 242 . . . . . . . . . . . . . . . . . . . . . . . . . . . . . . . . . . . . . (405) 557-7379
Counties Represented: Rogers (part), Tulsa (part), Wagoner (part)
Term Expires: 2016
E-mail: terry.odonnell@okhouse.gov
Committees: Criminal Justice and Corrections; Judiciary and Civil Procedure; Transportation
Education: Baylor BA; Tulsa 1989 JD

Representative **Charles L. Ortega** (R-District 52)
Room 442 . . . . . . . . . . . . . . . . . . . . . . . . . . . . . . . . . . . . . (405) 557-7369
Counties Represented: Greer (part), Harmon,          Dist: (580) 482-0259
Jackson, Kiowa (part)
Term Expires: 2016
1509 North Main, Altus, OK 73521
E-mail: charles.ortega@okhouse.gov
Committees: Appropriations and Budget; Business, Labor, and Retirement Laws; Energy and Natural Resources; Tourism and International Relations

Representative **Leslie Osborn** (R-District 47)
Room 303B . . . . . . . . . . . . . . . . . . . . . . . . . . . . . . . . . . (405) 557-7333
Counties Represented: Canadian (part), Grady (part)
Term Expires: 2016
P.O. Box 1200, Mustang, OK 73064
E-mail: leslie.osborn@okhouse.gov
Committees: Appropriations and Budget; Banking and Financial Services; Judiciary and Civil Procedure

Representative **Pat Ownbey** (R-District 48) Room 334 . . . . (405) 557-7326
Counties Represented: Carter (part), Garvin (part), Murray (part)
Term Expires: 2016
2303 Cloverleaf Place, Ardmore, OK 73401
E-mail: pat.ownbey@okhouse.gov
Committees: Appropriations and Budget; Children, Youth, and Family Services; Public Safety
Education: Oklahoma BSC

Representative **Scooter Park** (R-District 65) Room 338 . . . (405) 557-7305
Counties Represented: Caddo (part), Comanche (part), Cotton, Grady (part), Stephens (part)
Term Expires: 2016
E-mail: scooter.park@okhouse.gov
Committees: Agriculture and Rural Development; County and Municipal Government; Wildlife

Representative **David L. Perryman** (D-District 56)
Room 540 . . . . . . . . . . . . . . . . . . . . . . . . . . . . . . . . . . . . (405) 557-7401
Counties Represented: Caddo (part), Grady (part), Kiowa (part)
Term Expires: 2016
E-mail: david.perryman@okhouse.gov
Committees: Business, Labor, and Retirement Laws; Elections and Ethics

Representative **Pam Peterson** (R-District 67) Room 405 . . (405) 557-7341
Counties Represented: Tulsa (part)          Dist: (918) 289-3003
Term Expires: 2016
6528 East 101st, PMB 422, Tulsa, OK 74133
E-mail: pampeterson@okhouse.gov
Committees: Appropriations and Budget; Children, Youth, and Family Services; Criminal Justice and Corrections; Public Safety
Education: Oral Roberts 1977 BA

Representative **John Pfeiffer** (R-District 38) Room 301 . . . (405) 557-7332
Counties Represented: Garfield (part), Grant, Kay (part), Logan (part), Noble (part)
Term Expires: 2016
E-mail: john.pfeiffer@okhouse.gov
Committees: Agriculture and Rural Development; State Government Operations; Veterans and Military Affairs

Representative **Eric Proctor** (D-District 77) Room 540A . . . (405) 557-7410
Counties Represented: Rogers (part), Tulsa (part)
Term Expires: 2016
E-mail: eric.proctor@okhouse.gov
Committees: Banking and Financial Services; Energy and Natural Resources; State and Federal Relations; Transportation

Representative **R. C. Pruett** (D-District 19) Room 501 . . . . (405) 557-7382
Counties Represented: Atoka (part), Bryan (part), Choctaw, Pushmataha
Term Expires: 2016
P.O. Box 969, Antlers, OK 74523
E-mail: rcpruett@okhouse.gov
Committees: Public Safety; Rules; Tourism and International Relations; Utilities

Representative **Brian Renegar** (D-District 17) Room 504 . . (405) 557-7381
Counties Represented: Latimer, Leflore (part), Pittsburg (part)
Term Expires: 2016
E-mail: brian.renegar@okhouse.gov
Committees: Agriculture and Rural Development; Economic Development, Commerce and Real Estate; Public Safety
Education: Northeastern 1972 BS; Oklahoma State 1976 DVM

Representative **J. Michael "Mike" Ritze** (R-District 80)
Roon 433B . . . . . . . . . . . . . . . . . . . . . . . . . . . . . . . . . . . (405) 557-7338
Counties Represented: Tulsa (part), Wagoner (part)
Term Expires: 2016
18574 East 101st Street South, Broken Arrow, OK 74011
E-mail: mike.ritze@okhouse.gov
Committees: Long-Term Care and Senior Services; Public Health; Public Safety
Education: Northeast Missouri State BS; Kirksville Osteopathic DO

Representative **Dustin Roberts** (R-District 21)
Room 302B . . . . . . . . . . . . . . . . . . . . . . . . . . . . . . . . . . . (405) 557-7366
Counties Represented: Bryan (part)
Term Expires: 2016
E-mail: dustin.roberts@okhouse.gov
Committees: Economic Development, Commerce and Real Estate; Tourism and International Relations; Veterans and Military Affairs

Representative **Sean Roberts** (R-District 36) Room 250 . . . (405) 557-7322
Counties Represented: Osage (part), Tulsa (part)
Term Expires: 2016
E-mail: sean.roberts@okhouse.gov
Committees: County and Municipal Government; Energy and Natural Resources; Public Health

Representative **Michael Rogers** (R-District 98)
Room 300B . . . . . . . . . . . . . . . . . . . . . . . . . . . . . . . . . . . (405) 557-7362
Counties Represented: Tulsa (part), Wagoner (part)
Term Expires: 2016
E-mail: michael.rogers@okhouse.gov
Committees: Common Education; Elections and Ethics; Insurance

Representative **Wade Rousselot** (D-District 12)
Room 507 . . . . . . . . . . . . . . . . . . . . . . . . . . . . . . . . . . . . (405) 557-7388
Counties Represented: Wagoner (part)
Term Expires: 2016
5298 East 110th Street North, Wagoner, OK 74467
E-mail: waderousselot@okhouse.gov
Committees: Agriculture and Rural Development; Appropriations and Budget
Education: Oklahoma State 1981 BS

Representative **Todd Russ** (R-District 55) Room 300 . . . . . (405) 557-7312
Counties Represented: Beckham (part), Greer (part),     Dist: (580) 660-5100
Kiowa (part), Roger Mills, Washita
Term Expires: 2016
P.O. Box 98, Cordell, OK 73632
E-mail: todd.russ@okhouse.gov
Committees: Administrative Rules; Appropriations and Budget; Banking and Financial Services; Insurance

Representative
**Michael A. "Mike" Sanders** (R-District 59)
Room 205 . . . . . . . . . . . . . . . . . . . . . . . . . . . . . . . . . . . . (405) 557-7407
Counties Represented: Blaine (part), Canadian (part), Dewey, Kingfisher (part), Woodward (part)
Term Expires: 2016
E-mail: mike.sanders@okhouse.gov
Committees: Agriculture and Rural Development; Appropriations and Budget; Energy and Natural Resources
Education: Oklahoma Christian 1997 BS

Representative **Seneca Scott** (D-District 72) Room 510 . . . (405) 557-7391
Counties Represented: Tulsa (part)
Term Expires: 2016
3102 East Second Street, Tulsa, OK 74130
E-mail: seneca.scott@okhouse.gov
Committees: Energy and Natural Resources; Government Oversight and Accountability; State and Federal Relations
Education: Oklahoma

*(continued on next page)*

**Representatives** *continued*

**Representative Earl W. Sears** (R-District 11)
Room 432D . . . . . . . . . . . . . . . . . . . . . . . . . . . . . . . . . (405) 557-7358
Counties Represented: Rogers (part), Tulsa (part), Washington (part)
Term Expires: 2016
E-mail: earl.sears@okhouse.gov
Committees: Appropriations and Budget
Education: Northeastern State 1975 BS, 1982 MA

**Representative Mike Shelton** (D-District 97) Room 539 . . . (405) 557-7367
Counties Represented: Oklahoma (part)
Term Expires: 2016
4125 North Everest Avenue, Oklahoma City, OK 73111
E-mail: mikeshelton@okhouse.gov
Committees: Administrative Rules; Banking and Financial Services;
Insurance
Education: Langston BS

**Representative Ben Sherrer** (D-District 8) Room 500 . . . . . (405) 557-7364
Counties Represented: Mayes (part), Rogers (part), Wagoner (part)
Term Expires: 2016
123 North Hayden, Chouteau, OK 74337
E-mail: bensherrer@okhouse.gov
Committees: Appropriations and Budget; Children, Youth, and Family
Services; Criminal Justice and Corrections; Judiciary and Civil
Procedure

**Representative Jerry Shoemake** (D-District 16)
Rom 506 . . . . . . . . . . . . . . . . . . . . . . . . . . . . . . . . . . (405) 557-7373
Counties Represented: Muskogee (part), Okmulgee (part), Tulsa (part),
Wagoner (part)
Term Expires: 2016
15160 North 310 Road, Morris, OK 74445
E-mail: jerryshoemake@okhouse.gov
Committees: Agriculture and Rural Development; Rules; Veterans and
Military Affairs

**Representative Shane Stone** (D-District 89) Room 510A . (405) 557-7397
Counties Represented: Oklahoma (part)
Term Expires: 2016
E-mail: shane.stone@okhouse.gov
Committees: Business, Labor, and Retirement Laws; Common
Education; Insurance

**Representative Chuck Strohm** (R-District 69)
Room 300C . . . . . . . . . . . . . . . . . . . . . . . . . . . . . . . . (405) 557-7331
Counties Represented: Tulsa (part)
Term Expires: 2016
E-mail: chuck.strohm@okhouse.gov
Committees: Business, Labor, and Retirement Laws; Common
Education; Long-Term Care and Senior Services

**Representative Johnny Tadlock** (D-District 1)
Room 539B . . . . . . . . . . . . . . . . . . . . . . . . . . . . . . . . (405) 557-7363
Counties Represented: Leflore (part), McCurtain
Term Expires: 2016
E-mail: johnny.tadlock@okhouse.gov
Committees: County and Municipal Government; Criminal Justice and
Corrections; Government Oversight and Accountability

**Representative Todd Thomsen** (R-District 25)
Room 410 . . . . . . . . . . . . . . . . . . . . . . . . . . . . . . . . . (405) 557-7336
Counties Represented: Pontotoc
Term Expires: 2016
E-mail: todd.thomsen@okhouse.gov
Committees: Common Education; Energy and Natural Resources;
Utilities
Education: Oklahoma 1989

**Representative Steve Vaughan** (R-District 37)
Room 335 . . . . . . . . . . . . . . . . . . . . . . . . . . . . . . . . . (405) 557-7355
Counties Represented: Kay (part), Osage (part)
Term Expires: 2016
E-mail: steve.vaughan@okhouse.gov
Committees: Agriculture and Rural Development; Environmental Law;
Wildlife

**Representative Emily Virgin** (D-District 44) Room 500 . . . . (405) 557-7323
Counties Represented: Cleveland (part)
Term Expires: 2016
E-mail: emily.virgin@okhouse.gov
Committees: Higher Education and Career Technology; Judiciary and
Civil Procedure

**Representative Ken Walker** (R-District 70) Room 204 . . . . . (405) 557-7359
Counties Represented: Tulsa (part)
Term Expires: 2016
E-mail: ken.walker@okhouse.gov
Committees: Administrative Rules; Public Safety; State and Federal
Relations
Education: Baltimore Culinary; Oral Roberts (Attended)

**Representative Kevin Wallace** (R-District 32)
Room 246B . . . . . . . . . . . . . . . . . . . . . . . . . . . . . . . . (405) 557-7368
Counties Represented: Lincoln, Logan (part)
Term Expires: 2016
E-mail: kevin.wallace@okhouse.gov
Committees: Agriculture and Rural Development; Business, Labor, and
Retirement Laws; Wildlife

**Representative Weldon L. Watson** (R-District 79)
Room 406 . . . . . . . . . . . . . . . . . . . . . . . . . . . . . . . . . (405) 557-7330
Counties Represented: Tulsa (part)
Term Expires: 2016
E-mail: weldon.watson@okhouse.gov
Committees: Energy and Natural Resources; Rules; Utilities
Education: Oklahoma 1970 BA

**Representative Paul Wesselhoft** (R-District 54)
Room 328 . . . . . . . . . . . . . . . . . . . . . . . . . . . . . . . . . (405) 557-7343
Counties Represented: Cleveland (part), Oklahoma    Dist: (405) 794-9464
(part)
Term Expires: 2016
1105 Northeast 29th Street, Moore, OK 73160
E-mail: paulwesselhoft@okhouse.gov
Committees: Appropriations and Budget; Elections and Ethics; Energy
and Natural Resources; Public Safety
Education: Central Oklahoma 1972 BA; Southern Nazarene 1976 MA;
Gordon-Conwell 1979 MDiv

**Representative Cory T. Williams** (D-District 34)
Room 544 . . . . . . . . . . . . . . . . . . . . . . . . . . . . . . . . . (405) 557-7411
Counties Represented: Payne (part)
Term Expires: 2016
123 West Seventh Avenue, Suite 203, Stillwater, OK 74074
E-mail: cory.williams@okhouse.gov
Committees: Criminal Justice and Corrections; Environmental Law;
Higher Education and Career Technology
Education: Oklahoma State MA; Oklahoma City JD

**Representative Justin F. Wood** (R-District 26)
Room 202 . . . . . . . . . . . . . . . . . . . . . . . . . . . . . . . . . (405) 557-7345
Counties Represented: Pottawatomie (part)
Term Expires: 2016
E-mail: justin.wood@okhouse.gov
Committees: Alcohol, Tobacco, and Controlled Substances; Energy and
Natural Resources; Higher Education and Career Technology
Education: Central Oklahoma 2012 BA

**Representative Harold Wright** (R-District 57) Room 332 . . (405) 557-7325
Counties Represented: Beckham (part), Blaine (part), Caddo (part),
Canadian (part), Custer
Term Expires: 2016
10132 State Highway 54, Weatherford, OK 73096
E-mail: harold.wright@okhouse.gov
Committees: Agriculture and Rural Development; Appropriations and
Budget; Higher Education and Career Technology; Rules
Education: Southwestern Oklahoma St 1971 BA

**Representative George E. Young** (D-District 99)
Room 510B . . . . . . . . . . . . . . . . . . . . . . . . . . . . . . . . (405) 557-7393
Counties Represented: Oklahoma (part)
Term Expires: 2016
E-mail: george.young@okhouse.gov
Committees: Children, Youth, and Family Services; Long-Term Care
and Senior Services

# House Standing Committees
## Administrative Rules

| Majority Members | Minority Members |
|---|---|
| George E. Faught (R-14) *Chair* | Ed Cannaday (D-15) |
| John Michael Montgomery (R-62) | Mike Shelton (D-97) |
| *Vice Chair* | |
| Dan Fisher (R-60) | |
| Glen Mulready (R-68) | |
| Todd Russ (R-55) | |
| Ken Walker (R-70) | |

## Agriculture and Rural Development
**Majority Members**
John T. Enns (R-41) *Chair*
Scott R. Biggs (R-51) *Vice Chair*
Dennis Casey (R-35)
Jeff Coody (R-63)
Scooter Park (R-65)
John Pfeiffer (R-38)
Michael A. "Mike" Sanders (R-59)
Steve Vaughan (R-37)
Kevin Wallace (R-32)
Harold Wright (R-57)

**Minority Members**
Steve Kouplen (D-24)
Brian Renegar (D-17)
Wade Rousselot (D-12)
Jerry Shoemake (D-16)

## Alcohol, Tobacco, and Controlled Substances
**Majority Members**
David Derby (R-74) *Chair*
Doug Cox (R-5)
John T. Enns (R-41)
Randy Grau (R-81)
Jadine Nollan (R-66)
Justin F. Wood (R-26)

**Minority Members**
William Fourkiller (D-86)
*Vice Chair*
Claudia Griffith (D-45)

## Appropriations and Budget
**Majority Members**
Earl W. Sears (R-11) *Chair*
Dennis Casey (R-35) *Vice Chair*
John R. Bennett (R-2)
Lisa J. Billy (R-42)
Ann Coody (R-64)
Doug Cox (R-5)
Dennis Johnson (R-50)
Scott Martin (R-46)
Charles A. McCall III (R-22)
Mark E. McCullough (R-30)
Randy McDaniel (R-83)
Jason Nelson (R-87)
Charles L. Ortega (R-52)
Leslie Osborn (R-47)
Pat Ownbey (R-48)
Pam Peterson (R-67)
Todd Russ (R-55)
Michael A. "Mike" Sanders (R-59)
Paul Wesselhoft (R-54)
Harold Wright (R-57)

**Minority Members**
Mike Brown (D-4)
Chuck Hoskin (D-6)
Scott Inman (D-94)
Jeannie McDaniel (D-78)
Jerry McPeak (D-13)
Richard Daniel Morrissette (D-92)
Wade Rousselot (D-12)
Ben Sherrer (D-8)

## Banking and Financial Services
**Majority Members**
Todd Russ (R-55) *Chair*
James Leewright (R-29) *Vice Chair*
Scott Martin (R-46)
Charles A. McCall III (R-22)
Leslie Osborn (R-47)

**Minority Members**
Eric Proctor (D-77)
Mike Shelton (D-97)

## Business, Labor, and Retirement Laws
**Majority Members**
Randy McDaniel (R-83) *Chair*
Chuck Strohm (R-69) *Vice Chair*
Charles "Charlie" Joyner (R-95)
Mark McBride (R-53)
Tom Newell (R-28)
Charles L. Ortega (R-52)
Kevin Wallace (R-32)

**Minority Members**
William Fourkiller (D-86)
David L. Perryman (D-56)
Shane Stone (D-89)

## Children, Youth, and Family Services
**Majority Members**
Sally Kern (R-84) *Chair*
Pam Peterson (R-67) *Vice Chair*
John Paul Jordan (R-43)
Jason Nelson (R-87)
Tom Newell (R-28)
Pat Ownbey (R-48)

**Minority Members**
Ben Sherrer (D-8)
George E. Young (D-99)

## Common Education
**Majority Members**
Ann Coody (R-64) *Chair*
Michael Rogers (R-98) *Vice Chair*
Chad Caldwell (R-40)
Dennis Casey (R-35)
Dan Fisher (R-60)
Katie Henke (R-71)
John Paul Jordan (R-43)
Sally Kern (R-84)
Jason Nelson (R-87)
Jadine Nollan (R-66)
Chuck Strohm (R-69)
Todd Thomsen (R-25)

**Minority Members**
Ed Cannaday (D-15)
Donnie Condit (D-18)
Jeannie McDaniel (D-78)
Shane Stone (D-89)

## County and Municipal Government
**Majority Members**
Sean Roberts (R-36) *Chair*
Scooter Park (R-65) *Vice Chair*
Mike Christian (R-93)
Josh Cockroft (R-27)
Dan Kirby (R-75)
Jason W. Murphey (R-31)

**Minority Members**
Regina Goodwin (D-73)
Johnny Tadlock (D-1)

## Criminal Justice and Corrections
**Majority Members**
Pam Peterson (R-67) *Chair*
Terry S. O'Donnell (R-23)
*Vice Chair*
Scott R. Biggs (R-51)
Lisa J. Billy (R-42)
Bobby Cleveland (R-20)
Marian Cooksey (R-39)
Randy Grau (R-81)
Mark E. McCullough (R-30)

**Minority Members**
Cyndi Munson (D-85)
Ben Sherrer (D-8)
Johnny Tadlock (D-1)
Cory T. Williams (D-34)

## Economic Development, Commerce and Real Estate
**Majority Members**
Dan Kirby (R-75) *Chair*
Marian Cooksey (R-39) *Vice Chair*
Travis Dunlap (R-10)
Elise Hall (R-100)
Charles A. McCall III (R-22)
Randy McDaniel (R-83)
Dustin Roberts (R-21)

**Minority Members**
Regina Goodwin (D-73)
Richard Daniel Morrissette (D-92)
Brian Renegar (D-17)

## Elections and Ethics
**Majority Members**
Paul Wesselhoft (R-54) *Chair*
Gary W. Banz (R-101)
Charles "Charlie" Joyner (R-95)
Michael Rogers (R-98)

**Minority Members**
Donnie Condit (D-18) *Vice Chair*
David L. Perryman (D-56)

## Energy and Natural Resources
**Majority Members**
Weldon L. Watson (R-79) *Chair*
Mark McBride (R-53) *Vice Chair*
David Brumbaugh (R-76)
Kevin J. Calvey (R-82)
Marian Cooksey (R-39)
Jonathan David "Jon" Echols (R-91)
Tommy C. Hardin (R-49)
Dennis Johnson (R-50)
Charles L. Ortega (R-52)
Sean Roberts (R-36)
Michael A. "Mike" Sanders (R-59)
Todd Thomsen (R-25)
Paul Wesselhoft (R-54)
Justin F. Wood (R-26)

**Minority Members**
Mike Brown (D-4)
Scott Inman (D-94)
Steve Kouplen (D-24)
Jerry McPeak (D-13)
Eric Proctor (D-77)
Seneca Scott (D-72)

## Environmental Law

**Majority Members**
Kevin J. Calvey (R-82) *Chair*
Travis Dunlap (R-10) *Vice Chair*
Jeff Coody (R-63)
John Michael Montgomery (R-62)
Lewis H. Moore (R-96)
Steve Vaughan (R-37)

**Minority Members**
Jason Dunnington (D-88)
Cory T. Williams (D-34)

## Government Oversight and Accountability

**Majority Members**
Tom Newell (R-28) *Chair*
John Paul Jordan (R-43) *Vice Chair*
John R. Bennett (R-2)
Elise Hall (R-100)
James Leewright (R-29)

**Minority Members**
Seneca Scott (D-72)
Johnny Tadlock (D-1)

## Higher Education and Career Technology

**Majority Members**
Harold Wright (R-57) *Chair*
Justin F. Wood (R-26) *Vice Chair*
Dennis Casey (R-35)
Katie Henke (R-71)
Chris Kannady (R-91)
James Leewright (R-29)

**Minority Members**
Cyndi Munson (D-85)
Emily Virgin (D-44)
Cory T. Williams (D-34)

## Insurance

**Majority Members**
Glen Mulready (R-68) *Chair*
Jeff Coody (R-63) *Vice Chair*
Dan Kirby (R-75)
Randy McDaniel (R-83)
Lewis H. Moore (R-96)
Michael Rogers (R-98)
Todd Russ (R-55)

**Minority Members**
Steve Kouplen (D-24)
Mike Shelton (D-97)
Shane Stone (D-89)

## Judiciary and Civil Procedure

**Majority Members**
Randy Grau (R-81) *Chair*
Jonathan David "Jon" Echols (R-91) *Vice Chair*
Kevin J. Calvey (R-82)
Chris Kannady (R-91)
Mark E. McCullough (R-30)
Terry S. O'Donnell (R-23)
Leslie Osborn (R-47)

**Minority Members**
Richard Daniel Morrissette (D-92)
Ben Sherrer (D-8)
Emily Virgin (D-44)

## Long-Term Care and Senior Services

**Majority Members**
Jadine Nollan (R-66) *Chair*
Bobby Cleveland (R-20)
J. Michael "Mike" Ritze (R-80)
Chuck Strohm (R-69)

**Minority Members**
Jeannie McDaniel (D-78) *Vice Chair*
George E. Young (D-99)

## Public Health

**Majority Members**
J. Michael "Mike" Ritze (R-80) *Chair*
Elise Hall (R-100) *Vice Chair*
Doug Cox (R-5)
David Derby (R-74)
Jonathan David "Jon" Echols (R-91)
Glen Mulready (R-68)
Sean Roberts (R-36)

**Minority Members**
William Fourkiller (D-86)
Claudia Griffith (D-45)
Jeannie McDaniel (D-78)

## Public Safety

**Majority Members**
Mike Christian (R-93) *Chair*
Bobby Cleveland (R-20) *Vice Chair*
Scott R. Biggs (R-51)
David Derby (R-74)
Dennis Johnson (R-50)
Pat Ownbey (R-48)
Pam Peterson (R-67)
J. Michael "Mike" Ritze (R-80)
Ken Walker (R-70)
Paul Wesselhoft (R-54)

**Minority Members**
Ben Loring (D-7)
R. C. Pruett (D-19)
Brian Renegar (D-17)

## Rules

**Majority Members**
Tommy C. Hardin (R-49) *Chair*
Jason Nelson (R-87) *Vice Chair*
Gary W. Banz (R-101)
Chad Caldwell (R-40)
Chris Kannady (R-91)
Weldon L. Watson (R-79)
Harold Wright (R-57)

**Minority Members**
Donnie Condit (D-18)
R. C. Pruett (D-19)
Jerry Shoemake (D-16)

## State and Federal Relations

**Majority Members**
Lewis H. Moore (R-96) *Chair*
Dan Fisher (R-60) *Vice Chair*
Sally Kern (R-84)
Mark Lepak (R-9)
Jason W. Murphey (R-31)
Ken Walker (R-70)

**Minority Members**
Eric Proctor (D-77)
Seneca Scott (D-72)

## State Government Operations

**Majority Members**
Jason W. Murphey (R-31) *Chair*
Mark Lepak (R-9) *Vice Chair*
Josh Cockroft (R-27)
Scott Martin (R-46)
John Pfeiffer (R-38)

**Minority Members**
Jason Dunnington (D-88)
Richard Daniel Morrissette (D-92)

## Tourism and International Relations

**Majority Members**
Josh Cockroft (R-27) *Chair*
Gary W. Banz (R-101)
Travis Dunlap (R-10)
Mark Lepak (R-9)
John Michael Montgomery (R-62)
Charles L. Ortega (R-52)
Dustin Roberts (R-21)

**Minority Members**
R. C. Pruett (D-19) *Vice Chair*
Regina Goodwin (D-73)
Ben Loring (D-7)

## Transportation

**Majority Members**
Charles "Charlie" Joyner (R-95) *Chair*
William Casey Murdock (R-61) *Vice Chair*
John R. Bennett (R-2)
David Brumbaugh (R-76)
George E. Faught (R-14)
Katie Henke (R-71)
Terry S. O'Donnell (R-23)

**Minority Members**
Eric Proctor (D-77)
James Lockhart (D-3)
Jerry McPeak (D-13)

## Utilities

**Majority Members**
Todd Thomsen (R-25) *Chair*
David Brumbaugh (R-76) *Vice Chair*
Chad Caldwell (R-40)
Mike Christian (R-93)
Mark McBride (R-53)
William Casey Murdock (R-61)
Weldon L. Watson (R-79)

**Minority Members**
Ed Cannaday (D-15)
James Lockhart (D-3)
R. C. Pruett (D-19)

## Veterans and Military Affairs

**Majority Members**
Dustin Roberts (R-21) *Chair*
Ann Coody (R-64)
John T. Enns (R-41)
George E. Faught (R-14)
John Pfeiffer (R-38)

**Minority Members**
Jerry Shoemake (D-16) *Vice Chair*
Chuck Hoskin (D-6)
Cyndi Munson (D-85)

## Wildlife

**Majority Members**
Steve Vaughan (R-37) *Chair*
Kevin Wallace (R-32) *Vice Chair*
Tommy C. Hardin (R-49)
William Casey Murdock (R-61)
Scooter Park (R-65)

**Minority Members**
Mike Brown (D-4)
James Lockhart (D-3)

# Oregon Legislative Assembly

State Capitol, 900 Court Street, NE, Salem, OR 97301
Fax: (503) 373-1527  Internet: www.leg.state.or.us

## Oregon State Senate

State Capitol, 900 Court Street, NE, Salem, OR 97301
Tel: (503) 986-1851  Fax: (503) 986-1132  Fax: (503) 986-1080

President of the Senate **Peter Courtney** (D) . . . . . . . . . . . . .(503) 986-1600
   Education: Rhode Island 1965 BA, 1966 MPA; Boston U 1969 JD
President Pro Tempore **Diane Rosenbaum** (D) . . . . . . . . (503) 986-1721
   Education: Reed (Attended)
Majority Leader **Ginny Burdick** (D) . . . . . . . . . . . . . . . . . (503) 986-1718
   Education: U Puget Sound 1969 BA; Oregon 1973 MAJ
Deputy Majority Leader **Arnie Roblan** (D) . . . . . . . . . . . . .(503) 986-1705
   Education: U Washington 1971 BA; Oregon 1983 MA
Assistant Majority Leader **Michael E. Dembrow** (D) . . . . . (503) 986-1723
   Education: Connecticut BA; Indianapolis MA
Assistant Majority Leader **Sara A. Gelser** (D) . . . . . . . . . . (503) 986-1708
   Education: Earlham 1994 BA; Oregon State 1998 MAIS
Majority Whip **Mark Hass** (D) . . . . . . . . . . . . . . . . . . . . . (503) 986-1714
   Education: Oregon BS; American U 1982 MS
Majority Whip **Elizabeth Steiner Hayward** (D) . . . . . . . . . (503) 986-1717
   Education: Chicago 1985 BS; UMass (Amherst) 1991 MD
Minority Leader **Ted Ferrioli** (R) . . . . . . . . . . . . . . . . . . . (503) 986-1950
   Education: Oregon 1973 BA
Deputy Republican Caucus Leader **Brian J. Boquist** (R) . . (503) 986-1712
   Education: Western Oregon State 1985 BSA; Oregon State 1989 MBA
Deputy Republican Caucus Leader **Tim Knopp** (R) . . . . . . (503) 986-1727
Secretary of the Senate **Lori Brocker** . . . . . . . . . . . . . . . .(503) 986-1851
Deputy Secretary of the Senate **Cyndy Johnson** . . . . . . . . (503) 986-1851
   E-mail: cynthia.a.johnston@state.or.us
Democratic Caucus Administrator and Chief of Staff
  **Molly Woon** . . . . . . . . . . . . . . . . . . . . . . . . . . . . . . . .(503) 986-1700
Republican Caucus Administrator and Chief of Staff
  **Paul Rainey** . . . . . . . . . . . . . . . . . . . . . . . . . . . . . . . . (503) 986-1957
   E-mail: paul.rainey@state.or.us

## Senators

**Party Affiliation Statistics:** Republicans: 12, Democrats: 18

Senator **Herman Baertschiger, Jr.** (R-District 2) S-403 . . . (503) 986-1702
  Counties Represented: Jackson (part), Josephine (part)
  Term Expires: 2017
  E-mail: sen.hermanbaertschiger@state.or.us
  Committees: Education; Human Services and Early Childhood
Senator **Alan C. Bates** (D-District 3) Room S-205 . . . . . . (503) 986-1703
  Counties Represented: Jackson (part), Klamath   Dist: (541) 282-6502
  (part)
  Term Expires: 2019
  2859 State Street, Suite 101, Medford, OR 97504
  E-mail: sen.alanbates@state.or.us
  Education: Central Washington 1969 BS; Kansas City Osteopathic
Senator **Lee Beyer** (D-District 6) Room S-419 . . . . . . . . . .(503) 986-1706
  Counties Represented: Lane (part), Linn (part)
  Term Expires: 2019
  E-mail: sen.leebeyer@state.or.us
  Committees: Business, Transportation and Economic Development;
  Education; Rules
  Education: Oregon State 1974 BS
Senator **Brian J. Boquist** (R-District 12) Room S-305 . . . . (503) 986-1712
  Counties Represented: Benton (part), Marion (part), Polk (part),
  Washington (part), Yamhill (part)
  Term Expires: 2017
  E-mail: sen.brianboquist@state.or.us
  Committees: Finance and Revenue; Rules; Veterans' and Emergency
  Preparedness
Senator **Ginny Burdick** (D-District 18) Room S-213 . . . . . .(503) 986-1718
  Counties Represented: Clackamas (part), Multnomah (part), Washington
  (part)
  Term Expires: 2017
  E-mail: sen.ginnyburdick@state.or.us
  Committees: Joint Ways and Means; Judiciary; Rules
Senator **Peter Courtney** (D-District 11) Room S-201 . . . . . (503) 986-1600
  Counties Represented: Marion (part)   Fax: (503) 986-1004
  Term Expires: 2019
  E-mail: sen.petercourtney@state.or.us
  Committees: Human Services and Early Childhood; Veterans' and
  Emergency Preparedness

Senator **Michael E. Dembrow** (D-District 23)
  Room S-407 . . . . . . . . . . . . . . . . . . . . . . . . . . . . . . . . . (503) 986-1723
  Counties Represented: Multnomah (part)   Dist: (503) 281-0608
  Term Expires: 2017
  E-mail: sen.michaeldembrow@state.or.us
  Committees: Environment and Natural Resources; Human Services and
  Early Childhood; Workforce
Senator **Richard Devlin** (D-District 19) Room S-209 . . . . .(503) 986-1719
  Counties Represented: Clackamas (part), Multnomah (part), Washington
  (part)
  Term Expires: 2019
  E-mail: sen.richarddevlin@state.or.us
  Committees: Joint Audits; Joint Ways and Means
  Education: Portland State 1976 BS; Pepperdine 1980 MA
Senator **Chris Edwards** (D-District 7) Room S-405 . . . . . . (503) 986-1707
  Counties Represented: Lane (part)   Fax: (541) 744-7110
  Term Expires: 2019
  E-mail: sen.chrisedwards@state.or.us
  Committees: Conduct; Environment and Natural Resources; Finance
  and Revenue; Sustainable Transportation
  Education: Oregon State BA
Senator **Ted Ferrioli** (R-District 30) Room S-323 . . . . . . . .(503) 986-1950
  Counties Represented: Baker, Clackamas (part),   Tel: (541) 490-6528
  Deschutes (part), Grant, Harney, Jefferson, Lake (part), Malheur,
  Marion (part), Wasco (part), Wheeler
  Term Expires: 2017
  111 Skyline Drive, John Day, OR 97845
  E-mail: sen.tedferrioli@state.or.us
  Committees: Rules
  Affiliation: Executive Director, Malheur Timber Operators Incorporated
Senator **Sara A. Gelser** (D-District 8) . . . . . . . . . . . . . . . . .(503) 986-1708
  Counties Represented: Benton (part), Linn (part)
  Term Expires: 2017
  E-mail: sen.saragelser@state.or.us
  Committees: Education; Human Services and Early Childhood;
  Judiciary; Workforce
Senator **Fred Girod** (R-District 9) Room S-309 . . . . . . . . . (503) 986-1709
  Counties Represented: Clackamas (part), Linn   Dist: (503) 769-4322
  (part), Marion (part)
  Term Expires: 2017
  101 Fern Ridge Road, Stayton, OR 97383
  E-mail: sen.fredgirod@state.or.us
  Committees: Business, Transportation and Economic Development;
  Joint Ways and Means; Sustainable Transportation
  Education: Oregon Health DMD; Harvard MPA
Senator **William "Bill" Hansell** (R-District 29) S-423 . . . . .(503) 986-1729
  Counties Represented: Gilliam, Morrow, Sherman, Umatilla, Union,
  Wallowa, Wasco (part)
  Term Expires: 2017
  E-mail: sen.billhansell@state.or.us
  Committees: Conduct; Joint Ways and Means
  Education: Oregon BS; Harvard PMD
Senator **Mark Hass** (D-District 14) Room S-207 . . . . . . . . (503) 986-1714
  Counties Represented: Multnomah (part), Washington (part)
  Term Expires: 2017
  P.O. Box 536, Beaverton, OR 97075
  E-mail: sen.markhass@state.or.us
  Committees: Education; Finance and Revenue
Senator **Elizabeth "Betsy" Johnson** (D-District 16)
  Room S-209 . . . . . . . . . . . . . . . . . . . . . . . . . . . . . . . . . (503) 986-1716
  Counties Represented: Clatsop, Columbia,   Dist: (503) 543-4046
  Multnomah (part), Tillamook (part), Washington (part), Yamhill (part)
  Term Expires: 2019
  P.O. Box R, Scappoose, OR 97056
  E-mail: sen.betsyjohnson@state.or.us
  Committees: Joint Ways and Means; Sustainable Transportation
  Education: Carleton 1973 BA; Lewis & Clark 1977 JD
Senator **Tim Knopp** (R-District 27) S-309 . . . . . . . . . . . . . (503) 986-1727
  Counties Represented: Deschutes (part)
  Term Expires: 2017
  E-mail: sen.timknopp@state.or.us
  Committees: Education; Health Care; Workforce
Senator **Jeff Kruse** (R-District 1) Room S-315 . . . . . . . . . . (503) 986-1701
  Counties Represented: Coos (part), Curry, Douglas   Dist: (541) 580-3276
  (part), Jackson (part), Josephine (part)
  Term Expires: 2017
  636 Wild Iris Lane, Roseburg, OR 97470
  E-mail: sen.jeffkruse@state.or.us
  Committees: Education; Health Care; Judiciary; Sustainable
  Transportation
  Education: Willamette 1973 BS

*(continued on next page)*

**LEGISLATIVE BRANCH**

**Senators** *continued*

Senator **Laurie Monnes Anderson** (D-District 25)
Room S-413 . . . . . . . . . . . . . . . . . . . . . . . . . . . . . . . . . . . . . . (503) 986-1725
Counties Represented: Multnomah (part)
Term Expires: 2017
E-mail: sen.lauriemonnesanderson@state.or.us
Committees: Conduct; Health Care; Human Services and Early
Childhood; Veterans' and Emergency Preparedness
Education: Willamette 1968 BA; Colorado 1971 MA;
Radford 1981 BSN

Senator **Rod Monroe** (D-District 24) Room S-409 . . . . . . (503) 986-1724
Counties Represented: Clackamas (part),    Dist: (503) 760-4310
Multnomah (part)
Term Expires: 2019
7802 SE 111th Avenue, Portland, OR 97266
E-mail: sen.rodmonroe@state.or.us
Committees: Business, Transportation and Economic Development;
Joint Ways and Means
Education: Portland State 1965 BS, 1969 MA

Senator **Alan R. Olsen** (R-District 20) Room S-425 . . . . . . (503) 986-1720
Counties Represented: Clackamas (part), Marion    Dist: (503) 936-8605
(part)
Term Expires: 2019
P.O. Box 820, Canby, OR 97013
E-mail: sen.alanolsen@state.or.us
Committees: Environment and Natural Resources; Human Services and
Early Childhood; Veterans' and Emergency Preparedness
Education: Purdue BS

Senator **Floyd Prozanski** (D-District 4) Room S-417 . . . . . (503) 986-1704
Counties Represented: Douglas (part), Lane (part)    Dist: (541) 342-2447
Term Expires: 2019
P.O. Box 11511, Eugene, OR 97440
E-mail: sen.floydprozanski@state.or.us
Committees: Environment and Natural Resources; Judiciary
Education: Texas A&M 1977 BA; South Texas 1983 JD

Senator **Chuck Riley** (D-District 15) S-303 . . . . . . . . . . . . .(503) 986-1715
Counties Represented: Washington (part)
Term Expires: 2019
E-mail: sen.chuckriley@state.or.us
Committees: Business, Transportation and Economic Development;
Finance and Revenue; Joint Audits

Senator **Arnie Roblan** (D-District 5) S-417 . . . . . . . . . . . . . (503) 986-1705
Counties Represented: Coos (part), Douglas (part), Lane (part),
Lincoln, Polk (part), Tillamook (part), Yamhill (part)
Term Expires: 2017
E-mail: sen.arnieroblan@state.or.us
Committees: Education; Joint Ways and Means

Senator **Diane Rosenbaum** (D-District 21) Room S-223 . . (503) 986-1721
Counties Represented: Clackamas (part),    Dist: (503) 231-9970
Multnomah (part)
Term Expires: 2017
1125 Southeast Madison Street, Suite 100B, Portland, OR 97614
E-mail: sen.dianerosenbaum@state.or.us
Committees: Finance and Revenue; Rules; Workforce

Senator
**William Matthew "Chip" Shields** (D-District 22)
Room S-421 . . . . . . . . . . . . . . . . . . . . . . . . . . . . . . . . . . . . . . (503) 986-1722
Counties Represented: Multnomah (part)    Dist: (503) 231-2654
Term Expires: 2017
5313 North Vancouver Avenue, Portland, OR 97217
E-mail: sen.chipshields@state.or.us
Committees: Health Care; Joint Ways and Means
Education: Portland State MA

Senator **Elizabeth Steiner Hayward** (D-District 17) . . . . . .(503) 986-1717
Counties Represented: Multnomah (part), Washington (part)
Term Expires: 2017
900 Court Street Northeast, S-215, Salem, OR 97301
E-mail: sen.elizabethsteinerhayward@state.or.us
Committees: Health Care; Joint Ways and Means; Sustainable
Transportation

Senator **Kim Thatcher** (R-District 13) . . . . . . . . . . . . . . . . .(503) 986-1713
Counties Represented: Clackamas (part), Marion (part), Washington
(part), Yamhill (part)
Term Expires: 2017
E-mail: sen.kimthatcher@state.or.us
Committees: Judiciary; Workforce

Senator **Chuck Thomsen** (R-District 26) Room S-316 . . . . (503) 986-1726
Counties Represented: Clackamas (part), Hood River, Multnomah (part)
Term Expires: 2019
E-mail: sen.chuckthomsen@state.or.us
Committees: Business, Transportation and Economic Development;
Environment and Natural Resources; Joint Ways and Means
Education: Willamette BA

Senator **Doug Whitsett** (R-District 28) Room S-303 . . . . . (503) 986-1728
Counties Represented: Crook, Deschutes (part),    Dist: (541) 883-4006
Jackson (part), Klamath (part), Lake (part)
Term Expires: 2017
23131 North Poe Valley Road, Klamath Falls, OR 97603
E-mail: sen.dougwhitsett@state.or.us
Committees: Joint Ways and Means; Sustainable Transportation
Education: Central Oregon Comm Col AA;
Washington State 1967 DVM

Senator **Jackie Winters** (R-District 10) Room S-301 . . . . . (503) 986-1710
Counties Represented: Marion (part), Polk (part)
Term Expires: 2019
E-mail: sen.jackiewinters@state.or.us
Committees: Conduct; Joint Audits; Joint Ways and Means

# Senate Standing Committees

## Business, Transportation and Economic Development

| Majority Members | Minority Members |
|---|---|
| Lee Beyer (D-6) *Chair* | Fred Girod (R-9) *Vice Chair* |
| Rod Monroe (D-24) | Chuck Thomsen (R-26) |
| Chuck Riley (D-15) | |

## Conduct

| Majority Members | Minority Members |
|---|---|
| Laurie Monnes Anderson (D-25) *Chair* | William "Bill" Hansell (R-29) |
| Chris Edwards (D-7) | Jackie Winters (R-10) |

## Education

| Majority Members | Minority Members |
|---|---|
| Arnie Roblan (D-5) *Chair* | Tim Knopp (R-27) *Vice Chair* |
| Lee Beyer (D-6) | Herman Baertschiger, Jr. (R-2) |
| Sara A. Gelser (D-8) | Jeff Kruse (R-1) |
| Mark Hass (D-14) | |

## Environment and Natural Resources

| Majority Members | Minority Members |
|---|---|
| Chris Edwards (D-7) *Chair* | Alan R. Olsen (R-20) *Vice Chair* |
| Michael E. Dembrow (D-23) | Chuck Thomsen (R-26) |
| Floyd Prozanski (D-4) | |

## Finance and Revenue

| Majority Members | Minority Members |
|---|---|
| Mark Hass (D-14) *Chair* | Brian J. Boquist (R-12) *Vice Chair* |
| Chris Edwards (D-7) | |
| Chuck Riley (D-15) | |
| Diane Rosenbaum (D-21) | |

## Health Care

| Majority Members | Minority Members |
|---|---|
| Laurie Monnes Anderson (D-25) *Chair* | Jeff Kruse (R-1) *Vice Chair* |
| William Matthew "Chip" Shields (D-22) | Tim Knopp (R-27) |
| Elizabeth Steiner Hayward (D-17) | |

## Human Services and Early Childhood

| Majority Members | Minority Members |
|---|---|
| Sara A. Gelser (D-8) *Chair* | Herman Baertschiger, Jr. (R-2) *Vice Chair* |
| Peter Courtney (D-11) | Alan R. Olsen (R-20) |
| Michael E. Dembrow (D-23) | |
| Laurie Monnes Anderson (D-25) | |

## Judiciary

| Majority Members | Minority Members |
|---|---|
| Floyd Prozanski (D-4) *Chair* | Jeff Kruse (R-1) *Vice Chair* |
| Ginny Burdick (D-18) | Kim Thatcher (R-13) |
| Sara A. Gelser (D-8) | |

## Sustainable Transportation

**Majority Members**
Chris Edwards (D-7) *Chair*
Elizabeth "Betsy" Johnson (D-16)
Elizabeth Steiner Hayward (D-17)

**Minority Members**
Fred Girod (R-9) *Vice Chair*
Jeff Kruse (R-1)
Doug Whitsett (R-28)

## Rules

**Majority Members**
Diane Rosenbaum (D-21) *Chair*
Lee Beyer (D-6)
Ginny Burdick (D-18)

**Minority Members**
Ted Ferrioli (R-30) *Vice Chair*
Brian J. Boquist (R-12)

## Veterans' and Emergency Preparedness

**Majority Members**
Laurie Monnes Anderson (D-25)
 *Vice Chair*
Peter Courtney (D-11)

**Minority Members**
Brian J. Boquist (R-12) *Chair*
Alan R. Olsen (R-20)

## Workforce

**Majority Members**
Michael E. Dembrow (D-23) *Chair*
Sara A. Gelser (D-8)
Diane Rosenbaum (D-21)

**Minority Members**
Kim Thatcher (R-13) *Vice Chair*
Tim Knopp (R-27)

# Oregon House of Representatives

State Capitol, 900 Court Street, NE, Salem, OR 97301
Tel: (503) 986-1000  Internet: www.leg.state.or.us/house

Speaker of the House **Tina Kotek** (D) . . . . . . . . . . . . . . . . . (503) 986-1900
  Chief of Staff **Angela Wilhelms** . . . . . . . . . . . . . . . . . . . (503) 986-1400
    Education: Santa Clara U 2000 BS
Speaker Pro Tem **Tobias J. Read** (D) . . . . . . . . . . . . . . . . (503) 986-1427
  Education: Willamette 1997 AB; U Washington 2003 MBA
Majority Leader **Jennifer Williamson** (D) . . . . . . . . . . . . (503) 986-1436
  Education: Oregon 1996 BS; Willamette JD
Assistant Majority Leader (Policy)
  **Nancy Nathanson** (D) . . . . . . . . . . . . . . . . . . . . . . . . . . (503) 986-1413
Assistant Majority Leader (Politics) **David Gomberg** (D) . . (503) 986-1410
  Education: Oregon State 1976 BS, 1977 MAIS; Willamette 1981 MBA
Assistant Majority Leader (Politics) **Ann Lininger** (D) . . . . (503) 986-1438
  Education: Yale 1990 BA
Assistant Majority Leader (Politics)
  **Caddy McKeown** (D) . . . . . . . . . . . . . . . . . . . . . . . . . . . (503) 986-1409
  Education: Oregon; Oregon State
Majority Whip **Dan Rayfield** (D) . . . . . . . . . . . . . . . . . . . (503) 986-1416
Deputy Majority Whip **Barbara Smith Warner** (D) . . . . . . (503) 986-1000
  Education: Gannon 1989
Minority Leader **Michael "Mike" McLane** (R) . . . . . . . . . (503) 986-1455
  Education: Oregon State 1987 BS; Lewis & Clark 1990 JD
  Chief of Staff **Gary Wilhelms** . . . . . . . . . . . . . . . . . . . . (503) 986-1400
Deputy Minority Leader **Carl Wilson** (R) . . . . . . . . . . . . . (503) 986-1403
Assistant Minority Leader **Cliff Bentz** (R) . . . . . . . . . . . . . (503) 986-1460
  Education: Eastern Oregon State 1974 BS; Lewis & Clark 1977 JD
Assistant Minority Leader **John Davis** (R) . . . . . . . . . . . . . (503) 986-1426
  Education: George Fox U BA; Willamette JD
Assistant Minority Leader **Gene Whisnant** (R) . . . . . . . . . . (503) 986-1453
  Education: North Carolina 1966 BA; Arkansas 1976 MA
Minority Whip **Sherrie Sprenger** (R) . . . . . . . . . . . . . . . . (503) 986-1417
Deputy Minority Whip **Jodi L. Hack** (R) . . . . . . . . . . . . . . (503) 986-1419
Chief Clerk of the House **Timothy Sekerak** . . . . . . . . . . . (503) 986-1870
  E-mail: tim.sekerak@state.or.us

## Representatives

**Party Affiliation Statistics:** Republicans: 25, Democrats: 35

Representative **Jeff Barker** (D-District 28) Room H-480 . . . (503) 986-1428
  Counties Represented: Washington (part)
  Term Expires: 2017
  E-mail: rep.jeffbarker@state.or.us
  Committees: Judiciary
  Education: Portland State BS

Representative **Phil Barnhart** (D-District 11)
  Room H-383 . . . . . . . . . . . . . . . . . . . . . . . . . . . (503) 986-1411
  Counties Represented: Lane (part), Linn (part)   Dist: (541) 607-9207
  Term Expires: 2017                                  Fax: (541) 744-7110
  P.O. Box 71188, Eugene, OR 97401
  E-mail: rep.philbarnhart@state.or.us
  Committees: Revenue; Rules
  Education: Oregon BA, JD; California Psychology PhD
Representative **Greg Barreto** (R-District 58) . . . . . . . . . . . (503) 986-1458
  Counties Represented: Umatilla (part), Union, Wallowa
  Term Expires: 2017
  E-mail: rep.gregbarreto@state.or.us
  Committees: Agriculture and Natural Resources; Business and Labor;
  Education
Representative **Brent Barton** (D-District 40) H-275 . . . . . . (503) 986-1440
  Counties Represented: Clackamas (part)
  Term Expires: 2017
  E-mail: rep.brentbarton@state.or.us
  Committees: Business and Labor; Judiciary
  Education: Cambridge (UK); Stanford MA; Harvard JD
Representative **Cliff Bentz** (R-District 60) Room H-475 . . . (503) 986-1460
  Counties Represented: Baker, Grant, Harney, Lake   Dist: (541) 889-8866
  (part), Malheur
  Term Expires: 2017
  258 South Oregon Street, Ontario, OR 97914
  E-mail: rep.cliffbentz@state.or.us
  Committees: Energy and Environment; Revenue; Transportation and
  Economic Development
Representative
**Deborah "Debbie" Boone** (D-District 32)
  Room H-375 . . . . . . . . . . . . . . . . . . . . . . . . . . . (503) 986-1432
  Counties Represented: Clatsop, Tillamook (part),   Dist: (503) 717-9182
  Washington (part), Yamhill (part)
  Term Expires: 2017
  P. O. Box 928, Cannon Beach, OR 97110
  E-mail: rep.deborahboone@state.or.us
  Committees: Energy and Environment; Veterans and Emergency
  Preparedness
  Education: U Washington (Attended); Portland State BS
Representative **Peter Buckley** (D-District 5)
  Room H-272 . . . . . . . . . . . . . . . . . . . . . . . . . . . (503) 986-1405
  Counties Represented: Jackson (part), Klamath   Dist: (541) 488-9180
  (part)
  Term Expires: 2017
  71 Dewey Street, Ashland, OR 97520
  E-mail: rep.peterbuckley@state.or.us
  Committees: Joint Audits; Joint Ways and Means
  Education: U Santa Clara 1979 BFA
Representative **Knute Buehler** (R-District 54) . . . . . . . . . . (503) 986-1454
  Counties Represented: Deschutes (part)
  Term Expires: 2017
  E-mail: rep.knutebuehler@state.or.us
  Committees: Consumer Protection and Government Effectiveness;
  Health Care; Human Services and Housing
  Education: Oregon State BS; Oxford (UK) MA; Johns Hopkins MD
Representative **Brian L. Clem** (D-District 21)
  Room H-284 . . . . . . . . . . . . . . . . . . . . . . . . . . . (503) 986-1421
  Counties Represented: Marion (part)
  Term Expires: 2017
  E-mail: rep.brianclem@state.or.us
  Committees: Health Care; Rural Communities, Land Use, and Water
  Education: Oregon State BA
Representative **John Davis** (R-District 26) H-389 . . . . . . . . (503) 986-1426
  Counties Represented: Clackamas (part), Washington (part)
  Term Expires: 2017
  E-mail: rep.johndavis@state.or.us
  Committees: Revenue; Rural Communities, Land Use, and Water;
  Transportation and Economic Development
Representative **Margaret Doherty** (D-District 35)
  Room H-282 . . . . . . . . . . . . . . . . . . . . . . . . . . . (503) 986-1435
  Counties Represented: Clackamas (part), Multnomah (part), Washington
  (part)
  Term Expires: 2017
  E-mail: rep.margaretdoherty@state.or.us
  Committees: Business and Labor; Education; Transportation and
  Economic Development
  Education: Portland State BA; Lewis & Clark MA
Representative **Sal Esquivel** (R-District 6) Room H-483 . . . (503) 986-1406
  Counties Represented: Jackson (part)   Dist: (541) 734-4369
  Term Expires: 2017
  E-mail: rep.salesquivel@state.or.us
  Committees: Agriculture and Natural Resources; Business and Labor;
  Veterans and Emergency Preparedness

*(continued on next page)*

**LEGISLATIVE BRANCH**

**Representatives** *continued*

Representative **Paul Evans** (D-District 20) . . . . . . . . . . . . . (503) 986-1420
Counties Represented: Marion (part), Polk (part)
Term Expires: 2017
E-mail: rep.paulevans@state.or.us
Committees: Business and Labor; Human Services and Housing;
Veterans and Emergency Preparedness
Education: Western Oregon U 1992 BSPA

Representative **Shemia Fagan** (D-District 51) H-492 . . . . . (503) 986-1451
Counties Represented: Clackamas (part), Multnomah (part)
Term Expires: 2017
E-mail: rep.shemiafagan@state.or.us
Committees: Business and Labor; Consumer Protection and
Government Effectiveness
Education: Lewis & Clark JD

Representative **Lewis "Lew" Frederick** (D-District 43)
Room H-276 . . . . . . . . . . . . . . . . . . . . . . . . . . . . . . . . . (503) 986-1443
Counties Represented: Multnomah (part)
Term Expires: 2017
E-mail: rep.lewfrederick@state.or.us
Committees: Agriculture and Natural Resources; Education
Education: Earlham 1973 BA

Representative **Joe Gallegos** (D-District 30) H-484 . . . . . . (503) 986-1430
Counties Represented: Washington (part)
Term Expires: 2017
E-mail: rep.joegallegos@state.or.us
Committees: Consumer Protection and Government Effectiveness;
Higher Education, Innovation, and Workforce Development; Human
Services and Housing
Education: Denver 1978 PhD

Representative **Vic Gilliam** (R-District 18) Room H-389 . . . (503) 986-1418
Counties Represented: Clackamas (part), Marion (part)
Term Expires: 2017
E-mail: rep.vicgilliam@state.or.us
Committees: Rules; Rural Communities, Land Use, and Water

Representative **David Gomberg** (D-District 10) H-371 . . . . (503) 986-1410
Counties Represented: Lincoln (part), Polk (part), Tillamook (part),
Yamhill (part)
Term Expires: 2017
E-mail: rep.davidgomberg@state.or.us
Committees: Joint Ways and Means; Rural Communities, Land Use,
and Water

Representative **Chris Gorsek** (D-District 49) H-486 . . . . . . (503) 986-1449
Counties Represented: Multnomah (part)
Term Expires: 2017
E-mail: rep.chrisgorsek@state.or.us
Committees: Agriculture and Natural Resources; Transportation and
Economic Development
Education: Oregon 1989 BS, 1992 MA; Portland State 1998 PhD

Representative **Mitch Greenlick** (D-District 33)
Room H-492 . . . . . . . . . . . . . . . . . . . . . . . . . . . . . . . . . (503) 986-1433
Counties Represented: Multnomah (part),     Dist: (503) 297-2416
Washington (part)
Term Expires: 2017
712 Northwest Spring Avenue, Portland, OR 97229
E-mail: rep.mitchgreenlick@state.or.us
Committees: Conduct; Health Care; Judiciary
Education: Michigan PhD

Representative **Jodi L. Hack** (R-District 19) . . . . . . . . . . . . (503) 986-1419
Counties Represented: Marion (part)
Term Expires: 2017
E-mail: rep.jodihack@state.or.us
Committees: Education; Transportation and Economic Development

Representative **Cedric Hayden** (R-District 7) . . . . . . . . . . . (503) 986-1407
Counties Represented: Douglas (part), Lane (part)
Term Expires: 2017
E-mail: rep.cedrichayden@state.or.us
Committees: Health Care; Higher Education, Innovation, and Workforce
Development; Human Services and Housing

Representative **Dallas Heard** (R-District 2) . . . . . . . . . . . . . (503) 986-1402
Counties Represented: Douglas (part), Jackson (part), Josephine (part)
Term Expires: 2017
E-mail: rep.dallasheard@state.or.us
Committees: Business and Labor; Energy and Environment

Representative **Ken Helm** (D-District 34) . . . . . . . . . . . . . . (503) 986-1434
Counties Represented: Washington (part)
Term Expires: 2017
E-mail: rep.kenhelm@state.or.us
Committees: Energy and Environment; Rural Communities, Land Use,
and Water

Representative **Paul R. Holvey** (D-District 8)
Room H-275 . . . . . . . . . . . . . . . . . . . . . . . . . . . . . . . . . (503) 986-1408
Counties Represented: Lane (part)     Dist: (541) 344-5636
Term Expires: 2017
P.O. Box 51048, Eugene, OR 97405
E-mail: rep.paulholvey@state.or.us
Committees: Business and Labor; Consumer Protection and
Government Effectiveness; Energy and Environment

Representative **Val Hoyle** (D-District 14) Room H-283 . . . . (503) 986-1414
Counties Represented: Lane (part)
Term Expires: 2017
E-mail: rep.valhoyle@state.or.us
Committees: Rules

Representative **John E. Huffman, USA** (R-District 59)
Room H-476 . . . . . . . . . . . . . . . . . . . . . . . . . . . . . . . . . (503) 986-1459
Counties Represented: Clackamas (part), Deschutes    Dist: (541) 298-5959
(part), Jefferson, Marion (part), Wasco (part), Wheeler
Term Expires: 2017
P.O. Box 104, The Dalles, OR 97058
E-mail: rep.johnhuffman@state.or.us
Committees: Joint Ways and Means; Veterans and Emergency
Preparedness

Representative **Mark Johnson** (R-District 52)
Room H-489 . . . . . . . . . . . . . . . . . . . . . . . . . . . . . . . . . (503) 986-1452
Counties Represented: Clackamas (part), Hood River, Multnomah (part)
Term Expires: 2017
E-mail: rep.markjohnson@state.or.us
Committees: Energy and Environment; Higher Education, Innovation,
and Workforce Development; Revenue

Representative **Bill Kennemer** (R-District 39)
Room H-380 . . . . . . . . . . . . . . . . . . . . . . . . . . . . . . . . . (503) 986-1439
Counties Represented: Clackamas (part), Marion    Dist: (503) 263-4798
(part)
Term Expires: 2017
21041 South Highway 99 East, Oregon City, OR 97045
E-mail: rep.billkennemer@state.or.us
Committees: Business and Labor; Rules

Representative **Alissa Keny-Guyer** (D-District 46)
Room H-484 . . . . . . . . . . . . . . . . . . . . . . . . . . . . . . . . . (503) 986-1446
Counties Represented: Multnomah (part)
Term Expires: 2017
E-mail: rep.alissakenyguyer@state.or.us
Committees: Health Care; Human Services and Housing

Representative **Betty E. Komp** (D-District 22)
Room H-273 . . . . . . . . . . . . . . . . . . . . . . . . . . . . . . . . . (503) 986-1422
Counties Represented: Marion (part)
Term Expires: 2017
E-mail: rep.bettykomp@state.or.us
Committees: Joint Ways and Means

Representative **Tina Kotek** (D-District 44) Room H-395 . . . (503) 986-1900
Counties Represented: Multnomah (part)    Dist: (503) 986-1444
Term Expires: 2017
E-mail: rep.tinakotek@state.or.us
Committees: Joint Ways and Means

Representative **Wayne Krieger** (R-District 1)
Room H-381 . . . . . . . . . . . . . . . . . . . . . . . . . . . . . . . . . (503) 986-1401
Counties Represented: Coos (part), Curry, Douglas    Dist: (541) 247-7990
(part), Josephine (part)
Term Expires: 2017
95702 Skyview Ranch Road, Gold Beach, OR 97444
E-mail: rep.waynekrieger@state.or.us
Committees: Agriculture and Natural Resources; Judiciary

Representative **Ann Lininger** (D-District 38) H-283 . . . . . . (503) 986-1438
Counties Represented: Clackamas (part), Multnomah (part), Washington
(part)
Term Expires: 2017
E-mail: rep.annlininger@state.or.us
Committees: Judiciary; Revenue

Representative **John Lively** (D-District 12) H-488 . . . . . . . . (503) 986-1412
Counties Represented: Lane (part)
Term Expires: 2017
E-mail: rep.johnlively@state.or.us
Committees: Health Care; Transportation and Economic Development;
Veterans and Emergency Preparedness
Education: Oregon

Representative **Caddy McKeown** (D-District 9) H-376 . . . . (503) 986-1409
Counties Represented: Coos (part), Douglas (part), Lane (part), Lincoln
(part)
Term Expires: 2017
E-mail: rep.caddymckeown@state.or.us
Committees: Agriculture and Natural Resources; Higher Education,
Innovation, and Workforce Development; Transportation and Economic
Development

Representative **Susan McLain** (D-District 29) . . . . . . . . . . (503) 986-1429
Counties Represented: Washington (part)
Term Expires: 2017
E-mail: rep.susanmclain@state.or.us
Committees: Agriculture and Natural Resources; Education;
Transportation and Economic Development

Representative **Michael "Mike" McLane** (R-District 55)
Room H-385 . . . . . . . . . . . . . . . . . . . . . . . . . . . . . . . . . (503) 986-1455
Counties Represented: Crook, Deschutes (part),        Dist: (541) 233-4411
Jackson (part), Klamath (part), Lake (part)
Term Expires: 2017
E-mail: rep.mikemclane@state.or.us
Committees: Joint Ways and Means; Rules

Representative **Nancy Nathanson** (D-District 13)
Room H-280 . . . . . . . . . . . . . . . . . . . . . . . . . . . . . . . . . (503) 986-1413
Counties Represented: Lane (part)        Dist: (541) 343-2206
Term Expires: 2017
P.O. Box 41895, Eugene, OR 97404
E-mail: rep.nancynathanson@state.or.us
Committees: Conduct; Joint Audits; Joint Ways and Means

Representative **Mike Nearman** (R-District 23) . . . . . . . . . . (503) 986-1423
Counties Represented: Benton (part), Marion (part), Polk (part),
Yamhill (part)
Term Expires: 2017
E-mail: rep.mikenearman@state.or.us
Committees: Consumer Protection and Government Effectiveness;
Higher Education, Innovation, and Workforce Development

Representative **Rob Nosse** (D-District 42) H-274 . . . . . . . . (503) 986-1442
Counties Represented: Multnomah (part)
Term Expires: 2017
E-mail: rep.robnosse@state.or.us
Committees: Business and Labor; Health Care; Rules
Education: Miami U (OH)

Representative **Andy Olson** (R-District 15) Room H-478 . . (503) 986-1415
Counties Represented: Benton (part), Linn (part)        Dist: (541) 967-6576
Term Expires: 2017
PO Box 891, Albany, OR 97321
E-mail: rep.andyolson@state.or.us
Committees: Conduct; Judiciary
Education: George Fox U BHum

Representative **Julie Parrish** (R-District 37) Room H-386 . . (503) 986-1437
Counties Represented: Clackamas (part), Washington (part)
Term Expires: 2017
E-mail: rep.julieparrish@state.or.us
Committees: Human Services and Housing; Veterans and Emergency
Preparedness

Representative **Jessica Vega Pederson** (D-District 47)
H-490 . . . . . . . . . . . . . . . . . . . . . . . . . . . . . . . . . . . . . . (503) 986-1447
Counties Represented: Multnomah (part)
Term Expires: 2017
E-mail: rep.jessicavegapederson@state.or.us
Committees: Energy and Environment; Revenue
Education: Indiana 1996 (Attended); Loyola U (Chicago) BS

Representative **Carla C. Piluso** (D-District 50) . . . . . . . . . . (503) 986-1450
Counties Represented: Multnomah (part)
Term Expires: 2017
E-mail: rep.carlapiluso@state.or.us
Committees: Education; Human Services and Housing; Veterans and
Emergency Preparedness

Representative **Bill Post** (R-District 25) . . . . . . . . . . . . . . . (503) 986-1425
Counties Represented: Marion (part), Washington (part), Yamhill (part)
Term Expires: 2017
E-mail: rep.billpost@state.or.us
Committees: Judiciary; Rural Communities, Land Use, and Water

Representative **Dan Rayfield** (D-District 16) . . . . . . . . . . . . (503) 986-1416
Counties Represented: Benton (part)
Term Expires: 2017
E-mail: rep.danrayfield@state.or.us
Committees: Consumer Protection and Government Effectiveness; Joint
Ways and Means; Rules

Representative **Tobias J. Read** (D-District 27)
Room H-390 . . . . . . . . . . . . . . . . . . . . . . . . . . . . . . . . . (503) 986-1427
Counties Represented: Multnomah (part),        Dist: (503) 641-6800
Washington (part)
Term Expires: 2017
P.O. Box 2101, Beaverton, OR 97005
E-mail: rep.tobiasread@state.or.us
Committees: Higher Education, Innovation, and Workforce
Development; Joint Ways and Means; Revenue

Representative **Jeff Reardon** (D-District 48) H-491 . . . . . . (503) 986-1448
Counties Represented: Clackamas (part), Multnomah (part)
Term Expires: 2017
E-mail: rep.jeffreardon@state.or.us
Committees: Education; Energy and Environment; Higher Education,
Innovation, and Workforce Development
Education: Western Washington BE

Representative **Greg Smith** (R-District 57) Room H-482 . . (503) 986-1457
Counties Represented: Gilliam, Morrow, Sherman,        Dist: (541) 676-5154
Umatilla (part), Wasco (part)
Term Expires: 2017
P.O. Box 219, Heppner, OR 97836
E-mail: rep.gregsmith@state.or.us
Committees: Joint Ways and Means
Education: Eastern Oregon State BS

Representative **Barbara Smith Warner** (D-District 45)
Room H-487 . . . . . . . . . . . . . . . . . . . . . . . . . . . . . . . . . (503) 986-1000
Counties Represented: Multnomah (part)
Term Expires: 2017
E-mail: rep.barbarasmithwarner@state.or.us
Committees: Revenue; Rules

Representative **Sherrie Sprenger** (R-District 17)
Room H-473 . . . . . . . . . . . . . . . . . . . . . . . . . . . . . . . . . (503) 986-1417
Counties Represented: Linn (part), Marion (part)
Term Expires: 2017
E-mail: rep.sherriesprenger@state.or.us
Committees: Education; Judiciary

Representative **Duane A. Stark** (R-District 4) . . . . . . . . . . (503) 986-1404
Counties Represented: Jackson (part), Josephine (part)
Term Expires: 2017
E-mail: rep.duanestark@state.or.us
Committees: Consumer Protection and Government Effectiveness;
Human Services and Housing

Representative **Kathleen Taylor** (D-District 41) . . . . . . . . . (503) 986-1441
Counties Represented: Clackamas (part), Multnomah (part)
Term Expires: 2017
E-mail: rep.kathleentaylor@state.or.us
Committees: Human Services and Housing

Representative **Jim Weidner** (R-District 24)
Room H-387 . . . . . . . . . . . . . . . . . . . . . . . . . . . . . . . . . (503) 986-1424
Counties Represented: Washington (part), Yamhill (part)
Term Expires: 2017
E-mail: rep.jimweidner@state.or.us
Committees: Business and Labor; Energy and Environment; Health
Care

Representative **Gene Whisnant** (R-District 53)
Room H-471 . . . . . . . . . . . . . . . . . . . . . . . . . . . . . . . . . (503) 986-1453
Counties Represented: Deschutes (part)
Term Expires: 2017
E-mail: rep.genewhisnant@state.or.us
Committees: Higher Education, Innovation, and Workforce
Development; Joint Audits; Joint Ways and Means

Representative **Gail Whitsett** (R-District 56) H-474 . . . . . . (503) 986-1459
Counties Represented: Klamath (part), Lake (part)
Term Expires: 2017
E-mail: rep.gailwhitsett@state.or.us
Committees: Agriculture and Natural Resources; Conduct; Joint Ways
and Means; Revenue

Representative **Jennifer Williamson** (D-District 36)
H-372 . . . . . . . . . . . . . . . . . . . . . . . . . . . . . . . . . . . . . . (503) 986-1436
Counties Represented: Multnomah (part)
Term Expires: 2017
E-mail: rep.jenniferwilliamson@state.or.us
Committees: Higher Education, Innovation, and Workforce
Development; Joint Ways and Means; Judiciary

Representative **Carl Wilson** (R-District 3) . . . . . . . . . . . . . . (503) 986-1403
Counties Represented: Josephine (part)
Term Expires: 2017
E-mail: rep.carlwilson@state.or.us
Committees: Education; Rules

Representative **Brad Witt** (D-District 31) Room H-374 . . . . (503) 986-1431
Counties Represented: Columbia, Multnomah (part), Washington (part)
Term Expires: 2017
E-mail: rep.bradwitt@state.or.us
Committees: Agriculture and Natural Resources; Rural Communities,
Land Use, and Water

LEGISLATIVE BRANCH

# House Standing Committees

## Agriculture and Natural Resources

**Majority Members**
Brad Witt (D-31) *Chair*
Susan McLain (D-29) *Vice Chair*
Lewis "Lew" Frederick (D-43)
Chris Gorsek (D-49)
Caddy McKeown (D-9)

**Minority Members**
Wayne Krieger (R-1) *Vice Chair*
Greg Barreto (R-58)
Sal Esquivel (R-6)
Gail Whitsett (R-56)

## Business and Labor

**Majority Members**
Paul R. Holvey (D-8) *Chair*
Brent Barton (D-40) *Vice Chair*
Margaret Doherty (D-35)
Paul Evans (D-20)
Shemia Fagan (D-51)
Rob Nosse (D-42)

**Minority Members**
Bill Kennemer (R-39) *Vice Chair*
Greg Barreto (R-58)
Sal Esquivel (R-6)
Dallas Heard (R-2)
Jim Weidner (R-24)

## Conduct

**Majority Members**
Mitch Greenlick (D-33) *Chair*
Nancy Nathanson (D-13)

**Minority Members**
Andy Olson (R-15)
Gail Whitsett (R-56)

## Consumer Protection and Government Effectiveness

**Majority Members**
Shemia Fagan (D-51) *Chair*
Dan Rayfield (D-16) *Vice Chair*
Joe Gallegos (D-30)
Paul R. Holvey (D-8)

**Minority Members**
Knute Buehler (R-54) *Vice Chair*
Mike Nearman (R-23)
Duane A. Stark (R-4)

## Education

**Majority Members**
Margaret Doherty (D-35) *Chair*
Lewis "Lew" Frederick (D-43)
  *Vice Chair*
Susan McLain (D-29)
Carla C. Piluso (D-50)
Jeff Reardon (D-48)

**Minority Members**
Sherrie Sprenger (R-17) *Vice Chair*
Greg Barreto (R-58)
Jodi L. Hack (R-19)
Carl Wilson (R-3)

## Energy and Environment

**Majority Members**
Jessica Vega Pederson (D-47) *Chair*
Jeff Reardon (D-48) *Vice Chair*
Deborah "Debbie" Boone (D-32)
Ken Helm (D-34)
Paul R. Holvey (D-8)

**Minority Members**
Mark Johnson (R-52) *Vice Chair*
Cliff Bentz (R-60)
Dallas Heard (R-2)
Jim Weidner (R-24)

## Health Care

**Majority Members**
Mitch Greenlick (D-33) *Chair*
Rob Nosse (D-42) *Vice Chair*
Brian L. Clem (D-21)
Alissa Keny-Guyer (D-46)
John Lively (D-12)

**Minority Members**
Cedric Hayden (R-7) *Vice Chair*
Knute Buehler (R-54)
Jim Weidner (R-24)

## Higher Education, Innovation, and Workforce Development

**Majority Members**
Tobias J. Read (D-27) *Chair*
Joe Gallegos (D-30) *Vice Chair*
Caddy McKeown (D-9)
Jeff Reardon (D-48)
Jennifer Williamson (D-36)

**Minority Members**
Gene Whisant (R-53) *Vice Chair*
Cedric Hayden (R-7)
Mark Johnson (R-52)
Mike Nearman (R-23)

## Human Services and Housing

**Majority Members**
Alissa Keny-Guyer (D-46) *Chair*
Carla C. Piluso (D-50) *Vice Chair*
Paul Evans (D-20)
Joe Gallegos (D-30)
Kathleen Taylor (D-41)

**Minority Members**
Duane A. Stark (R-4) *Vice Chair*
Knute Buehler (R-54)
Cedric Hayden (R-7)
Julie Parrish (R-37)

## Judiciary

**Majority Members**
Jeff Barker (D-28) *Chair*
Jennifer Williamson (D-36)
  *Vice Chair*
Brent Barton (D-40)
Mitch Greenlick (D-33)
Ann Lininger (D-38)

**Minority Members**
Andy Olson (R-15) *Vice Chair*
Wayne Krieger (R-1)
Bill Post (R-25)
Sherrie Sprenger (R-17)

## Rural Communities, Land Use, and Water

**Majority Members**
Brian L. Clem (D-21) *Chair*
Ken Helm (D-34) *Vice Chair*
David Gomberg (D-10)
Brad Witt (D-31)

**Minority Members**
Bill Post (R-25) *Vice Chair*
John Davis (R-26)
Vic Gilliam (R-18)

## Revenue

**Majority Members**
Phil Barnhart (D-11) *Chair*
Jessica Vega Pederson (D-47)
  *Vice Chair*
Ann Lininger (D-38)
Tobias J. Read (D-27)
Barbara Smith Warner (D-45)

**Minority Members**
Cliff Bentz (R-60) *Vice Chair*
John Davis (R-26)
Mark Johnson (R-52)
Gail Whitsett (R-56)

## Rules

**Majority Members**
Val Hoyle (D-14) *Chair*
Barbara Smith Warner (D-45)
  *Vice Chair*
Phil Barnhart (D-11)
Rob Nosse (D-42)
Dan Rayfield (D-16)

**Minority Members**
Vic Gilliam (R-18) *Vice Chair*
Bill Kennemer (R-39)
Michael "Mike" McLane (R-55)
Carl Wilson (R-3)

## Transportation and Economic Development

**Majority Members**
Caddy McKeown (D-9) *Chair*
Chris Gorsek (D-49) *Vice Chair*
Margaret Doherty (D-35)
John Lively (D-12)
Susan McLain (D-29)

**Minority Members**
John Davis (R-26) *Vice Chair*
Cliff Bentz (R-60)
Jodi L. Hack (R-19)

## Veterans and Emergency Preparedness

**Majority Members**
John Lively (D-12) *Chair*
Deborah "Debbie" Boone (D-32)
  *Vice Chair*
Paul Evans (D-20)
Carla C. Piluso (D-50)

**Minority Members**
Sal Esquivel (R-6) *Vice Chair*
John E. Huffman (R-59)
Julie Parrish (R-37)

# Pennsylvania General Assembly

Capitol Building, Harrisburg, PA 17120
Internet: www.legis.state.pa.us

## Pennsylvania Senate

Capitol Building, Senate Post Office, Harrisburg, PA 17120
Tel: (717) 787-5920  Fax: (717) 772-2344

President of the Senate **Michael J. "Mike" Stack III** (D) . . (717) 787-3300
  E-mail: mstack@pa.gov
  Education: LaSalle Extension U 1987 BA; Villanova 1992 JD
President Pro Tem **Joseph B. Scarnati III** (R) . . . . . . . . . . (717) 787-7084
  Education: Penn State 1982
Majority Floor Leader **Jacob D. "Jake" Corman** (R). . . . . (717) 787-1377
  Education: Penn Col Tech 1990 AA; Penn State 1993 BA
Majority Whip **John R. Gordner** (R) . . . . . . . . . . . . . . . . . (717) 787-8928
  Education: Dickinson Law 1983 BA, 1987 JD
Majority Caucus Chairman
  **Robert B. "Bob" Mensch** (R) . . . . . . . . . . . . . . . . . . . . (717) 787-3110
  Education: Valley Forge Military 1965 AB
Majority Caucus Secretary **Richard L. Alloway II** (R). . . . . (717) 787-4651
  Education: Shippensburg 1993 BA
Majority Appropriations Committee Chairman
  **Patrick M. "Pat" Browne, CPA** (R) . . . . . . . . . . . . . . . (717) 787-1349
  Education: Notre Dame 1986 BA; Temple 1993 JD
Majority Policy Committee Chairman
  **David G. "Dave" Argall** (R). . . . . . . . . . . . . . . . . . . . . (717) 787-2637
  Education: Lycoming 1980 BA; Penn State 1993 MA, 2006 PhD
Majority Caucus Administrator
  **Charles T. "Chuck" McIlhinney, Jr.** (R) . . . . . . . . . . . . . (717) 787-7305
  Education: Bryant Col 1989 BS
Minority Floor Leader **Jay Costa, Jr.** (D). . . . . . . . . . . . . . (717) 787-7683
  Education: Indiana (PA) 1979 BA; Duquesne 1989 JD
Minority Whip **Anthony Hardy Williams** (D) . . . . . . . . . . (717) 787-5970
  Education: Penn State BA; Pennsylvania JD
Minority Caucus Chairman **Wayne D. Fontana** (D) . . . . . . (717) 787-5300
Minority Caucus Secretary
  **Lawrence M. "Larry" Farnese, Jr.** (D) . . . . . . . . . . . . . (717) 787-5662
  Education: Temple 1994 JD
Minority Caucus Administrator **John T. Yudichak** (D) . . . . (717) 787-7105
  Education: Penn State 1993 BA
Minority Appropriations Committee Chairman
  **Vincent J. Hughes** (D). . . . . . . . . . . . . . . . . . . . . . . . . (717) 787-7112
  Education: Temple (Attended)
Minority Policy Committee Chairman
  **Lisa M. Boscola** (D) . . . . . . . . . . . . . . . . . . . . . . . . . . (717) 787-4236
  Education: Villanova 1984 BA, 1985 MA
Secretary-Parliamentarian **Megan Martin** . . . . . . . . . . . . . (717) 787-5920
  E-mail: senatesecretary@os.pasen.gov
  Education: Delaware 1991 BA; Widener 1994 JD
Chief Clerk **Donetta M. D'Innocenzo** . . . . . . . . . . . . . . . . (717) 787-7163
  E-mail: ddinnocenzo@occ.pasen.gov
  Education: Shippensburg BA

## Senators

**Party Affiliation Statistics:** Republicans: 31, Democrats: 19

Senator **Richard L. Alloway II** (R-District 33) . . . . . . . . . . (717) 787-4651
  Counties Represented: Adams, Cumberland (part),  Fax: (717) 783-8657
  Franklin (part), York (part)
  Term Expires: 2016
  187 Main Capitol, P.O. Box 203033, Harrisburg, PA 17120-3033
  E-mail: alloway@pasen.gov
  Committees: Community, Economic, and Recreational Development;
  Game and Fisheries; Judiciary; Law and Justice; Rules and Executive
  Nominations; State Government
Senator **David G. "Dave" Argall** (R-District 29) . . . . . . . . (717) 787-2637
  Counties Represented: Berks (part), Schuylkill  Fax: (717) 783-8657
  Term Expires: 2016
  One West Centre Street, Mahanoy City, PA 17948
  E-mail: dargall@pasen.gov
  Committees: Aging and Youth; Agriculture and Rural Affairs;
  Appropriations; Community, Economic, and Recreational Development;
  Urban Affairs and Housing

Senator **Ryan P. Aument** (R-District 36) . . . . . . . . . . . . . . (717) 787-4420
  Counties Represented: Lancaster (part)  Dist: (717) 626-0036
  Term Expires: 2018  Fax: (717) 783-3156
  301 East Main Street, Lititz, PA 17543  Dist: (717) 627-1389
  E-mail: raument@pasen.gov
  Committees: Agriculture and Rural Affairs; Communications and
  Technology; Education; Finance; Public Health and Welfare; Veterans
  Affairs and Emergency Preparedness
  Education: Citadel 1999 BS
Senator **Lisa Baker** (R-District 20) . . . . . . . . . . . . . . . . . . (717) 787-7428
  Counties Represented: Luzerne (part), Pike,  Dist: (570) 675-3931
  Susquehanna (part), Wayne, Wyoming  (Dallas)
  Term Expires: 2018  Fax: (717) 787-9242
  22 Dallas Shopping Center, Dallas, PA 18612  Dist: (570) 674-5037
  E-mail: lbaker@pasen.gov
  Committees: Aging and Youth; Appropriations; Consumer Protection
  and Professional Licensure; Labor and Industry; Public Health and
  Welfare; Veterans Affairs and Emergency Preparedness
  Education: Shippensburg 1983 BA
Senator **Camera C. Bartolotta** (R-District 46) . . . . . . . . . . (717) 787-1463
  Counties Represented: Beaver (part), Greene,  Dist: (724) 746-3762
  Washington (part)  Fax: (717) 772-2108
  Term Expires: 2018  Dist: (724) 746-3797
  135 Technology Drive, Suite 202, Canonsburg, PA 15317
  E-mail: cbartolotta@pasen.gov
  Committees: Community, Economic, and Recreational Development;
  Environmental Resources and Energy; Transportation; Urban Affairs
  and Housing; Veterans Affairs and Emergency Preparedness
Senator **John P. Blake** (D-District 22) . . . . . . . . . . . . . . . . (717) 787-6481
  Counties Represented: Lackawanna, Luzerne  Dist: (570) 207-2881
  (part), Monroe (part)  Fax: (717) 783-5198
  Term Expires: 2018  Dist: (570) 207-2897
  409 Lackawanna Avenue, Suite 210, Scranton, PA 18503
  E-mail: senatorblake@pasenate.com
  Committees: Appropriations; Community, Economic, and Recreational
  Development; Environmental Resources and Energy; Finance; Local
  Government; Urban Affairs and Housing
  Education: Villanova 1983 BA; Marywood Col 1987 MSW;
  Scranton 2001 MBA
Senator **Lisa M. Boscola** (D-District 18) . . . . . . . . . . . . . . (717) 787-4236
  Counties Represented: Lehigh (part), Northampton  Dist: (610) 868-8667
  (part)  (Bethlehem)
  Term Expires: 2018  Fax: (717) 783-1257
  559 Main Street, Suite 270, Bethlehem, PA 18018  Dist: (610) 861-2184
  E-mail: boscola@pasenate.com
  Committees: Consumer Protection and Professional Licensure;
  Game and Fisheries; Judiciary; Rules and Executive Nominations;
  Transportation
Senator **James R. "Jim" Brewster** (D-District 45) . . . . . . . (717) 787-5580
  Counties Represented: Allegheny (part),  Dist: (412) 380-2242
  Westmoreland (part)  Fax: (717) 772-3588
  Term Expires: 2016  Dist: (412) 380-2249
  One Monroeville Center, 3824 Northern Pike, Suite 1015,
  Monroeville, PA 15146
  E-mail: brewster@pasenate.com
  Committees: Appropriations; Banking and Insurance; Game and
  Fisheries; Law and Justice; Transportation
  Education: California U (PA) BSEd
Senator **Michele Brooks** (R-District 50) . . . . . . . . . . . . . . (717) 787-1322
  Counties Represented: Crawford, Erie (part),  Dist: (724) 588-8911
  Mercer, Warren (part)  Fax: (717) 772-0577
  Term Expires: 2018  Dist: (724) 588-5464
  Three Greenville Plaza West, 100 Hadley Road, Suite Three,
  Greenville, PA 16125
  E-mail: mbrooks@pasen.gov
  Committees: Aging and Youth; Agriculture and Rural Affairs; Local
  Government; Rules and Executive Nominations; Urban Affairs and
  Housing
Senator **Patrick M. "Pat" Browne, CPA** (R-District 16) . . . (717) 787-1349
  Counties Represented: Lehigh (part)  Dist: (610) 821-8468
  Term Expires: 2018  (Allentown)
  702 Hamilton Street, Allentown, PA 18101  Fax: (717) 772-3458
  E-mail: pbrowne@pasen.gov  Dist: (610) 821-6798
  Committees: Appropriations; Banking and Insurance; Communications
  and Technology; Education; Finance; Transportation
Senator **Jacob D. "Jake" Corman** (R-District 34) . . . . . . . (717) 787-1377
  Counties Represented: Centre, Huntingdon (part),  Dist: (814) 355-0477
  Juniata, Mifflin  (Bellefonte)
  Term Expires: 2018  Fax: (717) 772-3146
  236 Match Factory Place, Bellefonte, PA 16823  Dist: (814) 355-6046
  E-mail: jcorman@pasen.gov
  Committees: Rules and Executive Nominations

*(continued on next page)*

LEGISLATIVE BRANCH

*Senators continued*

Senator **Jay Costa, Jr.** (D-District 43) . . . . . . . . . . . . . . . . (717) 787-7683
Counties Represented: Allegheny (part)    Dist: (412) 241-6690
Term Expires: 2016    (Pittsburgh)
1501 Ardmore Boulevard, Suite 403,    Fax: (717) 783-5976
Pittsburgh, PA 15221    Dist: (412) 731-2332
E-mail: costa@pasenate.com
Committees: Intergovernmental Operations; Local Government; Rules
and Executive Nominations; Veterans Affairs and Emergency
Preparedness

Senator **Andrew E. Dinniman** (D-District 19) . . . . . . . . . . (717) 787-5709
Counties Represented: Chester (part)    Dist: (610) 692-2112
Term Expires: 2016    (West Chester)
One North Church Street, West Chester, PA 19380    Fax: (717) 787-4384
E-mail: andy@pasenate.com    Dist: (610) 436-1721
Committees: Agriculture and Rural Affairs; Education; Environmental
Resources and Energy; Public Health and Welfare; State Government;
Veterans Affairs and Emergency Preparedness
Education: Connecticut 1966 BA; Maryland 1969 MA;
Penn State 1978 EdD

Senator **John H. Eichelberger, Jr.** (R-District 30) . . . . . . . (717) 787-5490
Counties Represented: Blair, Cumberland (part),    Dist: (814) 695-8386
Franklin (part), Fulton, Huntingdon (part)    (Hollidaysburg)
Term Expires: 2018    Fax: (717) 783-5192
309 Allegheny Street, Hollidaysburg, PA 16648    Dist: (814) 695-8398
E-mail: jeichelberger@pasen.gov
Committees: Appropriations; Banking and Insurance; Education;
Finance; Judiciary; Local Government
Education: Penn State 1985 BA

Senator
**Lawrence M. "Larry" Farnese, Jr.** (D-District 1) . . . . . . (717) 787-5662
Counties Represented: Philadelphia (part)    Dist: (215) 952-3121
Term Expires: 2016    Fax: (717) 787-4531
Main Capitol, P.O. Box 203001, Room 543,    Dist: (215) 952-3155
Harrisburg, PA 17120-3001
1802 South Broad Street, Philadelphia, PA 19145
E-mail: farnese@pasenate.com
Committees: Banking and Insurance; Community, Economic, and
Recreational Development; Consumer Protection and Professional
Licensure; Judiciary; Rules and Executive Nominations

Senator **Mike Folmer** (R-District 48) . . . . . . . . . . . . . . (717) 787-5708
Counties Represented: Dauphin (part), Lebanon,    Dist: (717) 274-6735
York (part)    (Lebanon)
Term Expires: 2018    Dist: (717) 274-7702
101 Municipal Building, 400 South Eighth Street,    Fax: (717) 787-3455
Lebanon, PA 17042
E-mail: mfolmer@pasen.gov
Committees: Communications and Technology; Education;
Intergovernmental Operations; Labor and Industry; Rules and Executive
Nominations; State Government
Education: Grace Col 1978 BA

Senator **Wayne D. Fontana** (D-District 42) . . . . . . . . . . . (717) 787-5300
Counties Represented: Allegheny (part)    Dist: (412) 344-2551
Term Expires: 2018    (Pittsburgh)
932 Brookline Boulevard,    Fax: (717) 772-5484
Pittsburgh, PA 15226-2106    Dist: (412) 344-3400
E-mail: fontana@pasenate.com    (Pittsburgh)
Committees: Communications and Technology; Community, Economic,
and Recreational Development; Law and Justice; Rules and Executive
Nominations; Urban Affairs and Housing

Senator **John R. Gordner** (R-District 27) . . . . . . . . . . . . . (717) 787-8928
Counties Represented: Columbia, Luzerne (part),    Dist: (570) 784-3464
Montour, Northumberland, Snyder    (Bloomsburg)
Term Expires: 2016    Fax: (717) 787-9715
603 West Main Street, Bloomsburg, PA 17815    Dist: (570) 784-9379
E-mail: jgordner@pasen.gov
Committees: Consumer Protection and Professional Licensure;
Judiciary; Rules and Executive Nominations; State Government;
Transportation

Senator **Stewart J. Greenleaf, Esq.** (R-District 12) . . . . . (717) 787-6599
Counties Represented: Bucks (part), Montgomery    Dist: (215) 657-7700
(part)    Fax: (717) 783-7328
Term Expires: 2018    Dist: (215) 657-1885
711 York Road, Willow Grove, PA 19090
E-mail: sgreenleaf@pasen.gov
Committees: Appropriations; Consumer Protection and Professional
Licensure; Intergovernmental Operations; Judiciary; Urban Affairs and
Housing
Education: Pennsylvania 1961 BA; Toledo 1966 JD

Senator **Arthur L. "Art" Haywood III** (D-District 4) . . . . . (717) 787-1427
Counties Represented: Montgomery (part),    Dist: (215) 517-1434
Philadelphia (part)    Fax: (717) 772-0572
Term Expires: 2018    Dist: (215) 517-1439
E-mail: senatorhaywood@pasenate.com
Committees: Aging and Youth; Communications and Technology;
Consumer Protection and Professional Licensure; Finance; Judiciary;
Public Health and Welfare; Urban Affairs and Housing

Senator **Vincent J. Hughes** (D-District 7) . . . . . . . . . . . . (717) 787-7112
Counties Represented: Montgomery (part),    Dist: (215) 879-7777
Philadelphia (part)    (Philadelphia)
Term Expires: 2016    Fax: (717) 772-0579
The Parkside Lofts, 4950 Parkside Avenue,    Dist: (215) 879-7778
Suite 300, Philadelphia, PA 19131
E-mail: hughes@pasenate.com
Committees: Appropriations; Intergovernmental Operations; Rules and
Executive Nominations

Senator **Scott E. Hutchinson** (R-District 21) . . . . . . . . . . . (717) 787-9684
Counties Represented: Butler (part), Clarion,    Dist: (814) 677-6345
Forest, Venango, Warren (part)    Fax: (717) 787-6088
Term Expires: 2016    Dist: (814) 677-6331
302 Seneca Street, Oil City, PA 16301
110 E. Diamond Street, Butler, PA 16001-5999
E-mail: shutchinson@pasen.gov
Committees: Environmental Resources and Energy; Finance; Local
Government; Public Health and Welfare; Veterans Affairs and
Emergency Preparedness
Education: Wharton 1983 BS

Senator **Thomas H. "Tom" Killion** (R-District 9) . . . . . . . (717) 787-4712
Counties Represented: Chester (part), Delaware    Dist: (610) 358-5183
(part)    Fax: (717) 783-7490
Term Expires: 2016    Fax: (610) 358-5184
E-mail: tkillion@pasen.gov

Senator **Shirley M. Kitchen** (D-District 3) . . . . . . . . . . . . . (717) 787-6735
Counties Represented: Philadelphia (part)    Dist: (215) 227-6161
Term Expires: 2016    (Philadelphia)
1701 West Lehigh Avenue, Suite 104,    Fax: (717) 772-0581
Philadelphia, PA 19132
E-mail: kitchen@pasenate.com
Committees: Agriculture and Rural Affairs; Public Health and Welfare;
Transportation; Urban Affairs and Housing
Education: Antioch U 1979 BA

Senator **Daylin Leach** (D-District 17) . . . . . . . . . . . . . . . . (717) 787-5544
Counties Represented: Delaware (part),    Dist: (610) 768-4200
Montgomery (part)    Fax: (610) 705-7741
Term Expires: 2016    Dist: (610) 768-4204
184 Main Capitol Building, P.O. Box 203017,
Harrisburg, PA 17120-3017
601 South Henderson Road, Suite 208, King of Prussia, PA 19406
E-mail: dleach@pasenate.com
Committees: Appropriations; Education; Environmental Resources and
Energy; Judiciary; Labor and Industry; State Government
Education: Temple 1983 BS; Houston 1986 JD

Senator **Thomas J. McGarrigle** (R-District 26) . . . . . . . . . (717) 787-1350
Counties Represented: Chester (part), Delaware    Dist: (610) 853-4100
(part)    Fax: (717) 787-0196
Term Expires: 2018    Dist: (610) 853-4136
5307 Township Line Road, Drexel Hill, PA 19026
E-mail: tmcgarrigle@pasen.gov
Committees: Aging and Youth; Banking and Insurance; Community,
Economic, and Recreational Development; Intergovernmental
Operations; Local Government
Education: Villanova 1975 BS, 1978 JD

Senator
**Charles T. "Chuck" McIlhinney, Jr.** (R-District 10) . . . . (717) 787-7305
Counties Represented: Bucks (part)    Dist: (215) 489-5000
Term Expires: 2018    (Doylestown)
22 South Main Street, Suite 220,    Fax: (717) 783-5962
Doylestown, PA 18901    Dist: (215) 489-5200
E-mail: cmcilhinney@pasen.gov
Committees: Game and Fisheries; Labor and Industry; Law and Justice;
Rules and Executive Nominations; State Government

Senator **Robert B. "Bob" Mensch** (R-District 24) . . . . . . . (717) 787-3110
Counties Represented: Berks (part), Bucks (part),    Dist: (215) 541-2388
Montgomery (part)    Fax: (717) 787-8004
Term Expires: 2018    Dist: (215) 541-2387
404 Main Street, Suite A, Pennsburg, PA 18073
E-mail: bmensch@pasen.gov
Committees: Aging and Youth; Appropriations; Game and Fisheries;
Public Health and Welfare; Veterans Affairs and Emergency
Preparedness

Senator **John C. Rafferty, Jr.** (R-District 44) . . . . . . . . . . . (717) 787-1398
  Counties Represented: Berks (part), Chester (part),    Dist: (610) 831-8830
  Montgomery (part)    (Collegeville)
  Term Expires: 2018    Fax: (717) 783-4587
  3818 Germantown Pike, Collegeville, PA 19426    Dist: (610) 831-8837
  E-mail: jrafferty@pasen.gov
  Committees: Appropriations; Consumer Protection and Professional
  Licensure; Judiciary; Law and Justice; Transportation
  Education: Pittsburgh 1975 BA; Beaver 1984 MA; Temple 1988 JD

Senator **Guy Reschenthaler** (R-District 37) . . . . . . . . . . . . (717) 787-5839
  Counties Represented: Allegheny (part), Washington (part)
  E-mail: greschenthaler@pasen.gov
  Committees: Community, Economic, and Recreational Development;
  Game and Fisheries; Intergovernmental Operations; Judiciary; Law and
  Justice

Senator **John P. Sabatina, Jr.** (D-District 5) . . . . . . . . . . . (717) 787-9608
  Counties Represented: Philadelphia (part)    Dist: (215) 281-2539
  Term Expires: 2016    Fax: (717) 772-2162
  12361 Academy Road, Philadelphia, PA 19154    Dist: (215) 281-2798
  E-mail: jsabatina@pasen.gov
  Committees: Aging and Youth; Communications and Technology;
  Judiciary; Labor and Industry; Veterans Affairs and Emergency
  Preparedness
  Education: Widener 1997 JD

Senator **Joseph B. Scarnati III** (R-District 25) . . . . . . . . . . (717) 787-7084
  Counties Represented: Cameron, Clearfield (part),    Dist: (814) 265-2030
  Clinton, Elk, Jefferson, McKean    (Warren)
  Term Expires: 2016    Fax: (717) 772-2755
  315 Second Avenue, Suite 203, Warren, PA 16365    Dist: (814) 265-2040
  E-mail: jscarnati@pasen.gov

Senator **Mario M. Scavello** (R-District 40) . . . . . . . . . . . . (717) 787-6123
  Counties Represented: Monroe (part), Northampton    Dist: (570) 620-4326
  (part)    Fax: (717) 772-3695
  Term Expires: 2018    Dist: (570) 620-4379
  2989 Route 611, Unit 103, Tannersville, PA 18372
  E-mail: mscavello@pasen.gov
  Committees: Appropriations; Consumer Protection and Professional
  Licensure; Game and Fisheries; Labor and Industry; Urban Affairs and
  Housing

Senator **Judith L. "Judy" Schwank** (D-District 11) . . . . . . (717) 787-8925
  Counties Represented: Berks (part)    Dist: (610) 929-2151
  Term Expires: 2016    Fax: (717) 772-0578
  1940 North 13th Street, Suite 232,    Dist: (610) 929-2576
  Reading, PA 19604
  E-mail: senatorschwank@pasenate.com
  Committees: Aging and Youth; Agriculture and Rural Affairs;
  Appropriations; Public Health and Welfare; State Government
  Education: Penn State 1982 MEd

Senator **Lloyd K. Smucker** (R-District 13) . . . . . . . . . . . . (717) 787-6535
  Counties Represented: Lancaster (part)    Dist: (717) 397-1309
  Term Expires: 2016    Fax: (717) 299-7798
  185 Main Capitol, Harrisburg, PA 17120-3013
  44 North Christian Street, Suite 100, Lancaster, PA 17602
  E-mail: lsmucker@pasen.gov
  Committees: Appropriations; Education; Intergovernmental Operations;
  Labor and Industry; Local Government; Public Health and Welfare
  Education: Lebanon Valley; Franklin & Marshall

Senator **Patrick J. Stefano** (R-District 32) . . . . . . . . . . . . (717) 787-7175
  Counties Represented: Fayette, Somerset,    Dist: (724) 626-1611
  Westmoreland (part)    Fax: (724) 626-1665
  Term Expires: 2018
  171 West Crawford Avenue, Second Floor, Connellsville, PA 15425
  E-mail: pstefano@pasen.gov
  Committees: Community, Economic, and Recreational Development;
  Game and Fisheries; Rules and Executive Nominations; State
  Government; Transportation

Senator **Christine M. Tartaglione** (D-District 2) . . . . . . . . (717) 787-1141
  Counties Represented: Philadelphia (part)    Dist: (215) 533-0440
  Term Expires: 2018    (Philadelphia)
  1061 Bridge Street, Philadelphia, PA 19124    Fax: (717) 787-7439
  E-mail: tartaglione@pasenate.com    Dist: (215) 560-2627
  Committees: Appropriations; Banking and    (Philadelphia)
  Insurance; Labor and Industry; Law and Justice; Veterans Affairs and
  Emergency Preparedness
  Education: Peirce Col 1980

Senator **Robert F. "Rob" Teplitz** (D-District 15) . . . . . . . . (717) 787-6801
  Counties Represented: Dauphin (part), Perry    Dist: (717) 232-2937
  Term Expires: 2016    Fax: (717) 783-3722
  46 Kline Village, Harrisburg, PA 17104    Dist: (717) 232-2656
  916 B Park Plaza, Halifax, PA 17032
  E-mail: rteplitz@pasenate.com
  Committees: Agriculture and Rural Affairs; Appropriations;
  Community, Economic, and Recreational Development; Education;
  Finance; Local Government
  Education: Franklin & Marshall BA; Cornell JD

Senator **Robert M. Tomlinson** (R-District 6) . . . . . . . . . . . (717) 787-5072
  Counties Represented: Bucks (part)    Dist: (215) 638-1784
  Term Expires: 2018    Fax: (215) 772-2991
  3207 Street Road, Bensalem, PA 19020    Dist: (215) 638-1786
  E-mail: rtomlinson@pasen.gov
  Committees: Community, Economic, and Recreational Development;
  Consumer Protection and Professional Licensure; Education; Rules and
  Executive Nominations; Transportation
  Education: West Chester 1970 BS

Senator **Patricia H. Vance** (R-District 31) . . . . . . . . . . . . . (717) 787-8524
  Counties Represented: Cumberland (part), York    Dist: (717) 975-1985
  (part)    (Camp Hill)
  Term Expires: 2016    Fax: (717) 772-0576
  3806 Market Street, Camp Hill, PA 17011    Dist: (717) 975-2247
  E-mail: vance@pasen.gov
  Committees: Appropriations; Banking and Insurance; Communications
  and Technology; Consumer Protection and Professional Licensure;
  Finance; Public Health and Welfare

Senator **Elder Vogel, Jr.** (R-District 47) . . . . . . . . . . . . . . (717) 787-3076
  Counties Represented: Beaver (part), Butler (part),    Dist: (724) 774-0444
  Lawrence    Fax: (717) 772-2756
  Term Expires: 2016    Dist: (724) 773-7384
  457 Main Capitol Building, P.O. Box 203047,
  Harrisburg, PA 17120-3047
  488 Adams Street, Rochester, PA 15074-1940
  E-mail: evogel@pasen.gov
  Committees: Agriculture and Rural Affairs; Appropriations; Banking
  and Insurance; Communications and Technology; Environmental
  Resources and Energy; Local Government

Senator **Randy Vulakovich** (R-District 38) . . . . . . . . . . . . (717) 787-6538
  Counties Represented: Allegheny (part)    Dist: (412) 487-6600
  Term Expires: 2018    Fax: (717) 787-8625
  300 Wetzel Road, Suite 302, Glenshaw, PA 15116    Dist: (412) 487-6607
  E-mail: rvulakovich@pasen.gov
  Committees: Aging and Youth; Appropriations; Communications and
  Technology; Judiciary; Transportation; Veterans Affairs and Emergency
  Preparedness

Senator **Scott Wagner** (R-District 28) . . . . . . . . . . . . . . . . (717) 787-3817
  Counties Represented: York (part)    Dist: (717) 846-2828
  Term Expires: 2018    Fax: (717) 783-1900
  218 North George Street, York, PA 17401    Dist: (717) 852-8478
  E-mail: swagner@pasen.gov
  Committees: Appropriations; Intergovernmental Operations; Labor and
  Industry; Transportation; Urban Affairs and Housing

Senator **Kim L. Ward** (R-District 39) . . . . . . . . . . . . . . . . . (717) 787-6063
  Counties Represented: Westmoreland (part)    Dist: (724) 537-7650
  Term Expires: 2016    Dist: (724) 600-7002
  Main Capitol, P.O. Box 203039, Room168,    Fax: (717) 772-0580
  Harrisburg, PA 17120-3039    Dist: (724) 600-7008
  766 East Pittsburgh Street, Suite 101,    Dist: (724) 537-7696
  Greensburg, PA 15601
  E-mail: kward@pasen.gov
  Committees: Agriculture and Rural Affairs; Appropriations; Banking
  and Insurance; Community, Economic, and Recreational Development;
  Environmental Resources and Energy; Finance

Senator **Donald C. White** (R-District 41) . . . . . . . . . . . . . . (717) 787-8724
  Counties Represented: Armstrong, Butler (part),    Dist: (724) 357-0151
  Indiana, Westmoreland (part)    (Indiana)
  Term Expires: 2016    Fax: (717) 772-1589
  618 Philadelphia Street, Indiana, PA 15701    Dist: (724) 357-0148
  E-mail: dwhite@pasen.gov
  Committees: Banking and Insurance; Environmental Resources and
  Energy; Law and Justice; Rules and Executive Nominations; State
  Government
  Education: Juniata 1972; Indiana (PA) 1977

*(continued on next page)*

**LEGISLATIVE BRANCH**

**Senators** *continued*

Senator **Sean Wiley** (D-District 49) . . . . . . . . . . . . . . . . . (717) 787-8927
Counties Represented: Erie (part)  Dist: (814) 453-2515
Term Expires: 2016  Fax: (717) 772-1588
1314 Griswold Plaza, Suite 100, Erie, PA 16501  Dist: (814) 871-4640
E-mail: swiley@pasenate.com
Committees: Aging and Youth; Appropriations; Banking and Insurance;
Community, Economic, and Recreational Development; Game and
Fisheries; Intergovernmental Operations
Education: DeVry U 1993 BS

Senator **Anthony Hardy Williams** (D-District 8) . . . . . . . . . (717) 787-5970
Counties Represented: Delaware (part), Philadelphia  Dist: (215) 492-2980
(part)  (Philadelphia)
Term Expires: 2018  Fax: (717) 772-0574
2901 Island Avenue, Suite 100,  Dist: (215) 492-2990
Philadelphia, PA 19153
E-mail: williams@pasenate.com
Committees: Communications and Technology; Education; Law and
Justice; Rules and Executive Nominations; State Government

Senator **John N. Wozniak** (D-District 35) . . . . . . . . . . . . . (717) 787-5400
Counties Represented: Bedford, Cambria, Clearfield  Dist: (814) 266-2277
(part)  (Johnstown)
Term Expires: 2016  Fax: (717) 772-0573
2307 Bedford Street, Johnstown, PA 15904  Dist: (814) 266-0057
E-mail: wozniak@pasenate.com
Committees: Appropriations; Consumer Protection and Professional
Licensure; Finance; Game and Fisheries; Intergovernmental Operations;
Transportation
Education: Pittsburgh 1978 BA

Senator **Gene Yaw** (R-District 23) . . . . . . . . . . . . . . . . . . . (717) 787-3280
Counties Represented: Bradford, Lycoming,  Dist: (570) 322-6457
Sullivan, Susquehanna (part), Union  Dist: (570) 265-7448
Term Expires: 2016  Fax: (717) 772-0575
457 Main Capitol, Senate Box 203023,  Dist: (570) 327-3703
Harrisburg, PA 17120-3023
330 Pine Street, Suite 204, Williamsport, PA 17701
1 Progress Plaza, Suite 13, Towanda, PA 18848
E-mail: gyaw@pasen.gov
Committees: Agriculture and Rural Affairs; Banking and Insurance;
Environmental Resources and Energy; Judiciary; Law and Justice;
Rules and Executive Nominations
Education: Lycoming 1970 BA; Washington College of Law 1973 JD

Senator **John T. Yudichak** (D-District 14) . . . . . . . . . . . . . (717) 787-7105
Counties Represented: Carbon, Luzerne (part)  Dist: (570) 883-4690
Term Expires: 2018  Fax: (717) 783-4141
1701 Wyoming Avenue, Exeter, PA 18643  Dist: (570) 883-4694
E-mail: yudichak@pasenate.com
Committees: Consumer Protection and Professional Licensure;
Environmental Resources and Energy; Labor and Industry; Local
Government

# Senate Standing Committees

## Aging and Youth

**Majority Members**
Michele Brooks (R-50) *Chair*
Randy Vulakovich (R-38)
*Vice Chair*
David G. "Dave" Argall (R-29)
Lisa Baker (R-20)
Thomas J. McGarrigle (R-26)
Robert B. "Bob" Mensch (R-24)

**Minority Members**
Arthur L. "Art" Haywood III (D-4)
*Minority Chair*
John P. Sabatina, Jr. (D-5)
Judith L. "Judy" Schwank (D-11)
Sean Wiley (D-49)

## Agriculture and Rural Affairs

**Majority Members**
Elder Vogel, Jr. (R-47) *Chair*
Michele Brooks (R-50) *Vice Chair*
David G. "Dave" Argall (R-29)
Ryan P. Aument (R-36)
Kim L. Ward (R-39)
Gene Yaw (R-23)

**Minority Members**
Judith L. "Judy" Schwank (D-11)
*Minority Chair*
Andrew E. Dinniman (D-19)
Shirley M. Kitchen (D-3)
Robert F. "Rob" Teplitz (D-15)

# Appropriations

**Majority Members**
Patrick M. "Pat" Browne (R-16)
*Chair*
Kim L. Ward (R-39) *Vice Chair*
David G. "Dave" Argall (R-29)
Lisa Baker (R-20)
John H. Eichelberger, Jr. (R-30)
Stewart J. Greenleaf (R-12)
Robert B. "Bob" Mensch (R-24)
John C. Rafferty, Jr. (R-44)
Mario M. Scavello (R-40)
Lloyd K. Smucker (R-13)
Patricia H. Vance (R-31)
Elder Vogel, Jr. (R-47)
Randy Vulakovich (R-38)
Scott Wagner (R-28)

**Minority Members**
Vincent J. Hughes (D-7)
*Minority Chair*
John P. Blake (D-22)
*Minority Vice Chair*
James R. "Jim" Brewster (D-45)
Daylin Leach (D-17)
Judith L. "Judy" Schwank (D-11)
Christine M. Tartaglione (D-2)
Robert F. "Rob" Teplitz (D-15)
Sean Wiley (D-49)
John N. Wozniak (D-35)

# Banking and Insurance

**Majority Members**
Donald C. White (R-41) *Chair*
John H. Eichelberger, Jr. (R-30)
*Vice Chair*
Patrick M. "Pat" Browne (R-16)
Thomas J. McGarrigle (R-26)
Patricia H. Vance (R-31)
Elder Vogel, Jr. (R-47)
Kim L. Ward (R-39)
Gene Yaw (R-23)

**Minority Members**
Sean Wiley (D-49) *Minority Chair*
James R. "Jim" Brewster (D-45)
Lawrence M. "Larry" Farnese, Jr.
(D-1)
Christine M. Tartaglione (D-2)

# Communications and Technology

**Majority Members**
Ryan P. Aument (R-36) *Chair*
Patricia H. Vance (R-31) *Vice Chair*
Patrick M. "Pat" Browne (R-16)
Mike Folmer (R-48)
Elder Vogel, Jr. (R-47)
Randy Vulakovich (R-38)

**Minority Members**
John P. Sabatina, Jr. (D-5)
*Minority Chair*
Wayne D. Fontana (D-42)
Arthur L. "Art" Haywood III (D-4)
Anthony Hardy Williams (D-8)

# Community, Economic, and Recreational Development

**Majority Members**
Kim L. Ward (R-39) *Chair*
Patrick J. Stefano (R-32) *Vice Chair*
Richard L. Alloway II (R-33)
David G. "Dave" Argall (R-29)
Camera C. Bartolotta (R-46)
Thomas J. McGarrigle (R-26)
Guy Reschenthaler (R-37)
Robert M. Tomlinson (R-6)

**Minority Members**
Lawrence M. "Larry"
Farnese, Jr. (D-1)
*Minority Chair*
John P. Blake (D-22)
Wayne D. Fontana (D-42)
Robert F. "Rob" Teplitz (D-15)
Sean Wiley (D-49)

# Consumer Protection and Professional Licensure

**Majority Members**
Robert M. Tomlinson (R-6) *Chair*
Mario M. Scavello (R-40)
*Vice Chair*
Lisa Baker (R-20)
John R. Gordner (R-27)
Stewart J. Greenleaf (R-12)
John C. Rafferty, Jr. (R-44)
Patricia H. Vance (R-31)

**Minority Members**
Lisa M. Boscola (D-18)
*Minority Chair*
Lawrence M. "Larry" Farnese, Jr.
(D-1)
Arthur L. "Art" Haywood III (D-4)
John N. Wozniak (D-35)
John T. Yudichak (D-14)

# Education

**Majority Members**
Lloyd K. Smucker (R-13) *Chair*
Mike Folmer (R-48) *Vice Chair*
Ryan P. Aument (R-36)
Patrick M. "Pat" Browne (R-16)
John H. Eichelberger, Jr. (R-30)
Robert M. Tomlinson (R-6)

**Minority Members**
Andrew E. Dinniman (D-19)
*Minority Chair*
Daylin Leach (D-17)
Robert F. "Rob" Teplitz (D-15)
Anthony Hardy Williams (D-8)

## Environmental Resources and Energy

**Majority Members**
Gene Yaw (R-23) *Chair*
Camera C. Bartolotta (R-46)
 *Vice Chair*
Scott E. Hutchinson (R-21)
Elder Vogel, Jr. (R-47)
Kim L. Ward (R-39)
Donald C. White (R-41)

**Minority Members**
John T. Yudichak (D-14)
 *Minority Chair*
John P. Blake (D-22)
Andrew E. Dinniman (D-19)
Daylin Leach (D-17)

## Finance

**Majority Members**
John H. Eichelberger, Jr. (R-30)
 *Chair*
Scott E. Hutchinson (R-21)
 *Vice Chair*
Ryan P. Aument (R-36)
Patrick M. "Pat" Browne (R-16)
Patricia H. Vance (R-31)
Kim L. Ward (R-39)

**Minority Members**
John P. Blake (D-22)
 *Minority Chair*
Arthur L. "Art" Haywood III (D-4)
Robert F. "Rob" Teplitz (D-15)
John N. Wozniak (D-35)

## Game and Fisheries

**Majority Members**
Mario M. Scavello (R-40) *Chair*
Charles T. "Chuck"
 McIlhinney, Jr. (R-10)
 *Vice Chair*
Richard L. Alloway II (R-33)
Robert B. "Bob" Mensch (R-24)
Guy Reschenthaler (R-37)
Patrick J. Stefano (R-32)

**Minority Members**
James R. "Jim" Brewster (D-45)
 *Minority Chair*
Lisa M. Boscola (D-18)
Sean Wiley (D-49)
John N. Wozniak (D-35)

## Intergovernmental Operations

**Majority Members**
Thomas J. McGarrigle (R-26) *Chair*
Stewart J. Greenleaf (R-12)
 *Vice Chair*
Mike Folmer (R-48)
Guy Reschenthaler (R-37)
Lloyd K. Smucker (R-13)
Scott Wagner (R-28)

**Minority Members**
Sean Wiley (D-49) *Minority Chair*
Jay Costa, Jr. (D-43)
Vincent J. Hughes (D-7)
John N. Wozniak (D-35)

## Judiciary

**Majority Members**
Stewart J. Greenleaf (R-12) *Chair*
John C. Rafferty, Jr. (R-44)
 *Vice Chair*
Richard L. Alloway II (R-33)
John H. Eichelberger, Jr. (R-30)
John R. Gordner (R-27)
Guy Reschenthaler (R-37)
Randy Vulakovich (R-38)
Gene Yaw (R-23)

**Minority Members**
Daylin Leach (D-17)
 *Minority Chair*
Lisa M. Boscola (D-18)
Lawrence M. "Larry" Farnese, Jr.
 (D-1)
Arthur L. "Art" Haywood III (D-4)
John P. Sabatina, Jr. (D-5)

## Labor and Industry

**Majority Members**
Lisa Baker (R-20) *Chair*
Scott Wagner (R-28) *Vice Chair*
Mike Folmer (R-48)
Charles T. "Chuck" McIlhinney, Jr.
 (R-10)
Mario M. Scavello (R-40)
Lloyd K. Smucker (R-13)

**Minority Members**
Christine M. Tartaglione (D-2)
 *Minority Chair*
Daylin Leach (D-17)
John P. Sabatina, Jr. (D-5)
John T. Yudichak (D-14)

## Law and Justice

**Majority Members**
Charles T. "Chuck"
 McIlhinney, Jr. (R-10)
 *Chair*
Richard L. Alloway II (R-33)
 *Vice Chair*
John C. Rafferty, Jr. (R-44)
Guy Reschenthaler (R-37)
Donald C. White (R-41)
Gene Yaw (R-23)

**Minority Members**
James R. "Jim" Brewster (D-45)
 *Minority Chair*
Wayne D. Fontana (D-42)
Christine M. Tartaglione (D-2)
Anthony Hardy Williams (D-8)

## Local Government

**Majority Members**
Scott E. Hutchinson (R-21) *Chair*
Thomas J. McGarrigle (R-26)
 *Vice Chair*
Michele Brooks (R-50)
John H. Eichelberger, Jr. (R-30)
Lloyd K. Smucker (R-13)
Elder Vogel, Jr. (R-47)

**Minority Members**
Robert F. "Rob" Teplitz (D-15)
 *Minority Chair*
John P. Blake (D-22)
Jay Costa, Jr. (D-43)
John T. Yudichak (D-14)

## Public Health and Welfare

**Majority Members**
Patricia H. Vance (R-31) *Chair*
Ryan P. Aument (R-36) *Vice Chair*
Lisa Baker (R-20)
Scott E. Hutchinson (R-21)
Robert B. "Bob" Mensch (R-24)
Lloyd K. Smucker (R-13)

**Minority Members**
Shirley M. Kitchen (D-3)
 *Minority Chair*
Andrew E. Dinniman (D-19)
Arthur L. "Art" Haywood III (D-4)
Judith L. "Judy" Schwank (D-11)

## Rules and Executive Nominations

**Majority Members**
Jacob D. "Jake" Corman (R-34)
 *Chair*
John R. Gordner (R-27) *Vice Chair*
Richard L. Alloway II (R-33)
Michele Brooks (R-50)
Mike Folmer (R-48)
Charles T. "Chuck" McIlhinney, Jr.
 (R-10)
Patrick J. Stefano (R-32)
Robert M. Tomlinson (R-6)
Donald C. White (R-41)
Gene Yaw (R-23)

**Minority Members**
Jay Costa, Jr. (D-43) *Minority Chair*
Lisa M. Boscola (D-18)
Lawrence M. "Larry" Farnese, Jr.
 (D-1)
Wayne D. Fontana (D-42)
Vincent J. Hughes (D-7)
Anthony Hardy Williams (D-8)

## State Government

**Majority Members**
Mike Folmer (R-48) *Chair*
John R. Gordner (R-27) *Vice Chair*
Richard L. Alloway II (R-33)
Charles T. "Chuck" McIlhinney, Jr.
 (R-10)
Patrick J. Stefano (R-32)
Donald C. White (R-41)

**Minority Members**
Anthony Hardy Williams (D-8)
 *Minority Chair*
Andrew E. Dinniman (D-19)
Daylin Leach (D-17)
Judith L. "Judy" Schwank (D-11)

## Transportation

**Majority Members**
John C. Rafferty, Jr. (R-44) *Chair*
Robert M. Tomlinson (R-6)
 *Vice Chair*
Camera C. Bartolotta (R-46)
Patrick M. "Pat" Browne (R-16)
John R. Gordner (R-27)
Patrick J. Stefano (R-32)
Randy Vulakovich (R-38)
Scott Wagner (R-28)

**Minority Members**
John N. Wozniak (D-35)
 *Minority Chair*
Lisa M. Boscola (D-18)
James R. "Jim" Brewster (D-45)
Shirley M. Kitchen (D-3)

## Urban Affairs and Housing

**Majority Members**
Scott Wagner (R-28) *Chair*
David G. "Dave" Argall (R-29)
 *Vice Chair*
Camera C. Bartolotta (R-46)
Michele Brooks (R-50)
Stewart J. Greenleaf (R-12)
Mario M. Scavello (R-40)

**Minority Members**
Wayne D. Fontana (D-42)
 *Minority Chair*
John P. Blake (D-22)
Arthur L. "Art" Haywood III (D-4)
Shirley M. Kitchen (D-3)

## Veterans Affairs and Emergency Preparedness

**Majority Members**
Randy Vulakovich (R-38) *Chair*
Robert B. "Bob" Mensch (R-24)
 *Vice Chair*
Ryan P. Aument (R-36)
Lisa Baker (R-20)
Camera C. Bartolotta (R-46)
Scott E. Hutchinson (R-21)

**Minority Members**
Jay Costa, Jr. (D-43) *Minority Chair*
Andrew E. Dinniman (D-19)
John P. Sabatina, Jr. (D-5)
Christine M. Tartaglione (D-2)

**LEGISLATIVE BRANCH**

# Pennsylvania House of Representatives

Capitol Building, House Box 202220, Harrisburg, PA 17120-2020
Tel: (717) 787-2372 Fax: (717) 787-4990

Speaker of the House **Mike Turzai** (R) . . . . . . . . . . . . . . . . (717) 772-9943
Majority Floor Leader **David "Dave" Reed** (R) . . . . . . . . . (717) 705-7173
Majority Whip **Bryan Cutler** (R) . . . . . . . . . . . . . . . . . . . (717) 783-6424
   Education: Lebanon Valley 2001 BS; Widener 2006 JD
Majority Caucus Chairman **Sandra J. Major** (R) . . . . . . . . (717) 783-2910
Majority Caucus Secretary **Donna Oberlander** (R) . . . . . . . (717) 772-9908
   Education: Clarion 1991 BA
Majority Caucus Administrator **Brian L. Ellis** (R) . . . . . . . (724) 283-5852
Majority Policy Committee Chairman
   **Kerry A. Benninghoff** (R) . . . . . . . . . . . . . . . . . . . . (717) 783-1918
Minority Floor Leader **Frank Dermody** (D) . . . . . . . . . . . . (717) 787-3566
   Education: Columbia 1973 BA; Indiana 1982 JD
Minority Whip **Michael K. Hanna, Sr.** (D) . . . . . . . . . . . . (717) 772-2283
   Education: Lock Haven 1977 BA; Pittsburgh 1980 JD
Minority Caucus Chairman **Dan B. Frankel** (D) . . . . . . . . . (717) 705-1875
   Education: Kenyon 1978 BA
Minority Caucus Secretary **Rosita C. Youngblood** (D) . . . . (717) 787-7727
   Education: Antioch U 1985 BA
Minority Caucus Administrator **Neal P. Goodman** (D) . . . . (717) 787-2798
Minority Policy Committee Chairman
   **P. Michael Sturla** (D) . . . . . . . . . . . . . . . . . . . . . . (717) 787-3555
   Education: Kansas 1979 BS
Parliamentarian **Clancy Myer** . . . . . . . . . . . . . . . . . . . . . (717) 787-8126
   Education: Penn State 1971 BS; Dickinson Law 1974 JD
Chief Clerk of the House **Dave Reddecliff** . . . . . . . . . . . . . (717) 787-2372

# Representatives

**Party Affiliation Statistics:** Republicans: 118, Democrats: 84,
Vacancies: 1

Representative **Leslie Acosta** (D-District 197) . . . . . . . . . . (717) 772-2004
   Counties Represented: Philadelphia (part)   Dist: (215) 457-5281
   Term Expires: 2016   Fax: (717) 780-4784
   511 West Courtland Street, Suite 197,   Dist: (215) 457-5285
   Philadelphia, PA 19140
   E-mail: lacosta@pahouse.net
   Committees: Appropriations; Children and Youth; Finance; Human
   Services; State Government
   Education: U Phoenix 2003 MBA
Representative **William F. "Bill" Adolph, Jr.**
   (R-District 165) . . . . . . . . . . . . . . . . . . . . (717) 787-1248 (Harrisburg)
   Counties Represented: Delaware (part)   Dist: (610) 544-9878
   Term Expires: 2016   (Springfield)
   920 W. Sproul Rd., Springfield, PA 19064   Fax: (717) 705-1835
   E-mail: wadolph@pahousegop.com   (Harrisburg)
   Committees: Appropriations; Committee on   Dist: (610) 338-2294
   Committees; Rules   (Springfield)
   Education: Christian Brothers U 1971 BA
Representative
   **Matthew E. Baker** (R-District 68) . . . . . . . . (717) 772-5371 (Harrisburg)
   Counties Represented: Bradford (part), Potter   Dist: (570) 724-1390
   (part), Tioga   (Wellsboro)
   Term Expires: 2016   Fax: (717) 705-1850
   74 Main St., Wellsboro, PA 16901   (Harrisburg)
   E-mail: mbaker@pahousegop.com   Dist: (570) 724-2168
   Committees: Health; Rules   (Wellsboro)
   Education: Elmira 1988 BS
Representative
   **Bryan E. Barbin, JD** (D-District 71) . . . . . . . (717) 783-1491 (Harrisburg)
   Counties Represented: Cambria (part), Somerset   Dist: (814) 536-9818
   (part)   (Johnstown)
   Term Expires: 2016   Tel: (814) 262-6112
   413 Main Street, Johnstown, PA 15901-1880   Fax: (717) 705-7001
   E-mail: bbarbin@pahouse.net   (Harrisburg)
   Committees: Environmental Resources and Energy;   Dist: (814) 539-8429
   Judiciary; Transportation; Veterans Affairs and   (Johnstown)
   Emergency Preparedness
   Education: Richmond 1979 BA; Pittsburgh 1982 JD

Representative
**Stephen E. Barrar** (R-District 160) . . . . . . . (717) 783-3038 (Harrisburg)
   Counties Represented: Chester (part), Delaware   Dist: (610) 485-7606
   (part)   (Boothwyn)
   Term Expires: 2016   Fax: (717) 787-7604
   3358 Chichester Avenue, Suite 13,   (Harrisburg)
   Boothwyn, PA 19061   Dist: (610) 485-8277
   E-mail: parep160@aol.com   (Boothwyn)
   Committees: Consumer Affairs; Veterans Affairs and Emergency
   Preparedness
Representative
**Kerry A. Benninghoff** (R-District 171) . . . . . (717) 783-1918 (Harrisburg)
   Counties Represented: Centre (part), Mifflin (part)   Dist: (814) 355-1300
   Term Expires: 2016   (Bellefonte)
   209 S. Allegheny St., Suite B, Bellefonte, PA 16823   Fax: (717) 260-6528
   E-mail: kbenning@pahousegop.com   (Harrisburg)
   Committees: Finance   Dist: (814) 355-3523
      (Bellefonte)
Representative **Ryan A. Bizzarro** (D-District 3) . . . . . . . . . (717) 772-2297
   Counties Represented: Erie (part)   Fax: (717) 780-4767
   Term Expires: 2016
   1101 Peninsula Drive, Erie, PA 16505
   E-mail: repbizzarro@pahouse.net
   Committees: Consumer Affairs; Insurance; Judiciary; Veterans Affairs
   and Emergency Preparedness
   Education: Edinboro 2008 BA; Gannon 2010 MPA
Representative **Stephen Bloom** (R-District 199) . . . . . . . . . (717) 772-2280
   Counties Represented: Cumberland (part)   Dist: (717) 249-1990
   Term Expires: 2016   Fax: (717) 249-8775
   1227 Ritner Highway, Carlisle, PA 17013
   E-mail: sbloom@pahousegop.com
   Committees: Agriculture and Rural Affairs; Environmental Resources
   and Energy; Finance; Labor and Industry
   Education: Penn State 1983 BS, 1987 JD
Representative
**Karen Boback, PhD** (R-District 117) . . . . . . . (717) 787-1117 (Harrisburg)
   Counties Represented: Lackawanna (part), Luzerne   Dist: (570) 868-7780
   (part), Wyoming   (Mountain Top)
   Term Expires: 2016   Dist: (570) 477-3752
   7844 Blue Ridge Trail, Mountain Top, PA 18707   (Sweet Valley)
   P.O. Box 330, Sweet Valley, PA 18656   Fax: (717) 705-1889
   E-mail: kboback@pahousegop.com   (Harrisburg)
   Committees: Agriculture and Rural Affairs;   Dist: (570) 868-4658
   Appropriations; Tourism and Recreational   (Mountain Top)
   Development; Veterans Affairs and Emergency   Dist: (570) 477-3468
   Preparedness   (Sweet Valley)
   Education: Col Misericordia BSElEd, MSE; Marywood U MSE;
   Pennsylvania PhD
Representative **Kevin J. Boyle** (D-District 172) . . . . . . . . . (717) 783-4944
   Counties Represented: Montgomery (part),   Dist: (215) 331-2600
   Philadelphia (part)   Fax: (215) 708-3135
   Term Expires: 2016
   7518 Frankford Avenue, Philadelphia, PA 19136
   E-mail: kjboyle@pahouse.net
   Committees: Finance; Health; Insurance; Liquor Control; Urban Affairs
   Education: LaSalle Extension U 2002 BA; Harvard 2005 MEd
Representative
**Matthew D. Bradford, JD** (D-District 70) . . . . . . . . . . . . (717) 772-2572
   Counties Represented: Montgomery (part)   Dist: (610) 270-1150
   Term Expires: 2016   (Norristown)
   117 B East Wing, P.O. Box 202070,   Fax: (717) 772-2360
   Harrisburg, PA 17120-2070   Dist: (717) 270-1895
   1846 Markley Street, Norristown, PA 19401   (Norristown)
   E-mail: mbradford@pahouse.net
   Committees: Appropriations; Finance; Gaming Oversight; Liquor
   Control; Local Government
   Education: Villanova BA, JD
Representative **Tim Briggs** (D-District 149) . . . . . . . . . . . . (717) 705-7011
   Counties Represented: Montgomery (part)   Dist: (610) 768-3135
   Term Expires: 2016   Fax: (610) 768-3112
   6-A East Wing, P.O. Box 202149, Harrisburg, PA 17120-2149
   E-mail: tbriggs@pahouse.net
   Committees: Appropriations; Environmental Resources and Energy;
   Judiciary; Professional Licensure; Transportation
   Education: West Chester 1992 BA; Temple 2004 JD
Representative **Rosemary M. Brown** (R-District 189) . . . . . (717) 260-6171
   Counties Represented: Monroe (part), Pike (part)   Dist: (570) 420-8301
   Term Expires: 2016   Fax: (570) 420-8304
   13 Seven Bridges Road/Route 209, East Stroudsburg, PA 18301
   E-mail: rbrown@pahousegop.com
   Committees: Education; Gaming Oversight; Professional Licensure;
   Veterans Affairs and Emergency Preparedness
   Education: Scranton 1992 BA

LEGISLATIVE BRANCH

LEGISLATIVE BRANCH

Representative **Vanessa Lowery Brown** (D-District 190). .(717) 783-3822
Counties Represented: Philadelphia (part)   Dist: (215) 879-6615
Term Expires: 2016   Fax: (215) 879-6616
330 Irvis Office Building, P.O. Box 202190,
Harrisburg, PA 17120-2190
E-mail: vbrown@pahouse.net
Committees: Agriculture and Rural Affairs; Health; State Government;
Tourism and Recreational Development; Urban Affairs

Representative **Donna Bullock** (D-District 195). . . . . . . . .(717) 787-3480
Counties Represented: Philadelphia (part)   Fax: (717) 772-9853
Term Expires: 2016
2839 W. Girard Avenue, Philadelphia, PA 19130
117A East Wing, PO Box 202195, Harrisburg, PA 17120-2195
E-mail: dbullock@pahouse.net
Committees: Aging and Older Adult Services; Appropriations; Liquor
Control; State Government

Representative **Frank Burns** (D-District 72) . . . . . . . . . . . .(717) 772-8056
Counties Represented: Cambria (part)   Dist: (814) 536-8400
Term Expires: 2016   (Johnstown)
104A East Wing, P.O. Box 202072,   Dist: (814) 467-9583
Harrisburg, PA 17120-2072   (Windber)
535 Fairfield Avenue, Johnstown, PA 15906   Dist: (814) 472-8021
E-mail: fburns@pahouse.net   (Ebensburg)
Committees: Consumer Affairs; Game and   Fax: (814) 533-2368
Fisheries; Liquor Control; Tourism and Recreational   (Johnstown)
Development   Dist: (814) 533-2476
Education: Pittsburgh (Johnstown) 1999 BA

Representative
**Thomas R. Caltagirone** (D-District 127) . . . (717) 787-3525 (Harrisburg)
Counties Represented: Berks (part)   Dist: (610) 376-1529
Term Expires: 2016   (Reading)
645 Penn Street, 2nd Floor, Reading, PA 19601   Fax: (717) 772-5401
E-mail: tcaltagi@pahouse.net   (Harrisburg)
Committees: Urban Affairs   Dist: (610) 378-4406
Education: Frederick 1967 BA   (Reading)

Representative **Mike Carroll** (D-District 118) . . (717) 787-3589 (Harrisburg)
Counties Represented: Lackawanna (part), Luzerne   Dist: (570) 655-4883
(part)   (Hughestown)
Term Expires: 2016   Dist: (610) 681-2940
42 Center Street, Hughestown, PA 18640   (Gilbert)
P.O. Box 619, Gilbert, PA 18331   Fax: (717) 780-4763
E-mail: mcarroll@pahouse.net   (Harrisburg)
Committees: Agriculture and Rural Affairs; Rules;   Dist: (570) 655-9110
Transportation   (Hughestown)
Education: Scranton BA   Dist: (610) 681-2943
   (Gilbert)

Representative
**Martin T. Causer** (R-District 67) . . . . . . . . . (717) 787-5075 (Harrisburg)
Counties Represented: Cameron, McKean, Potter   Dist: (814) 362-4400
(part)   (Bradford)
Term Expires: 2016   Fax: (717) 705-7021
78 Main Street, 1st Floor, Bradford, PA 16701   (Harrisburg)
E-mail: mcauser@pahousegop.com   Dist: (814) 362-4405
Committees: Agriculture and Rural Affairs;   (Bradford)
Environmental Resources and Energy

Representative **Jim Christiana** (R-District 15). . . . . . . . . . .(717) 260-6144
Counties Represented: Beaver (part), Washington   Dist: (724) 728-7655
(part)   Fax: (717) 260-6506
Term Expires: 2016
3468 Brodhead Road, Suite 9, Monaca, PA 15061
E-mail: jchristi@pahousegop.com
Committees: Appropriations; Education; Environmental Resources and
Energy; Professional Licensure
Education: Washington & Jefferson 2006

Representative
**Mark B. Cohen** (D-District 202) . . . . . . . . . . (717) 787-4117 (Harrisburg)
Counties Represented: Philadelphia (part)   Dist: (215) 924-0895
Term Expires: 2016   (Philadelphia)
6001 North Fifth Street, 2nd Floor,   Fax: (717) 787-6650
Philadelphia, PA 19120   (Harrisburg)
E-mail: mcohen@pahouse.net   Dist: (215) 924-8480
Committees: State Government   (Philadelphia)
Education: Pennsylvania 1970 BS; Widener 1993 JD;
Lebanon Valley 2000 MBA

Representative
**H. Scott Conklin** (D-District 77) . . . . . . . . . (717) 787-9473 (Harrisburg)
Counties Represented: Centre (part)   Dist: (814) 238-5477
Term Expires: 2016   (State College)
301 South Allen Street, Suite 102,   Dist: (814) 342-4872
State College, PA 16801   (Philipsburg)
209 East Presquesile Street, Philipsburg, PA 16866   Fax: (717) 780-4764
E-mail: sconklin@pahouse.net   (Harrisburg)
Committees: Children and Youth   Dist: (814) 863-3898
   (State College)
   Dist: (814) 342-4874
   (Philipsburg)

Representative **Tonyelle Cook-Artis** (D-District 200). . . . . .(717) 783-2178
Counties Represented: Philadelphia (part)   Dist: (215) 242-7300
Term Expires: 2016   Fax: (717) 783-9755
E-mail: tartis@pahouse.net   Dist: (215) 242-7303
Committees: Agriculture and Rural Affairs; Commerce; State
Government; Urban Affairs
Education: Bennett BA; George Washington

Representative **Becky Corbin** (R-District 155) . . . . . . . . . . .(717) 783-2520
Counties Represented: Chester (part)   Fax: (717) 782-2927
Term Expires: 2016
315 Gordon Drive, Exton, PA 19334
E-mail: bcorbin@pahousegop.com
Committees: Environmental Resources and Energy; Health; Liquor
Control; Urban Affairs
Education: Chatham 1974 BSChem

Representative **Dominic "Dom" Costa** (D-District 21). . . .(717) 783-9114
Counties Represented: Allegheny (part)   Dist: (412) 361-2040
Term Expires: 2016   (Pittsburgh)
109B East Wing, P.O. Box 202021,   Fax: (717) 780-4761
Harrisburg, PA 17120-2021   (Pittsburgh)
1808 Chislett Street, Pittsburgh, PA 15206
E-mail: repdomcosta@pahouse.net
Committees: Gaming Oversight; Insurance; Judiciary; Professional
Licensure; Rules; Veterans Affairs and Emergency Preparedness

Representative **Paul Costa** (D-District 34) . . . . (717) 783-1914 (Harrisburg)
Counties Represented: Allegheny (part)   Dist: (412) 824-3400
Term Expires: 2016   (Turtle Creek)
519 Penn Avenue, Turtle Creek, PA 15145   Fax: (717) 783-3180
E-mail: pcosta@pahouse.net   (Harrisburg)
Committees: Liquor Control; Rules   Dist: (412) 664-6420
Education: Point Park Col 1994 BS   (Turtle Creek)
   Fax: (717) 705-2564

Representative **Jim Cox** (R-District 129) . . . . . (717) 772-2435 (Harrisburg)
Counties Represented: Berks (part), Lancaster (part)   Dist: (610) 670-0139
Term Expires: 2016   (Sinkling Spring)
2909 Windmill Road, Suite 7,   Fax: (610) 927-3584
Sinking Spring, PA 19608   (Sinking Spring)
E-mail: jcox@pahousegop.com   Fax: (717) 260-6516
Committees: Health; Judiciary; Labor and Industry; Urban Affairs
Education: Pensacola Christian 1992 AB; Regent U 1996 JD

Representative **Angel Cruz** (D-District 180) . . . (717) 787-1407 (Harrisburg)
Counties Represented: Philadelphia (part)   Dist: (215) 291-5643
Term Expires: 2016   (Philadelphia)
2749 North 5th Street, Philadelphia, PA 19133   Fax: (717) 780-4769
E-mail: acruz@pahouse.net   (Harrisburg)
Committees: Human Services   Dist: (215) 291-5647
   (Philadelphia)

Representative **Lynda Schlegel Culver** (R-District 108) . . . (717) 787-3485
Counties Represented: Northumberland (part),   Dist: (570) 286-5885
Snyder (part)   Fax: (570) 988-1627
Term Expires: 2016
106 Arch Street, Sunbury, PA 17801
E-mail: lculver@pahousegop.com
Committees: Commerce; Insurance; Transportation; Urban Affairs;
Veterans Affairs and Emergency Preparedness
Education: Bloomsburg 1995 BA

Representative **Bryan Cutler** (R-District 100) . .(717) 783-6424 (Harrisburg)
Counties Represented: Lancaster (part)   Dist: (717) 786-4551
Term Expires: 2016   (Quarryville)
207 East State Street, Quarryville, PA 17566   Fax: (717) 786-3645
E-mail: bcutler@pahousegop.com   (Quarryville)
Committees: Committee on Committees; Rules   Fax: (717) 772-9859
   (Harrisburg)

*(continued on next page)*

LEGISLATIVE BRANCH

**Representatives** continued

Representative **Mary Jo Daley** (D-District 148) . . . . . . . . . (717) 787-9475
Counties Represented: Montgomery (part)      Fax: (717) 787-0861
Term Expires: 2016
815 Fayette Street, Suite 200, Conshohocken, PA 19428
E-mail: repmaryjodaley@pahouse.net
Committees: Aging and Older Adult Services; Appropriations; Finance;
Health; State Government
Education: Pennsylvania 1987 BBA, 2000 MPA;
Gwynedd-Mercy 1969 AS

Representative
**Peter J. Daley II** (D-District 49) . . . . . . . . . . (717) 783-9333 (Harrisburg)
Counties Represented: Fayette (part), Washington    Dist: (724) 379-5540
(part)                                             (Donora)
Term Expires: 2016                  Fax: (717) 783-7558
657 McKean Avenue, Donora, PA 15033       (Harrisburg)
E-mail: pdaley@pahouse.net          Dist: (724) 938-5354
Committees: Consumer Affairs               (Donora)
Education: California U (PA) 1972 BS, 1975 MA;
Pittsburgh 1983 MPA; Widener 1993 JD

Representative **Margo L. Davidson** (D-District 164) . . . . . . (717) 783-4907
Counties Represented: Delaware (part)     Dist: (610) 259-7016
Term Expires: 2016              Fax: (717) 780-4750
1500 Garrett Road, Suite 2D,       Dist: (610) 259-5575
Upper Darby, PA 19082
E-mail: repdavidson@pahouse.net
Committees: Agriculture and Rural Affairs; Finance; Insurance;
Tourism and Recreational Development; Veterans Affairs and
Emergency Preparedness
Education: Temple 1988 BA

Representative **Tina M. Davis** (D-District 141) . . . . . . . . . . (717) 783-4903
Counties Represented: Bucks (part)      Dist: (215) 943-8669
Term Expires: 2016
3611 Green Lane, Levittown, PA 19057
E-mail: repdavis@pahouse.net
Committees: Committee on Committees; Consumer Affairs; Gaming
Oversight; Insurance; Judiciary; Professional Licensure
Education: LaSalle Col (Canada) 1983 BA

Representative **Jason Dawkins** (D-District 179) . . . . . . . . (717) 787-1354
Counties Represented: Philadelphia (part)     Dist: (215) 744-7901
Term Expires: 2016
4915 Frankford Avenue, Philadelphia, PA 19107
E-mail: jdawkins@pahouse.net
Committees: Aging and Older Adult Services; Health; Human Services;
Judiciary; Urban Affairs

Representative **Gary Day** (R-District 187) . . . . . . . . . . . . . . (717) 787-3017
Counties Represented: Berks (part), Lehigh (part)    Dist: (610) 366-2330
Term Expires: 2016             Fax: (717) 705-1951
163A East Wing, P.O. Box 202187,     Dist: (610) 366-2333
Harrisburg, PA 17120-2187
6299 Route 309, Suite 302, New Tripoli, PA 18066
E-mail: gday@pahousegop.com
Committees: Appropriations; Health; Insurance
Education: Penn State 1990 BEc

Representative **Madeleine Dean** (D-District 153) . . . . . . . . (717) 783-7619
Counties Represented: Montgomery (part)    Dist: (215) 517-6800
Term Expires: 2016             Fax: (717) 780-4754
1175 Old York Road, Abington, PA 19001    Dist: (215) 517-6828
E-mail: mdean@pahouse.net
Committees: Appropriations; Ethics; Finance; Judiciary
Education: La Salle U 1981 BA; Widener 1984 JD

Representative **Daniel J. Deasy, Jr.** (D-District 27) . . . . . . (717) 772-8187
Counties Represented: Allegheny (part)     Dist: (412) 928-9514
Term Expires: 2016             Fax: (717) 565-3170
111B East Wing, P.O. Box 202027, Harrisburg, PA 17120-2027
436 South Main Street, Pittsburgh, PA 15220
E-mail: ddeasy@pahouse.net
Committees: Gaming Oversight; Professional Licensure; Tourism and
Recreational Development; Urban Affairs
Education: Pittsburgh

Representative **Pamela A. DeLissio** (D-District 194) . . . . . . (717) 783-4945
Counties Represented: Montgomery (part),    Dist: (215) 482-8726
Philadelphia (part)
Term Expires: 2016
6511 Ridge Avenue, Philadelphia, PA 19128
E-mail: repdelissio@pahouse.net
Committees: Aging and Older Adult Services; Agriculture and Rural
Affairs; Children and Youth; Health; State Government
Education: Penn State 1978 BS

Representative **Sheryl M. Delozier, MBA** (R-District 88) . . (717) 783-5282
Counties Represented: Cumberland (part)    Dist: (717) 761-4665
Term Expires: 2016             Fax: (717) 731-7126
164A East Wing, P.O. Box 202088, Harrisburg, PA 17120-2088
2929 Gettysburg Road, Suite 6, Camp Hill, PA 17011
E-mail: sdelozie@pahousegop.com
Committees: Consumer Affairs; Ethics; Judiciary; Labor and Industry;
Liquor Control
Education: Delaware BA; Penn State MBA

Representative **Anthony M. "Tony" DeLuca**
(D-District 32) . . . . . . . . . . . . . . . . . . . . . . . (717) 783-1011 (Harrisburg)
Counties Represented: Allegheny (part)     Dist: (412) 793-2448
Term Expires: 2016                        (Pittsburgh)
7205 Saltsburg Road, Pittsburgh, PA 15235    Fax: (717) 772-9937
E-mail: tdeluca@pahouse.net            (Harrisburg)
Committees: Insurance            Dist: (412) 793-7495
                                          (Pittsburgh)

Representative
**Frank Dermody** (D-District 33) . . . . . . . . . . (717) 787-3566 (Harrisburg)
Counties Represented: Allegheny (part),    Dist: (724) 274-4770
Westmoreland (part)                   (Cheswick)
Term Expires: 2016             Fax: (717) 787-8060
1331 Freeport Road, Suite 202,      (Harrisburg)
Cheswick, PA 15024           Dist: (724) 274-8814
E-mail: fdermody@pahouse.net        (Cheswick)
Committees: Rules

Representative **Russ Diamond** (R-District 102) . . . . . . . . . . (717) 787-2686
Counties Represented: Lebanon (part)     Dist: (717) 277-2101
Term Expires: 2016             Fax: (717) 277-2105
2230 Lebanon Valley, Lebanon, PA 17042
E-mail: rdiamond@pahousegop.com
Committees: Agriculture and Rural Affairs; Gaming Oversight; Human
Services; Tourism and Recreational Development

Representative
**Gene DiGirolamo** (R-District 18) . . . . . . . . (717) 783-7319 (Harrisburg)
Counties Represented: Bucks (part)      Dist: (215) 750-1017
Term Expires: 2016                    (Bensalem)
Neshaminy Valley Commons, 2444 Bristol Road,   Fax: (717) 772-2414
Bensalem, PA 19020           (Harrisburg)
E-mail: gdigirol@pahousegop.com     Dist: (215) 750-1295
Committees: Consumer Affairs; Human Services   (Bensalem)

Representative **Maria P. Donatucci** (D-District 185) . . . . . . (717) 783-8634
Counties Represented: Delaware (part), Philadelphia   Dist: (215) 468-1515
(part)                               (Philadelphia)
Term Expires: 2016             Fax: (717) 772-9888
2115 Oregon Avenue, Philadelphia, PA 19145   Dist: (215) 952-1164
E-mail: mdonatucci@pahouse.net
Committees: Appropriations; Labor and Industry; Liquor Control;
Transportation; Veterans Affairs and Emergency Preparedness

Representative **Michael J. Driscoll** (D-District 173) . . . . . . (717) 787-4331
Counties Represented: Philadelphia (part)    Dist: (215) 281-3414
Term Expires: 2016             Fax: (717) 772-9962
3294 Red Lion Road, Suite Three,     Dist: (215) 281-3418
Philadelphia, PA 19114
E-mail: mdriscoll@pahouse.net
Committees: Aging and Older Adult Services; Commerce; Human
Services; Insurance

Representative **George Dunbar** (R-District 56) . . . . . . . . . . (717) 260-6132
Counties Represented: Westmoreland (part)    Dist: (724) 744-0305
Term Expires: 2016             Fax: (717) 782-2880
2090 Harrison Avenue, Suite 4,     Dist: (724) 744-0380
Philadelphia, PA 15644
E-mail: gdunbar@pahousegop.com
Committees: Appropriations; Finance; Gaming Oversight; State
Government
Education: Robert Morris U (PA) 1993 BS

Representative **Cris Dush** (R-District 66) . . . . . . . . . . . . . . (717) 787-3845
Counties Represented: Indiana (part), Jefferson   Dist: (814) 849-8008
Term Expires: 2016             Fax: (717) 782-2946
73 South White Street, Suite Two,     Fax: (814) 849-6710
Brookville, PA 15825
E-mail: cdush@pahousegop.com
Committees: Aging and Older Adult Services; Commerce; Labor and
Industry; State Government

Representative **Brian L. Ellis** (R-District 11) . . . (717) 787-7686 (Harrisburg)
Counties Represented: Butler (part)      Dist: (724) 283-5852
Term Expires: 2016                    (Lyndora)
6 Chesapeake Place, Suite 200, Lyndora, PA 16045   Fax: (717) 782-2907
E-mail: bellis@pahousegop.com        (Harrisburg)
Committees: Committee on Committees; Ethics;   Dist: (724) 284-8253
Rules                                    (Lyndora)

Representative **Joe Emrick** (R-District 137) . . . . . . . . . . . . (717) 260-6159
Counties Represented: Northampton (part)                Dist: (570) 897-0401
Term Expires: 2016                                       Fax: (570) 897-0140
5 Mount Bethel Plaza, Mount Bethel, PA 18343
E-mail: jemrick@pahousegop.com
Committees: Agriculture and Rural Affairs; Game and Fisheries;
Human Services; Professional Licensure
Education: Lycoming 1993 BA; Kutztown 1999 MEd

Representative **Harold A. "Hal" English** (R-District 30) . . . (717) 260-6407
Counties Represented: Allegheny (part)                   Fax: (717) 783-5740
Term Expires: 2016
4290 William Flinn Highway, Suite 200, Allison Park, PA 15101
E-mail: henglish@pahousegop.com
Committees: Aging and Older Adult Services; Education; Game and
Fisheries; Tourism and Recreational Development
Education: West Virginia 1984 BS; Baltimore 1987 JD

Representative **Eli Evankovich** (R-District 54) . . . . . . . . . . (717) 260-6129
Counties Represented: Allegheny (part),                  Dist: (724) 387-1281
Westmoreland (part)                                             (Export)
Term Expires: 2016                                       Dist: (724) 335-2790
5648 William Penn Highway, Export, PA 15632              (New Kensington)
2400 Leechburg Road, New Kensington, PA 15068           Fax: (724) 387-1295
E-mail: eevankov@pahousegop.com                                (Export)
Committees: Consumer Affairs; Finance; Health;           Dist: (724) 335-2649
Insurance; Rules                                         (New Kensington)
Education: Pittsburgh 2005 BS

Representative
**Dwight Evans** (D-District 203) . . . . . . . . . . (717) 783-1540 (Harrisburg)
Counties Represented: Philadelphia (part)               Dist: (215) 549-0220
Term Expires: 2016                                            (Philadelphia)
7174 Ogontz Avenue, Philadelphia, PA 19138              Fax: (717) 787-2334
E-mail: devans@pahouse.net                                    (Harrisburg)
Education: La Salle U 1975 BS                            Dist: (215) 549-8965
                                                             (Philadelphia)

Representative
**Garth D. Everett** (R-District 84) . . . . . . . . . (717) 787-5270 (Harrisburg)
Counties Represented: Lycoming (part), Union            Dist: (570) 546-2084
(part)                                                        (Muncy)
Term Expires: 2016                                       Fax: (717) 772-9958
Penn Hills Plaza, 21 Kristi Road, Suite 2,                   (Harrisburg)
Muncy, PA 17756                                         Dist: (570) 546-5220
E-mail: geverett@pahousegop.com                              (Muncy)
Committees: Appropriations; Environmental Resources and Energy;
Game and Fisheries; Judiciary
Education: Penn State 1976 BS, 2000 JD

Representative
**Florindo J. "Flo" Fabrizio** (D-District 2) . . . (717) 787-4358 (Harrisburg)
Counties Represented: Erie (part)                       Dist: (814) 455-6319
Term Expires: 2016                                            (Erie)
1216 West 26th Street, Erie, PA 16508                   Fax: (717) 780-4774
E-mail: ffabrizi@pahouse.net                                 (Harrisburg)
Committees: Health; Rules                               Dist: (814) 455-6593
Education: Penn State 1966 BA;                                (Erie)
Edinboro 1969 MEd

Representative **Frank Farina** (D-District 112) . . . . . . . . . . . (717) 783-5043
Counties Represented: Lackawanna (part)                 Dist: (570) 876-1111
Term Expires: 2016                                      Fax: (570) 783-1231
423 Main Street, Eynon, PA 18403                        Dist: (570) 876-5304
E-mail: ffarina@pahouse.net
Committees: Aging and Older Adult Services; Game and Fisheries;
Labor and Industry; Local Government
Education: Penn State 1999 BS

Representative **Frank A. Farry** (R-District 142) . . . . . . . . . (717) 260-6140
Counties Represented: Bucks (part)                      Dist: (215) 752-6750
Term Expires: 2016                                      Fax: (215) 752-6754
52B East Wing, P.O. Box 202142, Harrisburg, PA 17120-2142
370 East Maple Avenue, Suite 102, Langhorne, PA 19047
E-mail: ffarry@pahousegop.com
Committees: Consumer Affairs; Health; Local Government; Veterans
Affairs and Emergency Preparedness
Education: Rutgers 1998 MS, 2000 JD

Representative **Mindy Fee** (R-District 37) . . . . . . . . . . . . . (717) 772-5290
Counties Represented: Lancaster (part)                  Fax: (717) 783-1904
Term Expires: 2016
47 Market Square, Manheim, PA 17545
E-mail: mfee@pahousegop.com
Committees: Agriculture and Rural Affairs; Game and Fisheries; Local
Government; Tourism and Recreational Development
Education: Millersville 1987 BA

Representative **Marty Flynn** (D-District 113) . . . . . . . . . . . . (717) 787-8981
Counties Represented: Lackawanna (part)                 Dist: (570) 342-4349
Term Expires: 2016                                      Fax: (717) 705-1958
409 North Main Street, Scranton, PA 18504               Dist: (570) 342-4353
E-mail: mflynn@pahouse.net
Committees: Commerce; Consumer Affairs; Game and Fisheries;
Gaming Oversight; Insurance
Education: Marywood U 1999 BS

Representative
**Dan B. Frankel** (D-District 23) . . . . . . . . . . . (717) 705-1875 (Harrisburg)
Counties Represented: Allegheny (part)                  Dist: (412) 422-1774
Term Expires: 2016                                            (Pittsburgh)
2345 Murray Avenue, Suite 205,                          Fax: (717) 705-2034
Pittsburgh, PA 15217                                         (Harrisburg)
E-mail: dfrankel@pahouse.net                            Dist: (412) 420-2011
Committees: Rules                                            (Pittsburgh)

Representative
**Robert L. Freeman** (D-District 136) . . . . . . . (717) 783-3815 (Harrisburg)
Counties Represented: Northampton (part)                Dist: (610) 253-5543
Term Expires: 2016                                           (Easton)
215 Northampton Street, Easton, PA 18042                Fax: (717) 783-2152
E-mail: rfreeman@pahouse.net                                (Harrisburg)
Committees: Local Government                             Dist: (610) 250-2645
Education: Moravian 1978 BA; Lehigh 1984 MA                 (Easton)

Representative **Matt Gabler** (R-District 75) . . . . . . . . . . . . (717) 260-6142
Counties Represented: Clearfield (part), Elk            Dist: (814) 781-6301
Term Expires: 2016                                      Dist: (814) 375-4688
150B East Wing, P.O. Box 202075,                        Fax: (717) 375-5955
Harrisburg, PA 17120-2075
53 South St. Marys Street, Suite 2, Saint Marys, PA 15857
DuBois Area Plaza, 1221 East DuBois Avenue, Suite 10,
DuBois, PA 15801
E-mail: mgabler@pahousegop.com
Committees: Environmental Resources and Energy; Finance; Game and
Fisheries; Rules; State Government
Education: Bucknell 2006 BA

Representative **Ed Gainey** (D-District 24) . . . . . . . . . . . . . (717) 783-1017
Counties Represented: Allegheny (part)                  Dist: (412) 665-5502
Term Expires: 2016
100 Sheridan Square, 3rd Floor, Pittsburgh, PA 15206
E-mail: egainey@pahouse.net
Committees: Appropriations; Gaming Oversight; Insurance;
Transportation; Urban Affairs
Education: Morgan State 1994 BSBusMgt

Representative
**John T. Galloway** (D-District 140) . . . . . . . . (717) 787-1292 (Harrisburg)
Counties Represented: Bucks (part)                      Dist: (215) 943-7206
Term Expires: 2016                                           (Levittown)
8610 New Falls Road, Levittown, PA 19054               Fax: (717) 780-4780
E-mail: jgalloway@pahouse.net                               (Harrisburg)
Committees: Appropriations; Labor and Industry;         Dist: (215) 943-2008
Professional Licensure                                      (Levittown)

Representative
**Marc J. Gergely** (D-District 35) . . . . . . . . . . (717) 783-1018 (Harrisburg)
Counties Represented: Allegheny (part)                  Dist: (412) 664-0035
Term Expires: 2016                                           (McKeesport)
1540 Lincoln Way, White Deer, PA 15131                 Fax: (717) 780-4779
E-mail: mgergely@pahouse.net                                (Harrisburg)
Committees: Labor and Industry                          Dist: (412) 664-0039
                                                            (McKeesport)

Representative
**Jaret A. Gibbons** (D-District 10) . . . . . . . . . (717) 705-2060 (Harrisburg)
Counties Represented: Beaver (part), Butler (part),     Dist: (724) 752-1133
Lawrence (part)                                             (Ellwood City)
Term Expires: 2016                                      Fax: (717) 780-4766
309 Fifth Street, Ellwood City, PA 16117                    (Harrisburg)
E-mail: jgibbons@pahouse.net                            Dist: (724) 752-3784
Committees: Commerce; Professional Licensure;              (Ellwood City)
Tourism and Recreational Development
Education: Duquesne 2003 BA; Pittsburgh 2006 JD

Representative **Mark M. Gillen** (R-District 128) . . . . . . . . . (717) 787-8550
Counties Represented: Berks (part), Lancaster (part)    Dist: (610) 775-5130
Term Expires: 2016                                      Fax: (610) 775-3736
29 Village Center Drive, Suite A-7, Reading, PA 19607
E-mail: mgillen@pahousegop.com
Committees: Aging and Older Adult Services; Education; Labor and
Industry; Veterans Affairs and Emergency Preparedness
Education: Bob Jones U 1987 BA; Kutztown 2008 MEd

*(continued on next page)*

**LEGISLATIVE BRANCH**

**Representatives** *continued*

**Representative**
**Keith Gillespie** (R-District 47) . . . . . . . . . . (717) 705-7167 (Harrisburg)
Counties Represented: York (part)     Dist: (717) 840-4711
Term Expires: 2016     (York)
4188 Lincoln Highway, York, PA 17406
E-mail: kgillesp@pahousegop.com     Fax: (717) 772-9869
Committees: Game and Fisheries; Professional     (Harrisburg)
Licensure     Dist: (717) 755-2896
    (York)

**Representative**
**Mauree Gingrich** (R-District 101) . . . . . . . . (717) 783-1815 (Harrisburg)
Counties Represented: Lebanon (part)     Dist: (717) 270-1905
Term Expires: 2016     (Cleona)
445 West Penn Avenue, Cleona, PA 17042
E-mail: mgingric@pahousegop.com     Fax: (717) 705-2569
Committees: Aging and Older Adult Services;     (Harrisburg)
Labor and Industry; Rules     Dist: (717) 270-1854
    (Cleona)

**Representative Robert W. "Bob" Godshall**
(R-District 53) . . . . . . . . . . . . . . . . . . . . . . . . (717) 783-6428 (Harrisburg)
Counties Represented: Montgomery (part)     Dist: (215) 368-3500
Term Expires: 2016     (Hatfield)
1702 Cowpath Road, Hatfield, PA 19440
E-mail: rgodshal@pahousegop.com     Fax: (717) 787-7424
Committees: Committee on Committees; Consumer     (Harrisburg)
Affairs; Insurance; Rules     Dist: (215) 361-4220
Education: Juniata 1955 BS     (Hatfield)

**Representative**
**Neal P. Goodman** (D-District 123) . . . . . . . (717) 787-2798 (Harrisburg)
Counties Represented: Schuylkill (part)     Dist: (570) 773-3075
Term Expires: 2016     (Mahanoy City)
39 Western Centre Street, P.O. Box 66,     Fax: (717) 772-9948
Mahanoy City, PA 17948     (Harrisburg)
E-mail: ngoodman@pahouse.net     Dist: (570) 773-3105
Committees: Rules     (Mahanoy City)

**Representative Keith J. Greiner, CPA** (R-District 43) . . . . . (717) 783-6422
Counties Represented: Lancaster (part)     Fax: (717) 782-2626
Term Expires: 2016
E-mail: kgreiner@pahousegop.com
Committees: Appropriations; Children and Youth; Commerce; Local
Government
Education: Penn State 1987 BSAcc

**Representative**
**Seth M. Grove** (R-District 196) . . . . . . . . . . (717) 783-2655 (Harrisburg)
Counties Represented: York (part)     Dist: (717) 767-3947
Term Expires: 2016     Fax: (717) 767-9857
1954 Carlisle Road, York, PA 17408
E-mail: sgrove@pahousegop.com
Committees: Appropriations; Education; Finance; Labor and Industry

**Representative**
**Marcia M. Hahn** (R-District 138) . . . . . . . . . . (610) 746-2100 (Nazareth)
Counties Represented: Northampton (part)     Fax: (610) 746-3803
Term Expires: 2016
354 West Moorestown Road, Nazareth, PA 18064
E-mail: mhahn@pahousegop.com
Committees: Agriculture and Rural Affairs; Commerce; Health;
Tourism and Recreational Development

**Representative**
**Michael K. Hanna, Sr.** (D-District 76) . . . . . (717) 772-2283 (Harrisburg)
Counties Represented: Centre (part), Clinton     Dist: (570) 748-5480
Term Expires: 2016     (Lock Haven)
29 Bellefonte Avenue, Lock Haven, PA 17745     Dist: (814) 353-8790
102 Turnpike Street, Milesburg, PA 16853     (Milesburg)
E-mail: mhanna@pahouse.net     Fax: (717) 787-4137
Committees: Rules     (Harrisburg)
    Dist: (570) 748-5328
    (Lock Haven)
    Dist: (814) 355-6056
    (Milesburg)

**Representative R. Ted Harhai** (D-District 58) . . (717) 772-2820 (Harrisburg)
Counties Represented: Westmoreland (part)     Dist: (724) 684-2939
Term Expires: 2016     (Monessen)
1200 Maronda Way, Suite 401,     Fax: (717) 772-0784
Monessen, PA 15062     (Harrisburg)
E-mail: tharhai@pahouse.net     Dist: (724) 684-6613
Committees: Game and Fisheries     (Monessen)
Education: Carnegie Mellon 1977 BA

**Representative**
**Julie Harhart** (R-District 183) . . . . . . . . . . . (717) 772-5398 (Harrisburg)
Counties Represented: Lehigh (part), Northampton     Dist: (610) 821-6924
(part)     (Whitehall)
Term Expires: 2016     Dist: (610) 760-9805
125 South Walnut Street, First Floor,     (Slatington)
Whitehall, PA 18052     Fax: (717) 783-7667
E-mail: jharhart@pahousegop.com     (Harrisburg)
Committees: Professional Licensure; Transportation     Dist: (610) 821-6927
    (Whitehall)
    Dist: (610) 821-6109
    (Slatington)

**Representative**
**Patrick J. Harkins** (D-District 1) . . . . . . . . . (717) 787-7406 (Harrisburg)
Counties Represented: Erie (part)     Dist: (814) 459-1949
Term Expires: 2016     (Erie)
460 East 26th Street, Erie, PA 16504     Fax: (717) 780-4775
E-mail: pharkins@pahouse.net     (Harrisburg)
Committees: Education; Game and Fisheries;     Dist: (814) 871-4854
Labor and Industry; Liquor Control; Rules; Veterans     (Erie)
Affairs and Emergency Preparedness

**Representative**
**Catherine "Kate" Harper** (R-District 61) . . . (717) 787-2801 (Harrisburg)
Counties Represented: Montgomery (part)     Dist: (610) 277-3230
Term Expires: 2016     (Blue Bell)
1515 Dekalb Pike, Suite 106, Blue Bell, PA 19422     Fax: (717) 787-2022
E-mail: kharper@pahousegop.com     (Harrisburg)
Committees: Local Government; Transportation     Dist: (610) 270-1677
    (Blue Bell)

**Representative**
**Adam C. Harris** (R-District 82) . . . . . . . . . . (717) 783-7830 (Harrisburg)
Counties Represented: Franklin (part), Juniata,     Dist: (717) 242-0423
Mifflin (part)     (Lewistown)
Term Expires: 2016     Dist: (717) 436-6001
3 Monument Square, Lewistown, PA 17044     (Mifflintown)
P.O. Box 393, Middleburg, PA 17842     Dist: (570) 837-1904
E-mail: aharris@pahousegop.com     (Middleburg)
Committees: Commerce; Rules     Fax: (717) 772-9869
Education: Susquehanna 1998 BA     (Harrisburg)
    Dist: (717) 242-2141
    (Lewistown)
    Dist: (717) 436-5362
    (Mifflintown)
    Dist: (570) 837-1923
    (Middleburg)

**Representative Jordan A. Harris** (D-District 186) . . . . . . . (717) 783-1792
Counties Represented: Philadelphia (part)     Fax: (717) 787-7172
Term Expires: 2016
1310 Point Breeze Ave., Philadelphia, PA 19145
E-mail: jharris@pahousegop.com
Committees: Agriculture and Rural Affairs; Environmental Resources
and Energy; Finance; Professional Licensure; Rules
Education: Millersville 2006 BA; Cabrini 2008 MEd

**Representative Doyle Heffley** (R-District 122) . . . . . . . . . . (717) 260-6139
Counties Represented: Carbon (part)     Dist: (610) 377-6363
Term Expires: 2016     Fax: (610) 377-5675
110 North Third Street, 2nd Floor, Lehighton, PA 18235
E-mail: dheffley@pahousegop.com
Committees: Game and Fisheries; Human Services; Tourism and
Recreational Development; Transportation

**Representative**
**Susan C. "Sue" Helm** (R-District 104) . . . . (717) 787-1230 (Harrisburg)
Counties Represented: Dauphin (part), Lebanon     Dist: (717) 651-0100
(part)     (Harrisburg)
Term Expires: 2016     Dist: (717) 362-1119
P.O. Box 559, Elizabethville, PA 17023     (Elizabethville)
E-mail: shelm@pahousegop.com     Fax: (717) 651-0801
Committees: Appropriations; Gaming Oversight;     (Harrisburg)
Tourism and Recreational Development; Urban     Dist: (717) 362-1009
Affairs     (Elizabethville)

**Representative Timothy "Tim" Hennessey**
(R-District 26) . . . . . . . . . . . . . . . . . . . . . . . . (717) 787-3431 (Harrisburg)
Counties Represented: Chester (part), Montgomery     Dist: (610) 380-8600
(part)     (Coatesville)
Term Expires: 2016     Fax: (717) 705-1849
1038 East Lincoln Highway, Coatesville, PA 19320     (Harrisburg)
E-mail: thenness@pahousegop.com     Dist: (610) 380-1777
Committees: Aging and Older Adult Services;     (Coatesville)
Transportation
Education: St Joseph Col 1969 BS; Villanova 1972 JD

Representative
**David S. Hickernell** (R-District 98) . . . . . . . . (717) 783-2076 (Harrisburg)
Counties Represented: Dauphin (part), Lancaster    Dist: (717) 684-5525
(part)    (Columbia)
Term Expires: 2016    Dist: (717) 367-5525
222 South Market Street, Suite 103,    (Elizabethtown)
Elizabethtown, PA 17022    Fax: (717) 705-1946
236 Locust Street, Columbia, PA 17512    (Harrisburg)
E-mail: dhickern@pahousegop.com    Dist: (717) 684-2538
Committees: Professional Licensure; Tourism    (Columbia)
and Recreational Development    Dist: (717) 367-6425
    (Elizabethtown)

Representative **Richard "Rich" Irvin** (R-District 81) . . . . . . (717) 787-3335
Counties Represented: Centre (part), Huntingdon,    Dist: (814) 644-2996
Mifflin (part)    Fax: (717) 782-2884
Term Expires: 2016    Dist: (814) 644-2999
E-mail: rirvin@pahousegop.com
Committees: Aging and Older Adult Services; Labor and Industry;
Local Government; State Government

Representative **R. Lee James** (R-District 64) . . . . . . . . . . . (717) 783-8188
Counties Represented: Butler (part), Venango
Term Expires: 2016
3220 State Route 257, Suite 8, Seneca, PA 16346
E-mail: rljames@pahousegop.com
Committees: Commerce; Environmental Resources and Energy;
Finance; Local Government; Rules; Veterans Affairs and Emergency
Preparedness
Education: Clarion 1974 BS, 1983 MBA

Representative **Barry J. Jozwiak** (R-District 5) . . . . . . . . . (717) 772-9940
Counties Represented: Berks (part)    Fax: (717) 782-2925
Term Expires: 2016
E-mail: bjozwiak@pahousegop.com
Committees: Aging and Older Adult Services; Game and Fisheries;
Judiciary; Veterans Affairs and Emergency Preparedness

Representative **Warren Kampf** (R-District 157) . . . . . . . . . (717) 260-6166
Counties Represented: Chester (part), Montgomery    Dist: (610) 251-2876
(part)    Fax: (717) 782-2888
Term Expires: 2016    Dist: (610) 640-2357
42 East Lancaster Avenue, Unit A, Paoli, PA 19301
E-mail: wkampf@pahousegop.com
Committees: Appropriations; Consumer Affairs; Insurance; Liquor
Control

Representative **Aaron D. Kaufer** (R-District 120) . . . . . . . . (717) 787-3798
Counties Represented: Luzerne (part)    Dist: (570) 283-1001
Term Expires: 2016    Fax: (717) 782-2950
161 Main Street, Suite 201, Luzerne, PA 18709    Dist: (570) 283-1008
E-mail: akaufer@pahousegop.com
Committees: Aging and Older Adult Services; Finance; Gaming
Oversight; Health

Representative
**Rob W. Kauffman** (R-District 89) . . . . . . . . (717) 705-2004 (Harrisburg)
Counties Represented: Franklin (part)    Dist: (717) 264-3943
Term Expires: 2016    (Chambersburg)
166 South Main Street, Chambersburg, PA 17201    Dist: (717) 532-1707
9974 Molly Pitcher Highway,    (Shippensburg)
Shippensburg, PA 17257    Fax: (717) 705-1951
E-mail: rkauffma@pahousegop.com    (Harrisburg)
Committees: Agriculture and Rural Affairs;    Dist: (717) 264-2893
Consumer Affairs; Rules; Tourism and Recreational    (Chambersburg)
Development; Urban Affairs    Dist: (717) 532-5043
    (Shippensburg)

Representative **Sid Michaels Kavulich** (D-District 114) . . . (717) 783-4874
Counties Represented: Lackawanna (part)    Dist: (570) 562-2350
Term Expires: 2016    (Taylor)
802 South Main Street, Scranton, PA 18517    Dist: (570) 254-9672
E-mail: skavulich@pahouse.net    (Scott Township)
Committees: Agriculture and Rural Affairs; Ethics;    Fax: (570) 562-2353
Finance; Gaming Oversight; Local Government;    (Taylor)
Tourism and Recreational Development

Representative **Fred Keller** (R-District 85) . . . . . . . . . . . . . (717) 787-3443
Counties Represented: Snyder (part), Union (part)    Dist: (570) 966-0052
Term Expires: 2016    Dist: (570) 837-0052
343 Chestnut Street, Suite 1, Mifflinville, PA 17844    Fax: (570) 966-0053
E-mail: fkeller@pahousegop.com
Committees: Appropriations; Children and Youth; Labor and Industry;
State Government

Representative
**Mark K. Keller** (R-District 86) . . . . . . . . . . . (717) 783-1593 (Harrisburg)
Counties Represented: Cumberland (part), Perry    Dist: (717) 582-8119
Term Expires: 2016    (New Bloomfield)
18 West Main Street, P.O. Box 9,    Dist: (717) 267-2047
New Bloomfield, PA 17068    (Chambersburg)
1720 Crottlestown Road, Chambersburg, PA 17201    Fax: (717) 705-7012
E-mail: mkeller@pahousegop.com    (Harrisburg)
Committees: Agriculture and Rural Affairs; Game    Dist: (717) 582-8979
and Fisheries; Judiciary; Transportation    (New Bloomfield)
    Dist: (717) 267-7024
    (Chambersburg)

Representative
**William F. Keller** (D-District 184) . . . . . . . . (717) 787-5774 (Harrisburg)
Counties Represented: Philadelphia (part)    Dist: (215) 271-9190
Term Expires: 2016    (Philadelphia)
1531 South Second Street, Philadelphia, PA 19147    Fax: (717) 705-2088
E-mail: wkeller@pahouse.net    (Harrisburg)
Committees: Transportation    Dist: (215) 952-1025
    (Philadelphia)

Representative **Patty H. Kim** (D-District 103) . . . . . . . . . . . (717) 783-9342
Counties Represented: Dauphin (part)    Fax: (717) 787-8957
Term Expires: 2016
8 South Front Street, Steelton, PA 17113
E-mail: pkim@pahouse.net
Committees: Children and Youth; Local Government; Urban Affairs
Education: Boston Col 1995 BA

Representative **Stephen Kinsey** (D-District 201) . . . . . . . . . (717) 787-3181
Counties Represented: Philadelphia (part)    Fax: (717) 772-4038
Term Expires: 2016
5537 Germantown Avenue, Philadelphia, PA 19144
E-mail: skinsey@pahouse.net
Committees: Appropriations; Committee on Committees; Finance;
Health; Human Services; Rules; Transportation
Education: West Chester 1981 BSEd; Eastern U 2002 MBA

Representative
**Thaddeus Kirkland** (D-District 159) . . . . . . . (717) 787-5881 (Harrisburg)
Counties Represented: Delaware (part)    Dist: (610) 876-6420
Term Expires: 2016    (Chester)
29 East Fifth Street, Chester, PA 19013    Fax: (717) 787-9074
E-mail: tkirklan@pahouse.net    (Harrisburg)
Education: Cheyney 1991 BA    Dist: (610) 447-3004
    (Chester)

Representative **Kate Anne Klunk** (R-District 169) . . . . . . . . (717) 787-4790
Counties Represented: York (part)    Dist: (717) 630-8942
Term Expires: 2016    Fax: (717) 630-9731
118 Carlisle Street, Hanover, PA 17331
E-mail: kklunk@pahousegop.com
Committees: Aging and Older Adult Services; Children and Youth;
Gaming Oversight; Judiciary

Representative **Jerry Knowles** (R-District 124) . . . . . . . . . (570) 668-1240
Counties Represented: Berks (part), Carbon (part),    Tel: (717) 787-9029
Schuylkill (part)    Fax: (570) 952-3374
Term Expires: 2016    Fax: (717) 783-3899
237 West Broad Street, Tamaqua, PA 18252
E-mail: jknowles@pahousegop.com
Committees: Finance; Professional Licensure; State Government; Urban
Affairs

Representative
**William C. "Bill" Kortz II** (D-District 38) . . . (717) 787-8175 (Harrisburg)
Counties Represented: Allegheny (part)    Dist: (412) 466-1940
Term Expires: 2016    (Dravosburg)
751 Pittsburgh McKeesport Boulevard,    Dist: (412) 866-2870
Dravosburg, PA 15034    (Pittsburgh)
5101 Old Clairton Road, Pittsburgh, PA 15236    Fax: (717) 780-4783
E-mail: wkortz@pahouse.net    (Harrisburg)
Committees: Commerce; Game and Fisheries;    Dist: (412) 460-3023
Gaming Oversight; Professional Licensure; Veterans    (Dravosburg)
Affairs and Emergency Preparedness    Dist: (412) 886-2871
Education: Indiana (PA) 1977 BA;    (Pittsburgh)
Duquesne 1988 MBA

Representative **Nick Kotik** (D-District 45) . . . . (412) 264-4260 (Coraopolis)
Counties Represented: Allegheny (part)    Dist: (412) 429-5091
Term Expires: 2016    (Carnegie)
1350 Fifth Avenue, Coraopolis, PA 15108    Dist: (717) 783-3780
115 East Main Street, Carnegie, PA 15108    (Harrisburg)
E-mail: nkotik@pahouse.net    Fax: (412) 269-2767
Committees: Gaming Oversight    (Coraopolis)
Education: Indiana (PA) 1972 BA    Dist: (412) 429-6310
    (Carnegie)
    Dist: (717) 780-4773
    (Harrisburg)

*(continued on next page)*

**Representatives** *continued*

Representative
**Leanne Krueger-Braneky** (D-District 161) ........... (717) 787-2372
Counties Represented: Delaware (part)
Term Expires: 2016
E-mail: lkrueger-braneky@pahouse.net,
Committees: Children and Youth; Environmental Resources and
Energy; Liquor Control

Representative **John A. Lawrence** (R-District 13) ........ (717) 260-6117
Counties Represented: Chester (part), Lancaster          Dist: (610) 869-1602
(part)                                                    Fax: (610) 869-1605
Term Expires: 2016
1 Commerce Boulevard, Second Floor, Suite 200,
West Grove, PA 19390
E-mail: jlawrenc@pahousegop.com
Committees: Agriculture and Rural Affairs; Commerce; Finance;
Health; Rules
Education: Penn State 2000 BS

Representative **Harry Lewis, Jr.** (R-District 74) ......... (717) 787-1806
Counties Represented: Chester (part)                     Dist: (610) 269-1289
Term Expires: 2016                                        Fax: (717) 782-2947
131 Wallace Avenue, Unit 14,                             Dist: (610) 269-1082
Downingtown, PA 19335
E-mail: hlewis@pahousegop.com
Committees: Children and Youth; Education; Urban Affairs

Representative
**Mark A. Longietti** (D-District 7) ........ (717) 772-4035 (Harrrisburg)
Counties Represented: Mercer (part)                      Dist: (724) 981-4655
Term Expires: 2016                                            (Hermitage)
2213 Shenango Valley Freeway, Unit 2-E,                  Fax: (717) 780-4785
Hermitage, PA 16148                                          (Harrisburg)
E-mail: mlongietti@pahouse.net                           Dist: (724) 981-6528
Committees: Aging and Older Adult Services;                  (Hermitage)
Commerce; Committee on Committees; Consumer Affairs; Education;
Ethics; Tourism and Recreational Development
Education: Westminster (PA) 1985 BA; Boston Col 1988 JD

Representative **Ryan E. Mackenzie** (R-District 134) ...... (717) 787-1000
Counties Represented: Berks (part), Lehigh (part)       Dist: (610) 965-9933
Term Expires: 2016                                       Fax: (717) 782-2893
1245 Chestnut Street, Unit 5, Emmaus, PA 18049          Dist: (610) 965-9174
E-mail: rmackenzie@pahousegop.com
Committees: Commerce; Environmental Resources and Energy;
Gaming Oversight; Labor and Industry; Tourism and Recreational
Development
Education: NYU 2004 BS; Harvard 2010 MBA

Representative
**John A. Maher III, CPA** (R-District 40) .... (717) 783-1522 (Harrisburg)
Counties Represented: Allegheny (part), Washington      Dist: (412) 831-8080
(part)                                                       (Upper St. Clair)
Term Expires: 2016                                       Fax: (717) 783-8332
711 Summerfield Commons, 2547 Washington                     (Harrisburg)
Road, Upper Saint Clair, PA 15241                       Dist: (412) 831-8083
E-mail: jmaher@pahousegop.com                                (Upper St. Clair)
Committees: Agriculture and Rural Affairs; Environmental Resources
and Energy; Professional Licensure
Education: Duke AB

Representative
**Tim Mahoney** (D-District 51) ............ (717) 772-2174 (Harrisburg)
Counties Represented: Fayette (part), Somerset          Dist: (724) 438-6100
(part)                                                       (Uniontown)
Term Expires: 2016                                       Dist: (724) 626-1164
66A Lebanon Avenue, Uniontown, PA 15401                      (Connellsville)
1402 Memorial Boulevard, Connellsville, PA 15425        Fax: (717) 780-4786
E-mail: tmahoney@pahouse.net                                 (Harrisburg)
Committees: Agriculture and Rural Affairs; Game          Dist: (724) 438-6104
and Fisheries; Liquor Control; Local Government;             (Uniontown)
Tourism and Recreational Development                     Dist: (724) 626-1165
                                                             (Connellsville)

Representative
**Sandra J. Major** (R-District 111) ........ (717) 783-2910 (Harrisburg)
Counties Represented: Susquehanna (part), Wayne         Dist: (570) 278-3374
(part)                                                       (Montrose)
Term Expires: 2016                                       Dist: (570) 836-5888
RR 7, Box 7186, Montrose, PA 18801                           (Tunkhannock)
130 North Bridge Street, Tunkhannock, PA 18657          Fax: (717) 783-2010
E-mail: smajor@pahousegop.com                                (Harrisburg)
Committees: Committee on Committees                      Dist: (570) 278-2952
                                                             (Montrose)

Representative **David M. Maloney, Sr.** (R-District 130) ... (717) 260-6161
Counties Represented: Berks (part)                      Dist: (610) 385-0704
Term Expires: 2016                                           (Douglassville)
46 East Philadelphia Avenue, Boyertown, PA 19512        Dist: (610) 369-3010
515 Old Swede Road, Suite B2,                                (Boyertown)
Douglassville, PA 19518                                 Fax: (610) 385-1176
E-mail: davidmaloneypa@gmail.com                             (Douglassville)
Committees: Children and Youth; Game and                Dist: (610) 369-3011
Fisheries; Labor and Industry; Local Government              (Boyertown)

Representative
**Joseph F. Markosek** (D-District 25) ....... (717) 783-1012 (Harrisburg)
Counties Represented: Allegheny (part)                  Dist: (412) 856-8284
Term Expires: 2016                                           (Monroeville)
Commerce Building, 4232 Northern Pike,                  Fax: (717) 705-1891
Suite 103, Monroeville, PA 15146                             (Harrisburg)
E-mail: jmarkose@pahouse.net                            Dist: (412) 374-9242
Committees: Appropriations; Rules                            (Monroeville)
Education: Notre Dame 1972 BA

Representative **Jim Marshall** (R-District 14) .. (717) 260-6432 (Harrisburg)
Counties Represented: Beaver (part), Butler (part)      Dist: (724) 847-1352
Term Expires: 2016                                           (Beaver Falls)
1122 Seventh Avenue, Beaver Falls, PA 15010             Fax: (717) 772-9869
E-mail: jmarshal@pahousegop.com                             (Harrisburg)
Committees: Appropriations; Environmental               Dist: (724) 847-5283
Resources and Energy; Transportation; Veterans               (Beaver Falls)
Affairs and Emergency Preparedness

Representative
**Ronald S. Marsico** (R-District 105) ....... (717) 783-2014 (Harrisburg)
Counties Represented: Dauphin (part)                    Dist: (717) 652-3721
Term Expires: 2016                                           (Harrisburg)
4401 Linglestown Road, Suite B,                         Fax: (717) 705-2010
Harrisburg, PA 17112                                        (Harrisburg)
E-mail: rmarsico@pahousegop.com                         Dist: (717) 652-6276
Committees: Judiciary; Transportation                        (Harrisburg)
Education: Ohio State 1971 BA

Representative **Kurt A. Masser** (R-District 107) ......... (717) 260-6134
Counties Represented: Columbia (part), Montour,         Dist: (570) 648-8017
Northumberland (part)                                    Fax: (570) 787-9463
Term Expires: 2016                                       Dist: (570) 644-7845
467 Industrial Park Road, Elysburg, PA 17824
E-mail: kmasser@pahousegop.com
Committees: Appropriations; Consumer Affairs; Gaming Oversight;
Liquor Control

Representative **Robert F. Matzie** (D-District 16) ......... (717) 787-4444
Counties Represented: Allegheny (part), Beaver          Dist: (724) 266-7774
(part)                                                   Dist: (412) 761-1701
Term Expires: 2016                                       Fax: (717) 780-4772
109A East Wing, P.O. Box 202016,                        Dist: (724) 266-7634
Harrisburg, PA 17120-2016                               Dist: (412) 761-1721
1240 Merchant Street, 1st Floor, Ambridge, PA 15003
Bellevue Satellite Office, 10 Hawley Avenue, Pittsburgh, PA 15202
E-mail: rmatzie@pahouse.net
Committees: Commerce; Consumer Affairs; Health; Insurance;
Transportation

Representative
**Stephen "Steve" McCarter** (D-District 154) .......... (717) 783-1079
Counties Represented: Montgomery (part)                 Fax: (717) 787-2713
Term Expires: 2016
215 S. Easton Road, Glenside, PA 19038
E-mail: repmccarter@pahouse.net
Committees: Children and Youth; Commerce; Education; Environmental
Resources and Energy; State Government

Representative **Joanna E. McClinton** (D-District 191) .... (717) 772-9850
Counties Represented: Delaware (part), Philadelphia     Fax: (717) 783-1516
(part)
Term Expires: 2016
6027 Ludlow Street, Unit A, Philadelphia, PA 19139
E-mail: jmcclinton@pahouse.net
Committees: Children and Youth; Human Services; Local Government

Representative **John D. McGinnis** (R-District 79) ........ (717) 787-6419
Counties Represented: Blair (part)                      Dist: (814) 946-7218
Term Expires: 2016                                       Fax: (717) 782-2923
1331 12th Avenue, Suite 104, Altoona, PA 16601          Dist: (814) 949-7915
E-mail: jmcginnis@pahousegop.com
Committees: Game and Fisheries; Local Government; Urban Affairs;
Veterans Affairs and Emergency Preparedness
Education: Notre Dame 1976 BA; Indiana (South Bend) 1987 MSBA;
Penn State 1993 PhD

Representative **Daniel T. McNeill** (D-District 133) . . . . . . . (717) 772-9902
Counties Represented: Lehigh (part)          Dist: (610) 266-1273
Term Expires: 2016                           Fax: (610) 266-2126
1080 Schadt Avenue, Whitehall, PA 18052
E-mail: dmcneill@pahouse.net
Committees: Agriculture and Rural Affairs; Finance; Labor and
Industry; Local Government; Professional Licensure

Representative **Steven C. Mentzer** (R-District 97) . . . . . . (717) 787-1776
Counties Represented: Lancaster (part)          Fax: (717) 705-2031
Term Expires: 2016
1555 Highlands Drive, Suite 110, Lititz, PA 17543
E-mail: smentzer@pahousegop.com
Committees: Aging and Older Adult Services; Insurance; Labor and
Industry
Education: Elizabethtown (Attended)

Representative
**Daryl D. Metcalfe** (R-District 12) . . . . . . . . . (717) 783-1707 (Harrisburg)
Counties Represented: Butler (part)          Dist: (724) 772-3110
Term Expires: 2016                           (Cranberry Township)
Municipal Building, 2525 Rochester Road,     Fax: (717) 787-4771
Suite 201, Cranberry Township, PA 16066         (Harrisburg)
E-mail: dmetcalf@pahousegop.com              Dist: (724) 772-2922
Committees: State Government                     (Cranberry Township)

Representative **Carl Walker Metzgar** (R-District 69) . . . . . . (717) 783-8756
Counties Represented: Bedford (part), Somerset    Dist: (814) 443-4230
(part)                                           Fax: (717) 787-2005
Term Expires: 2016                           Dist: (814) 443-3866
P.O. Box 147, Somerset, PA 15501
E-mail: cmetzgar@pahousegop.com
Committees: Commerce; Consumer Affairs; Environmental Resources
and Energy; Ethics
Education: Frostburg State U 2004 BS; Duquesne 2007 JD

Representative
**Nicholas A. "Nick" Miccarelli III** (R-District 162) . . . . . . (717) 787-3472
Counties Represented: Delaware (part)        Dist: (610) 534-1002
Term Expires: 2016                           Fax: (717) 772-5569
406 Irvis Office Building, P.O. Box 202162,  Dist: (610) 534-1710
Harrisburg, PA 17120-2162
605 East Chester Pike, Ridley Park, PA 19078
E-mail: nickmicc@pahousegop.com
Committees: Appropriations; Consumer Affairs; Gaming Oversight;
Liquor Control

Representative
**David R. Millard** (R-District 109) . . . . . . . . . (717) 783-1102 (Harrisburg)
Counties Represented: Columbia (part)        Dist: (570) 759-8734
Term Expires: 2016                              (Berwick)
904B Orange Street, Berwick, PA 18603        Dist: (570) 387-0246
605 West Main Street, Bloomsburg, PA 17815      (Bloomsburg)
E-mail: dmillard@pahousegop.com              Fax: (717) 772-0094
Committees: Agriculture and Rural Affairs;      (Harrisburg)
Appropriations; Professional Licensure; Tourism   Dist: (570) 759-8734
and Recreational Development                    (Berwick)
                                             Dist: (570) 387-4288
                                                (Bloomsburg)

Representative **Brett R. Miller** (R-District 41) . . . . . . . . . (717) 705-7161
Counties Represented: Lancaster (part)       Dist: (717) 295-5050
Term Expires: 2016                           Fax: (717) 295-5053
2938 Columbia Avenue, Suite 501, Lancaster, PA 17603
E-mail: bmiller@pahousegop.com
Committees: Children and Youth; Game and Fisheries; Local
Government; State Government

Representative **Daniel L. "Dan" Miller** (D-District 42) . . . . (717) 783-1850
Counties Represented: Allegheny (part)       Fax: (717) 780-4756
Term Expires: 2016
106B East Wing, Harrisburg, PA 17120-2042
E-mail: repmiller@pahouse.net
Committees: Children and Youth; Education; Human Services;
Judiciary
Education: Catholic U 2002 JD; Western Connecticut St 1997 BS

Representative
**Duane D. Milne** (R-District 167) . . . . . . . . . (717) 787-8579 (Harrisburg)
Counties Represented: Chester (part)         Dist: (610) 251-1070
Term Expires: 2016                              (Malvern)
18 East Lancaster Avenue, Malvern, PA 19355  Fax: (610) 251-1074
E-mail: dmilne@pahousegop.com                   (Malvern)
Committees: Appropriations; Commerce; Finance
Education: William & Mary 1995 BA; Delaware PhD

Representative **Dan Moul** (R-District 91) . . . . . (717) 783-5217 (Harrisburg)
Counties Represented: Adams (part)           Dist: (717) 334-3010
Term Expires: 2016                              (Gettysburg)
33-A West Middle Street, Gettysburg, PA 17325  Dist: (866) 646-4915
E-mail: dmoul@pahousegop.com                    (Gettysburg)
Committees: Agriculture and Rural Affairs;   Fax: (717) 334-8426
Children and Youth; Game and Fisheries; Tourism  (Gettysburg)
and Recreational Development

Representative **Gerald J. Mullery** (D-District 119) . . . . . . . (717) 783-4893
Counties Represented: Luzerne (part)         Dist: (570) 740-7031
Term Expires: 2016                           Fax: (570) 826-2584
156 South Market Street, Nanticoke, PA 18634
E-mail: repmullery@pahouse.net
Committees: Education; Game and Fisheries; Health; Judiciary; Local
Government
Education: King 1992 BA; Duquesne 1998 JD

Representative
**Thomas P. Murt** (R-District 152) . . . . . . . . . . (717) 787-6886 (Harrisburg)
Counties Represented: Montgomery (part),     Dist: (215) 674-3755
Philadelphia (part)                             (Hatboro)
Term Expires: 2016                           Fax: (215) 674-3021
19 South York Road, Hatboro, PA 19040           (Hatboro)
E-mail: tmurt@pahousegop.com
Committees: Human Services; Insurance; Labor and Industry; Urban
Affairs
Education: Penn State 1982 BS; La Salle U 1989 MA

Representative **Mark Mustio** (R-District 44) . . (717) 787-6651 (Harrisburg)
Counties Represented: Allegheny (part)       Dist: (412) 262-3780
Term Expires: 2016                              (Moon Township)
937 Beaver Grade Road, Moon Township, PA 15108  Dist: (412) 749-4727
519 Broad Street, Sewickley, PA 15143           (Sewickley)
E-mail: mmustio@pahousegop.com               Fax: (717) 783-3899
Committees: Appropriations; Committee on        (Harrisburg)
Committees; Environmental Resources and Energy;  Dist: (412) 262-3783
Liquor Control; Professional Licensure          (Moon Township)
                                             Dist: (412) 749-4730
                                                (Sewickley)

Representative **Edward "Ed" Neilson** (D-District 174) . . . . (717) 772-4032
Counties Represented: Philadelphia (part)    Fax: (717) 783-1579
Term Expires: 2016
E-mail: eneilson@pahouse.net
Committees: Game and Fisheries; Gaming Oversight; Transportation;
Urban Affairs
Education: St Joseph's U BA

Representative **Eric R. Nelson** (R-District 57) . . . . . . . . . . (717) 787-2372
Counties Represented: Westmoreland (part)
Term Expires: 2016
Committees: Aging and Older Adult Services; Gaming Oversight;
Human Services

Representative **Tedd C. Nesbit** (R-District 8) . . . . . . . . . . . (717) 783-6438
Counties Represented: Butler (part), Mercer (part)  Dist: (724) 458-4911
Term Expires: 2016                           Fax: (724) 782-2943
234 West Pine Street, Grove City, PA 16127   Dist: (724) 450-4104
E-mail: tnesbit@pahousegop.com
Committees: Children and Youth; Gaming Oversight; Judiciary

Representative **Brandon P. Neuman** (D-District 48) . . . . . . (717) 783-4834
Counties Represented: Washington (part)      Dist: (724) 743-7602
Term Expires: 2016                           Dist: (724) 743-7606
1825 Washington Road, Suite C,               Fax: (717) 705-1887
Washington, PA 15301
E-mail: bneuman@pahousegop.com
Committees: Agriculture and Rural Affairs; Consumer Affairs;
Environmental Resources and Energy; Judiciary; Labor and Industry
Education: Richmond 2005 BA; Pittsburgh 2006 MSL;
Duquesne 2009 JD

Representative
**Michael H. O'Brien** (D-District 175) . . . . . . . (717) 783-8098 (Harrisburg)
Counties Represented: Philadelphia (part)    Dist: (215) 503-3245
Term Expires: 2016                              (Philadelphia)
610 North Second Street, Philadelphia, PA 19123  Fax: (717) 780-4787
E-mail: mobrien@pahouse.net                     (Harrisburg)
Committees: Appropriations; Committee on      Dist: (215) 503-7850
Committees; Consumer Affairs; Education; Ethics;  (Philadelphia)
Health; State Government

Representative **Bernie O'Neill** (R-District 29) . . (717) 705-7170 (Harrisburg)
Counties Represented: Bucks (part)           Dist: (215) 441-2624
Term Expires: 2016                              (Warminster)
755 York Road, Suite 105, Warminster, PA 18974  Fax: (717) 783-3278
E-mail: boneill@pahousegop.com                  (Harrisburg)
Committees: Education                         Dist: (215) 441-2627
                                                (Warminster)

*(continued on next page)*

**Representatives** *continued*

Representative **Donna Oberlander** (R-District 63) . . . . . . . .(717) 772-9908
Counties Represented: Armstrong (part), Clarion,   Dist: (724) 783-6166
Forest (part)   Dist: (814) 226-9000
Term Expires: 2016   Fax: (717) 787-8215
405 Irvis Office Building, P.O. Box 202063,   Dist: (724) 783-6177
Harrisburg, PA 17120-2063   Dist: (814) 226-1614
160 South 2nd Street, Suite C, Clarion, PA 16214
E-mail: doberlan@pahousegop.com

Representative **Jason A. Ortitay** (R-District 46) . . . . . . . .(717) 787-1281
Counties Represented: Allegheny (part), Washington   Dist: (412) 221-5110
(part)   Fax: (412) 221-5113
Term Expires: 2016
275 Millers Run Road, Bridgeville, PA 15017
E-mail: jortitay@pahousegop.com
Committees: Aging and Older Adult Services; Gaming Oversight;
Human Services; Tourism and Recreational Development

Representative **David C. Parker** (R-District 115) . . . . . . . .(717) 787-3364
Counties Represented: Monroe (part)   Dist: (570) 420-2940
Term Expires: 2016   Fax: (570) 420-2944
411 Main Street, Suite 102-E, Stroudsburg, PA 18360
E-mail: dparker@pahousegop.com
Committees: Children and Youth; Commerce; Gaming Oversight

Representative
**Eddie Day Pashinski** (D-District 121) . . . . . .(717) 783-0686 (Harrisburg)
Counties Represented: Luzerne (part)   Dist: (570) 825-5934
Term Expires: 2016   (Wilkes Barre)
152 South Pennsylvania Avenue,   Fax: (717) 772-2284
Wilkes Barre, PA 18702   (Harrisburg)
E-mail: epashinski@pahouse.net   Dist: (570) 826-5436
Committees: Aging and Older Adult Services;   (Wilkes Barre)
Commerce; Human Services; Insurance; State Government
Education: Wilkes U BS; Penn State MA

Representative
**John D. Payne** (R-District 106) . . . . . . . . . .(717) 787-2684 (Harrisburg)
Counties Represented: Dauphin (part)   Dist: (717) 534-1323
Term Expires: 2016   (Hershey)
250 West Chocolate Avenue, Hershey, PA 17033   Fax: (717) 787-7557
E-mail: jpayne@pahousegop.com   (Harrisburg)
Committees: Committee on Committees; Gaming   Dist: (717) 534-1457
Oversight; Liquor Control   (Hershey)

Representative
**Michael Peifer** (R-District 139) . . . . . . . . . .(717) 783-2037 (Harrisburg)
Counties Represented: Pike (part), Wayne (part)   Dist: (570) 253-5533
Term Expires: 2016   (Honesdale)
32 Commercial Street, Honesdale, PA 18431   Fax: (717) 782-2910
E-mail: mpeifer@pahousegop.com   (Harrisburg)
Committees: Aging and Older Adult Services;   Dist: (570) 253-8046
Appropriations; Finance; Game and Fisheries   (Honesdale)
Education: Rider 1990 BS

Representative
**Joseph A. Petrarca** (D-District 55) . . . . . . . .(717) 787-5142 (Harrisburg)
Counties Represented: Armstrong (part), Indiana   Dist: (724) 567-6982
(part), Westmoreland (part)   (Vandergrift)
Term Expires: 2016   Fax: (717) 705-2014
239 Longfellow Street, Vandergrift, PA 15690   (Harrisburg)
E-mail: jpetrarc@pahouse.net   Dist: (724) 567-0006
Committees: Judiciary   (Vandergrift)
Education: St Vincent Col BS; Pittsburgh JD

Representative
**Scott A. Petri** (R-District 178) . . . . . . . . . . .(717) 787-9033 (Harrisburg)
Counties Represented: Bucks (part)   Dist: (215) 364-3414
Term Expires: 2016   (Richboro)
The Weather Vane, 95 Almshouse Road, Suite 303,   Fax: (717) 705-7012
Richboro, PA 18954   (Harrisburg)
E-mail: spetri@pahousegop.com   Dist: (215) 364-8626
Committees: Ethics; Liquor Control; Urban Affairs   (Richboro)
Education: Washington & Jefferson 1982 BA; Villanova 1985 JD

Representative **Kristin Lee Phillips-Hill** (R-District 93) . . . .(717) 783-8389
Counties Represented: York (part)   Dist: (717) 428-9889
Term Expires: 2016   Fax: (717) 771-1035
6872 Susquehanna Trail South, Jacobus, PA 17407
E-mail: khill@pahousegop.com
Committees: Children and Youth; Education; Health; State Government

Representative **Tina Pickett** (R-District 110) . . (717) 783-8238 (Harrisburg)
Counties Represented: Bradford (part), Sullivan,   Dist: (570) 265-3124
Susquehanna (part)   (Towanda)
Term Expires: 2016   Fax: (717) 787-0860
321 Main Street, Towanda, PA 18848   (Harrisburg)
E-mail: tpickett@pahousegop.com   Dist: (570) 265-9453
Committees: Committee on Committees; Consumer   (Towanda)
Affairs; Insurance; Rules

Representative **Jeffrey P. Pyle** (R-District 60) . . (717) 783-5327 (Harrisburg)
Counties Represented: Armstrong (part), Butler   Dist: (724) 763-3222
(part), Indiana (part)   (Ford City)
Term Expires: 2016   Dist: (724) 478-1050
409 Ford Street, Ford City, PA 16226   (Apollo)
208 1/2 North Railroad Avenue, Apollo, PA 15613   Dist: (724) 397-2961
289 Route 85 Highway, Home, PA 15747   (Home)
E-mail: jpyle@pahousegop.com   Fax: (717) 705-1921
Committees: Appropriations; Environmental   (Harrisburg)
Resources and Energy; Transportation   Dist: (724) 763-9788
Education: West Virginia 1986 BA;   (Ford City)
Indiana (PA) 1991 BS   Dist: (724) 478-1529
  (Apollo)
  Dist: (724) 397-2964
  (Home)

Representative **Thomas J. Quigley** (R-District 146) . . . . . .(717) 772-9963
Counties Represented: Montgomery (part)   Dist: (610) 792-1280
Term Expires: 2016   Fax: (717) 782-2951
E-mail: tquigley@pahousegop.com   Dist: (610) 792-1283
Committees: Consumer Affairs; Education; Finance; Human Services
Education: Philadelphia U 1986 BS, 1993 MBA

Representative
**Marguerite Quinn** (R-District 143) . . . . . . . .(717) 772-1413 (Harrisburg)
Counties Represented: Bucks (part)   Dist: (215) 489-2126
Term Expires: 2016   (Doylestown)
1032 North Easton Road,   Fax: (717) 783-3793
Doylestown, PA 18901-1055   (Harrisburg)
E-mail: mquinn@pahousegop.com   Dist: (215) 489-2129
Committees: Appropriations; Insurance; Professional   (Doylestown)
Licensure; Transportation
Education: St Joseph's U BA

Representative **Jack B. Rader, Jr.** (R-District 176) . . . . . . . .(717) 787-7732
Counties Represented: Monroe (part)   Dist: (570) 620-4341
Term Expires: 2016   Fax: (570) 620-4349
E-mail: jrader@pahousegop.com
Committees: Children and Youth; Human Services; Local Government;
Tourism and Recreational Development

Representative
**Kathy L. Rapp** (R-District 65) . . . . . . . . . . . .(717) 787-1367 (Harrisburg)
Counties Represented: Crawford (part), Forest   Dist: (814) 723-5203
(part), Warren   (Warren)
Term Expires: 2016   Fax: (717) 787-5854
404 Market Street, Warren, PA 16365   (Harrisburg)
E-mail: klrapp@pahousegop.com   Dist: (814) 728-3564
Committees: Education; Environmental Resources   (Warren)
and Energy; Finance; Veterans Affairs and Emergency Preparedness

Representative **Adam J. Ravenstahl** (D-District 20) . . . . . .(717) 787-5470
Counties Represented: Allegheny (part)   Fax: (717) 783-0407
Term Expires: 2016   Dist: (412) 761-2303
3689 California Avenue, Pittsburgh, PA 15212
E-mail: aravenstahl@pahousegop.com
Committees: Aging and Older Adult Services; Children and Youth;
Labor and Industry; Liquor Control; Veterans Affairs and Emergency
Preparedness
Education: Robert Morris U (PA) 2007 BS

Representative
**Harry A. Readshaw** (D-District 36) . . . . . . .(717) 783-0411 (Harrisburg)
Counties Represented: Allegheny (part)   Dist: (412) 881-4208
Term Expires: 2016   (Pittsburgh)
1917 Brownsville Road, Pittsburgh, PA 15210   Fax: (717) 705-2007
E-mail: hreadsha@pahouse.net   (Harrisburg)
Committees: Professional Licensure   Dist: (412) 886-2077
  (Pittsburgh)

Representative
**David "Dave" Reed** (R-District 62) . . . . . . . .(717) 705-7173 (Harrisburg)
Counties Represented: Indiana (part)   Dist: (724) 465-0220
Term Expires: 2016   (Indiana)
550 Philadelphia Street, Indiana, PA 15701   Fax: (717) 705-1947
E-mail: dreed@pahousegop.com   (Harrisburg)
Committees: Committee on Committees; Rules   Dist: (724) 465-0221
  (Indiana)

Representative **Mike Reese** (R-District 59) . . . . . . . . . . . . .(717) 783-9311
Counties Represented: Somerset (part),   Dist: (724) 423-6503
Westmoreland (part)   Fax: (717) 260-6502
Term Expires: 2016   Dist: (724) 423-2812
2203 Mount Pleasant Road, Mount Pleasant, PA 15666
P.O. Box 202059, Harrisburg, PA 17120-2059
E-mail: mreese@pahousegop.com
Committees: Agriculture and Rural Affairs; Committee on Committees;
Education; Liquor Control; Rules
Education: Duquesne 2000 BSEd; Seton Hall 2004 MBA

Representative **Mike Regan** (R-District 92) . . . . . . . . . . . . . (717) 783-8783
Counties Represented: Cumberland (part), York Dist: (717) 432-0792
(part) (Dillsburg)
Term Expires: 2016 Fax: (717) 782-2920
1 E. Harrisburg Street, Dillsburg, PA 17019 Fax: (717) 732-0795
412 Irvis Office Buiding, Harrisburg, PA 17120 (Dillsburg)
E-mail: mregan@pahousegop.com
Committees: Insurance; Judiciary; Liquor Control; Tourism
and Recreational Development; Veterans Affairs and Emergency
Preparedness
Education: Albright BS

Representative **Brad Roae** (R-District 6) . . . . . . (717) 787-2353 (Harrisburg)
Counties Represented: Crawford (part), Erie (part) Dist: (814) 827-6054
Term Expires: 2016 (Titusville)
109 South Washington Street, Titusville, PA 16354 Dist: (814) 336-1136
Downtown Mall, 900-920 Water Street, (Meadville)
Meadville, PA 16335 Fax: (717) 705-2032
E-mail: broae@pahousegop.com (Harrisburg)
Committees: Finance; Human Services; Insurance; Dist: (814) 878-5778
State Government (Titusville)
Dist: (814) 337-7680
(Meadville)

Representative
**James R. Roebuck, Jr.** (D-District 188) . . . . (717) 783-1000 (Harrisburg)
Counties Represented: Philadelphia (part) Dist: (215) 724-2227
Term Expires: 2016 (Philadelphia)
4712 Baltimore Avenue, Philadelphia, PA 19143 Fax: (717) 783-1665
E-mail: jroebuck@pahouse.net (Harrisburg)
Committees: Education Dist: (215) 724-2230
Education: Virginia Union 1966 BA; (Philadelphia)
Virginia 1969 MA, 1977 PhD

Representative **Chris Ross** (R-District 158) . . . (717) 783-1574 (Harrisburg)
Counties Represented: Chester (part) Dist: (610) 925-0555
Term Expires: 2016 (Unionville)
P.O. Box 835, Unionville, PA 19375 Fax: (717) 783-1589
E-mail: cross@pahousegop.com (Harrisburg)
Committees: Liquor Control; Urban Affairs Dist: (610) 925-5408
Education: Harvard 1974 AB (Unionville)

Representative
**William Gregory "Greg" Rothman** (R-District 87) . . . . (717) 787-2372
Counties Represented: Cumberland (part) Dist: (717) 795-6091
Term Expires: 2016
5521 Carlisle Pike, Suite 2-D, Mechanicsburg, PA 17050
E-mail: grothman@pahousegop.com
Committees: Children and Youth; Commerce; Urban Affairs
Education: UMass (Amherst) 1989 BS; Johns Hopkins 2005 MS

Representative **Mark Rozzi** (D-District 126) . . . . . . . . . . . . (717) 783-3290
Counties Represented: Berks (part) Fax: (717) 787-7517
Term Expires: 2016
4933 Kutztown Road, Temple, PA 19560
E-mail: mrozzi@pahouse.net
Committees: Appropriations; Children and Youth; Commerce; Gaming
Oversight; Human Services
Education: Kutztown 1996 BA

Representative **Rick Saccone** (R-District 39) . . . . . . . . . . . (717) 260-6122
Counties Represented: Allegheny (part), Washington Dist: (412) 653-1025
(part) Fax: (412) 653-1275
Term Expires: 2016
1002 Old Hickory Lane, Jefferson Hills, PA 15025
E-mail: rsaccone@pahousegop.com
Committees: Children and Youth; Judiciary; State Government;
Veterans Affairs and Emergency Preparedness
Education: Pittsburgh 2002 PhD

Representative
**Christopher Sainato** (D-District 9) . . . . . . . . (717) 772-2436 (Harrisburg)
Counties Represented: Lawrence (part) Dist: (724) 656-1112
Term Expires: 2016 (New Castle)
Z-Penn Building, 20 South Mercer Street, Fax: (717) 783-8536
New Castle, PA 16101 (Harrisburg)
E-mail: csainato@pahouse.net Dist: (724) 656-3352
Committees: Veterans Affairs and Emergency (New Castle)
Preparedness
Education: Youngstown State 1982 BS

Representative
**Steve Samuelson** (D-District 135) . . . . . . . . (717) 705-1881 (Harrisburg)
Counties Represented: Northampton (part) Dist: (610) 867-3890
Term Expires: 2016 (Bethlehem)
104 East Broad Street, Bethlehem, PA 18018 Fax: (717) 772-2469
E-mail: ssamuels@pahouse.net (Harrisburg)
Committees: Aging and Older Adult Services Dist: (610) 861-2104
(Bethlehem)

Representative
**Thomas R. "Tommy" Sankey III** (R-District 73) . . . . . . (717) 787-7099
Counties Represented: Cambria (part), Clearfield Dist: (814) 765-0609
(part) Fax: (717) 782-2922
Term Expires: 2016 Dist: (814) 765-0592
315 East Market Street, Suite B, Clearfield, PA 16830
E-mail: tsankey@pahousegop.com
Committees: Environmental Resources and Energy; Finance; Insurance;
Local Government; State Government
Education: St Francis U 2004 BSAcc

Representative
**Steven J. "Steve" Santarsiero** (D-District 31) . . . . . . . . (717) 787-5475
Counties Represented: Bucks (part) Dist: (215) 968-3975
Term Expires: 2016 Fax: (717) 787-6929
224 Irvis Office Building, P.O. Box 202031, Dist: (215) 968-4674
Harrisburg, PA 17120-2031
277 North Sycamore Street, Newton, PA 18940
E-mail: ssantarsiero@pahouse.net
Committees: Children and Youth; Education; Transportation
Education: Tufts 1987 BA; Pennsylvania 1992 JD;
Holy Family U 2006 MEd

Representative **James R. Santora** (R-District 163) . . . . . . (717) 783-8808
Counties Represented: Delaware (part) Dist: (610) 259-2820
Term Expires: 2016 Fax: (717) 782-2955
Six South Springfield Road, Dist: (610) 259-7019
Clifton Heights, PA 19018
E-mail: jsantora@pahousegop.com
Committees: Commerce; Gaming Oversight; Professional Licensure;
Urban Affairs

Representative **Lynwood W. Savage** (D-District 192) . . . . . (717) 783-2192
Counties Represented: Philadelphia (part)
Term Expires: 2016
E-mail: lsavage@pahouse.net
Committees: Aging and Older Adult Services; Agriculture and
Rural Affairs; Environmental Resources and Energy; Tourism and
Recreational Development

Representative
**Stanley E. "Stan" Saylor** (R-District 94) . . (717) 783-6426 (Harrisburg)
Counties Represented: York (part) Dist: (717) 244-9232
Term Expires: 2016 (Red Lion)
15 South Main Street, 2nd Floor, Fax: (717) 705-1849
Red Lion, PA 17356 (Harrisburg)
E-mail: ssaylor@pahousegop.com Dist: (717) 246-2387
Committees: Education (Red Lion)

Representative **Paul Schemel** (R-District 90) . . . . . . . . . . . . (717) 783-5218
Counties Represented: Franklin (part) Dist: (717) 749-7384
Term Expires: 2016 Fax: (717) 782-2903
1402 East Main Street, Waynesboro, PA 17268 Fax: (717) 762-4380
E-mail: pschemel@pahousegop.com
Committees: Aging and Older Adult Services; Commerce; Judiciary

Representative
**Michael H. "Mike" Schlossberg** (D-District 132) . . . . . . (717) 705-1869
Counties Represented: Lehigh (part)
Term Expires: 2016
2030 W. Tilghman Street, Allentown, PA 18104
E-mail: mschlossberg@pahouse.net
Committees: Education; Environmental Resources and Energy; Health;
Human Services; Transportation
Education: Muhlenberg 2005 BA; Lehigh 2006 MA

Representative **Kevin J. Schreiber** (D-District 95) . . . . . . . . (717) 787-7514
Counties Represented: York (part) Dist: (717) 848-9595
Term Expires: 2016 Fax: (717) 780-4765
53 E. North Street, Suite 3, York, PA 17401 Dist: (717) 848-1871
E-mail: repschreiber@pahouse.net
Committees: Appropriations; Education; Environmental Resources and
Energy; Local Government; Tourism and Recreational Development
Education: Penn State 2012 MPA

Representative **Peter G. Schweyer** (D-District 22) . . . . . . . (717) 787-2909
Counties Represented: Lehigh (part) Dist: (610) 791-6270
Term Expires: 2016 Fax: (717) 787-2176
1912 South Fourth Street, Allentown, PA 18103 Dist: (610) 791-6274
E-mail: pschweyer@pahouse.net
Committees: Appropriations; Consumer Affairs; Liquor Control; Urban
Affairs; Veterans Affairs and Emergency Preparedness

Representative **Justin J. Simmons** (R-District 131) . . . . . . (717) 783-1673
Counties Represented: Lehigh (part), Montgomery Dist: (610) 861-2069
(part), Northampton (part) Fax: (610) 861-2069
Term Expires: 2016
3606 Route 378, Suite A, Bethlehem, PA 18015
E-mail: jsimmons@pahousegop.com
Committees: Insurance; Liquor Control; Urban Affairs
Education: St Joseph's U 2008 BA

*(continued on next page)*

LEGISLATIVE BRANCH

**Representatives** *continued*

Representative **Brian K. Sims, JD** (D-District 182) . . . . . . . (717) 783-4072
Counties Represented: Philadelphia (part)     Fax: (717) 787-5066
Term Expires: 2016
21 S. 12th Street, Suite 182, Philadelphia, PA 19107
E-mail: bsims@pahouse.net
Committees: Commerce; Game and Fisheries; Human Services; State
Government; Tourism and Recreational Development
Education: Bloomsburg 2001 BSBA; Michigan State 2004 JD

Representative **Pam Snyder** (D-District 50) . . . . . . . . . . . . (717) 783-3797
Counties Represented: Fayette (part), Greene,    Fax: (717) 772-3605
Washington (part)
Term Expires: 2016
123 B East Wing, Harrisburg, PA 17120-2050
E-mail: psnyder@pahouse.net
Committees: Committee on Committees; Consumer Affairs;
Environmental Resources and Energy; Labor and Industry; Local
Government

Representative
**Curtis G. "Curt" Sonney** (R-District 4) . . . . (717) 783-9087 (Harrisburg)
Counties Represented: Erie (part)     Dist: (814) 664-9126
Term Expires: 2016     (Corry)
4457 Buffalo Road, Erie, PA 16510    Dist: (814) 897-2080
707 East Columbia Avenue, Corry, PA 16407     (Erie)
E-mail: csonney@pahousegop.com    Fax: (717) 787-2005
Committees: Appropriations; Insurance; Liquor     (Harrisburg)
Control; Professional Licensure     Dist: (814) 664-5857
    (Corry)
    Dist: (814) 897-2083
    (Erie)

Representative **Craig T. Staats** (R-District 145) . . . . . . . . . (717) 783-3154
Counties Represented: Bucks (part)     Dist: (215) 536-1434
Term Expires: 2016     Fax: (717) 260-6521
10 South Third Street, Quakertown, PA 18951    Dist: (215) 536-1437
E-mail: cstaats@pahousegop.com
Committees: Aging and Older Adult Services; Education; Human
Services; Liquor Control

Representative **Todd Stephens** (R-District 151) . . . . . . . . . (717) 260-6163
Counties Represented: Montgomery (part)     Dist: (215) 368-5165
Term Expires: 2016     Fax: (215) 368-5169
515 Stump Road, North Wales, PA 19454
E-mail: tstephen@pahousegop.com
Committees: Children and Youth; Consumer Affairs; Insurance;
Judiciary
Education: Shippensburg BA

Representative
**P. Michael Sturla** (D-District 96) . . . . . . . . . (717) 787-3555 (Harrisburg)
Counties Represented: Lancaster (part)     Dist: (717) 295-3157
Term Expires: 2016     (Lancaster)
The Griest Building, 8 North Queen Street,    Fax: (717) 705-1923
Suite 1100, Lancaster, PA 17603     (Harrisburg)
E-mail: Rep.MikeSturla@pahouse.net    Dist: (717) 295-7816
Committees: Rules     (Lancaster)

Representative **Will Tallman** (R-District 193) . . . . . . . . . . . (717) 783-8875
Counties Represented: Adams (part), Cumberland    Dist: (717) 633-1721
(part)     Fax: (717) 705-7012
Term Expires: 2016
5 East Wing, P.O. Box 202193, Harrisburg, PA 17120-2193
Hanover Station, 1157 Eichelberger Street, Unit 3A,
Hanover, PA 17331
E-mail: wtallman@pahousegop.com
Committees: Aging and Older Adult Services; Education; Veterans
Affairs and Emergency Preparedness

Representative
**John J. Taylor** (R-District 177) . . . . . . . . . . . (717) 787-3179 (Harrisburg)
Counties Represented: Philadelphia (part)     Dist: (215) 425-0901
Term Expires: 2016     (Philadelphia)
4725 Richmond Street, Philadelphia, PA 19137    Dist: (215) 744-2600
2901 East Thompson Street, Philadelphia, PA 19134     (Philadelphia)
E-mail: jtaylor@pahousegop.com    Fax: (215) 705-1850
Committees: Liquor Control; Transportation     (Harrisburg)
Education: Central Florida 1980 BS;    Dist: (215) 560-3996
Temple 1984 JD     (Philadelphia)
    Dist: (215) 744-2605
    (Philadelphia)

Representative
**W. Curtis Thomas** (D-District 181) . . . . . . . .(717) 787-9471 (Harrisburg)
Counties Represented: Philadelphia (part)     Dist: (215) 232-1203
Term Expires: 2016     (Philadelphia)
1348 West Girard Avenue, Philadelphia, PA 19123    Fax: (717) 787-7297
E-mail: cthomas@pahouse.net     (Harrisburg)
Committees: Commerce     Dist: (215) 232-1203
Education: Temple 1975 BS; Antioch U 1980 JD     (Philadelphia)

Representative **Mike Tobash** (R-District 125) . . . . . . . . . . . (717) 260-6148
Counties Represented: Dauphin (part), Schuylkill    Dist: (570) 385-8235
(part)     Fax: (570) 385-8238
Term Expires: 2016
988 East Main Street, Schuylkill Haven, PA 17972
E-mail: mtobash@pahousegop.com
Committees: Agriculture and Rural Affairs; Education; Insurance;
Veterans Affairs and Emergency Preparedness

Representative **Marcy Toepel** (R-District 147) . . . . . . . . . . (717) 787-9501
Counties Represented: Montgomery (part)     Res: (610) 287-4181
Term Expires: 2016     Fax: (610) 287-4182
105 Memorial Road and Route 29, Schnecksville, PA 19473
Irvis Office Building, Room 405, Harrisburg, PA 17120-2147
E-mail: mtoepel@pahousegop.com
Committees: Consumer Affairs; Health; Judiciary; Professional
Licensure

Representative **Tarah Toohil** (R-District 116) . . . . . . . . . . . (717) 260-6136
Counties Represented: Luzerne (part)     Dist: (570) 450-7905
Term Expires: 2016     Fax: (570) 459-3946
1 West Broad Street, Harrisburg, PA 17120-2116
E-mail: ttoohil@pahousegop.com
Committees: Children and Youth; Health; Judiciary; Local Government;
Rules

Representative **Jesse Topper** (R-District 78) . . . . . . . . . . . (717) 787-7076
Counties Represented: Bedford (part), Franklin    Fax: (717) 782-2933
(part), Fulton
Term Expires: 2016
133 South Richard Street, Bedford, PA 15522
E-mail: jtopper@pahousegop.com
Committees: Commerce; Health; Labor and Industry; State Government
Education: Frostburg State U

Representative **Dan Truitt** (R-District 156) . . . . . . . . . . . . (717) 260-6164
Counties Represented: Chester (part)     Dist: (610) 696-4990
Term Expires: 2016     Fax: (610) 738-2163
21 South Church Street, 1st Floor, West Chester, PA 19382
E-mail: dtruitt@pahousegop.com
Committees: Commerce; Education; Labor and Industry; State
Government

Representative **Mike Turzai** (R-District 28) . . . . (717) 772-9943 (Harrisburg)
Counties Represented: Allegheny (part)     Dist: (412) 369-2230
Term Expires: 2016     (Pittsburgh)
125 Hillvue Lane, First Floor, Pittsburgh, PA 15237    Fax: (717) 772-2470
E-mail: mturzai@pahousegop.com     (Harrisburg)
Committees: Committee on Committees; Rules    Dist: (412) 369-2236
    (Pittsburgh)

Representative
**Michael A. "Mike" Vereb** (R-District 150) . .(717) 705-7164 (Harrisburg)
Counties Represented: Montgomery (part)     Dist: (610) 409-2615
Term Expires: 2016     (Collegeville)
3950 Germantown Pike, Collegeville, PA 19426    Fax: (610) 409-2619
E-mail: mvereb@pahousegop.com     (Collegeville)
Committees: Appropriations; Judiciary; Veterans Affairs and
Emergency Preparedness

Representative
**Gregory S. Vitali** (D-District 166) . . . . . . . .(717) 787-7647 (Harrisburg)
Counties Represented: Delaware (part),     Dist: (610) 789-3900
Montgomery (part)     (Havertown)
Term Expires: 2016     Fax: (717) 705-2089
1001 East Darby Road, Havertown, PA 19083     (Harrisburg)
E-mail: gvitali@pahouse.net    Dist: (215) 560-4197
Committees: Environmental Resources and Energy     (Havertown)
Education: Villanova 1978 BS, 1981 JD

Representative **Judith F. "Judy" Ward** (R-District 80) . . . . (717) 787-9020
Counties Represented: Blair (part)     Dist: (814) 695-2398
Term Expires: 2016     Fax: (717) 260-6521
324 Allegheny Street, Hollidaysburg, PA 16648    Dist: (814) 946-7239
E-mail: jward@pahousegop.com
Committees: Health; Human Services; Labor and Industry; State
Government

Representative **Ryan Warner** (R-District 52) . . . . . . . . . . . (717) 787-1540
Counties Represented: Fayette (part), Westmoreland (part)
Term Expires: 2016
2152 University Drive, Mount Braddock, PA 15465
E-mail: rwarner@pahousegop.com
Committees: Game and Fisheries; Gaming Oversight; Human Services; Local Government
Dist: (724) 437-1105
Fax: (717) 782-2882
Dist: (724) 437-1106

Representative
**Katharine M. Watson** (R-District 144) . . . . . (717) 787-5452 (Harrisburg)
Counties Represented: Bucks (part)
Term Expires: 2016
1410 West Street Road, Warminster, PA 18974
E-mail: kwatson@pahousegop.com
Committees: Children and Youth; Rules; Transportation
Dist: (215) 674-0500 (Warminster)
Fax: (717) 783-8934 (Harrisburg)
Dist: (215) 674-0347 (Warminster)

Representative **Parke H. Wentling** (R-District 17) . . . . . . . . (717) 783-5008
Counties Represented: Crawford (part), Erie (part), Lawrence (part), Mercer (part)
Term Expires: 2016
142 Main Street, Suite 1W, Girard, PA 16417
E-mail: pwentling@pahousegop.com
Committees: Game and Fisheries; Human Services; Local Government
Dist: (814) 774-3105
Fax: (814) 705-1948
Dist: (814) 774-3108

Representative
**Jake Wheatley, Jr.** (D-District 19) . . . . . . . . (717) 783-3783 (Harrisburg)
Counties Represented: Allegheny (part)
Term Expires: 2016
2015-2017 Centre Avenue, Pittsburgh, PA 15219
E-mail: jwheatley@pahouse.net
Committees: Finance
Dist: (412) 471-7760 (Pittsburgh)
Fax: (717) 780-4753 (Harrisburg)
Dist: (412) 471-8056 (Pittsburgh)

Representative **Jeff C. Wheeland** (R-District 83) . . . . . . . . (717) 787-2885
Counties Represented: Lycoming (part)
Term Expires: 2016
349 Pine Street, Suite 1, Williamsport, PA 17701
E-mail: jwheeland@pahousegop.com
Committees: Commerce; Local Government; State Government; Urban Affairs
Fax: (717) 782-2948

Representative **Martina A. White** (R-District 170) . . . . . . . .(717) 787-2372
Counties Represented: Philadelphia (part)
Term Expires: 2016
E-mail: mwhite@pahousegop.com
Committees: Human Services; Judiciary; Urban Affairs
Education: Elizabethtown 2010 BSBA

Representative
**Rosita C. Youngblood** (D-District 198) . . . . (717) 787-7727 (Harrisburg)
Counties Represented: Philadelphia (part)
Term Expires: 2016
5736 Greene Street, Philadelphia, PA 19144
E-mail: ryoungbl@pahouse.net
Committees: Rules
Dist: (215) 849-6426 (Philadelphia)
Fax: (717) 772-1313 (Harrisburg)
Dist: (215) 849-5476 (Philadelphia)

Representative **David H. Zimmerman** (R-District 99) . . . . . (717) 787-3531
Counties Represented: Lancaster (part)
Term Expires: 2016
125 Peters Road, New Holland, PA 17557
E-mail: dzimmerman@pahousegop.com
Committees: Agriculture and Rural Affairs; Human Services; Local Government
Dist: (717) 351-1100
Fax: (717) 705-1986
Dist: (717) 351-1103

District 168 **(Vacant)** . . . . . . . . . . . . . . . . . . . . . . . . . . . . . (717) 787-2372
Note: A special election to fill this legislative vacancy will be held on July 12, 2016.

# House Standing Committees
## Aging and Older Adult Services

| Majority Members | Minority Members |
|---|---|
| Timothy "Tim" Hennessey (R-26) *Chair* | Steve Samuelson (D-135) *Democratic Chair* |
| Steven C. Mentzer (R-97) *Secretary* | Adam J. Ravenstahl (D-20) *Democratic Secretary* |
| Cris Dush (R-66) | Donna Bullock (D-195) |
| Harold A. "Hal" English (R-30) | Mary Jo Daley (D-148) |
| Mark M. Gillen (R-128) | Jason Dawkins (D-179) |
| Mauree Gingrich (R-101) | Pamela A. DeLissio (D-194) |
| Richard "Rich" Irvin (R-81) | Michael J. Driscoll (D-173) |
| Barry J. Jozwiak (R-5) | Frank Farina (D-112) |
| Aaron D. Kaufer (R-120) | Mark A. Longietti (D-7) |
| Kate Anne Klunk (R-169) | Eddie Day Pashinski (D-121) |
| Eric R. Nelson (R-57) | |

**Majority Members** *continued*
Jason A. Ortitay (R-46)
Michael Peifer (R-139)
Paul Schemel (R-90)
Craig T. Staats (R-145)
Will Tallman (R-193)

**Minority Members** *continued*
Lynwood W. Savage (D-192)

## Agriculture and Rural Affairs

| Majority Members | Minority Members |
|---|---|
| Martin T. Causer (R-67) *Chair* | Mike Carroll (D-118) *Democratic Chair* |
| Mark K. Keller (R-86) *Vice Chair* | Sid Michaels Kavulich (D-114) *Democratic Vice Chair* |
| David H. Zimmerman (R-99) *Secretary* | Brandon P. Neuman (D-48) *Democratic Secretary* |
| Stephen Bloom (R-199) | Vanessa Lowery Brown (D-190) |
| Karen Boback (R-117) | Tonyelle Cook-Artis (D-200) |
| Russ Diamond (R-102) | Margo L. Davidson (D-164) |
| Joe Emrick (R-137) | Pamela A. DeLissio (D-194) |
| Mindy Fee (R-37) | Lynwood W. Savage (D-192) |
| Marcia M. Hahn (R-138) | Jordan A. Harris (D-186) |
| Rob W. Kauffman (R-89) | Tim Mahoney (D-51) |
| John A. Lawrence (R-13) | Daniel T. McNeill (D-133) |
| John A. Maher III (R-40) | |
| David R. Millard (R-109) | |
| Dan Moul (R-91) | |
| Mike Reese (R-59) | |
| Mike Tobash (R-125) | |

## Appropriations

| Majority Members | Minority Members |
|---|---|
| William F. "Bill" Adolph, Jr. (R-165) *Chair* | Joseph F. Markosek (D-25) *Democratic Chair* |
| Mark Mustio (R-44) *Vice Chair* | Leslie Acosta (D-197) |
| Jeffrey P. Pyle (R-60) *Secretary* | Matthew D. Bradford (D-70) |
| Karen Boback (R-117) | Donna Bullock (D-195) |
| Jim Christiana (R-15) | Tim Briggs (D-149) |
| Gary Day (R-187) | Mary Jo Daley (D-148) |
| George Dunbar (R-56) | Madeleine Dean (D-153) |
| Garth D. Everett (R-84) | Maria P. Donatucci (D-185) |
| Keith J. Greiner (R-43) | Ed Gainey (D-24) |
| Seth M. Grove (R-196) | John T. Galloway (D-140) |
| Susan C. "Sue" Helm (R-104) | Stephen Kinsey (D-201) |
| Warren Kampf (R-157) | Michael H. O'Brien (D-175) |
| Fred Keller (R-85) | Mark Rozzi (D-126) |
| Jim Marshall (R-14) | Kevin J. Schreiber (D-95) |
| Kurt A. Masser (R-107) | Peter G. Schweyer (D-22) |
| Nicholas A. "Nick" Miccarelli III (R-162) | |
| David R. Millard (R-109) | |
| Duane D. Milne (R-167) | |
| Michael Peifer (R-139) | |
| Marguerite Quinn (R-143) | |
| Curtis G. "Curt" Sonney (R-4) | |
| Michael A. "Mike" Vereb (R-150) | |

## Children and Youth

| Majority Members | Minority Members |
|---|---|
| Katharine M. Watson (R-144) *Chair* | H. Scott Conklin (D-77) *Democratic Chair* |
| Dan Moul (R-91) *Vice Chair* | Mark Rozzi (D-126) *Democratic Secretary* |
| Tarah Toohil (R-116) *Secretary* | Leslie Acosta (D-197) |
| Keith J. Greiner (R-43) | Pamela A. DeLissio (D-194) |
| Kristin Lee Phillips-Hill (R-93) | Patty H. Kim (D-103) |
| Fred Keller (R-85) | Leanne Krueger-Braneky (D-161) |
| Kate Anne Klunk (R-169) | Stephen "Steve" McCarter (D-154) |
| Harry Lewis, Jr. (R-74) | Joanna E. McClinton (D-191) |
| David M. Maloney, Sr. (R-130) | Daniel L. "Dan" Miller (D-42) |
| Brett R. Miller (R-41) | Adam J. Ravenstahl (D-20) |
| Tedd C. Nesbit (R-8) | Steven J. "Steve" Santarsiero (D-31) |
| David C. Parker (R-115) | |
| Jack B. Rader, Jr. (R-176) | |
| William Gregory "Greg" Rothman (R-87) | |
| Rick Saccone (R-39) | |
| Todd Stephens (R-151) | |

## Commerce

**Majority Members**
Adam C. Harris (R-82) *Chair*
Ryan E. Mackenzie (R-134)
  *Secretary*
Lynda Schlegel Culver (R-108)
Cris Dush (R-66)
Keith J. Greiner (R-43)
Marcia M. Hahn (R-138)
R. Lee James (R-64)
John A. Lawrence (R-13)
Carl Walker Metzgar (R-69)
Duane D. Milne (R-167)
David C. Parker (R-115)
William Gregory "Greg" Rothman
  (R-87)
James R. Santora (R-163)
Paul Schemel (R-90)
Jesse Topper (R-78)
Dan Truitt (R-156)
Jeff C. Wheeland (R-83)

**Minority Members**
W. Curtis Thomas (D-181)
  *Democratic Chair*
Michael J. Driscoll (D-173)
  *Democratic Secretary*
Tonyelle Cook-Artis (D-200)
Marty Flynn (D-113)
Jaret A. Gibbons (D-10)
William C. "Bill" Kortz II (D-38)
Mark A. Longietti (D-7)
Robert F. Matzie (D-16)
Stephen "Steve" McCarter (D-154)
Eddie Day Pashinski (D-121)
Mark Rozzi (D-126)
Brian K. Sims (D-182)

## Committee on Committees

**Majority Members**
Robert W. "Bob" Godshall (R-53)
  *Chair*
William F. "Bill" Adolph, Jr.
  (R-165)
Bryan Cutler (R-100)
Brian L. Ellis (R-11)
Sandra J. Major (R-111)
Mark Mustio (R-44)
John D. Payne (R-106)
Tina Pickett (R-110)
David "Dave" Reed (R-62)
Mike Reese (R-59)
Mike Turzai (R-28)

**Minority Members**
Michael H. O'Brien (D-175)
  *Democratic Chair*
Tina M. Davis (D-141)
Stephen Kinsey (D-201)
Mark A. Longietti (D-7)
Pam Snyder (D-50)

## Consumer Affairs

**Majority Members**
Robert W. "Bob" Godshall (R-53)
  *Chair*
Warren Kampf (R-157) *Secretary*
Stephen E. Barrar (R-160)
Sheryl M. Delozier (R-88)
Gene DiGirolamo (R-18)
Eli Evankovich (R-54)
Frank A. Farry (R-142)
Rob W. Kauffman (R-89)
Kurt A. Masser (R-107)
Carl Walker Metzgar (R-69)
Nicholas A. "Nick" Miccarelli III
  (R-162)
Tina Pickett (R-110)
Thomas J. Quigley (R-146)
Todd Stephens (R-151)
Marcy Toepel (R-147)

**Minority Members**
Peter J. Daley II (D-49)
  *Democratic Chair*
Pam Snyder (D-50)
  *Democratic Secretary*
Ryan A. Bizzarro (D-3)
Frank Burns (D-72)
Tina M. Davis (D-141)
Marty Flynn (D-113)
Mark A. Longietti (D-7)
Robert F. Matzie (D-16)
Brandon P. Neuman (D-48)
Michael H. O'Brien (D-175)
Peter G. Schweyer (D-22)

## Education

**Majority Members**
Stanley E. "Stan" Saylor (R-94)
  *Chair*
Kristin Lee Phillips-Hill (R-93)
  *Secretary*
Rosemary M. Brown (R-189)
Jim Christiana (R-15)
Harold A. "Hal" English (R-30)
Mark M. Gillen (R-128)
Seth M. Grove (R-196)
Harry Lewis, Jr. (R-74)
Bernie O'Neill (R-29)
Thomas J. Quigley (R-146)
Kathy L. Rapp (R-65)
Mike Reese (R-59)
Craig T. Staats (R-145)
Will Tallman (R-193)
Mike Tobash (R-125)
Dan Truitt (R-156)

**Minority Members**
James R. Roebuck, Jr. (D-188)
  *Democratic Chair*
Steven J. "Steve" Santarsiero (D-31)
  *Democratic Secretary*
Patrick J. Harkins (D-1)
Mark A. Longietti (D-7)
Stephen "Steve" McCarter (D-154)
Daniel L. "Dan" Miller (D-42)
Gerald J. Mullery (D-119)
Michael H. O'Brien (D-175)
Michael H. "Mike" Schlossberg
  (D-132)
Kevin J. Schreiber (D-95)

## Environmental Resources and Energy

**Majority Members**
John A. Maher III (R-40) *Chair*
Ryan E. Mackenzie (R-134)
  *Secretary*
Stephen Bloom (R-199)
Martin T. Causer (R-67)
Jim Christiana (R-15)
Becky Corbin (R-155)
Garth D. Everett (R-84)
Matt Gabler (R-75)
R. Lee James (R-64)
Jim Marshall (R-14)
Carl Walker Metzgar (R-69)
Mark Mustio (R-44)
Jeffrey P. Pyle (R-60)
Kathy L. Rapp (R-65)
Thomas R. "Tommy" Sankey III
  (R-73)

**Minority Members**
Gregory S. Vitali (D-166)
  *Democratic Chair*
Bryan E. Barbin (D-71)
Tim Briggs (D-149)
Jordan A. Harris (D-186)
Leanne Krueger-Braneky (D-161)
Stephen "Steve" McCarter (D-154)
Brandon P. Neuman (D-48)
Lynwood W. Savage (D-192)
Michael H. "Mike" Schlossberg
  (D-132)
Kevin J. Schreiber (D-95)
Pam Snyder (D-50)

## Ethics

**Majority Members**
Scott A. Petri (R-178) *Chair*
Sheryl M. Delozier (R-88)
Brian L. Ellis (R-11)
Carl Walker Metzgar (R-69)

**Minority Members**
Mark A. Longietti (D-7)
  *Democratic Chair*
Madeleine Dean (D-153)
Sid Michaels Kavulich (D-114)
Michael H. O'Brien (D-175)

## Finance

**Majority Members**
Kerry A. Benninghoff (R-171)
  *Chair*
Michael Peifer (R-139) *Vice Chair*
George Dunbar (R-56) *Secretary*
Stephen Bloom (R-199)
Eli Evankovich (R-54)
Matt Gabler (R-75)
Seth M. Grove (R-196)
R. Lee James (R-64)
Aaron D. Kaufer (R-120)
Jerry Knowles (R-124)
John A. Lawrence (R-13)
Duane D. Milne (R-167)
Thomas J. Quigley (R-146)
Kathy L. Rapp (R-65)
Brad Roae (R-6)
Thomas R. "Tommy" Sankey III
  (R-73)

**Minority Members**
Jake Wheatley, Jr. (D-19)
  *Democratic Chair*
Madeleine Dean (D-153)
  *Democratic Vice Chair*
Margo L. Davidson (D-164)
  *Democratic Secretary*
Leslie Acosta (D-197)
Kevin J. Boyle (D-172)
Matthew D. Bradford (D-70)
Mary Jo Daley (D-148)
Jordan A. Harris (D-186)
Sid Michaels Kavulich (D-114)
Stephen Kinsey (D-201)
Daniel T. McNeill (D-133)

## Game and Fisheries

**Majority Members**
Keith Gillespie (R-47) *Chair*
Dan Moul (R-91) *Vice Chair*
Brett R. Miller (R-41) *Secretary*
Joe Emrick (R-137)
Harold A. "Hal" English (R-30)
Garth D. Everett (R-84)
Mindy Fee (R-37)
Matt Gabler (R-75)
Doyle Heffley (R-122)
Barry J. Jozwiak (R-5)
Mark K. Keller (R-86)
David M. Maloney, Sr. (R-130)
John D. McGinnis (R-79)
Michael Peifer (R-139)
Ryan Warner (R-52)
Parke H. Wentling (R-17)

**Minority Members**
R. Ted Harhai (D-58)
  *Democratic Chair*
Gerald J. Mullery (D-119)
  *Democratic Vice Chair*
Frank Farina (D-112)
  *Democratic Secretary*
Frank Burns (D-72)
Marty Flynn (D-113)
Patrick J. Harkins (D-1)
William C. "Bill" Kortz II (D-38)
Tim Mahoney (D-51)
Edward "Ed" Neilson (D-174)
Brian K. Sims (D-182)

## Gaming Oversight

**Majority Members**
John D. Payne (R-106) *Chair*
Susan C. "Sue" Helm (R-104)
  *Secretary*
Rosemary M. Brown (R-189)
Russ Diamond (R-102)
George Dunbar (R-56)
Aaron D. Kaufer (R-120)
Kate Anne Klunk (R-169)
Ryan E. Mackenzie (R-134)
Kurt A. Masser (R-107)
Nicholas A. "Nick" Miccarelli III
  (R-162)
Tedd C. Nesbit (R-8)
Jason A. Ortitay (R-46)
David C. Parker (R-115)
James R. Santora (R-163)
Eric R. Nelson (R-57)
Ryan Warner (R-52)

**Minority Members**
Nick Kotik (D-45)
  *Democratic Chair*
Dominic "Dom" Costa (D-21)
  *Democratic Vice Chair*
Tina M. Davis (D-141)
  *Democratic Secretary*
Matthew D. Bradford (D-70)
Daniel J. Deasy, Jr. (D-27)
Marty Flynn (D-113)
Ed Gainey (D-24)
Sid Michaels Kavulich (D-114)
William C. "Bill" Kortz II (D-38)
Edward "Ed" Neilson (D-174)
Mark Rozzi (D-126)

## Health

**Majority Members**
Matthew E. Baker (R-68) *Chair*
Kristin Lee Phillips-Hill (R-93)
  *Secretary*
Becky Corbin (R-155)
Jim Cox (R-129)
Gary Day (R-187)
Eli Evankovich (R-54)
Frank A. Farry (R-142)
Marcia M. Hahn (R-138)
Aaron D. Kaufer (R-120)
John A. Lawrence (R-13)
Marcy Toepel (R-147)
Tarah Toohil (R-116)
Jesse Topper (R-78)
Judith F. "Judy" Ward (R-80)

**Minority Members**
Florindo J. "Flo" Fabrizio (D-2)
  *Democratic Chair*
Mary Jo Daley (D-148)
  *Democratic Secretary*
Kevin J. Boyle (D-172)
Vanessa Lowery Brown (D-190)
Jason Dawkins (D-179)
Pamela A. DeLissio (D-194)
Stephen Kinsey (D-201)
Robert F. Matzie (D-16)
Gerald J. Mullery (D-119)
Michael H. O'Brien (D-175)
Michael H. "Mike" Schlossberg
  (D-132)

## Human Services

**Majority Members**
Gene DiGirolamo (R-18) *Chair*
Craig T. Staats (R-145) *Secretary*
Russ Diamond (R-102)
Joe Emrick (R-137)
Doyle Heffley (R-122)
Thomas P. Murt (R-152)
Eric R. Nelson (R-57)
Jason A. Ortitay (R-46)
Thomas J. Quigley (R-146)
Jack B. Rader, Jr. (R-176)
Brad Roae (R-6)
Judith F. "Judy" Ward (R-80)
Ryan Warner (R-52)
Parke H. Wentling (R-17)
Martina A. White (R-170)
David H. Zimmerman (R-99)

**Minority Members**
Angel Cruz (D-180)
  *Democratic Chair*
Leslie Acosta (D-197)
Jason Dawkins (D-179)
Michael J. Driscoll (D-173)
Stephen Kinsey (D-201)
Joanna E. McClinton (D-191)
Daniel L. "Dan" Miller (D-42)
Eddie Day Pashinski (D-121)
Mark Rozzi (D-126)
Michael H. "Mike" Schlossberg
  (D-132)
Brian K. Sims (D-182)

## Insurance

**Majority Members**
Tina Pickett (R-110) *Chair*
Marguerite Quinn (R-143)
  *Vice Chair*
Mike Regan (R-92) *Secretary*
Lynda Schlegel Culver (R-108)
Gary Day (R-187)
Eli Evankovich (R-54)
Robert W. "Bob" Godshall (R-53)
Warren Kampf (R-157)
Steven C. Mentzer (R-97)
Thomas P. Murt (R-152)
Brad Roae (R-6)
Thomas R. "Tommy" Sankey III
  (R-73)
Justin J. Simmons (R-131)
Curtis G. "Curt" Sonney (R-4)
Todd Stephens (R-151)
Mike Tobash (R-125)

**Minority Members**
Anthony M. "Tony" DeLuca (D-32)
  *Democratic Chair*
Dominic "Dom" Costa (D-21)
  *Democratic Vice Chair*
Eddie Day Pashinski (D-121)
  *Democratic Secretary*
Ryan A. Bizzarro (D-3)
Kevin J. Boyle (D-172)
Margo L. Davidson (D-164)
Tina M. Davis (D-141)
Michael J. Driscoll (D-173)
Marty Flynn (D-113)
Ed Gainey (D-24)
Robert F. Matzie (D-16)

## Judiciary

**Majority Members**
Ronald S. Marsico (R-105) *Chair*
Jim Cox (R-129)
Sheryl M. Delozier (R-88)
Garth D. Everett (R-84)
Barry J. Jozwiak (R-5)
Mark K. Keller (R-86)
Kate Anne Klunk (R-169)
Tedd C. Nesbit (R-8)
Mike Regan (R-92)
Rick Saccone (R-39)
Paul Schemel (R-90)
Todd Stephens (R-151)
Marcy Toepel (R-147)
Tarah Toohil (R-116)
Michael A. "Mike" Vereb (R-150)
Martina A. White (R-170)

**Minority Members**
Joseph A. Petrarca (D-55)
  *Democratic Chair*
Bryan E. Barbin (D-71)
Ryan A. Bizzarro (D-3)
Tim Briggs (D-149)
Dominic "Dom" Costa (D-21)
Tina M. Davis (D-141)
Jason Dawkins (D-179)
Madeleine Dean (D-153)
Daniel L. "Dan" Miller (D-42)
Gerald J. Mullery (D-119)
Brandon P. Neuman (D-48)

## Labor and Industry

**Majority Members**
Mauree Gingrich (R-101) *Chair*
Ryan E. Mackenzie (R-134)
  *Vice Chair*
Stephen Bloom (R-199) *Secretary*
Jim Cox (R-129)
Sheryl M. Delozier (R-88)
Cris Dush (R-66)
Mark M. Gillen (R-128)
Seth M. Grove (R-196)
Richard "Rich" Irvin (R-81)
Fred Keller (R-85)
David M. Maloney, Sr. (R-130)
Steven C. Mentzer (R-97)
Thomas P. Murt (R-152)
Jesse Topper (R-78)
Dan Truitt (R-156)
Judith F. "Judy" Ward (R-80)

**Minority Members**
Marc J. Gergely (D-35)
  *Democratic Chair*
John T. Galloway (D-140)
  *Democratic Vice Chair*
Patrick J. Harkins (D-1)
  *Democratic Secretary*
Maria P. Donatucci (D-185)
Frank Farina (D-112)
Daniel T. McNeill (D-133)
Brandon P. Neuman (D-48)
Adam J. Ravenstahl (D-20)
Pam Snyder (D-50)

## Liquor Control

**Majority Members**
Chris Ross (R-158) *Chair*
Becky Corbin (R-155) *Secretary*
Sheryl M. Delozier (R-88)
Warren Kampf (R-157)
Kurt A. Masser (R-107)
Nicholas A. "Nick" Miccarelli III
  (R-162)
Mark Mustio (R-44)
John D. Payne (R-106)
Scott A. Petri (R-178)
Mike Reese (R-59)
Mike Regan (R-92)
Justin J. Simmons (R-131)
Curtis G. "Curt" Sonney (R-4)
Craig T. Staats (R-145)
John J. Taylor (R-177)

**Minority Members**
Paul Costa (D-34)
  *Democratic Chair*
Frank Burns (D-72)
  *Democratic Secretary*
Kevin J. Boyle (D-172)
Matthew D. Bradford (D-70)
Donna Bullock (D-195)
Maria P. Donatucci (D-185)
Leanne Krueger-Braneky (D-161)
Patrick J. Harkins (D-1)
Tim Mahoney (D-51)
Adam J. Ravenstahl (D-20)
Peter G. Schweyer (D-22)

## Local Government

**Majority Members**
Catherine "Kate" Harper (R-61)
  *Chair*
Frank A. Farry (R-142) *Secretary*
Mindy Fee (R-37)
Keith J. Greiner (R-43)
Richard "Rich" Irvin (R-81)
R. Lee James (R-64)
David M. Maloney, Sr. (R-130)
John D. McGinnis (R-79)
Brett R. Miller (R-41)
Jack B. Rader, Jr. (R-176)
Thomas R. "Tommy" Sankey III
  (R-73)
Tarah Toohil (R-116)
Ryan Warner (R-52)
Parke H. Wentling (R-17)
Jeff C. Wheeland (R-83)
David H. Zimmerman (R-99)

**Minority Members**
Robert L. Freeman (D-136)
  *Democratic Chair*
Matthew D. Bradford (D-70)
Frank Farina (D-112)
Sid Michaels Kavulich (D-114)
Patty H. Kim (D-103)
Tim Mahoney (D-51)
Joanna E. McClinton (D-191)
Daniel T. McNeill (D-133)
Gerald J. Mullery (D-119)
Kevin J. Schreiber (D-95)
Pam Snyder (D-50)

## Professional Licensure

**Majority Members**
Julie Harhart (R-183) *Chair*
Joe Emrick (R-137) *Vice Chair*
Marcy Toepel (R-147) *Secretary*
Rosemary M. Brown (R-189)
Jim Christiana (R-15)
Keith Gillespie (R-47)
David S. Hickernell (R-98)
Jerry Knowles (R-124)
John A. Maher III (R-40)
David R. Millard (R-109)
Mark Mustio (R-44)
Marguerite Quinn (R-143)
James R. Santora (R-163)
Curtis G. "Curt" Sonney (R-4)

**Minority Members**
Harry A. Readshaw (D-36)
   *Democratic Chair*
William C. "Bill" Kortz II (D-38)
   *Democratic Vice Chair*
Jaret A. Gibbons (D-10)
   *Democratic Secretary*
Tim Briggs (D-149)
Dominic "Dom" Costa (D-21)
Tina M. Davis (D-141)
Daniel J. Deasy, Jr. (D-27)
John T. Galloway (D-140)
Jordan A. Harris (D-186)
Daniel T. McNeill (D-133)

## Rules

**Majority Members**
David "Dave" Reed (R-62) *Chair*
William F. "Bill" Adolph, Jr.
   (R-165)
Matthew E. Baker (R-68)
Bryan Cutler (R-100)
Brian L. Ellis (R-11)
Eli Evankovich (R-54)
Matt Gabler (R-75)
Mauree Gingrich (R-101)
Robert W. "Bob" Godshall (R-53)
Adam C. Harris (R-82)
R. Lee James (R-64)
Rob W. Kauffman (R-89)
John A. Lawrence (R-13)
Tina Pickett (R-110)
Mike Reese (R-59)
Tarah Toohil (R-116)
Mike Turzai (R-28)
Katharine M. Watson (R-144)

**Minority Members**
Mike Carroll (D-118)
Dominic "Dom" Costa (D-21)
Paul Costa (D-34)
Frank Dermody (D-33)
Florindo J. "Flo" Fabrizio (D-2)
Dan B. Frankel (D-23)
Neal P. Goodman (D-123)
Michael K. Hanna, Sr. (D-76)
Patrick J. Harkins (D-1)
Jordan A. Harris (D-186)
Stephen Kinsey (D-201)
Joseph F. Markosek (D-25)
P. Michael Sturla (D-96)
Rosita C. Youngblood (D-198)

## State Government

**Majority Members**
Daryl D. Metcalfe (R-12) *Chair*
George Dunbar (R-56)
Cris Dush (R-66)
Matt Gabler (R-75)
Richard "Rich" Irvin (R-81)
Fred Keller (R-85)
Jerry Knowles (R-124)
Brett R. Miller (R-41)
Kristin Lee Phillips-Hill (R-93)
Brad Roae (R-6)
Rick Saccone (R-39)
Thomas R. "Tommy" Sankey III
   (R-73)
Jesse Topper (R-78)
Dan Truitt (R-156)
Judith F. "Judy" Ward (R-80)
Jeff C. Wheeland (R-83)

**Minority Members**
Mark B. Cohen (D-202)
   *Democratic Chair*
Leslie Acosta (D-197)
   *Democratic Secretary*
Vanessa Lowery Brown (D-190)
Donna Bullock (D-195)
Tonyelle Cook-Artis (D-200)
Pamela A. DeLissio (D-194)
Mary Jo Daley (D-148)
Stephen "Steve" McCarter (D-154)
Michael H. O'Brien (D-175)
Eddie Day Pashinski (D-121)
Brian K. Sims (D-182)

## Tourism and Recreational Development

**Majority Members**
David S. Hickernell (R-98) *Chair*
Karen Boback (R-117)
Russ Diamond (R-102)
Harold A. "Hal" English (R-30)
Mindy Fee (R-37)
Marcia M. Hahn (R-138)
Doyle Heffley (R-122)
Susan C. "Sue" Helm (R-104)
Rob W. Kauffman (R-89)
Ryan E. Mackenzie (R-134)
David R. Millard (R-109)
Dan Moul (R-91)
Jason A. Ortitay (R-46)
Jack B. Rader, Jr. (R-176)
Mike Regan (R-92)

**Minority Members**
Jaret A. Gibbons (D-10)
   *Democratic Chair*
Vanessa Lowery Brown (D-190)
Frank Burns (D-72)
Margo L. Davidson (D-164)
Daniel J. Deasy, Jr. (D-27)
Sid Michaels Kavulich (D-114)
Mark A. Longietti (D-7)
Tim Mahoney (D-51)
Lynwood W. Savage (D-192)
Kevin J. Schreiber (D-95)
Brian K. Sims (D-182)

## Transportation

**Majority Members**
John J. Taylor (R-177) *Chair*
Lynda Schlegel Culver (R-108)
Julie Harhart (R-183)
Catherine "Kate" Harper (R-61)
Doyle Heffley (R-122)
Timothy "Tim" Hennessey (R-26)
Mark K. Keller (R-86)
Jim Marshall (R-14)
Ronald S. Marsico (R-105)
Jeffrey P. Pyle (R-60)
Marguerite Quinn (R-143)
Katharine M. Watson (R-144)

**Minority Members**
William F. Keller (D-184)
   *Democratic Chair*
Bryan E. Barbin (D-71)
Tim Briggs (D-149)
Mike Carroll (D-118)
Maria P. Donatucci (D-185)
Ed Gainey (D-24)
Stephen Kinsey (D-201)
Robert F. Matzie (D-16)
Edward "Ed" Neilson (D-174)
Steven J. "Steve" Santarsiero (D-31)
Michael H. "Mike" Schlossberg
   (D-132)

## Urban Affairs

**Majority Members**
Scott A. Petri (R-178) *Chair*
Harry Lewis, Jr. (R-74) *Secretary*
Becky Corbin (R-155)
Jim Cox (R-129)
Lynda Schlegel Culver (R-108)
Susan C. "Sue" Helm (R-104)
Rob W. Kauffman (R-89)
Jerry Knowles (R-124)
John D. McGinnis (R-79)
Thomas P. Murt (R-152)
Chris Ross (R-158)
William Gregory "Greg" Rothman
   (R-87)
James R. Santora (R-163)
Justin J. Simmons (R-131)
Jeff C. Wheeland (R-83)
Martina A. White (R-170)

**Minority Members**
Thomas R. Caltagirone (D-127)
   *Democratic Chair*
Kevin J. Boyle (D-172)
Vanessa Lowery Brown (D-190)
Jason Dawkins (D-179)
Daniel J. Deasy, Jr. (D-27)
Tonyelle Cook-Artis (D-200)
Ed Gainey (D-24)
Patty H. Kim (D-103)
Edward "Ed" Neilson (D-174)
Peter G. Schweyer (D-22)

## Veterans Affairs and Emergency Preparedness

**Majority Members**
Stephen E. Barrar (R-160) *Chair*
Karen Boback (R-117)
Rosemary M. Brown (R-189)
Lynda Schlegel Culver (R-108)
Frank A. Farry (R-142)
Mark M. Gillen (R-128)
R. Lee James (R-64)
Barry J. Jozwiak (R-5)
Jim Marshall (R-14)
John D. McGinnis (R-79)
Kathy L. Rapp (R-65)
Mike Regan (R-92)
Rick Saccone (R-39)
Will Tallman (R-193)
Mike Tobash (R-125)
Michael A. "Mike" Vereb (R-150)

**Minority Members**
Christopher Sainato (D-9)
   *Democratic Chair*
Bryan E. Barbin (D-71)
Ryan A. Bizzarro (D-3)
Dominic "Dom" Costa (D-21)
Margo L. Davidson (D-164)
Maria P. Donatucci (D-185)
Patrick J. Harkins (D-1)
William C. "Bill" Kortz II (D-38)
Adam J. Ravenstahl (D-20)
Peter G. Schweyer (D-22)

# Puerto Rico Legislative Assembly

**Note:** Members of the Puerto Rico Legislative Assembly are affiliated with the following political parties: Popular Democratic Party (PPD); New Progressive Party (NPP); and Puerto Rican Independence Party (PIP).

## Puerto Rico Senate

The Capitol, P.O. Box 9023431, San Juan, PR 00902-3431
Tel: (787) 724-2030  Fax: (787) 724-2010  Internet: www.senado.pr.gov
President of the Senate
  **Eduardo A. Bhatia Gautier** (PDP) . . . . . . . . . (787) 724-2030 ext. 3031
Vice President of the Senate
  **José Luis Dalmau Santiago** (PDP) . . . . . . . . (787) 724-2030 ext. 2317
Majority Leader
  **Aníbal José "Jossie" Torres** (PDP) . . . . . (787) 724-2030 ext. 2100
Majority Whip **Rossana López León** (PDP) . . . . (787) 724-2030 ext. 1020
Minority Leader **Lawrence "Larry" Seilhamer
  Rodríguez** (NPP) . . . . . . . . . . . . . . . . . . . . (787) 724-2030 ext. 1623
Minority Whip
  **Carmelo J. Ríos Santiago** (NPP) . . . . . . . . . (787) 724-2030 ext. 2214
Secretary of the Senate **Tania Barbarossa** . . . . . . (787) 724-2030 ext. 2742
  E-mail: tbarbarossa@senado.pr.gov          Fax: (787) 723-5413
Sergeant-at-Arms **Luis A. Ramos Rivera** . . . . . . . (787) 724-2030 ext. 2262
  E-mail: luramos@senado.pr.gov

## Senators

Senator
  **Eduardo A. Bhatia Gautier** (PDP-At Large) . . (787) 724-2030 ext. 3031
  Term Expires: 2017                        Fax: (787) 725-6511
  E-mail: ebhatia@senado.pr.gov
Senator
  **José Luis Dalmau Santiago** (PDP-At Large) . .(787) 724-2030 ext. 2357
  Term Expires: 2017                        Fax: (787) 726-8328
  E-mail: jldalmau@senado.pr.gov
  Committees: Ethics; Health and Nutrition
Senator **Maria de Lourdes Santiago Negrón**
  (PIP-At Large) . . . . . . . . . . . . . . . . . . . . . . . . (787) 724-2030 ext. 2704
  Term Expires: 2017
  E-mail: masantiago@senado.pr.gov
  Committees: Ethics
Senator **Antonio J. "Tony" Fas Alzamora**
  (PDP-At Large) . . . . . . . . . . . . . . . . . . . . . . . (787) 724-2030 ext. 2022
  Term Expires: 2017                        Fax: (787) 723-9810
  E-mail: afas@senado.pr.gov
  Committees: Culture, Tourism, Recreation and Sports and Globalization
  Education: Puerto Rico BS; Pontifical Catholic (Puerto Rico) 1972 JD
Senator **María Teresa "Maritere" González
  López** (PDP-District 4) . . . . . . . . . . . . . . . . . (787) 724-2030 ext. 2682
  Counties Represented: Aguadilla Municipio      Fax: (787) 722-2686
  Term Expires: 2017
  E-mail: mgonzalez@senado.pr.gov
  Committees: Civil Rights, Citizenship and Social Economy;
  Cooperatives, Small and Medium Enterprises and Micro-Enterprises;
  Culture, Tourism, Recreation and Sports and Globalization; Education;
  Government, Governmental Efficiency and Economic Innovation; Rural
  Development; Women's Affairs
Senator **Rossana López León** (PDP-At Large) . . (787) 724-2030 ext. 1020
  Term Expires: 2017                        Fax: (787) 977-4917
  E-mail: rolopez@senado.pr.gov
  Committees: Civil Rights, Citizenship and Social Economy; Rules;
  Women's Affairs
Senator **Ángel "Chayanne" Martínez
  Santiago** (NPP-District 3) . . . . . . . . . . . . . . . (787) 724-2030 ext. 2762
  Counties Represented: Arecibo Municipio        Fax: (787) 977-4739
  Term Expires: 2017
  E-mail: anmartinez@senado.pr.gov
  Committees: Agriculture, Food Security and Sustainability of the
  Southern Mountain Regions; Culture, Tourism, Recreation and Sports
  and Globalization; Health and Nutrition; Sustainable Communities and
  Housing

Senator
  **José Rafael Nadal Power** (PDP-District 1) . . . (787) 724-2030 ext. 2000
  Counties Represented: San Juan Municipio       Fax: (787) 721-8090
  Term Expires: 2017
  E-mail: jnadal@senado.pr.gov
  Committees: Budget and Appropriations; Cooperatives, Small and
  Medium Enterprises and Micro-Enterprises; Ethics; Health and
  Nutrition; Infrastructure, Transportation and Urban Development;
  Judiciary, Security and Veterans Affairs; Municipal Autonomy,
  Decentralization and Regionalization; Public Corporations and
  Public-Private Partnerships; Women's Affairs
Senator
  **Ramón Luis Nieves Pérez** (PDP-District 1) . . . (787) 724-2030 ext. 2207
  Counties Represented: San Juan Municipio       Fax: (787) 725-8007
  Term Expires: 2017
  E-mail: rnieves@senado.pr.gov
  Committees: Banking, Insurance and Telecommunications; Budget and
  Appropriations; Cooperatives, Small and Medium Enterprises and
  Micro-Enterprises; Education; Energy and Water Resources; Ethics;
  Judiciary, Security and Veterans Affairs; Women's Affairs; Workforce
  Development Consumer Affairs
  Education: Puerto Rico BA, JD
Senator **Margarita Nolasco Santiago**
  (NPP-At Large) . . . . . . . . . . . . . . . . . . . . . . . . (787) 724-2030 ext. 2909
  Term Expires: 2017
  E-mail: mnolasco@senado.pr.gov
  Committees: Education; Government, Governmental Efficiency and
  Economic Innovation; Infrastructure, Transportation and Urban
  Development; Rules; Women's Affairs
Senator
  **Migdalia Padilla Alvelo** (NPP-District 2) . . . . . (787) 724-2030 ext. 2221
  Counties Represented: Bayamon Municipio        Fax: (787) 725-6783
  Term Expires: 2017
  E-mail: mpadilla@senado.pr.gov
  Committees: Banking, Insurance and Telecommunications; Budget
  and Appropriations; Energy and Water Resources; Government,
  Governmental Efficiency and Economic Innovation; Women's Affairs;
  Workforce Development Consumer Affairs
Senator
  **Itzamar Peña Ramirez** (NPP-At Large) . . . . . . (787) 724-2030 ext. 2006
  Term Expires: 2017
  E-mail: ipena@senado.pr.gov
  Committees: Civil Rights, Citizenship and Social Economy; Ethics;
  Judiciary, Security and Veterans Affairs; Municipal Autonomy,
  Decentralization and Regionalization; Public Corporations and
  Public-Private Partnerships; Women's Affairs
Senator
  **Miguel A. Pereira Castillo** (PDP-District 6) . . . (787) 724-2030 ext. 2221
  Counties Represented: Guayama Municipio        Fax: (787) 721-8025
  Term Expires: 2017
  E-mail: mpereira@senado.pr.gov
  Committees: Agriculture, Food Security and Sustainability
  of the Southern Mountain Regions; Banking, Insurance and
  Telecommunications; Education; Ethics; Government, Governmental
  Efficiency and Economic Innovation; Judiciary, Security and Veterans
  Affairs; Public Corporations and Public-Private Partnerships
Senator **José "Joito" Pérez Rosa** (NPP-District 3) . . . . . . (787) 722-3460
  Counties Represented: Arecibo Municipio        Fax: (787) 725-3874
  Term Expires: 2017
  E-mail: josperez@senado.pr.gov
  Committees: Budget and Appropriations; Cooperatives, Small and
  Medium Enterprises and Micro-Enterprises; Environmental and Natural
  Resources; Rural Development
  Education: Pontifical Catholic (Puerto Rico) BA
Senator
  **Carmelo J. Ríos Santiago** (NPP-District 2) . . . (787) 724-2030 ext. 2214
  Counties Represented: Bayamon Municipio        Fax: (787) 722-6832
  Term Expires: 2017
  E-mail: crios@senado.pr.gov
Senator **Luis Daniel Rivera Filomeno**
  (PDP-District 8) . . . . . . . . . . . . . . . . . . . . . . . . (787) 724-2030 ext. 2928
  Counties Represented: Carolina Municipio       Fax: (787) 724-4069
  Term Expires: 2017
  E-mail: ldrivera@senado.pr.gov
  Committees: Budget and Appropriations; Civil Rights, Citizenship
  and Social Economy; Culture, Tourism, Recreation and Sports and
  Globalization; Environmental and Natural Resources; Health and
  Nutrition; Judiciary, Security and Veterans Affairs; Municipal
  Autonomy, Decentralization and Regionalization; Workforce
  Development Consumer Affairs

*(continued on next page)*

LEGISLATIVE BRANCH

**Senators** *continued*

Senator
**Thomas Rivera Schatz** (NPP-At Large) . . . . . . (787) 724-2030 ext. 3008
Term Expires: 2017
E-mail: trivera@senado.pr.gov

Senator **Pedro A. "Pedrito" Rodríguez**
**González** (PDP-District 8) . . . . . . . . . . . . . . . . .(787) 722-2030 ext. 2352
Counties Represented: Carolina Municipio     Fax: (787) 721-3211
Term Expires: 2017
E-mail: prodriguez@senado.pr.gov
Committees: Budget and Appropriations; Civil Rights, Citizenship and
Social Economy; Environmental and Natural Resources; Infrastructure,
Transportation and Urban Development; Rural Development;
Sustainable Communities and Housing

Senator
**Ángel M. Rodríguez Otero** (PDP-At Large) . . .(787) 724-2030 ext. 2343
Term Expires: 2017
E-mail: anrodriguez@senado.pr.gov
Committees: Agriculture, Food Security and Sustainability of the
Southern Mountain Regions; Civil Rights, Citizenship and Social
Economy; Cooperatives, Small and Medium Enterprises and
Micro-Enterprises; Culture, Tourism, Recreation and Sports and
Globalization; Education; Government, Governmental Efficiency and
Economic Innovation; Municipal Autonomy, Decentralization and
Regionalization; Public Corporations and Public-Private Partnerships;
Rural Development

Senator **Gilberto Rodríguez Valle, JD**
(PDP-District 4) . . . . . . . . . . . . . . . . . . . . . . . . (787) 724-2030 ext. 2346
Counties Represented: Aguadilla Municipio     Fax: (787) 725-6882
Term Expires: 2017
E-mail: girodriguez@senado.pr.gov
Committees: Agriculture, Food Security and Sustainability
of the Southern Mountain Regions; Banking, Insurance and
Telecommunications; Budget and Appropriations; Cooperatives, Small
and Medium Enterprises and Micro-Enterprises; Energy and Water
Resources; Ethics; Judiciary, Security and Veterans Affairs; Public
Corporations and Public-Private Partnerships; Rules
Education: Puerto Rico BA

Senator **Ángel R. Rosa Rodríguez, PhD**
(PDP-At Large) . . . . . . . . . . . . . . . . . . . . . . . . .(787) 722-3460 ext. 2006
Term Expires: 2017     Fax: (787) 721-4427
E-mail: arosa@senado.pr.gov
Committees: Budget and Appropriations; Cooperatives, Small and
Medium Enterprises and Micro-Enterprises; Culture, Tourism,
Recreation and Sports and Globalization; Education; Energy and Water
Resources; Government, Governmental Efficiency and Economic
Innovation; Health and Nutrition; Judiciary, Security and Veterans
Affairs
Education: Puerto Rico BSc; Boston U PhD

Senator **Ramón "Ramoncito" Ruiz Nieves**
(PDP-District 5) . . . . . . . . . . . . . . . . . . . . . . . . . (787) 722-2030 ext. 2955
Counties Represented: Ponce Municipio     Fax: (787) 722-1086
Term Expires: 2017
E-mail: rruiz@senado.pr.gov
Committees: Agriculture, Food Security and Sustainability
of the Southern Mountain Regions; Banking, Insurance and
Telecommunications; Government, Governmental Efficiency and
Economic Innovation; Judiciary, Security and Veterans Affairs; Rules;
Rural Development; Sustainable Communities and Housing; Women's
Affairs

Senator **Lawrence "Larry" Seilhamer**
**Rodríguez** (NPP-District 5) . . . . . . . . . . . . . . .(787) 724-2030 ext. 1623
Counties Represented: Ponce Municipio     Fax: (787) 977-3048
Term Expires: 2017
E-mail: lseilhamer@senado.pr.gov

Senator
**Jorge I. Suárez Cáceres** (PDP-At Large) . . . . . (787) 724-2030 ext. 2240
Term Expires: 2017     Fax: (787) 724-1361
E-mail: jsuarez@senado.pr.gov
Committees: Civil Rights, Citizenship and Social Economy;
Government, Governmental Efficiency and Economic Innovation;
Infrastructure, Transportation and Urban Development; Public
Corporations and Public-Private Partnerships; Sustainable Communities
and Housing; Workforce Development Consumer Affairs

Senator **Cirilo Tirado Rivera** (PDP-At Large) . . . .(787) 724-2030 ext. 2234
Term Expires: 2017     Fax: (787) 724-3446
E-mail: ctirado@senado.pr.gov
Committees: Budget and Appropriations; Culture, Tourism, Recreation
and Sports and Globalization; Environmental and Natural Resources;
Judiciary, Security and Veterans Affairs; Public Corporations and
Public-Private Partnerships; Sustainable Communities and Housing
Education: U Puerto Rico BA

Senator
**Aníbal José "Jossie" Torres** (PDP-At Large) . .(787) 724-2030 ext. 2100
Term Expires: 2017     Fax: (787) 725-9264
E-mail: ajtorress@senado.pr.gov
Committees: Rules

Senator
**Martín Vargas Morales** (PDP-District 5) . . . . . (787) 724-2030 ext. 2121
Counties Represented: Ponce Municipio     Fax: (787) 977-3078
Term Expires: 2017
E-mail: mvargas@senado.pr.gov
Committees: Education; Environmental and Natural Resources;
Government, Governmental Efficiency and Economic Innovation;
Infrastructure, Transportation and Urban Development; Municipal
Autonomy, Decentralization and Regionalization; Workforce
Development Consumer Affairs

# Senate Standing Committees

## Agriculture, Food Security and Sustainability of the Southern Mountain Regions

| **Majority Members** | **Minority Members** |
|---|---|
| Ramón "Ramoncito" Ruiz Nieves (PDP-5) *President* | Ángel "Chayanne" Martínez Santiago (NPP-3) |
| Miguel A. Pereira Castillo (PDP-6) *Vice President* | |
| Gilberto Rodríguez Valle (PDP-4) *Secretary* | |
| Ángel M. Rodriguez Otero (PDP) | |

## Banking, Insurance and Telecommunications

| **Majority Members** | **Minority Members** |
|---|---|
| Ramón Luis Nieves Pérez (PDP-1) *President* | Migdalia Padilla Alvelo (NPP-2) |
| Ramón "Ramoncito" Ruiz Nieves (PDP-5) *Vice President* | |
| Miguel A. Pereira Castillo (PDP-6) *Secretary* | |
| Gilberto Rodríguez Valle (PDP-4) | |

## Budget and Appropriations

| **Majority Members** | **Minority Members** |
|---|---|
| José Rafael Nadal Power (PDP-1) *President* | Migdalia Padilla Alvelo (NPP-2) |
| Ángel R. Rosa Rodríguez (PDP) *Vice President* | José "Joito" Pérez Rosa (NPP-3) |
| Cirilo Tirado Rivera (PDP) *Secretary* | |
| Ramón Luis Nieves Pérez (PDP-1) | |
| Luis Daniel Rivera Filomeno (PDP-8) | |
| Gilberto Rodríguez Valle (PDP-4) | |
| Pedro A. "Pedrito" Rodríguez González (PDP-8) | |

## Civil Rights, Citizenship and Social Economy

| **Majority Members** | **Minority Members** |
|---|---|
| Rossana López León (PDP) *President* | Itzamar Peña Ramìrez (NPP) |
| María Teresa "Maritere" González López (PDP-4) *Vice President* | |
| Pedro A. "Pedrito" Rodríguez González (PDP-8) *Secretary* | |
| Luis Daniel Rivera Filomeno (PDP-8) | |
| Ángel M. Rodriguez Otero (PDP) | |
| Jorge I. Suárez Cáceres (PDP) | |

## Cooperatives, Small and Medium Enterprises and Micro-Enterprises

**Majority Members**
Gilberto Rodríguez Valle (PDP-4)
*President*
Ángel R. Rosa Rodríguez (PDP)
*Vice President*
Ángel M. Rodriguez Otero (PDP)
*Secretary*
María Teresa "Maritere" González López (PDP-4)
José Rafael Nadal Power (PDP-1)
Ramón Luis Nieves Pérez (PDP-1)

**Minority Members**
José "Joito" Pérez Rosa (NPP-3)

## Culture, Tourism, Recreation and Sports and Globalization

**Majority Members**
Antonio J. "Tony" Fas Alzamora (PDP)
*President*
Ángel M. Rodriguez Otero (PDP)
*Vice President*
Cirilo Tirado Rivera (PDP)
*Secretary*
María Teresa "Maritere" González López (PDP-4)
Ángel R. Rosa Rodríguez (PDP)
Luis Daniel Rivera Filomeno (PDP-8)

**Minority Members**
Ángel "Chayanne" Martínez Santiago (NPP-3)

## Education

**Majority Members**
María Teresa "Maritere" González López (PDP-4)
*President*
Ángel R. Rosa Rodríguez (PDP)
*Vice President*
Ángel M. Rodriguez Otero (PDP)
*Secretary*
Miguel A. Pereira Castillo (PDP-6)
Ramón Luis Nieves Pérez (PDP-1)
Martín Vargas Morales (PDP-5)

**Minority Members**
Margarita Nolasco Santiago (NPP)

## Energy and Water Resources

**Majority Members**
Ramón Luis Nieves Pérez (PDP-1)
*President*
Ángel R. Rosa Rodríguez (PDP)
*Vice President*
Gilberto Rodríguez Valle (PDP-4)
*Secretary*

**Minority Members**
Migdalia Padilla Alvelo (NPP-2)

## Environmental and Natural Resources

**Majority Members**
Cirilo Tirado Rivera (PDP)
*President*
Martín Vargas Morales (PDP-5)
*Vice President*
Pedro A. "Pedrito" Rodríguez González (PDP-8)
*Secretary*
Luis Daniel Rivera Filomeno (PDP-8)

**Minority Members**
José "Joito" Pérez Rosa (NPP-3)

## Ethics

**Majority Members**
Miguel A. Pereira Castillo (PDP-6)
*President*
José Rafael Nadal Power (PDP-1)
*Vice President*
Gilberto Rodríguez Valle (PDP-4)
*Secretary*
José Luis Dalmau Santiago (PDP)
Ramón Luis Nieves Pérez (PDP-1)

**Minority Members**
Itzamar Peña Ramírez (NPP)
Maria de Lourdes Santiago Negrón (PIP)

## Government, Governmental Efficiency and Economic Innovation

**Majority Members**
Ángel R. Rosa Rodríguez (PDP)
*President*
Miguel A. Pereira Castillo (PDP-6)
*Vice President*
María Teresa "Maritere" González López (PDP-4)
*Secretary*
Jorge I. Suárez Cáceres (PDP)
Ángel M. Rodriguez Otero (PDP)
Martín Vargas Morales (PDP-5)
Ramón "Ramoncito" Ruiz Nieves (PDP-5)

**Minority Members**
Margarita Nolasco Santiago (NPP)
Migdalia Padilla Alvelo (NPP-2)

## Health and Nutrition

**Majority Members**
José Luis Dalmau Santiago (PDP)
*President*
Luis Daniel Rivera Filomeno (PDP-8)
*Vice President*
José Rafael Nadal Power (PDP-1)
*Secretary*
Ángel R. Rosa Rodríguez (PDP)

**Minority Members**
Ángel "Chayanne" Martínez Santiago (NPP-3)

## Infrastructure, Transportation and Urban Development

**Majority Members**
Pedro A. "Pedrito" Rodríguez González (PDP-8)
*President*
Jorge I. Suárez Cáceres (PDP)
*Vice President*
Martín Vargas Morales (PDP-5)
*Secretary*
José Rafael Nadal Power (PDP-1)

**Minority Members**
Margarita Nolasco Santiago (NPP)

## Judiciary, Security and Veterans Affairs

**Majority Members**
Miguel A. Pereira Castillo (PDP-6)
*President*
Gilberto Rodríguez Valle (PDP-4)
*Vice President*
Ramón Luis Nieves Pérez (PDP-1)
*Secretary*
José Rafael Nadal Power (PDP-1)
Luis Daniel Rivera Filomeno (PDP-8)
Ángel R. Rosa Rodríguez (PDP)
Ramón "Ramoncito" Ruiz Nieves (PDP-5)
Cirilo Tirado Rivera (PDP)

**Minority Members**
Itzamar Peña Ramirez (NPP)

## Municipal Autonomy, Decentralization and Regionalization

**Majority Members**
Martín Vargas Morales (PDP-5)
*President*
Ángel M. Rodriguez Otero (PDP)
*Vice President*
Luis Daniel Rivera Filomeno (PDP-8)
*Secretary*
José Rafael Nadal Power (PDP-1)

**Minority Members**
Itzamar Peña Ramìrez (NPP)

LEGISLATIVE BRANCH

## Public Corporations and Public-Private Partnerships

**Majority Members**
Ángel M. Rodriguez Otero (PDP)
*President*
Miguel A. Pereira Castillo (PDP-6)
*Vice President*
José Rafael Nadal Power (PDP-1)
*Secretary*
Gilberto Rodríguez Valle (PDP-4)
Jorge I. Suárez Cáceres (PDP)
Cirilo Tirado Rivera (PDP)

**Minority Members**
Itzamar Peña Ramìrez (NPP)

## Rules

**Majority Members**
Aníbal José "Jossie" Torres (PDP)
*President*
Rossana López León (PDP)
*Vice President*
Gilberto Rodríguez Valle (PDP-4)
*Secretary*
Ramón "Ramoncito" Ruiz Nieves
(PDP-5)

**Minority Members**
Margarita Nolasco Santiago (NPP)

## Rural Development

**Majority Members**
Ángel M. Rodriguez Otero (PDP)
*President*
Ramón "Ramoncito"
Ruiz Nieves (PDP-5)
*Vice President*
Pedro A. "Pedrito" Rodríguez
González (PDP-8)
*Secretary*
María Teresa "Maritere" González
López (PDP-4)

**Minority Members**
José "Joito" Pérez Rosa (NPP-3)

## Sustainable Communities and Housing

**Majority Members**
Jorge I. Suárez Cáceres (PDP)
*President*
Pedro A. "Pedrito" Rodríguez
González (PDP-8)
*Vice President*
Ramón "Ramoncito"
Ruiz Nieves (PDP-5)
*Secretary*
Cirilo Tirado Rivera (PDP)

**Minority Members**
Ángel "Chayanne" Martínez
Santiago (NPP-3)

## Women's Affairs

**Majority Members**
María Teresa "Maritere"
González López (PDP-4)
*President*
Rossana López León (PDP)
*Vice President*
Ramón Luis Nieves Pérez (PDP-1)
Ramón "Ramoncito" Ruiz Nieves
(PDP-5)
José Rafael Nadal Power (PDP-1)

**Minority Members**
Itzamar Peña Ramírez (NPP)
*Secretary*
Migdalia Padilla Alvelo (NPP-2)
Margarita Nolasco Santiago (NPP)

## Workforce Development Consumer Affairs

**Majority Members**
Luis Daniel Rivera
Filomeno (PDP-8)
*President*
Ramón Luis Nieves Pérez (PDP-1)
*Vice President*
Jorge I. Suárez Cáceres (PDP)
*Secretary*
Martín Vargas Morales (PDP-5)

**Minority Members**
Migdalia Padilla Alvelo (NPP-2)

# Puerto Rico House of Representatives

P.O. Box 922228, San Juan, PR 00902-2228
Tel: (787) 721-6040  Fax: (787) 723-2717

Speaker of the House **Jaime R. Perelló Borrás** (PDP) .... (787) 622-4953
  Education: Inter American 1998 BSc; Cambridge MEd
Speaker Pro Tem **Roberto Rivera Ruiz de Porras** (PDP) . . (787) 622-4893
Majority Leader
  **Carlos M. "Charlie" Hernández López** (PDP) ........ (787) 622-4896
Minority Leader **Jenniffer A. González Colón** (NPP) .... (787) 722-0458
Minority Whip
  **Carlos J. "Johnny" Méndez Nuñez** (NPP).........(787) 721-8011
Secretary of the House **Aileen Figueroa Vázquez** ....... (787) 722-0830
Fax: (787) 723-4342

# Representatives

Representative
  **Javier Aponte Dalmau** (PDP-District 38) .... (787) 721-6040 ext. 2421
  Counties Represented: Canovanas Municipio (part),  Fax: (787) 722-7780
  Carolina Municipio (part), Trujillo Alto Municipio (part)
  Term Expires: 2017
  E-mail: apontedalmau@camaraderepresentantes.org
  Committees: Agriculture, Natural Resources and Environmental Affairs;
  Consumer Affairs and Anti-Monopolistic Practices; Cooperatives
  and Non-Profits; Development of the Eastern Region; Development
  of the Metropolitan Region; Estate and Budget; Health; Small and
  Medium Sized Businesses, Trade Industry and Telecommunications;
  Socio-Economic Development and Planning
  Education: Puerto Rico BBA; Pontifical Catholic (Puerto Rico) JD
Representative
  **José F. Aponte Hernández** (NPP-At Large)...........(787) 722-1090
  Term Expires: 2017  Fax: (787) 722-5106
  E-mail: japonte@camaraderepresentantes.org
Representative
  **José L. Báez Rivera** (PDP-District 4) ........ (787) 721-6040 ext. 2713
  Counties Represented: San Juan Municipio (part)  Fax: (787) 724-6620
  Term Expires: 2017
  E-mail: jbaez@camaraderepresentantes.org
  Committees: Cooperatives and Non-Profits; Development of the
  Metropolitan Region; Federal and International Affairs and Veteran
  Affairs; Government; Health; Legal/Judicial Affairs; Public Safety
  and the Development of Initiatives Against Crime and Corruption;
  Transportation, Infrastructure and Recreation and Sports
  Education: Puerto Rico
Representative
  **Carlos A. Bianchi Angleró** (PDP-District 20) . . (787) 721-6040 ext. 2913
  Counties Represented: Cabo Rojo Municipio (part),  Fax: (787) 977-2456
  Hormigueros Municipio (part), Mayaguez Municipio (part), San
  German Municipio (part)
  Term Expires: 2017
  E-mail: cbianchi@camaraderepresentantes.org
  Committees: Ethics; Housing and Urban Development; Internal Affairs
Representative **Ángel Bulerín Ramos** (NPP-District 37) . . . (787) 723-6035
  Counties Represented: Canovanas Municipio (part),  Dist: (787) 256-2396
  Loiza Municipio, Rio Grande Municipio (part)  Fax: (787) 722-8905
  Term Expires: 2017  Dist: (787) 876-6916
  E-mail: abulerin@camaraderepresentantes.org
  Committees: Development of the Eastern Region; Housing and Urban
  Development; Municipal Affairs and Regionalization; Transportation,
  Infrastructure and Recreation and Sports
Representative **María Milagros**
  **Charbonier Laureano** (NPP-At Large).... (787) 721-6040 ext. 35773578
  Term Expires: 2017
  E-mail: mcharbonier@camaraderepresentantes.org
  Committees: Government; Health; Social Welfare and Poverty
  Eradication; Women Affairs and Equity
Representative
  **Ramón Luis Cruz Burgos** (PDP-District 34) .......... (787) 622-3802
  Counties Represented: Maunabo Municipio, Patillas Municipio, San
  Lorenzo Municipio (part), Yabucoa Municipio
  Term Expires: 2017
  E-mail: rcruz@camaraderepresentantes.org
  Committees: Agriculture, Natural Resources and Environmental Affairs;
  Cooperatives and Non-Profits; Development of the Eastern Region;
  Estate and Budget; Internal Affairs; Transportation, Infrastructure and
  Recreation and Sports

Representative **Efraín De Jesús**
  **Rodríguez** (PDP-District 19) . . . . . . . . . . . (787) 721-6040 ext. 21632380
  Counties Represented: Cabo Rojo Municipio (part),      Fax: (787) 722-4296
  Hormigueros Municipio (part), Mayaguez Municipio (part), San
  German Municipio (part)
  Term Expires: 2017
  E-mail: edejesus@camaraderepresentantes.org
  Committees: Development of the Western Region; Ethics; Government;
  Legal/Judicial Affairs; Municipal Affairs and Regionalization; Public
  Safety and the Development of Initiatives Against Crime and
  Corruption; Socio-Economic Development and Planning; Tourism
  Industry Development

Representative
  **José Aníbal Díaz Collazo** (PDP-District 29) . . . . . . . . . . (787) 721-6040
  Counties Represented: Cayey Municipio, Cidra Municipio
  Term Expires: 2017
  Committees: Integrated Development of the Southern Region

Representative
  **Narden Jaime Espinosa** (PDP-District 35) . . . . . . . . . . (787) 722-4992
  Counties Represented: Humacao Municipio, Las      Fax: (787) 622-4995
  Piedras Municipio (part), Naguabo Municipio
  Term Expires: 2017
  E-mail: njaime@camaraderepresentantes.org
  Committees: Development of the Eastern Region; Estate and
  Budget; Health; Housing and Urban Development; Internal Affairs;
  Socio-Economic Development and Planning; Transportation,
  Infrastructure and Recreation and Sports

Representative
  **Armando Franco Gonzalez** (PDP-District 17) . . . . . . . . (787) 721-6040
  Counties Represented: Aguadilla Municipio, Moca Municipio (part)
  Term Expires: 2017
  E-mail: afranco@camaraderepresentantes.org
  Committees: Development of the Western Region; Housing and Urban
  Development; Integrated Development of the Northern Region; Internal
  Affairs; Labor Affairs and Government Employees Retirement System;
  Transportation, Infrastructure and Recreation and Sports

Representative
  **Luisa "Piti" Gándara Menéndez** (PDP-At Large) . . . . . (787) 722-2494
  Term Expires: 2017      Fax: (787) 724-7025
  E-mail: lgandara@camaraderepresentantes.org
  Committees: Agriculture, Natural Resources and Environmental Affairs;
  Education for the Promotion of Arts and Culture; Federal and
  International Affairs and Veteran Affairs; Health; Social Welfare and
  Poverty Eradication; Tourism Industry Development; Women Affairs
  and Equity

Representative
  **Jenniffer A. González Colón** (NPP-At Large) . . . . . . . . (787) 722-0458
  Term Expires: 2017      Fax: (787) 722-6441
  E-mail: jgo@camaraderepresentantes.org

Representative
  **César Hernández Alfonzo** (PDP-District 15) . . . . . . . . . (787) 725-5115
  Counties Represented: Camuy Municipio, Hatillo Municipio (part),
  Quebradillas Municipio
  Term Expires: 2017
  E-mail: cehernandez@camaraderepresentantes.org
  Committees: Agriculture, Natural Resources and Environmental Affairs;
  Estate and Budget; Ethics; Health; Integrated Development of the
  Northern Region; Small and Medium Sized Businesses, Trade Industry
  and Telecommunications; Socio-Economic Development and Planning;
  Tourism Industry Development

Representative **Urayoán Hernández Alvarado**
  (NPP-District 26) . . . . . . . . . . . . . . . . . . . . . . (787) 721-6040 ext. 2046
  Counties Represented: Aibonito Municipio (part), Coamo Municipio
  (part), Juana Diaz Municipio (part), Salinas Municipio (part), Santa
  Isabel Municipio (part)
  Term Expires: 2017
  E-mail: uhernandez@camaraderepresentantes.org
  Committees: Agriculture, Natural Resources and Environmental Affairs;
  Development of the Central Southern Region; Integrated Development
  of the Southern Region; Tourism Industry Development

Representative **Carlos M. "Charlie" Hernández López**
  (PDP-At Large) . . . . . . . . . . . . . . . . . . . . . . . . . . . . . . (787) 622-4896
  Term Expires: 2017      Dist: (787) 805-5218
  E-mail: chernandez@camaraderepresentantes.org      Fax: (787) 622-4886
  Committees: Rules and Calendars Special Debate      Dist: (787) 833-2390

Representative
  **Rafael Hernández Montañez** (PDP-District 11) . . . . . . (787) 622-4877
  Counties Represented: Dorado Municipio, Vega Alta      Fax: (787) 622-4880
  Municipio (part), Vega Baja Municipio (part)
  Term Expires: 2017
  E-mail: rahernandez@camaraderepresentantes.org
  Committees: Development of the Metropolitan Region; Estate and
  Budget; Federal and International Affairs and Veteran Affairs;
  Government; Health; Housing and Urban Development; Transportation,
  Infrastructure and Recreation and Sports

Representative
  **Yashira Lebron Rodriguez** (NPP-District 8) . . . . . . . . . . (787) 721-6040
  Counties Represented: Bayamon Municipio (part)      Fax: (787) 622-4710
  Term Expires: 2017
  Committees: Social Welfare and Poverty Eradication; Women Affairs
  and Equity

Representative
  **Luis G. León Rodriguez** (NPP-District 24) . . . . . . . . . . . (787) 622-4965
  Counties Represented: Jayuya Municipio, Juana      Fax: (787) 725-3908
  Diaz Municipio (part), Ponce Municipio (part)
  Term Expires: 2017
  E-mail: lleon@camaraderepresentantes.org
  Committees: Federal and International Affairs and Veteran Affairs;
  Housing and Urban Development; Integrated Development of the
  Southern Region; Legal/Judicial Affairs

Representative **Ricardo "Ricky" Llerandi Cruz**
  (NPP-District 14) . . . . . . . . . . . . . . . . . . . . . . (787) 721-6040 ext. 2991
  Counties Represented: Arecibo Municipio (part), Hatillo Municipio
  (part)
  Term Expires: 2017
  E-mail: rllerandi@camaraderepresentantes.org
  Committees: Ethics; Health; Integrated Development of the Northern
  Region; Legal/Judicial Affairs; Tourism Industry Development

Representative
  **Brenda López de Arrarás** (PDP-At Large) . . . . . . . . . . . (787) 725-2771
  Term Expires: 2017      Fax: (787) 725-4290
  E-mail: blopez@camaraderepresentantes.org
  Committees: Agriculture, Natural Resources and Environmental
  Affairs; Education for the Promotion of Arts and Culture; Federal
  and International Affairs and Veteran Affairs; Internal Affairs;
  Legal/Judicial Affairs; Social Welfare and Poverty Eradication; Women
  Affairs and Equity

Representative **José L. López Munoz** (NPP-District 1) . . . (787) 723-2212
  Counties Represented: San Juan Municipio (part)      Tel: (787) 723-2161
  Term Expires: 2017      Fax: (787) 723-2004
  E-mail: nunolopez@camaraderepresentantes.org
  Committees: Development of the Metropolitan Region; Government;
  Internal Affairs; Socio-Economic Development and Planning

Representative **Ángel N. Matos García**
  (PDP-District 40) . . . . . . . . . . . . . . . . . . . . . (787) 721-6040 ext. 20362011
  Counties Represented: Carolina Municipio (part)
  Term Expires: 2017
  E-mail: amatos@camaraderepresentantes.org
  Committees: Consumer Affairs and Anti-Monopolistic Practices;
  Cooperatives and Non-Profits; Development of the Eastern Region;
  Federal and International Affairs and Veteran Affairs; Housing and
  Urban Development; Small and Medium Sized Businesses, Trade
  Industry and Telecommunications; Socio-Economic Development and
  Planning; Tourism Industry Development

Representative **Jose Enrique "Quiquito" Melendez**
  **Ortiz, Jr.** (NPP-At Large) . . . . . . . . . . . . . . . . . . . . . . . (787) 723-2489
  Term Expires: 2017
  E-mail: jem@camaraderepresentantes.org
  Committees: Consumer Affairs and Anti-Monopolistic Practices;
  Legal/Judicial Affairs; Transportation, Infrastructure and Recreation and
  Sports
  Education: Inter American BA;
  Pontifical Catholic (Puerto Rico) 2002 JD

Representative
  **Carlos J. "Johnny" Méndez Nuñez** (NPP-District 36) . .(787) 722-3539
  Counties Represented: Ceiba Municipio, Culebra      Fax: (787) 725-7444
  Municipio, Fajardo Municipio, Luquillo Municipio, Rio Grande
  Municipio (part), Vieques Municipio
  Term Expires: 2017
  E-mail: cmendez@camaraderepresentantes.org
  Committees: Ethics

*(continued on next page)*

**LEGISLATIVE BRANCH**

**LEGISLATIVE BRANCH**

**Representatives** *continued*

Representative **Lydia R. Méndez Silva** (PDP-District 21) . . (787) 722-0801
Counties Represented: Guanica Municipio, Lajas    Dist: (787) 873-5085
Municipio, Maricao Municipio, Sabana Grande    Fax: (787) 723-9551
Municipio, Yauco Municipio (part)    Dist: (787) 873-5085
Term Expires: 2017
E-mail: lmendez@camaraderepresentantes.org
Committees: Agriculture, Natural Resources and Environmental Affairs;
Development of the Western Region; Education for the Promotion of
Arts and Culture; Estate and Budget; Government; Health; Integrated
Development of the Southern Region; Social Welfare and Poverty
Eradication

Representative
**Ángel Muñoz Suarez** (NPP-District 37) . . . . . . (787) 721-6040 ext. 2940
Counties Represented: Canovanas Municipio (part), Loiza Municipio,
Rio Grande Municipio (part)
Term Expires: 2017
E-mail: amunoz@camaraderepresentantes.org
Committees: Agriculture, Natural Resources and Environmental
Affairs; Cooperatives and Non-Profits; Development of the Western
Region; Small and Medium Sized Businesses, Trade Industry and
Telecommunications

Representative **Manuel A. Natal Albelo** (PDP-At Large) . . (787) 721-8011
Term Expires: 2017    Tel: (787) 723-5758
E-mail: mnatal@camaraderepresentantes.org
Committees: Agriculture, Natural Resources and Environmental Affairs;
Consumer Affairs and Anti-Monopolistic Practices; Education for the
Promotion of Arts and Culture; Federal and International Affairs and
Veteran Affairs; Social Welfare and Poverty Eradication

Representative **Jorge Navarro Suárez** (NPP-District 5) . . . (787) 724-4464
Counties Represented: Guaynabo Municipio (part),    Fax: (787) 723-4711
San Juan Municipio (part)
Term Expires: 2017
E-mail: jnavarro@camaraderepresentantes.org
Committees: Consumer Affairs and Anti-Monopolistic Practices;
Development of the Metropolitan Region; Estate and Budget;
Socio-Economic Development and Planning

Representative **Luis R. "Narmito" Ortiz Lugo**
(PDP-District 30) . . . . . . . . . . . . . . . . . . . . . (787) 721-6040 ext. 2058
Counties Represented: Arroyo Municipio, Guayama Municipio, Salinas
Municipio (part)
Term Expires: 2017
E-mail: lortiz@camaraderepresentantes.org
Committees: Development of the Central Southern Region; Estate and
Budget; Housing and Urban Development; Integrated Development of
the Southern Region; Public Safety and the Development of Initiatives
Against Crime and Corruption; Tourism Industry Development;
Transportation, Infrastructure and Recreation and Sports

Representative
**Sonia I. Pacheco Irigoyen** (PDP-District 24) . . . . . . . . . (787) 721-6040
Counties Represented: Jayuya Municipio, Juana Diaz Municipio (part),
Ponce Municipio (part)
Term Expires: 2017
E-mail: spacheco@camaraderepresentantes.org
Committees: Cooperatives and Non-Profits; Development of the
Metropolitan Region; Education for the Promotion of Arts and Culture;
Labor Affairs and Government Employees Retirement System;
Municipal Affairs and Regionalization; Public Safety and the
Development of Initiatives Against Crime and Corruption; Small and
Medium Sized Businesses, Trade Industry and Telecommunications;
Social Welfare and Poverty Eradication; Socio-Economic Development
and Planning; Women Affairs and Equity

Representative
**Angel R. Peña Ramirez** (NPP-District 33) . . . . . . . . . . . (787) 721-4099
Counties Represented: Juncos Municipio, Las    Fax: (787) 724-7423
Piedras Municipio (part), San Lorenzo Municipio (part)
Term Expires: 2017
E-mail: anpena@camaraderepresentantes.org
Committees: Development of the Eastern Region; Internal Affairs;
Labor Affairs and Government Employees Retirement System;
Municipal Affairs and Regionalization

Representative **Jaime R. Perelló Borrás** (PDP-At Large) . . (787) 622-4953
Term Expires: 2017    Fax: (787) 622-4955
E-mail: jperello@camaraderepresentantes.org

Representative **Luis Pérez Ortiz** (NPP-District 7) . . . . . . . . (787) 724-6262
Counties Represented: Bayamon Municipio (part)    Dist: (787) 778-3888
Term Expires: 2017    Fax: (787) 723-2746
E-mail: lperez@camaraderepresentantes.org    Dist: (787) 778-3888
Committees: Development of the Western Region; Education for the
Promotion of Arts and Culture; Estate and Budget; Health; Housing
and Urban Development; Social Welfare and Poverty Eradication

Representative
**Waldemar Quiles Rodriguez** (NPP-District 22) . . . . . . . .(787) 725-9925
Counties Represented: Guayanilla Municipio,    Tel: (787) 721-8740
Penuelas Municipio, Ponce Municipio (part), Yauco    Fax: (787) 721-3644
Municipio (part)
Term Expires: 2017
E-mail: wquiles@camaraderepresentantes.org
Committees: Agriculture, Natural Resources and Environmental Affairs;
Estate and Budget; Health; Transportation, Infrastructure and
Recreation and Sports

Representative
**Maria de Lourdes Ramos Rivera** (NPP-At Large) . . . . . (787) 622-4379
Term Expires: 2017    Fax: (787) 622-4382
E-mail: lramos@camaraderepresentantes.org
Committees: Education for the Promotion of Arts and Culture; Ethics;
Government; Labor Affairs and Government Employees Retirement
System; Socio-Economic Development and Planning; Women Affairs
and Equity

Representative
**Rafael "June" Rivera Ortega** (NPP-District 28) . . . . . . . (787) 977-2417
Counties Represented: Barranquitas Municipio    Fax: (787) 977-2437
(part), Comerio Municipio, Corozal Municipio, Naranjito Municipio
Term Expires: 2017
E-mail: rarivera@camaraderepresentantes.org
Committees: Agriculture, Natural Resources and Environmental Affairs;
Cooperatives and Non-Profits; Development of the Central Southern
Region

Representative
**Roberto Rivera Ruiz de Porras** (PDP-District 39) . . . . . .(787) 622-4893
Counties Represented: Carolina Municipio (part),    Fax: (787) 622-4876
Trujillo Alto Municipio (part)
Term Expires: 2017
E-mail: rrivera@camaraderepresentantes.org
Committees: Ethics

Representative
**Gabriel Rodríguez Aguiló** (NPP-District 13) . . . . . . . . . (787) 723-0109
Counties Represented: Arecibo Municipio (part),    Dist: (787) 871-3190
Barceloneta Municipio, Ciales Municipio, Florida    Fax: (787) 721-8253
Municipio, Manati Municipio (part)    Dist: (787) 871-3915
Term Expires: 2017
E-mail: gfrodriguez@camaraderepresentantes.org
Committees: Agriculture, Natural Resources and Environmental Affairs;
Estate and Budget; Federal and International Affairs and Veteran
Affairs; Health; Internal Affairs

Representative
**Angel E. Rodríguez Miranda** (NPP-District 9) . . . . . . . . (787) 473-6825
Counties Represented: Bayamon Municipio (part),    Fax: (787) 725-4986
Toa Alta Municipio
Term Expires: 2017
E-mail: angrodriguez@camaraderepresentantes.org
Committees: Government; Public Safety and the Development of
Initiatives Against Crime and Corruption; Small and Medium Sized
Businesses, Trade Industry and Telecommunications

Representative **José "Rodriguez" Rodríguez Quiles**
(PDP-District 16) . . . . . . . . . . . . . . . . . . . . . . . . . . . . (787) 919-3025
Counties Represented: Isabela Municipio, Las Marias Municipio, San
Sebastian Municipio
Term Expires: 2017
E-mail: joserodriguez@camaraderepresentantes.org
Committees: Agriculture, Natural Resources and Environmental Affairs;
Development of the Western Region; Ethics; Government; Integrated
Development of the Northern Region; Labor Affairs and Government
Employees Retirement System; Legal/Judicial Affairs; Municipal
Affairs and Regionalization; Public Safety and the Development of
Initiatives Against Crime and Corruption; Transportation, Infrastructure
and Recreation and Sports

Representative
**Jesús Santa Rodríguez** (PDP-District 31) . . . . . . . . . . . (787) 721-6040
Counties Represented: Caguas Municipio (part), Gurabo Municipio
Term Expires: 2017
E-mail: jsanta@camaraderepresentantes.org
Committees: Development of the Central Southern Region; Estate and
Budget; Government; Labor Affairs and Government Employees
Retirement System; Municipal Affairs and Regionalization

Representative **Pedro Julio "Pellé" Santiago Guzman**
(NPP-District 10) . . . . . . . . . . . . . . . . . . . . . . . . . . . . (787) 721-6040
Counties Represented: Toa Baja Municipio
Term Expires: 2017
E-mail: psantiago@camaraderepresentantes.org
Committees: Education for the Promotion of Arts and Culture; Estate
and Budget; Government; Transportation, Infrastructure and Recreation
and Sports

Representative
**Antonio Luis "Tony" Soto Torres** (NPP-District 6) .... (787) 721-6040
Counties Represented: Bayamon Municipio (part), Catano Municipio, Guaynabo Municipio (part)
Term Expires: 2017
E-mail: ansoto@camaraderepresentantes.org
Committees: Estate and Budget; Small and Medium Sized Businesses, Trade Industry and Telecommunications; Tourism Industry Development; Transportation, Infrastructure and Recreation and Sports

Representative
**Héctor A. Torres Calderón** (NPP-District 12) ........ (787) 725-1216
Counties Represented: Manati Municipio (part), Fax: (787) 724-6620
Morovis Municipio, Vega Alta Municipio (part), Vega Baja Municipio (part)
Term Expires: 2017
E-mail: hetorres@camaraderepresentantes.org
Committees: Integrated Development of the Northern Region; Labor Affairs and Government Employees Retirement System; Municipal Affairs and Regionalization; Public Safety and the Development of Initiatives Against Crime and Corruption

Representative **Luis Raul Torres Cruz** (PDP-District 2) .... (787) 723-1816
Counties Represented: San Juan Municipio (part) Fax: (787) 722-3573
Term Expires: 2017
E-mail: ltorres@camaraderepresentantes.org
Committees: Estate and Budget; Government; Internal Affairs; Labor Affairs and Government Employees Retirement System; Small and Medium Sized Businesses, Trade Industry and Telecommunications; Tourism Industry Development

Representative
**Jose R. "Pito" Torres Ramirez** (PDP-District 27) ..... (787) 725-2698
Counties Represented: Aibonito Municipio (part), Fax: (787) 721-4556
Coamo Municipio (part), Juana Diaz Municipio (part), Salinas Municipio (part), Santa Isabel Municipio (part)
Term Expires: 2017
E-mail: jrtorres@camaraderepresentantes.org
Committees: Internal Affairs

Representative **Nelson Torres Yordán** (PDP-District 23) ... (787) 721-6040
Counties Represented: Ponce Municipio (part)
Term Expires: 2017
E-mail: njtorres@camaraderepresentantes.org
Committees: Consumer Affairs and Anti-Monopolistic Practices; Estate and Budget; Ethics; Government; Integrated Development of the Southern Region; Legal/Judicial Affairs

Representative **José M. "Conny" Varela Fernández**
(PDP-District 32) ................................. (787) 725-3928
Counties Represented: Caguas Municipio (part) Tel: (787) 722-4326
Term Expires: 2017 Dist: (787) 746-2077
E-mail: jvarela@camaraderepresentantes.org Fax: (787) 723-4679
Committees: Development of the Central Southern Dist: (787) 743-1477
Region; Development of the Eastern Region; Estate and Budget;
Government; Health; Internal Affairs; Labor Affairs and Government
Employees Retirement System; Legal/Judicial Affairs

Representative
**Victor Lorenzo Vassallo Anadón** (PDP-District 25) .... (787) 722-4290
Counties Represented: Barranquitas Municipio Fax: (787) 622-4952
(part), Coamo Municipio (part), Orocovis Municipio, Villalba Municipio
Term Expires: 2017
E-mail: vvasallo@camaraderepresentantes.org
Committees: Consumer Affairs and Anti-Monopolistic Practices; Development of the Central Southern Region; Health; Integrated Development of the Southern Region; Internal Affairs; Municipal Affairs and Regionalization; Small and Medium Sized Businesses, Trade Industry and Telecommunications; Transportation, Infrastructure and Recreation and Sports

Representative **Luis R. Vega Ramos** (PDP-At Large) ..... (787) 722-2494
Term Expires: 2017 Fax: (787) 724-7025
E-mail: lvega@camaraderepresentantes.org
Committees: Development of the Metropolitan Region; Education for the Promotion of Arts and Culture; Government; Health

# House Standing Committees
## Agriculture, Natural Resources and Environmental Affairs

| Majority Members | Minority Members |
| --- | --- |
| César Hernández Alfonzo (PDP-15) *President* | Urayoán Hernández Alvarado (NPP-26) |
| José "Rodriguez" Rodríguez Quiles (PDP-16) *Vice President* | Ángel Muñoz Suarez (NPP-37) |
| | Rafael "June" Rivera Ortega (NPP-28) |
| Lydia R. Méndez Silva (PDP-21) *Secretary* | Waldemar Quiles Rodriguez (NPP-22) |
| Javier Aponte Dalmau (PDP-38) | Gabriel Rodríguez Aguiló (NPP-13) |
| Ramón Luis Cruz Burgos (PDP-34) | |
| Luisa "Piti" Gándara Menéndez (PDP) | |
| Brenda López de Arrarás (PDP) | |
| Manuel A. Natal Albelo (PDP) | |

## Consumer Affairs and Anti-Monopolistic Practices

| Majority Members | Minority Members |
| --- | --- |
| Nelson Torres Yordán (PDP-23) *President* | Jose Enrique "Quiquito" Melendez Ortiz, Jr. (NPP) |
| Ángel N. Matos García (PDP-40) *Vice President* | Jorge Navarro Suárez (NPP-5) |
| Manuel A. Natal Albelo (PDP) *Secretary* | |
| Javier Aponte Dalmau (PDP-38) | |
| Victor Lorenzo Vassallo Anadón (PDP-25) | |

## Cooperatives and Non-Profits

| Majority Members | Minority Members |
| --- | --- |
| Sonia I. Pacheco Irigoyen (PDP-24) *President* | Ángel Muñoz Suarez (NPP-37) |
| José L. Báez Rivera (PDP-4) *Vice President* | Rafael "June" Rivera Ortega (NPP-28) |
| Javier Aponte Dalmau (PDP-38) | |
| Ramón Luis Cruz Burgos (PDP-34) | |
| Ángel N. Matos García (PDP-40) | |

## Development of the Central Southern Region

| Majority Members | Minority Members |
| --- | --- |
| Luis R. "Narmito" Ortiz Lugo (PDP-30) *President* | Urayoán Hernández Alvarado (NPP-26) |
| Jesús Santa Rodríguez (PDP-31) *Secretary* | Rafael "June" Rivera Ortega (NPP-28) |
| José M. "Conny" Varela Fernández (PDP-32) | |
| Victor Lorenzo Vassallo Anadón (PDP-25) | |

## Development of the Eastern Region

| Majority Members | Minority Members |
| --- | --- |
| Narden Jaime Espinosa (PDP-35) *President* | Ángel Bulerín Ramos (NPP-37) |
| Ramón Luis Cruz Burgos (PDP-34) *Vice President* | Angel R. Peña Ramirez (NPP-33) |
| Javier Aponte Dalmau (PDP-38) *Secretary* | |
| José M. "Conny" Varela Fernández (PDP-32) | |
| Ángel N. Matos García (PDP-40) | |

## Development of the Metropolitan Region

| Majority Members | Minority Members |
| --- | --- |
| Sonia I. Pacheco Irigoyen (PDP-24) *Acting President* | José L. López Munoz (NPP-1) |
| José L. Báez Rivera (PDP-4) *Vice President* | Jorge Navarro Suárez (NPP-5) |
| Luis R. Vega Ramos (PDP) *Secretary* | |
| Javier Aponte Dalmau (PDP-38) | |
| Rafael Hernández Montañez (PDP-11) | |

## Development of the Western Region

**Majority Members**
Efraín De Jesús
  Rodríguez (PDP-19)
  *President*
José "Rodriguez" Rodríguez
  Quiles (PDP-16)
  *Secretary*
Armando Franco Gonzalez
  (PDP-17)
Lydia R. Méndez Silva (PDP-21)

**Minority Members**
Ángel Muñoz Suarez (NPP-37)
Luis Pérez Ortiz (NPP-7)

## Education for the Promotion of Arts and Culture

**Majority Members**
Brenda López de Arrarás (PDP)
  *President*
Sonia I. Pacheco Irigoyen (PDP-24)
  *Vice President*
Luisa "Piti" Gándara
  Menéndez (PDP)
  *Secretary*
Lydia R. Méndez Silva (PDP-21)
Manuel A. Natal Albelo (PDP)
Luis R. Vega Ramos (PDP)

**Minority Members**
Luis Pérez Ortiz (NPP-7)
Maria de Lourdes Ramos Rivera
  (NPP)
Pedro Julio "Pellé" Santiago
  Guzman (NPP-10)

## Ethics

**Majority Members**
Nelson Torres Yordán (PDP-23)
  *President*
Carlos A. Bianchi
  Angleró (PDP-20)
  *Vice President*
César Hernández Alfonzo (PDP-15)
  *Secretary*
Efraín De Jesús Rodríguez
  (PDP-19)
Roberto Rivera Ruiz de Porras
  (PDP-39)
José "Rodriguez" Rodríguez Quiles
  (PDP-16)

**Minority Members**
Ricardo "Ricky" Llerandi Cruz
  (NPP-14)
Carlos J. "Johnny" Méndez Nuñez
  (NPP-36)
Maria de Lourdes Ramos Rivera
  (NPP)

## Estate and Budget

**Majority Members**
Rafael Hernández
  Montañez (PDP-11)
  *President*
César Hernández Alfonzo (PDP-15)
  *Vice President*
José M. "Conny" Varela
  Fernández (PDP-32)
  *Secretary*
Javier Aponte Dalmau (PDP-38)
Ramón Luis Cruz Burgos (PDP-34)
Narden Jaime Espinosa (PDP-35)
Lydia R. Méndez Silva (PDP-21)
Luis R. "Narmito" Ortiz Lugo
  (PDP-30)
Jesús Santa Rodríguez (PDP-31)
Luis Raul Torres Cruz (PDP-2)
Nelson Torres Yordán (PDP-23)

**Minority Members**
Jorge Navarro Suárez (NPP-5)
Luis Pérez Ortiz (NPP-7)
Waldemar Quiles Rodriguez
  (NPP-22)
Gabriel Rodríguez Aguiló (NPP-13)
Pedro Julio "Pellé" Santiago
  Guzman (NPP-10)
Antonio Luis "Tony" Soto Torres
  (NPP-6)

## Federal and International Affairs and Veteran Affairs

**Majority Members**
Ángel N. Matos García (PDP-40)
  *President*
Manuel A. Natal Albelo (PDP)
  *Vice President*
Rafael Hernández
  Montañez (PDP-11)
  *Secretary*
José L. Báez Rivera (PDP-4)
Luisa "Piti" Gándara Menéndez
  (PDP)
Brenda López de Arrarás (PDP)

**Minority Members**
Luis G. León Rodriguez (NPP-24)
Gabriel Rodríguez Aguiló (NPP-13)

## Government

**Majority Members**
José M. "Conny" Varela
  Fernández (PDP-32)
  *President*
José L. Báez Rivera (PDP-4)
  *Vice President*
Nelson Torres Yordán (PDP-23)
  *Secretary*
Efraín De Jesús Rodríguez
  (PDP-19)
Rafael Hernández Montañez
  (PDP-11)
Lydia R. Méndez Silva (PDP-21)
José "Rodriguez" Rodríguez Quiles
  (PDP-16)
Jesús Santa Rodríguez (PDP-31)
Luis Raul Torres Cruz (PDP-2)
Luis R. Vega Ramos (PDP)

**Minority Members**
María Milagros Charbonier
  Laureano (NPP)
José L. López Munoz (NPP-1)
Maria de Lourdes Ramos Rivera
  (NPP)
Angel E. Rodríguez Miranda
  (NPP-9)
Pedro Julio "Pellé" Santiago
  Guzman (NPP-10)

## Health

**Majority Members**
Lydia R. Méndez Silva (PDP-21)
  *President*
Luisa "Piti" Gándara
  Menéndez (PDP)
  *Vice President*
Narden Jaime Espinosa (PDP-35)
  *Secretary*
Javier Aponte Dalmau (PDP-38)
José L. Báez Rivera (PDP-4)
César Hernández Alfonzo (PDP-15)
Rafael Hernández Montañez
  (PDP-11)
José M. "Conny" Varela Fernández
  (PDP-32)
Victor Lorenzo Vassallo Anadón
  (PDP-25)
Luis R. Vega Ramos (PDP)

**Minority Members**
María Milagros Charbonier
  Laureano (NPP)
Ricardo "Ricky" Llerandi Cruz
  (NPP-14)
Luis Pérez Ortiz (NPP-7)
Waldemar Quiles Rodriguez
  (NPP-22)
Gabriel Rodríguez Aguiló (NPP-13)

## Housing and Urban Development

**Majority Members**
Carlos A. Bianchi
  Angleró (PDP-20)
  *President*
Armando Franco
  Gonzalez (PDP-17)
  *Vice President*
Luis R. "Narmito"
  Ortiz Lugo (PDP-30)
  *Secretary*
Rafael Hernández Montañez
  (PDP-11)
Narden Jaime Espinosa (PDP-35)
Ángel N. Matos García (PDP-40)

**Minority Members**
Ángel Bulerín Ramos (NPP-37)
Luis G. León Rodriguez (NPP-24)
Luis Pérez Ortiz (NPP-7)

## Integrated Development of the Northern Region

**Majority Members**
Armando Franco
  Gonzalez (PDP-17)
  *President*
César Hernández Alfonzo (PDP-15)
  *Vice President*
José "Rodriguez" Rodríguez
  Quiles (PDP-16)
  *Secretary*

**Minority Members**
Ricardo "Ricky" Llerandi Cruz
  (NPP-14)
Héctor A. Torres Calderón
  (NPP-12)

## Integrated Development of the Southern Region

**Majority Members**

Victor Lorenzo Vassallo Anadón (PDP-25)
*President*
Nelson Torres Yordán (PDP-23)
*Vice President*
Lydia R. Méndez Silva (PDP-21)
*Secretary*
José Aníbal Díaz Collazo (PDP-29)
Luis R. "Narmito" Ortiz Lugo (PDP-30)

**Minority Members**

Urayoán Hernández Alvarado (NPP-26)
Luis G. León Rodríguez (NPP-24)

## Internal Affairs

**Majority Members**

Jose R. "Pito" Torres Ramirez (PDP-27)
*President*
José M. "Conny" Varela Fernández (PDP-32)
*Vice President*
Luis Raul Torres Cruz (PDP-2)
*Secretary*
Carlos A. Bianchi Angleró (PDP-20)
Ramón Luis Cruz Burgos (PDP-34)
Narden Jaime Espinosa (PDP-35)
Armando Franco Gonzalez (PDP-17)
Brenda López de Arrarás (PDP)
Victor Lorenzo Vassallo Anadón (PDP-25)

**Minority Members**

José L. López Munoz (NPP-1)
Angel R. Peña Ramirez (NPP-33)
Gabriel Rodríguez Aguiló (NPP-13)

## Labor Affairs and Government Employees Retirement System

**Majority Members**

Jesús Santa Rodríguez (PDP-31)
*President*
Sonia I. Pacheco Irigoyen (PDP-24)
*Vice President*
Luis Raul Torres Cruz (PDP-2)
*Secretary*
Armando Franco Gonzalez (PDP-17)
José "Rodriguez" Rodríguez Quiles (PDP-16)
José M. "Conny" Varela Fernández (PDP-32)

**Minority Members**

Angel R. Peña Ramirez (NPP-33)
Maria de Lourdes Ramos Rivera (NPP)
Héctor A. Torres Calderón (NPP-12)

## Legal/Judicial Affairs

**Majority Members**

José L. Báez Rivera (PDP-4)
*Acting President*
Nelson Torres Yordán (PDP-23)
*Vice President*
Efraín De Jesús Rodríguez (PDP-19)
*Secretary*
Brenda López de Arrarás (PDP)
José "Rodriguez" Rodríguez Quiles (PDP-16)
José M. "Conny" Varela Fernández (PDP-32)

**Minority Members**

Luis G. León Rodríguez (NPP-24)
Ricardo "Ricky" Llerandi Cruz (NPP-14)
Jose Enrique "Quiquito" Melendez Ortiz, Jr. (NPP)

## Municipal Affairs and Regionalization

**Majority Members**

José "Rodriguez" Rodríguez Quiles (PDP-16)
*President*
Efraín De Jesús Rodríguez (PDP-19)
*Vice President*
Sonia I. Pacheco Irigoyen (PDP-24)
Jesús Santa Rodríguez (PDP-31)
Victor Lorenzo Vassallo Anadón (PDP-25)

**Minority Members**

Ángel Bulerín Ramos (NPP-37)
Angel R. Peña Ramirez (NPP-33)
Héctor A. Torres Calderón (NPP-12)

## Public Safety and the Development of Initiatives Against Crime and Corruption

**Majority Members**

José L. Báez Rivera (PDP-4)
*President*
José "Rodriguez" Rodríguez Quiles (PDP-16)
*Vice President*
Sonia I. Pacheco Irigoyen (PDP-24)
*Secretary*
Efraín de Jesús Rodríguez (PDP-19)
Luis R. "Narmito" Ortiz Lugo (PDP-30)

**Minority Members**

Angel E. Rodríguez Miranda (NPP-9)
Héctor A. Torres Calderón (NPP-12)

## Rules and Calendars Special Debate

**Majority Members**

Carlos M. "Charlie" Hernández López (PDP) *President*

## Small and Medium Sized Businesses, Trade Industry and Telecommunications

**Majority Members**

Javier Aponte Dalmau (PDP-38)
*President*
Luis Raul Torres Cruz (PDP-2)
*Vice President*
César Hernández Alfonzo (PDP-15)
*Secretary*
Ángel N. Matos García (PDP-40)
Sonia I. Pacheco Irigoyen (PDP-24)
Victor Lorenzo Vassallo Anadón (PDP-25)

**Minority Members**

Ángel Muñoz Suarez (NPP-37)
Angel E. Rodríguez Miranda (NPP-9)
Antonio Luis "Tony" Soto Torres (NPP-6)

## Socio-Economic Development and Planning

**Majority Members**

Javier Aponte Dalmau (PDP-38)
*Acting President*
Sonia I. Pacheco Irigoyen (PDP-24)
*Vice President*
Efraín De Jesús Rodríguez (PDP-19)
César Hernández Alfonzo (PDP-15)
*Secretary*
Narden Jaime Espinosa (PDP-35)
Ángel N. Matos García (PDP-40)

**Minority Members**

José L. López Munoz (NPP-1)
Jorge Navarro Suárez (NPP-5)
Maria de Lourdes Ramos Rivera (NPP)

## Social Welfare and Poverty Eradication

**Majority Members**

Luisa "Piti" Gándara Menéndez (PDP)
*President*
Lydia R. Méndez Silva (PDP-21)
*Vice President*
Brenda López de Arrarás (PDP)
*Secretary*
Manuel A. Natal Albelo (PDP)
Sonia I. Pacheco Irigoyen (PDP-24)

**Minority Members**

María Milagros Charbonier Laureano (NPP)
Yashira Lebron Rodriguez (NPP-8)
Luis Pérez Ortiz (NPP-7)

## Tourism Industry Development

**Majority Members**

Ángel N. Matos García (PDP-40)
*President*
Efraín De Jesús Rodríguez (PDP-19)
*Vice President*
Luisa "Piti" Gándara Menéndez (PDP)
*Secretary*
César Hernández Alfonzo (PDP-15)
Luis R. "Narmito" Ortiz Lugo (PDP-30)
Luis Raul Torres Cruz (PDP-2)

**Minority Members**

Urayoán Hernández Alvarado (NPP-26)
Ricardo "Ricky" Llerandi Cruz (NPP-14)
Antonio Luis "Tony" Soto Torres (NPP-6)

## Transportation, Infrastructure and Recreation and Sports

**Majority Members**

Ramón Luis Cruz Burgos (PDP-34)
*President*
Luis R. "Narmito"
Ortiz Lugo (PDP-30)
*Vice President*
José L. Báez Rivera (PDP-4)
Narden Jaime Espinosa (PDP-35)
Armando Franco Gonzalez
(PDP-17)
Rafael Hernández Montañez
(PDP-11)
José "Rodriguez" Rodríguez Quiles
(PDP-16)
Victor Lorenzo Vassallo Anadón
(PDP-25)

**Minority Members**

Ángel Bulerín Ramos (NPP-37)
Jose Enrique "Quiquito" Melendez
Ortiz, Jr. (NPP)
Waldemar Quiles Rodriguez
(NPP-22)
Pedro Julio "Pellé" Santiago
Guzman (NPP-10)
Antonio Luis "Tony" Soto Torres
(NPP-6)

## Women Affairs and Equity

**Majority Members**

Brenda López de Arrarás (PDP)
*President*
Sonia I. Pacheco Irigoyen (PDP-24)
*Vice President*
Luisa "Piti" Gándara Menéndez
(PDP)

**Minority Members**

María Milagros Charbonier
Laureano (NPP)
Yashira Lebron Rodriguez (NPP-8)
Maria de Lourdes Ramos Rivera
(NPP)

# Rhode Island General Assembly

State House, Providence, RI 02903
Tel: (401) 222-2000  Tel: (401) 222-6533 (Administration)
Internet: www.rilin.state.ri.us

## Rhode Island Senate

82 Smith Street, Providence, RI 02903
Tel: (401) 222-6655  Fax: (401) 222-2967

President of the Senate **M. Teresa Paiva Weed** (D)......(401) 222-6655
  Education: Columbus Law JD
President Pro Tempore **William A. Walaska** (D) .........(401) 751-5866
  Education: Providence 1968 BA; Williams 1973 BA;
  Providence 1987 MBA
Deputy President Pro Tempore **Harold M. Metts** (D) .....(401) 272-0112
  Education: Roger Williams 1970 BS; Rhode Island Col 1983 MEd
Majority Leader **Dominick J. Ruggerio** (D)............(401) 222-3310
  Education: Providence 1974 BS
Senior Deputy Majority Leader
  **James E. "Jamie" Doyle II** (D) ..................(401) 729-9988
  Education: Providence 1994
Majority Whip **Maryellen Goodwin** (D) ..............(401) 272-3102
Deputy Majority Whip **Frank S. Lombardo III** (D).......(401) 270-1379
Minority Leader **Dennis L. Algiere** (R) ...............(401) 222-2708
  Education: Providence 1982 BA; Northeastern MS
Minority Whip **Nicholas D. Kettle** (R)...............(401) 473-7784
Secretary of the Senate **Joseph R. Brady**..............(401) 276-5555

## Senators

**Party Affiliation Statistics:** Republicans: 5, Democrats: 32,
Independents: 1

Senator **Dennis L. Algiere** (R-District 38) ..............(401) 222-2708
  Counties Represented: Washington (part)
  Term Expires: 2017
  6 Elm Street, Westerly, RI 02891
  E-mail: sen-algiere@rilin.state.ri.us
Senator
  **Stephen R. "Steve" Archambault** (D-District 22) .....(401) 276-2599
  Counties Represented: Providence (part)
  Term Expires: 2017
  195 Whipple Road, Smithfield, RI 02917
  E-mail: sen-archambault@rilegislature.gov
  Committees: Environment and Agriculture; Government Oversight;
  Judiciary; Rules
  Education: American U 1990 BA; Salve Regina U 1996 MS;
  Roger Williams 2000 JD
Senator **Frank A. Ciccone III** (D-District 7) .............(401) 275-0949
  Counties Represented: Providence (part)
  Term Expires: 2017
  15 Mercy Street, Providence, RI 02909
  E-mail: sen-ciccone@rilin.state.ri.us
  Committees: Commerce; Labor
Senator **William J. Conley, Jr.** (D-District 18)...........(401) 438-1924
  Counties Represented: Providence (part)
  Term Expires: 2017
  3 Bridgham Court, Rumford, RI 02916
  E-mail: sen-conley@rilegislature.gov
  Committees: Environment and Agriculture; Judiciary
  Education: Boston Col BA; Columbus Law JD
Senator **Marc A. Cote** (D-District 24) ..................(401) 765-3360
  Counties Represented: Providence (part)
  Term Expires: 2017
  144 Woodland Rd., Woonsocket, RI 02895
  E-mail: sen-cote@rilegislature.gov
  Committees: Commerce; Special Legislation and Veterans' Affairs
  Education: Rhode Island 1975 BS; Babson 1977 MBA
Senator **Cynthia Armour Coyne** (D-District 32) .........(401) 222-6655
  Counties Represented: Bristol (part), Providence (part)
  Term Expires: 2017
  E-mail: sen-coyne@rilegislature.gov
  Committees: Environment and Agriculture; Health and Human Services

Senator **Elizabeth A. Crowley** (D-District 16) . . . . . . . . . . (401) 725-8526
Counties Represented: Providence (part)    Tel: (401) 222-1310
Term Expires: 2017
135 Perry Street, Central Falls, RI 02863
E-mail: sen-crowley@rilegislature.gov
Committees: Health and Human Services; Housing and Municipal
Government

Senator **Daniel DaPonte** (D-District 14) . . . . . . . . . . . . . . (401) 222-3438
Counties Represented: Providence (part)
Term Expires: 2017
52 Vine Street, Apartment 1, East Providence, RI 02914
E-mail: sen-daponte@rilegislature.gov
Committees: Education; Finance; Rules
Education: Rhode Island 2000 BS

Senator **Louis P. DiPalma** (D-District 12) . . . . . . . . . . . . . (401) 847-8540
Counties Represented: Newport (part)
Term Expires: 2017
24 Sail Court, Middletown, RI 02842
E-mail: sen-dipalma@rilegislature.gov
Committees: Education; Finance
Education: Bridgeport 1983 BS; Brown U 1989 ScM

Senator **James E. "Jamie" Doyle II** (D-District 8) . . . . . . . (401) 729-9988
Counties Represented: Providence (part)
Term Expires: 2017
8 Massasoit Avenue, Pawtucket, RI 02861
E-mail: sen-doyle@rilegislature.gov
Committees: Finance; Labor

Senator **Walter S. Felag, Jr.** (D-District 10) . . . . . . . . . . . . (401) 245-7521
Counties Represented: Bristol (part), Newport (part)    Tel: (401) 847-2260
Term Expires: 2017
51 Overhill Rd., Warren, RI 02885
E-mail: sen-felag@rilegislature.gov
Committees: Finance; Special Legislation and Veterans' Affairs
Education: Providence 1976 BA

Senator **Paul W. Fogarty** (D-District 23) . . . . . . . . . . . . . (401) 949-0895
Counties Represented: Providence (part)    Tel: (401) 276-5589
Term Expires: 2017
P.O. Box 37, Harmony, RI 02829
E-mail: sen-fogarty@rilin.state.ri.us
Committees: Commerce; Labor

Senator **Hanna M. Gallo** (D-District 27) . . . . . . . . . . . . . (401) 942-8566
Counties Represented: Kent (part), Providence (part)    Tel: (401) 222-4200
Term Expires: 2017
285 Meshanticut Valley Parkway, Cranston, RI 02920
E-mail: sen-gallo@rilegislature.gov
Committees: Commerce; Education
Education: Rhode Island 1995 BS, 1997 MS

Senator **Mark W. Gee** (R-District 35) . . . . . . . . . . . . . . . (401) 222-6655
Counties Represented: Kent (part), Washington (part)
Term Expires: 2017
E-mail: sen-gee@rilegislature.gov
Committees: Government Oversight

Senator **Gayle L. Goldin** (D-District 3) . . . . . . . . . . . . . . (401) 340-5050
Counties Represented: Providence (part)
Term Expires: 2017
P.O. Box 2722, Providence, RI 02906
E-mail: sen-goldin@rilegislature.gov
Committees: Environment and Agriculture; Health and Human Services
Education: McGill (Canada) 1993 BA; Tufts 1998 MPP

Senator **Maryellen Goodwin** (D-District 1) . . . . . . . . . . . . (401) 272-3102
Counties Represented: Providence (part)
Term Expires: 2017
325 Smith Street, Providence, RI 02908
E-mail: sen-goodwin@rilegislature.gov
Committees: Environment and Agriculture; Finance; Housing and
Municipal Government; Labor; Rules

Senator **Paul V. Jabour** (D-District 5) . . . . . . . . . . . . . . . (401) 751-3300
Counties Represented: Providence (part)    Tel: (401) 751-3301
Term Expires: 2017
529 Broadway, Providence, RI 02909
E-mail: sen-jabour@rilegislature.gov
Committees: Commerce; Government Oversight; Judiciary; Special
Legislation and Veterans' Affairs

Senator **Nicholas D. Kettle** (R-District 21) . . . . . . . . . . . . (401) 473-7784
Counties Represented: Kent (part), Providence (part)
Term Expires: 2017
5 Autumn Ridge Road, Coventry, RI 02816
E-mail: sen-kettle@rilegislature.gov
Committees: Education; Environment and Agriculture; Health and
Human Services; Health, Education and Welfare; Housing and
Municipal Government; Rules

Senator **Frank S. Lombardi** (D-District 26) . . . . . . . . . . . . (401) 453-3900
Counties Represented: Providence (part)
Term Expires: 2017
25 Briarbrooke Lane, Cranston, RI 02921
E-mail: sen-lombardi@rilegislature.gov
Committees: Judiciary; Labor; Rules
Education: Providence 1984 BSAcc; Northeastern 1998 JD

Senator **Frank S. Lombardo III** (D-District 25) . . . . . . . . . (401) 270-1379
Counties Represented: Providence (part)
Term Expires: 2017
68 Rollingwood Drive, Johnston, RI 02919
E-mail: sen-lombardo@rilegislature.gov
Committees: Commerce; Labor; Rules

Senator **Erin P. Lynch Prata** (D-District 31) . . . . . . . . . . . (401) 276-5562
Counties Represented: Kent (part), Providence (part)
Term Expires: 2017
State House, Room 314, Providence, RI 02903
28 Goodwin Street, Warwick, RI 02818
E-mail: sen-lynch@rilegislature.gov
Committees: Government Oversight; Judiciary; Rules; Special
Legislation and Veterans' Affairs
Education: Boston Col BA; Columbus Law JD

Senator **Michael J. McCaffrey** (D-District 29) . . . . . . . . . . (401) 739-7576
Counties Represented: Kent (part)    Tel: (401) 222-6625
Term Expires: 2017    Res: (401) 463-7444
115 Twin Oak Drive, Warwick, RI 02889
E-mail: sen-mccaffrey@rilegislature.gov
Committees: Housing and Municipal Government; Judiciary; Labor;
Rules
Education: Providence 1985 BS; Suffolk 1989 JD

Senator **Harold M. Metts** (D-District 6) . . . . . . . . . . . . . . (401) 272-0112
Counties Represented: Providence (part)    Res: (401) 456-9115
Term Expires: 2017
31 Tanner Street, Providence, RI 02907
E-mail: sen-metts@rilegislature.gov
Committees: Education; Judiciary

Senator **Joshua Miller** (D-District 28) . . . . . . . . . . . . . . . (401) 276-5582
Counties Represented: Providence (part)
Term Expires: 2017
41 Talbot Manor, Cranston, RI 02905
E-mail: sen-miller@rilegislature.gov
Committees: Education; Health and Human Services; Housing and
Municipal Government

Senator **Elaine J. Morgan** (R-District 34) . . . . . . . . . . . . . (401) 222-6655
Counties Represented: Kent (part), Washington (part)
Term Expires: 2017
E-mail: sen-morgan@rilegislature.gov
Committees: Commerce; Special Legislation and Veterans' Affairs

Senator **Donna M. Nesselbush** (D-District 15) . . . . . . . . . (401) 728-3244
Counties Represented: Providence (part)
Term Expires: 2017
181 Raleigh Avenue, Pawtucket, RI 02860
E-mail: sen-nesselbush@rilegislature.gov
Committees: Health and Human Services; Housing and Municipal
Government; Judiciary

Senator **Edward J. O'Neill** (I-District 17) . . . . . . . . . . . . . (401) 728-3295
Counties Represented: Providence (part)    Tel: (401) 524-5527
Term Expires: 2017
2 Lladnar Drive, Lincoln, RI 02863
E-mail: sen-oneill@rilegislature.gov
Committees: Education; Finance; Government Oversight

Senator **John A. Pagliarini, Jr.** (R-District 11) . . . . . . . . . . (401) 529-7599
Counties Represented: Bristol (part), Newport (part)
Term Expires: 2017
E-mail: sen-pagliarini@rilegislature.gov
Committees: Finance

Senator **M. Teresa Paiva Weed** (D-District 13) . . . . . . . . . (401) 222-6655
Counties Represented: Newport (part)
Term Expires: 2017
318 State House, Providence, RI 02903
48 Admiral Kalbfus, Newport, RI 02840
E-mail: sen-paivaweed@rilin.state.ri.us

Senator **Ryan William Pearson** (D-District 19) . . . . . . . . . (401) 276-5594
Counties Represented: Providence (part)    Tel: (401) 276-5555
Term Expires: 2017
1427 Diamond Hill Road, Cumberland, RI 02864
E-mail: sen-pearson@rilegislature.gov
Committees: Education; Finance; Government Oversight; Housing and
Municipal Government
Education: Providence BS

*(continued on next page)*

**Senators** *continued*

Senator **Roger A. Picard** (D-District 20) . . . . . . . . . . . . . . . (401) 769-4902
Counties Represented: Providence (part)
Term Expires: 2017
764 Mendon Road, Woonsocket, RI 02895
E-mail: sen-picard@rilin.state.ri.us
Committees: Commerce; Labor
Education: Rhode Island 1979 BA; Rhode Island Col 1995 MSW

Senator **Juan M. Pichardo** (D-District 2) . . . . . . . . . . . . . . (401) 461-2389
Counties Represented: Providence (part)          Tel: (401) 276-5599
Term Expires: 2017
229 Atlantic Avenue, Providence, RI 02907
E-mail: sen-pichardo@rilegislature.gov
Committees: Finance; Housing and Municipal Government; Special
Legislation and Veterans' Affairs

Senator **Leonidas P. "Lou" Raptakis** (D-District 33) . . . . . (401) 397-2720
Counties Represented: Kent (part)
Term Expires: 2017
2080 Nooseneck Hill Road, Coventry, RI 02816
E-mail: sen-raptakis@rilegislature.gov
Committees: Judiciary; Special Legislation and Veterans' Affairs
Education: Rhode Island Col 1985 BA

Senator **Dominick J. Ruggerio** (D-District 4) . . . . . . . . . . (401) 222-3310
Counties Represented: Providence (part)          Tel: (401) 276-2503
Term Expires: 2017                               Tel: (401) 751-1011
1046 Douglas Avenue, Providence, RI 02904       Res: (401) 331-6074
42 Countryside Dr., North Providence, RI 02904
E-mail: sen-ruggerio@rilin.state.ri.us

Senator **Adam J. Satchell** (D-District 9) . . . . . . . . . . . . . . (401) 615-5170
Counties Represented: Kent (part)
Term Expires: 2017
18 Wyman Street, West Warwick, RI 02893
E-mail: sen-satchell@rilegislature.gov
Committees: Education; Health and Human Services
Education: Merrimack 2003 BA; Rhode Island Col 2009

Senator **James C. Sheehan** (D-District 36) . . . . . . . . . . . . (401) 885-1988
Counties Represented: Washington (part)
Term Expires: 2017
40 Blueberry Lane, North Kingstown, RI 02852
E-mail: sen-sheehan@rilegislature.gov
Committees: Education; Government Oversight; Health and Human
Services
Education: Rhode Island 1988 BA; Catholic U 1992 MA

Senator **V. Susan Sosnowski** (D-District 37) . . . . . . . . . . (401) 783-7704
Counties Represented: Washington (part)          Tel: (401) 222-4200
Term Expires: 2017
680 Glen Rock Road, West Kingston, RI 02892
E-mail: sen-sosnowski@rilegislature.gov
Committees: Environment and Agriculture; Finance; Health and Human
Services

Senator **William A. Walaska** (D-District 30) . . . . . . . . . . . (401) 737-1065
Counties Represented: Kent (part)                Tel: (401) 751-5866
Term Expires: 2017
140 Aldrich Ave., Warwick, RI 02889
E-mail: sen-walaska@rilin.state.ri.us
Committees: Commerce; Environment and Agriculture
Affiliation: President, CEO WAL, Inc.

# Senate Standing Committees
## Commerce

| **Majority Members** | **Minority Members** |
|---|---|
| Roger A. Picard (D-20) | Elaine J. Morgan (R-34) |
| *Chairperson* | |
| William A. Walaska (D-30) | |
| *Vice Chairperson* | |
| Marc A. Cote (D-24) *Secretary* | |
| Frank A. Ciccone III (D-7) | |
| Paul W. Fogarty (D-23) | |
| Hanna M. Gallo (D-27) | |
| Paul V. Jabour (D-5) | |
| Frank S. Lombardo III (D-25) | |

## Education

| **Majority Members** | **Minority Members** |
|---|---|
| Hanna M. Gallo (D-27) | Nicholas D. Kettle (R-21) |
| *Chairperson* | |
| Harold M. Metts (D-6) | |
| *Vice Chairperson* | |
| Adam J. Satchell (D-9) *Secretary* | |
| Daniel DaPonte (D-14) | |
| Louis P. DiPalma (D-12) | |
| Joshua Miller (D-28) | |
| Ryan William Pearson (D-19) | |
| James C. Sheehan (D-36) | |

**Members**
Edward J. O'Neill (I-17)

## Environment and Agriculture

| **Majority Members** | **Minority Members** |
|---|---|
| V. Susan Sosnowski (D-37) | Nicholas D. Kettle (R-21) |
| *Chairperson* | |
| William J. Conley, Jr. (D-18) | |
| *Vice Chairperson* | |
| Gayle L. Goldin (D-3) *Secretary* | |
| Stephen R. "Steve" Archambault (D-22) | |
| Cynthia Armour Coyne (D-32) | |
| Maryellen Goodwin (D-1) | |
| William A. Walaska (D-30) | |

## Finance

| **Majority Members** | **Minority Members** |
|---|---|
| Daniel DaPonte (D-14) *Chairperson* | John A. Pagliarini, Jr. (R-11) |
| Louis P. DiPalma (D-12) | |
| *1st Vice Chairperson* | |
| Walter S. Felag, Jr. (D-10) | |
| *2nd Vice Chairperson* | |
| Ryan William Pearson (D-19) | |
| *Secretary* | |
| James E. "Jamie" Doyle II (D-8) | |
| Maryellen Goodwin (D-1) | |
| Juan M. Pichardo (D-2) | |
| V. Susan Sosnowski (D-37) | |

**Members**
Edward J. O'Neill (I-17)

## Government Oversight

| **Majority Members** | **Minority Members** |
|---|---|
| James C. Sheehan (D-36) | Mark W. Gee (R-35) |
| *Chairperson* | |
| Paul V. Jabour (D-5) | |
| *Vice Chairperson* | |
| Stephen R. "Steve" Archambault (D-22) | |
| Erin P. Lynch Prata (D-31) | |
| Ryan William Pearson (D-19) | |

**Members**
Edward J. O'Neill (I-17) *Secretary*

## Health and Human Services

| **Majority Members** | **Minority Members** |
|---|---|
| Joshua Miller (D-28) *Chairperson* | Nicholas D. Kettle (R-21) |
| Donna M. Nesselbush (D-15) | |
| *Vice Chairperson* | |
| James C. Sheehan (D-36) *Secretary* | |
| Cynthia Armour Coyne (D-32) | |
| Elizabeth A. Crowley (D-16) | |
| Gayle L. Goldin (D-3) | |
| Adam J. Satchell (D-9) | |
| V. Susan Sosnowski (D-37) | |

## Housing and Municipal Government

**Majority Members**
Juan M. Pichardo (D-2)
  *Chairperson*
Elizabeth A. Crowley (D-16)
  *Vice Chairperson*
Maryellen Goodwin (D-1)
Michael J. McCaffrey (D-29)
Joshua Miller (D-28)
Donna M. Nesselbush (D-15)
Ryan William Pearson (D-19)

**Minority Members**
Nicholas D. Kettle (R-21) *Secretary*

## Judiciary

**Majority Members**
Michael J. McCaffrey (D-29) *Chairperson*
Paul V. Jabour (D-5) *Vice Chairperson*
Erin P. Lynch Prata (D-31) *Secretary*
Stephen R. "Steve" Archambault (D-22)
William J. Conley, Jr. (D-18)
Frank S. Lombardi (D-26)
Harold M. Metts (D-6)
Donna M. Nesselbush (D-15)
Leonidas P. "Lou" Raptakis (D-33)

## Labor

**Majority Members**
Paul W. Fogarty (D-23) *Chairperson*
Frank A. Ciccone III (D-7) *Vice Chairperson*
Frank S. Lombardo III (D-25) *Secretary*
James E. "Jamie" Doyle II (D-8)
Maryellen Goodwin (D-1)
Frank S. Lombardi (D-26)
Michael J. McCaffrey (D-29)
Roger A. Picard (D-20)

## Rules

**Majority Members**
Erin P. Lynch Prata (D-31)
  *Chairperson*
Stephen R. "Steve"
  Archambault (D-22)
  *Vice Chairperson*
Frank S. Lombardi (D-26) *Secretary*
Daniel DaPonte (D-14)
Maryellen Goodwin (D-1)
Frank S. Lombardo III (D-25)
Michael J. McCaffrey (D-29)

**Minority Members**
Nicholas D. Kettle (R-21)

## Special Legislation and Veterans' Affairs

**Majority Members**
Walter S. Felag, Jr. (D-10)
  *Chairperson*
Erin P. Lynch Prata (D-31)
  *Vice Chairperson*
Leonidas P. "Lou" Raptakis (D-33)
  *Secretary*
Marc A. Cote (D-24)
Paul V. Jabour (D-5)
Juan M. Pichardo (D-2)

**Minority Members**
Elaine J. Morgan (R-34)

## Rhode Island House of Representatives

Tel: (401) 222-2466 Fax: (401) 222-1925
Speaker of the House **Nicholas A. Mattiello** (D) . . . . . . . . (401) 222-1478
  Chief of Staff **Leo Skenyon** . . . . . . . . . . . . . . . . . . . . . . . (401) 222-2466
Speaker Pro Tem **Robert B. Jacquard** (D). . . . . . . . . . . . . (401) 222-2466
  Education: Roger Williams 1984 BS, 1998 JD
Majority Leader **John J. DeSimone** (D) . . . . . . . . . . . . . . (401) 351-7373
  Education: Providence 1982 BA; Suffolk 1985 JD
Senior Deputy Majority Leader
  **Kenneth A. Marshall** (D). . . . . . . . . . . . . . . . . . . . . . . . (401) 254-1377
  Education: Bryant Col 1991 BA
Majority Whip **Stephen R. Ucci** (D) . . . . . . . . . . . . . . . . (401) 934-2121
  Education: New England 1996 JD
Deputy Majority Whip **Christopher R. Blazejewski** (D) . . (401) 484-8814
  Education: Harvard 2002 BA, 2005 JD

Minority Leader **Brian C. Newberry** (R) . . . . . . . . . . . . . . (401) 765-1069
  Education: Pennsylvania 1993 BA; Temple 1996 JD
Minority Whip **Joseph A. Trillo** (R) . . . . . . . . . . . . . . . . . (401) 222-2259
Clerk of the House **Francis McCabe** . . . . . . . . . . . . . . . . .(401) 222-1478
  Education: Rhode Island Col 1971 BA; New England 1991 JD

## Representatives

**Party Affiliation Statistics:** Republicans: 11, Democrats: 62,
Independents: 1, Vacancies: 1
Representative
  **Marvin L. Abney, USA (Ret)** (D-District 73) . . . . . . . . . (401) 487-1380
  Counties Represented: Newport (part)
  Term Expires: 2017
  12 Summer Street, Newport, RI 02840
  E-mail: rep-abney@rilegislature.gov
  Committees: Finance; Health, Education and Welfare; Veterans' Affairs
  Education: Austin State 1975 BPA; Webster 1982 MM
Representative **Mia A. Ackerman** (D-District 45) . . . . . . . (401) 658-0981
  Counties Represented: Providence (part)
  Term Expires: 2017
  6 Shelter Lane, Cumberland, RI 02864
  E-mail: rep-ackerman@rilegislature.gov
  Committees: Health, Education and Welfare; Municipal Government
  Education: SUNY (Binghamton) BA
Representative **Edith H. Ajello** (D-District 1). . . . . . . . . . . (401) 222-2466
  Counties Represented: Providence (part)    Res: (401) 274-7078
  Term Expires: 2017
  29 Benefit Street, Providence, RI 02904
  E-mail: rep-ajello@rilegislature.gov
  Committees: Judiciary
  Education: Bucknell 1966 BA
Representative **Joseph S. Almeida** (D-District 12) . . . . . . (401) 467-7033
  Counties Represented: Providence (part)
  Term Expires: 2017
  299 California Avenue, Providence, RI 02905
  E-mail: rep-almeida@rilegislature.gov
  Committees: Judiciary; Rules
  Education: Roger Williams 1990 BA
Representative **Gregg Amore** (D-District 65). . . . . . . . . . . (401) 339-9378
  Counties Represented: Providence (part)
  Term Expires: 2017
  73 Plymouth Road, East Providence, RI 02914
  E-mail: rep-amore@rilegislature.gov
  Committees: Finance; Health, Education and Welfare; Municipal
  Government
  Education: Providence BA; New England Col MPP
Representative **Samuel A. Azzinaro** (D-District 37) . . . . . . (401) 596-1434
  Counties Represented: Washington (part)
  Term Expires: 2017
  24 1st Street, Westerly, RI 02891
  E-mail: rep-azzinaro@rilegislature.gov
  Committees: Health, Education and Welfare; Rules; Veterans' Affairs
Representative **Jean Philippe Barros** (D-District 59) . . . . . (401) 475-1579
  Counties Represented: Providence (part)
  Term Expires: 2017
  One William Street, Pawtucket, RI 02860
  E-mail: rep-barros@rilegislature.gov
  Committees: Finance; Municipal Government
Representative **David A. Bennett, RN** (D-District 20) . . . . .(401) 648-1171
  Counties Represented: Kent (part), Providence (part)
  Term Expires: 2017
  27 Shippee Avenue, Warwick, RI 02886
  E-mail: rep-bennett@rilegislature.gov
  Committees: Environment and Natural Resources; Health, Education
  and Welfare; Municipal Government
  Education: Rhode Island Col 1987 BA
Representative
  **Christopher R. Blazejewski** (D-District 2). . . . . . . . . . .(401) 484-8814
  Counties Represented: Providence (part)
  Term Expires: 2017
  1 Thayer St, Providence, RI 02906
  E-mail: rep-blazejewski@rilegislature.gov
  Committees: Judiciary; Rules
Representative **Dennis M. Canario** (D-District 71) . . . . . . . (401) 683-4926
  Counties Represented: Newport (part)
  Term Expires: 2017
  64 Birchwood Drive, Portsmouth, RI 02871
  E-mail: rep-canario@rilegislature.gov
  Committees: Health, Education and Welfare; Judiciary; Veterans'
  Affairs
  Education: Roger Williams 1988 AS

*(continued on next page)*

**Representatives** *continued*

Representative **John M. Carnevale** (D-District 13) . . . . . . . (401) 274-1353
Counties Represented: Providence (part)
Term Expires: 2017
150 Barbara Street, Providence, RI 02909
E-mail: rep-carnevale@rilin.state.ri.us
Committees: Finance
Education: Roger Williams BSA

Representative **Lauren H. Carson** (D-District 75) . . . . . . . . (401) 523-1143
Counties Represented: Newport (part)
Term Expires: 2017
11 Willow Street, Room 5, Newport, RI 02840
E-mail: rep-carson@rilegislature.gov
Committees: Oversight; Small Business
Education: Rhode Island 1992 MB, 2008 MA

Representative
**Stephen M. "Steve" Casey** (D-District 50) . . . . . . . . . . (508) 942-0484
Counties Represented: Providence (part)
Term Expires: 2017
625 Park Avenue, Woonsocket, RI 02895
E-mail: rep-casey@rilegislature.gov
Committees: Corporations; Labor; Veterans' Affairs
Education: Boston Col 1990 BComm

Representative **Michael W. Chippendale** (R-District 40) . . (401) 497-4495
Counties Represented: Kent (part), Providence (part)
Term Expires: 2017
124A Johnston Road, Foster, RI 02825
E-mail: rep-chippendale@rilegislature.gov
Committees: Labor; Oversight; Rules

Representative **Arthur J. Corvese** (D-District 55) . . . . . . . . (401) 353-8695
Counties Represented: Providence (part)
Term Expires: 2017
234 Lexington Avenue, North Providence, RI 02904
E-mail: rep-corvese@rilegislature.gov
Committees: Health, Education and Welfare; Labor; Oversight; Rules
Education: Providence 1977 BS; New England Col 1981 OD

Representative **Doreen Marie Costa** (R-District 31) . . . . . . (401) 206-6891
Counties Represented: Washington (part)
Term Expires: 2017
39 Dyer Ave, North Kingstown, RI 02852
E-mail: rep-costa@rilegislature.gov
Committees: Judiciary; Veterans' Affairs

Representative **Gregory J. Costantino** (D-District 44) . . . . (401) 426-0284
Counties Represented: Providence (part)
Term Expires: 2017
21 Greenwood Lane, Lincoln, RI 02865
E-mail: rep-costantino@rilegislature.gov
Committees: Municipal Government
Education: Providence 1978 BA

Representative **David A. Coughlin, Jr.** (D-District 60) . . . . (401) 723-2670
Counties Represented: Providence (part)
Term Expires: 2017
Nine Armistice Boulevard, Pawtucket, RI 02860
E-mail: rep-coughlin@rilegislature.gov
Committees: Judiciary; Municipal Government

Representative **Robert E. Craven, Sr.** (D-District 32) . . . . . (401) 294-2222
Counties Represented: Washington (part)
Term Expires: 2017
25 Highland Road, Saunderstown, RI 02874
E-mail: rep-craven@rilegislature.gov
Committees: Judiciary; Municipal Government
Education: Rhode Island 1978 BA; New England 1983 JD

Representative **John J. DeSimone** (D-District 5) . . . . . . . . (401) 351-7373
Counties Represented: Providence (part)        Res: (401) 454-1400
Term Expires: 2017
735 Smith Street, Providence, RI 02904
E-mail: rep-desimone@rilin.state.ri.us

Representative **Grace Diaz** (D-District 11) . . . . . . . . . . . . . (401) 467-8413
Counties Represented: Providence (part)        Res: (401) 575-3641
Term Expires: 2017
45 Adelaide Avenue, Providence, RI 02907
E-mail: rep-diaz@rilegislature.gov
Committees: Health, Education and Welfare; Rules

Representative **John G. Edwards** (D-District 70) . . . . . . . . (401) 624-8879
Counties Represented: Newport (part)
Term Expires: 2017
69 South Avenue, Tiverton, RI 02878
E-mail: rep-edwards@rilegislature.gov
Committees: Judiciary; Labor; Oversight; Small Business
Education: Northeastern 1983 MA

Representative **Deborah A. Fellela** (D-District 43) . . . . . . . (401) 231-2014
Counties Represented: Providence (part)
Term Expires: 2017
3 Diaz Street, Johnston, RI 02919
E-mail: rep-fellela@rilegislature.gov
Committees: Labor; Veterans' Affairs

Representative **Blake Anthony Filippi** (I-District 36) . . . . . (401) 744-2242
Counties Represented: Washington (part)
Term Expires: 2017
E-mail: rep-filippi@rilegislature.gov
Committees: Environment and Natural Resources; Judiciary; Municipal Government

Representative **Kathleen A. Fogarty** (D-District 35) . . . . . . (401) 782-1919
Counties Represented: Washington (part)
Term Expires: 2017
50 Woodmark Way, Wakefield, RI 02879
E-mail: rep-fogarty@rilegislature.gov
Committees: Health, Education and Welfare; Municipal Government
Education: Providence 1987 BA

Representative **Antonio Giarrusso** (R-District 30) . . . . . . . .(401) 415-5390
Counties Represented: Kent (part)
Term Expires: 2017
5 Lenihan Lane, East Greenwich, RI 02818
E-mail: rep-giarrusso@rilegislature.gov
Committees: Finance; Labor
Education: Bryant Col (Attended)

Representative **Carol Hagan McEntee** (D-District 33) . . . . (401) 222-1478
Counties Represented: Washington (part)
Term Expires: 2017
E-mail: rep-mcentee@rilegislature.gov
Committees: Judiciary; Labor; Municipal Government

Representative **Arthur Handy** (D-District 18) . . . . . . . . . . .(401) 222-2466
Counties Represented: Providence (part)        Res: (401) 785-8996
Term Expires: 2017
26 Welfare Avenue, Cranston, RI 02910
E-mail: rep-handy@rilegislature.gov
Committees: Environment and Natural Resources; Health, Education and Welfare; Oversight; Small Business
Education: Miami 1990 BA

Representative **Joy Hearn** (D-District 66) . . . . . . . . . . . . . . (401) 247-9867
Counties Represented: Bristol (part), Providence (part)
Term Expires: 2017
23 Brentonwood Avenue, Barrington, RI 02806
E-mail: rep-hearn@rilegislature.gov
Committees: Finance; Municipal Government

Representative **Raymond A. Hull** (D-District 6) . . . . . . . . . (401) 272-4026
Counties Represented: Providence (part)
Term Expires: 2017
616 Mt. Pleasant Avenue, Providence, RI 02908
E-mail: rep-hull@rilin.state.ri.us
Committees: Environment and Natural Resources
Education: Roger Williams 1992 BA; Anna Maria 1999 MA

Representative **Robert B. Jacquard** (D-District 17) . . . . . . .(401) 222-2466
Counties Represented: Providence (part)        Res: (401) 943-7799
Term Expires: 2017
34 Sagamore Road, Cranston, RI 02920
E-mail: rep-jacquard@rilegislature.gov
Committees: Finance; Veterans' Affairs

Representative
**Raymond H. Johnston, Jr.** (D-District 61) . . . . . . . . . . . (401) 288-7248
Counties Represented: Providence (part)
Term Expires: 2017
102 Archer Street, Pawtucket, RI 02861
E-mail: rep-johnston@rilegislature.gov
Committees: Corporations; Municipal Government; Oversight
Education: Roger Williams (Attended)

Representative **Katherine S. Kazarian** (D-District 63) . . . . .(401) 438-1718
Counties Represented: Providence (part)
Term Expires: 2017
380 Pleasant Street, East Providence, RI 02916
E-mail: rep-kazarian@rilegislature.gov
Committees: Corporations; Rules
Education: Columbia 2012 BA

Representative **Cale P. Keable** (D-District 47) . . . . . . . . . . (401) 710-1239
Counties Represented: Providence (part)
Term Expires: 2017
66 South Main Street, Pascoag, RI 02859
E-mail: rep-keable@rilegislature.gov
Committees: Judiciary; Rules
Affiliation: Of Counsel, Partridge Snow & Hahn LLP
40 Westminster Street, Suite 1100, Providence, RI 02903
Education: Providence 1998 BA; Harvard 2001 JD

Representative **Brian Patrick Kennedy** (D-District 38) .... (401) 222-2466
Counties Represented: Washington (part)     Res: (401) 377-8818
Term Expires: 2017
P.O. Box 1001, Ashaway, RI 02804-0018
E-mail: rep-kennedy@rilin.state.ri.us
Committees: Corporations
Education: Providence 1983 BAGS; Anna Maria 1987 MBA

Representative **Robert B. Lancia** (R-District 16) ........ (401) 944-3315
Counties Represented: Providence (part)
Term Expires: 2017
25 Church Hill Drive, Cranston, RI 02920
E-mail: rep-lancia@rilegislature.gov
Committees: Health, Education and Welfare; Veterans' Affairs

Representative **Charlene M. Lima** (D-District 14) ........ (401) 222-2258
Counties Represented: Providence (part)     Tel: (401) 222-6595
Term Expires: 2017     Res: (401) 946-5707
455 Laurel Hill Avenue, Cranston, RI 02920
E-mail: rep-lima@rilegislature.gov
Committees: Corporations; Municipal Government; Rules
Education: Rhode Island 1975 BA

Representative **John Joseph Lombardi** (D-District 8) .... (401) 453-3900
Counties Represented: Providence (part)
Term Expires: 2017
48 Grove Street, Providence, RI 02909
E-mail: rep-lombardi@rilin.state.ri.us
Committees: Environment and Natural Resources; Small Business
Education: Rhode Island Col 1975 BA, 1982 MA; Suffolk 1987 JD

Representative **Karen L. MacBeth** (R-District 52) ........ (401) 333-5398
Counties Represented: Providence (part)
Term Expires: 2017
75 Newell Drive, Cumberland, RI 02864
E-mail: rep-macbeth@rilegislature.gov
Committees: Veterans' Affairs
Education: Rhode Island Col BS; Providence MA

Representative **Shelby Maldonado** (D-District 56) ....... (401) 340-8833
Counties Represented: Providence (part)
Term Expires: 2017
Six Washington Street, Central Falls, RI 02863
E-mail: rep-maldonado@rilegislature.gov
Committees: Health, Education and Welfare; Municipal Government;
Small Business

Representative **Jan P. Malik** (D-District 67) ............. (401) 247-1271
Counties Represented: Bristol (part)     Res: (401) 247-1733
Term Expires: 2017
23 Hezekiah Drive, Warren, RI 02885
E-mail: rep-malik@rilegislature.gov
Committees: Finance; Veterans' Affairs
Education: Dean AA

Representative **Michael J. Marcello** (D-District 41) ...... (401) 647-5905
Counties Represented: Providence (part)
Term Expires: 2017
P.O. Box 114, Scituate, RI 02857
E-mail: rep-marcello@rilin.state.ri.us
Committees: Corporations; Environment and Natural Resources

Representative **Kenneth A. Marshall** (D-District 68) ..... (401) 254-1377
Counties Represented: Bristol (part)
Term Expires: 2017
26 Harborview Avenue, Bristol, RI 02809
E-mail: rep-marshall@rilegislature.gov
Committees: Corporations; Finance; Labor; Municipal Government;
Rules

Representative **Nicholas A. Mattiello** (D-District 15) ..... (401) 222-1478
Counties Represented: Providence (part)     Res: (401) 461-5800
Term Expires: 2017
55 Pasture View Lane, Cranston, RI 02921
E-mail: rep-mattiello@rilin.state.ri.us

Representative **Daniel P. McKiernan** (D-District 7) ....... (401) 301-8678
Counties Represented: Providence (part)
Term Expires: 2017
122 Whitford Avenue, Providence, RI 02908
E-mail: rep-mckiernan@rilegislature.gov
Committees: Labor; Oversight; Small Business

Representative **James N. McLaughlin** (D-District 57) .... (401) 333-4946
Counties Represented: Providence (part)
Term Expires: 2017
15 Garden Street, Cumberland, RI 02864
E-mail: rep-mclaughlin@rilegislature.gov
Committees: Health, Education and Welfare; Veterans' Affairs

Representative **Joseph M. McNamara** (D-District 19) .... (401) 222-2466
Counties Represented: Kent (part), Providence (part)     Res: (401) 941-8319
Term Expires: 2017
23 Howie Avenue, Warwick, RI 02888
E-mail: rep-mcnamara@rilegislature.gov
Committees: Environment and Natural Resources; Health, Education
and Welfare; Labor
Education: Boston U BS; Providence MEd

Representative **Helio Melo** (D-District 64) .............. (401) 222-8028
Counties Represented: Providence (part)     Tel: (401) 435-0546
Term Expires: 2017
1187 South Broadway, East Providence, RI 02914
E-mail: rep-melo@rilegislature.gov
Committees: Environment and Natural Resources; Labor

Representative **Mary Duffy Messier** (D-District 62) ...... (401) 728-1682
Counties Represented: Providence (part)
Term Expires: 2017
25 Olympia Avenue, Pawtucket, RI 02861
E-mail: rep-messier@rilegislature.gov
Committees: Corporations; Veterans' Affairs

Representative **Patricia L. Morgan** (R-District 26) ........ (401) 222-2259
Counties Represented: Kent (part)
Term Expires: 2017
E-mail: rep-morgan@rilin.state.ri.us
Committees: Finance

Representative **Michael A. Morin** (D-District 49) ........ (401) 265-0910
Counties Represented: Providence (part)
Term Expires: 2017
180 Allen Street, Unit 202, Woonsocket, RI 02895
E-mail: rep-morin@rilegislature.gov
Committees: Corporations; Finance; Health, Education and Welfare;
Small Business
Education: Comm Col Rhode Island 2011 AAS

Representative **Robert A. Nardolillo** (R-District 28) ...... (401) 580-2500
Counties Represented: Kent (part)
Term Expires: 2017
960 Maple Valley Road, Greene, RI 02827
E-mail: rep-nardolillo@rilin.state.ri.us
Committees: Corporations; Small Business

Representative
**Eileen Slattery Naughton** (D-District 21) ............ (401) 222-2466
Counties Represented: Kent (part)     Res: (401) 738-7928
Term Expires: 2017
100 Old Homestead Road, Warwick, RI 02889
E-mail: rep-naughton@rilegislature.gov
Committees: Environment and Natural Resources; Finance; Veterans'
Affairs
Education: Amherst 1967 BA

Representative **Brian C. Newberry** (R-District 48) ....... (401) 765-1069
Counties Represented: Providence (part)
Term Expires: 2017
53 Follett Street, N. Smithfield, RI 02896
E-mail: rep-newberry@rilin.state.ri.us

Representative **Jared R. Nunes** (D-District 25) ........... (401) 821-8693
Counties Represented: Kent (part)
Term Expires: 2017
52 Phillip Street, Coventry, RI 02816
E-mail: rep-nunes@rilegislature.gov
Committees: Corporations; Labor; Small Business

Representative **William W. O'Brien** (D-District 54) ....... (401) 440-4063
Counties Represented: Providence (part)
Term Expires: 2017
626 Smithfield Road, North Providence, RI 02904
E-mail: rep-obrien@rilegislature.gov
Committees: Corporations; Environment and Natural Resources;
Oversight; Rules
Education: Rhode Island Col 1991 BA

Representative **Jeremiah T. O'Grady** (D-District 46) ...... (401) 725-7163
Counties Represented: Providence (part)
Term Expires: 2017
36 Lakeview Road, Lincoln, RI 02865
E-mail: rep-ogrady@rilegislature.gov
Committees: Corporations; Environment and Natural Resources;
Judiciary

Representative **Thomas A. Palangio** (D-District 3) ....... (401) 248-8877
Counties Represented: Providence (part)
Term Expires: 2017
718 Douglas Avenue, Providence, RI 02908
E-mail: rep-palangio@rilegislature.gov
Committees: Environment and Natural Resources; Labor; Oversight
Education: Rhode Island Col 1984

*(continued on next page)*

**Representatives** *continued*

Representative **Robert D. Phillips** (D-District 51) . . . . . . . (401) 762-2010
Counties Represented: Providence (part)
Term Expires: 2017
325 Dunlap Street, Woonsocket, RI 02895
E-mail: rep-phillips@rilin.state.ri.us
Committees: Small Business
Education: Rhode Island 2005 BSBA

Representative **Justin Price** (R-District 39) . . . . . . . . . . . . (401) 222-2259
Counties Represented: Washington (part)
Term Expires: 2017
214 Shannock Village Road, Richmond, RI 02875
E-mail: rep-price@rilegislature.gov
Committees: Environment and Natural Resources; Health, Education
and Welfare; Municipal Government

Representative **J. Aaron Regunberg** (D-District 4) . . . . . . . (401) 263-7770
Counties Represented: Providence (part)
Term Expires: 2017
62 Camp Street, Providence, RI 02906
E-mail: rep-regunberg@rilegislature.gov
Committees: Environment and Natural Resources; Health, Education
and Welfare

Representative **Daniel Patrick Reilly** (R-District 72) . . . . . . (401) 619-8734
Counties Represented: Newport (part)
Term Expires: 2017
14 Williams Street, Portsmouth, RI 02871
E-mail: rep-reilly@rilegislature.gov
Committees: Finance; Oversight; Rules

Representative **Sherry Roberts** (R-District 29) . . . . . . . . . . (401) 680-0128
Counties Represented: Kent (part)
Term Expires: 2017
22 Seminole Trail, West Greenwich, RI 02817
E-mail: rep-roberts@rilin.state.ri.us
Committees: Corporations; Small Business

Representative **Deborah L. Ruggiero** (D-District 74) . . . . . (401) 423-0444
Counties Represented: Newport (part)
Term Expires: 2017
78 Columbia Avenue, Jamestown, RI 02835
E-mail: rep-ruggiero@rilin.state.ri.us
Committees: Finance; Small Business
Education: Boston Col BA

Representative **Patricia A. Serpa** (D-District 27) . . . . . . . . . (401) 828-5687
Counties Represented: Kent (part)
Term Expires: 2017
194 Kimberly Lane, West Warwick, RI 02893
E-mail: rep-serpa@rilegislature.gov
Committees: Finance; Oversight
Education: Mount St Joseph BEd; Providence MEd

Representative **K. Joseph Shekarchi** (D-District 23) . . . . . . (401) 827-0100
Counties Represented: Kent (part)
Term Expires: 2017
33 College Hill Road, Warwick, RI 02886
E-mail: rep-shekarchi@rilegislature.gov
Committees: Labor
Education: Suffolk 1984 BA, 1990 JD

Representative **Scott A. Slater** (D-District 10) . . . . . . . . . . (401) 741-7641
Counties Represented: Providence (part)
Term Expires: 2017
74 Sawyer Street, Providence, RI 02907
E-mail: rep-slater@rilegislature.gov
Committees: Environment and Natural Resources; Finance; Oversight;
Rules

Representative **Joseph J. Solomon, Jr.** (D-District 22) . . . (401) 308-3904
Counties Represented: Kent (part)
Term Expires: 2017
703 West Shore Road, Warwick, RI 02889
E-mail: rep-solomon@rilegislature.gov
Committees: Veterans' Affairs

Representative **Teresa Ann Tanzi** (D-District 34) . . . . . . . . (401) 527-9468
Counties Represented: Washington (part)
Term Expires: 2017
P.O. Box 5134, Wakefield, RI 02880
E-mail: rep-tanzi@rilin.state.ri.us
Committees: Finance; Small Business

Representative **Carlos E. Tobon** (D-District 58) . . . . . . . . . (401) 365-4063
Counties Represented: Providence (part)
Term Expires: 2017
30 Bloomingdale Avenue, Pawtucket, RI 02860
E-mail: rep-tobon@rilegislature.gov
Committees: Environment and Natural Resources; Finance; Veterans'
Affairs

Representative **Joseph A. Trillo** (R-District 24) . . . . . . . . . (401) 222-2259
Counties Represented: Kent (part)                    Tel: (401) 826-9100
Term Expires: 2017                                   Res: (401) 885-3250
643 East Avenue, Warwick, RI 02886
E-mail: rep-trillo@rilin.state.ri.us
Committees: Corporations

Representative **Stephen R. Ucci** (D-District 42) . . . . . . . . . (401) 934-2121
Counties Represented: Providence (part)             Res: (401) 275-5559
Term Expires: 2017
42 John Street, Unit 2, Johnston, RI 02919
E-mail: rep-ucci@rilegislature.gov
Committees: Labor; Rules

Representative **Anastasia P. Williams** (D-District 9) . . . . . . (401) 222-2466
Counties Represented: Providence (part)             Res: (401) 272-8135
Term Expires: 2017
32 Hammond Street, Providence, RI 02909
E-mail: rep-williams@rilin.state.ri.us
Committees: Corporations

Representative **Thomas J. Winfield** (D-District 53) . . . . . . (401) 222-2466
Counties Represented: Providence (part)             Res: (401) 949-3356
Term Expires: 2017
4 Church St., Smithfield, RI 02828
E-mail: rep-winfield@rilegislature.gov
Committees: Labor; Oversight; Small Business

District 69 **(Vacant)** . . . . . . . . . . . . . . . . . . . . . . . . . . . . . . (401) 222-2466
Note: A general election to fill this legislative vacancy will be held on
November 8, 2016.

# House Standing Committees
## Corporations

**Majority Members**
Brian Patrick Kennedy (D-38)
*Chairperson*
William W. O'Brien (D-54)
*Vice Chairperson*
Mary Duffy Messier (D-62)
*Secretary*
Stephen M. "Steve" Casey (D-50)
Raymond H. Johnston, Jr. (D-61)
Katherine S. Kazarian (D-63)
Charlene M. Lima (D-14)
Michael J. Marcello (D-41)
Kenneth A. Marshall (D-68)
Michael A. Morin (D-49)
Jared R. Nunes (D-25)
Jeremiah T. O'Grady (D-46)
Anastasia P. Williams (D-9)

**Minority Members**
Robert A. Nardolillo (R-28)
Sherry Roberts (R-29)
Joseph A. Trillo (R-24)

## Environment and Natural Resources

**Majority Members**
Arthur Handy (D-18) *Chairperson*
David A. Bennett (D-20)
*Vice Chairperson*
Jeremiah T. O'Grady (D-46)
Raymond A. Hull (D-6)
John Joseph Lombardi (D-8)
Michael J. Marcello (D-41)
Joseph M. McNamara (D-19)
Helio Melo (D-64)
Eileen Slattery Naughton (D-21)
William W. O'Brien (D-54)
Thomas A. Palangio (D-3)
J. Aaron Regunberg (D-4)
Scott A. Slater (D-10)
Carlos E. Tobon (D-58)

**Minority Members**
Blake Anthony Filippi (I-36)
Justin Price (R-39)

## Finance

**Majority Members**
Marvin L. Abney (D-73)
*Chairperson*
Eileen Slattery Naughton (D-21)
*Deputy Chairperson*
John M. Carnevale (D-13)
*Vice Chairperson*
Robert B. Jacquard (D-17)
*Secretary*
Gregg Amore (D-65)

**Minority Members**
Antonio Giarrusso (R-30)
Patricia L. Morgan (R-26)
Daniel Patrick Reilly (R-72)

**Majority Members** *continued*

Jean Philippe Barros (D-59)
Joy Hearn (D-66)
Jan P. Malik (D-67)
Kenneth A. Marshall (D-68)
Michael A. Morin (D-49)
Deborah L. Ruggiero (D-74)
Patricia A. Serpa (D-27)
Scott A. Slater (D-10)
Teresa Ann Tanzi (D-34)
Carlos E. Tobon (D-58)

## Health, Education and Welfare

| **Majority Members** | **Minority Members** |
| --- | --- |
| Joseph M. McNamara (D-19) | Nicholas D. Kettle (R-21) |
| *Chairperson* | Robert B. Lancia (R-16) |
| Grace Diaz (D-11) | Justin Price (R-39) |
| *Deputy Chairperson* | |
| Samuel A. Azzinaro (D-37) | |
| *Vice Chairperson* | |
| Marvin L. Abney (D-73) | |
| Mia A. Ackerman (D-45) | |
| Gregg Amore (D-65) | |
| David A. Bennett (D-20) | |
| Dennis M. Canario (D-71) | |
| Arthur J. Corvese (D-55) | |
| Kathleen A. Fogarty (D-35) | |
| Arthur Handy (D-18) | |
| Shelby Maldonado (D-56) | |
| James N. McLaughlin (D-57) | |
| Michael A. Morin (D-49) | |
| J. Aaron Regunberg (D-4) | |

## Judiciary

| **Majority Members** | **Minority Members** |
| --- | --- |
| Cale P. Keable (D-47) *Chairperson* | Doreen Marie Costa (R-31) |
| Christopher R. Blazejewski (D-2) | *Vice Chairperson* |
| *Secretary* | Blake Anthony Filippi (I-36) |
| Edith H. Ajello (D-1) | |
| Joseph S. Almeida (D-12) | |
| Dennis M. Canario (D-71) | |
| David A. Coughlin, Jr. (D-60) | |
| Robert E. Craven, Sr. (D-32) | |
| John G. Edwards (D-70) | |
| Carol Hagan McEntee (D-33) | |
| Jeremiah T. O'Grady (D-46) | |

## Labor

| **Majority Members** | **Minority Members** |
| --- | --- |
| K. Joseph Shekarchi (D-23) | Michael W. Chippendale (R-40) |
| *Chairperson* | Antonio Giarrusso (R-30) |
| Thomas A. Palangio (D-3) | |
| *Vice Chairperson* | |
| Arthur J. Corvese (D-55) *Secretary* | |
| Stephen M. "Steve" Casey (D-50) | |
| John G. Edwards (D-70) | |
| Deborah A. Fellela (D-43) | |
| Carol Hagan McEntee (D-33) | |
| Kenneth A. Marshall (D-68) | |
| Daniel P. McKiernan (D-7) | |
| Joseph M. McNamara (D-19) | |
| Helio Melo (D-64) | |
| Jared R. Nunes (D-25) | |
| Stephen R. Ucci (D-42) | |
| Thomas J. Winfield (D-53) | |

## Municipal Government

| **Majority Members** | **Minority Members** |
| --- | --- |
| Robert E. Craven, Sr. (D-32) | Blake Anthony Filippi (I-36) |
| *Chairperson* | Justin Price (R-39) |
| Mia A. Ackerman (D-45) | |
| *Vice Chairperson* | |
| Raymond H. Johnston, Jr. (D-61) | |
| *Secretary* | |
| Gregg Amore (D-65) | |
| Jean Philippe Barros (D-59) | |
| David A. Bennett (D-20) | |

**Majority Members** *continued*

Gregory J. Costantino (D-44)
David A. Coughlin, Jr. (D-60)
Kathleen A. Fogarty (D-35)
Carol Hagan McEntee (D-33)
Joy Hearn (D-66)
Charlene M. Lima (D-14)
Shelby Maldonado (D-56)
Kenneth A. Marshall (D-68)

## Oversight

| **Majority Members** | **Minority Members** |
| --- | --- |
| Patricia A. Serpa (D-27) | Michael W. Chippendale (R-40) |
| *Chairperson* | *Co-Vice Chairperson* |
| Scott A. Slater (D-10) | Daniel Patrick Reilly (R-72) |
| *Co-Vice Chairperson* | |
| Raymond H. Johnston, Jr. (D-61) | |
| *Secretary* | |
| Lauren H. Carson (D-75) | |
| Arthur J. Corvese (D-55) | |
| John G. Edwards (D-70) | |
| Arthur Handy (D-18) | |
| Daniel P. McKiernan (D-7) | |
| William W. O'Brien (D-54) | |
| Thomas A. Palangio (D-3) | |
| Thomas J. Winfield (D-53) | |

## Rules

| **Majority Members** | **Minority Members** |
| --- | --- |
| Samuel A. Azzinaro (D-37) | Michael W. Chippendale (R-40) |
| *Chairperson* | Daniel Patrick Reilly (R-72) |
| Arthur J. Corvese (D-55) | |
| *Vice Chairperson* | |
| Grace Diaz (D-11) *Secretary* | |
| Joseph S. Almeida (D-12) | |
| Christopher R. Blazejewski (D-2) | |
| Katherine S. Kazarian (D-63) | |
| Cale P. Keable (D-47) | |
| Charlene M. Lima (D-14) | |
| Kenneth A. Marshall (D-68) | |
| William W. O'Brien (D-54) | |
| Scott A. Slater (D-10) | |
| Stephen R. Ucci (D-42) | |

## Small Business

| **Majority Members** | **Minority Members** |
| --- | --- |
| Deborah L. Ruggiero (D-74) | Robert A. Nardolillo (R-28) |
| *Chairperson* | Sherry Roberts (R-29) |
| Jared R. Nunes (D-25) | |
| *Vice Chairperson* | |
| Robert D. Phillips (D-51) *Secretary* | |
| Lauren H. Carson (D-75) | |
| John G. Edwards (D-70) | |
| Arthur Handy (D-18) | |
| John Joseph Lombardi (D-8) | |
| Shelby Maldonado (D-56) | |
| Daniel P. McKiernan (D-7) | |
| Michael A. Morin (D-49) | |
| Teresa Ann Tanzi (D-34) | |
| Thomas J. Winfield (D-53) | |

## Veterans' Affairs

| **Majority Members** | **Minority Members** |
| --- | --- |
| Jan P. Malik (D-67) *Chairperson* | Doreen Marie Costa (R-31) |
| Samuel A. Azzinaro (D-37) | Robert B. Lancia (R-16) |
| *Vice Chairperson* | Karen L. MacBeth (R-52) |
| Mary Duffy Messier (D-62) | |
| *Secretary* | |
| Marvin L. Abney (D-73) | |
| Dennis M. Canario (D-71) | |
| Stephen M. "Steve" Casey (D-50) | |
| Deborah A. Fellela (D-43) | |
| Robert B. Jacquard (D-17) | |
| James N. McLaughlin (D-57) | |
| Eileen Slattery Naughton (D-21) | |
| Joseph J. Solomon, Jr. (D-22) | |
| Carlos E. Tobon (D-58) | |

# South Carolina Legislature

223 Blatt Building, 1105 Pendleton Street, Columbia, SC 29201
Internet: www.scstatehouse.gov

## South Carolina Senate

Gressette Building, P.O. Box 142, Columbia, SC 29202
Tel: (803) 212-6200  Fax: (803) 212-6299  E-mail: scl@scsenate.org
Internet: www.scsenate.org

President of the Senate **Henry Dargan McMaster** (R) . . . . (803) 734-2080
   Education: South Carolina 1969 BA, 1973 JD
President Pro Tem **Hugh Kenneth Leatherman, Sr.** (R) . . (803) 212-6640
   Education: North Carolina State 1953 BS
Majority Leader **A. Shane Massey** (R) . . . . . . . . . . . . . . . (803) 212-6000
   Education: Clemson 1997 BA; South Carolina 2000 JD
Minority Leader **Nikki G. Setzler** (D) . . . . . . . . . . . . . . . (803) 212-6140
   Education: South Carolina 1968 BA, 1971 JD
Assistant Minority Leader
   **John Wesley Matthews, Jr.** (D) . . . . . . . . . . . . . . . . . . (803) 212-6056
Clerk and Director of Senate Research
   **Jeffrey S. Gossett** . . . . . . . . . . . . . . . . . . . . . . . . . . . . . (803) 212-6200
   E-mail: jeffgossett@scsenate.gov
   Education: South Carolina 1992 BA
Assistant Clerk **Kenneth M. Moffitt** . . . . . . . . . . . . . . . . . (803) 212-6300
   E-mail: kenmoffitt@scsenate.gov
Reading Clerk **John O. Wienges** . . . . . . . . . . . . . . . . . . . (803) 212-6200
   E-mail: johnwienges@scsenate.gov
   Education: South Carolina 1983 BA
Chaplain **Rev. James I. St. John** . . . . . . . . . . . . . . . . . . . (803) 212-6628
Sergeant-at-Arms **James R. Melton** . . . . . . . . . . . . . . . . . (803) 212-6730
   E-mail: jimmelton@scsenate.gov

## Senators

**Party Affiliation Statistics:** Republicans: 28, Democrats: 18

Senator **Thomas C. Alexander** (R-District 1) . . . . . . . . . . (803) 212-6220
   Counties Represented: Oconee, Pickens (part)   Dist: (864) 638-2988
   Term Expires: 2016   Res: (864) 638-2153
   150 Cleveland Dr., Walhalla, SC 29691
   E-mail: thomasalexander@scsenate.gov
   Committees: Banking and Insurance; Finance; Invitations; Joint Bond
   Review; Labor, Commerce and Industry; Medical Affairs
   Education: Anderson Col 1976 AA; Clemson 1978 BS
Senator **Karl B. Allen, JD** (D-District 7) . . . . . . . . . . . . . . (803) 212-6040
   Counties Represented: Greenville (part)
   Term Expires: 2016
   108 Lavinia Ave., Greenville, SC 29601
   E-mail: karlallen@scsenate.gov
   Committees: Corrections and Penology; Judiciary; Labor, Commerce
   and Industry; Rules; Transportation
   Education: South Carolina 1982 BA, 1986 JD
Senator **Sean Bennett** (R-District 38) . . . . . . . . . . . . . . . . (803) 212-6116
   Counties Represented: Berkeley (part), Charleston (part), Dorchester
   (part)
   Term Expires: 2016
   121 S. Cedar St., Summerville, SC 29483
   E-mail: seanbennett@scsenate.gov
   Committees: Banking and Insurance; Fish, Game and Forestry;
   Judiciary; Labor, Commerce and Industry; Transportation
   Education: South Carolina 1990 BA
Senator **Lee Bright** (R-District 12) . . . . . . . . . . . . . . . . . . (803) 212-6008
   Counties Represented: Greenville (part),   Tel: (864) 587-1800
   Spartanburg (part)   Res: (864) 576-6742
   Term Expires: 2016
   502 Gressette Building, Columbia, SC 29201
   P.O. Box 589, Roebuck, SC 29376
   E-mail: leebright@scsenate.gov
   Committees: Agriculture and Natural Resources; Banking and
   Insurance; General Committee; Judiciary; Labor, Commerce and
   Industry
Senator **Kevin L. Bryant** (R-District 3) . . . . . . . . . . . . . . . (803) 212-6320
   Counties Represented: Anderson (part)   Tel: (864) 202-8394
   Term Expires: 2016
   104-A North Avenue, Anderson, SC 29625
   E-mail: kevinbryant@scsenate.gov
   Committees: Agriculture and Natural Resources; Finance; General
   Committee; Labor, Commerce and Industry
   Education: Georgia 1989 BSPh

Senator **Paul G. Campbell, Jr.** (R-District 44) . . . . . . . . . . (843) 212-6016
   Counties Represented: Berkeley (part), Charleston   Res: (843) 569-0089
   (part), Dorchester (part)
   Term Expires: 2016
   150 Loganberry Circle, Goose Creek, SC 29445
   E-mail: paulcampbell@scsenate.gov
   Committees: Agriculture and Natural Resources; Corrections and
   Penology; Finance; General Committee; Invitations; Joint Bond Review;
   Transportation
   Education: Clemson 1968 BSChE; Jackson State U 1978 MBA
Senator **George E. "Chip" Campsen III** (R-District 43) . . . (803) 212-6016
   Counties Represented: Beaufort (part), Charleston   Tel: (843) 722-0123
   (part), Colleton (part)   Res: (843) 886-8454
   Term Expires: 2016
   360 Concord Street, Suite 201, Charleston, SC 29401
   E-mail: chipcampsen@scsenate.gov
   Committees: Corrections and Penology; Fish, Game and Forestry;
   Invitations; Judiciary; Rules; Transportation
   Education: South Carolina 1981 BS, 1988 JD, 1989 MS
Senator **Raymond E. Cleary III** (R-District 34) . . . . . . . . . (803) 212-6100
   Counties Represented: Charleston (part),   Tel: (843) 357-2234
   Georgetown (part), Horry (part)   Res: (843) 650-5100
   Term Expires: 2016
   3577 Marion Lane, Murrells Inlet, SC 29576
   E-mail: raycleary@scsenate.gov
   Committees: Finance; General Committee; Invitations; Labor,
   Commerce and Industry; Medical Affairs; Transportation
   Education: Ohio State 1970 BA, 1973 DDS
Senator **Creighton B. Coleman, JD** (D-District 17) . . . . . . (803) 212-6180
   Counties Represented: Chester, Fairfield, York (part)   Tel: (803) 635-6884
   Term Expires: 2016   Res: (803) 635-7066
   513 Gressette Building, Columbia, SC 29201
   P.O. Box 1006, Winnsboro, SC 29180
   E-mail: creightoncoleman@scsenate.gov
   Committees: Agriculture and Natural Resources; Fish, Game and
   Forestry; Judiciary; Medical Affairs; Rules
   Education: Citadel 1979 BA; South Carolina 1985 JD
Senator **Thomas D. "Tom" Corbin** (R-District 5) . . . . . . . . (803) 212-6100
   Counties Represented: Greenville (part), Spartanburg (part)
   Term Expires: 2016
   1139 Bailey Mill Rd., Travelers Rest, SC 29690
   E-mail: tomcorbin@scsenate.gov
   Committees: Fish, Game and Forestry; General Committee; Judiciary;
   Labor, Commerce and Industry; Rules
   Education: Clemson 1987 BS
Senator **John E. Courson** (R-District 20) . . . . . . . . . . . . . . (803) 212-6250
   Counties Represented: Lexington (part), Richland   Res: (803) 256-7853
   (part)
   Term Expires: 2016
   P.O. Box 142, Columbia, SC 29202
   E-mail: johncourson@scsenate.gov
   Committees: Banking and Insurance; Education; Ethics; Finance;
   Medical Affairs
Senator **Ronnie W. Cromer** (R-District 18) . . . . . . . . . . . . (803) 212-6330
   Counties Represented: Lexington (part), Newberry,   Tel: (803) 276-0990
   Union (part)   Res: (803) 364-3950
   Term Expires: 2016
   P.O. Box 378, Prosperity, SC 29127
   E-mail: ronniecromer@scsenate.gov
   Committees: Banking and Insurance; Finance; Fish, Game and Forestry;
   General Committee; Invitations; Rules
   Education: South Carolina 1973 BS
Senator **Thomas C. "Tom" Davis** (R-District 46) . . . . . . . . (803) 212-6008
   Counties Represented: Beaufort (part), Jasper (part)   Tel: (843) 252-8583
   Term Expires: 2016
   602 Gressette Building, Columbia, SC 29201
   P.O. Drawer 1107, Beaufort, SC 29901-1107
   E-mail: tomdavis@scsenate.gov
   Committees: Banking and Insurance; Finance; Labor, Commerce and
   Industry; Medical Affairs
   Education: Furman 1982 BA; Maryland Law 1985 JD
Senator **Michael L. "Mike" Fair** (R-District 6) . . . . . . . . . . (803) 212-6420
   Counties Represented: Greenville (part)   Tel: (864) 246-4257
   Term Expires: 2016
   P.O. Box 14632, Greenville, SC 29610
   211 Gressette Building, Columbia, SC 29201
   E-mail: mikefair@scsenate.gov
   Committees: Corrections and Penology; Education; Finance; Medical
   Affairs

**LEGISLATIVE BRANCH**

Senator **Michael W. "Mike" Gambrell** (R-District 4) . . . . . (864) 861-2222
Counties Represented: Abbeville (part), Anderson (part), Greenwood (part)
Term Expires: 2016
Education: Clemson 1980 BS
Senator
**Chauncey Klugh "Greg" Gregory** (R-District 16) . . . . . (803) 212-6024
Counties Represented: Lancaster (part), York (part)       Tel: (803) 289-6211
Term Expires: 2016                                        Res: (803) 283-4715
P.O. Box 700, Lancaster, SC 29721
E-mail: greggregory@scsenate.gov
Committees: Agriculture and Natural Resources; Fish, Game and Forestry; General Committee; Judiciary; Rules
Education: South Carolina 1985 BS
Senator **Lawrence K. "Larry" Grooms** (R-District 37) . . . (803) 212-6400
Counties Represented: Berkeley (part), Charleston (part)
Term Expires: 2016
203 Gressette Building, Columbia, SC 29201
E-mail: larrygrooms@scsenate.gov
Committees: Agriculture and Natural Resources; Corrections and Penology; Education; Finance; Transportation
Education: Clemson 1987 BS
Senator
**Robert Wesley "Wes" Hayes, Jr., JD** (R-District 15) . . (803) 212-6410
Counties Represented: York (part)                        Tel: (803) 324-2800
Term Expires: 2016                                       Res: (803) 328-8532
1486 Cureton Drive, Rock Hill, SC 29732
E-mail: roberthayes@scsenate.gov
Committees: Banking and Insurance; Education; Ethics; Finance; Medical Affairs
Education: West Point 1975 BS; South Carolina 1983 JD
Senator **Greg Hembree** (R-District 28) . . . . . . . . . . . . . . . . (803) 212-6016
Counties Represented: Dillon (part), Horry (part)
Term Expires: 2016
P.O. Box 944, Myrtle Beach, SC 29597
E-mail: greghembree@scsenate.gov
Committees: Agriculture and Natural Resources; Education; Fish, Game and Forestry; Judiciary; Transportation
Education: U Memphis 1982 BBA; South Carolina 1985 JD
Senator
**Charles Bradley "Brad" Hutto, JD** (D-District 40) . . . . . (803) 212-6140
Counties Represented: Allendale (part), Bamberg,         Tel: (803) 534-5218
Barnwell, Colleton (part), Hampton (part),               Res: (803) 536-1808
Orangeburg (part)
Term Expires: 2016
510 Gressette Building, Columbia, SC 29201
P.O. Box 1084, Orangeburg, SC 29116-1084
E-mail: bradhutto@scsenate.gov
Committees: Corrections and Penology; Education; Ethics; Fish, Game and Forestry; Judiciary; Medical Affairs
Education: South Carolina 1978 BA; Georgetown 1981 JD
Senator **Darrell Jackson** (D-District 21) . . . . . . . . . . . . . . (803) 212-6048
Counties Represented: Richland (part)                    Tel: (803) 771-0325
Term Expires: 2016                                       Res: (803) 776-6954
608 Motley Road, Hopkins, SC 29061
612 Gressette Building, Columbia, SC 29201
E-mail: darrelljackson@scsenate.gov
Committees: Banking and Insurance; Corrections and Penology; Education; Ethics; Finance; Medical Affairs
Education: Benedict 1979 BA
Senator **Kevin L. Johnson** (D-District 35) . . . . . . . . . . . . . (803) 212-6108
Counties Represented: Kershaw (part), Lee (part), Richland (part), Sumter (part)
Term Expires: 2016
P.O. Box 156, Manning, SC 29102
E-mail: kevinjohnson@scsenate.gov
Committees: General Committee; Judiciary; Labor, Commerce and Industry; Medical Affairs; Transportation
Education: South Carolina 1982 BS
Senator **Marlon E. Kimpson** (D-District 42) . . . . . . . . . . . (803) 212-6200
Counties Represented: Charleston (part), Dorchester (part)
Term Expires: 2016
612 Gressette Building, Columbia, SC 29201
E-mail: marlonkimpson@scsenate.gov
Committees: Corrections and Penology; General Committee; Invitations; Judiciary; Rules; Transportation
Education: Morehouse Col 1991 BA; South Carolina 1999 JD

Senator **Hugh Kenneth Leatherman, Sr.** (R-District 31) . . (803) 212-6640
Counties Represented: Darlington (part), Florence        Tel: (843) 662-0388
(part)                                                   Res: (843) 667-1152
Term Expires: 2016
1817 Pineland Avenue, Florence, SC 29501
111 Gressette Building, Columbia, SC 29201
Committees: Ethics; Finance; Interstate Cooperation; Joint Bond Review; Labor, Commerce and Industry; Rules; Transportation
Senator **Joel B. Lourie** (D-District 22) . . . . . . . . . . . . . . . . (803) 212-6116
Counties Represented: Kershaw (part), Richland           Res: (803) 787-5802
(part)
Term Expires: 2016
P.O. Box 6212, Columbia, SC 29260
601 Gressette Building, Columbia, SC 29201
E-mail: joellourie@scsenate.gov
Committees: Banking and Insurance; Corrections and Penology; Finance; General Committee; Medical Affairs
Education: South Carolina 1984 BA
Senator **Gerald Malloy** (D-District 29) . . . . . . . . . . . . . . . . (803) 212-6148
Counties Represented: Chesterfield (part),               Tel: (843) 339-3000
Darlington (part), Lee (part), Marlboro (part)           Res: (843) 332-5533
Term Expires: 2016
1216 Salem Road, Hartsville, SC 29550
512 Gressette Building, Columbia, SC 29201
E-mail: geraldmalloy@scsenate.gov
Committees: Banking and Insurance; Education; Invitations; Judiciary; Rules; Transportation
Education: South Carolina 1984 BS, 1988 JD
Senator **Larry A. Martin** (R-District 2) . . . . . . . . . . . . . . . . (803) 212-6610
Counties Represented: Pickens (part)                     Tel: (864) 306-2126
Term Expires: 2016                                       Res: (864) 878-6105
P.O. Box 247, Pickens, SC 29671
311 Gressette Building, Columbia, SC 29201
E-mail: larrymartin@scsenate.gov
Committees: Banking and Insurance; Education; Judiciary; Rules
Senator **Shane R. Martin** (R-District 13) . . . . . . . . . . . . . . (803) 212-6100
Counties Represented: Greenville (part),                 Res: (864) 597-1619
Spartanburg (part), Union (part)
Term Expires: 2016
501 Gressette Building, Columbia, SC 29201
2741 Glenn Springs Road, Spartanburg, SC 29302
E-mail: shanemartin@scsenate.gov
Committees: Corrections and Penology; Finance; General Committee; Medical Affairs; Rules
Education: Clemson 1994 BS, 1999 MS
Senator **A. Shane Massey** (R-District 25) . . . . . . . . . . . . . (803) 212-6000
Counties Represented: Aiken (part), Edgefield,           Tel: (803) 649-6200
Lexington (part), McCormick (part), Saluda (part)        Res: (803) 480-0419
Term Expires: 2016
608 Gressette Building, Columbia, SC 29201
P.O. Box 551, Edgefield, SC 29824
E-mail: shanemassey@scsenate.gov
Committees: Agriculture and Natural Resources; Corrections and Penology; Judiciary; Labor, Commerce and Industry; Rules
Senator **John Wesley Matthews, Jr.** (D-District 39) . . . . . (803) 212-6056
Counties Represented: Berkeley (part), Calhoun           Res: (803) 829-2383
(part), Colleton (part), Dorchester (part), Orangeburg (part)
Term Expires: 2016
613 Gressette Building, Columbia, SC 29201
P.O. Box 142, Columbia, SC 29202
E-mail: johnmatthews@scsenate.gov
Committees: Agriculture and Natural Resources; Banking and Insurance; Education; Ethics; Finance; Interstate Cooperation
Senator **Margie Bright Matthews** (D-District 45) . . . . . . . (803) 212-6056
Counties Represented: Allendale (part), Beaufort (part), Charleston (part), Colleton (part), Hampton (part), Jasper (part)
Term Expires: 2016
Committees: Agriculture and Natural Resources; Corrections and Penology; Fish, Game and Forestry; General Committee; Judiciary
Education: South Carolina 1985 BS, 1989 JD
Senator **J. Thomas McElveen III, JD** (D-District 35) . . . . . (803) 212-6200
Counties Represented: Kershaw (part), Lee (part), Richland (part), Sumter (part)
Term Expires: 2016
E-mail: thomasmcelveen@scsenate.gov
Committees: Agriculture and Natural Resources; Fish, Game and Forestry; General Committee; Invitations; Judiciary; Transportation
Education: Davidson 2000 BA; South Carolina 2003 JD

*(continued on next page)*

**Senators** *continued*

Senator **Floyd Nicholson** (D-District 10) . . . . . . . . . . . . . (803) 212-6000
Counties Represented: Abbeville (part), Greenwood       Tel: (864) 388-8377
(part), McCormick (part), Saluda (part)                Res: (864) 223-9460
Term Expires: 2016
610 Gressette Building, Columbia, SC 29201
527 Bryte Street, Greenwood, SC 29649
E-mail: floydnicholson@scsenate.gov
Committees: Education; Finance; General Committee; Labor,
Commerce and Industry; Medical Affairs
Education: South Carolina State 1972 BS

Senator **Harvey Smith Peeler, Jr.** (R-District 14) . . . . . . . . (803) 212-6430
Counties Represented: Cherokee, Spartanburg            Tel: (864) 489-9994
(part), Union (part), York (part)                      Res: (864) 489-3766
Term Expires: 2016
P.O. Box 742, Gaffney, SC 29342
213 Gressette Building, Columbia, SC 29201
E-mail: harveypeeler@scsenate.gov
Committees: Education; Ethics; Finance; Interstate Cooperation; Joint
Bond Review; Medical Affairs; Transportation
Affiliation: Vice President and General Manager, Peeler Jersey Farms,
Inc.
Education: Clemson 1970 BS

Senator **Luke A. Rankin** (R-District 33) . . . . . . . . . . . . . . (803) 212-6132
Counties Represented: Horry (part)                     Tel: (843) 248-2405
Term Expires: 2016                                     Res: (843) 626-6269
201 Beaty Street, Conway, SC 29526
508 Gressette Building, Columbia, SC 29201
E-mail: lukerankin@scsenate.gov
Committees: Banking and Insurance; Education; Ethics; Judiciary;
Transportation
Education: South Carolina 1984 BA, 1987 JD

Senator **Glenn G. Reese** (D-District 11) . . . . . . . . . . . . . . (803) 212-6108
Counties Represented: Spartanburg (part)               Tel: (864) 585-1956
Term Expires: 2016                                     Res: (864) 592-2984
507 Fagan Drive Lake Bowen, Inman, SC 29349
E-mail: glennreese@scsenate.gov
Committees: Banking and Insurance; Corrections and Penology; Ethics;
Finance; Interstate Cooperation; Invitations; Labor, Commerce and
Industry; Rules
Education: Auburn 1963 BA; Converse 1967 MA

Senator **Ronnie A. Sabb, JD** (D-District 32) . . . . . . . . . . . (803) 212-6032
Counties Represented: Berkeley (part), Florence (part), Georgetown
(part), Horry (part), Williamsburg
Term Expires: 2016
E-mail: ronniesabb@scsenate.gov
Committees: Agriculture and Natural Resources; Corrections and
Penology; Fish, Game and Forestry; Judiciary; Rules; Transportation

Senator **John L. Scott, Jr.** (D-District 19) . . . . . . . . . . . . (803) 212-6048
Counties Represented: Richland (part)                  Tel: (803) 733-5176
Term Expires: 2016                                     Res: (803) 786-2373
612 Gressette Building, Columbia, SC 29201
215 Elmont Drive, Columbia, SC 29203
E-mail: johnscott@scsenate.gov
Committees: Finance; Labor, Commerce and Industry; Medical Affairs;
Rules; Transportation
Education: South Carolina State 1975 BS

Senator **Nikki G. Setzler** (D-District 26) . . . . . . . . . . . . . (803) 212-6140
Counties Represented: Aiken (part), Calhoun            Tel: (803) 796-1285
(part), Lexington (part), Saluda (part)                Res: (803) 796-7563
Term Expires: 2016                                     Res: (803) 796-7573
1309 Canary Drive, West Columbia, SC 29169
E-mail: nikkisetzler@scsenate.gov
Committees: Banking and Insurance; Education; Ethics; Finance;
Interstate Cooperation; Labor, Commerce and Industry

Senator **Katrina Frye Shealy** (R-District 23) . . . . . . . . . . (803) 212-6056
Counties Represented: Lexington (part)
Term Expires: 2016
E-mail: katrinashealy@scsenate.gov
Committees: Agriculture and Natural Resources; Corrections and
Penology; Fish, Game and Forestry; General Committee; Judiciary

Senator **Vincent A. Sheheen** (D-District 27) . . . . . . . . . . . (803) 212-6124
Counties Represented: Chesterfield (part), Kershaw     Tel: (803) 432-4391
(part), Lancaster (part)
Term Expires: 2016
P.O. Drawer 10, Camden, SC 29020
E-mail: vincentsheheen@scsenate.gov
Committees: Agriculture and Natural Resources; Education; Fish, Game
and Forestry; General Committee
Education: Clemson 1993 BA; South Carolina 1995 JD

Senator **Paul R. Thurmond** (R-District 41) . . . . . . . . . . . . (803) 212-6172
Counties Represented: Charleston (part), Dorchester    Res: (843) 937-8000
(part)
Term Expires: 2016
601 White Chapel Circle, Charleston, SC 29412
E-mail: paulthurmond@scsenate.gov
Committees: Banking and Insurance; Education; Fish, Game and
Forestry; Judiciary; Medical Affairs
Education: Vanderbilt 1998 BS; South Carolina 2002 JD

Senator **Ross Turner** (R-District 8) . . . . . . . . . . . . . . . . (803) 212-6148
Counties Represented: Greenville (part)                Res: (864) 987-0596
Term Expires: 2016
P.O. Box 16703, Greenville, SC 29606
E-mail: rossturner@scsenate.gov
Committees: Corrections and Penology; Fish, Game and Forestry;
Judiciary; Labor, Commerce and Industry; Rules
Education: Clemson 1986 BS

Senator **Daniel B. Verdin III** (R-District 9) . . . . . . . . . . . . (803) 212-6230
Counties Represented: Greenville (part), Laurens       Tel: (864) 984-4129
Term Expires: 2016                                     Res: (864) 682-8914
P.O. Box 272, Laurens, SC 29360
E-mail: dannyverdin@scsenate.gov
Committees: Agriculture and Natural Resources; Corrections and
Penology; Finance; Invitations; Medical Affairs; Transportation
Affiliation: Owner, Verdin's Farm & Garden Center
Education: Bob Jones U 1986 BA

Senator **Kent M. Williams** (D-District 30) . . . . . . . . . . . . (803) 212-6000
Counties Represented: Dillon (part), Florence (part),  Tel: (843) 362-0307
Horry (part), Marion, Marlboro (part)
Term Expires: 2016
4205 Stirk Place, Marion, SC 29571
E-mail: kentwilliams@scsenate.gov
Committees: Agriculture and Natural Resources; Banking and
Insurance; Finance; Fish, Game and Forestry; Labor, Commerce and
Industry
Education: Florence-Darlington 1981 AS;
South Carolina State 1987 BS

Senator **Thomas R. "Tom" Young, Jr.** (R-District 24) . . . . (803) 212-6124
Counties Represented: Aiken (part)
Term Expires: 2016
P.O. Box 651, Aiken, SC 29802
E-mail: tomyoung@scsenate.gov
Committees: Agriculture and Natural Resources; Education; Fish, Game
and Forestry; General Committee; Judiciary; Rules
Education: South Carolina 1993 BA, 1996 JD

# Senate Standing Committees

## Agriculture and Natural Resources
Tel: (803) 212-6230  E-mail: sag@scsenate.org

| Majority Members | Minority Members |
|---|---|
| Daniel B. Verdin III (R-9) | Creighton B. Coleman (D-17) |
| *Chairman* | John Wesley Matthews, Jr. (D-39) |
| Lee Bright (R-12) | Margie Bright Matthews (D-45) |
| Kevin L. Bryant (R-3) | J. Thomas McElveen III (D-35) |
| Paul G. Campbell, Jr. (R-44) | Ronnie A. Sabb (D-32) |
| Chauncey Klugh "Greg" Gregory | Vincent A. Sheheen (D-27) |
| (R-16) | Kent M. Williams (D-30) |
| Lawrence K. "Larry" Grooms | |
| (R-37) | |
| Greg Hembree (R-28) | |
| A. Shane Massey (R-25) | |
| Katrina Frye Shealy (R-23) | |
| Thomas R. "Tom" Young, Jr. (R-24) | |

## Banking and Insurance
Tel: (803) 212-6240  E-mail: sbi@scsenate.org

| Majority Members | Minority Members |
|---|---|
| Robert Wesley "Wes" | Darrell Jackson (D-21) |
| Hayes, Jr. (R-15) | Joel B. Lourie (D-22) |
| *Chairman* | Gerald Malloy (D-29) |
| Thomas C. Alexander (R-1) | John Wesley Matthews, Jr. (D-39) |
| Sean Bennett (R-38) | Glenn G. Reese (D-11) |
| Lee Bright (R-12) | Nikki G. Setzler (D-26) |
| John E. Courson (R-20) | Kent M. Williams (D-30) |
| Ronnie W. Cromer (R-18) | |
| Thomas C. "Tom" Davis (R-46) | |
| Larry A. Martin (R-2) | |
| Luke A. Rankin (R-33) | |
| Paul R. Thurmond (R-41) | |

## Corrections and Penology

Tel: (803) 212-6420  E-mail: cp@scsenate.org

| Majority Members | Minority Members |
|---|---|
| Michael L. "Mike" Fair (R-6) *Chairman* | Karl B. Allen (D-7) |
| Paul G. Campbell, Jr. (R-44) | Charles Bradley "Brad" Hutto (D-40) |
| George E. "Chip" Campsen III (R-43) | Darrell Jackson (D-21) |
| Lawrence K. "Larry" Grooms (R-37) | Marlon E. Kimpson (D-42) |
| Shane R. Martin (R-13) | Joel B. Lourie (D-22) |
| A. Shane Massey (R-25) | Margie Bright Matthews (D-45) |
| Katrina Frye Shealy (R-23) | Glenn G. Reese (D-11) |
| Ross Turner (R-8) | Ronnie A. Sabb (D-32) |
| Daniel B. Verdin III (R-9) | |

## Education

Tel: (803) 212-6250  E-mail: edu@scsenate.org

| Majority Members | Minority Members |
|---|---|
| John E. Courson (R-20) *Chairman* | Charles Bradley "Brad" Hutto (D-40) |
| Michael L. "Mike" Fair (R-6) | Darrell Jackson (D-21) |
| Lawrence K. "Larry" Grooms (R-37) | Gerald Malloy (D-29) |
| Robert Wesley "Wes" Hayes, Jr. (R-15) | John Wesley Matthews, Jr. (D-39) |
| Greg Hembree (R-28) | Floyd Nicholson (D-10) |
| Larry A. Martin (R-2) | Nikki G. Setzler (D-26) |
| Harvey Smith Peeler, Jr. (R-14) | Vincent A. Sheheen (D-27) |
| Luke A. Rankin (R-33) | |
| Paul R. Thurmond (R-41) | |
| Thomas R. "Tom" Young, Jr. (R-24) | |

## Ethics

Tel: (803) 212-6410  E-mail: set@scsenate.org

| Majority Members | Minority Members |
|---|---|
| Luke A. Rankin (R-33) *Chairman* | Charles Bradley "Brad" Hutto (D-40) |
| John E. Courson (R-20) | Darrell Jackson (D-21) |
| Robert Wesley "Wes" Hayes, Jr. (R-15) | John Wesley Matthews, Jr. (D-39) |
| Hugh Kenneth Leatherman, Sr. (R-31) | Glenn G. Reese (D-11) |
| Harvey Smith Peeler, Jr. (R-14) | Nikki G. Setzler (D-26) |

## Finance

Tel: (803) 212-6640  E-mail: sfi@scsenate.org

| Majority Members | Minority Members |
|---|---|
| Hugh Kenneth Leatherman, Sr. (R-31) *Chairman* | Darrell Jackson (D-21) |
| Thomas C. Alexander (R-1) | Joel B. Lourie (D-22) |
| Kevin L. Bryant (R-3) | John Wesley Matthews, Jr. (D-39) |
| Paul G. Campbell, Jr. (R-44) | Floyd Nicholson (D-10) |
| Raymond E. Cleary III (R-34) | Glenn G. Reese (D-11) |
| John E. Courson (R-20) | John L. Scott, Jr. (D-19) |
| Ronnie W. Cromer (R-18) | Nikki G. Setzler (D-26) |
| Thomas C. "Tom" Davis (R-46) | Kent M. Williams (D-30) |
| Michael L. "Mike" Fair (R-6) | |
| Lawrence K. "Larry" Grooms (R-37) | |
| Robert Wesley "Wes" Hayes, Jr. (R-15) | |
| Shane R. Martin (R-13) | |
| Harvey Smith Peeler, Jr. (R-14) | |
| Daniel B. Verdin III (R-9) | |

## Fish, Game and Forestry

Tel: (803) 212-6330  E-mail: sfg@scsenate.org

| Majority Members | Minority Members |
|---|---|
| George E. "Chip" Campsen III (R-43) *Chairman* | Creighton B. Coleman (D-17) |
| Sean Bennett (R-38) | Charles Bradley "Brad" Hutto (D-40) |
| Thomas D. "Tom" Corbin (R-5) | Margie Bright Matthews (D-45) |
| Ronnie W. Cromer (R-18) | J. Thomas McElveen III (D-35) |
| Chauncey Klugh "Greg" Gregory (R-16) | Ronnie A. Sabb (D-32) |
| Greg Hembree (R-28) | Vincent A. Sheheen (D-27) |
| Katrina Frye Shealy (R-23) | Kent M. Williams (D-30) |
| Paul R. Thurmond (R-41) | |
| Ross Turner (R-8) | |
| Thomas R. "Tom" Young, Jr. (R-24) | |

## General Committee

Tel: (803) 212-6320  E-mail: sge@scsenate.org

| Majority Members | Minority Members |
|---|---|
| Kevin L. Bryant (R-3) *Chairman* | Kevin L. Johnson (D-35) |
| Lee Bright (R-12) | Marlon E. Kimpson (D-42) |
| Paul G. Campbell, Jr. (R-44) | Joel B. Lourie (D-22) |
| Raymond E. Cleary III (R-34) | Margie Bright Matthews (D-45) |
| Thomas D. "Tom" Corbin (R-5) | J. Thomas McElveen III (D-35) |
| Ronnie W. Cromer (R-18) | Floyd Nicholson (D-10) |
| Chauncey Klugh "Greg" Gregory (R-16) | Vincent A. Sheheen (D-27) |
| Shane R. Martin (R-13) | |
| Katrina Frye Shealy (R-23) | |
| Thomas R. "Tom" Young, Jr. (R-24) | |

## Interstate Cooperation

Tel: (803) 212-6350  E-mail: slc@scsenate.org

| Majority Members | Minority Members |
|---|---|
| Hugh Kenneth Leatherman, Sr. (R-31) *Chairman* | John Wesley Matthews, Jr. (D-39) |
| Harvey Smith Peeler, Jr. (R-14) | Glenn G. Reese (D-11) |
| | Nikki G. Setzler (D-26) |

## Invitations

Tel: (803) 212-6220  E-mail: siv@scsenate.org

| Majority Members | Minority Members |
|---|---|
| Raymond E. Cleary III (R-34) *Chairman* | Marlon E. Kimpson (D-42) |
| Thomas C. Alexander (R-1) | Gerald Malloy (D-29) |
| Paul G. Campbell, Jr. (R-44) | J. Thomas McElveen III (D-35) |
| George E. "Chip" Campsen III (R-43) | Glenn G. Reese (D-11) |
| Ronnie W. Cromer (R-18) | |
| Daniel B. Verdin III (R-9) | |

## Judiciary

Tel: (803) 212-6610  E-mail: sju@scsenate.org

| Majority Members | Minority Members |
|---|---|
| Larry A. Martin (R-2) *Chairman* | Karl B. Allen (D-7) |
| Sean Bennett (R-38) | Creighton B. Coleman (D-17) |
| Lee Bright (R-12) | Charles Bradley "Brad" Hutto (D-40) |
| George E. "Chip" Campsen III (R-43) | Kevin L. Johnson (D-35) |
| Thomas D. "Tom" Corbin (R-5) | Marlon E. Kimpson (D-42) |
| Chauncey Klugh "Greg" Gregory (R-16) | Gerald Malloy (D-29) |
| Greg Hembree (R-28) | Margie Bright Matthews (D-45) |
| A. Shane Massey (R-25) | J. Thomas McElveen III (D-35) |
| Luke A. Rankin (R-33) | Ronnie A. Sabb (D-32) |
| Katrina Frye Shealy (R-23) | |
| Paul R. Thurmond (R-41) | |
| Ross Turner (R-8) | |
| Thomas R. "Tom" Young, Jr. (R-24) | |

## Labor, Commerce and Industry

Tel: (803) 212-6350  E-mail: slc@scsenate.org

| Majority Members | Minority Members |
|---|---|
| Thomas C. Alexander (R-1) | Karl B. Allen (D-7) |
| *Chairman* | Kevin L. Johnson (D-35) |
| Sean Bennett (R-38) | Floyd Nicholson (D-10) |
| Lee Bright (R-12) | Glenn G. Reese (D-11) |
| Kevin L. Bryant (R-3) | John L. Scott, Jr. (D-19) |
| Raymond E. Cleary III (R-34) | Nikki G. Setzler (D-26) |
| Thomas D. "Tom" Corbin (R-5) | Kent M. Williams (D-30) |
| Thomas C. "Tom" Davis (R-46) | |
| Hugh Kenneth Leatherman, Sr. | |
| (R-31) | |
| A. Shane Massey (R-25) | |
| Ross Turner (R-8) | |

## Medical Affairs

Tel: (803) 212-6430  E-mail: med@scsenate.org

| Majority Members | Minority Members |
|---|---|
| Harvey Smith Peeler, Jr. (R-14) | Creighton B. Coleman (D-17) |
| *Chairman* | Charles Bradley "Brad" Hutto |
| Thomas C. Alexander (R-1) | (D-40) |
| Raymond E. Cleary III (R-34) | Darrell Jackson (D-21) |
| John E. Courson (R-20) | Kevin L. Johnson (D-35) |
| Thomas C. "Tom" Davis (R-46) | Joel B. Lourie (D-22) |
| Michael L. "Mike" Fair (R-6) | Floyd Nicholson (D-10) |
| Robert Wesley "Wes" Hayes, Jr. | John L. Scott, Jr. (D-19) |
| (R-15) | |
| Shane R. Martin (R-13) | |
| Paul R. Thurmond (R-41) | |
| Daniel B. Verdin III (R-9) | |

## Rules

Tel: (803) 212-6340  E-mail: sru@scsenate.org

| Majority Members | Minority Members |
|---|---|
| Ronnie W. Cromer (R-18) | Karl B. Allen (D-7) |
| *Chairman* | Creighton B. Coleman (D-17) |
| George E. "Chip" Campsen III | Marlon E. Kimpson (D-42) |
| (R-43) | Gerald Malloy (D-29) |
| Thomas D. "Tom" Corbin (R-5) | Glenn G. Reese (D-11) |
| Chauncey Klugh "Greg" Gregory | Ronnie A. Sabb (D-32) |
| (R-16) | John L. Scott, Jr. (D-19) |
| Hugh Kenneth Leatherman, Sr. | |
| (R-31) | |
| Larry A. Martin (R-2) | |
| Shane R. Martin (R-13) | |
| A. Shane Massey (R-25) | |
| Ross Turner (R-8) | |
| Thomas R. "Tom" Young, Jr. (R-24) | |

## Transportation

Tel: (803) 212-6400  E-mail: str@scsenate.org

| Majority Members | Minority Members |
|---|---|
| Lawrence K. "Larry" | Karl B. Allen (D-7) |
| Grooms (R-37) | Kevin L. Johnson (D-35) |
| *Chairman* | Marlon E. Kimpson (D-42) |
| Sean Bennett (R-38) | Gerald Malloy (D-29) |
| Paul G. Campbell, Jr. (R-44) | J. Thomas McElveen III (D-35) |
| George E. "Chip" Campsen III | Ronnie A. Sabb (D-32) |
| (R-43) | John L. Scott, Jr. (D-19) |
| Raymond E. Cleary III (R-34) | |
| Greg Hembree (R-28) | |
| Hugh Kenneth Leatherman, Sr. | |
| (R-31) | |
| Harvey Smith Peeler, Jr. (R-14) | |
| Luke A. Rankin (R-33) | |
| Daniel B. Verdin III (R-9) | |

# South Carolina House of Representatives

P.O. Box 11867, Columbia, SC 29211
Tel: (803) 734-2010  Fax: (803) 734-2925

Speaker of the House **James H. "Jay" Lucas, JD** (R) . . . . (803) 734-2701
  Education: South Carolina 1975 BA, 1981 MPA, 1987 JD

Speaker Pro Tempore
  **Thomas E. "Tommy" Pope, JD** (R) . . . . . . . . . . . . . . . (803) 212-6895
  Education: South Carolina 1984 BS, 1987 JD
Majority Leader **Bruce W. Bannister, JD** (R) . . . . . . . . . . (803) 734-3138
  Education: Davidson 1995 BA; South Carolina 1998 JD
Minority Leader **J. Todd Rutherford** (D) . . . . . . . . . . . . . (803) 734-9441
  Education: Howard U 1992 BA; South Carolina 1996 JD
Clerk of the House **Charles F. Reid** . . . . . . . . . . . . . . . . (803) 734-2010
  Education: Wofford 1990 BA;                    Tel: (803) 734-2403
  South Carolina 1993 JD
Reading Clerk **James L. M. "Bubba" Cromer, Jr.** . . . . . . . (803) 734-2010
Sergeant-at-Arms **Mitchell G. Dorman** . . . . . . . . . . . . . . (803) 734-2040

## Representatives

**Party Affiliation Statistics:** Republicans: 76, Democrats: 46,
Vacancies: 2

Representative **Terry Alexander** (D-District 59) . . . . . . . . . (843) 734-3004
  Counties Represented: Darlington (part), Florence      Tel: (843) 679-0694
  (part)
  Term Expires: 2016
  1646 Harris Court, Florence, SC 29501
  E-mail: terryalexander@schouse.gov
  Committees: Labor, Commerce and Industry
  Education: Francis Marion 1991 BA; Howard U 1998 MDiv
Representative **Merita A. "Rita" Allison** (R-District 36) . . . (803) 212-6788
  Counties Represented: Greenville (part),               Res: (864) 439-6255
  Spartanburg (part)
  Term Expires: 2016
  P.O. Box 93, Lyman, SC 29365
  E-mail: ritaallison@schouse.gov
  Committees: Education and Public Works
Representative **Carl L. Anderson** (D-District 103) . . . . . . . (803) 734-2933
  Counties Represented: Georgetown (part), Horry         Dist: (843) 546-5332
  (part), Williamsburg (part)
  Term Expires: 2016
  304C Blatt Building, Columbia, SC 29201
  PO Box 694, Georgetown, SC 29442
  E-mail: carlanderson@schouse.gov
  Committees: Labor, Commerce and Industry; Regulations and
  Administrative Procedures
  Education: Horry-Georgetown 1981 BBA; Francis Marion 2011 PhD
Representative
  **Michael A. "Mike" Anthony** (D-District 42) . . . . . . . . . (803) 734-3060
  Counties Represented: Laurens (part), Union            Res: (864) 427-3023
  Term Expires: 2016
  322 Mount Vernon Road, Union, SC 29379
  E-mail: michaelanthony@schouse.gov
  Committees: Rules; Ways and Means
  Education: Gardner-Webb BS
Representative **Todd K. Atwater** (R-District 87) . . . . . . . . . (803) 212-6924
  Counties Represented: Lexington (part)                 Tel: (803) 798-6207
  Term Expires: 2016
  PO Box 1056, Lexington, SC 29071-1056
  E-mail: toddatwater@schouse.gov
  Committees: Labor, Commerce and Industry; Rules
  Education: Wofford 1988 BS; South Carolina 1991 JD
Representative **Jimmy C. Bales** (D-District 80) . . . . . . . . . (803) 734-3058
  Counties Represented: Kershaw (part), Richland         Res: (803) 776-6416
  (part)
  Term Expires: 2016
  1515 Crossing Creek Road, Eastover, SC 29044
  E-mail: jimmybales@schouse.gov
  Committees: Invitations and Memorial Resolutions; Ways and Means
  Education: Columbia Col (SC) 1960 BA;
  East Tennessee State 1966 MA; South Carolina 1975 EdD
Representative **Nathan Ballentine** (R-District 71) . . . . . . . (803) 734-2969
  Counties Represented: Lexington (part), Richland       Res: (803) 732-1861
  (part)
  Term Expires: 2016
  324 Sienna Drive, Chapin, SC 29036
  E-mail: nathanballentine@schouse.gov
  Committees: Labor, Commerce and Industry; Legislative Oversight
  Education: South Carolina 1992 BS
Representative **Justin T. Bamberg** (D-District 90) . . . . . . . (803) 212-6907
  Counties Represented: Bamberg, Barnwell (part),        Res: (803) 682-2860
  Colleton (part)
  Term Expires: 2016
  216 Family Circle Drive, Columbia, SC 29003
  E-mail: justinbamberg@schouse.gov
  Committees: Medical, Military, Public and Municipal Affairs;
  Operations and Management of the House

Representative **Bruce W. Bannister, JD** (R-District 24) . . . (803) 734-3138
Counties Represented: Greenville (part)   Tel: (864) 298-0084
Term Expires: 2016
518B Blatt Building, Columbia, SC 29201
P.O. Box 10007, Greenville, SC 29603
E-mail: brucebannister@schouse.gov
Committees: Judiciary

Representative **Eric M. Bedingfield** (R-District 28) . . . . . . . (803) 734-2962
Counties Represented: Greenville (part)   Res: (864) 230-7044
Term Expires: 2016
945 Cooley Bridge Road, Belton, SC 29627
E-mail: ericbedingfield@schouse.gov
Committees: Labor, Commerce and Industry; Regulations and
Administrative Procedures
Education: Greenville Tech 1988 AA

Representative **Beth E. Bernstein, JD** (D-District 78) . . . . . (803) 212-6940
Counties Represented: Richland (part)
Term Expires: 2016
1019 Assembly Street, Columbia, SC 29201
E-mail: bethbernstein@schouse.gov
Committees: Ethics; Judiciary
Education: Georgia 1991 BA; South Carolina 1994 JD

Representative
**Kenneth A. "Kenny" Bingham** (R-District 89) . . . . . . . (803) 734-3114
Counties Represented: Lexington (part)   Dist: (803) 796-9300
Term Expires: 2016   Res: (803) 796-3582
P.O. Box 2025, Cayce, SC 29171
E-mail: kennybingham@schouse.gov
Committees: Ethics; Joint Bond Review; Ways and Means
Affiliation: Owner, American Engineering Consultants
Education: South Carolina 1984 BS

Representative
**William Knight "Bill" Bowers** (D-District 122) . . . . . . .(803) 734-2959
Counties Represented: Beaufort (part), Hampton,   Dist: (843) 914-2142
Jasper (part)   Res: (843) 632-5755
Term Expires: 2016
P.O. Box 686, Hampton, SC 29924
E-mail: billbowers@schouse.gov
Committees: Labor, Commerce and Industry; Legislative Oversight
Education: Clemson 1974 BS; South Carolina 1980 MBA, 1994 PhD

Representative **Jeffrey A. Bradley** (R-District 123) . . . . . . . (803) 212-6928
Counties Represented: Beaufort (part)   Res: (843) 342-6918
Term Expires: 2016
304 Seabrook Drive, Hilton Head Island, SC 29926
E-mail: jeffreybradley@schouse.gov
Committees: Education and Public Works

Representative **Norman Douglas "Doug" Brannon, JD**
(R-District 38) . . . . . . . . . . . . . . . . . . . . . . . . . . . . . . .(803) 212-6876
Counties Represented: Spartanburg (part)   Dist: (864) 573-0048
Term Expires: 2016
201 Clearwater Road, Landrum, SC 29356
E-mail: dougbrannon@schouse.gov
Committees: Judiciary
Education: South Carolina 1996 BS, 2000 JD

Representative **Grady A. Brown** (D-District 50) . . . . . . . . . (803) 734-2934
Counties Represented: Kershaw (part), Lee, Sumter   Dist: (803) 484-6832
(part)
Term Expires: 2016
420 South Main Street, Bishopville, SC 29010
E-mail: gradybrown@schouse.gov
Committees: Labor, Commerce and Industry; Rules

Representative **Robert L. Brown** (D-District 116) . . . . . . . (803) 734-3170
Counties Represented: Charleston (part), Colleton   Tel: (843) 889-6440
(part)   Res: (843) 889-8835
Term Expires: 2016
5925 Highway 162, Hollywood, SC 29449
E-mail: robertbrown@schouse.gov
Committees: Education and Public Works; Invitations and Memorial
Resolutions
Education: Trident Tech 1976 AS

Representative
**James Mikell "Mike" Burns** (R-District 17) . . . . . . . . . (803) 212-6891
Counties Represented: Greenville (part)   Res: (864) 895-5493
Term Expires: 2016
100 Old Locust Hill Road, Taylors, SC 29687
E-mail: jamesburns@schouse.gov
Committees: Agriculture, Natural Resources and Environmental Affairs

Representative
**William M. "Bill" Chumley** (R-District 35) . . . . . . . . . . (803) 212-6894
Counties Represented: Greenville (part),   Tel: (864) 303-2726
Spartanburg (part)   Res: (864) 433-9150
Term Expires: 2016
3303 Greenpond Rd, Woodruff, SC 29388
E-mail: billchumley@schouse.gov
Committees: Agriculture, Natural Resources and Environmental Affairs;
Regulations and Administrative Procedures

Representative **Gary E. Clary** (R-District 3) . . . . . . . . . . . . (803) 212-6908
Counties Represented: Pickens (part)   Res: (864) 654-5727
Term Expires: 2016
P.O. Box 1645, Clemson, SC 29633
E-mail: garyclary@schouse.gov
Committees: Education and Public Works; Legislative Oversight

Representative **Alan D. Clemmons, JD** (R-District 107) . . .(803) 734-3113
Counties Represented: Horry (part)   Dist: (843) 448-4246
Term Expires: 2016
1800-A North Oak Street, Myrtle Beach, SC 29577
E-mail: alanclemmons@schouse.gov
Committees: Rules; Ways and Means
Education: Coastal Carolina U 1982 BS; Hamline 1989 JD

Representative **William "Bill" Clyburn** (D-District 82) . . . . (803) 734-3033
Counties Represented: Aiken (part), Edgefield   Res: (803) 649-6167
(part), Saluda (part)
Term Expires: 2016
664 Edrie Street, Aiken, SC 29801
E-mail: billclyburn@schouse.gov
Committees: Ways and Means
Education: Allen 1964 BS; South Carolina 1975 MEd

Representative
**Gilda Cobb-Hunter, LISW** (D-District 66) . . . . . . . . . . . (803) 734-2809
Counties Represented: Orangeburg (part)   Dist: (803) 534-2448
Term Expires: 2016   Res: (803) 531-1257
4188 Five Chop Road, Orangeburg, SC 29115
P.O. Box 2263, Orangeburg, SC 29116
E-mail: gildacobbhunter@schouse.gov
Committees: Joint Bond Review; Ways and Means
Education: Florida A&M 1973 BS; Florida State 1978 MA

Representative **J. Derham Cole, Jr., JD** (R-District 32) . . . (803) 212-6790
Counties Represented: Spartanburg (part)   Tel: (864) 591-1113
Term Expires: 2016   Res: (864) 285-4732
P.O. Box 1467, Spartanburg, SC 29304
E-mail: derhamcole@schouse.gov
Committees: Ways and Means
Education: South Carolina 1999 BS, 2003 MA, 2003 JD

Representative **Neal Anthony Collins** (R-District 5) . . . . . . (803) 212-6913
Counties Represented: Pickens (part)   Dist: (864) 350-4175
Term Expires: 2016
P.O. Box 906, Easley, SC 29641
E-mail: nealcollins@schouse.gov
Committees: Education and Public Works
Education: Furman 2004 BA; South Carolina 2007 JD

Representative **Christopher A. Corley** (R-District 84) . . . . . (803) 212-6917
Counties Represented: Aiken (part)   Dist: (706) 925-3686
Term Expires: 2016   Res: (803) 634-1762
E-mail: christophercorley@schouse.gov
Committees: Medical, Military, Public and Municipal Affairs

Representative
**Heather Ammons Crawford** (R-District 68) . . . . . . . . . . (803) 212-6933
Counties Represented: Horry (part)
Term Expires: 2016
P.O. Box 31385, Myrtle Beach, SC 29588
E-mail: heathercrawford@schouse.gov
Committees: Labor, Commerce and Industry
Education: Francis Marion 2005 BS

Representative
**William E. "Bill" Crosby** (R-District 117) . . . . . . . . . . . (803) 212-6879
Counties Represented: Berkeley (part), Charleston   Res: (843) 553-2821
(part)
Term Expires: 2016
2680 Hanford Mills Lane, North Charleston, SC 29406
E-mail: billcrosby@schouse.gov
Committees: Agriculture, Natural Resources and Environmental Affairs;
Operations and Management of the House

Representative **Joseph S. "Joe" Daning** (R-District 92) . . (803) 734-2951
Counties Represented: Berkeley (part)   Res: (843) 553-9288
Term Expires: 2016
118 Queensbury Circle, Goose Creek, SC 29445
E-mail: joedaning@schouse.gov
Committees: Education and Public Works; Rules
Education: Trident Tech 1992 AA; Southern Illinois 1995 BS;
Webster 1999 MA

*(continued on next page)*

**Representatives** *continued*

Representative
**F. Gregory "Greg" Delleney, Jr.** (R-District 43) . . . . . . . (803) 734-3120
Counties Represented: Chester (part), York (part)    Tel: (803) 581-2211
Term Expires: 2016    Res: (803) 385-3580
P.O. Drawer 808, Chester, SC 29706
E-mail: gregdelleney@schouse.gov
Committees: Judiciary
Education: Citadel 1974 BA; Cumberland 1981 JD

Representative **Chandra E. Dillard, JD** (D-District 23) . . . . (803) 212-6791
Counties Represented: Greenville (part)    Tel: (864) 294-2503
Term Expires: 2016    Res: (864) 233-6549
5 Alleta Avenue, Greenville, SC 29607
E-mail: chandradillard@schouse.gov
Committees: Agriculture, Natural Resources and Environmental Affairs;
Ethics
Education: Winthrop 1987 BS; Walden 2008 MPA

Representative **MaryGail K. Douglas** (D-District 41) . . . . . (803) 212-6789
Counties Represented: Chester (part), Fairfield,    Res: (803) 635-9292
Richland (part)
Term Expires: 2016
56 Kabbad Road, Winnsboro, SC 29180
E-mail: marygaildouglas@schouse.gov
Committees: Medical, Military, Public and Municipal Affairs; Rules
Education: South Carolina 1972 BS

Representative **Greg D. Duckworth** (R-District 104) . . . . . . (803) 212-6918
Counties Represented: Horry (part)
Term Expires: 2016
2412 Watson Drive, North Myrtle Beach, SC 29582
E-mail: gregduckworth@schouse.gov
Committees: Agriculture, Natural Resources and Environmental Affairs

Representative **Shannon S. Erickson** (R-District 124) . . . . (803) 734-3261
Counties Represented: Beaufort (part)    Tel: (843) 986-1090
Term Expires: 2016
Blatt Building, 320C, Columbia, SC 29201
E-mail: shannonerickson@schouse.gov
Committees: Ways and Means
Education: South Carolina 1997 BA

Representative **Regina Raye Felder** (R-District 26) . . . . . . (803) 212-6892
Counties Represented: York (part)    Dist: (803) 547-6715
Term Expires: 2016
116 Mary Mack Lane, Fort Mill, SC 29715
E-mail: rayefelder@schouse.gov
Committees: Education and Public Works; Legislative Oversight
Education: Mercyhurst 1991 BBA; Limestone 1993 BS

Representative **Kirkman Finlay III** (R-District 75) . . . . . . . (803) 212-6943
Counties Represented: Richland (part)    Dist: (803) 748-1090
Term Expires: 2016    Res: (803) 695-9550
PO Box 11684, Columbia, SC 29211
E-mail: kirkmanfinlay@schouse.gov
Committees: Legislative Oversight
Education: Virginia BA

Representative
**P. Michael "Mike" Forrester** (R-District 34) . . . . . . . . . . (803) 212-6792
Counties Represented: Spartanburg (part)    Tel: (864) 592-6204
Term Expires: 2016    Res: (864) 595-1137
287 Creekridge Drive, Spartanburg, SC 29301
E-mail: mikeforrester@schouse.gov
Committees: Labor, Commerce and Industry; Regulations and
Administrative Procedures
Education: SUNY (Albany) BSB

Representative **Russell W. Fry** (R-District 106) . . . . . . . . . (803) 212-6781
Counties Represented: Horry (part)    Tel: (843) 488-5000
Term Expires: 2016
E-mail: russellfry@schouse.gov
Committees: Medical, Military, Public and Municipal Affairs
Education: South Carolina 2007 BA; Charleston Law 2011 JD

Representative
**Laurie Slade Funderburk, JD** (D-District 52) . . . . . . . . (803) 734-3044
Counties Represented: Kershaw (part)    Dist: (803) 432-0188
Term Expires: 2016    Res: (803) 432-4371
P.O. Box 188, Camden, SC 29021
E-mail: lauriefunderburk@schouse.gov
Committees: Judiciary; Legislative Oversight
Education: South Carolina 1997 BA, 2001 JD

Representative **Craig A. Gagnon, DC** (R-District 11) . . . . . (803) 212-6934
Counties Represented: Abbeville (part), Anderson    Dist: (864) 366-2024
(part)    Res: (864) 366-4112
Term Expires: 2016
504 Church Street, Abbeville, SC 29620
E-mail: craiggagnon@schouse.gov
Committees: Agriculture, Natural Resources and Environmental Affairs
Education: UMass (Lowell) 1978 (Attended);
Kennesaw Col 1981 (Attended)

Representative **J. Wayne George** (D-District 57) . . . . . . . . . (803) 212-6936
Counties Represented: Dillon (part), Horry (part),    Dist: (843) 464-6884
Marion (part)
Term Expires: 2016
223 Meadowview Lane, Mullins, SC 29574
E-mail: waynegeorge@schouse.gov
Committees: Education and Public Works; Regulations and
Administrative Procedures
Education: Morris Col BS

Representative **Wendell G. Gilliard** (D-District 111) . . . . . . (803) 212-6793
Counties Represented: Charleston (part)    Tel: (843) 209-3123
Term Expires: 2016    Res: (843) 402-9710
P.O. Box 31641, Charleston, SC 29417
E-mail: wendellgilliard@schouse.gov
Committees: Medical, Military, Public and Municipal Affairs;
Regulations and Administrative Procedures

Representative
**Stephen L. Goldfinch, Jr., JD** (R-District 108) . . . . . . . . (803) 212-6927
Counties Represented: Charleston (part),    Dist: (843) 357-9301
Georgetown (part)    Res: (803) 385-4302
Term Expires: 2016
PO Box 823, Murrells Inlet, SC 29576
E-mail: stephengoldfinch@schouse.gov
Committees: Judiciary
Education: Citadel 2004 BS, 2006 MBA; Charleston Law 2010 JD

Representative **Jerry N. Govan, Jr.** (D-District 95) . . . . . . . (803) 734-3012
Counties Represented: Orangeburg (part)    Tel: (803) 533-7976
Term Expires: 2016    Res: (803) 533-1158
P.O. Box 77, Orangeburg, SC 29116
E-mail: jerrygovan@schouse.gov
Committees: Education and Public Works; Operations and Management
of the House
Education: South Carolina State 1982 BA

Representative
**Daniel P. "Dan" Hamilton** (R-District 20) . . . . . . . . . . . (803) 212-6795
Counties Represented: Greenville (part)    Tel: (864) 527-7685
Term Expires: 2016    Res: (864) 244-0663
PO Box 6088, Greenville, SC 29606
E-mail: danhamilton@schouse.gov
Committees: Labor, Commerce and Industry

Representative **Kevin J. Hardee** (R-District 105) . . . . . . . . . (803) 212-6796
Counties Represented: Horry (part)    Res: (843) 455-3567
Term Expires: 2016
2088 Cane Branch, Loris, SC 29569
E-mail: kevinhardee@schouse.gov
Committees: Agriculture, Natural Resources and Environmental Affairs;
Interstate Cooperation
Education: Horry-Georgetown 1986

Representative
**Christopher R. "Chris" Hart, JD** (D-District 73) . . . . . . . (803) 734-3061
Counties Represented: Richland (part)    Res: (803) 771-7701
Term Expires: 2016
5219 Burke Avenue, Columbia, SC 29203
E-mail: chrishart@schouse.gov
Committees: Medical, Military, Public and Municipal Affairs
Education: Howard U 1997 BA; South Carolina 2000 JD

Representative **Jackie E. "Coach" Hayes** (D-District 55) . . (803) 734-3099
Counties Represented: Darlington (part), Dillon    Tel: (843) 841-3679
(part), Horry (part), Marlboro (part)    Res: (843) 774-6125
Term Expires: 2016
240 Bermuda Road, Dillon, SC 29536
E-mail: jackiehayes@schouse.gov
Committees: Rules; Ways and Means
Education: Catawba 1984 BA

Representative **Phyllis J. Henderson** (R-District 21) . . . . . . (803) 212-6883
Counties Represented: Greenville (part)    Tel: (864) 423-3149
Term Expires: 2016    Res: (864) 268-1081
110 Silver Creek Court, Greer, SC 29650
E-mail: phyllishenderson@schouse.gov
Committees: Labor, Commerce and Industry; Legislative Oversight
Education: Cincinnati 1982 BA

Representative
**Patricia M. "Pat" Henegan** (D-District 54) . . . . . . . . . . (803) 212-6896
Counties Represented: Chesterfield (part),     Res: (843) 479-7838
Darlington (part), Marlboro (part)
Term Expires: 2016
P.O. Box 41, Bennettsville, SC 29512
E-mail: patriciahenegan@schouse.gov
Committees: Interstate Cooperation; Medical, Military, Public and
Municipal Affairs

Representative
**William G. "Bill" Herbkersman** (R-District 118) . . . . . . (803) 734-3063
Counties Represented: Beaufort (part), Jasper (part)    Dist: (843) 757-7900
Term Expires: 2016                        Res: (843) 757-5424
896 May River Road, Bluffton, SC 29910-5833
E-mail: billherbkersman@schouse.gov
Committees: Rules; Ways and Means

Representative **Donna C. Hicks** (R-District 37) . . . . . . . . . (803) 212-6878
Counties Represented: Spartanburg (part)      Tel: (864) 804-4239
Term Expires: 2016
P.O. Box 161852, Boiling Springs, SC 29316
E-mail: donnawood@schouse.gov
Committees: Judiciary
Education: South Carolina 1998 BS; New Orleans Baptist 2002 MDiv,
2006 ThM

Representative **Jonathon D. Hill** (R-District 8) . . . . . . . . . (803) 212-6919
Counties Represented: Anderson (part)
Term Expires: 2016
1031 Double Springs Road, Townville, SC 29689
E-mail: jonathanhill@schouse.gov
Committees: Medical, Military, Public and Municipal Affairs

Representative **David R. Hiott** (R-District 4) . . . . . . . . . . . (803) 734-3323
Counties Represented: Pickens (part)       Dist: (864) 878-9832
Term Expires: 2016
P.O. Box 997, Pickens, SC 29671
E-mail: davidhiott@schouse.gov
Committees: Agriculture, Natural Resources and Environmental Affairs
Education: Central Wesleyan 1983 BA

Representative **William M. "Bill" Hixon** (R-District 83) . . . (803) 212-6898
Counties Represented: Aiken (part), Edgefield (part)    Tel: (803) 279-8855
Term Expires: 2016                        Res: (803) 278-0892
P.O. Box 7927, North Augusta, SC 29861
E-mail: billhixon@schouse.gov
Committees: Agriculture, Natural Resources and Environmental Affairs

Representative **Kenneth F. Hodges** (D-District 121) . . . . . . (803) 734-3062
Counties Represented: Beaufort (part), Colleton     Tel: (843) 525-9006
(part)
Term Expires: 2016
PO Box Drawer 355, Green Pond, SC 29446
E-mail: kennethhodges@schouse.gov
Committees: Agriculture, Natural Resources and Environmental Affairs
Education: Clarke 1977 BA; Interdenominational 1986 MDiv

Representative
**Jenny Anderson Horne, JD** (R-District 94) . . . . . . . . . . (803) 212-6871
Counties Represented: Charleston (part), Dorchester    Tel: (843) 873-1721
(part)
Term Expires: 2016
102 Perry Lane, Summerville, SC 29483
E-mail: jennyhorne@schouse.gov
Committees: Ethics; Judiciary
Education: South Carolina 1994 BA, 1997 JD

Representative **Lonnie Hosey** (D-District 91) . . . . . . . . . . . (803) 536-8903
Counties Represented: Allendale, Barnwell (part),    Res: (803) 259-1178
Orangeburg (part)
Term Expires: 2016
P.O. Box 423, Barnwell, SC 29812
E-mail: lonniehosey@schouse.gov
Committees: Regulations and Administrative Procedures; Ways and
Means
Affiliation: Director, Adult and Continuing Education Center, South
Carolina State University
300 College Street, NE, Orangeburg, SC 29117

Representative **Leon Howard** (D-District 76) . . . . . . . . . . . (803) 734-3046
Counties Represented: Richland (part)      Tel: (803) 254-9468
Term Expires: 2016                        Res: (803) 254-1216
2425 Barhamville Road, Columbia, SC 29204
E-mail: leonhoward@schouse.gov
Committees: Medical, Military, Public and Municipal Affairs
Education: Midlands Tech AA

Representative **Chip Huggins** (R-District 85) . . . . . . . . . . . (803) 734-2971
Counties Represented: Lexington (part)     Dist: (803) 732-2000
Term Expires: 2016                       Res: (803) 732-4418
308 Wayworth Court, Columbia, SC 29212
E-mail: chiphuggins@schouse.gov
Committees: Regulations and Administrative Procedures; Ways and
Means
Education: Winthrop 1987 BS

Representative
**Joseph H. "Joe" Jefferson, Jr.** (D-District 102) . . . . . . (803) 734-2936
Counties Represented: Berkeley (part), Dorchester    Dist: (843) 567-4386
(part)
Term Expires: 2016
1375 Colonial Maham Drive, Pineville, SC 29468
E-mail: josephjefferson@schouse.gov
Committees: Legislative Oversight; Medical, Military, Public and
Municipal Affairs
Education: Claflin 1970 BS

Representative
**Jeffrey E. "Jeff" Johnson** (R-District 58) . . . . . . . . . . . (803) 212-6946
Counties Represented: Horry (part)      Dist: (843) 488-5333
Term Expires: 2016                      Res: (843) 397-0079
7223 Pee Dee Highway, Conway, SC 29527
E-mail: jeffjohnson@schouse.gov
Committees: Education and Public Works

Representative
**Wallace H. "Jay" Jordan, Jr.** (R-District 63) . . . . . . . . (803) 212-6785
Counties Represented: Providence (part)
Term Expires: 2016
E-mail: wallacejordan@schouse.gov
Committees: Medical, Military, Public and Municipal Affairs
Education: Col Charleston; Charleston Law JD

Representative
**Ralph Shealy Kennedy, Jr., JD** (R-District 39) . . . . . . . (803) 212-6938
Counties Represented: Lexington (part), Saluda    Dist: (803) 532-4100
(part)                         Res: (803) 532-4003
Term Expires: 2016
617 Woodland Way, Leesville, SC 29070
E-mail: ralphkennedy@schouse.gov
Committees: Judiciary; Regulations and Administrative Procedures
Education: Clemson BS; South Carolina JD

Representative
**John Richard Christopher King** (D-District 49) . . . . . . . (803) 212-6873
Counties Represented: York (part)      Res: (803) 980-5454
Term Expires: 2016
P.O. Box 11555, Rock Hill, SC 29731
E-mail: johnking@schouse.gov
Committees: Education and Public Works; Ethics
Education: Strayer U 2006 MEd

Representative **Roger K. Kirby** (D-District 61) . . . . . . . . . . (803) 212-6947
Counties Represented: Florence (part), Marion    Dist: (843) 374-7653
(part)
Term Expires: 2016
1690 Johnsonville Highway, Lake City, SC 29560
E-mail: rogerkirby@schouse.gov
Committees: Agriculture, Natural Resources and Environmental Affairs

Representative **Patsy G. Knight** (D-District 97) . . . . . . . . . (803) 734-2960
Counties Represented: Colleton (part), Dorchester (part)
Term Expires: 2016
PO Box 663, St. George, SC 29477
E-mail: patsyknight@schouse.gov
Committees: Agriculture, Natural Resources and Environmental Affairs;
Operations and Management of the House

Representative
**Harry B. "Chip" Limehouse III** (R-District 110) . . . . . . . (803) 734-2977
Counties Represented: Charleston (part)     Tel: (843) 577-6242
Term Expires: 2016                      Res: (803) 252-0845
22 Menotti Street, Charleston, SC 29401
E-mail: chiplimehouse@schouse.gov
Committees: Joint Bond Review; Ways and Means
Education: South Carolina BA

Representative **Dwight A. Loftis** (R-District 19) . . . . . . . . (803) 734-3101
Counties Represented: Greenville (part)     Res: (864) 834-5760
Term Expires: 2016
P.O. Box 14784, Greenville, SC 29610
E-mail: dwightloftis@schouse.gov
Committees: Rules; Ways and Means
Education: North Greenville Col 1966 AA

*(continued on next page)*

LEGISLATIVE BRANCH

**Representatives** *continued*

Representative **Deborah A. Long, O.D.** (R-District 45) . . . . (803) 212-6874
Counties Represented: Lancaster (part), York (part)   Tel: (803) 417-7353
Term Expires: 2016   Res: (803) 547-5215
1115 John Short Road, Indian Land, SC 29707
E-mail: deborahlong@schouse.gov
Committees: Operations and Management of the House; Ways and Means
Education: North Carolina Greensboro 1976 BA;
Southern Col Optometry 1980 OD

Representative **Phillip D. Lowe** (R-District 60) . . . . . . . . . (803) 734-2975
Counties Represented: Darlington (part), Florence   Tel: (843) 662-1234
(part)
Term Expires: 2016
507 West Cheves Street, Florence, SC 29501
E-mail: philliplowe@schouse.gov
Committees: Ways and Means
Education: Medical U (SC) 1982 BS

Representative
**James H. "Jay" Lucas, JD** (R-District 65) . . . . . . . . . . (803) 734-2701
Counties Represented: Chesterfield (part),   Tel: (843) 332-5050
Darlington (part), Kershaw (part), Lancaster (part)   Res: (843) 383-9421
Term Expires: 2016
PO Box 1408, Hartsville, SC 29550
1744 Garland Drive, Hartsville, SC 29550
E-mail: jaylucas@schouse.gov
Committees: Operations and Management of the House

Representative **David James Mack III** (D-District 109) . . . . (803) 734-3192
Counties Represented: Charleston (part), Dorchester   Tel: (843) 225-4869
(part)   Res: (843) 760-0198
Term Expires: 2016
4340 Evanston Boulevard, North Charleston, SC 29418
E-mail: davidmack@schouse.gov
Committees: Labor, Commerce and Industry
Education: Howard U 1975 BS

Representative **Peter M. McCoy, Jr., JD** (R-District 115) . . (803) 212-6872
Counties Represented: Charleston (part)   Tel: (843) 628-2855
Term Expires: 2016   Res: (843) 452-4722
135 King Street, Charleston, SC 29401
E-mail: petermccoy@schouse.gov
Committees: Judiciary
Education: Hampden-Sydney 2001 BA; Regent U 2005 JD

Representative
**Joseph A. "Joe" McEachern** (D-District 77) . . . . . . . . . (803) 212-6875
Counties Represented: Richland (part)   Tel: (803) 735-1808
Term Expires: 2016   Res: (803) 786-8304
P.O. Box 3751, Columbia, SC 29230
E-mail: joemceachern@schouse.gov
Committees: Invitations and Memorial Resolutions; Judiciary

Representative **Cezar E. McKnight** (D-District 101) . . . . . . (803) 212-6926
Counties Represented: Clarendon (part),   Dist: (843) 374-4529
Williamsburg (part)   Res: (843) 372-3323
Term Expires: 2016
E-mail: cezarmcknight@schouse.gov
Committees: Medical, Military, Public and Municipal Affairs

Representative **Mia S. McLeod, JD** (D-District 79) . . . . . . (803) 212-6794
Counties Represented: Richland (part)   Tel: (803) 251-9476
Term Expires: 2016
PO Box 290692, Columbia, SC 29229
E-mail: mia@schouse.gov
Committees: Legislative Oversight; Medical, Military, Public and
Municipal Affairs
Education: South Carolina State 1990 BA; South Carolina 1995 JD

Representative
**Walton J. "Walt" McLeod III** (D-District 40) . . . . . . . . . (803) 734-3276
Counties Represented: Newberry   Tel: (803) 345-1538
Term Expires: 2016   Res: (803) 945-7461
308 Pomaria Street, Little Mountain, SC 29075
E-mail: waltmcleod@schouse.gov
Committees: Judiciary
Education: Yale 1959 BA; South Carolina 1964 LLB

Representative **James H. Merrill** (R-District 99) . . . . . . . . (803) 734-3072
Counties Represented: Berkeley (part), Charleston   Tel: (843) 849-7307
(part)   Res: (843) 849-7306
Term Expires: 2016
2401 Daniel Island Drive, Charleston, SC 29492
E-mail: jimmerrill@schouse.gov
Committees: Ways and Means
Education: South Carolina 1989 BA, 1992 MPA

Representative **Harold Mitchell, Jr.** (D-District 31) . . . . . . (803) 734-6638
Counties Represented: Spartanburg (part)   Res: (864) 279-4675
Term Expires: 2016
P.O. Box 3046, Spartanburg, SC 29304-3046
E-mail: haroldmitchell@schouse.gov
Committees: Education and Public Works; Interstate Cooperation
Affiliation: Executive Director, ReGenesis, Inc.
710 South Church Street #2, Spartanburg, SC 29306

Representative **Dennis Carroll Moss** (R-District 29) . . . . . . (803) 734-3073
Counties Represented: Cherokee (part), Chester   Tel: (864) 761-6353
(part), York (part)   Res: (864) 487-2121
Term Expires: 2016
306 Silver Circle, Gaffney, SC 29340
E-mail: dennismoss@schouse.gov
Committees: Invitations and Memorial Resolutions; Judiciary

Representative
**V. Stephen "Steve" Moss** (R-District 30) . . . . . . . . . . (803) 212-6885
Counties Represented: Cherokee (part), York (part)
Term Expires: 2016
104 Rains Road, Blacksburg, SC 29702
E-mail: stevemoss@schouse.gov
Committees: Agriculture, Natural Resources and Environmental Affairs
Education: Clemson 1972 BA

Representative
**Christopher J. "Chris" Murphy, JD** (R-District 98) . . . . (803) 212-6925
Counties Represented: Dorchester (part)   Tel: (843) 832-1120
Term Expires: 2016
4238 Persimmon Woods, North Charleston, SC 29420
E-mail: chrismurphy@schouse.gov
Committees: Judiciary; Regulations and Administrative Procedures
Education: Citadel 1990 BA; Mississippi 1995 JD

Representative **Wendy K. Nanney** (R-District 22) . . . . . . . . (803) 212-6877
Counties Represented: Greenville (part)   Tel: (864) 979-4735
Term Expires: 2016   Res: (864) 292-1523
124 Birnam Court, Greenville, SC 29615
E-mail: wendynanney@schouse.gov
Committees: Judiciary
Education: Bob Jones U 1987 BS

Representative **Joseph H. "Joe" Neal** (D-District 70) . . . . (803) 734-2804
Counties Represented: Richland (part), Sumter   Res: (803) 776-0353
(part)
Term Expires: 2016
P.O. Box 5, Hopkins, SC 29061
E-mail: joeneal@schouse.gov
Committees: Rules; Ways and Means
Affiliation: Vice President, New Horizon Systems, Inc.
Education: Benedict 1972 BA

Representative
**William Weston J. Newton, JD** (R-District 120) . . . . . . (803) 212-6942
Counties Represented: Beaufort (part), Jasper (part)   Dist: (843) 706-6111
Term Expires: 2016   Res: (843) 706-3880
83 Myrtle Island, Bluffton, SC 29910
E-mail: westonnewton@schouse.gov
Committees: Judiciary; Legislative Oversight
Education: Washington and Lee 1989 BA; South Carolina 1993 JD

Representative **Ralph W. Norman, Jr.** (R-District 48) . . . . . (803) 366-8141
Counties Represented: York (part)   Res: (803) 366-2819
Term Expires: 2016   Tel: (803) 212-6888
404C Blatt Building, Columbia, SC 29201   (Blatt Cola)
P.O. Box 36518, Rock Hill, SC 29732
E-mail: ralphnorman@schouse.gov
Committees: Labor, Commerce and Industry; Legislative Oversight
Education: Presbyterian Col 1975 BS

Representative **Russell L. Ott** (D-District 93) . . . . . . . . . . . (803) 212-6945
Counties Represented: Calhoun, Lexington (part), Orangeburg (part)
Term Expires: 2016
135 Ott Farm Trail, St. Matthews, SC 29135
E-mail: russellott@schouse.gov
Committees: Agriculture, Natural Resources and Environmental Affairs

Representative **J. Anne Parks** (D-District 12) . . . . . . . . . . . (803) 734-3069
Counties Represented: Greenwood (part),   Tel: (864) 229-3206
McCormick   Res: (864) 223-3193
Term Expires: 2016
P.O. Box 181, Greenwood, SC 29648
E-mail: anneparks@schouse.gov
Committees: Medical, Military, Public and Municipal Affairs
Education: Johnson C Smith 1976 BS

Representative **Michael A. "Mike" Pitts** (R-District 14) . . . (803) 734-2830
Counties Represented: Greenwood (part), Laurens   Tel: (864) 681-0238
(part)   Res: (864) 923-2925
Term Expires: 2016
372 Bucks Point Road, Laurens, SC 29360
E-mail: mikepitts@schouse.gov
Committees: Ethics; Ways and Means
Education: Greenville Tech 1978 AA; Lander 1985 BS

Representative
**Thomas E. "Tommy" Pope, JD** (R-District 47) . . . . . . . (803) 212-6895
Counties Represented: York (part)   Tel: (803) 324-7574
Term Expires: 2016
P.O. Box 471, York, SC 29745
E-mail: tommypope@schouse.gov

Representative
**Mandy D. Powers Norrell, JD** (D-District 44) . . . . . . . . (803) 212-6937
Counties Represented: Lancaster (part)   Dist: (803) 289-1800
Term Expires: 2016   Res: (803) 289-6409
PO Box 994, Lancaster, SC 29721
E-mail: mandynorrell@schouse.gov
Committees: Judiciary
Education: Furman 1995 BA; South Carolina 1997 JD

Representative **Joshua Putnam** (R-District 10) . . . . . . . . . (803) 212-6931
Counties Represented: Anderson (part), Greenville   Dist: (864) 238-9431
(part), Pickens (part)
Term Expires: 2016
P.O. Box 51542, Piedmont, SC 29673
E-mail: joshuaputman@schouse.gov
Committees: Education and Public Works; Legislative Oversight
Education: North Greenville U 2011 BS

Representative
**Richard M. "Rick" Quinn, Jr.** (R-District 69) . . . . . . . . (803) 212-6897
Counties Represented: Lexington (part)   Res: (803) 808-3964
Term Expires: 2016   Dist: (803) 799-8638
115 John Preston Drive, Lexington, SC 29072
E-mail: rickquinn@schouse.gov
Committees: Judiciary
Education: South Carolina 1994

Representative
**Dr. Robert L. Ridgeway III** (D-District 64) . . . . . . . . . . . (803) 212-6929
Counties Represented: Clarendon (part), Sumter   Res: (803) 938-3087
(part)
Term Expires: 2016
117 N. Brooks Street, Manning, SC 29102
E-mail: bobbyridgeway@schouse.gov
Committees: Legislative Oversight; Medical, Military, Public and
Municipal Affairs
Education: South Carolina State 1988 MD

Representative **Robert Shannon Riley** (R-District 13) . . . . (803) 212-6939
Counties Represented: Greenwood (part)   Res: (864) 992-4585
Term Expires: 2016
P.O. Box 212, Hodges, SC 29653
E-mail: shannonriley@schouse.gov
Committees: Agriculture, Natural Resources and Environmental Affairs;
Invitations and Memorial Resolutions
Education: Erskine 1996 BA

Representative **Samuel Rivers, Jr., PhD** (R-District 15) . . . (803) 212-6890
Counties Represented: Berkeley (part), Charleston   Dist: (843) 529-0390
(part)   Res: (843) 553-6448
Term Expires: 2016
PO Box 760, Goose Creek, SC 29445
E-mail: samuelrivers@schouse.gov
Committees: Education and Public Works; Legislative Oversight

Representative
**Leola C. Robinson-Simpson** (D-District 25) . . . . . . . . . (803) 212-6941
Counties Represented: Greenville (part)   Res: (864) 277-0232
Term Expires: 2016
19 Prince Avenue, Greenville, SC 29605
E-mail: leolarobinsonsimpson@schouse.gov
Committees: Medical, Military, Public and Municipal Affairs;
Regulations and Administrative Procedures
Education: York (NY) 1975 BA; Furman 1990 MEd

Representative **J. Todd Rutherford** (D-District 74) . . . . . . . (803) 734-9441
Counties Represented: Richland (part)   Tel: (803) 256-3003
Term Expires: 2016   Res: (803) 799-8633
P.O. Box 1452, Columbia, SC 29202
E-mail: toddrutherford@schouse.gov
Committees: Judiciary

Representative **Mike Ryhal** (R-District 56) . . . . . . . . . . . . . (803) 212-6935
Counties Represented: Horry (part)   Res: (843) 655-2452
Term Expires: 2016
8328 Juxa Drive, Myrtle Beach, SC 29579
E-mail: mikeryhal@schouse.gov
Committees: Labor, Commerce and Industry
Education: Geneva 1993 BS

Representative
**William E. "Bill" Sandifer III** (R-District 2) . . . . . . . . . . (803) 734-3015
Counties Represented: Oconee (part), Pickens (part)   Tel: (864) 885-2240
Term Expires: 2016   Res: (864) 882-1225
112 Cardinal Drive, Seneca, SC 29672
E-mail: billsandifer@schouse.gov
Committees: Labor, Commerce and Industry

Representative **J. Gary Simrill** (R-District 46) . . . . . . . . . . . (803) 734-3040
Counties Represented: York (part)   Tel: (803) 366-0445
Term Expires: 2016   Res: (803) 328-8089
1515 Alexander Road, Rock Hill, SC 29732
E-mail: garysimrill@schouse.gov
Committees: Ways and Means
Education: Winthrop 1991 BS

Representative **G. Murrell Smith, Jr., JD** (R-District 67) . . (803) 734-3042
Counties Represented: Sumter (part)   Tel: (803) 778-2471
Term Expires: 2016   Res: (803) 469-4416
P.O. Box 580, Sumter, SC 29151
E-mail: murrellsmith@schouse.gov
Committees: Ethics; Ways and Means
Education: Wofford 1990 BA; South Carolina 1993 JD

Representative **Garry R. Smith** (R-District 27) . . . . . . . . . (803) 734-3141
Counties Represented: Greenville (part)   Res: (864) 963-0337
Term Expires: 2016
210 Foxhound Road, Simpsonville, SC 29680
E-mail: garrysmith@schouse.gov
Committees: Operations and Management of the House; Ways and
Means
Education: South Carolina (Aiken) 1979 BA;
South Carolina State 1983 MPA

Representative
**James Emerson Smith, Jr., JD** (D-District 72) . . . . . . . (803) 734-2997
Counties Represented: Richland (part)   Tel: (803) 933-9800
Term Expires: 2016   Res: (803) 256-3582
P.O. Box 50333, Columbia, SC 29250
E-mail: james@jamessmith.com
Committees: Judiciary; Legislative Oversight
Education: South Carolina 1990 BA, 1995 JD

Representative
**F. Michael "Mike" Sottile** (R-District 112) . . . . . . . . . . (803) 212-6880
Counties Represented: Charleston (part)   Tel: (843) 884-3159
Term Expires: 2016   Res: (843) 886-8759
132 Sparrow Drive, Isle of Palms, SC 29451
E-mail: mikesottile@schouse.gov
Committees: Labor, Commerce and Industry; Rules

Representative **Lawrence Kit Spires** (R-District 96) . . . . . . (803) 734-3010
Counties Represented: Lexington (part)   Tel: (803) 606-5749
Term Expires: 2016   Res: (803) 894-4440
P.O. Box 396, Pelion, SC 29123
E-mail: kitspires@schouse.gov
Committees: Medical, Military, Public and Municipal Affairs; Rules
Education: South Carolina State 1976 BSPh

Representative
**Leonidas E. "Leon" Stavrinakis, JD** (D-District 119) . . (803) 734-3039
Counties Represented: Charleston (part)   Tel: (843) 724-1060
Term Expires: 2016   Res: (843) 573-0491
PO Box 30099, Charleston, SC 29417
E-mail: leonstav@schouse.gov
Committees: Ethics; Ways and Means
Education: Col Charleston 1988 BA; South Carolina 1992 JD

Representative **Tommy M. Stringer** (R-District 18) . . . . . . . (864) 877-9511
Counties Represented: Greenville (part)   Tel: (803) 212-6881
Term Expires: 2016
P.O. Box 2078, Greer, SC 29652
E-mail: tommystringer@schouse.gov
Committees: Education and Public Works; Legislative Oversight
Education: Bob Jones U 1989 BS

Representative
**Edward R. "Eddie" Tallon, Sr.** (R-District 33) . . . . . . . . (803) 212-6893
Counties Represented: Spartanburg (part)   Tel: (864) 380-8777
Term Expires: 2016   Res: (864) 596-1478
140 Bagwell Farm Road, Spartanburg, SC 29302
E-mail: eddietallon@schouse.gov
Committees: Judiciary
Education: Spartanburg Methodist 1970 AA; Limestone 1971 BA

*(continued on next page)*

**Representatives** *continued*

Representative **Bill Taylor** (R-District 86) . . . . . . . . . . . . . (803) 212-6923
Counties Represented: Aiken (part)          Tel: (803) 270-2012
Term Expires: 2016
P.O. Box 2646, Aiken, SC 29802
E-mail: billtaylor@schouse.gov
Committees: Education and Public Works; Legislative Oversight

Representative **Anne J. Thayer** (R-District 9) . . . . . . . . . . (803) 212-6889
Counties Represented: Anderson (part)        Tel: (864) 940-1696
Term Expires: 2016                           Res: (864) 224-2919
225 Ansonborough Plantation, Belton, SC 29627
E-mail: annethayer@schouse.gov
Committees: Judiciary; Rules
Education: Marycrest Col 1990 BA

Representative **Mary Tinkler** (D-District 114) . . . . . . . . . . (803) 212-6948
Counties Represented: Charleston (part), Dorchester   Dist: (843) 853-6055
(part)                                                Res: (843) 693-7125
Term Expires: 2016
1286 Winchester Drive, Charleston, SC 29407
E-mail: marytinkler@schouse.gov
Committees: Medical, Military, Public and Municipal Affairs

Representative **McLain R. "Mac" Toole** (R-District 88) . . . (803) 734-2973
Counties Represented: Lexington (part)       Tel: (803) 755-6542
Term Expires: 2016
180 Dogwood Circle, West Columbia, SC 29170
E-mail: mactoole@schouse.gov
Committees: Labor, Commerce and Industry; Operations and
Management of the House
Education: Midlands Tech 1966 AS

Representative **J. David Weeks, JD** (D-District 51) . . . . . . . (803) 734-3102
Counties Represented: Sumter (part)          Tel: (803) 775-5856
Term Expires: 2016                           Res: (803) 775-4228
2 Marlborough Court, Sumter, SC 29154
E-mail: davidweeks@schouse.gov
Committees: Ethics; Judiciary
Education: Morris Col 1975 BA; Howard U 1996 MEd;
South Carolina 1989 JD

Representative **Don L. Wells** (R-District 81) . . . . . . . . . . . . (803) 212-6884
Counties Represented: Aiken (part)           Dist: (803) 649-6233
Term Expires: 2016                           Res: (803) 643-3461
615 Cardinal Drive Aiken, Aiken, SC 29803
E-mail: donwells@schouse.gov
Committees: Education and Public Works; Regulations and
Administrative Procedures
Education: Tennessee Temple 1983 (Attended)

Representative
**Jackson Seth Whipper, JD** (D-District 113) . . . . . . . . . (803) 734-3191
Counties Represented: Charleston (part), Dorchester   Tel: (843) 740-7777
(part)                                                Res: (843) 744-1976
Term Expires: 2016
4592 Durant Avenue, North Charleston, SC 29405
E-mail: sethwhipper@schouse.gov
Committees: Judiciary
Education: South Carolina 1972 BA; North Carolina Central 1984 JD

Representative **W. Brian White** (R-District 6) . . . . . . . . . . (803) 734-3144
Counties Represented: Anderson (part)        Tel: (864) 260-4025
Term Expires: 2016
P.O. Box 970, Anderson, SC 29622
E-mail: brianwhite@schouse.gov
Committees: Joint Bond Review; Ways and Means
Affiliation: Vice President, White's Aviation

Representative
**William R. "Bill" Whitmire** (R-District 1) . . . . . . . . . . . (803) 734-3068
Counties Represented: Oconee (part)          Tel: (864) 638-4237
Term Expires: 2016                           Res: (864) 638-2970
P.O. Box 157, Walhalla, SC 29691
E-mail: billwhitmire@schouse.gov
Committees: Rules; Ways and Means
Education: Piedmont Col 1972 AB

Representative **Robert Q. Williams** (D-District 62) . . . . . . . (803) 734-3142
Counties Represented: Darlington (part), Florence    Tel: (843) 413-2791
(part)                                               Res: (843) 395-9408
Term Expires: 2016
2512 Holly Circle, Darlington, SC 29532
E-mail: robertwilliams@schouse.gov
Committees: Agriculture, Natural Resources and Environmental Affairs;
Legislative Oversight
Education: Troy State 2003 MPA

Representative **Mark N. Willis** (R-District 16) . . . . . . . . . . (803) 212-6882
Counties Represented: Greenville (part), Laurens   Tel: (864) 230-0135
(part)                                             Res: (864) 862-6179
Term Expires: 2016
201 Quillen Avenue, Fountain Inn, SC 29644
E-mail: markwillis@schouse.gov
Committees: Education and Public Works; Interstate Cooperation

Representative **Richard L. Yow** (R-District 53) . . . . . . . . . . (803) 212-6949
Counties Represented: Chesterfield (part), Lancaster   Dist: (843) 623-5001
(part)
Term Expires: 2016
200 W. Main Street, Chesterfield, SC 29709
E-mail: richardyow@schouse.gov
Committees: Interstate Cooperation; Medical, Military, Public and
Municipal Affairs

District 7 **(Vacant)** . . . . . . . . . . . . . . . . . . . . . . . . . . . . . . . (803) 734-2010
Note: A special election date has not yet been determined to fill this
legislative vacancy.

District 100 **(Vacant)** . . . . . . . . . . . . . . . . . . . . . . . . . . . . . (803) 734-2010
Note: A special election to fill this legislative vacancy will be held on
August 30, 2016.

# House Standing Committees

## Agriculture, Natural Resources and Environmental Affairs

| Majority Members | Minority Members |
|---|---|
| David R. Hiott (R-4) *Chair* | Chandra E. Dillard (D-23) |
| V. Stephen "Steve" Moss (R-30) | *2nd Vice Chair* |
| *1st Vice Chair* | Russell L. Ott (D-93) *Secretary* |
| James Mikell "Mike" Burns (R-17) | Kenneth F. Hodges (D-121) |
| William M. "Bill" Chumley (R-35) | Roger K. Kirby (D-61) |
| William E. "Bill" Crosby (R-117) | Patsy G. Knight (D-97) |
| Greg D. Duckworth (R-104) | Robert Q. Williams (D-62) |
| Craig A. Gagnon (R-11) | |
| Kevin J. Hardee (R-105) | |
| William M. "Bill" Hixon (R-83) | |
| Robert Shannon Riley (R-13) | |

## Education and Public Works

| Majority Members | Minority Members |
|---|---|
| Merita A. "Rita" Allison (R-36) | Robert L. Brown (D-116) |
| *Chair* | *2nd Vice Chair* |
| Regina Raye Felder (R-26) | J. Wayne George (D-57) |
| *1st Vice Chair* | Jerry N. Govan, Jr. (D-95) |
| Jeffrey A. Bradley (R-123) | John Richard Christopher King |
| Gary E. Clary (R-3) | (D-49) |
| Neal Anthony Collins (R-5) | Harold Mitchell, Jr. (D-31) |
| Joseph S. "Joe" Daning (R-92) | |
| Jeffrey E. "Jeff" Johnson (R-58) | |
| Joshua Putnam (R-10) | |
| Samuel Rivers, Jr. (R-15) | |
| Tommy M. Stringer (R-18) | |
| Bill Taylor (R-86) | |
| Don L. Wells (R-81) | |
| Mark N. Willis (R-16) | |

## Ethics

| Majority Members | Minority Members |
|---|---|
| Kenneth A. "Kenny" | J. David Weeks (D-51) *Vice Chair* |
| Bingham (R-89) | Beth E. Bernstein (D-78) |
| *Chair* | Chandra E. Dillard (D-23) |
| Michael A. "Mike" Pitts (R-14) | John Richard Christopher King |
| *Secretary* | (D-49) |
| Jenny Anderson Horne (R-94) | Leonidas E. "Leon" Stavrinakis |
| G. Murrell Smith, Jr. (R-67) | (D-119) |

## Interstate Cooperation

| Majority Members | Minority Members |
|---|---|
| Mark N. Willis (R-16) *Chair* | Patricia M. "Pat" Henegan (D-54) |
| Richard L. Yow (R-53) | *2nd Vice Chair* |
| *1st Vice Chair* | Harold Mitchell, Jr. (D-31) |
| Kevin J. Hardee (R-105) | |

## Invitations and Memorial Resolutions

**Majority Members**
Dennis Carroll Moss (R-29)
  *1st Vice Chair*
Robert Shannon Riley (R-13)

**Minority Members**
Jimmy C. Bales (D-80) *Chair*
Robert L. Brown (D-116)
  *2nd Vice Chair*
Joseph A. "Joe" McEachern (D-77)

## Judiciary

**Majority Members**
F. Gregory "Greg"
  Delleney, Jr. (R-43)
  *Chair*
Christopher J. "Chris"
  Murphy (R-98)
  *2nd Vice Chair*
Bruce W. Bannister (R-24)
Norman Douglas "Doug" Brannon
  (R-38)
Stephen L. Goldfinch, Jr. (R-108)
Donna C. Hicks (R-37)
Jenny Anderson Horne (R-94)
Ralph Shealy Kennedy, Jr. (R-39)
Peter M. McCoy, Jr. (R-115)
Dennis Carroll Moss (R-29)
Wendy K. Nanney (R-22)
William Weston J. Newton (R-120)
Richard M. "Rick" Quinn, Jr.
  (R-69)
Edward R. "Eddie" Tallon, Sr.
  (R-33)
Anne J. Thayer (R-9)

**Minority Members**
James Emerson Smith, Jr. (D-72)
  *1st Vice Chair*
Beth E. Bernstein (D-78)
Laurie Slade Funderburk (D-52)
Joseph A. "Joe" McEachern (D-77)
Walton J. "Walt" McLeod III (D-40)
Mandy D. Powers Norrell (D-44)
J. Todd Rutherford (D-74)
J. David Weeks (D-51)
Jackson Seth Whipper (D-113)

## Labor, Commerce and Industry

**Majority Members**
William E. "Bill" Sandifer III (R-2)
  *Chair*
F. Michael "Mike" Sottile (R-112)
  *2nd Vice Chair*
Todd K. Atwater (R-87)
Nathan Ballentine (R-71)
Eric M. Bedingfield (R-28)
Heather Ammons Crawford (R-68)
P. Michael "Mike" Forrester (R-34)
Daniel P. "Dan" Hamilton (R-20)
Phyllis J. Henderson (R-21)
Ralph W. Norman, Jr. (R-48)
Mike Ryhal (R-56)
McLain R. "Mac" Toole (R-88)

**Minority Members**
Grady A. Brown (D-50)
  *1st Vice Chair*
Terry Alexander (D-59)
Carl L. Anderson (D-103)
William Knight "Bill" Bowers
  (D-122)
David James Mack III (D-109)

## Legislative Oversight

**Majority Members**
William Weston J. Newton (R-120)
  *Chair*
Nathan Ballentine (R-71)
Gary E. Clary (R-3)
Regina Raye Felder (R-26)
Kirkman Finlay III (R-75)
Phyllis J. Henderson (R-21)
Ralph W. Norman, Jr. (R-48)
Joshua Putnam (R-10)
Samuel Rivers, Jr. (R-15)
Tommy M. Stringer (R-18)
Bill Taylor (R-86)

**Minority Members**
Laurie Slade Funderburk (D-52)
  *1st Vice Chair*
William Knight "Bill" Bowers
  (D-122)
Joseph H. "Joe" Jefferson, Jr.
  (D-102)
Mia S. McLeod (D-79)
Dr. Robert L. Ridgeway III (D-64)
James Emerson Smith, Jr. (D-72)
Robert Q. Williams (D-62)

## Medical, Military, Public and Municipal Affairs

**Majority Members**
Lawrence Kit Spires (R-96)
  *2nd Vice Chair*
Christopher A. Corley (R-84)
Russell W. Fry (R-106)
Jonathon D. Hill (R-8)
Wallace H. "Jay" Jordan, Jr. (R-63)
Richard L. Yow (R-53)

**Minority Members**
Leon Howard (D-76) *Chair*
J. Anne Parks (D-12) *1st Vice Chair*
Wendell G. Gilliard (D-111)
  *3rd Vice Chair*
Justin T. Bamberg (D-90)
MaryGail K. Douglas (D-41)
Christopher R. "Chris" Hart (D-73)
Patricia M. "Pat" Henegan (D-54)

**Minority Members** *continued*
Joseph H. "Joe" Jefferson, Jr.
  (D-102)
Cezar E. McKnight (D-101)
Mia S. McLeod (D-79)
Dr. Robert L. Ridgeway III (D-64)
Leola C. Robinson-Simpson (D-25)
Mary Tinkler (D-114)

## Operations and Management of the House

**Majority Members**
Garry R. Smith (R-27) *Chair*
McLain R. "Mac" Toole (R-88)
  *2nd Vice Chair*
William E. "Bill" Crosby (R-117)
Deborah A. Long (R-45)
James H. "Jay" Lucas (R-65)
  *Ex-Officio Member*

**Minority Members**
Jerry N. Govan, Jr. (D-95)
  *1st Vice Chair*
Patsy G. Knight (D-97)
  *Secretary-Treasurer*
Justin T. Bamberg (D-90)

## Regulations and Administrative Procedures

**Majority Members**
Eric M. Bedingfield (R-28) *Chair*
William M. "Bill" Chumley (R-35)
P. Michael "Mike" Forrester (R-34)
Chip Huggins (R-85)
Ralph Shealy Kennedy, Jr. (R-39)
Christopher J. "Chris" Murphy
  (R-98)
Don L. Wells (R-81)

**Minority Members**
Carl L. Anderson (D-103)
  *1st Vice Chair*
J. Wayne George (D-57)
Wendell G. Gilliard (D-111)
Lonnie Hosey (D-91)
Leola C. Robinson-Simpson (D-25)

## Rules

**Majority Members**
Alan D. Clemmons (R-107) *Chair*
Dwight A. Loftis (R-19) *Vice Chair*
Todd K. Atwater (R-87)
Joseph S. "Joe" Daning (R-92)
William G. "Bill" Herbkersman
  (R-118)
F. Michael "Mike" Sottile (R-112)
Lawrence Kit Spires (R-96)
Anne J. Thayer (R-9)
William R. "Bill" Whitmire (R-1)

**Minority Members**
Michael A. "Mike" Anthony (D-42)
Grady A. Brown (D-50)
MaryGail K. Douglas (D-41)
Jackie E. "Coach" Hayes (D-55)
Joseph H. "Joe" Neal (D-70)

## Ways and Means

**Majority Members**
W. Brian White (R-6) *Chair*
Harry B. "Chip"
  Limehouse III (R-110)
  *1st Vice Chair*
Michael A. "Mike" Pitts (R-14)
  *2nd Vice Chair*
Kenneth A. "Kenny" Bingham
  (R-89)
Alan D. Clemmons (R-107)
J. Derham Cole, Jr. (R-32)
Shannon S. Erickson (R-124)
William G. "Bill" Herbkersman
  (R-118)
Chip Huggins (R-85)
Deborah A. Long (R-45)
Dwight A. Loftis (R-19)
Phillip D. Lowe (R-60)
James H. Merrill (R-99)
J. Gary Simrill (R-46)
G. Murrell Smith, Jr. (R-67)
Garry R. Smith (R-27)
William R. "Bill" Whitmire (R-1)

**Minority Members**
William "Bill" Clyburn (D-82)
  *3rd Vice Chair*
Michael A. "Mike" Anthony (D-42)
Jimmy C. Bales (D-80)
Gilda Cobb-Hunter (D-66)
Jackie E. "Coach" Hayes (D-55)
Lonnie Hosey (D-91)
Joseph H. "Joe" Neal (D-70)
Leonidas E. "Leon" Stavrinakis
  (D-119)

# South Dakota Legislature

Capitol Building, 500 East Capitol Avenue, Pierre, SD 57501-5070
Tel: (605) 773-3251 Fax: (605) 773-6806 Internet: http://legis.state.sd.us

## South Dakota Senate

State Capitol, 500 East Capitol Avenue, Pierre, SD 57501-5070
Tel: (605) 773-3821 Tel: (605) 773-3251 (Legislative Research Council)
President of the Senate **Matthew "Matt" Michels** (R)
  Room A215 . . . . . . . . . . . . . . . . . . . . . . . . . . . . . . . (605) 773-3212
  Education: South Dakota 1980 BSN, 1982 BS, 1985 JD
President Pro Tem **Gary L. Cammack** (R) . . . . . . . . . . . . . (605) 985-5591
Majority Leader **Corey W. Brown** (R) . . . . . . . . . . . . . . . (605) 765-9550
Assistant Majority Leader **Jim White** (R) . . . . . . . . . . . . (605) 773-3821
  Education: North Dakota 1966 BS
Majority Whip **Ried Holien** (R) . . . . . . . . . . . . . . . . . . . . (605) 773-3821
Majority Whip **Ernie Otten, Jr.** (R) . . . . . . . . . . . . . . . . . (605) 773-3821
Majority Whip **Deb Soholt** (R) . . . . . . . . . . . . . . . . . . . . (605) 322-3490
  Education: North Dakota 1978 BN; South Dakota State 1990 MN
Minority Leader **Billie H. Sutton** (D) Room 301 . . . . . . . (605) 775-2641
Assistant Minority Leader **Troy Heinert** (D) . . . . . . . . . . (605) 319-6570
Minority Whip **Scott Parsley** (D) . . . . . . . . . . . . . . . . . . (605) 256-8004
Minority Whip **Jim Peterson** (D) . . . . . . . . . . . . . . . . . . (605) 623-4573
  Education: Augustana (SD) 1965 BA
Secretary of the Senate **Kay Johnson** . . . . . . . . . . . . . . . (605) 773-3825
  E-mail: kay.johnson@state.sd.us

## Senators

**Party Affiliation Statistics: Republicans: 27, Democrats: 8**

Senator **James A. "Jim" Bradford** (D-District 27) . . . . . . . (605) 773-3821
  Counties Represented: Bennett, Haakon, Jackson,      Res: (605) 685-4241
  Pennington (part), Shannon
  Term Expires: 2017
  P.O. Box 690, Pine Ridge, SD 57770-0690
  E-mail: sen.bradford@state.sd.us
  Committees: Commerce and Energy; Health and Human Services;
  Judiciary
Senator **Corey W. Brown** (R-District 23) . . . . . . . . . . . . . (605) 765-9550
  Counties Represented: Campbell, Edmunds, Faulk,      Res: (605) 769-0540
  Hand, McPherson, Potter, Spink (part), Walworth
  Term Expires: 2017
  316 South Potter Street, Gettysburg, SD 57442
  E-mail: sen.brown@state.sd.us
  Committees: Legislative Procedure; State Affairs
Senator **Gary L. Cammack** (R-District 29) . . . . . . . . . . . . (605) 985-5591
  Counties Represented: Butte (part), Meade (part),    Fax: (605) 985-5593
  Pennington (part)
  Term Expires: 2017
  P.O. Box 100, Union Center, SD 57787-0100
  E-mail: sen.cammack@state.sd.us
  Committees: Agriculture and Natural Resources; Taxation;
  Transportation
Senator **Dr. Richard Blake Curd, MD** (R-District 12) . . . . . (605) 339-8918
  Counties Represented: Lincoln (part), Minnehaha      Tel: (605) 331-5890
  (part)
  Term Expires: 2017
  38 S. Riverview Heights, Sioux Falls, SD 57105
  E-mail: sen.curd@state.sd.us
  Committees: Commerce and Energy; Education; Health and Human
  Services
  Education: Missouri (Kansas City), MD
Senator **Bob Ewing** (R-District 31) . . . . . . . . . . . . . . . . . (605) 773-3821
  Counties Represented: Lawrence                        Tel: (605) 642-9095
  Term Expires: 2017                                    Res: (605) 722-5559
  PO Box 607, Spearfish, SD 57783                       Fax: (605) 722-7269
  E-mail: sen.ewing@state.sd.us
  Committees: Agriculture and Natural Resources; Local Government;
  Taxation
Senator **Scott Fiegen** (R-District 25) . . . . . . . . . . . . . . . . (605) 428-5504
  Counties Represented: Minnehaha (part)               Tel: (605) 782-1724
  Term Expires: 2017
  203 E. 4th Street, Dell Rapids, SD 57022
  E-mail: sen.fiegen@state.sd.us
  Committees: Local Government; Taxation

Senator **Jason Frerichs** (D-District 1) . . . . . . . . . . . . . . . (605) 773-4494
  Counties Represented: Brown (part), Day, Marshall,   Res: (605) 949-2204
  Roberts
  Term Expires: 2017
  13507 465th Avenue, Wilmot, SD 57279-8027
  E-mail: sen.frerichs@state.sd.us
  Committees: Agriculture and Natural Resources; Education; Legislative
  Procedure; Taxation
Senator **Brock L. Greenfield** (R-District 2) . . . . . . . . . . . . (605) 450-1263
  Counties Represented: Brown (part), Clark, Hamlin,   Res: (605) 532-4088
  Spink (part)
  Term Expires: 2017
  507 N. Smith Street, Clark, SD 57225-1250
  E-mail: sen.greenfield@state.sd.us
  Committees: Commerce and Energy; Education; Taxation
Senator **Jenna Haggar** (R-District 10) . . . . . . . . . . . . . . . (605) 610-9779
  Counties Represented: Minnehaha (part)
  Term Expires: 2017
  PO Box 763, Sioux Falls, SD 57101
  E-mail: sen.haggar@state.sd.us
  Committees: Commerce and Energy; Local Government; Taxation
Senator **Terri Haverly** (R-District 35) . . . . . . . . . . . . . . . (605) 390-4616
  Counties Represented: Pennington (part)
  Term Expires: 2017
  22983 Candlelight Drive, Rapid City, SD 57703
  E-mail: sen.haverly@state.sd.us
  Committees: Appropriations; Joint Appropriations
Senator **Phyllis M. Heineman** (R-District 13) . . . . . . . . . . (605) 773-3821
  Counties Represented: Lincoln (part), Minnehaha      Res: (605) 339-2167
  (part)
  Term Expires: 2017
  2005 South Phillips, Sioux Falls, SD 57105-2939
  E-mail: sen.heineman@state.sd.us
  Committees: Appropriations; Government Operations and Audit; Joint
  Appropriations; Legislative Procedure
Senator **Troy Heinert** (D-District 26) . . . . . . . . . . . . . . . . (605) 319-6570
  Counties Represented: Brule, Buffalo, Jones,         Res: (605) 856-5045
  Lyman, Mellette, Todd
  Term Expires: 2017
  P.O. Box 348, Mission, SD 57555
  E-mail: sen.heinert@state.sd.us
  Committees: Health and Human Services; Judiciary; Local Government
Senator **Ried Holien** (R-District 5) . . . . . . . . . . . . . . . . . . (605) 773-3821
  Counties Represented: Codington (part)              Res: (605) 886-4330
  Term Expires: 2017
  P.O. Box 443, Watertown, SD 57201
  E-mail: sen.holien@state.sd.us
  Committees: Legislative Procedure; Local Government; State Affairs
Senator **Bernie Hunhoff** (D-District 18) . . . . . . . . . . . . . . (605) 665-6655
  Counties Represented: Yankton                        Res: (605) 665-2975
  Term Expires: 2017
  707 Riverside Drive, Yankton, SD 57078
  E-mail: sen.hunhoff@state.sd.us
  Committees: Education; Retirement Laws; State Affairs; Transportation
Senator **Phil Jensen** (R-District 33) . . . . . . . . . . . . . . . . . (605) 773-3821
  Counties Represented: Meade (part), Pennington       Res: (605) 343-1335
  (part)                                               Fax: (605) 343-1335
  Term Expires: 2017
  10215 Pioneer Avenue, Rapid City, SD 57702
  E-mail: sen.jensen@state.sd.us
  Committees: Agriculture and Natural Resources; Health and Human
  Services; Retirement Laws
  Education: Wichita State (Attended)
Senator **Jeff Monroe** (R-District 24) . . . . . . . . . . . . . . . . (605) 224-0264
  Counties Represented: Hughes, Hyde, Stanley, Sully   Res: (605) 222-7829
  Term Expires: 2017
  127 West Dakota Avenue, Pierre, SD 57501
  E-mail: sen.monroe@state.sd.us
  Committees: Judiciary; Taxation; Transportation
  Education: Nebraska 1978 BA
Senator **David Novstrup** (R-District 3) . . . . . . . . . . . . . . . (605) 225-8541
  Counties Represented: Brown (part)
  Term Expires: 2017
  1008 S. Wells Street, Aberdeen, SD 57401-7373
  E-mail: sen.davidnovstrup@state.sd.us
  Committees: Commerce and Energy; Government Operations and
  Audit; Judiciary
Senator **Angie Buhl O'Donnell** (D-District 15) . . . . . . . . . (605) 376-2512
  Counties Represented: Minnehaha (part)
  Term Expires: 2017
  521 N. Prairie, Sioux Falls, SD 57104
  E-mail: sen.buhl@state.sd.us
  Committees: Appropriations; Joint Appropriations

Senator **Betty Olson** (R-District 28) . . . . . . . . . . . . . . . . . . (605) 855-2824
Counties Represented: Butte (part), Corson, Dewey, Harding, Perkins, Ziebach
Term Expires: 2017
11919 SD Highway 79, Prairie City, SD 57649
E-mail: sen.bettyolson@state.sd.us
Committees: Agriculture and Natural Resources; Local Government

Senator **David M. Omdahl** (R-District 11) . . . . . . . . . . . . . (605) 323-0098
Counties Represented: Minnehaha (part)
Term Expires: 2017
P.O. Box 88235, Sioux Falls, SD 57109-8235
E-mail: sen.omdahl@state.sd.us
Committees: Appropriations; Joint Appropriations
Education: South Dakota Mines 1982 BSCE

Senator **Ernie Otten, Jr.** (R-District 6) . . . . . . . . . . . . . . . (605) 773-3821
Counties Represented: Lincoln (part)          Res: (605) 368-5716
Term Expires: 2017
46787 273rd Street, Tea, SD 57064-8024
E-mail: sen.otten@state.sd.us
Committees: State Affairs; Transportation

Senator **Scott Parsley** (D-District 8) . . . . . . . . . . . . . . . . . . (605) 256-8004
Counties Represented: Lake, Miner, Moody,    Res: (605) 256-4984
Sanborn                                       Fax: (605) 256-8057
Term Expires: 2017
103 N. Liberty Avenue, Madison, SD 57042-2706
E-mail: sen.parsley@state.sd.us
Committees: Appropriations; Joint Appropriations

Senator **Deb Peters** (R-District 9) . . . . . . . . . . . . . . . . . . . . (605) 773-3821
Counties Represented: Minnehaha (part)        Res: (605) 321-4168
Term Expires: 2017
705 North Sagehorn Drive, Hartford, SD 57033-2380
E-mail: sen.peters@state.sd.us
Committees: Appropriations; Government Operations and Audit; Joint Appropriations

Senator **Jim Peterson** (D-District 4) . . . . . . . . . . . . . . . . . . (605) 623-4573
Counties Represented: Brookings (part), Codington (part), Deuel, Grant
Term Expires: 2017
16952 482nd Avenue, Revillo, SD 57259-5208
E-mail: sen.peterson@state.sd.us
Committees: Agriculture and Natural Resources; Retirement Laws; Taxation; Transportation

Senator **Bruce E. Rampelberg** (R-District 30) . . . . . . . . . . (605) 348-3322
Counties Represented: Custer, Fall River,     Res: (605) 390-2165
Pennington (part)
Term Expires: 2017
13948 Lariat Road, Rapid City, SD 57702-7315
E-mail: sen.rampelberg@state.sd.us
Committees: Agriculture and Natural Resources; Education; Health and Human Services; Retirement Laws

Senator **Arthur L. Rusch** (R-District 17) . . . . . . . . . . . . . . (605) 624-8723
Counties Represented: Clay, Turner
Term Expires: 2017
P.O. Box 312, Vermillion, SD 57069-0312
E-mail: sen.rusch@state.sd.us
Committees: Agriculture and Natural Resources; Health and Human Services; Judiciary

Senator **William J. Shorma** (R-District 16) . . . . . . . . . . . . (605) 422-3282
Counties Represented: Lincoln (part), Union
Term Expires: 2017
21 Spanish Bay, Dakota Dunes, SD 57049
E-mail: sen.shorma@state.sd.us
Committees: Commerce and Energy; Health and Human Services; Transportation

Senator **Deb Soholt** (R-District 14) . . . . . . . . . . . . . . . . . . (605) 322-3490
Counties Represented: Minnehaha (part)        Res: (605) 321-5931
Term Expires: 2017
2628 E. Regency Court, Sioux Falls, SD 57103
E-mail: sen.soholt@state.sd.us
Committees: Education; Legislative Procedure; State Affairs

Senator **Alan D. Solano** (R-District 32) . . . . . . . . . . . . . . . (605) 343-7262
Counties Represented: Pennington (part)       Res: (605) 342-8974
Term Expires: 2017
3410 Wisconsin Avenue, Rapid City, SD 57701
E-mail: sen.solano@state.sd.us
Committees: Education; State Affairs; Transportation

Senator **Billie H. Sutton** (D-District 21) . . . . . . . . . . . . . . (605) 775-2641
Counties Represented: Bon Homme (part), Charles   Res: (605) 775-2110
Mix, Gregory, Tripp
Term Expires: 2017
919 Franklin Street, Burke, SD 57523
E-mail: sen.sutton@state.sd.us
Committees: Commerce and Energy; Government Operations and Audit; Legislative Procedure; Local Government; State Affairs

Senator **Larry J. Tidemann** (R-District 7) . . . . . . . . . . . . . (605) 773-3821
Counties Represented: Brookings (part)        Res: (605) 692-1267
Term Expires: 2017
251 Indian Hills Road, Brookings, SD 57006-3650
E-mail: sen.tidemann@state.sd.us
Committees: Appropriations; Government Operations and Audit; Joint Appropriations; Retirement Laws

Senator **Craig Tieszen** (R-District 34) . . . . . . . . . . . . . . . . (605) 773-3821
Counties Represented: Pennington (part)       Res: (605) 348-4990
Term Expires: 2017
3416 Brookside Drive, Rapid City, SD 57702-8118
E-mail: sen.tieszen@state.sd.us
Committees: Health and Human Services; Judiciary; Local Government

Senator **Bill L. Van Gerpen** (R-District 19) . . . . . . . . . . . . (605) 773-3821
Counties Represented: Bon Homme (part), Douglas,  Res: (605) 589-3064
Hanson, Hutchinson, McCook
Term Expires: 2017
1304 South Laurel Street Tyndall, Tyndall, SD 57066
E-mail: sen.vangerpen@state.sd.us
Committees: Appropriations; Joint Appropriations
Education: Southwestern Baptist 1979 MDiv

Senator **Mike Vehle** (R-District 20) . . . . . . . . . . . . . . . . . . (605) 773-3821
Counties Represented: Aurora, Davison, Jerauld   Res: (605) 996-5778
Term Expires: 2017
132 North Harmon Drive, Mitchell, SD 57301
E-mail: sen.vehle@state.sd.us
Committees: Agriculture and Natural Resources; Judiciary; Transportation

Senator **Jim White** (R-District 22) . . . . . . . . . . . . . . . . . . . (605) 773-3821
Counties Represented: Beadle, Kingsbury       Res: (605) 352-8184
Term Expires: 2017
1145 Beach Circle NE, Huron, SD 57350-4700
E-mail: sen.white@state.sd.us
Committees: Appropriations; Joint Appropriations

## Senate Standing Committees

### Agriculture and Natural Resources

| Majority Members | Minority Members |
|---|---|
| Gary L. Cammack (R-29) *Chair* | Jason Frerichs (D-1) |
| Betty Olson (R-28) *Vice Chair* | Jim Peterson (D-4) |
| Bob Ewing (R-31) | |
| Phil Jensen (R-33) | |
| Bruce E. Rampelberg (R-30) | |
| Arthur L. Rusch (R-17) | |
| Mike Vehle (R-20) | |

### Appropriations

| Majority Members | Minority Members |
|---|---|
| Deb Peters (R-9) *Chair* | Angie Buhl O'Donnell (D-15) |
| Larry J. Tidemann (R-7) *Vice Chair* | Scott Parsley (D-8) |
| Terri Haverly (R-35) | |
| Phyllis M. Heineman (R-13) | |
| David M. Omdahl (R-11) | |
| Bill L. Van Gerpen (R-19) | |
| Jim White (R-22) | |

### Commerce and Energy

| Majority Members | Minority Members |
|---|---|
| Dr. Richard Blake Curd (R-12) *Chair* | James A. "Jim" Bradford (D-27) |
| Brock L. Greenfield (R-2) *Vice Chair* | Billie H. Sutton (D-21) |
| Jenna Haggar (R-10) | |
| David Novstrup (R-3) | |
| William J. Shorma (R-16) | |

### Education

| Majority Members | Minority Members |
|---|---|
| Deb Soholt (R-14) *Chair* | Jason Frerichs (D-1) |
| Alan D. Solano (R-32) *Vice Chair* | Bernie Hunhoff (D-18) |
| Dr. Richard Blake Curd (R-12) | |
| Brock L. Greenfield (R-2) | |
| Bruce E. Rampelberg (R-30) | |

## Government Operations and Audit

| Majority Members | Minority Members |
|---|---|
| Larry J. Tidemann (R-7) *Chair* | Billie H. Sutton (D-21) |
| Phyllis M. Heineman (R-13) *Vice Chair* | |
| David Novstrup (R-3) | |
| Deb Peters (R-9) | |

## Health and Human Services

| Majority Members | Minority Members |
|---|---|
| Bruce E. Rampelberg (R-30) *Chair* | James A. "Jim" Bradford (D-27) |
| Craig Tieszen (R-34) *Vice Chair* | Troy Heinert (D-26) |
| Dr. Richard Blake Curd (R-12) | |
| Phil Jensen (R-33) | |
| Arthur L. Rusch (R-17) | |
| William J. Shorma (R-16) | |

## Judiciary

| Majority Members | Minority Members |
|---|---|
| Craig Tieszen (R-34) *Chair* | James A. "Jim" Bradford (D-27) |
| David Novstrup (R-3) *Vice Chair* | Troy Heinert (D-26) |
| Jeff Monroe (R-24) | |
| Arthur L. Rusch (R-17) | |
| Mike Vehle (R-20) | |

## Legislative Procedure

| Majority Members | Minority Members |
|---|---|
| Corey W. Brown (R-23) *Chair* | Jason Frerichs (D-1) |
| Phyllis M. Heineman (R-13) | Billie H. Sutton (D-21) |
| Ried Holien (R-5) | |
| Deb Soholt (R-14) | |

## Local Government

| Majority Members | Minority Members |
|---|---|
| Bob Ewing (R-31) *Chair* | Troy Heinert (D-26) |
| Ried Holien (R-5) *Vice Chair* | Billie H. Sutton (D-21) |
| Scott Fiegen (R-25) | |
| Jenna Haggar (R-10) | |
| Betty Olson (R-28) | |
| Craig Tieszen (R-34) | |

## Retirement Laws

| Majority Members | Minority Members |
|---|---|
| Bruce E. Rampelberg (R-30) *Chair* | Bernie Hunhoff (D-18) |
| Phil Jensen (R-33) *Vice Chair* | Jim Peterson (D-4) |
| Larry J. Tidemann (R-7) | |

## State Affairs

| Majority Members | Minority Members |
|---|---|
| Corey W. Brown (R-23) *Vice Chair* | Bernie Hunhoff (D-18) |
| Ried Holien (R-5) | Billie H. Sutton (D-21) |
| Ernie Otten, Jr. (R-6) | |
| Deb Soholt (R-14) | |
| Alan D. Solano (R-32) | |

## Taxation

| Majority Members | Minority Members |
|---|---|
| Jeff Monroe (R-24) *Chair* | Jason Frerichs (D-1) |
| Brock L. Greenfield (R-2) *Vice Chair* | Jim Peterson (D-4) |
| Gary L. Cammack (R-29) | |
| Bob Ewing (R-31) | |
| Scott Fiegen (R-25) | |
| Jenna Haggar (R-10) | |

## Transportation

| Majority Members | Minority Members |
|---|---|
| Mike Vehle (R-20) *Chair* | Bernie Hunhoff (D-18) |
| Jeff Monroe (R-24) *Vice Chair* | Jim Peterson (D-4) |
| Gary L. Cammack (R-29) | |
| Ernie Otten, Jr. (R-6) | |
| William J. Shorma (R-16) | |
| Alan D. Solano (R-32) | |

# South Dakota House of Representatives

State Capitol, 500 East Capitol Avenue, Pierre, SD 57501-5070
Tel: (605) 773-3851

Speaker of the House **Dean Wink** (R) . . . . . . . . . . . . . . . . . (605) 985-5240
Speaker Pro Tem **G. Mark Mickelson, CPA** (R) . . . . . . . . (605) 977-4873
  Education: South Dakota 1988 BSBA; Harvard 1993 JD
Majority Leader **Brian G. Gosch** (R) . . . . . . . . . . . . . . . (605) 719-3365
  Education: South Dakota 1993, 1996 JD
Assistant Majority Leader **Steven "Steve" Westra** (R) . . . (605) 336-2111
  Education: South Dakota State BSBA
Majority Whip **Jim Bolin** (R) . . . . . . . . . . . . . . . . . . . . . (605) 773-3851
Majority Whip **Kris Langer** (R) . . . . . . . . . . . . . . . . . . . . (605) 261-3620
Majority Whip **Mike Stevens** (R) . . . . . . . . . . . . . . . . . . (605) 665-5550
  Education: Bethel Col (MN) BA; South Dakota JD
Majority Whip **Don K. Haggar** (R) . . . . . . . . . . . . . . . . . (605) 360-8130
Minority Leader **Spencer Hawley** (D) . . . . . . . . . . . . . . . (605) 692-6223
Assistant Minority Leader **Julie A. Bartling** (D) . . . . . . . . (605) 775-2741
Minority Whip **Paula Hawks** (D) . . . . . . . . . . . . . . . . . . (605) 254-2440
  Education: South Dakota State 1998 BS; South Dakota 2008 MS
Minority Whip **Dean Schrempp** (D) . . . . . . . . . . . . . . . . (605) 365-7367
Chief Clerk of the House **Karen Gerdes** . . . . . . . . . . . . . . (605) 773-3251

## Representatives

**Party Affiliation Statistics:** Republicans: 58, Democrats: 12

Representative
**David L. Anderson, CPCU** (R-District 16) . . . . . . . . . . . (605) 764-5781
  Counties Represented: Lincoln (part), Union    Res: (605) 957-6510
  Term Expires: 2017    Fax: (605) 764-5447
  29177 477th Avenue, Hudson, SD 57304
  E-mail: rep.anderson@state.sd.us
  Committees: Appropriations; Joint Appropriations

Representative **Julie A. Bartling** (D-District 21) . . . . . . . . (605) 775-2741
  Counties Represented: Bon Homme (part), Charles Mix, Gregory, Tripp
  Term Expires: 2017
  28921 US Highway 18, Gregory, SD 57533
  E-mail: rep.bartling@state.sd.us
  Committees: Government Operations and Audit; State Affairs

Representative **Arch Beal** (R-District 12) . . . . . . . . . . . . . (605) 336-2988
  Counties Represented: Lincoln (part), Minnehaha  Res: (605) 336-3034
  (part)    Fax: (605) 336-6186
  Term Expires: 2017
  4815 N. Northview Avenue, Sioux Falls, SD 57107
  E-mail: rep.beal@state.sd.us
  Committees: Commerce and Energy; Taxation

Representative **Jim Bolin** (R-District 16) . . . . . . . . . . . . . (605) 773-3851
  Counties Represented: Lincoln (part), Union  Res: (605) 987-2630
  Term Expires: 2017
  403 West 11th Street, Canton, SD 57013-2418
  E-mail: rep.bolin@state.sd.us
  Committees: Retirement Laws; State Affairs; Transportation

Representative **Shawn Bordeaux** (D-District 26A) . . . . . . . (605) 856-8241
  Counties Represented: Mellette, Todd    Fax: (605) 856-4135
  Term Expires: 2017
  P.O. Box 283, Mission, SD 57555
  E-mail: rep.bordeaux@state.sd.us
  Committees: Appropriations; Joint Appropriations

Representative **Thomas J. Brunner** (R-District 29) . . . . . . . (605) 257-2336
  Counties Represented: Butte (part), Meade (part), Pennington (part)
  Term Expires: 2017
  E-mail: rep.brunner@state.sd.us
  Committees: Agriculture and Natural Resources

Representative
**Blaine B. "Chip" Campbell** (R-District 35) . . . . . . . . . . (605) 773-3851
  Counties Represented: Pennington (part)  Res: (605) 393-1645
  Term Expires: 2017    Tel: (605) 484-4848
  3480 Colvin Street, Rapid City, SD 57703
  E-mail: rep.campbell@state.sd.us
  Committees: Education; Health and Human Services

Representative **Kristin A. Conzet** (R-District 32) . . . . . . . . (605) 342-6658
  Counties Represented: Pennington (part)
  Term Expires: 2017
  273 Minnesota Street, Rapid City, SD 57701
  E-mail: rep.conzet@state.sd.us
  Committees: Health and Human Services; Local Government

Representative **Scott W. Craig** (R-District 33) . . . . . . (605) 877-1375 (Bus)
Counties Represented: Meade (part), Pennington    Res: (605) 342-0999
(part)
Term Expires: 2017
8556 Heather Drive, Rapid City, SD 57702-7710
E-mail: rep.craig@state.sd.us
Committees: Agriculture and Natural Resources; Local Government
Education: Azusa Pacific BA; Fuller Sem MA

Representative **Justin R. Cronin** (R-District 23) . . . . . . . . (605) 773-3851
Counties Represented: Campbell, Edmunds, Faulk,    Res: (605) 765-9325
Hand, McPherson, Potter, Spink (part), Walworth
Term Expires: 2017
PO Box 42, Gettysburg, SD 57442-0042
E-mail: rep.cronin@state.sd.us
Committees: Appropriations; Government Operations and Audit; Joint
Appropriations

Representative **Fred Deutsch** (R-District 4) . . . . . . . . . . . . (605) 886-8650
Counties Represented: Brookings (part), Codington    Res: (605) 882-3323
(part), Deuel, Grant
Term Expires: 2017
E-mail: rep.deutsch@state.sd.us
Committees: Commerce and Energy; Education

Representative **Lynne DiSanto** (R-District 35) . . . . . . . . . . (605) 389-0111
Counties Represented: Pennington (part)
Term Expires: 2017
4973 Hansen Lane, Rapid City, SD 57703
E-mail: rep.disanto@state.sd.us
Committees: Health and Human Services; Judiciary

Representative **Dan Dryden** (R-District 34) . . . . . . . . . . . . (605) 773-3851
Counties Represented: Pennington (part)    Res: (605) 721-2902
Term Expires: 2017    Fax: (605) 721-2902
2902 Tomahawk Drive, Rapid City, SD 57702-4250
E-mail: rep.dryden@state.sd.us
Committees: Appropriations; Government Operations and Audit; Joint
Appropriations

Representative **Mary Duvall** (R-District 24) . . . . . . . . . . . . (605) 224-4070
Counties Represented: Hughes, Hyde, Stanley, Sully
Term Expires: 2017
453, Pierre, SD 57501
E-mail: rep.duvall@state.sd.us
Committees: Taxation; Transportation
Education: South Dakota State 1985 BS

Representative **Dennis Feickert** (D-District 1) . . . . . . . . . . (605) 225-5844
Counties Represented: Brown (part), Day, Marshall,    Tel: (605) 773-3851
Roberts
Term Expires: 2017
38485 129th Street, Aberdeen, SD 57401-8386
E-mail: rep.feickert@state.sd.us
Committees: Agriculture and Natural Resources; Transportation

Representative **Peggy Gibson** (D-District 22) . . . . . . . . . . . (605) 352-9862
Counties Represented: Beadle, Kingsbury    Fax: (605) 353-9934
Term Expires: 2017
1010 Valley View Court, Huron, SD 57350
E-mail: rep.gibson@state.sd.us
Committees: Education; Judiciary

Representative **Brian G. Gosch** (R-District 32) . . . . . . . . . (605) 719-3365
Counties Represented: Pennington (part)    Fax: (605) 341-2439
Term Expires: 2017
312 Alta Vista Drive, Rapid City, SD 57701-2337
E-mail: rep.gosch@state.sd.us
Committees: Legislative Procedure; State Affairs
Affiliation: Attorney, South Dakota Advocacy Services
221 South Central Avenue, Pierre, SD 57501-2453

Representative **Lana Greenfield** (R-District 2) . . . . . . . . . . (605) 635-6996
Counties Represented: Brown (part), Clark, Hamlin,    Res: (605) 635-6932
Spink (part)
Term Expires: 2017
E-mail: lana.greenfield@gmail.com
Committees: Health and Human Services; Local Government

Representative **Don K. Haggar** (R-District 10) . . . . . . . . . . (605) 360-8130
Counties Represented: Minnehaha (part)
Term Expires: 2017
P.O. Box 1532, Sioux Falls, SD 57101
E-mail: rep.donhaggar@state.sd.us
Committees: State Affairs; Taxation

Representative **Michele Harrison** (R-District 23) . . . . . . . . (605) 845-5202
Counties Represented: Campbell, Edmunds, Faulk,    Res: (605) 850-9989
Hand, McPherson, Potter, Spink (part), Walworth
Term Expires: 2017
P.O. Box 303, Mobridge, SD 57601
E-mail: rep.harrison@state.sd.us
Committees: Agriculture and Natural Resources; Commerce and
Energy

Representative **Steven Haugaard** (R-District 10) . . . . . . . . (605) 334-1121
Counties Represented: Minnehaha (part)    Res: (605) 332-1171
Term Expires: 2017
47629 258th Street, Sioux Falls, SD 57104
E-mail: rep.haugaard@state.sd.us
Committees: Health and Human Services; Judiciary

Representative **Paula Hawks** (D-District 9) . . . . . . . . . . . . (605) 254-2440
Counties Represented: Minnehaha (part)
Term Expires: 2017
405 South Tessa Ave, Hartford, SD 57033
E-mail: rep.hawks@state.sd.us
Committees: Education; Local Government

Representative **Spencer Hawley** (D-District 7) . . . . . . . . . (605) 692-6223
Counties Represented: Brookings (part)    Res: (605) 692-9716
Term Expires: 2017    Fax: (605) 692-8321
1215 West 8th Street South, Brookings, SD 57006
E-mail: rep.hawley@state.sd.us
Committees: Commerce and Energy; Legislative Procedure; State
Affairs

Representative
**Dr. Leslie J. Heinemann, DDS** (R-District 8) . . . . . . . . (605) 997-3732
Counties Represented: Lake, Miner, Moody,    Fax: (605) 997-3799
Sanborn
Term Expires: 2017
47962 228th St., Flandreau, SD 57028-6701
E-mail: rep.heinemann@state.sd.us
Committees: Health and Human Services; Local Government
Education: Augustana (SD) BS; Loyola U (Chicago) 1981 MD

Representative **Thomas "Tom" Holmes** (R-District 14) . . . (605) 773-3851
Counties Represented: Minnehaha (part)
Term Expires: 2017
4709 Shields Avenue, Sioux Falls, SD 57103
E-mail: rep.holmes@state.sd.us
Committees: Education; Health and Human Services

Representative **Jean M. Hunhoff** (R-District 18) . . . . . . . . (605) 668-8312
Counties Represented: Yankton    Res: (605) 665-1463
Term Expires: 2017
2511 Mulligan Drive, Yankton, SD 57078
E-mail: rep.jeanhunhoff@state.sd.us
Committees: Appropriations; Government Operations and Audit; Joint
Appropriations

Representative **Roger W. Hunt** (R-District 25) . . . . . . . . . . (605) 582-2580
Counties Represented: Minnehaha (part)    Res: (605) 582-3865
Term Expires: 2017    Fax: (605) 582-2481
P.O. Box 827, Brandon, SD 57005
E-mail: rep.hunt@state.sd.us
Committees: Education; Government Operations and Audit; Judiciary;
Legislative Procedure

Representative **Alex Jensen** (R-District 12) . . . . . . . . . . . . (605) 212-4407
Counties Represented: Lincoln (part), Minnehaha (part)
Term Expires: 2017
5915 South Remington Place, Sioux Falls, SD 57108
E-mail: rep.jensen@state.sd.us
Committees: Appropriations; Joint Appropriations

Representative **Timothy R. "Tim" Johns** (R-District 31) . . (605) 717-2889
Counties Represented: Lawrence    Fax: (605) 717-0590
Term Expires: 2017
203 West Main Street, Lead, SD 57754
E-mail: rep.johns@state.sd.us
Committees: Education; Judiciary
Education: Northern State 1970 BA; South Dakota 1974 JD

Representative **Daniel M. "Dan" Kaiser** (R-District 3) . . . . (605) 228-4988
Counties Represented: Brown (part)
Term Expires: 2017
1415 Nicklaus Drive, Aberdeen, SD 57401-8822
E-mail: rep.kaiser@state.sd.us
Committees: Education; Transportation

Representative **Kevin Killer** (D-District 27) . . . . . . . . . . . . (605) 454-8105
Counties Represented: Bennett, Haakon, Jackson, Pennington (part),
Shannon
Term Expires: 2017
PO Box 322, Pine Ridge, SD 57770
E-mail: rep.killer@state.sd.us
Committees: Judiciary; Taxation

Representative **Patrick A. Kirschman** (D-District 15) . . . . . (605) 366-4798
Counties Represented: Minnehaha (part)
Term Expires: 2017
901 North Duluth Avenue #1, Sioux Falls, SD 57104
E-mail: rep.kirschman@state.sd.us
Committees: Commerce and Energy; Retirement Laws; Taxation

*(continued on next page)*

**Representatives** *continued*

Representative **Joshua M. Klumb** (R-District 20) . . . . . . . (605) 770-9708
Counties Represented: Aurora, Davison, Jerauld    Fax: (605) 996-1351
Term Expires: 2017
26296 401st Avenue, Mount Vernon, SD 57363
E-mail: rep.klumb@state.sd.us
Committees: Agriculture and Natural Resources; Education

Representative **Kris Langer** (R-District 25) . . . . . . . . . . . . (605) 261-3620
Counties Represented: Minnehaha (part)
Term Expires: 2017
320 West 9th Street, Dell Rapids, SD 57022-1582
E-mail: rep.langer@state.sd.us
Committees: Judiciary; State Affairs

Representative **Isaac Latterell** (R-District 6) . . . . . . . . . . . (605) 368-1002
Counties Represented: Lincoln (part)
Term Expires: 2017
P.O. Box 801, Tea, SD 57064
E-mail: rep.latterell@state.sd.us
Committees: Judiciary; Taxation
Education: Northern State BS

Representative **J. Sam Marty** (R-District 28B) . . . . . . . . . . (605) 866-4477
Counties Represented: Butte (part), Harding, Perkins
Term Expires: 2017
16692 Antelope Road, Prairie City, SD 57649
E-mail: rep.marty@state.sd.us
Committees: Agriculture and Natural Resources; Local Government

Representative **Elizabeth May** (R-District 27) . . . . . . . . . . (605) 455-2824
Counties Represented: Bennett, Haakon, Jackson,    Res: (605) 455-2588
Pennington (part), Shannon
Term Expires: 2017
20261 BIA 2, Kyle, SD 57752-7400
E-mail: rep.may@state.sd.us
Committees: Education; Taxation

Representative **Steven D. McCleerey** (D-District 1) . . . . . . (605) 698-3749
Counties Represented: Brown (part), Day, Marshall,    Res: (605) 698-7478
Roberts
Term Expires: 2017
45708 116th Street, Sisseton, SD 57262-7019
E-mail: rep.mccleerey@state.sd.us
Committees: Education; Retirement Laws

Representative **G. Mark Mickelson, CPA** (R-District 13) . . (605) 977-4873
Counties Represented: Lincoln (part), Minnehaha    Res: (605) 371-3365
(part)
Term Expires: 2017
2901 S. 5th Avenue, Sioux Falls, SD 57105
E-mail: rep.mickelson@state.sd.us
Committees: Judiciary; Legislative Procedure; State Affairs

Representative **Scott Munsterman** (R-District 7) . . . . . . . (877) 788-2883
Counties Represented: Brookings (part)    Res: (605) 697-5636
Term Expires: 2017
1133 West 8th Street, South, Brookings, SD 57006
E-mail: rep.munsterman@state.sd.us
Committees: Health and Human Services; State Affairs

Representative **Al Novstrup** (R-District 3) . . . . . . . . . . . . (605) 360-9711
Counties Represented: Brown (part)    Res: (605) 226-2505
Term Expires: 2017
1705 Northview Lane, Aberdeen, SD 57401-2268
E-mail: rep.novstrup@state.sd.us
Committees: Commerce and Energy; Taxation

Representative **Herman Otten** (R-District 6) . . . . . . . . . . . (605) 773-3251
Counties Represented: Lincoln (part)
Term Expires: 2017
P.O. Box 326, Tea, SD 57064-0325
E-mail: rep.otten@state.sd.us
Committees: Agriculture and Natural Resources; Local Government

Representative **Jeff Partridge** (R-District 34) . . . . . . . . . . (605) 301-4803
Counties Represented: Pennington (part)    Res: (605) 718-1912
Term Expires: 2017
7174 Prestwick Road, Rapid City, SD 57702
E-mail: rep.partridge@state.sd.us
Committees: Appropriations; Joint Appropriations

Representative **Kent S. Peterson** (R-District 19) . . . . . . . . (605) 425-3299
Counties Represented: Bon Homme (part), Douglas, Hanson,
Hutchinson, McCook
Term Expires: 2017
440 East Washington Avenue, Salem, SD 57058
Committees: Agriculture and Natural Resources; Judiciary

Representative **Lee Qualm** (R-District 21) . . . . . . . . . . . . (605) 337-3682
Counties Represented: Bon Homme (part), Charles Mix, Gregory, Tripp
Term Expires: 2017
27507 John Qualm Road, Platte, SD 57369
E-mail: rep.qualm@state.sd.us
Committees: Agriculture and Natural Resources; Local Government

Representative **Nancy Rasmussen** (R-District 17) . . . . . . . (605) 238-5221
Counties Represented: Clay, Turner    Res: (605) 238-5321
Term Expires: 2017
28639 458th Avenue, Hurley, SD 28639-6410
E-mail: rep.rasmussen@state.sd.us
Committees: Taxation; Transportation

Representative **Raymond "Ray" Ring** (D-District 17) . . . . (605) 675-9379
Counties Represented: Clay, Turner
Term Expires: 2017
607 Sterling Street, Vermillion, SD 57069-3453
E-mail: rep.ring@state.sd.us
Committees: Appropriations; Joint Appropriations
Education: St Benedict 1967 BS; Kansas 1973 MA, 1980 PhD

Representative **Fred W. Romkema** (R-District 31) . . . . . . . (605) 722-1432
Counties Represented: Lawrence
Term Expires: 2017
240 Fairway Drive, Spearfish, SD 57783
E-mail: rep.romkema@state.sd.us
Committees: Appropriations; Joint Appropriations

Representative **Tim G. Rounds** (R-District 25) . . . . . . . . . (605) 222-0695
Counties Represented: Minnehaha (part)    Res: (605) 224-6588
Term Expires: 2017
513 North Van Buren, Pierre, SD 57501
E-mail: rep.rounds@state.sd.us
Committees: Commerce and Energy; Retirement Laws; Transportation

Representative **Tona Rozum** (R-District 20) . . . . . . . . . . . (605) 996-8440
Counties Represented: Aurora, Davison, Jerauld    Res: (605) 996-2191
Term Expires: 2017    Fax: (605) 996-9699
87 South Harmon Drive, Mitchell, SD 57301
E-mail: rep.rozum@state.sd.us
Committees: Local Government; Taxation

Representative **Lance S. Russell** (R-District 30) . . . . . . . . . (605) 745-6871
Counties Represented: Custer, Fall River, Pennington (part)
Term Expires: 2017
1938 Lincoln Avenue, Hot Springs, SD 57747
E-mail: rep.russell@state.sd.us
Committees: Judiciary; Taxation

Representative **James G. Schaefer** (R-District 26B) . . . . . . (605) 869-2357
Counties Represented: Brule, Buffalo, Jones, Lyman    Fax: (605) 869-2312
Term Expires: 2017
23026 SD Highway 273, Kennebec, SD 57544
E-mail: rep.schaefer@state.sd.us
Committees: Agriculture and Natural Resources; Transportation

Representative **Lee Schoenbeck** (R-District 5) . . . . . . . . . . (605) 886-0010
Counties Represented: Codington (part)    Fax: (605) 886-0011
Term Expires: 2017
P.O. Box 1325, Watertown, SD 57201
E-mail: rep.schoenbeck@state.sd.us
Committees: Commerce and Energy; Legislative Procedure; Retirement
Laws; Transportation

Representative **Kyle Schoenfish** (R-District 19) . . . . . . . . . (605) 928-7241
Counties Represented: Bon Homme (part), Douglas,    Res: (605) 660-6468
Hanson, Hutchinson, McCook    Fax: (605) 928-1441
Term Expires: 2017
42472 Maxwell Road, Scotland, SD 57059
E-mail: rep.schoenfish@state.sd.us
Committees: Agriculture and Natural Resources; Local Government

Representative **Dean Schrempp** (D-District 28A) . . . . . . . . (605) 365-7367
Counties Represented: Corson, Dewey, Ziebach    Res: (605) 964-6541
Term Expires: 2017
E-mail: rep.schrempp@state.sd.us
Committees: Agriculture and Natural Resources; Transportation

Representative **Jacqueline Sly** (R-District 33) . . . . . . . . . . (605) 343-4956
Counties Represented: Meade (part), Pennington (part)
Term Expires: 2017
22560 Potter Road, Rapid City, SD 57702
E-mail: rep.sly@state.sd.us
Committees: Education; Health and Human Services

Representative **Karen Soli** (D-District 15) . . . . . . . . . . . . . (605) 338-5934
Counties Represented: Minnehaha (part)
Term Expires: 2017
810 West 6th Street, Sioux Falls, SD 57104-2904
E-mail: rep.soli@state.sd.us
Committees: Health and Human Services; Local Government
Education: St Olaf 1970 BA; Lutheran Sem (Canada) 1978 MDiv

LEGISLATIVE BRANCH

Representative **Roger D. Solum** (R-District 5) . . . . . . . . . . (605) 882-5284
  Counties Represented: Codington (part)   Res: (605) 882-7056
  Term Expires: 2017
  1333 Mayfair Drive, Watertown, SD 57201
  E-mail: rep.solum@state.sd.us
  Committees: State Affairs; Taxation
Representative **Jim Stalzer** (R-District 11) . . . . . . . . . . . . (605) 838-0354
  Counties Represented: Minnehaha (part)
  Term Expires: 2017
  5909 W. Bristol Drive, Sioux Falls, SD 57106-0660
  E-mail: rep.stalzer@state.sd.us
  Committees: Commerce and Energy; Transportation
  Education: National American U 1978 BSBA
Representative **Wayne H. Steinhauer** (R-District 9) . . . . . . (605) 773-3851
  Counties Represented: Anderson (part)
  Term Expires: 2017
  26581 East Shore Place, Hartford, SD 57033
  E-mail: repsteinhauer@gmail.com
  Committees: Commerce and Energy; Transportation
Representative **Mike Stevens** (R-District 18) . . . . . . . . . . . (605) 665-5550
  Counties Represented: Yankton   Res: (605) 661-0057
  Term Expires: 2017
  214 Marina Dell, Yankton, SD 57078
  E-mail: rep.stevens@state.sd.us
  Committees: Judiciary; State Affairs
Representative **Burt E. Tulson** (R-District 2) . . . . . . . . . . . (605) 785-3480
  Counties Represented: Brown (part), Clark, Hamlin, Spink (part)
  Term Expires: 2017
  44975 South Dakota Highway 28, Lake Norden, SD 57248
  E-mail: rep.tulson@state.sd.us
  Committees: Education; Local Government
Representative **Mike Verchio** (R-District 30) . . . . . . . . . . . (605) 574-2466
  Counties Represented: Custer, Fall River, Pennington (part)
  Term Expires: 2017
  289 Rainbow Ridge Court, Hill City, SD 57745
  E-mail: rep.verchio@state.sd.us
  Committees: State Affairs; Transportation
Representative **Dick Werner** (R-District 22) . . . . . . . . . . . . (605) 350-1371
  Counties Represented: Beadle, Kingsbury   Tel: (605) 353-0957
  Term Expires: 2017
  E-mail: rep.werner@state.sd.us
  Committees: Agriculture and Natural Resources; Transportation
  Education: South Dakota
Representative **Steven "Steve" Westra** (R-District 13) . . . (605) 336-2111
  Counties Represented: Lincoln (part), Minnehaha   Res: (605) 271-1623
  (part)
  Term Expires: 2017
  508 East Meadowlark Trail, Sioux Falls, SD 57108-2885
  E-mail: rep.westra@state.sd.us
  Committees: Judiciary; Legislative Procedure; State Affairs
Representative **John Wiik** (R-District 4) . . . . . . . . . . . . . . . (605) 862-8215
  Counties Represented: Brookings (part), Codington   Res: (605) 880-1440
  (part), Deuel, Grant   Fax: (605) 862-8909
  Term Expires: 2017
  P.O. Box 95, Big Stone City, SD 57216
  E-mail: rep.wiik@state.sd.us
  Committees: Commerce and Energy; Taxation
Representative **Mark K. Willadsen** (R-District 11) . . . . . . . . (605) 332-2130
  Counties Represented: Minnehaha (part)   Res: (605) 361-6104
  Term Expires: 2017
  7712 West Benelli Circle, Sioux Falls, SD 57106-7790
  E-mail: rep.willadsen@state.sd.us
  Committees: Commerce and Energy; Taxation
Representative **Dean Wink** (R-District 29) . . . . . . . . . . . . . (605) 985-5240
  Counties Represented: Butte (part), Meade (part),   Fax: (605) 985-5458
  Pennington (part)
  Term Expires: 2017
  P.O. Box 137, Howes, SD 57748-0137
  E-mail: rep.wink@state.sd.us
  Committees: Legislative Procedure; State Affairs
Representative **Mathew Wollmann** (R-District 8) . . . . . . . . (605) 480-3038
  Counties Represented: Lake, Miner, Moody, Sanborn
  Term Expires: 2017
  210 West Center Street, Apt. 302, Madison, SD 57042
  E-mail: rep.wollmann@state.sd.us
  Committees: Commerce and Energy; Education; Health and Human
  Services
Representative **Larry Zikmund** (R-District 14) . . . . . . . . . . (605) 373-0975
  Counties Represented: Minnehaha (part)
  Term Expires: 2017
  2405 East 52nd Street, Sioux Falls, SD 57103
  E-mail: rep.zikmund@state.sd.us
  Committees: Commerce and Energy; Education

# House Standing Committees
## Agriculture and Natural Resources

**Majority Members**
Lee Qualm (R-21) *Chair*
Joshua M. Klumb (R-20)
  *Vice Chair*
Thomas J. Brunner (R-29)
Scott W. Craig (R-33)
Michele Harrison (R-23)
J. Sam Marty (R-28B)
Herman Otten (R-6)
Kent S. Peterson (R-19)
James G. Schaefer (R-26B)
Kyle Schoenfish (R-19)
Dick Werner (R-22)

**Minority Members**
Dennis Feickert (D-1)
Dean Schrempp (D-28A)

## Appropriations

**Majority Members**
Justin R. Cronin (R-23) *Chair*
Dan Dryden (R-34) *Vice Chair*
David L. Anderson (R-16)
Jean M. Hunhoff (R-18)
Alex Jensen (R-12)
Jeff Partridge (R-34)
Fred W. Romkema (R-31)

**Minority Members**
Shawn Bordeaux (D-26A)
Raymond "Ray" Ring (D-17)

## Commerce and Energy

**Majority Members**
Tim G. Rounds (R-25) *Chair*
Lee Schoenbeck (R-5) *Vice Chair*
Arch Beal (R-12)
Fred Deutsch (R-4)
Michele Harrison (R-23)
Al Novstrup (R-3)
Jim Stalzer (R-11)
Wayne H. Steinhauer (R-9)
John Wiik (R-4)
Mark K. Willadsen (R-11)
Mathew Wollmann (R-8)
Larry Zikmund (R-14)

**Minority Members**
Spencer Hawley (D-7)
Patrick A. Kirschman (D-15)

## Education

**Majority Members**
Jacqueline Sly (R-33) *Chair*
Timothy R. "Tim" Johns (R-31)
  *Vice Chair*
Blaine B. "Chip" Campbell (R-35)
Fred Deutsch (R-4)
Thomas "Tom" Holmes (R-14)
Roger W. Hunt (R-25)
Daniel M. "Dan" Kaiser (R-3)
Joshua M. Klumb (R-20)
Elizabeth May (R-27)
Burt E. Tulson (R-2)
Mathew Wollmann (R-8)
Larry Zikmund (R-14)

**Minority Members**
Peggy Gibson (D-22)
Paula Hawks (D-9)
Steven D. McCleerey (D-1)

## Government Operations and Audit

**Majority Members**
Dan Dryden (R-34) *Chair*
Jean M. Hunhoff (R-18) *Vice Chair*
Justin R. Cronin (R-23)
Roger W. Hunt (R-25)

**Minority Members**
Julie A. Bartling (D-21)

## Health and Human Services

**Majority Members**
Scott Munsterman (R-7) *Chair*
Blaine B. "Chip" Campbell (R-35)
Kristin A. Conzet (R-32)
Lynne DiSanto (R-35)
Lana Greenfield (R-2)
Steven Haugaard (R-10)
Dr. Leslie J. Heinemann (R-8)
Thomas "Tom" Holmes (R-14)
Jacqueline Sly (R-33)
Mathew Wollmann (R-8)

**Minority Members**
Karen Soli (D-15)

**LEGISLATIVE BRANCH**

## Judiciary

**Majority Members**
G. Mark Mickelson (R-13) *Chair*
Mike Stevens (R-18) *Vice Chair*
Lynne DiSanto (R-35)
Steven Haugaard (R-10)
Roger W. Hunt (R-25)
Timothy R. "Tim" Johns (R-31)
Kris Langer (R-25)
Isaac Latterell (R-6)
Kent S. Peterson (R-19)
Lance S. Russell (R-30)
Steven "Steve" Westra (R-13)

**Minority Members**
Peggy Gibson (D-22)
Kevin Killer (D-27)

## Legislative Procedure

**Majority Members**
Dean Wink (R-29) *Chair*
G. Mark Mickelson (R-13)
  *Vice Chair*
Brian G. Gosch (R-32)
Roger W. Hunt (R-25)
Lee Schoenbeck (R-5)
Steven "Steve" Westra (R-13)

**Minority Members**
Spencer Hawley (D-7)

## Local Government

**Majority Members**
Kristin A. Conzet (R-32) *Chair*
Herman Otten (R-6) *Vice Chair*
Scott W. Craig (R-33)
Lana Greenfield (R-2)
Dr. Leslie J. Heinemann (R-8)
J. Sam Marty (R-28B)
Lee Qualm (R-21)
Tona Rozum (R-20)
Kyle Schoenfish (R-19)
Burt E. Tulson (R-2)

**Minority Members**
Paula Hawks (D-9)
Karen Soli (D-15)

## Retirement Laws

**Majority Members**
Jim Bolin (R-16) *Chair*
Tim G. Rounds (R-25) *Vice Chair*
Lee Schoenbeck (R-5)

**Minority Members**
Patrick A. Kirschman (D-15)
Steven D. McCleerey (D-1)

## State Affairs

**Majority Members**
Brian G. Gosch (R-32) *Chair*
Steven "Steve" Westra (R-13)
  *Vice Chair*
Jim Bolin (R-16)
Don K. Haggar (R-10)
Kris Langer (R-25)
G. Mark Mickelson (R-13)
Scott Munsterman (R-7)
Roger D. Solum (R-5)
Mike Stevens (R-18)
Mike Verchio (R-30)
Dean Wink (R-29)

**Minority Members**
Julie A. Bartling (D-21)
Spencer Hawley (D-7)

## Taxation

**Majority Members**
Roger D. Solum (R-5) *Chair*
Tona Rozum (R-20) *Vice Chair*
Arch Beal (R-12)
Mary Duvall (R-24)
Don K. Haggar (R-10)
Isaac Latterell (R-6)
Elizabeth May (R-27)
Al Novstrup (R-3)
Nancy Rasmussen (R-17)
Lance S. Russell (R-30)
John Wiik (R-4)
Mark K. Willadsen (R-11)

**Minority Members**
Kevin Killer (D-27)
Patrick A. Kirschman (D-15)

## Transportation

**Majority Members**
Mike Verchio (R-30) *Chair*
Mary Duvall (R-24) *Vice Chair*
Jim Bolin (R-16)
Daniel M. "Dan" Kaiser (R-3)
Nancy Rasmussen (R-17)
Tim G. Rounds (R-25)
James G. Schaefer (R-26B)
Lee Schoenbeck (R-5)
Jim Stalzer (R-11)
Wayne H. Steinhauer (R-9)
Dick Werner (R-22)

**Minority Members**
Dennis Feickert (D-1)
Dean Schrempp (D-28A)

# Tennessee General Assembly

State Capitol, 600 Charlotte Avenue, Nashville, TN 37243
Tel: (615) 741-1100

## Tennessee Senate

Tel: (615) 741-2730  Tel: (800) 449-8366  Fax: (615) 741-7100
Speaker of the Senate **Ronald Lynn "Ron" Ramsey** (R) . . (615) 741-4524
  Education: East Tennessee State 1978 BS
Speaker Pro Tem **Bo Watson** (R) . . . . . . . . . . . . . . . . . . . . (615) 741-3227
  Education: Tennessee BA
Deputy Speaker **Steve Southerland** (R) . . . . . . . . . . . . . . (615) 741-3851
Majority Leader **Mark Norris** (R) . . . . . . . . . . . . . . . . . . . (615) 741-1967
  Education: Denver JD
Majority Caucus Chairman **Bill Ketron** (R) . . . . . . . . . . . . (615) 741-6853
  Education: Mid Tennessee State 1976 BS
Minority Leader **Lee Harris** (D) . . . . . . . . . . . . . . . . . . . . (615) 741-1767
Minority Caucus Chairman **Jeffrey "Jeff" Yarbro** (D) . . . . (615) 741-3291
  Education: Harvard 1999 AB; Virginia 2004 JD
Chief Clerk of the Senate **Russell A. Humphrey** . . . . . . . . (615) 741-2730
  E-mail: russell.humphrey@capitol.tn.gov
  Education: Tennessee (Memphis) JD

## Senators

**Party Affiliation Statistics:** Republicans: 28, Democrats: 5

Senator **Paul Bailey** (R-District 15) . . . . . . . . . . . . . . . . . (615) 741-3978
  Counties Represented: Bledsoe, Cumberland,          Fax: (615) 253-0381
  Jackson, Overton, Putnam, White
  Term Expires: 2018
  E-mail: sen.paul.bailey@capitol.tn.gov
  Committees: Energy, Agriculture and Natural Resources; Government
  Operations; Transportation and Safety
  Education: Tennessee Tech
Senator **Mae Beavers** (R-District 17) . . . . . . . . . . . . . . . . (615) 741-2421
  Counties Represented: Cannon, Clay, DeKalb, Macon, Smith, Wilson
  Term Expires: 2018
  2020 Hunters Place, Mount Juliet, TN 37122
  E-mail: sen.mae.beavers@capitol.tn.gov
  Committees: Government Operations; Transportation and Safety
  Education: Trevecca Nazarene Col BS
Senator **Mike Bell** (R-District 9) . . . . . . . . . . . . . . . . . . . . (615) 741-1946
  Counties Represented: Bradley (part), McMinn, Meigs, Monroe, Polk
  Term Expires: 2018
  261 County Road 757, Riceville, TN 37370
  E-mail: sen.mike.bell@capitol.tn.gov
  Committees: Energy, Agriculture and Natural Resources; Government
  Operations; Joint Government Operations; Judiciary
Senator **Janice Bowling** (R-District 16) . . . . . . . . . . . . . . (615) 741-6694
  Counties Represented: Coffee, Franklin, Grundy, Marion, Sequatchie,
  Van Buren, Warren
  Term Expires: 2016
  2315 Ovoca Road, Tullahoma, TN 37388
  E-mail: sen.janice.bowling@capitol.tn.gov
  Committees: Government Operations; Joint Government Operations;
  Judiciary; Transportation and Safety
  Education: Auburn BS
Senator **Richard Briggs** (R-District 7) . . . . . . . . . . . . . . . . (615) 741-1766
  Counties Represented: Knox (part)          Fax: (615) 253-0199
  Term Expires: 2018
  E-mail: sen.richard.briggs@capitol.tn.gov
  Committees: Health and Welfare; State and Local Government
Senator **Dewey E. "Rusty" Crowe** (R-District 3) . . . . . . . . (615) 741-2468
  Counties Represented: Carter, Unicoi, Washington     Dist: (423) 926-8288
  Term Expires: 2018
  808 East Eighth Avenue, Johnson City, TN 37601
  E-mail: sen.rusty.crowe@capitol.tn.gov
  Committees: Education; Government Operations; Health and Welfare;
  Joint Government Operations
  Education: East Tennessee State BS; Atlanta JD
Senator **Steven "Steve" Dickerson** (R-District 20) . . . . . . (615) 741-6679
  Counties Represented: Davidson (part)
  Term Expires: 2016
  PO Box 120931, Nashville, TN 37214
  E-mail: sen.steven.dickerson@capitol.tn.gov
  Committees: Education; Finance, Ways and Means; State and Local
  Government
  Education: Sewanee BA; Wake Forest MD

Senator **R. Todd Gardenhire** (R-District 10) . . . . . . . . . . . (615) 741-6682
  Counties Represented: Bradley (part), Hamilton     Fax: (615) 253-0209
  (part)
  Term Expires: 2016
  P.O. Box 4506, Chattanooga, TN 37405
  E-mail: sen.todd.gardenhire@capitol.tn.gov
  Committees: Commerce and Labor; Education; Judiciary
  Education: Tennessee (Chattanooga) 1972 BSBusMgt
Senator **Dr. Mark E. Green, MD** (R-District 22) . . . . . . . . (615) 741-2374
  Counties Represented: Houston, Montgomery,     Fax: (615) 253-0193
  Stewart
  Term Expires: 2016
  1990 Madison Street, Suite 102, Clarksville, TN 37043
  E-mail: sen.mark.green@capitol.tn.gov
  Committees: Commerce and Labor; Energy, Agriculture and Natural
  Resources; State and Local Government
  Education: West Point 1986 BS; Wright State MD
Senator **Dolores R. Gresham** (R-District 26) . . . . . . . . . . . (615) 741-2368
  Counties Represented: Chester, Decatur, Fayette,     Fax: (901) 465-6330
  Hardeman, Hardin, Haywood, Henderson, McNairy
  Term Expires: 2016
  3515 Country Club Road, Somerville, TN 38068
  E-mail: sen.dolores.gresham@capitol.tn.gov
  Committees: Commerce and Labor; Education; Energy, Agriculture and
  Natural Resources
  Education: Incarnate Word Col BA; George Washington 1980 MS;
  Loyola U (New Orleans) MA
Senator **Ferrell Haile** (R-District 18) . . . . . . . . . . . . . . . . (615) 741-1999
  Counties Represented: Davidson (part), Sumner, Trousdale
  Term Expires: 2016
  1900 Cairo Road, Gallatin, TN 37066
  E-mail: sen.ferrell.haile@capitol.tn.gov
  Committees: Education; Finance, Ways and Means; Joint Government
  Operations
  Education: Lipscomb U; Tennessee 1970 BS
Senator **Thelma M. Harper** (D-District 19) . . . . . . . . . . . . (615) 741-2453
  Counties Represented: Davidson (part)          Dist: (615) 228-6466
  Term Expires: 2018
  P.O. Box 281047, Nashville, TN 37228
  E-mail: sen.thelma.harper@capitol.tn.gov
  Committees: Finance, Ways and Means; Joint Government Operations;
  State and Local Government
  Education: Tennessee State BS
Senator **Lee Harris** (D-District 29) . . . . . . . . . . . . . . . . . . (615) 741-1767
  Counties Represented: Shelby (part)          Fax: (615) 253-0357
  Term Expires: 2018
  E-mail: sen.lee.harris@capitol.tn.gov
  Committees: Energy, Agriculture and Natural Resources; Government
  Operations; Judiciary
Senator **Joey Hensley** (R-District 28) . . . . . . . . . . . . . . . . (615) 741-3100
  Counties Represented: Giles, Lawrence, Lewis,     Fax: (615) 253-0231
  Maury, Perry, Wayne
  Term Expires: 2016
  855 Summertown Highway, Hohenwald, TN 38462
  E-mail: sen.joey.hensley@capitol.tn.gov
  Committees: Education; Finance, Ways and Means; Health and Welfare
  Education: U Memphis BS; Tennessee (Memphis) MD
Senator **Ed Jackson** (R-District 27) . . . . . . . . . . . . . . . . . (615) 741-1810
  Counties Represented: Crockett, Dyer, Lake,     Fax: (615) 253-0179
  Lauderdale, Madison
  Term Expires: 2018
  E-mail: sen.ed.jackson@capitol.tn.gov
  Committees: Government Operations; Health and Welfare; State and
  Local Government
Senator **Jack Johnson** (R-District 23) . . . . . . . . . . . . . . . . (615) 741-2495
  Counties Represented: Williamson          Fax: (615) 253-0321
  Term Expires: 2018
  330 Franklin Road, Suite 135-A-178, Brentwood, TN 37027
  E-mail: sen.jack.johnson@capitol.tn.gov
  Committees: Commerce and Labor; State and Local Government
Senator **Brian K. Kelsey** (R-District 31) . . . . . . . . . . . . . . (615) 741-3036
  Counties Represented: Shelby (part)
  Term Expires: 2018
  110 East Mulberry Street, Suite 200, Collierville, TN 38017
  E-mail: sen.brian.kelsey@capitol.tn.gov
  Committees: Education; Government Operations; Judiciary
  Education: North Carolina BA; Georgetown JD

*(continued on next page)*

LEGISLATIVE BRANCH

**Senators** *continued*

Senator **Bill Ketron** (R-District 13) . . . . . . . . . . . . . . . . . . . (615) 741-6853
  Counties Represented: Rutherford (part)
  Term Expires: 2018
  12 Jefferson Square, 805 South Church Street,
  Murfreesboro, TN 37130
  E-mail: sen.bill.ketron@capitol.tn.gov
  Committees: Finance, Ways and Means; Joint Fiscal Review; State and
  Local Government

Senator **Sara Kyle** (D-District 30) . . . . . . . . . . . . . . . . . . . (615) 741-4167
  Counties Represented: Shelby (part)          Fax: (615) 253-0221
  Term Expires: 2018
  E-mail: sen.sara.kyle@capitol.tn.gov
  Committees: Joint Fiscal Review; Judiciary; Transportation and Safety
  Education: Austin Peay State 1975 BA; Nashville 1987 JD

Senator **Becky Duncan Massey** (R-District 6) . . . . . . . . . .(615) 741-1648
  Counties Represented: Knox (part)          Dist: (865) 693-7239
  Term Expires: 2016
  6932 Westland Drive, Knoxville, TN 37919
  E-mail: sen.becky.massey@capitol.tn.gov
  Committees: Health and Welfare; Joint Government Operations;
  Transportation and Safety

Senator **Randy McNally** (R-District 5) . . . . . . . . . . . . . . . (615) 741-6806
  Counties Represented: Anderson, Knox (part),     Dist: (865) 483-5544
  Loudon
  Term Expires: 2018
  94 Royal Troon Circle, Oak Ridge, TN 37830
  E-mail: sen.randy.mcnally@capitol.tn.gov
  Committees: Finance, Ways and Means; Health and Welfare; Joint
  Fiscal Review; Joint Pensions and Insurance
  Education: Memphis State 1967 BS

Senator **Frank S. Nicely** (R-District 8) . . . . . . . . . . . . . . . (615) 741-2061
  Counties Represented: Claiborne, Grainger, Hancock, Hawkins,
  Jefferson, Union
  Term Expires: 2016
  1023 Creek Road, Strawberry Plains, TN 37871
  E-mail: sen.frank.niceley@capitol.tn.gov
  Committees: Energy, Agriculture and Natural Resources; Transportation
  and Safety
  Education: Tennessee 1969 BS

Senator **Mark Norris** (R-District 32) . . . . . . . . . . . . . . . . . (615) 741-1967
  Counties Represented: Shelby (part), Tipton     Dist: (901) 524-5279
  Term Expires: 2016                    Fax: (615) 253-0194
  853 South Collierville - Arlington Road, Collierville, TN 38017
  E-mail: sen.mark.norris@capitol.tn.gov
  Committees: Finance, Ways and Means; Joint Pensions and Insurance;
  State and Local Government

Senator **Doug Overbey** (R-District 2) . . . . . . . . . . . . . . . . . (615) 741-0981
  Counties Represented: Blount, Sevier (part)     Dist: (865) 681-8236
  Term Expires: 2016
  1105 North Heritage Drive, Maryville, TN 37803
  E-mail: sen.doug.overbey@capitol.tn.gov
  Committees: Finance, Ways and Means; Health and Welfare; Joint
  Fiscal Review; Joint Pensions and Insurance; Judiciary
  Education: Carson-Newman 1976 BA; Tennessee 1979 JD

Senator **Ronald Lynn "Ron" Ramsey** (R-District 4) . . . . . (615) 741-4524
  Counties Represented: Johnson, Sullivan     Dist: (423) 323-8700
  Term Expires: 2016                    Fax: (615) 253-0197
  Legislative Plaza, 301 6th Avenue North, Suite 1, Nashville, TN 37243
  E-mail: lt.gov.ron.ramsey@capitol.tn.gov

Senator **Kerry Evan Roberts, CPA** (R-District 25) . . . . . . . .(615) 741-4499
  Counties Represented: Cheatham, Dickson,     Fax: (615) 253-0302
  Hickman, Humphreys, Robertson
  Term Expires: 2018
  E-mail: sen.kerry.roberts@capitol.tn.gov
  Committees: Energy, Agriculture and Natural Resources; Government
  Operations; Judiciary
  Education: Lipscomb U 1983 BS

Senator **Steve Southerland** (R-District 1) . . . . . . . . . . . . . (615) 741-3851
  Counties Represented: Cocke, Greene, Hamblen,     Dist: (423) 587-6167
  Sevier (part)                        Fax: (615) 253-0330
  Term Expires: 2018
  4648 Harbor Drive, Morristown, TN 37814
  E-mail: sen.steve.southerland@capitol.tn.gov
  Committees: Commerce and Labor; Energy, Agriculture and Natural
  Resources; Joint Fiscal Review; Transportation and Safety

Senator **John D. Stevens** (R-District 24) . . . . . . . . . . . . . . (615) 741-4576
  Counties Represented: Benton, Carroll, Gibson, Henry, Obion, Weakley
  Term Expires: 2016
  161 Court Square, Huntingdon, TN 38344
  E-mail: sen.john.stevens@capitol.tn.gov
  Committees: Finance, Ways and Means; Joint Government Operations;
  Judiciary
  Education: Tennessee (Martin) BA; U Memphis JD

Senator **Reginald Tate** (D-District 33) . . . . . . . . . . . . . . . (615) 741-2509
  Counties Represented: Shelby (part)          Fax: (615) 253-0167
  Term Expires: 2018
  War Memorial Building, 301 6th Avenue North, Suite 320,
  Nashville, TN 37243
  E-mail: sen.reginald.tate@capitol.tn.gov
  Committees: Commerce and Labor; Education; Finance, Ways and
  Means; Joint Fiscal Review

Senator **Jim D. Tracy** (R-District 14) . . . . . . . . . . . . . . . . .(615) 741-1066
  Counties Represented: Bedford, Lincoln, Marshall,     Fax: (615) 741-2255
  Moore, Rutherford (part)
  Term Expires: 2016
  106 Finch Lane, Shelbyville, TN 37160
  E-mail: sen.jim.tracy@capitol.tn.gov
  Committees: Commerce and Labor; Education; Joint Pensions and
  Insurance; Transportation and Safety
  Education: Martin U 1978 BS

Senator **Bo Watson** (R-District 11) . . . . . . . . . . . . . . . . . . (615) 741-3227
  Counties Represented: Hamilton (part)          Fax: (615) 253-0280
  Term Expires: 2018
  1607 Gunston Hall Road, Hixson, TN 37343
  E-mail: sen.bo.watson@capitol.tn.gov
  Committees: Commerce and Labor; Finance, Ways and Means; Health
  and Welfare; Joint Pensions and Insurance

Senator **Ken Yager** (R-District 12) . . . . . . . . . . . . . . . . . . . (615) 741-1449
  Counties Represented: Campbell, Fentress, Morgan,     Dist: (865) 285-9797
  Pickett, Rhea, Roane, Scott          Fax: (615) 253-0237
  Term Expires: 2016
  P.O. Box 684, Kingston, TN 37763
  E-mail: sen.ken.yager@capitol.tn.gov
  Committees: Commerce and Labor; Energy, Agriculture and Natural
  Resources; Joint Fiscal Review; State and Local Government
  Education: Tennessee (Martin) 1969 BA, 1972 MS;
  U Memphis 1977 JD

Senator **Jeffrey "Jeff" Yarbro** (D-District 21) . . . . . . . . . .(615) 741-3291
  Counties Represented: Davidson (part)          Fax: (615) 253-0198
  Term Expires: 2018
  E-mail: sen.jeff.yarbro@capitol.tn.gov
  Committees: Health and Welfare; Transportation and Safety

# Senate Standing Committees

## Commerce and Labor
11 Legislative Plaza, Nashville, TN 37243
Tel: (615) 741-7061

| **Majority Members** | **Minority Members** |
| --- | --- |
| Jack Johnson (R-23) *Chair* | Reginald Tate (D-33) |
| Dr. Mark E. Green (R-22) | |
| *1st Vice Chair* | |
| Jim D. Tracy (R-14) *2nd Vice Chair* | |
| R. Todd Gardenhire (R-10) | |
| Dolores R. Gresham (R-26) | |
| Steve Southerland (R-1) | |
| Bo Watson (R-11) | |
| Ken Yager (R-12) | |

## Education
War Memorial Building, 13 Legislative Plaza, Room 308,
Nashville, TN 37243
Tel: (615) 741-3038

| **Majority Members** | **Minority Members** |
| --- | --- |
| Dolores R. Gresham (R-26) *Chair* | Reginald Tate (D-33) *1st Vice Chair* |
| R. Todd Gardenhire (R-10) | |
| *2nd Vice Chair* | |
| Dewey E. "Rusty" Crowe (R-3) | |
| Steven "Steve" Dickerson (R-20) | |
| Ferrell Haile (R-18) | |
| Joey Hensley (R-28) | |
| Brian K. Kelsey (R-31) | |
| Jim D. Tracy (R-14) | |

## Energy, Agriculture and Natural Resources

10 Legislative Plaza, Nashville, TN 37243
Tel: (615) 741-6955

| Majority Members | Minority Members |
|---|---|
| Steve Southerland (R-1) *Chair* | Lee Harris (D-29) |
| Frank S. Nicely (R-8) | |
|   *1st Vice Chair* | |
| Paul Bailey (R-15) *2nd Vice Chair* | |
| Mike Bell (R-9) | |
| Dr. Mark E. Green (R-22) | |
| Dolores R. Gresham (R-26) | |
| Kerry Evan Roberts (R-25) | |
| Ken Yager (R-12) | |

## Finance, Ways and Means

War Memorial Building, Room 307, Nashville, TN 37243
Tel: (615) 741-9500

| Majority Members | Minority Members |
|---|---|
| Randy McNally (R-5) *Chair* | Thelma M. Harper (D-19) |
| Bo Watson (R-11) *1st Vice Chair* | Reginald Tate (D-33) |
| Doug Overbey (R-2) | |
|   *2nd Vice Chair* | |
| Steven "Steve" Dickerson (R-20) | |
| Ferrell Haile (R-18) | |
| Joey Hensley (R-28) | |
| Bill Ketron (R-13) | |
| Mark Norris (R-32) | |
| John D. Stevens (R-24) | |

## Government Operations

6A Legislative Plaza, Nashville, TN 37243
Tel: (615) 741-3642

| Majority Members | Minority Members |
|---|---|
| Mike Bell (R-9) *Chair* | Lee Harris (D-29) |
| Ed Jackson (R-27) *1st Vice Chair* | |
| Kerry Evan Roberts (R-25) | |
|   *2nd Vice Chair* | |
| Paul Bailey (R-15) | |
| Mae Beavers (R-17) | |
| Janice Bowling (R-16) | |
| Dewey E. "Rusty" Crowe (R-3) | |
| Brian K. Kelsey (R-31) | |

## Health and Welfare

8 Legislative Plaza, Nashville, TN 37243
Tel: (615) 741-7936

| Majority Members | Minority Members |
|---|---|
| Dewey E. "Rusty" Crowe (R-3) | Jeffrey "Jeff" Yarbro (D-21) |
|   *Chair* | |
| Bo Watson (R-11) *1st Vice Chair* | |
| Joey Hensley (R-28) | |
|   *2nd Vice Chair* | |
| Richard Briggs (R-7) | |
| Ed Jackson (R-27) | |
| Becky Duncan Massey (R-6) | |
| Randy McNally (R-5) | |
| Doug Overbey (R-2) | |

## Judiciary

7 Legislative Plaza, Nashville, TN 37243
Tel: (615) 741-7821

| Majority Members | Minority Members |
|---|---|
| Brian K. Kelsey (R-31) *Chair* | Lee Harris (D-29) |
| Doug Overbey (R-2) *1st Vice Chair* | Sara Kyle (D-30) |
| Janice Bowling (R-16) | |
|   *2nd Vice Chair* | |
| Mike Bell (R-9) | |
| R. Todd Gardenhire (R-10) | |
| Kerry Evan Roberts (R-25) | |
| John D. Stevens (R-24) | |

## State and Local Government

6 Legislative Plaza, Nashville, TN 37243
Tel: (615) 741-7891

| Majority Members | Minority Members |
|---|---|
| Ken Yager (R-12) *Chair* | Thelma M. Harper (D-19) |
| Steven "Steve" Dickerson (R-20) | |
|   *1st Vice Chair* | |
| Richard Briggs (R-7) | |
|   *2nd Vice Chair* | |
| Dr. Mark E. Green (R-22) | |
| Ed Jackson (R-27) | |
| Jack Johnson (R-23) | |
| Bill Ketron (R-13) | |
| Mark Norris (R-32) | |

## Transportation and Safety

2 Legislative Plaza, Nashville, TN 37243
Tel: (615) 741-7971

| Majority Members | Minority Members |
|---|---|
| Jim D. Tracy (R-14) *Chair* | Sara Kyle (D-30) |
| Mae Beavers (R-17) *1st Vice Chair* | Jeffrey "Jeff" Yarbro (D-21) |
| Frank S. Nicely (R-8) | |
|   *2nd Vice Chair* | |
| Paul Bailey (R-15) | |
| Janice Bowling (R-16) | |
| Becky Duncan Massey (R-6) | |
| Steve Southerland (R-1) | |

# Tennessee House of Representatives

Tel: (615) 741-2901  Fax: (615) 532-6973

Speaker of the House **Beth Halteman Harwell** (R) . . . . . . (615) 741-0709
  Education: David Lipscomb U BA; Vanderbilt PhD; George Peabody Col MS

Speaker Pro Tem **Curtis G. Johnson** (R) . . . . . . . . . . . . . . (615) 741-4341
  Education: Austin Peay State BBA

Deputy Speaker **Steve K. McDaniel** (R) . . . . . . . . . . . . . . (615) 741-0750
  Education: U Memphis 1973 BS

Majority Leader **Gerald McCormick** (R) . . . . . . . . . . . . . . (615) 741-2548

Assistant Majority Leader **Kevin D. Brooks** (R) . . . . . . . . . (615) 741-1350
  Education: Lee U 1990 BA

Majority Caucus Chairman **Glen Casada** (R) . . . . . . . . . . . (615) 741-4389
  Education: Western Kentucky BS

Assistant Majority Caucus Chairman **Dennis Powers** (R) . . (615) 741-3335
  Education: Tennessee BSBA

Majority Whip **Timothy Hill** (R) . . . . . . . . . . . . . . . . . . . . (615) 741-2050
  Education: East Tennessee State 2003 BSS

Majority Floor Leader **Sheila Butt** (R) . . . . . . . . . . . . . . . . (615) 741-3005
  Education: East Tennessee State BS

Assistant Majority Floor Leader **Jerry Sexton** (R) . . . . . . . (615) 741-2534

Majority Caucus Secretary **Dawn White** (R) . . . . . . . . . . . (615) 741-6849
  Education: Mid Tennessee State 1998 BS, 1999 MEd

Majority Caucus Treasurer **Tilman Goins** (R) . . . . . . . . . . (615) 741-6877
  Education: East Tennessee State BA, BS

Minority Leader **Craig Fitzhugh** (D) . . . . . . . . . . . . . . . . . (615) 741-2134
  Education: Tennessee 1972 BS, 1975 JD

Minority Leader Pro-Tempore
  **Joseph E. "Joe" Armstrong** (D) . . . . . . . . . . . . . . . . . (615) 741-0768
  Education: Tennessee 1981 BS

Assistant Minority Leader **Joe Towns, Jr.** (D) . . . . . . . . . . (615) 741-2189
  Education: LeMoyne-Owen BA; Arkansas MS

Minority Floor Leader **Jason Powell** (D) . . . . . . . . . . . . . . (615) 741-6861
  Education: Colorado BA; Tennessee State MPA

Minority Caucus Chairman **Mike Stewart** (D) . . . . . . . . . . (615) 741-2184

Minority Caucus Vice Chairman **Antonio Parkinson** (D) . . (615) 741-4575

Minority Caucus Secretary **Harold Moses Love, Jr.** (D) . . . (615) 741-3831
  Education: Tennessee State 1994; Vanderbilt 1998 MTS

Minority Caucus Treasurer **Karen D. Camper** (D) . . . . . . . (615) 741-1898
  Education: SUNY (Albany) AS

Minority Whip **JoAnne Favors** (D) . . . . . . . . . . . . . . . . . . (615) 741-2702

Chief Clerk of the House **Joe McCord** (R) . . . . . . . . . . . . . (615) 741-2901
  Education: Tennessee 1991 BA

**LEGISLATIVE BRANCH**

LEGISLATIVE BRANCH

# Representatives

**Party Affiliation Statistics:** Republicans: 73, Democrats: 26

**Representative Raumesh Akbari** (D-District 91) . . . . . . . . (901) 605-6918
Counties Represented: Shelby (part)
Term Expires: 2016
Legislative Plaza, 301 6th Avenue North, Suite 35,
Nashville, TN 37243
4276 Woodcrest, Memphis, TN 38111
E-mail: raumesh@lisaakbari.com
Committees: Criminal Justice
Education: Washington U (MO) 2006 BA; Saint Louis U 2009 JD

**Representative David Alexander** (R-District 39) . . . . . . . . (615) 741-8695
Counties Represented: Franklin (part), Marion    Fax: (615) 253-0314
(part), Moore
Term Expires: 2016
512 South High Street, Winchester, TN 37398
E-mail: rep.david.alexander@capitol.tn.gov
Committees: Finance, Ways and Means; Joint Pensions and Insurance;
Transportation
Education: Mississippi Col 1977 BA

**Representative
Joseph E. "Joe" Armstrong** (D-District 15) . . . . . . . . . (615) 741-0768
Counties Represented: Knox (part)    Dist: (865) 357-1524
Term Expires: 2016    Fax: (615) 253-0316
4708 Hilldale Lane, Knoxville, TN 37914
E-mail: rep.joe.armstrong@capitol.tn.gov
Committees: Finance, Ways and Means; Transportation

**Representative Bill Beck** (D-District 51) . . . . . . . . . . . . . (615) 741-3229
Counties Represented: Davidson (part)    Fax: (615) 253-0233
Term Expires: 2016
E-mail: rep.bill.beck@capitol.tn.gov
Committees: Civil Justice; Transportation

**Representative Harry R. Brooks** (R-District 19) . . . . . . . . . (615) 741-6879
Counties Represented: Knox (part)    Fax: (615) 253-0212
Term Expires: 2016
6600 Washington Pike, Knoxville, TN 37918
E-mail: rep.harry.brooks@capitol.tn.gov
Committees: Calendar and Rules; Education, Administration, and
Planning
Education: Carson-Newman 1969 BA; Tennessee MAC

**Representative Kevin D. Brooks** (R-District 24) . . . . . . . . . (615) 741-1350
Counties Represented: Bradley (part)    Fax: (615) 253-0346
Term Expires: 2016
P.O. Box 4801, Cleveland, TN 37320
E-mail: rep.kevin.brooks@capitol.tn.gov
Committees: Calendar and Rules; Education, Administration, and
Planning; Finance, Ways and Means

**Representative Sheila Butt** (R-District 64) . . . . . . . . . . . . (615) 741-3005
Counties Represented: Maury    Fax: (615) 253-0231
Term Expires: 2016
3870 Albert Matthews Road, Columbia, TN 38401
E-mail: rep.sheila.butt@capitol.tn.gov
Committees: Criminal Justice

**Representative David "Coach" Byrd** (R-District 71) . . . . . . (615) 741-2190
Counties Represented: Hardin, Lawrence (part),    Fax: (615) 253-0377
Lewis, Wayne
Term Expires: 2016
E-mail: rep.david.byrd@capitol.tn.gov
Committees: Agriculture and Natural Resources

**Representative Kent Calfee** (R-District 32) . . . . . . . . . . . (615) 741-7658
Counties Represented: Roane (part)    Fax: (615) 253-0163
Term Expires: 2016
476 Dogwood Valley Road, Kingston, TN 37763
E-mail: rep.kent.calfee@capitol.tn.gov
Committees: Business and Utilities; Education, Administration, and
Planning; Joint Pensions and Insurance
Education: East Tennessee State (Attended)

**Representative Karen D. Camper** (D-District 87) . . . . . . . . (615) 741-1898
Counties Represented: Shelby (part)    Dist: (901) 315-8899
Term Expires: 2016    Fax: (615) 253-0211
1184 Old Hickory Boulevard, Memphis, TN 38116-4334
E-mail: rep.karen.camper@capitol.tn.gov
Committees: Finance, Ways and Means; Joint Pensions and Insurance;
Transportation

**Representative Dale Carr** (R-District 12) . . . . . . . . . . . . . (615) 741-5981
Counties Represented: Sevier (part)    Fax: (615) 253-0303
Term Expires: 2016
2150 Murphys Chapel Drive, Sevierville, TN 37876
E-mail: rep.dale.carr@capitol.tn.gov
Committees: Local Government; Transportation
Education: Tennessee (Attended)

**Representative Mike Carter** (R-District 29) . . . . . . . . . . . . (615) 741-3025
Counties Represented: Hamilton (part)
Term Expires: 2016
War Memorial Building, 301 6th Avenue North, Suite G-3,
Nashville, TN 37243
E-mail: rep.mike.carter@capitol.tn.gov
Committees: Civil Justice; Finance, Ways and Means
Education: Mid Tennessee State 1975 BS; U Memphis 1978 JD

**Representative Glen Casada** (R-District 63) . . . . . . . . . . . (615) 741-4389
Counties Represented: Williamson (part)    Dist: (615) 943-7396
Term Expires: 2016    Fax: (615) 253-0229
3144 Natoma Circle, Thompsons Station, TN 37179
E-mail: rep.glen.casada@capitol.tn.gov
Committees: Calendar and Rules; Consumer and Human Resources;
Government Operations; Insurance and Banking; Joint Government
Operations

**Representative John Ray Clemmons** (D-District 55) . . . . . (615) 741-4410
Counties Represented: Davidson (part)    Fax: (615) 253-0202
Term Expires: 2016
E-mail: rep.john.ray.clemmons@capitol.tn.gov
Committees: Government Operations; Health

**Representative Jim Coley** (R-District 97) . . . . . . . . . . . . . (615) 741-8201
Counties Represented: Shelby (part)    Fax: (615) 253-0267
Term Expires: 2016
2498 Kenwood Lane, Bartlett, TN 38134
E-mail: rep.jim.coley@capitol.tn.gov
Committees: Civil Justice; Education, Administration, and Planning

**Representative Barbara W. Cooper** (D-District 86) . . . . . . (615) 741-4295
Counties Represented: Shelby (part)    Dist: (901) 578-7002
Term Expires: 2016    Fax: (615) 741-0327
99 North Main Street, Number 2105, Memphis, TN 38103
E-mail: rep.barbara.cooper@capitol.tn.gov
Committees: Finance, Ways and Means; Transportation
Education: Tennessee BS, MEd

**Representative Martin Daniel** (R-District 18) . . . . . . . . . . . (615) 741-2287
Counties Represented: Sevier (part)    Fax: (615) 253-0348
Term Expires: 2016
E-mail: rep.martin.daniel@capitol.tn.gov
Committees: Civil Justice

**Representative John J. DeBerry, Jr.** (D-District 90) . . . . . . (615) 741-2239
Counties Represented: Shelby (part)    Dist: (901) 725-0130
Term Expires: 2016    Fax: (615) 253-0294
1207 Sledge Street, Memphis, TN 38104
E-mail: rep.john.deberry@capitol.tn.gov
Committees: Education, Administration, and Planning; Health

**Representative Barry Doss** (R-District 70) . . . . . . . . . . . . . (615) 741-7476
Counties Represented: Giles, Lawrence (part)
Term Expires: 2016
War Memorial Building, 301 6th Avenue North, Suite 106,
Nashville, TN 37243
E-mail: rep.barry.doss@capitol.tn.gov
Committees: Business and Utilities; Health
Education: Tennessee 1985 BSAg

**Representative Kevin Dunlap** (D-District 43) . . . . . . . . . . . (615) 741-1963
Counties Represented: Grundy, Warren (part), White    Fax: (615) 253-0207
Term Expires: 2016
E-mail: rep.kevin.dunlap@capitol.tn.gov
Committees: Education, Administration, and Planning

**Representative Bill Dunn** (R-District 16) . . . . . . . . . . . . . . (615) 741-1721
Counties Represented: Knox (part)    Dist: (865) 687-4904
Term Expires: 2016    Fax: (615) 253-0276
5309 LaVesta Road, Knoxville, TN 37918
E-mail: rep.bill.dunn@capitol.tn.gov
Committees: Calendar and Rules; Finance, Ways and Means
Education: Tennessee BS, MS

**Representative Jeremy Durham** (R-District 65) . . . . . . . . . (615) 741-1864
Counties Represented: Williamson (part)    Fax: (615) 253-0228
Term Expires: 2016
802 Founders Pointe Boulevard, Franklin, TN 37064
E-mail: rep.jeremy.durham@capitol.tn.gov
Committees: Insurance and Banking; State Government
Education: Tennessee 2006 BA; U Memphis 2008 JD

**Representative Jimmy A. Eldridge** (R-District 73) . . . . . . . (615) 741-7475
Counties Represented: Madison (part)    Fax: (615) 253-0373
Term Expires: 2016
29 Emerald Lake Drive, Jackson, TN 38305
E-mail: rep.jimmy.eldridge@capitol.tn.gov
Committees: Calendar and Rules; Consumer and Human Resources;
Local Government
Education: Lambuth BS

Representative **Jeremy Faison** (R-District 11) . . . . . . . . . . (615) 741-6871
Counties Represented: Cocke, Greene (part),     Fax: (615) 253-0225
Jefferson (part)
Term Expires: 2016
1009 Country Mountain Road, Cosby, TN 37722
E-mail: rep.jeremy.faison@capitol.tn.gov
Committees: Calendar and Rules; Government Operations; Health
Education: Clearwater Christian

Representative **Andrew E. Farmer** (R-District 17) . . . . . . . (615) 741-4419
Counties Represented: Jefferson (part)
Term Expires: 2016
103 Commerce Street, Sevierville, TN 37862
E-mail: rep.andrew.farmer@capitol.tn.gov
Committees: Criminal Justice; Insurance and Banking
Education: East Tennessee State BBA; Thomas M Cooley JD

Representative **JoAnne Favors** (D-District 28) . . . . . . . . . . (615) 741-2702
Counties Represented: Hamilton (part)     Fax: (615) 253-0351
Term Expires: 2016
25 Legislative Plaza, Nashville, TN 37243
E-mail: rep.joanne.favors@capitol.tn.gov
Committees: Health; Insurance and Banking

Representative **Craig Fitzhugh** (D-District 82) . . . . . . . . . . (615) 741-2134
Counties Represented: Crockett, Haywood,     Dist: (731) 772-8978
Lauderdale     Fax: (615) 741-1446
Term Expires: 2016
135 South Alpine Street, Ripley, TN 38063
E-mail: rep.craig.fitzhugh@capitol.tn.gov
Committees: Calendar and Rules; Education, Administration, and
Planning; Finance, Ways and Means; Government Operations; Joint
Government Operations; Joint Pensions and Insurance

Representative **John W. Forgety** (R-District 23) . . . . . . . . (615) 741-1725
Counties Represented: McMinn, Monroe (part)     Fax: (615) 253-0309
Term Expires: 2016
120 County Road 447, Athens, TN 37303
E-mail: rep.john.forgety@capitol.tn.gov
Committees: Calendar and Rules; Civil Justice

Representative **Brenda Gilmore** (D-District 54) . . . . . . . . . (615) 741-1997
Counties Represented: Davidson (part)     Fax: (615) 253-0361
Term Expires: 2016
3009 Vista Valley Court, Nashville, TN 37218
E-mail: rep.brenda.gilmore@capitol.tn.gov
Committees: Finance, Ways and Means; Joint Fiscal Review
Education: Tennessee State 1984 BS; Vanderbilt 1988

Representative **Tilman Goins** (R-District 10) . . . . . . . . . . . (615) 741-6877
Counties Represented: Hamblen     Fax: (615) 253-0182
Term Expires: 2016
536 Valley View Drive, Morristown, TN 37813
E-mail: rep.tilman.goins@capitol.tn.gov
Committees: Business and Utilities; Criminal Justice

Representative **Marc Gravitt** (R-District 30) . . . . . . . . . . . . (615) 741-1934
Counties Represented: Hamilton (part)     Fax: (615) 253-0271
Term Expires: 2016
E-mail: rep.marc.gravitt@capitol.tn.gov
Committees: Local Government

Representative **Curtis Halford** (R-District 79) . . . . . . . . . . . (615) 741-7478
Counties Represented: Carroll (part), Gibson     Fax: (615) 253-0218
Term Expires: 2016
127 Old Dyer Trenton Road, Dyer, TN 38330
E-mail: rep.curtis.halford@capitol.tn.gov
Committees: Agriculture and Natural Resources; Calendar and Rules;
Government Operations; Joint Government Operations

Representative **G. A. Hardaway** (D-District 93) . . . . . . . . . (615) 741-5625
Counties Represented: Shelby (part)     Fax: (615) 253-0185
Term Expires: 2016
1243 Worthington Street, Memphis, TN 38114
E-mail: rep.ga.hardaway@capitol.tn.gov
Committees: Agriculture and Natural Resources; Consumer and Human
Resources; Joint Government Operations

Representative **Michael "Mike" Harrison** (R-District 9) . . . (615) 741-7480
Counties Represented: Hancock, Hawkins     Dist: (423) 235-6803
Term Expires: 2016     Fax: (615) 253-0307
115 Green Acres Drive, Rogersville, TN 37857
Committees: Finance, Ways and Means; Health; Joint Pensions and
Insurance

Representative **Beth Halteman Harwell** (R-District 56) . . . (615) 741-0709
Counties Represented: Davidson (part)     Dist: (615) 385-0357
Term Expires: 2016     Fax: (615) 741-4917
42 Wyn Oak, Nashville, TN 37205
E-mail: speaker.beth.harwell@capitol.tn.gov
Committees: Calendar and Rules

Representative **David B. Hawk** (R-District 5) . . . . . . . . . . . (615) 741-7482
Counties Represented: Greene (part)     Fax: (615) 253-0210
Term Expires: 2016
407 Crockett Avenue, Greeneville, TN 37745
E-mail: rep.david.hawk@capitol.tn.gov
Committees: Agriculture and Natural Resources; Finance, Ways and
Means

Representative **Patsy Hazlewood** (R-District 27) . . . . . . . . (615) 741-2746
Counties Represented: Hamilton (part)     Fax: (615) 253-0304
Term Expires: 2016
E-mail: rep.patsy.hazlewood@capitol.tn.gov
Committees: Finance, Ways and Means

Representative **Matthew Hill** (R-District 7) . . . . . . . . . . . . . (615) 741-2251
Counties Represented: Washington (part)     Fax: (615) 253-0299
Term Expires: 2016
216 Mockingbird Place, Jonesborough, TN 37659
E-mail: rep.matthew.hill@capitol.tn.gov
Committees: Finance, Ways and Means; Health
Education: East Tennessee State BS

Representative **Timothy Hill** (R-District 3) . . . . . . . . . . . . . (615) 741-2050
Counties Represented: Johnson
Term Expires: 2016
PO Box 3071, Blountville, TN 37617
E-mail: rep.timothy.hill@capitol.tn.gov
Committees: Business and Utilities; Calendar and Rules; Insurance and
Banking; Transportation

Representative **John B. Holsclaw, Jr.** (R-District 4) . . . . . . (615) 741-7450
Counties Represented: Carter, Unicoi     Fax: (615) 253-0310
Term Expires: 2016
E-mail: rep.john.holsclaw@capitol.tn.gov
Committees: Health

Representative **Andrew H. "Andy" Holt** (R-District 76) . . . (615) 741-7847
Counties Represented: Carroll (part), Obion (part),     Fax: (615) 253-0293
Weakley
Term Expires: 2016
461 Jewell Store Road, Dresden, TN 38225
E-mail: rep.andy.holt@capitol.tn.gov
Committees: Agriculture and Natural Resources; Local Government
Education: Tennessee 2004 BS; Tennessee (Martin) 2007 MBA

Representative **Dan Howell** (R-District 22) . . . . . . . . . . . . . (615) 741-7799
Counties Represented: Bradley (part), Meigs, Polk     Fax: (615) 253-0252
Term Expires: 2016
War Memorial Bldg., 301 6th Avenue North, Suite 112,
Nashville, TN 37243
E-mail: rep.dan.howell@capitol.tn.gov
Committees: Government Operations; Local Government

Representative **Bud Hulsey** (R-District 2) . . . . . . . . . . . . . . (615) 741-2886
Counties Represented: Sullivan (part)     Fax: (615) 253-0247
Term Expires: 2016
E-mail: rep.bud.hulsey@capitol.tn.gov
Committees: Agriculture and Natural Resources; State Government

Representative **Darren Jernigan** (D-District 60) . . . . . . . . . (615) 741-6959
Counties Represented: Davidson (part)
Term Expires: 2016
4837 Rainer Drive, Old Hickory, TN 37138
E-mail: rep.darren.jernigan@capitol.tn.gov
Committees: Health; State Government
Education: Austin Peay 1995 BS; Mid Tennessee State 2000

Representative **Curtis G. Johnson** (R-District 68) . . . . . . . . (615) 741-4341
Counties Represented: Montgomery (part)     Dist: (931) 358-3719
Term Expires: 2016     Fax: (615) 253-0269
2599 Memorial Drive, Clarksville, TN 37043
E-mail: rep.curtis.johnson@capitol.tn.gov
Committees: Calendar and Rules; Finance, Ways and Means;
Government Operations; Insurance and Banking; Joint Government
Operations

Representative **Sherry Jones** (D-District 59) . . . . . . . . . . . . (615) 741-2035
Counties Represented: Davidson (part)     Dist: (615) 832-4211
Term Expires: 2016     Fax: (615) 253-0290
4947 Sherman Oaks Road, Nashville, TN 37211
E-mail: rep.sherry.jones@capitol.tn.gov
Committees: Civil Justice; Health

Representative **Roger Kane** (R-District 89) . . . . . . . . . . . . . (615) 741-2010
Counties Represented: Knox (part)
Term Expires: 2016
7031 Cherry Grove Road, Knoxville, TN 37931
E-mail: rep.roger.kane@capitol.tn.gov
Committees: Insurance and Banking
Education: Houston BBA

*(continued on next page)*

LEGISLATIVE BRANCH

**Representatives** *continued*

Representative **Kelly Keisling** (R-District 38) . . . . . . . . . . . (615) 741-6852
Counties Represented: Clay, Fentress (part), Macon,        Fax: (615) 253-0234
Pickett, Scott
Term Expires: 2016
1042 Cordell Hull Memorial Drive, Byrdstown, TN 38549
E-mail: rep.kelly.keisling@capitol.tn.gov
Committees: Insurance and Banking; Transportation
Education: Belmont U

Representative **Sabi "Doc" Kumar** (R-District 66) . . . . . . (615) 741-2860
Counties Represented: Robertson        Fax: (615) 253-0283
Term Expires: 2016
E-mail: rep.sabi.kumar@capitol.tn.gov
Committees: Health

Representative **William G. Lamberth** (R-District 44) . . . . . (615) 741-1980
Counties Represented: Sumner (part)        Fax: (615) 253-0336
Term Expires: 2016
Legislative Plaza, 301 6th Avenue North, Suite 22,
Nashville, TN 37243
E-mail: rep.william.lamberth@capitol.tn.gov
Committees: Business and Utilities; Criminal Justice; State Government
Education: Tennessee 2001 BS; William & Mary 2004 JD

Representative **Mary Littleton** (R-District 78) . . . . . . . . . . (615) 741-7477
Counties Represented: Cheatham, Dickson (part)
Term Expires: 2016
104 Steven Nicks Drive, Dickson, TN 37055
E-mail: rep.mary.littleton@capitol.tn.gov
Committees: Health; State Government
Education: Tennessee (Martin) BS; Murray State U MPA

Representative **Ron Lollar** (R-District 99) . . . . . . . . . . . . . (615) 741-7084
Counties Represented: Shelby (part)        Fax: (615) 253-0294
Term Expires: 2016
7559 Olivia Hill Drive, Bartlett, TN 38133
E-mail: rep.ron.lollar@capitol.tn.gov
Committees: Agriculture and Natural Resources
Education: Austin Peay State 1975 BS

Representative **Harold Moses Love, Jr.** (D-District 58) . . . (615) 741-3831
Counties Represented: Davidson (part)        Fax: (615) 253-0323
Term Expires: 2016
2516 Buchanan Street, Nashville, TN 37208
E-mail: rep.harold.love@capitol.tn.gov

Representative **Jon C. Lundberg** (R-District 1) . . . . . . . . . . (615) 741-7623
Counties Represented: Sullivan (part)        Fax: (615) 253-0272
Term Expires: 2016
212 Skyline Drive, Bristol, TN 37620
E-mail: rep.jon.lundberg@capitol.tn.gov
Committees: Calendar and Rules; Civil Justice; Insurance and Banking

Representative **Susan M. Lynn** (R-District 57) . . . . . . . . . . (615) 741-7462
Counties Represented: Wilson (part)        Fax: (615) 253-0353
Term Expires: 2016
War Memorial Bldg., 301 6th Avenue North, Suite 104,
Nashville, TN 37243
1009 Cedarcreek Village Road, Nashville, TN 37243
E-mail: rep.susan.lynn@capitol.tn.gov
Committees: Consumer and Human Resources; Finance, Ways and
Means; Joint Fiscal Review

Representative **Pat Marsh** (R-District 62) . . . . . . . . . . . . . (615) 741-6824
Counties Represented: Bedford, Lincoln (part)        Fax: (615) 253-0344
Term Expires: 2016
War Memorial Building, 301 6th Avenue North, Room 110,
Nashville, TN 37243
E-mail: rep.pat.marsh@capitol.tn.gov
Committees: Agriculture and Natural Resources; Business and Utilities;
Calendar and Rules; Joint Fiscal Review

Representative **Judd Matheny** (R-District 47) . . . . . . . . . . (615) 741-7448
Counties Represented: Coffee, Warren (part)        Fax: (615) 253-0226
Term Expires: 2016
398 Vanguard Lane, Tullahoma, TN 37388
E-mail: rep.judd.matheny@capitol.tn.gov
Committees: Health; Insurance and Banking; Joint Government
Operations

Representative **Jimmy Matlock** (R-District 21) . . . . . . . . . . (615) 741-3736
Counties Represented: Loudon, Monroe (part)
Term Expires: 2016
190 Matlock Road, Lenoir City, TN 37771
E-mail: rep.jimmy.matlock@capitol.tn.gov
Committees: Calendar and Rules; Insurance and Banking;
Transportation

Representative **Gerald McCormick** (R-District 26) . . . . . . . (615) 741-2548
Counties Represented: Hamilton (part)        Fax: (615) 253-0305
Term Expires: 2016
P. O. Box 1087, Chattanooga, TN 37405
E-mail: rep.gerald.mccormick@capitol.tn.gov
Committees: Business and Utilities; Calendar and Rules; Finance, Ways
and Means; Government Operations; Joint Government Operations

Representative **Steve K. McDaniel** (R-District 72) . . . . . . . (615) 741-0750
Counties Represented: Chester, Decatur, Henderson,        Dist: (731) 968-7883
Perry        Fax: (615) 253-0213
Term Expires: 2016
97 Battleground Drive, Parker Crossroads, TN 38388
E-mail: rep.steve.mcdaniel@capitol.tn.gov
Committees: Agriculture and Natural Resources; Finance, Ways and
Means; Joint Pensions and Insurance

Representative **Steve K. McManus** (R-District 96) . . . . . . . (615) 741-1920
Counties Represented: Shelby (part)        Fax: (615) 253-0232
Term Expires: 2016
405 Riveredge Drive, Cordova, TN 38018
E-mail: rep.steve.mcmanus@capitol.tn.gov
Committees: Calendar and Rules; Finance, Ways and Means; Insurance
and Banking

Representative **Larry J. Miller** (D-District 88) . . . . . . . . . . (615) 741-4453
Counties Represented: Shelby (part)        Res: (901) 272-7884
Term Expires: 2016        Fax: (615) 253-0329
550 Techno Lane, Apartment 803, Memphis, TN 38105
E-mail: rep.larry.miller@capitol.tn.gov
Committees: Finance, Ways and Means; Local Government

Representative **Bo Mitchell** (D-District 50) . . . . . . . . . . . . . (615) 741-4317
Counties Represented: Davidson (part)
Term Expires: 2016
6421 Riverplace Drive, Nashville, TN 37221
E-mail: rep.bo.mitchell@capitol.tn.gov
Committees: Consumer and Human Resources; Finance, Ways and
Means
Education: David Lipscomb U 1992; Nashville 2003 JD

Representative **Debra Moody** (R-District 81) . . . . . . . . . . . (615) 741-3774
Counties Represented: Tipton
Term Expires: 2016
3176 Oil Mill Road, Covington, TN 38019
E-mail: rep.debra.moody@capitol.tn.gov
Committees: Agriculture and Natural Resources; Education,
Administration, and Planning
Education: Arkansas State (Attended); U Memphis (Attended)

Representative **Antonio Parkinson** (D-District 98) . . . . . . . (615) 741-4575
Counties Represented: Shelby (part)        Dist: (901) 570-5810
Term Expires: 2016        Fax: (615) 253-0347
301 6th Avenue North, Suite 36, Nashville, TN 37243
PO Box 281453, Memphis, TN 38168
E-mail: rep.antonio.parkinson@capitol.tn.gov
Committees: Calendar and Rules; Criminal Justice; Local Government

Representative **Joe Pitts** (D-District 67) . . . . . . . . . . . . . . . (615) 741-2043
Counties Represented: Montgomery (part)        Fax: (615) 253-0200
Term Expires: 2016
544 Hay Market Road, Clarksville, TN 37043
E-mail: rep.joe.pitts@capitol.tn.gov
Committees: Insurance and Banking

Representative **Mark Pody** (R-District 46) . . . . . . . . . . . . . (615) 741-7086
Counties Represented: Cannon, DeKalb (part),        Fax: (615) 253-0206
Wilson (part)
Term Expires: 2016
505 Windham Trail, Lebanon, TN 37090
E-mail: rep.mark.pody@capitol.tn.gov
Committees: Business and Utilities; Consumer and Human Resources;
Insurance and Banking

Representative **Jason Powell** (D-District 53) . . . . . . . . . . . (615) 741-6861
Counties Represented: Davidson (part)
Term Expires: 2016
371 Lynn Avenue, Nashville, TN 37211
E-mail: rep.jason.powell@capitol.tn.gov
Committees: Business and Utilities; State Government

Representative **Dennis Powers** (R-District 36) . . . . . . . . . . (615) 741-3335
Counties Represented: Anderson (part), Campbell,        Fax: (615) 253-0296
Union (part)
Term Expires: 2016
139 Preston Circle, Jacksboro, TN 37757
E-mail: rep.dennis.powers@capitol.tn.gov
Committees: Agriculture and Natural Resources; Insurance and
Banking

Representative **John D. Ragan** (R-District 33) . . . . . . . . . . (615) 741-4400
Counties Represented: Anderson (part)    Fax: (615) 253-0297
Term Expires: 2016
119 Morningside Drive, Oak Ridge, TN 37830
E-mail: rep.john.ragan@capitol.tn.gov
Committees: Government Operations; Joint Government Operations;
Transportation

Representative **Bob Ramsey** (R-District 20) . . . . . . . . . . . . (615) 741-3560
Counties Represented: Blount (part)    Fax: (615) 253-0376
Term Expires: 2016
2120 Middlewood Drive, Maryville, TN 37803
E-mail: rep.bob.ramsey@capitol.tn.gov
Committees: Calendar and Rules; Health; State Government

Representative **Jay D. Reedy** (R-District 74) . . . . . . . . . . . (615) 741-7098
Counties Represented: Houston, Humphreys,    Fax: (615) 253-0315
Montgomery (part)
Term Expires: 2016
E-mail: rep.jay.reedy@capitol.tn.gov
Committees: Agriculture and Natural Resources

Representative **Courtney Rogers** (R-District 45) . . . . . . . . (615) 741-3893
Counties Represented: Sumner (part)    Fax: (615) 253-0350
Term Expires: 2016
919 Conference Drive, Suite 4, Goodlettsville, TN 37072
E-mail: rep.courtney.rogers@capitol.tn.gov
Committees: Civil Justice; Transportation
Education: USC BS; Central Michigan MPA

Representative **Bill Sanderson** (R-District 77) . . . . . . . . . (615) 741-0718
Counties Represented: Dyer, Lake, Obion (part)    Fax: (615) 253-0214
Term Expires: 2016
3804 Concord Road, Kenton, TN 38233
E-mail: rep.bill.sanderson@capitol.tn.gov
Committees: Joint Fiscal Review; State Government; Transportation
Education: Lambuth 1981 BSBA

Representative
**Charles Michael Sargent, Jr.** (R-District 61) . . . . . . . . (615) 741-6808
Counties Represented: Williamson (part)    Dist: (615) 771-7222
Term Expires: 2016    Fax: (615) 253-0217
117 Ashton Park Boulevard, Franklin, TN 37067
E-mail: rep.charles.sargent@capitol.tn.gov
Committees: Calendar and Rules; Finance, Ways and Means; Insurance
and Banking; Joint Pensions and Insurance

Representative **Cameron Sexton** (R-District 25) . . . . . . . . (615) 741-2343
Counties Represented: Cumberland, Overton (part),    Fax: (615) 253-0230
Van Buren
Term Expires: 2016
186 Homestead Drive, Crossville, TN 38555
E-mail: rep.cameron.sexton@capitol.tn.gov
Committees: Business and Utilities; Calendar and Rules; Health; Local
Government
Education: Tennessee 1994 BA

Representative **Jerry Sexton** (R-District 35) . . . . . . . . . . . (615) 741-2534
Counties Represented: Claiborne, Grainger, Union    Fax: (615) 253-0273
(part)
Term Expires: 2016
E-mail: rep.jerry.sexton@capitol.tn.gov
Committees: Calendar and Rules; Transportation

Representative **Johnny W. Shaw** (D-District 80) . . . . . . . . (615) 741-4538
Counties Represented: Hardeman, Madison (part)    Dist: (731) 658-7689
Term Expires: 2016    Fax: (615) 253-0356
123 West Market Street, Bolivar, TN 38008    Dist: (731) 658-3408
P.O. Box 191, Bolivar, TN 38008
E-mail: rep.johnny.shaw@capitol.tn.gov
Committees: Agriculture and Natural Resources; Joint Fiscal Review;
State Government

Representative **David A. Shepard** (D-District 69) . . . . . . . (615) 741-3513
Counties Represented: Dickson (part), Hickman    Dist: (615) 446-9782
Term Expires: 2016    Fax: (615) 253-0244
204 McCreary Heights, Dickson, TN 37055
E-mail: rep.david.shepard@capitol.tn.gov
Committees: Insurance and Banking; Joint Fiscal Review; Local
Government
Education: Tennessee BS; Tennessee (Memphis) PharmD

Representative **Eddie Smith** (R-District 13) . . . . . . . . . . . . (615) 741-2031
Counties Represented: Knox (part)    Fax: (615) 253-0192
Term Expires: 2016
E-mail: rep.eddie.smith@capitol.tn.gov
Committees: Education, Administration, and Planning; Transportation

Representative **Mike Sparks** (R-District 49) . . . . . . . . . . . (615) 741-6829
Counties Represented: Rutherford (part)    Fax: (615) 253-0332
Term Expires: 2016
114 Woodland Drive, Smyrna, TN 37167
E-mail: rep.mike.sparks@capitol.tn.gov
Committees: Local Government

Representative **Billy Spivey** (R-District 92) . . . . . . . . . . . . (615) 741-4170
Counties Represented: Franklin (part), Lincoln (part), Marion (part),
Marshall
Term Expires: 2016
1523 Cornersville Highway, Lewisburg, TN 37091
E-mail: rep.billy.spivey@capitol.tn.gov
Committees: Local Government

Representative **Mike Stewart** (D-District 52) . . . . . . . . . . . (615) 741-2184
Counties Represented: Davidson (part)    Fax: (615) 253-0181
Term Expires: 2016
412 North 16th Street, Nashville, TN 37206
E-mail: rep.mike.stewart@capitol.tn.gov
Committees: Calendar and Rules; Criminal Justice; Government
Operations; Insurance and Banking

Representative **Art Swann** (R-District 8) . . . . . . . . . . . . . . (615) 741-5481
Counties Represented: Blount (part)    Fax: (615) 253-0220
Term Expires: 2016
3652 Wagon Wheel Road, Maryville, TN 37803
E-mail: rep.art.swann@capitol.tn.gov
Committees: Agriculture and Natural Resources; Business and Utilities
Education: Tennessee (Martin) 1975 BS

Representative **Bryan Terry** (R-District 48) . . . . . . . . . . . . (615) 741-2180
Counties Represented: Rutherford (part)    Fax: (615) 253-0372
Term Expires: 2016
E-mail: rep.bryan.terry@capitol.tn.gov
Committees: Consumer and Human Resources; Health

Representative **Curry Todd** (R-District 95) . . . . . . . . . . . . (615) 741-1866
Counties Represented: Shelby (part)    Dist: (901) 853-1348
Term Expires: 2016    Fax: (615) 253-0208
944 Hand Forth Cove, Collierville, TN 38017
E-mail: rep.curry.todd@capitol.tn.gov
Committees: Business and Utilities; Finance, Ways and Means; State
Government

Representative **Joe Towns, Jr.** (D-District 84) . . . . . . . . . . (615) 741-2189
Counties Represented: Shelby (part)    Dist: (901) 332-7009
Term Expires: 2016    Fax: (615) 253-0201
4528 St. Honore Drive, Memphis, TN 38116
E-mail: rep.joe.towns@capitol.tn.gov
Committees: Business and Utilities; Insurance and Banking

Representative **Ron Travis** (R-District 31) . . . . . . . . . . . . . (615) 741-1450
Counties Represented: Bledsoe, Rhea, Roane (part),    Fax: (615) 253-0262
Sequatchie
Term Expires: 2016
1318 Armstrong Ferry Road, Dayton, TN 37321
E-mail: rep.ron.travis@capitol.tn.gov
Committees: Consumer and Human Resources; Insurance and Banking;
Joint Fiscal Review

Representative **Johnnie R. Turner** (D-District 85) . . . . . . . (615) 741-6954
Counties Represented: Shelby (part)    Dist: (901) 785-6750
Term Expires: 2016    Fax: (615) 253-0339
752 West Levi Road, Memphis, TN 38109
E-mail: rep.johnnie.turner@capitol.tn.gov
Committees: Consumer and Human Resources; Education,
Administration, and Planning; Joint Government Operations

Representative **James "Micah" Van Huss** (R-District 6) . . (615) 741-1717
Counties Represented: Washington (part)    Fax: (615) 253-0301
Term Expires: 2016
1835 Sulphur Springs, Jonesborough, TN 37659
E-mail: rep.james.vanhuss@capitol.tn.gov
Committees: Criminal Justice; Local Government
Education: Pensacola Christian 2003 BS

Representative **Terri Lynn Weaver** (R-District 40) . . . . . . . (615) 741-2192
Counties Represented: DeKalb (part), Smith,    Fax: (615) 253-0378
Sumner (part), Trousdale
Term Expires: 2016
100 Seabowisha Lane, Lancaster, TN 38569
E-mail: rep.terri.lynn.weaver@capitol.tn.gov
Committees: Criminal Justice; Transportation

Representative **Dawn White** (R-District 37) . . . . . . . . . . . . (615) 741-6849
Counties Represented: Rutherford (part)    Fax: (615) 253-0264
Term Expires: 2016
1522 Riverview Drive, Murfreesboro, TN 37129
E-mail: rep.dawn.white@capitol.tn.gov
Committees: Business and Utilities; Education, Administration, and
Planning; Transportation

Representative **Mark White** (R-District 83) . . . . . . . . . . . . (615) 741-4415
Counties Represented: Shelby (part)    Fax: (615) 253-0349
Term Expires: 2016
6820 Talisman Cove, Memphis, TN 38119
E-mail: rep.mark.white@capitol.tn.gov
Committees: Consumer and Human Resources; Education,
Administration, and Planning; Joint Fiscal Review
Education: U Memphis 1974

**LEGISLATIVE BRANCH**

*(continued on next page)*

**Representatives** *continued*

Representative **Leigh Rosser Wilburn** (R-District 94) . . . . . (615) 741-6890
Counties Represented: Fayette      Fax: (615) 253-0380
Term Expires: 2016
Committees: Civil Justice; Health

Representative **Ryan Williams** (R-District 42) . . . . . . . . . . (615) 741-1875
Counties Represented: Putnam      Fax: (615) 253-0160
Term Expires: 2016
570 Pleasant Hill Drive, Cookeville, TN 38501
E-mail: rep.ryan.williams@capitol.tn.gov
Committees: Health
Education: Carson-Newman BS

Representative **John Mark Windle** (D-District 41) . . . . . . . (615) 741-1260
Counties Represented: Fentress (part), Jackson,    Dist: (931) 823-3970
Morgan, Overton (part)      Fax: (615) 253-0328
Term Expires: 2016
P.O. Box 707, Livingston, TN 38570
E-mail: rep.john.windle@capitol.tn.gov
Committees: Agriculture and Natural Resources; Transportation
Education: Tennessee BS, JD

Representative **Tim Wirgau** (R-District 75) . . . . . . . . . . . . (615) 741-6804
Counties Represented: Benton, Henry, Stewart    Fax: (615) 253-0239
Term Expires: 2016
245 Savannah Drive, Buchanan, TN 38222
E-mail: rep.tim.wirgau@capitol.tn.gov
Committees: Business and Utilities; Calendar and Rules; Joint Fiscal
Review; Local Government

Representative
**Richard B. "Rick" Womick** (R-District 34) . . . . . . . . . . . (615) 741-2804
Counties Represented: Rutherford (part)     Fax: (615) 253-0322
Term Expires: 2016
6015 Highway 99, Rockvale, TN 37153
E-mail: rep.rick.womick@capitol.tn.gov
Committees: Consumer and Human Resources; Education,
Administration, and Planning
Education: Dayton BSEd

Representative **Jason Zachary** (R-District 14) . . . . . . . . . . . (615) 741-2264
Counties Represented: Knox (part)
Term Expires: 2016
E-mail: rep.jason.zachary@capitol.tn.gov
Committees: Business and Utilities; Transportation

# House Standing Committees

## Agriculture and Natural Resources
23 Legislative Plaza, Nashville, TN 37243

| **Majority Members** | **Minority Members** |
|---|---|
| Curtis Halford (R-79) *Chair* | G. A. Hardaway (D-93) |
| Andrew H. "Andy" Holt (R-76) | Johnny W. Shaw (D-80) |
|   *Vice Chair* | John Mark Windle (D-41) |
| David "Coach" Byrd (R-71) | |
| David B. Hawk (R-5) | |
| Bud Hulsey (R-2) | |
| Ron Lollar (R-99) | |
| Pat Marsh (R-62) | |
| Steve K. McDaniel (R-72) | |
| Debra Moody (R-81) | |
| Dennis Powers (R-36) | |
| Jay D. Reedy (R-74) | |
| Art Swann (R-8) | |

## Business and Utilities
War Memorial Building, G - 19A, Nashville, TN 37243

| **Majority Members** | **Minority Members** |
|---|---|
| Pat Marsh (R-62) *Chair* | Jason Powell (D-53) |
| Tim Wirgau (R-75) *Vice Chair* | Joe Towns, Jr. (D-84) |
| Kent Calfee (R-32) | |
| Barry Doss (R-70) | |
| Tilman Goins (R-10) | |
| Timothy Hill (R-3) | |
| William G. Lamberth (R-44) | |
| Gerald McCormick (R-26) | |
| Mark Pody (R-46) | |
| Cameron Sexton (R-25) | |
| Art Swann (R-8) | |
| Curry Todd (R-95) | |
| Dawn White (R-37) | |
| Jason Zachary (R-14) | |

## Calendar and Rules
War Memorial Building, Room 212, Nashville, TN 37243

| **Majority Members** | **Minority Members** |
|---|---|
| Bill Dunn (R-16) *Chair* | Craig Fitzhugh (D-82) |
| Timothy Hill (R-3) *Vice Chair* | Antonio Parkinson (D-98) |
| Harry R. Brooks (R-19) | Mike Stewart (D-52) |
| Kevin D. Brooks (R-24) | |
| Glen Casada (R-63) | |
| Jimmy A. Eldridge (R-73) | |
| Jeremy Faison (R-11) | |
| John W. Forgety (R-23) | |
| Curtis Halford (R-79) | |
| Beth Halteman Harwell (R-56) | |
| Curtis G. Johnson (R-68) | |
| Jon C. Lundberg (R-1) | |
| Pat Marsh (R-62) | |
| Jimmy Matlock (R-21) | |
| Gerald McCormick (R-26) | |
| Steve K. McManus (R-96) | |
| Bob Ramsey (R-20) | |
| Charles Michael Sargent, Jr. (R-61) | |
| Cameron Sexton (R-25) | |
| Jerry Sexton (R-35) | |
| Tim Wirgau (R-75) | |

## Civil Justice
20 Legislative Plaza, Nashville, TN 37243

| **Majority Members** | **Minority Members** |
|---|---|
| Jon C. Lundberg (R-1) *Chair* | Bill Beck (D-51) |
| Mike Carter (R-29) *Vice Chair* | Sherry Jones (D-59) |
| Jim Coley (R-97) | |
| Martin Daniel (R-18) | |
| John W. Forgety (R-23) | |
| Courtney Rogers (R-45) | |
| Leigh Rosser Wilburn (R-94) | |

## Consumer and Human Resources
War Memorial Building, Nashville, TN 37243

| **Majority Members** | **Minority Members** |
|---|---|
| Jimmy A. Eldridge (R-73) *Chair* | G. A. Hardaway (D-93) |
| Mark Pody (R-46) *Vice Chair* | Bo Mitchell (D-50) |
| Glen Casada (R-63) | Johnnie R. Turner (D-85) |
| Susan M. Lynn (R-57) | |
| Bryan Terry (R-48) | |
| Ron Travis (R-31) | |
| Mark White (R-83) | |
| Richard B. "Rick" Womick (R-34) | |

## Criminal Justice
War Memorial Building, Room 112, Nashville, TN 37243

| **Majority Members** | **Minority Members** |
|---|---|
| William G. Lamberth (R-44) *Chair* | Raumesh Akbari (D-91) |
| James "Micah" Van Huss (R-6) | Antonio Parkinson (D-98) |
|   *Vice Chair* | Mike Stewart (D-52) |
| Sheila Butt (R-64) | |
| Andrew E. Farmer (R-17) | |
| Tilman Goins (R-10) | |
| Terri Lynn Weaver (R-40) | |

## Education, Administration, and Planning
War Memorial Building, Room 212, Nashville, TN 37243

| **Majority Members** | **Minority Members** |
|---|---|
| Harry R. Brooks (R-19) *Chair* | John J. DeBerry, Jr. (D-90) |
| Debra Moody (R-81) *Vice Chair* | Kevin Dunlap (D-43) |
| Kevin D. Brooks (R-24) | Craig Fitzhugh (D-82) |
| Kent Calfee (R-32) | Johnnie R. Turner (D-85) |
| Jim Coley (R-97) | |
| Eddie Smith (R-13) | |
| Dawn White (R-37) | |
| Mark White (R-83) | |
| Richard B. "Rick" Womick (R-34) | |

## Finance, Ways and Means
33 Legislative Plaza, Nashville, TN 37243

**Majority Members**
Charles Michael Sargent, Jr. (R-61) *Chair*
David Alexander (R-39) *Vice Chair*
Kevin D. Brooks (R-24)
Mike Carter (R-29)
Bill Dunn (R-16)
Michael "Mike" Harrison (R-9)
David B. Hawk (R-5)
Patsy Hazlewood (R-27)
Matthew Hill (R-7)
Curtis G. Johnson (R-68)
Susan M. Lynn (R-57)
Gerald McCormick (R-26)
Steve K. McDaniel (R-72)
Steve K. McManus (R-96)
Curry Todd (R-95)

**Minority Members**
Joseph E. "Joe" Armstrong (D-15)
Karen D. Camper (D-87)
Barbara W. Cooper (D-86)
Craig Fitzhugh (D-82)
Brenda Gilmore (D-54)
Larry J. Miller (D-88)
Bo Mitchell (D-50)

## Government Operations
War Memorial Buiding, Room 215, Nashville, TN 37243

**Majority Members**
Jeremy Faison (R-11) *Chair*
John D. Ragan (R-33) *Vice Chair*
Glen Casada (R-63)
Curtis Halford (R-79)
Dan Howell (R-22)
Curtis G. Johnson (R-68)
Gerald McCormick (R-26)

**Minority Members**
John Ray Clemmons (D-55)
Craig Fitzhugh (D-82)
Mike Stewart (D-52)

## Health
25 Legislative Plaza, Nashville, TN 37243

**Majority Members**
Cameron Sexton (R-25) *Chair*
Barry Doss (R-70) *Vice Chair*
Jeremy Faison (R-11)
Michael "Mike" Harrison (R-9)
Matthew Hill (R-7)
John B. Holsclaw, Jr. (R-4)
Sabi "Doc" Kumar (R-66)
Mary Littleton (R-78)
Judd Matheny (R-47)
Bob Ramsey (R-20)
Bryan Terry (R-48)
Leigh Rosser Wilburn (R-94)
Ryan Williams (R-42)

**Minority Members**
John Ray Clemmons (D-55)
John J. DeBerry, Jr. (D-90)
JoAnne Favors (D-28)
Darren Jernigan (D-60)
Sherry Jones (D-59)

## Insurance and Banking
20 Legislative Plaza, Nashville, TN 37243

**Majority Members**
Steve K. McManus (R-96) *Chair*
Ron Travis (R-31) *Vice Chair*
Glen Casada (R-63)
Jeremy Durham (R-65)
Andrew E. Farmer (R-17)
Timothy Hill (R-3)
Curtis G. Johnson (R-68)
Roger Kane (R-89)
Kelly Keisling (R-38)
Jon C. Lundberg (R-1)
Judd Matheny (R-47)
Jimmy Matlock (R-21)
Mark Pody (R-46)
Dennis Powers (R-36)
Charles Michael Sargent, Jr. (R-61)

**Minority Members**
JoAnne Favors (D-28)
Joe Pitts (D-67)
David A. Shepard (D-69)
Mike Stewart (D-52)
Joe Towns, Jr. (D-84)

## Local Government
23 Legislative Plaza, Nashville, TN 37243

**Majority Members**
Tim Wirgau (R-75) *Chair*
Mike Sparks (R-49) *Vice Chair*
Dale Carr (R-12)
Jimmy A. Eldridge (R-73)
Marc Gravitt (R-30)
Andrew H. "Andy" Holt (R-76)
Dan Howell (R-22)
Cameron Sexton (R-25)
Billy Spivey (R-92)
James "Micah" Van Huss (R-6)

**Minority Members**
Larry J. Miller (D-88)
Antonio Parkinson (D-98)
David A. Shepard (D-69)

## State Government
War Memorial Building, Room 209, Nashville, TN 37243

**Majority Members**
Bob Ramsey (R-20) *Chair*
Mary Littleton (R-78) *Vice Chair*
Jeremy Durham (R-65)
Bud Hulsey (R-2)
William G. Lamberth (R-44)
Bill Sanderson (R-77)
Curry Todd (R-95)

**Minority Members**
Darren Jernigan (D-60)
Jason Powell (D-53)
Johnny W. Shaw (D-80)

## Transportation
24 Legislative Plaza, Nashville, TN 37243

**Majority Members**
Jimmy Matlock (R-21) *Chair*
Courtney Rogers (R-45) *Vice Chair*
David Alexander (R-39)
Dale Carr (R-12)
Timothy Hill (R-3)
Kelly Keisling (R-38)
John D. Ragan (R-33)
Bill Sanderson (R-77)
Jerry Sexton (R-35)
Eddie Smith (R-13)
Terri Lynn Weaver (R-40)
Dawn White (R-37)
Jason Zachary (R-14)

**Minority Members**
Joseph E. "Joe" Armstrong (D-15)
Bill Beck (D-51)
Karen D. Camper (D-87)
Barbara W. Cooper (D-86)
John Mark Windle (D-41)

# Texas Legislature

State Capitol, 1100 North Congress Avenue, Austin, TX 78701
Tel: (512) 463-4630  Tel: (877) 824-7038 (In State)
Internet: www.legis.state.tx.us

## Texas State Senate

P.O. Box 12068, Austin, TX 78711
Tel: (512) 463-0100  TTY: (800) 735-2989  Fax: (512) 463-6034
Internet: www.senate.state.tx.us

President of the Senate **Dan Patrick** (R) . . . . . . . . . . . . . . (512) 463-0001
  Education: Maryland Baltimore County BA
President Pro Tem **Kevin Eltife** (R) . . . . . . . . . . . . . . . . . . (512) 463-0101
  Education: Texas BBA
Republican Caucus Chair **Paul Bettencourt** (R) . . . . . . . . (512) 463-0107
Democratic Caucus Chair **José R. Rodríguez** (D) . . . . . . . . (512) 463-0129
  Education: George Washington 1974 JD
Secretary of the Senate **Patsy Spaw** . . . . . . . . . . . . . . . . . . (512) 463-0100
  E-mail: patsy.spaw@senate.state.tx.us
  Education: St Edward's BA; Texas JD

## Senators

**Party Affiliation Statistics: Republicans: 20, Democrats: 11**

Senator **Paul Bettencourt** (R-District 7) . . . . . . . . . . . . . . (512) 463-0107
  Counties Represented: Harris (part)    Dist: (713) 464-0282
  Term Expires: January 8, 2019    Fax: (713) 461-0108
  1100 North Congress Avenue, Room E1.712, Austin, TX 78701
  11451 Katy Freeman, Suite 209, Houston, TX 77079
  E-mail: paul.bettencourt@senate.state.tx.us
  Committees: Education; Finance; Higher Education; Intergovernmental
  Relations
Senator **LTC Brian Birdwell, USA (Ret)** (R-District 22) . . . (512) 463-0122
  Counties Represented: Bosque, Ellis, Falls, Hill,    Dist: (254) 772-6225
  Hood, Johnson, McLennan, Navarro, Somervell,    (Waco Office)
  Tarrant (part)    Dist: (254) 573-9622
  Term Expires: January 10, 2017    (Granbury Office)
  900 Austin Avenue, Suite 500, Waco, TX 76701    Fax: (254) 776-2843
  1315 Waters Edge Drive, Suite 116-2,    (Waco Office)
  Granbury, TX 76048    Dist: (817) 579-7172
  E-mail: brian.birdwell@senate.state.tx.us    (Granbury Office)
  Committees: Finance; Natural Resources and Economic Development;
  Nominations; State Affairs; Veteran Affairs and Military Installations
  Education: Lamar 1984 BS; Missouri (Kansas City) 1996 MPA
Senator **Konni Burton** (R-District 10) . . . . . . . . . . . . . . . . (512) 463-0110
  Counties Represented: Tarrant (part)    Dist: (817) 882-8157
  Term Expires: January 8, 2019    Fax: (817) 882-8539
  1100 North Congress Avenue, Room GE.7, Austin, TX 78701
  933 West Weatherford Street, Suite 203, Fort Worth, TX 76102
  E-mail: konni.burton@senate.state.tx.us
  Committees: Criminal Justice; Higher Education; Nominations; Veteran
  Affairs and Military Installations
Senator **Donna Campbell** (R-District 25) . . . . . . . . . . . . . . (512) 463-0125
  Counties Represented: Bexar (part), Comal,    Dist: (210) 979-0013
  Guadalupe (part), Hays (part), Kendall, Travis (part)    Fax: (512) 463-7794
  Term Expires: January 8, 2019
  9601 McAllister Freeway, Suite 150, San Antonio, TX 78216
  E-mail: donna.campbell@senate.state.tx.us
  Committees: Administration; Education; Health and Human Services;
  Intergovernmental Relations; Veteran Affairs and Military Installations
  Education: Central State BS; Texas Woman's MN;
  Texas Tech 1989 MD
Senator **Brandon Creighton** (R-District 4) . . . . . . . . . . . . . (512) 463-0104
  Counties Represented: Chambers, Galveston (part),    Dist: (281) 292-4128
  Harris (part), Jefferson, Montgomery (part)    Fax: (281) 292-6253
  Term Expires: January 10, 2017
  2829 Technology Forest, Suite 240, The Woodlands, TX 77381
  E-mail: brandon.creighton@senate.state.tx.us
  Committees: Agriculture, Water, and Rural Affairs; Business and
  Commerce; Criminal Justice; State Affairs
  Education: Texas BA; Oklahoma City 1998 JD

Senator **Rodney Ellis** (D-District 13) . . . . . . . . . . . . . . . . . (512) 463-0113
  Counties Represented: Fort Bend (part), Harris    Dist: (713) 236-0306
  (part)    (Houston Office)
  Term Expires: January 10, 2017    Dist: (281) 261-2360
  440 Louisiana, Suite 575, Houston, TX 77002    (Missouri City
  2440 Texas Parkway, Suite 110,    Office)
  Missouri City, TX 77489    Fax: (512) 463-0006
  E-mail: rodney.ellis@senate.state.tx.us    Dist: (713) 236-0604
  Committees: Business and Commerce; State Affairs;    (Houston Office)
  Transportation    Dist: (281) 261-4726
  Affiliation: Director, Apex Securities, Inc.    (Missouri City
  333 Clay Street, #3010, Houston, TX 77002    Office)
  Education: Texas Southern 1975 BA; Texas 1977 MPA, 1979 JD
Senator **Kevin Eltife** (R-District 1) . . . . . . . . . . . . . . . . . . (512) 463-0101
  Counties Represented: Bowie, Camp, Cass,    Dist: (903) 596-9122
  Franklin, Gregg, Harrison, Lamar, Marion, Morris,    (Tyler Office)
  Panola, Red River, Rusk, Smith, Titus, Upshur,    Dist: (903) 753-8137
  Wood    (Longview Office)
  Term Expires: January 10, 2017    Fax: (512) 475-3751
  3304 South Broadway, Suite 103, Tyler, TX 75701    Dist: (903) 596-9189
  101 East Methvin, Suite 301, Longview, TX 75601    (Tyler Office)
  E-mail: kevin.eltife@senate.state.tx.us    Dist: (903) 753-8568
  Committees: Administration    (Longview Office)
Senator **Craig Estes** (R-District 30) . . . . . . . . . . . . . . . . . . (512) 463-0130
  Counties Represented: Archer, Clay, Collin    Dist: (940) 689-0191
  (part), Cooke, Denton (part), Erath, Grayson, Jack,    (Wichita Falls Office)
  Montague, Palo Pinto, Parker, Wichita, Wise, Young    Dist: (940) 898-0331
  Term Expires: January 8, 2019    (Denton Office)
  2525 Kell Boulevard, Suite 302,    Fax: (512) 463-8874
  Wichita Falls, TX 76308    Dist: (940) 689-0194
  4401 North I-H 35, Suite 202, Denton, TX 76207    (Wichita Falls Office)
  E-mail: craig.estes@senate.state.tx.us    Dist: (940) 898-0926
  Committees: Health and Human Services; Natural    (Denton Office)
  Resources and Economic Development; Nominations; State Affairs
  Education: Oral Roberts 1977 BS
Senator **Troy Fraser** (R-District 24) . . . . . . . . . . . . . . . . . . (512) 463-0124
  Counties Represented: Bandera, Bell, Blanco,    Dist: (254) 939-3562
  Brown, Burnet, Callahan, Comanche, Coryell,    (Belton Office)
  Gillespie, Hamilton, Kerr, Lampasas, Llano, Mills,    Dist: (325) 676-7404
  San Saba, Taylor (part), Travis (part)    (Abilene Office)
  Term Expires: January 10, 2017    Fax: (254) 939-7611
  1920 North Main, Suite 101, Belton, TX 76513    (Belton Office)
  500 Chestnut, Suite 810, Abilene, TX 79602    Dist: (325) 676-8060
  E-mail: troy.fraser@senate.state.tx.us    (Abilene Office)
  Committees: Natural Resources and Economic Development;
  Nominations; State Affairs; Transportation
  Affiliation: Founder and Former Chief Development Officer, Pal-Ex,
  Inc.
Senator **Sylvia R. Garcia** (D-District 6) . . . . . . . . . . . . . . . (512) 463-0106
  Counties Represented: Harris (part)    Dist: (713) 923-7575
  Term Expires: January 10, 2017    Fax: (713) 923-7676
  5425 Polk Street, Suite 125, Houston, TX 77023
  E-mail: sylvia.garcia@senate.state.tx.us
  Committees: Education; Intergovernmental Relations; Transportation;
  Veteran Affairs and Military Installations
  Education: Texas Woman's 1972 BSW; Texas Southern 1978 JD
Senator **Bob Hall** (R-District 2) . . . . . . . . . . . . . . . . . . . . . (512) 463-0102
  Counties Represented: Dallas (part), Delta, Fannin,    Dist: (972) 722-7945
  Hopkins, Hunt, Kaufman, Rains, Rockwall, Van    Fax: (512) 463-7202
  Zandt
  Term Expires: January 8, 2019
  1100 North Congress Avenue, Room E1.808, Austin, TX 78701
  Alliance Building #2, 6537 Horizon Road, Suite B-1,
  Rockwall, TX 75032
  E-mail: bob.hall@senate.state.tx.us
  Committees: Agriculture, Water, and Rural Affairs; Natural Resources
  and Economic Development; Transportation; Veteran Affairs and
  Military Installations
  Education: Citadel BSEE
Senator **Kelly Hancock** (R-District 9) . . . . . . . . . . . . . . . . (512) 463-0109
  Counties Represented: Dallas (part), Tarrant (part)    Dist: (817) 514-3804
  Term Expires: January 8, 2019    Fax: (817) 514-3806
  9121 Belshire Drive, Suite 200, North Richland Hills, TX 76182
  E-mail: kelly.hancock@senate.state.tx.us
  Committees: Administration; Business and Commerce; Finance; Natural
  Resources and Economic Development; Transportation
  Education: Baylor 1986 BBA

Senator **Juan "Chuy" Hinojosa** (D-District 20) . . . . . . . . . (512) 463-0120
Counties Represented: Brooks, Hidalgo (part),     Dist: (956) 972-1841
Jim Wells, Nueces (part)     (McAllen Office)
Term Expires: January 10, 2017     Dist: (361) 225-1200
612 Nolana Street, Suite 410-B,     (Corpus Christi
McAllen, TX 78504     Office)
2820 S.P.I.D, Sutie 291, Corpus Christi, TX 78415     Fax: (512) 463-0229
E-mail: juan.hinojosa@senate.state.tx.us     Dist: (956) 664-0602
Committees: Agriculture, Water, and Rural Affairs;     (McAllen Office)
Criminal Justice; Finance; Natural Resources     Dist: (361) 225-0119
and Economic Development     (Corpus Christi
Education: Texas Pan American 1970 BS;     Office)
Georgetown JD

Senator **Donald Huffines** (R-District 16) . . . . . . . . . . . . . . (512) 463-0116
Counties Represented: Dallas (part)     Dist: (214) 239-6131
Term Expires: January 8, 2019
8222 Douglas Avenue, Suite 675, Dallas, TX 75225
E-mail: don.huffines@senate.state.tx.us
Committees: Administration; Business and Commerce; Education;
Transportation
Education: Texas 1981

Senator **Joan Huffman** (R-District 17) . . . . . . . . . . . . . . . (512) 463-0117
Counties Represented: Brazoria (part), Fort Bend     Dist: (979) 480-0994
(part), Harris (part)     (Lake Jackson Office)
Term Expires: January 8, 2019     Fax: (979) 480-9122
129 Circle Way, Suite 101, Lake Jackson, TX 77566     (Lake Jackson Office)
E-mail: joan.huffman@senate.state.tx.us
Committees: Criminal Justice; Finance; State Affairs
Education: LSU 1979 BA; South Texas 1984 JD

Senator **Lois W. Kolkhorst** (R-District 18) . . . . . . . . . . . . (512) 463-0118
Counties Represented: Aransas, Austin, Burleson,     Dist: (979) 251-7888
Calhoun, Colorado, De Witt, Fayette, Fort Bend     Fax: (979) 251-7968
(part), Goliad, Gonzales, Harris (part), Jackson, Lavaca, Lee,
Matagorda, Nueces (part), Refugio, Victoria, Waller, Washington,
Wharton
Term Expires: January 10, 2017
1100 North Congress Avenue, Room 3E.2, Austin, TX 78701
2000 South Market Street, Suite 101, Brenham, TX 77833
E-mail: lois.kolkhorst@senate.state.tx.us
Committees: Agriculture, Water, and Rural Affairs; Education; Finance;
Health and Human Services; Transportation
Education: Texas Christian 1988 BA

Senator **Eddie Lucio, Jr.** (D-District 27) . . . . . . . . . . . . . . (512) 463-0127
Counties Represented: Cameron, Hidalgo (part),     Dist: (956) 548-0227
Kenedy, Kleberg, Willacy     (Brownsville Office)
Term Expires: January 10, 2017     Fax: (512) 463-0061
Seven North Park Plaza, Brownsville, TX 78521     Dist: (956) 548-0440
E-mail: eddie.lucio@senate.state.tx.us     (Brownsville Office)
Committees: Education; Intergovernmental Relations; Natural
Resources and Economic Development; Veteran Affairs and Military
Installations
Education: Texas Pan American BS

Senator **José Menéndez** (D-District 26) . . . . . . . . . . . . . . (512) 463-0126
Counties Represented: Bexar (part)     Dist: (210) 733-6604
Term Expires: January 10, 2017     Fax: (210) 733-6605
101 West Nueva, Suite 809, San Antonio, TX 78205
E-mail: jose.menendez@senate.state.tx.us
Committees: Criminal Justice; Higher Education; Intergovernmental
Relations
Education: Southern Methodist 1991 BA, 1991 BBA

Senator **Jane Nelson** (R-District 12) . . . . . . . . . . . . . . . . (512) 463-0112
Counties Represented: Denton (part), Tarrant (part)     Dist: (817) 424-3446
Term Expires: January 10, 2017     Dist: (817) 488-6648
1235 South Main Street, Suite 280,     Fax: (512) 463-0923
Grapevine, TX 76051
E-mail: jane.nelson@senate.state.tx.us
Committees: Finance; State Affairs
Education: North Texas 1972 BS

Senator **Robert Nichols** (R-District 3) . . . . . . . . . . . . . . . (512) 463-0103
Counties Represented: Anderson, Angelina,     Dist: (903) 589-3003
Cherokee, Hardin, Henderson, Houston, Jasper,     (Jacksonville Office)
Liberty, Montgomery (part), Nacogdoches, Newton,     Fax: (512) 463-1526
Orange, Polk, Sabine, San Augustine, San Jacinto,     Dist: (903) 589-0203
Shelby, Trinity, Tyler     (Jacksonville Office)
Term Expires: January 8, 2019
329 Neches Street, Jacksonville, TX 75766
E-mail: robert.nichols@senate.state.tx.us
Committees: Finance; Intergovernmental Relations; Natural Resources
and Economic Development; Transportation
Education: Lamar 1968 BS

Senator **Charles Lee Perry** (R-District 28) . . . . . . . . . . . . . (512) 463-0128
Counties Represented: Baylor, Borden, Childress,     Dist: (806) 783-9934
Coke, Coleman, Concho, Cottle, Crane, Crosby, Dawson, Dickens,
Eastland, Fisher, Floyd, Foard, Garza, Hale, Hardeman, Haskell,
Hockley, Irion, Jones, Kent, Kimble, King, Knox, Lamb, Lubbock,
Lynn, Mason, McCulloch, Menard, Mitchell, Motley, Nolan, Reagan,
Runnels, Schleicher, Scurry, Shackelford, Stephens, Sterling, Stonewall,
Sutton, Taylor (part), Terry, Throckmorton, Tom Green, Upton, Ward,
Wilbarger
Term Expires: January 10, 2017
11003 Quaker Avenue, Suite 101, Lubbock, TX 79424
E-mail: charles.perry@senate.state.tx.us
Committees: Agriculture, Water, and Rural Affairs; Criminal Justice;
Health and Human Services; Higher Education
Education: Texas Tech 1984 BBA

Senator **José R. Rodríguez** (D-District 29) . . . . . . . . . . . . (512) 463-0129
Counties Represented: Culberson, El Paso,     Dist: (915) 351-3500
Hudspeth, Jeff Davis, Presidio     Fax: (915) 351-3579
Term Expires: January 10, 2017
100 North Ochoa, Suite A, El Paso, TX 79901
E-mail: jose.rodriguez@senate.state.tx.us
Committees: Agriculture, Water, and Rural Affairs; Education; Health
and Human Services; Nominations; Veteran Affairs and Military
Installations

Senator **Charles Schwertner** (R-District 5) . . . . . . . . . . . . (512) 463-0105
Counties Represented: Brazos, Freestone, Grimes,     Fax: (512) 463-5713
Leon, Limestone, Madison, Milam, Robertson, Walker, Williamson
Term Expires: January 8, 2019
501 South Austin Avenue, Suite 1250, Georgetown, TX 78626
E-mail: charles.schwertner@senate.state.tx.us
Committees: Administration; Business and Commerce; Finance; Health
and Human Services; State Affairs
Education: Texas (Arlington) 1992 BPharm;
Texas (Galveston) 1997 MD

Senator **Kel Seliger** (R-District 31) . . . . . . . . . . . . . . . . . (512) 463-0131
Counties Represented: Andrews, Armstrong,     Dist: (806) 374-8994
Bailey, Briscoe, Carson, Castro, Cochran,     (Amarillo Office)
Collingsworth, Dallam, Deaf Smith, Donley, Ector,     Dist: (432) 268-9909
Gaines, Glasscock, Gray, Hall, Hansford, Hartley,     (Big Spring Office)
Hemphill, Howard, Hutchinson, Lipscomb, Loving,     Fax: (512) 475-3733
Martin, Midland, Moore, Ochiltree, Oldham,     Dist: (806) 374-4607
Parmer, Potter, Randall, Roberts, Sherman, Swisher,     (Amarillo Office)
Wheeler, Winkler, Yoakum     Dist: (432) 268-9899
Term Expires: January 8, 2019     (Big Spring Office)
PO Box 9155, Amarillo, TX 79105
410 South Taylor, Suite 1600, Amarillo, TX 79101
401 Austin, Suite 101, Big Spring, TX 79720
E-mail: kel.seliger@senate.state.tx.us
Committees: Business and Commerce; Education; Finance; Higher
Education; Natural Resources and Economic Development
Education: Dartmouth BA

Senator **Larry Taylor** (R-District 11) . . . . . . . . . . . . . . . . (512) 463-0111
Counties Represented: Brazoria (part), Galveston     Dist: (281) 485-9800
(part), Harris (part)     Fax: (281) 485-9804
Term Expires: January 10, 2017
6117 Broadway, Suite 122, Pearland, TX 77581
E-mail: larry.taylor@senate.state.tx.us
Committees: Business and Commerce; Education; Finance;
Intergovernmental Relations
Education: Baylor 1982 BBA

Senator **Van Taylor** (R-District 8) . . . . . . . . . . . . . . . . . . (512) 463-0108
Counties Represented: Collin (part), Dallas (part)     Dist: (972) 398-9416
Term Expires: January 8, 2019     Fax: (972) 398-9418
6301 Preston Road, Suite 700, Plano, TX 75024
E-mail: van.taylor@senate.state.tx.us
Committees: Education; Health and Human Services; Nominations;
Transportation
Education: Harvard 1995 BA, MBA

Senator **Carlos Uresti** (D-District 19) . . . . . . . . . . . . . . . (512) 463-0119
Counties Represented: Atascosa (part), Bexar     Dist: (210) 932-2568
(part), Brewster, Crockett, Dimmit, Edwards,     (San Antonio Office)
Frio, Kinney, Maverick, Medina, Pecos, Real,     Dist: (830) 758-0294
Reeves, Terrell, Uvalde, Val Verde, Zavala     (Eagle Pass Office)
Term Expires: January 10, 2017     Fax: (512) 463-1017
3315 Sidney Brooks Drive, Suite 100,     Dist: (210) 932-2572
San Antonio, TX 78235     (San Antonio Office)
501 Main Street, Suite 114, Eagle Pass, TX 78852     Dist: (830) 758-0402
E-mail: carlos.uresti@senate.state.tx.us     (Eagle Pass Office)
Committees: Administration; Finance; Health and Human Services;
Natural Resources and Economic Development
Education: St Mary's U (TX) 1985 BA, 1992 JD

*(continued on next page)*

LEGISLATIVE BRANCH

**Senators** *continued*

Senator **Kirk P. Watson** (D-District 14) . . . . . . . . . . . . . . . .(512) 463-0114
Counties Represented: Bastrop, Travis (part)        Fax: (512) 463-5949
Term Expires: January 8, 2019
E-mail: kirk.watson@senate.state.tx.us
Committees: Business and Commerce; Finance; Higher Education;
Nominations
Education: Baylor BA, 1981 JD

Senator **Royce West** (D-District 23) . . . . . . . . . . . . . . . . . .(512) 463-0123
Counties Represented: Dallas (part)              Dist: (214) 467-0123
Term Expires: January 8, 2019                    Dist: (214) 741-0123
5787 South Hampton Road, Suite 385,             Fax: (512) 463-0299
Dallas, TX 75232                                 Dist: (214) 467-0050
2612 Main Street, Suite 100, Dallas, TX 75226    Dist: (214) 749-7830
E-mail: royce.west@senate.state.tx.us
Committees: Administration; Education; Finance; Higher Education
Education: Texas (Arlington) BA, MA; Houston 1979 JD

Senator **John Whitmire** (D-District 15) . . . . . . . . . . . . . . .(512) 463-0115
Counties Represented: Harris (part)              Dist: (713) 864-8701
Term Expires: January 8, 2019                    Fax: (512) 475-3737
803 Yale Street, Houston, TX 77007               Dist: (713) 864-5287
E-mail: john.whitmire@senate.state.tx.us
Committees: Business and Commerce; Criminal Justice; Finance
Education: Houston BA, 1975 JD

Senator **Judith Zaffirini** (D-District 21) . . . . . . . . . . . . . . .(512) 463-0121
Counties Represented: Atascosa (part), Bee, Bexar    Dist: (956) 722-2293
(part), Caldwell, Duval, Guadalupe (part), Hays       (Laredo Office)
(part), Jim Hogg, Karnes, La Salle, Live Oak,        Fax: (512) 475-3738
McMullen, San Patricio, Starr, Travis (part), Webb,   Dist: (956) 727-4448
Wilson, Zapata                                        (Laredo Office)
Term Expires: January 10, 2017
1407 Washington Street, Laredo, TX 78042
E-mail: judith.zaffirini@senate.state.tx.us
Committees: Agriculture, Water, and Rural Affairs; Health and Human
Services; Natural Resources and Economic Development; State Affairs
Education: Texas BS, MA, PhD

# Senate Standing Committees
## Administration
Tel: (512) 463-0350

| **Majority Members** | **Minority Members** |
| --- | --- |
| Kelly Hancock (R-9) *Chair* | Carlos Uresti (D-19) *Vice Chair* |
| Donna Campbell (R-25) | Royce West (D-23) |
| Kevin Eltife (R-1) | |
| Donald Huffines (R-16) | |
| Charles Schwertner (R-5) | |

## Agriculture, Water, and Rural Affairs
Tel: (512) 463-0340

| **Majority Members** | **Minority Members** |
| --- | --- |
| Charles Lee Perry (R-28) *Chair* | Judith Zaffirini (D-21) *Vice Chair* |
| Brandon Creighton (R-4) | José R. Rodríguez (D-29) |
| Bob Hall (R-2) | Juan "Chuy" Hinojosa (D-20) |
| Lois W. Kolkhorst (R-18) | |

## Business and Commerce
Tel: (512) 463-0365

| **Majority Members** | **Minority Members** |
| --- | --- |
| Kelly Hancock (R-9) *Chair* | Rodney Ellis (D-13) |
| Brandon Creighton (R-4) | Kirk P. Watson (D-14) |
| *Vice Chair* | John Whitmire (D-15) |
| Donald Huffines (R-16) | |
| Charles Schwertner (R-5) | |
| Kel Seliger (R-31) | |
| Larry Taylor (R-11) | |

## Criminal Justice
Tel: (512) 463-0345

| **Majority Members** | **Minority Members** |
| --- | --- |
| Joan Huffman (R-17) *Vice Chair* | John Whitmire (D-15) *Chair* |
| Konni Burton (R-10) | Juan "Chuy" Hinojosa (D-20) |
| Brandon Creighton (R-4) | José Menéndez (D-26) |
| Charles Lee Perry (R-28) | |

## Education
Tel: (512) 463-0355

| **Majority Members** | **Minority Members** |
| --- | --- |
| Larry Taylor (R-11) *Chair* | Eddie Lucio, Jr. (D-27) *Vice Chair* |
| Paul Bettencourt (R-7) | Sylvia R. Garcia (D-6) |
| Donna Campbell (R-25) | José R. Rodríguez (D-29) |
| Donald Huffines (R-16) | Royce West (D-23) |
| Lois W. Kolkhorst (R-18) | |
| Kel Seliger (R-31) | |
| Van Taylor (R-8) | |

## Finance
Tel: (512) 463-0370

| **Majority Members** | **Minority Members** |
| --- | --- |
| Jane Nelson (R-12) *Chair* | Juan "Chuy" Hinojosa (D-20) |
| Paul Bettencourt (R-7) | *Vice Chair* |
| LTC Brian Birdwell (R-22) | Carlos Uresti (D-19) |
| Kelly Hancock (R-9) | Kirk P. Watson (D-14) |
| Joan Huffman (R-17) | Royce West (D-23) |
| Lois W. Kolkhorst (R-18) | John Whitmire (D-15) |
| Robert Nichols (R-3) | |
| Charles Schwertner (R-5) | |
| Kel Seliger (R-31) | |
| Larry Taylor (R-11) | |

## Health and Human Services
Tel: (512) 463-0360

| **Majority Members** | **Minority Members** |
| --- | --- |
| Charles Schwertner (R-5) *Chair* | José R. Rodríguez (D-29) |
| Lois W. Kolkhorst (R-18) | Carlos Uresti (D-19) |
| *Vice Chair* | Judith Zaffirini (D-21) |
| Donna Campbell (R-25) | |
| Craig Estes (R-30) | |
| Charles Lee Perry (R-28) | |
| Van Taylor (R-8) | |

## Higher Education
Tel: (512) 463-4788

| **Majority Members** | **Minority Members** |
| --- | --- |
| Kel Seliger (R-31) *Chair* | Royce West (D-23) *Vice Chair* |
| Paul Bettencourt (R-7) | José Menéndez (D-26) |
| Konni Burton (R-10) | Kirk P. Watson (D-14) |
| Charles Lee Perry (R-28) | |

## Intergovernmental Relations
Tel: (512) 463-2527

| **Majority Members** | **Minority Members** |
| --- | --- |
| Paul Bettencourt (R-7) *Vice Chair* | Eddie Lucio, Jr. (D-27) *Chair* |
| Donna Campbell (R-25) | Sylvia R. Garcia (D-6) |
| Robert Nichols (R-3) | José Menéndez (D-26) |
| Larry Taylor (R-11) | |

## Natural Resources and Economic Development
Tel: (512) 463-0390

| **Majority Members** | **Minority Members** |
| --- | --- |
| Craig Estes (R-30) *Chair* | Juan "Chuy" Hinojosa (D-20) |
| LTC Brian Birdwell (R-22) | Eddie Lucio, Jr. (D-27) |
| Troy Fraser (R-24) | Carlos Uresti (D-19) |
| Bob Hall (R-2) | Judith Zaffirini (D-21) |
| Kelly Hancock (R-9) | |
| Robert Nichols (R-3) | |
| Kel Seliger (R-31) | |

## Nominations
Tel: (512) 463-2084

| **Majority Members** | **Minority Members** |
| --- | --- |
| LTC Brian Birdwell (R-22) *Chair* | José R. Rodríguez (D-29) |
| Van Taylor (R-8) *Vice Chair* | Kirk P. Watson (D-14) |
| Konni Burton (R-10) | |
| Craig Estes (R-30) | |
| Troy Fraser (R-24) | |

## State Affairs
Tel: (512) 463-0380

**Majority Members**
Joan Huffman (R-17) *Chair*
LTC Brian Birdwell (R-22)
Brandon Creighton (R-4)
Craig Estes (R-30)
Troy Fraser (R-24)
Jane Nelson (R-12)
Charles Schwertner (R-5)

**Minority Members**
Rodney Ellis (D-13) *Vice Chair*
Judith Zaffirini (D-21)

## Transportation
Tel: (512) 463-0067

**Majority Members**
Robert Nichols (R-3) *Chair*
Donald Huffines (R-16) *Vice Chair*
Troy Fraser (R-24)
Bob Hall (R-2)
Kelly Hancock (R-9)
Lois W. Kolkhorst (R-18)
Van Taylor (R-8)

**Minority Members**
Rodney Ellis (D-13)
Sylvia R. Garcia (D-6)

## Veteran Affairs and Military Installations
Tel: (512) 463-2211

**Majority Members**
Donna Campbell (R-25) *Chair*
Konni Burton (R-10) *Vice Chair*
LTC Brian Birdwell (R-22)
Bob Hall (R-2)

**Minority Members**
Sylvia R. Garcia (D-6)
Eddie Lucio, Jr. (D-27)
José R. Rodríguez (D-29)

# Texas House of Representatives
1100 North Congress Avenue, Austin, TX 78701
P.O. Box 2910, Austin, TX 78768
Fax: (512) 463-5896  Internet: www.house.state.tx.us

Speaker of the House **Joe Straus III** (R) . . . . . . . . . . . . . . . (512) 463-1000
  Education: Vanderbilt BA
Speaker Pro Tem **Dennis Bonnen** (R) . . . . . . . . . . . . . . . (512) 463-0564
  Education: St Edward's 1994 BA
Minority Leader **Yvonne Davis** (D) . . . . . . . . . . . . . . . . . (512) 463-0598
  Education: Houston 1977 BS
Minority Caucus Chair **Chris Turner** (D) . . . . . . . . . . . . . (512) 463-0574
  Education: Texas 1996 BA
Chief Clerk of the House **Robert Haney** . . . . . . . . . . . . . (512) 463-0845
  E-mail: robert.haney@house.state.tx.us
Sergeant at Arms **Roderick Welsh** . . . . . . . . . . . . . . . . . (512) 463-0910
  E-mail: roderick.welsh@house.state.tx.us

## Representatives
**Party Affiliation Statistics:** Republicans: 99, Democrats: 50,
Vacancies: 1

Representative **Alma A. Allen** (D-District 131) . . . . . . . . . (512) 463-0744
  Counties Represented: Harris (part)          Dist: (713) 776-0505
  Term Expires: 2017                           Fax: (512) 463-0761
  10101 Fondren Road, Suite 500,               Dist: (713) 776-1490
  Houston, TX 77096
  E-mail: alma.allen@house.state.tx.us
  Committees: Corrections; House Administration; Public Education
  Education: Texas Southern BSEd, MA; Houston 1992 DEd
Representative **Roberto R. Alonzo** (D-District 104) . . . . . . (512) 463-0408
  Counties Represented: Dallas (part)          Dist: (214) 942-7104
  Term Expires: 2017                           Fax: (512) 463-1817
  312 West 12th Street, Suite A, Dallas, TX 75208   Dist: (214) 942-8104
  E-mail: roberto.alonzo@house.state.tx.us           (Dallas)
  Committees: Calendars; Higher Education; House Administration;
  Pensions
  Education: Texas 1980 BA; Texas Southern 1984 JD
Representative **Carol Alvarado** (D-District 145) . . . . . . . . . (512) 463-0732
  Counties Represented: Harris (part)          Dist: (713) 649-6563
  Term Expires: 2017                           Fax: (512) 463-4781
  2900 Woodridge Drive, Suite 305,             Dist: (713) 649-6454
  Houston, TX 77087
  E-mail: carol.alvarado@house.state.tx.us
  Committees: Rules and Resolutions; Special Purpose Districts; Urban
  Affairs
  Education: Houston BA, 2008 MBA

Representative **Rafael Anchia** (D-District 103) . . . . . . . . . . (512) 463-0746
  Counties Represented: Dallas (part)          Dist: (214) 943-6081
  Term Expires: 2017                                  (Dallas)
  1111 West Mockingbird Lane, Suite 1330,      Fax: (512) 473-0738
  Dallas, TX 75247                             Dist: (214) 200-0882
  E-mail: rafael.anchia@house.state.tx.us            (Dallas)
  Committees: Energy Resources; International Trade and
  Intergovernmental Affairs
  Education: Southern Methodist BA; Tulane 1993 JD
Representative **Charles "Doc" Anderson** (R-District 56) . . (512) 463-0135
  Counties Represented: McLennan (part)        Dist: (254) 754-3892
  Term Expires: 2017                                  (Waco)
  900 Austin Avenue, Suite 804, Waco, TX 76701   Fax: (512) 463-0642
  E-mail: charles.anderson@house.state.tx.us   Dist: (254) 754-1604
  Committees: Agriculture and Livestock; Economic    (Waco)
  and Small Business Development; State and Federal Power and
  Responsibility
  Education: Texas A&M BA, DVM
Representative **Rodney E. Anderson** (R-District 105) . . . . . (512) 463-0641
  Counties Represented: Dallas (part)          Dist: (469) 713-6581
  Term Expires: 2017                           Fax: (512) 463-0044
  800 West Airport Freeway, Suite 1100, Irving, TX 75062
  E-mail: rodney.anderson@house.state.tx.us
  Committees: International Trade and Intergovernmental Affairs; Urban
  Affairs
Representative **Trent Ashby** (R-District 57)
  Room E2.414 . . . . . . . . . . . . . . . . . . . . . . . . . . . . . . . (512) 463-0508
  Counties Represented: Angelina, Houston, Leon,   Fax: (512) 463-5896
  Madison, San Augustine, Trinity
  Term Expires: 2017
  E-mail: trent.ashby@house.state.tx.us
  Committees: Appropriations; House Administration; Natural Resources
  Education: Texas A&M 1996 BS
Representative **Jimmie Don Aycock** (R-District 54) . . . . . . (512) 463-0684
  Counties Represented: Bell (part), Lampasas   Fax: (512) 463-8987
  Term Expires: 2017
  2916 Illinois Avenue, Killeen, TX 76543
  E-mail: jimmie.aycock@house.state.tx.us
  Committees: Defense and Veterans' Affairs; Public Education
  Education: Texas A&M 1970 DVM
Representative **Cecil Bell, Jr.** (R-District 3)
  Room E2.720 . . . . . . . . . . . . . . . . . . . . . . . . . . . . . . . (512) 463-0650
  Counties Represented: Montgomery (part), Waller   Fax: (512) 463-0575
  Term Expires: 2017
  E-mail: cecil.bell@house.state.tx.us
  Committees: Appropriations; Land and Resource Management; Rules
  and Resolutions
Representative **Diego M. Bernal** (D-District 123) . . . . . . . . (512) 463-0532
  Counties Represented: Bexar (part)           Dist: (210) 308-9700
  Term Expires: 2017
  126 West Rector Street, Suite 114, San Antonio, TX 78216
  E-mail: diego.bernal@house.state.tx.us
  Committees: International Trade and Intergovernmental Affairs; Urban
  Affairs
  Education: Michigan 1999 BA, 2001 MSW, 2004 JD
Representative **Cesar J. Blanco** (D-District 76)
  Room E1.218 . . . . . . . . . . . . . . . . . . . . . . . . . . . . . . . (512) 463-0622
  Counties Represented: El Paso (part)         Fax: (512) 463-0931
  Term Expires: 2017
  E-mail: cesar.blanco@house.state.tx.us
  Committees: Defense and Veterans' Affairs; Public Health; Rules and
  Resolutions
Representative **Dwayne Bohac** (R-District 138) . . . . . . . . . (512) 463-0727
  Counties Represented: Harris (part)          Dist: (713) 460-2800
  Term Expires: 2017                           Fax: (512) 463-0681
  2600 Gessner, Suite 212, Austin, TX 77080    Dist: (713) 460-2822
  E-mail: dwayne.bohac@house.state.tx.us
  Committees: Public Education; Ways and Means
  Education: Texas A&M 1989 BS, 1990 BBA
Representative **Dennis Bonnen** (R-District 25) . . . . . . . . . (512) 463-0564
  Counties Represented: Brazoria (part), Matagorda   Dist: (979) 848-1770
  Term Expires: 2017                                  (Angleton)
  122 East Myrtle, Angleton, TX 77515          Fax: (512) 463-8414
  E-mail: dennis.bonnen@house.state.tx.us      Dist: (979) 849-3169
  Committees: Natural Resources; Ways and Means      (Angleton)
Representative **Greg Bonnen** (R-District 24) . . . . . . . . . . . (512) 463-0729
  Counties Represented: Galveston (part)       Dist: (281) 338-0924
  Term Expires: 2017
  174 Calder Road, Suite 116, League City, TX 77573
  E-mail: greg.bonnen@house.state.tx.us
  Committees: Appropriations; Insurance
  Education: Texas A&M 1988 BS; Texas (Galveston) 1992 MD

*(continued on next page)*

**LEGISLATIVE BRANCH**

**Representatives** *continued*

Representative **Cindy Burkett** (R-District 113)...........(512) 463-0464
  Counties Represented: Dallas (part)          Dist: (972) 683-6311
  Term Expires: 2017                            Fax: (512) 463-9295
  18601 LBJ Freeway, Suite 401, Mesquite, TX 75150
  P.O. Box 850792, Mesquite, TX 75185
  E-mail: cindy.burkett@house.state.tx.us
  Committees: Appropriations; Local and Consent Calendars;
  Transportation

Representative **DeWayne Burns** (R-District 58)
  Room E2.804 ..................................(512) 463-0538
  Counties Represented: Bosque, Johnson         Fax: (512) 463-0897
  Term Expires: 2017
  E-mail: dewayne.burns@house.state.tx.us
  Committees: Homeland Security and Public Safety; Natural Resources

Representative **Dustin Burrows** (R-District 83)
  Room E2.802 ..................................(512) 463-0542
  Counties Represented: Borden, Gaines, Lubbock  Fax: (512) 463-0671
  (part), Lynn, Mitchell, Scurry, Terry
  Term Expires: 2017
  E-mail: dustin.burrows@house.state.tx.us
  Committees: County Affairs; International Trade and Intergovernmental
  Affairs

Representative
  **Angie Chen Button, CPA** (R-District 112)...........(512) 463-0486
  Counties Represented: Dallas (part)           Dist: (972) 234-8980
  Term Expires: 2017                            Fax: (972) 470-0789
  1200 East Executive Drive, Suite 130, Richardson, TX 75081
  E-mail: angie.button@house.state.tx.us
  Committees: Economic and Small Business Development; Rules and
  Resolutions; Ways and Means
  Education: Texas (Dallas) MPFM

Representative **Terry Canales** (D-District 40)
  Room E2.816 ..................................(512) 463-0426
  Counties Represented: Hidalgo (part)          Fax: (512) 463-0043
  Term Expires: 2017
  E-mail: terry.canales@house.state.tx.us
  Committees: Criminal Jurisprudence; Energy Resources
  Education: St Mary's U (TX) 1973 JD

Representative **Giovanni Capriglione** (R-District 98)
  Room E1.412 ..................................(512) 463-0690
  Counties Represented: Tarrant (part)          Fax: (512) 477-5770
  Term Expires: 2017
  E-mail: giovanni.capriglione@house.state.tx.us
  Committees: Appropriations; Investments and Financial Services; Local
  and Consent Calendars
  Education: Santa Clara U 1995 BS, 2003 MBA

Representative **Travis Clardy** (R-District 11).............(512) 463-0592
  Counties Represented: Cherokee, Nacogdoches,  Dist: (936) 560-3982
  Rusk                                          Fax: (512) 463-8792
  Term Expires: 2017                            Dist: (936) 564-0051
  202 East Pilar, Room 310, Nacogdoches, TX 75961
  E-mail: travis.clardy@house.state.tx.us
  Committees: Higher Education; Judiciary and Civil Jurisprudence;
  Local and Consent Calendars; State and Federal Power and
  Responsibility
  Education: Abilene Christian 1984 BBA; Pepperdine 1988 JD

Representative **Garnet F. Coleman** (D-District 147) ......(512) 463-0524
  Counties Represented: Harris (part)           Dist: (713) 520-5355
  Term Expires: 2017                            Fax: (512) 463-1260
  5445 Alameda, Suite 501, Houston, TX 77004    Dist: (713) 520-1860
  E-mail: garnet.coleman@house.state.tx.us
  Committees: County Affairs; Public Health
  Education: St Thomas U 1990 BA

Representative **Nicole Collier** (D-District 95)
  Room E1.324 ..................................(512) 463-0716
  Counties Represented: Tarrant (part)          Fax: (512) 463-1516
  Term Expires: 2017
  E-mail: nicole.collier@house.state.tx.us
  Committees: Business and Industry; General Investigating and Ethics;
  Public Health
  Education: Houston 1996; Texas Wesleyan U 2001 JD

Representative **Byron Cook** (R-District 8) .............(512) 463-0730
  Counties Represented: Anderson, Freestone, Hill,  Fax: (512) 463-2506
  Navarro
  Term Expires: 2017
  P.O. Box 1397, Corsicana, TX 75151
  E-mail: byron.cook@house.state.tx.us
  Committees: Calendars; State Affairs

Representative **Thomas "Tom" Craddick** (R-District 82) . .(512) 463-1000
  Counties Represented: Crane, Dawson, Martin,   Dist: (432) 682-3000
  Midland, Upton                                 Fax: (512) 463-7722
  Term Expires: 2017                             Dist: (432) 684-4864
  500 West Texas, Suite 880, Midland, TX 79701
  E-mail: tom.craddick@house.state.tx.us
  Committees: Energy Resources; State Affairs
  Affiliation: Sales Representative, Mustang Mud, Inc.
  Education: Texas Tech 1965 BBA, 1966 MBA

Representative **Myra Crownover** (R-District 64) .........(512) 463-0582
  Counties Represented: Denton (part)            Dist: (940) 321-0013
  Term Expires: 2017                             Fax: (512) 463-0471
  P.O. Box 535, Lake Dallas, TX 75065-0535       Dist: (940) 497-0121
  E-mail: myra.crownover@house.state.tx.us
  Committees: Higher Education; Public Health
  Education: Southern Methodist BA; Texas A&M MA

Representative **John Cyrier** (R-District 17) Room E2.802 . .(512) 463-0682
  Counties Represented: Bastrop, Caldwell, Gonzales,  Fax: (512) 463-9955
  Karnes, Lee
  Term Expires: 2017
  E-mail: john.cyrier@house.state.tx.us
  Committees: Agriculture and Livestock; Land and Resource
  Management

Representative **Anthony "Tony" Dale** (R-District 136)
  Capitol Extension, Room E1.410 ...................(512) 463-0696
  Counties Represented: Williamson (part)        Fax: (512) 463-9333
  Term Expires: 2017
  E-mail: anthony.dale@house.state.tx.us
  Committees: Energy Resources; Homeland Security and Public Safety;
  Local and Consent Calendars
  Education: Ohio State 1992 BA

Representative **Drew Darby** (R-District 72) .............(512) 463-0331
  Counties Represented: Coke, Concho, Glasscock,  Dist: (325) 658-7313
  Howard, Irion, Reagan, Runnels, Sterling, Tom     (San Angelo)
  Green                                         Fax: (512) 499-3978
  Term Expires: 2017                            Dist: (325) 659-3762
  36 West Beauregard, Suite 517,                    (San Angelo)
  San Angelo, TX 76903
  E-mail: drew.darby@house.state.tx.us
  Committees: Energy Resources; Ways and Means
  Education: Texas BBA, 1971 JD

Representative **Sarah Davis** (R-District 134) ............(512) 463-0389
  Counties Represented: Harris (part)           Dist: (713) 521-4474
  Term Expires: 2017                            Fax: (512) 463-1374
  3100 Richmond Avenue, Suite 316,              Dist: (713) 521-4443
  Houston, TX 77098
  E-mail: sarah.davis@house.state.tx.us
  Committees: Appropriations; Calendars; General Investigating and
  Ethics; Public Health

Representative **Yvonne Davis** (D-District 111)...........(512) 463-0598
  Counties Represented: Dallas (part)           Dist: (214) 941-3895
  Term Expires: 2017                            Fax: (512) 463-2297
  5787 South Hampton Road, Suite 447,           Dist: (214) 941-6859
  Dallas, TX 75232
  E-mail: yvonne.davis@house.state.tx.us
  Committees: Redistricting; Transportation; Ways and Means

Representative **Joe D. Deshotel** (D-District 22).........(512) 463-0662
  Counties Represented: Jefferson (part)        Dist: (409) 724-0788
  Term Expires: 2017                            Fax: (512) 463-8381
  One Plaza Square, Suite 203,                  Dist: (409) 724-0750
  Port Arthur, TX 77642
  E-mail: joe.deshotel@house.state.tx.us
  Committees: Land and Resource Management; Public Education
  Education: Lamar 1974 BS; Texas Southern 1978 JD

Representative **Dawnna Dukes** (D-District 46) ..........(512) 463-0506
  Counties Represented: Travis (part)           Fax: (512) 463-7864
  Term Expires: 2017
  E-mail: dawnna.dukes@house.state.tx.us
  Committees: Appropriations; Culture, Recreation and Tourism;
  Emerging Issues in Texas Law Enforcement
  Education: Texas A&M 1986 BS

Representative **Harold V. Dutton, Jr.** (D-District 142).....(512) 463-0510
  Counties Represented: Harris (part)           Dist: (713) 692-9192
  Term Expires: 2017                            Fax: (512) 463-8333
  8799 North Loop East, Suite 305,              Dist: (713) 692-6791
  Houston, TX 77029
  E-mail: harold.dutton@house.state.tx.us
  Committees: Juvenile Justice and Family Issues; Public Education
  Education: Texas Southern 1966 BBA, 1991 JD

Representative **Gary Elkins** (R-District 135)............(512) 463-0722
  Counties Represented: Harris (part)          Dist: (832) 912-8380
  Term Expires: 2017                           Fax: (512) 463-2331
  9601 Jones Road, Suite 215, Houston, TX 77065   Dist: (832) 912-8879
  E-mail: gary.elkins@house.state.tx.us
  Committees: Government Transparency and Operation; Urban Affairs
  Education: SW Assemblies God BS

Representative **Wayne Faircloth** (R-District 23)
  Room E2.812 ......................................(512) 463-0502
  Counties Represented: Chambers, Galveston (part)   Fax: (512) 936-4260
  Term Expires: 2017
  E-mail: wayne.faircloth@house.state.tx.us
  Committees: Economic and Small Business Development; Rules and
  Resolutions; Special Purpose Districts

Representative **Patrick "Pat" Fallon** (R-District 106)
  Room E1.312 ......................................(512) 463-0694
  Counties Represented: Denton (part)          Fax: (512) 463-1130
  Term Expires: 2017
  E-mail: pat.fallon@house.state.tx.us
  Committees: Elections; Special Purpose Districts
  Education: Notre Dame 1990 BA

Representative **Marsha Farney** (R-District 20)
  Room E1.310 ......................................(512) 463-0309
  Counties Represented: Burnet, Milam, Williamson   Fax: (512) 463-0049
  (part)
  Term Expires: 2017
  E-mail: marsha.farney@house.state.tx.us
  Committees: House Administration; Public Education; State Affairs
  Education: Texas A&M (Commerce) BSEd, MSEd; Texas 2007 PhD

Representative **Jessica Christian Farrar** (D-District 148) .. (512) 463-0620
  Counties Represented: Harris (part)          Dist: (713) 691-6912
  Term Expires: 2017                           Fax: (512) 463-0894
  P.O. Box 30099, Houston, TX 77249            Dist: (713) 691-3363
  E-mail: jessica.farrar@house.state.tx.us
  Committees: Judiciary and Civil Jurisprudence; State Affairs
  Education: Houston 1995 BA

Representative **Allen Fletcher** (R-District 130)...........(512) 463-0661
  Counties Represented: Harris (part)          Dist: (281) 373-5454
  Term Expires: 2017                           Fax: (512) 463-4130
  Building Nine, 25222 Northwest Freeway,      Dist: (281) 373-5460
  Suite 199, Cypress, TX 77429
  E-mail: allen.fletcher@house.state.tx.us
  Committees: Business and Industry; Emerging Issues in Texas Law
  Enforcement; Transportation

Representative **Dan Flynn** (R-District 2)...............(512) 463-0880
  Counties Represented: Hopkins, Hunt, Van Zandt   Dist: (903) 567-0921
  Term Expires: 2017                           Fax: (512) 463-2188
  P.O. Box 999, Canton, TX 75103              Dist: (903) 567-0923
  E-mail: dan.flynn@house.state.tx.us
  Committees: Emerging Issues in Texas Law Enforcement; Investments
  and Financial Services; Pensions

Representative **James Frank** (R-District 69)
  Capitol Extension, Room E2.304..................(512) 463-0534
  Counties Represented: Archer, Baylor, Clay, Foard,   Fax: (512) 463-8161
  Knox, Wichita
  Term Expires: 2017
  E-mail: james.frank@house.state.tx.us
  Committees: Defense and Veterans' Affairs; Natural Resources
  Education: Texas A&M

Representative **John Frullo** (R-District 84)..............(512) 463-0676
  Counties Represented: Lubbock (part)         Dist: (806) 763-2366
  Term Expires: 2017                           Fax: (512) 463-0072
  4601 50th Street, Suite 216, Lubbock, TX 79414
  E-mail: john.frullo@house.state.tx.us
  Committees: Culture, Recreation and Tourism; Insurance

Representative **Rick Galindo** (R-District 117)
  Room E1.410 ......................................(512) 463-0269
  Counties Represented: Bexar (part)           Fax: (512) 463-1096
  Term Expires: 2017
  E-mail: rick.galindo@house.state.tx.us
  Committees: Government Transparency and Operation; Public
  Education
  Education: St Mary's U (TX)

Representative **Charlie Geren** (R-District 99)............(512) 463-0610
  Counties Represented: Tarrant (part)         Dist: (817) 783-8333
  Term Expires: 2017                           Fax: (512) 463-8310
  1011 Roberts Cutoff, River Oaks, TX 76114    Dist: (817) 738-8362
  E-mail: charlie.geren@house.state.tx.us
  Committees: Calendars; House Administration; Licensing and
  Administrative Procedures; State Affairs
  Education: Southern Methodist 1971 BBA

Representative **Helen Giddings** (D-District 109) .........(512) 463-0953
  Counties Represented: Dallas (part)          Dist: (972) 224-6795
  Term Expires: 2017                           Fax: (512) 463-5887
  1510 North Hampton, Suite 340, DeSoto, TX 75115   Dist: (972) 228-6796
  E-mail: helen.giddings@house.state.tx.us
  Committees: Appropriations; Calendars; State Affairs

Representative **Craig Goldman** (R-District 97)
  Room E2.720 ......................................(512) 463-0608
  Counties Represented: Tarrant (part)         Fax: (512) 463-8342
  Term Expires: 2017
  E-mail: craig.goldman@house.state.tx.us
  Committees: Elections; Licensing and Administrative Procedures
  Education: Texas BA

Representative **Larry Gonzales** (R-District 52)...........(512) 463-0670
  Counties Represented: Williamson (part)      Fax: (512) 463-1496
  Term Expires: 2017
  P.O. Box 2501, Round Rock, TX 78680
  E-mail: larry.gonzales@house.state.tx.us
  Committees: Appropriations; Government Transparency and Operation;
  Local and Consent Calendars; Redistricting
  Education: Texas 1993 BA

Representative **Mary E. Gonzalez** (D-District 75)
  Room E1.218 ......................................(512) 463-0613
  Counties Represented: El Paso (part)         Fax: (512) 463-1237
  Term Expires: 2017
  E-mail: mary.gonzalez@house.state.tx.us
  Committees: Agriculture and Livestock; Public Education
  Education: Texas; St Edward's 2009 MLA

Representative **R. D. "Bobby" Guerra** (D-District 41)
  Room E1.306 ......................................(512) 463-0578
  Counties Represented: Hidalgo (part)         Fax: (512) 463-1482
  Term Expires: 2017
  E-mail: bobby.guerra@house.state.tx
  Committees: Insurance; Local and Consent Calendars; Public Health
  Education: Texas Pan American; Texas Southern 1985 JD

Representative **Ryan Guillen** (D-District 31)............(512) 463-0416
  Counties Represented: Atascosa, Brooks, Duval,   Dist: (956) 716-4838
  Jim Hogg, Kenedy, La Salle, Live Oak, McMullen,   (Rio Grande City)
  Starr, Willacy                               Dist: (361) 701-9976
  Term Expires: 2017                           (Benavides)
  100 North FM 3167, Rio Grande City, TX 58582   Dist: (956) 794-1767
  E-mail: ryan.guillen@house.state.tx.us       (Laredo)
  Committees: Culture, Recreation and Tourism;   Fax: (512) 463-1012
  Licensing and Administrative Procedures      Dist: (956) 716-8129
  Education: Texas A&M BS                       (Rio Grande City)

Representative **Roland Gutierrez** (D-District 119).......(512) 463-0452
  Counties Represented: Bexar (part)           Dist: (210) 532-2758
  Term Expires: 2017                           Fax: (512) 463-1447
  3319 Sidney Brooks, San Antonio, TX 78235    Dist: (210) 532-3830
  E-mail: roland.gutierrez@house.state.tx.us
  Committees: Government Transparency and Operation; Licensing and
  Administrative Procedures; Local and Consent Calendars
  Education: Texas (San Antonio) 1995 BA; St Mary's U (TX) 1998 JD

Representative **Patricia Fincher Harless** (R-District 126) .. (512) 463-0496
  Counties Represented: Harris (part)          Dist: (281) 376-4114
  Term Expires: 2017                           Fax: (512) 463-1507
  6605 Cypresswood Drive, Suite 225,           Dist: (281) 826-0101
  Spring, TX 77379
  E-mail: patricia.harless@house.state.tx.us
  Committees: Calendars; State Affairs; Transportation
  Education: LeTourneau BS

Representative **Ana E. Hernandez** (D-District 143).......(512) 463-0614
  Counties Represented: Harris (part)          Dist: (713) 675-8596
  Term Expires: 2017                           Fax: (512) 463-0612
  1233 Mercury Drive, Houston, TX 77029        Dist: (713) 675-8599
  E-mail: ana.hernandez@house.state.tx.us
  Committees: Judiciary and Civil Jurisprudence; Pensions
  Education: Houston 2001 BA; Texas 2004 JD

Representative **Abel Herrero** (D-District 34)............(512) 463-0462
  Counties Represented: Nueces (part)          Dist: (361) 884-2277
  Term Expires: 2017                           Fax: (512) 463-1705
  606 North Carancahua, Suite 103A,            Dist: (361) 884-6706
  Corpus Christi, TX 78401
  E-mail: abel.herrero@house.state.tx.us
  Committees: Criminal Jurisprudence; Energy Resources
  Education: Texas A&M 1993 BA; Texas 1997 JD

Representative **Donna Howard** (D-District 48) .........(512) 463-0631
  Counties Represented: Travis (part)          Fax: (512) 463-0901
  Term Expires: 2017
  P.O. Box 2910, Austin, TX 78760
  E-mail: donna.howard@house.state.tx.us
  Committees: Appropriations; Higher Education; House Administration
  Education: Texas 1974 BS, 1977 MA

*(continued on next page)*

**LEGISLATIVE BRANCH**

**Representatives** *continued*

Representative
**Daniel G. "Dan" Huberty** (R-District 127) . . . . . . . . . . .(512) 463-0520
Counties Represented: Harris (part)　　　　Dist: (281) 360-9410
Term Expires: 2017　　　　　　　　　　　　Fax: (512) 463-1606
4501 Magnolia Cove, Suite 201, Kingwood, TX 77345
E-mail: dan.huberty@house.state.tx.us
Committees: Calendars; Public Education; State Affairs
Education: Cleveland State 1991 BBA; U Phoenix 1998 MBA

Representative **Bryan Hughes** (R-District 5) . . . . . . . . . . . .(512) 463-0271
Counties Represented: Camp, Morris, Rains,　Dist: (903) 935-1141
Smith (part), Titus, Wood　　　　　　　　　　　　　(Marshall)
Term Expires: 2017　　　　　　　　　　　Dist: (903) 569-8880
Harrison County Annex, 102 West Houston,　　　　　(Mineola)
Marshall, TX 75671
701 North Pacific Avenue, Mineola, TX 75773　Fax: (512) 463-1515
E-mail: bryan.hughes@house.state.tx.us　　　Dist: (903) 935-1142
Committees: Appropriations; Juvenile Justice　　　　　(Marshall)
and Family Issues　　　　　　　　　　　　Dist: (903) 569-8889
Education: Texas (Tyler) BBA; Baylor 1995 JD　　　　(Mineola)

Representative **Todd Hunter** (R-District 32) . . . . . . . . . . .(512) 463-0672
Counties Represented: Nueces (part)　　　Dist: (361) 949-4603
Term Expires: 2017　　　　　　　　　　　Fax: (361) 949-4364
15217 S.P.I.D., Suite 205, Corpus Christi, TX 78418
E-mail: todd.hunter@house.state.tx.us
Committees: Calendars; Criminal Jurisprudence; General Investigating
and Ethics; Redistricting; Urban Affairs
Education: Kansas 1975 BA; Southern Methodist 1978 JD

Representative **Jason Isaac** (R-District 45) Room E1.410 . .(512) 463-0647
Counties Represented: Blanco, Hays　　　　Fax: (512) 463-3573
Term Expires: 2017
E-mail: jason.isaac@house.state.tx.us
Committees: Economic and Small Business Development;
Environmental Regulation; Local and Consent Calendars

Representative **Celia Israel** (D-District 50) Room E1.406 . . (512) 463-0821
Counties Represented: Travis (part)
Term Expires: 2017
E-mail: celia.israel@house.state.tx.us
Committees: Elections; Transportation

Representative **Eric "EJ" Johnson** (D-District 100) . . . . . . (512) 463-0586
Counties Represented: Dallas (part)　　　Dist: (214) 565-5663
Term Expires: 2017　　　　　　　　　　　Fax: (512) 463-8147
1409 South Lamar, Suite 9, Dallas, TX 75215　Dist: (214) 565-5668
E-mail: eric.johnson@house.state.tx.us
Committees: Calendars; Economic and Small Business Development;
Homeland Security and Public Safety
Education: Harvard 1998 BA; Pennsylvania 2003 JD; Princeton MPAff

Representative **Jarvis D. Johnson** (D-District 139) . . . . . . (512) 463-4630
Counties Represented: Harris (part)
Term Expires: 2017
E-mail: jarvis.johnson@house.state.tx.us

Representative **Kyle J. Kacal** (R-District 12)
Room E2.704 . . . . . . . . . . . . . . . . . . . . . . . . . . . . . . . (512) 463-0412
Counties Represented: Brazos (part), Falls,　Fax: (512) 463-9059
Limestone, McLennan (part), Robertson
Term Expires: 2017
E-mail: kyle.kacal@house.state.tx.us
Committees: Environmental Regulation; Natural Resources; Rules and
Resolutions
Education: Texas A&M 1992 BA

Representative **James L. "Jim" Keffer** (R-District 60) . . . . (512) 463-0656
Counties Represented: Brown, Callahan, Coleman,　Dist: (800) 586-4515
Eastland, Hood, Palo Pinto, Shackelford, Stephens　Fax: (512) 478-8805
Term Expires: 2017
P.O. Box 857, Eastland, TX 76448
E-mail: james.keffer@house.state.tx.us
Committees: Energy Resources; Natural Resources; Redistricting
Affiliation: President, EBAA Iron Sales, Inc.
Education: Texas Tech 1975 BA

Representative **Mark Keough** (R-District 15)
Room E2.402 . . . . . . . . . . . . . . . . . . . . . . . . . . . . . . . (512) 463-0797
Counties Represented: Montgomery (part)　Fax: (512) 463-0898
Term Expires: 2017
E-mail: mark.keough@house.state.tx.us
Committees: Corrections; Human Services

Representative **Ken King** (R-District 88) . . . . . . . . . . . . . . (512) 463-0736
Counties Represented: Armstrong, Bailey, Briscoe,　Dist: (806) 323-8870
Castro, Cochran, Donley, Gray, Hale, Hansford,　Fax: (512) 463-0211
Hemphill, Hockley, Lamb, Lipscomb, Ochiltree, Roberts, Swisher,
Yoakum
Term Expires: 2017
P.O. Box 507, Canadian, TX 79014
E-mail: ken.king@house.state.tx.us
Committees: Calendars; Environmental Regulation; House
Administration; Public Education

Representative **Phil King** (R-District 61) . . . . . . . . . . . . . . (512) 463-0738
Counties Represented: Parker, Wise　　　Dist: (817) 596-4796
Term Expires: 2017　　　　　　　　　　　Fax: (512) 463-1957
2110 Fort Worth Highway, Weatherford, TX 76086　Dist: (817) 596-8375
E-mail: phil.king@house.state.tx.us
Committees: Energy Resources; Environmental Regulation; State and
Federal Power and Responsibility
Education: Dallas Baptist 1981 BA, 1986 MBA;
Texas Wesleyan U 1993 JD

Representative **Susan Lewis King** (R-District 71) . . . . . . . (512) 463-0718
Counties Represented: Jones, Nolan, Taylor　Dist: (325) 670-0384
Term Expires: 2017　　　　　　　　　　　Fax: (512) 463-0994
P.O. Box 2376, Abilene, TX 79604
E-mail: susan.king@house.state.tx.us
Committees: Defense and Veterans' Affairs; Human Services
Education: Texas 1976 BSN

Representative **Tracy O. King** (D-District 80) . . . . . . . . . . (512) 463-0194
Counties Represented: Dimmit, Frio, Uvalde,　Dist: (830) 773-0860
Webb (part), Zapata, Zavala　　　　　　　Fax: (512) 463-1220
Term Expires: 2017　　　　　　　　　　　Dist: (830) 757-0317
1995 Williams Street, Eagle Pass, TX 78852
E-mail: tracy.king@house.state.tx.us
Committees: Agriculture and Livestock; Natural Resources
Education: Texas A&M 1983 BS

Representative **Stephanie Klick** (R-District 91)
Room E2.716 . . . . . . . . . . . . . . . . . . . . . . . . . . . . . . . (512) 463-0599
Counties Represented: Tarrant (part)　　　Fax: (512) 463-0751
Term Expires: 2017
E-mail: stephanie.klick@house.state.tx.us
Committees: Human Services; Pensions
Education: Texas Christian 1981 BN

Representative **Linda Koop** (R-District 102)
Room E1.512 . . . . . . . . . . . . . . . . . . . . . . . . . . . . . . . (512) 463-0454
Counties Represented: Dallas (part)　　　Fax: (512) 463-1121
Term Expires: 2017
E-mail: linda.koop@house.state.tx.us
Committees: Appropriations; Emerging Issues in Texas Law
Enforcement; International Trade and Intergovernmental Affairs

Representative **Matt Krause** (R-District 93)
Room E1.424 . . . . . . . . . . . . . . . . . . . . . . . . . . . . . . . (512) 463-0562
Counties Represented: Tarrant (part)　　　Fax: (512) 463-2053
Term Expires: 2017
E-mail: matt.krause@house.state.tx.us
Committees: Corrections; Land and Resource Management
Education: Liberty 2007 JD

Representative **John Kuempel** (R-District 44) . . . . . . . . . . (512) 463-0602
Counties Represented: Guadalupe, Wilson　Dist: (830) 379-8732
Term Expires: 2017　　　　　　　　　　　Fax: (512) 480-0391
523 East Donegan, Suite 102, Seguin, TX 78155
E-mail: john.kuempel@house.state.tx.us
Committees: General Investigating and Ethics; Licensing and
Administrative Procedures; State Affairs
Education: Texas 1992

Representative **Brooks Landgraf** (R-District 81)
Room E1.312 . . . . . . . . . . . . . . . . . . . . . . . . . . . . . . . (512) 463-0546
Counties Represented: Andrews, Ector, Ward,　Fax: (512) 463-8067
Winkler
Term Expires: 2017
E-mail: brooks.landgraf@house.state.tx.us
Committees: Energy Resources; Investments and Financial Services
Education: Texas A&M 2003 BS

Representative **Lyle Larson** (R-District 122) . . . . . . . . . . . (512) 463-0646
Counties Represented: Bexar (part)　　　Dist: (210) 402-5402
Term Expires: 2017　　　　　　　　　　　Fax: (512) 463-0893
14607 San Pedro Avenue, Suite 180, San Antonio, TX 78232
E-mail: lyle.larson@house.state.tx.us
Committees: Calendars; Culture, Recreation and Tourism; General
Investigating and Ethics; Natural Resources
Education: Texas A&M 1981 BBA

Representative **Jodie Laubenberg** (R-District 89) . . . . . . . . (512) 463-0186
Counties Represented: Collin (part) Dist: (972) 424-6810
Term Expires: 2017 Fax: (512) 463-5896
206 North Murphy Road, Murphy, TX 75094
E-mail: jodie.laubenberg@house.state.tx.us
Committees: Elections; Judiciary and Civil Jurisprudence
Education: Texas 1980 BA

Representative **Jeff Leach** (R-District 67) Room E1.322 . . . (512) 463-0544
Counties Represented: Collin (part) Fax: (512) 463-9974
Term Expires: 2017
E-mail: jeff.leach@house.state.tx.us
Committees: Criminal Jurisprudence; Government Transparency and Operation
Education: Baylor 2005 BA; Southern Methodist 2008 JD

Representative **Oscar Longoria** (D-District 35)
Room E1.510 . . . . . . . . . . . . . . . . . . . . . . . . . . . . (512) 463-0645
Counties Represented: Cameron (part), Hidalgo Fax: (512) 463-0559
(part)
Term Expires: 2017
E-mail: oscar.longoria@house.state.tx.us
Committees: Appropriations; Investments and Financial Services
Education: Texas 2003 BS, 2007 JD

Representative
**Jose Manuel "J.M." Lozano** (R-District 43) . . . . . . . . . (512) 463-0463
Counties Represented: Bee, Jim Wells, Kleberg, Dist: (361) 595-1550
San Patricio Fax: (512) 463-1765
Term Expires: 2017 Dist: (361) 595-1755
635 East King Avenue, Kingsville, TX 78363
E-mail: jm.lozano@house.state.tx.us
Committees: Environmental Regulation; International Trade and Intergovernmental Affairs; Redistricting

Representative **Eddie Lucio III** (D-District 38) . . . . . . . . . . (512) 463-0606
Counties Represented: Cameron (part) Dist: (956) 542-2800
Term Expires: 2017 Fax: (512) 463-0660
1805 East Reuben M. Torres Boulevard, Suite B-27, Dist: (956) 542-2889
Brownsville, TX 78521
E-mail: eddie.lucio_iii@house.state.tx.us
Committees: Calendars; Land and Resource Management; Natural Resources
Education: Texas 2002 BBA, 2005 JD

Representative **John Lujan** (R-District 118) Room 4S.4 . . . (512) 463-0714
Counties Represented: Bexar (part) Fax: (512) 463-1458
Term Expires: 2017
E-mail: john.lujan@house.state.tx.us
Committees: County Affairs; Defense and Veterans' Affairs

Representative **Marisa Marquez** (D-District 77) . . . . . . . . . (512) 463-0638
Counties Represented: El Paso (part) Dist: (915) 532-2755
Term Expires: 2017 Fax: (512) 463-8908
310 North Mesa Street, Suite 906, El Paso, TX 79901
E-mail: marisa.marquez@house.state.tx.us
Committees: Appropriations; Culture, Recreation and Tourism; Emerging Issues in Texas Law Enforcement; House Administration
Education: Notre Dame 2000 BBA

Representative
**Armando "Mando" Martinez** (D-District 39) . . . . . . . . (512) 463-0530
Counties Represented: Hidalgo (part) Dist: (956) 447-9473
Term Expires: 2017 Fax: (512) 463-0849
800 West Railroad Street, Room H-111, Dist: (956) 447-8683
Weslaco, TX 78596
E-mail: mando.martinez@house.state.tx.us
Committees: Emerging Issues in Texas Law Enforcement; Higher Education; Transportation
Education: Texas Pan American 1998 BS

Representative **Trey Martinez-Fischer** (D-District 116) . . . . (512) 463-0616
Counties Represented: Bexar (part) Dist: (210) 737-7200
Term Expires: 2017 Fax: (512) 463-4873
1910 Fredericksburg Road, San Antonio, TX 78201 Dist: (210) 737-6700
E-mail: trey.martinez.fischer@house.state.tx.us
Committees: Special Purpose Districts; Ways and Means
Education: Texas (San Antonio) 1993 BA; CUNY 1994 MPA; Texas 1998 JD

Representative **Will Metcalf** (R-District 16)
Room E2.704 . . . . . . . . . . . . . . . . . . . . . . . . . . . . (512) 463-0726
Counties Represented: Montgomery (part) Fax: (512) 463-8428
Term Expires: 2017
E-mail: will.metcalf@house.state.tx.us
Committees: Economic and Small Business Development; Homeland Security and Public Safety
Education: Sam Houston State BS

Representative **Morgan Meyer** (R-District 108)
Room E1.418 . . . . . . . . . . . . . . . . . . . . . . . . . . . . (512) 463-0367
Counties Represented: Dallas (part) Fax: (512) 463-0078
Term Expires: 2017
E-mail: morgan.meyer@house.state.tx.us
Committees: Energy Resources; Insurance

Representative **Borris L. Miles** (D-District 146) . . . . . . . . . (512) 463-0518
Counties Represented: Harris (part) Dist: (713) 665-8322
Term Expires: 2017 Fax: (512) 463-0941
2656 South Loop West, Suite 265, Dist: (713) 665-0009
Houston, TX 77054
E-mail: borris.miles@house.state.tx.us
Committees: Appropriations; Licensing and Administrative Procedures; State and Federal Power and Responsibility

Representative **Doug Miller** (R-District 73) . . . . . . . . . . . . (512) 463-0325
Counties Represented: Comal, Gillespie, Kendall Dist: (830) 625-1313
Term Expires: 2017 Fax: (830) 625-1747
387 West Mill Street, New Braunfels, TX 78130
E-mail: doug.miller@house.state.tx.us
Committees: Licensing and Administrative Procedures; Special Purpose Districts
Education: Texas Southern 1976 BS

Representative **Rick Miller** (R-District 26) . . . . . . . . . . . . . (512) 463-0710
Counties Represented: Fort Bend (part) Fax: (512) 463-0711
Term Expires: 2017
130 Industrial Boulevard, Suite 126, Sugar Land, TX 77478
E-mail: rick.miller@house.state.tx.us
Committees: Appropriations; Public Health
Education: Naval Acad 1968 BS; Indust'l Col Armed Forces MS

Representative **Ina Minjarez** (D-District 124)
Room E2.708 . . . . . . . . . . . . . . . . . . . . . . . . . . . . (512) 463-0634
Counties Represented: Bexar (part) Fax: (512) 463-7668
Term Expires: 2017
E-mail: ina.minjarez@house.state.tx.us
Committees: State Affairs; Transportation

Representative **Joseph E. "Joe" Moody** (D-District 78)
Room E1.216 . . . . . . . . . . . . . . . . . . . . . . . . . . . . (512) 463-0728
Counties Represented: El Paso (part) Dist: (915) 532-3331
Term Expires: 2017 Fax: (512) 463-0397
E-mail: joe.moody@house.state.tx.us
Committees: Criminal Jurisprudence; General Investigating and Ethics; Homeland Security and Public Safety
Education: New Mexico State 2003 BA; Texas Tech 2006 JD

Representative **Geanie W. Morrison** (R-District 30) . . . . . . (512) 463-0456
Counties Represented: Aransas, Calhoun, De Dist: (361) 572-0196
Witt, Goliad, Refugio, Victoria Fax: (512) 476-3933
Term Expires: 2017 Dist: (361) 576-0747
1908 North Laurent, Suite 500, Victoria, TX 77901
E-mail: geanie.morrison@house.state.tx.us
Committees: Environmental Regulation; Higher Education

Representative **Sergio Muñoz, Jr.** (D-District 36) . . . . . . . . (512) 463-0704
Counties Represented: Hidalgo (part) Dist: (956) 584-8999
Term Expires: 2017 Fax: (512) 463-5364
121 East Tom Landry, Mission, TX 78572
E-mail: sergio.munoz@house.state.tx.us
Committees: Appropriations; Insurance; Local and Consent Calendars

Representative **Jim Murphy** (R-District 133)
Room E2.606 . . . . . . . . . . . . . . . . . . . . . . . . . . . . (512) 463-0815
Counties Represented: Harris (part) Dist: (855) 597-0662
Term Expires: 2017 Fax: (512) 463-8715
E-mail: jim.murphy@house.state.tx.us
Committees: Corrections; Ways and Means

Representative **Andrew S. Murr** (R-District 53)
Room E1.412 . . . . . . . . . . . . . . . . . . . . . . . . . . . . (512) 463-0536
Counties Represented: Bandera, Crockett, Edwards, Fax: (512) 463-1449
Kerr, Kimble, Llano, Mason, Medina, Menard, Real, Schleicher, Sutton
Term Expires: 2017
E-mail: andrew.murr@house.state.tx.us
Committees: Culture, Recreation and Tourism; Rules and Resolutions; Transportation

Representative **Elliott Naishtat** (D-District 49)
Room GW.16 . . . . . . . . . . . . . . . . . . . . . . . . . . . . (512) 463-0668
Counties Represented: Travis (part) Fax: (512) 463-8022
Term Expires: 2017
E-mail: elliott.naishtat@house.state.tx.us
Committees: Human Services; Public Health
Education: Queens Col (NY) 1965 BA; Texas 1972 MSSW, 1982 JD

*(continued on next page)*

**LEGISLATIVE BRANCH**

**Representatives** *continued*

Representative
**Alfonso "Poncho" Nevárez** (D-District 74)
Room E1.306 . . . . . . . . . . . . . . . . . . . . . . . . . . (512) 463-0566
Counties Represented: Brewster, Culberson,   Fax: (512) 236-9408
Hudspeth, Jeff Davis, Kinney, Loving, Maverick, Pecos, Presidio,
Reeves, Terrell, Val Verde
Term Expires: 2017
E-mail: poncho.nevarez@house.state.tx.us
Committees: Homeland Security and Public Safety; Local and Consent
Calendars; Natural Resources
Education: Texas 1994; Texas A&M International 1996 (Attended);
St Mary's U (TX) 1999 JD

Representative **Rene Oliveira** (D-District 37) . . . . . . . . . . . (512) 463-0640
Counties Represented: Cameron (part)   Dist: (956) 542-1828
Term Expires: 2017   Fax: (512) 463-8186
855 West Price Road, Suite 22,   Dist: (956) 542-1618
Brownsville, TX 78520
E-mail: rene.oliveira@house.state.tx.us
Committees: Business and Industry; Redistricting; State Affairs
Education: Texas BA, 1973 JD

Representative **John Otto** (R-District 18) . . . . . . . . . . . . . (512) 463-0570
Counties Represented: Liberty, San Jacinto, Walker   Dist: (936) 258-8135
Term Expires: 2017   Fax: (512) 463-0315
P.O. Box 965, Mont Belvieu, TX 77535   Dist: (936) 258-7190
E-mail: john.otto@house.state.tx.us
Committees: Appropriations
Education: Texas A&M BBA

Representative **Chris Paddie** (R-District 9) Room E2.412 . . (512) 463-0556
Counties Represented: Cass, Harrison, Marion,   Fax: (512) 463-5896
Panola, Sabine, Shelby
Term Expires: 2017
E-mail: chris.paddie@house.state.tx.us
Committees: Energy Resources; House Administration; Transportation
Education: Texas A&M

Representative **Tan Parker** (R-District 63) . . . . . . . . . . . . . (512) 463-0688
Counties Represented: Denton (part)   Dist: (972) 724-8477
Term Expires: 2017   Fax: (512) 480-0694
800 Parker Square, Suite 245, Flower Mound, TX 75028
E-mail: tan.parker@house.state.tx.us
Committees: Investments and Financial Services; Redistricting; State
and Federal Power and Responsibility; Ways and Means
Education: Dallas 1993 BA; London School Econ (UK) MS

Representative **Dennis Paul** (R-District 129)
Room E2.814 . . . . . . . . . . . . . . . . . . . . . . . . . . (512) 463-0734
Counties Represented: Harris (part)   Fax: (512) 479-6955
Term Expires: 2017
E-mail: dennis.paul@house.state.tx.us
Committees: Insurance; Pensions

Representative **Gilbert Peña** (R-District 144)
Room E1.416 . . . . . . . . . . . . . . . . . . . . . . . . . . (512) 463-0460
Counties Represented: Harris (part)   Fax: (512) 463-0763
Term Expires: 2017
E-mail: gilbert.pena@house.state.tx.us
Committees: Human Services; Juvenile Justice and Family Issues

Representative **Dade Phelan** (R-District 21)
Room E1.324 . . . . . . . . . . . . . . . . . . . . . . . . . . (512) 463-0706
Counties Represented: Jefferson (part), Orange   Fax: (512) 463-1861
Term Expires: 2017
E-mail: dade.phelan@house.state.tx.us
Committees: Appropriations; Elections

Representative **Larry Phillips** (R-District 62) . . . . . . . . . . . (512) 463-0297
Counties Represented: Delta, Fannin, Grayson   Dist: (903) 891-7297
Term Expires: 2017   Fax: (512) 463-1561
421 North Crockett Street, Sherman, TX 75090   Dist: (903) 870-0066
E-mail: larry.phillips@house.state.tx.us
Committees: Homeland Security and Public Safety; Transportation
Education: Baylor 1988 BBA; Houston 1990 JD

Representative **Joseph "Joe" Pickett** (D-District 79) . . . . . (512) 463-0596
Counties Represented: El Paso (part)   Dist: (915) 590-4349
Term Expires: 2017   Fax: (512) 463-6504
1790 Lee Trevino Drive, Suite 307,   Dist: (915) 590-4726
El Paso, TX 79936
E-mail: joe.pickett@house.state.tx.us
Committees: Investments and Financial Services; Redistricting;
Transportation

Representative **Walter "Four" Price** (R-District 87) . . . . . . (512) 463-0470
Counties Represented: Carson, Hutchinson, Moore,   Dist: (806) 374-8787
Potter, Sherman
Term Expires: 2017
600 South Tyler, Suite 1402, Amarillo, TX 12013
E-mail: four.price@house.state.tx.us
Committees: Appropriations; Calendars; Human Services
Education: Texas 1990 BBA; St Mary's U (TX) 1995 JD

Representative **John Raney** (R-District 14) . . . . . . . . . . . . (512) 463-0698
Counties Represented: Brazos (part)   Dist: (979) 260-5040
Term Expires: 2017   Fax: (512) 463-5109
1920 West Villa Maria Road, Suite 303,   Dist: (979) 260-5097
Bryan, TX 77807
E-mail: john.raney@house.state.tx.us
Committees: Appropriations; Higher Education; House Administration
Education: Texas A&M 1969 BBA

Representative **Richard Peña Raymond** (D-District 42) . . . (512) 463-0558
Counties Represented: Webb (part)   Dist: (956) 753-7722
Term Expires: 2017   Fax: (512) 463-6296
City Hall, 1110 Houston Street, Third Floor,   Dist: (956) 753-7729
Laredo, TX 78040
E-mail: richard.raymond@house.state.tx.us
Committees: Human Services; Judiciary and Civil Jurisprudence
Education: Texas BA, JD

Representative **Ron Reynolds** (D-District 27) . . . . . . . . . . (512) 463-0494
Counties Represented: Fort Bend (part)   Dist: (281) 208-3574
Term Expires: 2017   Fax: (512) 463-1403
2440 Texas Parkway, Suite 102,   Dist: (281) 208-3696
Missouri City, TX 77489
E-mail: ron.reynolds@house.state.tx.us
Committees: Elections; Environmental Regulation

Representative **Debbie Riddle** (R-District 150) . . . . . . . . . (512) 463-0572
Counties Represented: Harris (part)   Dist: (281) 537-5252
Term Expires: 2017   Fax: (512) 463-1908
3648 F.M. 1960 Road West, Suite 106,   Dist: (281) 537-8821
Houston, TX 77068
E-mail: debbie.riddle@house.state.tx.us
Committees: Calendars; Energy Resources; Juvenile Justice and Family
Issues
Education: Southwestern AA

Representative **Matt Rinaldi** (R-District 115)
Room E1.422 . . . . . . . . . . . . . . . . . . . . . . . . . . (512) 463-0468
Counties Represented: Dallas (part)   Fax: (512) 463-1044
Term Expires: 2017
E-mail: matt.rinaldi@house.state.tx.us
Committees: Agriculture and Livestock; Business and Industry

Representative **Eddie Rodriguez** (D-District 51) . . . . . . . . (512) 463-0674
Counties Represented: Travis (part)   Fax: (512) 463-0314
Term Expires: 2017   Dist: (512) 463-5896
E-mail: eddie.rodriguez@house.state.tx.us
Committees: Calendars; Economic and Small Business Development;
Environmental Regulation
Education: Texas 1995 BA, 2008 JD

Representative **Justin Rodriguez** (D-District 125) . . . . . . . (512) 463-0669
Counties Represented: Bexar (part)   Dist: (210) 521-7100
Term Expires: 2017   Fax: (512) 463-5074
5503 Grissom Road, Suite 105,   Dist: (210) 521-7101
San Antonio, TX 78238
E-mail: justin.rodriguez@house.state.tx.us
Committees: Appropriations; Pensions; Rules and Resolutions
Education: U Incarnate Word BBA; Wisconsin 2000 JD

Representative **Ramon Romero, Jr.** (D-District 90) . . . . . . (512) 463-0740
Counties Represented: Tarrant (part)   Fax: (512) 463-1075
Term Expires: 2017
1550 West Berry Street, Fort Worth, TX 76110
E-mail: ramon.romero@house.state.tx.us
Committees: Business and Industry; County Affairs

Representative **Toni Rose** (D-District 110) . . . . . . . . . . . . (512) 463-0664
Counties Represented: Dallas (part)   Fax: (512) 463-0476
Term Expires: 2017
E-mail: toni.rose@house.state.tx.us
Committees: Human Services; Juvenile Justice and Family Issues;
Rules and Resolutions
Education: Paul Quinn BS

Representative **Scott Sanford** (R-District 70)
Room E2.210 . . . . . . . . . . . . . . . . . . . . . . . . . . (512) 463-0356
Counties Represented: Collin (part)   Fax: (512) 463-0701
Term Expires: 2017
E-mail: scott.sanford@house.state.tx.us
Committees: Juvenile Justice and Family Issues; Land and Resource
Management
Education: Baylor BBA, 1988 MT

Representative **Matt Schaefer** (R-District 6) . . . . . . . . . . . (512) 463-0584
Counties Represented: Smith (part)          Dist: (903) 592-0900
Term Expires: 2017                          Fax: (903) 592-0902
200 East Ferguson, Suite 506, Tyler, TX 75702
E-mail: matt.schaefer@house.state.tx.us
Committees: Defense and Veterans' Affairs; Urban Affairs
Education: Texas Tech, 2005 JD

Representative **Leighton Schubert** (R-District 13) . . . . . . . (512) 463-0600
Counties Represented: Austin, Burleson, Colorado,   Fax: (512) 463-5240
Fayette, Grimes, Lavaca, Washington
Term Expires: 2017
E-mail: leighton.schubert@house.state.tx.us
Committees: Corrections; County Affairs

Representative **Mike Schofield** (R-District 132)
Room E2.316 . . . . . . . . . . . . . . . . . . . . . . . . . . . (512) 463-0528
Counties Represented: Harris (part)         Fax: (512) 463-7820
Term Expires: 2017
E-mail: mike.schofield@house.state.tx.us
Committees: Elections; Judiciary and Civil Jurisprudence

Representative **Matt Shaheen** (R-District 66)
Room E1.322 . . . . . . . . . . . . . . . . . . . . . . . . . . . (512) 463-0594
Counties Represented: Collin (part)         Fax: (512) 463-1021
Term Expires: 2017
E-mail: matt.shaheen@house.state.tx.us
Committees: Criminal Jurisprudence; Defense and Veterans' Affairs
Education: Randolph-Macon; Southern Methodist

Representative **Kenneth Sheets** (R-District 107) . . . . . . . . (512) 463-0244
Counties Represented: Dallas (part)         Dist: (214) 370-8305
Term Expires: 2017                          Fax: (512) 463-9967
6301 Gaston Avenue, Suite 536, Dallas, TX 75214   Dist: (214) 370-8475
E-mail: kenneth.sheets@house.state.tx.us
Committees: Insurance; Judiciary and Civil Jurisprudence; Local and
Consent Calendars

Representative **J.D. Sheffield** (R-District 59) . . . . . . . . . . (512) 463-0628
Counties Represented: Comanche, Coryell, Erath,   Fax: (512) 463-3644
Hamilton, McCulloch, Mills, San Saba, Somervell
Term Expires: 2017
P.O. Box 704, Gatesville, TX 76528
E-mail: j.d.sheffield@house.state.tx.us
Committees: Appropriations; Public Health; Rules and Resolutions
Education: Howard Payne; Texas Col MD

Representative **Ronald E. Simmons** (R-District 65) . . . . . . (512) 463-0478
Counties Represented: Denton (part)         Fax: (512) 463-2089
Term Expires: 2017
E-mail: ron.simmons@house.state.tx.us
Committees: Business and Industry; Transportation
Education: Dallas Baptist 1987 BBA

Representative **David Simpson** (R-District 7) . . . . . . . . . . (512) 463-0750
Counties Represented: Gregg, Upshur         Dist: (903) 553-9226
Term Expires: 2017                          Fax: (512) 463-9085
1705 Judson Road, Suite D2, Longview, TX 75601    Dist: (903) 553-9877
E-mail: david.simpson@house.state.tx.us
Committees: Agriculture and Livestock; Criminal Jurisprudence
Education: Vanderbilt 1983 BA

Representative **Wayne Smith** (R-District 128) . . . . . . . . . . (512) 463-0733
Counties Represented: Harris (part)         Dist: (832) 556-2002
Term Expires: 2017                          Fax: (512) 463-1323
909 Decker Drive, Room 104, Baytown, TX 77520     Dist: (832) 556-0319
E-mail: wayne.smith@house.state.tx.us
Committees: Culture, Recreation and Tourism; Licensing and
Administrative Procedures
Education: Texas (Arlington) BSCE

Representative **John T. Smithee** (R-District 86) . . . . . . . . (512) 463-0702
Counties Represented: Dallam, Deaf Smith, Hartley,   Dist: (806) 372-3327
Oldham, Parmer, Randall                     Fax: (512) 476-7016
Term Expires: 2017                          Dist: (806) 342-0327
320 South Polk Street, 1st Floor, Amarillo, TX 79101
E-mail: john.smithee@house.state.tx.us
Committees: Judiciary and Civil Jurisprudence; State Affairs
Education: West Texas State 1976 BBA; Texas Tech 1976 JD

Representative **Stuart Spitzer** (R-District 4)
Room E1.316 . . . . . . . . . . . . . . . . . . . . . . . . . . . (512) 463-0458
Counties Represented: Henderson (part), Kaufman   Fax: (512) 463-2040
Term Expires: 2017
E-mail: stuart.spitzer@house.state.tx.us
Committees: County Affairs; Human Services

Representative **Drew Springer** (R-District 68)
Room E2.410 . . . . . . . . . . . . . . . . . . . . . . . . . . . (512) 463-0526
Counties Represented: Childress, Collingsworth,   Fax: (512) 463-1011
Cooke, Cottle, Crosby, Dickens, Fisher, Floyd, Garza, Hall,
Hardeman, Haskell, Jack, Kent, King, Montague, Motley, Stonewall,
Throckmorton, Wheeler, Wilbarger, Young
Term Expires: 2017
E-mail: drew.springer@house.state.tx.us
Committees: Agriculture and Livestock; Local and Consent Calendars;
Ways and Means
Education: North Texas 1988 BSAcc

Representative **Phil Stephenson, CPA** (R-District 85)
Capitol Extension, Room E1.316 . . . . . . . . . . . . . . .(512) 463-0604
Counties Represented: Fort Bend (part), Jackson,   Fax: (512) 463-5244
Wharton
Term Expires: 2017
E-mail: phil.stephenson@house.state.tx.us
Committees: Investments and Financial Services; Pensions
Education: Texas Tech 1969 BAcc

Representative **Jonathan Stickland** (R-District 92) . . . . . . .(512) 463-0522
Counties Represented: Tarrant (part)        Fax: (512) 463-9529
Term Expires: 2017
E-mail: jonathan.stickland@house.state.tx.us
Committees: County Affairs; Special Purpose Districts
Education: Parkland (Attended)

Representative **Joe Straus III** (R-District 121) . . . . . . . . . . (512) 463-1000
Counties Represented: Bexar (part)          Dist: (210) 828-4411
Term Expires: 2017                          Fax: (512) 463-0675
7373 Broadway, Suite 202-A,                 Dist: (210) 832-9994
San Antonio, TX 78209
E-mail: joe.straus@speaker.state.tx.us

Representative **Ed Thompson** (R-District 29) . . . . . . . . . . (512) 463-0707
Counties Represented: Brazoria (part)       Fax: (512) 463-8717
Term Expires: 2017
2337 North Galveston Avenue, Pearland, TX 77581
E-mail: ed.thompson@house.state.tx.us
Committees: Environmental Regulation; Land and Resource
Management
Education: Houston BBA

Representative **Senfronia Thompson** (D-District 141) . . . .(512) 463-0720
Counties Represented: Harris (part)         Dist: (713) 633-3390
Term Expires: 2017                          Fax: (512) 463-6306
10527 Homestead Road, Houston, TX 77016     Dist: (713) 633-7830
E-mail: senfronia.thompson@house.state.tx.us
Committees: Judiciary and Civil Jurisprudence; Licensing and
Administrative Procedures; Local and Consent Calendars; Redistricting
Education: Texas Southern BS; Prairie View A&M MEd;
Texas Southern 1996 LLM

Representative **Tony Tinderholt** (R-District 94)
Room E1.216 . . . . . . . . . . . . . . . . . . . . . . . . . . . (512) 463-0624
Counties Represented: Tarrant (part)        Fax: (512) 463-8386
Term Expires: 2017
E-mail: tony.tinderholt@house.state.tx.us
Committees: Corrections; County Affairs

Representative **Chris Turner** (D-District 101) . . . . . . . . . . (512) 463-0574
Counties Represented: Tarrant (part)        Dist: (817) 459-2800
Term Expires: 2017                          Fax: (512) 463-1481
1600 East Pioneer Parkway, Suite 515,       Dist: (817) 459-7900
Arlington, TX 76010
E-mail: chris.turner@house.state.tx.us
Committees: General Investigating and Ethics; Higher Education; Ways
and Means

Representative **Scott Turner** (R-District 33) . . . . . . . . . . . (512) 463-0484
Counties Represented: Collin (part), Rockwall   Fax: (512) 463-7834
Term Expires: 2017
P.O. Box 667, Frisco, TX 75034
P.O. Box 92, Rockwall, TX 75087
E-mail: scott.turner@house.state.tx.us
Committees: Government Transparency and Operation; International
Trade and Intergovernmental Affairs
Education: Illinois 1995 BA

Representative **Gary VanDeaver** (R-District 1)
Room E1.310 . . . . . . . . . . . . . . . . . . . . . . . . . . . (512) 463-0692
Counties Represented: Bowie, Franklin, Lamar, Red   Fax: (512) 463-0902
River
Term Expires: 2017
E-mail: gary.vandeaver@house.state.tx.us
Committees: Appropriations; Public Education

*(continued on next page)*

**LEGISLATIVE BRANCH**

**Representatives** *continued*

Representative **Jason Villalba** (R-District 114)
Capitol Extension, Room E2.702 . . . . . . . . . . . . . . . . . . . .(512) 463-0576
  Counties Represented: Dallas (part)     Fax: (512) 463-7827
  Term Expires: 2017
  E-mail: jason.villalba@house.state.tx.us
  Committees: Business and Industry; Economic and Small Business
  Development
  Education: Baylor 1992 BBA; Texas 1996 JD

Representative **Hubert Vo** (D-District 149) . . . . . . . . . . . . .(512) 463-0568
  Counties Represented: Harris (part)     Dist: (281) 988-0212
  Term Expires: 2017     Fax: (512) 463-0548
  7474 South Kirkwood Street, Suite 202,     Dist: (281) 498-6905
  Houston, TX 77072
  E-mail: hubert.vo@house.state.tx.us
  Committees: Economic and Small Business Development; House
  Administration; Insurance
  Education: Houston 1983 MSME

Representative **Armando Walle** (D-District 140) . . . . . . . . .(512) 463-0924
  Counties Represented: Harris (part)     Dist: (713) 694-8620
  Term Expires: 2017     Fax: (512) 463-1510
  150 West Parker Road, Suite 700,     Dist: (713) 694-8613
  Houston, TX 77076
  E-mail: armando.walle@house.state.tx.us
  Committees: Appropriations; Government Transparency and Operation;
  State and Federal Power and Responsibility
  Education: Houston 2004 BS

Representative **James White** (R-District 19) . . . . . . . . . . . .(512) 463-0490
  Counties Represented: Hardin, Jasper, Newton,     Dist: (936) 634-2686
  Polk, Tyler     Fax: (512) 463-9059
  Term Expires: 2017     Dist: (936) 634-2683
  2915 Atkinson Drive, Lufkin, TX 75901
  E-mail: james.white@house.state.tx.us
  Committees: Corrections; Emerging Issues in Texas Law Enforcement;
  Juvenile Justice and Family Issues

Representative **Molly S. White** (R-District 55)
Room E2.702 . . . . . . . . . . . . . . . . . . . . . . . . . . . . . . . .(512) 463-0630
  Counties Represented: Bell (part)     Fax: (512) 463-0937
  Term Expires: 2017
  E-mail: molly.white@house.state.tx.us
  Committees: Homeland Security and Public Safety; Urban Affairs

Representative **Paul D. Workman** (R-District 47)
Room E1.216 . . . . . . . . . . . . . . . . . . . . . . . . . . . . . . . .(512) 463-0652
  Counties Represented: Travis (part)     Fax: (512) 463-0565
  Term Expires: 2017
  E-mail: paul.workman@house.state.tx.us
  Committees: Insurance; Natural Resources; State and Federal Power
  and Responsibility

Representative **John Wray** (R-District 10) Room E1.220 . . (512) 463-0516
  Counties Represented: Ellis, Henderson (part)     Fax: (512) 463-1051
  Term Expires: 2017
  E-mail: john.wray@house.state.tx.us
  Committees: Homeland Security and Public Safety; Ways and Means

Representative **Gene Wu** (D-District 137) . . . . . . . . . . . . . .(512) 463-0492
  Counties Represented: Harris (part)     Fax: (512) 463-1182
  Term Expires: 2017
  P.O. Box 742442, Houston, TX 77274
  E-mail: gene.wu@house.state.tx.us
  Committees: County Affairs; Energy Resources
  Education: Texas A&M BS; Texas MPP; South Texas JD

Representative **William "Bill" Zedler** (R-District 96) . . . . .(512) 463-0374
  Counties Represented: Tarrant (part)     Dist: (817) 483-1885
  Term Expires: 2017     Fax: (512) 463-0364
  5840 West Interstate 20, Suite 110,     Dist: (817) 478-1887
  Arlington, TX 76017
  E-mail: bill.zedler@house.state.tx.us
  Committees: Public Health; Special Purpose Districts
  Education: Sam Houston State BBA, MBA

Representative **John M. Zerwas, MD** (R-District 28) . . . . .(512) 463-0657
  Counties Represented: Fort Bend (part)     Tel: (888) 827-1560
  Term Expires: 2017     (Toll Free)
  9315 F.M. 1489, Suite C, Simonton, TX 77476     Dist: (281) 533-9042
  P.O. Box 434, Simonton, TX 77476-0434     Fax: (512) 236-0713
  E-mail: john.zerwas@house.state.tx.us     Dist: (281) 533-9049
  Committees: Higher Education; Public Health
  Education: Houston 1976; Baylor Col Medicine 1980 MD

District 120 **(Vacant)** . . . . . . . . . . . . . . . . . . . . . . . . . . . . .(512) 463-4630
  Note: A special runoff election to fill this legislative vacancy will be
  held on August 2, 2016.

# House Standing Committees
P.O. Box 2910, Austin, TX 78768-2910

## Agriculture and Livestock

| Majority Members | Minority Members |
| --- | --- |
| Charles "Doc" Anderson (R-56) *Vice Chair* | Tracy O. King (D-80) *Chair* |
| John Cyrier (R-17) | Mary E. Gonzalez (D-75) |
| Matt Rinaldi (R-115) | |
| David Simpson (R-7) | |
| Drew Springer (R-68) | |

## Appropriations

| Majority Members | Minority Members |
| --- | --- |
| John Otto (R-18) *Chair* | Dawnna Dukes (D-46) |
| Trent Ashby (R-57) | Helen Giddings (D-109) |
| Cecil Bell, Jr. (R-3) | Donna Howard (D-48) |
| Greg Bonnen (R-24) | Oscar Longoria (D-35) |
| Cindy Burkett (R-113) | Marisa Marquez (D-77) |
| Giovanni Capriglione (R-98) | Borris L. Miles (D-146) |
| Sarah Davis (R-134) | Sergio Muñoz, Jr. (D-36) |
| Larry Gonzales (R-52) | Justin Rodriguez (D-125) |
| Bryan Hughes (R-5) | Armando Walle (D-140) |
| Linda Koop (R-102) | |
| Rick Miller (R-26) | |
| Dade Phelan (R-21) | |
| Walter "Four" Price (R-87) | |
| John Raney (R-14) | |
| J.D. Sheffield (R-59) | |
| Gary VanDeaver (R-1) | |

## Business and Industry

| Majority Members | Minority Members |
| --- | --- |
| Ronald E. Simmons (R-65) *Vice Chair* | Rene Oliveira (D-37) *Chair* |
| Allen Fletcher (R-130) | Nicole Collier (D-95) |
| Matt Rinaldi (R-115) | Ramon Romero, Jr. (D-90) |
| Jason Villalba (R-114) | |

## Calendars

| Majority Members | Minority Members |
| --- | --- |
| Todd Hunter (R-32) *Chair* | Eddie Lucio III (D-38) *Vice Chair* |
| Byron Cook (R-8) | Roberto R. Alonzo (D-104) |
| Sarah Davis (R-134) | Helen Giddings (D-109) |
| Charlie Geren (R-99) | Eric "EJ" Johnson (D-100) |
| Patricia Fincher Harless (R-126) | Eddie Rodriguez (D-51) |
| Daniel G. "Dan" Huberty (R-127) | |
| Ken King (R-88) | |
| Lyle Larson (R-122) | |
| Walter "Four" Price (R-87) | |
| Debbie Riddle (R-150) | |

## Corrections

| Majority Members | Minority Members |
| --- | --- |
| Jim Murphy (R-133) *Chair* | Alma A. Allen (D-131) |
| James White (R-19) *Vice Chair* | |
| Mark Keough (R-15) | |
| Matt Krause (R-93) | |
| Leighton Schubert (R-13) | |
| Tony Tinderholt (R-94) | |

## County Affairs

| Majority Members | Minority Members |
| --- | --- |
| Dustin Burrows (R-83) | Garnet F. Coleman (D-147) *Chair* |
| John Lujan (R-118) | Ramon Romero, Jr. (D-90) |
| Leighton Schubert (R-13) | Gene Wu (D-137) |
| Stuart Spitzer (R-4) | |
| Jonathan Stickland (R-92) | |
| Tony Tinderholt (R-94) | |

## Criminal Jurisprudence

| Majority Members | Minority Members |
| --- | --- |
| Todd Hunter (R-32) | Abel Herrero (D-34) *Chair* |
| Jeff Leach (R-67) | Joseph E. "Joe" Moody (D-78) *Vice Chair* |
| Matt Shaheen (R-66) | |
| David Simpson (R-7) | Terry Canales (D-40) |

## Culture, Recreation and Tourism

**Majority Members**
John Frullo (R-84)
Lyle Larson (R-122)
Andrew S. Murr (R-53)
Wayne Smith (R-128)

**Minority Members**
Ryan Guillen (D-31) *Chair*
Dawnna Dukes (D-46) *Vice Chair*
Marisa Marquez (D-77)

## Defense and Veterans' Affairs

**Majority Members**
Susan Lewis King (R-71) *Chair*
James Frank (R-69) *Vice Chair*
Jimmie Don Aycock (R-54)
John Lujan (R-118)
Matt Schaefer (R-6)
Matt Shaheen (R-66)

**Minority Members**
Cesar J. Blanco (D-76)

## Economic and Small Business Development

**Majority Members**
Angie Chen Button (R-112) *Chair*
Charles "Doc" Anderson (R-56)
Wayne Faircloth (R-23)
Jason Isaac (R-45)
Will Metcalf (R-16)
Jason Villalba (R-114)

**Minority Members**
Eric "EJ" Johnson (D-100)
 *Vice Chair*
Eddie Rodriguez (D-51)
Hubert Vo (D-149)

## Elections

**Majority Members**
Jodie Laubenberg (R-89) *Chair*
Craig Goldman (R-97) *Vice Chair*
Patrick "Pat" Fallon (R-106)
Dade Phelan (R-21)
Mike Schofield (R-132)

**Minority Members**
Celia Israel (D-50)
Ron Reynolds (D-27)

## Energy Resources

**Majority Members**
Drew Darby (R-72) *Chair*
Chris Paddie (R-9) *Vice Chair*
Thomas "Tom" Craddick (R-82)
Anthony "Tony" Dale (R-136)
James L. "Jim" Keffer (R-60)
Phil King (R-61)
Brooks Landgraf (R-81)
Morgan Meyer (R-108)
Debbie Riddle (R-150)

**Minority Members**
Rafael Anchia (D-103)
Terry Canales (D-40)
Abel Herrero (D-34)
Gene Wu (D-137)

## Environmental Regulation

**Majority Members**
Geanie W. Morrison (R-30) *Chair*
Jason Isaac (R-45)
Kyle J. Kacal (R-12)
Ken King (R-88)
Phil King (R-61)
Jose Manuel "J.M." Lozano (R-43)
Ed Thompson (R-29)

**Minority Members**
Eddie Rodriguez (D-51) *Vice Chair*
Ron Reynolds (D-27)

## General Investigating and Ethics

**Majority Members**
John Kuempel (R-44) *Chair*
Sarah Davis (R-134)
Todd Hunter (R-32)
Lyle Larson (R-122)

**Minority Members**
Nicole Collier (D-95) *Vice Chair*
Joseph E. "Joe" Moody (D-78)
Chris Turner (D-101)

## Government Transparency and Operation

**Majority Members**
Gary Elkins (R-135) *Chair*
Rick Galindo (R-117)
Larry Gonzales (R-52)
Jeff Leach (R-67)
Scott Turner (R-33)

**Minority Members**
Armando Walle (D-140) *Vice Chair*
Roland Gutierrez (D-119)

## Higher Education

**Majority Members**
John M. Zerwas (R-28) *Chair*
Travis Clardy (R-11)
Myra Crownover (R-64)
Geanie W. Morrison (R-30)
John Raney (R-14)

**Minority Members**
Donna Howard (D-48) *Vice Chair*
Roberto R. Alonzo (D-104)
Armando "Mando" Martinez (D-39)
Chris Turner (D-101)

## Homeland Security and Public Safety

**Majority Members**
Larry Phillips (R-62) *Chair*
DeWayne Burns (R-58)
Anthony "Tony" Dale (R-136)
Will Metcalf (R-16)
Molly S. White (R-55)
John Wray (R-10)

**Minority Members**
Alfonso "Poncho" Nevárez (D-74)
 *Vice Chair*
Eric "EJ" Johnson (D-100)
Joseph E. "Joe" Moody (D-78)

## House Administration

**Majority Members**
Charlie Geren (R-99) *Chair*
Trent Ashby (R-57)
Marsha Farney (R-20)
Ken King (R-88)
Chris Paddie (R-9)
John Raney (R-14)

**Minority Members**
Marisa Marquez (D-77) *Vice Chair*
Alma A. Allen (D-131)
Roberto R. Alonzo (D-104)
Donna Howard (D-48)
Hubert Vo (D-149)

## Human Services

**Majority Members**
Mark Keough (R-15)
Susan Lewis King (R-71)
Stephanie Klick (R-91)
Gilbert Peña (R-144)
Walter "Four" Price (R-87)
Stuart Spitzer (R-4)

**Minority Members**
Richard Peña Raymond (D-42)
 *Chair*
Toni Rose (D-110) *Vice Chair*
Elliott Naishtat (D-49)

## Insurance

**Majority Members**
John Frullo (R-84) *Chair*
Greg Bonnen (R-24)
Morgan Meyer (R-108)
Dennis Paul (R-129)
Kenneth Sheets (R-107)
Paul D. Workman (R-47)

**Minority Members**
Sergio Muñoz, Jr. (D-36)
 *Vice Chair*
R. D. "Bobby" Guerra (D-41)
Hubert Vo (D-149)

## International Trade and Intergovernmental Affairs

**Majority Members**
Jose Manuel "J.M." Lozano (R-43)
 *Vice Chair*
Rodney E. Anderson (R-105)
Dustin Burrows (R-83)
Linda Koop (R-102)
Scott Turner (R-33)

**Minority Members**
Rafael Anchia (D-103) *Chair*
Diego M. Bernal (D-123)

## Investments and Financial Services

**Majority Members**
Tan Parker (R-63) *Chair*
Giovanni Capriglione (R-98)
Dan Flynn (R-2)
Brooks Landgraf (R-81)
Phil Stephenson (R-85)

**Minority Members**
Oscar Longoria (D-35) *Vice Chair*
Joseph "Joe" Pickett (D-79)

## Judiciary and Civil Jurisprudence

**Majority Members**
John T. Smithee (R-86) *Chair*
Travis Clardy (R-11)
Jodie Laubenberg (R-89)
Mike Schofield (R-132)
Kenneth Sheets (R-107)

**Minority Members**
Jessica Christian Farrar (D-148)
 *Vice Chair*
Ana E. Hernandez (D-143)
Richard Peña Raymond (D-42)
Senfronia Thompson (D-141)

## Juvenile Justice and Family Issues

**Majority Members**
Debbie Riddle (R-150) *Vice Chair*
Bryan Hughes (R-5)
Gilbert Peña (R-144)
Scott Sanford (R-70)
James White (R-19)

**Minority Members**
Harold V. Dutton, Jr. (D-142) *Chair*
Toni Rose (D-110)

## Land and Resource Management

| **Majority Members** | **Minority Members** |
| --- | --- |
| Ed Thompson (R-29) *Vice Chair* | Joe D. Deshotel (D-22) *Chair* |
| Cecil Bell, Jr. (R-3) | Eddie Lucio III (D-38) |
| John Cyrier (R-17) | |
| Matt Krause (R-93) | |
| Scott Sanford (R-70) | |

## Licensing and Administrative Procedures

| **Majority Members** | **Minority Members** |
| --- | --- |
| Wayne Smith (R-128) *Chair* | Roland Gutierrez (D-119) |
| Charlie Geren (R-99) | *Vice Chair* |
| Craig Goldman (R-97) | Ryan Guillen (D-31) |
| John Kuempel (R-44) | Borris L. Miles (D-146) |
| Doug Miller (R-73) | Senfronia Thompson (D-141) |

## Local and Consent Calendars

| **Majority Members** | **Minority Members** |
| --- | --- |
| Travis Clardy (R-11) *Vice Chair* | Senfronia Thompson (D-141) *Chair* |
| Cindy Burkett (R-113) | R. D. "Bobby" Guerra (D-41) |
| Giovanni Capriglione (R-98) | Roland Gutierrez (D-119) |
| Anthony "Tony" Dale (R-136) | Sergio Muñoz, Jr. (D-36) |
| Larry Gonzales (R-52) | Alfonso "Poncho" Nevárez (D-74) |
| Jason Isaac (R-45) | |
| Kenneth Sheets (R-107) | |
| Drew Springer (R-68) | |

## Natural Resources

| **Majority Members** | **Minority Members** |
| --- | --- |
| James L. "Jim" Keffer (R-60) *Chair* | Tracy O. King (D-80) |
| James Frank (R-69) *Vice Chair* | Eddie Lucio III (D-38) |
| Trent Ashby (R-57) | Alfonso "Poncho" Nevárez (D-74) |
| Dennis Bonnen (R-25) | |
| DeWayne Burns (R-58) | |
| Kyle J. Kacal (R-12) | |
| Lyle Larson (R-122) | |
| Paul D. Workman (R-47) | |

## Pensions

| **Majority Members** | **Minority Members** |
| --- | --- |
| Dan Flynn (R-2) *Chair* | Roberto R. Alonzo (D-104) |
| Stephanie Klick (R-91) | *Vice Chair* |
| Dennis Paul (R-129) | Ana E. Hernandez (D-143) |
| Phil Stephenson (R-85) | Justin Rodriguez (D-125) |

## Public Education

| **Majority Members** | **Minority Members** |
| --- | --- |
| Jimmie Don Aycock (R-54) *Chair* | Alma A. Allen (D-131) *Vice Chair* |
| Dwayne Bohac (R-138) | Joe D. Deshotel (D-22) |
| Marsha Farney (R-20) | Harold V. Dutton, Jr. (D-142) |
| Rick Galindo (R-117) | Mary E. Gonzalez (D-75) |
| Daniel G. "Dan" Huberty (R-127) | |
| Ken King (R-88) | |
| Gary VanDeaver (R-1) | |

## Public Health

| **Majority Members** | **Minority Members** |
| --- | --- |
| Myra Crownover (R-64) *Chair* | Elliott Naishtat (D-49) *Vice Chair* |
| Sarah Davis (R-134) | Cesar J. Blanco (D-76) |
| Rick Miller (R-26) | Garnet F. Coleman (D-147) |
| J.D. Sheffield (R-59) | Nicole Collier (D-95) |
| William "Bill" Zedler (R-96) | R. D. "Bobby" Guerra (D-41) |
| John M. Zerwas (R-28) | |

## Redistricting

| **Majority Members** | **Minority Members** |
| --- | --- |
| Jose Manuel "J.M." Lozano (R-43) *Chair* | Yvonne Davis (D-111) *Vice Chair* |
| Larry Gonzales (R-52) | Rene Oliveira (D-37) |
| Todd Hunter (R-32) | Joseph "Joe" Pickett (D-79) |
| James L. "Jim" Keffer (R-60) | Senfronia Thompson (D-141) |
| Tan Parker (R-63) | |

## Rules and Resolutions

| **Majority Members** | **Minority Members** |
| --- | --- |
| Kyle J. Kacal (R-12) *Vice Chair* | Carol Alvarado (D-145) |
| Cecil Bell, Jr. (R-3) | Cesar J. Blanco (D-76) |
| Angie Chen Button (R-112) | Justin Rodriguez (D-125) |
| Wayne Faircloth (R-23) | Toni Rose (D-110) |
| Andrew S. Murr (R-53) | |
| J.D. Sheffield (R-59) | |

## Special Purpose Districts

| **Majority Members** | **Minority Members** |
| --- | --- |
| Doug Miller (R-73) *Chair* | Carol Alvarado (D-145) *Vice Chair* |
| Wayne Faircloth (R-23) | Trey Martinez-Fischer (D-116) |
| Patrick "Pat" Fallon (R-106) | |
| Jonathan Stickland (R-92) | |
| William "Bill" Zedler (R-96) | |

## State Affairs

| **Majority Members** | **Minority Members** |
| --- | --- |
| Byron Cook (R-8) *Chair* | Helen Giddings (D-109) *Vice Chair* |
| Thomas "Tom" Craddick (R-82) | Jessica Christian Farrar (D-148) |
| Marsha Farney (R-20) | Ina Minjarez (D-124) |
| Charlie Geren (R-99) | Rene Oliveira (D-37) |
| Patricia Fincher Harless (R-126) | |
| Daniel G. "Dan" Huberty (R-127) | |
| John Kuempel (R-44) | |
| John T. Smithee (R-86) | |

## Transportation

| **Majority Members** | **Minority Members** |
| --- | --- |
| Cindy Burkett (R-113) | Joseph "Joe" Pickett (D-79) *Chair* |
| Allen Fletcher (R-130) | Armando "Mando" Martinez (D-39) |
| Patricia Fincher Harless (R-126) | *Vice Chair* |
| Andrew S. Murr (R-53) | Yvonne Davis (D-111) |
| Chris Paddie (R-9) | Celia Israel (D-50) |
| Larry Phillips (R-62) | Ina Minjarez (D-124) |
| Ronald E. Simmons (R-65) | |

## Urban Affairs

| **Majority Members** | **Minority Members** |
| --- | --- |
| Todd Hunter (R-32) *Vice Chair* | Carol Alvarado (D-145) *Chair* |
| Rodney E. Anderson (R-105) | Diego M. Bernal (D-123) |
| Gary Elkins (R-135) | |
| Matt Schaefer (R-6) | |
| Molly S. White (R-55) | |

## Ways and Means

| **Majority Members** | **Minority Members** |
| --- | --- |
| Dennis Bonnen (R-25) *Chair* | Yvonne Davis (D-111) *Vice Chair* |
| Dwayne Bohac (R-138) | Trey Martinez-Fischer (D-116) |
| Angie Chen Button (R-112) | Chris Turner (D-101) |
| Drew Darby (R-72) | |
| Jim Murphy (R-133) | |
| Tan Parker (R-63) | |
| Drew Springer (R-68) | |
| John Wray (R-10) | |

# Utah Legislature

350 North State Street, Salt Lake City, UT 84114
Internet: www.le.utah.gov

## Utah State Senate

350 North State Street, Suite 320, Salt Lake City, UT 84114
Tel: (801) 538-1035 TTY: (801) 326-1494 Fax: (801) 326-1475
E-mail: senate@le.state.ut.us

President of the Senate **Wayne L. Niederhauser** (R) ..... (801) 538-1035
   Education: Utah State BS, 1985 MS
Majority Leader **Ralph Okerlund** (R) .................. (435) 527-3370
   Education: Utah 1973 BS
Majority Whip **J. Stuart Adams** (R) .................. (801) 593-1776
   Education: Utah 1978 BA
Assistant Majority Whip **Peter C. Knudson** (R) ........ (435) 723-6366
   Education: U Pacific 1966 DDS; Loyola U (Chicago) 1969 MS
Minority Leader **Gene Davis** (D) .................... (801) 484-9428
   Education: LaSalle Extension U LLB
Minority Whip **Karen Mayne** (D) ..................... (801) 968-7756
Assistant Minority Whip **Luz Escamilla** (D)............(801) 521-0407
   Education: Utah 2000 BS, 2006 MPA
Minority Caucus Manager **Jim Dabakis** (D) ........... (801) 656-8269
   Education: BYU 1971 (Attended)
Secretary of the Senate **Leslie McLean**................(801) 538-1458
   E-mail: lmclean@le.utah.gov

## Senators

**Party Affiliation Statistics:** Republicans: 24, Democrats: 5

Senator **J. Stuart Adams** (R-District 22) .............. (801) 593-1776
   Counties Represented: Davis (part)   Fax: (801) 544-7676
   Term Expires: 2019
   3271 East 1875 North, Layton, UT 84040
   E-mail: jsadams@le.utah.gov
   Committees: Business and Labor; Joint Administrative Rules Review;
   Joint Executive Appropriations; Joint Health Reform Task Force;
   Joint Legislative Management; Transportation, Public Utilities and
   Technology

Senator **Curtis S. "Curt" Bramble** (R-District 16) ....... (801) 226-3663
   Counties Represented: Utah (part), Wasatch (part)   Fax: (801) 812-8297
   Term Expires: 2017
   3663 North 870 East, Provo, UT 84604
   E-mail: cbramble@le.utah.gov
   E-mail: curt@cbramble.com
   Committees: Business and Labor; Retirement and Independent Entities;
   Revenue and Taxation
   Education: BYU BS, MS

Senator **Allen M. Christensen** (R-District 19) ........... (801) 782-5600
   Counties Represented: Morgan (part), Summit (part), Weber (part)
   Term Expires: 2017
   1233 East 2550 North, Ogden, UT 84414
   E-mail: achristensen@le.utah.gov
   Committees: Ethics; Health and Human Services; Joint Health Reform
   Task Force; Natural Resources, Agriculture and Environment
   Education: U Pacific 1973 DDS

Senator **Jim Dabakis** (D-District 2) ................... (801) 656-8269
   Counties Represented: Salt Lake (part)
   Term Expires: 2019
   54 B Street, Salt Lake City, UT 84103
   E-mail: jdabakis@le.utah.gov
   Committees: Education; Joint Administrative Rules Review; Joint
   Executive Appropriations; Joint Legislative Management; Revenue and
   Taxation; Rules

Senator **Gene Davis** (D-District 3) ................... (801) 484-9428
   Counties Represented: Salt Lake (part)   Fax: (801) 484-9442
   Term Expires: 2019
   865 Parkway Avenue, Salt Lake City, UT 84106
   E-mail: gdavis@le.utah.gov
   Committees: Business and Labor; Ethics; Joint Administrative Rules
   Review; Joint Executive Appropriations; Joint Health Reform Task
   Force; Joint Legislative Management; Judiciary, Law Enforcement and
   Criminal Justice; Retirement and Independent Entities; Revenue and
   Taxation

Senator **Margaret Dayton** (R-District 15)...............(801) 221-0623
   Counties Represented: Utah (part)   Fax: (801) 221-2513
   Term Expires: 2019
   97 West Westview Drive, Orem, UT 84058
   E-mail: mdayton@le.utah.gov
   Committees: Government Operations and Political Subdivisions;
   Natural Resources, Agriculture and Environment; Retirement and
   Independent Entities
   Education: BYU 1972 BS

Senator **Luz Escamilla** (D-District 1) ................. (801) 521-0407
   Counties Represented: Salt Lake (part)
   Term Expires: 2017
   1004 North Morton Drive, Salt Lake City, UT 84116
   E-mail: lescamilla@le.utah.gov
   Committees: Ethics; Government Operations and Political Subdivisions;
   Health and Human Services; Joint Executive Appropriations; Joint
   Legislative Management; Joint Native American Legislative Liaison;
   Judiciary, Law Enforcement and Criminal Justice

Senator **Lincoln S. Fillmore** (R-District 10) ............. (801) 538-1035
   Counties Represented: Salt Lake (part)
   Term Expires: 2017
   E-mail: lfillmore@le.utah.gov
   Committees: Economic Development and Workforce Services;
   Education

Senator **Wayne A. Harper** (R-District 6) ............... (801) 566-5466
   Counties Represented: Salt Lake (part)
   Term Expires: 2017
   2094 Surrey Circle, Taylorsville, UT 84129
   E-mail: wharper@le.utah.gov
   Committees: Revenue and Taxation; Transportation, Public Utilities and
   Technology
   Education: BYU BA, MS

Senator **Deidre Henderson** (R-District 7)...............(801) 787-6197
   Counties Represented: Utah (part)
   Term Expires: 2017
   462 River Cross Road, Spanish Fork, UT 84660
   E-mail: dhenderson@le.utah.gov
   Committees: Business and Labor; Ethics; Revenue and Taxation; Rules
   Education: BYU

Senator **Lyle W. Hillyard** (R-District 25)...............(435) 752-2610
   Counties Represented: Cache (part), Rich   Res: (435) 753-0043
   Term Expires: 2017   Fax: (435) 753-8895
   595 South Riverwoods Parkway, Suite 100, Logan, UT 84321
   E-mail: lhillyard@le.utah.gov
   Committees: Government Operations and Political Subdivisions; Joint
   Executive Appropriations; Judiciary, Law Enforcement and Criminal
   Justice
   Education: Utah State 1965 BS; Utah 1967 JD

Senator **David P. Hinkins** (R-District 27) ............... (435) 748-2828
   Counties Represented: Carbon, Emery, Grand,   Res: (435) 384-5550
   San Juan, Utah (part), Wasatch (part)   Fax: (435) 748-2089
   Term Expires: 2017
   P.O. Box 485, Orangeville, UT 84537
   E-mail: dhinkins@le.utah.gov
   Committees: Government Operations and Political Subdivisions; Joint
   Native American Legislative Liaison; Rules; Transportation, Public
   Utilities and Technology

Senator **Jani Iwamoto** (D-District 4) ................. (801) 274-0496
   Counties Represented: Salt Lake (part)   Fax: (801) 274-0289
   Term Expires: 2019
   4760 Highland Drive, Suite 427, Salt Lake City, UT 84117
   E-mail: jiwamoto@le.utah.gov
   Committees: Economic Development and Workforce Services; Ethics;
   Joint Native American Legislative Liaison; Natural Resources,
   Agriculture and Environment
   Education: Utah BS; UC Davis 1985 JD

Senator **Alvin B. "Al" Jackson, Jr.** (R-District 14) ....... (801) 216-4479
   Counties Represented: Utah (part)   Fax: (801) 216-4589
   Term Expires: 2017
   6108 New London Street, Highland, UT 84003
   E-mail: abjackson@le.utah.gov
   Committees: Government Operations and Political Subdivisions;
   Transportation, Public Utilities and Technology
   Education: Embry-Riddle 1990 BS; Johns Hopkins 1999 MBA

Senator **Scott K. Jenkins** (R-District 20) .............. (801) 621-5412
   Counties Represented: Davis (part), Weber (part)   Res: (801) 731-5120
   Term Expires: 2017
   1950 North 4425 West, Plain City, UT 84404
   E-mail: sjenkins@le.utah.gov
   Committees: Economic Development and Workforce Services; Natural
   Resources, Agriculture and Environment
   Affiliation: Owner and Operator, Great Western Supply
   Education: Weber State 1974 AS

*(continued on next page)*

LEGISLATIVE BRANCH

**Senators** *continued*

Senator **Peter C. Knudson** (R-District 17) . . . . . . . . . . . . (435) 723-6366
Counties Represented: Box Elder, Cache (part),    Res: (435) 723-2035
Tooele (part)    Fax: (435) 723-6371
Term Expires: 2019
1209 Michelle Drive, Brigham City, UT 84302
E-mail: pknudson@le.utah.gov
Committees: Ethics; Health and Human Services; Joint Executive
Appropriations; Joint Health Reform Task Force; Joint Legislative
Management; Natural Resources, Agriculture and Environment; Rules

Senator **Mark Benson Madsen** (R-District 13) . . . . . . . . . (801) 360-9389
Counties Represented: Salt Lake (part), Utah (part)
Term Expires: 2017
1304 North Redwood Road, #321, Saratoga Springs, UT 84045
E-mail: mmadsen@le.utah.gov
Committees: Education; Joint Administrative Rules Review; Judiciary,
Law Enforcement and Criminal Justice; Rules
Education: George Mason 2000 BA; J Reuben Clark Law 2003 JD

Senator **Karen Mayne** (D-District 5) . . . . . . . . . . . . . . . . . (801) 968-7756
Counties Represented: Salt Lake (part)
Term Expires: 2019
5044 West Bannock Circle, West Valley City, UT 84120
E-mail: kmayne@le.utah.gov
Committees: Business and Labor; Economic Development and
Workforce Services; Ethics; Joint Executive Appropriations; Joint
Legislative Management; Retirement and Independent Entities; Rules;
Transportation, Public Utilities and Technology

Senator **Dr. F. Ann Millner** (R-District 18) . . . . . . . . . . . . . (801) 900-3897
Counties Represented: Davis (part), Morgan (part), Weber (part)
Term Expires: 2019
4287 Harrison Boulevard, Room 313, Ogden, UT 84403
E-mail: amillner@le.utah.gov
Committees: Economic Development and Workforce Services;
Education
Education: Tennessee BS; Southwest Texas State MS; BYU 1986 EdD

Senator **Wayne L. Niederhauser** (R-District 9) . . . . . . . . . (801) 538-1035
Counties Represented: Salt Lake (part)    Res: (801) 942-3398
Term Expires: 2019    Fax: (801) 283-7751
3182 East Granite Woods Lane, Sandy, UT 84092
E-mail: wniederhauser@le.utah.gov
Committees: Education; Joint Executive Appropriations; Joint
Legislative Management; Revenue and Taxation

Senator **Ralph Okerlund** (R-District 24) . . . . . . . . . . . . . . (435) 527-3370
Counties Represented: Beaver (part), Garfield, Juab, Kane, Millard,
Piute, Sanpete, Sevier, Utah (part), Wayne
Term Expires: 2017
248 South 500 West, Monroe, UT 84754
E-mail: rokerlund@le.utah.gov
Committees: Business and Labor; Economic Development and
Workforce Services; Joint Executive Appropriations; Joint Legislative
Management

Senator **Brian Shiozawa** (R-District 8) . . . . . . . . . . . . . . . . (801) 889-7450
Counties Represented: Salt Lake (part)
Term Expires: 2017
3177 Fort Union Boulevard, Salt Lake City, UT 84121
E-mail: bshiozawa@le.utah.gov
Committees: Health and Human Services; Natural Resources,
Agriculture and Environment
Education: Stanford BS; U Washington 1981 MD

Senator **Howard A. Stephenson** (R-District 11) . . . . . . . . (801) 972-8814
Counties Represented: Salt Lake (part), Utah (part)    Res: (801) 572-1038
Term Expires: 2019
1038 East 13590 South, Draper, UT 84020
E-mail: hstephenson@le.utah.gov
Committees: Education; Joint Administrative Rules Review; Revenue
and Taxation
Education: BYU 1975 BS, 1977 MPA

Senator **Jerry W. Stevenson** (R-District 21) . . . . . . . . . . . (801) 544-1211
Counties Represented: Davis (part)    Res: (801) 544-5172
Term Expires: 2019    Fax: (801) 546-6819
466 South 1700 West, Layton, UT 84041
E-mail: jwstevenson@le.utah.gov
Committees: Economic Development and Workforce Services;
Education; Ethics; Joint Executive Appropriations

Senator **Daniel W. Thatcher** (R-District 12) . . . . . . . . . . . (801) 759-4746
Counties Represented: Salt Lake (part), Tooele (part)
Term Expires: 2019
6352 West City Vistas Way, West Valley City, UT 84128
E-mail: dthatcher@le.utah.gov
Committees: Government Operations and Political Subdivisions;
Judiciary, Law Enforcement and Criminal Justice; Retirement and
Independent Entities

Senator **Stephen H. "Steve" Urquhart** (R-District 29) . . . (435) 668-7759
Counties Represented: Washington (part)    Fax: (435) 272-4484
Term Expires: 2017
634 East 1100 South, St. George, UT 84790
E-mail: surquhart@le.utah.gov
Committees: Education; Judiciary, Law Enforcement and Criminal
Justice; Rules
Education: Williams 1989; J Reuben Clark Law 1992 JD

Senator **Kevin T. Van Tassell** (R-District 26) . . . . . . . . . . (801) 789-7082
Counties Represented: Daggett, Duchesne, Summit    Res: (435) 789-0724
(part), Uintah, Wasatch (part)    Fax: (435) 789-8411
Term Expires: 2019
3424 West 1500 North, Vernal, UT 84078
E-mail: kvantassell@le.utah.gov
Committees: Health and Human Services; Joint Native American
Legislative Liaison; Rules; Transportation, Public Utilities and
Technology

Senator **Evan J. Vickers** (R-District 28) . . . . . . . . . . . . . . . (435) 586-9651
Counties Represented: Beaver (part), Iron,    Res: (435) 586-9561
Washington (part)    Fax: (435) 586-3473
Term Expires: 2019
2166 North Cobble Creek Drive, Cedar City, UT 84721
E-mail: evickers@le.utah.gov
Committees: Health and Human Services; Natural Resources,
Agriculture and Environment
Education: Utah 1977 BS

Senator **Todd Weiler** (R-District 23) . . . . . . . . . . . . . . . . . (801) 599-9823
Counties Represented: Davis (part), Salt Lake (part)    Fax: (801) 525-5327
Term Expires: 2017
1248 West 1900 South, Woods Cross, UT 84087
E-mail: tweiler@le.utah.gov
Committees: Business and Labor; Judiciary, Law Enforcement and
Criminal Justice; Retirement and Independent Entities; Rules
Education: BYU 1990 BS; J Reuben Clark Law 1996 JD

# Senate Standing Committees

## Business and Labor

| Majority Members | Minority Members |
| --- | --- |
| Curtis S. "Curt" Bramble (R-16) | Gene Davis (D-3) |
| *Chair* | Karen Mayne (D-5) |
| J. Stuart Adams (R-22) | |
| Deidre Henderson (R-7) | |
| Ralph Okerlund (R-24) | |
| Todd Weiler (R-23) | |

## Economic Development and Workforce Services

| Majority Members | Minority Members |
| --- | --- |
| Lincoln S. Fillmore (R-10) *Chair* | Jani Iwamoto (D-4) |
| Scott K. Jenkins (R-20) | Karen Mayne (D-5) |
| Dr. F. Ann Millner (R-18) | |
| Ralph Okerlund (R-24) | |
| Jerry W. Stevenson (R-21) | |

## Education

| Majority Members | Minority Members |
| --- | --- |
| Dr. F. Ann Millner (R-18) *Chair* | Jim Dabakis (D-2) |
| Lincoln S. Fillmore (R-10) | |
| Mark Benson Madsen (R-13) | |
| Wayne L. Niederhauser (R-9) | |
| Howard A. Stephenson (R-11) | |
| Jerry W. Stevenson (R-21) | |
| Stephen H. "Steve" Urquhart (R-29) | |

## Ethics

| Majority Members | Minority Members |
| --- | --- |
| Peter C. Knudson (R-17) *Chair* | Gene Davis (D-3) *Vice Chair* |
| Allen M. Christensen (R-19) | Luz Escamilla (D-1) |
| Deidre Henderson (R-7) | Jani Iwamoto (D-4) |
| Jerry W. Stevenson (R-21) | Karen Mayne (D-5) |

## Government Operations and Political Subdivisions

**Majority Members**
Margaret Dayton (R-15) *Chair*
Lyle W. Hillyard (R-25)
David P. Hinkins (R-27)
Alvin B. "Al" Jackson, Jr. (R-14)
Daniel W. Thatcher (R-12)

**Minority Members**
Luz Escamilla (D-1)

## Health and Human Services

**Majority Members**
Evan J. Vickers (R-28) *Chair*
Allen M. Christensen (R-19)
Peter C. Knudson (R-17)
Brian Shiozawa (R-8)
Kevin T. Van Tassell (R-26)

**Minority Members**
Luz Escamilla (D-1)

## Judiciary, Law Enforcement and Criminal Justice

**Majority Members**
Mark Benson Madsen (R-13) *Chair*
Lyle W. Hillyard (R-25)
Daniel W. Thatcher (R-12)
Stephen H. "Steve" Urquhart (R-29)
Todd Weiler (R-23)

**Minority Members**
Gene Davis (D-3)
Luz Escamilla (D-1)

## Natural Resources, Agriculture and Environment

**Majority Members**
Scott K. Jenkins (R-20) *Chair*
Allen M. Christensen (R-19)
Margaret Dayton (R-15)
Peter C. Knudson (R-17)
Brian Shiozawa (R-8)
Evan J. Vickers (R-28)

**Minority Members**
Jani Iwamoto (D-4)

## Retirement and Independent Entities

**Majority Members**
Todd Weiler (R-23) *Chair*
Curtis S. "Curt" Bramble (R-16)
Margaret Dayton (R-15)
Daniel W. Thatcher (R-12)

**Minority Members**
Gene Davis (D-3)
Karen Mayne (D-5)

## Revenue and Taxation

**Majority Members**
Deidre Henderson (R-7) *Chair*
Curtis S. "Curt" Bramble (R-16)
Wayne A. Harper (R-6)
Wayne L. Niederhauser (R-9)
Howard A. Stephenson (R-11)

**Minority Members**
Jim Dabakis (D-2)
Gene Davis (D-3)

## Rules

**Majority Members**
Kevin T. Van Tassell (R-26) *Chair*
Todd Weiler (R-23) *Vice Chair*
Deidre Henderson (R-7)
David P. Hinkins (R-27)
Peter C. Knudson (R-17)
Mark Benson Madsen (R-13)
Stephen H. "Steve" Urquhart (R-29)

**Minority Members**
Jim Dabakis (D-2)
Karen Mayne (D-5)

## Transportation, Public Utilities and Technology

**Majority Members**
Alvin B. "Al" Jackson, Jr. (R-14) *Chair*
J. Stuart Adams (R-22)
Wayne A. Harper (R-6)
David P. Hinkins (R-27)
Kevin T. Van Tassell (R-26)

**Minority Members**
Karen Mayne (D-5)

# Utah House of Representatives

350 North State Street, Suite 350, Salt Lake City, UT 84114
Tel: (801) 538-1029  Fax: (801) 326-1544

Speaker of the House **Gregory H. "Greg" Hughes** (R) . . . (801) 432-0362

Majority Leader **James A. "Jim" Dunnigan** (R) . . . . . . . . (801) 840-1800
  Education: Utah BS
Majority Whip **Francis D. Gibson** (R) . . . . . . . . . . . . . . . . (801) 491-3763
  Education: BYU BS; Houston MSW
Assistant Majority Whip **Brad R. Wilson** (R) . . . . . . . . . . .(801) 425-1028
  Education: Weber State BS
Minority Leader **Brian S. King** (D) . . . . . . . . . . . . . . . . . (801) 532-1739
  Education: Utah BS, 1985 JD
Minority Whip **Rebecca Chavez-Houck** (D) . . . . . . . . . . . (801) 891-9292
Assistant Minority Whip **Joel K. Briscoe** (D) . . . . . . . . . . (801) 946-9791
  Education: Utah 1982 BA
Minority Caucus Manager **Patrice Arent** (D) . . . . . . . . . . . (801) 889-7849
  Education: Utah 1978 BS; Cornell 1981 JD
Chief Clerk of the House **Sandy D. Tenney** . . . . . . . . . . . .(801) 538-1029
  E-mail: stenney@le.utah.gov

# Representatives

**Party Affiliation Statistics: Republicans: 63, Democrats: 12**

Representative
  **Jacob L. "Jake" Anderegg** (R-District 6) . . . . . . . . . . . . (801) 901-3580
  Counties Represented: Utah (part)
  Term Expires: 2017
  P.O. Box 934, Lehi, UT 84043-0934
  E-mail: janderegg@le.utah.gov
  Committees: Business and Labor; Rules; Transportation
  Education: BYU 2001 BS; Westminster (MO) 2005 MBA
Representative **Johnny Anderson** (R-District 34) . . . . . . . . (801) 898-1168
  Counties Represented: Salt Lake (part)
  Term Expires: 2017
  4289 South El Camino Street, Taylorsville, UT 84129
  E-mail: janderson34@le.utah.gov
  Committees: Political Subdivisions; Transportation
  Education: U Phoenix BS
Representative **Patrice Arent** (D-District 36) . . . . . . . . . . . (801) 889-7849
  Counties Represented: Salt Lake (part)        Res: (801) 272-1956
  Term Expires: 2017
  3665 East 3800 South, Salt Lake City, UT 84109
  E-mail: parent@le.utah.gov
  Committees: Ethics; Government Operations; Joint Executive
  Appropriations; Joint Legislative Management; Public Utilities and
  Technology
Representative **Stewart Barlow** (R-District 17) . . . . . . . . . (801) 544-4708
  Counties Represented: Davis (part)
  Term Expires: 2017
  940 Signal Hill, Fruit Heights, UT 84037
  E-mail: sbarlow@le.utah.gov
  Committees: Health and Human Services; Transportation
Representative **Joel K. Briscoe** (D-District 25) . . . . . . . . . .(801) 946-9791
  Counties Represented: Salt Lake (part)        Res: (801) 583-2281
  Term Expires: 2017
  1124 East 600 South, Salt Lake City, UT 84102
  E-mail: jbriscoe@le.utah.gov
  Committees: Joint Executive Appropriations; Joint Legislative
  Management; Natural Resources, Agriculture and Environment;
  Revenue and Taxation
Representative **Melvin R. "Mel" Brown** (R-District 53) . . . (435) 336-3309
  Counties Represented: Daggett, Duchesne (part), Morgan, Rich,
  Summit (part)
  Term Expires: 2017
  P.O. Box 697, Coalville, UT 84017
  E-mail: melbrown@le.utah.gov
  Committees: Health and Human Services; Natural Resources,
  Agriculture and Environment
Representative **Rebecca Chavez-Houck** (D-District 24) . . . (801) 891-9292
  Counties Represented: Salt Lake (part)        Res: (801) 608-4467
  Term Expires: 2017
  643 East 16th Avenue, Salt Lake City, UT 84103
  E-mail: rchouck@le.utah.gov
  Committees: Government Operations; Health and Human Services;
  Joint Executive Appropriations; Joint Health Reform Task Force; Joint
  Legislative Management
Representative **Scott H. Chew** (R-District 55) . . . . . . . . . . (435) 630-0221
  Counties Represented: Duchesne (part), Uintah
  Term Expires: 2017
  P.O. Box 182, Jensen, UT 84035
  E-mail: scottchew@le.utah.gov
  Committees: Natural Resources, Agriculture and Environment; Public
  Utilities and Technology

*(continued on next page)*

**LEGISLATIVE BRANCH**

**Representatives** *continued*

Representative **LaVar Christensen** (R-District 32) . . . . . . . (801) 572-9878
Counties Represented: Salt Lake (part)  Res: (801) 571-8603
Term Expires: 2017  Fax: (801) 572-9267
12308 South Raleigh Court, Draper, UT 84020
E-mail: lavarchristensen@le.utah.gov
Committees: Education; Joint Administrative Rules Review; Judiciary

Representative **Kay J. Christofferson** (R-District 56) . . . . . (801) 768-8914
Counties Represented: Utah (part)
Term Expires: 2017
1256 East 1500 North, Lehi, UT 84043
E-mail: kchristofferson@le.utah.gov
Committees: Public Utilities and Technology; Transportation
Education: BYU 1982 BCE

Representative **Kim Coleman** (R-District 42) . . . . . . . . . . . (801) 865-8970
Counties Represented: Salt Lake (part)
Term Expires: 2017
8303 South 5260 West, West Jordan, UT 84081
E-mail: kimcoleman@le.utah.gov
Committees: Education; Political Subdivisions

Representative **Fred C. Cox** (R-District 30) . . . . . . . . . . . . . (801) 966-2636
Counties Represented: Salt Lake (part)
Term Expires: 2017
4466 Early Duke Street, West Valley City, UT 84120
E-mail: fredcox@le.utah.gov
Committees: Government Operations; Judiciary

Representative **Rich Cunningham** (R-District 50) . . . . . . . . (801) 722-4942
Counties Represented: Salt Lake (part)
Term Expires: 2017
2568 West Horseshoe Circle, South Jordan, UT 84095
E-mail: rcunningham@le.utah.gov
Committees: Retirement and Independent Entities; Revenue and
Taxation; Transportation
Education: Eastern Utah (Attended); Indiana (PA) (Attended);
Utah (Attended)

Representative **Bruce Cutler** (R-District 44) . . . . . . . . . . . . (801) 556-4600
Counties Represented: Salt Lake (part)
Term Expires: 2017
6051 Mohican Circle, Murray, UT 84123
E-mail: brucecutler@le.utah.gov
Committees: Judiciary

Representative **Bradley M. Daw** (R-District 60) . . . . . . . . . . (801) 850-3608
Counties Represented: Utah (part)
Term Expires: 2017
842 East 280 South, Orem, UT 84097
E-mail: bdaw@le.utah.gov
Committees: Government Operations; Law Enforcement and Criminal
Justice
Education: BYU BS; San José State MS

Representative **Brad L. Dee** (R-District 11) . . . . . . . . . . . . . (801) 399-8623
Counties Represented: Davis (part), Weber (part)  Res: (801) 479-5495
Term Expires: 2017
111 West 5600 South, Ogden, UT 84405
E-mail: bdee@le.utah.gov
Committees: Joint Executive Appropriations; Public Utilities and
Technology; Transportation
Education: U Phoenix MA

Representative **Sophia M. DiCaro** (R-District 31) . . . . . . . . (801) 608-2570
Counties Represented: Salt Lake (part)
Term Expires: 2017
7147 Antelope Road, West Valley City, UT 84128
E-mail: sdicaro@le.utah.gov
Committees: Economic Development and Workforce Services;
Retirement and Independent Entities; Transportation
Education: Utah MPA

Representative **Jack R. Draxler** (R-District 3) . . . . . . . . . . . (435) 752-2668
Counties Represented: Cache (part)
Term Expires: 2017
1946 North 1650 East, North Logan, UT 84341
E-mail: jdraxler@le.utah.gov
Committees: Government Operations; Joint Native American
Legislative Liaison; Transportation

Representative **Susan "Sue" Duckworth** (D-District 22) . . (801) 250-0728
Counties Represented: Salt Lake (part)
Term Expires: 2017
2901 Merton Way, Magna, UT 84044
E-mail: sduckworth@le.utah.gov
Committees: Business and Labor; Natural Resources, Agriculture and
Environment; Retirement and Independent Entities

Representative
**James A. "Jim" Dunnigan** (R-District 39) . . . . . . . . . . (801) 840-1800
Counties Represented: Salt Lake (part)  Res: (801) 968-8594
Term Expires: 2017
3105 West 5400, South, Suite 6, Taylorsville, UT 84118
E-mail: jdunnigan@le.utah.gov
Committees: Business and Labor; Ethics; Joint Executive
Appropriations; Joint Health Reform Task Force; Joint Legislative
Management; Political Subdivisions

Representative
**Rebecca P. "Becky" Edwards** (R-District 20) . . . . . . . . (801) 554-1968
Counties Represented: Davis (part)
Term Expires: 2017
1121 Eaglewood Loop, North Salt Lake, UT 84054
E-mail: beckyedwards@le.utah.gov
Committees: Economic Development and Workforce Services; Public
Utilities and Technology
Education: BYU BS, MSW, MS

Representative **Steve Eliason** (R-District 45) . . . . . . . . . . . (801) 300-9844
Counties Represented: Salt Lake (part)
Term Expires: 2017
8157 South Grambling Way, Sandy, UT 84094
E-mail: seliason@le.utah.gov
Committees: Education; Law Enforcement and Criminal Justice;
Retirement and Independent Entities

Representative **Justin L. Fawson** (R-District 7) . . . . . . . . . (801) 781-0016
Counties Represented: Weber (part)
Term Expires: 2017
1205 East 2325 North, Ogden, UT 84414
E-mail: justinfawson@le.utah.gov
Committees: Education; Transportation
Education: Westminster (UT) 2004 BA; Capella U 2013 MBA

Representative **Gage Froerer** (R-District 8) . . . . . . . . . . . . (801) 745-0505
Counties Represented: Weber (part)
Term Expires: 2017
P.O. Box 379, Huntsville, UT 84317
E-mail: gfroerer@le.utah.gov
Committees: Business and Labor; Revenue and Taxation; Rules

Representative **Francis D. Gibson** (R-District 65) . . . . . . . . (801) 491-3763
Counties Represented: Utah (part)
Term Expires: 2017
208 South 680 West, Mapleton, UT 84664
E-mail: fgibson@le.utah.gov
Committees: Education; Joint Executive Appropriations; Joint Health
Reform Task Force; Joint Legislative Management

Representative **Brian M. Greene** (R-District 57) . . . . . . . . . (801) 358-1338
Counties Represented: Utah (part)
Term Expires: 2017
1113 East Mahogany Lane, Pleasant Grove, UT 84062
E-mail: bgreene@le.utah.gov
Committees: Judiciary; Revenue and Taxation
Education: BYU BA; J Reuben Clark Law 1995 JD

Representative **Keith Grover** (R-District 61) . . . . . . . . . . . . (801) 319-0170
Counties Represented: Utah (part)
Term Expires: 2017
1374 West 1940 North, Provo, UT 84604
E-mail: keithgrover@le.utah.gov
Committees: Government Operations; Public Utilities and Technology

Representative **Craig Hall** (R-District 33) . . . . . . . . . . . . . . (801) 573-1774
Counties Represented: Salt Lake (part)
Term Expires: 2017
3428 Harrisonwood Drive, West Valley City, UT 84119
E-mail: chall@le.utah.gov
Committees: Health and Human Services; Judiciary
Education: Utah State BA; Baylor JD

Representative
**Stephen G. "Steve" Handy** (R-District 16) . . . . . . . . . . (801) 979-8711
Counties Represented: Davis (part)
Term Expires: 2017
1355 East 625 North, Layton, UT 84040
E-mail: stevehandy@le.utah.gov
Committees: Ethics; Natural Resources, Agriculture and Environment;
Public Utilities and Technology
Education: Utah 1975 BA, 1978 MS

Representative **Timothy D. Hawkes** (R-District 18) . . . . . . (801) 294-4494
Counties Represented: Davis (part)
Term Expires: 2017
443 South 225 East, Centerville, UT 84014
E-mail: thawkes@le.utah.gov
Committees: Economic Development and Workforce Services; Natural
Resources, Agriculture and Environment

Representative **Lynn N. Hemingway** (D-District 40)......(801) 231-2153
Counties Represented: Salt Lake (part)
Term Expires: 2017
1513 Ashford Drive, Millcreek, UT 84124
E-mail: lhemingway@le.utah.gov
Committees: Political Subdivisions; Public Utilities and Technology;
Retirement and Independent Entities

Representative **Sandra Hollins** (D-District 23)...........(801) 363-4257
Counties Represented: Salt Lake (part)
Term Expires: 2017
518 North 800 West, Salt Lake City, UT 84116
E-mail: shollins@le.utah.gov
Committees: Health and Human Services; Law Enforcement and
Criminal Justice

Representative
**Gregory H. "Greg" Hughes** (R-District 51)...........(801) 432-0362
Counties Represented: Salt Lake (part)
Term Expires: 2017
472 Midlake Drive, Draper, UT 84020
E-mail: greghughes@le.utah.gov
Committees: Joint Executive Appropriations; Joint Legislative
Management

Representative **Eric K. Hutchings** (R-District 38).........(801) 963-2639
Counties Represented: Salt Lake (part)
Term Expires: 2017
5438 West Stony Ridge Circle, Kearns, UT 84118
E-mail: ehutchings@le.utah.gov
Committees: Education; Revenue and Taxation
Education: BYU BA

Representative **Don L. Ipson** (R-District 75)............(435) 674-6301
Counties Represented: Washington (part)          Res: (435) 673-8216
Term Expires: 2017
539 Diagonal Street, St. George, UT 84770
E-mail: dipson@le.utah.gov
Committees: Law Enforcement and Criminal Justice; Political
Subdivisions

Representative **Ken Ivory** (R-District 47) ..............(801) 571-5515
Counties Represented: Salt Lake (part)
Term Expires: 2017
8393 South 2010 West, West Jordan, UT 84088
E-mail: kivory@le.utah.gov
Committees: Public Utilities and Technology; Revenue and Taxation
Education: BYU 1989; Cal Western 1994

Representative
**Michael S. "Mike" Kennedy** (R-District 27) .........(801) 763-1376
Counties Represented: Utah (part)
Term Expires: 2017
659 East 200 North, Alpine, UT 84004
E-mail: mikekennedy@le.utah.gov
Committees: Health and Human Services; Joint Health Reform Task
Force; Political Subdivisions
Education: BYU 1994 BS; Michigan State 1998 MD;
J Reuben Clark Law 2007 JD

Representative **Brad King** (D-District 69) ..............(435) 637-7955
Counties Represented: Carbon, Duchesne (part), Emery (part), Grand
(part)
Term Expires: 2017
635 North 500 East, Price, UT 84501
E-mail: bradking@le.utah.gov
Committees: Business and Labor; Rules; Transportation
Education: BYU BS, MS

Representative **Brian S. King** (D-District 28) ...........(801) 532-1739
Counties Represented: Salt Lake (part), Summit          Res: (801) 583-5464
(part)
Term Expires: 2017
1855 Michigan Avenue, Salt Lake City, UT 84108
E-mail: briansking@le.utah.gov
Committees: Joint Executive Appropriations; Joint Legislative
Management; Judiciary; Revenue and Taxation

Representative **John Knotwell** (R-District 52)..........(801) 449-1834
Counties Represented: Salt Lake (part)
Term Expires: 2017
5328 West Shooters Ridge Circle, Herriman, UT 84096
E-mail: jknotwell@le.utah.gov
Committees: Business and Labor; Revenue and Taxation; Rules
Education: Utah Valley U 2000 AS; Utah 2009 BS

Representative **Bradley G. Last** (R-District 71) .........(435) 635-7334
Counties Represented: Iron (part), Washington (part)
Term Expires: 2017
1194 South 180 West, Hurricane, UT 84737
E-mail: blast@le.utah.gov
Committees: Economic Development and Workforce Services;
Education; Retirement and Independent Entities
Education: Utah BS, MBA

Representative **David E. Lifferth** (R-District 2)...........(801) 358-9124
Counties Represented: Utah (part)
Term Expires: 2017
8782 North Pinehurst Drive, Eagle Mountain, UT 84005
E-mail: dlifferth@le.utah.gov
Committees: Education; Transportation
Education: BYU 1991 BS

Representative **Dan McCay** (R-District 41).............(801) 560-0400
Counties Represented: Salt Lake (part)
Term Expires: 2017
3364 Kollman Way, Riverton, UT 84065
E-mail: dmccay@le.utah.gov
Committees: Education; Revenue and Taxation
Education: Utah State BE, MEd; Oregon JD

Representative **Kay L. McIff** (R-District 70) .............(435) 896-4461
Counties Represented: Emery (part), Grand (part), Sanpete (part),
Sevier (part)
Term Expires: 2017
225 North 100 East, Richfield, UT 84701
E-mail: kaymciff@le.utah.gov
Committees: Health and Human Services; Joint Native American
Legislative Liaison; Law Enforcement and Criminal Justice

Representative
**Michael K. "Mike" McKell** (R-District 66)...........(801) 210-1495
Counties Represented: Utah (part)
Term Expires: 2017
582 South 1750 East, Spanish Fork, UT 84660
E-mail: mmckell@le.utah.gov
Committees: Ethics; Natural Resources, Agriculture and Environment;
Revenue and Taxation
Education: Southern Utah BA; Idaho 2005 JD

Representative **Carol Spackman Moss** (D-District 37)....(801) 272-6507
Counties Represented: Salt Lake (part)
Term Expires: 2017
2712 East Kelly Lane, Salt Lake City, UT 84117
E-mail: csmoss@le.utah.gov
Committees: Education; Joint Administrative Rules Review; Rules;
Transportation
Education: Utah BA, MA

Representative **Merrill F. Nelson** (R-District 68) .........(801) 971-2172
Counties Represented: Beaver (part), Juab (part), Millard, Tooele (part),
Utah (part)
Term Expires: 2017
164 South 800 East, Grantsville, UT 84029
E-mail: mnelson@le.utah.gov
Committees: Government Operations; Judiciary
Education: BYU 1979 BS; J Reuben Clark Law 1982 JD

Representative **Michael E. "Mike" Noel** (R-District 73)...(435) 644-3996
Counties Represented: Beaver (part), Garfield, Kane, Piute, San Juan,
Sevier (part), Wayne
Term Expires: 2017
P.O. Box 301, Kanab, UT 84741
E-mail: mikenoel@kanab.net
Committees: Education; Ethics; Joint Native American Legislative
Liaison; Natural Resources, Agriculture and Environment; Rules
Education: Cal State (Fullerton) BA; South Dakota MA

Representative **Curtis "Curt" Oda** (R-District 14)........(801) 773-9796
Counties Represented: Davis (part)
Term Expires: 2017
P.O. Box 824, Clearfield, UT 84089
E-mail: coda@le.utah.gov
Committees: Economic Development and Workforce Services; Joint
Administrative Rules Review; Judiciary

Representative **Derrin Owens** (R-District 58)............(435) 851-1284
Counties Represented: Juab (part), Sanpete (part)
Term Expires: 2017
P.O. Box 127, Fountain Green, UT 84632
E-mail: derrinowens@le.utah.gov
Committees: Business and Labor; Natural Resources, Agriculture and
Environment

*(continued on next page)*

**LEGISLATIVE BRANCH**

LEGISLATIVE BRANCH

**Representatives** *continued*

Representative **Lee B. Perry** (R-District 29) . . . . . . . . . . . . (435) 734-2864
Counties Represented: Box Elder (part), Weber (part)
Term Expires: 2017
977 West 2390 South, Perry, UT 84302-4921
E-mail: leeperry@le.utah.gov
Committees: Government Operations; Natural Resources, Agriculture and Environment

Representative **Jeremy Peterson** (R-District 9) . . . . . . . . . (801) 392-5324
Counties Represented: Weber (part)
Term Expires: 2017
2227 Jefferson Avenue, Ogden, UT 84401
E-mail: jeremyapeterson@le.utah.gov
Committees: Law Enforcement and Criminal Justice; Revenue and Taxation

Representative **Val Peterson** (R-District 59) . . . . . . . . . . . . (801) 224-4473
Counties Represented: Utah (part)
Term Expires: 2017
528 West 1160 North, Orem, UT 84057
E-mail: vpeterson@le.utah.gov
Committees: Business and Labor; Government Operations

Representative **Dixon M. Pitcher** (R-District 10) . . . . . . . . (801) 476-0345
Counties Represented: Weber (part)          Res: (801) 476-8080
Term Expires: 2017
6470 Bybee Drive, Ogden, UT 84403
E-mail: dpitcher@le.utah.gov
Committees: Business and Labor; Political Subdivisions

Representative **Marie H. Poulson** (D-District 46) . . . . . . . . (801) 942-5390
Counties Represented: Salt Lake (part)
Term Expires: 2017
7037 Horizon Circle, Salt Lake City, UT 84121
E-mail: mariepoulson@le.utah.gov
Committees: Education; Ethics; Joint Health Reform Task Force; Joint Native American Legislative Liaison; Political Subdivisions; Retirement and Independent Entities
Education: BYU BA

Representative **Kraig Powell** (R-District 54) . . . . . . . . . . . . (435) 654-0501
Counties Represented: Summit (part), Wasatch
Term Expires: 2017
943 East 530 North, Heber City, UT 84032
E-mail: kraigpowell@le.utah.gov
Committees: Natural Resources, Agriculture and Environment; Political Subdivisions; Retirement and Independent Entities
Education: Willamette BA; Virginia MA, JD

Representative **Paul Ray** (R-District 13) . . . . . . . . . . . . . . . (801) 725-2719
Counties Represented: Davis (part)
Term Expires: 2017
P.O. Box 977, Clearfield, UT 84089
E-mail: pray@le.utah.gov
Committees: Health and Human Services; Law Enforcement and Criminal Justice

Representative **Edward H. Redd** (R-District 4) . . . . . . . . . (435) 752-3364
Counties Represented: Cache (part)
Term Expires: 2017
1675 East 1460 North, Logan, UT 84341
E-mail: eredd@le.utah.gov
Committees: Health and Human Services; Joint Health Reform Task Force; Law Enforcement and Criminal Justice
Education: BYU 1982 BA; Utah 1986 MD

Representative **Marc Roberts** (R-District 67) . . . . . . . . . . . . (801) 210-0155
Counties Represented: Utah (part)
Term Expires: 2017
383 East Salem Park Circle, Salem, UT 94653
E-mail: mroberts@le.utah.gov
Committees: Business and Labor; Law Enforcement and Criminal Justice
Education: BYU 2006 BCE

Representative **Angela Romero** (D-District 26) . . . . . . . . . (801) 722-4972
Counties Represented: Salt Lake (part)
Term Expires: 2017
1098 South Emergy Street, Salt Lake City, UT 84104
E-mail: angelaromero@le.utah.gov
Committees: Economic Development and Workforce Services; Ethics; Joint Native American Legislative Liaison; Law Enforcement and Criminal Justice
Education: Utah 1998 BA, 2010 MPA

Representative **Douglas "Doug" Sagers** (R-District 21) . . (435) 843-3754
Counties Represented: Tooele (part)          Res: (435) 882-0931
Term Expires: 2017
243 Home Town Court, Tooele, UT 84074
E-mail: dougsagers@le.utah.gov
Committees: Joint Native American Legislative Liaison; Natural Resources, Agriculture and Environment; Revenue and Taxation

Representative **Scott Sandall** (R-District 1) . . . . . . . . . . . . (435) 279-7551
Counties Represented: Box Elder (part), Cache (part)
Term Expires: 2017
635 North Hillcrest Circle, Tremonton, UT 84337
E-mail: ssandall@le.utah.gov
Committees: Economic Development and Workforce Services; Natural Resources, Agriculture and Environment

Representative **Dean Sanpei** (R-District 63) . . . . . . . . . . . . (801) 979-5711
Counties Represented: Utah (part)          Res: (801) 374-8995
Term Expires: 2017
2145 North 1450 East, Provo, UT 84604
E-mail: dsanpei@le.utah.gov
Committees: Government Operations; Joint Executive Appropriations; Joint Health Reform Task Force
Education: Hawaii BA; BYU 1998 MPA

Representative **Mike Schultz** (R-District 12) . . . . . . . . . . . . (801) 859-7713
Counties Represented: Davis (part), Weber (part)
Term Expires: 2017
2135 North 4500 West, Hooper, UT 84315
E-mail: mikeschultz@le.utah.gov
Committees: Business and Labor; Natural Resources, Agriculture and Environment; Rules

Representative **V. Lowry Snow** (R-District 74) . . . . . . . . . (435) 628-3688
Counties Represented: Washington (part)
Term Expires: 2017
912 West 1600 South, Suite B-200, St. George, UT 84770
E-mail: vlsnow@le.utah.gov
Committees: Education; Judiciary
Affiliation: Founding Partner, Snow Jensen & Reece, P.C.
912 W 1600, Suite B200, St. George, UT 84770

Representative **Robert M. Spendlove** (R-District 49) . . . . . (801) 560-5394
Counties Represented: Salt Lake (part)
Term Expires: 2017
8491 Treasure Mountain Drive, Sandy, UT 84093
E-mail: rspendlove@le.utah.gov
Committees: Economic Development and Workforce Services; Health and Human Services

Representative **Jon E. Stanard** (R-District 62) . . . . . . . . . . (435) 414-4631
Counties Represented: Washington (part)
Term Expires: 2017
P.O. Box 910772, St. George, UT 84791
E-mail: jstanard@le.utah.gov
Committees: Business and Labor; Revenue and Taxation; Rules
Education: Dixie 2003 BS

Representative **Keven J. Stratton** (R-District 48) . . . . . . . . (801) 225-3570
Counties Represented: Utah (part)
Term Expires: 2017
1313 East 800 North, Orem, UT 84097
E-mail: kstratton@le.utah.gov
Committees: Judiciary; Public Utilities and Technology

Representative **Earl Tanner** (R-District 43) . . . . . . . . . . . . . (801) 871-5388
Counties Represented: Salt Lake (part)
Term Expires: 2017
6672 Nottingham Circle, West Jordan, UT 84084
E-mail: earltanner@le.utah.gov
Committees: Law Enforcement and Criminal Justice; Public Utilities and Technology
Education: Utah BS, 1976 JD

Representative
**Norman K. "Norm" Thurston** (R-District 64) . . . . . . . . . (385) 399-9658
Counties Represented: Utah (part)
Term Expires: 2017
965 East Center Street, Provo, UT 84606
E-mail: normthurston@le.utah.gov
Committees: Health and Human Services; Political Subdivisions
Education: BYU 1991 BA; Princeton 1993 MA, 1995 PhD

Representative **Raymond "Ray" Ward** (R-District 19) . . . . (801) 294-6854
Counties Represented: Davis (part)
Term Expires: 2017
954 East Millbrook Way, Bountiful, UT 84010
E-mail: rayward@le.utah.gov
Committees: Health and Human Services; Political Subdivisions

Representative **R. Curt Webb** (R-District 5) . . . . . . . . . . . . (435) 753-2467
  Counties Represented: Cache (part)    Res: (435) 753-0215
  Term Expires: 2017
  65 West 100 North, Logan, UT 84321
  E-mail: curtwebb@le.utah.gov
  Committees: Business and Labor; Joint Administrative Rules Review;
  Political Subdivisions
  Education: Utah State BS

Representative **John R. Westwood** (R-District 72) . . . . . . (435) 590-1467
  Counties Represented: Iron (part)
  Term Expires: 2017
  751 South 2075 West, Cedar City, UT 84720
  E-mail: jwestwood@le.utah.gov
  Committees: Economic Development and Workforce Services;
  Retirement and Independent Entities; Transportation
  Education: Southern Utah 1977 BS

Representative **Mark A. Wheatley** (D-District 35) . . . . . . . (801) 264-8844
  Counties Represented: Salt Lake (part)
  Term Expires: 2017
  447 East Moss Creek Drive, Murray, UT 84107
  E-mail: markwheatley@le.utah.gov
  Committees: Economic Development and Workforce Services; Ethics;
  Joint Administrative Rules Review; Joint Native American Legislative
  Liaison; Judiciary
  Education: Westminster (UT) BS

Representative **Brad R. Wilson** (R-District 15) . . . . . . . . . . (801) 425-1028
  Counties Represented: Davis (part)
  Term Expires: 2017
  1423 Whispering Meadows Lane, Kaysville, UT 84037
  E-mail: bradwilson@le.utah.gov
  Committees: Business and Labor; Economic Development and
  Workforce Services; Joint Executive Appropriations; Joint Legislative
  Management

## House Standing Committees

### Business and Labor

| Majority Members | Minority Members |
| --- | --- |
| Val Peterson (R-59) *Chair* | Susan "Sue" Duckworth (D-22) |
| John Knotwell (R-52) *Vice Chair* | Brad King (D-69) |
| Jacob L. "Jake" Anderegg (R-6) | |
| James A. "Jim" Dunnigan (R-39) | |
| Gage Froerer (R-8) | |
| Derrin Owens (R-58) | |
| Dixon M. Pitcher (R-10) | |
| Marc Roberts (R-67) | |
| Mike Schultz (R-12) | |
| Jon E. Stanard (R-62) | |
| R. Curt Webb (R-5) | |
| Brad R. Wilson (R-15) | |

### Economic Development and Workforce Services

| Majority Members | Minority Members |
| --- | --- |
| Rebecca P. "Becky" Edwards (R-20) *Chair* | Angela Romero (D-26) |
| John R. Westwood (R-72) *Vice Chair* | Mark A. Wheatley (D-35) |
| Sophia M. DiCaro (R-31) | |
| Timothy D. Hawkes (R-18) | |
| Bradley G. Last (R-71) | |
| Curtis "Curt" Oda (R-14) | |
| Scott Sandall (R-1) | |
| Robert M. Spendlove (R-49) | |
| Brad R. Wilson (R-15) | |

### Education

| Majority Members | Minority Members |
| --- | --- |
| Bradley G. Last (R-71) *Chair* | Carol Spackman Moss (D-37) |
| V. Lowry Snow (R-74) *Vice Chair* | Marie H. Poulson (D-46) |
| LaVar Christensen (R-32) | |
| Kim Coleman (R-42) | |
| Steve Eliason (R-45) | |
| Justin L. Fawson (R-7) | |
| Francis D. Gibson (R-65) | |
| Eric K. Hutchings (R-38) | |
| David E. Lifferth (R-2) | |
| Dan McCay (R-41) | |
| Michael E. "Mike" Noel (R-73) | |

### Ethics

| Majority Members | Minority Members |
| --- | --- |
| Stephen G. "Steve" Handy (R-16) *Chair* | Patrice Arent (D-36) *Co-Chair* |
| James A. "Jim" Dunnigan (R-39) | Marie H. Poulson (D-46) |
| Michael K. "Mike" McKell (R-66) | Angela Romero (D-26) |
| Michael E. "Mike" Noel (R-73) | Mark A. Wheatley (D-35) |

### Government Operations

| Majority Members | Minority Members |
| --- | --- |
| Jack R. Draxler (R-3) *Chair* | Patrice Arent (D-36) |
| Bradley M. Daw (R-60) *Vice Chair* | Rebecca Chavez-Houck (D-24) |
| Fred C. Cox (R-30) | |
| Keith Grover (R-61) | |
| Merrill F. Nelson (R-68) | |
| Lee B. Perry (R-29) | |
| Val Peterson (R-59) | |
| Dean Sanpei (R-63) | |

### Health and Human Services

| Majority Members | Minority Members |
| --- | --- |
| Kay L. McIff (R-70) *Chair* | Rebecca Chavez-Houck (D-24) |
| Robert M. Spendlove (R-49) *Vice Chair* | Sandra Hollins (D-23) |
| Stewart Barlow (R-17) | |
| Melvin R. "Mel" Brown (R-53) | |
| Craig Hall (R-33) | |
| Michael S. "Mike" Kennedy (R-27) | |
| Paul Ray (R-13) | |
| Edward H. Redd (R-4) | |
| Norman K. "Norm" Thurston (R-64) | |
| Raymond "Ray" Ward (R-19) | |

### Judiciary

| Majority Members | Minority Members |
| --- | --- |
| LaVar Christensen (R-32) *Chair* | Brian S. King (D-28) |
| Merrill F. Nelson (R-68) *Vice Chair* | Mark A. Wheatley (D-35) |
| Fred C. Cox (R-30) | |
| Bruce Cutler (R-44) | |
| Brian M. Greene (R-57) | |
| Craig Hall (R-33) | |
| Curtis "Curt" Oda (R-14) | |
| V. Lowry Snow (R-74) | |
| Keven J. Stratton (R-48) | |

### Law Enforcement and Criminal Justice

| Majority Members | Minority Members |
| --- | --- |
| Don L. Ipson (R-75) *Chair* | Sandra Hollins (D-23) |
| Marc Roberts (R-67) *Vice Chair* | Angela Romero (D-26) |
| Bradley M. Daw (R-60) | |
| Steve Eliason (R-45) | |
| Kay L. McIff (R-70) | |
| Jeremy Peterson (R-9) | |
| Paul Ray (R-13) | |
| Edward H. Redd (R-4) | |
| Earl Tanner (R-43) | |

### Natural Resources, Agriculture and Environment

| Majority Members | Minority Members |
| --- | --- |
| Lee B. Perry (R-29) *Chair* | Joel K. Briscoe (D-25) |
| Douglas "Doug" Sagers (R-21) *Vice Chair* | Susan "Sue" Duckworth (D-22) |
| Melvin R. "Mel" Brown (R-53) | |
| Scott H. Chew (R-55) | |
| Stephen G. "Steve" Handy (R-16) | |
| Timothy D. Hawkes (R-18) | |
| Michael K. "Mike" McKell (R-66) | |
| Michael E. "Mike" Noel (R-73) | |
| Derrin Owens (R-58) | |
| Kraig Powell (R-54) | |
| Scott Sandall (R-1) | |
| Mike Schultz (R-12) | |

**LEGISLATIVE BRANCH**

## Political Subdivisions

**Majority Members**
R. Curt Webb (R-5) *Chair*
Kraig Powell (R-54) *Vice Chair*
Johnny Anderson (R-34)
Kim Coleman (R-42)
James A. "Jim" Dunnigan (R-39)
Don L. Ipson (R-75)
Michael S. "Mike" Kennedy (R-27)
Dixon M. Pitcher (R-10)
Norman K. "Norm" Thurston
  (R-64)
Raymond "Ray" Ward (R-19)

**Minority Members**
Lynn N. Hemingway (D-40)
Marie H. Poulson (D-46)

## Public Utilities and Technology

**Majority Members**
Ken Ivory (R-47) *Chair*
Stephen G. "Steve" Handy (R-16)
  *Vice Chair*
Scott H. Chew (R-55)
Kay J. Christofferson (R-56)
Brad L. Dee (R-11)
Rebecca P. "Becky" Edwards (R-20)
Keith Grover (R-61)
Keven J. Stratton (R-48)
Earl Tanner (R-43)

**Minority Members**
Patrice Arent (D-36)
Lynn N. Hemingway (D-40)

## Retirement and Independent Entities

**Majority Members**
Kraig Powell (R-54) *Chair*
Rich Cunningham (R-50)
  *Vice Chair*
Sophia M. DiCaro (R-31)
Steve Eliason (R-45)
Bradley G. Last (R-71)
John R. Westwood (R-72)

**Minority Members**
Susan "Sue" Duckworth (D-22)
Lynn N. Hemingway (D-40)
Marie H. Poulson (D-46)

## Revenue and Taxation

**Majority Members**
Dan McCay (R-41) *Chair*
Jeremy Peterson (R-9) *Vice Chair*
Rich Cunningham (R-50)
Gage Froerer (R-8)
Brian M. Greene (R-57)
Eric K. Hutchings (R-38)
Ken Ivory (R-47)
John Knotwell (R-52)
Michael K. "Mike" McKell (R-66)
Douglas "Doug" Sagers (R-21)
Jon E. Stanard (R-62)

**Minority Members**
Joel K. Briscoe (D-25)
Brian S. King (D-28)

## Rules

**Majority Members**
Michael E. "Mike" Noel (R-73)
  *Chair*
John Knotwell (R-52) *Vice Chair*
Jacob L. "Jake" Anderegg (R-6)
Gage Froerer (R-8)
Mike Schultz (R-12)
Jon E. Stanard (R-62)

**Minority Members**
Brad King (D-69)
Carol Spackman Moss (D-37)

## Transportation

**Majority Members**
Johnny Anderson (R-34) *Chair*
Jacob L. "Jake" Anderegg (R-6)
  *Vice Chair*
Stewart Barlow (R-17)
Kay J. Christofferson (R-56)
Rich Cunningham (R-50)
Brad L. Dee (R-11)
Sophia M. DiCaro (R-31)
Jack R. Draxler (R-3)
Justin L. Fawson (R-7)
David E. Lifferth (R-2)
John R. Westwood (R-72)

**Minority Members**
Brad King (D-69)
Carol Spackman Moss (D-37)

# Vermont General Assembly

State House, Montpelier, VT 05633
Tel: (802) 828-2228  Fax: (802) 828-2424  Internet: www.leg.state.vt.us

## Vermont Senate

Tel: (802) 828-2241

President of the Senate **Philip B. "Phil" Scott** (R) . . . . . . . (802) 828-2226
  Education: Vermont 1980 BS
President Pro Tem **John F. Campbell** (D) . . . . . . . . . . . . . (802) 295-6238
  Education: Florida 1976 BS; Southeastern U 1983 JD
Majority Leader **Philip Baruth** (D) . . . . . . . . . . . . . . . . . . . (802) 503-5266
  Education: Brown U 1984 BA
Assistant Majority Leader **Claire D. Ayer** (D). . . . . . . . . . . (802) 759-2748
  Education: Middlebury 1992 BA
Minority Leader **Joseph "Joe" Benning** (R) . . . . . . . . . . (802) 626-3600
  Education: Lyndon State 1979 BA
Assistant Minority Leader **William T. "Bill" Doyle** (R) . . . . (802) 223-2851
  Education: Princeton 1949 BS; Columbia 1955 MS, 1960 PhD
Secretary of the Senate **John H. Bloomer, Jr.** (R). . . . . . . . (802) 828-2241
  Education: Williams 1982 BA; Pennsylvania 1985 MA;
  Rutgers 1987 JD
Assistant Secretary of the Senate **Steven D. Marshall** . . . . (802) 828-2241
  E-mail: smarshall@leg.state.vt.us
  Education: Vermont 1974 BS; St Mary's U (TX) 1977 JD

## Senators

**Party Affiliation Statistics:** Republicans: 9, Democrats: 20,
Independents: 1

Senator **Timothy "Tim" Ashe** (D-Chittenden) . . . . . . . . . . (802) 318-0903
  Counties Represented: Chittenden (part)
  Term Expires: 2019
  45 Lakeview Terrace, Burlington, VT 05401
  E-mail: tashe@leg.state.vt.us
  E-mail: timashe@burlingtontelecom.net
  Committees: Finance; Joint Fiscal; Joint Legislative Justice Oversight;
  Judiciary
  Education: Vermont 1999; JFK School Govt 2004 MPP
Senator **Claire D. Ayer** (D-Addison) . . . . . . . . . . . . . . . . . (802) 759-2748
  Counties Represented: Addison
  Term Expires: 2019
  504 Thompson Hill Road, Weybridge, VT 05753
  E-mail: cayer@leg.state.vt.us
  Committees: Finance; Health and Welfare; Joint Fiscal; Joint Health
  Care Oversight; Joint Mental Health Oversight
Senator **Becca Balint** (D-Windham) . . . . . . . . . . . . . . . . . (802) 828-2241
  Counties Represented: Windham
  Term Expires: 2019
  271 South Main Street, Brandon, VT 05301
  E-mail: bbalint@leg.state.vt.us
  Committees: Economic Development, Housing and General Affairs;
  Institutions
Senator **Philip Baruth** (D-Chittenden) . . . . . . . . . . . . . . . . (802) 503-5266
  Counties Represented: Chittenden (part)
  Term Expires: 2019
  87 Curtis Avenue, Burlington, VT 05408
  E-mail: pbaruth@leg.state.vt.us
  Committees: Economic Development, Housing and General Affairs;
  Education; Joint Government Accountability; Rules
Senator **Joseph "Joe" Benning** (R-Caledonia) . . . . . . . . . (802) 626-3600
  Counties Represented: Caledonia
  Term Expires: 2019
  291 Happy Hill Road, Lyndonville, VT 05851
  E-mail: jbenning@leg.state.vt.us
  Committees: Government Operations; Joint Judicial Retention; Joint
  Judicial Rules; Judiciary; Rules
Senator **Christopher A. Bray** (D-Addison) . . . . . . . . . . . . (802) 453-4424
  Counties Represented: Addison          Fax: (802) 329-2256
  Term Expires: 2019
  829 South Street, New Haven, VT 05472
  E-mail: cbray@leg.state.vt.us
  Committees: Government Operations; Joint Energy; Joint Judicial
  Rules; Natural Resources and Energy
  Education: Vermont 1977 BA, 1991 MA

Senator **John F. Campbell** (D-Windsor) . . . . . . . . . . . . . . . (802) 295-6238
  Counties Represented: Windsor    Tel: (802) 295-1111
  Term Expires: 2019    Fax: (802) 295-6344
  P.O. Box 1306, Quechee, VT 05059
  E-mail: jcampbell@leg.state.vt.us
  E-mail: vt13@aol.com
  Committees: Agriculture; Appropriations; Institutions; Joint Judicial
  Rules; Joint Rules; Rules

Senator **Brian Campion** (D-Bennington) . . . . . . . . . . . . . . (802) 753-7705
  Counties Represented: Bennington
  Term Expires: 2019
  1292 West Road, Bennington, VT 05201
  E-mail: bcampion@leg.state.vt.us
  Committees: Education; Natural Resources and Energy

Senator **Brian Collamore** (R-Rutland) . . . . . . . . . . . . . . . . (802) 828-2241
  Counties Represented: Rutland
  Term Expires: 2019
  124 Patricia Lane, Rutland, VT 05701
  E-mail: bcollamore@leg.state.vt.us
  Committees: Government Operations; Health and Welfare

Senator **Ann E. Cummings** (D-Washington) . . . . . . . . . . . (802) 223-6043
  Counties Represented: Washington
  Term Expires: 2019
  24 Colonial Drive, Montpelier, VT 05602
  E-mail: acummings@leg.state.vt.us
  Committees: Economic Development, Housing and General Affairs;
  Education; Joint Government Accountability; Joint Transportation
  Oversight
  Education: St Michael's 1989 MSA

Senator **Dustin Allard Degree** (R-Franklin) . . . . . . . . . . . (802) 828-2241
  Counties Represented: Franklin
  Term Expires: 2019
  31 Bank Street, St. Albans, VT 05478
  E-mail: ddegree@leg.state.vt.us
  Committees: Education; Finance; Transportation

Senator **William T. "Bill" Doyle** (R-Washington) . . . . . . . . (802) 223-2851
  Counties Represented: Washington    Tel: (802) 635-2356
  Term Expires: 2019
  186 Murray Road, Montpelier, VT 05602
  E-mail: wdoyle@leg.state.vt.us
  Committees: Economic Development, Housing and General Affairs;
  Education
  Affiliation: Professor of Government, Johnson State College

Senator **Margaret K. "Peg" Flory** (R-Rutland) . . . . . . . . . (802) 483-6854
  Counties Represented: Rutland    Tel: (802) 775-3229
  Term Expires: 2019
  3011 U.S Route 7, Pittsford, VT 05763
  E-mail: pflory@leg.state.vt.us
  E-mail: mkf3229@yahoo.com
  Committees: Institutions; Joint Administrative Rules; Joint Judicial
  Retention; Joint Legislative Justice Oversight; Rules; Transportation
  Education: Southern Vermont 1968 AS; Champlain 1988 AS

Senator **M. Jane Kitchel** (D-Caledonia) . . . . . . . . . . . . . . (802) 684-3482
  Counties Represented: Caledonia
  Term Expires: 2019
  P.O. Box 82, Danville, VT 05828
  E-mail: janek45@hotmail.com
  E-mail: jkitchel@leg.state.vt.us
  Committees: Appropriations; Joint Fiscal; Joint Health Care Oversight;
  Joint Transportation Oversight; Transportation
  Education: Wilson Col 1976 AB

Senator **Virginia "Ginny" Lyons** (D-Chittenden) . . . . . . . . (802) 863-6129
  Counties Represented: Chittenden (part)
  Term Expires: 2019
  241 White Birch Lane, Williston, VT 05495
  E-mail: vlyons@leg.state.vt.us
  Committees: Finance; Health and Welfare; Joint Administrative Rules;
  Joint Energy; Joint Legislative Justice Oversight
  Education: Drew 1966 AB; Rutgers 1968 MS; Vermont 1988 PhD

Senator **Mark A. MacDonald** (D-Orange) . . . . . . . . . . . . . (802) 433-5867
  Counties Represented: Orange    Fax: (802) 433-1035
  Term Expires: 2019
  404 MacDonald Road, Williamstown, VT 05679
  E-mail: mmacdonald@leg.state.vt.us
  E-mail: senatormark@aol.com
  Committees: Finance; Joint Administrative Rules; Joint Energy; Natural
  Resources and Energy
  Education: UMass (Boston) 1972 BA

Senator
  **Richard T. "Dick" Mazza** (D-Grand Isle-Chittenden) . . . . (802) 863-1067
  Counties Represented: Chittenden (part), Grand Isle    Tel: (802) 862-4065
  Term Expires: 2019    Fax: (802) 859-9215
  777 West Lakeshore Drive, Colchester, VT 05446
  E-mail: rmazza@leg.state.vt.us
  Committees: Agriculture; Institutions; Joint Rules; Joint Transportation
  Oversight; Rules; Transportation

Senator **Norman H. McAllister** (R-Franklin) . . . . . . . . . . . (802) 285-6363
  Counties Represented: Franklin
  Note: On January 6, 2016, the Vermont Senate voted to suspend
  Senator Norman McAllister.
  Term Expires: 2019
  712 Hanna Road, Franklin, VT 05457
  E-mail: nmcallister@leg.state.vt.us
  Education: Vermont Tech 1971 AS

Senator **Richard J. "Dick" McCormack** (D-Windsor) . . . . . (802) 253-5497
  Counties Represented: Windsor
  Term Expires: 2019
  127 Cleveland Brook Road, Bethel, VT 05032
  E-mail: rmccormack@leg.state.vt.us
  E-mail: metcalf@sover.net
  Committees: Appropriations; Health and Welfare
  Education: Hofstra 1970 BA; Vermont Law MSEL

Senator **Kevin J. Mullin** (R-Rutland) . . . . . . . . . . . . . . . . . (802) 353-6770
  Counties Represented: Rutland
  Term Expires: 2019
  118 Oxyoke Drive, Rutland, VT 05701
  E-mail: kjmbjm@aol.com
  Committees: Economic Development, Housing and General Affairs;
  Finance; Joint Health Care Oversight
  Education: Castleton State BS

Senator **Alice W. Nitka** (D-Windsor) . . . . . . . . . . . . . . . . . (802) 228-8432
  Counties Represented: Windsor
  Term Expires: 2019
  P.O. Box 136, Ludlow, VT 05149-0136
  E-mail: anitka@leg.state.vt.us
  Committees: Appropriations; Joint Judicial Retention; Judiciary
  Education: Russell Sage 1967 BA

Senator **Anthony Pollina** (D-Washington) . . . . . . . . . . . . . (802) 229-5809
  Counties Represented: Washington
  Term Expires: 2019
  93 Story Road, North Middlesex, VT 05682
  E-mail: apollina@leg.state.vt.us
  Committees: Government Operations; Health and Welfare
  Education: Johnson State 1977 BA

Senator **Helen Riehle** (R-Chittenden) . . . . . . . . . . . . . . . . (802) 482-4382
  Counties Represented: Chittenden (part)    Dist: (802) 864-5460
  Term Expires: 2019
  E-mail: hriehle@leg.state.vt.us
  Committees: Education; Natural Resources and Energy
  Education: Vermont 1972 BS

Senator **John S. Rodgers** (D-Essex-Orleans) . . . . . . . . . . . (802) 525-4182
  Counties Represented: Essex, Orleans
  Term Expires: 2019
  624 Daniels Pond Road, Glover, VT 05839
  E-mail: jrodgers@leg.state.vt.us
  Committees: Institutions; Joint Mental Health Oversight; Natural
  Resources and Energy
  Education: New Hampshire Tech 1985 AS

Senator **Richard W. "Dick" Sears, Jr.** (D-Bennington) . . . . (802) 442-9139
  Counties Represented: Bennington
  Term Expires: 2019
  343 Matteson Road, North Bennington, VT 05257
  E-mail: rsears@leg.state.vt.us
  Committees: Appropriations; Joint Fiscal; Joint Judicial Rules; Joint
  Legislative Justice Oversight; Joint Rules; Judiciary
  Education: Vermont 1969 BA

Senator **Michael Sirotkin** (D-Chittenden) . . . . . . . . . . . . . (802) 999-4360
  Counties Represented: Chittenden (part)
  Term Expires: 2019
  80 Bartlett Bay Road, South Burlington, VT 05403
  E-mail: msirotkin@leg.state.vt.us
  Committees: Agriculture; Finance; Joint Judicial Retention
  Education: Wharton BS; Denver JD

Senator **Robert A. Starr, Jr.** (D-Essex-Orleans) . . . . . . . . . (802) 988-2877
  Counties Represented: Essex, Orleans
  Term Expires: 2019
  958 Route 105 West, North Troy, VT 05859
  E-mail: rstarr@leg.state.vt.us
  Committees: Agriculture; Appropriations
  Education: Vermont Tech 1963 AS

*(continued on next page)*

LEGISLATIVE BRANCH

**Senators** *continued*

Senator **Richard A. Westman** (R-Lamoille) . . . . . . . . . . . . (802) 644-2297
　Counties Represented: Lamoille
　Term Expires: 2019
　2439 Iron Gate Road, Cambridge, VT 05444
　E-mail: rawestman@gmail.com
　Committees: Finance; Joint Information Technology; Transportation
　Education: Johnson State 1982 BA

Senator **Jeanette K. White** (D-Windham) . . . . . . . . . . . . . . (802) 387-4379
　Counties Represented: Windham
　Term Expires: 2019
　35A Old Depot Road, Putney, VT 05346
　E-mail: jwhite@leg.state.vt.us
　Committees: Government Operations; Joint Government Accountability;
　Judiciary
　Education: Iowa 1965 BS

Senator **David Zuckerman** (P-Chittenden) . . . . . . . . . . . . . (802) 482-2199
　Counties Represented: Chittenden (part)
　Term Expires: 2019
　2093 Gilman Road, Hinesburg, VT 05461
　E-mail: dzuckerman@leg.state.vt.us
　Committees: Agriculture; Education
　Education: Vermont 1995 BA

## Senate Standing Committees

### Agriculture

**Majority Members** | **Members**
Robert A. Starr, Jr. (D) *Chair* | David Zuckerman (P) *Vice Chair*
John F. Campbell (D)
Richard T. "Dick" Mazza (D)
Michael Sirotkin (D)

### Appropriations

**Majority Members**
M. Jane Kitchel (D) *Chair*
Alice W. Nitka (D) *Vice Chair*
John F. Campbell (D)
Richard J. "Dick" McCormack (D)
Richard W. "Dick" Sears, Jr. (D)
Robert A. Starr, Jr. (D)

### Economic Development, Housing and General Affairs

**Majority Members** | **Minority Members**
Philip Baruth (D) *Vice Chair* | Kevin J. Mullin (R) *Chair*
Becca Balint (D) | William T. "Bill" Doyle (R)
Ann E. Cummings (D)

### Education

**Majority Members** | **Minority Members**
Ann E. Cummings (D) *Chair* | William T. "Bill" Doyle (R)
Philip Baruth (D) | 　*Vice Chair*
Brian Campion (D) | Dustin Allard Degree (R) *Clerk*
　| Helen Riehle (R)

**Members**
David Zuckerman (P)

### Finance

**Majority Members** | **Minority Members**
Timothy "Tim" Ashe (D) *Chair* | Dustin Allard Degree (R)
Mark A. MacDonald (D) | Kevin J. Mullin (R)
　*Vice Chair* | Richard A. Westman (R)
Claire D. Ayer (D)
Virginia "Ginny" Lyons (D)
Michael Sirotkin (D)

### Government Operations

**Majority Members** | **Minority Members**
Jeanette K. White (D) *Chair* | Joseph "Joe" Benning (R)
Anthony Pollina (D) *Vice Chair* | Brian Collamore (R)
Christopher A. Bray (D)

### Health and Welfare

**Majority Members** | **Minority Members**
Claire D. Ayer (D) *Chair* | Brian Collamore (R) *Clerk*
Virginia "Ginny" Lyons (D)
　*Vice Chair*
Anthony Pollina (D)
Richard J. "Dick" McCormack (D)

### Institutions

**Majority Members** | **Minority Members**
John S. Rodgers (D) *Vice Chair* | Margaret K. "Peg" Flory (R) *Chair*
Becca Balint (D)
John F. Campbell (D)
Richard T. "Dick" Mazza (D)

### Judiciary

**Majority Members** | **Minority Members**
Richard W. "Dick" Sears, Jr. (D) | Joseph "Joe" Benning (R)
　*Chair* | 　*Vice Chair*
Timothy "Tim" Ashe (D)
Alice W. Nitka (D)
Jeanette K. White (D)

### Natural Resources and Energy

**Majority Members** | **Minority Members**
Christopher A. Bray (D) *Chair* | Helen Riehle (R)
Brian Campion (D) *Clerk*
Mark A. MacDonald (D)
John S. Rodgers (D)

### Rules

**Majority Members** | **Minority Members**
John F. Campbell (D) *Chair* | Joseph "Joe" Benning (R)
Philip Baruth (D) *Vice Chair* | Margaret K. "Peg" Flory (R)
Richard T. "Dick" Mazza (D)

### Transportation

**Majority Members** | **Minority Members**
Richard T. "Dick" Mazza (D) *Chair* | Richard A. Westman (R) *Vice Chair*
M. Jane Kitchel (D) | Dustin Allard Degree (R)
　| Margaret K. "Peg" Flory (R)

## Vermont House of Representatives
Tel: (802) 828-2228

Speaker of the House **Shapleigh "Shap" Smith** (D) . . . . . (802) 828-2245
　E-mail: speaker@leg.state.vt.us
Majority Leader **William W. "Willem" Jewett** (D) . . . . . . (802) 388-0320
Assistant Majority Leader **Kathryn L. "Kate" Webb** (D) . . (802) 985-2789
　Education: Vermont 1975 BA, 1980 MS
Minority Leader **Donald H. Turner** (R) . . . . . . . . . . . . . . . (802) 893-1419
Assistant Minority Leader **Brian K. Savage** (R) . . . . . . . . . (802) 868-3566
Progressive Leader **Christopher Pearson** (P) . . . . . . . . . . (802) 860-3933
Assistant Progressive Leader **Susan Hatch Davis** (P) . . . . . (802) 439-5103
Clerk of the House **Donald G. Milne** . . . . . . . . . . . . . . . . . (802) 828-2247
　E-mail: don@leg.state.vt.us
　Education: New York Law 1959 LLB
Sergeant-at-Arms **Francis K. Brooks** (D) . . . . . . . . . . . . . . (802) 828-2228
　E-mail: fbrooks@leg.state.vt.us
　Education: Norwich 1967 BS; Clarkson Col 1974 MS

## Representatives

**Party Affiliation Statistics:** Republicans: 53, Democrats: 85,
Independents: 12, Vacancies: 1

Representative **Janet Ancel** (D-Washington-6) . . . . . . . . . . (802) 223-5350
　Counties Represented: Washington (part)
　Term Expires: 2017
　P.O. Box 123, Calais, VT 05648
　E-mail: janetancel@earthlink.net
　Committees: Joint Fiscal; Joint Transportation Oversight; Ways and
　Means

Representative **Robert L. Bancroft** (R-Chittenden-8-3) . . . . (802) 879-7386
　Counties Represented: Chittenden (part)
　Term Expires: 2017
　405 Brookside Road, Westford, VT 05494
　E-mail: bancroft.vt@gmail.com
　Committees: Health Care

Representative **John L. Bartholomew** (D-Windsor-1) . . . . .(802) 436-2151
 Counties Represented: Windsor (part)
 Term Expires: 2017
 23 Linden Road, Hartland, VT 05048
 E-mail: jbartholomew@leg.state.vt.us
 Committees: Agriculture and Forest Products

Representative **Fred K. Baser** (R-Addison-4) . . . . . . . . . . (802) 453-4391
 Counties Represented: Addison (part)
 Term Expires: 2017
 35 Mountain Street, Bristol, VT 05443
 E-mail: fbaser@leg.state.vt.us
 Committees: Commerce and Economic Development

Representative **Lynn Batchelor** (R-Orleans-1) . . . . . . . . . . (802) 873-3006
 Counties Represented: Orleans (part)
 Term Expires: 2017
 165 Beach Street, Derby Line, VT 05830
 E-mail: lbatchelor@leg.state.vt.us
 Committees: Corrections and Institutions

Representative **Scott Beck** (R-Caledonia-3) . . . . . . . . . . . . (802) 827-4436
 Counties Represented: Caledonia (part)
 Term Expires: 2017
 93 Overlook Drive, St. Johnsbury, VT 05819
 E-mail: sbeck@leg.state.vt.us
 Committees: Education

Representative **Steven Berry** (D-Bennington-4) . . . . . . . . . (802) 827-4436
 Counties Represented: Bennington (part)      Dist: (802) 362-5738
 Term Expires: 2017
 P.O. Box 858, Manchester, VT 05254
 E-mail: sberry@leg.state.vt.us
 Committees: Human Services

Representative
 **Stephen C. "Steve" Beyor** (R-Franklin-5) . . . . . . . . . . . (802) 868-3456
 Counties Represented: Franklin (part)
 Term Expires: 2017
 PO Box 287, Highgate Springs, VT 05460
 E-mail: sbeyor@leg.state.vt.us
 Committees: Fish, Wildlife and Water Resources

Representative
 **Clement J. "Clem" Bissonnette** (D-Chittenden-6-7) . . . (802) 655-9527
 Counties Represented: Chittenden (part)
 Term Expires: 2017
 11 Dufresne Drive, Winooski, VT 05404
 E-mail: cbissonnette@leg.state.vt.us
 Committees: Transportation

Representative **Bill Botzow** (D-Bennington-1) . . . . . . . . . . (802) 447-7717
 Counties Represented: Bennington (part)
 Term Expires: 2017
 1225 South Stream Road, Bennington, VT 05201
 E-mail: bbotzow@leg.state.vt.us
 E-mail: botzow@sover.net
 Committees: Commerce and Economic Development
 Education: Princeton 1968 BA

Representative
 **Carolyn Whitney Branagan** (R-Franklin-1) . . . . . . . . . . (802) 527-7694
 Counties Represented: Franklin (part)      Fax: (802) 524-9533
 Term Expires: 2017
 1295 Ballard Road, Georgia, VT 05478
 E-mail: cbranagan@leg.state.vt.us
 E-mail: cbranagan@comcast.net
 Committees: Joint Fiscal; Ways and Means

Representative **Patrick M. Brennan** (R-Chittenden-9-2) . . . (802) 863-3773
 Counties Represented: Chittenden (part)
 Term Expires: 2017
 P.O. Box 796, Colchester, VT 05446
 E-mail: pbrennan@leg.state.vt.us
 Committees: Joint Transportation Oversight; Transportation

Representative
 **Timothy "Tim" Briglin** (D-Windsor-Orange-2) . . . . . . . (802) 785-2414
 Counties Represented: Orange (part), Windsor (part)
 Term Expires: 2017
 459 Tucker Hill Road, Thetford Center, VT 05075
 E-mail: tbriglin@leg.state.vt.us
 Committees: Health Care

Representative **Cynthia M. Browning** (D-Bennington-4) . . (802) 375-9019
 Counties Represented: Bennington (part)
 Term Expires: 2017
 P.O. Box 389, Arlington, VT 05250
 E-mail: cbrowning@leg.state.vt.us
 Committees: Corrections and Institutions

Representative **Tom Burditt** (R-Rutland-2) . . . . . . . . . . . . . (802) 438-0031
 Counties Represented: Rutland (part)
 Term Expires: 2017
 1118 Clarendon Avenue, West Rutland, VT 05777
 E-mail: tburditt@leg.state.vt.us
 Committees: Judiciary

Representative **Mollie S. Burke** (P-Windham-2-2) . . . . . . . . (802) 257-4844
 Counties Represented: Windham (part)
 Term Expires: 2017
 62 West Street, Brattleboro, VT 05301
 E-mail: mburke@leg.state.vt.us
 Committees: Transportation

Representative **Sarah E. Buxton** (D-Windsor-Orange-1) . . . (802) 233-0274
 Counties Represented: Orange (part), Windsor (part)
 Term Expires: 2017
 318 Vermont Route 110, Suite 3, Tunbridge, VT 05077
 E-mail: sbuxton@leg.state.vt.us
 E-mail: sbuxton@gmail.com
 Committees: Education; Joint Administrative Rules

Representative **William "Bill" Canfield** (R-Rutland-3) . . . . (802) 265-4428
 Counties Represented: Rutland (part)
 Term Expires: 2017
 12 Pine Street, Fair Haven, VT 05743
 E-mail: wcanfield@leg.state.vt.us
 Committees: Ways and Means

Representative **Stephen A. Carr** (D-Rutland-6) . . . . . . . . . . (802) 247-3921
 Counties Represented: Rutland (part)
 Term Expires: 2017
 27 East Prospect Street, Brandon, VT 05733
 E-mail: scarr@leg.state.vt.us
 Committees: Commerce and Economic Development
 Education: Castleton State 1972 BA

Representative
 **Robin Chesnut-Tangerman** (P-Rutland-Bennington) . . . . (802) 235-2050
 Counties Represented: Bennington (part), Rutland (part)
 Term Expires: 2017
 72 Sundog Lane, Rutland, VT 05757
 E-mail: rchesnut-tangerman@leg.state.vt.us
 Committees: Joint Energy; Natural Resources and Energy

Representative **Kevin "Coach" Christie** (D-Windsor-4-2) . . (802) 295-1066
 Counties Represented: Windsor (part)
 Term Expires: 2017
 682 Christian Street, White River Junction, VT 05001
 E-mail: kchristie@leg.state.vt.us
 Committees: Education

Representative **Alison H. Clarkson** (D-Windsor-5) . . . . . . . (802) 457-4627
 Counties Represented: Windsor (part)
 Term Expires: 2017
 18 Golf Avenue, Woodstock, VT 05091
 E-mail: aclarkson@leg.state.vt.us
 Committees: Ways and Means

Representative **Joanna E. Cole** (D-Chittenden-6-1) . . . . . . . (802) 600-7175
 Counties Represented: Chittenden (part)
 Term Expires: 2017
 108 Rivers Edge Drive, Burlington, VT 08408
 E-mail: jcole@leg.state.vt.us
 Committees: Government Operations
 Education: Gaston 1983 AAS; North Carolina Charlotte 1986 BS,
 1988 MS; Drew 2001 MT

Representative **Jim Condon** (D-Chittenden-9-1) . . . . . . . . . (802) 655-5764
 Counties Represented: Chittenden (part)
 Term Expires: 2017
 500A Dalton Drive, Colchester, VT 05446
 E-mail: jcondon@leg.state.vt.us
 Committees: Ways and Means

Representative **Daniel F. Connor** (D-Franklin-6) . . . . . . . . . (802) 827-4436
 Counties Represented: Franklin (part)
 Term Expires: 2017
 4367 Route 36, Fairfield, VT 05455
 E-mail: dconnor@leg.state.vt.us
 Committees: Agriculture and Forest Products

Representative **Chip Conquest** (D-Orange-Caledonia) . . . . .(802) 757-3803
 Counties Represented: Caledonia (part), Orange (part)
 Term Expires: 2017
 409 Bible Hill Road, Wells River, VT 05081
 E-mail: cconquest@leg.state.vt.us
 E-mail: conquest@sover.net
 Committees: Joint Judicial Retention; Judiciary

*(continued on next page)*

**Representatives** *continued*

Representative **Sarah Copeland-Hanzas** (D-Orange-2) .... (802) 222-3536
Counties Represented: Orange (part)
Term Expires: 2017
P.O. Box 43, Bradford, VT 05033
E-mail: scopelandhanzas@leg.state.vt.us
Committees: Government Operations; Rules

Representative
**Timothy R. Corcoran II** (D-Bennington-2-1) .......... (802) 447-0929
Counties Represented: Bennington (part)
Term Expires: 2017
8 Corey Lane, Bennington, VT 05201
E-mail: tcorcoran@leg.state.vt.us
Committees: Transportation

Representative
**Lawrence P. "Larry" Cupoli** (R-Rutland-5-2) ......... (800) 322-5616
Counties Represented: Rutland (part)
Term Expires: 2017
57 Piedmont Pond Road, Rutland, VT 05701
E-mail: lcupoli@leg.state.vt.us
Committees: Education

Representative **Leigh J. Dakin** (D-Windsor-3-1) ......... (802) 828-2247
Counties Represented: Windsor (part)       Res: (802) 875-3456
Term Expires: 2017
P.O. Box 467, Chester, VT 05143
E-mail: ldakin@leg.state.vt.us
Committees: Health Care

Representative **Maureen P. Dakin** (D-Chittenden-9-2) ..... (802) 828-2247
Counties Represented: Chittenden (part)
Term Expires: 2017
E-mail: mdakin@leg.state.vt.us
Committees: Commerce and Economic Development
Education: Vermont 1972 BA; Trinity Col (VT) 1989 BA

Representative **Paul Dame** (R-Chittenden-8-2) .......... (802) 828-2228
Counties Represented: Chittenden (part)
Term Expires: 2017
P.O. Box 8852, Essex Junction, VT 05453
E-mail: pdame@leg.state.vt.us
Committees: Human Services

Representative **Susan Hatch Davis** (P-Orange-1) ....... (802) 439-5103
Counties Represented: Orange (part)       Tel: (802) 828-0911
Term Expires: 2017
75 Notchend Road, West Topsham, VT 05086
E-mail: sdavis@leg.state.vt.us
Committees: Corrections and Institutions; Joint Information Technology

Representative **David L. Deen** (D-Windham-4) .......... (802) 869-3116
Counties Represented: Windham (part)       Fax: (802) 869-1103
Term Expires: 2017
5607 Westminster West Road, Putney, VT 05346
E-mail: ddeen@leg.state.vt.us
Committees: Fish, Wildlife and Water Resources; Rules

Representative
**Dennis J. Devereux** (R-Rutland-Windsor-2) .......... (802) 259-2460
Counties Represented: Rutland (part), Windsor (part)
Term Expires: 2017
P.O. Box 1, Belmont, VT 05730
E-mail: ddevereux@leg.state.vt.us
Committees: Government Operations

Representative
**Eileen "Lynn" Dickinson** (R-Franklin-3-2) ........... (802) 524-3404
Counties Represented: Franklin (part)       Fax: (802) 527-3767
Term Expires: 2017
69 Button Road, St. Albans, VT 05478
E-mail: edickinson@leg.state.vt.us
Committees: Corrections and Institutions

Representative **Anne B. Donahue** (R-Washington-1) ...... (802) 485-6431
Counties Represented: Washington (part)
Term Expires: 2017
148 Donahue Drive, Northfield, VT 05663
E-mail: adonahue@leg.state.vt.us
Committees: Health Care; Joint Mental Health Oversight; Rules

Representative **Johannah Leddy Donovan**
(D-Chittenden-6-5) ........................ (802) 846-7245 ext. 105
Counties Represented: Chittenden (part)       Tel: (802) 863-4634
Term Expires: 2017
38 Bayview Street, Burlington, VT 05401
E-mail: jdonovan@leg.state.vt.us
Committees: Ways and Means
Education: Trinity Col (VT) 1967 BA

Representative **Alyson Eastman** (I-Addison-Rutland) ..... (802) 828-2247
Counties Represented: Addison (part), Rutland (part)
Term Expires: 2017
375 Mount Independence Road, Orwell, VT 05760
E-mail: aeastman@leg.state.vt.us
Committees: Agriculture and Forest Products

Representative **Alice M. Emmons** (D-Windsor-3-2) ...... (802) 885-5893
Counties Represented: Windsor (part)
Term Expires: 2017
318 Summer Street, Springfield, VT 05156
E-mail: aemmons@leg.state.vt.us
Committees: Corrections and Institutions; Joint Legislative Justice
Oversight
Education: New Hampshire 1977 BS

Representative **Debbie G. Evans** (D-Chittenden-8-1) ...... (802) 878-4317
Counties Represented: Chittenden (part)
Term Expires: 2017
53 Greenfield Road, Essex Junction, VT 05452
E-mail: devans@leg.state.vt.us
Committees: Government Operations

Representative **Peter J. Fagan** (R-Rutland-5-1) .......... (802) 342-1214
Counties Represented: Rutland (part)
Term Expires: 2017
17 Clinton Avenue, Rutland, VT 05701
E-mail: pfagan@leg.state.vt.us
Committees: Appropriations

Representative
**Martha A. "Marty" Feltus** (R-Caledonia-4) ........... (802) 626-9516
Counties Represented: Caledonia (part)
Term Expires: 2017
77 Old Coach Road, Lyndonville, VT 05851
E-mail: martyfeltus@gmail.com
Committees: Appropriations
Education: Beloit BA

Representative **Rachael Fields** (D-Bennington-2-1) ....... (802) 828-2247
Counties Represented: Bennington (part)
Term Expires: 2017
802 Overlea Road, Bennington, VT 05201
E-mail: rfields@leg.state.vt.us
Committees: Corrections and Institutions

Representative **Larry G. Fiske** (R-Franklin-7) ........... (802) 933-8410
Counties Represented: Franklin (part)
Term Expires: 2017
50 St. Albans Street, Enosburg Falls, VT 05450
E-mail: lfiske@leg.state.vt.us
Committees: Human Services

Representative
**Robert "Bob" Forguites** (D-Windsor-3-2) ............ (802) 886-2654
Counties Represented: Windsor (part)
Term Expires: 2017
P.O. Box 303, North Springfield, VT 05150
E-mail: rforguites@leg.state.vt.us
Committees: Natural Resources and Energy

Representative **William R. "Bill" Frank** (D-Chittenden-3) .. (802) 899-3136
Counties Represented: Chittenden (part)
Term Expires: 2017
19 Poker Hill Road, Underhill, VT 05489
E-mail: bill@repbillfrank.com
Committees: Judiciary

Representative **Patricia "Patsy" French**
(D-Orange-Washington-Addison) .................. (802) 728-9421
Counties Represented: Addison (part), Orange (part), Washington (part)
Term Expires: 2017
886 Harlow Hill, Randolph, VT 05060
E-mail: pfrench@leg.state.vt.us
Committees: Human Services; Joint Administrative Rules

Representative
**Douglas A. "Doug" Gage** (R-Rutland-5-4) ........... (802) 773-0616
Counties Represented: Rutland (part)
Term Expires: 2017
41 Hazel Street, Rutland, VT 05701
E-mail: dgage@leg.state.vt.us
Committees: Health Care

Representative **Marianna Gamache** (R-Franklin-4) ...... (802) 393-1169
Counties Represented: Franklin (part)       Fax: (802) 524-0305
Term Expires: 2017
P.O. Box 435, Swanton, VT 05488
E-mail: mgamache@leg.state.vt.us
Committees: Natural Resources and Energy

Representative **Diana Gonzalez** (P-Chittenden-6-7) . . . . . . . (802) 828-2247
Counties Represented: Chittenden (part)
Term Expires: 2017
27 LeClair Street, Winooski, VT 05404
E-mail: dgonzalez@leg.state.vt.us
Committees: General, Housing and Military Affairs

Representative **Maxine Jo Grad** (D-Washington-7) . . . . . . (802) 496-7667
Counties Represented: Washington (part)          Fax: (802) 496-6104
Term Expires: 2017
301 Paddy Hill Road, Moretown, VT 05660
E-mail: mgrad@leg.state.vt.us
Committees: Joint Legislative Justice Oversight; Judiciary
Education: Clark U 1982 BA, 1982 MA; Vermont Law 1985 JD,
1985 MSL

Representative **Rodney Graham** (R-Orange-1) . . . . . . . . . . (802) 433-6127
Counties Represented: Orange (part)
Term Expires: 2017
859 Graham Road, Williamstown, VT 05679
E-mail: rgraham@leg.state.vt.us
Committees: Agriculture and Forest Products

Representative **Adam Greshin** (I-Washington-7) . . . . . . . . (802) 583-3223
Counties Represented: Washington (part)
Term Expires: 2017
611 Eurich Pond Road, Warren, VT 05674
E-mail: agreshin@leg.state.vt.us
Committees: Ways and Means

Representative **Sandy Haas** (P-Windsor-Rutland) . . . . . . . . (802) 767-4751
Counties Represented: Rutland (part), Windsor (part)
Term Expires: 2017
360 South Main Street, Rochester, VT 05767
E-mail: shaas@leg.state.vt.us
Committees: Human Services; Joint Judicial Rules; Joint Legislative
Justice Oversight; Joint Rules

Representative **Helen Head** (D-Chittenden-7-3) . . . . . . . . . (802) 862-2267
Counties Represented: Chittenden (part)
Term Expires: 2017
65 East Terrace, South Burlington, VT 05403
E-mail: helen@helenhead.com
Committees: General, Housing and Military Affairs

Representative **Michael "Mike" Hebert** (R-Windham-1) . . . (802) 451-9088
Counties Represented: Windham (part)          Fax: (802) 254-3660
Term Expires: 2017
P.O. Box 120, Vernon, VT 05354
E-mail: mhebert@leg.state.vt.us
Committees: Natural Resources and Energy

Representative **Robert "Bob" Helm** (R-Rutland-3) . . . . . . . (802) 265-2145
Counties Represented: Rutland (part)          Tel: (802) 468-2222
Term Expires: 2017
647 Route 4A East, Fair Haven, VT 05743
E-mail: rhelm@leg.state.vt.us
Committees: Appropriations

Representative **Mark A. Higley** (R-Orleans-Lamoille) . . . . . (802) 744-6379
Counties Represented: Lamoille (part), Orleans (part)
Term Expires: 2017
P.O. Box 10, Lowell, VT 05847
E-mail: mhigley@leg.state.vt.us
Committees: Government Operations

Representative **Mary S. Hooper** (D-Washington-4) . . . . . . (802) 223-2892
Counties Represented: Washington (part)
Term Expires: 2017
882 North Street, Montpelier, VT 05602
E-mail: mhooper@leg.state.vt.us
Committees: Appropriations; Joint Legislative Justice Oversight; Joint
Mental Health Oversight

Representative **Ronald E. Hubert** (R-Chittenden-10) . . . . . . (802) 893-1368
Counties Represented: Chittenden (part)          Tel: (802) 893-4844
Term Expires: 2017                               Fax: (802) 893-3814
68 Woodcrest Circle, Milton, VT 05468
69 Middle Road, Milton, VT 05468
E-mail: rhubert@leg.state.vt.us
Committees: Government Operations

Representative **Mark A. Huntley** (D-Windsor-2) . . . . . . . . (802) 236-6722
Counties Represented: Windsor (part)
Term Expires: 2017
535 Center Road, Cavendish, VT 05142
E-mail: mhuntley@leg.state.vt.us
Committees: Fish, Wildlife and Water Resources; Transportation

Representative **Tim Jerman** (D-Chittenden-8-2) . . . . . . . . . (802) 878-2972
Counties Represented: Chittenden (part)
Term Expires: 2017
5 Sycamore Lane, Essex Junction, VT 05452
E-mail: tjerman@leg.state.vt.us
Committees: Education

Representative
**William W. "Willem" Jewett** (D-Addison-2) . . . . . . . . (802) 388-0320
Counties Represented: Addison (part)
Term Expires: 2017
P.O. Box 129, Ripton, VT 05766
E-mail: wjewett@leg.state.vt.us
Committees: Fish, Wildlife and Water Resources; Joint Judicial
Retention; Judiciary

Representative **Mitzi Johnson** (D-Grand Isle-Chittenden) . . (802) 363-4448
Counties Represented: Chittenden (part), Grand Isle
Term Expires: 2017
P.O. Box 144, South Hero, VT 05486
E-mail: mjohnson@leg.state.vt.us
Committees: Appropriations; Joint Fiscal

Representative
**Bernard C. "Bernie" Juskiewicz** (R-Lamoille-3) . . . . . . (802) 644-5606
Counties Represented: Lamoille (part)
Term Expires: 2017
668 North Cambridge Road, Cambridge, VT 05444
E-mail: bjuskiewicz@leg.state.vt.us
Internet: ilikemikevt.tumblr.com
Committees: Education
Education: Col Emporia 1966 BA

Representative **Kathleen C. Keenan** (D-Franklin-3-1) . . . . . (802) 524-5013
Counties Represented: Franklin (part)          Tel: (802) 524-1037
Term Expires: 2017
8 Thorpe Avenue, St. Albans, VT 05478
E-mail: kkeenan@leg.state.vt.us
Committees: Appropriations

Representative **Warren F. Kitzmiller** (D-Washington-4) . . . . (802) 229-0878
Counties Represented: Washington (part)
Term Expires: 2017
138 North Street, Montpelier, VT 05602
E-mail: wkitzmiller@leg.state.vt.us
Committees: Commerce and Economic Development

Representative **Anthony "Tony" Klein** (D-Washington-5) . . (802) 223-8926
Counties Represented: Washington (part)          Fax: (802) 224-9096
Term Expires: 2017
95 Powder Horn Glen Road, Montpelier, VT 05602
E-mail: tklein@leg.state.vt.us
Committees: Joint Energy; Natural Resources and Energy

Representative **Patti Komline** (R-Bennington-Rutland) . . . . (802) 867-4232
Counties Represented: Bennington (part), Rutland (part)
Term Expires: 2017
P.O. Box 781, Dorset, VT 05251
E-mail: pkomline@leg.state.vt.us
Committees: Ways and Means

Representative **Robert C. "Bob" Krebs, LS, PE**
(D-Grand Isle-Chittenden) . . . . . . . . . . . . . . . . . . . . . . . (802) 372-4567
Counties Represented: Chittenden (part), Grand Isle
Term Expires: 2017
134 East Shore Road, South Hero, VT 05486
E-mail: rkrebs@leg.state.vt.us
Committees: Fish, Wildlife and Water Resources; Joint Administrative
Rules
Education: Vermont

Representative **Jill Krowinski** (D-Chittenden-6-3) . . . . . . . . (802) 363-3907
Counties Represented: Chittenden (part)
Term Expires: 2017
27 Spring Street, Burlington, VT 05401
E-mail: jkrowinski@leg.state.vt.us
Committees: Human Services
Education: Pittsburgh 2002 BA

Representative **Rob LaClair** (R-Washington-2) . . . . . . . . . . (802) 476-9668
Counties Represented: Washington (part)
Term Expires: 2017
146 Airport Road, Barre, VT 05641
E-mail: rlaclair@leg.state.vt.us
Committees: Government Operations

Representative **Martin LaLonde** (D-Chittenden-7-1) . . . . . . (802) 863-3086
Counties Represented: Chittenden (part)
Term Expires: 2017
304 Four Sisters Road, South Burlington, VT 05403
E-mail: mlalonde@leg.state.vt.us
Committees: Judiciary

Representative **Diane Lanpher** (D-Addison-3) . . . . . . . . . . (802) 877-2230
Counties Represented: Addison (part)          Tel: (802) 860-6657
Term Expires: 2017
P.O. Box 165, Vergennes, VT 05491
E-mail: dlanpher@leg.state.vt.us
E-mail: dianelanpher@hotmail.com
Committees: Appropriations

*(continued on next page)*

**LEGISLATIVE BRANCH**

**Representatives** *continued*

Representative **Richard H. Lawrence** (R-Caledonia-4) .... (802) 626-5917
Counties Represented: Caledonia (part)          Tel: (802) 626-5538
Term Expires: 2017          Fax: (802) 626-8081
194 Bean Pond Road, Lyndonville, VT 05851
E-mail: rlawrence@leg.state.vt.us
E-mail: richlaw@kingcon.com
Committees: Agriculture and Forest Products

Representative
**Paul D. Lefebvre** (R-Essex-Caledonia-Orleans) ......... (802) 467-8338
Counties Represented: Caledonia (part), Essex (part), Orleans (part)
Term Expires: 2017
133 Water Street, Orleans, VT 05822
E-mail: plefebvre@leg.state.vt.us
Committees: Fish, Wildlife and Water Resources

Representative **Joan G. Lenes** (D-Chittenden-5-2) ....... (802) 985-8515
Counties Represented: Chittenden (part)          Fax: (802) 399-2671
Term Expires: 2017
197 Governor's Lane, Shelburne, VT 05482
E-mail: jlenes@leg.state.vt.us
E-mail: jglenes@aol.com
Committees: Corrections and Institutions

Representative **Patricia "Patti" Lewis** (R-Washington-1) .. (802) 223-6319
Counties Represented: Washington (part)
Term Expires: 2017
449 East Road, Berlin, VT 05641
E-mail: plewis@leg.state.vt.us
Committees: Government Operations

Representative
**William J. "Bill" Lippert, Jr.** (D-Chittenden-4-2) ....... (802) 482-3528
Counties Represented: Chittenden (part)
Term Expires: 2017
2751 Baldwin Road, Hinesburg, VT 05461
E-mail: wlippert@leg.state.vt.us
Committees: Health Care; Joint Fiscal; Joint Judicial Rules; Joint Rules
Education: Earlham 1972 BA; Antioch U 1979 MA

Representative **Emily Long** (D-Windham-5) ............ (802) 365-7360
Counties Represented: Windham (part)
Term Expires: 2017
239 Wiswall Hill Road, Newfane, VT 05345
E-mail: elong@leg.state.vt.us
Committees: Education

Representative **Gabrielle Lucke** (D-Windsor-4-2) ........ (802) 296-2690
Counties Represented: Windsor (part)
Term Expires: 2017
554 Campbell Street, White River Junction, VT 05001
E-mail: glucke@leg.state.vt.us
Committees: General, Housing and Military Affairs

Representative
**Terence "Terry" Macaig** (D-Chittenden-2) ........... (802) 878-3872
Counties Represented: Chittenden (part)
Term Expires: 2017
82 Pamela Court, Williston, VT 05495
E-mail: tmacaig@leg.state.vt.us
E-mail: macaig@msn.com
Committees: Corrections and Institutions

Representative **Ann Manwaring** (D-Windham-6) ........ (802) 464-2150
Counties Represented: Windham (part)
Term Expires: 2017
P.O. Box 1089, Wilmington, VT 05363
E-mail: amanwaring@leg.state.vt.us
Committees: Education; Joint Government Accountability

Representative **Michael J. Marcotte** (R-Orleans-2) ...... (802) 334-6302
Counties Represented: Orleans (part)          Tel: (802) 334-2132
Term Expires: 2017
106 Private Pond Road, Newport, VT 05855
E-mail: mmarcotte@leg.state.vt.us
E-mail: jimkwik@surfglobal.net
Committees: Commerce and Economic Development

Representative
**Marcia Robinson Martel** (R-Caledonia-1) ........... (802) 748-9134
Counties Represented: Caledonia (part)
Term Expires: 2017
E-mail: mmartel@leg.state.vt.us
Committees: Judiciary

Representative **Linda J. Martin** (D-Lamoille-2) ......... (802) 888-5654
Counties Represented: Lamoille (part)
Term Expires: 2017
P.O. Box 94, Wolcott, VT 05680
E-mail: lmartin@leg.state.vt.us
Committees: Government Operations

Representative
**James W. "Jim" Masland** (D-Windsor-Orange-2) ..... (802) 785-4146
Counties Represented: Orange (part), Windsor (part)
Term Expires: 2017
714 Pero Hill Road, Thetford Center, VT 05075
E-mail: jmasland@leg.state.vt.us
E-mail: jamesq56@yahoo.com
Committees: Ways and Means
Education: Stanford 1972 BA, 1972 MS

Representative
**Curtis A. "Curt" McCormack** (D-Chittenden-6-3) ..... (802) 318-2585
Counties Represented: Chittenden (part)
Term Expires: 2017
221 North Winooski Avenue, Burlington, VT 05401
E-mail: cmccormack@leg.state.vt.us
Committees: Transportation

Representative **Patricia A. McCoy** (R-Rutland-1) ......... (802) 828-2247
Counties Represented: Rutland (part)
Term Expires: 2017
1392 High Road, Poultney, VT 05764
E-mail: pmccoy@leg.state.vt.us
Committees: Human Services

Representative
**James "Jim" McCullough** (D-Chittenden-2) .......... (802) 878-2180
Counties Represented: Chittenden (part)          Tel: (802) 879-6001
Term Expires: 2017
592 Governor Chittendon Road, Williston, VT 05495
E-mail: jim_mccullough@myfairpoint.net
Committees: Fish, Wildlife and Water Resources

Representative
**Francis M. "Topper" McFaun** (R-Washington-2) ....... (802) 479-9843
Counties Represented: Washington (part)
Term Expires: 2017
97 Sunset Road, Barre, VT 05641
E-mail: fmcfaun@leg.state.vt.us
Committees: Human Services

Representative **Alice Miller** (D-Bennington-3) ........... (802) 442-9825
Counties Represented: Bennington (part)
Term Expires: 2017
88 Horton Hill Road, Shaftsbury, VT 05262
E-mail: amiller@leg.state.vt.us
Committees: Education
Education: Bennington 1960 BA; NYU 1964 MA

Representative **Kiah Morris** (D-Bennington-2-2) .......... (802) 828-2247
Counties Represented: Bennington (part)
Term Expires: 2017
P.O. Box 4705, Bennington, VT 05201
E-mail: kmorris@leg.state.vt.us
Committees: Health Care

Representative **Mary A. Morrissey** (R-Bennington-2-2) ... (802) 442-2092
Counties Represented: Bennington (part)
Term Expires: 2017
228 Dewey Street, Bennington, VT 05201
E-mail: mmorrissey@leg.state.vt.us
Committees: General, Housing and Military Affairs

Representative **Michael Mrowicki** (D-Windham-4) ...... (802) 387-8787
Counties Represented: Windham (part)          Tel: (802) 387-2120
Term Expires: 2017
299 South Pine Banks Road, Putney, VT 05346
E-mail: mmrowicki@leg.state.vt.us
Committees: Human Services

Representative **Barbara S. Murphy** (I-Franklin-2) ........ (802) 849-6545
Counties Represented: Franklin (part)
Term Expires: 2017
7 Lily Road, Fairfax, VT 05454
E-mail: bmurphy@leg.state.vt.us
Committees: Transportation

Representative **Linda K. Myers** (R-Chittenden-8-1) ...... (802) 878-3514
Counties Represented: Chittenden (part)
Term Expires: 2017
51 Forest Road, Essex Junction, VT 05452
E-mail: lmyers@leg.state.vt.us
Committees: Corrections and Institutions; Joint Administrative Rules

Representative **Betty A. Nuovo** (D-Addison-1) .......... (802) 388-2024
Counties Represented: Addison (part)
Term Expires: 2017
P.O. Box 1113, Middlebury, VT 05753
E-mail: bnuovo@leg.state.vt.us
Committees: Judiciary
Education: Bucknell 1953 BSEd

Representative **Anne Theresa O'Brien** (D-Chittenden-1) . . (802) 434-4250
Counties Represented: Chittenden (part)
Term Expires: 2017
2406 Hinesburg Road, Richmond, VT 05477
E-mail: aobrien@leg.state.vt.us
Committees: Appropriations
Education: Vermont 1982 BSN; St Michael's 1992 MS

Representative **Jean D.C. O'Sullivan** (D-Chittenden-6-2) . . (802) 658-0492
Counties Represented: Chittenden (part)
Term Expires: 2017
37 Village Green, Burlington, VT 05408
E-mail: josullivan@leg.state.vt.us
Committees: Commerce and Economic Development

Representative
**Oliver K. Olsen** (I-Windham-Bennington-Windsor) . . . . . (802) 585-5435
Counties Represented: Bennington (part), Windham (part), Windsor (part)
Term Expires: 2017
1320 Middletown Road, South Londonderry, VT 05155
E-mail: oliver@oliverolsen.com
Committees: Natural Resources and Energy

Representative **Corey Parent** (R-Franklin-3-1) . . . . . . . . . . (802) 370-0494
Counties Represented: Franklin (part)
Term Expires: 2017
160 North Main Street, Unit 3, St. Albans, VT 05478
E-mail: cparent@leg.state.vt.us
Committees: Commerce and Economic Development

Representative **Carolyn W. Partridge** (D-Windham-3) . . . . .(802) 874-4182
Counties Represented: Windham (part)
Term Expires: 2017
1612 Old Cheney Road, Windham, VT 05359
E-mail: cpartridge@leg.state.vt.us
E-mail: hoparwel@sover.net
Committees: Agriculture and Forest Products
Education: NYU 1971 BA

Representative **Avram Patt** (D-Lamoille-Washington) . . . . . (802) 223-1014
Counties Represented: Lamoille (part), Washington (part)
Term Expires: 2017
E-mail: apatt@leg.state.vt.us
Committees: Health Care

Representative **Albert "Chuck" Pearce** (R-Franklin-5) . . . . (802) 848-7813
Counties Represented: Franklin (part)
Term Expires: 2017
84 Magoon Road, Richford, VT 05476
E-mail: apearce@leg.state.vt.us
Committees: Appropriations

Representative **Christopher Pearson** (P-Chittenden-6-4) . . .(802) 860-3933
Counties Represented: Chittenden (part)
Term Expires: 2017
12 Brookes Avenue, Burlington, VT 05401
E-mail: cpearson@leg.state.vt.us
Committees: Health Care; Joint Health Care Oversight

Representative **Paul N. Poirier** (I-Washington-3) . . . . . . . . (802) 476-7870
Counties Represented: Washington (part)
Term Expires: 2017
33 Abbott Avenue, Barre, VT 05641
E-mail: ppoirier@leg.state.vt.us
Committees: Health Care
Education: Norwich 1970, 1974 MAEd

Representative **Dave Potter** (D-Rutland-2) . . . . . . . . . . . . . (802) 438-5385
Counties Represented: Rutland (part)
Term Expires: 2017
P.O. Box 426, North Clarendon, VT 05759
E-mail: dpotter@leg.state.vt.us
Committees: Transportation

Representative **Ann D. Pugh** (D-Chittenden-7-2) . . . . . . . . (802) 863-6705
Counties Represented: Chittenden (part)            Tel: (802) 656-8800
Term Expires: 2017
67 Bayberry Lane, South Burlington, VT 05403
E-mail: apugh@leg.state.vt.us
Committees: Human Services; Joint Mental Health Oversight
Education: Union Col (NY) 1974 BS; Vermont 1990 CAS

Representative **Joey Purvis** (R-Chittenden-9-1) . . . . . . . . . (802) 879-6110
Counties Represented: Chittenden (part)
Term Expires: 2017
364 Hidden Oaks Drive, Colchester, VT 05446
E-mail: jpurvis@leg.state.vt.us
Committees: Agriculture and Forest Products

Representative
**Constance N. "Connie" Quimby** (R-Essex-Caledonia) . .(802) 695-2575
Counties Represented: Caledonia (part), Essex (part)
Term Expires: 2017
579 Main Street, Concord, VT 05824
E-mail: cquimby@leg.state.vt.us
Committees: Fish, Wildlife and Water Resources; Transportation

Representative **Barbara Rachelson** (D-Chittenden-6-6) . . . .(802) 862-1290
Counties Represented: Chittenden (part)
Term Expires: 2017
205 Summit Street, Burlington, VT 05401
E-mail: brachelson@leg.state.vt.us
Committees: Joint Judicial Retention; Judiciary
Education: Brandeis 1978 BA; Michigan 1979 MSW

Representative **Kesha K. Ram** (D-Chittenden-6-4) . . . . . . . .(802) 881-4433
Counties Represented: Chittenden (part)
Term Expires: 2017
31 North Prospect Street, Burlington, VT 05401
E-mail: kram@leg.state.vt.us
Committees: Joint Information Technology; Natural Resources and Energy

Representative **Herbert "Herb" Russell** (D-Rutland-5-3) . . (802) 779-7370
Counties Represented: Rutland (part)
Term Expires: 2017
24 Griswold Drive, Rutland, VT 05701
E-mail: hfontrussell@leg.state.vt.us
Committees: Transportation

Representative
**Marjorie Q. Ryerson** (D-Orange-Washington-Addison) . . (802) 728-4127
Counties Represented: Addison (part), Orange (part), Washington (part)
Term Expires: 2017
36 Randolph Avenue, Randolph, VT 05060
E-mail: water05060@gmail.com
Committees: Agriculture and Forest Products

Representative **Brian K. Savage** (R-Franklin-4) . . . . . . . . . (802) 868-3566
Counties Represented: Franklin (part)            Tel: (802) 782-9314
Term Expires: 2017
17 Linda Avenue, Swanton, VT 05488
P.O. Box 232, Swanton, VT 05488
E-mail: bsavage@leg.state.vt.us
Committees: General, Housing and Military Affairs; Rules

Representative **Heidi E. Scheuermann** (R-Lamoille-1) . . . . (802) 253-2275
Counties Represented: Lamoille (part)
Term Expires: 2017
P.O. Box 908, Stowe, VT 05672
E-mail: hscheuermann@leg.state.vt.us
Committees: Commerce and Economic Development

Representative **David "Dave" Sharpe** (D-Addison-4) . . . . . (802) 453-2754
Counties Represented: Addison (part)
Term Expires: 2017
1209 Meehan Road, Bristol, VT 05443
E-mail: dsharpe@leg.state.vt.us
Committees: Education; Joint Fiscal

Representative **Charles "Butch" Shaw** (R-Rutland-6) . . . . (802) 433-2398
Counties Represented: Rutland (part)
Term Expires: 2017
910 Markowski Road, Florence, VT 05744
E-mail: bshaw@leg.state.vt.us
E-mail: butchshaws@aol.com
Committees: Corrections and Institutions; Joint Legislative Justice Oversight

Representative **Loren T. Shaw** (R-Orleans-1) . . . . . . . . . . . (802) 766-5022
Counties Represented: Orleans (part)
Term Expires: 2017
320 Foxwood Lane, Derby, VT 05829
E-mail: lshaw@leg.state.vt.us
Committees: Transportation

Representative **Amy Sheldon** (D-Addison-1) . . . . . . . . . . .(802) 828-2247
Counties Represented: Addison (part)
Term Expires: 2017
P.O. Box 311, Middlebury, VT 05740
E-mail: asheldon@leg.state.vt.us
Committees: Fish, Wildlife and Water Resources

Representative **Laura Sibilia** (I-Windham-Bennington) . . . . (802) 348-7131
Counties Represented: Bennington (part), Windham (part)
Term Expires: 2017
76 Cotton Mill Hill, Brattleboro, VT 05301
E-mail: lsibilia@leg.state.vt.us
Committees: Commerce and Economic Development

*(continued on next page)*

LEGISLATIVE BRANCH

**Representatives** *continued*

Representative **Harvey T. Smith** (R-Addison-5) . . . . . . . . . (802) 877-2712
Counties Represented: Addison (part)
Term Expires: 2017
2516 Lime Kiln Road, New Haven, VT 05472
E-mail: hsmith@leg.state.vt.us
Committees: Agriculture and Forest Products

Representative
**Shapleigh "Shap" Smith** (D-Lamoille-Washington) . . . . (802) 828-2245
Counties Represented: Lamoille (part), Washington (part)
Term Expires: 2017
115 State Street, Montpelier, VT 05633-5201
369 Farm Hill Road, Morrisville, VT 05701
E-mail: speaker@leg.state.vt.us
Committees: Joint Rules

Representative **Tom Stevens** (D-Washington-Chittenden) . . (802) 244-4164
Counties Represented: Chittenden (part), Washington (part)
Term Expires: 2017
12 Winooski Street, Waterbury, VT 05676
E-mail: tstevens@leg.state.vt.us
E-mail: tom@stevensvermont.com
Committees: General, Housing and Military Affairs

Representative **Vicki Strong** (R-Orleans-Caledonia) . . . . . . . (802) 754-2790
Counties Represented: Caledonia (part), Orleans (part)
Term Expires: 2017
1367 Creek Road, Irasburg, VT 05845
E-mail: vstrong@leg.state.vt.us
Committees: Judiciary

Representative **Valerie A. Stuart** (D-Windham-2-1) . . . . . . (802) 257-0249
Counties Represented: Windham (part)
Term Expires: 2017
520 Meadowbrook Road, Brattleboro, VT 05301
E-mail: vstuart@leg.state.vt.us
Committees: Commerce and Economic Development

Representative **Mary M. Sullivan** (D-Chittenden-6-5) . . . . . (802) 862-6632
Counties Represented: Chittenden (part)
Term Expires: 2017
84 Caroline Street, Burlington, VT 05401
E-mail: msullivan@leg.state.vt.us
Committees: Joint Energy; Natural Resources and Energy

Representative **Donna G. Sweaney** (D-Windsor-1) . . . . . . . (802) 674-5175
Counties Represented: Windsor (part)
Term Expires: 2017
2 Runnemede Lane, Windsor, VT 05089
E-mail: dsweaney@leg.state.vt.us
Committees: Government Operations; Joint Government Accountability
Education: Youngstown State 1966 BA; Hartford 1974 MEd

Representative **Job Tate** (R-Rutland-Windsor-1) . . . . . . . . . . (802) 558-5153
Counties Represented: Rutland (part), Windsor (part)
Term Expires: 2017
111 Birchwood Drive, #6, Mendon, VT 05701
E-mail: jtate@leg.state.vt.us
Committees: General, Housing and Military Affairs

Representative **Thomas Terenzini** (R-Rutland-4) . . . . . . . . (802) 855-1945
Counties Represented: Rutland (part)
Term Expires: 2017
34B Chasanna Drive, Rutland, VT 05701
E-mail: tterenzini@leg.state.vt.us
Committees: Fish, Wildlife and Water Resources

Representative **George W. Till** (D-Chittenden-3) . . . . . . . . . (802) 899-2984
Counties Represented: Chittenden (part)          Fax: (802) 878-6131
Term Expires: 2017
74 Foothills Drive, Jericho, VT 05465
E-mail: gtill@leg.state.vt.us
Committees: Joint Health Care Oversight; Ways and Means

Representative **Tristan D. Toleno** (D-Windham-2-3) . . . . . . (802) 579-5511
Counties Represented: Windham (part)
Term Expires: 2017
33 Highlawn Road, Brattleboro, VT 05301
E-mail: toleno@leg.state.vt.us
Committees: Corrections and Institutions
Education: Wesleyan U (Attended); Marlboro 2011 MBA

Representative **Catherine Beattie "Kitty" Toll**
(D-Caledonia-Washington) . . . . . . . . . . . . . . . . . . . . . (802) 684-3671
Counties Represented: Caledonia (part), Washington (part)
Term Expires: 2017
P.O. Box 192, Danville, VT 05828
E-mail: ktoll@leg.state.vt.us
E-mail: kittytoll@live.com
Committees: Appropriations; Joint Mental Health Oversight

Representative **Maida F. Townsend** (D-Chittenden-7-4) . . . (802) 862-7404
Counties Represented: Chittenden (part)
Term Expires: 2017
232 Patchen Road, South Burlington, VT 05403
E-mail: mtownsend@leg.state.vt.us
Committees: Government Operations

Representative
**Matthew "Matt" Trieber** (D-Windham-3) . . . . . . . . . . (802) 376-1134
Counties Represented: Windham (part)
Term Expires: 2017
82 Atkinson Street, Bellows Falls, VT 05060
E-mail: mtrieber@leg.state.vt.us
Committees: Appropriations

Representative **Joseph "Chip" Troiano** (D-Caledonia-2) . . (802) 533-7712
Counties Represented: Caledonia (part)
Term Expires: 2017
261 Hutchins Farm Road, East Hardwick, VT 05836
E-mail: ctroiano@leg.state.vt.us
Committees: Human Services

Representative **Donald H. Turner** (R-Chittenden-10) . . . . . . (802) 893-1419
Counties Represented: Chittenden (part)          Tel: (802) 373-5960
Term Expires: 2017                                Fax: (802) 893-3467
P.O. Box 487, Milton, VT 05468
E-mail: dturner@leg.state.vt.us
Committees: Agriculture and Forest Products; Rules

Representative **Warren Van Wyck** (R-Addison-3) . . . . . . . . (802) 877-2169
Counties Represented: Addison (part)             Tel: (802) 656-8421
Term Expires: 2017
University of Vermont, South Prospect Street, Burlington, VT 05401
E-mail: wvanwyck@leg.state.vt.us
Committees: Joint Energy; Natural Resources and Energy

Representative **Gary G. Viens** (R-Orleans-2) . . . . . . . . . . . (802) 323-2183
Counties Represented: Orleans (part)
Term Expires: 2017
50 Mountain View Drive, Newport, VT 05855
E-mail: gviens@leg.state.vt.us
Committees: Joint Judicial Retention; Judiciary

Representative **Tommy J. Walz** (D-Washington-3) . . . . . . . . (802) 476-7819
Counties Represented: Washington (part)
Term Expires: 2017
157 Camp Street, Barre, VT 05641
E-mail: twalz@leg.state.vt.us
Committees: General, Housing and Military Affairs
Education: Bowdoin 1967; Johann Goethe Universitat 1975;
Middlebury 1980

Representative
**Kathryn L. "Kate" Webb** (D-Chittenden-5-1) . . . . . . . . . (802) 985-2789
Counties Represented: Chittenden (part)
Term Expires: 2017
1611 Harbor Road, Shelburne, VT 05482
E-mail: kwebb@leg.state.vt.us
E-mail: klwebb22@mac.com
Committees: Fish, Wildlife and Water Resources; Rules

Representative **Janssen Willhoit** (R-Caledonia-3) . . . . . . . . (802) 431-5118
Counties Represented: Caledonia (part)
Term Expires: 2017
46 Hastings Hill, St. Johnsbury, VT 05819
E-mail: jwillhoit@leg.state.vt.us
Committees: Fish, Wildlife and Water Resources

Representative
**Theresa Wood** (D-Washington-Chittenden) . . . . . . . . . . . (802) 828-2228
Counties Represented: Chittenden (part), Washington (part)
Term Expires: 2017
E-mail: twood@leg.state.vt.us
Committees: Corrections and Institutions

Representative **Mark Woodward** (D-Lamoille-2) . . . . . . . . . (802) 635-7166
Counties Represented: Lamoille (part)
Term Expires: 2017
110 Woodward Road, Johnson, VT 05656
E-mail: mwoodward@leg.state.vt.us
Committees: Health Care

Representative **Kurt Wright** (R-Chittenden-6-1) . . . . . . . . . (802) 658-1410
Counties Represented: Chittenden (part)
Term Expires: 2017
31 Vine Street, Burlington, VT 05401
E-mail: kwright@leg.state.vt.us
Committees: Education

LEGISLATIVE BRANCH

Representative **Michael Yantachka** (D-Chittenden-4-1) . . . . (802) 425-3960
  Counties Represented: Chittenden (part)
  Term Expires: 2017
  393 Natures Way, Charlotte, VT 05445
  E-mail: myantachka@leg.state.vt.us
  Committees: Natural Resources and Energy
Representative
  **Samuel "Sam" Young** (D-Orleans-Caledonia) . . . . . . . . (802) 321-0365
  Counties Represented: Caledonia (part), Orleans (part)
  Term Expires: 2017
  P.O. Box 10, West Glover, VT 05875
  E-mail: syoung@leg.state.vt.us
  Committees: Joint Information Technology; Ways and Means
Representative **Teo Zagar** (D-Windsor-4-1) . . . . . . . . . . . . . (802) 558-3966
  Counties Represented: Windsor (part)          Tel: (802) 457-1317
  Term Expires: 2017
  PO Box 875, Barnard, VT 05031
  E-mail: tzagar@leg.state.vt.us
  Committees: Agriculture and Forest Products
  Education: Vermont; Hampshire

## House Standing Committees

### Agriculture and Forest Products

**Majority Members**
Carolyn W. Partridge (D) *Chair*
John L. Bartholomew (D)
  *Ranking Member*
Daniel F. Connor (D)
Marjorie Q. Ryerson (D)
Teo Zagar (D)

**Members**
Alyson Eastman (I)

**Minority Members**
Richard H. Lawrence (R)
  *Vice Chair*
Rodney Graham (R)
Joey Purvis (R)
Harvey T. Smith (R)
Donald H. Turner (R)

### Appropriations

**Majority Members**
Mitzi Johnson (D) *Chair*
Kathleen C. Keenan (D)
  *Ranking Member*
Mary S. Hooper (D)
Diane Lanpher (D)
Anne Theresa O'Brien (D)
Catherine Beattie "Kitty" Toll (D)
Matthew "Matt" Trieber (D)

**Minority Members**
Peter J. Fagan (R) *Vice Chair*
Martha A. "Marty" Feltus (R)
Robert "Bob" Helm (R)
Albert "Chuck" Pearce (R)

### Commerce and Economic Development

**Majority Members**
Bill Botzow (D) *Chair*
Warren F. Kitzmiller (D)
  *Ranking Member*
Stephen A. Carr (D)
Maureen P. Dakin (D)
Jean D.C. O'Sullivan (D)
Valerie A. Stuart (D)

**Members**
Laura Sibilia (I)

**Minority Members**
Michael J. Marcotte (R) *Vice Chair*
Fred K. Baser (R)
Corey Parent (R)
Heidi E. Scheuermann (R)

### Corrections and Institutions

**Majority Members**
Alice M. Emmons (D) *Chair*
Joan G. Lenes (D)
  *Ranking Member*
Cynthia M. Browning (D)
Rachael Fields (D)
Terence "Terry" Macaig (D)
Tristan D. Toleno (D)
Theresa Wood (D)

**Members**
Susan Hatch Davis (P)

**Minority Members**
Linda K. Myers (R) *Vice Chair*
Lynn Batchelor (R)
Eileen "Lynn" Dickinson (R)
Charles "Butch" Shaw (R)

### Education

**Majority Members**
David "Dave" Sharpe (D) *Chair*
Sarah E. Buxton (D) *Clerk*
Kevin "Coach" Christie (D)
  *Ranking Member*
Tim Jerman (D)
Emily Long (D)
Ann Manwaring (D)
Alice Miller (D)

**Minority Members**
Bernard C. "Bernie" Juskiewicz (R)
  *Vice Chair*
Scott Beck (R)
Lawrence P. "Larry" Cupoli (R)
Kurt Wright (R)

### Fish, Wildlife and Water Resources

**Majority Members**
David L. Deen (D) *Chair*
James "Jim" McCullough (D)
  *Vice Chair*
Mark A. Huntley (D)
William W. "Willem" Jewett (D)
Robert C. "Bob" Krebs (D)
Amy Sheldon (D)
Kathryn L. "Kate" Webb (D)

**Minority Members**
Stephen C. "Steve" Beyor (R)
  *Ranking Member*
Paul D. Lefebvre (R) *Clerk*
Constance N. "Connie" Quimby (R)
Thomas Terenzini (R)
Janssen Willhoit (R)

### General, Housing and Military Affairs

**Majority Members**
Helen Head (D) *Chair*
Tom Stevens (D) *Vice Chair*
Gabrielle Lucke (D) *Clerk*
Tommy J. Walz (D)

**Members**
Diana Gonzalez (P)

**Minority Members**
Brian K. Savage (R)
  *Ranking Member*
Mary A. Morrissey (R)
Job Tate (R)

### Government Operations

**Majority Members**
Donna G. Sweaney (D) *Chair*
Debbie G. Evans (D) *Vice Chair*
Joanna E. Cole (D)
Sarah Copeland-Hanzas (D)
Linda J. Martin (D)
Maida F. Townsend (D)

**Minority Members**
Dennis J. Devereux (R)
  *Ranking Member*
Mark A. Higley (R)
Ronald E. Hubert (R)
Rob LaClair (R)
Patricia "Patti" Lewis (R)

### Health Care

**Majority Members**
William J. "Bill" Lippert, Jr. (D)
  *Chair*
Leigh J. Dakin (D) *Clerk*
Timothy "Tim" Briglin (D)
Kiah Morris (D)
Avram Patt (D)
Mark Woodward (D)

**Members**
Christopher Pearson (P) *Vice Chair*
Paul N. Poirier (I)

**Minority Members**
Anne B. Donahue (R)
  *Ranking Member*
Douglas A. "Doug" Gage (R)
Robert L. Bancroft (R)

### Human Services

**Majority Members**
Ann D. Pugh (D) *Chair*
Patricia "Patsy" French (D)
Steven Berry (D)
Jill Krowinski (D)
Michael Mrowicki (D)
Joseph "Chip" Troiano (D)

**Members**
Sandy Haas (P) *Vice Chair*

**Minority Members**
Francis M. "Topper" McFaun (R)
  *Ranking Member*
Larry G. Fiske (R) *Clerk*
Paul Dame (R)
Patricia A. McCoy (R)

### Judiciary

**Majority Members**
Maxine Jo Grad (D) *Chair*
William W. "Willem" Jewett (D)
  *Vice Chair*
Chip Conquest (D)
William R. "Bill" Frank (D)
Martin LaLonde (D)
Betty A. Nuovo (D)
Barbara Rachelson (D)

**Minority Members**
Tom Burditt (R) *Ranking Member*
Vicki Strong (R) *Clerk*
Marcia Robinson Martel (R)
Gary G. Viens (R)

**LEGISLATIVE BRANCH**

## Natural Resources and Energy

**Majority Members**
Anthony "Tony" Klein (D) *Chair*
Kesha K. Ram (D) *Clerk*
Robert "Bob" Forguites (D)
Mary M. Sullivan (D)
Michael Yantachka (D)

**Members**
Robin Chesnut-Tangerman (P)
Oliver K. Olsen (I)

**Minority Members**
Michael "Mike" Hebert (R)
  *Ranking Member*
Marianna Gamache (R)
Warren Van Wyck (R)

## Rules

**Majority Members**
Sarah Copeland-Hanzas (D)
David L. Deen (D)
Kathryn L. "Kate" Webb (D)

**Minority Members**
Anne B. Donahue (R)
Brian K. Savage (R)
Donald H. Turner (R)

## Transportation

**Majority Members**
Dave Potter (D) *Vice Chair*
Timothy R. Corcoran II (D)
  *Ranking Member*
Mark A. Huntley (D) *Clerk*
Clement J. "Clem" Bissonnette (D)
Curtis A. "Curt" McCormack (D)
Herbert "Herb" Russell (D)

**Members**
Mollie S. Burke (P)
Barbara S. Murphy (I)

**Minority Members**
Patrick M. Brennan (R) *Chair*
Constance N. "Connie" Quimby (R)
Loren T. Shaw (R)

## Ways and Means

**Majority Members**
Janet Ancel (D) *Chair*
Johannah Leddy Donovan (D)
  *Ranking Member*
Alison H. Clarkson (D) *Clerk*
Jim Condon (D)
James W. "Jim" Masland (D)
George W. Till (D)
Samuel "Sam" Young (D)

**Members**
Adam Greshin (I)

**Minority Members**
Carolyn Whitney Branagan (R)
  *Vice Chair*
William "Bill" Canfield (R)
Patti Komline (R)

# Virgin Islands Unicameral Legislature

Capitol Building, Charlotte Amalie, St. Thomas, VI 00804
P.O. Box 1690, St. Thomas, VI 00804
Tel: (340) 774-0880  Fax: (340) 693-3635  Internet: www.legvi.org

## Virgin Islands Legislature

President of the Senate **Neville A. James** (D) . . . . . . . . . . (340) 774-0880
Vice President of the Senate **Janette Millin Young** (D) . . . (340) 712-3521
Secretary **Myron D. Jackson** (D) . . . . . . . . . . . . . . . . . . . . (340) 693-3537
  Education: Parsons Design
Majority Leader **Sammuel Sanes** (D) . . . . . . . . . . . . . . . . (340) 712-2310
  Education: Florida Memorial Col
Liaison to the United States Department of Interior
  Office of Insular Affairs **Myron D. Jackson** (D) . . . . . . . (340) 693-3537
Liaison to the White House **Kenneth L. Gittens** (D) . . . . . (340) 693-3537
  Education: John Jay Col 2000 AS; Columbia Southern 2008 BS,
  2011 MS

## Senators

**Party Affiliation Statistics:** Democrats: 11, Independents: 4

Senator **Marvin A. Blyden** (D-St. Thomas-St. John) . . . . . (340) 774-0880
  Counties Represented: St. John Island, St. Thomas Island
  Term Expires: 2017
  Committees: Culture, Historic Preservation, Youth and Recreation;
  Energy and Environment Protection; Finance; Health, Hospitals, and
  Human Services; Housing, Public Works, and Waste Management
Senator **Jean Forde** (D-St. Thomas-St. John) . . . . . . . . . . . (340) 774-0880
  Counties Represented: St. John Island, St. Thomas Island
  Term Expires: 2017
  Committees: Education and Workforce Development; Health, Hospitals,
  and Human Services; Homeland Security, Public Safety, and Justice;
  Housing, Public Works, and Waste Management
Senator **Novelle E. Francis, Jr.** (D-St. Croix) . . . . . . . . . . . (340) 774-0880
  Counties Represented: St. Croix Island
  Term Expires: 2017
  Committees: Culture, Historic Preservation, Youth and Recreation;
  Economic Development, Agriculture and Planning; Health, Hospitals,
  and Human Services; Homeland Security, Public Safety, and Justice;
  Rules and Judiciary
Senator **Kenneth L. Gittens** (D-St. Croix) . . . . . . . . . . . . . (340) 693-3537
  Counties Represented: St. Croix Island
  Term Expires: 2017
  E-mail: kenneth.gittens2k12@gmail.com
  Committees: Culture, Historic Preservation, Youth and Recreation;
  Education and Workforce Development; Homeland Security, Public
  Safety, and Justice; Housing, Public Works, and Waste Management;
  Rules and Judiciary
Senator **Clifford F. Graham** (D-St. Thomas-St. John) . . . . . (340) 693-3513
  Counties Represented: St. John Island, St. Thomas    Fax: (340) 693-3631
  Island
  Term Expires: 2017
  E-mail: cgraham@legvi.org
  Committees: Economic Development, Agriculture and Planning; Energy
  and Environment Protection; Finance; Housing, Public Works, and
  Waste Management
  Education: Hampton 1989 BS
Senator **Justin Harrigan, Sr.** (D-St. Thomas-St. John) . . . . (340) 774-0880
  Counties Represented: St. John Island, St. Thomas Island
  Term Expires: 2017
  Committees: Education and Workforce Development; Health, Hospitals,
  and Human Services; Homeland Security, Public Safety, and Justice;
  Rules and Judiciary; Veterans' Affairs
Senator **Myron D. Jackson** (D-St. Thomas-St. John) . . . . . (340) 693-3537
  Counties Represented: St. John Island, St. Thomas Island
  Term Expires: 2017
  E-mail: mjackson@legvi.org
  Committees: Culture, Historic Preservation, Youth and Recreation;
  Economic Development, Agriculture and Planning; Education and
  Workforce Development; Finance; Veterans' Affairs
Senator **Neville A. James** (D-St. Croix) . . . . . . . . . . . . . . . (340) 774-0880
  Counties Represented: St. Croix Island
  Term Expires: 2017
  Committees: Economic Development, Agriculture and Planning;
  Housing, Public Works, and Waste Management; Rules and Judiciary;
  Veterans' Affairs

**LEGISLATIVE BRANCH**

Senator **Almando "Rocky" Liburd** (I-At-Large) . . . . . . . . (340) 774-0880
Term Expires: 2017
Committees: Economic Development, Agriculture and Planning; Energy and Environment Protection; Health, Hospitals, and Human Services; Homeland Security, Public Safety, and Justice; Housing, Public Works, and Waste Management

Senator **Terrence "Positive" Nelson** (I-St. Croix) . . . . . . . (340) 712-2210
Counties Represented: St. Croix Island          Fax: (340) 712-2374
Term Expires: 2017
E-mail: tnelson@legvi.org
Committees: Culture, Historic Preservation, Youth and Recreation; Education and Workforce Development; Energy and Environment Protection; Finance; Veterans' Affairs

Senator **Nellie Rivera-O'Reilly** (I-St. Croix) . . . . . . . . . . . (340) 693-3507
Counties Represented: St. Croix Island          Fax: (340) 693-3641
Term Expires: 2017
E-mail: teamnellie@gmail.com
Committees: Culture, Historic Preservation, Youth and Recreation; Economic Development, Agriculture and Planning; Health, Hospitals, and Human Services; Homeland Security, Public Safety, and Justice; Rules and Judiciary

Senator **Tregenza Roach** (I-St. Thomas-St. John) . . . . . . . . (340) 693-3686
Counties Represented: St. John Island, St. Thomas          Fax: (340) 693-3660
Island
Term Expires: 2017
E-mail: troach@legvi.org
Committees: Economic Development, Agriculture and Planning; Education and Workforce Development; Finance; Housing, Public Works, and Waste Management; Veterans' Affairs
Education: Missouri 1981 BA; Connecticut 1989 JD

Senator **Sammuel Sanes** (D-St. Croix) . . . . . . . . . . . . . . (340) 712-2310
Counties Represented: St. Croix Island          Fax: (340) 712-2380
Term Expires: 2017
E-mail: sammuelsanes@yahoo.com
Committees: Culture, Historic Preservation, Youth and Recreation; Energy and Environment Protection; Finance; Homeland Security, Public Safety, and Justice; Veterans' Affairs

Senator **Kurt Vialet** (D-St. Croix) . . . . . . . . . . . . . . . . . . (340) 774-0880
Counties Represented: St. Croix Island
Term Expires: 2017
Committees: Economic Development, Agriculture and Planning; Education and Workforce Development; Energy and Environment Protection; Finance; Health, Hospitals, and Human Services

Senator **Janette Millin Young** (D-St. Thomas-St. John) . . . (340) 693-3521
Counties Represented: St. John Island, St. Thomas          Fax: (340) 693-3633
Island
Term Expires: 2017
E-mail: jyoung@legvi.org
Committees: Economic Development, Agriculture and Planning; Energy and Environment Protection; Rules and Judiciary; Veterans' Affairs

## Senate Standing Committees

### Culture, Historic Preservation, Youth and Recreation

| Majority Members | Minority Members |
| --- | --- |
| Myron D. Jackson (D) *Chair* | Terrence "Positive" Nelson (I) |
| Sammuel Sanes (D) *Vice Chair* | Nellie Rivera-O'Reilly (I) |
| Marvin A. Blyden (D) | |
| Novelle E. Francis, Jr. (D) | |
| Kenneth L. Gittens (D) | |

### Economic Development, Agriculture and Planning

| Majority Members | Minority Members |
| --- | --- |
| Janette Millin Young (D) *Chair* | Almando "Rocky" Liburd (I) |
| Novelle E. Francis, Jr. (D) | Nellie Rivera-O'Reilly (I) |
| *Vice Chair* | Tregenza Roach (I) |
| Clifford F. Graham (D) | |
| Myron D. Jackson (D) | |
| Neville A. James (D) | |
| Kurt Vialet (D) | |

### Education and Workforce Development

| Majority Members | Minority Members |
| --- | --- |
| Jean Forde (D) *Chair* | Terrence "Positive" Nelson (I) |
| Kurt Vialet (D) *Vice Chair* | Tregenza Roach (I) |
| Kenneth L. Gittens (D) | |
| Justin Harrigan, Sr. (D) | |
| Myron D. Jackson (D) | |

## Energy and Environment Protection

| Majority Members | Minority Members |
| --- | --- |
| Sammuel Sanes (D) *Chair* | Almando "Rocky" Liburd (I) |
| Marvin A. Blyden (D) *Vice Chair* | Terrence "Positive" Nelson (I) |
| Clifford F. Graham (D) | |
| Kurt Vialet (D) | |
| Janette Millin Young (D) | |

## Finance

| Majority Members | Minority Members |
| --- | --- |
| Clifford F. Graham (D) *Chair* | Terrence "Positive" Nelson (I) |
| Kurt Vialet (D) *Vice Chair* | Tregenza Roach (I) |
| Marvin A. Blyden (D) | |
| Myron D. Jackson (D) | |
| Sammuel Sanes (D) | |

## Health, Hospitals, and Human Services

| Majority Members | Minority Members |
| --- | --- |
| Kurt Vialet (D) *Chair* | Almando "Rocky" Liburd (I) |
| Justin Harrigan, Sr. (D) *Vice Chair* | Nellie Rivera-O'Reilly (I) |
| Marvin A. Blyden (D) | |
| Jean Forde (D) | |
| Novelle E. Francis, Jr. (D) | |

## Homeland Security, Public Safety, and Justice

| Majority Members | Minority Members |
| --- | --- |
| Novelle E. Francis, Jr. (D) *Chair* | Almando "Rocky" Liburd (I) |
| Kenneth L. Gittens (D) *Vice Chair* | Nellie Rivera-O'Reilly (I) |
| Jean Forde (D) | |
| Justin Harrigan, Sr. (D) | |
| Sammuel Sanes (D) | |

## Housing, Public Works, and Waste Management

| Majority Members | Minority Members |
| --- | --- |
| Marvin A. Blyden (D) *Chair* | Almando "Rocky" Liburd (I) |
| Clifford F. Graham (D) *Vice Chair* | Tregenza Roach (I) |
| Jean Forde (D) | |
| Kenneth L. Gittens (D) | |
| Neville A. James (D) | |

## Rules and Judiciary

| Majority Members | Minority Members |
| --- | --- |
| Kenneth L. Gittens (D) *Chair* | Nellie Rivera-O'Reilly (I) |
| Janette Millin Young (D) *Vice Chair* | |
| Novelle E. Francis, Jr. (D) | |
| Justin Harrigan, Sr. (D) | |
| Neville A. James (D) | |

## Veterans' Affairs

| Majority Members | Minority Members |
| --- | --- |
| Justin Harrigan, Sr. (D) *Chair* | Terrence "Positive" Nelson (I) |
| Myron D. Jackson (D) *Vice Chair* | Tregenza Roach (I) |
| Neville A. James (D) | |
| Sammuel Sanes (D) | |
| Janette Millin Young (D) | |

# Virginia General Assembly

P.O. Box 396, Richmond, VA 23218

## Virginia Senate

P.O. Box 396, Richmond, VA 23218
Tel: (804) 698-7410  Tel: (804) 698-7460 (Senate Support Services)
TTY: (804) 698-7419  Fax: (804) 698-7651

President of the Senate **Ralph S. Northam** (D) . . . . . . . . . (804) 786-2078
  E-mail: ltgov@ltgov.virginia.gov
  Education: VMI BS; Eastern Virginia Medical 1984 MD
President Pro Tem **Stephen D. Newman** (R) . . . . . . . . . . (804) 698-7523
  Education: Lynchburg
Majority Leader **Thomas K. Norment, Jr.** (R) . . . . . . . . . (804) 698-7503
  Education: VMI BA; William & Mary JD
Majority Whip **William M. "Bill" Stanley, Jr.** (R) . . . . . . . (804) 698-7520
  Education: Hampden-Sydney BS; UDC JD
Majority Caucus Chairman **Ryan T. McDougle** (R) . . . . . . (804) 698-7504
  Education: James Madison BS, BA; William & Mary JD
Majority Caucus Vice Chairman
  **Stephen D. Newman** (R) . . . . . . . . . . . . . . . . . . . . . (804) 698-7523
Minority Leader **Richard Lawrence "Dick" Saslaw** (D) . . (804) 698-7535
  Education: Maryland BSE
Minority Whip **John S. Edwards** (D) . . . . . . . . . . . . . . . (804) 698-7521
  Education: Princeton 1966 AB; Virginia 1970 JD
Minority Whip **Janet D. Howell** (D) . . . . . . . . . . . . . . . (804) 698-7532
  Education: Oberlin BA; Pennsylvania 1968 AM
Minority Caucus Chairman **A. Donald McEachin** (D) . . . . . (804) 698-7509
  Education: American U 1982 BS; Virginia 1986 JD;
  Virginia Union 2008 MDiv
Minority Caucus Vice Chair
  **John Chapman "Chap" Petersen** (D) . . . . . . . . . . . . . (804) 698-7534
  Education: Williams BA; Virginia JD
Clerk of the Senate **Susan Clarke Schaar** . . . . . . . . . . . . (804) 698-7400
  E-mail: sschaar@senate.virginia.gov

## Senators

**Party Affiliation Statistics:** Republicans: 21, Democrats: 18,
Vacancies: 1

Senator
  **Kenneth Cooper "Kenny" Alexander** (D-District 5) . . . (804) 698-7505
  Independent Cities Represented: Chesapeake (part),      Dist: (757) 223-1333
  Norfolk (part)
  Note: On May 3, 2016, Senator Kenneth Alexander was elected Mayor
  of the City of Norfolk, Virginia. Senator Alexander will depart from
  the Virginia Senate effective June 30, 2016.
  Term Expires: 2020
  120 West Berkley Avenue, Norfolk, VA 23523
  E-mail: district05@senate.virginia.gov
  Committees: Commerce and Labor; Finance; Transportation
  Education: Old Dominion BS; Norwich MA
Senator **George L. Barker** (D-District 39) . . . . . . . . . . . . (804) 698-7539
  Counties Represented: Fairfax (part), Prince William    Dist: (703) 303-1426
  (part)
  Independent Cities Represented: Alexandria (part), Alexandria (part)
  Term Expires: 2020
  P.O. Box 10527, Alexandria, VA 22310
  E-mail: district39@senate.virginia.gov
  Committees: Education and Health; Finance; General Laws and
  Technology
  Education: Harvard MS
Senator **Richard H. "Dick" Black** (R-District 13) . . . . . . . . (804) 698-7513
  Counties Represented: Loudoun (part), Prince         Dist: (703) 406-2951
  William (part)
  Term Expires: 2020
  P.O. Box 3026, Leesburg, VA 20177
  E-mail: district13@senate.virginia.gov
  Committees: Agriculture, Conservation and Natural Resources;
  Commerce and Labor; Education and Health; General Laws and
  Technology; Rehabilitation and Social Services
Senator **Charles W. "Bill" Carrico, Sr.** (R-District 40) . . . . (804) 698-7540
  Counties Represented: Grayson, Lee, Scott, Smyth      Dist: (276) 236-0098
  (part), Washington, Wise (part), Wythe (part)
  Independent Cities Represented: Bristol
  Term Expires: 2020
  PO Box 1100, Galax, VA 24333
  E-mail: district40@senate.virginia.gov
  Committees: Education and Health; Finance; Rules; Transportation

Senator **A. Benton "Ben" Chafin, Jr.** (R-District 38) . . . . (804) 698-7538
  Counties Represented: Bland, Buchanan, Dickenson,     Dist: (276) 889-1044
  Montgomery (part), Pulaski, Russell, Smyth (part), Tazewell, Wise
  (part)
  Independent Cities Represented: Norton, Radford
  Term Expires: 2020
  E-mail: district38@senate.virginia.gov
  Committees: Agriculture, Conservation and Natural Resources;
  Commerce and Labor; Courts of Justice; Privileges and Elections;
  Rehabilitation and Social Services
  Education: East Tennessee State 1982 BA; Richmond 1985 JD
Senator **Amanda F. Chase** (R-District 11) . . . . . . . . . . . . (804) 698-7511
  Counties Represented: Amelia, Chesterfield (part)     Dist: (804) 212-2005
  Independent Cities Represented: Colonial Heights
  Term Expires: 2020
  P.O. Box 5811, Midlothian, VA 23112
  E-mail: district11@senate.virginia.gov
  Committees: Education and Health; Local Government; Privileges and
  Elections; Transportation
Senator **John A. Cosgrove, Jr.** (R-District 14) . . . . . . . . . (804) 698-7514
  Counties Represented: Isle of Wight (part),          Dist: (757) 547-3422
  Southampton (part)                                   Fax: (804) 698-7651
  Independent Cities Represented: Chesapeake (part), Franklin (part),
  Portsmouth (part), Suffolk (part), Virginia Beach (part)
  Term Expires: 2020
  P.O. Box 15483, Chesapeake, VA 23328
  E-mail: district14@senate.virginia.gov
  Committees: Commerce and Labor; Education and Health; Local
  Government; Rehabilitation and Social Services; Transportation
  Education: Old Dominion 1985 BS
Senator **Rosalyn R. "Roz" Dance** (D-District 16) . . . . . . . (804) 698-7516
  Counties Represented: Chesterfield (part),           Dist: (804) 862-2922
  Dinwiddie (part), Prince George (part)
  Independent Cities Represented: Hopewell, Petersburg, Richmond (part)
  Term Expires: 2020
  E-mail: district16@senate.virginia.gov
  Committees: Agriculture, Conservation and Natural Resources;
  Commerce and Labor; Rehabilitation and Social Services; Rules
  Education: Virginia State 1986 BS; VCU 1994 MPA
Senator **R. Creigh Deeds** (D-District 25) . . . . . . . . . . . . (804) 698-7525
  Counties Represented: Albemarle (part), Alleghany,   Dist: (434) 296-5491
  Bath, Highland, Nelson, Rockbridge                   (Charlottesville)
  Independent Cities Represented: Buena Vista,         Dist: (540) 839-2473
  Charlottesville, Covington, Lexington                (Hot Springs)
  Term Expires: 2020                                   Fax: (434) 296-5949
  P.O. Box 5462, Charlottesville, VA 22905-5462        (Charlottesville)
  PO Drawer D, Hot Springs, VA 24445                   Fax: (540) 839-6306
  E-mail: district25@senate.virginia.gov              (Hot Springs)
  Committees: Courts of Justice; Privileges and Elections; Transportation
  Education: Concord Col 1980 BA; Wake Forest 1984 JD
Senator **William R. "Bill" DeSteph, Jr.** (R-District 8) . . . . (804) 698-7508
  Independent Cities Represented: Virginia Beach       Dist: (757) 321-8180
  (part)                                               Fax: (757) 631-6150
  Term Expires: 2020
  588 Central Drive, Virginia Beach, VA 23454
  E-mail: district08@senate.virginia.gov
  Committees: General Laws and Technology; Local Government;
  Privileges and Elections; Rehabilitation and Social Services;
  Transportation
  Education: Maryland 1994 BS
Senator **Siobhan S. Dunnavant** (R-District 12) . . . . . . . . (804) 698-7512
  Counties Represented: Hanover (part), Henrico        Dist: (804) 601-8151
  (part)
  Term Expires: 2020
  P.O. Box 70849, Henrico, VA 23255
  E-mail: district12@senate.virginia.gov
  Committees: Education and Health; Finance; Local Government
Senator **Adam P. Ebbin** (D-District 30) . . . . . . . . . . . . . . (804) 698-7530
  Counties Represented: Arlington (part), Fairfax      Dist: (571) 384-8957
  (part)
  Independent Cities Represented: Alexandria (part)
  Term Expires: 2020
  PO Box 26415, Alexandria, VA 22313
  E-mail: district30@senate.virginia.gov
  Committees: Agriculture, Conservation and Natural Resources; General
  Laws and Technology; Privileges and Elections
  Education: American U 1985 BA

Senator **John S. Edwards** (D-District 21) . . . . . . . . . . . . . (804) 698-7521
Counties Represented: Giles, Montgomery (part),   Dist: (540) 985-8690
Roanoke (part)   Fax: (540) 345-9950
Independent Cities Represented: Roanoke
Term Expires: 2020
P.O. Box 1179, Roanoke, VA 24006-1179
E-mail: district21@senate.virginia.gov
Committees: Courts of Justice; Privileges and Elections; Transportation

Senator **Barbara A. Favola** (D-District 31) . . . . . . . . . . . . (804) 698-7531
Counties Represented: Arlington (part), Fairfax   Dist: (703) 835-4845
(part), Loudoun (part)
Term Expires: 2020
2319 18th Street North, Arlington, VA 22201-3506
E-mail: district31@senate.virginia.gov
Committees: Local Government; Rehabilitation and Social Services;
Transportation
Education: St Joseph's Col (NY) 1977 BS; NYU 1980 MPA

Senator **Thomas A. "Tom" Garrett, Jr.** (R-District 22) . . . (804) 698-7522
Counties Represented: Amherst, Appomattox,   Dist: (434) 944-7770
Buckingham, Cumberland, Fluvanna, Goochland, Louisa (part), Prince
Edward
Independent Cities Represented: Lynchburg (part)
Term Expires: 2020
PO Box 66, Hadensville, VA 23067
E-mail: district22@senate.virginia.gov
Committees: Courts of Justice; Education and Health; General Laws
and Technology; Privileges and Elections; Transportation
Education: Richmond BA, JD

Senator **Emmett W. Hanger, Jr.** (R-District 24) . . . . . . . . (804) 698-7524
Counties Represented: Augusta, Culpeper (part),   Dist: (540) 885-6898
Greene, Madison, Rockingham (part)
Independent Cities Represented: Staunton, Waynesboro
Term Expires: 2020
P.O. Box 2, Mount Solon, VA 22843-0002
E-mail: district24@senate.virginia.gov
Committees: Agriculture, Conservation and Natural Resources; Finance;
Local Government; Rehabilitation and Social Services; Rules
Education: James Madison BS, MBA

Senator **Janet D. Howell** (D-District 32) . . . . . . . . . . . . . (804) 698-7532
Counties Represented: Arlington (part), Fairfax   Dist: (703) 709-8283
(part)
Term Expires: 2020
P.O. Box 2608, Reston, VA 20195-0608
E-mail: senhowell@gmail.com
E-mail: district32@senate.virginia.gov
Committees: Courts of Justice; Education and Health; Finance;
Privileges and Elections

Senator **Lynwood W. Lewis, Jr.** (D-District 6) . . . . . . . . . (804) 698-7506
Counties Represented: Accomack, Mathews,   Dist: (757) 787-1094
Northampton   Fax: (757) 787-2749
Independent Cities Represented: Norfolk (part), Virginia Beach (part)
Term Expires: 2020
P.O. Box 760, Accomac, VA 23301
E-mail: district06@senate.virginia.gov
Committees: Agriculture, Conservation and Natural Resources; Local
Government
Education: Hampden-Sydney 1984 BA; Richmond 1988 JD

Senator **Dr. Mamie E. Locke** (D-District 2) . . . . . . . . . . . (804) 698-7502
Counties Represented: York (part)   Dist: (757) 825-5880
Independent Cities Represented: Hampton (part),   Fax: (757) 825-7327
Newport News (part), Portsmouth (part)
Term Expires: 2020
P.O. Box 9048, Hampton, VA 23670
E-mail: district02@senate.virginia.gov
Committees: Education and Health; General Laws and Technology;
Rehabilitation and Social Services; Rules
Education: Tougaloo BA; Atlanta MA, PhD

Senator **L. Louise Lucas** (D-District 18) . . . . . . . . . . . . . (804) 698-7518
Counties Represented: Brunswick (part),   Dist: (757) 397-8209
Greensville, Isle of Wight (part), Southampton   Fax: (757) 966-9671
(part), Surry (part), Sussex
Independent Cities Represented: Chesapeake (part), Emporia, Franklin
(part), Portsmouth (part), Suffolk (part)
Term Expires: 2020
P.O. Box 700, Portsmouth, VA 23705-0700
E-mail: senlucas@aol.com
E-mail: district18@senate.virginia.gov
Committees: Commerce and Labor; Courts of Justice; Education and
Health; Finance
Education: Norfolk State BS, MA

Senator **David W. "Dave" Marsden** (D-District 37) . . . . . (804) 698-7537
Counties Represented: Fairfax (part)   Dist: (571) 249-3037
Term Expires: 2020
P.O. Box 10889, Burke, VA 22009
E-mail: district37@senate.virginia.gov
Committees: Agriculture, Conservation and Natural Resources;
Transportation
Education: Randolph-Macon

Senator **Ryan T. McDougle** (R-District 4) . . . . . . . . . . . . (804) 698-7504
Counties Represented: Caroline, Essex, Hanover   Dist: (804) 730-1026
(part), King George (part), Lancaster, Middlesex,   Fax: (804) 730-1051
Northumberland, Richmond, Spotsylvania (part), Westmoreland (part)
Term Expires: 2020
P.O. Box 187, Mechanicsville, VA 23111
E-mail: district04@senate.virginia.gov
Committees: Commerce and Labor; Courts of Justice; Finance;
Rehabilitation and Social Services; Rules

Senator **A. Donald McEachin** (D-District 9) . . . . . . . . . . . (804) 698-7509
Counties Represented: Hanover (part), Henrico   Dist: (804) 226-4111
(part)   Fax: (804) 226-8888
Independent Cities Represented: Richmond (part)
Term Expires: 2020
4719 Nine Mile Road, Richmond, VA 23223
E-mail: district09@senate.virginia.gov
Committees: Agriculture, Conservation and Natural Resources; Courts
of Justice; Privileges and Elections

Senator **Jeremy McPike** (D-District 29) . . . . . . . . . . . . . . (804) 698-7529
Counties Represented: Prince William (part)   Dist: (571) 316-0581
Independent Cities Represented: Manassas, Manassas Park
Term Expires: 2020
P.O. Box 2819, Woodbridge, VA 22195
E-mail: district29@senate.virginia.gov
Committees: General Laws and Technology; Local Government;
Rehabilitation and Social Services

Senator **Stephen D. Newman** (R-District 23) . . . . . . . . . . (804) 698-7523
Counties Represented: Bedford (part), Botetourt,   Dist: (434) 385-1065
Campbell (part), Craig, Roanoke (part)   Fax: (434) 485-8111
Independent Cities Represented: Bedford, Lynchburg (part)
Term Expires: 2020
P.O. Box 480, Forest, VA 24551
E-mail: district23@senate.virginia.gov
Committees: Commerce and Labor; Education and Health; Finance;
Rules; Transportation

Senator **Thomas K. Norment, Jr.** (R-District 3) . . . . . . . . (804) 698-7503
Counties Represented: Gloucester, Isle of Wight   Dist: (757) 259-7810
(part), James City (part), King and Queen, King   Fax: (757) 259-7812
William, New Kent, Surry (part), York (part)
Independent Cities Represented: Hampton (part), Poquoson, Suffolk
(part)
Term Expires: 2020
P.O. Box 6205, Williamsburg, VA 23188
E-mail: district03@senate.virginia.gov
Committees: Commerce and Labor; Courts of Justice; Finance; Rules

Senator **Mark D. Obenshain** (R-District 26) . . . . . . . . . . . (804) 698-7526
Counties Represented: Page, Rappahannock,   Dist: (540) 437-1451
Rockingham (part), Shenandoah, Warren   Fax: (540) 437-3101
Independent Cities Represented: Harrisonburg
Term Expires: 2020
P.O. Box 555, Harrisonburg, VA 22803
E-mail: district26@senate.virginia.gov
Committees: Agriculture, Conservation and Natural Resources;
Commerce and Labor; Courts of Justice; Finance; Rules
Education: Virginia Tech 1984 BA; Washington and Lee 1987 JD

Senator
**John Chapman "Chap" Petersen** (D-District 34) . . . . . (804) 698-7534
Counties Represented: Fairfax (part)   Dist: (703) 349-3361
Independent Cities Represented: Fairfax   Fax: (800) 635-9417
Term Expires: 2020
P.O. Box 1066, Fairfax, VA 22038
E-mail: district34@senate.virginia.gov
Committees: Agriculture, Conservation and Natural Resources;
Education and Health; General Laws and Technology; Rehabilitation
and Social Services

Senator **Bryce E. Reeves** (R-District 17) . . . . . . . . . . . . . (804) 698-7517
Counties Represented: Albemarle (part), Culpeper   Dist: (540) 645-8440
(part), Louisa (part), Orange, Spotsylvania (part)
Independent Cities Represented: Fredericksburg
Term Expires: 2020
PO Box 7021, Fredericksburg, VA 22404
E-mail: district17@senate.virginia.gov
Committees: Courts of Justice; General Laws and Technology;
Privileges and Elections; Rehabilitation and Social Services; Rules
Education: Texas A&M BS; George Mason 1999 MPA

*(continued on next page)*

**Senators** *continued*

Senator **Frank M. Ruff, Jr.** (R-District 15) . . . . . . . . . . . . . (804) 698-7515
Counties Represented: Brunswick (part), Campbell    Dist: (434) 374-5129
(part), Dinwiddie (part), Halifax (part), Lunenburg,    Fax: (434) 955-2224
Mecklenburg, Nottoway, Pittsylvania (part), Prince George (part)
Independent Cities Represented: Danville (part)
Term Expires: 2020
P.O. Box 332, Clarksville, VA 23927
E-mail: district15@senate.virginia.gov
Committees: Agriculture, Conservation and Natural Resources; Finance;
General Laws and Technology; Rules
Affiliation: President, Brentwood Manor Furnishings
Education: Richmond

Senator
**Richard Lawrence "Dick" Saslaw** (D-District 35) . . . . . (804) 698-7535
Counties Represented: Fairfax (part)    Dist: (703) 978-0200
Independent Cities Represented: Alexandria (part),    Fax: (703) 978-3032
Falls Church
Term Expires: 2020
P.O. Box 1856, Springfield, VA 22151-0856
E-mail: district35@senate.virginia.gov
Committees: Commerce and Labor; Courts of Justice; Education and
Health; Finance; Rules

Senator **William M. "Bill" Stanley, Jr.** (R-District 20) . . . . (804) 698-7520
Counties Represented: Carroll (part), Franklin    Dist: (540) 721-6028
(part), Halifax (part), Henry, Patrick, Pittsylvania    Fax: (540) 721-6405
(part)
Independent Cities Represented: Danville (part), Galax, Martinsville
Term Expires: 2020
13508 Booker T Washington Highway, Moneta, VA 24121
E-mail: district20@senate.virginia.gov
Committees: Agriculture, Conservation and Natural Resources;
Commerce and Labor; Courts of Justice; Local Government; Rules

Senator **Richard H. Stuart** (R-District 28) . . . . . . . . . . . . . (804) 698-7528
Counties Represented: King George (part), Prince    Dist: (804) 493-8892
William (part), Spotsylvania (part), Stafford (part),    Fax: (804) 493-8897
Westmoreland (part)
Term Expires: 2020
P.O. Box 1146, Montross, VA 22520
E-mail: district28@senate.virginia.gov
Committees: Agriculture, Conservation and Natural Resources;
Commerce and Labor; Courts of Justice; General Laws and
Technology; Rules
Education: Virginia Wesleyan BA

Senator **Glen H. Sturtevant, Jr.** (R-District 10) . . . . . . . . . (804) 698-7510
Counties Represented: Chesterfield (part), Powhatan    Dist: (804) 601-4046
Independent Cities Represented: Richmond (part)
Term Expires: 2020
P.O. Box 2535, Midlothian, VA 23113
E-mail: district10@senate.virginia.gov
Committees: Commerce and Labor; Courts of Justice; Local
Government; Privileges and Elections

Senator **David R. Suetterlein** (R-District 19) . . . . . . . . . . . (804) 698-7519
Counties Represented: Bedford (part), Carroll (part),    Dist: (540) 302-8486
Floyd, Franklin (part), Montgomery (part), Roanoke (part), Wythe
(part)
Independent Cities Represented: Salem
Term Expires: 2020
P.O. Box 20237, Roanoke, VA 24018
E-mail: district19@senate.virginia.gov
Committees: Agriculture, Conservation and Natural Resources;
Education and Health; General Laws and Technology; Transportation

Senator **Scott A. Surovell** (D-District 36) . . . . . . . . . . . . . (804) 698-7536
Counties Represented: Fairfax (part), Prince William    Dist: (571) 249-4484
(part), Stafford (part)    Fax: (571) 542-3741
Term Expires: 2020
P.O. Box 289, Mount Vernon, VA 22121
E-mail: district36@senate.virginia.gov
Committees: General Laws and Technology; Local Government;
Rehabilitation and Social Services
Education: James Madison 1993 BA; Virginia 1996 JD

Senator **Jill Holtzman Vogel** (R-District 27) . . . . . . . . . . . (804) 698-7527
Counties Represented: Clarke, Culpeper (part),    Dist: (540) 662-4551
Fauquier, Frederick, Loudoun (part), Stafford (part)    Fax: (540) 341-8809
Independent Cities Represented: Winchester
Term Expires: 2020
117 East Piccadilly Street, Suite 100-A, Winchester, VA 22601
E-mail: district27@senate.virginia.gov
Committees: Finance; General Laws and Technology; Privileges and
Elections; Rules
Education: William & Mary 1992 BA; DePaul 1995 JD

Senator **Frank W. Wagner** (R-District 7) . . . . . . . . . . . . . . (804) 698-7507
Independent Cities Represented: Norfolk (part),    Dist: (757) 228-3333
Virginia Beach (part)    Fax: (757) 244-7866
Term Expires: 2020
P.O. Box 68008, Virginia Beach, VA 23471
E-mail: district07@senate.virginia.gov
Committees: Commerce and Labor; Finance; Rehabilitation and Social
Services; Rules
Education: Naval Acad BS

Senator **Jennifer T. Wexton** (D-District 33) . . . . . . . . . . . . (804) 698-7533
Counties Represented: Fairfax (part), Loudoun    Dist: (703) 672-3696
(part)
Term Expires: 2020
20 West Market Street, Leesburg, VA 20176
E-mail: district33@senate.virginia.gov
Committees: General Laws and Technology; Rehabilitation and Social
Services; Transportation
Education: Maryland; William & Mary 1995 JD

District 1 **(Vacant)** . . . . . . . . . . . . . . . . . . . . . . . . . . . . . . . (804) 698-7410
Note: A special election to fill this legislative vacancy will be held on
November 8, 2016.

## Senate Standing Committees
Fax: (804) 698-7671

## Agriculture, Conservation and Natural Resources
Tel: (804) 698-7450

| **Majority Members** | **Minority Members** |
| --- | --- |
| Richard H. Stuart (R-28) *Chair* | Rosalyn R. "Roz" Dance (D-16) |
| Richard H. "Dick" Black (R-13) | Adam P. Ebbin (D-30) |
| A. Benton "Ben" Chafin, Jr. (R-38) | Lynwood W. Lewis, Jr. (D-6) |
| Emmett W. Hanger, Jr. (R-24) | David W. "Dave" Marsden (D-37) |
| Mark D. Obenshain (R-26) | A. Donald McEachin (D-9) |
| Frank M. Ruff, Jr. (R-15) | John Chapman "Chap" Petersen |
| William M. "Bill" Stanley, Jr. | (D-34) |
| (R-20) | |
| David R. Suetterlein (R-19) | |

## Commerce and Labor
Tel: (804) 698-7450

| **Majority Members** | **Minority Members** |
| --- | --- |
| Frank W. Wagner (R-7) *Chair* | Kenneth Cooper "Kenny" |
| Richard H. "Dick" Black (R-13) | Alexander (D-5) |
| A. Benton "Ben" Chafin, Jr. (R-38) | Rosalyn R. "Roz" Dance (D-16) |
| John A. Cosgrove, Jr. (R-14) | L. Louise Lucas (D-18) |
| Ryan T. McDougle (R-4) | Richard Lawrence "Dick" Saslaw |
| Stephen D. Newman (R-23) | (D-35) |
| Thomas K. Norment, Jr. (R-3) | |
| Mark D. Obenshain (R-26) | |
| William M. "Bill" Stanley, Jr. | |
| (R-20) | |
| Richard H. Stuart (R-28) | |
| Glen H. Sturtevant, Jr. (R-10) | |

## Courts of Justice
Tel: (804) 698-7450

| **Majority Members** | **Minority Members** |
| --- | --- |
| Mark D. Obenshain (R-26) *Chair* | R. Creigh Deeds (D-25) |
| A. Benton "Ben" Chafin, Jr. (R-38) | John S. Edwards (D-21) |
| Thomas A. "Tom" Garrett, Jr. | Janet D. Howell (D-32) |
| (R-22) | L. Louise Lucas (D-18) |
| Ryan T. McDougle (R-4) | A. Donald McEachin (D-9) |
| Thomas K. Norment, Jr. (R-3) | Richard Lawrence "Dick" Saslaw |
| Bryce E. Reeves (R-17) | (D-35) |
| William M. "Bill" Stanley, Jr. | |
| (R-20) | |
| Richard H. Stuart (R-28) | |
| Glen H. Sturtevant, Jr. (R-10) | |

LEGISLATIVE BRANCH

## Education and Health

Tel: (804) 698-7450

**Majority Members**
Stephen D. Newman (R-23) *Chair*
Richard H. "Dick" Black (R-13)
Charles W. "Bill" Carrico, Sr.
  (R-40)
Amanda F. Chase (R-11)
John A. Cosgrove, Jr. (R-14)
Siobhan S. Dunnavant (R-12)
Thomas A. "Tom" Garrett, Jr.
  (R-22)
David R. Suetterlein (R-19)

**Minority Members**
George L. Barker (D-39)
Janet D. Howell (D-32)
Dr. Mamie E. Locke (D-2)
L. Louise Lucas (D-18)
John Chapman "Chap" Petersen
  (D-34)
Richard Lawrence "Dick" Saslaw
  (D-35)

## Finance

Tel: (804) 698-7480

**Majority Members**
Emmett W. Hanger, Jr. (R-24)
  *Co-Chair*
Thomas K. Norment, Jr. (R-3)
  *Co-Chair*
Charles W. "Bill" Carrico, Sr.
  (R-40)
Siobhan S. Dunnavant (R-12)
Ryan T. McDougle (R-4)
Stephen D. Newman (R-23)
Mark D. Obenshain (R-26)
Frank M. Ruff, Jr. (R-15)
Jill Holtzman Vogel (R-27)
Frank W. Wagner (R-7)

**Minority Members**
Kenneth Cooper "Kenny"
  Alexander (D-5)
George L. Barker (D-39)
Janet D. Howell (D-32)
L. Louise Lucas (D-18)
Richard Lawrence "Dick" Saslaw
  (D-35)

## General Laws and Technology

Tel: (804) 698-7450

**Majority Members**
Frank M. Ruff, Jr. (R-15) *Chair*
Richard H. "Dick" Black (R-13)
William R. "Bill" DeSteph, Jr.
  (R-8)
Thomas A. "Tom" Garrett, Jr.
  (R-22)
Bryce E. Reeves (R-17)
Richard H. Stuart (R-28)
Jill Holtzman Vogel (R-27)
David R. Suetterlein (R-19)

**Minority Members**
George L. Barker (D-39)
Adam P. Ebbin (D-30)
Dr. Mamie E. Locke (D-2)
Jeremy McPike (D-29)
John Chapman "Chap" Petersen
  (D-34)
Scott A. Surovell (D-36)
Jennifer T. Wexton (D-33)

## Local Government

Tel: (804) 698-7450

**Majority Members**
William M. "Bill"
  Stanley, Jr. (R-20)
  *Chair*
Amanda F. Chase (R-11)
John A. Cosgrove, Jr. (R-14)
William R. "Bill" DeSteph, Jr.
  (R-8)
Siobhan S. Dunnavant (R-12)
Emmett W. Hanger, Jr. (R-24)
Glen H. Sturtevant, Jr. (R-10)

**Minority Members**
Lynwood W. Lewis, Jr. (D-6)
Barbara A. Favola (D-31)
Jeremy McPike (D-29)
Scott A. Surovell (D-36)

## Privileges and Elections

Tel: (804) 698-7450

**Majority Members**
Jill Holtzman Vogel (R-27) *Chair*
A. Benton "Ben" Chafin, Jr. (R-38)
Amanda F. Chase (R-11)
William R. "Bill" DeSteph, Jr.
  (R-8)
Thomas A. "Tom" Garrett, Jr.
  (R-22)
Bryce E. Reeves (R-17)
Glen H. Sturtevant, Jr. (R-10)

**Minority Members**
R. Creigh Deeds (D-25)
Adam P. Ebbin (D-30)
John S. Edwards (D-21)
Janet D. Howell (D-32)
A. Donald McEachin (D-9)

## Rehabilitation and Social Services

Tel: (804) 698-7450

**Majority Members**
Bryce E. Reeves (R-17) *Chair*
Richard H. "Dick" Black (R-13)
A. Benton "Ben" Chafin, Jr. (R-38)
John A. Cosgrove, Jr. (R-14)
William R. "Bill" DeSteph, Jr.
  (R-8)
Emmett W. Hanger, Jr. (R-24)
Ryan T. McDougle (R-4)
Frank W. Wagner (R-7)

**Minority Members**
Rosalyn R. "Roz" Dance (D-16)
Barbara A. Favola (D-31)
Dr. Mamie E. Locke (D-2)
Jeremy McPike (D-29)
John Chapman "Chap" Petersen
  (D-34)
Scott A. Surovell (D-36)
Jennifer T. Wexton (D-33)

## Rules

Tel: (804) 698-7450

**Majority Members**
Ryan T. McDougle (R-4) *Chair*
Charles W. "Bill" Carrico, Sr.
  (R-40)
Emmett W. Hanger, Jr. (R-24)
Stephen D. Newman (R-23)
Thomas K. Norment, Jr. (R-3)
Mark D. Obenshain (R-26)
Bryce E. Reeves (R-17)
Frank M. Ruff, Jr. (R-15)
William M. "Bill" Stanley, Jr.
  (R-20)
Richard H. Stuart (R-28)
Jill Holtzman Vogel (R-27)
Frank W. Wagner (R-7)

**Minority Members**
Rosalyn R. "Roz" Dance (D-16)
Dr. Mamie E. Locke (D-2)
Richard Lawrence "Dick" Saslaw
  (D-35)

## Transportation

Tel: (804) 698-7450

**Majority Members**
Charles W. "Bill"
  Carrico, Sr. (R-40)
  *Chair*
Amanda F. Chase (R-11)
John A. Cosgrove, Jr. (R-14)
William R. "Bill" DeSteph, Jr.
  (R-8)
Thomas A. "Tom" Garrett, Jr.
  (R-22)
Stephen D. Newman (R-23)
David R. Suetterlein (R-19)

**Minority Members**
Kenneth Cooper "Kenny"
  Alexander (D-5)
R. Creigh Deeds (D-25)
John S. Edwards (D-21)
Barbara A. Favola (D-31)
David W. "Dave" Marsden (D-37)
Jennifer T. Wexton (D-33)

# Virginia House of Delegates

P.O. Box 406, Richmond, VA 23218
Tel: (804) 698-1500  Tel: (877) 391-3228 (Toll Free)
TTY: (804) 786-2369  Fax: (804) 786-6310
E-mail: hinformation@house.state.vt.us

Speaker of the House **William J. "Bill" Howell** (R) . . . . . . (804) 698-1028
  Began Service: 1988
  Education: Richmond BS; Virginia JD
Majority Leader **M. Kirkland "Kirk" Cox** (R) . . . . . . . . . . (804) 698-1066
  Education: James Madison 1979 BS
Majority Caucus Chairman
  **Timothy D. "Tim" Hugo** (R) . . . . . . . . . . . . . . . . . . . . . . (804) 698-1040
  Education: William & Mary 1986 BA
Majority Whip **Jackson H. Miller** (R) . . . . . . . . . . . . . . . (804) 698-1050
  Education: VCU 1990 BS
Minority Leader **David J. Toscano** (D). . . . . . . . . . . . . . . .(804) 698-1057
  Education: Colgate 1968 BA; Boston Col 1972 MA; Virginia 1986 JD
Minority Caucus Chairman **Mark D. Sickles** (D) . . . . . . . . (804) 698-1043
Minority Caucus First Vice Chair
  **Jennifer L. "Jenn" McClellan** (D) . . . . . . . . . . . . . . . . (804) 698-1071
  Education: Richmond 1994 BA; Virginia 1997 JD
Minority Caucus Secretary **Betsy B. Carr** (D) . . . . . . . . . . (804) 698-1069
  Education: Hollins Col 1968 BA
Minority Caucus Treasurer **Jeion A. Ward** (D) . . . . . . . . . (804) 698-1092
Minority Caucus Sergeant at Arms
  **Rev. Delores L. McQuinn** (D) . . . . . . . . . . . . . . . . . . . . . (804) 698-1070
  Education: VCU; Virginia Union
Clerk of the House **Gary Paul Nardo** . . . . . . . . . . . . . . . . . (804) 698-1619
  E-mail: gpnardo@house.virginia.gov
  Education: William & Mary 1988 BA; VCU; Bristol U

*(continued on next page)*

LEGISLATIVE BRANCH

**Virginia House of Delegates** *continued*

Chief Technology Officer **Sharon A. Crouch Steidel** . . . (804) 698-1561
E-mail: scrouchsteidel@house.virginia.gov

# Delegates

**Party Affiliation Statistics:** Republicans: 66, Democrats: 34

Delegate **Leslie R. "Les" Adams** (R-District 16) . . . . . . . . (804) 698-1016
Counties Represented: Henry (part), Pittsylvania          Dist: (434) 432-2531
(part)
Independent Cities Represented: Martinsville
Term Expires: 2018
P.O. Box 459, Chatham, VA 24531
E-mail: delladams@house.virginia.gov
Committees: Courts of Justice; Privileges and Elections; Science and
Technology; Transportation
Education: Liberty 1996 BS; Richmond 1999 JD

Delegate **Lashrecse D. Aird** (D-District 63) . . . . . . . . . . . . (804) 698-1500
Counties Represented: Chesterfield (part), Dinwiddie (part), Prince
George (part)
Independent Cities Represented: Hopewell (part), Petersburg
Term Expires: 2018
E-mail: dellaird@house.virginia.gov
Committees: Finance; General Laws; Health, Welfare and Institutions

Delegate **David B. "Dave" Albo** (R-District 42) . . . . . . . . (804) 698-1042
Counties Represented: Fairfax (part)          Dist: (703) 451-3555
Term Expires: 2018          Fax: (804) 698-6742
6367 Rolling Mill Place, Suite 102, Springfield, VA 22152
E-mail: deldalbo@house.virginia.gov
Committees: Courts of Justice; General Laws; Privileges and Elections
Education: Virginia 1984 BA; Richmond 1988 JD

Delegate **Richard L. "Rich" Anderson** (R-District 51) . . . . (804) 698-1051
Counties Represented: Prince William (part)          Dist: (571) 264-9983
Term Expires: 2018          Fax: (804) 698-6751
PO Box 7926, Woodbridge, VA 22195
E-mail: delranderson@house.virginia.gov
Committees: Appropriations; General Laws; Science and Technology;
Transportation
Education: Virginia Tech 1979 BA; Webster 1982 BA

Delegate **Terry L. Austin** (R-District 19) . . . . . . . . . . . . . . (804) 698-1019
Counties Represented: Alleghany, Bedford (part),          Dist: (540) 254-1085
Botetourt (part)
Independent Cities Represented: Bedford, Covington
Term Expires: 2018
P.O. Box 398, Buchanan, VA 24066
E-mail: deltaustin@house.virginia.gov
Committees: Counties, Cities and Towns; Science and Technology;
Transportation

Delegate **Lamont Bagby** (D-District 74) . . . . . . . . . . . . . . (804) 698-1074
Counties Represented: Henrico (part)
Independent Cities Represented: Richmond (part)
Term Expires: 2018
E-mail: dellbagby@house.virginia.gov
Committees: Education; Transportation
Education: Norfolk State BS

Delegate **John J. Bell** (D-District 87) . . . . . . . . . . . . . . . . (804) 698-1087
Counties Represented: Loudoun (part), Prince William (part)
Term Expires: 2018
E-mail: deljbell@house.virginia.gov
Committees: Counties, Cities and Towns; Militia, Police and Public
Safety

Delegate **Richard P. "Dickie" Bell** (R-District 20) . . . . . . . . (804) 698-1020
Counties Represented: Augusta (part), Highland,          Dist: (540) 448-3999
Nelson (part)          Fax: (804) 698-6720
Independent Cities Represented: Staunton, Waynesboro
Term Expires: 2018
2620 Easton Drive, Staunton, VA 24401
PO Box 239, Staunton, VA 24401
E-mail: deldbell@house.virginia.gov
Committees: Education; Health, Welfare and Institutions
Education: James Madison 1988 BGS

Delegate **Robert B. "Rob" Bell III** (R-District 58) . . . . . . . . (804) 698-1058
Counties Represented: Albemarle (part), Fluvanna          Dist: (434) 245-8900
(part), Greene, Rockingham (part)          Fax: (804) 698-6758
Term Expires: 2018          Dist: (434) 245-8903
2309 Finch Court, Charlottesville, VA 22911
E-mail: delrbell@house.virginia.gov
Committees: Commerce and Labor; Courts of Justice; General Laws;
Health, Welfare and Institutions
Education: Virginia 1988 BA, 1995 JD

Delegate **Robert S. Bloxom, Jr.** (R-District 100) . . . . . . . . .(804) 698-1000
Counties Represented: Accomack, Northampton
Independent Cities Represented: Norfolk (part), Virginia Beach (part)
Term Expires: 2018
P.O. Box 27, Mappsville, VA 23407
E-mail: DelRBloxom@house.virginia.gov
Committees: Agriculture, Chesapeake and Natural Resources; Finance;
Science and Technology

Delegate **Jennifer B. Boysko** (D-District 86) . . . . . . . . . . . (804) 698-1086
Counties Represented: Fairfax (part), Loudoun (part)
Term Expires: 2018
E-mail: deljboysko@house.virginia.gov
Committees: Counties, Cities and Towns; Privileges and Elections

Delegate **David L. Bulova** (D-District 37) . . . . . . . . . . . . . . .(804) 698-1037
Counties Represented: Fairfax (part)          Dist: (703) 310-6752
Independent Cities Represented: Fairfax          Fax: (804) 698-6737
Term Expires: 2018          Dist: (888) 816-2660
P.O. Box 106, Fairfax Station, VA 22039
E-mail: deldbulova@house.virginia.gov
Committees: Agriculture, Chesapeake and Natural Resources;
Education; General Laws
Education: William & Mary 1991 BA; Virginia Tech 1996 MPA

Delegate **Kathy J. Byron** (R-District 22) . . . . . . . . . . . . . . (804) 698-1022
Counties Represented: Bedford (part), Campbell          Dist: (434) 582-1592
(part), Franklin (part)          Fax: (804) 698-6722
Independent Cities Represented: Lynchburg (part)
Term Expires: 2018
523 Leesville Road, Lynchburg, VA 24502
E-mail: delkbyron@house.virginia.gov
Committees: Commerce and Labor; Finance; Science and Technology
Affiliation: Chief Executive Officer, B&B Presentations, Inc.

Delegate **Jeffrey L. Campbell** (R-District 6) . . . . . . . . . . . . (804) 698-1006
Counties Represented: Carroll, Smyth (part), Wythe          Dist: (276) 783-8197
Term Expires: 2018
P.O. Box 1209, Saltville, VA 24370
E-mail: deljcampbell@house.virginia.gov
Committees: Counties, Cities and Towns; Courts of Justice; Science
and Technology
Education: Emory & Henry 1992 BA; Appalachian Law 2000 JD

Delegate **Betsy B. Carr** (D-District 69) . . . . . . . . . . . . . . . . (804) 698-1069
Counties Represented: Chesterfield (part)          Dist: (804) 698-1169
Independent Cities Represented: Richmond (part)          Fax: (804) 698-6769
Term Expires: 2018
E-mail: delbcarr@house.virginia.gov
Committees: Appropriations; General Laws; Rules; Transportation

Delegate **Benjamin L. "Ben" Cline** (R-District 24) . . . . . . . (804) 698-1024
Counties Represented: Amherst (part), Augusta          Dist: (434) 946-9908
(part), Bath, Rockbridge          Fax: (804) 698-6724
Independent Cities Represented: Buena Vista, Lexington
Term Expires: 2018
P.O. Box 1405, Amherst, VA 24521
E-mail: delbcline@house.virginia.gov
Committees: Commerce and Labor; Courts of Justice; Finance; Militia,
Police and Public Safety
Education: Bates 1994 BA; Richmond 2007 JD

Delegate **Mark L. Cole** (R-District 88) . . . . . . . . . . . . . . . . (804) 698-1088
Counties Represented: Fauquier (part), Spotsylvania          Dist: (540) 786-3402
(part), Stafford (part)          Fax: (804) 698-6788
Independent Cities Represented: Fredericksburg (part)
Term Expires: 2018
P.O. Box 41965, Fredericksburg, VA 22403
E-mail: delmcole@house.virginia.gov
Committees: Education; Finance; Privileges and Elections
Education: Western Kentucky 1980 BS;
Mary Washington Col 1993 BLS

Delegate **Christopher E. Collins** (R-District 29) . . . . . . . . . (804) 698-1029
Counties Represented: Frederick (part), Warren (part)
Independent Cities Represented: Winchester
Term Expires: 2018
E-mail: delccollins@house.virginia.gov
Committees: Counties, Cities and Towns; Courts of Justice

Delegate **M. Kirkland "Kirk" Cox** (R-District 66) . . . . . . . . (804) 698-1066
Counties Represented: Chesterfield (part)          Dist: (804) 526-5135
Independent Cities Represented: Colonial Heights          Fax: (804) 698-6766
Term Expires: 2018          Dist: (804) 526-3020
131 Old Brickhouse Lane, Colonial Heights, VA 23834
PO Box 1205, Colonial Heights, VA 23834
E-mail: delkcox@house.virginia.gov
Committees: Appropriations; Rules

Delegate **Glenn R. Davis, Jr.** (R-District 84) ............ (804) 698-1084
Independent Cities Represented: Virginia Beach    Dist: (757) 802-4980
(part)
Term Expires: 2018
1081 Nineteenth Street, Suite 201, Virginia Beach, VA 23451
E-mail: delgdavis@house.virginia.gov
Committees: Education; Militia, Police and Public Safety;
Transportation
Education: George Mason

Delegate **L. Mark Dudenhefer** (R-District 2) ........... (804) 698-1002
Counties Represented: Prince William (part), Stafford (part)
Term Expires: 2018
E-mail: delmdudenhefer@house.virginia.gov
Committees: Education; Science and Technology; Transportation
Education: LSU (New Orleans) 1974 BSE; Tulane 1987 MBA;
U Phoenix 2000 MCIS

Delegate **James E. Edmunds II** (R-District 60) ......... (804) 698-1060
Counties Represented: Campbell (part), Halifax,    Dist: (434) 476-0077
Prince Edward    Fax: (804) 698-6760
Term Expires: 2018    Dist: (434) 476-1370
455 Short Street, Sutie 204, South Boston, VA 24592
PO Box 1115, Halifax, VA 24558
E-mail: deljedmunds@house.virginia.gov
Committees: Agriculture, Chesapeake and Natural Resources; Health,
Welfare and Institutions; Militia, Police and Public Safety
Education: Averett U 1996 BS

Delegate **C. Matthew Fariss** (R-District 59) ............ (804) 698-1059
Counties Represented: Albemarle (part),    Dist: (434) 821-5929
Appomattox, Buckingham, Campbell (part), Nelson    Fax: (804) 698-6759
(part)    Dist: (434) 821-3580
Term Expires: 2018
243-C Livestock Road, Rustburg, VA 24588
E-mail: delmfariss@house.virginia.gov
Committees: Agriculture, Chesapeake and Natural Resources; Finance;
Militia, Police and Public Safety

Delegate **Peter F. Farrell** (R-District 56) ............... (804) 698-1056
Counties Represented: Goochland (part), Henrico    Dist: (804) 644-0266
(part), Louisa, Spotsylvania (part)    Fax: (804) 698-6756
Term Expires: 2018
P.O. Box 87, Richmond, VA 23218
E-mail: delpfarrell@house.virginia.gov
Committees: Commerce and Labor; Finance; Health, Welfare and
Institutions
Education: Virginia 2006 BA

Delegate **Eileen Filler-Corn** (D-District 41) ............ (804) 698-1041
Counties Represented: Fairfax (part)    Dist: (571) 249-3453
Term Expires: 2018    Fax: (804) 698-6741
PO Box 523082, Springfield, VA 22152
E-mail: delefiller-corn@house.virginia.gov
Committees: Commerce and Labor; Finance; Transportation
Education: Ithaca 1986 BA; Washington College of Law 1993 JD

Delegate **Hyland F. "Buddy" Fowler** (R-District 55) ..... (804) 698-1055
Counties Represented: Caroline (part), Hanover    Dist: (804) 305-8867
(part), Spotsylvania (part)
Term Expires: 2018
10321 Washington Highway, Glen Allen, VA 23059
E-mail: delbfowler@house.virginia.gov
Committees: Finance; Militia, Police and Public Safety; Privileges and
Elections
Education: Mary Washington Col 1995 BA

Delegate **Nicholas J. Freitas** (R-District 30) ........... (804) 698-1030
Counties Represented: Culpeper (part), Madison, Orange
Term Expires: 2018
E-mail: delnfreitas@house.virginia.gov
Committees: Finance; Science and Technology

Delegate **T. Scott Garrett** (R-District 23) .............. (804) 698-1023
Counties Represented: Amherst (part), Bedford    Dist: (434) 455-0243
(part)    Fax: (804) 698-6723
Independent Cities Represented: Lynchburg (part)
Term Expires: 2018
2255 Langhorne Road, Suite 4, Lynchburg, VA 24501
E-mail: delsgarrett@house.virginia.gov
Committees: Appropriations; Health, Welfare and Institutions;
Transportation
Education: Virginia 1978 BA, 1984 MD

Delegate **C. Todd Gilbert** (R-District 15) .............. (804) 698-1015
Counties Represented: Page, Rockingham (part),    Dist: (540) 459-7550
Shenandoah, Warren (part)    Fax: (804) 698-6715
Term Expires: 2018    Dist: (540) 459-7004
P.O. Box 309, Woodstock, VA 22664
E-mail: deltgilbert@house.virginia.gov
Committees: Courts of Justice; General Laws; Militia, Police and
Public Safety
Education: Virginia 1993 BA; Southern Methodist 1996 JD

Delegate **Thomas A. "Tag" Greason** (R-District 32) ..... (804) 698-1032
Counties Represented: Loudoun (part)    Dist: (703) 203-3203
Term Expires: 2018    Fax: (804) 698-6732
19309 Winmeade Drive, Lansdowne, VA 20176
PO Box 427, Lansdowne, VA 20176
E-mail: deltgreason@house.virginia.gov
Committees: Appropriations; Education; General Laws
Affiliation: Executive Vice President, Sales, QTS Realty Trust, Inc.
12851 Foster Street, Overland Park, KS 66213
Education: West Point 1993 BS; George Mason 2000 MBA

Delegate **Gregory David Habeeb** (R-District 8) ......... (804) 698-1008
Counties Represented: Craig, Montgomery (part),    Dist: (540) 915-2962
Roanoke (part)    Fax: (804) 698-6708
Independent Cities Represented: Salem
Term Expires: 2018
P.O. Box 882, Salem, VA 24153
E-mail: delghabeeb@house.virginia.gov
Committees: Commerce and Labor; Courts of Justice; Rules;
Transportation
Education: Wake Forest 1998 BA, 2001 JD

Delegate **Christopher T. Head** (R-District 17) .......... (804) 698-1017
Counties Represented: Botetourt (part), Roanoke    Dist: (540) 283-2839
(part)    Fax: (804) 698-6717
Independent Cities Represented: Roanoke (part)
Term Expires: 2018
P.O. Box 19130, Roanoke, VA 24019
E-mail: delchead@house.virginia.gov
Committees: Finance; Health, Welfare and Institutions; Militia, Police
and Public Safety
Education: Georgia 1985 BMus

Delegate **Gordon C. Helsel, Jr.** (R-District 91) ......... (804) 698-1091
Counties Represented: York (part)    Dist: (757) 969-9036
Independent Cities Represented: Hampton (part), Poquoson
Term Expires: 2018
P.O. Box 2571, Poquoson, VA 23662
E-mail: delghelsel@house.virginia.gov
Committees: General Laws; Health, Welfare and Institutions; Science
and Technology

Delegate **Stephen E. "Steve" Heretick** (D-District 79) ... (804) 698-1079
Independent Cities Represented: Norfolk (part), Portsmouth (part)
Term Expires: 2018
E-mail: delsheretick@house.virginia.gov
Committees: Counties, Cities and Towns; Science and Technology

Delegate **Charniele L. Herring** (D-District 46) .......... (804) 698-1046
Independent Cities Represented: Alexandria (part)    Dist: (703) 606-9705
Term Expires: 2018    Fax: (804) 698-6746
P.O. Box 11779, Alexandria, VA 22312
E-mail: delcherring@house.virginia.gov
Committees: Counties, Cities and Towns; Courts of Justice
Education: George Mason 1993 BA; Columbus Law 1997 JD

Delegate **Daun Sessoms Hester** (D-District 89) ......... (804) 698-1089
Independent Cities Represented: Norfolk (part)
Term Expires: 2018
1751 Church Street, Norfolk, VA 23504
E-mail: DelDHester@house.virginia.gov
Committees: Appropriations; Education; General Laws
Education: Virginia State BS; George Washington 1990 MA

Delegate **M. Keith Hodges** (R-District 98) .............. (804) 698-1098
Counties Represented: Essex, Gloucester, King and    Dist: (804) 277-9801
Queen, King William (part), Mathews, Middlesex    Fax: (804) 698-6798
Term Expires: 2018    Dist: (804) 695-0216
P.O. Box 928, Urbanna, VA 23175
E-mail: delkhodges@house.virginia.gov
Committees: Counties, Cities and Towns; General Laws; Health,
Welfare and Institutions
Education: Medical Col (VA) 1989 BSPh

*(continued on next page)*

LEGISLATIVE BRANCH

**Delegates** *continued*

Delegate **Patrick A. Hope** (D-District 47) . . . . . . . . . . . . . (804) 698-1047
  Counties Represented: Arlington (part)      Dist: (703) 486-1010
  Term Expires: 2018      Fax: (804) 698-6747
  P.O. Box 3148, Arlington, VA 22203      Dist: (703) 772-0120
  E-mail: delphope@house.virginia.gov
  Committees: Courts of Justice; Health, Welfare and Institutions; Militia, Police and Public Safety
  Education: St Mary's U (TX) 1993 BA; Catholic U 1996 MA; Columbus Law 2001 JD

Delegate **William J. "Bill" Howell** (R-District 28) . . . . . . . (804) 698-1028
  Counties Represented: Stafford (part)      Dist: (540) 371-1612
  Independent Cities Represented: Fredericksburg      Fax: (804) 698-6728
  (part)      Dist: (540) 371-7449
  Term Expires: 2018
  P.O. Box 8296, Fredericksburg, VA 22404-8296
  E-mail: delwhowell@house.virginia.gov
  Committees: Rules

Delegate **Timothy D. "Tim" Hugo** (R-District 40) . . . . . . . (804) 698-1040
  Counties Represented: Fairfax (part), Prince William      Dist: (703) 968-4101
  (part)      Fax: (804) 698-6740
  Term Expires: 2018
  P.O. Box 893, Centreville, VA 20122
  E-mail: delthugo@house.virginia.gov
  Committees: Commerce and Labor; Finance; Privileges and Elections; Transportation

Delegate **Riley Edward Ingram** (R-District 62) . . . . . . . . . (804) 698-1062
  Counties Represented: Chesterfield (part), Henrico      Dist: (804) 458-9873
  (part), Prince George (part)      Fax: (804) 698-6762
  Independent Cities Represented: Hopewell (part)      Dist: (804) 458-0621
  Term Expires: 2018
  3302 Oaklawn Boulevard, Hopewell, VA 23860
  E-mail: delringram@house.virginia.gov
  Committees: Appropriations; Counties, Cities and Towns; Privileges and Elections; Rules

Delegate **Matthew James** (D-District 80) . . . . . . . . . . . . . (804) 698-1080
  Independent Cities Represented: Chesapeake (part),      Dist: (757) 967-7583
  Norfolk (part), Portsmouth (part), Suffolk (part)      Fax: (804) 698-6780
  Term Expires: 2018
  P.O. Box 7487, Portsmouth, VA 23707
  E-mail: delmjames@house.virginia.gov
  Committees: Agriculture, Chesapeake and Natural Resources; Appropriations; Health, Welfare and Institutions
  Education: Hampton 1978 BA; Northwestern 1981 MBA

Delegate **S. Chris Jones** (R-District 76) . . . . . . . . . . . . . . (804) 698-1076
  Independent Cities Represented: Chesapeake      Dist: (757) 483-6242
  (part), Suffolk (part)      Fax: (804) 698-6776
  Term Expires: 2018      Dist: (757) 483-0722
  P.O. Box 5059, Suffolk, VA 23435-0059
  E-mail: delcjones@house.virginia.gov
  Committees: Appropriations; Privileges and Elections; Rules
  Education: Randolph-Macon 1980 BS; VCU 1982 BS

Delegate **Mark L. Keam** (D-District 35) . . . . . . . . . . . . . . (804) 698-1035
  Counties Represented: Fairfax (part)      Dist: (703) 350-3911
  Term Expires: 2018      Fax: (804) 698-6735
  P.O. Box 1134, Vienna, VA 22183-1134
  E-mail: delmkeam@house.virginia.gov
  Committees: Agriculture, Chesapeake and Natural Resources; Commerce and Labor; Education; Finance
  Education: UC Irvine 1989 BA; Hastings 1995 JD

Delegate **Terry G. Kilgore** (R-District 1) . . . . . . . . . . . . . (804) 698-1001
  Counties Represented: Lee, Scott, Wise (part)      Dist: (276) 386-7011
  Independent Cities Represented: Norton      Fax: (804) 698-6701
  Term Expires: 2018      Dist: (276) 386-2377
  P.O. Box 669, Gate City, VA 24251
  E-mail: deltkilgore@house.virginia.gov
  Committees: Commerce and Labor; Courts of Justice; Rules
  Education: Clinch Valley 1983 BA; William & Mary 1986 JD

Delegate **Barry D. Knight** (R-District 81) . . . . . . . . . . . . . (804) 698-1081
  Independent Cities Represented: Chesapeake      Dist: (757) 426-6387
  (part), Virginia Beach (part)      Fax: (804) 698-6781
  Term Expires: 2018      Dist: (757) 426-9091
  1852 Mill Landing Road, Virginia Beach, VA 23457
  E-mail: delbknight@house.virginia.gov
  Committees: Agriculture, Chesapeake and Natural Resources; Appropriations; General Laws; Rules

Delegate **Kaye Kory** (D-District 38) . . . . . . . . . . . . . . . . . (804) 698-1038
  Counties Represented: Fairfax (part)      Dist: (703) 354-6024
  Term Expires: 2018      Fax: (804) 698-6738
  6505 Waterway Drive, Falls Church, VA 22044
  E-mail: delkkory@house.virginia.gov
  Committees: Commerce and Labor; Finance; General Laws; Militia, Police and Public Safety
  Education: Miami U (OH) 1969 BA; Iowa; George Mason

Delegate **Paul E. Krizek** (D-District 44) . . . . . . . . . . . . . . (804) 698-1044
  Counties Represented: Fairfax (part)
  Term Expires: 2018
  E-mail: delpkrizek@house.virginia.gov
  Committees: Counties, Cities and Towns; Courts of Justice

Delegate **R. Steven "Steve" Landes** (R-District 25) . . . . . (804) 698-1025
  Counties Represented: Albemarle (part), Augusta      Dist: (540) 255-5335
  (part), Rockingham (part)      Fax: (804) 698-6725
  Term Expires: 2018      Dist: (540) 248-8434
  P.O. Box 12, Verona, VA 24482
  E-mail: delslandes@house.virginia.gov
  Committees: Appropriations; Education; Privileges and Elections; Rules
  Education: VCU 1983 BS

Delegate **David A. "Dave" LaRock** (R-District 33) . . . . . . . (804) 698-1033
  Counties Represented: Clarke (part), Frederick      Dist: (540) 751-8364
  (part), Loudoun (part)
  Term Expires: 2018
  P.O. Box 6, Hamilton, VA 20159
  E-mail: deldlarock@house.virginia.gov
  Committees: Education; Science and Technology; Transportation

Delegate **James A. "Jay" Leftwich** (R-District 78) . . . . . . (804) 698-1078
  Independent Cities Represented: Chesapeake (part)      Dist: (757) 382-4157
  Term Expires: 2018
  308 Cedar Lakes Drive, Chesapeake, VA 23322
  E-mail: deljleftwich@house.virginia.gov
  Committees: Courts of Justice; Education; General Laws; Science and Technology
  Education: James Madison 1985 BS; Richmond 1988 JD

Delegate **James M. "Jim" LeMunyon** (R-District 67) . . . . (804) 698-1067
  Counties Represented: Fairfax (part), Loudoun      Dist: (703) 264-1432
  (part)      Fax: (804) 698-6767
  Term Expires: 2018      Dist: (703) 264-1432
  PO Box 220962, Chantilly, VA 20153-0962
  E-mail: deljlemunyon@house.virginia.gov
  Committees: Education; General Laws; Transportation
  Education: Valparaiso 1981 BS; Wisconsin 1987 MS

Delegate **Mark H. Levine** (D-District 45) . . . . . . . . . . . . . (804) 698-1045
  Counties Represented: Arlington (part), Fairfax (part)
  Independent Cities Represented: Alexandria (part)
  Term Expires: 2018
  E-mail: delmlevine@house.virginia.gov
  Committees: Health, Welfare and Institutions; Science and Technology
  Education: Harvard; Yale JD

Delegate **Joseph C. "Joe" Lindsey** (D-District 90) . . . . . . (804) 698-1090
  Independent Cities Represented: Norfolk (part),      Dist: (757) 623-6522
  Virginia Beach (part)
  Term Expires: 2018
  E-mail: deljlindsey@house.virginia.gov
  Committees: Appropriations; Education; Privileges and Elections

Delegate **L. Scott "Scott" Lingamfelter** (R-District 31) . . (804) 698-1031
  Counties Represented: Fauquier (part), Prince      Dist: (703) 580-1294
  William (part)      Fax: (804) 698-6731
  Term Expires: 2018      Dist: (703) 590-7090
  5420 Lomax Way, Woodbridge, VA 22193
  E-mail: delslingamfelter@house.virginia.gov
  Committees: Appropriations; Education; Militia, Police and Public Safety
  Education: VMI 1973 BA; Virginia 1981 MA

Delegate **Alfonso H. Lopez** (D-District 49) . . . . . . . . . . . . (804) 698-1049
  Counties Represented: Arlington (part), Fairfax      Dist: (571) 336-2147
  (part)      Fax: (804) 698-6749
  Term Expires: 2018
  P.O. Box 40366, Arlington, VA 22204
  E-mail: delalopez@house.virginia.gov
  Committees: Agriculture, Chesapeake and Natural Resources; Militia, Police and Public Safety; Science and Technology
  Education: Vassar 1992 BA; Tulane 1995 JD

LEGISLATIVE BRANCH

Delegate **G. Manoli Loupassi** (R-District 68) . . . . . . . . . (804) 698-1068
Counties Represented: Chesterfield (part), Henrico    Dist: (804) 440-6223
(part)    Fax: (804) 698-6768
Independent Cities Represented: Richmond (part)
Term Expires: 2018
6002A West Broad Street, Suite 200, Richmond, VA 23230
E-mail: delmloupassi@house.virginia.gov
Committees: Commerce and Labor; Courts of Justice
Education: Washington and Lee 1989 BA; Richmond 1992 JD

Delegate
**Daniel W. "Danny" Marshall III** (R-District 14) . . . . . . . (804) 698-1014
Counties Represented: Henry (part), Pittsylvania    Dist: (434) 797-5861
(part)    Fax: (804) 698-6714
Independent Cities Represented: Danville    Dist: (434) 792-2642
Term Expires: 2018
P.O. Box 439, Danville, VA 24543
E-mail: deldmarshall@house.virginia.gov
Committees: Agriculture, Chesapeake and Natural Resources;
Commerce and Labor; Counties, Cities and Towns
Education: Averett U

Delegate **Robert G. "Bob" Marshall** (R-District 13) . . . . . (804) 698-1013
Counties Represented: Prince William (part)    Dist: (703) 853-4213
Independent Cities Represented: Manassas Park    Fax: (804) 698-6713
Term Expires: 2018
P.O. Box 421, Manassas, VA 20108-0421
E-mail: delbmarshall@house.virginia.gov
Committees: Counties, Cities and Towns; Finance; Science and
Technology
Education: Belmont Abbey 1969 BA; Cal State (Fullerton) 1991 MA

Delegate
**T. Montgomery "Monty" Mason** (D-District 93) . . . . . . (804) 698-1093
Counties Represented: James City (part), York (part)    Dist: (757) 229-9310
Independent Cities Represented: Newport News (part), Williamsburg
Term Expires: 2018
P.O. Box 232, Williamsburg, VA 23187
E-mail: delmmason@house.virginia.gov
Committees: Counties, Cities and Towns; Courts of Justice
Education: William & Mary 1989 BA

Delegate **James P. "Jimmie" Massie III** (R-District 72) . . (804) 698-1072
Counties Represented: Henrico (part)    Dist: (804) 377-0100
Term Expires: 2018    Fax: (804) 698-6772
P.O. Box 29598, Richmond, VA 23242
E-mail: deljmassie@house.virginia.gov
Committees: Appropriations; Education; Rules
Education: Virginia 1980 BA

Delegate **Jennifer L. "Jenn" McClellan** (D-District 71) . . . (804) 698-1071
Counties Represented: Henrico (part)    Dist: (804) 698-1171
Independent Cities Represented: Richmond (part)    Fax: (804) 698-6771
Term Expires: 2018    Dist: (804) 343-3642
E-mail: deljmcclellan@house.virginia.gov
Committees: Commerce and Labor; Courts of Justice; Education

Delegate **Rev. Delores L. McQuinn** (D-District 70) . . . . . . . (804) 698-1070
Counties Represented: Chesterfield (part), Henrico    Fax: (804) 698-6770
(part)
Independent Cities Represented: Richmond (part)
Term Expires: 2018
E-mail: deldmcquinn@house.virginia.gov
Committees: Appropriations; General Laws; Transportation

Delegate **Jackson H. Miller** (R-District 50) . . . . . . . . . . . (804) 698-1050
Counties Represented: Prince William (part)    Dist: (703) 244-6172
Independent Cities Represented: Manassas    Fax: (804) 698-6750
Term Expires: 2018
P.O. Box 10072, Manassas, VA 20108
E-mail: deljmiller@house.virginia.gov
Committees: Agriculture, Chesapeake and Natural Resources;
Commerce and Labor; Courts of Justice; Privileges and Elections

Delegate **J. Randall "Randy" Minchew** (R-District 10) . . . (804) 698-1010
Counties Represented: Clarke (part), Frederick    Dist: (703) 777-1570
(part), Loudoun (part)    Fax: (804) 698-6710
Term Expires: 2018    Dist: (703) 737-3632
P.O. Box 385, Leesburg, VA 20178
E-mail: delrminchew@house.virginia.gov
Committees: Courts of Justice; General Laws; Privileges and Elections;
Transportation
Education: Duke 1980 AB; Washington and Lee 1984 JD;
Virginia Theol Sem 2010 ThB

Delegate **Jason S. Miyares** (R-District 82) . . . . . . . . . . . . (804) 698-1082
Independent Cities Represented: Virginia Beach (part)
Term Expires: 2018
E-mail: deljmiyares@house.virginia.gov
Committees: Courts of Justice; Privileges and Elections
Education: James Madison; William & Mary 2005 JD

Delegate **James W. "Will" Morefield** (R-District 3) . . . . . (804) 698-1003
Counties Represented: Bland, Buchanan, Russell    Dist: (276) 345-4300
(part), Tazewell    Fax: (804) 698-6703
Term Expires: 2018
P.O. Box 828, North Tazewell, VA 24630
E-mail: deljmorefield@house.virginia.gov
Committees: Agriculture, Chesapeake and Natural Resources; Counties,
Cities and Towns; Militia, Police and Public Safety
Education: Midwestern State 2007 BAAS

Delegate **Richard L. "Rick" Morris** (R-District 64) . . . . . . . (804) 698-1064
Counties Represented: Isle of Wight (part), Prince    Dist: (757) 912-1644
George (part), Southampton (part), Surry (part),    Fax: (804) 698-6764
Sussex (part)
Independent Cities Represented: Franklin (part), Suffolk (part)
Term Expires: 2018
P.O. Box 128, Carrolton, VA 23314
E-mail: delrmorris@house.virginia.gov
Committees: Counties, Cities and Towns; Courts of Justice; Militia,
Police and Public Safety
Education: St Leo U 1998 BA; Regent U 2002 JD

Delegate **Kathleen J. Murphy** (D-District 34) . . . . . . . . . . (804) 698-1034
Counties Represented: Fairfax (part), Loudoun (part)
Term Expires: 2018
E-mail: delkmurphy@house.virginia.gov
Committees: Finance; Privileges and Elections

Delegate **John M. O'Bannon III** (R-District 73) . . . . . . . . . (804) 698-1073
Counties Represented: Henrico (part)    Dist: (804) 282-8640
Term Expires: 2018    Fax: (804) 698-6773
P.O. Box 70365, Richmond, VA 23255-0356    Dist: (804) 521-7837
E-mail: deljobannon@house.virginia.gov
Committees: Appropriations; Health, Welfare and Institutions;
Privileges and Elections
Education: Richmond 1969 BS; VCU 1973 MD

Delegate **Israel D. O'Quinn** (R-District 5) . . . . . . . . . . . . . (804) 698-1005
Counties Represented: Grayson, Smyth (part),    Dist: (276) 525-1311
Washington (part)    Fax: (804) 698-6705
Independent Cities Represented: Bristol, Galax
Term Expires: 2018
101 Martin Luther King Jr. Boulevard, Bristol, VA 24201
P.O. Box 16325, Bristol, VA 24209
E-mail: delioquinn@house.virginia.gov
Committees: Commerce and Labor; Militia, Police and Public Safety;
Privileges and Elections
Education: Emory & Henry 2002 BA

Delegate **Robert D. "Bobby" Orrock, Sr.** (R-District 54) . . (804) 698-1054
Counties Represented: Caroline (part), Spotsylvania    Dist: (540) 891-1322
(part)    Fax: (804) 698-6754
Term Expires: 2018
P.O. Box 458, Thornburg, VA 22565
E-mail: delborrock@house.virginia.gov
Committees: Agriculture, Chesapeake and Natural Resources; Finance;
Health, Welfare and Institutions; Rules
Education: Virginia Tech 1978 BS; Virginia State 1988 MS

Delegate
**Christopher Kilian "Chris" Peace** (R-District 97) . . . . . . (804) 698-1097
Counties Represented: Hanover (part), King William    Dist: (804) 730-3737
(part), New Kent    Fax: (804) 698-6797
Term Expires: 2018    Dist: (804) 730-5049
P.O. Box 819, Mechanicsville, VA 23111
E-mail: delcpeace@house.virginia.gov
Committees: Appropriations; General Laws; Health, Welfare and
Institutions
Education: Hampden-Sydney 1998 BA; Richmond 2002 JD

Delegate **Todd E. Pillion** (R-District 4) . . . . . . . . . . . . . . . (804) 698-1004
Counties Represented: Dickenson, Russell (part), Washington (part),
Wise (part)
Term Expires: 2018
E-mail: deltpillion@house.virginia.gov
Committees: Counties, Cities and Towns; Science and Technology;
Transportation

Delegate **Kenneth R. Plum** (D-District 36) . . . . . . . . . . . . (804) 698-1036
Counties Represented: Fairfax (part)    Dist: (703) 758-9733
Term Expires: 2018    Fax: (804) 698-6736
2073 Cobblestone Lane, Reston, VA 20191    Dist: (703) 391-0865
E-mail: delkplum@house.virginia.gov
Committees: Agriculture, Chesapeake and Natural Resources; Rules;
Science and Technology; Transportation
Education: Old Dominion BA; Virginia MEd

*(continued on next page)*

**Delegates** *continued*

**Delegate Brenda L. Pogge** (R-District 96) . . . . . . . . . . . . . (804) 698-1096
Counties Represented: James City (part), York (part)   Dist: (757) 223-9690
Term Expires: 2018   Fax: (804) 698-1196
P.O. Box 1386, Yorktown, VA 23692
E-mail: delbpogge@house.virginia.gov
Committees: Agriculture, Chesapeake and Natural Resources;
Education; Finance; Health, Welfare and Institutions

**Delegate Charles D. Poindexter** (R-District 9) . . . . . . . . . (804) 698-1009
Counties Represented: Franklin (part), Henry   Dist: (540) 576-2600
(part), Patrick   Fax: (804) 698-6709
Term Expires: 2018
P.O. Box 117, Glade Hill, VA 24092
E-mail: delcpoindexter@house.virginia.gov
Committees: Agriculture, Chesapeake and Natural Resources;
Appropriations; Counties, Cities and Towns
Education: Lynchburg 1964 BS; George Washington 1973 MSA

**Delegate Marcia S. "Cia" Price** (D-District 95) . . . . . . . . . .(804) 698-1095
Independent Cities Represented: Hampton (part), Newport News (part)
Term Expires: 2018
E-mail: delmprice@house.virginia.gov
Committees: Health, Welfare and Institutions; Privileges and Elections

**Delegate Margaret Bevans Ransone** (R-District 99) . . . . . (804) 698-1099
Counties Represented: Caroline (part), King   Dist: (804) 472-4181
George, Lancaster, Northumberland, Richmond,   Fax: (804) 786-6310
Westmoreland   Dist: (804) 493-8481
Term Expires: 2018
P.O. Box 358, Kinsale, VA 22488
E-mail: delmransone@house.virginia.gov
Committees: Agriculture, Chesapeake and Natural Resources;
Commerce and Labor; Privileges and Elections
Education: Randolph-Macon 2002 BA

**Delegate Salam "Sam" Rasoul** (D-District 11) . . . . . . . . (804) 698-1011
Independent Cities Represented: Roanoke (part)   Dist: (540) 904-6905
Term Expires: 2018
P.O. Box 13842, Roanoke, VA 24037
E-mail: delsrasoul@house.virginia.gov
Committees: Militia, Police and Public Safety; Privileges and Elections;
Science and Technology

**Delegate Roxann L. Robinson** (R-District 27) . . . . . . . . . .(804) 698-1027
Counties Represented: Chesterfield (part)   Dist: (804) 308-1534
Term Expires: 2018   Fax: (804) 698-6727
9409 Hull Street Road, Suite F-1, Richmond, VA 23236
E-mail: delrrobinson@house.virginia.gov
Committees: Education; General Laws; Health, Welfare and
Institutions; Science and Technology
Education: Fairmont State Col 1978 BS; Illinois Optometry BS

**Delegate Larry Nick "Nick" Rush** (R-District 7) . . . . . . . . (804) 698-1007
Counties Represented: Floyd, Montgomery (part),   Dist: (540) 382-7731
Pulaski (part)   Fax: (804) 698-6707
Term Expires: 2018
P.O. Box 1591, Christiansburg, VA 24068
E-mail: delnrush@house.virginia.gov
Committees: Appropriations; Militia, Police and Public Safety;
Privileges and Elections

**Delegate Mark D. Sickles** (D-District 43) . . . . . . . . . . . . . .(804) 698-1043
Counties Represented: Fairfax (part)   Dist: (703) 922-6440
Term Expires: 2018   Fax: (804) 698-6743
P.O. Box 10628, Franconia, VA 22310   Dist: (703) 922-6880
E-mail: delmsickles@house.virginia.gov
Committees: Appropriations; Health, Welfare and Institutions;
Privileges and Elections

**Delegate Marcus B. Simon** (D-District 53) . . . . . . . . . . . . (804) 698-1053
Counties Represented: Fairfax (part)   Dist: (571) 327-0053
Independent Cities Represented: Falls Church
Term Expires: 2018
P.O. Box 958, Falls Church, VA 22040
E-mail: delmsimon@house.virginia.gov
Committees: Militia, Police and Public Safety; Science and Technology
Education: West Virginia (Attended); NYU 1992 BA;
Washington College of Law 1999 JD

**Delegate Lionell Spruill, Sr.** (D-District 77) . . . . . . . . . . . .(804) 698-1077
Independent Cities Represented: Chesapeake   Dist: (757) 424-2178
(part), Suffolk (part)   Fax: (804) 698-6777
Term Expires: 2018   Dist: (757) 321-6646
P.O. Box 5403, Chesapeake, VA 23324
E-mail: dellspruill@house.virginia.gov
Committees: Commerce and Labor; Counties, Cities and Towns;
Health, Welfare and Institutions; Rules

**Delegate Christopher P. "Chris" Stolle** (R-District 83) . . . (804) 698-1083
Independent Cities Represented: Norfolk (part),   Dist: (757) 633-2080
Virginia Beach (part)   Fax: (804) 698-6783
Term Expires: 2018   Dist: (757) 512-8011
P.O. Box 5429, Virginia Beach, VA 23471
E-mail: delcstolle@house.virginia.gov
Committees: Appropriations; Counties, Cities and Towns; Health,
Welfare and Institutions
Education: Naval Acad 1981 BS; Uniformed Services 1988 MD;
William & Mary 2004 MBA

**Delegate Richard C. "Rip" Sullivan, Jr.** (D-District 48) . . .(804) 698-1048
Counties Represented: Arlington (part), Fairfax (part)
Term Expires: 2018
E-mail: delrsullivan@house.virginia.gov
Committees: Agriculture, Chesapeake and Natural Resources; Finance

**Delegate Scott W. Taylor** (R-District 85) . . . . . . . . . . . . . (804) 698-1085
Independent Cities Represented: Virginia Beach   Dist: (757) 422-4060
(part)
Term Expires: 2018
4001 - 117 VA Beach Boulevard, Box 731, Virginia Beach, VA 23452
E-mail: delstaylor@house.virginia.gov
Committees: Counties, Cities and Towns; Finance; Transportation
Education: Harvard 2014 ALB

**Delegate Luke E. Torian** (D-District 52) . . . . . . . . . . . . . . .(804) 698-1052
Counties Represented: Prince William (part)   Dist: (703) 785-2224
Term Expires: 2018   Fax: (804) 698-6752
4222 Fortuna Plaze, Suite 659, Dumfries, VA 22025
E-mail: delltorian@house.virginia.gov
Committees: Agriculture, Chesapeake and Natural Resources;
Appropriations; General Laws; Privileges and Elections
Education: Winston-Salem State 1980 BA; Virginia Union 1984 MDiv;
Howard U 1987 DMin

**Delegate David J. Toscano** (D-District 57) . . . . . . . . . . . . (804) 698-1057
Counties Represented: Albemarle (part)   Dist: (434) 220-1660
Independent Cities Represented: Charlottesville   Fax: (804) 698-6757
Term Expires: 2018
211 East High Street, Charlottesville, VA 22902
E-mail: deldtoscano@house.virginia.gov
Committees: Courts of Justice; Rules; Transportation

**Delegate Roslyn C. "Roz" Tyler** (D-District 75) . . . . . . . . (804) 698-1075
Counties Represented: Brunswick, Dinwiddie (part),   Dist: (434) 336-1710
Greensville, Isle of Wight (part), Lunenburg (part),   Fax: (804) 698-6775
Southampton (part), Surry (part), Sussex (part)
Independent Cities Represented: Emporia, Franklin (part)
Term Expires: 2018
25359 Blue Star Highway, Jarratt, VA 23867
E-mail: delrtyler@house.virginia.gov
Committees: Commerce and Labor; Education; Militia, Police and
Public Safety
Education: Virginia State 1982 BS; Old Dominion 1986 BS;
Virginia State 1995 MEd

**Delegate Ronald A. Villanueva** (R-District 21) . . . . . . . . . (804) 698-1021
Independent Cities Represented: Chesapeake   Dist: (757) 216-3883
(part), Virginia Beach (part)   Fax: (804) 698-6721
Term Expires: 2018   Dist: (757) 216-3885
P.O. Box 61106, Virginia Beach, VA 23466
E-mail: delrvillanueva@house.virginia.gov
Committees: Commerce and Labor; Science and Technology;
Transportation
Education: Old Dominion 1992 BA

**Delegate Jeion A. Ward** (D-District 92) . . . . . . . . . . . . . . . (804) 698-1092
Independent Cities Represented: Hampton (part)   Dist: (757) 827-5921
Term Expires: 2018   Fax: (804) 698-6792
P.O. Box 7310, Hampton, VA 23666   Dist: (757) 827-5311
E-mail: deljward@house.virginia.gov
Committees: Commerce and Labor; General Laws; Transportation

**Delegate R. Lee Ware, Jr.** (R-District 65) . . . . . . . . . . . . . .(804) 698-1065
Counties Represented: Chesterfield (part), Fluvanna   Dist: (804) 598-6696
(part), Goochland (part), Powhatan   Fax: (804) 698-6765
Term Expires: 2018
P.O. Box 689, Powhatan, VA 23139
E-mail: dellware@house.Virginia.gov
Committees: Agriculture, Chesapeake and Natural Resources;
Commerce and Labor; Finance; Rules
Education: Wheaton (IL) 1974 BA

**Delegate Vivian E. Watts** (D-District 39) . . . . . . . . . . . . . . (804) 698-1039
Counties Represented: Fairfax (part)   Dist: (703) 978-2989
Term Expires: 2018   Fax: (804) 698-6739
8717 Mary Lee Lane, Annandale, VA 22003   Dist: (703) 978-5762
E-mail: delvwatts@house.virginia.gov
Committees: Courts of Justice; Finance; Science and Technology
Education: Michigan 1962 BA

LEGISLATIVE BRANCH

Delegate **Michael J. Webert** (R-District 18) . . . . . . . . . . . (804) 698-1018
Counties Represented: Culpeper (part), Fauquier    Dist: (540) 999-8218
(part), Rappahannock, Warren (part)    Fax: (804) 698-6718
Term Expires: 2018
P.O. Box 631, Marshall, VA 20116
E-mail: delmwebert@house.virginia.gov
Committees: Agriculture, Chesapeake and Natural Resources; Counties,
Cities and Towns; Militia, Police and Public Safety
Education: Kent (Kent, CT) 1988 BA; George Mason 2010 BA

Delegate **Tony O. Wilt** (R-District 26) . . . . . . . . . . . . . . . . (804) 698-1026
Counties Represented: Rockingham (part)    Dist: (540) 208-0735
Independent Cities Represented: Harrisonburg    Fax: (804) 698-6726
Term Expires: 2018    Dist: (540) 437-1650
P.O. Box 1425, Harrisonburg, VA 22803
E-mail: deltwilt@house.virginia.gov
Committees: Agriculture, Chesapeake and Natural Resources; Counties,
Cities and Towns; Militia, Police and Public Safety

Delegate
**Thomas C. "Tommy" Wright, Jr.** (R-District 61) . . . . . (804) 698-1061
Counties Represented: Amelia, Cumberland,    Dist: (434) 696-3061
Lunenburg (part), Mecklenburg, Nottoway    Fax: (804) 698-6761
Term Expires: 2018    Dist: (434) 696-4061
P.O. Box 1323, Victoria, VA 23974
E-mail: deltwright@house.virginia.gov
Committees: Agriculture, Chesapeake and Natural Resources; General
Laws; Militia, Police and Public Safety

Delegate **David E. Yancey** (R-District 94) . . . . . . . . . . . . . (804) 698-1094
Independent Cities Represented: Newport News    Dist: (757) 897-3953
(part)    Fax: (804) 698-6794
Term Expires: 2018
PO Box 1163, Newport News, VA 23601
E-mail: deldyancey@house.virginia.gov
Committees: Commerce and Labor; Education; Transportation
Education: Georgia 1995 BA

Delegate **Joseph R. Yost** (R-District 12) . . . . . . . . . . . . . . (804) 698-1012
Counties Represented: Giles, Montgomery (part),    Dist: (540) 577-4984
Pulaski (part)    Fax: (804) 698-6712
Independent Cities Represented: Radford
Term Expires: 2018
P.O. Box 621, Blacksburg, VA 24063
E-mail: deljyost@house.virginia.gov
Committees: Education; General Laws; Health, Welfare and Institutions
Education: Radford 2006 BS, 2008 MA

# House Standing Committees

## Agriculture, Chesapeake and Natural Resources

**Majority Members**
Daniel W. "Danny"
   Marshall III (R-14)
   *Chair*
Charles D. Poindexter (R-9)
   *Vice Chair*
Robert S. Bloxom, Jr. (R-100)
James E. Edmunds II (R-60)
C. Matthew Fariss (R-59)
Barry D. Knight (R-81)
Jackson H. Miller (R-50)
James W. "Will" Morefield (R-3)
Robert D. "Bobby" Orrock, Sr.
   (R-54)
Brenda L. Pogge (R-96)
Margaret Bevans Ransone (R-99)
R. Lee Ware, Jr. (R-65)
Michael J. Webert (R-18)
Tony O. Wilt (R-26)
Thomas C. "Tommy" Wright, Jr.
   (R-61)

**Minority Members**
David L. Bulova (D-37)
Matthew James (D-80)
Mark L. Keam (D-35)
Alfonso H. Lopez (D-49)
Kenneth R. Plum (D-36)
Richard C. "Rip" Sullivan, Jr.
   (D-48)
Luke E. Torian (D-52)

## Appropriations

**Majority Members**
S. Chris Jones (R-76) *Chair*
R. Steven "Steve" Landes (R-25)
   *Vice Chair*
Richard L. "Rich" Anderson (R-51)
M. Kirkland "Kirk" Cox (R-66)
T. Scott Garrett (R-23)
Thomas A. "Tag" Greason (R-32)
Riley Edward Ingram (R-62)
Barry D. Knight (R-81)
L. Scott "Scott" Lingamfelter
   (R-31)
James P. "Jimmie" Massie III
   (R-72)
John M. O'Bannon III (R-73)
Christopher Kilian "Chris" Peace
   (R-97)
Charles D. Poindexter (R-9)
Larry Nick "Nick" Rush (R-7)
Christopher P. "Chris" Stolle (R-83)

**Minority Members**
Betsy B. Carr (D-69)
Daun Sessoms Hester (D-89)
Matthew James (D-80)
Joseph C. "Joe" Lindsey (D-90)
Rev. Delores L. McQuinn (D-70)
Mark D. Sickles (D-43)
Luke E. Torian (D-52)

## Commerce and Labor

**Majority Members**
Terry G. Kilgore (R-1) *Chair*
Kathy J. Byron (R-22) *Vice Chair*
Robert B. "Rob" Bell III (R-58)
Benjamin L. "Ben" Cline (R-24)
Peter F. Farrell (R-56)
Gregory David Habeeb (R-8)
Timothy D. "Tim" Hugo (R-40)
G. Manoli Loupassi (R-68)
Daniel W. "Danny" Marshall III
   (R-14)
Jackson H. Miller (R-50)
Israel D. O'Quinn (R-5)
Margaret Bevans Ransone (R-99)
Ronald A. Villanueva (R-21)
R. Lee Ware, Jr. (R-65)
David E. Yancey (R-94)

**Minority Members**
Eileen Filler-Corn (D-41)
Mark L. Keam (D-35)
Kaye Kory (D-38)
Jennifer L. "Jenn" McClellan
   (D-71)
Lionell Spruill, Sr. (D-77)
Roslyn C. "Roz" Tyler (D-75)
Jeion A. Ward (D-92)

## Counties, Cities and Towns

**Majority Members**
Riley Edward Ingram (R-62) *Chair*
Christopher P. "Chris" Stolle (R-83)
   *Vice Chair*
Terry L. Austin (R-19)
Jeffrey L. Campbell (R-6)
Christopher E. Collins (R-29)
M. Keith Hodges (R-98)
Daniel W. "Danny" Marshall III
   (R-14)
Robert G. "Bob" Marshall (R-13)
James W. "Will" Morefield (R-3)
Richard L. "Rick" Morris (R-64)
Todd E. Pillion (R-4)
Charles D. Poindexter (R-9)
Scott W. Taylor (R-85)
Michael J. Webert (R-18)
Tony O. Wilt (R-26)

**Minority Members**
John J. Bell (D-87)
Jennifer B. Boysko (D-86)
Stephen E. "Steve" Heretick (D-79)
Charniele L. Herring (D-46)
Paul E. Krizek (D-44)
T. Montgomery "Monty" Mason
   (D-93)
Lionell Spruill, Sr. (D-77)

## Courts of Justice

**Majority Members**
David B. "Dave" Albo (R-42)
   *Chairman*
Robert B. "Rob" Bell III (R-58)
   *Vice Chairman*
Leslie R. "Les" Adams (R-16)
Jeffrey L. Campbell (R-6)
Benjamin L. "Ben" Cline (R-24)
Christopher E. Collins (R-29)
C. Todd Gilbert (R-15)
Gregory David Habeeb (R-8)
Terry G. Kilgore (R-1)
James A. "Jay" Leftwich (R-78)
G. Manoli Loupassi (R-68)
Jackson H. Miller (R-50)

**Minority Members**
Charniele L. Herring (D-46)
Patrick A. Hope (D-47)
Paul E. Krizek (D-44)
T. Montgomery "Monty" Mason
   (D-93)
Jennifer L. "Jenn" McClellan
   (D-71)
David J. Toscano (D-57)
Vivian E. Watts (D-39)

*(continued on next page)*

**Courts of Justice** *continued*

**Majority Members** *continued*

J. Randall "Randy" Minchew (R-10)
Jason S. Miyares (R-82)
Richard L. "Rick" Morris (R-64)

## Education

| **Majority Members** | **Minority Members** |
|---|---|
| R. Steven "Steve" Landes (R-25) *Chair* | Lamont Bagby (D-74) |
| Brenda L. Pogge (R-96) *Vice Chair* | David L. Bulova (D-37) |
| Richard P. "Dickie" Bell (R-20) | Daun Sessoms Hester (D-89) |
| Mark L. Cole (R-88) | Mark L. Keam (D-35) |
| Glenn R. Davis, Jr. (R-84) | Joseph C. "Joe" Lindsey (D-90) |
| L. Mark Dudenhefer (R-2) | Jennifer L. "Jenn" McClellan |
| Thomas A. "Tag" Greason (R-32) | (D-71) |
| David A. "Dave" LaRock (R-33) | Roslyn C. "Roz" Tyler (D-75) |
| James A. "Jay" Leftwich (R-78) | |
| James M. "Jim" LeMunyon (R-67) | |
| L. Scott "Scott" Lingamfelter (R-31) | |
| James P. "Jimmie" Massie III (R-72) | |
| Roxann L. Robinson (R-27) | |
| David E. Yancey (R-94) | |
| Joseph R. Yost (R-12) | |

## Finance

| **Majority Members** | **Minority Members** |
|---|---|
| R. Lee Ware, Jr. (R-65) *Chair* | Lashrecse D. Aird (D-63) |
| Benjamin L. "Ben" Cline (R-24) *Vice Chair* | Eileen Filler-Corn (D-41) |
| Robert S. Bloxom, Jr. (R-100) | Mark L. Keam (D-35) |
| Kathy J. Byron (R-22) | Kaye Kory (D-38) |
| Mark L. Cole (R-88) | Kathleen J. Murphy (D-34) |
| C. Matthew Fariss (R-59) | Richard C. "Rip" Sullivan, Jr. |
| Peter F. Farrell (R-56) | (D-48) |
| Nicholas J. Freitas (R-30) | Vivian E. Watts (D-39) |
| Hyland F. "Buddy" Fowler (R-55) | |
| Christopher T. Head (R-17) | |
| Timothy D. "Tim" Hugo (R-40) | |
| Robert G. "Bob" Marshall (R-13) | |
| Robert D. "Bobby" Orrock, Sr. (R-54) | |
| Brenda L. Pogge (R-96) | |
| Scott W. Taylor (R-85) | |

## General Laws

| **Majority Members** | **Minority Members** |
|---|---|
| C. Todd Gilbert (R-15) *Chair* | Lashrecse D. Aird (D-63) |
| Christopher Kilian "Chris" Peace (R-97) *Vice Chair* | David L. Bulova (D-37) |
| David B. "Dave" Albo (R-42) | Betsy B. Carr (D-69) |
| Richard L. "Rich" Anderson (R-51) | Daun Sessoms Hester (D-89) |
| Thomas A. "Tag" Greason (R-32) | Kaye Kory (D-38) |
| Gordon C. Helsel, Jr. (R-91) | Rev. Delores L. McQuinn (D-70) |
| M. Keith Hodges (R-98) | Luke E. Torian (D-52) |
| Barry D. Knight (R-81) | Jeion A. Ward (D-92) |
| James A. "Jay" Leftwich (R-78) | |
| James M. "Jim" LeMunyon (R-67) | |
| Roxann L. Robinson (R-27) | |
| Robert B. "Rob" Bell III (R-58) | |
| Thomas C. "Tommy" Wright, Jr. (R-61) | |
| J. Randall "Randy" Minchew (R-10) | |
| Joseph R. Yost (R-12) | |

## Health, Welfare and Institutions

| **Majority Members** | **Minority Members** |
|---|---|
| Robert D. "Bobby" Orrock, Sr. (R-54) *Chair* | Lashrecse D. Aird (D-63) |
| John M. O'Bannon III (R-73) *Vice Chair* | Patrick A. Hope (D-47) |
| Richard P. "Dickie" Bell (R-20) | Matthew James (D-80) |
| Robert B. "Rob" Bell III (R-58) | Mark H. Levine (D-45) |
| James E. Edmunds II (R-60) | Marcia S. "Cia" Price (D-95) |
| Peter F. Farrell (R-56) | Mark D. Sickles (D-43) |
| T. Scott Garrett (R-23) | Lionell Spruill, Sr. (D-77) |
| Christopher T. Head (R-17) | |
| Gordon C. Helsel, Jr. (R-91) | |
| M. Keith Hodges (R-98) | |
| Christopher Kilian "Chris" Peace (R-97) | |
| Brenda L. Pogge (R-96) | |
| Roxann L. Robinson (R-27) | |
| Christopher P. "Chris" Stolle (R-83) | |
| Joseph R. Yost (R-12) | |

## Militia, Police and Public Safety

| **Majority Members** | **Minority Members** |
|---|---|
| L. Scott "Scott" Lingamfelter (R-31) *Chair* | John J. Bell (D-87) |
| Thomas C. "Tommy" Wright, Jr. (R-61) *Vice Chair* | Patrick A. Hope (D-47) |
| Benjamin L. "Ben" Cline (R-24) | Kaye Kory (D-38) |
| Glenn R. Davis, Jr. (R-84) | Alfonso H. Lopez (D-49) |
| James E. Edmunds II (R-60) | Salam "Sam" Rasoul (D-11) |
| C. Matthew Fariss (R-59) | Marcus B. Simon (D-53) |
| Hyland F. "Buddy" Fowler (R-55) | Roslyn C. "Roz" Tyler (D-75) |
| C. Todd Gilbert (R-15) | |
| Christopher T. Head (R-17) | |
| James W. "Will" Morefield (R-3) | |
| Richard L. "Rick" Morris (R-64) | |
| Israel D. O'Quinn (R-5) | |
| Larry Nick "Nick" Rush (R-7) | |
| Michael J. Webert (R-18) | |
| Tony O. Wilt (R-26) | |

## Privileges and Elections

| **Majority Members** | **Minority Members** |
|---|---|
| Mark L. Cole (R-88) *Chair* | Jennifer B. Boysko (D-86) |
| Jackson H. Miller (R-50) *Vice Chair* | Joseph C. "Joe" Lindsey (D-90) |
| Leslie R. "Les" Adams (R-16) | Kathleen J. Murphy (D-34) |
| David B. "Dave" Albo (R-42) | Marcia S. "Cia" Price (D-95) |
| Hyland F. "Buddy" Fowler (R-55) | Salam "Sam" Rasoul (D-11) |
| Timothy D. "Tim" Hugo (R-40) | Mark D. Sickles (D-43) |
| Riley Edward Ingram (R-62) | Luke E. Torian (D-52) |
| S. Chris Jones (R-76) | |
| R. Steven "Steve" Landes (R-25) | |
| J. Randall "Randy" Minchew (R-10) | |
| Jason S. Miyares (R-82) | |
| John M. O'Bannon III (R-73) | |
| Israel D. O'Quinn (R-5) | |
| Margaret Bevans Ransone (R-99) | |
| Larry Nick "Nick" Rush (R-7) | |

## Rules

| **Majority Members** | **Minority Members** |
|---|---|
| William J. "Bill" Howell (R-28) *Chair* | Betsy B. Carr (D-69) |
| M. Kirkland "Kirk" Cox (R-66) *Vice Chair* | Kenneth R. Plum (D-36) |
| Gregory David Habeeb (R-8) | Lionell Spruill, Sr. (D-77) |
| Riley Edward Ingram (R-62) | David J. Toscano (D-57) |
| S. Chris Jones (R-76) | |
| Terry G. Kilgore (R-1) | |
| Barry D. Knight (R-81) | |
| R. Steven "Steve" Landes (R-25) | |
| James P. "Jimmie" Massie III (R-72) | |

**Majority Members** *continued*

Robert D. "Bobby" Orrock, Sr.
 (R-54)
R. Lee Ware, Jr. (R-65)

## Science and Technology

| **Majority Members** | **Minority Members** |
|---|---|
| Richard L. "Rich" Anderson (R-51) | Stephen E. "Steve" Heretick (D-79) |
| *Chair* | Mark H. Levine (D-45) |
| Roxann L. Robinson (R-27) | Alfonso H. Lopez (D-49) |
| *Vice Chair* | Kenneth R. Plum (D-36) |
| Leslie R. "Les" Adams (R-16) | Salam "Sam" Rasoul (D-11) |
| Terry L. Austin (R-19) | Marcus B. Simon (D-53) |
| Robert S. Bloxom, Jr. (R-100) | Vivian E. Watts (D-39) |
| Kathy J. Byron (R-22) | |
| Jeffrey L. Campbell (R-6) | |
| L. Mark Dudenhefer (R-2) | |
| Nicholas J. Freitas (R-30) | |
| Gordon C. Helsel, Jr. (R-91) | |
| David A. "Dave" LaRock (R-33) | |
| James A. "Jay" Leftwich (R-78) | |
| Robert G. "Bob" Marshall (R-13) | |
| Todd E. Pillion (R-4) | |
| Ronald A. Villanueva (R-21) | |

## Transportation

| **Majority Members** | **Minority Members** |
|---|---|
| Ronald A. Villanueva (R-21) *Chair* | Lamont Bagby (D-74) |
| Timothy D. "Tim" Hugo (R-40) | Betsy B. Carr (D-69) |
| *Vice Chair* | Eileen Filler-Corn (D-41) |
| Leslie R. "Les" Adams (R-16) | Rev. Delores L. McQuinn (D-70) |
| Richard L. "Rich" Anderson (R-51) | Kenneth R. Plum (D-36) |
| Terry L. Austin (R-19) | David J. Toscano (D-57) |
| Glenn R. Davis, Jr. (R-84) | Jeion A. Ward (D-92) |
| L. Mark Dudenhefer (R-2) | |
| T. Scott Garrett (R-23) | |
| Gregory David Habeeb (R-8) | |
| David A. "Dave" LaRock (R-33) | |
| James M. "Jim" LeMunyon (R-67) | |
| J. Randall "Randy" Minchew (R-10) | |
| Todd E. Pillion (R-4) | |
| Scott W. Taylor (R-85) | |
| David E. Yancey (R-94) | |

# Washington Legislature

TTY: (800) 635-9993  Internet: www.leg.wa.gov

## Washington State Senate

P.O. Box 40482, Olympia, WA 98504-0482
Tel: (360) 786-7550  Fax: (360) 786-1999  TTY: (800) 635-9993

President of the Senate
 **Bradley Scott "Brad" Owen** (D) . . . . . . . . . . . . . . . . . (360) 786-7700
 Affiliation: Lieutenant Governor, Office of the Lieutenant Governor,
 State of Washington
 220 Legislative Building, 416 Sid Snyder Avenue, SW,
 Olympia, WA 98504
 Education: Walla Walla Col LittD
 Office Director **Ken Camp** . . . . . . . . . . . . . . . . . . . . . . . (360) 786-7714
  E-mail: ken.camp@leg.wa.gov
  Education: USC 1998 BA
President Pro Tem **Pam Roach** (R) . . . . . . . . . . . . . . . . . . (360) 786-7660
 Education: BYU 1970 BA
Vice President Pro Tem **Sharon Brown** (R) . . . . . . . . . . . (360) 786-7614
Majority Leader **Mark G. Schoesler** (R) . . . . . . . . . . . . . (360) 786-7620
Majority Deputy Leader **John E. Braun** (R) . . . . . . . . . . . (360) 786-7638
 Education: U Washington BS; Michigan MBA
Majority Floor Leader **Joe Fain** (R) . . . . . . . . . . . . . . . . . (360) 786-7692
 Education: Wisconsin BA; Seattle MBA, JD
Majority Deputy Floor Leader **Jim Honeyford** (R) . . . . . . (360) 786-7684
 Education: Central Washington BA, MEd
Majority Whip **Ann Rivers** (R) . . . . . . . . . . . . . . . . . . . . (360) 786-7634
Majority Assistant Whip **Mark Miloscia** (R) . . . . . . . . . . (360) 786-7658
 Education: Air Force Acad BS; North Dakota MBA; Chapman MA
Majority Caucus Chair **Linda Evans Parlette** (R) . . . . . . . . (360) 786-7622
 Education: Washington State 1968 BS
Majority Caucus Vice Chair **Jan Angel** (R) . . . . . . . . . . . (360) 786-7650
Democratic Leader **Sharon K. Nelson** (D) . . . . . . . . . . . . . (360) 786-7667
Democratic Deputy Leader **Andy Billig** (D) . . . . . . . . . . . (360) 786-7604
 Education: Georgetown BA
Democratic Floor Leader **Christine Rolfes** (D) . . . . . . . . . (360) 786-7644
 Education: Virginia BA; U Washington MPA
Democratic Assistant Floor Leader
 **Annette Cleveland** (D) . . . . . . . . . . . . . . . . . . . . . . . . (360) 786-7696
Democratic Whip **K. Cyrus Habib** (D) . . . . . . . . . . . . . . . (360) 786-7694
 Education: Columbia BA; Yale JD
Democratic Assistant Whip **Mark Mullet** (D) . . . . . . . . . . (360) 786-7608
 Education: Indiana BA; U Washington 2008 MA
Democratic Caucus Chair **Karen R. Fraser** (D) . . . . . . . . . (360) 786-7642
 Education: U Washington 1966 BA, 1969 MPA
Democratic Caucus Vice Chair **Rosemary McAuliffe** (D) . . (360) 786-7600
 Education: Seattle 1962 BS
Secretary of the Senate **Hunter Goodman** . . . . . . . . . . . . . (360) 786-7550
 E-mail: hunter.goodman@leg.wa.gov
Deputy Secretary **Pablo G. "Paul" Campos** . . . . . . . . . . . (360) 786-7501
 E-mail: paul.campos@leg.wa.gov
Sergeant-at-Arms **Andy Staubitz** . . . . . . . . . . . . . . . . . . . (360) 786-7547
 E-mail: andy.staubitz@leg.wa.gov

## Senators

**Party Affiliation Statistics:** Republicans: 25, Democrats: 24

Senator **Jan Angel** (R-District 26) . . . . . . . . . . . . . . . . . . . (360) 786-7650
 Counties Represented: Kitsap (part), Pierce (part)    Dist: (360) 443-2409
 Term Expires: 2019
 203A Irv Newhouse Building, Olympia, WA 98504
 1700 Southeast Mile Hill Drive, Suite 236,
 Port Orchard, WA 98366-3553
 E-mail: jan.angel@leg.wa.gov
 Committees: Financial Institutions, Housing and Insurance; Health
 Care; Trade and Economic Development
Senator **Barbara Bailey** (R-District 10) . . . . . . . . . . . . . . . (360) 786-7618
 Counties Represented: Island, Skagit (part), Snohomish (part)
 Term Expires: 2017
 109B Irv Newhouse Building, Olympia, WA 98504
 E-mail: barbara.bailey@leg.wa.gov
 Committees: Health Care; Higher Education; Rules; Ways and Means
 Education: SUNY (Albany) BS

*(continued on next page)*

**LEGISLATIVE BRANCH**

**Senators** *continued*

Senator **Michael "Mike" Baumgartner** (R-District 6) . . . . (360) 786-7610
Counties Represented: Spokane (part)    Dist: (509) 329-3740
Term Expires: 2019
Legislative Building, Room 404, Olympia, WA 98504
P. O. Box 40406, Olympia, WA 98504
901 North Monroe, Suite 222, Spokane, WA 99201
E-mail: michael.baumgartner@leg.wa.gov
Committees: Commerce and Labor; Health Care; Higher Education;
Transportation
Education: Washington State 1999 BSEc; Harvard MPA

Senator **Randi Becker** (R-District 2) . . . . . . . . . . . . . . . . . . (360) 786-7602
Counties Represented: Pierce (part), Thurston (part)
Term Expires: 2017
110 Irv Newhouse Building, Olympia, WA 98504-0402
PO Box 40402, Olympia, WA 98504-0402
E-mail: becker.randi@leg.wa.gov
Committees: Health Care; Ways and Means
Education: Green River Comm Col

Senator **Don Benton** (R-District 17) . . . . . . . . . . . . . . . . . . (360) 786-7632
Counties Represented: Clark (part)    Fax: (360) 786-7819
Term Expires: 2017
P.O. Box 40417, Vancouver, WA 98668
E-mail: benton.don@leg.wa.gov
Committees: Financial Institutions, Housing and Insurance;
Governmental Operations and Security; Rules; Transportation
Education: Concordia U (CA) BSBusMgt

Senator **Andy Billig** (D-District 3) . . . . . . . . . . . . . . . . . . . (360) 786-7604
Counties Represented: Spokane (part)    Dist: (509) 209-2427
Term Expires: 2017
412 Legislative Building, Olympia, WA 98504
25 West Main Avenue, Suite 237, Spokane, WA 99201-5090
E-mail: andy.billig@leg.wa.gov
Committees: Early Learning, K-12 Education; Rules; Ways and Means

Senator **John E. Braun** (R-District 20) . . . . . . . . . . . . . . . . (360) 786-7638
Counties Represented: Clark (part), Cowlitz (part), Lewis (part),
Thurston (part)
Term Expires: 2017
P.O. Box 40420, Olympia, WA 98504
E-mail: john.braun@leg.wa.gov
Committees: Commerce and Labor; Energy, Environment and
Telecommunications; Trade and Economic Development; Ways and
Means

Senator **Sharon Brown** (R-District 8) . . . . . . . . . . . . . . . . . (360) 786-7614
Counties Represented: Benton (part)
Term Expires: 2017
202 Irv Newhouse Building, Olympia, WA 98504
E-mail: sharon.brown@leg.wa.gov
Committees: Energy, Environment and Telecommunications; Health
Care; Trade and Economic Development; Ways and Means

Senator **Reuven Carlyle** (D-District 36) . . . . . . . . . . . . . . (360) 786-7814
Counties Represented: King (part)    Dist: (206) 216-3184
Term Expires: 2019
3131 Western Avenue, Seattle, WA 98121
E-mail: reuven.carlyle@leg.wa.gov
Committees: Higher Education; Trade and Economic Development;
Transportation

Senator **Maralyn Chase** (D-District 32) . . . . . . . . . . . . . . (360) 786-7662
Counties Represented: King (part), Snohomish    Dist: (206) 216-3200
(part)    Fax: (360) 786-7819
Term Expires: 2019
3131 Western Ave, Suite 421, Seattle, WA 98121
P. O. Box 40432, Olympia, WA 98504
E-mail: maralyn.chase@leg.wa.gov
Committees: Natural Resources and Parks; Rules; Trade and Economic
Development
Education: U Washington 1972 BA, 1974 MA

Senator **Annette Cleveland** (D-District 49) . . . . . . . . . . . . (360) 786-7696
Counties Represented: Clark (part)
Term Expires: 2017
220 John A. Cherberg Building, Olympia, WA 98504
E-mail: annette.cleveland@leg.wa.gov
Committees: Energy, Environment and Telecommunications; Health
Care; Transportation

Senator **Steve Conway** (D-District 29) . . . . . . . . . . . . . . . . (360) 786-7656
Counties Represented: Pierce (part)    Dist: (206) 366-2604
Term Expires: 2019
P. O. Box 40429, Olympia, WA 98504
E-mail: steve.conway@leg.wa.gov
Committees: Commerce and Labor; Health Care; Ways and Means
Education: Portland 1966 BS; Oregon 1969 MS, 1979 PhD

Senator **Bruce Dammeier** (R-District 25) . . . . . . . . . . . . . (360) 786-7648
Counties Represented: Pierce (part)    Dist: (360) 786-7550
Term Expires: 2017
205 Irv Newhouse Building, Olympia, WA 98504
101 South Meridian, Suite D, Puyallup, WA 98371
E-mail: bruce.dammeier@leg.wa.gov
Committees: Early Learning, K-12 Education; Health Care; Rules;
Ways and Means
Education: Naval Acad BS; U Washington MS

Senator **Brian Dansel** (R-District 7) . . . . . . . . . . . . . . . . . . (360) 786-7612
Counties Represented: Ferry, Okanogan (part), Pend    Dist: (509) 315-4312
Oreille, Spokane (part), Stevens
Term Expires: 2017
115B Irv Newhouse Building, Olympia, WA 98504
9507 N Division Street, Suite M3, Spokane, WA 99218
E-mail: brian.dansel@leg.wa.gov
Committees: Accountability and Reform; Agriculture, Water and Rural
Economic Development; Governmental Operations and Security;
Natural Resources and Parks

Senator **Jeannie Darneille** (D-District 27) . . . . . . . . . . . . . (360) 786-7652
Counties Represented: Pierce (part)
Term Expires: 2017
226 John A. Cherberg Building, Olympia, WA 98504
E-mail: jeannie.darneille@leg.wa.gov
Committees: Financial Institutions, Housing and Insurance; Human
Services, Mental Health, and Housing; Law and Justice
Education: Western Washington 1971 BA; Colorado State 1975 MA

Senator **Doug Ericksen** (R-District 42) . . . . . . . . . . . . . . . (360) 786-7682
Counties Represented: Whatcom (part)
Term Expires: 2019
P. O. Box 40442, Olympia, WA 98504
E-mail: doug.ericksen@leg.wa.gov
Committees: Energy, Environment and Telecommunications; Rules;
Trade and Economic Development; Transportation
Education: Cornell 1991 BA; Western Washington 1995 MA

Senator **Joe Fain** (R-District 47) . . . . . . . . . . . . . . . . . . . . . (360) 786-7692
Counties Represented: King (part)
Term Expires: 2019
P. O. Box 40447, Olympia, WA 98504
25 Second Street Northwest, Auburn, WA 98001
E-mail: joe.fain@leg.wa.gov
Committees: Early Learning, K-12 Education; Financial Institutions,
Housing and Insurance; Rules; Transportation

Senator **Karen R. Fraser** (D-District 22) . . . . . . . . . . . . . . (360) 786-7642
Counties Represented: Thurston (part)    Fax: (360) 786-1999
Term Expires: 2017
P.O. Box 40422, Olympia, WA 98504-0422
E-mail: fraser.karen@leg.wa.gov
Committees: Accountability and Reform; Rules; Ways and Means

Senator **David Frockt** (D-District 46) . . . . . . . . . . . . . . . . . (360) 729-3225
Counties Represented: King (part)    Dist: (206) 729-3243
Term Expires: 2017
PO Box 40446, Olympia, WA 98504-0446
155 Northeast 100th Street, Suite 218, Seattle, WA 98125
E-mail: david.frockt@leg.wa.gov
Committees: Health Care; Higher Education; Trade and Economic
Development
Education: Pennsylvania 1991 BA; UCLA 1998 JD

Senator **K. Cyrus Habib** (D-District 48) . . . . . . . . . . . . . . . (360) 786-7694
Counties Represented: King (part)    Dist: (425) 576-5189
Term Expires: 2019
P.O. Box 40448, Olympia, WA 98504
615 Market Street, Suite B, Kirkland, WA 98033
E-mail: cyrus.habib@leg.wa.gov
Committees: Energy, Environment and Telecommunications;
Governmental Operations and Security; Transportation

Senator **James E. "Jim" Hargrove** (D-District 24) . . . . . . (360) 786-7646
Counties Represented: Clallam, Grays Harbor    Dist: (360) 533-9477
(part), Jefferson    (Hoquaim)
Term Expires: 2017    Dist: (360) 457-2520
535 East 1st Street, P.O. Box 2496,    (Port Angeles)
Port Angeles, WA 98362    Res: (360) 532-4747
311 Seventh Street, Hoquiam, WA 98550    Fax: (360) 786-1323
E-mail: hargrove.jim@leg.wa.gov
Committees: Human Services, Mental Health, and Housing; Ways and
Means
Education: Oregon State 1976 BS

Senator **Bob Hasegawa** (D-District 11) . . . . . . . . . . . . . (360) 786-7616
Counties Represented: King (part)
Term Expires: 2017
223 John A. Cherberg Building, Olympia, WA 98504
E-mail: bob.hasegawa@leg.wa.gov
Committees: Commerce and Labor; Rules; Ways and Means
Education: Antioch U 2003 BA

Senator **Mike Hewitt** (R-District 16) . . . . . . . . . . . . . . (360) 786-7630
Counties Represented: Benton (part), Columbia,    Dist: (509) 545-2014
Franklin (part), Walla Walla    Fax: (360) 786-1266
Term Expires: 2017
P. O. Box 40416, Olympia, WA 98504
E-mail: hewitt.mike@leg.wa.gov
Committees: Natural Resources and Parks; Ways and Means

Senator **Andy Hill** (R-District 45) . . . . . . . . . . . . . . . . . (360) 786-7672
Counties Represented: King (part)
Term Expires: 2019
P. O. Box 40445, Olympia, WA 98504
E-mail: andy.hill@leg.wa.gov
Committees: Early Learning, K-12 Education; Ways and Means
Education: Colgate 1986 BS; Harvard 1990 MBA

Senator **Steve Hobbs** (D-District 44) . . . . . . . . . . . . . . (360) 786-7686
Counties Represented: Snohomish (part)    Dist: (425) 334-2092
Term Expires: 2019
P. O. Box 40444, Olympia, WA 98504
E-mail: hobbs.steve@leg.wa.gov
Committees: Agriculture, Water and Rural Economic Development;
Financial Institutions, Housing and Insurance; Transportation
Education: U Washington 1994 BA, 2011 MPA

Senator **Jim Honeyford** (R-District 15) . . . . . . . . . . . . (360) 786-7684
Counties Represented: Yakima (part)    Tel: (360) 786-7173
Term Expires: 2019    Fax: (360) 786-1999
100 Flagstone Lane, Sunnyside, WA 98944
E-mail: honeyford.jim@leg.wa.gov
Committees: Agriculture, Water and Rural Economic Development;
Energy, Environment and Telecommunications; Rules; Ways and Means

Senator **Pramila Jayapal** (D-District 37) . . . . . . . . . . . (360) 786-7688
Counties Represented: King (part)    Dist: (206) 435-7033
Term Expires: 2019
P.O. Box 40437, Olympia, WA 98504
1200 12th Avenue South, Eighth Floor, Seattle, WA 98144
E-mail: pramila.jayapal@leg.wa.gov
Committees: Accountability and Reform; Health Care; Transportation

Senator **Karen Keiser** (D-District 33) . . . . . . . . . . . . . . (360) 786-7664
Counties Represented: King (part)    Res: (253) 839-8694
Term Expires: 2019    Fax: (360) 786-1999
P. O. Box 40433, Olympia, WA 98504
E-mail: keiser.karen@leg.wa.gov
Committees: Commerce and Labor; Health Care; Ways and Means
Education: UC Berkeley 1969 BA, 1973 MA

Senator **Curtis King** (R-District 14) . . . . . . . . . . . . . . . (360) 786-7626
Counties Represented: Clark (part), Klickitat, Skamania, Yakima (part)
Term Expires: 2017
P.O. Box 40414, Olympia, WA 98504-0414
E-mail: king.curtis@leg.wa.gov
Committees: Commerce and Labor; Rules; Transportation
Education: U Washington BS; Furman MBA

Senator **Marko Liias** (D-District 21) . . . . . . . . . . . . . . . (360) 786-7640
Counties Represented: Snohomish (part)
Term Expires: 2019
213 John A. Cherberg Building, Olympia, WA 98504
E-mail: marko.liias@leg.wa.gov
Committees: Governmental Operations and Security; Higher Education;
Transportation

Senator **Steve Litzow** (R-District 41) . . . . . . . . . . . . . . (360) 786-7641
Counties Represented: King (part)    Tel: (425) 453-3076
Term Expires: 2017
P. O. Box 40441, Olympia, WA 98504
E-mail: steve.litzow@leg.wa.gov
Committees: Early Learning, K-12 Education; Financial Institutions,
Housing and Insurance; Transportation

Senator **Rosemary McAuliffe** (D-District 1) . . . . . . . . . . . (360) 786-7600
Counties Represented: King (part), Snohomish    Res: (425) 486-8397
(part)    Fax: (360) 786-1999
Term Expires: 2017    Dist: (425) 486-3120
P.O. Box 40401, Olympia, WA 98504-0401
E-mail: mcauliffe.rosemary@leg.wa.gov
Committees: Early Learning, K-12 Education; Natural Resources and
Parks

Senator **John R. McCoy** (D-District 38) . . . . . . . . . . . . . (360) 786-7674
Counties Represented: Snohomish (part)    Dist: (425) 257-1769
Term Expires: 2019
241 John A. Cherberg Building, Olympia, WA 98504
E-mail: john.mccoy@leg.wa.gov
Committees: Energy, Environment and Telecommunications;
Governmental Operations and Security; Trade and Economic
Development

Senator **Mark Miloscia** (R-District 30) . . . . . . . . . . . . . (360) 786-7658
Counties Represented: King (part), Pierce (part)
Term Expires: 2019
P.O. Box 40430, Olympia, WA 98504
33305 First Way SW, Suite B104, Federal Way, WA 98023
E-mail: mark.miloscia@leg.wa.gov
Committees: Accountability and Reform; Higher Education; Human
Services, Mental Health, and Housing; Transportation

Senator **Mark Mullet** (D-District 5) . . . . . . . . . . . . . . . (360) 786-7608
Counties Represented: King (part)
Term Expires: 2017
415 Legislative Building, Olympia, WA 98504
E-mail: mark.mullet@leg.wa.gov
Committees: Early Learning, K-12 Education; Financial Institutions,
Housing and Insurance; Rules

Senator **Sharon K. Nelson** (D-District 34) . . . . . . . . . . . (360) 786-7667
Counties Represented: King (part)    Dist: (206) 435-7032
Term Expires: 2019
P.O. Box 40434, Olympia, WA 98504
1200 12th Avenue South, 8th Floor, Seattle, WA 98144
E-mail: sharon.nelson@leg.wa.gov
Committees: Rules

Senator **Steve O'Ban** (R-District 28) . . . . . . . . . . . . . . . (360) 786-7654
Counties Represented: Pierce (part)
Term Expires: 2017
102 Irv Newhouse Building, Olympia, WA 98504
E-mail: steve.oban@leg.wa.gov
Committees: Human Services, Mental Health, and Housing; Law and
Justice; Ways and Means
Education: U Washington BA; Seattle JD

Senator **Mike Padden** (R-District 4) . . . . . . . . . . . . . . . (360) 786-7606
Counties Represented: Spokane (part)
Term Expires: 2017
P. O. Box 40404, Olympia, WA 98504
E-mail: padden.mike@leg.wa.gov
Committees: Accountability and Reform; Human Services, Mental
Health, and Housing; Law and Justice; Ways and Means

Senator **Linda Evans Parlette** (R-District 12) . . . . . . . . . . (360) 786-7622
Counties Represented: Chelan, Douglas, Grant    Dist: (509) 663-9702
(part), Okanogan (part)    Fax: (360) 786-1266
Term Expires: 2017    Dist: (509) 663-9703
Legislative Building, Room 305, Olympia, WA 98504
P.O. Box 40412, Olympia, WA 98504
E-mail: parlette.linda@leg.wa.gov
Committees: Health Care; Rules; Ways and Means

Senator **Kirk Pearson** (R-District 39) . . . . . . . . . . . . . . (360) 786-7676
Counties Represented: King (part), Skagit (part), Snohomish (part)
Term Expires: 2017
115D Irv Newhouse Building, Olympia, WA 98504
E-mail: kirk.pearson@leg.wa.gov
Committees: Governmental Operations and Security; Law and Justice;
Natural Resources and Parks; Rules
Education: Wenatchee Valley 1977 BA

Senator **Jamie Pedersen** (D-District 43) . . . . . . . . . . . . . (360) 786-7628
Counties Represented: King (part)
Term Expires: 2019
P. O. Box 40443, Olympia, WA 98504
E-mail: jamie.pedersen@leg.wa.gov
Committees: Financial Institutions, Housing and Insurance; Law and
Justice; Transportation
Education: Yale BA, JD

Senator **Kevin Ranker** (D-District 40) . . . . . . . . . . . . . . (360) 786-7678
Counties Represented: San Juan, Skagit (part), Whatcom (part)
Term Expires: 2017
P.O. Box 40440, Olympia, WA 98504-0440
E-mail: ranker.kevin@leg.wa.gov
Committees: Energy, Environment and Telecommunications; Ways and
Means

Senator **Ann Rivers** (R-District 18) . . . . . . . . . . . . . . . . (360) 786-7634
Counties Represented: Clark (part)    Res: (360) 576-1444
Term Expires: 2017
P.O. Box 40418, Olympia, WA 98504
E-mail: ann.rivers@leg.wa.gov
Committees: Early Learning, K-12 Education; Health Care; Rules;
Transportation

*(continued on next page)*

**LEGISLATIVE BRANCH**

**Senators** *continued*

Senator **Pam Roach** (R-District 31) . . . . . . . . . . . . . . . .(360) 786-7660
  Counties Represented: King (part), Pierce (part)
  Term Expires: 2019
  P.O. Box 650, Auburn, WA 98071
  E-mail: roach.pam@leg.wa.gov
  Committees: Financial Institutions, Housing and Insurance;
  Governmental Operations and Security; Law and Justice; Rules

Senator **Christine Rolfes** (D-District 23) . . . . . . . . . . . . . . (360) 786-7644
  Counties Represented: Kitsap (part)         Dist: (206) 780-7799
  Term Expires: 2017
  P.O. Box 40423, Olympia, WA 98504
  382 Wyatt Way Northeast, Bainbridge Island, WA 98110
  E-mail: christine.rolfes@leg.wa.gov
  Committees: Early Learning, K-12 Education; Rules; Ways and Means

Senator **Mark G. Schoesler** (R-District 9) . . . . . . . . . . . . . (360) 786-7620
  Counties Represented: Adams, Asotin, Franklin    Fax: (360) 786-1999
  (part), Garfield, Spokane (part), Whitman
  Term Expires: 2017
  Legislative Building, Room 307, Olympia, WA 98504
  P.O. Box 40409, Olympia, WA 98504
  E-mail: schoesler.mark@leg.wa.gov
  Committees: Rules; Ways and Means

Senator **Tim Sheldon** (D-District 35) . . . . . . . . . . . . . . . (360) 786-7668
  Counties Represented: Kitsap (part), Mason,    Res: (360) 877-5768
  Thurston (part)                 Fax: (360) 786-1999
  Note: Democrat Tim Sheldon caucused with the Republican Party
  during the 2016 legislative session.
  Term Expires: 2019
  P.O. Box 474, Hoodsport, WA 98548
  E-mail: sheldon.timothy@leg.wa.gov
  Committees: Energy, Environment and Telecommunications; Rules;
  Transportation
  Education: Pennsylvania 1969 BS; U Washington 1972 MBA

Senator **Dean A. Takko** (D-District 19) . . . . . . . . . . . . . . .(360) 786-7636
  Counties Represented: Cowlitz (part), Grays Harbor (part), Lewis
  (part), Pacific, Wahkiakum
  Term Expires: 2017
  E-mail: dean.takko@leg.wa.gov
  Committees: Agriculture, Water and Rural Economic Development;
  Governmental Operations and Security; Transportation
  Education: Lower Columbia 1970 AA; Western Washington 1972 BS

Senator **Judith "Judy" Warnick** (R-District 13) . . . . . . . . (360) 786-7624
  Counties Represented: Grant (part), Kittitas, Lincoln, Yakima (part)
  Term Expires: 2019
  P.O. Box 40413, Olympia, WA 98504
  E-mail: judith.warnick@leg.wa.gov
  Committees: Agriculture, Water and Rural Economic Development;
  Commerce and Labor; Natural Resources and Parks; Ways and Means

# Senate Standing Committees

P.O. Box 40466, Olympia, WA 98504
Tel: (360) 786-7400

## Accountability and Reform

| Majority Members | Minority Members |
|---|---|
| Mark Miloscia (R-30) *Chair* | Pramila Jayapal (D-37) |
| Mike Padden (R-4) *Vice Chair* | *Ranking Member* |
| Brian Dansel (R-7) | Karen R. Fraser (D-22) |

## Agriculture, Water and Rural Economic Development

| Majority Members | Minority Members |
|---|---|
| Judith "Judy" Warnick (R-13) *Chair* | Dean A. Takko (D-19) |
| Brian Dansel (R-7) *Vice Chair* | *Ranking Member* |
| Jim Honeyford (R-15) | Steve Hobbs (D-44) |

## Commerce and Labor

| Majority Members | Minority Members |
|---|---|
| Michael "Mike" Baumgartner (R-6) *Chair* | Bob Hasegawa (D-11) *Ranking Member* |
| John E. Braun (R-20) *Vice Chair* | Steve Conway (D-29) |
| Curtis King (R-14) | Karen Keiser (D-33) |
| Judith "Judy" Warnick (R-13) | |

## Early Learning, K-12 Education

| Majority Members | Minority Members |
|---|---|
| Steve Litzow (R-41) *Chair* | Rosemary McAuliffe (D-1) |
| Bruce Dammeier (R-25) *Vice Chair* | *Ranking Member* |
| Joe Fain (R-47) | Andy Billig (D-3) |
| Andy Hill (R-45) | Mark Mullet (D-5) |
| Ann Rivers (R-18) | Christine Rolfes (D-23) |

## Energy, Environment and Telecommunications

| Majority Members | Minority Members |
|---|---|
| Doug Ericksen (R-42) *Chair* | John R. McCoy (D-38) |
| Tim Sheldon (D-35) *Vice Chair* | *Ranking Member* |
| John E. Braun (R-20) | Annette Cleveland (D-49) |
| Sharon Brown (R-8) | K. Cyrus Habib (D-48) |
| Jim Honeyford (R-15) | Kevin Ranker (D-40) |

## Financial Institutions, Housing and Insurance

| Majority Members | Minority Members |
|---|---|
| Don Benton (R-17) *Chair* | Mark Mullet (D-5) |
| Jan Angel (R-26) *Vice Chair* | *Ranking Member* |
| Joe Fain (R-47) | Jeannie Darneille (D-27) |
| Steve Litzow (R-41) | Steve Hobbs (D-44) |
| Pam Roach (R-31) | Jamie Pedersen (D-43) |

## Governmental Operations and Security

| Majority Members | Minority Members |
|---|---|
| Pam Roach (R-31) *Chair* | Marko Liias (D-21) |
| Don Benton (R-17) *Vice Chair* | *Ranking Member* |
| Kirk Pearson (R-39) *Vice Chair* | K. Cyrus Habib (D-48) |
| Brian Dansel (R-7) | John R. McCoy (D-38) |
| | Dean A. Takko (D-19) |

## Health Care

| Majority Members | Minority Members |
|---|---|
| Randi Becker (R-2) *Chair* | David Frockt (D-46) |
| Bruce Dammeier (R-25) *Vice Chair* | *Ranking Member* |
| Jan Angel (R-26) | Annette Cleveland (D-49) |
| Barbara Bailey (R-10) | Steve Conway (D-29) |
| Michael "Mike" Baumgartner (R-6) | Pramila Jayapal (D-37) |
| Sharon Brown (R-8) | Karen Keiser (D-33) |
| Linda Evans Parlette (R-12) | |
| Ann Rivers (R-18) | |

## Higher Education

| Majority Members | Minority Members |
|---|---|
| Barbara Bailey (R-10) *Chair* | Reuven Carlyle (D-36) |
| Michael "Mike" Baumgartner (R-6) *Vice Chair* | David Frockt (D-46) |
| Mark Miloscia (R-30) | Marko Liias (D-21) |

## Human Services, Mental Health, and Housing

| Majority Members | Minority Members |
|---|---|
| Steve O'Ban (R-28) *Chair* | Jeannie Darneille (D-27) |
| Mark Miloscia (R-30) *Vice Chair* | *Ranking Member* |
| Mike Padden (R-4) | James E. "Jim" Hargrove (D-24) |

## Law and Justice

| Majority Members | Minority Members |
|---|---|
| Mike Padden (R-4) *Chair* | Jamie Pedersen (D-43) |
| Steve O'Ban (R-28) *Vice Chair* | *Ranking Member* |
| Kirk Pearson (R-39) | Jeannie Darneille (D-27) |
| Pam Roach (R-31) | |

## Natural Resources and Parks

| Majority Members | Minority Members |
|---|---|
| Kirk Pearson (R-39) *Chair* | Maralyn Chase (D-32) |
| Brian Dansel (R-7) *Vice Chair* | Rosemary McAuliffe (D-1) |
| Mike Hewitt (R-16) | |
| Judith "Judy" Warnick (R-13) | |

## Rules

**Majority Members**
Pam Roach (R-31) *Vice Chair*
Barbara Bailey (R-10)
Don Benton (R-17)
Bruce Dammeier (R-25)
Doug Ericksen (R-42)
Joe Fain (R-47)
Jim Honeyford (R-15)
Curtis King (R-14)
Linda Evans Parlette (R-12)
Kirk Pearson (R-39)
Ann Rivers (R-18)
Mark G. Schoesler (R-9)
Tim Sheldon (D-35)

**Minority Members**
Andy Billig (D-3)
Maralyn Chase (D-32)
Karen R. Fraser (D-22)
Bob Hasegawa (D-11)
Mark Mullet (D-5)
Sharon K. Nelson (D-34)
Christine Rolfes (D-23)

## Trade and Economic Development

**Majority Members**
Sharon Brown (R-8) *Chair*
John E. Braun (R-20) *Vice Chair*
Jan Angel (R-26)
Doug Ericksen (R-42)

**Minority Members**
Maralyn Chase (D-32)
   *Ranking Member*
Reuven Carlyle (D-36)
David Frockt (D-46)
John R. McCoy (D-38)

## Transportation

**Majority Members**
Curtis King (R-14) *Chair*
Don Benton (R-17) *Vice Chair*
Joe Fain (R-47) *Vice Chair*
Michael "Mike" Baumgartner (R-6)
Doug Ericksen (R-42)
Steve Litzow (R-41)
Mark Miloscia (R-30)
Ann Rivers (R-18)
Tim Sheldon (D-35)

**Minority Members**
Steve Hobbs (D-44)
   *Ranking Member*
Marko Liias (D-21)
   *Assistant Ranking Member*
Reuven Carlyle (D-36)
Annette Cleveland (D-49)
K. Cyrus Habib (D-48)
Pramila Jayapal (D-37)
Jamie Pedersen (D-43)
Dean A. Takko (D-19)

## Ways and Means

**Majority Members**
Andy Hill (R-45) *Chair*
John E. Braun (R-20) *Vice Chair*
Bruce Dammeier (R-25) *Vice Chair*
Jim Honeyford (R-15) *Vice Chair*
Barbara Bailey (R-10)
Randi Becker (R-2)
Sharon Brown (R-8)
Mike Hewitt (R-16)
Steve O'Ban (R-28)
Mike Padden (R-4)
Linda Evans Parlette (R-12)
Mark G. Schoesler (R-9)
Judith "Judy" Warnick (R-13)

**Minority Members**
James E. "Jim" Hargrove (D-24)
   *Ranking Member*
Karen Keiser (D-33)
   *Assistant Ranking Member*
Kevin Ranker (D-40)
   *Assistant Ranking Member*
Andy Billig (D-3)
Steve Conway (D-29)
Karen R. Fraser (D-22)
Bob Hasegawa (D-11)
Christine Rolfes (D-23)

# Washington House of Representatives

P.O. Box 40600, Olympia, WA 98504-0600
Tel: (360) 786-7573  Fax: (360) 786-7021

Speaker of the House **Frank Chopp** (D) . . . . . . . . . . . . . . . (360) 786-7920
   Education: U Washington 1975 BA
Speaker Pro Tempore **Jim Moeller** (D) . . . . . . . . . . . . . . (360) 786-7872
   Education: Washington State 1979 SB
Assistant Speaker Pro Tempore **Tina L. Orwall** (D) . . . . . . . (360) 786-7834
   Education: U Washington 1988 BS, 1991 MSW
Majority Leader **Pat Sullivan** (D) . . . . . . . . . . . . . . . . . . . (360) 786-7858
   Education: U Washington
Deputy Majority Leader **Larry Springer** (D) . . . . . . . . . . . (360) 786-7822
   Education: Western Washington 1969 BA; Oregon 1974 MS
Majority Floor Leader **Kristine Lytton** (D) . . . . . . . . . . . . . (360) 786-7800
Deputy Majority Floor Leader **Steve Bergquist** (D) . . . . . . (360) 786-7862
   Education: U Washington 2002 BA; Western Washington 2004 MA
Deputy Majority Floor Leader **Gael Tarleton** (D) . . . . . . . . (360) 786-7860
   Education: Georgetown 1981 BS, 1983 MA
Majority Whip **Kevin Van De Wege** (D) . . . . . . . . . . . . . . (360) 786-7916
   Education: Washington State 2002 BA
Deputy Majority Whip **Marcus Riccelli** (D) . . . . . . . . . . . . (360) 786-7888
   Education: Gonzaga 2000 BA; U Washington 2007 MPA

Deputy Majority Whip **Cindy Ryu** (D) . . . . . . . . . . . . . . . . (360) 786-7880
   Education: U Washington MS, MBA
Assistant Majority Whip **Joan McBride** (D) . . . . . . . . . . . . (360) 786-7848
Majority Caucus Chair **Eric Pettigrew** (D) . . . . . . . . . . . . (360) 786-7838
   Education: Oregon State 1981 BS; U Washington MSW
Minority Leader **Dan Kristiansen** (R) . . . . . . . . . . . . . . . . (360) 786-7967
Deputy Minority Leader **Joel Kretz** (R) . . . . . . . . . . . . . . (360) 786-7988
Minority Floor Leader **J. T. Wilcox** (R) . . . . . . . . . . . . . . (360) 786-7912
Assistant Minority Floor Leader **Matt Manweller** (R) . . . . (360) 786-7808
   Education: Whitman 1991 BS; Montana 1999 MA; Oregon 2003 PhD
Assistant Minority Floor Leader **Matt Shea** (R) . . . . . . . . (360) 786-7984
Minority Whip **Paul Harris** (R) . . . . . . . . . . . . . . . . . . . . (360) 786-7976
Assistant Minority Whip **Dan Griffey** (R) . . . . . . . . . . . . . (360) 786-7966
Assistant Minority Whip **Dave Hayes** (R) . . . . . . . . . . . . . (360) 786-7914
Assistant Minority Whip **Lynda Wilson** (R) . . . . . . . . . . . . (360) 786-7994
Minority Caucus Chair **Shelly Short** (R) . . . . . . . . . . . . . . (360) 786-7908
Minority Caucus Vice Chair **Joe Schmick** (R) . . . . . . . . . . (360) 786-7844
Chief Clerk of the House **Barbara Baker** . . . . . . . . . . . . . (360) 786-7751
   E-mail: baker_ba@leg.wa.gov
   Education: U Puget Sound JD

# Representatives

**Party Affiliation Statistics:** Republicans: 48, Democrats: 49, Vacancies: 1

Representative **Sherry V. Appleton** (D-District 23) . . . . . . . (360) 786-7934
   Counties Represented: Kitsap (part)
   Term Expires: 2017
   E-mail: sherry.appleton@leg.wa.gov
   Committees: Community Development, Housing, and Tribal Affairs;
   Public Safety; State Government
Representative **Andrew Barkis** (R-District 2) . . . . . . . . . . . (360) 786-7824
   Counties Represented: Pierce (part), Thurston (part)
   Term Expires: 2017
   E-mail: andrew.barkis@leg.wa.gov
   Committees: Business and Financial Services; Local Government
Representative **Steve Bergquist** (D-District 11) . . . . . . . . . (360) 786-7862
   Counties Represented: King (part)
   Term Expires: 2017
   E-mail: bergquist.steve@leg.wa.gov
   Committees: Education; Higher Education; State Government;
   Transportation
Representative **Brian E. Blake** (D-District 19) . . . . . . . . . . (360) 786-7870
   Counties Represented: Cowlitz (part), Grays Harbor      Dist: (360) 353-5241
   (part), Lewis (part), Pacific, Wahkiakum
   Term Expires: 2017
   1329 Broadway Street, Room 205, Longview, WA 98632
   E-mail: brian.blake@leg.wa.gov
   Committees: Agriculture and Natural Resources; Business and
   Financial Services; Commerce and Gaming
Representative **Vincent Buys** (R-District 42) . . . . . . . . . . . (360) 786-7854
   Counties Represented: Whatcom (part)
   Term Expires: 2017
   E-mail: vincent.buys@leg.wa.gov
   Committees: Agriculture and Natural Resources; Appropriations
Representative **Michelle Caldier** (R-District 26) . . . . . . . . . (360) 786-7802
   Counties Represented: Kitsap (part), Pierce (part)
   Term Expires: 2017
   John L. O'Brien Building, Room 417, Olympia, WA 98504
   E-mail: michelle.caldier@leg.wa.gov
   Committees: Education; General Government and Information
   Technology; Health Care and Wellness
Representative **Bruce Chandler** (R-District 15) . . . . . . . . . (360) 786-7960
   Counties Represented: Yakima (part)
   Term Expires: 2017
   E-mail: bruce.chandler@leg.wa.gov
   Committees: Agriculture and Natural Resources; Appropriations
Representative **Frank Chopp** (D-District 43) . . . . . . . . . . . (360) 786-7920
   Counties Represented: King (part)                  Dist: (206) 729-3223
   Term Expires: 2017                                 Fax: (206) 729-3220
   1200 12th Avenue South, Suite 801, Seattle, WA 98144
   E-mail: frank.chopp@leg.wa.gov
   Committees: Rules
   Affiliation: Executive Director, Fremont Public Association
Representative **Judy Clibborn** (D-District 41) . . . . . . . . . . (360) 786-7926
   Counties Represented: King (part)                  Tel: (425) 453-3075
   Term Expires: 2017
   1611 116th Avenue NE, Suite 206, Bellevue, WA 98004
   E-mail: judy.clibborn@leg.wa.gov
   Committees: Health Care and Wellness; Transportation

*(continued on next page)*

**Representatives** *continued*

Representative **Eileen L. Cody** (D-District 34) . . . . . . . . . . (360) 786-7978
Counties Represented: King (part)          Dist: (206) 389-2590
Term Expires: 2017
1200 12th Avenue South, Suite 801, Seattle, WA 98144
P.O. Box 16327, Seattle, WA 98116
E-mail: eileen.cody@leg.wa.gov
Committees: Appropriations; Health Care and Wellness

Representative **Cary Condotta** (R-District 12) . . . . . . . . . . (360) 786-7954
Counties Represented: Chelan, Douglas, Grant     Dist: (509) 664-1274
(part), Okanogan (part)
Term Expires: 2017
3021 G. S. Center Road, Suite C, Wenatchee, WA 98801
E-mail: cary.condotta@leg.wa.gov
Committees: Appropriations; Commerce and Gaming; Finance

Representative **Richard C. DeBolt** (R-District 20) . . . . . . . . (360) 786-7896
Counties Represented: Clark (part), Cowlitz (part), Lewis (part),
Thurston (part)
Term Expires: 2017
E-mail: richard.debolt@leg.wa.gov
Committees: Capital Budget; Health Care and Wellness; Technology
and Economic Development
Affiliation: Executive Director, Twin Cities Chamber of Commerce
Education: Wyoming BS

Representative **Tom Dent** (R-District 13) . . . . . . . . . . . . . . (360) 786-7932
Counties Represented: Grant (part), Kittitas, Lincoln, Yakima (part)
Term Expires: 2017
John L. O'Brien Building, Room 411, Olympia, WA 98504
E-mail: tom.dent@leg.wa.gov
Committees: Agriculture and Natural Resources; Appropriations; Early
Learning and Human Services

Representative **Mary Dye** (R-District 9) . . . . . . . . . . . . . . . (360) 786-7942
Counties Represented: Adams, Asotin, Franklin (part), Garfield,
Spokane (part), Whitman
Term Expires: 2017
432 John L. O'Brien Building, Olympia, WA 98504
E-mail: mary.dye@leg.wa.gov
Committees: Business and Financial Services; Environment

Representative **Jessyn Farrell** (D-District 46) . . . . . . . . . . . (360) 786-7818
Counties Represented: King (part)
Term Expires: 2017
E-mail: farrell.jessyn@leg.wa.gov
Committees: Environment; Rules; Transportation
Education: U Washington BA

Representative **Jake Fey** (D-District 27) . . . . . . . . . . . . . . . (360) 786-7974
Counties Represented: Pierce (part)          Dist: (253) 534-3233
Term Expires: 2017
7406 27th Street West, Suite 207, University Place, WA 98466
E-mail: fey.jake@leg.wa.gov
Committees: Environment; Technology and Economic Development;
Transportation
Education: U Washington BA; U Puget Sound MBA

Representative **Joe Fitzgibbon** (D-District 34) . . . . . . . . . (360) 786-7952
Counties Represented: King (part)          Dist: (206) 923-5475
Term Expires: 2017
219 First Avenue South, Seattle, WA 98116
E-mail: joe.fitzgibbon@leg.wa.gov
Committees: Environment; Finance; Local Government

Representative **Noel Frame** (D-District 36) . . . . . . . . . . . . (360) 786-7814
Counties Represented: King (part)
John L. O'Brien Building, Room 317, Olympia, WA 98504
E-mail: noel.frame@leg.wa.gov
Committees: Finance; Higher Education; State Government

Representative **Roger E. Goodman** (D-District 45) . . . . . . . (360) 786-7878
Counties Represented: King (part)          Dist: (425) 739-1810
Term Expires: 2017
615 Market Street, Suite B, Kirkland, WA 98033
E-mail: roger.goodman@leg.wa.gov
Committees: Environment; Judiciary; Public Safety
Education: Dartmouth 1983 AB; George Washington 1986 JD;
Harvard 1998 MPA

Representative **Mia Gregerson** (D-District 33) . . . . . . . . . . (360) 786-7868
Counties Represented: King (part)          Tel: (206) 423-1210
Term Expires: 2017
E-mail: mia.gregerson@leg.wa.gov
Committees: Labor; Local Government; Transportation
Education: U Washington BA

Representative **Dan Griffey** (R-District 35) . . . . . . . . . . . . . (360) 786-7966
Counties Represented: Kitsap (part), Mason, Thurston (part)
Term Expires: 2017
John L. O'Brien, Room 410, Olympia, WA 98504
E-mail: dan.griffey@leg.wa.gov
Committees: Education; Local Government; Public Safety

Representative **Larry Haler** (R-District 8) . . . . . . . . . . . . . . (360) 786-7986
Counties Represented: Benton (part)          Dist: (509) 372-7997
Term Expires: 2017
719 Jadwin Avenue, Suite 6, Richland, WA 99352
E-mail: larry.haler@leg.wa.gov
Committees: Appropriations; Higher Education; Judiciary; Rules
Education: City U (WA) 2001 MABA; Pacific Lutheran 1974 AB

Representative **Drew Hansen** (D-District 23) . . . . . . . . . . . (360) 786-7842
Counties Represented: Kitsap (part)
Term Expires: 2017
E-mail: drew.hansen@leg.wa.gov
Committees: Appropriations; Higher Education; Judiciary
Education: Harvard AB; Oxford (UK) 1997 BA; Yale 2000 JD

Representative **Mark Hargrove** (R-District 47) . . . . . . . . . . (360) 786-7918
Counties Represented: King (part)
Term Expires: 2017
E-mail: mark.hargrove@leg.wa.gov
Committees: Education; Higher Education; Transportation

Representative **Mark Harmsworth** (R-District 44) . . . . . . . (360) 786-7751
Counties Represented: Snohomish (part)
Term Expires: 2017
E-mail: mark.harmsworth@leg.wa.gov
Committees: Rules; Technology and Economic Development;
Transportation

Representative **Paul Harris** (R-District 17) . . . . . . . . . . . . . (360) 786-7976
Counties Represented: Clark (part)          Dist: (360) 260-6128
Term Expires: 2017
237 Northeast Chkalov Drive, Suite 106, Vancouver, WA 98684
E-mail: paul.harris@leg.wa.gov
Committees: Appropriations; Health Care and Wellness; Rules

Representative **Brad Hawkins** (R-District 12) . . . . . . . . . . (360) 786-7832
Counties Represented: Chelan, Douglas, Grant (part), Okanogan (part)
Term Expires: 2017
E-mail: hawkins.brad@leg.wa.gov
Committees: Community Development, Housing, and Tribal Affairs;
Early Learning and Human Services; State Government
Education: Central Washington 1999 BA;
George Washington 2001 MPA

Representative **Dave Hayes** (R-District 10) . . . . . . . . . . . . . (360) 786-7914
Counties Represented: Island, Skagit (part), Snohomish (part)
Term Expires: 2017
E-mail: hayes.dave@leg.wa.gov
Committees: Education; Public Safety; Transportation

Representative **Teri Hickel** (R-District 30) . . . . . . . . . . . . . (360) 786-7573
Counties Represented: King (part), Pierce (part)
Term Expires: 2017
E-mail: teri@terihickel.com
Committees: Community Development, Housing, and Tribal Affairs;
Rules; Transportation

Representative **Jeff Holy** (R-District 6) . . . . . . . . . . . . . . . . (360) 786-7962
Counties Represented: Spokane (part)
Term Expires: 2017
E-mail: holy.jeff@leg.wa.gov
Committees: Commerce and Gaming; Higher Education; State
Government
Education: Washington State BA; Gonzaga 1990 JD

Representative **Zachary "Zack" Hudgins** (D-District 11) . . (360) 786-7956
Counties Represented: King (part)          Dist: (206) 501-2233
Term Expires: 2017
8601 8th Avenue South, Suite 6, Seattle, WA 98108
E-mail: zack.hudgins@leg.wa.gov
Committees: Appropriations; General Government and Information
Technology; Technology and Economic Development

Representative **Samuel W. "Sam" Hunt** (D-District 22) . . (360) 786-7992
Counties Represented: Thurston (part)
Term Expires: 2017
E-mail: sam.hunt@leg.wa.gov
Committees: Appropriations; Education; State Government
Education: Washington State 1967 BA

Representative **Christopher Hurst** (D-District 31) . . . . . . . . (360) 786-7866
Counties Represented: King (part), Pierce (part)     Dist: (360) 825-4941
Term Expires: 2017
John L. O'Brien Building, Room 320, Olympia, WA 98504
1174 Myrtle Avenue, Enumclaw, WA 98022
E-mail: christopher.hurst@leg.wa.gov
Committees: Agriculture and Natural Resources; Business and
Financial Services; Commerce and Gaming

Representative **Laurie Jinkins** (D-District 27) . . . . . . . . . . (360) 786-7930
Counties Represented: Pierce (part)       Dist: (253) 566-5610
Term Expires: 2017
7406 27th Street West, Suite 207, University Place, WA 98466
E-mail: laurie.jinkins@leg.wa.gov
Committees: Appropriations; Health Care and Wellness; Judiciary
Education: Wisconsin 1985 BBA, 1987 MA; Seattle 1990 JD

Representative **Norm Johnson** (R-District 14) . . . . . . . . . . (360) 786-7810
Counties Represented: Clark (part), Klickitat,       Dist: (509) 454-7210
Skamania, Yakima (part)
Term Expires: 2017
421 North 20th Avenue, Suite A, Yakima, WA 98902
E-mail: norm.johnson@leg.wa.gov
Committees: Community Development, Housing, and Tribal Affairs;
Health Care and Wellness

Representative **Ruth Kagi** (D-District 32) . . . . . . . . . . . . . . (360) 786-7910
Counties Represented: King (part), Snohomish       Dist: (206) 366-2622
(part)       Fax: (206) 368-4693
Term Expires: 2017
15031 Aurora Avenue North, Suite 421, Shoreline, WA 98133
E-mail: ruth.kagi@leg.wa.gov
Committees: Appropriations; Early Learning and Human Services
Education: U Washington 1967 BA; Syracuse 1968 MPA

Representative **Christine Kilduff** (D-District 28) . . . . . . . . . (360) 786-7958
Counties Represented: Pierce (part)
Term Expires: 2017
John L. O'Brien Building, Room 331, Olympia, WA 98504
E-mail: christine.kilduff@leg.wa.gov
Committees: Capital Budget; Early Learning and Human Services;
Education; Judiciary

Representative **Steve Kirby** (D-District 29) . . . . . . . . . . . . (360) 786-7996
Counties Represented: Pierce (part)
Term Expires: 2017
E-mail: steve.kirby@leg.wa.gov
Committees: Business and Financial Services; Commerce and Gaming;
Judiciary

Representative **Brad Klippert** (R-District 8) . . . . . . . . . . . . (360) 786-7882
Counties Represented: Benton (part)       Dist: (509) 396-9838
Term Expires: 2017
3311 West Clearwater Avenue, Suite D108, Kennewick, WA 99336
E-mail: brad.klippert@leg.wa.gov
Committees: Education; Judiciary; Public Safety

Representative **Linda Kochmar** (R-District 30) . . . . . . . . . (360) 786-7898
Counties Represented: King (part), Pierce (part)       Dist: (206) 429-2378
Term Expires: 2017
33305 First Way SW, Suite B104, Federal Way, WA 98023
E-mail: kochmar.linda@leg.wa.gov
Committees: Business and Financial Services; Capital Budget;
Transportation

Representative **Joel Kretz** (R-District 7) . . . . . . . . . . . . . . . (360) 786-7988
Counties Represented: Ferry, Okanogan (part), Pend       Dist: (509) 826-7203
Oreille, Spokane (part), Stevens
Term Expires: 2017
20 North Main Street, Omak, WA 98841
P.O. Box I, Omak, WA 99841
E-mail: joel.kretz@leg.wa.gov
Committees: Agriculture and Natural Resources; Rules

Representative **Dan Kristiansen** (R-District 39) . . . . . . . . . (360) 786-7967
Counties Represented: King (part), Skagit (part), Snohomish (part)
Term Expires: 2017
E-mail: dan.kristiansen@leg.wa.gov
Committees: Rules

Representative **Patty Kuderer** (D-District 48) . . . . . . . . . . . (425) 453-3064
Counties Represented: King (part)
Term Expires: 2017
1611 116th Avenue NE, Suite 206, Bellevue, WA 98004
E-mail: kuderer.patty@leg.wa.gov
Committees: Education; General Government and Information
Technology; Judiciary

Representative **Kristine Lytton** (D-District 40) . . . . . . . . . . (360) 786-7800
Counties Represented: San Juan, Skagit (part),       Dist: (360) 676-2105
Whatcom (part)
Term Expires: 2017
Legislative Building, Suite 429A, Olympia, WA 98504
960 Harris Avenue, Suite 201, Bellingham, WA 98225
E-mail: kristine.lytton@leg.wa.gov
Committees: Agriculture and Natural Resources; Appropriations;
Education; Rules

Representative **Drew C. MacEwen** (R-District 35) . . . . . . . (360) 786-7902
Counties Represented: Kitsap (part), Mason, Thurston (part)
Term Expires: 2017
267 AA John L. O'Brien, JLOB 434, Olympia, WA 98504
E-mail: macewen.drew@leg.wa.gov
Committees: Appropriations; General Government and Information
Technology

Representative **Chad Magendanz** (R-District 5) . . . . . . . . . (360) 786-7876
Counties Represented: King (part)
Term Expires: 2017
E-mail: magendanz.chad@leg.wa.gov
Committees: Appropriations; Education; Technology and Economic
Development
Education: Cornell 1985 BS

Representative **Matt Manweller** (R-District 13) . . . . . . . . . . (360) 786-7808
Counties Represented: Grant (part), Kittitas, Lincoln, Yakima (part)
Term Expires: 2017
E-mail: manweller.matt@leg.wa.gov
Committees: Finance; Labor

Representative **Joan McBride** (D-District 48) . . . . . . . . . . . (360) 786-7848
Counties Represented: King (part)
Term Expires: 2017
John L. O'Brien Building, Room 335, Olympia, WA 98504
E-mail: joan.mcbride@leg.wa.gov
Committees: Environment; Local Government; Rules; Transportation

Representative **Gina McCabe** (R-District 14) . . . . . . . . . . . (360) 786-7856
Counties Represented: Clark (part), Klickitat, Skamania, Yakima (part)
Term Expires: 2017
John L. O'Brien Building, Room 431, Olympia, WA 98504
E-mail: gina.mccabe@leg.wa.gov
Committees: Business and Financial Services; General Government and
Information Technology; Labor

Representative **Bob McCaslin, Jr.** (R-District 4) . . . . . . . . . (360) 786-7820
Counties Represented: Spokane (part)
Term Expires: 2017
John L. O'Brien Building, Room 425, Olympia, WA 98504
E-mail: bob.mccaslin@leg.wa.gov
Committees: Early Learning and Human Services; Education; Local
Government

Representative **Jim Moeller** (D-District 49) . . . . . . . . . . . . . (360) 786-7872
Counties Represented: Clark (part)
Term Expires: 2017
E-mail: jim.moeller@leg.wa.gov
Committees: Health Care and Wellness; Labor; Rules; Transportation

Representative **Jeff Morris** (D-District 40) . . . . . . . . . . . . . . (360) 786-7970
Counties Represented: San Juan, Skagit (part),       Dist: (360) 588-6227
Whatcom (part)
Term Expires: 2017
2415 T Avenue, Suite 202, Anacortes, WA 98221
E-mail: jeff.morris@leg.wa.gov
Committees: General Government and Information Technology;
Technology and Economic Development; Transportation
Affiliation: Founder, J. Robert Morris Corp.
Education: Central Washington BA

Representative **Luis Moscoso** (D-District 1) . . . . . . . . . . . . . (360) 786-7900
Counties Represented: King (part), Snohomish       Dist: (425) 398-4212
(part)
Term Expires: 2017
817 238th Street Southeast, Suite L, Bothell, WA 98021
E-mail: luis.moscoso@leg.wa.gov
Committees: Commerce and Gaming; Public Safety; Transportation
Education: Iowa 1974 BA

Representative
**Richard Walter "Dick" Muri** (R-District 28) . . . . . . . . . (360) 786-7890
Counties Represented: Pierce (part)
Term Expires: 2017
930 Tacoma Avenue South, Room 1046, Tacoma, WA 98402
E-mail: dick.muri@leg.wa.gov
Committees: Education; Judiciary

Representative **Terry R. Nealey** (R-District 16) . . . . . . . . . . (360) 786-7828
Counties Represented: Benton (part), Columbia,       Dist: (509) 526-6284
Franklin (part), Walla Walla
Term Expires: 2017
26 East Main Street, Suite 205, Walla Walla, WA 99362
E-mail: terry.nealey@leg.wa.gov
Committees: Finance; Technology and Economic Development

*(continued on next page)*

**Representatives** *continued*

Representative **Ed Orcutt** (R-District 20) . . . . . . . . . . . . (360) 786-7812
Counties Represented: Clark (part), Cowlitz (part),      Dist: (360) 673-4978
Lewis (part), Thurston (part)                            Fax: (360) 673-4979
Term Expires: 2017
110 West Marine Drive, Kalama, WA 98625
P.O. Box 1820, Kalama, WA 98625
E-mail: ed.orcutt@leg.wa.gov
Committees: Agriculture and Natural Resources; Finance;
Transportation
Education: Maine 1984 AS; Idaho 1987 BS

Representative **Timm Ormsby** (D-District 3) . . . . . . . . . . . (360) 786-7946
Counties Represented: Spokane (part)                     Dist: (509) 458-2122
Term Expires: 2017
25 West Main Street, Suite 238, Spokane, WA 99201
E-mail: timm.ormsby@leg.wa.gov
Committees: Appropriations; Labor

Representative **Lillian Ortiz-Self** (D-District 21) . . . . . . . . (360) 786-7972
Counties Represented: Snohomish (part)
Term Expires: 2017
John L. O'Brien Building, Room 330, Olympia, WA 98504
E-mail: lillian.ortiz-self@leg.wa.gov
Committees: Early Learning and Human Services; Education;
Transportation

Representative **Tina L. Orwall** (D-District 33) . . . . . . . . . . (360) 786-7834
Counties Represented: King (part)                        Dist: (206) 824-5097
Term Expires: 2017                                       Fax: (206) 824-5098
22525 Marine View Drive South, Suite 204, Des Moines, WA 98198
E-mail: tina.orwall@leg.wa.gov
Committees: Education; Judiciary; Public Safety; Rules

Representative **Kevin Parker** (R-District 6) . . . . . . . . . . . . (360) 786-7922
Counties Represented: Spokane (part)                     Dist: (509) 455-7225
Term Expires: 2017
10 North Post Street, Suite 648, Spokane, WA 99201
E-mail: kevin.parker@leg.wa.gov
Committees: Appropriations

Representative **Strom Peterson** (D-District 21) . . . . . . . . . (360) 786-7950
Counties Represented: Snohomish (part)
Term Expires: 2017
John L. O'Brien Building, Room 324, Olympia, WA 98504
E-mail: strom.peterson@leg.wa.gov
Committees: Capital Budget; Environment; Local Government

Representative **Eric Pettigrew** (D-District 37) . . . . . . . . . . (360) 786-7838
Counties Represented: King (part)                        Dist: (206) 587-5543
Term Expires: 2017
219 First Avenue South, Suite 205, Seattle, WA 98144
E-mail: eric.pettigrew@leg.wa.gov
Committees: Agriculture and Natural Resources; Appropriations; Public
Safety; Rules

Representative **Liz Pike** (R-District 18) . . . . . . . . . . . . . . . (360) 786-7751
Counties Represented: Clark (part)
Term Expires: 2017
E-mail: liz.pike@leg.wa.gov
Committees: Environment; Local Government; Transportation

Representative **Gerry Pollet** (D-District 46) . . . . . . . . . . . (360) 786-7886
Counties Represented: King (part)                        Dist: (206) 729-3234
Term Expires: 2017
John L. O'Brien Building, Room 317, Olympia, WA 98504-0600
PO Box 40600, Olympia, WA 98504-0600
5031 University Way, NE, Suite 107, Seattle, WA 98105
E-mail: gerry.pollet@leg.wa.gov
Committees: Education; Finance; Higher Education

Representative **Chris Reykdal** (D-District 22) . . . . . . . . . . . (360) 786-7940
Counties Represented: Thurston (part)
Term Expires: 2017
E-mail: chris.reykdal@leg.wa.gov
Committees: Finance; Higher Education; Rules
Education: Washington State 1994 BA; North Carolina 1999 MA

Representative **Marcus Riccelli** (D-District 3) . . . . . . . . . . (360) 786-7888
Counties Represented: Spokane (part)
Term Expires: 2017
E-mail: riccelli.marcus@leg.wa.gov
Committees: Capital Budget; Health Care and Wellness; Transportation

Representative **June Robinson** (D-District 38) . . . . . . . . . . (360) 786-7864
Counties Represented: Snohomish (part)
Term Expires: 2017
John L. O'Brien Building, Room 332, Olympia, WA 98504-0600
E-mail: june.robinson@leg.wa.gov
Committees: Community Development, Housing, and Tribal Affairs;
Finance; Health Care and Wellness

Representative **Jay Rodne** (R-District 5) . . . . . . . . . . . . . . (360) 786-7852
Counties Represented: King (part)
Term Expires: 2017
E-mail: jay.rodne@leg.wa.gov
Committees: Health Care and Wellness; Judiciary; Transportation
Education: Gonzaga 1997 JD

Representative **J.D. Rossetti** (D-District 19) . . . . . . . . . . . (360) 786-7573
Counties Represented: Cowlitz (part), Grays Harbor (part), Lewis
(part), Pacific, Wahkiakum
Term Expires: 2017
E-mail: rossetti_ju@leg.wa.gov
Committees: Education; Technology and Economic Development;
Transportation

Representative **Cindy Ryu** (D-District 32) . . . . . . . . . . . . . (360) 786-7880
Counties Represented: King (part), Snohomish          Dist: (206) 366-2618
(part)
Term Expires: 2017
15031 Aurora Avenue North, Shoreline, WA 98133
E-mail: cindy.ryu@leg.wa.gov
Committees: Business and Financial Services; Finance; Rules;
Technology and Economic Development

Representative **Sharon Tomiko Santos** (D-District 37) . . . (360) 786-7944
Counties Represented: King (part)                     Dist: (206) 587-5549
Term Expires: 2017
1200 12th Avenue South, Suite 801, Seattle, WA 98144
P.O. Box 28992, Seattle, WA 98118-8992
E-mail: sharontomiko.santos@leg.wa.gov
Committees: Business and Financial Services; Education; Technology
and Economic Development
Education: Evergreen State 1985 BA; Northeastern 1988 MA

Representative **David Sawyer** (D-District 29) . . . . . . . . . . (360) 786-7906
Counties Represented: Pierce (part)
Term Expires: 2017
E-mail: sawyer.david@leg.wa.gov
Committees: Appropriations; Community Development, Housing, and
Tribal Affairs; Early Learning and Human Services
Education: Central Washington 2005 BA

Representative **Joe Schmick** (R-District 9) . . . . . . . . . . . . (360) 786-7844
Counties Represented: Adams, Asotin, Franklin (part), Garfield,
Spokane (part), Whitman
Term Expires: 2017
E-mail: joe.schmick@leg.wa.gov
Committees: Agriculture and Natural Resources; Appropriations; Health
Care and Wellness

Representative **Elizabeth Scott** (R-District 39) . . . . . . . . . (360) 786-7816
Counties Represented: King (part), Skagit (part), Snohomish (part)
Term Expires: 2017
John L. O'Brien Building, Room 436, Olympia, WA 98504
E-mail: scott.elizabeth@leg.wa.gov
Committees: Commerce and Gaming; Early Learning and Human
Services
Education: Seattle Pacific BA; Southern Illinois MA

Representative **Mike Sells** (D-District 38) . . . . . . . . . . . . . (360) 786-7840
Counties Represented: Snohomish (part)                Dist: (425) 257-2168
Term Expires: 2017
2812 Lombard Avenue, Suite 210, Everett, WA 98201
E-mail: mike.sells@leg.wa.gov
Committees: Higher Education; Labor; Transportation
Education: Central Washington 1967 BA

Representative **Tana Senn** (D-District 41) . . . . . . . . . . . . . (360) 786-7894
Counties Represented: King (part)
Term Expires: 2017
John L. O'Brien Building, Room 309, Olympia, WA 98504-0600
E-mail: tana.senn@leg.wa.gov
Committees: Appropriations; Early Learning and Human Services
Education: Columbia MPPA

Representative **Matt Shea** (R-District 4) . . . . . . . . . . . . . . (360) 786-7984
Counties Represented: Spokane (part)                  Dist: (509) 921-2353
Term Expires: 2017
502 South Sullivan Road, Suite 207, Spokane Valley, WA 99037
E-mail: matt.shea@leg.wa.gov
Committees: Environment; Judiciary; Transportation

Representative **Shelly Short** (R-District 7) . . . . . . . . . . . . (360) 786-7908
Counties Represented: Ferry, Okanogan (part), Pend   Dist: (509) 775-8047
Oreille, Spokane (part), Stevens
Term Expires: 2017
147 North Clarke Avenue, Suite 5, Republic, WA 99166
E-mail: shelly.short@leg.wa.gov
Committees: Environment; Health Care and Wellness; Rules

Representative **Norma Smith** (R-District 10) . . . . . . . . . . (360) 786-7884
 Counties Represented: Island, Skagit (part),  Dist: (360) 678-3604
 Snohomish (part)
 Term Expires: 2017
 22 Front Street, NW, Suite C, Coupeville, WA 98239
 P.O. Box 507, Coupeville, WA 98239
 E-mail: norma.smith@leg.wa.gov
 Committees: Capital Budget; Technology and Economic Development

Representative **Larry Springer** (D-District 45) . . . . . . . . . . (360) 786-7822
 Counties Represented: King (part)  Dist: (425) 739-1806
 Term Expires: 2017
 615 Market Street, Suite B, Kirkland, WA 98033
 E-mail: larry.springer@leg.wa.gov
 Committees: Appropriations; Education; Finance; Rules

Representative **Melanie Stambaugh** (R-District 25) . . . . . . (360) 786-7948
 Counties Represented: Pierce (part)
 Term Expires: 2017
 P.O. Box 40600, Olympia, WA 98504
 E-mail: melanie.stambaugh@leg.wa.gov
 Committees: Education; Higher Education; Rules

Representative **Derek Stanford** (D-District 1) . . . . . . . . . . (360) 786-7928
 Counties Represented: King (part), Snohomish  Dist: (425) 361-2283
 (part)
 Term Expires: 2017
 21818 66th Avenue West, Suite 14, Mountlake Terrace, WA 98043
 E-mail: derek.stanford@leg.wa.gov
 Committees: Agriculture and Natural Resources; Business and
 Financial Services; Capital Budget
 Education: Harvey Mudd 1993 MS; U Washington 1999 PhD

Representative **Drew Stokesbary** (R-District 31) . . . . . . . . (360) 786-7846
 Counties Represented: King (part), Pierce (part)
 Term Expires: 2017
 John L. O'Brien Building, Room 426, Olympia, WA 98504
 E-mail: drew.stokesbary@leg.wa.gov
 Committees: Finance; Judiciary

Representative **Pat Sullivan** (D-District 47) . . . . . . . . . . . . (360) 786-7858
 Counties Represented: King (part)
 Term Expires: 2017
 E-mail: pat.sullivan@leg.wa.gov
 Committees: Appropriations; Rules

Representative **Gael Tarleton** (D-District 36) . . . . . . . . . . . (360) 786-7860
 Counties Represented: King (part)
 Term Expires: 2017
 E-mail: tarleton.gael@leg.wa.gov
 Committees: Higher Education; Rules; Technology and Economic
 Development; Transportation

Representative **David V. Taylor** (R-District 15) . . . . . . . . . . (360) 786-7874
 Counties Represented: Yakima (part)
 Term Expires: 2017
 E-mail: david.taylor@leg.wa.gov
 Committees: Appropriations; Environment; Local Government

Representative **Steve Tharinger** (D-District 24) . . . . . . . . . . (360) 786-7904
 Counties Represented: Clallam, Grays Harbor (part), Jefferson
 Term Expires: 2017
 E-mail: steve.tharinger@leg.wa.gov
 Committees: Appropriations; Finance; Health Care and Wellness
 Education: Colorado Col BA

Representative **Kevin Van De Wege** (D-District 24) . . . . . . (360) 786-7916
 Counties Represented: Clallam, Grays Harbor (part),  Dist: (360) 582-9830
 Jefferson
 Term Expires: 2017
 64 Village Lane, Suite A, Sequim, WA 98382
 E-mail: kevin.vandewege@leg.wa.gov
 Committees: Agriculture and Natural Resources; Community
 Development, Housing, and Tribal Affairs; Health Care and Wellness;
 Rules

Representative **Luanne Van Werven** (R-District 42) . . . . . . (360) 786-7980
 Counties Represented: Whatcom (part)
 Term Expires: 2017
 John L. O'Brien Building, Room 419, Olympia, WA 98504
 E-mail: luanne.vanwerven@leg.wa.gov
 Committees: Appropriations; Higher Education; State Government

Representative **Brandon Vick** (R-District 18) . . . . . . . . . . . (360) 786-7850
 Counties Represented: Clark (part)
 Term Expires: 2017
 E-mail: vick.brandon@leg.wa.gov
 Committees: Business and Financial Services; Commerce and Gaming;
 Finance; General Government and Information Technology
 Education: Clarke AA; Washington State (Attended)

Representative
 **Brady Piñero Walkinshaw** (D-District 43) . . . . . . . . . . . (360) 786-7826
 Counties Represented: King (part)
 Term Expires: 2017
 5031 University Way, NE, Seattle, WA 98105
 E-mail: brady.walkinshaw@leg.wa.gov
 Committees: Appropriations; Early Learning and Human Services;
 Judiciary
 Education: Princeton 2006 AB

Representative **Maureen Walsh** (R-District 16) . . . . . . . . . (360) 786-7836
 Counties Represented: Benton (part), Columbia,  Dist: (509) 543-3325
 Franklin (part), Walla Walla
 Term Expires: 2017
 2815 St. Andrews Loop, Suite B-2, Pasco, WA 99302
 E-mail: maureen.walsh@leg.wa.gov
 Committees: Capital Budget; Early Learning and Human Services

Representative **J. T. Wilcox** (R-District 2) . . . . . . . . . . . . . (360) 786-7912
 Counties Represented: Pierce (part), Thurston (part)
 Term Expires: 2017
 E-mail: jt.wilcox@leg.wa.gov
 Committees: Appropriations; Finance; Rules

Representative **Lynda Wilson** (R-District 17) . . . . . . . . . . . (360) 786-7994
 Counties Represented: Clark (part)
 Term Expires: 2017
 John L. O'Brien Building, Room 318, Olympia, WA 98504
 E-mail: lynda.wilson@leg.wa.gov
 Committees: Public Safety; Transportation

Representative **Sharon Wylie** (D-District 49) . . . . . . . . . . . (360) 786-7924
 Counties Represented: Clark (part)
 Term Expires: 2017
 John L. O'Brien Building, Room 310, Olympia, WA 98504
 P.O. Box 40600, Olympia, WA 98504
 E-mail: sharon.wylie@leg.wa.gov
 Committees: Commerce and Gaming; Finance; Technology and
 Economic Development
 Education: UC Riverside 1973 BA

Representative **Jesse Young** (R-District 26) . . . . . . . . . . . . (360) 786-7964
 Counties Represented: Kitsap (part), Pierce (part)
 Term Expires: 2017
 John L. O'Brien Building, Room 431, Olympia, WA 98504
 E-mail: jesse.young@leg.wa.gov
 Committees: Rules; Technology and Economic Development;
 Transportation
 Education: Notre Dame

Representative **Hans Zeiger** (R-District 25) . . . . . . . . . . . . (360) 786-7968
 Counties Represented: Pierce (part)  Dist: (253) 840-4526
 Term Expires: 2017
 101 South Meridian, Suite D, Puyallup, WA 98371
 E-mail: hans.zeiger@leg.wa.gov
 Committees: Community Development, Housing, and Tribal Affairs;
 Higher Education; Rules; Transportation

District 44 **(Vacant)** . . . . . . . . . . . . . . . . . . . . . . . . . . . . . (360) 786-7573
 Note: The Democratic Party has not yet chosen a successor to fill this
 legislative vacancy.

## House Standing Committees

### Agriculture and Natural Resources

| **Majority Members** | **Minority Members** |
|---|---|
| Brian E. Blake (D-19) *Chair* | Vincent Buys (R-42) |
| Kristine Lytton (D-40) *Vice Chair* | *Ranking Minority Member* |
| Christopher Hurst (D-31) | Tom Dent (R-13) |
| Eric Pettigrew (D-37) | *Assistant Ranking Minority* |
| Derek Stanford (D-1) | *Member* |
| Kevin Van De Wege (D-24) | Bruce Chandler (R-15) |
| | Joel Kretz (R-7) |
| | Ed Orcutt (R-20) |
| | Joe Schmick (R-9) |

### Appropriations

| **Majority Members** | **Minority Members** |
|---|---|
| Timm Ormsby (D-3) *Vice Chair* | Bruce Chandler (R-15) |
| Eileen L. Cody (D-34) | *Ranking Minority Member* |
| Drew Hansen (D-23) | Kevin Parker (R-6) |
| Zachary "Zack" Hudgins (D-11) | *Assistant Ranking Minority* |
| Samuel W. "Sam" Hunt (D-22) | *Member* |
| Laurie Jinkins (D-27) | J. T. Wilcox (R-2) |
| Ruth Kagi (D-32) | *Assistant Ranking Minority* |
| Kristine Lytton (D-40) | *Member* |

*(continued on next page)*

LEGISLATIVE BRANCH

**Appropriations** *continued*

**Majority Members** *continued*

Eric Pettigrew (D-37)
David Sawyer (D-29)
Tana Senn (D-41)
Larry Springer (D-45)
Pat Sullivan (D-47)
Steve Tharinger (D-24)
Brady Piñero Walkinshaw (D-43)

**Minority Members** *continued*

Vincent Buys (R-42)
Cary Condotta (R-12)
Tom Dent (R-13)
Larry Haler (R-8)
Paul Harris (R-17)
Drew C. MacEwen (R-35)
Chad Magendanz (R-5)
Joe Schmick (R-9)
David V. Taylor (R-15)
Luanne Van Werven (R-42)

## Business and Financial Services

**Majority Members**

Steve Kirby (D-29) *Chair*
Cindy Ryu (D-32) *Vice Chair*
Brian E. Blake (D-19)
Christopher Hurst (D-31)
Sharon Tomiko Santos (D-37)
Derek Stanford (D-1)

**Minority Members**

Brandon Vick (R-18)
   *Ranking Minority Member*
Andrew Barkis (R-2)
Mary Dye (R-9)
Linda Kochmar (R-30)
Gina McCabe (R-14)

## Capital Budget

**Majority Members**

Derek Stanford (D-1) *Vice Chair*
Christine Kilduff (D-28)
Strom Peterson (D-21)
Marcus Riccelli (D-3)

**Minority Members**

Richard C. DeBolt (R-20)
   *Ranking Minority Member*
Norma Smith (R-10)
   *Assistant Ranking Minority Member*
Linda Kochmar (R-30)
Maureen Walsh (R-16)

## Commerce and Gaming

**Majority Members**

Christopher Hurst (D-31) *Chair*
Sharon Wylie (D-49) *Vice Chair*
Brian E. Blake (D-19)
Steve Kirby (D-29)
Luis Moscoso (D-1)

**Minority Members**

Cary Condotta (R-12)
   *Ranking Minority Member*
Jeff Holy (R-6)
   *Assistant Ranking Minority Member*
Elizabeth Scott (R-39)
Brandon Vick (R-18)

## Community Development, Housing, and Tribal Affairs

**Majority Members**

Sherry V. Appleton (D-23) *Chair*
June Robinson (D-38) *Vice Chair*
David Sawyer (D-29)
Kevin Van De Wege (D-24)

**Minority Members**

Norm Johnson (R-14)
   *Ranking Minority Member*
Hans Zeiger (R-25)
   *Assistant Ranking Minority Member*
Brad Hawkins (R-12)
Teri Hickel (R-30)

## Early Learning and Human Services

**Majority Members**

Ruth Kagi (D-32) *Chair*
Brady Piñero Walkinshaw (D-43)
   *Vice Chair*
Christine Kilduff (D-28)
Lillian Ortiz-Self (D-21)
David Sawyer (D-29)
Tana Senn (D-41)

**Minority Members**

Maureen Walsh (R-16)
   *Ranking Minority Member*
Elizabeth Scott (R-39)
   *Assistant Ranking Minority Member*
Tom Dent (R-13)
Brad Hawkins (R-12)
Bob McCaslin, Jr. (R-4)

## Education

**Majority Members**

Sharon Tomiko Santos (D-37) *Chair*
Lillian Ortiz-Self (D-21) *Vice Chair*
Steve Bergquist (D-11)
Samuel W. "Sam" Hunt (D-22)
Christine Kilduff (D-28)
Patty Kuderer (D-48)
Kristine Lytton (D-40)
Tina L. Orwall (D-33)
Gerry Pollet (D-46)

**Minority Members**

Chad Magendanz (R-5)
   *Ranking Minority Member*
Richard Walter "Dick" Muri (R-28)
   *Assistant Ranking Minority Member*
Melanie Stambaugh (R-25)
   *Assistant Ranking Minority Member*
Michelle Caldier (R-26)

**Majority Members** *continued*

J.D. Rossetti (D-19)
Larry Springer (D-45)

**Minority Members** *continued*

Dan Griffey (R-35)
Mark Hargrove (R-47)
Dave Hayes (R-10)
Brad Klippert (R-8)
Bob McCaslin, Jr. (R-4)

## Environment

**Majority Members**

Joe Fitzgibbon (D-34) *Chair*
Strom Peterson (D-21) *Vice Chair*
Jessyn Farrell (D-46)
Jake Fey (D-27)
Roger E. Goodman (D-45)
Joan McBride (D-48)

**Minority Members**

Matt Shea (R-4)
   *Ranking Minority Member*
Shelly Short (R-7)
   *Assistant Ranking Minority Member*
Mary Dye (R-9)
Liz Pike (R-18)
David V. Taylor (R-15)

## Finance

**Majority Members**

Steve Tharinger (D-24) *Vice Chair*
Joe Fitzgibbon (D-34)
Noel Frame (D-36)
Gerry Pollet (D-46)
Chris Reykdal (D-22)
June Robinson (D-38)
Cindy Ryu (D-32)
Larry Springer (D-45)
Sharon Wylie (D-49)

**Minority Members**

Terry R. Nealey (R-16)
   *Ranking Minority Member*
Ed Orcutt (R-20)
   *Assistant Ranking Minority Member*
Cary Condotta (R-12)
Matt Manweller (R-13)
Drew Stokesbary (R-31)
Brandon Vick (R-18)
J. T. Wilcox (R-2)

## General Government and Information Technology

**Majority Members**

Zachary "Zack" Hudgins (D-11)
   *Chair*
Patty Kuderer (D-48) *Vice Chair*
Jeff Morris (D-40)

**Minority Members**

Drew C. MacEwen (R-35)
   *Ranking Minority Member*
Michelle Caldier (R-26)
   *Assistant Ranking Minority Member*
Gina McCabe (R-14)
Brandon Vick (R-18)

## Health Care and Wellness

**Majority Members**

Eileen L. Cody (D-34) *Chair*
Marcus Riccelli (D-3) *Vice Chair*
Judy Clibborn (D-41)
Laurie Jinkins (D-27)
Jim Moeller (D-49)
June Robinson (D-38)
Steve Tharinger (D-24)
Kevin Van De Wege (D-24)

**Minority Members**

Joe Schmick (R-9)
   *Ranking Minority Member*
Paul Harris (R-17)
   *Assistant Ranking Minority Member*
Michelle Caldier (R-26)
Richard C. DeBolt (R-20)
Norm Johnson (R-14)
Jay Rodne (R-5)
Shelly Short (R-7)

## Higher Education

**Majority Members**

Drew Hansen (D-23) *Chair*
Gerry Pollet (D-46) *Vice Chair*
Steve Bergquist (D-11)
Noel Frame (D-36)
Chris Reykdal (D-22)
Mike Sells (D-38)
Gael Tarleton (D-36)

**Minority Members**

Hans Zeiger (R-25)
   *Ranking Minority Member*
Larry Haler (R-8)
   *Assistant Ranking Minority Member*
Mark Hargrove (R-47)
Jeff Holy (R-6)
Melanie Stambaugh (R-25)
Luanne Van Werven (R-42)

## Judiciary

**Majority Members**

Laurie Jinkins (D-27) *Chair*
Christine Kilduff (D-28) *Vice Chair*
Roger E. Goodman (D-45)
Drew Hansen (D-23)
Steve Kirby (D-29)
Patty Kuderer (D-48)
Tina L. Orwall (D-33)
Brady Piñero Walkinshaw (D-43)

**Minority Members**

Jay Rodne (R-5)
   *Ranking Minority Member*
Matt Shea (R-4)
   *Assistant Ranking Minority Member*
Larry Haler (R-8)
Brad Klippert (R-8)
Richard Walter "Dick" Muri (R-28)
Drew Stokesbary (R-31)

## Labor

**Majority Members**
Mike Sells (D-38) *Chair*
Mia Gregerson (D-33) *Vice Chair*
Jim Moeller (D-49)
Timm Ormsby (D-3)

**Minority Members**
Matt Manweller (R-13)
  *Ranking Minority Member*
Gina McCabe (R-14)

## Local Government

**Majority Members**
Mia Gregerson (D-33) *Vice Chair*
Joe Fitzgibbon (D-34)
Joan McBride (D-48)
Strom Peterson (D-21)

**Minority Members**
David V. Taylor (R-15)
  *Ranking Minority Member*
Dan Griffey (R-35)
  *Assistant Ranking Minority
  Member*
Andrew Barkis (R-2)
Bob McCaslin, Jr. (R-4)
Liz Pike (R-18)

## Public Safety

**Majority Members**
Roger E. Goodman (D-45) *Chair*
Tina L. Orwall (D-33) *Vice Chair*
Sherry V. Appleton (D-23)
Luis Moscoso (D-1)
Eric Pettigrew (D-37)

**Minority Members**
Brad Klippert (R-8)
  *Ranking Minority Member*
Dave Hayes (R-10)
  *Assistant Ranking Minority
  Member*
Dan Griffey (R-35)
Lynda Wilson (R-17)

## Rules

**Majority Members**
Frank Chopp (D-43) *Chair*
Jessyn Farrell (D-46)
Kristine Lytton (D-40)
Joan McBride (D-48)
Jim Moeller (D-49)
Tina L. Orwall (D-33)
Eric Pettigrew (D-37)
Chris Reykdal (D-22)
Cindy Ryu (D-32)
Larry Springer (D-45)
Pat Sullivan (D-47)
Gael Tarleton (D-36)
Kevin Van De Wege (D-24)

**Minority Members**
Larry Haler (R-8)
Mark Harmsworth (R-44)
Paul Harris (R-17)
Teri Hickel (R-30)
Joel Kretz (R-7)
Dan Kristiansen (R-39)
Shelly Short (R-7)
Melanie Stambaugh (R-25)
J. T. Wilcox (R-2)
Jesse Young (R-26)
Hans Zeiger (R-25)

## State Government

**Majority Members**
Samuel W. "Sam" Hunt (D-22)
  *Chair*
Steve Bergquist (D-11) *Vice Chair*
Sherry V. Appleton (D-23)
Noel Frame (D-36)

**Minority Members**
Jeff Holy (R-6)
  *Ranking Minority Member*
Luanne Van Werven (R-42)
  *Assistant Ranking Member*
Brad Hawkins (R-12)

## Technology and Economic Development

**Majority Members**
Jeff Morris (D-40) *Chair*
Gael Tarleton (D-36) *Vice Chair*
Jake Fey (D-27)
Zachary "Zack" Hudgins (D-11)
J.D. Rossetti (D-19)
Cindy Ryu (D-32)
Sharon Tomiko Santos (D-37)
Sharon Wylie (D-49)

**Minority Members**
Norma Smith (R-10)
  *Ranking Minority Member*
Richard C. DeBolt (R-20)
  *Assistant Ranking Minority
  Member*
Mark Harmsworth (R-44)
Chad Magendanz (R-5)
Terry R. Nealey (R-16)
Jesse Young (R-26)

## Transportation

**Majority Members**
Judy Clibborn (D-41) *Chair*
Jessyn Farrell (D-46) *Vice Chair*
Jake Fey (D-27) *Vice Chair*
Luis Moscoso (D-1) *Vice Chair*
Steve Bergquist (D-11)
Mia Gregerson (D-33)
Joan McBride (D-48)
Jim Moeller (D-49)
Jeff Morris (D-40)
Lillian Ortiz-Self (D-21)

**Minority Members**
Ed Orcutt (R-20)
  *Ranking Minority Member*
Mark Hargrove (R-47)
  *Assistant Ranking Minority
  Member*
Mark Harmsworth (R-44)
Dave Hayes (R-10)
Teri Hickel (R-30)
Linda Kochmar (R-30)
Liz Pike (R-18)

**Majority Members** *continued*
Marcus Riccelli (D-3)
J.D. Rossetti (D-19)
Mike Sells (D-38)
Gael Tarleton (D-36)

**Minority Members** *continued*
Jay Rodne (R-5)
Matt Shea (R-4)
Lynda Wilson (R-17)
Jesse Young (R-26)
Hans Zeiger (R-25)

**LEGISLATIVE BRANCH**

# West Virginia State Legislature

State Capitol, State Capitol Complex, Charleston, WV 25305
Tel: (304) 347-4836  Fax: (304) 347-4919  Internet: www.legis.state.wv.us

## West Virginia Senate

Tel: (304) 357-7800  Fax: (304) 357-7829

President of the Senate/Lieutenant Governor
**William P. "Bill" Cole III** (R) . . . . . . . . . . . . . . . . . . . . . (304) 357-7801
  Education: Northwood BA
President Pro Tempore **Donna J. Boley** (R) . . . . . . . . . . . . (304) 357-7905
Majority Leader **Mitch B. Carmichael** (R) . . . . . . . . . . . . (304) 357-7855
  Education: Marshall 1983 BBA
Majority Whip **Craig P. Blair** (R) . . . . . . . . . . . . . . . . . . . (304) 357-7867
Minority Leader **Jeffrey V. Kessler** (D) . . . . . . . . . . . . . . (304) 357-7902
  Education: West Liberty State 1977 BA; West Virginia 1981 JD
Minority Whip **John R. Unger** (D) . . . . . . . . . . . . . . . . . . (304) 357-7933
  Education: West Virginia 1993 BA; Oxford (UK) 2004 MA
Clerk of the Senate **Clark S. Barnes** (R) . . . . . . . . . . . . . . (304) 357-7800
  E-mail: clark.barnes@wvsenate.gov
  Education: Davis & Elkins 1976 AAS; West Virginia 1982 BA;
  Pensacola Christian 1987 MA
Sergeant-at-Arms **Howard Wellman** . . . . . . . . . . . . . . . . (304) 357-7800

## Senators

**Party Affiliation Statistics:** Republicans: 18, Democrats: 16

Senator **Robert G. "Bob" Ashley** (R-District 3) . . . . . . . . (304) 357-7970
  Counties Represented: Pleasants, Roane (part), Wirt, Wood
  Term Expires: 2016
  P.O. Box 823, Spencer, WV 25276
  E-mail: bob.ashley@wvsenate.gov
  Committees: Banking and Insurance; Confirmations; Economic
  Development; Health and Human Resources; Judiciary; Military;
  Natural Resources
  Education: Marshall 1975 BBA
Senator **Robert D. "Bob" Beach** (D-District 13)
  State Capitol Complex, Room 204W . . . . . . . . . . . . . . (304) 357-7919
  Counties Represented: Marion (part), Monongalia    Res: (304) 932-7170
  (part)
  Term Expires: 2018
  P.O. Box 1620, Morgantown, WV 26501
  E-mail: bob.beach@wvsenate.gov
  Committees: Agriculture and Rural Development; Education; Judiciary;
  Natural Resources; Transportation and Infrastructure
  Education: Fairmont State Col 2000 BA
Senator **Craig P. Blair** (R-District 15) . . . . . . . . . . . . . . . (304) 357-7867
  Counties Represented: Berkeley (part), Hampshire,    Tel: (304) 754-9031
  Mineral (part), Morgan    Res: (304) 754-5040
  Term Expires: 2016
  47 Wasser Drive, Martinsburg, WV 25403
  E-mail: craig.blair@wvsenate.gov
  Committees: Agriculture and Rural Development; Economic
  Development; Energy, Industry and Mining; Finance; Government
  Organization; Labor; Rules
Senator **Donna J. Boley** (R-District 3) . . . . . . . . . . . . . . . (304) 357-7905
  Counties Represented: Pleasants, Roane (part),    Res: (304) 684-3266
  Wirt, Wood    Fax: (304) 684-3266
  Term Expires: 2016
  2332 Greens Run Road, Saint Mary's, WV 26170
  E-mail: donna.boley@wvsenate.gov
  Committees: Agriculture and Rural Development; Confirmations;
  Education; Energy, Industry and Mining; Finance; Military;
  Transportation and Infrastructure
Senator **Gregory L. Boso** (R-District 11) . . . . . . . . . . . . . (304) 357-7973
  Counties Represented: Grant (part), Nicholas, Pendleton, Pocahontas,
  Randolph, Upshur, Webster
  Term Expires: 2016
  401 Main Street, Summersville, WV 26651
  E-mail: greg.boso@wvsenate.gov
  Committees: Confirmations; Energy, Industry and Mining; Enrolled
  Bills; Finance; Government Organization; Interstate Cooperation;
  Natural Resources
  Education: West Virginia Tech 1980

Senator **Mitch B. Carmichael** (R-District 4) . . . . . . . . . . . . (304) 357-7855
  Counties Represented: Jackson, Mason, Putnam    Res: (304) 372-4667
  (part), Roane (part)
  Term Expires: 2016
  18 Colonial Drive, Ripley, WV 25271
  E-mail: mitch.carmichael@wvsenate.gov
  Committees: Banking and Insurance; Education; Finance; Judiciary;
  Rules
Senator **Sue Cline** (R-District 9) Room 216W . . . . . . . . . . (304) 357-7807
  Counties Represented: McDowell (part), Raleigh, Wyoming
  Term Expires: 2016
  E-mail: sue.cline@wvsenate.gov
  Committees: Agriculture and Rural Development; Banking and
  Insurance; Economic Development; Education; Judiciary
Senator **William P. "Bill" Cole III** (R-District 6) . . . . . . . . . (304) 357-7801
  Counties Represented: McDowell (part), Mercer,    Tel: (304) 327-0511
  Mingo (part), Wayne (part)    Res: (304) 324-0040
  Term Expires: 2016
  404 Oakhurst Avenue, Bluefield, WV 24701
  E-mail: bill.cole@wvsenate.gov
  Committees: Rules
Senator **Douglas Eugene Facemire** (D-District 12)
  State Capitol Complex, Building One, Room 217-W . . . . . (304) 357-7845
  Counties Represented: Braxton, Clay, Gilmer (part),    Res: (304) 765-2231
  Harrison, Lewis
  Term Expires: 2016
  P.O. Box 215, Sutton, WV 26601
  E-mail: douglas.facemire@wvsenate.gov
  Committees: Banking and Insurance; Energy, Industry and Mining;
  Finance; Government Organization; Military; Natural Resources
Senator **Ryan James Ferns** (R-District 1) . . . . . . . . . . . . . (304) 357-7918
  Counties Represented: Brooke, Hancock, Marshall (part), Ohio
  Term Expires: 2018
  37 Jenna Way Drive, Wheeling, WV 26003
  E-mail: ryan.ferns@wvsenate.gov
  Committees: Banking and Insurance; Economic Development;
  Government Organization; Health and Human Resources; Judiciary;
  Labor
Senator **Ed Gaunch** (R-District 8) . . . . . . . . . . . . . . . . . . (304) 357-7841
  Counties Represented: Kanawha (part), Putnam (part)
  Term Expires: 2018
  524 Woodbridge Drive, Charleston, WV 25311
  E-mail: ed.gaunch@wvsenate.gov
  Committees: Banking and Insurance; Energy, Industry and Mining;
  Enrolled Bills; Government Organization; Interstate Cooperation;
  Judiciary; Labor; Pensions; Transportation and Infrastructure
Senator **William Michael "Mike" Hall** (R-District 4) . . . . . (304) 357-7901
  Counties Represented: Jackson, Mason, Putnam    Tel: (304) 549-8126
  (part), Roane (part)    Res: (304) 757-8249
  Term Expires: 2018
  76 Crystal Springs Drive, Winfield, WV 25213
  E-mail: mike.hall@wvsenate.gov
  Committees: Banking and Insurance; Education; Finance; Natural
  Resources; Pensions; Rules
  Education: Marshall 1970 BA
Senator **Robert Karnes** (R-District 11) Room 200W . . . . . . (304) 357-7906
  Counties Represented: Grant (part), Nicholas, Pendleton, Pocahontas,
  Randolph, Upshur, Webster
  Term Expires: 2018
  E-mail: robert.karnes@wvsenate.gov
  Committees: Agriculture and Rural Development; Education; Health
  and Human Resources; Interstate Cooperation; Judiciary; Labor;
  Natural Resources
Senator **Jeffrey V. Kessler** (D-District 2) . . . . . . . . . . . . . . (304) 357-7902
  Counties Represented: Calhoun, Doddridge, Gilmer    Res: (304) 843-1386
  (part), Marion (part), Marshall (part), Monongalia    Fax: (304) 845-9055
  (part), Ritchie, Tyler, Wetzel
  Term Expires: 2016
  607 Wheeling Avenue, Glen Dale, WV 26038
  E-mail: jeff.kessler@wvsenate.gov
  Committees: Confirmations; Economic Development; Finance; Rules
Senator **Arthur E. "Art" Kirkendoll** (D-District 7) . . . . . . . . (304) 357-7857
  Counties Represented: Boone, Lincoln, Logan,    Res: (304) 855-7418
  Mingo (part), Wayne (part)
  Term Expires: 2016
  P.O. Box 1227, Chapmanville, WV 25508
  E-mail: art.kirkendoll@wvsenate.gov
  Committees: Energy, Industry and Mining; Interstate Cooperation;
  Judiciary; Pensions; Transportation and Infrastructure

Senator **William Ramsey Laird IV** (D-District 10) . . . . . . . (304) 357-7849
  Counties Represented: Fayette, Greenbrier, Monroe,    Res: (304) 469-8055
  Summers
  Term Expires: 2016
  225 Highland Avenue, Oak Hill, WV 25901
  E-mail: william.laird@wvsenate.gov
  Committees: Agriculture and Rural Development; Education; Finance;
  Health and Human Resources; Labor; Military; Natural Resources
  Education: Concord Col BA; Marshall MA

Senator **Kent Leonhardt** (R-District 2) Room 200W . . . . . . (304) 357-7827
  Counties Represented: Calhoun, Doddridge, Gilmer (part), Marion
  (part), Marshall (part), Monongalia (part), Ritchie, Tyler, Wetzel
  Term Expires: 2018
  E-mail: kent.leonhardt@wvsenate.gov
  Committees: Agriculture and Rural Development; Government
  Organization; Health and Human Resources; Judiciary; Military;
  Natural Resources; Transportation and Infrastructure

Senator **Mark R. Maynard** (R-District 6) Room 206W . . . . (304) 357-7808
  Counties Represented: McDowell (part), Mercer, Mingo (part), Wayne
  (part)
  Term Expires: 2018
  E-mail: mark.maynard@wvsenate.gov
  Committees: Agriculture and Rural Development; Economic
  Development; Energy, Industry and Mining; Enrolled Bills; Government
  Organization; Interstate Cooperation; Judiciary; Labor; Natural
  Resources

Senator **Ronald F. "Ron" Miller** (D-District 10)
  State Capitol Complex, Room 229W . . . . . . . . . . . . . . . (304) 357-7954
  Counties Represented: Fayette, Greenbrier, Monroe,    Res: (304) 497-3184
  Summers
  Term Expires: 2018
  P.O. Box 359, HC34, Lewisburg, WV 24901
  E-mail: ronald.miller@wvsenate.gov
  Committees: Agriculture and Rural Development; Confirmations;
  Enrolled Bills; Government Organization; Judiciary; Natural Resources

Senator **Jeff Mullins** (R-District 9) Room 203W . . . . . . . . (304) 357-7831
  Counties Represented: McDowell (part), Raleigh, Wyoming
  Term Expires: 2018
  E-mail: jeff.mullins@wvsenate.gov
  Committees: Banking and Insurance; Confirmations; Economic
  Development; Energy, Industry and Mining; Finance; Government
  Organization; Pensions; Transportation and Infrastructure

Senator **Corey L. Palumbo** (D-District 17) . . . . . . . . . . . . . (304) 357-7854
  Counties Represented: Kanawha (part)    Res: (304) 746-7933
  Term Expires: 2016
  1206 Williamsburg Way, Charleston, WV 25314
  E-mail: corey.palumbo@wvsenate.gov
  Committees: Banking and Insurance; Confirmations; Government
  Organization; Health and Human Resources; Interstate Cooperation;
  Judiciary
  Education: West Virginia 1994 BA; North Carolina 1998 JD

Senator **Robert Hugh "Bob" Plymale** (D-District 5) . . . . . (304) 357-7937
  Counties Represented: Cabell, Wayne (part)    Res: (304) 453-6321
  Term Expires: 2016    Fax: (304) 696-6099
  206 Cliffview Drive, Huntington, WV 25704
  E-mail: robert.plymale@wvsenate.gov
  Committees: Confirmations; Economic Development; Education;
  Finance; Health and Human Resources; Pensions; Rules; Transportation
  and Infrastructure
  Education: Marshall 1978 BA

Senator **Roman W. Prezioso, Jr.** (D-District 13) . . . . . . . . (304) 357-7961
  Counties Represented: Marion (part), Monongalia    Res: (304) 366-5308
  (part)    Fax: (304) 366-2483
  Term Expires: 2016
  1806 Dogwood Drive, Fairmont, WV 26554
  E-mail: roman.prezioso@wvsenate.gov
  Committees: Banking and Insurance; Finance; Health and Human
  Resources; Labor; Rules
  Education: Fairmont State Col AB; West Virginia MS

Senator **Michael Romano** (D-District 12) . . . . . . . . . . . . . (304) 357-7904
  Counties Represented: Braxton, Clay, Gilmer (part), Harrison, Lewis
  Term Expires: 2018
  128 South 2nd Street, Clarksburg, WV 26301
  E-mail: mike.romano@wvsenate.gov
  Committees: Banking and Insurance; Economic Development;
  Education; Judiciary; Military

Senator **Herbert S. "Herb" Snyder** (D-District 16)
  State Capitol Complex, Building One, Room 217-W . . . . . (304) 357-7957
  Counties Represented: Berkeley (part), Jefferson    Tel: (304) 725-6174
  Term Expires: 2016
  P.O Box 400, Shenandoah Junction, WV 25442
  E-mail: herb.snyder@wvsenate.gov
  Committees: Banking and Insurance; Energy, Industry and Mining;
  Government Organization; Judiciary; Natural Resources
  Education: Shepherd Col 1977 BS

Senator **Ronny Douglas "Ron" Stollings** (D-District 7) . . (304) 357-7939
  Counties Represented: Boone, Lincoln, Logan,    Res: (304) 369-6194
  Mingo (part), Wayne (part)
  Term Expires: 2016
  P.O. Box 365, Madison, WV 25130
  E-mail: ron.stollings@wvsenate.gov
  Committees: Economic Development; Education; Finance; Health and
  Human Resources; Labor; Rules
  Education: West Virginia 1977 BA, 1978 MS; Marshall 1982 MD

Senator **Dave Sypolt** (R-District 14) . . . . . . . . . . . . . . . . . (304) 357-7914
  Counties Represented: Barbour, Grant (part), Hardy,    Res: (304) 698-5299
  Mineral (part), Monongalia (part), Preston, Taylor, Tucker
  Term Expires: 2018
  P.O. Box 5, Kingwood, WV 26537
  E-mail: dave.sypolt@wvsenate.gov
  Committees: Agriculture and Rural Development; Education; Energy,
  Industry and Mining; Finance; Military; Rules
  Education: Glenville State 1988 AS, 2004 BA

Senator **Tom Takubo** (R-District 17) . . . . . . . . . . . . . . . . . (304) 357-7990
  Counties Represented: Kanawha (part)
  Term Expires: 2018
  272 Creekstone Ridge, South Charleston, WV 25309
  E-mail: drtomtakubo@gmail.com
  Committees: Confirmations; Economic Development; Education;
  Finance; Health and Human Resources; Natural Resources

Senator **Charles S. Trump IV** (R-District 15) . . . . . . . . . . . (304) 357-7980
  Counties Represented: Berkeley (part), Hampshire, Mineral (part),
  Morgan
  Term Expires: 2018
  171 South Washington Street, Berkeley Springs, WV 25411
  E-mail: charles.trump@wvsenate.gov
  Committees: Banking and Insurance; Education; Health and Human
  Resources; Judiciary; Labor; Pensions; Rules

Senator **John R. Unger** (D-District 16) . . . . . . . . . . . . . . . (304) 357-7933
  Counties Represented: Berkeley (part), Jefferson    Res: (304) 263-5488
  Term Expires: 2016    Fax: (304) 263-3545
  P.O. Box 2415, Martinsburg, WV 25402
  E-mail: john.unger@wvsenate.gov
  Committees: Education; Enrolled Bills; Finance; Health and Human
  Resources; Interstate Cooperation; Pensions

Senator **Chris W. Walters** (R-District 8) . . . . . . . . . . . . . . (304) 357-7866
  Counties Represented: Kanawha (part), Putnam    Res: (304) 346-4823
  (part)
  Term Expires: 2016
  P.O. Box 1131, Poca, WV 25159
  E-mail: chris.walters@wvsenate.gov
  Committees: Economic Development; Finance; Government
  Organization; Health and Human Resources; Military; Transportation
  and Infrastructure
  Education: West Virginia 2010 BA

Senator **Robert Lynn "Bob" Williams** (D-District 14)
  State Capitol Complex, Building One, Room 209-W . . . . . (304) 357-7995
  Counties Represented: Barbour, Grant (part), Hardy,    Res: (304) 842-7161
  Mineral (part), Monongalia (part), Preston, Taylor, Tucker
  Term Expires: 2016
  P.O. Box 562, Grafton, WV 26354
  E-mail: bob.williams@wvsenate.gov
  Committees: Agriculture and Rural Development; Energy, Industry
  and Mining; Government Organization; Judiciary; Labor; Natural
  Resources; Rules
  Education: Fairmont State Col BS; West Virginia MS

Senator **Mike Woelfel** (D-District 5) . . . . . . . . . . . . . . . . . (304) 357-7956
  Counties Represented: Cabell, Wayne (part)
  Term Expires: 2018
  801 Eighth Street, Huntington, WV 25701
  E-mail: mike.woelfel@wvsenate.gov
  Committees: Agriculture and Rural Development; Banking and
  Insurance; Economic Development; Energy, Industry and Mining;
  Judiciary; Transportation and Infrastructure

*(continued on next page)*

LEGISLATIVE BRANCH

**Senators** *continued*

Senator **Jack Yost** (D-District 1) . . . . . . . . . . . . . . . . . . . . . (304) 357-7984
  Counties Represented: Brooke, Hancock, Marshall  Res: (304) 737-2720
  (part), Ohio
  Term Expires: 2016
  1413 Pleasant Avenue, Wellsburg, WV 26070
  E-mail: jack.yost@wvsenate.gov
  Committees: Economic Development; Energy, Industry and Mining;
  Finance; Government Organization; Labor; Military

# Senate Standing Committees
## Agriculture and Rural Development

| Majority Members | Minority Members |
|---|---|
| Robert Karnes (R-11) *Chair* | Robert D. "Bob" Beach (D-13) |
| Kent Leonhardt (R-2) *Vice Chair* | William Ramsey Laird IV (D-10) |
| Craig P. Blair (R-15) | Ronald F. "Ron" Miller (D-10) |
| Donna J. Boley (R-3) | Robert Lynn "Bob" Williams |
| Sue Cline (R-9) | (D-14) |
| Mark R. Maynard (R-6) | Mike Woelfel (D-5) |
| Dave Sypolt (R-14) | |

## Banking and Insurance

| Majority Members | Minority Members |
|---|---|
| Ed Gaunch (R-8) *Chair* | Douglas Eugene Facemire (D-12) |
| Robert G. "Bob" Ashley (R-3) | Corey L. Palumbo (D-17) |
| *Vice Chair* | Roman W. Prezioso, Jr. (D-13) |
| Mitch B. Carmichael (R-4) | Michael Romano (D-12) |
| Sue Cline (R-9) | Herbert S. "Herb" Snyder (D-16) |
| Ryan James Ferns (R-1) | Mike Woelfel (D-5) |
| William Michael "Mike" Hall (R-4) | |
| Jeff Mullins (R-9) | |
| Charles S. Trump IV (R-15) | |

## Confirmations

| Majority Members | Minority Members |
|---|---|
| Donna J. Boley (R-3) *Chair* | Jeffrey V. Kessler (D-2) |
| Jeff Mullins (R-9) *Vice Chair* | Ronald F. "Ron" Miller (D-10) |
| Robert G. "Bob" Ashley (R-3) | Corey L. Palumbo (D-17) |
| Gregory L. Boso (R-11) | Robert Hugh "Bob" Plymale (D-5) |
| Tom Takubo (R-17) | |

## Economic Development

| Majority Members | Minority Members |
|---|---|
| Tom Takubo (R-17) *Chair* | Jeffrey V. Kessler (D-2) |
| Ryan James Ferns (R-1) *Vice Chair* | Robert Hugh "Bob" Plymale (D-5) |
| Robert G. "Bob" Ashley (R-3) | Michael Romano (D-12) |
| Craig P. Blair (R-15) | Ronny Douglas "Ron" Stollings |
| Sue Cline (R-9) | (D-7) |
| Mark R. Maynard (R-6) | Mike Woelfel (D-5) |
| Jeff Mullins (R-9) | Jack Yost (D-1) |
| Chris W. Walters (R-8) | |

## Education

| Majority Members | Minority Members |
|---|---|
| Dave Sypolt (R-14) *Chair* | Robert D. "Bob" Beach (D-13) |
| Donna J. Boley (R-3) *Vice Chair* | William Ramsey Laird IV (D-10) |
| Mitch B. Carmichael (R-4) | Robert Hugh "Bob" Plymale (D-5) |
| Sue Cline (R-9) | Michael Romano (D-12) |
| William Michael "Mike" Hall (R-4) | Ronny Douglas "Ron" Stollings |
| Robert Karnes (R-11) | (D-7) |
| Tom Takubo (R-17) | John R. Unger (D-16) |
| Charles S. Trump IV (R-15) | |

## Energy, Industry and Mining

| Majority Members | Minority Members |
|---|---|
| Gregory L. Boso (R-11) *Chair* | Douglas Eugene Facemire (D-12) |
| Craig P. Blair (R-15) *Vice Chair* | Arthur E. "Art" Kirkendoll (D-7) |
| Donna J. Boley (R-3) | Herbert S. "Herb" Snyder (D-16) |
| Ed Gaunch (R-8) | Robert Lynn "Bob" Williams |
| Mark R. Maynard (R-6) | (D-14) |
| Jeff Mullins (R-9) | Mike Woelfel (D-5) |
| Dave Sypolt (R-14) | Jack Yost (D-1) |

## Enrolled Bills

| Majority Members | Minority Members |
|---|---|
| Mark R. Maynard (R-6) *Chair* | Ronald F. "Ron" Miller (D-10) |
| Ed Gaunch (R-8) *Vice Chair* | John R. Unger (D-16) |
| Gregory L. Boso (R-11) | |

## Finance

| Majority Members | Minority Members |
|---|---|
| William Michael "Mike" Hall (R-4) | Douglas Eugene Facemire (D-12) |
| *Chair* | Jeffrey V. Kessler (D-2) |
| Chris W. Walters (R-8) *Vice Chair* | William Ramsey Laird IV (D-10) |
| Craig P. Blair (R-15) | Robert Hugh "Bob" Plymale (D-5) |
| Donna J. Boley (R-3) | Roman W. Prezioso, Jr. (D-13) |
| Gregory L. Boso (R-11) | Ronny Douglas "Ron" Stollings |
| Mitch B. Carmichael (R-4) | (D-7) |
| Jeff Mullins (R-9) | John R. Unger (D-16) |
| Dave Sypolt (R-14) | Jack Yost (D-1) |
| Tom Takubo (R-17) | |

## Government Organization

| Majority Members | Minority Members |
|---|---|
| Craig P. Blair (R-15) *Chair* | Douglas Eugene Facemire (D-12) |
| Chris W. Walters (R-8) *Vice Chair* | Ronald F. "Ron" Miller (D-10) |
| Gregory L. Boso (R-11) | Corey L. Palumbo (D-17) |
| Ryan James Ferns (R-1) | Herbert S. "Herb" Snyder (D-16) |
| Ed Gaunch (R-8) | Robert Lynn "Bob" Williams |
| Kent Leonhardt (R-2) | (D-14) |
| Mark R. Maynard (R-6) | Jack Yost (D-1) |
| Jeff Mullins (R-9) | |

## Health and Human Resources

| Majority Members | Minority Members |
|---|---|
| Ryan James Ferns (R-1) *Chair* | William Ramsey Laird IV (D-10) |
| Tom Takubo (R-17) *Vice Chair* | Corey L. Palumbo (D-17) |
| Robert G. "Bob" Ashley (R-3) | Robert Hugh "Bob" Plymale (D-5) |
| Robert Karnes (R-11) | Roman W. Prezioso, Jr. (D-13) |
| Kent Leonhardt (R-2) | Ronny Douglas "Ron" Stollings |
| Charles S. Trump IV (R-15) | (D-7) |
| Chris W. Walters (R-8) | John R. Unger (D-16) |

## Interstate Cooperation

| Majority Members | Minority Members |
|---|---|
| Ed Gaunch (R-8) *Chair* | Arthur E. "Art" Kirkendoll (D-7) |
| Robert Karnes (R-11) *Vice Chair* | Corey L. Palumbo (D-17) |
| Gregory L. Boso (R-11) | John R. Unger (D-16) |
| Mark R. Maynard (R-6) | |

## Judiciary

| Majority Members | Minority Members |
|---|---|
| Charles S. Trump IV (R-15) *Chair* | Robert D. "Bob" Beach (D-13) |
| Ryan James Ferns (R-1) *Vice Chair* | Arthur E. "Art" Kirkendoll (D-7) |
| Robert G. "Bob" Ashley (R-3) | Ronald F. "Ron" Miller (D-10) |
| Mitch B. Carmichael (R-4) | Corey L. Palumbo (D-17) |
| Sue Cline (R-9) | Michael Romano (D-12) |
| Ed Gaunch (R-8) | Herbert S. "Herb" Snyder (D-16) |
| Robert Karnes (R-11) | Robert Lynn "Bob" Williams |
| Kent Leonhardt (R-2) | (D-14) |
| Mark R. Maynard (R-6) | Mike Woelfel (D-5) |

## Labor

| Majority Members | Minority Members |
|---|---|
| Ryan James Ferns (R-1) *Chair* | William Ramsey Laird IV (D-10) |
| Charles S. Trump IV (R-15) | Roman W. Prezioso, Jr. (D-13) |
| *Vice Chair* | Ronny Douglas "Ron" Stollings |
| Craig P. Blair (R-15) | (D-7) |
| Ed Gaunch (R-8) | Robert Lynn "Bob" Williams |
| Robert Karnes (R-11) | (D-14) |
| Mark R. Maynard (R-6) | Jack Yost (D-1) |

## Military

| Majority Members | Minority Members |
|---|---|
| Kent Leonhardt (R-2) *Chair* | Douglas Eugene Facemire (D-12) |
| Donna J. Boley (R-3) *Vice Chair* | William Ramsey Laird IV (D-10) |
| Robert G. "Bob" Ashley (R-3) | Michael Romano (D-12) |
| Dave Sypolt (R-14) | Jack Yost (D-1) |
| Chris W. Walters (R-8) | |

## Natural Resources

**Majority Members**
Robert Karnes (R-11) *Chair*
Mark R. Maynard (R-6) *Vice Chair*
Robert G. "Bob" Ashley (R-3)
Gregory L. Boso (R-11)
William Michael "Mike" Hall (R-4)
Kent Leonhardt (R-2)
Tom Takubo (R-17)

**Minority Members**
Robert D. "Bob" Beach (D-13)
Douglas Eugene Facemire (D-12)
William Ramsey Laird IV (D-10)
Ronald F. "Ron" Miller (D-10)
Herbert S. "Herb" Snyder (D-16)
Robert Lynn "Bob" Williams
(D-14)

## Pensions

**Majority Members**
Ed Gaunch (R-8) *Chair*
Charles S. Trump IV (R-15)
  *Vice Chair*
William Michael "Mike" Hall (R-4)
Jeff Mullins (R-9)

**Minority Members**
Arthur E. "Art" Kirkendoll (D-7)
Robert Hugh "Bob" Plymale (D-5)
John R. Unger (D-16)

## Rules

**Majority Members**
William P. "Bill" Cole III (R-6)
  *Chair*
Craig P. Blair (R-15)
Mitch B. Carmichael (R-4)
William Michael "Mike" Hall (R-4)
Dave Sypolt (R-14)
Charles S. Trump IV (R-15)

**Minority Members**
Jeffrey V. Kessler (D-2)
Robert Hugh "Bob" Plymale (D-5)
Roman W. Prezioso, Jr. (D-13)
Ronny Douglas "Ron" Stollings
(D-7)
Robert Lynn "Bob" Williams
(D-14)

## Transportation and Infrastructure

**Majority Members**
Chris W. Walters (R-8) *Chair*
Kent Leonhardt (R-2) *Vice Chair*
Donna J. Boley (R-3)
Ed Gaunch (R-8)
Jeff Mullins (R-9)

**Minority Members**
Robert D. "Bob" Beach (D-13)
Arthur E. "Art" Kirkendoll (D-7)
Robert Hugh "Bob" Plymale (D-5)
Mike Woelfel (D-5)

# West Virginia House of Delegates

Tel: (304) 340-3200  Fax: (304) 347-4819  TTY: (304) 347-4901

Speaker of the House
**Timothy Paul "Tim" Armstead** (R) . . . . . . . . . . . . . . . . . (304) 340-3210
  Education: Charleston 1987 BA; West Virginia 1990 JD
Speaker Pro Tem **Everette W. "Bill" Anderson, Jr.** (R) . . . (304) 340-3168
  Education: Marshall BA; West Virginia MA
Majority Leader **Daryl E. Cowles** (R) . . . . . . . . . . . . . . . . . (304) 340-3177
Majority Whip **John David O'Neal IV** (R) . . . . . . . . . . . . . . (304) 340-3164
Assistant Majority Whip **Danny Hamrick** (R) . . . . . . . . . . . (304) 340-3141
Assistant Majority Whip **Eric Lee Householder** (R) . . . . . . (304) 340-3274
Assistant Majority Whip **John B. "JB" McCuskey** (R) . . . (304) 340-3183
  Education: George Washington BA; West Virginia 2009 JD
Assistant Majority Whip **Randy E. Smith** (R) . . . . . . . . . . . (304) 340-3396
Assistant Majority Whip **Kelli Ann Sobonya** (R) . . . . . . . . (304) 340-3175
Minority Leader **Timothy R. "Tim" Miley** (D) . . . . . . . . . . (304) 340-3240
  Education: Southern Methodist BBA; Duquesne JD
Minority Whip **Michael "Mike" Caputo** (D) . . . . . . . . . . . (304) 340-3249
Assistant Minority Whip **Michael Thomas Ferro** (D) . . . . . (304) 340-3111
  Education: West Liberty State BA; West Virginia MA
Assistant Minority Whip **Clifton "Clif" Moore** (D) . . . . . . (304) 340-3165
  Education: West Virginia BA; Kennedy-Western MA, PhD
Assistant Minority Whip **David "Dave" Pethtel** (D) . . . . . . (304) 340-3158
  Education: Glenville State AB; West Virginia MA
Assistant Minority Whip
**Margaret Donaldson "Peggy" Smith** (D) . . . . . . . . . . (304) 340-3123
  Education: West Virginia Wesleyan BA; West Virginia MEd, JD
Clerk of the House **Steve Harrison** (R) . . . . . . . . . . . . . . . (304) 340-3200
  E-mail: house.clerk@wvhouse.gov
Sergeant-at-Arms **Marshall Clay** . . . . . . . . . . . . . . . . . . . . (304) 340-3200

# Delegates

**Party Affiliation Statistics:** Republicans: 64, Democrats: 36

Delegate **George "Boogie" Ambler** (R-District 42) . . . . . . (304) 340-3129
  Counties Represented: Greenbrier (part), Monroe    Res: (304) 647-4145
  (part)
  Term Expires: 2016
  Route 1 Box 315, Ronceverte, WV 24970-9741
  E-mail: george.ambler@wvhouse.gov
  Committees: Agriculture and Natural Resources; Education; Energy;
  Roads and Transportation
  Education: Bluefield State BS

Delegate
**Everette W. "Bill" Anderson, Jr.** (R-District 8)
  Building One, Room 151-R . . . . . . . . . . . . . . . . . . . . . . . (304) 340-3168
  Counties Represented: Wood (part)
  Term Expires: 2016
  E-mail: bill.anderson@wvhouse.gov
  Committees: Agriculture and Natural Resources; Energy; Finance;
  Political Subdivisions; Rules

Delegate
**Timothy Paul "Tim" Armstead** (R-District 40) . . . . . . . (304) 340-3210
  Counties Represented: Kanawha (part)    Tel: (304) 965-5169
  Term Expires: 2016
  5012 Elk River Road, Elkview, WV 25071
  E-mail: tim.armstead@wvhouse.gov
  Committees: Rules

Delegate **Karen "Lynne" Arvon** (R-District 31) . . . . . . . . (304) 340-3384
  Counties Represented: Raleigh (part)    Res: (304) 575-5066
  Term Expires: 2016
  101 Triangle Lane, Beckley, WV 25801
  E-mail: karen.arvon@wvhouse.gov
  Committees: Government Organization; Health and Human Resources;
  Roads and Transportation; Veterans Affairs and Homeland Security
  Education: Marshall AS; West Virginia State U BSBA

Delegate **Martin "Rick" Atkinson III** (R-District 11) . . . . . (304) 340-3185
  Counties Represented: Jackson (part), Roane
  Term Expires: 2016
  E-mail: martin.atkinson@wvhouse.gov
  Committees: Agriculture and Natural Resources; Government
  Organization; Health and Human Resources; Veterans Affairs and
  Homeland Security

Delegate **Mike Azinger** (R-District 10) . . . . . . . . . . . . . . . (304) 340-3202
  Counties Represented: Wood (part)
  Term Expires: 2016
  1007 51st Street, Vienna, WV 26105
  E-mail: mike.azinger@wvhouse.gov
  Committees: Banking and Insurance; Industry and Labor; Judiciary

Delegate **Mick Bates** (D-District 30) . . . . . . . . . . . . . . . . . (304) 340-3180
  Counties Represented: Raleigh (part), Wyoming (part)
  Term Expires: 2016
  P.O. Box 844, Beckley, WV 25801
  E-mail: mick.bates@wvhouse.gov
  Committees: Banking and Insurance; Finance; Health and Human
  Resources; Small Business Entrepreneurship and Economic
  Development

Delegate **Frank L. Blackwell** (D-District 25) . . . . . . . . . . . (304) 340-3163
  Counties Represented: Mercer (part), Wyoming (part)
  Term Expires: 2016
  1801 Moran Avenue, Mullens, WV 25882
  E-mail: frank.blackwell@wvhouse.gov
  Committees: Agriculture and Natural Resources; Education; Roads and
  Transportation

Delegate **Saira Blair** (R-District 59) . . . . . . . . . . . . . . . . . . (304) 340-3122
  Counties Represented: Berkeley (part), Morgan (part)
  Term Expires: 2016
  Building One, 1900 Kanawha Boulevard, State Capitol Complex,
  Room 219E, Charleston, WV 25305
  E-mail: saira.blair@wvhouse.gov
  Committees: Government Organization; Industry and Labor; Small
  Business Entrepreneurship and Economic Development

Delegate **Lawrence Brent Boggs** (D-District 34)
  State Capitol Complex, Room 258M . . . . . . . . . . . . . . . . . (304) 340-3142
  Counties Represented: Braxton, Gilmer (part)
  Term Expires: 2016
  E-mail: brent.boggs@wvhouse.gov
  Committees: Energy; Finance; Political Subdivisions; Roads and
  Transportation; Rules
  Education: Glenville State AS

*(continued on next page)*

LEGISLATIVE BRANCH

**LEGISLATIVE BRANCH**

**Delegates** *continued*

**Delegate Anna Border-Sheppard** (R-District 9)
Room 227E . . . . . . . . . . . . . . . . . . . . . . . . . . . . . . . .(304) 340-3136
Counties Represented: Wirt, Wood (part)
Term Expires: 2016
E-mail: anna.border@wvhouse.gov
Committees: Agriculture and Natural Resources; Energy; Government Organization; Senior Citizen Issues
Education: West Virginia BS

**Delegate Jim Butler** (R-District 14) . . . . . . . . . . . . . . . . .(304) 340-3199
Counties Represented: Mason (part), Putnam (part)    Res: (304) 675-3984
Term Expires: 2016
P.O. Box 296, Henderson, WV 25106
E-mail: jim.butler@wvhouse.gov
Committees: Finance; Political Subdivisions; Roads and Transportation

**Delegate Andrew Byrd** (D-District 35) . . . . . . . . . . . . . . . .(304) 340-3362
Counties Represented: Kanawha (part)
Term Expires: 2016
868 Whispering Way, South Charleston, WV 25303
E-mail: andrew.byrd@wvhouse.gov
Committees: Industry and Labor; Judiciary; Political Subdivisions; Veterans Affairs and Homeland Security

**Delegate Scott Cadle** (R-District 13) . . . . . . . . . . . . . . . . .(304) 340-3118
Counties Represented: Jackson (part), Mason    Tel: (304) 674-3953
(part), Putnam (part)    Res: (304) 882-3686
Term Expires: 2016
5558 Graham Station Road, Lavalette, WV 25253
E-mail: scott.cadle@wvhouse.gov
Committees: Agriculture and Natural Resources; Energy; Government Organization; Roads and Transportation
Education: Glenville State

**Delegate Denise Lynne Campbell** (D-District 43) . . . . . . .(304) 340-3145
Counties Represented: Pocahontas, Randolph (part)    Tel: (304) 636-1391
Term Expires: 2016
State Captol Complex, Room 151R, Charleston, WV 25305
E-mail: denise.campbell@wvhouse.gov
Committees: Agriculture and Natural Resources; Education; Health and Human Resources; Rules; Senior Citizen Issues

**Delegate Denny Ray Canterbury, Jr.** (R-District 42)
Room 212E . . . . . . . . . . . . . . . . . . . . . . . . . . . . . . . .(304) 340-3131
Counties Represented: Greenbrier (part), Monroe (part)
Term Expires: 2016
E-mail: ray.canterbury@wvhouse.gov
Committees: Agriculture and Natural Resources; Energy; Finance; Pensions and Retirement; Senior Citizen Issues

**Delegate Michael "Mike" Caputo** (D-District 50) . . . . . . . .(304) 340-3249
Counties Represented: Marion (part)    Tel: (304) 363-7500
Term Expires: 2016
310 Gaston Avenue, Fairmont, WV 26554
E-mail: mike.caputo@wvhouse.gov
Committees: Energy; Government Organization; Industry and Labor; Rules

**Delegate Roy G. Cooper** (R-District 28) Room 203E . . . . .(304) 340-3119
Counties Represented: Monroe (part), Summers    Res: (304) 466-5523
(part)
Term Expires: 2016
E-mail: roy.cooper@wvhouse.gov
Committees: Agriculture and Natural Resources; Education; Health and Human Resources; Veterans Affairs and Homeland Security
Education: Concord Col BS; Tidewater Comm Col AS

**Delegate Daryl E. Cowles** (R-District 58) Room 228M . . . .(304) 340-3177
Counties Represented: Hampshire (part), Morgan    Tel: (304) 258-1880
(part)
Term Expires: 2016
E-mail: daryl.cowles@wvhouse.gov
Committees: Industry and Labor; Political Subdivisions; Rules

**Delegate J. Frank Deem** (R-District 10) . . . . . . . . . . . . . . .(304) 340-3137
Counties Represented: Wood (part)
Term Expires: 2016
5518 Second Avenue, Vienna, WV 26105
E-mail: frank.deem@wvhouse.gov
Committees: Banking and Insurance; Judiciary; Senior Citizen Issues
Education: Marietta BS

**Delegate Walter Edwin Duke** (R-District 61) . . . . . . . . . . .(304) 340-3188
Counties Represented: Berkeley (part)
Term Expires: 2016
112 Tavern Road, Martinsburg, WV 25401
E-mail: walter.duke@wvhouse.gov
Committees: Education; Political Subdivisions; Senior Citizen Issues
Education: Shepherd U BA; West Virginia MA

**Delegate Jeffery "Jeff" Eldridge** (D-District 22) . . . . . . . .(304) 340-3113
Counties Represented: Boone (part), Lincoln    Tel: (304) 928-9728
(part), Logan (part), Putnam (part)    Res: (304) 756-3817
Term Expires: 2016
4754 Coal River Road, Alum Creek, WV 25003
E-mail: jeff.eldridge@wvhouse.gov
Committees: Agriculture and Natural Resources; Energy; Government Organization
Education: Marshall BA, MA

**Delegate Joe Carey Ellington, Jr.** (R-District 27)
Room 215E . . . . . . . . . . . . . . . . . . . . . . . . . . . . . . . .(304) 340-3172
Counties Represented: Mercer (part), Monroe (part),    Tel: (304) 425-3800
Summers (part)
Term Expires: 2016
E-mail: joe.ellington@wvhouse.gov
Committees: Education; Health and Human Resources; Industry and Labor; Interstate Cooperation; Small Business Entrepreneurship and Economic Development

**Delegate Paul Espinosa** (R-District 66) . . . . . . . . . . . . . . .(304) 340-3265
Counties Represented: Jefferson (part)    Res: (304) 728-8139
Term Expires: 2016
107 Hancock Court, Charles Town, WV 25414
E-mail: paul.espinosa@wvhouse.gov
Committees: Education; Finance; Roads and Transportation; Rules; Small Business Entrepreneurship and Economic Development
Education: West Virginia Wesleyan 1984 BA

**Delegate Allen Vincent Evans** (R-District 54) . . . . . . . . . .(304) 340-3399
Counties Represented: Grant, Mineral (part), Pendleton (part)
Term Expires: 2016
Charleston, WV 25305
HC 33, Box 3025, Dorcas, WV 26847
E-mail: allen.evans@wvhouse.gov
Committees: Agriculture and Natural Resources; Finance; Roads and Transportation

**Delegate David A. Evans** (R-District 4) . . . . . . . . . . . . . . .(304) 340-3151
Counties Represented: Marshall, Ohio (part)    Tel: (304) 780-8136
Term Expires: 2016    Res: (304) 686-3740
15 Pleasant Drive, Cameron, WV 26033
E-mail: david.evans@wvhouse.gov
Committees: Education; Energy; Roads and Transportation; Veterans Affairs and Homeland Security
Education: Glenville State 1967 AB; West Virginia MS

**Delegate Larry W. Faircloth** (R-District 60) . . . . . . . . . . . .(304) 340-3147
Counties Represented: Berkeley (part)    Tel: (304) 582-0087
Term Expires: 2016    Res: (304) 229-2975
186 Diamante Drive, Inwood, WV 25428
E-mail: larry.faircloth@wvhouse.gov
Committees: Government Organization; Health and Human Resources; Interstate Cooperation; Senior Citizen Issues; Small Business Entrepreneurship and Economic Development
Education: Shepherd U

**Delegate Tom Fast** (R-District 32) . . . . . . . . . . . . . . . . . . .(304) 340-3170
Counties Represented: Clay (part), Fayette, Kanawha (part), Nicholas (part), Raleigh (part)
Term Expires: 2016
P.O. Box 332, Fayetteville, WV 25840
E-mail: tom.fast@wvhouse.gov
Committees: Industry and Labor; Judiciary; Roads and Transportation

**Delegate Michael Thomas Ferro** (D-District 4)
Building One, Room 222-E . . . . . . . . . . . . . . . . . . . . . .(304) 340-3111
Counties Represented: Marshall, Ohio (part)
Term Expires: 2016
E-mail: mike.ferro@wvhouse.gov
Committees: Government Organization; Industry and Labor; Interstate Cooperation; Senior Citizen Issues; Veterans Affairs and Homeland Security

**Delegate William "Bill" Flanigan** (R-District 51) . . . . . . . .(304) 340-3153
Counties Represented: Monongalia (part)
Term Expires: 2016
250 Fred Street, Morgantown, WV 26501
E-mail: bill.flanigan@wvhouse.gov
Committees: Banking and Insurance; Government Organization; Small Business Entrepreneurship and Economic Development

**Delegate Barbara Evans Fleischauer** (D-District 51)
Room 231E . . . . . . . . . . . . . . . . . . . . . . . . . . . . . . . .(304) 340-3127
Counties Represented: Monongalia (part)    Tel: (304) 296-7035
Term Expires: 2016
E-mail: barbaraf@wvhouse.gov
Committees: Health and Human Resources; Judiciary; Rules; Veterans Affairs and Homeland Security
Education: Allegheny 1975 BA; West Virginia 1982 JD

Delegate **Shawn Fluharty** (D-District 3) . . . . . . . . . . . . . . (304) 340-3270
Counties Represented: Ohio (part)
Term Expires: 2016
42 Walnut Avenue, Wheeling, WV 26003
E-mail: shawn.fluharty@wvhouse.gov
Committees: Health and Human Resources; Industry and Labor;
Judiciary

Delegate **Michael "Mike" Folk** (R-District 63) . . . . . . . . . (304) 340-3350
Counties Represented: Berkeley (part)          Tel: (304) 279-6797
Term Expires: 2016                             Res: (304) 262-9530
1346 Swan Pond Road, Martinsburg, WV 25405
E-mail: michael.folk@wvhouse.gov
Committees: Agriculture and Natural Resources; Judiciary; Pensions
and Retirement; Political Subdivisions
Education: Shepherd Col 1992 BS; West Virginia 1994 MBA

Delegate **Geoff Foster** (R-District 15) . . . . . . . . . . . . . . . . .(304) 340-3121
Counties Represented: Putnam (part)
Term Expires: 2016
Ten Hawthorne Street, Winfield, WV 25213
E-mail: geoff.foster@wvhouse.gov
Committees: Judiciary; Roads and Transportation; Veterans Affairs and
Homeland Security

Delegate **Cindy Frich** (R-District 51) . . . . . . . . . . . . . . . . .(304) 340-3125
Counties Represented: Monongalia (part)        Res: (304) 599-1309
Term Expires: 2016
1248 Bakers Ridge Road, Morgantown, WV 26505
E-mail: cindy.frich@wvhouse.gov
Committees: Banking and Insurance; Finance; Veterans Affairs and
Homeland Security
Education: Miami U (OH) 1987 BA

Delegate
**Gary Martin "Marty" Gearheart** (R-District 27)
Room 200E-A . . . . . . . . . . . . . . . . . . . . . . . . . . . . . . . . . .(304) 340-3179
Counties Represented: Mercer (part), Monroe (part),   Tel: (304) 320-0879
Summers (part)
Term Expires: 2016
E-mail: marty.gearheart@wvhouse.gov
Committees: Finance; Political Subdivisions; Roads and Transportation

Delegate **Nancy Peoples Guthrie** (D-District 36) . . . . . . . . (304) 340-3156
Counties Represented: Kanawha (part)           Tel: (304) 925-4420
Term Expires: 2016
State Captol Complex, Charleston, WV 25305
E-mail: nancy.guthrie@wvhouse.gov
Committees: Agriculture and Natural Resources; Finance; Roads and
Transportation; Rules
Education: Penn State

Delegate **William David "Bill" Hamilton** (R-District 45)
Room 216E . . . . . . . . . . . . . . . . . . . . . . . . . . . . . . . . . . . .(304) 340-3167
Counties Represented: Upshur (part)            Tel: (304) 472-1532
Term Expires: 2016
E-mail: bill.hamilton@wvhouse.gov
Committees: Agriculture and Natural Resources; Finance; Pensions and
Retirement; Senior Citizen Issues

Delegate **Danny Hamrick** (R-District 48) . . . . . . . . . . . . . . (304) 340-3141
Counties Represented: Harrison, Taylor (part)   Res: (304) 647-4252
Term Expires: 2016
403 Elm Street, Clarksburg, WV 26301
E-mail: danny.hamrick@wvhouse.gov
Committees: Banking and Insurance; Education; Government
Organization; Interstate Cooperation; Roads and Transportation

Delegate **Roger Hanshaw** (R-District 3) Room 229E . . . . . (304) 340-3135
Counties Represented: Ohio (part)
Term Expires: 2016
E-mail: roger.hanshaw@wvhouse.gov
Committees: Judiciary; Political Subdivisions; Small Business
Entrepreneurship and Economic Development

Delegate **William G. "Bill" Hartman** (D-District 43) . . . . . (304) 340-3178
Counties Represented: Pocahontas, Randolph (part)   Tel: (304) 636-0400
Term Expires: 2016
1900 Kanawha Boulevard, State Capitol Complex,
Charleston, WV 25305
E-mail: bill.hartman@wvhouse.gov
Committees: Government Organization; Political Subdivisions; Senior
Citizen Issues; Small Business Entrepreneurship and Economic
Development
Education: West Virginia BA

Delegate **Kenneth P. Hicks** (D-District 19) . . . . . . . . . . . . . (304) 340-3155
Counties Represented: Wayne (part)
Term Expires: 2016
182 Hidden Valley Drive, Kenova, WV 25530
E-mail: ken.hicks@wvhouse.gov
Committees: Banking and Insurance; Education; Industry and Labor

Delegate **Jordan Hill** (R-District 41) . . . . . . . . . . . . . . . . . . (304) 340-3352
Counties Represented: Greenbrier (part), Nicholas (part)
Term Expires: 2016
1307 Webster Road, Suite 200, Summersville, WV 26651
E-mail: jordan.hill@wvhouse.gov
Committees: Government Organization; Health and Human Resources;
Senior Citizen Issues; Small Business Entrepreneurship and Economic
Development

Delegate **Sean Hornbuckle** (D-District 16) . . . . . . . . . . . . (304) 340-3395
Counties Represented: Cabell (part), Lincoln (part)
Term Expires: 2016
501 Sixth Avenue, Huntington, WV 25701
E-mail: sean.hornbuckle@wvhouse.gov
Committees: Education; Political Subdivisions; Small Business
Entrepreneurship and Economic Development; Veterans Affairs and
Homeland Security

Delegate **Eric Lee Householder** (R-District 64) . . . . . . . . . (304) 340-3274
Counties Represented: Berkeley (part)          Tel: (304) 261-9468
Term Expires: 2016
212 Snooks Lane, Martinsburg, WV 25405
E-mail: eric.householder@wvhouse.gov
Committees: Finance; Health and Human Resources; Industry and
Labor; Political Subdivisions

Delegate **Gary Gibson Howell** (R-District 56) . . . . . . . . . . .(304) 340-3192
Counties Represented: Mineral (part)           Tel: (304) 790-9022
Term Expires: 2016
P.O. Box 39, Keyser, WV 26726
E-mail: gary.howell@wvhouse.gov
Committees: Government Organization; Roads and Transportation;
Rules; Veterans Affairs and Homeland Security

Delegate **Michael Ihle** (R-District 13) . . . . . . . . . . . . . . . . .(304) 340-3146
Counties Represented: Jackson (part), Mason (part), Putnam (part)
Term Expires: 2016
507A Sand Street, Ravenswood, WV 26164
E-mail: michael.ihle@wvhouse.gov
Committees: Government Organization; Industry and Labor; Political
Subdivisions

Delegate **Lynwood "Woody" Ireland** (R-District 7) . . . . . .(304) 340-3195
Counties Represented: Pleasants (part), Ritchie
Term Expires: 2016
Building One, 1900 Kanawha Boulevard, State Capitol Complex,
Room 151-R, Charleston, WV 25305
E-mail: woody.ireland@wvhouse.gov
Committees: Agriculture and Natural Resources; Energy; Judiciary;
Rules; Veterans Affairs and Homeland Security
Education: West Virginia BS

Delegate **John R. Kelly** (R-District 10) Room 221E . . . . . . (304) 340-3394
Counties Represented: Wood (part)
Term Expires: 2016
2802 Brookview Street, Parkersburg, WV 26104
E-mail: john.kelly@wvhouse.gov
Committees: Education; Senior Citizen Issues; Small Business
Entrepreneurship and Economic Development; Veterans Affairs and
Homeland Security

Delegate **Kayla Kessinger** (R-District 32) Room 227E . . . . (304) 340-3197
Counties Represented: Clay (part), Fayette, Kanawha (part), Nicholas
(part), Raleigh (part)
Term Expires: 2016
1736 Kess Springs Court, Mount Hope, WV 26104
E-mail: kayla.kessinger@wvhouse.gov
Committees: Energy; Judiciary; Small Business Entrepreneurship and
Economic Development; Veterans Affairs and Homeland Security

Delegate **Brian Kurcaba** (R-District 51) . . . . . . . . . . . . . . . (304) 340-3173
Counties Represented: Monongalia (part)
Term Expires: 2016
P.O. Box 30, Morgantown, WV 26507
E-mail: brian.kurcaba@wvhouse.gov
Committees: Banking and Insurance; Education; Health and Human
Resources; Industry and Labor; Pensions and Retirement

Delegate **Patrick Lane** (R-District 38) . . . . . . . . . . . . . . . . . (304) 340-3252
Counties Represented: Kanawha (part), Putnam     Tel: (304) 545-5263
(part)
Term Expires: 2016
5402 Morning Dove Lane, Cross Lanes, WV 25313
E-mail: patrick.lane@wvhouse.gov
Committees: Health and Human Resources; Judiciary; Political
Subdivisions; Rules; Small Business Entrepreneurship and Economic
Development
Education: Concord Col 1996 BA; West Virginia 2000 JD

*(continued on next page)*

**Delegates** *continued*

Delegate **Linda Longstreth** (D-District 50) . . . . . . . . . . . . (304) 340-3124
Counties Represented: Marion (part)
Term Expires: 2016
804 Ohio Avenue, Fairmont, WV 26554
E-mail: linda.longstreth@wvhouse.gov
Committees: Finance; Health and Human Resources; Roads and
Transportation; Veterans Affairs and Homeland Security
Education: Fairmont State Col AB; West Virginia MS

Delegate **Dana L. Lynch** (D-District 44) . . . . . . . . . . . . . . . (304) 340-3916
Counties Represented: Nicholas (part), Randolph          Tel: (304) 644-1949
(part), Upshur (part), Webster                            Res: (304) 847-7233
Term Expires: 2016
176 Woodplant Road, Webster Springs, WV 26288
E-mail: dana.lynch@wvhouse.gov
Committees: Agriculture and Natural Resources; Energy; Government
Organization; Veterans Affairs and Homeland Security

Delegate **Timothy J. Manchin** (D-District 50)
Room 151R . . . . . . . . . . . . . . . . . . . . . . . . . . . . . . . . . . . . . (304) 340-3331
Counties Represented: Marion (part)          Tel: (304) 367-1862
Term Expires: 2016
E-mail: tmanchin@manchininjurylaw.com
Committees: Banking and Insurance; Industry and Labor; Judiciary;
Political Subdivisions; Rules; Small Business Entrepreneurship and
Economic Development
Education: West Virginia BS, JD

Delegate **Justin Marcum** (D-District 20)
Building One, Room 150R . . . . . . . . . . . . . . . . . . . . . . . . . (304) 340-3126
Counties Represented: Logan (part), Mingo (part)
Term Expires: 2016
E-mail: justin.marcum@wvhouse.gov
Committees: Judiciary; Pensions and Retirement
Education: Marshall; Appalachian Law JD

Delegate **John B. "JB" McCuskey** (R-District 35) . . . . . . (304) 340-3183
Counties Represented: Kanawha (part)          Res: (304) 282-4885
Term Expires: 2016
P.O. Box 11359, Charleston, WV 25339
E-mail: john.mccuskey@wvhouse.gov
Committees: Banking and Insurance; Energy; Industry and Labor;
Judiciary

Delegate **Patrick Riley "Pat" McGeehan** (R-District 1) . . . (304) 340-3397
Counties Represented: Brooke (part), Hancock
Term Expires: 2016
616 Florida Avenue, #5, Chester, WV 26034
E-mail: pat.mcgeehan@wvhouse.gov
Committees: Banking and Insurance; Government Organization;
Veterans Affairs and Homeland Security
Education: Air Force Acad 2003 BSE

Delegate **Timothy R. "Tim" Miley** (D-District 48) . . . . . . . (304) 340-3240
Counties Represented: Harrison, Taylor (part)          Tel: (304) 326-1800
Term Expires: 2016
23 Valley View Road, Bridgeport, WV 26330
E-mail: tim.miley@wvhouse.gov
Committees: Energy; Rules; Small Business Entrepreneurship and
Economic Development

Delegate **Carol Devine Miller** (R-District 16) . . . . . . . . . . . (304) 340-3176
Counties Represented: Cabell (part), Lincoln (part)          Tel: (304) 697-6540
Term Expires: 2016
1316 12th Street, Huntington, WV 25701
E-mail: carol.miller@wvhouse.gov
Committees: Agriculture and Natural Resources; Finance; Rules; Small
Business Entrepreneurship and Economic Development
Education: Columbia Col (SC) BS

Delegate **Michel Moffatt** (R-District 22) . . . . . . . . . . . . . . . (304) 340-3152
Counties Represented: Boone (part), Lincoln (part), Logan (part),
Putnam (part)
Term Expires: 2016
156 Jamestown Way, Hurricane, WV 25526
E-mail: michel.moffatt@wvhouse.gov
Committees: Government Organization; Political Subdivisions; Roads
and Transportation

Delegate **Clifton "Clif" Moore** (D-District 26)
Room 231E . . . . . . . . . . . . . . . . . . . . . . . . . . . . . . . . . . . . . (304) 340-3165
Counties Represented: McDowell (part), Mercer          Tel: (304) 436-8569
(part)
Term Expires: 2016
E-mail: clif.moore@wvhouse.gov
Committees: Banking and Insurance; Health and Human Resources;
Judiciary; Senior Citizen Issues

Delegate **James Hanly "Jim" Morgan** (D-District 16) . . . (304) 340-3277
Counties Represented: Cabell (part), Lincoln (part)          Tel: (304) 523-6120
Term Expires: 2016
P.O. Box 117, Huntington, WV 25706
E-mail: jim.morgan@wvhouse.gov
Committees: Banking and Insurance; Government Organization;
Political Subdivisions; Small Business Entrepreneurship and Economic
Development
Education: West Virginia 1959 BA

Delegate **Ricky Duane Moye** (D-District 29) Room 2R . . . (304) 340-3162
Counties Represented: Raleigh (part)          Tel: (304) 255-2932
Term Expires: 2016
E-mail: rickymoye@wvhouse.gov
Committees: Education; Finance; Political Subdivisions; Roads and
Transportation; Senior Citizen Issues

Delegate **Fredrik Eric Nelson, Jr.** (R-District 35) . . . . . . . . (304) 340-3230
Counties Represented: Kanawha (part)          Tel: (304) 343-5156
Term Expires: 2016
P.O. Box 186, Charleston, WV 25231
E-mail: nelson@wvhouse.gov
Committees: Banking and Insurance; Finance; Rules; Senior Citizen
Issues

Delegate **Joshua A. Nelson** (R-District 23) . . . . . . . . . . . . (304) 340-3184
Counties Represented: Boone (part), Raleigh (part)          Tel: (304) 928-7792
Term Expires: 2016                                          Res: (304) 369-7908
3712 Lick Creek Road, Danville, WV 25053
E-mail: joshua.nelson@wvhouse.gov
Committees: Energy; Government Organization; Industry and Labor;
Veterans Affairs and Homeland Security
Education: Liberty 2010 BS

Delegate **John David O'Neal IV** (R-District 28) . . . . . . . . . (304) 340-3164
Counties Represented: Monroe (part), Summers          Tel: (304) 894-8445
(part)
Term Expires: 2016
Eight Oriole Place, Beckley, WV 25801
E-mail: john.oneal@wvhouse.gov
Committees: Banking and Insurance; Finance; Political Subdivisions;
Rules

Delegate **John Overington** (R-District 62) . . . . . . . . . . . . . (304) 340-3148
Counties Represented: Berkeley (part)          Tel: (304) 274-1791
Term Expires: 2016
491 Hoffman Road, Martinsburg, WV 25401
E-mail: john@overington.com
Committees: Industry and Labor; Judiciary; Rules; Senior Citizen
Issues
Education: Washington Col 1969 BS

Delegate **Don C. Perdue** (D-District 19) . . . . . . . . . . . . . . . (304) 340-3269
Counties Represented: Wayne (part)          Tel: (304) 633-3870
Term Expires: 2016
Route One, Box 98, Prichard, WV 25555
E-mail: don.perdue@wvhouse.gov
Committees: Banking and Insurance; Education; Health and Human
Resources
Education: Marshall BS; Ohio Northern BS

Delegate **David G. Perry** (D-District 32) . . . . . . . . . . . . . . . (304) 340-3337
Counties Represented: Clay (part), Fayette, Kanawha (part), Nicholas
(part), Raleigh (part)
Term Expires: 2016
330 East Martin Avenue, Oak Hill, WV 25901
E-mail: d.perry@wvhouse.gov
Committees: Banking and Insurance; Education; Finance; Political
Subdivisions; Senior Citizen Issues
Education: Marshall AB, MA

Delegate **David "Dave" Pethtel** (D-District 5)
Room 230E . . . . . . . . . . . . . . . . . . . . . . . . . . . . . . . . . . . . . (304) 340-3158
Counties Represented: Monongalia (part), Wetzel          Tel: (304) 775-4221
Term Expires: 2016
P.O. Box 990, Hundred, WV 26575
E-mail: dave.pethtel@wvhouse.gov
Committees: Energy; Finance; Pensions and Retirement; Senior Citizen
Issues

Delegate **Rupert Wilson Phillips, Jr.** (D-District 24)
Room 150R . . . . . . . . . . . . . . . . . . . . . . . . . . . . . . . . . . . . . (304) 340-3174
Counties Represented: Boone (part), Logan (part),          Tel: (304) 687-9793
Raleigh (part), Wyoming (part)
Term Expires: 2016
E-mail: rupert.phillips@wvhouse.gov
Committees: Energy; Senior Citizen Issues

Delegate **Mike Pushkin** (D-District 37)................(304) 340-3106
  Counties Represented: Kanawha (part)
  Term Expires: 2016
  411-B Randolph Street, Charleston, WV 25302
  E-mail: mike.pushkin@wvhouse.gov
  Committees: Government Organization; Health and Human Resources;
  Industry and Labor; Veterans Affairs and Homeland Security

Delegate **Douglas Vernon Reynolds** (D-District 17) ..... (304) 340-3280
  Counties Represented: Cabell (part), Wayne (part)      Tel: (304) 522-9200
  Term Expires: 2016
  75 West Third Avenue, Huntington, WV 25701
  E-mail: delegatedoug@yahoo.com
  Committees: Energy; Finance; Industry and Labor; Roads and
  Transportation
  Education: Duke BA; West Virginia JD

Delegate **Ralph Rodighiero** (D-District 24)............(304) 340-3297
  Counties Represented: Boone (part), Logan (part), Raleigh (part),
  Wyoming (part)
  Term Expires: 2016
  142 Sayer Circle, Logan, WV 25601
  E-mail: ralph.rodighiero@wvhouse.gov
  Committees: Agriculture and Natural Resources; Education; Health and
  Human Resources

Delegate **Matthew Rohrbach** (R-District 17) ...........(304) 340-3221
  Counties Represented: Cabell (part), Wayne (part)
  Term Expires: 2016
  25 Kensington Lane, Huntington, WV 25705
  E-mail: matthew.rohrbach@wvhouse.gov
  Committees: Education; Health and Human Resources; Roads and
  Transportation; Senior Citizen Issues

Delegate
  **William Rogers "Roger" Romine** (R-District 6)
  Room 210E.......................................(304) 340-3226
  Counties Represented: Doddridge, Pleasants (part),      Tel: (304) 771-0018
  Tyler
  Term Expires: 2016
  E-mail: roger.romine@wvhouse.gov
  Committees: Agriculture and Natural Resources; Education; Energy;
  Interstate Cooperation; Senior Citizen Issues
  Education: Salem Col BS; West Virginia MA

Delegate **Ruth Rowan** (R-District 57) Room 210E .......(304) 340-3157
  Counties Represented: Hampshire (part), Mineral (part)
  Term Expires: 2016
  E-mail: ruth.rowan@wvhouse.gov
  Committees: Education; Senior Citizen Issues; Veterans Affairs and
  Homeland Security
  Education: California U (PA) BS; West Virginia MA

Delegate **Larry L. Rowe** (D-District 36) ...............(304) 340-3287
  Counties Represented: Kanawha (part)
  Term Expires: 2016
  202 Wayne Isaac Lane, Charleston, WV 25306
  E-mail: larry.rowe@wvhouse.gov
  Committees: Banking and Insurance; Industry and Labor; Judiciary;
  Small Business Entrepreneurship and Economic Development

Delegate **Steven Shaffer** (D-District 52) ..............(304) 340-3160
  Counties Represented: Preston (part)
  Term Expires: 2016
  P.O. Box 25, Tunnelton, WV 26444
  E-mail: steve.shaffer@wvhouse.gov
  Committees: Agriculture and Natural Resources; Judiciary; Senior
  Citizen Issues
  Education: Fairmont State U 2000 BS; West Virginia 2003 JD

Delegate **John Headley Shott** (R-District 27) ...........(304) 340-3252
  Counties Represented: Mercer (part), Monroe      Tel: (304) 327-0573
  (part), Summers (part)      Res: (304) 325-7534
  Term Expires: 2016
  422 Oakhurst Avenue, Bluefield, WV 24701
  E-mail: john.shott@wvhouse.gov
  Committees: Banking and Insurance; Industry and Labor; Judiciary;
  Rules
  Education: Davidson 1970 BA; North Carolina 1975 JD

Delegate **Stephen G. Skinner** (D-District 67) ...........(304) 340-3248
  Counties Represented: Jefferson (part)
  Term Expires: 2016
  P.O. Box 366, Shepherdstown, WV 25443
  E-mail: stephen.skinner@wvhouse.gov
  Committees: Banking and Insurance; Judiciary; Small Business
  Entrepreneurship and Economic Development
  Education: West Virginia Wesleyan 1990 BA; West Virginia 1994 JD

Delegate
**Margaret Donaldson "Peggy" Smith** (D-District 46)
  Room 6R........................................(304) 340-3123
  Counties Represented: Lewis, Upshur (part)
  Term Expires: 2016
  E-mail: peggydonaldsonsmith@wvhouse.gov
  Committees: Finance; Interstate Cooperation; Roads and Transportation;
  Veterans Affairs and Homeland Security

Delegate **Randy E. Smith** (R-District 53)..............(304) 340-3396
  Counties Represented: Preston (part), Tucker (part)      Tel: (304) 698-1621
  Term Expires: 2016      Res: (304) 789-6545
  442 Freeland Crosscut Road, Terra Alta, WV 26764
  E-mail: randy.smith@wvhouse.gov
  Committees: Agriculture and Natural Resources; Energy; Government
  Organization; Industry and Labor

Delegate **Kelli Ann Sobonya** (R-District 17) Room 207E..(304) 340-3175
  Counties Represented: Cabell (part), Wayne (part)      Tel: (304) 736-6655
  Term Expires: 2016
  E-mail: kelli.sobonya@wvhouse.gov
  Committees: Health and Human Resources; Industry and Labor;
  Judiciary; Political Subdivisions; Rules

Delegate **Isaac Sponaugle** (D-District 55)..............(304) 340-3154
  Counties Represented: Hardy, Pendleton (part)
  Term Expires: 2016
  P.O. Box 578, Franklin, WV 26807
  E-mail: isaac.sponaugle@wvhouse.gov
  Committees: Agriculture and Natural Resources; Government
  Organization; Roads and Transportation
  Education: West Virginia 2001 BSBA, 2004 JD

Delegate **Chris Stansbury** (R-District 35) ..............(304) 340-3340
  Counties Represented: Kanawha (part)
  Term Expires: 2016
  P.O. Box 18151, Charleston, WV 25303
  E-mail: chris.stansbury@wvhouse.gov
  Committees: Government Organization; Health and Human Resources;
  Political Subdivisions; Small Business Entrepreneurship and Economic
  Development

Delegate **Joe Statler** (R-District 51) Room 220E ........(304) 340-3900
  Counties Represented: Monongalia (part)
  Term Expires: 2016
  E-mail: joe.statler@wvhouse.gov
  Committees: Education; Energy; Industry and Labor; Roads and
  Transportation

Delegate **Erikka Lynn Storch** (R-District 3) Room 202E ..(304) 340-3378
  Counties Represented: Ohio (part)      Tel: (304) 232-7575
  Term Expires: 2016
  E-mail: erikka.storch@wvhouse.gov
  Committees: Energy; Finance; Interstate Cooperation; Political
  Subdivisions; Small Business Entrepreneurship and Economic
  Development

Delegate **Amy Summers** (R-District 49) Room 215E-A ...(304) 340-3139
  Counties Represented: Marion (part), Monongalia (part), Taylor (part)
  Term Expires: 2016
  E-mail: amy.summers@wvhouse.gov
  Committees: Agriculture and Natural Resources; Health and Human
  Resources; Judiciary

Delegate **Patsy Trecost II** (D-District 48)..............(304) 340-3102
  Counties Represented: Harrison, Taylor (part)
  Term Expires: 2016
  E-mail: patsy.trecost@wvhouse.gov
  Committees: Education; Political Subdivisions; Roads and
  Transportation; Veterans Affairs and Homeland Security

Delegate **Jill Upson** (R-District 65)...................(304) 340-3366
  Counties Represented: Jefferson (part)
  Term Expires: 2016
  336 Pebble Beach Drive, Charles Town, WV 25414
  E-mail: jill.upson@wvhouse.gov
  Committees: Banking and Insurance; Education; Energy; Veterans
  Affairs and Homeland Security

Delegate **Danny Wagner** (R-District 47)...............(304) 340-3398
  Counties Represented: Barbour, Tucker (part)
  Term Expires: 2016
  107 Keyes Avenue, Philippi, WV 26418
  E-mail: danny.wagner@wvhouse.gov
  Committees: Agriculture and Natural Resources; Education; Roads and
  Transportation; Veterans Affairs and Homeland Security

*(continued on next page)*

**LEGISLATIVE BRANCH**

**Delegates** *continued*

**Delegate Ronald N. "Ron" Walters** (R-District 39)
Room 212E . . . . . . . . . . . . . . . . . . . . . . . . . . . . . . . . . . . .(304) 340-3194
Counties Represented: Kanawha (part)          Tel: (304) 346-4823
Term Expires: 2016
E-mail: ron.walters@wvhouse.gov
Committees: Banking and Insurance; Finance; Pensions and Retirement;
Senior Citizen Issues
Education: Michigan BS

**Delegate Terry Waxman** (R-District 48) . . . . . . . . . . . . . .(304) 340-3171
Counties Represented: Harrison, Taylor (part)
Term Expires: 2016
49 Diamond Cove Road, Bridgeport, WV 26330
E-mail: terry.waxman@wvhouse.gov
Committees: Banking and Insurance; Finance; Health and Human
Resources; Small Business Entrepreneurship and Economic
Development

**Delegate Ryan Weld** (R-District 2) . . . . . . . . . . . . . . . . . .(304) 340-3367
Counties Represented: Brooke (part), Ohio (part)
Term Expires: 2016
2225 Marianna Street, Wellsburg, WV 26070
E-mail: ryan.weld@wvhouse.gov
Committees: Judiciary; Political Subdivisions; Veterans Affairs and
Homeland Security

**Delegate Steve Westfall** (R-District 12) . . . . . . . . . . . . . .(304) 340-3140
Counties Represented: Jackson (part)          Tel: (304) 372-9117
Term Expires: 2016                            Res: (304) 372-9315
450 South Church Street, Ripley, WV 25271
E-mail: steve.westfall@wvhouse.gov
Committees: Banking and Insurance; Education; Finance; Health and
Human Resources; Small Business Entrepreneurship and Economic
Development
Education: Glenville State BA

**Delegate Brad White** (R-District 36) . . . . . . . . . . . . . . . . .(304) 340-3138
Counties Represented: Kanawha (part)
Term Expires: 2016
P.O. Box 4779, Charleston, WV 25364
E-mail: brad.white@wvhouse.gov
Committees: Banking and Insurance; Health and Human Resources;
Industry and Labor; Senior Citizen Issues

**Delegate Phyllis White** (D-District 21) . . . . . . . . . . . . . . .(304) 340-3304
Counties Represented: McDowell (part), Mingo (part), Wyoming (part)
Term Expires: 2016
P.O. Box 1985, Gilbert, WV 25621
E-mail: phyllis.white@wvhouse.gov
Committees: Agriculture and Natural Resources; Energy; Government
Organization; Small Business Entrepreneurship and Economic
Development

**Delegate Mark Zatezalo** (R-District 1) . . . . . . . . . . . . . . .(304) 340-3120
Counties Represented: Brooke (part), Hancock
Term Expires: 2016
540 North 12th Street, Weirton, WV 26062
E-mail: mark.zatezalo@wvhouse.gov
Committees: Energy; Government Organization; Judiciary; Senior
Citizen Issues; Small Business Entrepreneurship and Economic
Development

# House Standing Committees
## Agriculture and Natural Resources

| Majority Members | Minority Members |
|---|---|
| Allen Vincent Evans (R-54) | Jeffery "Jeff" Eldridge (D-22) |
| *Chair, Agriculture* | *Minority Chair, Agriculture* |
| William Rogers | Isaac Sponaugle (D-55) |
| "Roger" Romine (R-6) | *Minority Vice Chair, Agriculture* |
| *Vice Chair, Agriculture* | Dana L. Lynch (D-44) |
| William David "Bill" | *Minority Chair, Natural* |
| Hamilton (R-45) | *Resources* |
| *Chair, Natural Resources* | Nancy Peoples Guthrie |
| George "Boogie" Ambler (R-42) | (D-36)*Minority Vice Chair,* |
| *Vice Chair, Natural Resources* | *Natural Resources* |
| Everette W. "Bill" Anderson, Jr. | Frank L. Blackwell (D-25) |
| (R-8) | Denise Lynne Campbell (D-43) |
| Martin "Rick" Atkinson III (R-11) | Ralph Rodighiero (D-24) |
| Anna Border-Sheppard (R-9) | Steven Shaffer (D-52) |
| Scott Cadle (R-13) | Phyllis White (D-21) |
| Denny Ray Canterbury, Jr. (R-42) | |
| Roy G. Cooper (R-28) | |
| Michael "Mike" Folk (R-63) | |

**Majority Members** *continued*
Lynwood "Woody" Ireland (R-7)
Carol Devine Miller (R-16)
Randy E. Smith (R-53)
Amy Summers (R-49)
Danny Wagner (R-47)

## Banking and Insurance

| Majority Members | Minority Members |
|---|---|
| Ronald N. "Ron" Walters (R-39) | Clifton "Clif" Moore (D-26) |
| *Chair, Banking* | *Minority Chair, Banking* |
| Cindy Frich (R-51) | James Hanly "Jim" Morgan (D-16) |
| *Vice Chair, Banking* | *Minority Vice Chair, Banking* |
| John B. "JB" McCuskey (R-35) | Stephen G. Skinner (D-67) |
| *Chair, Insurance* | *Minority Chair, Insurance* |
| Steve Westfall (R-12) | Mick Bates (D-30) |
| *Vice Chair, Insurance* | *Minority Vice Chair, Insurance* |
| Mike Azinger (R-10) | Kenneth P. Hicks (D-19) |
| J. Frank Deem (R-10) | Timothy J. Manchin (D-50) |
| William "Bill" Flanigan (R-51) | Don C. Perdue (D-19) |
| Danny Hamrick (R-48) | David G. Perry (D-32) |
| Brian Kurcaba (R-51) | Larry L. Rowe (D-36) |
| Patrick Riley "Pat" McGeehan | |
| (R-1) | |
| Fredrik Eric Nelson, Jr. (R-35) | |
| John David O'Neal IV (R-28) | |
| John Headley Shott (R-27) | |
| Jill Upson (R-65) | |
| Terry Waxman (R-48) | |
| Brad White (R-36) | |

## Education

| Majority Members | Minority Members |
|---|---|
| Paul Espinosa (R-66) *Chair* | David G. Perry (D-32) |
| Walter Edwin Duke (R-61) | *Minority Chair* |
| *Vice Chair* | Ricky Duane Moye (D-29) |
| George "Boogie" Ambler (R-42) | *Minority Vice Chair* |
| Roy G. Cooper (R-28) | Frank L. Blackwell (D-25) |
| Joe Carey Ellington, Jr. (R-27) | Denise Lynne Campbell (D-43) |
| David A. Evans (R-4) | Kenneth P. Hicks (D-19) |
| Danny Hamrick (R-48) | Sean Hornbuckle (D-16) |
| John R. Kelly (R-10) | Don C. Perdue (D-19) |
| Brian Kurcaba (R-51) | Ralph Rodighiero (D-24) |
| Matthew Rohrbach (R-17) | Patsy Trecost II (D-48) |
| William Rogers "Roger" Romine | |
| (R-6) | |
| Ruth Rowan (R-57) | |
| Joe Statler (R-51) | |
| Jill Upson (R-65) | |
| Danny Wagner (R-47) | |
| Steve Westfall (R-12) | |

## Energy

| Majority Members | Minority Members |
|---|---|
| Lynwood "Woody" Ireland (R-7) | Michael "Mike" Caputo (D-50) |
| *Chair* | *Minority Chair* |
| Randy E. Smith (R-53) *Vice Chair* | David "Dave" Pethtel (D-5) |
| George "Boogie" Ambler (R-42) | *Minority Vice Chair* |
| Everette W. "Bill" Anderson, Jr. | Lawrence Brent Boggs (D-34) |
| (R-8) | Jeffery "Jeff" Eldridge (D-22) |
| Anna Border-Sheppard (R-9) | Dana L. Lynch (D-44) |
| Scott Cadle (R-13) | Timothy R. "Tim" Miley (D-48) |
| Denny Ray Canterbury, Jr. (R-42) | Rupert Wilson Phillips, Jr. (D-24) |
| David A. Evans (R-4) | Douglas Vernon Reynolds (D-17) |
| Kayla Kessinger (R-32) | Phyllis White (D-21) |
| John B. "JB" McCuskey (R-35) | |
| Joshua A. Nelson (R-23) | |
| William Rogers "Roger" Romine | |
| (R-6) | |
| Joe Statler (R-51) | |
| Erikka Lynn Storch (R-3) | |
| Jill Upson (R-65) | |
| Mark Zatezalo (R-1) | |

# Finance

**Majority Members**
Fredrik Eric Nelson, Jr. (R-35)
*Chair*
Eric Lee Householder (R-64)
*Vice Chair*
Everette W. "Bill" Anderson, Jr.
(R-8)
Jim Butler (R-14)
Denny Ray Canterbury, Jr. (R-42)
Paul Espinosa (R-66)
Allen Vincent Evans (R-54)
Cindy Frich (R-51)
Gary Martin "Marty" Gearheart
(R-27)
William David "Bill" Hamilton
(R-45)
Carol Devine Miller (R-16)
John David O'Neal IV (R-28)
Erikka Lynn Storch (R-3)
Ronald N. "Ron" Walters (R-39)
Terry Waxman (R-48)
Steve Westfall (R-12)

**Minority Members**
Lawrence Brent Boggs (D-34)
*Minority Chair*
Nancy Peoples Guthrie (D-36)
*Minority Vice Chair*
Mick Bates (D-30)
Linda Longstreth (D-50)
Ricky Duane Moye (D-29)
David G. Perry (D-32)
David "Dave" Pethtel (D-5)
Douglas Vernon Reynolds (D-17)
Margaret Donaldson "Peggy" Smith
(D-46)

# Government Organization

**Majority Members**
Gary Gibson Howell (R-56) *Chair*
Karen "Lynne" Arvon (R-31)
*Vice Chair*
Martin "Rick" Atkinson III (R-11)
Saira Blair (R-59)
Anna Border-Sheppard (R-9)
Scott Cadle (R-13)
Larry W. Faircloth (R-60)
William "Bill" Flanigan (R-51)
Danny Hamrick (R-48)
Jordan Hill (R-41)
Michael Ihle (R-13)
Patrick Riley "Pat" McGeehan
(R-1)
Michel Moffatt (R-22)
Joshua A. Nelson (R-23)
Randy E. Smith (R-53)
Chris Stansbury (R-35)
Mark Zatezalo (R-1)

**Minority Members**
James Hanly "Jim" Morgan (D-16)
*Minority Chair*
Michael Thomas Ferro (D-4)
*Minority Vice Chair*
Michael "Mike" Caputo (D-50)
Jeffery "Jeff" Eldridge (D-22)
William G. "Bill" Hartman (D-43)
Dana L. Lynch (D-44)
Mike Pushkin (D-37)
Isaac Sponaugle (D-55)
Phyllis White (D-21)

# Health and Human Resources

**Majority Members**
Joe Carey Ellington, Jr. (R-27)
*Chair*
Amy Summers (R-49) *Vice Chair*
Karen "Lynne" Arvon (R-31)
Martin "Rick" Atkinson III (R-11)
Roy G. Cooper (R-28)
Larry W. Faircloth (R-60)
Jordan Hill (R-41)
Eric Lee Householder (R-64)
Brian Kurcaba (R-51)
Patrick Lane (R-38)
Matthew Rohrbach (R-17)
Kelli Ann Sobonya (R-17)
Chris Stansbury (R-35)
Terry Waxman (R-48)
Steve Westfall (R-12)
Brad White (R-36)

**Minority Members**
Barbara Evans Fleischauer (D-51)
*Minority Chair*
Denise Lynne Campbell (D-43)
*Minority Vice Chair*
Mick Bates (D-30)
Shawn Fluharty (D-3)
Linda Longstreth (D-50)
Clifton "Clif" Moore (D-26)
Don C. Perdue (D-19)
Mike Pushkin (D-37)
Ralph Rodighiero (D-24)

# Industry and Labor

**Majority Members**
John Overington (R-62) *Chair*
Kelli Ann Sobonya (R-17)
*Vice Chair*
Mike Azinger (R-10)
Saira Blair (R-59)
Daryl E. Cowles (R-58)
Joe Carey Ellington, Jr. (R-27)
Tom Fast (R-32)
Eric Lee Householder (R-64)

**Minority Members**
Michael Thomas Ferro (D-4)
*Minority Chair*
Shawn Fluharty (D-3)
*Minority Vice Chair*
Andrew Byrd (D-35)
Michael "Mike" Caputo (D-50)
Kenneth P. Hicks (D-19)
Timothy J. Manchin (D-50)
Mike Pushkin (D-37)

**Majority Members** *continued*
Michael Ihle (R-13)
Brian Kurcaba (R-51)
John B. "JB" McCuskey (R-35)
Joshua A. Nelson (R-23)
John Headley Shott (R-27)
Randy E. Smith (R-53)
Joe Statler (R-51)
Brad White (R-36)

**Minority Members** *continued*
Douglas Vernon Reynolds (D-17)
Larry L. Rowe (D-36)

# Interstate Cooperation

**Majority Members**
Erikka Lynn Storch (R-3) *Chair*
Larry W. Faircloth (R-60)
*Vice Chair*
Joe Carey Ellington, Jr. (R-27)
Danny Hamrick (R-48)
William Rogers "Roger" Romine
(R-6)

**Minority Members**
Michael Thomas Ferro (D-4)
Margaret Donaldson "Peggy" Smith
(D-46)

# Judiciary

**Majority Members**
John Headley Shott (R-27) *Chair*
Patrick Lane (R-38) *Vice Chair*
Mike Azinger (R-10)
J. Frank Deem (R-10)
Tom Fast (R-32)
Michael "Mike" Folk (R-63)
Geoff Foster (R-15)
Roger Hanshaw (R-3)
Lynwood "Woody" Ireland (R-7)
Kayla Kessinger (R-32)
John B. "JB" McCuskey (R-35)
John Overington (R-62)
Kelli Ann Sobonya (R-17)
Amy Summers (R-49)
Ryan Weld (R-2)
Mark Zatezalo (R-1)

**Minority Members**
Timothy J. Manchin (D-50)
*Minority Chair*
Stephen G. Skinner (D-67)
*Minority Vice Chair*
Andrew Byrd (D-35)
Barbara Evans Fleischauer (D-51)
Shawn Fluharty (D-3)
Justin Marcum (D-20)
Clifton "Clif" Moore (D-26)
Larry L. Rowe (D-36)
Steven Shaffer (D-52)

# Pensions and Retirement

**Majority Members**
Denny Ray Canterbury, Jr. (R-42)
*Chair*
Michael "Mike" Folk (R-63)
*Vice Chair*
William David "Bill" Hamilton
(R-45)
Brian Kurcaba (R-51)
Ronald N. "Ron" Walters (R-39)

**Minority Members**
Justin Marcum (D-20)
David "Dave" Pethtel (D-5)

# Political Subdivisions

**Majority Members**
Erikka Lynn Storch (R-3) *Chair*
Jim Butler (R-14) *Vice Chair*
Everette W. "Bill" Anderson, Jr.
(R-8)
Daryl E. Cowles (R-58)
Walter Edwin Duke (R-61)
Michael "Mike" Folk (R-63)
Gary Martin "Marty" Gearheart
(R-27)
Roger Hanshaw (R-3)
Eric Lee Householder (R-64)
Michael Ihle (R-13)
Patrick Lane (R-38)
Michel Moffatt (R-22)
John David O'Neal IV (R-28)
Kelli Ann Sobonya (R-17)
Chris Stansbury (R-35)
Ryan Weld (R-2)

**Minority Members**
Ricky Duane Moye (D-29)
*Minority Chair*
Patsy Trecost II (D-48)
*Minority Vice Chair*
Lawrence Brent Boggs (D-34)
Andrew Byrd (D-35)
William G. "Bill" Hartman (D-43)
Sean Hornbuckle (D-16)
Timothy J. Manchin (D-50)
James Hanly "Jim" Morgan (D-16)
David G. Perry (D-32)

## Roads and Transportation

**Majority Members**
Gary Martin "Marty"
  Gearheart (R-27)
  *Chair*
Danny Hamrick (R-48) *Vice Chair*
George "Boogie" Ambler (R-42)
Karen "Lynne" Arvon (R-31)
Jim Butler (R-14)
Scott Cadle (R-13)
Paul Espinosa (R-66)
Allen Vincent Evans (R-54)
David A. Evans (R-4)
Tom Fast (R-32)
Geoff Foster (R-15)
Gary Gibson Howell (R-56)
Michel Moffatt (R-22)
Matthew Rohrbach (R-17)
Joe Statler (R-51)
Danny Wagner (R-47)

**Minority Members**
Patsy Trecost II (D-48)
  *Minority Chair*
Nancy Peoples Guthrie (D-36)
  *Minority Vice Chair*
Frank L. Blackwell (D-25)
Lawrence Brent Boggs (D-34)
Linda Longstreth (D-50)
Ricky Duane Moye (D-29)
Douglas Vernon Reynolds (D-17)
Margaret Donaldson "Peggy" Smith
  (D-46)
Isaac Sponaugle (D-55)

## Rules

**Majority Members**
Timothy Paul "Tim"
  Armstead (R-40)
  *Chair*
Everette W. "Bill" Anderson, Jr.
  (R-8)
Daryl E. Cowles (R-58)
Paul Espinosa (R-66)
Gary Gibson Howell (R-56)
Lynwood "Woody" Ireland (R-7)
Patrick Lane (R-38)
Carol Devine Miller (R-16)
Fredrik Eric Nelson, Jr. (R-35)
John David O'Neal IV (R-28)
John Overington (R-62)
John Headley Shott (R-27)
Kelli Ann Sobonya (R-17)

**Minority Members**
Lawrence Brent Boggs (D-34)
Denise Lynne Campbell (D-43)
Michael "Mike" Caputo (D-50)
Barbara Evans Fleischauer (D-51)
Nancy Peoples Guthrie (D-36)
Timothy J. Manchin (D-50)
Timothy R. "Tim" Miley (D-48)

## Senior Citizen Issues

**Majority Members**
Ruth Rowan (R-57) *Chair*
Anna Border-Sheppard (R-9)
  *Vice Chair*
Denny Ray Canterbury, Jr. (R-42)
J. Frank Deem (R-10)
Walter Edwin Duke (R-61)
Larry W. Faircloth (R-60)
William David "Bill" Hamilton
  (R-45)
Jordan Hill (R-41)
John R. Kelly (R-10)
Fredrik Eric Nelson, Jr. (R-35)
John Overington (R-62)
Matthew Rohrbach (R-17)
William Rogers "Roger" Romine
  (R-6)
Ronald N. "Ron" Walters (R-39)
Brad White (R-36)
Mark Zatezalo (R-1)

**Minority Members**
Ricky Duane Moye (D-29)
  *Minority Chair*
David "Dave" Pethtel (D-5)
  *Minority Vice Chair*
Denise Lynne Campbell (D-43)
Michael Thomas Ferro (D-4)
William G. "Bill" Hartman (D-43)
Clifton "Clif" Moore (D-26)
David G. Perry (D-32)
Rupert Wilson Phillips, Jr. (D-24)
Steven Shaffer (D-52)

## Small Business Entrepreneurship and Economic Development

**Majority Members**
Carol Devine Miller (R-16) *Chair*
Jordan Hill (R-41) *Vice Chair*
Saira Blair (R-59)
Joe Carey Ellington, Jr. (R-27)
Paul Espinosa (R-66)
Larry W. Faircloth (R-60)
William "Bill" Flanigan (R-51)
Roger Hanshaw (R-3)
John R. Kelly (R-10)
Kayla Kessinger (R-32)
Patrick Lane (R-38)
Chris Stansbury (R-35)

**Minority Members**
Stephen G. Skinner (D-67)
  *Minority Chair*
Larry L. Rowe (D-36)
  *Minority Vice Chair*
Mick Bates (D-30)
William G. "Bill" Hartman (D-43)
Sean Hornbuckle (D-16)
Timothy J. Manchin (D-50)
Timothy R. "Tim" Miley (D-48)
James Hanly "Jim" Morgan (D-16)
Phyllis White (D-21)

**Majority Members** *continued*
Erikka Lynn Storch (R-3)
Terry Waxman (R-48)
Steve Westfall (R-12)
Mark Zatezalo (R-1)

## Veterans Affairs and Homeland Security

**Majority Members**
David A. Evans (R-4)
  *Chair, Homeland Security*
Joshua A. Nelson (R-23)
  *Chair, Veterans Affairs*
Patrick Riley "Pat"
  McGeehan (R-1)
  *Vice Chair, Homeland Security*
Roy G. Cooper (R-28)
  *Vice Chair, Veterans Affairs*
Martin "Rick" Atkinson III (R-11)
Karen "Lynne" Arvon (R-31)
Geoff Foster (R-15)
Cindy Frich (R-51)
Gary Gibson Howell (R-56)
Lynwood "Woody" Ireland (R-7)
John R. Kelly (R-10)
Kayla Kessinger (R-32)
Ruth Rowan (R-57)
Jill Upson (R-65)
Danny Wagner (R-47)
Ryan Weld (R-2)

**Minority Members**
Margaret Donaldson
  "Peggy" Smith (D-46)
  *Minority Chair, Homeland
  Security*
Linda Longstreth (D-50)
  *Minority Chair, Veterans Affairs*
Mike Pushkin (D-37)*Minority Vice
  Chair, Homeland Security*
Sean Hornbuckle (D-16)*Minority
  Vice Chair, Veterans Affairs*
Andrew Byrd (D-35)
Michael Thomas Ferro (D-4)
Barbara Evans Fleischauer (D-51)
Dana L. Lynch (D-44)
Patsy Trecost II (D-48)

LEGISLATIVE BRANCH

# Wisconsin Legislature

Tel: (608) 266-9960  Tel: (800) 362-9472 (Toll Free)

## Wisconsin State Senate

P.O. Box 7882, Madison, WI 53707-7882
Tel: (608) 266-2517  TTY: (800) 228-2115  Fax: (608) 266-0643

President of the Senate **Mary Lazich** (R) . . . . . . . . . . . . . . (608) 266-5400
  Education: Wisconsin (Milwaukee) BA
President Pro Tem **Rick Gudex** (R) . . . . . . . . . . . . . . . . . . (608) 266-5300
Majority Leader **Scott L. Fitzgerald** (R) . . . . . . . . . . . . . . (608) 266-5660
  Education: Wisconsin (Oshkosh) 1985 BS
Assistant Majority Leader **Leah Vukmir** (R) . . . . . . . . . . . (608) 266-2512
  Education: Marquette 1980 BS; Wisconsin 1983 MS
Majority Caucus Chairperson **Sheila E. Harsdorf** (R) . . . . . (608) 266-7745
  Education: Minnesota 1978 BS
Majority Caucus Vice Chairperson
  **Van H. Wanggaard** (R) . . . . . . . . . . . . . . . . . . . . . . . . . . (608) 266-1832
Minority Leader **Jennifer Shilling** (D) . . . . . . . . . . . . . . . (608) 266-5490
  Education: Wisconsin (La Crosse) 1992 BA
Assistant Minority Leader **David "Dave" Hansen** (D) . . . . (608) 266-5670
  Education: Wisconsin (Green Bay) 1971 BS
Minority Caucus Chairperson **Julie M. Lassa** (D) . . . . . . . . (608) 266-3123
  Education: Wisconsin (Stevens Point) 1993 BS
Minority Caucus Vice Chairperson
  **Kathleen Vinehout** (D) . . . . . . . . . . . . . . . . . . . . . . . . . (608) 266-8546
  Education: Southern Illinois 1980 BS; Saint Louis U 1982 MPH,
  1987 PhD
Chief Clerk of the Senate and Director of Operations
  **Jeffrey Renk** . . . . . . . . . . . . . . . . . . . . . . . . . . . . . . . . (608) 266-2517
Sergeant-at-Arms **Edward A. "Ted" Blazel** . . . . . . . . . . . (608) 266-1801
Fax: (608) 264-0716

## Senators

**Party Affiliation Statistics:** Republicans: 19, Democrats: 14

Senator **Janet Bewley** (D-District 25) . . . . . . . . . . . . . . . (608) 266-3510
  Counties Represented: Ashland, Barron (part), Bayfield, Burnett (part), Douglas, Dunn (part), Iron, Polk (part), Price, Sawyer (part), St. Croix (part), Vilas (part), Washburn
  Term Expires: 2019
  E-mail: sen.bewley@legis.wi.gov
  Committees: Education; Insurance, Housing, and Trade; Joint Legislative Audit; Universities and Technical Colleges
  Education: Case Western 1973; Maine 1977 MAdmin
Senator **Timothy W. "Tim" Carpenter** (D-District 3) . . . . . (608) 266-8535
  Counties Represented: Milwaukee (part)      Dist: (414) 383-9161
  Term Expires: 2019                          Fax: (608) 282-3543
  2957 South 38th Street, Milwaukee, WI 53215
  E-mail: sen.carpenter@legis.wisconsin.gov
  Committees: Health and Human Services; Joint Information Policy and Technology; Joint Tax Exemptions; Transportation and Veterans Affairs
  Education: Wisconsin (Milwaukee) BA
Senator **Robert L. Cowles** (R-District 2) . . . . . . . . . . . . . (608) 266-0484
  Counties Represented: Brown (part), Oconto (part),   Dist: (920) 448-5092
  Outagamie (part), Shawano (part), Waupaca (part)    Fax: (608) 267-0304
  Term Expires: 2017
  300 West St. Joseph Street, Unit 23, Green Bay, WI 54301
  E-mail: sen.cowles@legis.wisconsin.gov
  Committees: Joint Information Policy and Technology; Joint Legislative Audit; Natural Resources and Energy; Transportation and Veterans Affairs
  Education: Wisconsin (Green Bay) 1975 BS
Senator **Alberta Darling** (R-District 8) . . . . . . . . . . . . . . (608) 266-5830
  Counties Represented: Milwaukee (part), Ozaukee   Dist: (262) 250-9440
  (part), Washington (part), Waukesha (part)        Fax: (608) 267-0588
  Term Expires: 2017                                Dist: (262) 250-8510
  1325 West Dean Road, River Hills, WI 53217
  N88 W16621 Appleton Avenue, Suite 201, Menomonee Falls, WI 53051
  E-mail: sen.darling@legis.wisconsin.gov
  Committees: Economic Development and Commerce; Education; Finance; Joint Employment Relations; Joint Finance; Joint Legislative Audit; Joint Legislative Council
  Education: Wisconsin 1966 BS

Senator **Jon B. Erpenbach** (D-District 27) . . . . . . . . . . . . (608) 266-6670
  Counties Represented: Columbia (part), Dane    Dist: (888) 549-0027
  (part), Green (part), Iowa (part), Sauk (part)  Fax: (608) 266-2508
  Term Expires: 2019
  7194 Belle Fontaine Boulevard, Middleton, WI 53562
  E-mail: sen.erpenbach@legis.wisconsin.gov
  Committees: Agriculture, Small Business, and Tourism; Finance; Health and Human Services; Joint Finance; Joint Retirement Systems
Senator **Scott L. Fitzgerald** (R-District 13) . . . . . . . . . . . (608) 266-5660
  Counties Represented: Columbia (part), Dane (part),   Dist: (920) 386-2218
  Dodge (part), Jefferson (part), Washington (part),    Fax: (608) 267-6795
  Waukesha (part)
  Term Expires: 2019
  N4692 Maple Road, Juneau, WI 53039
  E-mail: sen.fitzgerald@legis.wisconsin.gov
  Committees: Joint Employment Relations; Joint Legislative Council; Joint Legislative Organization; Senate Organization
Senator **Rick Gudex** (R-District 18) . . . . . . . . . . . . . . . . (608) 266-5300
  Counties Represented: Dodge (part), Fond du Lac (part), Winnebago (part)
  Term Expires: 2017
  361 East Division Street, Fond du Lac, WI 54935
  E-mail: sen.gudex@legis.wisconsin.gov
  Committees: Economic Development and Commerce; Joint Legislative Council; Universities and Technical Colleges; Workforce Development, Public Works, and Military Affairs
Senator **David "Dave" Hansen** (D-District 30) . . . . . . . . . (608) 266-5670
  Counties Represented: Brown (part), Marinette   Dist: (920) 492-2200
  (part), Oconto (part)                           Fax: (608) 267-6791
  Term Expires: 2017
  3489 Blackwolf Run, Green Bay, WI 54311
  E-mail: sen.hansen@legis.wisconsin.gov
  Committees: Agriculture, Small Business, and Tourism; Joint Legislative Organization; Senate Organization; Transportation and Veterans Affairs; Universities and Technical Colleges
Senator **Nikiya Q. Harris Dodd** (D-District 6) . . . . . . . . . (608) 266-2500
  Counties Represented: Milwaukee (part)      Fax: (608) 266-7381
  Term Expires: 2017
  7060 North Presidio Drive, Unit G, Milwaukee, WI 53223
  E-mail: sen.harris@legis.wisconsin.gov
  Committees: Education Reform; Government Operations and Consumer Protection; Insurance, Housing, and Trade; Joint Law Revision; Joint Review of Administrative Rules; Public Benefit and Regulatory Reform
  Education: Wisconsin (Milwaukee) 2001 BS, 2007 MS
Senator **Sheila E. Harsdorf** (R-District 10) . . . . . . . . . . . (608) 266-7745
  Counties Represented: Burnett (part), Dunn (part),   Fax: (608) 267-0369
  Pierce (part), Polk (part), St. Croix (part)
  Term Expires: 2017
  N6627 County Road East, River Falls, WI 54022
  E-mail: sen.harsdorf@legis.wisconsin.gov
  Committees: Agriculture, Small Business, and Tourism; Education Reform; Finance; Joint Finance; Joint Information Policy and Technology; Public Benefit and Regulatory Reform; Universities and Technical Colleges
Senator **Chris Kapenga** (R-District 33) . . . . . . . . . . . . . . (608) 266-9174
  Counties Represented: Waukesha (part)       Fax: (608) 282-3699
  Term Expires: 2019
  N9W31035 Concord Court, Delafield, WI 53018
  E-mail: sen.kapenga@legis.wisconsin.gov
  Committees: Elections and Local Government; Government Operations and Consumer Protection; Public Benefit and Regulatory Reform
Senator **Christopher "Chris" Larson** (D-District 7) . . . . . . (608) 266-7505
  Counties Represented: Milwaukee (part)      Fax: (608) 282-3547
  Term Expires: 2019
  3261 South Herman Street, Milwaukee, WI 53207
  E-mail: sen.larson@legis.wisconsin.gov
  Committees: Education; Labor and Government Reform; Workforce Development, Public Works, and Military Affairs
  Education: Wisconsin (Milwaukee) 1997 BA
Senator **Frank G. Lasee** (R-District 1) . . . . . . . . . . . . . . . (608) 266-3512
  Counties Represented: Brown (part), Calumet (part),   Fax: (608) 267-6792
  Door, Kewaunee, Manitowoc (part), Outagamie (part)
  Term Expires: 2019
  1645 Swan Road, De Pere, WI 54115
  P. O. Box 7882, Madison, WI 53707
  E-mail: sen.lasee@legis.wisconsin.gov
  Committees: Insurance, Housing, and Trade; Joint Retirement Systems; Joint Review of Administrative Rules; Judiciary and Public Safety; Natural Resources and Energy
  Education: Wisconsin (Green Bay) 1986 BA

*(continued on next page)*

LEGISLATIVE BRANCH

**Senators** *continued*

**Senator Julie M. Lassa** (D-District 24). . . . . . . . . . . . . .(608) 266-3123
Counties Represented: Adams (part), Jackson (part),    Dist: (715) 342-0526
Monroe (part), Portage, Waushara (part), Wood    Fax: (608) 267-6797
(part)
Term Expires: 2017
4901 Beaver Dam Road, Stevens Point, WI 54481
E-mail: sen.lassa@legis.wisconsin.gov
Committees: Economic Development and Commerce; Revenue,
Financial Institutions, and Rural Issues; Workforce Development, Public
Works, and Military Affairs

**Senator Mary Lazich** (R-District 28). . . . . . . . . . . . . . . .(608) 266-5400
Counties Represented: Milwaukee (part), Racine    Dist: (414) 425-9452
(part), Walworth (part), Waukesha (part)    Fax: (608) 267-6790
Term Expires: 2017
4405 South 129th Street, New Berlin, WI 53153
E-mail: sen.lazich@legis.wisconsin.gov
Committees: Joint Employment Relations; Joint Legislative Audit; Joint
Legislative Council; Joint Legislative Organization; Senate Organization

**Senator Devin Lemahieu** (R-District 9). . . . . . . . . . . . . .(608) 266-2056
Counties Represented: Calumet (part), Manitowoc    Fax: (608) 282-3549
(part), Sheboygan (part)
Term Expires: 2019
21 South Eighth Street, Oostburg, WI 53070
E-mail: sen.lemahieu@legis.wisconsin.gov
Committees: Agriculture, Small Business, and Tourism; Elections and
Local Government; Government Operations and Consumer Protection;
Health and Human Services; Joint Review of Administrative Rules;
Joint Tax Exemptions

**Senator Howard L. Marklein** (R-District 17). . . . . . . . . . .(608) 266-0703
Counties Represented: Grant, Green (part), Iowa    Fax: (608) 282-3557
(part), Juneau (part), Lafayette, Monroe (part), Richland, Sauk (part),
Vernon (part)
Term Expires: 2019
S11665 Soeldner Road, Spring Green, WI 53588
E-mail: sen.marklein@legis.wi.gov
Committees: Finance; Joint Finance; Joint Retirement Systems; Labor
and Government Reform; Revenue, Financial Institutions, and Rural
Issues; Transportation and Veterans Affairs
Education: Wisconsin (Whitewater) 1976 BBA

**Senator Mark Miller** (D-District 16). . . . . . . . . . . . . . . .(608) 266-9170
Counties Represented: Dane (part)    Dist: (608) 221-2701
Term Expires: 2017    Fax: (608) 266-3556
4903 Roigan Terrace, Monona, WI 53716
E-mail: sen.miller@legis.wisconsin.gov
Committees: Elections and Local Government; Joint Legislative
Council; Joint Review of Administrative Rules; Natural Resources and
Energy; Public Benefit and Regulatory Reform
Education: Wisconsin 1973 BS

**Senator Terry Moulton** (R-District 23). . . . . . . . . . . . . . .(608) 266-7511
Counties Represented: Barron (part), Chippewa    Fax: (608) 282-3563
(part), Clark (part), Dunn (part), Eau Claire (part), Jackson (part),
Marathon (part), Trempealeau (part), Wood (part)
Term Expires: 2019
980 118th Street, Chippewa Falls, WI 54729
E-mail: sen.moulton@legis.wisconsin.gov
Committees: Agriculture, Small Business, and Tourism; Health and
Human Services; Joint Legislative Council; Sporting Heritage, Mining,
and Forestry

**Senator Stephen L. "Steve" Nass** (R-District 11). . . . . . .(608) 266-2635
Counties Represented: Jefferson (part), Kenosha    Fax: (608) 282-3551
(part), Racine (part), Rock (part), Walworth (part), Waukesha (part)
Term Expires: 2019
N8330 Jackson Road, Whitewater, WI 53190
E-mail: sen.nass@legis.wisconsin.gov
Committees: Education; Education Reform; Joint Review of
Administrative Rules; Labor and Government Reform; Public Benefit
and Regulatory Reform; Universities and Technical Colleges
Education: Wisconsin (Whitewater) 1978 BS, 1990 MS

**Senator Luther S. Olsen** (R-District 14). . . . . . . . . . . . . .(608) 266-0751
Counties Represented: Adams (part), Columbia    Dist: (715) 258-3830
(part), Dane (part), Dodge (part), Fond du Lac    Fax: (608) 267-4350
(part), Green Lake, Juneau (part), Marquette, Outagamie (part), Sauk
(part), Shawano (part), Waupaca (part), Waushara (part)
Term Expires: 2017
1023 Thomas Street, Ripon, WI 54971
E-mail: sen.olsen@legis.wisconsin.gov
Committees: Education; Finance; Insurance, Housing, and Trade; Joint
Finance; Natural Resources and Energy
Education: Wisconsin 1973 BS

**Senator Jerry Petrowski** (R-District 29). . . . . . . . . . . . . .(608) 266-2502
Counties Represented: Clark (part), Marathon (part),    Fax: (608) 267-9027
Rusk, Sawyer (part), Taylor, Wood (part)
Term Expires: 2019
720 North 136th Avenue, Marathon, WI 54448
E-mail: sen.petrowski@legis.wisconsin.gov
Committees: Agriculture, Small Business, and Tourism; Economic
Development and Commerce; Joint Legislative Council; Transportation
and Veterans Affairs

**Senator Janis A. Ringhand** (D-District 15). . . . . . . . . . . .(608) 266-2253
Counties Represented: Dane (part), Green (part),    Fax: (608) 282-3555
Jefferson (part), Rock (part), Walworth (part)
Term Expires: 2019
412 Fowler Circle, Evansville, WI 53536
E-mail: sen.ringhand@legis.wi.gov
Committees: Economic Development and Commerce; Revenue,
Financial Institutions, and Rural Issues

**Senator Fred A. Risser** (D-District 26). . . . . . . . . . . . . . .(608) 266-1627
Counties Represented: Dane (part)    Dist: (608) 238-5008
Term Expires: 2017    Fax: (608) 266-1629
100 Wisconsin Avenue, Unit 501, Madison, WI 53703
E-mail: sen.risser@legis.wisconsin.gov
Committees: Education; Elections and Local Government; Joint Law
Revision; Joint Legislative Council; Judiciary and Public Safety
Education: Oregon 1950 BA, 1952 LLB

**Senator Roger Roth, Jr.** (R-District 19). . . . . . . . . . . . . .(608) 266-0718
Counties Represented: Outagamie (part), Winnebago    Fax: (608) 282-3559
(part)
Term Expires: 2019
1910 West Charles Street, Appleton, WI 54914
E-mail: sen.roth@legis.wisconsin.gov
Committees: Insurance, Housing, and Trade; Joint Information Policy
and Technology; Sporting Heritage, Mining, and Forestry; Workforce
Development, Public Works, and Military Affairs
Education: Wisconsin (Oshkosh) 2001 BA

**Senator Jennifer Shilling** (D-District 32). . . . . . . . . . . . .(608) 266-5490
Counties Represented: Crawford, La Crosse, Monroe (part), Vernon
(part)
Term Expires: 2017
2608 Main Street, La Crosse, WI 54601
E-mail: sen.shilling@legis.wisconsin.gov
Committees: Joint Employment Relations; Joint Legislative Council;
Joint Legislative Organization; Senate Organization

**Senator Duey Stroebel** (R-District 20). . . . . . . . . . . . . . .(608) 267-2369
Counties Represented: Calumet (part), Fond du Lac    Dist: (888) 534-0060
(part), Ozaukee (part), Sheboygan (part), Washington (part)
Term Expires: 2017
2428 Covered Bridge Road, Saukville, WI 53080
E-mail: sen.stroebel@legis.wisconsin.gov
Committees: Government Operations and Consumer Protection;
Revenue, Financial Institutions, and Rural Issues; Workforce
Development, Public Works, and Military Affairs

**Senator Lena C. Taylor** (D-District 4). . . . . . . . . . . . . . . .(608) 266-5810
Counties Represented: Milwaukee (part)    Dist: (414) 342-7176
Term Expires: 2017    Fax: (608) 267-3544
1518 West Capitol, Milwaukee, WI 53206
E-mail: sen.taylor@legis.wisconsin.gov
Committees: Agriculture, Small Business, and Tourism; Finance; Joint
Finance; Joint Legislative Council; Joint Review on Criminal Penalties;
Judiciary and Public Safety
Education: Wisconsin (Milwaukee) 1990 BA; Southern Illinois 1993 JD

**Senator Thomas "Tom" Tiffany** (R-District 12). . . . . . . . .(608) 266-2509
Counties Represented: Florence, Forest, Langlade,    Fax: (608) 267-0309
Lincoln, Marathon (part), Marinette (part), Menominee, Oconto (part),
Oneida, Shawano (part), Vilas (part)
Term Expires: 2017
4973 Willow Dam Road, Hazelhurst, WI 54531
E-mail: sen.tiffany@legis.wi.gov
Committees: Agriculture, Small Business, and Tourism; Finance; Joint
Finance; Joint Law Revision; Joint Tax Exemptions; Revenue, Financial
Institutions, and Rural Issues; Sporting Heritage, Mining, and Forestry
Education: Wisconsin (Platteville) 1980 BS

**Senator Kathleen Vinehout** (D-District 31). . . . . . . . . . . .(608) 266-8546
Counties Represented: Buffalo, Chippewa (part),    Tel: (877) 763-6636
Dunn (part), Eau Claire (part), Jackson (part),    Fax: (608) 282-3571
Pepin, Pierce (part), St. Croix (part), Trempealeau (part)
Term Expires: 2019
W1490 Ceslar Valley Road, Alma, WI 54610
E-mail: sen.vinehout@legis.wisconsin.gov
Committees: Agriculture, Small Business, and Tourism; Education
Reform; Joint Information Policy and Technology; Joint Legislative
Audit; Sporting Heritage, Mining, and Forestry

LEGISLATIVE BRANCH

Senator **Leah Vukmir** (R-District 5) . . . . . . . . . . . . . . . . . (608) 266-2512
  Counties Represented: Milwaukee (part), Waukesha   Fax: (608) 267-0367
  (part)
  Term Expires: 2019
  2544 North 93rd Street, Wauwatosa, WI 53226
  E-mail: sen.vukmir@legis.wisconsin.gov
  Committees: Education; Finance; Health and Human Services; Joint
  Finance; Judiciary and Public Safety

Senator **Van H. Wanggaard** (R-District 21) . . . . . . . . . . . . (608) 266-1832
  Counties Represented: Kenosha (part), Racine   Fax: (608) 282-3561
  (part), Walworth (part)
  Term Expires: 2019
  1246 Blaine Avenue, Racine, WI 53405
  E-mail: sen.wanggaard@legis.wisconsin.gov
  Committees: Elections and Local Government; Joint Legislative
  Council; Joint Review on Criminal Penalties; Judiciary and Public
  Safety; Labor and Government Reform

Senator **Robert W. Wirch** (D-District 22) . . . . . . . . . . . . . (608) 267-8979
  Counties Represented: Kenosha (part), Racine (part)   Res: (262) 694-7379
  Term Expires: 2017   Fax: (608) 267-0984
  3007 Springbrook Road, Pleasant Prairie, WI 53158
  E-mail: sen.wirch@legis.wisconsin.gov
  Committees: Government Operations and Consumer Protection; Labor
  and Government Reform; Natural Resources and Energy; Sporting
  Heritage, Mining, and Forestry
  Education: Wisconsin (Parkside) 1970 BA

## Senate Standing Committees

### Agriculture, Small Business, and Tourism

| Majority Members | Minority Members |
|---|---|
| Terry Moulton (R-23) *Chair* | Jon B. Erpenbach (D-27) |
| Thomas "Tom" Tiffany (R-12) | David "Dave" Hansen (D-30) |
| *Vice Chair* | Lena C. Taylor (D-4) |
| Sheila E. Harsdorf (R-10) | Kathleen Vinehout (D-31) |
| Devin Lemahieu (R-9) | |
| Jerry Petrowski (R-29) | |

### Economic Development and Commerce

| Majority Members | Minority Members |
|---|---|
| Rick Gudex (R-18) *Chair* | Julie M. Lassa (D-24) |
| Jerry Petrowski (R-29) *Vice Chair* | Janis A. Ringhand (D-15) |
| Alberta Darling (R-8) | |

### Education

| Majority Members | Minority Members |
|---|---|
| Luther S. Olsen (R-14) *Chair* | Janet Bewley (D-25) |
| Alberta Darling (R-8) *Vice Chair* | Christopher "Chris" Larson (D-7) |
| Stephen L. "Steve" Nass (R-11) | Fred A. Risser (D-26) |
| Leah Vukmir (R-5) | |

### Education Reform

| Majority Members | Minority Members |
|---|---|
| Sheila E. Harsdorf (R-10) | Nikiya Q. Harris Dodd (D-6) |
| *Vice Chair* | Kathleen Vinehout (D-31) |
| Stephen L. "Steve" Nass (R-11) | |

### Elections and Local Government

| Majority Members | Minority Members |
|---|---|
| Devin Lemahieu (R-9) *Chair* | Mark Miller (D-16) |
| Chris Kapenga (R-33) *Vice Chair* | Fred A. Risser (D-26) |
| Van H. Wanggaard (R-21) | |

### Finance

| Majority Members | Minority Members |
|---|---|
| Alberta Darling (R-8) *Chair* | Jon B. Erpenbach (D-27) |
| Luther S. Olsen (R-14) *Vice Chair* | Lena C. Taylor (D-4) |
| Sheila E. Harsdorf (R-10) | |
| Howard L. Marklein (R-17) | |
| Thomas "Tom" Tiffany (R-12) | |
| Leah Vukmir (R-5) | |

### Government Operations and Consumer Protection

| Majority Members | Minority Members |
|---|---|
| Duey Stroebel (R-20) *Chair* | Nikiya Q. Harris Dodd (D-6) |
| Devin Lemahieu (R-9) *Vice Chair* | Robert W. Wirch (D-22) |
| Chris Kapenga (R-33) | |

### Health and Human Services

| Majority Members | Minority Members |
|---|---|
| Leah Vukmir (R-5) *Chair* | Timothy W. "Tim" Carpenter (D-3) |
| Terry Moulton (R-23) *Vice Chair* | Jon B. Erpenbach (D-27) |
| Devin Lemahieu (R-9) | |

### Insurance, Housing, and Trade

| Majority Members | Minority Members |
|---|---|
| Frank G. Lasee (R-1) *Chair* | Janet Bewley (D-25) |
| Luther S. Olsen (R-14) *Vice Chair* | Nikiya Q. Harris Dodd (D-6) |
| Roger Roth, Jr. (R-19) | |

### Judiciary and Public Safety

| Majority Members | Minority Members |
|---|---|
| Van H. Wanggaard (R-21) *Chair* | Fred A. Risser (D-26) |
| Leah Vukmir (R-5) *Vice Chair* | Lena C. Taylor (D-4) |
| Frank G. Lasee (R-1) | |

### Labor and Government Reform

| Majority Members | Minority Members |
|---|---|
| Stephen L. "Steve" Nass (R-11) *Chair* | Christopher "Chris" Larson (D-7) |
| Van H. Wanggaard (R-21) *Vice Chair* | Robert W. Wirch (D-22) |
| Howard L. Marklein (R-17) | |

### Natural Resources and Energy

| Majority Members | Minority Members |
|---|---|
| Robert L. Cowles (R-2) *Chair* | Mark Miller (D-16) |
| Frank G. Lasee (R-1) *Vice Chair* | Robert W. Wirch (D-22) |
| Luther S. Olsen (R-14) | |

### Public Benefit and Regulatory Reform

| Majority Members | Minority Members |
|---|---|
| Chris Kapenga (R-33) *Chair* | Nikiya Q. Harris Dodd (D-6) |
| Sheila E. Harsdorf (R-10) *Vice Chair* | Mark Miller (D-16) |
| Stephen L. "Steve" Nass (R-11) | |

### Revenue, Financial Institutions, and Rural Issues

| Majority Members | Minority Members |
|---|---|
| Howard L. Marklein (R-17) *Chair* | Julie M. Lassa (D-24) |
| Duey Stroebel (R-20) *Vice Chair* | Janis A. Ringhand (D-15) |
| Thomas "Tom" Tiffany (R-12) | |

### Senate Organization

| Majority Members | Minority Members |
|---|---|
| Scott L. Fitzgerald (R-13) *Chair* | David "Dave" Hansen (D-30) |
| Mary Lazich (R-28) | Jennifer Shilling (D-32) |

### Sporting Heritage, Mining, and Forestry

| Majority Members | Minority Members |
|---|---|
| Thomas "Tom" Tiffany (R-12) *Chair* | Robert W. Wirch (D-22) |
| Roger Roth, Jr. (R-19) *Vice Chair* | Kathleen Vinehout (D-31) |
| Terry Moulton (R-23) | |

### Transportation and Veterans Affairs

| Majority Members | Minority Members |
|---|---|
| Jerry Petrowski (R-29) *Chair* | Timothy W. "Tim" Carpenter (D-3) |
| Howard L. Marklein (R-17) *Vice Chair* | David "Dave" Hansen (D-30) |
| Robert L. Cowles (R-2) | |

### Universities and Technical Colleges

| Majority Members | Minority Members |
|---|---|
| Sheila E. Harsdorf (R-10) *Chair* | Janet Bewley (D-25) |
| Stephen L. "Steve" Nass (R-11) *Vice Chair* | David "Dave" Hansen (D-30) |
| Rick Gudex (R-18) | |

LEGISLATIVE BRANCH

## Workforce Development, Public Works, and Military Affairs

| Majority Members | Minority Members |
|---|---|
| Roger Roth, Jr. (R-19) *Chair* | Christopher "Chris" Larson (D-7) |
| Rick Gudex (R-18) *Vice Chair* | Julie M. Lassa (D-24) |
| Duey Stroebel (R-20) | |

# Wisconsin State Assembly

P.O. Box 8952, Madison, WI 53708

Tel: (608) 266-1501

Speaker of the Assembly **Robin Vos** (R) . . . . . . . . . . . . . . .(608) 266-3387

Speaker Pro Tem **Tyler August** (R) . . . . . . . . . . . . . . . . (608) 266-1190
  Education: Wisconsin (Eau Claire) (Attended); Wisconsin (Attended)

Majority Leader **Jim Steineke** (R) . . . . . . . . . . . . . . . . . . (608) 266-2418

Assistant Majority Leader **Daniel "Dan" Knodl** (R) . . . . . . (608) 266-3796

Majority Caucus Chair **John Murtha** (R) . . . . . . . . . . . . . .(608) 266-7683

Majority Caucus Vice Chair **Lee Nerison** (R) . . . . . . . . . . (608) 266-3534

Majority Caucus Secretary **Jessie Rodriguez** (R) . . . . . . . . (608) 266-0610

Majority Caucus Sergeant-at-Arms
  **Samantha Kerkman** (R) . . . . . . . . . . . . . . . . . . . . . . . (608) 266-2530
  Education: Wisconsin (Whitewater) 1996 BA

Minority Leader **Peter W. Barca** (D) . . . . . . . . . . . . . . . . (608) 266-5504
  Education: Wisconsin (Milwaukee) 1977 BS; Wisconsin 1983 MA

Assistant Minority Leader **Katrina Shankland** (D) . . . . . . . (608) 267-9649
  Education: Wisconsin 2009 BA

Minority Caucus Chair **Andy Jorgensen** (D) . . . . . . . . . . . .(608) 266-3790

Minority Caucus Vice Chair
  **Jocasta "Joey" Zamarripa** (D) . . . . . . . . . . . . . . . . . . .(608) 267-7669
  Education: Wisconsin (Milwaukee)

Minority Caucus Secretary **Beth M. Meyers** (D) . . . . . . . . .(608) 266-7690

Minority Caucus Sergeant-at-Arms **Josh Zepnick** (D) . . . . . (608) 266-1707
  Education: Wisconsin 1990 BA; Minnesota 1998 MA

Chief Clerk of the Assembly **Patrick Fuller** . . . . . . . . . . . . (608) 266-1501
  E-mail: patrick.fuller@legis.wisconsin.gov   Fax: (608) 266-5617
  Education: Toledo BE; Touro MBA

Sergeant-at-Arms **Anne Tonnon Byers** . . . . . . . . . . . . . . . .(608) 266-2004
  E-mail: anne.tonnonbyers@legis.wi.gov

# Representatives

**Party Affiliation Statistics:** Republicans: 63, Democrats: 36

Representative **Scott Allen** (R-District 97) . . . . . . . . . . . . . (608) 266-8580
  Counties Represented: Waukesha (part)   Fax: (608) 282-3697
  Term Expires: 2017
  S42 W25312 Dale Drive, Waukesha, WI 53189
  E-mail: rep.allen@legis.wisconsin.gov
  Committees: Environment and Forestry; Housing and Real Estate; Jobs and the Economy; Small Business Development; Veterans and Military Affairs

Representative **Tyler August** (R-District 32) . . . . . . . . . . . . (608) 226-1190
  Counties Represented: Kenosha (part), Racine   Fax: (608) 282-3632
  (part), Walworth (part)
  Term Expires: 2017
  116 Evelyn Lane, Unit 3A, Lake Geneva, WI 53147
  E-mail: rep.august@legis.wi.gov
  Committees: Assembly Organization; Insurance; Joint Law Revision; Joint Legislative Council; Joint Tax Exemptions; Rules

Representative **Joan Ballweg** (R-District 41) . . . . . . . . . . . . (608) 266-8077
  Counties Represented: Adams (part), Columbia   Dist: (920) 324-3537
  (part), Fond du Lac (part), Green Lake (part),   Fax: (608) 282-3641
  Juneau (part), Marquette (part), Sauk (part), Waushara (part)
  Term Expires: 2017
  170 West Summit Street, Markesan, WI 53946
  E-mail: rep.ballweg@legis.wisconsin.gov
  Committees: Colleges and Universities; Financial Institutions; Joint Legislative Council; Joint Review of Administrative Rules; Mental Health Reform; Rules; Tourism
  Education: Wisconsin (Stevens Point) 1974 BA

Representative **Peter W. Barca** (D-District 64) . . . . . . . . . . .(608) 266-5504
  Counties Represented: Kenosha (part), Racine (part)   Dist: (414) 552-8859
  Term Expires: 2017   Fax: (608) 282-3664
  1339 38th Avenue, Kenosha, WI 53144
  E-mail: rep.barca@legis.wisconsin.gov
  Committees: Assembly Organization; Joint Employment Relations; Joint Information Policy and Technology; Joint Legislative Council; Joint Legislative Organization; Rules

Representative **Mandela Barnes** (D-District 11) . . . . . . . . . (608) 266-3756
  Counties Represented: Milwaukee (part)   Fax: (608) 282-3611
  Term Expires: 2017
  4800 North Port Washington Road, Suite 205, Milwaukee, WI 53217
  E-mail: rep.barnes@legis.wisconsin.gov
  Committees: Corrections; Education; Jobs and the Economy; Small Business Development
  Education: Alabama A&M 2008 (Attended)

Representative **Terese E. Berceau** (D-District 77) . . . . . . . . (608) 266-3784
  Counties Represented: Dane (part)   Dist: (608) 225-8193
  Term Expires: 2017   Fax: (608) 282-3677
  4326 Somerset Lane, Madison, WI 53711
  E-mail: rep.berceau@legis.wisconsin.gov
  Committees: Campaigns and Elections; Colleges and Universities; Insurance; Joint Legislative Audit; Rules
  Education: Wisconsin 1973 BS

Representative
**Kathleen M. "Kathy" Bernier** (R-District 68) . . . . . . . . .(608) 266-9172
  Counties Represented: Chippewa (part), Clark   Fax: (608) 282-3668
  (part), Eau Claire (part), Jackson (part), Trempealeau (part)
  Term Expires: 2017
  10923 40th Avenue, Chippewa Falls, WI 54729
  E-mail: rep.bernier@legis.wi.gov
  Committees: Aging and Long-Term Care; Agriculture; Campaigns and Elections; Family Law; Mining and Rural Development; Workforce Development
  Education: Wisconsin (Eau Claire) BA

Representative **Jill Billings** (D-District 95) . . . . . . . . . . . . . (608) 266-5780
  Counties Represented: La Crosse (part)   Fax: (608) 282-3695
  Term Expires: 2017
  403 13th Street South, La Crosse, WI 54601
  E-mail: rep.billings@legis.wisconsin.gov
  Committees: Children and Families; Colleges and Universities; Interstate Affairs; Mining and Rural Development; Tourism
  Education: Augsburg 1989 BA

Representative **Mark Born** (R-District 39) . . . . . . . . . . . . . . (608) 266-2540
  Counties Represented: Dodge (part), Washington   Fax: (608) 282-3639
  (part)
  Term Expires: 2017
  121 Franklin Street, Beaver Dam, WI 53916
  E-mail: rep.born@legis.wi.gov
  Committees: Criminal Justice and Public Safety; Financial Institutions; Insurance; Natural Resources and Sporting Heritage; Public Benefit Reform; Rules; Tourism
  Education: Gustavus Adolphus 1998 BA

Representative **David Bowen** (D-District 10) . . . . . . . . . . . . (608) 266-7671
  Counties Represented: Milwaukee (part)   Fax: (608) 282-3610
  Term Expires: 2017
  4080 North 21st Street, #3, Milwaukee, WI 53209
  E-mail: rep.bowen@legis.wisconsin.gov
  Committees: Corrections; Small Business Development; Transportation; Workforce Development
  Education: Wisconsin (Milwaukee)

Representative **Janel Brandtjen** (R-District 22) . . . . . . . . . .(608) 267-2367
  Counties Represented: Milwaukee (part),   Fax: (608) 282-3622
  Washington (part), Waukesha (part)
  Term Expires: 2017
  N52 W16632 Oak Ridge Trail, Menomonee Falls, WI 53051
  E-mail: rep.brandtjen@legis.wisconsin.gov
  Committees: Children and Families; Corrections; Public Benefit Reform; State Affairs and Government Operations; Workforce Development

Representative **Edward "Ed" Brooks** (R-District 50) . . . . . (608) 266-8531
  Counties Represented: Juneau (part), Monroe   Dist: (608) 524-3902
  (part), Richland (part), Sauk (part), Vernon (part)   Fax: (608) 282-3650
  Term Expires: 2017
  S4311 Grote Hill Road, Reedsburg, WI 53959
  E-mail: rep.brooks@legis.wisconsin.gov
  Committees: Agriculture; Corrections; Interstate Affairs; Mining and Rural Development; Urban and Local Affairs
  Education: Wisconsin 1965 BS

Representative **Robert Brooks** (R-District 60) . . . . . . . . . . . (608) 267-2369
  Counties Represented: Ozaukee (part), Washington   Fax: (608) 282-3660
  (part)
  Term Expires: 2017
  204 East Dekora Street, Saukville, WI 53080
  E-mail: rep.rob.brooks@legis.wisconsin.gov
  Committees: Aging and Long-Term Care; Children and Families; Colleges and Universities; Education; Environment and Forestry; Housing and Real Estate

Representative **Jonathan Brostoff** (D-District 19) . . . . . . . (608) 266-0650
Counties Represented: Milwaukee (part)          Fax: (608) 282-3619
Term Expires: 2017
920 East Pleasant, #2, Milwaukee, WI 53212
E-mail: rep.brostoff@legis.wisconsin.gov
Committees: Aging and Long-Term Care; Financial Institutions; Mental
Health Reform; State Affairs and Government Operations; Ways and
Means

Representative **Dave Considine** (D-District 81) . . . . . . . . . (608) 266-7746
Counties Represented: Columbia (part), Dane (part),     Fax: (608) 282-3681
Iowa (part), Sauk (part)
Term Expires: 2017
N6194 Breezy Hill Road, Baraboo, WI 53913
E-mail: rep.considine@legis.wisconsin.gov
Committees: Agriculture; Education; Environment and Forestry; Mental
Health Reform; Mining and Rural Development

Representative **David "Dave" Craig** (R-District 83) . . . . . . (608) 266-3363
Counties Represented: Milwaukee (part), Racine     Fax: (608) 282-3683
(part), Walworth (part), Waukesha (part)
Term Expires: 2017
P.O. Box 323, Big Bend, WI 53103
E-mail: rep.craig@legis.wi.gov
Committees: Campaigns and Elections; Family Law; Financial
Institutions; Insurance; Public Benefit Reform; State Affairs and
Government Operations
Education: Wisconsin (Milwaukee) 2002 BA

Representative **Mary Czaja** (R-District 35) . . . . . . . . . . . . (608) 266-7694
Counties Represented: Langlade (part), Lincoln,     Fax: (608) 282-3635
Marathon (part), Oneida (part), Shawano (part)
Term Expires: 2017
W4587 Highway S, Apartment A, Irma, WI 54442
E-mail: rep.czaja@legis.wi.gov
Committees: Environment and Forestry; Finance; Joint Finance
Education: Wisconsin (River Falls) 1986 BS

Representative **Chris Danou** (D-District 92) . . . . . . . . . . . . (608) 266-7015
Counties Represented: Buffalo (part), Jackson     Dist: (608) 534-5016
(part), Trempealeau (part)                        Fax: (608) 282-3692
Term Expires: 2017
23951 8th Street, Trempealeau, WI 54661
E-mail: rep.danou@legis.wisconsin.gov
Committees: Agriculture; Insurance; Mining and Rural Development;
Natural Resources and Sporting Heritage; Transportation
Education: Wisconsin 1989 BA; American U 1991 MA;
Wisconsin (Stevens Point) 1997 MS

Representative **Steve Doyle** (D-District 94) . . . . . . . . . . . . (608) 266-0631
Counties Represented: La Crosse (part)          Fax: (608) 282-3694
Term Expires: 2017
N5525 Hauser Road, Onalaska, WI 54650
E-mail: rep.doyle@legis.wi.gov
Committees: Financial Institutions; Insurance; Joint Review on Criminal
Penalties; Small Business Development; Tourism
Education: Wisconsin (La Crosse) 1980 BA; Wisconsin 1986 JD

Representative **Cindi Duchow** (R-District 99) . . . . . . . . . . . (608) 266-3007
Counties Represented: Waukesha (part)          Tel: (888) 534-0099
Term Expires: 2017
E-mail: rep.duchow@legis.wisconsin.gov
Committees: Children and Families; Criminal Justice and Public Safety;
Education; Public Benefit Reform; Ways and Means
Education: Wisconsin

Representative **James Edming** (R-District 87) . . . . . . . . . . . (608) 266-7506
Counties Represented: Clark (part), Marathon (part),     Fax: (608) 282-3687
Rusk, Sawyer (part), Taylor
Term Expires: 2017
P.O. Box 8952, Madison, WI 53708-8952
E-mail: rep.edming@legis.wisconsin.gov
Committees: Environment and Forestry; Health; Natural Resources and
Sporting Heritage; Small Business Development; Veterans and Military
Affairs

Representative **Bob Gannon** (R-District 58) . . . . . . . . . . . . (608) 264-8486
Counties Represented: Washington (part)          Fax: (608) 282-3658
Term Expires: 2017
4833 Cedar Hills Drive, Slinger, WI 53086
E-mail: rep.gannon@legis.wisconsin.gov
Committees: Children and Families; Corrections; Insurance; Small
Business Development; State Affairs and Government Operations

Representative **Eric Genrich** (D-District 90) . . . . . . . . . . . . (608) 266-0616
Counties Represented: Brown (part)          Fax: (608) 282-3690
Term Expires: 2017
1089 Division Street, Green Bay, WI 54303
E-mail: rep.genrich@legis.wisconsin.gov
Committees: Education; Energy and Utilities; Financial Institutions;
Housing and Real Estate; Joint Information Policy and Technology;
Urban and Local Affairs
Education: Wisconsin 2002 BA; Wisconsin (Milwaukee) 2010 MLIS

Representative **Evan Goyke** (D-District 18) . . . . . . . . . . . . (608) 266-0645
Counties Represented: Milwaukee (part)          Fax: (608) 282-3618
Term Expires: 2017
2734 West State Street, Milwaukee, WI 53208
E-mail: rep.goyke@legis.wi.gov
Committees: Agriculture; Constitution and Ethics; Criminal Justice and
Public Safety; Judiciary; Public Benefit Reform; Veterans and Military
Affairs
Education: St John's U (MN) 2005 BA; Marquette 2009 JD

Representative **Dave Heaton** (R-District 85) . . . . . . . . . . . (608) 266-0654
Counties Represented: Marathon (part)          Fax: (608) 282-3685
Term Expires: 2017
8007 East Jefferson Street, Wausau, WI 54403
E-mail: rep.heaton@legis.wisconsin.gov
Committees: Children and Families; Consumer Protection; Judiciary;
Veterans and Military Affairs

Representative **Gary Hebl** (D-District 46) . . . . . . . . . . . . . . (608) 266-7678
Counties Represented: Dane (part)          Tel: (608) 837-7117
Term Expires: 2017                         Fax: (608) 282-3646
515 Scheuerell Lane, Sun Prairie, WI 53590
E-mail: rep.hebl@legis.wisconsin.gov
Committees: Environment and Forestry; Family Law; Joint Review of
Administrative Rules; Judiciary; Rules
Education: Wisconsin 1973 BA; Gonzaga 1976 JD

Representative **Dianne Hesselbein** (D-District 79) . . . . . . . (608) 266-5340
Counties Represented: Dane (part)          Fax: (608) 282-3679
Term Expires: 2017
1420 High Point Road, Middleton, WI 53562
E-mail: rep.hesselbein@legis.wi.gov
Committees: Colleges and Universities; Joint Tax Exemptions; Natural
Resources and Sporting Heritage; Veterans and Military Affairs
Education: Wisconsin (Oshkosh) 1993 BS; Edgewood 1996 MA

Representative **Gordon Hintz** (D-District 54) . . . . . . . . . . . (608) 266-2254
Counties Represented: Winnebago (part)          Dist: (920) 232-0805
Term Expires: 2017                               Fax: (608) 282-3654
1209 Waugoo Ave., Oshkosh, WI 54901
E-mail: rep.hintz@legis.wisconsin.gov
Committees: Finance; Joint Finance
Education: Hamline 1996 BA; Wisconsin 2001 MPA

Representative **Cody Horlacher** (R-District 33) . . . . . . . . . (608) 266-5715
Counties Represented: Jefferson (part), Walworth     Fax: (608) 282-3633
(part), Waukesha (part)
Term Expires: 2017
1254 Bear Pass, #7, Mukwonago, WI 53149
E-mail: rep.horlacher@legis.wisconsin.gov
Committees: Campaigns and Elections; Constitution and Ethics;
Criminal Justice and Public Safety; Education; Interstate Affairs;
Judiciary

Representative **Robert Hutton** (R-District 13) . . . . . . . . . . (608) 267-9836
Counties Represented: Milwaukee (part), Waukesha     Fax: (608) 282-3613
(part)
Term Expires: 2017
17785 Marseille Drive, Brookfield, WI 53045
E-mail: rep.hutton@legis.wi.gov
Committees: Constitution and Ethics; Corrections; Education; Small
Business Development; Urban and Local Affairs
Education: Wisconsin (Whitewater) 1990 BA

Representative **André Jacque** (R-District 2) . . . . . . . . . . . . (608) 266-9870
Counties Represented: Brown (part), Manitowoc     Fax: (608) 282-3602
(part), Outagamie (part)
Term Expires: 2017
1615 Lost Dauphin Road, De Pere, WI 54115
E-mail: rep.jacque@legis.wi.gov
Committees: Energy and Utilities; Interstate Affairs; Joint Review on
Criminal Penalties; Labor; Ways and Means

*(continued on next page)*

LEGISLATIVE BRANCH

**Representatives** *continued*

Representative **John Jagler** (R-District 37) . . . . . . . . . . . . (608) 266-9650
Counties Represented: Columbia (part), Dane (part),     Fax: (608) 282-3637
Dodge (part), Jefferson (part)
Term Expires: 2017
601 Clyman Street, Watertown, WI 53094
E-mail: rep.jagler@legis.wisconsin.gov
Committees: Constitution and Ethics; Education; Housing and Real
Estate; Insurance; Mental Health Reform; Rules; State Affairs and
Government Operations
Education: Wisconsin (Parkside) 1988 (Attended)

Representative **Adam Jarchow** (R-District 28) . . . . . . . . . (608) 267-2365
Counties Represented: Burnett (part), Polk (part),     Fax: (608) 282-3628
St. Croix (part)
Term Expires: 2017
971 Apple River Court, Balsam Lake, WI 54810
E-mail: rep.jarchow@legis.wisconsin.gov
Committees: Energy and Utilities; Financial Institutions; Tourism

Representative **La Tonya Johnson** (D-District 17) . . . . . . . . (608) 266-5580
Counties Represented: Milwaukee (part)     Fax: (608) 282-3617
Term Expires: 2017
2363 North 54th Street, Milwaukee, WI 53210
E-mail: rep.johnson@legis.wi.gov
Committees: Children and Families; Criminal Justice and Public Safety;
Family Law; Financial Institutions
Education: Tennessee State 1997 BS

Representative **Andy Jorgensen** (D-District 43) . . . . . . . . . (608) 266-3790
Counties Represented: Dane (part), Jefferson     Dist: (920) 563-7456
(part), Rock (part), Walworth (part)     Fax: (608) 282-3643
Term Expires: 2017
1148 Brown Drive, Milton, WI 53563
E-mail: rep.jorgensen@legis.wisconsin.gov
Committees: Agriculture; Assembly Organization; Colleges and
Universities; Public Benefit Reform; Rules; Small Business
Development

Representative **Robb Kahl** (D-District 47) . . . . . . . . . . . . . . (608) 266-8570
Counties Represented: Dane (part)     Fax: (608) 282-3647
Term Expires: 2017
5700 Winnequah Road, Monona, WI 53716
E-mail: rep.kahl@legis.wi.gov
Committees: Children and Families; Energy and Utilities; Insurance;
State Affairs and Government Operations; Transportation
Education: Ripon 1990 BA; Syracuse 1995 (Attended);
Wisconsin 1997 JD

Representative **Terry Katsma** (R-District 26) . . . . . . . . . . . (608) 266-0656
Counties Represented: Sheboygan (part)     Fax: (608) 282-3626
Term Expires: 2017
705 Erie Avenue, Oostburg, WI 53070
E-mail: rep.katsma@legis.wisconsin.gov
Committees: Consumer Protection; Financial Institutions; Housing and
Real Estate; Ways and Means; Workforce Development

Representative **Samantha Kerkman** (R-District 61) . . . . . . (608) 266-2530
Counties Represented: Kenosha (part)     Dist: (262) 279-1037
Term Expires: 2017     Fax: (608) 282-3661
P.O. Box 156, Powers Lake, WI 53159
E-mail: rep.kerkman@legis.wisconsin.gov
Committees: Children and Families; Interstate Affairs; Joint Legislative
Audit; Judiciary; Ways and Means

Representative
**Frederick P. "Fred" Kessler** (D-District 12) . . . . . . . . . . (608) 266-5813
Counties Represented: Milwaukee (part)     Dist: (414) 535-0266
Term Expires: 2017     Fax: (608) 282-3612
9312 West Clovernook Street, Milwaukee, WI 53224
E-mail: rep.kessler@legis.wisconsin.gov
Committees: Agriculture; Campaigns and Elections; Constitution and
Ethics; Criminal Justice and Public Safety
Education: Wisconsin 1962 BA, 1966 LLB

Representative **Joel Kitchens** (R-District 1) . . . . . . . . . . . . (608) 266-5350
Counties Represented: Brown (part), Door,     Fax: (608) 282-3601
Kewaunee, Manitowoc (part)
Term Expires: 2017
1117 Cove Road, Sturgeon Bay, WI 54235
E-mail: rep.kitchens@legis.wisconsin.gov
Committees: Agriculture; Education; Environment and Forestry;
Financial Institutions; Tourism; Workforce Development

Representative **Joel Kleefisch** (R-District 38) . . . . . . . . . . . (608) 266-8551
Counties Represented: Dane (part), Jefferson     Tel: (920) 474-3338
(part), Waukesha (part)     Fax: (608) 282-3638
Term Expires: 2017
W357 N6189 Spinnaker Drive, Oconomowoc, WI 53066
E-mail: rep.kleefisch@legis.wisconsin.gov
Committees: Corrections; Criminal Justice and Public Safety; Family
Law; Natural Resources and Sporting Heritage; State Affairs and
Government Operations; Tourism
Education: Pepperdine 1993 BA

Representative **Daniel "Dan" Knodl** (R-District 24) . . . . . . (608) 266-3796
Counties Represented: Milwaukee (part), Ozaukee     Dist: (262) 502-0118
(part), Washington (part), Waukesha (part)     Fax: (608) 282-3624
Term Expires: 2017
N101 W14475 Ridgefield Court, Germantown, WI 53022
E-mail: rep.knodl@legis.wisconsin.gov
Committees: Assembly Organization; Joint Legislative Council; Joint
Legislative Organization; Labor; Rules

Representative **Dean Knudson** (R-District 30) . . . . . . . . . . (608) 266-1526
Counties Represented: Pierce (part), St. Croix (part)     Fax: (608) 282-3630
Term Expires: 2017
1753 Laurel Avenue, Hudson, WI 54016
E-mail: rep.knudson@legis.wi.gov
Committees: Education; Finance; Joint Finance; Joint Review of
Administrative Rules

Representative **Debra Kolste** (D-District 44) . . . . . . . . . . . . (608) 266-7503
Counties Represented: Rock (part)     Fax: (608) 282-3644
Term Expires: 2017
4105 Park View Drive, Janesville, WI 53546
E-mail: rep.kolste@legis.wi.gov
Committees: Health; Public Benefit Reform; Transportation; Workforce
Development
Education: Nebraska 1975 BS

Representative **Dale Kooyenga** (R-District 14) . . . . . . . . . . (608) 266-9180
Counties Represented: Milwaukee (part), Waukesha     Fax: (608) 282-3614
(part)
Term Expires: 2017
15365 St. Therese Boulevard, Brookfield, WI 53005
E-mail: rep.kooyenga@legis.wi.gov
Committees: Finance; Joint Finance

Representative **Jesse Kremer** (R-District 59) . . . . . . . . . . . . (608) 266-9175
Counties Represented: Calumet (part), Fond du Lac     Fax: (608) 282-3659
(part), Sheboygan (part), Washington (part)
Term Expires: 2017
119 Hillcrest Road, Kewaskum, WI 53040
E-mail: rep.kremer@legis.wisconsin.gov
Committees: Constitution and Ethics; Criminal Justice and Public
Safety; Health; Mining and Rural Development; Public Benefit Reform

Representative **Scott Krug** (R-District 72) . . . . . . . . . . . . . . (608) 266-0215
Counties Represented: Adams (part), Portage (part),     Fax: (608) 282-3672
Waushara (part), Wood (part)
Term Expires: 2017
1414 Akron Avenue, Neshkoro, WI 54457
E-mail: rep.krug@legis.wi.gov
Committees: Colleges and Universities; Consumer Protection;
Environment and Forestry; Jobs and the Economy; Mining and Rural
Development; Public Benefit Reform

Representative **Mike Kuglitsch** (R-District 84) . . . . . . . . . . (608) 267-5158
Counties Represented: Milwaukee (part), Waukesha     Fax: (608) 282-3684
(part)
Term Expires: 2017
21865 West Tolbert Drive, New Berlin, WI 53146
E-mail: rep.kuglitsch@legis.wi.gov
Committees: Energy and Utilities; Jobs and the Economy; Joint
Retirement Systems; Labor; Rules; Workforce Development
Education: Wisconsin (Whitewater)

Representative
**Frederick Robert "Bob" Kulp** (R-District 69) . . . . . . . . . (608) 267-0280
Counties Represented: Clark (part), Marathon (part),     Fax: (608) 282-3669
Wood (part)
Term Expires: 2017
C4098 Pauline Lane, Stratford, WI 54484
E-mail: rep.kulp@legis.wi.gov
Committees: Jobs and the Economy; Labor; Mining and Rural
Development; State Affairs and Government Operations; Workforce
Development

Representative **Thomas "Tom" Larson** (R-District 67).....(608) 266-1194
Counties Represented: Barron (part), Chippewa    Fax: (608) 282-3667
(part), Dunn (part)
Term Expires: 2017
E9359 County Road N, Colfax, WI 54730
E-mail: rep.larson@legis.wi.gov
Committees: Energy and Utilities; Family Law; Judiciary; Mining and
Rural Development; Small Business Development; Transportation

Representative **Amy Loudenbeck** (R-District 31) ........ (608) 266-9967
Counties Represented: Rock (part), Walworth (part)    Fax: (608) 282-3631
Term Expires: 2017
10737 South State Road 140, Clinton, WI 53525
E-mail: rep.loudenbeck@legis.wisconsin.gov
Committees: Finance; Joint Finance; Joint Information Policy and
Technology
Education: Wisconsin 1991 BA

Representative **John Macco** (R-District 88) ............. (608) 266-0485
Counties Represented: Brown (part)    Fax: (608) 282-3688
Term Expires: 2017
P.O. Box 8953, Madison, WI 53708-8953
E-mail: rep.macco@legis.wisconsin.gov
Committees: Colleges and Universities; Jobs and the Economy; Joint
Legislative Audit; Transportation; Ways and Means

Representative **Cory Mason** (D-District 66) ............. (608) 266-0634
Counties Represented: Racine (part)    Dist: (262) 638-2362
Term Expires: 2017    Fax: (608) 282-3666
1948 Michigan Boulevard, Racine, WI 53402
E-mail: rep.mason@legis.wisconsin.gov
Committees: Environment and Forestry; Joint Legislative Council; Joint
Retirement Systems; Labor; Tourism

Representative **Beth M. Meyers** (D-District 74).........(608) 266-7690
Counties Represented: Ashland, Bayfield, Douglas    Fax: (608) 282-3674
(part), Iron, Price, Sawyer (part), Vilas (part)
Term Expires: 2017
36505 Aiken Road, Bayfield, WI 54814
E-mail: rep.meyers@legis.wisconsin.gov
Committees: Aging and Long-Term Care; Tourism; Transportation

Representative **Nick Milroy** (D-District 73).............(608) 266-0640
Counties Represented: Burnett (part), Douglas    Dist: (715) 392-8690
(part), Washburn (part)    Fax: (608) 282-3673
Term Expires: 2017
4543 South Sam Anderson Road, South Range, WI 54874
E-mail: rep.milroy@legis.wisconsin.gov
Committees: Environment and Forestry; Mining and Rural
Development; Natural Resources and Sporting Heritage; Veterans and
Military Affairs

Representative **Dave Murphy** (R-District 56) ...........(608) 266-7500
Counties Represented: Outagamie (part), Winnebago    Fax: (608) 282-3656
(part)
Term Expires: 2017
1777 Ivy Lane, Greenville, WI 54942
E-mail: rep.murphy@legis.wi.gov
Committees: Colleges and Universities; Education; Financial
Institutions; Housing and Real Estate; Joint Retirement Systems;
Workforce Development
Education: Wisconsin (Fox Valley) 1974 (Attended)

Representative **Jeffrey Mursau** (R-District 36)...........(608) 266-3780
Counties Represented: Forest (part), Langlade    Tel: (715) 854-3477
(part), Marinette (part), Menominee, Oconto (part),    Fax: (608) 282-3636
Shawano (part)
Term Expires: 2017
4 Oak Street, Crivitz, WI 54114
E-mail: rep.mursau@legis.wisconsin.gov
Committees: Environment and Forestry; Family Law; Mining and Rural
Development; Natural Resources and Sporting Heritage; Tourism

Representative **John Murtha** (R-District 29) ........... (608) 266-7683
Counties Represented: Dunn (part), St. Croix (part)    Dist: (715) 684-3508
Term Expires: 2017    Fax: (608) 282-3629
2283 20th Avenue, Baldwin, WI 54002
E-mail: rep.murtha@legis.wisconsin.gov
Committees: Assembly Organization; Housing and Real Estate; Joint
Legislative Council

Representative **Lee Nerison** (R-District 96) ............ (608) 266-3534
Counties Represented: Crawford, Monroe (part),    Dist: (608) 634-4562
Vernon (part)    Fax: (608) 282-3696
Term Expires: 2017
S3035 County Road B, Westby, WI 54667
E-mail: rep.nerison@legis.wisconsin.gov
Committees: Aging and Long-Term Care; Agriculture; Consumer
Protection; Natural Resources and Sporting Heritage; Veterans and
Military Affairs

Representative **Adam Neylon** (R-District 98) ...........(608) 266-5120
Counties Represented: Waukesha (part)    Fax: (608) 282-3698
Term Expires: 2017
294 Meadowcreek Court, Number 4, Pewaukee, WI 53072
E-mail: rep.neylon@legis.wi.gov
Committees: Children and Families; Consumer Protection; Energy and
Utilities; Jobs and the Economy; Public Benefit Reform

Representative **Todd Novak** (R-District 51) ............. (608) 266-7502
Counties Represented: Green (part), Iowa (part),    Fax: (608) 282-3651
Lafayette (part), Richland (part), Sauk (part)
Term Expires: 2017
202 West Division Street, Dodgeville, WI 53533
E-mail: rep.novak@legis.wisconsin.gov
Committees: Agriculture; Criminal Justice and Public Safety; Mental
Health Reform; Mining and Rural Development; Urban and Local
Affairs; Ways and Means

Representative **John Nygren** (R-District 89) ........... (608) 266-2343
Counties Represented: Brown (part), Marinette    Dist: (715) 732-4296
(part), Oconto (part)    Fax: (608) 282-3689
Term Expires: 2017
N2118 Keller Road, Marinette, WI 54143
E-mail: rep.nygren@legis.wisconsin.gov
Committees: Corrections; Finance; Joint Employment Relations; Joint
Finance; Joint Legislative Audit; Joint Legislative Council

Representative **Tod Ohnstad** (D-District 65) ........... (608) 266-0455
Counties Represented: Kenosha (part)    Fax: (608) 282-3665
Term Expires: 2017
3814 18th Avenue, Kenosha, WI 53140
E-mail: rep.ohnstad@legis.wi.gov
Committees: Jobs and the Economy; Labor; State Affairs and
Government Operations; Tourism; Ways and Means
Education: Wisconsin (Parkside) (Attended)

Representative **Alvin R. "Al" Ott** (R-District 3) ......... (608) 266-5831
Counties Represented: Calumet (part), Outagamie    Dist: (920) 989-1240
(part)    Fax: (608) 282-3603
Term Expires: 2017
W2168 Campground Road, Forest Junction, WI 54123-0112
P.O. Box 112, Forest Junction, WI 54123-0112
E-mail: rep.ott@legis.wisconsin.gov
Committees: Agriculture; Interstate Affairs; Natural Resources and
Sporting Heritage; Tourism; Transportation

Representative **Jim Ott** (R-District 23) ................. (608) 266-0486
Counties Represented: Milwaukee (part), Ozaukee    Dist: (262) 241-9411
(part)    Fax: (608) 282-3623
Term Expires: 2017
11743 N. Lakeshore Drive, Mequon, WI 53092
E-mail: rep.ottj@legis.wisconsin.gov
Committees: Constitution and Ethics; Criminal Justice and Public
Safety; Joint Law Revision; Joint Review of Administrative Rules;
Judiciary; Veterans and Military Affairs

Representative **Kevin Petersen** (R-District 40)...........(608) 266-3794
Counties Represented: Outagamie (part), Shawano    Dist: (715) 258-2474
(part), Waupaca (part), Waushara (part)    Fax: (608) 282-3640
Term Expires: 2017
N1433 Drivas Road, Waupaca, WI 54981
E-mail: rep.petersen@legis.wisconsin.gov
Committees: Energy and Utilities; Financial Institutions; Health;
Insurance; Joint Information Policy and Technology; Ways and Means

Representative **Warren Petryk** (R-District 93) ...........(608) 266-0660
Counties Represented: Buffalo (part), Dunn (part),    Fax: (608) 282-3693
Eau Claire (part), Pepin, Pierce (part), St. Croix (part)
Term Expires: 2017
S9840 Highway 93, Eleva, WI 54738
E-mail: rep.petryk@legis.wi.gov
Committees: Aging and Long-Term Care; Colleges and Universities;
Energy and Utilities; Insurance; Joint Information Policy and
Technology; Veterans and Military Affairs; Workforce Development

Representative **Sondy Pope** (D-District 80) ............. (608) 266-3520
Counties Represented: Dane (part), Green (part),    Dist: (608) 836-8737
Iowa (part)    Fax: (608) 282-3680
Term Expires: 2017
9262 Moen Road, Cross Plains, WI 53528
E-mail: rep.pope-roberts@legis.wisconsin.gov
Committees: Consumer Protection; Corrections; Education; Rules

Representative **Romaine Robert Quinn** (R-District 75) ... (608) 266-2519
Counties Represented: Barron (part), Burnett (part),    Fax: (608) 282-3675
Dunn (part), Polk (part), St. Croix (part), Washburn (part)
Term Expires: 2017
604 West Stout Street, Rice Lake, WI 54868
E-mail: rep.quinn@legis.wisconsin.gov
Committees: Aging and Long-Term Care; Colleges and Universities;
Education; Mining and Rural Development; Natural Resources and
Sporting Heritage; Urban and Local Affairs

*(continued on next page)*

**LEGISLATIVE BRANCH**

**Representatives** *continued*

Representative **Daniel Riemer** (D-District 7) . . . . . . . . . . (608) 266-1733
Counties Represented: Milwaukee (part)          Fax: (608) 282-3607
Term Expires: 2017
3053 South 39th Street, Milwaukee, WI 53215
E-mail: rep.riemer@legis.wi.gov
Committees: Health; Mental Health Reform; Veterans and Military
Affairs; Ways and Means; Workforce Development
Education: Chicago 2009 BA

Representative **Keith Ripp** (R-District 42) . . . . . . . . . . . . . (608) 266-3404
Counties Represented: Columbia (part), Dane (part),      Dist: (608) 849-4519
Dodge (part), Fond du Lac (part), Green Lake       Fax: (608) 282-3642
(part), Marquette (part)
Term Expires: 2017
7113 County Road V, Lodi, WI 53555
E-mail: rep.ripp@legis.wisconsin.gov
Committees: Agriculture; Natural Resources and Sporting Heritage;
State Affairs and Government Operations; Transportation; Workforce
Development

Representative **Jessie Rodriguez** (R-District 21) . . . . . . . . (608) 266-0610
Counties Represented: Milwaukee (part)          Fax: (608) 282-3621
Term Expires: 2017
9312 South 33rd Street, Franklin, WI 53132
E-mail: rep.rodriguez@legis.wi.gov
Committees: Children and Families; Colleges and Universities;
Criminal Justice and Public Safety; Education; Mental Health Reform

Representative **Mike Rohrkaste** (R-District 55) . . . . . . . . . (608) 266-5719
Counties Represented: Outagamie (part), Winnebago      Fax: (608) 282-3655
(part)
Term Expires: 2017
1417 Mahler Boulevard, Neenah, WI 54956
E-mail: rep.rohrkaste@legis.wisconsin.gov
Committees: Colleges and Universities; Health; Interstate Affairs; Jobs
and the Economy; Mental Health Reform

Representative **Joe Sanfelippo** (R-District 15) . . . . . . . . . . (608) 266-0620
Counties Represented: Milwaukee (part), Waukesha      Fax: (608) 282-3615
(part)
Term Expires: 2017
20770 W. Coffee Road, New Berlin, WI 53146
E-mail: rep.sanfelippo@legis.wi.gov
Committees: Campaigns and Elections; Financial Institutions; Health;
Mental Health Reform; Transportation
Education: Marquette 1984 (Attended)

Representative **Melissa Sargent** (D-District 48) . . . . . . . . (608) 266-0960
Counties Represented: Dane (part)          Fax: (608) 282-3648
Term Expires: 2017
1638 Mayfield Lane, Madison, WI 53704
E-mail: rep.sargent@legis.wi.gov
Committees: Aging and Long-Term Care; Energy and Utilities;
Financial Institutions; Joint Law Revision; Joint Legislative Audit;
Mental Health Reform; Small Business Development
Education: Wisconsin 1991 BA

Representative **Michael Schraa** (R-District 53) . . . . . . . . . (608) 267-7990
Counties Represented: Dodge (part), Fond du Lac      Fax: (608) 282-3653
(part), Winnebago (part)
Term Expires: 2017
220 Wyldeberry Lane, Oshkosh, WI 54904
E-mail: rep.schraa@legis.wi.gov
Committees: Finance; Joint Finance; Public Benefit Reform
Education: Wisconsin (Oshkosh) 1982 (Attended)

Representative **Katrina Shankland** (D-District 71) . . . . . . . (608) 267-9649
Counties Represented: Portage (part)          Fax: (608) 282-3671
Term Expires: 2017
833 Clark Street, Apt G, Stevens Point, WI 54481
E-mail: rep.shankland@legis.wi.gov
Committees: Assembly Organization; Joint Legislative Council; Joint
Legislative Organization; Joint Review of Administrative Rules; Natural
Resources and Sporting Heritage; Rules; Workforce Development

Representative **Christine Sinicki** (D-District 20) . . . . . . . . (608) 266-8588
Counties Represented: Milwaukee (part)          Dist: (414) 481-7667
Term Expires: 2017          Fax: (608) 282-3620
3132 South Indiana Avenue, Milwaukee, WI 53207
E-mail: rep.sinicki@legis.wisconsin.gov
Committees: Consumer Protection; Education; Labor; State Affairs and
Government Operations; Veterans and Military Affairs

Representative **Ken Skowronski** (R-District 82) . . . . . . . . (608) 266-8590
Counties Represented: Milwaukee (part)          Fax: (608) 282-3682
Term Expires: 2017
8642 South 116 Street, Franklin, WI 53132
E-mail: rep.skowronski@legis.wi.gov
Committees: Health; Natural Resources and Sporting Heritage; Small
Business Development; Urban and Local Affairs; Veterans and Military
Affairs

Representative **John Spiros** (R-District 86) . . . . . . . . . . . . . (608) 266-1182
Counties Represented: Marathon (part), Wood (part)      Fax: (608) 282-3686
Term Expires: 2017
1406 East Fillmore Street, Marshfield, WI 54449
E-mail: rep.spiros@legis.wi.gov
Committees: Criminal Justice and Public Safety; Labor; Transportation;
Ways and Means

Representative **Mark Spreitzer** (D-District 45) . . . . . . . . . . (608) 266-1192
Counties Represented: Green (part), Rock (part)      Fax: (608) 282-3645
Term Expires: 2017
1718 Henderson Avenue, Beloit, WI 53511
E-mail: rep.spreitzer@legis.wisconsin.gov
Committees: Jobs and the Economy; Mining and Rural Development;
Natural Resources and Sporting Heritage; Public Benefit Reform;
Workforce Development

Representative **David Steffen** (R-District 4) . . . . . . . . . . . . (608) 266-5840
Counties Represented: Brown (part)          Fax: (608) 282-3604
Term Expires: 2017
1320 Sunray Lane, Green Bay, WI 54313
E-mail: rep.steffen@legis.wisconsin.gov
Committees: Energy and Utilities; Insurance; Jobs and the Economy;
Urban and Local Affairs; Ways and Means

Representative **Jim Steineke** (R-District 5) . . . . . . . . . . . . (608) 266-2418
Counties Represented: Brown (part), Outagamie      Fax: (608) 282-3605
(part)
Term Expires: 2017
N2352 Vandenbroek Road, Kaukauna, WI 54130
E-mail: rep.steineke@legis.wi.gov
Committees: Assembly Organization; Joint Employment Relations;
Joint Legislative Council; Joint Legislative Organization; Rules

Representative **Amanda Stuck** (D-District 57) . . . . . . . . . . (608) 266-3070
Counties Represented: Outagamie (part), Winnebago      Fax: (608) 282-3657
(part)
Term Expires: 2017
1404 West Harriman Avenue, Appleton, WI 54911
E-mail: rep.stuck@legis.wisconsin.gov
Committees: Energy and Utilities; Environment and Forestry; Housing
and Real Estate; Jobs and the Economy

Representative **Lisa Subeck** (D-District 78) . . . . . . . . . . . . (608) 266-7521
Counties Represented: Dane (part)          Fax: (608) 282-3678
Term Expires: 2017
818 South Gammon Road, #4, Madison, WI 53719
E-mail: rep.subeck@legis.wisconsin.gov
Committees: Children and Families; Family Law; Health; Public Benefit
Reform; Urban and Local Affairs

Representative **Rob Swearingen** (R-District 34) . . . . . . . . (608) 266-7141
Counties Represented: Florence, Forest (part),      Fax: (608) 282-3634
Oneida (part), Vilas (part)
Term Expires: 2017
4485 Oakview Lane, Rhinelander, WI 54501
E-mail: rep.swearingen@legis.wi.gov
Committees: Environment and Forestry; Joint Tax Exemptions; Rules;
Small Business Development; State Affairs and Government
Operations; Tourism; Transportation

Representative **Gary Tauchen** (R-District 6) . . . . . . . . . . . . (608) 266-3097
Counties Represented: Brown (part), Oconto (part),      Dist: (715) 758-6181
Outagamie (part), Shawano (part), Waupaca (part)      Fax: (608) 282-3606
Term Expires: 2017
N3397 South Broadway Road, Bonduel, WI 54107
E-mail: rep.tauchen@legis.wisconsin.gov
Committees: Agriculture; Public Benefit Reform; Small Business
Development; State Affairs and Government Operations; Tourism

Representative **Chris Taylor** (D-District 76) . . . . . . . . . . . . (608) 266-5342
Counties Represented: Dane (part)          Fax: (608) 282-3676
Term Expires: 2017
2910 Oakridge Avenue, Madison, WI 53704
E-mail: rep.taylor@legis.wisconsin.gov
Committees: Finance; Joint Finance; Joint Law Revision; Joint
Legislative Council

Representative **Jeremy Thiesfeldt** (R-District 52) . . . . . . . . (608) 266-3156
Counties Represented: Fond du Lac (part)          Fax: (608) 282-3652
Term Expires: 2017
604 Sunset Lane, Fond du Lac, WI 54935
E-mail: rep.thiesfeldt@legis.wi.gov
Committees: Campaigns and Elections; Education; Family Law;
Judiciary; Transportation

Representative **Paul Tittl** (R-District 25) . . . . . . . . . . . . . . (608) 266-0315
Counties Represented: Calumet (part), Manitowoc     Fax: (608) 282-3625
(part)
Term Expires: 2017
2229 Rheaume Road, Manitowoc, WI 54220
E-mail: rep.tittl@legis.wi.gov
Committees: Health; Insurance; Jobs and the Economy; Mental Health
Reform; Natural Resources and Sporting Heritage; Veterans and
Military Affairs

Representative **Travis Tranel** (R-District 49) . . . . . . . . . . . . (608) 266-1170
Counties Represented: Grant, Iowa (part), Lafayette     Fax: (608) 282-3649
(part), Richland (part)
Term Expires: 2017
2231 Louisburg Road, Cuba City, WI 53807
E-mail: rep.tranel@legis.wi.gov
Committees: Agriculture; Colleges and Universities; Energy and
Utilities; Insurance; Small Business Development; Tourism

Representative **Nancy VanderMeer** (R-District 70) . . . . . . . (608) 266-8366
Counties Represented: Jackson (part), Monroe     Fax: (608) 282-3670
(part), Portage (part), Wood (part)
Term Expires: 2017
18940 Eden Avenue, Tomah, WI 54660
E-mail: rep.vandermeer@legis.wisconsin.gov
Committees: Agriculture; Consumer Protection; Mental Health Reform;
Mining and Rural Development; Small Business Development; Veterans
and Military Affairs

Representative **Tyler Vorpagel** (R-District 27) . . . . . . . . . . (608) 266-8530
Counties Represented: Calumet (part), Manitowoc     Fax: (608) 282-3627
(part), Sheboygan (part)
Term Expires: 2017
2418 Valley Road, Plymouth, WI 53073
E-mail: rep.vorpagel@legis.wisconsin.gov
Committees: Campaigns and Elections; Children and Families;
Public Benefit Reform; State Affairs and Government Operations;
Transportation

Representative **Robin Vos** (R-District 63) . . . . . . . . . . . . . . (608) 266-3387
Counties Represented: Racine (part), Walworth     Dist: (262) 514-2597
(part)     Fax: (608) 282-3663
Term Expires: 2017
960 Rock Ridge Road, Burlington, WI 53105
E-mail: rep.vos@legis.wisconsin.gov
Committees: Assembly Organization; Joint Employment Relations;
Joint Legislative Council; Joint Legislative Organization; Rules

Representative **Dana J. Wachs** (D-District 91) . . . . . . . . . . (608) 266-7461
Counties Represented: Chippewa (part), Eau Claire     Fax: (608) 282-3691
(part)
Term Expires: 2017
437 Lincoln Avenue, Eau Claire, WI 54701
E-mail: rep.wachs@legis.wi.gov
Committees: Colleges and Universities; Constitution and Ethics; Joint
Law Revision; Judiciary
Education: Valparaiso 1985 JD

Representative
**Thomas "Tom" Weatherston** (R-District 62) . . . . . . . . (608) 266-0731
Counties Represented: Racine (part)     Fax: (608) 282-3662
Term Expires: 2017
5300 Santa Anita Drive, Racine, WI 53402
E-mail: rep.weatherston@legis.wi.gov
Committees: Aging and Long-Term Care; Energy and Utilities;
Financial Institutions; Transportation; Veterans and Military Affairs;
Workforce Development
Education: SUNY Col (Buffalo) 1977 BS

Representative **Leon D. Young** (D-District 16) . . . . . . . . . . (608) 266-3786
Counties Represented: Milwaukee (part)     Dist: (414) 374-7414
Term Expires: 2017     Fax: (608) 282-3616
2224 N. 17th St., Milwaukee, WI 53205
E-mail: rep.young@legis.wisconsin.gov
Committees: Consumer Protection; Housing and Real Estate; Insurance;
Interstate Affairs; Urban and Local Affairs

Representative
**Jocasta "Joey" Zamarripa** (D-District 8) . . . . . . . . . . (608) 267-7669
Counties Represented: Milwaukee (part)     Dist: (414) 384-2786
Term Expires: 2017     Fax: (608) 282-3608
1645 South 12th Street, Milwaukee, WI 53204
E-mail: rep.zamarripa@legis.wisconsin.gov
Committees: Campaigns and Elections; Criminal Justice and Public
Safety; Health; Jobs and the Economy; State Affairs and Government
Operations

Representative **Josh Zepnick** (D-District 9) . . . . . . . . . . . . (608) 266-1707
Counties Represented: Milwaukee (part)     Dist: (414) 727-0841
Term Expires: 2017     Fax: (608) 282-3609
1921 W. Plainfield Avenue, Milwaukee, WI 53221
E-mail: rep.zepnick@legis.wisconsin.gov
Committees: Energy and Utilities; Financial Institutions; Interstate
Affairs; Ways and Means

# Assembly Standing Committees

## Aging and Long-Term Care

| Majority Members | Minority Members |
|---|---|
| Thomas "Tom" Weatherston (R-62) *Chair* | Jonathan Brostoff (D-19) |
| Romaine Robert Quinn (R-75) *Vice-Chair* | Beth M. Meyers (D-74) |
| Kathleen M. "Kathy" Bernier (R-68) | Melissa Sargent (D-48) |
| Robert Brooks (R-60) | |
| Lee Nerison (R-96) | |
| Warren Petryk (R-93) | |

## Agriculture

| Majority Members | Minority Members |
|---|---|
| Lee Nerison (R-96) *Chair* | Dave Considine (D-81) |
| Todd Novak (R-51) *Vice-Chair* | Chris Danou (D-92) |
| Kathleen M. "Kathy" Bernier (R-68) | Evan Goyke (D-18) |
| Edward "Ed" Brooks (R-50) | Andy Jorgensen (D-43) |
| Joel Kitchens (R-1) | Frederick P. "Fred" Kessler (D-12) |
| Alvin R. "Al" Ott (R-3) | |
| Keith Ripp (R-42) | |
| Gary Tauchen (R-6) | |
| Travis Tranel (R-49) | |
| Nancy VanderMeer (R-70) | |

## Assembly Organization

| Majority Members | Minority Members |
|---|---|
| Robin Vos (R-63) *Chair* | Peter W. Barca (D-64) |
| Jim Steineke (R-5) *Vice Chair* | Andy Jorgensen (D-43) |
| Tyler August (R-32) | Katrina Shankland (D-71) |
| Daniel "Dan" Knodl (R-24) | |
| John Murtha (R-29) | |

## Campaigns and Elections

| Majority Members | Minority Members |
|---|---|
| Kathleen M. "Kathy" Bernier (R-68) *Chair* | Terese E. Berceau (D-77) |
| | Frederick P. "Fred" Kessler (D-12) |
| Tyler Vorpagel (R-27) *Vice Chair* | Jocasta "Joey" Zamarripa (D-8) |
| David "Dave" Craig (R-83) | |
| Cody Horlacher (R-33) | |
| Joe Sanfelippo (R-15) | |
| Jeremy Thiesfeldt (R-52) | |

## Children and Families

| Majority Members | Minority Members |
|---|---|
| Jessie Rodriguez (R-21) *Chair* | Jill Billings (D-95) |
| Bob Gannon (R-58) *Vice-Chair* | La Tonya Johnson (D-17) |
| Janel Brandtjen (R-22) | Robb Kahl (D-47) |
| Robert Brooks (R-60) | Lisa Subeck (D-78) |
| Cindi Duchow (R-99) | |
| Dave Heaton (R-85) | |
| Samantha Kerkman (R-61) | |
| Adam Neylon (R-98) | |
| Tyler Vorpagel (R-27) | |

## Colleges and Universities

| Majority Members | Minority Members |
|---|---|
| Dave Murphy (R-56) *Chair* | Terese E. Berceau (D-77) |
| Robert Brooks (R-60) *Vice-Chair* | Jill Billings (D-95) |
| Joan Ballweg (R-41) | Dianne Hesselbein (D-79) |
| Scott Krug (R-72) | Andy Jorgensen (D-43) |
| John Macco (R-88) | Dana J. Wachs (D-91) |
| Warren Petryk (R-93) | |
| Romaine Robert Quinn (R-75) | |
| Jessie Rodriguez (R-21) | |
| Mike Rohrkaste (R-55) | |
| Travis Tranel (R-49) | |

## Constitution and Ethics

| Majority Members | Minority Members |
| --- | --- |
| Jim Ott (R-23) *Vice Chair* | Evan Goyke (D-18) |
| Cody Horlacher (R-33) | Frederick P. "Fred" Kessler (D-12) |
| Robert Hutton (R-13) | Dana J. Wachs (D-91) |
| John Jagler (R-37) | |
| Jesse Kremer (R-59) | |

## Consumer Protection

| Majority Members | Minority Members |
| --- | --- |
| Scott Krug (R-72) *Chair* | Sondy Pope (D-80) |
| Dave Heaton (R-85) *Vice-Chair* | Christine Sinicki (D-20) |
| Terry Katsma (R-26) | Leon D. Young (D-16) |
| Lee Nerison (R-96) | |
| Adam Neylon (R-98) | |
| Nancy VanderMeer (R-70) | |

## Corrections

| Majority Members | Minority Members |
| --- | --- |
| Robert Hutton (R-13) *Chair* | Mandela Barnes (D-11) |
| Janel Brandtjen (R-22) *Vice-Chair* | David Bowen (D-10) |
| Edward "Ed" Brooks (R-50) | Sondy Pope (D-80) |
| Bob Gannon (R-58) | |
| Joel Kleefisch (R-38) | |
| John Nygren (R-89) | |

## Criminal Justice and Public Safety

| Majority Members | Minority Members |
| --- | --- |
| Joel Kleefisch (R-38) *Chair* | Evan Goyke (D-18) |
| Jesse Kremer (R-59) *Vice-Chair* | La Tonya Johnson (D-17) |
| Mark Born (R-39) | Frederick P. "Fred" Kessler (D-12) |
| Cindi Duchow (R-99) | Jocasta "Joey" Zamarripa (D-8) |
| Cody Horlacher (R-33) | |
| Todd Novak (R-51) | |
| Jim Ott (R-23) | |
| Jessie Rodriguez (R-21) | |
| John Spiros (R-86) | |

## Education

| Majority Members | Minority Members |
| --- | --- |
| Jeremy Thiesfeldt (R-52) *Chair* | Mandela Barnes (D-11) |
| Joel Kitchens (R-1) *Vice-Chair* | Dave Considine (D-81) |
| Robert Brooks (R-60) | Eric Genrich (D-90) |
| Cindi Duchow (R-99) | Sondy Pope (D-80) |
| Cody Horlacher (R-33) | Christine Sinicki (D-20) |
| Robert Hutton (R-13) | |
| John Jagler (R-37) | |
| Dean Knudson (R-30) | |
| Dave Murphy (R-56) | |
| Romaine Robert Quinn (R-75) | |
| Jessie Rodriguez (R-21) | |

## Energy and Utilities

| Majority Members | Minority Members |
| --- | --- |
| Mike Kuglitsch (R-84) *Chair* | Eric Genrich (D-90) |
| David Steffen (R-4) *Vice-Chair* | Robb Kahl (D-47) |
| André Jacque (R-2) | Melissa Sargent (D-48) |
| Adam Jarchow (R-28) | Amanda Stuck (D-57) |
| Thomas "Tom" Larson (R-67) | Josh Zepnick (D-9) |
| Adam Neylon (R-98) | |
| Kevin Petersen (R-40) | |
| Warren Petryk (R-93) | |
| Travis Tranel (R-49) | |
| Thomas "Tom" Weatherston (R-62) | |

## Environment and Forestry

| Majority Members | Minority Members |
| --- | --- |
| Jeffrey Mursau (R-36) *Chair* | Dave Considine (D-81) |
| Scott Krug (R-72) *Vice Chair* | Gary Hebl (D-46) |
| Scott Allen (R-97) | Cory Mason (D-66) |
| Robert Brooks (R-60) | Nick Milroy (D-73) |
| Mary Czaja (R-35) | Amanda Stuck (D-57) |
| James Edming (R-87) | |
| Joel Kitchens (R-1) | |
| Rob Swearingen (R-34) | |

## Family Law

| Majority Members | Minority Members |
| --- | --- |
| Thomas "Tom" Larson (R-67) *Chair* | Gary Hebl (D-46) |
| Kathleen M. "Kathy" Bernier (R-68) *Vice Chair* | La Tonya Johnson (D-17) |
| David "Dave" Craig (R-83) | Lisa Subeck (D-78) |
| Joel Kleefisch (R-38) | |
| Jeffrey Mursau (R-36) | |
| Jeremy Thiesfeldt (R-52) | |

## Finance

| Majority Members | Minority Members |
| --- | --- |
| John Nygren (R-89) *Chair* | Gordon Hintz (D-54) |
| Dale Kooyenga (R-14) *Vice Chair* | Chris Taylor (D-76) |
| Mary Czaja (R-35) | |
| Dean Knudson (R-30) | |
| Amy Loudenbeck (R-31) | |
| Michael Schraa (R-53) | |

## Financial Institutions

| Majority Members | Minority Members |
| --- | --- |
| David "Dave" Craig (R-83) *Chair* | Jonathan Brostoff (D-19) |
| Terry Katsma (R-26) *Vice-Chair* | Steve Doyle (D-94) |
| Joan Ballweg (R-41) | Eric Genrich (D-90) |
| Mark Born (R-39) | La Tonya Johnson (D-17) |
| Adam Jarchow (R-28) | Melissa Sargent (D-48) |
| Joel Kitchens (R-1) | Josh Zepnick (D-9) |
| Dave Murphy (R-56) | |
| Kevin Petersen (R-40) | |
| Joe Sanfelippo (R-15) | |
| Thomas "Tom" Weatherston (R-62) | |

## Health

| Majority Members | Minority Members |
| --- | --- |
| Joe Sanfelippo (R-15) *Chair* | Debra Kolste (D-44) |
| Mike Rohrkaste (R-55) *Vice Chair* | Daniel Riemer (D-7) |
| James Edming (R-87) | Lisa Subeck (D-78) |
| Jesse Kremer (R-59) | Jocasta "Joey" Zamarripa (D-8) |
| Kevin Petersen (R-40) | |
| Ken Skowronski (R-82) | |
| Paul Tittl (R-25) | |

## Housing and Real Estate

| Majority Members | Minority Members |
| --- | --- |
| John Jagler (R-37) *Chair* | Eric Genrich (D-90) |
| Scott Allen (R-97) *Vice Chair* | Amanda Stuck (D-57) |
| Robert Brooks (R-60) | Leon D. Young (D-16) |
| Terry Katsma (R-26) | |
| Dave Murphy (R-56) | |
| John Murtha (R-29) | |

## Insurance

| Majority Members | Minority Members |
| --- | --- |
| Kevin Petersen (R-40) *Chair* | Terese E. Berceau (D-77) |
| Paul Tittl (R-25) *Vice Chair* | Chris Danou (D-92) |
| Tyler August (R-32) | Steve Doyle (D-94) |
| Mark Born (R-39) | Robb Kahl (D-47) |
| David "Dave" Craig (R-83) | Leon D. Young (D-16) |
| Bob Gannon (R-58) | |
| John Jagler (R-37) | |
| Warren Petryk (R-93) | |
| David Steffen (R-4) | |
| Travis Tranel (R-49) | |

## Interstate Affairs

| Majority Members | Minority Members |
| --- | --- |
| André Jacque (R-2) *Chair* | Jill Billings (D-95) *Vice Chair* |
| Edward "Ed" Brooks (R-50) | Leon D. Young (D-16) |
| Cody Horlacher (R-33) | Josh Zepnick (D-9) |
| Samantha Kerkman (R-61) | |
| Alvin R. "Al" Ott (R-3) | |
| Mike Rohrkaste (R-55) | |

## Jobs and the Economy

| Majority Members | Minority Members |
|---|---|
| Adam Neylon (R-98) *Chair* | Mandela Barnes (D-11) |
| Scott Krug (R-72) *Vice-Chair* | Tod Ohnstad (D-65) |
| Scott Allen (R-97) | Mark Spreitzer (D-45) |
| Mike Kuglitsch (R-84) | Amanda Stuck (D-57) |
| Frederick Robert "Bob" Kulp (R-69) | Jocasta "Joey" Zamarripa (D-8) |
| John Macco (R-88) | |
| Mike Rohrkaste (R-55) | |
| David Steffen (R-4) | |
| Paul Tittl (R-25) | |

## Judiciary

| Majority Members | Minority Members |
|---|---|
| Jim Ott (R-23) *Chair* | Evan Goyke (D-18) |
| Cody Horlacher (R-33) *Vice Chair* | Gary Hebl (D-46) |
| Dave Heaton (R-85) | Dana J. Wachs (D-91) |
| Samantha Kerkman (R-61) | |
| Thomas "Tom" Larson (R-67) | |
| Jeremy Thiesfeldt (R-52) | |

## Labor

| Majority Members | Minority Members |
|---|---|
| André Jacque (R-2) *Chair* | Cory Mason (D-66) |
| John Spiros (R-86) *Vice-Chair* | Tod Ohnstad (D-65) |
| Daniel "Dan" Knodl (R-24) | Christine Sinicki (D-20) |
| Mike Kuglitsch (R-84) | |
| Frederick Robert "Bob" Kulp (R-69) | |

## Mental Health Reform

| Majority Members | Minority Members |
|---|---|
| Paul Tittl (R-25) *Chair* | Jonathan Brostoff (D-19) |
| John Jagler (R-37) *Vice Chair* | Dave Considine (D-81) |
| Joan Ballweg (R-41) | Daniel Riemer (D-7) |
| Todd Novak (R-51) | Melissa Sargent (D-48) |
| Jessie Rodriguez (R-21) | |
| Mike Rohrkaste (R-55) | |
| Joe Sanfelippo (R-15) | |
| Nancy VanderMeer (R-70) | |

## Mining and Rural Development

| Majority Members | Minority Members |
|---|---|
| Frederick Robert "Bob" Kulp (R-69) *Chair* | Jill Billings (D-95) |
| Jeffrey Mursau (R-36) *Vice Chair* | Dave Considine (D-81) |
| Kathleen M. "Kathy" Bernier (R-68) | Chris Danou (D-92) |
| Edward "Ed" Brooks (R-50) | Nick Milroy (D-73) |
| Jesse Kremer (R-59) | Mark Spreitzer (D-45) |
| Scott Krug (R-72) | |
| Thomas "Tom" Larson (R-67) | |
| Todd Novak (R-51) | |
| Romaine Robert Quinn (R-75) | |
| Nancy VanderMeer (R-70) | |

## Natural Resources and Sporting Heritage

| Majority Members | Minority Members |
|---|---|
| Alvin R. "Al" Ott (R-3) *Chair* | Chris Danou (D-92) |
| Romaine Robert Quinn (R-75) *Vice Chair* | Dianne Hesselbein (D-79) |
| Mark Born (R-39) | Nick Milroy (D-73) |
| James Edming (R-87) | Katrina Shankland (D-71) |
| Joel Kleefisch (R-38) | Mark Spreitzer (D-45) |
| Jeffrey Mursau (R-36) | |
| Lee Nerison (R-96) | |
| Keith Ripp (R-42) | |
| Ken Skowronski (R-82) | |
| Paul Tittl (R-25) | |

## Public Benefit Reform

| Majority Members | Minority Members |
|---|---|
| Mark Born (R-39) *Chair* | Evan Goyke (D-18) |
| Cindi Duchow (R-99) *Vice Chair* | Andy Jorgensen (D-43) |
| Janel Brandtjen (R-22) | Debra Kolste (D-44) |
| David "Dave" Craig (R-83) | Mark Spreitzer (D-45) |
| Jesse Kremer (R-59) | Lisa Subeck (D-78) |
| Scott Krug (R-72) | |
| Adam Neylon (R-98) | |
| Michael Schraa (R-53) | |
| Gary Tauchen (R-6) | |
| Tyler Vorpagel (R-27) | |

## Rules

| Majority Members | Minority Members |
|---|---|
| Jim Steineke (R-5) *Chair* | Peter W. Barca (D-64) |
| Robin Vos (R-63) *Vice Chair* | Terese E. Berceau (D-77) |
| Tyler August (R-32) | Gary Hebl (D-46) |
| Joan Ballweg (R-41) | Andy Jorgensen (D-43) |
| Mark Born (R-39) | Sondy Pope (D-80) |
| John Jagler (R-37) | Katrina Shankland (D-71) |
| Daniel "Dan" Knodl (R-24) | |
| Mike Kuglitsch (R-84) | |
| Rob Swearingen (R-34) | |

## Small Business Development

| Majority Members | Minority Members |
|---|---|
| Gary Tauchen (R-6) *Chair* | Mandela Barnes (D-11) |
| James Edming (R-87) *Vice Chair* | David Bowen (D-10) |
| Scott Allen (R-97) | Steve Doyle (D-94) |
| Bob Gannon (R-58) | Andy Jorgensen (D-43) |
| Robert Hutton (R-13) | Melissa Sargent (D-48) |
| Thomas "Tom" Larson (R-67) | |
| Ken Skowronski (R-82) | |
| Rob Swearingen (R-34) | |
| Travis Tranel (R-49) | |
| Nancy VanderMeer (R-70) | |

## State Affairs and Government Operations

| Majority Members | Minority Members |
|---|---|
| Rob Swearingen (R-34) *Chair* | Jonathan Brostoff (D-19) |
| David "Dave" Craig (R-83) *Vice-Chair* | Robb Kahl (D-47) |
| Janel Brandtjen (R-22) | Tod Ohnstad (D-65) |
| Bob Gannon (R-58) | Christine Sinicki (D-20) |
| John Jagler (R-37) | Jocasta "Joey" Zamarripa (D-8) |
| Joel Kleefisch (R-38) | |
| Frederick Robert "Bob" Kulp (R-69) | |
| Keith Ripp (R-42) | |
| Gary Tauchen (R-6) | |
| Tyler Vorpagel (R-27) | |

## Tourism

| Majority Members | Minority Members |
|---|---|
| Travis Tranel (R-49) *Chair* | Jill Billings (D-95) |
| Adam Jarchow (R-28) *Vice Chair* | Steve Doyle (D-94) |
| Joan Ballweg (R-41) | Cory Mason (D-66) |
| Mark Born (R-39) | Beth M. Meyers (D-74) |
| Joel Kitchens (R-1) | Tod Ohnstad (D-65) |
| Joel Kleefisch (R-38) | |
| Jeffrey Mursau (R-36) | |
| Alvin R. "Al" Ott (R-3) | |
| Rob Swearingen (R-34) | |
| Gary Tauchen (R-6) | |

## Transportation

| Majority Members | Minority Members |
|---|---|
| Keith Ripp (R-42) *Chair* | David Bowen (D-10) |
| John Spiros (R-86) *Vice Chair* | Chris Danou (D-92) |
| Thomas "Tom" Larson (R-67) | Robb Kahl (D-47) |
| John Macco (R-88) | Debra Kolste (D-44) |
| Alvin R. "Al" Ott (R-3) | Beth M. Meyers (D-74) |
| Joe Sanfelippo (R-15) | |
| Rob Swearingen (R-34) | |
| Jeremy Thiesfeldt (R-52) | |
| Tyler Vorpagel (R-27) | |
| Thomas "Tom" Weatherston (R-62) | |

**LEGISLATIVE BRANCH**

## Urban and Local Affairs

| Majority Members | Minority Members |
| --- | --- |
| Edward "Ed" Brooks (R-50) *Chair* | Eric Genrich (D-90) |
| Robert Hutton (R-13) *Vice-Chair* | Lisa Subeck (D-78) |
| Todd Novak (R-51) | Leon D. Young (D-16) |
| Romaine Robert Quinn (R-75) | |
| David Steffen (R-4) | |
| Ken Skowronski (R-82) | |

## Veterans and Military Affairs

| Majority Members | Minority Members |
| --- | --- |
| Ken Skowronski (R-82) *Chair* | Evan Goyke (D-18) |
| Nancy VanderMeer (R-70) *Vice Chair* | Dianne Hesselbein (D-79) |
| Scott Allen (R-97) | Nick Milroy (D-73) |
| James Edming (R-87) | Daniel Riemer (D-7) |
| Dave Heaton (R-85) | Christine Sinicki (D-20) |
| Lee Nerison (R-96) | |
| Jim Ott (R-23) | |
| Warren Petryk (R-93) | |
| Paul Tittl (R-25) | |
| Thomas "Tom" Weatherston (R-62) | |

## Ways and Means

| Majority Members | Minority Members |
| --- | --- |
| John Spiros (R-86) *Chair* | Jonathan Brostoff (D-19) |
| John Macco (R-88) *Vice Chair* | Tod Ohnstad (D-65) |
| Cindi Duchow (R-99) | Daniel Riemer (D-7) |
| André Jacque (R-2) | Josh Zepnick (D-9) |
| Terry Katsma (R-26) | |
| Samantha Kerkman (R-61) | |
| Todd Novak (R-51) | |
| Kevin Petersen (R-40) | |
| David Steffen (R-4) | |

## Workforce Development

| Majority Members | Minority Members |
| --- | --- |
| Warren Petryk (R-93) *Chair* | David Bowen (D-10) |
| Thomas "Tom" Weatherston (R-62) *Vice Chair* | Debra Kolste (D-44) |
| Kathleen M. "Kathy" Bernier (R-68) | Daniel Riemer (D-7) |
| Janel Brandtjen (R-22) | Katrina Shankland (D-71) |
| Terry Katsma (R-26) | Mark Spreitzer (D-45) |
| Joel Kitchens (R-1) | |
| Mike Kuglitsch (R-84) | |
| Frederick Robert "Bob" Kulp (R-69) | |
| Dave Murphy (R-56) | |
| Keith Ripp (R-42) | |

# Wyoming Legislature

State Capitol, Cheyenne, WY 82002 (Mailing)
3001 E. Pershing Boulevard, Cheyenne, WY 82001 (Physical)
Tel: (307) 777-7881  Tel: (307) 777-8683  Tel: (866) 996-8683
Fax: (307) 777-5466  Internet: www.wyoleg.gov

## Wyoming Senate

Tel: (307) 777-7711  Tel: (307) 777-7881 (Legislative Services)

President of the Senate **Philip A. "Phil" Nicholas** (R) .... (307) 632-8957
  Education: Oregon State BS; Wyoming JD
Vice President of the Senate **Drew A. Perkins** (R) ....... (307) 856-0375
  Education: BYU 1980 BS; Southwestern 1983 MS; Wyoming 1992 JD
Majority Floor Leader **Eli Bebout** (R)................(307) 742-7140
  Education: Wyoming 1969 BS
Minority Floor Leader
  **Dr. Christopher J. "Chris" Rothfuss, PhD** (D)........ (307) 777-7711
  Education: Wyoming 1994 BA, 1996 MSChE; U Washington 2002 MS, 2002 PhD
Minority Whip **Bernadine L. Craft** (D)................(307) 382-1607
  Education: Utah BS, MS; Northern Colorado PhD
Minority Caucus Chair **John M. Hastert** (D)...........(307) 777-7881
Chief Clerk of the Senate **Ellen Thompson** ............(307) 777-7881

## Senators

**Party Affiliation Statistics:** Republicans: 26, Democrats: 4

Senator **James Lee "Jim" Anderson** (R-District 28).....(307) 265-4698
  Counties Represented: Natrona (part)
  Term Expires: 2017
  5941 South Cedar Street, Casper, WY 82601
  E-mail: jameslee.anderson@wyoleg.gov
  Committees: Minerals, Business and Economic Development; Travel, Recreation, Wildlife and Cultural Resources
  Education: Casper 1974 AS
Senator **Paul R. Barnard** (R-District 15) ...............(307) 789-9742
  Counties Represented: Uinta (part)          Fax: (307) 789-0077
  Term Expires: 2019
  246 Aspen Hills Court, Evanston, WY 82930
  E-mail: paul.barnard@wyoleg.gov
  Committees: Agriculture, Public Lands and Water Resources; Travel, Recreation, Wildlife and Cultural Resources
  Education: Pacific U 1974 BS, 1974 OD
Senator **Eli Bebout** (R-District 26) ...................(307) 856-0375
  Counties Represented: Fremont (part)
  Term Expires: 2017
  P.O. Box 112, Riverton, WY 82501
  E-mail: eli.bebout@wyoleg.gov
  Committees: Rules and Procedure
Senator **Brian Boner** (R-District 2) ...................(307) 359-0707
  Counties Represented: Converse (part), Platte
  Term Expires: 2017
  1078 Riverbend Drive, Douglas, WY 82633
  E-mail: brian.boner@wyoleg.gov
  Committees: Labor, Health and Social Services; Transportation, Highways and Military Affairs
  Education: Wyoming 2007 BS; Nebraska 2011 MBA
Senator **Bruce Burns** (R-District 21) ..................(307) 672-6491
  Counties Represented: Sheridan (part)       Fax: (307) 672-8808
  Term Expires: 2019
  P.O. Box 6027, Sheridan, WY 82801
  E-mail: bruce.burns@wyoleg.gov
  Committees: Appropriations
  Education: Colorado BA
Senator **Cale Case** (R-District 25) .....................(307) 332-7623
  Counties Represented: Fremont (part)
  Term Expires: 2019
  787 South Fourth Street, Lander, WY 82520
  E-mail: cale.case@wyoleg.gov
  Committees: Corporations, Elections and Political Subdivisions; Revenue
Senator **Leland Christensen** (R-District 17)............(307) 353-8204
  Counties Represented: Teton (part)
  Term Expires: 2019
  E-mail: leland.christensen@wyoleg.gov
  Committees: Agriculture, Public Lands and Water Resources; Judiciary

Senator **Henry H. R. "Hank" Coe** (R-District 18) . . . . . . . (307) 587-4655
  Counties Represented: Park (part)  Fax: (307) 527-6853
  Term Expires: 2017
  P.O. Box 1088, Cody, WY 82414
  E-mail: hank.coe@wyoleg.gov
  Committees: Education; Minerals, Business and Economic
  Development

Senator **Stan Cooper** (R-District 14) . . . . . . . . . . . . . . . . (307) 877-6450
  Counties Represented: Lincoln (part), Sublette (part), Sweetwater (part),
  Uinta (part)
  Term Expires: 2017
  417 Agate Street, Kemmerer, WY 83101
  E-mail: stan.cooper@wyoleg.gov
  Committees: Minerals, Business and Economic Development; Travel,
  Recreation, Wildlife and Cultural Resources
  Education: Utah State 1967 BS

Senator **Bernadine L. Craft** (D-District 12) . . . . . . . . . . . (307) 382-1607
  Counties Represented: Sweetwater (part)
  Term Expires: 2017
  P.O. Box 63, Rock Springs, WY 82902
  E-mail: bernadine.craft@wyoleg.gov
  Committees: Labor, Health and Social Services; Rules and Procedure;
  Travel, Recreation, Wildlife and Cultural Resources

Senator **Dan Dockstader** (R-District 16) . . . . . . . . . . . . . . (307) 886-1500
  Counties Represented: Lincoln (part), Sublette (part), Teton (part)
  Term Expires: 2017
  P.O. Box 129, Afton, WY 83110
  E-mail: dan.dockstader@wyoleg.gov
  Committees: Agriculture, Public Lands and Water Resources; Education
  Education: BYU BA

Senator **Ogden Driskill** (R-District 1) . . . . . . . . . . . . . . . . (307) 777-7881
  Counties Represented: Campbell (part), Crook, Weston (part)
  Term Expires: 2019
  P.O. Box 155, Devils Tower, WY 82714
  E-mail: ogden.driskill@wyoleg.gov
  Committees: Labor, Health and Social Services; Revenue
  Education: Casper 1980 AA

Senator **Fred Emerich** (R-District 5) . . . . . . . . . . . . . . . . . (307) 634-8783
  Counties Represented: Laramie (part)
  Term Expires: 2019
  P.O. Box 903, Cheyenne, WY 82003
  E-mail: fred.emerich@wyoleg.gov
  Committees: Agriculture, Public Lands and Water Resources;
  Transportation, Highways and Military Affairs
  Education: Wyoming 1968 BS; Colorado Col 1973 DVM

Senator **Floyd A. Esquibel** (D-District 8) . . . . . . . . . . . . . (307) 638-6529
  Counties Represented: Laramie (part)  Fax: (307) 632-6518
  Term Expires: 2017
  1222 West 31st Street, Cheyenne, WY 82001
  E-mail: floyd.esquibel@wyoleg.gov
  Committees: Journal; Judiciary; Transportation, Highways and Military
  Affairs
  Education: Wyoming 1966 BA; Denver 1972 MSW, 1975 JD

Senator **Gerald E. Geis** (R-District 20) . . . . . . . . . . . . . . . (307) 347-6443
  Counties Represented: Big Horn (part), Fremont (part), Hot Springs,
  Park (part), Washakie
  Term Expires: 2019
  600 Holly Avenue, Worland, WY 82401
  E-mail: gerald.geis@wyoleg.gov
  Committees: Agriculture, Public Lands and Water Resources

Senator **John M. Hastert** (D-District 13) . . . . . . . . . . . . . . (307) 871-1001
  Counties Represented: Sweetwater (part)
  Term Expires: 2019
  P.O. Box 472, Green River, WY 82935
  E-mail: john.hastert@wyoleg.gov
  Committees: Appropriations

Senator **Larry S. Hicks** (R-District 11) . . . . . . . . . . . . . . . (307) 383-7192
  Counties Represented: Albany (part), Carbon, Sweetwater (part)
  Term Expires: 2019
  P.O. Box 413, Baggs, WY 82321
  E-mail: larry.hicks@wyoleg.gov
  Committees: Corporations, Elections and Political Subdivisions;
  Judiciary
  Education: Wyoming 1983 BS; Montana 1986 MS; Wyoming PhD

Senator **Wayne H. Johnson** (R-District 6) . . . . . . . . . . . . (307) 635-2181
  Counties Represented: Goshen (part), Laramie (part)  Fax: (307) 635-2181
  Term Expires: 2017
  5502 Canyon Road, Cheyenne, WY 82009
  E-mail: wayne.johnson@wyoleg.gov
  Committees: Transportation, Highways and Military Affairs; Travel,
  Recreation, Wildlife and Cultural Resources
  Education: Utah State 1969 BS; Colorado 1970 MPA;
  Oklahoma 1973 MLS

Senator **Dave Kinskey** (R-District 22) . . . . . . . . . . . . . . . . (307) 673-5990
  Counties Represented: Johnson, Sheridan (part)
  Term Expires: 2017
  1 East Alger, #201, Sheridan, WY 82801
  E-mail: dave.kinskey@wyoleg.gov
  Committees: Judiciary; Revenue
  Education: Harvard 1979 BA; Wyoming 1982 JD

Senator **William R. "Bill" Landen** (R-District 27) . . . . . . . (307) 777-7711
  Counties Represented: Natrona (part)  Res: (307) 237-4067
  Term Expires: 2019
  2010 Kingsbury Avenue, Casper, WY 82609
  E-mail: bill.landen@wyoleg.gov
  Committees: Revenue
  Education: Casper AA; Wyoming 1978 BSJ, 1994 MPA

Senator **Curt Meier** (R-District 3) . . . . . . . . . . . . . . . . . . . . (307) 834-2344
  Counties Represented: Goshen (part), Niobrara, Weston (part)
  Term Expires: 2019
  4799 CR 18, LaGrange, WY 82221
  E-mail: curt.meier@wyoleg.gov
  Committees: Corporations, Elections and Political Subdivisions;
  Transportation, Highways and Military Affairs
  Education: Wyoming BS

Senator **Philip A. "Phil" Nicholas** (R-District 10) . . . . . . . (307) 742-7140
  Counties Represented: Albany (part)
  Term Expires: 2017
  P.O. Box 928, Laramie, WY 82073-0928
  E-mail: phil.nicholas@wyoleg.gov
  Committees: Rules and Procedure

Senator
  **Col Stephan A. Pappas, ARNG (Ret)** (R-District 7) . . . . (307) 637-5227
  Counties Represented: Laramie (part)
  Term Expires: 2019
  2617 E. Lincolnway, Suite A, Cheyenne, WY 82001
  E-mail: stephan.pappas@wyoleg.gov
  Committees: Corporations, Elections and Political Subdivisions;
  Education

Senator **Drew A. Perkins** (R-District 29) . . . . . . . . . . . . . . (307) 234-1274
  Counties Represented: Natrona (part)
  Term Expires: 2019
  1133 Granada Avenue, Casper, WY 82601
  E-mail: drew.perkins@wyoleg.gov
  Committees: Appropriations; Rules and Procedure

Senator **R. Ray Peterson** (R-District 19) . . . . . . . . . . . . . . (307) 548-6405
  Counties Represented: Big Horn (part), Park (part)  Fax: (307) 548-7470
  Term Expires: 2019
  P.O. Box 193, Cowley, WY 82420
  E-mail: ray.peterson@wyoleg.gov
  Committees: Labor, Health and Social Services; Revenue
  Education: BYU

Senator **Tony Ross** (R-District 4) . . . . . . . . . . . . . . . . . . . . (307) 632-8957
  Counties Represented: Laramie (part)  Fax: (307) 632-8960
  Term Expires: 2017
  2402 Pioneer Avenue, Cheyenne, WY 82001
  E-mail: tony.ross@wyoleg.gov
  Committees: Appropriations
  Education: U Puget Sound BS; Wyoming JD

Senator **Dr. Christopher J. "Chris" Rothfuss, PhD**
  (D-District 9) . . . . . . . . . . . . . . . . . . . . . . . . . . . . . . . . . . . (307) 777-7711
  Counties Represented: Albany (part)
  Term Expires: 2019
  E-mail: chris.rothfuss@wyoleg.gov
  Committees: Education; Minerals, Business and Economic
  Development; Rules and Procedure

Senator **Charles K. Scott** (R-District 30) . . . . . . . . . . . . . . (307) 473-2512
  Counties Represented: Natrona (part)
  Term Expires: 2017
  13900 State Highway 487, Casper, WY 82604
  E-mail: charles.scott@wyoleg.gov
  Committees: Corporations, Elections and Political Subdivisions; Labor,
  Health and Social Services
  Education: Harvard 1967 BA, 1969 MBA

Senator **Michael Von Flatern** (R-District 24) . . . . . . . . . . . (307) 686-2946
  Counties Represented: Campbell (part)
  Term Expires: 2017
  1318 Columbine Drive, Gillette, WY 82718
  E-mail: michael.vonflatern@wyoleg.gov
  Committees: Judiciary; Minerals, Business and Economic Development

*(continued on next page)*

LEGISLATIVE BRANCH

**Senators** *continued*

Senator **Jeff Wasserburger** (R-District 23) . . . . . . . . . . . . (307) 687-4534
Counties Represented: Campbell (part), Converse     Res: (307) 682-0936
(part)
Term Expires: 2019
4300 Longhorn Avenue, Gillette, WY 82718
E-mail: jeff.wasserburger@wyoleg.gov
Committees: Appropriations; Journal
Education: Chadron State BS; Wyoming MS

## Senate Standing Committees

### Agriculture, Public Lands and Water Resources

**Majority Members**
Gerald E. Geis (R-20) *Chairman*
Paul R. Barnard (R-15)
Leland Christensen (R-17)
Dan Dockstader (R-16)
Fred Emerich (R-5)

### Appropriations

**Majority Members**
Tony Ross (R-4) *Chairman*
Bruce Burns (R-21)
Drew A. Perkins (R-29)
Jeff Wasserburger (R-23)

**Minority Members**
John M. Hastert (D-13)

### Corporations, Elections and Political Subdivisions

**Majority Members**
Cale Case (R-25) *Chairman*
Larry S. Hicks (R-11)
Curt Meier (R-3)
Col Stephan A. Pappas (R-7)
Charles K. Scott (R-30)

### Education

**Majority Members**
Henry H. R. "Hank" Coe (R-18)
*Chairman*
Dan Dockstader (R-16)
Col Stephan A. Pappas (R-7)

**Minority Members**
Dr. Christopher J. "Chris" Rothfuss
(D-9)

### Journal

**Majority Members**
Jeff Wasserburger (R-23) *Chairman*

**Minority Members**
Floyd A. Esquibel (D-8)

### Judiciary

**Majority Members**
Leland Christensen (R-17)
*Chairman*
Larry S. Hicks (R-11)
Dave Kinskey (R-22)
Michael Von Flatern (R-24)

**Minority Members**
Floyd A. Esquibel (D-8)

### Labor, Health and Social Services

**Majority Members**
Charles K. Scott (R-30) *Chairman*
Brian Boner (R-2)
Ogden Driskill (R-1)
R. Ray Peterson (R-19)

**Minority Members**
Bernadine L. Craft (D-12)

### Minerals, Business and Economic Development

**Majority Members**
Michael Von Flatern (R-24)
*Chairman*
James Lee "Jim" Anderson (R-28)
Henry H. R. "Hank" Coe (R-18)
Stan Cooper (R-14)

**Minority Members**
Dr. Christopher J. "Chris" Rothfuss
(D-9)

### Revenue

**Majority Members**
R. Ray Peterson (R-19) *Chairman*
Cale Case (R-25)
Ogden Driskill (R-1)
Dave Kinskey (R-22)
William R. "Bill" Landen (R-27)

### Rules and Procedure

**Majority Members**
Philip A. "Phil" Nicholas (R-10)
*Chairman*
Eli Bebout (R-26)
Drew A. Perkins (R-29)

**Minority Members**
Bernadine L. Craft (D-12)
Dr. Christopher J. "Chris" Rothfuss
(D-9)

### Transportation, Highways and Military Affairs

**Majority Members**
Curt Meier (R-3) *Chairman*
Brian Boner (R-2)
Fred Emerich (R-5)
Wayne H. Johnson (R-6)

**Minority Members**
Floyd A. Esquibel (D-8)

### Travel, Recreation, Wildlife and Cultural Resources

**Majority Members**
Stan Cooper (R-14) *Chairman*
James Lee "Jim" Anderson (R-28)
Paul R. Barnard (R-15)
Wayne H. Johnson (R-6)

**Minority Members**
Bernadine L. Craft (D-12)

## Wyoming House of Representatives

Tel: (307) 777-7852  Fax: (307) 777-5466

Speaker of the House **Kermit Brown** (R) . . . . . . . . . . . . . . (307) 745-7358
Education: Wyoming BS, JD
Speaker Pro Tem **Tim Stubson** (R) . . . . . . . . . . . . . . . . . . . (307) 777-5520
Education: Wyoming 1993 BA, 1997 JD
Majority Floor Leader **Rosie Berger** (R) . . . . . . . . . . . . . . (307) 745-7358
Education: Regis U 1996 BSBA
Majority Whip **Hans Hunt** (R) . . . . . . . . . . . . . . . . . . . . . . (307) 265-2279
Minority Floor Leader **Mary A. Throne** (D) . . . . . . . . . . . . (307) 630-6728
Education: Princeton 1982 BA; Columbia 1988 JD
Minority Whip **Ken A. Esquibel** (D) . . . . . . . . . . . . . . . . . (307) 200-0859
Minority Caucus Chairman **James W. "Jim" Byrd** (D) . . . (307) 745-9251
Chief Clerk of the House **Patricia Benskin** . . . . . . . . . . . . (307) 777-7852

## Representatives

**Party Affiliation Statistics:** Republicans: 51, Democrats: 9

Representative **Jim Allen** (R-District 33) . . . . . . . . . . . . . . (307) 349-6784
Counties Represented: Fremont (part)
Term Expires: 2017
P.O. Box 243, Lander, WY 82520
E-mail: jim.allen@wyoleg.gov
Committees: Agriculture, Public Lands and Water Resources;
Transportation, Highways and Military Affairs
Representative **Mark Baker** (R-District 48) . . . . . . . . . . . . (307) 777-7852
Counties Represented: Sweetwater (part)
Term Expires: 2017
P.O. Box 3266, Rock Springs, WY 82902
E-mail: mark.baker@wyoleg.gov
Committees: Judiciary
Representative **Fred A. Baldwin** (R-District 18) . . . . . . . . (307) 877-3687
Counties Represented: Lincoln (part), Sweetwater (part), Uinta (part)
Term Expires: 2017
P.O. Box 1032, Kemmerer, WY 83101
E-mail: fred.baldwin@wyoleg.gov
Committees: Labor, Health and Social Services; Travel, Recreation,
Wildlife and Cultural Resources
Representative **Eric Barlow** (R-District 3) . . . . . . . . . . . . . (307) 777-7852
Counties Represented: Campbell (part), Converse (part)
Term Expires: 2017
P.O. Box 774, Green River, WY 82935
E-mail: eric.barlow@wyoleg.gov
Committees: Labor, Health and Social Services; Travel, Recreation,
Wildlife and Cultural Resources
Education: Colorado State 1998 DVM

Representative **Rosie Berger** (R-District 51)............(307) 777-5520
  Counties Represented: Sheridan (part)     Res: (307) 672-7600
  Term Expires: 2017
  P.O. Box 275, Big Horn, WY 82833
  E-mail: rosie.berger@wyoleg.gov
  Committees: Rules and Procedure

Representative
**Theodore "Jim" Blackburn** (R-District 42)..........(307) 514-4318
  Counties Represented: Laramie (part)
  Term Expires: 2017
  E-mail: jim.blackburn@wyoleg.gov
  Committees: Corporations, Elections and Political Subdivisions;
  Revenue

Representative **Stan Blake** (D-District 39)..............(307) 875-3779
  Counties Represented: Sweetwater (part)
  Term Expires: 2017
  P.O. Box 774, Green River, WY 82935
  E-mail: stan.blake@wyoleg.gov
  Committees: Agriculture, Public Lands and Water Resources;
  Transportation, Highways and Military Affairs

Representative **Kermit Brown** (R-District 14)..........(307) 745-7358
  Counties Represented: Albany (part)     Fax: (307) 745-7385
  Term Expires: 2017
  P.O. Box 817, Laramie, WY 82073
  E-mail: kermit.brown@wyoleg.gov
  Committees: Rules and Procedure

Representative
**Donald E. "Don" Burkhart, Jr.** (R-District 15).........(307) 324-6007
  Counties Represented: Carbon (part)
  Term Expires: 2017
  P.O. Box 852, Rawlins, WY 82301
  E-mail: donald.burkhart@wyoleg.gov
  Committees: Appropriations
  Education: John Carroll 1970 BS

Representative **James W. "Jim" Byrd** (D-District 44)....(307) 200-0859
  Counties Represented: Laramie (part)     Res: (307) 634-1746
  Term Expires: 2017
  2511 Snyder Avenue, Cheyenne, WY 82001
  E-mail: james.byrd@wyoleg.gov
  Committees: Corporations, Elections and Political Subdivisions;
  Minerals, Business and Economic Development

Representative **Rita Campbell** (R-District 34)...........(307) 856-4725
  Counties Represented: Fremont (part)
  Term Expires: 2017
  4 Riggs Road, Shoshoni, WY 82649
  E-mail: rita.campbell@wyoleg.gov
  Committees: Agriculture, Public Lands and Water Resources;
  Transportation, Highways and Military Affairs

Representative **Richard Cannady** (R-District 6).........(307) 436-5355
  Counties Represented: Converse (part)     Res: (307) 436-9794
  Term Expires: 2017
  P.O. Box 1597, Glenrock, WY 82637
  E-mail: richard.cannady@wyoleg.gov
  Committees: Minerals, Business and Economic Development;
  Transportation, Highways and Military Affairs

Representative **Scott Clem** (R-District 31)..............(307) 660-7141
  Counties Represented: Campbell (part)
  Term Expires: 2017
  1802 Limecreek Avenue, Gillette, WY 82716
  E-mail: scott.clem@wyoleg.gov
  Committees: Travel, Recreation, Wildlife and Cultural Resources

Representative **Cathy Connolly, JD** (D-District 13)......(307) 745-9251
  Counties Represented: Albany (part)
  Term Expires: 2017
  1321 Garfield, Laramie, WY 82070
  E-mail: cathy.connolly@wyoleg.gov
  Committees: Appropriations; Rules and Procedure
  Education: SUNY (Buffalo) 1991 JD, 1992 PhD

Representative **JoAnn Dayton** (D-District 17)...........(307) 382-5623
  Counties Represented: Sweetwater (part)
  Term Expires: 2017
  738 D Street, Rock Springs, WY 82901
  E-mail: joann.dayton@wyoleg.gov
  Committees: Labor, Health and Social Services; Revenue

Representative **Harlan Edmonds** (R-District 12).........(307) 214-8125
  Counties Represented: Laramie (part)
  Term Expires: 2017
  P.O. Box 2904, Cheyenne, WY 82003
  E-mail: harlan.edmonds@wyoleg.gov
  Committees: Labor, Health and Social Services; Minerals, Business and
  Economic Development

Representative **Roy Edwards** (R-District 53)............(307) 682-4131
  Counties Represented: Campbell (part)
  Term Expires: 2017
  205 East Sunset Drive, Gillette, WY 82716
  E-mail: roy.edwards@wyoleg.gov
  Committees: Revenue

Representative **John Eklund, Jr.** (R-District 10).........(307) 246-3251
  Counties Represented: Goshen (part), Laramie (part)
  Term Expires: 2017
  2918 Torrington Highway, Cheyenne, WY 82009
  E-mail: john.eklund@wyoleg.gov
  Committees: Agriculture, Public Lands and Water Resources;
  Transportation, Highways and Military Affairs
  Education: Wyoming 1974 BS

Representative **Ken A. Esquibel** (D-District 41).........(307) 630-6096
  Counties Represented: Laramie (part)
  Term Expires: 2017
  3121 Spruce Court, Cheyenne, WY 82001
  E-mail: ken.esquibel@wyoleg.gov
  Committees: Judiciary

Representative **John L. Freeman** (D-District 60).........(307) 875-7378
  Counties Represented: Sweetwater (part)
  Term Expires: 2017
  2340 North Carolina Way, Green River, WY 82935
  E-mail: john.freeman@wyoleg.gov
  Committees: Education; Travel, Recreation, Wildlife and Cultural
  Resources
  Education: Wyoming 1978 BA

Representative **Gerald S. Gay** (R-District 36)...........(307) 265-5187
  Counties Represented: Natrona (part)
  Term Expires: 2017
  364 South Socony Place, Casper, WY 82609
  E-mail: gerald.gay@wyoleg.gov
  Committees: Corporations, Elections and Political Subdivisions;
  Minerals, Business and Economic Development; Travel, Recreation,
  Wildlife and Cultural Resources
  Education: Casper 1977 AS; Wyoming 1980 BSChE

Representative
**Michael D. "Mike" Greear** (R-District 27)...........(307) 347-9801
  Counties Represented: Big Horn (part), Washakie   Tel: (307) 388-3399
  Term Expires: 2017     Fax: (307) 347-2859
  P.O. Box 542, Worland, WY 82401
  E-mail: mike.greear@wyoleg.gov
  Committees: Appropriations; Rules and Procedure
  Education: Wyoming 1991 BS, 1994 JD

Representative **Marti Halverson** (R-District 22).........(307) 777-7852
  Counties Represented: Lincoln (part), Sublette (part), Teton (part)
  Term Expires: 2017
  P.O. Box 5009, Etna, WY 83118
  E-mail: marti.halverson@wyoleg.gov
  Committees: Judiciary

Representative **Steve Harshman** (R-District 37).........(307) 777-5520
  Counties Represented: Natrona (part)     Res: (307) 262-8075
  Term Expires: 2017
  P.O. Box 40136, Casper, WY 82604
  E-mail: steve.harshman@wyoleg.gov
  Committees: Appropriations
  Education: Black Hills State BSEd; Oregon State MSE

Representative **Elaine Harvey** (R-District 26)............(307) 777-5520
  Counties Represented: Big Horn (part), Park (part)  Res: (307) 548-7866
  Term Expires: 2017
  792 Garfield Avenue, Lovell, WY 82431
  E-mail: elaine.harvey@wyoleg.gov
  Committees: Labor, Health and Social Services

Representative **Hans Hunt** (R-District 2)..............(307) 746-4063
  Counties Represented: Goshen (part), Niobrara, Weston (part)
  Term Expires: 2017
  1347 Old Highway 85, Newcastle, WY 82701
  E-mail: hans.hunt@wyoleg.gov
  Committees: Agriculture, Public Lands and Water Resources;
  Education; Rules and Procedure

Representative **Allen Jaggi** (R-District 19).............(307) 786-2817
  Counties Represented: Uinta (part)
  Term Expires: 2017
  P.O. Box 326, Lyman, WY 82937
  E-mail: allen.jaggi@wyoleg.gov
  Committees: Agriculture, Public Lands and Water Resources
  Education: Utah State 1968 BA

*(continued on next page)*

**LEGISLATIVE BRANCH**

**LEGISLATIVE BRANCH**

**Representatives** *continued*

Representative **Mark Jennings** (R-District 30) . . . . . . . . . . (307) 461-0697
Counties Represented: Sheridan (part)
Term Expires: 2017
765 West Timberline Drive, Sheridan, WY 82801
E-mail: mark.jennings@wyoleg.gov
Committees: Corporations, Elections and Political Subdivisions;
Revenue

Representative **Norine A. Kasperik** (R-District 32) . . . . . . . (307) 257-7875
Counties Represented: Campbell (part)
Term Expires: 2017
664 Par Drive, Gillette, WY 82718
E-mail: norine.kasperik@wyoleg.gov
Committees: Labor, Health and Social Services; Minerals, Business and
Economic Development
Education: Regis U 1992 BS; Mary Hardin-Baylor 2007 BS

Representative **Mark Kinner** (R-District 29) . . . . . . . . . . . . (307) 674-4777
Counties Represented: Sheridan (part)
Term Expires: 2017
456 Sumner Street, Sheridan, WY 82801
E-mail: mark.kinner@wyoleg.gov
Committees: Education; Revenue

Representative **Dan R. Kirkbride** (R-District 4) . . . . . . . . . (307) 777-7852
Counties Represented: Converse (part), Platte
Term Expires: 2017
P.O. Box 37, Chugwater, WY 82210
E-mail: dan.kirkbride@wyoleg.gov
Committees: Corporations, Elections and Political Subdivisions; Travel,
Recreation, Wildlife and Cultural Resources
Education: Wyoming 1975 BSJ

Representative **Kendell Kroeker** (R-District 35) . . . . . . . . . (307) 777-7881
Counties Represented: Natrona (part)
Term Expires: 2017
P.O. Box 354, Evansville, WY 82636
E-mail: kendell.kroeker@wyoleg.gov
Committees: Judiciary
Education: Colorado 1995 BSBA

Representative **Samuel P. "Sam" Krone** (R-District 24) . . . (307) 587-4530
Counties Represented: Park (part)
Term Expires: 2017
P.O. Box 2481, Cody, WY 82414
E-mail: samuel.krone@wyoleg.gov
Committees: Judiciary
Education: Wyoming 1998 BS, 2001 JD

Representative **Lloyd Charles Larsen** (R-District 54) . . . . . (307) 332-4617
Counties Represented: Fremont (part)
Term Expires: 2017
1076 South 2nd Street, Lander, WY 82520
E-mail: lloyd.larsen@wyoleg.gov
Committees: Labor, Health and Social Services; Minerals, Business and
Economic Development

Representative **Dan Laursen** (R-District 25) . . . . . . . . . . . . (307) 754-9805
Counties Represented: Park (part)
Term Expires: 2017
478 Road 8, Powell, WY 82435
E-mail: dan.laursen@wyoleg.gov
Committees: Agriculture, Public Lands and Water Resources; Rules and
Procedure; Travel, Recreation, Wildlife and Cultural Resources

Representative **Tyler Lindholm** (R-District 1) . . . . . . . . . . . (307) 283-1891
Counties Represented: Crook, Weston (part)
Term Expires: 2017
P.O. Box 691, Sundance, WY 82729
E-mail: tyler.lindholm@wyoleg.gov
Committees: Agriculture, Public Lands and Water Resources;
Corporations, Elections and Political Subdivisions

Representative
**Thomas A. "Tom" Lockhart** (R-District 57) . . . . . . . . . (307) 472-4116
Counties Represented: Natrona (part)          Fax: (307) 237-2441
Term Expires: 2017
770 East 12th, Casper, WY 82601
E-mail: tom.lockhart@wyoleg.gov
Committees: Minerals, Business and Economic Development
Education: Wyoming BSEE; Portland State MBA

Representative **Carl R. "Bunky" Loucks** (R-District 59) . . . (307) 237-6804
Counties Represented: Natrona (part)          Fax: (307) 472-7368
Term Expires: 2017
1555 West Coffman Avenue, Casper, WY 82604
E-mail: bunky.loucks@wyoleg.gov
Committees: Revenue; Transportation, Highways and Military Affairs

Representative
**Michael K. "Mike" Madden** (R-District 40) . . . . . . . . . . (307) 684-9356
Counties Represented: Johnson, Sheridan (part)
Term Expires: 2017
63 Langdon Road, Buffalo, WY 82935
E-mail: mike.madden@wyoleg.gov
Committees: Revenue; Rules and Procedure
Education: South Dakota State BS; Iowa State PhD

Representative **Robert McKim** (R-District 21) . . . . . . . . . . (307) 885-3733
Counties Represented: Lincoln (part)
Term Expires: 2017
10964 Highway 238, Afton, WY 83110-9746
E-mail: robert.mckim@wyoleg.gov
Committees: Agriculture, Public Lands and Water Resources
Education: BYU 1971 BS

Representative **David R. Miller** (R-District 55) . . . . . . . . . . (307) 857-5789
Counties Represented: Fremont (part)          Fax: (307) 857-2833
Term Expires: 2017
2420 Watt Court, Riverton, WY 82501
E-mail: david.miller@wyoleg.gov
Committees: Judiciary

Representative **Glenn Moniz** (R-District 46) . . . . . . . . . . . (307) 745-4711
Counties Represented: Albany (part)
Term Expires: 2017
P.O. Box 784, Laramie, WY 82073
E-mail: glenn.moniz@wyoleg.gov
Committees: Appropriations; Rules and Procedure

Representative **Bob Nicholas** (R-District 8) . . . . . . . . . . . . (307) 634-2994
Counties Represented: Laramie (part)          Fax: (307) 635-7155
Term Expires: 2017
6225 Mountainview Drive, Cheyenne, WY 82009
E-mail: bob.nicholas@wyoleg.gov
Committees: Appropriations
Education: Wyoming 1982 BA, 1985 JD

Representative **David Northrup** (R-District 50) . . . . . . . . . (307) 777-7852
Counties Represented: Park (part)
Term Expires: 2017
799 Lane 13, Powell, WY 82435
E-mail: david.northrup@wyoleg.gov
Committees: Education; Rules and Procedure

Representative **Jerry D. Paxton** (R-District 47) . . . . . . . . . (307) 777-7852
Counties Represented: Albany (part), Carbon (part),     Res: (307) 327-5373
Sweetwater (part)
Term Expires: 2017
P.O. Box 692, Encampment, WY 82325
E-mail: jerry.paxton@wyoleg.gov
Committees: Corporations, Elections and Political Subdivisions;
Education
Education: Wyoming 1984 MS

Representative **Charles F. Pelkey** (D-District 45) . . . . . . . . (307) 920-0542
Counties Represented: Albany (part)
Term Expires: 2017
311 South Fourth Street, Laramie, WY 82070
E-mail: charles.pelkey@wyoleg.gov
Committees: Judiciary

Representative **Ruth Ann Petroff** (R-District 16) . . . . . . . . (307) 734-9446
Counties Represented: Teton (part)            Fax: (307) 734-9476
Term Expires: 2017
P.O. Box 2764, Jackson, WY 83001
E-mail: ruth.petroff@wyoleg.gov
Committees: Rules and Procedure; Travel, Recreation, Wildlife and
Cultural Resources

Representative **Garry C. Piiparinen** (R-District 49) . . . . . . . (307) 777-7852
Counties Represented: Uinta (part)
Term Expires: 2017
112 Freedom Drive, Evansville, WY 82930
E-mail: garry.piiparinen@wyoleg.gov
Committees: Education

Representative **William "Bill" Pownall** (R-District 52) . . . . (307) 777-7852
Counties Represented: Campbell (part)
Term Expires: 2017
P.O. Box 273, Gillette, WY 82717
E-mail: bill.pownall@wyoleg.gov
Committees: Judiciary

Representative **Tom Reeder** (R-District 58) . . . . . . . . . . . . (307) 235-0404
Counties Represented: Natrona (part)
Term Expires: 2017
P.O. Box 40046, Casper, WY 82604
E-mail: tom.reeder@wyoleg.gov
Committees: Revenue; Transportation, Highways and Military Affairs

Representative **Andy Schwartz** (D-District 23) . . . . . . . . . (307) 413-6464
  Counties Represented: Teton (part)
  Term Expires: 2017
  P.O. Box 2654, Jackson, WY 83001
  E-mail: andy.schwartz@wyoleg.gov
  Committees: Journal; Labor, Health and Social Services; Travel,
  Recreation, Wildlife and Cultural Resources
Representative **Albert Sommers** (R-District 20) . . . . . . . . (307) 777-7852
  Counties Represented: Sublette (part)
  Term Expires: 2017
  P.O. Box 1608, Pinedale, WY 82941
  E-mail: albert.sommers@wyoleg.gov
  Committees: Education; Minerals, Business and Economic
  Development
  Education: Wyoming 1981 BS
Representative **Cheri E. Steinmetz** (R-District 5) . . . . . . . (307) 837-3006
  Counties Represented: Goshen (part)
  Term Expires: 2017
  P.O. Box 101, Lingle, WY 82223
  E-mail: cheri.steinmetz@wyoleg.gov
  Committees: Journal; Travel, Recreation, Wildlife and Cultural
  Resources
Representative **Tim Stubson** (R-District 56) . . . . . . . . . . . (307) 265-2279
  Counties Represented: Natrona (part)
  Term Expires: 2017
  1645 S. Chestnut, Casper, WY 82601
  E-mail: tim.stubson@wyoleg.gov
  Committees: Appropriations; Rules and Procedure
Representative **Mary A. Throne** (D-District 11) . . . . . . . . . (307) 630-6728
  Counties Represented: Laramie (part)
  Term Expires: 2017
  P.O. Box 828, Cheyenne, WY 82003
  E-mail: mary.throne@wyoleg.gov
  Committees: Education; Rules and Procedure
Representative **Tom Walters** (R-District 38) . . . . . . . . . . . . (307) 777-7852
  Counties Represented: Natrona (part)
  Term Expires: 2017
  14700 Highway 220, Casper, WY 82604
  E-mail: tom.walters@wyoleg.gov
  Committees: Minerals, Business and Economic Development; Rules
  and Procedure; Transportation, Highways and Military Affairs
  Education: Wyoming 1998
Representative **Sue Wilson** (R-District 7) . . . . . . . . . . . . . . (307) 777-7852
  Counties Represented: Laramie (part)
  Term Expires: 2017
  P.O. Box 21035, Cheyenne, WY 82003
  E-mail: sue.wilson@wyoleg.gov
  Committees: Labor, Health and Social Services; Revenue
Representative **Nathan Winters** (R-District 28) . . . . . . . . . (307) 777-7852
  Counties Represented: Big Horn (part), Fremont (part), Hot Springs,
  Park (part)
  Term Expires: 2017
  106 Mountain View, Thermopolis, WY 82443
  E-mail: nathan.winters@wyoleg.gov
  Committees: Judiciary
Representative **Dan Zwonitzer** (R-District 43) . . . . . . . . . . . (307) 214-7826
  Counties Represented: Laramie (part)
  Term Expires: 2017
  521 Cottonwood, Cheyenne, WY 82001
  E-mail: dan.zwonitzer@wyoleg.gov
  Committees: Corporations, Elections and Political Subdivisions
Representative
  **David L. "Dave" Zwonitzer** (R-District 9) . . . . . . . . . . . (307) 630-1955
  Counties Represented: Laramie (part)
  Term Expires: 2017
  4204 Del Range Boulevard, Cheyenne, WY 82009
  E-mail: david.zwonitzer@wyoleg.gov
  Committees: Transportation, Highways and Military Affairs

## House Standing Committees
### Agriculture, Public Lands and Water Resources

| Majority Members | Minority Members |
| --- | --- |
| Robert McKim (R-21) *Chair* | Stan Blake (D-39) |
| Jim Allen (R-33) | |
| Rita Campbell (R-34) | |
| John Eklund, Jr. (R-10) | |
| Hans Hunt (R-2) | |
| Allen Jaggi (R-19) | |
| Dan Laursen (R-25) | |
| Tyler Lindholm (R-1) | |

## Appropriations

| Majority Members | Minority Members |
| --- | --- |
| Steve Harshman (R-37) *Chair* | Cathy Connolly (D-13) |
| Donald E. "Don" Burkhart, Jr. (R-15) | |
| Michael D. "Mike" Greear (R-27) | |
| Glenn Moniz (R-46) | |
| Bob Nicholas (R-8) | |
| Tim Stubson (R-56) | |

## Corporations, Elections and Political Subdivisions

| Majority Members | Minority Members |
| --- | --- |
| Dan Zwonitzer (R-43) *Chair* | James W. "Jim" Byrd (D-44) |
| Theodore "Jim" Blackburn (R-42) | |
| Gerald S. Gay (R-36) | |
| Mark Jennings (R-30) | |
| Dan R. Kirkbride (R-4) | |
| Tyler Lindholm (R-1) | |
| Jerry D. Paxton (R-47) | |

## Education

| Majority Members | Minority Members |
| --- | --- |
| David Northrup (R-50) *Chair* | John L. Freeman (D-60) |
| Hans Hunt (R-2) | Mary A. Throne (D-11) |
| Mark Kinner (R-29) | |
| Jerry D. Paxton (R-47) | |
| Garry C. Piiparinen (R-49) | |
| Albert Sommers (R-20) | |

## Journal

| Majority Members | Minority Members |
| --- | --- |
| Cheri E. Steinmetz (R-5) *Chair* | Andy Schwartz (D-23) |

## Judiciary

| Majority Members | Minority Members |
| --- | --- |
| David R. Miller (R-55) *Chair* | Ken A. Esquibel (D-41) |
| Mark Baker (R-48) | Charles F. Pelkey (D-45) |
| Marti Halverson (R-22) | |
| Kendell Kroeker (R-35) | |
| Samuel P. "Sam" Krone (R-24) | |
| William "Bill" Pownall (R-52) | |
| Nathan Winters (R-28) | |

## Labor, Health and Social Services

| Majority Members | Minority Members |
| --- | --- |
| Elaine Harvey (R-26) *Chair* | JoAnn Dayton (D-17) |
| Fred A. Baldwin (R-18) | Andy Schwartz (D-23) |
| Eric Barlow (R-3) | |
| Harlan Edmonds (R-12) | |
| Norine A. Kasperik (R-32) | |
| Lloyd Charles Larsen (R-54) | |
| Sue Wilson (R-7) | |

## Minerals, Business and Economic Development

| Majority Members | Minority Members |
| --- | --- |
| Thomas A. "Tom" Lockhart (R-57) *Chair* | James W. "Jim" Byrd (D-44) |
| Richard Cannady (R-6) | |
| Harlan Edmonds (R-12) | |
| Gerald S. Gay (R-36) | |
| Norine A. Kasperik (R-32) | |
| Lloyd Charles Larsen (R-54) | |
| Albert Sommers (R-20) | |
| Tom Walters (R-38) | |

**LEGISLATIVE BRANCH**

## Revenue

**Majority Members**
Michael K. "Mike" Madden (R-40)
   *Chair*
Theodore "Jim" Blackburn (R-42)
Roy Edwards (R-53)
Mark Jennings (R-30)
Mark Kinner (R-29)
Carl R. "Bunky" Loucks (R-59)
Tom Reeder (R-58)
Sue Wilson (R-7)

**Minority Members**
JoAnn Dayton (D-17)

## Rules and Procedure

**Majority Members**
Kermit Brown (R-14) *Chair*
Rosie Berger (R-51)
Michael D. "Mike" Greear (R-27)
Hans Hunt (R-2)
Dan Laursen (R-25)
Michael K. "Mike" Madden (R-40)
Glenn Moniz (R-46)
David Northrup (R-50)
Ruth Ann Petroff (R-16)
Tim Stubson (R-56)
Tom Walters (R-38)

**Minority Members**
Cathy Connolly (D-13)
Mary A. Throne (D-11)

## Transportation, Highways and Military Affairs

**Majority Members**
David L. "Dave" Zwonitzer (R-9)
   *Chair*
Jim Allen (R-33)
Rita Campbell (R-34)
Richard Cannady (R-6)
John Eklund, Jr. (R-10)
Carl R. "Bunky" Loucks (R-59)
Tom Reeder (R-58)
Tom Walters (R-38)

**Minority Members**
Stan Blake (D-39)

## Travel, Recreation, Wildlife and Cultural Resources

**Majority Members**
Ruth Ann Petroff (R-16) *Chair*
Fred A. Baldwin (R-18)
Eric Barlow (R-3)
Scott Clem (R-31)
Gerald S. Gay (R-36)
Dan R. Kirkbride (R-4)
Dan Laursen (R-25)
Cheri E. Steinmetz (R-5)

**Minority Members**
John L. Freeman (D-60)
Andy Schwartz (D-23)

# Indexes

# Subject Index

This index lists all organizations by subject.

**SUBJECT INDEX**

**SUBJECT INDEX**

SUBJECT INDEX

SUBJECT INDEX

SUBJECT INDEX

## Environment *continued*

Environmental Protection Bureau (RI), 416
Environmental Protection Division (GA), 115
Environmental Quality (CA), 584
Environmental Quality (LA), 736
Environmental Quality Board (PR), 412
Environmental Quality Board (WV), 516
Environmental Quality Commission (KY), 185
Environmental Quality Control (SC), 423
Environmental Quality Department (VA), 495
Environmental Regulation (TX), 1037
Environmental Resources and Energy (PA), 965, 978
Environmental Safety and Toxic Materials (CA), 591
Environmental Services Division (IA), 171
Environmental Services Division (SD), 432
Environmental Solutions Division (OR), 392
Executive Director's Office (TX), 457
Executive Office of Energy and Environmental Affairs (MA), 235
Field Operations Office (PA), 403
Global Warming and Climate Change (MA), 775
Guam Environmental Protection Agency (GU), 125
Health, Insurance and Environment (CO), 598
Illinois Environmental Protection Agency (IL), 151
Indiana Department of Environmental Management (IN), 157
Information Technology Division (NM), 322
Kansas Department of Health and Environment (KS), 177
Laboratory Environmental Assessment Program (OR), 392
Legal Services Office (TX), 458
Livestock Environmental Permitting Program (OH), 368
Marine Resources (MS), 814
Michigan Department of Natural Resources (MI), 251
Mississippi Department of Environmental Quality (MS), 265
Missouri Department of Conservation (MO), 278
Natural and Environmental Resources Department (PR), 412
Natural Resources, Agriculture and Environment (UT), 1045
Natural Resources and Environment (GA), 650
Natural Resources and Environment (IA), 702
Natural Resources and Environment (KY), 732
Natural Resources and Environment (LA), 743
Natural Resources and Environmental Control (DE), 614
Natural Resources and Environmental Programs (NY), 332
Nebraska Department of Environmental Quality (NE), 290
New Mexico Environment Department (NM), 322
Office of Administration (NY), 333
Office of Air Resources, Climate Change and Energy (NY), 333
Office of Community Engagement (MS), 265
Office of Environmental Adjudication (IN), 161
Office of Environmental Compliance (LA), 201
Office of Environmental Health Services (WV), 518
Office of Environmental Justice (NY), 333

## Environment *continued*

Office of Environmental Quality Control (HI), 130
Office of Environmental Services (LA), 201
Office of Management and Finance (LA), 201
Office of Natural Resources (NY), 333
Office of Public Protection and Regional Affairs (NY), 333
Office of Remediation and Materials Management (NY), 333
Office of Technical Assistance and Technology (MA), 236
Office of the Secretary of Energy and Environment (OK), 378
Oklahoma Conservation Commission (OK), 386
Oklahoma Department of Environmental Quality (OK), 380
Oklahoma Department of Wildlife Conservation (OK), 384
Operations Division (OR), 392
Pesticide Programs Division (CA), 40
Programs (WA), 503
Realty and Environmental Planning Office (IL), 148
Regulatory Programs (FL), 101
Resource Conservation Office (IL), 148
Resources and Environment (ID), 663
Rural Affairs and Environment (AZ), 567
Science Services Administration (MD), 219
Tennessee Department of Environment and Conservation (TN), 441
Texas Commission on Environmental Quality (TX), 457
Utah Department of Environmental Quality (UT), 471

### Clean Air

Air and Radiation Management Administration (MD), 219
Air Quality Board (WV), 516
Air Resources Management Division (FL), 101
Bureau of Air Quality (ME), 210
Division of Air Quality (UT), 471
Office of Air (TX), 458
Office of Air Resources, Climate Change and Energy (NY), 333
Operations Division (OR), 392
Safety, Consumer Protection and Clean Air (NY), 335
Waste, Air, Radiation and Remediation (PA), 403

### Clean or Green Technology, CleanTech, GreenTech

Global Warming and Climate Change (MA), 775

### Climate Change, Global Warming

Global Warming and Climate Change (MA), 766, 775
Office of Air Resources, Climate Change and Energy (NY), 333
State Climatology Office (SC), 425

### Conservation

Agriculture and Conservation (IL), 682
Agriculture, Conservation and Forestry (AL), 545
Alabama Department of Conservation and Natural Resources (AL), 4
Appropriations - Agriculture, Conservation and Natural Resources (MO), 827
Coastal Resources Division (GA), 115
Conservation and Natural Resources (MO), 828
Conservation and Recreation Division (IA), 171
Conservation and Technical Services (PA), 402
Conservation Commission (MO), 278

## Environment *continued*

Department of Conservation and Natural Resources (PA), 402
Department of Environmental Conservation (AK), 12
Department of Environmental Conservation (NY), 333
Department of Environmental Protection (WV), 515
Department of Land Conservation and Development (OR), 393
Department of Resources, Recycling and Recovery (CA), 40
Division of Conservation (KY), 186
Environmental Conservation (NY), 892, 904
Land, Water and Conservation Division (SC), 425
Maine Department of Agriculture, Conservation and Forestry (ME), 209
Missouri Department of Conservation (MO), 278
Office of Conservation (LA), 202
Office of Resource Conservation (MD), 218
Oklahoma Wildlife Conservation Commission (OK), 384
Recreation and Conservation Office (WA), 507
Resource Conservation and Forestry Division (SD), 432
Soil Conservation Division (IA), 168
Vermont Housing and Conservation Board (VT), 480
Washington State Conservation Commission (WA), 507

### Energy Conservation, Energy Efficiency

Division of Oil and Gas Conservation (KY), 186
Energy and Water Resources (PR), 983
North Dakota Public Service Commission (ND), 365

### Environmental Sustainability, Green Living

Agriculture, Food Security and Sustainability of the Southern Mountain Regions (PR), 982
Global Warming and Climate Change (MA), 766, 775
Massachusetts Environmental Policy Act (MEPA) Office (MA), 236
Renewable Energy and Sustainability (IL), 685
Sustainability and Energy Division (DC), 96
Sustainable Transportation (OR), 957

### Land Management

Administration (HI), 133
Agricultural Land Preservation Foundation (MD), 218
Board of University and School Lands (ND), 363
Bonding, Capital Expenditures and State Assets (MA), 766
California State Lands Commission (CA), 54
Department of Land and Natural Resources (HI), 131
Department of Land Management (GU), 124
Department of State Lands (OR), 394
Division of Mining, Land and Water (AK), 15
Environmental Solutions Division (OR), 392
Farmland Preservation Office (OH), 368
Forestry, Fire and State Lands Division (UT), 473
Land and Recreational Services (FL), 101
Land and Resource Management (TX), 1038
Land Division (WI), 528
Land Management Office (IL), 148

## Environment *continued*

Land Management Team (IN), 159
Land Survey Division (HI), 128
Land Use Management (NJ), 311
Land, Water and Conservation Division (SC), 425
Office of Hawaiian Affairs (HI), 133
Office of the Commissioner of State Lands (AR), 36
Rural Communities, Land Use, and Water (OR), 960
State Board of Land Commissioners (CO), 62
State Lands Division (FL), 101
Texas General Land Office (TX), 468
Water and Land (HI), 661
Water, Land, and Agriculture (HI), 656

### Natural Resources

Administrative Management Team (IN), 159
Agency of Natural Resources (VT), 481
Agricultural Resources Division (ID), 137
Agriculture (IN), 689
Agriculture (KY), 725
Agriculture and Forestry (AL), 552
Agriculture and Natural Resources (KS), 720
Agriculture and Natural Resources (NJ), 878
Agriculture and Natural Resources (OR), 960
Agriculture and Natural Resources (SC), 1000
Agriculture and Natural Resources (SD), 1011, 1015
Agriculture and Natural Resources (TN), 1024
Agriculture and Natural Resources (WA), 1077
Agriculture and Natural Resources Budget (KS), 720
Agriculture and Rural Development (IN), 696
Agriculture, Chesapeake and Natural Resources (VA), 1067
Agriculture/Environment/Natural Resources (NC), 910
Agriculture, Food Production and Outdoor Resources (MO), 818
Agriculture, Livestock and Natural Resources (CO), 598
Agriculture, Natural Resources, and Energy (CO), 595
Agriculture, Natural Resources and Environmental Affairs (PR), 987
Agriculture, Natural Resources and Environmental Affairs (SC), 1008
Alabama Department of Conservation and Natural Resources (AL), 4
Alaska Department of Natural Resources (AK), 15
Appropriations - Agriculture, Conservation and Natural Resources (MO), 827
Appropriations - Natural and Economic Resources (NC), 911
Arizona State Land Department (AZ), 24
Chief Legal Counsel's Office (IN), 160
Community Resource Development Division (ME), 212
Conservation and Natural Resources (MO), 828
Department for Natural Resources (KY), 185
Department of Conservation and Natural Resources (NV), 297
Department of Conservation and Natural Resources (PA), 402
Department of Conservation and Recreation (MA), 235
Department of Environment and Natural Resources (NC), 348
Department of Environment and Natural Resources (SD), 432

**SUBJECT INDEX**

SUBJECT INDEX

**SUBJECT INDEX**

SUBJECT INDEX

**SUBJECT INDEX**

SUBJECT INDEX

**SUBJECT INDEX**

## Media

Arts, Entertainment, Sports, Tourism and Internet Media (CA), 591

## Medicaid

Alabama Medicaid Agency (AL), 6
Bureau for Medical Services (WV), 517
Bureau of Health Services Financing (Medicaid) (LA), 201
Department for Medicaid Services (KY), 189
Department of Health Care Finance (DC), 92
Department of Medicaid (OH), 370
Division of Health Care Finance (KS), 177
Division of Medicaid (MS), 268
Division of Medicaid and Health Financing (UT), 472
Division of Medicaid and Long Term Care (NE), 290
Division of Medical Assistance (NC), 349
Health Programs (SC), 424
Medicaid (MS), 805, 814
Medicaid (OH), 936
Medicaid Division (ID), 136
Medicaid Eligibility and Beneficiary Services (SC), 424
Medicaid Fraud and Abuse Control Division (KY), 196
Medicaid Fraud Control Unit (CT), 73
Medicaid Fraud Control Unit (NM), 328
Medicaid Fraud Control Unit (NY), 343
Medicaid Fraud Control Unit (TX), 467
Medicaid Fraud Control Unit (WY), 535
Medical Assistance Division (NM), 324
Medical Assistance Plans Division (GA), 113
Medical Assistance Services Board (VA), 494
Office of Medicaid (MA), 236
Office of Medicaid Business and Policy (NH), 305
Office of the Deputy Commissioner for Medicaid and Health Care Policy (AK), 13
Office of the Medicaid Inspector General (NY), 332
Quality Assurance Division (MT), 285
TennCare Bureau (TN), 442

## Metals, Minerals

Department of Mineral Resources (ND), 362
Mines and Minerals Office (IL), 148
Surface Mine Board (WV), 516

## Mines, Mining

Arizona State Mine Inspector (AZ), 22
Division of Mine Permits (KY), 186
Division of Mine Safety (KY), 186
Division of Mining, Land and Water (AK), 15
Energy, Industry and Mining (WV), 1082
Jobs and the Economy (WI), 1101
Mining and Outdoor Recreation Policy (MN), 799
Mining and Rural Development (WI), 1101
Office of Miners' Health Safety and Training (WV), 515
Oil, Gas and Mining Division (UT), 473
Oklahoma Department of Mines (OK), 382
Sporting Heritage, Mining, and Forestry (WI), 1093

## Minority Affairs

Department of Chamorro Affairs (GU), 124
Governors Office of Minority Affairs (AL), 3
Office of Diversity, Equity, and Opportunity (RI), 414
Office of Multicultural Affairs (UT), 472
Office on African Affairs (DC), 84
Office on Asian and Pacific Islander Affairs (DC), 84

### African-American Affairs

Office on African American Affairs (DC), 89

### Native American Affairs

Division of Indian Affairs (UT), 472
Government, Elections, and Indian Affairs (NM), 886
Governor's Office of Indian Affairs (WA), 501
Indian Affairs Department (NM), 324

### Native Hawaiian Affairs

Department of Hawaiian Home Lands (HI), 133
Hawaiian Affairs (HI), 656
Hawaiian Homes Commission (HI), 133
Ocean, Marine Resources and Hawaiian Affairs (HI), 660
Tourism and International Affairs (HI), 656

## Natural Disasters

Office of Disaster Assistance and Petroleum Management (AS), 20

## Nonprofit, Philanthropy

Cooperatives and Non-Profits (PR), 987

## Outdoors

Mining and Outdoor Recreation Policy (MN), 799

## Pharmaceuticals

Georgia Drugs and Narcotics Agency (GA), 116
Health Regulation and Licensing Administration (DC), 91
Oregon Board of Pharmacy (OR), 398
Pharmaceutical Control Division (DC), 92

## Policy, Planning

Agriculture Policy (MN), 797
Budget and Policy (TX), 452
Budget and Program Planning Office (MT), 281
Budget, Planning and Analysis (OR), 392
Capital Investment, Planning and Grant Administration (NJ), 314
Center for Policy, Planning and Evaluation (DC), 91
Criminal Justice Planning Agency (AS), 20
Department of Government Efficiency and Financial Planning (IN), 161
Department of Health Care Policy and Financing (CO), 60
Department of Planning (MD), 223
Department of Planning and Budget (AS), 19
Division of Planning and Development (KS), 178
Division of Policy (KS), 179
Economic Development, Agriculture and Planning (VI), 1057
Education (FL), 630
Education Innovation Policy (MN), 798
Education Policy (AL), 552

**Policy, Planning** *continued*

Environment and Natural Resources Policy and Finance (MN), 798
Environment and Planning (TN), 446
Epidemiology and Health Planning Division (KY), 189
Financial Management, Budget, and Policy Office (MS), 265
Global Warming and Climate Change (MA), 775
Government Operations and Elections Policy (MN), 798
Governor's Office of Management and Budget (UT), 469
Governor's Office of Policy and Planning (PA), 400
Greater Minnesota Economic and Workforce Development Policy (MN), 798
Higher Education Policy and Finance (MN), 799
Higher Education Policy Commission (WV), 522
Indiana Criminal Justice Institute (IN), 164
Job Growth and Energy Affordability Policy and Finance (MN), 799
Media and Graphics (ME), 213
Mining and Outdoor Recreation Policy (MN), 799
Modal Planning and Program Management Division (MN), 261
New Hampshire Office of Energy and Planning (NH), 302
Office of External Affairs and Policy (GA), 118
Office of Facility Planning and Control (LA), 199
Office of Grants, Policy and Statistics (MD), 224
Office of Health Planning (GA), 113
Office of Health Policy (KY), 188
Office of Health Policy and Planning (MS), 268
Office of Intermodal Planning (MS), 273
Office of Medicaid Business and Policy (NH), 305
Office of Multimodal Programming (LA), 204
Office of Planning and Budget (GA), 112
Office of Planning and Budget (LA), 199
Office of Planning and Programming (IL), 150
Office of Planning and Research (CA), 38
Office of Policy and Budget (FL), 99
Office of Policy and Management (CT), 67
Office of Policy, Planning and Statistics (IL), 149
Office of Policy, Research and Legislative Affairs (CO), 59
Office of Policy, Research and Regulatory Reform (CO), 63
Office of State Assessment (NY), 345
Office of State Planning and Budgeting (CO), 60
Office of Strategic Planning and Policy Development (NY), 338
Office of the Deputy Commissioner for Medicaid and Health Care Policy (AK), 13
Office on Women's Policy and Initiatives (DC), 84
Planning (PA), 407
Planning and Assessment Division (IN), 159
Planning and Finance Division (IA), 170
Planning and Modal Programs (CA), 50
Planning Board (PR), 412
Planning Data and Analysis (MD), 223
Planning Division (OH), 373
Planning, Programming and Modal Division (IA), 173
Policy Analysis and Government Accountability (DE), 618

**Policy, Planning** *continued*

Policy and Legislative Services (OH), 373
Policy, Communications, and Administration Office (CO), 61
Policy Office (OH), 366
Policy Office (PA), 403
Policy Office (SC), 422
Policy Research Office (NE), 288
Post Audit and Oversight (MA), 775
Program and Policy (ND), 360
Public Safety and Crime Prevention Policy and Finance (MN), 799
Realty and Environmental Planning Office (IL), 148
Socio-Economic Development and Planning (PR), 989
State Health Planning and Development Agency (HI), 130
State Planning and Community Affairs (GA), 651
Steering and Policy (MA), 766
Steering, Policy and Scheduling (MA), 775
Tax and Fiscal Policy (IN), 691
Transportation Planning Bureau (MI), 253
Transportation Policy (OH), 373
Transportation Policy and Finance (MN), 799
Transportation Systems Planning Bureau (ME), 213
Unemployment Compensation Program (PA), 405
Vision 2020 (KS), 722
Water Policy and Ecosystem Restoration (FL), 101

## Poverty

Social Welfare and Poverty Eradication (PR), 989

## Printing

Publication and Regulations Division (MA), 243

## Public Administration

Judiciary, Rules and Administration (ID), 668
Office of Public Advocacy (AK), 11
Public and Municipal Affairs (NH), 852
Public Rights Division (CA), 57

### Public Policy

Office of Grants, Policy and Statistics (MD), 224
Public Benefit and Regulatory Reform (WI), 1093
Public Policy (IN), 691, 698

### Public Safety

Alaska Department of Public Safety (AK), 16
Amusement Ride Safety Division (OH), 367
Appropriations - Justice and Public Safety (NC), 911
Appropriations - Public Safety (IL), 683
Appropriations - Public Safety and Corrections (MO), 828
Arizona Department of Public Safety (AZ), 25
Armed Services, Veterans Affairs and Public Safety (OH), 941
Colorado Department of Public Safety (CO), 63
Criminal Justice and Public Safety (NH), 868
Criminal Justice and Public Safety (WI), 1100
Dam Safety and Floodplain Management Division (VA), 495
Department of Emergency Services and Public Protection (CT), 70
Department of Fire Prevention and Electrical Safety (WY), 536
Department of Fire Services (MA), 241

**SUBJECT INDEX**

SUBJECT INDEX

**SUBJECT INDEX**

# Name Index

This index lists all individuals in the directory alphabetically by last name.

Alexander, Dr. David C., 312
Alexander, Greg, 139
Alexander, Gwen, 233
Alexander, Jake, 351
Alexander, Jay, 506
Alexander, Jennifer, 257, 276
Alexander, John M., Jr., 907, 910, 911, 912, 913
Alexander, Julie, 159
Alexander, Julie Horn, 249
Alexander, Kelly M., Jr., 913, 920, 921, 922, 923, 924
Alexander, Kenneth Cooper "Kenny", 1058, 1060, 1061
Alexander, Kimberly, 637, 647, 649
Alexander, Kristin, 464
Alexander, Louise, 546, 552, 553
Alexander, Mark, 81
Alexander, Mont, 426
Alexander, Sheila, 113
Alexander, Stephanie, 16
Alexander, Terry, 1002, 1009
Alexander, Thomas C., 998, 1000, 1001, 1002
Alexander, Yvette M., 86
Alfaro, Ricard, 411
Alfaro, Sandra, 51
Alferman, Justin, 819, 828, 829, 830, 831
Alfond, Justin L., 744
Alford, Debbie D., 119
Alford, Lisa, 5
Alford, Robert, 347
Alford, Steve, 713, 720, 721, 722
Alford, Susan, 427
Alger, Jenifer, 282
Algiere, Dennis L., 990
Alhija, Hussain, 219
Alicea, Caroletta C., 853, 868
Alim, Fahizah, 39
Alke, Debbie, 285
Alkhatib, Suhair, 225
Alkire, LtCol Steve, 536
Allain, Robert L. "Bret", 733, 736
Allan, Jon, 247
Allan, Jonathan, 392
Alland, Alexandra, 244
Allard, Chandra, 244
Allard, David, 403, 413
Allbaugh, Joe M., 379
Allegeier, Linda, 537
Allen Mitchell, Chaunda, 198
Allen-Picone, Susan, 478
Allen, Alesia, 6
Allen, Alma A., 1029, 1036, 1037, 1038
Allen, Amanda, 216
Allen, Barbara, 473
Allen, Benjamin "Ben", 581, 584, 585
Allen, Bradley G., 338
Allen, Brice, 446
Allen, Bruce, 326
Allen, Carlton "Turner", 119
Allen, Cathryn, 373
Allen, Charles, 86
Allen, Chaz, 699, 702, 703
Allen, Christy, 451
Allen, C. Richard, 116
Allen, Deborah, 152
Allen, Denise, 157
Allen, Diane B., 871, 873
Allen, Dixie, 475
Allen, Doug, 387
Allen, Capt Dyana K., 483
Allen, Faimealelei Anthony Fue, 562, 563, 564

Allen, Gary, 371
Allen, Gerald, 543, 545, 546
Allen, Glenn, 120
Allen, Heather, 61
Allen, James, 331, 380
Allen, James E. "Trey", 118
Allen, James F., 335
Allen, Jamey, 379
Allen, Janeill, 472
Allen, Jeff J., 477
Allen, Jeffrey, 342
Allen, Jim, 1104, 1107, 1108
Allen, John, 339
Allen, John M., 568, 570
Allen, Jordan, 444
Allen, Joyce, 528
Allen, Julie A., 280
Allen, Kara K., 199
Allen, Kara M., 330
Allen, Karl B., 998, 1001, 1002
Allen, Kathleen, 200
Allen, Kathy M., 364
Allen, Kimbol, 140
Allen, Larry, 140, 267
Allen, Lawrence Alvin, Jr., 456
Allen, Leesa M., 405
Allen, Lisa, 278
Allen, Loranda, 120
Allen, Lucy, 264
Allen, Mark, 266, 944, 946, 947
Allen, Maryellen, 194
Allen, Mary M., 853, 869
Allen, Michael J., 208, 209
Allen, Patrick, 391
Allen, Patty, 154
Allen, Ray, 529
Allen, Richard "Rick", 11
Allen, Robert, 452
Allen, Sandi, 331
Allen, Sarah, 128
Allen, Scott, 1094, 1100, 1101, 1102
Allen, Sheila, 385
Allen, Steve, 446
Allen, Susan, 791, 797, 798
Allen, Susan "Sue", 820, 828, 829, 831
Allen, Sylvia, 565, 567
Allen, Tim, 388
Allen, Tracy, 154
Allen, Travis, 585, 586, 591, 592
Allenson, David, 419
Alletto, Michelle, 201
Alley, Andrea, 52
Alley, Ann, 158
Alley, Lisa Marie, 50
Alley, Robert, 746
Allie, Brian, 257
Allis, Richard "Rick", 474
Allison, Constance, 452
Allison, Dustin, 275
Allison, James "Jim", 449
Allison, Jason M., 104
Allison, Kathleen, 51
Allison, Mary B., 183
Allison, Merita A. "Rita", 1002, 1008
Allison, Stephen, 637, 646, 648, 649, 651
Allman, Kimberly A. "Kim", 157, 159
Allmeroth, Becky, 278
Alloway, Richard L., II, 961, 964, 965
Allred, Glenda, 9
Allred, Paul, 471
Allwood, Paul, 257
Almager, Kristy, 466
Almanza, Esteban, 38
Almeida, Joseph S., 993, 997
Almeida, Raul, 502
Almeida, Tony, 346

Almy, Susan W., 853, 870
Alonzo-Diaz, Lupe, 46
Alonzo, Roberto R., 1029, 1036, 1037, 1038
Alonzo, Rosie, 135
Alosio, Vaifale Akeli, 560
Alpert, Gary, 310
Alston, LTC Jeffrey, 528
Alston, Lela, 568, 570
Alston, Lolita, 85
Alston, Dr. Samuel, 428
Alter, Marcey, 113
Alteri, Sean, 185
Althaus, Ullyssa, 393
Althoff, George, 527
Althoff, Pamela J., 669, 673, 674, 675
Altholz, Rochelle, 495
Altier, Mark, 376
Altieri, Michael, 235
Altig, Stephanie, 140, 142
Alting, Ronnie J., 687, 690, 691
Altland, Sharon, 401
Altmaier, David, 107
Altman, Daniel, 157
Altman, Gary H., 313
Altman, Jeff, 273
Altman, Rachele, 398
Altman, BG Steve, 172
Altman, Thad, 619, 621, 622, 623
Altobello, Emil "Buddy", Jr., 601, 602, 609, 610, 611
Altshuler, Katie Gumerson, 378
Aluise, Eric B., 515
Alund, Christopher, 335
Alvarado-Ramos, Lourdes E. "Alfie", 506
Alvarado, Asuncion, 89
Alvarado, Carol, 1029, 1038
Alvarado, Ralph, 723, 725, 726
Alvarado, Robert "Bob", 50
Alvarez, Andres, 490
Alvarez, Daniel, 581
Alvarez, Danielle M., 104
Alvarez, Frank, 49
Alvarez, Julian, 465
Alvaro, Brad, 136
Alves, David, 419
Alves, John, 69
Alves, Sheila, 498
Alvey, Michael, 185
Alvey, Scott, 193
Alvey, Shannon, 473
Alvino, Suzanne, 310
Alvis, Julie, 47
Alviti, Peter, 418
Alvord, Alan, 41
Alvord, Melanie A., 453
Alwine, Bob, 446
Alworth, Tom, 340
Amacher, Gina, 260
Amadon, Roger, 850
Amajor, Chuks, 468
Aman, Andre, 289
Aman, William "Bill", 601, 602, 608, 610, 611
Amann, Kathleen, 48
Amato, Maria, 95
Ambach, Craig, 435
Ambler, George "Boogie", 1083, 1088, 1090
Ambre, Melissa K., 157
Ambrose, Colleen, 283
Ambrose, Robert P., 303
Ambrose, Suzanne, 43
Ambrozic, Jane, 171
Amburgey, Jeffrey A., 520
Amedée, Beryl Adams, 737, 742, 743
Amedore, George A., Jr., 887, 891, 892, 893, 894
Ameen, Effie, 593
Ameh, Eci, 505

Amell-Jackson, Stephanie, 427
Amerman, Bill, 928, 932, 933
Amerson, Ellen, 147
Amerson, Ryan, 154
Ames, Chuck, 222
Ames, Gregory H., 282
Ames, Richard, 853, 870
Amgwert, Bonnie, 292
Amick, Valerie E., 514
Amini, Gordon, 389
Aminpour, Farhad, 235
Amis, Sonya M., 270
Amituana'i, Vailoata Eteuati, 562, 563, 564, 565
Ammon, Keith, 853, 869
Ammons, Carol, 675, 682, 683, 684, 685, 686
Ammons, David "Dave", 511
Ammons, James R., 26
Ammons, Jennifer, 113
Ammons, Natalie, 116
Ammons, Randy J., 458
Amo, Gabriel F., Jr., 413
Amodeo, John P., 343
Amon, Corey, 315
Amonett, Jane, 440
Amore, Gregg, 993, 996, 997
Amoroso, Joseph, 312
Amoroso, Rhonda K., 354
Amour, Celeste, 56
Amstutz, Ron, 937, 943
Amundson, COL Michael, 171
Amy, Barbara, 12
Amy, Dr. Brian, 91
Ananich, Jim, 776, 778
Anaya, Mike, 328
Ancel, Janet, 1048, 1056
Ancel, Sarah, 164
Anchia, Rafael, 1029, 1037
Andaya, Athena E., 180
Andel, David, 152
Anderegg, Jacob L. "Jake", 1041, 1045, 1046
Anders, Ira, 820, 829, 830, 831
Anders, John F. "Andy", 737, 742, 743
Andersen, COL Brett W., 291
Andersen, Daniel D., 477
Andersen, Paul, 285
Anderson, Alexander, 108
Anderson, Alan, 358
Anderson, Anita M., 263
Anderson, Bert, 928, 932
Anderson, Betsy, 539
Anderson, Beverly, 290
Anderson, Bill, 699, 701, 702, 703
Anderson, Blake, 472
Anderson, Brittany, 500
Anderson, Dr. Bruce, 131
Anderson, Bruce D., 786, 789, 790
Anderson, Camille, 477
Anderson, Carla, 140
Anderson, Carl L., 1002, 1009
Anderson, Chad, 791, 797, 798, 799
Anderson, Charles "Doc", 1029, 1036, 1037
Anderson, Charles E. "Chuck", 403
Anderson, Christine "Chris", 12
Anderson, Craig, 477
Anderson, Curtis Stovall "Curt", 756, 762
Anderson, Dan, 260
Anderson, Daniel D. "Dan", 261
Anderson, Danielle, 45
Anderson, Darran, 464

Anderson, Dave, 135, 529
Anderson, Capt. David, 394
Anderson, David L., 1012, 1015
Anderson, Deborah, 188
Anderson, Denise, 256
Anderson, Dennis Paul, 847, 849, 850
Anderson, Dick, 928, 932
Anderson, Dirk, 481
Anderson, D. Kamili, 88
Anderson, Donovan, 98
Anderson, Ellen, 334
Anderson, Elliot T., 847, 849
Anderson, Eloise, 526
Anderson, Eric, 312
Anderson, Eric R., 138
Anderson, Everette W. "Bill", Jr., 1083, 1088, 1089, 1090
Anderson, Freya, 17
Anderson, Gail, 301
Anderson, Gary, 239
Anderson, Glenn N. "Andy", 439
Anderson, Gordon, 455
Anderson, Heather, 398
Anderson, Howard C., Jr., 925, 927
Anderson, James Lee "Jim", 1102, 1104
Anderson, Janice, 315
Anderson, Jeffrey R. "Jeff", 141
Anderson, Jennifer M., 66
Anderson, Jeramey, 806, 814, 815
Anderson, Joel, 278, 581, 584, 585
Anderson, John L., 61
Anderson, Johnny, 198, 1041, 1046
Anderson, Joyce, 203
Anderson, Julia, 263
Anderson, Kathryn, 527
Anderson, Keith A., 88, 93
Anderson, Kenneth W., Jr., 463
Anderson, Kent, 163
Anderson, Kevin, 356
Anderson, Laura, 396
Anderson, Laury, 261
Anderson, Layne, 36
Anderson, Leslie, 210
Anderson, Lori, 358
Anderson, Madhu, 247
Anderson, Maggie, 360
Anderson, Maria, 92
Anderson, Mark, 439, 494, 791, 797, 799
Anderson, BG Mark, 528
Anderson, Marti, 703, 707, 708, 709
Anderson, Mary, 507
Anderson, Monique M., 220
Anderson, Neil, 669, 672, 673, 674, 675
Anderson, Neil A., 664, 667, 668
Anderson, Oskar, 528
Anderson, Pamela, 928, 933
Anderson, Pat, 408
Anderson, Patrick, 944, 946, 947
Anderson, Paul, 297
Anderson, Paul H., 791, 797, 798
Anderson, Peggy, 5
Anderson, Peggy L., 361
Anderson, Rachel LeBaron, 507
Anderson, Richard L. "Rich", 1062, 1067, 1068, 1069
Anderson, Robert, 100
Anderson, Rodney, 288
Anderson, Rodney E., 1029, 1037, 1038

NAME INDEX

Blake, Stan, 1105, 1107, 1108
Blake, Todd, 427
Blakely, Matthew, 247
Blanch, Blake, 165
Blanchard, Bob, 211
Blanchard, Brian, 105
Blanchard, Clark, 47
Blanchard, Jennifer, 258
Blanchard, Peter J., 210
Blanchette, Lisa, 415
Blanco, Cesar J., 1029, 1037, 1038
Blanco, Daniel A., 138
Blanco, Rafael, 412
Bland, Doug, 326
Bland, Gilbert T., 492
Bland, Todd R., 45
Blaney, CW3 Samuel, 113
Blank, Brian V., 193
Blank, Simon, 109
Blankenbush, Kenneth, 895, 902, 903, 905, 906
Blankenhorn, Randall S., 149
Blankenship, Denise, 282
Blankenship, Kathy, 200
Blankenship, Tim, 516
Blankinship, Steven, 320
Blas, Frank F., Jr., 652, 653, 654
Blas, Paula M., 124
Blas, Raymond F.Y., Sr., 125
Blasdel, Mark, 832, 835
Blassingame, Janice, 93
Blatt, Eric, 481
Blatt, Michele, 523
Blatter, Therron, 471
Blaz, Anthony ''Tony'', 124
Blazejewski, Christopher R., 993, 997
Blazel, Edward A. ''Ted'', 1091
Blazer, Lesli, 381
Bledsoe, Cecile, 572, 574
Bledsoe, Craig, 137, 142
Bledsoe, Grace, 457
Bledsoe, Robert, 62
Bleiwas, Kenneth, 343
Blessing, Buck, 62
Blessing, Louis W., III, 937, 941, 942
Blessing, Matthew, 526
Blessing, Rebecca, 183
Blessing, Rondee, 142
Blessinger, Christine, 157
Blevins, Dewey, 186
Blevins, Donald W. ''Don'', Jr., 194
Blevins, Johnny, 380
Blevins, Patricia M. ''Patti'', 612, 613, 614
Blinman, Eric, 321
Blinn, Katie, 511
Blizzard, Samantha, 221
Block, Andrew K., Jr., 497
Block, Edward ''Eddie'', 455
Block, Elliott, 40
Block, Joan H., 233
Block, Martin ''Marty'', 582, 584
Block, Matthew, 198
Blocker, Michele, 271
Blocker, Col. Tyree C., 408
Bloczynski, Ann, 533
Blomstedt, Matthew L., 295
Bloom, Major Mike, 394
Bloom, Phil, 159
Bloom, Richard, 586, 591, 592, 593
Bloom, Stephen ''Steve'', 397
Bloom, Stephen, 966, 977, 978, 979
Bloomer, John H., Jr., 1046
Bloomfield, Dave, 842, 844
Blosser, Amy, 181

Blotter, Shelley, 297
Blount, David, 800, 803, 804, 805
Blount, Ferrell, 351
Blount, Katie, 264
Blow, Jean, 433
Blowman, David, 77
Bloxom, Robert S., Jr., 1062, 1067, 1068, 1069
Bludworth, Sabrina, 327
Blue, Celia J., 418
Blue, Daniel Terry ''Dan'', Jr., 907, 908, 910, 911, 912, 913
Blue, Dominic L., 241
Bluemink, Elizabeth, 15
Bluhm, Cheryl, 144
Blumberg, Lester, 237
Blume, Lydia, 746, 752
Blumenthal, David D., 317
Blumhagen, Michele, 363
Blumstein, Andrée Sophia, 450
Blunk, COL Don, 141
Blust, John M., 914, 920, 921, 922, 923, 924
Bly, David, 791, 797, 798
Blyden, Marvin A., 1056, 1057
Boal, Carmine R., 703
Boal, Kimberly A., 407
Board, Yvonne, 189
Boardman, Ellen O., 97
Boardman, Michael, 208
Boback, Karen, 966, 977, 980
Bobchak, Rose, 321
Bobertz, Shannon, 425
Bobinsky, Marcella J., 305
Bocage, Guy, 315
Boccella, John, 171
Bocchino, Mike, 602, 608, 609, 610
Boccieri, John A., 937, 943
Bodie, Cindy, 367
Bodin, Erik, 494
Bodine, Tom, 365
Bodisch, Robert S. ''Duke'', 463
Bodner, Darrin, 402
Bodvake, Ron, 429
Boe, Tracy, 928, 932, 933
Boeger, Karen, 274
Boehm, Ralph G., 854, 868
Boehm, Ryan, 231
Boehme, Kimberly, 494
Boehmer, Darrell, 155
Boehning, Randy, 928, 932
Boekhaus, Mike, 178
Boerboom, Jim, 255
Boers, Greg, 52
Boerwinkle, M-Sgt. Matthew, 153
Boes, Richard, 478
Boesiger, Bess, 294
Boessen, Arlene, 280
Boettcher, Andrew, 253
Boettcher, Benjamin, 76
Boffetti, James T., 302
Boffy, Holly, 207
Bogatz, James A. ''Jim'', 291
Bogdan, Wendy, 47
Bogdanoff, Peter, 510
Boger, Jennifer, 409
Boggess, Leslie S., 519
Boggs, Ben, 184
Boggs, Kristin, 937, 943
Boggs, Kristin A., 515
Boggs, Larry, 944, 946, 947
Boggs, Lawrence Brent, 1083, 1088, 1089, 1090
Bograd, Michael B. E., 265
Bohac, Bridget C., 457
Bohac, MajGen Daryl, 291
Bohac, Dwayne, 1029, 1038
Bohac, Kenneth F., 186
Bohan, James, 402
Bohannon, Brad, 119

Bohannon, David, 220
Bohannon, Stephen, 326
Bohard, Jerri L., 395
Bohle, Karen, 225
Bohlin, Daniel, 533
Bohn, Ralph, 471
Bohnhoff, Jean, 144
Bohon, Jim, 39
Bohringer, Richard, 532
Boisclair, Shawn, 69
Boisvert, Louise, 211
Boisvert, Tracey L., 302
Bol, Marsha, 321
Boland, David J., 332
Bolar, Bettie, 174
Bolcas, Michael A., 191
Bolden, Michael, 267
Bolden, Stephanie T., 615, 617, 618
Bolding, Reginald, Jr., 568, 570
Boldra, Sue Ellen, 713, 720, 722
Boldt, Ken, 63
Bolduc, BrigGen Gerard, 209
Boldyga, Nicholas A., 767, 775
Bolea, Brent A., 218
Bolender, Melanie P., 376
Boles, James L. ''Jamie'', Jr., 913, 914, 920, 921, 922, 923, 924
Boley, Donna J., 1080, 1082, 1083
Bolin, Bradley S., 675
Bolin, Jim, 1012, 1016
Boling, Brian, 392
Bolinsky, Mitch, 602, 608, 609
Bolkcom, Joseph L. ''Joe'', 699, 701, 702, 703
Boll, Lorna Hemp, 531
Bollier, Barbara, 713, 720, 721, 722
Bolling, Melinda M., 93
Bolling, Susanne, 344
Boltjes, Todd, 56
Bolton, Barry, 384
Bolton, Jennifer, 470
Bolton, Yvonne P., 70
Bolyard, David H., 521
Bolz, Kate, 842, 844
Bomar, MAJ Stephen S. ''Steve'', 393
Bomgar, Joel, 806, 813, 814, 815, 816
Bonacic, John J., 887, 891, 892, 893
Bonacquist, Mark, 336
Bonar, David L., 80
Bonaventura, Mary Beth, 156
Bonaventure, Carla, 206
Boncore, Joseph A., 763
Bond, Darren, 399
Bond, Heather, 113
Bond, James, 533
Bond, Janis, 268
Bond, Patrick, 3
Bond, Robert P., 471
Bond, Stefanie, 169
Bond, Stephanie J., 519
Bondi, Pamela J. ''Pam'', 106, 108
Bondon, Jack, 820, 829
Bonds, Anita, 86
Bonds, Craig, 462
Bone, Dr. George H., 227
Bonebrake, Terry D., 399
Boner, Brian, 1102, 1104
Bonfert, Diane, 193
Bonham, Charlton H. ''Chuck'', 47
Bonham, Virgil, 382
Bonilla, Mary, 39
Bonilla, Susan, 41, 586, 591, 592, 593
Bonini, Colin R. J., 612, 614

Bonlender, Brian N., 502, 508
Bonnen, Dennis, 1029, 1038
Bonnen, Greg, 1029, 1036, 1037
Bonnet, Jerry, 166
Bonner, Amy, 76
Bonner, Dr. Charlene M., 241
Bonnet, Terri E., 786, 789, 790
Bonnett, Lisa, 151
Bonnett, Victor G., 520
Bonnot, Ken, 276
Bonoff, Terri E., 786, 789, 790
Bonsack, Deborah, 90
Bonsall, Molly, 24
Bonsignore, Ruth, 241
Bonta, Rob, 586, 591, 592
Bontrager, Chad, 176
Bonvechio, Jeffrey, 95
Booher, Darwin L., 776, 778
Book, Thomas Todd, 375
Bookard, Sonya, 426
Booker, Ashley, 262
Booker, Cleopatra, 495
Booker, Joe W., Jr., 321
Boomhower, Dan, 262
Boone, Christine, 382
Boone, Deborah ''Debbie'', 957, 960
Boone, Douglas, 382
Boone, Jerry, 335
Boone, Lee Anne Bruce, 381
Boone, Susan, 268
Boone, Susan M., 423
Booras, Efstathia, 854, 870
Boornazian, Richard, 311
Boose, Terry, 937, 941, 943
Booth, Deanne, 435
Booth, John, 484
Booth, Lisa, 185
Booth, Quincy, 95
Booth, Roger, 162
Booth, Thomas M. ''Tommy'', Jr., 273
Boothe, Alan C., 547, 553, 554
Boothe, Susan, 368
Boots, David, 153
Boots, Phil L., 687, 690, 691
Booyse, Anthony, 474
Boozer, F. Vernon, 227
Boozer, Young J., III, 9
Bopp, Dawn, 159
Boquist, Brian J., 955, 956, 957
Borchers, Kim, 175
Bordeaux, Shawn, 1012, 1015
Bordelon, Adrienne, 200
Bordelon, Elizabeth, 205
Borden, Brian, 117
Borden, David A., 854, 870
Borden, Richelle, 390
Borden, Steve, 447
Borden, W. Allen, 441
Bordenet, John, 854, 868
Border-Sheppard, Anna, 1084, 1088, 1089, 1090
Borders, Bruce A., 692, 697, 698
Borders, Maj Christopher, 141
Bordner, Thomas, 406
Bordonaro, Nicole, 407
Borello, Daryl, 391
Boren, Marie, 456
Boresi, Susan, 280
Borg, Dean, 51
Borg, Joseph P. ''Joe'', 7
Borger-Gilligan, Frank, 439
Borja, Carleen, 124
Borja, Michael J.B., 124
Bork, Daniel P., 186
Borkowski, Kaelene, 435
Born, John, 371

Born, Mark, 1094, 1100, 1101
Borns, Dan, 23
Borochoff, Robert ''Bob'', 459
Borrego, JC, 322
Borrego, Valerie J., 328
Borrelli, Sonny, 568, 571
Borrowman, John, 297
Borski, Heather, 472
Borstel, Charles, 239
Bortner, Dan, 159
Bortner, Nathan, 404
Bortolazzo, Dawne, 48
Bortolin, Gregory, 301
Borud, Matt, 135
Borunda, Luis E., 217
Borup, Susan, 62
Bosack, Tabbitha, 403
Boschee, Joshua A., 928, 932, 933
Boscola, Lisa M., 961, 964, 965
Boshears-Davis, Deborah, 441
Bosler, Keely, 37
Bosley, Barbara, 521
Bosley, John, 97
Bosma, Brian C., 691, 692
Boso, Gregory L., 1080, 1082, 1083
Boss, Frederick M., 399
Boss, Rebecca, 419
Bosse, Bob, 436
Bosse, MAJ Paul A., 209
Bossier, Shonita, 192
Bossio, Rose, 505
Bossman, Daria, 432
Bosso, Luke, 156
Bostock, Bob, 311
Boston, Brooke, 454
Bostrom, Mark, 284
Boswell, Dr. Cary F., 5
Boswell, Jamie, 121
Boswell, Leonard L., 172
Boteler, Kathy, 270
Botelho, Bo, 288, 289
Botello, Armando, 49
Bothfeld, Diane, 479
Botka, Bruce, 507
Bott, John C., 209
Bottenfield, Tim, 285
Botting, Matthew, 38
Bottrell, Marilyn, 288
Botts, Lyndsay, 446
Botzow, Bill, 1049, 1055
Boubary, Kelly, 367
Boubique, Jocelyn, 55
Boucek, Frank, 25
Bouchard, Alisha, 235
Bouchard, Linda Shapiro, 216
Bouchard, COL Michael, 209
Bouche, Frank, 25
Boucher, Antonietta ''Toni'', 599
Boucher, Antonietta, 609, 610, 612
Boucher, John, 10
Boucher, Kenneth ''K.R.'', 159
Boudin Frost, Miranda, 6
Boudreau, Ann, 532
Boudreau, Christopher, 212
Boudreau, Steven, 419
Boudreaux, Gerald, 733, 736
Bouey, Stephen M. ''Steve'', 66
Bouffard, Rodney, 209
Boughn, Jay, 282
Bougie, Deliverance, 161
Bouie, Joseph, Jr., 737, 743, 744
Boukus, Elizabeth A. ''Betty'', 601, 602, 609, 611
Bouldin, Amanda, 854, 870
Boulet, David, 202

Brinkley, David R., 218
Brinkley, Capt. Patrick D., 409
Brinkman, Keith, 104
Brinkman, Scott W., 182
Brinkman, Thomas E. "Tom", Jr., 938, 941, 942, 943
Brinks, Winnie, 779, 784, 785
Brinly, Beth A., 182
Brinn, W. T., 348
Brinningstaull, Dawn, 252
Brinson, Bob, 350
Brinson, Jack, 356
Brisbo, Andrew, 250
Briscoe, Carla, 186
Briscoe, Joel K., 1041, 1045, 1046
Briscoe, John W., 278
Briscoe, Lynn, 502
Brisé, Ronald A. "Ron", 107
Briseno, Coco, 50
Brislin, Jennifer Feldman, 189
Brisson, William D., 914, 920, 922, 923, 924
Bristol, Susan, 242
Bristow, David, 293
Brito, Dr. Arturo, 311, 312
Britt, Art, 356
Britt, Don, 328
Britt, Gregory "Greg", 497
Britt, Renee, 266
Britt, Rufus, 422
Britt, Sylmia, 44
Brittingham, Devashree, 80
Brittingham, Nan, 219
Britton, Kathleen, 476
Britton, Sam, 273
Brnovich, Mark, 27
Broadaway, Mary, 575, 580
Broadfield, Dawne, 414
Broadhead, Ronald, 326
Broadie, Harriett, 93
Broadrick, Bruce, 638, 648, 649
Broadwater, Chris, 738, 743, 744
Broadwater, M. Kathleen, 225
Broady-Rudd, Sandra E., 526
Brochin, James "Jim", 753, 755, 756
Brock, Andrew C., 907, 908, 910, 911, 912, 913
Brock, Caroline, 206
Brock, Chris, 375
Brock, Cindy, 136
Brock, Larry R., 191
Brock, Robert, 147
Brockamp, Kim, 391
Brocker, Lori, 955
Brockman, Cecil Antonio, 914, 920, 921, 922, 924
Brockman, Donna, 184
Brockman, Joe, 277
Brockman, Kelly, 441
Brockway, Buzz, 638, 646, 647, 648, 649
Brodehl, Randy, 836, 840
Broden, John E., 687, 690, 691
Brodeur, Brenda, 414
Brodeur, Jason T., 624, 630
Brodeur, Mark, 420
Brodeur, Paul, 767, 775
Brodie, Angus, 512
Brodie, Katie, 134
Brodie, Margaret, 13
Brody, Mark, 914, 920, 921, 923
Brody, Terrence S., 309
Broeker, Roberta, 278
Broersma, Barbara, 444
Broessel, Kristi, 248
Brogan, Richard, 447

Brogan, Susanne, 230
Brogan, Victoria R., 311
Brohl, Barbara J., 64
Brokaw, Toni, 374
Brom, Evan, 24
Bromirski, Timothy, 338
Bromwell, Eric M., 757, 762
Bronner, David G., 8
Bronson, Harry B., 895, 902, 904, 905, 906, 907
Brookbank, Diane, 528
Brookes, Brady, 155
Brookins, Linda, 458
Brookman, Monica, 243
Brookman, Pam, 193
Brooks, Benjamin T., Sr., 757, 762
Brooks, Bob, 186
Brooks, Bonnie, 426
Brooks, Corey, 944, 946, 947
Brooks, Daniel E., 321
Brooks, Darren, 103
Brooks, Delece A., 119
Brooks, Doris Flores, 125
Brooks, Edward "Ed", 1094, 1099, 1100, 1101, 1102
Brooks, Francis K., 1048
Brooks, Harry R., 1020, 1024
Brooks, Heidi, 746
Brooks, Jim, 101
Brooks, K. Allen, 302
Brooks, Kara, 155
Brooks, Katharine, 344
Brooks, Kathryn, 489
Brooks, Kevin A., 12
Brooks, Kevin D., 1019, 1020, 1024, 1025
Brooks, Kris, 78
Brooks, Linda, 315
Brooks, Lisa, 332
Brooks, Michele, 961, 964, 965
Brooks, M. Linda, 120
Brooks, Patty Pansing, 842, 844
Brooks, Paul, 185
Brooks, Rick, 417
Brooks, Robert, 1094, 1099, 1100
Brooks, Ron, 193
Brooks, Samantha, 21
Brooks, Sarah, 44
Brooks, Stephen, 189
Brooks, Taineshia, 421
Broomfield, Tyrone, 33
Brophy McGee, Kate, 568, 570
Brophy, Michelle, 419
Brophy, Theresa A., 217
Brosch, Chris, 76
Brossoie, Nicole, 312
Brostoff, Jonathan, 1095, 1099, 1100, 1101, 1102
Brothers, Ronald "Ron", 225
Brothers, Rudolph, 465
Brough, Aaron, 476
Brough, William P. "Bill", 586, 591, 592, 593
Brougham Freeman, Leslie, 201
Broughton, James W. C. "Jimmy", 346
Broughton, Ron, 161
Broun, Joal, 357
Brouse, Lorrie, 439
Broussard, Billy, 204
Broussard, Earl, Jr., 461
Broussard, John J., 206
Broussard, Col. Joseph, 204
Brower, Mike, 185
Brower, Tom, 657, 659, 660, 661
Brown-Bland, ToNola, 353
Brown Glisson, Vickie Yates, 188

Brown-McCreery, Heidi, 151
Brown-Powers, Timi, 703, 708, 709
Brown-Whitfield, Cheryl A., 224
Brown, Adam, 676, 682, 683, 684, 685, 686
Brown, Alice T., 199
Brown, Alison, 273
Brown, Anne, 81
Brown, Anne Gust, 37
Brown, Beau, 6
Brown, Bill, 268, 944, 946, 947
Brown, Blair, 233
Brown, Bob, 836, 840, 841
Brown, Brandon, 203
Brown, Brenda, 121
Brown, Bryce, 506
Brown, Carol J., 482
Brown, Carolyn, 194
Brown, Cassie, 455
Brown, Catherine F. "Cathy", 274
Brown, Cathrynn N., 883, 886
Brown, Cecil C., 273
Brown, Chad, 33
Brown, Chad M., 738, 743
Brown, Charles, 270
Brown, Charlie, 352, 692, 698
Brown, Cheryl R., 586, 591, 592, 593
Brown, Chris, 807, 812, 813, 814, 815, 854, 869
Brown, Chris A., 874, 879
Brown, Chuck, 439
Brown, Dr. Chuck Carr, 200
Brown, Cloria, 820, 828, 829, 830
Brown, Corey W., 1010, 1012
Brown, Craig C., 22
Brown, Curtis, 496
Brown, Dan, 120
Brown, Danny, 42
Brown, Dan W., 816, 818, 819
Brown, Darren, 214
Brown, David "Dave", 168
Brown, David A., 69
Brown, David E., 494
Brown, David L., 351
Brown, David M. "Dave", 786, 789
Brown, Dean, 15
Brown, Debbie, 619
Brown, Debra, 58
Brown, Dee L., 832, 835
Brown, Derek, 397
Brown, Donald C., 60
Brown, Donna, 162
Brown, Doris, 202
Brown, Dorothy, 384
Brown, Duane, 854, 868
Brown, Edmund Gerald "Jerry", Jr., 37
Brown, Edna R., 934, 935, 936, 937
Brown, Elizabeth "Liz", 687, 690
Brown, Eric, 246
Brown, Faith, 481
Brown, Gary, 344, 494
Brown, George, 105
Brown, George A., Jr., 726, 731, 732
Brown, Gerard, 92
Brown, Gladys M., 407
Brown, Grady A., 1003, 1009
Brown, Gregory, 223
Brown, Harry, 907, 908, 910, 911, 912, 913
Brown, Henderson J., 97
Brown, Hollie, 473
Brown, Jacinta, 18
Brown, CSM James M., 160

Brown, James R., 190
Brown, James S., 508
Brown, Jason, 429
Brown, Jason, III, 343
Brown, Jason R., 91
Brown, Jayme, 369
Brown, Jeffrey, 8
Brown, Jennifer, 472
Brown, J. Michael, 195
Brown, JoAnn, 116
Brown, Joanne M. Salas, 125
Brown, Joe, 474
Brown, Joe W., 447
Brown, J. Paul, 595, 598
Brown, Julie Imanuel, 107
Brown, Karen, 351, 498
Brown, Karilyn, 575, 580
Brown, Kate, 390
Brown, Katie L., 392
Brown, Kermit, 1104, 1105, 1108
Brown, Kevin, 232, 403
Brown, Kevin C., 183
Brown, Kevin M., 319
Brown, Koven L., 547, 552
Brown, Kyle M., 60
Brown, LaKimbre, 89
Brown, Larry, 62
Brown, Layna, 523
Brown, Linda C., 192
Brown, Lynn, 507
Brown, Marcus L., 400
Brown, Marie A., 423
Brown, Marty, 509
Brown, Mary Elizabeth, 264
Brown, Matthew, 7, 86, 97
Brown, Max, 502
Brown, Maj M. Caitlin, 104
Brown, Melanie L., 247
Brown, Melvin R. "Mel", 1041, 1045
Brown, Mike, 948, 953, 954
Brown, Monica J., 90
Brown, Natascha, 229
Brown, Nathan, 190
Brown, Nicholas, 501
Brown, Nicole, 356
Brown, Pamela "Pam", 854, 870
Brown, Paula, 267
Brown, Peg, 64
Brown, Phil, 158
Brown, Philip "Phil", 593
Brown, Quanta, 369
Brown, Rayne, 914, 920, 921, 922, 923, 924
Brown, Rebecca, 9
Brown, Rebecca A., 854, 868
Brown, Renysha, 150
Brown, Rich, 779
Brown, Richard D. "Ric", 492
Brown, Robert L., 1003, 1008, 1009
Brown, Robert L., Jr., 121
Brown, Rosemary M., 966, 978, 979, 980
Brown, Ryan, 164, 260
Brown, Sandra "Sandy", 177
Brown, Sarah, 169
Brown, Scott, 171
Brown, Sean, 479
Brown, Sharon, 1069, 1070, 1072, 1073
Brown, Sheryll, 380
Brown, Stacy E., 522
Brown, Stephen, 52
Brown, Steve, 443
Brown, Taylor, 833, 834, 835
Brown, Terry, 499
Brown, Terry R., 738, 742, 743, 744
Brown, Thomas "Tom", 193
Brown, Tiffany, 406

Brown, Tim, 385
Brown, Timothy N. "Tim", 692, 698
Brown, Tim W., 938, 942, 943
Brown, Todd F., 392
Brown, Tracy, 157
Brown, Troy E., 734, 736, 737
Brown, Vanessa Lowery, 967, 977, 979, 980
Brown, Vaughn, 104
Brown, Vince, 55
Brown, Wanda, 820, 829, 830
Brown, William Hogan, 430
Brown, Zach, 836, 840, 841
Brownback, Samuel Dale "Sam", 175
Browne, Capt. Avery A., 50
Browne, Felix, 240
Browne, Mark, 64
Browne, Patrick M. "Pat", 961, 964, 965
Browne, Victor, 487
Brownfield, Jeffrey V. "Jeff", 56
Brownfield, Michael "Mike", 246
Browning, Cynthia M., 1049, 1055
Browning, David, 273
Browning, Debbie A., 513
Browning, H. Butch, Jr., 203
Browning, John, 105
Browning, Kristopher, 110
Browning, Lynne, 198
Browning, Nickey Reed, 800, 803, 804
Browning, Sarah, 307
Browning, Tommy, 267
Brownsberger, William N., 763, 766, 767
Broxson, Douglas Vaughn "Doug", 624, 630
Broyles, Tommy, 456
Broz-Vaughn, Mary C., 491
Broz, Jerry, 288
Bruce, David, 247
Bruce, Col. Mark, 179
Bruce, Patsy, 449
Bruce, Roger B., 638, 648, 649, 650
Bruce, Terry, 709, 712
Bruch, Eli, 85
Bruchman, Rob, 714, 720, 721, 722
Bruckner, Henry P., 132
Bruder, Connie, 164
Brudvik, Len, 510
Bruebaker, Gary, 509
Brueggeman, Barbara, 275
Brueggemann, Sheri, 299
Bruen, Kevin, 332
Bruff, Mike, 353
Brumbaugh, David, 947, 948, 953, 954
Brumfield, Myles, 203
Brumley, Gretchen, 88
Brun, Robert, 234
Bruncati, James, 312
Brune, Gary J., 314
Brunell, Duane, 213
Brunelle, Mike, 400
Bruner, Ann, 504
Bruner, Laura, 217, 221
Bruner, Mike, 5
Bruner, Richard "Dick", 173
Brunetti, Rick, 177
Bruni, Louis A., 309
Bruni, Maria C., 147
Brunk, Jared, 146
Brunker, Maureen, 531
Brunkow, Jennifer, 177
Brunner, Charles, 779, 784, 785
Brunner, Ryan, 437

Brunner, Thomas J., 1012, 1015
Bruno, Anthony, 69
Bruno, Delila, 283
Bruno, Mark, 281
Bruno, Rhonda, 379
Bruno, Ruth, 59
Bruns, Pat, 376
Brunson, Jeana, 105
Brunson, Teresa, 9
Brunt, James, 335
Brush, Darin, 476
Bruun, Bech K., 466
Bryan, Albert, Jr., 485
Bryan, Bill, 347
Bryan, Hob, 800, 803, 804, 805
Bryan, Jerry, 109
Bryan, Laura, 207
Bryan, Nicole, 184
Bryan, Robert P. "Rob", III, 914, 920, 921, 923, 924
Bryan, Tony, 381
Bryant Kuhns, Christie, 938, 942, 943
Bryant, Angela R., 908, 910, 911, 912
Bryant, Charlie, 445
Bryant, David, 179
Bryant, Dewey Phillip "Phil", 264
Bryant, Eileen, 344
Bryant, Elizabeth, 166
Bryant, John, 100
Bryant, Kevin L., 998, 1000, 1001, 1002
Bryant, Linda, 500
Bryant, Mark E., 747, 752
Bryant, Michael D., 464
Bryant, Michael G., 349
Bryant, Nancy, 180
Bryant, Neil, 397
Bryant, Rob, 539
Bryant, Robert W. "Bob", 395
Bryant, Roger, 516
Bryant, Terri, 676, 683, 685, 686
Bryant, Wendy, 46
Bryant, William "Bill", 35
Bryant, William Bradley "Brad", 118
Bryars, Debra, 149
Bryce, Philip A., 306
Bryce, Terry, 380
Brycki, Paul, 602, 609, 610
Brymer, David, 458
Bryson, Charles, 444
Bryson, Col. Homer, 113
Bucar, Stephen A., 409
Bucari, Louis, 71
Bucci, Joseph A., 418
Bucci, Matthew J. "Matt", 413
Bucco, Anthony M. "Tony", Jr., 874, 878
Bucco, Anthony R., 871, 873
Buchanan, Bill, 347
Buchanan, Derek W., 109
Buchanan, Doug, 94
Buchanan, Gary, 311
Buchanan, Irma, 439
Buchanan, Kendall, 424
Buchanan, Matthew, 426
Buchholtz, Chelsea, 466
Buchholz, Russ, 361
Buchta, David, 186
Buchwald, David, 895, 903, 904, 905, 906
Buchy, Jim "Jim", 937, 938, 941, 942, 943
Buck-Taylor, Cecilia, 602, 609, 610
Buck, Debbie, 137
Buck, James "Jim", 389
Buck, James R. "Jim", 687, 690, 691

Buck, Karen, 338
Buck, Mike, 118
Buck, Perry L., 595, 596, 598
Buck, Steven L., 384
Buckel, Jason C., 757, 763
Buckland, Andrew Russell, 747
Bucklen, Kristopher, 402
Buckler, Lauren, 220
Buckles, Ed, 149
Buckley, Alan, 164
Buckley, Daphne L., 270
Buckley, Deirdre, 236
Buckley, Eric, 190
Buckley, Erica, 344
Buckley, Jack, 236
Buckley, Kim, 429
Buckley, Peter, 957
Buckley, Pola A., 215
Buckley, Tim, 231
Buckman, John, 159
Buckmaster, Bruce, 396
Buckner-Webb, Cherie, 661, 663, 664
Buckner, Debbie G., 637, 638, 650, 651
Buckner, Janet P., 596, 598
Buckner, La Tasha, 195
Buckner, LaTasha, 192
Buckner, Tara L., 516
Buco, Thomas "Tom", 854, 869
Bucy, Pamela "Pam", 283
Buczynski, Fran, 307
Budell, Russell, 101
Budler, Joanne M. "Jo", 180
Budoff, Jennifer, 86
Budzik, Matthew, 74
Bueche, James, 203
Buehler, Knute, 957, 960
Buehler, Nathan, 396
Buell, Dean, 299
Buell, Tonia, 506
Buerger, David, 532
Buesing, Carl, 526
Bueter, Fred, 251
Buettner, Ellen, 381
Buff, Mark, 497
Buffi, Deborah B., 416
Buffington, Doug, 520
Buffington, Miriam L., 158
Buffkin, Karen K., 67
Buford, Tom, 723, 725
Bugg, J. Bruce, 464
Buggs, David, 462
Bugher, Robert, 156
Buhl O'Donnell, Angie, 1010, 1011
Buhl, Lynn Yerges, 219
Buhnerkempe, John, 148
Buhs, Caleb, 252
Buick, David A., 253
Buis, Rodney, 183
Buki-Dabby, Maya, 233
Bukowski, Ray, 311
Bulerín Ramos, Ángel, 984, 987, 988, 989, 990
Bull, John M.R., 496
Bull, LeAnne, 5
Bullard, Bruce, 144
Bullard, Dwight M., 619, 621, 622, 623
Bullard, COL Kevin, 271
Bullard, Lori, 446
Bullard, Steve, 195
Bullen, Peyton, 439
Bullerman, Heather M., 435
Bullinger, Kenan, 360
Bullock, Al, 222
Bullock, Donna, 967, 977, 979, 980
Bullock, Jeffrey W. "Jeff", 79
Bullock, Kevin, 370
Bullock, Steve, 281
Bulluck, Joyce, 356
Bulot, Dr. James, 114

Bulova, David L., 1062, 1067, 1068
Bulwinkle, LTC Marion A., III, 430
Bumgardner, Aundré, 602, 609, 612
Bumgardner, Dana, 914, 920, 922, 923, 924
Bumgarner, Kami, 270
Bump, Benjamin "Ben", 538
Bump, Joel, 160
Bump, Suzanne M., 244
Bumpus, Robert, 317
Bumstead, Jon, 779, 780, 784
Bunch, Regina, 726, 732, 733
Bundy, Seth, 274
Bunker, Joshua, 260
Bunn, David A., 47
Bunten, Elysia C., 322
Buntin, Charles, 6
Bunting, Nina Lou, 82
Buntrock, Rhonda, 433
Buono, Victor, 80
Burack, Thomas S. "Tom", 304
Buras, Rennie J., II, 205
Burbank, Scott, 8
Burbidge, Marianne, 473
Burch, Clayton, 523
Burch, Denise, 488
Burch, Michael, 355
Burch, Thomas J. "Tom", 726, 732, 733
Burchill, Kiyomi, 43
Burckhard, Randy, 925, 927
Burckle, Ed, 322
Burden, Col Gregg, 179
Burdeshaw, Jane Elizabeth, 5
Burdette, Brian K., 118
Burdette, J. Keith, 513, 514
Burdette, Patricia A., 513
Burdette, Randall P., 498
Burdick, Brett, 497
Burdick, Ginny, 955, 956, 957
Burditt, Tom, 1049, 1055
Burger, Steve, 292
Burges, Judy M., 565, 567
Burgess, Bradley Warren, 382
Burgess, Daniel, 235
Burgess, Daniel "Danny", 624, 630
Burgess, Thomas A., 225
Burget, Niomi, 175
Burgin, Gina, 492
Burgin, Jean, 726
Burgos, Robin, 225
Burgoyne, Grant, 661, 663
Burhop, Dave, 498
Burk, Curtis, 472
Burk, Jim, 432
Burk, Kathy G., 268
Burk, Michelle, 368
Burkart, Kristin, 537
Burke, Alexander, 144
Burke, Autumn R., 585, 586, 591, 592
Burke, Belit, 393
Burke, Bradley, 178
Burke, Chari, 159
Burke, Daniel J., 675, 676, 683, 684
Burke, David E. "Dave", 934, 935, 936
Burke, Dean, 632, 634, 635
Burke, Edward L., 408
Burke, Kelly M., 676, 682, 683, 684, 685, 686
Burke, Mollie S., 1049, 1056
Burke, Monte, 207
Burke, Robert E., 478
Burke, Ronald, 106
Burke, Susan, 473

Burke, Yvonne Brathwaite, 50
Burkes, Aaron, 36
Burkes, Rebecca, 31
Burket, Lee, 410
Burkett-Lewis, Dionne, 84
Burkett, Charlene, 156
Burkett, Cindy, 1030, 1036, 1038
Burkhalter, Dallas, 138
Burkhalter, Mark, 121
Burkhart-Wilson, Tabitha, 189
Burkhart, Donald E. "Don", Jr., 1105, 1107
Burkley, Tony, 938, 941, 942, 943
Burks, BrigGen William R., 298
Burleigh, Richard, 136, 142
Burley, Dana M., 874
Burley, Dr. Howard, 445
Burling, Dennis, 290
Burlison, Eric, 820, 828, 829, 830
Burman, Bonnie Kantor, 367
Burman, Diane X., 342
Burnand, Mary Beth, 235
Burne, Brian T., 213
Burnell, Barry, 135
Burnett, A.G., 300
Burnett, Cedric, 807, 812, 813, 814, 815
Burnett, Christopher, 468
Burnett, David, 572, 574
Burnett, George, 388
Burnett, Jerry, 16
Burnett, Michelle, 419
Burnett, Miles, 41
Burnett, Tom, 836, 840
Burnham, Bobbie, 256
Burnham, David, 417
Burns, Anthony, 325
Burns, Bill, 134
Burns, Bob, 820, 830, 831, 832
Burns, Bruce, 1102, 1104
Burns, Craig M., 493
Burns, David C., 744, 746
Burns, David E. "Dave", 210
Burns, DeWayne, 1030, 1037, 1038
Burns, Edmund, 342
Burns, Frank, 967, 978, 979, 980
Burns, George, 297
Burns, Gordon, 39
Burns, James Mikell "Mike", 1003, 1008
Burns, Jim, 135
Burns, Johnnie, 261
Burns, Jon G., 637, 638, 646, 647, 648, 650, 651
Burns, Kimberly M., 222
Burns, Marlies, 476
Burns, Randall, 13
Burns, Robert "Bob", 26
Burns, Roxie, 396
Burns, Susan "Sue", 369
Burns, Timothy P. "Tim", 341
Burnsed, Genia, 121
Burnside, Andrew, 261
Buroker, Brenda, 158
Burr, Justin P., 914, 920, 921, 922, 923, 924
Burr, Sue, 57
Burrage, J. David, 382
Burrage, Steve, 387
Burrell, Cheryl, 414
Burris, Alec, 16
Burris, Amy Cannizaro, 204
Burris, Patricia, 82
Burroughs, James C., II, 255
Burroughs, Tom, 713, 714, 720, 721
Burrows Kleats, Leila, 322

Burrows, Dustin, 1030, 1036, 1037
Burrus, Peter, 499
Burshem, Craig, 495
Burstein, Christine, 747, 752
Burt, A. Keith, 386
Burt, John A., 854, 868
Burt, Robert "Robby", 273
Burt, Roy, 324
Burt, William F. "Bill", 880, 882
Burtenshaw, Alaina, 300
Burtenshaw, Van, 664, 667, 668
Burton, Alan R., 210
Burton, Anastasia, 286
Burton, Beth, 120
Burton, Charles W. "Woody", 692, 697, 698
Burton, Colleen, 624, 630
Burton, Daniel, 477
Burton, Diane, 250
Burton, Jack, 12
Burton, Jeff, 190
Burton, MG Jefferson S., 476
Burton, Kimiko, 43
Burton, Konni, 1026, 1028, 1029
Burton, Nathan, 451
Burton, Ronald "Ron", 325
Burton, Scott, 35
Burton, Sharron, 192
Burton, Terry Clark, 800, 801, 803, 804, 805
Burton, Wayne M., 854, 868
Burzichelli, John J., 874, 878, 879
Bus, Alida, 12
Busby, Charles, 807, 812, 813, 815
Busby, Pamela, 447
Buscemi, Beverly A.H., 422
Busch, Kathy, 181
Busch, Michael Erin, 756, 757
Buschatzke, Thomas, 25
Buschfort, Valeria, 14
Buschman, Sara, 526
Buse, Christopher "Chris", 262
Busey, Jennifer, 393, 399
Bush, Amy, 449
Bush, Anita, 299
Bush, Carol, 466, 854, 868
Bush, Charles, 186, 193
Bush, David, 534
Bush, D. Michael, 537
Bush, George Prescott, 468
Bush, Jeffrey L. "Jeff", 516
Bush, Melinda, 670, 673, 674, 675
Bush, Patrick, 77
Bushek, Brian, 340
Bushell, Gerrard P., 340
Bushey, Kim, 480
Bushman, Kirk, 285
Bushnell, Richard, 207
Bushweller, Brian J., 612, 613, 614
Buskey, James E., 547, 552, 553, 554
Buss, Brittany, 536
Bussa, Mike, 372
Bussey, Celina, 326
Bussey, Nicholas, 292
Bussman, Paul, 543, 545, 546
Bustamante Adams, Irene, 847, 849, 850
Bustamante, Jereima "Jeri", 99
Butani, Rachna, 97
Butay, Jade, 132
Butcher, Clay, 13
Butcher, Loarie H., 514
Butcher, Loita C., 519
Butcher, Mike, 251
Butcher, Ronald K., 317

Butera, John, 208
Butler, Albert, 801, 803, 804, 805
Butler, Cindy K., 521
Butler, Craig W., 373
Butler, Deborah, 357
Butler, Denver "Denny", 726, 731, 732, 733
Butler, Edward A., 854, 868
Butler, George W. "Bo", 119
Butler, Gloria S., 632, 635, 636, 637
Butler, James "Jim", 42, 938, 942
Butler, Dr. Jay C., 14
Butler, Jim, 1084, 1089, 1090
Butler, John Mark, 121
Butler, Julie, 299
Butler, Larry B., 603, 609, 610
Butler, Mack, 547, 552, 553, 554
Butler, Marc W., 895, 902, 904, 905, 906
Butler, Marla, 147
Butler, Michael, 820, 828, 829, 831
Butler, Mickey, 444
Butler, Pat, 308
Butler, Patricia, 70
Butler, Robert "Bob", 117
Butler, Rosetta R., 224
Butler, Sarah, 192
Butler, Thomas F., 461
Butler, Major Thomas P., 409
Butler, Timothy A., 120
Butler, Timothy J. "Tim", 676, 684, 685, 686
Butler, Col. Tom, 286
Butler, Tommy, 286
Butler, Wesley J., 262
Butola, Andrea, 418
Butt, Sheila, 1019, 1020, 1024
Butterfield, Cleon P., 477
Butters, COL Dennis, 6
Butterworth, Ann, 450
Butterworth, Gary, 62
Butterworth, MG James B. "Jim", 111
Butterworth, Sharon Swift, 460
Button, Angie Chen, 1030, 1037, 1038
Button, Glendon, 481
Button, Lewis, III, 74
Buttrey, Edward, 832, 833, 835
Butzlaff, Nathan, 10
Buuck, Adam, 120
Buxton, John, 213
Buxton, Sarah E., 1049, 1055
Buxton, Susan, 141
Buys, Vincent, 1073, 1077, 1078
Buzard, Kimberley, 468
Buzbee, Richard, 30
Buzzard, Alice Jo, 516
Byard, Jeff, 6
Byard, Jim, Jr., 4
Byars, Louis, 118
Bydalek, Dave, 294
Bye, Beth, 599, 608, 609, 610, 611
Bye, Pam, 3
Byer, Von W., 456
Byers, Jonathan, 364
Byers, Katie, 163
Byers, Terri, 130
Byers, Dr. William "Dubs", 33
Bynum, Jeff, 267
Bynum, Sharon, 428
Byrd, Andrew, 1084, 1089, 1090

Byrd, Cindy, 389
Byrd, David "Coach", 1020, 1024
Byrd, Isaac, 120
Byrd, James W. "Jim", 1104, 1105, 1107
Byrd, Larry, 807, 812, 813, 814, 815
Byrd, Melisa, 92
Byrd, Warren, 207
Byrd, Wendell, 780, 784, 785
Byrne, Alice Ann, 5
Byrne, Andrea, 539
Byrne, Brendan T., Jr., 315
Byrne, David B., 3
Byrne, Dennis, 537
Byrne, Emily, 478
Byrne, Jess, 135
Byrne, Mary, 315
Byrne, Robert, 57
Byrne, Sean M., 337
Byrnes, Joshua, 703, 707, 708, 709
Byrnes, Tracy, 166
Byron, Cyril, Jr., 87
Byron, Frank A., 854, 869
Byron, Gary, 603, 609, 610
Byron, Kathy J., 1062, 1067, 1068, 1069
Byron, Shawn, 307
Byron, Tom, 105
Byrum, Dr. Beverly, 367
Byrum, Marvin, 4
Bzdyra, Michael, 71


**C**

Cabe, Becky, 184
Cabello, Homero, 454
Cabello, John M., 676, 683, 685, 686
Cabezas, James I., 229
Cabral, Antonio F. D., 767, 775
Cabrera, Misael, 23
Cachares, Ray, 153
Cachola, Romy M., 657, 659, 660, 661
Cachuela, Brenda, 224
Cadena, Micaela, 321
Cadigan, William J. "Bill", 152
Cadle, Col Michael O., 518
Cadle, Scott, 1084, 1088, 1089, 1090
Cadman, Bill, 593
Cadotte, Mark, 394
Cadovius, Nicole M., 69
Cadreche, Dr. Marina, 440
Cafaro, Capri S., 934, 935, 936, 937
Caferro, Mary M., 833, 834, 835
Cage, Caleb, 296, 299
Cage, Celena, 201
Cagigal, David, 526
Cagle, Bobby, 114
Cagle, Casey, 117, 119, 631
Cagle, Karen, 45
Cahill, Alexandra "Alex", 235
Cahill, Daniel F. "Dan", 768, 775
Cahill, Edward M., 334
Cahill, John, 178
Cahill, Kevin, 339
Cahill, Kevin A., 895, 904, 905, 907
Cahill, Michael, 854, 869
Cahill, Timothy, 237
Cahoon, Amy, 247
Cail, Hodari, 231
Cain, Allan, 461
Cain, C. Camille, 452
Cain, Charlene, 323
Cain, Emma, 535
Cain, Jim, 236
Cain, Keli, 380

Cain, Shawn, 220
Cain, Staci, 189
Cain, Tracy, 464
Caine, Justin, 248
Caines, Jeff, 391
Caisido, Marie, 323
Caissie, Jennie L., 231
Cajero Bedford, Olivia, 565, 567
Cajigal, Ferdinand, 132
Cajindos, Justin, 154
Calabrese-Benton, Tisha, 442
Calabretta, Daniel J., 37
Calahan, Tamy, 62
Calametti, Karen, 6
Calamia, Gerald, 313
Calcote, Sharon, 206
Caldero Lopez, Col. Jose, 412
Calderon, Alissandra, 146
Calderon, Ian Charles, 585, 586, 591, 592
Calderon, Miguel, 150
Caldier, Michelle, 1073, 1078
Caldwell, Alicia, 61
Caldwell, Brittany, 425
Caldwell, Chad, 948, 953, 954
Caldwell, Donna, 137
Caldwell, Doug M., 494
Caldwell, Johnnie, Jr., 638, 646, 647, 649
Caldwell, Krissa, 397
Caldwell, Matthew H. "Matt", 624, 631
Caldwell, Michael, 638, 647, 651
Caldwell, Ronald "Ron", 572, 574
Caldwell, Steven P. "Steve", 97
Calendar, Marcia, 6
Calfee, Kent, 1020, 1024
Calhoun, Cathy, 335
Calhoun, Cori, 260
Calhoun, Credell, 807, 813, 814, 815, 816
Calhoun, Dustin, 373
Calhoun, John, 101
Calhoun, BG Michael A., 104
Calhoun, Rosemary, 114
Cali-Pitts, Jacqueline A., 854, 870
Cali, Laura N., 391
Caligiuri, Richard "Rick", 257
Calio, Kevin, 78
Calisle, Lisa, 242
Calkins, Ronald "Ron", 33
Call, Bowen "Bo", 471
Callahan, COL Christopher P., 419
Callahan, Jamie, 37
Callahan, Melissa, 202
Callahan, Robin, 236
Callahan, Shirley, 250
Callahan, Victor, 277
Callaway, Douglas D., 105
Calley, Brian, 246, 776
Callier, Helen, 461
Callinan, Marianne, 237
Callison, Jeffrey, 51
Callton, Mike, 780, 784, 785
Callum, Rhonda, 220
Caltagirone, Thomas R., 967, 980
Calter, Thomas J., III, 768, 775
Calvey, Kevin J., 948, 953, 954
Calvo, Edward Baza "Eddie", 123
Calvo, Jose "Joey", 123
Calvo, Mark, 123
Camacho, David, 124
Camacho, John, 125

Cambrom, Elizabeth, 438
Camden, Allison, 506
Cameron, Amy, 48
Cameron, Brett, 22
Cameron, Casey, 474
Cameron, David, 481
Cameron, Dean L., 136
Cameron, Guy E., 534
Camillo, Fred, 603, 608, 609
Cammack, Gary L., 1010, 1011, 1012
Cammack, Martin "Marty", 259
Camp, Alissa, 154
Camp, Ken, 510, 1069
Camp, Tim, 423
Campanale, Kate, 768, 775
Campanella, Leslie, 44
Campanile, Nicholas "Nick", 101
Campbell-Street, Cherrell, 444
Campbell, Allison, 338
Campbell, Alyson, 277
Campbell, Barbara, 184
Campbell, Blaine B. "Chip", 1012, 1015
Campbell, Carla J., 514
Campbell, Crystal, 207
Campbell, Daniel, 220
Campbell, Daphne D., 624, 630
Campbell, Denise Lynne, 1084, 1088, 1089, 1090
Campbell, Donna, 37, 1026, 1028, 1029
Campbell, Fred, 34
Campbell, Jack, 145
Campbell, James J., Sr., 747
Campbell, MAJ Jason, 434
Campbell, J. Brent, 202
Campbell, Jeffrey L., 1062, 1067, 1069
Campbell, Jennifer, 314, 424
Campbell, John, 272
Campbell, John F., 1046, 1047, 1048
Campbell, Joseph, 250
Campbell, Kathy, 842, 844
Campbell, Kimberly L., 807, 812, 814, 815
Campbell, Larry L., 714, 721, 722
Campbell, Linda Dean, 768, 775
Campbell, Lori, 13, 150
Campbell, Martha, 450
Campbell, Melinda S., 516
Campbell, Mick, 276
Campbell, Nicole, 454, 467
Campbell, Noel, 568, 571
Campbell, Paul G., Jr., 998, 1000, 1001, 1002
Campbell, Ray, 233
Campbell, Richard, 144
Campbell, Richard H. "Dick", 747
Campbell, Rita, 1105, 1107, 1108
Campbell, Col Shelley R., 536
Campbell, Thomas W., 522
Campbell, Tom, 925, 927
Camper, Karen D., 1019, 1020, 1025
Campion, Brian, 1047, 1048
Campos-Vergara, Maria, 43
Campos, Carlos, 150
Campos, Eva, 327
Campos, Nora E., 586, 591, 592
Campos, Pablo G. "Paul", 1069
Campos, Pete, 880, 882
Campos, Shelby, 390
Campsen, George E. "Chip", III, 998, 1001, 1002
Camuso, Paul A., 233

Canaan, Jeff, 503
Canaca, Jorge, 26
Canaday, Nicholas, 455
Canales, Terry, 1030, 1036, 1037
Canario, Dennis M., 993, 997
Canary, Leura Garrett, 8
Canavaggio, George, 116
Canavero, Steve, 300
Cancel, Alice, 895, 903, 905, 906
Candelaria, Jacob R., 880, 882
Candelaria, Juan R., 601, 603, 608, 609, 610, 611
Candelora, Vincent J. "Vinny", 601, 603, 609, 610, 611
Canelaria, Mia, 323
Canepa, Jim, 373
Canfield, Edward J., 780, 784
Canfield, Greg, 3
Canfield, Jack, 514
Canfield, William "Bill", 1049, 1056
Cannaday, Dr. Billy K., Jr., 492
Cannaday, Ed, 948, 952, 953, 954
Cannady, Eric M., 87
Cannady, Richard, 1105, 1107, 1108
Cannady, Tom, 190
Cannella, Anthony, 582, 584, 585
Canney, Jeff, 327
Canning, Kevin, 81
Cannon, Ben, 397
Cannon, Gus, 464
Cannon, Mike, 423
Cannon, Nancy, 430
Cannon, Park, 638
Cannon, Timothy H. "Tim", 100
Cannon, Major Timothy J., 109
Canole, Michael, 418
Canter, Laura, 245
Canterbury, Denny Ray, Jr., 1084, 1088, 1089, 1090
Canto, Doreen Napua, 133
Canton, Amy, 378
Cantor, Raymond, 310
Cantoria, Filomena, 123
Cantrell, Chris, 291
Cantrell, Courtney, 349
Cantrell, Don, 423
Cantrell, Wesley E. "Wes", 638, 647, 649, 650
Cantu, Major Eliseo "Al", Jr., 465
Cantu, Jeannette, 466
Cantwell, James M., 768, 775
Cantwell, Mari, 44
Canzoneri, Mike, 104
Capacci, George, 506
Capezza, Thomas A., 336
Caplan, Jesse M., 236
Caple, Wendi, 77
Caplis, Ed, 285
Capp, James, 115
Cappel-Chmidling, Marcelle, 177
Cappello, Stephen, 88
Capper, Patrick, 502
Cappone, Mark, 373
Capps, Scott, 352
Capriglione, Giovanni, 1030, 1036, 1037, 1038
Caputo, Michael "Mike", 1083, 1084, 1088, 1089, 1090
Caputo, Ralph R., 874, 878, 879
Caraballo, Aracelis, 120

**NAME INDEX**

Chun, Calvert, 132
Chung, Christina, 46
Church, Jeff, 140
Church, Robert, 23
Church, Ryan, 260
Church, Tom, 327
Churchill, Ellington C., Jr., 221
Churchill, Julie M., 210
Churchill, Patricia, 280
Churchill, Shareese DeLeaver, 216
Chute, Christine, 398
Chytka, LTC Matt, 351
Cialone, Josephine, 350
Ciardullo, Mark, 178
Cias, Judy M., 58
Ciattarelli, Jack M., 874, 875, 878, 879
Cibrik, Sharon L., 518
Cicak, Kevin, 405
Cicatiello, Judith L., 370
Ciccocioppo, Barry, 409
Ciccone, Frank A., III, 990, 992, 993
Ciccone, Kimberly, 335
Cicero, Robert "Bob", 185
Cichos, Mark, 435
Cierpiot, Mike, 819, 821, 827, 829, 831
Cignarale, Anthony "Tony", 56
Ciliberti, Barrie S., 757, 762
Cilley, Jacalyn L. "Jackie", 855, 868
Cills, COL Linda, 485
Cimaglio, Barbara, 480
Cimino, Joseph, 496
Cimino, Victoria, 306
Cincotta, David, 380
Cintron, Roberto, 486
Cioppa, Eric A., 212
Ciotola, Carol, 414
Cipiti, Nicholas, 372
Cirelli, Connie, 419
Cirigliano, Vincent, 232
Cirish, Daria, 68
Cirrito, Christopher, 465
Ciscomani, Juan, 21
Cisneros, Carlos R., 880, 882
Cisse, Lubona "Lulu", 191
Cissell, Jackie, 155
Citro, COL Albert, 78
Ciulu, Maddy, 221
Clabaugh, Gerd W., 172
Claeys, Jeremy "J.R.", 714, 720, 722
Claeys, Thomas, 364
Clagg, Kevin, 384
Claggett, Steve, 348
Clahchischilliage, Sharon E., 883, 885, 886
Clairmont, Toby L., 130
Claitor, Dan, 734, 736
Claman, Matthew W. "Matt", 557, 560
Clancy, James "Jim", Jr., 458
Clanton, Jeff, 160
Clapper, Scott, 80
Claps, Rocco J., 147
Clardy, Travis, 1030, 1037, 1038
Clarey, Patricia T. "Pat", 43
Claridge, Kevin, 101
Clark, Alan, 572, 574
Clark, Alex, 216
Clark, Arthur, 123
Clark, Brenda, 444
Clark, Bryant W., 807, 812, 813, 814, 815, 816
Clark, Cameron R. "Cam", 159
Clark, Carol, 340
Clark, Charles, 503
Clark, Chris, 188

Clark, Christy, 282, 836, 840, 841
Clark, Cindy J., 520
Clark, Clayton, 480
Clark, Daniel, 169
Clark, David, 87, 115, 475, 639, 647, 650, 651
Clark, David A., 101
Clark, Dawn, 530
Clark, Delisa, 423
Clark, Eric, 188
Clark, Gary F., 101
Clark, Gerard, 105
Clark, Heath N., 639, 647, 650
Clark, Lt. Col. Jack, 4
Clark, Jason, 465
Clark, Karen, 791, 797, 798, 799
Clark, Ken, 568, 570, 571
Clark, Larry, 300
Clark, Lawrence "Larry", 403, 727, 731, 732, 733
Clark, Leah, 137
Clark, Linda, 233
Clark, Dr. Linda, 139
Clark, Lisa, 479
Clark, Liz, 555
Clark, Liza, 431
Clark, Lonnie G., 714, 720, 722
Clark, Marilee, 72
Clark, Mark A., 507
Clark, Martha Fuller, 851, 852
Clark, Mary E., 237
Clark, Matt, 216
Clark, Michael, 453
Clark, Nancy, 455
Clark, Patricia, 71
Clark, Paula M., 210
Clark, Perry B., 723, 725, 726
Clark, Robert, 427
Clark, Robert A. "Robbie", 383
Clark, Robert B. "Ben", III, 908, 911, 912, 913
Clark, Sarah L., 403
Clark, Stuart, 503
Clark, Thomas, 357
Clark, Tina, 520
Clark, Valerie, 639, 646, 647, 648, 651
Clark, Vaughn, 379
Clark, Virginia, 48
Clarke-Reed, Gwyndolen "Gwyn", 624, 630
Clarke, Adline C., 547, 552, 553
Clarke, Adrienne, 337
Clarke, Alyce Griffin, 807, 812, 813, 815, 816
Clarke, Betsy, 257
Clarke, Caroline, 313
Clarke, Eugene S. "Buck", 801, 803, 804, 805
Clarke, Harold W., 497
Clarke, Jennifer, 415
Clarke, Larry, 196
Clarke, Michael, 332
Clarke, Scott D., 146
Clarke, Stephanie Schardin, 322
Clarke, Thomas L. "Tom", 515
Clarkowski, Lynn, 260
Clarkson, Alison H., 1049, 1056
Clarkson, Johnathan, 44
Claros, Evelyn, 123
Clary, Gary E., 1003, 1008, 1009
Clary, Holly, 490
Clary, Jan, 205
Clasen, Michael, 478
Claudio, Lorna, 30
Clausen, Greg D., 786, 789, 790

Clauser, David, 178
Clausing, Jan, 177
Clawson, Terry, 457
Claxton, Jeff, 454
Clay, Kendra, 34
Clay, Kimberly, 193
Clay, Marshall, 1083
Clay, Patricia "Trish", 522
Clay, Reed, 452
Clayborne, James F., Jr., 669, 670, 673, 674
Clayman, Jennifer L., 62
Clayton, Amanda, 176
Clayton, Christina, 119
Clayton, Gwendolyn, 117
Clayton, Stephanie, 714, 720, 721, 722
Clearwater, Karen, 395
Cleary, Joseph "Jay", 222
Cleary, Raymond E., III, 998, 1001, 1002
Cleeves, Ben, 178
Cleland, Meredith, 426
Clem, Brian L., 957, 960
Clem, Scott, 1105, 1108
Clemens, Jeff, 619, 621, 622
Clemenson, Randall "Randy", 170
Clement, Elizabeth "Beth", 246
Clemente, Paul, 780, 784, 785
Clements, Marlon, 110
Clements, Scott, 270
Clemmer, Ann V., 32
Clemmons, Alan D., 1003, 1009
Clemmons, John Ray, 1020, 1025
Clemonds, Bruce, 277
Clemons, David, 241
Clemons, Erik, 73
Clemons, Kelley, 441
Clenchy, Brooke, 234
Clendenin, Stephanie, 46
Clendenin, William "Bill", 425
Clere, Edward D. "Ed", 692, 698
Cleveland, Annette, 1069, 1070, 1072, 1073
Cleveland, Bobby, 948, 953, 954
Cleveland, George G., 914, 920, 921, 922, 923, 924
Cleveland, Dr. Philip, 7
Clevenger, Anna, 165
Clevenger, Brian, 219
Clevlen, Linda M., 457
Clezie, Lane, 138
Clibborn, Judy, 1073, 1078, 1079
Cliburn, Christie, 271
Clifford, Denise, 503
Clifford, Tom, 322, 327
Clift, Bob, 105
Clift, Claire J., 845
Clifton, Brandon, 166
Clifton, Harold D., 516
Clifton, LTC Mark, 381
Clifton, Robert D., 875, 879
Clifton, Sandra V., 46
Clinch, Frank, 284
Cline, Benjamin L. "Ben", 1062, 1067, 1068
Cline, Chris, 276
Cline, Paul, 471
Cline, Raechelle, 526
Cline, Sue, 1080, 1082
Cline, Terry L., 378, 380
Clingan-Fischer, Deanna, 167
Clippinger, Luke, 757, 762
Clocker, Joseph F., 224
Clokey, Micah, 324
Cloninger, Bret, 22
Cloonen, Katherine "Kate", 677, 682, 684, 685, 686
Close, Bryan, 386

Close, Jim, 260
Close, Matt, 368
Cloud, Cynthia I., 539
Clouden, Percival, 487
Clough, Frank, 307
Clough, Mark, 135
Clouse, Steve, 547, 553, 554
Cloutier, Catherine A., 612, 614
Cloutier, John R., 855, 869
Clover Adams, Jamie, 247
Clow, Bryan, 148
Clow, Lance W., 664, 667, 668
Clowes, Dana, 241
Cluck, COL Damon N., 33
Cluster, John W. E., Jr., 757, 762
Clyburn, Casey, 424
Clyburn, William "Bill", 1003, 1009
Clyde, Kathleen, 938, 942, 943
Clyne, Pamela J., 319
Cmelik, Kevin, 171
Coakley, Ann, 528
Coash, Colby, 842, 844, 845
Coates, John, 101
Coatney, Denise, 175
Coatney, Michael, 292
Coats, Kara S., 78
Coba, Katy, 391
Cobb-Hunter, Gilda, 1003, 1009
Cobb, Beckie Stockstill, 457
Cobb, Deborah, 193
Cobb, Deirdre Webster, 315
Cobb, Jeff, 776
Cobb, Michael A., 394
Cobb, Paula L., 101
Cobb, Regina, 568, 570, 571
Cobb, Dr. Robert, 120
Cobb, Steven, 418
Cobb, Tireka, 199
Cobbs, Jackie, 201
Cobbs, Nicholas, 86
Cobey, William W. "Bill", Jr., 354
Coble, Jerry, 351
Coble, Susan, 404
Cobos, Andrew J., 468
Cocca, John, 24
Cochran, Alexander, 331
Cochran, Brad J., 518
Cochran, Christopher, 50
Cochran, Connie, 495
Cochran, Cory, 157
Cochran, John, 337
Cochran, Karin, 348
Cochran, Patrick "Pat", 164
Cochran, Tom, 780, 784, 785
Cochran, Victoria, 496
Cochrane, Karl, 291
Cochrane, Larry, 507
Cockerham, Angela, 807, 812, 813, 814, 816
Cockrill, Harold D., 507
Cockroft, Josh, 948, 953, 954
Cockrum, Stacy, 49
Codey, Richard J., 871, 873
Cody, Eileen L., 1074, 1077, 1078
Cody, Julie, 395
Cody, Preston W., 509
Coe, Henry H. R. "Hank", 1103, 1104
Coe, Michael, 852
Coe, Peggy, 378
Coffelt, Todd, 171
Coffer, Lara, 457
Coffey, Gwen, 447
Coffey, James, 855, 869
Coffey, Ludell Neill, 448
Coffey, Primrose, 493
Coffey, Rodney, 193
Coffin, Ann, 104

Coffin, Jim, 537
Coffina, Scott A., 309
Coffman, Cynthia H., 65
Coffman, Deborah, 34
Coffrin, Betty, 152
Cofield, Tamara, 9
Cofone, Paula M., 414
Cofrancesco, Peter J., III, 319
Cogan, Jennifer, 428
Coggburn, William, 385
Coghill, John B., Jr., 555, 556, 557
Cohan, Jennifer L., 80
Cohen, Alan, 855, 870
Cohen, Ben, 273
Cohen, Hal, 479, 480
Cohen, Harvey, 341
Cohen, Jeffrey P., 480
Cohen, Marcie, 96
Cohen, Mark B., 967, 980
Cohen, Michael, 41, 43, 51, 54
Cohen, Michael D., 338
Cohen, Randy L., 72
Cohen, Richard J. "Dick", 786, 789, 790
Cohen, Robert S., 103
Cohen, Roger, 314
Cohen, Roger J., 406
Cohen, Tracey, 88
Cohen, Wendy H., 154
Cohenour, Jill, 833, 834, 835
Cohn, Barbara, 337
Cohoon, Dennis M., 703, 708, 709
Coia, Robin Melfi, 417
Coit, Janet, 416
Coker, Lynda, 114
Coker, Seth, 112
Colbeck, Patrick, 776, 778, 779
Colbert, Col Christopher H., 156
Colbert, Eliz, 354
Colcord, Elizabeth, 351
Cole, Chris, 481
Cole, David N., 307
Cole, Janet, 418
Cole, Janie M., 517
Cole, J. Derham, Jr., 1003, 1009
Cole, Jean, 536
Cole, COL Jimmy L., 445
Cole, Joanna E., 1049, 1055
Cole, Kirk, 460
Cole, Lori A., 290
Cole, Mark L., 1062, 1068
Cole, Michael E., 74
Cole, Mike, 442
Cole, Phillip "Phil", 387
Cole, Randy, 375
Cole, Ronnie, 449
Cole, Sheena, 361
Cole, Triston, 780, 784, 785
Cole, Washington, 270
Cole, William P. "Bill", III, 1080, 1083
Coleman-Evans, Merika, 547, 553
Coleman, Brooks P., Jr., 639, 646, 647, 649, 650
Coleman, Cara L., 494
Coleman, Cedric, 190
Coleman, Creighton B., 998, 1000, 1001, 1002
Coleman, Dan, 57
Coleman, Derek H., 514
Coleman, Doug, 568, 570, 571
Coleman, Eric D., 599, 609, 610, 611
Coleman, Garey E., 599
Coleman, Garnet F., 1030, 1036, 1038
Coleman, Jacqueline, 91
Coleman, Jerry, 365
Coleman, Joel, 476

Coleman, John F., Jr., 407
Coleman, John G., Jr., 223
Coleman, Karen, 334
Coleman, Kathy C., 516
Coleman, Kim, 1042, 1045, 1046
Coleman, Lawrence, 507
Coleman, Linda, 543, 545, 546
Coleman, Maida J., 275
Coleman, Maureen A., 341
Coleman, Mike V., 519
Coleman, Moniko, 495
Coleman, Phil, 183
Coleman, Randy W., 522
Coleman, Renee, 98
Coleman, R. James "Jim", 140
Coleman, Rob, 468
Coleman, Rodney, 352
Coleman, Ryan, 231
Coleman, Sam, 488
Coleman, Sara Otte, 359
Coleman, Todd E., 188
Coleman, Tonomey, 241
Coles, Dr. John Davies, 91
Coletti, Joe, 347
Coley, Jim, 1020, 1024
Coley, Paul, 102
Coley, Timothy, 26
Coley, William P. "Bill", II, 934, 935, 936
Colgan, Brian, 153
Collada, Andrew, 40
Collamore, Brian, 1047, 1048
Colleary, Kathleen, 232
Collens, Valdamier, 485
Colleran, Michael J., 214
Collett, Johnny, 183
Collie, Megan, 10
Collier-Montgomery, Cecily E., 98
Collier, Bryan, 465
Collier, Clark, 23
Collier, Janice, 143
Collier, Lisa, 468
Collier, Nicole, 1030, 1036, 1037, 1038
Collier, Olivia, 348
Collier, Richard, 451
Collier, Stephanie, 424
Collier, Weldon, 110
Colligan, John, Jr., 497
Collings, Kim, 186
Collins-Day, Patricia, 45
Collins-Smith, Linda, 572, 574
Collins, A.L. "Buddy", 354
Collins, MG Augustus L. "Leon", 271
Collins, Belinda, 42
Collins, Benjamin, 95
Collins, Cari D., 275
Collins, Charlie, 575, 580
Collins, Chris, 349
Collins, Christopher, 324
Collins, Christopher E., 1062, 1067
Collins, Crystal, 448
Collins, Dawn, 27
Collins, Del, 430
Collins, Donna, 415
Collins, Frank, III, 99
Collins, Gary, 380
Collins, Gary E., 664, 667, 668
Collins, Gary L., 79
Collins, Hubert, 727, 732, 733
Collins, Jacqueline Y. "Jacqui", 670, 673, 674, 675
Collins, James L., 75
Collins, Jeffrey L. "Jeff", 914, 920, 922, 923, 924
Collins, Jim, 248
Collins, John, II, 54
Collins, Josh, 256

Collins, J. Sparb, 364
Collins, Leight D., 226
Collins, Lennie, 351
Collins, Lori, 184, 480
Collins, Maura, 479
Collins, Meghan Speakes, 107
Collins, Michael J., 228
Collins, Michael L., 376
Collins, Neal Anthony, 1003, 1008
Collins, Nick, 768, 775
Collins, Patrick, 62
Collins, Paul, 267
Collins, Richard G., 615, 617, 618
Collins, Ronald F., 744, 746
Collins, Sheri, 402
Collins, BG Stephen D., 195
Collins, Steve, 726
Collins, Terri, 547, 552, 554
Collins, Vendella M., 248
Collinwood, Kathleen McConkie, 470
Collison, Craig, 261
Colliton, Jeff, 508
Colman, Loren, 258
Colman, Rebecca, 338
Colmenero, Angela, 467
Colmers, John M., 227
Colo, Xavier, 228
Colomb, Yvonne, 734, 736
Colombo, Gino, 514
Colon-Padilla, Ricardo, 412
Colón Rondón, Idalia, 411
Colón, Carmen I., 70
Colón, José, 94
Colón, Lisa, 139
Colón, Luis A., 61
Colon, Noel, 335
Colon, William, 69
Colona, Mike, 821, 828, 829, 830, 831
Colonna, Jerome E., 397
Colsch, Michael, 152
Colston, Barbara, 109
Coltharp, Harold, 526
Colton, William, 894, 895, 903, 904, 905, 906, 907
Coluci, Kevin, 242
Columbia, Charles, 190
Columbus, Kristen E., 248
Colver, Jim, 557, 559, 560
Colville, Chris, 497
Colvin, Brittney, 371
Colvin, Jody, 203
Colvin, Leland, 427
Colvin, Theresa M., 218
Colyer, Jeffrey W. "Jeff", 175
Comai, Stephanie, 252
Combee, Neil, 624, 630, 631
Combs, Brenn, 190
Combs, Del, 190
Combs, Drew, 363
Combs, Heather, 192
Combs, Kevin, 224
Combs, Leslie A., 727, 731, 732, 733
Combs, Linda Morrison, 347
Combs, Mallie, 516
Combs, Margaret D., 194
Combs, Marvin, 186
Combs, Ryan, 350
Combs, Steve, 499
Combs, Tina H., 522
Combs, William, 389
Comeau, Ed, 855, 868
Comeau, J. Michael, 243
Comeaux, Toby, 200
Comen, Jeffrey, 218
Comer, Carol, 157
Comer, Challey, 332
Comer, Christine, 61
Comer, Cindy, 499
Comer, Mike, 523
Comer, Ralph, 446
Comer, Valerie V., 514
Comer, William, 16

Comes, Rachel, 432
Comfort, Cameron, 505
Comfort, Paul W., 225
Comins, Daniel, 338
Commons, Geoff, 482
Compton, Beth, 147
Compton, Keith, 538
Compton, Liz E., 110
Compton, Mark, 410
Compton, Tiffanye, 34
Comrie, Leroy G., Jr., 888, 891, 892, 893, 894
Comstock, Heather, 78
Comtois, Guy, 855, 869
Conant, James "Jim", 178
Conaway, Frank M., Jr., 757, 762
Conaway, Herbert C. "Herb", Jr., 874, 875, 878, 879
Conaway, Joann, 80
Concannon, Sean M., 400
Concannon, Susan, 714, 720, 721
Concannon, William, 233
Conde, Doug, 142
Condit, Donnie, 948, 953, 954
Conditt, Margaret, 938, 942, 943
Condon, Andrew, 70
Condon, Jim, 1049, 1056
Condon, Patricia A., 208
Condon, Sean, 394
Condos, James C. "Jim", 483
Condos, Nick, 52
Condotta, Cary, 1074, 1078
Condra, Gary, 506
Condrey, Ronnie, 355
Cone, Marc A., 210
Cone, Nancy, 307
Cone, Rachel Davis, 105
Coney, Brad, 201
Coney, Sgt Nicholas, 113
Conger, Robert, 316
Congo, Richard, 97
Conilogue, Alan, 135
Conklin, Allison, 369
Conklin, Cindy, 68
Conklin, Clark, 288
Conklin, H. Scott, 967, 977
Conklin, Tiffany E., 54
Conklin, Col Timothy, 62
Conley, Barb, 21
Conley, Jayson, 165
Conley, Kevin, 355
Conley, Patricia, 81
Conley, William J., Jr., 990, 992, 993
Conlin, Robert J. "Bob", 532
Conlin, Zachary, 110
Conlon, Tom, 416
Conmay, Patrick "Pat", 299
Conn, Amanda, 229
Conn, Debra, 505
Connealy, Chris, 455
Connell, David W., 114
Connell, Kathy I., 65
Connell, Patrick "Pat", 833, 835
Connell, Paul, 533
Connelley, Maria S., 124
Connelly, Marjorie M. "Marge", 492
Connelly, Michael G., 670, 673, 674
Connelly, Steven A. "Steve", 217
Conner, Dede, 183
Conner, Kevin, 149
Conner, Pat, 441
Conner, Todd, 81
Conners, Lisa B. "Betty", 226
Conners, Trish, 108
Connett, Brian, 297
Connick, Patrick, 738, 743

Connolly, Cathy, 1105, 1107, 1108
Connolly, Elizabeth "Beth", 312
Connolly, Lora, 43, 44
Connolly, Michael, 344
Connolly, Sandy, 262
Connolly, LTC Sean M., 72
Connor, Colin, 237
Connor, Daniel F., 1049, 1055
Connor, Michael, 303
Connors, Christopher J., 871, 873
Connors, Henry "Hap", 498
Connors, Steve, 76
Connors, Tom, 479
Conover, Barry C., 475
Conquest, Chip, 1049, 1055
Conrad-Saydah, Ashley, 39
Conrad, Debra, 914, 920, 921, 922, 923
Conrad, Jerri, 297
Conrad, Jerry L., 521
Conrad, Joan, 168
Conrad, Larry J., 514
Conrad, Michael, 94
Conrad, Nathan, 531
Conrad, Peter G., 223
Conroy, Deborah O'Keefe, 677, 683, 684, 685, 686
Conroy, Kevin D., 217
Conroy, Robert, 214
Conroy, Theresa W., 603, 611, 612
Cons, Manuel, 45
Considine, Bob, 311
Considine, Dave, 1095, 1099, 1100, 1101
Considine, John "Jack", 791, 797, 799
Considine, Matthew, 484
Constable, Richard E. "Rich", III, 316
Constangy, Bill "Billy", 346
Consuegra, William, 329
Contarino, Joseph, 417
Conti, Kathleen, 596, 598
Conti, Lisa, 109
Conti, Trisha, 482
Contine, Deonne, 299
Contorelli, Matthew, 24
Contreras-Madera, Griselda, 298
Contreras, Carlos, 457
Contreras, Guadalupe Chavira "Lupe", 565, 566, 567
Contris, Kim, 504
Converse, Larry, 855, 869
Conway, James, 337
Conway, Karen, 511
Conway, Kathie, 821, 828, 829, 831
Conway, Pat, 821, 827, 828, 829, 831
Conway, Scott, 231
Conway, Sean, 295
Conway, Steve, 508, 699, 1070, 1072, 1073
Conway, COL William T., 303
Conzet, Kristin A., 1012, 1015, 1016
Coody, Ann, 948, 953, 954
Coody, Jeff, 948, 953, 954
Cook-Artis, Tonyelle, 967, 977, 978, 980
Cook, Allen W., 855, 868
Cook, Amanda, 185
Cook, Andrew C. "Andy", 533
Cook, Anthony "Tony", 692, 697, 698
Cook, Bill, 908, 910, 911, 912
Cook, Bob, 387
Cook, Brenda, 310

Cook, Byron, 1030, 1036, 1038
Cook, Charmaine, 328
Cook, Cheryl L., 401
Cook, David, 183, 300
Cook, David A., 631
Cook, Dwight, 925, 927
Cook, Eddie, Jr., 8
Cook, Erika, 169
Cook, Greg, 537
Cook, Gregory W., 514
Cook, Jennifer R., 175
Cook, John, 197
Cook, Jo Marie, 110
Cook, Jon, 12
Cook, Julie, 535
Cook, Kelly, 458
Cook, Mark, 190
Cook, Meghan, 350
Cook, Michael, 380
Cook, Michael H., 494
Cook, Michelle L., 601, 603, 608, 609, 610, 611
Cook, Nicole, 96
Cook, Rob, 836, 840, 841
Cook, Robert, 267, 429, 508
Cook, Rollin E., 470
Cook, Scott, 139
Cook, Sherry, 457
Cook, Steve, 479
Cook, Tanya, 842, 844
Cook, Thomas J., 77
Cook, Vivian E., 896, 903, 905, 906, 907
Cook, Zachary J., 883, 886
Cooke, John B., 593, 595
Cooke, Kevin, 639, 646, 649, 650, 651
Cooke, Margret R., 237
Cooke, Paul L., 63
Cooksey, Marian, 948, 953
Cookson, Gay, 472
Cookson, Steve, 821, 828, 829, 830
Cooley, Belinda, 7
Cooley, Gordon M., 222
Cooley, Ken, 587, 591, 592, 593
Coombes, Terri L., 153
Coombs, John, 85
Coomer, Christian, 639, 646, 647, 649, 650, 651
Coon, David, 531
Coon, Kathy, 539
Coone, Brenda, 5
Cooney, Mark, 348
Cooney, Mary Ann, 305
Cooney, Mary R., 855, 870
Cooney, Michael R. "Mike", 286
Coonradt, Anne, 344
Coons, Stefanie, 394
Cooper Melmed, Jacki, 59
Cooper, Alisa, 316
Cooper, Anthony S., 430
Cooper, Barbara W., 1020, 1025
Cooper, Belle Mead, 422
Cooper, Charles G., 459
Cooper, James "Jim", 585, 587, 591, 592
Cooper, Janice E., 747
Cooper, Jennifer, 36, 155
Cooper, John, 572, 574
Cooper, John R., 5
Cooper, Jon, 502
Cooper, Joseph A. "Joe", Jr., 349
Cooper, Korey, 440
Cooper, Leah, 520
Cooper, Lisa, 449
Cooper, Rick W., 491
Cooper, Roy A., 356
Cooper, Roy G., 1084, 1088, 1089, 1090
Cooper, Sharon, 639, 648, 649, 650
Cooper, Stan, 1103, 1104
Cooper, Tanya, 107

NAME INDEX

Dickinson, Stewart, 347
Dickman, Jill, 847, 849, 850
Dickson, Laura, 266
Dickson, Sydnee, 476
Dickson, Tom, 639, 646, 647, 649, 650
DiCola, Stacy, 420
DiCostanzo, Kristi, 17
DiDomenico, Sal, 764, 766, 767
Diebel, Margaret "Maggie", 257
Diefenthaler, Andrew, 495
Diegnan, Patrick J., Jr., 871, 873
Diehl, Geoffrey "Geoff", 769, 775
Diehl, Sherrie, 218
Diep, Man, 470
Diepenbrock, Martha, 48
Dierks, Diana K., 714, 720, 721, 722
Dietl, Paul D., 233
Dietrich, Mark, 135
Dietrich, Roxie, 365
Dietz, Kristi, 527
Dietz, Megan, 511
Diez, Pam, 202
DiFranco, Debbie, 855, 868
Diggs, Kimberly, 95
DiGiacomo, Heather, 103
DiGiacomo, Tom, 105
Digilio-Grimes, Catherine, 491
DiGirolamo, Gene, 968, 978, 979
Dilan, Erik Martin, 896, 903, 904, 905
Dilan, Martin Malave, 887, 888, 892, 893, 894
Dilges, Jason, 435
Dill, Brian, 112
Dill, James F., 745
Dill, Lawrence, 132
Dillard, Chandra E., 1004, 1008
Dillard, Cynthia S., 8
Dillard, James H., II, 492
Dillard, Mary Ellen, 273
Dillavou, Mitchell J. "Mitch", 173
Dilling, Donald, 179
Dillingham, Kathleen Jackson, 747
Dillon, Brian, 68
Dillon, Erin, 367
Dillon, Patricia A., 601, 603, 608, 609, 610
Dillon, Patty, 406
Dillon, Stephen, 454
Dills, Kelly, 275
Dilmore, Cory D., 101
Dilsaver, Steven, 535
Dilzer, Daniel E., 72
DiMaio, John, 874, 875, 878
Dimas, James, 147
DiMauro, Lissa, 416
DiMemmo, Joe, 404
DiMezza, Rich, 337
DiMichele, Donna Longo, 414
Dimick, Lori, 165
Dimond, Doug, 438
DiNapoli, Thomas P. "Tom", 342
Dineen, Kate, 330
Dines, George B., Jr., 87
Dines, James Mitchell "Jim", 883, 886
Ding, George, 345
Dingess, Tom L., 519
Dingley, Mark A., 413
Dingus, Angela, 369
DiNitto, Joseph A., 415
Diniz, Rui, 415
Dinniman, Andrew E., 408, 962, 964, 965
D'Innocenzo, Donetta M., 961

Dinowitz, Jeffrey, 896, 903, 904, 905, 906
Dinubilo, Cathleen, 56
Dion, Mark N., 747
DiOrio, Dr. Mary, 368
DiPalma, Louis P., 991, 992
DiPietro, David J., 896, 903, 904, 905, 906, 907
Dipko, John A., 529
DiPrimio, Joseph J., 222
DiRico, James, 241
Dirks, Brian, 510
DiRocco, Dominick, 309
Diruocco, Luciana, 479
DiSanto, Lynne, 1013, 1015, 1016
Disare, Jeremy, 339
DiSesa, Len, 856, 868
Dishong, Randy, 352
DiSilvestro, Linda A., 856, 869
DiSimoni, Michael, 319
Dismang, Jonathan, 572, 574
Dismukes, Jeffrey, 381
DiStefano, Louis, 418
Distefano, Michael, 202
Ditmer, Charles, 423
Dittmer, Robert "Bob", 162
Ditto, Jessica, 182
Ditto, Will, 372
Dittoe, Mike, 937
DiVirgilio, Bobbi, 78
Divita, Marilyn, 515
Dix, Amy, 211
Dix, Bill C., 699, 700, 702
Dix, Doug, 434
Dixon, Angela, 342
Dixon, April, 177
Dixon, Bob, 817, 819
Dixon, Deborah Butler, 807, 812, 813, 814, 815, 816
Dixon, Jimmy, 915, 920, 921, 922, 923
Dixon, Joe, 24
Dixon, Katherine Z., 224
Dixon, Kelly, 380
Dixon, Morgan, 530
Dixon, Sage, 665, 667, 668, 669
Dixon, Stanley, 372
Dixon, Susan, 170
Dixon, Yvonne T., 98
Dizney-Spencer, Dieuwke, 136
DiZoglio, Diana, 769, 775
Djurovich, Alexandra, 262
Dlugolecki, David, 340
Do, David, 84
Doades, Matt, 158
Doak, John D., 389
Doaks, Tracy, 350
Doan, Erin, 256
Doan, Scott, 323
Doan, Tran, 358
Doane-Selmier, Stacy, 157
Doane, Alan, 836, 840, 841
Doane, Michelle, 140
Dobbins, Caleb, 307
Dobbins, Dr. Kenneth W. "Ken", 278
Dobbs, Dr. Thomas E., III, 268
Dobson, Amy, 10
Dobson, Brenda, 172
Dobson, Josh, 915, 920, 921, 922, 924
Dobson, Kathy, 58
Dobson, Richard, 186
Dockendorff, Annie, 21
Dockery, David T., 265
Dockery, Col William D., 445
Dockham, Jerry C., 353
Dockstader, Dan, 1103, 1104
Dockstader, Scott, 173
Dockter, Jason, 929, 932
Dockter, Rebecca, 283
Dodd, Bill, 587, 591, 593
Dodd, Melva, 371

Dodd, Stephanie, 376
Dodds, Bryan, 260
Dodds, Ginny, 262
Dodge, George, Jr., 883, 885, 886
Dodgen, April, 116
Dodrill, Chris S., 523
Dodson, Anastasia, 44
Dodson, Cathy, 367
Dodson, Debbie, 498
Dodson, Denny E., 519
Dodson, Tracy, 352
Doe, Shari, 360
Doehl, Col Robert, 14
Doely, Leslie, 283
Doerflinger, Preston L., 378, 385
Doering, David A. "Dave", 276
Doerr, Mark, 138
Doestsch, George L., Jr., 227
Dofflemyer, Major Norman "Bill", 229
Dogan, Shamed, 821, 829, 831
Doheny, Michael, 240
Doherty, David, 856, 868
Doherty, Ed, 234
Doherty, Margaret, 957, 960
Doherty, Michael J., 871, 873
Dohman, Ramona L., 259
Dohrman, Dean A., 821, 828, 829, 830, 831, 832
Dohrman, Tami, 504
Dohrmann, BG Alan S., 359, 362
Doke, Robert, 379
Dolan, Jim, 347
Dolan, Tracy, 480
Dolcino, Chiara, 305
Dold, BG Scott A., 176
Dolecheck, Cecil, 704, 707, 708
Dolezal, Charles J., 368
Doll, John, 714, 721, 722
Dollar, Matt, 640, 646, 648, 649
Dollar, Nelson, 915, 920, 921, 922, 923, 924
Dollar, Terri, 466
Dollinger, Susan, 363
Dollman, Sean, 27
Doman, Andrew, 142
Dombrowski, Sandra "Sandy", 301
Domingo, Rey, 132
Domingue, Darin, 199
Dominguez, Claricel "Joe", 669
Dominguez, Larry J., 329
Dominguéz, Martha M., 456
Dominic, Joe, 57
Domogalla, Kevin G., 292
Donahue, Anne B., 1050, 1055, 1056
Donahue, Daniel M., 769, 775
Donahue, James A., III, 409
Donahue, John Leo "Jack", 734, 736, 737
Donahue, Kevin, 85, 94
Donahue, Mike, 307
Donahue, Patricia, 307
Donahue, Shauna, 220
Donahue, Susan "Sue", 566, 567
Donald, Brenda, 90
Donald, James E., 118
Donald, Odie, II, 93
Donaldson, Leah, 101
Donaldson, Pat, 139
Donaldson, Polly, 93
Donaldson, Terence, 443
Donaldson, Tim, 476
Donaldson, William, 111
Donati, Beverly G., 490

Donato, Paul J., 767, 769, 775
Donato, Stephanie, 337
Donatucci, Maria P., 968, 977, 979, 980
Doncavage, Todd L., 262
Dondorf, Robert, 332
Donegan, Susan L., 481
Donelon, James J. "Jim", 206
Donlon, Thomas, 69
Donmoyer, Kristen, 401
Donnals, Jennifer, 438
Donnan, Chanda, 252
Donnellan, Kevin, 22
Donnelly, Jennifer, 393
Donnelly, John, 47
Donnelly, Kenneth J., 763, 764, 766, 767
Donnelly, Mary Jane, 77
Donnelly, Pete, 116
Donner, Dennis, 291
Donoghue, Eileen M., 764, 766, 767
Donoho, Victor, 446
Donohue, Charlie, 297
Donohue, Elizabeth "Liz", 67
Donohue, Jeffery M., 727, 731, 732
Donohue, Nicholas "Nick", 498
Donovan, Cynthia D. "Cindy", 159
Donovan, Daniel, 856, 869
Donovan, Eric T., 237
Donovan, Jack, 307
Donovan, Kelly, 343
Donovan, Kerry, 593, 595
Donovan, Kirsten, 502
Donovan, Leslie D. "Les", Sr., 710, 712, 713
Donovan, Judith, 90
Donovan, Johannah Leddy, 1050, 1056
Donovan, Pete, 285
Donovan, Robert E., 420
Donovan, Thomas A. "Tom", 136
Donovan, Thomas J., 302
Donta, Michael "Mike", 191
Doody, Stephen, 235, 334
Dooker, Charles, 193
Doolan, Pamela, 72
Dooley, Diana S., 43
Dooley, Michael, 402
Dooley, Shawn, 769, 775
Dooling, Timothy V., 244
Dooling, Vicki, 847, 849
Doolittle, Trent, 327
Doom, Jennifer, 192
Doore, Donna R., 747
Doory, Ann Marie, 228
Dore, Tim, 596, 598
Doredant, Sharon, 104
Dorman, Greg, 62
Dorman, Mitchell G., 1002
Dorman, Pamala, 493
Dorman, Dr. Steve, 323
Dormin, John, 335
Dormire, Dave, 275
Dormsjo, Leif A., 94
Dorn, Randolf "Randy", 511, 512
Dorn, Robert, 24
Dornfeld, Joanna, 255
Dorschner, Dale, 257
Dorsey, Christi, 91
Dorsey, J. Van Lear, 227
Dorsey, Susan Y. "Syd", 491
Dorsey, Tynesia, 369
Dortch-Okara, Barbara, 245
Dortch, Jarvis, 808, 812, 813, 814, 815
Dortch, Tina, 5
Dory, Traci, 298

Dosch, Mark A., 929, 932, 933
Doser, BG Zachary, 298
Doss, Barry, 1020, 1024, 1025
Doss, Bill, 272
Doss, Phillip "Phil", 450
Dossett, J.J., 944, 946, 947
Dossett, Michael, 195
Dossett, Myron B., 727, 731, 733
Dossett, Rhonda, 382
Doster, Kelly, 459
Dosunmu, Basil, 444
Doten, Becca, 55
Dotson, James "Jim", 574, 576, 580, 581
Dotson, Richard, 493
Dotterer, Dwight, 218
Doty, Beverly Nicholson, 486
Doty, Sally, 801, 803, 804, 805
Dotzenrod, Jim, 925, 927, 928
Dotzler, William A. "Bill", Jr., 699, 700, 701, 702, 703
Doucet, Brad D., 203
Doucette, Fred, 856, 869
Dougall, John, 477
Dougan, Dorn, 419
Dougan, John, 280
Dougherty, Carolyn, 385
Dougherty, Debbie, 436
Dougherty, Malcolm, 49
Dougherty, Stephanie, 49
Doughty, B. J., 446
Doughty, Dale, 213
Douglas, Brad T., 519
Douglas, Charlotte Vining, 574, 576, 580, 581
Douglas, Dan M., 576, 580
Douglas, Debra, 307
Douglas, Demetrius, 640, 647, 648, 649
Douglas, Diane, 28
Douglas, Jeff, 42
Douglas, Jerry, 386
Douglas, Jim, 293
Douglas, Karen, 48
Douglas, Mallie C., 87
Douglas, MaryGail K., 1004, 1009
Douglas, Parker, 477
Douglas, Susan, 494
Doukas, Dave, 71
Douthit, Scotty Dale, 35
Dove, Willie, 713, 714, 720, 721
Dovilla, Michael D. "Mike", 937, 938, 942, 943
Dovre, Dawn, 433
Dovre, Travis, 431
Dow, Diane, 311
Dow, Thomas E., 327
Dowd, Anita, 184
Dowd, Anne Marie, 245
Dowd, Michael, 496
Dowd, Patrick, 502
Dowe, Carlton "Ital", 487
Dowell, Doug, 187
Dowling, Anne Melissa, 146
Dowling, David C., 495
Dowling, Dax, 506
Dowling, Gary, 71
Dowling, Stephanie, 26
Downey, Caroline J., 336
Downey, Joann, 875, 878, 879
Downey, Matthew "Matt", 342
Downing, Benjamin Brackett, 764, 766, 767
Downing, Michael, 275
Downing, Patrick, 8
Downing, Tani Pack, 470
Downs, Gregory C., 35

**NAME INDEX**

Downs, Herb F., 211
Downs, Noranne, 105
Doyle, Brooke, 237
Doyle, James E. "Jamie", II, 990, 991, 992, 993
Doyle, John, 44
Doyle, Karen, 213
Doyle, Kevin M., 194
Doyle, Loren, 418
Doyle, Maureen, 253
Doyle, Paul R., 599, 609, 610, 611
Doyle, Robert, III, 108
Doyle, Robert John, 519
Doyle, Steve, 1095, 1100, 1101
Doyle, William T. "Bill", 1046, 1047, 1048
Dozier, Gregory C., 113
Dozier, Mustaafa, 97
Dozier, Sarah, 348
Draa, Ronald "Ron", 103
Drabicki, Judith, 333
Dragon, Paul, 479
Drake, Brad, 625, 631
Drake, Dan, 104
Drake, Dickie, 548, 553, 554
Drake, Jay, 346
Drake, Linda, 512
Drake, Michael, 336
Drake, Michael J. "Mike", 154
Drake, Ron, 76
Drake, Sara, 57
Drane, Hardy, 82
Drankiewicz, Douglas D., 527
Drapala, William, 381
Draper, Sarah, 115
Draper, Tom, 278
Draut, Ken, 183
Drawdy, Larry, 271
Draxler, Jack R., 1042, 1045, 1046
Drazkowski, Steve, 792, 799
Dreasky, Logan, 249
Drenner, Karla Lea, 640, 648, 650
Dreslin, Sally, 334
Dressel, Meredith, 530
Dressel, Roderick O., 340
Dresslar, Tom, 38
Dressler, Ronald, 474
Drew, Barry T., 410
Drew, Catherine, 305
Drew, Kathleen, 504
Drew, Timothy, 304
Drewes, Rik, 436
Drews, Christopher, 453
Drexler, Kim, 80
Dreyzehner, Dr. John J., 443
Driedger, Kevin, 254
Driehaus, Denise, 938, 942, 943
Driggs, Adam, 566, 567
Drinkwater, Sarah, 397
Driscoll, David, 15
Driscoll, Matthew J., 335
Driscoll, Michael J., 968, 977, 978, 979
Driscoll, Robyn, 832, 833, 835
Driskell, Gretchen, 780, 784
Driskell, Roger L., 150
Driskill, Joseph L., 275, 279
Driskill, Ogden, 1103, 1104
Driver, Greg, 347
Drizos, Stephen, 402
Droge, Heather, 180
Droste, Amy M., 247
Droste, LeAnn, 250
Drown, R. Trevor, 576, 580, 581
Drown, Stuart, 41
Drozdoff, Leo, 297
Drozt, Thomas, 225
Drucker, Judith, 315
Druker, Dave, 153

Drummond, Barbara, 548, 552, 553, 554
Drummond, Harriet, 557, 559
Drumwright, Kathy, 495
Drury, Scott R., 677, 683, 685
Dryden, Dan, 1013, 1015
Dryden, David, 80
Drygas, Heidi, 14
Dryjanski, Andrew, 154
Drysdale, Donald L., 47
Dryzga, Daniel, 317
D'Souza, Anita, 468
D'Souza, Anita Butani, 96
Duane, Michael, 483
Duarte, Darren, 240
Duarte, Joseph "Joe", 856, 869
Dubitsky, Adam, 216
Dubitsky, Doug, 603, 609, 610, 611
Dubnow, Jared Melamed, 143
DuBois, Michelle M., 769, 775
DuBose, Bobby B., 625, 630
Dubow, Jason, 223
Dubray, Rick, 451
Ducay, Robert, 43
Ducey, Douglas A. "Doug", 21
Duchesne, Robert S., 747
Duchette, André G., 214
Duchow, Cindi, 1095, 1099, 1100, 1101, 1102
Duchscherer, Brian, 362
Duckett, Charles Kenneth "Chuck", 346
Ducklett, Greg, 451
Duckworth, Greg D., 1004, 1008
Duckworth, Iona, 354
Duckworth, Roderic, 108
Duckworth, Susan "Sue", 1042, 1045, 1046
Ducote, Stephanie, 203
Ducrest, John P., 199
Duda, Pat, 480
Dudden, Marcia, 332
Dudek, Elizabeth "Liz", 106
Dudenhefer, L. Mark, 1063, 1068, 1069
Dudgeon, Mike, 640, 646, 647, 648, 650
Dudik, Kimberly, 836, 840, 841
Dudish, Kimberly "Kim", 455
Dudlek, Joe, 76
Dudley, Christine T., 145
Dudley, Dwight Richard, 625, 630
Dudley, Jahala, 478
Dudley, Kelly, 120
Duecker, Jonathan A., 409
Duenas, Christopher M. "Chris", 123
Duenas, Joseph W., 124
Duenwald, Catherine, 435
Duer, D. Holbrook, 401
Duff, Eileen, 231
Duff, Robert "Bob", 599, 609, 611
Duffey, Mike, 938, 941, 942
Duffy, Amy, 426
Duffy, Charles M., 510
Duffy, Jennifer, 314
Duffy, Leanne, 64
Duffy, Michael, 161
Dufour, Christine, 258
DuFour, Deb, 435
Dufurrena, Timothy, 297
Dugan, Jennifer, 256
Dugan, Mike, 631, 632, 635, 636, 637
Dugan, Molly, 223
Dugger, Jim, 25

Dugger, Tony, 821, 829, 831
Duggins, Ralph H., 462
Duginske, James, 83
Duh, Kai-Ing, 228
Duke, Walter Edwin, 1084, 1088, 1089, 1090
Dukes, Billy, Jr., 425
Dukes, Dawnna, 1030, 1036, 1037
Dukes, Timothy D., 615, 617, 618
Dukes, Winfred J., 640, 646, 647, 651
Dumais, Kathleen M., 757, 762, 763
Dumais, Russell, 856, 870
Dumaran, Gene, 132
DuMond, Melissa, 50
Dunahoo, Emory, Jr., 640, 646, 647, 648, 649, 651
Dunahoo, Sandra K. "Sandy", 195
Dunaski, Mark A., 259
Dunaway, Patty, 194
Dunbar, Denise, 90
Dunbar, MajGen Donald P., 528
Dunbar, George, 968, 977, 978, 979, 980
Dunbar, Nelia, 43
Dunbar, Scott, 112
Duncan, Ben, 424
Duncan, Bill, 308
Duncan, Daniel, 120
Duncan, David, 40
Duncan, Emily, 165
Duncan, Gary, 278
Duncan, Geoff L., 640, 647, 649, 650, 651
Duncan, John, 225, 445
Duncan, John E., 439
Duncan, Kelly, 432
Duncan, Nancy, 252
Duncan, Robert W. "Bob", 496
Duncan, Sandi, 448
Duncan, Sharon, 141
Duncan, Valerie, 425
Duncan, Wesley, 301
Dungan, Casey, 442
Dungey, Cynthia C., 369
Dunham, Doug, 25
Dunham, Mark, 415
Dunigan, Andy, 156
Dunkel, Aaron, 177
Dunkel, Nancy A., 704, 707, 708, 709
Dunkelberger, Scott, 401
Dunkin, Kenneth "Ken", 677, 683, 684, 686
Dunlap, Cary, 535
Dunlap, Kevin, 1020, 1024
Dunlap, Matthew "Matt", 215
Dunlap, Melissa Wheeler, 429
Dunlap, Travis, 949, 953, 954
Dunleavy, John, 481, 483
Dunleavy, Martin J., 601
Dunleavy, Mike J., 555, 556, 557
Dunn, Annette, 173
Dunn, Aubrey, 328
Dunn, Barbara, 502
Dunn, Bill, 1020, 1024, 1025
Dunn, Bruce, 374
Dunn, Cynthia Adams "Cindy", 402
Dunn, Dennis, 120
Dunn, Emily, 121
Dunn, Jason, 184
Dunn, Col Jefferson S. "Jeff", 4
Dunn, Jess, 172
Dunn, Jill C., 521
Dunn, John, 190

Dunn, Kathleen "Katie", 305
Dunn, Leo L., 408
Dunn, Lucetta A. "Lucy", 50
Dunn, Matthew, 154
Dunn, Priscilla, 543, 545, 546
Dunn, Randy D., 821, 828, 829
Dunn, Richard "Rick", 112, 115
Dunn, S. Terence "Terry", 380
Dunnavant, Siobhan S., 1058, 1061
Dunne, Cynthia J., 599
Dunnigan, Erik, 182
Dunnigan, James A. "Jim", 1041, 1042, 1045, 1046
Dunnington, Jason, 949, 954
Dunphy, Larry C., 747
Dunphy, Michelle Ann, 747
Dunstan, Col Floyd W., 62
Dunstan, Roger, 54
Dunwell, Mary Ann, 285, 836, 841
DuPlessis, Jim, 727, 732
DuPont, Henry "Hank", Jr., 176
DuPont, Michael R., 317
DuPre, Dan, 425
Dupre, Sheila M., 241
Dupree, Cindy, 446
Duprey, Janet L., 896, 903, 904, 905, 906, 907
Dupuy, Lt. Col. Charles "Charlie", 203
Dupuy, Jason, 214
Dura, Arlene, 360
Duran, Crisanta, 595, 596
Duran, Diana, 290
Duran, Ofelia, 64
Duran, Roberta, 323
Durand, Brian, 67
Durand, LouOma, 505
Durant, Chan Tei, 85
Durant, Peter J., 769, 775
Durbin, Lawrence E., 493
Durden, Cheryl, 90
Durden, Lisa, 119
Durden, Veronda L., 460
Durgin, MaryAnn, 420
Durhal, Fred, III, 780, 784
Durham, Deborah V. "Debi", 173
Durham, Fred, 23
Durham, Jeremy, 1020, 1025
Durham, Steve, 65
Durham, William F., 515
Durish, Dena, 301
Durivage, Catherine A., 256
Durkee, Janet, 76
Durkin, Jim, 675, 677
Durkin, Thomas J., 245
Durr, Eric, 336
Durrance, Justin K., 120
Durrum, Kim, 188
Durso, Emily, 89
Durusau, Mary, 206
Duryea, Elizabeth, 68
Dusablon, Glenn, 417
Dusenberry, Joe S., Jr., 426
Dush, Cris, 968, 977, 978, 979, 980
Dussault, RADM Kathleen M., 300
Dusse, Barry, 199
Dusseault, Charles R. "Chuck", 307
Dutton, Catherine, 159
Dutton, Dick, 384
Dutton, Erica, 406
Dutton, Harold V., Jr., 1030, 1037, 1038
Dutton, Marcy, 152
Duttweiler, Jonathan, 113
Duvall, Betty, 397
Duvall, Mary, 1013, 1016

Duvieilh, Cheryl, 203
Duwve, Dr. Joan, 158
Dvorak, Ryan M., 691, 693, 697, 698
Dvorin, Jeffrey "Jeff", 344
Dvorsky, Robert E., 700, 701, 702
Dwelle, Terry L., 360
Dwertman, James, 371
Dwight, Stephen, 738, 742, 743, 744
Dwinell, Steven E. "Steve", 109
Dworkin, Jonathon, 75
Dwyer, Carole, 415
Dwyer, Chris, 404
Dwyer, Elizabeth Kelleher, 414
Dwyer, James, 225
Dwyer, James J., 769, 775
Dwyer, William F. "Bill", 303
Dyches, Kim, 471
Dyckman, Mark, 149
Dye, Carol, 248
Dye, Charles R. "Randy", 514
Dye, Mary, 1074, 1078
Dyer-Webster, Debra, 145
Dyer, Jay, 452
Dyer, Tom, 37
Dygon, John, 109
Dykema, Angela, 296
Dykema, Carolyn C., 769, 775
Dykema, Linda, 248
Dyslin, Daniel, 147
Dyson, Robert R., 341
Dyson, Tom, 148
Dzamov, Nik, 373
Dzamov, Satch, 373
Dzialo, BrigGen Matthew J., 419
Dziedzic, Kari, 786, 790
Dziedzic, Marianne, 74
Dzielak, David J., 268
Dzurenda, James, 297

**E**

Eads, Diana, 190
Eads, Lance, 576, 580
Eagle, Dane, 625, 630
Eakins, James, 385
Eakins, Kari, 539
Ealum, Christy, 6
Ealum, Darrel Bush, 640, 647, 648, 651
Earick, Dr. Mary, 308
Earl, Caryn, 401
Earl, Chris, 477
Earle, Beverly Miller, 915, 920, 922, 923
Earle, Fredericka, 97
Earle, Jonice, 94
Earle, Steven M., 344
Earley-Jeter, Marcey, 366
Earley, Stephen, 345
Earls, Lisa, 121
Early, Darin, 420
Early, Todd, 463
Earnest, Brent, 324
Earp, James, 50, 138
Easland, Rebecca "Becky", 525
Easley, Catherine Gatewood, 182
Easley, Kaci, 488
Eason, Cheryl, 43
Eason, Lisa, 112
East, Lt. Col. Danny, 159
Easter, Mandy, 169
Eastlick, Jay, 279
Eastman, Alyson, 1050, 1055
Eastman, Eric, 856, 870
Eastman, Jennifer, 219
Eastman, Kathy, 209
Easton, Lee-Ann, 296

**NAME INDEX**

Enoch, Donald ''Don'', 17
Enright, Scott Edward, 132, 133
Enright, Thomas, 206
Enriquez, Monica, 27
Ensor, Catherine J., 220
Enstrom, Mona, 271
Entlicher, Sue, 822, 827, 829, 830, 831
Entringer, Robert J., 359
Entzel, Suzie, 363
Epel, Joshua B., 64
Epes, Berthell, 92
Eppler, David, 230
Epps, James ''Bubber'', 637, 640, 646, 649, 650, 651
Epps, Joyce, 403
Epstein, Jeffrey M., 351
Epstein, Ronald L. ''Ron'', 335
Epting, Pamela P., 107
Erbele, Robert S., 925, 927, 928
Erdelyi, Joseph, 479
Erdey, Dale M., 734, 736, 737
Erdmann, Sarah, 507
Erdos, Lanny, 371
Erfe, Scott, 69
Erhardt, Ron, 792, 799
Erick, Candice, 110
Ericksen, Doug, 1070, 1072, 1073
Erickson, Amy, 11
Erickson, John, 158
Erickson, Kris, 431
Erickson, Lars, 506
Erickson, Lynell, 436
Erickson, Neal, 294
Erickson, Shannon S., 1004, 1009
Erickson, Sheila, 489
Erickson, Sondra, 792, 798, 799
Erickson, Tom, 11
Erickson, Travis, 13
Ericson, Benjamin, 235
Ericson, Scott, 470
Erker, Rodger, 387
Erlandsen, Dana J., 529
Erlewine, Kristi, 376
Ernest, Stephen, 255
Ernst, Dr. Mark, 145
Erpelding, Mathew, 664, 665, 667, 668, 669
Erpenbach, Jon B., 1091, 1093
Erquiaga, Dale A.R., 296
Erreca, Erik, 40
Errington, Sue, 693, 697, 698
Erskine, Andrea L., 211
Erste, Louis, 118
Ertman, Denise, 505
Ervin, Paris, 154
Ervin, Peter, 192
Erway, Kristen, 404
Erwin, David, 526
Erwin, James L. ''Jim'', 190
Erwin, Scott, 203
Esau, Keith, 715, 721, 722
Escamilla, Luz, 1039, 1040, 1041
Escareño, Leslie Bingham, 454
Escobar, Karen, 53
Escobar, Rodney, 451
Esera, Tuiasina Siolosega, 560, 561, 562
Esgar, Daneya, 596, 598
Espaillat, Adriano, 888, 891, 892, 893
Espaldon, James V. ''Jim'', 652, 653, 654
Esparza, Mike, 468
Esparza, Raul R., III, 145
Esperance, Jay, 432
Espero, Will, 654, 656

Espich, Jeffrey K. ''Jeff'', 155
Espie, David, 225
Espinda, Nolan, 131
Espino, Marc, 45
Espinola, Dr. Aurelio A., 125
Espinosa Trujillo, Amber, 323
Espinosa, Narden Jaime, 985, 987, 988, 989, 990
Espinosa, Paul, 1084, 1088, 1089, 1090
Espinoza, Angel, 328
Espinoza, Diego, 568, 570
Espinoza, Nora, 883, 886
Espinoza, Robert, 322
Espinoza, Valerie L., 329
Espling, Eleanor M. ''Ellie'', 746, 747, 752
Esposito, Anthony, 145
Esposito, Georgia, 498
Esposito, Louis P. ''Lou'', Jr., 601, 603, 610, 611
Esquibel, Floyd A., 1103, 1104
Esquibel, José A., 66
Esquibel, Ken A., 1104, 1105, 1107
Esquivel, Emanuel Joaquin, 47
Esquivel, Sal, 957, 960
Esser, Eric, 529
Essig, Don, 135
Essmann, Jeff, 837, 840, 841
Estep, Denise, 220
Estep, Jeffrey D., 519
Estes-Smargiassi, Stephen, 245
Estes, Bud, 715, 721
Estes, Craig, 1026, 1028, 1029
Estes, Jeffrey C., 511
Estes, Maia Hunt, 85
Estes, Ron, 180
Esteves, Gina, 454
Estevez, Eric P., 856, 869
Estrada, Luis, 222
Estrada, Marie, 328
Etheridge, Deb, 14
Etheridge, Jamie, 442
Etheridge, Jay, 108
Etheridge, Julie, 273
Etheridge, Robert W., 457
Etue, Col. Kriste Kibbey, 252
Eubanks, Dan, 808, 812, 813, 815, 816
Eubanks, James C., 267
Eubanks, Jon Scott, 574, 576, 580
Eubanks, Martin, 421
Eugenis, Cameron, 153
Eum, Shawn C., 216
Eure, Casey, 808, 812, 813, 814, 815
Eustace, Timothy J., 874, 875, 878, 879
Evangelista, Frank, 67
Evangelista, Jodi, 310
Evangelista, Laura, 333
Evangelos, Jeffrey, 747, 752
Evankovich, Eli, 969, 978, 979, 980
Evans, Allen Vincent, 1084, 1088, 1089, 1090
Evans, Arthur, 136
Evans, Bill, 76
Evans, Carole, 76
Evans, Carrie, 386
Evans, Cindy, 657, 660, 661
Evans, David A., 1084, 1088, 1090
Evans, Debbie G., 1050, 1055
Evans, Drew, 260
Evans, Dwight, 969
Evans, Edward L. ''Ed'', 380

Evans, Ellen, 508, 511
Evans, Gloria, 353
Evans, Greg, 105, 434
Evans, Harold, 333
Evans, Jack, 76, 86, 323
Evans, Jeff, 168, 338
Evans, Jennifer, 473
Evans, Jeremy, 54
Evans, Jim, 54
Evans, Joel, 337
Evans, John C., 348
Evans, Kenneth, 92
Evans, Laine, 152
Evans, Dr. L. C. ''Buster'', 113
Evans, Lisa, 396
Evans, Lora A., 478
Evans, Marcus C., Jr., 677, 682, 683, 684, 686
Evans, Mary Alice, 129
Evans, Michael T., 808, 812, 813, 815, 816
Evans, Mike, 120
Evans, Pam, 260
Evans, Paul, 958, 960
Evans, Randall, 159
Evans, Richard ''Rich'', 394
Evans, Robert Emil ''Bob'', 808, 812, 813, 814, 815
Evans, Ruth, 8
Evans, Stacey, 640, 646, 649, 650
Evans, Stephanie, 89
Evans, Terra, 55
Evans, Thomas, 426
Evans, Thomas R. ''Tom'', 420
Evans, Tim, 121
Evans, Timothy, 94
Evatt, Angela, 221
Eve, Holly Law, 489
Evenson, Tom, 525
Everatt, Betty L., 208
Everett, Brent H., 471
Everett, Carole, 227
Everett, Courtney, 166
Everett, Garth D., 969, 977, 978, 979
Everett, H. Doug, 121
Everett, Justin, 596, 598
Everidge-Frey, Carolyn, 377
Everitt, Bob, 508
Evers, Anthony ''Tony'', 533
Evers, Greg, 619, 622, 623
Evers, Valerie, 276
Eversley, Melissa, 90
Everson, Melvin, 116
Eves, Mark W., 746, 747, 752
Ewald, Michael, 380
Ewart, Tom, 428
Ewer, David, 282
Ewing, Bob, 1010, 1011, 1012
Ewing, Eric W., 524
Ewing, Julie, 472
Ewing, Maureen, 420
Ewing, LTC Todd, 195
Ewy, John L., 715, 720, 721, 722
Excell, Steve, 511
Exline, Nancy N., 517
Extine, Doug, 511
Exum, Tracey, 441
Eyer, Tamara ''Tammi'', 247
Ezelle, Robert, 505
Ezeocha, Kaitlyn, 145
Ezray, Michelle, 56
Ezzell, Candy Spence, 883, 885, 886

**F**

Fa'ai'usao, Don, 18
Fa'au'uga, Alo, 560, 561, 562
Faber, Keith L., 934, 936

Fabian, Dan, 790, 792, 797, 798, 799
Fabrizio, Florindo J. ''Flo'', 969, 979, 980
Facemire, Douglas Eugene, 1080, 1082, 1083
Facemyer, Les, 514
Facey, Heather, 100
Facey, Tom, 832, 833, 835
Factor, Laura, 373
Fadell, Elizabeth, 532
Fadipe, Charlotte, 39
Fagan, Bob, 268
Fagan, Peter J., 1050, 1055
Fagan, Renny, 61
Fagan, Shemia, 958, 960
Fagergren, Mark, 470
Faherty, Sean, 233
Fahy, Patricia, 896, 903, 904, 905, 906
Faiivae, Susana, 20
Failautusi, Gaea Perefoti, 560, 561, 562
Fails, SgtMaj Rachel L., 171
Fain, Joe, 1069, 1070, 1072, 1073
Fair, Michael L. ''Mike'', 998, 1001, 1002
Fair, Reginald ''Reggie'', 38
Fairbanks, David, 100
Fairbanks, Joseph, 380
Fairbourn, LTC Steven A., 476
Faircloth, Chuck, 106
Faircloth, John, 915, 920, 921, 922, 923, 924
Faircloth, Larry W., 1084, 1089, 1090
Faircloth, Sherry, 109
Faircloth, Wayne, 1031, 1037, 1038
Fairrow, Veran, 443
Faison, Barry, 499
Faison, Jeremy, 1021, 1024, 1025
Faivre, Gay, 52
Fajardo, Kelly K., 883, 886
Fala, Robert A., 514
Falcicchio, John, 83
Falcon, Antonio, 460
Falcon, Kimberly ''Kim'', 282
Falcon, Mark E., 202
Falcone, David J., 244
Falcone, Henry, 69
Falconer, R. Reid, 738, 743
Falepo, Soloalii, 18
Fales, Deborah A., 212
Faley, Andrea, 64
Falk, Frances, 60
Falkenbury, Jamey, 355
Fallaw, Anthony ''Tony'', 427
Fallaw, Chuck, 430
Fallin, Lynn N., 131
Fallin, Mary, 378
Fallon, Christopher, 240
Fallon, Patrick ''Pat'', 1031, 1037, 1038
Falls, Kathe, 200
Falls, Martin, 353
Falsetti, Rachel, 50
Falstad, David, 530
Falter, Michael ''Mike'', 148
Falvay, Sheri, 249
Falzome, Sam, 479
Falzon, Dr. Andrew L., 318
Fan, Dr. Nancy H., 77
Fanczi, Steve, 117
Fandel, Linda Lantor, 167
Fandl, Maria, 477
Fanelli, Susan, 45
Fanene, Jonathan, 19
Fanion, Gerald, Jr., 440
Fann, Karen, 568, 570, 571
Fannin, James R. ''Jim'', 734, 736, 737
Fant, Julian ''Jay'', 625, 630

Farabough, David, 34
Faraca, Tony, 141
Farago, Nichole ''Nikki'', 258
Farber, Elizabeth G., 514
Fardig, David, 404
Farhoumand, Kazem, 418
Farias, Dr. Fred, III, 465
Farina, Frank, 969, 977, 978, 979
Farina, Raymond, 337
Faris, Pam, 780, 784
Fariss, C. Matthew, 1063, 1067, 1068
Farkas, Brian, 524
Farley-Bouvier, Tricia, 769, 775
Farley, Adrian, 57
Farley, Allen, 548, 552, 553, 554
Farley, Edward, 83
Farley, Gary, 439
Farley, Glenn, 22
Farley, Hugh T., 887, 888, 891, 892, 893, 894
Farley, James, 14
Farley, Michael, 136
Farley, Patricia, 845, 846, 847
Farley, Robert, 419
Farley, Shawn O., 518
Farley, Steve, 565, 566, 567
Farmer-Butterfield, Jean, 915, 920, 921, 922, 923
Farmer, Alec, 32
Farmer, Andrew E., 1021, 1024, 1025
Farmer, David A., 519
Farmer, Joseph L., 376
Farmer, Raymond G. ''Ray'', 424
Farmer, Thomas, 448
Farnese, Lawrence M. ''Larry'', Jr., 961, 962, 964, 965
Farney, Marsha, 1031, 1037, 1038
Farnham, Douglas, 479
Farnham, BrigGen Douglas, 209
Farnham, Nichi S., 210
Farnsworth, Bill, 134
Farnsworth, David Christian ''Dave'', 566, 567
Farnsworth, Debbie R., 141
Farnsworth, Deborah, 414
Farnsworth, Edwin W. ''Eddie'', 568, 570, 571
Farnsworth, George, 40
Farnsworth, James, 280
Farnsworth, Richard R., 748
Farquhar, Dr. Andy, 4
Farran, Yusuf Elias, 457
Farrar, Janet, 537
Farrar, Jessica Christian, 1031, 1037, 1038
Farrell, Cynthia ''Cindy'', 261
Farrell, Debora, 213
Farrell, Herman D., Jr., 896, 906, 907
Farrell, Jessyn, 1074, 1078, 1079
Farrell, Michael, 57
Farrell, Peter F., 1063, 1067, 1068
Farrell, Robert W., 490
Farrell, Tom, 311
Farren, Mike, 520
Farrer, Joe, 576, 580
Farrin, Bradlee Thomas, 748
Farrington, Jeff, 780, 784, 785
Farris, Carol D., 49
Farris, Lori, 196
Farris, Ray, 440
Farris, Robert, 117
Farrow, Joseph A., 50

**NAME INDEX**

Fitzgerald, Timothy, 97
Fitzgibbon, Joe, 1074, 1078, 1079
FitzGibbon, Megan, 262
Fitzhugh, Craig, 1019, 1021, 1024, 1025
Fitzmartin, Megan, 366
Fitzmaurice, Michael T., 244
Fitzpatrick, Daniel J., 369
Fitzpatrick, Dr. Joseph, 209
Fitzpatrick, Kevin, 154
Fitzpatrick, Dr. Lisa, 92
Fitzpatrick, Michael J., 896, 905, 907
Fitzpatrick, Perry, 96
Fitzpatrick, Scott, 822, 828, 829, 830
Fitzpatrick, Steve, 837, 840, 841
Fitzpatrick, Thomas Okuda, 497
Fitzsimmons, Elizabeth "Liz", 218
Fitzwater, Paul, 822, 828, 829, 830
Fitzwater, Travis, 822, 830, 831
Fjeseth, Blair, 286
Flach, Andrew, 143
Flachsbarth, Brett, 178
Flack, Michael A., 374
Flagstad, Judy, 437
Flahaven, Kathleen, 154
Flahaven, Roger, 153
Flaherty, Joseph J., 415
Flaherty, Col. W. Steven, 498
Flake, David, 33
Flakoll, Tim, 925, 927, 928
Flanagain, Jessica, 288
Flanagan, Allison, 184
Flanagan, Beverly, 157
Flanagan, Jack, 856, 869, 870
Flanagan, James "Jim", 445
Flanagan, Jennifer L., 764
Flanagan, John J., 887, 888, 893
Flanagan, Joseph, 229
Flanagan, Kathleen, 235
Flanagan, Kathy, 483
Flanagan, Kevin, 367
Flanagan, Paul E., 317
Flanagan, Peggy, 792, 798, 799
Flanagan, Robert L. "Bob", 756, 757, 762
Flanagan, Susan C., 422
Flanagan, Dr. Timothy J., 61
Flanagan, William E., 389
Flanders, Donald H. "Don", 856, 868
Flanigan, Tom, 822, 828, 829, 831
Flanigan, William "Bill", 1084, 1088, 1089, 1090
Flannagan, Deborah K., 121
Flasch, COL Adam R., 223
Flather, Fred, 147
Flax, Anita, 419
Fleeharty, Jack, 149
Fleener, Craig, 10
Fleenor, Lowell, 538
Fleenor, Robert, 384
Fleetham, Jeffrey, 25
Fleetwood, Susan, 347
Fleggas, Speros J., 347
Fleig, Joshua, 200
Fleischauer, Barbara Evans, 1084, 1089, 1090
Fleischauer, Donna, 404
Fleischer, Mark, 334
Fleischman, David, 369
Fleischmann, Andrew M., 603, 608, 609
Fleming, Barry A., 640, 648, 649, 650
Fleming, Charles, 117
Fleming, David L., 225

Fleming, Emily J., 514
Fleming, Jim, 360
Fleming, Lauren, 467
Fleming, Patrick, 539
Fleming, Patrick J., 213
Fleming, Paul, 441
Fleming, Rhonda, 463
Fleming, Shelly, 389
Fleming, Stephani, 250
Fleming, Tim, 119
Fleps, Christina, 95
Fletcher, Allen, 1031, 1036, 1038
Fletcher, David G. "Dave", 474
Fletcher, Jada J., 221
Fletcher, Michael R., 495
Fletcher, Rhonda, 213
Fletcher, Roland G., 219
Fletcher, Sharon, 370
Fletcher, Tamala, 461
Flewellen, Bert, 113
Flexer, Mae, 599, 600, 608, 610, 612
Flick, Jo, 286
Flickinger, Sandra, 395
Flinn, Joyce, 169
Flinn, Richard D., Jr., 407
Flint, Arwen, 56
Flint, Glen, 294
Flint, Steve, 333
Flippo, Scott, 572, 574
Fliss, Mary, 509
Floberg, Mike, 178
Flock, Denise K., 258
Floden, Stacy, 191
Flodmand, Richard, 315
Flohr, Dave, 361
Flomenbaum, Mark A., 214
Flood, Byron, 273
Flood, Cheryl, 109
Flood, Jennifer R., 391
Flood, Kelly, 727, 731, 732
Flood, Nathan, 402
Flood, Patrick, 442
Flood, Rebecca, 263
Flora, Jerilyn D. "Jeri", 100
Floren, Livvy R., 601, 603, 609, 610
Florence, Doug, 148
Florentz, Tammy, 435
Flores, Amanda, 59
Flores, Anitere, 620, 621, 622, 623
Flores, Carmen, 467
Flores, Edgar R., 848, 849
Flores, John, 154
Flores, K. Joseph "Joe", 493
Flores, Manny, Jr., 462
Flores, Dr. Val, 65
Florio, Mike, 54
Flory, Cathye, 376
Flory, Katrina, 367
Flory, Margaret K. "Peg", 1047, 1048
Flowers, Cynthia, 5
Flowers, Falita, 114
Flowers, Larry L., 368
Flowers, Mary E., 678, 683, 684, 685, 686
Flowers, Stephanie, 572, 574
Flowers, Tom, 283
Flowers, Vivian L., 576, 580
Floyd, David W., 727, 732, 733
Floyd, Dorinda R., 94
Floyd, Elmer, 915, 920, 921, 922, 923, 924
Floyd, Hugh, 640, 647, 648
Floyd, Johnny Wilson, 121
Floyd, Kay, 944, 946, 947
Floyd, Pam, 511
Floyd, Tiffany, 135
Fludd, Virgil, 637, 640, 647, 648, 650, 651
Fluharty, Shawn, 1085, 1089
Flygare, Jill, 472

Flynn, Dan, 1031, 1037, 1038
Flynn, Erin, 436
Flynn, Heather, 339
Flynn, Joseph, 482
Flynn, Julie, 215
Flynn, Keith W., 482
Flynn, Kelly, 837, 840, 841
Flynn, Larry, 285
Flynn, Laurie, 244
Flynn, Marty, 969, 978, 979
Flynn, Michael C., 373
Flynn, Ryan, 322
Foca, Chris, 495
Foehr, Lisa, 415
Foerschler, Sharon, 299
Fogarty, Charles J. "Charlie", 416
Fogarty, Kathleen A., 994, 997
Fogarty, Paul W., 991, 992, 993
Fogels, Edmund J. "Ed", 15
Fogle, Brian, 279
Foglia, Linda, 341
Foglia, Philip, 332
Fogue, Andrea, 391
Foil, Franklin J., 739, 742, 743
Folden, William "Bill", 758, 762
Foley, Brad, 213
Foley, Diana J., 301
Foley, Katherine, 70
Foley, Mike, 288, 294, 842
Foley, Robert, 210, 748, 752
Folger, Col. Gary, 16
Folino, Kelley, 143
Folio, Michael J., 521
Folk, Michael "Mike", 1085, 1088, 1089
Folmer, Mike, 962, 964, 965
Folse, Lela M., 206
Folsom, Mayra, 102
Foltz, Carol, 238
Fondeur, Jennifer, 413
Fondon, Cheryl Lynn, 3
Fonfara, John W., 599, 600, 609, 611
Fong, George, 340
Fong, Michael, 56
Fons, Brandon, 266
Fontaine, Elizabeth K., 245
Fontaine, Paula, 419
Fontaine, Robert, 227
Fontana, Wayne D., 961, 962, 964, 965
Fontenot, Tom, 88
Fontes, Jennifer McCrory, 348
Fonts, Sean, 417
Foor, Amanda, 159
Foote, Kathleen, 57
Foote, Mike, 595, 596, 598
Forbes, Carlene, 84
Forbes, Eugene, 304
Forbes, John, 704, 707, 708
Forbes, Jonathan J., 66
Forbes, Peter Craig, 375
Forbes, Peter J., 238
Forbess, Debra, 103
Forby, Gary F., 670, 673, 674, 684
Ford-Jenrette, Keisha, 118
Ford, Aaron D., 845, 846, 847
Ford, Angela, 356
Ford, Anne, 506
Ford, Carl, 915, 920, 921, 922, 923, 924
Ford, Craig, 546, 548, 552, 554
Ford, Dave, 371
Ford, Emily, 11
Ford, James E., 354
Ford, Joel D. M., 908, 910, 911, 912, 913
Ford, John, 945, 946, 947
Ford, Jon, 688, 690, 691

Ford, LaShawn K., 678, 682, 683, 684, 685, 686
Ford, Lula Mae, 152
Ford, Mikah, 110
Ford, Monica, 139
Ford, Ramie, 267
Ford, Susan, 852, 856, 869
Ford, Walter, 69
Ford, William, 531
Forde, Jean, 1056, 1057
Fordyce, Richard, 274
Fordyce, Thomas G., 465
Forehand, Joy, 326
Foreman, Kelly, 190
Foreman, Kevin J., 519
Foreman, Rebecca, 71
Forese, Thomas "Tom", 26
Forest, Armand D., 856, 869
Forest, Dan, 354, 355, 907
Forest, Kristen R., 391
Forestal, Daniel "Dan", 693, 696, 698
Foresti, Jessica, 54
Forgety, John W., 1021, 1024
Forgione, Donald, 101
Forguites, Robert "Bob", 1050, 1056
Forino, Donna M., 340
Forkner, Albert L., 535
Forkner, Justin, 158
Forlano, Laurie, 494
Forlini, Anthony, 780, 784, 785
Forman, Sarah Jane, 88
Formby, Mark S., 808, 813, 814, 815, 816
Formica, Paul, 599, 600, 608, 609, 611
Fornario, Jana, 366
Fornaro, Jack A., 317
Forniss, Beatrice M., 4
Fornshell, Anne, 372
Forren, Jerry A., 522
Forrer, Mindy, 180
Forrest, Joseph, 386
Forrest, Karen, 13
Forrest, Sharon, 17
Forrester, Darby, 5
Forrester, Jeanie, 851, 852
Forrester, P. Michael "Mike", 1004, 1009
Forrester, Reid K., 279
Forristall, Greg, 704, 708, 709
Forrister, Larry, 350
Forry, Linda Dorcena, 764, 766
Forsaith, Andy, 528
Forschino, Anthony, 25
Forse, Don, 468
Forshee, Elizabeth "Beth", 418
Forshey, Dr. Tony, 367
Forslund, Thomas O. "Tom", 536
Forster, Daniel "Dan", 115
Forster, Deidre, 536
Forster, Nathan, 242
Forstner, Nathaniel, 246
Forsythe, Anne, 489
Fort, Joanne Doddy, 97
Fort, Vincent D., 631, 632, 635, 636, 637
Forte, A.J., 322
Forte, Grover Berry, 548, 552
Fortes, Robert, 239
Fortier-Hollow, Sandra, 233
Fortier, Breean, 232
Fortier, Joanne, 304
Fortier, Lisa, 385
Fortin, Michael W., 209
Fortmann, John, 150
Fortner, Mike, 678, 683, 684, 685, 686
Fortney, Matt, 531
Fortson, Brian, 32
Fortune, Anthony W., 96

Forward, Rob, 364
Foshee, David, 422
Fosler, Dixie, 103
Foss, Craig, 137
Foss, Darsi, 528
Fossitt, Rhonda, 250
Foster-Lee, Isha, 84
Foster, Becki, 379
Foster, Beckie, 510
Foster, Ben, 199
Foster, Darius, 6
Foster, David, 449
Foster, Ed, 22
Foster, Gary, 242
Foster, Geoff, 1085, 1089, 1090
Foster, Helen Diane, 336
Foster, Jacqueline, 113
Foster, James D., 4
Foster, Joseph A., 302
Foster, Joseph S., 284
Foster, Julie, 201
Foster, Kelly, 183
Foster, LaToya, 84
Foster, Linda D., 493
Foster, Michael W., Jr., 101
Foster, Neal, 557, 560
Foster, Robert, 808, 812, 813, 814, 815, 816
Foster, Sally, 423
Fothergill, John J., 857, 869
Fotinos, Charissa, 509
Fotinos, Shawn, 292
Fouberg, Glenna N., 432
Fountain, Brennon, 76
Fountain, BrigGen David R., 476
Fountain, Sandra, 352
Fourcade, Jim, 387
Fourkiller, William, 949, 953, 954
Fournet, Kaye, 205
Fournier, Normand, 241
Foushee, Valerie P., 908, 910, 911, 912, 913
Foust, David, 94
Fowden, Mark, 536
Fowle, Lori, 748
Fowler, Alicia, 49
Fowler, Hyland F. "Buddy", 1063, 1068
Fowler, Kathy, 189
Fowler, Kent, 52
Fowler, Mark, 4
Fowler, Micaela, 11
Fowler, Michael, 27
Fowler, Russell "Rusty", 160
Fowler, Sarah, 376
Fowler, Scott, 148
Fowlkes-Bridges, Bernadette, 225
Fowlkes, Earl D., Jr., 86
Fox, A.J., 274
Fox, BrigGen Bryan, 284
Fox, Charles E., 407
Fox, Daniel J., 601, 604, 609, 610, 611
Fox, Gloria L., 769, 775
Fox, Heidi, 106
Fox, BG Jack R., 326
Fox, Jan, 380
Fox, Joseph A., 388
Fox, Joy, 413
Fox, Katja, 305
Fox, Nicole B., 842, 844
Fox, Randy, 439
Fox, Timothy C. "Tim", 286
Foxley, Theresa A., 469
Foxman, Richard, 146
Foy, Bettye, 159
Foy, Joy, 269
Fraase, Karen, 144
Fradel, Jennifer, 318
Frady, Beth W., 102
Fraker, Lyndall, 822, 830, 831, 832
Frakes, Scott, 289

Gaines, Randal L., 739, 742, 743
Gaines, Robert, 313
Gaines, Ruth Ann, 704, 708, 709
Gaines, Tawanna P., 758, 762, 763
Gaines, Ted, 581, 582, 584, 585
Gaines, Wallica, 493
Gainey, Ed, 969, 977, 979, 980
Gaither, Keith, 442
Gaj, Robert, 417
Gajos, Ronald, 152
Gajwani, Seema, 83
Galbally, Sarah, 400
Galbato, Joe, 446
Galdieri, Emelia A., 303
Gale, John A., 294, 295
Gale, Susan, 22
Galea'i, Alfonso P., 20
Galea'i, Dr. Seth, 20
Galef, Sandra R. "Sandy", 897, 903, 904, 905, 906
Galgiani, Cathleen, 582, 584, 585
Galifianakis, Manuel "Mike", III, 117
Galimba, Michelle, 132
Galindo, David W., 458
Galindo, Laura, 324
Galindo, Rick, 1031, 1037, 1038
Galinskie, Amanda, 75
Gall, Renae L., 361
Gallagher, Brian S., 857, 870
Gallagher, Carla, 247
Gallagher, Carrie Meek, 333
Gallagher, Dennis, 299
Gallagher, Gabrielle, 310
Gallagher, Greg, 365
Gallagher, James, 585, 587, 591, 592
Gallagher, John G., 214
Gallagher, Kathleen, 237
Gallagher, Kevin, 413
Gallagher, Linda J., 715, 720, 722
Gallagher, Lynn, 323
Gallagher, Mary L., 239
Gallagher, Patrick, 162
Gallagher, Ryan, 160
Gallahorn, Kenny, 16
Gallardo, Sandra, 43
Galleger, Laura, 110
Gallegos, David M., 883, 886
Gallegos, Doreen Y., 883, 885, 886
Gallegos, Erin, 66
Gallegos, Joe, 958, 960
Gallegos, Ralph, 328
Gallegos, Sergio, 26
Gallegos, Valerie, 328
Galles, Lori, 535
Gallien, Kirk, 204
Gallivan, Patrick M., 888, 891, 892, 893, 894
Gallman, Jodi, 426
Gallo, Glenna, 476
Gallo, Hanna M., 991, 992
Gallo, Dr. Maria, 133
Galloway, John T., 969, 977, 979, 980
Galloway, Nicole, 280
Galo, Anna B., 462
Galuski, Monica, 454
Galuteria, Brickwood, 654, 655, 656
Galvano, Bill, 619, 620, 621, 622, 623
Galvin, Mary M., 72
Galvin, Susan, 418
Galvin, William C., 769, 775
Galvin, William Francis, 243

Gamache, Marianna, 1050, 1056
Gamage, Charlene, 209
Gambineri, Mara K., 102
Gamble, Dr. Janice Murray, 428
Gambrell, Charles William "Bill", 429
Gambrell, John "Eric", 465
Gambrell, Michael W. "Mike", 999
Gamelgaard, Samantha, 396
Gamette, Matthew, 140
Gamez, Annette, 248
Gammon, BrigGen Kenneth L., 476
Gándara Menéndez, Luisa "Piti", 985, 987, 988, 989, 990
Gandy, Rachel, 3
Gane, Brad, 115
Ganeriwala, Manju S., 493
Ganjehsani, Warren, 426
Gann, Thomas H. "Tom", 454
Gannon, Bob, 1095, 1099, 1100, 1101
Gannon, Elaine Freeman, 822, 828, 829, 831
Gannon, John L., 665, 667, 668
Gannon, Leslie, 190
Gannon, William M., 857, 868
Gannuch, Craig, 201
Gant, Aaron, 423
Gant, Carol, 319
Gantt, David F., 897, 904, 906, 907
Gaoteote, Tamaaiga P., 19
Gara, Les S., 557, 560
Garay, Marcos, 22
Garballey, Sean, 770, 775
Garbarino, Andrew R., 897, 904, 905, 906
Garber, Randy, 715, 720, 721, 722
Garceau, Annemarie, 338
García Padilla, Alejandro Javier, 411
Garcia Richard, Stephanie, 883, 885, 886
Garcia, Alison, 357
Garcia, Ana, 239
Garcia, Anthony "Tony", 104
Garcia, Cristina, 587, 591, 592, 593
García, Daniela, 780, 784, 785
Garcia, David A., 222
Garcia, Eduardo, 587, 591, 592, 593
Garcia, Elba, 89
Garcia, Eleazar, 466
Garcia, Ernest, 459
Garcia, Jeanette Autobee, 61
Garcia, Joe, 323, 455
Garcia, Joseph D., 513
Garcia, Leroy M., Jr., 594, 595
Garcia, Martina X., 324
Garcia, Mia, 27
García, Miguel P., 883, 886
Garcia, Norma, 455
Garcia, Ramiro, Jr., 458
Garcia, Rene, 464, 620, 621, 622
Garcia, Sylvia R., 1026, 1028, 1029
Gard, Allison, 62
Gard, Howard A. "Hal", 395
Gard, Lisa, 169
Gardenhire, Ricki, 192
Gardenhire, R. Todd, 1017, 1018, 1019
Gardenswartz, Alissa, 66
Gardiner, Andy, 619, 620

Gardner, Berta, 555, 556, 557
Gardner, Carrice, 126
Gardner, Colleen Crawford, 343
Gardner, Craig, 206, 340
Gardner, David M., 848, 849
Gardner, George E., Jr., 489
Gardner, Janice S., 857, 868
Gardner, Keith J., 320
Gardner, Kimberly M., 822, 827, 828, 829, 830, 831
Gardner, Pat, 640, 646, 648, 650, 651
Gardner, Randy L., 934, 935, 936
Gardner, Rick L., 359
Gardner, Tracie M., 330
Gardner, William D. "Bill", 261
Gardner, William M. "Bill", 303
Garduño, Lauren, 464
Gargasz, Carolyn M., 857, 868
Gargus, Melissa B., 6
Garidel, Dudley J., Jr., 207
Garinger, Gail, 242
Garino, Peter, 418
Garland, Alice, 355
Garland, Denise, 209
Garland, Julie, 57
Garland, Dr. Rebecca, 354
Garlick, Denise C., 770
Garn, Jacob W. "Jake", 473
Garner Walters, Marketa, 199
Garner, Aaron, 156
Garner, Dale, 171
Garner, Frank, 837, 841
Garner, Katie, 247
Garner, Marcia, 444
Garnett, Alec, 596, 598
Garnett, Kensil K., 150
Garofalo, Pat, 792, 798, 799, 800
Garofalo, Raymond "Ray", 739, 743
Garraty, Teresa, 218
Garrett, Barbara, 42
Garrett, Connie, 105
Garrett, James, 490
Garrett, J. Daniel, 548, 552, 554
Garrett, Joe, 5
Garrett, Julian B., 700, 701, 702
Garrett, LaTanya, 780, 784
Garrett, Matthew, 394
Garrett, Michelle, 328
Garrett, Rob, 242
Garrett, Thomas A. "Tom", Jr., 1059, 1060, 1061
Garrett, Col Tommy L., 842, 844, 845
Garrett, T. Scott, 1063, 1067, 1068, 1069
Garrettson, Gordon, 226
Garrick, Sean M., 85
Garrido, Carolyn, 125
Garringer, LTC Richard D., 33
Garrison, Charlotte, 203
Garrison, Dennis, 520
Garrison, Douglas, 156
Garrison, Earl, 944, 945, 946, 947
Garrison, Jackie, 200
Garrison, James, 27
Garrison, John, 353
Garriss, M. Dwayne, 120
Garry, Colleen M., 770, 775
Gartland, Lavin, 112
Garvey, Dennis, 442
Garvey, James D. "Jim", Jr., 207
Garvey, Kevin, 163
Garvey, Michael S. "Mike", 159

Gary, Timothy, 528
Garza, Jon, 454
Garza, Rick J., 510
Garza, Thomas R. "Rick", 453
Garza, Tim, 47, 48
Gasaway, Dan, 640, 647, 648, 649, 650
Gasaway, John M., 305
Gasber, Greg, 529
Gaskill, Mary, 703, 704, 707, 708, 709
Gaskins, Anthony A., 223
Gaskins, Clyde, 109
Gaskins, Greg, 357
Gaspard, Brett, 182
Gaspard, Greg, 205
Gasper, Russ, 289
Gass, Rita, 49
Gassman, Tedd, 704, 708
Gastinell, Sherri, 53
Gaston, Ben, 268
Gaston, Fred, 444
Gaston, Michael, 418
Gaston, Sharon, 457
Gaston, Victor, 546, 548, 553, 554
Gastreich, Kathy, 503
Gates, Angie M., 83
Gates, Brett, 367
Gates, Judy, 213
Gates, Mickey, 576, 580
Gates, Pamela B., 4
Gates, LTC Randall K., 483
Gates, Robert R., 64
Gates, Scott, 180
Gates, Sylvester James, Jr., 228
Gates, Timothy E., 406
Gattenby, Will, 388
Gatti, Ryan, 734, 736
Gattine, Drew, 748
Gattis, Lynn, 557, 560
Gatto, Mike, 588, 591, 592, 593
Gatz, Tim, 382
Gau, David, 58
Gaudion, Julien, 403
Gaudreault, Major Mike, 294
Gaul, Linda, 460
Gault, Chris, 112
Gaunch, Ed, 1080, 1082, 1083
Gauss, Mark, 145
Gauthier, Greta, 263
Gauthier, Paul, 335
Gautreaux, Ashley, 206
Gautreaux, Sid, 199
Gautz, Chris, 247
Gauvin, Russell J., 213
Gavel, Robert, 222
Gavelek, Ben, 165
Gavin, Anne-Harvin, 428
Gavin, Bradley "Brad", 158
Gavin, Diane P., 273
Gavin, James "Jim", 162
Gavrilis, John, 225
Gay-Dagnogo, Sherry, 780, 784
Gay, Debbie, 118
Gay, Gerald S., 1105, 1107, 1108
Gay, Stephanie, 381
Gayhart, Renee, 13
Gaynor, Peter T., 419
Gazelka, Paul E., 786, 787, 789, 790
Gearhart, Rose Marie, 369
Gearheart, Gary Martin "Marty", 1085, 1089, 1090
Geary, Charles, 285
Geary, Patricia J., 345
Geathers, Heidi, 510
Gebauer, Keith, 20
Gebhardt, Karl, 373
Gecker, Daniel A. "Dan", 492

Geddes, Robert L. "Bob", 134
Geddings, Anne, 34
Gedstad, Eric, 244
Gee, Gavin M., 135
Gee, Lucy, 102
Gee, Mark W., 991, 992
Gee, Dr. Rebekah E., 201
Geer, Pat, 115
Gehringer, Zachary, 391
Gehrke, Stephen, 503
Geier, Roberta, 81
Geiger, Bernice, 325
Geiger, Joseph N. "Joe", 515
Geiger, Peter E., 210
Geiger, Tony, 272
Geigis, Priscilla E., 235
Geiogue, Hal, 54
Geis, Gerald E., 1103, 1104
Geiselman, J. Wesley, 318
Geisenberger, Richard J. "Rick", 79
Geisreiter, Kurt, 510
Geiss, Erika, 780, 784, 785
Geissler, George, 379
Gelber, Eric, 44
Geldart, Christopher T., 95
Gelinas, David, 307
Geller, Joseph S. "Joe", 625, 630
Gellermann, AnnaLisa, 512
Gelser, Sara A., 955, 956, 957
Genardo, Kim, 347
Gendreau, Cal, 361
Gendreau, Gisgie Dávila, 251
Genesi, Nicolas, 120
Genest, Robert, 417
Genga, Henry J., 601, 604, 608, 609, 611
Gengarella, Patrick, 418
Genovese, Anthony F. "Tony", 314
Genrich, Eric, 1095, 1100, 1102
Gensterblum, Sherri, 249
Gentile, Carmine, 770, 775
Gentile, Linda M., 601, 604, 609, 610, 611
Gentile, Lou, 934, 935, 936, 937
Gentner, William E., III, 448
Gentry-Wiseman, Michelle, 148
Gentry, Linda E., 498
Gentry, Nate, 882, 883, 886
George, Biju, 97
George, Camille, 480
George, Catherine E., 302
George, Cindy, 161
George, Claudia D., 514
George, Darryl, 486
George, Deborah "Deb", 418
George, Janet L., 237
George, Jim, 219
George, J. Wayne, 1004, 1008, 1009
George, Kristi, 515
George, Lewis C., 370
George, Pamela "Pam", 450
George, Rebecca, 501
George, Rodney, 14
George, Thomas "Tom", 489
George, Tony, 176
Geraci, Brian, 229
Geraghty, Tim, 262
Gerard, Jerome D., 209
Gerard, Katie, 505
Gerardi, Debra R., 75
Gerberding, Evan, 39
Gerbes, John A. "Jack", 218
Gerdes, Karen, 1012
Geren, Charlie, 1031, 1036, 1037, 1038

Gerentine, Richard A., 340
Gergely, Marc J., 969, 979
Gerhardt, Terri, 367
Gerhart, Col. Michael T., Jr., 363
Gerhart, Nick, 168
Gerhold, Sara, 71
Gering, Catherine, 413
Gerke, Randy, 293
Gerke, Scott, 106
Gerlach, Andy, 434
Gerlach, Kendra, 349
Gerlin, Simon R., 245
Gerlt, Kim, 276
Germaine, Kreh, 284
German, MajGen Anthony P., 336
Germany, Cheryl, 119
Gerovich, Sule Calikoglu, 228
Gerratana, Theresa Bielinski "Terry", 599, 600, 608, 610, 611
Gerregano, David, 445
Gerringer, William, 357
Gerrish, Karen, 748
Gerrish, Merrily S., 238
Gerstein, Terri, 344
Gerstenfeld, David K., 391
Gervais, George, 209
Gerzofsky, Stan J., 745, 746
Geschwind, Lynnette Marie, 260
Gestrin, Terry, 665, 668, 669
Getchel, Dan, 260
Getchell, Chip, 213
Getsinger, Neal, 427
Getty, Joseph M., 216
Getz, Roger, 435
Getzie, Peter, 405
Geyer, Chris, 373
Ghartey Ogundimu, Lisa, 338
Ghazi, Sue, 97
Ghielmetti, James C., 50
Ghilarducci, Mark S., 40
Ghini, Charles, 109
Ghosh, Tista, 63
Ghrist, Jefferson L., 758, 762
Giachetti, Steven, 87
Giambrone, Steven, 202
Giampaolo, Steven, 64
Gianakos, Brad, 290
Gianaris, Michael N., 887, 888, 892, 893
Gianato, James J. "Jimmy", 519
Giani, Francine A., 470
Giannini, Bill, 439
Gianoulias, Bill, 282
GiaQuinta, Phillip K. "Phil", 691, 693, 697, 698
Giardina, Tony, 331
Giarrrusso, John, 241
Giarrusso, Antonio, 994, 996, 997
Gibbons, Jaret A., 969, 978, 980
Gibbons, Lesley Ann, 45
Gibbons, Richard, 403, 404
Gibbons, William L. "Bill", 445
Gibbs, Catherine, 161
Gibbs, John, 467
Gibbs, Karl, 808, 812, 814, 816
Gibbs, Marc, 152, 665, 667, 668
Gibbs, Margaret "Marty", 196
Gibellina, Emily, 143
Gibler, Tracie, 167
Giblin, Charles, 316
Giblin, Thomas P., 874, 875, 879
Gibson-Beltz, Cathy, 289
Gibson, Arian, 91

Gibson, Audrey, 620, 622, 623
Gibson, Carroll, 723, 725, 726
Gibson, Davis, 299
Gibson, Emily, 440
Gibson, Francis D., 1041, 1042, 1045
Gibson, Greg L., 165
Gibson, Jackson, 327
Gibson, Jess, 156
Gibson, Julie, 275
Gibson, Karen, 258
Gibson, Ladd, 427
Gibson, Mark, 371
Gibson, Marlena, 81
Gibson, Paul, 239
Gibson, Peggy, 1013, 1015, 1016
Gibson, Sarah, 288
Gibson, Sherray, 97
Gibson, Stacie, 249
Gibson, Stacy, 445
Gibson, Thomas "Tom", 46
Gibson, Ventris Cassandra, 96
Gibson, Wade, 420
Gibson, Zackary, 99
Gick, Dale, 159
Giddens, Danny, 348
Giddings, Helen, 1031, 1036, 1038
Gideon, Sara, 746, 748, 752
Gidge, Kenneth N., 857, 868
Giegler, Janice R., 601, 604, 609, 611, 612
Gieseke, Mark Allen, 261
Giesen, Cheri L., 362
Giesler, Gregory, 197
Giessel, Catherine, 555, 556
Gifford, Jeff, 385
Gifford, Lisa, 386
Gifford, Shannon, 65
Gifford, Susan Williams, 767, 770, 775
Giglio, David, 507
Giglio, Joseph M. "Joe", 894, 897, 902, 903, 904
Giguere, Paul, 213
Gilbert, Alan "Al", 263
Gilbert, Carol Anne, 221
Gilbert, C. Todd, 1063, 1067, 1068
Gilbert, LTC Dan, 155
Gilbert, Deirdre, 212
Gilbert, Dudley, 379
Gilbert, Jennifer, 302
Gilbert, Mark, 269
Gilbert, Paul E., 748
Gilbreth, Donna, 304
Gilchrist, Corinne, 156
Gilchrist, David, 401
Gilchrist, James W. "Jim", 758, 762
Gilchrist, Jane Ammons, 356
Gilchrist, Lauren, 255
Gilchrist, Shannon, 207
Gile, Audra, 176
Gile, Mary Stuart, 857, 868
Giles, Robert F. "Bob", 319
Gilford, Steven R., 152
Gilg, Kerstin, 214
Gilkey, Ann, 286
Gill, Amy, 406
Gill, Charles "Chuck", 314
Gill, Dr. James R., 67
Gill, Jeff, 161
Gill, Laurie R., 436
Gill, Michael "Mike", 98
Gill, Nia H., 871, 873
Gill, R. Michael "Mike", 218
Gill, Rosa U., 913, 915, 920, 921, 922, 923
Gill, Tierney, 533
Gill, Tracy Ann, 395
Gillam, Jeremy, 574, 576, 580
Gillan, James W., 125
Gillard, Carl, 640

Gillard, Major Chris, 266
Gillen, Mark M., 969, 977, 978, 979, 980
Gillen, Michele S., 245
Gillenwater, Kelley J., 516
Gillert, Thomas, 388
Gillespie, Cynthia D. "Cindy", 32
Gillespie, Erin, 100
Gillespie, Glenn, 79
Gillespie, James, 168
Gillespie, Joshua E., 157
Gillespie, Keith, 970, 978, 980
Gillespie, Mitch, 348
Gillespie, Tonya, 520
Gillespie, William H., 516
Gillett, Mark, 538
Gillett, Stacy, 502
Gillette, John Kelly, III, 459
Gilliam-Johnson, Patrice, 78
Gilliam, Cynthia "Cindy", 355
Gilliam, BG Harrison B., 518
Gilliam, Vic, 958, 960
Gilliard, Wendell G., 1004, 1009
Gilligan, Sheri, 641, 647, 648, 650
Gillihan, Lori, 43
Gillihan, Richard, 42, 43
Gilliland, Cameron, 136
Gilliland, Kathleen R., 65
Gilliland, Mike, 252
Gilliland, Nikki, 176
Gillim, Mack, 186
Gilling-Weber, Lana, 290
Gillis, Greer Johnson, 94
Gillis, Kathaleen, 405
Gillis, Larry B., 191
Gillis, Laura, 192
Gillispie, Sandra, 524
Gillway, James S., 748, 752
Gilman, Phyllis, 193
Gilman, Steven, 457
Gilman, Wendy, 302
Gilmore, Benjamin, 226
Gilmore, Brenda, 1021, 1025
Gilmore, David, 100
Gilmore, Janet, 455
Gilmore, Jon, 29
Gilmore, Kathy, 292
Gilmore, Phyllis, 177
Gilmour, Campbell M. "Cam", 506
Giltner, Phil, 332
Gimlin, Rick, 299
Gimmel, Richard F., 183
Ginal, Joann, 596, 598
Gingerich, David, 401
Gingerich, Jade Ann, 219
Gingrich, Mauree, 970, 977, 979, 980
Gingrow-Shaw, Mary, 215
Ginn, Frank, 632, 635, 636, 637
Ginn, Lesli, 455
Ginn, Mary F., 202
Ginn, Major Randy, 266
Ginsberg, Barry, 335
Ginter, Timothy E. "Tim", 938, 942, 943
Ginzler, Phyllis, 748, 752
Gionet, Edmond D., 857, 869
Giordano, John, 311
Giordano, Robert, 314
Gipe, Lisa, 407
Gipp, Charles R. "Chuck", 171
Gipson, Alexis J., 302
Gipson, Andrew "Andy", 808, 812, 813, 814, 815
Gipson, Connie, 51
Gipson, Hannibal McNeil "Mac", Jr., 7
Gipson, Mike A., 585, 588, 591, 592, 593

Gipson, Monica, 157
Giraldo, Gustavo, 152
Girantino, Kim, 76
Girard, Kate, 284
Girdler, Christopher "Chris", 723, 725
Girod, Fred, 955, 956, 957
Girouard, Spencer, 280
Giroux, Andy, 208
Giroux, Edward A. "Ed", 415
Girten, Janet M., 63
Gisclair, Jerry "Truck", 739, 742, 743, 744
Gish, Joan Wasser, 233
Gissler, Layne A., 289
Gist, Lawrence "Larry", 465
Gittens, Kenneth L., 1056, 1057
Gittins, Rex, 291
Gittisriboongul, Alvin, 43
Gittlen, Russell, 242
Givan, Juandalynn "Lee Lee", 548, 552, 553
Given, Gale Y., 513
Givens, David P., 723, 725
Givens, Dr. F. Lynwood, 464
Givens, Jimmy D., 380
Givens, Kevin N., 151
Givens, Stephanie, 422
Givner, Jennifer, 338
Gizaw, Seyoum, 97
Gjessing, Catherine, 481
Gjonaj, Mark, 897, 903, 906
Gladden, Lisa A., 753, 755
Gladstone, Carol, 232
Glady, Michelle, 100
Glandon, Donna, 384
Glanton, Mike, Sr., 641, 646, 647, 650
Glantz, Tonya, 419
Glardon, Ben, 781, 784, 785
Glascock, Stephen, 204
Glaser, Wayne, 361
Glasper, Marcus, 505
Glass, David L. "Dave", 310
Glass, Glen, 758, 762
Glass, Karen E., 237
Glassheim, Eliot, 929, 932
Glassman, Sarah, 238
Glassman, Steven, 344
Glatt, L. David, 360
Glause, Paul Thomas "Tom", 536
Glazer, Steven M. "Steve", 582, 584, 585
Glazier, Mark, 158
Gleason, Arthur L., Jr., 196
Gleason, Eric, 464
Gleason, Judith I. "Judy", 309
Gleason, Thomas R., 244
Gleckler, Bryan, 146
Gledhill, Lynda, 41, 42, 43
Glen, Alan, 50
Glen, Robert A., 80
Glenn-Hood, Karen, 218
Glenn, Cheryl D., 758, 762
Glenn, Enid, 530
Glenn, Gary, 428, 781, 784, 785
Glenn, Jim, 727, 731, 732, 733
Glenn, Sandra Dungee, 408
Glenn, Scott, 130
Glennon, Barry, Jr., 303
Glennon, Greg, 483
Glick, Armand, 473
Glick, C. Susan "Sue", 688, 689, 690, 691
Glick, Deborah J., 897, 904, 905, 906, 907
Glick, Michael, 154
Glick, Pam, 537
Glimm, Carl, 837, 840
Glisson, BG Michael J., 148

Gloak, Geoffrey T., 335
Gloe, Monty, 435
Gloor, Mike, 842, 844, 845
Glover, Barb, 275
Glover, Bobby, 33
Glover, Cedric B., 739, 743
Glover, Dana, 464
Glover, Eugene P., 24
Glover, Paul, 350
Glover, Rusty, 543, 545, 546
Glover, Ruth, 179
Glover, Samuel B., 427
Gluckman, Judah, 86
Glunt, Steven, 402
Glymph, James E., 87
Gnodtke, John, 247
Gobble, Chris, 446
Gobble, Tim, 449
Gobeil, Judge Elizabeth D., 119
Gober, Dennis, 384
Gobi, Anne M., 764, 766
Gobin, Anne R., 70
Goble, Jim, 384
Goble, Phil, 471
Goddard, Johnnie, 177
Goddard, Randy, 169
Goddin, Karen Wilde, 396
Godel, Eric, 361
Godfrey, Allen, 269
Godfrey, Gerad, 10
Godfrey, Gwenn, 101
Godfrey, Lynda, 101
Godfrey, Mary, 190
Godfrey, Rob, 421
Godfrey, Robert D. "Bob", 601, 604, 609, 610, 611
Godialis, Christopher, 73
Godin, Eric, 108
Godkin, Caroline, 47
Godowsky, Steven H., 77
Godsey Valente, Maureen, 244
Godshall, Robert W. "Bob", 970, 978, 979, 980
Godwin, Anne, 347
Godwin, Aubrey V., 26
Godwin, Larry, 446
Goe, Christina, 286
Goehring, Doug Charles, 362, 365
Goertz, Keith, 333
Goesling, Dr. William H. "Bill", 139
Goetcheus, Christopher, 238
Goetsch, Warren, 144
Goettsch, Craig A., 168
Goetz, Jennifer A., 408
Goetz, Katie, 329
Goff, Angele, 496
Goff, Jane, 65
Goff, Dr. Kendra F., 102
Goff, Kevin, 8
Goff, 1LT Preston, 271
Gogal, Mark, 349
Gogarty, Maurice, 104
Goggin, Greg, 213
Goggins, Tameka, 121
Goheen, Pam, 499
Goico, Mario, 713, 715, 720, 721, 722
Goicoechea, Dan, 142
Goicoechea, Dr. Julian Joesep, 297
Goicoechea, Peter J. "Pete", 845, 846, 847
Goike, Ken, 781, 785
Goings, Michelle, 304
Goins, Jenny, 191
Goins, Mark, 451
Goins, Michael, 196
Goins, Steve, 442
Goins, Tilman, 1019, 1021, 1024
Gold, Judi, 84
Goldberg, David, 152
Goldberg, Deborah B., 244
Goldberg, Evan L., 55

Goldberg, Jack R., 72
Goldberg, Richard "Rich", 143
Golden, Daniel, 396
Golden, James, 496
Golden, Jared, 748
Golden, Jodi, 152
Golden, Martin J., 887, 888, 891, 892, 893, 894
Golden, Mekell L., 518
Golden, Robyn H., 417
Golden, Tammy, 443
Golden, Thomas A., Jr., 770
Golden, Tim, 121
Golden, Violet Ann, 486
Golder, Ed, 251
Golderese, Matthew, 413
Goldfeder, Phillip, 897, 902, 903, 904, 905, 906
Goldfinch, Stephen L., Jr., 1004, 1009
Goldin, Gayle L., 991, 992
Goldman, Allan, 114
Goldman, Craig, 1031, 1037, 1038
Goldman, Jared, 44
Goldman, Lauren A., 243
Goldman, Mike, 452
Goldmark, Peter J., 512
Goldner, Paul, 35
Goldsborough, David, 226
Goldsmith, Fred, 95
Goldstein, Louisa H., 225
Goldstein, Mark, 223
Goley, Jeffrey, 852, 857, 868
Golick, Rich, 641, 646, 649, 650
Golightly, Andrew, 280
Gollott, Tommy Arlin, 801, 803, 804, 805
Golombek, Ellen, 61
Gomberg, David, 957, 958, 960
Gomes, Edwin A. "Ed", 599, 600, 611, 612
Gomez, Bealquin "Bill", 883, 885, 886
Gomez, Cynthia, 37, 131
Gomez, Elena, 45
Gomez, Jaime, 66
Gomez, Jessica, 396
Gomez, Jimmy, 588, 592, 593
Gomez, Joe E., 329
Gomez, Joel "Nico", 386
Gomez, Jose, 499
Gomez, Richard, 476
Gomez, Rosa, 45
Gómez, Saúl, 46
Gomez, Steven "Steve", 481
Goncalves, Kimberly, 46
Gonroff, Jennifer, 343
Gonzales, Anne, 939, 942
Gonzales, Audrey, 324
Gonzales, Danielle, 324
Gonzales, Estela, 41
Gonzales, Gilbert, 38
Gonzales, Greg, 442
Gonzales, Justin, 576, 580
Gonzales, Larry, 1031, 1036, 1037, 1038
Gonzales, Linda, 324
Gonzales, Oona, 326
Gonzales, Roberto J. "Bobby", 883, 885, 886
Gonzales, Sally Ann, 569, 570, 571
Gonzales, Veronica, 321
González Colón, Jenniffer A., 984, 985
Gonzalez-Cortes, Martha, 247
González López, María Teresa "Maritere", 981, 982, 983, 984
González Ortiz, Jesus Manuel, 411

Gonzalez-Sánchez, Arlene, 337
Gonzalez, Anna, 397
Gonzalez, Ben, 455
Gonzalez, Carlos, 770
Gonzalez, Carlos E., 857, 869
Gonzalez, Diana, 1051, 1055
Gonzalez, Joseph A. "Jody", 459
Gonzalez, Julio, 625, 630
Gonzalez, Juvencio, 409
Gonzalez, Liz, 56
Gonzalez, Lorena S., 588, 591, 592
Gonzalez, Lori, 507
Gonzalez, Martin, 56
Gonzalez, Mary E., 1031, 1036, 1038
Gonzalez, Miguel, 56
Gonzalez, Minnie, 601, 604, 608, 610, 611
Gonzalez, Pedro "Pete", 26
Gonzalez, Ramon, Jr., 715, 720, 722
Goo, Wesley, 49
Gooch, James, Jr., 727, 731, 732, 733
Gooch, Steve, 473, 631, 632, 635, 636, 637
Gooch, Teresa P., 497
Good, Alicia, 416
Good, Ann, 253
Good, Cayanna, 119
Good, Mindy, 90
Good, Tina, 70
Goodale, BG John, 141
Goodbarn, Thomas W., 292
Goode, Adam A., 748
Goode, Jesse, 86
Goodell, Andrew, 897, 903, 904, 905, 906
Goodell, David, 422
Goodell, Walter, 482
Goodheart, Daniel, 209
Goodie, Sharon, 86
Goodin, Don, 182
Goodin, Terry A., 693, 698
Goodloe, Major Mark, 179
Goodman, Carmen, 158
Goodman, David, 368
Goodman, Hunter, 1069
Goodman, Ken, 915, 921, 922, 923, 924
Goodman, Marna, 147
Goodman, Neal P., 966, 970, 980
Goodman, Rebecca, 196
Goodman, Roger E., 1074, 1078, 1079
Goodman, Stephanie, 455
Goodman, Tara, 108
Goodmann, Peter, 185
Goodpaster, Rusty K., 164
Goodrum, Brent, 15
Goodson, Barbara, 198
Goodson, Stephen, 134
Goodson, Tom, 626
Goodwin, Amy Shuler, 513, 514
Goodwin, Barbara J. "Barb", 787, 789, 790
Goodwin, Chris, 264
Goodwin, JB, 454
Goodwin, John, 385
Goodwin, Kathleen Huffman "Kay", 515
Goodwin, Maryellen, 990, 991, 992, 993
Goodwin, Michael R., 214
Goodwin, Regina, 949, 953, 954
Goodwin, Rob, 117
Goodwin, Wanda T., 94
Goodwin, Wayne, 355
Googe, Laurie, 193
Gookin, MAJ Chris, 483
Gookin, Eric, 174
Goolsby, Ashley, 353

Goolsby, Carl, 354
Gopalpur, Kanth, 396
Gorbea, Nellie M., 420
Gordner, John R., 961, 962, 964, 965
Gordon-Booth, Jehan A., 675, 678, 683, 684, 685
Gordon, Alan, 55
Gordon, Bruce, 260
Gordon, Darin J., 442
Gordon, David, 186
Gordon, Deborah, 448
Gordon, Donovan, 340
Gordon, CSM James R., 156
Gordon, J. Craig, 641, 647, 648, 650, 651
Gordon, Jeff, 468
Gordon, Kenneth I., 770, 775
Gordon, Lana, 178
Gordon, Lincoln Dwayne, 67
Gordon, Lisa, 338
Gordon, Mark, 539
Gordon, Pamela S., 857, 869
Gordon, Richard E. "Dick", 857, 868
Gordon, Richard S., 588, 591, 592, 593
Gordon, Rick, 498
Gordon, Robert M., 871, 873, 874
Gordon, Ronald B. "Ron", 469
Gordon, Scott, 181
Gordon, Tori, 29
Gordy, Tracey, 223
Gore, Mollie, 428
Gore, Suzanne, 494
Gore, Yvonne, 370
Gorham, David, 171, 172
Gorka, Chris, 342
Gorley, Rebecca, 280
Gorman, Mary J., 857, 868
Gormely, Tana, 286
Gormley, William T., 494
Gorniak, Dr. Jan M., 85
Gornnert, Jennifer Z., 303
Gorrell, Neil, 503
Gorsek, Chris, 958, 960
Gorst, Cathy J., 533
Gortmaker, Bryan, 436
Gosar, Pete, 539
Gosch, Brian G., 1012, 1013, 1016
Goshgarian, Kasper M., 238
Gosling, Doug, 307
Goss, Ashley, 178
Gossage, Bill, 576, 580
Gossage, Chloe, 346
Gosselin, Lisa, 479
Gossett, Jeffrey S., 998
Gotcher, Dr. T. Mark, 34
Gothard, Robin L., 524
Gotschall, June, 16
Gott, Melissa, 208
Gottfried, Richard N., 897, 905, 906
Gottlieb, Mark, 529
Gottling, Suzanne H. "Sue", 857, 870
Gottschalk, Deborah I., 77
Gouak, Sarah, 452
Goucher, Patricia "Pat", 223
Goudelocke, Owen, 206
Goulard, Frank, 397
Gould, Celia R., 137
Gould, Corinne, 438
Gould, Jeff, 138
Gould, Linda, 857, 870
Gould, Michael, 82
Goulet, Denis, 305
Goulet, Sara, 404
Goulette, Bill, 857, 868
Gouris, Tom, 454
Govan, Jerry N., Jr., 1004, 1008, 1009
Gove, DiAnne C., 874, 875, 879

Gove, Sarah, 392
Gowan, David M., Sr., 567, 569, 571
Gowen, Ernest L., 152
Gowen, Larry J., 103
Gowen, BG Timothy E. "Tim", 223
Gower, Michael F., 391
Goya, Sandra, 130
Goyette, Martin, 57
Goyke, Evan, 1095, 1099, 1100, 1101, 1102
Grab, Christopher, 489
Grab, Mark, 404
Graber, Kirstin P., 59
Grabinger, John, 925, 927
Grable, Sherry, 5
Grace, Janet, 70
Graci, Joseph P. "Joe", 402
Gracz, Gregory L. "Greg", 525
Grad, Maxine Jo, 1051, 1055
Gradillas, Ricardo, 95
Grady, Thomas "Tom", 107
Graeber, Jan, 455
Graf, Alfred "Al", 897, 903, 904, 905
Graf, Keith, 453
Graf, Sandy, 442
Graf, Thomas M., 245
Grafe, Doug, 398
Grafton, Ed, 516
Graham, Arthur L. "Art", 107
Graham, Charles, 915, 920, 921, 922, 923, 924
Graham, Clifford F., 1056, 1057
Graham, Derrick W., 727, 731, 732, 733
Graham, George W., Jr., 915, 920, 921, 924
Graham, Jackie B., 5
Graham, Jane, 161
Graham, Jeff, 464
Graham, Jesse, 272
Graham, Kellie, 288
Graham, Lisa, 162
Graham, Richard A. "Rick", 116
Graham, Robert, 487, 857
Graham, Robin, 93
Graham, Rodney, 1051, 1055
Graham, Ronald L., 490
Graham, Scott, 116
Graham, Sharon L., 214
Graham, Vickie, 445
Graham, Walter, 109
Graham, William R., Jr., 232
Grainger, Kristen, 390
Grammer, Robin L., Jr., 758, 762
Granda, Ximena, 151
Grandon, James, 408
Grange, Michael, 471
Grange, Natalie, 476
Granger, Jennie, 407
Granger, Noel, 345
Granger, Norman L. "Norm", 174
Grannis, Alexander B. "Pete", 342
Grant, Britt C., 119
Grant, Cathy, 235
Grant, Charles W., 499
Grant, David, 51
Grant, Derek, 535
Grant, Donna E., 215
Grant, Gay M., 748
Grant, BG James, 313
Grant, James W. "J.W.", 626, 631
Grant, Jeffrey D., 22
Grant, Jennifer, 109
Grant, Jerry, 82
Grant, Ken, 533
Grant, Kevin R., 379

Grant, Linda, 96
Grant, Linda S., 215
Grant, Loreen, 190
Grant, Michael, 240
Grant, Major Paul, 427
Grant, Rebecca, 214
Grant, Tammy, 145
Grant, Troy, 448
Grantham, Don A., 121
Grantham, Kevin J., 594, 595
Granwehr, Bernardo, 174
Grasel, Laurie, 99
Grasser, Daniel, 529
Grassini, Anthony, 415
Grassley, Patrick "Pat", 704, 707, 708
Grate, Jonathan, 190
Gratwick, Geoffrey, 745, 746
Gratz, Steve, 377
Grau, Randy, 949, 953, 954
Graulty, Reynaldo D., 133
Graven, Lisa, 386
Graves, Catherine, 56
Graves, Devin S., 386
Graves, Devon, 54
Graves, James, 8
Graves, Jerry, 187
Graves, Joseph, 781, 784, 785
Graves, Laurie, 480
Graves, Nathan, 538
Graves, Roger, 271
Gravino, Ronald "Ron", 317
Gravitt, Marc, 1021, 1025
Gravley, Micah, 641, 647, 649, 650
Gray-Johnson, Tanguler, 114
Gray, Adam C., 588, 591
Gray, Andy, 282
Gray, Anthony "Tony", 456
Gray, Barbara, 339
Gray, Cheryl, 382
Gray, Cindy, 496
Gray, Elizabeth I., 307
Gray, Gary, 220
Gray, Gregory, 259
Gray, Harold, 80
Gray, Ieisha, 92
Gray, James, 520
Gray, James P., 858, 868
Gray, John, 310
Gray, Jonathan, 462
Gray, Julia, 524
Gray, Kari, 534
Gray, Kelsey, 508
Gray, Laura, 478
Gray, Lisa, 25
Gray, Lynn, 386
Gray, Lyons, 353
Gray, Michael John, 574, 576, 580
Gray, Michelle, 577, 580, 581
Gray, Patricia, 446
Gray, Rebecca, 395
Gray, Richard D., 74
Gray, Rick, 569, 570, 571
Gray, Ronald E., 615, 617, 618
Gray, Stephen, 372
Gray, Steven, 366, 372
Gray, Tabitha I., 206
Gray, Dr. Teri Quinn, 82
Gray, Terrence, 416
Gray, Tommy, 120
Gray, Torrey J., 212
Gray, Ty, 26
Grayson, Jeff, 371
Graziano, Joanne, 232
Greaney, Andrew Michael, 316
Greason, Thomas A. "Tag", 1063, 1067, 1068
Greco, Bob, 236
Greear, Michael D. "Mike", 1105, 1107, 1108

Greef, Edward, 837, 840, 841
Greeley, John, 455
Green-Wright, Suzette, 473
Green, Dr. Adam S., 522
Green, Alan K., 822, 828, 830, 831
Green, Allyson, 429
Green, Anthony "Tony", 162
Green, Arthur R. "Rick", 97
Green, Babatunde, 72
Green, Charles, 490
Green, Chris, 502, 527
Green, Christopher "Chris", 110
Green, Dana, 109
Green, David, 468
Green, Dennis, 858, 868
Green, Doug, 939, 942, 943
Green, Elkins, 314
Green, Gayle, 395
Green, Gerald "Jerry", 874, 875, 879
Green, Jeffrey A. "Jeff", 514
Green, Josh, 654, 655, 656
Green, Justin B., 101
Green, Kathy, 59
Green, Larry, 534
Green, Leonard B., 419
Green, Loretta E., 538
Green, Marci D., 309
Green, Mark, 9, 112
Green, Dr. Mark E., 1017, 1018, 1019
Green, Marta, 44
Green, Mary Ann, 8
Green, Melisa J., 517
Green, Michael C. "Mike", 336
Green, Michael I., 522
Green, Mike, 776, 778, 779
Green, Orville, 135
Green, Paul D., 383
Green, Paul J., 246
Green, Scott A., 82
Green, Stephen M., 96
Green, Steve, 792, 798, 799
Green, Tony, 398
Green, Trecina, 270
Green, Tyler R., 477
Green, Whitney, 30
Greenbeck-Marsh, Donna, 229
Greenberg, Marjorie L., 29
Greenberg, Melissa, 338
Greenberg, Scott B., 24
Greene-Ross, Karen, 55
Greene, Brian, 535
Greene, Brian M., 1042, 1045, 1046
Greene, Carol Bowen, 519
Greene, Christine, 115
Greene, Courtney, 173
Greene, Crystal, 397
Greene, Gerald E., 641, 646, 647, 650, 651
Greene, James, 45
Greene, John, 104
Greene, Johnny, 95
Greene, Judith, 413
Greene, Lamar, 85
Greene, Rebecca, 213
Greene, Ricky E., Jr., 352
Greeney, Bill, 22
Greenfield, Brock L., 1010, 1011, 1012
Greenfield, Lana, 1013, 1015, 1016
Greenfield, Marion, 495
Greenfield, Steven J., 482
Greenleaf, Stewart J., 962, 964, 965
Greenlick, Mitch, 958, 960
Greenslade, Adam L., 375
Greenspan, Barbara, 154

Greenstein, Linda R., 871, 872, 873
Greenwald, Louis D., 874, 875
Greenwalt, Chris, 505
Greenwalt, Kristi, 90
Greenwell, Meghan, 193
Greenwood, Geoff, 171
Greenwood, Randall Adam, 748
Greer, Jeff, 728, 731, 732, 733
Greer, Lynn, 548, 553, 554
Greer, Marty, 194
Greeson, James L., 158
Greff, Peter, 536
Gregerson, Mia, 1074, 1079
Gregg, Adam, 170
Gregg, Jodi Murray, 72
Gregg, Randall, 250
Gregoire, Danielle W., 770
Gregor, David M., 77
Gregor, Karin, 167
Gregory, Chauncey Klugh "Greg", 999, 1000, 1001, 1002
Gregory, Pamela, 217
Gregory, Rebecca A. "Becky", 466
Gregory, Retha, 273
Gregory, Sara Beth, 196
Gregory, Scott, 42
Gregory, Vincent, 776, 778, 779
Gregson, Gay, 449
Greiberis, Patricia "Tricia", 284
Greig, Christine, 781, 784, 785
Greimel, Tim, 779, 781, 784
Greiner, Jill, 300
Greiner, Keith J., 970, 977, 978, 979
Grenier, Dennis, 535
Grenier, James "Jim", 858, 868
Grenvik, Craig, 537
Gresham, Caryn, 515
Gresham, Dolores R., 1017, 1018, 1019
Gresham, Earl, 189
Greshin, Adam, 1051, 1056
Gresko, Joe, 604, 609, 610
Greve, Thomas, 81
Grey, Cheryl, 282
Grey, Laura, 59
Grey, Leslie M., 408
Grey, Todd C., 472
Gribble, Marybeth, 439
Grief, Gary, 462
Griego, Antoinette, 323
Griego, Robert, 321
Grier, Annette, 489
Grier, John T. "JT", 499
Griese, BG Kevin R., 434
Griesmer, Heidi, 373
Griesmer, Tim, 66
Griff, Holly, 143
Griffey, Dan, 1073, 1074, 1078, 1079
Griffin, Alisha, 44
Griffin, Anjali, 430
Griffin, Ann "AJ", 944, 945, 946, 947
Griffin, Barbara, 858, 868
Griffin, Caroline V., 340
Griffin, David, 349
Griffin, Gail, 565, 566, 567
Griffin, Greg, 117
Griffin, Jenni, 474
Griffin, LTC J. Timothy "Tim", 35, 572
Griffin, Kathleen, 338
Griffin, Kevin, 475
Griffin, Laura, 266
Griffin, Marianne, 532
Griffin, Mary E., 451, 858, 870
Griffin, Michael, 315

Griffin, Michelle, 34
Griffin, Reg, 114
Griffin, Rory, 34
Griffin, Tina, 508
Griffin, William E., 483
Griffith-Peterson, Heather, 460
Griffith, Claudia, 949, 953, 954
Griffith, Donovan, 151
Griffith, Field, 499
Griffith, Lynne, 506
Griffith, Patti, 476
Griffith, Zack, 445
Griffiths, Gilbert R., 408
Griffo, Joseph A., 887, 888, 891, 892, 893
Grigg, Herbert, 486
Grigg, Phil, 503
Griggs, Ron, 880, 882
Grigsby Jackson, Diane, 147
Grigsby, Brooke, 6
Grigsby, Geri, 187
Grigsby, COL Steven T., 6
Grijalva, Nancy, 248
Grim, Karen, 499
Grimaldi, Paul, 418
Grimes, Albert, 244
Grimes, Alison, 194, 196
Grimes, Derek, 161
Grimes, Jefferson, 464
Grimes, Pamela, 77
Grimm, Rita C., 173
Grimmie, Robert, 313
Grimsley, Denise, 619, 620, 621, 622, 623
Grimsley, Dexter, 548, 552, 554
Grinder, COL Many-Bears, 447
Grinstead, Alan, 76
Grisham, Brian, 439, 440
Grisier, Chad, 179
Gritton, Jesse, 190
Groban, Joshua, 37
Groce, Kay, 29
Grodhaus, Mike, 366
Grodin, Nancy S., 227
Groeber, Patricia M., 336
Groen, Warren, 858, 868
Groendyke, John D., 384
Groene, Michael, 842, 844
Groeneweg, Major Keith, 537
Groenwegen, Nancy G., 342
Groeschl, David, 137
Groff, Marybeth, 241
Grogan, Ron, 297
Grogg, Tim A., 156
Groginsky, Elizabeth, 88
Groh, Caitlin, 153
Groh, Sandra, 26
Grohman, Martin, 748
Groleau, Gary, 308
Groll, Heather R., 338
Grondel, Darrin, 509
Gronstal, Michael E. "Mike", 699, 700, 702
Gronvall, Tamar N., 256
Groom, Dennis, 76
Groomes, Diane, 85
Grooms, Lawrence K. "Larry", 999, 1000, 1001, 1002
Grooms, Ronald T., 688, 690, 691
Grose, Keni, 285
Groskurth, Dean C., 289
Gross, William D., 405
Grosserode, Amanda, 715, 720
Grossman-Garber, Deborah, 415
Grossman, Andrea, 236
Grossman, Cheryl L., 939, 942, 943
Grossman, Gail, 237
Grossman, Parrell D., 364
Grosso, David, 86

Grost, Lisa, 249
Groth, Jenifer, 159
Groth, Sue, 261
Grothier, Loni, 361
Grotz, Donna, 162
Grout, Douglas E., 304
Grove, Monte, 395
Grove, Seth M., 970, 977, 978, 979
Grove, Shannon L., 588, 591, 592
Grove, Wendy, 377
Groveman, Jon, 481
Grover, Keith, 1042, 1045, 1046
Groves, Sara, 286
Grovom, Lindsey, 836
Grubb, Courtney, 502
Grubb, Mark A., 79
Grubbs, Roe, 266
Gruber, Victoria L., 753
Gruenhagen, Glenn, 792, 797, 798, 799
Grugin, Pat, 194
Grumbles, Benjamin H. "Ben", 219
Grundler, Judy, 274
Grundstrom, Lisa, 257
Gruner, Jane, 298
Gruzesky, Sandy, 186
Grygar, Katie, 35
Grzyb, Shari, 68
Guadagno, Kimberly M. "Kim", 317, 319
Guadarrama, Joaquin, 467
Guardino, Carl, 50
Guay, Kim, 13
Guberman, David A., 240
Gudex, Rick, 1091, 1093, 1094
Gudlin, Mark, 447
Gudmundson, Gary, 372
Gudvangen, Peggy, 363
Güity-Guevara, Julio, 84
Guenther, Judy, 510
Guerard, Krissie, 257
Guerette, C. Lee, 858, 869
Guerin, J. Michael, 232
Guerin, Stacey K., 748
Guerin, Stewart, 206
Guerin, Tracy, 507
Guerra, R. D. "Bobby", 1031, 1037, 1038
Guerra, Sandra, 72
Guerra, Vanessa, 781, 784, 785
Guerrant, Kyle, 254
Guerrera, Antonio "Tony", 604, 608, 612
Guerrero Pérez, Carmen R., 412
Guerrero, Susana, 319
Guerrero, Vincent Leon, 123
Guerrier, JoShonda, 100
Guertin, Thom, 414
Guess, Tom, 496
Guest, Andrea, 78
Guest, Staci, 116
Guettler, Vera, 7
Gugel, Thomas H., 226
Guggisberg, Ron, 929, 932, 933
Guglielmo, Anthony "Tony", 599, 600
Guglielmo, Anthony, 609, 611
Guhman, Betty Anderson, 29
Guice, Jeffrey S. "Jeff", 808, 813, 814, 815, 816
Guice, Lee, 189
Guice, W. David, 351
Guichard, Maryanne, 504
Guido, Christopher, 243
Guido, Mary, 50
Guidry, David, 202
Guidry, Dr. Jimmy, 201
Guilbeaux, Chris, 198
Guilford, Michele, 496
Guilfoy, Joanna, 142

Guilfoyle, Patrice, 270
Guillen, Rene, 21
Guillen, Ryan, 1031, 1037, 1038
Guillory, Sammy, 200
Guillory, Shaydra, 205
Guilmette, David W., 215
Guinn, John E. "Johnny", 739, 742, 743, 744
Guinn, Luther, 30
Guion, Kevin J., 423
Guivetchi, Kamyar, 48
Gulick, Lia, 247
Gullette, Susan, 450
Gulley, Kevin, 161
Gulliams, Scott, 201
Gullickson, Stephanie, 365
Gully, Ed, 489
Gumbley, James, 418
Gummels, Joan, 280
Gundersen, Daniel C. "Dan", 492
Gunderson, Kelly, 442
Gunderson, Terry, 259
Gunlock, Thomas W., 376
Gunn, Kenneth "Ken", 495
Gunn, Philip, 806, 808, 812, 815
Gunn, Rick, 908, 911, 912, 913
Gunn, Theresa, 53
Gunn, William E., 430
Gunnarson, Heather, 474
Gunnell, Peter A.J., 366
Gunson, Karen, 394
Gunter-Smith, Dr. Pamela J., 408
Gunter, Teena, 379
Gunter, William A., 4
Guntharp, Steve, 33
Gunther, Aileen M., 897, 902, 904, 905, 906
Gunther, Bob, 793, 797, 798, 799, 800
Gunthrop, Genie, 229
Gupta, Rahul, 517
Gupton, Garry, 193
Gurney, Gardner S., 342
Gurr, Jenifer, 60
Gurr, Peter, 18
Gursky, Gregory, 254
Gusciora, Reed, 874, 875, 878, 879
Gustafson, Stan, 704, 708, 709
Gustafson, Victor, 130
Gustavson, Donald G. "Don", 845, 846, 847
Gustus, Toni, 237
Guth, Dennis, 700, 702
Gutherz, Christy, 265
Guthrie, Camille E., 429
Guthrie, LTC Jacqueline "Jackie", 528
Guthrie, Janelle, 503
Guthrie, Jim, 662, 663
Guthrie, Joseph "Joe", 858, 869
Guthrie, Lesley, 460
Guthrie, Nancy Peoples, 1085, 1088, 1089, 1090
Guthrie, Tawana, 112
Gutier, Alberto, 21
Gutierrez-Scaccetti, Diane, 105
Gutierrez, Ana Sol, 758, 762
Gutierrez, Beatriz, 70
Gutierrez, Cathy, 454
Gutierrez, David, 48
Gutierrez, Fernando, 392
Gutierrez, Ingrid, 84
Gutierrez, Julia, 413
Gutierrez, Julissa, 331
Gutierrez, Rafael, 148
Gutierrez, Roland, 1031, 1037, 1038
Gutierrez, Sergio, 39
Gutkin, Steve, 318
Gutknecht, Kevin G., 260

**NAME INDEX**

NAME INDEX

Holstine, Mark D., 516
Holston, David, 369
Holstrom, Gabe, 574
Holt, Andrew H. "Andy", 1021, 1024, 1025
Holt, Angie, 115
Holt, Chad, 11
Holt, Darryl, 488
Holt, David, 945, 946, 947
Holt, Erin, 441
Holt, Kenneth C. "Ken", 221
Holt, Kyle, 431
Holt, Larry G., 464
Holt, L. Todd, 456
Holt, Maude, 92
Holt, Phillip, 459
Holt, Steven, 705, 708, 709
Holtam, Sheryl, 447
Holton, Andrew, 357
Holton, Anne, 491
Holtrop, Ann, 148
Holtz, Dan, 116
Holtz, Deb A., 258
Holtzclaw, Bill, 543, 545, 546
Holtzclaw, Derek, 337
Holtzclaw, James, 665, 667, 668, 669
Holvey, Paul R., 958, 960
Holy, Jeff, 1074, 1078, 1079
Holyfield, Jeffrey L. "Jeff", 254
Holz, Charles "Chuck", 705, 707, 708, 709
Holzapfel, James W., 872, 873, 874
Holzman, Dr. Gregory S., 285
Holzmann, Frank P., 464
Holzmiller, Jay, 507
Holzrichter, Mitch, 143
Holzworth, Brenda, 360
Hommes, Harold, 168
Hommrich, Bonnie, 438
Honan, Kevin G., 770
Honchar, James A., 400
Hone, Jay, 322
Honerman, James, 259
Honeycutt, Michael, 458
Honeycutt, Mike, 283
Honeyford, Jim, 1069, 1071, 1072, 1073
Honeywell, Kristi, 435
Honeywill, Sara, 116
Hong, Glenn, 132
Honig, Elie, 318
Honigberg, Martin P., 308
Honoré Thomas, Desireé W., 198
Honorow, Helen G., 308
Honsowitz, Keelie, 249
Hood, Aaron, 160
Hood, Anthony J., 96
Hood, Dirk, 291
Hood, James Matthew "Jim", 272
Hood, Jane, 428
Hood, Jeffrey, 23
Hood, Joe, 112
Hood, Joey, 809, 812, 814, 815, 816
Hood, Kimberly K., 469
Hood, Lakeisha, 110
Hood, Morris W., III, 776, 778
Hood, Philip Alan, 35
Hood, Ronald E. "Ron", 939, 941, 942, 943
Hood, Roseyn, 65
Hood, Tom B., 269
Hook, Mary, 192
Hooker, Mark, 30
Hooker, Patrick, 330
Hooker, Sylvia, 119
Hooker, Thomas "Tom", 781, 784, 785
Hooks, Wilbur "Buddy", 445

Hookstra, Inga L., 289
Hoomani, John, 347
Hooper-Bears, Cindy, 180
Hooper, Earlene, 894, 897, 904, 906, 907
Hooper, Jan, 396
Hooper, John, III, 58
Hooper, Mary S., 1051, 1055
Hooper, Phil, 357
Hoover, Brian H., 407
Hoover, Cathy, 503
Hoover, Jeanne Marie, 87
Hoover, Jeffrey H., 726, 728, 731, 732
Hoover, Kay, 12
Hoover, Tonya L., 47
Hopcroft, Thomas, 234
Hope, Kylee, 163
Hope, Patrick A., 1064, 1067, 1068
Hopgood, Hoon-Yung, 776, 778, 779
Hopkins-Staten, Theresa, 73
Hopkins, Carlos L., 488
Hopkins, Frank X., 289
Hopkins, Garth, 51
Hopkins, Kristopher N., 514
Hopkins, Lisa, 523
Hopkins, Marsha, 113
Hopkins, Mary, 537
Hopkins, Raymond E., 493
Hopkins, Shae, 184
Hopkins, Steve, 809, 813, 814, 815, 816
Hopmann, Randy, 464
Hopp, Clark, 12
Hoppe, Joe, 793, 798, 799
Hoppe, Mark, 178
Hopper, David, 158
Hopper, Dean, 325
Hopper, Donald, 162
Hopper, Gary S., 859, 869
Hopper, Jimmy, 438
Hoppmann, Gerald W., 187
Hopson, W. Briggs, III, 801, 803, 804, 805
Hora, Cindy, 154
Horan, James, 334
Horan, Kevin, 809, 812, 813, 814
Horan, Mark, 535
Horan, Maura Hughes, 72
Horbaczewski, Jan, 457
Horent, Eric, 200
Horgas, Major William A., 408
Horhn, John, 801, 803, 804, 805
Horie, Wayne M., 128
Horlacher, Cody, 1095, 1099, 1100, 1101
Horlander, Dennis, 728, 731, 732
Horman, Wendy, 665, 667, 668
Horn, Adria, 209
Horn, Craig, 916, 920, 921, 922, 923
Horn, David M., 511
Horn, Julie, 214
Horn, Kenneth, 777, 778, 779
Horn, Nicole, 6
Horn, Stephanie, 511
Horn, Wally E., 700, 702
Horn, Werner D., 859, 870
Hornbacher, Wade, 156
Hornback, Paul, 723, 725
Hornberger, Kevin Bailey, 758, 763
Hornbrook, Michael J., 245
Hornbuckle, Sean, 1085, 1088, 1089, 1090
Hornby, Catharine, 232
Horne, Daniel, 494
Horne, Jenny Anderson, 1005, 1008, 1009
Horne, John, 185

Horne, Stephen A., 809, 813, 814, 816
Hornick, June, 225
Hornsby, Joey, 103
Hornsby, Dr. Kathryn, 116
Hornstein, Frank, 793, 798, 799
Horoski, John, 312
Horrigan, Timothy "Tim", 859, 869
Horsch, Dwight, 140
Horseman, Ron, 189
Horsley, Todd, 499
Horsman, John, 79
Horst, Deena L., 181
Horstman, Terry, 146
Hortman, Melissa, 790, 793, 799
Horton, Lt. Derick, 428
Horton, Dodie, 739, 743, 744
Horton, Jerome E., 58
Horton, Keith, 115, 154
Horton, Melissa, 199
Horton, Robert "Bob", 4
Horton, Rusti, 661
Horton, Tara, 13
Horton, William R., 925
Horvath, Gary, 255
Horvath, Lori, 368
Horvath, COL Stefanie K., 259
Hosemann, C. Delbert, Jr., 271
Hoser, William K., 480
Hosey, Lonnie, 1005, 1009
Hosford, SGM Robert, 104
Hosford, Russell, 623
Hoshijo, Leonard, 131
Hoskin, Chuck, 948, 949, 953, 954
Hosking, Donna, 480
Hoskins, Anne E., 228
Hoskins, Denny L., 819, 823, 830
Hoskinson, Buddy, 184
Hosmer, Andrew, 851, 852
Hosmer, Mary, 280
Hostetler, Deb, 288
Hostetter, Gregory, 401
Hottinger, Jay, 934, 936, 937
Hottman, Hagen, 314
Hotz, Robert W., 293
Houchens, Gary W., 183
Houchin, Erin, 688, 690, 691
Houchlei, COL Timothy "Tim", 251
Houdek, Sherry, 365
Houdyshell, Michael, 434
Hougaard, Rob, 470
Hough, Lincoln, 823, 828, 830, 831
Hough, Michael J., 754, 756
Hough, R. "Matt", 408
Houghtaling, Eric, 876, 878, 879
Houghton, Jay D., 823, 827, 828
Houghton, Marella, 199
Houlihan, William C., 530
House, B. B., 273
House, Brenda C., 421
House, Douglas, 577, 580
House, Melvin, 371
House, Ronald "Rin", 148
Householder, Eric Lee, 1083, 1085, 1089
Houser, Michael, 716, 721, 722
Housley, Karin, 787, 789, 790
Houston, Annazette, 448
Houston, Jim, 52
Houston, Melissa McLawhorn, 389
Houston, Penny, 641, 647, 651
Houston, Robin, 251

Houston, Roderick A., 716, 721, 722
Houston, Scott, 430
Houston, Vincent, 467
Hove, Stephanie, 527
Hoven, Brian E., 833, 834, 835
Hovey-Wright, Marcia, 781, 784
Hovish, Leon, 345
Howard-Hogan, Ina, 241
Howard, Burley, 147
Howard, Carolyn J. B., 756, 758, 763
Howard, Chris M., 267
Howard, Cluster, 728, 731, 732
Howard, David, 93, 833, 834, 835
Howard, Dennis W., 218
Howard, Donna, 1031, 1036, 1037
Howard, Elizabeth, 489
Howard, Frank A., 740, 742, 744
Howard, Henry "Wayne", 641, 646, 647, 648, 649
Howard, Jack, 220
Howard, Jenny, 441
Howard, Joshua B., 354
Howard, Joy, 391
Howard, J.P., 86
Howard, Julia Craven, 916, 920, 921, 922, 923
Howard, Kenneth B. "Ken", 348
Howard, Laura, 77
Howard, Leon, 1005, 1009
Howard, Matthew "Matt", 100
Howard, Paul S., 519
Howard, Ralph A., 549, 553, 554
Howard, Randall F., 366
Howard, Raymond, 859, 868
Howard, Regina A., 226
Howard, Sara, 843, 844
Howard, Seth, 758, 762
Howarth, Joe, 876, 878, 879
Howatt, Robert, 80
Howe, Curtis, 454
Howe, Elin M., 237
Howe, Jeff, 793, 798, 799
Howell-Thomas, Lourdes O., 103
Howell, Algie T., Jr., 498
Howell, Claudia, 664
Howell, Dan, 112, 1021, 1025
Howell, Deborah, 485
Howell, Donald, 142
Howell, Dr. Eleanor, 350
Howell, Gary, 781, 784
Howell, Gary Gibson, 1085, 1089, 1090
Howell, Janet D., 1058, 1059, 1060, 1061
Howell, Jenna, 434
Howell, Kelly, 16
Howell, Kevin D., 354
Howell, Marge, 352
Howell, Monique, 164
Howell, Rob, 164
Howell, Sam, 267
Howell, Steve, 157
Howell, Suzanne, 249
Howell, Thomas P., 400
Howell, Timothy, 92
Howell, William J. "Bill", 1061, 1064, 1068
Howells, Kelley A., 229
Howes, Constance A., 417
Howgate, James C., II, 115
Howitt, Steven S., 770
Howland, Scott R., 50
Howle, Elaine M., 53
Howrylak, Martin, 781, 784, 785
Howse, Ronald "Ron", 105

Howse, Stephanie, 939, 942, 943
Howze, Richard "Dickie", 199
Hoxie, Dean, 416
Hoxie, CSM John, 453
Hoy, Monica L., 278
Hoydick, Laura, 601, 604, 608, 609, 611
Hoye, Patrick, 172
Hoyer, MG James A., 518
Hoyer, John A., 519
Hoyle, Dennis E., 419
Hoyle, Val, 958, 960
Hoylman, Brad, 889, 891, 892, 893
Hoyt, Marilyn, 432
Hoyt, Ryan, 203
Hoyt, Thomas "Tom", 366
Hoyt, William B. "Sam", III, 341
Hrepich, Kathleen, 44
Hritz-Seifts, Nancy, 340
Hronek, Col J. Peter, 283
Hsu, Baron, 95
Hua-Ly, Thuy, 509
Huang, David, 168
Hubbard, Drew, 89
Hubbard, Mike, 278, 546, 549, 553
Hubbard, Penny V., 823, 829, 830, 831
Hubbard, Quatro, 496
Hubbard, Sam, 264
Hubbell, Brian L., 749
Hubenak, Priscilla M., 467
Huber, Daniel, 172
Hubert, Ronald E., 1051, 1055
Huberty, Daniel G. "Dan", 1032, 1036, 1038
Hubman, David, 345
Hubrecht, Tila, 823, 829, 830, 831
Huckabay, C. Todd, 382
Hudachko, Tom, 472
Huddleston, Mac, 809, 812, 813, 814, 815
Huddleston, Robert E., 809, 812, 813, 816
Hudgens, Abbie, 445
Hudgens, Major Kevin, 140
Hudgens, Ralph T., 120
Hudgins, Zachary "Zack", 1074, 1077, 1078, 1079
Hudina, Alan, 512
Hudson-Beckham, Antoinnette, 95
Hudson, Beverly A., 403
Hudson, Billy, 801, 803, 804, 805, 806
Hudson, Brian A., Sr., 407
Hudson, Cynthia, 500
Hudson, Deborah D., 615, 617, 618
Hudson, Edwin K., 261
Hudson, Heather, 413
Hudson, Kathleen, 6
Hudson, Mark, 389
Hudson, Matt, 623, 626, 630
Hudson, Lt. Col. Monroe, 79
Hudson, Roger, 66
Hudspeth, James, 471
Huebert, Steve, 716, 720, 721, 722
Huebsch, Michael D. "Mike", 531
Huelle, James M., 336
Huerta, Avdiel, 467
Huertas, Joe, 439
Hueso, Ben, 582, 584, 585
Huether, Leigh Ann, 359
Huff, Andrew I., 281
Huff, John M., 276
Huff, Robert "Bob", 41, 582, 584
Huff, Russell, 457
Huff, Ryan, 292
Huff, Shawn, 39

Jesiel, Sheri L., 679, 683, 684, 685, 686
Jeske, Ken, 391
Jesperson, Kevin, 318
Jessen, Alan, 53
Jessop-Folau, Mitzie, 19
Jessop, Harla, 435
Jessup, Harvey, 424
Jeter, Charles, 913, 916, 920, 921, 922, 923, 924
Jeter, George, 357
Jeter, Jere, 438
Jeter, Tracey, 491
Jeter, Vanessa, 354
Jett, Cheryl, 447
Jett, Joe, 577, 580
Jett, Michael, 160
Jett, Skylar, 137
Jeudy, Jean L., 859, 868
Jewett, William W. "Willem", 1048, 1051, 1055
Jiggetts, Yolanda, 220
Jimenez, Angelica M., 874, 876, 878, 879
Jimenez, Esther, 37
Jimenez, Henry, 84
Jimenez, Jose, 144
Jindal, Raj, 205
Jinings, Jon, 393
Jinkins, Laurie, 1075, 1077, 1078
Jinnette, Melanie, 423
Jobe, Cory, 146
Jochimsen, Kenda, 169
Jochum, Pam, 699, 700, 702, 703
Joens, Dave, 153
Joffrion, Liza, 446
Johannessen, Robert L., 201
Johansen, Lawrence A., 307
Johansen, Paul R., 514
Johanson, Aaron Ling, 657, 660, 661
Johns-Brown, Lonnie, 512
Johns, Mark, 898, 902, 903, 904, 905
Johns, Rebecca "Becky", 440
Johns, Ronnie S., 734, 736
Johns, Timothy R. "Tim", 1013, 1015, 1016
Johnsen, Gladys, 859, 870
Johnson-Aten, Bonnie, 482
Johnson-Clarke, Fern, 91
Johnson-Woods, Kim, 56
Johnson, Adria, 189
Johnson, Alan L., 468
Johnson, Alesa G., 183
Johnson, Alice M., 787, 789, 790
Johnson, Alicia, 507
Johnson, Allen, 360
Johnson, Amy, 11
Johnson, Amy L., 105
Johnson, Anna, 386
Johnson, Anne, 51
Johnson, Anne M., 470
Johnson, Anwar, 152
Johnson, Bertram Courtney "Bert", 777, 778, 779
Johnson, Betty, 291
Johnson, Blake, 573, 574
Johnson, Brad, 285
Johnson, Brad T., 471
Johnson, Brenda, 364
Johnson, Brian, 793, 798, 799
Johnson, Cato, 449
Johnson, Cecilia, 28
Johnson, Charles, 461
Johnson, Charles E. "Chuck", 258
Johnson, Cheryl, 181
Johnson, Cheryl K., 527
Johnson, Chris, 162, 809, 812, 813, 815
Johnson, Christopher K., 745

Johnson, Christopher L. "Chris", 191
Johnson, Clark, 793, 797, 798, 799
Johnson, Craig, 328
Johnson, Craig W., 558, 560
Johnson, Curtis G., 1019, 1021, 1024, 1025
Johnson, Curtis M., 523
Johnson, Cyndy, 955
Johnson, Dacia, 396
Johnson, Dan G., 662, 663
Johnson, Darnisa, 35
Johnson, Darryl L., 146
Johnson, David, 271, 573, 574
Johnson, David J. "Dave", 700, 702
Johnson, Deb, 209
Johnson, Debbie, 26
Johnson, Deborah George, 85
Johnson, Delus, 819, 823, 827, 829, 830
Johnson, Denise, 228
Johnson, Dennis, 929, 932, 949, 953, 954
Johnson, Dewayne, 447
Johnson, Dicky, 33
Johnson, Donald, 203
Johnson, BrigGen Donald L., 445
Johnson, Donna R., 82
Johnson, Doreathea, 39
Johnson, Doreen Wonda, 884, 886
Johnson, Elizabeth "Betsy", 396
Johnson, Elizabeth, 421
Johnson, Elizabeth "Betsy", 955, 957
Johnson, Elvernoy H., 233
Johnson, Eric, 107, 859, 870
Johnson, Eric "EJ", 1032, 1036, 1037
Johnson, Eric M., 297
Johnson, Faith S., 462
Johnson, Finos "Buddy", 574
Johnson, Franklin, 485
Johnson, Freddie L., 374
Johnson, Gary L., 259
Johnson, Gordon M., 874, 876, 878, 879
Johnson, G.R., 77
Johnson, Gregory C. "Greg", 226
Johnson, Gregory K., 193
Johnson, Greta, 939, 941, 942, 943
Johnson, Grindly R., 498
Johnson, Herma, 524
Johnson, Jack, 1017, 1018, 1019
Johnson, Jacob C., 202
Johnson, James, 161, 247
Johnson, James A., 404
Johnson, James J., 615, 617, 618
Johnson, Jan, 168, 515
Johnson, Jane E., 100
Johnson, Jarvis D., 1032
Johnson, Jay, 148, 430
Johnson, Col. J. Bret, 277
Johnson, Jean, 44
Johnson, Jeanette, 525
Johnson, Jeffrey A., 409
Johnson, Jeffrey C., 123
Johnson, Jeffrey E. "Jeff", 1005, 1008
Johnson, Jennifer A., 475
Johnson, Jerome, 89
Johnson, Jerry, 843, 844
Johnson, Jessica, 441
Johnson, JoAnn M., 168
Johnson, Joel, 781, 784, 785
Johnson, Jon, 477
Johnson, J.P. "Bob", 577, 580

Johnson, Justin G., 478
Johnson, Karen, 44
Johnson, Kate, 471
Johnson, Kathleen "Kathy", 15
Johnson, Kathy, 8
Johnson, Kay, 1010
Johnson, Ken, 549, 553, 554
Johnson, Kerri, 538
Johnson, Kevin L., 999, 1001, 1002
Johnson, Kirk, 445
Johnson, La Tonya, 1096, 1099, 1100
Johnson, Larry, 134
Johnson, Larry, Jr., 167
Johnson, Laura, 22, 137
Johnson, Leanne, 428
Johnson, Leigh, 70
Johnson, Lillian, 96
Johnson, Linda, 536
Johnson, Linda P., 916, 920, 921, 922, 923, 924
Johnson, Louise, 424
Johnson, Lydia, 401
Johnson, Lynn Skene, 69
Johnson, Manson B., 460
Johnson, Manuela, 158
Johnson, Maria, 104
Johnson, Mark, 283, 502, 958, 960
Johnson, Marlo D., 247
Johnson, Marva, 107
Johnson, Mary, 201, 276
Johnson, Mary C., 929, 932, 933
Johnson, Michael "Mike", 740, 743
Johnson, Michael Allan, 258
Johnson, Mitzi, 1051, 1055
Johnson, Monique, 91
Johnson, Nancy, 57
Johnson, Natasha, 312
Johnson, Nathan, 52, 509
Johnson, Nicholas, 76
Johnson, Norm, 1075, 1078
Johnson, Norman K., 477
Johnson, Peggy, 326, 504
Johnson, Phil, 371
Johnson, Richard, 195
Johnson, COL Richard F., 241
Johnson, Rick, 383
Johnson, Rob, 438
Johnson, Robert, 158
Johnson, Robert A., 740, 743, 744
Johnson, Robert E., 234
Johnson, Robert L., III, 809, 813, 814, 815, 816
Johnson, Robin, 390
Johnson, Rod, 294
Johnson, Ronald, Jr., 116
Johnson, Ronald G. "Ron", 549, 552, 553
Johnson, Ronald T., 25
Johnson, Ruth, 251
Johnson, Schorr, 357
Johnson, Scott, 118
Johnson, Sheldon, 793, 798, 799
Johnson, Shelly, 200
Johnson, Sheryl, 92
Johnson, Sid, 112
Johnson, Siobhan, 149
Johnson, Sonia, 229
Johnson, S. Quinton, 616, 617, 618
Johnson, Steve, 66
Johnson, Sgt Steve L., 363
Johnson, Steven, 83, 248, 369
Johnson, Steven C., 716, 720, 722
Johnson, Stewart, 355
Johnson, Susan M., 601, 604, 608, 609, 610
Johnson, Tami, 502

Johnson, Teresa J. "Terry", 436
Johnson, Terry, 300, 939, 941, 942, 943
Johnson, Thomas W., 375
Johnson, Capt. Tim, 325
Johnson, Tina, 380
Johnson, Todd, 160
Johnson, Venus, 56
Johnson, Virginia Hurt, 346
Johnson, Vona, 436
Johnson, Wayne E., 354
Johnson, Wayne H., 1103, 1104
Johnson, Col Wendy, 291
Johnson, William, Jr., 222
Johnson, BrigGen Zane R., 498
Johnston, Britnee, 474
Johnston, Clay, 266
Johnston, Dan, 504
Johnston, Dennis, 477
Johnston, Drew, 390
Johnston, Erik, 488
Johnston, Kathryn, 347
Johnston, Keith, 352
Johnston, Laurel A., 126
Johnston, Michael, 110
Johnston, Michael "Mike", 594, 595
Johnston, Nancy, 274
Johnston, Nancy A., 259
Johnston, Raymond H., Jr., 994, 996, 997
Johnston, Ric, 134
Johnston, Richard, 242
Johnston, Russell, 234
Johnston, Tom, 371
Johnstone, Cecil Alice, 535
Johnstone, Martin E., 194
Joiner, Amber, 848, 849
Joiner, James, 31
Joiner, Tonya, 201
Jolicoeur, Edwin G., 501
Jolley, Clark, 945, 946, 947
Jolley, John, 534
Jolliffe, Nick, 363
Jolly, Linwood, 94
Jolly, Russell, 802, 803, 804
Jolly, Tierra, 88
Jonas, Jill, 529
Jonas, Michael, 315
Jondahl, Kimberly, 363
Jones-Hendrickson, Simon, 485
Jones-Jezz, Petrina, 444
Jones-Sawyer, Reginald Byron, Sr., 588, 592
Jones, Adrienne A., 756, 759, 762, 763
Jones, Allison, 255
Jones, Annette, 52, 252
Jones, Ashley, 347
Jones, Bert, 917, 920, 921, 922, 923
Jones, Bill, 462
Jones, Bob, 50
Jones, Bradley H., Jr., 767, 771
Jones, Brent A., 848, 849
Jones, Brian W., 588, 591, 592, 593
Jones, Bryan L., 427
Jones, Burt, 633, 635, 636, 637
Jones, Caleb, 823, 828, 830, 831
Jones, Cammy, 467
Jones, Candice, 147
Jones, Carmen, 439
Jones, Caroline C., 459
Jones, Carolyn, 376
Jones, Charles, 89
Jones, COL Charlie, 195
Jones, Cheryl, 178
Jones, Claire, 430
Jones, Colette, 487
Jones, Connie L., 259
Jones, Crys, 557

Jones, C. Todd, 376
Jones, Curtis, 4
Jones, Cynthia B. "Cindi", 494
Jones, Dan, 161
Jones, Dana, 48
Jones, Daniel Y., 25
Jones, Darlene, 158
Jones, Dave, 56
Jones, David, 449, 477
Jones, David M., 349
Jones, Deborah, 97
Jones, Dee, 347
Jones, Del-Gratia, 429
Jones, Delisa, 272
Jones, Diana, 389
Jones, Dick, 716, 721
Jones, Donald "Don", 837, 840
Jones, Donna, 182
Jones, Douglas, 13
Jones, Elaine P., 212
Jones, Elise, 113
Jones, Elizabeth, 422
Jones, Emanuel, 633, 635, 636
Jones, Emil, III, 671, 673, 674, 675
Jones, Fred, 480
Jones, Gary A., 388
Jones, Gary L., 207
Jones, Harold V., II, 633, 636
Jones, Harry, 402
Jones, Henry, 43
Jones, Hugh R., 127
Jones, Jack F., 325
Jones, James M. "Mike", 537
Jones, Jan, 637, 642, 647, 648, 649, 650
Jones, Jana, 510
Jones, Janet, 62
Jones, Jason, 103, 184
Jones, J.B. "Jeff", 642, 649, 650
Jones, Jeff C., 446
Jones, Jenelle, 513
Jones, Johanna Barba, 314
Jones, John, 463
Jones, Major Johnnie, 115
Jones, Joseph B. "Joe", 135, 142
Jones, Julia M., 520
Jones, Julie L., 100
Jones, Kelsie E., 450
Jones, COL Kenneth H., 445
Jones, Kenneth T. "Ken", 102
Jones, Kent L., 473
Jones, Kevin, 179, 716, 720, 721, 722
Jones, Kimberly, 485
Jones, Kindanne, 388
Jones, Kira Orange, 207
Jones, Kristi, 38
Jones, Krystal, 531
Jones, LaDawn, 642, 647, 649, 650, 651
Jones, Laura, 859, 868
Jones, Leigh Ann Apple, 450
Jones, Leon, Jr., 32
Jones, Lisa, 438
Jones, Llew, 833, 835
Jones, Lorraine, 27
Jones, Louis, 224
Jones, Louise, 193
Jones, Lyndajo, 35
Jones, Machelle, 116
Jones, Mark, 88
Jones, Mark Lawton, 381
Jones, Marty, 245
Jones, Matt, 593, 594, 595
Jones, Matthew "Matt", 151
Jones, Maurice A., 490
Jones, Megan, 705, 708
Jones, Melvin, 445
Jones, Mia L., 623, 626, 630

NAME INDEX

NAME INDEX

Kiesler, Laura, 419
Kiffmeyer, Mary, 787, 789, 790
Kifowit, Mark, 507
Kifowit, Stephanie A., 679, 682, 684, 685
Kigel, Beth R., 105
Kightlinger, Lon, 433
Kihuen, Ruben J., 845, 846, 847
Kikendall, Kathleen A., 247
Kilduff, Christine, 1075, 1078
Kiley, Beth, 303
Kilgore, Terry G., 1064, 1067, 1068
Killeen, Tom, 201
Killer, Kevin, 1013, 1016
Killian, Mark W., 22
Killingsworth, Patti, 442
Killion, Thomas H. "Tom", 962
Killough, Norma R., 247
Kilmartin, Peter F., 420
Kilpatrick, Charles A., 499
Kilpatrick, Pam, 346
Kilpatrick, Tanna, 379
Kilzer, Ralph L., 925, 927, 928
Kim, Daniel C., 41
Kim, Donna Mercado, 655, 656
Kim, Elizabeth O. "Betsy", 126
Kim, Helen J., 147
Kim, H. Tina, 342
Kim, Ji Sook "Lisa", 129
Kim, John J., 151
Kim, BrigGen Joseph K. "Joe", 132
Kim, Kevin, 335
Kim, Mark T., 97
Kim, Myong-Ae, 152
Kim, Patty H., 971, 977, 979, 980
Kim, Peter, 53
Kim, Ronald T., 898, 903, 904, 905, 906
Kim, Sarah, 244
Kim, Susan M., 126
Kim, Yong-ki, 97
Kim, Young O., 588, 591, 592, 593
Kimball, Gregg, 492
Kimbell, Emily, 184
Kimbler, Debra, 523
Kimbriel, Todd, 455
Kimbrough, Charles, 379
Kimichik, Alan, 248
Kimmet, Lisa, 286
Kimpson, Marlon E., 999, 1001, 1002
Kimpson, Milton, 426
Kimsey, Karen, 494
Kincaid, Lori, 308
Kincaid, Michael, 31
Kincaid, Nancy, 56
Kincannon, Christie, 276
Kincer, Shawna, 196
Kindall, Clare, 74
Kinder, Bruce, 435
Kinder, Peter D., 279, 816
Kindsvatter, Robert W. "Rob", 349
Kine, Thomas, 258
Kiner, David William, 601, 604, 610, 611
King Bynum, Barbara, 62
King, April, 117
King, Avis, 119
King, Brad, 1043, 1045, 1046
King, Brian S., 1041, 1043, 1045, 1046
King, Bryan, 93
King, Bryan B., 573, 574
King, Chris, 19
King, Courtney, 13

King, Curtis, 1071, 1072, 1073
King, LTC Cynthia "Cindi", 430
King, David, 355
King, Don, 447
King, Ed, 160
King, Garret, 92
King, James, Jr., 217
King, Jane Anderson, 466
King, Jason, 297
King, Jeff, 709, 710, 712, 713
King, John, 422
King, John A. "Jack", 240
King, John Richard Christopher, 1005, 1008
King, Kate, 21
King, Ken, 1032, 1036, 1037, 1038
King, Kevin, 332
King, Kim, 728, 731, 733
King, Laticia A., 353
King, Lesley, 423
King, Lisa, 333
King, Marcus, 146
King, Martha Jane, 728, 731, 733
King, Mary-Lee, 235
King, Michael D., 347
King, Mike, 178
King, Nancy J., 753, 754, 755
King, Pamela, 376
King, Phil, 1032, 1037
King, Philip, 907
King, Phylis K., 665, 667, 669
King, Rachel, 114
King, Rachel L., 113
King, Col Robert, 173
King, Robert L. "Bob", 183
King, Robin, 25
King, Scott, 178
King, Sharon L., 112
King, S. Nick, 823, 828, 830, 831
King, Stephen, 290
King, LTC Steven, 195
King, Susan, 252
King, Susan Lewis, 1032, 1037
King, Taroub, 100
King, Tom, 273
King, Tracy O., 1032, 1036, 1038
Kingery, Beverly E., 522
Kinghorn, David, 140
Kingsberry, Cassandra, 91
Kingsland, C. William, 314
Kingsland, Elizabeth, 297
Kingsley, Fredrick, 232
Kingston, Shawn A., 221
Kinimaka, Pratt M., 132
Kinkade, Bill, 809, 812, 813, 816
Kinkade, Brian D., 277
Kinkade, Cynthia, 381
Kinkade, Mark D., 145
Kinlow, Eugene, 84
Kinman, Barney, 189
Kinnaird, Melissa J., 517
Kinnemore, Lisa, 118
Kinner, Mark, 1106, 1107, 1108
Kinney, David L., 389
Kinney, E Wally, 466
Kinney, Jonathan L., 749
Kinney, Kevin, 700, 701, 702
Kinney, MaryAnne, 749
Kinney, Robin, 186
Kinnison, Mark, 382
Kinser, Cynthia E., 450
Kinsey, Jon, 448
Kinsey, Philip, 286
Kinsey, Robin, 109
Kinsey, Stephen, 971, 977, 978, 979, 980

Kinskey, Dave, 1103, 1104
Kinsman, Arthur, 240
Kintner, Bill, 843, 844
Kintner, Lauren, 288
Kintop, Jeff, 296
Kinzer, Donna, 228
Kinzler, Tiffany, 136
Kipke, Nicholaus R., 756, 759, 762, 763
Kipling, LTC Lesley E., 497
Kipp, George G., III, 837, 840, 841
Kirbach, Gerald, 145
Kirbey, Harold, 276
Kirby, Cathy, 250
Kirby, Chris, 200
Kirby, Dan, 949, 953, 954
Kirby, David F., 355
Kirby, Dean, 802, 803, 804, 805
Kirby, Jay, 60
Kirby, Karla, 96
Kirby, CMSgt Lawrence W. "Larry", 80
Kirby, Michelle R., 488
Kirby, Roger K., 1005, 1008
Kirby, Steve, 1075, 1078
Kirby, Todd, 195
Kirby, Tom, 642, 646, 648, 650, 651
Kirchen, Jennifer V., 258
Kirchhofer, Cynthia L. "Cindy", 694, 697, 698
Kirk, Carolyn, 238
Kirk, Dan, 116
Kirk, G.M. "Greg", 631, 633, 634, 635, 636, 637
Kirk, Joe, 446
Kirk, Lloyd, 380
Kirk, Vernon, 77
Kirkbride, Dan R., 1106, 1107, 1108
Kirkegaard, Donald A. "Don", 432
Kirkegard, Leroy, 283
Kirkendoll, Arthur E. "Art", 1080, 1082, 1083
Kirkham, Jon, 45
Kirkham, Terry, 139
Kirkland, Lydia, 408
Kirkland, Thaddeus, 971
Kirkpatrick Justice, Katie, 198
Kirkpatrick, Joe, 444
Kirkpatrick, Rich A., 406
Kirkpatrick, Travis, 384
Kirkton, Jeanne, 823, 828, 830, 831
Kirner, Randall "Randy", 848, 849, 850
Kirschenbaum, Mickey, 298
Kirschman, Patrick A., 1013, 1015, 1016
Kirst, Dr. Michael W., 57
Kirtley, Brian, 383
Kirtman, Nathaniel "Nate", III, 54
Kiser, Brian E., 187
Kiser, Todd E., 473
Kish, Kevin, 39
Kishaba, Kathie, 48
Kisko, Kathleen M., 319
Kiss, Melinda, 520
Kiss, Robert S. "Bob", 519
Kissee-Sandoval, Catherine J., 54
Kissel, John A., 599, 600, 608, 610, 611
Kissinger, Mark, 334
Kisthardt, Major Adam M., 408
Kitamura, Ken N., 131
Kitaoka, Tracy S., 127
Kitchel, M. Jane, 1047, 1048
Kitchen, Shirley M., 962, 964, 965
Kitchen, Stefanie, 421
Kitchens, Joel, 1096, 1099, 1100, 1101, 1102

Kitchens, Sharon L., 493
Kitchens, Teresa C., 427
Kitchner, Roseanne, 335
Kito, Sam, III, 557, 558, 560
Kitsis, Ted, 307
Kitsu, Mary, 132
Kittel, Scott, 108
Kittleman, Trent M., 759, 762
Kittrel, Barbara, 222
Kitzmiller, Warren F., 1051, 1055
Kivela, John, 781, 784, 785
Kixmiller, Kate, 159
Kizer, Richard S., 428, 429
Kjellander, Paul, 138
Klaeren, Lisa, 251
Klare, Amy K., 399
Klarer, Erin, 187
Klarides, Themis, 601, 604, 611
Klarin, Paul, 393
Klarman, Ginny, 349
Klaskin, Rochelle H., 532
Klaskin, Seth, 73
Klausmeier, Katherine A., 753, 754, 755, 756
Klausmeier, Tracy, 473
Klavas, Sarah, 529
Klee, Robert, 70
Kleeb, Marvin G., 717, 720, 722
Kleefisch, Joel, 1096, 1100, 1101
Kleefisch, Rebecca, 533
Klein, Anthony "Tony", 1051, 1056
Klein, Chris, 76
Klein, Heidi, 480
Klein, James "Jim", 150
Klein, Jarad, 703, 705, 707, 708, 709
Klein, Jay, 188
Klein, Jeffrey D. "Jeff", 887, 889
Klein, Jerry, 925, 926, 927, 928
Klein, Jill, 12
Klein, Johann, 373
Klein, Kevin, 63
Klein, Matthew M. "Matt", 930, 932, 933
Klein, Russell B., 66
Klein, Sarah, 531
Klein, Thomas H., 144
Kleinfelter, Janet M., 450
Kleinheider, Adam, 450
Kleinschmidt, Tim, 454
Klejewski, Julie, 259
Klemin, Lawrence R., 930, 933
Klenklen, Chris, 274
Klett, Joseph, 319
Klett, Stephanie, 529
Kleven, Kayla, 358
Klick, Stephanie, 1032, 1037, 1038
Klier, Frank, 169
Kliethermes, Rich, 274
Klima, Cindy, 152
Klimas, Tyler, 296
Klimke-Armatoski, Cindy, 532
Kline, Gregory J., 335
Kline, Howard, 196
Kline, Jolene, 361
Kline, Richard, 248
Kline, Scot L., 483
Klingenberg, Greg, 50
Klingenschmitt, Gordon, 596, 598
Klinger, Joseph G., 150
Klinker, Sheila, 694, 696, 697, 698
Klipfel, Bryan R., 363
Kliphuis, Travis, 322
Klippel, Andrew, 344
Klippert, Brad, 1075, 1078, 1079

Kloc, Hy, 665, 668
Klodowski, Emily, 137
Kloewer, Susan, 169
Klokkenga, Steve W., 154
Klontz, Diane, 502, 508
Kloo, Kenneth "Ken", 311
Kloos, Eric, 256
Klopott, Freeman, 340
Klotz, Mark, 333
Kluck, Erich, 210
Klug, Ron, 334
Klumb, Joshua M., 1014, 1015
Klunk, Kate Anne, 971, 977, 979
Kluttz, Susan W., 348
Kluzak, Martha, 210
Knaebe, Diana, 147
Knapik, Daniel, 235
Knapp, Allen, 494
Knapp, Chuck, 175
Knapp, Dennis, 251
Knapp, Karl, 48
Knapp, Renee, 437
Knapp, Wendy, 164
Knatterud, LaRhae, 258
Knecht, Ron, 301
Knedler, Michael, 174
Kneeland, Kailean, 394
Kneip, Robert C., 108
Knepper, John G., Jr., 534
Knesal, Robert, 269
Knezek, David M., Jr., 776, 777, 778, 779
Knicely, E. L., 490
Knickerbocker, Kal, 110
Knies, Grant, 156
Knight, Angela, 507
Knight, Barry D., 1064, 1067, 1068
Knight, Charles K., 66
Knight, David, 642, 647, 648, 650, 651
Knight, Ed, 428
Knight, John F., Jr., 549, 553, 554
Knight, Karl, 486
Knight, Kristopher, 77
Knight, Lisa, 446
Knight, Lloyd, 137
Knight, Patsy G., 1005, 1008, 1009
Knight, Randy, 485
Knight, CMSgt Robbie, 271
Knight, Wayne, 205
Knighten, Arlene D., 207
Knighten, Kendra, 134
Knighton, James L., 225
Knippa, Jon, 468
Knipper, Stephen "Steve", 195
Knirk, Maria, 332
Knittle, Julie, 504
Knoblach, Jim, 794, 799
Knoch, Tammy, 385
Knodl, Daniel "Dan", 1094, 1096, 1099, 1101
Knoedl, Mike, 35
Knollenberg, Martin J. "Marty", 777, 778, 779
Knopic, Joseph, 407
Knopp, Tim, 955, 956, 957
Knott, Aaron S., 399
Knott, James J., 292
Knotts, Christopher P., 203
Knotts, Tony, 759, 762
Knotwell, John, 1043, 1045, 1046
Knowles, Camila, 112
Knowles, Dennis, 292
Knowles, Jerry, 971, 978, 980
Knowles, Kyky, 320
Knowles, Robert, 860, 869
Knox, Forrest J., 710, 712, 713
Knox, Lynne, 70

Knudsen, Austin, 836, 837, 840, 841
Knudsen, Chris, 57
Knudsen, Michaelene, 278
Knudson, Dean, 1096, 1100
Knudson, Peter C., 1039, 1040, 1041
Knudson, Steve, 526
Knuffman, Nathan, 346
Knupp, Jim, 26
Knutson, Janell, 530
Knutson, LTC Ray, 359
Kobach, Kris W., 180
Koban, Pam, 448
Kobayashi, Bertrand A., Jr., 658, 660
Kobelt, Teresa, 368
Koch, Eric Allan, 691, 694, 697, 698
Koch, Gary G., 375
Koch, Karl C., 174
Koch, Lona "Grace", 40
Koch, Mark, 408
Koch, Matt, 493
Koch, Paul, 421
Koch, Will, 38
Kocher, Harold P., 361
Kochmar, Linda, 1075, 1078, 1079
Kocian, Aaron, 467
Kocot, Peter V., 771, 775
Koczera, Robert M., 771, 775
Kodira, Umesh, 52
Koebel, LaDonna, 190
Koehler, David M., 671, 672, 673, 674, 675
Koehler, Kyle, 939, 941, 942
Koeleveld, Celeste L.M., 334
Koenen, Lyle J., 786, 787, 789, 790
Koenig, Adam, 728, 731, 732
Koenig, Andrew, 823, 829, 830, 831
Koenig, Carol, 453
Koenig, Phil, 530
Koenigsmann, Carl, 333
Koepp, Glenn, 733
Koerner, Jeff, 101
Koessl, Wayne, 531
Koester, Kevin, 705, 708, 709
Koester, Randy, 156
Kofi, Ntsiful-Amissah, 338
Kofron, Scot, 536
Kohatsu, Dr. Neal, 44
Kohler, COL Charles S., 223
Kohler, Mark F., 74
Kohler, Pat A., 504
Kohorst, Kathleen, 173
Kohrman, Arthur F., 148, 149
Koko, Puletuimalo Dick "Puletu", 562, 563, 564, 565
Kokoruda, Noreen S., 604, 608, 609
Kolb, Brian M., 894, 898, 906
Kolb, Bruce, 162
Kolcum, Lt. Col. Dan, 371
Koleski, Dan, 324
Koleszar, Theresa, 163
Kolhoff, John, 250
Kolig, Erich, 225
Kolkhorst, Lois W., 1027, 1028, 1029
Kolkmeyer, Glenn, 823, 829, 831
Kollen, Bart, 70
Kollman, Amber, 59
Kollner, Cynthia "Cindy", 218
Kolman, Marc, 323
Kolodziej, Walter, 860, 869
Kolowski, Rick, 843, 844

Kolste, Debra, 1096, 1100, 1101, 1102
Kolterman, Mark, 843, 844
Komatsu, Ken, 24
Komline, Patti, 1051, 1056
Komp, Betty E., 958
Koncilja, Frances Ann, 64
Konenkamp, Matt, 431
Konesky, Mari, 258
Kong, Sam Satoru, 658, 659, 660, 661
Kongstvedt, Peter R., 494
Konieczny, Karen, 153
Koning, Daniel J., 326
Konkol, Louie, 140
Konsowski, Chris, 228
Kontio, Larry, 258
Kooi, Mike, 112
Kooiker, John, 705, 708, 709
Koolaee, Mehdi, 85
Koon, Denise, 427
Koon, Holly, 511
Koon, Jack, 113
Koon, J. Michael, 516
Koonts, Sarah, 348
Koontz, Veronica, 190
Koop, Linda, 1032, 1036, 1037
Koopman, Roger, 285
Kooser, David, 374
Kooyenga, Dale, 1096, 1100
Kopacki, CSM Jared J., 298
Kopca, Justin, 90
Kopec, Matthew, 569, 571
Kopetz, Kevin, 68
Kopkash, Ginger, 311
Kopp, Kathy, 525
Kopp, Nancy K., 230
Kopp, Tamara W., 276
Koppel, James G., 258
Koppelman, Ben, 930, 932
Koppelman, Kim, 930, 933
Kopycinski, Julie, 457
Kordenbrock, William R. "Bill", 251
Koreski, John, 391
Korman, Bart, 823, 827, 831
Korman, Joe, 404
Korman, Marc A., 759, 762
Korn, Susan, 392
Kornbrek, Glenn, 266
Kornegay, Chrystal, 238
Kornegay, Steven, 357
Kornfield, Victoria P. "Tori", 749
Korolyk, Peter, 76
Korte, Daron, 256
Korthuis-Smith, Wendy, 502
Korty, Tina, 159
Kortz, William C. "Bill", II, 971, 978, 979, 980
Kory, Kaye, 1064, 1067, 1068
Korycinski, Robert, 338
Koscielniak, Denise, 325
Kosin, Jared C., 13
Kosir, Marilyn, 262
Kosowski, Robert L., 781, 784, 785
Koss, Cindy, 389
Koss, Sherrie, 24
Kossack, Andrew J., 161
Kosse, Myra, 360
Kost, Bryan G., 424
Kostboth, Paul, 431
Koster, Chris, 280
Kostroun, David, 453
Koszalka, Doug, 404
Kotchman, Larry A., 364
Kotek, Tina, 957, 958
Kotik, Nick, 971, 979
Kotowski, Frank R., 860, 869
Kotze, Alexandra, 259
Kouchi, Ronald D. "Ron", 654, 655
Koudelka, Kirk, 263
Kouplen, Steve, 948, 950, 953, 954

Kouri, Harry "Trey", III, 386
Koutsoubos, Gary, 251
Kovacs, Paul D., 152
Kovar, Annette, 290
Kovar, Mark A., 292
Kovarik, Lynda, 149
Kowach, Jim, 178
Kowalenko, Henry, 149
Kowalko, John A., Jr., 616, 617, 618
Kowall, Michael W. "Mike", 776, 777, 778, 779
Kowalski, Nikki, 343
Kowalski, Randy, 146
Kowert, Cynthia J., 66
Kozak, Susan, 168
Kozel, Colleen, 433
Kozera, Steve, 251
Koznick, Jon, 794, 799
Kraayenbrink, Tim, 700, 701, 702
Kradjel, Rachel, 458
Kraft-Tharp, Tracy, 596, 598
Kraft, Ian, 536
Kraft, Randy, 532
Krakora, Joseph E., 315
Kramer, Benjamin F., 759, 762
Kramer, Chris, 169
Kramer, Kristine, 171
Kramer, Rona E., 217
Kraner, James C., 517
Kranich, Steve, 285
Krask, David, 219
Krassler, Suzanne, 72
Kratky, Michele, 823, 827, 828, 829, 830, 831
Kraus, Jacob, 263
Kraus, Tammy, 232
Kraus, Will, 817, 818, 819
Krause, Catherine, 301
Krause, J. Winston, 462
Krause, Kirk, 249
Krause, Larry, 282
Krause, Matt, 1032, 1036, 1038
Krause, Mike, 438
Kravalis, John, 339
Krawiec, Joyce R., 909, 911, 912, 913
Kraynak, Jessica, 106
Kreafle, Mark, 225
Kreamer, Sally, 168
Krebbs, Brett, 148
Krebs, Corey, 359
Krebs, Robert C. "Bob", 1051, 1055
Krebs, Shantel, 436
Krebs, Susan W., 759, 762
Krebsbach, Karen K., 926, 927
Kreider, Reid, 225
Kreider, Rick, 178
Kreidler, Mike, 512
Kreidt, Gary, 930, 932
Kreipke, Adrienne, 311
Kreiss-Tomkins, Jonathan, 558, 560
Kreiswirth, Barry, 85
Kreitler, Jennifer, 512
Kreitner, Morgan, 143
Kreizenbeck, Karin, 298
Kremer, Jesse, 1096, 1100, 1101
Kremer, Mary F., 396
Kremlick, Lindsey, 421
Kresha, Ron, 790, 794, 798, 799
Kressig, Bob M., 705, 708, 709
Kretschmar, William E., 930, 933
Kretz, Joel, 1073, 1075, 1077, 1079
Kretzler, Laurene R., 894
Kreutzer, Rick, 45
Krevda, Stefanie, 160

Kricker, Maja, 354
Krieg, Barbara A., 130
Krieg, Gail D., 259
Krieg, Ginger, 203
Krieg, William L. "Bill", 699
Krieger, Wayne, 958, 960
Kriete, Elizabeth, 136
Krimm, Carol L., 759, 762
Krise, Stephen, 382
Krishnan, Venkat, 114
Krist, Robert "Bob", 843, 844, 845
Kristan, Margaret, 527, 528
Kristiansen, Dan, 1073, 1075, 1079
Krivda, George E., Jr., 68
Krizek, Paul E., 1064, 1067
Krob, Gary, 169
Kroeker, Kendell, 1106, 1107
Kroff, Paul, 472
Krogseng, Kari Lynn, 52
Kroll, Kerry, 280
Krom, Daniel "Dan", 261
Kron, Michael, 399
Krone, Samuel P. "Sam", 1106, 1107
Kroninger, Deborah, 374
Kropf, Jim, 507
Kropp, LTC Allysa A., 497
Krout-Greenberg, Natalie, 52
Krow, Julie, 61
Krowinski, Jill, 1051, 1055
Krucoff, Barney, 222
Krueger-Braneky, Leanne, 972, 977, 978, 979
Krueger, Brian, 530
Krueger, Carl, 533
Krueger, Liz, 889, 891, 892, 893
Krug, Scott, 1096, 1099, 1100, 1101
Kruger, Charles B. "Chuck", 749
Kruger, Kirby, 360
Krupp, Adam, 163
Kruse, Amy A., 287
Kruse, Dennis K., 688, 690, 691
Kruse, I. Lise, 359
Kruse, Jeff, 955, 956, 957
Kruse, Kim, 16
Kruse, Marjorie A., 372
Kruse, Mark, 99
Krzycki, Kim, 290
Kubacki, Joe, 565
Kubinski, Mark, 139, 142
Kubitz, James W., 12
Kubu, Jeff, 429
Kucab, A. Robert, 353
Kuch, Bill, 860, 869
Kucinic, Vinko, 372
Kuczynski, Thomas, 97
Kudelka, Lesia, 424
Kuderer, Patty, 1075, 1078
Kudna, Sherry A., 391
Kuehn, Faith B., 76
Kuehn, John L., 843, 844
Kuehn, Col Michael, 171
Kuempel, John, 1032, 1037, 1038
Kueper, Marilyn, 153
Kuester, Geoff, 161
Kuether, Annie, 717, 720, 721, 722
Kuffman, Kelly, 368
Kuglitsch, Mike, 1096, 1100, 1101, 1102
Kuhn, Beth, 184
Kuhn, David A., 314
Kuhns, Michael, 210
Kula, Angela, 473
Kulesa, Kathy, 360
Kulik, Janelyn, 158
Kulik, Stephen, 771, 775
Kulmacz, Douglas, 69
Kulp, Frederick Robert "Bob", 1096, 1101, 1102

Kumabe, Clyde K., 128
Kumar, Sabi "Doc", 1022, 1025
Kumari, Cara, 444
Kumiega, Walter A., III, 749, 752
Kunde, Twila, 323
Kundrat, Michael, 226
Kunkel, Barbara, 250
Kunstman, William G., 131
Kuntz, William H., Jr., 461
Kunz, Amy, 130
Kunz, Greg, 136
Kunze, Stephanie, 939, 942
Kupchick, Brenda L., 605, 609, 610
Kuraoka, Craig I., 128
Kurata, James K., 128
Kurcaba, Brian, 1085, 1088, 1089
Kurita, Rosalind, 443
Kurjan Cook, Joanne, 387
Kurk, Neal M., 860, 869
Kurkjian, Luella H., 128
Kurlovich, Tatsiana, 97
Kurnick, Rick, 153
Kuroda, Kevin R., 657
Kuros, Kevin J., 771, 775
Kurose, Ruthann, 510
Kurth, Tom, 15
Kurtz, Randy, 151
Kushnir, Bernie, 537
Kusian, Tami, 174
Kutschbach, Kim, 366
Kutschma, Larry, 533
Kutsukos, John, 72
Kuttel, Jeanne, 48
Kuttikrishnan, Damodaran "Damu", 104
Kutzer, Wayne, 362
Kuzma, Abigail, 165
Kuzma, Jennifer, 302
Kuzmenchuk, Sergei V., 221
Kvam, Jay, 299
Kvas, Micole, 363
Kyle, Frederick, 494
Kyle, Sara, 1018, 1019
Kynoch, Robert, 103
Kyrillos, Joseph M. "Joe", Jr., 872, 873
Kyvik, Tara S., 104
Kyzer, Bryan, 425

**L**

La Belle, Bruce, 40
La Follette, Douglas, 533
La Rosa, Mike, 626, 630, 631
Labarge, BrigGen Timothy J., 336
LaBarre, Melinda A., 152
LaBauve, Yvette, 199
LaBonte, Kathy A., 304
Labore, Reggan, 433
LaBoy, Charles, 227
Labrie, Terri, 431
Labriola, David K., 601, 605, 610, 612
Lacewell, Linda A., 330, 331
Lacey, Clinton, 92
Lacey, Roy, 662, 663, 664
Lacey, Tammy, 285
Lachance, David, 215
LaChance, Joseph, 860, 870
Lackey, Tom, 588, 591, 592
Lacks, Jeff, 117
LaClair, Jolinda H., 479
LaClair, Rob, 1051, 1055
LaCost, Danielle M., 527
LaCour, Kim, 198
Lacroix, Kristin, 235
LaCrosse, Joanne, 345
Lacy, Gareth, 37
Lacy, J. Kevin, 352
Lacy, Lafayette, 277
Lacy, Peter L., 163
Ladatto, Donnie, 206

Ladd, Allison, 93
Ladd, Brittany, 145
Ladd, David, 241
Ladd, James R. ''Jim'', 501
Ladd, Karen, 303
Ladd, Roderick M. ''Rick'', Jr., 860, 868
Ladine, Bret, 38
Ladley, CMSgt Tammy S., 141
Ladner, John ''Timmy'', 809, 812, 813, 814, 816
Ladner, Robert ''Don'', 103
Ladyman, Jack, 577, 580, 581
Laesch, Steve, 530
Lafaele, Keniseli, 18
LaFaver, Jeremy, 823, 828, 829, 830
Laferriere, William H. ''Bill'', 479
Laffen, Lonnie J., 926, 927
Lafferty, Stephen W. ''Steve'', 759, 762
LaFlamme, Pete, 481
LaFlamme, Cpl Rick, 211
LaFleur, Donald, 364
LaFleur, Eric, 734, 736
Lafon, Dwayne, 44
LaFontaine, Andrea, 781, 784, 785
LaForme, Brian, 401
LaFountain, Lloyd P., III, 212
Lafreniere, Steven P., 5
LaFromboise, Josh, 282
Lagace, Nicole, 420
Lagana, Joseph, 876, 878, 879
Laganelli, COL John F., 425
Lagerberg, Brian, 506
Lagoe, Wanda, 356
Lagos, George, 307
LaGrand, David, 781, 785
LaGrande, Susan, 47
Lahm, Rhonda, 291
Lahr, Eric, 333
Lahti, Natalie, 141
Laidlaw, Anne, 31
Laigast, Guy, 205
Laine, Carolyn, 794, 798, 799
Lair, Mike, 823, 829, 830, 831
Laird, Barbara J., 417
Laird, Joel, Jr., 9
Laird, John, 46
Laird, Linea, 506
Laird, Tony, 537
Laird, William Ramsey, IV, 1081, 1082, 1083
Lajoie, Michael P., 69
Lajoie, Michel A., 749
Lakat, Michael, 312
Lake, Bob, 285
Lake, Donald Pete, 521
Lake, Edward, 381
Lake, Peter M., 466
Lakeman, Brenda, 76
Lakey, Todd M., 661, 662, 663, 664
Lally-Green, Maureen E., The Honorable, 408
Lally, Christine J., 39
Lally, Donald J., Jr., 413
Lally, Kendres, 69
Lalo, Julie, 403
LaLonde, Martin, 1051, 1055
Lalor, Kieran Michael, 898, 903, 904, 906, 907
Lam, Clarence, 759, 762
Lam, Trey, 386
Lamar, John Thomas ''Trey'', III, 809, 812, 813, 814, 815, 816
LaMar, Samantha, 193
LaMarco, Ray, 335
LaMarr, Catherine, 74

Lamb, Jason, 280
Lamb, Leah Ann, 471
Lamb, Lisa, 190
Lamb, Michael E., 11, 12
Lamb, Molly, 149
Lamb, Todd, 378, 383, 388
Lambe, BrigGen Scott, 430
Lambert-Harding, Denise, 316
Lambert, Alva M., 6
Lambert, Bradley C. ''Butch'', 491
Lambert, E. David, III, 314
Lambert, Eddie J., 734, 736
Lambert, Gary, 233
Lambert, Gayle, 283
Lambert, Judith ''Judy'', 440
Lambert, Keith, 250
Lambert, Kent D., 594, 595
Lambert, Mandy, 182
Lambert, Mark, 468
Lambert, Melissa, 29
Lambert, Pamela ''Pam'', 32
Lambert, Ray, 364
Lambert, Scott, 164
Lambert, Tammi, 85
Lambert, Tricia, 307
Lambert, William, 307
Lamberth, William G., 1022, 1024, 1025
Lamberti, Jeffrey M. ''Jeff'', 171
Lambeth, Donny C., 917, 920, 921, 922, 924
Lamia, Tonya, 146
Lamkins, Mark, 532
Lamkins, Susan, 414
Lamm, Debra, 837, 840, 841
Lammers, Kelly, 289
Lamone, Linda H., 229
Lamont, Robert J., 520
Lamorena, Alberto A. ''Tony'', V, 123, 124
Lamoureux, Michael, 29
Lampe, Robert, 168
Lampen, Barbara, 341
Lampert, Robert O. ''Bob'', 535
Lamphere, JoAnn, 339
Lampitt, Pamela Rosen, 874, 876, 878, 879
Lampkin, MarQuaita, 272
Lampkin, Sheilla E., 577, 580
Lampton, Lucius M., 268
Lanane, Timothy S., 687, 688, 690, 691
Lancia, Robert B., 995, 997
Lanciaux, Michelle, 414
Land, Lewis, 326
Land, Mitchell, 117
Land, R. Bruce, 876, 879
Land, Samantha, 100
Land, Walter ''Walt'', 110
Landante, Ernest, 310
Landefeld, Mike, 496
Landek, Steven M., 671, 673, 674, 675
Landen, Michael, 323
Landen, William R. ''Bill'', 1103, 1104
Lander, Jerry, 159
Landerfelt, Jeffery, 301
Landers, Wes, 440
Landes, R. Steven ''Steve'', 1064, 1067, 1068
Landgraf, Brooks, 1032, 1037
Landgraf, Lois, 595, 596, 598
Landgraf, Rita M., 77
Landis, Al, 939, 941, 942
Landis, Frank E., Jr., 294
Landis, Jeremy, 371
Landon, Ed G., 221
Landon, John, 705, 707, 708, 709

Landon, Lt. Col. Walter F. ''Pete'', 216
Landreman, Steven, 527
Landroche, J. B., 119
Landrum, Major Jamie, 425
Landrum, Col William M., III, 186
Landry, Barry, 207
Landry, Jeffrey M. ''Jeff'', 205
Landry, Nancy, 740, 743
Landry, Steve, 213
Landry, Col. Terry, 740, 742, 744
Landry, Tia, 502
Landry, Todd, 204
Landsberg, James E. ''Jim'', 100
Landwehr, Thomas J. ''Tom'', 259
Landy, Anita, 22
Lane, B.R., 148
Lane, Colleen K., 25
Lane, Greg, 511
Lane, James, 94
Lane, Joanne, 102
Lane, Marilyn, 782, 784, 785
Lane, Marla S., 277
Lane, Michael R., 146
Lane, Patrick, 1085, 1089, 1090
Lane, Patrick W., 388
Lane, Shelley B., 209
Lane, Susan, 234
Lane, Sylvia, 95
Laney, Terrance, 84
Laney, Tonya, 298
Lanford, Mike, 272
Lang, Judith, 310
Lang, Kellie, 186
Lang, Lisa, 184
Lang, Louis I. ''Lou'', 675, 679, 686
Lang, Mike L., 838, 840, 841
Lang, Sarah, 907
Lang, Tanara, 382
Lang, Timothy N. ''Tim'', 502
Langan, Julie, 496
Langdon, James, 526
Langdon, James H., Jr., 917, 920, 921, 922, 923, 924
Lange, Kelly Ann, 173
Lange, Lorie, 530
Lange, Michael, 537
Lange, Scott, 383
Langehaug, Myron, 362
Langeluttig, Jackie, 97
Langen, Cynthia ''Cindy'', 61
Langen, Sue, 506
Langer, Kris, 1012, 1014, 1016
Langer, Lt. Col. Matthew, 260
Langham, Diane, 265
Langham, Jeff, 7
Langhorne, Diane, 224
Langhorst, David R., 137
Langianese, Sally, 402
Langkilde, Fagafaga D., 19
Langlais, Mary Jane, 414
Langlais, Robert ''Bob'', 417
Langley, Brian D., 745, 746
Langley, Gregory, 201
Langley, Kristie, 536
Langley, Silma-del, 415
Langrehr, Jocelyn C., 78
Langston, Jennifer, 103
Langston, Kevin, 114
Langton, Belinda, 427
Langton, Edward J. ''Ed'', 268
Langyel, Michael, 531
Lanham, Craig, 515
Lanham, Julie, 157

Lani, Andrea, 210
Lanier, Cathy L., 85
Lanier, David, 46
Lanier, Ronald L., 493
Lanigan, Gary, 310
Laning, Rose, 358
Laning, Vernon R., 930, 932, 933
Lankford, Karen, 447
Lanni, Walter J., 417
Lannin, Anna, 289
Lannom, Dave, 446
Lanouette, Bob, 504
Lanphear, Kathleen M., 417
Lanphear, Laurie P., 484
Lanpher, Diane, 1051, 1055
Lansdowne, Heather, 176
Lanston, Meg, 356
Lant, Bill, 824, 829, 830, 831, 832
Lantagne, Bryan, 244
Lanterman, Linda, 179
Lantrip, Peggy, 202
Lantz, Brittoni, 389
Lantz, Kaci, 451
Lanza, Andrew J., 887, 889, 891, 892, 893
Laoyan, Gem, 47
LaPalm, Ernie, 504
LaPanne, Susan, 415
LaPerle, Albert, 484
LaPierre, Paul, 72
Lapington, Joann, 324
LaPlante, Gary, 209
LaPlante, Vern, 258
Lapoint, Jana, 210
LaPointe, Clara, 305
Lapointe, Timothy L., 173
LaPorte, Edward, 319
LaPorte, Leo, 252
Lapp, David S., 220
LaPrade, Elizabeth, 117
Lapso, Alex, 371
Lara, David, 336
Lara, Ricardo, 583, 584
Lardie, Keri, 247
Lareau, Meggie, 490
Large, Robert, 177
Largent, Lisa, 512
LaRiccia, Dominic F., 642, 646, 648, 651
Larisey, Michael, 205
LaRiviere, Kathleen L. ''Khaki'', 488
Larkin-Thomason, Tracy, 299
Larkin, Gina, 152
Larkin, Jonathan, 569, 570, 571
Larkin, Margaret, 338
Larkin, William J., Jr., 889, 892, 893, 894
LaRocca, Debra, 205
LaRock, David A. ''Dave'', 1064, 1068, 1069
LaRock, Jean-Daniel ''J. D.'', 234
LaRose, Frank, 935, 936, 937
Larrañaga, Larry A., 884, 885, 886
Larrimore, Edmond ''Ed'', 219
Larscheid, Joe, 171
Larsen, Cliff, 833, 835
Larsen, Dee, 477
Larsen, Kara, 506
Larsen, Ken A., 508
Larsen, Lillian ''Lillie'', 294
Larsen, Lloyd Charles, 1106, 1107
Larsen, Michael, 135
Larsen, Missy, 477
Larsen, Oley, 926, 927
Larsen, Dr. Randall, 168
Larsen, Ronda, 297
Larson, Caitlin, 166
Larson, Charles W., Sr., 174

Larson, Christopher ''Chris'', 1091, 1093, 1094
Larson, Debbi, 262
Larson, Diane, 930, 932, 933
Larson, Eric, 104
Larson, Glenn, 528
Larson, Jeffrey P. ''Jeff'', 22
Larson, Judy, 431
Larson, Lauren, 64, 301
Larson, Lori, 292
Larson, Lyle, 1032, 1036, 1037, 1038
Larson, Robert, 395
Larson, Stephen, 168
Larson, Susan E., 292
Larson, Thomas ''Tom'', 1097, 1100, 1101
Larson, Timothy D. ''Tim'', 599, 600, 608, 609, 610
Larson, Tyson, 843, 844
LaSalvia, Rocco, 154
Lasee, Frank G., 1091, 1093
Lasher, Geralyn, 248
Lashore, Patricia, 529
Lashua, C. Vane, 340
Lashway, Patricia, 505
Laskey, Frederick A., 245
Lasky, Bette R., 851, 852
Lasky, Lisa, 420
Laslesnieski, LTC Tom, 113
Lasley, Ann E., 349
Laslovich, Jesse, 286
Lassa, Julie M., 1091, 1092, 1093, 1094
Lassiter, Mark, 90
Lassiter, Steve, 354
Lassiter, William, 351
Last, Bradley G., 1043, 1045, 1046
Lastinger, Derrick, 120
Lastra Power, Alberto, 412
Laszloffy, Sarah, 836, 838, 840, 841
Latham, Catina, 146
Latham, Michael, 332
Latham, Rebecca, 326
Lathan, Tiffany, 357
Lathrop, Angela, 170
Lathrop, COL Jon, 52
Latimer, George S., 889, 891, 892, 893
Latimer, Jeanne W., 462
Latimer, Jeremy, 499
Latimer, William E., 388
Latino, Vincent ''Vince'', 204
Latombe, Lynn, 461
LaTourette, Sarah, 939, 941, 942, 943
Lattanzio, Virginia, 340
Latterell, Isaac, 1014, 1016
Lattimore, Jada, 447
Lattner, Tim, 105
Lattuca, Charles, 225
LaTurner, Jacob, 710, 712, 713
Latuseck, Sarah, 256
Latvala, Christopher ''Chris'', 626, 630
Latvala, Jack, 620, 621, 622, 623
Latz, Ronald ''Ron'', 787, 789, 790
Lau, Girard D., 127
Lau, Lynette, 127
Lau, Stephen, 38
Laube, Cheryl, 567
Laubenberg, Jodie, 1033, 1037
Laubert, Beverley E., 367
Laucher, Joel, 56
Laucirica, BG Donald, 62
Laudato, Paul J., 340
Lauderman, Richard, 496
Laue, Brant M., 175
Lauer, Jeanie, 824, 828, 831

NAME INDEX

Minutola, Lisa, 81
Minutola, Nicole, 314
Mira, Belchior, 489
Miramant, David, 745, 746
Miranda, Catherine H., 566, 567
Miranda, César R., 412
Miranda, Frank, 406
Miranda, Rys, 16
Mirante, Laura, 67
Mirbaba, Melody, 66
Miro, Joseph E., 616, 617
Mirra, Leonard, 772, 775
Mirshahi, Mohammad, 499
Mirth, Brad, 383
Misa, Elizabeth J., 334
Miserez, Robert V. "Bob", 275
Mishler, Ryan D., 687, 688, 690, 691
Misisualapa, Tialavea, 560, 561, 562
Misjak, Karen, 173
Misjak, Pauline, 253
Miskell, Maulid, 64
Mitcheff, Dr. Michael, 156
Mitchell, Alice, 121
Mitchell, Antoinette S., 88
Mitchell, Bill, 675, 680, 683, 684, 685
Mitchell, Billy, 637, 643, 648, 650
Mitchell, Bo, 1022, 1024, 1025
Mitchell, Bradley, 422
Mitchell, Christian L., 680, 684, 685, 686
Mitchell, Darin, 569, 570, 571
Mitchell, Darryl, 112
Mitchell, David, 169
Mitchell, David A., 498
Mitchell, Deven, 16
Mitchell, Doug, 282
Mitchell, Fay, 348
Mitchell, Harold, Jr., 1006, 1008
Mitchell, Holly J., 583, 584, 585
Mitchell, Col James "Jay", 324
Mitchell, Jay, 290
Mitchell, Jennifer L., 499
Mitchell, Joe, 149
Mitchell, John L., Jr., 616, 617, 618
Mitchell, John W., 177
Mitchell, Judy, 534
Mitchell, Keiffer Jackson, Jr., 216
Mitchell, Kelly, 166
Mitchell, Kip, 213
Mitchell, Kristen, 502
Mitchell, Mandi, 200
Mitchell, Mark B., 340
Mitchell, Matthew M. "Matt", 101
Mitchell, Monica, 13
Mitchell, Dr. Patricia "Pat", 347
Mitchell, Dr. Rick L., 493
Mitchell, Dr. Roger A., Jr., 85
Mitchell, Rolundia, 42
Mitchell, Ronnie, 289
Mitchell, Sam, 4
Mitchell, Savannah, 33
Mitchell, Sedrick V., 48
Mitchell, Stephanie, 444
Mitchell, Suzanne, 32
Mitchell, Terese, 260
Mitchell, Theodore Bear, I, 752
Mitchell, Van T., 220
Mitsch Bush, Diane E., 597, 598
Mitskog, Alisa, 930, 932
Mitten, Gina, 819, 825, 828, 829, 830

Mittenthal, Matthew, 343
Mittnacht, Marcia, 234
Miwa, Jim, 127
Mix, Dave, 364
Mix, Leslie, 204
Mixson, Karen, 191
Miyagi, MajGen Vern T., 130
Miyamoto, Douglas, 535
Miyamoto, Keith, 129
Miyares, Jason S., 1065, 1068
Miyasato, Colleen O., 132
Mizbani, Reza, 337
Mizell, Beth, 735, 736
Mizelle, Virginia "Ginny", 265
Mizukami, Pam, 49
Mizuno, Derek, 129
Mizuno, John M., 657, 658, 660
Mizzell, Hope, 425
Mlacnik, Laura, 150
Mlynarczyk, Peter C., 72
Moak, Debbie, 21
Moats, Ronald M., 520
Moazez, Monica, 301
Moberly, John, 196
Mobley, Sheila, 95
Mobley, Tricia, 373
Moccia, Kim, 255
Mock, Allen R., 517
Mock, Corey, 928, 930, 932, 933
Modrell, Joan, 291
Moe, Mary Sheehy, 833, 835
Moe, Nelson, 498
Moe, Tami, 530
Moed, Justin, 694, 696, 697
Moeger, Cathy, 263
Moeller, Anna, 680, 682, 683, 684, 685
Moeller, Jim, 1073, 1075, 1078, 1079
Moewe, Mary, 440
Moffatt, John, 114
Moffatt, Michel, 1086, 1089, 1090
Moffatt, Stephen, 232
Moffet, Greg, 62
Moffett-Massey, Sharon, 252
Moffett, Howard M., 862, 870
Moffett, COL James P. "Pat", 536
Moffett, Phil, 729, 732
Moffett, Donald L., 680, 682, 683, 684, 685, 686
Moffitt, Jennifer Lester, 52
Moffitt, Kelly, 27
Moffitt, Kenneth M., 998
Moga Bryant, Catherine, 348
Mogni, John, 232
Mohamed, Mohamed A., 87
Mohan, Anthony J., 221
Mohedano, Corky, 193
Mohney, Kirk F., 214
Mohr Peterson, Judy, 131
Mohr, Gary C., 372
Mohr, Janet L., 256
Mohr, Vicki, 381
Moidja, Sharon, 444
Moiola, Teresa, 299
Mojica, Katty, 234
Mojica, Maria I., 73
Molamphy, Patrick, 352
Molchanow, Karen, 408
Mole, Lois Park, 422
Molea, Marcus, 367
Moliga, Lolo Matalasi, 18
Moliga, Vaetasi
  Tuumolimoli Saena
  "Tuua", 563, 564, 565
Molin, Chris, 399
Molina, LaRonda, 379
Molinari, Jennifer, 445
Moline, Stephen, 167
Molisee, Samantha, 300

Molke, Currie, 527
Mollenkamp, John R., 277
Moller, Mary Rae, 390
Molloy, Andrew "Drew", 497
Molloy, Juel T. R., 485
Molloy, Rueben, 486
Molnar, Janice, 338
Mom, Rady, 772
Mommsen, Norlin, 706, 707, 708
Mompeller, Andy, 103
Monaghan, Dan, 326
Monaghan, Kimberly, 750, 752
Monahan-Cummings, Carol, 40
Monahan, Christopher "Chris", 404
Monahan, Dena, 480
Monahan, Col Edward C., 191
Monahan, Francis J., 497
Monahan, John, 313
Monahan, J. Stephen "Steve", 481
Monahan, Lauren, 235
Monegan, Walter, III, 16
Money, Mari, 151
Moneyham, Laura, 103
Monforte, John, 325
Monforton, Matthew, 838, 840, 841
Monge, Elaine, 238
Mongeon, Karin, 361
Mongeon, Ron, 210
Mongold, Susan, 497
Mongon, Christina, 312
Monhollon, Rusty, 279
Moniz, Glenn, 1106, 1107, 1108
Monk, C. Kevin, 205
Monk, Emily, 145
Monks, Jason, 666, 667, 669
Monnes Anderson, Laurie, 956, 957
Monning, William W. "Bill", 581, 583, 584, 585
Monroe Wesley, Erin, 198
Monroe, Andrienne, 300
Monroe, Dani, 234
Monroe, Jeff, 1010, 1012
Monroe, John, 177
Monroe, Nicole, 500
Monroe, Rod, 956
Monsen, Alda, 82
Monson, Brian, 135
Monson, Charles, 337
Monson, David, 930, 932
Monsour, Alex, 810, 812, 813, 814, 815
Montague, Janice, 217
Montalvo, Jorge, 331
Montanaro, Maria, 419
Montano, Dani, 184
Montano, Elizabeth, 325
Montecillo, Genise, 825, 828, 829
Montell, Brad, 729, 731, 733
Montenegro, Steve B., 567, 569, 570, 571
Monterroza, Erika, 46
Montesano, Debra, 6
Montesano, Michael A., 894, 899, 903, 904, 905, 906
Montet, Ricky, 199
Montez, Tracy, 39
Montford, Bill, 620, 621, 622, 623
Montgomery, Eric, 180
Montgomery, Erin, 216
Montgomery, Jesse, 147
Montgomery, John Michael, 950, 952, 954
Montgomery, Joseph, 371
Montgomery, Paula, 219
Montgomery, Phil, 531
Montgomery, Richard, 449

Montgomery, Capt. Scot, 537
Montgomery, Tom, 387
Montgomery, Velmanette, 889, 891, 892, 893
Montigny, Mark C., 763, 765, 766
Montinola, Peter, 123
Montoucet, Jack, 741, 743, 744
Montoya, Bill, 322
Montoya, Debbie, 325
Montoya, Karen Louise, 329
Montoya, Kenneth, 396
Montoya, Mary, 322
Montoya, Paul, 321
Montoya, Rodney D., 884, 886
Montoya, Rudy, 467
Moody, Christa, 274
Moody, Conny, 149
Moody, Craig, 383
Moody, Debra, 1022, 1024
Moody, Edward, 365
Moody, Joseph E. "Joe", 1033, 1036, 1037
Moody, Michael E., 246
Moody, Patrick, 9
Moody, Robert J. "Bobby", 268
Moon, David, 760, 762
Moon, Jason, 250
Moon, Jeff, 163
Moon, Mike, 825, 827, 830, 831
Moon, Lt. Col. Randy, 179
Moon, Robert, 339
Moonen, Matthew W., 750, 752
Mooney, Arnold, 550, 553, 554
Mooney, Gail, 930, 932
Mooney, John, 227
Mooney, Joseph, 71
Mooney, Patrick M., 325
Moore-Hudnall, Cassandra, 55
Moore Smeal, Shirley R., 402
Moore, Adam, 266
Moore, Alan, 372
Moore, Alice E., 236
Moore, Allan, 471
Moore, Barry, 550, 552, 553
Moore, Beth, 190
Moore, Brian, 402, 706, 707, 708, 709
Moore, Brian M., 416
Moore, Bryan T., 205
Moore, Cassandra, 271
Moore, LTC Charles, 141
Moore, Clifton "Clif", 1083, 1086, 1088, 1089, 1090
Moore, Danielle, 184
Moore, David "Doc", 838, 840
Moore, David J., 192
Moore, David T., 127
Moore, Delicia, 87
Moore, Dewayne, 381
Moore, Diane, 473
Moore, Donna, 528
Moore, Douglas, 68
Moore, Douglas L., 508
Moore, Edmond, 7
Moore, Ed W., 393
Moore, Eric L., 392
Moore, Eric S., 427
Moore, Eva, 147
Moore, Frederick "Eric", 832, 833, 834, 835
Moore, Garrett W., 499
Moore, Gary, 136
Moore, Glynis, 75
Moore, Harold E., 493
Moore, Holly M., 386
Moore, Hunter, 21
Moore, Jamillah, 54

Moore, Jim, 272
Moore, Jim M., 446
Moore, John, 848, 849
Moore, John L., 810, 812, 813, 814, 815
Moore, Joseph D. "Joe", 22
Moore, Josh, 862, 868
Moore, Julia George, 205
Moore, Karhlton, 371
Moore, Kevin, 150, 163, 527
Moore, Kim, 187
Moore, Lauren, 182
Moore, Lewis H., 950, 954
Moore, Lloyd H., 6
Moore, Lucinda M. "Luci", 395
Moore, Marie, 381
Moore, Marilyn, 599, 600, 609, 610, 611
Moore, Marjorie, 472
Moore, Mark, 250
Moore, Mary, 550, 553, 554
Moore, Matt, 459
Moore, Michael O., 765, 766, 767
Moore, Mike C., 442
Moore, Pierce, 264
Moore, Randy, 491
Moore, Robert, 459
Moore, Robert S., Jr., 32
Moore, Rodney, 190
Moore, Rodney W., 917, 920, 921, 922, 923, 924
Moore, Roz, 198
Moore, Russell, 27
Moore, Sabrina, 422
Moore, Sarah H., 6
Moore, Shawn, 80
Moore, Spencer R., 114
Moore, Steve, 30
Moore, Tara, 439
Moore, Thomas A., 520
Moore, Tim, 729, 732, 733
Moore, Tim K., 913, 917
Moore, Tom, 706, 708, 709
Moore, Toni, 348
Moore, T. Suzette, 220
Moore, Valerie, 190
Moore, Victor A., 509
Moore, Virgil, 138
Moore, Virginia, 184
Moore, William "Bill", 45
Moorefield, Michael, 280
Moorehead, Morris D., 487
Moores, Mark, 881, 882
Moorlach, John M.W., 583, 584, 585
Moorse, John, 256
Moosally, Fred, 98
Moose, Timothy "Tim", 351
Moracco, Nathan, 258
Moraitis, George R., Jr., 627, 630
Morales, Howie C., 881, 882
Morales, Jeffrey "Jeff", 50
Morales, Joe, 60
Morales, Marice I., 760, 762
Morales, Raquel, 454
Moran, Bernie, 433
Moran, Brian J., 496
Moran, Daniel P., 465
Moran, Denise, 443
Moran, Frank A., 772, 775
Moran, Gary, 235
Moran, Mary, 158
Moran, Michael J., 772, 775
Moran, Pamela R., 492
Moran, Patricia, 313
Moran, Philip, 802, 803, 804, 805, 806
Moran, Rena, 795, 798
Moran, Susan "Sue", 248
Morante, Teri, 250
Morath, Michael "Mike", 456
Morawski, Lisa, 391
Morazzini, Zackery P., 41
Moreau, Jacques, 418

Novstrup, Al, 1014, 1015, 1016
Novstrup, David, 1010, 1011, 1012
Nowak, Ellen E., 530
Nowakowski, Tammy, 382
Nowlan, Lynette, 25
Nowlin, Darlene, 92
Noyce, Dr. Pendred, 234
Noyes, Richard "Rick", 292
Nozzolio, Michael F., 887, 889, 891, 892, 893, 894
Nua, Motusa Tuileama, 19
Nuckles, Kim P., 513
Nuckols, Christina, 488
Nudelman, Elizabeth, 17
Nuding, Tim, 144
Nunes, Brandon, 45
Nunes, Jared R., 995, 996, 997
Nunes, Katherine, 151
Nunev, Jason, 393
Nunez, Alicia, 68
Nuñez, Andy, 884, 885, 886
Nunez, Daniel, 96
Nunez, Gus, 296
Nuñez, Jeanette M., 627, 630
Nungesser, William H. "Billy", 205
Nunley, Michael, 321
Nunn, Christopher, 112
Nunn, Zach, 703, 706, 707, 708, 709
Nunnally, Zaneta, 163
Nunnelly, Mark E., 231, 232
Nuovo, Betty A., 1052, 1055
Nussbaum, Sarah, 275
Nutt, Bennie, 265
Nutting, Robert W., 750
Nuxoll, Sheryl L., 662, 663
Nyberg, David "Dave", 246
Nybo, Chris, 672, 673, 674, 675
Nye, Mark, 666, 668
Nye, Rich, 476
Nygent-Hill, Jennifer, 487
Nygren, John, 1097, 1100
Nyhan, Keith, 305
Nyhan, Kevin, 307
Nyland, Dennis, 281

## O

Oakar, Mary Rose, 376
Oakeley, Timothy N., 321
Oakes, Rebecca L., 60
Oakey, Brian, 137
Oakley, Nathan, 270
Oaks, Chelsie, 539
Oaks, Nathaniel T., 760, 762
Oaks, Robert C. "Bob", 899, 906, 907
Oban, Erin, 926, 927
O'Ban, Steve, 1071, 1072, 1073
O'Banner, Major Jimmy, 266
O'Bannon, Lt. Col. Curtis, 191
O'Bannon, Daniel, 470
O'Bannon, John M., III, 1065, 1067, 1068
O'Barr, Kevin, 356
Obeng, Yaw, 368
Obenshain, Mark D., 1059, 1060, 1061
Ober, David L., 691, 695, 697, 698
Ober, Lynne M., 862, 869
Ober, Russell T., III, 862, 869, 870
Oberg, Julianne A. "Julie", 217
Oberholtzer, Todd, 369
Oberlander, Donna, 966, 974
Obermiller, Gary, 371
Obernolte, Jay, 585, 589, 591, 593

Oberoi, Chirjeev, 161
Oberweis, James D. "Jim", 672, 673, 674, 675
Obhof, Larry J., Jr., 934, 935, 936
Obiol, Carla, 356
O'Boyle, Peter A., 426
O'Brien, Anne Theresa, 1053, 1055
O'Brien, Brenda J., 253
O'Brien, Carol Higgins, 240
O'Brien, Christopher "Chris", 228
O'Brien, Connie, 717, 720, 721, 722
O'Brien, Elizabeth "Liz", 299
O'Brien, Kennedy, 310
O'Brien, Kerri J., 335
O'Brien, Kevin P., 306
O'Brien, Margaret, 776, 777, 778, 779
O'Brien, Michael B., Sr., 862, 870
O'Brien, Michael H., 941, 973, 977, 978, 979, 980
O'Brien, Michael J., 940, 941, 942
O'Brien, Sandy, 79
O'Brien, Sean, 13, 531, 940, 941, 942, 943
O'Brien, Victoria, 13
O'Brien, Wende, 260
O'Brien, William L. "Bill", 862
O'Brien, William W., 995, 996, 997
Obuchowski, Joel, 334
Obuchowski, Michael J., 478
O'Callaghan, David, 236
O'Callaghan, Jean, 114
Ochoa, Patricia "Patti", 38
Ochrym, Ronald. G. "Ron", 342
Ockfen, Ken, 137
O'Clair, Terry, 360
O'Connell, David, 926, 927
O'Connell, Frank, 116
O'Connell, Robert E., Jr., 215
O'Connell, Shaunna, 772, 775
O'Connell, Sophie, 419
O'Connell, Thomas B. "Tom", 281
O'Connor-Bennett, Sarah, 149
O'Connor-Hebert, Megan, 339
O'Connor Ives, Kathleen, 765, 766, 767, 775
O'Connor, Angela, 236
O'Connor, Anne V., 256
O'Connor, Beth A., 750
O'Connor, Bob, 235
O'Connor, Christine, 418
O'Connor, Clifford "Cliff", 114
O'Connor, Diane, 262
O'Connor, George, 234
O'Connor, John, 862, 868
O'Connor, Kevin, 339
O'Connor, Patrick, 765
O'Connor, Reba D., 490
O'Connor, Roxanne, 536
Oda, Curtis "Curt", 1043, 1045
O'Day, James J., 772
O'Dea, Tom, 606, 610, 611, 612
O'Dell, Brad, 325
Odell, Gregory, 308
O'Dell, John, 60
Oden, Jeremy H., 9
Odett, Judy, 252
Odiorne, Jim, 512
Odom, Eleanor, 424
Odom, Jayme, 148
O'Donnell, Ann, 375

O'Donnell, Anthony J. "Tony", 760, 762, 763
O'Donnell, Daniel J., 899, 903, 904, 906
O'Donnell, Kelly, 401
O'Donnell, Michael, II, 711, 712, 713
O'Donnell, Patrick, 589, 591, 592, 593
O'Donnell, Patrick J., 842
O'Donnell, Steven G., 417
O'Donnell, Terry S., 951, 953, 954
O'Donoghue, Laura, 348
O'Driscoll, Tim, 795, 798, 799
Oechsner, Troy, 333
Oedekoven, Dr. Dustin, 431, 436
Oehler, Anna, 532
Oehlke, Dave, 926, 927
Oelslager, W. Scott, 935, 936
Oettel, William, 76
Offenbecher, Richard "Rick", 529
Ogami, Jack H., 394
Ogata, Lloyd T., 128
Ogilvie, Moy, 72
Ogilvie, Stephen, 470
Ogle, LtCol Jody, 518
Oglesby, Robert E. "Bob", 442
O'Grady, Elaine, 481
O'Grady, Jeremiah T., 995, 996, 997
O'Grady, Vincent P., 227
Ohaegbu, Nkiruka Catherine, 38
O'Halloran, Nancy, 399
O'Hanlon, Katie, 413
O'Hara, Erin, 441
Ohara, Patricia T., 127
O'Hare, James P., 334
O'Hearne, Andrew S., 862, 868
O'Hern, Cassandra, 259
O'Hern, Thomas M. "Tom", 262
Ohle, Maureen G., 152
Ohlemiller, Marcia L., 399
Ohlko, Holly, 67
Ohm, Bill, 862, 870
Ohno, Takashi, 658, 659, 660, 661
Ohnstad, Tod, 1097, 1101, 1102
O'Holleran, Jennie P., 488
O'Holleran, Kevin, 500
O'Holleran, Molly, 294
Ohorilko, Brian, 170
Ohrenschall, James, 848, 849
Oie, Claude R., 292
Oie, Mary Jo, 292
Oimoen, John E., 150
Ojakian, Mark E., 73
Ojiri, Scott M., 128
Okabe, Wil, 126
Okahara, BrigGen Ryan T., 130
Okamoto, Clifford, 46
Okamoto, George, 40
Okashima, Ryan, 50
O'Keefe, Brian, 533
O'Keefe, Robert, 467
Okerlund, Jennifer, 137
Okerlund, Ralph, 1039, 1040
O'Kief, Jennifer, 141
Okimoto, Kay M., 129
Okorafor, Ngozi, 147
Okraska, Jennifer, 404
Okrent, Betty, 338
Oksman, G. Timothy, 500
Okubo, Janice, 130
Okun, Ruthanne, 250
Okwuosa, Chisorom, 44
Olah, L. Elaine, 328
Olanoff, Beth, 409

Olanolan, Beulah, 132
Oldenberg, Glenda, 284
Oldenburg, William J. "Bill", 307
Oldfield, Mark, 40
Oldson, Jo, 706, 707, 708, 709
O'Leary, Donna, 305, 343
O'Leary, Meg, 282
O'Leary, Michael "Mike", 372
O'Leary, Sarah, 372
O'Leary, Terence "Terry", 330
O'Leary, William G. "Bill", 12
Oleka, OJ, 196
Olenick, Bruce, 135
Olenick, Michael, 107
Olens, Samuel S. "Sam", 117, 119
Olgiati, Susan L., 319
Olige, Angela, 454
Oligmueller, Gerry A., 288
Oligny, Jeffrey, 862, 868
Oline, Kathy, 505
Oliphint, Kim, 48
Oliva, Jose R., 627, 630, 631
Oliva, Steve, 435
Olivares-Castain, Stacie, 56
Olivas, Esther, 22
Olivas, Jeanne, 192
Olive, Karen, 443
Olive, Lawrence, 486
Oliveira, Rene, 1034, 1036, 1038
Oliver, Gathelyn, 447
Oliver, Javon, 90
Oliver, Jeff, 66
Oliver, Jim, 186
Oliver, Karl, 810, 812, 813, 814, 815, 816
Oliver, Kristina J., 515
Oliver, Lee Ann, 364
Oliver, Lindsey, 208
Oliver, Mary Margaret, 643, 646, 648, 649, 650
Oliver, Merril, 216
Oliver, Col. Michael, 426
Oliver, Paulina, 299
Oliver, Shane, 434
Oliver, Sheila Y., 874, 877, 878, 879
Oliver, Steven, 387
Oliver, Valerie, 443
Oliver, William J., 204
Olivera, Gregg, 316
Oller, Sean-Marie, 482
Olmstead, LtCol Candis, 14
Olpadwala, Sarosh, 93
Olse, Kathleen "Katie", 460
Olsen, Alan R., 956, 957
Olsen, Andrea, 838, 840, 841
Olsen, Christian, 29
Olsen, Greg, 337
Olsen, Kristin, 589, 591, 592
Olsen, Luther S., 526, 1092, 1093
Olsen, Melodie, 509
Olsen, Mike, 292
Olsen, Nancy, 536
Olsen, Oliver K., 1053, 1056
Olsen, Regg, 471
Olsen, Steven, 142
Olson-Collins, Cheryll, 527
Olson-Morgan, Janne, 43
Olson, Andy, 959, 960
Olson, Betty, 1011, 1012
Olson, Carol, 174
Olson, Christian, 29
Olson, Christopher D., 930, 932, 933
Olson, Daniel M. "Dan", 103
Olson, Dawn M., 260
Olson, Debbie, 152
Olson, Dennis W., 256

Olson, Donald "Donny", 556
Olson, Hope, 364
Olson, Jessica, 467
Olson, Judy, 328
Olson, Justin D., 569, 570, 571
Olson, Karen, 263
Olson, Kevin, 283
Olson, COL Kevin, 259
Olson, Kristin, 99
Olson, Kurt E., 558, 560
Olson, Margaret, 360
Olson, Nathan, 511
Olson, Renee, 298
Olson, Rick, 706, 708, 709
Olson, Robert S. "Rob", 711, 712, 713
Olson, Sanjay, 528
Olson, Tina, 538
Olstad, Janet, 257
Olszewski, Albert, 838, 840, 841
Olthoff, Julie, 695, 696, 697
Olvera, Rene, 466
O'Malley, Bernadette, 244
O'Malley, Jennifer, 158
O'Malley, Jim, 530
O'Malley, John A., 241
Oman, Jesse, 262
Oman, Leni, 506
O'Mara, Thomas F. "Tom", 890, 891, 892, 893, 894
Omdahl, David M., 1011
Omishakin, Toks, 446
Omisore, Diji, 87
Ommen, Doug, 168
Omotoso, Olufemi, 88
O'Nan, Ronnie, 194
Onder, Robert F. "Bob", 816, 817, 818, 819
Ondiek, Baraka, 87
O'Neal, Bill, 425
O'Neal, Christopher J. "Chris", 400
O'Neal, David, 133
O'Neal, John David, IV, 1083, 1086, 1088, 1089, 1090
O'Neil, Diedre, 388
O'Neil, William "Bill", 862, 869
O'Neill, Arthur J., 601, 606, 608, 610, 611
O'Neill, Bernie, 973, 978
O'Neill, Bill B., 881, 882
O'Neill, Brendan J., 81
O'Neill, Brian, 312
O'Neill, Colin, 209
O'Neill, Edward J., 991, 992
O'Neill, Jayson, 282
O'Neill, John J., III, 226
O'Neill, Marion, 795, 798, 799
O'Neill, Philip "P.K.", 848, 849
O'Neill, Terrence M., 74
Ong, Augustinus, 305
Ong, Michael, 128
Ong, Nicole, 22
Ong, Thomas L. "Tom", 518
Onifade, Dr. Tiffiani, 110
Onishi, Richard, 658, 659, 660, 661
Onken, Blake, 290
Onkst, Wayne, 184
Ono, Jeffrey T., 129
Onofrio, Ben, 469
Onstad, Kenton, 928, 931, 933
Onstad, Nels, 256
Onstott, Matthew, 324
Ooten, David, 383
Ooten, Michelann, 380
Openshaw, Cheryl, 499
Opheikens, Cassandra, 472
Opitz, Wolfgang, 511
Opper, Richard, 284

Piccione, Jason, 39
Pichardo, Juan M., 992, 993
Pichardo, Victor M., 900, 903, 905, 906
Pick, Brian, 89
Pickelman, Barton G., 251
Pickels, J. Hunter, 221
Pickens, Mary Jane, 513
Picker, Michael, 54
Pickering, Marvin, 486
Pickering, Richard, 326
Pickering, Robert, 273
Pickering, Stacey E., 272
Pickett, Andrew, 404
Pickett, Diane, 101
Pickett, Joseph "Joe", 1034, 1037, 1038
Pickett, Richard A., 750
Pickett, Robert M. "Bob", 11
Pickett, Tina, 974, 978, 979, 980
Picone, Joseph, 206
Pieciak, Michael, 481
Piecuch, Stanley W., 209
Piepenbrink, Bradley O., 99
Pier, Steve, 467
Pierce, Alicia, 467
Pierce, Amilyn, 27
Pierce, Bobby J., 572, 573, 574
Pierce, Dave, 76
Pierce, David E., 236
Pierce, David M., 851, 852
Pierce, David W., 863, 869
Pierce, Drusilla, 221
Pierce, Garland E., 913, 918, 920, 921, 922
Pierce, Greg, 537
Pierce, Jeff, 435
Pierce, Jeffrey, 750
Pierce, Katrina, 50
Pierce, Matt, 695, 697, 698
Pierce, Roxanna, 451
Pierce, Steve, 566, 567
Pierce, Susan M., 515
Pierce, Teresa, 750, 752
Pierce, Zachary M., 60
Pierceall, Tracy, 151
Pierpont, Jon, 474
Pierpont, Ruth L., 340
Pierre, Vincent J., 741, 743, 744
Pierson-McDaniels, Monica, 202
Pierson, Brandi, 286
Pierson, Donald, Jr., 200
Pierson, Erika L., 85
Pierson, Gordon, Jr., 839, 840, 841
Pierson, Justin, 434
Pierson, Nels, 796, 797, 798
Pierson, Tommie, 825, 827, 829, 830
Pierson, Wayne, 443
Pietras, Chet, 159
Pietzman, Randy, 825, 828, 829, 830, 831
Pigler, Carmen, 87
Pigman, Dr. Cary, 627, 630
Pignatelli, William Smitty, 773, 775
Pigott, Bill, 810, 812, 813, 814
Pigott, Bruno L., 157
Piiparinen, Garry C., 1106, 1107
Pike, Jennifer, 134
Pike, Linda, 140
Pike, Liz, 1076, 1078, 1079
Pike, Patricia, 825, 827, 828, 830, 831
Pilato, Steve, 516
Pilcher-Cook, Mary, 711, 712
Pilipchuk, John, 352
Pilkenton, Kathy, 106
Pillion, Todd E., 1065, 1067, 1069

Pillo, Cynthia M., 518
Pilo, Randel, 531
Pilon, Ray, 627, 631
Piluso, Carla C., 959, 960
Pimentel, Eligio Cerda, 152
Pimlott, Ken, 47
Pinaula, Benny, 123
Pine, Aimee, 154
Pine, Howard, 318
Ping, Timothy, 159
Pinkard, Eugene, 89
Pinkney, Tanya T., 217
Pinkston Sutton, Janie, 351
Pinney, Brian, 507
Pino, Raul, 71
Pinocci, Randy, 839, 840, 841
Pinsky, Paul G., 754, 755
Pinto, David, 796, 798, 799
Pinto, Greg, 148
Pinto, John, 881, 882
Pintor-Marin, Eliana, 877, 878, 879
Piotrowicz, Linda, 68
Piper, Adam, 429
Piper, Emily Johnson, 258
Piper, Wendy, 863, 869
Pippin, Capt. Eric, 179
Pipsair, Sophia, 203
Pirkle, Clay, 643, 646, 650, 651
Pirner, Steven M., 432
Pirtle, Cliff R., 881, 882
Pisani, Christine, 136
Pisano, Amanda, 313
Pisarik, Holly Gillespie, 421
Pisaturo, Laura, 415
Pisca, Jeremy, 142
Piscitelli, Chris, 227
Piscopo, John E., 601, 606, 609, 611
Pishon, Mark, 163
Pistner, Linda M., 214
Pitcher, Dixon M., 1044, 1045, 1046
Pitcher, Rebecca Clark, 144
Pitcock, Josh, 155
Pitkin, Jeffrey J. "Jeff", 340
Pitman, Laura, 380
Pitney, Pat, 10
Pitre, Joseph A., 863, 869
Pitrof, Karrie, 392
Pitrolo, James L. "Jim", 517
Pitsch, Mathew W. "Mat", 578, 580
Pitt, M. Stephen, 182
Pitt, Nancy, 250
Pittard, William S. "Steve", 499
Pittelkau, Judy, 508
Pittell, Stacie, 96
Pittinger, Brook, 497
Pittman, Anastasia A., 944, 945, 946, 947
Pittman, Dionne, 117
Pittman, James A., 83
Pittman, Kitty, 381
Pittman, Larry, 918, 920, 921, 922, 924
Pittman, Lee "Trip", 544, 545, 546
Pitts, Joe, 1022, 1025
Pitts, Michael A. "Mike", 1007, 1008, 1009
Pitts, Patricia S. "Patty", 491
Pitts, Robert, 524
Piwowarski, Barbara, 146
Piwowarski, CSM David A., 336
Pizarro, Ray, 462
Pizzetta, Harold, 272
Pizzini, Lynne, 282
Pizzuti, Sandy, 257
Place, Andrew G., 407
Place, Whitney, 255
Plaeger-Brockway, Roy, 504

Plaistowe, Franklin, 507
Plakon, Scott, 627, 630
Plano, Bart, 225
Plantz, Anna M., 514
Plasencia, Rene, 627, 630
Plassio, William, 402
Plastiras, James, 334
Platt, Andrew Joseph, 760, 763
Platt, Brent, 473
Platt, Nicholas, 109
Platt, Rick, 472
Plawecki, Julie, 782, 784, 785
Player, J. Darrin, 427
Plazibat, Stephen, 154
Pleasanton, Kristin, 79
Pleger, Steve, 112
Plessinger, Gretl, 103
Plier, Jimmy, 6
Plinski, Sarah, 150
Plocher, Dean, 826, 828, 829, 830
Plondin, Amy, 509
Plotkin, Adam, 532
Plouck, Tracy J., 370
Plowden, Mark W., 429
Plum, Kenneth R., 1065, 1067, 1068, 1069
Plumb, Ron, 443
Plumlee, Celeste, 569, 570
Plumley, Jewell, 524
Plummer, Einon, 372
Plummer, Perry, 306
Plung, Dan, 512
Plunk, Lauren, 450
Plunket, Paul, 459
Plunkett, Alan, 160
Plunkett, Brent, 166
Pluta, Stefan, 434
Plutro, Beth A., 494
Plyant, Stan R., 6
Plymale, Robert Hugh "Bob", 1081, 1082, 1083
Pocino, Raymond M., 317
Poddar, Keshav, 413
Podesta, Alexis, 38
Podunovich, Anastasiya, 14
Pody, Mark, 1022, 1024, 1025
Poe, Jim, 161
Poe, Raymond, 144
Poedubicky, Gary, 318
Poftak, Steve, 242
Pogemiller, Lawrence J. "Larry", 262
Pogge, Brenda L., 1066, 1067, 1068
Pogue, Jeffrey "Jeff", 826, 828, 830, 831
Pogue, Kenneth, 51
Pogue, Tonya, 389
Pogue, Troy D., 157
Pohl, Allan, 250
Pohuski, Linda, 230
Poindexter, Charles D., 1066, 1067
Pointer, David, 315
Poirier, Elizabeth A., 767, 773, 775
Poirier, Paul N., 1053, 1055
Poitevint, Scott, 113
Pokarney, Bruce A., 391
Poke, Irvin, 250
Poklemba, John J., 342
Polak, Lorraine, 436
Polasek, Joseph, 528
Polasik, Misty, 53
Polatty, Jan, 423
Polen, Terry L., 516
Poleski, Earl, 782, 784
Polin, Greg, 244
Polishook, Lewis, 331
Politi-Corrigan, Jen, 61
Polito, Karyn E., 242
Polito, Tawny, 296
Polizos, Dimitri, 550, 552, 553
Polk, Bert, 424

Polk, Beryl, 268
Polk, John A., 802, 803, 804, 805
Pollack, Stephanie, 241, 242
Pollard, Aaron, 435
Pollard, John, 261
Pollard, Lisa, 303
Pollard, Randy D., 143
Pollard, Tim, 193
Pollert, Chet, 931, 932
Polles, Sam, 267
Pollet, Gerry, 1076, 1078
Pollina, Anthony, 1047, 1048
Pollio, Christine, 69
Pollock, Daniel "Dan", 257
Pollock, Greg, 468
Polston, Chip, 196
Polzin, Cindy, 525
Pomerleau, Lilo, 456
Pomnichowski, Jennifer "JP", 834, 835
Ponds, Annette, 449
Ponozzo, Kristi, 283
Pontones, Pam, 158
Pool, Ray, 388
Pool, Vicki L., 166
Poole, Bill R., 550, 553, 554
Poole, Danette, 495
Poole, Joel, 280
Poole, Kendell, 446
Poole, Sheila J., 337
Poole, Major William, 425
Poolman, Nicole, 926, 927
Poore, Nicole, 613, 614
Poore, Pete, 427
Popadak, Heather O., 209
Popat, Sajeed, 91
Pope, Beverly, 110
Pope, Bill, 272
Pope, Christopher S., 839, 840, 841
Pope, Diana, 117
Pope, Jerry, 471
Pope, Jon, 134
Pope, J. Rogers, 741, 743, 744
Pope, Peggy J., 519
Pope, Sondy, 1097, 1100, 1101
Pope, Thomas E. "Tommy", 1002, 1007
Popkin, Ben, 355
Popoff, Christine M., 391
Poppe, Cheryl L., 237
Poppe, Jeanne, 796, 797, 798, 800
Poppell, Chad, 103
Poppell, James "Jim", 100
Popplewell, Celeste, 186
Porett, Matthew, 256
Porteous, Alexander E. "Alec", 211
Porter, Alyce, 136
Porter, Amy, 71
Porter, Coy, 474
Porter, David J., 463
Porter, Dennis, 135
Porter, Elizabeth W., 627, 630
Porter, BG Greg, 536
Porter, Gregory W. "Greg", 695, 697, 698
Porter, Holly, 76
Porter, James, 482
Porter, Jim, 181
Porter, Leslie, 321
Porter, Louis, 481
Porter, Marjorie, 863, 869
Porter, Robyn A., 606, 608, 610
Porter, Todd, 931, 932
Porter, Torome, 264
Porter, William, 339
Porter, William W., 243
Porterfield, Carrie, 110
Portmann, Jennifer, 193
Ports, James F. "Jim", Jr., 224

Portzer, Tiffany, 335
Posewitz, Andrew, 286
Possley, Maura, 153
Post, Aubrey, 107
Post, Bill, 959, 960
Post, Jennifer, 335
Post, Kerri, 104
Post, Lisa, 154
Posthumus Lyons, Lisa, 782, 784, 785
Posthumus, Richard "Dick", 246
Postman, David, 501
Postolowski, John J., 64
Pote, Ken, 211
Potesta, Jay K., 165
Pothier, Karl, 222
Potteiger, Michael C., 408
Potter-Blair, Kimberly, 190
Potter, Charles, Jr., 616, 617, 618
Potter, Cora, 120
Potter, Dave, 1053, 1056
Potter, Dena, 489
Potter, Karen, 81
Potter, Linda, 186
Potter, Milton, 487
Potter, Osbert, 485
Potter, Roberta, 56
Pottorf, Ron, 372
Potts, Rachel, 275
Potucek, John, 863, 870
Poturalski, James "Jim", 160
Potvin, Paula, 233
Potvin, Phil, 782, 784
Pou, Nellie, 872, 873
Pouha, Feki, 657, 658, 660, 661
Poulin, Michael J., 215
Pouliot, Dee Ann, 307
Pouliot, Matthew G. "Matt", 750
Poulson, Marie H., 1044, 1045, 1046
Pouncey, Lola T., 102
Pourhosseini, Faizi, 42
Povich, Lon F., 231
Povis, Audrey D., 391
Powdrell-Culbert, Jane E., 884, 886
Powell, Alan, 643, 647, 648, 649, 650
Powell, Allan, 424
Powell, Bobby, 628, 630
Powell, Brent L., 810, 813, 814, 815, 816
Powell, Dr. Brett, 32
Powell, Duane, 257
Powell, Jason, 1019, 1022, 1024, 1025
Powell, Jay, 643, 647, 648, 649, 650, 651
Powell, Jeffrey, 509
Powell, Jeffrey H., 96
Powell, Kevin, 443
Powell, Kraig, 1044, 1045, 1046
Powell, Larry R., 711, 712, 713
Powell, Mark, 157
Powell, Mark S., 217
Powell, Marta B., 510
Powell, Mike, 467
Powell, Col. Ralph, 140
Powell, Randy, 718, 721
Powell, Dr. Rayan, 367
Powell, Rudy, 105
Powell, Lt. Col. Russell, 115
Powell, Sean P., 218
Powell, Sheree, 381
Powell, Tony K., 102
Powell, Travis, 183
Powell, Tyler, 378
Powell, Tyrone, 400
Powelson, Robert F., 407
Power, Greg, 359
Power, LeAnn, 73
Power, Scott, 348

Rinn, Christopher, 312
Riordan, CPT Emily P., 303
Ríos Santiago, Carmelo J., 981
Rios, George, 462
Rios, Rebecca, 567, 570, 571
Rioux, John L., 212
Ripko, Megan, 63
Ripley, Rick, 834, 835
Ripoli, Kim, 416
Ripp, Jeffrey, 531
Ripp, Keith, 1098, 1099, 1101, 1102
Rippel, Leon, 74
Ris, Lauren, 62
Risby, Dr. Emile, 112
Risch, Jay, 527
Risch, Patricia, 312
Rise, Donna, 282
Riser, Hartwell Neil, Jr., 735, 736, 737
Risher, Chris, 444
Riske, Laura, 527
Risoni, Dario, 298
Risser, Fred A., 1092, 1093
Ristow, Nate, 529
Rita, Angie, 424
Rita, Robert "Bob", 680, 683, 684, 686
Ritchie, Jeremiah, 320
Ritchie, Monica, 265
Ritchie, Patricia, 890, 891, 892, 893, 894
Ritenour, Rhodes B., 500
Ritter, Cathy, 59
Ritter, Kristin, 509
Ritter, Matthew D., 606, 608, 611
Ritter, Stacia, 410
Ritter, Stefan, 116
Ritz, Glenda, 157
Ritze, J. Michael "Mike", 951, 954
Ritzman, James D., 407
Ritzman, Capt. Jeff, 172
Rius, Dr. Ana, 412
Rivard, Adrien "Bo", III, 107
Rivard, Dee L., 78
Rivard, Jim, 184
Rivas, Albert, 51
Rivera Filomeno, Luis Daniel, 981, 982, 983, 984
Rivera-O'Reilly, Nellie, 1057
Rivera Ortega, Rafael "June", 986, 987
Rivera Rocafort, Ingrid, 411
Rivera Ruiz de Porras, Roberto, 984, 986, 988
Rivera Schatz, Thomas, 982
Rivera, German, 70
Rivera, Greg, 154
Rivera, Gustavo, 887, 890, 892, 893
Rivera, José, 894, 900, 902, 905, 906
Rivera, Lonny, 376
Rivera, Mayte, 239
Rivera, Orlando E., 102
Rivera, Pedro A., 408, 409
Rivera, Randy, 453
Rivera, Robert, 462
Rivero, Tony, 570
Rivers, Ann, 1069, 1071, 1072, 1073
Rivers, Samuel, Jr., 1007, 1008, 1009
Rives, David, 397
Riviere, Gil, 655, 656
Rizer, Col Kenneth R. "Ken", 706, 707, 708
Rizk, Jim, 457
Rizzo, John Joseph, 819, 826, 828, 829, 830, 831
Rizzo, Linda, 106
Rizzo, Madeline, 339
Rizzs, Jill, 153

Roach, Michael, 316
Roach, Mintha, 448
Roach, Pam, 1069, 1072, 1073
Roach, Tregenza, 1057
Roae, Brad, 975, 978, 979, 980
Roark, Jerry, 321
Roark, Robin O., 454
Robach, Joseph E., 890, 892, 893, 894
Robb, Jack, 299
Robbins, Brent, 206
Robbins, Danny, 384
Robbins, David, 326
Robbins, Robert D. "Robby", 427
Robbins, Steve C., 391
Robbins, Zachary, 490
Roberge-Wentzell, Dianna, 73
Roberson, Ann S., 424
Roberson, Kenneth L. "Ken", 628, 630
Roberson, Lyod B. "Rob", 810, 813, 814, 815
Roberson, Michael, 845, 846, 847
Roberson, Terry, 173
Robert, Melinda, 200
Roberts-Davis, Alice, 255
Roberts, Brett, 783, 784, 785
Roberts, Bruce, 50
Roberts, Byron R., 423
Roberts, Carol R., 863, 868
Roberts, Charles, III, 107
Roberts, Cheryl J., 494
Roberts, Chuck, 515
Roberts, Dan, 33
Roberts, Darwin, 511
Roberts, Dustin, 951, 953, 954
Roberts, E. J., 269
Roberts, Elizabeth H., 418
Roberts, Ellen S., 593, 594, 595
Roberts, Gary "Bud", 31
Roberts, Georgia, 64
Roberts, Greg, 339
Roberts, Guy, 479
Roberts, Hunter, 431
Roberts, Jacque, 42
Roberts, John, 183
Roberts, John S., 252
Roberts, Ken A., 138
Roberts, Kerry Evan, 1018, 1019
Roberts, Lt. Col. Kris Edward, 864, 870
Roberts, Lane, 277
Roberts, Lily, 29
Roberts, Linda, 367
Roberts, Linda A., 94
Roberts, Lon E., 527
Roberts, Lonnie, 449
Roberts, Marc, 1044, 1045
Roberts, Matthew, 27, 150
Roberts, Melissa, 60
Roberts, Melissa B., 527
Roberts, Patrick, 353
Roberts, Patti, 46
Roberts, Richard H., 445
Roberts, Rodney A. "Rod", 170
Roberts, Ronald, 72
Roberts, Samuel D. "Sam", 340
Roberts, Sarah, 783, 784
Roberts, Sean, 951, 953, 954
Roberts, Sherry, 996, 997
Roberts, Shirrell, 4
Roberts, Steve, 181
Roberts, Sydney R., 153
Roberts, Thom, 444
Roberts, Tom, 179
Roberts, Wally, 176
Roberts, Walt, 453
Robertson, Allison, 453
Robertson, April L., 517

Robertson, David B., 776, 777, 778, 779
Robertson, Jeff, 384
Robertson, Jessica, 156
Robertson, Judy, 32
Robertson, Ken, 499
Robertson, Lance, 381
Robertson, Stephen W. "Steve", 159
Robertson, Timothy N. "Tim", 864, 868
Robeson, Miriam E., 165
Robey, Toya, 183
Robins, Connie, 502
Robins, Leah, 236
Robins, Tom, 378
Robinson-Simpson, Leola C., 1007, 1009
Robinson, Alan, 408
Robinson, Albert L., 724, 725, 726
Robinson, Annette M., 900, 902, 903, 905, 906
Robinson, A. Shane, 760, 762
Robinson, Barbara, 457
Robinson, Barbara A., 760, 762
Robinson, Bonnie, 159
Robinson, Brian, 93
Robinson, Daryl, 119
Robinson, David, 497
Robinson, Debbie, 510
Robinson, Dennis R., 317, 319
Robinson, Dr. Edmondo J., 77
Robinson, George, 137
Robinson, George S., 918, 921, 922, 923, 924
Robinson, Gladys Ashe, 907, 909, 910, 911, 912
Robinson, LTC Hazel L., 225
Robinson, Herman, 201
Robinson, Hunter, 355
Robinson, Janelle, 220
Robinson, BG Jessie Roy, 271
Robinson, Joe, 379
Robinson, Josephine Bias, 89
Robinson, June, 1076, 1078
Robinson, Karen, 256
Robinson, Karina, 55
Robinson, Kimberly Lewis, 203
Robinson, Kirk, 502
Robinson, Larry J., 926, 927, 928
Robinson, Dr. Loren K., 404
Robinson, Mary, 401
Robinson, Mikelle, 248
Robinson, Natalie, 165
Robinson, Oliver, 550, 552, 553
Robinson, Pam, 296
Robinson, Pamela, 535
Robinson, Randy, 508
Robinson, Rose Mary, 783, 785
Robinson, Roxann L., 1066, 1068, 1069
Robinson, Scott, 507
Robinson, Suzette, 94
Robinson, Thomas "Tom", 440
Robinson, Tiffany P., 221
Robinson, Troy, 187
Robinson, Turhan, 220
Robinson, Valerie, 90
Robinson, William, 50
Robinson, William C., 521
Robison, Mark, 381
Robitaille, Karen, 241
Roblan, Arnie, 955, 956
Robleto, Rich, 107
Robson, Bob, 567, 570, 571

Roby, Mike, 116
Robyn, Angie Heffner, 280
Rocca, Tory, 777, 778, 779
Rocchio, Robert, 418
Rocco, Janice, 56
Roch, Dennis J., 884, 885, 886
Roche, Tim, 338
Rochford, Dennis, 77
Rock-Burns, Kathryn, 69
Rock, Deborah, 248
Rock, Erin Geraghty, 103
Rock, Michael, 235
Rock, Rob Basler, 420
Rock, Timothy T., 519
Rockeman, Karl, 360
Rockensuess, Brian, 157
Rockwell, Meredith, 376
Rockwell, Rebecca L., 475
Roda, Ann, 402
Roda, Patricia, 238
Roddenberry, Delbert, 352
Roddy, Margo, 258
Roddy, Peter, 38
Roddy, Robin M., 81
Roddy, Steve, 467
Rodefeld, Nels, 384
Rodeghero, Andrew, 164
Rodeheaver, Grant, 506
Rodekohr, Debbie, 535
Rodella, Debbie A., 884, 886
Rodemack, Dave, 476
Rodeman, Steve P., 398
Roden, Ryan, 538
Roden, Shane, 826, 828, 829, 831
Rodewald, Catherine, 461
Rodgers, Adrienne, 102
Rodgers, Alexsis, 500
Rodgers, Don W., 196
Rodgers, Ervan D., 375
Rodgers, Homer, 204
Rodgers, James, 334
Rodgers, John S., 1047, 1048
Rodgers, Rachel, 184
Rodighiero, Ralph, 1087, 1088, 1089
Rodin, Martin, 464
Rodne, Jay, 1076, 1078, 1079
Rodrigue, Dave, 307
Rodrigues, David M., 417
Rodrigues, Joseph "Joe", 44
Rodrigues, Joseph, 420
Rodrigues, Michael J., 763, 765, 766
Rodrigues, Nancy, 489
Rodrigues, Ray Wesley, 628, 630
Rodríguez Aguiló, Gabriel, 986, 987, 988, 989
Rodríguez González, Pedro A. "Pedrito", 982, 983, 984
Rodriguez-Gregg, Maria, 877, 878, 879
Rodríguez Miranda, Angel E., 986, 988, 989
Rodriguez Otero, Ángel M., 982, 983, 984
Rodríguez Quiles, José "Rodríguez", 986, 987, 988, 989, 990
Rodríguez Valle, Gilberto, 982, 983, 984
Rodriguez, Carlos, 342, 475
Rodriguez, Catherine, 64
Rodriguez, Dr. Christopher, 318
Rodriguez, Dennis G., Jr., 652, 653, 654
Rodriguez, Diane, 61
Rodriguez, Dorothy "Duffy", 322
Rodriguez, Eddie, 1034, 1036, 1037

Rodriguez, Freddie, 590, 591, 592, 593
Rodriguez, Grace Arupo, 38
Rodriguez, Jessie, 1094, 1098, 1099, 1100, 1101
Rodriguez, Jose, 504
Rodríguez, José Javier, 628, 630, 631
Rodríguez, José R., 1026, 1027, 1028, 1029
Rodriguez, Julio, 146
Rodriguez, Justin, 1034, 1036, 1038
Rodriguez, Lisa, 504
Rodriguez, Marcos, 502
Rodriguez, Mark, 42
Rodriguez, Nancy, 881, 882
Rodriguez, Penny, 207
Rodriguez, Reyes, 411
Rodriguez, Robert A., 530
Rodriguez, Robert J., 900, 903, 905, 906, 907
Rodriguez, Roberto "Bob", 190
Rodriguez, Rose, 331
Rodriguez, Tim, 215
Rodriguez, Wendy, 459
Rodriquez, Matthew "Matt", 39
Rodvik, Karsten, 12
Roe, Josh, 176
Roeber, Rebecca, 826, 829, 830, 831
Roebuck, James R., Jr., 408, 975, 978
Roederer, David, 171
Roegner, Kristina, 940, 941, 943
Roegner, Rob, 356
Roehrdanz, Charles "Chuck", 263
Roehrich, Marcus, 361
Roeker, Rebecca, 529
Roemer, Tim, 24
Roeske, Capt. Eric, 260
Roethle, Alana, 179
Rogers-Sirten, Ronnie E., 444
Rogers, Allison, 414
Rogers, Angie, 206
Rogers, Bathsheba, 199
Rogers, Beth, 428
Rogers, Bill, 278
Rogers, Brian, 396
Rogers, Carl W., 644, 647, 648, 649, 650
Rogers, Christopher, 158
Rogers, Courtney, 1023, 1024, 1025
Rogers, Dale, 726
Rogers, David, 6
Rogers, David M., 773, 775
Rogers, Earline S., 687, 689, 690, 691
Rogers, Greg, 34, 458
Rogers, Hazelle P. "Hazel", 623, 628, 630
Rogers, Jerry, 471
Rogers, John, 281, 415
Rogers, John B., 213
Rogers, John H., 773, 775
Rogers, John M., 940, 943
Rogers, John W., Jr., 550, 554
Rogers, June, 8
Rogers, Karen Field, 77
Rogers, Katherine D., 864, 869
Rogers, Keith, 197
Rogers, Kyndall, 29
Rogers, Margaret Ellis, 810, 812, 815, 816
Rogers, Megan, 275
Rogers, Michael, 951, 953, 954
Rogers, Randy, 382
Rogers, Ray, 810, 812, 813, 814, 815, 816
Rogers, Richard, 264

NAME INDEX

Soto Torres, Antonio Luis "Tony", 987, 988, 989, 990
Soto, Cynthia, 681, 682, 683, 684
Soto, Darren, 621, 622, 623
Soto, Nery Adames, 411
Sotoa, Aliitama, 19
Sottile, F. Michael "Mike", 1007, 1009
Soublet, Brian, 49
Soucek, Dan, 910, 911, 912
Soucy, Donna M., 851, 852
Soucy, Timothy M., 865, 870
Souede, Benjamin, 390
Soufer, Eric, 343
Souki, Joseph M., 657, 659
Soules, William P., 881, 882
Soulier, Bennett J., 205
Soura, Christian L., 423
South, Dwalia Sherree, 268
South, Jeffrey "Jeff", 150
South, Kyle, 551, 553, 554
Southerland, Steve, 1017, 1018, 1019
Southern, Beth, 524
Southern, Justin, 524
Southern, Timothy "Tim", 433
Southworth, Adrienne, 195
Southworth, Peter, 37
Southworth, Tom, 865, 870
Souza, Debbie, 419
Souza, Kathleen F., 865, 868
Souza, Mary, 663
Sowada, Kate, 193
Sowell, Wayne, 322
Sowersby, Beverly "Bev", 338
Sox, Stephanie, 421
Space, F. Parker, 877, 878, 879
Spacek, David T., 150
Spackman, Gary, 137
Spadaccini, Matthew, 314
Spadoni, Wendy, 31
Spagnola, Joshua, 106
Spalding, Teresa, 249
Spalj, Mike, 56
Spalla, Jim, 105
Spallone, James Field, 73
Spang, Judith T., 865, 870
Spangler, Donna, 471
Spangler, Marcia, 172
Spangler, Matt, 393
Spann-Downing, Tracy, 91
Spann-Nicholas, Wonza, 225
Spann, Caprice G., 340
Spannknebel, Paul, 136
Spano, Jake, 263
Spano, Jim, 56
Spano, COL Robert, 52
Spano, Ross, 629, 630
Spanos, Peter, 865, 869
Sparing, BG Robert A. "Bob", 284
Sparks, Abigail "Abby", 445
Sparks, Cassie, 177
Sparks, Catherine "Cathy", 416
Sparks, Cheryl M., 226
Sparks, Dan, 788, 789, 790
Sparks, Eric S., 26
Sparks, John, 944, 946, 947
Sparks, Michael F., 4
Sparks, Mike, 1023, 1025
Sparks, Mitchell, 395
Sparrow, Craig, 434
Spartz-Campbell, Tracy, 13
Sparveri, Gloria, 73
Spaulding, Col. Gene, 102
Spaulding, Jim, 87
Spaulding, Randy, 509
Spaw, Patsy, 1026
Speaks, Nelda, 579, 580, 581
Spear, Ken, 537

Speares, Scott, 425
Spearman, Molly M., 422
Spearman, Pastor Patricia "Pat", 846, 847
Spears, Amanda, 191
Spears, David B., 491
Spears, Linda, 236
Spears, Mable, 98
Speciale, Michael, 918, 920, 921, 922, 923, 924
Speech, Tom, 528
Speedy, Michael "Mike", 696, 697, 698
Speer, Alfred W., 737
Speer, Don, 187
Speer, Jacob, 164
Speers, Jay, 343
Speigle, Dan, 511
Speir, John, 229
Speliotis, Theodore C., 773, 774
Spellman, Debra, 56
Spellman, Maribeth, 478
Spence, Douglas H., 519
Spence, Jon, 141
Spence, Logan, 467
Spence, Stephen E., 514
Spencer, Bob, 137
Spencer, Bryan, 827, 829, 831
Spencer, Carl, 832
Spencer, Gabe, 508
Spencer, Garth A., Jr., 75
Spencer, Jason, 58, 645, 648, 649, 650, 651
Spencer, L. Grace, 874, 877, 878
Spencer, Lisa, 443
Spencer, COL Thomas, 303
Spencer, COL Tracy, 381
Spendlove, Robert M., 1044, 1045
Sperbeck, Erika, 56
Spespy, Julia, 99
Speyerer, Diane, 440
Spicher, Wendy S., 401
Spicola, Ashley, 99
Spicola, William, 99
Spiegel, Ellen Barre, 848, 849
Spiegelman, Jeffrey N., 617, 618
Spielberg, Leah, 60
Spiess, Rebecca, 63
Spila, Danielle, 407
Spilka, Karen E., 765, 766, 767
Spill, Jeffrey D., 303
Spillane, Ann, 153
Spillane, James, 865, 869
Spillane, Shaun, 53
Spillars, Andrea, 274
Spilman, Ronald "Ron", 322
Spindler, Robin, 289
Spires, Kim, 428
Spires, Lawrence Kit, 1007, 1009
Spiros, John, 1098, 1100, 1101, 1102
Spitzberg, Sam, 340
Spitzer, Stuart, 1035, 1036, 1037
Spitzley, John, 249
Spivey, Billy, 1023, 1025
Splinter, Garth L., 386
Spohnholz, Ivy, 559, 560
Sponaugle, Isaac, 1087, 1088, 1089, 1090
Sponholtz, Warren, 101
Sponseller, Bart, 528
Sponseller, Roger, 391
Spooner, Renee, 475
Sporlein, Barbara, 262
Spotts, M. Caroline, 691
Spottswood, Robert A., 107
Sprager, Meghan, 530
Sprague, Dale R., 865, 869
Sprague, Kaitlyn, 231

Sprague, Robert, 941, 942
Spraker, Kelly, 490
Spratling, Boyd, 297
Spratt, Tyrone, 256
Spreitzer, Mark, 1098, 1101, 1102
Sprengeler, Stacy, 537
Sprenger, Sherrie, 957, 959, 960
Spriggs, Sareeta, 84
Spriggs, Timothy, 95
Springer, Christine, 26
Springer, Darren M., 478
Springer, Drew, 1035, 1036, 1038
Springer, Gary, 398
Springer, Katherine "Katie", 165
Springer, Larry, 1073, 1077, 1078, 1079
Springer, Ryan, 91
Springer, Tina, 298
Springsteen, John, 12
Sprinkle, Michael "Mike", 848, 849, 850
Sproat, James P., 339
Sproat, Scott, 380
Sprowls, Chris, 629, 630
Spruill, Chet, 349
Spruill, Jack, 120
Spruill, Lionell, Sr., 1066, 1067, 1068
Spurling, James, 53
Squadron, Daniel, 887, 891, 892, 893, 894
Squatrito, Jerome, 417
Squires, Keith, 474
Sreden, Noa Ann, 210
Srednicki, Edward B., 240
Sredzinski, J.P., 607, 609, 611
S'Renco, Drew, 386
Srinivasan, Prasad, 607, 609, 611
St. Amour, Kenneth, 482
St. Germain, Karen Gaudet, 203
St. Martin, Michael, 417
Staab, Joy, 527
Staats, Craig T., 976, 977, 978, 979
Stabler, Stan, 4
Stachon, Eva, 153
Stack, Brian P., 872, 873
Stack, Michael J. "Mike", III, 409, 961
Stackhouse, Major Diane M., 409
Stackpole, Matthew, 320
Stacks, Robert "Bob", 178
Stacks, Sherri, 574
Stadelman, Chris, 513
Stadelman, Steve, 672, 673, 674, 675
Stadick Smith, Mary, 432
Staed, Art, 706, 708, 709
Staffanson, Scott, 839, 840, 841
Stafford, Cynthia A., 629, 630
Stafford, Lorna, 394
Stafstrom, Steven, 607, 609, 610
Stafursky, Josh, 288
Stagg, Joy D., 430
Stagg, Robert B., 496
Stagnolia, Reecie D., 183
Stah-Cooper, Sue, 342
Staheli, Andrea, 471
Stahle, Diane, 171
Staiert, Suzanne, 66
Stair, LaVonne, 358
Stakem, Bernard "Bernie", 406
Stakem, James J., 227
Staks, Kathleen, 62
Staley, Cory, 149
Staley, Danny, 350
Stall, Linda, 44

Stall, Robert, 537
Stallworth, Charles L. "Charlie", 601, 607, 608, 609, 610
Stalzer, Jim, 1015, 1016
Stam, Paul, 913, 919, 920, 921, 922, 923, 924
Stamas, Jim, 776, 777, 778, 779
Stambaugh, Melanie, 1077, 1078, 1079
Stamnas, Peter, 307
Stamp, Clay B., 216
Stanard, Jon E., 1044, 1045, 1046
Stanard, Michael J., 274
Stancil, Elmer, 118
Stancil, Steven L. "Steve", 117
Stanczyk, Major Russell, 294
Standifer, Selena, 273
Standridge, David, 551, 552, 553
Standridge, Greg, 573, 574
Standridge, Rob, 944, 946, 947
Stanek, Cate, 60
Stanerson, Quentin, 707, 708, 709
Staneski, Pam, 607, 608, 609, 612
Stanevich, Ron L., 521
Stanfield, Mary, 63
Stanfield, Meredith, 103
Stanfield, Reginald, 221
Stanford, Bronwyn, 100
Stanford, Derek, 1077, 1078
Stanford, Susan, 462
Stang, Charles, 366
Stanger, COL Christopher S., 33
Stangl, Karin, 328
Staniforth, Jonathan, 536
Stanislaus, Dr. Angeline, 279
Stanislaus, Selvi, 43
Stanislawski, Gary, 946, 947
Stanko, Ronald "Ron", III, 400
Stanley, Amanda, 159, 162
Stanley, Christina, 67
Stanley, Craig, 386
Stanley, Donald, 171
Stanley, Spencer, 386
Stanley, Stephen S., 751
Stanley, Thomas M., 774, 775
Stanley, Vicki, 351
Stanley, Warren, 50
Stanley, William M. "Bill", Jr., 1058, 1060, 1061
Stansbury, Chris, 1087, 1089, 1090
Stansbury, Kayla, 177
Stanton, Bettye, 450
Stanton, Cheryl M., 423
Stanton, Tammy, 443
Stanton, Terry, 253
Stanton, Ty, 402
Staples, Gary V., 811, 812, 815
Staples, Kelly, 189
Staples, Dr. Steven R., 491
Staples, Theresa, 63
Stapleton, Sheryl Williams, 882, 885, 886
Stapleton, Trey, 108
Stapleton, Walker R., 66
Stapp, Jennie, 286
Stapp, Susan, 56
Stargel, Kelli, 621, 622, 623
Starghill, Catherine, 313
Stark, Cindy, 137
Stark, Duane A., 959, 960
Stark, Jim, 160
Stark, Regina, 511
Stark, Richard N. "Rick", 629, 630

Stark, Suzanne, 61
Starkey, David, 430
Starkey, Elayne, 75
Starkey, Jonathan, 81
Starks, Ann, 7
Starks, David, 48
Starks, Dennis J., 94
Starnes, Anthony "Tony", 445
Starnes, Sandra, 107
Starr, Amy, 292
Starr, Brantley, 467
Starr, Chuck, 290
Starr, Jenny, 260
Starr, Mark, 45
Starr, Robert A., Jr., 1047, 1048
Starr, Sanford, 370
Starry, Joe, 156
Statham, Kevin, 382
Statkus, Carol A., 534
Statler, James F., 187
Statler, Joe, 1087, 1088, 1089, 1090
Staton, Lt. Col. David, 203
Staton, Donna Hill, 230
Staton, W. Rick, 519
Statton, Jerry, 387
Staubitz, Andy, 1069
Staudt, Quinn L., 331
Stauffacher, Bob, 538
Stauffer, Kent T., 344
Stausboll, Anne, 43
Stavisky, Toby Ann, 887, 891, 892, 893, 894
Stavrinakis, Leonidas E. "Leon", 1007, 1008, 1009
Steadman, M. Patrick "Pat", 594, 595
Steagall, Todd, 427
Steans, Heather A., 672, 673, 674
Steanson, Howard L., 176
Stearn, R. Gwenn, 420
Stearns, Chris, 508
Stearns, David, 538
Stearns, Paul, 751
Steavens, Erik, 464
Stebbins, Katie, 238
Steben, Robert "Bob", 173
Stec, Daniel G., 901, 903, 904, 906
Steck, Phillip G. "Phil", 901, 903, 905, 907
Steckelberg, Larry, 253
Steckler, Tom, 110
Steckman, Sharon S., 703, 707, 708, 709
Stedman, Bert, 556, 557
Stedman, Stuart West, 465
Steece, Richard, 443
Steed, Robert E., 477
Steele Danner, Kathleen "Katie", 276
Steele, Brent E., 687, 689, 690, 691
Steele, Elizabeth, 245
Steele, Fitz, 730, 731, 732, 733
Steele, Fred, 390
Steele, Georgia, 116
Steele, Jen, 201
Steele, Jim, 10
Steele, Peter, 208
Steele, Steven, 485
Steele, Susan, 533
Steele, Tracy L., 36
Steeley, James H., 407
Steen, Fred Franklin, II, 346
Steen, Ida Clement, 457
Steen, John T., Jr., 465
Steen, John Thomas, III, 463
Steenberg, Tom, 839, 840, 841
Steenblock, Terri, 260
Steenson, Naomi R., 392
Steer, Susan, 368
Stefan, Michael "Mike", 404

Thompson, Christine "Chris", 481
Thompson, Cindy, 421
Thompson, Curt, 634, 635, 636
Thompson, Darwin, 478
Thompson, David "Dave", 788, 789, 790
Thompson, COL David E., 195
Thompson, Dawn, 79
Thompson, Deborah, 440
Thompson, Ed, 1035, 1037, 1038
Thompson, Ed J., 344
Thompson, Ellen, 1102
Thompson, Erin, 326
Thompson, Francis C., 735, 736
Thompson, Gary L., 518
Thompson, Geraldine F. "Geri", 621, 622, 623
Thompson, Jason, 268
Thompson, Jeff, 667, 668
Thompson, Jeffrey A. "Jeff", 696, 697, 698
Thompson, Jeffrey S., 171
Thompson, Jennifer B., 272
Thompson, John J., 162
Thompson, J.S. "Bud", 198
Thompson, Julio A., 483
Thompson, Kelli S., 532
Thompson, Kendra, 193
Thompson, Kent, 719, 721, 722
Thompson, Kevin, 50
Thompson, Lakisha, 91
Thompson, LaTrece, 156
Thompson, Lei S., 19
Thompson, Lisa, 253
Thompson, Lisa M., 518
Thompson, Lowell, 260
Thompson, Marcus, 96
Thompson, Margaret, 408
Thompson, Maria S., 350
Thompson, Mark "Mat", 120
Thompson, Mark, 146, 223
Thompson, Mary Jo, 514
Thompson, Megan, 176
Thompson, Michael "Mike", 533
Thompson, Michael C. "Mike", 378, 382
Thompson, Michelle, 489
Thompson, Mick, 379, 383, 386
Thompson, Mike, 291
Thompson, Nicki Ann, 131
Thompson, Nikki D., 259
Thompson, Patti, 151
Thompson, Paul, 120, 388
Thompson, Perry, 483
Thompson, Roger, 946, 947
Thompson, Ruth, 450
Thompson, Ryan J., 370
Thompson, Sakina, 90
Thompson, Samuel D., 872, 873
Thompson, Sandi, 450
Thompson, Sandra, 8
Thompson, Scott, 380
Thompson, Sean, 310
Thompson, Senfronia, 1035, 1037, 1038
Thompson, Shawn, 342
Thompson, Sheryl D., 249
Thompson, Sid, 398
Thompson, Steve M., 559, 560
Thompson, Thomas N. "Tommy", 730, 731, 732, 733
Thompson, Tony, 88
Thompson, Troy, 403
Thompson, Tyrone, 848, 849
Thompson, Willie R., 268
Thomsen, Chuck, 956
Thomsen, Paul, 300

Thomsen, Todd, 952, 953, 954
Thomson, Donald, 435
Thomson, Herb, 213
Thomson, John C., 70
Thomson, Lisa A., 423
Thomson, Margaret, 167
Thomson, Michael D. "Mike", 279
Thomson, Will, 62
Thoreson, Blair, 931, 932
Thorley, Wayne, 301
Thornbrue, Janette, 385
Thornhill, Carla, 272
Thornhill, Curtis, 267
Thornley, Jared, 150
Thornquist, John, 502
Thornton, Amy, 179
Thornton, Charles, 84
Thornton, David, 263
Thornton, Joseph C., 518
Thornton, William "Bill", 279
Thornton, William, 279
Thorpe, Bob, 570, 571
Thorpe, Jeannie, 499
Thorson, Beth, 454
Thorson, Len C., 363
Thottam, Benny, 344
Thrasher, James "Jim", 440
Three Stars, Lenore, 508
Threedy, David E., 501
Threlkel, Peter, 398
Threlkeld, Ray, 154
Threlkeld, Wendy, 428
Throener, Sara, 170
Throne, Mary A., 1104, 1107, 1108
Thronson, Eric, 51
Thronson, Stuart, 505
Throwe, Joanne M., 223
Thrower, Pat, 388
Thuet, Chad, 262
Thuma, Jennifer, 165
Thurber, Katie, 291
Thurlow, Dan, 597, 598
Thurman, David, 442
Thurman, Duane, 509
Thurman, Kim, 273
Thurmond, Paul R., 1000, 1001, 1002
Thurmond, Tony, 590, 591, 592
Thurnau, Carl, 345
Thurness, Codi, 176
Thurston, John M., 36
Thurston, Lindsay Hughes, 196
Thurston, Neva G., 278
Thurston, Norman K. "Norm", 1044, 1045, 1046
Tibbitts-Nutt, Monica, 242
Ticehurst, Susan, 866, 869
Tiche, Eric, 53
Tichota, Ken, 289
Tidball-Zeltinger, Brenda, 434
Tidball, Jennifer, 277
Tidemann, Larry J., 1011, 1012
Tidwell, Donna G., 443
Tidwell, Norman, 447
Tiedemann, Gina, 112
Tiedje, Marjorie, 13
Tiemeyer, Richard, 278
Tierney, James M., 333
Tierney, Karyn, 33
Tieszen, Craig, 1011, 1012
Tietz, Pam, 508
Tietze, Annie, 719, 720, 721, 722
Tiffany, Gabriel, 47
Tiffany, Thomas "Tom", 1092, 1093
Tifimalae Ale, Ale, 20
Tilden, Dr. John D., 247
Tilei, Laupule, 19
Till, Angela, 3

Till, George W., 1054, 1056
Tiller, Stephanie R., 518
Tillery, Ann, 291
Tillett, Rochelle, 505
Tilley, John C., 189
Tillison, Paula, 385
Tillman, Charmin, 267
Tillman, Jerry W., 907, 910, 911, 912
Tillman, Sherry, 94
Tilly, David, 169
Tilly, Megan, 388
Tilsen, Josh L., 262
Tilton, Ben, 866, 869
Tilton, Cathy, 559, 560
Tilton, Franklin T., 866, 869
Tilton, Rio, 866, 868
Timberger, David, 458
Timberlake, Daniel S. "Dan", 493
Timberlake, James, 468
Timberlake, Jeffrey L., 751, 752
Timbs, Wheeler Timothy "Tim", III, 268
Timian, Robert, 359
Timilty, James E., 766, 767
Timilty, Walter F., Jr., 774, 775
Timm, Patricia, 294
Timmerman, Chad, 161
Timmerman, Kristi, 439
Timmons, Brock, 121
Timmons, BrigGen Carol, 78
Timmons, Michael, 751, 752
Timmons, Capt. Paul, 382
Timmons, Saree, 16
Timmons, Scott, 501
Timmons, Trevor, 66
Timony, Erin D., 523
Timpf, Edward A., 253
Tincher, David R., 513
Tincher, Deborah, 520
Tincher, Jaime, 255
Tindell, Sean J., 803, 804, 805
Tinderholt, Tony, 1035, 1036
Tine, Paul, 919, 920, 921, 922, 923, 924
Ting, David, 40
Ting, Philip Y. "Phil", 590, 591, 592, 593
Tingerthal, Mary, 262
Tingle, Casey, 198
Tinitali, Dr. Matautu "Peter", 19
Tinker, Scott W., 457
Tinkham, COL Cynthia, 381
Tinkler, Mary, 1008, 1009
Tinsley-Talabi, Alberta, 783, 784
Tinsley, Karen, 369
Tinsley, Sue, 286
Tippets, John H., 135
Tipping-Spitz, Ryan D., 751
Tippins, Lindsey, 634, 635, 636, 637
Tipton, James A., 730, 731
Tipton, Roy M., 273
Tirado Rivera, Cirilo, 982, 983, 984
Tirocchi, Lisa, 417
Titone, Matthew, 902, 904, 905, 906, 907
Tittl, Paul, 1099, 1100, 1101, 1102
Tittle, Christy, 160
Titus, Michele R., 902, 903, 904, 905
Titus, Robin L., 849, 850
Titus, Sally, 170
Titze, Tina, 434
Tivnan, Kevin M., 233
Tivnan, Maureen, 481
To, Trang, 54
Toal, Russell, 324
Tobash, Mike, 976, 977, 978, 979, 980

Tobe, Richard, 341
Tobia, John, 629, 630
Tobias, Priscilla, 150
Tobin, Andrew M. "Andy", 26
Tobin, L. Michael, 532
Tobon, Carlos E., 996, 997
Toche, Diana, 51
Todacheene, Heidi, 324
Todaro, Don, 254
Todd, Brandon T., 86
Todd, Connie, 361
Todd, Curry, 1023, 1024, 1025
Todd, Cynthia, 451
Todd, David, 438
Todd, David P., 401
Todd, James, 719, 721, 722
Todd, Nancy J., 594, 595
Todd, Patricia, 551, 552, 554
Todd, Sheridan, 536
Todman, Adrianne, 97
Todman, Rochelle, 485
Todorovich, Jessica, 504
Toepel, Marcy, 976, 978, 979, 980
Tofau, Gaoteote Palaie, 560, 561
Tofiga-Matagi, Ruth, 19
Toguchi, Pamela A., 131
Tokioka, James Kunane, 659, 660, 661
Tokuda, Jill N., 655, 656
Tolbert, Shannon, 439
Toleno, Tristan D., 1054, 1055
Tolkoff, Andrew, 345
Toll, Catherine Beattie "Kitty", 1054, 1055
Toll, Sandi, 331
Tollefsrud, Tim, 432
Tolley, Karen, 220
Tolley, Lisa, 349
Tollison, Gray, 803, 804, 805, 806
Tolliver, Doris, 156
Tolman, Dave, 140
Tolmich, Kevin, 113
Tolson, Deborah L., 221
Tolson, Karen, 83
Tolstad, Ron, 364
Tom, Kerry, 130
Tom, Maeley L., 43
Toman, Nathan P., 931, 932, 933
Tomasi, Tom R., 481
Tomassini, Phil, 406
Tomassone, Joseph "Joe", 338
Tomassoni, David J., 262, 788, 789, 790
Tomblin, Earl Ray, 513
Tomczak, Karen, 349
Tome, Rachelle, 210
Tomes, Jim, 687, 689, 690, 691
Tomlin, Alexandria "Alex", 321
Tomlin, Christopher, 314
Tomlinson, Christopher "Chris", 117, 118
TomLinson, Danny, 60
Tomlinson, Michele, 139
Tomlinson, Robert M., 963, 964, 965
Tommelleo, Donna, 70
Tompkin, Cheryl R., 41
Tonaki, Donna, 129
Tonaki, John M., 129
Tondee, Sharon Renee, 99
Toner, Ed, 289
Toner, Paul F., 234
Toner, Stacy, 13
Toney, Bruce, 465
Toney, Dr. Denise, 489
Toney, Ellyn, 203
Tong, Amy, 42
Tong, Tu, 262

Tong, William M., 607, 609, 610
Tongate, Butch, 322
Tonkovich, Alexa, 12
Tonnon Byers, Anne, 1094
Tonumaipe'a, Ueligitone, 19
Toohil, Tarah, 976, 977, 979, 980
Tooker, Megan, 174
Toole, McLain R. "Mac", 1008, 1009
Toole, Robert W., 386
Toole, Steve, 357
Tooley, Michael T., 285
Toombs, Kwasi, 520
Toomer, Raymond, 338
Toomey, Bill, 518
Toomey, Bob, 421
Toomey, Timothy J., Jr., 774
Toone, Robert E. "Robin", Jr., 242
Toopetlook, John, 17
Topol, Amy, 110
Topper, Curtis "Curt", 403
Topper, Jesse, 976, 978, 979, 980
Toppin, Gina, 95
Tops, Terrell, 85
Torbett, John A., 919, 920, 921, 923, 924
Torgersen, Carl, 48
Torgerson, Loren, 512
Torgerson, Mark, 14
Torgerson, Sharon, 236
Torian, Luke E., 1066, 1067, 1068
Torkelson, Paul, 797, 798, 799, 800
Torlakson, Thomas "Tom", 42, 58
Torlone, Kathy A., 520
Tormey, Ed, 171
Tornillo, Robert, 108
Tornini, Ruben, 386
Toro, Matthew, 419
Toro, Pamela J., 414
Torpey, Mark R., 340
Torr, Gerald R. "Jerry", 696, 697, 698
Torraco, Lisa A., 881, 882
Torre, Greg, 114
Torrence, Terri, 265
Torres Barreto, Brenda, 330
Torres Calderón, Héctor A., 987, 988, 989
Torres Cruz, Luis Raul, 987, 988, 989
Torres-Diaz, Miguel, 412
Torres Ramírez, Jose R. "Pito", 987, 989
Torres Ray, Patricia, 788, 789, 790
Torres Yordán, Nelson, 987, 988, 989
Torres, Aníbal José "Jossie", 981, 982, 984
Torres, Annjenette, 325
Torres, Daniel, 37
Torres, Henry, 116
Torres, Jared, 100
Torres, Jesse, 38
Torres, Linda, 310
Torres, Lori A., 521
Torres, Mary Camacho, 652, 653, 654
Torres, Michael, 45
Torres, Victor Manuel "Vic", Jr., 629, 630
Torres, Vincent A., 320
Torrey, Kim, 179
Torrijos, Javier, 81
Toryanski, Kim Wherry, 141
Tosado, Jose F., 774, 775
Toscano, David J., 1061, 1066, 1067, 1068, 1069
Tosh, Dwight, 579, 580, 581
Toteff, Sally, 503
Touchet-Morgan, Elizabeth, 203

Vignati, Joe, 115
Vigneau, Paul, 241
Vigue, Michael "Mike", 16
Vikram, Abhisek, 409
Villa, Anne G., 200
Villa, Dan J., 281
Villa, David, 532
Villa, Susan, 40
Villaflor, Bienvenido C., 654
Villagrana, Hector, 147
Villalba, Jason, 1036, 1037
Villalpando, Nick, 455
Villanueva-Matkovich, Karen, 516
Villanueva, Ronald A., 1066, 1067, 1069
Villegas-Reimers, Eleonora, 233
Vincelli, Nick, 356
Vincent, Chas V., 834, 835
Vincent, Gregory, 67
Vincent, Jaclyn, 227
Vincent, John, 532
Vincent, Maria, 256
Vincent, Micah, 161
Vincent, Michael, 127
Vincent, RoseLee, 774
Vinehout, Kathleen, 1091, 1092, 1093
Vines, John T., 579, 580
Viniard, Scott, 147
Vinson, Lori, 247
Vinson, Patricia, 5
Vinson, Stevi, 382
Viola, John, 235
Viola, John J., 615, 617, 618
Virbel, Jay, 51
Virgin, Emily, 952, 954
Viscoli, Sergio J., 321
Vise, Ryan, 452
Viswanathan, Karthik, 232
Vitale, A. Nino, 941, 943
Vitale, Joseph F., 873
Vitali, Gregory S., 976, 978
Vivao, Reno, 20
Vivian, Rob, 309
Vlaminck, Jeff, 261
Vo, Hubert, 1036, 1037
Vocke, Judge Timothy, 532
Vodicka, Steve, 289
Vogel, Bob, 797, 798, 799
Vogel, Elder, Jr., 963, 964, 965
Vogel, Jeannie, 438
Vogel, Jeff, 176
Vogel, Jeffrey C. "Jeff", 535
Vogel, Jill Holtzman, 1060, 1061
Vogel, Nancy, 46
Vogelpohl, Carl, 35
Vogler, Hank, 297
Vogt, David Edward, III, 761, 762
Vogt, Jeff, 260
Voigt, David, 263
Voigt, Faleosina, 19
Voitier, Doris, 207
Volesky, Mike, 283
Volk, Amy Fern, 745
Volkman, Dr. David, 409
Volodarski, Alex, 117
Volpe, Maria, 416
Volturo, Stephanie, 81
Volz, James, 483
Von Flatern, Michael, 1103, 1104
von Gillern, R. Brad, 295
Von Moll, David A., 493
von Pier, Lisa, 310
Von Ruden, Mary, 531
Von Steigleder, Eric, 491
von Tagen, William "Bill", 142
von Wolffradt, Robert "Bob", 171, 173
Vonderheide, Michael, 322
Vonderweidt, Chris, 212

Vontz, Kathi, 295
VonWeisenstein, LTC Thomas W., 445
Voorhees, Robert F., 313
Voorhies, Edwin, 372
Vorachek, Amy, 359
Vorona, Nancy, 498
Vorpagel, Tyler, 1099, 1101
Vorsiek, Brenda L., 105
Vorters, Dian M., 41
Vos, Robin, 1094, 1099, 1101
Vosberg, Myles, 365
Vosburg, Chad, 204
Vosburg, Christie Henke, 39
Vosburg, Kurt R., 292
Vose, Michael, 867, 870
Voss, Chris, 235
Vosters, Jonathan "Jon", 536
Vouk, Elizabeth, 319
Vourvopoulos, Karen, 369
Vovokes, Michael, 404
Vowell, Jeff, 110
Voyles, Larry D., 26
Vrabely, Joseph, 73
Vu, Kim, 292
Vuckovich, Gene, 834, 835
Vukmir, Leah, 1091, 1093
Vulakovich, Randy, 963, 964, 965
Vullo, Maria T., 333, 341
Vura-Weis, Lisa, 413
Vyncke, Rick, 60

**W**

Waalkes, Marie L., 252
Wachs, Dana J., 1099, 1100, 1101
Wachter, Michelle, 526
Wack, Wendy, 473
Waddell, Anthony L., 97
Waddell, Joyce, 910, 911, 912, 913
Waddell, Julie, 161
Waddell, Ken, 919, 920, 921, 922, 923, 924
Waddell, Michael, 385
Waddell, Tiffany, 217
Waddell, Tim, 173
Waddle, Daniel J., 292
Wade, Brent, 458
Wade, Chris, 76
Wade, Dale, 12
Wade, Dotti L., 94
Wade, Katharine L. "Katie", 70
Wade, Leroy, 279
Wade, Mark, 427
Wade, Pat, 444
Wade, Richard, 467
Wade, Ronn, 220
Wade, Stephen, 510
Wade, Dr. Trudy, 910, 911, 912, 913
Wadhams, Emily E., 480
Wadlington, Terry, 372
Wadsworth, Nathan, 752
Wadsworth, Tim, 551, 552, 553, 554
Wagaman, Jeff, 180
Wagenius, Jean, 797, 798, 799, 800
Wagenseller, Elizabeth Gerloff "Liz", 409
Waggoner, Connie, 148
Waggoner, J. T. "Jabo", 544, 545, 546
Waggoner, Lt. Col. Larry, 266
Waggoner, Olivia, 434
Wagle, Susan, 709, 711, 712
Wagley, Marisa Lopez, 455
Wagner, A.J., 376
Wagner, Bruce, 214
Wagner, Bryan W., 489
Wagner, Camille, 37
Wagner, Carol, 395

Wagner, Danny, 1087, 1088, 1090
Wagner, Don, 506
Wagner, Donald P. "Don", 590, 591, 592, 593
Wagner, Eric, 79, 146
Wagner, Frank W., 1060, 1061
Wagner, J. Harold, 153
Wagner, Joseph F., 774, 775
Wagner, Ken, 415
Wagner, Mark, 362
Wagner, Nick, 168
Wagner, Dr. Nick, 367
Wagner, Robert, 247
Wagner, Robin, 201
Wagner, Rod G., 293
Wagner, R. Thomas "Tom", Jr., 82
Wagner, Scott, 963, 964, 965
Wagner, Todd, 256
Wagoner, Kirk B., 839, 840, 841
Wagoner, Toby D., 517
Wagstaff, Tina, 357
Wahl, Jason, 364
Wahl, Kathy, 249
Wahl, Richard, 168
Wahley, Rex, 349
Wahlgren, Wesley W., 292
Wahlin, Tim, 363
Waihe'e, John D., IV, 133
Wainscott, Heather, 189
Wainwright, Dale, 465
Wainwright, George L., Jr., 353
Waite, Shawn N., 394
Waites, Keisha, 645, 649, 650, 651
Waites, Robert G. "Bobby", 264
Waites, Thad F., 268
Wakai, Glenn, 655, 656
Wakayama, Kevin, 132
Wakefield, Nedra, 121
Wakefield, Victor, 300
Wakeham, Joanne, 494
Wakeland, Rich, 463
Wakeling, Brian, 299
Wakeman, Marjorie, 70
Waki, David "Dave", 391
Walachy, Mary E., 293
Walaska, William A., 990, 992
Walb, Valerie, 371
Walborn, Gene, 285
Walburn, Julie, 368
Walcott, Cynthia "Cindy", 479
Wald, Donnita, 365
Wald, Sherri, 436
Walden-Newman, Michael, 293
Walden, Michael, 445
Waldron, Marie, 585, 590, 591, 592, 593
Waldron, Marijane K., 515
Waldron, Martha, 235
Waldrop, Alan, 466
Waldrop, Dr. Karen, 193
Waldrop, Major Tommy, 115
Waldstreicher, Jeffrey D. "Jeff", 761, 762
Walela, Irene Mary, 45
Walend, Trudi, 346
Wales, Gus, 199
Walisky, Irene, 471
Walke, Peter, 330
Walkenhorst, Steve, 477
Walker-Tolles, Erin, 13
Walker, Alexandra J., 60
Walker, Brady, 218
Walker, Brent H., 521
Walker, Bruce, 522
Walker, Caroline "Callie", 110
Walker, Christopher, 120

Walker, Claude E., 485
Walker, Cliff, 8
Walker, David Stevenson, 355
Walker, Deborah, 279
Walker, Debra, 8, 156, 355
Walker, Earl, 266
Walker, Elda, 384
Walker, Ernie R., 72
Walker, George, 355
Walker, Greg, 689, 690, 691
Walker, James "Jim", 394
Walker, Jamie, 16
Walker, Jason, 176
Walker, Jay, 761, 763
Walker, Jeff, 466
Walker, Jim, 268
Walker, Johnnie, 97
Walker, John W., 579, 580, 581
Walker, Jonathan, 199
Walker, Joseph, 475
Walker, Joy R., 753
Walker, Justin, 273
Walker, Ken, 952, 954
Walker, Kenneth, 811, 812, 813, 816
Walker, Kevin, 315
Walker, Larry, III, 634, 636, 637
Walker, Latrice, 902, 903, 904, 905
Walker, Lisa, 451
Walker, Mark, 372
Walker, Mary, 115, 446
Walker, Melissa, 323
Walker, Nate, 827, 829, 830, 832
Walker, Pamela, 350
Walker, Dr. Robert B., 522
Walker, Robert Lee, 496
Walker, Ron, 277
Walker, Ronald L. "Ron", II, 240
Walker, Roxann, 36
Walker, Scott K., 525, 526
Walker, Shawn, 497
Walker, Steve, 85
Walker, Steven, 271
Walker, Susan, 324
Walker, Susan V., 442
Walker, Suzanne, 164
Walker, Tammie, 13
Walker, Todd, 368, 375
Walker, Toni Edmonds, 607, 608, 610
Walker, Wayne, 9
Walker, BG William, 98
Walker, William M. "Bill", 10
Walkinshaw, Brady Piñero, 1077, 1078
Wall, Ann, 357
Wall, Ashbel T., II, 414
Wall, Janet G., 867, 869
Wall, Jeff, 57
Wall, MAJ Robert S., 417
Wall, Dr. Sharon, 429
Wall, Tod, 378
Wall, William, 440
Wallace, Antoinette, 368
Wallace, Dave, 579, 580
Wallace, Dawn, 21
Wallace, Lt Cdr Deborah, 111
Wallace, Edward "Ed", 173
Wallace, Elizabeth, 154
Wallace, James P., 217
Wallace, Jimmy, 451
Wallace, Kevin, 952, 953, 954
Wallace, Kim, 440
Wallace, La Quita, 45
Wallace, Larry, 57
Wallace, Litesa E., 681, 682, 683, 684, 685
Wallace, Marian, 467
Wallace, Maynard, 279
Wallace, Meghan, 75

Wallace, Monna, 241
Wallace, Raymond A. "Ray", 752
Wallace, Sonja, 34
Wallace, Steven, 140
Wallack, Anya Rader, 419
Walle, Armando, 1036, 1037
Wallen, Karen, 141
Waller-Dakwa, Stacey K., 9
Waller, Joshua, 122
Waller, Melissa, 357
Waller, Patricia, 98
Waller, Shelley, 384
Waller, Travis, 470
Wallin-Rohmann, Andrea, 42
Wallin, Jeffrey, 482
Wallin, John, 595
Wallin, Warren, 342
Wallingford, Wayne, 818, 819
Wallman, Kris, 931, 932, 933
Wallner, Mary Jane, 867, 869, 870
Walrath, Col Justin, 536
Walsh, Bennett, 238
Walsh, Chris, 774, 775
Walsh, Debra, 369
Walsh, Edward, 332
Walsh, Jason, 16
Walsh, John J., 246
Walsh, Kimberly A., 517
Walsh, Lawrence "Larry", Jr., 682, 683, 685, 686
Walsh, Linda, 13
Walsh, Maureen, 1077, 1078
Walsh, Michael A., 402
Walsh, Pamela "Pam", 302
Walsh, Regina "Gina", 816, 818, 819
Walsh, Robert M., Jr., 867, 869
Walsh, Rosa, 100
Walsh, Thomas, 774
Walsh, Thomas C., 867, 870
Walston, Charles, 351
Walston, Tom, 455
Walsworth, Mike A., 735, 736, 737
Walter, Chris, 53
Walter, Kelly, 153
Walter, Marissa, 366
Walter, Raymond W. "Ray", 902, 904, 905, 907
Walters, Betty, 17
Walters, Chip, 466
Walters, Chris W., 1081, 1082, 1083
Walters, Denise, 137
Walters, Joe, 497
Walters, Karen Stapf, 37, 58
Walters, Kevin, 439
Walters, Lyndsey, 143
Walters, Nancy, 262
Walters, Rebecca, 466
Walters, Ronald N. "Ron", 1088, 1089, 1090
Walters, Ryan, 190
Walters, Sheila K., 128
Walters, Tom, 1107, 1108
Walters, LTC Travis, 453
Walther, Larry W., 30
Walton Gray, Rochelle, 827, 830, 831
Walton, Doug, 106
Walton, John, 310
Walton, Leann, 159
Walton, Richard L., 499
Waltz, Brent, 689, 690, 691
Walz, Tommy J., 1054, 1055
Wambles, Don, 9
Wamsley, Scott, 248
Wandalowski, Quinn, 228
Wandell, Daniel C., 243
Wang, Cindy, 115
Wang, Lena L., 132
Wang, Yumei, 392

Weithman, Tom, 498
Weixel, Gordon, 361
Weizenbaum, Jon, 460
Welborn, Jeffrey W., 840, 841
Welch, Andrew J. "Andy", III, 646, 647, 649, 650
Welch, Bernadette, 445
Welch, David A., 867, 868
Welch, Emanuel Chris, 682, 683, 684, 685
Welch, James T., 766
Welch, Jim, 180
Welch, Leslie, 27
Welch, Liz, 800
Welch, Reginald, 265
Welch, Shawn, 259
Welch, William F., 763
Welcome, Shawn, 200
Weld, Ryan, 1088, 1089, 1090
Weldon, Tom, Jr., 637, 646, 647, 649, 650
Weldy, Pete, 157
Welk, Paul, 364
Welker, David M., 517
Welker, Dora, 152
Welker, Todd, 507, 512
Welks, Keith, 410
Wellborn, Sam M., 121
Welling, Kyleen, 165
Wellman, Dan, 150
Wellman, Howard, 1080
Wellner, Lt. Neil, 172
Wells, Alicia, 233
Wells, Cathy, 205
Wells, David, 154
Wells, Don L., 1008, 1009
Wells, Dr. Eden, 249
Wells, Elisa, 267
Wells, Florence, 495
Wells, James R. "Jim", 296
Wells, John, 273
Wells, Keith, 296
Wells, Ken, 398
Wells, Kevin, 210
Wells, Ralign T., 225
Wells, Todd A., 303
Wells, Tommy, 93
Wells, W. Andrew "Andy", Jr., 910, 911, 912
Wells, William L., 424
Welsch, Danika, 167
Welsh, Eileen, 79
Welsh, Col Gent, 505
Welsh, Joan W., 752
Welsh, Roderick, 1029
Wendland, Tim, 135
Wendtland, Kyle J., 535
Wenerowicz, Michael, 402
Weng-Gutierrez, Julie, 57
Weninger, Hal, 362
Weninger, Jeff, 570, 571
Wenk, Gordon, 247
Wenke, BrigGen Donald S., 15
Wensil, Lisa B., 520
Wente, Judy, 22
Wentling, Parke H., 977, 978, 979
Wentworth, Jason, 235
Wentzel, Paul H., Jr., 401
Wentzlass, Col James L., 259
Weprin, David I., 894, 902, 903, 904, 905, 907
Weprin, Mark S., 331
Werk, Elliot, 138
Werkheiser, William A. "Bill", 646, 648, 649, 651
Werman, Jeb, 512
Werner, David, 111
Werner, Dick, 1015, 1016
Werner, Keith E., 350
Wernert, John J., III, 162
Wersal, Lori, 532
Wertzler, Jon, 182
Werwie, Cullen, 526

Wery-Tagaban, Nicole, 11
Wesco, Timothy "Tim", 696, 697, 698
Wesley, Roy W., 53
Wesley, Serena, 390
Wesley, Steven, 77
Wesolowski, TeNeathia, 339
Wessel-Kroeschell, Beth, 707, 708, 709
Wesselhoft, Paul, 952, 953, 954
Wessels, Sue, 139
Wessler, Michael, 244
Wesson, James A., 496
West, Betsy, 354
West, Bruce, 259
West, Carol, 218
West, Christopher R., 761, 762
West, Felicia, 33
West, Gary, 439
West, Gary L., 439
West, Jim, 509
West, Johnathan R. "John", 218
West, Katie, 80
West, Kimberly, 242
West, Madeleine, 62
West, Michael, 259
West, Monieca, 32
West, Roger, 919, 920, 922, 924
West, Royce, 1028
West, Scott, 191
West, Sejal, 445
West, Stephen "Steve", 724, 725
West, Steven M., 477
West, Susan T., 198
West, Thomas M. "Tom", 184
West, William, 420
Westbrook, Jolette A., 236
Westby, Darin, 537
Westby, Kurt, 70
Westby, Misha, 534
Westerberg, Richard, 139
Westerfield, Whitney H., 724, 725, 726
Westerfield, William, 537
Western, Deea L., 456
Western, Jennifer, 529
Western, Kevin, 260
Westfall, Lana, 488
Westfall, BG Ronald A., 155
Westfall, Steve, 1088, 1089, 1090
Westin, Susan B., 398
Westlund, Roy A., 221
Westman, Richard A., 1048
Weston, Bruce, 374
Weston, Dennis, 13
Weston, Doris, 200
Weston, Michael, 45
Westra, Steven "Steve", 1012, 1015, 1016
Westrick-Corbin, Sara, 162
Westrin, James E., 297
Westrom, Susan, 731, 732
Westrom, Torrey, 789, 790
Westrup, Evan, 37
Westwood, Brad, 472
Westwood, John R., 1045, 1046
Weteling, Stephanie, 474
Wetlaufer, Jon, 170
Wetmore, Lou, 352
Wetz, Max, 361
Wetzel, Dale, 365
Wetzel, John E., 402
Wexton, Jennifer T., 1060, 1061
Weyand, Jason M., 397
Weyers, John, III, 191
Weyler, Kenneth L., 867, 869
Weyrich, Bob, 431
Whalen, Joseph F., 450
Whalen, Susan, 70

Whaley, Bernice, 75
Whaley, Chris A., 81
Whaley, James, 281
Whaley, Patricia, 113
Wharton, A. C., Jr., 448
Whatley, Kim M., 83
Whatley, Tom, 545, 546
Wheat, Thomas Craig, 460
Wheatley, Jake, Jr., 977, 978
Wheatley, Kimberly, 77
Wheatley, Mark A., 1045
Wheatly, Lt. Russ, 140
Wheaton, Bob, 248
Wheaton, Linda, 39
Wheeland, Jeff C., 977, 978, 979, 980
Wheeler, Barbara M., 682, 683, 684, 685
Wheeler, Bruce, 567, 570, 571
Wheeler, Cindy, 389
Wheeler, Clara Belle, 489
Wheeler, Dara, 49
Wheeler, David K. "Dave", 308
Wheeler, Deborah H., 867, 869
Wheeler, James R., 440
Wheeler, Janet, 531
Wheeler, Dr. J. Gary, 31
Wheeler, Jim, 847, 849
Wheeler, John, 284
Wheeler, Karen L., 539
Wheeler, Keith, 682, 683, 685, 686
Wheeler, Lisa, 46
Wheeler, Mary Gwen, 183
Wheeler, Sandy C., 391
Wheeler, Ted, 397, 399
Wheeler, Tom, 451
Whelan, Abigail, 797, 798, 799
Whelan, James "Jim", 873
Whelan, Margaret, 26
Whelan, Maureen, 77
Whelan, Timothy R. "Tim", 774
Whetstone, Eldon, 158
Whetstone, King, 401
Whidden, Christine, 69
Whilby, Leroy, 110
Whinnery, Melanie, 343
Whipper, Jackson Seth, 1008, 1009
Whipple, Brandon, 713, 719, 720, 722
Whipple, Craig, 481
Whipps Lee, Susannah, 774
Whisenhunt, Robert "Sterling", 102
Whisler, Eric, 438
Whisman, Ginnie, 368
Whisnant, Gene, 957, 959, 960
Whiston, Brian J., 254
Whitaker, David, 425
Whitaker, David Jeffrey, 574, 579, 580
Whitaker, Grant S., 477
Whitaker, Norris "Jim", 10
Whitaker, Scott, 191
Whitcomb, Dana, 338
Whitcomb, Kellie, 157
Whitcomb, Walter, 209
White, Lt. Col. Adam, 203
White, Andrew A. "Andy", 852, 867, 869
White, Ann, 476
White, Bill, 278
White, Brad, 502, 1088, 1089, 1090
White, Chris, 331
White, Cris A., 66
White, Daisy Sloan, 461
White, Dawn, 1019, 1023, 1024, 1025
White, Donald C., 963, 964, 965
White, Dustin Michael, 752

White, Eugene E., 515
White, Gannet N., 214
White, Sgt George M., 753
White, Glen, 291
White, Gordon, 503
White, Gregory, 238
White, Ingrid E., 303
White, Jacob, 505
White, James, 1036, 1037
White, James J., 225
White, LTC James W. "Jim", 172
White, Jason, 811, 812, 813, 814, 815, 816
White, Jay, 271
White, Jeanette K., 1048
White, Jesse, 153
White, Jill, 473
White, Jim, 1010, 1011
White, John C., 207
White, Jordan A., 475
White, Karen Farmer, 408
White, Kate, 49
White, Kenneth, 327
White, Kent B., 462
White, Kerry E., 840, 841
White, Larry, 205
White, Mack A. "Bodi", Jr., 736
White, Malinda Brumfield, 742, 743, 744
White, Mamie V., 494
White, Mark, 1023, 1024
White, Martina A., 977, 979, 980
White, Megan, 506
White, Michael, 221
White, Molly L., 276
White, Molly S., 1036, 1037, 1038
White, Nancy, 240
White, Patrice, 95
White, Patricia J., 513
White, Phyllis, 1088, 1089, 1090
White, Rev. Ralph, 448
White, Rueyenne, 489
White, Sadicka, 368
White, Sarah C., 441
White, Stephanie, 388
White, Stephen A., 235
White, Tammy, 162
White, Terri, 381
White, Thomas, 449
White, Timothy, 93
White, Timothy A., 202
White, Todd, 253
White, W. Brian, 1008, 1009
White, William, 493
White, William "Bill", 827, 828, 830
White, William M. "Bill", 522
White, William P., 408
Whiteford, Mary, 783, 785
Whitehead, Jerry, 140
Whitehead, Shana, 152
Whitehouse, Don, 506
Whitehouse, Elizabeth, 192
Whitehouse, Joshua, 867
Whitehouse, Peter, 373
Whitehurst, David K., 496
Whitener, Tim J., 517
Whitfield, Melissa, 31
Whitfield, Patricia "Tricia", 394
Whitfield, Paul, 108
Whitford, COL John, 71
Whitford, Lea, 834, 835
Whitham, Jonathan, 158
Whiting, Teresa, 472
Whitley, David, 452
Whitley, Jane, 214
Whitley, Kim, 191
Whitley, Onetta, 272
Whitley, Richard, 298
Whitlock, Marthagem, 445
Whitlock, Tivy, 459

Whitlow, CMSgt James B., 62
Whitman, Henry "Hank", 460
Whitmarsh, Theresa, 509
Whitmer, Joe, 22
Whitmer, John, 719, 721
Whitmire, Chris, 919, 920, 921, 922, 923, 924
Whitmire, John, 1028
Whitmire, Matthew, 165
Whitmire, William R. "Bill", 1008, 1009
Whitney, Jessica, 171
Whitney, Joli A., 398
Whitney, Judith, 483
Whitney, Katie, 479
Whitney, Linda, 53
Whitney, Marilyn, 134
Whitney, Mark, 115
Whitsett, Doug, 956, 957
Whitsett, Gail, 959, 960
Whitson, Terry L., 158
Whitt, Charise, 299
Whitt, Jelani, 97
Whitt, Rhonda, 440
Whittacre, Dan, 352
Whittaker, Jetta, 14
Whittaker, Robert L. "Bob", 191
Whittaker, Dr. Terry M., 82
Whittall-Scherfee, Laura, 39
Whittemore, Rodney L., 746
Whitten, Mark, 102
Whittier, Scott, 210
Whittington, Kay, 265
Whitver, Jack, 699, 701, 702
Whitworth, Kent, 193
Whorton, Isaac, 551, 552, 553
Whorton, Ritchie, 551, 552, 553
Whyte, Dan, 285
Wiant, Dr. Linda, 113
Wichmann, Chris, 535
Wick, Arne, 284
Wicker, Jordan, 155
Wicker, Kelly, 501
Wicker, Thomas A., 271
Wickersham, Kimberly, 429
Wickersheim, Michael, 100
Wickert, Matthew, 518
Wickes, Barry, 402
Wickham-Hurley, Zenita, 230
Wickham, Angela, 136
Wickham, Betsy, 106
Wickham, Cynthia "Cyndi", 394
Wickliffe, Bill, 197
Wickman, Blake, 135
Wide, James, 156
Wideman, Suellen, 220
Widerburg, Gary, 475
Widley, Robyn R., 256
Widom, Chester A. "Chet", 42
Wiebe, Wade, 178
Wiebers, Ann, 170
Wiechman, Marie, 293
Wieck, Colleen A., 255
Wieckowski, Bob, 583, 584, 585
Wiedmaier, Dr. Cheryl, 30
Wieferich, Bradley "Brad", 253
Wiegmann, William, 404
Wieland, Paul, 818, 819
Wielechowski, Bill, 556, 557
Wiemann, John D., 827, 828, 829, 830
Wiencek, Tami, 167
Wieneke, Chris, 147
Wienges, John O., 998
Wierzba, Aimee, 531
Wiese, Deborah, 248
Wieske, J. P., 525
Wiesman, John M., 504
Wiessmann, Robin L., 401

**NAME INDEX**

Wilson, Phil, 512
Wilson, Rhonda, 102
Wilson, Ric, 440
Wilson, Richard, 268, 450
Wilson, Robert, 538
Wilson, Robert B. "Bob", 101
Wilson, Roger, 289, 372, 504
Wilson, Sara Redding, 489
Wilson, Scott, 47
Wilson, Shawn D., 203
Wilson, Sheila, 174
Wilson, Shelley, 372
Wilson, Stephanie, 164
Wilson, Sue, 1107, 1108
Wilson, Sylvan, 370
Wilson, Tammie, 559, 560
Wilson, Tammie Hall, 429
Wilson, Terri L., 374
Wilson, Tim, 94
Wilson, Vicki, 149
Wilson, Wanda Young, 449
Wilson, William, 156
Wilson, William J. "Billy", 198
Wilt, Mike, 384
Wilt, Ronald, 406
Wilt, Tony O., 1067, 1068
Wiltgen, David, 531
Wiltshire, Lisa M., 370
Wilz, Greg, 359
Wimberly, Benjie E., 874, 878, 879
Wimbley, Jason, 44
Wimmer, Matt, 136
Wims-Campbell, Carolyn L., 181
Wimsatt, Michael J., 304
Winans, Joby, 504
Winch, Lt. Col. David E., 82
Winchester, Martin, 456
Winckler, Cindy L., 707, 708, 709
Winder, Chuck, 661, 663, 664
Winder, Phillip, 76
Winder, Sundee, 202
Windholz, JoAnn, 598
Windle, John Mark, 1024, 1025
Windley, Paula, 352
Windschitl, Matt W., 703, 707, 708, 709
Windy Boy, Jonathan, 834, 835
Wine, John, 180
Wines, Larissa M., 522
Winfield, Brian, 44
Winfield, Gary A., 599, 601, 608, 609, 610, 611
Winfield, Thomas J., 996, 997
Winfree, Jana, 380
Wingate, Thomas P., 465
Winger, Christine Jennifer, 682, 684, 685, 686
Winger, Nicole, 55
Winges-Yanez, Kristin, 398
Wingfield, Betsey C., 70
Wingfield, Will, 160
Wingo, Kurtis, 370
Wingo, Rich, 552, 553, 554
Wink, Dean, 1012, 1015, 1016
Winkel, Vickie, 135
Winkelman, John, 293
Winkler, Jerry, 476
Winkley, Mary, 52
Winn, Dr. Valdenia, 719, 720, 721
Winning, Rich, 372
Winokur, Michelle M. D., 108
Winslow, Dallas, 80
Winsor, Tom J., 752
Winston, Wyman, 531
Winter, Brad D., 328
Winter, Colleen, 433

Winter, Faith, 598
Winter, Larry, 118
Winter, Michael, 96
Winter, Trish, 328
Winters, Aaron, 143
Winters, Andria, 145
Winters, Christopher D. "Chris", 483
Winters, Dennis, 530
Winters, Gwen, 268
Winters, Jackie, 956
Winters, Janine "Jan", 247
Winters, Lance, 57
Winters, Nathan, 1107
Winters, Shelley, 307
Winters, Tammy, 171
Winters, Thomas R., 375
Wintrow, Melissa, 667, 668, 669
Wirch, Robert W., 1093
Wire, Lisa, 434
Wire, Ronald "Ron", 435
Wirgau, Tim, 1024, 1025
Wirth, Peter, 882
Wirths, Harold J. "Hal", 313
Wisch, Eric, 512
Wisch, Joshua A., 127
Wisdom, Leslie, 480
Wise, Ann, 200
Wise, Beth, 352
Wise, Brian, 367
Wise, Dana, 79
Wise, George Maxwell "Max", 725, 726
Wise, Howard F., 367
Wise, Neville, 189
Wise, Pat, 285
Wise, Rachel, 294
Wise, Ryan, 169, 174
Wise, Sandra, 444
Wise, Stan, 121
Wise, Tristan, 502
Wise, Vickie, 196
Wise, Zackary "Zack", 426
Wiseman, Chris, 60
Wiseman, Jack D., 515
Wiseman, Steven A. "Steve", 517
Wisian, MajGen Kenneth W., 468
Wisloski, Stephen, 484
Wisniewski, John S., 874, 878, 879
Wist, Cole, 598
Witham, Jennifer, 360
Witherill, Donald T., 210
Withers, Jan, 349
Withers, Randall, 204
Withers, Richard, 39
Witherspoon, Jeanne, 154
Witherspoon, Tammy, 803, 804, 805
Withrow, Jay W., 490
Withrow, Patti J., 519
Witkos, Kevin, 599, 601, 610, 611
Witkowski, Ron, 842
Witt, Brad, 959, 960
Witt, Brett, 425
Witt, Craig M., 299
Witt, Lyndsay, 358
Witte, Jeff M., 329
Witten, Margaret, 120
Wittenberg, Doreen A., 304
Wittenberg, Joyce, 283
Wittenberg, Robert, 783, 784, 785
Witter, Susan E. "Susie", 498
Wittich, Art, 840, 841
Wittig, Larry A., 408
Wittman, John, 452
Witty, Patrick "Pat", 200
Witzel, John, 295
Wivell, William J. "Bill", 762
Wobensmith, John Casper, 217

Wodiska, Joan E., 492
Wodnik, Loraine, 283
Woehler, Kerri, 506
Woelfel, Mike, 1081, 1082, 1083
Woerner, Carrie, 902, 906, 907
Wohlers, Jason Bliss, 417
Wohlman, Matthew J., 255
Woitkun, Steven J., 867, 868
Wojahn, Beth, 321
Wojcicki Jimenez, Sara, 682, 683, 685
Wojcieszyn, Sally, 75
Wojtenko, Russell, Jr., 313
Wolanski, Lori, 211
Wolcott, Gary, 211
Wolf, Ben, 103
Wolf, Clayton, 462
Wolf, Daniel A. "Dan", 766
Wolf, Kay, 711, 712, 713
Wolf, Lindsey, 467
Wolf, Michael J., 79
Wolf, Richard, 226
Wolf, Steve, 399
Wolf, Terry, 852, 867, 868
Wolf, Thomas W. "Tom", 400
Wolfe Moore, Kathy, 720, 721, 722
Wolfe, Chuck, 194
Wolfe, David W., 874, 878
Wolfe, Larry, 129
Wolfe, Linda, 77
Wolfe, Mark, 461
Wolfe, Mary Lynn, 707, 708, 709
Wolfe, Meagan, 532
Wolfe, Robert, 152
Wolfe, Tina, 119
Wolff, Cheryl, 288
Wolff, Jonathan, 57
Wolff, Lori, 136
Wolfgang, Douglas, 401
Wolfgram, Darlene, 360
Wolfingbarger, Brentton, 83
Wolford, Jamion A., 523
Wolford, Scott, 473
Wolk, Larry, 63
Wolk, Lois, 581, 584, 585
Wolken, Cynthia, 834, 835
Wolkins, David A., 696, 697, 698
Wolley, Gregory J., 396
Wollmann, Mathew, 1015
Wolock, Ellen, 317
Womack, Mona S., 188
Womack, Reece, 387
Womack, Richard, 579, 580, 581
Womer, Jonathan, 414
Womick, Richard B. "Rick", 1024
Won Pat, Judith T., 652, 653, 654
Won, Delmond J., 129
Wong-Hernandez, Jacqueline, 52
Wong-Martinusen, Collin, 55
Wong Tomiyasu, Danette, 131
Wong, Angela, 282
Wong, Barry, 21
Wong, Brian, 240
Wong, Donald H., 774, 775
Wong, Herbert S., 227
Wong, Martha, 464
Wong, Rachael S., 131
Wong, San, 170
Wong, Sharon N., 128
Woo-Sam, Mark, 46
Woo, Richard Y., 226
Wood-Lenderman, Stacia, 34
Wood, Barbara, 279
Wood, Beth A., 355
Wood, Brandon, 461
Wood, Clarice, 87
Wood, Curtis M., 240

Wood, Cynthia "Cindy", 267
Wood, David, 827, 828, 829, 831
Wood, Franny, 235
Wood, Fred, 667, 668
Wood, J. Barry, 161
Wood, Jennifer L., 418
Wood, Jim, 590, 591, 592
Wood, Joe T., Jr., 117
Wood, John, 629, 630
Wood, Jonathan, 344
Wood, Joseph, 35
Wood, Justin F., 952, 953, 954
Wood, Leonard "Rob", 13
Wood, Mary, 509
Wood, Melinda, 133
Wood, Michael, 336, 391
Wood, Natalie, 299
Wood, Pamela "Pam", 456
Wood, Randy, 552, 553, 554
Wood, Robert, 468
Wood, Spencer, 367
Wood, Stephen J., 752
Wood, Terrie E., 608, 609, 610, 611
Wood, Theresa, 1054, 1055
Wood, Tom, 336
Wood, William J. "Bill", 288, 289
Woodall, Daniel, 76
Woodall, Jason, 440
Woodall, Jeremy, 395
Woodard, Alan, 351
Woodard, Jeff, 546
Woodard, Michael "Mike", 910, 911, 912
Woodburn, Jeff, 850, 851, 852
Woodburn, Jeffrey S., 99
Woodbury, David, 867, 869
Woodbury, Melissa, 849
Woodcock, Chandler E., 211
Woodcock, Marsha, 200
Woodell, Capt. Scott, 115
Woodford, Emma, 386
Woodhouse, Joyce, 845, 846
Woodland, Kenneth M., 244
Woodrick, Jim, 264
Woodrow, Jeremy, 16
Woodrow, Mel, 387
Woodruff, Candice, 452
Woodruff, Carlton, 25
Woodruff, Trevor, 460
Woodrum, Jo Ann, 427
Woodrum, Mitchell E. "Mitch", 514
Woods, Brett F., 321
Woods, Douglas, 57
Woods, Elizabeth, 403
Woods, Jill, 91
Woods, Jon, 574
Woods, Kanda, 387
Woods, Karima, 92
Woods, Laura, 595
Woods, Lesha, 203
Woods, Lester, 278
Woods, Maggie, 193
Woods, Monica, 106
Woods, Pat, 882
Woods, Patrick, 510
Woods, Richard Lee, 118
Woods, Samantha, 191
Woods, Shelita, 199
Woods, Dr. Stephen T., 374
Woods, Steve, 45
Woods, Susan, 409
Woods, Tom, 840, 841
Woods, Wally, 194
Woods, CSM William D., 62
Woodside, Diana, 402
Woodsome, David, 746
Woodson, Justin H., 659, 660, 661
Woodson, Lorraine, 237
Woodson, Steve, 534
Woodson, Tonya E., 500

Woodward, Lauri, 312
Woodward, Mark, 387, 1054, 1055
Woodward, Marvin M., 117
Woodward, Spud, 115
Woodwell, Keith, 470
Woodworth, CW4 Jim, 483
Woodworth, Joanne, 150
Woody, Elizabeth M. "Marsi", 140
Wool, Adam, 559, 560
Woolard, Christopher "Chris", 376
Wooldridge, Lynette, 188
Wooley, Bob, 885, 886
Woolf, Brandon, 142
Woolf, Jim, 139
Woolfolk, COL Edmund W "Ned", Jr., 104
Woolley, Dan, 498
Woon, Molly, 955
Woosley, Bishop, 31
Wooster, Dr. James H., 314
Wooten, Adrienne, 812, 813, 814, 815
Wooten, Amy, 441
Wooten, Greg, 138
Wooten, James Michael "Mike", 427
Wooten, Michael "Mike", 95
Wooten, Vicki S., 421
Worcester, Lacie, 178
Worden, Amy, 403
Worden, Bradd, 33
Wordlaw, John, 43
Workman, Kelly A., 514
Workman, Paul D., 1036, 1037, 1038
Workman, Ritch, 629, 630, 631
Workman, Todd, 179
Workman, Wayne, 253
Worlds, Gwendolyn, 110
Worley, Kevin, 11
Wormley, Richelle, 311
Worrell, Alice, 370
Worrell, Ritchie, 444
Worsley, Bob, 566, 567
Wortham, CSM Douglas J., 259
Worthan, Gary, 707, 709
Worthy, Kimberly, 283
Wortley, Jay, 254
Wortman, David, 145
Wospil, Thomas "Tom", 314
Wozniak, Angela, 902, 903, 905, 906
Wozniak, John N., 964, 965
Wray, Jerry, 372
Wray, John, 1036, 1037, 1038
Wray, Michael H., 919, 920, 921, 922, 923, 924
Wreh, J Michael, 418
Wren, Anthony "Tony", 299
Wren, Jennifer, 120
Wrenn, William L. "Bill", 304
Wresinski, David, 253
Wright-McMurray, Sonja, 30
Wright Yeskoo, Marcia, 494
Wright, April, 80
Wright, Brandon P., 223
Wright, Dr. Carey M., 270
Wright, Cindy, 9
Wright, Craig, 304
Wright, Crystal, 323
Wright, Dalton, 279
Wright, David, 341
Wright, David L., 448
Wright, Debbie J., 6
Wright, Dennis, 334
Wright, Donald S. "Ted.", 867, 870
Wright, Emily, 11
Wright, Flint, 297